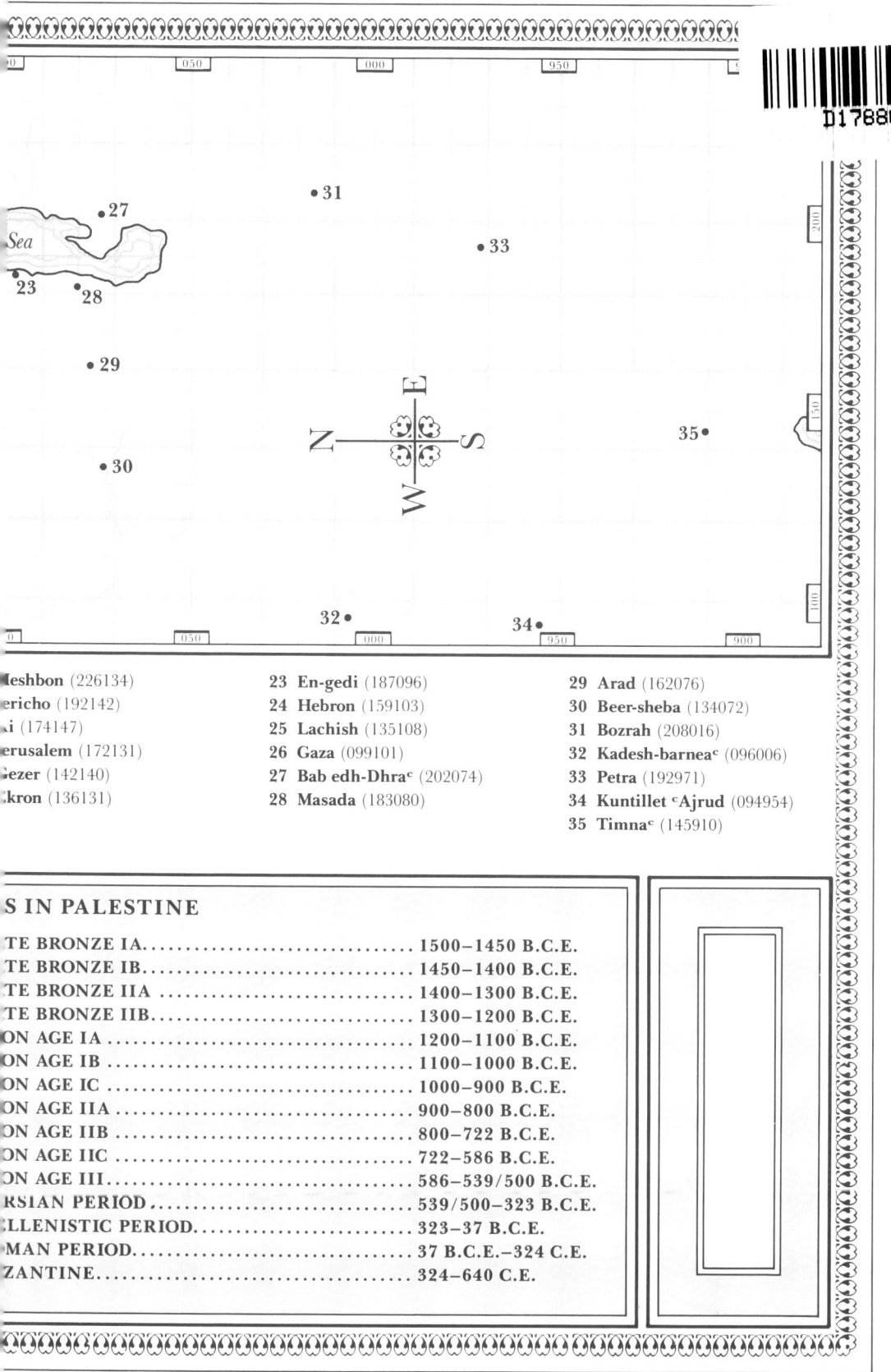

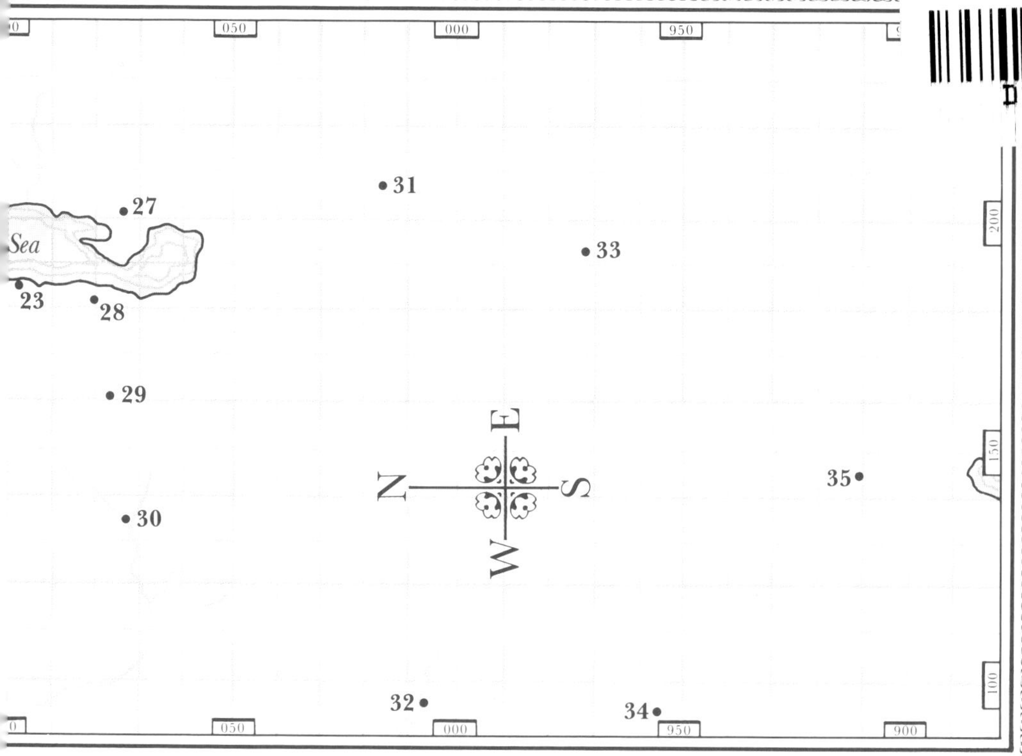

leshbon (226134)
ericho (192142)
i (174147)
erusalem (172131)
ezer (142140)
kron (136131)

23 **En-gedi** (187096)
24 **Hebron** (159103)
25 **Lachish** (135108)
26 **Gaza** (099101)
27 **Bab edh-Dhra**[c] (202074)
28 **Masada** (183080)

29 **Arad** (162076)
30 **Beer-sheba** (134072)
31 **Bozrah** (208016)
32 **Kadesh-barnea**[c] (096006)
33 **Petra** (192971)
34 **Kuntillet** [c]**Ajrud** (094954)
35 **Timna**[c] (145910)

S IN PALESTINE

TE BRONZE IA	1500–1450 B.C.E.
TE BRONZE IB	1450–1400 B.C.E.
TE BRONZE IIA	1400–1300 B.C.E.
TE BRONZE IIB	1300–1200 B.C.E.
ON AGE IA	1200–1100 B.C.E.
ON AGE IB	1100–1000 B.C.E.
ON AGE IC	1000–900 B.C.E.
ON AGE IIA	900–800 B.C.E.
ON AGE IIB	800–722 B.C.E.
ON AGE IIC	722–586 B.C.E.
ON AGE III	586–539/500 B.C.E.
RSIAN PERIOD	539/500–323 B.C.E.
LLENISTIC PERIOD	323–37 B.C.E.
MAN PERIOD	37 B.C.E.–324 C.E.
ZANTINE	324–640 C.E.

THE ANCHOR BIBLE DICTIONARY

THE ANCHOR BIBLE DICTIONARY

VOLUME 4
K–N

David Noel Freedman
EDITOR-IN-CHIEF

ASSOCIATE EDITORS
Gary A. Herion • David F. Graf
John David Pleins

MANAGING EDITOR
Astrid B. Beck

ABD

DOUBLEDAY
NEW YORK • LONDON • TORONTO • SYDNEY • AUCKLAND

THE ANCHOR BIBLE DICTIONARY: VOLUME 4
PUBLISHED BY DOUBLEDAY
a division of Bantam Doubleday Dell Publishing Group, Inc.
666 Fifth Avenue, New York, New York 10103

DESIGN BY Stanley S. Drate/Folio Graphics Company, Inc.

Library of Congress Cataloging-in-Publication Data
Anchor Bible dictionary / David Noel Freedman, editor-in-chief;
associate editors, Gary A. Herion, David F. Graf, John David Pleins;
managing editor, Astrid B. Beck.
—1st ed.
p. cm.
Includes bibliographical references.
1. Bible—Dictionaries. I. Freedman, David Noel, 1922– .
BS440.A54 1992
220.3—dc20 91-8385
CIP

Vol. 1 ISBN 0-385-19351-3
Vol. 2 ISBN 0-385-19360-2
Vol. 3 ISBN 0-385-19361-0
Vol. 4 ISBN 0-385-19362-9
Vol. 5 ISBN 0-385-19363-7
Vol. 6 ISBN 0-385-26190-X

10 9 8 7 6 5 4 3 2 1

FIRST EDITION

CONSULTANTS

HANS DIETER BETZ (Greco-Roman Religion)
Shailer Mathews Professor of NT Studies, University of Chicago

JAMES H. CHARLESWORTH (Apocrypha and Pseudepigrapha)
George L. Collord Professor of NT Language and Literature, Princeton Theological Seminary

FRANK MOORE CROSS (Old Testament)
Hancock Professor of Hebrew and Other Oriental Languages, Harvard University

WILLIAM G. DEVER (Archaeology)
Professor of Near Eastern Archaeology and Anthropology, University of Arizona

A. KIRK GRAYSON (Mesopotamia and Assyriology)
Professor, University of Toronto

PETER MACHINIST (Bible and Ancient Near East)
Professor of Near Eastern Languages and Civilizations, Harvard University

ABRAHAM J. MALHERBE (New Testament)
Buckingham Professor of New Testament Criticism and Interpretation, The Divinity School, Yale University

BIRGER A. PEARSON (Early Christianity)
Professor of Religious Studies, University of California at Santa Barbara

JACK M. SASSON (Bible and Ancient Near East)
Professor in Religious Studies, University of North Carolina

WILLIAM R. SCHOEDEL (Early Christian Literature)
University of Illinois at Urbana-Champaign

EDITORIAL STAFF

EDITOR-IN-CHIEF:
David Noel Freedman

ASSOCIATE EDITORS:
Gary A. Herion
David F. Graf
John David Pleins

MANAGING EDITOR:
Astrid B. Beck

ASSISTANT EDITOR:
Philip C. Schmitz

PRODUCTION EDITOR:
Leslie Barkley

ASSISTANTS TO THE EDITOR:
Mark J. Fretz
Herbert Grether
John Huddlestun
John Kutsko
Dale Manor
Paul Mirecki
James Mueller
David R. Seely
William Ward
Harry Weeks

PRODUCTION ASSISTANTS:
Carol Herion
Dennis Moser

LIST OF ABBREVIATIONS

1 Apoc. Jas.	*First Apocalypse of James* (NHC V,*3*)
1 Chr	1 Chronicles
1 Clem.	*1 Clement*
1 Cor	1 Corinthians
1 En.	*1 Enoch (Ethiopic Apocalypse)*
1 Esdr	1 Esdras
1 John	1 John
1 Kgdms	1 Samuel (LXX)
1 Kgs	1 Kings
1 Macc	1 Maccabees
1 Pet	1 Peter
1 Sam	1 Samuel
1 Thess	1 Thessalonians
1 Tim	1 Timothy
1Q, 2Q, 3Q, etc.	Numbered caves of Qumran, yielding written material; followed by abbreviation of biblical or apocryphal book
1QapGen	*Genesis Apocryphon* of Qumran Cave 1
1QH	*Hôdāyôt (Thanksgiving Hymns)* from Qumran Cave 1
1QIsa[a, b]	First or second copy of Isaiah from Qumran Cave 1
1QM	*Milḥāmāh (War Scroll)*
1QpHab	*Pesher on Habakkuk* from Qumran Cave 1
1QS	*Serek hayyaḥad (Rule of the Community, Manual of Discipline)*
1QSa	Appendix A *(Rule of the Congregation)* to 1QS
1QSb	Appendix B *(Blessings)* to 1QS
1st	first
2 Apoc. Jas.	*Second Apocalypse of James* (NHC V,*4*)
2 Bar.	*2 Baruch (Syriac Apocalypse)*
2 Chr	2 Chronicles
2 Clem.	*2 Clement*
2 Cor	2 Corinthians
2 En.	*2 Enoch (Slavonic Apocalypse)*
2 Esdr	2 Esdras
2 John	2 John
2 Kgdms	2 Samuel (LXX)
2 Kgs	2 Kings
2 Macc	2 Maccabees
2 Pet	2 Peter
2 Sam	2 Samuel
2 Thess	2 Thessalonians
2 Tim	2 Timothy
2d	second
3 Bar.	*3 Baruch (Greek Apocalypse)*
3 Cor.	*3 Corinthians*
3 En.	*3 Enoch (Hebrew Apocalypse)*
3 John	3 John
3 Kgdms	1 Kings (LXX)
3 Macc.	*3 Maccabees*
3d	third
3Q15	Copper Scroll from Qumran Cave 3
4 Bar.	*4 Baruch*
4 Ezra	*4 Ezra*
4 Kgdms	2 Kings (LXX)
4 Macc.	*4 Maccabees*
4QFlor	*Florilegium* (or *Eschatological Midrashim*) from Qumran Cave 4
4QMess ar	Aramaic "Messianic" text from Qumran Cave 4
4QPhyl	Phylacteries from Qumran Cave 4
4QPrNab	Prayer of Nabonidus from Qumran Cave 4
4QTestim	*Testimonia* text from Qumran Cave 4
4QTLevi	*Testament of Levi* from Qumran Cave 4
5 Apoc. Syr. Pss.	*Five Apocryphal Syriac Psalms*
5 Macc.	*5 Maccabees*
11QMelch	*Melchizedek* text from Qumran Cave 11
11QtgJob	*Targum of Job* from Qumran Cave 11
A	Codex Alexandrinus
ÄA	Ägyptologische Abhandlungen
AA	*Archäologischer Anzeiger*, Berlin
AAL	*Afroasiatic Linguistics*, Malibu, CA

AANLM	*Atti dell'Accademia Nazionale dei Lincei, Memorie, Classe di scienze morali, storiche e filologiche*, ser. 8
AANLR	*Atti dell'Accademia Nazionale dei Lincei, Rendiconti, Classe di scienze morali, storiche e filologiche*, ser. 8
AARAS	American Academy of Religion Academy Series
AARASR	American Academy of Religion Aids for the Study of Religion
AARCRS	American Academy of Religion Classics in Religious Studies
AARSR	American Academy of Religion Studies in Religion
AARTT	American Academy of Religion Texts and Translations
AASF	Annales Academiae Scientarum Fennicae, Helsinki
AASOR	Annual of the American Schools of Oriental Research
ÄAT	Ägypten und Altes Testament
AAWLM	*Abhandlungen der Akademie der Wissenschaften und der Literatur Mainz*
AB	Anchor Bible
ABAW	Abhandlungen der Bayerischen Akademie der Wissenschaften
AbB	Altbabylonische Briefe in Umschrift und Übersetzung, ed. F. R. Kraus. Leiden, 1964–
abbr.	abbreviated, abbreviation
ABD	*Anchor Bible Dictionary*
ABIUSJH	*Annual of Bar-Ilan University Studies in Judaica and the Humanities*
ABL	*Assyrian and Babylonian Letters*, 14 vols., ed. R. F. Harper. Chicago, 1892–1914
ABLA	M. Noth. 1971. *Aufsätze zur biblischen Landes- und Altertumskunde*, ed. H. W. Wolff. Neukirchen-Vluyn
ʿAbod. Zar.	*ʿAboda Zara*
ʾAbot	*ʾAbot*
ʾAbot R. Nat.	*ʾAbot de Rabbi Nathan*
Abr	Philo, *De Abrahamo*
ABR	*Australian Biblical Review*
ABRMW	H. Graf Reventlow. 1985. *The Authority of the Bible and the Rise of the Modern World.* Trans. J. Bowden. Philadelphia
AbrN	*Abr-Nahrain*
absol.	absolute
AcApos	*Acta Apostolorum Apocrypha.* 3 vols. Hildesheim, 1959
ACF	*Annuaire du Collège de France*, Paris
ACNT	Augsburg Commentary on the New Testament
AcOr	*Acta orientalia*
AcOrASH	*Acta orientalia Academiae Scientiarum Hungaricae*
ACR	*American Classical Review*
AcSum	*Acta Sumerologica*
act.	active
Acts	Acts (or Acts of the Apostles)
Acts Andr.	*Acts of Andrew*
Acts Andr. Mth.	*Acts of Andrew and Matthias*
Acts Andr. Paul	*Acts of Andrew and Paul*
Acts Barn.	*Acts of Barnabas*
Acts Jas.	*Acts of James the Great*
Acts John	*Acts of John*
Acts John Pro.	*Acts of John (by Prochorus)*
Acts Paul	*Acts of Paul*
Acts Pet.	*Acts of Peter*
Acts Pet. (Slav.)	*Slavonic Acts of Peter*
Acts Pet. 12 Apost.	*Acts of Peter and the Twelve Apostles* (NHC VI,*1*)
Acts Pet. Andr.	*Acts of Peter and Andrew*
Acts Pet. Paul	*Acts of Peter and Paul*
Acts Phil.	*Acts of Philip*
Acts Phil. (Syr.)	*Acts of Philip (Syriac)*
Acts Pil.	*Acts of Pilate*
Acts Thad.	*Acts of Thaddaeus*
Acts Thom.	*Acts of Thomas*
ActSS	*Acta Sanctorum*
ACW	Ancient Christian Writers
A.D.	*anno domini* (year)
ad loc.	*ad locum* (at the place)
ADAIK	Abhandlungen des deutschen archäologischen Instituts, Kairo
ADAJ	*Annual of the Department of Antiquities of Jordan*
Add Dan	Additions to Daniel
Add Esth	Additions to Esther
ADFU	Ausgrabungen der Deutschen Forschungsgemeinschaft in Uruk-Warka
adj.	adjective
ADOG	*Abhandlungen der Deutschen Orient-Gesellschaft*, Berlin
ADPV	Abhandlungen des Deutschen Palästina-Vereins
adv.	adverb
AE	*L'année épigraphique* [cited by year and no. of text]
AEB	*Annual Egyptological Bibliography*
Aeg	*Aegyptus: Revista italiana di egittologia e papirologia*
AEHE IV	*Annuaire de l'École pratique des Hautes Études*, IVe section, Sc. hist. et philol., Paris
AEHE V	*Annuaire de l'École pratique des Hautes Études*, V^{e} section, Sc. relig., Paris

AEHL	*Archaeological Excavations in the Holy Land,* ed. A. Negev. Englewood Cliffs, NJ, 1980
AEL	M. Lichtheim. 1971–80. *Ancient Egyptian Literature.* 3 vols. Berkeley
AER	*American Ecclesiastical Review*
AESH	B. Trigger, B. J. Kemp, D. O'Connor, and A. B. Lloyd. 1983. *Ancient Egypt: A Social History.* Cambridge
Aet	Philo, *De aeternitate mundi*
Aev	*Aevum: Rassegna di scienze storiche linguistiche e filologiche*
ÄF	Ägyptologische Forschungen
AFER	*African Ecclesiastical Review,* Eldoret, Kenya
AfL	*Archiv für Liturgiewissenschaft,* Regensburg
AFNW	*Arbeitsgemeinschaft für Forschung des Landes Nordrhein-Westfalen,* Cologne
AfO	*Archiv für Orientforschung,* Graz
AfrTJ	*Africa Theological Journal,* Arusha, Tanzania
AgAp	Josephus, *Against Apion (= Contra Apionem)*
ʾAg. Ber.	*ʾAggadat Berešit*
AGJU	Arbeiten zur Geschichte des antiken Judentums und des Urchristentums
Agr	Philo, *De agricultura*
AGSU	Arbeiten zur Geschichte des Spätjudentums und Urchristentums
AH	*An Aramaic Handbook,* ed. F. Rosenthal, 2 vols. Wiesbaden, 1967
Ah.	*Ahiqar*
AHAW	Abhandlungen der Heidelberger Akademie der Wissenschaften
AHG	B. Albrektson. 1967. *History and the Gods.* ConBOT 1. Lund
AHR	*American Historical Review*
AHW	*Akkadisches Handwörterbuch,* ed. W. von Soden. 3 vols. Wiesbaden, 1965–81
AI	Arad Inscription [cited according to Y. Aharoni. 1981. *Arad Inscriptions,* Jerusalem]
AION	*Annali dell'Istituto orientali di Napoli*
AIPHOS	*Annuaire de l'Institut de philologie et d'histoire orientales et slaves*
AIR	*Ancient Israelite Religion: Essays in Honor of Frank Moore Cross,* ed. P. D. Miller, P. D. Hanson, and S. D. McBride. Philadelphia, 1987
AIS	I. Finkelstein. 1988. *The Archaeology of the Israelite Settlement.* Jerusalem
AJA	*American Journal of Archaeology*
AJAS	*American Journal of Arabic Studies*
AJBA	*Australian Journal of Biblical Archaeology*
AJBI	Annual of the Japanese Biblical Institute, Tokyo
AJP	*American Journal of Philology*
AJSL	*American Journal of Semitic Languages and Literatures*
AJT	*American Journal of Theology*
Akk	Akkadian
AKM	*Abhandlungen zur Kunde des Morgenlandes (Leipzig)*
AL	*The Assyrian Laws,* ed. G. R. Driver and J. C. Miles. Oxford, 1935
ALBO	Analecta lovaniensia biblica et orientalia
ALGHJ	Arbeiten zur Literatur und Geschichte des hellenistischen Judentums
Allogenes	*Allogenes* (NHC XI,*3*)
Altertum	*Das Altertum,* Berlin
ALUOS	Annual of Leeds University Oriental Society
Am	*America,* New York
AmBenR	*American Benedictine Review*
AMI	Archäologische Mitteilungen aus Iran
Amos	Amos
AMT	R. C. Thompson. 1923. *Assyrian Medical Texts.* Oxford
AN	J. J. Stamm. 1939. *Die akkadische Namengebung.* MVÄG 44. Berlin
AnBib	Analecta Biblica
AnBoll	*Analecta Bollandiana*
AncIsr	R. de Vaux, 1961. *Ancient Israel: Its Life and Institutions.* Trans. J. McHugh. London. Repr. New York, 1965
ANE	Ancient Near East(ern)
ANEP	*Ancient Near East in Pictures Relating to the Old Testament,* 2d ed. with suppl., ed. J. B. Pritchard, Princeton, 1969
ANET	*Ancient Near Eastern Texts Relating to the Old Testament,* 3d ed. with suppl., ed. J. B. Pritchard, Princeton, 1969
ANF	The Ante-Nicene Fathers
Ang	*Angelicum,* Rome
ANHMW	*Annalen des Naturhistorische Museum in Wien*
Anim	Philo, *De animalibus*
Anon. Sam.	*Anonymous Samaritan Text*
AnOr	Analecta orientalia
ANQ	*Andover Newton Quarterly*
ANRW	*Aufstieg und Niedergang der römischen Welt,* ed. H. Temporini and W. Haase, Berlin, 1972–
AnSt	*Anatolian Studies*
Ant	Josephus, *Jewish Antiquities (= Antiquitates Judaicae)*
AntCl	*L'antiquité classique*

ANTF	Arbeiten zur neutestamentlichen Textforschung
ANTJ	Arbeiten zum Neuen Testament und Judentum
Anton	*Antonianum*
Anuario	*Anuario de Filología,* Barcelona
ANVAO	Avhandlinger utgitt av det Norske Videnskaps-Akademi i Oslo
AO	Der Alte Orient
AOAT	Alter Orient und Altes Testament
AOATS	Alter Orient und Altes Testament Sonderreihe
AÖAW	*Anzeiger der Österreichischer Akademie der Wissenschaften,* Vienna
AOB[2]	*Altorientalische Bilder zum Alten Testament,* 2d ed., ed. H. Gressman. Berlin and Leipzig, 1927
AOBib	Altorientalische Bibliothek
AoF	*Altorientalische Forschungen*
AOS	American Oriental Series
AOSTS	American Oriental Society Translation Series
AOT[2]	*Altorientalische Texte zum Alten Testament,* 2d ed., ed. H. Gressman. Berlin and Leipzig, 1926
AP	*L'année philologique*
Ap. Ezek.	*Apocryphon of Ezekiel*
Ap. Jas.	*Apocryphon of James* (NHC I,2)
Ap. John	*Apocryphon of John* (NHC II,*1*; III,*1*; IV,*1*)
APAACS	American Philological Association American Classical Studies
APAPM	American Philological Association Philological Monographs
APAT	*Die Apokryphen und Pseudepigraphen des Alten Testaments,* 2 vols., ed. E. Kautzch. Tübingen, 1900. Repr. 1975
APAW	*Abhandlungen der Preussischen Akademie der Wissenschaft*
APEF	*Annual of the Palestine Exploration Fund*
APNM	H. B. Hoffman. 1965. *Amorite Personal Names in the Mari Texts.* Baltimore
Apoc. Ab.	*Apocalypse of Abraham*
Apoc. Adam	*Apocalypse of Adam* (NHC V,*5*)
Apoc. Dan.	*Apocalypse of Daniel*
Apoc. Dosith.	*Apocalypse of Dositheus*
Apoc. El.	*Apocalypse of Elijah*
Apoc. Ezek.	*Apocalypse of Ezekiel*
Apoc. Messos	*Apocalypse of Messos*
Apoc. Mos.	*Apocalypse of Moses*
Apoc. Paul	*Apocalypse of Paul* (NHC V,*2*)
Apoc. Pet.	*Apocalypse of Peter* (NHC VII,*3*)
Apoc. Sedr.	*Apocalypse of Sedrach*
Apoc. Thom.	*Apocalypse of Thomas*
Apoc. Vir.	*Apocalypses of the Virgin*
Apoc. Zeph.	*Apocalypse of Zephaniah*
Apoc. Zos.	*Apocalypse of Zosimus*
Apocr.	*Apocryphal, Apocrypha*
Apol Jud	Philo, *Apologia pro Iudaeis*
Apos.	Apostolic, Apostles
Apos. Con.	*Apostolic Constitutions and Canons*
APOT	*Apocrypha and Pseudepigrapha of the Old Testament,* 2 vols., ed. R. H. Charles. Oxford, 1913
Ar	Arabic
AR	Archaeological Reports
ᶜArak.	*ᶜArakin*
Aram	Aramaic
ArbT	*Arbeitzen zur Theologie,* Stuttgart
Arch	*Archaeology*
ArchEleph	B. Porten. 1968. *Archives from Elephantine.* Berkeley
ArchPal	W. F. Albright. 1960. *The Archaeology of Palestine.* 3d rev. ed. Harmondsworth. Repr. Gloucester, MA, 1971
ARE	*Ancient Records of Egypt,* 5 vols., ed. J. H. Breasted. Chicago, 1906. Repr. New York, 1962
ARET	Archivi reali di Ebla, Testi
ARG	*Archiv für Reformationsgeschichte*
ARI	W. F. Albright. 1968. *Archaeology and the Religion of Israel.* 5th ed. Baltimore
Aris. Ex.	*Aristeas the Exegete*
Aristob.	*Aristobulus*
ARM	Archives royales de Mari
ARMT	Archives royals de Mari: transcriptions et traductions
ARNA	*Ancient Records from North Arabia,* ed. F. V. Winnett and W. L. Reed. Toronto, 1970
ArOr	*Archiv orientální*
art.	article
Art.	*Artapanus*
ARW	*Archiv für Religionswissenschaft*
AS	Assyriological Studies
ASAE	*Annales du Service des antiquités de l'Egypte*
ASAW	*Abhandlungen der Sächsischen Akademie der Wissenschaften in Leipzig*
Asc. Jas.	*Ascents of James*
Ascen. Is.	*Ascension of Isaiah*
Asclepius	*Asclepius 21–29* (NHC VI,*8*)
ASNU	Acta seminarii neotestamentici upsaliensis
ASORDS	American Schools of Oriental Research Dissertation Series

ASORMS	American Schools of Oriental Research Monograph Series
ASP	American Studies in Papyrology
ASS	*Acta sanctae sedis*
AsSeign	*Assemblées du Seigneur*
ASSR	*Archives des sciences sociales des religions*
Assum. Mos.	*Assumption of Moses*
Assum. Vir.	*Assumption of the Virgin*
Assur	*Assur,* Malibu, CA
ASTI	*Annual of the Swedish Theological Institute*
ASV	American Standard Version
ATAbh	Alttestamentliche Abhandlungen
ATANT	Abhandlungen zur Theologie des Alten und Neuen Testaments
ATAT	Arbeiten zu Text und Sprache im Alten Testament
ATD	Das Alte Testament Deutsch
ATDan	Acta theologica danica
ATG	*Archivo Teológico Granadino,* Granada
ATJ	*Ashland Theological Journal,* Ashland, OH
ATR	*Anglican Theological Review,* Evanston, IL
Aug	*Augustinianum,* Rome
AulaOr	*Aula Orientalis,* Barcelona
AuS	G. Dalman. 1928–42. *Arbeit und Sitte in Palästina.* 7 vols. BFCT 14, 17, 27, 29, 33, 36, 41. Gütersloh, 1928. Repr. Hildesheim, 1964
AusBR	*Australian Biblical Review*
AUSS	*Andrews University Seminary Studies,* Berrien Springs, MI
Auth. Teach.	*Authoritative Teaching* (NHC VI,*3*)
AUU	Acta universitatis upsaliensis
AV	Authorized Version
AW	*The Ancient World,* Chicago
AWEAT	Archiv für wissenschaftliche Erforschung des Alten Testaments
B	Codex Vaticanus
b. (Talm.)	Babylonian (Talmud) = "Babli"
B. Bat.	*Baba Batra*
B. Meṣ.	*Baba Meṣiʿa*
B. Qam.	*Baba Qamma*
BA	*Biblical Archaeologist*
Bab.	Babylonian
BAC	Biblioteca de autores cristianos
BAEO	Boletín de la asociación españala des orientalistas
BAfO	*Beihefte zur Archiv für Orientforschung,* Graz
BAGD	W. Bauer, W. F. Arndt, F. W. Gingrich, and F. W. Danker. 1979. *Greek-English Lexicon of the New Testament.* 2d ed. Chicago
BAIAS	*Bulletin of the Anglo-Israel Archaeological Society,* London
BANE	*The Bible in the Ancient Near East,* ed. G. E. Wright. Garden City, NY, 1961. Repr. Winona Lake, IN, 1979
Bar	Baruch
BAR	*Biblical Archaeologist Reader*
Bar.	*Baraita*
BARev	*Biblical Archaeology Review*
BARIS	British Archaeological Reports, International Series
Barn.	*Epistle of Barnabas*
BASOR	*Bulletin of the American Schools of Oriental Research*
BASORSup	BASOR Supplement
BASP	*Bulletin of the American Society of Papyrologists*
BASPSup	Bulletin of the American Society of Papyrologists Supplement
BAss	Beiträge zur Assyriologie und semitischen Sprachwissenschaft
BAT	Die Botschaft des Alten Testaments
BBB	Bonner biblische Beiträge
BBC	Broadman Bible Commentary
BBET	Beiträge zur biblischen Exegese und Theologie
BBLAK	*Beiträge zur biblischen Landes- und Altertumskunde,* Stuttgart
B.C.	before Christ
BC	Biblical Commentary, ed. C. F. Keil and F. Delitzsch. Edinburgh.
B.C.E.	before the common (or Christian) era
BCH	*Bulletin du correspondance hellénique*
BCNHE	Bibliothèque copte de Nag Hammadi Section Études
BCNHT	Bibliothèque copte de Nag Hammadi Section Textes
BCPE	*Bulletin de Centre Protestant d'Études,* Geneva
BDB	F. Brown, S. R. Driver, and C. A. Briggs. 1907. *A Hebrew and English Lexicon of the Old Testament.* Oxford
BDF	F. Blass, A. Debrunner, and R. W. Funk. 1961. *A Greek Grammar of the New Testament and Other Early Christian Literature.* Chicago
BDR	F. Blass, A. Debrunner, and F. Rehkopf. 1984. *Grammatik des neutestamentlichen Griechisch.* 16th ed. Göttingen
BE	*Bulletin epigraphique,* ed. P. Gauthier. Paris
BE	Bibliothèque d'étude (Institut français d'Archéologie orientale)
BEFAR	Bibliothèque des Écoles françaises d'Athènes et de Rome
Bek.	*Bekorot*
Bel	Bel and the Dragon
Bened	*Benedictina,* Rome

BeO	*Bibbia e oriente,* Bornato
Ber.	*Berakot*
Berytus	*Berytus,* Beirut, Lebanon
BES	*Bulletin of the Egyptological Seminar,* Chico, CA
Beṣa	*Beṣa (= Yom Ṭob)*
Beth Mikra	*Beth Mikra,* Jerusalem
BETL	Bibliotheca ephemeridum theologicarum lovaniensium
BEvT	Beiträge zur evangelischen Theologie
BFCT	Beiträge zur Förderung christlicher Theologie
BGBE	Beiträge zur Geschichte der biblischen Exegese
BGU	*Berlin Griechische Urkunden*
BHG	*Bibliotheca Hagiographica Graeca.* Brussels, 1909
BHH	*Biblisch-Historisches Handwörterbuch,* ed. B. Reicke and L. Rost. Göttingen, 1962
BHI	J. Bright. 1981. *A History of Israel.* 3d ed. Philadelphia
BHK	*Biblia hebraica,* 3d ed., ed. R. Kittel
BHNTC	Black's/Harper's New Testament Commentaries
BHS	*Biblia hebraica stuttgartensia*
BHT	Beiträge zur historischen Theologie
BIATC	*Bulletin d'information de l'Académie de Théologie Catholique,* Warsaw
Bib	*Biblica,* Rome
BibAT	*Biblical Archeology Today: Proceedings of the International Congress on Biblical Archaeology, Jerusalem, April 1984.* Jerusalem, 1985
BibB	Biblische Beiträge
BibBh	*Biblebhashyam,* Kerala, India
bibliog.	bibliography
BibOr	Biblica et orientalia
BibS(F)	Biblische Studien (Freiburg, 1895–)
BibS(N)	Biblische Studien (Neukirchen, 1951–)
BIES	*Bulletin of the Israel Exploration Society (= Yediot)*
BIFAO	*Bulletin de l'institute français d'archéologie orientale,* Cairo
Bij	*Bijdragen: Tijdschrift voor Filosofie en Theologie,* Amsterdam
Bik.	*Bikkurim*
BiMes	Bibliotheca Mesopotamica
BIN	*Babylonian Inscriptions in the Collection of James B. Nies,* New Haven, 1917–54
BiOr	*Bibliotheca Orientalis,* Leiden
BIOSCS	*Bulletin of the International Organization for Septuagint and Cognate Studies*
BJPES	*Bulletin of the Jewish Palestine Exploration Society (= Yediot;* later *BIES)*
BJRL	*Bulletin of the John Rylands University Library of Manchester*
BJS	Brown Judaic Studies
BK	*Bibel und Kirche,* Stuttgart
BK	E. Bresciani and M. Kamil. 1966. Le lettere aramaiche di Hermopoli. *AANLM* 12/5: 357–428
bk.	book
Bk. Barn.	*Book of the Resurrection of Christ by Barnabas the Apostle*
Bk. Elch.	*Book of Elchasai*
Bk. Noah	*Book of Noah*
BKAT	Biblischer Kommentar: Altes Testament
BLE	*Bulletin de littérature ecclésiastique,* Toulouse
BLe	H. Bauer and P. Leander. 1918–22. *Historische Grammatik der hebräischen Sprache.* Halle, Repr. Hildesheim, 1962
BLit	*Bibel und Liturgie,* Klosterneuburg
BMAP	E. G. Kraeling. 1953. *The Brooklyn Museum Aramaic Papyri.* New Haven. Repr. 1969
BMMA	*Bulletin of the Metropolitan Museum of Art*
BMQ	*British Museum Quarterly*
BMS	*The Bible in Modern Scholarship,* ed. J. P. Hyatt. Nashville, 1965
BN	*Biblische Notizen,* Bamberg
Bo	Unpublished Boğazköy tablets (with catalog number)
BOSA	*Bulletin on Sumerian Agriculture,* Cambridge
B.P.	before (the) present (time)
BR	*Biblical Research,* Chicago
BRev	*Bible Review*
BRevuo	*Biblia Revuo,* Ravenna
BRL	K. Galling. 1937. *Biblisches Reallexikon.* Tübingen
BRM	*Babylonian Records in the Library of J. Pierpont Morgan,* ed. A. T. Clay, New York, 1912–23
BSac	*Bibliotheca Sacra*
BSAW	*Berichte über die Verhandlungen der Sächsischen Akademie der Wissenschaften zu Leipzig,* phil.-hist. Kl.
BSC	Bible Study Commentary
BSFE	*Bulletin de la Société française d'égyptologie*
BSOAS	*Bulletin of the School of Oriental and African Studies*
BTAVO	Beihefte zum Tübinger Atlas des Vorderen Orients
BTB	*Biblical Theology Bulletin*
BTF	*Bangalore Theological Forum,* Bangalore

BTNT	R. Bultmann. 1955. *Theology of the New Testament.* 2 vols. Trans. K. Grobel. New York and London
BToday	*Bible Today,* Collegeville, MN
BTrans	*Bible Translator,* Aberdeen
BTS	*Bible et terre sainte*
BTZ	*Berliner Theologische Zeitschrift*
BU	Biblische Untersuchungen
BuA	B. Meissner. 1920–25. *Babylonien und Assyrien.* 2 vols. Heidelberg
Burg	*Burgense,* Burgos, Spain
BurH	*Buried History,* Melbourne, Australia
BVC	*Bible et vie chrétienne*
BWANT	Beiträge zur Wissenschaft vom Alten und Neuen Testament
BWL	W. G. Lambert. 1960. *Babylonian Wisdom Literature.* Oxford
ByF	*Biblia y Fe,* Madrid, Spain
BZ	*Biblische Zeitschrift,* Paderborn
BZAW	Beihefte zur *ZAW*
BZNW	Beihefte zur *ZNW*
BZRGG	Beihefte zur *ZRGG*
BZVO	Berliner Beitrage zum Vorderen Orient
C	Codex Ephraemi
C&AH	*Catastrophism and Ancient History,* Los Angeles
ca.	*circa* (about, approximately)
CaByr	*Cahiers de Byrsa*
CAD	*The Assyrian Dictionary of the Oriental Institute of the University of Chicago*
CaE	*Cahiers Evangile,* Paris
CAH	*Cambridge Ancient History*
CahRB	Cahiers de la Revue biblique
CahThéol	Cahiers Théologiques
CaJ	*Cahiers de Josephologie,* Montreal
Cant	Song of Songs (or Canticles)
CaNum	*Cahiers de Numismatique,* Bologna
CAP	A. E. Cowley. 1923. *Aramaic Papyri of the Fifth Century B.C.* Oxford [cited by document number]
CAT	Commentaire de l'Ancient Testament
Cath	*Catholica,* Münster
Cav. Tr.	*Cave of Treasures*
CB	*Cultura biblica*
CBC	Cambridge Bible Commentary on the New English Bible
CBQ	*Catholic Biblical Quarterly,* Washington, DC
CBQMS	Catholic Biblical Quarterly Monograph Series
CBSC	Cambridge Bible for Schools and Colleges
CC	*Cross Currents,* West Nyack, NY
CCath	Corpus Catholicorum
CCER	*Cahiers du Cercle Ernest Renan,* Paris
CChr	Corpus Christianorum
CD	Cairo (Genizah), Damascus Document [= S. Schechter, *Documents of Jewish Sectaries,* vol. 1, *Fragments of a Zadokite Work,* Cambridge, 1910. Repr. New York, 1970]
CdÉ	*Chronique d'Égypte,* Brussels
C.E.	common (or Christian) era
Cerinthus	*Cerinthus*
cf.	*confer,* compare
CGTC	Cambridge Greek Testament Commentary
CGTSC	Cambridge Greek Testament for Schools and Colleges
CH	*Church History*
CH	Code of Hammurabi [cited according to G. R. Driver and J. C. Miles, eds. 1952–55. *The Babylonian Laws.* 2 vols. Oxford]
CHAL	*A Concise Hebrew and Aramaic Lexicon of the Old Testament,* ed. W. L. Holladay. Grand Rapids, 1971
chap(s).	chapter(s)
CHB	*The Cambridge History of the Bible,* 3 vols., ed. P. R. Ackroyd, G. W. M. Lampe, and S. L. Greenslade. Cambridge, 1963–70
CHD	Chicago Hittite Dictionary
Cher	Philo, *De cherubim*
CHI	*Cambridge History of Iran*
CHJ	*The Cambridge History of Judaism,* ed. W. D. Davies and L. Finkelstein. Cambridge, 1984–
CHR	*Catholic Historical Review*
CHSP	*Center for Hermeneutical Studies Protocol Series,* Berkeley, CA
CIG	*Corpus inscriptionum graecarum*
CII	*Corpus inscriptionum indicarum*
CIJ	*Corpvs inscriptionvm ivdaicarvm,* ed. J. B. Frey. Sussidi allo studio delle antichità cristiane, pub. per cura del Pontificio istituto di archeologia cristiana 1, 3. Vatican City, 1936–52
CIL	*Corpus inscriptionum latinarum*
CIS	*Corpus inscriptionum semiticarum*
CiuD	*Ciudad de Dios,* Madrid
CJ	*Concordia Journal,* St. Louis, MO
CJT	*Canadian Journal of Theology*
CL	*Communautés et Liturgies,* Ottignies, Belgium
CL	Code of Lipit-Ishtar [R. R. Steele. 1948. The Code of Lipit-Ishtar. *AJA* 52: 425–50]
Cl. Mal.	*Cleodemus Malchus*
CLA	*Canon Law Abstracts,* Melrose, Scotland
cm	centimeter(s)

CMHE	F. M. Cross. 1973. *Canaanite Myth and Hebrew Epic.* Cambridge, MA
CMIB	*Canadian Mediterranean Institute Bulletin,* Ottawa
CNFI	*Christian News From Israel,* Jerusalem, Israel
CNS	*Cristianesimo nella Storia,* Bologna, Italy
CNT	Commentaire du Nouveau Testament
CO	*Commentationes orientales,* Leiden
Col	Colossians
col(s).	column(s)
Coll	*Collationes,* Brugge, Belgium
Colloquium	*Colloquium,* Auckland/Sydney
ColT	*Collectanea Theologica,* Warsaw
comp.	compiled, compiler
ComViat	*Communio Viatorum,* Prague
ConBNT	Coniectanea biblica, New Testament
ConBOT	Coniectanea biblica, Old Testament
Concilium	Concilium
Conf	Philo, *De confusione linguarum*
Congr	Philo, *De congressu eruditionis gratia*
conj.	conjunction; conjugation
ConNT	*Coniectanea neotestamentica*
constr.	construction; construct
ContiRossini	K. Conti Rossini. 1931. *Chrestomathia Arabica meridionalis ephigraphica,* Rome
COut	Commentaar op het Oude Testament
CP	*Classical Philology*
CPJ	*Corpus papyrorum Judicarum,* ed. A. Tcherikover. 3 vols. Cambridge, MA, 1957–64
CQ	*Church Quarterly*
CQR	*Church Quarterly Review*
CR	*Clergy Review,* London
CRAIBL	*Comptes rendus de l'Académie des inscriptions et belles-lettres*
CRBR	*Critical Review of Books in Religion*
CRINT	Compendia rerum iudaicarum ad novum testamentum
CRRA	*Compte Rendu de . . . Recontre Assyriologique Internationale*
Crux	*Crux,* Vancouver, BC
CS	*Chicago Studies,* Mundelein, IL
CSCO	Corpus scriptorum christianorum orientalium
CSEL	Corpus scriptorum ecclesiasticorum latinorum
CSR	*Christian Scholars Review,* Houghton, NY
CT	*Cuneiform Texts from Babylonian Tablets . . . in the British Museum,* London, 1896–
CT	*The Egyptian Coffin Texts,* ed. A. de Buck and A. H. Gardiner. Chicago, 1935–47
CTA	A. Herdner. 1963. *Corpus des tablettes en cunéiformes alphabétiques découvertes à Ras Shamra-Ugarit de 1929 à 1939.* MRS 10. Paris
CTAED	S. Ahituv. 1984. *Canaanite Toponyms in Ancient Egyptian Documents.* Jerusalem
CTH	E. Laroche. 1971. *Catalogue des textes hittites.* Paris
CThM	Calwer Theologische Monographien
CTJ	*Calvin Theological Journal,* Grand Rapids, MI
CTM	*Concordia Theological Monthly*
CToday	*Christianity Today,* Carol Stream, IL
CTQ	*Concordia Theological Quarterly,* Fort Wayne, IN
CTSAP	*Catholic Theological Society of America Proceedings,* New York
CTSSR	College Theology Society Studies in Religion
CU	Code of Ur-Nammu [J. J. Finkelstein. 1960. The Laws of Ur-Nammu. *JCS* 14: 66–82; F. Yildiz. 1981. A Tablet of Codex Ur-Nammu from Sippar. *Or* 58: 87–97]
CurTM	*Currents in Theology and Mission,* Chicago
D	"Deuteronomic" source; or Codex Bezae
DACL	*Dictionnaire d'archéologie chrétienne et de liturgie*
DAGR	*Dictionnaire des antiquités grecques et romaines d'après les textes et les monuments,* ed. C. Daremberg and E. Saglio. 4 vols. Paris, 1877–1919
Dan	Daniel
DB	*Dictionnaire de la Bible,* 5 vols., ed. F. Vigouroux. Paris, 1895–1912
DBAT	*Dielheimer Blätter zum Alten Testament*
DBM	*Deltion Biblikon Meleton,* Athens
DBSup	*Dictionnaire de la Bible, Supplément,* ed. L. Pirot, A. Robert, H. Cazelles, and A. Feuillet. Paris, 1928–
DBTh	*Dictionary of Biblical Theology,* 2d ed., ed. X. Léon-Dufour. Trans. E. M. Stewart. New York, 1973
DC	*Doctor Communis,* Vatican City
DD	*Dor le Dor,* Jerusalem
DDSR	*Duke Divinity School Review*
Dec	Philo, *De decalogo*
Dem.	*Demetrius (the Chronographer)*
Dem.	*Demai*
Deo	Philo, *De Deo*
Der. Er. Rab.	*Derek Ereṣ Rabba*
Der. Er. Zuṭ.	*Derek Ereṣ Zuṭa*
Deut	Deuteronomy

DH	Deuteronomistic History/Historian
DHRP	Dissertationes ad historiam religionum pertinentes
Diakonia	*Diakonia,* Vienna
Dial. Sav.	*Dialogue of the Savior* (NHC III,5)
Dial. Trypho	Justin, *Dialogue with Trypho*
Did	*Didaskalia,* Portugal
Did.	*Didache*
Diogn.	*Epistle to Diognetes*
Direction	*Direction,* Fresno, CA
Disc. 8–9	*Discourse on the Eighth and Ninth* (NHC VI,6)
DISO	C.-F. Jean and J. Hoftijzer. 1965. *Dictionnaire des inscriptions sémitiques de l'ouest.* Leiden
diss.	dissertation
div.	division
Div	*Divinitas,* Vatican City
DivT	*Divus Thomas,* Piacenza, Italy
DJD	Discoveries in the Judean Desert
DL	*Doctrine and Life,* Dublin
DMOA	Documenta et Monumenta Orientis Antiqui
DN	divine name
DÖAW	*Denkschriften der Österreichischer Akademie der Wissenschaften,* Vienna
DOSA	J. Biella. 1982. *Dictionary of Old South Arabic: Sabaean Dialect.* HSS 25. Chico, CA
DOTT	*Documents from Old Testament Times,* ed. D. W. Thomas. Edinburgh, 1958. Repr. New York, 1961
DRev	*The Downside Review,* Bath
DS	Denzinger-Schönmetzer, *Enchiridion symbolorum*
DTC	*Dictionnaire de théologie catholique*
DTT	*Dansk Teologisk Tidsskrift,* Copenhagen
DunRev	*Dunwoodie Review*
E	east(ern); or "Elohist" source
EA	Tell el-Amarna tablets [cited from J. A. Knudtzon, O. Weber, and E. Ebeling, *Die El-Amarna Tafeln,* 2 vols., VAB 2, Leipzig, 1915; and A. F. Rainey, *El-Amarna Tablets 359–379: Supplement to J. A. Knudtzon, Die El-Amarna Tafeln,* 2d rev. ed., AOAT 8, Kevelaer and Neukirchen-Vluyn, 1970]
EAEHL	*Encyclopedia of Archaeological Excavations in the Holy Land,* 4 vols., ed. M. Avi-Yonah, 1975
EAJET	*East Africa Journal of Evangelical Theology,* Machakos, Kenya
EAJT	*East Asia Journal of Theology,* Singapore
EB	Early Bronze (Age); or Echter Bibel
EBib	Études bibliques
Ebr	Philo, *De ebrietate*
Ec	*The Ecumenist,* New York, NY
Eccl *or* Qoh	Ecclesiastes or Qoheleth
EcR	*The Ecumenical Review,* Geneva
Ecu	*Ecumenismo,* Ravenna, Italy
ed.	editor(s); edition; edited by
ED	Early Dynastic period
ᶜEd.	*ᶜEduyyot*
EDB	*Encyclopedic Dictionary of the Bible,* ed. and trans. L. F. Hartman. New York, 1963
e.g.	*exempli gratia* (for example)
Eg	Egyptian
ÉgT	*Église et Théologie,* Ottawa
EHAT	Exegetisches Handbuch zum Alten Testament
EHI	R. de Vaux. 1978. *The Early History of Israel.* Trans. D. Smith. Philadelphia
EHS	Einleitung in die Heilige Schrift
EI	*Eretz Israel*
EJ	*Encyclopedia Judaica,* 10 vols., ed. J. Klutzkin and I. Elbogen. Berlin, 1928–34
EKKNT	Evangelisch-katholischer Kommentar zum Neuen Testament
EKL	*Evangelisches Kirchenlexikon*
El. Mod.	*Eldad and Modad*
EM	*Ephemerides Mexicanae,* Mexico City
Emm	*Emmanuel,* New York
EncBib	*Encyclopaedia Biblica,* ed. T. K. Cheyne. London, 1800–1903. 2d ed. 1958
EncBibBarc	*Enciclopedia de la Biblia,* ed. A. Diez Macho and S. Bartina. Barcelona, 1963–65
EncBrit	*Encyclopaedia Britannica*
EnchBib	*Enchiridion biblicum*
EncJud	*Encyclopaedia Judaica* (1971)
EncMiqr	*Entsiqlopēdiā Miqrāʾīt-Encyclopaedia Biblica,* Jerusalem, 1950–
EncRel	*Encyclopedia of Religion,* 16 vols., ed. M. Eliade. New York, 1987
Eng	English
Entr	*Encounter,* Indianapolis, IN
Ep Jer	Epistle of Jeremiah
Ep. Alex.	*Epistle to the Alexandrians*
Ep. Apos.	*Epistle to the Apostles*
Ep. Barn.	*Epistle of Barnabas*
Ep. Chr. Abg.	*Epistle of Christ and Abgar*
Ep. Chr. Heav.	*Epistle of Christ from Heaven*
Ep. Lao.	*Epistle to the Laodiceans*
Ep. Lent.	*Epistle of Lentulus*
Ep. Paul Sen.	*Epistles of Paul and Seneca*

Ep. Pet. Phil.	*Letter of Peter to Philip* (NHC VIII,*2*)
Ep. Pol.	*Epistles of Polycarp*
Ep. Tit. (Apoc.)	*Apocryphal Epistle of Titus*
Eph	Ephesians
Eph.	see *Ign. Eph.*
EphC	*Ephemerides Carmelitica,* Rome
Ephem	M. Lidzbarski. 1900–15. *Ephemeris für semitische Epigraphik.* 3 vols. Giessen
EphLit	*Ephemerides Liturgicae,* Rome
EphMar	*Ephemerides Mariologicae,* Madrid
EPRO	Études préliminaires aux religions orientales dans l'Empire romain
ER	*Epworth Review,* London
ErbAuf	*Erbe und Auftrag*
ERE	*Encyclopaedia of Religion and Ethics,* 12 vols., ed. J. Hastings. Edinburgh and New York, 1908–22
ErFor	Erträge der Forschung
ErfThSt	Erfurter Theologische Studien
ErJb	*Eranos Jahrbuch*
ERT	*Evangelical Review of Theology,* Exeter
ᶜErub.	*ᶜErubin*
Escr Vedat	*Escritos del Vedat,* Torrente
esp.	especially
EspVie	*Esprit et Vie.,* Langres
EstBib	*Estudios Bíblicos,* Madrid
EstEcl	*Estudios Eclesiásticos,* Barcelona
EstFranc	*Estudios Franciscanos,* Barcelona
Esth	Esther
EstTeo	*Estudios Teológicos,* São Leopoldo, Brazil
ET	English translation
et al.	*et alii* (and others)
etc.	*et cetera* (and so forth)
Eth	Ethiopic
ETL	*Ephemerides Theologicae Lovanienses,* Louvain
ETOT	W. Eichrodt. 1961–67. *Theology of the Old Testament.* 2 vols. Trans. J. A. Baker. Philadelphia
ÉTR	*Études théologiques et Religieuses,* Montpellier, France
Études	*Études,* Paris
Eugnostos	*Eugnostos the Blessed* (NHC III,*3*; V,*1*)
EuntDoc	*Euntes Docete,* Rome
Eup.	*Eupolemus*
EV(V)	English version(s)
EvJ	*Evangelical Journal,* Myerstown, PA
EvK	Evangelische Kommentare
EvQ	*Evangelical Quarterly,* Derbyshire
EvT	*Evangelische Theologie,* Munich
EWNT	*Exegetisches Wörterbuch zum Neuen Testament,* ed. H. Balz and G. Schneider
Ex	*Explor,* Evanston, IL
ExB	Expositor's Bible
Exeg. Soul	*Exegesis on the Soul* (NHC II,*6*)
Exod	Exodus
ExpTim	*Expository Times,* Surrey
Ezek	Ezekiel
Ezek. Trag.	*Ezekiel the Tragedian*
Ezra	Ezra
f(f).	following page(s)
FAS	Freiburger Altorientalische Studien
FB	Forschuung zur Bibel
FBBS	Facet Books, Biblical Series
FC	Fathers of the Church
fc.	forthcoming (publication)
fem.	feminine; female
FFNT	Foundations and Facets: New Testament
FGLP	Forschungen zur Geschichte und Lehre des Protestantismus
FGrH	F. Jacoby. *Die Fragmente der griechischen Historiker.* 2d ed. 3 vols. in 10 pts. Leiden, 1957–64 [cited by fragment no.]
FH	*Fides et Historia,* Grand Rapids
fig(s).	figure(s)
FKT	*Forum Katholische Theologie,* Aschaffenburg
fl.	*floruit* (flourished)
Flacc	Philo, *In Flaccum*
FoiVie	*Foi et Vie,* Paris
Fond	*Fondamenti,* Bresica
Forum	*Forum,* Bonner, MT
FOTL	Forms of Old Testament Literature
FR	Freiburger Rundbrief
Fran	*Franciscanum,* Bogotá
Frg. Tg.	*Fragmentary Targum*
Frgs. Hist. Wrks.	*Fragments of Historical Works*
Frgs. Poet. Wrks.	*Fragments of Poetic Works*
FRLANT	Forschungen zur Religion und Literatur des Alten und Neuen Testaments
Frm.	*Fragments* (NHC XII,*3*)
FSAC	W. F. Albright. 1957. *From the Stone Age to Christianity.* 2d ed., repr. Garden City, NY
FTS	Freiburger Theologische Studien
FuF	*Forschungen und Fortschritte,* Berlin
Fuga	Philo, *De fuga et inventione*
Fund	*Fundamentum,* Riehen, Switzerland
Furrow	*Furrow,* Maynooth
FWSDFML	*Funk and Wagnall's Standard Dictionary of Folklore, Mythology and Legend*
FZPT	*Freiburger Zeitschrift für Philosophie und Theologie,* Fribourg
GAG	W. von Soden. 1969. *Grundriss der akkadischen Grammatik samt Ergänzungsheft.* AnOr 33/47. Rome

Gaium	Philo, *Legatio ad Gaium*
Gal	Galatians
GARI	A. K. Grayson. 1972. *Assyrian Royal Inscriptions.* RANE. Wiesbaden
GB	D. Baly. 1974. *The Geography of the Bible.* 2d ed. New York
GBS	Guides to Biblical Scholarship
GCS	Griechischen christlichen Schriftsteller
Gem.	*Gemara*
Gen	Genesis
GesB	W. Gesenius. *Hebräisches und aramäisches Handwörterbuch,* 17th ed., ed. F. Buhl. Berlin, 1921
GGR	M. P. Nilsson. *Geschichte der griechische Religion.* 2 vols. 2d ed. Munich, 1961
GHBW	R. R. Wilson. 1977. *Genealogy and History in the Biblical World.* YNER 7. New Haven
Gig	Philo, *De gigantibus*
Giṭ.	*Giṭṭin*
GJV	E. Schürer. 1901–9. *Geschichte des jüdisches Volkes im Zeitalter Jesu Christi.* Leipzig. Repr. Hildesheim, 1970
Gk	Greek
GK	*Gesenius' Hebräische Grammatik,* 28th ed., ed. by E. Kautzsch. Leipzig, 1909. Repr. Hildesheim, 1962
Gk. Apoc. Ezra	*Greek Apocalypse of Ezra*
GKB	G. Bergsträsser. 1918–29. *Hebräische Grammatik mit Benutzung der von E. Kautzsch bearbeiteten 28. Auflage von Wilhelm Gesenius' hebräischer Grammatik.* 2 vols. Leipzig. Repr. Hildesheim, 1962
GKC	*Gesenius' Hebrew Grammar,* 28th ed., ed. E. Kautzsch. Trans. A. E. Cowley. Oxford, 1910
GLECS	*Comptes Rendus du Groupe Linguistique d'Études Chamito-Sémitiques,* Paris
GM	*Göttinger Miszellen*
GN	geographical name
GNB	Good News Bible
GNC	Good News Commentary
GNS	Good News Studies
GNT	Grundrisse zum Neuen Testament
GO	Göttinger Orientforschungen
Gos. Barn.	*Gospel of Barnabas*
Gos. Bart.	*Gospel of Bartholomew*
Gos. Bas.	*Gospel of Basilides*
Gos. Bir. Mary	*Gospel of the Birth of Mary*
Gos. Eb.	*Gospel of the Ebionites*
Gos. Eg.	*Gospel of the Egyptians* (NHC III,*2*; IV,*2*)
Gos. Eve	*Gospel of Eve*
Gos. Gam.	*Gospel of Gamaliel*
Gos. Heb.	*Gospel of the Hebrews*
Gos. Inf.	*Infancy Gospels*
Gos. Inf. (Arab)	*Arabic Gospel of the Infancy*
Gos. Inf. (Arm)	*Armenian Gospel of the Infancy*
Gos. John (Apocr.)	*Apocryphal Gospel of John*
Gos. Marcion	*Gospel of Marcion*
Gos. Mary	*Gospel of Mary*
Gos. Naass.	*Gospel of the Naassenes*
Gos. Naz.	*Gospel of the Nazarenes*
Gos. Nic.	*Gospel of Nicodemus*
Gos. Pet.	*Gospel of Peter*
Gos. Phil.	*Gospel of Philip* (NHC II,*3*)
Gos. Thom.	*Gospel According to Thomas* (NHC II,*2*)
Gos. Trad. Mth.	*Gospel and Traditions of Matthias*
Gos. Truth	*Gospel of Truth* (NHC I,*3*; XII,*2*)
GOTR	*Greek Orthodox Theological Review,* Brookline, MA
GP	F. M. Abel. 1933. *Géographie de la Palestine,* 2 vols. Paris
GRBS	*Greek, Roman and Byzantine Studies,* Durham, NC
Great Pow.	*The Concept of Our Great Power* (NHC VI,*4*)
Greg	*Gregorianum,* Rome
GSAT	*Gesammelte Studien zum Alten Testament,* Munich
GTA	Göttinger theologische Arbeiten
GTJ	*Grace Theological Journal,* Winona Lake, IN
GTT	*Gereformeerd Theologisch Tijdschrift,* Netherlands
GTTOT	J. J. Simons. 1959. *The Geographical and Topographical Texts of the Old Testament.* Francisci Scholten memoriae dedicata 2. Leiden
GuL	*Geist und Leben,* Munich
GVG	C. Brockelmann. 1903–13. *Grundriss der vergleichenden Grammatik der semitischen Sprachen.* 2 vols. Berlin. Repr. 1961
ha.	hectares
Hab	Habakkuk
HAB	*Harper's Atlas of the Bible*
HÄB	Hildesheimer ägyptologische Beiträge
HAD	*Hebrew and Aramaic Dictionary of the OT,* ed. G. Fohrer. Trans W. Johnstone. Berlin, 1973
Hag	Haggai
Ḥag.	*Ḥagiga*
HAIJ	J. M. Miller and J. H. Hayes. 1986. *A History of Ancient Israel and Judah.* Philadelphia
Ḥal.	*Ḥalla*
HALAT	*Hebräisches und aramäisches Lexikon zum Alten Testament,* ed. W. Baumgartner et al.
HAR	*Hebrew Annual Review*

HAT	Handbuch zum Alten Testament
HAW	Handbuch der Altertumswissenschaft
HBC	*Harper's Bible Commentary*
HBD	*Harper's Bible Dictionary,* ed. P. J. Achtemeier. San Francisco, 1985
HBT	*Horizons in Biblical Theology,* Pittsburgh, PA
HDB	*Dictionary of the Bible,* 4 vols., ed. by J. Hastings et al. Edinburgh and New York, 1899–1904. Rev. by F. C. Grant and H. H. Rowley, 1963
HDR	Harvard Dissertations in Religion
HDS	Harvard Dissertation Series
Hdt.	Herodotus
Heb	Hebrew; Epistle to the Hebrews
Heb. Apoc. El.	*Hebrew Apocalypse of Elijah*
Hec. Ab	*Hecataeus of Abdera*
Hel. Syn. Pr.	*Hellenistic Synagogal Prayers*
Hen	*Henoch,* Torino, Italy
Heres	Philo, *Quis rerum divinarum heres*
Herm	*Hermathena,* Dublin, Ireland
Herm. Man.	*Hermas, Mandate*
Herm. Sim.	*Hermas, Similitude*
Herm. Vis.	*Hermas, Vision*
Hermeneia	Hermeneia: A Critical and Historical Commentary on the Bible
Ḥev	Naḥal Ḥever texts
HeyJ	*The Heythrop Journal,* London
HG	J. Friedrich. 1959. *Die hethitischen Gesetze.* DMOA 7. Leiden
HGB	Z. Kallai. 1986. *Historical Geography of the Bible.* Leiden
HHI	S. Herrmann. 1975. *A History of Israel in Old Testament Times.* 2d ed. Philadelphia
HibJ	*Hibbert Journal*
HIOTP	H. Jagersma. 1983. *A History of Israel in the Old Testament Period.* Trans. J. Bowden. Philadelphia
Hist. Eccl.	Eusebius, *Historia ecclesiastica* (= *Church History*)
Hist. Jos.	*History of Joseph*
Hist. Jos. Carp.	*History of Joseph the Carpenter*
Hist. Rech.	*History of the Rechabites*
Hit	Hittite
HJP[1]	E. Schürer. *The History of the Jewish People in the Time of Jesus Christ,* 5 vols., trans. J. Macpherson, S. Taylor, and P. Christie. Edinburgh, 1886–90
HJP[2]	E. Schürer. *The History of the Jewish People in the Age of Jesus Christ,* 3 vols., ed. and trans. G. Vermes et al. Edinburgh, 1973–87
HKAT	Handkommentar zum Alten Testament
HKL	R. Borger. 1967–75. *Handbuch der Keilschriftliteratur.* 3 vols. Berlin
HKNT	Handkommentar zum Neuen Testament
HL	Hittite Laws [*ANET,* 188–97]
HM	*Hamizrah Hehadash/Near East,* Jerusalem
HNT	Handbuch zum Neuen Testament
HNTC	Harper's NT Commentaries
HO	Handbuch der Orientalistik
Hokhma	*Hokhma,* La Sarraz, Switzerland
Hor	*Horizons,* Villanova, PA
Hor.	*Horayot*
Hos	Hosea
HPR	*Homiletic and Pastoral Review,* New York
HPT	M. Noth. 1981. *A History of Pentateuchal Traditions.* Trans. B. Anderson. Chico, CA
HR	*History of Religions,* Chicago
HS	*Hebrew Studies,* Madison, WI
HSAO	*Heidelberger Studien zum Alten Orient.* Wiesbaden, 1967
HSAT	*Die heilige Schrift des Alten Testaments,* 4th ed., ed. E. Kautzsch and A. Bertholet. Tübingen, 1922–23
HSCL	Harvard Studies in Comparative Literature
HSCP	*Harvard Studies in Classical Philology,* Cambridge, MA
HSM	Harvard Semitic Monographs
HSS	Harvard Semitic Studies
HTKNT	Herders theologischer Kommentar zum Neuen Testament
HTR	*Harvard Theological Review*
HTS	Harvard Theological Studies
HUCA	*Hebrew Union College Annual,* Cincinnati
Ḥul.	*Ḥullin*
Hymn Dance	*Hymn of the Dance*
Hyp. Arch.	*Hypostasis of the Archons* (NHC II,*4*)
Hypo	Philo, *Hypothetica*
Hypsiph.	*Hypsiphrone* (NHC XI,*4*)
IB	*Interpreter's Bible*
IBC	Interpretation: A Bible Commentary for Teaching and Preaching
ibid.	*ibidem* (in the same place)
IBS	*Irish Biblical Studies,* Belfast
ICC	International Critical Commentary
IDB	*Interpreter's Dictionary of the Bible,* ed. G. A. Buttrick. 4 vols. Nashville, 1962
IDBSup	*Interpreter's Dictionary of the Bible Supplementary Volume,* ed. K. Crim. Nashville, 1976
IEJ	*Israel Exploration Journal,* Jerusalem
IG	*Inscriptiones Graecae*
IGRR	*Inscriptiones Graecae ad res Romanas pertinentes,* ed. R. Cagnat, J. Toutain, et al. 3 vols. Paris, 1901–27. Repr. Rome, 1964

Ign. Eph.	*Ignatius, Letter to the Ephesians*
Ign. Magn.	*Ignatius, Letter to the Magnesians*
Ign. Phld.	*Ignatius, Letter to the Philadelphians*
Ign. Pol.	*Ignatius, Letter to the Polycarp*
Ign. Rom.	*Ignatius, Letter to the Romans*
Ign. Symrn.	*Ignatius, Letter to the Smyrnaeans*
Ign. Trall.	*Ignatius, Letter to the Trallians*
IGLS	Jalabert, L., and Mouterde, R. 1929–. *Inscriptions grecques et latines de la Syrie.* 6 vols. Paris.
IGSK	Inschriften griechischer Städte aus Kleinasien
IJH	*Israelite and Judean History,* ed. J. Hayes and M. Miller. OTL. Philadelphia, 1977
IJT	*Indian Journal of Theology,* Calcutta
IKirZ	*Internationale Kirchliche Zeitschrift,* Bern
ILS	*Inscriptiones Latinae selectae,* ed. H. Dessau. 3 vols. in 5 pts. Berlin, 1892–1916. Repr.
Imm	*Immanuel,* Jerusalem
impf.	imperfect
impv.	imperative
inf.	infinitive
Inf. Gos. Thom.	*Infancy Gospel of Thomas*
INJ	*Israel Numismatic Journal,* Jerusalem
Int	*Interpretation,* Richmond, VA
Interp. Know.	*Interpretation of Knowledge* (NHC XI,*1*)
IOS	*Israel Oriental Studies*
IOTS	B. S. Childs. 1979. *Introduction to the Old Testament as Scripture.* Philadelphia
IPN	M. Noth. 1928. *Die israelitischen Personennamen.* BWANT 3/10. Stuttgart. Repr. Hildesheim, 1966
Iraq	*Iraq*
Irénikon	*Irénikon*
IRT	Issues in Religion and Theology
Isa	Isaiah
ISBE	*International Standard Bible Encyclopedia,* 2d ed., ed. G. W. Bromiley
ISEELA	*Instituto Superior de Estudios Eclesiasticos Libro Anual,* Mexico City
Istina	*Istina,* Paris
ITC	International Theological Commentary
ITQ	*Irish Theological Quarterly,* Maynooth
ITS	*Indian Theological Studies,* Bangalore
IvEph	*Die Inschriften von Ephesos,* ed. H. Wankel. 8 vols. IGSK 11–15
j. (*Talm.*)	Jerusalem (Talmud)
J	"Yahwist" source
JA	*Journal asiatique*
JAAR	*Journal of the American Academy of Religion*
JAC	*Jahrbuch für Antike und Christentum*
Jan. Jam.	*Jannes and Jambres*
JANES	*Journal of the Ancient Near Eastern Society of Columbia University,* New York
JAOS	*Journal of the American Oriental Society,* New Haven
JAOSSup	Journal of the American Oriental Society Supplement
JARCE	*Journal of the American Research Center in Egypt,* Boston
Jas	James
JAS	*Journal of Asian Studies*
JB	Jerusalem Bible
JBC	*The Jerome Biblical Commentary,* ed. R. E. Brown, J. A. Fitzmyer, and R. E. Murphy. 2 vols. in 1. Englewood Cliffs, NJ, 1968
JBL	*Journal of Biblical Literature*
JBR	*Journal of Bible and Religion,* Boston
JCS	*Journal of Cuneiform Studies*
JDAI	*Jahrbuch des deutschen archäologischen Instituts*
JDS	Judean Desert Studies
Jdt	Judith
JEA	*Journal of Egyptian Archaeology,* London
Jeev	*Jeevadhara,* Kottayam, Kerala, India
JEH	*Journal of Ecclesiastical History,* London
JEnc	*The Jewish Encyclopaedia,* 12 vols., ed. I. Singer et al. New York, 1901–6
JEOL	*Jaarbericht Vooraziatisch-Egyptisch Gezelschap "Ex Oriente Lux"*
Jer	Jeremiah
JES	*Journal of Ecumenical Studies,* Philadelphia
JESHO	*Journal of the Economic and Social History of the Orient,* Leiden
JETS	*Journal of the Evangelical Theological Society*
JFA	*Journal of Field Archaeology*
JFSR	*Journal of Feminist Studies in Religion,* Atlanta
JHNES	Johns Hopkins Near Eastern Studies
JHS	*Journal of Hellenic Studies,* London
JIBS	*Journal of Indian and Buddhist Studies*
JIPh	*Journal of Indian Philosophy*
JITC	*Journal of the Interdenominational Theological Center,* Atlanta
JJS	*Journal of Jewish Studies,* Oxford
JLA	*The Jewish Law Annual,* Leiden
JMES	*Journal of Middle Eastern Studies*
JMS	*Journal of Mithraic Studies*
JNES	*Journal of Near Eastern Studies,* Chicago
JNSL	*Journal of Northwest Semitic Languages,* Stellenbosch

Job	Job
Joel	Joel
John	John
Jonah	Jonah
Jos	Philo, *De Iosepho*
Jos. or Joseph.	Josephus
Jos. Asen.	*Joseph and Asenath*
Josh	Joshua
JPOS	*Journal of Palestine Oriental Society,* Jerusalem
JPSV	Jewish Publication Society Version
JPT	*Journal of Psychology and Theology,* La Mirada, CA
JQR	*Jewish Quarterly Review*
JQRMS	Jewish Quarterly Review Monograph Series
JR	*Journal of Religion,* Chicago
JRAI	*Journal of the Royal Anthropological Institute*
JRAS	*Journal of the Royal Asiatic Society*
JRE	*Journal of Religious Ethics*
JRelS	*Journal of Religious Studies,* Cleveland, OH
JRH	*Journal of Religious History*
JRS	*Journal of Roman Studies,* London
JRT	*Journal of Religious Thought,* Washington, DC
JSHRZ	Jüdische Schriften aus hellenistisch-römischer Zeit
JSJ	*Journal for the Study of Judaism,* Leiden
JSNT	*Journal for the Study of the New Testament,* Sheffield
JSNTSup	Journal for the Study of the New Testament Supplement Series
JSOT	*Journal for the Study of the Old Testament,* Sheffield
JSOTSup	Journal for the Study of the Old Testament Supplement Series
JSP	*Journal for the Study of the Pseudepigrapha*
JSPSup	Journal for the Study of the Pseudepigrapha Supplement
JSS	*Journal of Semitic Studies,* Manchester
JSSEA	*Journal of the Society for the Study of Egyptian Antiquities,* Mississauga, Ontario
JSSR	*Journal for the Scientific Study of Religion*
JTC	*Journal for Theology and the Church*
JTS	*Journal of Theological Studies,* Oxford
JTSoA	*Journal of Theology for Southern Africa,* Cape Town, South Africa
Jub.	*Jubilees*
Judaica	*Judaica: Beiträge zum Verständnis . . .*
Judaism	*Judaism,* New York
Jude	Jude
Judg	Judges
JW	Josephus, *The Jewish War (= Bellum Judaicum)*
JWH	*Journal of World History*
K	Kethib
K	Tablets in the Kouyunjik collection of the British Museum [cited by number]
KAI	*Kanaanäische und aramäische Inschriften,* 3 vols., ed. H. Donner and W. Röllig, Wiesbaden: Otto Harrassowitz, 1962
Kairos	*Kairos,* Salzburg
KAJ	*Keilschrifttexte aus Assur juristischen Inhalts,* ed. E. Ebeling. WVDOG 50. Leipzig, 1927
Kalla	*Kalla*
KAR	*Keilschrifttexte aus Assur religiösen Inhalts,* ed. E. Ebeling. WVDOG 28/34. Leipzig, 1919–23
KAT	Kommentar zum Alten Testament
KAV	*Keilschrifttexte aus Assur verschiedenen Inhalts,* ed. O. Schroeder. WVDOG 35. Leipzig, 1920
KB	*Keilschriftliche Bibliothek,* ed. E. Schrader. Berlin, 1889–1915
KB	L. Koehler and W. Baumgartner. 1953. *Lexicon in Veteris Testamenti libros.* Leiden; *Supplementum ad Lexicon in Veteris Testamenti libros.* Leiden, 1958
KBANT	Kommentare und Beiträge zum Alten und Neuen Testament
KBo	*Keilschrifttexte aus Boghazköi.* WVDOG 30/36/68–70/72– . Leipzig, 1916–23; Berlin, 1954–
KD	*Kerygma und Dogma,* Göttingen
KEHAT	*Kurzgefasstes exegetisches Handbuch zum Alten Testament,* ed. O. F. Fridelin, Leipzig, 1812–96
Kelim	*Kelim*
Ker.	*Keritot*
Ketub.	*Ketubot*
KG	H. Frankfort. 1948. *Kingship and the Gods.* Chicago. Repr. 1978
KHC	*Kurzer Handcommentar zum Alten Testament,* ed. K. Marti. Tübingen
Kil.	*Kilʾayim*
KJV	King James Version
KK	*Katorikku Kenkyu,* Tokyo, Japan
Klosterman	E. Klosterman. 1904. *Eusebius Das Onomastikon der Biblischen Ortsnamen.* Leipzig. Repr. 1966
KlPauly	*Der Kleine Pauly,* ed. K. Zeigler–W. Sontheimer, Stuttgart, 1964
KlSchr	*Kleine Schriften* (A. Alt, 1953–59, 1964 [3d ed.]; O. Eissfeldt, 1963–68; K. Ellinger, 1966)

KlT	Kleine Texte
km	kilometer(s)
KRI	K. Kitchen. 1968– . *Ramesside Inscriptions, Historical and Biographical.* 7 vols. Oxford
KRI	Y. Kaufmann. 1960. *The Religion of Israel.* Trans. M. Greenberg. New York
KTR	*King's Theological Review,* London
KTU	*Keilalphabetischen Texte aus Ugarit,* vol. 1, ed. M. Dietrich, O. Loretz, and J. Sanmartín. AOAT 24. Kevelaer and Neukirchen-Vluyn, 1976
KUB	Staatliche Museen zu Berlin, Voderasiatische Abteilung (later Deutsche Orient-Gesellschaft) *Keilschrifturkunden aus Boghazköi,* 1921–
LÄ	*Lexikon der Ägyptologie,* eds. W. Helck and E. Otto, Wiesbaden, 1972
L. A. B.	*Liber Antiquitatum Biblicarum*
Lad. Jac.	*Ladder of Jacob*
LAE	*The Literature of Ancient Egypt,* ed. W. K. Simpson. New Haven, 1972
L. A. E.	*Life of Adam and Eve*
Lam	Lamentations
Lane	E. W. Lane. 1863–93. *An Arabic-English Lexicon.* 8 vols. London. Repr. 1968
LAPO	Littératures anciennes du Proche-Orient
LAR	D. D. Luckenbill. 1926–27. *Ancient Records of Assyria and Babylonia.* Chicago
LÄS	Leipziger ägyptologische Studien
LAS	D. D. Luckenbill. 1924. *Annals of Sennacherib.* OIP 2. Chicago
LASBF	*Liber Annuus Studii Biblici Franciscani,* Jerusalem
Lat	Latin
Lat	*Lateranum,* Vatican City
Laur	*Laurentianum,* Rome
LavTP	*Laval Théologique et Philosophique,* Quebec
LB	Late Bronze (Age)
LB	*Linguistica Biblica,* Bonn
LBAT	*Late Babylonian Astronomical and Related Texts,* ed. T. G. Pinches and A. Sachs. Providence, RI, 1955
LBHG	Y. Aharoni. 1979. *The Land of the Bible,* 3d ed., rev. and enl. by A. F. Rainey. Philadelphia, 1979
LBS	Library of Biblical Studies
LCC	Library of Christian Classics
LCL	Loeb Classical Library
LD	Lectio divina
LE	Laws of Eshnunna [A. Goetze. 1956. *The Laws of Eshnunna.* AASOR 31. New Haven; *ANET,* 161–63]
Leg All I–III	Philo, *Legum allegoriae* I–III
Leš	*Lešonénu*
Let. Aris.	*Letter of Aristeas*
Lev	Leviticus
Levant	*Levant,* London
LexLingAeth	A. Dillmann. 1865. *Lexicon linguae aethiopicae.* Leipzig. Repr. New York, 1955; Osnabruck, 1970
LexSyr	C. Brockelmann. 1928. *Lexicon Syriacum.* 2d ed. Halle. Repr.
LHA	F. Zorrell. 1966. *Lexicon Hebraicum et Aramaicum Veteris Testamenti.* Rome
Life	Josephus, *Life (= Vita)*
List	*Listening: Journal of Religion and Culture,* River Forest, IL
lit.	literally
Liv. Pro.	*Lives of the Prophets*
LL	*The Living Light,* Washington, DC
LLAVT	*Lexicon Linguae aramaicae Veteris Testamenti documentis antiquis illustratum.* E. Vogt. 1971. Rome
loc. cit.	*loco citato* (in the place cited)
Lost Tr.	*The Lost Tribes*
LPGL	G. W. H. Lampe. 1961–68. *A Patristic Greek Lexicon.* Oxford
LQ	*Lutheran Quarterly*
LR	*Lutherische Rundschau*
LS	*Louvain Studies,* Louvain
LSJM	H. G. Liddell and R. Scott. 1968. *A Greek-English Lexicon.* rev. ed., ed. H. S. Jones and R. McKenzie. Oxford
LSS	Leipziger Semitistische Studien
LTJ	*Lutheran Theological Journal,* Adelaide, S. Australia
LTK	*Lexikon für Theologie und Kirche*
LTP	*Laval Théologique et Philosophique*
LTQ	*Lexington Theological Quarterly,* Lexington, KY
LUÅ	Lunds universitets årsskrift
Luc	Lucianic recension
Luke	Luke
LumVie	*Lumière et Vie,* Lyons, France
LumVit	*Lumen Vitae,* Brussels
LW	*Lutheran World*
LXX	Septuagint
m	meter(s)
MA	Middle Assyrian
Maarav	*Maarav,* Santa Monica, CA
Maᶜaś.	*Maᶜaśerot*
Maᶜaś. Š.	*Maᶜaśer Šeni*
MABL	*The Moody Atlas of Bible Lands,* ed. B. J. Beitzel. Chicago, 1985
Magn.	see *Ign. Magn.*
MaisDieu	*Maison-Dieu,* Paris

Mak.	*Makkot*
Makš.	*Makširin* (= *Mašqin*)
Mal	Malachi
MAL	Middle Assyrian Laws
MAMA	*Monumenta Asiae Minoris Antiqua,* vol. 1, ed. W. M. Calder and J. M. R. Cormack. Publications of the American Society for Archaeological Research in Asia Minor. Manchester, 1928. Vol. 3, ed. J. Keil and A. Wilhelm, 1931. Vol. 4, ed. W. H. Buckler, W. M. Calder, W. K. C. Guthrie, 1933. Vol. 5, ed. C. W. M. Cox and A. Cameron, 1937. Vol. 6, ed. W. H. Buckler and W. M. Calder, 1939
Man	*Manuscripta,* St. Louis, MO
MANE	*Monographs on the Ancient Near East,* Malibu, CA
Mansrea	*Mansrea,* Madrid
MAOG	Mitteilungen der Altorientalischen Gesellschaft, Leipzig
Marianum	*Marianum,* Rome
Mark	Mark
Marsanes	*Marsanes* (NHC XI,*1*)
MarSt	*Marian Studies,* Dayton, OH
Mart. Bart.	*Martyrdom of Bartholomew*
Mart. Is.	*Martyrdom of Isaiah*
Mart. Mt.	*Martyrdom of Matthew*
Mart. Paul	*Martyrdom of Paul*
Mat. Pet.	*Martyrdom of Peter*
Mart. Pet. Paul	*Martyrdom of Peter and Paul*
Mart. Phil.	*Martyrdom of Philip*
Mart. Pol.	*Martyrdom of Polycarp*
Mas	Masada texts
MÄS	Münchner Ägyptologische Studien
masc.	masculine
Matt	Matthew
May	*Mayéutica,* Marcilla (Navarra), Spain
MB	Middle Bronze (Age)
MB	*Le Monde de la Bible*
MBA	Y. Aharoni and M. Avi-Yonah. 1977. *The Macmillan Bible Atlas.* Rev. ed. New York
MC	*Miscelánea Comillas,* Madrid
MCBW	R. K. Harrison. 1985. *Major Cities of the Biblical World.* New York, 1985
McCQ	*McCormick Quarterly*
MD	E. S. Drower and R. Macuch. 1963. *Mandaic Dictionary.* Oxford
MDAIK	Mitteilungen des deutschen archäologischen Instituts, Kairo
MDOG	Mitteilungen der deutschen Orient-Gesellschaft
MDP	Mémoires de la délégation en Perse
MedHab	Epigraphic Expedition, *Medinet Habu.* OIP 8 (1930), 9 (1932), Chicago
Meg.	*Megilla*
Meᶜil.	*Meᶜila*
Mek.	*Mekilta*
Melch.	*Melchizedek* (NHC IX,*1*)
Melkon	*Melkon*
MelT	*Melita Theologica,* Rabat, Malta
Mem. Apos.	*Memoria of Apostles*
Menaḥ.	*Menaḥot*
MEOL	*Medeelingen en Verhandelingen van het Vooraziatisch-Egyptisch Gezelschap "Ex Oriente Lux,"* Leiden
Mer	*Merleg,* Munich
MeyerK	H. A. W. Meyer, Kritisch-exegetischer Kommentar über das Neue Testament
MGWJ	*Monatsschrift für Geschichte und Wissenschaft des Judentums*
mi.	mile(s)
Mic	Micah
Mid.	*Middot*
Midr.	*Midraš;* cited with usual abbreviation for biblical book; but *Midr. Qoh.* = *Midraš Qohelet*
MIFAO	Mémoires publiés par les membres de l'Institut français d'archéologie orientale du Caire
Migr	Philo, *De migratione Abrahami*
MIO	*Mitteilungen des Instituts für Orientforschung,* Berlin
Miqw.	*Miqwaʾot*
Mird	Khirbet Mird texts
misc.	miscellaneous
MM	J. H. Moulton and G. Milligan. 1914–30. *The Vocabulary of the Greek Testament Illustrated from the Papyri and other Non-Literary Sources.* London. Repr. Grand Rapids, 1949
MNTC	Moffatt NT Commentary
ModChurch	*Modern Churchman,* Leominster, UK
Moᶜed	*Moᶜed*
Moᶜed Qaṭ.	*Moᶜed Qaṭan*
Month	*Month,* London
MPAIBL	*Mémoires présentés à l'Académie des inscriptions et belles-lettres*
MPAT	*A Manual of Palestinian Aramaic Texts,* ed. J. A. Fitzmyer and D. J. Harrington. BibOr 34. Rome, 1978
MRR	*The Magistrates of the Roman Republic,* ed. T. R. S. Broughton and M. L. Patterson. 2 vols. Philological Monographs 15. 1951–52. Suppl., 1960
MRS	Mission de Ras Shamra
ms (pl. mss)	manuscript(s)
MScRel	*Mélanges de science religieuse,* Lille
MSD	Materials for the Sumerian Dictionary
MSL	*Materialen zum sumerischen Lexikon,* Rome, 1937–

MSR	*Mélanges de Science Religieuse,* Lille
MSU	Mitteilungen des Septuaginta-Unternehmens
MT	Masoretic Text
MTS	Marburger Theologische Studien
MTZ	*Münchner theologische Zeitschrift*
Mur	Wadi Murabbaᶜat texts
Mus	*Le Muséon: Revue d'Études Orientales,* Paris
MUSJ	*Mélanges de l'Université Saint-Joseph*
Mut	Philo, *De mutatione nominum*
MVAG	Mitteilungen der vorder-asiatisch-ägyptischen Gesellschaft
N	north(ern)
n(n).	note(s)
NA	Neo-Assyrian
NAB	New American Bible
Nah	Nahum
NARCE	*Newsletter of the American Research Center in Egypt*
NASB	New American Standard Bible
Našim	*Našim*
NAWG	*Nachrichten der Akademie der Wissenschaften in Göttingen*
Nazir	*Nazir*
NB	Neo-Babylonian
N.B.	*nota bene* (note well)
NBD	*The New Bible Dictionary,* 2d ed., ed. J. D. Douglas and N. Hillyer. Leicester and Wheaton, IL
NCBC	New Century Bible Commentary
NCCHS	*New Catholic Commentary on Holy Scripture,* ed. R. D. Fuller et al.
NCE	*New Catholic Encyclopedia,* ed. M. R. P. McGuire et al.
NCH	M. Noth. 1986. *The Chronicler's History.* Trans. H. G. M. Williamson. JSOTSup 51. Sheffield [translates chaps. 14–25 of *ÜgS*]
NC1BC	New Clarendon Bible Commentary
NDH	M. Noth. 1981. *The Deuteronomistic History.* Trans. H. G. M. Williamson. JSOTSup 15. Sheffield [translates chaps. 1–13 of *ÜgS*]
NDIEC	*New Documents Illustrating Early Christianity,* ed. G. H. K. Horsley. Macquarie University, 1976– [= 1981–]
NE	northeast(ern)
NE	M. Lidzbarski. 1898. *Handbuch der nordsemitischen Epigraphik.* 2 vols. Weimar
NEB	New English Bible, Oxford, 1961–70
NEBib	Neue Echter Bibel
Ned.	*Nedarim*
NedTTs	*Nederlands Theologisch Tijdschrift,* The Hague
Neg.	*Negaᶜim*
Neh	Nehemiah
Neot	*Neotestamentica,* Stellenbosch
NETR	*The Near East School of Theology Theological Review,* Beirut
neut.	neuter
Nez.	*Neziqin*
NFT	New Frontiers in Theology
NGTT	*Nederduits Gereformeerde Teologiese Tydskrif,* Stellenbosch
NHC	Nag Hammadi Codex
NHI	M. Noth. 1960. *The History of Israel.* 2d ed. Trans. S. Godman, rev. P. R. Ackroyd. London
NHL	*The Nag Hammadi Library in English,* 3d ed., ed. J. M. Robinson. San Francisco, 1988
NHS	Nag Hammadi Studies
NHT	S. R. Driver. 1913. *Notes on the Hebrew Text and the Topography of the Books of Samuel.* 2d ed. Oxford
NICNT	New International Commentary on the New Testament
NICOT	New International Commentary on the Old Testament
Nid.	*Niddah*
NIDNTT	*New International Dictionary of New Testament Theology,* 3 vols., ed. C. Brown. Grand Rapids, 1975–78
NIGTC	New International Greek Testament Commentary
NIV	New International Version
NJB	New Jerusalem Bible
NJBC	*New Jerome Bible Commentary*
NJPSV	New Jewish Publication Society Version
NKJV	New King James Version
NKZ	*Neue kirchliche Zeitschrift*
no.	number
Norea	*The Thought of Norea* (NHC IX,2)
NorTT	*Norsk Teologisk Tidsskrift,* Oslo, Norway
NovT	*Novum Testamentum,* Leiden
*NovTG*²⁶	*Novum Testamentum Graece,* ed. E. Nestle and K. Aland. 26th ed. Stuttgart, 1979
NovTSup	Novum Testamentum Supplements
NPNF	Nicene and Post-Nicene Fathers
NRSV	New Revised Standard Version
NRT	*La nouvelle revue théologique*
n.s.	new series
NSSEA	*Newsletter of the Society for the Study of Egyptian Antiquities*
NT	New Testament
NTA	*New Testament Abstracts*

NTAbh	Neutestamentliche Abhandlungen
NTApocr	E. Henneke. *New Testament Apocrypha,* ed. W. Schneemelcher. Trans. R. McL. Wilson. 2 vols. Philadelphia, 1963–65
NTC	B. S. Childs. 1985. *The New Testament as Canon: An Introduction.* Philadelphia, 1985
NTCS	*Newsletter for Targumic and Cognate Studies,* Toronto
NTD	Das Neue Testament Deutsch
NTF	Neutestamentliche Forschungen
NTHIP	W. G. Kümmel. 1972. *The New Testament: The History of the Investigation of Its Problems.* Trans. S. M. Gilmour and H. C. Kee. Nashville
NTL	New Testament Library
NTM	New Testament Message
NTOA	Novum Testamentum et Orbis Antiquus
NTS	*New Testament Studies,* Cambridge, MA
NTT	*Nieuw theologisch Tijdschrift*
NTTS	New Testament Tools and Studies
Num	Numbers
Numen	*Numen: International Review for the History of Religions,* Leiden
NV	*Nova et Vetera,* Geneva
NW	northwest(ern)
NWDB	*The New Westminster Dictionary of the Bible,* ed. H. S. Gehman. Philadelphia, 1970
OA	Old Assyrian
OAkk	Old Akkadian
OB	Old Babylonian
Obad	Obadiah
OBO	Orbis biblicus et orientalis
ÖBS	Österreichische biblische Studien
OBT	Overtures to Biblical Theology
OC	*One in Christ,* London
OCA	Orientalia christiana analecta
OCD	*Oxford Classical Dictionary*
OCP	*Orientalia Christiana Periodica,* Rome
Odes Sol.	*Odes of Solomon*
OECT	*Oxford Editions of Cuneiform Texts,* ed. S. Langdon, 1923–
OED	*Oxford English Dictionary*
OG	Old Greek
OGIS	*Orientis graeci inscriptiones selectae,* ed. W. Dittenberger. 2 vols. Leipzig, 1903–5
Ohol.	*Oholot*
OIC	Oriental Institute Communications
OIP	Oriental Institute Publications
OL	Old Latin
OLA	Orientalia Lovaniensia Analecta
OLP	*Orientalia lovaniensia periodica*
OLZ	*Orientalistische Literaturzeitung,* Berlin
OMRO	*Oudheidkundige Medeelingen uit het Rijks-Museum van Oudheden te Leiden*
Onomast.	Eusebius, *Onomasticon*
Op	Philo, *De opificio mundi*
OP	*Occasional Papers on the Near East,* Malibu, CA
op. cit.	*opere citato* ([in] the work cited)
Or	*Orientalia*
ᶜOr.	*ᶜOrla*
OrAnt	*Oriens antiquus*
OrBibLov	Orientalia et biblica lovaniensia
OrChr	*Oriens christianus*
Orig. World	*On the Origin of the World* (NHC II,*5*; XIII,*2*)
OrSyr	*L'orient syrien*
o.s.	old series
OstStud	*Ostkirchliche Studien,* Würzburg
OT	Old Testament
OTA	*Old Testament Abstracts*
OTE	*Old Testament Essays,* Pretoria
OTG	Old Testament Guides
OTG	*The Old Testament in Greek according to the Text of Codex Vaticanus,* ed. A. E. Brooke, N. McLean, and H. St. J. Thackeray. Cambridge, 1906–40
ÖTK	Ökumenischer Taschenbuch-Kommentar
OTL	Old Testament Library
OTM	Old Testament Message
OTP	*Old Testament Pseudepigrapha,* 2 vols., ed. J. Charlesworth. Garden City, NY, 1983–87
OTS	*Oudtestamentische Studiën*
p	Pesher (commentary)
P	"Priestly" source
p(p).	page(s); past
PÄ	*Probleme der Ägyptologie,* Leiden
PAAJR	*Proceedings of the American Academy for Jewish Research,* Philadelphia
Pal.	*Palestinian*
Pal. Tgs.	*Palestinian Targums*
PalCl	*Palestra del Clero*
par(s).	paragraph(s); (gospel) parallel(s)
Para	*Para*
Paraph. Shem	*Paraphrase of Shem* (NHC VII,*1*)
part.	participle
pass.	passive
passim	throughout
PBA	*Proceedings of the British Academy,* Oxford

PBS	University Museum, University of Pennsylvania, *Publications of the Babylonian Section,* Philadelphia
PCB	*Peake's Commentary on the Bible,* rev. ed., ed. M. Black and H. H. Rowley. New York, 1962
P.E.	Eusebius, *Praeparatio evangelica*
Peʾa	*Peʾa*
PEFA	Palestine Exploration Fund Annual
PEFQS	*Palestine Exploration Fund Quarterly Statement*
PEGLAMBS	*Proceedings of the Eastern Great Lakes and Midwest Biblical Societies*
PEGLBS	*Proceedings of the Eastern Great Lakes Biblical Society*
PEQ	*Palestine Exploration Quarterly,* London
perf.	perfect
Pers	Persian
Pesaḥ.	*Pesaḥim*
Pesiq. R.	*Pesiqta Rabbati*
Pesiq. Rab Kah.	*Pesiqta de Rab Kahana*
PG	J. Migne, *Patrologia graeca*
PGM	*Papyri graecae magicae,* 3 vols., ed. K. Preisendanz. Leipzig, 1928–41
Ph. E. Poet	*Philo the Epic Poet*
PhEW	*Philosophy East and West*
Phil	Philippians
Phil.-hist. Kl.	Philosophische-historische Klasse
Phld.	see *Ign. Phld.*
Phlm	Philemon
PHOE	G. von Rad. 1966. *The Problem of the Hexateuch and Other Essays.* Trans. E. Dicken. Edinburgh and New York
Phoen	Phoenician
PhönWest	*Phönizier im Westen,* ed. H. G. Neimeyer. Madrider Beiträge 8. Mainz, 1982
PhRev	*Philosophical Review*
PI	J. Pedersen. 1926–40. *Israel: Its Life and Culture.* 2 vols. Copenhagen
PIBA	*Proceedings of the Irish Biblical Association,* Dublin
PIOL	Publications de l'Institut orientaliste de Louvain
PIR	*Prosopographia imperii Romani saec. I.II.III,* 3 vols., ed. E. Klebs, H. Dessau, and P. von Rohden. Berlin, 1897–98
PIR²	*Prosopographia imperii Romani saec. I.II.III,* 2d ed., ed. E. Groag, A. Stein, and L. Petersen. 5 vols. Berlin and Leipzig, 1933–
Pirqe R. El.	*Pirqe Rabbi Eliezer*
P. J.	*Paraleipomena Jeremiou*
PJ	*Palästina-Jahrbuch*
PL	J. Migne, *Patrologia latina*
pl.	plural
pl(s).	plate(s)
Plant	Philo, *De plantatione*
Plato Rep.	*Plato: Republic 588B–589B* (NHC VI,*5*)
PMR	Charlesworth, J. H. 1976. *The Pseudepigrapha and Modern Research.* SCS 7. Missoula, MT
PN	personal name
PN A	Pottery Neolithic A
PN B	Pottery Neolithic B
PNPI	J. K. Stark. 1971. *Personal Names in Palmyrene Inscriptions.* Oxford
PNPPI	F. Benz. 1972. *Personal Names in the Phoenician and Punic Inscriptions.* Studia Pohl 8. Rome
PNTC	Pelican New Testament Commentaries
PO	Patrologia orientalis
Pol.	see *Ign. Pol.*
Post	Philo, *De posteritate Caini*
POTT	*Peoples of Old Testament Times,* ed. D. J. Wiseman. Oxford, 1973
POuT	De Prediking van het Oude Testament
PPN A	Pre-Pottery Neolithic A
PPN B	Pre-Pottery Neolithic B
Pr Azar	Prayer of Azariah
Pr. Jac.	*Prayer of Jacob*
Pr. Jos.	*Prayer of Joseph*
Pr Man	Prayer of Manasseh
Pr. Mos.	*Prayer of Moses*
Pr. Paul	*Prayer of the Apostle Paul* (NHC I,*1*)
Pr. Thanks.	*The Prayer of Thanksgiving* (NHC VI,7)
Praem	Philo, *De praemiis et poeniis*
Praep. Evang.	Eusebius, *Praeparatio evangelica*
Pre. Pet.	*Preaching of Peter*
Presbyterion	*Presbyterion,* St. Louis, MO
Prism	*Prism,* St. Paul, MN
Pro	*Proyección,* Granada, Spain
Prob	Philo, *Probus*
Procl	Proclamation Commentaries
Proof	*Prooftexts: A Journal of Jewish Literary History*
Prot. Jas.	*Protevangelium of James*
Prov	Proverbs
Provid I–II	Philo, *De providentia* I–II
PRS	*Perspectives in Religious Studies,* Macon, GA
PRU	*Le Palais Royal d'Ugarit,* ed. C. F. A. Schaeffer and J. Nougayrol. Paris
Ps(s)	Psalm(s)
Ps-Abd.	*Apostolic History of Pseudo-Abdias*
PSB	*Princeton Seminary Bulletin,* Princeton, NJ
PSBA	*Proceedings of the Society of Biblical Archaeology*
Ps-Clem.	*Pseudo-Clementines*

Ps-Eup.	*Pseudo-Eupolemus*
Ps-Hec.	*Pseudo-Hecataeus*
Ps-Mt.	*Gospel of Pseudo-Matthew*
Ps-Orph.	*Pseudo-Orpheus*
Ps-Philo	*Pseudo-Philo*
Ps-Phoc.	*Pseudo-Phocylides*
Pss. Sol.	*Psalms of Solomon*
PSt	*Process Studies,* Claremont, CA
PSTJ	*Perkins (School of Theology) Journal,* Dallas, TX
PT	*Perspectiva Teológica,* Venda Nova, Brazil
pt.	part
PThS	*Pretoria Theological Studies,* Leiden
PTMS	Pittsburgh Theological Monograph Series
PTU	F. Gröndahl. 1967. *Die Personennamen der Texte aus Ugarit.* Studia Pohl 1. Rome
Pun	Punic
PVTG	Pseudepigrapha Veteris Testamenti graece
PW	A. Pauly–G. Wissowa, *Real-Encyclopädie der classischen Altertumswissenschaft,* Stuttgart, 1839–; supplements, 1903–56, 11 vols.; 2d series, 1914–48
PWCJS	*Proceedings of the . . . World Congress of Jewish Studies*
PWSup	Supplement to PW
Pyr	K. Sethe. 1908–32. *Die altägyptischen Pyramidentexte.* 4 vols. Leipzig. Repr. Hildesheim, 1969
Q	Qere; "Q"-source; Qumran texts (e.g., 4QTestim)
Qad	*Qadmoniot,* Jerusalem
QD	Quaestiones disputatae
QDAP	*Quarterly of the Department of Antiquities in Palestine*
QHBT	*Qumran and the History of the Biblical Text,* ed. F. M. Cross and S. Talmon. Cambridge, MA, 1975
Qidd.	*Qiddušin*
Qinnim	*Qinnim*
QL	Qumran Literature
Qod.	*Qodašin*
Qoh or Eccl	Qoheleth or Ecclesiastes
Quaes Ex I–II	Philo, *Quaestiones et solutiones in Exodum* I–II
Quaes Gen I–IV	Philo, *Quaestiones et solutiones in Genesin* I–IV
Ques. Ezra	*Questions of Ezra*
Quod Det	Philo, *Quod deterius potiori insidiari soleat*
Quod Deus	Philo, *Quod deus immutabilis sit*
Quod Omn	Philo, *Quod omnis probus liber sit*
R	H. C. Rawlinson. 1861–1909. *The Cuneiform Inscriptions of Western Asia.* London
RA	*Revue d'Assyriologie et d'Archéologie orientale,* Paris
RAB	J. Rogerson. 1985. *Atlas of the Bible.* New York
Rab.	*Rabbah* (following abbreviation for biblical book: *Gen. Rab.* = *Genesis Rabbah*)
RAC	*Reallexikon für Antike und Christentum,* 10 vols., ed. T. Klauser, Stuttgart, 1950–78
RANE	Records of the Ancient Near East
RÄR	H. Bonnet. 1952. *Reallexikon der ägyptischen Religionsgeschichte.* Berlin
RArch	*Revue archéologique*
RasT	*Rassegna di Teologia,* Naples
RAT	*Revue Africaine de Théologie,* Kinshasa Limete, Zaire
RazFe	*Razón y Fe,* Madrid
RB	*Revue biblique,* Paris
RBén	*Revue bénédictine,* Maredsous
RBI	*Rivista biblica italiana,* Brescia
RBR	*Ricerche Bibliche e Religiose*
RCB	*Revista de Cultura Biblica,* São Paulo, Brazil
RCT	*Revista Catalana de Teología,* Barcelona, Spain
RDAC	*Report of the Department of Antiquities, Cyprus,* Nicosia
RdÉ	*Revue d'égyptologie*
RdM	*Die Religionen der Menschheit,* ed. C. M. Schröder, Stuttgart
RE	*Realencyklopädie für protestantische Theologie und Kirche,* 3d ed., ed. A. Hauck. Leipzig, 1897–1913
REA	*Revue des études anciennes*
REAug	*Revue des études augustiniennes,* Paris
REB	*Revista Eclesiástica Brasileira,* Brazil
RechBib	Recherches bibliques
RefRev	*Reformed Review,* Holland, MI
RefTR	*Reformed Theological Review,* Melbourne
REJ	*Revue des études juives,* Paris
RelArts	Religion and the Arts
RelLond	*Religion,* London, 1971–
RelNY	*Religion,* New York
RelS	*Religious Studies,* London
RelSoc	*Religion and Society*
RelSRev	*Religious Studies Review*
Renovatio	*Renovatio,* Bonn
repr.	reprint, reprinted
RES	*Revue des études sémitiques,* Paris
RES	*Répertoire d'épigraphie sémitique* [cited by number]

ResABib	Die Reste der altlateinische Bibel
ResQ	*Restoration Quarterly,* Abilene, TX
Rev	Revelation
Rev. Ezra	*Revelation of Ezra*
Rev. Steph.	*Revelation of Stephen*
RevExp	*Review and Expositor,* Louisville, KY
RevistB	*Revista Bíblica,* Buenos Aires
RevistEspir	*Revista de Espritualidad,* Madrid
RevQ	*Revue de Qumran,* Paris
RevRef	*La Revue Réformée,* Aix en Provence
RevRel	*Review for Religious,* St. Louis, MO
RevScRel	*Revue des sciences religieuses,* Strasbourg
RevSém	*Revue sémitique*
RevThom	*Revue thomiste,* Toulouse
RGG	*Religion in Geschichte und Gegenwart*
RGTC	*Répertoire géographique des textes cunéiformes,* 8 vols., ed. W. Röllig. BTAVO B7. Wiesbaden
RHA	*Revue hittite et asianique*
RHE	*Revue d'histoire ecclésiastique,* Louvain
RHLR	*Revue d'histoire et de littérature religieuses,* Paris
RHPR	*Revue d'histoire et de philosophie religieuses,* Strasbourg
RHR	*Revue de l'histoire des religions,* Paris
RIC	*The Roman Imperial Coinage,* ed. H. Mattingly et al. London, 1923–81
RIC[2]	*The Roman Imperial Coinage,* 2d ed., ed. C. H. V. Sutherland and R. A. G. Carson. London, 1984–
RIDA	*Revue internationale des droits de l'antiquité*
RIH	J. de Rouge. 1877–78. *Inscriptions hiéroglyphiques copiées en Egypte.* 3 vols. Études égyptologiques 9–11. Paris
RivArCr	*Rivista di archeologia cristiana,* Rome
RivB	*Rivista biblica,* Bologna
RLA	*Reallexikon der Assyriologie,* ed. G. Ebeling et al. Berlin, 1932–
RLT	*Revista Latinoamericana de Teologia,* San Salvador
RNAB	see *RAB*
RNT	Regenesburger Neues Testament
RocTKan	*Roczniki Teologiczno-Kanoniczne,* Lublin
Rom	Romans
Rom.	see *Ign. Rom.*
Roš Hš.	*Roš Haššana*
ROTT	G. von Rad. 1962–65. *Old Testament Theology.* 2 vols. Trans. D. M. G. Stalker. New York
RP	*Revue de philologie*
RQ	*Römische Quartalschrift für christliche Altertumskunde und Kirchengeschichte,* Vatican City
RR	*Review of Religion*
RS	*Ras Shamra*
RSLR	*Rivista di storia letteratura religiosa,* Turin
RSO	*Rivista degli studi orientali*
RSPT	*Revue des sciences philosophiques et théolgiques,* Paris
RSR	*Recherches de science religieuse,* Paris
RST	*Religious Studies and Theology,* Edmonton, Alberta
RSV	Revised Standard Version
RT	*Recueil de travaux relatifs à la philologie et à l'archéologie égyptiennes et assyriennes*
RTAM	*Recherches de Theologie Ancienne et Médiévale*
RTL	*Revue théologique de Louvain*
RTP	*Revue de théologie et de philosophie,* Lausanne
RUO	*Revue de l'université d'Ottawa*
Ruth	Ruth
RV	Revised Version
RVV	Religionsgeschichtliche Versuche und Vorarbeiten
Ry	G. Ryckmans. 1927–59. Inscriptions sudarabes I–XVII. *Mus* 40–72 [cited by no. of text]
S	south(ern)
S. ʿOlam Rab.	*Seder ʿOlam Rabbah*
Šabb.	*Šabbat*
SacDoc	*Sacra Doctrina,* Bologna
SacEr	*Sacris Erudiri: Jaarboek voor Godsdienstwetenschappen,* Brugge, Belgium
Sacr	Philo, *De sacrificiis Abelis et Caini*
SAHG	A. Falkenstein and W. von Soden. 1953. *Sumerische und akkadische Hymnen und Gebete.* Zurich
SAK	*Studien zur Altägyptischen Kultur,* Hamburg
Sal	*Salesianum,* Rome
Salman	*Salmanticensis,* Salamanca
Sam. Pent.	Samaritan Pentateuch
Sam. Tg.	*Samaritan Targum*
SamOstr	Samaria Ostracon/Ostraca
SANE	*Sources From the Ancient Near East,* Malibu, CA
Sanh.	*Sanhedrin*
SANT	Studien zum Alten und Neuen Testament
SAOC	Studies in Ancient Oriental Civilization
Sap	*Sapienza,* Naples
SAQ	Sammlung ausgewählter kirchen-und dogmengeschichtlicher Quellenschriften

SAT	*Die Schriften des Alten Testaments in Auswahl,* ed. and trans. H. Gunkel et al. Göttingen
SB	Sources bibliques
SBA	Studies in Biblical Archaeology
SBAW	Sitzungsberichten der (königlichen) bayerischen Akademie der Wissenschaften
SBB	Stuttgarter biblische Beiträge
SBibB	*Studies in Bibliography and Booklore,* Cincinnati, OH
SBJ	La sainte bible de Jérusalem
SBLABS	Society of Biblical Literature Archaeology and Biblical Studies
SBLAS	Society of Biblical Literature Aramaic Studies
SBLASP	Society of Biblical Literature Abstracts and Seminar Papers
SBLBAC	Society of Biblical Literature The Bible in American Culture
SBLBMI	Society of Biblical Literature The Bible and Its Modern Interpreters
SBLBSNA	Society of Biblical Literature Biblical Scholarship in North America
SBLDS	Society of Biblical Literature Dissertation Series
SBLMasS	Society of Biblical Literature Masoretic Studies
SBLMS	Society of Biblical Literature Monograph Series
SBLNTGF	Society of Biblical Literature: The New Testament in the Greek Fathers
SBLRBS	Society of Biblical Literature: Resources for Biblical Study
SBLSBS	Society of Biblical Literature: Sources for Biblical Study
SBLSCS	Society of Biblical Literature: Septuagint and Cognate Studies
SBLSP	*Society of Biblical Literature Seminar Papers*
SBLSS	Society of Biblical Literature: Semeia Studies
SBLTT	Society of Biblical Literature: Texts and Translations
SBLWAW	Society of Biblical Literature: Writings of the Ancient World
SBM	Stuttgarter biblische Monographien
SBS	Stuttgarter Bibelstudien
SBT	Studies in Biblical Theology
SC	Sources chrétiennes
SCCNH	*Studies on the Civilization and Culture of Nuzi and the Hurrians,* 2 vols., ed. D. I. Owen and M. A. Morrison. Winona Lake, IN, 1981–87
ScEccl	*Sciences ecclésiatiques*
ScEs	*Science et esprit,* Montreal
SCHNT	Studia ad corpus hellenisticum novi testamenti
Scr	*Scripture*
SCR	*Studies in Comparative Religion*
ScrB	*Scripture Bulletin*
ScrC	*Scripture in Church,* Dublin
ScrHier	*Scripta Hierosolymitana,* Jerusalem
Scrip	*Scriptorium,* Brussels
Scriptura	*Scriptura,* Stellenbosch
ScrT	*Scripta Theologica,* Barañain/Pamplona
SCS	Septuagint and Cognate Studies
ScuolC	*Scuola Cattolica,* Milan
SD	Studies and Documents
SDB	*Smith's Dictionary of the Bible,* ed. H. B. Hackett. Boston, 1880
SE	southeast(ern)
SE	*Studia Evangelica I, II, III* (= TU 73 [1959], 87 [1964], 88 [1964], etc.)
SEÅ	*Svensk Exegetisk Årsbok*
Search	*Search,* Dublin
Šeb.	*Šebiʿit*
Šebu.	*Šebuʿot*
sec.	section
Sec. Gos. Mk.	*Secret Gospel of Mark*
SecondCent	*Second Century,* Macon, GA
Sef	*Sefarad,* Madrid
SEG	*Supplementum Epigraphicum Graecum,* ed. J. J. E. Hondius. Leiden, 1923–
Sem	*Semitica,* Paris
Ṣem.	*Ṣemaḥot*
Semeia	*Semeia,* Chico, CA
SemiotBib	*Sémiotique et Bible,* Lyon
Semitics	*Semitics,* Pretoria
Sent. Sextus	*Sentences of Sextus* (NHC XII,*1*)
Šeqal.	*Šeqalim*
Seux	J. M. Seux. 1968. *Epithètes Royales Akkadiennes et Sumériennes.* Paris
SGL	A. Falkenstein. 1959. *Sumerische Götterlieder.* Heidelberg
SGV	*Sammlung gemeinverständlicher Vorträge und Schriften aus dem Gebiet der Theologie und Religionsgeschichte,* Tübingen
SHAW	Sitzungsberichte der Heidelberger Akademie der Wissenschaften
Shep. Herm.	*Shepherd of Hermas*
SHIB	R. M. Grant and D. Tracy. 1984. *A Short History of the Interpretation of the Bible.* 2d ed. Philadelphia
Shofar	*Shofar,* West Lafayette, IN
SHR	Studies in the History of Religions
SHT	Studies in Historical Theology

Sib. Or.	*Sibylline Oracles*
SICV	*Sylloge inscriptionum Christianorum veterum musei Vaticani,* ed. H. Zilliacus. Acta instituti Romani Finlandiae 1/1–2. Rome
SIDÅ	Scripta Instituti Donneriana Åboensis, Stockholm
SIDJC	*Service International de Documentation Judéo-chrétienne,* Rome
SIG[3]	*Sylloge Inscriptionum Graecarum,* ed. W. Dittenberger. 3d ed. Leipzig
SII	*Studies in Islam,* New Delhi
sing.	singular
Sipra	*Sipra*
Sipre	*Sipre*
Sir	Ecclesiasticus *or* Wisdom of Jesus Ben-Sira
SIRIS	*Sylloge inscriptionum religionis Isiacae et Serapicae,* ed. L. Vidman. RVV 28. Berlin, 1969
SJ	Studia Judaica
SJLA	Studies in Judaism in Late Antiquity
SJOT	*Scandinavian Journal of the Old Testament*
SJT	*Scottish Journal of Theology,* Edinburgh
SkrifK	*Skrif en Kerk,* Pretoria
SLAG	*Schriften der Luther-Agricola-Gesellschaft* (Finland)
SLJT	*Saint Luke's Journal of Theology,* Sewanee, TN
SMEA	*Studi Micenei ed Egeo-Anatolici*
SMS	*Syro-Mesopotamian Studies,* Malibu, CA
SMSR	*Studi e materiali di storia delle religioni*
Smyrn.	see *Ign. Smyrn.*
SNT	Studien zum Neuen Testament
SNTSMS	Society for New Testament Studies Monograph Series
SNTU	*Studien zum Neuen Testament und seiner Umwelt,* Linz
SNVAO	*Skrifter utgitt av det Norske Videnskaps-Akademi i Oslo*
SO	Symbolae osloenses
SÖAW	*Sitzungsberichte der Österreichen Akademie der Wissenschaften*
Sobr	Philo, *De sobrietate*
Somn I–II	Philo, *De somniis* I–II
SonB	Soncino Books of the Bible
Sop.	*Soperim*
Soph. Jes. Chr.	*Sophia of Jesus Christ* (NHC III,*4*)
Soṭa	*Soṭa*
SOTSBooklist	*Society for Old Testament Study Booklist*
SOTSMS	Society for Old Testament Study Monograph Series
Sou	*Soundings,* Nashville
SPap	*Studia papyrologica*
SPAW	Sitzungsberichte der preussischen Akademie der Wissenschaften
SPB	Studia postbiblica
Spec Leg I–IV	Philo, *De specialibus legibus* I–IV
SPhil	*Studia Philonica,* Chicago
SPIB	*Scripta Pontificii Instituti Biblici,* Rome
SpT	*Spirituality Today,* Dubuque, IA
SQAW	Schriften und Quellen der alten Welt
SR	*Studies in Religion/Sciences religieuses,* Waterloo, Ontario
SS	Studi semitici
SSAOI	*Sacra Scriptura Antiquitatibus Orientalibus Illustrata,* Rome
SSEA	Society for the Study of Egyptian Antiquities
SSN	*Studia Semitica Neerlandica,* Assen
SSS	Semitic Study Series
St	*Studium,* Madrid
ST	*Studia theologica*
STÅ	*Svendk teologisk årsskrift*
StadtrChr	P. Lampe. 1987. *Die stadtrömischen Christen in den ersten beiden Jahrhunderten.* WUNT 2/18. Tübingen
StANT	*Studien zum Alten und Neuen Testament,* Munich
StBT	*Studien zu den Boğazköy-Texten,* Wiesbaden
StDI	Studia et Documenta ad Iura Orientis Antiqui Pertinenti
STDJ	Studies on the Texts of the Desert of Judah
StEb	*Studi Eblaiti,* Rome
StEc	*Studi Ecumenici,* Verona, Italy
Steles Seth	*Three Steles of Seth* (NHC VII,*5*)
StFS	*Studia Francisci Scholten,* Leiden
STK	*Svensk teologisk kvartalskrift,* Lund
STL	Studia theologica Ludensia
StLtg	*Studia Liturgica,* Rotterdam
StMiss	*Studia Missionalia,* Rome
StOr	*Studia Orientalia,* Helsinki
StOvet	*Studium Ovetense,* Oviedo
StPat	*Studia Patavina,* Padua, Italy
StPatr	*Studia Patristica*
StPhilon	*Studia Philonica*
Str	*Stromata,* San Miguel, Argentina
Str-B	H. L. Strack and P. Billerbeck. 1922–61. *Kommentar zum NT aus Talmud und Midrasch.* 6 vols. Munich
STT	*The Sultantepe Tablets,* 2 vols., ed. O. R. Gurney, J. J. Finkelstein, and P. Hulin. Occasional Publications of the British School of Archaeology at Ankara 3, 7. London, 1957–64

StTh	*Studia Theologica*
StudBib	Studia biblica
StudBT	*Studia biblica et theologica,* Guilford, CT
Studium	*Studium,* Madrid
StudNeot	Studia neotestamentica, Studia
StudOr	Studia orientalia
StudPhoen	Studia Phoenicia [I–VIII]
STV	*Studia theologica varsaviensia*
Sukk.	*Sukka*
Sum	Sumerian
SUNT	Studien zur Umwelt des Neuen Testaments
suppl.	supplement
Sus	Susanna
SVF	*Stoicorum veterum fragmenta,* ed. J. von Arnim. 4 vols. Leipzig, 1903–24. Repr. Stuttgart, 1966; New York, 1986
SVTP	Studia in Veteris Testamenti pseudepigrapha
SVTQ	*St. Vladimir's Theological Quarterly,* Tuckahoe, NY
SW	southwest(ern)
SWBA	Social World of Biblical Antiquity
SwJT	*Southwestern Journal of Theology,* Fort Worth, TX
SWP	*Survey of Western Palestine:* *SWP* 1 = C. R. Conder and H. H. Kitchener. 1881. *Galilee.* London. *SWP* 2 = C. R. Conder and H. H. Kitchener. 1882. *Samaria.* London. *SWP* 3 = C. R. Conder and H. H. Kitchener. 1883. *Judaea.* London. *SWP* 4 = E. H. Palmer. 1881. *Arabic and English Name Lists.* London. *SWP* 5 = C. Wilson and C. Warren. 1881. *Special Papers.* London. *SWP* 6 = C. Warren and C. Warren, 1884. *Jerusalem.* London. *SWP* 7 = H. B. Tristram. 1884. *The Fauna and Flora of Palestine.* London.
SymBU	Symbolae biblicae upsalienses
Syr	Syriac
Syr	*Syria: Revue d'Art Oriental et d'Archéologie,* Paris
Syr. Men.	*Syriac Menander*
SZ	*Stimmen der Zeit,* Munich
T. 12 P.	*Testaments of the Twelve Patriarchs*
T. Ab.	*Testament of Abraham*
T. Adam	*Testament of Adam*
T. Ash.	*Testament of Asher*
T. Benj.	*Testament of Benjamin*
T. Dan.	*Testament of Daniel*
T. Gad	*Testament of Gad*
T. Hez.	*Testament of Hezekiah*

T. Isaac	*Testament of Isaac*
T. Iss.	*Testament of Issachar*
T. Jac.	*Testament of Jacob*
T. Job	*Testament of Job*
T. Jos.	*Testament of Joseph*
T. Jud.	*Testament of Judah*
T. Levi	*Testament of Levi*
T. Mos.	*Testament of Moses*
T. Naph.	*Testament of Naphtali*
T. Reu.	*Testament of Reuben*
T. Sim.	*Testament of Simeon*
T. Sol.	*Testament of Solomon*
Ṭ. Yom	*Ṭebul Yom*
T. Zeb.	*Testament of Zebulun*
TA	*Tel Aviv,* Tel Aviv
Taʿan.	*Taʿanit*
TAD	B. Porten and A. Yardeni. 1986. *Textbook of Aramaic Documents from Ancient Egypt.* Jerusalem *TAD* A = vol. 1, *Letters* *TAD* B = vol. 2, *Contracts* *TAD* C = vol. 3, *Literature and Lists* *TAD* D = vol. 4, *Fragments and Inscriptions*
TAik	*Teologinen Aikakauskirja,* Helsinki
Talm.	*Talmud*
TAM	*Tituli Asiae Minoris*
Tamid	*Tamid*
TAPA	*Transactions of the American Philological Association*
TAPhS	*Transactions of the American Philosophical Society,* Philadelphia
TBC	Torch Bible Commentary
TBei	*Theologische Beiträge,* Wuppertal
TBl	*Theologische Blätter*
TBT	*The Bible Today,* Collegeville, MN
TBü	Theologische Bücherei
TCGNT	B. M. Metzger. 1971. *A Textual Commentary on the Greek New Testament,* United Bible Societies
TCL	*Textes cunéiforms du Musée du Louvre,* Paris, 1910–
TCS	Texts from Cuneiform Sources: TCS 1 = E. Sollberger. 1966. *Business and Administrative Correspondence Under the Kings of Ur.* Locust Valley, NY. TCS 2 = R. Biggs. 1967. *ŠÀ.ZI.GA: Ancient Mesopotamian Potency Incantations.* TCS 3 = Å. Sjöberg, E. Bergmann, and G. Gragg. 1969. *The Collection of the Sumerian Temple Hymns.* TCS 4 = E. Leichty. 1970. *The Omen Series šumma izbu.* TCS 5 = A. K. Grayson. 1975. *Assyrian and Babylonian Chronicles.*

TD	*Theology Digest,* St. Louis, MO
TDNT	*Theological Dictionary of the New Testament,* 10 vols., ed. G. Kittel and G. Friedrich. Trans. G. W. Bromiley. Grand Rapids, 1964–76
TDOT	*Theological Dictionary of the Old Testament,* ed. G. J. Botterweck, H. Ringgren, and H. J. Fabry. Trans. J. T. Willis, G. W. Bromiley, and D. E. Green. Grand Rapids, 1974–
TE	*Theologica Evangelica,* Pretoria
Teach. Silv.	*Teachings of Silvanus* (NHC VII,*4*)
Tem.	*Temura*
Temenos	*Temenos: Studies in Comparative Religion,* Helsinki
Ter	*Teresianum,* Rome
Ter.	*Terumot*
Test	*Testimonianze,* Florence
Testim. Truth	*Testimony of Truth* (NHC IX,*3*)
TEV	Today's English Version
TextsS	Texts and Studies
TF	*Theologische Forschung*
Tg. Esth. I	*First Targum of Esther*
Tg. Esth. II	*Second Targum of Esther*
Tg. Isa.	*Targum of Isaiah*
Tg. Ket.	*Targum of the Writings*
Tg. Neb.	*Targum of the Prophets*
Tg. Neof.	*Targum Neofiti I*
Tg. Onq.	*Targum Onqelos*
Tg. Ps.-J.	*Targum Pseudo-Jonathan*
Tg. Yer. I	*Targum Yerušalmi I*
Tg. Yer. II	*Targum Yerušalmi II*
TGI	K. Galling. 1950. *Textbuch zur Geschichte Israels.* 2d ed. Tübingen
TGl	*Theologie und Glaube,* Paderborn
Thal.	*Thallus*
ThArb	*Theologische Arbeiten,* Berlin
THAT	*Theologisches Handwörterbuch zum Alten Testament,* 2 vols., ed. E. Jenni and C. Westermann. Munich, 1971–76
ThEd	*Theological Educator,* New Orleans
ThEH	*Theologische Existenz Heute,* Munich
Them	*Themelios,* Madison, WI
Theod.	*Theodotus*
Theology	*Theology,* London
THeth	Texte der Hethiter
ThH	*Théologie historique*
THKNT	Theologischer Handkommentar zum Neuen Testament
Thom. Cont.	*Book of Thomas the Contender* (NHC II,*7*)
Thomist	*Thomist,* Washington, D.C.
ThPh	*Theologie und Philosophie,* Freiburg
ThStud	Theologische Studien
Thund.	*The Thunder: Perfect Mind* (NHC VI,*2*)
ThV	*Theologische Versuche,* Berlin
ThViat	*Theologia Viatorum,* Berlin
TijdTheol	*Tijdschrift voor Theologie,* Nijmegen
Titus	Titus
TJ	*Trinity Journal,* Deerfield, IL
TJT	*Toronto Journal of Theology*
TLZ	*Theologische Literaturzeitung*
TNB	*The New Blackfriars,* Oxford
TNTC	Tyndale New Testament Commentary
Tob	Tobit
Ṭohar.	*Ṭoharot*
TOTC	Tyndale Old Testament Commentary
TP	*Theologie und Philosophie*
TPNAH	J. D. Fowler. 1988. *Theophoric Personal Names in Ancient Hebrew.* JSOTSup 49. Sheffield
TPQ	*Theologisch-Praktische Quartalschrift,* Austria
TQ	*Theologische Quartalschrift*
TR	P. Lucau. *Textes Religieux Égyptiens,* 1, Paris
Trad	*Tradition,* New York
Traditio	*Traditio,* New York
Trall.	see *Ign. Trall.*
TRE	*Theologische Realenzyklopädie*
Treat. Res.	*Treatise on Resurrection* (NHC I,*4*)
Treat. Seth	*Second Treatise of the Great Seth* (NHC VII,*2*)
Treat. Shem	*Treatise of Shem*
TRev	*Theologische Revue*
Tri. Trac.	*Tripartite Tractate* (NHC I,*5*)
Trim. Prot.	*Trimorphic Protennoia* (NHC XIII,*1*)
TRu	*Theologische Rundschau,* Tübingen
TS	*Theological Studies,* Washington, DC
TSK	*Theologische Studien und Kritiken*
TSSI	J. C. L. Gibson. 1971–82. *Textbook of Syrian Semitic Inscriptions.* 3 vols. Oxford
TT	*Teologisk Tidsskrift*
TTKi	*Tidsskrift for Teologie og Kirke,* Oslo, Norway
TTKY	*Türk Tarih Kurumu Kongresi Yayĭnlari.* Ankara
TToday	*Theology Today,* Princeton, NJ
TTS	Trierer Theologische Studien
TTZ	*Trierer theologische Zeitschrift*
TU	Texte und Untersuchungen
TUAT	Texte aus der Umwelt des Alten Testaments
TV	*Teología y Vida,* Santiago, Chile
TvT	*Tijdschrift voor Theologie,* Nijmegen, The Netherlands

TWAT	*Theologisches Wörterbuch zum Alten Testament,* ed. G. J. Botterweck, H. Ringgren, and H. J. Fabry. Stuttgart, 1970–
TWNT	*Theologisches Wörterbuch zum Neuen Testament,* 8 vols., ed. G. Kittel and G. Friedrich. Stuttgart, 1933–69
TynBul	*Tyndale Bulletin*
TZ	*Theologische Zeitschrift,* Basel, Switzerland
UBSGNT	*United Bible Societies Greek New Testament*
UCPNES	University of California Publications in Near Eastern Studies
UCPSP	University of California Publications in Semitic Philology
UET	Ur Excavations: Texts
UF	*Ugarit-Forschungen*
Ug	Ugaritic
UGAÄ	Untersuchungen zur Geschichte und Altertumskunde Aegyptens
ÜgS	M. Noth. 1967. *Überlieferungsgeschichtliche Studien.* 3d ed. Tübingen
UNT	Untersuchungen zum Neuen Testament
ʿUq.	*ʿUqṣin*
Urk. IV	*Urkunden des ägyptischen Altertums.* Abt. IV, *Urkunden der 18. Dynastie,* ed. K. Sethe and W. Helck. 22 fasc. Leipzig, 1903–58
US	*Una Sancta*
USQR	*Union Seminary Quarterly Review,* New York, NY
UT	C. H. Gordon. 1965. *Ugaritic Textbook.* AnOr 38. Rome; suppl. 1967
UUÅ	*Uppsala universitets Årsskrift*
v(v)	verse(s)
VAB	*Vorderasiatische Bibliothek,* Leipzig, 1907–16
Val. Exp.	*A Valentinian Exposition* (NHC XI,2)
VAT	Vorderasiatische Abteilung, Thontafelsammlung, Staatliche Musee zu Berlin
VC	*Vigiliae christianae*
VCaro	*Verbum caro*
VD	*Verbum domini*
VE	*Vox Evangilica*
VetChr	*Vetera Christianum,* Bari
VF	*Verkündigung und Forschung*
Vg	Vulgate
Vid	*Vidyajyoti,* Delhi
VigChrist	*Vigiliao Christianae*
VIO	Veröffentlichung der Institut für Orientforschung
Virt	Philo, *De virtutibus*
Vis. Ezra	*Vision of Ezra*
Vis. Is.	*Vision of Isaiah*
Vis. Paul	*Vision of Paul*
Vita	*Vita Adae et Evae*
Vita C	Eusebius, *Vita Constantini*
Vita Cont	Philo, *De vita contemplativa*
Vita Mos I–II	Philo, *De vita Mosis* I–II
VKGNT	*Vollständige Konkordanz zum griechischen Neuen Testament,* ed. K. Aland
VL	Vetus Latina
vol(s).	volume(s)
Vorsokr.	*Fragmente der Vorsokrater,* 4th ed., ed. H. Diels. Berlin, 1922
VR	*Vox Reformata,* Geelong, Victoria, Australia
VS	Vorderasiatische Schriftdenkmäler der königlichen Museen zu Berlin
VSpir	*Vie spirituelle,* Paris
VT	*Vetus Testamentum,* Leiden
VTSup	Vetus Testamentum Supplements
W	west(ern)
WA	["Weimar Ausgabe," =] *D. Martin Luthers Werke: Kritische Gesamtausgabe,* ed. J. K. F. Knaake et al. Weimar, 1883–
Way	*The Way,* London
WbÄS	A. Erman and H. Grapow. 1926–31. *Wörterbuch der ägyptischen Sprache.* 7 vols. Leipzig. Repr. 1963
WBC	World Bible Commentary
WBKL	Wiener Beitrage zur Kulturgeschichte und Linguistik
WbMyth	*Wörterbuch der Mythologie,* ed. H. W. Haussig, Stuttgart, 1961
WC	Westminster Commentaries, London
WD	*Wort und Dienst*
WDB	*Westminster Dictionary of the Bible*
Wehr	H. Wehr. 1976. *A Dictionary of Modern Written Arabic,* 3d ed., ed. J. M. Cowen. Ithaca
WF	Wege der Forschung
WGI	J. Wellhausen. 1878. *Geschichte Israels.* Berlin [see also *WPGI* and *WPHI*]
WHAB	*Westminster Historical Atlas of the Bible*
Whitaker	R. E. Whitaker. 1972. *A Concordance of the Ugaritic Literature.* Cambridge, MA
WHJP	*World History of the Jewish People*
Wis	Wisdom of Solomon
WLSGF	*The Word of the Lord Shall Go Forth: Essays in Honor of David Noel Freedman,* eds. C. L. Meyers and M. O'Connor. Winona Lake, IN, 1983
WMANT	Wissenschaftliche Monographien zum Alten und Neuen Testament
WO	*Die Welt des Orients*
WoAr	*World Archaeology*
Wor	*Worship,* Collegeville, MN
WordWorld	*Word and World,* St. Paul, MN
WPGI	J. Wellhausen. 1895. *Prolegomena zur Geschichte Israels.* 4th ed. Berlin

WPHI	J. Wellhausen. 1885. *Prolegomena to the History of Israel.* 2 vols. Trans. J. S. Black and A. Menzies. Edinburgh. Repr. Cleveland 1957; Gloucester, MA, 1973
WS	*World and Spirit,* Petersham, MA
WTJ	*Westminster Theological Journal,* Philadelphia, PA
WTM	J. Levy. 1924. *Wörterbuch über die Talmudim und Midraschim.* 5 vols. 2d ed., ed. L. Goldschmidt. Leipzig. Repr. 1963
WTS	E. Littmann and M. Höfner. 1962. *Wörterbuch der Tigre-Sprache.* Wiesbaden
WuD	*Wort und Dienst,* Bielefeld
WUNT	Wissenschaftliche Untersuchungen zum Neuen Testament
WUS	J. Aistleitner. 1974. *Wörterbuch der ugaritischen Sprache.* 4th ed., ed. O. Eissfeldt. BSAW 106/3. Berlin
WuW	*Wissenschaft und Weisheit,* Mönchengladbach
WVDOG	*Wissenschaftliche Veröffentlichungen der Deutschen Orient-Gesellschaft*
WW	*Word & World,* Fort Lee, NJ
WZ	*Wissenschaftliche Zeitschrift*
WZKM	*Wiener Zeitschrift für die Kunde des Morgenlandes*
WZKSO	*Wiener Zeitschrift für die Kunde Süd- und Ostasiens*
Yad.	*Yadayim*
Yal.	*Yalqut*
Yebam.	*Yebamot*
Yem. Tg.	*Yemenite Targum*
YES	Yale Egyptological Studies
YGC	W. F. Albright. 1969. *Yahweh and the Gods of Canaan.* Garden City, NY. Repr. Winona Lake, IN, 1990
YJS	*Yale Judaica Series,* New Haven
YNER	Yale Near Eastern Researches
Yoma	*Yoma (= Kippurim)*
YOS	Yale Oriental Series
y. (Talm.)	Jerusalem (Talmud) = "Yerushalmi"
ZA	*Zeitschrift für Assyriologie*
Zabim	*Zabim*
ZAH	*Zeitschrift für Althebräistic*
ZÄS	*Zeitschrift für Ägyptische Sprache und Altertumskunde*
ZAW	*Zeitschrift für die alttestamentliche Wissenschaft,* Berlin
ZB	Zürcher Bibelkommentare
ZDMG	*Zeitschrift der deutschen morgenländischen Gesellschaft*
ZDPV	*Zeitschrift des deutschen Palästina-Vereins*
Zebaḥ.	*Zebaḥim*
Zech	Zechariah
ZEE	*Zeitschrift für evangelische Ethik*
Zeph	Zephaniah
Zer.	*Zeraʿim*
ZHT	*Zeitschrift für historische Theologie*
ZKG	*Zeitschrift für Kirchengeschichte*
ZKT	*Zeitschrift für katholische Theologie,* Innsbruck
ZMR	*Zeitschrift für Missionskunde und Religionswissenschaft*
ZNW	*Zeitschrift für die neutestamentliche Wissenschaft*
Zost.	*Zostrianos* (NHC VIII,*1*)
ZPE	*Zeitschrift für Papyrologie und Epigraphik*
ZPKT	*Zeitschrift für Philosophie und Katholische Theologie*
ZRGG	*Zeitschrift für Religions- und Geistesgeschichte,* Erlangen
ZST	*Zeitschrift für systematische Theologie*
ZTK	*Zeitschrift für Theologie und Kirche*
ZWT	*Zeitschrift für wissenschaftliche Theologie*
ZycMysl	*Zycie i Mysl*

K

KAB [Heb *qab*]. See WEIGHTS AND MEASURES.

KABZEEL (PLACE) [Heb *qabṣĕʾēl*]. Var. JEKABZEEL. A city in S Judah listed as part of Judah's inheritance (Josh 15:21). It was known traditionally for supplying great warriors (see 2 Sam 23:20 and 1 Chr 11:22). The Chronicler lists Kabzeel as one of the towns reoccupied after the Exile (1 Chr 11:22). The variant Jekabzeel mentioned in Neh 11:25 is most likely the same city. According to Aharoni (*LBHG* [1967 ed]: 295–98) we can identify Kabzeel-Jekabzeel with Tell Gharreh (M.R. 148071) midway between Beer-sheba and Arad. See IRA, TEL. He also suggested that the town was probably named after a man or clan (*LBHG* [1967 ed]: 97). Since, however, the Bible does not mention any people with a similar name, it is just as likely that the name arose from its root meaning, "a gathering place"; compare the modern Hebrew word *kibbutz* denoting a collective farm or settlement.

Tom Wayne Willett

KADESH-BARNEA (PLACE) [Heb *qādēš barnēaʿ*]. Var. KADESH; KEDESH; MERIBATH-KADESH. A site in N Sinai where the Israelites camped before their entrance into Canaan. It was also known simply as Kadesh (Num 13:26; cf. Deut 1:19) or Kedesh (Josh 15:23). The first part of the name of the site appears to derive from the Hebrew root *qdš*, referring to "holiness" or "separateness"; the meaning of the second element is unknown. According to Gen 14:7, Kadesh-barnea was the scene of Chedorlaomer's defeat of the Amalekites, when it was also known as Enmishpat. Kadesh-barnea was the site of some significant developments in Israel's history. After their departure from Mt. Sinai, the Israelites traveled to Kadesh-barnea, from whence the twelve spies were sent into Canaan; as a result of Israel's discouragement and ensuing complaints when they heard the report of ten of the spies, Yahweh sentenced Israel to wander in the wilderness for forty years (Numbers 13–14). It was at Kadesh-barnea that Miriam, sister of Moses and Aaron, died and was buried (Num 20:1). It was also the setting where Moses disobeyed Yahweh's command when he struck the rock to provide water rather than speaking to it (Num 20:2–13); this disobedience was the basis for Moses' exclusion from entry into the promised land. After Israel's entrance into Canaan, the site is mentioned as part of the S border of Judah (Josh 15:1–3).

A. Location

During the early 1800s, the search for Kadesh-barnea concentrated in the Arabah because of the reference in Num 20:16, which places the site on the border of Edom. The search shifted W in the latter part of the century because of problems correlating the Arabah locations with the geographical descriptions in the Bible. Some suggested that Kadesh-barnea should be identified with ʿAin Qedeis, an oasis in the N Sinai which also seemed to preserve the name of the site. However, the name apparently did not preserve any real tradition, since ʿAin Qedeis, too, failed to conform to the biblical descriptions of the site and its location. In 1905 N. Schmidt (1910) recognized that the biblical texts conformed better with remains near ʿAin el-Qudeirat (M.R. 096006) and suggested that this was the region in which Kadesh-barnea should be located. C. L. Woolley and T. E. Lawrence (1914–15) made an extensive study of the region soon after and confirmed Schmidt's conclusion, and their identification has essentially been universally accepted since.

The site now recognized as Kadesh-barnea is located near ʿAin el-Qudeirat in the Wadi el-ʿAin. It rests near the junction of a road leading from Suez to Beer-sheba/Hebron and the road branching from the Via Maris near el-Arish leading to ʿAqaba. This area is now the largest oasis in the N Sinai and has a spring that produces about 40 m^3 of water per hour (Dothan 1965).

B. Excavation History

Woolley and Lawrence conducted a three-day excavation at the site in 1914, enough to provide a basic outline of the upper fortress. M. Dothan reexcavated the site in 1956 and discovered the Persian levels as well as two fortresses dating from the Iron Age II. The excavations by R. Cohen in 1972–82 supplied significant additional detail to the earlier excavations.

1. The Earliest Fortress. The excavations revealed three superimposed fortresses dating from the 10th century B.C. to the 7th–6th century B.C., followed by some Persian occupation. The bottom fortress lay under some 5 m of debris and was a large (ca. 27 m diameter) oval fortress with casemate outer walls. It rested on the E edge of the site and was later bisected by the upper two fortresses. A large multiroom building was located separate from the oval fortress to the W (i.e., under and just inside the NW corner of the upper two levels). It contained a room (ca. 4 m by 6 m) with stone benches lining the walls. The ceramic collection of this stratum was characteristically 10th century B.C., but consisted of wheel-made pottery and a handmade pottery often found in the Negeb now referred to as "Negebite" ware. The ceramic repertoire included large pithoi storejars, juglets, flasks, lamps, kraters, cooking pots, various sizes of bowls, and chalices. Among the small finds were three iron arrowheads and an "eye of Horus," along with a faience statuette.

The date of the ceramic collection and layout of the site are consistent to suggest that the fortress was constructed during the time of Solomon. It was probably one of a series of fortresses built to protect the S border of Israel. Perhaps it was destroyed during the raids into Canaan by Shishak (cf. 1 Kgs 14:25–28).

2. The Middle Fortress. After an occupational gap of about two centuries, the site (in contrast to the other fortresses along the S border) was rebuilt. The new construction neither followed nor reused the earlier remains. The new fortress was rectangular (ca. 60 × 40 m) and had solid walls (ca. 4 m thick). Eight projecting towers were incorporated into its design with one at each corner and one at the midpoint along each of the walls. See Fig. KAD.01. The walls were in turn protected by a defensive complex consisting of an earth glacis which sloped down to a retaining wall about 2.5 m high, beyond which was a 4-m-wide moat measuring 2.5 m deep.

A wide street (ca. 3.5 m) bisected the interior of the fortress. While there were buildings on both sides of the street, some special features were on the W end of the fortress. In the NW corner (built over the remains of the separated large building with stone benches of the earlier period) was a building in which were found mudbrick installations with traces of fire and large numbers of animal bones. Immediately across the street to the S was a cistern with a 10-m-diameter shaft, which was lined on the lower levels with large stones and plaster. Twenty-five steps descended into the cistern providing access. The cistern was fed from the spring outside the fortress to the S via a plastered conduit which carried the water under the rampart. The cistern had a capacity of ca. 180 m^3. Just to the E of the cistern was a large rectangular room (ca. 5.5 m by 3.8 m) which may have been a silo; a smaller (ca. 2 m diameter) circular silo was nearby.

Outside the fortress on the N were located several round granaries (which contained a fairly large number of camel bones) and a room attached to the fortress in which was found an oven with a complete handmade cooking pot inside of it. The ceramics of this fortress, like that of the lower fortress, exhibited a mixture of wheel-made pottery (typically 8th–7th centuries B.C.) and handmade Negebite ware.

Uzziah may have directed the construction of this fortress; he tried to fortify the S part of Judah (2 Chr 26:10). Its destruction apparently came at the end of Manasseh's reign in the middle of the 7th century B.C.

3. The Upper Fortress. The upper fortress followed essentially the same external plan as the middle fortress with the exception that the outer walls were casemate instead of solid. See Fig. KAD.01. The glacis and moat continued in use. The interior layout of the fortress changed, although the cistern continued in use (however, from a higher level). In the NW corner the special character of the architecture continued and the excavators found

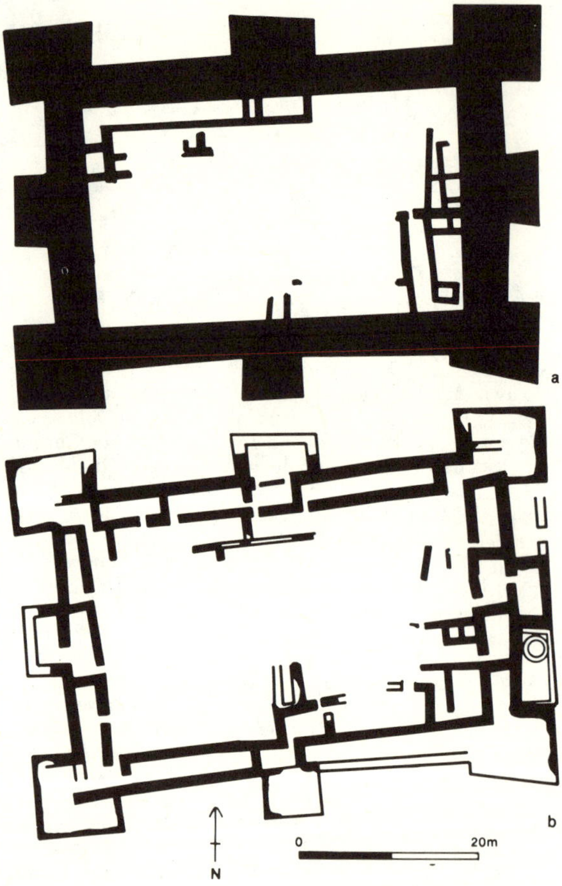

KAD.01. Fortress at Kadesh-barnea: *a*, middle fortress plan—8th–7th century B.C.E.; *b*, upper fortress plan—7th–6th century B.C.E. *(Redrawn from Cohen 1979: 74, fig. 11)*

three rectangular rooms which opened onto a large stone pavement. On the pavement stood a large circular structure (ca. 1.9 m) built of mudbrick and preserved to a height of ca. 1.2 m. This structure was filled with a thick layer of ashes and next to it were found a small incense burner, many ceramic vessels, and animal bones. In view of the kinds of finds located in the NW quadrant and the special architectural features (e.g., the stone benches along the walls in the lowest level; cf. Dever 1987) it might be suggested that this constituted a shrine either for the personnel of the site or for the region. This stratum also yielded a typical collection of wheel-made and handmade Negebite ceramic pieces of the 7th century B.C. In addition, ceramic figurine fragments of the head of a horse and a pinch-face male were found which may originally have been part of a "horse and rider" figurine.

Cohen suggests that this fortress was built during the time of Josiah and that it was destroyed as part of Nebuchadnezzar's campaign when he destroyed Jerusalem (1983: XVII).

4. Persian Period. The site was reoccupied during the Persian period with no apparent architectural addition or repair to the defensive walls. The occupants apparently lived in some of the remaining casemate rooms and, as was common for the Persian period, dug various pits on the site.

5. Ostraca. Several ostraca have been found, most indicating some kind of accounting system. It is unclear whether the hieratic numbers were for actual accounting purposes or represented student exercises. Of special significance, however, are the appearances of a sign for the shekel; a reference from the Persian levels to a *gerah* (the smallest Hebrew unit of weight measurement, ca. 0.50 gram); references to a "thousand" (*ʾalep*) and to "thousands" (*ʾalepîm*); what appears to be a fragment of an abecedary with the Hebrew sequence of *zayin, ḥet, ṭet;* and a reference to a sherd of unclear context to an *ʾeškār* (perhaps an allusion to an offering or gift [cf. Ps 72:10]).

C. Peculiarities and Problems

A peculiar feature of the site is the fact that no gate has been found to provide access to the inside. While the upper fortress had experienced some erosion, it seems clear from the nature of the glacis and lower ramparts that there was no typical gate into the fortress. Nor has the middle fortress yielded evidence of a gate. The lower fortress may have had one, but the excavations have not been extensive enough to locate it. Perhaps access was via ladders, which would have eliminated the weakness of a break in the wall for a gate.

A beleaguering point is the fact that the excavations have produced no evidence of a large number of people having stayed at the site any time during when the Exodus is postulated to have occurred. While there are remains of settlements in the vicinity from the EB II period (Beit-Arieh and Gophna 1976; 1981), these are obviously much too early to have anything to do with the Israelites. There are at least three lines by which to address this dilemma: (1) perhaps the site is not Kadesh-barnea of the Hebrew Bible; (2) evidence may yet be unearthed to corroborate the presence of a large group of people in the LB/Iron Age, since the excavations have not exhausted the site; or (3) a growing number of scholars suggest that the Exodus, at least in the way the Hebrew Bible portrays the event, did not occur, in which case one should not necessarily expect to find evidence of Israel's LB/early Iron Age I occupation.

Bibliography

Beit-Arieh, I., and Gophna, R. 1976. Early Bronze Age II Sties in Wadi el-Qudeirat (Kadesh-barnea). *TA* 3: 142–50.

———. 1981. The Early Bronze Age II Settlement at ʿAin el-Qudeirat (1980–1981). *TA* 8: 128–35.

Cohen, R. 1976. Notes and News. Kadesh-Barnea, 1976. *IEJ* 26: 201–2.

———. 1979. The Iron Age Fortresses in the Central Negev. *BASOR* 236: 61–79.

———. 1980. Notes and News. Kadesh-Barnea, 1979. *IEJ* 30: 235–36.

———. 1981. Excavations at Kadesh-Barnea, 1976–1978. *BA* 44: 93–107.

———. 1982. Notes and News. Kadesh-Barnea, 1980. *IEJ* 32: 70–71.

———. 1983. *Kadesh-barnea.* Jerusalem.

Dever, W. G. 1987. The Contribution of Archaeology to the Study of Canaanite and Early Israelite Religion. Pp. 209–47 in *AIR*.

Dothan, M. 1965. The Fortress at Kadesh-Barnea. *IEJ* 15: 134–51.

———. 1977. Kadesh-Barnea. *EAEHL* 3: 697–98.

Schmidt, N. 1910. Kadesh Barnea. *JBL* 29: 61–76.

Woolley, C. L., and Lawrence, T. E. 1914–15. *The Wilderness of Zin.* PEFA 3. London.

DALE W. MANOR

KADESH-ON-THE-ORONTES. A city located strategically alongside the Orontes River in Syria on the site of Tell Nebi Mend (34° 34′ N; 36° 33′ E), and which flourished in the LB Age. Its inhabitants apparently included Hurrian, Aryan, and Semitic elements. The earliest mention of the city is in the annals of Thutmose III (1479–1425 B.C.), who conquered it. Although the Hittite Šuppiluliumas (1375–1335 B.C.) reduced Shutatarra, king of Kadesh, to a vassal, a number of Amarna Letters indicate that Aitakama, son of Shutatarra, also pursued relations with Amenhotep IV (1353–1335 B.C.). Aitakama was eventually assassinated by his pro-Hittite son Ariteshub. Despite conquest by the Egyptian king Seti I (1306–1290 B.C.), Kadesh was an ally of the Hittites by the time of the Battle of Kadesh (ca. 1285 B.C.).

The Battle of Kadesh resulted from the attempt of Rameses II (1290–1224 B.C.) to wrest the city from Muwatallis the Hittite. The Egyptian army was divided into four divisions named Amon, Re, Ptah, and Sutekh. A few miles S of Kadesh, two enemy spies, disguised as deserters, misled Rameses into thinking that the Hittite army had fled toward Aleppo, about 120 miles to the N. In fact, the Hittite army, perhaps 20,000 strong, was hiding on the E side of Kadesh. Shortly after the Amon division, commanded by Rameses himself, had set up a temporary rendezvous camp NW of Kadesh, the Hittite chariotry pounced upon the Re division which was still SW of Kadesh en route to the campsite. The Re division fled toward Rameses' position where he, with the aid of brilliant leadership and mercenaries who arrived just in time, successfully rallied his troops after the initial chaos. But the outcome was at best a stalemate for Rameses, and he eventually settled for a truce which included Hittite control of Kadesh. See also Klengel 1969: 139–77.

The Egyptians commemorated the battle in two extraordinarily detailed written versions and in captioned pictographic reliefs. J. Breasted (*ARE* 3: 124, 135–36, 142) and M. Lichtheim (*AEL* 2: 57–60), among others, designate one of the written versions as the prose Record (or the Bulletin) and the other as the Poem. A. Gardiner (1960), however, argued that both accounts should be classified as prose. Based on a study of the form and genres of Egyptian military documents, A. Spalinger (1983: 153–73, 238) concludes that both "Bulletin" and "Poem" are poor labels, and that one should include military diary traditions in any discussion of the genre of the accounts of the battle.

Archaeological excavations by M. Pezard in 1921 and 1922 produced the Stele of Seti I, and a flawed report (edited posthumously) which suggested significant occupation of Kadesh between the end of the LB and the onset of the Seleucid period (cf. Noth, 1948: 233). However, the invasion of the Sea Peoples ca. 1200 seems to have ended the historical record of Kadesh, and it remained unoccupied until a city named Laodicea was built on the remains during the Seleucid era.

Bibliography

Gardiner, A. H. 1960. *The Kadesh Inscription of Ramesses II.* Oxford.

Klengel, H. 1969. *Geschichte Syriens im 2. Jahrtausend v. u. Z.* Part 2. Berlin.

Noth, M. 1948. Die Stadt Kades am Orontes in der Geschichte des zweiten Jahrtausends v. Chr. *WO* 1: 223–33.

Pezard, M. 1931. *Qadesh.* Paris.

Spalinger, A. J. 1983. *Aspects of the Military Documents of the Ancient Egyptians.* New Haven.

Hector Avalos

KADMIEL (PERSON) [Heb *qadmîʾēl*]. A Levite associated with various activities during and following the return from Exile, although it has been suggested that the name appears primarily as a designation of a levitical family (Brockington *Ezra, Nehemiah and Esther* NCBC, 60). Concerning the return itself, Kadmiel made his way to Jerusalem with Zerubbabel (Ezra 2:40; Neh 7:43; 12:8; 1 Esdr 5:26). Though the genealogical records in this case are somewhat unclear (Myers *Ezra, Nehemiah* AB, 13), he was one of only a few Levites who did so (Williamson *Ezra, Nehemiah* WBC, 35). In helping to establish the postexilic community, Kadmiel served in a supervisory role during the rebuilding of the temple (Ezra 3:9; 1 Esdr 5:58), led worship in the public ceremonies prior to the establishment of the new covenant (Neh 9:4), and supported this covenant by "sealing" it (Neh 10:10—Eng 10:9). Finally, in an appended list in Nehemiah, Kadmiel is characterized as a man of praise and thanksgiving (Neh 12:24).

Terry L. Brensinger

KADMONITES [Heb *qadmōnî*]. One of ten groups of people found in a list of pre-Israelite inhabitants of the land promised to Abraham (Gen 15:19). Literally translated the name would be "Easterners." Koehler and Baumgartner (*HALAT* 3: 1002) identify this group with the *bĕnê qedem* "people of the East" (Gen 29:1; Judg 6:3, 33; 7:12; 8:10; 1 Kgs 5:10; Isa 11:14; Jer 49:28; Ezek 25:4, 10; Job 1:3). The latter "ethnographic collective name" is used "for the Syro-Arabian desert, mainly nomads or seminomads" (*GTTOT,* 13). While the translational equivalents of these two expressions are nearly identical and the expressions arise from the same root *qdm,* "east", it is not certain that they refer to the same people. Since the term "Kadmonites" is only found in Gen 15:19, the best indication of its meaning can be determined from its placement within the list. Ishida (1979: 483–84) suggests that the list of nations in Gen 15:19–21 is geographically arranged from S to N and reflects the extent of the Davidic empire. He thinks that the first three names of the list (Kenites, Kenizzites, Kadmonites) "represent the foreign elements in the South whose absorption into the tribe of Judah was complete by the time of David" (1979: 484).

Bibliography

Clements, R. 1967. *Abraham and David, Genesis 15 and its Meaning for Israelite Tradition.* SBT n.s. 5. London.

Ishida, T. 1979. The Structure and Historical Implications of the Lists of Pre-Israelite Nations. *Bib* 60: 461–90.

Stephen A. Reed

KAIN (PLACE) [Heb *qayin*]. Appears in the enumeration of cities in districts belonging to Judah (Josh 15:57). Its grouping with several other towns of fairly certain identification, namely Maon, Carmel, Ziph, and Juttah, leads to a plausible identification of Kain with en-Nebi Yaqin (M.R. 164100). However, LXX in Josh 15:57 omits the name Kain and counts only nine cities in its list rather than ten as in the MT. Then possibly Kain in the MT should be understood as a genitive which was added to qualify the preceding proper noun Zanoah (i.e., Zanoah of Kain, i.e., Zanoah of the Kenites) in order to distinguish it from the Zanoah of Josh 15:34. If this is correct, Kain must be understood as the singular collective noun for Kenites. Both the interpretations as a collective noun and as a proper place name have been applied to *qayin* in Num 24:33 and Judg 4:11.

Wesley I. Toews

KAIWAN (DEITY). See SAKKUTH AND KAIWAN (DEITIES).

KALLAI (PERSON) [Heb *qallāy*]. A head of a priestly family mentioned only in Neh 12:20 as one of some 20 priestly heads serving in the days of Joiakim (vv 12–21). Recently, H. G. M. Williamson (*Ezra, Nehemiah* WBC, 359–60) has argued that this list probably predates the transcription of the similar list found in vv 1–7 of the same chapter. See AMOK. The name "Kallai," as well as all the other names which follow Malluchi (i.e., the entirety of vv 14a–21), are omitted in the major LXX manuscripts. A similar situation obtains for the LXX of vv 1–7.

Commentators are generally agreed that the list of priestly families found in vv 12–21 is composite in nature, the last six families (vv 19–21) representing a secondary addition to the list to bring it into closer conformity with the actual priestly hierarchy in later times. Thus, the name "Kallai" may well not have appeared at all on the original list. Furthermore, Williamson (*Ezra, Nehemiah* WBC, 357, n. 20a) suspects that the Heb *qallāy,* otherwise unattested, represents a scribal device to fill a gap which had resulted from the loss of a name from the list (note that a name is clearly lacking after Miniamin in v 17). Elsewhere (*Ezra, Nehemiah* WBC, 343, n. 8a) he points to a number of doubtful passages in which rhyming names are set next to each other, probably as an attempt to salvage some meaning from a corrupt text. The line "of Sallai, Kallai" (Neh 12:20a) may thus fall into this category as well. If the name "Kallai" is to be retained as authentic, it may best be explained as an abbreviation of a fuller name such as the "Kelaiah" of Ezra 10:23 (see Bowman *IB* 3: 788).

William H. Barnes

KAMON (PLACE) [Heb *qāmôn*]. The burial place of Jair the Gileadite (Judg 10:5), one of the minor judges of Israel. One might expect that if Jair was a Gileadite, he was from Gilead in Transjordan, and perhaps he was buried in his place of origin (*EHI,* 787). Keil and Delitzsch (n.d., 372–73) offer an alternate assumption, however, that since Jair judged Israel (i.e., not just Gilead), he may very well have been living in, and buried in, Cisjordan. Eusebius and Jerome cited Kammona in the Esdraelon, possibly the Cyamon (Gk *Kyamōn*) of Judith 7:3, possibly Tell Qeimun (M.R. 160230), the Jokmeam of 1 Kgs 4:12. Most interpreters, however, look toward Gilead. This thought is heightened by Judg 10:4, which tells us he had 30 sons who had 30 cities, called Havvoth-jair, "the villages of Jair." These "tent cities" are referred to in Num 32:41, where Jair the son of Manasseh conquered their villages (of Gilead?) and called them Havvoth-jair. This Jair was Machir's grandson (1 Chr 2:21–23), great-grandson of Manasseh, and thus great-great-grandson of Joseph, son of Jacob. Deut 3:14 tells of his conquest of Argob, that is Bashan, and that he called the villages Havvoth-jair. Some scholars think these verses all refer to the same man while others think the conqueror and the judge are two different people. There is a further problem in the identification of Gilead, which some see as N of the Yarmuk, i.e., Bashan as in Deut 3:14. Some see it as S of the Jabbok River while most see it as N of the Jabbok, S of the Yarmuk. That puts Kamon in this area if it is related to Jair as "Gileadite." The name is preserved in Qamm (M.R. 218221) and Qumeim, halfway between the Sea of Galilee and Ramoth-gilead. These two villages are on either side of the present road, about 6 and 7 miles respectively S-SE of Umm Qeis (M.R. 214229), on the way to modern Irbid (Beth-arbel [M.R. 229218], Hos 10:14). There is no archaeological evidence here for the Iron Age. The area was not settled before the Roman period. Kamon has also been identified with Qanawat in Jabal Druze but others think this is much too far E. Simons (*GTTOT,* 134) suggested Krak-Canatha between Dera'a and Souweida. It may also be the name of a clan territory. Jdt 4:4 refers to Kona, which has been suggested as Qoman. Simons (*GTTOT,* 298, 497) does not agree. It is too obviously a literary adaptation of Gen 14:15, though one can note the word there is Hobah. Polybius' *History* 5.70, 12, refers to Kamoun, a site taken by Antiochus in his war with Ptolemy Philopator. The reference follows immediately after his capture of Scythopolis and in conjunction with his conquest of Pella, Abila, Gadara, etc., in Gilead (Gehman *NWDB,* 533). The site is identified with Hanzir, 5 miles E of Pella (M.R. 207206). It is N of the Jabbok. Iron Age I and Hellenistic type potsherds have been found on the site.

Bibliography

Keil, C. F., and Delitzsch, F. n.d. *Joshua, Judges, Ruth.* Vol. 2 of *Commentary on the Old Testament.* Trans. J. Martin. Grand Rapids. Repr. 1986.
Ottosson, M. 1969. *Gilead: Tradition and History.* Lund.

HENRY O. THOMPSON

KANAH (PLACE) [Heb *qānâ*]. This name is used for both a town (Josh 19:28) and a river or stream (Josh 16:8; 17:9).

1. The latter is usually identified with the Wadi Qanah, though Kallai (*HGB,* 153) has pointed out there is no proof of this. It is just the similarity of names (Robinson 1856: 3.135; *SWP* 2: 299; *SWP* 4: 248). Biblically it is the natural boundary between the Hebrew tribes of Ephraim and Manasseh. The biblical description is that it is a wadi running W from the watershed at the head of the Micmethath valley 4 miles SW of Shechem. It flows W past Tappuah. When it enters the Sharon plain, it becomes today the Wadi Yasin, passes S of the Arab village of Jaljuliya (M.R. 145173; Gilgal, Josh 12:23?) and turns NW. Then it turns 90 degrees to join with the Wadi el-Ishkar which flows SW to join the Wadi Aujeh (the modern Yarkon River) near Tell el-Mukhmar, an Iron Age mound (Danelius 1958: 38). The Yarkon flows W-SW past Tell el-Qasileh (M.R. 130167) and reaches the sea 3.5 miles N of Joppa (Jaffa/Tel Aviv), between Joppa and Arsuf (Apollonia). Kanah means "reeds." Guerin, influenced by the reeds, argues in favor of Nehr al-Falik 5 miles N of Arsuf. He identified it with Nahr el-Kasab, the river of reeds, mentioned by Beha ad-Din, a Muslim historian. But this last must be the Nahr el-Mafjir (M.R. 193143), 13 miles further N (Ewing *ISBE* 3: 1789). Eva Danelius was curious about the 90 degree turn into the Ishkar. Local tradition said the wadi once ran N of Jaljuliya. She found that W. M. Thomson (1893) cited Kitto that the river Arsuf which enters the sea between Em Khalid and El Haram is the biblical Kanah. There is no river Arsuf now. El Haram is the mosque of Sidna Ali near Arsuf. She traced the Kanah's mouth to 1.5 miles N of Arsuf, 11.5 miles N of Joppa. Thus Ephraim reached further N than the current drain of the Wadi Qanah today.

2. Josh 19:24–31 describes the territory allotted to the tribe of Asher. Some interpreters see the S border touching the Carmel range while others see it reaching S of Carmel to below Dor. Asher's E border followed Zebulun and then Naphtali. The border continues in the N to Cabul (v 27), Ebron, Rehob, Hammon, Kanah, as far as Sidon the Great (v 28). Most commentators relate Kanah to Qana between Tibnin and Tyre, 7 miles SE of Tyre (*HGB,* 212; *GP* 2: 412). This is the *q-n* of Egyptian lists: Thutmose III (no. 26); Seti I; Rameses II (1290–1224 B.C.) 8th-year reliefs (*ANET,* 256). This site is distinguished from the NT site of Cana of Galilee, 9 miles NE of Nazareth, today's Khirbet Qana (M.R. 178247; not Kafr Canna), the native place of the apostle Nathanael (John 21:2) and the site of Jesus' first miracle (John 2:1–11; 4:46–54).

Bibliography

Danelius, E. 1958. The Boundary of Ephraim and Manasseh in the Western Plain. *PEQ* 90: 32–43.
Robinson, E. 1856. *Biblical Researches in Palestine,* 2d ed. 3 vols. London.
Thomson, W. M. 1893. *The Land of the Book.* London.

HENRY O. THOMPSON

KAP. The eleventh letter of the Hebrew alphabet.

KAPPA. The tenth letter of the Greek alphabet.

KAREAH (PERSON) [Heb *qārēaḥ*]. The father of Johanan and Jonathan, two of the captains of the Judean forces in the open country (2 Kgs 25:23; Jer 40:8). These captains, including the sons of Kareah, approached Gedeliah shortly after the Exile of 587 B.C., and Gedeliah urged their cooperation with the Babylonians. Apart from his sons, nothing else is known of Kareah. The LXX lacks Jonathan and includes only Johanan as the son of Kareah. Jonathan could have easily been dropped from the text through haplography (Carroll *Jeremiah* OTL, 703). In Jeremiah 41–43, the narrative mentions only Johanan, son of Kareah (Jer 41:11; 42:1, 8; 43:2), and Jonathan is not mentioned apart from Jer 40:8. It is perhaps because Jonathan plays no role in the subsequent narrative that the RSV follows the LXX at Jer 40:8, and identifies only Johanan as the son of Kareah. In Hebrew, the name means "bald."

JOHN M. BRACKE

KARKA (PLACE) [Heb *qarqaʿ*]. A station named in the description of the extreme southern border of the tribal allotment of Judah (Josh 15:3). This place, whose name perhaps means "floor" (of earth?), is located between Addar and Azmon. The absence of Karka in Numbers 34, a parallel passage, is presumably a scribal error. The location of this ancient border station is unknown, although Aharoni (*LBHG,* 665) has proposed a tentative identification with Ain Qoseimeh (M.R. 089007), one of three small wells in the vicinity of the oasis of ʿAin el-Qudeirat (Kadesh-barnea?).

WADE R. KOTTER

KARKOR (PLACE) [Heb *qarqōr*]. According to Judg 8:10, Zebah and Zalmunna, the kings of Midian, were in Karkor. Gideon had surprised the Midianites with his 300 men in the famous story in Judges 7. The Midianites fled across the Jordan and Gideon pursued them, indicating that Karkor is in Transjordan. The hosts of Midian had been decimated, but there were still 15,000 who could regroup under their chiefs Zebah and Zalmunna. Apparently they did not think they would be pursued, for they relaxed and did not even post a guard. However, Gideon followed the caravan route E of Nobah and Jogbehah, attacked the army, and captured the two kings.

Karkor means simply "ground." The location of the site is often considered unknown. Some have suggested it is the Karkara or Qarqar S of Hamath, mentioned by Shalmaneser III (*ANET,* 278–79) and Sargon II (*ANET,* 285). Simons (*GTTOT,* 295) suggests this indicates that it was a popular name. However, this Qarqar is located in the N, while the context of Judg 8:10–13 suggests that the site was not only in Transjordan but that Gideon and his troops were traveling E, not N. Simons notes that while the location is unknown, v 11 places it on or near the N-S desert highway, roughly on the same line as the pilgrim highway from Damascus to Mecca. Thus it passed E of Jogbehah, and Gideon pursued his quarry E of Nobah and Jogbehah. This puts Qarqar on the Wadi Sirhan in the N Hegaz, 150 miles from Jogbehah and 50 miles SE of the oasis of Azraq. To Simons, this is not a probable location. But Myers (*IB* 2: 746) accepts the Sirhan location as do Boling (*Judges* AB, 156) and Aharoni (*LBHG,* 241). Keil and Delitzsch (n.d., 353) cite Eusebius and Jerome on their identification of Karkor with the castle of Carcaria, a day's journey from Petra. Keil considers that wrong, since it is too far. The ruins of Nowakis and Jebeiha are NW of Amman. Burckhardt (1822: 612) mentioned a ruin in the neighborhood called Karkagheisch, on the left side of the road from Salt to Amman, 1.5 hours NW of Amman. This would seem to be a more logical place for the Karkor of Judg 8:10. Myers (*IB* 2) relates Jogbehah in Num 32:35 to Jubeihat (M.R. 231159), 15 miles SE of Penuel. Nobah (Num 32:42) was nearby. Boling claims Nobah's location is unknown but relates Jogbehah to Khirbet el-Ajbeihat, 7 miles NW of Amman.

Bibliography

Burckhardt, J. L. 1822. *Travels in Syria and the Holy Land.* London.

Keil, C. F., and Delitzsch, F. n.d. *Joshua, Judges, Ruth.* Vol. 2 of *Commentary on the Old Testament.* Trans. J. Martin. Grand Rapids. Repr. 1986.

HENRY O. THOMPSON

KARNAIM (PLACE) [Heb *qarnayīm*]. See ASHTEROTH-KARNAIM (PLACE).

KARTAH (PLACE) [Heb *qartâ*]. Levitical city assigned to the tribe of Zebulun, which appears in Josh 21:34. There is no parallel to Kartah in the Zebulun listing in 1 Chronicles 6, nor does the city appear outside of Joshua 21. In 1 Chronicles 6 only two cities are named: Rimmono and Tabor, neither of which are mentioned in Joshua 21. There is no record of Kartah in any nonbiblical texts and consequently there are many problems surrounding the identification of this site.

Albright (*ARI,* 209) maintained that the Zebulun list of levitical cities in Joshua is "curiously corrupt." Kartah, he argued, is a repeat of Kartan from Naphtali two verses above. Albright argued that the Chronicles variant of Tabor was correct, eliminating Kartah altogether. Following Albright, Aharoni (*LBHG,* 237) reconstructed the thirty-eighth "original" levitical city as [Chisloth?]-tabor, and identified Chisloth-tabor with Iksal, a city approximately 5 km due W of Mt. Tabor.

It seems probable that in Joshua, Kartah is a repetition from the Naphtali list, and that the Chronicler has preserved the original listing. There is good reason to identify the Tabor of 1 Chr 6:62—Eng 6:77 with Chisloth-tabor. In Josh 19:12, the boundary of Zebulun is described as going "eastward toward the sunrise to the boundary of Chisloth-tabor"; hence Chisloth-tabor is on the E boundary of Zebulun.

Iksal (M.R. 180232) is located on the E edge of the Esdraelon Plain on a low rocky ridge. Immediately to the N are the hills of the lower Galilee. The focus of all archaeological work at Iksal has been on rock-cut tombs and caves, although the earliest date given to the tombs is Roman. There is no indication of any earlier occupation at Iksal.

While Albright argued for Tabor on textual critical

grounds, Abel (*GP*, 299), Wright (*WHAB*, 123), and Peterson (1977: 114–15) concentrated on geographical issues. There is evidence geographically to support Iksal as the levitical city in Zebulun. The major drawback to Iksal is the lack of archaeological information dating to the Iron or LB periods. Until there is further archaeological work done at Iksal, the ancient occupation of this possible site for Chisloth-tabor remains unknown.

Bibliography

Boling, R. 1985. Levitical Cities: Archaeology and Texts. Pp. 23–32 in *Biblical and Related Studies Presented to Samuel Iwry*. Winona Lake, IN.

Mazar, B. 1957. The Cities of the Priests and the Levites. *VTSup* 7: 193–205.

Peterson, J. L. 1977. *A Topographical Surface Survey of the Levitical "Cities" of Joshua 21 and I Chronicles 6*. Diss. Seabury-Western Theological Seminary.

Robinson, E. 1841. *Biblical Researches in Palestine*. Vol. 2. Boston.

JOHN L. PETERSON

KARTAN (PLACE) [Heb *qartân*]. Third levitical city mentioned in the Joshua list for Naphtali (21:32). In 1 Chr 6:61—Eng 6:76 the third Naphtali city is Kiriathaim. Aharoni (*LBHG*, 105) interprets this as a variation on the same name. Years before, Albright (1945: 72) had argued the same position by maintaining the name is preserved in its Galilaean dialectical form in the Chronicler. The only OT reference to Kartan (Kiriathaim) is in the Levitical City lists. It does not appear in the Naphtali distribution list of Joshua nor is it mentioned in any nonbiblical lists. There is no agreement among scholars when it comes to identifying Kartan with an ancient site. However, there are two tells considered possible candidates: Khirbet el-Quneitireh (Tell Raqqat) and Khirbet el-Qureiyeh.

Tell Raqqat (M.R. 199245) has been tentatively identified as Kartan by Aharoni (*LBHG*, 380). It is located 1 km N of modern Tiberias on a hill rising just above Ain el-Fulîyeh. There are impressive sightlines from Tell Raqqat. Extending to the N is the coast of the Sea of Galilee. Here the important Via Maris trade route connected with the Trunk Highway between Egypt and Damascus at Hazor. Directly to the NW of Tell Raqqat is the narrow Arbel Pass, flanked by mountains on both sides. To the S of Tell Raqqat the coastal road continues through Tiberias and Hammath.

Tell Raqqat was mentioned by early geographers, but very few descriptions of the site were given. E. Robinson (1841: 394) passed Tell Raqqat on his visit to the Galilee in 1838, but did not give any details. G. A. Smith (1899: 289–90) commented that Tiberias occupied the site or the neighborhood of Tell Raqqat. There have been numerous visits to the site by archaeologists. Albright (1926: 26) made the first identification at the site by identifying the EB and MB periods. He then argued that the Iron Age town was either under the Bronze Age site or under modern-day Tiberias. In 1949 R. Amiran identified Iron Age pottery. In 1952 an excavation was conducted at Tell Raqqat by the Israel Department of Antiquities (see Aharoni 1953). EB, MB, LB, much Iron Age and a few Persian, Byzantine, and Arab pottery was identified. The levitical city survey made the same identification (except for the Persian) and found each century in Iron I and Iron II represented. In his levitical city study, Peterson (1977: 95) suggested that Tell Raqqat was biblical Hammath, dating from the EB period to Iron II inclusively. During the Roman period Hammath moved to Hammân Ṭabrîyeh, where it flourished during the Roman and Byzantine periods.

Khirbet el-Qureiyeh has been identified with biblical Kartan by G. E. Wright (*WHAB*, 125) and J. Simons (*GTTOT*, 206). The tell is located just N of the present boundary of Israel in the Lebanese mountains of upper Galilee. Khirbet el-Qureiyeh is approximately 6 km W and 1 km N of Tell Qades. This site is close to Aytarun (M.R. 194280), a Lebanese village 3 km N and 3 km W of the present boundary. Because of the plateaus and mountains in upper Galilee, transportation is difficult. The nearest road passing to the S is at Tell Qades. It is not surprising that no geographer ever mentioned Khirbet el-Qureiyeh in their travels.

Nevertheless, following G. E. Wright, Peterson and more recently Boling (1985: 25) have identified Kartan with Khirbet el-Qureiyeh, a site located in the NW section of Naphtali, only a few km from Asher and within 20 km of the Phoenician city, Tyre.

Bibliography

Aharoni, Y. 1953. Tel Raqqat. Trans. H. Katzenstein. Report to the Department of Antiquities. Jerusalem.

Albright, W. F. 1926. The Jordan Valley in the Bronze Age. *AASOR* 6. New Haven, CT.

———. 1945. The List of Levitic Cities. Pp. 49–73 in *Louis Ginzberg Jubilee Volume*. New York.

Amiran, R. 1949. Tel Raqqat, Trans. H. Katzenstein. Report to the Department of Antiquities. Jerusalem.

Boling, R. 1985. Levitical Cities: Archaeology and Texts. Pp. 23–32 in *Biblical and Related Studies*. Winona Lake, IN.

Peterson, J. L. 1977. *A Topographical Surface Survey of the Levitical "Cities" of Joshua 21 and I Chronicles 6*. Diss. Seabury-Western Theological Seminary.

Robinson, E. 1841. *Biblical Researches in Palestine*. Vol. 2. Boston.

Smith, G. A. 1899. *The Historical Geography of the Holy Land*. 6th ed. New York.

JOHN L. PETERSON

KASHRUTH. See MEAL CUSTOMS (JEWISH DIETARY LAWS).

KASSITE LANGUAGE. See LANGUAGES (INTRODUCTORY SURVEY).

KATTATH (PLACE) [Heb *qaṭṭāt*]. A town in the territory of the tribe of Zebulun (Josh 19:15). The majority of scholars equate Kattath with the Kitron of Judg 1:30, since both toponyms occur in verses which also mention the town of Nahalal (see Boling *Judges* AB, 445). However, Kallai (*HGB*, 418) notes that there is no reason to assume that the two toponyms are either variants of or derived via scribal errors from a single original place name.

Abel (*GP* 2: 415) took note of traditions which located

Kattath at Kh. Qutteneh (M.R. 153226). While both the ancient and modern names are superficially similar, the ruin is located on the SW slopes of Mt. Carmel, well outside the area which the tribe of Zebulun seems to have controlled. The exact location of Kattath remains unknown, but Aharoni suggested that the NW edge of the Jezreel Valley is the region in which Kattath should be sought (*LBHG,* 235).

MELVIN HUNT

KEBARA CAVE (M.R. 144218). Kebara Cave is to date the southernmost of the known prehistoric cave sites on Mt. Carmel. It is located on its W flanks, about 3 km from the Mediterranean Sea, and 13 km S of *Naḥal Ha-Meʿarot* (Wadi el-Mughara). The cave is situated 60 m above sea level and consists of a large hall, with an open chimney, 20 m above, in the ceiling.

The Kebara Cave was discovered by M. Stekelis in 1929. A trial sounding was conducted in 1930 by D. Garrod and T. D. McCown which revealed Natufian remains. F. Turville-Petre and D. Baines conducted additional excavations the following year.

The stratigraphy in the cave, established by Turville-Petre and synthesized after his death by Garrod, is as follows: layer A: Bronze Age to Recent; layer B: Lower Natufian; layer C: Kebaran; layers D_1 and D_2: Aurignacian; layer E: Aurignacian; and layer F: Levalloiso-Mousterian.

Further excavations were conducted between 1951 and 1965 by M. Stekelis, who noticed that the stratified remains dip markedly toward the center of the cave. His excavations concentrated on the Upper Paleolithic (Aurignacian) layers and especially the Mousterian levels, to a depth of 8.5 m below the surface. The bedrock was not reached.

Since 1982, Kebara Cave is being excavated by a Joint Israeli-French team, headed by O. Bar-Yosef, B. Vandermeersch, and B. Arensburg.

The following geologically based units have been established: I–III Upper Paleolithic; IV–VI Transitional Period (or industry of a mixed nature); and VII–XIII Mousterian.

Kebara gave its name to an Epipaleolithic flint industry—the Kebaran—typified by predominantly microlithic tools.

Layer A, the most recent stratum, contained sherds from the Bronze Age to recent times.

Layer B is attributed to the Lower Natufian. A collective burial pit was uncovered which contained adult and infant skeletons. Noteworthy among the flint tools were the numerous sickle blades and lunates, many of which were retouched with Helewan retouch. The rich assemblage of bone tools included points, bipoints, hooks, harpoons, needles, combs, and four sickle hafts decorated with carved animal heads. The jewelry consisted of pear-shaped bone pendants, pierced bones, teeth, and shells. Among the basalt objects, some were decorated.

Layer C consists of the Kebaran industry with microliths greatly outnumbering normal-sized tools. Among the microliths, a characteristic backed bladelet, obliquely truncated, known by the name "Kebaran bladelet" is well represented.

Layers D and E are assigned to the local Aurignacian. Layer D, with its two sublayers, parallels the Upper Paleolithic IV of the Neuville division. It is characterized by many-nosed and steep scrapers.

Layer E parallels the Upper Paleolithic III and is characterized by a large number of El-Wad points, and a decrease in the number of the Aurignacian scrapers. One of the main characteristics of the Aurignacian levels is a preponderance of large circular hearths, with remains of charred animal bones.

Layer F is assigned to an upper phase of the Mousterian. Several living floors were distinguished, marked by hearths with charcoal and ashes, broken animal bones and teeth, as well as numerous flint tools. A concentration of refuse along the walls marked the kitchen midden areas. Gazelle, *Dama, Capra sp.,* and *Cervus elaphus* were the most common animals hunted.

The flint industry is characterized by a high proportion of well-made delicate flakes, blades, and points in Levalloisian technique as well as many side scrapers of various types.

A C_{14} date of 41,000 ± 1,000 B.P. was obtained for the upper part of the Mousterian layer.

In 1965 at a lower level, the buried skeleton of a 7-month-old infant with Neanderthal characteristics was unearthed. Another Neanderthal skeleton, that of a young man, was found in a recent excavation in unit XI.

The overall picture which emerges from the finds is that the Kebara Cave served as a multi-activity center—as a home base, a workshop for tool making, and as a burial site.

Bibliography

Bar-Yosef, O. 1982. Kebara Cave. *Archaeological Newsletter* 82: 10–11 (in Hebrew).

Bar-Yosef, O., and Vandermeersch, B. 1983. Kebara Cave. *Archaeological Newsletter* 83: 21–22 (in Hebrew).

Bate, D. M. A. 1932. A Note on the Fauna of the Athlit Caves. *JRAI* 62: 277–79.

Davis, S. 1977. The Ungulate Remains from Kebara Cave. *EI* 13: 150–63.

Garrod, D. A. E. 1954. Excavations at the Mugharet Kebara, Mount Carmel, 1931: The Aurignacian Industries. *Proceedings of the Prehistoric Society* 20: 155–92.

Saxson, E. C. 1974. The Mobile Herding Economy of Kebarah Cave, Mt. Carmel: An Economic Analysis of the Faunal Remains. *Journal of Archaeological Science* 1: 27–45.

Schick, T., and Stekelis, M. 1977. Mousterian Assemblages in Kebara Cave, Mount Carmel. *EI* 13: 97–149.

Smith, P., and Arensburg, B. 1977. A Mousterian Skeleton from Kebara Cave. *EI* 13: 164–76.

Stekelis, M. 1952. Notes and News: Kebbara. *IEJ* 2: 142.

———. 1953. Notes and News: Kabbara. *IEJ* 3: 262.

———. 1955. Kabbara. *RB* 62: 84–85.

———. 1956. Nouvelles fouilles dans la Grotte de Kébarah. Pp. 385–89 in *Congressos Internationales de Ciencias Prehistoricas Y Protohistoricas, Madrid 1954.* Zaragoza.

———. 1964. Kebara Cave. *IEJ* 14: 277.

———. 1977. Kebara Cave. *EAEHL* 3: 699–702.

Turville-Petre, F. 1932. Excavations in the Mugharet el-Kebarah. *JRAI* 62: 271–76.

Ziffer, D. 1978. A Re-evaluation of the Upper-Palaeolithic Industry at Kebara Cave and their place in the Aurignacian Culture of the Levant. *Paléorient* 4: 273–93.

TAMAR SCHICK

KEDAR (PERSON) [Heb *qēdār*]. The second son of Ishmael (Gen 25:13; 1 Chr 1:29). The "sons of Ishmael" constituted a group of N Arabian tribes who flourished from the 8th through the 4th centuries B.C. Kedar, attested from 738 B.C. well into the Hellenistic period, was the most powerful among them (Eph'al 1982: 223–27; Knauf 1989: 66, 96–108). See ISHMAELITES.

In Assyrian and Neo-Babylonian texts, the name of the tribe is given as *Qidr, Qidar/Qidâr, Qadr, Qadar/Qadâr,* and *Qudar/Qudâr* (Eph'al 1982: 223–24). As a personal name, *qdr* occurs in Safaitic, Thamudic, Nabatean *(qdrw),* and Standard Arabic (*Qidr* and *Qudâr*). Among more recent bedouin tribes, there were *Qudêriyyah* and *Qudêrât.* The names are derived from Ar *qadara* "to decree" or "to possess power"; this etymology matches the role played by the tribe of Kedar within the Ishmaelite confederacy (Knauf 1989: 66).

In Jer 2:10 (late 7th century B.C.), Kedar and the *Kittîm* ("Cypriots," Greeks) mark the E and the W end of the world as it was known to the prophet. Jer 49:28–33, an "oracle against a proud desert power" (Dumbrell 1972), may reflect Nebuchadnezzar's Arabian campaign of 599/598 B.C. Kedar is mentioned in the heading and in the introduction of the oracle only (v 28), and may belong to its final editing rather than to its first utterance. Verses 29–33 call the inhabitants of the desert, who own camels, sheep, and tents, "kingdom of Hazor" (v 28), "inhabitants of Hazor" (v 30), and "Hazor" (v 33). "Hazor" does not refer to the well-known city in N Palestine, but to "the country of *ḥăṣērîm,*" hamlets and/or fortified enclosures (cf. Gen 25:16; Isa 42:11). The description of the Arab hair style in Jer 49:32 refers back to Jer 25:23–24, where the expression "the people with the edge of their hair cropped" denotes the bedouin. Iconographically, this "Arabian hairdress" is well attested from the 6th century B.C. to the 1st century A.D. (Knauf 1989: 103 n. 564).

Ezek 27:21, a part of the list dealing with the "trade partners of Tyre," credits the "princes of Kedar" with delivering sheep to the Phoenicians. Because this list still considers Edom to be a flourishing area (27:16), it should antedate Edom's conquest by Nabonidus in 553/552 B.C. For "Trito-Isaiah," the Kedarites are still paradigmatic sheep-breeders, Isa 60:7 (late 6th century B.C.). Knauf (1989: 109) assumes that "Kedar and Nebaioth" in Isa 60:7 already refer to the Nabateans, who, as a clan or a subtribe of Kedar, had immigrated into Edom in the course of the 6th century. A cuneiform tablet from Ṭawîlân near Petra, dated to the 1st year of Darius (probably Darius I, i.e., 521/520 B.C.), contains a contract for the delivery of small cattle to Harran in N Syria (Dalley 1984).

"Deutero-Isaiah," who believes Kedar to live in the desert as well as between rocks and mountains (Isa 42:11), may equally have located Kedar in the country that previously was Edom (the LXX renders *yšby slʿ* "rock-people" as "inhabitants of Petra"). No firm date can be proposed for Isa 21:16–17. The two verses announce Kedar's doom within three years, and characterize the Kedarites as bowmen (v 17; cf. Gen 21:20). These verses form an appendix (in prose and of unknown date) to the poetical oracle "on the wilderness" (Isa 21:13–15), which may comment on Nabonidus' march of conquest in 552 B.C. (Galling 1963; Lindsay 1976). The author of this appendix may have added his note on Kedar, because he missed the bedouin in 21:13–15, where only two N Arabian cities, Dedan and Tema, are mentioned. Relations between Tema and Kedar are documented in Babylonian cuneiform correspondence (*UET* IV 167, 5–11; Ebeling 1949: 163–64, #303; Knauf 1989: 75, n. 393), and in an Aramaic inscription on a jar (5th/4th centuries B.C.) found at Tema (Livingstone et al. 1983: 108), which reads: "1 wine. Kedar."

Psalm 120 is either a lament by an exile in bedouin country (cf. the arrows and the charcoal from juniper wood, a typical plant of the N Arabian desert [v 4]), or a complaint by a peaceful mind who compares his compatriots (in postexilic Jerusalem?) to bloodthirsty bedouin (vv 2–7). Meshech, evoked in parallel to the "tents of Kedar" in v 5, may not refer to a region in Asia Minor (as in Gen 10:2; Ezek 27:13; 32:26; 38:2; 39:1), but rather to a clan or subtribe of Kedar, Ar **Mâsik* (Knauf 1989: 72, n. 363).

Geshem, Nehemiah's adversary (see GESHEM) who controlled S Palestine and Sinai, S Transjordan and NW Arabia around the middle of the 5th century B.C., originated from the tribe of Kedar, according to an inscription left behind at Tell el-Maskhûta by his son (Dumbrell 1971). The realm of these two Kedarites comprised all of the later *Arabia Petraea.* This observation lends support to the assumption that the Nabateans emerged out of the Kedarites. Two texts from the 3d century B.C. refer to the Nabateans under the name of Kedar: Cant 1:5 and the Minaean "lists of hierodules".

Cant 1:5 mentions the black tents of the tribes of Kedar and *Shalmah* (see SHALMA, which MT vocalizes as "Solomon"). In the 3d century B.C., Shalmah was a tribe to the S of the Nabateans. This does not leave many choices among the contemporary Arab tribes for the identification of Kedar.

The so-called Minaean "lists of hierodules" (for the texts, cf. Garbini 1974: 115–24, M 392–97) are actually epigraphic marriage certificates, set up in the main temple of the Minaean capital by merchants from one of their trading colonies in Arabia or on the shores of the Mediterranean who had married women from their guest country and now publicly announced their marriages back at home. These lists, mainly from the 3d century B.C., contain all the "addresses" of their trading partners known from other sources—with the exception of the Nabateans. All major native cities or tribes of the wives can be identified—with the exception of Kedar, who occur three times in these lists. Thus, from Cant 1:5 and the Minaean lists it can be concluded that the Nabateans were known as Kedarites to at least some of their neighbors as late as the 3d century B.C. (Knauf 1989: 106–8).

Pliny the Elder is the last author who referred to Kedar. According to *HN* 5. 11(12), 65, the *Cedrei* live S of the Sinai peninsula, the *Cauchbei* (sic!) E of them, and both have the Nabateans for neighbors. This geography does not make sense. Pliny may quote a source from the 4th/3d centuries B.C. which he did not fully understand. His source may have tried to depict the emancipation of the new Nabatean tribe from its previous subordinate role within the tribe of Kedar.

Bibliography

Dalley, S. 1984. The Cuneiforn Tablet from Tell Tawilan. *Levant* 16: 19–22.

Dumbrell, W. J. 1971. The Tell el-Maskhuta Bowls and the "Kingdom" of Qedar in the Persian Period. *BASOR* 203: 33–44.

———. 1972. Jeremiah 49, 29–33. An Oracle Against a Proud Desert Power. *AJBA* 1/5: 99–109.

Ebeling, E. 1949. *Neubabylonische Briefe. ABAW* N.F. 30. Munich.

Eph'al, I. 1982. *The Ancient Arabs. Nomads on the Borders of the Fertile Crescent, 9th–5th Centuries B.C.* Jerusalem.

Galling, K. 1963. Jesaja 21 im Lichte der neuen Nabonidtexte. Pp. 49–62 in *Tradition und Situation* (A. Weiser festschrift). Göttingen.

Garbini, G. 1974. *Iscrizioni sudarabiche, I: Iscrizioni minee.* Ricerche X. Naples.

Knauf, E. A. 1989. *Ismael.* 2d ed. ADPV. Wiesbaden.

Lindsay, J. 1976. The Babylonian Kings and Edom, 605–550 B.C. *PEQ* 108: 23–39.

Livingstone, A., et al. 1983. Taima': Recent Soundings and New Inscribed Material. *Atlal* 7: 102–16.

ERNST AXEL KNAUF

KEDEMAH (PERSON) [Heb *qēdmâ*]. A son of Ishmael (Gen 25:15; 1 Chr 1:31). All the sons of Ishmael are prominent N Arabian tribes or cities of the 1st millennium B.C. (see ISHMAELITES), more or less amply attested as such in both biblical and extrabiblical sources—with the exception of Kedemah. For Kedemah as a personal name, one may compare Ar (and Safaitic) *Qudâmah.* Because Kedemah figures last in the list of Ishmael's twelve sons, the name can be interpreted as a personification of the "people of the East" (Heb *qedem;* see EAST, PEOPLE OF THE) which was added to the sons of Ishmael in order to make them number twelve (Knauf 1989: 81).

Bibliography

Knauf, E. A. 1989. *Ishmael.* 2d ed. ADPV. Wiesbaden.

ERNST AXEL KNAUF

KEDEMOTH (PLACE) [Heb *qĕdēmôt*]. Third levitical city allotted to the tribe of Reuben. In Josh 21:37, Kedemoth is missing from the MT and the verse must be reconstructed. In 1 Chr 6:64—Eng 6:79, the verse is intact. Besides the two references to Kedemoth as a levitical city, it appears in two other verses in the OT. In Deut 2:26, Moses sends messengers "from the wilderness of Kedemoth" to Sihon in an attempt to receive permission for the Hebrews to pass through Sihon's land. This request is denied. It is important to note the phrase "wilderness of Kedemoth," for this is one of the few geographical descriptions given relating to this city. The other reference to Kedemoth is in the distribution/inheritance list of Reuben in Josh 13:18, which supplies no additional information.

Outside of the OT, only Eusebius (*Onomast.* 114: 5–6) in the 4th century makes reference to this levitical city. Briefly he restates Deut 2:26, asserting that Moses sent messengers from the wilderness of Kedemoth to Sihon, king of the Amorites. As early as Eusebius, the exact location of this site was probably lost and no further mention is made of the site until modern geographers started to associate different archaeological sites with the biblical city.

There is not universal agreement regarding the location of biblical Kedemoth and the geographers give their suggestions tentatively. Kedemoth is a town situated N of the Arnon. It is probably an outpost toward the desert. It is impossible to define its location more precisely. Three possible sites are usually considered to be Kedemoth: Qasr ez-Zaᶜferan, es-Saliyeh, and er-Remeil.

There are two Qasr ez-Zaᶜferans, located about 1 km apart. The mounds are approximately 10 to 12 km to the E of Khirbet Libb and 4 to 5 km to the NNW of Tell el-Medeiyineh. Both are located in a group of low hills and although the other hills do not seem to be fortified, these two mounds were.

The most N mound was the main settlement; this Glueck has called Qasr ez-Zaᶜferan I. It is the larger of the two sites, and a Nabatean fortress had been built on the foundation of an earlier and larger structure. The pottery found at Qasr ez-Zaᶜferan I was Early Iron I, Early Iron II and Nabatean.

Qasr ez-Zaᶜferan II is located about 1 km S of ez-Zaᶜferan I. There is also a large Nabatean fortress built with the same type of blocks as the fortress at ez-Zaᶜferan. Most of the sherds found belonged to the Nabatean period, together with plain and painted Byzantine. A few sherds could be dated to Early Iron I. Glueck (1934: 30) argued that the Iron I sherds were carried to ez-Zaᶜferan II, as he believed the site was not actually occupied during Early Iron I. There were also decorated Moabite sherds. The most serious argument against this identification has been raised by van Zyl (1960: 75, 85). He has maintained that Qasr ez-Zaᶜferan is located too far to the N and would like to see it placed more to the SE. Van Zyl argues this on the grounds of Num 21:13 and Deut 2:26, that Kedemoth should be located N of the Arnon River on the E edge of the desert. The site he proposes for biblical Kedemoth is es-Saliyeh.

Es-Saliyeh is located N of Qasr Abu el-Kharaq on the N side of Wadi Salieyh. It is a large site, situated on a rise at the S edge of a fertile plateau. Presumably, es-Saliyeh depended upon the cultivation of its arable land. At the site there remain many ruined buildings, cisterns, and low mounds, dating to the early Iron Age and rebuilt by the Nabateans. The pottery found at es-Saliyeh has included LB, Early Iron I–II and Nabatean sherds. Van Zyl maintains that es-Saliyeh is biblical Kedemoth because it borders the desert. Although the description in the MT does not explicitly state that Kedemoth borders the desert (the reference need not be to more than pasture lands), the argument is interesting particularly because es-Saliyeh lies right on the W edge of the Desert of Kedemoth.

The third suggestion for the location of biblical Kedemoth is er-Remeil, situated about 3.5 km SW of Khirbet el-Medeiyineh. From the S it overlooks the Wadi re-Remeil, which is an extension of the Wadi eth-Themed. Positioned on a high point, er-Remeil can be seen for kilometers in all directions. At this site we have another example of the extensive fortress system in Moab during the Iron Age. The pottery that has been identified at er-Rumeil dates to the 9th and 8th centuries B.C.

The levitical city Kedemoth was probably located at es-Saliyeh. The biblical texts regarding this city are scanty and there are no references to it outside of the Bible; however, Van Zyl's reconstruction is convincing. See Peterson 1977: 671–86.

Bibliography

Anderson, B. W. 1964. *Archaeological Newsletter #3, 1963–64*. Jerusalem.

Glueck, N. 1934. Explorations in Eastern Palestine I. *AASOR* 14. Philadelphia.

Musil, A. 1907. *Arabica Petraea*. Vol. 2. Vienna.

Peterson, J. L. 1977. *A Topographical Surface Survey of the Levitical "Cities" of Joshua 21 and I Chronicles 6*. Diss. Seabury-Western Theological Seminary.

Zyl, A. H. van. 1960. *The Moabites*. Leiden.

JOHN L. PETERSON

KEDESH (PLACE) [Heb *qedeš*]. **1.** A variant form of KADESH-BARNEA.

2. A levitical city in Issachar (1 Chr 6:57), assigned to the sons of Gershon. The parallel version (Josh 21:28) is KISHION; therefore, some scholars maintained that the version in 1 Chr 6:57 is a corruption inspired by Kedesh in Galilee in 1 Chr 6:61.

Scholars supporting the version of 1 Chr 6:57 identify Kedesh with Tell Abu Kudeis, a small mound in the Jezreel valley between Taanach and Megiddo. Some scholars advanced the theory that this mound should also be identified with Kedesh near where Sisera was killed (Judg 4:11). Others maintain that this event occurred near Kedesh in Naphtali (see #3 below), where also Barak would have gathered his people in the battle against Sisera (Judg 4:6). However, this latter view has been rejected by scholars who maintain that the two are different localities and that Kedesh in Naphtali should be located near the plain of Zaanaim (literally "Alon Besananim," Judg 4:11) which is between Mount Tabor and the Jordan river. They claim that it is implausible that Sisera fled "on his feet" (Judg 4:17) all the way to Kedesh in Naphtali, which was among Israelite possessions. In addition, Judg 5:19 places the battle "in Taanach by the waters of Megiddo," which supports the identification of Tel Abu Kudeis with the place where Sisera died.

The excavations in Tel Abu Kudeis revealed finds dating from the 12th century B.C.E. (which is, according to many, the date of the Deborah War) to the 9th century B.C.E. Among the finds in level IV (9th century), are a sanctuary and a four-horn altar which testify to a tradition of a sacred place. See also Kallai *HGB*, 228, 232–35, 472; *Historical Ency. of Palestine* 4: 816 (in Hebrew); *EAEHL* 3: 702–3.

Bibliography

Stern, E. 1969. Excavations at Kedesh, (Tell Abu Kudeis), *Qadmoniot* 2. 95–97 (in Hebrew).

Stern, E., and Beith-Arieh, Y. 1973. Excavations at Kedesh, (Tell Abu Kudeish). Pp. 93–122 in *Excavations and Researches*. Tell Aviv.

RAMI ARAV

3. The first levitical city mentioned in the Naphtali distribution in Galilee. Besides occurring in the levitical city lists of Josh 21:32 and 1 Chr 6:61—Eng 6:76, Kedesh is one of the Cities of Refuge (Josh 20:7). It appears as one of the cities given in the allotment to Naphtali (Josh 19:37). In other OT accounts the king of Kedesh was defeated by Joshua (Josh 12:22), although Noth (*Josua* HAT, 73) argues that this Kedesh must be identified with the Kedesh in the Jezreel valley. Kedesh was the home of Barak (Judg 4:6) and it is where Deborah and Barak gathered their followers for the battle with Sisera (Judg 4:1–10). Aharoni (*LBHG*, 223–24) associates the Kedesh in Naphtali of the Deborah narrative with Kh. Qedish (M.R. 202237). 2 Kgs 15:29 tells how Tiglath-pileser, during the reign of Pekah, captured Kedesh and took the people captive. It was here that Jonathan Maccabeus defeated the army of Demetrius (1 Macc 11:63, 73) and it is mentioned in Josephus (*JW* 2.459) as being a Tyrian village.

There is basic agreement that Kedesh in Galilee is to be identified with Tell Qades (M.R. 200279), located in the hill country NW of Lake Huleh in upper Galilee. It lies in the E zone overlooking the N part of the Jordan valley. Tell Qades' location is strategic for the whole Galilee region. It stands at one end of a small but fertile plain. This area has spacious tablelands with an abundance of springs. The highest parts of upper Galilee are mountainous, making habitation difficult and transportation nearly impossible. One of the major roads from the Jordan valley to the Phoenician coast passed by Tell Qades leading W to Abdon and Achzib in the Acco Plain. This was a rugged road—the climb out of the Jordan valley is steep and treacherous, while the continuation of the road in the mountains as it passes Tell Qades on its way to the W coast is difficult. This was nevertheless one of the major lines of communication, making Kedesh one of the most important cities in upper Galilee.

E. Robinson (1841: 355) first identified Tell Qades with biblical Kedesh in Naphtali. He made his identification by associating the name of Tell Qades with biblical Kedesh. The early geographers, including C. W. Wilson, C. R. Conder, and H. H. Kitchener (*SWP* 1: 228) and Guérin (1880: 355–62), all concentrated their efforts on the tombs and mausoleums. It was not until Albright's visit in 1925 (1925: 12) that the different historical periods were identified. Since Albright there have been numerous surveys and soundings conducted at Tell Qades, including a probe conducted by Y. Aharoni (1953: 263). The occupations that have been identified through probes and surveys include the EB, MB, LB, Iron I, Iron II, Hellenistic, Roman, and Arab periods. See also Peterson 1977: 67–76.

Tell Qades is one of the most northern sites associated with the levitical cities W of the Jordan. This means that this refuge city was not only strategically located geographically, but it was also an important communication center between the Canaanites/Phoenicians/Tyrians and Israel. See also QADES, TELL.

Bibliography

Aharoni, Y. 1953. News and Notes. *IEJ* 3: 261–68.

Albright, W. F. 1925. Bronze Age Mounds of Northern Palestine and the Hauran: The Spring Trip of the School in Jerusalem. *BASOR* 19: 5–19.

Guérin, M. V. 1880. *Description Géographique, historique et archéologique de la Palestine.* Paris.
Peterson, J. L. 1977. A Topographical Surface Survey of the Levitical "Cities" of Joshua 21 and 1 Chronicles 6. Th.D. diss. Evanston.
Robinson, E. 1841. *Biblical Researches in Palestine.* Vol. 3. Boston.

JOHN L. PETERSON

KEDRON (PLACE) [Gk *Kedrōn*]. A town fortified by Cendebeus, one of the commanders of Antiochus VII, who wanted to use the town as a staging area for raids against Judea ca. 139–138 B.C. (1 Macc 15:38–41). This action provoked a military response from Simon the Maccabee and his sons, who routed Cendebeus' forces and forced them to retreat to Kedron (1 Macc 16:1–9); it is not clear whether Kedron was then destroyed by the Maccabean force (v 10 seems to imply that only Azotus was burned; but see Goldstein, *1 Maccabees* AB, 522). The passages clearly indicate that Kedron was in the coastal plain (15:38) located in the vicinity of Jamnia and Azotus (Ashdod), not too far from Gazara (=Gezer). Abel *(GP)* was the first to identify Kedron with the village of Qaṭrā (M.R. 129136), which may be derived from an original Qiṭron (*GTTOT,* 147). Such a location would have accommodated military forays up the Sorek valley into the Shephelah and W hill country of Judah.

GARY A. HERION

KEFAR BIRᶜAM (M.R. 189272). The Arabic name for a Roman ruin NW of Gush Halav (see GISCALA) and just NE of Sasa, located alongside an abandoned Maronite village. Birᶜam is the site where two ancient synagogues have been reported. One of these has not survived but was said by medieval Jewish travelers to be in the village. When H. Kohl and C. Watzinger surveyed the site in 1905, the remains of the synagogue in the town had already been lost. The discussion, therefore, focuses only on the restored remains of the synagogue just S of the modern village.

The site is not mentioned in any ancient sources, but was doubtless a very important Jewish town by the 3d century C.E. (Middle Roman times). Gush Halav is one of very few other settlements in this general area to have had two synagogues, which underscores the importance of the settlement. Depending on the identification of ancient MEIRON with Mero of Josephus, it is possible that Birᶜam was outside the borders of Israel and was in the municipality of Tyre (Avi-Yonah 1977: 134), which might explain its absence in ancient sources.

The synagogue was restored by the Israel Department of Antiquities and is maintained by the National Parks Authority, but no excavation report on the site exists. It is a monumental basilical structure 15.2 m wide and 20 m long, with a triple doorway on its S facade that is oriented S toward Jerusalem. A well-preserved porch, 5.35 m wide and supported by eight columns, runs the length of the facade. In conception and design the synagogue is similar to Meiron, which also has a porch at the S end. The facade wall of the synagogue is particularly well-preserved and is constructed of ashlar stones. The central portal, 2.65 m high and 1.42 m wide, is elegant with its lintel depicting two Winged victories bearing a wreath. The figures, however, have been purposefully destroyed. Windows have been placed above each of the three portals; on the sill of the E window is the Hebrew inscription: "Built by Eliezer Son of Yudan."

The interior of the building is paved with large flagstones. Only one column and several pedestals were found *in situ.* Judging from the pedestals and capitals found in the porch, the columns had attic bases and the capitals were molded with ovolo, cavetto, and abacus. The central nave is surrounded by aisles on all three sides. Two rows of six columns run N–S, and two additional columns close the N end where two heart-shaped columns stand in the corners. Although Avigad (1977: 707) follows Kohl and Watzinger in drawing an entrance on the E wall, it is not clear that there is justification for it (Kohl and Watzinger 1916: Pl. XII). Indeed, the Israelis have restored the W wall with a side entrance. No remains of any upper story were found.

The synagogue is among the best-preserved ruins in all of Israel today and presents a dramatic picture of the remnants of the Galilean highland culture from Roman times.

Bibliography

Amiran, R. 1956. A Fragment of Ornamental Relief from Kefar Barᶜam. *IEJ* 6: 239–45.
Avigad, N. 1977. Kefar Birᶜam. *EAEHL* 3: 704–7.
Avi-Yonah, M. 1977. *The Holy Land: From the Persian to the Arab Conquests (536 B.C. to A.D. 640).* Grand Rapids.
Chiat, M. J. S. 1982. *Handbook of Synagogue Architecture.* Brown Judaic Studies 29. Chico, CA.
Kohl, H., and Watzinger, C. 1916. Antike Synagogen in Galileae. *WVDOG* 89–100.

ERIC M. MEYERS

KEFAR GILᶜADI (M.R. 203294). A modern kibbutz in the extreme N of Israel ca. 20 km E of Tyre. Two sites have long been known in the area—the large mound N of the kibbutz where the former Arab village of Abil el-Qamḥ once stood (M.R. 204296; identified with biblical Abel-beth-maacah, *GP* 2: 354), and Khirbet Niḥa, which lies NW of the kibbutz and was occupied from the 1st century B.C. on. In 1957 a survey was conducted in the area surrounding this kibbutz, revealing the existence of three new sites: (1) a site NE of the Rawaḥina spring which yielded Neolithic and Chalcolithic remains (see A below); (2) an area of tombs and mausoleums S of the kibbutz, called Givat ha-Shoket (see B below); and (3) a small, flat mound near a spring S of Givat ha-Shoket (see C below).

A. The Rawaḥina Spring Site

During excavations in 1957 and 1962, an area of 200 square dunams was exposed containing four distinguishable strata (3 Chalcolithic and 1 Neolithic). The top stratum (I) contained the lower portions of round stone silos, the pottery of which resembles Ghassulian ware. In strata II–III were uncovered foundations of a building containing pottery similar to the Chalcolithic ware of Jericho VIII and Wadi Rabah (level II).

Stratum IV contained two older occupation phases: IVa (the upper phase) contained both a wall over 1 m thick built of large rubble stone, and a clay fertility figurine; IVb (the lower and oldest phase) rested on virgin soil. The flint tools (axes, adzes, hoes, blades, sickle blades, arrowheads, and spearheads) were similar in both phases, and most of the pottery from both phases resembles the "dark-faced burnished ware" known from Cilicia and the Amuq plain (see Hole 1959). In phase IVb were found sherds of cord-marked ware known from excavations at Tabat el-Ḥamam in N Syria (Braidwood 1940). Radiocarbon tests of charcoal from that phase fixed a date of ca. 6900 B.C. (± 320 years), thus the pottery from this phase represents some of the earliest found in the ancient Near East, roughly comparable in date to the earliest pottery excavated at Chatal Hüyük in Anatolia. These Neolithic remains found near the Rawaḥina spring are much closer in character to those found in Neolithic sites in Lebanon and Syria than are those excavated further S in Palestine (Kaplan 1959).

B. The Givat Ha-Shoket Mausoleum

The excavations here in 1961 exposed the lower part of a Roman period mausoleum (9 × 9 m) with walls 1.8 m thick (Kaplan 1967). Three superimposed layers of burials were found on the floor. The topmost level (stratum I) yielded an empty sarcophagus, with the name "Hezekiah" inscribed on one of its short sides.

The intermediate level (stratum II) included a complex of 7 rectangular graves filling a cavity below the floor of the mausoleum. Although most of the graves contained coffins made of thin lead sheets, one had a heavy lead coffin ornamented with reliefs depicting Hercules in a gabled frame, a roaring lion also in a gabled frame, Corinthian columns, and panels depicting grape clusters, vine tendrils, and birds. Inside it was found a rare gold diadem inlaid with semiprecious stones and also a gold chain bracelet with greenish stones. Several glass vessels of the 3d century A.D. were found in some of the graves.

The lower level (stratum III), stratigraphically underlying the 7 graves, yielded a marble sarcophagus partly concealed in the rock. One of its long sides bore a Gk inscription (painted in red) with the name "Heraklides." Inside was a sheet-lead coffin (actually the inner lining of a wooden coffin) containing a human skeleton.

This stratigraphy suggests that the mausoleum was actually used for burials in two separate periods. Hezekiah's sarcophagus actually constitutes the oldest artifact in the mausoleum; indeed, the mausoleum seems to have been built originally to preserve it, probably by Heraklides, his son, who hoped to be buried there himself. Apparently when the pit was dug for Heraklides' own sarcophagus, Hezekiah's was shifted aside and then later restored to its original place. This first period dates not later than the Severan dynasty (A.D. 193–235), and accounts for the remains in strata I and III. The second period begins in the time of Diocletian, when the first graves in stratum II were dug beneath the floor of the mausoleum ca. A.D. 290–295; the final grave was probably dug ca. A.D. 310. Once again, the sarcophagus of Hezekiah was moved aside during the digging of these tombs, and later was returned to its original location (thus its final stratigraphic position *above* stratum II).

C. The Mound S of Givat Ha-Shoket

This small mound was occupied mainly in the Israelite period, and may well be biblical Janoah, one of the towns in Naphtali conquered by Tiglath-pileser III (2 Kgs 15:29). This identification is based both on the fact that Janoah appears in the biblical list after Ijon and Abel-beth-maachah, and before Kedesh and Hazor, and on the similarity between its name and that of Khirbet Niḥa nearby (which was only occupied from the 1st century B.C. on, when the area of Givat ha-Shoket served as its cemetery).

Bibliography

Braidwood, R. and L. 1940. Report on Two Sondages on the Coast of Syria South of Tartous. *Syria* 21: 183–226.

Hole, F. 1959. A Reanalysis of Basal Tabbat al-Hamman. *Syria* 36: 149–83.

Kaplan, J. 1959. The Neolithic Pottery of Palestine. *BASOR* 156: 15–22.

———. 1967. A Mausoleum at Kfar Giladi. *EI* 8: 104–113 (in Hebrew).

JACOB KAPLAN

KEHELATHAH (PLACE) [Heb *qĕhelātâ*]. The seventh encampment of the Israelites after leaving the wilderness of Sinai, as listed in Num 33:22–23, where it is placed between Rissah and Mount Shepher. Many scholars suggest that this is a duplicate for Makheloth in Num 33:25–26, since LXX preserves very similar names for both: Makellath in 33:22–23 and Makeloth in 33:25–26 (*GTTOT,* 256). Both names also have similar meanings, "assembly," or the like. A suggested location is Kuntilet Ajjrud, also called Kuntilet Qraye (*GP,* 214; M.R. 094956). For a discussion of the location of any of the places associated with the journey of the Israelites from Egypt through Sinai, see DOPHKAH.

Bibliography

Beit-Arieh, I. 1988. The Route Through Sinai—Why the Israelites Fleeing Egypt Went South. *BARev* 15/3: 28–37.

JEFFREY R. ZORN

KEILAH (PLACE) [Heb *qĕʿîlâ*]. A fortified town of Judah (Josh 15:44; Kallai HGB, 335). Keilah was located in the E part of the Shephelah about 13.5 km NW of Hebron. The important role Keilah played in OT history is reflected in references to the site both in the Bible (Josh 15:44; 1 Samuel 23; 1 Chr 4:29; Neh 3:17–18) and the Amarna Tablets. Today scholars identify the ancient town with the present-day site of Kh. Qila (M.R. 150113; Aharoni *LBHG,* 123; Kallai *HGB,* 381, 385).

During the Amarna period, Keilah was caught in a struggle between two Canaanite city-state kings, Shuwardata of Hebron, and Abdu-Ḫeba of Jerusalem. Located near the border between the two regions, the troops of Keilah became part of Shuwardata's military force as he made encroachments on Abdu-Ḫeba's territory. Abdu-Ḫeba, who saw Shuwardata's tactics as a violation of the agreement between the city-states and Egypt, protested the violation and the use of the troops of Keilah, and appealed for assistance to the king of Egypt (*ANET,* 489, nos. 289 and 290; Aharoni *LBHG,* 174).

Several features combined to make Keilah an important site at different times in biblical history. It was located in the E or upper part of the Shephelah, the band of the Shephelah nearest the central hill country. It was situated on a N-S route which connected a number of sites in the E Shephelah (*RAB,* 85, 87). It was a fortified town which had "gates and bars" (1 Sam 23:7), perhaps part of a line of fortresses running N and S in the E Shephelah. Also, the E Shephelah, including the area in which Keilah was located, most likely was forested. Perhaps for this reason the area around Keilah was not heavily populated, especially during the 2d millennium B.C.E. (*RAB,* 86). However, the thickets of the forest offered protection for those seeking refuge.

David attempted to use Keilah as his headquarters and a place of refuge from Saul. He gained control of the site in a battle with the Philistines who had attacked the town and robbed the threshing floors of the inhabitants (1 Sam 23:1–6). However, his attempted plan was foiled by the citizens of Keilah, who apparently were loyal to the authority of Saul (1 Sam 23:7–13).

During the period of the divided kingdom, Keilah, along with eight other towns, was a part of the district of Mareshah (*LBHG,* 353). During the period of restoration, the Persian period, Keilah was a district capital near the SW border of the province of Judah, a province which had been drastically reduced in size (*LBHG,* 416–18). Apparently Keilah and other towns in that district were repaired and resettled by the returnees from Babylonian territory (Neh 3:17–18). According to Eusebius, the prophet Habakkuk was buried at Keilah.

LAMOINE F. DEVRIES

KEISAN, TELL (M.R. 164253). A site in the middle of the plain of Acre.

A. Name and Identification

The modern Arabic name of the site, Tell Keisan, may signify "of treachery" and is attested from the 12th century onward in Arab chronicles. It presumably refers to a military event now forgotten. None of the proposed identifications of Keisan with a biblical city is convincing. Kishion in Josh 19:20 (R. Dussaud and A. Alt) relies on the similarity of sound with Tel Qison (or Kison) read on certain maps, but the name is mistaken; besides, the Kishon runs much farther to the S. The same comment applies to Allammelech (Josh 19:26): the wadi of that name passes too far to the S. Achshaph (Josh 19:25) is a more serious candidate, since it is often mentioned in association with Acco. See ACHSHAPH. The papyrus Anastasi I speaks of Achshaph and seems to place it to the S of Acco, which is not the case with Tell Keisan, and implies that a city separates the two, which is not possible. But this Egyptian text is not easy to interpret. Another possibility is Mishal (Josh 19:26; Y. Aharoni), but no argument supports this view; three or four other cities mentioned in the list of Joshua are also possible candidates, but there is no means of deciding among them. Therefore any reference to the Bible is problematic, and it is best to be somewhat cautious. It is probable that this region was never under Israelite control. The lists in Joshua owe a great deal to later redactors, and may derive from a register of postexilic Jewish communities. One theory suggests that Keisan was one of the twenty cities granted by Solomon to the king of Tyre (1 Kgs 9:11–13), and hence belonged to the region of Kabul. There is a village with this name about 8 km from Keisan, but it is unclear if it should be identified with the Kabul of 1 Kings 9:10–14. The text of Kings mentions Kabul in Galilee without any further details. According to the list in Joshua 19, Kabul is situated rather to the N, in what is now S Lebanon. The village of Kabul is the Cabor of the Crusaders, which may reflect an older place name close to the Arabic *kebir,* for example, and would suggest that the Kabul of today is a recent name. In any case, the Bible tells us that Solomon's gift did not please the king of Tyre, which would not fit the agricultural and commercial wealth of the plain of Acco. What is true is that Keisan belongs to the frontier region between the hills of lower Galilee and the coast (S Phoenicia).

B. Description

The tell is an imposing mass in the heart of the plain of Acco. The flat, oval summit (250 m × 300 m) dominates the plain at a height of 28 m. It is 8 km from the sea as the crow flies, and only 4 km from the hills of lower Galilee. Prehistoric inhabitants occupied the site when it was only a rocky knoll near the swamps and the riverbank which provided abundant game. Later its position in the center of the fertile plain would make it an excellent agricultural site. Hunting (both birds and animals) and fishing in the marshes, rich agricultural land, close proximity to both sea and mountain, meant that Keisan was an important link between the herdsmen of the hill country and the traders of the coast. This contributed to its prosperity throughout three millennia, a prosperity founded on a balanced economy integrating all systems of exchange. Keisan was a rich market town at the crossroads of highways leading from Tell Abu Hawam (Haifa) to Hazor and Damascus, and from Acco to Megiddo, Beth-shan and Transjordan.

C. History of Excavations

An English expedition in 1935 and 1936 directed by J. Garstang and A. Rowe was interrupted by the disturbances in Palestine at that time: much damage was done, and the expedition house was burned down. Even worse, most of the documents and finds which had been taken to Liverpool, the headquarters of the expedition, were destroyed by bombing in 1941. In 1970, the Ecole Biblique conducted 8 campaigns between 1971 and 1980 under the successive direction of J. Prignaud, J. Briend, and J.-B. Humbert.

D. The Results of the Excavations

The English excavation had shown that the town was founded at the beginning of the EB, when it enjoyed its greatest extension, within mudbrick ramparts.

In the MB, the city was less extensive, but had a cyclopean rampart about halfway down the slope. The well, more than 20 m deep, was dug at the foot of the tell in the

MB and has continued to provide water in such quantity that it served for irrigating nearby gardens until the beginning of this century. From this time come the structural blocks which bear Egyptian hieroglyphs which may date from the campaign of Seti I, who marched from Megiddo toward Tyre and Sidon in 1303 B.C.

The excavations in 1936 revealed a prosperous settlement in the 13th century and throughout Iron Age I, but suggested a complete gap for Iron Age II, after 900 B.C. The Ecole Biblique was particularly interested in the period from 1200 B.C. Its findings confirmed the importance of Iron Age I, but were able to show continuity of occupation from that time until the 2d century B.C.

The deepest level (13) lay under a thick destruction layer. The pottery fits perfectly into the LB tradition, but also has specific features of Iron Age I. It is a transitional style. The presence of Mycenaean IIIC shows that Sea Peoples had settled in the area before the destruction of Keisan. The destruction may have been the result of a new wave of Sea Peoples looking for somewhere to settle, but it may equally have been due to some local struggle, which apparently characterized the entire LB period. This level is the one which sees the beginning of the Iron Age, and it would appear that in archaeology there is no *event* which marks the transition from Bronze to Iron.

The following level (12) certainly belonged to another group whose hold on the site was precarious: the structures are modest, and the first sherds called "Philistine" make their appearance. Before the end of the 12th century, the town was solidly reconstructed (level 11), but was occupied for only a short time. It was soon destroyed or abandoned, and was only redeveloped with poor structures of mudbrick, at three or four stages during the first half of the 11th century. Under some influence difficult to define, reconstruction was undertaken vigorously (level 9) and in accordance with an elaborate scheme of town planning: series of module-type houses forming a solid line at the top of the slope, arranged to prevent the incursion of raiders into the city which was without a rampart. The module was divided into two or four compartments which had some affinity with the "four-room house" which was to be characteristic of the Iron Age. A type of pottery appeared which integrated Cypriot and Levantine features with the earlier basis inherited from the Mycenaeans. In fact, throughout the entire Iron Age I, the Palestinian coast constantly received new population groups and influences coming by way of the sea. The prosperity attested in the 11th century witnesses to a period of peace and an undeniably successful economy. The exceptional thickness of sediments from Iron I contrasts with the thinness of those from other sites of the region for the same period. This is probably because Keisan, positioned inland from the coast while dominating a rich territory, became the refuge-site in a period of prolonged disturbance. Regardless, level 9 was eventually destroyed by fire ca. 1000 B.C. marking the end of a period of prosperity which had lasted for a millennium. The final examples of the "Philistine" pottery disappeared. It would be arbitrary to see in the destruction of Keisan the effects of the campaign of King David in the N of Palestine, which is of questionable historicity. Instead, the destruction should be seen as the work of a tide of Aramean nomads who, at a moment when the Levant was destabilized, came up against Galilee and the rich kingdom of Tyre to which Keisan belonged.

The renewal of occupation (level 8) occurred immediately, but once again was undistinguished, bearing a clear Phoenician imprint. Still, the modest scale of the settlement is striking: Keisan was a little village on the edge of the kingdom of Tyre during the period of the Israelite monarchy (levels 7, 6, 5). This interpretation reflects the results of archaeological investigation into the whole of this region. Despite several cities which are better constructed—the so-called "Solomonic" cities—the sites of ancient Israel never recovered the prosperity they had enjoyed in the Bronze Age.

For this reason, the upswing which followed the Neo-Assyrian occupation (level 4) looks like a real renaissance. It is known that the new power practiced systematic displacement of populations. Keisan, although there is no trace of destruction, was reconstructed according to a totally new plan, and with smaller houses. Possibly a group deported by the imperial power was the new blood which Keisan needed. In any case, the quantity, quality, and novelty of the pottery undeniably marks a radical change. However, the influence comes not from the E but from the N. The influence of Phoenicia was never greater, and the same is true of its openness to Cyprus. The administration of the conquerors was tolerant but nonetheless effective, as inferred from a cuneiform tablet giving a list of rations for workers; overseas trade was certainly encouraged. Each house excavated contained at least one of the large loop-handled amphoras which have been found in great number in the chariot tombs of Cyprus in the 7th century B.C. It is not known what they held, in spite of the brief inscriptions which are sometimes on them; oil was exported from Palestine. Keisan belonged to a region which was like a Cypriot commercial "factory." There are abundant remains of new types of jars: smaller, lighter, better baked, with the strength required for overseas trade; these have been found in 7th century B.C. contexts as far as the coasts of Spain and the Atlantic coast of Morocco, and show the vitality of the commercial ports of the Levant.

However, two consecutive destructions affected the site—perhaps punitive expeditions of Assurbanipal in the middle of the 7th century. It is possible that a gap in occupation preceded the Persian period (level 3).

Keisan was rebuilt, but it ceased to be an administrative center. However, its function was an interchange between the hill country and the sea continued for several centuries of peace, which favored commerce. The link with the Mediterranean remained essential, and trade with the Greek islands and the coasts of Asia expanded continuously until the 3d century. With the creation of Acco/Ptolemais as regional capital, Keisan became nothing more that a suburb of this great Hellenistic port (level 2).

Keisan was finally abandoned before the end of the 2d century B.C. The campaign of Simon Maccabeus against Ptolemais in 163 B.C. may have rendered the final deathblow. Keisan did, however, have two revivals, the first during the time of Justinian, when a church was built on the summit (level 1); the second, when Saladin chose the strategic point which dominates Acre from which to direct the siege of 1189.

Bibliography

Briend, J., and Humbert, J.-B. 1980. *Tell Keisan 1971–1976, Une cité phénicienne en Galilée.* Paris.

Humbert, J.-B. 1982. Notes and News: Tell Keisan, 1979, 1980. *IEJ* 32: 61–64.

Sigrist, R. M. 1982. Une tablette cunéiforme de Tell Keisan. *IEJ* 32: 32–35.

Spycket A. 1973. Le culte du Dieu-Lune à Tell Keisan. *RB* 80/3: 384–95.

JEAN-BAPTISTE HUMBERT

KELAIAH (PERSON) [Heb *qēlāyāh*]. Var. KELITA. One of the Levites who married a foreign woman during the era of Ezra's mission (Ezra 10:23 = 1 Esdr 9:23). The text indicates that Kelaiah is also known as Kelita *(qĕlîṭāʾ)*. Even Noth, in his exhaustive study of Hebrew names, concedes that the meaning of the name is uncertain (*IPN* 256). For further discussion, see BEDEIAH.

JEFFREY A. FAGER

KELITA (PERSON) [Heb *qĕlîṭāʾ*]. Var. KELAIAH. One of the Levites who, along with various priests and laymen, listened to Ezra and agreed to renounce their foreign wives and children (Ezra 10:23; 1 Esdr 9:23). Kelita's legacy, however, is not limited simply to the renunciation of mixed marriages. He was among those who provided interpretive assistance during the great reading of the Law in the time of Ezra (Neh 8:7; 1 Esdr 9:48). In addition, following the public confession of sin concerning Israel's past failings, he joined in with other officials and laity in supporting and "sealing" a new covenant (Neh 10:11—Eng 10:10). According to Ezra 10:23 and 1 Esdr 9:23, Kelita is a name associated with a certain Kelaiah (Heb *qēlāyāh*). Rather than being a gloss mistakenly identifying two otherwise distinct individuals, Kelita appears to be a descriptive nickname indicating a crippled or stunted condition (see root *qālaṭ, BDB,* 886). Once the nickname is provided, the real name goes unmentioned.

TERRY L. BRENSINGER

KEMUEL (PERSON) [Heb *qĕmûʾēl*]. Three individuals mentioned in the Hebrew Bible have this name, the origin and meaning of which are not known. The transcription of the name is also unclear, as evidenced by the rendition of *Samouel* in the LXX (Vatican). There do not seem to be any occurrences of the name in extrabiblical literature (*IPN,* 256).

1. The son of Nahor, father of Aram (Gen 22:21).

2. The son of Shiphtan, a leader of the tribe of Ephraim appointed to help distribute the land to the children of Israel (Num 34:24).

3. The father of Hashabiah, a leader of the Levites who served King David (1 Chr 27:17).

RAPHAEL I. PANITZ

KENAN (PERSON) [Heb *qênān*]. Var. CAINAN. Son of Enosh, when Enosh was 90 years old (Gen 5:9–14). When Kenan was 70 years old, his son Mahalalel was born. Kenan lived a total of 910 years. The similarity of names in the genealogies of Genesis 4 and 5 has led to comparison of Kenan with Cain of Genesis 4. Just as Cain was the son of Adam (whose name means "man, humanity"), so Kenan was the son of Enosh (whose name also means "man, humanity"; Wilson 1977: 161 n. 63).

The first three consonants of both Cain and Kenan are the same, *qyn* (see CAIN). Kenan differs from Cain in the addition of a *nun* at the end of the name, vocalized *-ān* in the MT (and in all versions). Such an ending, along with *-ōn,* is common in West Semitic personal names of all periods (Noth *IPN,* 38; Huffmon *APNM,* 135–38; Sivan 1984: 97; Silverman 1985: 125). Suggestions have been made to identify this ending with a diminutive sense (Noth *IPN,* 38) and to render Kenan as "little Cain," i.e., a second Cain (Diakonoff 1982: 17). However, Noth's other examples need not be interpreted as diminutives. Instead, the general identification of *-ān* as a hypocoristic suffix better accords with the evidence.

Perhaps this shortened "Cain" name should be compared with Tubal-Cain. See TUBAL-CAIN. If Tubal-Cain is to be understood as a two-element name (rather than as two separate names), it demonstrates the existence of longer constructions in names using the *qyn* element. Therefore, Kenan could be a hypocoristic form of a longer name. For another use of the *-ān* ending in a Genesis 1–11 personal name, see HARAN (PERSON). A deity bearing the same name as Kenan *(qynn)* is attested in Sabean inscriptions in Old South Arabic (Ryckmans 1934: 30).

Bibliography

Diakonoff, I. M. 1982. Father Adam. Pp. 16–24 in *Rencontre assyriologique internationale 28, Wien 6–10 Juli 1981.* AfO Beiheft 19. Vienna.

Ryckmans, G. 1934. *Les noms propres sud-sémitiques.* Vol. 1, *Répertoire analytique.* Louvain.

Silverman, M. H. 1985. *Religious Values in the Jewish Proper Names at Elephantine.* AOAT 217. Kevelaer and Neukirchen-Vluyn.

Sivan, D. 1984. *Grammatical Analysis and Glossary of the Northwest Semitic Vocables in Akkadian Texts of the 15th–13th C.B.C. from Canaan and Syria.* AOAT 214. Kevelaer and Neukirchen-Vluyn.

Wilson, R. R. 1977. *Genealogy and History in the Biblical World.* YNER 7. New Haven and London.

RICHARD S. HESS

KENATH (PLACE) [Heb *qĕnat*]. A town in Bashan which was taken by the Manassite Nobah, whose name was given to the site (Num 32:42). In a later campaign against Gilead, after the division of the Israelite monarchy, Geshur and Aram captured Kenath (1 Chr 2:23). Because the Gadite settlement of Jogbehah is mentioned both in Num 32:35, in the same context as Kenath (v 42), and in Judg 8:11, on the same caravan route as Nobah, it is possible that Kenath and Nobah were alternative regional designations or local place names. Kallai (1983) concludes that Nobah is a region which encompasses other localities, including Kenath. See HAVVOTH-JAIR; JOGBEHAH; NOBAH (PLACE).

The name Kenath appears in the Egyptian Execration Texts, an itinerary of Thutmose III, and the Amarna Tablets. In later times Kenath was known as Kanatha, one of the Decapolis. Though it is sometimes linked with

Kerak-Kanata, Kenath is possibly identified with El Qanawât, located about 3 miles NE of Es Suweīdiya, Syria.

Bibliography

Kallai, Z. 1983. Conquest and Settlement of Transjordan. *ZDPV* 99: 100–18.

GERALD L. MATTINGLY
PAUL NIMRAH FRANKLYN

KENAZ (PERSON) [Heb *qĕnaz*]. KENIZZITE. **1.** The son of Eliphaz, the firstborn son of Esau and Adah (Gen 36:11; 1 Chr 1:36), who functioned as an Edomite clan chief (Gen 36:15, 42; 1 Chr 1:53). Though Kenaz of Gen 36:11 is ordinarily understood to be the eponymous ancestor of the Kenizzites (Gen 15:19), this connection is not buttressed by hard evidence.

2. The younger brother of Caleb and father of Othniel (Josh 15:17; Judg 1:13; 3:9, 11). In 1 Chr 4:13 Kenaz is credited with a second son, Seraiah.

3. The grandson of Caleb through Elah (1 Chr 4:15). The plural gentilic adjective "Kenizzites" surfaces but once in the OT (Gen 15:19), within a promise that Yahweh makes to Abraham in a theophany. Listed in second position, just after the Kenites, this is one of ten peoples whose land Yahweh intends to deliver to Abraham's descendants. In the singular form, this gentilic adjective is thrice attested (Num 32:12; Josh 14:6, 14) in the phrase "Caleb the son of Jephunneh the Kenizzite." This predication probably should be associated with the Kenizzites of Gen 15:19.

The Kenizzites were a non-Israelite ethnic group that presumably penetrated the Negeb from the SE. What little is known about them emerges mainly from a consideration of their wider geopolitical context. Toward the close of the LB Age and the onset of the Iron Age (ca. 1300–1100 B.C.E.), the S portion of Palestine's central hill country was occupied by diverse tribal groups. These included the Judahites, the Calebites, the Othnielites, the Simeonites, the Korahites, the Jerahmeelites, the Kenites, as well as the Kenizzites. Though scholars lack the necessary data for reconstructing the early history of these tribes in any detail, it is nonetheless clear that, owing to the prominence of David and the increasingly sturdy position of the tribe of Judah from whence he came, these S tribes were eventually subsumed under the category of "Greater Judah" (*HAIJ,* 103). From the narrative in Numbers 13–14, we may infer that the Calebites settled into the city of Hebron and subjected its quite promising agricultural environs to their advantage. In Josh 15:13–19 (and Judg 1:11–15, its parallel), the spotlight falls on the Othnielites. We are told that Othniel, the son of Kenaz, the younger brother of Caleb, took possession of the city of Debir (Tell Beit Mirsim?) SW of Hebron. Though the text is too laconic to be of much help to biblical historians, it does attest that the Othnielites, residing in the hill country directly SW of Hebron, clustered around Debir. To the SE of Hebron, the Kenites held sway in the vicinity of Arad (Judg 1:16). The precise extent of the territories claimed by the Calebites, the Othnielites, and the Kenites is unknowable, and, as de Vaux (*EHI,* 538) observes, there was some territorial overlap.

Several biblical genealogies denote that the Kenizzites, Calebites, and Othnielites were closely related tribal groups, and that from their tent encampments along the foothills of S Palestine, all three maintained intimate associations with their eastern Edomite neighbors. Caleb and Othniel are both recognized for their genealogical linkage with Kenaz. In Num 32:12 and Josh 14:6, 14, Caleb is identified as "the son of Jephunneh the Kenizzite," and in Judg 1:13 and 3:9, Othniel is said to be "the son of Kenaz, Caleb's younger brother." Kenaz, in turn, takes his place in the Edomite genealogy of Genesis 36. Finally, in the Wadi Arabah, a region rich in mineral deposits to the S of the Dead Sea, the Kenizzites cultivated close ties with the Kenites, from whom they undoubtedly learned the art of mining and metallurgy (Glueck 1940: 83). In due course, the Kenizzites and other neighboring S tribal groups became thoroughly absorbed by Judah.

Bibliography

Glueck, N. 1940. *The Other Side of the Jordan.* New Haven.
———. 1959. *Rivers in the Desert.* New York.

J. KENNETH KUNTZ

KENITES [Heb *qênî*]. The Kenites—or more correctly the Qenites—were a community or clan whose ancestry was traced to an eponym, biblical Cain (Heb *qayin*). The Kenites constituted a non-Israelite group, frequenting the wilderness near Sinai, that may have been responsible for mediating the religion of Israel's god, Yhwh, to Moses. This view is conjectural, based on hints in legendary texts about Israel's history before or just after its entry into the land. It locates the era of Kenite influence in an era largely inaccessible to archaeologists, epigraphers, and historians—a time Abraham Malamat rightly calls the era of Israel's "proto-history" (1983; cf. Soggin 1979).

A. Kenites as Cain's Descendants
B. Kenites in the Iron Age
C. Kenites and Israelite Proto-History

A. Kenites as Cain's Descendants

Our knowledge of the Kenites in the Iron Age, when Israel occupied its land, is limited to a few texts only (Josh 15:57; Judges 4–5; Judg 1:16; 1 Sam 15:6; 27:10; 30:29; 1 Chr 2:55). There has been widespread agreement that the etymology of the term "Kenite" implies that the Kenites were itinerant smiths (*AncIsr,* 478–79; *ARI,* 96): the root, *qyn,* can form the basis for words meaning "to forge," or "a metal-worker," in Arabic, Syriac, and Palmyrene. A derived term designates part of a spear (2 Sam 21:16; Wyatt 1986: 89); the context suggests a spearhead (of ca. 6.5 lbs), but it may be the shaft, in which case the root is unrelated (cf. CAD *qanû*). Proponents of this hypothesis observe that Gen 4:22 identifies Tubal-cain, a descendant of Cain *(qyn),* as the founder and "patron saint" of metallurgy. The element "Tubal" is to be explained on the basis of the fact that Tabal was a renowned center of metallurgy in SE Cappadocia (see Elat 1977: 53).

It seems most probable that it was the wordplay with Cain's name *(qyn)*—a root having to do with artisanship—that led the biblical narrator (J) in Genesis 4 (or his oral sources) to identify a scion of Cain as the first metallurgist, and to give him a name reminiscent of that of Tabal. Thus, another form of the root, *qynh,* denotes a song of lament (this, too, has a parallel in Arabic); thus another of Lamech's offspring in Gen 4:21 becomes the archetypal musician. The name Cain is attested both as a Nabatean personal name (J. T. Milik and J. Starcky *apud ARNA* 146:23; 157:107:3; 108:2) and, with preformative *ʾalep,* as a Sabean clan name (*DOSA,* 454). It is uncertain, then, if the biblical Kenites are named after an occupation (tinkerer or songster?) or if they drew their appellation from a particular figure. Even if it began as an occupational term, by the time of our texts it had an ethnic denotation—and may bear no relation to the economic activity of Kenites in Canaan.

This alternative does not refute the assumption that the Kenites were itinerant tinkerers and musical specialists. One of Cain's offspring, after all, is the "father of those who dwell with tents and cattle" (Gen 4:20), a condition characterizing the later Kenites (see below). On the other hand, Cain himself (or, originally, possibly Enoch) is said to have built the first walled town (Gen 4:17: *bnh* + town); yet Kenites were not sedentary.

In essence, the Kenite traditions in Gen 4:17–24 depict Cain as a prime culture-hero, an almost Promethean figure in the development of the civilized arts (cf. Wyatt 1986). Cain is the first human horticulturalist (Gen 4:2), and therefore the author of the first technological advance (cf. Marx and Engels 1938: 7). Yhwh, like Aeschylus' Zeus quite possibly intent on retarding human development (cf. Gen 3:22; 6:3; 11:6, all J), rejects the fruits of Cain's labor, and prefers the products of husbandry (Gen 4:3–4). He condemns Cain, ironically, to a nomadic existence as punishment for murder (4:8–12).

Although outcasts, Kenites pioneer the arts of city building, tent dwelling, herding, music, and metal work, as well as agriculture. One might infer from P's account, in which Cain's line is folded into Seth's (Genesis 5—with the order and the gutturals garbled), that the Kenites of Genesis 4 should have been eradicated in the Flood. This is, however, far from being J's implication, despite the fact that he deliberately provides for two branches of descent from Adam (Gen 4:25–26): the accursed, yet protected Kenites (and Gen 4:15, 24) mediate the blessings of civilization to all humankind. This apparent inconsistency is one of the reasons critics have sometimes attempted to discover a prehistory in the J materials, including a core of "nomadic" tribal traditions (as Beltz 1974).

B. Kenites in the Iron Age

The oldest information about the Kenites is preserved in the Song of Deborah (Judg 5:24–27). There, Jael is "the woman of the Kenite *ḥbr.*" The late prose interpretation of the song, in Judges 4 (Halpern 1988), takes *ḥbr* to be the name of an individual, Heber (Jael's husband). But it may equally denote the "community" of the Kenites, identical to the nomadic unit of the Mari *ḥibrum* (Malamat 1962: 144–46).

In the Song of Deborah, it is certain at any rate that the Kenites dwell in tents and pasture dairy herds: Jael is praised above "[other] women of the tent" as distinct from women in houses (Judg 5:24); and, when Sisera, the general of the Canaanite army, asks for a drink, she serves him milk in a ceramic krater, possibly with human or animal figures (5:25), like wares found at Iron I Tell en-Nasbeh, Tell Beit Mirsim, and, most recently, Shiloh (Finkelstein, Bunimovitz, and Lederman 1985: 135) and Tell el-Hammah (Cahill, Lipton, and Tarler 1988). Clearly conceived of as non-Israelite even in this early context, Jael is an archetypal Kenite. It merits remark that her camp can be no farther S than the Jezreel valley; the Song of Deborah does not even hint that such a N location is in any sense inappropriate for a Kenite.

The Judges 4 prose interpretation of Judg 5:24–27 stems either from the hand of the Deuteronomistic Historian, in the late 7th century B.C.E., or from a slightly older source (ca. 700). It retains the elements of Kenite dairy production, their residence in tents, and their status as "allies" of the Israelites (hence the need to explain why Sisera would take refuge among them—4:17; Halpern 1988). It does adduce a nomad's wineskin rather than mention a ceramic krater (Judg 4:19). It adds, too, the implication that Jael was the proprietress of her own tent (4:17)—it was normal, among polygamous pastoralists, for each wife to preside over her own establishment, in a discrete tent, a convention also visible in the Jacob cycle (Gen 30:16). For discretion's sake, this remains the practice today. But most of all, the late prose source feels compelled to explain that Jael's camp had wandered N (to the vicinity of Kedesh in Naphtali in the far N, in the prose interpretation), away from the standard pastures of the Kenite community (4:11). By the time of the prose writer, the Kenites were identified chiefly with the S.

A few other sources confirm these conclusions from the Song of Deborah. An oracle of Balaam in Num 24:21–22 speaks of the age-old residence of Cain in "the rock," or perhaps Sela in Edom—an interesting comment given that the only Kenite personal name surely known to us in the historical period, Jael, means "mountain goat." Balaam's oracle is linked to another on Amalek, another S community. 1 Sam 15:5–6, in a pre-Deuteronomistic source of 1 Samuel, relates that Saul met Kenites in the company of Amalekites at the "city of Amalek" S of Carmel in SE Judah (cf. 1 Sam 15:5, 12). Saul spared the Kenites, Amalek's fellow-travelers, because of earlier relations between the Kenites and Israel. Like Gen 15:19, a late piece, and the other passages cited to this point, 1 Samuel 15 identifies the Kenites as alien to Israel. The linkage to Amalek is of special interest, since Amalek was Judah's great competitor, in the 11th century B.C.E. for the desert hinterland of the S hill country.

The location of the Kenites in the SE (on the border of Judah with Edom) is attested in texts from various eras. In the 7th century, Josh 15:22, 57 (on the date, see Alt 1925) locate settlements named Kinah (Heb *qînâ*) and Kain (Heb *qayin*) in the southernmost and southeastern reaches of Judah. Judg 1:16 also locates the descendants of the Kenite in the SE: this Deuteronomistic passage, which may stem from an earlier source, has a group of Kenites descended from Moses' in-laws joining the Judahites in conquests S of Arad (cf. Num 10:29–32). The Kenites start from "the city of palms"—probably Jericho (Deut 34:3; 2 Chr 28:15), but identified in the Talmud with Zoar (*m. Yebam.* 16:7). Here again the Kenites appear as collaborators, on the border with Edom (cf. also Boling *Judges* AB, 57; *YGC,* 40–42).

Two earlier texts, 1 Sam 27:10 and 30:29, probably refer not to Kenites in the S, but to Kenizzites (so LXX and 4QSam[a]).

In sum, the Kenites are identifiable as an Iron Age pastoral community occupying the wilderness S and E of Arad. The reference in Judg 5:24–27 might tempt us to suppose that, in search of summer pastures, they sometimes migrated as far N as the Jezreel, or even to the S end of the Bekaa Valley (Judges 4). But the language of Judg 4:11 has another implication: Heber "had separated" from the Kenites, from the children of Hobab, Moses' in-law. The issue here is lineage fission—the Kenites in the N were a branch community of those near Arad.

1 Chr 2:55 confirms this inference. It speaks of a Kenite migration to Judah (to Jabez; cf. 1 Chr 4:9–10) from "Hammath, the father of the house of Rechab." This must be in the N. The only known Hammath in Israelite territory was located on Naphtalite soil (Josh 19:35; probably Tell el-Hamma [M.R. 197197], 12 km S of Beth-shan; cf. Hammon in 1 Chr 6:61). It may have been "Hammath of the house of Rechab" (cf. Jer 35:18, "house of the Rechabites"; note Levenson 1976 on the communal nature of Rechab): the Rechabites originated in the N (2 Kgs 10:15, 23); and, in the mid-9th century B.C.E., they developed a regimen of ascetic nonagricultural nomadism (Jer 35:6–10). It is almost as though the Rechabites had assumed the status of the accursed Cain (Gen 4:11–12), doomed to live without tillage because of his earlier carnage. The Rechabites may therefore have been a lineage of a N Kenite community. Even if they were not, connubium between them and the Kenites is not difficult to imagine. Eventually, some of the Rechabites also found their way into Judah, where the depredations of Nebuchadnezzar induced them ultimately to take refuge in Jerusalem (Jer 35:11). The Kenite encampment at Jabez was probably related to the Rechabite withdrawal to Judah.

Because the Kenites near Arad were linked to Moses (Judg 1:16; 4:11) and Moses' in-laws were linked to a Midianite priesthood (Exod 2:17–21; 3:1; 18:1–5), B. Mazar (1965) has argued that the Kenites presided at the well-known Israelite sanctuary at Arad (see Aharoni 1968: 27–28), as well as at a high place in the vicinity of Kedesh in Naphtali (Judg 4:11). Mazar's view has attracted widespread support. However, there is no sure sign of a *temenos* at Arad before the shrine built by David or Solomon; this would have been served by the priestly agents of the United Monarchy. Judg 1:16 speaks of a Kenite presence *south* of Arad, not in it (*VGC,* 40–41 n. 82), and later ostraca at Arad attest to the presence of Korahites, among other (Aaronid?) priestly elements, but give no indication of a Kenite role there (see *AI* 49, 50, 54). There may be further indications that the Midianite-Kenite cultic tradition called for a tent (not a stone) shrine (below, C), much as Solomon had to incorporate the earlier Israelite tent into his cultic establishment. The links between any Kenites related to Moses and the Arad temple are in fact unsubstantiated (Ussishkin 1988).

There are, however, indications that the Kenites enjoyed a certain status as ritual specialists or as the beneficiaries of a special relationship with Yhwh. The marking of their eponym, Cain, and Yhwh's promise of divine protection to him (Gen 4:15) were apparently elements projected back into prehistory by the later Kenites—the elements were appropriated by Yahwistic tradition. It would be erroneous to revert to the notion of a "desert ideal" embodied by the Kenites and Rechabites, among others—S. Talmon (1966: 31–37) has shown the bankruptcy of that theory. But it is interesting to note that the "mark of Cain" has a parallel in what seems to be a prophetic hairstyle or tonsure (2 Kgs 2:23; 1 Kgs 20:37–41; Ezek 9:4–8; cf. Zech 13:4, 6, with allusions to Elijah and to Amos). This was probably a mark (like the Akkadian *abbuttu;* see Mendelsohn 1932: 31–37) of Yhwh's proprietorship (cf. Deut 6:8; Ezek 9:4–6), though another sort of mutilation (as Exod 21:6; Deut 15:17) is also possible. That the prophet was thought to enjoy personal protection comparable to Cain's is a convention of Israelite social usage evinced in various passages (including 1 Kgs 20:35–36; 22:26–28; Jer 26:16).

Like the Kenites, prophets sometimes claimed to have been torn from the land. Properly, the Levites were also landless (Deut 18:1), and like pastoral nomads may have had common pastures (as Lev 25:34). The association of landlessness with murder is of course explicit in the case of Cain. It leads to the accusation leveled against the eponym of Levi as well (and Simeon) in Gen 34:25–31; 49:5–7. It is probably no coincidence, then, that in the national folklore the archetypal Levite, Moses, begins his career as a murderer (Exod 2:11–12)—of a foreigner, not a brother. Moses' face, too, was reputed in one tradition to have been disfigured (Exod 34:29–35, P), again through an encounter with Yhwh.

Both some prophets (Hos 12:14; Jer 15:1) and some Levites (*CMHE,* 195–215) traced their guilds to Moses—Elijah's flight to Horeb recapitulates Moses' epiphany there on the same understanding (1 Kgs 19:8–19). The paradigmatic revelation is, of course, that at Sinai, in the pasturelands of Moses' Midianite-Kenite father-in-law (Exod 3:1). Sinai is also the locus of Levi's first commission, according to an anti-Aaronic Levitic tradition (Exodus 32). All these links between certain strands of Israelite prophecy, the Levitic orders, and the Kenites center on the person of Moses. This suggests that there was a strong strain of primitivism connected with Moses in the Israelite cult. It reached a height, perhaps, in the mid-9th century during the careers of Elijah, Elisha, and Jonadab ben-Rechab. The Kenites either served as a model for primitivist movements or themselves embodied one. In either case, they will have enjoyed a sacral cachet that distinguished them from other pastoral nomads on the fringes of Judah and Israel.

In sum, the Kenites of Iron II Israel appear to have been a pastoral community, with a mixed dairy and meat production strategy (see Hesse 1986: 22 for an example), focused on lands in the vicinity of Arad. The rise of Kenite settlements in the 7th century suggests the regularization of their commerce with the state. This was presumably part of Manasseh's and Josiah's systematic resettlement of the hinterland in that era; and Kenite caravans may have played a substantial role in channeling the S trade through Jerusalem and the Assyrian province of Samerina (further, Halpern fc.). Nevertheless, the Balaam oracle also suggests that some Kenites were deported by Assyria (Num 24:22), presumably during a Sargonid campaign in Arabia, but possibly as early as Tiglath-pileser III's war with the Arabs in 734–733. The priestly or cultic dimensions of the Kenite clan were probably restricted to shrines along the pilgrimage route to Mt. Sinai—Kadesh-barnea, perhaps, and Sinai itself. Other than the name, Yhwh of Teman, represented at Kuntillet ʾAjrud, their ministry has left no plain residue in the archaeological or biblical record.

C. Kenites and Israelite Proto-History

The relationship specifically between the Kenites and Moses is explicit in two texts only, both Deuteronomistic (or just earlier): Judg 1:16 and 4:11. These speak of "Hobab, the father-in-law of Moses." In the Pentateuch, Moses' father-in-law is named variously as Jethro (Exod 3:1; 18:1—E) or Reuel (Exod 2:18; Num 10:29—J). There have been various attempts to reconcile these differences (see Albright 1963). The most successful has been that which identifies Reuel in J (Exod 2:18; Num 10:29) as a scribal insertion meant to sustain a harmonization that makes both Jethro and Hobab not the father-in-law (*ḥtn,* vocalized *ḥōtēn*) but the brothers-in-law (*ḥtn,* vocalized *ḥātān*) of Moses (Bacon 1891: 111–12). In fact, the dissonance arises from variants in the oral tradition, probably based on familiarity with different groups of S nomads; it is probable, however, that the Judges texts reflect a misreading of J in Num 10:29 ("Hobab the son of Reuel the father-in-law of Moses") to imply that Hobab, not Reuel (as Exod 2:18), was the father's name. In any event, an easier harmonization would be to attribute to Moses more than a single wife.

Despite their difference on the name of Moses' father-in-law, the pentateuchal sources concur that Moses' in-laws were "Midianites." This element is absent from the texts in Judges, which describe Hobab as a Kenite. Scholars circumvent the problem by placing the Kenites in an early Midianite league (Dumbrell 1975; see Rowley 1950: 152–53), just as later (1 Sam 15:6) they came to be affiliated with Amalek. There is no evidence for or against this view (see further below).

The fact that J and E locate Moses' first encounter with Yhwh during his residence among his Midianite in-laws, and the fact that J speaks of Yahwism long before Moses, while E and P claim the name Yhwh was first revealed at Sinai (Horeb), spawned a thesis in the 19th century that Yhwh was a Kenite or Midianite deity. This thesis, which has consistently found staunch advocates, is commonly called the Kenite or Midianite hypothesis (for its history, starting with F. W. Ghillany writing under the pseudonym R. von der Alm in 1862, see Rowley 1950: 151ff.; 1963; cf. de Vaux 1969). Recent supporters cite possible Egyptian references, in the 14th–13th centuries B.C.E., to a "Yhwh Bedouin Land" (see *CTAED,* 121–22), perhaps near a place named Reuel and thus associated with Kenites (Weinfeld 1987: 305). This suggests worship of the god, somewhere in the region of Edom, before the development of a nation, Israel (Freedman 1987: 329; Weinfeld 1987: 309–10). Yhwh, after all, in the earliest Israelite poetry, was "the one of Sinai" (Judg 5:5), who marched to Israel's rescue from the Edomite southland (Judg 5:4; Deut 33:2). However, there is some question (Astour 1979: 30) as to whether the Egyptian epigraphs refer to the god Yhwh or to an abbreviated personal name (of the known form, Yahwi-DN).

Two archaeological arguments for the Kenite hypothesis merit brief attention. The excavations at biblical Timna, just N of Eilat, uncovered a 12th-century B.C.E. temple. This temple was characterized by what archaeologists call "Midianite" pottery. And, it was apparently a tent-shrine, much like the tabernacle in the biblical tradition. Inside it, the excavators uncovered a copper snake (Rothenberg 1972: 151–62). Curiously, the only zoomorphic icon associated with Moses in any source earlier than P is a copper snake called Nehushtan (2 Kgs 18:4; Num 21:9). The tent-shrine, if that indeed is what it was, is not altogether unexpected on the desert fringe, but it may be that Israel's notions of its early cult were in part shaped by Midianite-Kenite models. Snakes, too, were common icons in the Mediterranean basin: bronze serpent figurines have also been found at Megiddo (LB IIB), Hazor (LB IIA and IIB), Gezer (MB and LB IIA) and Tel Mevorakh (LB IIA), and it will not do to make too much of the coincidence (Stern 1984: 21–22 and Dever 1987: 230 supply further references).

The other archaeological indication of an early Israelite-Kenite nexus is even more circumstantial: the floruit of Midianite culture in the era of Israel's emergence into history. It is increasingly evident that, in the absence of a national state in LB II-Iron IA Edom, a mercantile culture, based in the region of Qurayyah, dominated NW Arabia (Rothenberg and Glass 1983: 101–14). This culture, identified on the basis of biblical evidence as Midianite, sent out tendrils through S Canaan to the coast and Egypt, and along the King's Highway at least as far as Amman.

Synthesizing this data, Cross has suggested (in an unpublished paper) that an Israelite Exodus through or sojourn in Edom would have meant important contacts with Midian. Further, any migration northward in Transjordan toward the traditional Reubenite springboard for the invasion of Canaan must have followed the routes controlled by Midianite traders. Cross has also added an entirely fresh dimension to the literary case for a Kenite influence. He argues that Levites who looked to Moses as the founder of their order preserved memories both of the association between Moses and Midian (in J and E) and of Moses' activity in the area of Reuben in Transjordan. In the Mesha stele, and in the tradition that Moses declaimed Deuteronomy from the valley opposite Beth-peor, Cross finds evidence of an Iron II Israelite shrine in Reuben, in territory verging on that of the old Midianite confederacy.

More significantly, Cross has identified amid a welter of polemic against other Levites in the Aaronid source in the Pentateuch (Lev 10:1–7; Numbers 16–17) a strong strain denouncing precisely the Midianite traditions of the Mosaic (Mushite) Levites. J and E speak of Moses' marriage without any hint of censure—this, despite the fact that J's portrait of the serpent in the Garden of Eden (Genesis 3) does not, on the whole, commend itself as sympathetic to E's Mosaic snake icon (further below; contrast Soggin 1975: 99–102 on J as anti-Canaanite). But in Num 25:6–15, the Aaronid source (P) assails the Midianites as those who debauched Israel in the plain of Moab at Baal-peor: it was by taking action against the Midianites that Phinehas, the son of Aaron, secured an eternal priestly franchise to his line. Similarly, P portrays the Midianites as Israel's archenemies in Num 31:1–12; in this text, P even reverses the generally positive view that J and E take of Balaam because of Balaam's association with the villains of Numbers 25 (Num 22:7). P has a strong dislike for Midian, and holds it in the same sort of contempt that J (Exod 17:8–14) and Deuteronomy (25:17) reserved for the Amalekites: the Midianites are the first object of Israelite Holy War.

Cross has found more than P's polemic. He has found a riposte to it in the E source: E is the probable purveyor of the most open attack on Aaron in the Bible, the story of the golden calf in Exodus 32; it is the source of the story of Moses' snake, Nehushtan (Num 21:4–9). E also has links to Deuteronomy and is probably to be identified wth the Mushites (Friedman 1987). In Numbers 12, E recounts a story in which Aaron and Miriam denounce Moses' marriage to a Cushite wife—Cross identifies her as stemming from Cushan, a clan of the Midianite confederacy. Yhwh intervenes decisively on Moses' behalf. A more direct response to the Aaronid assaults on Midian could hardly be written (*CMHE,* 198–206).

To Cross's argument, we may add the consideration that P's polemic against Midian can have had no relevance whatsoever in P's own time: the Midianite league disappeared at the end of the 12th century, and Israelites attributed its demise to Gideon (Judges 7–8), whose victory Isaiah holds up as a model act of Yhwh (9:3; 10:26). In fact, Midian had flourished in a commercial condominium with Egypt. With the withdrawal of the Egyptian empire into Africa in the mid-12th century B.C.E. and the rise of new kingdoms in Canaan and Transjordan—the successor-states to Asian Egypt—trade languished, and Midian lost her middleman monopoly to inland hills centers to the N (for the archaeological data, note Sauer 1986: 10). This is the political background to the regularization of the Negeb settlements in the 11th century B.C.E., when increasing settlement by elements like the Kenizzites gradually led to the imposition of state authority from the N (cf. Finkelstein 1984). In any event, the only Midianites of which P could have known in Iron II were those in the background of the Mushite priesthoods. Thus, P treats Midian on the model of Amalek solely to attack his cultic competitors.

Cross's analysis of the literature suggests that the Mushite-Midianite network was a fixture of early Israelite tradition. Aaronic priests attacked it, as a target in their ongoing exchange with Mushites—P, alone among the pentateuchal sources, gives no hint of a link between Moses and Midian. And Mushite orders defended the connection, openly in Numbers 12. The ground for this tradition has been exposed in excavations in Israel, Egypt, S Transjordan, and the Hejaz. Some theological interaction between the Transjordanian and Israelite settlers who homesteaded the Canaanite hills in Iron I and the traders of S Edom and N Arabia must therefore be conceded.

There are two points, however, on which the Kenite hypothesis requires qualification. The first is minor. Mushite traditions of kinship with the Midianites cannot be traced back tangibly to the period in which Midian still cohered as a local power. There is always the possibility, therefore, that recollections of Midianite domination in the region inspired the tradition. Too much weight should not be accorded this alternative; but it is worth remembering that the folklore is not history, and stops short of being authoritative testimony.

The second point is more significant. Numbers 12 speaks of a Cushite wife of Moses, not a Kenite. And J and E tie Moses to Midian. Similarly, Hab 3:7 employs Midian and Cushan as poetic complements. Conversely, 1 Samuel 15, which speaks rather cryptically of a Kenite bond with all Israel in the course of the Exodus, associates the Kenites with Amalek, not Midian. Amalek was another tribe or clan in the southlands of 11th-century Edom and Judah. What fuses Midian to the Kenites, and the Kenites to Moses (note *EHI,* 331)?

The two (Deuteronomistic) texts that explicitly describe an unmediated relationship between Moses and the Kenites (Judg 1:16; 4:11) tie Moses to a Hobab. J, in Num 10:29, identifies Hobab as a "son of Reuel, the Midianite." Reuel, incidentally, was the name of another (non-Amalekite) Edomite tribe (Gen 36:13, 17; further, Weinfeld 1987: 305 on the place name in a topographic list of Rameses III). It is possible that the invocation specifically of the Kenites, rather than the Midianites (or others) generally, represents a skillful parry to the Aaronid thrust against Midian. The Kenites in the Iron Age were celebrated aliens of the Israelites (see A above), who had produced the folk-heroine Jael. Appealing to the Kenites as the S nomadic party from whom Moses took his wife will have stilled the polemical rapier. Thus, the early traditions (J, E) are vague about the distinctive identity of Moses' in-laws. The version set out in Judg 1:16 and 4:11 may have appropriated actual Kenite claims; it may reflect cultic cooperation between Kenites and Levites in the S; it may even reflect Kenite exploitation of the pilgrimage routes to Kedesh and Sinai. Whether it preserves an authentic recollection remains an open question.

If one can speak with any assurance about any aspect of the Exodus, then the group that experienced Egyptian bondage or the succor at the sea (Exod 15:1–18) furnished a national myth, a national identity, for the Iron I Israelites. In disseminating this myth, the landless Levites became Israel's primary ritual specialists. Since these priests brought with them a gospel of a god located at Sinai, in Midian, it is reasonable to look for their concrete origins there: in the national folklore, naturally, their forebear had to be an Israelite; the memory of involvement with Midianite elements (or S nomadic elements) was preserved with that of the home of their god. Later, their traditions of connubium with Midianites came under the guns of the Aaronid temple priesthood. By that time, however, their history, and their old cultic practice, were fixed in doctrine.

Bibliography

Aharoni, Y. 1968. Arad: Its Inscriptions and Temple. *BA* 31: 2–32.

Albright, W. F. 1963. Jethro, Hobab and Reuel in Early Hebrew Tradition. *CBQ* 25: 1–11.

Alt, A. 1925. Judas Gaue unter Josia. *PJ* 21: 100–116.

Astour, M. C. 1979. Yahweh in Egyptian Topographical Lists. Pp. 17–33 in *Festschrift Elmer Edel,* ed. M. Görg and E. Puesch. Bamborg.

Bacon, B. W. 1891. JE in the Middle Books of the Pentateuch II. *JBL* 10: 107–130.

Beltz, W. 1974. *Die Kaleb-Traditionen im Alten Testament.* BWANT 18. Stuttgart.
Cahill, J.; Lipton, G.; and Tarler, D. 1988. Tell el-Ḥammah. *IEJ* 38: 191–94.
Dever, W. G. 1987. The Contribution of Archaeology to the Study of Canaanite and Early Israelite Religion. Pp. 209–247 in *AIR.*
Dumbrell, W. 1975. Midian—A Land or a League? *VT* 25: 323–37.
Elat, M. 1977. *Economic Relations in the Lands of the Bible c. 1000–539 B.C.* Jerusalem.
Finkelstein, I. 1984. The Iron Age "Fortresses" of the Negev Highlands. *TA* 11: 189–209.
Finkelstein, I.; Bunimovitz, S.; and Lederman, Z. 1985. Excavations at Shiloh 1981–1984: Preliminary Report. *TA* 12: 123–80.
Freedman, D. N. 1987. "Who Is Like Thee Among the Gods?" The Religion of Early Israel. Pp. 315–35 in *AIR.*
Friedman, R. E. 1987. *Who Wrote the Bible?* New York.
Halpern, B. 1988. *The First Historians.* San Francisco.
———. 1989. The Iron Gods of Israelite History. In *The Bible and the Ancient Near East Revisited,* ed. J. A. Hackett and P. Machinist. Decatur.
———. fc. The States and the Lineages in Judah in the Seventh Century B.C.E. In *Law and Its Social Setting in the Ancient Mediterranean World,* ed. B. Halpern and D. W. Hobson.
Hesse, B. 1986. Animal Use at Tel Miqne-Ekron in the Bronze Age and Iron Age. *BASOR* 264: 17–27.
Levenson, J. D. 1976. On the Promise to the Rechabites. *CBQ* 38: 508–14.
Malamat, A. 1962. Mari and the Bible. *JAOS* 82: 143–150.
———. 1983. Die Frühgeschichte Israels—eine methodologische Studie. *TZ* 39: 1–16.
Marx, K., and Engels, F. 1938. *The German Ideology.* Parts 1 and 3. Marxist-Leninist Library 17. London.
Mazar, B. 1965. The Sanctuary of Arad and the Family of Hobab the Kenite. *JNES* 24: 297–303.
Mendelsohn, I. 1932. *Legal Aspects of Slavery in Babylonia, Assyria and Palestine.* Williamsport, PA.
Rothenberg, B. 1972. *Timna. Valley of the Biblical Copper Mines.* London.
Rothenberg, B., and Glass, J. 1983. The Midianite Pottery. Pp. 65–124 in *Midian, Moab and Edom,* ed. J. F. A. Sawyer and D. J. A. Clines. JSOTSup 24. Sheffield.
Rowley, H. H. 1950. *From Joseph to Joshua.* Schweich Lectures, 1948. London.
———. 1963. Moses and Monotheism. Pp. 35–73 in *From Moses to Qumran.* London.
Sauer, J. A. 1986. Transjordan in the Bronze and Iron Ages: A Critique of Glueck's Synthesis. *BASOR* 263: 1–26.
Soggin, J. A. 1975. The Fall of Man in the Third Chapter of Genesis. Pp. 88–111 in *Old Testament and Oriental Studies.* BibOr 29. Rome.
———. 1979. The History of Israel—A Study in Some Questions of Method. *EI* 14: 44*–51*.
Stern, E. 1984. *Excavations at Tel Mevorakh (1973–1976).* Pt. 2, *The Bronze Age.* Qedem 18. Jerusalem.
Talmon, S. 1966. The "Desert Motif" in the Bible and in Qumran Literature. Pp. 31–63 in *Biblical Motifs. Origins and Transformations,* ed. A. Altmann. Cambridge, MA.
Ussishkin, D. 1988. The Date of the Judaean Shrine at Arad. *IEJ* 38: 142–57.
Vaux, R. de. 1969. Sur l'origine kénite ou madianite du yahvisme. *EI* 9: 28–32.
Weinfeld, M. 1987. The Tribal League at Sinai. Pp. 303–314 in *AIR.*
Wyatt, N. 1986. Cain's Wife. *Folklore* 97: 88–95.

BARUCH HALPERN

KENIZZITE [Heb *qĕnîzzî*]. See KENAZ (PERSON).

KERAK (M.R. 217066). A site in ancient Moab situated above Wadi el-Kerak which drains the Moabite plateau into the Jordan valley (this site should not be confused with Kh. Kerak on the SW shore of the Galilee, which has proved important in ceramic typology and chronology of the EB period; see KHIRBET KERAK WARE and BETH-YERAH).

A. Name and Identification

The Arabic name *al-Karak* derives from Aramaic *karkā* "the walled town, city"; the root *krk,* meaning "to circumvent; to enclose," is peculiar to Aramaic. The name of the site in the Hellenistic-Roman-Byzantine periods was **Karakmōbā* "the fortress-city of Moab," attested, in various spellings (*Charach-, Charak-*) since Claudius Ptolemaeus (middle of 2d century A.D.; cf. Canova 1954: LXI). Presumably, the name **Karakmōbā* derives from the Persian period, when Aramaic was the official language of the administration.

The Moabite name of Kerak is unknown. Generally, the Moabite city (or cities) of Kir (Isa 15:1), Kir-heres (Jer 48:31, 36; Isa 16:11), and Kir-hareseth (Isa 16:7; 2 Kgs 3:25) are identified with Kerak (Musil 1907: 58; Glueck 1935: 4; Abel, *GP* 2: 418–19). This, however, is difficult to prove. Kir occurs only once (Isa 15:1), where it stands in parallelism with Ar. If Ar refers to a landscape, not to a city, Kir was probably the capital of this district. In Moabite, **qīr* denotes "city" (*KAI* 181.11, 12, 24, 29). Ar was probably the region between Wadi Mūjib and Wadi el-Ḥasā (Weippert 1979: 18); its natural center is er-Rabbah, ancient Rabbathmoba. Kir-heres/Hareseth is used parallel to "Moab" in Isa 16:7, 11; Jer 48:31, 36. In Jer 46:38, "Moab" is a designation of a city, too, i.e., the capital city of Moab, which is in accordance with Late Assyrian and Neo-Babylonian usage. These texts attest that Kir-heres/Hareseth was, at a time, the capital of Moab. They do not say much about its location. The same holds true for 2 Kgs 3:25. In 2 Kgs 3:4–27, only vv 4–6 contain reliable information (Bartlett 1983: 145). What really happened in this war is documented in the inscription of Mesha (*KAI* 181). According to this inscription, Dibon was the capital of Moab in Mesha's days. If one should look for Kir-heres/Hareseth S of Wadi Mūjib, both er-Rabbah and el-Kerak are reasonable candidates for the location (cf. Iron Age evidence from er-Rabbah; Miller 1982). Only excavations at both sites could help to settle the question. *Qîr Ḥăreśet/Ḥereś* probably means "city of the woodland" (cf. Arabic *ḥirš* "wood"). If the absence of large-scale Iron Age settlement activity in the Wadi el-Kerak means that the wadi slopes were wooded in the Iron Age, the name could be an argument in favor of Kerak. There is, however, not enough information available from the Moabite plateau for the Iron Age. On the other hand, Kerak lay off the major roads of the Iron Age and the Roman-Byzantine periods; er-Rabba did not (Worschech and Knauf 1985).

B. Description

Kerak occupies the upper ridge of a spur protruding into Wadi el-Kerak from the S. Steep slopes on the N, E, and W sides protect the settlement. A moat excavated by the Crusaders on the S side separates the town from the ridge, and adds to its natural strength. Apart from this, and according to the Madaba mosaic map, Byzantine Kerak had the same extent as had the Crusader through Ottoman city, the wall of which is still preserved. In order to reach their fields on the Moabite plateau or in Wadi el-Kerak, the inhabitants of Kerak had to cover wide distances. In the last century, some spent their summers in tents on their fields. For water, they depended on cisterns, or brought water from springs in Wadi el-Kerak.

C. History of Exploration

The archaeological data for the history of Kerak and the upper part of Wadi el-Kerak consists of only surface surveys. From 1896 to 1902, A. Musil spent several months in Kerak and left an unsurpassed account of the ethnography of the late Ottoman city, and the topography and ecology of its surroundings (Musil 1907: 45–62 and passim). W. F. Albright visited Kerak in 1924 (Albright 1924: 10–11), and N. Glueck passed there in 1934 (Glueck 1935: 4). Both picked up "Moabite" (that is 9th/8th through 6th/5th centuries B.C.) and later pottery from the site. From 1936 to 1939, R. Canova, an Italian classicist lived in Kerak and collected inscriptions, mostly Greek Byzantine tombstones, from the city and its vicinity (Bagatti 1978). Canova's book (Canova 1954) is the only historical and archaeological monograph published on Kerak until now. The upper part of Wadi el-Kerak, the immediate environment of the site, was surveyed by J. M. Miller's survey of the Moabite plateau in 1982, by H. Donner and E. A. Knauf in 1983 (Donner and Knauf 1985), by S. Mittmann and E. A. Knauf in spring 1984, and by U. Worschech and E. A. Knauf in summer 1984 (Worschech 1985: 61).

D. History of Occupation

In the late Ottoman period, the whole area between Wadi Mūjib and Wadi el-Ḥasā was known as *arḍ el-Kerak* "the land of Kerak" (Musil 1907: 1). This reflects the fact that Kerak was the center of that region in times of insecurity and instability, when permanent settlement retreated into the wadis W of the plateau. In times of high security and high density of settlements on the plateau, the natural center of this region was er-Rabbah, Rabbathmoba "the capital of Moab."

The EB Age predecessor of Kerak, a walled town, is situated W of Kerak in Wadi el-Kerak, overlooking ʿAin es-Sārah, and was called Khirbet ez-Zuṭṭ until recently (today eṣ-Ṣāliḥīyeh). Evidence for MB, LB, and early Iron Age occupation is sparse in Wadi el-Kerak, which was, however, intensely settled by agricultural communities from the Nabatean through the Ottoman period (1st–20th centuries A.D.). Kerak must have been a major city since, at least, the 9th century B.C. This is attested by a fragment of a Moabite royal inscription, probably left by Mesha (Reed and Winnett 1963; Freedman 1964), and by fragments of Iron Age monumental architectural decoration from Kerak (a lion's relief in basalt; Canova 1954: 8) and from ʿAin es-Sārah below Kerak (a proto-aeolic capital; Donner and Knauf 1985). Note, however, that the wadi system to the N of Wadi el-Kerak, Wadi Ibn Ḥammād, was not under Moabite control until the time of Mesha (*KAI* 181.31–33; Worschech and Knauf 1986: 84–85). If Kerak had not been already the administrative center of its region at the end of the Moabite kingdom, it became the center in the Persian period (539/520–332 B.C.). This seems to be attested by the name of the site in classical antiquity (see above), and may indirectly be attested by an inscription in official Aramaic, dated to the fifteenth year of some ruler (probably Ptolemaeus II), which contains a remarkable number of Arabic names and words (Milik 1959: 330–41; Lipiński 1975: 261–62). Both with their seat of administration, and their language of administration (on a local level), the Ptolemies may have taken over Persian usage.

Nabatean presence at Kerak is attested by the fragment of a half-bust with parallels at Petra, Kh. et-Tannūr, and Kh. el-Mesheirfeh (Musil 1907: 53 fig. 18). Charachmoba had the status of a *polis* at the time of Hadrian, and minted coins under Elagabal (Piccirillo and Spijkerman 1978: 108–15). In the Byzantine period, Kerak became a bishopric. The regional center of the Arḍ el-Kerak in the Roman, Byzantine, and Umayyad periods, however, was er-Rabbah. The center shifted back to Kerak with the Crusaders in 1142 (Mayer 1987). Regained by the Muslims in 1188, Kerak remained the administrative center for S Jordan throughout the Ayyubid, Mamluk, and Ottoman periods (Bakhit 1982).

Bibliography

Albright, W. F. 1924. The Archaeological Results of an Expedition to Moab and the Dead Sea. *BASOR* 14: 2–12.

Bagatti, B. 1978. In Memoriam Reginetta Canova: A Pioneer Archaeologist in Jordan. *ADAJ* 22: 181–82.

Bakhit, M. A. 1982. Jordan in Perspective: The Mamluk-Ottoman Period. Pp. 361–62 in *Studies in the History and Archaeology of Jordan I,* ed. A. Hadidi. Amman.

Bartlett, J. R. 1983. The 'United' Campaign against Moab in 2 Kings 3:4–27. Pp. 135–46 in *Midian, Moab and Edom,* ed. J. F. A. Sawyer and D. J. A. Clines. JSOTSup 24. Sheffield.

Canova, R. 1954. *Iscrizioni e monumenti protocristiani del paese di Moab.* Sussidi allo studio delle antichità cristiane 4. Vatican.

Donner, H., and Knauf, E. A. 1985. Chronique archéologique: Ghōr eṣ-Ṣāfī et Wādī l-Kerak. *RB* 92: 429–30.

Freedman, D. N. 1964. A Second Mesha Inscription. *BASOR* 175: 50–51.

Glueck, N. 1935. *Explorations in Eastern Palestine II.* AASOR 15. New Haven.

Lipiński, E. 1975. Nordsemitische Texte aus dem 1.Jt.v.Chr. Pp. 245–84 in *Religionsgeschichtliches Textbuch zum Alten Testament.* Grundrisse zum Alten Testament 1. Göttingen.

Mayer, H. E. 1987. The Crusader Lordship of Kerak and Shaubak. Some Preliminary Remarks. Pp. 199–204 in *Studies in the History and Archaeology of Jordan III,* ed. A. Hadidi. Amman.

Milik, J. T. 1959. Nouvelles inscriptions sémitiques et grecques du pays du Moab. *LASBF* 9: 330–58.

Miller, J. M. 1982. Recent Archaeological Developments Relevant to Ancient Moab. Pp. 169–73 in *Studies in the History and Archaeology of Jordan I,* ed. A. Hadidi. Amman.

Musil, A. 1907. *Arabia Petraea I.* Vienna.
Piccirillo, M., and Spijkerman, A. 1978. *The Coins of the Decapolis and Provincia Arabia.* SBF.CMa 25. Jerusalem.
Reed, W. L., and Winnett, F. V. 1963. A Fragment of an Early Moabite Inscription from Kerak. *BASOR* 172: 1–9.
Weippert, M. 1979. The Israelite "Conquest" and the Evidence from Transjordan. Pp. 15–34 in *Symposia,* ed. F. M. Cross. Cambridge, MA.
Worschech, U. F. Ch. 1985. *Northwest Arḍ el-Kerak 1983 and 1984: A Preliminary Report.* BN Beiheft 2. Munich.
Worschech, U., and Knauf, E. A. 1985. Alte Strassen in der nordwestlichen Arḍ el-Kerak. *ZDPV* 101: 128–33.
———. 1986. Dimon und Horonaim. *BN* 31: 70–95.

ERNST AXEL KNAUF

KEREN-HAPPUCH (PERSON) [Heb *qeren happûk*]. The third of Job's daughters born to him after the restoration of his fortunes (42:14). The name means literally "horn of antimony" (cf. Driver and Gray, *Job* ICC). The typical Hebrew word for "horn" here certainly means "container" or "flask" (cf. 1 Sam 16:1 and 1 Kgs 1:39 for analogous usages). "Antimony" is a black powder still used as mascara to darken the edges of the eyes in order to contrast with the natural color of the eye. Note Jezebel's failed attempt to woo the maniacal Jehu by "painting her eyes" (2 Kgs 9:30) and Jeremiah's scornful description of the evil Jerusalem as a harlot, seeking to "enlarge your eyes with paint" (Jer 4:30). As in the names of her two sisters, "Turtle-dove" and "Cassia," the name Keren-Happuch appears to have been chosen to refer to the beauty and charm of the girl: "In all the land no women were found more beautiful than Job's daughters" (42:15). See also JEMIMAH; KEZIAH.

JOHN C. HOLBERT

KERIOTH (PLACE) [Heb *qĕrîyôt*]. Hebrew word for "cities" and a proper noun, a well fortified town in Moab's tableland mentioned in oracles of Jeremiah (48:24, 41) and Amos (2:2). Although the use of definite articles in Jer 48:41 and Amos 2:2 seem to support the LXX's translation "the cities," in Amos 2:2, it is probable that all three appearances of Kerioth in the OT refer to the name of a town. Most decisive is the reference to Mesha's dragging of the *ariel* of Ataroth before Kemosh at Kerioth (Mesha Inscription, line 13). A number of archaeological sites have been identified with ancient Kerioth, including el-Qereiyat (M.R. 215105), SE of Kh. ʿAṭṭarus, and Kh. Aleiyan (M.R. 233104), NE of Dhiban.

GERALD L. MATTINGLY

KERIOTH-HEZRON (PLACE) [Heb *qĕrîyôt ḥeṣrôn*]. A settlement of the tribe of Judah (Josh 15:25). Kerioth-hezron is only mentioned this one time, where it is listed among the settlements occupied by Judah in the aftermath of the conquest. Though the present literary context of the Judean town list is set in the period of Joshua, its original setting was as part of a post-Solomonic administrative division of the S kingdom. The date for the establishment of this system is debated, with suggestions ranging from the early 9th to the late 7th centuries B.C. Kerioth-hezron is in the southernmost district of Judah, the Negeb.

The location of Kerioth-hezron is problematic. In the list it is placed between Hazor-hadattah and Amam. Some scholars read these as separate names, Kerioth (and) Hezron, assuming that a *waw* has been lost. Hazor-hadattah means "New Hazor," and Kerioth-hezron is qualified by "that is, Hazor." It seems that the author intended to make clear that he was referring to two towns in the same region with similar names. The name means "towns of Hezron." Hezron was a descendent of Judah (1 Chr 2:3, 5); his sons, Jerahmeel, Ram, and Caleb all settled to the south of Jerusalem (1 Chr 2:9). If Aharoni is correct, the Jerahmeelites settled in the vicinity of Arad (1979: 216), while Caleb centered around Hebron (Josh 14:6–15). Kerioth-hezron may lie between Hebron and Arad. A possible location is Khirbet el-Qaryatein, 8.5 km north of Arad (M.R. 161083). See also *GP* and *LBHG.*

Bibliography

Cross, F. M., and Wright, G. E. 1956. The Boundary and Province Lists of the Kingdom of Judah. *JBL* 75: 202–26.

JEFFREY R. ZORN

KERMES INSECT. See ZOOLOGY.

KEROS (PERSON) [Heb *qîrōs*]. A temple servant who was the progenitor of a family which returned from Babylon with Zerubabbel (Ezra 2:44 = Neh 7:47 = 1 Esdr 5:29 [Gk *kēras*]).

MICHAEL DAVID MCGEHEE

KERYGMA PETROU. See PETER, PREACHING OF.

KETAB (PERSON) [Gk *Kētab*]. A temple servant who was the progenitor of a family which returned from Babylon with Zerubbabel (1 Esdr 5:30). Although 1 Esdras is often assumed to have been compiled from Ezra and Nehemiah, this family does not appear in their lists of returning exiles (see Ezra 2:46; Neh 7:48). Differences such as this raise questions about the literary relationships among the texts.

MICHAEL DAVID MCGEHEE

KETHIB AND QERE. A variance in the Masoretic Text between "what is written" (Heb *kĕtîb*) in the consonantal text and "what is read" (Heb *qĕrê*) according to the tradition of vocalization. These variances arose for a variety of reasons over the centuries of textual transmission, and are noted in several sources. The causes and classifications Kethib and Qere notations figure significantly in the biblical scholar's understanding of the transmission and interpretation of the Hebrew Bible. See MASORETIC TEXT.

A. Terminology
B. Sources
  1. Marginal notes
  2. Masoretic lists
C. Origins of *kĕtîb* (K) and *qĕrê* (Q) Notes
D. Classes and Causes of K/Q Variations
  1. Nonstandard Orthography in the K
  2. Variations Due to Language Change
  3. Scribal Errors in the K
  4. Scribal Errors in the Parent Text of the Q
  5. Variant Textual Traditions
  6. Epexegetical Alterations of the K

A. Terminology

The words *kĕtîb* and *qĕrê* are Masoretic terms used with reference to texts in the Hebrew Bible in which the received reading tradition, the *qĕrê,* suggests an orthography which is at variance with what is written in the consonantal text, the *kĕtîb.* The difference in orthography is usually more substantial than the placement of vowel letters, but *kĕtîb* and *qĕrê* notes will comment on unusual cases of *mālēʾ* (full) or *ḥāsēr* (defective) spellings.

The words *kĕtîb* and *qĕrê* are Aram *Peʿil* participles meaning "what is written" and "what is read," respectively. The traditional pronunciation of the word *qry* as *qĕrî* arose by analogy with the vocalization of the word *ktyb.* The term *qry* has been interpreted both as an imperative form and as a participle. Its identity as a passive participle can be determined, however, by analogy with the use of the term *ktyb* in Masoretic notes of the type *ktybn wlʾ qryyn* (plural for: "written but not read").

The following abbreviations will be used in this article:

A	The Aleppo Codex
C	The codex of the Prophets found in the Cairo Geniza
K	*kĕtîb*
K/Q	*kĕtîb* and *qĕrê*
L	Leningrad Codex B 19A
Mp	Masora parva
Q	*qĕrê*

B. Sources

There are two major sources for identifying instances of K/Q variations: (1) notes in the Mp of the Hebrew Bible; (2) independent Masoretic lists of K/Q situations. In addition, the various mss and editions provide instances of the class known as *qĕrê perpetuum* "perpetual *qĕrê,*" as well as unnoted cases resembling those identified in sources (1) and (2).

The class of *qĕrê perpetuum* comprises words never subject to K/Q notes, although their pronunciation implies an orthography different from the written text. It includes three proper names: the Tetragrammaton *yhwh* (pronounced *ʾădōnay*), Jerusalem, and Issachar. The pronunciation of *hwʾ* as *hîʾ* in the Pentateuch is often considered to be another *qĕrê perpetuum,* but this depends on the ms. In L, *hwʾ* is subject to a Q note in the Mp of the Pentateuch four times: Lev 6:18, 22; 13:20; Deut 13:16.

1. Marginal notes. Marginal annotations of K/Q situations do not appear in synagogue scrolls because these scrolls can contain only the unvocalized consonantal text if they are to be used liturgically. Some early pointed mss also do not mark K/Q situations. Examples of K/Q notes in the Mp of various mss may be found in Fig. KET.01.

a. Tiberian. It is the K/Q notes of the Mp from the Tiberian tradition which are most often referred to in discussions about *kĕtîb* and *qĕrê.* The manner in which they appear has been described in detail by Yeivin (1980 §§93–97). K/Q notes do not stand out from other Masoretic notes in the Mp of fully developed Tiberian mss. In less developed or complete mss, K/Q notes stand out as a class. They are the only kind of note from the Mp to be recorded in most printed editions. Some editions note the Q by printing it in the margin with its vocalization and leave the corresponding K unvocalized. Mss associate the vowels of the Q with the corresponding K and leave the consonants of the Q in the margin unvocalized. In either case, it is understood that the vowels in question belong to the Q and not the K (Yeivin 1980 §§94, 97).

K/Q readings are usually recorded by placing a small circle (the typical indicator of a note in the Mp) over the K with a marginal note indicating the Q reading over the word *qry* which appears in the margin of mss either written in full (infrequently) or in abbreviated form (commonly). It is typical for the entire wording of the Q to be recorded in mss like L and A, but some of their K/Q notes record

	Mp	Ketib	Ms	Text
a.	היא ק̇	הוא	L	Lev 6:18
	י̇ קר̇	הוא	L	Lev 6:22
b.	ו̇ ידעתי ק̇	ידעת	L	Job 42:1
	ידעתי קרי	ידעת	A	Job 42:1
c.	קראת ק	קראתי	L	Jer 3:4
	י̇ יתיר	דברתי	L	Jer 3:5
d.	אמרו ק̇	אמר	L	1 Sam 13:19
	סיבר̇ יב̇	ויאמר	L	Num 32:25
	(one of twelve cases where the plural is suggested)			
e.	למשסה ק̇	למשוסה	L	Isa 42:24
	י̇ קרי	למשוסה	A	Isa 42:24
	ו̇ יתי̇	למשוסה	C	Isa 42:24
f.	ו̇ יתיר יעבר ק̇	יעבור־	L	Isa 26:20
	ז̇ מ̇ל	יעבור־	A, C	Isa 26:20
	(one of seven cases written *mālēʾ*)			
g.	ו̇	לםרב	206	Isa 9:6
		ושחצומה	203	Jos 19:22
	ת̇ו̇	נשתה	208	Jer 2:15
h.	ב̇	בת		
	פחדיו ק	פחדו	or qu 680	Job 40:17
	פחדיו	בת		
	ק̇	פחדו	or 2373	Job 40:17

KET.01. Chart of *kĕtîb* and *qĕrê* notes from the Masora parva.

only the letter of syllable actually affected by the Q (see Fig. KET.01a). Earlier mss are more likely to have abbreviated citations. So, e.g., C has more partial Q citations than L or A.

Another K/Q indicator is the marginal sign that resembles a somewhat thick and elongated *zayin* or final *nun* (see Fig. KET.01b). It is usually dotted. This sign is also found in mss with Palestinian and Babylonian pointing. Neither the origin nor the distribution of this sign have been adequately explained. Despite various efforts to identify it as an abbreviation, the sign may simply be a mark which happens to look like a final *nun* or a *zayin.* Its distribution is puzzling. For example, in L of the former prophets, it is only found at Judg 20:13. It occurs twice in the book of Psalms (Pss 105:28; 129:3), but thirteen times in Job. Printed editions often neglect to record it (but cf. *BHK* on Judg 20:13). They either register only the term *qry* which usually accompanies this sign or substitute a note using *qry* for the original as, e.g., Job 39:30 in *BHK* and *BHS.*

Some notes use the word Heb *yattîr* "additional, superfluous," and its abbreviations to mark a Q form (see Fig. KET.01c). This term is not as common as *qĕrê* and is limited to cases in which the *kĕtîb* has a letter which is not heard in the pronunciation of the text. Manuscripts will not only vary internally with regard to the use of *qry* or *ytyr,* but will also differ between themselves in the use of this term (see Fig. KET.01e).

The terms *qry* and *ytyr,* and the *nun*-like sign may all be considered formal markers of cases of K/Q variance. K/Q cases are also subject to other forms of Masoretic notation. Fig. KET.01d records the use of the Masoretic term *sĕbîr* (pl. = *sĕbîrîn*) to mark a situation which may also be subject to a K/Q note. The significance of *sbyr* has been debated. It was likely used to mark an unusual phrase or word in the *kĕtîb* and to warn against a correction to another form (Barr 1981: 23–24). The terms *qry* and *sbyr* can be distinguished by the source of error they refer to in L. K/Q notes mark passages where the reading tradition might lead a scribe to alter the K, but the *sbyr* also marks places where a correction might be motivated by unusual syntax in the text such as a lack of agreement in gender or number (e.g., Gen 19:23; Num 13:22; 1 Kgs 22:43). The number of *sbyr* notes in different mss varies and it is not uncommon to find one ms list as a *sbyr* what another ms records as a *qry* (Yeivin 1980 §109).

Even within a single ms, a situation may be recorded in one place with a K/Q note and in another with different Masoretic terminology. This is particularly true of cases involving vowel letters. The Mp of L on Gen 13:3 marks the unusual spelling of Heb *ʾhlh* meaning "his tent" with the note "*waw* is read." But elsewhere, the Mp notes that the word *ʾhlh* appears four times with the vowel letter *he* standing for *ḥolem* (Gen 9:21; 12:8; 35:21). Different mss will also vary in the designation of cases of unusual or defective spellings as K/Q situations (see Fig. KET.01f).

Manuscripts can also vary in their placement of the vowels of the Q in conjunction with the consonants of the K. This is most obvious when K/Q notes point to a case of inverted consonants. The preference in a ms like L is to place the vowels in the order that they are found in the Q. Manuscript A, however, prefers to invert the vowels in order to place them under their proper consonants. This difference between A and L stems from the disagreement between Karaite and Rabbinate Masoretes as to whether only the consonantal text was given to Moses at Sinai, or whether the divine revelation also disclosed the vowel signs and accents. The latter position was held by the Karaites (and so also by A), whereas L generally follows the Rabbinate line (Yeivin 1962: 146–49).

It is well known that mss and editions of the Hebrew Bible differ in the number of K/Q notes which they contain in their Mp. A major reason for this inconsistency arises from the fact that K/Q examples are not noted systematically in the Mp. In L, for example, the K/Q on *nʿr* / *nʿrh* is faithfully noted in Deuteronomy 22 but never in Genesis 24. Through the centuries there has been a trend toward greater systematization of the various texts of the Masorah found in the mss. The body of K/Q notes published by Jacob ben Hayyim in the second Rabbinic Bible is a compilation of those found in various mss. Ginsburg's collation of editions found anywhere from 901 to 1353 recorded K/Q notes (Ginsburg 1869: 723). In the case of L, a fairly accurate facsimile of the Mp may be found in *BHK.* The edition of the Mp prepared for *BHS* adds many more K/Q notes in an effort to harmonize the notes of the Mp with those of the *masora finalis* and *masora magna* of L. But students using *BHS* are apt to arrive at a false impression about the number of K/Q notes the Mp of L contains and also about the manner in which some of them are registered.

b. Palestinian. Evidence for the manner in which K/Q notes appear in the margin of Palestinian mss has been collected by Revell (1977: 238–47). Examples of this tradition are found in Fig. KET.01g. It is common to find the marginal mark which resembles a (dotted) *zayin* or final *nun* used with no further note. K/Q notes may also consist only of a dot or double dot over the affected part of the K with no further note or only two dots written beside the line containing the K. There are also a number of cases where the double dot or *nun*-like mark occur in conjunction with the dot(s) over the K. Where the consonants of the Q were originally recorded in the margin, abbreviated citations of the Q slightly exceed full citations of the Q. Palestinian biblical mss represent a popular text type which shows little independence from the Tiberian tradition in their Masoretic notes (Revell 1974: 87).

c. Babylonian. Babylonian mss show various degrees of independence from the Tiberian tradition. To date, no comprehensive study of their K/Q notes has been published. The texts on which these remarks are based were published by Kahle (1913). The Babylonian tradition has a variety of ways in which it records K/Q cases; only the more frequent will be described here. Instead of the Tiberian circle, the supralinear marker is usually an abbreviation of the term *ktyb.* The marginal note records the corresponding Q with the abbreviation for *ktyb* above it and the abbreviation for *qry* below it. Babylonian mss may point the Q as well as the K. It is not uncommon for a ms simply to register the *qry* in the margin and leave the *ktyb* unmarked.

Babylonian mss are important to compare with Tiberian texts because many of them stem from the schools of Masoretes identified as the *madinḥāʾê* (Easterners), whereas the Tiberian schools tend to represent the *maʿarbāʾê* (Westerners). Most of the recorded differences between the Easterners and the Westerners are matters of K/Q (see, e.g., the list of Gordis 1937: 214–15). Variations attributed to the Easterners and Westerners in the standard Masoretic list affect about 10 percent of K/Q situations in the Prophets and Writings. But the proportion of disagreement on K/Q readings between Babylonian and Tiberian mss is even greater (Yeivin 1980 §96).

2. Masoretic lists. Testimony to the oldest independent list of K/Q variants is found in *b. Ned.* 37b:

> Rabbi Isaac said, "The pronunciation of the scribes (*mqrʾ swprym*), the omissions of the scribes (*ʿyṭwr swprym*), words read which are not written in the text (*qryyn wlʾ ktybn*), and words written in the text but not read (*ktybn wlʾ qryyn*) are a law of Moses from Sinai."

The text continues with examples of each of these classes. R. Isaac belonged to the third generation of ʾAmoraim and taught in Babylon toward the close of the 3d century C.E.

The K/Q classes of "read but not written," and "written but not read" are also mentioned in tractate *Sop.* (6: 8–9). *Sop.* was compiled sometime after the final redaction of the Babylonian Talmud. It is usually dated to the Gaonic period about the middle of the 8th century C.E. *Sop.* also lists the following K/Q situations: words written *lʾ* but read as *lw* and vice versa (6: 5–6), the K/Q *yʿwl* / *yʿyl* (6: 7), words written in the singular but pronounced as plural (7: 1), words written with a *he* which is not pronounced and vice versa (7: 2), words written as one word but read as two and vice versa (7: 3), and words spelled with a *waw* but read as with a *yod* vowel letter (7: 4). Similar lists also occur in the collative lists of the *masora magna.* Lists of this kind are rare in the *masora magna* of L, but see, e.g., no. 782 in Weil's edition (1971): "Fourteen words written with the vowel letter *he* but read with the vowel letter *waw.*" The systematic compilation of lists of this kind eventually resulted in independent Masoretic treatises of the type known as *ʾoklah weʾoklah* (Lyons 1974: 62). Lists of K/Q situations are prominent in these treatises. See, e.g., lists nos. 80, 81, 97–100, and 105–59 in the edition of Frensdorff (1972), originally published in 1864.

C. Origins of *kĕtîb* (K) and *qĕrê* (Q) Notes

Discussion of the origins of K/Q notes must distinguish the question about how the notations of K/Q situations came to be composed, from questions concerning the origins of the variations they record. The position taken here is that the K/Q variations represent alternate traditions, each accepted in a certain circle. The K represents the written tradition accepted by the scribes who copied the consonantal text, while the Q represents the oral reading tradition accepted by the readers and synagogue schools (Breuer 1981: 261). K/Q notes, whether recorded in lists or in the Mp of mss, are the work of the Masoretes, the scholars who produced the first pointed biblical mss. The Masoretic scribes knew by heart what was to be read, the Q. Precisely where the Q did not agree with the K, there was a danger that the Q might affect the orthography of the K. Hence, passages were noted where the Q suggested an orthography at variance with the K. This is in accord with the dominant character of Masoretic operations which throughout are meant to safeguard the copying of the consonantal text (Barr 1981: 36–37).

Two arguments can be advanced in favor of the view that the Masoretes are the creators of K/Q notes. First, there is no evidence for marginal notations of K/Q cases before the time of the Masoretes. Second, the K/Q notes in the Mp cannot be divorced in either terminology or function from the bulk of Masoretic activity.

The argument from manuscript evidence is weakened because of the gap in evidence between the finds of the Dead Sea Scrolls and the earliest Masoretic mss. It is noteworthy, however, that biblical mss found among the Dead Sea Scrolls contain no system of marginal notation corresponding to K/Q situations. The evidence of the early versions does not shed any light on this problem, either. There is no decisive preference shown in the LXX for either the K or the Q (Yeivin 1980 §106). The Targums prefer the Q (Sperber 1973: 132–33). But this is to be expected given their origins as translations of the synagogue readings. Several passages in rabbinic literature show knowledge of discrepancies between the consonantal text and the received reading tradition. Some even use the formula "it is written, but we read," e.g., *b. Menaḥ.* 89b on Lev 23:13; *ʿErub.* 26a on 2 Kgs 20:4; cf. also *Gen. Rab.* 34:8 on Gen 8:17 (for further examples see Bamberger 1923: 232–39; Yeivin 1980 §105). But the evidence falls short of indicating that the rabbis knew about the presence of marginal notes to the K.

Positive evidence for the Masoretic origins of K/Q notes comes from a consideration of their form and function. They are written in the same script and form as other notes in the Mp. The functional vocabulary applied to K/Q cases is also applied to other situations in the Mp. For instance, the note on *šmnt* in L at Num 3:29 reads, "defective in the whole Bible and always read (*qry*) in this way with one exception." The note on *wph* in Josh 18:8 reads "occurs twice, once written (*ktyb*) *pe he* and once written *pe ʾalep.*" This is a common kind of note in the Mp.

As with other types of notes in the Mp, a number of K/Q notes are at odds with the details of the text. In L, Exod 16:7, Ezek 6:3, and Ezra 10:44 have a Q which equals the K. Other texts have notes which are erroneous, such as those on Ps 99:6 and Dan 2:35 in L. These kinds of inconsistencies indicate that K/Q notes were not simply derived from the ms to which they were attached. The majority were probably taken from older sources transmitted in Masoretic circles (Rubinstein 1961: 129–30).

One must also consider the fact that K/Q readings figure prominently in Masoretic lists of the collative type. The composition of *Sop.* points to the beginning of Masoretic work as the enumeration of various known features of the orthography of the consonantal text and their arrangement into lists (Yeivin 1980 §150). It is significant that this same tractate has a number of lists of K/Q situations. It is likely that the various details of the Mp including those of K/Q were first transmitted in Masoretic lists (Rubinstein 1965: 16–17). Many of these lists probably first circulated orally before they were written down, either in the form of the Mp or *masora magna* (Lyons 1974: 63–64).

The view articulated here is in opposition to two other opinions about the origin of K/Q notes: (1) that the marginal Q notes are the result of a process of manuscript collation and represent a record of variant readings; (2) that the Q notes were meant to correct the K where it was supposed to be in error. These theories are not mutually exclusive and some have proposed that the collection of K/Q notes is a result of both ms collation and correction.

The collation theory was first put forward by David Kimḥi (ca. 1160–1235). Kimḥi suggested in his introduction to the Former Prophets that Ezra found the state of biblical mss in disarray because of the Babylonian exile. Variant readings were resolved by the device of the K/Q notes inserted in the ms margin. Theories related to this view have been prominent in later critical scholarship (Bamberger 1930: 39–41; Gordis 1937: 9–12). In this century, both Gordis (1937) and Orlinsky (1960) have proposed theories of ms collation to explain the origins of the K/Q notes in the Mp. A suggestive text they (and others) have pointed to in this regard has been the report of *j. Taʿan.* 4: 2:68a and its parallels (Talmon 1962: 16–17):

> Three scrolls of the Torah were found in the Temple Court: the *mʿwnh* scroll, the *zʿṭwṭy* scroll, and the *hyʾ* scroll. In one of them they found written *mʿwn ʾlhy qdm* (Deut 33:27) and in the other two they found written *mʿwnh*; they adopted the reading of the two and discarded the reading of the one. In one they found written *wyšlḥ ʾt zʿṭwṭy bny yśrʾl* (Exod 24:5) and in the other two they found written *wyšlḥ ʾt nʿry bny yśrʾl*; they adopted the two and discarded the one. In one they found *hyʾ* written nine times, and in the other two they found it written eleven times; they adopted the two and discarded the one.

Gordis's theory of a pre-Masoretic collation is vulnerable to the observations about the Masoretic origins of K/Q notes made above. Orlinsky was more sensitive to the relationship between the placement of notes in the Mp and the beginning of Masoretic activity than Gordis. But it is highly uncertain that ms collation was a characteristic type of Masoretic activity as he suggests (Barr 1981: 21). Recent study of the report of the three scrolls has denied that it speaks of ms collation, but instead reports on the process whereby three nonconforming scrolls were discarded from use (Talmon 1962: 15–18). A related problem is the presence of just one Q for each K in the Mp. It would be quite natural for the transmission process to generate multiple variants for a single text (Rubinstein 1959: 128). In fact, the existence of just one Q for any K is a difficulty for all collation theories. It is explained, however, by the assumption that the Masoretes combined the reading tradition they knew with the ms they chose to point. There need only be one Q for each K because the reading tradition was considered in relation to only one ms.

Sperber contended that most of the Hebrew Bible was transmitted in two recensions, one of which is represented by the K and the other which is represented by the Q (1943: 299–311). The scribes sought to preserve the details of these two recensions when they standardized the MT. They used the technique of K/Q to preserve one recension in the K and the other in the Q. It is possible that some K/Q readings are derived from different recensions (see D.5 below). But this idea is no explanation for the composition of K/Q notes, nor can it be extrapolated into a general principle which will explain the origins of all the variants the K/Q system records.

The first to propose the correction theory was Abrabanel (ca. 1437–1508) in the introduction to his commentary on Jeremiah. He suggested that Ezra and his followers found that the sacred books contained irregular expressions, and loose and ungrammatical phrases arising from carelessness and ignorance of the inspired writers. These were corrected by the Q notes found in the Mp. Modern support for the view that K/Q notes are the result of critical work on erroneous readings usually uses the correction theory as a supplement to the textual collation theory (e.g., Ginsburg 1869: 723–24; Würthwein 1979: 17–18).

A decisive blow to the correction theory arises from the probability that the K/Q notes are the work of the Masoretes. The Masoretes labored to preserve the text as accurately as possible in the form in which they received it. Correction of the text is incompatible with the goals of Masoretic activity (Gordis 1937: 19–20). It is likely, however, that some variants recorded in the K/Q system are corrections or alterations which originated in the reading tradition (see D.6 below).

D. Classes and Causes of K/Q Variations

The classification of K/Q cases can proceed on two separate levels. First, K/Q readings may be described formally, i.e., in terms of the orthographic differences that they entail. Second, K/Q situations may be classified in terms of the various reasons for their creation. It will often happen that variants which show similarity on the level of form will have arisen due to different pressures on the K and Q traditions.

Masoretic lists of the collative type contain formal descriptions of K/Q variations. Elias Levita (1538: 182–95) suggested a sevenfold division of K/Q variants which is still useful: (a) letters of words read in the Q but not written in the K and vice versa; (b) letters interchanged between the K and Q; (c) transpositions of letters (metathesis); (d) two words in sequence with the first having a letter belonging to the second and vice versa; (e) words read but not written and vice versa; (f) expressions written as one word but pronounced as two and vice versa; (g) substitutions or euphemisms. A catalogue of K/Q readings classified according to this system appears in Bamberger (1923: 221–29). More modern attempts at classifications have generally combined analyses of the formal distinctions between K/Q readings and their causes. Among the most notable are those of Ginsburg (1869), Gordis (1937), and Barr (1981).

A traditional view of the origin of the K/Q notes holds that the Q represents the ordinary meaning of the text while the K represents some hidden or mystical meaning. Both were regarded by this view as equally inspired and to have originated with Moses. It is apparent, however, that the divergences between the K and the Q are the result of a long and complex history of transmission. The variations recorded by the K/Q system are due to a number of different causes. These include textual variations, dialectical differences, and correctional and epexegetical tendencies of the Q. Others are recorded because the K was written before the spelling conventions marked by the Q were standardized.

A detailed account of the etiology for each K/Q situation in a ms like L demands a book-length study, but no such work has appeared since it was undertaken by Gordis. The kinds of pressures which have created K/Q readings are generally indicated below. The examples have been taken from the Mp of L. In every case, they are only illustrative and are not to be taken as exhaustive.

1. Nonstandard Orthography in the K. A large number of K/Q notes record divergences in the orthography of the K and are meant to prevent correction of the K to the standard orthography of the word pronounced in the Q. These notes affect cases like the following:

a. 3 masc. sing. suffix on plural nouns. For example, *mṭbᶜtw* / *mṭbᶜtyw* Exod 28:28. Lachish letter 3:18 contains the spelling *wᵓnšw* meaning "and his men." It is likely that the K is a traditional consonantal spelling of the later full orthography which the Q indicates is standard (Orlinsky 1943: 271–72).

b. Unusual mālēᵓ spellings. Examples include notes on words spelled with a double *yod* and a defective *ḥolem,* e.g., *ṣbyym* / *ṣbwym* Gen 14:8; *ḥolem* marked by *ᵓalep,* e.g., *lᵓ* / *lw* Exod 21:8; and *šureq* marked by *he,* e.g., Lev 21:5.

c. Unusual ḥaser spellings. Note *lk* / *lkh* in Num 23:13. Another candidate which might be included here is the variation *nᶜr* / *nᶜrh* in Deuteronomy 22. It is possible, however, that this example could be better analyzed as a lexical variant (see sec. D.2. below) in which the epicene *nᶜr* found in the K has been resolved into its feminine counterpart in the Q.

2. Variations Due to Language Change. This class contains important evidence for dating the relative age of the language represented by the Q. For instance, in the case of the reading tradition for biblical Aramaic, it can be shown that it represents a language similar to the Aramaic of the Dead Sea Scrolls. But some features of the Q point to a later form of that dialect (Morrow and Clarke 1986: 421–22).

a. Phonological shifts. This class refers to shifts in sound which have not resulted in morphological change in the inflection of the word. Examples include:

(1) Quiescence. Note that *hqlyᵓ* (1 Sam 17:17) and *wšyṣyᵓ* (Ezra 6:15) are both examples of words which have the annotation *ytyrᵓ* "superfluous *ᵓalep*" in the Mp. The danger that such a word might be written without the silent consonant can be illustrated by the K/Q on *mby* / *mbyᵓ* in Jer 39:16.

(2) Reduction of *ḥolem.* A number of phrases with one major stress are marked by joining the words in question together with *maqqep.* It is typical in this situation for the /o/ vowel to reduce from tone-long *ḥolem* to *qameṣ qaṭan,* e.g., *lšᵓwl* (1 Sam 22:15) and *yᶜbwr* (Isa 26:20). It is possible that the vocalization of *bmwty* in Deut 32:13 has also arisen because of a stress shift (BDB, 119). Another explanation could be suggested, however, on the basis of orthography found in 1QIsa[a] where the vowel letter *waw* is used to mark short vowels (see Kutscher 1974: 147–48).

(3) Dissimilation of the consonant *yod* to *ᵓalep* when preceded by *qameṣ* and followed by another vowel in biblical Aramaic. This shift occurs in nouns which are in the feminine absolute state, e.g., *rbyᶜyh* / *rbyᶜᵓh* (Dan 2:40); in the masculine determined state, e.g., *kśdyᵓ* / *kśdᵓh* (Dan 5:30); and in many plural gentilics, e.g., *lkśdyᵓ* / *lkśdᵓy* (Dan 2:5).

b. Morphological Shifts. Examples include:

(1) Replacement of the archaic 3 fem. pl. ending. For example, *špkh* / *špkw* (Deut 21:7); *nṣth* / *nṣtw* (Jer 2:15).

(2) Loss of the archaic 2 fem. sing. ending. It is not clear whether the K in all cases represents a form that was pronounced when it was written or whether the ending had already fallen out of use. Typical forms include *wᵓty* / *wᵓt* (Judg 17:2); *lmdty* / *lmdt* (Jer 2:33).

(3) Replacement of the 3 fem. sing., 2 masc. sing., and 1 person pl. suffix forms on plural nouns with their singular counterparts in biblical Aramaic. For example, *brglyh* / *brglh* (Dan 7:7); *lᶜbdyk* / *lᶜbdk* (Dan 2:4); *ᵓytynᵓ* / *ᵓytnᵓ* (Dan 3:18).

c. Dialectical Variants. A number of differences between the K and Q amount to variations in word formation with no change in semantic meaning. It often is difficult to determine whether the choice made in the Q is textually based or dialectical, i.e., the Q arose from a dialect of Hebrew that preferred a different form of the word than found in the K. Nominal variants of this sort include the alternation of *qrwᵓ* / *qryᵓ* in Num 1:16; 26:9; *ᵓswr* / *ᵓsyr* in Gen 39:20 and *šbyt* / *sbwt* in Ezek 16:53. Dialectical differences may also be implied by the K/Q notes on variants between *Qal* and *Hipᶜil* forms of the root *lwn* in Exod 16:2; Num 14:36; and 16:11. Cf. also *wyyrš* / *wywrš* in Num 21:32.

3. Scribal Errors in the K. A number of K/Q situations seem to have arisen because of scribal errors in the K. Barr cites 1 Sam 4:13, 1 Kgs 22:49, and Ezek 25:7 as examples of scribal error in the K (1981: 34–35). Typical errors include haplography, e.g., *wyšthw* / *wyšthww* (Gen 27:29); *bnymn* / *bny bnymn* (Judg 20:13); errors in word division, e.g., *ᵓšdt* / *ᵓš dt* (Deut 33:2); *mnhsᶜrh* / *mn hsᶜrh* (Job 38:1); and metathesis, e.g., *wtrᵓnh* / *wtᵓrnh* (1 Sam 14:27).

K/Q variants have also arisen because of confusion in the writing of consonants. It is possible that some K/Q arose as two different interpretations of an ambiguous grapheme (Barr 1981: 27–28). For example, *waw* and *yod* are often indistinguishable in the Dead Sea Scrolls. Common consonantal confusions include:

a. *waw* / *yod* interchange, e.g., *tnwᵓwn* / *tnyᵓwn* (Num 32:7). The Q is correct, the root *nwᵓ* is only used in the *Hipᶜil* in biblical Hebrew; cf. Num 32:9.

b. *reš* / *dalet* interchange, e.g., *ᵓᶜbd* / *ᵓᶜbwr* (Jer 2:20). The consonants *reš* and *dalet* are easily confused in most Hebrew scripts.

c. *bet* / *kap* interchange, e.g., *wybw* / *wykw* (2 Kgs 3:24).

4. Scribal Errors in the Parent Text of the Q. This is less frequent than the incidence of scribal errors in the K. A number of difficult cases in the vocalization of the Q suggest that its tradents took as authoritative a ms or ms tradition which had an error. A case in point is the alternation *rbyt* / *rbt* in Dan 4:19. There is no justification for the 3 fem. sing. suggested by the Q and it appears to be based on an error (Morrow and Clarke 1986: 416). See also McCarthy's discussion of the Q *bᶜyny* in 2 Sam 16:12 (1981: 81–83).

5. Variant Textual Traditions. This possibility is suggested by the Masoretic lists of words read but not written and words written but not read. The early form of the list of words read but not written in *Ned.* 37b mentions seven cases: 2 Sam 8:3; 16:23; Jer 31:38; 50:29; Ruth 2:11 (*ʾt*); 3:5, 17. The standard list contains ten examples. There is no reference to Ruth 2:11 and the list is augmented with Judg 20:13; 2 Sam 18:20; 2 Kgs 19:31, 37. The early form of the list of words written but not read has five examples: Deut 6:25 (*zʾt*); 2 Kgs 5:18; Jer 51:3; Ezek 48:16; Ruth 3:12. The standard list has eight examples. It leaves out Deut 6:25 and adds 2 Sam 13:33; 15:21; Jer 38:16; 39:12 (*IDBSup,* 719). These texts have to be examined on a case by case basis to determine if an authentic textual variant underlies each one. Nevertheless, the tradition in general indicates the probability that the Q and K diverge at times because of different textual traditions.

Evidence of textual traditions in the K/Q also seems indicated where the Q of Samuel and Kings is in many cases the K of Chronicles and no Q is recorded there. Compare, e.g., 2 Sam 23:8–9, 13, 15–16, 18, 20–21 and 1 Chr 11:11–12, 15, 17–18, 20, 22–23. Sperber took this kind of correspondence as evidence that the Q was based on a recension of the Deuteronomistic History separate from the K (1943: 303–9).

6. Epexegetical Alterations of the K. Some K/Q variations are probably the result of alterations by the tradents of the Q in order to clarify the meaning of the text. Classes of epexegetical alterations include:

a. Grammatical Corrections. A probable case of grammatical correction is attested in the alternation of *whyh* / *whyw* when the subject is *twṣʾwt* as in Num 34:3; Josh 15:4; 18:12, 14, 19. The K agrees with the Q in Num 34:9 and Josh 17:18; cf. also Josh 19:29. Gordis considered this variant to be due to the loss of the archaic 3 fem. pl. ending (1937: 104–5). But a verb does not have to agree with its subject in number or gender in biblical Hebrew if it precedes it (*GKC* §145o). These Q readings are likely a correction to a simpler grammatical form which anticipates the kind of change the Masoretic *sbyr* notes aim to prevent.

This class may also include certain cases of variation between short and long imperfect forms, e.g., Josh 7:21; Jer 3:7; 17:8; and gender variations such as *ʾḥd* / *ʾḥt* in 2 Sam 23:8 and *hwʾ* / *hyʾ* in Isa 30:33. The latter alternation is similar to the preference shown for pronouncing 3 fem. pl. verbs and suffixes in the Q of biblical Aramaic. See, e.g., *npqw* / *npqh* (Dan 5:5); *bynyhwn* / *bynyhyn* (Dan 7:8).

b. Euphemisms. One form of this kind of alteration is the euphemistic replacement of words based on roots such as *šgl* and *ʿpl* with milder forms, cf. Deut 28:27, 30; 1 Sam 5:6, 12. The K/Q *šnʾw* / *śnʾy* in 2 Sam 5:8 has probably resulted from a desire to protect David's character (McCarthy 1981: 230–31). A euphemistic substitution can also be found in the alternation of *bgd* / *bʾ gd* in Gen 30:11. Both of these Q readings were likely generated in a manner similar to the midrashic *ʾal tiqrê* ("do not read") technique. According to McCarthy (1981: 166), similar techniques generated most of the readings now preserved in the rabbinic lists of the "emendations of the scribes" (*tiqqûnê sôpĕrîm*).

c. Expansions. An expansion in the Q may be indicated by the prepositional phrase *ʾly* in Ruth 3:5, 17 found in the lists of words read but not written. The addition of *waw* in the Q is attested in Lam 5:3, 5. This kind of expansionary tendency is often found in the versions. The rabbinic tradition of the "corrections of the scribes" (*ʿiṭṭûrê sôpĕrîm*) is related to this phenomenon.

Bibliography

Bamberger, S. 1923. Die Bedeutung der Qeri Kethib. *Jahrbuch der Jüdisch-Literarischen Gesellschaft* 15: 217–65.

———. 1930. Die Bedeutung der Qeri Kethib (Fortsetzung). *Jahrbuch der Jüdisch-Literarischen Gesellschaft* 21: 39–88.

Barr, J. 1981. A New Look at Kethib-Qere. *OTS* 21: 19–37.

Breuer, M. 1981. Written, Read, and Chanted. *Leš* 45: 260–69 (in Hebrew).

Fassberg, S. E. 1989. The Origin of the *Ketib/Qere* in the Aramaic Portions of Ezra and Daniel. *VT* 39: 1–12.

Frensdorff, S. 1972. *Das Buch Ochlah W'ochlah.* New York.

Ginsburg, C. D. 1869. Keri and Kethiv. Vol. 2, pp. 719–26 in *A Cyclopaedia of Biblical Literature.* Edinburgh.

Gordis, R. 1937. *The Biblical Text in the Making.* Philadelphia. Repr. 1971, New York.

Kahle, P. 1913. *Masoreten des Ostens.* Hildesheim. Repr. 1966.

Kutscher, E. Y. 1974. *The Language and Linguistic Background of the Isaiah Scroll.* STDJ 6. Leiden.

Levita, E. 1538. *Massoreth ha-Massoreth,* ed. C. D. Ginsburg, 1867. Repr. in *Jacob Ben Chajim Ibn Adonijah's Introduction to the Rabbinic Bible and the Massoreth ha-Massoreth of Elias Levita.* New York, 1968.

Lyons, D. 1974. The Collative Tiberian Masorah: A Preliminary Study. Pp. 55–66 in *1972 and 1973 Proceedings of the IOMS.* SBLMasS 1. Missoula, MT.

McCarthy, C. 1981. *The Tiqqune Sopherim.* OBO 36. Göttingen.

Morrow, W. S., and Clarke, E. G. 1986. The *Ketib/Qere* in the Aramaic Portions of Ezra and Daniel. *VT* 36: 406–22.

Orlinsky, H. M. 1940. Problems of Kethib-Qere. *JAOS* 60: 30–45.

———. 1943. The Biblical Prepositions *táḥaṯ, bēn, báʿaḏ* and Pronouns *ʾănû* (or *ʾanū*), *zoʾtâh.* *HUCA* 17: 267–92.

———. 1960. The Origin of the Kethib-Qere System: A New Approach. *VTSup* 7: 184–92.

Revell, E. J. 1974. The Relation of the Palestinian to the Tiberian Massora. Pp. 87–97 in *1972 and 1973 Proceedings of the IOMS.* SBLMasS 1. Missoula, MT.

———. 1977. *Biblical texts with Palestinian Pointing and their Accents.* SBLMasS 4. Missoula, MT.

Rubinstein, A. 1959. A Kethib-Qere Problem in the Light of the Isaiah Scroll. *JSS* 4: 127–33.

———. 1961. Singularities in the Massorah of the Leningrad codex (B19a). *JJS* 12: 123–31.

———. 1965. The Problem of Errors in the Massorah Parva of Codex B19a. *Sef* 25: 16–26.

Sperber, A. 1943. Problems of the Masora. *HUCA* 17: 293–394.

———. 1973. *The Bible In Aramaic.* Vol. 4B. Leiden.

Talmon, S. 1962. The Three Scrolls of the Law that Were Found in the Temple Court. *Textus* 2: 14–27.

Weil, G. E. 1971. *Massorah Gedolah Iuxta Codicem Leningradensem B 19a.* Vol. 1. Rome.

Würthwein, E. 1979. *The Text of the Old Testament.* 4th ed. Grand Rapids.

Yeivin, I. 1962. The Vocalization of Qere-Kethiv in A. *Textus* 2: 146–49.

———. 1980. *Introduction to the Tiberian Masorah.* SBLMasS 5. Missoula, MT.

William S. Morrow

KETHUBIM. The third section of the Jewish division of the Hebrew Bible meaning "writings" (Heb *kĕtûbîm*), known also as the Hagiographa from the Greek term meaning "holy writings." This division includes the books of Psalms, Job, Proverbs, Ruth, Canticles (Song of Solomon), Qoheleth (Ecclesiastes), Lamentations, Esther, Daniel, Ezra, Nehemiah, and 1–2 Chronicles.

KETURAH (PERSON) [Heb *qĕṭûrâ*]. The third wife of Abraham, after Sarah and Hagar (Gen 25:1–4; 1 Chr 1:32–33). As far as they can be identified, her children and grandchildren were prominent Arabian or Aramean tribes or cities. See MEDAN; MIDIAN; ISHBAK; SHUAH; SHEBA; DEDAN. Medan, Midian, Dedan, and Sheba/Saba were situated along the "incense route" through W Arabia, and Shuah was involved in Sabean commerce as early as the second half of the 8th century B.C. "Keturah" is not attested as a personal name. It is reasonable to suggest that Keturah is a personification of the incense trade (cf. Heb *qĕṭōret* "incense"; *qĕṭôrâ* "incense offering"; Ephᶜal 1982: 231–33). Within a concept of geography in terms of genealogy as it is encountered in the OT, Keturah links to Abraham those Arabian tribes and cities which were not included among the descendants of Hagar.

The date of the geographical list constituted by the "sons of Keturah" is difficult to ascertain. Whereas some of its elements, like the "sons of Midian" (Gen 25:4), may antedate the 8th century B.C. (Knauf 1988: 85–86), the list as a whole presupposes the establishment of the "incense route" in the course of the 8th century B.C. Because it does not mention the Minaeans, who gained supremacy over the Arabian trade in the 4th century B.C., the list can be assumed to have been finalized before 400 B.C. (Knauf 1988: 168).

Bibliography

Ephᶜal, I. 1982. *The Ancient Arabs.* Jerusalem and Leiden.
Knauf, E. A. 1988. *Midian.* ADPV. Wiesbaden.

ERNST AXEL KNAUF

KEYS OF THE KINGDOM. In Matt 16:19 the giving over of the "keys of the kingdom of heaven" (*tas kleidas tēs basileias tōn ouranōn*) is part of the three-part promise of Jesus to Peter, who had confessed Jesus to be "the Christ, the Son of the living God." As the Petrine confession represents a post-Easter formulation of the Church's Easter faith, so the promise made to Peter reflects Matthew's understanding of the Church and relates to the ecclesiastic situation after the Resurrection.

The logion of v 19 is but loosely linked to the image of the Church built on Peter (Cephas)—the "rock." The imagery of the building is maintained but the metaphor is mixed. In v 19 Peter is depicted as one having the power of a householder, the image of the keys having been evoked by the image of the gates of Hades. Nonetheless, the mixed metaphors incline many scholars to think that the two sayings (vv 18, 19) enjoyed an independent existence at some point in the existence of the Palestinian Jewish-Christian church.

Some hold that v 19 alludes to Isa 22:15–25, in which an oracle is expressed apropos of Eliakim, the successor to the deposed Shebna: "I will place on his shoulder the key of the house of David; he shall open, and none shall shut; and he shall shut, and none shall open" (Isa 22:22). In this case, Peter would appear to fulfill something of a prime ministerial role in the kingdom of heaven. Allusion is certainly made to the Isaian text in Rev 3:7 ("the holy one, the true one, who has the key to David, who opens and no one shall shut, who shuts and no one opens"), apparently in reference to Jesus. In an earlier passage (Rev 1:18), Revelation had described Jesus as having the keys of Death and Hades. There is, however, no clear reference to Isaiah 22 in Matt 16:19 and the attempted Aramaic retroversions would seem to argue against its plausibility.

In Jewish tradition, the key of David refers to the authority of the teachers of the Law. Luke cites a Q tradition in which reference is made to a key (the key of knowledge in Luke's formulation) held by lawyers (Luke 11:52). The Matthean version of the saying, a woe addressed to the scribes and Pharisees "because you shut the kingdom of heaven against men; for you neither enter yourselves, nor allow those who would enter to go in" (Matt 23:13), without explicit reference to a key, serves as a negative parallel to Matt 16:19. Thus "the keys of the kingdom of heaven" would seem to indicate that Peter enjoyed an authority like that of the teachers of the Law, but in contradistinction to them. He represents something of a chief rabbi for the Matthean community.

The present wording of Matt 16:19a, specified and reinforced by the binding and loosing logion of v 19b–c, is clearly a Matthean formulation ("kingdom of heaven"). The emphasis of the image is primarily positive; its primary reference is to a power allowing entrance into the kingdom. The Matthean language may be compared with the earlier eschatological understanding whereby entrance into the kingdom is effected by means of belief in the gospel which had been preached. Matthew's phraseology affirms the eschatological significance of Peter's commission to preach. In its post-resurrectional setting, the image symbolizes Peter's plenipotentiary authority over the Church and may well also have reference to Peter's power to gather the community together, to interpret the Scriptures, and to exercise various disciplinary functions within the community. The household imagery affirms Peter's full power over the Church and confirms that the exercise of that power is sanctioned by the risen One. See also *TDNT* 3: 744–53.

Bibliography

Raymond, E.; Donfried, K. P.; and Reumann, J., eds. 1973. *Peter in the New Testament.* Minneapolis.
Schnackenburg, R. 1981. Das Vollmachtswort vom Binden und Losen, traditionsgeschichtlich gesehen. Pp. 141–57 in *Kontinuität und Einheit,* ed. P.-G. Müller and W. Stenger. Freiburg.

RAYMOND F. COLLINS

KEZIAH (PERSON) [Heb *qĕṣîᶜâ*]. The second of Job's daughters born to him after the restoration of his fortunes (42:14). The name means "cassia plant," and refers to the aromatic cassia which is mentioned in Ps 45:9 [—Eng 45:8] along with myrrh and aloes. The principle ancient versions are agreed in this identification, the LXX reading *kesia* and the Vulgate *cassia.* Dhorme (1967) assumes that the reference is to the aromatic cassia which is today called cinnamon or canella. Not only do the names of Job's daughters refer in some way to their beauty and charm, but the three together present assonantal relationships. Jemimah and Keziah clearly offer final syllabic rhyme, while Keziah and Keren-happuch offer first syllable assonance. See also JEMIMAH; KEREN-HAPPUCH.

Bibliography

Dhorme, E. 1967. *A Commentary on the Book of Job.* London.

JOHN C. HOLBERT

KHAFAJE. A site in Iraq on the left bank of the Diyala river, SE of tell Asmar. Particularly vigorous clandestine excavations shortly after the first World War brought this region of the lower branch of the Diyala to the attention of the scientific community, and the Oriental Institute of the University of Chicago decided in 1929 to explore four of its principal tells: Asmar, Ischaeli, Agrab, and Khafaje.

The latter site, formed of a group of three principal hills (A, B-C and D) of unequal importance and belonging to different periods, has proved to be quite rich. P. Delougaz directed the research for the first seven expeditions under the sponsorship of the Oriental Institute (1930 to 1937) and under a joint expedition of the University Museum of the University of Pennsylvania and the American Schools of Oriental Research for the two final campaigns in 1937 and 1938.

Tell D, about 400 m by 250 m, has been only minimally explored; it contains, apparently, the ruins of a small fortress and two temples, one dedicated to Sin. The name of this installation is unknown.

Tell B-C, of larger dimensions (more than 500 m by 400 m) is a fortress built by the son of Hammurabi and known by the name of *Dur-Samsuiluna* ("fortress of Samsuiluna"). Behind an enclosure wall of 5 m thickness, a large residence of 1200 square m has been found, but the excavations have not been continued long enough to give a precise image of the installation.

It is tell A that has been the object of the most thorough research. Oblong in shape (about 900 m by 400 m), the city that it contains was known at the end of the 3d millennium by the name "Tuttub." However, its history results more from knowledge gathered from archaeological finds than from textual sources, which have not been found in great number. Its origins are found in the Predynastic period, without doubt during the phase generally known by the name of Jemdet-Nasr, about 3000 B.C.E.; it is during this period that the five first phases of the temple of Sin are dated. It is possible that the city was most often under the control of Eshnunna (tell Asmar), but it is impossible to know the course of events for this early period. However, its real importance, at least if one trusts the monuments that have been unearthed, dates from the Early Dynastic Period, when the improvements to the Oval Temple show that the city possessed the means to undertake works of enormous size. It is to this period that the largest number of discovered monuments belong. But following this period, the city again enjoyed real importance, at least during certain periods. The foundations of a large edifice dated from the Agade period found in the N part of the city show that it still felt the need to construct buildings that clearly fell into the category of palaces. In addition, around 1900 Tuttub freed itself from the natural dominance of Eshnunna, its neighbor, and for about thirty years knew independence. The incorporation of the region into the empire of Hammurabi, in the 18th century, was accompanied by a weakening and a growing poverty that proved the end to urban life in Tuttub as in all the other neighboring cities.

The major ruin is clearly the Oval Temple. The first of the sanctuaries of this type to have been found in Mesopotamia, it presents an organization that expresses spatially the progression from the profane toward the sacred by a progressive elevation of the levels of occupation. The general form, irregular, is created by an approximately ellipsoidal enclosure of 74 m by 54 m oriented NW-SE about 40 cm higher than the surrounding surface; one reaches this slightly elevated level by a single entrance to the NW that gives onto an open space tightly associated with D House located to the N between the two enclosures. Almost facing the entrance, a monumental doorway allows one to enter into an almost concentric second enclosure in which a stairway of four steps marks a new level of elevation. One then arrives in a large trapezoidal courtyard with rooms located all around its perimeter. Two functions were without doubt intended: to allow the completion of rites that took place outdoors and to allow access to the terrace six meters above that takes up all of the SE part; although no trace has been found, a temple which formed the apex of the progression was probably located on the summit.

Among the material remains that have been collected are several stone statuettes, a votive plaque, and a group of three standing copper statuettes on a circular pedestal with four feet. We do not know the name of the deity worshiped in the Oval Temple, but the sanctuary seems to be characteristic of the Early Dynastic Period. It was built during the course of the second phase of the period (ED II) and seems to have been in use up until the empire of Agade, having undergone several reconstructions and alterations.

The Temple of Sin is located about 50 m to the E; it is in reality a small sanctuary whose notoriety comes more from the minute study undertaken by the excavators than from the importance of the location. The oldest phase recovered goes back to the Jemdet-Nasr period and the most recent has been fixed at the end of the Early Dynastic; ten major architectural phases allow us to follow the evolution of the small urban temple and its alterations; the most important part consists of a rectangular room NW-SE equipped with a platform built against the NW wall (the location of the throne of the god) and sometimes parallelepiped or cylindrical pedestals (probably offering tables). The adjoining structures were located along the two sides; toward the E extended a courtyard that was important for the course of the history of the building. Also of note is a third temple dedicated to Nintu, and above all, the very curious small walled quarter of which the significance is not very well understood.

Bibliography

Delougaz, P. 1940. *The Oval Temple at Khafajah.* OIP 53. Chicago.

Delougaz, P., and Lloyd, S. 1942. *Pre-sargonid Temples in the Diyala Region.* OIP 57. Chicago.

Delougaz, P.; Hill, D.; and Lloyd, S. 1967. *Private Houses and Graves in the Diyala Region.* OIP 88. Chicago.

Frankfort, H. 1942. *Sculpture of the Third Millennium B.C. from Tell Asmar and Khafajah.* OIP 57. Chicago.

———. 1943. *More Sculpture from the Diyala Region.* OIP 60. Chicago.

Heinrich, E. 1982. *Die Tempel und Heiligtümer im alten Mesopotamien.* Berlin.

JEAN-CL. MARGUERON
Trans. Stephen Rosoff

KHALIL, RAMAT EL-. See RAMAT EL-KHALIL (M.R. 160107).

KHELEIFEH, TELL EL- (M.R. 147884). The site of Tell el-Kheleifeh is located approximately 500 m from the N shore of the Gulf of Aqaba, roughly equidistant between modern Eilat and Aqaba. This low mudbrick mound was first surveyed in 1933 by the German explorer Fritz Frank, who identified the site with biblical Ezion-geber (Frank 1934). Having conducted a surface survey of Tell el-Kheleifeh in 1937, Nelson Glueck directed three seasons of excavation (1938–1940) and discerned six major periods of occupation with three subphases (Glueck 1938a; 1938b; 1939; 1940a; 1965). The occupational horizons were dated between the Iron I and Persian periods. Glueck accepted Frank's identification of Tell el-Kheleifeh with biblical Ezion-geber and, though some uncertainty is reflected in his field records and later publications, the equation remained the underlying premise for the interpretation of the site's occupational history.

A reappraisal of Glueck's excavations in light of advances in the science of archaeology, particularly refinements in pottery typology, has suggested the need for significant refinement and revision of his conclusions (Pratico 1982; 1985). The most important datum involves revision of the site's chronological horizons as indicated by the study of the pottery. The site's pottery cannot be dated earlier than the 9th century B.C., and this early limit is suggested only by isolated forms. The horizon as a whole appears to date between the 8th and early 6th centuries B.C. with a presence attested as late as the 4th century B.C. The horizons of the site's architectural traditions are too broad to provide definitive chronological refinement. Tell el-Kheleifeh, therefore, provides no clear archaeological indications, ceramic or architectural, for an identification with Ezion-geber of Israel's wilderness traditions (Num 33:35–36), the 10th century (1 Kgs 9:26–28), or the 9th century (1 Kgs 22:47–48).

Tell el-Kheleifeh was occupied in two major architectural phases: casemate fortress and fortified settlement. The earliest phase consisted of a casemate square (approximately 45 m on each side) which surrounded a courtyard that was apparently devoid of architecture with the exception of one monumental building (13.20 × 12.30 m), constructed on the "four-room" plan. Glueck originally identified this structure as a smelting furnace but later abandoned this interpretation, designating the building as a citadel. The best architectural parallels to the earliest phase are provided by the casemate fortresses of the central Negeb (Cohen 1979; cf. also 1970; 1976; Meshel 1975; 1977). The latter are generally dated to the 10th century B.C., a date which is not consistent with the suggested chronology of the extant Tell el-Kheleifeh pottery. Unfortunately, Glueck's methodology and recording system preclude precise determination of the date of the casemate fortresses phase.

After the destruction of the casemate fortress, the plan of Tell el-Kheleifeh was radically changed. The fortress was replaced by a significantly larger settlement with an offsets/insets wall and a four-chambered gateway. A large section of the earlier casemate fortress was retained, creating an inner enclosure or courtyard in the NW quadrant of the new offsets/insets plan. The N and W perimeters of the earlier casemate wall were now outside the offsets/insets fortification which also destroyed a portion of the N wall of the four-room building.

The plan of the fortified settlement phase is best paralleled by the citadels of Tell Arad X–VIII (Herzog et al. 1984). Similar features include an element of monumental architecture in the NW corner (though dissimilar in function), a main N-S street on the settlement's E side, inner-wall structures of similar plan and function, a gateway of the four-chambered plan and the offsets/insets fortification which created similar dimensions for each of the settlements.

The pottery which can be associated with the levels of the offsets/insets settlement dates between the 8th and early 6th centuries B.C. These dates are also indicated by certain of the epigraphic materials and studies in comparative architecture. Though the data are lean, both architectural and ceramic, the occupational history of Tell el-Kheleifeh continued beyond the Iron Age, perhaps as late as the 4th century B.C.

The identification of Tell el-Kheleifeh is both an archaeological and a historical problem. One may argue the identification from the perspectives of possibility or probability, but the problem of verification precludes examination of the site in the context of biblical Ezion-geber and/or Elath. The biblical notices pertaining to these two sites are of special importance, however, for providing a rough chronological framework relative to Judean or Edomite control or influence over the region. The methodological prerequisite for the reappraisal of Glueck's excavations must be the demand for uncensored archaeological data. Tell el-Kheleifeh must be allowed to tell its own story in its own language. Allowing Glueck's data to speak apart from the historical contours of Ezion-geber and Elath has produced a significantly different version for this chapter in the study of Syro-Palestinian archaeology.

Bibliography

Cohen, R. 1970. ᶜAtar Haroᶜa. *Atiqot* (Hebrew Series) 6: 6–24.

———. 1976. Excavations at Ḥorvat Ḥaluqim. *Atiqot* (English Series) 11: 34–50.

———. 1979. The Iron Age Fortresses in the Central Negev. *BASOR* 236: 61–79.

———. 1981. Excavations at Kadesh-barnea, 1976–1978. *BA* 44: 93–104.
Frank, F. 1934. Aus der ʿArabah, I: Tell el-Chlēfi. *ZDPV* 57: 243–45.
Glueck, N. 1938a. The First Campaign at Tell el-Kheleifeh (Ezion-Geber). *BASOR* 71: 3–17.
———. 1938b. The Topography and History of Ezion-Geber and Elath. *BASOR* 72: 2–13.
———. 1939. The Second Campaign at Tell el-Kheleifeh (Ezion-Geber: Elath). *BASOR* 75: 8–22.
———. 1940a. The Third Season of Excavation at Tell el-Kheleifeh. *BASOR* 79: 2–18.
———. 1940b. Ostraca from Elath. *BASOR* 80: 3–10.
———. 1941. Ostraca from Elath. *BASOR* 82: 3–11.
———. 1965. Ezion-geber. *BA* 28: 70–87.
———. 1967. Some Edomite Pottery from Tell el-Kheleifeh, Parts I and II. *BASOR* 188: 8–38.
———. 1969. Some Ezion-Geber: Elath Iron II Pottery. *EI* 9: 51–59.
———. 1971a. Iron II Kenite and Edomite Pottery. *Perspective* 12: 45–56.
———. 1971b. Tell el-Kheleifeh Inscriptions. Pp. 225–42 in *Near Eastern Studies in Honor of William Foxwell Albright,* ed. H. Goedicke. Baltimore.
Herzog, Z. et al. 1984. The Israelite Fortress at Arad. *BASOR* 254: 1–34.
Meshel, Z. 1975. On the Problem of Tell el-Kheleifeh, Elath and Ezion-Geber. *EI* 12: 49–56.
———. 1977. Ḥorvat Ritma—An Iron Age Fortress in the Negev Highlands. *TA* 4: 110–35.
Pratico, G. 1982. Tell el-Kheleifeh 1938–1940: A Forthcoming Reappraisal. *BA* 45/2: 120–21.
———. 1985. Nelson Glueck's 1938–1940 Excavations at Tell el-Kheleifeh: A Reappraisal. *BASOR* 259: 1–32.

Gary D. Pratico

KHIRBET. Geographic names containing the element "khirbet," meaning "ruin," may be found alphabetized under the second element of the name; for example: ISKANDER, KHIRBET; ADER, KHIRBET.

KHIRBET KERAK WARE. This term designates a distinctive assemblage of ceramic forms found at a number of sites in Palestine, Syria, and E Anatolia dating to the EB III. The name "Khirbet Kerak Ware" was given to this pottery group by W. F. Albright in the 1930s when the ware was first found in large quantities on the SW shore of the Sea of Galilee at the site of Khirbet Kerak, now known as BETH-YERAH (M.R. 204235), one of the major international trade centers of the EB III. (Kh. Kerak should not be confused with the Jordanian site of KERAK.)

A. Forms and Decoration

Smaller forms include upright-sided and sinuous-sided bowls. Sinuous-sided pots and kraters have been found among the larger vessels. A third category includes conical lids, biconical stands, and U-shaped pot stands.

Khirbet Kerak Ware is distinguished by its bidirectional burnished-surface and "metallic" ware, yet especially larger vessels are frequently made of poorly levigated clay often with some medium to large inclusions. It seems that only small upright-sided bowls had a slip applied before burnishing. Lids and U-shaped stands were usually left unburnished.

The sinuous-sided bowls, sinuous-sided pots and kraters have brownish-orange to brown rims and interior surfaces, while the exterior, excluding the rim, is black. The upright-sided bowls are brownish-orange over the entire surface. The surface colors of the lids and U-shaped stands ranges from tan to gray.

Decorations range from simple knobs and lines (esp. on the smaller bowls) to chevrons, spirals, and polygons (esp. on larger pots and kraters) to anthropoid faces on the U-shaped stands. The decorations are made before the burnish is applied and may be either fluted or raised, although there are a few examples where the decoration was etched through the burnished surface after the vessel was fired.

B. Provenience of Khirbet Kerak Ware

The earliest extant Khirbet Kerak Ware, dated ca. 2800 B.C.E., was found in E Anatolia and S Russia and bears many similarities to E Anatolian polished ware of the era immediately preceding (Amiran 1952; Lamb 1954; Burney 1958). The pottery appeared suddenly in N Canaan ca. 2700 B.C.E. during EB IIIa (Hennessy 1967; Callaway 1972). Scholars postulate that KKW appeared in Canaan either as an import from the Trans-Caucasus region or as a result of a major migration of an ethnic group (possibly the Hurrians; Burney 1958) from this region through Syria to N Canaan with settlement along some of the region's major trade routes. Significant quantities have been found as well at sites in the Ḥabur and 'Amuq regions of N Syria, at the Syrian coastal site of Ugarit and at several sites in the N Jordan valley and the Esdraelon Plain in N Canaan. Smaller quantities have been found at peripheral sites.

Assemblages of KKW found at various Canaanite sites show some unique variations in technique which set them apart from the wares found in Syria and Anatolia. Furthermore, some standard Canaanite forms (e.g., hole-mouth jars and simple bowls) were incorporated into the KKW repertoire at certain Canaanite sites through the application of the specialized burnishing and color typical of this ware. Both these features would indicate that the KKW found in Canaan was not imported from Syria and Anatolia.

Testing by neutron activation analysis and petrographic analysis of KKW found at Palestinian and Syrian sites has indicated that wherever this pottery is found in significant quantities, nearly all of it was manufactured locally at or near the site. It seems in the light of the few nonlocal sherds found at sites such as Beth-Yerah that perhaps initially some vessels were imported to Canaanite sites before local manufacture of the ware was established. Meager quantities have been found at S Canaanite sites. Initial testing of pieces from sites such as Jericho indicates that the pottery was not locally made but rather imported from major production centers in N Canaan. (viz., Beth-Yerah).

KKW remains one of the main diagnostic pottery forms

in determining EB III levels at archaeological tells in the Levant today.

Bibliography

Albright, W. F. 1926. The Jordan Valley in the Bronze Age. *AASOR* 6: 13–74.

Amiran, R. 1952. Anatolia and Palestine. *IEJ* 2: 89–103.

———. 1969. *Ancient Pottery of the Holy Land.* Jerusalem.

Burney, C. A. 1958. Eastern Anatolia in the Chalcolithic and Early Bronze Age. *AnSt* 8: 157–209.

Callaway, J. 1972. *The Early Bronze Age Sanctuary at Ai (et-Tell).* London.

———. 1980. *The Early Bronze Age Citadel and Lower City at Ai (et-Tell).* Cambridge, MA.

Chazan, M., and McGovern, P. E. 1984. Khirbet Kerak Pottery at Beth Shan: Technological Evidence for Local Manufacture? *Masca* 3: 20–24.

Esse, D., and Hopke, P. K. 1986. Levantine Trade in the Early Bronze Age. Pp. 327–39 in *Proceedings of the 24th International Archaeometry Symposium,* ed. J. S. Olin and M. J. Blackmun. Washington, D.C.

Hennessy, J. B. 1967. *The Foreign Relations of Palestine during the Early Bronze Age.* London.

Lamb, W. 1954. The Culture of North-East Anatolia and its Neighbours. *AnSt* 4: 21–32.

STEPHEN J. PFANN

KHORSABAD. The name of a village in N Iraq which designates the site of ancient Dur-Sharrukin (fortress of Sargon), a city founded by Sargon II of Assyria. The work began around 713 B.C. and the city was inaugurated in 707 B.C. as the capital of the empire; but it was never finished because Sargon II died in 705 B.C. and his successor Sennacherib, abandoned the city to return to Nineveh.

The site is famous for the profusion of discoveries that have been found there, and also because it was there that the very first digs were conducted in Mesopotamia. In fact, P. E. Botta, the French consul in Mosul in 1842, who was actively interested in orientalism, decided to dig at the site of Nineveh, neighbor of Mosul and soon after at Khorsabad, 15 kms N-NE of the Assyrian capital; it was a matter therefore of finding real proof of this Assyrian civilization, known only up to that time in biblical sources (the campaigns of Sennacherib, Ezekiel's prophecies and the adventures of Jonah) and through a few superficial discoveries that aroused curiosity without bringing any solutions to the questions that were being asked on the origins of Christianity and Judaism. Nevertheless the initial research conducted at Nineveh was deceiving, while the works being conducted at Khorsabad were crowned with success: on the third day monumental *bas-reliefs* filled with inscriptions were found.

The reverberations of these initial discoveries were sufficient for Paris to begin proceedings with *la Porte* in order to insure the continuation of exploration and sent Flandin to secure the design and the unearthing of the monuments uncovered. The first excavation, finished in October 1844, was accompanied by the shipment of the recovered reliefs to France and the opening of the Assyrian museum in the Louvre palace. V. Place in 1852 again took up the exploration in the tells of the Assyrian triangle and most particularly at Khorsabad; he brought to light an important part of the Sargon Palace, but most of the reliefs and statues he found were lost in a shipwreck in 1855 at Korna, near the confluence of the Tigris and the Euphrates. The Khorsabad tell was not explored for more than 60 years after that. It was the University of Chicago that decided to take up again the excavations in 1928; the most active digs took place from 1930–35 under the direction of G. Loud. These excavations revolved around the region of the Sargon Palace, a gate to the city and the old city itself. Finally a few research and conservation works were conducted on the site these last few years by the Iraqis.

The old city measures 1800 m × 1700 m and is enclosed behind an enclosure of 24 meters thick (in coarse bricks on top of a stone bedrock). We do not really know the interior organization of the city since the dig only explored small areas; however, we were able to enumerate the existence of seven doors in two facing walls, the north face possessing only one. On the western flank closely linked to the enclosure and in the proximity of the fifth door, the palace of the heir-apparent, Sennacherib, was found on a terrace. On the north face, straddling the enclosure, a terrace was installed that supported the great palace of Sargon. A ziggurat was found more than 40 m high and with layered paints (white, black, purple, and blue) which was dedicated to six divinities: Sin, Adad, Ea, Shamash, Ninurta, and Ningal. At the foot of this terrace was an area of private houses, enclosed by a wall opened toward the city by two monumental gates, where there had been constructed the great residences attributed to members of the royal family and the great dignitaries of the empire. The temple of Nabu, set on a terrace that was connected to the one that supported the great royal palace by a stone bridge, rose up between these residences.

The Sargon palace was planned according to the fundamental principles of Assyrian residences. A great public courtyard, approximately square in shape, containing the majority of administrative annexes consisted of the first unit; it had access to a rectangular courtyard decorated with orthostats in relief.

The renown of Dur-Sharrukin derives, without doubt, less from architecture than the bas-reliefs and monumental full-relief sculpture that were discovered, like the androcephalous bulls. Starting with the first dig and during the course of the excavations that followed on this site, an extraordinary dossier of Assyrian art was brought to light. The court scenes, the religious themes, and the representations of war, all meaning to glorify or protect the sovereign, are at the same time creations of rare quality by sculptors from the Assyrian period.

The epigraphic harvest from the excavations was just as important. The inscriptions on the bas-reliefs or on the doorway flagstones, the list of the Assyrian kings (more than 100 sovereigns between the beginning of the 2d millennium and the 8th century) provide an incomparable source for the history of the Assyrian empire.

Bibliography

Botta, P. E., and Flandin, E. 1849–50. *Monuments de Ninive.* 5 vols. Paris.

Loud, G. 1936–38. *Khorsabad.* 2 vols. Chicago.

Place, V. 1867–70. *Ninive et l'Assyrie.* 3 vols. Paris.

JEAN-CL. MARGUERON
Trans. Stephen Rosoff

KIBROTH-HATTAAVAH (PLACE) [Heb *qibrot hatta'awâ*]. The first encampment of the Israelites, after leaving the wilderness of Sinai, as listed in Num 33:16–17, where it is placed between the wilderness of Sinai and Hazeroth. After leaving Sinai, the Israelites complained to Moses about a lack of meat (Num 11:4–6). When Moses brought this before his God, the Lord caused a flock of quails to fall to the ground near the Israelite camp. Though they were able to feast now, a great plague from God came upon them even as they were eating, killing many people. It is this incident which gave the site its name: "The Graves of Craving" (Num 11:31–35, Deut 9:22). Unfortunately the name does not help in the identification of the site. A suggested location is Rueis el-Ebeirig, NE of Jebel Musa, and between the latter site and ʿAin el-Hazerah, often identified with Hazeroth, the next station in the list (*GP*, 214, 417; Palmer 1872: 212–14, 252, 418–19, 423; *GTTOT*, 255 and note 224; M.R. 076797). For a discussion of the location of any of the places associated with the journey of the Israelites from Egypt through Sinai, see DOPHKAH.

Bibliography

Beit-Arieh, I. 1988. The Route Through Sinai—Why the Israelites Fleeing Egypt Went South. *BARev* 15/3: 28–37.
Palmer, E. H. 1872. *The Desert of the Exodus.* New York.

JEFFREY R. ZORN

KIBZAIM (PLACE) [Heb *qibṣayim*]. Third Levitical city in the Ephraim list (Josh 21:22). The parallel city in the Levitical City list in 1 Chronicles is Jokmeam (1 Chr 6:52—Eng 6:68). Albright (1945: 67–68) has argued through a text-critical study that Kibzaim and Jokmeam are individual cities, but B. Mazar (1957: 198) has argued that the place name Jokmeam was taken from the name of the Levitic family who settled there. In his list, Mazar reads Jokmeam for Kibzaim. Both Kibzaim and Jokmeam appear only once in the OT; in each instance it is in a Levitical City list. There is no reference to either city in any extra-biblical sources. Because these two cities are so obscure, any identification becomes speculative. See JOKMEAM.

Tell el-Qusin (M.R. 167182) has been identified as biblical Kibzaim by Abel (*GP*, 417), but Y. Aharoni (*LBHG*, 325) has identified the site with the Samaria Ostraca's Kozah. The site is located 2 km N and 9 km W of Nablus. About 5 km due N of Qusin is Sebaste (biblical Samaria). Situated on a mountain, Qusin is surrounded by a broad, major valley. On its E and N sides is the important Nablus-Jenin road. In the valley to the W and S is a Wadi that joins other wadies which flow to the Mediterranean. There have been a few surveys conducted at Tell el-Qusin revealing pottery from the EB, Iron I, Iron II, Persian, Byzantine, and Ottoman periods. One serious problem with the identification of Qusin with biblical Kibzaim is that Qusin clearly lies in the tribe of Manasseh, not in Ephraim. Consequently this identification is not acceptable, and Aharoni's suggestion that Tell el-Qusin is Kozah is more likely correct.

Z. Kallai has identified Tell esh-Sheikh Dhiâb (M.R. 190161) with biblical Jokmeam. It is located in the Judean Desert, 22 km N of Jericho and 2.5 km NW of Khirbet Faṣâyil. The tell is situated at the foot of the Judean hills on the edge of the Jordan River valley about 9 km due W of the river. Tell esh-Sheikh Dhiâb is surrounded on three sides (N, S, W) by hills, while the flat valley lies to the E. Between Sheikh Dhiâb and the W mountains is the Wadi Faṣâyil. There have been some archaeological surveys conducted at Tell esh-Sheikh Dhiâb and a wide distribution of pottery has been found including Chalcolithic, EB, MB, Iron I, Iron II, Hellenistic, Roman, Byzantine, and Arabic.

The third city to have been identified with biblical Kibzaim and/or Jokmeam is Tell el-Mazar (M.R. 196171). Mazar (1957: 198) has been a leading exponent favoring the identification of biblical Kibzaim/Jokmeam with Tell el-Mazar. Mazar thinks that Kibzaim and Jokmeam are one and the same city, claiming that the settlement of Kibzaim was called Jokmeam after the family of Levites living there. This family, the Jekameamites, were descendants of the priestly family of Hebron. Mazar points out that "the same town" is mentioned in 1 Kgs 4:12. It is located on "the extreme S border of the fifth administrative district of Solomon." A problem with this text is that this city is located in Zebulun and its name has been understood to be a scribal error for Jokmeam. Therefore Mazar harmonizes the 2 lists by simply stating that Kibzaim changed to Jokmeam by the time of the Chronicler because the city took on the name of the levitical family that had originally settled Kibzaim.

Tell el-Mazar is located near the lower end of the widening plain of the Wadi el-Farʿah, which merges with the plain of the W side of the Jordan Valley. Because the Wadi el-Farʿah flows continuously it irrigates the land along its sides as well as the rich fields of the merged plains of the Wadi el-Farʿah and the Jordan Valley. Tell Mazar controlled the highway leading to the hill country by way of Wadi el-Farʿah and the highway to Transjordan via Wadi Zerqa. It was also on a N–S route which ran on the W side of the Jordan Ghôr. The archaeological surveys that have been conducted at Tell el-Mazar indicate occupation during the Iron I, Iron II, Hellenistic, Roman, Byzantine, and Arab periods.

With regard to the problem of Kibzaim/Jokmeam, Kallai's suggestion that Jokmeam is to be identified with Tell esh-Sheikh Dhiâb is the most probable identification. This would then associate with Tell el-Mazar, a site that has a longer occupational history, with the border town of Ataroth in Josh 16:7, although Ataroth like Jokmeam is mentioned only once in the Bible. Simon's recommendation that Tell Qusin is biblical Kibzaim is unacceptable on geographical grounds, which strengthens, if not proves, the opinion that Kibzaim and Jokmeam are separate cities. As a result Kibzaim goes unidentified while Jokmeam and Tell esh-Sheikh Dhiâb are associated together as one of the eastern cities in Ephraim. See Peterson 1977: 249–74.

Bibliography

Albright, W. F. 1945. The List of Levitic Cities. Pp. 49–73 in *Louis Ginzberg Jubilee Volume on the Occasion of his Seventieth Birthday.* New York.
Glueck, N. 1951. Explorations in Eastern Palestine. *AASOR* 25–28. New Haven, CT.
Kallai, Z. 1967. *The Tribes of Israel.* Jerusalem.

Mazar, B. 1957. The Cities of the Priests and the Levites. *VTSup* 7: 193–205.

Peterson, J. L. 1977. *A Topographical Surface Survey of the Levitical "Cities" of Joshua 21 and I Chronicles 6.* Diss. Seabury-Western Theological Seminary.

JOHN L. PETERSON

KID. See ZOOLOGY.

KIDRON, BROOK OF (PLACE) [Heb *naḥal qidrôn*]. A valley just E of the old walled city of Jerusalem, separating it from the Mount of Olives. The valley descends from the N, just W of Mt. Scopus, past St. Stephen's Gate of the Old City where it is known in modern Arabic as Wadi Sitti Maryam (Valley of St. Mary, since the traditional tomb of Mary is in the wadi). It continues southward as Wadi en-Nar ("Valley of Fire," because of its dry, parched wadi bed during most of the year, excepting in times of heavy rain). The name *qidrôn* apparently means "dark," "not clear," or "turbid" because of stirred up sediment. It is first mentioned in the OT in 2 Sam 15:23. After joining with the Hinnom Valley, S of Jerusalem, Kidron then courses SE into the wilderness of Judea and empties into the Dead Sea about 10 miles S of the mouth of the Jordan. Because of debris accumulation, the Kidron Valley is 10–50 feet higher than in ancient times.

In the times of the OT kings, the Kidron Valley was probably identified with, at least in part, the King's Garden (2 Kgs 25:4; Neh 3:15); the kings apparently owned land in the area. Water which flowed down the W side of the Kidron Valley through the water channel, and water which may have been diverted from the Siloam tunnel of Hezekiah (2 Kgs 20:20) watered the S end of the Kidron Valley near its confluence with the Hinnom Valley to produce a lush garden (cf. the "palace garden," 2 Kgs 21:18).

That the Kidron was also known as the King's Valley (seemingly located close to Jerusalem, possibly E of it, cf. Gen 14:17–18, and in which Absalom set up his monumental pillar, 2 Sam 18:18) is problematic. The Bible does not make this identification explicit, and the association can only be inferred as associated with En-rogel which is at the lower end of the Kidron (see Mazar 1975: 156). It might be argued that the name "King's Valley" derived from its proximity just E of the palace of David in the City of David (2 Sam 5:9; cf. 1 Kgs 3:1) on the W slopes of the Kidron Valley and S of where the temple platform was later constructed. Of the location of the Valley of the Kings, Josephus only indicates (*Ant* 7.243) that in it Absalom set up a marble column two stadia (ca. 1,200 feet) from Jerusalem, but from which direction from the city and from which part of the city he does not say.

Since David "was buried in the City of David" (1 Kgs 2:10; i.e., in the neighborhood of the city where the royal family owned property) and the kings of Judah during the Divided Monarchy were often buried there as well, it is possible that these royal tombs can be identified with some in the Kidron Valley. The City of David in which a number of kings are said to have been buried (cf. 1 Kgs 2:10; 11:43; 14:31; 15:8; 15:24; 22:50; 2 Kgs 8:24; 9:28; 12:21; 15:7; etc.) was on the SE ridge between the Kidron and Tyropoeon Valleys, just N of the modern Pool of Siloam. In this locale, in the S part of the City of David, near the E wall and along the W slope of the Kidron, R. Weill in 1913–14 found a group of four tombs horizontally cut into the bedrock, two with vertical shafts, and one with a stone bench to hold a coffin. These may be the tombs of David mentioned in Neh 3:15 near "the stairs that go down from the City of David," and it may be the place where Hezekiah was buried "in the ascent of the tombs of the sons of David" (2 Chr 32:33), "that is, the crest of the ridge" (Mazar 1975: 183). Many scholars believe that these were the royal burial tombs (although this is uncertain), and that they are to be distinguished from the other tombs recently found on the E slope of the W hill, opposite the temple platform (see Mazar 1975: 183). See below for discussion of tombs on the E slope of the Kidron Valley.

The Kidron Valley was also famous for the Gihon (meaning, "a bursting forth," "gusher") Spring, also called in Arabic today, Ain Sitti Maryam, "Spring of Mary," located at the foot of the City of David on the W slope of the valley. In ancient times the Gihon was the primary water supply for Jerusalem. Hezekiah eventually directed the spring's flow by digging a tunnel (Hezekiah's Tunnel) to a pool at the S end of the City of David (2 Kgs 20:20), and blocked "the upper outlet of the Gihon Spring" (2 Chr 32:30), which suggests that part of the water could have been diverted to help irrigate the Kidron Valley gardens. See SILOAM, POOL OF.

On the E side of the Kidron Valley, opposite the City of David, is the modern village of Silwan, in the middle of which are the remains of ancient tombs, some of monumental character, which were the burial places for certain royal officials and perhaps for some of the kings of Judah. One such tomb, showing evidence of Egyptian influence, is called in Arabic, "The Tomb of the Daughter of Pharaoh" (Mare 1987: 116; but it is unknown who was actually buried in it). Other ancient tombs, from the MB and LB, have been found opposite the walled city of Jerusalem in the Dominus Flevit area (Mare 1987: 44–46), and still other ancient tombs (EB and Iron Age II) have been found on the W side of the valley below the temple platform (Mare 1987: 45). At the lower end of the Kidron Valley, at its confluence with the Hinnom Valley, is the spring En-rogel, perhaps also part of a royal irrigation source.

The Kidron Valley was considered the E boundary of Jerusalem, and when David crossed the Kidron to escape the rebellion of his son, Absalom (2 Sam 15:23), he passed beyond the jurisdiction of the city; beyond the valley, on the Mount of Olives, David was among friends (2 Sam 15:32). This E boundary jurisdiction is also emphasized in the warning Solomon gave to Shimei that he not leave Jerusalem and cross the Kidron, lest he die (1 Kgs 2:37).

In the Kidron Valley and on its E slopes, opposite Jerusalem and the City of David, foreign cult worship was practiced in defiance of the worship of the Lord. At a place called the Mount of Corruption (cf. 2 Kgs 23:13; see CORRUPTION, MOUNT OF), probably on the S slope of the Mount of Olives near modern Silwan, Solomon desecrated the name of the Lord by erecting cult high places for Ashtoreth, Chemosh, and Molech (1 Kgs 11:7) which Josiah later destroyed (2 Kgs 23:13). In the same valley, King Asa buried the Asherah that his grandmother, the queen mother Maacah, had set up (1 Kgs 15:13). Here, too, Hezekiah took all the cult objects that represented unclean worship out of the temple of the Lord (2 Chr 29:16), and further "removed the altars that were in Jerusalem, and all the altars for burning incense they took away and threw into the Kidron Valley" (2 Chr 30:14). The high priest, Hilkiah, under orders from Josiah, took the Asherah from the temple and burned it in the Kidron Valley (2 Kgs 23:6) and destroyed the altars that the kings of Judah had built on the roof near the upper chamber of Ahaz, and also the altars Manassah had erected in the two courts of the temple (2 Kgs 23:12).

Hezekiah's purge of false worship from the temple was either incomplete, or heathen practices were reintroduced after Hezekiah's time, because Josiah later removed from the temple "all the articles made for Baal and Asherah and all the starry hosts" (i.e., heathen astral cults) and he "burned them outside Jerusalem in the fields of the Kidron" (2 Kgs 23:4). The desecration of these "fields," along with their use as a place of burial may have been viewed as a place of desolation similar to how the Hinnom Valley was viewed (Jer 7:32).

In the NT the Kidron Valley is only mentioned in John 18:1, which tells how Jesus crossed it and went into an olive grove at Gethsemane (Matt 26:36), at the foot of the Mount of Olives. In this same valley not far S of Gethsemane, Jesus must have passed the funerary monuments now popularly known as the tombs of Jehoshaphat, Absalom, James the Less, and Zachariah—tombs, however, which are misnamed and were actually built in the period from the second half of the 2d century B.C. to the first half of the 1st century A.D. (Mare 1987: 194–97).

The Kidron Valley has also been identified by Jews, Christians, and Muslims with the Valley of Jehoshaphat and associated with the final judgment. See JEHOSHAPHAT, VALLEY OF. Some have associated the Kidron Valley with Ezekiel's future river (Ezekiel 47) flowing E and S from Jerusalem to the Dead Sea.

Bibliography

Finegan, J. 1969. *The Archeology of the New Testament.* Princeton.

Mare, W. H. 1987. *The Archaeology of the Jerusalem Area.* Grand Rapids.

Mazar, B. 1975. *The Mountain of the Lord.* New York.

Simons, J. 1952. *Jerusalem in the Old Testament.* Leiden.

Smith, G. A. 1907, 1908. *Jerusalem, I and II.* London.

W. HAROLD MARE

KILAN (PERSON) [Gk *Kilan*]. Progenitor of a family which returned from Babylon with Zerubbabel (1 Esdr 5:15). Although 1 Esdras is often assumed to have been compiled from Ezra and Nehemiah, this family does not appear in their lists of returning exiles (see Ezra 2:16; Neh 7:21). Differences such as this raise questions about the literary relationships among the texts.

MICHAEL DAVID MCGEHEE

KILN [Heb *kibšān*]. The Hebrew word for kiln comes from the root *kābaš,* "to subdue," "bring into bondage," and is used three times in the OT: Gen 19:28, Exod 9:8, 10, and Exod 19:18. In Gen 19:28, the smoke from the burning cities of Sodom and Gomorrah rose like the smoke from a *kibšān*. Similarly, in Exod 19:18, the smoke from Mt. Sinai rose like the smoke from a *kibšān*. When a kiln is being fired, smoke rises rapidly from the exit flue due to the high velocity of the hot exhaust gases. These descriptions, therefore, most likely refer to smoke that was being forced into the air by means of hot gases. There is always abundant ash in the vicinity of a kiln as a result of the combustion of the various materials used as fuel. It was the ash from a *kibšān* which Moses sprinkled before Pharaoh in Exod 9:10 and which caused boils to break out on man and beast.

Two types of pottery kilns were used in ancient Palestine: the vertical or up-draft kiln and the horizontal or down-draft kiln. The vertical kiln was by far the most frequently used type. Both the vertical and horizontal kiln had all the elements of a modern kiln: a fire box where fuel is burned and heat generated, a chamber where the pottery is placed and which retains heat, and a flue or exit from which the spent gases escape. This arrangement creates a draft that pulls air into the fire box and moves hot gases through the stacked vessels and out the exit flue. Heat is transferred directly to the vessels by convection and indirectly by radiation after the surfaces of the walls of the kiln become red hot (Rhodes 1968: 13, 15).

The vertical kiln reached its definitive design form in the EB Age and has remained more or less unchanged to the present day. In this design, the vessels to be fired are placed in a chamber above a fire box, the two being separated by a partition floor supported by a wall or central pillar. See Fig. KIL.01. A fire is built in the entrance to the fire box. Hot gases then rise through flue holes in the partition floor, pass through the stack of vessels in the upper chamber and out the vent at the top, thus the designation "up-draft" kiln. Temperatures in the kiln are controlled by the intensity of the fire and the amount of draft. The draft can be regulated by adjusting the size of the air inlet opening, the size of the flue holes in the partition floor (before firing) and the size of the exit flue. For examples of well-preserved vertical kilns from the biblical period, see Pritchard 1978: 117–23 and Van Beek 1977: 172–73 (pictured in Rye 1981: fig. 1). For a description of a contemporary vertical kiln in the Middle East today, see Franken 1969: 94–95.

A major shortcoming of the vertical kiln is that it is difficult to maintain a constant temperature throughout the pottery chamber. As a result, there is often uneven firing of the wares. In the horizontal kiln, which represents a more sophisticated design than the simple up-draft kiln, this difficulty is overcome. Its design differs from the vertical kiln in that the elements are arranged along a horizontal rather than a vertical axis. See Fig. KIL.01. A fire box is located at the front and an exit flue at the back. In between, the vessels are stacked in a chamber for firing. A baffle or a row of pots is placed at the back of the fire box so as to direct the hot gases to the top of the pottery chamber. The gases are then drawn down through the stack of pots and out the exit flue, leading to the designation "down draft" kiln (Scott 1965: 382, 393; Rye 1981: 100).

Constant temperature is maintained in the pottery

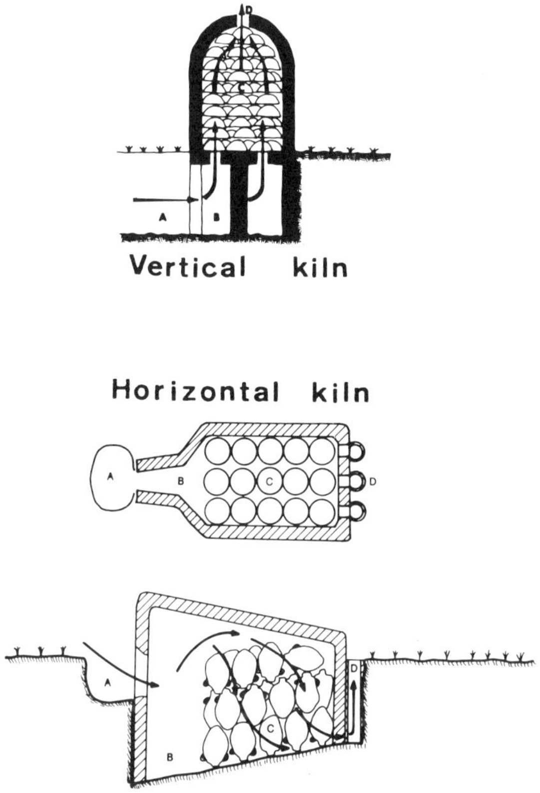

KIL.01. Schematic cross-sections of pottery kilns: *A*, stoking pit; *B*, fire box; *C*, pottery chamber; *D*, exit flue. *(Drawing by B. G. Wood)*

chamber of a horizontal kiln by diminishing the cross section in going from the front of the kiln to the back. This is accomplished by reducing the height or width of the pottery chamber, or both. Thus, as the gases cool as heat is transferred to the vessels, the velocity of the gases increases. This results in a more even amount of heat being transferred to all vessels in the chamber, regardless of location (Rhodes 1968: 20). As with the vertical kiln, the draft of the horizontal kiln can be controlled by adjusting the size of the air inlet opening and the exit flue. For examples of horizontal kilns from the biblical period, see Dothan 1971: 92. For contemporary examples of horizontal kilns, see Foster 1956: 396–97 and Hankey 1968: 30, 31.

Bibliography

Delcroix, G., and Huot, J.-L. 1972. Les Fours Dits "de Potier" dans l'Orient Ancient. *Syr* 49: 35–95.

Dothan, M. 1971. *Ashdod 2–3: The Second and Third Seasons of Excavations, 1963, 1965. Antiqot* 9–10 (English Series).

Foster, G. M. 1956. Pottery-Making in Bengal. *Southwestern Journal of Anthropology* 12: 395–405.

Franken, H. J. 1969. *Excavations at Tell Deir ᶜAllā 1: A Stratigraphical and Analytical Study of the Early Iron Age Pottery*. Leiden.

Hankey, V. 1968. Pottery Making at Beit Shebab, Lebanon. *PEQ* 100: 27–32.

Pritchard, J. B. 1978. *Recovering Sarepta, a Phoenician City*. Princeton.

Rhodes, D. 1968. *Kilns: Design, Construction and Operation*. Philadelphia.

Rye, O. S. 1981. *Pottery Technology: Principles and Reconstruction*. Manuals on Archaeology 4. Washington.

Scott, L. 1965. Pottery. Vol. 1, pp. 376–412 in *A History of Technology*, ed. C. Singer, E. J. Holmyard, and A. R. Hall. London.

Van Beek, G. W. 1977. Tel Gamma 1975–1976. *IEJ* 27: 171–76.

Bryant G. Wood

KINAH (PLACE) [Heb *qînâ*]. A town (Josh 15:22) mentioned in a list of cities (Josh 15:21–62) which presumably derives from the time of Josiah. The LXX, which reads *kina* in the Codex Alexandrinus and, by metathesis, *Ikam* in the Codex Vaticanus, perhaps also refers to this site in addition to the MT in the list of Simeonite cities (Josh 19:2–8), where *keimath* is mentioned (Kallai *HGB*, 352). Among other sites mentioned, Kinah was situated in the Negeb, on the Edomite border (Josh 15:21–32). Because of the possibility that a site may receive a new name while the old name persists in its immediate vicinity (Aharoni *LBHG* [1967 ed], 112) it is likely that the Wādi el-Q̣ēni points to biblical Kinah. An earlier suggestion located Kinah at Kh. Ṭaiyīb (M.R. 163081), about 5 km N–NE of the present city of Arad (Aharoni 1970: 21). In recent times Kinah has frequently been connected with Kh. Ghazze (Heb Ḥorvat ᶜUza, M.R. 165068), 6.5 km SW of Arad. See UZA, HORVAT.

In the time of Josiah, the *khirbe* was a strategically important site along Judah's SE border on the road to Edom (Keel and Küchler 1982: 233–34). This site, which consisted of a sizable fortress and an open settlement in the 7th to 6th centuries B.C. (Aharoni 1958: 33–35), dominates the Wādi el-Q̣ēni. The excavations conducted there since 1982 have yielded ostraca comparable with those found in Arad (Beit-Arieh and Cresson 1985: 96). Reconstruction of one of the Arad sherds mentions Kinah along with Arad as logistic centers of the area (Aharoni 1981: 46–49). The name "Kinah" may reflect colonization by Kenites of the E part of the Beer-sheba depression.

When the Seleucid army under Antiochus XII lost a battle with the Nabateans S of the Judean mountains (Josephus, *Ant* 13.387–91; *JW* 1.99–102), the remnant of the army retired to 'a village called Kana' (*Ant* 13.391; *JW* 1.102). The site of this retreat, which probably took place in 86/85 B.C., could have been the biblical Kinah (*GP* 2: 149).

Bibliography

Aharoni, Y. 1958. The Negeb of Judah. *IEJ* 8: 26–38.

———. 1970. Three Hebrew Ostraca from Arad. *BASOR* 197: 16–42.

———. 1981. *Arad Inscriptions*. Jerusalem.

Beit-Arieh, I., and Cresson, B. 1985. An Edomite Ostracon from Ḥorvat ᶜUza. *TA* 12: 96–101.
Keel, O., and Küchler, M. 1982. *Orte und landschaften der Bible,* vol. 2. Zürich.

RÜDIGER LIWAK

KING AND KINGSHIP. The term "king" is used as a title to refer to a male sovereign ruler who exercises authority over a defined territorial area, the state. The position of the king may be purely or partly hereditary or, as in some cases, elective. The king acts as a central symbol for the territory and population he rules over, as well as symbolizing its prosperity, fertility, and security. Kingship refers variously to the rank, authority, or office and dignity of the king, including the exercise of power over the subjects of the state. These two terms are applied to states which vary considerably in degree of social development, size of population or territorial extent. They are used of small agrarian polities of the past which have centered on a sovereign ruler as well as of much larger monarchies, including modern industrialized societies.

The inauguration and development of kingship in Israel was one of the most significant episodes in its history, affecting the formation and transformation of traditions now preserved within the Hebrew Bible. King and kingship have had a profound influence on the history of the community, its religious and literary traditions. The monarchies of Israel and Judah lasted little more than four centuries, were small in comparison with the surrounding riverine cultures of Egypt and Mesopotamia, but left an indelible mark upon the religious traditions of mankind. The ideology which grew up around Israelite and Judean kingship proved to be of immense significance for the development of messianic beliefs which have shaped major world religious traditions. An understanding of king and kingship in Israel forms part of the broader investigation of social anthropologists and historians into the formation and development of early state societies. It is also an essential element in trying to understand and appreciate the religious movements and ideas which culminated in the formation of the canon of the Hebrew Bible.

A. The Definition and Nature of Kingship
B. The Introduction of Kingship into Israel
C. The Formation of the State
D. Royal Ideology
E. Yahweh as King
F. The Royal Ideal
G. The Nature of the King
H. The Nature of Israelite Kingship
I. Royal Religion and Ideology
J. The Temple-Palace Complex
K. Royal Propaganda

A. The Definition and Nature of Kingship

Monarchy is the most common form of government in agrarian societies throughout history. The development of the state with the king as the central symbolic figure represents a major stage in the evolution of political systems. The king was responsible for the maintenance of law and order within a defined territory through the use of a professional and permanent military force and a dedicated central bureaucracy. There is considerable evidence for Israel to suggest that the bureaucracy was modeled upon Egyptian patterns (Mettinger 1971; Heaton 1974). Such states were politically centralized societies based on social stratification and specialization and dependent upon the extraction of an agricultural surplus from the peasantry in order to provide for the subsistence needs of the royal elite and its religious and political specialists. The king had the power to command the payment of various forms of taxation, the rendering of services, and the obeying of law. The central bureaucracy provided a means whereby the king was able to control the various levels of government responsible for the military, economic, legal, and ritual activities of a network of urban centers and villages within the territorial boundaries of the state.

The king as the *owner* of the institutions of the state was able to control the agrarian economy. Probably the most important aspect of kingship therefore in an agrarian society was the ownership of agricultural land. The development of a monarchy meant in reality the transfer of sovereignty over agricultural land from the villages to the king. In practice, arable land was granted to various royal functionaries (cf. 1 Samuel 22) as hereditary estates, securing patrimonial land tenure in return for taxes and military service. Alternatively, prebendal land grants were made to various officials as payment for their duties in the central administration of the state. Although in theory such prebendal estates were in return for official duties, it was not uncommon for such lands to become hereditary. Elite landlords extracted from their peasant cultivators as much as 50 percent or more of all produce in the form of taxation and rent. They in turn paid taxes, rent and labor to the king. Such systems of land tenure and taxation maintained and reinforced the distribution of power and privilege of a stratified agrarian society such as the kingdoms of Israel and Judah.

The Hebrew Bible uses derivatives of the root *mlk* to denote this form of government. *Melek* is the designation for a "king," whereas other derivatives of the root *mlk* denote "kingship," "kingdom," "to be king/reign," etc. The notion of "dominion" or "rule" is also expressed by the root *mšl.* It is interesting, in light of the above discussion, to note that the basic meaning of the Arabic root *mlk* is "to own completely" and may indicate a similar basic meaning of the Hebrew *melek.* It is an intriguing feature of Semitic languages that Hebrew has *melek* for "king" and *śar* for "official," "prince," while Akkadian has *šarru* "king" and *māliku* "counsellor" (Mettinger 1976: 296). The noun *melek* is used frequently in the Hebrew Bible to refer to neighboring or foreign monarchies, including Canaanite city states, Philistia, Ammon, Edom, Moab, Hamath, Aram, Tyre, etc. The most frequent usage, however, is reserved for the ruler of the kingdoms of Judah and Israel.

In the biblical traditions which relate to the introduction of kingship into Israel, Saul is anointed by Samuel as *nāgîd* over Israel (1 Sam 9:16; 10:1). The meaning of the noun *nāgîd* has proven to be particularly elusive and engendered a long yet inconclusive debate. Alt (1966) concluded that it referred to one who was designated to be leader by Yahweh, wheras *melek* designated an office conferred by the people's acclaim. Richter's extensive treatment (1965) concluded that the term underwent a complex development: it was originally a pre-monarchic title for a military leader and denoted a position quite distinct from *melek.* Cross (*CMHE,* 220–21), following an earlier suggestion of Albright, appeals to the Aramaic Sefire inscriptions for his view that *nāgîd* means commander. He emphasizes continuity with the charismatic leadership of the judges, as opposed to the dynastic kingship of David and Solomon designated by the term *melek.* Ishida (1977: 50) rejects the view that it was originally a title for the charismatic war leader in the pre-monarchic period. Instead he concludes that it denotes the "king designate" of Yahweh. Similarly Mettinger (1976: 151–84), who offers a thorough review of previous literature, suggests that it was originally a secular term for the "crown prince" designated by the reigning king; its theological use as a divine designation came later. Recently, Flanagan (1981: 67) has advocated the view that *nāgîd* indicates the chiefly power of Saul and David prior to the emergence of the early state and a fully developed kingship.

B. The Introduction of Kingship into Israel

The complex processes which led to the introduction of kingship, that is, the formation of an Israelite state, have continued to generate scholarly debate and research. Discussions of how kingship was introduced into Israel can be divided into two broad categories. The most common approach has been and continues to be a literary investigation and analysis of the traditions within the Hebrew Bible which relate to the rise of the monarchy. In recent years reconstructions of the formation of an Israelite state have drawn more extensively and consciously on social scientific studies and methods, particularly anthropological studies of state formation. This has given rise to alternative approaches which do not necessarily rely upon detailed literary analysis of biblical texts. This type of work has focused upon the links between environment, economy, trade, demography, settlement patterns, and so on, as part of the processes which culminated in the rise of an Israelite state and the introduction of kingship into Israel (Gottwald 1986; Frick 1986; Chaney 1986; Coote and Whitelam 1986).

The classical work of Alt (1966) has been influential in shaping the debate on the nature of the formation of an Israelite state in Palestine. His investigations were based upon a detailed treatment of biblical and extrabiblical material combined with an analysis of topography. According to Alt, Israel had gradually infiltrated into the scarcely populated hinterland of the hill country over a protracted period of time, possibly centuries. The areas where Israel settled were dictated by the military superiority of the city-states of the lowlands which were much too strong for the Israelites to confront. The rise of an Israelite state was the direct result of the threat posed by Philistine domination (1966: 183, 188, 195–96). This is a view that has proven to be extremely influential in the history of scholarship since it is reiterated in the majority of standard textbooks on the history of Israel.

For Alt, Saul's charismatic leadership was the starting point of the inauguration of kingship into Israel, but this was a title conferred by public acclaim. Initially it was designed as a defensive response to the Philistine threat and did not involve any notion of hereditary kingship. Alt sees this as a major change brought about during the reigns of David and Solomon in an attempt to hold together through a personal union the kingdoms of Israel and Judah along with the city-state monarchies of Ziklag and Jerusalem. A further suggestion of Alt, which still remains to be properly investigated, was that the initial structure of the Israelite state found its closest parallels in the near contemporary east Jordanian states of Ammon, Moab, and Edom.

Detailed studies of biblical texts pertaining to the introduction of kingship into Israel have formed a major part of the research effort into this area. It has long been a basic assumption that 1 Samuel 7–15 contains a valuable though complex account of the introduction of the monarchy in Israel. It is also widely acknowledged that the utilization of this material is made difficult by its composite nature and theological interpretation of the introduction of kingship. The history of the analysis of these chapters has been dominated by attempts to identify various literary strata. The traditional identification of two sources, one early and pro-monarchical (1 Sam 9:1–19:16; 11:1–11, 15; 13–14) and the other late and anti-monarchical (1 Sam 7:3–17; 8; 10:17–27; 11:12–14), has dominated the discussion of this narrative complex. Despite various refinements of this source-critical analysis or subsequent attempts to find three sources, it has remained influential in the discussion. It has also been assumed that 1 Sam 11:1–15 preserves the most authentic account of how Saul became king, although recent literary studies have raised serious questions about the use of such material for historical reconstruction.

The combination of Alt's view that kingship was the result of external pressure and interpretations of biblical material as anti-monarchic has led to widespread acceptance of the notion that the monarchy was an institution alien to early Israel. These arguments take various forms but all depend to a large extent upon the interpretation of texts within the books of Judges and Samuel. From this point of view Israel is described as a theocracy ruled by the heavenly king who endowed various earthly "judges" with charismatic power to deliver the community from foreign oppressors. The refusal of Gideon to accept the offer of a dynastic form of kingship (Judg 8:22–23) is seen as central evidence for a rejection of a dynastic monarchy by early Israel. The abortive attempt at monarchy by Abimelech (Judges 9) and Jotham's parable (Judg 9:7–15) against the nature of earthly kingship are used as corroborative evidence of this opposition to kingship. The acceptance of the existence of anti-monarchic passages in 1 Samuel 8–12 is central to this idea that early Israel was opposed to the introduction of a monarchy. From this point of view the monarchy is seen as an institution "alien" to Israel's origins and its essential nature. However, as with the discussion of the "anti-monarchic" material in 1 Samuel 8–12, scholars disagree on the dating of the Judges material. Views differ as to whether it is late Deuteronomistic material or reflects contemporary concerns about the nature of kingship as opposed to some theocratic nature of early Israel. Furthermore, Buccellati (1967) demonstrated that the conception of Israelite kingship as alien denies the dynamics of internal social development.

Ishida (1977: 30) accepts the theological shaping of the narratives but argues that they accurately reflect the sectional/factional conflicts involved in the development of new political situations. They reflect the dynamic development of social and political conditions. This is in line with Mendelsohn's influential view (1958), based upon comparisons with Ugaritic evidence, that 1 Samuel 8 reflects contemporary opposition to the introduction of monarchy. Crüsemann (1978), drawing upon anthropological studies of segmentary societies from the work of Sigrist, also sees the opposition to the inauguration to kingship as contemporary with the monarchy rather than as a late Deuteronomic redaction. Popular unrest during the reign of David provided fertile ground for the growth of anti-monarchical literature. The anti-monarchic attitude, he believes, stems from the opposition of segmentary societies to centralization and was expressed more fully during the Solomonic era.

The growth of interest in the potential and utilization of social scientific research for biblical studies has led to new ways of viewing the nature and development of Israelite kingship. Recent changes in approaches to ways of reading biblical narratives, especially new literary and canonical studies, have combined with this renewed interest in the application of social scientific methods and research to open up the debate on how the Israelite state arose. An important area of recent study has focused on the transition from pre-state Israel to the formation of a state with an hereditary kingship and its centralized institutions.

C. The Formation of the State

The evolutionary anthropologist E. Service (1962; 1975) was responsible for identifying the stages of development of sociopolitical societies through increasingly more complex forms. He identified four stages of development: band, tribe, chiefdom, and state. He subsequently realized that bands and tribes were practically indistinguishable. In particular, the study of such segmentary societies, especially chiefdoms, has been utilized in order to shed light on the crucial period of the transition from tribal confederation to state. Flanagan (1981) has argued on the basis of a study of biblical genealogies in comparison with anthropological studies that the periods of Saul and David were chiefdoms. Similarly, Frick (1979; 1985; 1986) has tested information about chiefdoms against the biblical data and has produced an extensive treatment of early Israel as a chiefdom. Such studies have identified important areas of future research which ought to add to our understanding of the complex developments which led eventually to the early monarchy in Israel.

Anthropological studies on state formation have also been used to suggest new ways of understanding the introduction of kingship into Israel. A variety of studies of Israelite state formation (Frick 1985; 1986; Coote and Whitelam 1986; 1987; Hauer 1986) suggest that the rise of the Israelite monarchy was due to a complex interrelationship of different factors. They all call into question the standard view that the origin of the Israelite state was due to Philistine pressure alone. In effect they stress the importance of internal developments in combination with various external pressures.

Hauer (1986), Coote and Whitelam (1986; 1987) and Otto (1986) draw upon a modified version of Carneiro's theory (1970) that circumscription had an important role to play in state origins. They emphasize the environmental and social constraints which operated as a counterweight against the tendency to disintegrate and eventually led to centralization. The geographical and social location of early Israel in the central highlands and southern Palestine was circumscribed by semiarid steppe and desert regions along with the network of lowland city-states, the Philistines, the Midianites, and the Amalekites. Frick (1985: 136–88) and Coote and Whitelam (1986; 1987), following Marfoe (1980), have drawn attention to the importance of highland farming strategies, such as terracing and intensive orchard cultivation, which demanded long-term investment, as important factors in the process of centralization. These studies also identify the pressure of demographic growth on circumscribed resources as an important factor in agricultural intensification which contributed to the move toward centralization and eventually resulted in the introduction of kingship into Israel.

The emphasis upon the complex interrelationship between various internal and external factors extends the study of the rise of kingship beyond many traditional approaches to understanding the biblical text. Future research, dependent to a large extent upon archaeological work at present being conducted in the region, needs to shed light on the relationship between the inauguration of kingship in Israel and the rise of almost simultaneous state formations in Edom, Moab, and Ammon.

D. Royal Ideology

One of the distinguishing features of early agrarian states is the way in which a network of beliefs grew up around and in association with the king. The justification and legitimation of the king's rule was of paramount importance. The dissemination of a royal ideology containing important images, attitudes, and ideals associated with kingship was carried out by a centralized bureaucracy and specialists. Such ideals of kingship can be found in literary traditions, ceremonial, and iconography in many different societies. The scepter (Ps 45:6), the crown (2 Sam 1:10; 2 Kgs 11:12; Pss 89:39; 132:18), and the throne (2 Sam 14:9; 1 Kgs 2:12) were all important symbols of kingship expressing the justness and legitimacy of the king's reign. Royal or official state religion was a crucial element in the legitimization and reinforcement of the social structure with its distribution of power and privilege.

The Hebrew Bible provides the major source for understanding the central elements of Israelite royal ideology. Archaeological material offers important, though limited evidence, which adds to this understanding. Attempts to reconstruct royal ideology remain tentative due to the fragmentary stature of the source material and continuing disputes over the dates or use of texts. The justification of kingship with its centralized social structure was based upon a guarantee of order, security, prosperity, fertility, etc., in return for loyalty and subservience. The manner and means by which such royal ideology was disseminated to the population of the state or even to potential enemies outside the territorial boundaries is also an important aspect of the study of king and kingship in Israel.

A vast wealth of textual and iconographic material dealing with kingship has been preserved from many different ANE societies spanning a vast geographical and temporal expanse. This material reveals many important formal correspondences covering ideas of kingship in these different societies. British and Scandinavian scholars (Hooke 1933; 1935; 1958; Engnell 1943; Widengren 1955), the so-called "myth and ritual" and Uppsala schools, tried to identify a common cultic pattern of divine kingship throughout the ANE. Their work provides an important landmark in the debate on the divine or sacral nature of the king and the various rites and ceremonies of kingship. Their conclusions, however, have been challenged by subsequent scholarship (Frankfort 1948).

It is important to remember that the formal similarities in the ideal picture of kingship throughout the ANE do not necessarily mean that the practical application and understanding of the functions of the king would have been the same in all societies. Particular ideologies were part of whole social systems and must be understood as far as possible in systemic terms before cross-cultural comparisons can be meaningfully carried out (Chaney 1986). Our evidence for Judean and Israelite royal ideology is fragmentary and often difficult to interpret; it is not even clear what differences there were between the two kingdoms. It is of immense value to be able to compare this evidence with material from similar agrarian kingships in order to suggest questions and lines of research into the organization and dynamics of the whole social system under consideration. But it is essential to consider differences as well as mere formal similarities since various factors such as environmental constraints may have played an important part in shaping different ways in which monarchies functioned.

E. Yahweh as King

One of the most important features of kingship in many different societies is the concept of the deity as king and the relationship with the earthly occupant of the throne. Thus the study of Yahweh's kingship has important implications for understanding the concepts of king and kingship in Israelite thought. The origin and nature of the concept of Yahweh's kingship in Israel has been the source of considerable debate. It is a matter of some controversy whether or not the idea was an important feature of Israelite religion from an early date. References to Yahweh as king in the Pentateuch and Deuteronomistic History (Exod 15:18; Num 23:21; Judg 8:23; 1 Sam 8:7; 10:19; 12:12) are notoriously difficult to date. It is a common concept throughout the Near East that the god, or high god, was the king of the state or polity. This was an important element of royal ideologies since the king ruled as the earthly representative of his god. In general terms it can be said that the earthly king's rule, or at least the ideal aspects of kingship, was merely a reflection of the heavenly king's rule.

The theme of Yahweh's kingship is given its most explicit treatment in the Psalter and, to a lesser extent, in the prophetic literature of the Hebrew Bible. H. Gunkel's (and J. Begrich 1933) classic study of psalm types identified Psalms 47, 93, and 96–99 as Enthronement Psalms celebrating Yahweh's kingship. He has been followed by H.-J. Kraus (1951) and C. Westermann (1965) in seeing these psalms as late and eschatological. In contrast, S. Mowinckel's pioneering study (1922, 1962) remains influential. He extended this category of psalms to include Psalms 95 and 100 while Mowinckel also pointed out that a number of other psalms were closely associated with this group in subject matter (Psalms 8; 15; 24; 29; 33; 46; 48; 50; 66a; 75; 76; 81; 82; 84; 87; 114; 118; 132; 149; as well as Exod 15:1–18). Furthermore, he produced a strong case for seeing these psalms as part of the important monarchic autumn festival.

The Enthronement Psalms deal with Yahweh's accession to his royal throne and exercise of royal power over the divine council, creation, and Israel. Yahweh is declared as king (Pss 47:6–8; 93:1; 96:10; 97:1; 98:6; 99:1), by virtue of his victory over the forces of chaos as represented by the primeval waters (Ps 93:3–4). Yahweh is able to subdue all opposition and guarantee the security of Israel (Pss 47:3–4, 8–9; 97:3, 7, 9; 98:2; 99:1–2). The guarantee of order, *mišpāṭ,* peace, security and well-being, is fundamental to Yahweh's kingship. He is depicted as the divine Judge (Pss 96:10–13; 97:2, 8; 98:9; 99:4). The theme of Yahweh's kingship is developed in very similar terms in the large collection of psalms which Mowinckel associated with the Enthronement Psalms. Yahweh's claim to kingship stems from his victory over the waters of chaos or rebellious sea monsters (Pss 74:12–14; 89:10–11) as well as earthly opponents (Pss 48:3–4; 68:30). He is the king of the gods in the divine council and responsible for the guarantee of justice and peace among the underprivileged (Psalm 82; cf. Deuteronomy 32). The very base of his throne is established upon justice and righteousness (Ps 89:14). Yahweh as king is able to order and sustain his creation (Pss 24:1; 74:15–17; 89:11–12; 29; 68:9).

The recurrent phrase *yhwh mālak,* announcing Yahweh's kingship, is a feature of the Enthronement Psalms. The translation and meaning of this phrase has been the subject of considerable debate. Kraus, following Gunkel, believed that the verb was a prophetic perfect which pointed to an eschatological understanding of these psalms. Mowinckel believed that it referred to something new and important that had just taken place, and therefore he translated it as "Yahweh has become king" (see also Lipiński 1963). Others argue that it refers to an enduring and lasting condition and ought to be translated as "Yahweh is king." Gray (1979: 20–25) has a good discussion of the various suggestions. It may be better to think of psalms which celebrate Yahweh's enduring kingship since theologically there is not a time when Yahweh was not king (Ps 93:2). In the context of the canon as a whole, rather than a supposed historical context, all aspects of this phrase as past, present, and future combine in the assertion that Yahweh was, is, and continues to be king.

Mowinckel's reconstruction of a New Year Enthronement festival to celebrate Yahweh's kingship has become one of the landmarks of biblical scholarship. The so-called "myth and ritual school" drew upon his research in extending the discussion of the nature of this Israelite festival with a comparison of similar ideas and themes elsewhere in the ANE, particularly the Babylonian *akītu* festival. Mowinckel identified the celebration of Yahweh's enthronement at the New Year Festival with the Feast of Tabernacles (*Sukkoth*). The debate has continued as to the nature and main characteristics of this festival. A. Weiser (1962), for instance, interpreted the Enthronement Psalms in the context of a Covenant festival which celebrated the Exodus at the central sanctuary of the Israelite league. Kraus (1951) envisages the celebration of Yahweh's kingship at a royal Zion-festival which celebrated the divine election of Jerusalem and the Davidic dynasty. For him, as for Gunkel, the emphasis upon the kingship of Yahweh did not take place until after the end of the Davidic dynasty in 587 B.C.E. However, Mowinckel's arguments have carried the greatest support in locating the celebration of Yahweh's kingship at the great autumnal festival of the New Year in the Jerusalem temple. The principal aspects of this celebration were the kingship of Yahweh, the defeat of the waters of chaos, the creation of the world, and the defeat of Israel's enemies. The Enthronement Psalms present Yahweh as the Divine Warrior who subdues the waters of chaos and then rises to judge the earth and thereby guarantee justice and order.

The prophetic literature treats similar themes of Yahweh's kingship. Although this is not always explicit in various oracles such ideas clearly underlie much of the prophetic material. The themes of Yahweh's kingship, his victory over the primeval forces of chaos, the defeat of earthly enemies, and the salvation of Israel all feature in this literature (Isa 24:21–23; 41:21–24; 44:6–7; 52:7; Jer 10:6–10; Zech 14:9, 16–17; Zeph 3:14–19). The concept of the Day of Yahweh, which has been particularly controversial in biblical scholarship, treats ideas similar to the conception of Yahweh's kingship in the Enthronement Psalms. A notable feature of the use of these ideas in the prophetic literature is that the twin themes of salvation and judgment, including of course the judgment and punishment of Israel, are closely related. The complex nature of prophetic literature with the interweaving of oracles and later interpretations makes it notoriously difficult to try to date individual passages. However, clearly Yahweh's royal attributes as Divine Warrior and Judge remain important themes in Israel's religious traditions as preserved in the Hebrew Bible.

F. The Royal Ideal

The expectation that the king's ideal attributes correspond to the central elements of Yahweh's kingship reflects the importance of religious legitimation in the establishment and maintenance of royal power in early agrarian states. The royal psalms (Psalms 2; 45; 72; 101; 110), which were identified by Gunkel, provide the clearest evidence for the main themes of Israelite, or rather Davidic royal ideology. Once again Mowinckel extended this group of psalms (Psalms 28; 44; 60; 61; 63; 64; 66; 68; 80; 83; 118; and 1 Sam 2:1–10) and argued that they had their setting at the great autumnal festival. Eaton (1976) and Mettinger (1976) have recently reassessed this material and argued for the inclusion of a wider range of material, including 2 Sam 23:1–7, as evidence for the royal ideal. The greatest problems of interpretation stem from disagreements over how to understand the nature of the language applied to the king: whether it is to be taken literally or to be understood as court hyperbole. The history of this debate also covers attempts to reconstruct the use of this material at the autumn or other festivals.

Considerations of the king's precise role in cultic rites have again formed part of the extensive yet inconclusive debate on the reconstruction of the great autumnal festival as a celebration of Yahweh's kingship. Johnson (1967) and Eaton (1976) are recent representatives of the view that the king took part in a great sacral drama of humiliation and then glorification as part of the annual renewal of kingship. Their views represent a more moderate position than the earlier advocates of the myth and ritual school who saw this drama as being linked to the king's divine nature. Considerable doubt surrounds attempts to reconstruct the autumn festival and its central features (Mettinger 1976: 3–4, 308). However, it is generally recognized that most of the royal psalms and associated material, as hymns from the royal sanctuary, provide crucial evidence for the complex of beliefs associated with the king in Israel.

The king was the central symbol of the social system. His prime function was the establishment and maintenance of order throughout the kingdom. The king's functions as warrior (1 Sam 8:20), judge (1 Sam 8:5; 2 Sam 12:1–15; 14:1–24; 15:1–6; 1 Kgs 3; 21:1–20; 2 Chr 19:4–11), and priest (1 Sam 13:10; 14:33–35; 2 Sam 6:13, 17; 24:25; 1 Kgs 3:4, 15; 8:62; 9:25; 12:32; 13:1; etc.) are all interrelated elements of this fundamental task. They were all essential to the maintenance of a divinely ordained order which was conceived of in cosmic terms and covered all aspects of a society's and individual's existence. This notion of kingship is evidenced from vast literary deposits throughout the ANE from Mesopotamia, through Syria-Palestine to Egypt over many centuries. Royal Sumerian hymns, the well-known prologues and epilogues to the law codes of Lipit-Ishtar and Hammurabi, and various royal inscriptions and documents from Egypt offer a strikingly similar view of the nature of kingship. Lipit-Ishtar of Sumer was divinely commissioned by Anu and Enlil "to establish justice in the land, to banish complaints, to turn back enmity and rebellion by the force of arms, (and) to bring well-being to the Sumerians and Akkadians" (*ANET*, 159). The prologue to Hammurabi's law code later echoed almost exactly this understanding of the kingly task.

In Mesopotamia the term *mēšarum* designated divine, cosmic order as the responsibility of the king, while in Egypt the Pharaoh was responsible for preserving *maʿat*. The true exercise of his duty as warrior was to protect and defend the state against internal and external military threat; as judge, to guarantee order through the establishment of justice; and as priest, to guarantee cultic order, so that the well-being of the kingdom was maintained through the fulfillment of the wishes of the divine realm. Both *mēšarum* and *maʿat* are often translated by the term "justice." Both terms, however, have a much wider connotation than the normal meaning of the English word justice. They denote the importance of "justice," "order," and "truth" for the whole of society and entail the notions of well-being, fertility, and prosperity. They are the gifts of the gods to the king who is the earthly representative of the divine realm and charged with the task of ushering in *mēšarum/maʿat* on his accession to the throne.

The importance of this idea in Egyptian royal ideology is illustrated in the myth of creation. Re was celebrated as expelling the powers of chaos through his act of creation.

The establishment of *maʿat,* also personified as the daughter of Re, was fundamental to the very structure of creation. The Pharaoh as "Lord of *maʿat,*" an epithet given to Re, preserved and protected Re's creation. The constant threat to world order posed by the powers of chaos was realized at the time of the Pharoah's death. The accession of a new Pharaoh to the throne expelled chaos and reestablished *maʿat.*

In Mesopotamia, the Babylonian creation epic *enuma elish* functioned as a justification for monarchy. It illustrates similar ideas about the ideal nature of kingship. There Marduk, who proves himself fit to be king of the gods, expels chaos by defeating the sea monster Tiamat in a dramatic battle. The law codes and other royal inscriptions provide the clearest evidence for the king's duty to establish and maintain a divinely ordained order. The Ugaritic legends of Krt and Aqht along with more fragmentary royal inscriptions throughout the Levant point to the widespread acceptance of similar ideas about the ideal nature of the king.

The Israelite royal psalms witness to similar notions about the functions of kingship. Psalm 72 is generally, though not universally, accepted as part of the enthronement ceremony of the king thereby proclaiming the ideal aspirations and hopes for the new reign. This psalm embodies most of the main elements of the ideals of kingship. The request (Ps 72:1–2) that the king be granted the divine gift of justice, *mišpāṭ,* is tied to the fertility and prosperity of the nation as a whole. His basic duty is then to preserve and protect the order and harmony of the kingdom and thereby the whole of Yahweh's creation (Ps 72:3, 5–7, 15–17). He is promised universal dominion and the defeat of his enemies, i.e., the defeat and expulsion of chaos (Ps 72:8–11). All these themes are found expressed in the other royal psalms and associated material in the Hebrew Bible. The king is the fount of justice (Pss 45:4, 6; 101; 2 Sam 23:3), fertility and prosperity (Pss 45:2, 8–9; 111:3; 2 Sam 23:4), and order (Pss 45:3; 101; 110:1–2, 5–7; 89:21–23; 2 Sam 23:6–7).

G. The Nature of the King

These themes of justice and fertility, the maintenance of cosmic and natural order, and universal dominion are the same themes and attributes of Yahweh's kingship celebrated in the Enthronement Psalms. The nature of the precise relationship between Yahweh and the king has been the subject of an intense and extensive debate. A major difficulty here is whether the exulted language of the royal psalms is to be taken literally or treated as court style or hyperbole.

The claim is advanced in a number of royal psalms and other texts that the king was the "son" or "first-born" of Yahweh, while Yahweh was the "father" of the king (Pss 2:7; 89:27; 2 Sam 7:14; cf. Isa 9:6). This is clearly an important ideological claim which underlies the right of the occupant of the throne to rule on behalf of the deity of the state. The precise meaning of such claims is the subject of an unresolved dispute. Scholars such as Hooke (1933; 1935; 1958), Engnell (1943) and Widengren (1955) defended the position that the Israelite king was of divine descent. Their appeals to analogous beliefs throughout the ANE have been decisively challenged. It is conceded that the Egyptian Pharaoh was believed to have been the offspring of Re and worshipped as the incarnation of Horus, Osiris, and Seth. Frankfort (1948) has been the most influential in challenging similar interpretations of Mesopotamian material. The Hittite king it is argued was not deified until after his death. One of the epithets of Keret at Ugarit was the "offspring of El." But Gray (1969; 1979), and others, deny any notion of the divine nature of the Ugaritic king, the emphasis rather being upon his sacral status.

The evidence within the Hebrew Bible for Israelite beliefs about the nature of the king is particularly problematic. The well-known *crux interpretum* in Ps 45:6 has figured prominently in this debate. The problem is whether or not the king was addressed as and thought to be "god" (*ʾĕlohîm*). Those who deny he was a god-king offer various explanations as to the understanding of the MT. The most common of which are to take this term as an adjective referring to the king's "divine throne," to argue for textual corruption through haplography, or to assume that the verse contains an ellipsis. Similar problems arise with Isa 9:6 which G. von Rad (1966) saw as analogous to the Egyptian royal protocol containing the Pharaoh's throne names at the time of his coronation. Suggestions that the king was addressed as "mighty god" (*ʾēl gibbôr*) have been strongly contested. Alternative explanations understand the term in a metaphorical rather than literal sense as referring to the king's special nature which sets him apart from the human sphere (cf. Isa 10:21; Jer 32:18).

This is also a common understanding of the "father"-"son" relationship between Yahweh and the king. Thus the decree of Yahweh in Ps 2:7 that "You are my son, today I have begotten you" is interpreted as a formula of adoption on the day of the king's coronation. The king is understood to have a special relationship with Yahweh which sets him apart from other mortals. However, this divine sonship is an expression of the sacral importance and functions of the king rather than the expression of a belief in the divine nature of the king. The divine qualities of the king, his god-like abilities, are referred to frequently (2 Sam 14:17, 20; 1 Kgs 3:4–15; 16–28; 4:29–34; 10:1–9, 24; Isa 11:2–4). Mettinger (1976: 260–75) represents the more general understanding that the king's divine sonship was not understood in mythological terms as literally a divine descent, but rather an expression of a special relationship which began only at the time of the king's accession to the throne. Frick has recently (1986: 32) suggested on the basis of African comparisons that it was the kingship rather than the king which was thought to be divine. The fact that the prophetic material does not attack royal claims to divinity is often cited as crucial, even if silent, evidence that the king in Israel was not understood to be divine.

It is more common to talk of the sacral nature of the king. This finds expression particularly in the ritual of anointing which accompanies the coronation. There are only two brief descriptions of the royal enthronement ceremony in the Hebrew Bible (1 Kgs 1:32–40; 2 Kings 11). The proclamation of the king as "the anointed of Yahweh" (*māšîaḥ yhwh*; 2 Sam 24:6, 10; 26:9, 11, 16, 23; 2 Sam 1:14, 16) implies the inviolable and sacrosanct nature of the king's person (cf. 2 Sam 19:21–22; 1 Kgs

21:10, 13). The term is used most frequently in the Hebrew Bible to refer to the Davidic king in Judah, although it is used in other contexts of various individuals. However, there is no consensus as to the specific significance of the rite. Kutsch (1963) remains the most extensive treatment of the rite and its significance throughout the ANE where it ranges in use from the transfer of property to the delegation of authority. Mettinger (1976: 185–94) has a useful review of previous literature on the subject. He identifies a development in the Israelite rite of anointing the king from a secular authorization by the people to a divine designation through the priest. The title was clearly an important ideological claim to the king's legitimacy and right to rule. It is closely linked in this respect to the divine promise of a Davidic dynasty in perpetuity (2 Sam 7:8–16; Ps 89:19–37).

The kingly ideal of the royal psalms, the special character of the king through his unique relationship with Yahweh, and the title *māšîaḥ yhwh* provided the foundations for the development of messianic beliefs of later Judaism and Christianity. The ideal of a future ruler in prophetic oracles was coached in royal terms (Isa 9:6–7; 11:1–5; Jer 23:5–6; Mic 5:2–4; Zech 9:9–10). Later messianic expectations had their origins in the process of reinterpretation of this ideal and the promises to the Davidic dynasty following the traumatic defeat and loss of kingship at the hands of the Babylonians in 587 B.C.E.

H. The Nature of Israelite Kingship

There has been considerable debate about the precise nature of kingship in Israel: whether or not it was dynastic or charismatic, elective or absolute. Alt put forward the view that the monarchy of Saul was charismatic and that the N kingdom of Israel did not accept the dynastic principle until the time of Omri. This influential idea shaped a great deal of scholarly research into many different aspects of the nature of Israelite kingship. It has been decisively overturned by Buccellati (1967) and Ishida (1977) who provide extrabiblical and biblical evidence (1 Sam 20:31; 2 Sam 2:8–11; 1 Kgs 14:10–14; 15:28–29; 16:3–4, 7, 11–12) that a dynastic understanding of kingship was a basic feature of ancient Near Eastern, including early Israelite, kingship.

Israelite kingship is frequently seen as governed or restrained by covenantal obligations. Von Rad (1966) identified the problematic *ʿēdût* of the coronation ceremony (2 Kgs 11:12) with the Egyptian royal protocol containing throne names and the rights and duties of kingship. The term *ḥoq* (Ps 2:7) and *ʿēdût* are frequently understood as some form of document or inscription containing the rights of kingship or the terms of the Davidic covenant. This is often compared with the *mišpāṭ* of the kingdom (1 Sam 10:25; cf. 8:11) and the so-called law of the king (Deut 17:14–20) as evidence for a constitutional understanding of Israelite kingship. Halpern (1981) provides an extensive treatment of the various aspects of this problem. He concludes that Judean and Israelite monarchies were determined by legal constraints.

Many of these passages are extremely ambiguous and notoriously difficult to date. The repeated use of the root *špṭ* in 1 Samuel 8 and 10:25, with its dual meaning of "govern" and "judge," clearly represents the basic functions of kingship in early agrarian states. However, the negative tone of these passages and Deut 17:14–20, whether a Deuteronomistic assessment of kingship or not, illustrates the striking differentiation between the ideal presentation of the duties of kingship and the stark reality of a society subject to the widespread powers of a highly centralized agrarian monarchy. Whitelam (1979) offers an extensive survey of royal influence and effect upon the administration of justice (cf. Macholz 1972a, b). There is no consensus on the question of whether or not the king promulgated law or radically reorganized the judicial system. Given the problematic nature of the evidence it is inevitable that many questions concerning the exact nature of the principles governing Israelite and Judean kingship will remain unsolved.

I. Royal Religion and Ideology

One of the most striking features of all early agrarian states, from Egypt and Mesopotamia to the Indus Valley and Mesoamerica, was the use of religion to establish and preserve the exercise of royal power in a centrally organized society. The *enuma eliš* is one of the best known state foundation myths which legitimizes the royal status quo. Israelite kingship was no exception in using state religion to legitimize and maintain royal rule (see Ahlström 1982). The king, as noted above, was presented as the chosen of the deity with the right to rule on earth as the god's representative. He was responsible for the organization and administration of the cult including cultic reform (1 Kgs 15:12–15; 2 Kgs 18:1–7; 22:3–23:23).

The Hebrew Bible provides ample evidence of syncretistic elements of royal and popular religion during the monarchic period (Jer 44:17–18; 2:27; Ezek 20:30–31; Mic 5:13–14; 2 Kgs 21:7; etc.). The sustained condemnation of royal religious apostasy from the theological perspective of the Deuteronomistic Historian and the prophetic critique of the cult (Amos 5:21–27; Isa 1:10–17; Jeremiah 7; etc.) illustrate clearly this feature of the ritual system. Archaeological evidence from various Israelite shrines, the inscriptions from Kuntillet Ajrud, and, to some extent, the evidence from Elephantine have added significantly to the understanding of cultic practices during the monarchic period. The syncretistic royal cult is seen by many as further evidence that kingship was alien to early Israel. Mendenhall (1975) has strongly advocated this position with his assessment of the monarchy under David and Solomon as representing a rapid reversion to LB Age paganism. The reconstruction of a premonarchic Israelite cult is difficult and controversial thus making it difficult to draw comparisons with later monarchic developments. Further research is needed to ascertain how the royal cult with all its syncretistic features functioned within Israelite society as a whole.

J. The Temple-Palace Complex

One of the major responsibilities of ANE kingship was the provision of a temple for the god of the state. This act of temple building provided the symbolic expression of the god as the guarantor of the state and the dynasty (2 Sam 5:12). The temple above all else defined the political, economic, and religious center. It was, thereby, a symbolic statement of the king's relationship with the god and his divine right to rule. The temple, among other things represented heaven upon earth (Ps 1:4). As the dwelling place of the deity upon earth, situated next to the king's palace and part of the same complex, it symbolized the king's special relationship with the divine world and the political and religious center of the state. In Judah, this was expressed in the royal Davidic ideology of a double election of Jerusalem as the dwelling place of Yahweh and the promise to David of a dynasty in perpetuity (2 Sam 7:1–17; Ps 89:1–37). Similarly Jeroboam's renovation and promotion of Bethel in the north was a statement of his own sovereignty and special relationship with the deity of the state.

The temple-palace complex was the central, organizing, unifying institution in the ANE. It not only legitimated the political role of the king but was central to the economic structure of the state (1 Kings 5–9). The maintenance of the ritual system of the temple formed part of the king's control of the state economy. The state cult required a heavy investment of labor and resources. But it also drew vast resources to the royal court and cult as tribute, taxation, and sacrificial inputs. In return, the royal cult system was presented ideologically as a guarantee of fertility and prosperity for the general population.

A vast literature has been devoted to the Solomonic temple in Jerusalem (Businck 1970; Gutmann 1976). Much of the discussion has focused on the ancient Near Eastern prototypes and architectural patterns. In recent years, more interest has been shown in examining how the temple and its rites formed an essential element of the political ideology of the royal state (Meyers 1983; Lundquist 1982; Whitelam 1986). Foreign patterns and symbols were appropriated by and mediated through the royal bureaucracy in order to symbolize fundamental aspects of the king's relation to the deity. The symbolic aspects of the temple and palace were extremely complex and worked on many different levels. The fortified exterior of the Solomonic temple was visual and immediately conveyed the important notion of power and authority (Meyers 1983). By contrast, the complex iconography of the interior, portraying more sophisticated images of the king's importance, was seen only by the royal court, urban elite, and religious functionaries.

K. Royal Propaganda

Royal ideology was disseminated in a number of ways and directed at many different audiences. The reigns of David and Solomon were typical of early state formations in the development of monumental art and architecture. The investment of labor and vast resources in the building of royal fortifications, temple-palace complexes, and other public buildings was repaid by their importance in displaying the king's might, power, and wealth to all potential enemies. The visibility, simplicity, and size provided impressive displays of royal power. The use of ashlar masonry in the Solomonic gates at Megiddo and Gezer and its use in other royal buildings offered striking and immediate images of the king's power. The other most common architectural feature of royal buildings was the so-called Proto-Aeolic capital found at Jerusalem, Hazor, Megiddo, Samaria, and Ramat Rahel. These features were important symbols of royal power and the king's right to rule. The royal fortifications made explicit the protection offered by the state against external and internal military threat. Border fortifications were important symbols of the king's power which guaranteed protection while at the same time defined the limits of the state.

The use of literary material to propagate and disseminate royal ideology is less well understood and less secure. The so-called Succession Narrative (1 Samuel 9–1 Kings 2) was seen by Rost (1982) as Solomonic propaganda. It has recently been compared, along with other material in the books of Samuel, with the Hittite "apology of Hattusilis" which seeks to legitimize a usurper to the throne (McCarter 1980; 1981; Whitelam 1984). Recent development in new literary and canonical studies have challenged long held presuppositions about the social location of biblical texts or how they can be used for historical reconstruction. This forms part of a continuing debate which will shape much future research into the nature of kingship in early Israel.

Bibliography

Ahlström, G. W. 1982. *Royal Administration and National Religion in Ancient Palestine.* Leiden.

Alt, A. 1966. The Formation of the Israelite State in Palestine. Pp. 171–237 in *Essays in Old Testament History and Religion.* Oxford.

Buccellati, G. 1967. *Cities and Nations of Ancient Syria.* Rome.

Businck, T. A. 1970. *Der Tempel von Jerusalem.* Vol. 1, *Der Tempel Salomos.* Leiden.

Carneiro, R. L. 1970. A Theory of the Origins of the State. *Science* 169: 733–38.

Chaney, M. L. 1986. Systemic Study of the Israelite Monarchy. *Semeia* 37: 53–76.

Coote, R. B., and Whitelam, K. W. 1986. The Emergence of Israel: Social Transformation and State Formation following the Decline in Late Bronze Age Trade. *Semeia* 37: 107–47.

———. 1987. *The Emergence of Early Israel in Historical Perspective.* Sheffield.

Crüsemann, F. 1978. *Der Widerstand gegen des Königtum.* Neukirchen-Vluyn.

Eaton, J. H. 1976. *Kingship and the Psalms.* London.

Engnell, M. 1943. *Studies in Divine Kingship in the Ancient Near East.* Uppsala.

Flanagan, J. 1981. Chiefs in Israel. *JSOT* 20: 47–73.

Frankfort, H. 1948. *Kingship and the Gods.* Chicago.

Frick, F. 1979. Religion and Sociopolitical Structure in Early Israel: an Ethno-Archaeological Approach. *SBLSP,* 233–53.

———. 1985. *The Formation of the State in Ancient Israel.* Sheffield.

———. 1986. Social Science Methods and Theories of Significance for the Study of the Israelite Monarchy: A Critical Review Essay. *Semeia* 37: 9–52.

Gottwald, N. K. 1986. The Participation of Free Agrarians in the Introduction of Monarchy to Ancient Israel. *Semeia* 37: 77–106.

Gray, J. 1969. Sacral Kingship in Ugarit. *Ugaritica* 6: 289–302.

———. 1979. *The Biblical Doctrine of the Reign of God.* Edinburgh.

Gunkel, H., and Begrich, J. 1933. *Einleitung in die Psalmen.* Göttingen.

Gutmann, J. 1976. *The Temple of Solomon.* Missoula, MT.

Halpern, B. 1981. *The Constitution of the Monarchy in Israel.* Chico, CA.

Hauer, C. 1986. From Alt to Anthropology: The Rise of the Israelite State. *JSOT* 36: 3–15.

Heaton, E. W. 1974. *Solomon's New Men: The Emergence of Ancient Israel as a National State.* London.
Hooke, S. 1933. *Myth and Ritual.* London.
———. 1935. *The Labyrinth.* London.
———. 1958. *Myth, Ritual and Kingship.* London.
Ishida, T. 1977. *The Royal Dynasties in Ancient Israel.* Berlin.
Johnson, A. R. 1967. *Sacral Kingship in Ancient Israel.* Cardiff.
Kraus, H.-J. 1951. *Die Königsherrshaft Gottes im Alten Testament.* Tübingen.
Kutsch, E. 1963. *Salbung als Rechtsakt in Alten Testament und in Alten Orient.* Berlin.
Lipiński, E. 1963. Yāhweh mâlāk. *Biblica* 44: 455–60.
———. 1965. *La royauté de Yahwé dans le poésie et le culte de l'ancien Israël.* Brussels.
Lundquist, J. 1982. The Legitimizing Role of the Temple in the Origin of the State. *SBLSP.*
Macholz, G. C. 1972a. Die Stellung des Königs in der israelitischen Gerichtsverfassung. *ZAW* 84: 157–82.
———. 1972b. Zur Geschichte der Justizorganisation in Juda. *ZAW* 84: 314–40.
Marfoe, L. 1980. The Integrative Transformation: Patterns of Socio-Economic Organisation in Southern Syria. *BASOR* 234: 1–42.
McCarter, P. K. 1980. The Apology of David. *JBL* 90: 489–504.
———. 1981. "Plots True or False." The Succession Narrative as Court Apologetic. *Int* 35: 355–67.
Mendelsohn, I. 1958. Samuel's Denunciation of Kingship in the Light of Akkadien Documents from Ugarit. *BASOR* 143: 17–32.
Mendenhall, G. E. 1975. The Monarchy. *Int* 29: 155–70.
Mettinger, T. N. D. 1971. *Solomonic State Officials: A Study of the Civil Government Officials of the Israelite Monarchy.* Lund.
———. 1976. *King and Messiah. The Civil and Sacral Legitimation of the Israelite Kings.* Lund.
Meyers, C. 1983. Jachim and Boaz in Religious and Political Perspective. *CBQ* 45: 167–78.
Mowinckel, S. 1922. *Psalmenstudien II.* Oslo.
———. 1962. *The Psalms in Israel's Worship.* 2 vol. Trans. D. R. Ap-Thomas. Oxford.
Otto, E. 1986. Gibt es Zusammenhänge Zwischen Bevölkerungswachstum, Staatsbildung und Kulturentwicklung in eisenzeitlichen Israel? In *Regulation, Manipulation und Explosion der Bevölkerungsdichte,* ed. O. Kraus. Göttingen.
Rad, G. von. 1966. The Royal Ritual in Judah. In *The Problem of the Hexateuch and Other Essays.* Edinburgh.
Richter, W. 1965. Die *nāgīd*-Formel. *BZ* 9: 71–84.
Rost, L. 1982. *The Succession to the Throne of David.* Sheffield.
Service, E. R. 1962. *Primitive Social Organization.* New York.
———. 1975. *The Origins of the State and Civilization.* New York.
Weiser, A. 1962. *The Psalms.* Philadelphia.
Westermann, C. 1965. *The Praise of God in the Psalms.* London.
Whitelam, K. W. 1979. *The Just King: Monarchical Judical Authority in Ancient Israel.* Sheffield.
———. 1984. The Defence of David. *JSOT* 29: 61–87.
———. 1986. The Symbols of Power: Aspects of Royal Propaganda in the United Monarchy. *BA* 49: 166–73.
Widengren, G. 1955. *Sakrales Königtum im Alten Testament und im Judentum.* Stuttgart.

KEITH W. WHITELAM

KING JAMES VERSION. See VERSIONS, ENGLISH.

KING'S GARDEN (PLACE) [Heb *gan hammelek*]. A garden area in the Kidron Valley near the City of David, just below the terraced structures of the city, near the wall of the Pool of Siloam (Neh 3:15), near the gate between the two walls (Jer 39:4; 52:7). It, no doubt, extended just E and S of the City of David to take advantage of the intermittent flow of water coming down from the Kidron brook. It also took advantage of "the gently flowing waters of Shiloah" (Isa 8:6) coming from the water channel which had been cut along the W side of the valley. Other sources of water were the overflow from the Pool of Siloam (which was fed from the Gihon waters coming through Hezekiah's Tunnel; 2 Kgs 20:20; 2 Chr 32:30 [Mare 1987: 123]), and water issuing from the spring En-rogel (cf. Josephus *Ant* 9.10,4 §225) near the confluence of the Kidron and the Hinnom Valleys (cf. Mare 1987: 108, 176; Simons 1952: 109, 127, 193).

Bibliography

Mare, W. H. 1987. *Archaeology of the Jerusalem Area.* Grand Rapids.
Simons, J. 1952. *Jerusalem in the Old Testament.* Leiden.

W. HAROLD MARE

KING'S HIGHWAY (PLACE) [Heb *derek hammelek*]. The great roadway traversing the Transjordan from N to S along the desert border, connecting Damascus with the Gulf of Aqabah. The name is derived from the OT (Num 20:17; 21:22) and may not have been the actual name for the route, but rather a reference to an official road otherwise known as "the highway" (Num 20:16). The N section of the highway was known as "the way of Bashan" because the road went from Heshbon to Ashtaroth, the capital of Bashan (Num 21:33; Deut 3:1). The King's Highway facilitated the export of precious perfumes from S Arabia and competed for international commerce with the *Via Maris* (or "the way of the sea"), the other important international highway which crossed Palestine along the Mediterranean coast.

The earliest biblical reference to the King's Highway was the campaign described in Genesis 14. Under the leadership of Chedorlaomer, king of Elam, the four kings of the north campaigned from Ashtaroth and Karnaim in Bashan, to Ham in N Gilead, then to Shaveh-kiriathaim on the Moabite plateau, to the southernmost point of Elath on the Gulf of Aqabah and then back to Enmishpat (Kadesh-barnea). Ashtaroth, Karnaim, and Elath were located on the highway, and Ham was not far from it. Kiriathaim was more to the W (see Josh 13:19) and the location of Shaveh is unknown.

The King's Highway was also mentioned in connection with the wilderness wanderings, as the Israelites marched from Kadesh-barnea to the plains of Moab opposite Jericho (Num 21:10; 33:43–49). At Kadesh-barnea the Israelites asked permission to use the roadway (Num 20:19; 21:22), but were refused access by the kings of Edom (Num 20:14–21) and Moab (Judg 11:17; see also Num 21:21–35) and were forced to seek an alternate route (Num 21:4; Deut 2:8). Some scholars, relying on speculative identifications of several sites listed in the biblical itinerary, believe that the Israelites marched from Kadesh-barnea across the N end of Edom and then followed the

King's Highway northward. If correct, then the stations listed in Num 21:11–20 and 33:44–46 must also have been located along the King's Highway.

The alternate route, however, went "by the way of the Red Sea, to go around the land of Edom" (Num 21:4; cf. Judg 11:18). The Israelites moved from Kadesh-barnea S to Elath and then N to the southern end of Edom. From there they traveled on an alternate route located E of the King's Highway, called "the way of the wilderness of Edom" and "the way of the wilderness of Moab," along the fringes of the desert (Deut 2:8; not according to RSV). This eastern route paralleled the King's Highway and circumnavigated the four major wadis and their deep canyons: the Yarmuk, the Jabbok, the Arnon, and the Zered. "The way of the wilderness of Edom" and "the way of the wilderness of Moab" followed the most convenient topographical line, the same course that the modern railroad follows, avoiding the difficult fords on the King's Highway. The alternate road rejoined the King's Highway at Rabbath-ammon, a strategic site for controlling both routes. The disadvantage of this route was that it was farther out in the desert, where settlements and water supplies were sparse.

Because of the special military and economic advantages afforded by the King's Highway, the route became a strategic focalpoint in Israel's later political controversies. David secured absolute control over this important roadway (2 Chr 19:7; see also 1 Kgs 4:24) and Solomon capitalized on the new avenue of trade to the S (1 Kgs 9:26–10:22; 2 Chr 8:17–9:21). After the death of Solomon, both the Moabites (2 Kgs 1:1; 3:4–27; and the Mesha Stele) and the Edomites (2 Kgs 8:20–22; 2 Chr 21:8–10) regained temporary control over the highway. Their control was eclipsed by the Arameans who, under Ben-hadad I and Hazael, expanded their authority in the Transjordan to include the King's Highway (2 Kgs 10:32–33; see Mazar 1962: 103–8). After the decline of the Arameans, both Israel (2 Kgs 14:25, 28) and Judah (2 Kgs 14:7; cf. however, 2 Kgs 14:7–14 and 2 Chr 25:5–24; and see 2 Kgs 14:22; 2 Chr 26:2) regained control of the King's Highway.

The road maintained its significance throughout antiquity. When the Assyrians conquered Damascus and the Transjordan, the King's Highway also opened avenues to Arabia. The road was rebuilt by the Roman Emperor Trajan in 106 C.E. A modern road known as the Tariq es-Sultani follows the same route as the ancient road.

Bibliography

Mazar, B. 1962. The Aramean Empire and Its Relations with Israel. *BA* 25: 98–120.

SCOTT T. CARROLL

KING'S POOL (PLACE) [Heb *bĕrēkat hammelek*]. According to Neh 2:14, the King's Pool was in the vicinity of the Fountain Gate, which from its name is to be connected with a source of water, no doubt the spring En-rogel in the Kidron Valley. The Water Gate was farther N in the vicinity of the Gihon Spring (Neh 3:26; Simons 1952: 121). The Fountain Gate is mentioned again in Neh 3:15 in connection with the wall of the Pool of Siloam. Thus the Pool of Siloam and the King's Pool seem to be alternative names for the same reservoir located near the King's Garden, the overflow of which would supply additional water to that garden (Mare 1987: 123; Simons 1952: 193). The King's Pool appropriately continued to carry that designation into Nehemiah's time, no doubt because Hezekiah, the king, was its builder (2 Kgs 20:20).

Bibliography

Mare, W. H. 1987. *Archaeology of the Jerusalem Area.* Grand Rapids.
Simons, J. 1952. *Jerusalem in the Old Testament.* Leiden.

W. HAROLD MARE

KING'S VALLEY (PLACE). See SHAVEH, VALLEY OF; KIDRON, BROOK OF.

KINGDOM OF GOD, KINGDOM OF HEAVEN. The "Kingdom of God/Heaven" is a subject of major importance in the Bible for two primary reasons: its frequency in the first three canonical (synoptic) gospels of the NT, and the conviction that it stands at the very center of the message of the historical Jesus. Its meaning, which is derived from a world of oriental monarchs and monarchies that is very different from modern Western democracies, has been interpreted in various ways. Historically it has been associated with the future state of the resurrected, immortal blessed; the Church; monastic contemplation; mystical ecstasy; pious religious experience; the progressively redeemed society inspired by love; the future transformation of this world; apocalyptic hope for the next world; and an open-ended symbol possible of many interpretations.

This entry explores this concept in two articles. The first surveys the concept of the "Kingdom of God/Heaven" as it is presented in the Hebrew Bible, in early Judaism, and in the Greco-Roman world. The second surveys its use in the New Testament and in other early Christian writings.

OT, EARLY JUDAISM, AND HELLENISTIC USAGE

A. Linguistic Considerations
B. The Old Testament
C. Daniel and Palestinian Pseudepigrapha
 1. Daniel
 2. *Jubilees* 1:28
 3. *1 Enoch*
 4. *Psalms of Solomon*
 5. *Testament of Moses*
 6. *Testaments of the Twelve Patriarchs*
 7. Summary
D. The Dead Sea Scrolls
E. Josephus
F. Jewish Prayers
 1. The Kaddish Prayer
 2. Benediction Eleven of the Synagogue Prayers
G. Rabbinic Literature
 1. Mekilta de-Rabbi Ishmael on Exodus
 2. Sipre Leviticus 20:26
 3. Sipre Deuteronomy 113
 4. Talmuds
 5. Targums

H. Hellenistic Kingship
I. The Stoics and Cynics
J. Literature of the Jewish Diaspora
   1. Tobit, Additions to Esther, 2 Maccabees, *3 Maccabees*
   2. *Sibylline Oracles*
   3. *4 Maccabees*
   4. The Wisdom of Solomon
   5. Philo of Alexandria

A. Linguistic Considerations

"The Kingdom of God" literally translates Gk *hē basileia tou theou,* and is found in NT texts, especially Mark, Luke, and Acts. The variant preferred by Matthew, "the Kingdom of Heaven," or literally, "the Kingdom of the Heavens" (Gk *hē basileia tōn ouranōn*), corresponds to Heb *malkût šāmayîm* or Aram *malkûtāʾ dišmayāʾ*. The conventional argument is that the plural "heavens" in this variant does not refer simply to the transcendent realm, but is a "circumlocution," an expression which avoids uttering or writing the Divine Name (YHWH); if so, "the Kingdom of (the) Heaven(s)" is equivalent to "the Kingdom of God" (Dalman). There are other equivalent Jewish and NT expressions, for example, "the Kingdom" and "the Kingdom of the Father." It has usually been argued that the "Kingdom of God/Heaven" is not primarily spatial, territorial, political, or national; therefore, it should be translated as "kingly rule," "reign," or "sovereignty" rather than "kingdom" (Dalman). While this view still predominates, it has recently been challenged (Koch; Buchanon; see below). Even if one maintains this view, the political, economic, and social dimensions of ancient oriental kingship by way of analogy must not be forgotten.

B. The Old Testament

The expression "Kingdom of Heaven" (Heb *malkût šāmayîm*) is not found in the OT; this fact has led some scholars to deny its importance in that literature. However, the expression "Kingdom of YHWH" does occur (1 Chr 28:5; 2 Chr 13:8) and there are a few indirect references to YHWH's kingdom by means of a personal pronoun (1 Chr 17:14; Pss 103:19; 145:11, 12, 13) or the equivalent (Ps 22:28; Obad 21; 1 Chr 29:11; cf. Aram Dan 4:3, 34; 7:27 + 2:44). There are also many passages which refer to YHWH as "king" *(melek)* or as "reigning" (*yimlōk,* etc.). These passages indicate that God was imagined as the reigning king over Israel, all peoples, and, indeed, nature itself. Thus, other scholars have concluded that although the exact phrase is missing, the *idea* of the Kingdom of God is present, indeed even widespread, in the Hebrew Scriptures (Bright; Patrick; Schnackenburg; Perrin).

The idea of the Kingdom of God in the Hebrew Scriptures has usually been related to a widespread polytheistic nature myth among the peoples of ANE monarchies; that is, in creating the world, God acted as a primordial, sacral king who defeated the evil powers. God then sustained his creation by making the land fertile. Expressions of the Israelite adaptation of this nature myth are enshrined in certain "enthronement psalms" (Pss 47, 93, 96–99) which have as a frequent refrain, "YHWH has become king!" (e.g., Pss 93:1; 96:10; 97:1). These psalms were probably recited in Israel's adaptation of an annual New Year's festival when the actual reigning, earthly king was enthroned. If so, a certain correlation between heavenly and earthly kings is implied. However, for the Israelites there was only one God, YHWH, who had delivered his people from bondage in Egypt and had given them the promised land (Deut 6:20–24; 26:5b–10; Josh 24:2b–13). YHWH reigned as king not only over nature, but also over history when he redeemed and sustained his people (Exod 15; Isa 30:7; 41:9; Pss 87:4; 89:11; 136). The myth had clear national-political overtones.

The implied Kingdom of God was not equivalent to the kingdom of Israel. Though Israel adapted Near Eastern ideas of "divine kingship" for the earthly king, God and the king were not identical; the god/king of the world was also the god/king over the people of Israel, and therefore superior to any earthly "divine king." Correspondingly, there was also tension between these two kingdoms. Moreover, the prophets were often critical of the monarchy. In this context, there developed a hope for a better Kingdom of God in the future (Isa 33:22; 52:7–11). The prophet Isaiah wrote: "For YHWH is our judge, YHWH is our lawgiver, YHWH is our king; he will save us" (33:22).

C. Daniel and Palestinian Pseudepigrapha

Most of this literature is strongly dominated by apocalyptic eschatology, the major exception being the *Psalms of Solomon.* Interestingly, that document contains the only precise reference to "the Kingdom of God" (*Ps. Sol.* 17:3). As in the case of the Hebrew Scriptures, some scholars conclude from the single reference that the apocrypha and the pseudepigrapha are not very important for understanding the Kingdom of God; as in the case of the Hebrew Scriptures, however, others argue that the *idea* of the Kingdom of God is implied in general kingdom references and references to God as king, largely in apocalyptic contexts (Lattke; Collins). See APOCALYPSES AND APOCALYPTICISM.

1. Daniel. Canonical Daniel is considered here primarily because of its late date (ca. 165 B.C.E.) and the apocalyptic orientation of its last six chaps. Daniel contains three types of Kingdom references (Collins). (a) Daniel 1–6 portrays the schema of four world kingdoms succeeded by a final, eternal, *earthly* kingdom "set up" by God (Dan 2:44; cf. Daniel 7; cf. the Roman chronicler, Aemilius Sura, ca. 175 B.C.E.; *Syb. Or.* 4, 1st century B.C.E.), which is presumably the Jewish nation. (b) This human kingdom can be distinguished from the "everlasting kingdom" of God superior to all human kingdoms (Dan 4:25); it is mentioned in short hymns of the same section (4:3 = Aram 3:33; 4:34–35 = Aram 4:31–32; 6:26) and shows influence of the enthronement psalms (see above). (c) The four-kingdoms scheme is taken up again in the apocalyptic section (Daniel 7–12) where they are represented as beasts from the sea (the "combat myth"), but now they are succeeded by everlasting "dominion, glory, and kingdom" conferred by God, the Ancient of Days, on "one like a Son of Man" (7:13–14); subsequently this kingdom is received by "the Holy Ones of the Most High" who are to possess it forever, and to whom all other kingdoms are subject (7:18; cf. 7:27). In Daniel, the Son of Man seems to be identified with the "Holy Ones," but who are they? The Jewish people as a whole? A sect of pious, righteous Jews, that is, the *hasîdîm* or "Holy Ones" (1 Macc 1:62–63; 2:29–42; 2 Macc

14:6; cf. Dan 11:33–35; 12)? The angels in the likeness of human beings (Dan 8:13; *1 En.* 14:22–23), with the Son of Man as Michael, Israel's heavenly representative (cf. 1QM 17:7; Collins)? If the latter is correct, the earthly rule of the Jewish people would be paralleled by the heavenly rule of the angels. To make matters more complicated, all three Kingdom ideas seem to merge in Daniel 7.

2. *Jubilees* 1:28. The book of *Jubilees* (mid-2d century B.C. Palestinian Jewish document originally written in Hebrew; fragments from the QL) refers in 1:28 to God as a "king" who rules "upon Mount Zion forever and ever."

3. *1 Enoch*. There are various ideas about the final period of history in the composite work called *1 Enoch* (early 2d century to the late 1st century B.C.E.). (a) In the Book of Watchers (*1 En.* 1–36), the elect people of God, including those who are resurrected (*1 En.* 22), will live in a final paradisiacal state on earth where God, whose throne is on a mountain, is an "eternal King," "King of Kings," or "King of the Universe" (9:4; 25:7; 12:3; 25:3–5; 27:3). (b) In the Book of Dream Visions (*1 En.* 83–90) God is addressed in prayer as follows: "Lord King, great and powerful in your majesty, Lord of the whole creation of heaven, King of Kings and God of the whole world" (*1 En.* 84:2). (c) In the Animal Apocalypse (*1 En.* 85–90) the Lord judges and then sits on his earthly throne "in the pleasant land" (Israel), a transformation of the earth which seems to involve a resurrection (*1 En.* 90:20). (d) In the Apocalypse of Weeks (*1 En.* 93:1–10; 91:12–17) there is reference to both historical and eschatological temples, judgment, and the final consummation. (e) The Book of the Similitudes (*1 En.* 37–71; probably early 1st century C.E.) is the most apocalyptic and closely related to Daniel. In it, the Lord of Spirits, who is once called "King (Lord?) over all kings" (63:4; cf. Dan 4:29), sets the Son of Man on his throne of glory (68:1; 62:5; cf. 69:29). "That Son of Man," who is also "messiah," assumes traditional kingly functions (in heaven? cf. 48:10; 52:4) and judges and destroys all the earthly kings (cf. 46:4–5; 48:4–5; 62–63).

In short, in *1 Enoch* God is called king and the Son of Man is a king/"messiah." There are several paradisiacal states mentioned, and there is great stress on the final judgment of all the kings and kingdoms of the world by both figures.

4. *Psalms of Solomon*. The *Psalms of Solomon* (63 B.C.E.; Gk and Syr extant; original Heb) speaks of the now familiar themes of God as "king of the heavens, judging even kings and rulers" (*Pss. Sol.* 2:30) and God as "Lord, our king for evermore" (17:1). Most important, it contains the only explicit reference in the apocryphal and pseudepigraphal literature to the precise expression "the Kingdom of God": "And the Kingdom of God is forever over the nations in judgment" (17:3; cf. Exod 15:18 and sec. G.5 below). Thereafter, the messiah-king, the "Son of David," is prophesied to rule over a restored national-earthly kingdom (Duling 1973). The question is how this important "Kingdom of God" reference should be interpreted. Because of the Son of David's role, it has been usually taken in a national-political sense; yet, because nationalistic ideas fade in the rest of the passage (17:33–38) and there are some apocalyptic emphases in relation to resurrection of the dead (3:12; 13:11; 14:3; 15:13) and to the superiority of God's rule over earthly kingdoms (e.g., 17:7, 22–25), the Kingdom has also been interpreted apocalyptically (Perrin 1963).

5. *Testament of Moses*. The *Testament of Moses* (from the Maccabean period down to the period contemporary with Jesus) purports to be Moses' last words to his successor Joshua (cf. Deuteronomy 31–34). It comes close to the apocalypse genre and it is full of predictions about the future. The portrayal of the history of Israel as a revelation of sin and punishment (*T. Mos.* 2–7) culminates in eschatological crisis (perhaps the persecution of Antiochus IV Epiphanes beginning in 168 B.C.E.) and the martyrdom of a certain Taxo (8–9; cf. the *maśkîlîm*, "those who are wise," in Dan 11:35), whose death seems to bring on God's apocalyptic judgment. This is followed by an eschatological hymn (*T. Mos.* 10) which stresses the destruction of the evil one, cosmic apocalyptic events, and the exaltation of Israel to the heavens (10:9; cf. Daniel 12). The eschatological hymn contains the most important verses for the Kingdom:

> (1) Then *his/God's/Kingdom* will appear throughout his whole creation.
> Then the devil will have an end.
> Yea, sorrow will be led away with him.
> . . . .
> (3) For the Heavenly One will arise from his kingly throne.
> Yea, he will go forth from his holy habitation with indignation and wrath on behalf of his sons.
> (*T. Mos.* 10:1, 3, trans. J. Priest)

Again, when the Kingdom appears, there will be destruction; as with Daniel and the *Similitudes of Enoch*, it is brought about by God and his angels, not by a human agent.

6. *Testaments of the Twelve Patriarchs*. The composite Testaments (2d century B.C.E.? probably written in Greek; contain Jewish elements and Christian redaction) are especially known for their two messiahs conception. In the *Testament of Benjamin* 9:1 "the kingdom of the Lord" will be taken from "among you" because (with few exceptions) "you will be sexually promiscuous like the promiscuity of the Sodomites." In 10:7 the patriarchs will be raised up over their respective tribes and prostrate themselves before "the King of heaven" *(basileus tōn ouranōn)*, after which the general resurrection and judgment occur. The *Testament of Dan* 5:7–13 is an apocalyptic eschatological poem in which God wins his war against Beliar and grants paradisiacal peace to his saints in the New Jerusalem. The last verse, which shows some signs of Christian reworking, includes the passing reference:

> The Holy One of Israel will rule over *(basileuon)* them (in humility and poverty,
> and he who trusts in him shall reign in truth in the heavens.)
> (*T. Dan.* 5:13, trans. H. C. Kee)

7. Summary. Palestinian Jewish literature, with the exception of the *Psalms of Solomon*, is heavily dominated by apocalyptic eschatology; this literature contains casual references to God as king, to his heavenly and universal reign, to the superiority of his (or the Son of Man's) reign over human kingdoms, to the final judgment, and to the final paradisiacal state of his people, usually (though not always) on earth. The only explicit reference to the expression "the Kingdom of God," *Pss. Sol.* 17:3, occurs in a mildly nationalistic text, which nonetheless has some apocalyptic overtones; thus, some scholars have also interpreted the reference apocalyptically.

It should be noted that there is a social significance to the Kingdom references in this literature. The major theme is the ultimate vindication of the persecuted "elect" against the powerful and mighty kingdoms of the world. These "elect" represent the perceived negative social experience ("alienation," "anomie"), if not the actual persecution, of marginal groups/sects.

D. The Dead Sea Scrolls

The Dead Sea Scrolls (latter 2d century B.C.E. to 1st century C.E.; mainly Heb; also Aram, Gk) contain several terms for "kingdom," that is, *malkût* (ca. 15 times); *mĕlukāh* (twice); *mamlākāh* (once); *memšālāh* (31 times); *miśrāh* (3 times) (Viviano 1987a).

Although a number of these are references to the kingdoms of this world, there are eleven references to God as "king" *(melek)* (e.g., 1QH 10.8, a hymn) and there occurs the verb "to reign" (Heb *mālak*) in a citation of Exodus 15:18, "Yah/w/eh will reign *(yimlôk)* for ever and ever" (4QFlor. 1:3, a commentary; cf. 1QM 12:3?). One also finds the "dominion" *(mamšālāh)* of God over all things in contrast to the rule of the demon Beliel (1QS 1:18, 23–24; 2:19–21; cf. 1QS 9:24: *mimšol*; cf. Viviano 1987a).

The main and most important references to God as king and to his kingdom are in the *War Scroll* (Lattke; Viviano 1987a). There God is called "King of Honor" (1QM 12:8; cf. 19:1) and perhaps "King of Kings" (14:6 based on 4QMa). There is also mention of the eschatological kingdom of *Israel* in Jerusalem, a kingdom established by the priestly Prince of the Congregation. Thus, "kingdom" is also associated with peace, justice, and a purified cult in a renewed temple (Exod 19:6; 1QM 12:3, 16; 19:8; cf. 1QSb 3–5; 10:12; 17:8). Closest to the NT "Kingdom of God" language are the statements, "And to the God of Israel shall be the Kingdom, and by the saints of his people will he display might" (1QM 6:6) and, "You, O God, resplendent in the glory of *your Kingdom* . . . (1QM 12:7). Thus, God will intervene on behalf of his people—in the latter case through his angels—in the war against earthly kingdoms, and he will establish a kingdom of justice (12:10) and blessing (12:12). The key passage (1QM 12:7–15) probably closes with the earthly rule of God's people, Israel, over the nations (1QM 12:16–17, damaged; cf. 1QM 19:8, also damaged). This would imply a correlation between the kingdom of God and the earthly kingdom of a purified Israel, a distinctly political connotation.

The political dimension of the War Scroll recalls the defeat of "Manasseh" (= Alexander Jannaeus 103–76 B.C.E.?) in the final age (cf. 4QpNah 3:10–4:9) and, of course, the Davidic messianism of the scrolls: "For to him / the Messiah of Israel / and to his seed was granted the covenant of kingship over his people for everlasting generations" (4QPB 1:4; cf. 4QFlor. 10–13).

The social dimensions of the Kingdom are also clear, especially in the following example: "The Master shall bless the Prince of the Congregation . . . and shall renew for him the covenant of the community that he may establish the kingdom of his people forever, / that he may judge the poor with righteousness and / dispense justice with / equity to the oppressed / of the land . . ." (1QSb 5:20–21).

In summary, the Dead Sea Scrolls contain references to God as King and Israel as an eschatological Kingdom. There is, nonetheless, a nationalistic expectation in which God intervenes on behalf of his people, and a promise of a renewed covenant in which there will be justice and peace for the poor and oppressed. As with the apocalyptic literature, the correlation between the Kingdom and a purified, priest-directed Israel ruling over the nations reflects the perceived negative social experience of a marginal group, presumably the Essenes (see C, above).

E. Josephus

The ancient Jewish historian Josephus has many references to the words "king" and "kingdom," especially in relation to a political office or government over a territory (citations in Buchanon). Some modern scholars have argued that among the revolutionary "Zealots" the Kingdom of God must have been conceived in this-worldly terms, that is, as equivalent to the people of God politically liberated from Rome (e.g., Brandon; Hengel). While this reconstruction has merit in the light of Jewish ideas in general, there are two major problems: (1) the surviving writings of Josephus contain no explicit Kingdom of God sayings in relation to revolutionary movements; and (2) the scholarly convention of positing a single, ongoing revolutionary Zealot movement in 1st-century Palestine has been challenged.

F. Jewish Prayers

1. The Kaddish Prayer. This Aramaic synagogue prayer reads:

> Magnified and sanctified be his great name in the world
> that he has created according to his will.
> May he establish his Kingdom *(malkûtêḥ)* in your
> lifetime and in your days and in your lifetime of all
> the house of Israel, even speedily and at a near time.

The Kaddish represents an eschatological hope for the establishment (not "coming") of "his (= God's) Kingdom" in the near future. The major question is its date. The prayer is preserved in the more formal Aramaic of the later Rabbinic schools (Elbogen) and is not specifically mentioned as part of the synagogue liturgy before the 6th century C.E. (*EncJud* 10: 661). Yet, the prayer contains simple eschatological ideas, does not mention the destruction of the Temple, and is similar to other early Jewish prayers, as well as to the Lord's Prayer (Matt 6:10; Luke 11:21). Thus, the Kaddish remains a possible, but debated, parallel to the Kingdom of God teaching in the Lord's prayer (Matt 6:10 = Luke 11:2).

2. Benediction Eleven of the Synagogue Prayers. In the eschatological portions (petitions 10–14) of the synagogue prayers called the "Eighteen Benedictions" (*Shemoneh Esreh,* or *Amidah*), Benediction Eleven speaks of a future time when Israel will no longer be under foreign domination, when YHWH will be king: "Restore our judges as of old and our counsellors as in the beginning; put away from us sorrow and sighing; and be alone King *(ûmĕlôk)* over us, O Y-Y, in mercy and compassion, in grace and justice! Blessed art You, O Y-Y, a king *(melek)* who loves grace and righteousness." There is no explicit reference to the "Kingdom of God." More distinctive and therefore probably more noteworthy is the fourteenth benediction, which expresses hope for the Kingdom of the Messiah from the house of David (Lattke).

G. Rabbinic Literature

The Rabbis often referred to God as King and to His kingdom in nonpolitical terms. Their most frequent and characteristic expression is "to take the yoke of the Kingdom of Heaven upon oneself," which refers especially to difficulties incurred by those who confess the oneness of God in the *Shemaᶜ* (Deut 6:4–9) and accept the demands of Torah. While the Rabbinic literature in general is later than the NT, it is argued that a few of these references may date back to the late 1st century C.E. (Dalman; Lattke; Chilton 1978, 1979). In any case, some of the earliest references are found in the following documents.

1. Mekilta de-Rabbi Ishmael on Exodus. In material ascribed to Rabbi Eliezar ben Hyrcanos, student of Rabbi Yohanan ben Zakkai (a 1st century Palestinian teacher), this commentary on Exod 17:14 states, "R. Eleazar says: When will the name of these people (= Israel's enemies, the Amalekites) be blotted out? At the time when idolatry will be eradicated together with its worshippers, and God will be recognized throughout the world as the One, *and His kingdom will be established for all eternity*" (Lauterbach). This comment is followed by quotations of Zech 14:3, 9 (cf. *Tg. Zech.* 14:9). Here, the Kingdom seems to be universal.

2. Sipre Leviticus 20:26. Rabbi Eleazar ben Azariah (ca. 100 C.E.) is said to have spoken of "the yoke of the Kingdom" as attempting not to transgress the purity laws.

3. Sipre Deuteronomy 113. This commentary on Deuteronomy states that the manifestation of God's rule began with Abraham: "Before our father Abraham came into the world, God was, as it were, only the King of heaven: but when Abraham came, he made Him King over heaven and earth."

4. Talmuds. Rabbi Yohanan ben Zakkai (ca. 80 C.E.) is said to have contrasted "the yoke of the Kingdom of Heaven" with "the yoke of flesh and blood," that is, human governments (*y. Qidd.* 59b). Rabbi Gamaliel II from the early 2d century C.E. is said to have spoken about the "yoke" of the Kingdom in terms of monotheism as confessed by reciting the *Shemaᶜ* (Deut 6:4–9) and the commandments (cf. Str-B 1: 177); An example is found in *b. Ber.* 2.2, from about 150 C.E.:

> R. Joshua b. Korḥa said: Why does the section *Hear, O Israel* (Deut 6:4–9) precede / the section / *And it shall come to pass if ye shall harken / diligently to my commandments/?*—so that a man may first take upon himself the yoke of the Kingdom of Heaven *(ᶜôl malkût šāmayîm)* and afterward take upon him the yoke of the commandments *(ᶜôl miṣôt).*

5. Targums. Over a period of several centuries beginning already in pre-70 C.E. Temple days, Aramaic paraphrases of the Hebrew text were made for Aramaic-speaking Jews of the synagogues who no longer understood classical Hebrew. Eventually, under the direction of the Rabbis, these were set down in writing. In contrast to the rarity of *explicit* "Kingdom of God/Heaven" references in the Jewish literature discussed so far, the Latter Prophets Targum (the Targum Jonathan) has ten explicit references to "the Kingdom of YHWH" (esp. *malkûtāʾ daY-Y*) in 8 contexts (*Tg. Isa.* 24:23; 31:4; 40:9; 52:7; *Tg. Ezek.* 7:7, 10; *Tg. Obad.* 21; *Tg. Mic.* 4:7, 8; *Tg. Zech.* 14:9). The Palestinian *Targum Neofiti* I on the Pentateuch, which may be basically pre-Christian (McNamara), comments on the Exodus at the Red Sea (*Tg. Exod.* 15:18): "For His (= the Holy One's) is the crown of kingship; and He is the King of kings in this world, and His is the kingship in the world to come. And His it is and shall be for ever and ever" (cf. *Tg. Onkelos Exod.* 15:18; Mekilta Rabbi Nathan Exod 15:18; *Pss. Sol.* 17:3). The relative frequency of "Kingdom of God" language in the Targums, the fact that the expression is not associated with the Law (as in the remaining Rabbinic literature, see above), and the eschatological tone of the paraphrases are striking and have revived discussion about the possible relation of these paraphrases to sayings attributed to Jesus in the NT (Chilton; Koch; Buchanon).

The *Targum Jonathan* adds "Kingdom of Y-Y" or "Kingdom of your God" to the Hebrew text. In Heb Zech 14:9 the catchword "king" *(melek)* in "YHWH will be king over all the earth" (on "that day," the day of judgment) evokes the "Kingdom of God" interpretation: *"the Kingdom of God (malkûtāʾ daY-Y) will be revealed on earth to all humankind in the future";* that is, the fact that YHWH will reign in the future is interpreted to mean that an already present reign of God will be made manifest universally in the future. A reference to Zech 14:9 in relation to the Kingdom in Mekilta Exod 17:14 suggests that the Targumic interpretation may be from the 1st century.

In Obad 21 the term "kingdom" in the Hebrew text ("the kingdom *(hammelûkāʾ)* shall be the Lord's") is rendered *"the Kingdom of God (malkûtāʾ daY-Y) will be revealed upon all the dwellers of the earth,"* a similar wording as in *Tg. Zech.* 14:9, suggesting a common tradition. In both passages, the Kingdom is universal, as it is in Mekilta Exodus.

In the four Isaiah passages, three contain no *m-l-k* ("to reign") root in the original Hebrew. Yet, the Targum consistently renders the activity of YHWH as "Kingdom of God" *(malkûtāʾ daY-Y).* The phrase "YHWH of hosts will descend to fight upon Mount Zion" in Hebrew Isa 31:4 is again seen as a future revelation of the Kingdom, that is, "the kingdom of Y-Y of hosts *will be revealed to dwell* on Mount Zion." The link of the Kingdom with YHWH and the revelation on Mount Zion is found again in *Tg. Isa.* 24:23 where "YHWH of hosts will reign *(mālak)* on Mount Zion" becomes "the *Kingdom* of God *(malkûtāʾ daY-Y)* of hosts will *be revealed* on Mount Zion." Similarly, "behold your God" spoken by the herald of good tidings (to?) Zion/Jerusalem in Hebrew Isa 40:9 becomes *"the Kingdom of* your (pl.) God is *revealed*" (followed by God's self-revelation "in power"; cf. Mark 9:1) and "Your God reigns" in Hebrew Isa 52:7, spoken by the one who publishes salvation and says to Zion, is given almost the same exact paraphrase ("your" is sing.). In these Isaiah Targums, the place of revelation, Mount Zion, is clear and the imagery sounds more militaristic.

The final passages are in Ezekiel and Micah. In Ezek 7:7(10) your "doom (crown?) has come (to you)" in reference to the day of the Lord is rendered "the *kingdom* is *revealed upon* you." In Mic 4:7b, 8, the context is a prophecy about Israel's glorious future and the restoration of the Davidic throne. This is clearly a more nationalistic context and both Biblical and Targumic texts deserve to be quoted in full:

7b) and the Lord will reign *(mālak)* upon them in
Mount Zion
from this time forth and for evermore.
8) And you, O tower of the flock,
hill of the daughter of Zion,
to you it will come,
the former dominion *(memšālā')* will come,
the kingdom *(mamleket)* of the daughter of Jerusalem.

The Targum paraphrases:

> and *the kingdom of* Y-Y will *be revealed* upon them in Mount Zion
> from this time forth and for evermore.
> and you, *Messiah of Israel that is hidden from before the sins of the congregation of Zion,*
> to you *the kingdom* is about to come,
> even the former dominion will come *to* the kingdom of the *congregation* of Jerusalem.

In this more complex interpretation, there are three references to the kingdom: (1) the familiar Kingdom of God revealed on Mount Zion some time in the future; (2) the kingdom which will "come to" the "Messiah of Israel" who is currently hidden because of the sins of "the congregation of Zion"; and (3) the kingdom of the "congregation of Jerusalem" to which the "former dominion" "will come." It would appear that the kingdom that comes to the Messiah is equivalent to the "former dominion" which comes to the Kingdom of the congregation of Israel, and that both are related to the eschatological Kingdom of God to be revealed on Mount Zion, but hindered because of the sins of the congregation of Zion. In other words, the Kingdom of God, the Kingdom of the Messiah, and the dominion of Israel over the nations are related (Koch). The question here is whether this overtly nationalistic text is early enough to belong with the others (so Chilton).

H. Hellenistic Kingship

In the period of classical Greece, the major idea about *basileia* ("kingdom," "rule") was that the (philosopher-) king transcends common law; he is subject to a higher, Natural Law. By the Hellenistic Age, this view was modified in the light of ideologies about oriental Divine Kingship and Hellenistic absolute monarchies (Goodenough). Pythagorean philosophical fragments concluded that the king *is* the higher law, or Animate Law; he is one who represents and reveals divine Natural Law in his kingdom. He is therefore divine, and acts as a god in leading the military, dispensing justice, and carrying out his priestly functions as leader of the religious cult.

> Now the king bears the same relation to the city-state *(polis)* as God to the world; and the city-state *(polis)* is in the same relation to the world as the king is to God. For the city-state, made as it is by a harmonizing together of many different elements, is an imitation of the order and harmony of the world, while the king who has an absolute rulership, and is himself Animate Law, has been metamorphosed into a deity among men. (Diotogenes *On Kingship,* quoted by Stob. 4.7.61 [Goodenough, 68]).

Such a king is not subject to passion; he is subject to virtue. He is a "wise man," a "lawful imitator and servant of God" (Pseudo-Sthenidas in Stob. 4.7.63 [Goodenough, 73–74]). In a passage which seems to bring together traditional Greek ideas and oriental sun symbolism, the Pythagorean Ecphantus stated,

> . . . the earthly king can fall short in no particular of the virtue of the heavenly king; but just as the king is an alien and foreign thing which has come down from heaven to man, so anyone would suppose that his virtues were the work of God, and have become the king's through God (Stob. 4.7.66 [Goodenough, 77–78]).

Plutarch concluded that the king is not only the incarnation of the Law; he is the incarnation of the divine Logos (*Ad principem ineruditum* in *Mor.* 10 [LCL]). In short, "rule/kingdom" *(basileia)* became a projected metaphor for the virtuous rule of the superior being.

I. The Stoics and Cynics

Stoics and Cynics applied the popular Hellenistic philosophical ideas about the king to the wise man. For the Stoics, the sage was the only true king; the city-state *(polis)* was blessed and stable if it had a sage in it.

The Cynic sage could be portrayed as a king, his kingdom being a countercultural "kingdom" *(basileia;* Höistad). He was "sent" by God to correct the human predicament and offer true enlightenment. Correspondingly, the true king was typified by such countercultural virtues; the tyrant was typified by vices (Epic. *Disc.* 3.22.63, 76, 80). Since the sage lived "according to (true) nature" *(kata physin)* or was governed by the *logos* or *sophia,* and embodied a *basileia* of countercultural virtue, in some sense he was divine; there is no mention, however, of "Kingdom *of God.*"

J. Literature of the Jewish Diaspora

In the literature of the Jewish people outside of Palestine, the idea of the reign of God as king is quite prevalent, though the expression is rare (Wis 10:10; Philo *Spec Leg* 4.164; cf. Wis 6:4). Sometimes the idea has an apocalyptic sense. In more philosophical texts, it reflects Hellenistic kingship and wisdom philosophy and it takes on spiritual or ethical connotations.

1. Tobit, Additions to Esther, 2 Maccabees, *3 Maccabees.* Hellenistic Jewish prayers address God as King. A prayer in Tobit (originally Aram; before 200 B.C.E.; uncertain provenance, although probably from the Diaspora [Nickelsburg]) refers to God as "King of the ages" (13:6, 10), "King of heaven" (13:7, 11), and "the great King" (13:15). Similarly, in prayers in the Additions to Esther 13:9–17 (originally Heb?) God's name is added to Esther when Mordecai addresses him as "O Lord God and King, God of Abraham . . ." (13:15) and Esther calls him "our King" (14:3b) and "O King of the gods and Master of all dominion" (14:12). 2 Maccabees (Gk; perhaps 1st century B.C.E. Egypt) contains a priestly sacrificial prayer in 1:24–29 which begins, "O Lord, Lord God, Creator of all things, who art awe-inspiring and strong and just and merciful, who alone art King *(basileus)*. . . ." In general, God is the creator, lawgiver, and just judge and is called the "King of the Universe" (7:9: *tou kosmoubasileus*), as he is throughout Jewish liturgical prayer. In this case he will raise the martyrs who died for the Torah (probably under Antiochus IV Epiphanes); he is also called "King of Kings" (13:4) as one who has control over history. In *3 Maccabees* (composite Gk; probably early 1st century B.C.E. Egypt) the prayer of Simon the High Priest addresses God as "Lord, Lord, King of the heavens, ruler of all creation, holy among the holy ones, sovereign, conqueror of all . . ." (2:2), and the prayer of Eleazar begins, "King, great in power, Most High, all-conquering God, who governs the whole creation with mercy . . ." (6:2).

2. *Sibylline Oracles.* Most of the third oracle of the *Sibylline Oracles* (composite; from the 2d century B.C.E. to the 7th century C.E.; Diaspora) comes from 2d century B.C.E. Diaspora Egypt (Collins). Like Daniel, it has a list of world kingdoms (*Sib. Or.* 3:156–61), as well as historical kings of deliverance (e.g., 3:286 [Cyrus]; 3:192–93 [Ptolemy VI?]). Also, God "the Great (immortal) King" (3:55, 499, 560, 616, 716, 808) will raise up an eschatological kingdom that is apparently different from the reigns of the historical kings, but it is nonetheless an earthly kingdom with the Jerusalem temple as the goal of pilgrimage for all nations (3:767–95). A late addition close to the time of Christianity (after the Roman conquest of Egypt, 31 B.C.E.) expects that "the most great kingdom of the immortal King will become manifest over men" (3:47–48), be ruled by a "holy prince" (perhaps a Jewish messiah), and be the occasion for "the judgment of the Great King, immortal God" (3:56). Such ideas are somewhat like those found in the Targums.

The fourth oracle (ca. 80 C.E.) has the schema of four world kingdoms in a context of apocalyptic destruction, resurrection, and final judgment, but it does not have a final "Kingdom of God." A final addition to the fifth oracle inserted just before the Diaspora Revolt in 115 C.E. tells of judgment brought by "a certain king sent from God" (5:108), and later he is said to descend from heaven and to refashion Jerusalem (5:414–28). However, it is finally God who is the King (5:499), and the dominant emphasis is on his universal eschatological kingdom, an earthly kingdom with its center at Jerusalem.

3. *4 Maccabees.* In *4 Maccabees* (Greek; probably 1st century C.E.; possibly Antioch), if man lives his life by the Law, which is given to the intellect, he will "reign over a kingdom" characterized by the four cardinal virtues (2:23). Eleazar, who stoically follows the Law in opposition to tyrant and torture, is called "great king, ruler of the passions" (7:10).

4. The Wisdom of Solomon. In the Wisdom of Solomon (Gk; 1st century B.C.E. Egypt or Syria) a sage who identifies himself with Solomon combines apocalyptic (1:1–6:11) and wisdom (6:12–9:18) materials with God's acts of judgment in history (10–19). The document contrasts the tyrants without wisdom, who oppress their innocent righteous victims, with the eternal order of God's creation as characterized by hidden wisdom and the conviction that God will surely vindicate his people. The Lord will "overturn the thrones of rulers" (5:23) and eternally "reign over" the resurrected righteous who will judge the nations and "rule over" the peoples (3:8; 5:16). Addressing the fictional "kings of the earth" (6:1) as "servants of His (= the Lord's) Kingdom" who did not rule rightly (6:4), the sage shows that those monarchs who desire wisdom will receive it (6:9–11) and will participate in God's Kingdom after death:

6:17) The beginning of wisdom is the most sincere
desire for instruction
and concern for instruction is love of her,
18) and love of her is the keeping of her laws,
and giving heed to her laws is assurance of
immortality,
19) and immortality brings one near to God;
20) so the desire for wisdom leads to a kingdom
(basileia).

The advice follows: "honor wisdom that you may reign for ever" (Wis 6:21).

In the "book of wisdom," as the history of Israel's saints and sinners shows, Jacob is praised by being shown "the Kingdom of God":

10:9) Wisdom rescued from troubles those who served
her.
10) When a righteous man fled from his brother's
wrath,
she guided him on straight paths;
she showed him the Kingdom of God *(basileia tou
theou),*
and gave him knowledge of angels. . . .

In short, the Wisdom of Solomon, while influenced by apocalyptic ideas reminiscent of Daniel, does not expect a Kingdom of God on earth; rather, the Kingdom of God tends to be identified with wisdom and righteousness, and thus with immortality granted to those who have virtue. The influence of Hellenistic popular philosophy is apparent.

5. Philo of Alexandria. The Kingdom in writings of Philo of Alexandria, a contemporary of Jesus, also betrays the influence of Hellenistic popular philosophy. The term "kingdom" *(basileia)* can refer to the control exercised by the mind *(nous)* or wisdom *(sophia)* over the sage. This *basileia* is also equivalent to "wisdom" *(sophia)* or "virtue" *(aretē)*; a life lived in accord with it can be designated "kingdom of the sage" *(basileia tou sophou)*, which is superior to the *basileia* of empirical kings (*TDNT* 1; Mack; cf. *Migr Abr* 197; *Som* 2.244). Thus, "God grants the kingdom of the sage *(basileia tou sophou)*, and the man of excellence receives it," and as a result, "he [the sage] brings no harm to anyone, but the acquisition and enjoyment of good things to all his subjects, to whom he is the herald of peace and order" (*Abr* 261).

Philo also mentions the "Kingdom of God." Since the requirements of the Mosaic Torah are consistent with the patterns of the created order *(physis)*, the wise king will "write" a copy of the Torah on his soul; in so doing, he takes on the image of the "archetype, the Kingdom of God" (*Spec Leg* 4.164; cf. *Mut Nom* 135; *Som* 285).

Bibliography

(See the end of the next article).

DENNIS C. DULING

NEW TESTAMENT AND EARLY CHRISTIAN LITERATURE

A. Gospel of Mark
B. *Secret Gospel of Mark*
C. Gospel of Matthew
D. Luke-Acts
E. Johannine Literature
F. "Q" Source
G. *Gospel of Thomas*
H. The Historical Jesus and the Kingdom
 1. The Political Kingdom
 2. The Kingdom and Present Ethical Action
 3. The Future Apocalyptic Kingdom
 4. The Modified Apocalyptic Kingdom
 5. The Atemporal Kingdom
 6. The Kingdom, Wisdom, and Gnosticism
 7. Summary
I. The Writings of Paul
J. The Pauline School
 1. 2 Thessalonians
 2. Colossians
 3. Ephesians
 4. 2 Timothy
K. Other Canonical Christian Literature
 1. James
 2. Hebrews
 3. Revelation
 4. 2 Peter
L. Patristic Literature: A Summary

A. Gospel of Mark

The Gospel of Mark contains 20 references to the word "kingdom," 14 of which are to the "Kingdom of God" and 6 to the word "king" *(basileus)* as ironic references to Jesus. Mark 1:14–15 states: "Now after John was arrested, Jesus came into Galilee, preaching the gospel of God, and saying, 'The time is fulfilled, and the Kingdom of God is at hand *(ēngiken)*; repent, and believe in the gospel.' " Location and technical vocabulary suggest that this saying is "Markan" and programmatic. The perfect tense in Greek *(ēngiken)* is *past* with *present* implications; yet, the *future* is implied insofar as the Kingdom is not yet present with full apocalyptic "power" (cf. 9:1; 14:25; 15:43). The temporal ambiguity may also suggest that the Kingdom has symbolic meaning, as does "Galilee" (Kelber). This tension about time also corresponds to the Kingdom's presence as mysteriously hidden, incomprehensible to outsiders, such as religious authorities, but revealed to insiders (Mark 4:10–12 [Isa 6:9–10]; 4:26–29; 4:30–32; contrast *Gos. Thom.* 20; 21). However, the boundaries about insiders/outsiders become uncertain (4:31–8:21) when Jesus encounters resistance from his family (6:1–6a; cf. 3:20–35) and misunderstanding from his disciples (6:52; 8:17, 21).

The central section (8:22–10:56) contains a key apocalyptic saying, Mark 9:1: "Truly, I say to you, there are some standing here who will never taste death before they see the Kingdom of God come *(elēlythyian)* in power." This unusual "seeing" the Kingdom "come (perfect participle *elēlythyian)* in power" was composed by Mark with the advent of the Son of Man (8:38; 13:20) and the Messianic Banquet (14:25) in mind (Perrin 1967). What has been "at hand" and mysteriously present but hidden will be seen in the future in its apocalyptic fullness.

There are six other Kingdom sayings in this central section (9:47; 10:14, 15; 10:23, 24, 25). The apocalyptic goal of the "way" that goes through suffering service is the Kingdom (9:47; 10:15, 23, 24, 25). To "enter," one must not be led into (individual?) temptation (9:47) and one must be childlike (Mark 10:14, 15). While one saying about "entering" is clearly future (10:15), baptismal symbolism (10:14: "hinder," cf. Acts 8:36 and 10:47; 10:15: the simile "like a child"; "enter," cf. John 3:3, 5; cf. also Matt 18:3; *Gos. Thom.* 22), the quality of "possessing" the Kingdom (Mark 10:14; cf. Matt 5:3), and the likelihood that the Markan author changed the language to "receiving the Kingdom" (10:15; cf. "receiving *the child*" in Mark 9:37; Luke 18:17; Matt 18:5; cf. also 10:40) suggest the continuing present dimension. Within the same central section, Mark elaborates the story of the rich young man (Mark 10:17–22) with two Kingdom sayings (10:23, 24b) about the difficulty of "entering" the kingdom on the part of those who have riches. He then adds the well-known aphorism, "It is easier for a camel to go through the eye of a needle than for a rich man to enter the Kingdom of God" (Mark 10:25). In the final, Jerusalem section (11:1–16:8), the "good scribe" who is "not far" from the Kingdom by agreeing with Jesus' summation of the Law as love of God and neighbor (Mark 12:34) seems to mark an added ethical dimension to the Kingdom of God. In short, "entering" the Kingdom has present dimensions and requires an "ethic" which reverses accepted social norms: "But many that are first will be last, and the last first" (10:31).

The last saying of Jesus is in the concluding frame of a discipleship section (Donahue 1973) of the Last Supper scene, Mark 14:25: "Truly I say to you, I shall not drink again of the fruit of the vine until that day when I drink it new in the Kingdom of God." "That day" shows that Jesus' final Passover anticipates another, future meal "in the Kingdom of God." It is not clear whether the disciples will be present (contrast Matt 26:29).

The final Kingdom saying says that Joseph of Arimathea was also "looking for the Kingdom of God" (15:42). This is apparently an apocalyptic reference.

The most eschatological (9:1; 14:25), christological (1:15), and communal (4:11) Kingdom sayings have been composed by Mark himself. The coming of God's mysterious Kingdom is set within a larger apocalyptic drama extending from the prophets to the End (Perrin and Duling; Mack). It will reach its fullest expression in the future. However, it is already mysteriously present in the work and words of Jesus Christ, God's suffering Son, an authoritative and powerful miracle worker, preacher, and teacher from Galilee. He overcomes demonic opposition but is temporarily defeated by a human political opposition (Ambrozic; Kelber). This special quality of kingship is revered in the Greco-Roman world in general and Judaism in particular (Robbins). It is present to those who in contrast to the outsiders understand and follow Jesus, that is, those who love the one God and the neighbor as oneself, who are childlike, and who resist temptation. Does Mark intend to include the disciples (Weeden and Kelber vs. Kee and Tannehill 1977)? Does mysterious presence of the Kingdom persist into the writer's time, or is it past and future, and therefore absent for the period of the writer (Boring 1987)?

B. *Secret Gospel of Mark*

In a recently discovered letter of Clement of Alexandria, Clement describes a "more-spiritual gospel" of Mark written for the instruction of the initiated (M. Smith 1973a; 1973b), the "Secret Gospel of Mark." See MARK, SECRET GOSPEL OF. Some modern critics speculate that perhaps canonical Mark and *Secret Mark* came from a common tradition (M. Smith 1973a; 1973b), or that canonical Mark was a purged form of "Secret Mark" (M. Smith; Koester 1983; Crossan 1985; contrast Brown 1974). If so, *Secret Mark* was earlier, not later, than canonical Mark.

Clement quotes from a passage in *Secret Mark* not found in canonical Mark at 10:34; there is also reference back to this passage in his version of 10:46. The new passage is related to the Lazarus episode in John (John 11; cf. M. Smith 1973a; Brown 1974). It tells about the arrival of the Jesus group at Bethany, the request of a woman for Jesus' help in relation to her young brother who had died ("Son of David, have mercy on me," cf. Mark 10:47–48), the resuscitation of the youth who was rich and loved Jesus, Jesus' command that "after six days" (cf. Mark 9:2) the youth came to Jesus at night "wearing a linen cloth over his naked body," Jesus' teaching "the mystery of the kingdom of God" (cf. Mark 4:10–12), and Jesus' departure to the other side of the Jordan.

Teaching the mystery of the Kingdom of God in this context seems to imply some connection with a nocturnal initiation rite of baptism, as well as what was believed to have been Jesus' own baptismal practice (esp. the baptism sayings in Mark 10:38–39; cf. also the "young man" who fled from the garden naked, Mark 14:51–52; 1 Cor 2:7; Eph 1:9–13; 5:32; 6:19; *Gos. Thom.* 37, 62; Hipp. *Trad. ap.* 21). It may therefore shed light on various baptismal practices related to the kingdom (M. Smith 1973a; 1973b; Koester 1983; Crossan 1985; J. Smith; see A, above; and below).

C. Gospel of Matthew

Statistically, a commanding 54 references to "kingdom" and 38 to "Kingdom of Heaven/God" or its equivalents are scattered throughout Matthew. The vast majority of these are to "Kingdom of Heaven" (32 references; 4 "Kingdom of God" references). All are spoken by, or related to, Jesus but one (Matt 3:2: John the Baptist), and the majority are located in Matthew's five great discourses (30 references). God is given the widespread oriental designation "Great King" only in Matt 5:35 (cf. 22:2, 7, 11, 13). The gospel affirms that Jesus is descended from David, addressed as "Son of David" usually in healing contexts (Duling 1978), and is mockingly called "King of the Jews/Israel" in the trial scene (chap. 27) and "the King" by Jerusalem crowds (21:5). The future, judging Son of Man, who is correlated with "the least of these," is also called "the King" in his kingdom (25:34, 40).

Matthew has a special emphasis on preaching "the gospel of the Kingdom." Key summaries (4:23; 9:35; cf. 5–7; 8–9) emphasize that Jesus was a Galilean wanderer who went about teaching in "their" synagogues, preaching "the gospel of the Kingdom," and "healing every disease and infirmity among the people." Jesus is preeminently preacher and teacher of "the gospel of the Kingdom" (cf. 10:7; 28:20). However, when Matthew also says that this gospel ". . . will be preached throughout the whole world as a testimony to the nations" (24:14; cf. 26:13), the later gentile mission is in view. In such sayings, the Kingdom preaching *of* Jesus merges with the Kingdom preaching *about* Jesus himself.

Jesus' inaugural proclamation, "Repent, for the Kingdom of Heaven is at hand *(ēngiken)*" (4:17; cf. Mark 1:15) and the Baptist's anticipation of this proclamation (3:2; cf. Q) show that the future Kingdom is in some sense already present both spatially and temporally (Kingsbury), especially with reference to the God who "draws near" in his Son who, in turn, is now known on earth (1:23; 18:20; 28:20). There are a few other past/present sayings that imply christology. Matthew 11:12 states: "From the days of John the Baptist until now the Kingdom of Heaven has suffered violence *(biazetai),* and those of violence *(biastai)* snatch it away *(harpazousin).*" Matthew reinterprets this Q saying (= Luke 16:16) probably to refer to demonic forces and their human agents which "snatch away" (cf. 12:29 *harpasai* and 13:19 *harpazei*) the Kingdom in the interim between John and Jesus. In another slightly modified saying from Q, Jesus defends himself against a "witchcraft" accusation (Neyrey): "But if it is by the Spirit of God that I cast out demons, then the Kingdom of God has come upon *(ephthasen)* you." These sayings should be compared to those which stress the "present earthly" Son of Man (8:20; 9:6; 11:19; 12:8, 32; 13:37), the "suffering" Son of Man (17:22; 20:18–19; cf. 16:21), the risen "Lord" as object of worship (8:2, 6, 8, 25; 14:28, 30; 15:22; 17:15; 20:30?, 31, 33), the ironic references to Jesus as earthly king (2:2; 27:11, 29, 37, 42), and the correlation of the King/Son of man with those who are unfortunate (25:34, 40; cf. 5:3, 10). Certain parables also imply the growth of the Kingdom from small beginnings (e.g., 13:33, the leaven [Q]). Presumably Jesus and his teaching are also present to Matthew's church (Kingsbury and Meier). This conclusion has been taken one step further by claiming that "the gospel of the Kingdom" also refers to Matthew's *literary document,* a "capsule-summary" of his work (Kingsbury; Matt 13:19; cf. Mark 4:15).

Most frequent and more dominating in Matthew are the eschatological sayings (5:19 [twice], 20; 6:10; 7:10, 21; 8:11, 12; 13:38, 41, 43, 47; 16:28; 18:1, 3; 19:23, 24?;

21:31?; 23:13?; 25:1; 26:29). Jesus' prayer, "Thy Kingdom come" from Q (Matt 6:10 = Luke 11:2), falls into this category. A number of sayings extend the Markan metaphor of "entering" the Kingdom in the future (5:20; 7:21; 18:3; 19:23, 24; 23:13; cf. 7:14; 18:8, 9 ["life"]; 25:21, 23 ["the joy of your master"]; cf. also "shut" [23:13] and "narrow gate" [7:13]). Quite distinctive are those future sayings that refer to an alternative Kingdom, especially of the apocalyptic Son of Man (13:41; 16:28; cf. 20:21) who is the final judge. An example is, "The Son of man will send his angels, and they will gather out of *his Kingdom* all causes of sin and all evil-doers and throw them into the furnace of fire; there men will weep and gnash their teeth. Then the righteous will shine like the sun in *the Kingdom of their Father*" (13:41–43a). Here, the Kingdom of the Son of Man seems to be a provisional Kingdom which includes both righteous and unrighteous; it is presumably the Matthaean community. It is distinct from the Kingdom of the Father which will include only "the righteous." This view is supported by the parable of the Last Judgment (25:31) where the Son of Man, who is "King" (25:34, 40), will separate the sheep from the goats. Only "the righteous" will inherit "the Kingdom prepared . . . from the foundation of the world" and that is because of their good works (25:34–46). Other parables of the Kingdom reinforce the distinction between insiders and outsiders at the eschatological judgment (e.g., the weeds, 13:24–30; the net, 13:47–50; the ten maidens, 25:1–13).

There are also Kingdom sayings with ethical and communal implications. The joy of finding and/or risking all can be found in the parables (13:44, 45). The works, or "fruits" (e.g., 7:16, 20) of "the righteous" who will ultimately be permitted to "enter" are measured by the standard of "righteousness" typified by Jesus who fulfills all righteousness (3:15) or by John the Baptist who is believed by the tax collectors and harlots (21:31–32). The norm is the "higher righteousness" (5:17–20; 21:23, 32, 43). "Therefore I tell you, the Kingdom of God will be taken away from you and given to a nation producing the fruits of it" (21:43; 27:25). Those who are not worthy (22:1–14) or who cannot humble themselves like children (18:3–4) and, despite positive hints about the urban rich (esp. 5:3), "the rich" (19:23, 24) will have special difficulty entering the Kingdom. The Kingdom of God is also opposed by supernatural forces, namely, the Kingdom of Satan (12:26), the "Tempter" (4:3) or "Evil One" (6:13; 13:19). This opposition is highlighted by the continual battle between Jesus and Satan (12:25–37).

Despite the spurning of "offices" found in Judaism (23:8–12), the Kingdom sayings in Matthew can be related to an inevitable institutionalization in the Matthaean community. For example, there are authoritative roles, functions, and corresponding social structures that include discipline (esp. 16:19; cf. 18:15–20; Duling 1987).

In summary, the Kingdom of Heaven in Matthew is the message of Jesus (and John the Baptist), but also the message about Jesus. It is anticipated in the present which flows from the past, and it grows mysteriously; it is anticipated in the Matthaean community, which shows some hints of emerging institutionalism, but the Church is not yet the Kingdom. It is therefore temporal and primarily eschatological and christological. However, it is also spatial. It "draws near" with Jesus; it is some place the righteous will "enter." The prerequisites for "entering" are ethical: with Jesus (and John) as models, it is imperative to strive for the higher righteousness and "bear fruit," which implies concern for those who have been dealt a bad hand (Matt 25:40). Those who are outsiders, primarily Pharisaic opponents, are dominated by the Kingdom of Satan.

D. Luke-Acts

The term "kingdom" occurs 46 times in the gospel and 8 times in Acts. The most common expression is "the Kingdom of God" (Luke: 32 references; Acts: 6 references; 10 from Mark, 8 from Q, 17 with no parallels). In the gospel, all Kingdom sayings are spoken by Jesus except 3 (Luke 1:33; 4:5; 19:11); in Acts the sayings are generally continuations of Jesus' preaching by the apostles, especially Paul. "King" *(basileus)* occurs in the gospel 11 times, in Acts 20 times. Most are references to earthly kings. Jesus himself is called "king" only in (false) charges (Luke 23:2, 3; Acts 17:7), mocking contexts (Luke 23:37, 38), or the Jerusalem crowds' acclamation (Luke 19:38). Yet, Luke-Acts claims that Jesus is descended from King David and, through the resurrection/exaltation, the recipient of the royal promises to David and his sons (Luke 1:32; 3:31; Acts 2:30; 13:22–23, 33–40).

The first reference to the Kingdom in Luke-Acts is Luke 4:43: "I must preach the good news of the Kingdom of God to the *other cities* also; for I was sent for this purpose" (4:43). Despite the reference to "other cities," it is striking that earlier programmatic passages at Nazareth and Capernaum (4:31–37) do not explicitly refer to the Kingdom (contrast Mark 1:15 and Matt 4:17). Moreover, the reference is casual; it comes late in the narrative; and it lacks Mark's and Matthew's characteristic language (Kingdom "at hand," *ēngiken*). This shift in perspective demands explanation. One approach has been to relate the Lukan Kingdom to the Lukan "history of salvation" (Conzelmann modified; cf. Perrin-Duling). A key Lukan reformulation of a Q saying (see F below) at Luke 16:16 reads: "The law and the prophets were *until* John; *since then* the good news of the Kingdom of God is preached, and every one enters it violently" (cf. Acts 10:37–38; 13:25). The "law and the prophets" mark out the old era of Israel; the Baptist marks a transition (Luke 1–2) to the new era of the Kingdom proclamation ("since then"); and the Ascension marks another transition to the era of the Church (Luke 24:51, P^{75}). Creation occurs at the very beginning (Acts 14, 17) and the Parousia and Judgment will be in the *distant* future (e.g., Acts 1:6–7; 10:42). See PAROUSIA. Correspondingly, the Kingdom is associated with the period of Jesus and the continuing proclamation of simply "the Kingdom" by the apostles in the Church (Luke 9:2; Q [?] 9:60; cf. Acts 8:12; 20:25; 28:23, 31). Other generalized sayings in which Jesus "proclaims," "brings," and/or "speaks about" the Kingdom confirm this perspective (Luke 8:1; 9:11; Acts 1:3).

There are, to be sure, traditional sayings from the tradition that speak of, or imply, that the Kingdom of God is future (Luke 13:28–29 [Q]; 18:24–25 = Mark 10:23; cf. the future Kingdom of Jesus in Luke 22:29, 30; 23:42), and some speak of its "nearness." However, the two types are not usually correlated. For example, "The Kingdom of

God has come near *(ēngiken)* to you" (Luke 10:9) is what the disciples are supposed to say *after they heal the sick* (similarly, 10:11). An apparent exception to this tendency is the Son of Man's coming in a cloud with power and great glory (Luke 21:27 = Mark 13:24) in connection with the Kingdom: "when you see these things taking place [the withered fig tree], you know that the Kingdom of God is near *(engus)*. Truly I say to you, this generation will not pass away till all has taken place" (Luke 21:31–33; cf. 21:35). Nonetheless, the actual time of the "return" of the Son of Man is not quite clear (21:7–26, 32–33), especially if "this generation" refers to Luke's generation.

Observations about the "coming" of the Kingdom produce a similar result. Two traditional sayings (11:2 [Q]: "Your Kingdom come"; 22:18 [Mark 14:25]: ". . . I shall not drink of the fruit of the vine until the Kingdom of God comes") do not stress its nearness. While Luke maintains a traditional apocalyptic Son of Man saying (9:26: "taste before death"; cf. Mark 8:38; Matt 16:27–28), he appears to avoid the apocalyptic Kingdom "come in power" (= Mark 9:1) and to add a "presentizing" expression (9:23: taking up one's cross daily; see however 21:27). Luke 17:20–21, makes a similar point: "Being asked by the Pharisees when the Kingdom of God was coming, he answered them, "The Kingdom of God is not coming with signs to be observed; (21) nor will they say, 'Lo, here it is!' or 'There!' for behold, the Kingdom of God is in the midst of you *(entos hymōn)*." The context deals with the day(s) of the Son of Man (17:22–24), but some delay is expected (17:25) and the Kingdom saying rejects (merely preliminary? [see H.3 below]) apocalyptic signs (the resurrection at Jerusalem? cf. 17:11; 19:11); the Kingdom is already present "among you." Luke 19:11 may be related: "As they [the crowd, cf. 19:3] heard these things, he proceeded to tell a parable, because he was near to Jerusalem, and because they supposed that the kingdom of God was to appear *(anaphainō)* immediately." The parable of the pounds that follows (19:11–27; cf. Matt 25:14–30) implies a delay of the Parousia: "Trade with these [pounds] until I come." In addition, the Q saying in Luke 11:20, "But if it is by the finger of God that I cast out demons, then the Kingdom of God has come upon *(ephthasen)* you," associates the presence of the Kingdom with miracle working (cf. Luke 9:2; 9:11; 10:9). For Luke the Kingdom is not tied to the delayed Parousia; indeed, "seeing the Kingdom" suggests some other perception—perhaps the Transfiguration (9:26, 32), or the "power" of the Holy Spirit (Luke 4:16–30, the Spirit only on Jesus, cf. healing in 10:9 and 11:20; Acts 1:8, the Spirit on the community).

Luke also builds upon his sources to stress that the Kingdom has ethical implications. "Seeking" his Kingdom as a priority reduces anxiety for material things which nonetheless will accrue (12:31, from Q); the Father "gives" the Kingdom to the "little flock" that sells possessions, shows charity to the poor, and the like (12:32, expanded from a Q context); the Kingdom of God "belongs" to the little children (18:16; Mark 10:14); whoever does not "receive" the Kingdom of God like a child shall not "enter" it (18:24; Mark 10:15); it is easier for a camel to go through the eye of a needle than for a rich man to "enter" the Kingdom of God (18:25); finally, the wandering follower who leaves home and family "for the sake of the Kingdom of God" (Mark 10:29: "for the sake of the gospel!") has a reward that illustrates present-future tension in Luke-Acts, for he will ". . . receive manifold more in this time, and in the age to come eternal life" (18:29).

Finally, Luke's Kingdom of God points to a view of Jesus, a group, and ethics. The initial Kingdom saying in 4:43 could subtly imply what has been said and done at Nazareth and Capernaum after all (see above), that is, the arrival of the Spirit-filled prophet-Messiah who preaches good news to the poor, release to the captives, recovering of sight to the blind, liberty of the oppressed, the acceptable year of the Lord, and healing for the gentiles (4:16–30, at Nazareth); and who works miracles (4:31–41, at Capernaum) (Völkel; Merk; Tannehill 1986). To be a witness to Jesus means to continue this sort of "Kingdom" proclamation (Luke 9:60; 10:9; Acts 1:8; 8:12; 19:8; 20:25; 28:23, 31); but it is also to bear witness to the Proclaimer who is the prophet-Messiah, the one who suffers, dies, rises, and ascends in fulfillment of the Scripture (Luke 24:26–27; Acts 17:3; 28:23, 31): the risen and exalted Lord Jesus Christ (Acts 8:12; 28:23, 31). At the same time, continuing the Kingdom proclamation and living it as Jesus lived it "daily"—one "enters" the Kingdom through tribulations (Acts 14:22)—brings with it a passionate concern for political, social, and economic realities of Christians of all walks of life, especially women, the poor, the sick, and imprisoned. Perhaps the Lukan author is a client who, of all the gospel writers, wishes to legitimate to his "most excellent" patron Theophilus (Luke 1:3; Acts 1:1) an urban social group that is moving beyond its sectarian beginnings toward some "ecclesiastical" organization in the mainstream of society (cf. Esler).

E. Johannine Literature

The explicit language of the Kingdom of God in the gospel of John is limited to two sayings (3:3, 5) and three virtually equivalent sayings about "my (= Jesus') Kingdom" in one verse (18:36). God is not called "King," but there are 15 direct references and one indirect reference to Jesus as "King"; most of these have a questioning or mocking (ironic) sense.

In John 3 Nicodemus claims that Jesus' signs show that Jesus has been sent from God (3:1–8). Jesus responds: "Truly, truly, I say to you, unless one is born *anōthen* ("again" or "from above") he cannot *see* the Kingdom of God" (3:3). Nicodemus understands *anōthen* in the sense of being born "again" literally from the womb (3:4). Jesus reinterprets: "Truly, truly, I say to you, unless one is born *of water and the Spirit,* he cannot *enter* the Kingdom of God" (3:5). Most interpreters agree that the evangelist had access to a Jesus tradition about "seeing"/"entering" the Kingdom of God (John 3:3; cf. Mark 9:1; 10:15; Matt 18:3; Luke 18:17) and that he interpreted it in terms of his view of Jesus as the "Man from heaven" (Meeks 1972). Either the evangelist interpreted "born *anōthen*" as a nonliteral "born again" in the sense of "born of the Spirit" (3:5), which he then related to his belief about the descending-ascending Son of Man (3:10–21), and a later ecclesiastical redactor added "water and" to make the connection with baptism (Bultmann); or the tradition already included "water and" in relation to baptism (see A and B above, and also below) and he reinterpreted born *anōthen* to mean either "born from above" in the sense of begotten by a heavenly Father "from above," just as Jesus/Son of Man (3:9–21, 31–36; Brown *John 1–12* AB), or as an eschatological cleansing and heavenly instruction; that is, as the agency of the Law has now been replaced by the agency of Jesus (Lindars).

Whether related to the tradition of baptism or not, the evangelist interprets "to see" or "to enter" the Kingdom of God as to be born *anōthen,* for the Son is born *anōthen* (3:31), as the Spirit is *anōthen* (John 14–16). The meaning is present-spatial, not future-temporal (cf. Barrett). Thus, Jesus responds to Pilate's political question about his status as "king": "*My* kingdom is not of this world" (18:36). Similarly, while Jesus is confessed and hailed as "king of Israel" (1:49; 12:13), he is already "king of the Jews" in some ironic sense (18; 19). For the believer, to "see" or "enter" the Kingdom of God is to have "eternal life" (3:15, 16)—*already.* This Johannine viewpoint may reflect a Johannine "otherworldly" sect (Meeks 1972), though there have also been attempts to connect this group with other early Christian groups (Brown 1974).

Why is the Kingdom teaching so sparse in the Fourth Gospel? The usual suggestion is that John has little or no futuristic eschatology. Another possibility is that the Kingdom is sometimes being used negatively by competing gnostic groups within the Johannine circle (Hodgson).

F. "Q" Source

Scholars who accept the Two Source Theory reconstruct a source behind Matthew and Luke called "Q" and designate chapter and verse in it with the Lukan chapter and verse. Apart from a general Kingdom reference (Q 4:5), Q contains 8 or 9 explicit references to the Kingdom of God, two variations (Q 12:31 P^{45}; 11:2), two sayings often defended as Q sayings (Luke 9:60; 9:62), and another saying which probably implies a reference to the Kingdom of God (Q 12:2).

The first clear Kingdom of God reference is the beatitude "blessed are you poor for yours is the Kingdom of God" (Q 6:20). Beatitudes are a form of wisdom instruction, and wisdom instruction normally reinforces accepted social norms and values. This beatitude, however, is an "anti-beatitude" (Betz) that subverts values about poverty and riches; it supports a "radical wisdom of the Kingdom" (Kloppenborg). Some scholars are reminded of the Cynics' countercultural idealization of poverty (Theissen; Mack; otherwise Horsley 1987; see H.6). The following three Q beatitudes (hunger, sorrow, and persecution) are also "anti-beatitudes." All four point to a community that experiences itself as poor, hungry, sorrowful, and persecuted.

The next Kingdom saying is Q 7:28, "I tell you, among those born of women none is greater than John; yet he who is least in the Kingdom of God (Matt 11:11b: Kingdom of Heaven) is greater than he" (Q 7:28; cf. *Gos. Thom.* 46b). The emphasis of the latter part of this saying is on the higher value of the one who is least in the Kingdom (probably not Jesus). The inclusion of John in the former part of the saying corresponds to the earlier form of Q 16:16 in Matthew 11:12: "From the days of John the Baptist until now the Kingdom of Heaven has suffered violence *(biazetai),* and men of violence *(biastai)* take it by force." In this form, John, like Jesus/Son of Man, is a Kingdom envoy against the violent opponents (see C), just as he joins Jesus against the outsiders ("this generation") in his preaching of repentance and judgment (Q 3:16–17).

Luke 9:60, "Leave the dead to bury their own dead; but as for you, go and proclaim the Kingdom of God" (if it is in Q) is part of an instruction on discipleship and mission modeled on the homeless Son of Man (Q 9:58; cf. Q 9:57–62; 10:2–16, 21–24). This saying subverts the social norm to bury one's parents (*m. Ber.* 3:1). Similarly, Luke 9:62 juxtaposed to Luke 9:61 (if they are in Q) states that the one who follows the homeless Jesus and who is fit for the Kingdom need not bid farewell to the family, as did Elisha (1 Kgs 19:19–21). Both sayings express the "radical wisdom of the Kingdom."

The command to the disciples to heal and to say, "The Kingdom of God has come near to you" (Q 10:9) is similar in form and content to Q 11:20, "But if it is by the finger of God that I cast out demons, then the Kingdom of God has come upon you." Here the Kingdom is manifest by Jesus' exorcisms (cf. also Q 7:22; cf. 4:1–13; 7:7–8; 17:6). In the first saying, miracle working is associated with the homeless, provisionless, wandering missionary (Q 10:2–12); in the second, the opponents label Jesus' exorcisms as the deeds of Beelzebul (Q 11:15–19). Jesus is defended by counter-labeling: "this generation" which rejects Jesus' Kingdom preaching and miracle working activity is in league with Beelzebul and deserves judgment (Q 11:29–32). The opposition between God's and Satan's Kingdoms has apocalyptic overtones.

"Your (sing.) Kingdom come" (Q 11:2) is an address to God as Father. It begins a section on prayer in which God as patron provides for the daily needs of community members, and its orientation is future (contrast Q 11:20; cf. 19:9). If it is correlated with "Give us each day our daily bread" (Q 11:3; cf. Q 12:22–31), it points to a way of life.

Q 13:28 and 13:29 are better represented by the single, unified saying in Matthew 8:11–12: "I tell you, many will come from east and west and sit at table with Abraham, Isaac, and Jacob in the Kingdom of Heaven, while the sons of the Kingdom will be thrown into the outer darkness; there men will weep and gnash their teeth." This prophetic pronouncement states that the "sons of the Kingdom," probably Israel, will be excluded from the Kingdom, but that the gentiles will be included; presumably the mission to the gentiles is in view (cf. Q 7:1–10; 10:13–15; 11:31–32). Preaching in the gentile mission (Q 12:2–7) stresses that which is hidden (Q 12:2), perhaps an implied reference to the Kingdom; it would then be related to the Kingdom parables, the Mustard Seed (Q 13:18) and the Leaven (Q 13:20), which stress that what is small and hidden will grow to large proportions.

It has been generally recognized that Q is dominated by two types of material, wisdom sayings and prophetic/apocalyptic sayings; these are probably two literary strata (Lührmann; Jacobson; Kloppenborg). The conventional argument is that the prophetic/apocalyptic sayings are earlier (e.g., Schultz), a view often correlated with the historical Jesus as an apocalyptic prophet (see H.3 and H.4). Recently, it has also been argued on the analogy of the *Gospel of Thomas* (see G) that most of the eschatology and especially the apocalyptic Son of Man is a later accretion to Q (Koester). Another analysis (Kloppenborg) says that six "wisdom speeches" portraying Jesus as a teacher (Q1) may have been later modified by apocalyptic words and prophetic announcements of judgment against "this generation" (attributed to the Baptist and Jesus/Son of Man), by openness to the gentiles, and by the Deuteronomic perspective that God punishes an impenitent Israel (Q2). Wisdom teaching has been transformed by conflict with the synagogue into apocalyptic/prophetic polemic. The temptation story (Q 4:1–13) pushes the genre toward historical "biography" (Q3; contrast *Gos. Thom.*). There are ten Kingdom sayings in the earlier "wisdom speeches" stratum (Q 6:20; 9:60; 9:62; 10:9; 11:2; [12:2]; 13:18; 13:20; 13:28; 13:29) and three in the "announcement of judgment" stratum (7:28; 11:20; 16:16). Other scholars, however, claim that some of the wisdom sayings were actually spoken by early Christian *prophets* (Boring 1982).

In any case, the Kingdom is related to a radical, nonnormative ethic of a group that affirms the virtues of voluntary poverty, nonviolence, love of enemies, and discipleship as a separation from family and home, ideas perhaps reminiscent of Cynic virtues. Other apocalyptic/prophetic sayings of Q appear to be correlated with the rejection of Jesus (and John) by "this generation" (= Israel), especially the rejection of Jesus' preaching and miracle working as manifestations of that Kingdom. Implied is a rejection of God, wisdom, the prophets sent to Israel, and indeed the Q preachers/healers themselves, for whom Jesus as Son of Man is a role model. While the ostensible recipients of such sayings are outsiders ("this generation"), the actual recipients are undoubtedly insiders, the members of the "Q community," which experiences itself as a totally committed, elect group which is rejected, persecuted, and in protest against normative society (and other groups).

G. *Gospel of Thomas*

Of the 114 sayings attributed to Jesus in the Coptic *Gospel of Thomas* (1st century C.E. Syria or Egypt?) about 20% (22 sayings) refer explicitly to the "Kingdom of Heaven/God." The form of expression often varies from synoptic usage, often in the same saying, and the *Gos. Thom.* also has Kingdom references where the Synoptic Gospel sayings have none and vice versa. The most frequent expression is simply "the Kingdom" (12 references), then "the kingdom of the (my) Father" (7 references), while the more familiar "Kingdom of Heaven" occurs only 3 times.

It is striking that the Kingdom in *Gos. Thom.* is not apocalyptic. In *Gos. Thom.* 3a, the "Kingdom *within* you (pl.)" clearly refers to knowledge *within,* or knowledge of the self (cf. Luke 17:21; *Gos. Mary* 8:14–21). However, in *Gos. Thom.* 3b the Kingdom is also "*outside of* you (pl.)." *Gos. Thom.* 113, which explicitly denies apocalyptic eschatology, also claims that the Kingdom is *without,* that is "spread out upon the earth" where it awaits discovery. Non-apocalyptic, mysterious presence is also found in other sayings (*Gos. Thom.* 18; 51). Most scholars have concluded that such references imply the gnostic "knowledge" *(gnōsis).* However, wisdom alone is also possible (Davies), especially when *Gos. Thom.* 3b seems to know a wisdom midrash based on Deut 30:10–15 in which wisdom and light are both *within* the wise man and *throughout all creation* (cf. Job 28:12–15; Bar 3:29–4:1; Sir 1:1–10, 14; also Rom 10:5–10).

The cluster of sayings around *Gos. Thom.* 3 (e.g., *Gos. Thom.* 2–6) shows that it is important to "seek and find" the mysteriously present Kingdom (cf. *Gos. Thom.* 27, 49, 76) and this activity can also refer to seeking and finding Jesus, who is wisdom, light, and the "Living One" (*Gos. Thom.* 24, 38, 43, 52, 59, 77, 80, 91, 92, 94, 108). When one does find it (him), (s)he becomes childlike, has "Life," and is faced with ethical demands (King). *Gos. Thom.* 49, unique to *Gos. Thom.,* adds, "Jesus said, 'Blessed are the solitary and the elect, for you will find the Kingdom. For you are from it and to it you will return' "; and *Gos. Thom.* 82 states, "Jesus said, 'He who is near me is near the fire, and he who is far from me is far from the Kingdom.' "

"Entering the Kingdom" in reference to becoming like children in *Gos. Thom.* 22 (from "Thomas" himself, so King) probably symbolizes the initiation of the Thomas group by baptism. A primitive baptismal practice (cf. Jewish proselyte baptism and the Hellenistic Mysteries) also lies behind *Gos. Thom.* 37 and 21: the disciples undress, are naked and are unashamed, tread upon their garments, and become like little children, all of which symbolizes a return to the primal innocence and sinlessness of Adam and Eve in the Garden prior to the Fall (J. Smith; Meeks 1982; cf. Gen 3:15; cf. 1 Cor 12:13; Gal 3:28; Col 3:11). Becoming a child in *Gos. Thom.* 22 is becoming a "single one" (cf. *Gos. Thom.* 4, 16, 23; probably redactional, so Davies), a status which denies the dualities of "the world," especially male and female. Being "acquainted with the Kingdom" as a little child is also being superior to the Baptist (cf. esp. Luke 7:24–35 = Matt 11:7–19).

In connection with "entering the Kingdom," *Gos. Thom.* 114 must be considered: "Simon Peter said to them, 'Let Mary leave us, because women are not worthy of the Life.' Jesus said, 'Look, I shall guide her so that I will make her male, in order that she also may become a living spirit, being like you males. For every woman who makes herself male will enter the Kingdom of Heaven." This saying has been interpreted as an original male androgyny, as a contrast between this world ("the female") and the spirit ("the male"), and as a reference to celibacy (cf. King). It might imply that there were women in the Thomas group. Yet, it may be an addition since it does not accord with the denial of male (as well as female) sexuality in the androgyny of *Gos. Thom.* 22 (Davies).

Further impressions about the Kingdom and the Thomas group can be discovered by looking at four cases where *Gos. Thom.* adds Kingdom references to traditions paralleled in the synoptics (21, 99, 103, 107; Cameron; King). In the Lost Sheep (107; cf. Luke 15:3 = Matt 18:12), "finding" the "largest sheep" is probably redactional (cf. 8:1: "large fish"; 20: "large branch"; 96: "large loaves"; Cameron). It has usually been interpreted as *gnōsis* (Gärtner), though again it may be wisdom (Davies). A group emphasis is to be found in *Gos. Thom.* 21:3 and the related beatitude in 103 (the Thief in the Night; cf. Matt 24:42–44 = Luke 12:39–40; Mark 3:27; Matt 12:29) which are concerned with the identification of the Kingdom with "house" that must be protected from outsiders (not apocalyptic "watching"). The last of the four sayings, *Gos. Thom.* 99, states that those who "enter the Kingdom" are the true brothers and mother who do God's will (cf. Mark 3:31–35 = Matt 12:46–50 = Luke 8:19–21). Other ethical emphases are the demand for strictness in fasting in order to "find" the Kingdom (*Gos. Thom.* 27 [= POxy 1]) and "Thomas'" antibusiness theme tacked on to the parable of the Banquet: "Businessmen and merchants shall not enter the places of my Father" (*Gos. Thom.* 64:2; cf. 54; Luke 6:20; Matt 5:3).

Of the fourteen Thomas parables, nine refer explicitly to the Kingdom and three of them are unique to *Gos. Thom.* (21:1; 97; 98). *Gos. Thom.* 21:1 (Children in the Field) is one of two key baptism passages (cf. *Gos. Thom.* 37); it fits the childlike innocence of "entering" the Kingdom group by baptism (J. Smith). The loss of meal from the broken-handled jar in *Gos. Thom.* 97 might refer to the wise person's ability to see what is foolish (King). The parable of the Sword in *Gos. Thom.* 98 seems to refer to the wise person's preparation for overcoming powerful enemies, that is, it reflects conflict with outsiders.

Turning to Matthean parallels, the Weeds with its reference to the future harvest in *Gos. Thom.* 57 (= Matt 13:24–30) lacks Matthew's allegorical, apocalyptic associations (Matt 13:36–43); it probably refers simply to the wise person's dealing craftily with enemies. The Pearl in *Gos. Thom.* 76:1 is given an ascetic conclusion that points to spiritual wealth (76:2: "the treasure which does not perish"; contrast Matt 13:45). The Treasure in *Gos. Thom.* 109 is usually considered to be a gnostic interpretation of Matt 13:44 (cf. also *Midr. Cant.* 4:12 and Aesop's fables; Grant and Freedman) because the father and the son "did not know" about the treasure (see, however, Hedrick); if "lending at interest" at the conclusion is taken literally, not "spiritually," it sharply conflicts with *Gos. Thom.* 95 (cf. *Gos. Thom.* 64:2; 54).

The two parables which parallel Q are the Leaven (*Gos. Thom.* 96:1; cf. Luke 13:20–21 = Matt 13:33) and the Lost Sheep (*Gos. Thom.* 107; cf. Luke 15:4–7 = Matt 18:12–13). The "large loaves" in the former and the "largest sheep" in the latter are redactional and refer (if not to *gnōsis* then) to wisdom. The theme of "searching" for the largest sheep also recalls seeking and finding wisdom (cf. "finding" the "large fish").

Finally, the Mustard Seed in *Gos. Thom.* 20 (Mark 4:30–32 = Matt 13:31–32 = Luke 13:18–19), which takes the form of an "aphoristic dialogue" (Crossan 1983), does not have the OT allusions found in the synoptics (Dan 4:21; Ezek 17:23 or 31:6). This has been taken as "gnosticizing" ("plowed ground" = gnostic laboring; "large branch" = the "heavenly man"; tiny seed = *gnōsis*; cf. Montefiore and Turner). However, one could also interpret the tiny seed as wisdom (again, the "large branch," cf. 8:1; 96:1; 107). This is the only Thomas parable which compares the Kingdom to an inanimate object (R. Cameron), reinforcing the possibility that the Kingdom in *Gos. Thom.* implies "belonging to the group/community" (King).

In summary, the Kingdom in *Gos. Thom.*, as in the gospel of John, is a present reality. It has usually been associated with gnostic "knowledge"; a current alternative is to see it as wisdom, especially since the Kingdom is not only within the self but outside the self. Many metaphors express this mysterious theme, for example, the notion of "largeness." Group overtones and ethical norms abound. "Entering the Kingdom" seems to be analogous to entering the Thomas group by means of baptism. The resulting new life is expressed as becoming a "single one," a status equivalent to the innocent child who, like Adam and Eve in the Garden before the Fall, is not characterized by the dualities of "the world." Presumably, the initiated insider has "found" the Kingdom that is within and without, and at the same time (s)he is mysteriously unified with Jesus. Finally, the purity of the group is defended against outsiders.

H. The Historical Jesus and the Kingdom

The attempt to interpret the Kingdom of God in the message and life of Jesus demands critical correlation of meanings of the Kingdom of God in Jesus' environment, in the Christian Gospels and Acts, and in Jesus' teaching critically reconstructed. There are many obstacles, notably the relative paucity of explicit "Kingdom of God" sayings in non-Christian texts and the centrality of the Kingdom in the Christian evangelists, who do not define it and indeed contribute to its form and content. The question of Jesus' teaching concerning the Kingdom of God is therefore part of a larger "question of the historical Jesus." See JESUS.

1. The Political Kingdom. There have been two major approaches to the political view of Jesus' Kingdom teaching: (1) setting Jesus within the political movements of 1st century Palestine and (2) comparing his teaching to analogous Kingdom sayings found in the Aramaic Targums politically interpreted. These approaches can overlap.

The first approach attempts to trace the history of the revolutionary "Zealot" movement in Josephus; it then views Jesus in relation to that history (esp. Brandon; cf. Bammel and Moule). Accordingly, Christian evangelists in the late 1st century C.E. transformed the revolutionist Jesus into a nonpolitical pacifist because they feared that Christianity would be confused with the Jews who had recently revolted against Rome (66–70 C.E.). Remnants of Jesus as revolutionist can nevertheless be found, for example, crucifixion between two "brigands" for sedition, the *titulus* "King of the Jews," and a disciple named Simon the "Zealot" (Luke 6:15; Acts 1:13). It is inferred that Jesus' Kingdom was of necessity political.

A second, more moderate, approach stresses the Targum Jonathan to Isaiah (Koch; cf. already Reimarus; also Buchanon). The two Kingdoms in the Targum—the eschatological "self-revelation" of the Kingdom of God in the present and the future eschatological Kingdom that "comes to" the Messiah related to the dominion of Jerusalem over the nations—is a reflective separation (cf. also Matthew and Paul) of what Jesus had blended together when he spoke of the eschatological presence, yet "coming," of the Kingdom of God (Koch, based esp. on *Tg. Mic.* 4:7).

Both approaches have been combined in an even more extreme position: the Kingdom of Heaven was a code word for God's *political* restoration of the Davidic kingdom with Jesus as king and his followers as his chief counselors (Buchanon).

The political-historical approach boldly accepts political realism and faces the apolitical redactional tendencies in the Gospels. Its weaknesses are: (1) it neglects the *teaching* of Jesus (e.g., Matt 5:44, "Love your enemies . . ."; the parables); (2) Josephus does not refer to "the Kingdom of God"; (3) there may have been no ongoing, unified Zealot movement in Palestine (M. Smith 1971; Horsley and Hanson); and (4) the traditional characterization of Galilee as revolutionary may be inaccurate (cf. e.g., Freyne; Mack). The use of the Targums has the advantage that they contain ten Jewish references to "the Kingdom of God" (Koch; Chilton) which may have political overtones (Koch). The difficulties are: (1) dating the references (esp. *Tg. Mic.* 4:7) and (2) the extent of the political nuances (cf. Chilton). Radical political reconstructions (Buchanon) face the same difficulties. A more subtle approach relates *God's* ultimate overthrow of repressive political forces to Jesus' *nonviolent social-economic-religious* revolution (e.g., Horsley; Sanders' "restoration theology"; cf. Borg; see H.3).

2. The Kingdom and Present Ethical Action. The present ethical approach has drawn on the rabbinic literature and the present-oriented sayings of Jesus (Dalman; Dodd; Vermes; Flusser). If freedom from the yoke of Rome (*Tg. Zech.* 14:9) had not yet happened because Israel had failed to keep "the yoke of the Torah" (*Tg. Ezek.* 2:10; *Sipre Deut.* 32:29), the Kingdom of Heaven among the rabbis was nonapocalyptic and anti-Zealot (Flusser; cf. *Abot de Rabbi Nathan; Mekilta of Rabbi Nathan* on Exod 15:18; *t. Soṭa* 14:4 [1st century C.E.]; *Ketub.* 66b). Yet, individuals who take the yoke of the Torah upon themselves may be members of the Kingdom already in the present (*Pirqe Abot* 3:6; see Flusser).

The best-known approach to the Jesus-related and present Kingdom is called "realized eschatology" (Dodd; cf. Flusser). This position claims that Jesus' present sayings (e.g., *ephthasen,* "has come," Luke 11:20) are determinative for his future sayings (e.g., *engiken,* "at hand," Mark 1:15). For example, "repent, for the Kingdom of Heaven is at hand" (Mark 1:15) means that human beings should work for the Kingdom; or the future messianic banquet (Matt 8:11 = Luke 13:28; Mark 14:25) means "the transcendental order beyond time and space" (Dodd). The parables of the Kingdom demonstrate its presence; ethics provide a "moral ideal" for those who have already accepted it. Thus, the emphasis lies on the Kingdom "in the midst of you" (Luke 17:21) or that "has come upon you" (Luke 11:20); it has suffered violence since the days of John the Baptist (Matt 11:12). Related approaches have gone in two directions: either an individual submission to God (Vermes) or a social message for the poor, the hungry, the meek, the mourners, and the persecuted (Matt 5:3–6, 10 = Luke 6:20–22; Flusser).

This position rightly stresses the present ethical implications of the Kingdom. However, the "transcendental order beyond time and space" sounds too Platonic (see, however, *T. Mos.* 10). There are other questions. The present ethical emphasis may not be timeless and does not easily fit apocalyptic eschatology; there is considerable caution about using mostly later rabbinic texts about the Law for interpreting Jesus; and some suspect that modern, democratic ethical ideals about individual equality and social welfare may have influenced these interpretations.

3. The Future Apocalyptic Kingdom. The dominant alternative of the last century has been to stress the context of Jewish apocalyptic eschatology for the Kingdom: *God,* not revolutionary human beings, will act to redeem his people in the *future* by judging worldly kingdoms, destroying his people's Satanic enemies, and reversing the present order of the world. Either Jesus' apocalyptic *sayings* (esp. Weiss; in part, Hiers; see H.4) or his apocalyptic *life* (Schweitzer; Sanders; in part, Hiers) is emphasized.

The key *sayings* speak of the Kingdom "at hand" interpreted apocalyptically (*ēngiken* in Mark 1:15; Matt 4:17; 10:7; Luke 10:9; 10:11; and *engus estin* in Luke 21:31): the Kingdom coming "in power" (Mark 9:1); drinking wine new in the Kingdom of God (Mark 14:25 = Matt 26:29; cf. Luke 22:18); and for some, related passages about the apocalyptic Son of Man, the defeat of Satan in exorcisms, the signs of the End, and final judgment. The "present" sayings cause more difficulty. The Kingdom "has come" *(ephthasen)* is interpreted in a future sense (Aramaic *mĕtāʾ*; so Weiss; cf. Luke 10:9) and "has come [*ephthasen*] upon you" by exorcisms (Luke 11:20 = Matt 12:28) is said to mean *preparation* for the nearness of the Kingdom, not presence. The Kingdom ". . . not coming with signs to be observed . . ." (Luke 17:20–21a) denies only *accompanying* signs; and the Kingdom "in the midst of you" (17:21b) can refer to the future in Aramaic. Finally, the difficult saying about the Kingdom's suffering violence since John (Matt 11:12 = Luke 16:16) can mean that between John and Jesus there was a period of tribulation followed by the final victory of God's Kingdom on earth (Hiers). The parables make a contrast between present and near future.

In the classic approach called "thoroughgoing eschatology" (Schweitzer), Jesus' whole *life* was so absorbed by his expectation of the coming Kingdom that he sought to *bring it about* by taking the preliminary "messianic woes" upon himself in his suffering passion. Jesus' ethics meant repentance *before the End,* or "interim ethics."

A recent apocalyptic approach to Jesus' *life* stresses that the dominant scholarly focus on unique *sayings* predisposes the interpreter to see Jesus as a teacher isolated from Judaism; also, it does not explain why he was executed as an insurrectionist (Sanders). The key event in Jesus' life was his overturning the tables in the Jerusalem temple (Mark 11:15–19 = Matt 21:12–13 = Luke 19:45–48) interpreted as a prophetic, symbolic act about temple destruction (cf. Mark 13:1–2 = Matt 24:1–3 = Luke 21:5–7; 14:57–58 = Matt 26:60b–61). This event was consistent with "Jewish restoration theology." While sayings in general are less important, the significant ones deal with the usual apocalyptic themes. Related *Kingdom* sayings are "entering" the Kingdom (Matt 7:21; Mark 10:15 = Matt 18:3 = Luke 18:17; Mark 10:23 = Matt 19:23 = Luke 18:24); "Thy Kingdom come" (Matt 6:10 = Luke 11:2); sitting at Jesus' right hand in the Kingdom (Matt 20:21; cf. Mark 10:37 ["glory"]); drinking new wine in the Kingdom (Mark 14:25 = Matt 26:29 = Luke 22:18); and a parable (Matt 20:1–16). "Present" Kingdom sayings (Luke 11:20 = Matt 12:28; Luke 17:21) are either less important or interpreted as future (Matt 11:11–12 = Luke 7:28).

Decisive for this view are the "almost indisputable" facts of eschatological setting for John, Jesus, and the early apostles. Jesus was a "restoration prophet," or an "eschatological charismatic" who held a version of "Jewish restoration theology" (cf. Theudas and "the Egyptian," *Ant* 20.97, 169–70). However, the Kingdom was not conceived in military/political terms (cf. e.g., Horsley; contrast Buchanon).

Two general questions about the apocalyptic approach constantly arise: (1) Was the apocalyptic ethos in 1st century Palestinian Judaism as widespread and dominant? (2) If it was, did Jesus' teaching and life conform to it, or were he and/or his teaching distinctive (the form critical "criterion of dissimilarity")? Specifically, how determinative should the temple "cleansing" story be for the meaning of the Kingdom (Evans)?

4. The Modified Apocalyptic Kingdom. Many 20th century critics have accepted a modified "reduced apocalyptic" position (Bultmann 1958). Correspondingly, Jesus rejected the usual cosmic signs by stressing the imminence of the Kingdom, and by seeing his own prophetic, but non-Messianic, activity as the sign of its dawning, though not yet present, character—an "already, not yet" emphasis. Thus, Jesus summoned hearers to repent, warned them of impending disaster, proclaimed deliverance to those who heeded the message, anticipated the Kingdom in his meals (Luke 22:15–18); while the Kingdom was wholly future, he affirmed that it was already dawning in his exorcisms (Luke 11:20: "has come"), was "in the midst of" the people (Luke 17:21), and offered hope to the poor, hungry, and weeping (Luke 6:20–21). There is a dialectic between present and future; one is in the crisis of decision in such a way that chronological time is collapsed into each new existential moment of decision (the "NOW").

A modification of this position (Perrin 1963) concludes that of both Judaism and the teaching of Jesus the following can be stated: (1) *malkût(ā)* referred to the "kingly rule" of God (Dalman); (2) the Kingdom was an apocalyptic "concept" (Weiss) centered on two central themes: (a) God's final and decisive intervention in human history and human experience and (b) the resulting final state of the redeemed. The major difference between Judaism and Jesus is that Jesus used the Kingdom of God expression and returned to the *prophetic* understanding which avoided linear, apocalyptic time schemes. Again, a tension between present and future exists; it is part of the existential experience of the individual hearer. The ethics of the Kingdom is a response to the experience of this tension.

Some judge that these views destroy the futurity of the apocalyptic Kingdom and that they are too existentialistic and individualistic; others note that the focus on *distinctive sayings* isolates Jesus from Judaism (esp. Sanders). Nonetheless, many modifications and variations of this view exist. A somewhat related view has arisen in more recent literary and Targumic interpretations.

5. The Atemporal Kingdom. There is a distinction between literal language with one-to-one meanings and open-ended language with a variety of possible meanings, that is, between "sign" and "symbol" (Ricoeur) or "steno symbol" and "tensive symbol" (Wheelwright). It is possible similarly to distinguish between apocalyptic "sign" (Jewish and early Christian texts) and the Kingdom "symbol" (Jesus) limited only by the constraints of Israel's cultural myth (see Perrin 1976). This "literary turn" has been paralleled by renewed doubt about the extent of apocalyptic eschatology on Jesus (see above and H.6). The most important sayings are the traditionally "present" ones (e.g., Luke 11:20; 17:20–21; Matt 11:12). This perspective is also related to other literary discussions in NT study such as symbol and myth (Wilder), parable as metaphor (Funk) or "aesthetic object" (Via), and the language of "reversal" which shatters the world of accepted values (Crossan 1973). Correspondingly, the Kingdom of God symbol challenged Jesus' hearers to take the myth of God's activity on behalf of his people with renewed seriousness (Perrin 1976).

While the contrast between Jewish/early Christian apocalyptic "sign" and Jesus' Kingdom "symbol" has been too sharply drawn (Perrin 1976 admitted that the Kingdom in the Kaddish prayer is a symbol), and there is disagreement about whether the whole phrase "Kingdom of God" is a symbol, this interpretation of the Kingdom has produced a number of responses (cf. Duling 1984). One view attempts to correlate atemporal "structuralist" readings of certain parables with "present" Kingdom sayings to arrive at a preconceptual, intuitive insight into the Kingdom symbol as that which shatters one's familiar world and creates a new world; this, it is said, was Jesus' experience of God (Scott; cf. Crossan 1973). Another possibility (Breech) draws on the three most important "present" sayings (Luke 11:20; 17:20–21; Matt 11:12) and recategorizes other sayings (Luke 9:62; Mark 10:15, 23b, 25) to demonstrate that Jesus did not "shatter the world" but was a poet who taught about Palestinian peasant life with gentle humor (cf. Wilder), "demythologized" the Kingdom (cf. Perrin 1963), and shattered *religious expectation.* These atemporal, literary orientations to Jesus' Kingdom teaching are important for bringing out the richness of Jesus' Kingdom language. The problem some scholars see is that they, like existentialist interpretations before them, do not always take seriously enough the ancient, concrete, sociohistorical context.

Finally, the distinctive Targumic Kingdom passages have also been interpreted in an atemporal manner (Chilton 1978, 1979). Accordingly, the Targum's most nationalistic-political interpretation (*Tg. Mic.* 4:7–8) is a late 4th-century C.E. narrowing of the earlier Targumic interpretations. These stress that the Kingdom points to a revelation of a dynamic, powerful, personal God who was and is and is to come (cf. Isa 41:4) and who acts on behalf of his people. As such, they can be seen to cohere with Jesus' atemporal, nonpolitical Kingdom teaching. However, others have taken the Kingdom sayings in the Targums in a more political sense (Koch; Buchanon).

6. The Kingdom, Wisdom, and Gnosticism. Curiously, the modern literary atemporal approach to the kingdom has a distant analogy in the internalized Kingdom of the *Gospel of Thomas,* which contains no apocalyptic Son of Man expectation or apocalyptic kingdom sayings (see G above). The question is whether *Gos. Thom.* is a "gnosticizing" interpretation and elaboration of Jesus' most original sayings (Koester) or a wisdom interpretation (Davies).

A somewhat different wisdom orientation to the Kingdom built on popular (esp. Cynic) philosophy has emerged (Mack 1988). It draws on recent archaeology (Meyers and Strange) and the study of pre-70 C.E. Judaism (Smith 1978; Neusner) to establish that Galilee was *not* dominated by the three factors usually said to influence Jesus' view of the Kingdom: politically revolutionary Zealots, Pharisaic/rabbinic legal-ethical teaching, and apocalyptic fervor.

Rather, Galilee had become "an epitome of Hellenistic culture" (Mack 1988). If the earliest literary stratum of Q was wisdom (Kloppenborg); if certain of Jesus' proverbs were "countercultural"; if Jesus' pronouncements were Greek *chreiai,* that is, clever wisdom sayings which challenge accepted norms and values; and if Jesus' wisdom can be described as "aphoristic," that is, short sayings that were formally like proverbs, but unlike proverbs in challenging ancestral authority and conventional wisdom with individual authority and personal insight (Crossan 1983)—then perhaps Jesus might be seen in relation to a popularized combination of Cynic "metic" wisdom and Hebrew wisdom. Among the Cynics the sage is "King," and the sage's countercultural wisdom and itinerant vocation become a special sort of "Kingdom." If correct, the conventional view of Jesus as the prophet of the apocalyptic Kingdom was a later, imaginative creation of early Christian communities whose group formation involved opposition from and toward outsiders, that is, the synagogue (esp. the gospel of Mark). This perspective about Jesus is said to cohere with his three major "present" Kingdom sayings (Luke 11:20; 17:20–21; Matt 11:12).

Debate about this recent interpretation should continue in the following areas: Will the non-apocalyptic *Gos. Thom.* bear the weight some give it? What is the relative importance of Q and/or its wisdom stratum for Jesus' Kingdom teaching? Can one reduce the influence of the Pharisaic Jews in the Galilee of Jesus' day (see Saldarini)? Will archaeology so revolutionize discussions of S Galilee that one can really see it as an "epitome of Hellenistic culture" (see Freyne)? Will the dominating apocalyptic/prophetic perspective be so easily removed from discussions of the Kingdom (see Boring)? To what extent are countercultural wisdom and countercultural prophecy cut from the same or similar cloth?

7. Summary. The discussion of the Kingdom of God in the life and teaching of Jesus has been dominated in modern times by the extent to which its meaning has been determined by Jewish apocalyptic eschatology. The both/and, present/future "reduced apocalyptic" view of Jesus' Kingdom sayings that emerged as a consensus in a previous generation can still be found, but the contours of alternative positions have also surfaced. The radical political perspective on Jesus' Kingdom teaching is still current, but it remains a minority position; if a more modest version related to social, economic, and religious factors continues to be developed, it will not have the advantage of parallel Kingdom references in Josephus; Kingdom *ideas* in the apocryphal and pseudepigraphical literature and/or eschatological Kingdom *sayings* in the Targums will have to fill in the gap, but they must contend with dating issues, especially in the case of *Tg. Mic.* 4:7–8.

The more extreme apocalyptic position on Jesus' *life* as a basis for his Kingdom *teaching* has persisted as a minority position. A modified alternative to this perspective has been developed in relation to "Jewish restoration theology." Its advantage is the general apocalyptic context of much of early Judaism and early Christianity; its major difficulty is sustaining a perspective on Jesus' life in the face of critical methods that argue that the apocalyptic flavor of the Synoptic Gospels derives from early Christianity.

The "ethical" interpretations of the Kingdom still persist, and there is every indication that they will be developed further by those interested in the social dimensions of the Jesus group/movement and various early Christian groups/movements. It is interesting to note that the present sayings on which the ethical approaches have been based have also been correlated with "countercultural" wisdom in relation to the early strata of Q and in some cases the gnostic trajectory). All countercultural challenges to normative values have ethical implications, as the traditional prophetic interpretations have indicated.

Finally, the atemporal literary approaches now abound, especially in North America. While the sociohistorical dimension in these perspectives has been somewhat muted, in part they have emerged as a warning that all interpretations, from the evangelists to the present, will never totally contain the full import of Jesus' message about the Kingdom of God.

I. The Writings of Paul

Three of Paul's seven undisputed letters contain six explicit references to "Kingdom of God," and two other references to the Kingdom in relation to God. Four of the six references refer to "inheriting the Kingdom" (1 Cor 6:9, 10; 15:50; Gal 5:21). Distinctive form (the definite article "the" *(hē)* is missing and the use of "inherit" in Gal 5:21 is unique to Galatians; cf. Matt 25:34; cf. 19:29; Mark 10:17 = Luke 10:25; Luke 18:18) and common content (all four sayings are apocalyptic) point to a stereotyped pre-Pauline tradition. In 1 Cor 15:50, "flesh and blood cannot inherit the Kingdom of God" refers to the future resurrection of the transformed, spiritual body. The two references in 1 Cor 6:9–10 and one in Galatians 5:21 point to the future apocalyptic judgment in the form of a "threat" saying: "the unrighteous," characterized by vices, "will not inherit" the Kingdom of God (unless they have been "washed," 1 Cor 6:11); implied is that those characterized by virtues will inherit the Kingdom (Gal 5:22–23). This moral division implies group boundaries marked by rites of entry, that is, baptism (cf. Rom 6:1–6; Gal 3:28; 1 Cor 5:9–13; Meeks 1982).

1 Cor 15:24 is also apocalyptic and implies an anticipatory Kingdom, that is, the reign of Christ: "Then comes the end when he delivers the Kingdom to God the Father after destroying every rule and every authority and power." The anticipatory Kingdom may also be implied in 1 Thess 2:12 in a possible baptism context *(axios;* cf. Phil 1:27): "We exhorted each one of you and encouraged you and charged you to lead a life worthy of God, who calls you into his own Kingdom and glory." The anticipatory presence of the Kingdom is implied again in Paul's attempt to steer the middle course between the extremes of asceticism and libertinism in food practices (cf. Theissen 1982); the "antithetical definition formula" (Haufe) says: "For the Kingdom of God is not food and drink but righteousness and peace and joy in the Holy Spirit" (Rom 14:17). In a similar formula, 1 Cor 4:20 states: "For the Kingdom of God does not consist in talk but in power." Here the positive reference is apparently to miracle working (esp. 2 Cor 12:12; cf. Mark 9:1; Luke 11:20 = Matt 12:28).

In short, the undisputed writings of Paul point to a tension between the present, anticipatory "Kingdom of

Christ," which in some passages seems to imply an anticipatory "Kingdom of God," and the future apocalyptic consummation of the Kingdom of God at the End. Because the contexts often imply baptism, Paul has probably remolded baptismal traditions about the Kingdom for proclamations and exhortations related to group boundaries (Donfried; Meeks 1982).

J. The Pauline School

1. 2 Thessalonians. In a highly apocalyptic context about judgment "in that day" (2 Thess 1:10), the Paulinist hopes that the recipients of the letter may be made "worthy" *(axios)* of the Kingdom of God for which they are suffering (1:5). Here, the future Kingdom dominates, but is correlated with present suffering in the group.

2. Colossians. In contrast, Colossians 1:13–14 introduces the Colossians hymn about the present reign of the cosmic Christ (Col 1:15–20): "he has delivered us from the dominion of darkness and transferred us to the Kingdom of his beloved Son, in whom we have redemption, the forgiveness of sins" (Col 1:13–14). Here, the Christians already possess citizenship in "the Kingdom of the beloved Son" in so far as they are "saints of light" who are victorious over darkness; perhaps the terms "part" *(tēn merida),* "lot" *(tou klērou),* and "saints of light" in the previous verse (Col 1:12) imply heavenly communion with angelic beings (cf. Heb *gōral,* "lot" in QL). In any case, purity and group boundaries are present, although "the kingdom of the beloved Son" is more comprehensive than the church. The same meaning seems to be present in the expression "fellow workers for the Kingdom of God" (Col 4:11).

3. Ephesians. The christology of Christ's present, cosmic reign and its implications for the growing institution have also influenced Eph 5:5: "Be sure of this, that no fornicator or impure man, or one who is covetous (that is, an idolator), has any inheritance in the Kingdom of Christ and of God." The Kingdom of Christ and the Kingdom of God again overlap and are already present, albeit in hidden form; group purity is in view (on "inheriting" the Kingdom in Paul, see I above).

4. 2 Timothy. Finally, in 2 Tim 4:1 Christ's function as final judge does not clearly distinguish the eschatological Kingdom of Christ from the eschatological Kingdom of God: "I charge you in the presence of God and of Christ Jesus who is to judge the living and the dead, and by his appearing and his kingdom." In 2 Tim 4:18 the author says, "The Lord will rescue me from every evil and save me for his heavenly kingdom. To him be the glory for ever and ever. Amen." Here the author contrasts his present perilous existence on earth with hope for the future after death.

The writings of the Pauline School show that tension between the Kingdom of Christ and the Kingdom of God has often become somewhat muted. In 2 Thessalonians the focus seems to be totally future; this view resurfaces in 2 Timothy. In Colossians and Ephesians, however, the focus is present, and that is consistent with the cosmic Christ and the developing institution of the church. Finally, in Colossians, Ephesians, and 2 Timothy the two Kingdoms seem to merge, although not completely.

K. Other Canonical Christian Literature

1. James. In the form of a rhetorical question (Jas 2:5), the literal poor "before the world" are "rich" with respect to faith and "heirs of the kingdom which he has promised to those who love him" (cf. 1:9–11 [Isa 40:6; Jer 9:23–24]; 2:5–12; 5:1–6). They are also models of the pious who endure under trial (1:12; texts in Dibelius-Greeven). The theme has strong roots in the Jewish Scriptures and writings, as well as in the Lukan form of the teaching of Jesus (Luke 6:20). The Kingdom saying has apocalyptic overtones ("heirs"; "promised") and social implications (rich and poor).

2. Hebrews. In Heb 12:28, the pilgrim people are being warned to be grateful for receiving "a kingdom that cannot be shaken." As the context makes clear (cf. Heb 12:26–27, [Hag 2:6]), "what has been shaken" refers to transitory earthly copies or shadows of the true, eternal heavenly realities that are already provisionally present for Christians, to be consummated only in the future (11:27; cf. 2:5; 6:5; 9:11; 10:1; 13:14). The response should be "acceptable worship, with reverence and awe; for our God is a consuming fire." Otherwise, Scriptural language about "thy (= God's) Kingdom" which is "forever" (Ps. 45:6) is used in relation to the Son (Heb 1:8; cf. manuscript variations) who is a priest according to the order of Melchizedek, the "*king* of Salem, priest of the Most High God," the "*king* of righteousness," "the *king* of peace" (Heb 7:1–2). Finally, some heroes of faith are described as those who have conquered (earthly) kingdoms and enforced justice (11:33).

3. Revelation. Only two of the nine explicit references to the term "kingdom" in the book of Revelation refer to God (11:15; 12:10). Nonetheless, royal symbolism pervades the book and the heavenly Jerusalem (Rev 21:1–22:5) has been equated with the cosmic Kingdom of God (Schnackenburg).

God, Christ, the witnesses/martyrs, and earthly rulers are portrayed in royal terms. God is a great king sitting on his throne in the heavenly courtroom (Revelation 4). He is praised by the persecuted martyrs in heaven as the "King of the nations (ages?)," an apparent reference to the pilgrimage of the nations to Mount Zion (15:3–4 [Jer 10:7; Ps 86:9; Isa 2:1–2; cf. Mic 4:1–4; Jer 16:19]). Jesus Christ, the slain lamb (3:21; 22:3; chap. 5) who "has conquered" by his death, is also enthroned on God's throne. He is the royal Davidic king (esp. 17:14; 21:7; 22:16), "the prince of the kings of the earth" (1:5; cf. 15:3 [some manuscripts]), "King of kings," and "Lord of lords" (17:14; 19:16; cf. Deut 10:17). Correspondingly, at the trumpet call of the seventh angel the kingdom of the world will be transformed into the "Kingdom of our Lord and of his Christ" who will reign forever (11:15; cf. 10:7). In another vision (12:1–17), "the Kingdom of our God," accompanied with the salvation, the power, and "the authority of his Christ" (12:10), "have come" when Satan and his angels have been cast down from heaven to the earth. Since the Kingdom of God and the Kingdom of the Messiah seem to be coterminous (cf. 3:21; 22:1, 3), the question must be raised whether the 1,000-year "millennial reign" of Christ (20:1–6) is an interregnum before the final Kingdom of God (Schnackenburg).

Finally, the one who conquers, loves his followers, and

has freed them from their sins by his blood, makes *them* a "kingdom, priests to his God and Father" (1:5b–6) or "a kingdom and priests to our God" (5:10; cf. 20:6; Exod 19:6; Isa 61:6; *Jub.* 16:18); "they shall reign on earth" (5:10; cf. 20:6; 22:5). While their struggle with the earthly kingdoms persists in the present, they will have a share in the final reign of God and Christ. This appears to be anticipated when John of Patmos shares the "kingdom" of those to whom he writes, those who are enduring tribulation and patient endurance under the temporary sway of the kingdoms of the earth (1:9).

In summary, when the powers of Satan are defeated, the Kingdom of God and of his Christ that now rule in heaven will prevail over the earthly kingdoms that are temporarily under the power of the Beast (16:10; 17:12, 17–18); it will be a cosmic reign over heaven, earth, and the underworld; it will transform the kingdoms of the world, will be centered in the new Jerusalem on earth, and rule will be shared with the faithful (3:21; 22:3–5). Apocalyptic religious themes related to perceived experiences of political, social, and economic oppression lead to the strongest political implications about the Kingdom of God in the NT.

4. 2 Peter. An attempt to reassert the apocalyptic expectation and hope in the face of the delay of the Parousia and against "false teachers" is found in 2 Pet 3:1–13. In 2 Pet 1:10–11 those who are zealous in the calling—purity in the group is highlighted—are promised "an entrance into the eternal kingdom of our Lord and Savior Jesus Christ" (cf. 3:13, 18). Though this "entering" language is familiar from the Gospels (e.g., Mark 10:15 = Matt 18:3 = Luke 18:17; John 3:5), it is the kingdom of Christ, the Patron/Benefactor, that is stressed (cf. Eph 5:5).

L. Patristic Literature: A Summary

Many of the Kingdom references in the Church Fathers are quotations and allusions from the Bible (Lampe; Ferguson; Viviano 1987b). In the early period (2d century), statements generally fall into three categories. First, there are polemics against various opponents to show that the Christians are the true heirs of the Kingdom (e.g., Just. *Dial.* 140; Iren. *haer.* 3.21.9; cf. Matt 8:11–13). Second, there are polemics against the gnostic tendency to see the Kingdom as interior (e.g., Hipp. *haer.* 5.2–3; *2 Clem.* 12). Third, there is the opposite tendency, namely, apologetics show that the Christian view of the Kingdom is not politically subversive, even though "kingdom" is the normal word for "empire" (e.g., *1 Clem.* 61:1; Athenag. *Leg.* 18). In the two latter cases, the eschatological, heavenly, angelic nature of the Kingdom is generally emphasized (e.g., *1 Clem.* 42:3; *Did.* 16; Ign *Eph.* 16:1; Polyc. *Phil.* 5:3; *2 Clem.* 11:7; Hegesippus in Eus. *Hist. Eccl.* 3.20.4), though millennialist views of an interregnum on earth occasionally appear (Papias in Eus. *Hist. Eccl.* 3.39.12). In all of these cases an emerging corporate self-definition occurs. It may also be that Christian use of pagan wisdom sayings brought about a reference to wisdom as the Kingdom of God (*Sent. Sex.* 311).

With 3d century Origen there was a shift to a more internal, spiritual-mystical meaning of the Kingdom (*or.* 25); with the Constantinian era and the legitimate acceptance of Christianity, earthly political dimensions of the Kingdom were correlated with the Empire; and with Augustine's *City of God* a correlation of the present Church with the millennial Kingdom was introduced, despite the possibility that chaff was mixed with the wheat, and despite the possibility that those outside the Church might ultimately be in the final, heavenly, perfected Kingdom (cf. 20:9).

Bibliography

Ambrozic, A. M. 1972. *The Hidden Kingdom.* Washington.
Bacon, B. W. 1930. *Studies in Matthew.* London.
Baird, J. A. 1982. *Rediscovering the Power of the Gospel. Jesus' Theology of the Kingdom.* Wooster, OH.
Bammel, E., and Moule, C. F. D. 1984. *Jesus and the Politics of His Day.* Cambridge.
Barrett, C. K. 1962. *The Gospel According to St. John.* London.
Beasley-Murray, G. R. 1968. John 3:3, 5. Baptism, Spirit, and the Kingdom. *ExpTim* 97: 167–70.
———. 1986. *Jesus and the Kingdom of God.* Grand Rapids.
Betz, H. D. 1985. *Essays on the Sermon on the Mount.* Philadelphia.
Borg, M. J. 1984. *Conflict, Holiness and Politics in the Teachings of Jesus.* SBEC 5. New York.
Boring, M. E. 1982. *Sayings of the Risen Jesus.* Cambridge.
———. 1987. The Kingdom of God in Mark. Pp. 131–45 in Willis 1987.
Brandon, S. G. F. 1967. *Jesus and the Zealots.* New York.
Bright, J. 1953. *The Kingdom of God.* New York.
Brown, R. 1974. The Relation of "The Secret Gospel of Mark" to the Fourth Gospel. *CBQ* 36: 466–85.
Buchanon, G. W. 1983. *Jesus: The King and His Kingdom.* Macon, GA.
Bultmann, R. 1958. *Jesus and the Word.* Trans. L. P. Smith and E. H. Lantero. New York.
———. 1966. *The Gospel According to John. A Commentary.* Trans. G. R. Beasley-Murray, R. W. N. Hoare, and J. K. Riches. Philadelphia.
Cameron, P. S. 1984. *Violence and the Kingdom: The Interpretation of Matthew 11:12.* Frankfurt.
Cameron, R. 1986. Parable and Interpretation in the Gospel of Thomas. *Forum* 2/2: 3–39.
Chilton, B. 1978. Regnum Dei Deus Est. *SJT* 31: 261–70.
———. 1979. *God in Strength—Jesus' Announcement of the Kingdom.* SUNT 1. Linz.
———. 1983. *The Glory of Israel.* JSOTSupp 23. Sheffield.
———. 1984. *The Kingdom of God.* Philadelphia.
Chilton, B., and McDonald, J. I. H. 1987. *Jesus and the Ethics of the Kingdom.* Grand Rapids.
Collins, J. J. 1987. The Kingdom of God in the Apocrypha and Pseudepigrapha. Pp. 81–95 in Willis 1987.
Componovo, O. 1984. *Königtum, Königsherrschaft und Reich Gottes in den frühjüdischen Schriften.* OBO 58. Göttingen.
Conzelmann, H. 1960. *The Theology of St. Luke.* Trans. G. Buswell. New York.
Crossan, J. D. 1973. *In Parables.* New York.
———. 1983. *In Fragments: The Aphorisms of Jesus.* San Francisco.
———. 1985. *Four Other Gospels.* Minneapolis.
Dalman, G. 1902. *The Words of Jesus.* Trans. D. M. Kay. Edinburgh.
Davies, S. L. 1983. *The Gospel of Thomas and Christian Wisdom.* New York.
Dodd, C. H. 1961. *The Parables of the Kingdom.* Rev. ed. New York.
Donahue, J. 1973. *Are You the Christ?* SBLDS 10. Missoula, MT.
———. 1988. *The Gospel in Parable.* Philadelphia.

Donfried, K. P. 1987. The Kingdom of God in Paul. Pp. 175–90 in Willis 1987.
Duling, D. 1973. The Promises to David and Their Entrance into Early Christianity—Nailing Down a Likely Hypothesis. *NTS* 20: 55–57.
———. 1978. The Therapeutic Son of David in Matthew's Gospel. *NTS* 24: 392–410.
———. 1982. The Kingdom of God in the Teaching of Jesus. *Word World* 2: 117–26.
———. 1984. Norman Perrin and the Kingdom of God: Review and Response. *JR* 64: 468–83.
———. 1987. Binding and Loosing (Matt 16:19; 18:18; John 20:23). *Forum* 3/4: 3–31.
Edwards, R. A. 1976. *A Theology of Q.* Philadelphia.
Elbogen, I. 1913. *Der jüdische Gottesdienst in seiner geschichtlichen Entwicklung.* Leipzig.
Esler, P. H. 1987. *Community and Gospel in Luke-Acts.* Cambridge.
Evans, C. A. 1989. Jesus' Action in the Temple: Cleansing or Portent of Destruction? *CBQ* 51: 237–70.
Ferguson, E. 1987. The Kingdom of God in Early Patristic Literature. Pp. 191–208 in Willis 1987.
Flusser, D. 1969. *Jesus.* Trans. R. Walls. New York.
Freyne, S. 1988. *Galilee, Jesus and the Gospels.* Philadelphia.
Gager, J. 1975. *Kingdom and Community.* Englewood Cliffs, NJ.
Gärtner, B. 1961. *The Theology of the Gospel According to Thomas.* New York.
Goodenough, E. R. 1928. The Political Philosophy of Hellenistic Kingship. *Yale Classical Series* 1: 55–102.
Grant, R. M., and Freedman, D. N. 1960. *The Secret Sayings of Jesus.* London.
Haufe, G. 1985. Reich Gottes bei Paulus und in der Jesus Tradition. *NTS* 31: 467–72.
Hedrick, C. 1986. The Treasure Parable in Matthew and Thomas. *Forum* 2/2: 41–56.
Hengel, M. 1961. *Die Zealoten.* Leiden.
Hiers, R. H. 1970. *The Kingdom of God in the Synoptic Tradition.* Gainesville, FL.
Hill, D. 1981. Towards an Understanding of the Kingdom of God. *IBS* 3: 62–76.
Hodgson, R. 1987. The Kingdom of God in the School of St. John. Pp. 163–74 in Willis 1987.
Höistad, R. 1948. *Cynic Hero and Cynic King: Studies in the Cynic Conception of Man.* Lund.
Horsley, R. A. 1987. *Jesus and the Spiral of Violence.* San Francisco.
Horsley, R. A., and Hanson, J. S. 1985. *Bandits, Prophets, and Messiahs.* Minneapolis.
Jacobson, A. 1982. The Literary Unity of Q. *JBL* 101: 365–89.
Jeremias, J. 1971. *New Testament Theology.* Trans. J. Bowden. New York.
Johnson, G. 1984. "Kingdom of God" Sayings in Paul's Letters. Pp. 143–56 in *From Jesus to Paul. Studies in Honour of Francis Wright Beare,* ed. P. Richardson and J. Hurd. Waterloo, Ontario.
Kee, H. C. 1977. *Community of the New Age.* Philadelphia.
Kelber, W. 1974. *The Kingdom in Mark.* Philadelphia.
King, K. 1987. Kingdom in the Gospel of Thomas. *Forum* 3/1: 48–97.
Kingsbury, J. D. 1975. *Matthew: Structure, Christology, Kingdom.* Philadelphia.
———. 1988. *Matthew as Story.* 2d ed. Philadelphia.
Klein, G. 1970. "Reich Gottes" als biblischer Zentralbegriff. *EvT* 30: 642–70.
Kloppenborg, J. S. 1987. *The Formation of Q.* Philadelphia.
Koch, K. 1978. Offenbaren wird sich das Reich Gottes. *NTS* 25: 158–65.
Koester, H. 1971. One Jesus and Four Primitive Gospels. Pp. 158–204 in Robinson and Koester 1971.
———. 1983. History and Development of Mark's Gospel. Pp. 35–57 in *Colloquy on New Testament Studies: A Time for Reappraisal and Fresh Approaches,* ed. B. Corley. Macon, GA.
Kretzer, A. 1964. *Jesus and the Kingdom.* New York.
———. 1971. *Die Herrschaft der Himmel und die Söhne des Reiches.* SBM 10. Stuttgart.
Ladd, G. E. 1962. The Kingdom of God—Reign or Realm? *JBL* 81: 230–38.
———. 1964. *Jesus and the Kingdom.* New York.
Lampe, G. W. H. 1948. Some Notes on the Significance of *Basileia tou Theou, Basileia Christou* in the Greek Fathers. *JTS* 49: 58–73.
Lattke, M. 1984. On the Jewish Background of the Concept "Kingdom of God." Pp. 72–91 in Chilton 1984.
Lauterbach, J. Z. 1961. *Mekilta de-Rabbi Ishmael.* 3 vols. Philadelphia.
Lindars, B. 1981. John and the Synoptic Gospels: A Test Case. *NTS* 27: 287–94.
Lundström, G. 1963. *The Kingdom of God in the Teaching of Jesus.* Trans. J. Bulman. Edinburgh.
Mack, B. 1987. The Kingdom Sayings in Mark. *Forum* 3/1: 3–47.
———. 1988. *A Myth of Innocence: Mark and Christian Origins.* Philadelphia.
Malina, B., and Neyrey, J. 1988. *Calling Jesus Names: The Social Value of Labels in Matthew.* Sonoma, CA.
McNamara, M. 1972. *Targum and Testament.* Grand Rapids.
Meeks, W. 1972. The Man from Heaven in Johannine Sectarianism. *JBL* 91: 44–72.
———. 1982. *The First Urban Christians.* New Haven.
Meier, J. P. 1976. *Law and History in Matthew's Gospel.* AnBib 71. Rome.
Merk, O. 1975. Das Reich Gottes in den lukanischen Schriften. Pp. 201–20 in *Jesus und Paulus. Festschrift G. Kümmel,* ed. E. Ellis and E. Grässer. Göttingen.
Merklein, H. 1984. *Jesu Botschaft von der Gottesherrschaft.* 2d. ed. Stuttgart.
Meyers, E. M., and Strange, J. F. 1981. *Archeology, the Rabbis, and Early Christianity.* Nashville.
Montefiore, H. 1961. A Comparison of the Parables of the Gospel According to Thomas and of the Synoptic Gospels. *NTS* 7: 220–48.
Montefiore, H., and Turner, H. E. W. 1962. *Thomas and the Evangelists.* SBT 35. London.
Moxnes, H. 1988. *The Economy of the Kingdom.* OBT. Philadelphia.
Neusner, J. 1973. *From Politics to Piety.* Englewood Cliffs, NJ.
Neyrey, J. 1988. Jesus the Witch: Witchcraft Accusations in Matthew 12. Pp. 1–32 in Malina and Neyrey 1988.
Nickelsburg, G. W. E. 1981. *Jewish Literature Between the Bible and the Midrash.* Philadelphia.
Noack, B. 1948. *Das Gottesreich bei Lukas.* SymBU 10. Uppsala.
Oakman, D. 1986. *Jesus and the Economic Questions of His Day.* Studies in Bible and Early Christianity. Lewistown, NY.
Pamment, M. 1981. The Kingdom of Heaven According to the First Gospel. *NTS* 27: 211–32.
Patrick, D. 1987. The Kingdom of God in the Old Testament. Pp. 67–79 in Willis 1987.

Perrin, N. 1963. *The Kingdom of God in the Teaching of Jesus.* Philadelphia.
———. 1967. *Rediscovering the Teaching of Jesus.* London.
———. 1976. *Jesus and the Language of the Kingdom.* Philadelphia.
Perrin, N., and Duling, D. 1982. *The New Testament: An Introduction.* New York.
Reimarus, S. H. 1779. *Concerning the Intention of Jesus and His Teaching.* Trans. R. S. Fraser. Pp. 59–269 in *Reimarus: Fragments.* Ed. L. E. Keck. Philadelphia (1970).
Ricoeur, P. 1969. *The Symbolism of Evil.* Trans. E. Buchanan. Boston.
Robbins, V. 1984. *Jesus the Teacher.* Philadelphia.
Robinson, J. M. 1971. LOGOI SOPHON: On the Gattung of Q. Pp. 71–113 in Robinson and Koester 1971.
Robinson, J. M., and Koester, H. 1971. *Trajectories Through Early Christianity.* Philadelphia.
Saldarini, A. 1988. *Pharisees, Scribes, and Sadducees in Palestinian Society.* Wilmington, DE.
Sanders, E. P. 1985. *Jesus and Judaism.* Philadelphia.
Schnackenburg, R. 1963. *God's Rule and Kingdom.* New York.
Schultz, S. 1972. *Die Spruchquelle der Evangelisten.* Zürich.
Schürmann, H. 1982. Das Zeugnis der Redenquelle für die Basileia-Verkündigung Jesu. Pp. 121–200 in *Logia. Les Paroles de Jésus—The Sayings of Jesus: Mémorial Joseph Coppens. Ed. J. Delober. BETL 59. Leuven.*
Schweitzer, A. 1901. *The Mystery of the Kingdom of God.* Trans. W. Lowrie. Repr. New York 1950.
Scott, B. B. 1981. *Jesus: Symbol-Maker for the Kingdom.* Philadelphia.
Smalley, S. S. 1973. Spirit, Kingdom and Prayer in Luke-Acts. *NovT* 15: 59ff.
Smith, J. Z. 1965. The Garments of Shame. *HR* 5: 217–38.
Smith, M. 1971. Zealots and Sicarii: Their Origins and Relations. *HTR* 64: 1–19.
———. 1973a. *Clement of Alexandria and a Secret Gospel of Mark.* Cambridge, MA.
———. 1973b. *The Secret Gospel.* New York.
———. 1978. *Jesus the Magician.* New York.
———. 1982. Clement of Alexandria and Secret Mark: The Score at the End of the First Decade. *HTR* 75: 449–61.
Tannehill, R. C. 1977. The Disciples in Mark: The Function of a Narrative Role. *JR* 57: 134–57.
———. 1986. *The Narrative Unity of Luke-Acts.* Philadelphia.
Theissen, G. 1977. *Sociology of Early Palestinian Christianity.* Philadelphia.
———. 1982. The Strong and Weak in Corinth: A Sociological Analysis of a Theological Quarrel. Pp. 121–43 in *The Social Setting of Pauline Christianity: Essays on Corinth.* Philadelphia.
Vaage, L. 1986. The Kingdom of God in Q. Unpublished paper distributed to the Jesus Seminar, Notre Dame, 1986.
Vassiliadis, P. 1978. The Nature and Extent of the Q Document. *NovT* 20: 49–73.
Vermes, G. 1975. *Jesus the Jew.* London.
———. 1983. *Jesus and the World of Judaism.* London.
Viviano, B. 1987a. The Kingdom of God in the Qumran Literature. Pp. 97–107 in Willis 1987.
———. 1987b. *The Kingdom of God in History.* GNS. Wilmington, DE.
Völkel, M. 1974. Zur Deutung des "Reiches Gottes" bei Lukas. *ZNW* 65: 57–70.
Weiss, J. 1892. *Jesus' Proclamation of the Kingdom of God.* Trans. R. H. Hiers and D. L. Holland. Philadelphia (1971).
Wheelwright, P. 1968. *The Burning Fountain: A Study in the Language of Symbolism.* Bloomington, IN.
Wieser, T. 1962. Kingdom and Church in Luke-Acts. Diss. Union Theological Seminary. New York.
Willis, W. 1987. *The Kingdom of God in 20th-Century Interpretation.* Peabody, MA.

DENNIS C. DULING

KINGDOMS, BOOKS OF. The four books (1–4 Kingdoms) in the LXX which correspond to what is more commonly known as 1–2 Samuel through 1–2 Kings. Also called the Books of Reigns.

KINGFISHER. See ZOOLOGY.

KINGS, BOOK OF 1–2. The eleventh and twelfth books in the Bible (Catholic and Protestant canons). In the Jewish canon Kings is found in the second division of the Hebrew Bible, known as *nĕbîʾîm,* "Prophets," where it constitutes the fourth book of the "Former Prophets," after Joshua, Judges, and Samuel.

A. Title and Place in the Canon
B. Outline
C. Sources and Text
  1. Sources
  2. Text
D. Chronology
E. Literary Structure in Kings and Kings as Literature
  1. Literary Structure
  2. Themes
  3. Characterization
  4. Genres
F. History and Historiography in Kings
  1. Religion in Judah and Israel
  2. Kings and Rulers
  3. Military History
G. Theology
  1. Deity
  2. History

A. Title and Place in the Canon

The division of Kings into two books is an artificial one from the standpoint of contents (the history of King Ahaziah of Israel bridges the gap, 1 Kgs 22:51–2 Kgs 1:18); like the books of Samuel, the two books of Kings were originally one. In the textual tradition of the Hebrew Bible, this practice is attested no earlier than certain medieval manuscripts, and it first appears in print in Daniel Bomberg's *Biblia Rabbinica* (1516–17), explicitly under the influence of non-Jewish versions, presumably the LXX (Greek) and Vg (Latin) (Ginsburg 1966: 930–31; Bedouelle 1989: 78). Likewise, the separation between Samuel and Kings does not reflect a genuine change in subject matter as the narrative of 1 Kings 1–2 forms a natural continuation of the characters and events in 2 Samuel 9–20. Gk mss of the Lucianic recension place the division between Samuel and Kings at 1 Kgs 2:11, after the death of David. Some scholars believe that a change in Gk translators occurs at that point, and conclude therefore that Kings originally began at 1 Kgs 2:12 (Thackeray 1923: 18–19); others find the Lucianic evidence inconclusive and surmise that the text began elsewhere (Tov 1984: 117). The tradition of beginning the book of Kings at 1 Kgs 1:1 is ancient. The earliest known Heb manuscripts of Kings, some leather fragments preserved among the Dead Sea scrolls, were copied no earlier than the 1st century B.C.E. and appear to indicate that the scroll began at 1 Kgs 1:1 (Milik, 1962: 171–72; Shenkel, 1968: 123). The Septuagint presents the books of Samuel and Kings under the rubric of *Basileiōn a-d,* "1–4 Reigns"; Kings comprise the third and fourth books of this unity, corresponding to *tertius, quartus Regum liber* (3 and 4 Kings) of the Vg. In the Peshiṭta (Syriac tradition), "3 Kings" ends at 2 Kgs 2:18 (Gottlieb and Hammershaimb 1976: i).

In Christian and Jewish canons, the books comprising the "Former Prophets" recount a theological history of the nation, beginning with the conquest of the land of Canaan in Joshua and concluding with the destruction of Jerusalem and the Babylonian Exile in 2 Kings. This "history" is couched in terms of a pattern of prophecy and fulfillment that accepts as normative the Law of Moses as promulgated in Deuteronomy.

B. Outline

1. The Reign of Solomon (1 Kgs 1:1–11:43)
   a. Solomon's Securing of the Throne and The Death of David (1 Kgs 1:1–2:46)
   b. Solomon's Reign (1 Kgs 3:1–11:43)
      (1) Solomon the Wise (1 Kgs 3:1–4:34)
      (2) Solomon's Construction of the Temple and His Palaces in Jerusalem (1 Kgs 5:1–7:51)
      (3) Solomon's Dedication of the Temple (1 Kgs 8:1–66)
      (4) Incidents from the Reign of Solomon: Theophany, Forced Levy, Visit of the Queen of Sheba, Economic Exploits (1 Kgs 9:1–10:29)
      (5) Solomon the Foolish (1 Kgs 11:1–43)
2. Synoptic History of the Divided Monarchy to the Fall of the Northern Kingdom (1 Kgs 12:1–2 Kgs 17:41)
   a. Division of Solomon's Kingdom (1 Kgs 12:1–13:34)
      (1) Division of the Kingdom: Rehoboam, King of Judah, and Jeroboam I, King of Israel (1 Kgs 12:1–20)
      (2) Prophecy of Shemaiah in Judah and Response (1 Kgs 12:21–24)
      (3) The Sin of Jeroboam I (1 Kgs 12:25–33)
      (4) Prophetic Polemics Against the Northern Kingdom and the House of Jeroboam I (1 Kgs 13:1–14:20)
   b. Synchronized History of the Divided Monarchy to the Elijah Stories (1 Kgs 14:21–16:34)
      (1) Rehoboam, Abijam, and Asa, Kings of Judah (1 Kgs 14:21–15:24)
      (2) Nadab, Baasha, Elah, Zimri, Omri, and Ahab, Kings of Israel (1 Kgs 15:25–16:34)
   c. The Elijah Cycle (1 Kgs 17:1–2 Kgs 1:18)
      (1) The Elijah Stories: Three-Year Drought, Raising of the Phoenician Widow's Son, Contest on Mount Carmel, Flight to Horeb, Call of Elisha, Episode of Naboth's Vineyard (1 Kgs 17:1–19:21; 21:1–29)
      (2) Prophetic Stories Surrounding the Syro-Israelite Wars: Ben-Hadad, King of Syria; Ahab, King of Israel; Jehoshaphat, King of Judah; the Prophet Micaiah versus the False Prophets (1 Kgs 20:1–43; 22:1–40)
      (3) Jehoshaphat, King of Judah (1 Kgs 22:41–50)
      (4) Ahaziah, King of Israel (1 Kgs 22:51–2 Kgs 1:18)
   d. The Elisha Cycle (2 Kgs 2:1–8:29)
      (1) The Prophetic Succession From Elijah to Elisha (2 Kgs 2:1–25)
      (2) Joram (Jehoram), King of Israel (2 Kgs 3:1–27)
      (3) The Elisha Stories (2 Kgs 4:1–8:15; 9:1–3; 13:14–21)
      (4) Jehoram (Joram) and Ahaziah, Kings of Judah (2 Kgs 8:16–29)
   e. Synchronized History of the Divided Monarchy to the Fall of Israel (2 Kgs 9:1–17:41)
      (1) Jehu, King of Israel (2 Kgs 9:1–10:36)
      (2) Athaliah, Queen of Judah and the Accession and Reign of Joash, King of Judah (2 Kgs 11:1–12:21)
      (3) Jehoahaz and Jehoash, Kings of Israel; the Death of Elisha the Prophet (2 Kgs 13:1–25)
      (4) Amaziah, King of Judah (2 Kgs 14:1–22)
      (5) Jeroboam II, King of Israel (2 Kgs 14:23–29)
      (6) Azariah (Uzziah), King of Judah (2 Kgs 15:1–7)
      (7) Zechariah, Shallum, Menahem, Pekahiah, and Pekah, Kings of Israel: Assyrian Aggression (2 Kgs 15:8–31)
      (8) Jotham and Ahaz, Kings of Judah (2 Kgs 15:32–16:20)
      (9) Hoshea, King of Israel, and the Fall of Israel to the Assyrians; Theological Rationale for the Fall; Samaritan Origins (2 Kgs 17:1–41)
3. The Kingdom of Judah from Hezekiah to the Babylonian Exile (2 Kgs 18:1–25:30)
   a. Hezekiah, King of Judah: Religious Reform and Assyrian Invasion; Isaiah the Prophet (2 Kgs 18:1–20:21)
   b. Manasseh and Amon, Kings of Judah (2 Kgs 21:1–26)
   c. Josiah, King of Judah: Discovery of the Book of the Law and Religious Reform (2 Kgs 22:1–23:30)
   d. Jehoahaz, Jehoiakim, Jehoiachin, and Zedekiah, Kings of Judah: Babylonian Aggression and Fall of Jerusalem (2 Kgs 23:31–25:21)
   e. Judah Under Babylonian Administration: Gedaliah (2 Kgs 25:22–26)
   f. In Babylon, in Exile: Upgrading of Jehoiachin, King of Judah, from Prison to House Arrest (2 Kgs 25:27–30)

C. Sources and Text

1. Sources. The book of Kings deals with events covering roughly 400 years of Palestinian history. Like any historical work, its narrative account is based on a variety of sources, some of which are identified in the text, though most are not. These sources have been subject to sustained editing and literary adaptation, which result in a creative and unique literary composition whose very complexity continues to baffle those who would surgically isolate the original sources from the document called Kings that appears in the Bible. To further complicate matters, it is widely agreed that Kings is but part of a larger composition in the Hebrew Bible conventionally known as the Deuteronomistic History (Deuteronomy–2 Kings) in which the key religio-political ideals of Deuteronomy are used to describe and judge the checkered "history" of the People of Israel, from the conquest of Canaan to the fall of Judah to the Babylonians. It is well to emphasize at the outset that there is no manuscript evidence for a discrete "Deuteronomistic History" or sundry pre-deuteronomistic sources; they are working hypotheses the tentativeness of which is illustrated by the proliferation of theories and concomitant lack of consensus among scholars today.

a. Sources Identified in Kings. Kings makes reference to three sources of information: the "Book of the Deeds of Solomon" (1 Kgs 11:41), the "Book of the Daily Deeds/Chronicles of the Kings of Judah" (1 Kgs 14:29; 15:7, 23; 22:45, etc.), and the "Book of the Daily Deeds/Chronicles of the Kings of Israel" (1 Kgs 14:19; 15:31; 16:5, 14, etc.). Formulaic expressions used when these sources are cited indicate that the biblical information is to be understood as an extract from a larger work; no trace of the corresponding original and independent work is known to exist. Scholars have long assumed that the genre of these sources is comparable to other ANE historical archives such as Egyptian, Persian and Hellenistic daybooks maintained by court functionaries (Van Seters 1981: 175–76).

Again, it is commonly supposed that the kings of Judah and Israel maintained state archives in the form of annals that recorded such events as royal accessions and deaths, military campaigns and invasions, monumental building enterprises, and perhaps records from the state cult, including prophecies and royally sponsored innovations. Actual chronographic records of particular kings with notices of significant political and cultic events are extensively attested for the Neo-Babylonian kings (TCS 5: 70–111). It is also likely that "king-lists," probably analogous to specimens recovered from Mesopotamia, were compiled at some point for the rulers of Judah and Israel. Judging from the heterogeneous information supplied in 1 Kings, one should not automatically assume that the "Book of the Deeds of Solomon" was of the same genre as the two previously mentioned "Books of the Daily Deeds." The former contains an account of Solomon's reign and includes extensive cultic and building data (1 Kgs 6:1–8:66), contradictory figures for teams of forced labor (1 Kgs 5:16 vs. 9:23), lists of high officials and taxation districts (1 Kgs 4:1–19), trade and foreign relations (1 Kgs 5:1–12; 10:1–29); visions and folkloristic accounts of his "wisdom" (1 Kgs 3:3–28; 4:29–34; 9:1–9) and an itemized condemnation and sentence for apostasy (1 Kgs 11:1–40). Efforts to precisely describe the authorship, extent, and genre of these three pre-deuteronomistic sources must remain in the realm of conjecture.

The Talmud ascribes the authorship of Kings to the prophet Jeremiah (*B. Bat.* 15a; Montgomery and Gehman *Kings* ICC, 1), in keeping with a tendency to legitimate scriptural sources by attributing them to notable "literary" figures in the Hebrew Bible (compare Solomon). Attempts to identify the occupation of the author or authors of Kings ("scribe," "priest," "court official," "Wisdom teacher," etc.) are part and parcel with the task of identifying the sources, the editor(s) of the sources, and their original purpose or genre ("king-list," "prophetic history," "temple records," "programmatic reform document," etc.).

b. Source criticism. Wellhausen, building on the insights of Kuenen, argued that composition of a Deuteronomistic History (DtrH) from a welter of pre-existing sources was inspired by the religious reform of Josiah (ca. 621), which was itself motivated by the discovery of the book of Deuteronomy hidden in the temple. The tradition that the "book of the law" which was found in the Jerusalem temple at the time of Josiah was part of the canonical Deuteronomy is at least as ancient as Origen and entered the modern critical arena through de Wette's dissertation of 1805. According to Wellhausen, the compiler of DtrH, for the book of Kings, created a chronological framework by inserting a formula at the beginning and conclusion of the narrative accounts of the Judahite and Israelite kings, thus synchronizing their reigns and providing other information of a historical nature, in addition to giving a "verdict" regarding the cultic purity of their reign. The compiler was also responsible for a number of extended narratives in the form of commentaries which reflect the judgments of history in accordance with the religious tenets of Deuteronomy, specifically, the uncompromising demands for Yahwistic monotheism. Since the "glamor" of Josiah's reform colored the balance of the composition, the major redaction of DtrH, including Kings, probably took place no later than 600 B.C.E. (Wellhausen 1889: 298–301). An "appendix," carrying the history of the Judahite monarchy from the death of Josiah to the release of Jehoiachin from prison ca. 561 B.C.E., and other features scattered throughout Kings indicate a redaction during the Exile. Wellhausen related the Exilic redaction of Kings to the activity of the Priestly source in the "Hexateuch" (Genesis-Joshua). Much of the source-critical work dealing with DtrH by Wellhausen and scholars influenced by him was concerned with demonstrating the continuity of Pentateuchal sources from Joshua through 2 Kings ("JEDP").

Contrary to Wellhausen's belief, deuteronomistic language and theology is diagnostic neither of authorship nor of date of composition. Close parallels to "deuteronomistic theology" can be found in the Mesha Stone (Moab, 9th century) and Assurbanipal's annals (Assyria, 7th century). Deuteronomistic catchphrases and theology are readily imitated, as witness Tobit, 1 Maccabees, and *Jubilees,* Jewish texts of the Persian and Hellenistic period.

According to Noth, Deuteronomy through 2 Kings was authored by an individual or individuals from the point of view of the Deuteronomic Law. Earlier collections of pre-deuteronomistic narratives that dealt with key moments and figures in the history of Israel were assembled into a larger unified work, DtrH, during the Exile by a Judean author. Noth's analysis concluded that the sources identified by Wellhausen in Genesis through Numbers (J,E,P) had no intrinsic continuity with those found in Joshua through Kings; the general theological coherence and repetitive phraseology in Deuteronomy through 2 Kings led him to attribute it to the work of a single editor (*NDH,* 9–12). Although scholars before Noth had posited an Exilic redaction for Kings (König 1893: 267–69), none had made such an elegant argument for the unity of the composition. Evidence for this single work stems primarily from a linguistic analysis of repeated phrases and terminology, and secondarily from the chronological schema and the series of speeches and evaluations which reflect the theology of Deuteronomy. The Deuteronomistic Historian (DTR) was at his greatest liberty to express his theological evaluation in the book of Kings. The inconsistencies in DtrH that fuel the redaction-critical approach were attributed by Noth to DTR's respect for his sources (Noth NDH, 84), as well as to materials inserted by post-DTR redactors which conflicted with the underlying DtrH.

Childs (*IOTS,* 286–87) registers three major critiques of Noth: (1) objection to the proposition that DtrH was composed by a single author with a unified historical and theological outlook; (2) the problem with the dating of DTR; the majority opinion at the moment is pushing for a considerable portion of preexilic redaction and perhaps authorship; and (3) dissatisfaction with Noth's thesis regarding DTR's supposed concentration on the negative lesson of history. Von Rad, for example, championed the view that the dynastic promise to David informs the entire work, concluding with an optimistic notice of the release of Jehoiachin from prison, while H. W. Wolff (1975: 90–100) argues that the theme of the necessity of repentance and "return" to Yahweh is central to the author.

Smend and his followers propose a threefold redactional process for the deuteronomistic history during the Exile. Unlike Noth, the Smend school locates the inconsistencies and perceived internal contradictions in DtrH (Smend's DtrG) in the activity of two redactors with unified theological agendas (Smend 1978: 120–25; 134–39). The first, DtrP, opposed the monarchy (contrary to DtrH) and added both prophetic comments and extended speeches to DtrH (Dietrich 1972: 107–109; 134–48). Likewise, the final redactor, DtrN, made contributions which attempted to moderate the anti-monarchic stance of DtrP by insisting that the Davidic dynasty would endure if the sacred Law was maintained (Veijola 1975: 138–42). The presupposition which guides the redaction-critical efforts of this school entails the assumption that DtrH was without internal contradictions as a theological and historical work. Contradictions present in the canonical Kings are explained as "additions" of two exilic redactors at odds with the thought of DtrH, and assumes both DtrP and DtrN are subject to detection, with varying degrees of certainty, by the modern redaction critic. Halpern challenges the Smend school and similar approaches by posing the question why, if the goal of the later redactors DtrP and DtrN was to reform the message of the source, they did not completely rewrite it instead of juxtaposing conflicting narratives (1988: 112).

Cross's enormously popular thesis represents a revival of the critical assumptions of Wellhausen and Kuenen that dominated the field up to the publication of Noth's seminal study. For Cross, DtrH was composition of a redactor during the reign of Josiah, king of Judah; it originally ended with 2 Kgs 23:25. This redactor, whom Cross identifies as Dtr^1, emphasized a "call" for the "return" to Yahwistic monotheism, the unconditional promise of eternal kingship made to the Davidic lineage, and the consequences of the "sin of Jeroboam" for the Northern Kingdom (Cross *CMHE,* 278–85; 287–89). Noth's understanding of the emphasis on national judgment in DtrH is challenged by Cross's notion of Dtr^1 as embodying a call for return to Yahwistic monotheism under Josiah and a reunification of the Divided Monarchy. Dtr^2, the exilic redactor(s) that updated Dtr^1, made the promise of "eternal" kingship to the Davidids conditional on their fidelity to Yahweh, thus providing a theological retreat for the political disasters of the Exile. Dtr^2 blames the fall of Jerusalem on the inexpiable sin of Manasseh, a feint by which the redactor could "salvage" the theology of the Josianic Reform without implicating the kings of Judah that followed Josiah with abrogating his efforts at reform (*CMHE,* 285–87; Halpern 1988: 113–14). The viability of Cross's Dtr^1 rides on his construction of the religious and political aims of the Josianic reform and its chronology; any challenge to the theory's historicity would seriously undermine its credibility.

Several studies have investigated the possibility of predeuteronomistic redaction in Kings, that is, the nature and extent of the editorial work on the sources available to DTR prior to the composition of DtrH. Jepsen believed that ca. 580 B.C.E. a priestly redactor composed a history of the monarchy extending from Solomon to Hezekiah by combining "political" sources which contained a record of Solomon's rule, a synchronized history of the Divided Kingdom, and a "priestly" record from Jerusalem (Jepsen 1956: 10, 22–23, 106). Primarily on the basis of lexical evidence and regnal formulas, Helga Weippert seeks to demonstrate a threefold redaction of Kings. The first redaction predated DtrH, for it covered the history of the Divided Kingdom from Jehoshaphat of Judah and Joram of Israel down to Ahaz of Judah and Hoshea of Israel; she concludes it was compiled during the reign of Hezekiah (Weippert 1972: 319–23). Lemaire, building on the work of Weippert, finds evidence of a composition written at the time of Jehoshaphat in the mid-9th century; he proposes seven levels of redaction in Kings (1986: 232).

The sizable corpus of prophetic narratives in Samuel-Kings has suggested to some the existence of a pre-deuteronomistic "prophetic history." Garbini, analyzing several literary motifs, posits the existence of a narrative created during the reign of Jehu of Israel. Citing examples from Judges 9 through 2 Kings 10, he concludes that it was composed by a prophetic school opposed to the monarchy (Garbini 1979: 31–35). Building on the research of McCarter and Veijola, McKenzie offers another theory regarding an 8th-century prophetic source, arguing that most of 1 Kgs 17–2 Kgs 13 was composed by a "Prophetic Historian" (McKenzie 1985: 216).

Both Hoffmann and Van Seters understand DtrH to be a unified work produced by an author living in the postexilic period. Hoffmann sees cultic reform as the major theme of DtrH; the composition was intended as an object lesson to foster religious conformity within the postexilic Jewish community by rehearsing the history of the political disasters that befell the people of Israel whenever they compromised their fidelity to Yahweh. Hoffmann is pessimistic about the possibility of isolating pre-deuteronomistic sources in DtrH due to the author's thoroughgoing integration and stylization of his sources (1980: 316–17). Van Seters studies the compositional technique of DTR in light of the historiography of Herodotus and parallels from the ANE. He sees the inconsistencies in DtrH as reflecting the author's tolerance of inconsistency in his sources (Van Seters 1983: 258–64; 320–21). Rofé finds evidence for a postexilic dating of the accounts of Ahab's Syrian wars and the Naboth's Vineyard incident (1 Kgs 20:1–21:1–16); he argues that the formation of the Former Prophets is more adequately viewed as a process lasting some 400 years, from the 8th century to the latter end of the Persian period (1988: 103).

Peckham describes two levels of redaction in DtrH. The first (Dtr^1) is pre-deuteronomistic and preexilic in composition; it focused on the Davidic dynasty and the law of centralization and extended from Deuteronomy through 2 Kings 19:37 (Hezekiah, king of Judah). The second redaction (Dtr^2) culminated in Genesis through 2 Kgs 25, building on forms of the classic Pentateuchal sources J, E, and P: "the principal author and historian is Dtr^2, who rewrote these sources as the history of Israel from creation to the fall of Jerusalem" (Peckham 1985: 1). Other recent studies attempt to relate the formation of the Pentateuch to the activity of DTR (O'Brien 1989: 18, n. 54). Provan, on the basis of the regnal formulas and the treatment of the *bāmôt* ("high places, sanctuaries"), also posits a twofold redaction of DtrH: the first, probably Josianic in date, begins with Judges 17–21 or 1 Samuel 1 and concludes with 2 Kings 19 (Hezekiah); its major theme is cult centralization, and it concludes with the portrayal of Hezekiah as a second David. The second redaction was exilic and endeavored to bring the history of Judah up to date by blaming the Exile on the apostasy of the Judean kings (Provan 1988: 171–73).

The burgeoning diversity of conjectures regarding sources and dating does not inspire confidence in the historical reliability of source- and redaction-critical efforts in Kings. One detects a current readiness on the part of many scholars to isolate pre-deuteronomistic redaction (= sources) in Kings; there is, at the same, an impressive scholarly constituency arguing for a postexilic dating for much of the Former Prophets.

2. Text. Textual criticism has as "its highest achievable end the reconstruction of the biblical text in the form in which it was current during a certain period" (Mulder 1988: 103). It is likely that the MT represents but one of the Hebrew texts in circulation during the 4th and 3d centuries B.C.E. Textual criticism is useful for correcting errors in the transmission of the MT and establishing the textual traditions behind the versions of the Hebrew Bible; there is no justification, however, for employing the tools of textual criticism to recover the "autograph" or "Urtext" of any part of the Hebrew Bible. Normally, the salient manuscripts are limited to Heb, Gk, Aram, Syr, Lat, and, in the case of the Pentateuch, Samaritan.

a. General Textual History of the Hebrew Bible. The discovery of the Dead Sea scrolls in 1947 pushed the date of the earliest known manuscripts of the Hebrew Bible back a thousand years to the 3d century B.C.E. Surprisingly, textual analysis of these manuscripts demonstrated that major variants in text traditions, assumed to have been created by the rigorous standardization of canonic texts in Jewish and Christian circles around the 1st and 2d centuries A.D., were actually well developed centuries earlier. Variations from the MT attested principally in the Gk versions preserve a record of the development of the pre-MT of the Hebrew Bible (Talmon *QHBT,* 1–5). It should be emphasized that the "autograph text" of Kings, in the unlikely event that one ever existed at all, in light of the documented plethora of sources and editorial hands, would perforce date to a period preceding the divergent textual traditions preserved in the Dead Sea manuscripts.

b. Manuscript Tradition of Kings: Heb, Gk, Lat, Aram, Syr. The Heb manuscripts of Kings recovered from Qumran, unlike the extensive remains of the Samuel scrolls, consist of a series of leather and papyrus fragments that rarely add up to a discernible column from the original scroll. Texts identified and published to date include, from cave 5Q, 1 Kgs 1:1, 16–17, 27–37 (Milik 1962: 171–72); from 6Q, 1 Kgs 3:12–14; 12:28–31; 22:28–31; 2 Kgs 5:26; 6:32; 7:8–10; 7:20–8:5; 9:1–2; 10:19–21 (Baillet 1962: 107–12). Unpublished portions of a scroll from 4Q of 1 Kgs 7 and 8 reportedly remain in the possession of Frank Moore Cross (Shenkel 1968: 123, n. 14). Unfortunately, the paucity of Kings manuscript attestations from Qumran provides scant hope for resolving the current scholarly debate over the value of the Gk witnesses for correcting the MT; it is incautious to extrapolate, from Qumran, the same textual history for Kings from what is known of Samuel.

The findings at Qumran have served to reemphasize the importance of the Gk witnesses for research on the early textual tradition of the Hebrew Bible. An influential theory championed by Cross and his students is that of the "three local recensions texts" to explain the textual history of the Hebrew Bible between the 5th and 1st centuries B.C.E. Cross postulates a "proto-Hebrew" text of the Bible as the source of Palestinian and Babylonian recensions for use by local Jewish communities no later than 400 B.C.E. The Palestinian recension was, ultimately, the textual source of the Samaritan Pentateuch, whereas the Babylonian recension culminated in the "proto-MT." The earliest Gk versions were translations of a Heb text prepared for Egyptian Jews from the Palestinian recension. Texts based on the Palestinian recension are "characterized by conflation, glosses, synoptic additions, and other evidence of intense scribal activity" (Cross *QHBT,* 283). Cross claims that the LXX version of Samuel-Kings was prepared from an Egyptian Heb text that gained independence from its parent Palestinian tradition not later than 300 B.C.E. and which was "updated" in the 2d or 1st century B.C.E. by correcting it against Heb manuscripts in the Palestinian textual tradition. This "updating" of the LXX is recoverable today in part from "proto-Lucian" manuscripts. Cross contends that, since the Gk manuscript tradition that attests to the "proto-Lucianic" recension of the Hebrew Bible preserves readings from a translation of a Heb text predating the final form of the MT, and, since the MT of Samuel-Kings shows extensive textual corruption, "proto-Lucianic" readings may be profitably used to reconstruct a more pristine text for these books (Cross *QHBT,* 191–92;

Klein 1974: 27–50). This approach has been most assiduously applied to the textual study of Samuel because of the extensive Heb manuscript corpus from Qumran (4QSam), a substantial portion of which agrees with "proto-Lucian" against the MT and the LXX.

Cross's "three local recensions texts" theory has come under heavy criticism in recent scholarship, due in part to its presuppositions regarding the scribal activities of Babylonian Jews from the Persian Period to the Common Era, of which virtually nothing is known, and to the theory's over-simplification. According to Tov, in addition to the Heb text-forms which correspond to the LXX, the Samaritan Pentateuch, and the MT which has been found at Qumran (Cross's Egyptian, Palestinian, and Babylonian recensional traditions, respectively), one and possibly three other text-forms have been identified (Mulder 1988: 102, 104). The utility of "proto-Lucian" for textual criticism of the Hebrew Bible was recognized long before the discovery of the Dead Sea scrolls, and therefore is not dependent on the validity of the "three local recensions texts" theory (Marcos 1984: 169; Tov 1988: 186–87).

There is considerable ongoing debate about the nature of the Gk versions of Kings and their usefulness for textual criticism. The LXX varies from the MT in both arrangement and content; compare the order of 1 Kgs 4–11 and 20–21 (LXX) (Swete 1914: 232). The LXX account of Jeroboam I and the division of the United Monarchy (1 Kgs 12:24a–z) supplies novel and sometimes contradictory information to the account found in the MT and elsewhere in the LXX. The summarizing "miscellanies" regarding Solomon's reign found after 1 Kgs 2:35 and 2:46 (LXX) have no consecutive counterparts in the MT. As an illustration of the use of the LXX and "proto-Lucian" for text-critical work in Kings, consider 1 Kgs 22:32 "and they turned against him to fight, and Jehoshaphat cried out" (MT); "and they surrounded him to fight, and Jehoshaphat cried out" (LXX); "and they surrounded him to fight, and Jehoshaphat cried out, and the Lord saved him" ("proto-Lucian"); 1 Chr 18:31 "and they surrounded him to fight, and Jehoshaphat cried out, and Yahweh saved him" (MT) (Klein 1974: 50). While "proto-Lucian" Kings agrees with MT Chronicles against MT and LXX Kings, little is gained by accepting the longer text over the shorter.

There are weighty objections to the rather optimistic view that text-critical work favoring Gk versions can often restore a more "pristine" Heb text for Kings. Substantial departures from the MT, such as 1 Kgs 12:24a–z (LXX), generally provide better evidence of midrashic reworkings of the Heb text than solid clues for "textual archaeology" (Gooding 1967, 1976; Evans 1983). Gooding in particular has argued that the extensive rearrangement of the text found in the LXX (and "proto-Lucian") reflects a desire on the part of the translator to portray Solomon as wise, greatly enhancing the evil character of Jeroboam I while tending to whitewash the flaws of David, Solomon, and, curiously, Ahab (Gooding 1969). The Lucianic reading of 2 Kgs 17:2 "corrects" the MT's slightly positive evaluation of Hoshea, the last king of Israel, making him the most wicked Israelite king of all and therefore patently deserving of a doomed kingdom (Burney 1903: 329). It would be rash to assume that wherever "proto-Lucian" and other witnesses to the oldest traditions of Gk translations of Kings diverge from the MT the latter should be brought into conformity with the former. The integrity of textual criticism depends upon examination of each verse, variant by variant, using all versional evidence at one's disposal, raising the possibility at each step that a given textual variant may be due to theological or literary polishing, as well as the usual alterations due to the accumulation of errors and erring corrections.

The OL version of Kings was based primarily, though not exclusively, on the Gk translations, and provides an important witness to Lucianic readings (Burney 1903: xxxv–xxxvi; Trebolle Barrera 1986: 94; Kedar 1988: 308–11). The Vg, Jerome's authoritative Lat translation of the Old and New Testament (ca. 390–405 C.E.), is based on a Heb text identical or very similar to the MT for the books of Kings, though in places it is evident Jerome was influenced by the OL and various earlier Gk versions (White 1902: 883–85; Driver *NHT,* liv). Claims that he was particularly dependent on the Gk version known as Symmachus are exaggerated (Kedar 1988: 323).

The Targum (= Aramaic translation) of Former Prophets, Targum Jonathan, is clearly based on the same textual tradition as the MT; unlike most Targums of the Hebrew Bible, it generally avoids extended midrashic expansions of the underlying text, adhering instead to a literalistic style of translation. The basic translation of Targum Jonathan was probably made before 135 C.E., in Palestine, although redaction may have continued in Babylonia up to the Arab conquest (Burney 1903: xxxi–xxxii; Harrington and Saldarini 1987: 3–4; Smolar and Aberbach 1983: xxviii).

The Peshiṭta (Syriac version) of Former Prophets is not attested in manuscript before the 6th century C.E. In general, it is thought that the Heb textual tradition underlying the Peshiṭta is very close to or identical with the MT. Some scholars stress the possibility that, for Peshiṭta Pentateuch and possibly other portions of the Bible, translators worked from Targums and not directly from the MT. Berlinger, in one of the few studies devoted exclusively to Peshiṭta Kings, adduced evidence that the translator consulted Targum Jonathan in difficult places (Dirksen 1988: 258, 291; on manuscript families in Peshiṭta Kings and their chronology, see Dirksen 1989).

D. Chronology

1 and 2 Kings offers a variety of chronological notices regarding the reigns of the kings of Judah and Israel and contemporary events in the surrounding kingdoms. The rigid regnal formulas that give the work its distinctive historical ambience provide two complementary systems of dating: (1) the total span of years covered by the reign of each king, e.g., "Amaziah the son of Ahab . . . reigned two years over Israel" (1 Kgs 22:51), and (2) a synchronism between the accession date of the king of one kingdom and the contemporary regnal date of the other, e.g. "Amaziah . . . began to reign over Israel in Samaria in the seventeenth year of Jehoshaphat, king of Judah . . ." (1 Kgs 22:51). Other dates include "internal" developments, such as the time from the Exodus to the founding of the Jerusalem Temple by Solomon (1 Kgs 6:1), international events, e.g., Pharaoh Shishak's invasion of Palestine

(1 Kgs 14:25), and the age of a king at the time of accession, e.g., "Jehoshaphat was thirty-five years old when he began to reign . . ." (1 Kgs 22:42).

A few minutes' labor with a hand calculator will convince the reader not only of serious discrepancies between tallies of the individual regnal years of the kings of Judah and Israel but of outright contradictions between different citations of the same chronological event. For example, 143 years and seven months is the total for the reigns of the Israelite kings from Jehu through Hoshea; for the corresponding reigns in Judah, the tally is 166 years. Joram (Jehoram) of Israel began his reign in the eighteenth year of Jehoshaphat of Judah in 2 Kgs 3:1. In 2 Kgs 1:17, the same Joram is said to begin his reign in the second year of the son of Jehoshaphat. Omri came to the throne of Israel in the thirty-first year of Asa of Judah and is said to have reigned twelve years (1 Kgs 16:23). Omri's son is said to have become king in the thirty-eighth year of Asa (1 Kgs 16:29); but 31 years + 12 years = 38 years. Furthermore, Asa reportedly ruled only forty-one years (1 Kgs 15:10). If the information in 1 Kgs 15:10 is accurate, Asa had been dead at least a year before Omri's son ascended the throne.

Critical scholarship has adopted three major approaches to the vexatious arithmetic of Kings. The first operates on the suspicion that the dates were a product of free composition and numerological speculation; these dates were fabricated to fill in a largely fictional scheme of cultic and national "history" extending from creation to the Exile (Genesis–2 Kings) and to endow the text with an air of historical verisimilitude (Begrich 1929: 10–15). Few modern scholars would unreservedly subscribe to this approach; most would claim that the number of correspondences between datable ANE and biblical events outweighs the limited evidence of purely typological schematization like 1 Kgs 6:1. A less draconian form of this stratagem assumes that the author(s) in their lack of concern with precise chronography rounded off the figures of the reigns at will.

The second approach, which has won widespread acceptance today, accepts as axiomatic that the figures of the MT, or the textual traditions underlying it, are basically correct; this is to say, the regnal dates in Kings can somehow be made to correspond to an absolute chronology (B.C.E.). There are essentially three ways this axiom has resulted in concrete scholarship. (1) The first method maintains that discrepant figures are due to textual corruptions and subsequent scribal efforts at correction. The usual solution is to amend the text by accepting the accuracy of a given date and, from that Archimedean point, "adjusting" all figures perceived to be in error until a coherent sequence of reigns for each kingdom is established (Burney 1903: xli–xliv). Practitioners of this method frequently rely on the handful of events that can be more or less correlated with extra-biblical sources, e.g. the Battle of Qarqar, in which Ahab, King of Israel, participated (853 B.C.E.); the first Fall of Jerusalem to the Babylonians (March 16, 597 B.C.E.). (2) The second method assumes that regnal years were reckoned from different calendars in use during the Divided Monarchy; one began at Tishri, the indigenous autumnal New Year, the other in the Spring (Nisan); there is an ongoing debate as to whether Israel used one system and Judah another, and if so, how the chronology of Kings is affected (Thiele 1983: 51–54). In accordance with Assyro-Babylonian practice, the regnal dates of a king were calculated from the date of the first New Year that fell within his reign until his death; the days, weeks, or months of his reign that elapsed before that first New Year were not formally ascribed to his reign. It is maintained that many discrepancies in the MT can be explained by breaking the silence of the biblical text regarding regnal antedating and postdating, and by noting when the change occurred from a Tishri to a Nisan calendar (Hayes and Hooker 1988: 12–15; 87–88). While it is generally accepted that the earliest calendar in use during the Divided Monarchy was based on a Tishri New Year and that Nisan dating was used in Palestine during the Persian Period, there is no compelling biblical indication that a formal change in calendar occurred during the reign of Josiah (contra Hayes and Hooker 1988: 87) or any other king of Judah or Israel (Mowinckel 1932: 175); this method of reconciling the regnal dates in Kings must be viewed as highly speculative. (3) The third and last major methodological variation within this approach assumes the existence of co-regencies (when a king and his successor held joint rule), most plausibly for the reigns of David and Solomon (1 Kgs 1:38–40; 2:10–12) and Ahaziah (Uzziah) and Jotham (2 Kgs 15:5); the years of the co-regency were ascribed to both kings, thus throwing off the total (Begrich 1929: 44–54). Thiele identifies a total of 9 co-regencies and overlapping reigns for the kings of Judah and Israel (1983: 61–65). Although co-regencies are attested at various times and places in the ANE, a lack of consensus regarding their indication in the biblical text limits the usefulness of this assumption for disentangling the chronology of Kings. More sophisticated studies employ all of these approaches.

Proponents of the third approach to dating in Kings acknowledge the seriousness of the chronological incoherence of the MT but argue that the OG version bears witness to a separate Heb textual tradition that is primary; the chronology in the MT is derivative and secondary (Burney 1903: xli; Shenkel 1968: 37–42; 109–11). Critics of this approach focus on the selective use made by its advocates of the Gk textual tradition, e.g., from Omri of Israel (1 Kgs 16:23) to Joram of Israel (2 Kgs 1:18 [LXX]). Critics also stress the strong possibility that the internal coherence of this tradition reflects a later effort at making sense of the same or a similar chronological system preserved in the MT, and provides no independent witness (Thiele 1983: 88–101).

Although chronological information useful for ordering events and determining length of reigns is found in Kings, efforts to comprehensively convert the dates in Kings to absolute dating (B.C.E.) yield results which are approximate at best. A fact lost sight of in most studies of chronology in Kings is the nature of the text: it is a *theological* history; a precise and accurate exposition of historical events was not the primary concern of the authors. For example, Kings can distort its sources in the service of making a theological point. Sennacherib, the Assyrian king whose emissary blasphemed Yahweh, dies in the temple of his god at the hands of his sons immediately following his siege of Jerusalem (= 701 B.C.E.) according to 2 Kgs

19:36–37; in fact, the historical Sennacherib died in 681 B.C.E. Literary juxtaposition situates the rise of Solomon's "adversaries" *(śāṭān)* (Hadad the Edomite, Rezon the Syrian, and Jeroboam the Ephraimite) in his sinful old age (1 Kgs 11:14–40). These political scourges expressed proof of Yahweh's displeasure over Solomon's cultic infidelity in his dotage (1 Kgs 11:9–13), whereas, as historical threats to the political order, they probably dated anywhere from Solomon's accession to his death.

E. Literary Structure in Kings and Kings as Literature

1 and 2 Kings has earned an undeserved reputation as a pedestrian assemblage of names and numbers. The composition as a whole gives evidence of meticulous attention to detail through a unifying structure and schematization of themes; it contains a wealth of character sketches, nuanced dialogue, and dramatic scenes of a high order of literary finesse that reward a sensitive reading.

1. Literary Structure. 1–2 Kings is organized chronologically by reign. The distinct historiographic format of Kings derives from the stereotyped regnal formula which brackets the entry and exit of most monarchs on the historical scene. As a literary device, the repetitive enumeration of the vital statistics of the kings of Judah and Israel, dynast and usurper alike, reinforces the inexorable march of their kingdoms toward the fulfillment of prophesied doom. For the kings of Israel, a representative accession formula is:

> In the *x* year of PN (proper name), king of Judah, PN the son of PN began to reign over all Israel at Tirzah/Samaria, and reigned for *x* years. He did what was evil in the eyes of Yahweh.

Jehu is given no accession formula (2 Kgs 9–10:36). For the death of an Israelite king, with minor variations,

> Now the rest of the deeds of PN, and all that he did, are they not written in the Book of the Daily Deeds of the Kings of Israel? And PN slept with his fathers, and was buried at Tirzah/Samaria; and PN (his son) reigned in his stead.

For the accession of a king of Judah, the formula reads

> PN the son of PN began to reign over Judah in the *x* year of PN king of Israel. PN was *x* years old when he began to reign, and he reigned *x* years in Jerusalem. His mother's name was PN the daughter of PN. And PN did what was good/evil in the eyes of Yahweh.

Athaliah the Omride is given no accession formula (2 Kgs 11:1–20). For the death of a king of Judah,

> Now the rest of the deeds of PN, and all that he did, are they not written in the Book of the Daily Deeds of the Kings of Judah? PN slept with his fathers, and was buried with his fathers in the city of David his father; and PN his son reigned in his stead.

In overall structure, the contents of Kings are organized into three sections: the reign of Solomon (1 Kgs 1:1–11:43), a synoptic history of the Divided Monarchy to the fall of the Northern Kingdom (1 Kgs 12:1–2 Kgs 17:41), and the Kingdom of Judah alone, from Hezekiah to the Babylonian Exile (2 Kgs 18:1–25:30). Savran (1987: 148–49) describes a chiastic structure of leading themes that lends the work a dynamic literary and theological unity:

A	Solomon/United Monarchy	1 Kgs 1:1–11:25
B	Jeroboam/Rehoboam; division of kingdom	1 Kgs 11:26–14:31
C	kings of Judah/Israel	1 Kgs 15:1–16:22
D	Omride dynasty; rise and fall of Baal cult in Israel and Judah	1 Kgs 16:23–2 Kgs 12
C′	kings of Judah/Israel	2 Kgs 13–16
B′	fall of Northern Kingdom	2 Kings 17
A′	kingdom of Judah	2 Kings 18–25

The framing sections *A* and *A′* focus on the rise and fall of the Davidic dynasty (the promising accession of Solomon [1 Kgs 3–10] in contrast to the inglorious fates of Zedekiah and Jehoiachin [2 Kgs 24–25]) and the parallel fortunes of the national shrine in Jerusalem (the founding of the Temple by Solomon [1 Kgs 6–8] versus its desecration by Manasseh [2 Kgs 21], including a brief repristinization by Josiah [2 Kgs 22–23] and systematic destruction by the Babylonians [2 Kgs 25]).

Sections *B* and *B′* mimic the fate of Judah as they chronicle the genesis of the "sin of Jeroboam" and its divinely ordained outcome in the fall of the Northern Kingdom. Jeroboam, chosen king by God through prophetic proxy, fatally poisons his legacy by consecrating the notorious golden calves as a breakaway cult for his newly founded kingdom (1 Kgs 11:35–39; 12:25–33). The Northern Kingdom suffered its misfortune on account of the "sin of Jeroboam" (2 Kgs 17:21–23); like her sister nation, Judah, she was laid waste and led into exile by a Mesopotamian superpower. Sections *C* and *C′* dwell on the warlike relations between Israel and Judah through most of the Divided Monarchy; chronologically, the balance of their history as competing states is compressed into these five pithy chapters.

Section *D* is the literary pivot of the work; roughly forty years of history, one-tenth of the total covered in Kings, occupies over one-third of the chapters in 1–2 Kings. At issue in this crucial section is the history of the royal sponsorship of the Baal cult in Israel and Judah and the prophetic and priestly response. The Baal cult is founded by the ruling Omrides under Phoenician influence in a manner reminiscent of Jeroboam's apostasy; ultimately it is violently extirpated in Israel at prophetic initiative (2 Kings 9–10) and, in Judah, under the leadership of a priest (2 Kings 11). The Elijah and Elisha cycles (1 Kgs 17:1–2 Kgs 8:29) are extended collections of miracle stories that pit the faithful prophets of Yahweh against the idolatrous policies of Israel; whether the prophets lead the king to military triumph or humiliatingly denounce his crimes, the superiority of the "men of God" to the forces of the crown is never in question. As Savran observes, the depiction of the prophetic succession from Elijah to Elisha, at the heart of this section (2 Kings 2), is unique in the Hebrew Bible and underscores the enduring prophetic "mission" bearing the irresistible Word of God to the fluctuating succession of temporal monarchs (1987: 149).

2. Themes. a. "Right Cult" versus "Wrong Cult." Major speeches and dramatic confrontations in Kings, such as Solomon's dedicatory prayer (1 Kgs 8:23–60), the *ex eventu* prophecy against Jeroboam (1 Kgs 13:1–10), Elijah's contest with the prophets of Baal on Mt. Carmel (1 Kgs 18:20–40), the fall of the Northern Kingdom (2 Kgs 17:7–18) and the Rabshakeh's address to Jerusalem (2 Kgs 18:19–25; 27–35), center on the opposition between the stringent demands of monotheistic Yahwism and competing religious traditions. The ecumenical spirit is utterly condemned. The king of Judah who wins highest marks after the archetypal king David is Josiah, whose meritorious conduct centered on his ejection of non-Yahwistic paraphernalia and practices from the Temple and who reinstituted the Passover (2 Kgs 23:1–25). The worst king was Manasseh, who viciously "made Judah to sin with his idols" (2 Kgs 21:11) by promoting a plethora of non-Yahwistic religious practices. The fundamental and ultimately fatal illegitimacy of the Northern Kingdom is due to the "sin of Jeroboam," that is, a national cult neither purely Yahwistic (by the standards of DTR) nor centralized in Jerusalem.

b. Jerusalem Temple. The object of the cult was Yahweh; "the city which thou [Yahweh] has chosen, and the house which I [Solomon] have built for thy name" is Jerusalem and its Temple (1 Kgs 8:48). Half of Solomon's reign in 1 Kings is taken up with the building preparation, description, and dedication of the Temple (5:1–9:9). Its construction demonstrates Solomon's obedience to Yahweh and the fulfillment of Yahweh's promise to David. In Kings, the Temple which contains the Ark of the Covenant concretely symbolizes the reciprocal covenant between the descendants of David and Yahweh, namely, that in exchange for the exclusive worship of Yahweh he (Yahweh) would preserve the Kingdom of Judah. The violation of the Temple's covenantal function by Manasseh's introduction of non-Yahwistic cults is credited with its destruction by the Babylonians as divinely sanctioned punishment (2 Kgs 21:10–15; 23:26–27).

c. Prophecy and Fulfillment. In contrast to the prophetic corpus in the Hebrew Bible, virtually every prophecy (by a true prophet) in Kings is pointedly linked with its fulfillment in the realm of history. The repeated actualization of the prophetic word of God in the face of political opposition serves to drive home the theological lessons of the author. Four prophecies dominate the work: (1) the promise made to David by Nathan the prophet that a descendent shall rule over his kingdom and build a temple to Yahweh (2 Sam 7:11–16) (fulfilled by the accession of Solomon to the throne and the construction of the Jerusalem Temple); (2) the prophet Ahijah's prediction of the division of the United Monarchy by reason of Solomon's apostasy (1 Kgs 11:29–39); (3) the prophet Ahijah's prediction of the fall and exile of Israel as due to the "sin of Jeroboam" (1 Kgs 14:15–16); (4) the fall and exile of Judah, predicted by the prophet Isaiah (2 Kgs 20:17–18) and the prophetess Huldah (2 Kgs 22:16–17) (Savran 1987: 161). The famous *ex eventu* prophecy in 1 Kgs 13:1–10, supposedly uttered at the time of Jeroboam I, forecast Josiah's "cult reform" at Bethel some three hundred years later and is melodramatically drawn to Josiah's attention in 2 Kgs 23:16–18.

d. Dynastic Promise. The promise made to David in 2 Sam 7:11–13, that Yahweh will establish the throne of his descendants "forever," is made conditional on the conduct of the king in 1 Kgs 9:4–7 and is used to justify the persistence of the nation through external dangers and cultic defections. The restructuring of the original prophecy transforms the destruction of the Southern Kingdom into an object lesson illustrating the horrifying consequence of royal disloyalty to Yahweh (2 Kgs 21:10–15). The idealized figure of David, a paragon of fidelity to Yahweh, is held up as a template for the reigns of several kings and as a summary judgment in their regnal formula: "and he [Josiah] did what was right in the eyes of Yahweh, and walked in all the way of David his father" (2 Kgs 22:2).

3. Characterization. a. Yahweh. In Kings, Yahweh speaks in Deuteronomic theology, whether imparted directly (1 Kgs 3:11–14; 9:3–9; 2 Kgs 23:27) or through the lips of the prophets (1 Kgs 11:31–39; 13:3; 14:7–11; etc.). Unlike the two-dimensional human personae in Kings whose emotions and motivations are rarely described, the mind and feelings of Yahweh are unambiguously transparent to the author. Yahweh is pleased (1 Kgs 3:10), angry (1 Kgs 11:9, etc.), or jealous (1 Kgs 14:22). He is moved to act out of loyalty or concern (1 Kgs 11:12; 2 Kgs 13:4); most extraordinarily of all, Yahweh's motivations and influence over the affairs of history are specifiable (2 Kgs 10:32; 17:18, 20; 24:3–4; Nelson 1988: 45–46). Prophets routinely bear the message of God to human ears; Yahweh communicates only once through the written word (the book of the law found in the Temple, 2 Kgs 22:19; 23:3). Exceptionally, Yahweh addresses Solomon directly through the medium of dreams (1 Kgs 3:11–14; 9:3–9).

b. Solomon. The reign of Solomon, like that of his father David, is literarily partitioned into two phases: "good king" and "bad king." Initially Solomon exemplifies the ideal king by the standards of the ANE: he fosters the national cult by building a temple in his capital city and establishing a sacrificial system (1 Kgs 5:1–8:66), he promotes the cause of justice (the trial of two harlots, 1 Kgs 3:16–27), he brings political peace, military might, and economic prosperity to his realm (1 Kgs 4:24–26; 10:14–29), and he is supernaturally endowed with wisdom (1 Kgs 3:3–28; 4:29–34; 10:23–25). After he secures the throne by the customary assassination of rival claimants (1 Kgs 2:23–25; Athaliah is condemned for the same practice in 2 Kgs 11), he leads an exemplary career as a pious and hugely successful monarch until he dedicates the Temple. In his second vision at Gibeon a warning note is sounded: if Solomon or his descendants prove unfaithful to Yahweh, the kingdom and its temple will fall (1 Kgs 9:6–9). In spite of, or perhaps at the price of the international prestige, luxury, and wealth that accrued to him (1 Kgs 9:10–10:29), Solomon's foreign policy led him to cultic shipwreck. In 1 Kgs 11:1–40 Solomon in his old age becomes the "bad king": he commits apostasy to accommodate his foreign wives and incurs the displeasure of Yahweh (11:9–13) which, by literary juxtaposition, led to the creation of two international and one domestic adversaries at the close of his career (11:14–40).

c. Elijah. At several points the figure of Elijah the prophet is pointedly cast as a second Moses. Elijah is the greatest exponent of inflexible Yahwistic monotheism in Kings; both the lone figures of Moses and Elijah stalwartly represent the true faith in defiance of the overwhelming might of pagan nations, pharaonic Egypt and Omride Israel. Elijah's public contest against the pagan god and prophets on Mt. Carmel echoes the episode of the Golden Calf in the Wilderness; both figures lead the People of Israel to renew their covenant with Yahweh (1 Kgs 18:19–40; Exod 32). Both Elijah and Moses journey to Mt. Horeb at divine summons and there experience a theophany (1 Kgs 19:1–18; Exod 3:1–4:17; 33:17–23). The description of the succession of Elijah by Elisha as prophetic leader, complete with Elisha's parting of the Jordan and crossing over to Jericho from Transjordan, duplicates Moses' commissioning of Joshua and the latter's entry into the Promised Land (2 Kgs 2:1–15; Num 27:12–27; Josh 1–3). Even the deaths of Elijah and Moses are mysteries shrouded in divine silence (2 Kgs 2:1–18; Deut 34:1–6; Carroll 1969: 409–10; Carlson 1969: 437–39).

d. Women. In the main, women who engage in power politics in Kings are assigned a negative role. An exception is Bathsheba, the mother of Solomon, who engineered her son's succession to David's kingdom; she is portrayed as acting under the direction of Nathan, a faithful Yahwistic prophet, and thus escapes censure (1 Kgs 1:11–31). The Queen of Sheba serves as a foil to lend spectacle to Solomon's international importance and legendary wisdom (1 Kgs 10:1–13). Thereafter, women of temporal authority in Kings live to commit idolatry. Solomon's foreign wives lead the once-wise king into apostasy in his dotage (1 Kgs 11:1–10). Jezebel, a Phoenician princess who married into the Omride House of Israel, arguably bears the most flagrantly wicked personality in the Hebrew Bible. In contrast to her husband, Ahab, she is shrewd, decisive, ruthless, and terrifying in her machinations against Yahwism and traditional Israelite values, and she is held responsible for inciting Ahab to do evil (1 Kgs 18:19; 19:1–3; 21:1–26). At the command of the arch-Yahwist Jehu, she dies with a flair, hurling a sophisticated double entendre at her murderer (2 Kgs 9:31). Athaliah, daughter of Jezebel and the only reigning queen of Judah, supports a Baal cult in Jerusalem and attempts to wipe out the Davidic dynasty (2 Kings 11). She alone of Judahite monarchs is not introduced with the customary regnal formula: her royal credentials are impugned through silence.

4. Genres. a. Miracle Stories. Although the heaviest concentration of miracle stories in Kings occurs in the Elijah and Elisha cycles, miraculous events liberally pepper the narrative. Form critical approaches to miracle stories (legenda) usually emphasize their folkloristic kernel, which has often been "sophisticated" by adding a moral or having it demonstrate a loftier theological value. Virtually every miracle story in Kings strives to magnify or legitimate the figure of a prophet by demonstrating his ability to exercise control over supernatural phenomena. One hundred soldiers and their disrespectful captains are consumed by fire called down from heaven by Elijah, showing one and all that he is a "man of God" (2 Kgs 1:9–12). Several miracle stories appear to function primarily as aretalogies, stories intended simply to glorify the figure of a prophet as a wonder worker. Forty-two children are mangled by bears for pestering a prophet (2 Kgs 2:23–24); a borrowed axehead lost in water is caused to float (2 Kgs 6:1–7); a corpse is revivified because it touches the bones of Elisha (2 Kgs 13:21). Other stories use the miraculous as a didactic measure to win belief in the living God (Rofé 1974: 145). The divine vindication of the prophet Elijah over the prophets of Baal on Mount Carmel cause "all the people of Israel" to declare "Yahweh, he is God; Yahweh, he is God" (1 Kgs 18:39). Elijah resurrects a dead child in the name of Yahweh (1 Kgs 17:21–22); evidence of the miracle prompts the revived child's mother to confess, "Now I know that you are a man of God, and that the word of Yahweh in your mouth is true" (17:24). In 2 Kings 5 the Syrian Naaman is cured of his leprosy by washing in a river at the direction of Elisha; his response: "Behold, I know that there is no God in all the earth but in Israel" (5:15). The miraculous destruction of the altar at Bethel and withering of King Jeroboam I's hand in 1 Kings 13 is dramatically linked by prophecy to the activity of Josiah of Judah in Bethel some three hundred years later; literarily, this prophetic vignette tethers the careers of Jeroboam I, chief architect of cultic mischief in the Northern Kingdom, and Josiah, the reformer-king extraordinaire of Judah.

b. Legitimation Apologetic. 2 Kings 11 describes how the Omride Athaliah came to power in Judah by massacring all potential Davidic claimants to the throne—all but one, Joash, who was hidden by an aunt in the Jerusalem Temple for six years with the cooperation of the priest Jehoiada. In Joash's seventh year Jehoiada engineered a coup d'état by revealing him to troops loyal to David and "the people of the land." Historically, the concealment of an infant in the royal chapel for six years from Athaliah and her followers is improbable, to say the least. The form of the story follows a literary pattern attested other places in the Hebrew Bible (Moses, Hadad of Edom in 1 Kgs 11:14–22) and in the ancient world, namely, the Tale of the Hero Exposed at Birth. A child of noble birth must be abandoned; it is saved from certain death, raised by a human, adopted by royalty (a Davidic princess) and a servitor of a god (a priest of Yahweh); ultimately he becomes king. Versions of this tale were used to support the royal claims of Sargon II, Cyrus, and various pseudo-sons of Nabonidus, probably all usurpers: it is a stock legitimation birth narrative for royal pretenders (Handy 1988).

c. The Cult Reform. Positively evaluated cult reforms in Kings (Asa, Jehu, Joash/Jehoiada, Hezekiah, Josiah) inevitably show a return to "traditional" religion (monotheistic Yahwism). They are never depicted as capricious innovations undertaken at the king's whimsy or as religio-political capitulations to foreign powers. The validity of the greatest cult reform, that of Josiah's, is guaranteed by the prophetess Huldah (2 Kgs 22:14–20); comparable texts in Assyrian sources validate a projected reform through a series of favorable omens. Negatively evaluated cult reforms (Jeroboam I, Ahab, Ahaz, Manasseh) entail innovation or a return to Canaanite practices by introducing a plurality of deities and rites into the preexisting (Yahwistic) cultus. Such innovations, unsanctioned by prophet or priest, force the hapless people into sin (1 Kgs 12:30; 2 Kgs 21:16). Since every Israelite king, including Jehu (2 Kgs 10:31), was guilty of the "sin of Jeroboam" (the fostering of

Yahwism and other cults outside a Jerusalem context), they were all religious innovators in the literary historiography of Kings.

The narrative of the "anti-reformer" Manasseh of Judah in 2 Kgs 21:1–18 shows evidence of thematic patterning from the perspective of the Josianic reform; Manasseh (re-)introduces into the Jersualem cult the same triad of non-Yahwistic deities that Josiah removes, Baal, Asherah, and the Host of Heaven (2 Kgs 21:3; 23:4). The literary portrait of Manasseh has been executed in such a manner as to cause him to appear as the evil antitype of Josiah, the depths of his cultic apostasy adding luster by contrast to Josiah's return to "old time religion" (Hoffmann 1980: 162–67; Spieckermann 1982: 163). The destruction of the high places, sacred pillars and female cult image in Hezekiah's reform (2 Kgs 18:4) is a stock figure in Kings which clashes harshly with the apostasy of Manasseh; Hezekiah's political resistance to the pagan Assyrians and their contempt for his reform (2 Kgs 18:19–25) theologically prepares the way for the thoroughgoing purge of foreign cults by Josiah.

F. History and Historiography in Kings

1 and 2 Kings is a theological history; it does not attempt to offer an objective or dispassionate reportage of the "facts." Its authors were primarily concerned with the didactic possibilities of the reigns of their kings for illustrating the interplay of the divine and human wills in light of the present (the Jewish community for whom Kings was written). A "history" in the modern academic sense of the word denotes, among other things, a document that consciously and critically weighs the accuracy of its sources and makes no appeal to supernatural causation as a means of explaining the course of historical events. As the title intimates, Kings provides historical datum on the reigns of Israel's and Judah's monarchs; names and dates follow chronologically, interspersed with domestic and international events deemed salient by the author. In common with other historical works from antiquity, private conversations (Jezebel and Ahab, 1 Kgs 21:5–7), prayers (Hezekiah alone in the Temple, 2 Kgs 19:14–19), and actions of which no record could reasonably be expected to exist, miracles (the blinding and capture by Elisha of a Syrian army, 2 Kgs 6:11–23) and miraculous interpretations of events (the withdrawal of the Assyrian siege from Jerusalem, 2 Kgs 19:35–36) are integral to the literary artistry of the composition. Despite the focus on the royal court and national cult, Kings provides only isolated notice of national economic status; social, political, and military history; international relations; achievements in the arts; or even utilitarian material culture—what people wore, slept on, and cooked their meals in. Likewise, as a "history" devoted to the interaction of king and cult, there is surprisingly little information on the priesthood and other temple functionaries, specific oracles or omens by which the will of the national god influenced military and political decisions of the monarchy, the fiscal apparatus governing the organic relationship between royal taxes, tribute, and temple revenues, etc.

1 and 2 Chronicles is also a theological history of the Chosen People, beginning with Adam and concluding with Cyrus' Edict to the Judahite exiles. Because its synoptic narrative of the Divided Monarchy provides details "missing" in 1–2 Kings, generations of historians have selectively utilized it to create a conflated or harmonized image of "sacred history." More so than DTR, the Chronicler altered his sources and introduced *midrašim* to "rectify" his historical datum according to the exigencies of his theological program; the historical value of Chronicles is slender, and should be used with great caution for the purposes of historical reconstruction.

The relatively meagre success of Syro-Palestinian archaeology at verifying or refuting various historical assertions in Kings turns upon the nature of material remains surviving from antiquity and upon the particular interests of the authors that guided their selection of topics for inclusion in the text. The most conspicuous remains to date are traces of monumental architecture unearthed or exposed at the site of large urban centers (generally *tells*), for instance, the stone foundations of city walls, gates, palaces. Unfortunately, such vestiges of the past, when bereft of inscriptions or representative artwork that would positively identify the rulers who ordered their construction, are historically ambiguous. The organics preferred for writing Hebrew (wood, leather, papyrus) decompose rapidly in the climate of Palestine outside the immediate environs of the Dead Sea; hence, the predictable paucity of textual remains from the period of Kings unearthed by Syro-Palestinian archaeologists. The modern typologies developed to account for the chronological and geographical progression of pottery designs rarely, if ever, are subtle enough to distinguish between the reigns of specific Israelite and Judahite kings; thus, potsherds alone will not provide the criteria necessary for distinguishing whether, for instance, the Hazor city gates of Stratum X were built by Solomon, or Ahab, or perhaps even Jeroboam II.

1. Religion in Judah and Israel. The guiding concerns of the authors of Kings were focused upon the illustration of a pattern of prophecy and fulfillment from rise to fall of the kingdoms of Israel and Judah, specifically, the fidelity of the rulers and people to the religio-political vision outlined in Deuteronomy. The monumental remains that one would expect to correspond to the descriptions provided in Kings, for example, the elaborate specifications of the temple of Solomon and the royal palace in Jerusalem (1 Kings 6–7, clearly the dominant architectural achievements in the text), cannot be verified due to the legal and political impossibility of conducting archaeological investigations on the site of the central Temple Mount. The construction of the Temple was reportedly a collaborative Phoenicio-Israelite enterprise; the iconography of its decoration and ornamentation described in Kings (cherubim, lions, bulls, floral motifs, pomegranates, palm trees, 1 Kgs 6:23–7:37) is consonant with known Phoenician and North Syrian artistic traditions, as is the design of the floor plan (Busink 1970: 261–67).

The biblical portrayal of the Solomonic Temple as exclusively devoted to Yahweh worship from its inauguration to its destruction, with sharply defined "paganizing" interludes, is both anachronistic and tendentious. Archaeological research does not support the notion that monotheistic Yahwism was normative for either the people or rulers of the Divided Monarchy. Clay figurines (most frequently of bulls, horses, and nude women), probably cultic in origin, have been excavated in profusion at Jerusalem and at other urban sites in Palestine in contexts sufficiently diverse to rule out the likelihood that they were manufactured exclusively during the reigns of religiously "permissive" kings like Ahab and Manasseh (Ahlström 1984: 136–38). Similarly, research in onomastics (the formation of proper names) for the period indicates the great popularity that the national god Yahweh enjoyed as the divine element in proper names in both Judah and Israel, but not to the exclusion of other divine names (Tigay 1986: 37–41); a comparable onomastic milieu prevailed in other contemporary West Semitic kingdoms. Reports of cult centralization in Jerusalem during the reigns of Hezekiah (2 Kgs 18:22) and Josiah (2 Kgs 23:5–14, 24) are neither confirmed nor challenged by excavation findings (Ussishkin 1988: 156).

Regarding the historical verisimilitude of the presentation of the cult in Kings, the Baal cult is a case in point. According to literary division *D* (1 Kgs 16:23–2 Kings 12), following Savran, this cult in Israel received royal patronage under the Omrides, only to be bloodily purged from the land under the fanatical usurper Jehu (2 Kgs 10:18–28). In Judah, the Jerusalem temple to Baal, sanctioned if not erected by Athaliah, Omride scion, was said to have been destroyed by a popular movement led by a Yahwistic priest (2 Kings 11). The historiography of Kings therefore intimates that a full-blown Baal cult lasted around forty years, revived later by Manasseh in Judah, only to be liquidated by the reformer-king Josiah. In Syro-Palestine, Baal worship is a documented fact from at least ca. 1500 B.C.E. to 200 C.E. There is ample evidence both from Kings itself and from archaeological research that the state cults of both Judah and Israel were cults of many gods, with Yahweh at the apex of both pantheons throughout the Divided Monarchy (Ahlström 1982: 69–71; 1984: 137; Lemche 1988: 229; Mulder 1989: 55–58). There is a virtual flood of recent scholarship acknowledging the worship of the goddess Asherah alongside Yahweh in Judah (Day 1986: 391–99).

2. Kings and Rulers. Generally speaking, the names and order of reigns of the monarchs of Israel and Judah in Kings are historically accurate. The chronological proximity, prevailing political relationship between the two Kingdoms, kinship, and identical names of Joram of Israel and Jehoram (Joram) of Judah (2 Kgs 1:17; 8:16, 25) have suggested to some scholars that the two are one and the same person; perhaps the biblical historiographers were confused (Miller and Hayes 1986: 280–82). Failure to provide Jehu of Israel and Athaliah of Judah with standard regnal formulas may reflect dramatic license (the Israelite Jehu alone is anointed as king by Yahwistic prophet (2 Kgs 9:6) or the author's covert polemic against their right to the throne, 2 Kgs 11:1–3. From both biblical and epigraphic evidence, it has been suggested that Gedaliah, appointed to rule Judah by the Babylonians following the deportation of king Zedekiah to Babylon, was actually installed as a vassal king (2 Kgs 25:22–25; Miller and Hayes 1986: 421–24). The reluctance of the author of Kings to call non-Davidic rulers of Judah "king" (or "queen") may account for Gedaliah's curious lack of titles (*RSV* supplies "governor" in 2 Kgs 25:22, 23).

Determination of the historicity of particular events in Kings is realistically restricted to rational inference from what is known from the better documented Egyptian and Mesopotamian kingdoms to the internal affairs of the relatively obscure West Semitic kingdoms of Judah and Israel. Most studies on Kings draw attention to the notable disparity between the substantial military and political achievements of Omri and Ahab of Israel, which are known from excavations and textual sources (Assyrian and Moabite), and the Bible's cryptic (six verses for Omri, 1 Kgs 16:23–28) or pointedly unflattering accounts of their reigns (six chapters on Ahab, most of which contrast his personal and political weaknesses with the effective dynamism of the prophet Elijah, 1 Kgs 16:29–22:40). The Elijah and Elisha cycles are coterminous with the reigns of the Omrides and Jehu; the overriding goal of the author to subordinate political to prophetic power led to the inclusion or composition of much folkloristic material, rendering the actual sequence of historical events difficult or impossible to recover (1 Kings 17–2 Kings 10). Hezekiah, whose headstrong foreign policy provoked Assyrian military countermoves which brought Judah to the brink of national destruction and the reduction of its territory to Jerusalem and its environs, "did what was right in the eyes of Yahweh" (2 Kgs 18:3). His son Manasseh held the reins of state longer than any other Judahite king and successfully steered his kingdom as an Assyrian vassal-state through the various administrations of Sennacherib, Esarhaddon, and Assurbanipal. It is extremely likely that, like other Assyrian vassals, it was both expedient and obligatory for Manasseh to support Assyrian cults and practices in the Jerusalem Temple and elsewhere (Spieckermann 1982: 170, 319–22; Würthwein *Könige* ATD, 441–42); perhaps for this, and for returning the national cult to the status quo that existed before Hezekiah's cultic innovations, his reign incurs the severest condemnation of any ruler in Kings (2 Kgs 21:1–18; Ahlström 1982: 75–81).

It is to the credit of DTR as an historian that the informing Deuteronomic principles of reward for obedience and prophetic fulfillment were set aside for Josiah of Judah, the prize example in Kings of aggressive obedience to the Deuteronomic ideology. The king is struck down on the battlefield, apparently giving the lie to Huldah's prophecy (2 Kgs 23:29–30; 22:20).

3. Military History. Painting with the broadest possible strokes, the outline of military and political history set forth in Kings appears to correspond to what really happened. The Solomonic "Empire" (the actual extent and value of Solomon's geographical holdings may have been subject to considerable exaggeration in the Hebrew Bible) arose in the Western Asian power vacuum following an eclipse of the Egyptian, Hittite, and Assyrian superpowers. The effective division of the imperial heartland into two rival kingdoms, Israel and Judah, resulted in swiftly shifting alliances and vassalships between them and their neighboring states (Philistine, Phoenician, Aramaean, Ammonite, Moabite, Edomite), moves characteristic of small nations jockeying for power and survival. The expansion of the two Mesopotamian conquest nations, Assyria and Babylonia, led ultimately to lopsided military confrontations in which the territories of both Israel and Judah were devastated, their capital cities destroyed, and their populations subjected to mass deportation, all time-tested measures calculated to break down political resistance and national identity.

The account of Pharaoh Shishak's invasion of Palestine in 1 Kgs 14:25–26 mentions only Jerusalem and the booty he carried off from the Temple and palace; the literary nuancing of the narrative emphasizes the political weakness of Rehoboam, Solomon's unworthy successor (1 Kgs 14:27–30). The Egyptian account of the invasion fails to mention Jerusalem; it lists more cities taken in the territories of Israel and Syria than in Judah. The biblical historiographer appears to have been more anxious to portray Shishak's activity in Palestine as a blow to Rehoboam's prestige than as a significant military incident for the fledgling Northern Kingdom (*ANET,* 263–64; *LBHG,* 323–30; Ahlström 1982: 56–57). The date given in Kings, "the fifth year of King Rehoboam," cannot be tested due to chronological uncertainties in both Egyptian and Hebrew sources.

The date, geography and identity of the kings involved in the central Syro-Israelite wars are tentative by reason of the highly legendary nature of the biblical narratives (the Elijah and Elisha cycles), coupled with the anonymous titling of the "King of Israel" in 1 Kings 20 (use of Ahab's name is probably secondary); 22:1–36; 2 Kgs 6:8–7:20; 8:7–15. The royal Syrian names Ben-Hadad (Aramaean Bar-Hadad) and Hazael, attested in extra-biblical sources, were probably held by more than one ruler in Kings; a clear succession of kings of Damascus from the Rezon associated with Solomon (10th century, 1 Kgs 11:23–25) to the Rezin associated with Pekah of Israel (late 8th century, 2 Kgs 15:37) is impossible to determine. The relative military strength and weakness of the Syro-Palestinian states prior to the western campaigns of Tiglath-pileser III in the 8th century are difficult to assess; the contradictory state of military preparedness imputed to Ahab's Israel by the historiography of 1 Kgs 20–22:40 is decidedly at odds with the rank of Ahab in the international coalition described in the Kurkh Monolith of Shalmaneser III (Borger 1984: 360–62). Descriptions of Syro-Israelite military confrontations in Kings outside the Elijah-Elisha cycles (1 Kgs 15:16–22; 2 Kgs 12:17–16:9) are probably more historically informative than those within the cycles; see Miller and Hayes (1986: 250–87).

The terse description of the fall of the Northern Kingdom to the Assyrians (2 Kgs 17:1–6) and subsequent happenings in the province of *Samerina* (2 Kgs 17:24–41) telescope a number of events. Although Shalmaneser V probably captured the capital city, Samaria, in 722, the city had to be retaken in 720 by Sargon II, who was responsible for the massive deportations of the kingdom's inhabitants. The account of the cultic mixing of the Yahwism and idolatry practiced by the natives and newly imported aliens under the unnamed "King of Assyria" in 2 Kgs 17:24–33 is an anachronistic and polemic description of the origins of the Samaritans.

Kings appears to describe two separate campaigns of Sennacherib against Judah: in the first, 2 Kgs 18:13–16, a victorious Sennacherib receives submission from Hezekiah and booty stripped from palace and temple; in the second, 2 Kgs 18:17–19:37, a high official from the Assyrian court, cognizant of Hezekiah's cult reforms, parleys with the defenders in the local Palestinian dialect. The prophet Isaiah emboldens the Judahite king to resist; the Assyrian army is miraculously slaughtered by the angel of Yahweh; Sennacherib returns empty-handed to Nineveh, to be ingloriously slain by his sons "in the house of Nisroch, his god" (2 Kgs 19:37). Assyrian and Babylonian sources provide no reasonable justification for supposing that Sennacherib undertook a second campaign to Palestine after 701 B.C.E.; it is quite clear that at that time Judah was conquered by a savagely punitive military offensive (Ussishkin 1982: 19–58; 67–126), and that Hezekiah purchased his capital city, Jerusalem, and his life by paying a massive bribe to the Assyrian king and offering submission (for the Assyrian annal account of Sennacherib's third campaign, see Borger 1984: 388–90). The two biblical accounts each provide selected items of accurate information regarding the same historical campaign, even though the "miraculous" delivery of Jerusalem in the second account, and probably the dramatic rhetoric of the Rabshakeh's speeches, are theologically motivated fiction.

The surrender of Jerusalem to Nebuchadnezzar II and capture of Jehoiachin (2 Kgs 24:10–17) is datable in cuneiform sources to March 16, 597 B.C.E. (Cogan and Tadmor *II Kings* AB, 311). The biblical account of the subsequent sack of Jerusalem and second Judahite exile (2 Kgs 24:18–25:21; Jer 39:1–14; 52:1–27) is the only extensive documentation to survive; excavations at various fortified cities in Judah bear witness to the punitive devastation wrought by the Babylonians. "The fall of the city [Jerusalem] and the exile of many of its citizens marked a watershed in Judean history and have left fissure marks radiating throughout the Hebrew Scriptures" (Miller and Hayes 1986: 416).

G. Theology

1. Deity. The god, Yahweh, that was worshipped in the Solomonic Temple of Jerusalem was the only living God; belief in any other god or goddess was both illusory and sinful; compare the story of Elijah versus the prophets of Baal on Mount Carmel (1 Kgs 18:19–40), and Hezekiah's prayer, a transparent example of Deuteronomic theology (2 Kgs 19:14–19). Yahweh is god of all nations, a point ironically driven home in the speech of the Assyrian Rabshakeh (2 Kgs 18:25); Yahweh's forgiveness is available to the faithful even in exile (1 Kgs 8:46–53). The most heinous of sins committed in Kings are cultic (tolerance and proliferation of non-Yahwistic worship), not ethical (murder, theft, perjury). In the historiography of Kings, monotheistic Yahwism dates to the time of Moses; "later" paganizing rulers of Israel and Judah consistently ignored the example of David and "orthodox" prophetic exhortations.

2. History. Deuteronomic theology is rooted in the particular historical circumstances of a western Asiatic people. The infidelity of the kings and people of Israel was punished according to Deuteronomic law "in order to demonstrate how Israel's continual disobedience to the laws of God finally caused the nation to be destroyed through divine judgment" (*IOTS,* 286). It is fairly said that, in Kings, history is how the prophets see it. The Divine Will, against which humans cannot successfully resist, is made known through the prophets (2 Kgs 17:13; 21:10–

15) and through Deuteronomic law (2 Kgs 22:16). Nevertheless, history and Deuteronomic theology engage in sporadic conflict: God lies through the prophets (1 Kgs 22:19–23); unconditional dynastic promises are modified (1 Kgs 9:4–9); Josiah, the one king who fulfills the Deuteronomic law "with all his heart, and with all his soul and with all his might" (2 Kgs 23:23) dies before a heathen Pharaoh. The raw and ambiguous stuff of history, even that of the Chosen People, occasionally overflows the boundaries fixed by the theological agenda of the author(s) of Kings.

Bibliography

Ahlström, G. W. 1982. *Royal Administration and National Religion in Ancient Palestine.* Studies in the History of the Ancient Near East 1. Leiden.

———. 1984. An Archaeological Picture of Iron Age Religions in Ancient Palestine. *StOr* 55: 115–45.

Baillet, M. 1962. Textes des Grottes 2Q, 3Q, 6Q, 7Q à 10Q. *DJD* 3: 45–164.

Bedouelle, G. 1989. L'accès à la Bible du milieu du XVe siècle aux environs de 1530. Pp. 17–121 in *Le temps des Réformes et la Bible,* ed. G. Bedouelle and B. Roussel. Bible de tous les temps 5. Paris.

Begrich, J. 1929. *Die Chronologie der Könige von Israel und Juda und die Quellen des Rahmens der Königesbücher.* BHT 3. Tübingen.

Borger, R. 1984. Historische Texte in akkadischer Sprache aus Babylonien und Assyrien. *TUAT* 1/4: 354–410.

Burney, C. F. 1903. *Notes on the Hebrew Text of the Book of Kings.* Oxford.

Busink, T. A. 1970. *Der Tempel von Jerusalem,* vol. 1. Leiden.

Carlson, R. A. 1969. Élie à l'Horeb. *VT* 19: 416–39.

Carroll, R. P. 1969. The Elijah-Elisha Sagas: Some Remarks on Prophetic Succession in Ancient Israel. *VT* 19: 400–15.

Day, J. 1986. Asherah in the Hebrew Bible and Northwest Semitic Literature. *JBL* 105: 385–408.

Dietrich, W. 1972. *Prophetie und Geschichte.* FRLANT 108. Göttingen.

Dirksen, P. B. 1988. The Old Testament Peshitta. Pp. 255–97 in Mulder, ed. 1988.

———. 1989. Some Remarks in Connection with the Peshiṭta of Kings. *OTS* 25: 22–28.

Evans, C. D. 1983. Naram-Sin and Jeroboam: The Archetypal *Unheilsherrscher* in Mesopotamian and Biblical Historiography. Pp. 97–125 in *Scripture in Context II,* ed. W. W. Hallo, J. C. Moyer, and L. G. Perdue. Winona Lake, IN.

Garbini, G. 1979. 'Narrativa della successione' o 'storia dei rei'? *Henoch* 1: 19–41.

Ginsburg, C. D. 1966. *Introduction to the Massoretico-Critical Edition of the Hebrew Bible.* New York [originally published in 1897].

Gooding, D. W. 1967. The Septuagint's Rival Versions of Jeroboam's Rise to Power. *VT* 17: 173–89.

———. 1969. Problems of Text and Midrash in the Third Book of Reigns. *Textus* 7: 1–29.

———. 1976. *Relics of Ancient Exegesis: A Study of the Miscellanies in 3 Reigns 2.* Cambridge.

Gottlieb, H., and Hammershaimb, E. 1976. *The Book of Kings.* The Old Testament in Syriac According to the Peshiṭta Version 2/4. Leiden.

Halpern, B. 1988. *The First Historians.* San Francisco.

Handy, L. K. 1988. Speaking of Babies in the Temple. *PEGLAMBS* 8: 155–65.

Harrington, D. J., and Saldarini, A. J., eds. 1987. *Targum Jonathan of the Former Prophets.* Aramaic Bible 10. Wilmington, DE.

Hayes, J. H., and Hooker, P. K. 1988. *A New Chronology for the Kings of Israel and Judah and Its Implications for Biblical History and Literature.* Atlanta.

Hoffmann, H.-D. 1980. *Reform und Reformen.* ATANT 66. Zurich.

Jepsen, A. 1956. *Die Quellen des Königsbuches.* 2d ed. Halle.

Kedar, B. 1988. The Latin Translations. Pp. 299–338 in Mulder, ed. 1988.

Klein, R. W. 1974. *Textual Criticism of the Old Testament.* Philadelphia.

König, E. 1893. *Einleitung in das Alte Testament.* Sammlung theologischer Handbücher 2/1. Bonn.

Lemaire, A. 1986. Vers L'histoire de la Rédaction des Livres des Rois. *ZAW* 98: 221–35.

Lemche, N. P. 1988. *Ancient Israel: A New History of Israelite Society.* Biblical Seminar 5. Sheffield.

Marcos, N. Fernández. 1984. The Lucianic Text in the Books of Kingdoms: from Lagarde to the Textual Pluralism. Pp. 161–74 in *De Septuaginta: Studies in Honour of John William Wevers,* ed. A. Pietersma and C. Cox. Mississauga, Ontario.

McKenzie, S. L. 1985. The Prophetic History and the Redaction of Kings. *HAR* 9: 203–20.

Milik, J. T. 1962. Textes de la Grotte 5Q. *DJD* 3: 167–97.

Miller, J. M., and Hayes, J. H. 1986. *A History of Ancient Israel and Judah.* Philadelphia.

Mowinckel, S. 1932. "Die Chronologie der israelitischen und jüdischen Könige." *Acta Orientalia* 10: 161–277.

Mulder, M. J. 1988. The Transmission of the Biblical Text. Pp. 87–135 in Mulder, ed. 1988.

———. 1989. Solomon's Temple and YHWH's Exclusivity. *OTS* 25: 49–62.

Mulder, M. J., ed. 1988. *Mikra: Text, Translation, Reading and Interpretation of the Hebrew Bible in Ancient Judaism and Early Christianity.* CRINT 2/1. Philadelphia and Assen.

Nelson, R. D. 1988. The Anatomy of the Book of Kings. *JSOT* 40: 39–48.

O'Brien, M. A. 1989. *The Deuteronomistic History Hypothesis: A Reassessment.* OBO 92. Freiburg.

Peckham, B. 1985. *The Composition of the Deuteronomistic History.* HSM 35.

Provan, I. W. 1988. *Hezekiah and the Book of Kings.* BZAW 172. Berlin.

Rofé, A. 1974. Classes in the prophetical stories: Didactic legenda and parable. *VTSup* 26: 143–64.

———. 1988. The Vineyard of Naboth: The Origin and Message of the Story. *VT* 38: 89–104.

Savran, G. 1987. 1 and 2 Kings. Pp. 146–64 in *The Literary Guide to the Bible,* ed. R. Alter and F. Kermode. Cambridge, MA.

Shenkel, J. D. 1968. *Chronology and Recensional Development in the Greek Text of Kings.* HSM 1. Cambridge, MA.

Smend, R. 1978. *Die Entstehung des Alten Testaments.* Theologische Wissenschaft 1. Stuttgart.

Smolar, L., and Aberbach, M. 1983. *Studies in Targum Jonathan to the Prophets.* New York and Baltimore.

Spieckermann, H. 1982. *Juda unter Assur in der Sargonidenzeit.* FRLANT 129. Göttingen.

Swete, H. B. 1914. *An Introduction to the Old Testament in Greek.* 2d ed. Cambridge.

Thackeray, H. St. J. 1923. *Septuagint and Jewish Worship.* 2d ed. Schweich Lectures, 1920. London.

Thiele, E. R. 1983. *The Mysterious Numbers of the Hebrew Kings.* 3d ed. Grand Rapids.

Tigay, J. H. 1986. *You Shall Have No Other Gods.* HSS 31. Atlanta.
Tov, E. 1984. The LXX Additions (Miscellanies) in 1 Kings 2 (3 Reigns 2). *Textus* 11: 89–118.
———. 1988. The Septuagint. Pp. 161–88 in Mulder, ed. 1988.
Trebolle Barrera, J. C. 1986. Old Latin, Old Greek and Old Hebrew in the Books of Kings (1 Ki. 18:27 and 2 Ki. 20:11). *Textus* 13: 85–94.
Ussishkin, D. 1982. *The Conquest of Lachish by Sennacherib.* Tel Aviv University Publications of the Institute of Archaeology 6. Tel Aviv.
———. 1988. The Date of the Judaean Shrine at Arad. *IEJ* 38: 142–57.
Van Seters, J. 1981. Histories and Historians of the Ancient Near East: The Israelites," *Or* n.s. 50: 137–85.
———. 1983. *In Search of History.* New Haven.
Veijola, T. 1975. *Die Ewige Dynastie.* AASF B 193. Helsinki.
Weippert, H. 1972. Die 'deuteronomistischen' Beurteilungen der Könige von Israel und Juda und das Problem der Redaktion der Königsbücher. Bib 53: 301–39.
Wellhausen, J. 1889. *Die Composition des Hexateuchs und der historischen Bücher des Alten Testaments.* 2d ed. Berlin.
White, H. J. 1902. Vulgate. *HDB* 4: 873–90.
Wolff, H. W. 1975. The Kerygma of the Deuteronomic Historical Work. Pp. 83–100 in *The Vitality of Old Testament Traditions,* ed. W. Brueggemann and H. W. Wolff. Atlanta.

STEVEN W. HOLLOWAY

KINGSHIP, SACRAL. See SACRAL KINGSHIP.

KINSHIP. See FAMILY.

KIR (PLACE) [Heb *qîr*]. Apparently the name of two places mentioned in the Hebrew Bible. The word *qîr* in Hebrew means "wall," but in Moabite it means "city."

1. A Moabite town (Isa 15:1), probably the same as Kir-Hareseth (Isa 16:7), modern Kerak. Although the LXX of Isa 15:1 has *to teichos,* "the wall, fortress," most translations regard Heb *qîr* as a proper name. Isaiah introduced his oracle against Kir by referring to the sudden destruction of Ar and Kir; the former is often identified with Rabbah, but this is far from certain. Thus, after citing two of Moab's most important towns, Isaiah 15–16 lists many other Moabite places names, all of which stand under Yahweh's judgment.

GERALD L. MATTINGLY

2. The original home of the Arameans (Amos 9:7), and the place to which they were exiled by the Assyrians (2 Kgs 16:9; cf. Amos 1:5). Kir is also mentioned (along with Elam) in Isa 22:6. LXX^A translates Kir as the Libyan Cyrene in 2 Kgs 16:9 (followed by Vg), but otherwise Kir is not a place in the LXX. For this verse, in place of the proper name, the Greek has *apōkisen,* "removed." It has *ek bothrou* for Amos 9:7: God brought the Syrians "from the deep (the ditch, the pit)." This could be an enclosure for the reception of exiles, or it could be the writer's sense of humor, his opinion of the enemy Arameans. The Greek for Amos 1:5 is *epiklētos:* the Syrians shall be led captive. The LXX of Isa 22:6 describes a "gathering" (Gk *synagōgē*) for battle.

John Gray (*1 and 2 Kings* OTL, 633) identified *qîr* "as a common noun, 'the city,' i.e., the Assyrian capital Nineveh, cf. Istambul, a corruption of *eis ten polin* ('to the city'). The Assyrians regularly referred to their holy city of Assur as 'the City,' and the deportation to 'the City' may refer to dedication of prisoners of war. There is, we think, no connection with *qîr* named in Amos 9:7 as the original home of the Arameans. This we regard as a corruption of qeraqir, cf. Arabic broken plural, meaning 'waterholes' or oases of the North Arabian steppe." The origins of or the native land of the Arameans (Amos 9:7) is obscure so this verse is not helpful in itself. Assyro-Babylonian literature of the 14th century B.C. refers to Arimi, or Ahlame, nomads wandering in the wilderness W of Mesopotamia (Gehman *NWDB,* 57). Arameans appear in the fourth-year records (*ANET,* 275) of Tiglath-pileser I (1115–1077). May (*Amos* OTL, 157–58) notes the migration of Arameans into the area in the early 12th century. Such data would not rule out an Aramean origin in the desert near S Mesopotamia as more or less "adjacent" to today's Iran.

Prophetic oracles were poetry, however, and perhaps Amos's metaphor should not be taken too literally. He was making a theological point about God's power over various people and lands, and God's concern with others, not just the Israelites. There may also be a threat (Amos 1:5) that as the Syrians can be sent back to where they came from, so can the Israelites (cf. Gordon *IDB* 3: 36). May (*Amos* OTL, 31) offers the interpretation that Yahweh will send the Arameans back to Kir, obliterating their accomplishments, "the complete abrogation of the proud political history of the Arameans" (Wolff *Joel and Amos* Hermeneia, 157). Yahweh makes history and cancels it.

It has been suggested that Elam and Kir in Isa 22:6 are sources of mercenaries in the Assyrian army. The association of the two countries suggest proximity in geography, but Amos 9:7 has Egypt, Caphtor (Crete?), and Kir together, so one might doubt the proximity as necessary. Still, one could guess Kir is a country in Mesopotamia on the basis of Isa 22:6. Isa 21:2 relates Elam and Media, so this might strengthen the proximity view of Elam and Kir in Isa 22:6. Gehman (*NWDB,* 540) noted the identification of Kir with the plain between the Tigris River and Elam. Astour (*IDBSup,* 524) relates *qîr,* West Semitic for "wall," with the Akk *duru,* as a translation of the city-name Der, E of the lower Tigris, on the main road from Elam to Babylon. Tiglath-pileser III (745–727 B.C.) transferred its citizens to Damascus in 738, and in 732 exiled Damascus citizens to Duru. In the Neo-Babylonian period, it was the capital of the province of Gutium. Its governor, Gubaru, joined Cyrus and was the first with his troops to enter Babylon in 539. If this identification of the biblical Kir is correct, one would expect that among Gubaru's troops were descendants of the Damascenes from 732 B.C.

Several scholars have suggested the identification of Kir as a country by the river Kur (*Kuros, Kurros*) which begins in N Armenia, runs into the Araxes, and flows to the Caspian Sea (Keil n.d.a., 404; n.d.b. 244–45). Another alternate suggestion for Kir is the one noted above by Gehman. Kir may be the mountain region, el-Kaiyara, a range that marks the N boundary of Syria.

Bibliography
Keil, C. F. n.d.a. *1–2 Kings.* Vol. 3 of *Commentary on The Old Testament.* Trans. J. Martin. Grand Rapids. Repr. 1980.
———. n.d.b. *The Twelve Minor Prophets.* Vol. 10 of *Commentary on The Old Testament.* Trans. J. Martin. Grand Rapids. Repr. 1986.
HENRY O. THOMPSON

KIR-HARESETH (PLACE) [Heb *qîr ḥărešet*]. A capital of ancient Moab identified with modern Kerak (M.R. 217066), located ca. 17 miles S of the Arnon and 11 miles E of the Dead Sea. Strategically located on a promontory that overlooks the Dead Sea, Kerak sits astride a major intersection of the King's Highway and the E–W road across the plateau. This position has witnessed many important events in the region's history, in the days of Mesha (2 Kgs 3:25–27), during the Crusades, and into the present. Kir-hareseth is mentioned in Isa 16:7, and Kir-heres, an alternate name, appears in the oracles of Isa 16:11 and Jer 48:31, 36. KIR (Isa 15:1) is probably the same town.
GERALD L. MATTINGLY

KIRIATH-ARBA (PLACE) [Heb *qiryat ʾarbaʿ*]. The former name of Hebron (cf. Gen 23:2; Josh 14:15; Judg 1:10; etc). This name is associated with several significant events. The death of Sarah is placed here, and she is buried in the nearby Cave of Machpelah (Gen 23:2). Jacob/Israel comes to Kiriath-arba (here also identified as Mamre) and there witnesses his father Isaac's death (Gen 35:27). Kiriath-arba/Hebron is given to Caleb on account of his faithfulness in the episode of the aborted southern invasion of Canaan (see the narrative at Numbers 13 and 14). Here it is noted that the one after whom this city is named was one of the Anakim, who were said to be especially imposing (Josh 14:15, cf. Num 13:32–33). This information is repeated in Josh 15:13, where Caleb's portion is shown to be among the people of Judah. Kiriath-arba is specifically placed in the hill district of Judah (Josh 15:54), is said to be a City of Refuge (Josh 20:7), and is reassigned as a Levitical City (Josh 21:11–12). In a postexilic text, the equation of Kiriath-arba with Hebron is no longer made when the city is listed as one of those in which the returning exiles lived (Neh 11:25).

The name "Kiriath-arba" means "city of four," perhaps a reference to a cluster of four cities in the Hebron area (Aner, Eshcol, Mamre, and Hebron; see Boling *Joshua* AB, 358, and the citation there) or a veiled divine name having Babylonian or Hurrian elements (on the first see Burney 1918: 43–44; on the second, see Blenkinsopp 1972: 113 n. 9). On the issue of the Levitical Cities, see Hauer 1982 and the bibliography cited there.

Bibliography
Blenkinsopp, J. 1972. *Gibeon and Israel.* Cambridge.
Burney, C. F. 1918. *The Book of Judges.* London.
Hammond, R. C. 1966. Hebron. *RB* 73: 566–69, pl. 39a.
———. 1968. Hebron. *RB* 73: 253–58, fig. 6, pl. 30.
Hauer, D. 1982. David and the Levites. *JSOT* 23: 33–54.
JEFFRIES M. HAMILTON

KIRIATH-BAAL (PLACE) [Heb *qīryat baʿal*]. See KIRIATH-JEARIM.

KIRIATH-HUZOTH (PLACE) [Heb *qiryat ḥūṣôt*]. The city to which Balak first took Balaam following the latter's arrival in Moabite territory (Num 22:39). Once there, Balak offered sacrifices prior to Balaam's oracular activity (Num 22:41–24:25). Although the precise location of Kiriath-huzoth defies identification, it was apparently near Bamoth-baal (Num 22:41). Joshua 13:17 places Bamoth-baal in the tableland of Heshbon, territory then allotted to the tribe of Reuben. The City of Moab (Num 22:36), from which Barak and Balaam left on their way to Kiriath-huzoth, apparently was located near the Arnon River, and Kiriath-huzoth was probably situated somewhere between it and Bamoth-baal to the N. If so, Balak led Balaam into territory once lost by Moab to the Amorite king Sihon (Num 21:26) and which had been since regained by Moab or neutralized by the Israelites.

According to Rabbinic tradition, Kiriath-huzoth can be identified with a certain Bîrôšâ, perhaps the site of el-Barrishî near Rabbah *(Tg. Jonathan).* However, such a location is seemingly too far N to suit the description in Numbers 22. More reasonable is Abel's suggestion of el-Qeryeh, situated some 7.5 miles NE of Dibon (*GP* 2: 421). For Heb *qiryat ḥūṣôt* ("city of streets"), the LXX reads *poleis epauleōn* ("city of residences"). Probably behind this translation stands an original Heb *qîryat ḥăṣērōt* ("city of courts").
TERRY L. BRENSINGER

KIRIATH-JEARIM (PLACE) [Heb *qiryat yĕʿārîm*). Var. KIRIATHARIM; KIRIATH-BAAL. A city which lay at the intersection of the boundary of Judah (Josh 15:9) and the W boundary of Benjamin (Josh 18:14 and 18:28). Kiriath-jearim is listed in the cities of Judah in the hill country district (Josh 15:60). Kiriath-jearim was also associated with the original tribal claim of Dan who encamped there on their way to Laish/Dan (Judg 18:12). The site has been identified as modern Tell el-Achar, about 8 miles N of Jerusalem (Cooke 1925; McCarter *1 Samuel* AB, 137).

Kiriath-jearim figures prominently in two narratives, the pact with the Gibeonites (Joshua 9 and 10) and the narrative about the Ark of the Covenant (esp. 1 Samuel 6 and 7). In the first of these stories, Kiriath-jearim appears as one of the cities from which the Gibeonites came (Josh 9:17; the other cities are Gibeon, Chephirah, and Beeroth). Together these cities controlled the northwest approaches to Jerusalem (Boling *Joshua* AB, 266). It would appear that there are two different versions of this incident, one which records an account of treaty relations with indigenous elements, and another which explains this treaty as the result of duplicity on the part of the Gibeonites.

Kiriath-jearim appears in the narrative of the wanderings of the Ark following its capture by the Philistines as the city to which the Ark was sent upon its return by the Philistines (1 Sam 6:19–7:2). From the fact that the Ark was sent to Kiriath-jearim it may be inferred that the city was a cultic center of at least a minor sort. From here the Ark was taken by David to Jerusalem (2 Sam 6:2, where

"Baalah" is to be taken as a reference to Kiriath-jearim—cf. Josh 15:9, 1 Chr 13:6, and the textual analysis in McCarter *1 Samuel* AB, 162–63). The transfer of the Ark from Kiriath-jearim to Jerusalem is also mentioned in 2 Chr 1:4.

In addition to 2 Sam 6:2 mentioned above, Kiriath-jearim is referred to as "Baalah" in Josh 15:9 and as "Kiriath-Baal" in Josh 15:60 and 18:14. The first of these names can be rendered "wife" or "lady," with reference to the goddess Asherah/Anat/etc. (Boling *Joshua* AB, 369), and the second can be taken as an example of demythologizing, where Canaanite god and goddess elements in place-names are replaced by more palatable substitutes. As it stands, "Kiriath-jearim" means "city of woods" (*BDB*, 900). See the discussion in Boling *Joshua* AB, 267, 369.

Kiriath-jearim is also listed as the hometown of Jeremiah's rival Uriah (Jer 26:20), thus confirming its cultic stature; and as a city in the census of the returned exiles (Neh 7:29; cf. Ezra 2:25 where it appears as Kiriatharim).

Bibliography

Cooke, F. T. 1925. The Site of Kiriath-Jearim. AASOR 5: 105–120.

JEFFRIES M. HAMILTON

KIRIATH-SANNAH (PLACE) [Heb *qiryat-sannâ*]. According to Josh 15:49, the former name of the city of Debir. Precisely because this reading is problematic, Noth (1935: 44–50) assumed that the text indeed originally listed Kiriath-sannah, and that the equation with Debir was a later gloss. Orlinski (1939) offered a rebuttal, noting that the LXX reads *polis grammatōn hautē (estin) Dabir,* "city of books, i.e., Debir." Elsewhere the LXX uses *polis grammatōn* ("city of books") to render "Kiriath-sepher," which is elsewhere identified as the former name of Debir (Josh 15:15–17). The reading of *qryt-snh* is therefore probably erroneous, and the text probably originally read "Kiriath-sepher."

Bibliography

Noth, M. 1935. Zur historischen Geographie Südjudäas. *JPOS* 15: 44–50.
Orlinski, H. 1939. The Supposed *Qiryat Sannah* of Joshua 15:49. *JBL* 58: 255–61.

GARY A. HERION

KIRIATH-SEPHER (PLACE) [Heb *qiryat-sēper*]. Alternative name of a Canaanite, and later Judahite, town located in the SW hill country of Judah. It later became known as Debir. The name Kiriath-Sepher means something like "scribe town" or perhaps "town of the treaty-stele" (Boling and Wright *Joshua* AB, 293). The only OT passages to use the ancient name (Josh 15:15–16 = Judg 1:11–12) tell us that Caleb, following his capture of Hebron, promised the hand of his daughter Achsah to whomever would take Kiriath-Sepher/Debir. This task is said to have been accomplished by Caleb's nephew Othniel (Josh 15:17 = Judg 1:13). Although these verses show signs of subsequent editorial activity, they most likely depend on an ancient tradition which may well record the memory of actual historical events (Boling and Wright *Joshua* AB, 373–76). See DEBIR (PLACE) for a discussion of the controversy surrounding the location of this ancient town.

WADE R. KOTTER

KIRIATHAIM (PLACE) [Heb *qiryātayīm*]. **1.** A town in Moab's tableland assigned to the tribe of Reuben (Num 32:37; Josh 13:19). The Mesha Inscription (line 10) says that Mesha rebuilt Kiriathaim; this town was still in Moabite hands when Jeremiah (48:1, 23) and Ezekiel (25:9) pronounced oracles against Moab. A number of sites have been identified as ancient Kiriathaim: (a) el-Qereiyat (M.R. 215105), ca. 5 miles NW of Dhiban; (b) Kh. el Qureiyeh, ca. 6 miles W of Medeba; (c) Qaryat el-Mekhaiyet (M.R. 220128), ca. 3 miles WNW of Medeba; and (d) Jalul, ca. 3 miles E of Medeba. Shaveh-kiriathaim, the "plain of Kiriathaim" (Gen 14:5) may be associated with the Kiriathaim in the territory of Reuben.

2. A levitical city in the territory of Naphtali (I Chr 6:76), probably the same as Kartan (Josh 21:32), probably identified with modern Kh. el-Qureiyeh.

GERALD L. MATTINGLY

KIRIATHARIM (PLACE). See KIRIATH-JEARIM.

KISH (PERSON) [Heb *qîš*]. The name of five individuals. Its etymology is uncertain. One proposal relates it to Akk *qāšu,* "bestow," and *qīštu,* "gift" (*IPN,* 171 n. 3). Another relates it to *qyšh/qyšʾ* in the Aramaic inscriptions from Higr and compares it with the Arabic tribal and personal name *qais* (Nöldeke 1886: 167).

1. The father of Saul, first king of Israel; Kish is likewise the son of Abiel and brother of Ner. He was a member of the Benjaminite clan of Matri (1 Sam 10:21). His patrimonial land holdings appear to have been located at Zela, where he was buried (2 Sam 21:14).

Kish achieved the status of *gibbôr ḥayil,* "wealthy citizen" or "member of the landed, taxable class of citizenry" (1 Sam 9:1). The phrase is frequently used to describe elite military ranking as well as possession of material substance and social status (McKane 1957–58: 28–31). It seems likely that military officers and mercenaries received landed property and the associated gentry status in return for their military service and loyalty to a liege majesty (Weber 1952: 16–18, 24–25, 47, contra McKane 1957–58: 32–33). Kish probably earned his status as a landowner of social standing through mercenary service to the ruler(s) of an unnamed city-state within Benjamin (1 Sam 9:1). The city in question could have been Gibeon, particularly in light of the report in 1 Chr 8:33 and 9:39 that Kish was a descendant of the founder of Gibeon.

Since it is likely that the Saulide genealogy in Chronicles was artificially grafted onto a list of postexilic clans who resettled the site (see NER), the historicity of Kish's association with the city must remain uncertain, even if probable. Saul's confiscation of Gibeonite land during his reign (2 Sam 21:1–3) would have led to the acquisition of royal estates in the city, though it is not clear whether they could have become part of his inherited estate (Ben-Barak 1981: 79–84). If some of these lands were included among the holdings of Saul that David restored to Meribaal (2 Sam 9:7; 19:29) and which would then have been passed on to his descendants, the Chronicler might have been familiar with the association of the Saulide family with Gibeon and could have assumed that Saul's ancestors began that association.

2. The son of Mahli and brother of Eleazer, who was a member of the levitical division of Merari. His eldest son apparently was Jerahmeel (1 Chr 24:29). Kish is reported to have been among the Levites who were numbered in a census in the days of David. He is to have served at the "house of Yahweh," the main sanctuary in Jerusalem. His sons are said to have married their female cousins, the daughters of Eleazer, to preserve the line of Mahli (1 Chr 23:21–23). Many consider the intermarriage to fulfill the guidelines laid out in Num 36:6–9 in the case of Zelophehad's daughters (i.e., Curtis and Madsen *Chronicles* ICC, 265; Williamson *Chronicles* NCBC, 161). However, the provision in Numbers is designed to maintain inherited property within its traditional tribe. Since Levites were government agents (Ahlström 1982: 47–51) and were not to have received patrimonial lands (Deut 18:1–8; Josh 13:14), intermarriage would seem to make more sense as an adaptation of the Levirate law in Deut 25:5–10, which is designed to perpetuate a family line through the marriage of a widow to the dead husband's brother.

3. The son of Abdi and a Levite belonging to the division of Merari (2 Chr 29:12). He is to have participated in the cleansing of the temple in Jerusalem in response to Hezekiah's command to reconsecrate the sanctuary and remove its impurities after its temporary closure by his predecessor Ahaz (2 Chr 28:24–26; 29:6–7). He is one of two representatives for Merari and is said to have assembled his brethren (29:15), suggesting that he was in a position of authority within his levitical division at the time. The list of fourteen Levites among which his name appears seems to be a stylized presentation designed to show how all the main branches of the levitical families responded equally to Hezekiah's command and worked together (Williamson *Chronicles* NCBC, 354). Two representatives each are assigned to the four main levitical divisions of Kohath, Merari, Gershom, and Elizaphan (see 1 Chr 15:4–10 for the less familiar Elizaphan) and the three families of levitical singers, Asaph, Heman, and Jeduthun.

Following the standard ideology of the Chronicler, the Levites serve as subordinates to the priests. They were to have been restricted to the cleansing of the temple court area, while the priests cleansed the innermost part of the sanctuary (29:15). The Levites were then to have disposed of the refuse gathered by the priests from the inner sanctuary by removing it to the Kidron Valley (29:16), a long-standing burial ground (i.e., 2 Kgs 23:6) whose associated impurity made it a logical nearby dumping ground for the impure material.

4. A Benjaminite named as a distant relative of Esther; he was to have been the great-grandfather of Mordecai who adopted and reared Esther, the daughter of his uncle Abihail, after she was orphaned (Esth 2:5).

The accuracy of the genealogy given for Mordecai in Esth 2:5 has been debated. Some have accepted it as a genuine list of Mordecai's immediate three forebears (i.e., Cassel 1888: 52–53; Hoschander 1923: 17; Gerlemann *Esther* BKAT, 77). Others, following Josephus and the creators of the Targums of the book, have regarded Shimei and Kish to have been remote ancestors, Kish the father of Saul (1 Sam 9:1; 14:51; 1 Chr 8:33) and Shimei the Benjaminite rebel in the days of David (2 Sam 16:5; 1 Kgs 2:8, 36, 40). While accepting Jair possibly to be Mordecai's actual father, they believe that the author of Esther deliberately skipped over intermediate genealogical links to highlight Mordecai's well-known ancestors and so foreshadow the new face-off between Saul's descendant and Haman, the descendant of Agag, king of the Amalekites (Haupt 1907–08: 115; Paton *Esther* ICC, 176–78; *Esther* KAT, 299; Moore *Esther* AB, 19; R. Gordis 1974: 27). In 1 Samuel 15, Saul had been ordered by God to exterminate Agag and all his people and possessions but reportedly had spared his enemy's life. In Esther, his descendant Mordecai causes Agag's descendant to be killed, leading to a belated literary fulfillment of the divine command to Saul made centuries earlier.

Kish's identity as Mordecai's great-grandfather or the father of King Saul is further influenced by how one understands the grammatical force of the relative pronoun *ʾăšer* that begins v 6, following Kish's name and the phrase *ʾîš yĕmînî*, "a (Ben)jaminite man." Most agree that the relative pronoun must modify Kish, the subject of the sentence, understanding the intervening three-generation genealogy to be, in effect, a parenthetical statement interrupting normal narrative flow. However, since *ʾăšer* is thought to have developed from a demonstrative pronoun that would have stood immediately after the noun to which it referred (GKC, §138), grammatically, *ʾăšer* would most logically refer to the immediately preceeding phrase, "a Benjaminite man," which in turn is in apposition to the name Kish. Mordecai has already been identified as a Jew at the beginning of v 5 and so needs no further introduction as a Benjaminite. In addition, if the relative clause introduced by *ʾăšer* is associated with Mordecai, it results in a man who is over 116 years old at the time of the story, the reign of Xerxes (465–425 B.C.), since the person is question was part of the first wave of deportation in the wake of Jehoiachin's surrender in March, 597 B.C.E. (2 Kgs 24:10–17). By contrast, in having the relative clause modify Kish, the span from the first deportation to the early reign of Xerxes is bridged by four generations, a very plausible situation. Others have emphasized as well that had Kish, the father of King Saul, been Mordecai's intended ancestor, the author almost certainly would have referred to Saul by name to formalize the connection (i.e. Cassel 1888: 53; Hoschander 1923: 17).

Mordecai's ancestor Kish would have been considered a member of the army, the court, the temple staff, or the artisans of Jerusalem exiled with Jehoiachin, and would have been a fellow exile with the prophet Ezekiel. His family tree strongly suggests that he was to have been understood to have been a Levite, a member of the Merari division. He is said to have been the father of Shimei and the grandfather of Jair, in addition to his relations to Mordecai and Abihail. The name Kish appears elsewhere in 1 Chr 6:44, 23:21–23 and 2 Chr 29:12 as a clan or personal name associated with Merari. Shimei is listed as a clan of Merari in 1 Chr 6:29, while Abihail is the patronymic of the leader of the divisions of Merari during the idealized wilderness wanderings in Num 3:35. In light of the apparent attempt to root Esther's family in levitical Merari origins, the fictional nature of her family tree is likely. Thus Kish may not have been a real person who was exiled under Jehoiachin, but may represent a use of the Merarite clan of Kish to represent a fictitious ancestor.

In addition to the clear links with Merari, Esther's relatives have connections with Saul. Kish was Saul's father and is specifically named as a Benjaminite in 1 Sam 9:1. Shimei was a Benjaminite who cursed David as he fled Jerusalem during Absalom's coup and accused him of exterminating the Saulide royal family (2 Sam 16:5; 1 Kgs 2:8, 36, 40), while Jair recalls the site of Kiriath-Jearim, the reported site of the Ark during Saul's reign (1 Sam 7:1–2). When combined with the characterization of Haman as "the Agagite" (3:1), it is difficult to escape the allusions to 1 Samuel 15, as many have noted.

However, the secondary nature of the Saulide links needs to be considered carefully. The Greek rendering of Haman's epithet does not presume Hebrew *hʾggy,* "the Agagite," but rather, *hgʾgy,* "the Goagite," or *hbgy,* "the Bagoite," depending on the manuscript. The first seems to reflect a Persian title of honor meaning "man of authority" (Cassel 1888: 89), while the second seems to be related to the Persian word *baga,* "God" (Hoschander 1923: 22; contrast Haupt 1907–08: 123). In the context of the story it would be most appropriate for Haman to bear a title of Persian origin, since he is a court official. Therefore it seems likely that his original title was corrupted through letter transposition to read "the Agagite," which in turn may have led to the secondary association of Mordecai's forefather Kish with his well-known namesake the father of King Saul. With this development the appositive phrase "man of (Ben)jamin" at the end of v 6 may have been secondarily inserted in order to allude to Saul's genealogy in 1 Sam 9:1. It should be noted that the identical phrase *ʾîš yĕmînî,* without the *ben* element, occurs after Aphiah, and while intended to refer to the first of seven generations (see BECORATH), may have been mistaken by a scribe or copyist to refer back redundantly to Kish. The proposed insertion would have reinforced for the perceptive reader the resulting play on the Saul-Agag story in 1 Samuel 15, while obscuring the original Merarite connections.

5. The son of Jeiel and founder of the postexilic settlement at Gibeon (1 Chr 8:29–30; 9:35–36). His status as the premonarchic founder of the site (Williamson *Chronicles* NCBC, 85–86) or its postexilic rebuilder is often considered unclear (Rudolph *Chronikbücher* HAT, 80; Myers *1 Chronicles* AB, 62). However, his postexilic context is apparent from the remark that he and his sons lived opposite their kinsmen in Jerusalem (8:32; 9:38). The comment presumes the lot-casting procedure used to resettle Jerusalem in Neh 11:1–2, which would have removed the unnamed kinsmen from their recently resettled home in Gibeon to the former capital city as part of an official provincial decree or decision. Many of the tribal genealogies in 1 Chronicles 2–9 contain late "updates" that provide information about the population of the postexilic community of Jehud. It is conceivable that he was a distant descendant of Kish ben Abiel and that he was named after his forefather. His choice to resettle Gibeon may have been due to his preexilic ancestral links to the site.

Bibliography

Ahlström, G. 1982. *Royal Administration and National Religion in Ancient Palestine.* Leiden.

Ben-Barak, Z. 1981. Meribaal and the System of Land Grants in Ancient Israel. *Bib.* 62: 73–91.

Cassel, P. 1888. *An Explanatory Commentary on Esther.* Trans. A. Bernstein. Clark's Foreign Theological Library. Edinburgh.

Gordis, R. 1974. *Megillat Esther.* New York.

Haupt, P. 1907–08. Critical Notes on Esther. *AJSL* 24: 97–186.

Hoschander, J. 1923. *The Book of Esther in the Light of History.* Philadelphia.

McKane, W. 1957–58. The *Gibbôr Ḥayil* in the Israelite Community. *Glasgow University Oriental Society Transactions* 17: 28–37.

Nöldeke, T. 1886. Review of *Kinship and Marriage in Early Arabia,* by W. Robertson Smith. *ZDMG* 40: 148–87.

Weber, M. 1952. *Ancient Judaism.* Trans. H. H. Gerth and D. Martindale. Glencoe, IL.

DIANA V. EDELMAN

KISH (PLACE). Ancient city of Babylonia, situated on a now dead branch of the Euphrates, 15 kms E of Babylon. This city does not appear in biblical texts, but it draws its prestige from the role it played during the Early Dynastic periods (first half of the 3d millennium), for the appeal it held for the Mesopotamian sovereigns (the title of King of Kish), and for the longevity of its existence.

The site is formed from a series of tells of fairly substantial size. They cover a primarily E–W band for nearly 5 km in length and more than 1.5 km in width. The principal ones are el-Khazneh, el-Oheimir, and the Ingharra group, bordered to the N by the Bender tell and to the S by the A tell; others, designated by letters, were the objects of important varied research. It has been shown in excavations conducted by different teams and by MacGuire Gibson, that in its present state, these tells do not represent in any way the old city within its natural limits, but that we can recognize there the vestiges of the changes of an urban habitat through the vicissitudes of a long existence, linked to the transfer of natural water lanes and to the construction of canals. It is, therefore, impossible to present a clear image of the configuration, of the limits and of the ancient city's organization.

Visited by many travelers in the 19th century, the site was identified with the ancient city of Kish by G. Smith in 1873. Clandestine digs which took place at the beginning of the 20th century brought to the market an abundance of cuneiform tablets. That prompted Abby H. de Genouillac to excavate there at the beginning of 1912. After the First World War, exploration started up again from 1923 to 1933 by the Herbert Weld and Field Museum of Natural History of Chicago, under the successive direction of S. Langdon, E. Mackay, and C. Watelin. Unfortunately, the results were incompletely published and indicate a mediocre archaeological standard.

The beginnings of the ancient city go back to the end of the 4th millennium or to the beginning of the 3d, that is to say, to the last predynastic phase, according to the major sounding taken from the west of Ingharra tell. According to the king-lists, certainly compiled at a fairly late date, it is at Kish that Kingship descended from heaven and was given to men; it is thus that these same lists attribute four dynasties to the ancient city. This could show that the remembrance of a repeated domination of the city over the Babylonian world, perhaps expanded to Sumer on certain occasions, was maintained under a mythic form and would explain also the prestige wielded by the title of king of Kish over the larger part of the great Mesopotamian sovereigns; it is also thought that one can recognize in these remembrances indications of the role played by the city in the development of the monarchic power in Mesopotamia. It is from Kish again that tradition has Sargon leaving for Akkad when engaged in the formation of his empire. Moreover, archaeology seems to confirm the importance of the city in this period. It is in effect at the end of ED II and at the beginning of ED III that one must fix two important monuments of the city: Palace A and the "Plano-Convex Building" that represent two of the oldest examples of monumental civil architecture; the cemetery that was located in the ruins of the palace also belongs to the end of the same period. But the transfer of the capital from Kish to Akkad by Sargon marks, in fact, the end of the primacy of the old city that will henceforth play a rather small role up until the Sassanids. The archaeological evidence attests to some fairly important installations from the Old Babylonian period (tell el-Oheimir) with habitation and ziggurat, diverse installations, tombs and a Neo-Babylonian fort in tells X and W, and ziggurats and particularly imposing temples from the same period as at Ingharra, an undoubtedly Parthian fortress in the Bender tell, and finally, palaces and Sassanid residences in tell H. The longevity of the installation is thus remarkable, but the quarters seem to have been displaced over the course of time, and the city never regained its great importance—not even, it seems, during the period of the large temples from the Ingharra tell.

Among the monuments worthy of attention, one must note Palace A and the Plano-Convex Building because they are perhaps the oldest remains of royal architecture. Of the first, which takes its name from the small tell that contained its ruins, only two buildings have been found on the sides of a mostly open space: a majestic staircase created the entrance to the northern building, a four-columned portico, the façade of the second. They appeared to be independent, but in reality, links existed from one building to the other on the level of the first floor; the staircases show that this floor extended over the entire surface of the buildings, and the architectural analysis leads one to place the apartments and the reception rooms there, the ground floor having been occupied by stores and services. The room with four columns of the southern building owes this particularity to the fact that it had to support a wall on the upper level and not, as has long been thought, because it had some kind of special function. The Plano-Convex Building, located more than 1500 m to the N of the palace in an isolated setting, is also very incomplete; its organization is apparently more confused, but one can make out the principles that govern the monumental architecture of the Early Dynastic periods. Even if nothing proves it with certainty, it is traditional to consider both of these buildings as palaces: in any case they offer no religious characteristics.

On the other hand, the buildings unearthed by Genouillac, Mackay, and Watelin on the Ingharra tell are two temples from the Neo-Babylonian period, perhaps constructed by Nebuchadnezzar (4th century) of large dimensions and conceived according to a classical plan for the period: in the center a large, almost square courtyard surrounded by a simple or double crown of elongated rooms (annex chapels, treasuries, stores, priests' rooms) with a cella on the facing side, eventually preceded by an antecella with a cultic niche. Two ziggurats were closely associated with these two temples.

The site has given few important objects. One will note, however, some fairly rich funerary material for the Early Dynastic periods (in particular, tombs containing vases, weapons, copper bridles) and the Neo-Babylonian period.

Bibliography

Genouillac, H. de. 1924–25. *Premières recherches archéologiques à Kich.* Paris.

Gibson, M. 1972. *The City and Area of Kish.* Miami.

Langdon, S., and Watelin, L. C. 1930–34. *Excavations at Kish.* Vols. 1, 3, 4. Paris.

Mackay, E. 1925. *Report on the Excavations of the "A" Cemetery at Kish, Mesopotamia, I.* Chicago.

———. 1929. *A Sumerian Palace and the "A" Cemetery at Kish, Mesopotamia, II.* Chicago.

Margueron, J. C. 1982. *Recherches sur les palais mésopotamiens de l'âge du Bronze.* Paris.

Moorey, P. R. S. 1976. *The Oxford-Chicago Excavations at Kish (1923–33).* Oxford.

JEAN-CL. MARGUERON
Trans. Stephen Rosoff

KISHI (PERSON) [Heb *qîšî*]. See KUSHAIAH (PERSON).

KISHION (PLACE) [Heb *qišyôn*]. Levitical city allotted to the Gershonites and found in the distribution list to Issachar (Josh 19:20; 21:28). There is no parallel to Kishion in the Levitical City list in 1 Chronicles. Outside of the biblical record there is one possible reference to Kishion, in the Thutmose III list of conquered towns. *q-š-n* is the thirty-seventh city in this 15th century Egyptian list (Yeiven 1950) and it has been identified with biblical Kishion. Because of the uncertainty of the location of Kishion, there is wide disagreement about with which tell it should be associated. Three sites are usually considered to be candidates for Kishion: Tell el-Ajjul, Tell el-Muqarqash, and Khirbet Qasyûn.

Tell el-Ajjul (M.R. 185225) has been identified as a possible site for biblical Kishion by Abel (*GP,* 61–62, 422–23). The tell is located 2 km SW of En-dor, 7 km SSW of Mt. Tabor. The view rivals that of Mt. Tabor, with the entire Esdraelon Plain to the crest of the Jordan rift seen to the N, E, and W. There are several wadis cutting the surface of the land, indicating a plentiful water supply around the tell. Ajjul is magnificent, but the tell is all but sherdless; however, there is scanty evidence of ancient structures. The archaeological surveys conducted at Ajjul indicate occupation during Iron I, Iron II, Roman/Byzantine, Hellenistic, and Medieval periods.

Albright (1926: 231) was the first to identify Tell el-Muqarqash (M.R. 194228) with biblical Kishion. Originally Albright (1923: 12) had associated the site with Beth-shemesh, but he changed his position in 1926 in favor of Kishion. Albright used *qšn* in the Thutmose list as one of the determinatives in choosing Tell el-Muqarqash, just as Abel had done with Tell el-Ajjul. Muqarqash is located 7 km SE of Mt. Tabor, on the Wadi esh-Sherrar, at the junction of two valleys. The land around the tell is rich agriculturally and there is an excellent water supply for it is here that the Wadi Siran empties its waters into Wadi esh-Sherrar. The archaeological surveys conducted at Muqarqash have found occupation at the site during the Iron I, Iron II, and Byzantine periods.

The third site associated with biblical Kishion is Khirbet Qasyûn (M.R. 187229). Aharoni (*LBHG*, 148) has been the exponent of this identification, although he identifies it with a question mark in the campaign list of Thutmose III. He arrived at his conclusion by associating the name in the Thutmose list *(q-š-n)* with "Tell Qisyon." However, there is a problem. The name Khirbet Qasyûn is recent. The older 1:20,000 Palestine map calls the site El-Khirba. It was not until 1946 that Zimbalist (1946) discovered the site and first proposed its identification with the biblical Kishion.

Khirbet Qasyûn is located 2 km S of the base of Mt. Tabor in the Esdraelon Plain. The land around Qasyûn is important for understanding this site because it stands so much in the shadow of Mt. Tabor. There are three mounds that make up Khirbet Qasyûn: the one to the E is the lowest and smallest of the three; the one to the NNW and the one to the W with a S appendage are of equal height. Six different archaeological surveys have been conducted at Khirbet Qasyûn and pottery has been identified from the EB, MB, LB, Iron I, Iron II, Hellenistic and Roman/Byzantine periods. If the old Arabic root of this tell had been associated with Qasyûn, there would be good reason to associate it with biblical Kishion. However, because the original name was el-Khirba, there is no strong reason to make this identification. Overall, Tell el-Muqarqash is the preferred site for biblical Kishion. See also Peterson 1977: 141–65; Saarisalo 1927–28: 68.

Bibliography

Albright, W. F. 1923. Some Archaeological and Topographical Results of a Trip through Palestine. *BASOR* 11: 3–14.

———. 1926. The Topography of the Tribe of Issachar. *ZAW* 44: 225–36.

Peterson, J. L. 1977. *A Topographical Surface Survey of the Levitical "Cities" of Joshua 21 and I Chronicles 6.* Diss. Seabury-Western Theological Seminary.

Saarisalo, A. 1927–28. *The Boundary Between Issachar and Naphtali.* Helsinki.

Yeivin, S. 1950. The Third District in Tuthmosis III. List of Palestino-Syrian Towns. *JEA* 36: 51–62.

Zimbalist, N. 1946–47. Kishon and Kishyon. *BIES* 13 (English summary).

JOHN L. PETERSON

KISHON (PLACE) [Heb *qîšôn*]. A river mentioned in the Bible in connection with the battle of Deborah (Judg 4:7, 13; 5:21; Ps 83:10 [—Eng 83:9]) and with the contest between Elijah and the Priests of Baal on Mt. Carmel (1 Kgs 18:40). The usual identification is with Wadi al-Muqatta that drains the Jezreel westward, flowing N of the Carmel reaching the Mediterranean at Haifa. In modern Hebrew this had been named Kishon River.

However, Zori (Zimbalist) suggested that the Kishon of the battle of Deborah is to be identified with Wadi el-Bira (Nahal Tabor) that flows E from Mt. Tabor to the Jordan (Zimbalist 1946–47). A site close to the sources of this river is called Tel Kishyon (M.R. 187229). En-dor, associated with the battle of Deborah (Ps 83:11—Eng 83:10), is in the same region. It is apparently this river that appears on Hieronymus' map as the river Kishon (Rohricht 1890: map 12), and in the 14th century Eshtori ha-Parhi noted that this river was called *qison* in Arabic, and thus he also identified it as the Kishon (Edelman 1852: 21b, 47a). Both Zori and Eshtori ha-Parhi imply that there were two rivers by the name of Kishon. Most scholars, however, believe there was only one river; taking the phrase "Taanach on the waters of Megiddo" (Judg 5:19) as evidence that the battle of Deborah took place near these towns, they insist that the River Kishon should be located in the same vicinity. This also accords with the lower section of the same river being the Kishon of 1 Kings 18 (i.e., near Mt. Carmel).

In the song of Deborah, the Kishon appears in poetic parallelism with Heb *nahal qĕdûmîm* (AV "ancient river"; RSV "onrushing torrent"). Abel suggests that the version in LXX A and other manuscripts, Kaduseim, is closer to the original, and understands this to have designated "the river of Kadesh," suggesting that "Kadesh" here is Tell abu Qudeis (M.R. 170218) between Megiddo and Taanach (*GP*, I: 469). Similarly, Abel suggests that the river Pacida/Pagida, Pliny's alternative name for the river Belus (*HN* V.17–75), is the Kishon and that it is perhaps the Latin translation of Kishon (both connected to the meaning "to lay a trap").

The name Kishon does not appear in the descriptions of the tribal territories in Joshua, but sections of Wadi el-Muqatta (the Kishon) were almost certainly the border between Asher and Manasseh (there called Shihor-Libnath; Josh 19:26), the border between Zebulun and Manasseh ("the river that is before Jokneam"; Josh 19:11), and perhaps also the border between Issachar and Manasseh.

Bibliography

Edelman, H., ed. 1852. *Pharchi (Parchi), Caftor wa-Pherach.* Berlin (in Hebrew). Repr. 1959.

Rohricht, R. 1890. *Bibliotheca Geographica Palaestinae.* Berlin.

Zimbalist (Zori), N. 1946–47. Kishon and Kishyon. *Bulletin of the Jewish Palestine Exploration Society* 13: 28–33 (Hebrew with Eng summary).

RAFAEL FRANKEL

KISS (NT). Placing the lips upon a person or thing as a mark of homage or affection. It is a common phenomenon in many religions; generally directed towards inanimate objects (*RGG*³, 4: 190). Early Christian sources confine their prescriptions of the kiss to a greeting between two people. Its practice within community strengthens the ties of affection that exist in the fellowship.

A. NT Usage

The noun "kiss" *(philēma)* is mentioned seven times in the NT. Two of these occurrences are in Luke: Jesus suggests to Simon his host that he expected a welcoming kiss from him when he entered his house (7:45), and asks Judas about kissing the Son of Man when he was handed over (22:48). The other NT occurrences of the noun appear in connection with the verb "greet" in the imperative mood: four times in Paul (*philēma hagion* "holy kiss": Rom 16:16; 1 Cor 16:20; 2 Cor 13:12; 1 Thess 5:26), and once in 1 Pet 5:14 (where it is called the *philēma agapēs,* "kiss of love." The verb *kataphileō* appears six times—once each in Matthew (26:49) and Mark (14:45) in connection with Judas, and three times in Luke: the woman who expressed her love to Jesus is commended for kissing his feet (7:38, 45); and the father greets the returning prodigal by falling upon his neck and kissing him (15:20). Acts portrays Paul's emotional farewell from the Ephesian elders: "they wrapped their arms around Paul and kissed him" (20:37). In these two instances it includes an embrace and the placing of the lips of one person on either the lips or the cheek of another. One case involves a woman kissing a man; the rest presumably refer to men kissing each other. Only the heterosexual instance has possible erotic connotations; all are public.

B. The Kiss in Ancient Judaism

There is no agreement on the origins or significance of this practice in Judaism or Christianity. Hofmann (1938) first gave the kiss major attention and concluded that its roots were animistic and that the holy kiss was a means of conveying power from one person to another. Blank (*IDB* 3: 40) describes the holy kiss as a "ceremonious greeting comparable to the practice reflected in the OT." Perella takes it primarily in a liturgical sense, as conveying the Holy Spirit (1969: 18–23), or related to prayer (so also Stählin *TDNT* 9: 139).

Analogies have been sought in the practices of Judaism, but without shedding much light on Jewish practices of the Second Temple period. Josephus uses the noun *philēma* four times exclusively in the death scene at Masada, when the fathers bid farewell to their loved ones before they massacre them (*JW* 7.391). In the Hebrew Bible it is said that Jacob kissed Rachel at their first meeting (Gen 29:11). The story created problems; some Jewish commentators explained that Jacob subsequently wept because those who saw him kiss Rachel insinuated that he would introduce some new form of licentiousness. (John Calvin was so offended by the story that he insisted the biblical text must have inverted the order; *first* Jacob introduced himself and then he kissed Rachel!) In Josephus it is Rachel that weeps, and there is no kiss, although Jacob is "overcome with love for the maid" and "amazed" at her beauty, and Rachel "flung her arms around Jacob" (*Ant* 1.288–91). When Jacob and his family left without notice, Laban complained that he was not even able to kiss his daughters and grandchildren farewell (Gen 31:28). There are two other instances in which the kiss crosses the sexual barrier without censure: one is in Esther's encounter with King Artaxerxes, a pagan although her husband (AddEsth 15:8–12); the other concerns Raguel, who kissed his daughter (Tob 10:12). There is no evidence that non-relatives could kiss each other without censure.

In Judaism three types of kisses were considered valid: the kiss of reverence, the kiss of reunion or reconciliation (Gen 45:15), and the kiss of farewell. No general admonition to kiss each other is to be found in Jewish sources (Low 1921). The highly symbolic use of the kiss in Philo does not lead to the conclusion that the kiss of peace was practiced as a "formal and ceremonial institution of the Jewish synagogue" (Perella 1969: 15–16).

The story of *Joseph and Asenath* (Burchard 1983) has the fullest range of references to the kiss. It is certainly pre-Christian, although there are Christian interpolations. Asenath greets her parents with a kiss (4:1) and her father in turn kisses her (4:7). When Joseph arrives, her father urges her first to greet Joseph. After they have exchanged greetings he urges her, "Go and kiss your brother." As she moves toward Joseph to kiss him, Joseph stretches forth his right hand, lays it between her breasts, and says: "It is not fitting for a god-fearing man who blesses the living God with his lips . . . to kiss a foreign woman . . ." (8:4–5). He goes on: "But a god-fearing man will kiss his mother, and his sisters born of his mother, and the sisters related to him, and the wife he sleeps with, who bless the living God with their mouth. Similarly it is not proper for a god-fearing woman to kiss a strange man, for it is an abomination before God" (8:6–7).

The male custodians of Asenath show no reluctance to kiss her when she is depressed (18:3). After her conversion to Judaism, Joseph kisses Asenath without hesitation. Indeed, the scene of their reunion—while dominated by the three kisses by which he imparts the spirits of life, wisdom, and truth—distinguishes clearly between their warm greeting, embraces and the kiss itself. The interaction between erotic motifs and others is finely drawn.

In the quasi-enthronement scene (20:1–4) Asenath's willingness to serve Joseph as a slave are natural steps toward the climax in which the erotic dimensions of the feet washing interact with the servant motif. Joseph draws Asenath by the right hand and kisses her (hand?), and she kisses his head and takes her place by his right hand on the throne. In the betrothal scene Pharaoh "turned them around to face each other and led their mouths towards each other and brought their lips together and they kissed each other" (21:7). In a similar vein, when Asenath first met Jacob, he called her to himself, blessed her, kissed her, and she "stretched out her hands and she put her arms around the neck of Jacob . . . and kissed him" (22:9). Finally, in her attempts to moderate the anger of Joseph's brother, Simeon, she "stretched out her right hand and touched the beard of Simon and kissed him" and was able to persuade him to act kindly toward his enemies. Levi likewise kissed her hand as he recognized that she was interested in the life and not the death of the enemies (28:14–15). The kiss appears here as a reverential greeting, a part of a reunion, as an act with erotic overtones, and as a part of a reconciliation.

We conclude that by the first century the kiss was not seen as a merely formal act by devout Jews. Like Egyptian men and women who would not kiss Greek lips defiled by animal sacrifice (Herodotus 2.41) and later Christians who would not kiss pagans, Jews had also set restrictions. At the same time the freedom of expressing feelings of warmth and intimacy is evident in *Joseph and Asenath.* In the Second Temple period it is quite probable that among Jews the public kiss was not generally practiced: one commentary on Genesis (*Gen.Rab.* 70 [45b]) writes: "In general kissing leads to immorality: there are however three exceptions, namely kissing someone to honour that person [Samuel kissing Saul, 1 Sam 10:5], or kissing upon seeing someone after a long absence [Aaron kissed Moses, Exod 4:27], and the farewell kiss [as when Orpah kissed Naomi (Ruth 1:14)]." R. Tanchuma added the kissing of relatives: Jacob kissed Rachel (Gen 29:11; Str-B 1.995–96). Kissing of a cultic object is rejected (1 Kgs 19:18), and Hosea (13:2) ridicules those who even kiss calves while they slaughter people. Job is proud that he has not even kissed his hand in homage to idols (Job 31:26–27).

C. The Kiss in Greco-Roman Society

In Greco-Roman society the role of the public kiss changes with the levels of society and geographic location. It is reported that the elder Cato cast Manilius out of the Senate because he kissed his wife in the presence of his daughters. He allowed his wife to hug him only during a thunderstorm, and expressed his delight when Jupiter thundered! (Plut. *Cato* 17E). Julius Caesar is said to have been kissed by his mother on the way to the polls (Suetonius 13), and later, Clement of Alexandria (*Paed.* 3.12) rules that a man is never to kiss his wife in the presence of domestics, and never even to greet her in the presence of slaves.

Greco-Roman society treated the public kiss, both hetero- and homosexual, with considerable reticence (PWSup 5: 513). Dio Chrysostom portrays the return of a young lad from the hunt who gives his betrothed a kiss with the hare he has caught (*Orat.* 7:67). But Dio, when he approached and kissed the two hunters with whom he had been reunited, was ridiculed, and he "understood that in the cities people do not kiss one another" (*Orat.* 7:59).

The kiss is practiced at a time of reunion of loved ones or after a long period of separation. A special place seems to have belonged to the kiss exchanged by slaves who discovered their spiritual kinship as slaves (Aristophanes *Frogs* 754), and a newly inducted robber chief was greeted with a kiss of welcome (Apul. *Met.* 7.9). Plutarch (*Mor.: Bravery of Women* 244) seeks to explain the Roman custom of women kissing their kinsmen "on their lips," and wonders whether it was a way for men to test whether their wives had been drinking wine in their absence, or a sign of reconciliation after the Trojan women burned their ships to end their wandering (where he appeals to Aristotle [Frag. 609]); or something bestowed on women as a sign of privilege bringing honor and power in the household, or finally as a "token of kinship" in which "affection proceeded only so far as a kiss" (265B–E).

Plutarch's life of Fabius Maximus contains an incident in which Minucius admits that he is not competent to lead and goes over to Fabius' tent. There, after a speech, he embraces Fabius and kisses him. The soldiers do the same thing and embrace each other and kiss each other. Joy reigns in the whole encampment (18). Clearly the kiss serves here to confirm reconciliation.

Whatever the Greco-Roman world did to encourage or discourage kissing, it cannot be described as a source of the Pauline admonition. It may however be the case (as Thraede [1968–69: 143, n. 48] suggests) that the public kiss of greeting was becoming the fashion in the early imperial period. If public kissing was becoming a formal custom, it may have been easier for the church to make the public kiss into a group rule and provide it with a deeper motivation.

D. The Holy Kiss

There is general agreement that the "holy kiss" had its origin in the practice which emerged in the early church among the believers themselves, with the impetus probably coming from the shape of their life with Jesus himself. Nothing analogous to it is to be found among any Greco-Roman societies, nor indeed at Qumran. Lowrie (1955: 242), following Cabrol (*DACL* 2: 117–30), has suggested that Jesus originated the practice. Judas kissed Jesus in the garden, a sign which would convey one message to outsiders but would be the usual form of greeting and hence arouse no suspicions to the inside group. Others see the beginnings of the kiss in the post-resurrection appearances (Benko 1986: 82). While clearly the erotic kiss is virtually unmentioned in the NT, there is no polemic against it.

The Song of Songs, which most explicitly lauds the erotic kiss, was interpreted in 1st-century Judaism as an allegory. Christianity also did not find the Song's uninhibited affirmation of the kiss as a means of erotic communication of love congenial. The kiss as an erotic form of communication had an uneasy place in the canon. The OT scriptures warn of the dangers of the "woman's kiss" (Prov 7:13) but also depict its erotic delights without inhibition (Cant 1:2; 8:1; note that the latter sees the kiss as an unshameful public act).

The erotic element is present in Luke 7:36–50, where objection is taken to Jesus' allowing his feet to be publicly kissed by a woman (cf. Ov. *Ars* 2.534; Epict. *Disc.* 4.1.17). Interpreters are inclined to interpret the woman's continued kissing of Jesus' feet as an act of gratitude (Godet 1887: 357) or more frequently as an act of reverence (Marshall *Luke* NICNT, 309). Stählin affirms that "the kiss is the decisive embodiment of *agape*" and that the "significance of the whole event is here gathered up in the kiss (*TDNT* 9: 138–46). Few follow Schlatter's view that Luke saw it as an act of "expressing her burning love for Jesus in response to the way he had expressed to her his singular authority" (Schlatter 1960: 264). It would be incorrect to describe her action as an erotic act; nevertheless, her act itself and Jesus' acceptance of it, in the light of his reference to it as he criticizes his host's lack of grace, borders on the public display of affection decried in Proverbs and praised in the love poems of Song of Songs. Jesus risked receiving kisses of love from a person of unsavory reputation.

In contrast, the free and uninhibited exchange of kisses with maidens as part of an evening of play which leads to sleeping together "as a brother, not as a husband" with relative strangers depicted in the Shepherd of Hermas seeks to prove something quite different. Is it that the erotic element has been conquered as an enemy? (*Herm. Sim.* 9:11). Equally difficult to interpret is the *Gospel of Philip*'s affirmation: "It is by a kiss that the perfect conceive and give birth. For this reason we also kiss one another. We receive conception from the grace which is in each other" (59). The same Gospel reports that Jesus kissed Mary Magdalene often on her mouth and that the other disciples were offended (63–64; Perella 1969: 18–23).

Paul four times urges his readers to practice the "holy kiss" (not the "kiss of peace" as the NEB renders it in each of the four passages). Ethical teachers are not noted for urging people to kiss; many, following the Stoics, attained stature by showing people the value of and means whereby they could restrain expressions of ardor. Paul puts no restrictions on his command. In the earliest instance, the conclusion of 1 Thessalonians, with the request to his readers to pray for him, then adds: "Greet all the brethren *en philēmati hagiō* (with a holy kiss)" (5:26). The second half of this sentence is not to be used to narrow the meaning of the first half (Lightfoot 1902: 90); *all* members of the community are meant here, not merely the elders or the males.

In the remaining three references in the letters to Corinth and Rome he urges them to greet "each other" with the holy kiss. Since this admonition is in the midst of a discussion of greetings to and from others, it seems evident that the reason for this imperative is to assure that the mutual greeting not be neglected. The frequency of the imperative suggests that this new practice needs encouragement.

The social context of the practice involves the form of salutations emerging among the first Christians. Each of the occurrences of the "holy kiss" appears in the context of greetings, and Paul appears to have taken leadership in establishing literary greetings; indeed, he may well have been the first to draw up lists of people to greet (*TDNT* 1: 495). He was certainly the first popular ethical teacher known to instruct members of a mixed social group to greet each other with a kiss.

The addition of the adjective *hagios* clearly puts the Pauline admonition in a class by itself. It is a "sacred kiss." The imperative need not be limited to one's own gender for the protection of the holy kiss resides in what it communicates. It was not an erotic act, but an act meant to express *agapē*, as 1 Peter saw clearly. Paul is as liberated in attitudes toward women as Jesus himself had been, and in comparison with his Jewish and Hellenistic moralists, only Musonius Rufus comes close to him (Klassen 1984). In each of the instances in which heterosexual kissing is done in biblical narratives the male takes the initiative, except in Luke. Paul opens the door to a situation in which a woman will give a man unrelated to her a holy kiss in public.

Thraede concludes that the common thread in all five cases of the holy kiss is its position at the conclusion of a letter (1968–69). Four times in greetings appearing in the postscript it is embedded in variants of commands to greet people. Of the seven genuine Pauline letters, four have this command. Hofmann's suggestion "that the demand can only be followed when the church is gathered and hears the letter read. . . . in the assembly of the congregation in worship" (Hofmann 1938: 23–24) restricts the admonition too narrowly. It is more likely that Paul saw the holy kiss as something Christians should practice wherever they met. The most frequent meeting place would be the assemblies several times a week, but it can hardly be restricted to one context, not even to those times of worship associated with the action of the Holy Spirit (Kreider 1987: 31). There is certainly no evidence in the NT that it was connected with the Eucharist; indeed that connection does not appear until Justin Martyr.

The holy kiss is to be seen in a living context of people who are building a new social reality, rather than in restrictive eucharistic or liturgical terms, laden as these terms are in any case with centuries of dispute and controversy (Selwyn 1952: 244). Before we describe it as "one of the most ancient of rituals" (Bigg *1 Peter* ICC, 198) we must try to understand how it departs from 1st-century usage and what purpose it was meant to serve.

Wayne Meeks (1974: 182) has isolated the revolutionary concept of humanity expressed in Gal 3:28 and affirmed in baptism. Paul draws the concept of holiness into the regular workaday world in which people live out the oneness which they have experienced in baptism and the church. If the Christians at Philippi and elsewhere were to be greeted as "saints" (4:21), the "holy kiss" is nothing more than the kiss which "saints" give each other when they meet. The admonitions to kiss one another serve to stress the liberty to express without inhibition to all people of whatever background, rank or gender, the ardor of *agape* in any context. The "holy kiss" is a public declaration of the affirmation of faith: "In Christ there is neither male nor female, Jew nor Greek, slave nor free" (Gal 3:28).

Bibliography

Benko, S. 1986. *Pagan Rome and the Early Christians.* Bloomington, IN.

Burchard, C. 1983. *Joseph und Asenath.* JSHRZ 2/4. Gütersloh.

Godet, F. L. 1887. *Commentary on the Gospel of Luke.* Grand Rapids.

Hofmann, K.-M. 1938. *Philema Hagion.* BFCT 2/38. Göttingen.

Klassen, W. 1984. Musonius Rufus, Jesus and Paul: Three First Century Feminists. Pp. 185–202 in *From Jesus to Paul: Studies in Honour of Francis Wright Beare,* ed. P. Richardson and J. Hurd. Waterloo, Ontario.

Kreider, E. 1987. Let the Faithful Greet Each Other: The Kiss of Peace. *Conrad Grebel Review* 5: 28–49.

Lightfoot, J. B. 1902. *Notes on the Epistles of St. Paul.* London.

Low, I. 1921. Der Kuss. *MGWJ* 65: 253–76; 323–49.

Lowrie, W. 1955. The Kiss of Peace. *TToday* 12: 236–42.

Meeks, W. 1974. The Image of the Androgyne: Some Uses of a Symbol in Earliest Christianity. *HR* 13: 165–208.

Meissner, B. 1934. *Der Kuss im alten Orient.* SPAW 28: 914–30. Berlin.

Perella, N. J. 1969. *The Kiss Sacred and Profane.* Berkeley.

Selwyn, E. G. 1952. *The First Epistle of St. Peter.* London.

Schlatter, A. 1960. *Der Evangelium des Lukas.* 2d ed. Stuttgart.

Schnider, F., and Stenger, W. 1987. *Studien zum neutestamentlichen Briefformular.* NTTS 11. Leiden.

Thraede, K. 1968–69. Ursprünge und Formen des 'Heiligen Kusses' im frühen Christentum. *JAC* 11–12: 124–80.

William Klassen

KITE. See ZOOLOGY (FAUNA).

KITRON (PLACE) [Heb *qiṭrôn*]. A town in the territory of Zebulun from which the Israelites were unable to expel the Canaanite inhabitants (Judg 1:30). Kitron is often equated with the Kattath of Josh 19:15 (*LBHG,* 235), because both occur only in passages with Nahalal. Kallai has noted, however, that there are neither compelling textual nor linguistic reasons to equate the two towns, which he believes should be considered separately (*HGB,* 418). The statement that the Israelites could not conquer the town led Albright to argue that it must be located in a plain, where the Canaanites could be assumed to hold the military advantage (1921–22). Despite a lack of evidence to indicate that Zebulun control extended into the Plain of Acco, Albright located Kitron at Tell Qurdaneh/Tel Afeq (M.R. 160250), while Abel (*GP* 2: 423) supported the suggestion to locate Kitron at Tell el-Far (M.R. 160242). It seems unlikely that the location of Zebulunite towns should be found in the Plain of Acco. Aharoni's suggestion to seek Kitron's location along the fringes of the NW Jezreel Valley seems more plausible.

Bibliography

Albright, W. F. 1921–22. Contributions to the Historical Geography of Palestine. AASOR 2–3: 1–46.

MELVIN HUNT

KITTIM [Heb *kittîm*]. In the Table of Nations, the word refers to the descendants of Javan (Gen 10:4; cf. 1 Chr 1:7), but in other passages, the word refers to a place (cf. Num 24:24; Dan 11:30; 1 Macc 1:1).

The Kittim are descendants of Javan, grandson of Noah through Japheth, according to the Table of Nations (Gen 10:4; and the parallel genealogy in 1 Chr 1:7). They are associated with peoples from the region of the Aegean and the E Mediterranean. Balaam notes this maritime link in his fourth oracle (Num 24:24), where he predicts that ships from Kittim will cause difficulties for Assur, apparently the Assyrians, and Eber, possibly ancestors of the Hebrews (see Gen 10:21–25). This likely refers to the incursion of the Sea Peoples into the Levant during the 13th century B.C. Daniel 11:30 also mentions ships of the Kittim, and Jer 2:10 and Ezek 27:6 refer to its maritime setting. In the last text, their area is a source of wood used in the construction of Phoenician ships. It is also to be the source of the news of the destruction of the main Phoenician city, Tyre, according to Isa 23:1. Its distance from Phoenicia is stressed in Isa 23:12, since even flight to that far place will not provide refuge. Distance is also stressed in Jer 2:10.

The Heb term is apparently derived from the name of the town of Kition (Phoen *kt* or *kty;* Eg *ktn;* cf. Josephus *Ant* 1.28), which is near modern Larnaca on the south-central coast of Cyprus. It was a site of major importance from at least the Bronze Age (Barnett 1975: 370, 376). Some of the OT references could refer to the city itself, but the term seems to have expanded its scope to cover the entire area (Num 24:24; Isa 23:1; Ezek 27:6).

Even further expansion of the term is evident in some of the early versions of the OT and in the Apocrypha. 1 Macc 1:1 refers to Kittim as the birthplace of Alexander the Great, who is identified in that verse as "Alexander of Macedonia." The term has thus expanded its usage westward to signify the Greek peninsula. It is even further extended by the Targum Onkelos in its reading of Kittim in Num 24:24 as Rome. The Vulgate reads this verse as Italy, as it also does Ezek 27:6 and Dan 11:30. It seems that the term might have become proverbial, referring to a location or people far distant from Israel's customary purview, much as Timbuktu is used in American English. This would well fit the context of Num 24:24, Isa 23:12, Jer 2:10, and Dan 11:30. The Syriac Peshitta also stressed the geographical distance of Kittim by reading it as China (Cathay).

In the ostraca from the late 7th century B.C. found at Arad in the Judean desert, mention is made of Kittim with Greek names (Aharoni 1968:11). This could point to the existence of Greek, if not Cypriot, soldiers in the service of the Israelite king, Josiah.

The Midrash Pesher of Habakkuk reflects the historical and socioreligious context of its Essene authors during the Roman occupation of Palestine. The Pesher interprets the Chaldeans who will oppress Israel according to the canonical Habakkuk text (1:6) as the Kittim (2.12). In the Pesher, these Kittim have dominion over an Israel which is apostate in the eyes of the separatist Qumran community. These Kittim will come from far coastlands to inflict atrocities on all peoples (3.9–11), and their power will cause universal fear (3.4). Their distant maritime homeland and their apparent domination of Israel at the time of the Pesher itself support the interpretation of the Kittim as the Romans. Some propose a Syrian identification, but this locale does not appear to be sufficiently distant to fit the context (Brownlee 1979: 70).

Kittim are also mentioned in *Jub* 24:28–29, where they seem to be an archetypical, ultimate enemy who will confront the Philistines as the result of a curse upon them. No clear understanding of their identity, however, is possible from the context.

Bibliography

Aharoni, Y. 1968. Arad: Its Inscriptions and Temple. *BA* 31: 2–32.
Barnett, R. D. 1975. Sea Peoples. *CAH*² 3:359–78.
Brownlee, W. H. 1979. *The Midrash Pesher of Habakkuk.* Chico, CA.

DAVID W. BAKER

KNOWLEDGE, INTERPRETATION OF (NHC XI,*1*). The first of two Valentinian tractates occupying the first half of Nag Hammadi Codex XI, and written in the first of the two scribal hands responsible for the inscription of that codex. The language of composition is a rather standard Subakhmimic dialect of the Coptic language, bearing many resemblances to the compositional language of Codex I (the "Jung Codex"), whose inscriptional hand is quite similar to that of Codex XI, and whose contents are for the most part also Valentinian. The text bears a subscript title (and evidence of a superscript title as well) "The Interpretation of Knowledge," which, however, does not reappear elsewhere in the body of the tractate, nor is there any reference made to it elsewhere in ancient literature. The entire ms has suffered extensive damage, necessitating extensive reconstruction.

The style and structure of *Interp. Know.* is that of a

homily, perhaps meant to be delivered during a service of worship. Frequently the author speaks in the second person plural, as if addressing a congregation of which he is a member. The content of the last third of *Interp. Know.* seems aimed at a community which the author regards as beset with jealousy over the issue of spiritual gifts possessed by some members but not others, such as the ability to address the congregation. Those who possess such gifts seem to regard those who do not as ignorant, while the latter regard the former with envy.

The author attacks this situation by reminding the congregation that the oneness of the divine Father and the humiliation undergone by the Savior, as well as his offer of forgiveness of sins and release from death, are the true criteria for the behavior and attitude of the members toward one another. Using Paul's metaphor of church as the body and its members, as well as the deutero-Pauline metaphor of Christ as the head of the body, the author reminds them that, in spite of the diversity of gifts, all participate in the same body and head. Indeed, all together share the same power and grace which enables some to speak and others to understand. Therefore, any demonstration of jealousy or hate is a sign of ignorance and unwillingness to receive the grace of the Savior, which ought to be gratefully received even if it is manifested through the spiritual gifts of certain of the members. As plants have roots which are entirely intermingled, but may have many fruits, all should become equal, like the roots.

Throughout *Interp. Know.*, the author illustrates these points with passages drawn from the NT gospels (especially Matthew), which are mainly used to characterize the teaching of the Savior in the first half of the tractate, and in the second half, which is mostly parenetical in content, from the Pauline letters (especially Romans and 1 Corinthians), as well as the deutero-Pauline letters Colossians and Ephesians. The passages selected are topically arranged, often conflated with one another, and generally quoted imprecisely, as if from memory.

Most importantly, although the author clearly uses the theological terminology common to most early Christian texts, extensive use is also made of Valentinian Christian terminology and theology to illustrate certain points. For example, *Interp. Know.* begins with a distinction between those who believe because of signs and wonders and appearances of the resurrected Jesus in corporeal form, and those who can envision the presence of the Savior apart from such aids, a notion common to the Gospel of John and most gnostic Christianity. Nevertheless, the author maintains the superiority of both these approaches to a total lack of faith on the part of ordinary people who inhabit the "world" ("the place of unbelief and death"). The text then goes on to discuss what appears to be the descent of Sophia (i.e., Lady Wisdom, here called "word" and "virgin") and her receipt of a "husband," apparently the Savior, his encasing the unformed offspring of Sophia into "nets of flesh" subject to the "energies," and his subsequent descent and crucifixion: "And he was crucified and died—not his own death, for he did not deserve to be killed because of the Church of mortals. They removed him so that they might keep him in the Church. And he answered her with humiliations." The text then goes on to distinguish between two teachers, a teacher of immortality, and another teacher who uses the scriptures to teach us "about our death," presumably the Demiurge or Creator God of the OT. Instead, the good teacher, the Savior, teaches about the true and only Father; he teaches what seems to be the female seed of Sophia to accept not an earthly form, but rather the form that exists with the Father. In his redemptive descent, the Savior has "become small" and taken on a "garment of condemnation" (a visible form) in order to bear his members (the seed) aloft on his "shoulders," in order that they might enter the divine world "through the rib whence you came" (meaning to undergo a separation of the spirit from the beastly passions, a play on John 19:34; cf. Clement of Alexandria *Exc. Thdot.* 42.2; 61.3). It is Sophia who provided the flesh in which the Savior appeared, and which received the descending "majesty" (Gk *megethos*) so that the Savior might enter the "one who was disgraced" (i.e., the visible Jesus) for the salvation of the seed. The author also distinguishes between the salvific activity of the visible Jesus ("the one who was reproached") from that of "the one who was redeemed": from the former, believers receive forgiveness of sins; from the latter they receive grace. Such concepts are thoroughly at home in Valentinianism, especially in such texts as *The Gospel of Truth* (NHC I,*3:* 16,31–43,24) and Clement of Alexandria's *Excerpts from Theodotus.*

Throughout *Interp. Know.* the author seems to distinguish between ordinary Christians (in Valentinian terms, the "psychics" or "called") and Christians possessed of a higher insight (in Valentinian terms, the "pneumatics" or "elect"). The former believe through visible signs and see salvation as granted by the visible Savior, while the latter already possess a natural vision of the Savior independent of the witness to his corporeal passion and resurrection and seem already to live in the aeonic Church. Nevertheless, the essential point scored by the author is that both groups have the same Savior, and although some now already experience salvation, when the "consummation" occurs (apparently when Sophia is "completed" by (i.e., joined with) the Savior, "the [psychic] seeds that remain will endure until the All is separated and takes shape" (by the union of the aeonic male angels brought by the Savior with the female [psychic] seed produced by the Savior from Sophia's passions). Thus there should be no divisiveness in the Church, since all have the same Savior, and thus all will be saved eventually.

Given these characteristics, one would tend to place *Interp. Know.* at a point after the rise of a corpus of Christian writings which included minimally one or more gospels, a collection of Pauline and deutero-Pauline letters, and the development of an exegetical technique that would be widely recognized in Valentinian circles, say around A.D. 200, but before the composition of most of the Nag Hammadi Codices, around A.D. 350.

Bibliography

Koschorke, K. 1978. *Die Polemik der Gnostiker gegen das kirchliche Christentum.* Leiden.

———. 1979. Eine neugefundene gnostiche Gemeindordnung. *ZTK* 76: 30–60.

Pagels, E. H. 1977. The Interpretation of Knowledge: Introduction. *NHL,* 427.

———. 1988. The Interpretation of Knowledge (NHC XI,*1,* 1,1–

21,35): Introduction. *Nag Hammadi Codices XI, XII and XIII,* ed. C. W. Hedrick. Leiden.
Turner, J. D. 1977. The Interpretation of Knowledge. English translation. *NHL,* 427–34.
———. 1988. The Interpretation of Knowledge (NHC XI,*1,* 1,1–21,35): Coptic Text, English Translation and Critical Notes. *Nag Hammadi Codices XI, XII and XIII,* C. W. Hedrick. Leiden.

JOHN D. TURNER

KNOWLEDGE, TREE OF. See TREE OF KNOWLEDGE AND TREE OF LIFE.

KOA [Heb *qôaᶜ*]. People mentioned in a military setting in Ezek 23:23. It forms a pair with SHOA. It is equally unknown apart from this passage, where it is named as part of the Babylonian army. Generally it is tentatively identified with the Quti, but the lack of phonetic correspondence presents an overwhelming difficulty (Zadok 1978: 179; Hallo *RLA* 3: 719). Eichrodt (*Ezekiel* OTL, 328) recognized wordplay in the three names Pekod (punishment), Shoa (cry for help), and Koa, which he related to shrieking. Although it is unlikely that a related verb occurs in the OT (Baumgartner *HALAT* 3: 1042), one may cite the postbiblical Heb *qiᶜqēaᶜ* "cackle" (cf. Syr *qĕᶜâ* "cry out"). Seemingly it was this desire for artistic paronomasia that caused a distortion of the name, so that the prophet could draw a passionate picture of Judah's fate.

From the 3d millennium the Quti, also known as "Guti" and so "Gutians," were established and vigorous denizens of an area E of the Tigris, on both sides of the Lower Zab, although by the 1st millennium the term tended to be geographical rather than gentilic and was used more vaguely of the Transtigridian region (Hallo *RLA* 3: 718–19). It was the Babylonian governor of the Guti, Ugbaru, who went over to the Persian king Cyrus and captured Babylon for him. See SHOA for fuller treatment.

Bibliography

Zadok, R. 1978. West-Semitic Toponyms in Assyrian and Babylonian Sources. Pp. 163–79 in *Studies in Bible and the Ancient Near East,* ed. Y. Avishur. Jerusalem.

LESLIE C. ALLEN

KOHATH (PERSON) [Heb *qĕhāt; qŏhāt*]. KOHATHITE. A son of Levi, i.e., a tribe of Levites. The name, vocalized in some Hebrew mss *qŏhāt* but in most *qĕhāt,* is of uncertain etymology. It seems cognate to the Ugaritic name *ʾAqht* and syllabic *A-qá-tum* (Nougayrol 1965: 34); perhaps it is related to the Phoenician name rendered in Egyptian as *ỉ3wmqht3* (Albright 1928: 245) and to the late Hebrew name *to(w)qhat* (2 Chr 34:22). The root might be *qht,* but it would be otherwise unknown in Semitic. The Hebrew root *qhy,* "to be blunt," is a possible source, but the sense would be odd for a personal name. Since hollow roots are known to replace the middle radical with *he* in Aramaic (e.g., Aram *rhṭ,* Heb *rwṣ*), we cannot rule out the roots *qwt* and *qwy,* which in Arabic connote "sustenance" and "power." Most likely, however, the root is *yqh,* for the loss of an initial *yod* and the addition of a feminine suffix would form the infinitive construct of such roots. For example, the root *yld* generates *ledet, lat* (< **lidt*), and *lēdâ* (< **lidat*), or the root *yᶜd* both *ᶜēt* (< **ᶜidt*) and *ᶜēdâ* (< **ᶜidat*). Similarly, a root *yqh* might have had archaic infinitives **qiht* and **qihat.* The former would ordinarily have become **qahat* and the latter **qēhâ.* But the form **qiht* might also have, irregularly, become *qĕhat;* note that *dĕbaš* and *šĕʾār* probably come from **dibš* and **šiʾr.* Another possibility is that by Philippi's "law" **qiht* > **qaht,* which came to be pronounced **qāt;* in this case *qĕhāt* would be a development analogous to *bĕʾēr* < **bēr.* By any explanation the vocalization *qĕhāt* is to be preferred to *qŏhāt;* note that the LXX has *Kaath.* At any rate the root *yqh* also appears in Hebrew in the construct noun *yqht* (Gen 49:10); some discern another example in Prov 30:17, but see Thomas (1941) and Greenfield (1958: 212ff.). The root *yqh* seems to mean "to obey" or "command," for such are the senses of *wqh* in Arabic and Old South Arabic; the latter even has a noun *qht* meaning "command" or "obedience" (*DOSA,* 144–45). Akk *waqû,* "await," might also be a cognate, but it could also be a metathetic variant of *quʾʾu* (Heb *qiwwâ*) with the same meaning. If *yqh* is the root of the names Kohath, Tokhath, and Aqhat, they probably mean "obedience."

We know nothing of Kohath the son of Levi save his lifespan of 133 years (Exod 6:18). But he is in fact the personification of a clan, not an historical individual. The rest of our discussion will hence be devoted to the clan of Kohath.

The three sons of Levi according to the Zadokite genealogies were Gershon, Kohath, and Merari (Gen 46:11; Exod 6:16; Num 3:17; 26:57; 1 Chr 5:27—Eng 6:2; 6:1—Eng 6:16; 23:6). Ordinarily this order would imply that the Kohathites were of secondary rank, yet the Zadokite priests of Jerusalem claimed descent from Aaron, the eldest son of Amram, the eldest son of Kohath. Furthermore, their duties in the desert and the location of their cities show that Kohath was the most important levitical tribe during the monarchy, and so they precede the Gershonites, as in Num 4:24–45; 1 Chr 15:5–7; 2 Chr 29:12. One supposes that the genealogy crystallized in a day before the Kohathite ascendency, when either the Aaronides had not yet gained supremacy or had not affiliated themselves with Kohath. Of these possibilities the former is more likely; otherwise, why would the Aaronides revise their place in the genealogy and not reverse the order Gershon, Kohath?

According to priestly tradition, the Kohathites of the desert period, except for the house of Amram (Num 3:38), camped on the S side of the Tabernacle (Num 3:29). Their duty was to transport by hand the most sacred paraphernalia—ark, table, candelabra, altars, etc. (Num 3:31; 4:15–20; 7:9)—once they had been safely wrapped by the Aaronide priests (Num 4:5–15, 17–20). At that time the clan supposedly numbered 8,600 males more than one month old (Num 3:28), or 2,750 between the ages of 30 and 50, the career ages of cultic personnel (Num 4:36). It is believed that these census figures originate in later Israelite history.

Similarly, the assignment to the tribe of Levi of 48 cities, ascribed to the age of Joshua by the Bible, probably derives from the 8th century (Peterson 1977; Boling *Joshua* AB, 492–97). Be that as it may, to the various subclans of

Kohath the following are assigned: to the house of Aaron, thirteen cities in the S heartland of Judah, Simeon, and Benjamin, including the Judean capital Hebron and the cult city Gibeon (Josh 21:4, 10–19; 1 Chr 6:39–45—Eng vv 54–60); to the rest of Kohath, ten towns in Ephraim, Dan, and Manasseh, including the old national center Shechem (Josh 21:5, 20–26; 1 Chr 6:46, 51–55—Eng vv 61, 66–70). In other words, as might be expected, the Aaronides were based in the S, and the Kohathites as a whole were ensconced in the center of the country.

The Kohathites periodically appear in the Chronicler's survey of history. These materials, largely genealogical, are often of dubious authenticity, as the same individuals may appear as contemporaries of both David and Hezekiah, or Josiah and Ezra. The following is a report of what Chronicles says, but much of it may not reflect preexilic tradition.

First, Samuel is supposed to be a member of the house of Korah, according to the two genealogies in 1 Chr 6:7–13, 18–23. This may well be accurate, for 1 Sam 1:1 says only that Elkanah was an Ephraimite, i.e., that his family came from the area of Bethlehem, Kiriath-jearim, and Gedor in Judah. Hence they might be either Judahites or S Levites that migrated to the N. If the Chronicler is correct, the house of Kohath looms all the larger in Israelite history: besides the priests of Jerusalem, the prophet Samuel belongs in its ranks.

The second of the above-mentioned genealogies takes us into David's time, when Heman the singer, Samuel's grandson, serves in David's tent (1 Chr 6:18—Eng v 33). 1 Chr 15:5–10 says that one Uriel leads 120 Kohathite priests. This passage follows a different schema from the genealogical passages, inasmuch as Kohath, Merari, Gershon, Elizaphan, Hebron, and Uzziel are accorded equal status (v 11). 1 Chr 24:20–25 lists the subdivisions of the Kohathite Levites (to be distinguished from the Aaronide Amramites, the priests); note that Hebron must be restored to the beginning of v 23. The four Kohathite families are also included among the Levites keeping the sacred treasury in David's time (1 Chr 26:23).

Under Jehoshaphat we hear of Kohathites and Korahites together singing Yahweh's praises (2 Chr 20:19); here it does not seem that Korah is a family of Kohath as in the genealogies.

In Hezekiah's time the leader of the Kohathites is said to have been Joel the son of Azariah (2 Chr 29:12). Here Kohath, Merari, Gershon, Elizaphan, Heman, and Jeduthun seem to be of equal status (vv 12–14).

Josiah employs Zechariah and Mushullam of the house of Kohath to make music during his reconstruction of the Temple (2 Chr 34:12). In fact these men are probably Levites of Ezra's day (Ezra 8:16; Neh 8:4) retrojected into the 7th century.

Finally, in the restoration Kohathites are in charge of the Sabbath bread (1 Chr 9:32). However, the more reliable sources in Ezra and Nehemiah do not refer to the house of Kohath.

The genealogies ascribe to Kohath four sons; i.e., the Kohathites consisted of four sub-clans: Amram, Yizhar, Hebron, and Uzziel (Exod 6:18; Num 3:19, 27; 1 Chr 5:28—Eng 6:2; 6:3—Eng v 18; 23:12). 1 Chr 6:7—Eng v 22 lists one Amminadab as a sub-clan of Kohath, but this seems to be an error; we expect instead Izhar (the reading of Greek Codex Alexandrinus), elsewhere the father of Korah (Exod 6:21; Num 16:1; 1 Chr 6:22–23—Eng vv 37–38). The error could have arisen from the graphic similarity of Amram and Amminadab (admittedly slight), or perhaps Amminadab is an intrusion from the genealogy of Uzziel (1 Chr 15:10). Otherwise the sources are unanimous as to the composition of the house of Kohath.

The major ambiguities concerning the house of Kohath are its relation to the house of Amram and the relation of the house of Amram to the priesthood. The problem is analogous to the relation of the priests and Levites: at times they are opposed groups, at times the priests are the chief Levites. And just as some believed that all Levites were entitled to priesthood (see LEVITES AND PRIESTS), it seems that the Aaronides contested with other Kohathites the right to sacrifice to Yahweh, for Korah is of the house of Kohath (Num 16:1). In other words, the term "Kohathite," like "Levites," has both an inclusive and an exclusive sense. When used exclusively these terms refer only to nonpriestly members of the group in question. Hence while Elizaphan, the son of Uzziel, is the leader of the Kohathites in the desert (Num 3:30; note the prominence of Elizaphan in 1 Chr 15:8 and 2 Chr 29:13) the supreme leader of all the Levites is Eleazar, the son of Aaron. In Numbers 4, while the Kohathites are allowed to carry the holy paraphernalia, they must first be wrapped by the Aaronides. Joshua 21 and 1 Chronicles 6, in the list of levitical cities, take care to distinguish the Aaronides from "the rest of the sons of Kohath." 1 Chr 23:13–14 makes it clear that while the Aaronide half of the house of Amram is set apart by Yahweh to be his priests, the Mosaic half is reckoned to the Levites.

It may be that the figure of Amram was a creation of the genealogist to link Moses and Aaron; in the older, Elohistic source, it is unlikely that they are considered actual brothers, but rather fellow members of the tribe Levi (Exod 4:14). Thus it is probable that in older traditions Amram was not the father of *both* Moses and Aaron.

Since all our genealogical information on the Levites comes from the Aaronide priests of Jerusalem (note that Exod 2:1 does not even tell us the name of Moses' parents), we do not know how others organized the levitic clans. Surely there were differences, since location in a genealogy is a reflection of social status. As noted above, that Kohath is the second son of Levi is thus a telling admission that another group of Levites, the Gershonites, made a widely accepted claim to preeminence among the clans of Levi.

Bibliography

Albright, W. F. 1928. The Egyptian Empire in Asia in the Twenty-first Century B.C. *JPOS* 8: 223–56.

Cody, A. 1969. *A History of the Old Testament Priesthood.* AnBib 35. Rome.

Greenfield, J. C. 1958. Lexicographical Notes I. *HUCA* 29: 203–28.

Gunneweg, A. H. J. 1965. *Leviten und Priester.* Göttingen.

Möhlenbrink, K. 1934. Die levitischen Überlieferungen des Alten Testaments. *ZAW* 52: 184–231.

Moor, J. de. 1969. Review of F. Grondahl, *Die Personennamen der Texte aus Ugarit. BiOr* 26: 105–108.

Nougayrol, J. 1965. "Vocalises" et "Syllabes en Liberté" à Ugarit. Pp. 29–39 in *Studies in Honor of Benno Landsberger on His*

Seventy-Fifth Birthday, ed. H. G. Güterbock and T. Jacobsen. AS 16. Chicago.
Peterson, J. L. 1977. *A Topographical Surface Survey of the Levitical "Cities" of Joshua 21 and 1 Chronicles 6.* Th.D. Diss. Seabury-Western Theological Seminary.
Thomas, D. W. 1941. A Note on *li(y)qăhat* in Proverbs xxx. 17. *JTS* 42: 154–55.

William H. Propp

KOLA (PLACE) [Gk *Kōla*]. A site mentioned in the book of Judith, otherwise unknown (Jdt 15:4). It is possible that the site should be equated with Kona (Jdt 4:4), but this identification is unclear. See KONA. According to the passage in which it appears, Kola must be fairly close to Bethuliah. See BETHULIA. The text gives no other clues as to its location. The site is sometimes equated with Holon (Josh 15:21; 21:15), a village in the hill country of Judah, usually located SW of Hebron. See HOLON. This location is probably incorrect for Kola, since Bethuliah is in the Samaritan hill country. Given the genre of the book of Judith, it is probable that the name is fictitious.

Sidnie Ann White

KOLAIAH (PERSON) [Heb *qôlāyāh*]. **1.** The father of Pedaiah and an ancestor of Sallu, a Benjaminite and provincial leader who agreed to settle in Jerusalem (Neh 11:7). Although Sallu's line is referred to in both the list in Nehemiah 11 and 1 Chronicles 9 (cf. v 7), Kolaiah is not mentioned. This, like other differences in the two lists, suggest that there is no direct literary relationship between the two lists (contra Kellermann 1966: 208–27 and Mowinckel 1964: 146–47). Some, however, have conjectured that both writers were dependent upon common archival materials (*HSAT* 2: 42–43; Brockington *Ezra, Nehemiah and Esther* Century Bible, 187; cf. Myers *Ezra-Nehemiah* AB, 185). In any event, the presence of Kolaiah in the list provides no further evidence of use in resolving the problem. The name may mean "voice of Yahweh" (cf. *IDB* 3: 49). If, however, it is an alternative pronunciation for the name Kolaiah, which is found in the LXX of Ezr 10:23, then it may be more difficult to be certain of the name's significance (Brockington *Ezra, Nehemiah and Esther* Century Bible, 189). The latter may mean "accepted" or even "dwarf" (Brockington Ibid., 115).

2. Father of the false prophet Ahab, who is mentioned in Jer 29:21.

Bibliography

Kellermann, U. 1966. Die Listen in Nehemia 11 eine Dokummentation aus den letzten Jahren des Reiches Juda? *ZDPV* 82: 209–27.
Mowinckel, S. 1964. *Studien zu dem Buche Ezra-Nehemia I: Die nachchronistische Redaktion des Buches. Des Listen.* Skrifter utgitt av Det Norske Videnskaps-Akademii Oslo. Oslo.

Frederick W. Schmidt

KOM, KHIRBET EL- (M.R. 146104). A strategically important fortified town-site in the Judean hill country, W. of Hebron, situated at the head of the small Wâdī eṣ-Ṣaffar near the Wâdī Qubeibeh (Naḥal Lachish), one of the main access routes from the coastal plain to Hebron and the central hill country. From the standpoint of economic and political geography it is associated with the Shephelah (Dorsey 1980: 189; Rainey 1980). Lachish (11 km to the W-NW) is plainly visible from Kh. el-Kom.

ARCHAEOLOGY

A. Identification

The Arabic name means "ruins of the pile/heap," although a derivation from *qawm,* "fellow tribesmen, kindred: tribe, race, people, nation" is not impossible. The modern names of the site (an alternative name of Tell ᵓAbyad, referring to the white color of the local Senonian chalk outcroppings, was also offered by local informants) give no clue to its ancient name. A likely candidate is Makkedah (Josh 10:10–29; 12:16; 15:41), described by Eusebius as lying 8 Roman miles to the E of Eleutheropolis (Beit Jibrîn; *Onomast.* 126.22–25); the name may be preserved in transmuted form by Kh. Beit Maqdûm, less than 1 km away (Holzinger 1901: 39, et alia, cited in Dorsey 1980: 188; cf. also Rainey 1980: 196–97). This latter site is, indeed, very close to 8 Roman miles SE of Beit Jibrîn.

Survey work in the area indicates that the earliest occupation for Kh. Beit Maqdûm is Iron IIB, but the bulk of the pottery stems from the Byzantine period and later (Kochavi 1972: 60, 83–84, Site 136, listed as Kh. Beit Maqdûs; cf. Dorsey 1980: 190 n. 7), which suggests a possible shift of the name from a defunct site (Kh. el-Kôm) to a nearby living one in late antiquity. A further point to support the identity of Kh. el-Kom with Makkedah is the fact that the region is characterized by karstic caverns, fitting the character of Makkedah as narrated in Josh 10:16–27, in which five Canaanite kings initially found refuge, and where they eventually were buried. Against the identification is the fact that, despite extensive survey and excavation, Kh. el-Kôm has yielded no trace of LB occupation (cf. Josh 12:16), nor any trace of Iron Age I. Since all but one (Josh 15:37–41) of the biblical traditions involving Makkedah are set in the Conquest period, the lack of LB/Iron Age I remains poses a serious problem for the identification, or one must be prepared to ignore much of what the book of Joshua says about the S Conquest tradition; the tradition may instead reflect relationships as understood in later times (the list of "the kings of the land" cited in Josh 12:9–24 also includes the king of Arad, which was similarly unoccupied for more than a millennium prior to its Iron I resettlement).

The proposed identification of Kh. el-Kôm with biblical Shaphir (Mic 1:1), based upon the Arabic Wâdī eṣ Ṣaffar (Abel *GP* 2: 447–48), is more tenuous, since, as Dorsey points out (1980: 192), biblical *š* should become Arabic *s,* or, rarely, *š,* but not *ṣ.*

B. Ancient Significance

Kh. el-Kôm's significance in the EB II–IV has yet to be worked out. However, during the Iron Age II, probably beginning already in the late 10th/early 9th century (Holladay 1970: 176–77), the strongly fortified site probably formed part of the overall defensive network guarding the approaches to Hebron and thence to Jerusalem. If the identification with Makkedah is accepted, Josh 15:37–41 places the site in the S administrative district of the Shephelah (Rainey 1980: 194–97). Olive presses (not *in situ*) found at Kh. el-Kôm indicate one important aspect of the Iron II site's economy, linking it in this respect to nearby Tell Beit Mirsim and the Philistine site of Ekron (cf. Gitin and Dothan 1987: 206–21). The site was deserted or, at best, lightly occupied during the Persian period, but was reoccupied and refortified during the Hellenistic Period (Holladay 1970; 1971)—possibly as briefly as from ca. 332 or 301 B.C. to 276 B.C. (Geraty 1983: 546). During this period, Kh. el-Kôm seems to have been a pacifying element of the Greek central administration, projecting government power into an area of Idumean strength (Geraty 1983: 546; cf. Amiran 1953: 68–78). Personal names witnessed in the Kh. el-Kôm ostraca (below) include those of Arabic, Aramean, Edomite, Egyptian, Greek, Jewish, and Nabatean origin (Geraty 1983: 545–46), testifying to a polyglot, multicultural environment suitable to a quasi-frontier setting, and probably implying trade linkages with more distant areas.

Although at least two strong wells of modest antiquity are located within a 1-km radius, the Iron II town depended heavily upon cisterns carved in the soft chalky rock, which does not require lime plaster linings. Large underground stables/sheepfolds at the site and elsewhere in the vicinity seem to derive from the Hellenistic period and may indicate a major pastoralist orientation during that period. It is most likely, however, that some or all of them were originally large cisterns. In that case, irrigation gardening may have played a role in the site's subsistence strategy. Byzantine surface remains occur in the region, particularly at Kh. Beit Maqdum, but neither the Israeli survey, the earlier salvage work, nor the 1971 Canadian excavations found any evidence of occupation of that period at Kh. el-Kôm, thus reducing the probability that the outsized cisterns/stables were of Byzantine origin.

C. Significance to Modern Scholarship

Apart from its general economic and strategic implications, and pending publication of the pottery and small finds, Kh. el-Kôm's chief importance to modern scholarship derives from: (1) inscriptions discovered prior to and during the course of salvage work in the Iron Age II cemetery (Dever 1970); (2) a collection of ostraca from the Hellenistic village (Geraty 1983); and (3) the publication to two of the more than 100 Iron II tombs discovered by tomb robbers at the site (Dever 1970).

The most important Israelite inscriptions are from tombs. Inscriptions 1 and 2, respectively on the left of the doorway and over the doorway to Chamber 3 of Tomb 1, read: "Belonging to ʿOphai, the son of Nethanyahu, (is) this tomb chamber" (Dever 1970: 151–56); and "belonging to ʿUzza, son [or daughter] of Nethanyahu" (Dever 1970: 156–58; Barag 1970: 216–18). Inscription 3, from Tomb 1, is the second longest funerary inscription (after the Royal Steward's Tomb inscription; Avigad 1953) yet discovered from the OT period. Together with the accompanying deeply incised and strangely inverted "hand of Fatimah" motif, the inscription constitutes one of the most important contemporary literary testimonies to syncretistic or heterodox Judean religious practices (Dever 1984: 22, 30–31; Zevit 1984; Holladay 1987: 275–80; see also PALESTINIAN FUNERARY INSCRIPTIONS). This evidence derives, minimally, from the last years of the Judean monarchy, or, maximally, from the period stretching from the late 8th century to the early 6th century. Although most of the inscription is clear, a detailed reading of the inscription is difficult (Dever 1970: 159–69). Following, for the most part, Z. Zevit (1984: 43–46), it reads:

[Belonging to] Uryahu, the prosperous, his inscription.
Blessed by Uryahu by YHWH
  and from his enemies, Oh Asherata, save him.
  By Abiyahu.
[?] ?? and to Asherata
[?] A[she]rata

Other Judean inscriptions were purchased in the antiquities market and have been traced to the site. These include a typical 8th–7th century Judean wine decanter with *lyḥml,* "belonging to Yaḥmu/ol," deeply incised upon the shoulder; a late Judean folded-rim bowl with *ʾl,* "El" or "God," incised on the interior, just below the rim; and a group of 11 inscribed late Judean weights (Dever 1970: 169–87). An internally burnished saucer of uncertain origin bearing the inscription *lšl* on its base has also provisionally been linked to Kh. el-Kôm (Lemaire 1977).

The Hellenistic ostraca, collectively termed the "Khirbet el-Kôm Ostraca," consist of two ostraca from fill operations connected with the Hellenistic rebuilding of the town's defenses, plus a small household archive of six ostraca which includes a wholly Greek ostracon and the first bilingual Aramaic (Edomite?)-Greek ostracon yet found in Palestine (Geraty 1975; 1981; 1983).

The bilingual docket records a loan made by one *Qôsyadaʿ,* an Edomite (or, at this time, Idumean) *kapēlos,* or, possibly, "publican," to the Greek *Nikēratos* (for a varying interpretation, cf. Skaist 1978). Of special significance is the exact dating of the transaction: "the 12th of *Tammuz* (*Panēmos* in the Greek section), year 6." The year date probably refers to the 6th year of Ptolemy II Philadelphus, i.e., 277 B.C. (Geraty 1983: 545). Found lying on the floor of an abandoned Hellenistic house, together with numerous loom weights, it probably comes from the final years of the site's occupation. Other data, mostly onomastic, gleaned from the ostraca have already been cited above.

The multichambered Iron Age II tombs, particularly Tomb I, with its carefully carved body recesses, are valuable extensions to the S tomb typology already known from Tell en-Naṣbeh, the environs of Jerusalem, Beth-shemesh, Lachish, Kh. Beit Lei, Dhahriyeh *(Tell ez-Zaherîyeh),* and Tel Ḥalif.

D. History of Excavation and Site History

Initial salvage work at the site was conducted in 1967 by W. G. Dever, after antiquities appearing on the market earlier in the year had been traced back to Kh. el-Kôm. Further salvage excavations, which sought to provide firm archaeological contexts for the Iron II epigraphic, funerary, and ceramic remains discovered by Dever (1970), were conducted in 1971 by J. S. Holladay, Jr., accompanied by J. Strange (Holladay 1970; 1971). The results of the three major excavation areas, all on the perimeter of the tell, harmonize well with the archaeological profiles of other Shephelah sites such as Tell ᶜAitun and Tell Beit Mirsim.

Field 1 was in an olive orchard just inside the easternmost walled area, where EB II–III levels were discovered within 15 cm of the present surface. This area also included Hellenistic and Iron II intrusions, including a one-room (wine?) cellar and an early bottle-shaped cistern, in which was a good collection of (provisionally dated) 9th-century pottery. The Iron II town wall proved to have been set in an open-sided trench dug to bedrock and appears to have been the first fortification wall at the site.

Field 2 was to the S, beneath a threshing floor. This area yielded Hellenistic remains (courtyards and casemate rooms butted the defensive wall system) beneath which were late Iron Age II remains; EB and Chalcolithic materials were then found on the underlying rock surface. Some of the series of Judean weights published by Dever purportedly came from an area only 20 or 30 m farther W.

Field 3 lay some 200 m farther E, in the area of the town gate. A two-entry (two-roomed with benches) gate of the late Iron Age II period succeeded an earlier, probably originally four-roomed, gateway of the early Iron Age II period. In its last Iron II phase, Kh. el-Kôm was fortified with a solid "offsets"-style wall not entirely dissimilar to the "offsets" wall at Tell Arad or Tell en-Naṣbeh. The Iron II gate was rebuilt and refurbished at the beginning of the Hellenistic occupation of the site. This town-site, though substantial and well built, was short lived, probably beginning soon after either 332 B.C. or 301 B.C., and was possibly abandoned as early as 276 B.C. (Geraty 1983: 546). The site remained deserted until its reoccupation during the post–World War I *pax britannica* (Amiran 1953: 68–78, 205–09).

Bibliography

Amiran, D. H. K. 1953. The Pattern of Settlement in Palestine. *IEJ* 3: 68–72, 202–208, 257–60.

Avigad, N. 1953. The Epitaph of a Royal Steward from Silwan Village. *IEJ* 3: 137–52.

Barag, D. 1970. Note on an Inscription from Khirbet el-Qôm. *IEJ* 20: 216–18.

Dever, W. G. 1970. Iron Age Epigraphic Material from the Area of Khirbet el-Kôm. *HUCA* 40–41: 139–204.

———. 1984. Asherah, Consort of Yahweh? New Evidence from Kuntillet Ajrud. *BASOR* 255: 21–37.

Dorsey, D. A. 1980. The Location of Biblical Makkedah. *TA* 7: 185–93.

Geraty, L. T. 1975. The Khirbet el-Kôm Bilingual Ostracon. *BASOR* 220: 55–61.

———. 1981. Recent Suggestions on the Bilingual Ostracon from Khirbet el-Kôm. *AUSS* 19: 137–40.

———. 1983. The Historical, Linguistic, and Biblical Significance of the Khirbet el-Kôm Ostraca. Pp. 545–48 in *The Word of the Lord Shall Go Forth,* ed. C. L. Meyers and M. O'Connor. Winona Lake, IN.

Gitin, S., and Dothan, T. 1987. The Rise and Fall of Ekron of the Philistines. *BA* 50: 197–222.

Holladay, J. S., Jr. 1970. Notes and News: Khirbet el-Qôm. *IEJ* 20: 175–77.

———. 1971. Chronique archéologique: Khirbet el-Kôm. *RB* 78: 593–95.

———. 1987. Religion in Israel and Judah Under the Monarchy: An Explicitly Archaeological Approach. Pp. 249–99 in *AIR*.

Holzinger, H. 1901. *Das Buch Joshua*. KHC 6.

Kochavi, M., ed. 1972. *Judaea, Samaria, and the Golan, Archaeological Survey 1967–1968*. Jerusalem (in Hebrew).

Lemaire, A. 1977. Inscription paléo-hébraique sur une assiete. *Semitica* 27: 21–22.

Rainey, A. F. 1980. The Administrative Division of the Shephelah. *TA* 7: 194–202.

Skaist, A. 1978. A Note on the Bilingual Ostracon from Khirbet el-Kôm. *IEJ* 28: 106–108.

Zevit, Z. 1984. The Khirbet el-Qôm Inscription Mentioning a Goddess. *BASOR* 255: 39–47.

JOHN S. HOLLADAY, JR.

OSTRACA

Khirbet el-Kôm is the modern Arabic name given to a village that overlies an ancient site that goes back to the EB Age. It is situated almost midway between Hebron and Lachish, overlooking the Shephelah of S Palestine (M.R. 146104; also known as Khirbet el-Qôm). It first came to the attention of archaeologists when large-scale robbing of antiquities occurred after the outbreak of the Arab-Israeli hostilities in 1967. Late that year, W. G. Dever undertook a salvage excavation of some Iron Age tombs in the vicinity and published the Iron Age epigraphic finds (1969–70). In order to set these important Hebrew inscriptions in their stratigraphic context before further robbing, and before new building in the modern village precluded excavation of the occupational levels of the ancient town proper, John S. Holladay, Jr., undertook new salvage work in 1971 (1971: 175–77), choosing three widely separated fields on the W, S, and E edges of the village for detailed stratigraphic investigation. Eight ostraca came from the latter two, Field II (S) consisting primarily of a Hellenistic structure rebuilt on the foundations of an Iron Age structure against the city wall, and Field III (E) a Hellenistic rebuilding of an Iron Age city gate.

Ostraca numbers 1–6 came from a single room in the final phase of a Hellenistic structure rebuilt on Iron Age foundations against the city wall (Field II), and appear to be records from the archives of Qos-yadaᶜ bin Hannaʾ, an Idumean moneylender (called a *kapēlos* in one of the inscriptions). The locus from which the first four ostraca came was delimited laterally by the four walls of the structure's "west room," entered from another room to the E. To judge from the support pillar or pedestal (built up of large superimposed stones) in the center of this room, it had probably been roofed, perhaps even with a second floor. When this superstructure collapsed, it filled the (approximately) 2.5-m-square room with debris to a depth of 80 cm. The lower half of this detritus was the locus from which ostraca numbers 5 and 6 came, the change in locus numbers having been made when it had become certain that excavation of the room's last living surface had begun. The field reading of the sherds from the upper locus included undistinguished, EB, Iron Age II, Persian, and Hellenistic, though the call for the sherds from the lower locus and especially the floor itself was confined to undistinguished and Hellenistic. In addition to these sherds, many of which yielded restorable vessels, bone and various types of organic material were found, along with a chalkstone loomweight, ten unbaked clay loomweights, two whetstones, a worked bone instrument, fragments of a large chalkstone basin, a fragment of light greenish-blue faience, and the following iron objects: nail, spatula (?), point, and tanged blade.

The script of ostraca numbers 1, 2, 4, and 5 is Aramaic, though the language is ostensibly Edomite. The script and language of number 6 is Greek. Perhaps of greatest interest is number 3, a 9-line bilingual (Edomite and Greek) which contains a double date in a 6th year of an unspecified king or era. The combined evidence of Aramaic and Greek paleography along with other chronological factors suggest the 6th year of Ptolemy II Philadelphus: 277 B.C. Thus these ostraca provide the first firm 3d-century peg for the Palestinian Aramaic and Greek scripts—a notable contribution to LXX text criticism and the palaeographical study of the manuscripts from Qumran.

Ostraca numbers 7 and 8 came from foundation trenches of the initial Hellenistic rebuild of the Iron Age city gate in Field III. Though the inscriptions are poorly preserved, they are clearly in an Aramaic script of the late 4th century B.C.

These ostraca are among the few primary sources for the history of Palestine, its life, language, and onomasticon in the late 4th and early 3d centuries. Judging from the apparent language and name of the *kapēlos*, we have what is our first primary evidence of Edomite (or by this time, Idumaean) presence in the area. Whatever his exact profession as a *kapēlos*, it appears to have brought Qos-yadaᶜ into contact with Nabateans, Arameans, Jews (?), Greeks, Arabs, and Egyptians (to judge from the personal names mentioned in the ostraca). Though the script of the ostraca appears to be similar, if not identical, with Aramaic, their locale, the Qos name of the *kapēlos*, the use of *bn* rather than *br*, and *Hiphᶜil* rather than *ʾAphᶜel*, suggest a strong Canaanite influence if not a full-blown Edomite dialect. Ostraca numbers 3 and 6 may be the earliest extant indigenous Greek inscriptions to be found in Palestine. The evidence of the corpus must be considered when defining the Greek term *kapēlos*. Though normally translated something like "retailer" or "peddler," perhaps its meaning must now include in its scope the profession implied in the ostraca, i.e., "moneylender." This may have a bearing on the usage of the word in Isa 1:22 (LXX) and 2 Cor 2:17.

Bibliography

Dever, W. G. 1969–70. Iron Age Epigraphic Material from the Area of Khirbet el-Kôm. *HUCA* 40–41: 139–204.

Geraty, L. T. 1972. The Third Century B.C. Ostraca from Khirbet el-Kom. Ph.D. diss., Harvard.

———. 1975. The Khirbet el-Kom Bilingual Ostracon. *BASOR* 220: 55–61.

———. 1981. Recent Suggestions on the Bilingual Ostracon from Khirbet el-Kom. *AUSS* 19: 137–40.

———. The Historical, Linguistic, and Biblical Significance of the Khirbet el-Kom Ostraca. Pp. 545–48 in *WLSGF*.

Holladay, J. S., Jr. 1971. Notes and News: Khirbet el-Qôm. *IEJ* 21: 175–77.

LAWRENCE T. GERATY

KONA (PLACE) [Gk *Kōna*]. A site mentioned in the book of Judith which is otherwise unknown (Jdt 4:4). Kona is one of the towns which prepares to meet the onslaught of Holofernes as he comes down from the N. It is located, according to the author of Judith, N of Jerusalem. The name was early corrupted in certain Greek manuscripts to "villages" (Gk *kōmas*), indicating that the name was unfamiliar from a very early period (see also Old Latin^S, Syriac). Stummer (1947: 16) makes a tentative identification with Kamon, the village in Gilead of the judge Jair (Judg 10:5). See KAMON. He identifies this with modern Qamm, 3 miles N of Taiyibeh (M.R. 218221). Aharoni and Avi-Yonah *(MBA)* also indicate this as a possibility, as well as Camus, according to Polybius one of the cities conquered by Antiochus III (Polyb. 5.54–56). Camus is located NE of Pella. These identifications are possible only if one accepts the equation Kona equals Kamon. Given the genre of the book of Judith, it is entirely possible that the name is fictitious.

Bibliography

Stummer, F. 1947. *Geographie des Buches Judith.* Bibelwissenschaftliche Reihe, Heft 3. Stuttgart.

SIDNIE ANN WHITE

KORAH (PERSON) [Heb *qōraḥ*]. KORAHITES. Names based on **qrḥ*, "bald, bald head," are frequently attested in Semitic languages. In addition to several individuals named Korah, there is also the biblical Kareah, Qrḥ in Ugaritic and Arad Ostracon 49:2; Akkadian *Qar-ḫa-a* and *Qa-ri-ḫi;* Thamudic Qrḥ; Nabatean Qrḥ, Qrḥw, Qrḥh; and Arabic Qāriḥ, Qarāḥ, etc.

1. Son of Esau and Oholibamah (Gen 36:5, 14, 18; 1 Chr 1:35). However, Gen 36:16 lists him as a son of Eliphaz, and therefore Esau's grandson. He is credited with being one of the "tribal chiefs" (Heb *ʾallûpîm*) of Edom, and as such his name probably represents a tribe or clan within the Esauite/Edomite tribal system.

ULRICH HÜBNER

2. One of the principal families involved in leadership in the Jerusalem temple. The earliest attestation to the role of the Korahites is perhaps to be seen in 2 Chr 20:19, where the Korahites are listed alongside the Kohathites as leading the people in praise. Though it is generally assumed that the temple arrangements as projected by Chronicles are postexilic, this reference must date to a time prior to the development of the formal postexilic levitical genealogy. Here the Korahites and the Kohathites are parallel and equal participants in the cultic leadership, a state that conflicts with the later tradition which establishes Kohath as one of the primary eponyms of levitical leadership and the Korahites as but one sub-subgroup of the Kohathites.

The note in Num 26:58 likewise reflects a relatively early tradition, listing the family of Korah as one of five major levitical families. Already, however, we most likely see a development in which the levitical families of Gershon, Kohath, and Merari have established themselves as dominant phratries, and the major families—Libni, Hebron, Mahli, Mushi, and Korah—are understood to be the major representatives of these phratries. According to the genealogy of Exodus 6, Libni is the son of Gershom, Hebron of Kohath, Mahli and Mushi of Merari, and Korah the grandson of Kohath.

The early importance of the Korahites in Israelite worship is also attested to by the numerous psalms derived from the "Korahite Psalter" (Psalms 42, 44–49, 84–85, 87–88). The "prophesying" of an Asaphite Levite (2 Chr 20:14–17), along with the connection of both Korah and Asaph to cultic psalmody, has led many to make a connection between preexilic cultic prophecy and the development of the postexilic temple offices.

The early prominence of the Korahites in the postexilic (and possibly already preexilic) temple apparently faded during subsequent generations. Although there is genealogical instability, the dominant tradition establishes them as a sub-subgroup of the Kohathites. The various genealogies are as follows:

Exod 6:18 presents the shortest genealogy:
Kohath → Izhar → Korah, with the sons of Korah listed horizontally as Assir, Elkanah, and Abiasaph

1 Chr 6:22–24 extends the horizontal dimension vertically:
Kohath → Amminadab → Korah → Assir → Elkanah → Ebiasaph → Assir → Tahath → Uriel → Uzziah → Shaul

1 Chr 6:31 presents an even lengthier vertical genealogy:
Kohath → Izhar → Korah → Ebiasaph → Assir → Tahath → Zephaniah → Azariah → Joel → Elkanah → Amasai → Mahath → Elkanah → Zuph → Toah → Eliel → Jeroham → Elkanah → Samuel → Joel → Heman the Singer

In all three genealogies Korah is listed in third position in the Kohathite phratry. Although some would attempt to locate Korah's origins outside of the tribe of Levi, and although these genealogies obviously attest to variation in the tradition, noticably with regard to the name of Korah's father and the horizontal vs. vertical treatment of his "sons," there is little reason to deny him levitical status.

There is significant evidence, however, that the status of the Kohathites was diminished in the later postexilic period. In 1 Chr 23:12–20 a genealogy of the Kohathites is once again presented, but now with Korah conspicuously absent (v 18; cf. 24:22).

This reduction of the Kohathites to oblivion is likely the subject of the polemic underlying the major story of Korah and his followers in Numbers 16. It is generally acknowledged that the narrative in Numbers 16 is a composite of at least two stories: an Epic tradition (JE) concerning the civil/political conflict between Dathan and Abiram, in which they charge Moses with "making himself a prince" over the people (v 13); and a priestly tradition concerning the cultic/religious conflict between the Korahites and Aaron over the exclusive claims of Aaron to the priesthood (v 3). Some would further seek to distinguish between an early priestly narrative and a later priestly editing of the entire complex. What is clear, however, is that in this priestly narrative the Korahites have dared to challenge the exclusivity of the Aaronide claims to the priesthood and, as a result of a trial by ordeal, are consumed by the very fire which they desire to usurp (v 35). Although some have sought to place the origins of the story of Korah in the period of the early monarchy, this priestly narrative is certainly to be understood as attesting to the intense struggle for the control of temple prerogatives in the postexilic community. It is generally assumed that the Levites had full priestly authority in preexilic Israel, but that with Deuteronomy and Josiah's reform movement there ensued a tremendous power struggle which was eventually won by the Zadokite priests. The postexilic "settlement" may have broadened this to include some non-Zadokites, who were now subsumed, along with the Zadokites themselves, into a newly contrived "Aaronide" genealogy. Whether the Korahites were among former groups of levitical priestly groups who went into exile or whether they were a prominent levitical group which functioned in Palestine during the exile (so Budd *Numbers* WBC, 190) is unclear. What is clear, however, is that the Korahites were among the major losers in this power struggle. The genealogy in Exod 6:16–25 suggests that the tradition located the Korahites as the "cousins" of the Aaronides, i.e., they were very close to the center of power—but not close enough. The social struggle between the Korahites and the Aaronides concluded with the Aaronides consolidating their power and the Korahites reduced further and further to the periphery. In spite of the obviously contrived note in Num 26:11, the clear message of the priestly propaganda in Numbers 16 is that the Korahites were on the verge of social extinction, reduced to gatekeepers (1 Chr 9:19; 26:1, 19) and temple bakers (1 Chr 9:31). Any other Levites who would encroach upon Aaronide prerogatives would meet the same fate. They have the altar covering, hammered out of the 250 censers of Korah's followers, as a witness.

3. A member in the genealogy of Caleb, according to 1 Chr 2:43 (Caleb → Mesha → Hebron → Korah; but contrast 2:18–19). Given the number of geographical place names in the genealogies of 1 Chronicles 2, the name Korah might likewise be taken as the name of a city. Though the tradition clearly associates Caleb with the city of Hebron, it is not necessary to assume that Korah must have been in the same environs. In fact, the genealogies of 1 Chr 2:18–24 suggest that a genealogical relationship was thought to exist between Judah and Gilead. Given such ambiguity, it is possible that the note in 1 Chr 12:1–7 might be accurate. There the town of Korah is associated with the tribe of Benjamin. According to this text, it is from this town, as from the other Benjaminite towns of Gibeah, Anathoth, Gibeon, and Gederah, that several of Saul's kinfolk defected to David's ranks at Ziklag. However, this tradition has no attestation in the Deuteronomistic History, and may reflect a late and spurious tradition.

Bibliography

Coats, G. W. 1968. *Rebellion in the Wilderness.* Nashville.
Cody, A. 1969. *A History of Old Testament Priesthood.* Rome.
Liver, J. 1961. Korah, Dathan and Abiram. *Studies in the Bible,* ed. C. Rabin. *ScrHier* 8. Jerusalem.
Wanke, G. 1966. *Die Zionstheologie der Korachiten.* BZAW 97. Berlin.

Rodney R. Hutton

KORE (PERSON) [Heb *qôrē*ʾ]. Two individuals in the Hebrew Bible bear this name. The name Kore, "partridge" (possibly onomatopoeic from the cooing of the bird, or else to be translated, "caller, calling-bird," from the Heb root *qārā*ʾ, "to call"), probably belongs to the category of animal names used as nicknames (cf. *IPN,* 229–30; McCullough *IDB* 3: 661).

1. A Levite of the house of Korah, ancestor of the temple gatekeepers Meshelemiah (1 Chr 26:1) and Shallum (9:19). Although both Meshelemiah and Shallum are placed in the time of David (cf. 25:1; also cf. Meshelemiah, where it is argued that both names probably refer to the same person), another (?) Shallum (apparently the one mentioned in 9:17, as well as in Ezra 2:42 = Neh 7:45) is probably to be dated to after the Babylonian Exile, over 300 years later (cf. also 1 Chr 9:1–2). One may note at this juncture the remarkable blending of at least four different epochs of Israelite and Judahite history to be found in 1 Chronicles 9: the wilderness period (vv 19–20), the time of Samuel (v 22), the time of David (vv 21–22), and the postexilic time of composition of the list (vv 2, 17). It should be noted in passing that the so-called "Chronicler," despite the title which biblical scholarship has commonly assigned to the author of this work, is evidently far more concerned with emphasizing the levitical origins of the various cultic functionaries of the postexilic period, than he is with chronological exactitude (cf. Braun *1 Chronicles* WBC 136–37).

2. A Levite, son of Imnah, keeper of the east gate in the days of King Hezekiah (2 Chr 31:14). Possibly he was named after the Davidic Kore (see above), also a Levite, whose son Shallum likewise was stationed at the east gate (1 Chr 9:17–19; but see above concerning v 17), a position of some prominence (Williamson *1 and 2 Chronicles* NCBC, 376). For an analogous duplication of levitic names in the 10th and the 8th centuries, see ABDI. Evidently, the 8th-century Kore was a man of great trust, for he was given charge not only of the freewill offerings presented to the temple (for the priests stationed in Jerusalem), but also the distribution of the priestly and levitical portions in the outlying "cities of the priests" (2 Chr 31:15; cf. 1 Chr 6:39–45—Eng 6:54–60; also Dillard *2 Chronicles* WBC, 251; and Myers *2 Chronicles* AB, 184). In this latter task, he was assisted by six officials, presumably all Levites as well (2 Chr 31:15–16), although the text is somewhat unclear (cf. Williamson *1 and 2 Chronicles* NCBC, 376–77). In any case, Kore son of Imnah is yet another example of a prominent and upright Levite from the period of the monarchy, by means of which the Chronicler is able to contrast levitical faithfulness (one of his favorite themes) with the lack of the same among the priests (cf., e.g., his sharp comment in 2 Chr 29:34, again referring to the days of Hezekiah).

WILLIAM H. BARNES

KOSHER. See MEAL CUSTOMS (JEWISH DIETARY LAWS).

KOZ (PERSON) [Heb *qôṣ*]. Listed among the descendants of Judah (1 Chr 4:8). Nothing is otherwise known of him. The abrupt appearance of the name in the genealogy suggests to some commentators that it has dropped out as a result of haplography and should be appended to the end of 1 Chr 4:7 (Curtis *Chronicles* ICC, 107; Williamson *Chronicles* NCBC, 59).

H. C. LO

KUE (PLACE) [Heb *qōweh; qōwē*ʾ]. Name of a Neo-Hittite kingdom which occupied a fertile lowland area in SE Turkey (classical Cilicia *campestris*) during the first half of the 1st millennium B.C.E. It was bordered by the Taurus mountains on the N, by the Mediterranean on the S, and by the Amanus Mountains in the E. Access was controlled by the Cilician Gates in the Taurus Mountains and by the Syro-Cilician Gates in the Amanus range. Kue (Akk *qu-we*) was inhabited by Luwian and Hurrian populations which sometimes called themselves Danunites, a word related to Adana, the name of a chief city. Kue has been subsumed under various names, including Kizzuwatna in the Hittite period (1650–1200) and Cilicia (Gk *Kilikia*—cf. *Ḫilakku,* the Akk name of an ethnic group in Kue) in the Greco-Roman period.

Although some older versions (e.g., KJV) do not render it as a place-name, Kue is now recognized as the place from which Solomon procured horses in 1 Kgs 10:28 (= 2 Chr 1:16). However, the extent to which 1 Kgs 10:28 may be used to reconstruct Solomon's trading activities is a matter of dispute. According to Y. Ikeda (1982), 1 Kgs 10:28 provides solid evidence that Solomon held a dominant position as a middleman who supplied horses from Kue and chariots from Egypt to a wide range of kingdoms. D. Schley (1987), in contrast, views the passage as poetic hyperbole from which little of historical value may be extracted.

Kue was part of the anti-Assyrian coalition at the Battle of Qarqar in 853, and Shalmaneser III (860–825) attempted to subdue Kue in 839, at which time it was ruled by Kate. Shalmaneser installed Kirri, brother of Kate after two more campaigns in 834 and 833. Kue joined Arpad in a somewhat successful alliance against Adad-nirari III in 796, but Urikki of Kue paid tribute to Tiglath-pileser in 732. In 715 Sargon (722–705) helped Kue to regain territory lost to Midas of Phrygia, and by 709 it was clearly an Assyrian province governed by Ashur-sharra-usur. Although Sennacherib deported some of its people to Assyria after Kue's revolt (ca. 700), Assyrian sources suggest that his control, and that of Esarhaddon and Ashurbanipal, was intermittent and short-lived.

An important, but controversial, source for the history of Kue is the Luwian-Phoenician bilingual inscription found in 1946–47 at Karatepe, a hilltop site by the Ceyhan River in Turkey. The text commemorates the founding of the city of Azitawaddiya and the promotion of Azitawadda by Awarikus king of Adana and member of the Muksas dynasty. Whether Awarikus is to be identified with Urikki, the king of Kue contemporaneous with Tiglath-pileser and Sargon, is still debated. Also controversial are the proposed dates which have ranged from before 860 to after 705.

Neo-Babylonian records designate Neo-Hittite Kue as Khume, but its political status remains unclear during this period. Nebuchadrezzar claims to have conquered Cilicia around 592, but it is not certain that Kue/Khume was subsumed under Cilicia at that time. Cilicia, under various kings named Syennesis, had some independence during the Persian period. During the Greco-Roman period, however, the area once occupied by Kue became known almost exclusively as Cilicia, and only bare traces of its Neo-Hittite past remained. See also *CAH*² 3/1: 372–441.

Bibliography

Goetze, A. 1962. Cilicians. *JCS* 16: 48–58.

Ikeda, Y. 1982. Solomon's Trade in Horses and Chariots in its International Setting. Pp. 215–238 in *Studies in the Period of David and Solomon and Other Essays,* ed. Tomoo Ishida. Winona Lake, IN.

Schley, D. D. 1987. 1 Kings 10:26–29: A Reconsideration. *JBL* 106: 595–601.

HECTOR AVALOS

KUNTILLET ʿAJRUD (M.R. 094954). The Arabic name, meaning "hill of the water-source," of a site located in N Sinai. Ruins of the site date to the 8th century B.C. (the time of the Israelite monarchy), and various remains suggest that it served as some sort of a religious center. Of particular significance are inscriptional references to "Yahweh of Samaria and his Asherah" and to "Yahweh of Teman," which provide important evidence of the complex nature of Israelite religion during the OT period (Meshel 1979; and relevant articles in *AIR*.

A. Location
B. Initial Exploration of the Site
C. Recent Excavations
 1. Structural and Pottery Remains
  a. The Western Structure
  b. The Eastern Structure
 2. Textile Remains
 3. Epigraphic Remains
 4. Artistic Remains
D. Conclusion

A. Location

Kuntillet ʿAjrûd is located approximately 50 km south of Kadesh-barnea and about 15 km W of Darb el-Ghazza, a road which since antiquity has run N–S, connecting Quseima and Kadesh-barnea to Elat and S Sinai. The isolated hill rises prominently from the broad valley of Wadi Quraiya (or "wadi of the small building"), which forms a natural W–E route. See Fig. KUN.01. The top of the hill is a long and narrow plateau, and the actual ruins are found at its W end. At the foot of the hill there is a concentration of shallow wells providing one of the few reliable sources of water in this arid and isolated area. These wells made this site an important crossroads in the past—a fact also recorded on old maps of the modern period. The combination of water and crossroads undoubtedly contributed to the selection of the site for a small settlement.

B. Initial Exploration of the Site

The site has long been known to travelers. Edward Palmer, one of the first explorers of Sinai, visited the site in 1869. He arranged an exploratory dig at the site during which the first written find was discovered: the letter *ʾalef* incised on a fragment, which Palmer mistook for a Greek *alpha.* Palmer erred greatly in dating the site, and identified it with the Roman "Gypsaria," which on the "Tabula Peutingeriana" appears between "Elusa" (Halutza) and "Aila" (Eilat).

In 1902 the surveyor H. Musil visited the site. He arrived after hearing a rumor about the discovery of an ancient inscription there. He described in colorful detail the violent confrontation with the local bedouin, who tried to stop him from ascending the hill (since they considered it to be a sacred place). Prof. Beno Rothenberg visited the site after the Six-Day War in 1967, and dated it correctly to the Israelite period. Dr. Ze'ev Meshel visited in 1970 and later directed three seasons of excavation at the site (October 1975–April 1976).

C. Recent Excavations

1. Structural and Pottery Remains. The site contains two structures: a main structure (A) spanning the width of the W end of the plateau; and a secondary structure (B) 10 meters to its E. The structures differ greatly from one another in the state of their preservation. See Fig. KUN.02.

a. The Western Structure. The walls of structure A are at points preserved to a height of 1.5 meters. The building itself extends over an area of approximately 15 × 25 meters. It is rectangular, with four corner rooms protruding outward (resembling "towers") and with indirect entry from a small eastern vestibule. The plan initially seems to resemble a small fortress, similar in appearance to the Israelite citadel-with-towers found at Kadesh-barnea, Arad, and ʿUza. Structure A differs, however, in a number of important respects: it lacks the casemate walls typical of these fortresses, and its remains are unusual for a fortress and suggest a different type of function altogether.

Structure A was entered through a small exterior court area (locus 15) surrounded by stone benches. The benches, floor, and walls were plastered with white plaster. Some of the pieces of plaster that were in the debris on the floor were adorned with colorful pictures of a figure sitting on a throne and various floral motifs. It seems that part of the inner walls of this exterior court area were colorfully adorned at a specific height above that which was preserved.

From the court area, one entered the main structure proper by first passing through a small gate room (locus 5), turning left into a narrow room divided into two wings, whose walls were surrounded by plastered stone benches. This "bench room" (locus 6) extends N–S across the entire width of the building and apparently was the most important part of the site. The plastered stone benches take up most of the area, with only a narrow passage remaining between them, suggesting that the main function of the room is to be associated with the benches, not the passageway. An additional function is suggested by the manner in which the wings of the bench room are connected to the two corner rooms at their respective ends (loci 7 and 13). These have no usual doorway but instead are connected to the bench room by very narrow "windows" whose sills are formed by the lateral benches themselves. By examining

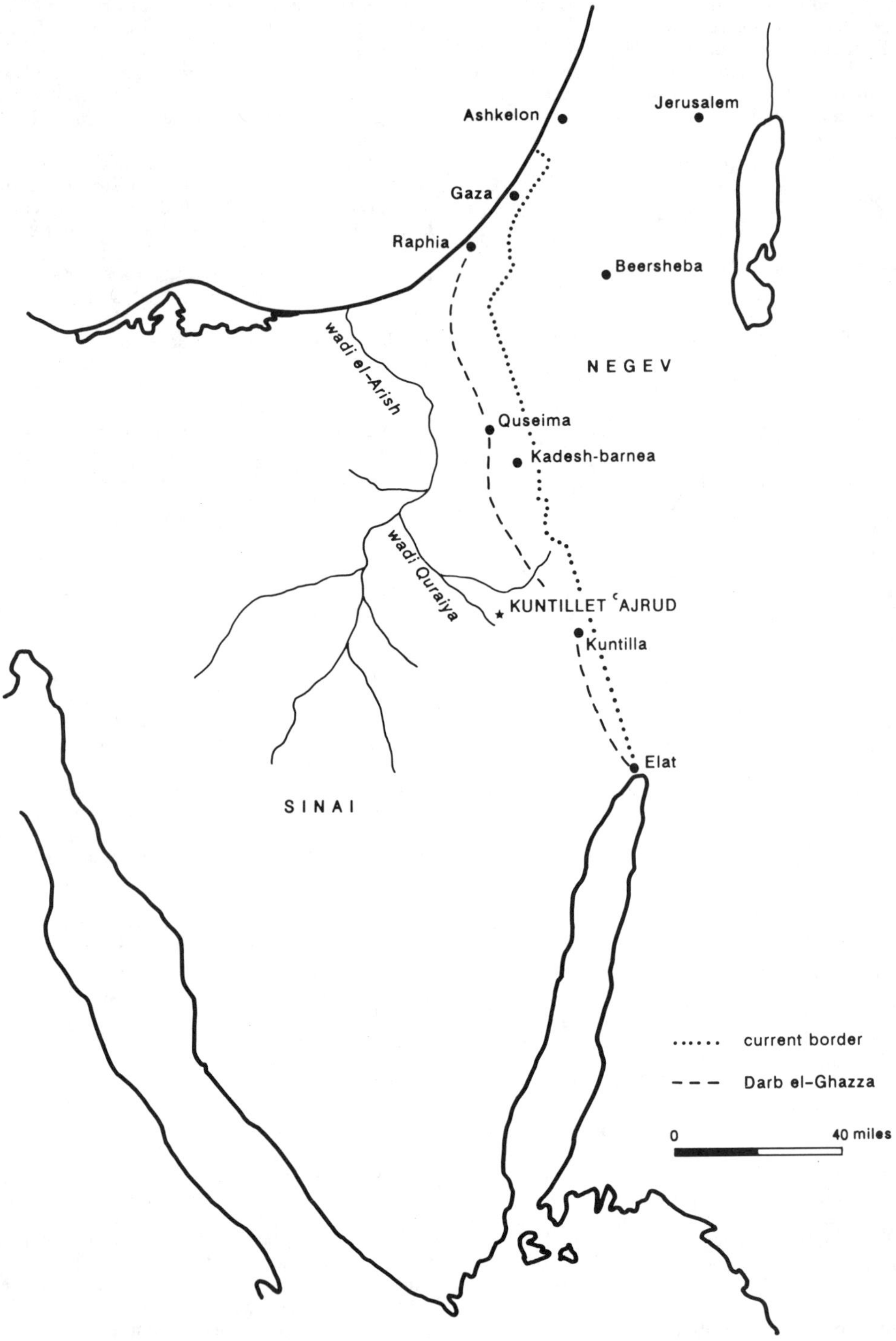

KUN.01. Regional map of Kuntillet ᶜAjrud.

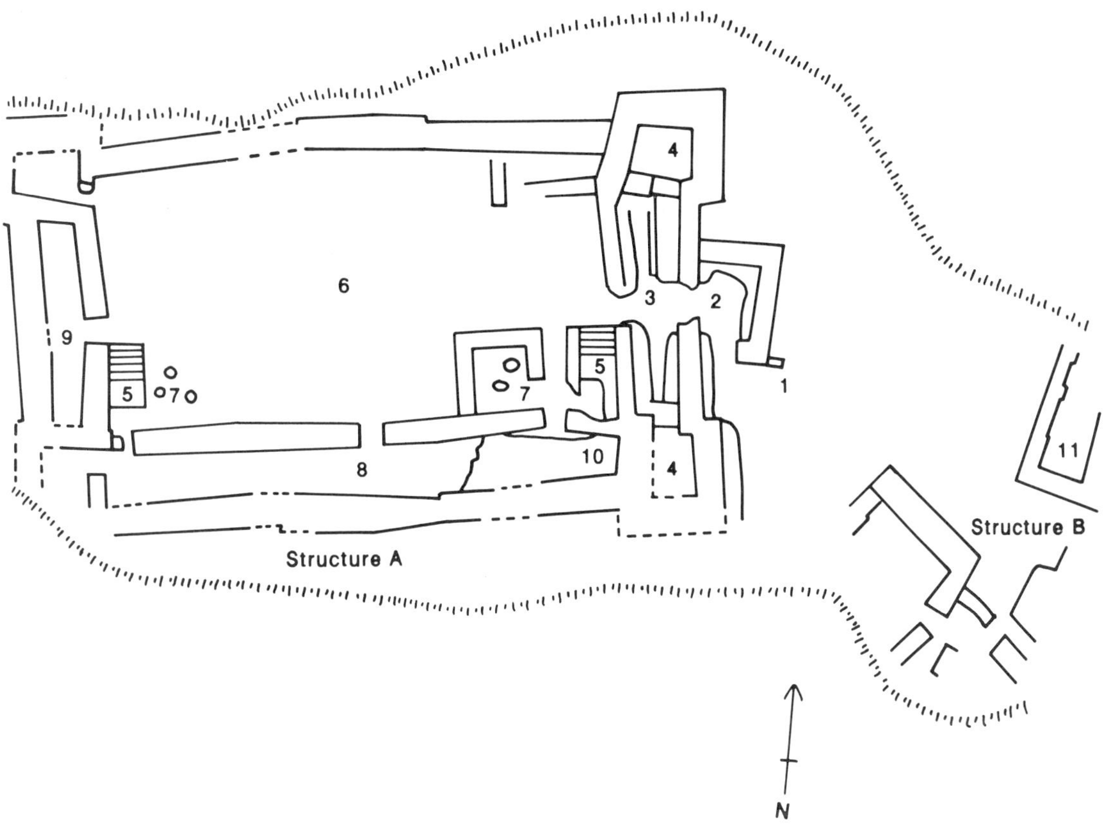

KUN.02. Site plan of Kuntillet ʿAjrud. *1,* entrance court (locus 15); *2,* gateroom (locus 5); *3,* "bench-room" (locus 6); *4,* depositories (loci 7 and 13); *5,* stairways; *6,* main courtyard; *7,* "kitchens" (loci 51 and 101); *8,* south storeroom; *9,* west storeroom; *10,* cellar (locus 8); *11,* long room (locus 159). *(Redrawn from Z. Meshel 1978)*

these benches it became clear that they had been constructed in a second phase, thus partially blocking the small openings that were present in the first phase of the building. Apparently these openings were merely structural features serving no other purposes, and the first phase was merely the stage of the building's construction.

The fragments of plaster that had dropped from the walls of the bench room included two Hebrew inscriptions written in Phoenician script. A part of a third inscription was found *in situ* about 1.5 m above the floor level on the N doorpost of the entrance leading to the main courtyard of structure A. This, along with other evidence discovered near other doorways (see below), possibly testifies to the sort of practice advocated in Deut 6:9—"And you shall write them upon the doorposts of your house, and on your gates."

In addition to these plaster inscriptions, most of the other significant finds were discovered in the bench room, in the corner rooms abutting its two wings, and in adjoining parts of the structure. These included two large pithoi adorned with inscriptions and pictures (see 3.e below), and stone bowls of various sizes, four of which had the names of donors incised on their rims (see 3.c). In general, the pottery in this part of the structure was comprised essentially of small vessels such as flasks, lamps, juglets, and bowls, quite different from the pottery found in the other rooms of the structure (primarily pithoi and storage jars). The bulk of the pottery was found in the two corner rooms, which perhaps served as *favissa* depositories for vessels that initially had been displayed on the benches. The bench room's design and its remains (particularly the inscriptional remains—see below) suggest that here travelers could honor the Israelite god by offering various items to him.

The two long rooms to the S and W of the main courtyard served as storerooms for hoarding food supplies: in fact, the bases of the pithoi and large storage jars housed here were discovered still *in situ,* firmly embedded in the hard-earth floor and covered by the fragments of their own upper parts. Names, inscriptions, and letters of the alphabet were written on the shoulders of many of these larger vessels (see 3.a–b below). These vessels were stored so compactly that it is difficult to imagine how someone could have moved about to sort through them.

The larger pithoi (1 meter in height and more than 0.5 meter in diameter) were concentrated mainly in the W storeroom, from one end to the other. At the E end of the S storeroom the builders took advantage of the natural depression in the bedrock to construct a type of cellar (locus 8). Among the items that had either fallen or been tossed into the cellar were a large woven sieve, whole pomegranates, fragments of wooden containers, and many tree branches that served as rafters. Next to the entrance of the S storeroom was found a large stone bowl bearing an inscription (see 3.c below), apparently dragged here from the bench room area. Among the debris around the entrance to the W storeroom were discovered fragments of another plaster inscription. One could guess that originally it, too, was written on the doorpost. (A picture drawn in red, black, and yellow was also discovered on one of the stones of the doorpost of the S storeroom.)

The main courtyard was essentially empty except for two "kitchens" (loci 51, 101) at the SW and SE corners near flights of stairs apparently leading to the roof. In each "kitchen" were found three ovens which, judging from their respective floor levels, were used consecutively, not simultaneously. It is difficult to determine how long each oven was in service, but it is safe to assume that the oven sequence corresponds to the total time-span the site was occupied.

Structure A is well preserved, making it possible to ascertain some interesting details about its construction. The walls were built of unhewn chalk cut from local deposits. At a height of about 1.2 m a middle layer of (mostly tamarisk) branches was placed lengthwise and crosswise, thereby strengthening the wall by forming an intermediate layer separating the lower course of stone from the upper one. This technique was obviously well known since it was used in the construction of the Jerusalem temple (1 Kgs 7:12), although at Kuntillet ʿAjrûd this technique was obviously applied on a more modest scale. A superior whitewashed plaster covered the walls, floors, and benches of the entry complex and the bench room, but all the other walls were covered in mud plaster mixed with straw. The ceilings were made of branches of local trees, most of which were found in the debris of the rooms. It seems that the entire structure was built with a single, preplanned design and a specific purpose already in mind. The dimensions and orientation of the structure were laid out with respect to the oblong surface of the plateau. The actual construction, however, was not perfect: the lines of the walls are not straight, the widths of the rooms are not uniform, and the two wings of the bench room are far from symmetrical.

b. The Eastern Structure. In contrast to structure A, structure B is poorly preserved, and its layout and design have not become clear. The white plaster that covered all its remaining parts and the many decorated plaster fragments found in its debris (particularly near doorways), however, suggests that the building was elegantly adorned with murals. It is possible that this was an anterior entrance to the main structure; it is also possible that this structure is an E wing to an entrance courtyard between the two structures. Although it seems unlikely, it is furthermore possible that the two structures were not contemporaneous and that the E structure slightly preceeded the W one.

In the N part of structure B was a long room that originally extended to the edge of the plateau (locus 159); its floor and walls were covered with white plaster. The entrance to the room was from the W; the doorway was indicated by two pillasters projecting out from the line of the wall, around which were found fragments of decorated plaster. Some traces of walls from the S part of the structure also remained.

Because the site was occupied for a relatively brief time span, the large mass of pottery discovered there presents interesting analysis. If the site indeed can be dated to ca. 800 B.C.E., then the pottery corpus from Kuntillet ʿAjrûd could serve as an important comparative standard for identifying contemporaneous levels at other sites. Analysis of similar pottery forms suggest that four different areas could have been a source for most of the pottery types: the S coast, central Judah, the N kingdom of Israel (i.e., Ephraim), and Phoenicia. Surprisingly, the site yielded no "Negeb-type pottery" supposedly associated with the nomadic inhabitants of the area.

2. Textile Remains. Kuntillet ʿAjrûd is unique in that it yields textile remains from the period of the Israelite monarchy. About one hundred cloth fragments, almost all of linen (only seven of wool) were discovered among the ruins. A. Sheffer (1978) details the superior quality of the threads and the unique characteristics of the fabrics. It has been noted that, in violation of biblical law (Lev 19:9; Deut 22:9–11), some of these fabrics were made by combining wool and linen (on one piece red woolen threads were interwoven with blue linen ones.) Loom weights and wooden beams found at the site confirm the possibility that actual weaving was done there. In light of the preponderance of linen fabrics from the site, it is worth pointing out that according to the OT the "holy garments" of the Jerusalem priests were supposed to be woven of linen (Ezek 44:17–18). The Bible also indicates that weaving activities were often associated with cultic establishments (2 Kgs 23:17). These factors, in addition to the inscriptional remains, suggest that the site was inhabited by priests.

3. Epigraphic Remains. The most important finds attesting to the significance, uniqueness, and nature of the site are the Hebrew inscriptions and pictures. The inscriptions, some written in ancient Hebrew script and some written in Phoenician script, can be categorized as follows:

a. Letters incised on pottery prior to firing. On the shoulders of most of the pithoi recovered from (mainly the storerooms of) the site—and only on this type of vessel—are one or two letters. The most frequent letter is the *ʾalef,* while the letter *yod* is more scarce, and twice the combination *qop-reš* appears. Thus far we know about similar inscriptions only from the excavations of the City of David (Jerusalem); incisions of the letter *ṭet* were found there also on the shoulders of an identical type of pithoi. This strengthens the assumption that these letters are abbreviations indicating types of offerings and "tithes," a practice described a millennium later in the Mishna (*Maʿaser Sheni* 4:11) and Tosefta (*Maʿaser Sheni* 5:6). Thus it is possible that *qop-reš* indicates *qorbān* ("offering"), that *yod* indicates *maʿăśēr* ("tithe"), and that *ʾalef* indicates "first harvest," either in a temporal or superlative sense. In any case, the letters were incised prior to firing. Neutron activation examination of the clay of the pithoi proved that they were made in the vicinity of Jerusalem. This perhaps reinforces the suggestion that priests lived at the site and received supplies in the forms of these sacrifices and tithes.

b. Inscriptions incised on the pottery subsequent to firing. Among the seven such inscriptions written on the shoulders of storage jars are four reading *lśrʿr,* obviously to be read *leśar ʿîr,* "(belonging or were sent) to a city official" (i.e., an official in charge of the place). It is thought that at least part of the supply was consigned to him or registered at the site in his name.

c. Inscriptions incised on the rims of stone bowls. Among the four inscriptions of this type, the most complete one reads: *lʿbdyw bn ʿdnh brk hʾ lyhw,* "(was given) by Obadio son of Adnah; may he be blessed by YHW(H)." These stone bowls were apparently dedicated to the god of Israel by donors who sought his blessings.

d. Inscriptions written in ink on plaster walls. Fragments of three such graffiti inscriptions, written in Phoenician script but in the Hebrew language, were found in the bench room, while parts of another two, written in ancient Hebrew script, were found in the debris of the entrance to the W storeroom. Only one inscription was found *in situ* on the N doorpost of the opening leading from the bench room to the courtyard, but it was the most fragmentary and faded. Several phrases could be read on the second, two-line inscription:

[. . . *y*]*ʾrk(w).ym(y)m.wyšbʿw*[. . .]*tnw.l*[*y*]*hwh*[ ]*tymn.wl*
[ ]*ʾšrt*[*h*]
[. . .]*hyṭ(y)b.yhwh.hty*[*mn.wʾšrth* . . .]

This is a blessing or prayer addressed to "Yahweh of Teman and his Asherah." The third inscription is obviously a piece of an ancient theophany describing the revelation of God in language echoing the OT:

. . .]*/wbzr(w)ḥ.ʾl.br*[. . .
. . .]*/wyms(w)n.hr(y)m/wyd(w)k(w)n.gbn(wny)m*[. . .
. . .]*wšdš.ʾly*[. . .
. . .]*lbrk.bʿl.by(w)m mlḥ*[*mh*]
. . .]*lsm(.)ʾl.by(w)m mlḥ*[*mh*]

It is noteworthy that Baal and God (Heb *ʾēl*) are mentioned here in poetic parallelism, in connection to a possible reference to a "day of war" *(yôm milḥamâ).*

e. Inscriptions (and pictures) written on pottery. The main examplars of this type are two large pithoi decorated with inscriptions and pictures in red ink. They were found (broken), one in the bench room and the other at the E end of the adjoining courtyard. The large pithoi had been used as convenient surfaces for writing and drawing. It is reasonable to suppose that the pithoi had been moved here for that purpose from the storerooms, since on their respective shoulders were also incised the letters *ʾalef* and *qop-reš.*

Among the inscriptions are four repetitions of the alphabet, with the letter *pe* preceding the letter *ʿayin* and not following it. There is also a list of personal names, as well as a text containing phrases echoed in the OT:

kl ʾšr ysʾ(y)l mʾ(y)š ḥ(w)nn h(w)ʾ[ ]*wntn lh yhwh klbbh*

There are two blessings written on pottery which on the one hand resemble typical epistolary-greeting formulas, and on the other hand resemble the priestly benediction. One of these (see Fig. KUN.03) was written above two figures of the (Egyptian-in-origin) god Bes, and may be reconstructed as follows:

ʾmr ʾ[*šy*]*w hm*[*l*]*k ʾmr lyhl*[ ]*wlywʿśh wl*[ ] *brkt(y) ʾtkm*
lyhwh šmrn wlʾšrth.

If this reconstruction is sound, it is possible that we have in *ʾšyw hmlk* a transposition of the name *ywʾš,* Joash, referring to the king *(hmlk)* of Israel who reigned from Samaria (ca. 801–786 B.C.E.), perhaps providing an important synchronism for dating the site. The second blessing reads: *ʾmr ʾmryw ʾmr lʾd(w)ny h*[ ]*l*[ ] *ʾt(h) brktk lyhwh t(y)mn wlʾšrth ybrkk wyšmrk wyhy ʿm ʾd(w)ny* [. . .]. These inscriptions, with their references to "Yahweh of Samaria (or of Teman) and his Asherah," have generated a great deal of scholarly discussion (see Meshel 1979: Dever 1984; and discussions in *AIR*). Not only do they shed light on the cultic and religious character of the site, but they also provide revealing glimpses into the history of Israelite religion.

4. Artistic Remains. The quantity and variety of pictorial and decorative art found at Kuntillet ʿAjrûd were unprecedented for an Israelite site. This art was drawn on the plaster of the walls, on doorposts, on pottery (primarily on the two large pithoi mentioned above), and also on one of the stones in the jamb of the central opening to the S storeroom.

The two pithoi depict various divine, human, and animal figures. On one of them, beside two representations of the god Bes, a female figure is portrayed seated and playing a lyre. See Fig. KUN.03. The familiar "tree of life flanked by two goats" motif is also found on this vessel, as well as pictures of a lion, a procession of animals, and a cow licking the tail of a suckling calf. On the other vessel are depicted five figures raising their hands in a gesture of prayer, and an archer raising a bow. Even though most of these artistic motifs are well known from the Syro-Phoenician world, the actual renderings themselves are here very crude and perhaps also reflect "Arab" N desert influence. Despite their lack of artistic proficiency, the Kuntillet ʿAjrûd artists were familiar with and influenced by the prevailing art styles of the time, and they appreciated the significance of duplicating those styles. In short, the pictures are an expression of "folk art" as opposed to professional "court art."

Just as the inscriptions on the pithoi were not all written by the same person on one specific occasion, so also the pictures seem to reflect various hands. While it is difficult to draw definitive conclusions about such things, it has been suggested that, according to style and line, three different artists can be identified, at least one of whom drew on both pithoi (Beck 1982).

The plaster art (in black, red, and yellow ink) differs in some respects from that drawn on the pithoi, primarily in being more decorative in character. From the E building (structure B) were recovered many fragments of decorative art: a running pattern (perhaps a frame) surrounded by two rows of lotus flowers and two rows of intertwined circles; a geometric checkerboard pattern with red and

KUN.03. Drawings and inscriptions on a pithos—Kuntillet ʿAjrud. *(Courtesy of Z. Meshel)*

yellow squares; but also a picture of people standing atop a fortified wall. The fragments of plaster found near the exterior court of structure A (locus 15) were restored revealing a large red, black, and yellow picture of a figure sitting on a throne smelling a lotus flower. (A third picture of a figure sitting on a throne was also discovered on a pottery fragment.) Some fragments revealed that in several sections there were at least two layers of plaster one over the other.

There is no clear answer to whether or not the artist responsible for the decorative art on the plaster also drew the pictorial scenes on the pithoi; while the Syro-Phoenician artistic influence is common to both, the technical quality of the plaster art is superior to that of the pithoi art, and the respective subject matters tend to be different. Most of the artistic parallels are dated to the 9th–7th centuries, generally corroborating the conclusion that the site was occupied around the year 800 B.C.E.

D. Conclusion

The unusual finds (especially the inscriptions and pictures) testify to the uniqueness of the site. The subject matter of the inscriptions, the references to various deities, and the presence of dedicated vessels all suggest that Kuntillet ʿAjrûd was a religious center; however, the lack of things usually associated with ritual sacrifice (e.g., altars) and the architectural layout of the site indicate that the remains are not those of a temple. It appears that the site may have served as a "wayside shrine" that, due to its location, was associated with journeys of the Israelite kings to Elat and to Ezion-geber, and perhaps also with the travels of pilgrims to S Sinai. These were able to journey S along the Darb el-Ghazza from Kadesh-barnea, stopping at the place to make dedications to Israel's god in the bench room of the main building.

The strong N (Israelite, not Judean) influence in the remains seems to connect Kuntillet ʿAjrûd with the N kingdom of Israel or with one of the Judean kings closely aligned with the N kingdom of Israel. This N influence is evident in the reference to "Yahweh of Samaria," in the Phoenician-style writing, in the cosmopolitan style and motifs of the decorative and pictorial artwork, in the pottery types, and in the onomastic conventions (names ending in *-yau,* and not *-yahu*). The site, occupied for only a few years, was likely inhabited by a small group of priests dispatched from the N kingdom of Israel with an officer *(śr ʿr)* at their head. They were sustained by the various sacrifices and tithes that were sent as provisions primarily from Judah; in return, they rendered their cultic services to travelers.

The date of the site, determined by typological and paleographic analysis, and by the need to identify an historical period in which N Israelite influence over Judah was especially strong, points to the period after the death of Jehoshaphat of Judah (ca. 850 B.C.E.). The reigns of Jehoram, Ahaziah, and Athaliah (between 850 and 837 B.C.E.) seem distinct possibilities. However, the period of Joash king of Israel (ca. 801–786 B.C.E.), who captured Amaziah king of Judah, broke down the wall of Jerusalem, and seized the treasures of the Jerusalem temple and palace (2 Kgs 14:1–16 = 2 Chr 25:1–24) seems especially well suited. This would be reinforced if the reconstruction of *ʾšyw hmlk* on the top line of the Bes figurine inscription indeed is a reference to Joash. It may tentatively be suggested that Joash intended to gain direct access to the Red Sea, and that this was the reason for the war between the two kings. The victory of Joash is reflected in the construction of the buildings at Kuntillet ʿAjrûd, and accounts for the concurrent references to the "Yahweh of Samaria" and the "Yahweh of Teman"; i.e., Samaria's god (as well as its king) having dominion over the entire region through which one reached "Teman" (meaning "the far south").

Bibliography

Beck, P. 1982. The Drawings from Horvat Teiman (Kuntillet Ajrûd). *TA* 9: 3–86.

Dever, W. G. 1984. Asherah, Consort of Yahweh? *BASOR* 255: 21–37.

Meshel, Z. 1978. Kuntillet ʿAjrûd: A Religious Centre from the time of the Judaean monarchy on the border of Sinai. Israel Museum Catalogue, no. 175.

———. 1979. Did Yahweh Have a Consort? The New Religious Inscriptions from Sinai. *BARev* 5/2: 24–34.

Sheffer, A. 1978. The Textiles. In Meshel 1978.

ZEEV MESHEL

KUSH (PLACE). From the early 12th Dynasty the name Kush applied to the territory lying S of Semna at the 2d cataract on the Nile river, and was often paired with *Wawat* (Lower Nubia) between the 1st and 2d cataracts (Posener 1958). The name was later extended as a term for Nubia in general. Both the region and its inhabitants are mentioned a number of times in the Bible; see CUSH (PERSON) and ETHIOPIA (PLACE).

A. Early History

The appearance of Kush in Egyptian texts is probably to be associated with the dominance of a people known as the C-group or *Medja* (Arkell 1961: 46–48; Emery 1965: 133–35). The threat of these barbarians to Egyptian interests in the S explains the efforts expended by Amenemhet I and Senwosret I (20th cent. B.C.) to reconquer *Wawat* (Trigger 1965: 94) and to secure the land between the two cataracts by means of fortresses (Reisner 1960; Emery 1965: 143–45). The tribes of Kush figure most prominently of all foreign peoples in the Execration Texts of the 12th and 13th Dynasties (Posener 1940; 1987), an indication of Egyptian inability to control the land S of the 2d cataract. Roughly contemporary with the Hyksos conquest of the lower Nile valley and delta, most of the Nubian forts erected by the Egyptians were destroyed, and Egyptian monuments either effaced or carried off by the Nubians to adorn their own towns. Thereafter, while the Hyksos ruled from Avaris, an amorphous kingdom is attested in the territory S of the 1st cataract, governed by a "ruler of Kush" and centered upon the site of Kerma, 35 miles N of Dongola (Säve-söderbergh 1956; Smith 1976: 80–83; Wenig, *LÄ* 3: 409–10). An erstwhile ally of Hyksos power in the delta, Kush was subjected to repeated attacks by the early kings of the 18th Dynasty, and under Thutmose I (ca. 1525–1514 B.C.) was finally brought under Egyptian control as far S as Hagar el-Merwa. While records of punitive campaigns appear sporadically throughout the New Kingdom, e.g., under Hatshepsut, Thutmose IV, Amenophis III, Akhenaten, Tutankhamun, and Rameses II, these were in the main "training" razzias, intended as much to "blood" the troops as to quell revolts.

B. Kush Under the Egyptian Empire

By the close of the reign of Thutmose III (ca. 1504–1451 B.C.) the political role of the Nubian chieftains had been terminated in favor of an administration modeled on that of Egypt. From the rank of a lowly fortress commandant, appointed *ad hoc* to run the new territorial acquisitions in the S, had developed the office of "King's son of the Southern Countries" (later "King's Son of Kush"), a viceroy responsible directly to the king and holding the cabinet rank of "king's scribe" (Habachi 1981: 65–110; *LÄ* 3: 630–40). From certainly the middle of the 18th Dynasty, the viceroy of Kush was placed in charge of the gold-producing regions of the S, with jurisdiction from the 3d nome of Upper Egypt *(Nekhen)* to the S limit of Egyptian control at *Karoy* (Habachi *LÄ* 3: 630). The viceroy's headquarters was usually located at Aniba, and its presence was indicated by the rock shrines across the river at Kasr Ibrim.

The viceroy enjoyed the services of two deputy governors, one for Kush and the other for Wawat; and the administration was divided into departments similar to those in Egypt: treasury, granary, livestock, mines, defense (cf. the "garrison of Kush"), etc. (Reisner 1960; Donadoni, in Endesfelder et al 1977). The countryside was organized in Egyptian fashion into towns and townships administered by mayors. The natural resources and farm produce of Kush loom large in the annual imposts of the Egyptian empire and include large amounts of gold, grain, cattle, incense, ebony, ivory, and slaves (Emery 1965: 184–85; Adams 1981).

Apart from the influence of bureaucratic models and the damaging effect of Egypt's insatiety, Kush under the empire felt the impact of Egyptian culture and religion as did no other part of the ancient world (O'Connor, *AESH* 260–64). This influence radiated from the large, land-owning temples constructed during the New Kingdom along the Nile, each dedicated to the worship of the royal genius, and each functioning as a focus for a colonial settlement (Säve-söderbergh 1941: 200–203). While native gods were not suppressed, they were overshadowed by the cult of Amun transplanted from Thebes to Debod, Wady es-Sebua, and (especially) Gebel Barkal. Egyptian colonists in moderate numbers were found in Kush, and their presence aided in the acculturation of the natives to Egyptian civilization, including burial practices, a process all but complete by the end of the New Kingdom (O'Connor,

AESH 263–65; Säve-söderbergh 1969). In addition to Egyptians, it became customary to exile captive Asiatics or recalcitrant Apiru to Kush (Habachi 1981: 185–96) while Nubians were called N to Egypt and her Asiatic empire to serve as domestics, settlers, and policemen (Klengel, in Endesfelder et al 1977).

Textual and archaeological evidence of Egyptian control of Kush ceases abruptly under Rameses XI (ca. 1106–1076 B.C.), and during the civil war involving the king and the last known functioning viceroy, Paynehsi. Thereafter, for three centuries settlements lay abandoned, trade lapsed, and between the first two cataracts population declined (Trigger 1965: 112–14).

C. 25th Dynasty (ca. 780–656 B.C.)

Kush, as the term is used in the OT ("Cush") and other textual sources of Iron II date, refers to the political and cultural entity which took shape in Napata (Gebel Barkal) in the early first millennium B.C., and contributed the 25th dynasty to Egyptian history (Leclant 1985). Although attested in the cemetery at Kurru (Dunham 1950) from the early 9th century B.C., the ruling family of the resuscitated Kushite state does not come into the light of history until the ruler Alara of the early 8th century B.C. (Arkell 1961: 116). Thereafter, the geopolitical thrust of Kushite history was for two centuries toward the N exactly coincident with the counterthrust of Assyria W and S toward the Nile. The hegemony of the Nubian ruler Kashta (mid-8th cent.) was acknowledged at Elephantine, as was that of his successor Piankhy (ca. 735–712 B.C.) at Thebes and later as far N as the Dakhleh oasis. Piankhy, through a successful military campaign as far N as Memphis, terminated the erstwhile attempt by Tefnakht, prince of Sais, to reunite Egypt by main force. His brother Shabako (712–698 B.C.) completed the task by invading Egypt (711 B.C.), killing Bocchoris (Bakhenranef), Tefnakht's son (= 24th Dyn.), and annexing the country to Kush (Redford 1985).

The 25th Dynasty replaced the quiescent foreign policy of the later Libyan dynasts with its own northward expansion. Kush intervened forcefully and unexpectedly at Eltekeh (701 B.C.), battling Sennacherib to a standstill; Shebitku (698–690 B.C.) broadcast his designs in Asia in his titulary (Redford 1985: 14, fig. 3). The Kawa inventory lists prove that Taharqa (690–664 B.C.) campaigned actively in western Asia during the first decade of his reign (Spalinger 1978), maintaining alliances with the Phoenician cities (Katzenstein 1973: 263–65). The awareness of the strength and fighting potential of the Kushites which appears suddenly in the Bible (Isa 18:1; Jer 46:9; Ezek 38:5, etc.) dates from these halcyon days of 25th Dynasty dominion.

Culturally the 25th Dynasty of indigenous Nubian origin, with a heavy overlay of acquired Egyptian traits. Although subject in the past to debate (Arkell 1961: 114–15; Emery 1965: 208), the royal family probably sprang from the line of local chieftains long since converted to the worship of Amun of Napata. The old-fashioned piety and fanatical puritanism displayed by the ruling family, characteristic of proselytes, explains the contempt with which they regarded the Egyptians of their time. While many aspects of Napatan culture (e.g., burial practices; Lloyd, *AESH* 269) continue to show native derivation, the kings aped the pharaohs by carving triumphal texts in the Egyptian language and script and by adorning their temples with reliefs in Egyptian style. In art, the 25th Dynasty enjoyed the inspiration of surviving New Kingdom monuments in the S (Wenig 1978: 56, 63), and rapidly became the exponent of the new "archaizing" style (Redford 1986: 328–31).

Egypt under the Kushites experienced a political and cultural revival. Control over the Thebaid was secured, in mimicry of the 23rd Dynasty, by the appointment of a Kushite princess to the office of Divine Worshipper of Amun at Thebes, and Kushites or local sympathizers to municipal and priestly offices in that city (Leclant 1954; 1961; Habachi 1981: 247–57). No major change was effected in the political system in Lower and Middle Egypt, the "Libyan" dynasts being allowed to retain their patrimonies (Yoyotte 1961). Their relatives, however, were transplanted to Kush in the temple service of local gods. Thebes underwent a building boom during the regime of the 25th Dynasty (Leclant 1965), and temples were generously endowed. The army was greatly favored, thriving under royal patronage.

D. Withdrawal and Decline

In spite of his spirited involvement in W Asian affairs, Taharqa found it strategically impossible to prevent the Assyrians from massing in S Palestine. After a successful defense of the delta against Esarhaddon in 674 B.C., Taharqa was defeated by the Assyrians in 671 and forced to flee S. The country was again invaded in 666 and 663 B.C. (Spalinger 1974a; 1974b). From safe havens in Napata and Thebes, both Taharqa and his successor Tanwetaman attempted to regain lost ground (Burstein 1984), but were quickly ejected by the Assyrians. Lacking any popular support in Middle Egypt or the delta, the 25th Dynasty could only stand by and watch as the descendants of Bocchoris, whom Shabako had put to death, eased out the Assyrians and reunited Egypt from Sais in the N.

The history of Kush after 663 B.C. is a melancholy tale of successive defeats and ultimate isolation in the S. Psamtik (Psammetichus) I, founder of the 26th Dynasty, wrested Thebes from Kush in 656 B.C. (Caminos 1964) and planted a frontier garrison at Elephantine, now transformed once again into the effectual point of demarcation between Egypt and Kush. Necho II (610–595 B.C.) dispatched a punitive expedition against Kush, while the great invasion of Psamtik II in 593 B.C. completely defeated the Kushite forces and resulted in the destruction of Napata (Sauneron and Yoyotte 1952; Habachi 1981: 259–69). It is perhaps as a consequence of this defeat that Kushite slaves found their way into Asia (cf. Jer 38:7). Subsequently the monuments of the 25th Dynasty in Egypt were desecrated and their memory anathematized. The descendants of the 25th Dynasty, after the destruction of Napata, came increasingly to favor a S location (Meroe) as their capital, although the necropoleis at Napata were not immediately given up (Arkell 1961: 144–73). Increasingly cut off in their S fastness, the kings of Kush presided over a declining culture, graphically reflected in the progressive degeneration of those things ultimately borrowed from Egypt, i.e., script, art, and architecture.

Among classical authors and in the Bible, recollection of

Kush (RSV "Cush," "Ethiopia") and the 25th Dynasty is garbled. The name "Kush" is seldom found in classical authors (who preferred the slightly pejorative "Aethiopia"), although it has survived in Near Eastern and African traditions. See also ETHIOPIA (PLACE). Taharqa is remembered as a conqueror (Strabo 15.1.6), but dated too early (2 Kgs 19:9; Avaux 1973); Shabako and Shebitku are remembered erroneously as tribal eponyms (Astour 1965). The defection of a mercenary garrison from Elephantine to Kush lived on in tradition (Hdt. 2.30), but was wrongly dated. The strong impression Kush of the 25th Dynasty had made fostered the anachronistic appearance of Kushites in much earlier history. For example, Joab in the 10th cent. B.C. is given a Kushite runner (2 Sam 18:21–23—cf. their reputation as swift runners under Taharqa; Moussa 1981), and a dubious Kushite "invasion" by an otherwise unknown Zerah is conjured up for the early 9th century B.C. (2 Chr 14:9–13). It is uncertain whether the marriage of Moses to a "Cushite woman" (Num 12:1) derives from a tradition of Bronze Age date, or is a late anachronism (Shinan 1978); certainly Judaic apologia of Ptolemaic times dwell heavily on a fanciful campaign of Moses against Ethiopia (Rajak 1978), possibly constructed solely on the basis of the passage in Numbers (Collins, *OTP* 2: 895, n. 45).

The presence of Egyptian monuments of ostensible antiquity on the Sudanese Nile and the "Egyptian" appearance of Meroitic culture gave rise in some circles to the late Hellenistic belief that Egyptian civilization had come from Kush. In the polemical romance literature of the Persian and Ptolemaic periods, Kush figures as the refuge whither the defeated pharaoh flees and whence he emerges to expel the foreigners from Egypt (Redford 1986: 276–96).

Bibliography

Adams, W. Y. 1977. *Nubia, Corridor to Africa.* London.

———. 1981. Ecology and Economy in the Empire of Kush. *ZÄS* 108: 1ff.

Arkell, A. J. 1961. *A History of the Sudan to 1821.* London.

Astour, M. 1965. Sabtah and Sabtecah. *JBL* 84: 422–25.

Avaux, A. 1973. La mention de Taharqa en II Rois 19, 9, Isaie 37, 9. *Annuaire de l'institut de philologie et d'histoire orientales et slaves* 20: 31ff.

Burstein, S. M. 1984. Psamtek I and the End of Nubian Domination in Egypt. *JSSEA* 14: 31–35.

Caminos, R. A. 1964. The Nitocris Adoption Stela. *JEA* 50: 71–101.

Dunham, D. 1950. *The Royal Cemeteries of Kush.* Vol. 1. Boston.

Emery, W. B. 1965. *Egypt in Nubia.* London.

Endesfelder, E. et al., eds. 1977. *Ägypten und Kusch* (Festschrift F. Hintze). Berlin.

Habachi, L. 1981. *Sixteen Studies on Lower Nubia.* ASAESup 23. Cairo.

Katzenstein, H. J. 1973. *The History of Tyre.* Jerusalem.

Leclant, J. 1954. *Enquêtes sur les sacerdoces et les sanctuaires égyptiens a l'époque dite "éthiopienne."* Cairo.

———. 1961. *Montouemhat, quatrième prophète d'Amon et prince de la ville.* Cairo.

———. 1965. *Recherches sur les monuments thébains de la XXVe dynastie dite "éthiopienne."* Cairo.

———. 1985. Égypte et Koush: la XXVe dynastie dite éthiopienne. Pp. 595–99 in *Annuaire de College de France 1984–85.*

Moussa, M. 1981. A Stela of Taharqa from the Desert Road at Dahshur. *MDAIK* 37: 331–33.

Posener, G. 1940. *Princes et pays d'Asie et de Nubie.* Bruxelles.

———. 1958. Pour une localisation du pays Koush au moyen empire. *Kush* 6: 39–68.

———. 1987. *Cinq figures d'envoûtement.* Cairo.

Rajak, T. 1978. Moses in Ethiopia: Legend and Literature. *JJS* 29: 111–22.

Redford, D. B. 1985. Sais and the Kushite Invasions of the 8th Cent. B.C. *JARCE* 22: 5–15.

———. 1986. *King-Lists, Annals and Daybooks.* Toronto.

Reisner, G. A. 1960. The Egyptian Forts from Halfa to Semna. *Kush* 8: 11–24.

Sauneron, S., and Yoyotte, J. 1952. La campagne nubienne de Psammétique II et sa signification historique. *BIFAO* 50: 157–207.

Säve-söderbergh, T. 1941. *Ägypten und Nubien.* Lund.

———. 1956. The Nubian Kingdom of the Second Intermediate Period. *Kush* 4: 54–61.

———. 1969. Die Akkulturation der nubischen C-Gruppe im Neuen Reich. *ZDMG* (Suppl. 1) 17: 2–20.

Shinan, A. 1978. Moses and the Ethiopian Woman. *ScrHier* 27: 66–78.

Smith, H. S. 1976. *The Fortress of Buhen: The Inscriptions.* London.

Spalinger, A. J. 1974a. Esarhaddon and Egypt: An Analysis of the First Invasion of Egypt. *Or* 43: 295–326.

———. 1974b. Ashurbanipal and Egypt: a Source Study. *JAOS* 94: 316–28.

———. 1978. The Foreign Policy of Egypt Preceding the Assyrian Conquest. *CdÉ* 53: 22–47.

Trigger, B. G. 1965. *History and Settlement of Lower Nubia.* New Haven.

———. 1976. *Nubia Under the Pharaohs.* London.

Wenig, S. 1978. *Africa in Antiquity.* Vol. 2. New York.

Yoyotte, J. 1961. Les principautés du Delta au temps de l'anarchie libyenne. *MIFAO* 66: 121–81.

DONALD B. REDFORD

KUSHAIAH (PERSON) [Heb *qûšāyāhû*]. Var. KISHI. A Levite, a descendant of Merari and father of Ethan (1 Chr 15:17). Kushaiah should probably be identified with Kishi of 1 Chr 6:29—Eng 6:44. The LXX supports identifying Kushaiah with Kishi, reading *kisaiou* in 1 Chr 15:17 and *kisai* in 1 Chr 6:29—Eng 6:44. The same person may be mentioned in 2 Chr 29:12, which speaks of Kish the son of Abdi. The origin of the name Kushaiah is unknown; Noth (*IPN,* 32) suggested that it was an imperative form but was unable to isolate the root word.

TOM WAYNE WILLETT

L

L. The abbreviation used in NT source criticism for the solely Lukan material in the Synoptic Gospels. See SYNOPTIC PROBLEM.

LAADAH (PERSON) [Heb *laʿdâ*]. An individual of the tribe of Judah, from the line of Shelah (1 Chr 4:21). He was the son of Er, though not the Er who was the firstborn of Judah. He is called the father of Mareshah. Mareshah in this case might denote a son or a city which has been identified as Tell Sandahannah (M.R. 140111) in the Shephelah.

David Channing Smith

LABAN (PERSON) [Heb *lābān*]. Name of the son of Bethuel (Gen 28:5). In Gen 29:5 he is called "the son of Nahor"; however, this expression should be understood in the sense of "grandson" or "descendant." According to the genealogy given in the book of Genesis, Terah was the father of Abraham (Abram), Nahor, and Haran (Gen 11:27). Nahor, through his wife Milcah, was the father of eight children (Gen 22:20–22). His eighth son, Bethuel, was the father of Rebekah (Gen 22:23) and of Laban (Gen 25:20). Laban was the father of Leah and Rachel (Gen 29:16); Leah and Rachel later became Jacob's wives. He also had several sons (Gen 30:35; 31:1) who probably were born after Jacob joined Laban's family through his marriage to Leah and Rachel. Noth has said that this genealogy was artificially created in order to show the kinship between the Israelites and the Arameans (Noth *HPT,* 217).

Laban lived in the "city of Nahor" (Gen 24:10), which in several places is identified with Haran (Gen 27:43; 29:4). The same area is also identified as Paddan-aram (28:2, 5). He is called an Aramean (25:20; 28:5; 31:20, 24). Jacob is also called an Aramean in Deut 26:5. This designation may express affinity between the early Israelites and the Aramean tribes.

Laban first appears in the stories of Abraham. After the death of Sarah (Gen 23:1–20), Abraham tried to find a wife for his son Isaac. Abraham sent his servant Eliezer, a Damascene slave (Gen 15:2–3), to go to Aram-naharaim (Mesopotamia) to find a wife for his son (Gen 24:1–9). Eliezer went to the city of Nahor (Gen 24:10) and went to the house of Bethuel to obtain his daughter Rebekah as a wife for Isaac. Laban met Eliezer, invited him to come to his house, and provided for the needs of his animals (Gen 24:28–32). Laban is an active participant in the transaction that led Rebekah to go with Eliezer to the land of Canaan. The picture of Laban portrayed on this occasion is that of a man who acted out of self interest and ambitious desires (Gen 24:30, 53).

Laban appears next in the Jacob cycle. When Jacob fled from his father's house to escape the wrath of his brother Esau (Gen 27:41–45), he went to the house of Laban, his uncle. Jacob lived with and worked for Laban twenty years as a herdsman (Gen 31:38, 41). For seven of these years Jacob worked to obtain Rachel as his wife, and for another seven he worked with the same purpose because Laban had deceived Jacob on his wedding night and had given him Leah, his oldest daughter. Jacob worked another six years caring for Laban's herd. Recent archaeological discoveries have contributed much information to the understanding of the Jacob-Laban narratives. Scholars have seen in the relationship between Jacob and Laban some parallels with the adoption and marriage customs practiced in northern Mesopotamia as recorded in the Nuzi tablets, but this view has been challenged by Van Seters (1969). Morrison (1983: 156) has said that the agreement between Jacob and Laban, sealed by these marriages, bears "a strong resemblance to Old Babylonian herding contracts." The basic element of this contract was Jacob's promise to work as a herdsman for Laban in return for his two wives and certain types of livestock.

After having lived with Laban twenty years, Jacob became a very rich man. Laban and his sons "did not regard him with favor as before" (Gen 31:2). For this reason Jacob fled with his wives, his sons, and his flocks to return to the land of Canaan. When Laban heard that Jacob had fled and had apparently stolen his household gods (Teraphim, Gen 31:19), he went after Jacob and met him at Gilead, in Transjordan (Gen 31:25). Scholars have debated whether possession of these household gods indicated possession of inheritance rights as indicated in some Nuzi texts (Greenberg 1962). At that time God appeared to Laban in a dream (Gen 31:24) admonishing him not to harm Jacob. When Laban met Jacob they entered into a covenant. According to Noth (*HPT,* 92), this covenant probably represents an early boundary agreement between Israelites and Arameans which settled border disputes over territory claimed in Transjordan by both groups (Gen 31:52). The covenant was sealed by an oath when Laban called on the God of Nahor and Jacob called on the God of Abraham, the gods of their fathers (Gen 31:53) as their witnesses to the covenant (Alt 1968: 23–24). A monument celebrating the event was erected. Laban called it in Aramaic Jegar-sahadutha (*yĕgar śahădûtāʾ*), and Jacob called it in Hebrew Galeed (*galʿēd*). Both words mean "heap of witness."

Bibliography

Alt, A. 1968. The God of the Fathers. Pp. 1–100 in *Essays on Old Testament History and Religion.* Garden City, NY.

Daube, D., and Yaron, R. 1956. Jacob's Reception of Laban. *JSS* 1: 60–62.

Greenberg, M. 1962. Another Look at Rachel's Theft of the Teraphim. *JBL* 81: 239–48.

Morrison, M. A. 1983. The Jacob and Laban Narrative in Light of Near Eastern Sources. *BA* 46: 155–64.

Van Seters, J. 1969. Jacob's Marriages and Ancient Near East Customs: A Reexamination. *HTR* 62: 377–95.

CLAUDE F. MARIOTTINI

LABAN (PLACE) [Heb *lābān*]. One of the Exodus encampments of the Israelites, mentioned in only a very general way in Deut 1:1 along with Hazeroth and Dizahab, suggesting that it be located somewhere in the Sinai. It may be the same as the Libnah listed in Num 33:20–21 between Rimmon-perez and Rissah, which is the sixth Israelite encampment after leaving the wilderness of Sinai. However, in Deuteronomy, Laban is listed before Hazeroth, while in Numbers, Hazeroth precedes Libnah; this is not a serious difficulty because the organizing principles of the two lists are not clear. It may also be that they are two different stations. If the equation is accepted, a possible location is in the wadi el-Beidha, which like Laban means "whiteness" (*GP,* 214; M.R. 122925). For a discussion of the location of any of the places associated with the journey of the Israelites from Egypt through Sinai, see DOPHKAH.

Bibliography

Beit-Arieh, I. 1988. The Route Through Sinai—Why the Israelites Fleeing Egypt Went South. *BARev* 15/3: 28–37.

JEFFREY R. ZORN

LACCUNUS (PERSON) [Gk *Lakkounos*]. One of the sons of Addi who returned with Ezra (1 Esdr 9:31). He was one of the Israelites who had foreign wives and had to put them away with their children in accordance with Ezra's reform. The name does not appear in the parallel list in the book of Ezra (cf. 10:30).

JIN HEE HAN

LACE. See DRESS AND ORNAMENTATION.

LACEDAEMONIANS. The Lacedaemonians were inhabitants of the Greek Pelopponese. Lacedaemonia, later called Sparta, was originally the name of a city-state settled during the Dorian invasion (ca. 1000 B.C.E.). Sparta supplanted Lacedaemonia as the capital of the SE Peloponese and the region was then known as Laconia. After the Spartans conquered the Messenians to their west in the 7th century, the combined territory was subsequently known as Lacedaemonia. The name "Lacedaemonians" is found only once in the LXX (2 Macc 5:9), and the name "Sparta" is likewise referred to once (1 Macc 14:16); however, "Spartans" occurs nine times in 1 Maccabees 12–15.

There are several factors that seem to indicate that the Jews of Jerusalem cultivated political contacts with the Lacedaemonians. Friendly relations between Jerusalem and Sparta existed from the time of the high priesthood of Onias I (320–290 B.C.E.). Surprisingly, the Jews claimed that the Lacedaemonians were common descendants from Abraham (1 Macc 12:21). Jason, the high priest, sought refuge among the Jews of Sparta after his failure to occupy Jerusalem (2 Macc 5:9; and Jos. *Ant* 12. 5.1.238; and 15.3.1.). A letter from Jonathan to the Spartans and their reply in 146 B.C.E. may suggest that the Maccabeans sought to reestablish relations with the Lacedaemonians (1 Macc 12:6–18; and Jos. *Ant* 13:5.8; and 12.4.10). A brief letter from the Spartan authorities to Simon, the high priest and Jonathon's successor, appears in 1 Macc 14:20–22. Finally, the letter sent to the nations requesting the recipients to abstain from further hostilities against the Jews specifically names Sparta (1 Macc 15:23; and Jos. *Ant* 14.8.5). The Maccabean Jewish political agenda was motivated in part by the fact that Jewish settlements existed in the Peloponese from the 2d century B.C.E. and partially because of the positive political and philosophical benefits of having contacts with mainland Greek culture as opposed to Syrian Hellenism.

SCOTT T. CARROLL

LACHISH (PLACE) [Heb *lākîš*]. A central biblical city in the Shephelah. Its king participated in the coalition of the S kings against Joshua and the Israelites, and it became the object of one of Israel's sieges (Josh 10). Rehoboam fortified the city after the division of the kingdom (2 Chr 11:9), and it was later the scene of the assassination of Amaziah (2 Kgs 14:19). When Sennacherib attacked Judah, it was while he was besieging Lachish that he sent the Rabshakeh to Hezekiah to try to intimidate him into surrender (2 Kgs 18:14–17; 19:8). Sennacherib later commemorated his conquest of Lachish by paneling the walls of one of the rooms of his palace in Nineveh with scenes of the siege. The city is mentioned in Jer 34:7 as one of two (with Azekah) cities in Judah still to hold out against the armies of Nebuchadnezzar.

A. Site and Identification
B. History of Excavations
  1. Wellcome-Marston Expedition
  2. Aharoni's Excavations
  3. Renewed Excavations
C. Summary of Excavations
  1. Neolithic, Chalcolithic, and Early Bronze
  2. Early Bronze IV
  3. Middle Bronze Age
  4. Late Bronze Age
  5. Iron Age
  6. Post-Iron Age

A. Site and Identification

The ancient city is represented by a major mound, Tell ed-Duweir, now called Tel Lachish (M.R. 135108). The site (including the slopes) covers an area of ca. 30 acres. Water was obtained from wells, one of which was uncovered at the NE corner of the site. Lachish is situated near Nahal Lachish (Wadi Ghafr), along which extended a main route from the coastal plain to the Hebron hills.

In 1878 Conder suggested the identification of ancient Lachish with Tell el-Hesi. This identification was later supported by the discovery there of a cuneiform letter apparently sent from Lachish and dated to the el-Amarna period. In 1929 Albright proposed the identification of Lachish with Tell el-Duweir. He based his suggestion on Eusebius (*Onomast.* 120.20), who states that Lachish was a village located on the 7th mile, along the road from Eleutheropolis (Beth-Guvrin) to Gaza. All archaeological data recovered from Tel Lachish support Albright's suggestion, which is generally accepted today. However, the identification is based solely on circumstantial evidence, hence the dissenting views (see Ahlström 1980 and response by Davies 1982).

B. History of Excavations

1. Wellcome-Marston Expedition. Large-scale excavations were initiated in 1932 by a British expedition directed by J. L. Starkey, ably aided by L. Harding and O. Tufnell. The expedition was financed by Sir Henry Wellcome, and later by him and Sir Charles Marston. The excavations came to an end in 1938, following Starkey's murder by bandits. Starkey published only brief preliminary excavation reports (Starkey 1933; 1934; 1935; 1936; 1937a; 1937b; Inge 1938), and Tufnell later completed the publication work (Tufnell 1953; Tufnell, Inge, and Harding 1940; Tufnell et al. 1958).

The British excavations were carried out both on the site and in the surrounding areas. The NW corner of the site was excavated to prepare a location to dump the soil from the excavations on the summit. The shoot constructed at this point and the huge dump indicate to the present-day visitor the large scale of the digging carried out here. The Levels II–I city gates, outer revetment, Level I Residency and Solar Shrine, Great Shaft, Judean palace-fort, and the Fosse Temple at the bottom of the NW corner are the most important remains uncovered on the mound proper. In addition, a sectional trench was cut at the NE corner and remains of the earlier periods were uncovered at the NE slope. In 1935, the "Lachish letters" were recovered in the city gate—undoubtedly Starkey's most important discovery. Large areas were cleared outside the site, uncovering numerous tombs from different periods, as well as Bronze Age settlements on the hills to the W and N of the site. Starkey and his associates were trained by Flinders Petrie, and followed his methods. Considering its time, it was an excellent excavation, and hardly any of Starkey's stratigraphic observations and conclusions (with the exception of the Assyrian siege ramp) were changed in the course of the renewed excavations.

2. Aharoni's Excavations. Excavations limited in scope and scale were carried out by Y. Aharoni in the Solar Shrine area in 1966 and 1968 (Aharoni 1975). Aharoni was at that time excavating at Arad, and believed that the ground plan of the Judean shrine uncovered at Arad resembled that of the Solar Shrine. This theory prompted the excavation at Lachish. Various remains of Levels VI to I were uncovered beneath the Solar Shrine, the most important of them the Level V Cult Room.

3. Renewed Excavations. In 1973, systematic excavations were renewed at Lachish aiming at a long-term study of the site and its material culture (Ussishkin 1978; 1983). The excavations are directed by D. Ussishkin and have largely continued adjacent to Starkey's excavated areas on the mound. The expedition pays particular attention to excavation methodology and combines the baulk/debris-layer method (known as the Wheeler-Kenyon method) and the locus-to-architecture method (known as the horizontal method).

The main excavation field is Area S, a long, narrow section cutting through the upper edge of the mound on its W side. See Fig. LAC.01 The plan is to reach virgin soil; the work, however, progresses slowly, and so far, excavations have reached the LB strata. Other excavation fields include Area P—the Judean palace-fort and monumental Bronze Age structures beneath its N end; Area D near the SE corner of the palace-fort; Area G—the Judean city-gates; and Area R—a sectional trench at the SW corner of the site where the Assyrian army forced its way into the city in 701 B.C. A comprehensive reconstruction program of the Judean city-gate is also being carried out. In addition, Y. Dagan has conducted a comprehensive surface survey of the surrounding region.

In order to maintain continuity from one excavation to the next, the renewed excavations have used the British system in dividing into city levels and its enumeration system for Levels VI–I. However, for the stratigraphy beneath Level VI, the strata must be renumbered since it is impossible to accommodate all the MB and LB strata within Starkey's Levels VIII and VII. The renumbering will be completed as soon as the relevant strata are uncovered and studied in Area S, which serves as the key excavation area for determining the site's stratigraphy. So far, with the excavation and study of the stratum underlying Level VI in area S, it has been labeled "Level VII." Temporarily, all strata in Area P beneath Level VI have been labeled P-1 to P-5.

C. Summary of Excavations

1. Neolithic, Chalcolithic, and Early Bronze. Prehistoric flint implements were recovered in the surrounding area. A group of flint implements recovered on the mound (Rosen 1988–89) probably indicate the existence of a Pottery Neolithic site in one of the surrounding valleys.

Ghassulian pottery fragments recovered on the site probably indicate that the mound was already settled during the Chalcolithic/Ghassulian period. Remains from the end of the Chalcolithic and the beginning of the EB were recovered by the British on the NE slope of the mound and at the NW settlement extending on the ridge NW of the mound. The people settled in caves, artificially enlarged and transformed into comfortable dwellings, which contained sunken hearths and lined storage pits. A dolmen found on the NW ridge probably relates to that settlement.

We may assume that during EB II–III the mound was extensively settled, but very little is known at present about it. Remains from this period were found in Starkey's NE section, in Area D at the center of the site, and in tombs.

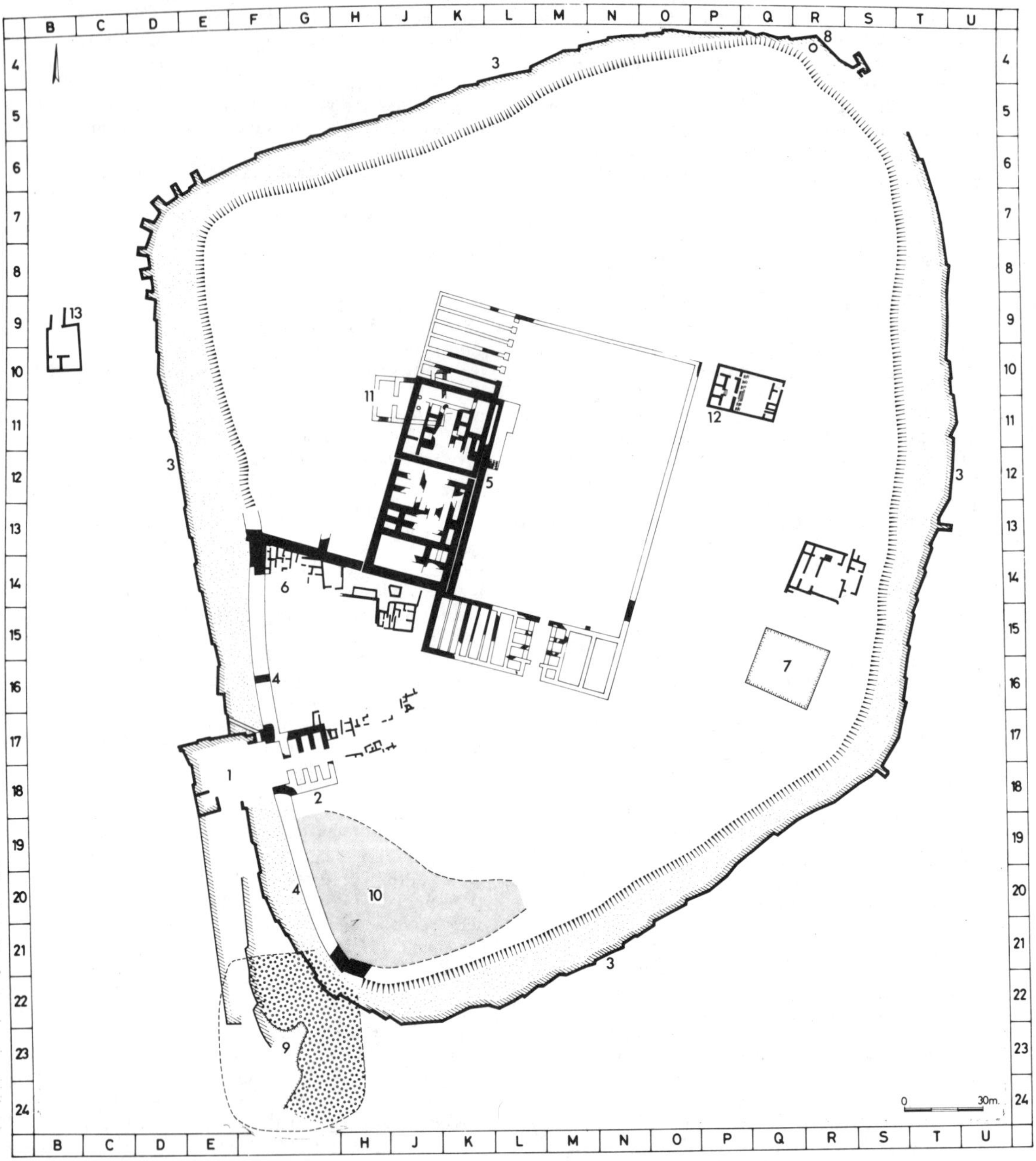

LAC.01. Site plan of Tel Lachish: *1,* outer city gate; *2,* inner city gate—Level IV–III; *3,* outer revetment wall; *4,* main city wall; *5,* palace-fort complex—Level III; *6,* sectional trench (Area S); *7,* Great Shaft; *8,* Well; *9,* siege ramp; *10,* counter-ramp; *11,* acropolis temple; *12,* Solar Shrine; *13,* Fosse Temple. *(Courtesy of D. Ussishkin)*

Much EB pottery, including numerous fragments of KHIRBET KERAK WARE, was recovered from the debris the early defenders used to build the counter-ramp in 701 B.C. (see below).

2. Early Bronze IV

During this period (also labeled MB I or EB–MB Intermediate Period), the mound was apparently abandoned, and settlement seems to have shifted to surrounding ridges. Caves in Area 1500, and part of the NW settlement located on the ridge to the W of the mound, which included a number of domestic buildings, were uncovered by the British. Notably, a group of small copper ingots was also found there. A large burial ground (Cemetery 2000) extended along the slope of the ridge to the N of the settlement, on which 120 rock-cut tombs were uncovered, few of them intact. Many of the tombs were too small to contain more than a single tightly flexed body, and nearly all traces of human remains have disappeared.

3. Middle Bronze Age. Relatively little is known about the MB city. In fact, all the remains so far excavated date to MB II–III (=MB IIB–C), and nothing is known about the settlement in MB I. The excavated remains include the fortifications, the palace, a cult place, Starkey's Level VIII in the NE section, and tombs.

A glacis was erected around the city, becoming the core of the present impressive shape of the site with its steep slopes and angled corners. The glacis was studied by the British near the NW corner. It was composed of nearly horizontal layers of fill capped by a lime-plastered sloping surface. Significantly, a freestanding city wall, topping the glacis along the upper edge of the site, was not found at this point. A fosse was cut in the rock along the bottom of the glacis at least along the W side of the mound.

The center of the site was crowned by a huge palace. Its NW wing was uncovered in Area P (Level P-4); most of the edifice extends beneath the later Judean palace-fort and its courtyard. The palace is characterized by massive brick walls, and it is built above an earlier edifice of a similar nature (Level P-5). A number of huge stone slabs incorporated in the palace's walls and floors probably originate in the earlier edifice. The palace was destroyed by a severe fire which marks the end of the MB city. Following the destruction, the palace was reoccupied, and some rooms were used for industrial purposes (Level P-3).

Remains of a cult place were uncovered in Area D, near the SW corner of the Judean palace-fort. The structure was mostly destroyed, but votive pottery and concentrations of animal bones were recovered. Tombs of that period were excavated by the British, noticeable among them Tomb 1502, which contained a dagger bearing an inscription in Canaanite alphabetic script.

4. Late Bronze Age. Immediately following the destruction of the MB city the settlement apparently dwindled and deteriorated, and only later did it gradually develop and regain its importance, culminating in the final Canaanite city of Level VI. Lachish is mentioned in Papyrus Hermitage 1116A dated to the 19th or 20th year of Amenhotep II (1427–1402 B.C.), which is the earliest reference to the city in an external source. The papyrus records presentations by Egyptian officials of grain and beer to envoys of various Canaanite cities, including Lachish (Weinstein 1981: 13). A number of cuneiform letters found in el-Amarna and dating to the 14th century B.C. were sent from Lachish. Another cuniform letter from that period, sent from an Egyptian official probably residing at Lachish to his superior, was found at Tell el-Hesi. Apparently, as testified by these letters, during the el-

Chronological Table (Dates B.C.)

Periods and Dates	Lachish Levels	Special Data
Pottery Neolithic		Site in vicinity
Chalcolithic-EB IVA (3500–2200)		Settlement on mound
EB IVB-C (2200–2000)		Area 1500; cemetery 2000; NW settlement
MB I (2000–1800)	?	
MB II–III (1800–1550);	Starkey's L. VIII [P-5, P-4]	
	.... ca. 1550; destruction by fire	
LB I (1550–1400)		Fosse Temple I
LB IIA (1400–1300)	Starkey's L. VII	Fosse Temple II
LB IIB (1300–1200)	Level VII [P-1]	Fosse Temple III
	.... ca. 1200; destruction by fire	
Iron Age IA-B (1200–1130)	Level VI	
	.... ca. 1150–1130; destruction by fire	
Iron Age IB (1130–1000)	Gap in settlement	
Iron Age IC (1000–930)	Level V	United Monarchy
	.... ca. 925; destruction by fire (?)	
Iron Age IIA-C (930–586)	Level IV	Divided Monarchy
	Level III	
	.... 701; destruction by fire	
	Gap in settlement	
	Level II	
	.... 588/586; destruction by fire	
Babylonian-Hellenistic (586–31)	Level I	

Amarna period Lachish was one of the most important city-states in southern Canaan.

Significantly, Lachish may have been unfortified throughout the LB Age. It seems that the MB fortifications were no longer in use, and a temple was thus erected in the disused fosse (see below). Remains of buildings along the edge of the site assigned to Levels VII and VI, dated to the 13th to 12th centuries B.C., were uncovered in Starkey's sectional trench in the NE corner and in Area S. Those buildings prove that a proper city wall had not been erected during that period, but it is possible that the buildings along the edge of the mound were in fact connected to one another and formed a fortified belt. However, during the 14th century B.C., the entire excavated area up to the edge of the mound in Area S formed an open, undeveloped field; hence, at least during the el-Amarna period Lachish was not fortified either by a city wall or a belt of buildings.

Relatively little is known about the settlement on the summit between the end of the MB and Level VII. Some remains were uncovered in the NE section (Starkey's Level VII), in Area P (Levels P-3 and P-2), and beneath Level VII in Area S.

Some time after the destruction of the MB city a small sanctuary was founded in the disused fosse near the NW corner of the site (Tufnell, Inge, and Harding 1940). It was later rebuilt twice, its three phases labeled by the British as Fosse Temples I to III. The original temple was a modest structure; it formed a rectangle oriented along a N-S axis, measuring ca. 10 by 5 m with subsidiary rooms on the W and N. An altar in the form of a bench with three projections adjoined the S wall of the shrine. Many of the finds were uncovered in *favissae* surrounding the building. The finds from Fosse Temple I include an imported Mycenaean kylix and beautiful "bichrome ware" vessels. Ca. 1400 B.C. the original sanctuary was replaced by Fosse Temple II. The position of the building was maintained, but the new structure was much larger in size and a new chamber was added on the S side. A number of benches for placing offerings were constructed along the walls of the main hall.

The remains of Level VII domestic structures in Area A (and possibly Level P-1 in Area P) and Fosse Temple III represent the 13th-century city (Ussishkin 1985). It was destroyed by fire. Fosse Temple III resembled the previous one, but had an enlarged altar and an additional room on the S side; many rich finds were uncovered beneath its destruction debris. They include a group of carved ivories, faience vessels, and Egyptian scarabs and jewelry.

Level VI represents the last, prosperous Canaanite city probably built shortly after the destruction of Level VII. Level VI shows a cultural continuity from Level VII, but the city was rebuilt along entirely different lines: in Area S the Level VII domestic structures were replaced by a public building; the fosse temple was not rebuilt, and a new temple was built in the acropolis, possibly as part of the royal compound.

Level VI shows strong affinities with Egypt during the reign of Rameses III (1182–1151 B.C.—low chronology of Wente and Van Siclen). The Egyptian presence is primarily indicated by a number of bowl fragments inscribed in hieratic script. Goldwasser (1982; 1984) recently restudied these bowls in conjunction with the hieratic bowls from Tel Sera[c]. The bowls constitute the documentation of the *šmw* (harvest tax) paid to an Egyptian religious institution, probably associated with a local temple (such as the Level VI temple). According to Goldwasser, the recording of the harvest tax on votive bowls reflects the economic exploitation of S Canaan by the Egyptian authorities via the religious establishment. This would imply that Lachish was under direct Egyptian control, together with S Canaan. The strong connections with Egypt are also reflected in the architecture of the acropolis temple, in the bronze object bearing a cartouche of Rameses III found in the city gate area (see below), and in two anthropoid clay coffins, one bearing a pseudo-hieroglyphic inscription, found in a tomb near the mound.

The main complex of the acropolis temple consists of an antechamber, the main hall, and the cella, as one ascends the slope. The entrances to the three units are built along a straight axis, oriented W–E, passing through the center of the main complex. See Fig. LAC.02. The main hall is rectangular, measuring ca. 16 by 13 m. Two massive columns bases found in the center of the main hall indicate that the roof, spanned by cedar of Lebanon beams (Clamer and Ussishkin 1977: 73), was supported by two columns. A monumental staircase made of stone slabs led the way to the cella. Three octagonal columns found here apparently flanked two niches built along the wall to the left of the staircase. Numerous fragments of painted plaster indicate that parts of the walls in the hall were decorated. The finds are few since the rich equipment of the temple seems to have been vandalized and robbed prior to when the temple was set on fire. Of special interest is a gold plaque portraying a nude Canaanite goddess standing on a horse (Clamer 1980). This plaque, and a graffito depicting a standing god(?), apparently indicate that this was a Canaanite (rather than Egyptian) sanctuary.

The layout of the acropolis temple (like that of the Level VI temple at Beth-shan) originates in Egypt. Its plan resembles shrines in el-Amarna and in the workmen's camp at Deir el-Medina (Bruyère 1948; 1952). The best analogy is Chapel G at Deir el-Medineh, which although smaller in size, consists of an antechamber, a main hall with two central columns and cella, with the entrances aligned along a central axis (Bruyère 1952: 21–27, Pls. I, V–VI). Many other elements in the temple, such as the octagonal columns, the staircase, and the painted plaster, and many of the finds, also originate in Egypt. Finally, it seems that the temple, having three units and entrances along a single, straight axis, was built according to a plan which later served as a prototype for Solomon's temple in Jerusalem. Significantly, however, unlike the acropolis temple, Solomon's temple was oriented from E–W, with its entrance facing E. The two massive columns in the main hall of the acropolis temple can illustrate the biblical account of the Philistine temple of Dagon in Gaze which was pulled down by Samson (Judg 16:23–30).

No Philistine painted pottery—neither monochrome (the so-called "locally made Mycenaean IIIC:1b") nor bichrome pottery—was found in any of the excavations, except for a few sherds in a cave on the N slope which

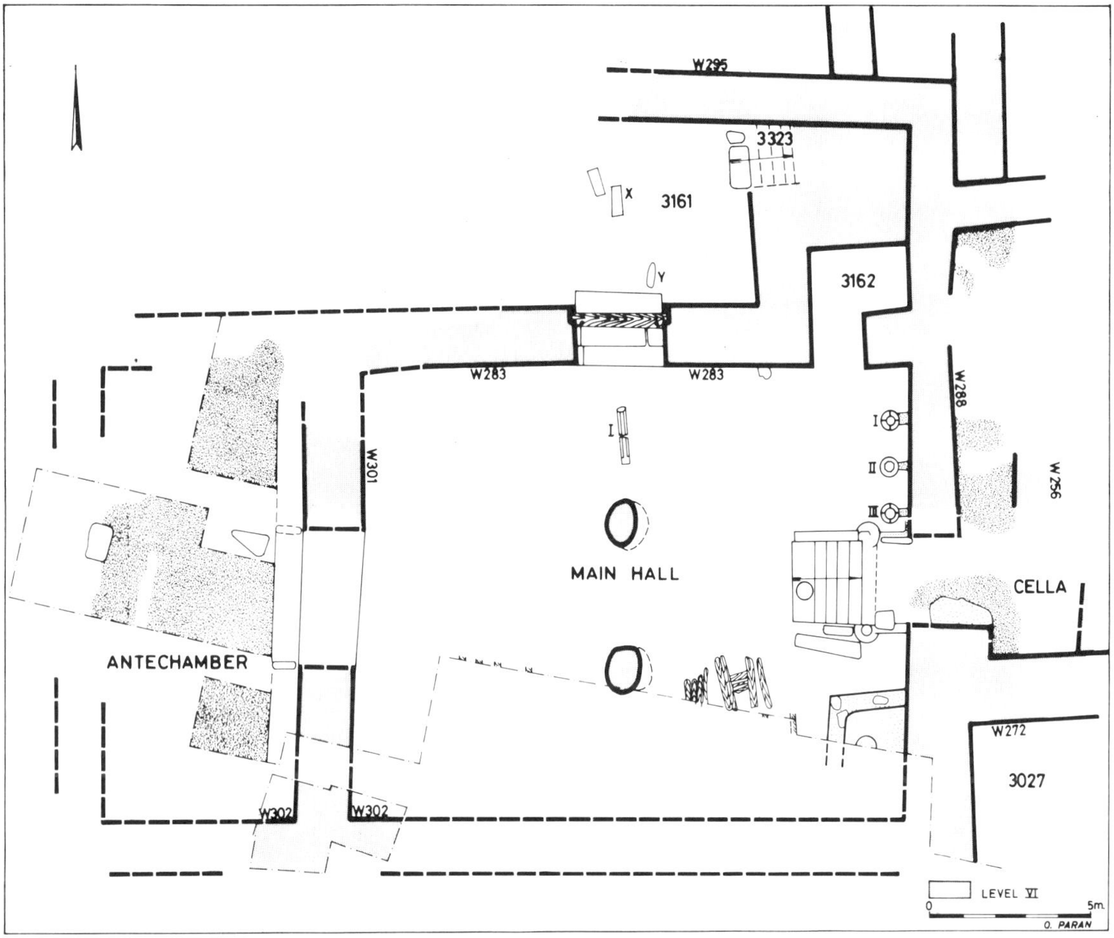

LAC.02. Acropolis temple at Tel Lachish: ground plan of main complex. *(Courtesy of D. Ussishkin)*

apparently remained open following the destruction of Level VI. This fact seems to have far-reaching implications. Tel Lachish lies only a short distance from both the coastal plain and from two significant Philistine centers—Tel Miqne and Tel Zafit (identified with ancient Ekron and Gath, respectively). Philistine bichrome pottery, however, was found at sites further inland from Tel Lachish, for example at Tel Beth-shemesh, Tel Eton, and Tell Beit Mirsim. Considering the geographical position and the size and prosperity of the Level VI city, it is difficult to imagine that nearby Philistine cities could have coexisted with Lachish without some Philistine pottery reaching the latter. Hence it appears that Lachish was not settled at the time that painted Philistine pottery was produced in the nearby region, and that this pottery dates in the main to the period following the destruction of Level VI, i.e., to the last third of the 12th century B.C., or even later (see below).

The Level VI city was destroyed by fire. The destruction was complete and the population liquidated or driven out. Following the catastrophe, the site was abandoned until the 10th century B.C.

A cache of bronze objects, which included a broken object bearing a cartouche of Rameses III, was found in a probe cut beneath the Judean city gate. The cache was sealed beneath the destruction debris of Level VI, and hence this destruction could have occurred either during the later part of the reign of Rameses III (1182–1151

B.C.—low chronology of Wente and Van Siclen) or later. It seems possible that the sudden downfall of Lachish coincided with the Egyptian loss of control over S Canaan ca. 1130 B.C. Without Egyptian protection, Lachish became easy prey for attack.

Evidence for the sudden destruction was found in Area S. The Level VI public edifice seems to have been turned to living quarters for refugees prior to its destruction. Human remains sealed beneath the destruction debris included bones of an adult, two children and an infant, apparently trapped when the catastrophe occurred.

With the absence of inscriptions, the identity of the conquering enemy remains a matter of speculation. One suggestion (Tufnell 1953: 52) is that the Level VI city was destroyed by the Sea Peoples. In that case the complete destruction and subsequent abandonment of the site could be compared to the fate of Alalakh and Ugarit, whose final destructions are attributed to the invading Sea Peoples. The founding of Philistine Ekron nearby and the diffusion of Philistine pottery in the region can easily be explained if it is assumed that they destroyed Canaanite Lachish. As a corollary to such a reconstruction, the invasion of the Sea Peoples was a prime factor in the collapse of Egyptian authority and military control over S Canaan, which left unfortified cities such as Lachish completely vulnerable.

The second possibility, argued by Albright (1937: 23–24; 1939: 20–22), is that the Level VI city was destroyed by the Israelites, as described in Josh 10:31–32. The biblical description fits the archaeological data: a large Canaanite city destroyed by fire; absence of fortifications, enabling the conquest of the city in a swift attack; and complete desertion of the razed city explained by the annihilation of the populace. On the other hand, the motive for the destruction remains obscure, since the Israelites did not settle here, nor in the surrounding region, until a much later date.

Consequently, the adoption or rejection of this possibility depends largely on whether or not the biblical source is accepted as having a sound historical basis. Acceptance of this viewpoint, however, leads to two corollaries: (1) A cardinal event in the biblical tradition of the Israelite conquest is thus dated to the middle of the 12th century B.C. or even later; and (2) Canaanite Hazor was destroyed in the 13th century, and no later than 1230 B.C. If it is assumed that Hazor was also conquered by the Israelites in accordance with Josh 11:10–11, the biblical description of a swift campaign by Joshua's forces is then incompatible with the archaeological evidence for the destruction of two major Canaanite cities which were separated by about a century.

Seven or eight brief inscriptions written in Canaanite alphabetic script were recovered at Lachish (see most recent summary by Puech 1986–87), thus making it the cardinal site in Canaan proper for the study of this script. The earliest inscription, engraved on a bronze dagger blade found in a MB tomb, contains four signs. It is best read vertically as *trnz,* possibly a name. An important inscription is painted on the shoulder of a ewer found in Fosse Temple II. The best reading to date is that of Cross (1954: 19–21): "Mattan. An offering to my lady ʾElat." A two-line fragmentary inscription was recently found in Level VI in Area S (Ussishkin 1983: 155–57, fig. 25). The two lines are read in boustraphedon fashion by Cross (1984) and Puech (1986–87).

5. Iron Age. a. Level V. Following a long period of abandonment a new settlement was established. Remains of small domestic buildings were uncovered in different parts of the site. The settlement was not fortified, but building remains uncovered in Area S indicate the possibility that the settlement was protected by a belt of houses located along the upper periphery.

A cult room was uncovered by Aharoni (1975) in the Solar Shrine area. The cultic equipment included a stone altar, four pottery incense burners, and a number of pottery chalices. Aharoni also identified cultic remains in the open area beside the room, including a stone stele and *favissae.* The cult room was destroyed by an intense fire, and remains of the Level V destruction could also be discerned in Area S.

The construction and destruction dates of Level V cannot be fixed with certainty as long as the dating of the red-slipped, irregularly burnished pottery which characterizes this city level remains problematic. It seems that Level V dates to the period of the United Monarchy, and its destruction is usually ascribed to Shishak's campaign in ca. 925 B.C.

b. Level IV. Level IV marks the construction of a large fortified city, making Lachish the strongest and most important city in Judah after Jerusalem. The construction of Level IV cannot be dated on the basis of archaeological data. It seems that the decision to turn Lachish into a fortified city followed new strategic needs of Judah arising as a result of the division of the United Monarchy. If that is so, the foundation of Level IV should be ascribed to one of the earlier kings of Judah, possibly Rehoboam (928–911 B.C.), Asa (908–867 B.C.), or Jehoshaphat (870–846 B.C.).

Lachish is mentioned in 2 Chr 1:5–12, 23 as one of the cities fortified by Rehoboam. This reference has recently been explained in four different ways. First, it was suggested that the entire list dates to the reign of Hezekiah (Naʾaman 1986) or Josiah (Fritz 1981). Second, it was suggested by Aharoni (1975: 41) and Yadin (1980: 21–22) that Level IV should be ascribed to Rehoboam. Third, Ussishkin indicates that the Level IV city represents an exceptionally strong Judean fort; it is difficult to associate it with Rehoboam's list in which Lachish is named among fifteen fortified towns, most of which are of secondary importance. The archaeological data agrees with the dating of Level IV to Rehoboam's reign, irrespective of the period from which the text may derive. Fourth, it was suggested by Tufnell (1953: 53–54) and by Ussishkin (1978: 93) that Palace A should be ascribed to Rehoboam. This suggestion was based on the stratigraphic assumption that Palace A (i.e., Podium A) was a monumental structure antedating the construction of Palace B in Level IV. Hence the conclusion that Palace A was an isolated fortress built at a later phase of Level V, and that it should be identified with Rehoboam's fortifications. It now appears that Palace A was an integral part of Palace B (see below).

Lachish was surrounded by a massive fortification system. The sole city gate was on the SW side. An ascending roadway led from the bottom of the site to an outer city gate, constructed as a bastion projecting from the line of the slope. Behind the outer gate the passage led through a courtyard to an inner gate, a large, six-chambered gatehouse. An outer revetment surrounded the site halfway down the slope; it supported a glacis which reached the bottom of the main city wall extending along the upper periphery of the site. The outer revetment apparently functioned as an outer obstacle preventing attackers from reaching the main wall, and except for a few places it was not manned in a time of siege.

The center of the city was crowned by the palace-fort (Palace B), obviously the seat of the Judean governor. The edifice was built on a raised foundation podium, and is all that remains after the superstructure was totally destroyed in antiquity. The foundation podium has two parts, labeled Podia A and B by the British. It is generally believed that Podium A represents an earlier edifice, Palace A, which was later incorporated into Palace B (whose present remains thus include Podia A and B). Some now believe that Podium A was an integral part of Palace B and that it is separated from Podium B and constructed in a different style for technical reasons.

Palace B had two annexed buildings—one on the N, which was probably a storehouse, and one on the S, which was either a storehouse or a stable (see below). The latter was labeled "government storehouse" by Starkey. A massive "enclosure wall" connected the SW corner of Palace B and the main city wall. The surface of the ground in this area sloped towards the city wall and was lime plastered.

The large, square "Great Shaft" hewn in the rock was uncovered by the British on the E side of the site. Since it is ca. 22.5 m deep, some have suggested that it is an unfinished water system, but it seems more likely that it was the quarry which supplied stones for the Level IV structures. A well ca. 44 m deep was uncovered near the outer revetment at the NE edge of the site, and probably formed the main water source of the city.

No domestic structures dating to the earlier phase of Level IV were uncovered. A house dated to the later phase of this level was uncovered in Area S, indicating that as time passed people started to settle in the garrison city.

2 Kgs 14:19 and 2 Chr 25:27 reveal that when a rebellion broke out in Jerusalem against Amaziah (798–769 B.C.), he fled to Lachish and was killed there by the rebels. Apparently when Amaziah saw that Jerusalem was lost to the rebels he fled to the next most important fortified city in Judah.

All the monumental structures (except the city walls), as well as the domestic building in Area S, were rebuilt in Level III, indicating their destruction at the end of Level IV. However, no remains of a willful destruction were discerned. M. Kochavi raised the possibility (oral information) that the destruction of Level IV resulted from an earthquake, e.g., the earthquake which occurred ca. 760 B.C., during the reign of Uzziah (Amos 1:1; Zech 14:5).

c. Level III. Level III is marked by the rebuilding of the city gate, the palace-fort complex, and the enclosure wall. See Fig. LAC.03. More people apparently settled at Lachish and a large number of domestic buildings have been uncovered in the area S of the palace fort and the enclosure wall. Various structures flanked the roadway leading from the city gate to the palace-fort.

Most impressive is the enlarged palace-fort complex. Podea A and B of the former Palace B, were extended by the addition of Podium C, which served as the foundation for the construction of the new edifice, Palace C. It is the largest structure so far known in ancient Israel, measuring ca. 76 by 36 m. The superstructure did not survive except some sections of flooring. The entrance was through a monumental staircase. The palace-fort and the two annexed buildings opened into a large paved courtyard surrounded by a stone fence which was added on the E side.

The S annexed building is of special interest. The Level IV "government storehouse" contained two rectangular units, each divided into three subunits. In Level III the structure ("Building 1034") was rebuilt and enlarged and had four such units. The building resembles the "stable compounds" in Megiddo (Lamon and Shipton 1939: 32–47), and thus also the "storehouse" at Tel Beer-sheba (Herzog 1973: 23–30). The Megiddo buildings were identified at the time as stables for horses, but this suggestion was contested by Pritchard (1970), and later by Aharoni (1982) and Herzog (1973: 26–30), who interpreted the Tel Beer-sheba building as a storehouse. Herr (1988) suggested that these buildings served as marketplaces. In following the argumentation of Yadin (1976) and Holladay (1986), we believe that these buildings—and hence the S annexed building at Lachish as well—were stables for horses.

The above assumption leads to further conclusions. In following Lamon and Shipton (1939: 35), it seems that the Level III stables which opened into a large courtyard housed chariotry units, the spacious courtyard serving as training and parading ground for the chariots. On the basis of the Megiddo and Tel Beer-sheba structures, it can be estimated that each unit in the Lachish building could house about 25 horses, hence the conclusion that the Level IV Judean garrison included a unit of 50 cavalry horses, while the Level III garrison included a chariotry unit of 50 chariots and 100 horses. The assumed connection of the Level III city with chariots fits the lamentation of Micah (Mic 1:13), who associates Lachish with chariots, and to the portrayal in the Lachish reliefs (see below) of burning vehicles, probably chariots, being thrown by the defenders on the Assyrian attackers. The importance of the assumed Lachish chariot unit in the Judean army is apparent in view of the fact that the written sources hardly refer to cavalry and chariotry units in Judah, and their relative weakness during this period is implied from Isaiah (Isa 31:1) and from the speech of Rabshakeh (2 Kgs 18:23–24; Isa 36:8–9).

(1) The Assyrian Conquest. It is now generally agreed (Ussishkin 1977) that the Level III city was conquered and destroyed by Sennacherib king of Assyria in 701 B.C. In Judah, Sennacherib attacked Lachish before turning to Jerusalem. He established his headquarters at Lachish (2 Kgs 18:14, 17; Isa 36:2, 37:8; 2 Chr 32:9) and from there sent a task force to challenge Hezekiah in Jerusalem. This fact as well as the "Lachish reliefs" (see below) prove the special military importance of Lachish during that period. The destruction of the Level III city was complete, and its inhabitants were deported. The desolate site was probably included in that part of Judah which was turned over by Sennacherib to the Philistine kings.

Remains of the destruction by fire were discerned in all

LAC.03. Reconstruction of Lachish—Level III. *(Drawing by J. Dekel, redrawn with additions from sketch by H. H. McWilliams in 1933, courtesy of D. Ussishkin)*

Level III structures. Large amounts of pottery vessels were sealed beneath the debris. This well-dated assemblage forms a basis for dating the pottery of Judah in that period (Aharoni and Aharoni 1976; Zimhoni fc.).

The main Assyrian attack was carried out in the SW corner of the city, and the archaeological discoveries in this area enable us to reconstruct the battle which took place (Ussishkin fc.). Deep valleys surrounded Lachish on all sides except for the SW corner, where a topographical saddle connected the site with the neighboring hillock. The fortifications were especially strong at this point, the outer revetment merging with the main city wall, together forming a massive tower. Still, the SW corner was the most vulnerable and most logical point of Lachish to assault. It seems that the site of the Assyrian camp can be restored with much certainty on the hillock to the SW, opposite the SW corner of the site, where the modern village is now situated. However, no remains of the assumed camp could be found there.

A huge siege ramp was laid by the Assyrians at the southwest corner, this being the oldest siege ramp and the only Assyrian one which is known today. See Fig. LAC.04. Unfortunately, a large part of it was removed unknowingly by the British expedition. The siege ramp was 70–75 m wide and 50–60 m long along its central axis, and its top reached the outer revetment wall. It was made of boulders probably collected in the surrounding fields and heaped against the slope of the mound. It is estimated that between 13,000 and 19,000 tons of stone were dumped here. The stones of the upper layer of the ramp were found stuck together by hard mortar to create a compact surface. The upper edge of the ramp was crowned with an earth platform which provided a level platform on which the siege machines could stand at the foot of the wall.

When the defenders saw the Assyrians laying a siege ramp, they laid a counter-ramp along the inside of the city wall, opposite the siege ramp. It was ca. 120 m long, and its apex rose ca. 3 m above the top of the city wall, thus creating a new defense line higher than the previous one. The counter-ramp is composed of layers of debris (taken from the earlier levels of the mound) and layers of limestone chips dumped in an orderly manner.

Once the fortification line along the top of the walls collapsed, the Assyrians raised the siege ramp above the outer revetment, a move which enabled them to attack the new defense line erected on top of the counter-ramp. The second stage of the siege ramp is also composed of boulders, many of which show signs of burning.

Remains of weapons, ammunition, and equipment were found in the excavation, mostly at the foot of the city wall.

LAC.04. Assyrian siege ramp and SW corner of Tel Lachish. *(Photograph by Y. Weinberg, courtesy of D. Ussishkin)*

They include a bronze helmet crest, scales of armor, sling stones, many iron arrowheads (850 arrowheads were found near the city wall at the point of attack), and a number of bone carved arrowheads. A fragment of an iron chain (ca. 37 cm long) and 12 large perforated stones were found near the point of attack and apparently were used by the defenders to attack and unbalance the siege machines. Each of the perforated stones weighs 100–200 kg, and remains of burnt ropes were discovered in the holes of two of them. These stones hung on ropes and probably were dropped from the top of the wall on the siege machines, or were moved to and fro like a pendulum in an attempt to damage them.

A mass burial which possibly was associated with the Assyrian conquest was uncovered by Starkey in several of the caves on the W slope of the mound. Disarticulated skeletons were dumped in a disorderly manner. Strewn throughout the bone deposits was pottery that indicated a date after 701 B.C. for the mass burials. It was estimated that about 1500 individuals were buried here. A total of 695 skulls were brought to London and studied by Risdon (1939). They belonged to men, women, and children—obviously civilians. Curiously, the crania indicate these people bore a close racial resemblance to the population of Egypt at that time. Three of the skulls were trepanned; one man survived long enough after the operation for the bone to heal while the other two men died shortly after the surgical procedure.

(2) The "Lachish Reliefs." When Sennacherib constructed his royal palace at Nineveh (Kuyunjik), he commissioned a set of stone reliefs to commemorate the conquest of Lachish. The reliefs decorated the walls of a large room (No. XXXVI) which had a central position in a large ceremonial unit of the palace. The architectural position of the reliefs, their length, and detailed portrayals emphasize the special importance of this victory for Sennacherib. Layard excavated part of the palace between 1847 and 1851. He uncovered Room XXXVI and brought most of the Lachish reliefs to the British Museum in London (Layard 1853a: Pls. 20–24; 1853b; Paterson 1915: Pls. 68–76; Ussishkin 1982: 67–118).

The Lachish reliefs covered all the walls of the rectangular room. The total length of the entire series was 26.85 m while the length of the presently preserved dado is ca. 18.85 m. From left to right the series depicted Assyrian horses and charioteers (this part is now missing), Assyrian infantry attacking the city, the besieged city (portrayed in the center of the series opposite the entrance to the room), Assyrian soldiers carrying booty and the deported Lachishites leaving their city, Judean captives, Sennacherib sitting on his throne facing Lachish, the royal tent and chariots, and the Assyrian camp.

The attacked city is shown in much detail. In the center is the city gate attacked by a siege machine, and to its right is the main siege ramp, on which six siege machines are deployed. A large structure, probably the palace-fort, is shown above the city gate. The city walls, manned by Judean warriors, are shown at both ends of the city. An analysis of the relief leads to the conclusion that the artist, although limited by the possibilities of the Assyrian schematic style, attempted to portray a realistic view of the city (Barnett 1958; Ussishkin 1980; 1982: 118–26). Lachish is shown as if viewed from a certain point located on the slope of the hillock SW of the mound. This point seems to be where Sennacherib sat on his throne, probably in front of the Assyrian camp, and commanded his army assailing the walls. Accordingly, I believe that the relief portrays Lachish as viewed by the Assyrian monarch from his command post, and in fact he is depicted in the relief sitting on his throne and facing the city. However, see ICONOGRAPHY.

(3) Royal Judean Storage Jars. Tel Lachish is a cardinal site for the study of the royal seal impressions for three reasons: (1) they were found in datable stratigraphic contexts; (2) some of the storage jars which carried them could be restored; and (3) at Lachish were recovered more stamped handles than in any other site. By 1983, 383 royal stamps and 54 "private" stamps from Lachish were counted (Ussishkin 1983: 163–64). Of the royal stamps, 85.9% were of the four-winged type, about two thirds of the latter bearing the city name Hebron.

All seal impressions were stamped on handles of storage jars of Type 484 according to Tufnell's classification (1953: 315–16; Pl. 95:484). See Fig. LAC.05. While some of these storage jars were stamped, many others were not stamped at all. One group of unstamped jars slightly differs from the typical ones, but is certainly related to them (Zimhoni fc.). A neutron activation analysis (Mommsen, Perlman, and Yellin 1984) indicated that the Type 484 storage jars were all made of similar clay from the region of the Shephelah, hence the conclusion that they were all produced in one center not far from Lachish. Lemaire's observation (1981) that only 22 seals, divided into six series, were used in stamping the jars, supports this conclusion.

Ten stamped royal jars, as well as numerous unstamped ones, could be restored, and allow the following conclusions. First, all kinds of jars—those bearing a four-winged symbol, those bearing a two-winged one, and those unstamped—were used concurrently. Second, all of them were found in Level III rooms sealed beneath the destruction debris (Lance 1971). Hence it is clear that they were produced during the reign of Hezekiah, shortly before 701 B.C. (Ussishkin 1977). This datum fits Na'aman's views (1979; 1986) that the royal storage jars were produced by the government of Judah as part of the preparations to meet the Assyrian invasion. Third, the measured capacity of the stamped jars is not uniform (between 39.75 and 51.80 liters), an indication that the stamps were not a royal guarantee of capacity. Fourth, there is no consistent pattern nor any uniform ruling for the application of stamps onto the four handles of each jar. Fifth, a "private stamp" was sometimes impressed together with a royal stamp on the same jar (Ussishkin 1976), supporting the conclusion that owners of the "private stamps" were either officials associated with the jars' production center, or potters at that center (Diringer 1949). Significantly, as noticed by Zimhoni (fc.), a large part of both the royal, and "private" impressions were carelessly applied and apparently were not meant to be read later. See STAMPS, ROYAL JAR HANDLE.

d. Level II. Following a period of abandonment, the settlement was renewed and refortified, probably during the reign of Josiah (639–609 B.C.). The Level II town was poorer and sparsely populated and its fortifications weaker than those of Level III.

A smaller city gate complex was built on the ruins of the former one. A rectangular courtyard separated the outer and inner gates, and a number of rooms opened into it. The "Lachish letters" (see below) uncovered in one of those rooms hint that the city's headquarters was located here. The outer revetment was apparently repaired and a new main city wall constructed of stone extended above the ruins of the previous one. The palace-fort was not rebuilt, and its ruins loomed in the center of the city.

A number of small houses, mostly of domestic character, were uncovered along the E side of the ruined palace-fort, in the Solar Shrine area, near the city gate, and in the SW corner of the site, but many other areas were found devoid of Level II remains.

Level II was destroyed by fire during the Babylonian conquest of Judah in 588/6 B.C. Jeremiah (34:7) mentions Lachish as one of the Judean strongholds attacked by Nebuchadnezzar. Large assemblages of pottery vessels were sealed beneath the destruction debris of the buildings, forming an indicative assemblage of the first decade of the 6th century B.C. (Aharoni and Aharoni 1976; Zimhoni fc.). Of special interest are storage jars whose handles are stamped by a rosette emblem; 23 of these stamped handles were found at Lachish.

e. Hebrew Inscriptions. While hardly any inscriptions were found in association with Level III (except for the royal seal impressions) a relatively large number of Hebrew ostraca, inscriptions on pottery vessels, bullae, Hebrew seals, and inscribed weights were found in Level II. Most important are the "Lachish letters" found sealed beneath the destruction debris in a room in the city gate complex (Torczyner et al. 1938; Lemaire 1977). These ostraca represent correspondence most of which were addressed to "my lord Yaush," an army commander at Lachish, shortly before the Babylonian destruction. They were sent by a subordinate stationed at some point where he could watch the signals from Azekah and Lachish. Recently Yadin (1984) suggested that the "Lachish letters" are in fact copies or drafts of letters sent from Lachish to the commander in Jerusalem. A few inscriptions on vessels were

LAC.05. Reconstructed storage jars from Tel Lachish, found in a burned storeroom—Level III. *(Photograph by A. Hay, courtesy of D. Ussishkin)*

found in the Level II storerooms near the city gate (Ussishkin 1978: 81–88; Lemaire 1980); two of them define types of wine kept in the vessels. Two jar inscriptions from Lachish mention dates, "in the fourth" and "in the ninth"—probably regnal years of Zedekiah king of Judah. Finally, seventeen bullae stamped with Hebrew seal impressions still bearing traces of papyri and strings on the reverse side were found by Aharoni (1975) in a juglet in a Level II building.

6. Post-Iron Age. a. Level I. This level spans the Babylonian, Persian, and the beginning of the Hellenistic periods. The settlement was probably abandoned for a while following the Level II destruction. Judeans returning from the Babylonian exile settled here (Neh 11:30), and during the Persian period Lachish was rebuilt as a governmental center. The city gate and city wall were restored, and a palace (the Residency), a temple (the Solar Shrine), and a few large buildings were erected on the summit.

The Residency was constructed on the foundation podium of the Judean palace-fort, which was cleared of the debris of the Palace C superstructure. However, the new edifice was smaller than the previous one. The building contained a large, square court and two porticoes opened to it. Hence its plan combined that of an Assyrian open-court house and a N Syrian *bit-hilani.* The square column bases in the porticos are cut in Persian style. At the end of Level I the Residency was settled by squatters. The Solar Shrine, measuring ca. 27 by 17 m, was built NE of the Residency in similar style, and both were probably contemporary. Its entrance faced E, hence the name given by Starkey. A bronze lamp and a limestone altar are the most important finds from the shrine. Among the finds from Level I are imported Greek pottery and many small stone incense altars found in caves at the foot of the mound.

The settlement came to an end during the earlier part of the Hellenistic period. The settlement pattern shifted to Marissa, and then to Eleutheropolis (Beth-Govrin). The reason for this shift is not clear. The Roman road from Eleutheropolis to Gaza passed near Lachish (as stated by Eusebius), and a segment of the road was uncovered by Starkey; other segments were recently identified and surveyed by Y. Dagan (oral information).

A large number of coins from different periods were found on the surface of the tell, indicating that the summit was continuously cultivated. Some areas of the summit contained burials termed "medieval graves" by the British. They were usually devoid of any burial offerings, and their date is unknown. The latest remains of the site are trenches, cartridges, and coins from Israel's War of Independence in 1948 A.D., when an Israeli unit was stationed on the tell.

Bibliography

Aharoni, M., and Aharoni, Y. 1976. The Stratification of Judahite Sites in the 8th and 7th Centuries B.C.E. *BASOR* 224: 73–90.

Aharoni, Y. 1975. *Investigations at Lachish, The Sanctuary and the Residency (Lachish V).* Tel Aviv.

———. 1982. *The Archaeology of the Land of Israel.* Philadelphia.

Ahlström, G. W. 1980. Is Tell ed-Duweir Ancient Lachish? *PEQ* 112: 7–9.

Albright, W. F. 1937. Further Light on the History of Israel from Lachish and Megiddo. *BASOR* 68: 22–26.

———. 1939. The Israelite Conquest of Canaan in the Light of Archaeology. *BASOR* 74: 11–23.

Barnett, R. D. 1958. The Siege of Lachish. *IEJ* 8: 161–64.

Bruyère, B. 1948. *Rapport sur les fouilles de Deir el Médineh (1935–1940).* Fouilles de l'Institut Français du Caire sous la direction de M. Ch. Kuentz, Tome XX. Cairo.

———. 1952. *Rapport sur les fouilles de Deir el Médineh (Années 1945–1946 et 1946–1947).* Fouilles de l'Institut Français du Caire sous la direction de M. Ch Kuentz, Tome XXI. Cairo.

Clamer, C. 1980. A Gold Plaque from Tel Lachish. *TA* 7: 152–62.

Clamer, C., and Ussishkin, D. 1977. A Canaanite Temple at Tell Lachish. *BA* 40/2: 71–76.

Cross, F. M. 1954. The Evolution of the Proto-Canaanite Alphabet. *BASOR* 134: 15–24.

———. 1984. An Old Canaanite Inscription Recently Found at Lachish. *TA* 11: 71–76.
Davies, G. I. 1982. Tell ed-Duweir = Ancient Lachish: A Response to G. W. Ahlström. *PEQ* 114: 25–28.
Diringer, D. 1949. The Royal Jar-Handle Stamps of Ancient Judah. *BA* 12: 70–86.
Fritz, V. 1981. The 'List of Rehoboam's Fortresses' in 2 Chr 11:5–12—A Document from the Time of Josiah. *EI* 15: 46*–53* (English).
Goldwasser, O. 1982. The Lachish Hieratic Bowl Once Again. *TA* 9: 137–38.
———. 1984. Hieratic Inscriptions from Tel Sera^{c} in Southern Canaan. *TA* 11: 77–93.
Herr, L. G. 1988. Tripartite Pillared Buildings and the Market Place in Iron Age Palestine. *BASOR* 272: 47–67.
Herzog, Z. 1973. The Storehouses. Pp. 23–30 in *Beer-sheba I,* ed. Y. Aharoni. Tel Aviv.
Holladay, J. S., Jr. 1986. The Stables of Ancient Israel. Pp. 103–66 in *The Archaeology of Jordan and other Sites, Presented to Siegfried H. Horn,* ed. L. T. Geraty and L. G. Herr. Berrien Springs, MI.
Inge, C. H. 1938. Excavations at Tell ed-Duweir. *PEQ,* 240–56.
Lamon, R. S., and Shipton, G. M. 1939. *Megiddo I.* OIP 42. Chicago.
Lance, H. D. 1971. The Royal Stamps and the Kingdom of Josiah. *HTR* 64: 315–32.
Layard, A. H. 1853a. *A Second Series of the Monuments of Nineveh.* London.
———. 1853b. *Discoveries in the Ruins of Nineveh and Babylon.* London.
Lemaire, A. 1977. *Inscriptions hébraiques.* Vol. 1, *Les ostraca.* Paris.
———. 1980. A Note on Inscription XXX from Lachish. *TA* 7: 92–94.
———. 1981. Classification des estampilles royales Judéennes. *EI* 15: 54*–60*.
Mommsen, H.; Perlman, I.; and Yellin, J. 1984. The Provenience of the *lmlk* Jars. *IEJ* 34: 89–113.
Na$^{\supset}$aman, N. 1979. Sennacherib's Campaign to Judah and the Date of the *LMLK* stamps. *VT* 29: 61–86.
———. 1986. Hezekiah's Fortified Cities and the *LMLK* stamps. *BASOR* 261: 5–21.
Paterson, A. 1915. *Assyrian Sculptures, Palace of Sinacherib.* The Hague.
Pritchard, J. B. 1970. The Megiddo Stables: A Reassessment. Pp. 268–76 in *Near Eastern Archaeology in the Twentieth Century,* ed. J. A. Sanders. Garden City, NY.
Puech, E. 1986–87. The Canaanite Inscriptions of Lachish and Their Religious Background. *TA* 13–14: 13–25.
Risdon, D. L. 1939. A Study of the Cranial and Other Human Remains from Palestine Excavated at Tell Duweir (Lachish) by the Wellcome-Marston Archaeological Research Expedition. *Biometrika* 35: 99–165.
Rosen, S. 1988–89. Pottery Neolithic Flint Artifacts from Tell Lachish. *TA* 15–16: 193–96.
Starkey, J. L. 1933. A Lecture Delivered at the Rooms of the Palestine Exploration Fund, on June 22nd, 1933. *PEQ,* 190–99.
———. 1934. Excavations at Tell El Duweir, 1933–1934. *PEQ,* 164–75.
———. 1935. Excavations at Tell El Duweir, 1934–1935. *PEQ* 198–207.
———. 1936. Excavations at Tell el Duweir, 1935–36. *PEQ,* 178–89.
———. 1937a. Lachish as illustrating Bible History. *PEQ,* 171–79.
———. 1937b. Excavations at Tell ed Duweir. *PEQ,* 228–41.
Torczyner, H., et al. 1938. *Lachish I, The Lachish Letters.* London.
Tufnell, O. 1953. *Lachish III, The Iron Age.* London.
Tufnell, O.; Inge, C. H.; and Harding, G. L. 1940. *Lachish II, The Fosse Temple.* London.
Tufnell, O., et al. 1958. *Lachish IV, The Bronze Age.* London.
Ussishkin, D. 1976. Royal Judean Storage Jars and Private Seal Impressions. *BASOR* 223: 1–13.
———. 1977. The Destruction of Lachish by Sennacherib and the Dating of the Royal Judean Storage Jars. *TA* 4: 28–60.
———. 1978. Excavations at Tel Lachish—1973–1977, Preliminary Report. *TA* 5: 1–97.
———. 1980. The "Lachish Reliefs" and the City of Lachish. *IEJ* 30: 174–95.
———. 1982. *The Conquest of Lachish by Sennacherib.* Tel Aviv.
———. 1983. Excavations at Tel Lachish—1978–1983, Second Preliminary Report. *TA* 10: 97–175.
———. 1985. Levels VII and VI at Tel Lachish and the End of the Late Bronze Age in Canaan. Pp. 213–30 in *Palestine in the Bronze and Iron Ages,* ed. J. N. Tubb. London.
———. fc. The Assyrian Attack on Lachish: The Archaeological Evidence from the Southwest Corner of the Site. *TA* 17.
Weinstein, J. M. 1981. The Egyptian Empire in Palestine: A Reassessment. *BASOR* 241: 1–28.
Yadin, Y. 1976. The Megiddo Stables. Pp. 249–52 in *Magnalia Dei: The Mighty Acts of God,* ed. F. M. Cross; W. E. Lemke; and P. D. Miller, Jr. Garden City, N.Y.
———. 1980. A Rejoinder. *BASOR* 239: 19–23.
———. 1984. The Lachish Letters: Originals or Copies and Drafts? Pp. 179–86 in *Recent Archaeology in the Land of Israel,* ed. H. Shanks and B. Mazar. Washington.
Zimhoni, O. fc. Two Ceramic Assemblages from Lachish Levels III and II. *TA* 17.

David Ussishkin

LACHISH LETTERS. In the course of the six archaeological excavations conducted by the Wellcome-Marston Archaeological Research Expedition at Tell ed-Duweir (ancient Lachish) between 1932 and 1938, twenty-one inscribed ostraca were found which, together with another ostracon discovered by Y. Aharoni in 1966 at the site of the city's so-called "Solar Shrine," perhaps comprise the single most significant corpus of Hebrew epigraphic material to have thus far come to light. All the ostraca appear to date to the last phase of Judahite occupation (Level 2), thus to the city destroyed in Nebuchadrezzar's conquest of Judah in 586 B.C.E. Their contribution to the study of ancient Hebrew—paleography and orthography, grammar and syntax—and its epistolographic tradition is surpassed only by their historical value as a witness to the situation prevailing in Judah during the final days of the Davidic State.

In the *editio princeps,* Torczyner (1938) labeled, albeit loosely, the eighteen ostraca recovered in 1935 just inside the city's outer-gate "letters." However, they and the ostraca of 1938 (nos. 19–21) and 1966 (no. 22) represent a heterogeneous collection. Nos. 10, 14, 15, and 21 are practically unreadable (Lemaire 1977: 139); while no. 20 is in fact an inscription on a jar, having been found together with other fragments of the same storage vessel just E of the palace-fortress (Lemaire 1977: 134–35). Since of the ostraca that remain, nos. 1, 11, 19, and 22 are lists of proper names, composed for administrative purposes, this leaves only nos. 2–6, 8–9, 12–13, and 16–18 that may with some confidence be identified as letters or parts thereof (Pardee 1982: 12). While several ostraca (nos. 2, 6–8, 18) originally came from the same pot and apparently were written by the same hand, the enormous quantity of jar fragments found with them, many blackened by fire (Torczyner 1938: 11), gives little endorsement to the search for a unitary explanatory context for these or a majority of the preserved ostraca (Pardee 1982: 77).

Among the ostraca discovered in 1935, nos. 1–15 and 18 belong to a single cache taken from the burnt deposit of a room adjoining the outer gate, plausibly identified as the guardroom. As such, it was a place where messages are likely to have been received by the commander of the fortress (Starkey 1938: 11–12). Indeed, where the relationship between sender and recipient can be determined, the letters belonging to this group appear to be addressed without exception from an inferior to a superior. Regrettably, the inferior is mentioned only once by name, in no. 3:1 identified as Hoshaiah; three times, however, in nos. 2:1, 3:2, and 6:1, the recipient is identified as Yaosh, who may, on the basis of allusions contained in the letters as well as the address "my lord," reasonably be identified as the commander of the fortress itself. Broadly speaking, the letters, where sufficiently preserved to permit a decision, are of the nature of military correspondence (Pardee 1982: 159), revealing Yaosh's wide-ranging involvement in, and concern for, administrative, political, and military issues of local and national importance.

A. Language

The language of the letters reflects throughout the popular Hebrew spoken in Judah in the early 6th century. Here we may call attention to the noncontraction of diphthongs, characteristic of the south, as well as to the use of shorter, popular grammatical speech forms, reflected in many portions of the MT's consonantal text. New to the Hebrew lexicon are several items found in the letters, such as the expression *ᶜt kym,* "right now," (2:3) or *lnṣḥ,* "ever," (3:10); rare Hebrew words are also found, as *dlt* (4:3), indicating some type of writing material, or *mśʾt* (4:10), used for "fire signal." Of interest are the occurrences of the formula of courtesy *my ᶜbdk klb ky,* "Who is your servant (but) a dog that . . . ," used by an inferior addressing Yaosh (2:3–4), and the oath formula *ḥyhwh,* "As Yahweh lives . . ." (3:9). While generally the orthography reflects preexilic practice in the use *matres lectionis,* at least one instance of an internal *mater lectionis* (viz. *hᶜyrh,* 4:7), in a context where the reading is undisputed, indicates the onset of postexilic practice, found also sporadically in the Arad Ostraca.

The Lachish Letters, though characteristically allusive in their subject matter rather than discursive, provide, because of their length and relatively nonstereotypical language, an important source for the study of Hebrew grammar and syntax in the early sixth century B.C.E. In its use of long and elaborate syntactical structures, the language of the letters is in fact reminiscent of the Deuteronomist and especially the prose style of Jeremiah. This puts an additional burden upon the modern translator/interpreter. For a straightforward analysis is encumbered by the necessity of reconstructing a context for the letters' characteristically elliptical phraseology (a context presumed alike by the original sender and receiver) and by the limitations on analysis the ostraca's state of preservation imposes.

B. Epistolography

The Lachish Letters, though limited to communications from an inferior to a superior submitting reports or requesting directives, furnish valuable data on current epistolary style and practice. In addition to the variety of greeting formulas employed (e.g., "May Yahweh have my lord hear good news right now, right now . . ." 2:1–3), several formal features immediately stand out. The *praescriptio* consists of (1) an address ("to my lord"), with or without the name of the recipient, and lacking (except in one letter) the name of the sender, followed by the greeting (above); or (2) simply a greeting formula without an address. The body of the letter is then introduced either by the familiar transitional particle *wᶜt,* "and now," or, unique to Lachish, the formula noted above, "Who is your servant (but) a dog that . . . ." No closing formulas, such as emerge in the letters of the Bar Kokhba period, follow the body of the letter proper.

C. Historical Significance

The most important of the letters historically are nos. 3, 4, and 6. While none of the allusions or names contained in them, with the possible exception of no. 4, can be correlated precisely with biblical personages or events, the letters mirror to a remarkable degree the troubled atmosphere prevailing in Judah on the eve of its conquest, transparent in the biblical account of the prophet Jeremiah.

Letter no. 3, a letter of Hoshaiah to Yaosh and the longest Hebrew letter dating to the monarchy, appears to report in fact on just the sort of embassy to obtain Egyptian assistance alluded to in Ezek 17:15 and against which Jeremiah (37:7) railed so vehemently. "And to your servant it has been reported that the general of the army, Coniah, son of Elnathan, has gone down to enter Egypt, and he has sent to fetch from here Hodaviah, the son of Ahijah, and his men" (13–18). Could Coniah, son of Elnathan, mentioned here, be related to Elnathan, son of Achbor, sent by King Jehoiakim to Egypt to arrest the prophet Uriah (Jer 26:22)? The letter concludes with the tantalizing report that Hoshaiah is dispatching to Yaosh the letter of one Tobiah, the servant of the king, that came to a man by the name of Shallum through the mediation of an unnamed prophet, containing the message "Beware!" Unfortunately, it is impossible to specify the object of this laconic warning; and although the prophet employed to convey the letter may have been known both to Hoshaiah and Yaosh, every attempt to identify him with a biblical prophet must remain hypothetical. The impression conveyed by the letter generally of intense political maneuvering and factional disunity, nevertheless, accords well with what we know from the Bible.

The most intriguing of all the letters is no. 4, even if the interpretation of its enigmatic contents has been the subject of considerable dispute. At issue are, in particular, two statements made in the body of the letter which, on one interpretation, allude to the abandonment of Beth-harapid (4–6), an outpost of unknown location, and to the fall of Azekah, ten miles north of Lachish, mentioned in Jer 34:6–7 as one of two fortresses including Lachish left remaining to Judah before Jerusalem's fall: "And may (my lord) know that we are watching for the signals of Lachish according to all the signs which my lord gave. For we do not see Azekah" (10–13). If so, this letter must date to the final critical phase of the Babylonian campaign, shortly before the capture of Lachish itself. But on another, if less accepted reading, the letter may simply allude to preparations for imminent invasion, i.e., the evacuation of small towns and the testing of a system of fire signals to warn of the enemy's advance (Pardee 1982: 95).

The interpretation of no. 6 is problematic as well, because at several key points in the letter the writing is almost totally effaced. But the unquestionable reference in lines 5–6 to the negative effect that certain statements being made are having on the situation makes probable an allusion to the circulation of letters from high-placed Judean officials that were demoralizing in the face of the Babylonian threat. This accords with what we know in the Bible both of Zedekiah's own vacillation in the rebellion and of the support Jeremiah received from influential members of Judah's nobility.

It can only be hoped that technical advances in the instrumentation used for epigraphic analysis will in the future enable scholars to refine their conclusions concerning these and other matters of interpretation, making possible a fuller appreciation of this important corpus of ancient Hebrew letters and documents.

The texts of selected Lachish letters are available with German translation and notes in *KAI,* 192–99. English translations include *ANET,* 322 (by W. F. Albright), and, with Hebrew text and notes, *TSSI* 1: 32–49.

Bibliography

Aharoni, Y. 1968. Trial Excavation in the 'Solar Shrine' at Lachish: Preliminary Report. *IEJ* 18: 157–69.

Cross, F. M., Jr., and Freedman, D. N. 1952. *Early Hebrew Orthography: A Study of the Epigraphic Evidence.* AOS 36. New Haven.

Diringer, D. 1953. Early Hebrew Inscriptions. Pp. 331–59 in *The Iron Age,* ed. O. Tufnell et al. Lachish III. London.

Lemaire, A. 1977. *Inscriptions hébraïques.* Vol. 1, *Les ostraca.* LAPO 9. Paris.

Michaud, H. 1957. Les ostraca de Lakiš conservés à Londres. *Syria* 34: 39–60.

Pardee, D. 1982. *Handbook of Ancient Hebrew Letters.* SBLSBS 15. Chico, CA.

Starkey, J. L. 1938. The Discovery. Pp. 11–14 in Torczyner 1938.

Torczyner, H., ed. 1938. *The Lachish Letters.* Lachish I. London.

ROBERT A. DI VITO

LADAN (PERSON) [Heb *laʿdān*]. **1.** A descendant of Ephraim and therefore a descendant of Joshua, the hero of the Conquest (1 Chr 7:26). Ladan is the son of Tahan and father of Ammihud. The only other listing of the Ephraimite clan is in Num 26:35–36, and Ladan is not found there. However, some of the names prior to Ammihud are found in the Numbers passage.

2. A Gershonite Levite (1 Chr 23:7–8; 26:21). Gershon is elsewhere in the OT Gershom, indicating perhaps divergent authorship. Gershon, Kohath, and Merari were the sons of Levi. The first son of Gershon is otherwise Libni (1 Chr 6:2—Eng 6:17; Exod 6:17; Num 3:21) but Ladan in 1 Chr 23:7–8 and 26:21. Ladan has three sons: Jehiel, Zetham, and Joel, according to 23:8. Libni (6:5—Eng 6:20) has one son, Jahath (cf. 23:10). This Jehiel is found also in 1 Chr 26:21–22 (spelled Jehieli) as a Gershonite whose sons Zetham and Joel were over the treasuries of Yahweh's temple. The phrase "these were the heads of the family of Ladan" (1 Chr 23:9) seems out of place and requires some textual emendations (Myers *1 Chronicles* AB, 158).

M. STEPHEN DAVIS

LADDER OF TYRE (PLACE) [Gk *klimax Tyrou*]. A distinctive geofeature which marked the N boundary of the Seleucid eparchy of Paralia over which Antiochus VI made Simon Maccabeus responsible (1 Macc 11:59; *Ant* 13.5.5. §146). Josephus, in locating Simon's territory, described the Ladder of Tyre as being 100 stadia N of Acre and the highest mountain in Galilee and Carmel (*JW* 2.10.2). This feature along the coast was also reportedly the northernmost boundary of the harvest of murex shells used in the production of purple dye (Totius Orbis Descriptio 29). The description which includes Carmel is problematic since Mt. Carmel, at 550 m, is higher than the ridges N of Acre which have a maximum elevation of 300 m. However, N of the plain of Acre there are several precipitous promontories which extend into the Mediterranean. These ridges prevented easy communication between Acre and Tyre along the coast. The climbing involved in traversing this route may have been the origin of the toponym "Ladder of Tyre." It has also been observed that when viewed collectively from the S, these ridges provide an image of rungs whereby one may ascend to Tyre. The promontories Ras Musheirefeh, Ras en-Nakurah, and Ras el-ʿAbyadh separately are all possible candidates for this location. Simons (*GTTOT,* 416) assigns the toponym "Ladder of Tyre" as a collective name for the series of promontories S of Tyre that extend into the Mediterranean.

ROBERT W. SMITH

LADY, ELECT. See ELECT LADY.

LAEL (PERSON) [Heb *lāʾēl*]. According to Num 3:24, the father of Eliasaph, the leader of the Gershonite subdivision (father's house) of the tribe of Levi. Noth (*IPN,* 32, 153) proposed a translation of the name such as "belonging to God," or "God's special possession," and suggested that it expressed a close relation between God and the name bearer while attributing no particular aspect to that relation.

RICHARD D. WEIS

LAGASH. The name of an important Sumerian city-state from the 3d millennium of which two urban centers have been found and partially excavated: Tello (= Girsu) and el-Hiba (= Lagash). Tello was the first site to produce important vestiges of Sumerian civilization. In 1877, E. de Sarzec, French Vice-Consul in Bassorah, having learned that statues had been found by clandestine excavators, undertook excavations there. At the end of the first four seasons, he announced in 1881 the importance of his discoveries. Up until his death in 1900, he had led eleven excavations in all. G. Cros continued exploration from 1903 to 1909 (four excavations), then H. de Genouillac returned to the site three times from 1929 to 1931 and A. Parrot led two digs there from 1931 to 1933. These twenty excavations have brought to light rich and varied material (statues, steles, cylinder seals, tablets, etc.) that for a long time have been the base of our knowledge of Sumerian civilization. However, much is still unknown about the city and its architecture. Between the regular excavations, clandestine digs devastated the site and dumped onto the market thousands of objects and tablets whose origins were unknown. But this destructive pillaging is not the only thing responsible: research was often conducted without careful methods, without knowledge of the unbaked brick architecture and without consideration of stratigraphy. Thus it is more the objects and tablets that allow one to talk about Tello than the archaeology itself.

However, exploration recently undertaken at El-Hiba, if it is continued, will help in compensating for certain gaps in the archaeological knowledge. This site, the largest of the S tells with more than 500 hectares, is found about 20 km to the NE of Tello. It was excavated for the first time in 1887 by R. Koldewey, who found only a large necropolis there. In 1968 an American group engaged in a systematic study of the site, and thus far five excavations have been conducted under the direction of V. E. Crawford and D. P. Hansen, the first four in 1968–69, 1970–71, 1972–73, and 1975–76. The results have still been published only partially, but the research deals in particular with two sanctuaries from the Early Dynastic period that show the interest there will be to continue the exploration.

The work and the study of the tablets suggest that Lagash was a state composed of several urban centers; the capital was without doubt in El-Hiba itself, but Tello-Girsu during antiquity was certainly (if one refers to its extended area and the quality of the finds found by the French team) a city of equal importance, perhaps with a more religious vocation.

It is during the 3d millennium that Lagash played a large role. The site of Tello had been occupied since the Ubaid period, and material from Uruk and Jemdet Nasr have been found. It is, however, impossible to evaluate the role of the importance of the city during this long period. It is during the Early Dynastic III period that the inscriptions bring to light the active role played by certain of the *ensi* (i.e., rulers) of Lagash, some of whom are Urnanshe, Eannatum, Entemena and Urukagina. The famous Stele of the Vultures (now in the Louvre Museum) that was drawn up to commemorate the victory of Lagash over Umma, illustrate thus the territorial rivalries and the certainly tumultuous life of the cities of Sumer. The rich and varied material—statuettes, most often fragmentary reliefs, sometimes called New Year plaques; masses of sculpted armaments, like that of Mesilim; different arms and tools out of bronze; the very beautiful Entemena vase, in silver, on which a leontocephalous eagle linking animals was engraved four times; fragments of engraved shell; cylindrical seals; foundation figurines, etc.—come without doubt for the most part from the temple consecrated to the principal god Ningirsu; the architecture of this temple is unfortunately practically unknown. At El-Hiba, however, the beginning of excavations at the Ibgal Temple of the goddess Inanna looks like a promising example of religious architecture; the last of the three levels seems to link the building to a series of oval or circular temples. At El-Hiba, the Ibgal of Inanna, of which the last phase was built by Eannatum, and the Bagara of Ningirsu are still very rare examples of the real importance of the city. The Old Akkadian period does not seem to have left marked traces, but at Lagash one finds evidence of Gudea and the beginning of the Neo-Sumerian renaissance after the dark age of Guti around 2150 B.C. The reconstruction of the temple of Ningirsu at Tello is known to us only through texts (cylinder A of Gudea); it clearly reveals important commercial trade relations because materials from the mountains of Amanus were brought to the site as well as from the gulf countries of Magan and Meluhha. But what shows at the same time, the real strength and originality of Lagash at this moment, is the collection of diorite statues of Gudea. The hydraulic works that have been unearthed on the eastern tell of Tello also clearly show the high degree of technology attained by the Sumerian civilization.

However, it is not Lagash but Ur that becomes the center of the empire and the focus of the Sumerian renaissance. With the Ur III period, Lagash is no longer an important center, but nevertheless, Tello and El-Hiba have provided architectural material that attests to a relative survival of the city during the course of the second and first millennia. See also *RLA* sub "Lagash."

Bibliography

Biggs, R. D. 1974. *Inscriptions from Al-Hiba-Lagash, the 1st and 2d Seasons.* BibMes 3. Malibu.

Crawford, V. E. 1972. Excavations in the Swamps of Sumer. *Expedition* 14/2: 12–20.

———. 1974. Lagash. *Iraq* 36: 29–35.

Hansen, D. P. 1970. Al-Hiba, 1968–1969: A Preliminary Report. *Artibus Asiae* 32/4: 243–50.

———. 1973. Al-Hiba, 1970–1971, a Preliminary Report. *Artibus Asiae* 35: 62–70.

Parrot, A. 1948. *Tello.* Paris.

Thureau-Dangin, F., and Delaporte, L. 1910–21. *Inventaire des tablettes de Tello.* 5 vols. Paris.

JEAN-CL. MARGUERON
Trans. Stephen Rosoff

LAHAD (PERSON) [Heb *lāhad*]. Listed among the descendants of Judah (1 Chr 4:2). Nothing is otherwise known of him.

LAHAV (PLACE). See HALIF, TEL.

LAHMAM (PLACE) [Heb *laḥmām*]. Town situated in the Shephelah, or lowlands, of Judah (Josh 15:40), within the same district as Lachish. Although the MT reads *laḥmās,* the vast majority of manuscripts support reading a final *mem,* which is easily confused with *samek,* especially in the square script (Boling and Wright *Joshua* AB, 380). This settlement is listed among the towns within the tribal allotment of Judah (Josh 15:21–62). The ancient settlement is most probably to be located at Khirbet el-Lahm (Boling and Wright *Joshua* AB, 386), located approximately 4.5 km S of Beit Jibrin (M.R. 140108).

WADE R. KOTTER

LAHMI (PERSON) [Heb *laḥmî*]. A Philistine, the brother of Goliath the Gittite, slain by Elhanan according to 1 Chr 20:5. The parallel passage in 2 Sam 21:19 depicts Elhanan as the slayer not of Goliath's brother but of Goliath himself, which would appear to contradict the information in 1 Samuel 17, in which David vanquishes Goliath. However, in spite of attempts to identify David and Elhanan and thereby relieve a tension in the biblical text (see GOLIATH), it is most often felt that the name of Goliath is secondary in 1 Sam 17:4 and 23. Thus the question is whether Elhanan slew Goliath or his brother, Lahmi. Where the MT of 2 Sam 21:19 refers to Elhanan as "the Bethlehemite" *bêt hallaḥmî ʾēt,* 1 Chr 20:5 reads the object "Lahmi, the brother of" *ʾet-laḥmî ʾăḥî,* in which the *laḥmî* element of "Bethlehemite" has become an independent personal noun. In this case it appears most likely that 2 Sam 21:19 preserves the original version. Williamson (*Chronicles* NCBC, 142) cautions against automatically assuming that the Chronicler deliberately changed his source in order to relieve the tension between the deed ascribed to David in 1 Samuel 17 and the one ascribed to Elhanan in 2 Samuel 21 and raises the possibility that the Chronicler may have been attempting to make comprehensible a difficult *Vorlage.*

CARL S. EHRLICH

LAISH (PERSON) [Heb *layiš*]. Father of Palti, the husband of Michal, the daughter of Saul (1 Sam 25:44, 2 Sam 3:15 [ketib *lwš*]). Michal had been previously married to David, but after he fell into disfavor with Saul, the Israelite king gave his daughter to the son of Laish. When David assumed the kingship, Michal was returned to him, with Palti experiencing much grief. The name "Laish" means "lion," the use of animal names not being an uncommon practice in Israel. The person was named because of a particular trait of the animal that was valued (Noth *IPN,* 229–30). Laish came from Gallim, which was probably located in Benjamin, on a route on which the Assyrian army advanced to Jerusalem in the late 8th century B.C. (cf. Isa 10:30).

STEPHEN G. DEMPSTER

LAISH (PLACE) [Heb *layiš*]. Var. LESHEM. A city in the extreme N of Canaan (M.R. 211294) that at least a part of the Israelite tribe of Dan (cf. Mazar 1960) attacked and conquered and made their new home (Judges 18). Josh 19:47 mentions that the name of the site before the appearance of the Danites was Leshem (Heb *lešem*) instead of Laish. However, according to both accounts, the Danites renamed the town Dan after their ancestral heritage (Judg 18:29; Josh 19:47). Malamat (1970: 171) says simply that the Joshua account is "possibly corrupt," while Boling and Wright (*Joshua* AB, 466) suggest that in Leshem the "final *m* may be enclitic." The LXX offers some differences from the MT account of Joshua, and in an amplified discussion states that Dan was unable to settle in their allotment and that the tribe of Judah conquered *Lachis* naming it *Lasendak* (LXX Josh 19:48). This reference tends to imply that the site was located in S Canaan. It is unclear if Judah then gave the town to Dan. Earlier extrabiblical historical accounts and archaeological excavations make clear that the city of Laish (and the later city of Dan) should be located in the far N of Canaan.

Laish is mentioned as one of the objects of the Egyptian curses in the Execration Texts (Posener 1940: E59) in a context along with Hazor; it is also mentioned in the royal archives at Mari, also in association with Hazor (Malamat 1970). The Mari text records the shipment of ca. 8.33 minas (ca. 4.5 kg) of tin to Laish (Malamat 1971). Additionally, the excavations have discovered an inscription whose reconstructed reading appears to be a dedication to the god who was at Dan. The inscription was written in Greek and Aramaic, and Biran suggests that it dates from the early 2d century B.C. (1981a: 145–47).

Laish is N of the Huleh basin, on a main branch road which passes from the Mediterranean inland to Damascus and Syria. Copious perennial springs surround the site and combine to become one of the tributaries of the Jordan river.

The excavations at Laish (see more detailed discussion in DAN [PLACE]) have provided indications of a significant (ca. 50 acres) EB II–III settlement (Biran 1987: 101–102), but the exposure has not been extensive enough to clarify the nature of the social organization. The MB city, however, is represented in both domestic (Biran *EAEHL* 1: 315–16) and monumental architecture, as well as tombs. The excavations have uncovered an impressively built MB tomb with a rich collection of wares, which Biran suggests was associated with one of the high ranking families of the city (1986: 173–79). The MB city was protected with a massive sloping earth rampart which had been laid against a stone core. On the SE corner of the fortification system was found an intact arched mudbrick city gate and tower complex (Biran 1981b). This gate and fortification system may have belonged to the city mentioned in both the Mari and Execration Texts. Furthermore, the reference to Dan in Gen 14:14, when Abraham pursued the four kings of Mesopotamia to rescue his nephew, Lot, may be an allusion to the city associated with this fortification system (Biran 1984: 19). (Obviously, the reference in Genesis is to "Laish"; the reference to "Dan" is an anachronism, since the town did not receive that name until much later.) Surprisingly, the gate complex was apparently deliberately buried, probably because of foundational or structural defects (Biran 1984: 7–9).

While Laish was not the largest site in the area (cf. Hazor at over 700 dunams), it was still large (ca. 200 dunams), implying a sizable population. That the rulers of Laish were able to organize and command crews to construct the ramparts and gate complex, then bury the gate and perhaps construct another elsewhere, implies the presence of a strong, centralized ruling power. Such power might be that to which the Egyptians were reacting when they cited the city of Laish in their Execration Texts. The importation of a large quantity of tin from Mari also implies it had economic power, probably as a center of metallurgy and as a redistribution center for finished products. LB Laish is attested in Thutmose III's list of Canaanite cities (No. 31: *ANET,* 242), but evidence of his campaign at Laish has not been located in the excavations. One find, however, indicates contact with Egypt during this period: a red granite statuette of a seated man, inscribed with the name Nefertem. The style is indicative of the 19th Dyn. (ca. 14th century B.C.; Biran 1987: 105). The richness of LB Laish can be inferred from the Mycenaean tomb (387) with its ceramic repertoire of imported wares (Biran 1974: 34) which in turn "presupposes the existence of a large and wealthy community in the 14th–13th centuries B.C." (Biran 1980: 172–73). Some areas of stratified LB remains have come to light, and in one was found an exquisite ceramic plaque of a dancer playing a lute (Biran 1986: 168–73). It is unclear exactly what defenses the LB community had, since none have been located for this period—apparently they relied upon the old MB fortification ramparts (Biran 1969: 122–23; 1987: 104). Perhaps a weakened fortification system is part of what is reflected in the analysis by the spies in Judg 18:7, which describes the people of Laish as those who "dwelt in security, . . . quiet and unsuspecting." The phrase that the people of Laish lived "after the manner of the Sidonians" (Heb *kĕmišpat ṣidōnîm*) has been interpreted generally either to refer to commercial enterprises as the basis of the economy (cf. Moore *Judges* ICC: 390) or to a non-military and peaceful nature (cf. Boling *Judges* AB, 260, 263; Klein 1988: 156–57).

It was against this LB city that the Danites mustered their forces; the city apparently received no defensive assistance from their neighboring powers (Judg 18:7, 28). The text states that the Danites burned the town (v 27), but no evidence for a widespread destruction by fire on this transitional horizon has been found at the site. There is, however, evidence of a change as seen in the sudden appearance of numerous pits and the collar-rim storejar. Biran suggests that these features might indicate the appearance of the Danites (Biran 1987: 105–06).

Bibliography

Biran, A. 1969. Notes and News: Tel Dan. *IEJ* 19: 121–23.

———. 1974. Tel Dan. *BA* 37: 26–51.

———. 1980. Tell Dan Five Years Later. *BA* 43: 168–82.

———. 1981a. To the God who is in Dan. Pp. 142–51 in *Temples and High Places in Biblical Times,* ed. A. Biran. Jerusalem.

———. 1981b. The Discovery of the Middle Bronze Age Gate at Dan. *BA* 44: 139–44.

———. 1984. The Triple-Arched Gate of Laish at Tel Dan. *IEJ* 34: 1–19.

———. 1986. The Dancer from Dan, the Empty Tomb and the Altar Room. *IEJ* 36: 168–87.

———. 1987. Dan. Pp. 101–11 in *Archaeology and Biblical Interpretation,* ed. L. G. Perdue, L. E. Toombs, and G. L. Johnson. Atlanta.

Klein, L. R. 1988. *The Triumph of Irony in the Book of Judges.* JSOTSup 68. Sheffield.

Malamat, A. 1970. Canaan and the Mari Texts. Pp. 164–77 in *Near Eastern Archaeology in the Twentieth Century,* ed. J. A. Sanders. Garden City, NY.

———. 1971. Syro-Palestinian Destination in a Mari Tin Inventory. *IEJ* 21: 31–38.

———. 1985. Mari and Early Israel. Pp. 235–43 in *BibAT.*

Mazar, B. 1960. The Cities of the Territory of Dan. *IEJ* 10: 65–77.

Posener, G. 1940. *Princes et pays d'Asie et de Nubie.* Brussels.

DALE W. MANOR

LAISHAH

LAISHAH (PLACE) [Heb *layšâ*]. A site NE of Jerusalem (Isa 10:30). It is mentioned in a text in which an "enemy from the north" launches a surprise attack on Jerusalem along a byway which runs E of the main road from Shechem to Jerusalem. The discussion as to whether Isa 10:27b–34 reflects a real event or is a visionary anticipation (Wildberger *Jesaja* BK [1–12], 425–29), may be based on a false alternative, since it is conceivable that both military and cultic recollections could have been combined (Christensen 1976: 395–97), and so together have influenced expectations of the future (Clements 1980: 118–19). The redactional structure of Isaiah 10 makes it likely that the Assyrians were the enemy in question (see vv 5–15, 33–34).

The identification of Laishah with el-ʿIsāwīje (M.R. 174134), which has been continuously suggested since it was first proposed by Dalman (1916: 53–54), is based on uncertain etymological considerations. Dalman thought that Laishah was Arabic misunderstood as el-ʿAyšā (i.e., feminine proper name plus definite article) and then confused with ʿIsa (Esau, Jesus). However, topographical and archaeological reasons exclude the almost inaccessible el-ʿIsāwīje. Other sites in the vicinity of Jerusalem are to be preferred, in particular probably (Donner 1968: 54) Kh. Rās et-Tawīl (M.R. 173138).

Bibliography

Christensen, D. L. 1976. The March of Conquest in Isaiah X 27c–34. *VT* 26: 385–409.

Clements, R. E. 1980. *Isaiah 1–39.* NCBC 23/1. Grand Rapids.

Dalman, G. 1916. Palästinische Wege und die Bedrohung Jerusalems nach Jesaja 10. *PJ* 12: 34–57.

Donner, H. 1968. Der Feind aus dem Norden. Topographische und archäologische Erwägungen zu Jes. 10, 27b–34. *ZDPV* 84: 46–54.

RÜDIGER LIWAK

LAKKUM

LAKKUM (PLACE) [Heb *laqqûm*]. A town in the allotment of Naphtali (Josh 19:33). Lakkum appears in a list of border sites, and it is the last site mentioned in an apparent line along Wadi Fajjas toward the Jordan river. Most scholars identify Lakkum with Khirbet el-Mansurah (M.R. 202233), about 11 miles NW of Tiberias (see, for instance, Woudstra 1981: 291). W. S. LaSor (*ISBE* 3: 61), however, notes that "this location seems too far from the Jordan."

Bibliography

Woudstra, M. H. 1981. *The Book of Joshua.* Grand Rapids, MI.

DAVID SALTER WILLIAMS

LAMB. The common sheep (*ovis aries*) has been domesticated in various subspecies for 8,000 years, beginning in western Asia. As one of the first animals to be domesticated, the sheep is also the most completely domesticated—indeed, hyperdomesticated—of all animals. Though several species of wild sheep survive, feral sheep—that is, escaped domesticated sheep living in the wild—are unknown. Domesticated sheep never truly escape, they merely stray, for sheep without a shepherd are incapable of surviving. Food, water, defense against predators, even reproduction—for all these, the sheep requires human intervention and assistance. And in this regard, the sheep is more "human" than any other animal. That is, culture has replaced nature in the sheep's life as it has in the life of humankind. Sheep need human care as humans need human care, and this isomorphism of need proved a powerful stimulus to the religious imagination first of Ancient Israel and later of Early Christianity.

A. The Lamb in the Mind of Ancient Israel

The literary imagination of Ancient Israel was not, in general, a fabulist imagination. The sentimental, didactic spirit of Aesop is Greek, not Israelite. With a very few exceptions, there are no talking animals in the OT, and certainly no animal protagonists, no animals with private lives or personalities. The one extremely striking exception to this rule is the 23d Psalm, in which the Psalmist speak as a sheep—"The Lord is my shepherd," etc.—and recounts the various ways in which his vulnerabilities are respected. Sheep will not drink from streams, only from pools; therefore, "By restful waters he leads me." They will not lower their heads into buckets or troughs; therefore, "My cup is overflowing." The animal husbandry in this psalm has often been discussed. Less often noted is the evidence it provides of the unique appeal of the sheep as a psychological surrogate for human weakness and innocent helplessness.

The equation of sheep with man is striking as well in the story of the binding of Isaac. Here, of course, the equation is not one of grown sheep and adult man but of lamb and child, the young of both species being alike in their touching inability to tell friend from foe. "God will provide the lamb," Abraham says to Isaac (Gen 22:8), all the while expecting to slay his son. Isaac believes his father, trusting just as the lamb, anthropomorphized, seems to trust when it is led unresisting to the slaughterground.

The equation of lamb and child is made in another way at 2 Sam 12:3–4: "The poor man had nothing but a ewe lamb, one only, a small one he had bought. This he fed, and it grew up with him and his children, eating his bread, drinking from his cup, sleeping on his breast; it was like a daughter to him." Here, the prophet Nathan is comparing Uriah the Hittite's love for his wife Bathsheba to the love a poor man might feel for a cherished lamb. King David, who has abused Uriah by seducing Bathsheba, is overwhelmed by the parable—overwhelmed as he could not have been if, in the Israelite cultural context, quasiparental fondness for a lamb were outlandish or repulsive.

These examples, though suggestive, prove only that the lamb was available as a metaphor to the Ancient Israelite literary mind. They do not prove that it was heavily used. Ancient Israel was a pastoral nation; and most of the time, when the OT makes reference to a lamb, it is a real lamb that is intended.

This is notably true of the Passover lamb of Exodus 12. At Yahweh's instruction, the Israelites slay a lamb and splash its blood on their lintels so that Yahweh will "pass over" their houses when he passes through Egypt slaying the firstborn of the land. The lamb's blood is a signal here, not a symbol. And as for the relationship between Yahweh and the slain lamb, it is one of simple instrumentality. Indeed, Yahweh in these chapters of the OT is supremely unlamblike. The slaying of the firstborn of Egypt is the first of his great acts as the Divine Warrior, leading his people Israel to victory over Egypt. Two chapters later, after the crossing of the Red Sea, Moses exults (Exod 15:1–3): "Yahweh I sing: he has covered himself in glory,/ Horse and rider he has thrown into the sea . . . Yahweh is a warrior; Yahweh is his name."

In Yahweh's covenant with Israel, provision is made (Exodus 29; Numbers 28 and 29) for the sacrifice of lambs at various times, including the annual commemoration of Passover itself. Nowhere in the covenant, however, is the suggestion ever remotely made that Yahweh himself is or has any special relationship—much less anything approaching identification—with the sacrificial lamb (or with any other sacrificial animals). Yahweh, though "a God of tenderness and compassion, slow to wrath, rich in kindness and faithfulness" (Exod 34:6), remains a warrior. On the rare occasions when the OT uses animal imagery to speak of him, the imagery it chooses is appropriate to his central identity; thus, lion imagery in Isa 31:4; Jer 49:19; 50:44; Hos 5:14; Amos 1:2; 11:10; 13:7ff. To this general statement there is just one highly circumscribed but still striking exception.

The exception is the work of the writer whom biblical scholarship calls "Deutero-Isaiah," the author of Isaiah 40–55. These chapters contain a much-discussed set of "Servant Songs," in which redemption and victory are promised to a suffering servant of Yahweh, a victim almost certainly to be identified with Israel. A crucial passage in one of these songs (Isa 53:6–7) reads:

> We had all gone astray like sheep,
> each taking his own way,
> and Yahweh burdened him
> with the sins of all of us.
> Harshly dealt with, he bore it humbly,
> he never opened his mouth
> like a lamb that is led to the slaughterhouse,
> like a sheep that is dumb before its shearers
> never opening its mouth.

The lamb in this passage is not to be identified with the paschal (Passover) lamb of Israel. The sufferer who is compared to the lamb is not necessarily to be identified with the Messiah. Neither the lamb nor the servant is by any means to be identified with Yahweh himself. The passage remains a pregnant one, however, because of the imaginative advance it makes in employing the lamb as a metaphor and a matrix for thought. More than just an innocent sufferer, the lamb here is a surrogate sufferer; not just a blameless victim, then, but also in some way a vicarious victim. The broad compatibility of this metaphor with the victim-substitution stories of the binding of Isaac and the sparing of the firstborn of Israel is clear, but there is a difference. Here the center of sympathy is, remarkably, the lamb rather than Isaac unbound or the Sons of Israel unslain. The same emotional displacement occurs in the 23d Psalm, but there, "I" am a cherished sheep, while here, "he" is a slain lamb, a shorn sheep.

B. The Lamb of God in Early Christianity

Growth and development in any religious tradition typically proceed by the progressive expansion of once minor motifs and the corresponding neglect of once major ones. The expansion of the lamb motif is an extraordinary example of this process.

The New Testament—in fact, Christianity itself—is an interpretation of the death of Jesus in the light of the Hebrew scriptures. From the beginning, Christians have differed somewhat in their interpretations of that death; but the interpretation that, early and late, has attracted most adherents is that found in the Johannine literature; that is, in the Fourth Gospel, the letters of John, and the book of Revelation.

It is in this body of literature that we find expressed the theological understanding of the death of Jesus that was already embodied in Christian ritual at the time when Paul began his own reflection upon Jesus and upon Christian practice as he found it (cf. 1 Cor 5:7–8). In its final bold form, Johannine thought interprets the death of Jesus as a reenactment of God's redemption of Israel out of captivity in Egypt. But in this new redemption, (1) Israel is the entire human race, (2) Egypt is human sinfulness and oppression, and (3) the Redeemer (God) and the instrument of redemption (the Paschal Lamb) are mutually identified by being jointly identified with the person of Jesus Christ slain and risen.

The radical inversions of the Johannine soteriology provided a way for Jesus' disciples to understand the horror of his execution as a paradoxical accomplishment rather than as a simple defeat. But this was not the only reason for the success of this interpretation. At the start of the Christian era, Judaism, though old as a national religion, was relatively young as an international religion. The Johannine theology, as a reconceptualization of Jewish revelation, succeeded in part because it addressed two major conflicts affecting Judaism as lived and practiced in settings of permanent diaspora. If Paul was the Apostle to the gentiles and Luke the gentile Evangelist, John (or the Johannine School) served as the Evangelist of the Jewish Diaspora.

The Johannine inversions arose as an imaginative synthesis of scriptural references to the lamb with remembered facts about the life and, above all, the death of Jesus. In John 1:29–36, John the Baptist addresses Jesus as "the Lamb of God" in a passage written deliberately to link OT passages and motifs that, as we have noted, were originally separate: the Paschal Lamb and the lamblike Suffering Servant. Later in the Fourth Gospel, Jesus emphasizes that his life will be comprehensible only in his death, "when I am lifted up" (John 12:32). His crucifixion, at Passover, is described in a way that repeatedly draws attention to the season and underlines his identity as a new Passover victim; thus the Evangelist emphasizes his unprotesting, lamblike silence (19:9) and the fact that his bones, like those of the Paschal Lamb, are not broken (19:36).

The Fourth Gospel is also, among the four gospels, the one that goes furthest toward identifying Jesus with God: "In the beginning was the Word. The Word was with God, and the Word was God" (John 1:1); "The Father and I are one" (10:30); and similar statements. Students of the Johannine literature distinguish stages in this identification, but the direction is clear from the start. The sheep/man isomorphism that remained, for the most part, undeveloped in the OT is exploited in this part of the NT as the character of the messiah is expanded downward to identity with the sacrificial animal and upward to identity with God Himself.

It is in the book of Revelation, however, that the nearest approach is made and the fullest expression given to what we might call Christianity's mystical syllogism:

> Jesus is the Lamb.
> Jesus is God.
> Therefore, the Lamb is God.

Twenty-nine of the thirty-four NT occurrences of "lamb" occur in this book, which is called "apocalypsis" or "revelation," not only and perhaps not principally because of what it reveals about the course of events in (or beyond) the Roman Empire but because of what it reveals about the identity and character of God. The book of Revelation is the culminating theophany of the NT; and like the theophany on Mount Sinai, it follows, interprets, and memorializes a preceding drama of redemption.

By opening with John's letters to the seven churches of Asia Minor, the book of Revelation proclaims its own literary identity as a work addressed to the larger Mediterranean ecumene where the Jewish Diaspora and, dependent upon it, the new Christian Church resides. Immediately following this, in Revelation 4–5, comes the opening, and utterly decisive, portion of the theophany: God entrusts the Scroll of the Seven Seals—in effect, history itself—to the Lamb, and the Lamb himself is then worshipped as inseparable and practically indistinguishable from God: "In my vision, I heard the sound of an immense number of angels gathered round the throne and the animals and the elders; there were ten thousand times ten thousand of them and thousands upon thousands, shouting, 'The Lamb that was sacrificed is worthy to be given power, riches, wisdom, strength, honor, glory, and blessing.' Then I heard all the living things in creation—everything that lives in the air, and on the ground, and under the ground, and in the sea, crying, 'To the One who is sitting on the throne and to the Lamb, be all praise, honor, glory and power, for ever and ever.' And the four animals said, 'Amen'; and the elders prostrated themselves to worship" (Rev 5:11–14).

At one level, the book of Revelation is a triumphant, theophanic epilogue to the Johannine passion narrative. At another, it is a profoundly ironic conclusion to the Bible as a whole. For though the Lamb is honored as God, God is nonetheless inseparable henceforth from the Lamb—a sacrificed, slain lamb (Rev 5:6), to whom all history and humankind have now been entrusted. Though the preexilic prophets presented the Babylonian Captivity as the judgment and action of God rather than the defeat of God, Israel had to struggle to retain her faith in God's power as the centuries passed and no redemption comparable to the Exodus was forthcoming. Had God abandoned his Chosen People, or was he perhaps as helpless as they? The NT vision of the Lamb-God, truly triumphant but truly slain, is one kind of answer.

Taken as a vision of the end of time, the book of Revelation seems to pair with the book of Genesis as the end pairs with the beginning. But the central preoccupation of the Bible is not with temporal beginnings and endings. It is rather with histories of betrayal, revenge and oppression, on the one hand, and histories of covenant fidelity, forgiveness and liberation, on the other. If human history in general is an endless cycle of violence, one crime begetting another and another, how can the cycle ever be broken? It can be broken—the Johannine interpretation of the death of Jesus hints (if it does not quite propose)—if and only if the ultimately responsible party, God himself, pays the ultimate price in a sacrificial, atoning death.

Since all individual acts of violence are justified by reference to prior acts of violence, all are ultimately unsuccessful as they fail to return to the beginning of the chain. By the same token, once this return to the source of violence has been accomplished by an act of divine violence against God, no further, individual, human acts of retribution are necessary and therefore none are justified. The ultimate vengeance has already been exacted. It is thus that the Lamb of God "takes away the sin of the world" (John 1:19), thus that we are "washed in the blood of the Lamb" (Rev 7:14). The covenant of the blood of the Lamb promises victory to those who, like the Lamb, are unable to tell friend from foe.

And this covenant—the marriage of the Lamb to "the new Jerusalem, coming down from God out of heaven" (Rev 21:2)—is to embrace all humankind. When the covenant formula of Ezekiel is quoted a verse later—"They shall be his people, and he will be their God" (Rev 21:3; Ezek 27:37), language once restricted to Israel is used, quite pointedly, without such restriction. Diaspora Judaism faced an obvious inner tension on this point: its God claimed general jurisdiction over humankind but acknowledged a particular responsibility for Israel. That tension was to be addressed in various ways as the history of Jewish thought continued to unfold in overwhelmingly gentile settings. Johannine Christianity addressed the same tension by a radical broadening of the divine responsibility. In effect, after the Gospel According to John identifies a new redemptive event in the death and resurrection of Jesus, the book of Revelation writes a new covenant and builds a new ritual around it. (Cf. 1 Cor 5:7: "Christ, our Passover, has been sacrificed; therefore let us keep the feast.")

The process by which, on the one hand, Jesus was identified with the pre-existent God and, on the other, God Himself was reconceived as simultaneously a warrior and a victim, was largely but not entirely complete by the end of the NT period (for an example of its use in early proselytism, see Acts 8:26–40). Its further trajectory in the history of the early Church may be charted, in part, iconographically. By the 4th century, no motif, including that of the cross itself, is more prominent than that of the Lamb, and none is presented in more highly interpreted, content-laden ways. The Lamb is often seen holding the pennon of victory crooked in one of its forelegs. In the apse of Old St. Peter's in Rome, the Lamb stands before the empty cross. In the church of Sts. Cosmas and Damian, Rome, the Lamb is portrayed, after Revelation 22, on a mount from which flow streams of living water. These and other Lamb motifs appear again and again in 4th-century Spain, France, Germany, and Italy.

The Lamb motif has remained prominent into modern times in the popular piety of all branches of Christianity. The Eastern Orthodox church imprints the Lamb on its communion bread. The Roman Catholic church, at least until the Second Vatican Council, employed a sacramental called the "Agnus Dei," blessed wax in a lambskin packet. The popular hymnody of the Protestant churches cherishes the Lamb motif as no other ("Washed in the Blood of the Lamb" and many other hymns).

The same motif, however, has inspired stupendous Byzantine mosaics and such masterpieces of music as the opening antiphonal lament of J. S. Bach's "St. Matthew Passion" and the "Hallelujah Chorus" of Frederick Handel's "Messiah." If there is one adjective that one would not think of applying to that chorus, it is "ironic." And yet the notion of the God-Man, Redeemer-Victim, Warrior-Lamb is inescapably paradoxical and even ironic, with an irony that must surely have been appreciated by the artist who first put the victory pennon in the lamb's tiny foreleg and surely was appreciated by the author of the Fourth Gospel whose Jesus, the only deeply and repeatedly ironic voice in the entire Bible, was its creator.

Bibliography

Brown, R. E. 1979. *The Community of the Beloved Disciple.* New York.

Collins, A. Y. 1976. *The Combat Myth in the Book of Revelation.* HDR. Missoula, MT.

Cullman, O. 1975. *Der johanneischer Kreis.* Stuttgart.

Farrar, A. 1986. *A Rebirth of Images: The Making of St. John's Apocalypse.* New York.

Feuillet, A. 1965. *Johannine Studies.* New York.

Girard, R. 1977. *Violence and the Sacred.* Stanford.

———. 1986. *The Scapegoat.* Baltimore.

———. 1987. *Things Hidden Since the Foundation of the World.* Stanford.

Haag, H. 1971. *Vom alten zum neuen Pascha: Geschichte und Theologie des Osterfestes.* Stuttgart.

Hohnjec, N. 1980. *Das Lamm—tó arnión in der Offenbarung des Johannes.* Rome.

Keel, O. 1977. *The Symbolism of the Biblical World: Ancient Near Eastern Iconography and the Book of Psalms.* New York.

Robert, P., de. 1968. *Le Berger d'Israel: Essai sur le thème pastoral dans l'ancien testament.* Neuchatel.

Schüssler Fiorenza, E. 1984. *The Book of Revelation: Justice and Judgement.* Philadelphia.

Segal, J. B. 1963. *The Hebrew Passover from the Earliest Times to AD 70.* London.

Sill, G. G. 1975. *Handbook of Symbols in Christian Art.* New York.

Taeger, J.-W. 1988. *Johannesapokalypse und johanneischer Kreis.* Berlin.

Westermann, C. 1980. *The Psalms: Structure, Content and Message.* Minneapolis.

———. 1981. *Sprache und Struktur der Prophetie Deuterojesajas.* Stuttgart.

JOHN R. MILES

LAMBDA. The eleventh letter of the Greek alphabet.

LAME, LAMENESS. Lameness may be defined as a compromised ability to walk or otherwise use limbs due to any of several pathological or other crippling conditions. Lameness may result from (1) trauma, as in healed breaks with malunion of the bone; (2) metabolic diseases; (3) nutritional diseases, such as rickets (vitamin D deficiency); (4) degenerative diseases, such as arthritis; (5) congenital defects of the skeleton, such as the dysplasias; and (6) infectious diseases, such as polio. In modern times "lameness" might include minor problems such as limping or periodic gimpiness. However, a study of the biblical examples of lameness indicate that severe crippling disability is meant by the various terms discussed here. This is made clear by several descriptions of lameness. The legs of the lame hung uselessly (Prov 26:7, the Hebrew of which is difficult, perhaps meaning "drawn up," thus "unequal in length"). Lameness required the victim to ride animals instead of walking (2 Sam 19:26). Lameness so disabled victims that they lay around markets and city gates of Jerusalem begging and annoying travelers (2 Sam 5:6), often having to be carried by family members to strategic locations daily in order to beg for alms (Acts 3:1–3). One NT period lame man was unable to set himself in the waters of the pool of Bethesda at the moment of the healing surge even after attempts to do so for many years (John 5:3).

A. Lameness in the OT

The OT uses several words to denote lameness or a crippled condition. Most common is the Hebrew *pisēaḥ*, "lame" (for which the LXX translates *xōlos*). Also found is *nākēh*, "stricken, wounded"; *ḥoreb*, "withered"; and *ṣelaᶜ*, "limping, stumbling." Also, three men of the name *Pāsēaḥ*, literally "Limper," are known in the Bible (1 Chr 4:12; Ezra 2:49 [= Neh 7:51]; Neh 3:6). However, it is difficult at best to establish any diagnostic inferences which may be associated with these terms. *Ḥoreb* (lit. "dried up") seems to mean "withered," or something similar, apparently used as a reference to shrunken, emaciated, or retracted muscles (Zech 11:17), but this term is rarely used in the Hebrew Bible with reference to physiology. *Nākēh* seems clearer in meaning but is very general, indicating only that the lame person has been smitten or afflicted in the limbs, etc. (2 Sam 4:4, 9:3; Ps 35:15). *Pisēaḥ*, "lame," is particularly unclear etymologically. Verbal forms of the root are used to describe lameness of traumatic origin in 2 Sam 4:4, but in 1 Kgs 18:26 apparently to describe a type of ritual dance (?) or ritual staggering (?) near the altar of Baal, but the sense of this verse is admittedly difficult. The Arabic cognate *fasaḫa* means "to be dislocated without breaking the bones." *Ṣelaᶜ*, "limping," "staggering," is often used figuratively of downfall or calamity (Ps 38:18; Jer 20:10; Job 18:12). The etymology here is very uncertain also, but if related to the Hebrew verb *ṣālaᶜ*1, it may originally have implied curvature, bent or bowed limbs. Clearly, it is difficult or impossible to reliably define any particular kind or cause of lameness, from a medical diagnostic point of view, of most of the Hebrew words which encompass the meaning "lameness" or "crippling."

Lameness occurs in several contexts in the OT. In levitical law, descendants of Aaron were unacceptable for the priesthood, but not impure, if they were lame or disfigured (Lev 21:16–18). Similarly sacrificial animals were also excluded as the burnt offering if lame (Deut 15:19–21), although they could still be used for certain personal offerings. Elsewhere, Mephibosheth, Jonathan's son, "fell and was [permanently] lame/crippled in both feet"—clearly lameness of traumatic etiology (2 Sam 4:4, 9:3, 19:27). In the OT as with the NT, most instances of lameness are mentioned paired together with blindness, revealing the impact of both conditions upon society and underscoring their severity. Both conditions made the victim dependent upon society, both were utterly incurable, both prevented the victim from being productive and self-sustaining. Thus the lame and the blind were an annoyance to visitors to Jerusalem probably because of their ceaseless begging for donations (2 Sam 5:6). The lame (and blind) were subjected to scorn and were outcasts of society (Jer 31:8). However, Job the Perfect was "eyes to the blind and feet to the lame" (Job 29:15), reflecting sympathetic and humanistic elements toward the disabled in late OT thought, a theme appearing also in the NT and Pseudepigrapha. Visionary pronouncements look to the day when even "the lame [being slow and stumbling] will be able to carry off loot [with the swiftness of a thief]," and that eventually "the lame will leap [with agileness] like a stag" (Isa 33:23, 35:6). In Jer 31:8 the lame will be included among the previously dispersed masses of returning Israel.

B. Lameness in the NT

In later Greek, *xōlos,* which indicates "lameness," or better, "crippling," is used of both legs (feet) and also arms (hands). In the NT the terminology of lame or crippling conditions is still more vague than that of the OT in terms of medical derivations and understanding, except where a particular verse may expatiate on a specific kind of lameness. In the NT, unlike the OT, the majority of instances of lameness occur within the context of miraculous healings of such permanently disabled victims. Reports of miraculous healings of the lame and blind at the hand of Jesus circulated periodically (Matt 11:5, 15:31, 21:14, etc.), and the Apostle Paul once healed a lame man as well (Acts 14:8). Jesus encouraged his followers not to invite their influential friends to elaborate dinners, but rather beggars, the lame and crippled (Luke 14:12–13). The lame often sought healing influences from the pool of Bethesda, whose waters were believed to possess healing properties (John 5:3). Congenital crippling is twice clearly mentioned in the NT, where each victim was "lame from his mother's womb, who never had walked" (Acts 3:1–3, 14:8). The lame were carried daily by family members to the gate of the (second) temple, where they loitered or lay begging for donations from pious worshippers (Acts 3:1–3).

C. Lameness in the Pseudepigrapha

Generally, the character of lameness as presented above does not change in pseudepigraphic texts. *Second Ezra* 2:21 commands "do not ridicule a lame man, protect the maimed" (cf. also *4 Ezra* 2:21). In the extant fragments of the *Apocryphon of Ezekiel,* preserved in Clement of Alexandria, *Paedogogus* 1:9[a], God promises healing to the lame (*OTP* 1: 495), and in the eschatological portions of the *Sibylline Oracles* (8: 206), the oracle also promises swift racing to the lame (*OTP* 1: 423). The pairing of lameness with blindness is very apparent in the "Story of the Lame Man and the Blind Man" found in the *Apocryphon of Ezekiel* (*OTP* 1: 487).

D. The Archaeological Context of Lameness

Soft tissues with associated injury and disease which may result in lameness are usually not recovered with excavated skeletal remains. Except for some human remains from Egypt (i.e., mummies), only skeletal defects which resulted in lameness and crippling would be expected to survive in ancient burials. There are many examples. The archaeological survey of Nubia produced skeletons with a variety of conditions, especially improperly set and healed broken bones, which were probably a common cause of lameness and crippling (Smith and Wood-Jones 1910; El-Batrawi 1935). Simple osteoarthritis ("wear-and-tear" arthritis associated with age) also no doubt occasionally accounted for some instances of lameness. Infectious diseases also were responsible for some forms of lameness. Pharaoh Siptah, whose mummy is in the Cairo Museum, clearly was crippled probably as a result of polio (Harris and Wente 1980: 293–95 and Plates 8.25–26). The sculpture and art of the ancient Egyptians also provides evidence of various conditions which made their victims lame. A good example is stela A from the 18th Dyn. which depicts the lame priest Ruma with a disfigured lower leg, also typical of polio (Wells 1964: 269 and plate 44).

Occasionally, the presence of ancient human remains is unnecessary for the demonstration of crippling or lameness, and from Palestine there is one unusual example. While the skeleton of the famous Babata from the time of Bar Kokhba and the Second Revolt has never been identified, most of her personal belongings, including the largest single cache of personal documents ever found in Palestine, have been found in the famous Cave of Letters in Nahal Hever. See BAR KOKHBA (LETTERS). Among them were her sandals, of which one was normally fashioned, the other oddly misshaped to conform to the peculiar contours of her pathologically defective foot. Clearly the famous Babata had a crippling condition (Yadin 1963).

E. Conclusion

Apparently all the examples of "lameness" in the Bible actually refer to severe crippling disabilities and not to cases of minor limping. However, most of the examples of lameness are so vaguely described that accurate diagnosis of the cause is impossible and only the incurable and chronic nature of the crippling conditions are obvious.

Bibliography

Batrawi, A. M. el-. 1935. *Report on the Human Remains.* Mission archeologigue de Nubie 1929–1934. Cairo.

Harris, J. E., and Wente, E. F., eds. 1980. *An X-Ray Atlas of the Royal Mummies.* Chicago.

Smith, G. E., and Wood-Jones, F. 1910. *The Archeological Survey of Nubia: Report for 1907–1908.* Vol. 2, *Report on the Human Remains.* Cairo.

Wells, C. 1964. *Bones, Bodies and Disease.* London.

Yadin, Y. 1963. *The Finds from the Bar-Kokhba Period in the Cave Letters.* Jerusalem.

RICHARD N. JONES

LAMECH (PERSON) [Heb *lemek; lāmek*]. **1.** Son of Methushael, husband of Adah and Zillah, and father of Jabal, Jubal, Tubal-cain, and Naamah; a descendant of Cain (Gen 4:18–24). No clearly negative evaluation is given of this first reported case of polygamy, even though it is a deviation from the norm (Wenham *Genesis 1–15* WBC, 112). The Song of Lamech, addressed to his wives, describes Lamech's expectation of seventy-sevenfold vengeance against whomsoever would assault him, above and beyond the sevenfold vengeance to be taken against anyone who slays Cain (cf. Gen 4:15). The repetition of these sevens and Lamech's being the seventh in Adam's line makes it difficult to avoid the impression that the number is intended to convey the idea of completion (Cassuto 1961: 243; Sasson 1978: 173). With Lamech, his family, and his song, there is a completion of the Cainite line. The references to Cain in the names of the offspring and in the poem form both a literary inclusio and, in the case of the poem, supposedly a culmination of the murderous character trait of this line.

Studies have noted the emphasis upon metalworking associated with Cain's son, Tubal-Cain, and the Kenite background of the genealogy (Sawyer 1986: 159–64). They have associated the poem with a sword, to which songs were dedicated in ancient Mesopotamia and among nomads (Speiser *Genesis* AB, 37; Westermann 1984: 334–37). However, the association of poem with sword is not clear from the text. Gevirtz (1963:25) understood the song as a statement of great pride in murderous vengeance and a taunting mockery of subsequent retribution. He also observed a gradual disintegration of correspondences in the word pairs of each of the couplets in the poem. Thus the parallelism of the first couplet (Adah and Zillah / wives of Lamech; hear my voice / give ear to my speech) is the closest, while that of the third couplet (seven / seventy-seven; Cain / Lamech) is the least similar (cf. Stuart 1976: 97, 99). The "man" (*ʾîš*) and the "boy" (*yeled*) of the second couplet represent a single individual: a youth in his prime (Cassuto 1961: 242; Gevirtz 1963: 30–34; Wenham *Genesis 1–15* WBC, 114).

The root *l-m-k* does not exist in West Semitic. The Arabic *ylmk,* "strong man," has been compared (*HALAT* 2: 505), as has the Sumerian LUMGA, the title of the god Ea as patron of music (Landersdorfer 1916: 19; Gabriel 1959: 415; Westermann 1984: 329), and the Akkadian *lumakku,* the title of a priest of lower rank appearing in lexical texts (Cassuto 1961: 233). A few personal names with an *l-m-k* element are found in the 3d millennium B.C. (Gevirtz 1963: 26), and at Mari in the 2d millennium B.C. (Limet 1976: 161).

2. Son of Methuselah, when Methuselah was 187 years old (Gen 5:25–31). At 182 years of age, Lamech sired Noah. In the *Genesis Apocryphon* (1 QapGen cols. I–V), Lamech is portrayed as being concerned about the paternity of his son, Noah, until he is reassured by his wife, Bat-Enosh, and by Enoch (Fitzmyer 1966: 69–87). As with the

Cainite Lamech of Genesis 4, the number seven here plays an important role: Lamech lives 777 years, and he is seventh from Enosh in the line of Seth (Jacob 1934: 166–67; Cassuto 1961: 243). While a common origin for both Lamechs has been posited, it is clear that the present text makes a stark distinction between the two: the descendant of Cain lusted for vengeance, the father of Noah hoped.

The normal genealogical formula describing the line of Seth in Genesis 5 is interrupted in the description of Lamech to note that Lamech verbalized this hope when naming his son Noah. He foretold that Noah would bring rest from the labor and toil of "our hands out of the ground which Yahweh has cursed" (v 29). It is not clear from the text that Lamech thereby expected his son either to be a "messianic" deliverer or that he would restore the world to an Edenic state. Source critics have usually understood v 29 to be a J gloss in an otherwise P genealogy (von Rad *Genesis* OTL, 72). In the context of Genesis 6–9, Noah indeed provides Lamech's posterity with "comfort" (Parunak 1975; *TWAT* 5: 366–84) by serving as the agent of humanity's deliverance from the flood by making a sacrifice that prompted Yahweh to promise never again to curse the land, and by instituting the practice of viticulture (Gen 8:20–22; cf. Skinner *Genesis* ICC, 133–34; Clines 1972–73; Wenham *Genesis 1–15* WBC, 128–29).

Bibliography

Cassuto, U. 1961. *A Commentary on the Book of Genesis.* Pt. 1, *From Adam to Noah.* Trans. I. Abrahams. Jerusalem.

Clines, D. J. A. 1972–73. Noah's Flood, 1: The Theology of the Flood Narrative. *Faith and Thought* 100/2: 128–45.

Fitzmyer, J. A. 1966. *The* Genesis Apocryphon *of Qumran Cave I.* Rome.

Gabriel, J. 1959. Die Kainitengenealogie. Gn 4, 17–24. *Bib* 40: 409–27.

Gevirtz, S, 1963. Lamech's Song to His Wives. Pp. 25–34 in *Patterns in the Early Poetry of Israel.* SAOC 32. Chicago.

Jacob, B. 1934. *Das Erste Buch der Tora: Genesis übersetzt und erklärt.* Berlin. Repr. New York.

Landersdorfer, S. 1916. *Sumerisches Sprachgut im Alten Testament.* BWANT 21. Leipzig.

Limet, H. 1976. *Textes administratifs de l'époque des* šakkanakku. ARM 19. Paris.

Parunak, H. V. D. 1975. A Semantic Survey of *NḤM. CBQ* 56: 512–32.

Sasson, J. M. 1978. A Genealogical "Convention" in Biblical Chronography? *ZAW* 90: 171–85.

Sawyer, J. F. A. 1986. Cain and Hephaestus. Possible Relics of Metalworking Traditions in Genesis 4. *AbrN* 24: 155–66.

Stuart, D. K. 1976. *Studies in Early Hebrew Meter.* HSM 13. Missoula, MT.

Westermann, C. 1984. *Genesis 1–11: A Commentary.* Trans. J. J. Scullion. Minneapolis.

RICHARD S. HESS

LAMED. The twelfth letter of the Hebrew alphabet.

LAMENTATIONS, BOOK OF. Lamentations consists of a series of five poems on the destruction of Jerusalem in 586 B.C. The poems do not narrate in order the events of the fall of the city, but through a variety of speakers they give vivid short pictures of the horrors of the siege and its aftermath, reflect on the causes of the calamity, and appeal for mercy to the God who brought about the ruin of his own city and temple. In later Jewish liturgical practice, Lamentations was associated with the 9th of Ab, when various destructions of the state, the city, and the temple are commemorated, and this practice may go back to earliest exilic times (see Jer 41:5; Zech 7:3–5; 8:19).

A. Contents and Plan of the Book
B. The Name of the Book
C. Place in the Canon
D. Date
E. Authorship
F. Place of Composition
G. Acrostic Form
H. Meter, Parallelism, and Other Aspects of Poetics
I. Relation to Sumerian Laments
J. Text

A. Contents and Plan of the Book

Neither narrative nor logical sequence is a dominant feature in contributing structure to Lamentations, where acrostics are of greater formal importance, and thus the poems are hard to outline and summarize without giving a false impression. Yet there are elements of plot and plan in the book.

Chapter one is a depiction of the anguish of Zion, the holy city, moving from an observer's point of view (vv 1–11) to the outcry of the city itself (vv 12–22). The principal themes of the book are announced in this first poem, including the paradox of the God who turns on his own city and temple, the elect people who are rejected, and the interplay of individual and community experience of suffering and reflection on its causes.

Chapter two is much like chapter one, but is occupied more with a statement of the cause of the city's destruction ("the Lord became an enemy," v 5), and does not make much use of the technique of personifying the city or community as a single suffering individual. Since God himself has been the destroyer, the city must "cry from the heart to the Lord!" (v 18).

Chapter three is marked as climactic within the book by its formal elaborateness. The speaker is an individual, so that this poem in its own way returns to a theme announced already in chapter one. However, the city here is not the bereaved mother, but an anonymous male ("I am the man who has been through trouble," v 1). Though opinions differ as to precisely how this figure is to be understood, it is clear that the poem impressively presents a spiritual progress: a sufferer achieves patient faith (vv 1–39) and calls on his people to share his return to God (vv 40–41), ending in a prayer of the whole community for relief of suffering (vv 42–66).

Chapter four is a return to depiction of the horrors of the siege and the fall of the city, a series of vignettes without tight structure, ending in an imprecation against the Edomites (treacherous allies) and a blessing on Zion (vv 21–22). Coming after chapter three, it suggests that the heights of spiritual renewal envisioned in that chapter are as yet hopes and aspirations rather than present realities for the suffering people.

Chapter five is a fitting liturgical close to the book. It has many features in common with the communal laments which occur in the book of Psalms (44; 60; 74; 79; 80; 83; 89), and culminates, like them, in an appeal to God for help. Even so, the pronounced stress on the persistence of the present misery makes it much like the other four poems in the book.

B. The Name of the Book

The English title "Lamentations" goes back through the Latin (*threni*) and Greek (*threnoi*) to a Hebrew title, *qînôt,* meaning "laments," attested in the Babylonian Talmud (*b. Bat.* 14b) and elsewhere in early Rabbinic writings. In the Hebrew Bible, as commonly in Jewish tradition, the book is titled *ʾekah,* "How!", from its first word, a practice attested for other books of the Pentateuch (thus Heb *bĕrēšît,* "In the beginning" = Genesis, etc.) and the book of Proverbs (Heb *mišlê,* "The proverbs of . . .").

Often manuscripts of ancient Bible translations or printed editions add, after the initial "Lamentations," the words "of Jeremiah" or "of Jeremiah the prophet," expressing a very common tradition concerning the authorship of the work.

C. Place in the Canon

There is no attested ancient controversy over whether Lamentations should be included in the canon, but there is considerable difference as to its position, a matter related to traditions concerning authorship.

In the common Jewish threefold division of the scriptures, the book always is placed somewhere among the "Writings" (*Ketubim*), though its exact location within that group has varied. The Babylonian Talmud (*b. Bat.* 14b) knows of an order of the Writings that is approximately chronological, so that Lamentations is set after books supposed to be by Solomon and just before other supposedly exilic or postexilic books, Daniel and Esther. More commonly, Lamentations is classed as one of the five short books called the *Megillot,* the "Scrolls." Within that group it is placed either "chronologically" (thus Ruth, Song of Songs, Ecclesiastes, Lamentations, Esther), or liturgically, following the order of the festivals with which each Scroll is associated in developed liturgical practice, beginning with Passover; in this latter case the order is Song of Songs (Passover), Ruth (Weeks; *Shabuoth*; Pentecost), Lamentations (the Ninth of Ab), Ecclesiastes (Sukkoth; Booths), and Esther (Purim).

The other, markedly different, ordering puts Lamentations after the book of Jeremiah, as though by that prophet (often another work associated with Jeremiah, Baruch, comes between the two). This positioning is found already in Septuagint manuscripts and is continued in the Latin Vulgate and generally in English Bibles. From Josephus' description of the canon (*AgAp* 1.8) it can be inferred that such an order was known to him, and presumably to other Jews of his time (1st century C.E.) as well.

D. Date

Although there is no evidence outside the book itself that permits us to date its composition, and though the rather nonspecific historical references within the book only dictate that it was written after the fall of Jerusalem in 586 B.C., the traditional and common-sense view remains the most plausible, that is, that Lamentations as a whole was completed not long after the siege and destruction of the city by the Babylonians. The horrors of the siege seem to be vividly present to the memory of the author or authors, and no turn of fortunes for the shattered people has occurred or is expected in the near future. Thus a date after 586 and well before 538, when Cyrus permitted the Jews to return from exile, is most likely, though Ackroyd (1973) justly emphasizes that our evidence for dating, especially chaps. 3–5, is extremely slender.

Scholars have attempted to date the composition of the five poems relative to one another, based on historical references or stylistic characteristics (see for example, Rudolph *Ruth-Hohe Lied-Klagelieder* KAT), but the evidence at our disposal is probably insufficient to make any such attempt widely convincing.

E. Authorship

Although one very ancient tradition ascribes Lamentations to Jeremiah, practically unanimous modern critical opinion holds the book to be anonymous. Before examining the issue, it is in place to observe that the authorship is not decisively important for understanding these poems of lament, because their author, whoever he was, expresses the historical experience of a community more than the personal experiences or opinions of one individual, and, as emphasized by Lanahan (1974), assumes a variety of *personae,* or speaking voices.

Nothing in the Bible expressly attributes our canonical book of Lamentations to Jeremiah the prophet, but the seeds for such an ascription are present in the general tendency to ascribe originally anonymous works to prominent figures, such as Moses, David, Solomon, and in the statement that Jeremiah, a "weeping" prophet (Jer 9:1–Heb 3:23), who lived through the fall of Jerusalem, wrote a "lament" or "laments" (2 Chr 35:25) over Josiah. Perhaps it is from such origins that there grows the ascription found already in the LXX, at the head of the book: ". . . Jeremiah sat weeping and composed this lament over Jerusalem and said. . . ." The LXX order of books associates it with Jeremiah. In various ways the Targum, the Syriac (Peshitta), and Vulgate make the same ascription to Jeremiah, as do the Babylonian Talmud (*B. Bat.* 15a) and other rabbinic works, which quote the book in the form: "Jeremiah says. . . ."

As noted above, the Hebrew Bible itself does not place Lamentations with the book of Jeremiah, a tradition continued in some uncommon but ancient listings of the books of Scripture. This impressive evidence of the book's original anonymity is bolstered by critical examination of the content of the book, for while it is not impossible that Jeremiah could have written it, some of its ideas seem implausible or incongruous as coming from him. In the question of reliance on help from foreign powers, contrast Lam 4:17, which refers to the poignant longing of the people ("we") for aid from Egypt, with Jer 2:18 or 37:5–10, where the prophet denounces alliances and predicts their failure; on the destruction of the temple, compare

Lam 1:10, with its reference to God's forbidding nations to enter the sanctuary, with Jer 7:14, where the prophet in God's name predicted this dire event; in Lam 4:20 King Zedekiah is "the breath of our nostrils, the anointed of Yahweh," on whom the common hopes of the people depended, while in Jer 37:17 the prophet clearly predicted his capture by the Babylonians. Could Jeremiah, active as a prophet through this whole tragic time, have lamented, "Her prophets find no vision from Yahweh"? (2:9). (Studies made to date of lexical and grammatical usage of the book are not conclusive as to authorship.) In the end it seems much easier to suppose that a series of anonymous compositions, whether by one poet or by several, came to be attributed to Jeremiah, early but erroneously, than to suppose that a genuine work by the prophet came to be separated from his name. Beyond this it has proved impossible to suggest a plausible alternate as author, or to determine whether only one person or several are involved. Similarly, recent examinations of the theological traditions on which the book draws, by Kraus (*Klagelieder* BKAT) and Gottwald (1962), leading to depictions of the author(s) as from among the priests or cult prophets of Jerusalem, are best regarded as to some degree plausible but not conclusive. More extreme, and less convincing, is the theory of Brunet (1968), according to which Lamentations is a kind of polemic against Jeremiah.

F. Place of Composition

Either Lamentations was written in Judah, the view that no doubt would be first to suggest itself to a reader, or it was written by a Jew in exile somewhere else who happened to know what was going on in Judah and was more interested in conditions there than in Babylon, Egypt, or wherever he was. One may argue about probabilities in this matter, but very little is at stake for the interpretation of the book.

G. Acrostic Form

All five poems in Lamentations are formally related in some way to the alphabet. This is least noticeable in chap. 5, which conforms to the alphabet only in having 22 lines, one for each letter in the Hebrew alphabet. (The attempt of Bergler [1977] to find a word acrostic in chap. 5 is strained and unconvincing.) In chaps. 1 and 2 each stanza has three lines, and the initial word of the first stanza begins with the first letter of the alphabet (*ʾalep*), the second stanza begins with a word starting with the second letter (*bet*), and so on through the alphabet. Chapter 4 follows the same scheme but has two-line stanzas. The most elaborate acrostic is chap. 3, with three-line stanzas in which each line begins with the appropriate letter: three *ʾalep* lines, three *bet* lines, and so on.

It is likely that biblical alphabetic acrostics (aside from Lamentations 1–4, Psalms 9–10, 25, 34, 37, 111, 112, 119, 145, and Prov 31:10–31, which are complete or nearly complete acrostics) owe their origin ultimately to Mesopotamian acrostics, of which extant examples predate any datable biblical acrostics, though Akkadian acrostics are, of course, syllabic rather than alphabetic. The general idea of conforming poetic structure to the writing system or a meaningful sequence of the initial signs of poetic lines arose first in Mesopotamia.

The purpose of the acrostic form with relation to Lamentations is uncertain. It has been proposed, on the basis of observed use of acrostics in literature generally, that the acrostic is to aid the memory, or display artistic skill, or express the notion of completeness, as if to imply that everything from start to finish has been said, and each of these views is to some degree plausible. Aesthetically, it seems that the somewhat rigid bounds which the acrostic sets contribute a desirable limit to a subject matter that might otherwise run on and on. One might compare the function of sonnet form in Italian or English literature. An unintended effect of the acrostic form has been that it makes Lamentations a favorite starting point for modern scholarly investigation of Hebrew poetic form and diction, including metrical studies, since the fundamental question of where lines begin and end is largely settled by the acrostic pattern (Freedman 1972).

In the MT, the order of the letters in chaps. 2, 3, and 4 is different from the usual Hebrew order; here *pe* comes before *ʿayin* (as if, in an English acrostic, *p* were put before *o*). In a recently published Qumran manuscript of Lamentations this divergent order is found also in chap. 1, though it cannot be automatically assumed that this represents the original reading, the author's intention. The Greek of Proverbs 31 and Psalm 34 seems also to reflect this divergent order. A very early ostracon containing the alphabet, published by Kochavi (1977; cf. Demsky 1977), of about 1200 B.C.E., from a site in Judah, and abecedaries of about 800 B.C.E.—from Kuntillet ʿAjrud in the S Negev (see Meshel 1978) also have the order *pe-ʿayin*, and it has been supposed that in them and in Lamentations we have evidence of an authentic early Hebrew tradition of alphabetic order divergent from the Ugaritic and Phoenician order that became dominant. Naveh (1978), however, justly cautions that, at least in the earlier ostracon, the writing is unskilled in the extreme, and that in it there is another reversal of order, *ḥet-zayin,* which is simply a mistake by the schoolboy writer.

H. Meter, Parallelism, and Other Aspects of Poetics

The surprisingly large place in studies of Hebrew poetics occupied by Lamentations is in part due to its dominantly acrostic form, and to a peculiarity of meter first described by Budde (1882). Budde discovered in Lamentations chaps. 1–4 (5 is different) a poetic line of two unequal parts, the first one longer by at least one word. Moreover, Budde held that this unbalanced rhythm was specifically related to the lament, and named it *qinah* meter.

Budde himself recognized in Lamentations the presence of numerous lines diverging from this pattern, and others have argued for still more balanced lines in the book, but it remains true that the unbalanced line is dominant. On the other hand, it seems less certain that this rhythm was necessarily associated with laments in ancient Hebrew usage, for laments occur without this rhythm (e.g., 2 Sam 1:17–27) and the rhythm occurs outside of laments. Since Budde's time, of course, many attempts have been made to present more refined and accurate theories of Hebrew meter, involving counting of accents, or, most recently, syllables; although many of these discussions have involved Lamentations significantly, they are best studies in the larger context of Hebrew poetics as a whole; in broad outline, Budde's discovery remains valid. The more refined and minute study of Freedman (1972), based on counting of syllables, confirms that Budde was correct in isolating chaps. 1–4 (acrostic chapters as following distinctive metrical practices.

In addition to its distinctively metrical character, Lamentations, like other biblical Hebrew poetry, exhibits a pervasive parallelism between poetic units (cola or lines). Moreover, the word order in the sentences of Lamentations diverges markedly from patterns of order in prose (Hillers 1974). It is plausible to suppose that unusual word orders are employed for the sake of rhythm or parallelism, but this cannot yet be demonstrated.

Cross (1983) attempts to exploit a contrast of Lamentations, as written poetry, with earlier oral poetry, but such a contrast has proved most problematic even in branches of literature where oral and written composition can be directly observed, and in ancient Hebrew literature (and Near Eastern literature in general) there is even less by way of an observable basis for such a distinction.

Like other biblical writings, especially poetic compositions, Lamentations has been restudied with profit from the point of view of recently discovered Northwest Semitic writings, especially Ugaritic, with an effect on our views of text, language, and poetics. Such an approach is represented, in varying degrees, in Dahood (1978), McDaniel (1968a; 1968b), and Hillers (*Lamentations* AB).

I. Relation to Sumerian Laments

Gunkel (1929) attempted to relate Lamentations to the genre of funeral songs discussed earlier by Jahnow (1923), but since the five chapters of Lamentations all seem to be late and impure examples of the type, as he himself stated, this sort of form-critical approach has not proved especially decisive for understanding the book.

A more striking association of Lamentations with a specific literary tradition was proposed by the biblical scholar Kraus (*Klagelieder* BKAT), and from the Assyriological point of view especially by the Sumerologist S. N. Kramer (1969; *ANET,* 611–19). Lamentations is supposed to descend from an ultimately Sumerian tradition of laments over ruined cities and temples.

There are now five principal extant compositions belonging to the Sumerian literary genre "Lament over the ruined city and temple," including laments over Ur, Sumer and Ur, Nippur, Eridu, and Uruk, composed during the Isin-Larsa period (1950–1700 B.C.E.) and thereafter copied as part of the Old Babylonian scribal school curriculum. Several may presently be studied in translations by Kramer (1969; *ANET,* 611–19) and Green (1978; 1984), and editions and translations of others are forthcoming (see Gwaltney 1983). These earliest Sumerian city-laments are related to a general Mesopotamian literary and liturgical tradition of congregational laments that continues down to Seleucid times (see Kutscher 1975; Cohen 1981). Gwaltney (1983) sees in these "lineal descendants" of the older city-laments the link between the ultimately Sumerian tradition and the biblical book of Lamentations.

In assessing the relation of the early Sumerian laments to the biblical book, note that the recurrent historical situation which evokes these poems is extraordinarily close: a city, in the sense of a focus of a human and divine community, has been destroyed by enemies; paradoxically it has been allowed to perish by its own god(s), the result being a physical, social, and spiritual crisis. There are frequent and striking resemblances in details of expression between these compositions (and the related "Curse of Agade"; see Cooper 1983) and the biblical Lamentations. On the other hand, as stressed by McDaniel (1968a; 1968b), the great similarity of the subject matter would be expected inevitably to produce many resemblances in form even if there were no literary influence or connection involved. And the whole question cannot be discussed apart from a clear general conception of the relation between Mesopotamian and Israelite literature (Hillers *Lamentations,* AB; Tigay 1976), which is not presently available. In detail, note that the major Sumerian laments may contain a reversal of fortunes: the god turns his favor to the people again, the city flourishes as never before, and similar good things happen, as in the "lament" over Nippur, where the joyful part of the poem is about twice as long as the complaint; this element, of course, is entirely absent from the biblical book. In any case, however, it remains true that it is most instructive for the student of the biblical Lamentations to read them together with Sumerian laments, if only as a reminder of how much historical and religious experience Israel shared with other ancient Near Eastern communities.

J. Text

In the book of Lamentations the MT itself seems to be in a good state of preservation. The ancient versions offer little help in clearing up difficulties since they give a text not essentially different from the traditional Hebrew text; this conclusion has emerged from prolonged and intensive study of the text of Lamentations, culminating in the recent works of Rudolph (1938), Albrektson (1963), and Gottlieb (1978). Some new insight into how this situation came about is provided by recent theoretical views on the history of the Hebrew text and versions, and new manuscript evidence.

According to one recent theory held in various forms by Barthèlemy (1963: 33, 138–60) and Cross (1964: 233), the Greek text of Lamentations belongs to the so-called *kaige* recension, a type of Greek text which has deliberately been brought into line with the emerging Masoretic text, the result being that it is of little use in correcting the Hebrew. (The Septuagint text has recently been re-edited by Ziegler [1976]). Among the Dead Sea scrolls so far published is one sizable manuscript containing portions of chap. 1 (4QLam[a]; see Cross 1983), with notable variants from the Masoretic text; perhaps in time this will yield a new view of the early textual history of the book, in the context of study of the Qumran biblical text as a whole. There are also several fragments of the canonical book (3QLam; 5QLama, 5QLamb) and two sectarian compositions (4Q179 = 4QapLam; 4Q501) which weave in significant bits of the text.

Bibliography

Ackroyd, P. 1973. Review of Hillers, *Lamentations,* AB. *Int* 27: 223–26.

Albrektson, B. 1963. *Studies in the Text and Theology of the Book of Lamentations.* STL 21. Lund.

Barthélemy, J.-D. 1963. *Les dévanciers d'Aquila.* VTSup 10. Leiden.
Bergler, S. 1977. Threni V—Nur ein alphabetisierendes Lied?—Versuch einer Deutung. *VT* 27: 304–20.
Brunet, G. 1968. *Les lamentations contre Jérémie: Réinterpretation des quatre premières lamentations.* Bibliothèque de L'École des Hautes Études, Section des Sciences Réligieuses 75. Paris.
Budde, K. 1882. Das hebräische Klagelied. *ZAW* 2: 1–52.
Cohen, M. 1981. *Sumerian Hymnology: The Ershemma.* HUCASup 2. Cincinnati.
———. 1988. *The Canonical Lamentations of Mesopotamia.* 2 vols. Potomac, MD.
Cooper, J. 1983. *The Curse of Agade.* Baltimore.
Cross, F. M. 1964. The History of the Biblical Text in the Light of Discoveries in the Judaean Desert. *HTR* 57.
———. 1983. Studies in the Structure of Hebrew Verse: The Prosody of Lamentations 1:1–22. *WLSGF,* pp. 129–53.
Dahood, M. 1978. New Readings in Lamentations. *Bib* 59: 174–97.
Demsky, A. 1977. A Proto-Canaanite Abecedary Dating from the Period of the Judges and its Implications for the History of the Alphabet. *TA* 4:14–27.
Freedman, D. N. 1972. Acrostics and Metrics in Hebrew Poetry. *HTR* 65: 367–92. Repr. pp. 40–76 in *Pottery, Poetry, and Prophecy.* Winona Lake, IN, 1980.
Gottlieb, H. 1978. *A Study on the Text of Lamentations.* Acta Jutlandica 48, Theology Series 12. Aarhus.
Gottwald, N. 1962. *Studies in the Book of Lamentations.* Rev. ed. SBT 14. London.
Green, M. 1975. *Eridu in Sumerian Literature.* Ph.D. diss. Chicago.
———. 1978. The Eridu Lament. *JCS* 30: 127–69.
———. 1984. The Uruk Lament. *JAOS* 104: 253–79.
Gunkel, H. 1929. Klagelieder Jeremiae. *RGG*² 3: 1049–52.
Gwaltney, W. 1983. The Biblical Book of Lamentations in the Context of Near Eastern Literature. Pp. 191–211 in *Scripture in Context II,* ed. W. Hallo, J. Moyer, and L. Perdue. Winona Lake, IN.
Hillers, D. 1974. Observations on Syntax and Meter in Lamentations. Pp. 265–70 in *A Light unto My Path,* ed. H. Bream, R. Heim, and C. Moore. Philadelphia.
Jahnow, H. 1923. *Das hebräische Leichenlied im Rahmen der Völkerdichtung.* BZAW 36. Giessen.
Kochavi, M . 1977. An Ostracon of the Period of the Judges from ʿIsbet Sartah. *TA* 4: 1–13.
Kramer, S. N. 1969. Lamentation over the Destruction of Nippur. *Eretz-Israel* 9. Jerusalem.
Kutscher, R. 1975. *On Angry Sea (a-ab-ba hu-luh-ha): The History of a Sumerian Congregational Lament.* New Haven.
Lanahan, W. 1974. The Speaking Voice in the Book of Lamentations. *JBL* 93: 41–49.
McDaniel, T. 1968a. The Alleged Sumerian Influence upon Lamentations. *VT* 18: 198–209.
———. 1968b. Philological Studies in Lamentations. *Bib* 49: 27–53; 199–220.
Meshel, Z. 1978. *Kuntillet ʿAjrud—A Religious Centre from the Time of the Judaean Monarchy on the Border of Sinai.* Israel Museum Catalogue 175. Jerusalem.
Naveh, J. 1978. Some Considerations on the Ostracon from ʿIzbet Sartah. *IEJ* 28: 31–35.
Rudolph, W. 1938. Der Text der Klagelieder. *ZAW* 52: 101–22.
Shea, W. 1979. The *qinah* Structure of the Book of Lamentations. *Bib* 60: 103–7.
Tigay, J. 1976. Review of *Lamentations* AB, by Hillers. *JNES* 35: 140–43.
Westermann, C. 1954. Struktur und Geschichte der Klage im Alten Testament. *ZAW* 66: 44–80.
Ziegler, J. 1976. *Ieremias, Baruch, Threni, Epistula Ieremiae* (Göttingen Septuagint). 2d ed. Göttingen.

DELBERT R. HILLERS

LAMPSTAND [Heb *mĕnôrâ*]. (In some English versions of the Bible the Hebrew *mĕnôrâ* is translated by the anachronistic word "candlestick.") Since lamps were the normal source of light other than daylight in the biblical world, one would expect stands to hold them to have been items of everyday usage. The furniture of a room described in 2 Kgs 4:10 includes a lampstand; and many examples of ceramic stands, at least some of which might be construed as lampstands, have been found in archaeological excavations. However, lampstands have rarely been found, archaeologically, in domestic contexts (Smith 1964: 9–11). Aside from the 2 Kings passage, all the biblical mentions of lampstands refer to golden objects used in sacred contexts.

Lampstands as receptacles for light-giving vessels were part of the sacred furniture in the central Israelite shrines or sanctuaries described in the Bible. The light given off by the lamps served to illuminate the interior of the sanctuary, and it also functioned as part of a set of ritual objects or acts, appealing to all the senses, that were part of the established priestly ritual (Haran 1978: 208–21). However, the lights or lamps were not the same as the stands on which they were placed. The nature of those stands varied during the long history of ancient Israel's cultic institutions.

A. Tabernacle Lampstand

The earliest of Israel's lampstand traditions belongs to pre-temple times, that is, to the tent or tabernacle associated with the premonarchic period. Of the forty-one occurrences of "lampstand" in the Hebrew Bible, more of them (26) deal with the tabernacle menorah or lampstand than with those of the subsequent Israelite shrines (either the Jerusalem temple built by Solomon and continuing, though with alterations over the centuries, until the destruction of Jerusalem; or the restored temple built in the early postexilic period and remodeled or rebuilt several times thereafter until the Roman destruction of Jerusalem in 70 C.E.).

The lampstand of the tabernacle (*miškān*) is mentioned in various places in the priestly writings of the Pentateuch, but the chief descriptive passages are found in the tabernacle texts of Exodus (Exod 25:31–40 and 37:17–24). Although the priestly texts in their final form are probably exilic or postexilic in date, biblical scholarship has established the greater antiquity of much of the priestly material, including traditions dealing with the tabernacle. Thorough study of the lampstand texts, from the perspectives of philosophy, archaeology, and art history, has established a basic reality for that biblical artifact that can be located in the Mosaic era, the end of the LB Age (see Meyers 1976: 182–84 and *passim*).

The Hebrew word for lampstand is ambiguous in what it represents in the priestly texts. Sometimes (e.g., Exod 26:35; 40:4; Num 8:2–3), it indicates a branched object, that is, a central shaft with three branches coming forth from each side. This arrangement produces seven receptacles for lamps: one on each of the six branches, and one on the central shaft. At other points the biblical references to the tabernacle lampstand (as in Exod 25:31–35; 37:17–21), refer only to the central shaft, which constitutes the actual stand for the lamps, with the branches thus being part of the symbolic shape of the appurtenance but not part of its functional aspect.

The latter instances make it clear that the seven lamps associated with the lampstand are not themselves to be construed as being physically part of the lampstand. They are discrete objects, and in at least two instances (Exod 27:20; Lev 24:2–3, and perhaps also Exod 25:37) a tradition of a single lamp rather than seven lamps can be discerned. In the case of both the seven lamps and the single one, these actual light sources were to be placed on the central shaft or stand and *not* on the end of the branches (see Lev 24:4). The idea of a seven-branched lampstand is the result of early post-biblical Jewish interpretations (in graphic and textual sources) of the Exodus texts, but it is not intrinsic to the biblical description itself.

The existence of apparently contradictory information about the number of lamps can be related to the conflation of two sanctuary traditions, the tent of meeting and the tabernacle. The single-lamp passages contain references to the tent of meeting, whereas the seven lamp texts are in the context of tabernacle data.

The biblical descriptions of the lampstand contain many technical terms that are very specific in their meaning and that help reconstruct the form of the object, the workmanship used in fashioning it, as well as its symbolic value. Perhaps the key to understanding its fundamental form and identity is the pair of words, *yarēk wĕqāneh,* that designate the central shaft, or lampstand proper. This pair, mistakenly translated "base and shaft" by the RSV, is actually a hendiadys denoting a cylindrical form that flares outward at its lower end, thereby forming a stable base. This feature makes it possible for the lampstand to be freestanding. There is no description of a tripodal or of a stepped base, one or the other of which appear in nearly all post-biblical descriptions or depictions of the lampstand.

Its basic cylindrical form, flaring at the bottom and possibly also at the top, places the lampstand typologically within the category of stands recovered in ceramic form in archaeological excavations in Palestine and appearing, in metal and stone form, in artistic renderings all over the ANE. Such stands were used to hold a variety of vessels, such as bowls, jars, incense dishes, offering platters, and, of course, lamps.

The other technical terms used to describe the whole lampstand are noteworthy for being part of the vocabulary of plant forms in ancient Israel. Moreover, the botanical aspects of the terminology relate to features of graphic renderings of plant forms especially as they appear in Egyptian art. The very term *qāneh,* representing "branch" and also appearing in the pair of words for the central shaft described above, is a generic word for "reed." It specifies the *arundo donax,* or Persian reed, a gigantic grass commonly found along the edges of bodies of water or water courses, the latter exemplified by the Nile. In nearly all other, nonpriestly biblical texts mentioning this reed, it has an Egyptian context and even symbolized Egypt (as in Isa 36:6 = 2 Kgs 18:21).

Another pair, *kaptōr wĕperah,* is best translated as a hendiadys: "floral capital" rather than RSV "capital and flower." It, too, is botanical in its vocabulary and Egyptian in its artistic orientation. These floral capitals, along with the somewhat enigmatic rounded bowls (*gĕbi ʿîm*) with almond-shaped inlay, were repeated three times on each branch and four times on the central shaft. This repetition functions as an artistic motif conveying permanence or continuity.

The presence of botanical terms, and the basic central shaft-plus-six-branches form, give the impression of a tree-shaped object. As such—and apart from its functional role as a holder of lamp(s)—the lampstand constitutes a conventional form appearing in depictions widespread in NE iconography (see Perrot 1937; Vincent 1924). This convention is derived from a stylized tree of life design and symbolizes such themes as the fertility of nature and the sustenance of life. The specific form of the branched lampstand of Exodus is closest to examples that are found at the end of the LB Age, or the age of Moses. See also TREE OF KNOWLEDGE AND TREE OF LIFE.

Since most ANE examples of the tree of life motif apparently represent the fertility-granting and life-giving powers of various deities, the presence of such a form in the aniconographic Israelite cult can perhaps be construed as the use of a powerful religious symbol to represent the presence of the unseen God of Israel. As a demythologized tree symbol, it served along with other aspects of the tabernacle, as God's residence, to assure God's availability to the Israelites or their priestly representatives.

The technology involved in shaping this complex appurtenance is not perfectly understood. The material, "pure gold," puts the lampstand in the category of furnishings for the interior of the tabernacle. It also points to a kind of metallurgy associated with Egyptian workmanship (Meyers 1976: 41–43). The fact that the lampstand was to be made all of one piece indicates the usage of sheet gold, or gold foil, which probably would have been shaped by a rubbing process (*miqšâ*) over a wooden form.

B. Lampstands of Solomon's Temple

The image of a single, branched lampstand, vivid from the tabernacle texts and from postbiblical Jewish art, should not obscure the fact that the temple built by Solomon in Jerusalem contained ten lampstands (1 Kgs 7:49 = 2 Chr 4:7). Furthermore, there is no indication that those objects were branched. The only detail of their shape is the mention of their "flowers." The Solomonic lampstands were probably the cylindrical stands with flaring bottoms and tops that are represented in the central shaft of the tabernacle stand. The lamps that rested on these stands in the Jerusalem temple were likely to have been the seven-spouted bowl lamps typically found in cultic contexts in archaeological strata of the Iron II period, the time of the Solomonic temple. Not only does the temple lampstand differ in number and decoration from the one described in Exodus; it also involved a different technological tradition. The "pure gold" for the Solomonic stands is indicated by a term different from that used for the tabernacle lampstand. The term in Kings is related to the Tyrian workmanship of the Jerusalem temple.

Without the branches, and with ten stands being used, it is doubtful that the symbolic value of these lampstands was the same as for the single tabernacle one. Rather, the light-giving property of the lamps they held apparently was their most significant attribute. Arboreal symbolism in the Jerusalem temple was present in other forms: in the trees carved on the cedar panels (1 Kgs 6:15, 18, 29) and cypress door (1 Kgs 6:34–35), and perhaps also in a sacred grove in the temple precincts (cf. Ps 52:8).

The lampstands commissioned by Solomon are not mentioned again in the Hebrew Bible. A possible exception is Jer 52:17. However, since that passage lists "lampstands" in an inventory of minor cultic appurtenances or utensils, it is doubtful that the main sanctuary lampstands are meant. Thus it is difficult to know whether or not the original ten lampstands of gold survived until the Babylonian conquest of 587 B.C.E. They may have been replaced during one of the periodic refurbishings of the temple (Meyers 1981), or they may have been relinquished in an earlier Judean encounter with a foreign power.

C. Postexilic Lampstands

The temple was restored early in the postexilic period, in the late 6th century, under the guidance of the prophets Haggai and Zechariah and under the leadership of the governor Zerubbabel and the chief priest Joshua. But the Bible gives no indication that the reestablished temple contained one or more lampstands. Most of our information about the cultic furniture of the rebuilt temple comes from extrabiblical sources, such as Philo, Josephus, the Talmud, and graphic renderings (Meyers 1979). Such sources from late in the postexilic period, or even after the destruction of the rebuilt temple in 70 C.E., are more likely to reflect the last known temple lampstand, since the restored temple was itself rebuilt at least several times (cf. 1 Macc 1:21; 4:49), most grandly in its last existing form as the Herodian temple. Those sources preserve a single lampstand tradition.

The nature and number of lampstands at the beginning of the postbiblical period may, however, be informed by one prophetic passage, Zech 4:1–6 and 11–14, which predates the completion of the temple restoration project. Zechariah's vision includes a golden lampstand. The description of the stand, which has its own complex and to some extent fanciful terminology, clearly depicts a single lampstand and not ten of them. In that sense, it relies upon the pentateuchal traditions. Such a reliance is typical of many of the characteristics of the semi-autonomous community established in Judah in the late 6th century. Zechariah apparently envisioned the rebuilt temple with a lampstand just like the one presented in the tabernacle texts. But such an appurtenance would have been fabricated according to Persian period or late Iron Age styles and technologies rather than according to archaic LB or early Iron Age ones (see Meyers and Meyers, *Haggai, Zechariah 1–8* AB, 227–40).

Zechariah's lampstand has its idiosyncratic qualities. On a symbolic level, it seems to combine the importance of the tree-of-life form of the tabernacle tradition with the light-giving aspects of the temple stands. The former is represented in Zechariah's vision by the presence of two olive trees flanking the golden lampstand. And the latter is expressed in the prophet's explanation of the symbolic value of the seven seven-spouted lamps resting on the stand (for which no branches are mentioned): "These seven are the eyes of Yahweh which range through all the earth" (Zech 4:10b).

Whether or not Zechariah's vision was ever translated into reality cannot be established except in the fact that the single lampstand tradition resumes by the time of the Roman conquest of Jerusalem in 70 C.E. However, the idea of visionary and symbolic temple furnishings gets played out once more, and extravagantly, in Revelation (1:12, 13, 20; 2:1; 11:4). There, the golden lampstands are seven in number (except in 11:4). The sacred number seven is combined with the sacred furniture of the temple in the apocalyptic imagery of this NT book.

Bibliography

Haran, M. 1978. *Temples and Temple Service in Ancient Israel.* Oxford.

Meyers, C. 1976. *The Tabernacle Menorah.* Missoula, MT.

———. 1979. Was There a Seven-Branched Menorah in Solomon's Temple? *BARev* 5: 46–57.

———. 1981. The Elusive Temple. *BA* 45: 33–42.

Perrot, N. 1937. Les representationes le l'arbre sacré sur les monuments de Mesopotamie et de l'Élam. *Babyloniaca* 17: 5–144.

Smith, R. H. 1964. The Household Lamps of Palestine in Old Testament Times. *BA* 27: 1–31.

Vincent, L. H. 1924. La peinture céramique Palestinienne. *Syria* 5: 81–107.

CAROL MEYERS

LANCE. See WEAPONS AND IMPLEMENTS OF WARFARE.

LAND. The frequent occurrence of various terms designating land, and the central role land plays in certain narratives, testify to the importance of this concept in the Bible. But while the concept is ubiquitous, the different units of the OT provide various ideological perspectives and theological nuances. Similarly, while the use of this term in the NT displays an awareness of the centrality of this concept, its meaning is further transformed through the motivations of its individual authors.

A. Old Testament
  1. Terminology
  2. Israel's Land
  3. Theology: The Land Theme in the OT
B. New Testament
  1. Terminology
  2. Theology

A. Old Testament

1. Terminology. In the vast majority of instances (RSV ca. 1620 times) "land" translates Hebrew *ʾereṣ*, a word that can also be rendered by "earth" (RSV ca. 660 times), "ground" (RSV 107 times), "country" (RSV 83 times) and by several less frequent terms (see EARTH for cognates and for a discussion of original meaning). In addition, "land" frequently translates *ʾădāmâ* (RSV ca. 105 times), also rendered "ground" (RSV 67 times), "earth" (RSV 37 times), "soil" (RSV 6 times), "country" (RSV 2 times), and occasionally, *śadeh* (usually rendered "field"). In spite of their frequent rendition by the same English "land," *ʾereṣ* and *ʾădāmâ* are seldom synonyms (never, according to Rost [1965: 77, 80], but Plöger [1967: 128] offers a few exceptions for Deut 4:38, 40; 11:8f.; 12:1; 26:2, 15).

"Land" is the usual translation of *ʾereṣ* when it refers to (a) a specific geographical region (e.g., "land of Ararat," 2 Kgs 19:37), or (b) the territory of a specific people (e.g., "land of the Kenites," Gen 15:19); while "earth" is the usual translation when *ʾereṣ* refers to the realm of human habitation (generally EARTH). The plural *(ʾărāṣôt)* is compatible with this usage, though relatively infrequent (ca. 70 times; e.g., Gen 41:54). In some instances, however, the translation of *ʾereṣ* as "earth" or "land" will depend on more complex exegetical decisions (e.g., Lev 25:23).

In the majority of instances of type b, the land in question is identified in some way as promised to, claimed, or possessed by Israel or a part of Israel (e.g., "land of Judah," Deut 34:2), although the explicit designation "land of Israel" is rare (see below). At other times, genitive combinations or adjectival phrases characterize the extent and quality of the land (e.g., "the whole land," Gen 13:9; "fatness of the land," Gen 27:28; "fertile" [lit. "good"] land, Judg 18:9). Often "land" locates a group of people (e.g., "elders of the land," Gen 50:7). On occasion, "land" can be personified (e.g., "captivity of the land," Judg 18:30; "the land rested," Josh 3:11; "the land mourns," Hos 4:3).

ʾădāmâ is primarily a nonpolitical term designating the agricultural land that sustains a sedentary population, in contrast to "wilderness" *(midbār)*, while *ʾereṣ* includes the latter (Rost 1965: 77, 81). As such, *ʾădāmâ* is usually owned by a person (head of household) or group (e.g., "your/their land," Deut 7:13). God's ultimate ownership is assumed and expressed (Isa 14:2 [*ʾadmat YHWH*], cf. Hos 9:3; Josh 22:4 [*ʾereṣ ʾăḥuzzatkem*]), and Israel owns it by virtue of his gift (Deut 26:15). The expression "land of Israel" *(ʾadmat yiśrāʾēl)*, however, is peculiar to Ezekiel (16 times), which Rost (1965: 78) takes to express the nonpolitical nature of that prophet's land expectations. While all agricultural land forms a collective unity—there is only one instance of the plural *(ʾădāmôt*, Ps 49:12—Eng 49:11); the reference in numerous OT contexts is to the portion of Israel or subgroups of Israel. In this respect, *ʾădāmâ*, like *ʾereṣ*, is a key term sustaining the OT's land theology.

2. Israel's Land. a. Israel's Relationship to the Land. In the majority of contexts, "land" is identified as the land to which Israel has a claim (see "Theology," below). It is characterized as anticipated (e.g., "the whole land before you," Gen 13:9), as highly desirable and praiseworthy (Deut 8:7–10), as the "good land" (especially in Deuteronomy), and as a "land flowing with milk and honey" (e.g., Exod 3:17).

Parenthetically, the two common English designations "Promised Land" and "Holy Land," though correctly expressing central theological concerns (see "Theology," below), are not characteristic for the OT. The Hebrew language has no words for "promise, to promise"; where such occur in Eng translation (e.g., Deut 9:28, RSV), they usually render the common Hebrew verbs "to speak" or "to say." The term "Holy Land" *(ʾadmat haqqōdeš)* occurs only in Zech 2:16—Eng 2:12, with reference to the eschatological future, and then in 2 Macc 1:7 (cf. Davies 1974: 29f.; Hanhart 1983: 128, 130). Its holiness, where expressed or implied, is not an inherent status, but totally dependent on God's decision to be present in or withdraw from it.

The most frequent designation of the land is also a reminder that it did not belong to Israel originally: "land of Canaan/the Canaanites" (JE,P, e.g., Gen. 12:5; 23:2; seldom in Deuteronomy [Deut 1:7; 11:30; 32:49]). Frequently this point is made in a formulaic listing of the original owners:

> I promise that I will bring you up out of the affliction of Egypt, to the land of the Canaanites, the Hittites, the Amorites, the Perizzites, the Hivites, and the Jebusites, a land flowing with milk and honey. (Exod 3:17)

This listing appears in the earliest Pentateuchal sources already, but finds its echoes elsewhere within and beyond the Pentateuch, up to the time of Ezra (9:1) and Nehemiah (9:8). In the majority of cases, the list contains six members, generally those of Exod 3:17 (above), with the Canaanites, Amorites, and Hittites vying for first position, and the Jebusites almost always at the end. However, the list never became a fixed formula; it ranges from three members (Exod 23:28) to ten (Gen 15:19f.), with variations in nations listed and in their order. Thus it is safe to assume that it is not merely repeated as a cliché, but gives evidence of ongoing reflection in Israel on the fact that nations other than Israel were the original owners of the land (see "Theology," below). Of course, this previous ownership can be expressed with reference to one nation only, above all, the Canaanites (e.g., Josh 17:16) but sometimes the Amorites (Num 21:31), though it appears that the latter are frequently limited as to residency (e.g., east of the Jordan, Josh 7:7; the hill country, Num 13:29; etc.).

This previous ownership and Israel's subsequent acquisition of the land, are appropriately expressed by a characteristic verbal vocabulary. God promises (*ʾāmar* [lit., "says"], *dābar* [lit., "speaks"; *Piʿel*]) or swears *(šābaʿ [Nipʿal])* to bring Israel into the land *(bôʾ [Hipʿil])*, or to give the land to Israel *(nātan)*. Israel is to go (go up, enter) into the land *(bôʾ, ʿālâ)*, go over [the Jordan] into the land *(ʿābar)*, possess the land *(yāraš)*, receive the land as inheritance *(naḥălâ)*, divide the land *(ḥālaq [Nipʿal])*, and dwell in the land *(yāšab)*. Thus Israel receives a land not originally her own, by God's initiative and agency, but cooperates in its takeover. (Of course, there are many passages that simply assume Israel's eventual acquisition of the land and refer to the latter, in some way or other, as Israel's land, either by possessive adjectives [e.g., "your land," Deut 28:24], or by contextual implication.)

Israel's relationship to this land is further characterized by the nouns "inheritance" *(naḥălâ)*, "possession" *(ʾăḥuzzâ)*, and "rest" *(mĕnûḥâ)*, together with their respective verbal stems. "Inheritance" designates the land as transferred to Israel by God without the right of sale (Wanke *THAT* 2: 56; cf. 1 Kings 21:3f.). The emphasis falls on God as the one who has authority to dispose of land belonging to him, and on Israel's inalienable right to retain such land as God confers.

As to the nature of the transfer, two interpretations have been proposed: (a) Scholars generally have derived *naḥălâ* from the realm of inheritance law; (therefore the Eng "inheritance"). (b) Forshey (1973), on the other hand, has plausibly argued for the origination of *naḥălâ* as a term of special land tenure granted by a feudal lord to a devoted servant as a fief. Since such a fief was hereditary, the term was eventually extended to include the meaning "inheritance" in later OT sources. He cautions, however, that the root *nḥl* has very wide connotations, making it impossible to interpret it in terms of a single model (235). In either case, the giving of *naḥălâ* points to a very personal bond between God and Israel, rather than to an impersonal commercial, legal, or military transaction.

The transfer itself is described variously as made to the tribes of Israel with their subdivisions, or to Israel as a whole. Division of the *naḥălâ* among the tribes is found mainly in Numbers (e.g., 26:52–56), Joshua (e.g., 11:23; 13:7–8), and Ezekiel (e.g., 48:29). It is to take place by lot (e.g., Num 26:55; Josh 1:23; Ezek 45:1) each tribal unit receiving its "allotment" (*ḥeleq;* e.g., Josh 11:23). Only the Levites are excluded from this distribution; their inheritance consists of the tithe (e.g., Num 18:21–26; 26:62), certain cities (e.g., Num 35:2; Josh 14:4), their share in the sacrifices (e.g., Josh 13:14; Deut 18:1f.), and ultimately God and his service (e.g., Josh 13:33; 18:7; Deut 10:8f.; cf. Ezek 44:28). The apportioning of the *naḥălâ* to Israel as a whole is found mainly in Deuteronomy (e.g., 4:38; 12:9; 15:4). Occasionally, *naḥălâ* refers to the land holdings of individual Israelite household heads (e.g., Josh 4:9; 1 Kgs 21:3f.; Ruth 4:5, 10).

Less frequent is the designation of the land as God's *naḥălâ,* probably with reference to his claim to original ownership (e.g., 1 Sam 26:19; Jer 2:7; just as Israel, his people, is often called his *naḥălâ,* e.g., Deut 4:20; 32:8f.). Forshey (1973: 236f.) points out, further, that the reference to Israel as God's *naḥălâ,* largely exilic, may have been a theological means to link the people closely to Yahweh in spite of their removal from the land. He suggests the translation "possession" as appropriate for most instances.

Another term defining Israel's relationship to the land as acquired ownership is "possession" (*ʾăḥuzzâ*). Its verbal root "seize, grasp, take hold" suggests again that the land, now Israel's "possession," had once been in other hands. The land of Canaan was given by God to Israel as its possession (e.g., Lev 14:34; Deut 32:49). Like *naḥălâ,* it can refer to the land holding of Israel as a whole or of individual tribes, clans, and households. In most instances it refers to land and real estate that is handed down through the generations and should not be sold (e.g., Lev 25:10ff. *passim;* 27:22–24). Sometimes, however, it is extended to include property generally. Its closeness to "land" and "inheritance" is expressed in such construct phrases as "land of your possession" (RSV: "your land;" *ʾereṣ ʾăḥuzzatkem;* Josh 22:19), "inheritance of their possession" (*naḥălat ʾăḥuzzātām;* Num 35:2), and "the possession of our inheritance" (*ʾăḥuzzat naḥălātēnû;* Num 32:32). In spite of their closeness of connotation, however, *naḥălâ* and *ʾăḥuzzâ* are not fully synonymous; *ʾăḥuzzâ* is the more general, juridicially abstract concept designating possession of land (Horst 1961: 155).

The land is also the destination of Israel's wandering, and as such, its place of rest. Both the verbal expression "give rest" (*nûaḥ, Hipʿil*) and its nominal derivative "rest" (*mĕnûḥâ*) express this, particularly within Deuteronomic-Deuteronomistic theology. As a distinctive aspect of God's land promise, rest can be expected by Israel only upon crossing the Jordan and occupying the heartland of Canaan (Deut 12:9f.; 25:19; cf. 3:20, see below). There God grants rest to his people in stages, beginning with the conquest (Josh 1:13, 15; 11:44; 22:4; 23:1) and culminating in the era of David and Solomon (2 Sam 7:1, 11; 1 Kgs 5:4; 8:56). The essence of this rest is "tangible peace granted to a nation plagued by enemies and weary of wandering" (von Rad 1966b: 155). Just as the land can be called God's inheritance, the land (and particularly the temple) can also be called his rest (Ps 95:11; 2 Chr 6:41). That Israel's access to God's gift of rest is contingent on faithfulness and endangered by rebellion, is the warning of Ps 95:11.

While the concepts inheritance, possession, and rest emphasize the divine intention and authorization for Israel to possess this land and find rest in it, other texts maintain God's ultimate ownership of the land, and Israel's calling to live in it as "strangers and sojourners" (*gērîm wĕtôšābîm*) in the land/on the earth (Lev 25:23; cf. Josh 22:19; Pss 24:1; 39:13—Eng 39:12; 119:19; Jer 2:7; 16:18).

However, the eventually expected appellation of the land acquired by Israel as "land of Israel" (*ʾereṣ yiśrāʾēl*) occurs only once in an older text (1 Sam 13:19, besides a few references to the N kingdom only), 3 times in Ezekiel (27:17; 40:2; 47:18; for *ʾadmat yiśrāʾēl,* see above), and 5 times in Chronicles (1 Chr 13:2 [MT pl.]; 22:2; 2 Chr 2:17—Eng 2:16; 30:25; 34:7). Wildberger (1956: 407, n. 15) sees this as a conscious, theologically motivated avoidance of a known term, while Ohler (1979: 58) ponders whether Israel was unable to perceive this "land" as a unity. The latter seems highly unlikely, however, in view of Israel's focused land theology (see below). Israel's contingent hold on a land not originally hers may have been the theological motivation for the reserve in the use of "land of Israel," but we cannot be sure.

b. The Extent of Israel's Land. A perplexing question concerns the extent of Israel's land. Two comprehensive "maps" are respectively reflected in many passages:

1. Num 34:1–12 explicitly defines the "land of Canaan" as extending from the Brook of Egypt (*naḥlâ miṣrayim*) to the Entrance of Hamath (*lĕbôʾ ḥĕmāt*), and from the Jordan/Dead Sea to the Mediterranean Sea. East Jordan is excluded. Many passages and events mark Israel's crossing of the Jordan as the beginning of the occupation (e.g., Deut 12:10; Josh 5:10–12). Numbers 32 and Joshua 22 offer a legitimation of the actual settlement of parts of East Jordan (called "unclean," in contrast to Canaan, "the LORD's land," Josh 22:19) by Israelite tribes.

2. Deut 11:24 offers much broader boundaries, including East and West Jordan, "from the River, the river Euphrates, to the western sea." In keeping with this picture, Deuteronomy 2 promises East Jordan, except the territories of Moab and Ammon, to Israel and sees the

crossing of the Arnon as the beginning of Israel's holy war of conquest against the nations. The settlement of Israelite tribes in East Jordan apparently presents no problem (Deut 3:12–20; Josh 13:8–12).

Weinfeld (1983: 59–75, esp. 65f., leaning on B. Mazar and R. de Vaux) has plausibly argued that the first "map" (Num 34:1–12) represents Israel's older, pre-deuteronomic claim, patterned on the old Egyptian province of Canaan as it emerged after the battle of Kadesh (ca. 1285 B.C.). It is reflected, in addition to the texts mentioned, in Josh 13:4; Judg 3:3; 1 Kgs 8:65; 2 Kgs 14:25; Amos 6:14; and it also offered the blueprint for Ezekiel's vision (Ezek 47:16–20). The second "map" (Deut 11:24), in this schema, originated in the expansive era of the Davidic-Solomonic empire, was formulated in grand, utopian ancient Near Eastern royal terminology (river to river, sea to sea, etc.), and received its final crystallization by "the so-called Deuteronomic author or school" in the Josianic era. This perspective is reflected or presupposed, besides the passages listed, in Gen 15:18; Exod 23:31; Pss 72:8; 80:12—Eng 80:11; 89:26—Eng 89:25; Josh 1:4; Deut 1:7; Zech 9:10; and others.

The characterization of map 2 as Deuteronomic is not without problems, however. Diepold (1972: 29–41, 56–64) distinguishes between a land limitation to West Jordan in Deuteronomy, with occasional redactional additions taking the wider view (e.g., 11:24), and a perspective of the Deuteronomistic History (including most of Deuteronomy 1–3 and 34) that envisions the land to include East Jordan up to the Euphrates. Numerous literary-critical decisions underlie both hypotheses, and it seems doubtful whether we can reach clear territorial definitions for Israel's land beyond conclusions for a particular canonical document or a limited historical context and period.

It is significant that several, especially later, documents exhibit much less well-defined geographical conceptions of the land. Thus Jeremiah, with his prominent theology of land (Diepold 1972: 105–39, 155–76; Martens 1972; Brueggemann 1974; Epp-Tiessen 1981; Zimmerli 1985), reflected little on its extent, assuming it to be basically the West Jordan area where the people of God actually lived, while the Deuteronomistic additions to Jeremiah reflect the remnant area of Judah, together with the lost southern territories of the Shephelah, the hill country, and the Negeb (Diepold 1972: 54f., 70f.). In the postexilic era, limited terms like "Judah and Jerusalem" increasingly describe the land (e.g., Ezra 4:6). The very freedom with which the documents and their redactors vary in their perspectives indicates that the concept of Israel's land is held together by an inner core of identity (see "Theology," below) rather than by geographical or ideological definition.

For our geographical understanding of Israel's land in the OT generally, a multiple perspective must be maintained: its heartland was the West Jordan region "from Dan to Beersheba" (e.g., Judg 20:1), with the exclusion of more or less of the Mediterranean coastal plain. Based on the reality of settlement and political control, the East Jordan region, excluding Edom, Moab, and Ammon, was generally also included. Occasionally, perhaps inspired by the extent of David's kingdom, all the lands up to the Euphrates were included in visionary statements (e.g., Deut 1:6–8; 11:24; Josh 1:3–4).

3. Theology: The Land Theme in the OT. The land theme is so ubiquitous that it may have greater claim to be the central motif in the OT than any other, including "covenant" (cf. the theological surveys of Wildberger 1956: 404–22; von Waldow 1974: 493–508; Davies 1974; and esp. Brueggemann 1977). It is nuanced differently in different books and compositional units, yet the tensions thus created are never such as to deflect altogether from a broad central narrative thrust pervading the canonical documents. An attempt will be made to sketch that narrative. Historical, form-critical, and traditio-historical matters will be considered from time to time.

a. The Pentateuch. The Pentateuchal narrative identifies the earth *(ʾereṣ)* as God's creation (Gen 1:1, 9f.), intended to be the source of all plant and animal life (1:11, 24), and as the habitat for human beings who are to administer it (1:28f.). Through his very name, the collective "Adam" *(ʾādām),* and the image of his formation "of dust from the ground" *(ʾădāmâ),* the human creature is closely linked to the soil (2:7). He is to experience it first in the garden graciously provided by God (2:8). To "till and keep" (lit. "to serve and watch over") this garden is to be his (after the creation of woman, their) task as God's steward(s), enjoying its produce within God-set limits (2:15–17). When humans claim the master role, "like God" (3:1–7), their task of filling the earth and caring for it is encumbered by a "heavy burden" *(ʿiṣṣābôn,* RSV: "pain" in 3:16, "toil" in 3:17); they are driven from the garden (3:22–24), but their task remains, and the earth (land) will continue to be the source of their livelihood (3:19, 23).

Abel and Cain continue this task as "keeper of sheep" and "tiller of the ground" *(ʿōbēd ʾădāmâ).* When Cain spills his brother's blood, however, he becomes "cursed from the ground," the latter no longer yielding "its strength" to him; paradigmatically for later "defilers" of the land, he becomes "a fugitive and a wanderer on the earth *(bāʾāreṣ),*" though not without God's protection (4:8–16). Sin continues to endanger human existence on the earth through the great Flood, God preserving only a remnant of animate life (6:5–7:24). God graciously confirms the human commission to fill and administer the earth (8:17; 9:1–2, 7), promising that he "will never again curse the ground *(hāʾădāmâ)* because of man" (8:21). A repeated human effort at establishing an autonomous identity ("a name") through entrenching themselves geographically by building "a city, and a tower with its top in the heavens" evokes the judgment of God who "scattered them abroad from there over the face of the earth *(hāʾāreṣ)*" (11:1–9).

In this manner, the two traditionally assumed literary sources J and P intertwine in the Primaeval History (Genesis 1–11) to present a theology in which land is God's gracious gift and task for humanity under the sovereign rule of God. These are constantly threatened by the human tendency to seek autonomous rule over the land, resulting in its loss and in a life of uprooted wandering, but it is precisely then that God's grace and protection become most palpable. Thus a dialectic results, between "landedness" as God's greatest gift and man's greatest temptation, and "landlessness" as God's judgment and yet the context for the highest experience of God's grace

(Brueggemann 1977 *passim*). It is this paradox that governs much of the subsequent land motif in the OT.

Abraham is promised a great name, many descendants, and God's blessing, on the provision that he uproot himself from his Mesopotamian homeland to go "to the land that I will show you" (12:1–3). The unknown land sought by Abraham in faith is later identified as Canaan (12:6–7), and the promise of its possession is repeated to Abraham and his descendants throughout the Pentateuch (Gen 13:15; 15:7, 18; 17:8; 22:17; 26:3; 28:4, 13; 35:12; 48:4; 50:24; Exod 3:8; 6:4–8; 13:5; 32:13; 33:1; Num 10:29; 14:23; 32:11; Deut 6:18, 23; 8:1; 9:5, 28; 10:11; 11:8–9, 21; 26:3, 15; 28:11; 31:7, 20; 34:4; cf. Josh 1:6; 5:6; Judg 2:1). Nonetheless, Abraham, Isaac, and Jacob live in the land as sojourners (Gen 17:8; 23:4; 26:3; 28:4; 35:27; 36:7; 37:1; Exod 6:4), until the family of Jacob/Israel, overtly driven by famine, but on a deeper level, guided by God, leaves Canaan again to settle in Egypt. Only a burial plot, the field and cave of Machpelah, bought by Abraham to bury Sarah, becomes their permanent possession in Canaan, and therewith a proleptic sign of the fulfillment of God's promise (Genesis 23). In Egypt, Israel multiplies to become a great people in accordance with God's promise, in the fertile but foreign land of Goshen (Gen 47:5–6; Exodus 1).

According to A. Alt's widely accepted characterization of Patriarchal religion (Alt 1966b), the land promise originated in the faith of seminomadic groups that the God of the Father would grant them land, in a limited context and in their own lifetime. R. C. Clements (1967: 23–46), partly based on Cross (1962) and others, sees the historical kernel of the land promise in an ancient covenant in which the El-deity (possibly El Shaddai) at Mamre, as owner of that territory, promises the land of the Kenites, Kenizzites, and Kadmonites to Abraham and his descendants. This promise was eventually extended to all of Judah and, through David, to all Israel and the whole land of Canaan. As such, it became the dominant theological theme of the Hexateuch, the expectation of immediate fulfillment having been advanced to the conquest under Joshua and to the Davidic-Solomonic era (Clements 1967: 57; von Rad 1966d: 83).

The book of Exodus introduces the Israelites as a numerous people enslaved in a foreign land (Exodus 1). Moses becomes God's chosen instrument to lead them out of Egypt toward the goal of the land promised to the Patriarchs (Exod 3:7–8; 6:2–8). The faithlessness and murmuring of the people prevents a direct entry into Canaan, however (Numbers 14; 26:63–65; 32:6–15; Deut 2:14–15), and results in forty years of wilderness wanderings with untold hardships, until the rebelling generation has died and a new generation stands at the Jordan, on the brink of entering the land. Moses is merely allowed to see it from afar (Deut 34:1–5). Yet this very time in the wilderness becomes a time of experiencing God's constant presence and preservation, including the conclusion of the covenant with God at Mt. Sinai and the receiving of the covenant laws he requires Israel to keep. Many of the latter regulate Israel's life in the promised land, which is also called God's own property (Lev 25:23). Among them are the laws governing the sabbath year (Exod 23:10–11; Lev 25:1–7), the jubilee year (Lev 25:8–55), and first fruits (*bikkûrîm;* Exod 23:16, 19; 34:22, 26; Lev 2:12; 28:26; *rēʾšît,* Lev 23:10; Num 18:12; Deut 18:4; 26:10).

The law codes now embedded in the covenant narrative are of diverse historical origin but are gathered here as covenantal law of Moses to indicate that their authority ultimately derives from the will of God. G. von Rad (1966d, followed by W. D. Davies [1974: 15–35] and others) has pointed out that the themes of "promised land" and "Yahweh's land" may be derived from originally separate traditions. The former was introduced into the Pentateuch by the Yahwist (see above). The latter, at home in the cult and the legal materials, may go back to the Canaanite view that each land belongs to its own god (thus von Waldow 1974: 494), though von Rad (1966d: 88) prefers to think of an early, Yahwistic origin. (For the synthesis of R. C. Clements [1967: 27–28], see above.) Whatever its origin, the concept of Yahweh's ownerships of the land of Canaan has been integrated fully into the biblical faith that God rules/owns the whole world, including Canaan (e.g., Exod 19:5). An important theological consequence of the notion of Yahweh's ownership of this specific land has remained highly effective in the Old Testament's land theology, namely, the notion that the Israelites (and by extrapolation, all humans) are "strangers and sojourners" *(gērîm wĕtôšābîm),* or in modern terms, God's long-term guests on his land/earth (Lev 25:23; Ps 39:13—Eng 39:12; 1 Chr 29:15; cf. Heb 11:13; 1 Pet 2:11).

b. Deuteronomy. In the form of three farewell speeches of Moses (Deuteronomy 1–4; 5–28; 29–30) in the plains of Moab on the eve of crossing the Jordan into the promised land, Deuteronomy recasts the preceding narrative into its own distinctive theological mold, with the land at its center (Plöger 1967: 60–100; Diepold 1972: 76–104).

According to M. Noth *(NDH)* and many others after him, it seems likely that the first speech of Moses (Deuteronomy 1–4) was prefixed to an older version of Deuteronomy by the Deuteronomistic Historian and consequently reflects the perspectives of the Deuteronomistic History (see below). God is about to fulfill his oath sworn to the fathers by bringing Israel into the land to inherit it. While Israel is to participate actively by going into it to take possession of it, the success will depend totally on God. He will subdue the former owners of the land and give it to Israel as a gift. It is a good land, praiseworthy in most glowing terms (e.g., Deut 8:7–9). It is the tangible token of God's faithfulness, the concrete expression of the covenant relationship, and the goal of Israel's wanderings where the people will find rest (12:9). But the land, like the original garden of Eden, constitutes a task for Israel. Its careful administration according to covenant law (rehearsed in chaps. 12–26), in single-hearted love and devotion to God will sustain Israel's claim to its possession and its blessings (e.g., 6:4–15; 8:11–20; 11:26–32; 28). Any deviation from God's statutes, commandments, and ordinances, and in particular the sin of idolatry that characterized the previous owners, will swiftly bring down on Israel the covenant curses, the last and worst of which is a return to Egypt (28:68). Thus the land becomes the touchstone for life or death; it is given out of God's free grace, but retained by means of obedience.

In a few passages (e.g., Deut 6:17–18) it appears as if keeping the law is already a precondition for receiving the land, but P. Diepold is surely right in suggesting that Deuteronomy addresses a people already committed voluntarily to the Sinai covenant; this people is not called to initial commitment now, but to ethical earnestness. The actual keeping of the laws of Deuteronomy, however, makes sense only in the land (Diepold 1972: 90–102).

It is noteworthy that the Pentateuch/Torah ends at the Jordan, stopping short of the actual occupation of the land, especially since the "small historical credos" or summaries (von Rad 1966c; e.g., Deut 26:5b–9) always include the occupation. Scholars have accounted for this in three main ways:

1. Some refuse to recognize the "Pentateuch" as the legitimate delimitation, preferring to include the book of Joshua, featuring the conquest, into a "Hexateuch" (von Rad 1966a).

2. Others assume, with Noth (*HPT,* 16), that the conquest theme was eliminated from the older Pentateuchal sources in the Priestly redaction. It survived, however, through the incorporation of older conquest materials into the Deuteronomistic History.

3. Most recently, R. Rendtorff (1985: 162f.) has argued that the Deuteronomic-Deuteronomistic school prepared the (probably first) collection of Pentateuchal materials, as well as that of the subsequent books, initially "without any fundamental break."

Whatever the literary prehistory may have been, the present delimitation must surely be seen (with J. A. Sanders 1972: 25–53; cf. also Rendtorff 1985: 162f.), as a deliberate canonical decision by a community that had lost the land again, but was able to define its identity as a landless people in terms of a still unfulfilled greater promise that lay in the future. Thus the actual occupation of the land from the time of Joshua to the loss of the land in 722 and 587 B.C., was relegated to the status of "foretaste," with the ultimate fulfillment still ahead, in the (eschatological) future.

c. The Deuteronomistic History. The Deuteronomistic History (Joshua, Judges, Samuel, Kings) in its final overall redactional unity, constitutes an assessment of Israel's performance in the land and of God's inevitable response to it (Noth *NDH,* 89–99). The book of Joshua presents the occupation of the land as a swift and total subjection of the Canaanites in a holy war waged by Yahweh, who gives the land to Israel (chaps. 1–12). At his command, Joshua distributes the land to each tribe, clan, and family (chaps. 13–22).

According to the historical reconstruction of A. Alt (1966a) and M. Noth (*NHI,* 68–84), no such massive conquest took place. Instead, various seminomadic elements of the later "Israel" infiltrated the settled agricultural areas, acquiring peacefully (therefore the technical term *Landnahme*) the more sparsely populated areas in the course of their search for pasture.

This reconstruction has, in turn, been challenged by the "revolutionary" theory proposed, in different forms, by G. Mendenhall (1962: 66–87) and N. Gottwald (1979: 210–220). Both assume that the eventual control of the land by the "tribes of Yahweh" (Gottwald's term) was achieved through some form of takeover of the socially stratified Canaanite city states by the combined onslaught of disadvantaged elements in the population seeking the establishment of an egalitarian society, joining forces "with a nuclear group of invaders and/or infiltrators from the desert" (Gottwald 1979: 210). As no consensus in this matter has emerged, all discussion must necessarily proceed again and again from the canonical data.

In the book of Judges, allowance is made for unconquered Canaanite enclaves (1:19–35; 3:1–6). Israel's hold on the land is repeatedly threatened by enemies, as a direct result of the people's disloyalty to Yahweh. Repentance prompts Yahweh to raise a deliverer ("judge") who leads Israel in defeating the enemy in holy war and continues to "judge" Israel until the cycle repeats itself (e.g., Judg 3:7–11). In the Samson stories (chaps. 13–16), increasing pressure from the Philistines is felt, while Israel is in a state of lawlessness and decay (chaps. 17–21).

This sets the stage for the introduction of kingship, leading to the extensive empire of David and Solomon (2 Samuel 2–1 Kings 11), the division of that empire into the kingdoms of Israel and Judah (1 Kings 12), the eventual defeat of these, and the exiling of their populations by the Assyrians and Babylonians in 722 and 587 B.C., respectively. In his long and nuanced account, the final author of the Deuteronomistic History assesses Israel's faithfulness or unfaithfulness to Yahweh, applying especially the yardstick of David's loyalty to Yahweh to all subsequent kings. This results in the demonstration of the inevitability of the loss of the land. Israel, led by all its kings from Jeroboam I on, had embarked on a course of apostasy (summarized in 2 Kings 17). While the indictment of Israel is generally for idolatry, the story of Ahab's criminal acquisition of Naboth's "inheritance" (*naḥălâ;* 1 Kings 21) makes clear that Canaanite perspectives constituted a significant threat to Yahwistic land laws and land theology. For Judah, periods of relative faithfulness, especially under Hezekiah (2 Kgs 18:1–8) and Josiah (2 Kgs 22:1–23:28), were outweighed by persistent unfaithfulness, peaking in the era of Manasseh (2 Kgs 21:1–18; 23:26–27). Yahweh could not but revoke the gift of the land and cast his people into exile and captivity, as formerly in Egypt. Some scholars find in the Deuteronomistic History intimations of hope for a future restoration (Brueggemann 1968; von Rad *ROTT:* 1.343, 346; Wolff 1966: 131–58), while others see in it a theodicy of Yahweh's final judgment (Noth *NDH,* 97–99).

d. Chronicles. Based largely on the Deuteronomistic History, Chronicles nevertheless yields a considerably different, much less central view of the land. The era of Joshua and the Judges is reflected only in certain genealogical references to names. There is no conquest; Joshua is mentioned briefly as living in the land (1 Chr 7:27). While the kings after David and Solomon are scrupulously assessed as to their faithfulness, the Chronicler does not survey by this means the vast panorama of Israel's covenant faithfulness in the land, as the Deuteronomic Historian does, but depicts instead the meticulous justice of God in the life of each king (*ROTT:* 1.348–50). That the Chronicler does not deny the cumulative impetus of a history of sin towards the loss of the land, and that he sees the restoration under Cyrus as the effect of God's grace to an Israel that had served its time in exile "until the land had enjoyed its sabbaths," is evidenced in his concluding words

(2 Chr 36:15–23). Nevertheless, these themes seem marginal rather than central.

S. Japhet (1979: 205–218) has argued that the Chronicler intentionally presents a history of Israel which, in contrast to most OT sources, pictures a "people of Israel in the land of Israel, as a continuous and uninterrupted reality from Jacob/Israel on" (218). Japhet may be right respecting the Chronicler's assumptions, but considering the relatively few and obscure clues on which she builds her case, it is hard to accept the deliberate intentionality she attributes to the Chronicler in this respect.

e. The Literary Prophets to the End of the Exile. Although the literary prophets stand outside the flow of the large narrative complexes (Pentateuch, Deuteronomistic History, Chronicler's History), they provide distinctive supplementary perspectives. Land is of central theological importance to all of them. Furthermore, they are historically correlated with that narrative by their (editorially supplied) headings. The emergence of a powerful class of landowners oppressing and/or displacing the small peasant from his inherited portion *(naḥălâ)* is the common indictment by Amos (3:9–10; 5:11; 6:4–7; 8:4, 6), Isaiah (3:13–15; 5:9–10; 10:1–2) and Micah (2:1–4; 3:1–3; 7:2–3), following Elijah's condemnation of Ahab's violence against Naboth (see above). All presuppose an obligation to administer in God's land a justice that involves equitable distribution of the land and its fruits. For Amos and Micah, this responsibility is rooted in God's expulsion of the previous inhabitants and his gift of the land to Israel coming out of Egypt (Amos 2:9; 9:7; Mic 6:4–5). For Isaiah, Israel's responsibility emerges from a pristine state of righteousness of Jerusalem/Zion. Amos and Micah announce God's judgment in the form of land loss and exile (Amos 4:1–3; 5:27; 6:7; 7:11; 9:4, 9, 15; Mic 1:16; 2:4; 4:10; 5:2—Eng 5:3), while Isaiah emphasizes the humiliation of Jerusalem (and Judah) through Assyrian military onslaught (1:7–9, 24–25; 3:18–26; 5:26–30; 7:20; 10:5–6; etc.).

Hosea and Jeremiah, steeped in the exodus tradition (Hos 2:17—Eng 2:15; 11:1; 12:14—Eng 12:14; 13:4; Jer 2:6; 7:22, 25; 31:32), extol an ideal time in the wilderness (Hos 2:16–17—Eng 2:14–15; 9:10; 13:5; Jer 2:2, 6; cf. 31:2–3), and indict the people for unfaithfulness in the land (Hos 2:3–17—Eng 2:1–15; 4:1–3, etc.). For Hosea, and for Jeremiah in his wake, this unfaithfulness takes the form of Canaanite or syncretistic fertility worship (Baalism) that seeks to ensure the fertility of the land through magical, often sexual, rites (Hos 2:7–15—Eng 2:5–13; 4:14–15; 7:16; 9:10; 11:2; 13:1–2; Jer 2:4–8, 20–25; 3:1–5, 6–10; 5:7–8; 13:20–27). The theme of social justice plays a lesser role in Hosea (4:1–3; 10:12–13; 12:7–9—Eng 12:6–8), but reemerges prominently in Jeremiah (2:34–35; 5:28; 6:13; 7:9; 21:12; 22:3, 13–17). Like Amos and Micah, both prophets announce God's judgment in the form of land devastation, loss, and exile (Hos 8:13; 9:3, 6, 17; 10:6; 11:5; Jer 4:23–28; 5:14–17; 8:10; 9:10, 11–15—Eng 9:11, 12–16; 10:18–22; 12:7–13; 13:24; 15:2, 14; 38:2; etc.).

The books of Amos, Micah, Hosea, and Jeremiah visualize a return of the people to the land (Amos 9:9–15; Hos 3:5; 11:11; Mic 4:6–7; 5:2–3—Eng 5:3–4; 7:11, 14, 15–20; Jer 12:15; 16:14–15; 23:7–8; 29:10–14; 30:1–3, 10–11; 31; 32:15 [for a full listing and discussion, see Martens 1972]), while Isaiah mainly projects the purification and exaltation of Jerusalem/Zion as the center of God's rule over the whole earth (2:2–4 = Mic 4:1–3; 4:2–6; 8:23–9:6—Eng 9:1–7; 10:20–27; 11:6–9; 12; 16:4–5; 17:12–14; 19:16–25; etc.).

A reminder is in order that we are sketching the picture offered by the canonical texts. The statement in the previous paragraph particularly takes into account many passages judged by various scholars to be secondary: the conclusion of Amos (9:11–15); Hos 2:18–25—Eng 2:16–23; Isa 2:2–4; Micah 4–5; Jeremiah 30–33; and others. In the case of Isaiah, the canonical combination of the words of the Jerusalem prophet with later prophecies, primarily in chaps. 40–66, not only strengthens the emphasis on restoration, but fuses the theme of purification and exaltation of Jerusalem with that of return from exile by way of a new exodus (see below).

The whole range of prophetic motifs discussed so far is appropriated, shaped, and expanded in the book of Ezekiel. Taking up the Abrahamic promise (33:24; cf. 20:42), Israel's origins in foreign lands (16:3, 45), and her stay in Egypt (20; 23:3), while scarcely mentioning a conquest (cf. 20:28), the book highlights Israel's unfaithfulness through idolatry (6:1–7, 13; 8; 14:1–11; 16:15–22) as the basis for land loss and exile. It gives less attention to social injustice (but cf. 22:6–12). Characteristically for Ezekiel the land is "Israel's land"; both *ʾereṣ* and *ʾădāmâ* are used (with the same meaning, according to Zimmerli 1985: 255). It is described lovingly as "the most glorious of all lands" (20:6; cf. Jer 3:19; Dan 8:9; 11:16, 41, 45; Zimmerli 1985: 253). Yahweh's future, however, according to Ezekiel (and Jeremiah before him, cf. Jeremiah 29) lies with those who have taken up exile (11:15–16). They will be "revived" by Yahweh (37:1–14) and will return to the land (11:17–21; 20:40–44; 34:11–16; 37:15–28 [for a full listing and discussion, cf. Martens 1972]). In fact, Yahweh himself has taken leave of his house and his city to "emigrate" with the exiles (chaps. 8–11) and will return with them eventually to the temple (43:1–5) in a land restored according to the elaborate blueprint laid out in chaps. 47–48. The latter is a combination of a realistically reconstituted Israel with images of supramundane symbolism. Central to it is the equitable distribution of the land to all Israel, including the sojourners (47:13–23), according to a tribal pattern grouped around the sanctuary (48:1–29).

Deutero-Isaiah (Isaiah 40–55) also announces to the exiles in Babylon the dawning of a new age, patterned typologically on Israel's salvation history, from creation to the occupation of the land (Anderson 1962: 177–95). While the accent falls on the new exodus, the salient land motifs of the Pentateuch and Joshua, combined with the significance of Zion in Jerusalemite theology (cf. Isa 2:2–4), play an important role. A new Israel redeemed from Babylon (48:20–21) will be led by God through a wilderness, turned into a Garden of Eden (40:3–5; 41:17–20; 42:14–16; 43:14–21; 48:21; 51:3) into her own land (49:8–12). There Jerusalem/Zion will become the exalted center for the whole earth (49:14–18; 52:1–10), when the Lord takes up residence in it (52:8; cf. Ezek 43:1–5).

f. The Postexilic Era. With its translation into an eschatological future, as seen in Ezekiel and Deutero-Isaiah and adumbrated in earlier prophets (cf. Hos 2:18–25—Eng 2:16–23; Isa 11:6–9), the OT's land theme has reached its ultimate narrative limit. There can be no expectation of its further extension once a redeemed people finds eschatological rest in the presence of God. This, together with the loss of sovereign control of the land by the Jews, accounts for the fact that "in the literature of the postexilic period there is an undeniable relocation of interest away from the land to the broadly human" (Davies 1974: 115; see pp. 110–15, he refers specifically to the books of Job, Proverbs, Ecclesiastes, Song of Songs, Esther, Jonah, and parts of Daniel).

This is only a partial picture, however. Their eschatological horizons did not preclude Ezekiel and Deutero-Isaiah from linking their prophecies to a concrete return to Palestine. Jeremiah had stated in totally non-eschatological terms that "houses and fields and vineyards shall again be bought in this land" (32:15) after an exile of 70 years (25:11–12; 29:10). Consequently, the Edict of Cyrus (Ezra 1:2–4; 6:1–5) and the subsequent return and rebuilding of a Jewish presence around Jerusalem and the temple (Ezra, Nehemiah) could at least in part be considered as fulfilment of prophecy and as a sign of God's impending universal rule.

Hanson (1979: 209–211, and throughout) has made it plausible that sociological tensions between a dominant priestly party and a suppressed visionary party in postexilic Jerusalem increasingly drove the latter from a "realized eschatology" to apocalyptic, eschatological expectations.

Hanhart (1983: 128–30) distinguishes between an early and a late postexilic phase. The former (basically the Persian period) is marked by the joy over the newly received land after a penance of 70 years that had restored to the land the sabbath years withheld earlier (2 Chr 36:21–23). The latter (basically the Greek period) is marked by a renewed lament over the impending punishment of Jerusalem for her guilt newly incurred after the exile (Isa 27:9–11).

However one thinks of these analyses, they support the observation that the land-motif remained of highest importance in the postexilic era. This is further supported if we remember that the Priestly source of the Tetrateuch was completed in the postexilic era (as Davies also notes, 1974: 115), and that the canonization process that gave preeminence to the land-dominated Pentateuch/Torah also falls into this era.

One must ask, further, whether the postexilic shift of emphasis "from the land to the broadly human" (Davies, see above), to the extent that it is valid, really represents a shift away from the land. Where Israel's relationship to the nations (Jonah, if it is postexilic) is treated, or where existence in the diaspora is shown to be possible and even positive, as in Esther and Daniel, the land is still the reference point for Israel's identity. For late postexilic prophecy (Deutero-Zechariah; Isaiah 24–27), Hanhart (1983: 131–33) has pointed out the significance of a new fluidity between the meaning of *ʾereṣ* as "land" and "earth." God's judgment and salvation of the *ʾereṣ* (of Israel, in the remnant form of Judah/Jerusalem) becomes increasingly a sign of God's acts with *ʾereṣ* (the whole earth). As Hanhart (1983: 128) remarks, "Die geschichtliche Erfahrung der nach-exilischen Prophetie ist das leidende Land als Symbol der leidenden Erde, ihre eschatologische Schau ist das erlöste Land als Symbol der erlösten Erde."

This is further illustrated in Joel (assuming a postexilic date), where the locust plague befalls the land (of Israel), but extends (from 2:1 on) to the whole earth (Hanhart 1983: 137, n. 3).

B. New Testament

1. Terminology. In most instances (RSV 43 times), "land" renders Greek *gē,* the standard LXX equivalent of both *ʾereṣ* and *ʾădāmâ.* Gk *gē* can also mean "earth" (see EARTH), "country, region" and "soil, ground." As translations of *gē,* "land" occurs in the following usages: (a) "Land of Israel" (Matt 2:20f.); (b) "land + name" (Sodom and Gomorrah, Matt 10:15; 11:24; Judea, John 3:22; Chaldeans, Acts 7:4; Canaan, Acts 13:19; Egypt, Acts 13:17; Jude 5); (c) "land" in contrast to water/sea (Matt 14:24, 34; Mark 4:1; 6:47, 53; Luke 5:3, 11; 8:27; John 6:21; 21:8, 9; Acts 27:43f.; Heb 11:29; Rev 10:2, 5, 8); (d) "land" as territory, area (Matt 27:45 = Mark 15:33 = Luke 23:44 [possibly "earth"]; Luke 4:25; Acts 27:39); (e) "land" as "ground, soil" (Luke 14:35; Heb 6:7); and (f) "this land" (Acts 7:4); and (g) "land of promise" (Heb 11:9).

In seven further instances, "land" occurs in a quotation or paraphrase from the OT: Matt 2:6 ("land of Judah," Mic 5:1—Eng 5:2); 4:15 ("land of Zebulun, land of Naphtali," Isa 8:23—Eng 9:1); Acts 7:3 ("the land which I will show you," Gen 12:1); Acts 7:6 ("aliens in a land belonging to others," Gen 15:13), Acts 7:29 ("land of Midian," Exod 2:15), Acts 7:40 ("land of Egypt," Exod 32:1); and Heb 8:9 ("land of Egypt," Jer 31:32).

As translation of *ʾagros,* "land" occurs three times in the combination "house(s) or/and . . . lands" (Matt 19:29; Mark 10:29f.). "Land" renders *chōra* in the phrases "the land of a rich man" (Luke 12:16) and "they were nearing land" (Acts 27:27), and *chōrion* in four instances treats land as an economic commodity (Acts 4:34; 5:3, 8; 28:7). Further, three occurrences of land in the RSV are supplied by the translators on the basis of the context (Luke 4:26; Acts 27:14; 2 Cor 10:16). In addition, *tēn gēn* in Matt 5:5, usually translated "earth," could possibly be rendered "land."

2. Theology. Apart from the introduction of OT land perspectives carried forward in quotations or allusions from the OT introduced for reasons other than their land theology, only four texts warrant any scrutiny for possible theological implications:

a. In Matt 2:20f. the angel of the Lord tells Joseph, "Take the child and his mother with you and go back to the land of Israel" (*eis gēn ʾIsraēl;* v 20), and Joseph complies immediately (v 21). Here we encounter twice the expression "land of Israel" (equivalent to Heb *ʾereṣ yiśrāʾēl*) so conspicuously avoided in the OT (see above). While no overt theological interpretation is offered, it seems certain that a parallelism between the journey of Israel's messiah and the earlier journey of Israel from Egypt to the promised land, now "Israel's land," is intended (cf. 2:15 and Hos 11:1). In that case, this naming of the land would appear to suggest a certain continuing validity of the OT's theological meaning of that land.

b. The third beatitude calls the meek happy, "for they shall inherit the earth/land" (*tēn gēn,* Matt 5:5). As all the beatitudes characterize citizenship in the kingdom of God, G. Strecker (1983: 193) may be right in considering the land to be spiritualized here (cf. Mark 10:14; Luke 22:28–30). On the other hand, a certain realism of land ownership could also be in view, although the extent of such kingdom-land (Israel? the earth?) remains undefined.

c. "Land" occurs six times in Stephen's speech in Acts 7 (vv 3, 4, 4, 6, 29, 40), where Stephen's Jewish hearers are reminded of their history of wandering between Mesopotamia and Egypt. While Stephen affirms the promise of the land to Abraham (vv 3, 17) and its divinely empowered conquest by Joshua (v 45), it is possible to see in his speech a certain negative slant against Judaism's claim to the land. Abraham did not experience the fulfillment of the land promise (v 5). Israel's time of closeness to God was the wilderness period (vv 44–45). Their stay in the land was marked by idolatry leading to exile, and the building of the Temple by Solomon seems an ill-considered, if not rebellious, act of confining the Lord of the universe (vv 47–51; Townsend 1972: 12).

d. Finally, the "land of promise" to Abraham is mentioned in Heb 11:9 (his "inheritance," v 8), but only for the purpose of reinterpretation. In keeping with the theology of Hebrews (see below), the writer emphasizes that Abraham and the other patriarchs were "strangers and exiles on the earth" (*ʾepi tēs gēs;* also "upon the land"), "seeking a homeland" *(patrida,* v 14), and "a better country, that is, a heavenly one" (v 16). Here the land realism of the OT is totally dissolved, not only for the NT era, but even retrospectively for Abraham.

These four texts, then, suggest both continuity and transformation in the NT's response to the OT's land theology. This observation will be confirmed by our study of certain less direct evidence (below). The paucity of theological material identifiable by the key word "land" raises the question whether that theme, so ubiquitous in the OT, has lost its significance in the NT, or whether it comes to expression in different ways. W. D. Davies, having pointed out the meager occurrence of specific references to the land in the Apocrypha, the Pseudepigrapha, and the Qumran scrolls (1974: 49), finds in an extensive investigation (1974: 49–158) that a "certainty of the ultimately indissoluble connection between Israel and the land was living and widespread in the world within which Christianity emerged" (1974: 157). Might the same not be true of emerging Christianity and its Scriptures? A full investigation would transcend the scope of this article; only a few directions can be indicated here in a sampling way. In doing so, we will focus on the canonical sources, rejecting (with Davies 1974: 336–44, Hengel 1971, Klassen 1984: 72–109, and others) the notion that the "historical" Jesus had zealotlike, violent insurrectionist (Brandon 1967) or less violent but nevertheless also revolutionary (Townsend 1972) aspirations to liberate the land from Roman rule.

On the side of the NT's continuity with the OT's land motifs, the following observations are pertinent:

a. The Gospels portray Jesus as a Jew linked genealogically (Matt 1:1–17, 20; Luke 3:23–37), but also geographically (Matt 2:1–6; Luke 2:4) to Israel generally and to the lineage and kingship of David in particular (e.g., Matt 9:27; cf. Rom 1:3). Despite the significance of other places (and Galilee as a whole; see below), Jerusalem retained a central importance in his ministry. He carried out his ministry within the approximate boundaries of OT "Israel," including Judah (Alt 1961), limiting his mission to the "house of Israel" (Matt 10:5–6; 15:24; Manson 1964), highlighting this limitation by occasional and conscious extensions of it to gentiles and/or gentile territory (e.g., Matt 8:5–13 = Luke 7:1–10; Mark 7:24–30 = Matt 15:21–28). The fact that the extension of his mission to the gentiles by the early Church seemed radical and tension-filled (Acts 10; 15) confirms the above characterization of the ministry of Jesus.

b. The Jesus of the Gospels also lived as a Jew with respect to the law, the synagogue and the Temple (e.g., Matt 5:17–18; Luke 2:49; 4:16; 6:6–7; 22:8). Again, his departures from Pharisaic-Rabbinic perspectives at some points, mainly (though not only) relating to the Sabbath (e.g., Mark 3:1–6 and parallels), merely highlights his extensive acceptance of the law with its close links to land and Temple. These departures are part of the tradition of reinterpretation in light of either their earlier and original, or their final, eschatological significance. In this faithfulness to the law, he was again followed by the early Church (Acts 2:46; 3:1; 5:42; 21:20; Gal 2:7–9), and by Jewish (Ebionite) Christians for a long time (Strecker 1983: 196–99). The reduction of legal obligations for gentiles took the form of a spirit-guided innovation (Acts 10; 15) which resulted in a theologico-geographical parallel existence of Jewish and gentile Christianity, rather than the abrogation of the OT and Jewish geographical-legal *realia* (Davies' term).

c. The extension of the gospel to the gentiles is in itself not a contravention of OT land theology, but can be seen as the development or fulfillment, even in geographical terms, of a variety of OT motifs, such as the Abrahamic blessing for the nations (Gen 12:3). God's concern for the nations as expressed in the prophetic "foreign nations oracles" (e.g., Amos 1:3–2:3), in the book of Jonah, and especially in the theme of the eschatological significance of God's work in and with Israel for all nations (e.g., Isa 2:2–4 = Mic 4:1–3; Isa 19:23–25; 49:6; 56:7).

d. Even the conscious and innovative extension, most evident in the missionary activity of Paul, retains Jerusalem as its starting point (Acts 1:8; 2; 8:1; 11:27) and, in a certain sense, its center (Acts 8:14; 9:26–30, cf. Gal 1:18–19; 15:1–35; 16:4). For himself, as a Jew, Paul retains the validity of the law and the Temple (Acts 21:17–26), albeit with some modifications, such as table-fellowship with the gentiles (Gal 2:11–14). Most significant is his apparent validation of the eschatological significance of the Jerusalem Temple in 2 Thess 2:4 (Davies 1974: 193f.).

On the other hand, new approaches to land and land-related motifs in the NT are patently clear. Three types of evidence can be distinguished: abrogation, symbolization, and transformation and extension. It goes without saying that the boundaries between these usages are often fluid.

a. Abrogation of the OT's land theology or aspects thereof, in explicit terms, is not frequent in the NT. It finds its clearest expression in Hebrews. Here, even the historical promise of land to Abraham, though acknowledged (11:8–16), is retroactively redirected to "a better country, that is, a heavenly one" (11:16, see above). Elsewhere, the land is excluded from the Abrahamic promise

(6:13). While the fall of Jericho is mentioned (11:30), the occupation of the land is omitted. The saints are described as "strangers and exiles" (11:13), "wandering over deserts and mountains, and in dens and caves of the earth (or land?)" (11:38). Strangers and exiles does not mean here long-term guests in God's land (cf. Lev 25:23, see above), but geographically footloose wanderers toward eternity. Israel's covenant, law, cultus, and priesthood are shadows of their higher, heavenly parallels and must pass away (8:13). Christ is the heavenly high priest after the order of Melchizedek, who is "without father or mother or genealogy," being "king of Salem, that is king of peace," i.e., no longer the earthly city of Gen 14:18 (7:2–3). Christ the high priest, who died "outside the gate" (13:12) as a one-time sacrifice, officiates in a "heavenly sanctuary" (8:5), also called "Mt. Zion . . . the heavenly Jerusalem" (12:22), where he will give rest [the OT equivalent of the promised land, see above] to the saved (chaps. 2–3). In everything, the *realia* of the OT are bracketed out as ephemeral shadows of nongeographical, nonphysical eternal realities.

Possibly the rejection of the Temple in the speech of Stephen (Acts 7; see above) expresses a similar perspective.

We must also list here, however, the fact that the references to land promises and land theology, so ubiquitous in the OT, are mentioned sparingly, as already discussed.

There are aspects of the theology of Paul that may belong here, too. Davies (1974: 164–220) notes that Paul, as a Jew, must have been keenly aware of the *realia* of Judaism, and that it is therefore the more remarkable that he hardly refers to the land or to any theological significance of geography. Abraham is, for him, the model of faith leading to righteousness. "Paul ignores completely the territorial aspect of the promise" (Davies 1974: 178). Davies sees this not only as absence of concern for the land, but as deliberate rejection. The land-related law, for Paul, is an interlude, now completed, between the universal promise to Abraham and its fulfillment in Jesus Christ (p. 179). Davies can speak of the "deterritorializing of the promise," which is now "located," not in a place but in the person of Jesus Christ (p. 179). While all this is undoubtedly true, we will need to return to Paul in our next two sections.

b. Symbolization. We are concerned here with NT uses of the OT's land motifs in such a way as to carry forward their meanings without their geographical realism. For the most part, the new meanings are anchored either in Jesus and his church, or in an eschatological, transcendent future. The common denominator for both is the (present and/or future) kingdom of God. In the context of Hebrews, we already noted the transformation of "land," "Mt. Zion," "inheritance," and "rest" into images of heavenly salvation. "Wilderness" (some translations: "lonely place") becomes the context of temptation (e.g., Matt 4:1–11 = Luke 4:1–13), but also of encounter with God (e.g., Luke 5:16). "Mountain" signifies manifestation of God (e.g., Mark 9:2–8 = Matt 17:1–8 = Luke 9:28–36), while "sea" symbolizes the unruly powers to be subjected to God's rule (e.g., Mark 4:35–41 = Matt 8:23–27 = Luke 8:22–25). "Temple" is, especially for Paul, the presence of God in the believer and the church (e.g., 1 Cor 3:16f.; but cf. our discussion of 2 Thess 2:4, above). "Jerusalem/Zion" comes to mean the eternal goal of the Christian's pilgrimage, the ultimate presence of God (Heb 11:10; 12:22; Rev 21:1–4).

In the gospel of John, the meaning of land motifs is repeatedly projected onto the person of Jesus. He, not Jacob's well, is the source of life-giving water (4:7–15). He, not the Pool of Bethesda, offers healing (5:2–9). He is the bread of life, the manna in the wilderness (6:31–35). His body is the Temple that will be destroyed and resurrected (2:18–21).

With less recourse to geographical terminology, Paul also focuses the land promises of the OT on Jesus, who is the entrance to the believers' inheritance (Gal 3:29–4:7), and in whom the promise to Abraham is fulfilled (Gal 3:15–18; Rom 4:16). While his "localization" of many of the OT's land-related *realia* (goal of promise, inheritance) "in Christ" can be seen as a rejection of the theological relevance of place, it is also true that the incarnate Christ himself represents a certain realism of geographical presence associated with the places of his ministry and the memories that attach to them. This realism of the incarnation then continues in the presence of the resurrected Christ in his body, the church, and its members, repeatedly referred to as "temple" by Paul (1 Cor 3:16–17; Davies 1974: 187).

Davies also recognizes this new realism in Christ, both geographical and transcendent, and finds in it the common denominator for the twofold emphasis to which his extensive investigation of land theology in the Pauline, Synoptic, Johannine (gospel) materials and of Jesus himself leads him: (1) "It is justifiable to speak of the *realia* [land, Jerusalem, Temple] of Judaism as being 'spiritualized' in the Christian dispensation" (Davies 1974: 366). (2) As Jesus had lived in a particular land, "the space and spaces which he occupied took on significance, so that the *realia* of Judaism continued as *realia* in Christianity" (366). The "reconciling principle," for Davies (367), is the person of Jesus Christ: "The New Testament finds holy space wherever Christ is or has been; it personalizes 'holy space' in Christ."

c. Transformation and Extension. In his conclusions just presented, and throughout his investigation, Davies partly acknowledges but largely deemphasizes or rejects a new theologico-geographical realism in the NT. This new "geography of faith" appears to the present writer to be the theologically most significant legacy of the OT's land themes in the NT (Janzen 1973). We noted above that Jesus' limitation of his mission to "Israel" suggests a certain intentionality in the geographical pattern of his ministry. There is a wealth of evidence in the gospels, in Acts, and in the Pauline writings that such an intentionality far exceeded the mere limitation of Jesus' own mission, and later expansion of it, into the gentile world. It appears that Jesus and the early Church, far from being aterritorial in theology, believed and lived out a new theologico-geographical realism. This consisted, in part, of the acceptance of earlier Israelite-Jewish *realia* (see above); in part, of the transformation of these, not only into symbolic meanings (see above), but into new geographical patterns and perspectives; and in part, of the creation of new geographical *realia* for faith.

The most prominent proposal in this direction is the so-called Lohmeyer-Lightfoot Theory (Lohmeyer 1936;

Lightfoot 1937), which finds in Mark, and less prominently in Matthew, a geographical theology centering in Galilee as the new "holy land." There Jesus began his ministry, called his disciples, experienced the transfiguration. Galileans were his first followers, and became almost synonymous with "Christians." Jerusalem was the place of opposition and rejection. While the resurrection took place in Jerusalem, the parousia would come in Galilee (Mark 14:28; 16:7). There the church was founded. It was the land that dwelt in darkness, but saw a great light (Matt 4:15–16, cf. Isa 8:23–9:1—Eng 9:1–2).

Davies (1974: 221–43) and G. Stemberger (1974: 409–38) reject this thesis as a "uniform pattern" (Stemberger 1974: 435), but Stemberger, has to admit "a certain emphasis on Galilee in the gospels" (435). "That Christ had chosen to exercise his ministry in Galilee, this fact underlined the paradox of the incarnation. . . . It is precisely to the despised and lowly people that Christ comes" (436), Galilee being of low regard in that time. Whether or not the many ramifications of the Lohmeyer-Lightfoot theory can be substantiated or not, is less important than the now widely recognized fact that a new, Christian geographical realism is at work here, taking up the OT notion of the election of a geographical area, but no longer attaching such election to the land as understood in the OT.

For the gospel of Luke, H. Conzelmann (1961: 18–94) has demonstrated a remarkably rich and nuanced geographical symbolism as the carrier of that gospel's theological message. In contrast to Mark and Matthew, Jerusalem, rather than Galilee, is the goal and focus of Jesus' mission. His Galilean ministry serves the purpose of gathering witnesses (almost synonymous with "Galileans") who will travel with him to Jerusalem. They become witnesses by way of election. Jesus' natural relatives do not qualify as such. Rejected in his home town, Nazareth, Jesus chooses Capernaum, a town without sacred history, as the center of his activity, foreshadowing the movement of the gospel from Jews to Gentiles, presented later in the book of Acts.

In a long journey symbolizing his acceptance of his passion, Jesus reaches Jerusalem, where all prophets must die. He enters the city in a non-eschatological, nonpolitical act and cleanses the Temple, signifying the Church's claim to be the true Israel (Conzelmann 1961: 75). Contrary to the disciples' mistaken notion, however, Jerusalem is not the place of the parousia; the latter is still in the distant future. Instead, it is the place of the birth of the Church, from which witnesses will be led by the Spirit into all the world, a story told in Acts.

For the gospel of John, Nazareth, and in a sense, all Galilee, is the carrier of the *scandalon* of the incarnation. Over against Jesus' origin in Nazareth and Galilee, from where nothing good (1:46), and certainly no eschatological figure (7:41, 52), is expected, stands the evidence that he is from above (8:23). This is recognized by the Galileans, who receive him (1:43–51; 2:11; 4:45, 53–54), and to a lesser degree by the Samaritans (4:39–42). Meeks (1966: 165) points out that, on the other hand, "the journeys to Jerusalem in John, symbolize the coming of the redeemer to 'his own' and his rejection by them, while the emphasized movement from Judea to Galilee (especially 4:43–54) symbolizes the redeemer's acceptance by others, who thereby become truly 'children of God,' the real Israel." Once again, a new "sacred geography" has become the carrier of Christology.

It is less important whether the analyses of the theologico-geographical patterning of the gospels, sketched here in barest outline, can be substantiated in the forms presented. Nor are we concerned here with the precise relationship of the geographical data of the life of the "historical" Jesus to their theological interpretations in the different gospels. The important observation in our investigation of the NT's response to the OT's land theology consists of seeing considerable evidence for the significance of geography in the NT's theology. Regions, places, and journeys remain means capable of being drawn into God's service, i.e., of becoming "holy."

Instead of a static acceptance of the "holy land" and the "holy places" of the OT, the NT sees God as drawing geographical *realia,* old and new, into his service in connection with his new self-revelation in Jesus Christ. This divine employment of geography continues in the early Church, as presented in Acts. There it is the Spirit that effects the spread of the gospel from Jerusalem (in keeping with Lukan geographical theology) to "all Judea, Samaria, and to the ends of the earth" (Acts 1:8), in a divinely led and empowered geographical strategy (see also Acts 13:1–4; 16:6–10; 19:21; Gal 2:1–2; Matt 28:28). New lands and places are chosen, thereby becoming "holy." A certain static land theology has been broken open in such a way as to designate all places on the map as potentially holy, contingent on God's election through the Spirit (cf. Exod 20:24).

It is in this sense also that John 4:23 must be understood. To worship God "in spirit and in truth" is not to negate the ongoing significance of place in favor of an interiorized or otherworldly faith. It means to recognize the potential of all lands and places—of the whole ecosystem—to be chosen by the transcendent God of the Bible to work signs of his election and presence.

Bibliography

Alt, A. 1961. *Where Jesus Worked: Towns and Villages of Galilee.* Trans. K. Grayston. London.

———. 1966a. The Settlement of the Israelites in Palestine. Pp. 133–69 in *Essays on Old Testament History and Religion.* Trans. R. A. Wilson. Oxford.

———. 1966b. The God of the Fathers. Pp. 1–77 in *Essays on Old Testament History and Religion.* Trans. R. A. Wilson. Oxford.

Anderson, B. W. 1962. Exodus Typology in Second Isaiah. Pp. 177–95 in *Israel's Prophetic Heritage,* ed. B. W. Anderson and W. Harrelson. Garden City, NY.

Betz, O. 1970. Israel bei Jesus und im Neuen Testament. Pp. 275–89 in Eckert, Levinson, and Stöhr, eds. 1970.

Brandon, S. G. F. 1967. *Jesus and the Zealots.* Manchester.

Brueggemann, W. 1968. The Kerygma of the Deuteronomistic Historian. *Int* 22: 387–402.

———. 1972. Weariness, Exile and Chaos. *CBQ* 34: 19–31.

———. 1974. Israel's Sense of Place in Jeremiah. Pp. 149–65 in *Rhetorical Criticism,* ed. J. J. Jackson and M. Kessler. PTMS 1. Pittsburgh.

———. 1977. *The Land: Place as Gift, Promise and Challenge in Biblical Faith.* OBT 1. Philadelphia.

———. 1980. On Land-losing and Land-receiving. *Crux* 19: 166–73.

Clements, R. 1967. *Abraham and David: Genesis 15 and its Meaning for Israelite Tradition.* SBT 2/5. London.

Conzelmann, H. 1961. *The Theology of St. Luke.* Trans. G. Buswell. New York.

Cross, F. M. 1962. Yahweh and the God of the Patriarchs. *HTR* 55: 225–59.

Davies, W. D. 1974. *The Gospel and the Land: Early Christianity and Jewish Territorial Doctrine.* Berkeley.

Diepold, P. 1972. *Israel's Land.* BWANT 5th ser. 15. Stuttgart.

Eckert, W. P.; Levinson, N. P.; and Stöhr, M., eds. 1970. *Jüdisches Volk-gelobtes Land.* Abhandlungen zum christlich-jüdischen Dialog 3. Munich.

Epp-Tiessen, D. J. 1981. *Jeremiah's Theology of Land.* M.A. thesis University of Manitoba.

Forshey, H. O. 1973. *The Hebrew Root NHL and Its Semitic Cognates.* Ph.D. diss. Harvard.

Gerlemann, G. 1977. Nutzrecht und Wohnrecht. Zur Bedeutung von *ʾăḥuzzâ* und *naḥălâ.* *ZAW* 89: 313–25.

Gottwald, N. 1979. *The Tribes of Yahweh.* Maryknoll, NY.

Hanhart, R. 1983. Das Land in der spätnachexilischen Prophetie. Pp. 126–40 in Strecker, ed. 1983.

Hanson, P. D. 1979. *The Dawn of Apocalyptic.* Rev. ed. Philadelphia.

Hengel, W. 1971. *Was Jesus a Revolutionist?* FBBS 28. Trans. W. Klassen. Philadelphia.

Horst, F. 1961. Zwei Begriffe für Eigentum (Besitz): *naḥălâ* und *ʾăḥuzzâ.* Pp. 135–56 in *Verbannung und Heimkehr,* ed. A. Kuschke. Tübingen.

Janzen, W. 1973. Geography of Faith: A Christian Perspective on the Meaning of Places. *Studies in Religion/Sciences Religieuses* 3: 166–82. Repr. 137–57 in *Still in the Image.* Institute of Mennonite Studies Series 6. Newton, KS, 1982.

Japhet, S. 1979. Conquest and Settlement in Chronicles. *JBL* 98: 205–18.

———. 1983. People and Land in the Restoration Period. Pp. 103–25 in Strecker, ed. 1983.

Kaiser, W. C., Jr. 1973. The Promise Theme and the Theology of Rest. *BSac* 130: 135–50.

Kartveit, M. 1989. *Motive und Schichten der Landtheologie in I Chronik 1–9.* Stockholm.

Klassen, W. 1984. *Love of Enemies.* OBT 15. Philadelphia.

Lightfoot, R. H. 1937. *Locality and Doctrine in the Gospels.* New York.

Lohfink, W. 1967. *Die Landverheissung als Eid: Eine Studie zu Genesis 15.* SBS 28. Stuttgart.

Lohmeyer, E. 1936. *Galiläa und Jerusalem.* Göttingen.

Manson, T. W. 1964. *Only to the House of Israel? Jews and Non-Jews.* FBBS 9. Philadelphia.

Marguardt, F.-W. 1975. *Die Juden und ihr Land.* Hamburg.

Martens, E. 1972. *Motivations for the Promise of Israel's Restoration to the Land in Jeremiah and Ezekiel.* Ph.D. diss. Claremont.

Meeks, W. A. 1966. Galilee and Judea in the Fourth Gospel. *JBL* 85: 159–69.

Mendels, D. 1987. *The Land of Israel as a Political Concept in Hasmonean Literature.* Texte und Studien zum Antiken Judentum 15. Tübingen.

Mendenhall, G. E. 1962. The Hebrew Conquest of Palestine. *BA* 25: 66–87. Repr. *BAR* 3: 100–20.

Minear, P. S. 1983. Holy People, Holy Land, Holy City: The Genesis and Genius of Christian Attitudes. *Int* 37: 18–31.

Ohler, A. 1979. *Israel, Volk und Land.* Stuttgart.

———. 1981. Landbesitz-Teilhabe am Gotteserbe. *BK* 36: 201–6.

Perlitt, J. 1983. Motive und Schichten der Landtheologie im Deuteronomium. Pp. 46–58 in Strecker, ed. 1983.

Plöger, J. G. 1967. *Literarkritische, formgeschichtliche und stilkritische Untersuchungen zum Deuteronomium.* Bonn.

Rad, G. von. 1966a. *The Problem of the Hexateuch and Other Essays.* Trans. E. W. T. Dicken. Edinburgh.

———. 1966b. There Remains Still a Rest for the People of God: An Investigation of a Biblical Conception. Pp. 94–102 in von Rad 1966a.

———. 1966c. The Form-Critical Problem of the Pentateuch. Pp. 1–78 in von Rad 1966a.

———. 1966d. The Promised Land and Yahweh's Land in the Hexateuch. Pp. 79–93 in von Rad 1966a.

Rendtorff, R. 1970. Das Land Israel im Wandel der Alttestamentlichen Geschichte. Pp. 153–68 in Eckert, Levinson, and Stöhr, eds. 1970.

———. 1975. *Israel und sein Land.* ThEH 188. Munich.

———. 1985. *The Old Testament: An Introduction.* Trans. J. Bowden. Philadelphia.

Robinson, W. C., Jr. 1960. The Theological Context for Interpreting Luke's Travel Narrative (9:51ff.). *JBL* 79: 20–31.

———. 1964. *Der Weg des Herrn. Studien zur Geschichte und Eschatologie im Lukas-Evangelium.* Wissenschaftliche Beiträge zur kirchlich-evangelischen Lehre 36. Hamburg-Bergstedt.

Rost, L. 1965. Die Bezeichnungen für Land und Volk im Alten Testament. Pp. 76–101 in *Das kleine Credo und andere Studien zum Alten Testament.* Heidelberg.

Sanders, J. A. 1972. *Torah and Canon.* Philadelphia.

Schmid, H. H. 1970. Messiaserwartung und Rückkehr in das Land Israel nach dem Alten Testament. Pp. 188–96 in Eckert, Levinson, and Stöhr, eds. 1970.

Seebas, H. 1977. Landverheissungen an die Väter. *EvT* 37: 210–29.

Stegemann, H. 1983. "Das Land" in der Tempelrolle und in anderen Texten aus den Qumranfunden. Pp. 154–71 in Strecker, ed. 1983.

Stemberger, G. 1974. Galilee—Land of Salvation? Appendix IV, pp. 409–38 in Davies 1974.

Strecker, G. 1983. Das Land in frühchristlicher Zeit. Pp. 188–200 in Strecker, ed. 1983.

Strecker, G., ed. 1983. *Das Land Israel in biblischer Zeit.* GTA 25. Göttingen.

Townsend, T. J. 1972. Israel's Land Promises under the New Covenant. Paper prepared for the Commission on Faith and Order of the National Council of Churches of Christ.

Waldow, H. E. von. 1974. Israel and Her Land: Some Theological Considerations. Pp. 493–508 in *A Light to My Path,* ed. N. Bream, R. D. Heim, and C. A. Moore. Philadelphia.

Weinfeld, M. 1983. The Extent of the Promised Land—the Status of Transjordan. Pp. 59–75 in Strecker, ed. 1983.

Wildberger, H. 1956. Israel und sein Land. *EvT* 16: 404–22.

Williamson, H. G. M. 1977. *Israel in the Books of Chronicles.* Cambridge.

Wirth, W. 1970. Die Bedeutung der biblischen Landverheissung für die Christen. Pp. 312–21 in Eckert, Levinson, and Stöhr, eds. 1970.

Wolff, H. W. 1966. The Kerygma of the Yahwist. *Int* 20: 131–58.

Zimmerli, W. 1985. The "Land" in the Pre-Exilic and Early Post-Exilic Prophets. Pp. 247–62 in *Understanding the Word,* ed. T. Butler, E. W. Conrad, and B. C. Ollenburger. JSOTSup 37. Sheffield.

W. Janzen

LAND LAWS. See LAW, BIBLICAL AND ANE; also FAMILY.

LANGUAGES. This entry examines the various languages that are associated with the biblical text and the ANE and Mediterranean cultures of which the biblical writers were a part. It consists of 16 separate articles, the first of which provides a systematic survey and overview of the plethora of languages that constituted the ancient world of the Bible. There follow articles on Akkadian, Aramaic, Byblos Syllabic, Coptic, Egyptian, Ethiopic, Greek, Hebrew, Hittite, Hurrian, the languages of Iran, Latin, Phoenician, South Arabian, and Ugaritic.

INTRODUCTORY SURVEY

The many languages attested in the ANE records are most conveniently surveyed according to their classification into language families.

A. The Afroasiatic Language Family
  1. The Semitic Languages
    a. East Semitic
    b. West Semitic
      (1) South Semitic
      (2) Central Semitic
  2. Egyptian
B. The Indo-European Language Family
  1. Anatolian
  2. Indo-Iranian (Aryan)
  3. Hellenic
  4. Phrygian
C. Hurrian and Urartian
  1. Hurrian
  2. Urartian
D. Other Languages
  1. Sumerian
  2. Elamite
  3. Qutian
  4. Hattic
  5. Kassite
E. Undeciphered Languages and Scripts
  1. Cretan and Cypriot Scripts
  2. Byblian Hieroglyphs
  3. Deir ʿAllā Clay Tablets
  4. Meroitic

A. The Afroasiatic Language Family

For much of the ancient period the most widespread group of languages spoken in the Near East was the Semitic group, which will be described in detail below. The Semitic languages constitute one branch of a large language family now usually called Afroasiatic (or Afrasian; formerly Hamito-Semitic). The Afroasiatic family comprises six branches: (1) *Semitic* (see below, A.1); (2) *Egyptian* (see below, A.2); (3) *Berber:* several modern languages and dialects distributed across N Africa from Egypt to Mauritania, such as *Shilḥ, Tamazight, Kabyle,* and *Tuareg* (in which an early consonantal alphabet continues to be used); perhaps also an ancient language, often called *Numidian,* attested in alphabetic (consonantal) inscriptions from Libya, one of which is dated 139 B.C.E. (despite the existence of a few Numidian-Punic and Numidian-Latin bilinguals, the language remains virtually unintelligible); (4) *Cushitic:* a group of some 40 languages spoken by about 15 million people in east central Africa (Ethiopia, Somalia, Kenya), such as *Oromo, Somali, Afar-Saho, Sidamo, Agaw,* and *Beja;* no ancient representatives of this branch are attested; (5) *Omotic:* about 40 languages spoken by just over a million people, mostly in W Ethiopia; previously classified as, and still considered by some scholars to be, a western subbranch of Cushitic; no ancient Omotic languages received written form; and (6) *Chadic:* a large group containing at least 125 languages in several subgroups spoken in W Africa (Cameroun, Chad, Niger, Nigeria); the most important member is *Hausa,* spoken by about 25 million people in Nigeria, Niger, and elsewhere; none of the Chadic languages is attested before the modern period.

1. The Semitic Languages. Semitic, a relatively close-knit family of highly inflected languages, has the longest recorded history of any linguistic group, spanning the period from the mid-3d millennium B.C.E. with Akkadian and Eblaite to the present day with Arabic, Amharic, and Hebrew. See Fig. LAN.01.

The Proto-Semitic phonological repertoire may be reconstructed as having contained three vowels, *a, i, u,* which could occur short or long *(ā, ī, ū),* and 29 consonants (all still distinguished in Old South Arabian); the consonants may be arranged according to their probable phonetic features as follows (traditional symbols appear in parentheses; Faber 1985, 1989):

Reconstruction of Probable Phonological Features of the Proto-Semitic Consonants

manner	stops			affricates			fricatives			approximants	nasals
place	voiced	voiceless	emphatic	voiced	voiceless	emphatic	voiced	voiceless	emphatic	voiced	voiced
bilabial	*b*	*p*								*w*	*m*
interdental							ð	θ	θʾ (θ̣)		
dental	*d*	*t*	*tʾ (ṭ)*							*r*	*n*
alveolar central				*d͜z (z)*	*t͜s (s)*	*t͜sʾ (ṣ)*		*s (š)*			
alveolar lateral						*(t)͜ɬ (ð̣)*		*ɬ (ś)*		*l*	
palatal										*y*	
velar	*g*	*k*	*kʾ (q)*				γ *(ġ)*	*x (ḫ)*			
pharyngeal							ʿ	*ḥ*			
glottal		ʾ						*h*			

Semitic morphology is strongly characterized, especially in its verbal forms, by what are termed discontinuous morphemes, which usually consist of three consonants; for example, the semantic field "to rule" is conveyed in Hebrew (and other Semitic languages) by the consonant sequence *m-l-k;* precise meaning and morphological information is conveyed by various modifications to this sequence, as in *timlōk,* "you (m.s.) will rule"; *himlîk,* "he caused to rule"; *melek,* "king"; *malkâ,* "queen"; *mĕlûkâ,* "kingship"; and *mamlākâ,* "kingdom."

Nouns in Proto-Semitic may be reconstructed as having three inflectional cases, each marked in the singular by one of the short vowels: e.g., nominative **baᶜlum,* "lord," genitive **baᶜlim,* and accusative **baᶜlam.* The final *-m* on these forms (⟶ *-n* in Arabic) originally marked the form as free, or not bound to a following genitive element, as opposed to the bound, or construct, form, as in **baᶜlu baytim,* "lord (nom.) of the house," or **baᶜlu-kă,* "your (masc. sing.) lord (nom.)." The noun exhibits two genders, masculine and feminine, the latter usually marked by one of a set of allomorphs, the most common of which are *-at* and *-t,* as in **baᶜlum,* "lord," and **baᶜlatum,* "lady." There are three numbers, singular, dual, and plural. Plurals are marked either by external endings, probably proper only to adjectives at first, as in **šalimum,* "whole," masc. pl. nom. **šalimūna* (gen.-acc. *-īna;* ⟶ *-ūma*/*-īma* in some languages), fem. pl. nom. **šalimātum* (gen.-acc. *-ātim*), or by modification of the pattern, as in classical Ethiopic (Geᶜez) *dabr,* "mountain," pl. *ʾadbār* (broken plurals; vestiges of this feature remain in languages that have otherwise generalized the external pl. markers, as in Hebrew *gibᶜâ* < **gibᶜatum,* "hill," pl. *gĕbāᶜōt* < **gibaᶜātum*).

The finite forms of the verb in early Semitic were undoubtedly very similar to the Akkadian preterite and durative forms, i.e., two conjugations inflected with prefixes (and suffixes in certain persons): a perfective form that functioned both as a past tense and as an injunctive (jussive), as in **yaqbir,* "he buried, may he bury" (m. pl. **yaqbirū,* "they buried, may they bury," 2fs **taqbirī,* "you buried, may you bury," etc.); and an imperfective form in which the middle consonant of the root was doubled, as in **yvqabbar,* "he buries, will bury" (m. pl. **yvqabbarū,* "they . . ."; 2fs **tvqabbarī,* "you . . ."). In addition, each verbal stem had associated with it an adjective (e.g., **qabir-,* "buried") that could be inflected by means of subject pronoun suffixes to form a predication, as in **qabir-a,* "he is/was buried"; **qabir-at,* "she . . ."; **qabir-(ā)kŭ,* "I . . ."; **qabir-tă,* "you (m.s.) . . ." Verbal roots also usually occurred in a number of stems characterized by internal changes, by prefixes (some of which became infixes in some languages), or by a combination of these features: e.g., **yišlam,* "he became whole," vs. **yušallim,* "he made whole"; **yaᶜbur,* "he went across," vs. **yušaᶜbir* (in some languages **yuhaᶜbir*), "he took across." The number and actual shape of these verbal stems varies among the languages, and their precise reconstruction in the proto-language remains unclear.

Many schemes of classification have been proposed during the course of research on Semitic during the last century and more. In the following outline the attested Semitic branches and languages will be presented essentially according to the genetic classification suggested by R. Hetzron (1976), with minor modifications.

a. East Semitic. This earliest-attested branch of Semitic includes only Akkadian and Eblaite. *Akkadian* was the language of the Semitic people of ancient Mesopotamia. Although it is not clear when the first speakers of Akkadian arrived in Mesopotamia, the earliest texts containing Akkadian material date from about 2600 B.C.E. Akkadian is written from left to right in the logo-syllabic cuneiform script borrowed from the unrelated Sumerian language (see below, D.1.). The long history of the language comprises a number of dialects: in the earliest period, ca. 2600–1950, the various regional dialects are collectively labeled *Old Akkadian;* thereafter, the *Assyrian* language in N Mesopotamia is differentiated from the *Babylonian* language in S Mesopotamia, and both Assyrian and Babylonian are further subdivided chronologically into Old (1950–1500), Middle (1500–1000), and Neo- (1000–625) phases; after the demise of Assyria and its language in ca. 625, Late Babylonian continues until the 1st century C.E., when the last Akkadian texts were written. See the separate entry on Akkadian (below).

Eblaite (also Eblaic) is the Semitic language of the Syrian city of Ebla, attested on cuneiform tablets dating to the 24th–23rd centuries B.C.E. Considered by some, especially when its discovery was first announced in the mid-1970s, to be an early diəlect of NW Semitic, it now seems more likely that Eblaite is most closely related to Akkadian, since it shares a number of significant linguistic innovations with the latter. The difficulties of Eblaite orthographic practice, which often differs from its contemporary Mesopotamian counterpart, continue to make both readings and classification difficult, however.

b. West Semitic. A major linguistic innovation that sets the rest of the Semitic family apart from the Eastern branch is the development of the verbal adjective with a subject suffix pronoun, as in **qabir-a,* "he is/was buried," into an active, perfective verb form, often with a vowel change: **qabar-a,* "he (has) buried." This development is attested in all "West Semitic" languages, that is, all Semitic languages apart from Akkadian and Eblaite. The earlier perfective form **yaqbir* was usually retained in its injunctive sense, "let him bury"; in some languages it also continued as a past-tense form, though now in secondary constructions, such as the Hebrew consecutive form *way-yiqbōr,* "and he buried." "West Semitic" can be subdivided into South Semitic and Central Semitic languages.

(1) South Semitic. The South Semitic languages exhibit the innovative perfective form **qabara.* The suffixes denoting the first person singular and all second persons of this form in South Semitic have *-k-,* whereas in the Central Semitic languages (see (2) below) these suffixes have *-t-:* compare classical Ethiopic (Geᶜez) *qabarku,* "I buried," *qabarka,* "you (m.s.) buried;" Mehri (Modern South Arabian) *qəbə́rk,* "I/you (m.s.) buried;" but Arabic *qabartu,* "I buried," *qabarta,* "you (m.s.) buried." In a more significant distinction, the South Semitic branch, unlike the Central, retains the early Semitic imperfective form, as in the following forms for "he buries": Geᶜez *yeqabber,* Mehri *yəqáwbər* (< **yəqōbər,* in which the originally doubled middle **-bb-* has been simplified); but Arabic *yaqbiru.* South

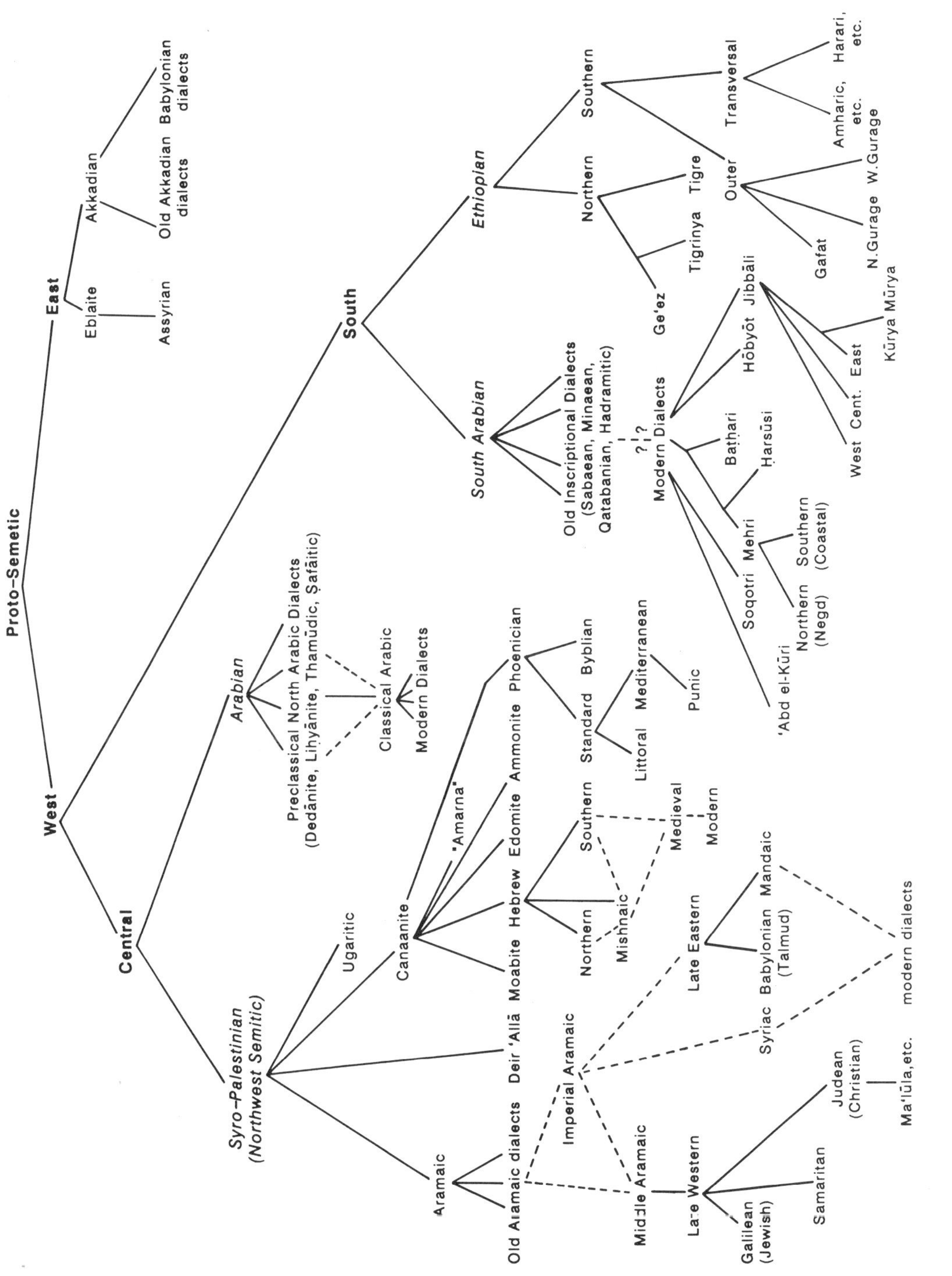

LAN.01. Chart showing the genetic classifications of the various Semitic languages.

Semitic comprises two subbranches, the South Arabian and the Ethiopian.

(a) South Arabian. There are two groups of South Arabian languages, ancient and modern. The relatedness of the two groups has often been assumed, partly because they overlap to some extent geographically and partly for sounder linguistic reasons, such as shared items of vocabulary and, in some instances, of morphology. Recently, however, the classification of the ancient group as part of the South branch of Semitic, and thus as closely related (or even ancestral) to the modern group, has been called into question with the suggestion that it belongs rather to Central Semitic (Voigt 1987).

The Old (or Epigraphic) South Arabian languages, for which the collective term *Ṣayhadic* has recently been proposed (Beeston 1984), are the following: *Sabaean* (or Sabaic; 6th century B.C.E., perhaps earlier, to 6th century C.E.); *Minaean* (or Minaic; 4th–2d centuries B.C.E.); *Qatabanian* (Qatabanic; 5th or 4th century B.C.E. to 3d C.E.); *Ḥaḍramitic* (4th century B.C.E. to 3d C.E.). These languages are attested in several thousand inscriptions, most of which have been found in the area covered by today's Yemen, although a few inscriptions have also come to light elsewhere in Arabia and even in Egypt, in old trading colonies. The best represented of the languages by far is Sabean, the other languages each being attested by a relative handful of inscriptions. The majority of the inscriptions are monumental in character, written boustrophedon in the earliest texts but consistently right to left thereafter, in a lapidary alphabetic script in which all 29 of the original Proto-Semitic consonants are distinctly represented. A few texts, however, are written in a cursive script that is not fully deciphered. The script is essentially consonantal in nature, although it is likely that *w* and *y* are used in some instances for *ū* and *ī*, respectively. Both the classification of these languages, which are usually regarded as part of South Semitic, and the nature of their relationship to the Modern South Arabian languages require further investigation. See the separate entry on South Arabian languages (below).

Modern South Arabian languages, currently spoken in Mahra province in Yemen and in Dhofar province in W Oman, probably share a common ancestor within the South Semitic branch. The languages are *Mehri,* with some 60,000 speakers of several dialects (including *Northern* or *Negd, Southern* or *Coastal;* note also the closely related *Ḥarsūsi,* and *Baṯḥari*); *Jibbāli* (formerly also referred to as Śḥeri or, incorrectly, as Šḥawri), with about 5,000 speakers (again, with several dialects, including that of the *Kūrya Mūrya* islands); *Soqoṭri,* with about 6,000 speakers on the islands of Soqoṭra, and *ʿAbd el-Kūri* (a subdialect); and *Hōbyōt,* with a small but indeterminate number of speakers. These languages are of considerable importance for the reconstruction of early Semitic, but have until recently not received the scholarly attention they deserve because of the uncertain reliability of the information about them; this situation began to improve greatly in recent years with the work of the late T. M. Johnstone. The languages have been known to Western scholarship only since the mid-19th century; they have no ancient forms, unless they may be considered direct descendants of one or more of the inscriptional Old South Arabian languages. As has been noted, however, the relationship between the ancient and modern groups is not clear. Two significant features argue for a close connection, at least with the Old South Arabian language Ḥaḍramitic: the form of the third person pronouns may be reconstructed for common Modern South Arabian as having begun with **ś* in the masc. and **s* in the fem., a curious pairing otherwise found in Semitic only in Ḥaḍramitic; the Modern South Arabian languages share with Ḥaḍramitic the preposition *h-,* "to, for."

(b) Ethiopian. Although no Ethiopian Semitic is attested before the common era, it is likely that the ancestor of these languages, which was closely related to the ancestor of the Modern South Arabian languages (and perhaps of the Old South Arabian tongues as well; see above), arrived in the horn of E Africa from the Arabian peninsula early in the 1st millennium B.C.E. Ethiopian Semitic has two subbranches, a northern and a southern; all of the languages exhibit some degree of influence from the Cushite language family, but the influence is markedly greater in the southern branch.

Northern Ethiopian comprises two modern languages, *Tigre* and *Tigrinya* (spoken in the northern Ethiopian provinces of Eritrea and Tigre), and, of greater importance to biblical studies, *Geʿez* (classical Ethiopic), the literary language of the Ethiopian Christian church. Literary Geʿez was probably based on the spoken language of Aksum in N Ethiopia, shortly after the Christianization of the country in the 4th century. In addition to a few monumental inscriptions from the 4th century and earlier, Geʿez is represented by an extensive Christian literature, much of it composed between the 5th and 10th centuries; at that time the spoken language probably died out with the fall of the Aksum empire, but Geʿez continued to be used in a frozen literary form until recent times. Much of the literature is either translated from or based on models in other languages (especially Greek), but there is also a large corpus of material composed in Geʿez. The earliest inscriptions are written in the Old South Arabian monumental script; the latter was adapted to a manuscript form (written from left to right) and furnished with diacritics to represent all but one of the Geʿez vowels distinctly. Most Geʿez manuscripts that have been preserved date back only to the 14th century, although a few may be from as early as the 12th or even the 11th century. See the separate entry on Ethiopic (below).

South Ethiopic comprises some 20 languages in two main subbranches (each of which has further divisions), including *Amharic,* the national language of modern Ethiopia, attested as a written language (in the Geʿez script) since the 16th century C.E.; *Harari,* the language of the city of Harar; *Gafat,* which recently died out; *Chaha;* and others.

(2) Central Semitic. The Central branch of Semitic shares with South Semitic the form *qabara* as an active perfective verb. As noted above, it differs from South Semitic in marking the first person singular and all second persons of that form by suffixes with *-t-* (as in Arabic *qabarta* and Hebrew *qābartā,* "you (m.s.) buried") rather than by suffixes with *-k-*. More importantly, Central Semitic exhibits a new form for the imperfective verb, the middle radical of which is not doubled (vs. South, East, and Proto-Semitic), and in which singular forms end in *-u* while masc. pl. forms end in *-ūna,* as in Arabic *yaqbiru,* "he buries," and *yaqbirūna,* "they (m.) bury." The origin of this imperfective is probably to be sought in the old subordinate (subjunctive) form attested in Akkadian (**yaqbir-u,* "who buried"; Hamori 1973). In Hebrew with the loss of final short vowels, the Central Semitic distinction between perfective/jussive **yaqbir,* "let him bury," and imperfective **yaqbiru,* "he buries," was lost in most verbs, as in *yiqbōr,* with both meanings; some verb types preserve the distinction, however, such as *yāqûm* < **yaqūmu,* "he stands," vs. *yāqōm* < **yaqum,* "may he stand"; *yibneh* < **yabniyu,* "he builds," vs. *yíben* < **yabni(y),* "let him build"; the alternative plural form *yiqbĕrûn,* "they will bury," which is always imperfective (i.e., never used for jussive or consecutive past tense; Hoftijzer 1985), also reflects the Central Semitic plural *yaqbirūna.*

The internal classification of the Central Semitic languages is a much debated topic. The scheme presented here suggests a bipartite division of Central Semitic into an Arabian branch and a Syro-Palestinian branch, the latter essentially consisting of the languages traditionally referred to as "Northwest Semitic."

(a) Arabian. The Arabian branch of Central Semitic comprises classical Arabic along with its antecedent inscriptional dialects and its colloquial spoken descendants.

Pre-Islamic inscriptions that are written in alphabetic scripts derived from the Old South Arabian and that exhibit close linguistic affinities with later classical Arabic are termed *Old* (or *Early*) *North Arabic.* Several dialects are distinguished: *Thamūdic,* comprising some 1,000 graffiti found in W and central N Arabia (especially in Midian), from the 6th century B.C.E. to the 4th century C.E., and including *Taymanite,* an early sub-branch in a special script found around the oasis of Tayma; *Dedānite* and later *Liḥyānite* inscriptions from the oasis of al-ʿUlā, ancient Dedān (NW Arabia), from the 5th or 6th century B.C.E.; *Ṣafāʾitic,* attested in over 15,000 graffiti, found in the region E of Damascus as far as Dura Europos and S to the northernmost reaches of modern Saudi Arabia, and dating from the 1st century B.C.E. to the 3d century C.E.; *Ḥasaean* (or Ḥasāʾitic), thus far some 30 texts, mostly funerary inscriptions, from al-Ḥasā in NE Saudi Arabia near the Persian Gulf.

Classical *Arabic,* the literary language of Islam, originated in the poetic *koinē* of the pre-Islamic and early Islamic Arabs, with influence from the Qurʾān, which exhibits features of the dialect of Mecca spoken by Muḥammad. The classical period of this language was the 8th and 9th centuries C.E. during which time it was systematized and standardized by grammarians in the cities of Kufa and Basra. Modern standard literary Arabic essentially exhibits the classical grammar, with updated vocabulary. Throughout the history of literary Arabic, the grammar of which was more or less fixed, spoken dialects have naturally existed and developed over time. Today there are many spoken forms of Arabic, often mutually unintelligible; these dialects have not usually received written form. Instances of literary Arabic that exhibit the influence of the spoken dialects are termed Middle Arabic.

Arabic is written from right to left with an alphabet that was borrowed from the Aramaic script used by the Nabateans (Arabic speakers who wrote in Aramaic) and modified to include six additional consonantal phonemes; in the consonantal script ʾ, *w,* and *y* are normally used to represent the long vowels *ā, ū,* and *ī,* respectively. In the 8th century the use of diacritics to indicate vowels, doubling, and other features was borrowed from Syriac.

(b) Syro-Palestinian ("Northwest Semitic"). The languages in this branch all share at least two linguistic innovations vis-à-vis common Central Semitic. One is the change of initial **w* to **y,* as in **warada* > **yarada* (> Hebrew *yārad*), "he descended," and **warx* > **yarx* (> Hebrew *yeraḥ*), "month." A more significant innovation occurred in the morphology: for the large group of monosyllabic triradical nouns, that is, *qatl, qitl,* and *qutl* forms, plurals came to be formed regularly and obligatorily by both inserting *a* between the second and third radicals and affixing the external plural markers (thus, *qatalūna, qitalātum,* and the like; cf. Hebrew *melek* < **malk-,* "king;" pl. *mĕlākîm* < **malakīma*).

(i) Early Dialects and Names, including "Amorite." The term *Amorite* is commonly used to refer to the large number of Semitic personal names attested in cuneiform sources from the late 3d and early 2d millennia B.C.E. that exhibit non-Akkadian, i.e., "West Semitic," features. The most recent collection lists over 6,000 such names (Gelb et al. 1980). Because some of the names exhibit typical NW Semitic features, such as the change of initial **w* to *y* (as in *ia-di-du-um,* "beloved," <√**wdd, ia-qa-rum,* "precious," <√**wqr*), the entire corpus of names is often labeled Northwest Semitic. But the corpus presents many severe practical difficulties from a linguistic point of view: it is negatively defined, simply as non-Akkadian Semitic; it spans the entire Near East and half a millennium; and it is not subject to normal linguistic tests for meaning, structure, and development, since names may lack any firm connection to the language spoken by their bearer. It is likely, therefore, that these names represent not a single language, or even necessarily a continuum of closely related dialects, but rather a diverse set of languages. It is a priori quite possibly, for example, that only some of the names reflect dialects that may be classified as Central Semitic, and only a subset of those as Northwest Semitic. (That some dialectal variations are exhibited by the names themselves has long been known.) Thus, since "Amorite" is not a linguistic unity, or even, perhaps, a linguistic entity, it is difficult to say anything meaningful about phonology, morphology, or classification that would obtain across the entire set of names.

Other early West Semitic names are attested in Egyptian sources, such as the Execration Texts (vases and statuettes inscribed with the names of foreign vassals, including Syro-Palestinian rulers, 20th–19th centuries B.C.E.), and lists of slaves' names (18th century). Among these names, many of which resemble many of those described above from cuneiform sources, are some with specifically NW Semitic features, such as initial **w* > *y* (e.g., *yqȝʿmw,* probably for */yaqar-ʿammu/,* "ʿAmmu-is-precious," with *yaqar* < **waqar*). Syro-Palestinian place names also appear in Egyptian texts over a long span of time, and these also provide some information about the history of the Semitic dialects in that area.

Inscriptions from both Palestine and the Sinai in an early, pictographic alphabet are generally held to reflect an archaic form of NW Semitic. The inscriptions found in Palestine probably date to the 17th–13th centuries B.C.E.; the date of those found at Serābīṭ el-Khādem in the Sinai is uncertain (15th century?). While a few letter combinations can be read with some confidence, such as *lbʿlt,* "for the Lady," much of the interpretation of these inscriptions remains uncertain.

Late Bronze period Akkadian texts from sites in Syria and Palestine contain many non-Akkadian Semitic names and, occasionally, non-Akkadian Semitic common words and constructions, reflecting the scribes' native languages. The problems discussed above in connection with the earlier "Amorite" names also apply to these forms, especially to the names. For the common words, particularly when they appear as glosses, there is at least a linguistic context on which to base an interpretation. Again, however, it is difficult to differentiate the various languages and dialects that are undoubtedly reflected in these texts; some forms in texts found at el-Amarna in Egypt exhibit distinctly Canaanite features, for which see under (iii) below.

(ii) Ugaritic. The language of the ancient city of Ugarit (modern Ras Shamra), *Ugaritic* was written from left to right on clay tablets with an indigenous alphabetic cuneiform script. The total number of texts and fragments published to date is over 1,100, all of them written during the 14th and 13th centuries B.C.E., although some may be copies of earlier compositions. The largest group are the economic or administrative texts; other genres attested are literary texts (myths and epics), rituals, letters, and a few contracts. Because the Ugaritic alphabet did not normally indicate vowels (except with the glottal stop ʾ), much of the phonology and morphology of Ugaritic is only partly understood. Some evidence for the vocalization of Ugaritic is provided by over 300 non-Akkadian words that appear in Akkadian texts found at Ras Shamra that were written by local scribes; these forms display features of the scribes' native language.

The classification of Ugaritic as a NW Semitic language is generally accepted. Its position within NW Semitic, however, has been a matter of considerable debate; some scholars consider Ugaritic to be a dialect of Canaanite, while others, noting that it does not participate in a number of Canaanite innovations (see (iii) below), argue that Ugaritic represents a separate branch of NW Semitic distinct from both Canaanite and Aramaic. See the separate entry on Ugaritic (below).

(iii) Canaanite. The Canaanite languages may be identified as those sharing the following innovations: the change of common NW Semitic **qattila* and **haqtila* to **qittila* and **hiqtila* in the perfects of the so-called "intensive" and causative conjugations, respectively (cf. Hebrew *Piʿēl* and *Hipʿîl*); the change of the first person sg. pronoun, originally **ʾanākū̆,* first to **ʾanōkū̆* with the unconditioned change of **ā* > **ō* (the "Canaanite shift") and then to **ʾanōkī̆* with dissimilation, and the concomitant (and more significant) change of **-tū̆* to **-tī̆* as the marker of the first person sg. in the suffix conjugation (i.e., **qabartū̆* ⟶ **qabartī̆,* "I buried"; cf. Hebrew *qābartî*); and the generalization of the allomorph **-nū̆* for the first person plural, originally proper only to the independent pronoun and the suffix conjugation, now as the possessive suffix and the accusative suffix as well (i.e., as the suffix, respectively, on nouns and verbs, as in Hebrew *sûsēnû,* "our horse," and *šĕmārānû,* "he guarded us"). Apart from the Canaanite evidence in the Akkadian Amarna letters, the various Canaanite languages begin to be recorded in the first half of the 1st millennium B.C.E., all written from right to left in a 22-letter consonantal alphabet developed by the Phoenicians.

Among the Akkadian texts found at the site of el-Amarna (ancient Akhetaten) in Egypt were many letters from the mayors of the Egyptian king's vassal cities in Syria and Palestine. The language of the letters from some of these cities, such as Byblos, Gezer, Jerusalem, and Shechem, is a kind of creole in which the vocabulary is mostly Akkadian (with some local words and phrases) but the morphology and the syntax reflect the local NW Semitic dialects. In some instances the presence of one or more of the diagnostic innovations noted above identifies the underlying dialects as Canaanite: *ru-šu-nu /rōšu-nū̆/,* "our head" (EA 264:18, provenance uncertain; cf. Hebrew *rō(ʾ)š-ēnû,* vs. Akkadian *rēš-ni*); *a-nu-ki /ʾanōkī̆/,* "I" (EA 287:66, 69, from Jerusalem; cf. Heb. *ʾānōkî* vs. Akk. *anāku*) and *mu-še-er-ti,* "I sent" (with *-ti* for "I"; ibid.: 53); *ḫi-iḫ-bi-e [hiḫbiʾe]* < */hiḫbiʾa/,* "he concealed" (EA 256:7, from Piḫilu/Pella; cf. Hebrew *hiḥbîʾ*).

Phoenician is the language of the Phoenician city-states of Byblos, Tyre, Sidon, and others, and of their surrounding areas and colonies. While the dialects of the various cities differed from one another to some degree, the Byblos dialect, the earliest attested, exhibits enough idiosyncrasies to be considered a branch of Phoenician separate from the others, which may be termed "Standard." Byblian texts are attested from the 10th century B.C.E., to the 1st century C.E.; Standard Phoenician inscriptions from Phoenicia proper, from Syria, and from the Mediterranean date from the 9th to 2d centuries B.C.E. The Phoenician dialect of the Tyrian colony at Carthage (Phoenician **qart ḥadašt,* "new city") and its colonies is *Punic,* attested from the 5th century B.C.E.; after the fall of Carthage in 146 B.C.E., inscriptions are referred to as Neo-Punic. The Phoenicians originated the 22-letter form of the linear alphabet later borrowed by speakers of other 1st-millennium languages, including Hebrew and Aramaic. See the separate entry on Phoenician (below).

Hebrew, by far the best-known Canaanite language, is first attested in epigraphic sources in the late 10th century B.C.E. Parts of the biblical text, however, particularly the older poetry, may stem from as early as the 12th century B.C.E.; the dialect (or dialects) represented by this early biblical material, which may be termed *Archaic Hebrew,* exhibits a number of distinctive features lost in most later Hebrew texts. The term *Classical Hebrew* may be used to denote biblical and epigraphic texts written from the beginning of the monarchy until the exile, while post-exilic texts, which show a number of linguistic developments, may be referred to as *Late Classical Hebrew.* The inscriptional remains give evidence of at least two main dialects of Hebrew during the biblical period, a S dialect, also called Judean, and a N dialect, also called Israelean. Dialectal distinctions were undoubtedly also present in biblical texts originally as well, but editorial harmonizing has tended to neutralize such distinctions, so that a relatively uniform language is reflected, probably the standard official Jerusalem dialect; nevertheless, some dialect variation remains, particularly in certain books, such as Job and Ecclesiastes.

Hebrew probably ceased to be a spoken language of daily life in most areas, replaced by Aramaic, a century or more before the turn of the era. The *Middle Hebrew* period, from the 2d century B.C.E. to the 5th C.E., comprises the Hebrew of texts found at Qumran, Samaritan Hebrew, and the Hebrew of the Mishna, each of which reflects a distinct dialect (or several dialects). Qumran Hebrew is a literary dialect, for the most part a deliberate attempt to reproduce the Late Classical language, though elements of the vernacular often appear. Mishnaic Hebrew, on the other hand, does not descend directly from classical Hebrew, at least not from the standard Jerusalem dialect of most of the Bible; rather, it is a written version of a vernacular language that probably reflects the continuation of a separate Hebrew dialect strain, with some connections to earlier northern Hebrew. In the *Medieval* period Hebrew continued as a written language, with writers drawing on both biblical and Mishnaic Hebrew to create a wide variety of literature. In the last century Hebrew was revived as a spoken language, and *Modern Hebrew* thrives today as the language of the state of Israel. See the separate entry on Hebrew (below).

Moabite is attested in one well-preserved 34-line inscription, promulgated by the Moabite king Mesha in the mid-9th century B.C.E., and in two small fragments (one of which is also by Mesha); there are also a number of seals from Moab that bear individual's names (ca. 9th–6th centuries). Although it exhibits a number of distinctive features, Moabite is considered by many scholars to be the language most similar to biblical Hebrew. The *Ammonite* language is known from fewer than a dozen inscriptions dating from the 9th to 6th centuries B.C.E., although there are also over a hundred seals bearing names that have been identified as Ammonite on paleographical or semantic grounds, or on the basis of their find-spots. *Edomite,* attested only in a very small number of ostraca and perhaps in names on a few seals (ca. 8th–6th centuries B.C.E.), is poorly known because of the meager corpus; it appears to be very closely related to Hebrew and Moabite. See also EPIGRAPHY, TRANSJORDANIAN.

(iv) Aramaic. All Aramaic dialects exhibit the following shared linguistic innovations, among others: the change of what was probably a vocalic *$*\underset{\circ}{n}$* to **r* in the words for "son," "daughter," and "two" (e.g., for "son": **bṇ* > **bir;* Testen 1985); the generalization of **-nā̆* as the suffix of the first person plural in all environments, in contradistinction to Canaanite **-nū̆* (see above); the rise of a new causative-reflexive conjugation, **hittaqtal* (vs. earlier Semitic **(v)štaqtala);* and the loss of the passive *n*-stem (as in the Hebrew *Nipᶜal*). All Aramaic dialects except for the modern spoken languages are written from right to left in the 22-letter alphabet borrowed from the Phoenicians, although there are many paleographical variants of the script among the forms of the language.

Old Aramaic, as the earliest phase of the language is known, is attested in a small number of inscriptions, some of them quite long, from the mid-9th century to the 6th century B.C.E., beginning with the bilingual Akkadian-Aramaic stele from Tell Fakhariya in N Syria. Most of these inscriptions exhibit one or more idiosyncratic linguistic features relative to the others, indicating dialectal diversity rather than the presence of any standard dialect.

Aramaic became an official language during the Persian Empire (6th–4th centuries B.C.E.), a development that both widened the use of the language and yielded a standard dialect, called *Official* or *Imperial Aramaic,* which is attested in a large number of texts on papyrus found in Egypt (some written in Egypt, some, e.g., in Persia) and Palestine; the *Biblical Aramaic* of the book of Ezra may also be placed here. After the breakup of the Persian empire, dialectal variation among Aramaic text groups became prominent once again.

The period from the 3d century B.C.E. to the 2d century C.E. has yielded a large number of Aramaic texts, which collectively may be labeled *Middle Aramaic;* inscriptional dialects of this period from Syria and Transjordan are *Nabatean, Palmyrene, Ḥatran,* and *Old Syriac* (the latter based on the dialect spoken in and around the city of Edessa). In Palestine a written dialect that has been termed *Standard Literary Aramaic* is attested in the Aramaic of the biblical book of Daniel, in the many texts in Aramaic from Qumran, and in the Aramaic of Targums Onqelos and Jonathan. Other Palestinian Aramaic texts of this period are the Bar Kokhba letters, tomb inscriptions, and words and phrases quoted in the Mishnah and the Christian New Testament. Scattered texts have also been found, e.g., in Egypt and as far afield as Afghanistan.

From the 3d century C.E. on we may distinguish three main branches of *Late Aramaic:* (1) *Late Western Aramaic* comprises *Galilean* (or *Jewish*) *Aramaic,* the language of the Palestinian Talmud, Midrashim, and Targums, as well as synagogue and funerary inscriptions; *Judean* or *Christian Palestinian Aramaic* (also called Syro-Palestinian or Palestinian Syriac); and *Samaritan Aramaic.* (2) *Late Eastern Aramaic* comprises *Babylonian Aramaic,* the language of the Babylonian Talmud; *Mandaic,* the language of the gnostic Mandaeans in S Babylonia; and the dialect of a substantial number of magical incantations on bowls, from the 4th–7th centuries C.E. (3) Literary *Syriac,* based on Old Syriac and exhibiting features found in both Western and Eastern Aramaic, is the language of a vast Christian literature from the 4th to 13th centuries C.E. An eastern (Nestorian) and a western (Jacobite) dialect are recognized. Syriac began to decline as a spoken language with the spread of Islam in the 7th century, and eventually it died out.

Modern Aramaic languages continue to be spoken in pockets of communities in various parts of the Near East and, as the result of relatively recent migrations, in countries like the Soviet Union, Sweden, and the United States. Four main branches of Neo-Aramaic dialects are known: *Western,* spoken only in three villages NE of Damascus (Christian Maᶜlūla and Muslim Jubbᶜadīn and Baḫᶜa); *Central,* consisting of *Ṭuroyo* (several dialects) and *Mlaḥsō,* spoken in villages in SE Turkey; *Eastern* (also called *Neo-Syriac,* although there is no direct link with classical Syriac), a large group of often significantly divergent dialects spoken by several hundred thousand people, originally in and near Kurdistan but now widely scattered; and *Neo-Mandaic,* which is spoken by a small number of Mandaeans in

Ahwāz in W Iran. See the separate entry on Aramaic (below).

(v) Other. The dialect of a long but fragmentary alphabetic inscription on plaster found at Deir ʿAlla in Jordan, dated to the mid-8th century B.C.E., has variously been labeled Canaanite and Aramaic by scholars. The reason for the debate is that the dialect exhibits features found in both of those language groups. It seems unlikely, however, that any of those features may be considered significant shared innovations; rather, there is no clear evidence in the Deir ʿAlla text for any of the diagnostic features listed above for Canaanite and for Aramaic. Thus, from the point of view of genetic linguistic classification, it is probably better to conclude that the Deir ʿAlla dialect is neither Canaanite nor Aramaic, but rather continues still another, independent branch of NW Semitic. It is likely that there were other dialects in the 1st millennium, thus far undiscovered, that were likewise unaffected by the innovations that characterize either Canaanite or Aramaic, spoken in communities away from the large Aramaic- and Canaanite-speaking centers. See also DEIR ʿALLA.

2. Egyptian. The second main branch (and the earliest-attested member) of the Afroasiatic language family—and history's second-earliest recorded language (after Sumerian; see D.1. below)—is *Egyptian,* the language of the inhabitants of ancient Egypt. Several chronological phases of the Egyptian language may be distinguished: *Old Egyptian,* in dynasties I–VIII (ca. 3100–2160); *Middle Egyptian* in dynasties IX–XVII (ca. 2160–1567); *New* (or *Late*) *Egyptian* in dynasties XVIII–XXX and later (ca. 1567 B.C.E.–394 C.E.); *Demotic,* the language of texts written in demotic script (see below), which overlaps New Egyptian in part, appearing from dynasty XXV to the late Roman period (ca. 715 B.C.E.–470 C.E.); and *Coptic,* from the 3d to 16th centuries C.E., possibly later. That there were also geographical variations of dialect in all of these periods is certain, but directly evidenced only for Coptic; for the earlier stages of the language only a standard dialect normally received written form. The Egyptians probably borrowed the idea of writing from the Sumerians, but the script devised by them was completely indigenous. The hieroglyphic script, in which the original pictographs remain fully recognizable, remained in use for monumental texts and on papyrus from the earliest period until after the turn of the era; hieratic, a cursive script attested from the Old Kingdom on in which the pictographs become stylized to the point where they are not recognizable, was used for writing more quickly with a reed pen; demotic script, which first appeared in the late 8th century B.C.E., was a still more cursive form of writing derived from hieratic. Coptic, the late stage of the Egyptian language spoken by the Christian Copts, was written with the Greek alphabet to which seven additional letters, derived from hieroglyphs, were added to represent sounds not found in Greek.

For the genetic relationship between Egyptian and Semitic, we may point to a number of morphological features, such as the independent pronoun *ỉnk,* "I" (cf. Akkadian *anāku,* Hebrew *ʾānōkî*); the pronominal suffixes *-ỉ,* "my;" *-k,* "your" (m. sg.), and *-n,* "our" (cf. Hebrew *-î/-ya, -kā, -nû,* respectively); the form called the Old Perfective, as in *snb. kwỉ,* "I being healthy," which corresponds formally and semantically to the Akkadian predicative verbal adjective ("stative"), as in *šalm-āku,* "I am healthy." The remoteness of the Egyptian-Semitic relationship, on the other hand, may be illustrated by noting the extreme dearth of clear cognates between the vocabularies of the two language groups. See the separate entries on Egyptian language and writing and on Coptic (below).

B. The Indo-European Language Family

Of the many branches of this vast family (in chronological order of attestation: Anatolian, Indo-Iranian, Hellenic, Italic, Celtic, Germanic, Armenian, Tocharian, Balto-Slavic, Albanian; in addition there are several minor, unclassified languages), only a few are represented in ancient Near East documents.

1. Anatolian. The most prominent member of this branch is *Hittite,* the earliest Indo-European language attested. Though the term "Hittite" is current in modern scholarly usage, the language was called Nesite by its speakers; it is not to be confused with the autochthonous, unrelated Hattic language (see D.4. below). Hittite was the language of the Indo-Europeans who settled in central Anatolia, and it became the language of the Hittite kingdom. Some 25,000 texts span the 18th to 13th centuries B.C.E.; these include historical texts, laws and legal texts, letters mythological texts, rituals and cultic texts, hymns and prayers, omens, and economic documents. The vast majority of these texts, which were written on clay tablets with the logo-syllabic cuneiform system indigenous to Mesopotamia, were discovered at the site of Boğazköy, ancient Ḫattusas, capital of the Hittite empire. See the separate entry on Hittite (below).

Two other Anatolian Indo-European languages attested in the cuneiform texts found at Boğazköy are *Palaic* (from Palā in NW Anatolia; texts from ca. 1650–1400) and *Luwian* (or *Luvian;* from Luwiya, later Arzawa, in W Anatolia; ca. 1400–1200), in which a few rituals and other religious texts are written; Luwian texts outnumber those in Palaic, but the number of both pales in comparison to the large corpus of Hittite texts. A dialect of Luwian is also written with an indigenous hieroglyphic script appearing on Hittite empire seals beginning in the 15th century B.C.E. and especially on N Syrian monuments from the 10th to 8th centuries B.C.E. The longest text in this *Hieroglyphic Luwian* (formerly termed "Hieroglyphic Hittite") apears in an 8th-century bilingual inscription (with Phoenician) from Karatepe in Cilicia.

Also attested in the 1st millennium B.C.E. are several members of the Anatolian family written in alphabetic scripts. *Lydian,* the language of Lydia on the W coast of Asia Minor, is attested in some 100 inscriptions, mostly epitaphs from Sardis dating from the 5th (or perhaps the 6th) to 4th centuries; there are in addition two Lydian-Greek bilinguals and a longer Lydian-Aramaic bilingual. Lydian is written from right to left in a script derived from Greek. *Lycian,* the language of Lycia in SW Asia Minor, is preserved in about 100 coin legends and 150 epitaphs from the 5th and 4th centuries, many of the latter Lycian-Greek bilinguals; an important historical inscription in an archaic form of Lycian appears on a stele from Xanthos, and a trilingual Lycian-Greek-Aramaic text, a decree establishing a new cult, was found near the same site in A.D.

1973. The Lycian script is likewise derived from Greek, and while similar (though not identical) to the Lydian, it is written from left to right. Inscriptions from Caria in SW Asia Minor (between Lydia and Lycia), and several graffiti from Egypt and Nubia in the same script, have been labeled *Carian.* Like the Lydian and Lycian, the Carian script appears to be derived for the most part from Greek, although there are many deviations. The more than 100 inscriptions, nearly all of which are very brief (although one text is 14 lines long), date to the 7th or early 6th century B.C.E. The Carian language as known from names and from a few glosses in Greek texts remains very poorly understood but has recently been shown to belong to the Anatolian branch of Indo-European. For Phrygian, see B.4. below.

2. Indo-Iranian (Aryan). A number of Indo-Iranian and divine names (such as Indra and Varuna) appear in Hurrian (see C.1.) royal names and other Hurrian contexts from the mid-2d millennium B.C.E. In addition, a tractate dealing with horse training, written in Hittite by a Hurrian specialist, contains several Indo-Iranian technical terms, as do some forms, also concerning horses, found in Akkadian texts written at the Hurrian site of Nuzi. A few of these terms found their way into some of the Semitic languages, as probably in *maryanni,* "charioteer," in Ugaritic. The historical and cultural implications of the presence of these Indo-Iranian forms in Hurro-Hittite contexts are debated. The Indic stock of this large branch (Sanskrit, Prakrit, and their descendants) had otherwise little impact on the linguistic landscape of the ANE.

Two Old Iranian languages are well attested. *Avestan* is an E variety of Iranian in which are written, in a script ultimately derived from Aramaic, sacred Zoroastrian texts, some of which (the Gāthā's) may go back to 600 B.C.E. *Old Persian,* a SW variety of Iranian appearing from the reign of Darius (522–486 B.C.E.) to that of Artaxerxes III (359–338), was one of the official languages the Achaemenid rulers of the Persian empire used for royal inscriptions; it is written in a reduced cuneiform script (only 42 signs: 36 syllabic, 5 word-signs, 1 word divider). Old Persian is the ancestor of the Middle Iranian languages, whose main representative is *Pahlavi,* the language of the Parthians (250 B.C. to 226 C.E.) and Sassanians (226–652 C.E.) and a large corpus of Zoroastrian texts. Other Old Iranian languages, such as *Median* (the language of the Medes), *Parthian,* and *Scythian,* remain sparsely attested and poorly understood. See the separate entry on the languages of Iran (below).

3. Hellenic. This branch of Indo-European contains only the various dialects of the *Greek* language. The earliest dialect attested, now usually termed Mycenaean Greek, was written on clay tablets in the syllabic script called Linear B (deciphered in 1952; for Linear A and other Cretan scripts, see E.2. below). The script contains 87 syllabic signs and a number of ideograms. Over 4,500 Linear B tablets, dating from the end of the 14th to the beginning of the 12th century B.C.E., have been discovered at Knossos in Crete, at Pylos, Tiryns, and Mycenae in the Peloponnese, and at Thebes, Eleusis, and Orchomenos in central Greece. Most of the texts are inventories of personnel, animals, rations, weapons, and the like.

The Homeric poems may have been written down as early as 800 B.C.E., while the earliest alphabetic Greek inscriptions attested thus far date to the late 8th century B.C.E. Linguists recognize a number of Greek dialects, the most prominent of which are Aeolic, Doric, and Ionic-Attic; the Attic branch of the latter, the dialect of Athens, yielded the *koinē* or "common" Greek of the Hellenistic period, and the Greek of the Christian New Testament. See the separate entry on Greek (below).

4. Phrygian. The language of ancient Phrygia, with its capital at Gordion in W central Asia Minor, is recorded in two groups of inscriptions. *Old Phrygian,* written in a native alphabet derived from the Greek, consists of over 90 inscriptions from the 8th to the 4th centuries B.C.E.; inscriptions may be written from left to right, from right to left, or boustrophedon. *New* or *Late Phrygian* appears in some 110 texts from the 2d and 3d centuries C.E., written in the Greek alphabet. Although it is an Indo-European language that was spoken in Asia Minor, Phrygian is not a member of the Anatolian branch (see B.1. above). Phrygian seems for now to constitute a separate branch, although the ancient Greeks and some modern linguists consider it to be related to *Thracian,* a poorly attested Indo-European language spoken in W Asia Minor and in the E Balkans, in a Thraco-Phrygian branch. Some also believe Phrygian and Thracian to be related to Armenian.

C. Hurrian and Urartian

Although these two extinct languages are not closely related, their common ancestry is now well established. The classification of Hurro-Urartian as a branch of one of the Caucasian language groups, especially the NE Caucasian languages, has been proposed but not proved. The Hurro-Urartian group contributed a number of loanwords to Hittite, Akkadian, and a very early stage of Old Armenian.

1. Hurrian. Texts in the language of the ancient Hurrians (biblical Horites) are attested from the 20th to the 12th centuries B.C.E. from several sites in N Syria and Anatolia, including Mari, Ugarit, Emar, and especially Ḫattusas (modern Boğazköy). Like most 2d-millennium languages, Hurrian was usually written in Mesopotamian-style syllabic cuneiform, although a few texts from Ugarit were also written in that city's indigenous alphabetic cuneiform script. The longest Hurrian text, which until recently was the source of most of our understanding of Hurrian grammar, is a 500-line letter sent by Tushratta, king of Mittanni, to the Egyptian pharaoh Amenophis III early in the 14th century. The majority of Hurrian texts are cultic in nature, although a few mythological and other literary texts, some omens, and a small number of lexical texts are also attested. Despite many advances, not a few details of Hurrian grammar and vocabulary have remained obscure; a long bilingual Hurrian-Hittite literary text, recently discovered at Ḫattusas, is expected to elucidate some of the difficulties, however. See the separate entry on Hurrian (below).

2. Urartian. The language of the kingdom of Urarṭu (near Lake Van in E Turkey; cf. biblical Ararat), *Urartian* is attested in texts dating from the end of the 9th century to the beginning of the 6th century B.C.E. The majority of the texts—several hundred in number—are monumental royal inscriptions in stone (building inscriptions, dedications, and, rarely, annals), whereas only some 20 Urartian clay tablets, administrative in content, have been published. While most texts are written in Mesopotamian cuneiform, Urartian was also recorded in two hieroglyphic scripts, a local variety that remains poorly understood, and, at one site (Altintepe), the Anatolian variety used for Luwian (see B.1. above).

D. Other Languages

A number of languages of the ANE, some of them well documented, appear to be isolates, that is, languages with no known relatives. They are presented in this section in the chronological order of their appearance.

1. Sumerian. The first written language, Sumerian was the language of early inhabitants of S Mesopotamia. Sumerian texts are attested beginning in the Uruk IV period, ca. 3100 B.C.E. Although the writing of the earliest texts is almost entirely pictographic, so that the underlying language is not obvious, the use of a few signs for homonymous words, such as *gi,* "reed," for *gi,* "to return," assures us that the language of these texts is in fact Sumerian. Much of the earliest textual material, however, is extremely difficult to understand, since it exhibits many signs that did not survive into later periods. Further, for much of the early period, the scribes used the writing system to record not the exact pronunciation, morphology, and syntax of a text but rather the main items or catchwords, as a mnemonic device; thus, much of the structure of the language must be reconstructed from later texts written when the scribes were more often not native Sumerian speakers but rather Akkadian speakers who had learned Sumerian as a dead, literary language. The earliest writing was pictographic, inscribed in clay tablets, but it evolved over the centuries into cuneiform—wedge-shaped signs impressed into clay with a reed stylus. The Sumerian cuneiform system was eventually borrowed by speakers of Akkadian, Eblaite, Hurrian and Urartian, Hittite, and Elamite to write their languages.

Sumerian may be divided into several chronological phases: *Old Sumerian,* from the earliest period to about 2100, which includes texts from Lagash and other sites dating to the Early Dynastic III period (26th–24th centuries), texts from the Sargonic period (23d–22d centuries), and inscriptions of Gudea, ruler of Lagash in the late 22d century; *Neo-Sumerian,* ca. 2100–1900, which comprises the vast numbers of administrative and legal documents of the Ur III dynasty, and other texts; and *Late Sumerian,* from 1900 on. The date of the death of Sumerian as a spoken language is debated, but it was almost certainly a strictly literary language by the end of the Old Babylonian period (ca. 1900–1600); some scholars have argued that Sumerian had died out as a living language already by the Ur III period (ca. 2100–2000).

The most commonly attested dialect of Sumerian is called *eme-gir*$_{15}$, which may mean "princely language." Another dialect is the *eme-sal,* which may mean "thin language" (or "fine" or "high-pitched"), used in some literary texts when the speaker is a woman or a *gala* (lamentation) priest. Regional dialects undoubtedly also existed, but are not evidenced in the textual material.

A wide variety of Sumerian texts is attested. Economic texts, attested already in the earliest period, are by far the largest group, comprising perhaps some 90 percent of Sumerian documents. Both legal texts and royal inscriptions are recorded from the Early Dynastic period on. There are many genres of literary texts: myths, epics, proverbs, hymns, prayers, and incantations. The various series of lexical lists, the dictionary- and encyclopedia-style texts by which the Sumerian scholars organized their knowledge and taught their writing system, appear by 3000; later, Akkadian scribes used these series, to which they appended glosses in their own language, to learn Sumerian.

Sumerian is an agglutinative language, i.e., one that combines discrete morphemes more or less unaltered in chains to form words, as in *é dumu-(a)n(i)-ak-a,* literally "house son-his-of-in" for "in his son's house." Sumerian also exhibits ergative constructions, in which the case of the subject of an intransitive verb is the same as that of the object of a transitive verb, as in the endingless *(-ø)* form *é,* "house," in the following examples: *lugal-e é-ø in-dù,* literally "king-by (= by the king) house was-built" for "the king built the house"; *é-ø ba-šub,* "the house collapsed."

2. Elamite. Elamite was the language of the early inhabitants of Elam, an area of SW Iran corresponding roughly to the modern province of Khuzistan. Scholars divide the attested history of the Elamite language into four periods. *Old Elamite,* beginning in the 23d century, comprises a very small number of texts, one of which is a document mentioning the Old Akkadian ruler Naram-Sin. *Middle Elamite* dates to the 13th–11th centuries, when Elam was a major political power in the Near East; with rare exception the many texts from this period, from the sites of Susa and Choga Zanbil (and others), are royal building and votive inscriptions on bricks (one of which is an Elamite-Akkadian bilingual), although a few royal historical texts also occur. After a gap of several centuries in which no Elamite texts are attested, *Neo-Elamite* texts begin to appear in the 8th century B.C.E. In addition to the genres found in the Middle Elamite corpus, Neo-Elamite also comprises several hundred administrative texts from Susa, over 30 letters, and a literary text containing omens. The Elamite language continued in use after the fall of the last indigenous Elamite dynasty about 640 B.C.E., and a few texts are also known from the period when Elam was under Babylonian rule in the 6th century. Under the Achaemenid dynasty, Elamite was an official language alongside Old Persian and Babylonian. *Achaemenid Elamite* is attested in over 3,000 administrative tablets from Persepolis, a few letters, and several dozen trilingual royal inscriptions; the latter, in Old Persian, Babylonian, and Elamite, provided the foundation for the decipherment of these languages during the last century. The longest and most important trilingual is the rock inscription of Darius I (522–486) at Behistun; the Elamite version is over 300 lines long. The last Elamite inscriptions date to the mid-4th century B.C.E.

Elamite inscriptions from the 23d century onward are written in the logo-syllabic cuneiform script borrowed from the Elamites' neighbors in Mesopotamia. Another writing system, an indigenous pictographic script called Proto-Elamite, was used in Elam during the 3d millennium on tablets from Susa, Tepe Yahya, and Tall-i Malyan (Anshan), among others. It is first attested on economic tablets found in archaeological strata dated to about 3000, and later on royal inscriptions from the Old Akkadian period (ca. 23d/22d century); in the latter period it sometimes appears on monuments that also bear cuneiform Akkadian inscriptions. Since the Proto-Elamite script remains essentially undeciphered, it is not certain that the language represented is in fact Elamite. A genetic connection between Elamite and the Dravidian language family in India has occasionally been suggested, but has not gained general acceptance.

3. Qutian. The language of the Quti(um) (Guti[um]) tribes of the central Zagros mountain region is referred to as Qutian. Since no texts written in Qutian have been found, virtually nothing is known about the language. It is attested only in a small number of entries in Mesopotamian synonym lists that cite foreign words, and in several dozen personal names in the Sumerian king list and a few other texts from the end of the 3d and beginning of the 2d millennia; it may also be the source of a few substratum vocabulary items in Sumerian.

4. Hattic. Hattic is the name given to the language of the pre-Indo-European (i.e., pre-Hittite-speaking) inhabitants of N central Anatolia in the 3d and early 2d millennia. Hattic was transmitted by its linguistic supplanters, the Hittites, as a religious language, the language of the local central Anatolian gods. Thus, Hattic texts, all of which come from Boğazköy, ancient Ḫattusas, span the same period of time as that covered by Hittite (18th–13th centuries), and are likewise written in Mesopotamian cuneiform. Other evidence for Hattic is found in proper names, both in Hittite texts and in the earlier Old Assyrian texts from the Anatolian trading colony at Kültepe (ancient Kanesh; 19th–18th centuries). All Hattic texts are of a religious character; they include rituals for temple foundations and consecrations, myths, incantations, prayers, festivals, songs, antiphonies, litanies, and invocations of deities. Hattic material often appears as recitations within Hittite texts, and in some instances, Hattic texts are provided with Hittite translations. Since such translations are frequently of dubious precision, and since copies of Hattic texts are often full of errors, it seems likely that, at least by the period of the Hittite empire (from the 14th century), Hattic was learned by the Hittite scribes as a dead language; it is quite possible, however, that away from Ḫattusas (especially to the NE) Hattic continued to be spoken until a much later time.

Because of the fragmentary nature of most texts containing Hattic, and because of the uncertain reliability of the Hittite translations in the bilingual texts, our understanding of Hattic grammar and vocabulary remains very limited, although it is clear that Hattic had a strong influence on the grammar and vocabulary of the Indo-European Hittite and Palaic languages (less so on Luwian) that replaced it in central Anatolia. Attempts to classify Hattic as a member of one or another of the Caucasian language groups have been made, but in the poor state of our present knowledge of Hattic, such a genetic relationship is not demonstrable.

5. Kassite. The language of the Kassites, a people from the central Zagros mountains (modern Luristan), some of whose members established a dynasty that ruled Babylonia for over 400 years (16th–12th centuries), remains poorly documented and poorly understood. As is true of Qutian, there are neither texts nor complete sentences written entirely in Kassite. The most important sources for Kassite are a vocabulary text giving 16 divine names and 32 common nouns in Kassite with their Akkadian equivalents; a tablet from the library of Assurbanipal (7th century) that lists non-Akkadian royal and other personal names, some of them Kassite, with Akkadian equivalents; over a dozen Akkadian texts from the Kassite period involving horse breeding and containing a number of Kassite terms having to do with horses; and a few Kassite words found in other Akkadian lexical texts or as loanwords into Akkadian. In addition to these sources, many Kassite personal, geographical, and divine names appear in Mesopotamian texts, especially during the Kassite period, but also occasionally earlier in the Old Babylonian period and later into the 1st millennium.

E. Undeciphered Languages and Scripts

A number of scripts attested in the ANE and Mediterranean remain undeciphered, and the languages they represent are unknown. In other cases the script can be read but the language still escapes our understanding. Some of the more prominent of these challenges are reviewed briefly here in the likely chronological order of their first appearance.

1. Cretan and Cypriot Scripts. *Cretan Hieroglyphic,* the first writing to appear on the island of Crete, dates from the 20th to 17th centuries B.C.E. and has some 140 signs; inscriptions most often appear on stone seals, more rarely on clay. From this script, or one similar to it, there developed two cursive linear scripts that are normally inscribed on clay tablets. The later of these, *Linear B,* records Mycenaean Greek, as noted above (B.3.). The earlier script, referred to as *Linear A,* has some 80 syllabic signs as well as ideograms. Since many of the signs correspond to signs in Linear B, much of Linear A can be read with some confidence, but the small number of texts (only 200–300 tablets, the largest number from Haghia Triada, a palace in S Crete), their brevity, and the lack of bilinguals have led to much debate concerning both the interpretation of the texts in general and even the language they record; the language has been identified, among other suggestions, as a form of NW Semitic, as a dialect of Luwian (Anatolian Indo-European), and as Greek, but none of these identifications has gained wide acceptance. Linear A, which began to appear in the 18th century, continued in use until the end of Minoan civilization, about 1450 B.C.E.

A small number of texts found at sites on Crete and dating to the 6th to 3d centuries B.C.E. are written in Greek characters, but record a language, usually called *Eteocretan,* that has resisted interpretation, despite the existence of a few bilinguals with Greek translations. The relationship between Eteocretan and the language or languages represented by Cretan Hieroglyphic and Linear A also remains uncertain.

The *Phaistos Disk* is a round clay tablet 6½ inches in diameter discovered during excavations at the palace of Phaistos in S Crete in 1908 and dated stratigraphically to the 17th century B.C.E. The disk is inscribed on both sides with a pictographic script that is not apparently related to other Cretan scripts. The number of individual pictographs used on the disk is 45, a fact that suggests a syllabic script. The most noteworthy aspect of the writing is that the signs were not incised or drawn into the clay, but rather made by impressing stamps, in history's first example of movable type. None of the numerous attempts at deciphering the relatively short text has gained acceptance; the language of the inscription has thus also remained unknown.

Sites in Cyprus have yielded a small number of texts on clay dating from about 1500 to 1150 in a syllabic script (written from left to right), related to those used on Crete (particularly Linear A) and termed *Cypro-Minoan,* apparently an adaptation of the Cretan writing for the recording of an autochthonous Cypriot language, which remains undeciphered. The Cypro-Minoan script forms an intermediary link between the Cretan scripts and another, later *Cypriot* or *Eteo-Cypriot* syllabic script, usually written from right to left; while one such inscription dates to the 11th century and a few to the 8th, most are attested from the 6th to 1st centuries B.C.E. The majority of the texts written in this scrit record a dialect of Greek (sometimes, especially later, with bilinguals in standard Greek), but a few are in a still-undeciphered, probably indigenous language.

2. Byblian Hieroglyphs. A group of nine or ten texts was discovered in Byblos between 1928 and 1932. The texts stem from the Bronze Age, but a more precise dating has not been possible. The inscriptions, written on stone and bronze and ranging in length from 3 to 41 lines, are written in a hieroglyphic script apparently derived, ultimately, from the Egyptian. The number of distinct signs is variously thought to be from fewer than 65 to more than 100, but both extremes indicate that the script is largely syllabic in nature. The language is usually assumed to be Semitic, though not on any sound linguistic basis. An attempted decipherment has recently appeared (Mendenhall 1985), in which it is claimed that the inscriptions date to the late 3d millennium and reflect an archaic form of West Semitic; however, reviewers have not found the decipherment plausible. See the separate entry on Byblos Syllabic (below).

3. Deir ᶜAlla Clay Tablets. Three inscribed rectangular clay tablets dating to about 1200 B.C.E. were discovered in 1964 at the site of Deir ᶜAlla in Jordan. The number of characters attested in the three inscriptions is over 50, so that the script was most probably syllabic in nature. Some of the characters resemble the earlier Cretan Linear A script, but whether there is in fact a connection between the two remains unclear. The inscriptions and their language are as yet undeciphered.

4. Meroitic. Meroitic is a language recorded in inscriptions from the ancient kingdom of Meroë in lower Nubia from the 1st century B.C.E. to the 3d or 4th century C.E. The script exists in two varieties: a lapidary, in which the signs are hieroglyphs borrowed from Egyptian, and a cursive. The writing contains only 23 characters and is thus essentially alphabetic in nature. The phonetic values of the signs are known, so that the texts can be read, but certain interpretation of them has so far remained elusive, partly because of the absence of bilinguals and partly because the language represented by the inscriptions has not been successfully shown to be related to any other.

Bibliography

In addition to the bibliographies included in the following articles, the items below should be noted.

General

Diakonoff, I. M. 1967. *Jazyki drevnej Perednej Azii* (The Languages of the Ancient Near East). Moscow.

Friedrich, J. 1957. *Extinct Languages.* Trans. F. Gaynor. New York.

Gelb, I. J. 1963. *A Study of Writing.* 2d ed. Chicago.

Afroasiatic

Cohen, D., ed. 1988. *Les langues chamito-sémitiques.* Pt. 3 of *Les langues dans le monde ancien et moderne,* ed. J. Perrot. Paris.

Cohen, M. 1947. *Essai comparatif sur le vocabulaire et la phonétique du chamito-sémitique.* Paris.

Diakonoff, I. M. 1988. *Afrasian Languages.* Moscow.

Hetzron, R. 1987. Afroasiatic Languages. Pp. 645–53 in *The World's Major Languages,* ed. B. Comrie. New York.

Hodge, C. T. 1970. Afroasiatic: An overview. Pp. 237–54 in *Current Trends in Linguistics.* Vol. 6, *Linguistics in South West Asia and North Africa,* ed. T. A. Sebeok. The Hague.

Rössler, O. 1950. Verbalbau und Verbalflexion in den semitohamitischen Sprachen: Vorstudien zu einer vergleichenden semitohamitischen Grammatik. *ZDMG* 100: 461–514 = The Structure and Inflection of the Verb in the Semito-Hamitic Languages: Preliminary Studies for a Comparative Semito-Hamitic Grammar. Pp. 679–748 in *Bono Homini Donum,* ed. Y. Arbeitman and A. R. Bomhard. Amsterdam, 1981.

Sasse, H.-J.; Störk, L.; and Wolff, E. 1981. Afroasiatisch. Pp. 129–262 in *Die Sprachen Afrikas,* ed. B. Heine, T. C. Shadeberg, and E. Wolff. Hamburg.

Semitic

Baumstark, A.; Brockelmann, C.; et al. 1964. *Semitistik.* HO 1/3. Leiden.

Bergsträsser, G. 1928. *Einführung in die semitischen Sprachen.* Munich. = *Introduction to the Semitic Languages.* Trans. P. T. Daniels. Winona Lake, IN, 1983.

Bomhard, A. R. 1988. The Reconstruction of the Proto-Semitic Consonant System. Pp. 113–40 in *Fucus: A Semitic/Afrasian Gathering in Remembrance of Albert Ehrman,* ed. Y. L. Arbeitman. Amsterdam.

Brockelmann, C. 1908–13. *Grundriss der vergleichenden Grammatik der semitischen Sprachen.* 2 vols. Berlin.

Faber, A. 1985. Akkadian Evidence for Proto-Semitic Affricates. *JCS* 37: 101–7.

———. 1989. On the Nature of Proto-Semitic **l. JAOS* 109: 33–36.

Gray, L. H. 1934. *Introduction to Semitic Comparative Linguistics.* New York.

Hamori, A. 1973. A Note on *yaqtulu* in East and West Semitic. *AO* 41: 319–24.

Hetzron, R. 1974. La division des langues sémitiques. Pp. 181–94 in *Actes du premier Congrès international de linguistique sémitique et chamito-sémitique, Paris 16–19 juillet 1969,* ed. A. Caquot and D. Cohen. The Hague.

———. 1976. Two principles of genetic reconstruction. *Lingua* 38: 89–108.

———. 1987. Semitic Languages. Pp. 654–63 in *The World's Major Languages,* ed. B. Comrie. Oxford.

Hoftijzer, J. 1985. *The Function and Use of the Imperfect Forms with Nun Paragogicum in Classical Hebrew.* SSN 21. Assen.

Hospers, J. H. 1973. *A Basic Bibliography for the Study of the Semitic Languages*. 2 vols. Leiden.
Kuryłowicz, J. 1973. *Studies in Semitic Grammar and Metrics*. London.
Moscati, S., ed. 1964. *An Introduction to the Comparative Grammar of the Semitic Languages: Phonology and Morphology*. Wiesbaden.
Sasse, H.-J. 1981. Die semitischen Sprachen. Pp. 225–38 in *Die Sprachen Afrika,* ed. B. Heine, T. C. Shadeberg, and E. Wolff. Hamburg.
Schramm, G. M. 1971. The Semitic Languages: An Overview. Pp. 257–60 in *Current Trends in Linguistics*. Vol. 6, *Linguistics in South West Asia and North Africa*, ed. T. A. Sebeok. The Hague.
Ullendorff, E. 1970. Comparative Semitics. Pp. 261–73 in *Current Trends in Linguistics*. Vol. 6, *Linguistics in South West Asia and North Africa*, ed. T. A. Sebeok. The Hague.
Voigt, R. M. 1987. The Classification of Central Semitic. *JSS* 32: 1–21.

Old North Arabic and Classical Arabic

Altheim, F., and Stiehl, R. 1964–69. *Die Araber in der Alten Welt*. 5 vols. Berlin.
Branden, A. van den 1950. *Les inscriptions thamoudéennes*. Bibliothèque du Muséon 25. Louvain.
———. 1962. *Les inscriptions dédanites*. Beirut.
Brockelmann, C. 1964. Das Arabische und seine Mundarten. Pp. 207–45 in *Semitistik*. HO 1/3. Leiden.
Caskell, W. 1954. *Lihyan und Lihyanisch*. Cologne.
Diem, W. 1980. Die genealogische Stellung des Arabischen in den semitischen Sprachen. Pp. 65–85 in *Studien aus Arabistik und Semitistik Anton Spitaler zum siebzigsten Geburtstag von seinen Schülern überreicht*, ed. W. Diem and S. Wild. Wiesbaden.
Fischer, W. 1987. *Grammatik des klassischen Arabisch*. 2d ed. Wiesbaden.
Fischer, W., ed. 1982. *Grundriss der Arabischen Philologie*. Vol. 1, *Sprachwissenschaft*. Wiesbaden.
Fischer, W., and Jastrow, O. 1980. *Handbuch der arabischen Dialekte*. Wiesbaden.
Jamme, A. 1966. Ḥasaean Inscriptions from Northeastern Saudi Arabia. Pp. 63–82 in idem, *Sabaean and Ḥasaean Inscriptions from Saudi Arabia*. 5523. Rome.
Rabin, C. 1951. *Ancient West-Arabian*. London.
Ryckmans, G., ed. 1950. *Corpus Inscriptionum Semiticarum*. Vol. 5, *Inscriptiones saracenicas continens*. Paris.
Winnett, F. W. 1937. *A Study of the Lihyanite and Thamudic Inscriptions*. Toronto.
Winnett, F. W., and Reed, W. L. 1970. *Ancient Records from North Arabia*. Near and Middle East Series 6. Toronto.

Syro-Palestinian (NW) Semitic

Blau, J. 1978. Hebrew and North West Semitic: Reflections on the Classification of the Semitic Languages. *HAR* 2: 21–44.
Garbini, G. 1960. *Il semitico di nord-ovest*. Naples.
Garr, W. R. 1985. *Dialect Geography of Syria-Palestine, 1000–586, B.C.E.* Philadelphia.
Ginsberg, H. L. 1970. The Northwest Semitic Languages. *WHJP* 2: 102–24.
Greenfield, J. C. 1969. Amurrite, Ugaritic and Canaanite. Pp. 92ff. in *Proceedings of the International Conference on Semitic Studies, held in Jerusalem, 19–23 July 1969*. Jerusalem.
Huehnergard, J. fc. Recent Research on Northwest Semitic Grammar. In *The Bible and the Ancient Near East Revisited*, ed. J. Hackett et al. ASOR/SBL Archaeology and Biblical Studies 2. Atlanta.
Kaufman, S. A. 1988. The Classification of the North West Semitic Dialects of the Biblical Period and Some Implications Thereof. *PWCJS* 9: 41–57.
Moran, W. L. 1961. The Hebrew Language in its Northwest Semitic Background. *BANE*, 54–72.

Early Dialects and Names, including "Amorite"

Aḥituv, S. 1984. *Canaanite Toponyms in Ancient Egyptian Documents*. Jerusalem.
Albright, W. F. 1934. *The Vocalization of the Egyptian Syllabic Orthography*. AOS 6. New Haven.
———. 1969. *The Proto-Sinaitic Inscriptions and Their Decipherment*. HTS 22. 2d ed. Cambridge, MA.
Buccellati, G. 1966. *Amorites of the Ur III Period*. Rome.
Gelb, I. J. 1958. La lingua degli amoriti. *AANLR* 13: 143–64.
———. 1961. The Early History of the West Semitic Peoples. *JCS* 15: 27–47.
Gelb, I. J., et al. 1980. *Computer-Aided Analysis of Amorite*. AS 21. Chicago.
Huehnergard, J. 1987. Northwest Semitic Vocabulary in Akkadian Texts. *JAOS* 107: 713–25.
Huffmon, H. B. 1965. *Amorite Personal Names in the Mari Texts*. Baltimore.
Krahmalkov, C. R. 1965. Studies in Amorite Grammar. Diss., Harvard.
Sivan, D. 1984. *Grammatical Analysis and Glossary of the Northwest Semitic Vocables in Akkadian Texts of the 15th–13th C.B.C. from Canaan and Syria*. AOAT 214. Kevelaer and Neukirchen-Vluyn.

Canaanite

Harris, Z. S. 1939. *Development of the Canaanite Dialects*. AOS 16. New Haven.
Israel, F. 1984. Geographic Linguistics and Canaanite Dialects. Pp. 363–87 in *Current Progress in Afro-Asiatic Linguistics: Papers of the Third International Hamito-Semitic Congress*, ed. J. Bynon. Amsterdam.

El-Amarna Canaanite

Böhl, F. M. T. de Liagre. 1909. *Die Sprache der Amarnabriefe mit besonderer Berücksichtigung der Kanaanismen*. LSS 5/2. Leipzig.
Ebeling, E. 1912. Das Verbum der El-Amarna Briefen. *BAss* 8/2: 39–79.
Moran, W. L. 1950. A Syntactical Study of the Dialect of Byblos as Reflected in the Amarna Tablets. Diss. Johns Hopkins.
———. 1960. Early Canaanite *yaqtula*. *Or* 29: 1–19.
Rainey, A. F. 1973. Reflections on the Suffix Conjugation in West Semitized Amarna Tablets. *UF* 5: 235–62.
———. 1975. Morphology and the Prefix-Tenses of West Semitized el-ʿAmarna Tablets. *UF* 7: 395–426.
———. 1986. The Ancient Hebrew Prefix Conjugation in the Light of Amarna Canaanite. *HS* 27: 4–19.
———. fc. The Prefix-Conjugation Patterns of Early Northwest Semitic. In *Festschrift W.L. Moran*, ed. T. Abusch, J. Huehnergard, and P. Steinkeller. Harvard Semitic Studies. Atlanta.

Moabite

Dearman, A., ed. 1989. *Studies in the Mesha Inscription and Moab*. ASOR/SBL Archaeology and Biblical Studies 2. Atlanta.

Ammonite

Aufrecht, W. E. 1987. The Ammonite Language of the Iron Age (review article of Jackson 1983). *BASOR* 266: 85–95.

Israel, F. 1979. The Language of the Ammonites. *OLP* 10: 143–59.
Jackson, K. P. 1983. *The Ammonite Language of the Iron Age.* HSM 27. Chico, CA.

Edomite

Beit-Arieh, L., and Cresson, B. 1985. An Edomite Ostracon from Ḥorvat ᶜUza. *TA* 12: 96–101.
Israel, F. 1979. Miscellanea idumea. *RBI* 27: 171–203.

Aramaic

Testen, D. 1985. The Significance of Aramaic $r < *n$. *JNES* 44: 143–46.

Indo-European

Baldi, P. 1983. *An Introduction to the Indo-European Languages.* Carbondale, IL.
Brugmann, K., and Delbrück, B. 1906–30. *Grundriss der vergleichenden Grammatik der indogermanischen Sprachen.* 2d ed. 5 vols. Strasbourg. Repr. 1967.
Cowgill, W., and Mayrhofer, M. 1986. *Indogermanische Grammatik.* I/1: *Einleitung,* and I/2 *Lautlehre* [*Segmentale Phonologie des Indogermanischen*]. Heidelberg.
Krahe, H. 1966–69. *Indogermanische Sprachwissenschaft.* 2 vols. Sammlung Göschen 59, 64. Berlin.
Kuryłowicz, J. 1968. *Indogermanische Grammatik.* Vol. 2, *Akzent und Ablaut.* Heidelberg.
Lockwood, W. B. 1969. *Indo-European Philology: Historical and Comparative.* London.
Meillet, A. 1937. *Introduction à l'étude comparative des langues indo-européennes.* Paris. Repr. 1964.
Schmalstieg, W. R. 1980. *Indo-European Linguistics: A New Synthesis.* University Park, PA.
Szemerényi, O. 1989. *Einführung in die vergleichende Sprachwissenschaft.* 3d ed. Darmstadt.
Watkins, C. 1969. *Indogermanische Grammatik.* Vol. 3, pt. 1, *Formenlehre: Geschichte der indogermanischen Verbalflexion.* Heidelberg.

Anatolian Languages

Kammenhuber, A. 1975. The Linguistic Situation of the 2nd Millennium B.C. in Ancient Anatolia. Pp. 116–20 in I. J. Gelb et al., *Proceedings of the Symposium on the Undeciphered Languages, held in London 25–27 July 1973* = *JRAS* 1975: 95–209.

Palaic

Carruba, O. 1970. *Das Palaische: Texte, Grammatik, Lexikon.* StBT 10. Wiesbaden.
———. 1972. *Beiträge zum Palaischen.* Nederlands Historisch-Archaeologisch Instituut in het Nabije Oosten, Uitgaven, 31. Istanbul.
Kammenhuber, A. 1959a. Das Palaische: Texte und Wortschatz. *RHA* 64: 1–92.
———. 1959b. Esquisse de grammaire palaïte. *Bulletin de la Société linguistique de Paris* 54: 18–45.
Melchert, H. C. 1984. Notes on Palaic. *Zeitschrift für vergleichende Sprachforschung* 97: 22–43.

Luwian

Laroche, E. 1959. *Dictionnaire de la langue louvite.* Bibliothèque archéologique et historique de l'Institut Français de l'Archéologie d'Istanbul 6. Paris.
Otten, H. 1953a. *Luvische Texte in Umschrift.* Deutsche Akademie der Wissenschaften zu Berlin, Institut für Orientforschung, Veröffentlichungen 17. Berlin.
———. 1953b. *Zur grammatikalischen und lexikalischen Bestimmung des Luvischen.* Deutsche Akademie der Wissenschaften zu Berlin, Institut für Orientforschung, Veröffentlichungen 19. Berlin.
Starke, F. 1985. *Die keilschrift-luwischen Texte in Umschrift.* StBT 30. Wiesbaden.

Hieroglyphic Luwian

Hawkins, J. D. fc. *The Hieroglyphic Luwian Inscriptions of the Iron Age.* 3 vols. Berlin.
Hawkins, J. D., and Morpurgo-Davies, A. 1975. Hieroglyphic Hittite: Some New Readings and their Consequences. Pp. 121–33 in I. J. Gelb et al., *Proceedings of the Symposium on the Undeciphered Languages, held in London 25–27 July 1973* = *JRAS* 1975: 95–209.
Hawkins, J. D.; and Morpurgo-Davies, A.; and Neumann, G. 1973. *Hittite Hieroglyphs and Luwian: New Evidence for the Connection.* NAWG. Göttingen.
Laroche, E. 1960. *Les hiéroglyphes hittites.* Vol. 1, *L'écriture.* Paris.
Meriggi, P. 1962. *Hieroglyphisch-hethitisches Glossar.* 2d ed. Wiesbaden.
———. 1966–67. *Manuale di eteo geroglifico.* 2 vols. Incunabula graeca 13, 14. Rome.

Lydian

Carruba, O. 1963. Lydisch und Lyder. *MIO* 8: 383–408.
———. 1969. Zur Grammatik des Lydischen. In *Studi in onore de Piero Meriggi, Athenaum* 47: 39–83.
Gusmani, R. 1964. *Lydisches Wörterbuch, mit grammatischer Skizze und Inschriftensammlung.* Heidelberg. Ergänzungsheft 1, 1980; 2, 1982; 3, 1986.
———. 1975. Die lydische Sprache. Pp. 134–42 in I. J. Gelb et al., *Proceedings of the Symposium on the Undeciphered Languages, held in London 25–27 July 1973* = *JRAS* 1975: 95–209.
Heubeck, A. 1959. *Lydiaka; Untersuchungen zu Schrift, Sprache und Götternamen der Lyder.* Erlanger Forschungen A/9. Erlangen.
———. 1969. Lydisch. Pp. 397–427 in *Altkleinasiatische Sprachen,* ed. J. Friedrich. HO 1/2/1–2/2. Leiden.

Lycian

Kalinkas, E. 1901. *Tituli Lyciae lingua Lycia conscripti.* Tituli Asiae Minoris 1. Vienna.
Melchert, H. C. 1989. *Lycian lexicon.* Lexica anatolica 1. Chapel Hill, NC.
Neumann, G. 1969. Lykisch. Pp. 358–96 in *Altkleinasiatische Sprachen,* ed. J. Friedrich et al. HO 1/2/1–2/2. Leiden.
———. 1979. *Neufunde lykischer Inschriften seit 1901.* DÖAW 135. Ergänzungsbände zu den tituli Asiae Minoris 7. Vienna.
Metzger, H.; Laroche E.; and Dupont-Sommer, A. 1974. La stèle trilingue récemment découverte au Létoon de Xanthos. *CRAIBL* 1974: 82–93, 115–25, 132–49.

Carian

Ray, J. 1990. An Outline of Carian Grammar. *Kadmos* 29: 54–83.

Phrygian

Brixhe, C., and Lejeune, M. 1984. *Corpus des inscriptions paléo-phrygiennes.* Institut Français d'Études Anatoliennes. Paris.
Diakonov, I. M., and Neroznak, V. P. 1985. *Phrygian.* Anatolian and Caucasian Studies. Delmar, NY.

Haas, O. 1966. *Die phrygischen Sprachdenkmäler.* Linguistique balkanique 10. Sofia.
Neumann, G. 1988. *Phrygisch und Griechisch.* SÖAW 499. Vienna.
Werner, R. 1969. Die Phryger und ihre Sprache. *BiOr* 26: 177–82.

Indo-Iranian

Bartholomae, C. 1895–96. *Grundriss der iranischen Philologie.* 2 vols. Strasbourg.
———. 1904. *Altiranische Wörterbuch.* Strasbourg. Repr. 1979.
Kammenhuber, A. 1968. *Die Arier im Vorderen Orient.* Heidelberg.
Mayhofer, M. 1966. *Die Indo-Arier im Alten Vorderasien.* Wiesbaden.
———. 1986–. *Etymologisches Wörterbuch des Altindoarischen.* Indogermanische Bibliothek. Heidelberg.

Avestan

Schlerath, B. 1968–. *Awesta-Wörterbuch.* 2 vols. thus far. Wiesbaden.

Mycenaean Greek (Linear B)

Chadwick, J. 1970. *The Decipherment of Linear B.* 2d ed. Cambridge.
———. 1987. *Linear B and Related Scripts.* Reading the Past 1. Berkeley.
Hooker, J. T. 1980. *Linear B: An Introduction.* Bristol.
Morpurgo-Davies, A., and Duhoux, Y., eds. 1985. *Linear B: A 1984 Survey.* Bibliothèque des Cahiers de l'Institut de Linguistique de Louvain 26. Louvain-la-Neuve.
Palmer, L. R. 1963. *The Interpretation of Mycenaean Greek Texts.* Oxford.
Ventris, M., and Chadwick, J. 1973. *Documents in Mycenaean Greek.* 2d ed. Cambridge.

Hurrian and Urartian

Barnett, R. D. 1974. The Hieroglyphic Writing of Urartu. Pp. 43–55 in *Anatolian Studies Presented to Hans Gustav Güterbock on the Occasion of his 65th Birthday,* ed. K. Bittel, P. H. J. Houwink ten Cate, and E. Reiner. Istanbul.
Klein, J. J. 1974. Urartian Hieroglyphic Inscriptions from Altintepe. *AnSt* 24: 77–94.
Speiser, E. A. 1941. *Introduction to Hurrian.* AASOR 20. New Haven.
Zimansky, P. E. 1985. *Ecology and Empire: The Structure of the Urartian State.* Studies in Ancient Oriental Civilization 41. Chicago.

Sumerian

Civil, M. 1973. The Sumerian Writing System: Some Problems. *Or* 42: 21–34.
Cooper, J. R. 1973. Sumerian and Akkadian in Sumer and Akkad. *Or* 42: 239–46.
Deimel, A. 1928–50. *Šumerisches Lexikon.* 4 pts., 7 vols. Rome.
Diakonoff, I. M. 1975. Ancient Writing and Ancient Written Language. Pp. 99–121 in *Sumerological Studies in Honor of Thorkild Jacobsen on his Seventieth Birthday June 7, 1974,* ed. S. Lieberman. AS 20. Chicago.
Falkenstein, A. 1936. *Archäische Texte aus Uruk.* Ausgrabungen der Deutschen Forschungsgemeinschaft in Uruk-Warka 2. Berlin.
———. 1949–50. *Grammatik der Sprache Gudeas von Lagaš.* 2 vols. AnOr 28–29, 29A. Rome. Ergänzungsheft (AnOr 29A) by D. O. Edzard, W. Farber, and W. R. Mayer, 1978.
———. 1959. *Das Sumerische.* HO 1/2/1–2/1. Leiden.
Jacobsen, T. 1988a. Sumerian Grammar Today. *JAOS* 108: 123–33.
———. 1988b. The Sumerian Verbal Core. *ZA* 78: 161–220.
Landsberger, B., et al. 1937–. *Materialen zum sumerischen Lexikon/Materials for the Sumerian Lexicon.* 16 vols. to date. Rome.
Poebel, A. 1923. *Grundzüge der sumerischen Grammatik.* Rostocker Orientalistische Studien 1. Rostock.
Sjöberg, Å., et al. 1984–. *The Sumerian Dictionary of the University Museum of the University of Pennsylvania.* Philadelphia.
Thomsen, M.-L. 1987. *The Sumerian Language: An Introduction to Its History and Grammatical Structure.* 2d ed. Mesopotamia: Copenhagen Studies in Assyriology 10. Copenhagen.

Elamite

Cameron, G. G. 1948. *Persepolis Treasury Tablets.* OIP 55. Chicago.
———. 1960. The Elamite Version of the Bisitun Inscriptions. *JCS* 14: 59–68.
Grillot-Susini, F., and Roche, C. 1987. *Éléments de grammaire élamite.* Paris.
Hallock, R. T. 1969. *Persepolis Fortification Tablets.* OIP 92. Chicago.
Hinz, W. 1975. Problems of Linear Elamite. Pp. 106–15 in I. J. Gelb et al., *Proceedings of the Symposium on the Undeciphered Languages, held in London 25–27 July 1973 = JRAS* 1975: 95–209.
Hinz, W., and Koch, H. 1987. *Elamisches Wörterbuch.* 2 vols. AMI Ergäzungsband 17. Berlin.
Labat, R. 1950–51. Structure de la langue élamite (État présent de la question). *Conférences de l'Institut de linguistique de l'Université de Paris* 9: 23–42.
McAlpin, D. W. 1981. Proto-Elamo-Dravidian: The Evidence and its Implications. *TAPhS* 71: 63–83.
Meriggi, P. 1971–74. *La scrittura proto-elamica.* 3 vols. Rome.
Paper, H. H. 1955. The Phonology and Morphology of Royal Achaemenid Elamite. Diss., Michigan.
Reiner, E. 1969. The Elamite Language. Pp. 54–118 in J. Friedrich et al., *Altkleinasiatische Sprachen.* HO 1/2/1–2/2. Leiden.
Weissbach, F. H. 1911. *Die Keilinschriften der Achämeniden.* VAB 3. Leipzig.

Qutian

Hallo, W. W. 1971. Gutium. *RLA* 3: 708–20.

Hattic

Girbal, C. 1986. *Beiträge zur Grammatik des Hattischen.* Europäische Hochschulschriften 21/50. Frankfurt am Main.
Kammenhuber, A. 1969. Das Hattische. Pp. 428–546 in J. Friedrich et al., *Altkleinasiatische Sprachen.* HO 1/2/1–2/2. Leiden.
Schuster, H.-S. 1974. *Die Ḫattisch-hethitischen Bilinguen.* Leiden.

Kassite

Balkan, K. 1954. *Kassitenstudien.* Vol. 1, *Die Sprache der Kassiten.* Trans. F. R. Kraus. AOS 37. New Haven.
Brinkman, J. A. 1980. Kassiten. *RLA* 5: 464–73.
Jaritz, K. 1957. Die kassitischen Sprachreste. *Anthropos* 52: 850–98.

Minoan Linear A

Best, J., and Woudhuizen, F., eds. 1988. *Ancient Scripts from Crete and Cyprus.* Publications of the Henri Frankfort Foundation 9. Leiden.
Chadwick, J. 1957. Introduction to the Problems of "Minoan Linear A." Pp. 143–47 in I. J. Gelb et al., *Proceedings of the Symposium on the Undeciphered Languages, held in London 25–27 July 1973 = JRAS* 1975: 95–209.
Duhoux, Y., ed. 1978. *Études minoennes I: Le linéaire A.* Louvain.
Godart, L., and Oliver, J.-P. 1976–85. *Recueil des inscriptions en linéar A.* 5 vols. Paris.
Gordon, C. H. 1966. *Evidence for the Minoan Language.* Ventnor, NJ.

Hooker, J. T. 1975. Problems and Methods in the Decipherment of Linear A. Pp. 164–72 in I. J. Gelb et al., *Proceedings of the Symposium on the Undeciphered Languages, held in London 25–27 July 1973* = *JRAS* 1975: 95–209.

Eteocretan

Duhoux, Y. 1982. *L'étéocrétois: Les textes—la langue.* Amsterdam.

Phaestos Disk

Duhoux, Y. 1977. *Le disque de Phaestos: Archéologie, épigraphie, édition critique, index.* Louvain.

Olivier, J.-P. 1975. *Le disque de Phaistos.* Athens.

Cypro-Minoan; Cypriot

Masson, O. 1961. *Les inscriptions chypriotes syllabiques.* Paris.

JOHN HUEHNERGARD

AKKADIAN

Akkadian was a Semitic language spoken and written in ancient Mesopotamia in the pre-Christian period. Abundant documents written in the various dialects of Akkadian have been recovered by archaeologists. The language is usually classified as East Semitic, in distinction to West Semitic languages such as Hebrew, Aramaic, Amorite, and Arabic. The name "Akkadian" derives from the city of Akkad, the seat of a Semitic-speaking dynasty in S Mesopotamia in the mid-3d millennium B.C.; occasionally, both in antiquity and in modern times, the language has also been called Assyrian or Babylonian, from its two major dialects.

A. Introduction
B. Third-Millennium Akkadian
C. Early Second-Millennium Dialects
  1. Old Babylonian
  2. Old Assyrian
D. Late Second-Millennium Dialects
  1. "Standard Babylonian"
  2. Middle Babylonian/Assyrian and Peripheral Dialects
E. First-Millennium Akkadian
  1. Neo-Babylonian and Neo-Assyrian
  2. Late Babylonian

A. Introduction

Akkadian is the oldest-known Semitic language, attested in texts spanning a period of over 2,600 years. The language was the vehicle of a highly developed and historically minded culture that made extensive use of writing; for this reason, and because documents written in it were generally inscribed on virtually indestructible clay tablets rather than on more perishable material such as papyrus, Akkadian textual documentation is the most extensive we possess for any ancient Semitic language, containing literary and religious works, lists of Akkadian and Sumerian words and grammatical forms and other learned compilations, and political, legal, economic, and personal records (for a full survey of Akkadian texts see *HKL* and Reiner 1978).

In the 3d millennium, speakers of Akkadian in Mesopotamia lived alongside the Sumerians, whose language is unrelated to Semitic or any other known language family. Sumerian is attested in texts from as early as ca. 3000 B.C., and it probably survived as a spoken language until ca. 1700 B.C. or later. The relationship between Sumerians and Akkadians has been compared to that between the ancient Romans and the peoples of medieval Europe: Sumerian culture, religion, scholarship, and language left a lasting impression on Akkadian language and culture (von Soden 1960). For example, the cuneiform writing system which had originally been used to write Sumerian was adapted to write Akkadian, and, with relatively minor modifications, it remained in use for over two and a half millennia. This system, originally comprising a larger number of signs, was reduced to some 600 signs by ca. 2000 B.C.; many of these were pictographic in origin, while others appear to have been conventional schematic representations of words. Inscribed with a stylus on clay tablets, the signs gradually acquired a characteristically "cuneiform" ("wedge-shaped") appearance. The signs often have multiple values, with the context indicating which value is actually being used; they may represent either words ("king," "old," "come," etc.) or syllables used to write words phonetically (*ba, ab, bab,* etc.). The complexity of this writing system resulted in the restriction of its use to a professional scribal and scholarly class, but in their hands it became the instrument of a millennial tradition of learning and record-keeping. In the course of time, the same system was borrowed to write other languages such as Hurrian, Hittite, and Urartian.

The Akkadian language and culture were unknown or forgotten in classical and medieval times. Occasional isolated cuneiform texts were made known in Europe during the 17th and 18th centuries, but in substance the discovery, publication, and decipherment of Akkadian texts was the achievement of the mid and late 19th century. The major figures involved in this decipherment included the German G. F. Grotefend, the Irishman E. Hincks, and the Englishman H. C. Rawlinson. Building upon prior advances in the decipherment of Old Persian and beginning with trilingual Akkadian/Old Persian/Elamite texts (such as the Behistun Inscription), these and other scholars during the 1840s and 1850s determined that the Akkadian inscriptions represented a Semitic language related to Arabic and Hebrew, that the signs could have multiple values, and that they represented not simple consonants (as in Hebrew or Arabic script) but either syllables or complete words. Once an initial identification of sign values had been achieved, further interpretation of texts was aided both by sign lists and word lists found at Nineveh in the 1840s, and by the similarity of many Akkadian lexemes with those of Hebrew and Arabic. By the late 1850s a fairly accurate interpretation of historical texts was possible, and further research moved on to comprehensive lexicology and to the publication and interpretation of the continually increasing textual corpus of Akkadian. (On the history of decipherment, see Kramer 1963: 6–32.)

In the long history of its attestation, Akkadian naturally underwent changes, and it is customary to distinguish various dialectical forms of it, both in its homeland and in other linguistic areas to which the use of Akkadian spread. The following paragraphs will survey this evolution.

B. Third-Millennium Akkadian

The first stage in the history of the Akkadian language is the Old Akkadian period. The language is first attested in personal names found in texts of the Fara period, ca. 2600 B.C. (Biggs 1967), but from ca. 2350 to 1950 B.C. we find texts fully written in Old Akkadian (OAkk; Gelb 1957: 3). Within this span, the period producing the greatest number of extant texts is that of the dynasty of Sargon of Akkad (ca. 2350–2150 B.C.). Prior to this we have only occasional texts, and afterwards there was a temporary return to the use of Sumerian in official documents. With the exception of a few religious texts, these OAkk writings cannot be truly classified as "literary"; they consist mainly of historical and dedicatory inscriptions of royal and private persons and letters, as well as economic, administrative, and legal texts. The writing system had not yet been given the precision it would later have in the expression of Akkadian phonemes: initial homorganic voiced and voiceless stops were still not graphically distinguished from one another (e.g., the same sign is used to write the syllables *da, ta,* and *ṭa,* etc.), the later aleph sign representing the glottal stop in conjunction with a vowel was not yet in use, and consonant doubling and vowel length were not normally represented. For the linguistic historian and the comparative Semitist, the OAkk texts are important because they exemplify early phonological and morphological characteristics of the language that would later be lost, such as the presence of Semitic *ś* and ʿ (which would later be merged with other phonemes), the absence of later vowel contraction, and the use of a productive dual.

C. Early Second-Millennium Dialects

1. Old Babylonian. In 2d-millennium texts we find the first attested dialect differentiation between southern Akkadian (Babylonian) and northern Akkadian (Assyrian). Old Babylonian (OB), the earliest form taken by the southern dialect, is found in texts dating from ca. 1950 B.C. to the end of the dynasty of Hammurabi of Babylon, ca. 1530 B.C. The period of Hammurabi himself and his immediate predecessors and successors is especially important because it was associated with the establishment of a careful chancery style of writing Akkadian, an innovation that affected the writing of royal and private inscriptions, letters, and business and administrative documents. Here, syllabic writing was generally preferred to logographic, and a number of signs current in OAkk were dropped from active use: preliminary measures were taken to distinguish initial voiced, voiceless, and emphatic stops; new means of representing the aleph were devised; and double consonants were normally represented graphically. Within OB itself, regional subdialectic traits are discernible in Mari, Elam, the Diyala area, and elsewhere. This was a time of great literary productivity: epics, hymns, and prayers were written in a somewhat more archaic form of OB (the so-called hymnic-epic dialect: von Soden 1931–33; Groneberg 1971) which was to remain an ideal literary standard throughout the remaining history of the language.

Because of its internal consistency and its later literary influence, OB is generally regarded as the classical stage of Akkadian; therefore, a brief description of its characteristics will indicate the principle characteristics of classical Akkadian. The *phonemic inventory* of Akkadian is reduced, by comparison with that of other Semitic languages such as classical Arabic. The vowels include long and short *a, e, i,* and *u;* consonants are ʾ (aleph), *b, d, g, ḫ, y, k, l, m, n, p, q, r, s, ṣ (ṣade), š (šin), t, ṭ (ṭet), w,* and *z.* Pronunciation of vowels is similar to that of vowels in Latin or German; that of consonants resembles English except for ʾ (glottal stop), *ḫ* (velar, like *ch* in German *ach*), *š* (= sh), and the velarized or "emphatic" consonants *q, ṣ,* and *ṭ*. Nominal and verbal roots are generally triconsonantal. Verbs are conjugated in four main stems: a basic stem, a stem with doubled second-root consonant (corresponding to Heb *Piʿel,* and denoting plurality or intensity), a causative stem with infix *š,* and a passive stem with infix *n.* Each of these stems, and other stems derived from them, may have the following forms: present or durative, preterite or punctual, perfect, atemporal stative, imperative, infinitive, and active and passive participle. In the noun, masculine and feminine are distinguished, the latter usually marked by a morpheme *-t.* The noun has singular, plural, and vestigial remains of an earlier, regularly used dual. There are three cases (nominative, genitive, and accusative) marked by different final vowels (or case endings: *-u, -i, -a*). Most case endings also include a final, nonfunctional *-m* ("mimation"), a feature which disappears in Akkadian after the OB period (Reiner 1966 and 1970; von Soden *GAG;* Riemschneider 1977: Caplice 1988).

2. Old Assyrian. Although Old Assyrian (OA) is contemporaneous with OB, the OA texts that have been discovered so far were written within a more restricted period (1950–1750 B.C.). Aside from a single incantation and a few royal inscriptions from the capital city Aššur, all OA texts are letters and business documents found at Kültepe and other Assyrian merchant colonies in W Anatolia. The writing system has a more restricted battery of signs than that used in the south, and is more archaic in its external form. The signs are also less informative: as in OAkk, initial homorganic voiced and voiceless stops are still represented by the same sign, and consonant doubling is not regularly indicated. The language is also more conservative than OB, particularly in resisting vocalic contraction. A persistent characteristic of Assyrian in all periods is the so-called Assyrian vowel harmony: short *a* in an open syllable is assimilated to the vowel of the following syllable: thus, the Assyrian equivalent of Babylonian *iṣbatu, ittaṣi,* would be *iṣbutu, ittiṣi.* It is noteworthy that Assyrian literary texts of all periods, whether copies of imported Babylonian texts or native Assyrian compositions (including the increasingly lengthy inscriptions of Assyrian kings), generally employ the Babylonian dialect, with occasional grammatical Assyrianisms (see Hecker 1968).

D. Late Second-Millennium Dialects

1. "Standard Babylonian." The Kassite domination of Babylonia that began after the downfall of the Hammurabi dynasty (ca. 1595 B.C.) disrupted literary and other scribal activities; consequently, the second half of the 2d millennium is generally not very well represented in direct textual remains. Nevertheless, this was clearly a period of great importance in the history of the Akkadian language and literature, involving a sifting of the OB literary inheritance. Some texts were discarded, presumably, at least in part, for theological reasons; others were reformulated in a new and standardized "canonical" form that henceforth remained normative as long as texts were written in Akkadian (von Soden 1953). These literary texts were couched in a form of Akkadian usually called "Standard Babylonian" (in German, *jungbabylonisch*), a specifically literary "dialect" loosely modeled on the OB literary language. The most noteworthy divergences of Standard Babylonian (SB) from OB are the loss of mimation in noun and pronoun and the reduction of case endings to *-u* for nominative and accusative singular, *-i* for genitive singular, and *-ī* or *-ē* for all cases of plural. Though influenced in these and sometimes in other ways by the contemporary spoken language, which increasingly diverged from it, SB remained in essence the norm for almost all literary and religious works until the end of Akkadian literary production. Texts in SB, although sparse in number for the remainder of the 2d millennium, increase thereafter, particularly in the 8th and 7th centuries. The library assembled by Assurbanipal at Nineveh (ca. 625 B.C.), and excavated by Layard, Rassam, and others, is a particularly rich source of such literary texts.

2. Middle Babylonian/Assyrian and Peripheral Dialects. In contrast to the "Standard Babylonian," which was primarily a literary dialect, Middle Babylonian (MB) and Middle Assyrian (MA) represent spoken vernacular dialects of S and N Mesopotamia in the second half of the 2d millennium (ca. 1530–1000 B.C.). Middle Babylonian (Aro 1955 and 1957) is rather sparsely attested in day-to-day documents such as letters and contracts. Middle Assyrian (Mayer 1971) is somewhat better attested, in a law code (cf. *ANET,* 180–8), rituals, a series of harem decrees, letters, and some royal inscriptions. It was in this period that Akkadian came to be used as an international lingua franca in Egypt, Syria-Palestine, Anatolia, Iran, and N Mesopotamian Hurrian centers like Nuzi. Texts discovered at sites such as el-Amarna, Ugarit, Boghazköy, and Nuzi attest the so-called "peripheral dialects" of Akkadian, in which the Akkadian sources contain aspects of the respective local language of the scribes. Texts of this period, whether from Mesopotamia or the peripheral areas, are most strikingly distinguished from those of the preceding area by (1) consonantal shifts—for example, *š* before a dental or another sibilant becomes *l* (e.g., OB *išten, ušziz* becomes MB/MA *ilten, ulziz*), (2) loss of mimation, and (3) toward the end of the millennium, loss of functionally distinct case endings. There are also some noteworthy differences between MA and MB: MA reflects (1) vowel harmony—for example, initial *wa-* becomes *u-*, and *š* before a labial becomes *s* (e.g. OB *wašbat* in MA becomes *usbat*), and (2) velarization or partial assimilation of infixed *t* to preceding *q* (Bab *iqtanarrab* = Ass *iqṭanarrab*).

E. First-Millennium Akkadian

1. Neo-Babylonian and Neo-Assyrian (ca. 1000–625 B.C.). Ending with the fall of the Assyrian kingdom, these dialects are attested mainly in letters and contracts, though Neo-Assyrian (NA) was also used in treaties and occasionally in literary and religious texts. Both dialects show the increasing influence of Aramaic, especially in the loss of case endings, the adoption of the Aram preposition *la,* "to, from," and replacement of *nīnu,* "we," by *anīnu* under influence of Aram *ʾ^{a}naḥnā.* Assyrian continued to be more resistant to change than Babylonian; thus, vowel contraction in final positions or in hollow verbs is resisted in the sequences *ia, iu, ua* (e.g., Bab *bikâ, annû, ikân* remain uncontracted in Ass *bikiā, anniu, ikūan*).

2. Late Babylonian (615 B.C.–1st century A.D.). This is the language of the Chaldean, Persian, and Seleucid-Arsacid periods. It is even more strongly influenced by Aramaic and is found in royal inscriptions, letters, and economic documents. The Greek language became used increasingly by the Babylonian upper class after the Macedonian conquest of Babylon (333 B.C.), and Akkadian documents become increasingly scarce, their use being limited mainly to the dwindling temple complexes that tried in vain to preserve and promote the old ways. The very last attested cuneiform documents date to ca. A.D. 50 and deal mostly with astrological subjects.

Bibliography

Aro, J. 1955. *Studien zur mittelbabylonischen Grammatik.* StudOr 20. Helsinki.

———. 1957. *Glossar zu den mittelbabylonischen Briefen.* StudOr 22. Helsinki.

Bergsträsser, G. 1983. Akkadian. Pp. 25–49 in *Introduction to the Semitic Languages.* Trans. P. T. Daniels. Winona Lake, IN.

Berkooz, M. 1937. *The Nuzi Dialect of Akkadian.* Language Dissertations 23. Philadelphia.

Biggs, R. D. 1967. Semitic Names in the Fara Period. *Or* n.s. 36: 55–66.

Böhl, F. M. T. de Liagre 1909. *Die Sprache der Amarnabriefe.* LSS 5/2. Leipzig.

Caplice, R. 1988. *Introduction to Akkadian.* 3d rev. ed. Rome.

Gelb, I. J. 1957. *Old Akkadian Writing and Grammar.* MSD 2. 2d ed. Rev. and enl. Chicago.

———. 1969. *Sequential Reconstruction of Proto-Akkadian.* AS 18. Chicago.

Gordon, C. H. 1938. The Dialect of the Nuzu Tablets. *Or* n.s. 7: 32–68, 215–32.

Groneberg, B. R. M. 1971. *Untersuchungen zum hymnisch-epischen Dialekt der altbabylonischen Texte.* Diss., Münster.

———. 1987. *Syntax, Morphologie und Stil der jungbabylonischen "hymnischen" Literatur.* Vol. 1: *Grammatik.* Freiburger Altorientalische Studien 14/1. Wiesbaden.

Hecker, K. 1968. *Grammatik der Kültepe-Texte.* AnOr 44. Rome.

Kramer, S. N. 1963. *The Sumerians.* Chicago.

Labat, R. 1932. *L'akkadien de Boghaz-Köi.* Bordeaux.

Mayer, W. 1971. *Untersuchungen zur Grammatik des Mittelassyrischen.* AOAT 2. Kevelaer.

Reiner, E. 1966. *A Linguistic Analysis of Akkadian.* Janua linguarum. Series practica 21. The Hague.

———. 1970. Akkadian. Pp. 274–303 in *Current Trends in Linguistics,* ed. T. A. Sebeok. Paris.

———. 1978. Die akkadische Literatur. Vol. 1. Pp. 151–210 in *Altorientalische Literaturen: Neues Handbuch der Literaturwissenschaft,* ed. W. Röllig. Wiesbaden.

Riemschneider, K. 1977. *An Akkadian Grammar.* Trans. T. A. Caldwell, J. N. Ostwalt, and J. F. X. Sheehan. Marquette.

Soden, W. von 1931–33. Der hymnisch-epische Dialekt des Akkadischen. *ZA* 40: 163–227; 41: 90–183.

———. 1953. Das Problem der zeitlichen Einordnung akkadischer Literaturwerke. *MDOG* 85: 14–26.

———. 1960. *Zweisprachigkeit in der geistigen Kultur Babyloniens.* SÖAW 235/1. Vienna.
———. 1965–81. *Akkadisches Handwörterbuch.* Wiesbaden.
Ungnad, A., and Matous, L. 1964. *Grammatik des Akkadischen.* 4th ed. Munich.
Wilhelm, G. 1970. *Untersuchungen zum Hurro-Akkadischen von Nuzi.* AOAT 9. Kevelaer and Neukirchen-Vluyn.

RICHARD I. CAPLICE

ARAMAIC

Aramaic is the best-attested and longest-attested member of the NW Semitic subfamily of languages (which also includes *inter alia* Hebrew, Phoenician, Ugaritic, Moabite, Ammonite, and Edomite). The relatively small proportion of the biblical text preserved in an Aramaic original (Dan 2:4–7:28; Ezra 4:8–68 and 7:12–26; Jeremiah 10:11; Gen 31:47 [two words] as well as isolated words and phrases in Christian Scriptures) belies the importance of this language for biblical studies and for religious studies in general, for Aramaic was the primary international language of literature and communication throughout the Near East from ca. 600 B.C.E. to ca. 700 C.E. and was the major spoken language of Palestine, Syria, and Mesopotamia in the formative periods of Christianity and rabbinic Judaism.

Jesus and his disciples, according to the stories in the Gospels, spoke Aramaic. Parts of the later books of the Hebrew Bible, as well as portions of the Gospels and Acts, are often thought to be translations from Aramaic originals, but even if not they are undoubtedly strongly "Aramaized" in their diction. Late biblical Hebrew and rabbinic Hebrew were heavily influenced by Aramaic in both grammar and vocabulary. Two of the major translation traditions of the Hebrew Bible—the Syriac Peshitta and the Jewish Targums—are in Aramaic, as are substantial portions of rabbinic literature, the entire literary corpus of Syriac Christianity, and that of the Mandaeans (a non-Christian gnostic sect of S Mesopotamia). After the Moslem conquest, Arabic gradually displaced Aramaic as the literary and colloquial language of the Near East. Isolated pockets of Modern Aramaic speech still remain to this day, and the study and use of classical Syriac as a learned, religious language has never stopped. Indeed, it has witnessed somewhat of a revival in recent decades (see *EJ* 3: 259–87).

A. The Periods and Sources of Aramaic
  1. Old Aramaic
  2. Imperial Aramaic
  3. Middle Aramaic
  4. Late Aramaic
  5. Modern Aramaic
B. Linguistic Overview
  1. Old Aramaic
  2. Imperial Aramaic
  3. Later Dialects

A. The Periods and Sources of Aramaic

Aramaic is attested over a period of almost 3,000 years, during which time there occurred great changes of grammar, lexical stock, and usage. It has generally proved helpful for analysis to divide the several Aramaic dialects into periods, groups, and subgroups based both on chronology and geography. Although no universally accepted scheme of such classificatory phases exists, and new discoveries regularly alter our picture—especially for the sparsely attested older dialects—the general shape of the outline is clear. The following scheme represents that adopted by the major research project in the field—the Comprehensive Aramaic Lexicon—and incorporates discoveries through the mid-1980s.

1. Old Aramaic (to ca. 612 B.C.E.). This period witnessed the rise of the Arameans as a major force in ANE history, the adoption of their language as an international language of diplomacy in the latter days of the Neo-Assyrian Empire, and the dispersal of Aramaic-speaking peoples from Egypt to Lower Mesopotamia as a result of the Assyrian policies of deportation. The scattered and generally brief remains of inscriptions on imperishable materials preserved from these times are enough to demonstrate that an international standard dialect had not yet been developed. The extant texts may be grouped into several dialects:

a. Standard Syrian (or Western Old Aramaic). These inscriptions, of very limited chronological (mid-9th to end of 8th century B.C.E.) and geographic spread (within a radius of about 100 km centered on Aleppo) include:

BR-HDD: A brief dedication of a stela to Melqart (the god of Tyre) by BR-HDD, king of Aram.

Zakkur: A stela dedicated to the god Iluwer by Zakkur, king of Hamath. Its text is reminiscent of many of the Psalms of Thanksgiving.

Sefire: Three stelae containing the text of a treaty between Matiʿel, king of Arpad, and BR-GʾYH, king of KTK, apparently the governor of one of the Neo-Assyrian Syrian provinces (perhaps Šamši-Ilu of Bit-Adini [Lemaire and Durand 1984]). This text is our best extrabiblical source for the West Semitic tradition of covenantal blessings and curses.

Nerab: Funeral stelae of two priests of the moon-god, Śehr.

BR-RKB: See Samalian, below.

b. Samalian. At modern Zinçirli, dynasts of the Neo-Hittite kingdom of Samʾal (also referred to by some scholars as Yaʾudi) wrote their dedicatory inscriptions first in Phoenician (KLMW), then in a local, highly idiosyncratic Aramaic dialect (the so-called Hadad and PNMW inscriptions), and, finally, in standard, Syrian Old Aramaic (BR-RKB).

c. Fakhariyah. A bilingual, Neo-Assyrian and Aramaic inscription on a statue. The script and orthography of this inscription are of major importance for the history of the alphabet (Kaufman 1986).

d. Mesopotamian. Primarily consists of brief economic and legal texts and endorsements scratched on clay tablets (Fales 1986; Kaufman 1989). Not surprisingly, both the Fakhariyah and Mesopotamian dialects evidence a substantial amount of Akkadian influence.

e. Deir ʿAlla. This important but fragmentary text, painted on the plaster walls of a cultic installation, recounts a vision of "Balaam, son of Beor," the Transjordanian prophet known from Numbers 22–24. The fact that some scholars classify the language of this text as a Canaanite, rather than an Aramaic, dialect, illustrates that there is no demonstrable dividing line (or, in linguistic terms, a bundle of isoglosses) separating Canaanite and Aramaic at this time. See DEIR ʿALLA (TEXTS).

2. Imperial Aramaic (or "Official Aramaic"; to ca. 200 B.C.E.). During this period Aramaic spread far beyond the borders of its native lands over the vast territories of the Neo-Babylonian and even larger Persian empires—from Upper Egypt to Asia Minor and eastward to the Indian subcontinent. Unfortunately, only a remnant of the undoubtedly once vast corpus of administrative documents, records, and letters that held these empires together has been preserved, for such texts were written in ink on perishable materials, in sharp contrast to the more durable cuneiform clay tablets of earlier W Asiatic cultures. (A single syllabic cuneiform Aramaic text, an incantation from Uruk, is known. Though from Hellenistic times, its archaizing language may be ascribed to this period.) Isolated monumental stone inscriptions have been found in the various peripheral regions (e.g., Sheik Fadl in Egypt, Teima in Arabia, Daskyleion in Asia Minor), but none, surprisingly enough, in the core regions of Syria and Mesopotamia.

The bulk of the finds, however, is from Egypt, where the dry climate led to the preservation of papyrus and leather along with the expected ostraca and stone inscriptions. The major Egyptian finds are (1) papyrus archives of the Jewish military garrison at Elephantine/Syene (including deeds of sale, marriage contracts, formal letters to the authorities in Jerusalem, and fragments of literary materials); (2) the correspondence of the Persian satrap of Egypt, Arsames; (3) a packet of letters sent to family members residing at Syene and Luxor, discovered at Hermopolis; and (4) Saqqarah: a late-7th-century papyrus letter from a Philistine king (perhaps of Ekron) asking help of pharaoh against the king of Babylon; and legal and economic records on papyri and ostraca from the 5th and 4th centuries.

The Aramaic "official" letters in the book of Ezra are almost certainly composed in Imperial Aramaic, for both their language and their epistolary style are appropriate to the period.

More fascinating for their historical context than their content are the fragmentary papyrus deeds of sale, dating from mid-4th-century Samaria, discovered in a cave of the Wadi Daliyeh, near Jericho, along with the skeletons of about 200 people who had apparently fled from the approaching Macedonian army. See DALIYEH, WADI ED- (M.R. 189155).

From a linguistic perspective, what characterizes this period above all is that it witnessed the development of a literary, standard form of both the language and its orthography—an ideal to be strived for, at least in literary texts and formal documents. The model for this standard appears to have been Babylonian Aramaic as spoken and written by educated Persians. This ideal, in the guise of Standard Literary Aramaic, was to last more than a thousand years.

3. Middle Aramaic (to ca. 250 C.E.). In the Hellenistic and Roman periods, Greek replaced Aramaic as the administrative language of the Near East, while in the various Aramaic-speaking regions the dialects began to develop independently of one another. Written Aramaic, however, as is the case with most written languages, by providing a somewhat artificial, cross-dialectal uniformity, continued to serve as a vehicle of communication within and among the various groups. For this purpose, the literary standard developed in the previous period, Standard Literary Aramaic, was used, but lexical and grammatical differences based on the language(s) and dialect(s) of the local population are always evident. It is helpful to divide the texts surviving from this period into two major categories: epigraphic and canonical.

a. Epigraphic. (1) Palmyrene: dedicatory and honorific inscriptions and a decree of duty tariffs from the independent Syrian desert oasis trading city of Tadmor/Palmyra (earliest: 33 B.C.E.). Many of the texts are Greek bilinguals.

(2) Nabatean: tomb and votive texts from the Arab kingdom of Petra (earliest: 170 B.C.E.). A hoard of legal papyri from the Bar Kokhba period was discovered in one of the Naḥal Ḥever caves.

(3) Hatran: dedicatory inscriptions from the important, 2d-century C.E. Parthian kingdom of Hatra. A smaller, similar group was found at nearby Assur.

(4) Other: isolated inscriptions from Syria (especially Dura-Europos), Asia Minor, Armenia, Georgia, Media, Parthia, Persia, and Babylonia. Archival materials from the Judean desert are also to be placed here.

b. Canonical. (1) Daniel. The Aramaic portions of this biblical book (in contrast to the material in Ezra) clearly belong to this dialect rather than to Imperial Aramaic.

(2) Jewish Literary Aramaic. (a) Qumran. Among the Dead Sea Scrolls, much (if not most) of the nonsectarian, parabiblical material is in Aramaic. This includes the *Genesis Apocryphon,* the *Targum of Job,* the books of *Enoch,* and the *Testament of Levi.*

(b) Targum Onkelos/Jonathan. Although the only reliable mss stem ultimately from the Babylonian academies, the consonantal texts of Targum Onkelos to the Torah and Jonathan to the Prophets apparently originated in Palestine in this period.

(c) Legal Formulas. Preserved in rabbinic literature are texts and formulas of an authentic Aramaic tradition.

(3) Middle Iranian Ideograms. After a brief flirtation with cuneiform for their monumental inscriptions ("Old Persian"), the Persians adopted the Aramaic script for writing their language; and, perhaps under the cuneiform model, in both Parthian and Pehlevi, Aramaic ideograms were used to indicate some Persian lexical units.

(4) Demotic Material. Also, apparently, from the earliest part of this period is the Aramaic material preserved in the demotic script on papyrus Amherst 63, which includes several hymns in a mixed Canaanite/Aramaic dialect and, in relatively good Aramaic, the lengthy story of the conflict between the two royal Assyrian brothers Asshurbanipal and Shamashshumukin. The decipherment of this material has been a slow process, but it is already clear that many unexpected features appear in the Aramaic of this text. Since Standard Literary Aramaic is very much a function of orthographic tradition, the occurrence here of such unexpected forms should not be a great surprise.

4. Late Aramaic (to ca. 1200 C.E.). The bulk of our

evidence for Aramaic comes from the vast literature and occasional inscriptions of this period. During the early centuries of this period Aramaic dialects were still widely spoken. During the second half of this period, however, Arabic had already displaced Aramaic as the spoken language of much of the population. Consequently, many of our texts were composed and/or transmitted by persons whose Aramaic dialect was only a learned language. Although the dialects of this period were previously divided into two branches (Eastern and Western), it now seems best to think rather of three: Palestinian, Syrian, and Babylonian.

a. Palestinian. (1) **Jewish.** (a) Inscriptions (mostly from synagogues); (b) Targumic: the dialect of the Palestinian Targums (Neofiti, Genizah fragments, and the Fragment Targum); (c) Galilean: the dialect of the Talmud and midrashim of Palestine (so-called "Yerushalmi").

(2) Christian. Christian Palestinian Aramaic is attested in a small group of inscriptions, bible translations, and liturgical lectionaries from the Judean region written in Syriac script.

(3) Samaritan. Two different translations of the Torah, liturgical poetry, and some literary/exegetical works are preserved from this group. The reading tradition of the modern Samaritan priests is a valuable linguistic source here, as it is for their Hebrew tradition.

b. Syrian. (1) Syriac. The liturgical language of Eastern Christianity is by far the best documented Aramaic dialect. A vast and varied literature in two (Eastern/Nestorian, Western/Jacobite) dialects and orthographies has been preserved, as well as small collections of epigraphic and archival materials. The orthography of Syriac is based on Standard Literary Aramaic, while its lexicon and grammar are primarily that of the city of Edessa.

(2) Late Jewish Literary Aramaic. This literary dialect, only recently recognized, served for the composition of Aramaic parabiblical and liturgical texts (the best known of them being Targum Pseudo-Jonathan, Targum Psalms, and the canonical Targum of Job) and in some cases (Tobit and perhaps others) for the translation into Aramaic of works whose presumed Hebrew or Aramaic original had been lost. Like other literary dialects, it borrows heavily from its forebears, in this case Biblical Aramaic, Jewish Literary Aramaic, Jewish Palestinian Aramaic, and Jewish Babylonian Aramaic. Like most rabbinic materials, the texts have suffered greatly in transmission and often give the impression of massive inconsistency. Recent studies have revealed, however, that this is a real, albeit literary dialect with its own grammar and lexicon, whose lexical affinities point to a close relationship with the Syriac-speaking region.

c. Babylonian. (1) Jewish. The spoken language of the Jews of Babylonia, preserved primarily in large parts of the Babylonian Talmud. Slightly different dialects are found on "magic bowls" (incantations written on pottery bowls) and in the halakic literature of the post-Talmudic Babylonian sages *(gaʾonîm)*. The written and oral traditions of the Jews of Yemen are particularly important sources for this material.

(2) Mandaic. The spoken and literary language of a non-Christian gnostic sect. The sect itself is generally thought to have Palestinian origins, but its language is totally at home in Mesopotamia.

5. Modern Aramaic (to the present day). These dialects can be divided into the same three geographic groups.

a. Western. Here Aramaic is still spoken only in the town of Ma'lula (ca. 30 miles NNE of Damascus) and surrounding villages. The vocabulary is heavily Arabized.

b. Syrian. Western Syrian (Turoyo) is the language of Jacobite Christians in the region of Tur-ʿAbdin in SE Turkey. This dialect is the descendant of something very like classical Syriac. Eastern Syrian is spoken in the Kurdistani regions of Iraq, Iran, Turkey, and Azerbaijan by Christians and, formerly, by Jews. Substantial communities of the former are now found in North America. The Jewish speakers have mostly settled in Israel. These dialects are widely spoken by their respective communities and have been studied extensively during the past century. It has become clear that they are not the descendants of any known literary Aramaic dialect.

c. Babylonian. Mandaic is still used, at least until recently, by some Mandaeans in southernmost Iraq and adjacent areas in Iran.

In addition, in recent years classical Syriac has undergone somewhat of a revival as a learned vehicle of communication for Syriac Christians, both in the Middle East and among immigrant communities in Europe and North America.

B. Linguistic Overview

The following summary presupposes a basic acquaintance with the structure of Aramaic's better known cognate language, Biblical Hebrew.

1. Old Aramaic. a. Phonology. In this period the Proto-Semitic phonemic inventory survives virtually unchanged, though some minor changes in articulation seem to be indicated. Since the linear consonantal alphabet used for Aramaic, borrowed from a Canaanite/Phoenician source, had only 22 graphemes, however, several of the characters had to be polyphonous: Thus

šin indicates: *š*, *ś*, and *ṯ*.
samek (at Fakhariyah only) indicates both *s* and *ṯ*.
zayin indicates *z* and *ḏ*.
ṣade indicates *ṣ* and *ẓ*.
qop indicates *q* and *ḍ* (probably a velar spirant by this time).
ḥet indicates *ḥ* and *ḫ*.
ʿayin indicates ʿ and *ġ*.

That these consonantal phonemes still survived (rather than having merged with their graphic equivalent) is surmised largely on the basis of their independent histories in the subsequent dialects. In the case of *ḫ and ġ*, however, evidence for their existence is primarily extrapolated from the fact that they are still regularly distinguished in the demotic papyrus (see above). The result of these orthographic choices is (with the exception of *qop*) to give these texts an appearance very similar to that of Canaanite, a fact that has led some scholars to unwarranted claims of Canaanite influence in grammar, vocabulary, and style. The consonant *nun* is assimilated to a following consonant: *ʾt*, "you."

b. Morphology. (1) Nouns. The most notable difference between Aramaic and the other NW Semitic dialects is the presence of the suffixed definite article *-ā(ʾ)*. Probably in origin the same form as the Hebrew and Phoenician *ha-*, the suffixation of this deictic element gives Aramaic the appearance of having three noun states (absolute, construct, emphatic [or determined]) rather than two (absolute and construct) as in Hebrew. The morphology of noun affixes is set out paradigmatically in Table 1.

	absolute	construct	emphatic
m. sg.	*mlk*	*mlk*	*mlkʾ*
m. pl.	*mlkn (-īn)*	*mlky (-ay)*	*mlkyʾ (-ayyāʾ)*
f. sg.	*mlkh (-a[h])*	*mlkt (-at)*	*mlktʾ (-atāʾ)*
f. pl.	*mlkn (-ān)*	*mlkt (-āt)*	*mlktʾ (-ātāʾ)*

Note, vis-à-vis Hebrew, the final *nun* as opposed to Hebrew *mem* in the m. pl. abs. and likewise the *nun* in the f. pl. abs. instead of the expected *taw*. Standard Old Aramaic does seem to use the *taw* f. pl. for attributive adjectives, however; thus *lhyt*, "bad" (Sefire III:2).

It is in its noun morphology where the Samalian dialect differs most markedly from the other early Aramaic dialects. It uses no orthographically indicated definite article and has f. pl. in *-t*. Its most distinctive feature, however, is surely the absence of *nunation* on the plural accompanying the retention of case distinction; thus *ʾlhw* is nominative, while *ʾlhy* is the oblique (accusative/genitive) form for "gods." The Deir ʿAlla plaster text yields no evidence of a definite article.

(2) Verbs. The three basic conjugations (stems) are the basic stem (*Peʿal: katab/yiktub*, etc.), factitive stem (*Paʿel: kattib*), and causative stem (*Hapʿel: haktib*). Passives are expressed by internal vowel modification of the active form (presumably using the vowel pattern *u-a* in the derived conjugations as in Hebrew; Middle Aramaic has a basic passive stem *Peʿīl* in the perfect—identical with the passive participle—but no evidence for such a form is found this early.) No certain *Nipʿal* is attested in normative Aramaic, though it does occur at Deir ʿAlla and, possibly, in Samalian. Reflexive/middle stems with a *taw* augment (*ʾtpʿl*), which will soon begin to replace the internal passives, are still rare in this period. At Fakhariyah, the reflexive of the basic stem still has infixed *taw*, as in Arabic and Ugaritic. Attested verb formatives are shown in Table 2.

Suffixing formatives:

	sing.	pl.
1c	*–t*	*–n*
2m	*–t*	*–tm*
3m		*–w*
3f	*–t*	

Prefixing/suffixing formatives:

1c	*ʾ–*	*n–*
2m	*t–*	*t– –n*
3m	*y–*	*y– –n*
3f	*t–*	*y– –n*

Additionally, a separate jussive form exists, differing morphologically (and orthographically) from the imperfect in its absence of nunation in the 3 m pl. and 2 m pl. (and, presumably, the 2 f. s, as in later Aramaic) and in final weak roots, where the imperfect ends in *-h* (presumably /ē/), the jussive in *-y* (probably, simply /ī/). The two forms are also distinct when they have pronominal suffixes, where (as in Hebrew) the imperfect inserts the so-called "energic" *nun* between the stem and the suffix, while the jussive does not. Samalian uses jussive-like forms for the imperfect as well (cf. Heb *yktbw*). In Fakhariyah, Mesopotamian, and Samalian, the 3d person jussive may take a *lamed* preformative instead of a *yod* (cf. the Akkadian precative), a form that was to be the ancestor of the later *l-/n-* preformative of the E Aramaic dialects. It is now clear that the so-called "imperfect consecutive" narrative tense was common to Old Syrian Aramaic and Hebrew. Its former designation "converted imperfect" is a misnomer. It is a remnant of the archaic prefixing preterite tense surviving from some earlier stage of the Semitic languages and still to be found in Old Aramaic (in the Zakkur inscription and at Deir ʿAlla, but not at Samʾal). It is one of many grammatical and lexical isoglosses in respect to which Hebrew groups with Aramaic rather than Phoenician.

In its nominal forms, too, Old Aramaic now appears to be much closer to Hebrew than previously thought. In Syrian Old Aramaic a distinct "infinitive absolute" is attested (cf. Sefire III:2 *hskr thskrhm*, "you shall certainly hand them over"). The infinitive absolute is formed without suffixes; in contrast, the "construct" infinitives (verbal nouns) of the derived stems have a feminine ending (*ḥzyh*, "*to see*": *lhmtty*, "to kill me"). Pronouns suffixed to these construct infinitives are morphologically like affixes to nouns rather than affixes to verbs. In the basic stem, Fakhariyah has infinitives with the *mem* preformative (known from later Aramaic), whereas the other dialects (again like Hebrew) have so far yielded only forms without the *mem*. On the other hand, at Fakhariyah the derived stem verbal noun seems to be without feminine ending. The *Peʿal* passive participle is *Peʿīl* (cf. Heb *Pāʿûl*).

c. Syntax. The various verbal forms are used in constructions virtually identical to constructions found in classical Hebrew prose, although the word order is, perhaps, a bit more free. Except for the Fakhariyah bilingual, the distinctive verb-final word order of formal Imperial Aramaic has not yet made its appearance. Only in Fakhariyah and Mesopotamian do we encounter genitive constructions using the old determinative pronoun (later, the relative) *zy* (*d̲ī* > *dī* > *d-*). Complex definite direct objects may be introduced by the particle *ʾyt* (*ʾiyāt* > *yt* in later Western Aramaic; cf. Hebrew *ʾet*). Verbal phrases subordinated to a main verb use the verbal noun if the relationship is telic, but otherwise the imperfect seems to be preferred. This gives rise to the distinctive double negative *lʾkhl lʾšlḥ*, "I shall not be able to send."

2. Imperial Aramaic. a. Phonology. The graphic representation of consonants begins to change noticeably, presumably as a result of phoneme mergers and the ensuing or concomitant introduction of the spirantization of stops (the "rafe" pronunciation of the *begad-kepat* consonants in Hebrew, a phenomenon surely due to Aramaic influence). Though in this period archaizing orthographies are common (particularly with *z* for historical *ḏ* and *q* for original *ḍ*), the language here starts to employ the consonantal inventory it will have in subsequent dialects. These mergers are: *ṯ > t, ḏ > d, ḏ̣* > ʿ, *ẓ > ṣ, ḫ > ḥ* (though in some dialects the reverse may have been the case), *ġ* > ʿ. The initial tendency for *ś* to merge with *s* probably can also be ascribed to this period, since it is common to all subsequent dialects. The other distinctively Aramaic phonological feature—the reduction of short vowels in open unstressed syllables—also seems to have had its start in this period, at least for *i/u* vowels.

A noteworthy feature of the formal language (the base of Standard Literary Aramaic) is frequent nasalization, a process whose orthographic manifestation is the dissimilation of long ("doubled") consonants into *nun* + consonant. In some of these forms—e.g., *ʾnt(h), "you"*—the *nun* is etymologically correct but had been assimilated in Old Aramaic. In others (e.g., *mndʿ*, "knowledge"), it is strictly a phonetic phenomenon.

b. Morphology. The semi-demotic language of the personal letters evidences features that are later to appear in the formal language: weakening of the *Hapʿel (hktb/yhktb)* to *apʿel (ʾktb/yktb),* and substitution of *nun* for *mem* on the plural pronominal suffixes. The later Western Aramaic features of *-n* on the 3 pl. perfect of IIIy verbs and *mem* preformative of derived stem infinitives are also found. Changes in the formal language include the simplification of the infinitive to a single form *(Peʿal mktb),* the use of 3 m. pl. forms for 3 f. pl, and the first appearance of the determined plural ending *-ē*. This form appears first on gentilics and collectives, and later, in the Eastern dialects, will replace *-ayyā* as the normal ending of the masculine plural.

c. Syntax. Morphosyntactic developments characterizing Imperial Aramaic involve the restriction of some features of the language and the expansion of others. The use of internal passives is limited in favor of the *ʾt-* preformative stems (only *ʾetpeʿel* and *ʾetpaʿal* are attested in this period). Internal passives seem to have survived the longest in the causative conjugation. Biblical Aramaic word-initial *ht-* is probably a Hebraism.

The imperative/jussive contrast is sporadically neutralized. The participle, used only as a substantive in Old Aramaic, is employed as a present tense verb. In personal letters a compound tense develops which uses the participle with forms of the verb *hwy,* "to be"; this compound tense becomes common in the later dialects. The "imperfect consecutive" disappears as a narrative tense.

The distribution of particles undergoes considerable change. The particle *ʾyt* (later *yt*), which marks definite direct objects, is supplanted by the prefix *l-* affixed to the object. Use of *dy/zy* (later Aramaic *d-*) as a determined pronoun marking genitival constructions becomes widespread.

Word order remains generally unchanged in the demotic and archival materials. In the formal language of the official letters (and in Biblical Aramaic), however, verb final constructions become very common, probably due to the influence of Persian, an Indo-European language.

3. Later Dialects. a. Phonology. Short vowels in unstressed syllables are reduced and, in some cases, totally elided. The vocalization traditions indicate that in the period after the loss of final case vowels, stress was generally on the final syllable of the word, although the modern dialects (and some reading traditions) show a strong tendency toward penultimate stress (the phonological situation that had obtained prior to the loss of those vowels). Weakening of the laryngeal/pharyngeal consonants is characteristic both of Palestinian dialects (Samaritan and some Galilean) and of Babylonian. In Syriac and Babylonian, final unstressed long vowels are elided, as are final liquids, nasals, and interdentals in Babylonian.

Characteristic of all Aramaic dialects, indeed of all Semitic languages, is variation of vowel quality in different environments of stress and syllable length, even though such changes are indicated only irregularly in the schemes of vowel pointing introduced in Late Aramaic. Typically, front and back vowels are raised in closed stressed syllables and lowered in closed unstressed syllables. In Western Syriac, all mid and low long vowels are raised; thus *ō > ū, ē > ī,* and *ā > ō.* In some dialects simplification of diphthongs is similarly conditioned; in others (notably Syriac), *ay* and *aw* are tenaciously preserved (almost certainly due to secondary restoration) in the reading traditions.

b. Morphology. In Hatran, Syriac (occasionally in Palmyrene), and Babylonian, *-ē* has become the normal m. pl. emphatic suffix.

The *Hapʿel* reflexive/passive *ʾettapʿal* (< *ʾethapʿal*) occurs in all later branches of Aramaic. After the demise of the internal passives, then, the following symmetrical pattern of stem formation is distinctive to Aramaic:

Basic:	*kĕṯaḇ*	*ʾeṯkĕṯeḇ*
Factitive:	*katteḇ*	*ʾeṯkattaḇ*
Causative:	*ʾaḵteḇ*	*ʾettaḵtaḇ*

Though a substantial group of derived stems with the prefixes *š-* and *s-* occur, some borrowed from Akkadian, others, no doubt, survivals from an earlier stage of the language (e.g., *šaḵlel,* "to complete"; *šaʿbeḏ,* "to enslave"), the *Šapʿel* is not a productive causative conjugation in Aramaic.

The infinitives of the derived stems continue to show substantial variation, e.g., for the *Hapʿel:*

SLA	*ʾaḵtāḇā*	(*ʾaḵtāḇū-* before suffixes)
Western	*maḵtāḇā*	(but *ʾaḵtāḇā* as a verbal noun)
Syriac	*maḵtāḇū*	
Babyl.	*ʾaḵtōḇē*	(also in proto-Eastern Neo-Aram.)

As the original participle *(kāṯeḇ)* becomes a tense, a new, nominal participle *kāṯōḇ* frequently appears.

In Babylonian, the precative preformative *l-* is the normal prefix of the preformative tense (sometimes *n-*), while in Classical Syriac *n-* (presumably simply a phonetic variant of *l-*) is used.

In Palestinian Jewish Targumic and Galilean the prefix of the 1 c.s. imperfect is *n-* (instead of *ʾ-*).

c. Syntax. In Eastern Aramaic the system of nominal states is restructured so that the emphatic (old determined) form becomes the normal form of the noun. Thus *malkā* means "the king" or "a king." The old absolute is preserved in predicate nominatives and distributive constructions, as well as with numerals. The use of both the construct state and the bound form with pronominal suffixes becomes more and more limited over time. Palestinian Jewish Targumic tends to avoid the use of pronominal suffixes on verbs as well.

Internal passives, at first limited to the perfect, are finally replaced by the ʾt- stems.

In most dialects, participles have eventually become a full-fledged present, even displacing the imperfect as a general present-future. (The imperfect, then, is restricted to use as a modal form.) In Syrian and Babylonian the pronouns are joined enclitically to the participle as subject markers: *kāṯeḇ* + *ʾănā* > *kāṯeḇnā*. (In Western Aramaic the pronouns preceded the participle; this is the origin of the present-future forms at Maʿlula.)

Proto-Eastern Neo-Aramaic develops a new past tense from the passive participle that totally displaces the old perfect: *kĕtīb-lī*, "I wrote." Ultimately, the present-future system is reshaped as well: The present-future (old participle) entirely displaces the old imperfect, and new present tense forms are developed.

Bibliography

A detailed survey and complete bibliography can be found in:

Beyer, K. 1986. *The Aramaic Language.* Trans. J. F. Healey. Göttingen.

Additional important works follow below.

Fales, F. M. 1986. *Aramaic Epigraphs on Clay Tablets of the Neo-Assyrian Period.* SS n.s. 2. Rome.

Greenfield, J. C. 1985. Aramaic in the Achaemenian Empire. *CAH* 2: 698–713.

———. 1987. Aramaic. ii: Iranian Loanwords in Early Aramaic. *Encyclopaedia Iranica* 2/3: 256–59.

Kaufman, S. A. 1974. *The Akkadian Influences on Aramaic.* AS 19. Chicago.

———. 1986. The Pitfalls of Typology. *HUCA* 57: 1–14.

———. 1989. Assyro-Aramaica (Review of Fales 1986). *JAOS* 109: 97–102.

Lemaire, A., and Durand, J.-M. 1984. *Les inscriptions araméens de Sfire et l'Assyrie de Shamshi-Ilu.* Geneva.

Lemosin Martal, R. 1983. *El libro de Ester y el Iran antiguo: Studio filologica-derasico de vocabolas arameoelamitas persas.* Madrid.

Naveh, J. 1985. *Amulets and Magic Bowls.* Jerusalem.

Rosenthal, F. 1981. Aramaic. i: General. *Encyclopaedia Iranica* 2/3: 250–56.

Shaked, S., ed. 1982. *Irano-Judaica.* Jerusalem.

———. 1985. Bagdāna, King of the Demons, and other Iranian Terms in Babylonian Aramaic magic. *Acta Iranica* 25: 511–25.

Stephen A. Kaufman

BYBLOS SYLLABIC INSCRIPTIONS

A group of inscriptions excavated by a French expedition to Byblos (modern Jebeil) between 1929 and 1932. The tiny corpus consists of three monumental inscriptions on stone (one of which is undeciphered, and probably in a different language or writing system than the others), and six stamped with a blunt chisel on copper plates or "spatulas." Two more inscriptions in a related but undecipherable system were discovered in further excavations in 1982. From the meager archaeological evidence available, and from internal evidence, the texts represent the dialect of Byblos (and presumably of the E Mediterranean coastal region) of the late phases of the EB Age, though the texts themselves may date as late as the Egyptian 12th Dynasty (the date assigned by the excavator M. Dunand), but certainly no later than ca. 1800 B.C. The texts were very well published in 1945 (Dunand). Though an attempt at decipherment was published in 1952 by E. Dhorme, it was not accepted since it made no attempt to identify the vowels and the syllabary included an entirely unacceptable number of variant signs for the same consonant. The content as read yielded no new information of any significance and consisted of vague ritual formulas mentioning mostly Egyptian deities. An attempt at linguistic analysis by Sobelmann (1961) was useless and did not attempt an actual reading of a single sign. In 1985 after decades of work on the texts, George E. Mendenhall published a decipherment and tentative translation of the texts, with a number of improved readings based on infrared photographs of the texts, as well as a grammatical analysis.

A. The Writing System

As Professor Dunand abundantly illustrated in his publication of the texts, the syllabary is clearly inspired by the Egyptian hieroglyphic system, and in fact it is the most important link known between the hieroglyphs and the Canaanite alphabet that scholars have sought since the 19th century, though not all of the syllabic signs can be thus explained. The texts yield 64 different signs, all except two of which designate a consonant (24 in all) plus a following vowel *a, i,* or *u.* See Fig. LAN. 02. One sign has been read as a ligature that yields a closed syllable, and another sign seems to designate a vowelless, i.e., alphabetic, final *mim.* Because of the consonant + vowel nature of the syllabary, neither closed syllables nor doubled consonants can be indicated directly. As also in the Eblaite and the Mycenaean Linear B systems, there are numerous instances of "dead vowels." This occurs when a syllabic sign was used to indicate a consonant only, usually when a closed syllable was called for by the grammatical context. It is quite probable that this usage was later extended to drop the notation of vowels entirely, resulting in the much simpler Canaanite alphabetic system.

The signs in this syllabic system very probably were originally pictographic representations of common objects, and a number are identical to Egyptian hieroglyphs, indicating the close relationship. Yet already in this archaic writing system many of the signs had already become so stylized or abbreviated that the original pictograph is either entirely unrecognizable or can be presumed only from later alphabetic forms, especially the Proto-Sinaitic signary that is typologically much more archaic. The first consonant-vowel syllable in the name of the object represented became the phonetic value of the sign—the acrophonic principle.

Most of the signs of the later Canaanite, Proto-Sinaitic, and Eastern (i.e., pre-Islamic Arabic) alphabets derive either from the Byblos syllabic set or from some closely related source. It is especially intriguing and significant that the Canaanite and Eastern alphabets in several cases used different signs from the same series, since there were theoretically three signs for each consonant *(Ca, Ci, Cu).*

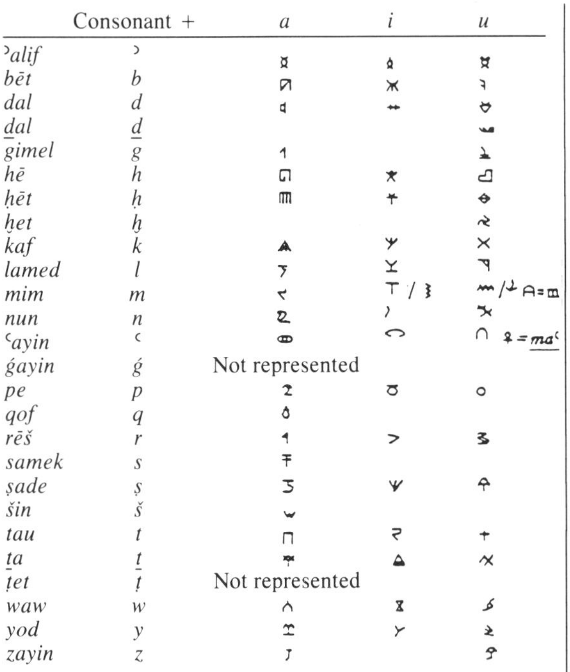
Consonant + a i u
ʾalif ʾ
bēt b
dal d
dal d
gimel g
hē h
ḥēt ḥ
ḫet ḫ
kaf k
lamed l
mim m
nun n
ʿayin ʿ
ǵayin ǵ Not represented
pe p
qof q
rēš r
samek s
ṣade ṣ
šin š
tau t
ta t
ṭet ṭ Not represented
waw w
yod y
zayin z
= maʿ

LAN.02. Chart of Byblos syllabary. *(Adapted from Mendenhall 1985: 19, table 3)*

For example, for the consonant /d/ the Canaanite alphabet used the syllabic sign for phonetic *du,* which represented a fish ("Old Coastal Semitic" [see below] *dugg* became Canaanite *dag*), in form a triangle (i.e., delta) with tail fins. The Eastern alphabets used the *da* sign, which actually represented a door leaf. The later loss of any connection between phonetic value and pictorial representation is indicated by the fact that the Canaanites gave the door *name (dalet/delta)* to the fish sign. Similarly, for the consonant /p/, the Canaanite alphabet continued the use of a highly abbreviated form of the *pa* sign (of unknown meaning), while the Eastern alphabets used the *pu* sign, a circle that doubtless represented the mouth saying *pu.* Similarly, for *ṣade* the Canaanite alphabet used the *ṣa* sign, which perhaps represented a scimitar, while the Eastern alphabet used the *ṣi* sign, which represented a growing vegetative shoot (Heb *ṣîṣ*).

In view of the similar syllabic structure and the similarity of some signs, it is probable that the Minoan/Mycenean linear systems were dependent at least by stimulus diffusion upon the Byblos syllabic system.

B. The Language

The language itself is termed "Old Coastal Semitic" (OCS) to distinguish it from Canaanite and Ugaritic. The contrasts to Ugaritic in every way are so great that they cannot be placed in the same category. The language of these texts is very archaic and pristine, in the sense that there is very little in the language that can be derived from some earlier form, while a very large amount can be seen to be that from which later Arabic and Canaanite forms or meanings derived. Thus it furnishes the basis for understanding the process of language change and language blending that resulted in the Canaanite language of the MB and LB periods. This process of hybridization (or blending, or creolization—all three terms have been used to describe a very well-known process in historical linguistics) took place some time between 2000 and 1700 B.C. and resulted in a new language termed "Canaanite" that was not structurally a continuity of either language complex involved. The linguistic influence that brought an end to OCS in the urban populations of the E Mediterranean coastal region was certainly a complex of "inland dialects" from N and NE Syria, especially Amorite. This process was in turn the result of still poorly understood events that attended the destruction of the EB Age urban civilizations of the coastal region, and the influx of populations from inland Syria who, at least by the 18th century, had become politically dominant in the coastal regions, as the Amorites had also become in 19th-century Mesopotamia.

These enormous linguistic changes that resulted in the Ugaritic and other Canaanite dialects were the major reason why these texts were not deciphered decades ago. Everyone who worked on them assumed that the language would have to be much like Phoenician (Dhorme) or Ugaritic. In fact, Ugaritic was almost entirely irrelevant and useless to the decipherment process, but various Arabic sources were astonishingly productive of meaningful cognates. A sample of the vocabulary indicates that 52 percent of the lexical items have Arabic cognates, while only 13 percent are Common Semitic. Approximately 25 percent of the vocabulary can be classified as Common West Semitic (which now, of course, includes pre-Islamic Arabic, Ethiopic, and Classical Arabic), and 10 percent of the vocabulary have no identifiable external cognates, which is to be expected from such an archaic dialect.

Only 24 consonants are attested over against the 30 alphabetic signs (actually only 27 different consonants) of Ugaritic, and 29 in pre-Islamic Arabic. A major reason for the reduced number of signs is the sharply limited number of velarized consonants (so-called "emphatics"). Only the *ṣade* and the *qof* are present, and the elaboration of velarization is thus seen to be a later linguistic development yielding the *ṭeth, ẓa,* and *dad.* It is of course possible that the extremely small corpus by accident did not include words with some of these consonants, but no other writing system of the time includes specific signs for these missing consonants, as well as for the *ǵayin* which also does not occur in these documents.

The "hollow verbs" *(mediae waw/yod)* of later Semitic dialects are purely triconsonantal, with the *w* written when preceded and followed by a vowel. It is often represented as zero in a syllable containing a /u/ vowel, as in the *figura etymologica ḥa-wu-bu + ma ta-ḥū-ba + m* (probably reflecting a theoretical original **ta-aḥ-wu-ba + m*), "you are certainly guilty." Diphthongs are written as two syllables, as in *ba-yi-ta + hu,* "his house," but several roots that later yield diphthongs have a medial /he/ instead of *waw/yod,* as in *ya-tu-ha-ʿ[i]-hi-du,* "they have bound themselves by covenant," and the startling form *ra-ha-ʿa,* "he has done evil." This proves that the Hebrew roots listed as *rʿ* and *ršʿ* are the same root, derived from two very archaic dialects at a time when the contrast between /h/ and /s/ was still operative (as in the *s*- and *h*- causatives in Old South Arabic dialects).

The verbal system is very complex, as one would expect from such an archaic dialect, and its description needs further study. It is very probable that there is a tense contrast between the present-future form *ya-qa-ta-lu* and the preterite *ya-qa-ti-lu,* as in E Semitic and Ethiopic. There are a variety of verbal nouns, as in Arabic, and their translation is often very difficult, even when the root meaning is reasonably clear. There are causatives written with both the /s/ sign and with the /h/.

C. The Contents

The stone inscriptions were in poor condition and very difficult to decipher, but what could be gained from them fits well with their probable function as building inscriptions or dedications. The copper inscriptions are all legal or political in nature, and this is to be expected because valuable copper was used for the preservation of written documents that were presumably very important to the persons involved.

The longest document (Text D) is something akin to a political constitution issued by the king, beginning with the phrase: *ha-wa-tū ḥu-ru-ba-ʿi-l(u),* "the words of Hur-Baal," exactly the introductory formula used by Hittite kings in their international suzerainty treaties at least half a millennium later. The document also contains in archaic and terse form most of the elements of the later treaty form (see COVENANT), including the curses and blessings, and a reference to the king's prior mighty acts.

Other documents include one certain (and another probable) marriage contract, in which the bride is designated by a passive participle *ru-ḥi-ma-tu,* "betrothed" (lit. "beloved"). The same word is used in Hos 1:6. The longer document seems to include a blessing formula, but more interestingly a threat against anyone who mistreats the *ra-ḥi-ma-ta* (cf. Judg 5:30), for which the only parallel known so far is found in the Jacob narrative at Gen 31:50.

One spatula records the elevation of a certain citizen to the status of *ra-ba-ṣu-ti,* "commissarship," and another records the solution of a legal dispute by an oracular response that stems from a deity named *ṭi-nu-ta,* doubtless the much later Carthaginian goddess Tanit. Aside from the inclusion of *ba-ʿil* in the royal name, the only other reference to a deity in the entire corpus is in the political constitution (Text D), where the punishment of a malefactor is to be carried out by his *li-ʾi-mu+hu,* which is taken to be his deified ancestor(s). This cultural feature that implies ancestor worship is also illustrated by the obelisk temple of Byblos, which includes steles of the *naos* type in which figures of the deceased were placed.

These texts have yielded an abundance of insights into the archaic language, thought patterns, and culture of the EB Age coastal region. Perhaps even more important is the demonstration of certain cultural and linguistic patterns or forms that were attested millennia later in radically different geographical and cultural contexts. In view of the fact that there is no evidence for any population in the Arabian peninsula in those regions contiguous to the highly populated Syro-Palestinian areas between the end of the Chalcolithic and the end of the LB ages, there can be little doubt that the Arabic complex of languages had its origins in the coastal regions of Lebanon and Palestine in the highly developed culture of the W Semitic EB Age. As is so often the case, the purest illustration of pristine language was preserved not in the place of origin but in what paleobotanists term "relict" areas, in this case the isolation of the Arabian desert and the fringe areas of the Fertile Crescent.

Bibliography

Dhorme, E. 1948. Déchiffrement des inscriptions pseudo-hiéroglyphiques de Byblos. *Syria* 25: 1–35.

Dunand, M. 1945. *Byblia Grammata.* Beirut.

Mendenhall, G. 1985. *The Syllabic Inscriptions from Byblos.* Beirut.

Sobelmann, H. 1961. The Proto-Byblian Inscriptions: A Fresh Approach. *JSS:* 226–45.

George E. Mendenhall

COPTIC LANGUAGE

The native language of Egypt as attested in manuscripts surviving from the 3d century C.E. onward, expressed in a writing system fundamentally different from that of the older Egyptian scripts. Coptic is the last phase in the long history of the Egyptian language, which gave way gradually to Arabic beginning in about the 11th century.

In addition to being the language of a region prominent throughout antiquity, Coptic is important to students of the Christian Bible in two principal respects. First, Coptic manuscripts preserve many noncanonical early Christian books that survive in no other language, or survive only imperfectly apart from Coptic. Such books are precious remains of the diverse literary tradition out of which the Bible was formed, providing valuable information about the intellectual and social milieu of early Christianity. Some of these books, most notably *The Gospel of Thomas, The Apocryphon of James,* and *The Dialogue of the Savior,* are essential sources for the study of Jesus' sayings. See also THOMAS, GOSPEL OF (NHC II,*2*); JAMES, APOCRYPHON OF (NHC I,*2*); and DIALOGUE OF THE SAVIOR (NHC III,*5*). Second, since the LXX and the NT were being translated into Coptic during the 3d century C.E., the Coptic version is based on Gk mss which are significantly older than the vast majority of extant witnesses. The Coptic evidence has yet to be applied systematically to the textual criticism of the Greek Bible.

A. Old Coptic
B. Standardization of the Coptic Alphabet and Birth of Coptic Literature
   1. Probable Role of the Christian Mission
   2. Dialectology
   3. Numerous Early Dialects and the Status of Sahidic as a Standard
C. Death of Egyptian
D. Growth of Coptic Studies and Egyptology in Europe
E. The Coptic Writing System
F. Grammar
   1. Basic Sentence Types
   2. Object Incorporation
   3. Sentence Conversion
   4. Cleft Sentence
   5. Adjectival Modification
   6. Other Features

G. Coptic Today
H. Basic Reference Works

A. Old Coptic

When Alexander the Great wrested control of Egypt from the Persians in 332 B.C.E., two standards of written Egyptian were current: Middle Egyptian, the classical stage of the language written in the hieroglyphic and hieratic scripts, and Demotic, a more recent development written in the demotic script. The three scripts in use were graphically related forms of a single complicated writing system. They were the tools of scribes and priests whose conservative professions perpetuated their use into the 5th century C.E. But the two linguistic stages expressed in these scripts were largely fossilized, left behind by the spoken language as it continued to evolve (Sethe 1925). Alexander's successors in Egypt established Greek as the country's primary administrative language and nurtured the spread of Hellenism and the growth of Alexandria into an international center of Hellenistic learning. A knowledge of Greek became a prerequisite for economic, social, and intellectual advancement. Greek remained the dominant language even after Egypt was conquered by the Romans in 30 B.C.E. Egyptian as spoken by the mass of peasants was a language without a written form.

Greek not only conveyed political and cultural prestige, but also it was written in an alphabetic script superior in any practical sense to the Egyptian writing system. It is not surprising that people soon began to experiment with using the Greek alphabet to transliterate Egyptian (Quaegebeur 1982). By the 2d century C.E., alphabets made up of mixtures of Greek and demotic characters were being used by some scribes to transliterate Egyptian magical and astrological texts. About a dozen such texts survive, dating from the first four centuries C.E. (Griffith 1901; Kasser 1980–81: 237–70; Satzinger 1984). Although these texts are grouped under the heading "Old Coptic," they are diverse linguistically, and it is doubtful that any of them were much more representative of the contemporary spoken language than were other Egyptian texts of the same period written in the hieroglyphic, hieratic, or demotic scripts. The Old Coptic texts seem to be products of the same scribal circles that were perpetuating Egypt's archaic literary tradition.

B. Standardization of the Coptic Alphabet and Birth of Coptic Literature

The Coptic alphabet is a standardized form of the Old Coptic scripts; it comprises the entire Greek alphabet and several letters derived from the demotic script. See Fig. LAN. 03. But in contrast to its Old Coptic antecedents, the Coptic alphabet was used to represent the spoken language of the time, and thus it ushered in a new epoch in the history of Egyptian literature.

1. Probable Role of the Christian Mission. There is no direct evidence for when, where, and by whom the standardization of the Coptic alphabet was brought about. The oldest surviving Coptic manuscripts were copied in the 3d and 4th centuries C.E. They are mostly translations of books from the Bible, like an early 4th-century papyrus codex in the British Library that contains Deuteronomy, Jonah, Acts, and the beginning of *The Apocalypse of Elijah*

The Coptic Alphabet

numerical value	character	transliteration	pronunciation (Worrell 1934: 84–88)
1	ⲁ	*a*	"Mann" (German)
2	ⲃ	*b*	voiced bilabial fricative
3	ⲅ	*g*	"smoky" (=ⲕ)
4	ⲇ	*d*	"smutty" (=ⲧ)
5	ⲉ	*e*	"let"
[6	ⲋ	used only as a numeral]	
7	ⲍ	*z*	"seep" (=ⲥ)
8	ⲏ	*ē*	"Tee" (German)
9	ⲑ	*th*	"pot-hole" (=ⲧϩ)
10	ⲓ (ⲉⲓ = ï)	*i (ei)*	"schien" (German), "trip," "yet"
20	ⲕ	*k*	"smoky"
30	ⲗ	*l*	"lieb" (German)
40	ⲙ	*m*	"meet"
50	ⲛ	*n*	"neat"
60	ⲝ	*ks*	"smokes" (=ⲕⲥ)
70	ⲟ	*o*	"not" (British)
80	ⲡ	*p*	"sappy"
100	ⲣ	*r*	"rund" (German)
200	ⲥ	*s*	"seep"
300	ⲧ	*t*	"smutty"
400	ⲩ (ⲟⲩ)	*u (ou)*	"Huhn" (German), "put," "wet"
500	ⲫ	*ph*	"sap-hole" (=ⲡϩ)
600	ⲭ	*kh*	"smoke-hole" (=ⲕϩ)
700	ⲯ	*ps*	"saps" (=ⲡⲥ)
800	ⲱ	*ō*	"Bohne" (German)
	ϣ	*š*	"sheep"
90	ϥ	*f*	voiceless bilabial fricative
	ϩ	*h*	"heap"
	ϫ	*j*	"posture"
	ϭ	*č*	"vacuum"
	ϯ	*ti*	"smutty" (=ⲧⲓ)
[900	⳨	used only as a numeral and as a monogram for ⲧⲁⲩⲣ]	
Achmimic adds:			
	ⳉ	*ḫ*	"ach" (German)
Bohairic adds:			
	ϧ, ϧ	*ḫ*	"ach" (German)

LAN.03. Table of Coptic alphabet.

(Layton 1987: 3–5). The evidence of such manuscripts suggests that the impetus to provide colloquial Egyptian with a new written form came from the Christian mission (Steindorff 1950; Kasser 1962). The first Egyptian Christians no doubt spoke Greek, and at some point the new religion won converts who spoke both Greek and Egyptian. Probably beginning in the later part of the 2d century, the Christian mission reached deeper into the population and embraced native Egyptians who knew little or no Greek. In order to win these converts, it was necessary to express the Christian message orally in Egyptian. To a religious movement increasingly dependent on an authoritative corpus of writings, the advantages of having written translations of the Holy Scriptures would have been obvious.

The rudiments of a new writing system were already available in the Old Coptic scripts. But the early Coptic translators' use of the new alphabet was far more sophisticated than any previous attempts, and the growing Church was an institution that could promote the use of the alphabet and maintain a standard. Nevertheless, the initial translation of the Bible was not necessarily the result of a centralized and carefully planned effort; rather, it seems that various translators, working independently, prepared a variety of translations using the new alphabetic writing system. Only later were those translations revised into a more or less standard version. Since the oldest Coptic literature also includes translations of gnostic and Manichaean books, the possibility cannot be ruled out entirely that the standardization of the alphabet was the work of some heterodox or even heretical religious group, against whom orthodox Christians entered into literary competition. But even if this was the case, the evidence of the surviving manuscripts leaves no doubt that Coptic literature reached its maturity in the care of the Christian Church and the allied monastic movement.

Early in the 4th century, a tradition of literacy in Coptic was established by the Pachomian monastic communities, and the few surviving works of Pachomius himself (d. 346) mark a rebirth of Egyptian literature (Orlandi 1986: 53–74). The large number of Coptic manuscripts that survive from the 4th century, as well as the variety they display in dialect and content, indicates both the vitality of the new literary movement and the diversity of those who participated in it. Much of this activity involved translating selected works from Greek. Biblical books, apocrypha, and patristic and hagiographic works always predominated. From the beginning, Coptic literature was almost exclusively religious and largely Christian. The first native author to utilize fully the rhetorical potential of Coptic was the monastic leader Shenoute, a skillful stylist and fiery orator whose numerous sermons and letters were composed during the later decades of the 4th century and the first half of the 5th. After the Council of Chalcedon in 451, the increasingly isolated and nationalistic character of the Egyptian Monophysite church motivated a modest but steady flow of original Coptic literature, at least in part consciously opposed to pro-Chalcedonian literary activity in Greek.

2. Dialectology. The question of the genesis of the Coptic writing system is related to the problem of Coptic dialects. In so far as the new alphabet was a system of phonetic transcription, it facilitated the written representation of differences among varieties of the spoken language. At first sight, the manuscripts surviving from the first several centuries of the Coptic period display what may seem to be a chaotic assortment of orthographic, morphological, and syntactic variants. But the apparent chaos can be reduced significantly by a careful sorting of the manuscripts according to linguistic criteria, the resultant groups presumably representing dialects of Coptic. Precisely how many dialects are to be defined by such a procedure is a matter of dispute, depending on differences both of theory and of method. Locating the dialects geographically is also problematic, because more often than not the provenance of a given work or manuscript is uncertain. But since the habitable part of Egypt south of the Nile Delta is the relatively thin strip of land lining the river valley, it is reasonable to suppose that a linear arrangement of the dialects according to their degrees of similarity to one another will reflect their geographical distribution along this part of the Nile. Numerical evaluations of distinctive dialectal features make it possible to construct a serial ranking of this sort, and the dialect map that emerges generally corroborates the conclusions that can be drawn from other types of evidence (Worrell 1934: 63–143; Kahle 1954: 1: 193–290; Vergote 1961; Kasser 1980–81; Hintze 1984; Funk 1988).

So far as can be judged from their written expression, the difference between the variety of Coptic spoken in the Nile Delta and that spoken in the south probably was great enough to have impeded communication between speakers from those two regions, but not so great as to have disguised the fact that they were speaking the same language (compare dialects *B* and *L5* in Table 1). Presumably, the variation in the language spoken along the Nile between the two extremities was gradual enough to form a dialect continuum. It is likely that Coptic literature was born in a limited number of restricted locales along this continuum: in cities, where roughly uniform ways of speaking would have been recognized locally as "normal." These local norms of speech were expressed in writing with varying degrees of orthographic consistency. What can be recognized as "dialects" in the manuscripts are these norms of written Coptic, representing the speech norms of specific nodes on the Egyptian dialect continuum.

Table 1
Coptic Dialectal Versions of John 3:14–15

(B)	*ouoh*	*m-*	*ph-*	*rēti*	*et-*	*a-*	*mōusēs*	*čes-*
(F4)	*auō*	*kata-*	*t-*	*hē*	*et-*	*a-*	*mōusēs*	*jisi*
(S)	*auō*	*kata-*	*t-*	*he*	*ent-*	*a-*	*mōusēs*	*jise*
(L5)	*auō*	*kata-*	*t-*	*he*	*nt-*	*a-*	*mōusēs*	*jise*
	and	according to-	the-	manner	REL-	PAST-	Moses	raise

(B)		*pi-*	*hofnhrēi*	*hi-*	*p-*	*šafe*		*pai-*			*rēti*	*hōti pe*
(F4)	*m-*	*pi-*	*haf*	*hi-*	*t-*	*erēmos*	*n-*	*tei-*			*hē*	*hōti*
(S)	*m-*	*p-*	*hof*	*hn-*	*t-*	*erēmos*		*taei*	*te*	*t-*	*he*	*haps*
(LF)	*m-*	*p-*	*haf*	*hi-*	*p-*	*jaeie*		*teei*	*te*	*t-*	*he*	
	OBJ-	the-	serpent	in-	the-	wilderness		this	is	the-	manner	

(B)	*ntou-*	*čes-*		*p-*	*šēri*	*m-*	*ph-*	*rōmi*	*hina*
(F4)	*nse-*	*jisi*	*m-*	*p-*	*šēli*	*m-*	*p-*	*lōmi*	*hina*
(S)	*etreu-*	*jest-*		*p-*	*šēre*	*m-*	*p-*	*rōme*	*jekaas*
(L5)	*etouna-*	*jise*	*m-*	*p-*	*šēre*	*m-*	*p-*	*rōme*	*jekase*
	REL/they/going to-	raise	OBJ-	the-	son	of-	the-	man	so that

(B)	*ouon*	*niben*	*eth-*		*nahti*	*ero-f*	*ntef-*	*či*
(F4)	*ouan*	*nibi*	*et-ne-l-*		*pisteuin*	*ela-f*	*nf-*	*ji*
(S)	*ouon*	*nim*	*et-*		*pisteue*	*ero-f*	*efe-*	*kō*
(L5)	*ouan*	*nim*	*et-*	*r-*	*pisteue*	*ara-f*	*efna-*	*kou*
	one	every	REL-do-		believe	in-him	FOCUS/he/going to-	put

(B)			*m-*	*pi-*	*ōnẖ*	*n-*		*eneh*
(F4)			*n-*	*ou-*	*ōnh*	*n-*	*ša-*	*eneh*
(S)	*na-f hraei*	*nhēt-f*	*n-*	*ou-*	*ōnh*		*ša-*	*eneh*
(L5)	*ne-f*	*nhēt-f*	*n-*	*ou-*	*ōōnh*		*ša-*	*anēhe*
	to-him	in-him	OBJ-	a-	life		to-	eternity

Note: *F4* is an early form of *F*; the translation is of the *L5* version (OBJ = preposition marking direct object; REL = relative converter).

3. Numerous Early Dialects and the Status of Sahidic as a Standard. The number of dialects discernible in the earliest extant Coptic literature has increased steadily with the continual discovery and publication of previously unknown manuscripts. At present it is possible to distinguish more than a dozen dialects (Funk 1988). The extent to which these dialects are attested varies considerably, from isolated fragments to quantities of complete manuscripts. It is difficult to know whether the varying degrees of attestation are reflections of the relative literary productivity of the different dialects or simply accidents of preservation.

The vast majority of early Coptic manuscripts are written in the Sahidic dialect (sometimes called Thebaic in older scholarship; abbreviated *S*). The wide diffusion of this dialect is indicative of its status as a literary standard. *S* was well suited to the role of literary standard because of its dialectal neutrality: it shared many features with the other dialects, and relatively few of its features were peculiar to itself. Assuming that *S* was a local dialect at the beginning of the Coptic period, it would probably have been spoken in the area south of Oxyrhynchus (modern El Bahnasa) and roughly midway between the two extreme poles of the dialect continuum, hence perhaps around Hermopolis (modern El Ashmûnein). There are reasons, however, for assuming that *S* was already a widely used colloquial standard before the Coptic period. If so, probably it had ceased to coincide exactly with the local dialect from which it developed, and hence this parent dialect cannot necessarily be located on the basis of the Coptic evidence alone (Satzinger 1985). It also follows from this assumption that the initial center of the diffusion of *S* as a literary standard cannot be determined on purely linguistic grounds; in any case, soon there were multiple centers of its diffusion.

Most of the other Coptic dialects did not survive as literary vehicles beyond the 6th century. Nonetheless, there is relatively extensive attestation for enough of them to indicate that people in various cities took an active interest in the dissemination of Coptic literature in local varieties of the language. Oxyrhynchite (also called Middle Egyptian; abbreviated *M*) was the dialect of middle Egypt, around Oxyrhynchus. The southernmost dialect was Achmimic *(A)*, a standardization of the language as spoken around Panopolis (modern Akhmîm) or farther south. Locating *A* is complicated by the question of its relationship to the dialect of a peculiar manuscript of Proverbs that may date from as early as the 3d century C.E. (Kasser 1960; 1982: 67 n. 1). This manuscript displays an alphabet and an orthographic system quite different from the other Coptic dialects, and strikingly reminiscent of the Old Coptic scripts. But the language of the manuscript is indisputably a dialect of Coptic (known as dialect *P*), most similar to *A* but similar also to dialects north of *A* on the dialect continuum. The problem is raised (Nagel 1965) by linguistic parallels in later nonliterary texts found in situ that show that *P* was probably the dialect of Thebes (modern Luxor). If so, *A* would seem to have been centered still farther south, a possibility contradicted by evidence for locating it at Panopolis, or even at Thebes.

On the dialect continuum south of *S* but north of *A* and *P*, hence in the region around Lycopolis (modern Asyût), there were three dialects similar enough to one another that initially scholars grouped them under a single name: Subachmimic (also called Lycopolitan; the three dialects are distinguished as *L4, L5,* and *L6;* Funk 1985). Whereas *L5* and the other early dialects that coexisted with *S* were used for the most part to translate books of the Bible and a selection of noncanonical early Christian works, the two other Lycopolitan dialects were used extensively for translating gnostic *(L6)* and Manichaean *(L4)* works. It is possible that the disappearance of *L4* and *L6* as literary vehicles was due to the Church's organized suppression of the kind of literature with which they are associated, but probably the general disappearance of early dialects as literary vehicles reflected the dominance of *S* and the resultant development of a literary culture increasingly independent of the actual spoken language of any given region.

Faiyumic (sometimes called Bashmuric or Middle Egyptian in older scholarship; abbreviated *F*) was the dialect of the Faiyûm Oasis (around Arsinoe, modern El Faiyûm). Bohairic (sometimes called Memphitic, or simply Coptic, in older scholarship; abbreviated *B*) was the dialect of the Nile Delta, at least in its western part. Both of these dialects were used for early translations of the Bible, but unlike most of the other early dialects, they continued in use beyond the 6th century. Because the Egyptian climate is much less conducive to the preservation of manuscripts in the Nile Delta than in southern Egypt, early evidence for *B* is particularly scarce, especially from before the 8th century.

C. Death of Egyptian

Despite the remarkable growth of Coptic literature, Greek continued to be the primary language of Egypt's literary culture. It was not until Egypt was conquered by the Arabs in A.D. 641 that Greek slipped at last from its dominant status. Literary activity in Coptic continued unabated (Orlandi 1986: 75–81), and its use also for personal correspondence and business documents increased dramatically. But now the language of the rulers was Arabic, and their initial religious tolerance soon waned. By the end of the 8th century, Coptic was beginning to wither under persecution along with the religion that had given it its written expression. Two centuries later, literacy in Coptic was becoming a rarity. In the meantime, the Bohairic dialect had achieved a degree of standardization comparable to that of Sahidic. Partly through translations from the latter dialect, Bohairic and Faiyumic literature had begun to blossom. As Egyptian now began to die out, it was the Church in the narrowest sense that was the last bastion of Coptic literature. Bohairic, the dialect of the region that was home to the central authority of the Church, lived longest.

In an effort to preserve some knowledge of their dying language, a series of scholars, beginning in the 11th century, undertook to compile Arabic glossaries of Coptic words, accompanied by simple observations on Coptic grammar, written in Arabic. The unsophisticated grammatical tradition thus born in the Bohairic dialect lasted until the 14th century, but it soon served as no more than an aid to the proper translation of Coptic texts into Arabic (Mallon 1906–7; Samir 1986). After a written history of more than four thousand years the Egyptian language was dead, leaving Arabic as the language of Egypt, as it is today.

Egyptian Christianity, however, was not abolished, and Bohairic Coptic remained the official liturgical language of the Egyptian church. But although the priests continued to pronounce at least parts of their services in Coptic, gradually even in church Arabic became the primary tongue. Still, the Egyptian Christians' reverence for Coptic as the language of their religion meant that monastic scribes continued to copy and preserve Coptic manuscripts, now mostly with accompanying Arabic translations, and hence they made possible a significantly different survival of their ancestral language, a survival outside of Egypt.

D. Growth of Coptic Studies and Egyptology in Europe

The Vatican's collection of oriental manuscripts seems already to have included a small number of Coptic-Arabic bilinguals when the library was founded by Pope Nicholas V in the middle of the 15th century. These are the first Coptic manuscripts of which there is any certain record in Europe. It is likely that they were brought to Italy by the Coptic delegates to the Council of Florence in A.D. 1441 (Levi della Vida 1939: 29–88; the oldest certain attestation of Coptic manuscripts in the Vatican collection dates from 1481). From this period onward there was frequent contact between the Roman and Coptic churches, and soon Coptic became a subject of interest to scholars studying oriental languages.

The first published accounts of Coptic appeared early in the 16th century (Postel 1538; Ambrogio 1539). At this time, a knowledge of Coptic amounted to little more than a knowledge of the Coptic alphabet. The first manuscript to be brought from Egypt to Europe containing a copy of one of the medieval Coptic-Arabic grammatical works written as the Egyptian language was dying did not arrive until 1591. Giovanni Battista Raimondi (d. 1614), director of the Typographia Medicea in Rome, dreamed of using this Coptic manuscript and others to rescue the Egyptian language from oblivion and to prepare a printed edition of the Coptic Bible, but his dreams came to nothing and the manuscripts he had assembled were neglected (Saltini 1860; Levi della Vida 1939: 263–68).

When the Italian pilgrim Pietro della Valle (1586–1652) returned to Rome from the Far East in 1626, his collection of oriental manuscripts included several Coptic-Arabic bilinguals that he had acquired in Egypt near the start of his journey a decade before. Two of his manuscripts were anthologies of several of the medieval Coptic-Arabic grammatical works, similar to the manuscript that had inspired Raimondi. Della Valle, too, having recognized at once the importance of such books for the recovery of the lost language of Egypt, entrusted the edition and translation of the more substantial grammatical manuscript to Tommaso Obicini, a specialist in Arabic. In preparation for the publication of Obicini's work, della Valle oversaw the production of a font of movable Coptic type at the printing press of the Sacra Congregatio de Propaganda Fide (Emmel 1987). But although Obicini made significant progress, he died in 1632 without having completed his work, and somehow his notes disappeared (not to be discovered until three hundred years later; van Lantschoot 1948).

In the meantime, the publication of della Valle's manuscript had been awaited with eagerness by an eminent patron of scholarship, Nicolas Claude Fabri de Peiresc (1580–1637), who had tried to arrange for the inclusion of Coptic among the languages of the great Polyglot Bible then in preparation in Paris (Gravit 1938). Although the study of Coptic progressed too slowly for this particular ambition to be realized, in 1643 it was one of Peiresc's protégés who finally published an edition of the Coptic grammatical manuscript in della Valle's collection (Kircher 1643). The editor was Athanasius Kircher (1602–1680), who thus laid the foundations on which the study of Egyptian would eventually grow into a scholarly discipline in Europe (Quatremère 1808: 45–109, 294–98).

The medieval grammars were soon surpassed by insights drawn from the study of increasingly large numbers of Coptic manuscripts brought out of Egypt. By the beginning of the 19th century, when the Rosetta Stone was first being studied, Coptic was well enough known that it could play a crucial role in the decipherment of texts written in the older Egyptian scripts. Toward the end of that century, the study of the entire history of Egyptian was put on a firm footing by Adolf Erman (1854–1937) and the "Berlin School" of Egyptology, where the fundamental importance of Coptic for the study of the earlier stages of Egyptian was fully recognized (Polotsky 1987: 14–15). In recent decades, the most fruitful work on Coptic has been a quest, pioneered by H. J. Polotsky, for a comprehensive synchronic description of its grammatical system (Polotsky 1971: 99–271, 341–438; 1968; 1970; 1985a; 1985b; 1988).

E. The Coptic Writing System

The Coptic alphabet is illustrated in Fig. LAN. 03. The alphabet represented seven vowels *(a, e, ē, i, o, u, ō),* two of which *(i, u)* also had corresponding consonantal values, and fourteen distinct consonants (fifteen in Achmimic and Bohairic). It is not known exactly how Coptic was pronounced. The inventors of the Coptic writing system took over the Greek alphabet according to its classical values, and it may be supposed that pronouncing Coptic texts according to those values will yield a reasonable reconstruction of how Coptic sounded, at least about the time it was first given written expression. However, even after this pronunciation is modified on the basis of the internal evidence of Coptic manuscripts, it no doubt remains approximate at best.

The care with which the Coptic writing system was initially worked out is illustrated by one orthographic feature in particular. Coptic scribes did not usually leave space between words. It was a peculiarity of Coptic that this way of writing often resulted in strings of consonants, the correct articulation of which may not have been immediately obvious. To alleviate this problem, a diacritical mark placed above the line of writing was used to mark syllables formed not with vowels but with syllabic consonants (like the syllabic n in the second syllable of "button"). For example, in Sahidic *hmpkōhtmpfčntf,* "superlinear strokes" placed over *hm, ht, m, pf, čn,* and *tf* indicate the syllabification *hm-pkō-ht-m-pf-čn-tf.*

F. Grammar

The extensive attestation of the Sahidic dialect, both chronologically and in content, as well as its dialectal neutrality, makes it the most appropriate starting point for learning Coptic. It is on Sahidic that the following brief description of some Coptic grammatical features is based. In the examples, dashes separate morphemes that combine into a prosodic unit, which is generally defined by a single accented syllable. Abbreviations for citing nonbiblical examples follow Crum (1939); OT references follow the numbering of the LXX (ed. Rahlfs).

1. Basic Sentence Types. Coptic displays at least four basic sentence types. The *tripartite sentence,* or *verbal sentence,* contains three basic elements, in a fixed order: a "conjugation base" encoding information such as tense; a subject (either a noun phrase or a pronoun); and a verb (infinitive).

(1) *a-p-noute* *ti* *na-u* *n-saoul*
PAST-the-god give to-them OBJ-Saul
"God gave them Saul." (Acts 13:21)

(2) *a-f-ti* *na-u* *n-ou-oeik*
PAST-he-give to-them OBJ-a-bread
"He gave them bread." (John 6:31)

There are four "sentence conjugation bases," with distinct affirmative and negative forms (e.g., the negative of *a-* is *mpe-*): (1) *perfect* ("he gave, he has given"); (2) *"not yet"* (negative only, "he has not yet given"); (3) *aorist* ("he gives," by nature, or whenever certain circumstances obtain; not a present tense); (4) *future,* known as "Energetic Future" or, unhappily, "Third Future" ("he will give," but mostly used in constructions where it has modal meanings such as "he might give"). There is also a set of "clause conjugation bases," which are used in the same pattern (the "Tripartite Conjugation Pattern": base + subject + verb), but which form dependent clauses and are negatived by an additional morpheme *(tm-)*: (1) *conjunctive* (various uses, most often in some sense continuative of a grammatical structure in a preceding clause); (2) *future conjunctive* (". . . and he will give"); (3) *temporal* ("when he had given . . ."); (4)*"until"* (". . . until he gives"); (5) *conditional* ("when/if he gives . . ."); (6) *protatic* ("if he gives . . ."; Shisha-Halevy 1974); and (7) *apodotic* (". . . then he gives"; Shisha-Halevy 1973). The tripartite pattern occurs in exx. 1, 2, 13–15, 18–22, and 24.

The *bipartite sentence* (the "Bipartite Conjugation Pattern") contains two basic elements, in a fixed order: a subject (either a noun phrase or a pronoun), and one of four types of predicate. The predicate is either adverbial (mostly locative prepositional phrases; ex. 3), or an infinitive (exx. 4, 16–20), or a *stative* (exx. 6, 23, 25), or the verbal auxiliary *na-* (exx. 7, 8). The bipartite sentence serves as a present tense, as do the two remaining sentence types.

(3) *f-hm-p-jaeie*
he-in-the-wilderness
"He is in the wilderness." (Matt 24:26)

(4) *p-joeis* *sooun* *n-te-hiē* *n-n-dikaios*
the-lord know OBJ-the-way of-the-righteous
"The Lord knows the way of the righteous." (Ps 1:6)

The stative (also called *qualitative*) is a verb form used only in the bipartite sentence; generally it has the meaning of a statal passive. In exx. 5 and 6 the infinitive *tajro* ("steady") is compared with the stative *tajrēu* ("in the state of having been *steadied*").

(5) *f-tajro* *m-p-hēt* *m-p-rōme*
it-steady OBJ-the-heart of-the-man
"It steadies man's heart." (ShA 1 429)

(6) *pef-hēt* *tajrēu*
his-heart steadied
"His heart is steady." (Ps 111:8–Eng 112:8)

The verbal auxiliary *na-* ("going to"), followed by a verb (infinitive only, never stative), is used in the bipartite sentence to form the most common expression of the future.

(7) *f-na-ti* *nē-tn* *n-ke-paraklētos*
he-going to-give to-you OBJ-another-counselor
"He will give you another Counselor." (John 14:16)

The bipartite sentence and the two remaining sentence types are negatived by a discontinuous morpheme.

(8) *n-f-na-ti an m-pef-ouoein*
NEG-it-going to-give NEG OBJ-its-light
"It will not give its light." (Mark 13:24)

The *nominal sentence* is constructed around a set of personal pronouns that serve as subjects in the pattern. For the first and second persons, these pronouns are proclitic forms of the independent personal pronouns; they precede the nominal predicate.

(9) *ntk-ou-šonte*
you-a-thornbush
"You are a thornbush." (ShMIF 23 42)

For the third person, the subject pronouns are a suppletive group, morphologically related to the definite article and the demonstratives; they follow the predicate.

(10) *na-snēu ne*
my-brothers they
"They are my brothers." (ShMIF 23 41)

The third-person type of nominal sentence serves, at least formally, as the nucleus of a more complex expanded type, in which the subject pronoun sometimes functions simply as a copula.

(11) *p-hēbs m-p-sōma pe p-bal*
the-lamp of-the-body it the-eye
"The eye is the lamp of the body." (Matt 6:22)

The fourth basic sentence type is defined by a small group of predicates, mostly expressive of qualities, that take a nominal or pronominal subject as a suffix.

(12) *nanou-paei*
be good-this
"This is good." (1 Tim 2:3)

2. Object Incorporation. The defining property of a syntactically transitive verb in Coptic is the ability of its infinitive to incorporate a direct object.

(13) *a-apa pesunthios nej-p-daimōnion ebol*
PAST-Apa Pesunthios cast-the-demon outward
"Apa Pesunthios cast out the demon." (Bap 114)

(14) *a-f-noj-ou ebol*
PAST-he-cast-them outward
"He cast them out." (Mark 1:34)

If the direct object of a transitive verb is not incorporated, it is marked by a preposition (*n-* with nouns, *mmo-* with pronouns).

(15) *n-f-nouje ebol n-n-daimonion*
CONJUNCTIVE-he-cast outward OBJ-the-demons
". . . and he will cast out the demons." (BMar 239)

(16) *k-nouje mmo-ou ebol*
you-cast OBJ-them outward
"You are casting them out." (BMar)

Incorporation is the rule when the direct object is a noun without any article; such nouns are devoid of gender and number and generally have a nonreferential or generic meaning.

(17) *ti-nej-daimonion ebol*
I-cast-demon outward
"I cast out demons." ("I exorcise.") (Luke 13:32)

As a rule, incorporation occurs in the bipartite sentence only in the latter circumstance. But in the tripartite sentence, pronominal direct objects, too, are most often incorporated, and there is variation between incorporation and nonincorporation of the direct object when it is a noun with an article (definite or indefinite).

3. Sentence Conversion. A remarkable feature of Coptic grammar is the way in which a basic sentence can be *converted* (or *transposed*) by prefixes into: (1) *preterit* time; (2) an adverbial *(circumstantial)* clause; (3) a *relative* clause; or (4) a focalizing construction (called a "Second Tense," in contrast to an unconverted "first" tense). The preterit conversion serves primarily to provide background information relevant to a larger context. Ex. 18 is preceded immediately by the narrative statement, "We came to Miletus."

(18) *ne-a-paulos gar krine . . . ne-f-čepē gar . . .*
PRET-PAST-Paul for decide . . . PRET-he-hasten for . . .
"For Paul had decided . . . ; for he was hastening . . ." (Acts 20:16)

The circumstantial conversion forms a subordinate clause with a wide variety of uses (the converter encoding something like "the circumstances being that . . .").

(19) *a-f-šaje e-f-smou e-p-noute*
PAST-he-speak CIRC-he-bless OBJ-the-god
"He spoke, blessing God." (Luke 1:64)

(20) *eti e-f-šaje a-p-alektōr moute*
still CIRC-he-speak PAST-the-cock crow
"While he was still speaking, the cock crowed." (Luke 22:60)

The relative conversion forms a clause that is subordinate to a preceding definite antecedent; as a rule, the antecedent is represented in the relative clause itself by a pronoun. Compare ex. 22 with ex. 21.

(21) *a-n-daimonion ei ebol hm-p-rōme*
PAST-the-demons come outward from-the-man
"The demons came out of the man." (Luke 8:33)

(22) *p-rōme ent-a-n-daimonion ei ebol nhēt-f*
the-man REL-PAST-the-demons come outward from-him
"the man from whom the demons had gone" (Luke 8:38)

The function of the second tense conversion is to focus on, or emphasize, an adverbial element in the sentence. Like the preterit conversion, the use of a second tense usually depends on a context larger than a single sentence. In the following example, the focus is on the prepositional phrase *e-p-satanas*. Compare the statement, "You belong to Satan," with ex. 23.

(23) *e-k-ēp e-p-satanas*
FOCUS-you-belong to-the-Satan
"It is to Satan that you belong." (ShMIF 23 40)

4. Cleft Sentence. The combination of a relative clause with a nominal sentence of the type illustrated in ex. 10 creates a cleft sentence in which a nominal or pronominal constituent is focalized. Compare the statement, "The Lord your God has chosen you," with ex. 24.

(24) *ntok pe ent-a-p-joeis pek-noute sotp-k*
you it REL-PAST-the-lord your-god choose-you
"It is you that the Lord your God has chosen." (Deut 7:6)

5. Adjectival Modification. The Coptic lexicon contains very few words that can be classed as adjectives. Adjectival modification of a noun is achieved by syntactic means: a relative or circumstantial clause (depending on whether the noun is definitely determined or not);

(25) *hen-šaje e-u-šoueit*
some-words CIRC-they-vain
"vain words" (Eph 5:6)

or an indefinitely determined noun in a nominal sentence;

(26) *hen-epra ne neei-šaje*
some-vanity they these-words
"These words are vain." (ShC 73 206)

or the relational preposition *n-* with a nondetermined noun.

(27) *nek-šaje n-epra*
your-words RELATION-vanity
"your vain words" (ShMIF 23 42)

6. Other Features. The case-roles of the various participants in the action of a verb are marked either by position (syntactic subject, incorporated direct object) or by prepositions (exx. 1, 2, etc.). The passive in progress is expressed by the use of a nonreferential third-person-plural subject: "they are choosing him" = "he is being chosen." Interrogative sentences are formed by using interrogative pronouns or particles, without altering the word order of the basic sentence types. Imperative sentences are formed by using infinitives apart from conjugation, with object incorporation occurring as it does in the tripartite pattern.

G. Coptic Today

The study of Coptic remains an essential part of the discipline of Egyptology. But because the content of Coptic literature is primarily relevant to the history of Christianity, Coptology (also called Coptic Studies) has begun to emerge as a distinct discipline with close ties to Egyptology on the one hand and to biblical and Christian historical studies on the other. A movement to revive Coptic as a spoken language was begun by Egyptian Christians late in the 19th century; the Egyptian church now urges its adherents to learn a modified form of the Bohairic dialect, as yet with only qualified success.

II. Basic Reference Works

Comprehensive bibliographies of Coptic Studies are Kammerer 1950; Simon, Quecke, and du Bourguet 1949–76; and Biedenkopf-Ziehner 1972–80. T. Orlandi's *Coptic Bibliography* (Rome: Centro Italiano Microfiches), issued on microfiche, is updated biannually by printed supplements and entirely revised in annual editions.

The standard and indispensable dictionary of Coptic is Crum 1939. Of more specialized interest are Černý 1975; Westendorf 1965–77; and Vycichl 1983. Smith 1983 is convenient for beginners. There is as yet no dictionary of the large number of words borrowed by Coptic from Greek.

Overall, the best Coptic grammar is still Stern 1880, but fundamental advances have been made by Polotsky (especially 1944; 1960; 1962; 1988), all of whose works are essential. Possibly seminal is Shisha-Halevy 1986. Lambdin 1983 is helpful for beginners.

Students of the Coptic versions of the Bible must consult scattered editions of individual manuscripts, essential guides to which are Vaschalde 1919–33; Till 1959; Nagel 1983–84; Nagel 1984b; and Schmitz and Mink 1986. Lefort, Wilmet, and Draguet 1950–60 is a useful concordance to the Sahidic NT.

Bibliography

Ambrogio, T. 1539. *Introductio in Chaldaicam Linguam, Syriacam, atque Armenicam, and Decem Alias Linguas.* Pavia.

Biedenkopf-Ziehner, A. 1972–80. Koptologische Literaturübersicht. *Enchoria* 2: 103–36; 3: 95–152; 4: 141–55; 5: 151–79; 6: 93–119; 8.2: 51–72; 10: 151–83.

Breydenbach, B. von. 1486. *Peregrinationes in Terram Sanctam.* Mainz.

Černý, J. 1975. *A Coptic Etymological Dictionary.* Cambridge.

Crum, W. E. 1939. *A Coptic Dictionary.* Oxford.

Emmel, S. 1987. Specimens of Coptic Type from the Sacra Congregatio de Propaganda Fide in Rome. *Yale University Library Gazette* 61: 96–104.

Funk, W.-P. 1985. How Closely Related Are the Subakhmimic Dialects? *ZÄS* 112: 124–39.

———. 1988. Dialects Wanting Homes: A Numerical Approach to the Early Varieties of Coptic. In *Historical Dialectology: Regional and Social,* ed. J. Fisiak. Berlin.

Gravit, F. W. 1938. Peiresc et les études coptes en France au XVIIe siècle. *Bulletin de la Société d'Archéologie Copte* 4: 1–22.

Griffith, F. L. 1901. The Date of the Old Coptic Texts and Their Relation to Christian Coptic. *ZÄS* 39: 78–82.

Hintze, F. 1984. Eine Klassifizierung der koptischen Dialekte. Pp. 411–32 in *Studien zu Sprache and Religion Ägyptens,* vol. 1, ed. F. Junge et al. Göttingen.

Kahle, P. E. 1954. *Bala'izah: Coptic Texts from Deir el-Bala'izah in Upper Egypt.* 2 vols. Oxford.

Kammerer, W. 1950. *A Coptic Bibliography.* University of Michigan General Library Publications 7. Ann Arbor.

Kasser, R. 1960. *Papyrus Bodmer VI: Livre des Proverbes.* CSCO 194 (Copt. 27). Louvain.

———. 1962. Les origines du christianisme égyptien. *RTP* 95: 11–28.

———. 1980–81. Prolégomènes à un essai de classification systématique des dialectes et subdialectes coptes selon les critères de la phonétique. *Mus* 93: 53–112, 237–97; 94: 91–152.

———. 1982. Le dialecte protosaïdique de Thèbes. *Archiv für Papyrusforschung und verwandte Gebiete* 28: 67–81.

Kircher, A. 1643. *Lingua Aegyptiaca Restituta.* Rome.

Lambdin, T. O. 1983. *Introduction to Sahidic Coptic.* Macon.

Lantschoot, A. van. 1948. *Un précurseur d'Athanase Kircher: Thomas Obicini et la scala Vat. copte 71.* Bibliothèque du *Muséon* 22. Louvain.

Layton, B. 1987. *Catalogue of Coptic Literary Manuscripts in the British Library Acquired Since the Year 1906.* London.
Lefort, L. T.; Wilmet, M.; and Draguet, R. 1950–60 *Concordance du Nouveau Testament sahidique.* 5 vols. CSCO 124, 173, 183, 185, 196 (Subs. 1, 11, 13, 15, 16). Louvain.
Levi della Vida, G. 1939. *Ricerche sulla formazione del più antico fondo dei manoscritti orientali della Biblioteca Vaticana.* Studi e testi 92. Vatican City.
Mallon, A. 1906–7. Une école de savants égyptiens au Moyen Age. *MUSJ* 1: 109–31; 2: 213–64.
Nagel, P. 1965. Der frühkoptische Dialekt von Theben. Pp. 30–49 in *Koptologische Studien in der DDR,* ed. P. Nagel. *Wissenschaftliche Zeitschrift der Martin-Luther-Universität Halle-Wittenberg,* Sonderheft. Halle.
———. 1983–84. Studien zur Textüberlieferung des sahidischen Alten Testaments. *ZÄS* 110: 51–74; 111: 138–64.
———. 1984a (ed.). *Graeco-Coptica: Griechen und Kopten im byzantinischen Ägypten.* Martin-Luther-Universität Halle-Wittenberg Wissenschaftliche Beiträge 48. Halle.
———. 1984b. Griechisch-koptische Bilinguen des Alten Testaments. Pp. 231–57 in Nagel 1984a.
———. 1989. Editionen koptischer Bibeltexte seit Till 1960. *Archiv für Papyrusforschung und verwandte Gebiete* 35: 43–100.
Orlandi, T. 1986. Coptic Literature. Pp. 51–81 in Pearson and Goehring 1986.
———. 1990. *Coptic Bibliography.* Rome.
Pearson, B. A., and Goehring, J. E., eds. 1986. *The Roots of Egyptian Christianity.* Philadelphia.
Polotsky, H. J. 1944. *Études de syntaxe copte.* Cairo: Société d'Archéologie Copte. (= 1971: 102–207)
———. 1960. The Coptic Conjugation System. *Or* 29: 392–422. (= 1971: 238–68)
———. 1962. Nominalsatz und Cleft Sentence im Koptischen. *Or* 31: 413–30. (= 1971: 418–35)
———. 1968. The "Weak" Plural Article in Bohairic. *JEA* 54: 243–45.
———. 1970. Coptic. Pp. 558–70 in *Linguistics in South West Asia and North Africa,* ed. T. A. Sebeok. Current Trends in Linguistics 6. The Hague.
———. 1971. *Collected Papers.* Jerusalem.
———. 1985a. Die koptischen Possessiva. *Enchoria* 13: 89–96.
———. 1985b. Verbalaspekte im Koptischen. *Göttinger Miszellen* 88: 19–23.
———. 1987. Egyptology, Coptic Studies and the Egyptian Language. Pp. 5–21 in *Lingua Sapientissima,* ed. J. D. Ray. Cambridge.
———. 1988–90. *Grundlagen des koptischen Satzbaus.* 2 vols. ASP 27, 29. Decatur, IL.
Postel, G. 1538. *Linguarum Duodecim Characteribus Differentium Alphabetum, Introductio, ac Legendi Modus Longè Facilimus.* Paris.
Quaegebeur, J. 1982. De la préhistoire de l'écriture copte. *OLP* 13: 125–36.
Quatremère, É. 1808. *Recherches critiques et historiques sur la langue et la littérature de l'Égypte.* Paris.
Saltini, G. E. 1860. Della Stamperia Orientale Medicea e di Giovan Battista Raimondi memoria compilata sui documenti dell'Archivio Centrale di Stato. *Giornale storico degli Archivi Toscani* 4: 257–308.
Samir, K. 1986. Arabic Sources for Early Egyptian Christianity. Pp. 82–97 in Pearson and Goehring 1986.
Satzinger, H. 1984. Die altkoptischen Texte als Zeugnisse der Beziehungen zwischen Ägyptern und Griechen. Pp. 137–46 in Nagel 1984a.
———. 1985. On the Origin of the Sahidic Dialect. Pp. 307–12 in *Acts of the Second International Congress of Coptic Studies,* ed. T. Orlandi and F. Wisse. Rome.
Schmitz, F.-J., and Mink, G. 1986. *Liste der koptischen Handschriften des Neuen Testaments.* ANTF 8. Berlin.
Sethe, K. 1925. Das Verhältnis zwischen Demotisch und Koptisch und seine Lehren für die Geschichte der ägyptischen Sprache. *ZDMG* 79: 290–316.
Shisha-Halevy, A. 1973. Apodotic *efsōtm:* A Hitherto Unnoticed Late Coptic, Tripartite Pattern Conjugation-Form and its Diachronic Perspective. *Mus* 86: 455–66.
———. 1974. Protatic *efsōtm:* A Hitherto Unnoticed Coptic Tripartite Conjugation-Form and its Diachronic Connections. *Or* 43: 369–81.
———. 1986. *Coptic Grammatical Categories: Structural Studies in the Syntax of Shenoutean Sahidic.* AnOr 53. Rome.
Simon, J.; Quecke, H.; and du Bourguet, P. 1949–76. Bibliographie copte. Regularly published in *Orientalia* 18–45.
Smith, R. 1983. *A Concise Coptic-English Lexicon.* Grand Rapids.
Steindorff, G. 1950. Bemerkungen über die Anfänge der koptischen Sprache und Literatur. Pp. 189–214 in *Coptic Studies in Honor of Walter Ewing Crum,* ed. M. Malinine. Bulletin of the Byzantine Institute 2. Boston.
Stern, L. 1880. *Koptische Grammatik.* Leipzig: Weigel. Repr. Osnabrück: Biblio Verlag, 1971.
Till, W. C. 1959. Coptic Biblical Texts Published After Vaschalde's Lists. *BJRL* 42: 220–40.
Vaschalde, A. 1919–33. Ce qui a été publié des versions coptes de la Bible. *RB* 28: 220–43, 513–31; 29: 91–106, 241–58; 30: 237–46; 31: 81–88, 234–58; *Mus* 43: 409–31; 45: 117–56; 46: 299–313.
Vergote, J. 1961. Les dialectes dans le domaine égyptien. *CdÉ* 36: 237–49.
Vycichl, W. 1983. *Dictionnaire étymologique de la langue copte.* Louvain.
Westendorf, W. 1965–77. *Koptisches Handwörterbuch.* Heidelberg.
Worrell, W. H. 1934. *Coptic Sounds.* University of Michigan Studies, Humanistic Series 26. Ann Arbor.

STEPHEN EMMEL

EGYPTIAN LANGUAGE AND WRITING

A. Linguistic Position
B. History
C. Writing
D. Phonology
E. Grammar

A. Linguistic Position

Egyptian is a member of the Afroasiatic language group, occupying one of the five or six main branches of this linguistic family (Semitic, Berber, Egyptian, Cushitic, Chadic, and possibly Omotic). Unlike the other branches, Egyptian is represented by a single language.

In most respects, Egyptian seems closest to the Asiatic (Semitic) languages—possibly only because our knowledge of the African languages is both poorer and from a much later historical era than either Egyptian or Semitic. Egyptian exhibits many common Afroasiatic features: (1) consonantal root structures; (2) masculine/feminine gender, with feminine marked by final *-t;* (3) plural in *-w* (m.) and *-wt* (f.); (4) independent and suffixed pronouns: e.g., *jnk,* "I," *-j,* "my"; (5) stative (qualitative) form of the verb: e.g., *ḥtp.kw,* "I am content"; and (6) lexical morphological features, such as nouns of instrument in *m-*, causative stem in *s-*, reflexive stem in *n-*.

Unlike African languages, Egyptian shares with Semitic a predominantly triconsonantal root structure (close to two thirds of all verb roots in one representative early text corpus) and an active dual (m. *-wj,* f. *-tj*). The vocalic patterns of many of its nouns, where these can be reconstructed, are also similar to those of Semitic nouns: for example, an active participle with the pattern *ā-i,* as in **ḥātip,* "content," reflected in cuneiform *ḫa-ti-ip* (Osing 1976: 128).

Unlike Semitic, Egyptian has no known case system and no prefixed verbal conjugation. Several of its features are found in African but not Semitic languages: (1) an "indirect" genitival construction, with the adjectival form of the preposition *jn,* "to, for": e.g., *prw jnj sn.k,* "house of (belonging to) your brother"; the direct genitival construct is also common *(prw sn.k);* (2) roots with two to six radicals, many with full or partial reduplication: e.g., *sn,* "kiss, smell," *snsn,* "associate with"; *ṯhn,* "shine," *ṯhnhn* "glitter"; and (3) passive forms with reduplicated final radical: e.g., *ḫmmj,* "unknown," from *ḫm,* "not know"; *nḥmm,* "will be taken," from *nḥm,* "take" (productive only in the oldest stage of Egyptian).

Egyptian has a vocabulary of about a hundred roots found also in Berber and Cushitic languages: for example, *gmj,* "find" = Berber *egmi,* "seek"; *nfr,* "perfect, good" = Bedja *nefir,* "pleasant." A few hieroglyphic phonograms reflect an earlier Semitic vocabulary that has been supplanted in historical times by native or non-Semitic words: for instance, Egyptian *ḏrt,* "hand" (related to the root *nḏr,* "grasp"), replacing earlier **jd* (preserved in the hieroglyph of a human hand, with the value *d;* also in the word *djw,* "five"); or Egyptian *jrt,* "eye" (possibly related to Cushitic and Chadic *il/iil* "eye"), replacing earlier **ʿ(j)n* (reflected in the hieroglyph of a human eye, used in writing the word *ʿn,* "beautiful").

B. History

Egyptian comprises two major historical phases (see section E below), each of which is represented by several distinct stages of development.

The language first appears in writing about 3300 B.C., in proper names, titles, and captions. Its first continuous text—essentially an expanded list of one individual's titles—dates from the end of Dynasty 3 (ca. 2750 B.C.) and marks the beginning of Old Egyptian, the earliest well-known stage of the language. Old Egyptian is preserved in tomb biographies, royal decrees, and an extensive series of religious (funerary) texts. It is roughly contemporary with the historical period of the Old Kingdom (OK) (Dyn. 3–6, ca. 2800–2300 B.C.).

Old Egyptian is closely related to the second major stage, that of Middle Egyptian. Also known as Classical Egyptian, this stage is represented in nearly every genre of Egyptian text: letters, accounts, stories, official and biographical inscriptions, and religious texts. As a living language, it spanned the period from the end of the OK approximately to the beginning of the New Kingdom (Dyn. 6–17, ca. 2300–1600 B.C.). Even when replaced in the popular, and later written, speech it remained the language of temple and official inscriptions throughout the history of pagan Egypt. In the New Kingdom (NK) (Dyn. 18–19, ca. 1600–1200 B.C.) and later, its grammar and vocabulary were heavily influenced by that of the contemporary language, but in most respects it retained the features of its classical stage of the Middle Kingdom (MK; Dyn. 12, ca. 2000–1800 B.C.).

The earlier historical phase represented by Old and Middle Egyptian differs significantly from that of the later, and final, phase of the language. Elements of this final phase are already visible in the colloquial speech (insofar as it was recorded) at the end of the MK, if not before. It first entered the written language as one of the reforms instituted by the "heretic" pharaoh Akhenaten, at the end of Dyn. 18 (ca. 1350 B.C.). Its earliest written stage, known as Late Egyptian, became the language of all but monumental inscriptions from the Ramesside to Saite periods (Dyn. 19–26, ca. 1300–650 B.C.).

For much of its 600-year history, Late Egyptian gives the impression of reflecting fairly closely the contemporary colloquial idiom. Under the pharaoh Psamtik (Psammetichus) I (ca. 650 B.C.), a new script was introduced, reflecting also newer grammatical features. This script and its stage of the language are known as Demotic ("popular"). True to its name, Demotic was at first used for commercial and other everyday documents, but under the Ptolemies (after 332 B.C.). it was expanded to religious and literary genres as well. Demotic remained in use alongside the monumental language until the middle of the 5th century A.D.

With the advent of Christianity, the pagan associations of the older scripts prompted the adoption of a new writing system based on the Greek alphabet. Both the alphabet and the language written in it—the final stage of Egyptian—are known as Coptic (probably from Greek *aigyptios,* "Egyptian," itself a rendering of Egyptian *ḥwt-kꜣ-ptḥ,* a designation of ancient Memphis). The Coptic alphabet first appears in magical papyri from the end of the 1st century A.D., where it was added to the (vowelless) Demotic to ensure proper pronunciation of key words. It was adopted as a full-fledged writing system in the 3d century A.D., when it was used for Egyptian translations of the Bible and for other Christian texts.

Coptic was influenced by Greek not only in its alphabet but also in vocabulary. Some two thousand Greek words appear in Coptic, replacing or supplementing older native words. Coptic is also the first stage of Egyptian to show clear dialectical variants, mostly in morphology and phonology. Differences in dialect probably existed throughout Egyptian history—one text of Dyn. 19 (ca. 1200 B.C.) describes obscure phraseology as being "like the speech of a Delta man with a man from Aswan"—but they are concealed by both the standardized nature and the purely consonantal structure of earlier scripts. Some seven major and eight minor Coptic dialects have been identified. Of these, Saidic (from Arabic *al-ṣaʿīd,* "Southern Egypt") was the major ecclesiastical and literary dialect from the 4th to 10th centuries A.D. In the 10th century, Bohairic (from Arabic *al-buḥairah,* "Northern Egypt") was adopted as the official language of the Coptic Church, and it eventually supplanted the other dialects. Bohairic remains the liturgical language of the Church today, but Coptic disappeared as a spoken language probably by the 15th century A.D. Knowledge of Coptic, however, provided the key to the modern recovery of the earlier language, beginning with Jean-François Champollion's decipherment of the Rosetta Stone in the early 19th century.

C. Writing

Egyptian is written in one of four major scripts: hieroglyphic, hieratic, Demotic, and Coptic. With the exception of Coptic, all represent the consonantal rather than the full phonological structure of the spoken language, a feature that Egyptian shares with Semitic writing systems. The vocalized forms preserved in Coptic—and, to a lesser extent, in older cuneiform transcriptions—allow for partial reconstruction of earlier phonology: for example, Coptic *šmoun,* "eight" < **ḫamān˘w,* which is reflected in cuneiform *ḫa-ma-an* (Osing 1976: 476).

Hieroglyphic is both the earliest and most widely attested script. It appears as early as the predynastic period (before 3200 B.C.) and remained in use until the 5th century A.D. Both the system and the orthography of its signs seem to have been first standardized at the beginning of the OK. Hieroglyphic writing consists essentially of two kinds of signs: ideograms, representing things, actions, or concepts; and phonograms, representing sounds. The simplest—and probably the first—ideograms are those that depict concrete things or actions, such as a scarab beetle ("beetle") or a pair of striding legs ("walk, move"). More abstract images are conveyed by an extended use of signs from this inventory, on the rebus principle: for example, the scarab beetle (*ḫprr,* "beetle") is used to write words with the root *ḫpr,* "develop."

Phonograms were developed on the same principle. These represent one or more consonantal sounds: for example, the sign for [p] (a reed stool) from **pǎj,* "stool" (Coptic *pai*), or that for [r] (a human mouth) from **rǎj,* "mouth" (Coptic *ro*), but also biliteral *pr* (a simple house plan) from **pār˘w,* "house" (Coptic *pōr,* cuneiform *pa-ru* [Osing 1976: 477]).

In all, about five hundred signs were in common use in Classical Egyptian hieroglyphic. Words could be written ideographically (usually only for concrete things, such as *prw,* "house") or purely phonographically; but most often the two values were combined, as in HOUSE-PLAN *(pr)* plus MOUTH *(r)* plus WALKING-LEGS, for *pr(j),* "go forth." Ideograms are often placed at the end of words spelled with phonograms, as "determinatives" indicating the genus or kind of action to which the word refers (for instance, the walking-legs sign in the preceding example).

Hieroglyphic writing employs no marks of punctuation. Texts could be written left to right or right to left, either horizontally or in vertical columns. The signs usually face the direction from which the text is read. The Egyptians did not distinguish hieroglyphic writing from other representations of reality, such as statues or scenes in relief. Both were a *tjt,* "symbol," rather than an accurate representation of reality. Hieroglyphic signs were often carved with the same detail as other pictorial elements of a scene. Conversely, statues or relief representations were themselves a kind of hieroglyph, a phenomenon most often illustrated in the animal-headed Egyptian gods—as, for instance, in the beetle-headed human form representing *ḫprj,* "the Developing One" (a form of the sun-god). Hieroglyphic was generally employed on the same kinds of permanent media used for representations, usually carved or painted on stone or wood. It remained the preferred form for monumental inscriptions throughout Egyptian history. With rare exceptions, only the early phase of the language (Old-Middle/Classical Egyptian) is written in hieroglyphs.

A simpler form of the hieroglyphic signs was used for writing on less permanent media, such as papyri, with reed pen and ink. This, in turn, was probably (though not demonstrably) the origin of hieratic, a purely cursive form of hieroglyphic. For the most part, hieratic bears the same relationship to hieroglyphic that modern handwriting does to printing. Hieratic was written from right to left, usually in horizontal lines, in ink on materials such as papyri, ostraca, linen, and leather. Hieratic signs are attested almost as early as hieroglyphic. By the time of the MK (and probably earlier), hieratic was the standard script for letters, accounts, and literature; most of the great literary works of Classical Egyptian are preserved in hieratic. It was also the writing system that Egyptian scribes learned first. Both Old and Middle Egyptian are represented in hieratic, and Late Egyptian almost exclusively so.

By the 21st Dyn. (ca. 1000 B.C.), administrative hieratic had developed a hand significantly different from that of other hieratic documents. Called "abnormal hieratic," this script was in use until the Saite period (Dyn. 26, ca. 650 B.C.), when it was replaced by Demotic, which developed from it. Demotic writing is characterized by extremely brief signs and numerous ligatures. Though ultimately based on hieroglyphic, it bears no resemblance to the original signs. Demotic is also the sole script of the stage of the language with the same name. Hieratic, like hieroglyphic, remained in use alongside the newer writing, but it was reserved primarily for religious papyri written in the older (semi-Classical language. Like hieratic, Demotic was written from right to left, with pen and ink, primarily on perishable materials. Occasionally, however, it was used to inscribe official documents on stone—as in the decree of Ptolemy V Epiphanes (196 B.C.) on the Rosetta Stone, carved in both hieroglyphic and Demotic as well as Greek.

Although they were aware of the syllabic, and later alphabetic, scripts of Semitic languages, the Egyptians never reduced the inventory of their own signs to either a syllabary or an alphabet. Several times in its history Egyptian did develop a system for rendering the phonology of foreign names and loanwords with groups of signs, sometimes equivalent to monosyllabic Egyptian words: for example, *jj-šꜣ-pj-jꜣ-r'* (Dyn. 18, ca. 1500 B.C.) = Canaanite **yašūp-ʾil* (Albright 1934: 34). Hieroglyphic also seems to be the basis of the Proto-Sinaitic script, in which some thirty signs were used to form an alphabet for writing a non-Egyptian language. Although the language and precise date of Proto-Sinaitic are still uncertain, the alphabet itself seems to have been created acrophonically based on Semitic counterparts of the words represented by the Egyptian signs: for example, the hieroglyph of a man's head (Eg *tpj,* "head") for [r] (Semitic *ra'š,* "head"). The apparent similarity of this script to Proto-Canaanite suggests that it may be the origin of the principle of alphabetic writing (Giveon *LA* 4: 1156–59).

The Egyptian language itself was written alphabetically in its final stage. Coptic uses the 24 letters of the Greek alphabet, plus seven derived from Demotic, primarily for sounds not present in Greek (*š, f, h, ḫ, c* = $[t^y]$, *g* = $[k^y/t^{yh}]$, and a monogram for *ti*).

D. Phonology

Although Coptic is the first stage of Egyptian to record vowels as well as consonants, the vocalic inventory of earlier stages has been reconstructed with the help of Coptic and older cuneiform transcriptions. Egyptian seems to have shared the common Semitic vowels [a], [i], and [u]. Length was determined by morphology, with long vowels in open stressed syllables, short vowels in closed stressed syllables, and indeterminate vowels elsewhere: e.g., **jˇrăk* > *erok,* "to you" (m.s.), **jˇraṯˇn* > *erōtn,* "to you" (pl.). Sometime between Dyn. 19 and 25 (ca. 1200–700 B.C.), the language underwent a general vowel-shift from the original system to that found in Coptic (*ă* > *ŏ, ĭ* > *ă, ŭ* > *ĕ;* and *ā* > *ō/ū, ī* > *ī/ē, ū* > *ē*).

The earliest stages of the language display 24 consonants, transcribed as follows: *ꜣ, j* (or *ỉ*), *ꜥ, w, b, p, f, m, n, r, h, ḥ, ḫ, ẖ, z* (or *s*), *s* (or *ś*), *š, q* (or *ḳ*), *g, t, ṯ, d, ḏ*. In Coptic these have been reduced to 14 or 15 in most dialects: *b, p, f, m, n, r/l, h/ḫ, s, š, k, g* = $[k^y]$, *t, c* = $[t^y]$, with original *ꜣ, ꜥ,* and *j* occasionally reflected in doubled vowels (e.g., **ḥāꜥˇs* > *hōōs,* "herself"). Coptic descendants of *j* (where preserved) and *w* are phonologically equivalent to vocalic [ī] (/ei/) and [ū] (/ou/): e.g., *ouōbš* < **wābiḫ,* "white" (adjective), but *oubáš* < **wˇbáḫ,* "become white" (infinitive). This may have been true of *j* and *w* in earlier stages as well, since both are often omitted in writing (like vowels).

The gradual reduction of the original 24-consonant inventory to that of Coptic is visible historically. By Middle Egyptian, *z* is no longer phonologically distinct from *s,* and *ṯ* and *ḏ* show evidence of reduction to *t* and *d,* respectively, in some words. Late Egyptian reflects the beginnings of both the eventual loss of the voiced stops—*d* > *t, ḏ* > *ṯ, g* > *k;* Coptic *b* is probably a (voiceless?) labial spirant—and the reduction of the four spirants *h, ḥ, ḫ, ẖ* to one or two (*h* or *h/ḫ,* depending on dialect).

The original sound of many Egyptian consonants is uncertain. That transcribed as *ꜣ* is generally thought to have been a glottal stop (*ʾalep*), but in Semitic loanwords in Old and Middle Egyptian it appears to correspond to Semitic [r]: for example, *kꜣnw,* later *kꜣmw,* "vineyard" = Semitic *karm.* In Coptic, however, its reflex is usually zero: e.g., **ꜣāpˇd* > *ōbt,* "bird," **wāꜣˇḏ* > *ouōt,* "fresh," as well as **kaꜣmˇw* > *gōm.* The correspondence between *ꜣ* and Semitic [r] may not indicate so much a value like [r] for *ꜣ* as a dissimilarity between Semitic [r] and Egyptian /r/.

The consonant transliterated *r* corresponds to *r* or *l* in Semitic loanwords in Late Egyptian (e.g., *jbꜣrjj* = Canaanite *'abir,* "stallion") and in Coptic reflexes of Egyptian words, where the distinction between *r* and *l* is partly dialectical (**rāmˇṯ,* "man" > Saidic *rōme,* Fayumic *lōmi*). Already in Old Egyptian, *r* seems to be regularly altered to *ꜣ* or *j* in syllable-final position (though this is not always reflected in writing): e.g., *ḏrt* (**ḏārˇt*) > Coptic *tōre,* "hand," but *ḏꜣt.k* (**ḏărtˇk*) > *tootk,* "your hand"; *ḥqr* (**ḥˇqăr*) > *hko,* "hunger," but *ḥqr.tj* (**ḥˇqărtˇj*) > *hkoeit,* "hungry." The consonant [l] may have existed in dialects earlier than Coptic, but it is not represented phonemically in writing before Demotic (unless older /r/ = [l]?). Coptic *l* derives from earlier *n* (e.g., *las* <**nĭs,* "tongue" = Semitic *lis*) as well as from earlier *r.* Earlier scripts may represent [l] by the groups *ꜣn* and (in Late Egyptian) *nr:* for example, *dng/dꜣg/dꜣng,* "dwarf" (= **dlg?*); *bnr* > Coptic *bol,* "out."

The consonants *z* and *s* are generally thought to represent the voiced/voiceless spirants [z] and [s], but *z* has also been analyzed as [ts]. Since [z], if present, would seem to have been the only voiced spirant (other than pharyngeal ꜥ) in the original inventory, the phoneme *z* may instead have represented an original voiceless [th], later assimilated to [s] as in many colloquial Arabic dialects. The consonant *ẖ* is equivalent to *š* in the oldest stage (dialect?) of the language, but by Middle Egyptian it has become a distinct phoneme. Its value is generally assumed to have been similar to that of [ç] (*ch* in German *ich*), while *ḫ* represented [x] (*ch* in German *ach*). But the two may also have represented a consonantal pair distinguished by palatalization (*ḫ* = [x] vs. *ẖ* = $[x^y]$), or voiced/voiceless spirants *ḫ* = [gh] (Arabic *ghain*) and *ẖ* = [x].

The three original consonants *q, k,* and *g* are reduced in Coptic to the voiceless stop [k] or its palatalized counterpart *g* = $[k^y]$, with *q* generally > Saidic *k, k* > *k* or *g,* and *g* > *g* or *k.* These correspondences suggest an original distinction *q* = [g] (later > [k] when the voiced stops were lost), *k* = [k], and *g* = $[k^y]$. The three are generally interpreted, however, as uvular [q] (Arabic *qaf*) and velar [k] and [g], respectively.

Similarly, the pairs *d/t* and *ḏ/ṯ* are thought to have represented the voiced/voiceless dental stops [d]/[t] and their palatalized counterparts $[d^y]/[t^y]$. But *d/t* have also been analyzed as the voiceless stops [ṭ]/[t], with *ḏ/ṯ* their palatalized alternants [ç̣]/[c], where [ṭ] and [ç̣] are similar to Ethiopic [ṭ] and $[ṭ^y]$, respectively. In words in which they have not coalesced with *d/t,* the pair *ḏ/ṯ* generally corresponds to Coptic *c* = $[t^y]$, a palatalized counterpart of Coptic *t* (< *d/t*).

Finally, the Bohairic dialect of Coptic also uses aspiration as a phonological feature in the stops: *p* vs. p^h, *t* vs. t^h, *k* vs. k^h, and *c* vs. c^h, where the aspirated letters are represented by Greek *phi, theta,* and *chi,* and the Coptic letter *gima* (= Saidic $[k^y]$). The extent to which this feature may have existed in earlier dialects or stages of the language is unknown, but its existence in Coptic suggests that it may also underlie some of the phonological alternants of the older scripts.

E. Grammar

The elements of Egyptian syntax can be grouped into four parts of speech: noun, adjective, adverb, and verb.

The noun category includes both nouns and pronouns. Gender is marked lexically (zero, *-w,* or *-j* for masculine; *-t* for feminine). Plural and dual number is indicated phonologically by *-w* and *-wj* for masculine, *-wt* and *-tj* for feminine: *sn,* "brother," *snw,* "brothers," *snwj,* "two brothers"; *snt,* "sister," *snwt,* "sisters," *sntj,* "two sisters." Syntactic usage is marked by position in the sentence or phrase rather than by case. Genitival relationships may be indicated by direct conjunction of two nouns (probably accompanied by changes in stress and phonology), or by suffix pronouns: e.g., *prw sn.j,* "house of my brother." Two nouns may also be linked by the "indirect" genitive (see section A above). The accusative (verbal object) is distinguished by position. Personal pronouns generally correspond to those found in Semitic languages: *jnk,* "I" (proclitic), *wj,* "I, me" (enclitic), *-j,* "my" (affixed).

Egyptian adjectives are for the most part noun equivalents and can be used independently as nouns. Those that modify a preceding noun agree with it in gender and (less regularly) number. Direct modification is a construction that disappeared gradually in the history of the language. By the advent of Coptic, most attributive adjectives had been replaced by a genitival or relative construction: e.g., *snt ꜥꜣt,* "big sister" = Coptic *nog n-sōne,* literally "big-one of sister."

The category of adverb includes primitive adverbs (*dj,* "here"), prepositional adverbs (*jmj,* "there," from *m,* "in"), and prepositional phrases (*m nwt tn,* "in this village"). Nouns and verbs can also function syntactically as adverbs.

The category of verb encompasses all verb forms, including those that function syntactically as nouns, adjectives, or adverbs. The earliest inventory includes five categories of inflection: (1) the suffix conjugation, in which morphological features, and pronominal subjects, are signaled by suffixes: *ꜥnḫ.s,* "she lives," *ꜥnḫ.n.s,* "she has lived"; (2) the stative (old perfective), corresponding in form to the Afroasiatic stative/qualitative: *ꜥnḫ.tj,* "she is alive"; (3) the imperative: *ꜥnḫ,* "live!"; (4) the attributive forms, including participles and relative forms: *ꜥnḫt,* "(she) who lives," *nwt ꜥnḫt.s jmj,* "village in which she lives"; and (5) the infinitival forms: *ꜥnḫ,* "to live." By the time of Coptic, these had been reduced to two productive forms—the infinitive and stative—for most verbs.

All four syntactic elements can function as sentence predicates. Nominal sentences, with the pattern *A B,* are statements of identity. Either element can be a noun or pronoun: *jnk sn.k,* "I (am) your brother"; *pen-son pe,* "He (is) our brother" (Gen 37:27). The bipartite pattern is often expanded by means of the enclitic pronoun *pw* > *pe* (3 m.s.): *snt.k pw spdt,* "Your sister (is) Sothis"; *pai pe pasnof,* "This (is) my blood" (Matt 26:28).

Statements of quality are expressed by adjectival sentences, a variant of the bipartite nominal pattern in which the first element is an immutable (m.s.) adjective: *mꜣꜥ sj,* "She (is) correct." These are primarily a feature of Old to Late Egyptian. In Demotic they are replaced by a form of the adjective-verb; and in Coptic by a nominal-sentence construction in which the adjective is treated as an undefined noun: *ou-me te,* "It (is) correct" (literally, "a correct one"; John 5:32).

Sentences with adverbial predicates are essentially statements of location or state. These follow the pattern *A Adv: sn.k dj* = *pek-son tai,* "Your brother (is) here."

Verbal predicates express action. Strictly speaking, such sentences are those in which the word order is verb-subject-object-adverb and in which the verb itself is predicate: *qd sn.j prw.f m nwt tn,* "My brother built his house in this village" (literally, "build brother–my house–his in village this"). Various forms of the verb, however, can also function as nominal, adjectival, or adverbial predicate in other, "nonverbal" sentences: *mrr.f jrr.f,* "When he likes, he acts" (literally, "That-he-likes [is] that-he-acts," an *A B* nominal sentence), *ḥꜥ sw,* "He is jubilant" (an adjectival sentence, in which *ḥꜥ* is an active participle), *tek-sōne onh,* "Your sister is alive" (an adverbial sentence, in which *onh* is the stative form of *ōnh,* "live").

Historically, the Egyptian language shows two dominant, and related, trends. One of these is the gradual loss of the (pure) verbal sentence. Earlier verb forms are replaced by "pseudoverbal" constructions built largely on the adverbial-sentence pattern: *ꜥnḫ.s,* "She lives" > *st ḥr ꜥnḫ* = Coptic *s-ōnh,* literally "She (is) upon living"; *ꜥnḫt,* "(she) who lives" > *ntt ḥr ꜥnḫ* = Coptic *et-ōnh,* literally "(she) who (is) upon living."

The second historical trend, coincident with the first, is the replacement of synthetic forms (marked by internal changes) to analytic ones (marked by the accretion of discrete morphemes): *ꜥnḫ.s,* "May she live" > Demotic *my-jr.s-ꜥnḫ* = Coptic *mares-ōnh,* literally "Let her-do living." This historical process affected not only verbs but other parts of speech as well: e.g., *sn.k,* "your brother" > *pꜣjj.k sn* = Coptic *pek-son,* literally "the-your brother."

On the basis of these changes, the language can be divided into a synthetic phase, represented by Old/Middle Egyptian, and an analytic phase, visible in Late Egyptian through Coptic. Because all Egyptian scripts except Coptic do not fully reveal a word's morphology, the grammar of the analytic phase is more visible, and therefore better understood, than that of its synthetic ancestor. In Old and Middle Egyptian, the existence of inflected forms is deduced through morphological changes that may be visible in one or more—but not all—root classes. The attributive forms of the verb, for example, are known to have distinguished two synthetic forms (labeled "perfective" and "imperfective") because of the alternation of unmarked vs. geminated forms visible primarily in final-*j* roots: e.g., (f.s.) active participles *mst* and *msst,* from *msj,* "give birth."

The major questions still unanswered in the study of Egyptian grammar have to do with the number and meaning of inflected forms that were present in the suffix conjugation of Old and Middle Egyptian. The simplest written form of this verbal category, called the *sḏm.f* (based on the paradigm verb *sḏm,* "hear"), probably conceals at least four distinct forms in the earliest stage of the language. All four are visible in the irregular verb *jnj,* "fetch" (*jn.f, jnn.f, jnt.f,* and *jnw.f*), but most roots show only one, two, or three written forms: *sḏm.f,* "he hears" (root *sḏm*); *mꜣ.f* vs. *mꜣꜣ.f,* "he sees" (root *mꜣꜣ*); *msj.s* vs. *mss.s* vs. *msjw.s,* "she gives birth" (root *msj*). Of these, one form (*jnt.f* / *mꜣ.f* / *msj.s*) expresses the subjunctive (jussive, optative, etc.). The form in final *w,* with its paradigmatic counterparts (*jnw.f* / *mꜣꜣ.f* / *msjw.s*), seems to be a future tense, later replaced by the subjunctive and an analytic form.

The remaining two *sḏm.f* forms are distinguished primarily by the presence of gemination in some roots: *jn.f* / *mꜣ.f* / *msj.s* vs. *jnn.f* / *mꜣꜣ.f* / *mss.s.* By analogy with the attributive forms, these were originally thought to express a contrast between "perfective" (completed or single actions) and "imperfective" (incomplete or multiple actions), respectively. In the analytic verbal systems, however, there is a major syntactic distinction, reflected morphologically, between forms in which the focus of attention is on the verbal action itself ("First Tenses") and those in which it is directed to an adverbial adjunct ("Second Tenses"): e.g., Demotic *jw.f-hy r-ḥr.f* > Coptic *f-hi ehraf,* "It falls on him," vs. *jjr.f-hy r-ḥr.f* > Coptic *ef-hi ehraf,* "It is on him that it falls." The latter appears to be syntactically an adverbial-predicate construction in which a nominal (attributive) form of the verb functions as subject to the adverbial phrase: literally, "How/That it falls (is) on him." The same distinction has been proposed for the synthetic verb: e.g., *hꜣ.f ḥr.f,* "It descends on him," vs. *hꜣꜣ.f ḥr.f,* "It is on him that it descends."

There is a good deal of evidence in favor of this analysis, and the model of the analytic tenses has become widely accepted for the synthetic verbal system as well. More recently, however, questions have been raised as to the adequacy of the analytic model to explain all observable features of the synthetic forms (Englund and Frandsen 1987). The forms of the analytic verb distinguish primarily time (e.g., past, present, future) and syntactic function. In contrast, those of the synthetic verb seem to express primarily aspect (e.g., completed vs. incomplete) and mood (indicative, subjunctive). When and how the synthetic verb developed the features visible in its analytic descendants are questions that have yet to be fully answered.

Bibliography

Albright, W. F. 1934. *The Vocalization of the Egyptian Syllabic Orthography.* AOS 5. New Haven.

Allen, J. P. 1984. *The Inflection of the Verb in the Pyramid Texts.* Bibliotheca Aegyptia 2. Malibu, CA.

Černý, J., and Groll, S. I. 1984. *A Late Egyptian Grammar.* 3d ed. Studia Pohl: Series Maior 4. Rome.

Diakonoff, I. M. 1965. *Semito-Hamitic Languages.* Moscow.

Edel, E. 1955–64. *Altägyptische Grammatik.* 2 vols. AnOr 34, 39. Rome.

Edgerton, W. F. 1947. Stress, Vowel Quantity, and Syllable Division in Egyptian. *JNES* 6: 1–17.

———. 1951. Early Egyptian Dialect Interrelationships. *BASOR* 122: 9–12.

Englund, G., and Frandsen, P. J. 1987. *Crossroad (Chaos or the Beginning of a New Paradigm).* CNI Publications 1. Copenhagen.

Fecht, G. 1960. *Wortakzent und Silbenstruktur.* ÄF 21. Glückstadt.

Frandsen, P. J. 1974. *An Outline of the Late Egyptian Verbal System.* Copenhagen.

Gardiner, A. 1957. *Egyptian Grammar.* 3d ed. Rev. London.

Johnson, J. H. 1976. *The Demotic Verbal System.* SAOC 38. Chicago.

Junge, F. 1978. *Syntax der Mitteläg yptischen Literatursprache.* Mainz/Rhein.

Lacau, P. 1970. *Études d'égyptologie.* Vol. 1, *Phonétique égyptienne ancienne.* Bibliothèque d'Étude 41. Cairo.

Lefebvre, G. 1955. *Grammaire de l'égyptien classique.* 2d ed. BE 12. Cairo.

Loprieno, A. 1986. *Das Verbalsystem im Ägyptischen und im Semitischen.* Göttinger Orientforschungen 4/17. Wiesbaden.

Osing, J. 1976. *Die Nominalbildung des Ägyptischen.* Mainz/Rhein.

Polotsky, H. J. 1944. *Études de syntaxe copte.* Cairo.

———. 1976. Les transpositions du verbe en égyptien classique. *IOS* 6: 1–50.

Schenkel, W. 1975. *Die altägyptische Suffixkonjugation.* ÄA 32. Wiesbaden.

Till, W. C. 1931. *Koptische Dialektgrammatik.* Munich.

———. 1966. *Koptische Grammatik.* 3d ed. Leipzig.

Vergote, J. 1973–83. *Grammaire copte.* 2 vols. Louvain.

Vernus, P. 1988. L'égypto-copte. Pp. 161–206 in *Les langues dans le monde ancien et moderne,* pt. 3, ed. D. Cohen. Paris.

JAMES P. ALLEN

ETHIOPIC

The study of the Semitic Ethiopic dialects has become an important discipline in the Near Eastern field. As W. Leslau (1959) has noted, these dialects can be divided into two groups: North Ethiopic (abbreviated hereafter NE) and South Ethiopic (abbreviated hereafter SE). NE includes Geez, which is the oldest dialect, and two modern dialects, Tigré and Tigrinya. SE comprises Amharic, Argobba, Harari, Gafat, and Guragé. Gurагé is a dialect cluster, and for typological reasons this cluster has been called "Gunnān-Gurагé" by R. Hetzron (1977). All the Ethiopic dialects exhibit features which comparative linguists find worthy of note. A few of these features, which will be discussed below, include an important difference between the morphology of the basic verb types of NE and SE, the development of a direct object suffix in NE and SE, and the existence of a main verb marker forms in SE.

A. The *Qatala* and *Qattala* Verb Stems

Two of the basic verb types of Ethiopic have been described by T. Lambdin (1978) as follows:

G verbs—simple root + stem vowel pattern: G = Grundstamm (basic stem).

D verbs—root + doubling (D) of the second radical + stem vowel pattern.

The perfect tense of G verbs (often described by linguists as *qatala*) in NE is characterized by a single middle consonant, whereas in many of the SE dialects the perfect tense of G verbs has a doubled middle radical (described by linguists as *qattala*). The pattern of the G perfect in NE is found in other Semitic languages, but the SE pattern with a geminated middle radical is not attested elsewhere. For the purposes of comparative Semitic philology, it is important to determine whether the doubling which occurs in the SE G perfect is a Proto-Semitic phenomenon or merely a characteristic which can be explained by a development within SE itself.

This problem of gemination is depicted by the following table, which gives the G and D patterns of the perfect and imperfect tenses in Geez (a NE dialect) and Amharic (a SE dialect):

	Geez (NE)		Amharic (SE)	
	G	D	G	D
Perfect	*qatala*	*qattala*	*qattala*	*qattala*
Imperfect	*yeqattel*	*yeqēttel*	*yeqatl*	*yeqattel*

In addition to the different NE and SE stem patterns for the G perfect, one can also see from the table that in the NE the G imperfect has a doubled middle radical (*ye* is a prefix), whereas in SE the same form has a single middle radical. It should be noted that in two NE dialects, Tigrinya and Tigré, the geminated middle radical of the G imperfect is simplified when subject suffixes are added. W. Leslau (1953) uses this phenomenon as one of his major arguments in favor of the secondary nature of the *yeqattel* form in Ethiopic. His suggestion that the form **yeqatl(u)* be reconstructed as the PE G imperfect is based on his view that **yeqatl(u)* can be derived from Proto-Semitic **yaqtulu* and on the fact that certain SE dialects have a *yeqatlu* imperfect form. However, it is possible that the *-u* of the SE imperfect form is related to the complicated problem of main verb markers, which will be discussed below and, therefore, should not be traced back to Proto-Semitic. H. Nyberg (1932), J. Polotsky (1949), and R. Hetzron (1972), on the other hand, have suggested that the NE *yeqattel* form is primary and that the loss of gemination in the SE G imperfect is related to the phonetic principle underlying the loss of gemination which occurs in the G imperfect of Tigrinya and Tigré as the result of adding suffixes. According to this view, the loss of gemination, originally associated only with the addition of suffixes, spread to all forms of the G imperfect in SE. However, the phenomenon of the loss of gemination in the G imperfect as the result of adding suffixes is probably restricted to Tigrinya and Tigré and, therefore, does not shed light on the development of SE *yeqatl.* Thus, it is necessary to seek an explanation which would account for both the loss of gemination in the SE G imperfect and the introduction of this characteristic in the G perfect. It is likely that the D perfect of Proto-SE changed from **qattala* to **qēttala,* as suggested by Polotsky (1938), since this form is actually attested in some of the SE dialects. As a result of this change, *ē* became the stem vowel of both the D perfect and imperfect as opposed to the G stem vowel *a.* It was at this point that an analogy may have occurred between the perfect and imperfect form of G and D verbs, affecting the form of the G imperfect:

D		G
**qēttala : *yeqēttel*	::	**qatala : *yeqatel*

The result of this analogy would have been the simplification of the geminated middle consonant of the G imperfect *(yeqatel).* At this early stage of Se, the G and D stems for the perfect and imperfect tenses could be symbolically described as follows: G (s s) and D (d d). However, evidence from the SE dialect Endegen, as described by W. Leslau (1976), suggests that a phonological process contributed to the collapse of the contrast G (s s) /D (d d). In this dialect, the G perfect normally has a simple middle radical *(qatala),* but there are, nevertheless, some G perfect forms with a geminated middle consonant. These verbs appear to be historically related to verbs whose last radical was *ʾ, *ʿ, or **ḥ.* These final radicals were evidently assimilated by the middle radical, resulting in the gemination of the middle radical. It is likely that a similar development occurred in the proto-stages of other SE dialects, but in these dialects, the perfect with a geminated middle radical was standardized for all root types.

B. The Direct Object Suffix

In Ethiopic, the pronominal object of a transitive verb is regularly expressed by a suffix attached directly to the verb. The forms of the direct object suffix in Geez (a NE dialect) are as follows: 1 c.s. *-ni,* 2 m.s. *-ka,* 2 f.s. *-ki,* 3 m.s. *-o/-hu,* 3 f.s. *-ā/-hā,* 1 c.pl. *-na,* 2 m.pl. *-kemu,* 2 f.pl. *-ken,* 3 m.pl. *-omu/-homu,* 3 f.pl. *-on/-hon.* Thus, in order to say, "They found me," one would attach the suffix *-ni* to *rakabu,* resulting in the form *rakabuni.* In SE, some of the forms of the direct object suffix differ considerably from the forms in Geez. This divergence is due primarily to the influence of two types of copulative elements which can be described as the *n* copula and the *t* copula. The *n* copula of SE is historically related to the Geez introductory particle *na-,* which is used to prepose and emphasize a pronominal element. Examples of this inflected particle are *naya* and *nayo,* meaning "as for me" and "as for him" respectively. The *t* copula originated in sentences employing the third person pronoun *wet* as a neutralized copula, which was reduced to *t* because of its enclitic nature: **āna- *wet* > **āna- *t,* "It is I." Both the *n* and *t* copulas were inflected for all persons and numbers. In order to see the influence of the copula on the SE direct object suffix forms, one can cite some of the attested suffixal forms in two SE dialects, Amharic and Chaha. In Amharic, the *t* copula was influential. For example, the original form **-ā* of the 3 f.s. direct object suffix was replaced by the 3 f.s. ending *-āt* of the copula. The 3 m.s. direct object allomorph *-t,* which is used after subject suffixes ending in *-u,* is also related to the copula. Since there is evidence of a *t* copula in Old Amharic (Goldenberg 1976), it is reasonable to assume that the *t* of 3 f.s. *-āt* and the 3 m.s. *t* which is added to *-u* reflect the old *t* copula. In Chaha, it was the *n* copula which affected the forms of the direct object suffix, as can be seen from the following list: 2 m.s. *-nāka,* 2 f.s. *-nāxi,* 3 m.s. *-ne,* 3 f.s. *-nā,* 1 c.pl. *-nda,* 2 c.pl. *-nāku,* 3 c.pl. *-no.*

C. Main Verb Marker Forms in SE

One of the major differences between the verbal inflection of NE and SE is the introduction of main verb markers in SE. In the SE dialect Chaha, the perfect always ends in *-m* when it is in a positive main clause. In a subordinate or negative clause, the final *-m* of the perfect is omitted, as the following examples show:

(1) Main clause: *naqaram,* "he pulled out";
(2) Subordinate clause: *ya-naqara,* "he who pulled out";
(3) Negative clause: *an-naqara,* "he did not pull out."

It is well known that the morphological distinction between main and subordinate verbs exists in the Cushitic languages, and since SE has a Cushitic substratum, it is reasonable to assume that main verb marking, as a morphological category, was borrowed by SE from Cushitic (Hetzron 1972). However, it is difficult to establish the origin of the actual forms of the main verb markers as they exist in SE. R. Hetzron (1972) has stated that some of the SE dialects used the Proto-Semitic imperfect elements **-u* and **-na/-ni* for main verb markers. In order to support this theory, Hetzron compares the SE dialects which have imperfect forms ending in *-u* with Arabic which has the imperfect form *yaqtulu,* pl. *yaqtulūna.* Such a theory would necessitate the reconstruction of **yaqtulu* for Proto-Ethiopic, but since there is no trace whatever of such a form in the linguistically conservative northern dialects, including ancient Geez, and no certain evidence for such a form elsewhere in the southern languages, it seems methodologically implausible to reconstruct **yaqtulu* for Proto-Ethiopic.

It is possible that the copula was one of the sources of the main verb marker forms in SE. The use of this form of the copula as a main verb marker may have originated in the cleft sentence construction. For example, in Soddo the relative verb form (i.e., *ya* + subordinate perfect or subordinate relative imperfect) combined with the copula *(e)n* is used for a simple statement in which no relative meaning is involved. The following example of this construction is taken from W. Leslau (1968):

> *zi addiya ba ṭobbeyā mula yaššila-n,* "this river was known all over Ethiopia"; lit. "this river in Ethiopia everywhere that was known it is."

Since this cleft sentence construction functions as a main sentence, it is possible that the copula *-n* which was attached to the verb was felt to be a main verb marker, and it should be noted that a final *-n* appears on some forms of Soddo main verbs. Another possible source for main verb markers is the form of the definite article as attached to the verb of a relative clause modifying a definite noun. The 3 f.s. and 1 c.s. perfect forms of Soddo verbs in relative clauses modifying an indefinite noun are as follows:

	Definite	Indefinite
3 f.s.	*yaqattalatti*	*yaqattalat*
1 c.s.	*yaqattalki*	*yaqattalkw*

The initial *ya-* of the above forms is the relative pronoun. According to Leslau (1968), the final *-i* of the definite forms is the article. A final *-i* also appears on the 3 f.s. and 1 c.s. forms of the Soddo main perfect, *qattalatti* and *qattalki,* respectively. The subordinate counterparts of these forms are 3 f.s. *qattalat* and 1 c.s. *qattalkw,* which are identical to the 3 f.s. and 1 c.s. forms of the perfect in a relative clause modifying an indefinite noun.

Finally, it should be noted that the main verb marker *-m,* mentioned above, may be related to the emphatic particle *-ma* of Geez and *-m* of Amharic. Thus, there are several possible sources within Ethiopic for the forms of the main verb markers. It is, therefore, unnecessary to look to Proto-Semitic for the origins of these forms.

Bibliography

Dillmann, A. 1857. *Grammatik der äthiopischen Sprache.* Leipzig.

Goldenberg, G. 1976. A copula *t* in Old Amharic. *IOS* 6: 131–37.

Hetzron, R. 1972. *Ethiopian Semitic: Studies in Classification.* Manchester.

———. 1977. *The Gunnän-Guragé Languages.* Naples.

Lambdin, T. 1978. *Introduction to Classical Ethiopic (Geʿez).* Ann Arbor.

Leslau, W. 1953. The Imperfect in South-East Semitic. *JAOS* 73: 164–66.

———. 1959. A Preliminary Description of Argobba. *Annales d'Ethiopie* 3: 251–73.

———. 1968. *Ethiopians Speak: Studies in Cultural Background.* Vol. 3, *Soddo.* Berkeley.

———. 1976. The Triradicals in the Guragé Dialect of Endegen. *IOS* 6: 138–54.

Nyberg, H. S. 1932. Review of G. Bergsträsser, *Einführung in die semitischen Sprachen. Göttingen gelehrte Anzeigen* 3: 104–15.

Polotsky, J. H. 1938. Études de grammaire gouragué. *Bulletin de la Société de linguistique de Paris* 39: 137–75.

———. 1949. Review of Leslau's *Gafat Documents. JAOS* 69: 36–41.

H. Lee Perkins

GREEK

The Greek language has played several roles in connection with the Bible of Jews and Christians. Apart from the fact that the Greeks and their language are mentioned in it, there occur first of all some Greek loanwords in the later books of the Masoretic Text (MT). Second, Greek is the language of one of the oldest versions of the OT, the Septuagint (LXX), which was probably antedated only by the earliest Aramaic Targums. It is, furthermore, the original language of some additional books in the LXX canon not included in the MT canon. See also CANON. Finally, it is Greek in which the NT has come down to us, parts of which (Pauline letters) are undoubtedly to be seen as original compositions. As the order of these different aspects reflects the increasing importance of Greek with regard to the Jewish people, it will be appropriate to subdivide this article in accordance with it.

A. Greek in the Hebrew-Aramaic Bible and in Palestine
B. Greek in Egypt and as the Language of the LXX
C. Koine Greek
D. The LXX as Translation
E. The Greek of the LXX
 1. Phonology
 2. Morphology
 3. Syntax and Semantics
F. Greek as the Language of the NT
G. The Greek of the NT
H. Atticism

A. Greek in the Hebrew-Aramaic Bible and in Palestine

Among the very first loanwords taken over from a foreign language is usually the name of that language and that of its speakers, although it often escapes notice that foreign names are to be considered as loans, too. The name of a foreign people may actually be (that is, within the foreign country itself) the name only of part of the nation as a whole, such as a well-known tribe or a still smaller subgroup. Further, it is also usual for such names to be completely adapted to the nature of the receptor language. These three general remarks apply also to the name by which Greece or the Greeks are known in the Hebrew Bible, *Yāwān,* who is mentioned by the author of Genesis in the Table of Nations (10:4–5; cf. 1 Chr 1:5–7); see also JAVAN (PERSON) as one of Noah's grandsons together with his offspring, ". . . each with his language, by their families, in their nations" (Gen 10:4). The name *Yāwān,* the first Greek loanword known in Hebrew, is the name of the eponymous ancestor of all the Greeks, although he is the same as *Iōn,* the ancestor only of one of the Greek tribes, the Ionians, who are called *Iaones* by Homer (*Il.* 13.685). The name must have been taken over at a rather early date because it still contains the *w,* a sound which died out before the date of the earliest Ionic-Attic inscriptions and literary texts, and before the subsequent vowel-contraction could have taken place; that is, before *Iawon had become *Iōn.*

In the OT, *Yāwān* is further mentioned by Ezekiel as one of the commercial partners of Phoenician Tyre (27:13), and the "sons of the Ionians" (Heb *bĕnê-hayyĕwānîm*) are reported by the prophet Joel to have bought Jewish slaves from the Phoenicians and the Philistines (4:6). Finally, Alexander the Great is called in Daniel "the king of *Yāwān*" (8:21). In the Assyrian language, Ionia is referred to as *māt Yaman.* The usurper *Yamani,* who ascended the throne of Ashdod and fled to Egypt in 711 B.C. before the advancing Sargon II, may have been a Greek who was given a familiar name (nickname) after his nationality. Greeks, whose actual presence in Palestine before the Exile can at least be assumed, were the mercenary soldiers of King Josiah who are mentioned several times as *Kittiyīm* in the Arad ostraca, and they may have been Greeks from *Kition* in Cyprus; in fact, the *Kittîm* figure as sons of *Yawan* in Gen 10:4. A Greek visitor to Palestine who is known by name is Antimenidas, an elder brother of the lyric poet Alcaeus. He fought in the Babylonian army and was probably involved in one of Nebuchadnezzar's campaigns against Ashkelon.

Two further Greek loanwords in the OT are names of coins, *ʾădarkōnîm* or "darics" and *darkĕmônîm* or "drachmae." Both words have in common that they were taken over in the genitive plural, *dareikōn* and *darchmōn,* as the genitive of price happens to be the case in which names of coins most often appear in bills and contracts. To these genitives was then added the Hebrew plural ending *-îm.* As the "daric" was a coin that was originally called after Darius I, its appearance in the history of King David half a millennium earlier is grossly anachronistic in 1 Chr 29:7, whereas its occurrence in Ezra 8:27 is unsurprising; the mention of "drachmae," however, in Neh 7:69–71 is also against the historical context. As the final redaction of all three books—Ezra, Nehemiah, and Chronicles—is dated to the first part of the Hellenistic period (350–300 B.C.), the use of these Greek words in Hebrew texts is easily explained by the fact that Greek was then the official language of Palestine as a province of the Macedonian Empire, the language of all legal and professional texts.

After Alexander's arrival in Palestine, a number of Greek towns were founded and colonized and some existing towns reorganized after the model of the polis, especially in the territory that was later called the DECAPOLIS (Ten-City League), which soon became a flourishing center of Hellenistic culture. It brought forth such a famous man as Menippus of Gadara (fl. 275 B.C.), the Cynic author whose writings have been influential throughout antiquity and inspired Varro and Lucian. Instances of towns with Greek names are *Dion,* called after the holy city of the Macedonians at the N foot of Mt. Olympus; *Pella,* formerly Paḫel, but renamed after the Macedonians' royal residence; further *Skythopolis* (Beth-Shan); and somewhat later *Philadelphia,* called after Ptolemy II Philadelphus, the new name of Rabbah "of the children of ʿAmmon." The other parts of Palestine, Galilee, Samaria, Philistia, and Idumea (south of Judea) were also subject to a constantly increasing Hellenization, as is shown for Idumea, for instance, by the many tombs with Greek inscriptions at Marissa. Even the relatively small area inhabited by Jews—Jerusalem and the surrounding districts—could not resist this strong cultural influence, which was officially stimulated. Many priests belonged to the "Hellenistic" party. The high priests Jason (till 172 B.C.) and his successor Menelaus even adopted Greek names; so also did the somewhat earlier rabbi, Antigonus of Socho (ca. 200 B.C.), one of the "fathers" quoted in *Pirqê-Abôt* (1:3); his pupil Boethus; the Jewish envoys sent to Rome and Sparta; and their fathers, Numenius son of Antiochus and Antipater son of Jason (1 Macc 12:16). All of these persons, of course, had Hebrew names as well, but were better known by their Greek names.

The Maccabean uprising, therefore, was not so much directed against the Hellenistic culture as such, which, moreover, was then already over a hundred and sixty years old, but it was triggered off when Antiochus IV went as far as endeavoring to Hellenize the Jerusalem temple and its cult. In this connection, it is a telling detail that the only Jew who predicts the downfall of this Hellenistic king, the author of the book of Daniel (7:25–27), does not refrain from using Greek words in the Aramaic text. When he tells about the musical instruments that Nebuchadnezzar's musicians are playing (3:5–7), four of the six instruments mentioned bear Greek names: *qaytĕrōs (kitharis), sabbĕkāʾ (sambykē), pĕsantērîn (psaltērion), sumpōnyāh (symphōnia);* it is true, however, that *kitharis* and *sambykē,* in their turn, may be very old loanwords in Greek as well. It seems a bit improbable to assume that these words were deliberately introduced here to lend an unfavorable color to the whole pagan pageant of the gold idol, because in that case the author would have taken care to use a Greek word for the idol itself.

It is not surprising, therefore, that according to some indications Jerusalem was the place where Jewish knowledge of the Greek language was concentrated, and where it was taught. According to the legendary *Letter of Aristeas,* which relates the story of the origin of the LXX, the translation was made for the library of King Ptolemy II (ca. 275 B.C.) by seventy-two Jewish priests who had been summoned to come to Alexandria from Jerusalem. Although this story is certainly etiological fiction pretending to be history, the presuppositions on which it rests cannot be too wild, and the most central presupposition is of course that Jerusalem priests knew Greek. See SEPTUAGINT.

A further indication is given by the postscript added to the LXX version of the book of Esther. It runs as follows: "In the 4th year of the reign of King Ptolemy and Cleopatra, Dositheus, who said that he was a priest and a Levite, and his son Ptolemaeus have brought the foregoing Purim letter, which they said was sent and had been translated by Lysimachus son of Ptolemaeus of the people of Jerusalem" (Esth 10:3[l]). If this refers to the first Ptolemy who married a Cleopatra, the king must be Ptolemy V, who started reigning in 204 B.C., but who married Cleopatra only in 194, so the 4th year of their joint rule would be around 190 B.C. Several Ptolemies after him, however, also had wives called Cleopatra, and a later date is therefore quite possible, such as 114 B.C. (Ptolemy VIII) or 77 B.C. (Ptolemy XII).

The Second Book of Maccabees, too, was sent as a festal letter to the "Jewish brethren in Egypt" by their brothers in Jerusalem and Judea, at least according to the letter prefixed to this book (1:1). This letter is dated to the 188th year of the Seleucids (124–123 B.C.), and it also mentions an earlier letter written in 143–142 B.C.

These three testimonies all point in the same direction; namely, that Jerusalem was a center of Jewish teaching and mastery of the Greek language, and that it functioned in maintaining contacts with the Greek-speaking Jews in the Diaspora, especially with those living in Egypt.

B. Greek in Egypt and as the Language of the LXX

Much more pronounced was the role which Greek played in Egypt in connection with the Jews. With the arrival of Alexander the Great (332 B.C.), Greek had of course become the official language of Egypt, but great numbers of Greeks had been in Egypt earlier than in Palestine. Apart from such incidental visits as the legendary sojourns of Helen and Menelaus (*Od.* 3.300) and of Pythagoras (D.L. 8.3), more regular contacts seem to have started with the settlement of merchants from Miletus and the subsequent foundation of their trading center in Naucratis on the W Canopic branch of the Nile (ca. 650 B.C.). Charaxus, brother of the poetess Sappho, is known to have been there on business. Around 560 B.C., the pharaoh Amasis (Ahmose) made this harbor the only place where Greeks were allowed to trade in Egypt, and it continued as such well into the Roman period. In addition to these merchants, many Ionian soldiers stayed in the country, serving as mercenaries in the army of the king of the 26th Dyn.: Greek armies and generals (Chabrias; King Agesilaus of Sparta) were also employed by the 29th and 30th Dyn.

The presence of a large number of Jews in Egypt before the Hellenistic period is likewise an established fact. The prophet Jeremiah was forced to settle there, together with many others who had remained in Palestine after the Exile (Jer 43:5–7). Possibly, however, the book of Deuteronomy, which reflects King Josiah's legal reform, implies that one of his predecessors (that is before 640 B.C.) had bought horses in Egypt and paid with Israelite slaves (17:16). The Aramaic papyri from Elephantine, too, show that a Jewish garrison was stationed there at the southernmost border of Egypt during the 5th century. And finally, the *Letter of Aristeas* (12–14) makes mention of many Jewish prisoners of war who were taken to Egypt by Ptolemy I (323–283 B.C.).

When Alexandria, which had at first been founded only as a harbor for the Macedonian navy, was chosen instead of Memphis as the capital of Ptolemaic Egypt soon after 323 B.C., it rapidly expanded into a cosmopolis. It was natural for foreigners, such as Greeks and Jews, to concentrate there, although many of them also lived and worked in the country. Quite naturally, in order to communicate they made use of the official language of the new rulers rather than the vernacular Egyptian or Aramaic. The Elephantine papyri show that the Jews in Egypt in their daily life had given up Hebrew for Aramaic, the language of the Persian government, and no doubt they continued to use Aramaic for some time among themselves after Egypt had been liberated from Persian rule. The fact, however, that the Hebrew OT had to be translated into Greek shows that after some time many of them no longer understood Hebrew and Aramaic and could not make use of Aramaic Targums (if they ever had them in Egypt in this early period).

According to *Aristeas,* Ptolemy II motivated the creation of the LXX version with two arguments. First, he wanted the library at Alexandria to contain a copy of the Jewish law. This may reflect the historical reality of a specific juridical need: the king may have wished to enable his officials to consult that law code to which such large minorities in Egypt and Palestine—which then formed part of his kingdom—constantly referred.

Second, it is expressly stated that Ptolemy wanted to bestow a favor through it (the LXX) upon the freed Jewish slaves living in Egypt, on the Jews in the Diaspora, and on those yet to be born (*Aristeas* 38; Jos. *Ant* 12.48). This makes sense only if it reflects a reality in which many if not most Jews outside of Palestine could not (or could not sufficiently) read and understand the Hebrew Torah, but spoke and were well versed in Greek. In fact, Aristeas at the end of his letter relates how the completed Greek version was read in Alexandria to the assembled Jews, who approved of it and even asked for a copy (*Aristeas* 308; Jos. *Ant* 12.107–8).

C. Koine Greek

The language of the LXX is not the Ionian dialect of the merchants from Miletus who dwelt in Naucratis, nor that of the inscriptions which the Ionian soldiers of Psammetichus II (594–588) scratched in the legs of the colossal statue of Ramesses II when they got as far S as Abū-Simbel (*SIG* no. 1); rather, it is the language which Alexander's army half a century earlier had imported to Palestine, Egypt, and the whole Near East as far as the river Indus. It was the mainly Attic idiom which in that army served to bridge the dialectical differences between the Macedonians, Thessalians, Athenians, and other Greeks of whom it was composed, and it was for that reason called the *koinē dialektos* or "common dialect" in contradistinction to the local dialects such as Doric and Boeotian. Koine Greek did not arise, however, within the Macedonian army or owe its existence to Hellenism; rather, the preexistence of Koine Greek itself was one of the historical factors which made the phenomenon of Hellenism possible. This new function of Attic had not so much to do with the status it had acquired as a literary language as with the situation within the Delian Confederacy in which Athens played such a prominent role that it could impose its own dialect as some kind of lingua franca on the other members. As a common vehicle of communication, it functioned mainly in the mercantile sector and could also be used in mixed Greek expeditions of a military character, such as the Anabasis of which Xenophon reports. It soon started to replace the other dialects in their homelands, beginning with its nearest of kin, the Ionian dialect, but not without taking over a number of the other dialect's peculiarities—especially that of the Macedonians, whose dialect—though today considered Greek—was most aberrant and stood in the need of such a common dialect. Koine Greek was therefore adopted by the royal court and the army. In fact, the army with which Alexander crossed over into Asia could not have functioned well without Koine Greek, for more than half of the soldiers had been recruited outside of Macedonia proper and came from different parts of Greece.

When the Attic of the classical period adopted its new role, it did not remain unaltered; it began to show slight traces of what in linguistics is called a process of *creolization.* This means that in circumstances in which a group of people who speak different dialects or languages has to adopt one of these as its common language, the language or dialect chosen is simplified to the extent that the categories (sounds, forms, word order) that have no equivalent or are not found in the replaced languages are abandoned.

This meant that Attic, when taken over by other Greeks, had to drop some of its phonological peculiarities. The clusters *-tt-* and *-rr-* shifted in favor of what the majority of dialects had, *-ss-* and *-rs-*, in such words as *thalassa, prassō,* and *arsēn, tharseō.* It gave up the peculiar declension of *leōs, neōs* for the regularly declined *laos, naos;* the curious second- and third-person aorist optatives in *-seias* and *-seie(n)* were replaced by the more normal in *-sais* and *-sai.* Since the language used by merchants, sailors, and soldiers could hardly be considered the literary or standard variety, the tendencies present in the substandard language go unchecked when it is adopted and spoken by foreigners. This, then, may account for such phenomena as the loss of the dual number (which was already a fact in some other dialects as well), the tendency to restrict the use of the optative to head clauses, the increasing use of plural verbs with neuter plural subjects, and the re-use or re-implication in the same sentence of a noun or pronoun that had already been used in the genitive absolute. A contribution stemming from the commercial sector is probably the standardization of the compound numerals between "ten" and "twenty": *hennea kai deka, henneakaideka,* and *henos deontes/-a eikosi* all became *deka-hennea* in accordance with *eikosi-hennea,* but *deka-heis* and *deka-dyo* did not endure; their successors *hendeka* and *dōdeka* are still used in Modern Greek.

Somewhat later (ca. 300 B.C.) was the persistent replacement of the third-person plural of the imperatives in *-ntōn* and *-sthōn* by those ending in *-tōsan* and *-sthōsan,* although these had already been used by Euripides and Thucydides (but not in official texts of treaties).

The vocabulary also changed, subject as it was to an inevitable evolution. It affected even such ordinary words as *hyei,* "it rains," and *naus,* "ship," which were gradually replaced by *brechei* and *ploion; naus* probably disappeared because it had such an irregular declension. Many new words were also made, especially in the governmental sphere: *achyropraktōr,* "collector of chaff(-tax)"; *archiphylakitēs,* "commandant of the police"; *sitologos,* "keeper of the public granary"; and *toparchēs,* "governor of a district," among others.

D. The LXX as Translation

It seems logical, and it is certainly probable, that the Pentateuch was the first section of the OT to be translated; and, in accordance with *Aristeas* 30 ("the books of the Law of the Jews together with a few others"), that it was translated en bloc (ca. 275 B.C.). Whether or not the "translation" may in reality have been a process of compilation and revision of earlier endeavors, the fact remains that the Greek of the Pentateuch is of far better quality than the Greek of the other translated books, which is always of a lesser quality and sometimes inferior (as is the Greek of Jeremiah 29–51). The language of the Pentateuch is to a certain extent uniform in that it contains specific renderings for some Hebrew words and phrases which are absent in the books translated later. In these there is not only much less uniformity, but within a number of books (1–4 Kingdoms, Jeremiah, Ezekiel), portions can be discerned which are the work of different translators using various methods and styles of translation. See also SEPTUAGINT.

As translations may range from literal to paraphrasing, it stands to reason that they betray the Hebrew original more or less according to the same scale. There are even parts of books in which Hebrew words have been allowed to stand transliterated (untranslated); for instance, in Jeremiah 29–51. The words *mābôʾ haššĕlîšî,* "the third entrance," at Jer 38:14 in the MT are represented by *oikian aselisi* at 45:14 in the LXX. Apparently the translator knew how to vocalize his model but not what to do with the word in the context. A very curious instance is the phrase *hōy Adōn,* "Alas, lord!" at 34:5, which was evidently considered as Greek in Hebrew letters, since it is matched by *heōs hądou* (41:5; B,S,A). In the first part, however, of Jeremiah LXX, which is a much better translation, the same phrase has been rendered by the correct *oimmoi Kyrie* at 22:18 (*oimmoi* is a frequent spelling in LXX mss for *oimoi*). Of course there are also cases of nontranslation which are quite justified, such as *hin* and *oiphi* in Num 15:4, these being transliterations of *hin* and *ʾêpâ,* because these measures had no exact equivalents in the Greek world.

Furthermore, there are translations which are too literal or stereotypical to make good sense. Ps 77:54 reads *oros hagiasmatos autou,* "the mountain of His sanctification," which perhaps renders *har-qodšô,* "His Holy mountain" (MT has here *gĕbûl-qodšô,* "His holy land"). Since *ʾānōkî* or *ʾănî,* "I," must sometimes in nominal sentences be translated by "I am," some books (Judges, 2-3-4 Kingdoms) wrongly translate *ʾānōkî* + verb by *egō eimi* + verb (Judg 6:18: *egō eimi kathēsomai*). The infinitive *lēʾmōr* can in most cases (that is, when the speaker is subject of the sentence) be rendered by *legōn,* "saying." Where this is not so, the LXX often has *legōn* in an ungrammatical way; e.g., Gen 22:20 (*anēngelē tǫ Abraam legontes,* "the message was brought to Abraham that . . ."; cf. Rev 11:1) and Gen 45:16 (*kai dieboēthē hē phōnē eis ton oikon Pharaō legontes*; cf. Rev 4:1), in which the participle has the wrong number and gender. Finally, throughout the LXX the Hebrew infinitive absolute is rendered by the un-Greek combination of participle with finite verb of the same stem; e.g., Exod 3:4 (*idōn eidon,* "I have *certainly* seen"; cf. Eph 5:5).

Apart from such Hebraistic translations, there is in *all* the translated books a much simpler and more monotonous word order than in nonbiblical Greek, and a style full of repetitions, through which the original Hebrew is still more or less visible.

All these phenomena together certainly distinguish the Greek used in the translation of the LXX and of many books of the Apocrypha from Greek as it was written by non-Jews. It does not, however, mean that this idiom is to be regarded as the written reflection of a special Jewish dialect of Greek, comparable to Yiddish (spoken) in Eastern Europe among German Jews) and Judeo-Spanish (used in Saloniki). The retaining of the Hebrew word order and of many Hebrew turns certainly stems from the desire to render the Torah as faithfully as possible. This is also proved by the translator Aquila, who went much further in this respect and apparently wanted to correct the LXX on a number of points. The best known instance is his rendition of the Heb accusative particle *ʾet* by *syn* with accusative (Gen 1:1), because elsewhere *ʾet* can indeed mean "with." At Isa 9:5 he translated *ʾăbî-ʿad*, "father of eternity," by *patēr eti* because *ʿad* means (1) "eternity" and (2) "still, yet." On the other hand, when Jewish authors do not translate but do compose their works in Greek (as did Philo of Alexandria and St. Paul) the occurrence of Semitisms is either zero or very incidental, and their word order is as varied as that used by native Greeks. Within the LXX canon itself, the nontranslations of 2-3-4 Maccabees are written in excellent idiomatic Greek. The Fourth Book of Maccabees, which was written toward the end of the 1st century A.D., even follows the Atticistic literary mode of imitating the Attic of the classical period and reintroducing old-fashioned grammar and vocabulary. Hence, the author of *4 Maccabees* has used *-tt-* again in such words as *glottan* (10:17, 21), but used *glossa* at 10:19, and used the optative in subordinate clauses (9:27; 19:1; 11:13).

All this does not of course rule out the possibility that some Jews had an accent when speaking Greek. Josephus himself confesses that he never succeeded in acquiring a correct pronunciation of Greek (*Ant* 20.263). And of course, in accordance with the extent to which the foreign language was mastered by a specific individual, that person may have used many, few or no Semitisms at all.

E. The Greek of the LXX

1. Phonology. The LXX mss do not reflect the orthography of the autographs but that of their own times (4th century A.D. or later). Only the Greco-Egyptian papyri of the Ptolemaic period can give an impression of the phonetic changes that were taking place when the LXX was being made. It appears then that *ei* and *i* were confused in the 3d century B.C., as were *oi* and *ō*, and that "iota adscript" was disappearing; there had been confusion between *ai* and *e* and between *oi* and *y* since the 2d century B.C. So the earliest mss of the LXX Pentateuch may have contained only the former group of confusions, and those of the later translated books may have had all of them. However, the further confusion of *ei-i* and *ē* in Bible mss dates back only to the 2d century A.D. and cannot, therefore, have figured in any LXX or NT autographs. In a single case, the mss tradition appears to be trustworthy as far as orthography goes. That is, where the mss have *-tt-* instead of *-ss-* in such later Atticistic works as *4 Maccabees* (and not only in the comparatives *kreittōn* and *elattōn,* which were more often exceptional in this respect).

2. Morphology. Here, the trustworthiness of the mss is much greater, as appears from the fact that they have transmitted phenomena that are practically restricted to the LXX in Greek literature, such as the third-plural ending *-osan* for *-on* in second aorists, which in its turn was later generally replaced by *-an.* The LXX mss then bear witness to the following formal peculiarities:

a. Declension. First-declension nouns in *-ra* and fem. perf. participles in *-uia* have gen. sing. in *-ēs* and dat. sing. in *-ē* like *thalassa.* In the second declension, there are fluctuations between types *(ho) hippos* and (third declension) *(to) oros;* vocative of *theos* is *thee;* Attic second-declension *leōs, neōs* replaced by *laos, naos; nous, chous* are declined like *bous,* hence gen. sing. *noos* (even in *4 Macc* 1:35) and dat. sing. *noi; ostoun* and *osteon* occur both, but gen. sing. *osteou* and dat. sg. *osteǭ* are usually uncontracted. Third declension acc. sing. sometimes *-an,* and that of adjectives and personal names in *-ēs* is *-ēn;* acc. sing. masc. of *pas* sometimes *pan;* acc. pl. sometimes in *-es,* especially *tessares* (on the analogy of nom. and acc. *treis*) and in participles (2 Esdr 23:15 B); acc. pl. of type *basileus: -eas* and *-eis;* acc. pl. of *bous* and type *pitys: -as;* the adjective *plērēs* is often an indeclinable; the dual number has been given up in all declensions.

b. Reduplication. Under Hebrew influence, substantives are sometimes reduplicated, having a distributive value, e.g., Exod 8:10 (MT 8:14)—*kai synēgagon autous thimōnias-thimōnias,* "and they gathered them [the dead frogs] together in heaps" (cf. Mark 6:39–49 under Aramaic influence), or a generalizing value, e.g., Lev 17:3—*anthrōpos-anthrōpos tōn huiōn Israēl* "every man of the sons of Israel." Doubled adjectives have an intensive value, as in Isa 26:20—*mikron hoson-hoson,* "a very short time" (cf. Luke 5:3 D; Heb 10:37).

c. Numerals. *Deka-treis,* etc., and *treiskaidekatos,* etc., have replaced *treiskaideka* and *tritos kai dekatos;* only *hendeka* is found, not *deka-heis,* but *dōdeka* and *deka-dyo* occur side by side. Reduplicated numerals have a distributive value, e.g., Gen 7:2–3: *hepta-hepta* and *dyo-dyo,* "each time seven," "each time two" (cf. Mark 6:7); doubled numerals occurred, however, also in nonbiblical Greek: Soph *frg.* 201 *(Eris) mian-mian.*

d. Verbs. *Personal endings.* The dual number has completely disappeared. The endings of the second aorist *-on, -es,* etc., are often replaced by *-a, -as,* etc., the third person being in *-an* or in *-osan,* as in Gen 18:8: *ephagosan;* in the imperfect such replacements are rare, as in Judg 6:3 (B): *anebainan,* and Jer 5:26: *synelambanosan;* the ending *-san* is also found in imperfects of contracts—Job 1:4 (B*, S*): *epoiousan,* and Judg 11:5 (A): *epolemousan,* and in optatives—Deut 33:16: *elthoisan,* and Deut 1:44: *poiēsaisan;* and it has completely replaced the older endings of the third-person-plural imperatives, both active and medio-passive, as in Gen 1:14: *estōsan,* Lev 20:10: *thanatousthōsan,* and Gen 1:14: *genēthētōsan.* The third-person plural of the perfect in *-asi* could be replaced by *-an,* as in Deut 11:7 (B): *heōrakan.*

Tenses. Present-Imperfect: beginning merging of *-aō* and *-eō* in contracted verbs, as in 2 Macc 7:7 (A): *epērōtoun;* verbs in *-mi* are changed into verbs in *-ō: hista(n)ō, titheō, didoō.* Aorist: compounds of *-agō* may have regular aorists in *-ēa;* verbs in *-ainō* and *-airō* always have aorists in *-ana, -ara;* there is a preference for passive aorists without *-th-,* like *ekrybēn, epeskepēn.* Perfect-Pluperfect: *-n-* before *-metha, -menos,* etc., no longer changes into *-sy-;* as in Num 5:13: *memiammenē;* in the pluperfect the characteristic ending is *-(k)ei-* in all persons, and the augment is often absent. Augment: *boulomai, dynamai, thelō,* and *mellō* have *ē-;* the temporal augment is often absent in verbs beginning with *aut(o)-, eu-,* and *oi-;* incidentally, verbs have two augments, as in Jer 47:7: *parakatetheto* (cf. Mark 3:5).

e. Hebrew Influence? In the field of Greek forms proper, hardly anything can be ascribed to Hebrew influence except for the reduplication of substantives. It is possible that the use of the expression *kol-zākār,* "all that is male," in some contexts together for persons and animals such as cattle and sheep, which happen to be referred to in Greek by neuter words *(probata, ktēnē),* induced the translators to choose the *neuter* adjective *pan arsenikon.* Due to the lexical meaning "male" of the whole expression, it was probably misunderstood at times as also having the masculine grammatical gender. This could easily happen in passages such as Gen 34:15, where *pan arsenikon* follows upon and refers to *pas arsēn* (34:14), and this may have led to the use of *pan* as acc. sing. masc., for instance, in Dan 11:37 (Theod): *epi pan theon.*

3. Syntax and Semantics. a. Substantives. *Number.* The singular may be generic in the somewhat restricted sense that it indicates all the representatives of the kind that happen to be present in the situation, as in Exod 8:2—*kai anebibasthē ho batrachos kai ekalypsen tēn gēn Aigyptou,* "and the *frogs* came up [out of the Nile] and covered the land of Egypt"; in such cases, the accompanying verb is sometimes in the plural, as in Judg 15:10 (B)—*kai eipan anēr Iouda,* and (A)—*kai eipan autois pas anēr Iouda.*

Nominative. Used with the article as vocative, as in Aristophanes and Plato, but much more frequently due to Hebrew, e.g., 3 Kgdms 18:26—*epakouson hēmōn ho Baal.* The nom. can also be used at the head of a sentence to indicate the "topic," which is then followed by a "comment" clause containing a resumptive pronoun, as in Ps 102(103):15—*anthrōpos, hōsei chortos hai hēmerai autou,* "man, like grass (are) his days." Contrary to Greek usage, appositions sometimes stand in the nom. case without congruity with the antecedent, as in Gen 11:29—"and the name of the wife of Nachor (was) Melcha, the daughter *of* Harran, the father *(patēr)* of Melcha and the father *(patēr)* of Jescha," with *patēr* used both times instead of *patros* (cf. Rev 1:5; 2:20).

Genitive. The genitive absolute indicates circumstances that are different from those of either the subject or the (in)direct object of the sentence. Very incidentally, however, the circumstances of subject or object are also referred to in Classical Greek by a gen. abs. (Plato *Resp.* 8.547b *biazomenōn . . . hōmologēsan*), but in Koine Greek this usage became quite normal; hence, Dan 8:1—"and I saw *(eidon)* . . . when I was in Susa *(emou ontos),*" and Tob 1:4 (B,A)—"when I was *(hote ēmēn)* in my country . . . when I was still young *(neōterou mou ontos).*"

Dative and accusative. Often used with verbs of the same stem or with verbs having a roughly equivalent meaning, in order to render the Hebrew absolute infinitives and cognate objects, as in Gen 2:17—*thanatǭ apothaneisthe,* "you will certainly die" (cf. Exod 19:12: *thanatǭ teleutēsei*), and Gen 27:33—*exestē . . . ekstasin megalēn* (cf. Judg 15:8—*epataxen . . . plēgēn megalēn*—and Luke 2:9).

Comparison of Adjectives. The comparative form has both the comparative and the superlative values: *meizōn* = "greater," "greatest," while the superlative form has only the "elative" value: *megistos* = "very great." Since *proteros* and *eschateros,* however, have fallen into disuse, *prōtos,* besides meaning "first," also means "earlier"; and *eschatos,* besides meaning "last," also means "later." Moreover, the positive degree can also function as comparative in accordance with Hebrew, which has no degrees of comparison, as in Gen 49:12—"his teeth are whiter *(leukoi)* than *(ē)* milk"; Exod 8:11—"the Lord is greater *(megas)* than *(para)* all the gods"; Ruth 4:15—"who is better *(agathē)* for you than *(hyper)* seven sons" (cf. Mark 9:43, 45, 47; Luke 13:2).

Pronouns. Personal. LXX Greek shows an overuse of personal pronouns (genitives after substantives, accusatives after verbs) which is due to the frequency of the Hebrew pronominal suffixes. *Possessives. Emos, sos,* etc., have been replaced generally by the genitives of the personal pronouns, except in the book of Proverbs. *Reflexives. Heautous,* etc., are also used for "ourselves" and "yourselves." Typical Hebrew is the use of "his soul" and "his bones" as reflexive pronouns.

Relatives. The former difference between the indispensable relative *hos, hē, ho* and the dispensable *hostis, hētis, hoti* is being given up. The use of the so-called "resumptive" personal pronouns and adverbs with relative pronouns is due to the fact that Hebrew has no relative pronoun but does have a relative conjunction *(ʾăšer),* as in Gen 1:11—*xylon . . . poioun karpon, hou to sperma autou en autǭ;* Gen 33:19—*agrou, hou estēsen ekei tēn skēnēn;* Deut 9:28—*tēn gēn, hothen exēgages hēmas ekeithen* (cf. Mark 7:25; Rev 3:8; 12:16).

Demonstratives. Fem. *hautē* may have neuter value like Hebrew fem. *zōt,* as in Judg 15:7 (B)—"if you do this" *(houtōs tautēn,* MT *kā-zōt).*

Definite Article. Used in the sing. to indicate (1) a representative of the whole kind, Amos 5:19—"as if a man fled from a lion *(tou leontos)* and a bear *(hē arkos)* met him . . . and a serpent *(ho ophis)* bit him"; (2) all representatives present of the kind, as in Exod 8:2—*kai anebibasthe ho batrachos kai ekalypsen ten gen Aigyptou.* Nouns followed by depending gentitives may lack the article because the Hebrew construct state never has it, as in Nah 1:1—*biblion horaseōs Naoum* (lit. "book of vision of Nahum"). The article *tou* with the infinitive, which was frequent in Thucydides, is used freely with final-consecutive or explicative force (Ps 26(27):4), sometimes even with such verbs as *dynamai* (Ps 39(40):13) and *archomai* (2 Chr 3:1).

Indefinite Pronouns. "Nobody, no one" is *ou/mē . . . pas* or *pas . . . ou/mē* in accordance with Hebrew *lō . . . kōl* or *kōl . . . lō.*

b. Verbs. *General.* Frequently with prepositions instead of oblique cases only, in accordance with Hebrew, as in Judg 21:7—*omnuein en* (cf. Matt 5:34). Finite forms are often replaced by *eimi, ginomai,* or *hyparchō* with participle. This is also classical, but in the LXX more frequent under Hebrew influence, as in Gen 4:14—*esomai stenōn kai tremōn.* Some intransitive verbs are used also as causatives in the LXX, as in Judg 9:6 (A,B)—"and they made Abimelech king *(ebasileusan),*" and 4 Kgdms 17:21: "and he made them sin *(exhēmarten).*"

Middle and Passive. The tendency is to use in fut. and aor. either the middle or the passive form only; the passive forms may then have also the reflexive value. There is also a tendency to replace fut. middle deponents like *akousomai* by an active like *akousō.*

Tense. The fut. ind. is often used to express a command like the Hebrew jussive, as in Exod 8:1—*eiselthe pros Pharaō kai ereis autō,* "you will go before pharaoh and you will say to him . . ."

Moods. The optative tends to be restricted to the expression of wishes, the conjunctive taking its place in subordinate clauses, except in the Atticistic *4 Maccabees.* Participles are often used as finite verbs, e.g., Judg 13:19—"and Manoe and his wife were watching" (*blepontes* only). Participles and infinitives may be continued not by a coordinated part. or inf. but by a finite verb, e.g., Isa 14:17—*ho theis tēn oikoumenēn holēn erēmon kai tas poleis katheilen* (cf. Rev 1:5–6). Participles are often combined with finite verbs of the same stem to render the Hebrew infinitive absolute: Gen 22:17—*eulogōn eulogēsō se kai plēthynōn plēthynō to sperma sou.*

c. Prepositions. The tendency is to drop semantic distinctions when combinable with different cases, like *epi* with gen., dat., or acc. The preposition *apo* is used with gen. often instead of partitive gen. only; *para* and *hyper* with acc. express comparative value of positive degree; *eis* with acc. is confused with *en* plus dat.: Gen 37:17—"and he found them in *(eis)* Dothaim," and Exod 4:21—"which I gave into your hands" *(en tais chersin sou); en* with dat. is often circumstantial-instrumental, ousting *meta* and *syn:* Exod 6:1—*en gar cheiri krataią exapostelei autous.* New prepositions, mostly compounds and all with gen. case: *apanōthen, hypokatōthen, (ap-, kat-)enanti, (kat-)enōpion, opisō, katopisthen, kyklothen;* translated from Hebrew: *ana, apo, kata, pro* with *prosōpou* or *porsōpon* and followed by genitive.

d. Conjunctions, Particles. Direct questions are introduced by *ei*: Gen 17:17—*ei tō hekatontaetei genēsetai,* "will there be born (a child) to a hundred-year-old?"; *ei* also introduces negative, *ei mē* positive oaths: Gen 14:23—*ei . . . lēmpsomai,* "that I shall certainly not accept"; in relative clauses *ean* is often equivalent to *an,* e.g., in Gen 2:19 and NT passim.

In the LXX there is a definite overuse of *kai,* "and," because Hebrew favors *wĕ-,* "and," above temporal, causal, final-consecutive, and other conjunctions, and because *kai* also renders the initial *wa-* of the OT narrative tense *wayyiqtōl.* Hence, *kai* is frequent, heading almost every sentence in Genesis. The frequency of *kai* is probably a Hebraism in Revelation.) The frequent Hebrew deictic word *hinnê* is rendered by *idou:* Amos 7:1, 4, 7, 8. Because Biblical Hebrew hardly ever uses a special construction for reported speech, the conjunction *hoti,* if it is used at all, is a *hoti recitativum* (i.e., introducing indirect discourse): Gen 12:13—*eipón oun hoti adelphē autou eimi,* "say then: 'I am his sister' " (the MT is different in that it has indirect speech in the choice of the pronoun and personal suffix: *ʾimrî-nāʾ ʾăḥōtî ʾāt,* "say you are my sister"); very common therefore are concatenations of direct speech such as Exod 9:1—"And the Lord said to Moses: 'Go to pharaoh and say to him: "Thus speaks the Lord, the god of the Hebrews: 'let my people go so that they may serve Me' " ' ".

e. Word Order. It is in this field together with that of style that the underlying Hebrew exercises its influence most strongly. It is essentially a V S O (verb-subject-object) language, with deviations in contrastive clauses, and it is the frequency of this order in the LXX which strikes an experienced reader as un-Greek, not the order as such. Furthermore, the order in noun groups is absolutely fixed: dependent genitives, adjectives, and demonstratives always follow the substantive and in this order, which in translation-Greek results in, e.g., Dan 4:5— (Theod) *pneuma theou hagion*—and Dan 3:28 (LXX)—*tēn polin sou tēn hagian* (cf. Rom 7:24—*ek tou sōmatos tou thanatou toutou* "from this body of death," where the demonstrative pron. is attributive to *sōmatos*).

f. Style. One of the most characteristic features of the Hebrew style is that it favors repetitions. Whereas a native Greek would probably have written at Gen 12:1 something like **ek tēs sēs gēs, syngeneias te kai patrikou oikou,* it is the typical Hebrew repetition of preposition, article, and personal suffix which is reproduced in the LXX: *exelthe ek tēs gēs sou kai ek tēs syngeneias sou kai ek tou oikou tou patros sou,* "He departed from his land, and from his kinfolk, and from the house of his father." Compare also the repetition of "all" in Gen 8:1—"and God remembered Noah and *all* the animals and *all* the cattle and *all* the birds and *all* the reptiles"—after these different categories have already been mentioned, each time preceded by "all," in 7:14, and the repetition of the degrees of relationship at Gen 11:31, which have already been demonstrated in 11:27–28. Even where such pieces may stem from different sources, a Greek compiler would have taken care to cancel things already mentioned. But repetition, be it by synonyms or another means, is even the structural principle of Hebrew poetry. There are three doublets in the two opening lines of Lamech's Song in Gen 4:23:

> Ada and Sella, listen to my voice,
> wives of Lamech, give ear to my words.

A further characteristic of Hebrew style is the mentioning of every stage of a series of successive actions. Hence in Gen 11:31, it is not said that "Terah led Abram out of Chaldea" but that "Terah *took* Abram . . . and led them out" (cf. the verb *lambanō* also in Mark 14:22 and Rev 10:9); frequent, too, are such sequences as "he spoke and said," "he called and said," and "it happened that" followed by the principal event (*kai egeneto* in various constructions).

It is this relative monotony in word order, the repetitive style, the mention of things that may be taken for granted, and also the marked frequency of nominal (verbless) sentences and phrases, which make the Greek of the translated LXX books so different from the nonbiblical Greek style and also from that of the nontranslations in the LXX canon like 2-3-4 Maccabees.

g. Vocabulary. It stands to reason that there were also changes in vocabulary, either because new words were coined and new senses were attributed to words already in use, or because specific words became more frequent than before while others fell into disuse. New words are *bdelygma* (to *bdelyssomai*) in Lev 5:2; *enōtizomai,* specially coined to match *akouō* in Lamech's Song in Gen 4:23; *thysiastērion* (to *thysia*) in Gen 8:20; *peritomē* (to *peritemno*) in Gen 17:13; and *sabbatizō* in Exod 16:30. New senses are carried by *kibōtos,* "ark" (of Noah), in Gen 6:14; *dēloi* in Num 27:21 or *dēlōsis* in Lev 8:18, meaning "the Urim"; *prostithēmi,* "to go on with" or "to do further," in Gen 4:2; and *hypsēla,* "offering heights," in 3 Kgdms 3:2.

More frequent through the Israelitic-Jewish context are *alsē,* "sacred groves," in Deut 7:5; *kibotos,* "ark" (of testimony) in Exod 25:9(10); *ho Pantokratōr* in 2 Kgdms 5:10; *peritemnō* in Gen 17:10; and *skēnē tou martyriou* in Exod 27:21. Finally, some expressions have been rendered word for word into Greek, e.g., Gen 23:15—*ana meson emou kai sou ti an eiē touto?*—and 3 Kgdms 17:18—*ti emoi kai soi?* (cf. Mark 1:24 and John 2:4, but also Epictetus 1.22, 15—*ti moi kai autō?*).

F. Greek as the Language of the NT

In Palestine, only Jerusalem and some territory around it constituted a center of Jewish population, to which some districts in Galilee were later added. In its earliest years, the Hasmonean state might have done without Greek alongside Hebrew as an official language, but as soon as the boundaries were extended this meant that Hellenistic towns and territories were added to it, such as Philistia, Idumea, Samaria, and parts of Galilee, and that the use of Greek was an inevitable necessity. In fact, the Hasmonean princes soon started to adopt additional Greek names and to strike bilingual coinage. Their rule did not prove a break in Hellenism; Palestine was no less affected by Greek culture than the other countries in the Near East. It produced a number of Hellenistic scholars: Menippus and Meleager of Gadara; the philosophers Philodemus, also from Gadara, and Antiochus of Ashkelon (teacher to Cicero); and, from the latter town also, the grammarians Dorotheus and Ptolemy; and still others.

King Herod I was an enthusiastic promoter of Greek culture, and he embellished Jerusalem and many other towns with theatres, colonnades, and aqueducts in the Hellenistic style. In the 1st century A.D., the country was Hellenized to the extent that the usual way of communication between the different population groups can only have been Greek, and because Greek was at least understood by a wandering preacher like Jesus, who met with Decapolitans (Matt 4:25) and Diaspora Jews (John 12:20–21; cf. 7:35), and who had many Greek followers according to Josephus (*Ant* 18.63). It should not therefore come as a surprise that some of the NT authors were able to write excellent Greek. Paul, for example, probably went at a very young age from Tarsus to Jerusalem and learned Greek there; and James, supposedly Jesus' brother, could have learned the language. Because the NT, as we have it, was addressed to the Western Diaspora, which spoke Greek, it was written in that language, even the letter that went as far west as Rome. The Jews there also used Greek, as is shown by their inscriptions in the catacombs and by Theodotus, son of Vettenus, a Jew who returned from Italy (where his father, an archisynagogue, got his Latin name) and built a synagogue complex in Jerusalem of which the memorial inscription in Greek is still extant (*CIJ* no. 1404). In fact, even among the Jews in Palestine, Greek was a current idiom. The majority of the ossuaries (bone containers) found around Jerusalem are inscribed in Greek (the minority are inscribed in Hebrew-Aramaic), and the tomb of the so-called "Goliath family" contained coffins with both Greek and Hebrew inscriptions. See PALESTINIAN FUNERARY INSCRIPTIONS.

G. The Greek of the NT

The Greek of the NT shows the same diversity and differences in quality as the books making up the LXX canon. Original compositions like Paul's and James' letters and the Epistle to the Hebrews are in good Greek, relatively free of Semitisms; the Letter of Jude even overdoes the un-Hebraistic word order by placing as many adjectives, participles, and genitives as possible with the substantives. Writings which at least partly depend on an oral Aramaic tradition, such as the Gospels, show the influence of that language in the confusion of relative and final-consecutive clauses due to the ambiguous particle *di-*, which may head both. Finally, the mastery of Greek by the author of Revelation, which of all NT books is most strongly suspected to be a translation, must simply be classified as insufficient; the author uses participles as finite verbs and incongruent appositions in the nominative, and his word order and style as well as his overuse of *kai* betray a very strong Semitic influence. All the NT books, however, have Hebraisms in the quotations from either the LXX or other versions like Theodotion (Acts 7:34—*idōn eidon*—from Exod 3:7, and many more).

As compared with what must have been the phonology of the later LXX books, we must assume that the NT autographs showed about the same development in that all diphthongs had become monophthongs, and the difference between long and short vowels had been leveled. Almost all the morphological and syntactical peculiarities of LXX Greek are also to be found in the NT with very few exceptions, such as *pan* as acc. sg. masc. and *egō eimi* for *egō*. Some trends, however, have gone further, like the normalization and simplification of the verb system: the future of verbs in *-azō* and *-izō* is no longer (as in the LXX), in *-aō* and *-ieō*, but in *-asō* and *-isō*; future participles and infinitives are practically absent; aor. ind. and perf. inf. are beginning to merge, as is shown for instance by 1 John 1:1—*ho heōrakamen . . . ho etheasametha*. The demonstrative pronoun *hode, hēde, tode,* which was still current in the LXX, is falling into disuse in the NT.

In the field of vocabulary, the NT favors some specific terms, but without developing a separate "Christian language." More frequently used than elsewhere are such words as *baptizein, euangelion, euangelizesthai, aphesis, aphiein* ("to forgive"), *stauros,* and *Christos*. Neologisms are perhaps *aposynagōgos*—"expelled from the synagogue" (John 9:22), *kardiognōstēs*—"knower of hearts" (Acts 1:24), *moschopoiein*—"to make a golden calf" (Acts 7:41), and *phagos*—"glutton" (Matt 11:19). Christian loanwords from Hebrew are *amēn, hallēlouia,* and *hōsanna*.

H. Atticism

Like the latest books of the LXX canon, the whole NT was written in the period of beginning Atticism. Apart from such incidental cases as *-tt-* in *elatton* and *kreittonos* in Heb 7:7, both of which may have been permanent exceptions, it is only Acts which shows some Atticistic tendencies. It is here only that the old-fashioned word *naun* is used (27:41) by the side of *ploion* (27:37, 39, 44), that optatives are found in dependent clauses (17:27; 27:12, 39), and that the obsolete future participles (8:27; 22:5; 24:11, 17) and future infinitives (11:28; 24:15; 27:10) are mainly present in the NT.

Only the author of Acts varies his style in accordance with the Greek stylistic ideal, which manifests itself in his use of alternating synonyms in one and the same context. In the story of Ananias and Sapphira (5:1–11) and its introduction (4:32–37), he uses three different words for "to sell": *pōleō* (4:34, 37), *pipraskō* (4:34; 5:4), and *apodidomai* (5:8); in the pericope of the apostles' imprisonment there are three words for "prison": *tērēsis dēmosia* (5:18), *phylakē* (5:19, 22), and *desmōterion* (5:21, 23). Compare in the story of the jailkeeper in Philippi the words *phylakē* (16:23, 24, 27) and *desmoterion* (16:26); the use of *naus* besides *ploion* may also be a case in point. He has two words for "many": *polloi* and *hikanoi,* two for "one another": *heautous* (28:29) and *allēlous* and the expression *allos pros allon* (2:12), two words for "other": *allos* and *heteros,* three for "to be": *eimi, ginomai,* and *hyparchō,* and there are some six for "the next day": *hē aurion, hē epaurion, hē hetera, hē epiousa, hē echomenē hemēra,* and *deuteraioi.* It is even thinkable that such a variant as *ēlthamen* (28:14) between *ēlthomen* (28:13) and *eisēlthomen* (28:16) goes back to the original and was deliberately chosen; compare also the shift from 1st declension sg. *Lystran* (14:6 and 16:1) to 2d declension pl. *Lystrois* (14:7 and 16:2). The variation between *Ierousalēm* and *Hierosolyma* has an extra dimension: the former is mainly used in contexts where in reality the conversation should be assumed to have been carried on in Aramaic (with some exceptions).

This stylistic tendency then may shed some light on the literary taste of both the author and Theophilus, his first addressee. Nevertheless, there are also Semitisms in Acts, such as the frequency of the periphrastic conjugation (1:10, 13, 14; 2:5, and elsewhere; on these, see Fitzmyer *Luke I–IX* AB).

Bibliography

Koine Greek

Debrunner, A., and Scherer, A. 1969. *Geschichte der griechischen Sprache.* Vol. 2, *Grundfragen und Grundzüge des nachklassischen Griechisch.* Sammlung Göschen 114/114a. Berlin.

Dieterich, K. 1898. *Untersuchungen zur Geschichte der griechischen Sprache.* New York. Repr. 1970.

Radermacher, L. 1947. *Koine.* SÖAW 224/5. Vienna.

Thumb, A. 1901. *Die griechische Sprache im Zeitalter des Hellenismus.* Strasbourg.

Linguistic

Neumann, F., and Untermann, J. 1980. *Die Sprachen im römischen Reich der Kaiserzeit.* Beihefte der Bonner Jahrbücher 40. Bonn.

LXX Greek

Conybeare, F. C., and Stock, St. G. 1905. *A Grammar of Septuagint Greek.* Repr. Grand Rapids, 1980.

Thackeray, H. St. J. 1909. *A Grammar of the Old Testament in Greek according to the Septuagint.* Vol. 1, *Introduction, orthography and accidence.* Repr. New York, 1978.

Ptolemaic Greek

Mayser, E., and Schmoll, H. 1970. *Grammatik der griechischen Papyri aus der Ptolemäerzeit.* 2d ed. Berlin.

Teodorson, S.-T. 1977. *The Phonology of Ptolemaic Koine.* Studia Graeca et Latina Gothoburgensia 36. Lund.

NT Greek

Blass, F.; Debrunner, A.; and Funk, R. W. 1961. *A Greek Grammar of the New Testament and of Other Early Christian Literature.* Chicago.

Radermacher, L. 1925. *Neutestamentliche Grammatik.* HNT 1. Tübingen.

NT Semitisms

Black, M. 1967. *An Aramaic Approach to the Gospels and Acts.* Oxford.

Mussies, G. 1971. *The Morphology of Koine Greek as Used in the Apocalypse of St. John. A Study in Bilingualism.* NovTSup 27. Leiden.

Thompson, S. 1985. *The Apocalypse and Semitic Syntax.* SNTSMS 52. Cambridge.

Wilcox, M. 1967. *The Semitisms of Acts.* Oxford.

Zimmerman, F. 1979. *The Aramaic Origin of the Four Gospels.* New York.

Atticism

Frösén, J. 1974. *Prolegomena to a Study of the Greek Language in the First Centuries A.D. The Problem of Koiné and Atticism.* Helsinki.

Schmid, W. 1887–96. *Der Attizismus in seinen Hauptvertretern von Dionysius von Halikarnass bis auf den zweiten Philostratus.* 4 vols. Stuttgart.

Imperial Greek

Gignac, F. T. 1976–81. *A Grammar of the Greek Papyri of the Roman and Byzantine Periods.* Testi e Documenti per lo studio dell'Antichita 55. Milan.

GERARD MUSSIES

HEBREW

Hebrew is the language of the Old Testament/Hebrew Bible and of Judaism since antiquity. It is the language of a vast literature, religious and secular, spanning three millennia.

A. Hebrew as a Language Name
B. Linguistic Affiliation
  1. Afroasiatic
  2. Semitic
  3. Northwest Semitic
C. Early History of Hebrew
  1. Prehistory
  2. Iron Age Hebrew
  3. Persian and Hellenistic Periods
D. Structural Overview
  1. Phonology
  2. Grammatical Features
  3. Parts of Speech
  4. Morphological Typology
E. Hebrew Literature
F. Hebrew Language Scholarship

A. Hebrew as a Language Name

The subject of this article has been commonly called Hebrew by its own community only during the last thousand years or so. The earliest biblical reference to the Hebrew language names it "the language of Canaan" (Isa 19:18), and aptly so, since Hebrew is the best attested and best known form of Canaanite. Elsewhere in the Bible (2 Kgs 18:26, 28 = Isa 26:13 = 2 Chr 32:18; Isa 36:11; Neh 13:24), the language is referred to as *yehûdît,* "Judahite" or "Jewish," in contrast to Aramaic, which by then had emerged as a medium of international trade and diplomacy. In the literature of later antiquity, the language is usually called "the holy tongue," with reference to the biblical corpus, and the "tongue of the sages," when referring to the language of the oral tradition—what is called rabbinic or mishnaic or tannaitic Hebrew. It is here that we come across the first explicit reference to divergent literary styles.

When the term *ʿibrî,* "Hebrew," appears in the Bible (e.g., Gen 39:14; 41:12; Exod 2:11; Jon 1:9), it does not refer to a language but rather to an ethnicity. It occurs almost always as a synonym of the more commonly encountered "sons of Israel" when the in-group came in contact with the out-group. Only with reference to the categorization of native-born versus foreign slaves does it appear as an in-group ethnic term (Exod 21:2; Deut 15:12). While the term "Hebrew" as a language reference appears in the Talmud, it very rarely refers to what we call Hebrew. In one citation, most opinions assert that this reference to "Hebrew" refers to some outland dialect of Aramaic (*b. Meg.* 18a; see Rashi's commentary *ad loc.*). Another possibility is that this specific reference is to the Georgian language, the term *ʿibrî,* "Hebrew," being used because of its similarity to the term the Greeks used for these people, the *Iberatoi.* In medieval Hebrew, such updating of biblical toponyms and ethnic labels on the basis of vague phonetic similarity was commonplace. The designation *Gomer* for Germany is an example.

The designation "Hebrew" appears in the Talmud in one other linguistic context, referring to the old Canaanite alphabet, which is called "Hebrew writing" as contrasted with "Assyrian writing" (*b. Meg.* 3a). The newer alphabetic style, at least in the shape of its letters, replaced the older one throughout the Near East during the early Persian Empire period, evolving into the "square character" and its cursive derivatives which are in use today. See HEBREW SCRIPTS.

Curiously enough, the term "Hebrew" as the in-group common reference to its language is a borrowing from Arabic, first introduced by Saadia Gaon (882–942 C.E.) in his grammatical writings (Skoss 1955). The new designation entered the Hebrew language only when Jews began to write their grammatical studies in their own language a few centuries later.

The entire extent of the Canaanite language area was a narrow belt along the E Mediterranean shoreline, stretching from N Syria southward to the Sinai. Phoenician is the usual designation for the Canaanite spoken north of Israel, although the Phoenician colonizers of North Africa called themselves Canaanites and named their new country, centering around Carthage, Canaan. See PHOENICIA, HISTORY OF.

Other than as the language of ancient Phoenician colonialism, Canaanite never assumed a major role in the ancient world. Rome defeated its archrival Carthage in the west, and in the Levant Aramaic, originally used east of the Phoenician hill country, gradually spread its domain. As the language of the Jews, Hebrew was the mother tongue of only Jerusalem and its environs at the beginning of the Common Era. In the northern domains of the expanded Hasmonean Kingdom of Judea a form of Aramaic was spoken, simply because the local population carried on the speech habits of their ancestors who were converted to Judaism during the reign of John Hyrcanus I. The Idumeans to the south, who had been converted at about the same time, continued to speak their ancestral Canaanite tongue.

Hebrew probably ceased to be a living language (in the sense of a community mother tongue) around the year 200 C.E. as the result of the Bar Kokhba disaster, when the population of Judea was decimated and the survivors fled northward to the Galilee.

Judging from the literary evidence, however, the survivors were not really aware of what was happening to them linguistically, for the Aramaic which they spoke as a family language was symbiotically linked to the Hebrew they continued to use for more formal purposes. Hebrew and the several varieties of Aramaic, quite distinct from each other as languages in every other way, now were treated as mere styles of one community language. These same speakers, nonetheless, always regarded the Syriac variety of Aramaic to be a separate language.

Hebrew qua Hebrew continued throughout the ages as the medium of intense literary activity and also as a spoken lingua franca. It was revived as a mother tongue late in the 19th and early in the 20th centuries.

GENE SCHRAMM

B. Linguistic Affiliation

1. Afroasiatic. The family of languages to which Hebrew belongs is grouped by linguists in a phylum called Afroasiatic. The geographical range of Afroasiatic covers northern and central Africa and western Asia. In time, Afroasiatic languages are attested from the 3d millennium B.C.E. (although some languages of the phylum must have existed for at least a millennium before this) until the present (on the classification of Afroasiatic, see Ruhlen 1987).

The Afroasiatic phylum has five or six members: Egyptian (later called Coptic, now extinct) and Berber in N Africa, the Chadic family (whose best-known member is Hausa) in sub-Saharan Africa, the Cushitic-Omotic family in the Horn of Africa, and the Semitic family, which includes Arabic and Hebrew. Many of the features of Semitic languages in general and of Hebrew in particular are best viewed in the larger context of Afroasiatic affiliation.

2. Semitic. Hebrew belongs to the family of Afroasiatic languages commonly referred to as Semitic languages. The major division of this family is between East Semitic and West Semitic (on the classification of Semitic languages, see the introductory survey at the beginning of this entry). East Semitic incorporates the group of dialects called Akkadian; West Semitic includes the Northwest Semitic languages, Arabic, and South Semitic.

3. Northwest Semitic. The Northwest Semitic languages comprise the Canaanite group and Aramaic. Evidence for early Northwest Semitic begins in the 3d millennium (if one admits some of the features of the language of Ebla) and continues to the end of the LB II period (around 1200 B.C.E.; see especially the article on Ugaritic below). Some of the distinctive features of Canaanite can be observed in these early Northwest Semitic samples, but the distinction between Canaanite and Aramaic remains difficult to impose until the Iron II period. A recent survey concludes that the Iron Age languages of Syria-Palestine are best viewed as a continuum having Phoenician as one of its poles and Aramaic as the other (Garr 1985: 229). Hebrew is probably to be located near the center of this cline (Waltke and O'Connor 1990: 8–9 n. 20).

The Canaanite languages include Phoenician (which distinguishes the minority dialect of Byblos from the more widespread dialect of Tyre and Sidon), Hebrew (which distinguishes a northern dialect, probably centered in Samaria, from a southern, the dialect of Jerusalem and Judah), Ammonite, Moabite, and Edomite. The language of the Deir ʿAlla texts should perhaps also be included. See DEIR ʿALLA, TELL (TEXTS).

C. Early History of Hebrew

1. Prehistory. The upheavals which rearranged the political geography of Syria-Palestine during the transition from LB II to Iron I (that is, about 1400–1200 B.C.E.) produced corresponding changes in the linguistic map. It is probably during this period that Hebrew can be said to have emerged as a distinct language (although the continuity of many earlier Northwest Semitic features must not be ignored).

Some poetic passages of the Hebrew Bible (e.g., Exodus 15; Judges 5) have been dated to this early period on the basis of certain archaic features of their language, but no extrabiblical text identifiable as Hebrew survives from this period. (A very useful handbook of dated inscriptional texts is that compiled by Jaroš [1982]; texts 1–7 of this collection date from LB I to the end of LB II. The bibliography by Suder [1984] is incomplete and already passing out of date; the Chronological Index of Inscriptions [pp. 113–20] is nonetheless a helpful guide. The most important recent study of early alphabetic texts is by E. Puech [1986]; the interest of Puech's investigation is the development of the writing system rather than the language. Older handbooks include *KAI* 182–200; *TSSI* vol. 1.)

2. Iron Age Hebrew. The earliest written evidence of Hebrew comes from the archaeological period Iron IIB–C (800–586 B.C.E.). Hebrew must have existed as a spoken language earlier, and texts were undoubtedly composed in it; but none survives (beyond some archaic portions of the Hebrew Bible). Smelik (1987: 9) considers the archaeological record sufficient to warrant the conclusion that writing was not used widely in Israel until the 8th century, literacy being restricted before that time to the royal court and select officials.

During the Iron Age, Hebrew existed in at least two dialects: northern, or "Israelian" (a term coined by H. L. Ginsberg), and southern, or "Judahite." Evidence of the northern dialect is epigraphic and spotty; the southern dialect, by contrast, is abundantly attested in inscriptions and much of the text of the Hebrew Bible.

Israelian Hebrew is the language of the Samaria ostraca, administrative documents written on pottery fragments unearthed during excavation of the northern capital. See SAMARIA (PLACE). The ostraca fall into two groups, datable to 795–794 B.C.E. and 776 B.C.E., respectively (Jaroš 1982: 57). Their texts are brief and formulaic, offering a poor sample of the language. But their consistent use of the date formula *bšt (h)-* (followed by a number or numerals), "In (the) year x," shows that the language, at least with respect to this formulaic feature, follows the usage of Phoenician as opposed to Judahite, which employs the form *šnh* for "year" (see *DISO,* 312–13). Other inscriptions found in the region of the N kingdom may also give evidence of the language (see, e.g., *TSSI,* vol. 1, pp. 15–20).

J. W. Wesselius has recently (1987) asserted that the language of the Deir ʿAlla texts is Israelian Hebrew, and that the fragments of a story about Balaam written in ink on plaster found at the site constitute the first-known literary text in the language of the N kingdom. Morphological details of those texts make the argument linguistically problematic, and its acceptance must await the verdict of scholarly judgment.

With the deportation of the N kingdom in 722 B.C.E., Israelian Hebrew became a negligible dialect, and it eventually vanished altogether.

The dialect of Judah can be recognized in inscriptions from numerous sites. A seven-line inscription on a limestone tablet discovered at Gezer in 1908 is frequently called the "Gezer Calendar" because it appears to tally the months of the year according to agricultural activities conducted in successive seasons. Although its language is often said to be Hebrew, it exhibits morphological features distinct from other samples of (Judahite) Hebrew, both epigraphic and biblical (see *KAI,* vol. 2, pp. 181–82; *TSSI* 1: 1–2 ["an archaic Hebrew dialect"]; Jaroš 1982 no.11 [pp. 37–38]).

The inscription on a privately owned scarab of uncertain provenance dates paleographically to the late 10th or early 9th century B.C.E. (Jaroš 1982 no. 13 [pp. 39–40]). The Yahwistic name of its owner, *zryhw,* is spelled in a manner characteristic of later Judahite and may warrant the linguistic classification of the two-word text as "Hebrew."

The corpus of extant Hebrew (the term will be used hereinafter for the dialect of Judah unless otherwise specified) expands considerably in the 8th century B.C.E. Inscribed seals, benedictions, and letters written in ink on pottery fragments (ostraca), and commemorative and funerary texts engraved in stone show the language in use in public and private contexts, in religious and more "secular" settings, at "official" and "unofficial" levels. Major texts include the SILOAM INSCRIPTION from Jerusalem, the tomb inscription from Khirbet el-Qom (see PALESTINIAN FUNERARY INSCRIPTIONS), letters from ARAD, and the LACHISH LETTERS.

The language of these nonbiblical Hebrew texts is not appreciably different from the stratum called Classical Hebrew found throughout the Primary History and in segments of the Major Prophets from the Hebrew Bible. The inscriptional record thus places beyond cavil the conclusion that the MT preserves significant samples of the language of Iron Age Judah in its successive phases. There are, however, indications that the phonological analysis represented in the Masoretic vocalization of the consonantal text is at many points a later adaptation of earlier speech traditions (see D.1. below).

Extrabiblical Hebrew offers an important control on attempts at relative and absolute dating of the linguistic strata of biblical books. The diachronic study of morphological and syntactic features permits limited statements about changes in the language over time (Adams and Adams 1977 is an example; Kutscher 1982 is a posthumously published attempt at a continuous history of Hebrew; see the further comments by Waltke and O'Connor [1990: 13–15]). The extent and significance of linguistic change as it affected Hebrew can be assessed variously; attention to change, however, need not divert the reader of biblical texts from the evident continuity of the language.

3. Persian and Hellenistic Periods. A broad distinction can be made between Classical Hebrew, by which is meant essentially the language of Judah before the Babylonian Exile (586 B.C.E.), and Late Biblical Hebrew (LBH), by which is meant essentially Hebrew of the Persian period (the term has gained currency since its use by Polzin 1976). The typology of LBH developed by Polzin has more recently been extended to a larger corpus of biblical texts by A. Hill (*WLSGF,* 77–89), tracing a body of characteristic features of LBH in the postexilic prophets. The coordination of relative with absolute dates ventured in Hill's study must remain tentative (as the author cautions [p. 84]), but such studies show the importance of diachronic arguments in the linguistic analysis of Hebrew.

Some of the distinctive features of LBH are attributable to the increased use of Aramaic by speakers of Hebrew after the Exile. There is evidence from the biblical text itself of concern to preserve the speech community of the "language of Judah" from the influence of Canaanite languages other than Hebrew (Neh 13:24; the "language of Ashdod" might have been Aramaic, but the peculiar designation suggests a Canaanite dialect). The statement in Neh 8:8 that the law of God was read "clearly" (Heb *mĕpôraš;* RSV marg. "with interpretation") has been taken to mean that in the postexilic period Classical Hebrew was no longer fully intelligible to the general populace.

Hebrew continued in use as a literary language in the Hellenistic period, and biblical books perhaps to be dated in this period show evidence of further linguistic change. The language of Qohelet has occasioned much study; the book's content contributes to the impression of Hellenistic influence (on the language, see Delsman 1982 and Fredericks 1988 [against late dating], but note the demurral of Schoors 1989). The Song of Songs is almost commonly set in the Hellenistic period, largely on the basis of linguistic arguments (see, e.g., Eissfeldt 1965: 490, 766). Esther is probably also a product of the Hellenistic age (Eissfeldt 1965: 510). The date of the Hebrew portions of Daniel has been a point of controversy; a date after 167 B.C.E. is generally held. See DANIEL, BOOK OF.

The book of Ecclesiasticus, or the Wisdom of Jesus the Son of Sirach (or Ben Sira), was composed in Hebrew about 180 B.C.E., but the Hebrew text was neglected for centuries and rediscovered only in modern times (Di Lella 1966; Skehan and Di Lella *Wisdom of Ben Sira* AB, 51–61). A Greek translation produced by Ben Sira's grandson after 132 B.C.E. is included among the books of the Apocrypha.

PHILIP C. SCHMITZ

D. Structural Overview

1. Phonology. Properly speaking, this description deals primarily with the orthographic system, with educated guesses as to what the language may have sounded like at any one time in any given location.

The West Semitic alphabet in which Hebrew is written consists of twenty-two signs, representing six glides, two resonants, and fourteen obstruents. The glides are usually transcribed as /w/ for the rounded labial, /y/ for the unrounded palatal, and /ʾ, h, ḥ, ʿ/ for the glottals; the resonants are /r/ and /l/. Most authorities assume, on the basis of Greek and Latin letter transcriptions and comparative Semitic correspondences, that the broad sound values approximate those of Arabic. The obstruents are the two nasals /m/ and /n/, and thirteen orals, divided into the categories of labial, dental, palatal, and velar, intersected by the oppositions of stop:fricative and plain:emphatic.

Almost all authorities agree on the schematization of the sound values of the Tiberian Hebrew consonantal system shown in Table 1.

Table 1: The Obstruents

labial	dental	palatal	velar
p	t ṭ s ṣ	š	k q
b	d z		g
m	n		

The tradition of pronouncing Hebrew reflected in the Tiberian Masora divided the six plain stopped obstruents into twelve, with an additional stop:spirant opposition: /p:f, b:v, t:t̲, d:d̲, k:x/, and /g:ḡ/. Originally, the realization of these six letters as either stops or spirants was predictable in terms of the immediate phonological environment: when following a vowel and not geminated, the spirant was sounded, while the stop was the default realization. But in time, with modifications occurring in the syllabic structure, the situation changed, and the consonantal inventory was increased marginally as a result.

The status of the sibilants is another area of disagreement, and for good reason, because there are many indications, in Hebrew as well as in other Semitic languages, of persistent instability in the silibant inventory. The Tiberian Masora distinguishes two consonants for the second-to-last letter of the alphabet: with a diacritic dot to the upper left, the letter is called *śin* and is transcribed as /ś/; with a diacritic dot to the right, it is called *šin* and is transcribed as /š/.

Together with the letter *samek,* there is no doubt that the three entities reflect a Proto-Semitic system of three separate phonemes. Whether or not the three were ever realized as separate phonemes in Hebrew is not as clear. The several traditions of liturgical pronunciation show different variations on the realization of these letters. In some instances, the three are merged into two sounds, in others into one. One Moroccan pronunciation tradition, for example, has *śin* and *šin* leveled as /š/ in opposition to *samek,* which is realized as /s/; the Samaritan tradition agrees with the Moroccan in this instance. One Lithuanian variety of Ashkenazic pronunciation levels all three to /s/. The classical payyetanic poet Qallir (6th century?) rhymes all three, although the precise realization is not to be recovered. No surviving liturgical tradition exhibits three separate sounds; nor is there any evidence that such a threefold realization ever existed in Hebrew. The prevalent traditions suggest that the Tiberians pronounced *śin* and *samek* both as /s/, as opposed to *šin,* which they sounded as /š/.

The letters transcribed with subdots (to include /q/, which is frequently transcribed as /ḳ/), called emphatics, are usually considered to have been pharyngealized or velarized, on the order of the Arabic cognate sounds. Greek letter transcriptions, both from Hebrew to Greek and from Greek to Hebrew, suggest that they differed from the plain counterparts in that aspiration was lacking as a coarticulatory feature, and this certainly agrees with the Arabic evidence.

The glottal glides are interpreted as the equivalents of the cognate Arabic sounds; there is certain evidence indicating that the merging of these four sounds took place independently in many areas at different times, resulting in either two or even one sound for the four letters.

The schematization of the full inventory of the Hebrew alphabet as modified by the Tiberian consonantal diacritics, counting *śin* and *samek* as homophonous graphemes, is shown in Table 2.

Table 2: The Twenty-two Letters and Their Sound Values

labial		dental					palatal	velar		glottal	
p	f	t	ṯ	ṭ	s	ṣ	š	k	x	ʾ	h
b	v	d	ḏ		z			g	ḡ	ḥ	ʿ
m				n							
			r	l							
w							y				

The vocalic system of the Tiberians can be interpreted in conflicting ways. Nine essential vowel diacritics exist, most of which are named in accordance with the manner of their articulation. The term *ḥîreq,* for example, meaning "cleft," is the name of the diacritic representing the high front vowel /i/; *šûreq,* meaning "whistle," designates the high back rounded vowel /u/; *pataḥ,* meaning "open," is the name of the low (or open) vowel /a/.

There is considerable disagreement whether or not the two vowel signs *šûreq* and *qibbuṣ* represent contrastive long and short varieties of /u/, and this question is tied into the overall issue of constrastive vowel length for Tiberian Hebrew. Vocalic length for Hebrew is not mentioned at all until the 13th-century grammar of Radaq, and it is quite certain that he was describing a morphophonemic feature. But later interpretations of Radaq's description, possibly influenced by features of Latin and Arabic, ascribed phonemic vowel length to the Tiberian system, in spite of contradictory evidence from the medieval tradition of metrics. Furthermore, no Jewish pronunciation tradition shows any evidence of phonemic vowel length.

In this connection, the status of the four Tiberian *šĕwâ* signs is to be considered as well. The Tiberians themselves describe the sounds represented by these symbols in a way that suggests very strongly that they were open transitions rather than true vowels. With these considerations, therefore, the probability is very great that the Tiberian vowel system was a seven-fold one, schematized in Table 3.

Table 3: The Tiberian Vowels

Front	Back
i	u
e	o
ɛ	ə
a	

Besides the diacritics added to indicate consonantal modification and those introduced to represent the vocalic inventory, another set of diacritics were devised to represent in portmanteau fashion the features of stress and intonation. Two such systems exist, one specific to the three books of Psalms, Proverbs, and Job, and the other for the remaining twenty-one books of the Jewish canon. These *ṭĕʿāmîm* or "accents" evolved in time to serve as cantillation symbols in the performance tradition, although the musical values for the former subsystem have been completely lost.

2. Grammatical Features. Features of the Hebrew language include both agreement and switch concord of grammatical gender and number within the phrase and within the clause. Two grammatical genders, typically labeled "masculine" and "feminine," exist. There are three grammatical numbers, a singular referring to one of a kind and a plural referring to two or more, plus a marginal dual category referring to two and only two of a kind. The dual is restricted in its occurrence to a very short list of nouns of measure, although a similarly formed plural suffix denoting bilateral symmetry also exists for nouns referring to paired body parts.

Gender and number are signaled in both the nominal and verbal systems. Noun phrases typically exhibit total agreement of gender and number, with the head noun governing the attributive and demonstrative adjectives. The numerical phrase, however, exhibits the relatively rare feature of switch concord, in which the gender assignment of the head noun and the numerical qualifier have opposite genders.

In the clause, the subject governs the verb, which agrees with it at least in part. When the subject is a binomial and follows the verb, the verb frequently agrees with only the first term of the binomial; when the verb follows the subject, the agreement is complete. Examples of both types may be found in the opening verses of Exodus 15 and Judges 5. In the former citation, the verb agrees with the initial noun "Moses" and is masculine singular; in the latter, it is feminine singular, agreeing with "Deborah." The second verb in each sequence is masculine plural, governed by the plurality inherent in the binomial expression. The gender of the plural verb exhibits yet another feature, namely the neutrality of the "masculine" gender, a neutrality held to be universal for all languages in which a binary gender system is linked to sex. Thus, while the two genders are labeled "masculine" and "feminine," the "masculine" is in reality an unassigned category.

The finite verbal system shows both prefixed and suffixed personal paradigms. For the last century and more, many authorities have viewed the content of the finite verb to be aspectual rather than tense, denoting actions as finished or ongoing rather than in past or present-future time. The native grammatical tradition, however, drawing on Arabic grammatical theory and models since the early Middle Ages, always described the verb system in terms of tense. More recent linguistic analyses would tend to favor the medieval assessment. Of particular interest, especially in biblical literature and medieval belletristic texts, is the apparent flip-flop of prefixing (present-future) and suffixing (past) forms in coordinated verb phrases, referred to as the *waw*-conversive or *waw*-consecutive phenomenon. In reality, what happens is an optional but very frequent sequence of tense situation which results in the neutralization of tense reference in coordinated verbs. This neutralization of time reference is extended in poetry as well to juxtaposed clauses without explicit coordination.

3. Parts of Speech. The Hebrew language distinguishes the following word classes and subclasses in a formal manner.

a. Nominals. Nominals are all words that may occur as the subject of a clause and include the principal subclasses of pronouns, proper nouns, and substantives. Personal pronouns, interrogatives, and demonstratives are partially analyzable and are defined by lists. Personal names, also partially analyzable, are characterized by gender assignment and absence of pluralization or dependency. Substantives are subdivided into nouns of variable gender and nouns of assigned gender.

b. Verbals. Verbals comprise those items that may occur as the heads of predicate phrases, include the existentials, adjectives and verbs per se.

The existentials comprise a short list of expressions denoting existence or being and constitute a rudimentary present tense system for biblical style and the basis of derivation for a full present tense system for later Hebrew. Adjectives are primarily participles, which is to say verbal in their derivation, although there are several adjectival categories that are derived from nouns. Adjectives thus differ from nouns of variable gender (words like "king" and "queen," "horse" and "mare") syntactically.

The finite verbal system consists of two indicative sets, a direct command imperative limited to the second persons, and a parallel but partial indirect command, the jussive/cohortative system. One of the indicative paradigms is formed by personal prefixes and gender/number suffixes added to a stem; the other is formed by a fused set of personal and gender/number suffixes associated with a second verb stem. The imperative is formed by gender/number suffixes attached to a stem marginally different from the prefixed indicative verb, while the jussive/cohortative is formed by the addition of personal prefixes as well as gender/number suffixes.

Nonfinite forms of the verb include verbal adverbs (the "absolute" infinitives of traditional grammars) and the true ("construct") infinitive.

c. Enumeratives. The enumeratives include an adjective for the word "one," a defective noun of symmetry for the word "two," substantives for the higher items, including "hundred," "thousand," and "myriad," and true numerals for the items between "three" and the multiples of ten. Switch concord occurs as the distinctive syntactic feature in numerical phrases between "three" and "nineteen."

d. Particles. The term particle is the traditional designation for all residual classes that are neither analyzable nor derivable. This includes the categories of coordinating conjunctions, adverbials, subordinators, and relativizers. The conjunctions and relativizers are defined only by list.

e. Adverbials. Other than those adverbs that are derived within the verbal system, this category includes a short list of unanalyzable forms, quantifiers like "also" and "even," and temporals such as "then" and "now."

4. Morphological Typology. For the past millennium, grammatical and lexicographical tradition has described all verbs and most nouns as being derived from stems that in turn are formed by the interdigitation of a consonantal root expressing lexical content and a vocalic pattern, with an optional augment, expressing grammatical content. This typology bears a superficial resemblance to the structures "begin-began-begun," familiar from English. A residue of the nominals and the rest of the word classes are not analyzable in this manner but are contiguous linear entities. This typology has been held for all of the Semitic languages until recently; the newer opposing view has favored the notion that the derivation of words proceeds from a linear contiguous root modified by affixation and apophony, i.e., a regular substitution of sounds that inherently signals change in grammatical meaning (Kuryłowicz 1964).

E. Hebrew Literature

Literary activity in the Hebrew language has been going on without significant interruption for a period of more than three thousand years, producing a rich and variegated corpus of material that has very few peers in terms of its contribution to world civilization.

It should come as no surprise that during its long history the Hebrew language has undergone many changes. When we categorize the recorded differences of grammatical usage within the framework of a literary chronology, the familiar divisions of biblical, Tannaitic, medieval, and modern literary periods emerge, most frequently considered to be discrete entities with clear boundaries. Grammars have been written accounting for biblical and Tannaitic Hebrew and, most recently, for the modern language as well, sometimes giving the impression that the literatures of these different eras have little to do with each other and that the grammatical differences typical of each period are consistent and distinctive enough to warrant separate grammatical treatment. Without denying the partial validity of these observations at all, one might suggest that the conventional conclusions appear to be somewhat off target.

The language of the biblical Hebrew corpus, which is virtually all that has been preserved from the first thousand years of literary activity, is first of all not a standardized language. It is actually specious to think in terms of biblical Hebrew as anything other than a literary reference without making serious qualifications. True enough, a standard of language has emerged from within the biblical corpus, but this standard is partially the product of the medieval grammarians and partly that of the poets, chroniclers, critics, commentators, and others who determined literary usage and style only much later on in history. And this standard, to be sure, is based only on the most frequently occurring morphological and syntactic constructions found in biblical prose narrative text, with some admixture of Tannaitic norms.

The standardized distillate that has come to be known as biblical Hebrew has had an enormous impact on later literary Hebrew, since the literary corpus with which it has been confused has never ceased to be primary in its own influence on later generations. But if there is really an older corpus of Hebrew literature that embodies a normative language of sorts, it is that of Jewish liturgy. The collections of prayer, embodied in the *Siddur* (order of prayer) and the *Mahzor* (cycle of prayer), originated during the period of the Second Commonwealth and are largely attributed to Ezra the Scribe, the men of the Great Synagogue, and their successors. Liturgy first appears in crystallized form much later on in the Gaonic age—from the time of the completion of the Babylonian Talmud until the high Middle Ages, roughly the period between 600 and 1100 C.E.

The *Siddur* has been the primary textbook of elementary education throughout the Jewish world for centuries. Containing as it does large segments of biblical as well as Mishnaic material together with the prayers and blessings themselves, it combines religious instruction with an introduction to the language and its literature. The Jewish child received his training from a text that was largely composed in a standardized language but that also included other, nonstandardized styles.

Literacy in Hebrew, prior to the period of generalized secular public eduction, was the norm for the male in Jewish communities almost without exception. In addition to the daily, Sabbath, and festival prayers, the Jewish boy studied the Pentateuch and the Prophets and, in this connection, learned to read and utilize the works of the principal commentators. Once the essentials had been acquired, studies in the Mishnah were added, followed shortly by intensive reading of the essential tractates of the Babylonian Talmud, again with the principal commentaries. This much was the basic curriculum. Advanced students then went on to study the codes of law, generally to receive rabbinic ordination. The Babylonian Talmud is written principally in a late form of eastern Aramaic, a language quite different from Hebrew, although still genetically related to it. Yet students did not study Aramaic as another language; nor did they even study Hebrew in a formal way. They learned these languages as they learned and mastered the literature. So thorough was the linguistic internalization that if any consciousness came to the surface, a text was identified as Aramaic or Hebrew not because of the overt linguistic signs but because of identification with the source corpus. The language symbiosis first encountered in the 3d century thus continued on even in other areas and other speech communities.

It would be too much to claim that only the grammarians were fully aware of the not so subtle differences between Hebrew and Aramaic or between one variety of Hebrew and another. It is quite likely, however, that the grammarians were the only ones who really cared and paid attention to things of that sort. Consider how often the ordinary user of English or any other language thinks that the language he or she speaks and hears in conversation is really grammatically the same as the one heard on the TV news programs or read in the morning newspaper.

This is not a trivial point to make. If the medieval Jewish poet wrote a masterpiece in a language he did not speak, he was the peer of his Moslem counterpart who also wrote his masterpiece in an Arabic he did not speak. And many a medieval Jew was equally as much at ease in literary Hebrew as in literary Arabic. To belabor this a bit more, it is no exaggeration to say that the language of choice in the literature of medieval Spain, whether Hebrew, Arabic, or a Romance tongue, was dictated by the literary genre and not by the speech community to which the author belonged. Epics were composed in Gallego, troubador ballads in Catalan, and chronicles in Aragonese. Castillian, it appears, was reserved for the most prosaic and least artistic purposes for a very long period of time.

In the medieval Jewish community, genre likewise imposed its dictates. Chronicles were written in loose imitation of the biblical prose narratives, poetry in a stricter biblical style, and legal literature in a style reminiscent sometimes of straight Mishnaic usage, and at other times in the Babylonian Talmudic mixture of Aramaic and Hebrew. Philosophical treatises were composed in Arabic until necessity imposed the switch to Hebrew late in the 12th century.

The age of the Bible comprises the first thousand years of Hebrew literary history. Jewish tradition attributes the earliest texts of the Bible to Moses, and biblical critical scholarship will agree with this, at least in part. Most critics are in agreement that the latest biblical texts come from the age of the Hasmonean dynasty, a little more than halfway through the period of the Second Commonwealth. The Bible makes mention of other books that we know of by name only. A handful of inscriptions from the First Temple period are known to us through archaeological digs, and more recently the Hebrew text of the apocryphal Ecclesiasticus was twice discovered. But except for the liturgical material ascribed by the Talmud to Ezra and the men of the Great Synagogue, the contents of the Hebrew Bible remain the legacy of this long period of time.

The Bible itself comes down in several stages and processes. The Pentateuch was possibly a canonical text by the time the First Temple was destroyed, and the books of the Prophets may have achieved official recognition during the Persian period. We simply do not know for sure. The works composing the Hagiographa, the third and last division of the Bible according to Jewish tradition, were not formally admitted to the canon until some twenty years after the destruction of the Second Temple. Certain elements of the Hagiographa, including the psalms that had been incorporated into the temple liturgy, had already received at least de facto recognition as canonical texts. But it was the Sanhedrin at Yahweh in the year 90 C.E. that put the final stamp of approval to Ruth and Esther, for example, and excluded Ecclesiasticus and Judith from the Scriptures.

At about the same time that Ben Sira composed Ecclesiasticus in excellent imitation of classical biblical style (that is, about 180 B.C.E.), a newer literature began to emerge. This was the literature of what has come to be known as Tannaitic Hebrew, named after the masters of the Mishnah, its principal classical text, although the earliest midrashic works were not only older but more numerous.

This newer literature was originally an oral one. Just when it was committed to writing is not really certain. Mishnaic material was redacted by Rabbi Akiba just prior to the Bar Kokhba disaster, and a second redaction took place at the hands of Rabbi Meir a generation or so later. The final text of "Our Mishnah," as it is referred to, is the work of Rabbi Judah the Prince at some time between 200 and 225 C.E. But the Mishnah may not have been committed to writing until its text became the focus of the Jerusalem and Babylonian Talmuds, which means the period between the years 400 and 500 C.E., or even somewhat later.

Tannaitic literature is quite different from biblical literature. Some morphological and syntactic constructions of high frequency in the corpus of the Bible hardly occur in the Mishnah, and there are structures typical of tannaitic literature that are rare or lacking in the Bible. But these differences, upon close examination, turn out to be far more trivial than startling, because the underlying grammatical processes are quite the same. Thus, the important difference is more stylistic than grammatical.

One example will suffice for the moment. There are two relative pronouns in the language, a longer form and a shorter prefixed one. In biblical text, the longer form is the one more frequently encountered. The shorter form occurs both in the earliest and latest contributions to the corpus, but appears only in poetic text. In the Mishnah, the situation is reversed. The short form is the norm, almost to the exclusion of the longer one, and the poetic overtones have completely disappeared.

Tannaitic style is characterized by a terseness that is surprising to those brought up in biblical literature. Clauses are very frequently juxtaposed without intervening conjunctions, and "little" grammatical function words tend to undergo ellipsis, producing an effect that may be viewed impressionistically as telegraphic. The aphorisms of the popular Mishnaic tractate *Pirqe ʾAbot (Chapters of the Fathers)* resemble the book of Proverbs in content alone. Otherwise, they are entirely different in style, being prosaic rather than poetic, and lacking the cadences, the phonological play, and tightness of encoding so typical of biblical Wisdom Literature.

Tannaitic prose narratives (the genre of the Aggadah) tend to be more dramatic than their biblical counterparts and startlingly different. The same terseness is there, but they are illuminated by the juxtaposition of biblical quotes embedded in the narrative fabric—one important reason why it is impossible to appreciate tannaitic literature without a thorough grounding in the Bible. The reverse is also very true. Tannaitic reworking of biblical material is so innovative that the reader is constantly faced with astonishing new ways of interpreting the older body of literature. A marvelous tannaitic statement, for example, takes the superscription of Psalm 92 to mean that the Sabbath Day personified was coauthor of the poem together with Adam!

The Tannaitic Age is also the period of early liturgical compilation. Some of the daily and sabbath prayers are quoted at least in part in the Talmud, and the last chapter of the Mishnaic tractate *Pesaḥim* is essentially a detailed outline of the Haggadah of Passover, still in use today. Mystical treatises and mystical poems begin to appear during this period, and a recently discovered handbook on magic reveals a less lofty kind of spirituality, providing instruction on how to win a horse race or upstage one's rival in love, all in good imitation of Mishnaic style (Margalioth 1966). This is also the period of the recently discovered Dead Sea Scrolls (on the language of which see Qimron 1986).

This period of late antiquity, just prior to the emergence of Islam, evidences a revolution in poetic style. Some of the early mystical poems produced at this time and later incorporated into the liturgy show the earliest evidence of experimentation with end-of-line rhyme incorporated within a metrical matrix of strict word count. By the early or mid 6th century, rhyme is already highly conventionalized, as demonstrated by the compositions of Elazar ha-Qallir and his purported teacher Yannai, who inaugurated a brand new style and school of esoteric and highly innovative poetry that dominated the literary scene for some five centuries. A second literary revolution was launched by Saadia Gaon in the late 9th and early 10th centuries. An Egyptian by birth, coming from an obscure community in the Fayyum oasis, Saadia propelled himself into the middle of a battle for supremacy waged between the rabbis of Baghdad and Jerusalem and ended up as the controversial but masterful Gaon of Sura, the first and perhaps only non-Babylonian known to have held this prestigious office. Saadia was a superb Arabist, as is apparent from his literary output, and he loved Arabic poetry. He found the older Qallirian style of Hebrew versification to be tiresome, for that school of poetry had by now outlived its creativity through sheer longevity.

Saadia was a master not only of Arabic literature but of Arabic grammarianship as well. He wrote, in Arabic, the first grammatical description of Hebrew, which included the earliest known grammatical statements comparing Hebrew, Arabic, and Aramaic. He produced, as well, the first dictionary of the Hebrew language—and a rhyming dictionary at that—for the benefit of his contemporary poets who lacked, in his estimation, the imaginativeness and good taste required for successful metrical composition. Saadia wrote, also in Arabic, some of the earliest commentaries on the Bible and the earliest commentary to the Mishnah. He translated the entire Bible into Arabic, a translation long used by oriental communities. In addition, Saadia produced some Hebrew poetry, considered by some to be quite good in quality though never reaching the majestic heights of his literary heirs.

Along with the standard curriculum in Jewish Law, Saadia taught metrics. Among his more talented students was a certain Dunash ibn Labrat who came to Baghdad from his native Morocco and, upon completion of his studies, returned to the West and settled in Spain. Joining the Jewish community of Cordova, the capital of the Omayyad caliphate in Andalusia, he attached himself to the court of Ḥisdai ibn Shaprut, a grandee and leader of the Jewish community, ultimately to become Hishdai's principal protégé. Dunash was certainly not the first person to write Hebrew poetry in Spain, but he was to become the first poet of the new Spanish school, which, in turn, dominated the literary scene for the next five centuries.

The Golden Age in Spain was an age of classical revival. Where the Qallirian style was highly idiosyncratic, neither biblical nor mishnaic nor anything else really, the poets of Spain, following Saadia's metrical preferences as taught to them by Dunash, adhered very closely to biblical style. Their poetry had the added features of rhyme—inherited essentially from the Qallirians but modified according to Saadianic conventions—and of meter, borrowed from the Arabic and adapted, again via Saadia, to suit Hebrew syllabic structure.

From Andalusia, the neoclassical style spread, first northward to Christian Spain and the Provence, and then to Italy, N France, England, and Germany. The Spanish school was far more creative and flexible than the older Qallirian school had been. Influences from the poetic styles of the non-Jewish environment are apparent in the girdle songs written in imitation of the colloquial Arabic style, troubador ballads in the Provençal model, and sonnets of the Petrarchian school that begin to appear in Hebrew a full generation before Petrarch himself. In addition to the metrical compositions, both secular and liturgical, there arose a new literature of the romance, a Hebrew translational link in a literary chain that began in India, advanced to Persia and then the Arab world, and wound up in the picaresque novel of Romance Spain.

Throughout all of this time, we see chronicles and books of family pedigree, mystical tracts, the ever-growing legal literature, the biblical and Talmudic commentaries, and the supercommentaries. Not much of it was to be passed down to modern times directly. Communities declined and simply disappeared; others suffered persecution and destruction or banishment. Books were burned. Quite understandably, there were priorities, and these dictated, on the whole, that only that material of first-rank community importance—whatever was legal and religious in significance rather than secular or frivolous—be preserved.

The chance discovery of an obscure Cairo synagogue by a pair of English lady tourists a century ago, however, released a flood of documents of immeasurable importance. The contents of the Cairo Geniza constitute one of the most remarkable documentary finds in recent history, far larger and far more significant than the more famous Dead Sea discoveries. Many of its documents, now scattered in libraries from Leningrad to San Francisco, have been published; many more remain waiting for scholars trained and motivated to carry on.

As Christian Europe approached its Renaissance, the Jewish world turned increasingly inward. Although secular literary activity continued, it steadily decreased in both quantity and quality and, by the 18th century, came virtually to a standstill. The French Revolution, which inaugurated the period of modern Jewish history, had little immediate and direct influence on Hebrew literary activity. But by the end of the 19th century, a new literary revival, centered in Russia and spreading from there to Ottoman Palestine, was on the upswing.

This literary revival coincided with but was not limited to the rise of political Zionism. Nor is it to be completely equated with the parallel and contemporary revival of Hebrew as a colloquial mother tongue, with which it is often confused. The revival of spoken Hebrew is most commonly associated with the figure of Eliezer Ben Yehudah, who certainly undertook to speak nothing but Hebrew upon settling in Jerusalem. But although Hebrew did in fact become the language of his family and of some of his friends and neighbors, the rebirth of the colloquial had other origins, more mundane and more pragmatic in scope.

For centuries, Hebrew had been used as a spoken language, as a lingua franca for Jews who chanced to come together but possessed no common mother tongue. By the middle of the 19th century, before the rise of Zionism, the Jews of Jerusalem, crowded into the smallest quarter of the Old City, constituted a majority of that town's population. Predominantly Sephardic in origin, they possessed as a community no common language. Some spoke Ladino, the descendant of preexilic Spanish, others Persian, and others one or another form of colloquial Arabic.

Of necessity, Hebrew was the language of the marketplace. Had the population been essentially Ashkenazic, perhaps Yiddish would have served instead. The prevailing demography, however, dictated not only Hebrew to be the language of the community, but also Hebrew as pronounced in the Sephardic manner. Hebrew thus remained the language of the marketplace in Jerusalem and the other principal towns, like Hebron, Tiberias, Zefat, and Jaffa. Its colloquial revival succeeded because Hebrew became the exclusive language of the nursery in the early Zionist settlements. While these early settlers—the parents—struggled with a language they knew perhaps bookishly well, their offspring acquired this new Hebrew fluently from the cradle.

The desire to establish Hebrew as the national language did not go unchallenged. Yiddish was a serious contender, but the Zionist dream won out with the aid of socialist experimentation. The language struggle was over by 1925, the year in which the Hebrew University was inaugurated.

Modern Hebrew literature began with a short period of intense experimentation in the belletristic use of a language that had not been artistically exercised for some time. The initial efforts do not measure up to the quality of material produced in the parallel Yiddish literary movement, but an updated standard literary language rapidly emerged, and writers were publishing in every genre imaginable. The success of the modern Hebrew literary revival was recently crowned by the recognition implicit in naming the late S. Y. Agnon to the fellowship of Nobel laureates.

Linguists are not surprised, and may even be delighted, to observe that Hebrew has since taken on a new life of its own. Originally based on a literary standard slightly modified by usage in the old *yĕšîbôt,* the colloquial has undergone a complete transformation. A rich literature is once again being produced by writers who speak Hebrew as their mother tongue but write in a language quite as different as any literary language when compared with its colloquial analogue.

F. Hebrew Language Scholarship

The history and evolution of the biblical text is not all that there is to tell. Hebrew was originally written in an alphabet of twenty-two letters that essentially represented only consonants. The vowels of Hebrew were not systematically represented in writing, since they were only sporadically hinted at by the ambivalent use of the letters cognate to English "w" and "y." Dialectal differences certainly existed; these are mentioned both in the Bible and in the Talmud. We have no way of knowing what the language sounded like; we are limited to formulating educated guesses as to the phonetic properties of the consonants, the vowels, and the other features (including the prosodies). In the course of time, the language underwent change, as do all languages. Changes in the consonantism and the vowel system continued, even after the language ceased to be the mother tongue of a Jewish community. These occurred in spite of the fact that the public reading of the biblical text was rigorously bound by a strict oral tradition.

There existed a class of professional memorizers, some who specialized in the biblical text, called Qaraʾim, "readers," and others who specialized in the legal traditions, called Tannaʾim, "repeaters." The recitation tradition was supposed to be rigorous and unchanging, but the Talmud provides information indicating that some "readers" were less skilled than others and rendered spurious readings (*B. Bat.* 30a). More important to our purposes, the tradition of oral recitation proliferated into traditions that tended to diverge as do language dialects, and indeed must have diverged according to the natural development of different liturgical dialects in various parts of the Jewish world. To the best of our knowledge, by the end of the 8th century C.E., there were three principal dialect areas. In the Mediterranean basin, Hebrew was pronounced with a five-vowel system. Further to the east, in Baghdad, Hebrew was a six-vowel language. The final product of biblical redaction, that which we call the Tiberian Masoretic text, is based on a seven-vowel dialect (Schramm 1964).

It is commonly and erroneously believed that the Masoretes, who produced the definitive biblical text, applied the vowel signs, accents, and other diacritics in their redaction according to their understanding of the text. While they certainly had an exegetical tradition on which to rely, the results of their labors indicate that they operated in a very different way. Certainly, the text that they produced is full of difficult readings, some of which would have been certainly replaced by simpler equivalents, if this were indeed the way they worked. That they employed a very different method of operation is to be seen in many ways.

The Tiberian annotational apparatus includes many comments, expressed in various specific ways, that all translate into the modern editorial term *sic*. Other comments present alternative renderings. In all instances, these readings point not to an intellectual choice between variants but to an effort at preserving a received tradition. Their intention was not to create a text based on a standardized language but rather to preserve and transmit a performance standard. The only intellectual decision they made was to record as faithfully as possible the pronunciation tradition that they considered to be the most prestigious (Ben-Asher 1879).

The biblical corpus has always been viewed as consisting of two separate coequal domains, namely the manuscript (written) tradition and the performance (oral) tradition. In copying a Torah scroll, the scribe was bound to copy his text as a virtual facsimile of all other authorized Torah scrolls, with leeway to do little more than reduce or enlarge the page size of the parchment leaves. Everything else had to be true and exact and scaled to the template. The copyist faithfully began each line with the same first word, ended each line with the exact last word, and included the same number of lines and the same blank spaces which indicated the pericopes. An oversized letter was reproduced as oversized, a minuscule was copied as a minuscule. Upside-down letters, backward letters, and flawed letters—all were faithfully reproduced as seen. Even the mysterious dots that appear here and there over letters were copied. A Torah scroll that failed to be a faithful replica of its authentic prototype was unfit for use and had to be duly corrected.

The performance tradition was equally demanding. The synagogue functionary, the reader who was appointed to cantillate the biblical text, had to pronounce the consonants, vowels, stresses, and junctures in the manner that he learned from his teacher. Any error in performance was corrected immediately before the lection could be resumed. But since the text was "read," only the oral tradition was to be committed to memory, and the reader was required to follow along the manuscript with a pointer. The rote memorization of the performance tradition by the professional reader was as sacrosanct in its domain as was the scribal fidelity to the written tradition.

The task of the Masoretes in producing their redaction was not a mindless one. Without having the benefit of any explicit phonological theory, they analyzed the sound system of the liturgical tradition they ultimately chose and invented graphic symbols to represent the sounds together with an apparatus of marginal notes to call attention to all sorts of oddities and significant statistical occurrences. They also left a sophisticated literature to accompany their redaction in the form of commentary (Ben-Asher 1879). It is clear from this literature that what they accomplished was in every way an old school linguistic phonemic analysis.

The Tiberian Masoretes were not alone in their endeavors. Parallel efforts were under way in Baghdad, where a slightly different liturgical tradition served as the base. The Tiberians, however, were far more rigorous in their method, and this is why their text became quickly and almost universally the text of preference in all of the communities throughout the Diaspora. As adopted by different communities, however, the new orthography was pronounced in accordance with the native performance tradition. The Tiberian orthography, true to its liturgical base, was not representative of the actual pronunciation in the communities to which it spread.

There is a question as to what motivated the production of a Masoretic text to begin with. It is not really reasonable to believe that these labors were undertaken because the professional readers were dying out, as is assumed by some. Professional readers exist to this very day. Their training is far less arduous, but that is becaue they can rely on the printed MT, a visual aid their spiritual ancestors bequeathed to them. Moreover, they can enjoy the benefits of today's technology, which provides the cantillation model via tape recordings.

Far more reasonable is the possibility that the activity of the Masoretes was provoked by the religious controversies of their day. The obvious causal factor is Karaism, a sect in the spiritual paradigm of the Sadducees who were in authority a thousand years earlier. The Karaites (a later designation, but etymologically the same as the term used to designate the professional "readers") rejected the validity of the Oral Law and the rabbinic establishment whose authority was based on the Talmud. Karaite jurisprudence was a fundamentalist one, returning to the biblical text alone as the source of all law, supplemented only by explicit rules for permissible exegesis. The need for a definitive biblical text, with complete representation of all the meaningful phonological segments, was an urgent one for both sides in this religious schism. Indeed there are those scholars who believe the Masoretes were themselves Karaites.

While this may have been the case (although the evidence is far from conclusive), there would have been no Masoretic Text at all save for this sectarian split. The initial grammarians who rose in the wake of the Masoretes were in all likelihood Karaite as well, as were the very first authors of the commentaries. Rabbanite scholars, spiritual heirs to the Pharisees, fought fire with fire and proceeded to write their own grammars and commentaries very soon thereafter.

In their methodology, the Masoretes were indebted to the Syrian Christian scholars who performed a similar task in their community and to the Moslems who provided an orthographic vocalism for the Quran. What the Masoretes accomplished, however, was far beyond that which was produced by their teachers.

This same religious schism produced the first Hebrew grammatical studies and dictionaries. And here, too, there is an indebtedness to the world of Islam. Just as the early Islamicized Persians needed grammars of Arabic and dictionaries for their nascent religious needs, the Karaites, having rejected the entire body of oral tradition, needed grammars and dictionaries for the parsing and understanding of biblical text.

They produced the earliest grammatical works, which were written in Arabic and based on the grammatical model provided for Arabic. To take the place of rabbanite midrash, the Karaites produced the first biblical commentaries, a genre similarly borrowed from Islam and also written in Arabic. The rabbanites entered the polemic fray very quickly, under the leadership of Saadia Gaon, whose grammatical works received widespread attention (Skoss 1955).

R. Shlomo Yiṣḥaqi—better known by his acronym Rashi—who lived in the French Rhineland a century later, cites Saadia as well as the Karaite scholar Yefet ben Ali very frequently in his biblical commentary, the earliest to be written in Hebrew. It is not known whether Rashi knew Arabic or whether he had the benefit of Hebrew translations, but within another century other Jewish scholars were writing grammars and producing dictionaries in Hebrew. Foremost of these was R. David Qimḥi (1160–1235 C.E.), known by his acronym Radaq, whose *Mikhlol (Compendium)* was one of the most sophisticated grammars yet produced and whose lexicon *Sefer ha-Shorashim* (Book of Roots) remained the standard dictionary for a very long time.

Radaq's most significant contribution was a brilliant statement of the Hebrew vowel system that ironically was soon completely misinterpreted. He was the first grammarian to write about long and short vowels in Hebrew. From his discussion and especially from the examples he cites, it is evident that he is thinking in terms of what we today call morphophonemic length, not phonetic or phonemic length. While the metrical conventions he knew exceedingly well recognized long and short syllables for Hebrew versification, the short syllables were *šĕwâ* syllables, not syllables containing vowels. All vowels, except for certain instances of the high back rounded vowel u, when this vowel was treated as a *šĕwâ,* were metrically equal. For Radaq, a short vowel was one that was reducible to *šĕwâ* upon the operation of the several morphological processes. The identical vowel in another environment that was not reducible to *šĕwâ* was what he considered to be a long vowel.

What may have transformed Radaq's contribution into a serious misunderstanding was the result of two factors. The first was the translation of the *Mikhlol* into Latin, in which language phonemic vowel length was real. The second was the introduction of Arabic studies into Christian Europe. Arabic, unlike Hebrew, has phonemic vowel length. Somehow, and this view has unfortunately persisted to our very day, Arabic came to be regarded as the model of what a Semitic language ought to be. It was therefore natural to believe that Hebrew had to have a vowel structure very much like that of Arabic.

More recently, biblical studies in European scholarly circles have stimulated additional grammatical and lexicographic productivity. Foremost is the name of Gesenius, whose works in both areas have undergone several editions, including the most recent editions by other scholars who have recognized their indebtedness to Gesenius by making his name the generic equivalent of biblical Hebrew grammars and dictionaries. (The grammars: in German, GK, GKB; in English, GKC. The lexicons: in German, GesB; in English, BDB. Recent study of Hebrew is surveyed by Waldman [1989]).

Grammatical consideration of Tannaitic Hebrew has come into its own only recently with the publication of a reference grammar first in Hebrew and later in an English translation (Segal 1927). Studies in modern Hebrew are primarily, but not exclusively, the product of Israeli scholars, many of whom worked under the aegis of the Vaad ha-Lashon (the Language Council) in the days of the British Mandate, and of the National Language Academy since the independence of Israel.

Bibliography

Adams, W. J., Jr., and Adams, L. L. 1977. Language Drift and the Dating of Biblical Passages. *HS* 18: 160–64.

Ben-Asher, A. 1879. *Dikduke Ha-Te'amim,* ed. S. Baer and H. L. Strack. Leipzig.

Carmi, T., ed. 1981. *The Penguin Book of Hebrew Verse.* New York.

Coffin, E. A. 1968. *Ibn Janah's Grammar of Hebrew.* Diss., Michigan.

Delsman, W. C. 1982. Zur Sprache des Buches Koheleth. Pp. 341–65 in *Von Kanaan bis Kerala,* ed. W. C. Delsman et al. AOAT 211. Kevelaer and Neukirchen-Vluyn.

Di Lella, A. 1966. *The Hebrew Text of Sirach.* The Hague.

Eissfeldt, O. 1965. *The Old Testament: An Introduction.* Trans. P. R. Ackroyd. New York.

Fredericks, D. C. 1988. *Qoheleth's Language.* Ancient Near Eastern Texts and Studies 3. Lewiston, NY.

Garr, W. R. 1985. *Dialect Geography of Syria-Palestine, 1000–586 B.C.E.* Philadelphia.

Hrushovski, B. 1981. Notes on the Systems of Hebrew Versification. Pp. 57–75 in Carmi 1981.

Jaroš, K. 1982. *Hundert Inschriften aus Kanaan und Israel.* Fribourg.

Kahle, P. 1947. *The Cairo Geniza.* London.

Kuryłowicz, J. 1964. *L'apophonie en sémitique.* Cracow.

Kutscher, E. Y. 1982. *A History of the Hebrew Language.* Ed. R. Kutscher. Jerusalem.

Margalioth, M. 1966. *Sepher ha-Razim.* Jerusalem.

Polzin, R. 1976. *Late Biblical Hebrew.* HSM 12. Missoula, MT.

Puech, E. 1986. Origine de l'alphabet: documents en alphabet linéaire et cunéiforme du IIe millénaire. *RB* 93: 161–213.
Qimron, E. 1986. *The Hebrew of the Dead Sea Scrolls.* Atlanta.
Ruhlen, M. 1987. *A Guide to the World's Languages.* Vol. 1, *Classification.* Stanford.
Schoors, A. 1989. Review of Fredericks 1988. *JBL* 108: 698–700.
Schramm, G. M. 1964. *The Graphemes of Tiberian Hebrew.* Berkeley.
Segal, M. H. 1927. *Mishnaic Hebrew.* Oxford.
Skoss, S. L. 1955. *Saadia Gaon, The Earliest Hebrew Grammarian.* Philadelphia.
Smelik, K. A. D. 1987. *Historische Dokumente aus dem alten Israel.* Trans. H. Weippert. Göttingen.
Suder, R. W. 1984. *Hebrew Inscriptions: A Classified Bibliography.* Cranbury, NJ; Mississauga, Ont.; and London.
Waldman, N. 1989. *The Recent Study of Hebrew.* Winona Lake, IN.
Waltke, B., and O'Connor, M. 1990. *An Introduction to Biblical Hebrew Syntax.* Winona Lake, IN.
Wesselius, J. W. 1987. Thoughts about Balaam: The Historical Background of the Deir Alla Inscription on Plaster. *BiOr* 44: 589–99.

Gene M. Schramm

HITTITE

The language generally known today as "Hittite" was actually referred to by its speakers as "Nesite," after the city of Kaneš/Neša (modern Kültepe, near Kayseri in central Turkey). Early researchers naturally, but prematurely, assigned the appellation "Hittite" to the language of the Hittite state, but the ancients themselves applied this term to the indigenous tongue of central Anatolia, which was gradually supplanted by Indo-European languages during the early 2d millennium B.C. Since this fact became known only after much had already been written about "Hittite," the designation has been retained for the Indo-European idiom, while the earlier language in Anatolia is now called "Hattic" (Güterbock 1959).

Hittite is the earliest attested member of the Indo-European language family, documented by cuneiform tablets written during the 17th through the 13th centuries B.C. Hittite is also the best known representative of the Anatolian branch of Indo-European, which also includes Palaic and Luwian from the 2d millennium, as well as Lydian and Lycian of the Classical period. It is now known that the "Hieroglyphic Hittite" employed in Syria and SE Anatolia in the early 1st millennium is actually a dialect of the older Luwian. Finally, while certainly an Indo-European language spoken in Anatolia, Phrygian entered this area later and is not closely related to these tongues. The poorly understood Carian and Etruscan languages are no longer generally assigned to the Indo-European family (Kammenhuber 1969: 134–61; Oettinger 1978).

Some controversy exists over the relationship of the Anatolian group to the other Indo-European languages. Most authorities hold that Anatolian is a branch on a equal footing with all other subfamilies, such as Indo-Iranian or Germanic (Kammenhuber 1961). Adherents of the "Indo-Hittite hypothesis," however, stress that a number of grammatical features set Anatolian apart from the remainder of the family; these features include the extremely simple morphology of the verb and the absence of a feminine gender from the nominal inflection. This situation might be explained by postulating the separation of Anatolian from the language group at a very early time, leaving the common ancestor of the other tongues a significant period of independent development before additional divergence occurred (Cowgill 1975). That is, Anatolian is perhaps an "aunt" rather than a "sister" of the other branches of Indo-European. The matter remains for the moment unresolved.

The bulk of the Hittite material, an estimated 25,000 tablets and fragments, has been recovered from the ruins of a single city, the Hittite capital Ḫattuša. Today, this is the site of the Turkish village of Boğazköy (Boğazkale), located approximately 100 miles E of Ankara. A few texts have also been found at Maşat Höyük in Turkey (Alp 1980), at Ras Shamra/Ugarit and Meskene/Emar in Syria (Laroche 1980), and at other scattered locations.

Two Hittite letters were among the tablets discovered in 1887 at Tell el-Amarna in Egypt (Knudtzon 1902), and explorations conducted by E. Chantre at Boğazköy in 1893–1894 produced a number of fragments in this language, but philological research into Hittite began in earnest only after the excavations of H. Winkler and Th. Makridi at the Hittite capital from 1906 through 1912 (Bittel 1970: 7–10). In 1915 the decipherment of Hittite was announced (Hrozný 1915), and as a result of the efforts of such pioneers as B. Hrozný, E. Forrer, F. Sommer, J. Friedrich, A. Goetze, E. Sturtevant, and H. Ehelolf, great progress was soon made in publishing the textual material, recovering the basic grammar of Hittite, translating important groups of texts, and analyzing the language from the perspective of Indo-European linguistics. Today, it is possible to understand most Hittite texts, although some uncertainties, chiefly lexical and phonological, remain.

Initial study of the Hittite documents was made easier by the scribal practice of indicating many words by an Akkadian or Sumerian writing ("ideogram"), rather than by spelling them phonetically in Hittite. Since the Mesopotamian languages were already well understood, it was often possible to discern the basic content of a text before Hittite had been fully deciphered. A negative consequence of this scribal habit, however, is that we still remain uncertain about a number of very common Hittite words, such as those for "son" and "horse," for which ideograms were consistently employed. While the graphic representation of Hittite abounds with "Sumerograms" and "Akkadograms," the language itself was little influenced by these Mesopotamian idioms. On the other hand, the Hittite lexicon was greatly enriched by borrowings from Hattic (chiefly in the area of political institutions), from Hurrian (particularly in the religious sphere), and from the closely related Luwian.

The tablets found at Boğazköy were originally written to serve the needs of the government of the Hittite kings in all its aspects, religious and secular. Therefore, texts of greatly varied genre were produced (Güterbock 1964; Laroche 1971), although most ephemeral economic documents were inscribed on wood, which perished long ago (Otten 1955: 79–80). Attested are royal and bureaucratic correspondence, as well as administrative documents such as land grants and instructions for officials. The Hittite kings issued a law code and contracted treaties with vassals and equals. They extolled their manly deeds in annals and justified their conduct before the gods in prayers. Other religious texts recovered include programs for the ceremonies of the state cult and rituals for life crises such as birth and death. Additional rituals were intended to counteract sorcery, disease, or other misfortune. Records of divination make up another large group of texts. Finally, scholarly material employed in scribal education presents translations of foreign literature, as well as such portions of the Mesopotamian scribal curriculum as lexical texts and astrological handbooks (Beckman 1983). Much of this scholarly material is bilingual (Akkadian-Hittite) or trilingual (Sumerian-Akkadian-Hittite) in form. In addition, a significant number of the Boğazköy texts were composed in whole or in part in foreign languages—in Akkadian, Hattic, Hurrian, Luwian, or Palaic (Forrer 1919).

The Indo-European migrations into Anatolia probably took place during the second half of the 3d millennium B.C., but opinion is divided as to just when speakers of Hittite arrived, as well as to the direction from which they came. In any case, the appearance of Hittite personal names and loanwords of Hittite origin in Akkadian documents of the Assyrian trading colonies demonstrates their presence by the 19th century B.C. (Macqueen 1986: 26–35). It is significant that the variety of cuneiform script employed in Hittite texts differs entirely from that used by the Assyrian merchants. The cuneiform of the Boğazköy texts resembles most closely the systems of early 2d millennium N Syria, from which it was probably imported by the Hittite kings of the 17th century who campaigned successfully in this area (Laroche 1978: 739–48). It seems that speakers of Anatolian had been illiterate before this time.

The tablets composing the Hittite archives were to a large extent broken and scattered about Ḫattuša in antiquity, as a result not only of the destruction which brought the Hittite period to an end, but also because of the rebuilding efforts of later inhabitants of the site (Otten 1955: 71–74). This state of affairs, combined with the absence of a native chronological system in the cuneiform records, forced scholars initially to date texts entirely on the basis of an interpretation of their contents. Since Hittite rulers shared a rather small number of throne names, and many texts contain no proper nouns at all, this situation was unsatisfactory.

However, in 1952 a fragmentary tablet displaying peculiarities of script and presentation of text was discovered in an archaeologically certain Old Hittite level at Boğazköy (Otten 1953). This key has allowed scholars to identify other pieces sharing these formal characteristics as products of the earliest period of Hittite literacy. In turn, the distinctive textual features of Old Hittite texts—grammar, orthography, lexicon—may be abstracted from this corpus. Finally, this process makes it possible to recognize later manuscripts of earlier compositions, since scribes seldom modernized completely the material which they recopied. Thus bodies of texts belonging to the Old Hittite (17th and 16th centuries), Middle Hittite (15th century), and New Hittite (14th and 13th centuries) periods of the language have been established (Neu and Rüster 1973; Košak 1980). Although significant differences of opinion persist among Hittitologists concerning details (Heinhold-Krahmer et al. 1979), it is along such lines that much of the most important recent research in Hittite has been carried out.

Bibliography

Alp, S. 1980. Die hethitischen Tontafelentdeckungen auf dem Maşat-Höyük. Vorläufiger Bericht. *Türk Tarih Kurumu Belleten* 173: 25–59.

Beckman, G. 1983. Mesopotamians and Mesopotamian Learning at Ḫattuša. *JCS* 35: 97–114.

Bittel, K. 1970. *Hattusha: The Capital of the Hittites.* New York.

Cowgill, W. 1975. More Evidence for Indo-Hittite: The Tense-Aspect Systems. Pp. 557–70 in *Proceedings of the Eleventh International Congress of Linguists* (1970). Bologna.

Forrer, E. 1919. Die acht Sprachen der Boghazköi-Inschriften. *SPAW* 53: 1029–41.

Friedrich, T. 1932. *Kleinasiatische Sprachdenkmäler.* Kleine Texte 163. Berlin.

Güterbock, H. G. 1959. Toward a Definition of the Term Hittite. *Oriens* 10: 233–39.

———. 1964. A View of Hittite Literature. *JAOS* 84: 107–15.

Heinhold-Krahmer, S., et al. 1979. *Probleme der Textdatierung in der Hethitologie.* Texte der Hethiter 11. Heidelberg.

Hrozný, B. 1915. Die Lösung des hethitischen Problems. *MDOG* 56: 17–50.

Kammenhuber, A. 1961. Zur Stellung des Hethitisch-Luvischen innerhalb der indogermanischen Gemeinsprache. *Zeitschrift für vergleichende Sprachforschung* 77: 31–75.

———. 1969. Hethitisch, Palaisch, Luwisch und Hieroglyphenluwisch. Pp. 119–357 in *Altkleinasiatische Sprachen,* ed. J. Friedrich et al. HO 1/2/1–2/2. Leiden.

Knudtzon, J. 1902. *Die zwei Arzawa-Briefe: Die ältesten Urkunden in indo-germanischer Sprache.* Leipzig.

Košak, S. 1980. Dating of Hittite Texts: A Test. *AnSt* 30: 31–39.

Laroche, E. 1971. *Catalogue des textes hittites.* Paris.

———. 1972. Linguistique asianique. Pp. 112–35 in *Acta Mycenaea,* ed. M. Ruipérez. Salamanca.

———. 1978. Problèmes de l'écriture cunéiforme hittite. *Annali di Scuola Normale Superiore di Pisa,* Cl. di lettere e filosofia 3/8/3: 739–53.

———. 1980. Emar, étape entre Babylone et le Hatti. Pp. 235–44 in *Le moyen Euphrat,* ed. J. Margueron. Strasbourg.

Macqueen, J. 1986. *The Hittites and Their Contemporaries in Asia Minor.* Rev. ed. New York.

Neu, E., and Rüster, C. 1973. Zur Datierung hethitischer Texte. Pp. 221–42 in *Festschrift Heinrich Otten,* ed. E. Neu and C. Rüster. Wiesbaden.

Oettinger, N. 1978. Die Gliederung des anatolischen Sprachgebietes. *Zeitschrift für vergleichende Sprachforschung* 92: 74–92.

Otten, H. 1953. Die inschriftlichen Funde [der Ausgrabungen in Boğazköy im Jahre 1952]. *MDOG* 86: 59–64.

———. 1955. Bibliotheken im Alten Orient. *Altertum* 1: 67–81.

Grammars

Friedrich, J. 1960. *Hethitisches Elementarbuch.* 2d ed. Pt. 1. Heidelberg.

Meriggi, P. 1980. Schizzo grammaticale dell'Anatolico. *AANLR* 8/24/3: 243–409.

Rosenkranz, B. 1978. *Vergleichende Untersuchungen der altanatolischen Sprachen.* The Hague.

Sturtevant, E., and Hahn, E. 1951. *A Comparative Grammar of the Hittite Language.* 2d ed. Philadelphia.

Dictionaries

Friedrich, J. 1952. *Hethitisches Wörterbuch.* 1st ed. Heidelberg. (Supplements appeared in 1957, 1961, and 1965.)

Friedrich, J., and Kammenhuber, A. 1975–. *Hethitisches Wörterbuch.* 2d ed. Heidelberg.

Güterbock, H. G., and Hoffner, H., eds. 1980–. *The Hittite Dictionary of the Oriental Institute of the University of Chicago.* Chicago.

Puhvel, J. 1984–. *Hittite Etymological Dictionary.* New York.

Tischler, J. 1977–. *Hethitisches Etymologisches Glossar.* Innsbruck.

GARY BECKMAN

HURRIAN

Hurrian is the name of the language spoken and written by the ancient Hurrians. The earliest Hurrian text dates to the first half of the 20th century B.C.E. (late Akkad or Ur III period); inscribed on a limestone tablet held by a bronze lion, it records a temple foundation by Tish-atal of Urkish. Among the thousands of Akkadian (Old Babylonian) texts from Mari, dating to the 18th century, were also found seven Hurrian texts; most of these are cultic in nature, although one is a fragment of a royal letter. The longest Hurrian text is a letter of nearly 500 lines sent by Tushratta, king of Mittanni, to the Egyptian pharaoh Amenophis III in the first half of the 14th century; the letter is the only Hurrian text in the famous archive of cuneiform texts found at el-Amarna in Egypt (see further below). The largest number of Hurrian texts have been found among the clay tablets excavated at Boğazköy, ancient Hattusas, the capital of the Hittite empire; the majority of these texts, which date to the 14th–13th centuries B.C.E., are rituals, although there are some omens and a few mythological texts. The Syrian seaport of Ugarit, where texts in Sumerian, Akkadian, Hittite, Egyptian, and the local Ugaritic language have been unearthed, has also yielded a significant number of Hurrian texts from the same period as those found at Boğazköy. Some 40 of the Ugarit texts, like Hurrian texts from other sites, are written in the same logo-syllabic cuneiform script as the Mesopotamian languages (Sumerian and Akkadian) and Hittite; of these, 30 cultic texts and one letter are written entirely in Hurrian, but there are also a short Hurrian-Akkadian bilingual literary text, a Sumerian-Hurrian bilingual lexical text, and several exemplars of a Sumerian-Akkadian-Hurrian-Ugaritic vocabulary. Besides the syllabic cuneiform texts, however, Ugarit has yielded a few Hurrian texts written in the indigenous alphabetic cuneiform. Excavations during the 1970s at the site of Emar on the Euphrates also produced a few Hurrian divination texts written in Mesopotamian cuneiform and dating to the 14th–13th centuries. In addition to the texts listed here that are actually written in Hurrian, the phonology, morphology, syntax, and vocabulary of Hurrian are also present to varying degrees as substrate influences in the grammar of the Akkadian texts written by scribes in the latter half of the 2d millennium at sites such as Alalakh, Emar, Hattusas, Nuzi, and Ugarit, and in the el-Amarna letters of the Mittannian king Tushratta. Hurrian personal names also abound in texts from sites across N Mesopotamia and Syria as well as Anatolia through much of the 2d millennium B.C.E.

Despite the relatively large number of texts found, Hurrian vocabulary and grammar, and therefore Hurrian texts, have remained imperfectly understood. This circumstance has been the result of two factors. One difficulty is that Hurrian has as its only certain linguistic relative Urartian, the language of Urarṭu around Lake Van (E Turkey), attested in the 9th–6th centuries B.C.E. (There have also been attempts to classify Hurrian and Urartian as a branch of the Caucasian languages; the connection, if valid, is very remote.) While comparison with Urartian can help to clarify some Hurrian features, Urartian is not a direct descendant of Hurrian and is itself not fully understood. The linguistic isolation of Hurrian and Urartian means that researchers cannot look to similar related languages to explicate features of grammar. In such cases, a sufficiently long bilingual text is usually needed to serve as a key to the language. Until recently much of the reconstruction of the grammar of Hurrian was accomplished on the basis of the very long Hurrian letter of Tushratta found at el-Amarna in Egypt (see above). Because that text deals with many of the same diplomatic issues that concern the Akkadian texts in the el-Amarna corpus, a close reading of frequently occurring parallel Akkadian and Hurrian phrases has enabled scholars to ascertain many of the features of Hurrian morphology and syntax, though many uncertainties have persisted. In the 1983 and 1985 excavations at Boğazköy/Hattusas, however, a multitablet bilingual Hurrian-Hittite literary text dating to about 1400 B.C.E. was discovered (Otten and Rüster 1991); comparison of the Hurrian text with its well-understood Hittite translation promises to clarify many points of Hurrian grammar and to add considerably to our knowledge of the Hurrian lexicon.

Bibliography

Adler, H.-P. 1976. *Das Akkadische des Königs Tušratta von Mitanni.* AOAT 201. Kevelaer and Neukirchen-Vluyn.

Bush, F. W. 1964. *A Grammar of the Hurrian Language.* Diss., Brandeis.

Chačikjan, M. L. 1985. *Churritskij i urartskij jazyki.* Erevan.

Diakonoff, I. M. 1971. *Hurrisch und Urartäisch.* Münchener Studien zur Sprachwissenschaft 6. Munich.

Diakonoff, I. M., and Starostin, S. A. 1986. *Hurro-Urartian as an Eastern Caucasian Language.* Munich.

Hass, V., ed. 1988. *Hurriter und Hurritisch.* Xenia: Konstanzer Althistorische Vorträge und Forschungen 21; Konstanzer Altorientalische Symposien 2. Constance.

Huehnergard, J. 1989. *The Akkadian of Ugarit.* Harvard Semitic Studies 34. Atlanta.

Laroche, E. 1980. *Glossaire de la langue hourrite.* Paris. Originally *Revue hittite et asianique* 34–35, 1976–77.

———. 1982. Documents hittites et hourrites. Pp. 53–63 in *Meskéné-Emar: Dix ans de travaux 1972–1982,* ed. D. Beyer. Paris.

Melikišvili, G. A. 1971. *Die urartäische Sprache.* Studia Pohl 7. Rome.

Neu, E. 1988. *Das Hurritische: Eine altorientalische Sprache in neuem Licht.* Akademie der Wissenschaften und der Literatur, Abhandlungen der Geistes- und Sozialwissenschaftlichen Kl. Mainz. Akademie der Wissenschaften und der Literatur. Stuttgart.

Otten, H., and Rüster, C. 1991. *Keilschrifttexte aus Boghazköi.* Vol. 32. Berlin.

Salvini, M. 1978. Hourrite et urartéen. Pp. 157–72 in *Les Hourrites:*

Actes de la xxive Recontre Assyriologique Internationale, Paris 1977. Paris. (= *Revue Hittite et Asianique* 36).

Speiser, E. A. 1941. *Introduction to Hurrian.* AASOR 20. New Haven.

Wilhelm, G. 1970. *Untersuchungen zum Hurro-Akkadischen von Nuzi.* AOAT 9. Kevelaer.

———. 1982. *Grundzüge der Geschichte und Kultur der Hurriter.* Darmstadt.

———. 1987. [translation of letter 24]. Pp. 139–51 in *Les lettres d'el-Amarna: Correspondance diplomatique du pharaon,* ed. W. L. Moran with V. Haas and G. Wilhelm. Paris.

JOHN HUEHNERGARD

LANGUAGES OF ANCIENT IRAN

The ancient empires of the Iranian-speaking Medes and Achaemenids (559–330 B.C.) and, following the interregnum of Alexander and the Seleucids, the empires of the Parthians (247 B.C.–A.D. 227), and Sassanians (227–651 A.D.), all of which spanned the entire Near East at one time or another, played a major role in the political, intellectual, and religious history of the ANE, and thus in Judaism, Christianity, and the gnostic religions of the Mandaeans and Manichaeism. This role was continued to a lesser degree by Iranian dynasties after Islamization in the middle of the 7th century A.D. Jewish, Christian, and Mandaean communities have remained in these areas since antiquity.

The Iranian languages belong to the Indo-Iranian (Aryan) branch of Indo-European languages (see Schmitt 1987). Originating in central Asia, speakers of Iranian began to spread from about 1000 B.C. throughout the southern parts of Eurasia from China to Europe, and eventually entered the Iranian plateau and Afghanistan (Grantovskij 1970; Ghirshman 1977; Burrow 1973; Mayrhofer 1974). Today, Iranian languages are concentrated in Iran and Afghanistan, but are also found in the Caucasus, central Asia, W China, on the Arab side of the Persian Gulf, and in Iraq, Syria, and Turkey (Geiger and Kuhn 1895–1904; Schmitt 1989; Spuler, 1958; Rastorgueva 1975; Abaev et al. 1979–82; Oranskij 1977). The most numerous non-Iranian languages are Turkic, and these have permeated central Asia and large areas of Afghanistan and Iran (some 20 percent of the Iranian population).

A. Old Iranian
B. Middle Iranian Languages
C. New Iranian Languages
D. Diachrony
E. Religious Minorities
F. Language Contact
G. Aramaic
H. Writing Systems

A. Old Iranian

The court language (often called Old Persian) of the Achaemenid dynasty is represented by a rather limited corpus of inscriptions and is based on the local language of the SW Iranian province of Parsa (Greek *persis,* "Persia," modern Fars; Kent 1953; Brandenstein and Mayrhofer 1964). Avestan (probably a calque on Greek *epistēmē,* "received knowledge"), the sacred language of the Zoroastrians was originally spoken perhaps in NE Iran or central Asia and is represented by a much more extensive corpus of texts, ranging from the Gathas of Zarathustra (of uncertain date, but possibly 1000 B.C.) to texts composed by priests during late-Achaemenid and possibly later times. The oldest preserved mss date from the 13th century A.D. (Jackson 1892; Reichelt 1909; Beekes 1988). Median, spoken in central Iran and the language of the predecessors of the Achaemenids (see Mayrhofer 1968), and other Old Iranian languages such as Scythian in S Russia and Old Parthian in E Iran, are known only by a small number of words and names scattered throughout the writings of other languages.

B. Middle Iranian Languages

Middle Iranian languages show a clear dialectal division into West Iranian, viz. Parthian and Middle Persian, and East Iranian, represented by the remainder. Parthian was the official language of the Parthians and was spoken in NE and probably also NW Iran. There are also extensive texts in Manichaean Parthian found in Chinese Turkistan which evidence the continuation of Parthian as one of the languages of the Manichaean Church in E Iran and central Asia until about the 10th century A.D. (Ghilain 1939; Heston 1976; Brunner 1977). Middle Persian, the official language of the Sassanians (227–651 A.D.) and thus also of their state religion, Zorastrianism, is also attested in various forms, the most extensive texts being written in so-called (Book-) Pahlavi. Most of these date from the 9th century A.D. but represent an earlier stage of the language. This language was also used by Christians. Middle Persian was one of the church languages of the Manichaeans in E Iran and central Asia, Mani (d. 277 A.D.) himself having composed a book in this language for Shapur I. The language continued to be used until the 11th century A.D. in both churches, as evidenced, for example, by the signatures of witnesses on a copperplate grant to the Syrian Church in S India (possibly 9th century A.D.) and by some local dynasties (Nyberg 1964, 1974; Heston 1976; Brunner 1977; MacKenzie 1971).

The eastern Middle Iranian languages, viz. Alanian, Khwarezmian (Henning 1955; Heston 1976), Sogdian (Gershevitch 1954), Saka (Emmerick 1968), and Skytho-Sarmatian and Bactrian (Humbach 1966), were spoken from S Russia to central Asia (including N Afghanistan), and in western China.

C. New Iranian Languages

(New) Persian emerged after Islamization as the dominant language of Persia. It was, and largely still is, the lingua franca in most of these areas, and it also was the adopted court language of the Mogul sultanate of Delhi in India (1526–1857 A.D.). It is spoken in a number of varieties, the three most important of which are Iranian Persian (Windfuhr 1979; Lazard 1963), Dari in Afghanistan, and Tajiki in Soviet Tajikistan. Together with other Perside dialects, these constitute the so-called "Southwest" Iranian dialects. The other West Iranian dialects include Kurdish in the W and NW, from the Soviet Caucasus, E Turkey, E Syria, and N Iraq to NW Iran, and scattered through much of Iran (MacKenzie 1961), and Baluchi in the east, stretching from the city of Merv in Soviet Turkmenistan to the Gulf into S Afghanistan and Pakistan (Elfenbein 1966).

East Iranian dialects include isolated Ossetic, the successor of Alanian, in the N Caucasus (Abaev 1964). The remainder are located in Afghanistan, the Hindukush, and the Pamirs, most importantly Pashto, the official language of Afghanistan besides Persian, which is found in SE Afghanistan and in neighboring regions of Pakistan (Morgenstierne 1927; Penzl 1955).

D. Diachrony

Linguistically, the Old Iranian languages continue the highly inflectional character of Indo-European. The tendency toward simplification is already seen in Old Persian in the 4th century B.C., largely concomitant with a shift in stress patterns, such that the original synthetic inflection was largely lost and replaced by analytic constructions. Middle Persian and Parthian are the result of those changes. The existence of masculine/feminine gender in several modern dialects of NW Iran shows that these dialects are a continuation of Old and Middle languages which must have been distinct from Middle Persian and Parthian. Similarly, the modern East Iranian languages continue the inherited inflection to some degree. On the other hand, all modern languages and dialects, including Persian, developed new formations and categorical distinctions, resulting in radically restructured morphosemantic verbal and case systems (Tedesco 1921; Lentz 1926; Windfuhr 1975).

E. Religious Minorities

Of the old religious minorities, the Zoroastrians, concentrated in the desert cities of Yazd and Kerman, have retained their central W Iranian dialect. The Armenian and Georgian Christians in and near the central city of Esfahan have retained their Indo-European Armenian and Caucasian Georgian language, respectively.

Many Jewish communities have adopted Persian. Judeo-Persian has a long-standing literary history. In fact, the oldest preserved texts in New Persian are written in the Hebrew script: a private letter from the 8th century A.D., found near Khotan in Chinese Turkistan; three brief inscriptions, dated 752 A.D., found in E Afghanistan; and a 9th-century inscription found in S India in Travancore. These texts are evidence for the use of the new vernacular by minorities as opposed to the continued official use of Pahlavi, Sogdian, and of course the new dominant language, Arabic. Many contemporary Jewish communities in Iran have retained the local Iranian dialects (Lazard 1968, 1974), while the Muslim population switched to Persian. Of particular interest is a "secret" language, called Loteraʾi, which is used by Jews throughout Iran (Yarshater 1977). While the nominal and verbal morphology is Iranian (usually the local dialect), the vocabulary is replete with Semitic words, mostly Hebrew but also Aramaic. It appears that the latter reflects the original situation, which may go back to antiquity, while the former were absorbed later. Compare, for example, the following sentence in Loteraʾi with the same in the dialect of Golpayegan (compare Book-Pahlavi, below):

ANNI BĀY-un b(e)-EZ-on xiābān, š-on vā-(e)-EZ -on
mon g -un be -š -on xiābān, š-on o var-e -gard-on
I want to go out (lit. in the street); I shall go and return.

Yarshater (1977: 2) analyzes this as follows: ANNI < Heb *ʾani,* "I"; BĀY < Aram *bāy,* "want"; EZ < Aram/Heb *ʿzl,* "to go." Golpaygani *-un/-on* is a first singular ending, *be-* a subjunctive prefix, *vā-/var-* is verbal prefix "back," *e-* is an imperfective prefix, here marking the future.

F. Language Contact

In view of the fact that Old Iranian and much of Middle Iranian is not well attested, Iranian loans in contemporary non-Iranian languages are an important source for the diachrony and dialectology of Iranian linguistics. Those languages include Elamite, the language of the predecessors of the Achaemenids in Fars and one of the administrative languages at Persepolis (Paper 1955), Akkadian, Armenian (since Achaemenid times), and, to a lesser degree, Old Egyptian, Greek, Lydian and Lycian, Latin, Indic, and, later, Arabic (Mayrhofer 1971; Schmitt 1973; Hinz 1975; Mayrhofer 1978; Schmitt 1978; Rossi 1981).

G. Aramaic

The Neo-Aramaic dialects of the contemporary Jewish, Christian, and Mandaean minorities and the Iranian languages form one of the most striking cases of linguistic symbiosis. It has lasted for some 2,500 years, with both Aramaic and Iranian fairly well known throughout this time. The most decisive event in this relationship was the adoption of Aramaic as the administrative language of the Achaemenid empire. While Aramaic influence on Iranian is limited (Weryho 1971), the main recipient was Eastern Aramaic from the 6th century B.C. on, most noticeably in the lexicon with many of the typically Indo-European Iranian compounds, most dramatically in Babylonian Middle Aramaic. Included were not only Iranian names and titles but also administrative, military, and everyday terms (e.g., *dt* [Dan 6:8, etc.] < OP *dāta,* "law, justice," and the compound noun *dtbrʾ* [Dan 3:2–3] < OP *dāta-bāra,* "judge"). They are found in the Aramaic parts of Daniel and Ezra (also in the Hebrew of Ezra, Esther, Nehemiah, and Daniel; i.e., the books dealing with the Achaemenid period), and in Aramaic inscriptions and other texts found throughout the empire from Egypt, Asia Minor, and the Caucasus all the way to Afghanistan. Included in this group are texts on papyrus and leather from Egypt, such as the so-called Driver documents (13 letters, apparently sent to Egypt from Babylonia or Persia in the later 5th century B.C., which are replete with Old Persian loans), a translation of two royal inscriptions, the administrative clay tablets from Persepolis, and legends on coins, seals, mortars, and pestles. Middle Iranian loanwords are found in the rabbinic writings of Babylon such as the Talmud and the Midrash, in Babylonian magic texts, and in Christian writings in E Syriac. The majority of these Middle Iranian loans are not Persian but NW Iranian, reflecting the Parthian dialect of the Arsacid rulers, and possibly also symbiotic Iranian dialects. That is the case with the Neo-Aramaic dialects in Iranian and Iraqi Kurdistan today, which naturally show much greater interference from neighboring Iranian dialects such as Kurdish (Telegdi 1935).

Linguistically more significant, this contact led to the radical restructuring of the East Aramaic tense system. Specifically, Old Persian had developed a new periphrastic past tense based on the perfect participle in which the agent (subject) is expressed not by the direct (nominative) case but by the oblique (dative/genitive) case, whereas the patient (direct object) is in the direct case and/or marked by the personal ending. This also developed in East Aramaic, e.g., OP *mana kṛtam asti,* "I have made," lit. "to, by me made it is," and E Aram. *šmyᶜ-ly,* "I have heard," where the participle *šmyᶜ* is followed by *ly,* which is from *l-y,* originally "by, to me" (Kutscher 1977: 70–89; Polotzky 1979. This past tense construction, later confined to transitive-causative verbs, is not to be mistaken as a "passive," which continued to exist, was not confined to the past, and did not allow the mention of the agent.)

H. Writing Systems

Most Iranian scripts are varieties of, and developments from, Aramaic. See ARAMAIC SCRIPT. The exceptions are the 36 signs of the Old Persian cuneiform (Diakonoff 1970; LeCoq 1974; Windfuhr 1970), Bactrian written in a variety of the Greek alphabet (evidence for the Greek intermezzo in Afghanistan and central Asia), and Saka, which is written in a form of central Asian Brahmi, the origin of which is still debated. Religion played a major part in the adoption or use of a script. Thus, with Mani being a native speaker of Aramaic, Manichaean Parthian and Middle Persian are written in a script most similar to Aramaic. Khwarezmian and Buddhist Sogdian are written in another form of Aramaic, Manichaean Sogdian is in the Manichaean script, and Christian Sogdian is written in the Syriac script.

Quite early Aramaic began to be used heterographically so that Aramaic words, not infrequently in inflected forms, could stand as symbols for Iranian ones. Later, Iranian endings, or parts of Iranian words, began to be added as a mnemonic device. The final stage of Sassanian Middle Persian writing, i.e., the cursive Book-Pahlavi of the Zoroastrian writings, mostly dating from the 9th century, still retains many heterographs. For example:

GBRʾ	ZY	*pyl*	TMH	*dyt*	MN-W	LWT-H	*gwspn-dʾn*	*pd*	*dšt*	*kwp*	YḤWWNt	ḤWH-*d*
mard	*ī*	*pīr*	*anōh*	*dīd*	*kē*	*abāg*	*gospandān*	*pad*	*dašt*	*kōf*	*būd*	*hēnd*

"There he saw some old men who lived on plains and mountains with their sheep" (Brunner 1977: 4). The adjectival construct with GBRʾ ZY *pyl* stands for Persian */mard ī pīr/,* "man-relational marker-old" = "old man," TMH for */anōh/,* "there," MN-W for */kē/,* "who," LWT-H for */abāg/,* "with," *t* in YḤWWNt to mark participial *t* and *d* to mark the third person plural copula */hēnd/* in the periphrastic past YḤWWNt ḤWH-*d* for */būt hēnd/,* "they were, have been."

In this writing system, the letter shapes had partially merged so that the original 22 letters were reduced to 14. (On the development of the Middle Iranian scripts, specifically Book-Pahlavi, see Henning *apud* Spuler 1958: 21–40; Kutscher 1970: 393–99; Nyberg 1974 2: 1–7, Humbach 1974; Humbach and Skjaervo 1983 3/2: 132–9; Delauney 1985). In order to record the then orthodox pronunciation of the sacred Avestan texts as accurately as possible, an ingenious Avestan alphabet was invented during Sassanid times (possibly the 6th century A.D.), based on the Book-Pahlavi script. Its 48 (originally 60) signs distinguish not only long and short vowels but also minute conditioned variants of the consonants, aspiration, palatalization, etc. (Morgenstierne 1942; Windfuhr 1972).

Finally, Late Khwarezmian is written in Arabic. In fact, the Arabic script is now used for all literary modern Iranian languages except those used in the Soviet Union.

Bibliography

Abaev, V. I. 1964. *A Grammatical Sketch of Ossetic.* Trans. S. Hill. The Hague.

Abaev, V. I.; Bogoljubov, M. N.; and Rastorgueva, V. S., eds. 1979–82. *Osnovy iranskogo jazykoznanija* [Foundations of Iranian linguistics]. 3 vols. Moscow.

Beekes, R. S. P. 1988. *A Grammar of Gatha-Avestan.* Leiden.

Brandenstein, W., and Mayrhofer, M. 1964. *Handbuch des Altpersischen.* Wiesbaden.

Brunner, C. 1977. *A Syntax of Western Middle Iranian.* Delmar, NY.

Burrow, T. 1973. The Proto-Indoaryans. *JRAS* 1973: 123–40.

Delauney, J. A. 1985. L'araméen d'Empire et les débuts de l'écriture en Asie Centrale. *Acta Iranica* 2: 219–36.

Diakonoff, I. M. 1970. The Origin of the 'Old Persian' Writing System and the Ancient Oriental Epigraphic and Annalistic Traditions. Pp. 98–124 in *W. B. Henning Memorial Volume,* ed. M. Boyce and I. Gershevitch. London.

Elfenbein, J. H. 1966. *The Baluchi Language: A Dialectology with Texts.* London.

Emmerick, R. E. 1968. *Saka Grammatical Studies.* London.

Geiger, W., and Kuhn, E., eds. 1895–1904. *Grundriss der Iranischen Philologie.* Vol. 1. Strasbourg.

Gershevitch, I. 1954. *A Grammar of Manichaean Sogdian.* Oxford.

Ghilain, A. 1939. *Essai sur la langue parthe, son système verbal d'après les textes manichéens du Turkestan oriental.* Louvain.

Ghirshman, R. 1977. *L'Iran et la migration des Indo-Aryéns et des Iraniens.* Leiden.

Grantovskij, E. A. 1970. *Rannaja istorija iranskikh plemen Perednej Azii* [The early history of the Iranian peoples of SW Asia]. Moscow.

Henning, W. B. 1933. Das Verbum des Mittelpersischen der Turfanfragmente. *Zeitschrift für Indologie und Iranistik* 9: 158–253.

———. 1955. The Khwarezmian Language. Pp. 421–36 in *Symbolae in Honorem Zekidi Veledi Togan.* Istanbul.

Heston, W. 1976. *Selected Problems in 5th to 10th Cent. Iranian Syntax.* Diss., Pennsylvania.

Hinz, W. 1975. *Altiranisches Sprachgut der Nebenüberlieferungen.* Wiesbaden.

Humbach, H. 1966. *Baktrische Sprachdenkmäler,* Teil 1, mit Beiträgen von Adolf Grohmann. Wiesbaden.

———. 1974. Aramaeo-Iranian and Pahlavi. *Acta Iranica* 1/2: 237–44.

Humbach, H., and Skjaervo, P. O. 1983. *The Sassanian Inscription of Paikuli.* Wiesbaden.

Jackson, A. V. W. 1892. *An Avesta Grammar in Comparison with Sanskrit.* Stuttgart.

Kent, R. 1953. *Old Persian: Grammar, Texts, Lexicon.* 2d rev. ed. New Haven.

Kutscher, E. 1970. Aramaic. Pp. 347–412 in *Current Trends in Linguistics* 6. Ed. T. Sebeok. The Hague.

———. 1977. *Hebrew and Aramaic Studies,* ed. Z. Ben-Ḥayyim, A. Dotan, and G. Sarfatti. Jerusalem.

Lazard, G. 1963. *La langue des plus anciens monuments de la prose persane.* Paris.

———. 1968. La dialectologie du judéo-persan. *Studies in Bibliography and Booklore* 8: 77–98.
———. 1974. Judeo-Persian ii. Language. *Encyclopedia of Islam* 4: 308–13.
LeCoq, P. 1974. La langue des inscriptions achémenides. *Acta Iranica* 2: 55–62.
Lentz, W. 1926. Die nordiranischen Elemente in der neupersischen Literatursprache bei Firdōsi. *Zeitschrift für Indologie und Iranistik* 2/4: 251–316.
MacKenzie, D. 1961–62. *Kurdish Dialect Studies.* 2 vols. London.
———. 1971. *A Concise Pahlavi Dictionary.* London.
Mayrhofer, M. 1968. Die Rekonstruktion des Medischen. *AÖAW* 105: 1–22.
———. 1971. *Aus der Namenwelt Alt-Irans. Die zentrale Rolle der Namensforschung in der Linguistik des Alt-Iranischen.* Innsbruck.
———. 1974. *Die Arier im Vorderen Orient.* SÖAW 294/3. Vienna.
———. 1978. Die Nebenüberlieferung des Altwestiranischen. Zu einem Buche von Walther Hinz. *AfO* 25: 179–84.
Morgenstierne, G. 1927. *An Etymological Vocabulary of Pashto.* Skrifter utgitt av det Norske Videnskaps-Akademi i Oslo 2. Oslo.
———. 1942. Orthography and Sound-System of the Avesta. *Norsk Tidsskrift for Sprogvidenskab* 12: 30–82.
Nyberg, H. S. 1964, 1974. *A Manual of Pahlavi.* Wiesbaden.
Oranskij, I. M. 1977. *Les langues iraniennes.* Trans. J. Blau. Institut d'Études Iraniennes de l'Université de la Sorbonne nouvelle. Documents et ouvrages de reference 1. Paris.
Paper, H. H. 1955. *The Phonology and Morphology of Royal Achaemenid Elamite.* Ann Arbor.
Penzl, H. 1955. *A Grammar of Pashto: A Descriptive Study of the Dialect of Kandahar, Afghanistan.* Washington, DC.
Polotsky, H. 1979. Verbs with Two Objects in Modern Syriac (Urmi). *IOS* 9: 204–27.
Rastorgueva, V. S., ed. 1975. *Opyt istoriko-tipologicheskogo issledovanija iraniskikh jazykov* [A tentative historical-typical study of Iranian languages]. 2 vols. Moscow.
Reichelt, H. 1909. *Awestisches Elementarbuch.* Heidelberg. Repr. 1978.
Rossi, A. 1981. La varietà linguistica nell'Iran achemenide. *AION* 1981/3: 141–196.
Schmitt, R. 1973. Der heutige Stand der altiranischen Namenforschung. *Orbis* 22: 248–60.
———. 1978. Fragen der Anthroponomastik des achämenidischen Volkerstaates. *ZDMG* 128: 116–124.
———. 1987. Aryans. *Encyclopedia Iranica,* vol. 2, fasc. 7: 684–7. London.
Schmitt, R., ed. 1989. *Compendium Linguarum Iranicarum.* Wiesbaden.
Spuler, B., ed. 1958. *Iranistik,* I: *Linguistik. Handbuch der Orientalistik,* I, IV. Leiden.
Tedesco, P. 1921. Dialektologie der westiranischen Turfantexte. *Monde Oriental 15:* 184–258.
Telegdi, S. 1935. Essai sur la phonétique des emprunts iraniens en araméen talmudique. *JA* 226: 177–256.
Weryho, J. W. 1971. Syriac Influences on Sassanian Iran. *Folio Orientalia* 13: 299–321.
Windfuhr, G. 1970. Notes on the Old Persian Script. *Indo-Iranian Journal* 13: 121–25.
———. 1972. Diacritic and Distinctive Features in Avestan. *JAOS* 91: 104–25.
———. 1975. Isoglosses: A Sketch on Persians and Parthians, Kurds and Medes. *Acta Iranica* 5: 457–72.
———. 1979. *Persian Grammar: History and State of Its Research.* The Hague.
Yarshater, E. 1977. The Hybrid Language of the Jewish Communities of Persia. *JAOS* 97/1: 1–7.

GERNOT L. WINDFUHR

LATIN

Originally the language of Latium, the region of Italy in which Rome is situated. It became the dominant language of the W Mediterranean with the expansion of Roman power. Colloquial or "Vulgar" Latin, spoken in various provinces of the Roman Empire, in the course of time developed into the Romance languages of France, Spain, Portugal, Italy, Switzerland, and Romania.

A. The Latin Language

Latin belongs to the Italic branch of the Indo-European (IE) family of languages. The Italic branch comprised both Q and P languages or dialects, according to how the unvoiced Indo-European labiovelar sound was represented by *qu* (as in Lat *quattuor,* "four," from IE **q^wetwor*) or by *p* (as in Oscan *petora,* Umbrian *petur,* "four"); Latin was a Q language.

IE intervocalic *s* became *r* in Latin; thus the genitive plural of *ā*-stems (IE **āsōm*) became *-arum* (contrast Gk *-aōn,* contracting to *-ōn,* with the disappearance of intervocalic *s*).

Of the IE cases, Latin retains the ablative, not only in its original ablative sense (denoting separation) but in the instrumental sense as well. The locative survives in place names and in a few common nouns (e.g., *domi,* "at home").

Latin forms the genitive singular of *o*-stems in *-ī,* which was taken over also by *ā*-stems (the ending *-ae,* as in *aqua vitae,* was formerly a dissyllable, *-āī*). The original IE genitive singular of *ā*-stems survives in *paterfamilias.*

Latin has no definite article; the situations in which its absence leads to ambiguity are fewer than might be expected. (The translator of the Rheims NT of 1582 used the Latin Vg as his base, but paid regard to the Gk text when deciding whether or not to use the Eng definite article.)

The Latin passive is formed by the addition of *-r* (e.g., *amor,* "I am loved," alongside *amo,* "I love"), as in other Italic languages or dialects and the neighboring Celtic languages and also in the remote Hittite and Tocharian languages.

The aorist (past historic) and perfect tenses have fallen together into one Latin form, called the perfect; e.g., *amavi* means either "I loved" or "I have loved."

Except in deponent verbs (verbs passive in form but active in meaning), Latin has no perfect participle active. In the NT this gives rise to some theological problems: in Heb 1:3, for example, the Gk aorist participle, "having made purification," is rendered in Vg by the present participle, "making purification," which obscures, or indeed contradicts, the point which the author intends to make.

Latin was the official language of Roman colonies in the east and west alike, and it was the language of the Roman armies wherever they were stationed; but in the E Mediterranean, Greek was never displaced from its position as the language of culture and general communication which it had held since Alexander the Great's conquests.

B. Latin Literature

The earliest specimens of Latin writing are inscriptions dating from the 5th century B.C. onward. Latin literature in the proper sense begins in the second half of the 3d century B.C., with Livius Andronicus, who translated Homer's *Odyssey* into Latin, and Naevius, author of an epic poem on the Punic War. Both of these authors used the native Saturnian meter, but it was soon displaced by imported Greek meters like the hexameter, used by Ennius (239–169 B.C.) for his *Annales,* an epic poem on the history of Rome. In the same period, Plautus and Terence presented the motifs and techniques of the Attic New Comedy in Latin dress.

But Roman genius made sure that Latin literature was no mere copy of Greek models but had a character and distinction of its own. Lucretius (*ca.* 55 B.C.) bent the hexameter to didactic use in his six books *On the Nature of Things,* an exposition of Epicurean philosophy. Cicero (d. 43 B.C.), in his orations, letters, and philosophical treatises, raised Latin prose to a level which has remained unsurpassed. Virgil's *Aeneid* (between 29 and 19 B.C.), for all its indebtedness to Homeric epic poetry, is an independent work of genius. Horace (65–8 B.C.) has by his *Odes* endeared himself to appreciative readers of all succeeding generations. Livy (59 B.C.–A.D. 17) wrote the history of Rome in 142 volumes, of which 35 are extant. These are some of the names which justify the description of this phase of Latin literature as the golden age.

To the silver age belong the philospher and tragedian Seneca (d. A.D. 65), his nephew the epic writer Lucan, the encyclopedist Pliny the Elder (d. A.D. 79), and his nephew the letter writer Pliny the Younger; the satirist Juvenal; Tacitus, Rome's greatest historian; the biographer Suetonius; and Apuleius, whose *Golden Ass* is a splendid example of early novel-writing. There was a falling away of literary power in the following generations, but new life was breathed into Latin prose by the Latin church fathers.

C. Latin in the NT

Latin plays only a marginal role in the NT. It was one of the three languages of the "title" fastened above Jesus' head on the cross (John 19:20). There is a sprinkling of loanwords from Latin in the Greek NT: *assarius,* "penny" (Matt 10:29; Luke 12:6); *census,* "taxes" (Mark 12:14, etc.); *centurio,* "centurion" (Mark 15:39); *colonia,* "colony" (Acts 16:12); *custodia,* "guard" (Matt 27:65); *denarius* (Mark 6:37, etc.); *flagello,* "scourge" (Mark 15:15 = Matt 27:26); *forum* (Acts 28:15); *legio,* "legion" (Mark 5:9, etc.); *libertinus,* "freedman" (Acts 6:9); *linteum,* "towel" (John 13:4–5); *macellum,* "meat market" (1 Cor 10:25); *membrana,* "parchment" (2 Tim 4:13); *mille* (sc. *passus*), "mile" (Matt 5:41); *modius,* "bushel" (Mark 4:21 = Matt 5:15 = Luke 11:33); *paenula,* "cloak" (2 Tim 4:13); *praetorium,* "palace," "praetorian, guard" (Mark 15:16 = Matt 27:27; John 18:28, etc.; Acts 23:35; Phil 1:13); *quadrans,* "penny" (Matt 5:26; Mark 12:42); *semicinctium,* "apron" (Acts 19:12); *sicarius,* "assassin" (Acts 21:38); *speculator,* "soldier of the guard" (Mark 6:27; found also as a loanword in rabbinical Heb *spiglaṭor,* with the same sense, "executioner"), *sudarium,* "napkin," "handkerchief" (Luke 19:20; John 11:44; 20:7; Acts 19:12); *taberna,* "tavern" (Acts 28:15); *titulus,* "title" (John 19:19–20).

Paul may have been able to claim his citizenship rights in Latin, *civis Romanus sum* (cf. Acts 16:37; 22:25; 25:11). He would have heard Latin spoken in Roman colonies such as Philippi and Corinth (although his chief associations were with Greek-speaking residents) and in his contacts with the Roman army. When he planned to evangelize Spain (Rom 15:24, 29) he must have been prepared to use Latin as his regular means of communication there; perhaps it was to gain fluency in it that he visited the Latin-speaking province of Illyricum (Rom 15:19). In Rome, however, Greek would serve him adequately: the city was completely bilingual, and the Roman church was Greek-speaking until the end of the 2d century.

D. Latin in the Church

Latin appears to have come first into Christian use in the Roman province of Africa, whose capital city, Carthage, became a Roman colony in 146 B.C. It was here that the first Latin Christian literature appeared, preeminently the writings of Tertullian of Carthage, which belong to the years A.D. 196–212. Parts, at least, of the Bible were available in a Latin version in Africa in the last quarter of the 2d century. In 180, the church of Scillium, near Carthage, possessed a copy (evidently in Latin) of Paul's letters. Tertullian quotes extensively from the Latin scriptures and Cyprian, bishop of Carthage (249–257), uses a practically complete Latin Bible.

Pope Victor I (ca. A.D. 190) is said to have been the first Latin-speaking bishop of Rome (Hier. *Vir. Ill.* 34). The first substantial contribution to Latin Christian literature produced in Rome was Novatian's treatise *On the Trinity* (ca. A.D. 250).

In the following centuries, Latin literature was enriched by a succession of gifted Christian writers, including Hilary, bishop of Poitiers (d. 367), author of the work *On the Trinity;* Ambrose, bishop of Milan (339–397), preacher and exegete; Jerome, who produced (among many other things) the first Latin translation of the OT direct from Hebrew; Pelagius (ca. 350–430), commentator on Paul's letters and the first British author; and Augustine of Hippo (354–430), "assuredly the greatest man that ever wrote Latin" (Souter 1927: 139), whose intellectual and spiritual powers, finding expression in a long succession of outstanding treatises and letters, have to this day exercised a profound influence on Christian thinking in the Western tradition.

Throughout W Europe for many centuries, Latin remained the language of church, law, and scholarship. Moreover, outstanding literary works in prose and poetry continued to appear in Latin until the 18th century. In his *Ecclesiastical History of the English People (Historia ecclesiastica gentis Anglorum),* Bede of Jarrow (673–735), a man of wide and deep learning, showed himself a master of the historian's art. The Irish scholar Johannes Scotus Erigena (815–877), translator of Pseudo-Dionysius' *Celestial Hierarchy* into Latin, produced original philosophical studies. Abelard (1079–1142) showed his best literary qualities in his letters and hymns rather than in his controversial writings.

Although in the reformed churches Latin was largely displaced by the vernacular tongues, it continued to be used as a literary medium. Luther and Calvin wrote in Latin as well as in German and French, respectively; and in the following century, John Milton wrote in Latin (both prose and poetry) as well as in English. Only in the second half of the 20th century, with the encouragement of vernacular liturgy, has Latin ceased to be the invariable liturgical language in the Roman Catholic Church.

Bibliography

Campenhausen, H. von. 1964. *The Fathers of the Latin Church.* Trans. M. Hoffmann. London.

Metzger, B. M. 1977. The Latin Versions. Pp. 285–374 in *The Early Versions of the New Testament.* Oxford.

Palmer, L. R. 1954. *The Latin Language.* London.

Rose, H. J. 1949. *A Handbook of Latin Literature, from the Earliest Times to the Death of St. Augustine.* 2d rev. ed. London.

Souter, A. 1927. *The Earliest Latin Commentaries on the Epistles of St. Paul.* Oxford.

Sparks, H. F. D. 1940. The Latin Bible. Pp. 100–127 in *The Bible in Its Ancient and English Versions,* ed. H. W. Robinson. Oxford.

F. F. Bruce

PHOENICIAN

The term Phoenician properly denotes those dialects of Canaanite spoken in antiquity in the region of the Lebanon (Phoenicia). Canaanite, called "the speech of Canaan" by its native speakers (Isa 19:18), was the indigenous Northwest Semitic language of all ancient Lebanon and the biblical land of Canaan. To the Canaanite family of languages also belonged the regional dialects of Judean (Hebrew), Moabite, Ammonite, and Edomite. Two dialects of Phoenician Canaanite are known: Byblian, the language of the city-state of Byblos, and Tyro-Sidonian, that of the city-states of Tyre and Sidon and their dependencies in central and S Lebanon. With the political and economic ascendancy in Phoenicia of Tyre and Sidon in the 1st millennium B.C.E., Tyro-Sidonian Phoenician emerged as the common language or *koinē* of all Phoenicians; although Byblian continued to be the official tongue of the city of Byblos, its linguistic importance was negligible. Trade and overseas expansion, already in process at the end of the 2d millennium B.C.E., carried and transplanted Tyro-Sidonian Phoenician far beyond Phoenicia to Cyprus, Greece, N Africa, SW Spain and the Balearic Islands, W Sicily, Sardinia, and Malta. Western Phoenician (Punic), the language of the Carthaginian state and its vast empire, rivaled in importance Greek and Latin in classical antiquity; it survived in N Africa well into the Christian period, counting among its native speakers the Roman emperor Septimius Severus, the poet Apuleius, and the Church Father Augustine of Hippo.

Classical Phoenician, specifically the Tyro-Sidonian (TS) of Lebanon proper and the Phoenician kingdoms and communities in Cyprus and Greece, was essentially similar to Hebrew (Heb) except for minor dialectal differences. Accordingly, the relatedness of TS and Heb may be described succinctly in terms of these differences.

A. Alphabet and Writing

Phoenician was written in a regional variety of the Proto-Sinaitic linear alphabet especially adapted to its 22-consonant inventory. It was this 22-letter alphabet, together with the Phoenician names of the letters, that was subsequently borrowed by other Canaanite-speaking peoples, including the Israelites, and by the Arameans and later the Greeks. Phoenician orthography was always purely consonantal; although the system of the *matres lectionis* (vowel letters) used in Hebrew, Moabite, and Aramaic was known to the Phoenicians, it was rarely used by them.

B. Phonology

The phoneme /z/ was pronounced [zd] or [zz], and /ṣ/ was pronounced [st], [ts], or [ss]. Proto-Semitic /š ś s/ had fallen together as [s], as in the Ephraimite dialect of Canaanite (see Judg 12:4–6); thus, the absence of the sound [š], which made it impossible for the Ephraimite to "pronounce correctly" Judean /šibbólet/, made it possible for St. Augustine to relate Punic *salus* [salūs] = Heb /šalōš/, "three, trinity," to Latin *salūs,* "salvation" (see Aug. *Ad Rom.* inch. Exp. 13). Phoenician did, however, represent the reflexes of /š ś/ by the alphabet letter *š;* only rarely by the letter *s.* The Proto-Semitic vowel /a/ had three reflexes in Phoenician: (1) [a] in an open unstressed syllable, (2) [e] or [i] in a closed unstressed syllable, and (3) commonly but not always [o] in a stressed syllable: TS /hessūs/ = Heb /hassūs/, "the horse"; TS /banó/ = Heb /baná/, "he built." Proto-Canaanite /ō/ had the reflexes (1) [ō] in a closed unstressed syllable and (2) [ū] in an open unstressed and commonly but not always in a closed stressed syllable: TS /dōbrīm/ = Heb /dōbĕrīm/, "they say"; TS /dūbér/ = Heb /dōbér/, "he says"; TS /śanūt/ = Heb /šānōt/, "years." The Proto-Semitic diphthongs /aw/ and /ay/ were contracted to [ō] or [ū] and [ē] or [ī], respectively, under all conditions.

C. Noun and Adjective

The feminine singular afformative is always /-ót/: TS /milkót/ = Heb /malká/, "queen." The nouns "father" and "brother" have the stems /ʾabū-/ and /ʾaḥū-/, respectively, in the construct state and with suffixal pronouns: TS /ʾabūnóm/ = Heb /ʾăbīhém/, "their father." Some nouns have forms different from those in Hebrew in the singular and plural: TS /śatt/ = Heb /šaná/, "year"; TS /ʾīsīm/ = Heb /ʾănāšīm/, "men"; TS /māqūmīm/ = Heb /mĕqōmōt/, "places." Some nouns common in TS are uncommon or unknown in Heb: the word for "gold" is /hārūṣ/, the common Heb word /zāhāb/ being unattested; "foot" is always /paʿm/, never /regel/; "great," "large," is /ʾiddīr/ or /kibbīr/, never /gādôl/; "small" is /ṣaʿīr/, never /qāṭān/; and "beautiful" is /śippīr/, not /yāpe/.

D. Pronouns

For "I" TS has /ʾānīki/ = Heb /ʾānōkî/; "you" (second masculine singular) was /ʾátta/, with stress on the initial syllable, in contrast to Heb ultima-stressed /ʾattā/. For "they" TS has the common gender pronoun *hmt* (pronunciation unknown). The possessive pronoun "our" is /-ón(u)/ = Heb /-énu/, and "your" (masculine plural) is /-kom/ = Heb /-kem/. In the third person, the TS possessive pronouns have complementary forms: /-o/, "his," /-a/, "her," and /-óm/, "their" (common gender), are used when the nouns are in the nominative or accusative case, but /-i/, "his, her," and /-nóm/, "their," are used when in the genitive case. When the noun ends in a vowel, the forms are /-yò/, "his"; /-yà/, "her"; and /-nom/, "their." The demonstrative pronouns are /zde/ and /zdō/ for the masculine and feminine singular, respectively, and /ʾillī/ for the common plural; when used adjectivally, the demonstratives follow the noun and do not as a rule receive the definite article: TS /heqqart zdō/ = Heb /haqqiryâ hazzōt/. The relative pronoun is /ʾīś/ = Heb /ʾăšer/; unlike its Heb counterpart, it is regularly used with participles. For "all, every, each," TS has /kil(l)/, corresponding to Heb /kol(l)/. TS does not have the adjective /ʾaḥēr/, "other, another," of Heb; "another" is expressed either by the adjective /zor/ or the ordinal /śenī/, and "the other" by the construct plural noun *ʾḥry* (pronunciation unknown): TS /ʾarūn zor/ or /ʾarūn śenī/, "another coffin," = Heb /ʾārôn ʾaḥēr/; TS *ʾḥry hbtm* = Heb /habbātîm haʾăḥērîm/, "the other houses."

E. Verb

The suffixing form (past perfective) of the causative stem in TS is /yiCCeC/ = Heb /hiCCiC/: TS /yiqdeś/ = Heb /hiqdīš/, "he dedicated." The third feminine singular of the suffixing form (past perfective) of all classes of verbs, including III*y*, ends in /-a/: TS /baná/ = Heb / bānĕtâ/, "she built." A distinction in inflection between indicative and nonindicative exists in the second and third person plural of the prefixing form of the verb: /yelekūn/, "they will go" (indicative) but /yelekū/, "let them go!" (jussive). The form /wayyiCCoC/ of Heb expressing past perfective action is unknown in TS; instead, TS uses the infinitive absolute with following subject (noun or independent personal pronoun): TS /(wa) katūb ʾānīki/ = Heb /wāʾ ektōb/, "I wrote." TS makes extensive use of the infinitive construct /liCCūC/ as a surrogate for the future tense, the jussive, and the imperative. Some verbs in TS have forms somewhat different from those in Hebrew: TS /yaton/ = Heb /nātan/, "he gave"; TS /ḥawo/ = Heb /ḥāyâ/, "he lived." Some verbs in TS are uncommon or unknown in Hebrew and vice versa: TS /ṭ-n-ʾ/ (*Qal, Piʿel* and *Yipʿel*), "to set up"; TS /ḥ-z-y/ = Heb /r-ʾ-y/, "to see" (unknown in TS); TS /k-n/ (*Qal*) = Heb /h-y-y/, "to be"; TS /ḥ-m-d/ and /ḥ-b-b/ (*Yipʿel*) = Heb /ʾ-h-b/, "to love" (unknown in TS); TS /p-ʿ-l/ = Heb /ʿ-ś-y/, "to do, make."

F. Other Parts of Speech

The preposition *b-* /bi-/ has the free variant *ʾb-* /ʾef-/, with prothetic vowel and spirantization of the bilabial, as well as the predictable variant *bn-* before suffixal pronouns: TS *bn* /bVnó/ = Heb /bō/, "in him." The preposition /ʿal/ has the free variant /ʿalt/, with excrescent -t. TS does not have the preposition /ʿim/ of Hebrew, using rather /ʾit(t)/. The conjunction /ʾô/, "or," of Hebrew is unknown, with TS using /ʾim/ instead. For "in order that," TS has *lkn* (pronunciation unknown) = Heb /lĕmáʿan/. The negative particle *lʾ* /lō/ of Heb is unknown; TS uses /ʾī/, /bal/, or /ʾībál/ to negate the indicative mood. For the accusative particle TS has the complementary forms *ʾt* /ʾot/, used immediately before a noun with possessive pronoun, and *ʾyt* (pronunciation unknown) used in all other cases; the accusative particle governs the genitive case of the noun, which must then receive the appropriate form of the possessive pronoun.

Bibliography

Grammars

Branden, A. van den. 1969. *Grammaire Phénicienne.* Beirut.

Friedrich, J., and Rollig, W. 1970. *Phonizisch-punische Grammatik.* 2d ed. AnOr 46. Rome.

Harris, Z. S. 1936. *A Grammar of the Phoenician Language.* AOS 8. New Haven.

Segert, S. 1976. *A Grammar of Phoenician and Punic.* Munich.

Dictionaries

Fuentes Estanol, M.-J. 1980. *Vocabulario Fenicio.* Biblioteca Fenicia 1. Barcelona.

Harris, Z. S. 1936. Glossary of Phoenician. Pp. 73–156 in Harris 1936.

Jean, C. F., and Hoftijzer, J. 1962. *Dictionnaire des Inscriptions Sémitiques de l'Ouest.* Leiden.

Tomback, R. S. 1980. *A Comparative Semitic Lexicon of the Phoenician and Punic Languages.* SBLDS 32. Missoula, MT.

CHARLES R. KRAHMALKOV

PRE-ISLAMIC SOUTH ARABIAN

For the present purpose, South Arabia is approximately congruous with modern N and S Yemen (the Yemen Arab Republic and the People's Democratic Republic of Yemen). In this area there are many thousands of inscriptions dating from some time in the first half of the 1st millennium B.C. down to the mid-6th century A.D. Almost all of those anterior to the latter 3d century A.D. are drafted in four languages commonly called Minaic, Sabaic, Qatabanic, and Hadramitic, on the basis of a listing of the four most important *folks (ethnē)* of S Arabia by the 3d-century B.C. Greek geographer Eratosthenes. Inscriptions in the first three cluster in the valleys and montane plains draining into the sand desert called by Arab geographers the Ṣayhad (on modern maps Ramlat al-Sabʿatayn); and even the Hadramites, whose inscriptions are rather widely spread in the E part of the domain, had their "metropolis" Shabwa not in the Wadi Hadramawt proper but on the E border of the Ṣayhad. It is thus convenient to group these four languages as "Ṣayhadic," rather than "Old (or Epigraphic) South Arabian," because a few inscriptions have been found, mostly to the south of the Ṣayhadic area, in a still undeciphered language which is certainly none of the four known Ṣayhadic languages.

At the NW end of the Ṣayhadic belt, the Wadi Jawf is linguistically divided, with Minaic in the E part and Sabaic in the W part; Sabaic also covers a large area comprising the high plateaus S of the Wadi Jawf, and the oases at a lower level E of the high plateau area, including the Sabaean "metropolis" Marib. Qatabanic is centered on the Wadis Ḥarīb and Bayḥān with the area S thereof.

Some Ṣayhadic texts are found well outside the S Arabian area: notably at Dedan (modern al-Ulā), where there was a Minaean trading establishment, and at Samhar (modern Khor Rori), a little east of Sallalah in what is now part of the sultanate of Oman. Additionally, there is a very small scattering of inscriptions spread over an even more extensive area: those in Egypt and the Mediterranean island of Delos reflect S Arabian trading interests; those in central Arabia are a result of military expeditions.

The earliest South Arabian inscriptions known are Sabaic; use of the other three languages began (so far as their epigraphic record goes) slightly later, and continued in the case of Minaic down to about 100 B.C., in the case of Qatabanic and Hadramitic to about the beginning of the 3d century A.D. Sabaic continued in use through the 4th to 6th centuries, but with features which suggest that it may by that time have been developing into something more like a "learned" prestigious language than one actively spoken. Because in that period the political control of the whole of S Arabia was in the hands of the so-called Tubba^c kings, who were of Himyarite stock, it is possible that Sabaic was yielding to Himyaritic: this is an Arabian dialect, albeit one rather more divergent than most from the general average of Arabic dialects, and showing more archaic features.

Muslim writers were acquainted with the history of only the three centuries immediately preceding Islam, and consequently applied the term Himyaritic to all pre-Islamic inscriptions (and other material remains); European scholars of the 19th century tended to echo this, by calling all Ṣayhadic texts "Himyaritic," but this is a complete misnomer.

All S Arabian pre-Islamic languages are written in the South Arabian variety of the South Semitic alphabet, including 29 letters, in contrast with the limited repertory of 22 letters found in the Phoenician-Hebrew-Aramaic group of alphabets. But the two script families did share a common origin in the remote past. Other members of the South Semitic script family are the old North Arabian scripts and Ethiopic (the latter deriving apparently directly from South Arabian). But the South Arabian script was not limited to rendering South Arabian languages, whether Ṣayhadic or another; it was also used for Hasaitic (an old-Arabian language of the al-Ḥasā area in E Arabia), and for Arabic in Qaryat al-Faw (an important caravan city on the route linking Najran with NE Arabia); although the few inscriptions from Najran appear to be Sabaic, the population probably spoke Arabic, using Sabaic as a prestigious language in the same way that the Arabic speakers of Palmyra used Aramaic for epigraphic purposes.

Alongside the monumental variety of South Arabian script, we now have a handful of documents on wood in a highly cursive script (based, however, on the monumental script) and apparently used for epistolary purposes. This script is extremely difficult to read, and though work is now proceeding on decipherment of the texts, it will be a long time before satisfactory results can be expected.

The South Arabian alphabet is basically consonantal, with no notation for short vowels and none for long *ā* (apart from a single instance, a late text of the Tubba^c period in which the Jewish name Yahuda is spelt in Aramaic fashion as *Yhwdʾ*); it remains disputable to what extent *w* and *y* may have been used as vowel letters. Nor is there in general any notation for consonant length (a lack found also in Ethiopic, despite the fact that the latter has evolved a system of vowel notation); Minaic texts, however, do show some half-dozen words in which duplication of a consonant may plausibly be thought to represent length of the consonant, as in Greek, although this manner of noting the feature is totally unknown in any other Semitic alphabetic script. All this manifestly places severe restrictions on our knowledge of the linguistic structures.

The Ṣayhadic languages are unmistakably Semitic, but they are made distinct from all other Semitic languages by the use of an affixed *-n* (in Hadramitic *-hn*) with the function of a definite article, so that Arabic speakers consciously equated it with their own prefixed *al-*. Also noteworthy is the maintenance of three unvoiced sibilant phonemes, a feature shared with a group of languages still spoken today in the Sallalah region and the island of Socotra, of which the main representative is Mahri; these possess besides /s/ and /š/ a further phoneme with lateral articulation (rather like Welsh /ll/). So far as cognates in other Semitic languages can be detected, over 80 percent of the cases show the following correspondences:

Ṣayhadic	**Mahric**	**Hebrew**	**Arabic**
s^1	/š/	*š (šin)*	*s*
s^2	lateral /ś/	*ś (śin)*	*š*
s^3	/s/	*s (samek)*	*s*

The shape of the letter s^3 closely resembles that of a Northwest Semitic *samek* at the beginning of the 1st millennium B.C.; and while the shape of s^2 is that of the ambiguous Northwest Semitic *śin/šin,* the cognates suggest that its value was that of the *śin*—whatever that may have been. The extra letter shape would thus have been s^1, which looks like a differentiated version of *s*.

The other letters additional to the 22-letter alphabet are the six which Arabic has over and above the latter, and their shapes are mainly secondarily developed forms: *ġ* based on *g*, *ḏ* on *d*, *ḫ* on *h*, *ḍ* on *ṭ*, *ẓ* on *ṣ* (indeed, these two often interchange), and *ṯ* for which rather oddly the closest resemblance in shape is *y*.

Another general feature of Ṣayhadic is frequent assimilation of *n* to a following consonant (other than a laryngeal or glottal) when the two are continuous. Assimilated and nonassimilated spellings, however, are almost equally common.

Within the Ṣayhadic family, there is a cleavage between Sabaic and the other three. Sabaic has *h-* as the prefix of the causative verb-stem and *-h-* in third person affix pronouns (cf. Heb *Hip^{c}īl, -oh, -ah, -hem*), while the others have s^1 (cf. Akkad *šaprus, -šu, -šum;* Syr *šap^{c}el;* Mahric causative verb-stem in *š-* and sibilant pronoun affixes). Some texts, however, show a mixture of both sibilant and *h* forms; and, as elements in personal names, *h-* verb-stem formations are almost universal. The verb-stem formant *h-* is retained in the imperfect and the participle (in contrast with Hebrew).

A peculiarity of Hadramitic is loss of phonemic distinction between s^3 and *ṯ*, and between *z* and *ḏ*, so that the two letters in each pair are used indifferently. Also notable in Hadramitic is a consonantal differentiation in the third person sing. affix pronoun: masc. -s^1, fem. -s^3 or *ṯ* (paralleled in Mahric by masc. *-š*, fem. -s); elsewhere in Ṣayhadic the consonantal base of these pronouns is uniform for both genders.

Qatabanic has a *b-* prefix for the indicative imperfect verb, without which the verb has a jussive or optative force.

Imperfects in *b-* occur sporadically in Minaic, but without sufficient evidence of their value.

In earlier Sabaic, and in the other three languages, the numeral 3 has the form *s^2lt(t)*, but in Sabaic from about the 1st century A.D. this is replaced by *tlt(t)*. One notes that the noun-stem affix which appears in Ugaritic and Akkadian as *-t* is in Ṣayhadic always so spelt, and never (as in the Hebrew and Arabic non-construct forms) with *-h*.

There are some traces of a verbal perfect-tense inflection with first person sing. and second persons marked by *-k*, as is the case in Ethiopic and Mahric, in Himyaritic (where it may be due to the Ṣayhadic substratum), and in some of the present-day Arabic dialects of Yemen (presumably inherited from Himyaritic).

The Marib area and the highlands west of it exhibit what may be termed standard Sabaic; but to the north and south there are texts showing dialectal peculiarities. One such dialect, for which textual evidence in any quantity has only just become available, is that of the Radmān folk, in the southeast corner of present-day N Yemen around the town of Radāʿ, and thus in close proximity to the Qatabanic area; as might be expected, this shows some admixture of forms recalling Qatabanic. Another dialect is evidenced in a small group of texts from around Haram in the Wadi Jawf, which have the preposition *mn*, "from," whereas in all other parts of the Ṣayhadic domain "from" is expressed exclusively by *bn* (very common) or *ln* (occasionally in Sabaic); it can be surmised that these forms are expansions with the differentiated meaning "from" as well as, respectively, "in, at" and "to, for." Ṣayhadic has only one preposition meaning "to, for" covering the ranges of Hebrew *lĕ-*, Arabic *li-* and Hebrew *ʾel*, and Arabic *ʾilā:* this preposition is in Sabaic and Qatabanic *l-*, in Minaic *k-*, in Hadramitic *h-*.

Sabaic, and to a partial extent Minaic, has two imperfect verb forms, one simple, the other characterized by affixed *-n*. While the latter is often used in main verbs with a jussive or optative sense, it also occurs frequently in subordinate clauses of all kinds, including relative ones; it is thus in no way parallel functionally to the Arabic "energetic" *-n* forms.

In its use of nominal "broken" or internal plurals, Ṣayhadic outdoes all other Semitic languages; such plurals are almost universally used, even for denominals in *-y;* e.g., *ṣrwḥy*, "man of Ṣirwāḥ," pl. *ʾṣrḥ*, where Arabic would admit only *Ṣirwāḥiyyūn*. Barely a dozen Ṣayhadic nouns, such as *bn*, "son," *ym*, "day," etc., are attested with external masc. pl. forms, additionally to internal ones.

A feature to which the term "consecutive infinitive" has been applied is that where two or more verbs are immediately (without intervening words) coordinated with each other, the normal rule is that only the first exhibits the appropriate morphological markers of the finite verb in respect to gender, number, and tense, while the following ones are devoid of those markers, thus showing a quasi-infinitival form, although semantically they have the same gender, number, and tense implications as the leading verb.

Lack of vocalization is especially frustrating in regard to the verbal system. The graphic forms show only a base-stem *fʿl* and derivative stems *hfʿl/s^1fʿl*, *tfʿl*, *ftʿl* and *s^1tfʿl* (and a few Minaic examples of *fʿʿl*, see above). A **nfʿl* stem is completely unattested; but it has to be noted that in Mahric and Ethiopic the *n-* prefix stem is confined to verbs from quadriliteral roots, of which only one is attested in Ṣayhadic, and that is a *hfʿl* stem. It remains uncertain how far these graphic forms may conceal a variety of vocalizations; though one Sabaic form at least, *ts^2m* (from root *s^2ym*), might be thought to demonstrate a *tafaʿla* stem, which exists in Ethiopic though not in Arabic. At all events, one must not allow the inadequate graphic evidence to mislead one into inferring that the verb system had more similarity to the Arabic one than to the Ethiopic or Mahric systems.

Relatively little work has been done so far on syntax. One does, however, gain the general impression that Ṣayhadic had a fairly close resemblance to Arabic in this domain, with a few notable exceptions. It is regular for two or more substantives to govern a single genitive jointly, contrary to the classical Arabic rule that the form "the (X + Y) of Z" must be rephrased as "the X of Z and its Y." An asyndetic relative clause, or a prepositional phrase qualifying a substantive, may be treated like genitives in that the governing substantive has the morphological form of a "construct" (i.e., a substantive followed by a possessive pronoun or another substantive in the genitive), whereas this feature is in Arabic generally restricted to cases where the governing substantive is a time word (e.g., *sanata māta*, "the year he died").

A lexical survey is hampered by the interpretational divergencies (sometimes bizarrely extreme) among scholars. Many of these have tended to pillage Lane's *Arabic Lexicon* in their search for cognates, with too little regard for the fact that the medieval Arab lexicographers (on whose work Lane is based) often cite as the meaning of a word a connotation derivable solely from a particular context and quite inapplicable outside that context. Nor should it be forgotten that the bulk of our inscriptions antedate Arabic by at least half a millennium, in which time there is ample scope for substantial semantic shifts. But subject to these cautions, it is true that the tendency in the last few decades, for scholars to have recourse increasingly to the vocabulary of Arabic for explaining Ṣayhadic, has had considerable pragmatic success.

The Ṣayhadic lexicon retains some old Semitic words that have totally disappeared from the Arabic vocabulary, such as *ʾbn*, "stone," and *ʿḍ*, "wood." Sabaic *lbʾ*, "lion, lioness," survives in Arabic only in the feminine *labuʾah*, while what has now become the *vox propria* for "lion" in Arabic, *ʾasad*, is revealed as originating in a metaphor by Ṣayhadic *ʾs^1d*, "warrior." Minaic *rtkl* has the same sense as Hebrew and Aramaic *rkl*, "to trade," whereas Arabic *rakala* means only "to kick." Ṣayhadic *kwr*, "mountain," and *nwd*, "wind," survive at the present day in Yemeni dialectical usage, though unknown in standard Arabic or in any other Semitic language.

Both the Ethiopic and the Mahric languages have provided useful materials: *ftḥ*, "lawsuit," recalls Ethiopic *fätäḥ*, "law"; the numeral *ṭd*, "one," exists in Mahri as *ṭad;* and *ḥbr* (designating something that damages crops) is better connected with Jibbali (Mahric) *ḥor* < *ḥbr*, "cold," than, as hitherto thought, with Hebrew *ḥĕbĕr*, "sorcery." Sometimes the search for cognates is fruitless: when we read in a Minaic inscription on a sarcophagus, "This sarcophagus is that of so-and-so . . . who *fqr* in the 22d year of Ptolemy," it is absurd to suppose that the verb can mean anything except "died," although this sense of the root is found nowhere else in Semitic.

As might be expected, Sabaic vocabulary of the 4th–6th centuries shows an increasing convergence with Arabic. One interesting example is the root meaning "join together": in normal everyday Arabic this is *ǧamaʿa,* which, however, makes its first epigraphic appearance in the 6th century A.D.; earlier Ṣayhadic appears (judging from derivatives) to have used in this sense *krb,* while in Arabic *karaba* means "draw near, approximate," with a secondary development "to oppress," and then "to grieve" (transitive).

In the 4th–6th centuries we encounter also a certain number of loanwords, mainly from Syriac; e.g., *bʿt,* "church"; $qs^{1}s^{1}$, "Christian priest" (Syriac *qĕšišo*); *brk,* "bless." Before that period loanwords are decidedly sparse. In some early texts we have a priestly title *ʾfklt* (pl.), Akk *apkallu;* in the 2d–3d centuries A.D., *ṭf,* "tablet," Akk (ultimately Sum) *ṭuppu.* Also of this latter period are a few terms evidently still considered foreign, and applied only with reference to non-Ṣayhadic-speaking peoples: Habashite (Abyssinian) military contingents are referred to as *ʾḥzb* (Ethiopic *ḥĕzb*), and among the spoils taken from Habashites are listed *dglmt,* "bracelets, anklets," (Ethiopic *dĕgĕlma*).

Considered overall, the content of the Ṣayhadic monumental inscriptions is starkly archival in character: building records, dedications, funerary texts, legal enactments, "victory" texts, and so forth. They are uniformly drafted in the third person, and we have less than half a dozen showing a first or second person form; the cursive texts may be expected eventually to enlarge our knowledge in this respect. But the 1st–3d centuries A.D., which are much more amply documented than any other period, provide us with a large number of texts recording the presentation of votive offerings to deities, and these throw valuable light on everyday life. There is a small group of so-called "pentitential" texts, recording expiation for ritual offenses, particularly against ritual purity; the rules inferable from these bear a strong likeness to purity codes prevalent throughout the ANE. (On the modern languages of this region, see the Introductory Survey at the beginning of this entry.)

Bibliography

South Semitic

Avanzini, A.; Marrassini, P.; and Leslau, W. 1973. South Arabian and Ethiopic Lexicography. Pp. 161–81 in *Studies on Semitic Lexicography,* ed. P. Fronzaroli. Quaderni di Semitistica 2. Florence.

Leslau, W. 1943. South-East Semitic (Ethiopic and South-Arabic). *JAOS* 63: 4–14.

———. 1970. Ethiopic and South Arabian. Pp. 467–527 in *Current Trends in Linguistics.* Vol. 6, *Linguistics in South West Asia and North Africa,* ed. T. A. Sebeok. The Hague.

Müller, W. W. 1964. Über Beziehungen zwischen den neusüdarabischen und den abessinischen Sprachen. *JSS* 9: 50–55.

Old South Arabian (Ṣayhadic)

Beeston, A. F. L. 1984. *Sabaic Grammar.* Journal of Semitic Studies Monograph 6. Manchester.

———. 1987. Apologia for "Ṣayhadic." *Proceedings of the Seminar for Arabian Studies* 17: 13–14.

Beeston, A. F. L.; Ghul, M. A.; Müller, W. W.; and Ryckmans, J. 1982. *Sabaic Dictionary (English-French-Arabic).* Louvain.

Ryckmans, J. 1971. Les confessions publiques sabéenes. In *AION* 32.

Modern South Arabian Languages

Bender, M. L. 1970. A Preliminary Investigation of South Arabian. Vol. 2, pp. 26–37 in *Proceedings of the Third International Conference on Ethiopian Studies, Addis Ababa 1966.* Addis Ababa.

Bittner, M. 1909–15. *Studien zur Laut- und Formenlehre der Mehri-Sprache in Südarabien.* Sitzungsberichte der kaiserliche Akademie der Wissenschaften in Wien, phil-hist. Kl., 162/5, 168/2, 172/5, 174/4, 176/1, 178/2, 178/3.

———. 1913–18. *Vorstudien zur Grammatik und zum Wörterbuche der Soqoṭri-Sprache.* Sitzungsberichte der kaiserliche Akademie der Wissenschaften in Wien, phil-hist. Kl., 173/4, 186/4, 186/5.

———. 1916–17. *Studien zur Šḫauri-Sprache in den Bergen von Ḍofâr am Persischen Meerbusen.* Sitzungsberichte der kaiserliche Akademie der Wissenschaften in Wien, phil-hist. Kl., 179/2, 179/4, 179/5, 183/5.

Christian, V. 1944. *Die Stellung des Mehri innerhalb der semitischen Sprachen.* Sitzungsberichte der kaiserliche Akademie der Wissenschaften in Wien, phil-hist. Kl., 222/3.

Jahn, A. 1905. *Grammatik der Mehri-Sprache in Südarabien.* Sitzungsberichte der kaiserliche Akademie der Wissenschaften in Wien, phil-hist. Kl., 150/6.

Johnstone, T. M. 1975. The Modern South Arabian languages. *AAL* 1/5: 1–29 = 93–121.

———. 1977. *Ḥarsūsi Lexicon and English-Ḥarsūsi Word-List.* Oxford.

———. 1981. *Jibbāli Lexicon.* Oxford.

———. 1986. Mahrī. *The Encyclopedia of Islam, New Edition* 6: 84–85.

———. 1987. *Mehri Lexicon and English-Mehri Word-List.* London.

Leslau, W. 1938. *Lexique Soqoṭri (sudarabique moderne) avec comparaisons et explications étymologiques.* Paris.

———. 1946. *Modern South Arabic Languages: A Bibliography.* New York.

———. 1947. Four Modern South Arabic Languages. *Word* 3: 180–203.

Lonnet, A. 1986. The Modern South Arabian Languages in the P.D.R. of Yemen. *Proceedings of the Seminar for Arabian Studies* 18: 49–55.

Lonnet, A., and Simeone-Senelle, M.-C. 1983. Observations phonétiques et phonologiques sur les consonnes d'un dialecte mehri. *Matériaux arabes et sudarabiques* 1983: 187–218.

Wagner, E. 1953. *Syntax der Mehri-Sprache unter Berücksichtigung auch der anderen neusüdarabischen Sprachen.* Deutsche Akademie der Wissenschaften zu Berlin, Institut für Orientforschung, Veröffentlichungen 13. Berlin.

A. F. L. BEESTON

UGARITIC

The native language employed in the city and kingdom of Ugarit in the LB Age is called Ugaritic.

A. Languages in Ugarit
B. The Language
  1. Classification
  2. Script, Phonology, and Vocalization

3. Principal Features
4. Geographical Distribution
C. Relation to Biblical Hebrew

A. Languages in Ugarit

During the LB Age, the city-state of Ugarit flourished as a cosmopolitan center of trade and commerce. As a result of its international character, several languages and various scripts were employed in the city. In addition to the native language, Ugaritic, evidence has survived of use at the same time of Akkadian, Hittite, Hurrian, and other languages. Some of these (e.g., Akkadian) were principally employed in the context of international trade and diplomacy; others (e.g., Hurrian) may reflect the mixed ethnic population within the city-state. The variety of languages was paralleled by the use of various scripts, including alphabetic cuneiform (used especially for Ugaritic itself), syllabic cuneiform, and hieroglyphic. Our knowledge of languages employed in Ugarit is based entirely on inscriptions, which include both archival texts and short inscriptions on monuments, tools, and other items. The multilingual context of the city-state had an influence on the native language, revealed both in loanwords and occasional grammatical forms. In addition, a few quadrilingual vocabularies have survived, in which Hurrian, Sumerian, and Akkadian equivalents of Ugaritic words are provided. One must suppose that professional scribes at Ugarit would have been multilingual in order to function properly in their profession.

B. The Language

1. Classification. The Semitic languages are commonly classified into three principal groups on a broadly geographical basis which corresponds conveniently, though not exactly, to linguistic divisions: East Semitic, Northwest Semitic, and South Semitic. There is general agreement that Ugaritic is a Northwest Semitic language, although there is continuing debate as to the precise subclassification of Ugaritic within the Northwest Semitic grouping. Some scholars assign Ugaritic to the "Canaanite" division of Northwest Semitic, though in fact the use of this term for languages of the 2d millennium B.C., like Ugaritic, involves historical and geographical difficulties. It is better to restrict its use, at least as a linguistic term, to the period after 1000 B.C., when the Northwest Semitic languages are known with certainty to have been split into two groups, Canaanite (i.e., Hebrew, Phoenician, Moabite) and Aramaic. Ugaritic does not, in fact, share all the characteristics of the later Canaanite. Thus one of these characteristics is the shifting of long stressed /a/ vowels to long /o/. For example, the feminine plural noun-ending in /-āt/ becomes /-ōt/. Ugaritic does not share this feature, whereas Hebrew does. In this context it is wiser to regard Ugaritic simply as a pre-Canaanite Northwest Semitic language.

There is no doubt, however, that Ugaritic has many affinities, both lexical and grammatical, with such languages as biblical Hebrew, Phoenician, and Moabite. It also has some affinities with Aramaic (for example, the shifting of the Proto-Semitic consonant /ḏ/ to /d/, against Hebrew /z/ and some lexica). We should note also links with the earlier Amorite (known to us only through personal names of the Mari period) and evidence of continuity with Eblaite. In summary, despite uncertainty over the subclassification of Ugaritic, it is agreed that it shares much with biblical Hebrew: a large, common lexical stock, certain fundamental grammatical similarities, and some common features of idiom and style.

2. Script, Phonology, and Vocalization. The native language of Ugarit had its own script, a form of alphabetic cuneiform, probably invented by the scribes of Ugarit, perhaps in the 15th century B.C. It combines the graphic principles of syllabic cuneiform (i.e., wedge-shaped marks on clay), with which the scribes of Syria were familiar, with the principle of the consonantal alphabet, which may have been learned from Byblos in the S. There were other, linear, consonantal scripts in use in the mid-2d millennium B.C., including the "Proto-Sinaitic" scripts of Sinai and Palestine. The normal Ugaritic script, written left to right, employed 30 symbols, though a shorter form of the alphabet, written right to left, has survived in a few texts (see below). The Ugaritic script tradition died out when the city was destroyed or soon afterwards and the innovative center of script development shifted S to Phoenicia.

The consonantal Ugaritic alphabet employs a wider range of symbols and represents a wider range of consonants than have survived in biblical Hebrew. Separate signs, for example for /ḥ/ and /ḫ/ and /ʿ/ and /ǵ/, suggest a phonology akin to Arabic rather than Hebrew (though there is evidence that Hebrew had more sounds than the Hebrew script could adequately represent). Vowels were not normally separately represented in the Ugaritic script. Hence, one cannot describe the script as alphabetic in the modern sense: it was left to the Greeks to develop an alphabet which included consonants *and* vowels as separate signs. Ugaritic is thus like Hebrew (for which the elaborate vocalization system was developed in the postbiblical period). However, in Ugaritic the letter *ʾalep*, the glottal stop, was written in three different forms to indicate the accompanying vowel. This, along with some Ugaritic texts and word lists written in the syllabic script normally used for Akkadian (a script which *does* represent vowels), enables us to establish a fairly clear idea of the vocalization of Ugaritic words. This vocalization is partly based on comparative Semitic grammar, especially comparison with Akkadian and Arabic.

3. Principal Features. Although the settlement of Ugarit goes back to the Neolithic period, and its importance grew from ca. 2000 B.C., all our sources of information on the linguistic situation in Ugarit come from the LB Age, ca. 1400–1200 B.C. This is too short a period of time, given the limited sources, in which to trace precisely chronological developments and change in the Ugaritic language. Some of the Ugaritic texts, because of their conservative nature, may preserve archaic linguistic features; a few of the administrative texts, from the last years of Ugarit prior to its destruction, reflect later modifications in the form of the language. Although Ugaritic ceased to be used after ca. 1200 B.C., it may be noted that Ugaritic had a direct linguistic and literary heir in Phoenician (of which relatively little is preserved) and some features of ancient Ugaritic are claimed to survive in the Arabic of the nearby modern city of Latakia (Badre et al. 1976: 105, 116, 125). From the perspective of comparative studies with the Bible, it needs to be remembered that all the evidence of Ugaritic is considerably earlier than any of the direct evidence for Hebrew.

More than 1,300 texts in the Ugaritic language have been recovered from Ras Shamra and nearby sites. The majority of these texts (economic, administrative, etc.) are in a standard form of the Ugaritic language, although the prose style is often abbreviated, almost shorthand, in the manner of such texts. A more elevated form of the language, marked by literary style and elegance, is found in the poetic texts (approximately 50 in number, though some are very long) and in some prose texts, such as letters and descriptions of religious rituals, many of which were found in royal and priestly archives. These texts of distinctive poetic style were probably the work of professional scribes, with the more mundane economic and practical texts reflecting the needs of merchants and administrators.

Unvocalized Ugaritic in transliteration looks very similar to unvocalized Hebrew in transliteration. There are, however, some major grammatical differences in addition to the phonological differences already alluded to. Nouns have case endings (as in Classical Arabic and Akkadian). Reconstruction, based on the methods of recovering vocalization referred to above, allows us to distinguish, for example, nominative, accusative, and genitive singular (/kussiʾu/, /kussiʾa/, /kussiʾi/, "chair, throne"). The dual is fully operative in Ugaritic. Another obvious feature is the absence of any definite article. The verbal "tenses" (if they can be so called) are perfect *qtl* and imperfect *yqṭl* as in Hebrew, Arabic, etc., though the use of the two is complex. The *yqṭl* form is frequently used for descriptions of past events, especially when one verb follows another in a descriptive sequence. In vocabulary, Ugaritic shares much with the Canaanite languages, though there are also many words shared with Akkadian. Some may be loanwords; others may go back to a much earlier stratum of Syrian Semitic, having been used already in Eblaite.

The poetic style of the literary texts (mythology and legends) shares the characteristics of Semitic poetry throughout the ANE and especially of the Northwest Semitic area. A notable feature of the poetic texts is the dominance of various forms of parallelism, together with related features such as formulaic language and the use of conventional word pairs in poetic parallel. Although the texts that have survived in the Ugaritic language provide some insight into the written forms of the language, they provide only partial understanding of what might have been the spoken forms of Ugaritic in everyday life.

4. Geographical Distribution. Inscriptions in the Ugaritic script and closely related scripts have been found over a wide area, but the evidence is hard to interpret. It is not always possible to be sure that an inscription in the Ugaritic script is in the Ugaritic language, since the inscriptions from outside Ugarit itself are invariably very short. One, from Sarepta, is thought to be in Phoenician. Nor is it possible to be sure that Ugaritic was normally used in the place where such an inscription has been found, since the particular text might be the product of an expatriate Ugaritian or the result of trade.

In general terms, Ugaritic was used in the city-state of Ugarit. The boundaries of the state changed from time to time, but they may have extended as far N as the Jebel el-ʿAqra (later Mt. Casius), E into the Orontes valley, and S as far as Tell Sukas (on the coast south of Latakia). Within this broad geographical area, inscriptions in Ugaritic have been found at Ras Shamra (Ugarit itself), Minet el-Beida (the nearby port), Ras Ibn Hani (a few km SW), and Tell Sukas. All these inscriptions (with the exception of three from Ras Shamra) are in the longer, conventional alphabet and presumably reflect the standard dialect of Ugaritic. A text in a variant form of the short alphabet, written right to left, was found at Tell Nebi Mend (ancient Qadesh) in the Orontes valley (Millard 1976: 459–60); whether this region was ever part of the kingdom of Ugarit is uncertain, though the dialect represented by the inscription may differ slightly from that in use in Ugarit itself.

Further inscriptions in the Ugaritic script have been found in regions that were never part of the kingdom of Ugarit (Craigie 1983: 153–57): Tell Taanach, Mt. Tabor, Kamid el-Loz, Beth Shemesh, and Sarepta. All these inscriptions are in a shorter form of the alphabetic cuneiform script, some reading left to right (Sarepta, Tell Taanach), some reading right to left (Mt. Tabor, Beth Shemesh), or some reading in both directions (Kamid el-Loz).

During a Swedish excavation at Hala Sultan Tekke in S Cyprus (1981), a silver bowl was discovered containing a short inscription in a form of the Ugaritic script. It is by no means certain, however, that Ugaritic was spoken in Cyprus (except, perhaps, by Ugaritic merchants), and the bowl was probably imported from the nearby Syrian coast. (See further Bordreuil 1983: 7–15.)

C. Relation to Biblical Hebrew

Despite the debate over classification, the rediscovery of the Ugaritic language has been of immense value for the study of biblical Hebrew (and vice versa). In the area of lexicography, a knowledge of Ugaritic words has frequently shed light on the meaning of otherwise obscure Hebrew words. To give but one example, in Prov 26:23 the obscurity of the Hebrew text has been resolved on the basis of recognition of the fact that a Hebrew scribe had at some stage corrupted a word corresponding to Ugaritic *spsg*, "glaze." The importance of Ugaritic in this context will be clear from the consultation of modern commentaries on biblical books, especially poetic books. Perhaps the 3-volume Psalms commentary in the AB series by Mitchell Dahood is the richest in the application of Ugaritic material to the elucidation of biblical Hebrew texts. Dahood's new meanings for Hebrew words were not always well enough supported by Hebrew evidence from context, but his approach is reflected in numerous monographs on individual OT books.

In the study of grammar (e.g., the forms and function of verbs, the usage of prepositions), Ugaritic has illuminated our knowledge of Hebrew, particularly with respect to archaic forms. Features like the rarity of the definite article and the use of the imperfect verb form for past action are seen also in Hebrew poetry. Hebrew's strange switching of verb forms in the "*wāw*-consecutive" may be partly explicable from comparison with Ugaritic. There are traces of case endings in Classical Hebrew: the /-īm/ masculine plural ending contains within it the /-ī/ which was originally an oblique case ending matched by a nominative /-ū/. The Hebrew prepositions have been the subject of renewed study in the light of Ugaritic usage.

The parallelism of Ugaritic poetry, the use of formulaic language and idiomatic expressions, and other features have contributed greatly to the study of Hebrew poetry. The Ugaritic language is a particularly valuable resource in the study of archaic and poetic aspects of the Hebrew Bible.

Bibliography

Aartun, K. 1974–78. *Die Partikeln des Ugaritischen.* AOAT 21–22. Neukirchen-Vluyn.

Aistleitner, J. 1974. *Wörterbuch der Ugaritischen Sprache.* 4th ed. Berlin.

Badre, L.; Bordeuil, P.; Mudarres, J.; ᶜAjjan, L.; and Vitale, R. 1976. Notes ougaritiques I. *Syria* 53: 95–125.

Bordreuil, P. 1983. Cunéiformes alphabétiques non canoniques II: à propos de l'épigraphe de Hala Sultan Tekké. *Semitica* 33: 7–15.

Brockelmann, C. 1964. Die kanaanäische Dialekte mit dem Ugaritischen. Pp. 40–58 in *Semitistik,* ed. B. Spuler. HO 3. Leiden.

Craigie, P. C. 1983. Ugarit, Canaan and Israel. *TynBul* 35: 145–68.

Gordon, C. H. 1965. *Ugaritic Textbook.* AnOr 38. Rome.

Millard, A. R. 1976. A Text in a Shorter Cuneiform Alphabet from Tell Nebi Mend. *UF* 8: 459–60.

Moran, W. L. 1961. The Hebrew Language in Its Northwest Semitic Background. Pp. 54–72 in *BANE.* London.

Pardee, D. 1975–79. The Preposition in Ugaritic. *UF* 7: 329–78; 8: 215–322; 9: 205–31; 11: 685–92.

Rabin, C. 1963. The Origin of Subdivisions in Semitic. Pp. 104–15 in *Hebrew and Semitic Studies,* ed. D. W. Thomas and W. D. McHardy. Oxford.

Segert, S. 1984. *A Basic Grammar of the Ugaritic Language.* Berkeley.

Watson, W. G. E. 1984. *Classical Hebrew Poetry: A Guide to Its Techniques.* Sheffield.

John F. Healey
Peter C. Craigie

LAODICEA (PLACE) [Gk *Laodikeia*]. A city in the Lycus valley of SW Phrygia, hence called *Laodicea ad Lycum* to distinguish it from other cities of the same name.

A. The Hellenistic and Roman City
B. Jewish Settlement
C. The Church of Laodicea

A. The Hellenistic and Roman City

Laodicea was founded by the Seleucid king Antiochus II and named in honor of his wife, Laodice, between his accession to the throne in 261 B.C. and his divorcing her in 253 B.C. According to the elder Pliny (*HN* 5.105), it was built on the site of an older settlement first called Diospolis and later Rhoas. The name Diospolis ("city of Zeus") might reflect the fact that Zeus was the chief deity of the place, as he was of Laodicea.

Laodicea stands on the S bank of the Lycus (modern Çürük-su), between two lesser streams, the Asopus (modern Gumuş-çay) on the W and the Capsus (modern Başli-çay) on the E. It is situated 10 or 11 miles downstream from Colossae and 6 miles S of Hierapolis. At Laodicea a northbound road left the Iconium-Ephesus highway and ran by Hierapolis to Philadelphia and the Hermus valley. The ruins of Laodicea are plainly visible 5 miles N of Denizli, between the villages of Eskihisar to the S and Goncali to the N.

One of the earliest appearances of Laodicea in history was when Achaeus, rebelling against his cousin Antiochus III, had himself crowned king there in 220 B.C. (Polyb. 5.57.5). The city rapidly increased in importance, to the point where it rivaled and then surpassed its older neighbor Colossae.

By the Peace of Apamea, imposed by the Romans on the Seleucids in 188 B.C., the region in which Laodicea lay was transferred from Seleucid sovereignty to that of the kings of Pergamum. When the kingdom of Pergamum, bequeathed by its last ruler to the Romans, was reconstituted as the Roman province of Asia, Laodicea and its neighbors were thenceforth under Roman control (129 B.C.).

Laodicea was one of the few cities of Asia to hold out against Mithridates VI, king of Pontus, when he overran the province in 88 B.C. It similarly held out against Labienus when he invaded the province at the head of a Parthian army in 40 B.C.; as a reward for the city's loyalty to Rome, Mark Antony conferred Roman citizenship on several leading Laodiceans.

Laodicea belonged to a *conventus,* or assize district, to which Hierapolis, Hydrela, Themisonium, and Cibyra also belonged. Although it was called the Cibyratic *conventus,* its court actually met at Laodicea (Plin. *HN* 5.105). From Cicero, to whose jurisdiction Laodicea and the other cities of the Cibyratic *conventus* belonged during his proconsulship of Cilicia (51–50 B.C.), we learn that it was a center of financial and banking operations (*Att.* 5.15; *Fam.* 3.5), as well as a place where gladiatorial shows were to be seen (*Att.* 6.3.9). Strabo (12.8.16) attests its economic prosperity at the beginning of the 1st century A.D.

Laodicea suffered severely from earthquakes. One is recorded in the principate of Augustus: the case for relieving the Laodiceans, with the people of Thyatira and Chios, was presented to the Roman senate by Tiberius, the emperor's stepson (Suet. *Tib.* 8). A later earthquake in A.D. 60 devastated the area. Laodicea was destroyed, but was rebuilt from its own resources without state assistance (Tac. *Ann.* 14.27.1).

In addition to its natural resources, Laodicea profited from the munificence of some of its leading citizens, among whom special mention is made of Hieron, who in the 1st century B.C. bequeathed over 2,000 talents to the city and adorned it with many fine public works, and of the family of Zeno the orator (Strab. 12.8.16). Zeno led the Laodiceans in their resistance to Labienus, and he was the first of them to be rewarded with Roman citizenship by Antony: he figures thenceforward as Marcus Antonius Zeno.

The family of Zeno enjoyed a brief period of splendor. His son Polemon, who had aided his father in resisting Labienus, was appointed by Antony king of Cilicia Tracheia, which he ruled from Iconium; after Antony's defeat and death (30 B.C.), he made his peace with Octavian (the future Emperor Augustus), who made him king of Pontus and the Bosporus.

Laodicea was noted for its textile products: the local wool, said to be even softer than that of Miletus, was raven-black in color—the result, according to Vitruvius (*De Arch.* 8.3.14), of the water drunk by the sheep. It appears, moreover, to have been the chief medical center of Phrygia. Its medical school may have been sponsored by the temple of the Anatolian deity Mēn Karou, about 13 miles W of the city. There is no evidence for the suggestion made by Ramsay (1895: 52) that Mēn Karou was Hellenized as Asklēpios. Neither is there positive evidence for the frequently repeated statement (as in Ramsay 1909: 419) that the "eyesalve" *(kollyrion)* produced in Laodicea (cf. Rev 3:18) was a preparation made from powdered Phrygian stone, recommended by Galen (*De sanitate tuenda* 6.12) as a specific for eye complaints, though it was quite possibly so.

Over and above their worship of Zeus and Mēn, the Laodiceans consulted the oracle of Apollo at Klaros in Ionia, to which they sent an annual delegation. The title *neōkoros,* "temple warden" (cf. Acts 19:35), was conferred on the city by Commodus (180–192) for its devotion to the imperial cult; the title was withdrawn after his death but restored by Caracalla (211–218) in the form "*Neōkoros* of Commodus and Caracalla."

With the reorganization of the Roman Empire toward the end of the 4th century A.D., Laodicea became the seat of government of the newly established province of Phrygia Pacatiana, mentioned in the endnote to 1 Timothy in later manuscripts and the KJV: "The first to Timothy was written from Laodicea, which is the chiefest city of Phrygia Pacatiana."

The site was partly excavated in 1961–1963 by an archaeological party from Laval University in Quebec, led by Jean des Gagniers. In particular, they completely cleared the nymphaeum, or public fountain house (des Gagniers 1969). The water supply for this came from the spring now called Başpinar in the upper part of Denizli: an aqueduct (part of which still survives) carried the water from that spring by force of gravity to a clearing basin on the S side of Laodicea, and from there it was piped under pressure (Weber 1898–1904) to a water tower that fed a water basin and feeding chambers, which in turn fed the fountains.

The nymphaeum, which apparently dates from the early 3d century A.D., contained a life-size statue of Isia. It was repeatedly reconstructed. The square water basin in the SW quarter was converted into a closed chamber that served as a Christian meeting place.

Other recognizable structures include an odeum or council chamber, two theaters (a larger one of Greek date and a smaller one of Roman date), the gymnasium (less probably a bathhouse) with a dedicatory inscription to Hadrian and his wife Sabina (A.D. 123/124), and an "amphitheatral" stadium (as it is called in inscriptions) of the exceptional length of 380 yards, dedicated to Vespasian by a wealthy citizen in A.D. 79 and formally consecrated by the proconsul of Asia (father of the future Emperor Trajan). This stadium was used not only for athletic contests but also for gladiatorial shows.

The tower-flanked triple arch, at what is now called the Ephesian Gate, W of the city, was dedicated to Domitian (A.D. 81–96). Practically all the recognizable buildings are of later date than the earthquake of A.D. 60.

In A.D. 494, there was another devastating earthquake, from which Laodicea seems never to have recovered, although it survived after a fashion until the Turkish conquest.

B. Jewish Settlement

When Antiochus III, shortly after 213 B.C., settled 2,000 Jewish families from Babylonia in Lydia and Phrygia, to help to stabilize those two disaffected and recently reconquered areas of his empire (Joseph. *Ant* 12.149), many of them evidently made their home in Laodicea. Laodicea was one of the centers to which the proceeds of the half-shekel tax paid annually by male Jews in the area were brought for transmission. In 62 B.C., the half-shekels brought together in Laodicea amounted to the equivalent of 20 Roman pounds (Cic. *Flac.* 68); from this it has been calculated that over 9,000 half-shekels were collected in and around Laodicea. The Jewish population of Laodicea and its vicinity must have been considerable.

According to Josephus (*Ant* 14.241–3), the magistrates of Laodicea sent a letter ca. 45 B.C. to a high Roman official, probably the proconsul of Asia, confirming that, in accordance with his instructions, they would not impede the liberty of Jewish residents to observe the Sabbath and other practices of their religion.

C. The Church of Laodicea

Laodicea was probably evangelized, with the other cities of the Lycus valley, during Paul's Ephesian ministry (Acts 19:10)—not by Paul in person but, it appears, by his colleague Epaphras (Col 4:13). Nevertheless, Paul regarded those cities as part of his appointed mission field, and he had a sense of pastoral responsibility for their churches (Col 2:1). He mentions the church of Laodicea in his letter to the Colossians: he asks the Colossian Christians to convey his greetings to those in Laodicea (among whom "Nympha and the church in her house" are specially mentioned), and he directs that this letter be read also in the Laodicean church, and that the Colossians read "the letter from Laodicea" (Col 4:16). The "letter from Laodicea" (possibly a letter of Paul's to be procured by the Colossian church "from Laodicea") is unknown to us: it has been suggested, not implausibly, that it was destroyed in the earthquake of A.D. 60. The letter has been identified with the canonical Letter to the Ephesians; this identification, first made by Marcion (ca. A.D. 144), has little probability. Later an apocryphal "Letter to the Laodiceans" (a mere cento of Pauline phrases) enjoyed a wide circulation in Western Europe; a Middle English version of it appears in several copies of the Wycliffite NT. It ceased to be included among the NT writings from the Reformation onward.

The church of Laodicea was one of the seven churches of Asia addressed in Revelation. In the letter to Laodicea (Rev 3:14–22), the church is rebuked for allowing the wealth and comfort enjoyed by the Laodiceans in general to blunt the edge of its Christian confession: materially affluent and self-sufficient, it was spiritually "wretched, pitiable, poor, blind and naked." The city's economic prosperity, eye ointment, and wool could do nothing to help this spiritual destitution. The lukewarmness for which, thanks to this letter, the name of Laodicea has become proverbial, may reflect the condition of the city's water supply. The water supplied by the spring at Başpinar, it is suggested, was tepid and nauseous by the time it was piped to Laodicea, unlike the therapeutic hot water of Hierapolis or the refreshing cold water of Colossae (Rudwick and Green 1958); hence the Lord's words, "Would that you were cold or hot!"

The warning was apparently effective: the church of Laodicea continued for long to maintain its Christian witness. Between A.D. 161 and 167 a bishop of Laodicea, Sagaris by name, suffered martyrdom. In his time, said Melito, bishop of Sardis, at the beginning of his *Easter Festival,* there was much debate at Laodicea about the proper day for the celebration of Easter (Euseb. *Hist. Eccl.* 4.26.3). Sagaris was a Quartodeciman, holding (with Melito himself and other church leaders in the province of Asia, including Polycarp, bishop of Smyrna) that Easter should coincide with the Jewish Passover, on Nisan 14, regardless of the day of the week, in opposition to the growing body of Christian opinion which held that Easter should always be celebrated on the first day of the week, on which Jesus rose from the dead. Sagaris' part in the debate is invoked by Polycrates, bishop of Ephesus, another champion of the Quartodeciman position, in a letter on the subject which he addressed ca. A.D. 190 to Victor, bishop of Rome (Euseb. *Hist. Eccl.* 5.24.5). Polycrates and other Quartodecimans appealed to the precedent of John, the beloved disciple, who spent his last years in the province of Asia.

A church synod held at Laodicea around A.D. 363 promulgated 60 rulings—the Canons of Laodicea—which were acknowledged by later church councils as a basis for canon law.

Bibliography

Bean, G. E. 1971. *Turkey beyond the Maeander.* London.

Buckler, W. H., and Calder, W. M., eds. 1939. *Monumenta Asiae Minoris Antiqua.* Vol. 6. Manchester.

des Gagniers, J. 1969. *Laodicée du Lycos: Le nymphée, Campagnes 1961–1963.* Quebec.

Hemer, C. J. 1986. *The Letters to the Seven Churches of Asia in Their Local Setting.* JSNTSup 11. Sheffield.

Magie, D. 1950. *Roman Rule in Asia Minor,* 2 vols. Princeton.

Ramsay, W. M. 1895. *The Cities and Bishoprics of Phrygia.* Vol. 1. Oxford.

———. 1909. *The Letters to the Seven Churches of Asia and Their Place in the Plan of the Apocalypse.* London.

Rudwick, M. J. S., and Green, E. M. B. 1958. The Laodicean Lukewarmness. *ExpTim* 69: 176–78.

Weber, G. 1898–1904. Die Hochdruck Wasserleitung von Laodicea ad Lycum. *Jahrbuch des kaiserlich-deutschen archäologischen Instituts* 13: 1–13; 19: 95–96.

Yamauchi, E. 1980. *The Archaeology of New Testament Cities in Western Asia Minor.* Grand Rapids.

F. F. BRUCE

LAODICEANS, EPISTLE TO THE. (1) A letter specified in Col 4:16 to be obtained from Laodicea and read by the Christians of Colossae; and (2) an apocryphal letter attributed to Paul and purporting to be the letter of Col 4:16, found in numerous medieval Latin and some Western vernacular mss of the NT.

The reference in Col 4:16 to a letter which the Colossians were to obtain "from Laodicea" has created a puzzle which has not yet received a generally accepted solution. From the 2d century to the present, there have been numerous endeavors to identify this letter, ranging from Marcion's retitling of Ephesians as Laodiceans (Tertullian, *Adv. Marc.* 5:17) to the denial that the letter ever existed. However, throughout the medieval period it was widely identified in the West with the apocryphal Letter to the Laodiceans. (See Enslin *IDB* 3: 71–72.)

A. The Apocryphal Letter to the Laodiceans

From the 4th century on, various patristic voices, both Eastern and Western, warned of a fraudulent Letter to the Laodiceans circulating under Paul's name (references, with texts, in Pink 1925: 179–82). While no such letter appears in any ancient NT Greek manuscript, an apocryphal Letter to the Laodiceans was known in the Eastern Church at least as early as Theodore of Mopsuestia (ca. 350–428 C.E.). He declared it inauthentic on the grounds that Col 4:16 does not refer to a letter written by Paul but to a (lost) letter from the Laodiceans to Paul. This view became normative in the Eastern Church.

It was otherwise in the West. Numerous Latin and some vernacular mss from the 6th to the 15th centuries contain an *ad Laodicenses* in varying positions among the Pauline letters (partial list of mss in Lightfoot 1884: 280–83). Although no explicit canonical claims were ever made for it (Gregory the Great, ca. 540–604 C.E., came close with his statement that Paul wrote 15 letters; *Moralia in Job* 35: 20), the manuscript evidence demonstrates that Laodiceans was considered genuine by a large portion of Western Christendom, despite the dominant tradition of a 14-letter Pauline corpus and the pronouncement of the Second Council of Nicaea (787 C.E.) against this "fabricated epistle."

During the 16th century, Laodiceans lost much of its popularity. The matter was officially settled for the Roman Catholics by the publication of a list of biblical books (*De Canonicis Scripturis,* 1546 C.E.) from which Laodiceans was excluded by the Council of Trent (1545–1563 C.E.). The letter also fell into disfavor among the Protestants, who perhaps were influenced by the disdain with which Erasmus (1469–1536 C.E.) regarded it; and so, for the first time, all major branches of the Church were united in declaring Laodiceans non-Pauline.

Yet, a few voices continued to speak in its defense. For example, the letter was included in Elias Hutter's Polyglot NT (1599 C.E.). The Heb, Gk, and Lat texts of Laodiceans in this publication were edited, revised, and republished in 1661 C.E. (Ebied 1966: 247). This latter edition perhaps was the original from which the triglot Laodiceans, discovered in the 1960s, was copied and published in 1679 C.E. (Ebied 1966: 243–44).

Modern scholars, however, are unanimous in regarding the apocryphal Laodiceans as a forgery. Its origins lie in a time well beyond the 1st century, and whatever value it may have relates to the later interpretation of Paul, not to Paul himself. Harnack (1924: 134–49) held it to be the Laodiceans mentioned in the Muratorian Canon (see also Quispel 1950). There, two letters, *ad Laudicenses* and *ad Alexandrinos,* are said to have been forged in Paul's name to promote Marcion's heresy *(finctae ad haeresem Marcionis).* To many scholars, however, it is not obvious that the apocryphal Laodiceans contains any of Marcion's distinctive emphases, even if it does incorporate some of his textual emendations to Paul's letters, as Harnack claimed. On the other hand, there is no evidence outside the Muratorian Canon of a second apocryphal Laodiceans.

The origin of the apocryphal letter is not later than the 4th century; it was known by Theodore of Mopsuestia, as noted above, and others, including Jerome (ca. 342–420 C.E.) and Augustine (354–430 C.E.). If the Muratorian Canon comes from the 4th-century East rather than the 2d-century West (Sundberg 1973), then there is no testimony to the letter's existence prior to the 4th century. Opinion is divided regarding a Lat or a Gk original, though the evidence for the latter is substantial (Lightfoot 1884: 289–91).

Slightly shorter than Philemon, Laodiceans is basically a collection of sentences and phrases from Paul's letters (critical Lat text and his translation into Gk in Lightfoot 1884: 285–92; Eng translation in James 1924: 478–79, Schneemelcher 1965: 131–32). The epistle's opening—"Paul, an apostle not of men and not through man, but through Jesus Christ . . ."—is obviously an echo of Gal 1:1. Dependence on Philippians is particularly evident: "For my life is in Christ and to die is joy" (v 8; cf. Phil 1:21); "And what is pure, true, proper, just and lovely, do" (v 15; cf. Phil 4:8); "That you may have the same love and be of one mind" (v 9b; cf. Phil 2:2). Most telling of all is the conclusion: "And see that this epistle is read to the Colossians and that of the Colossians among you"—obviously designed to reflect Col 4:16, "And when this letter has been read among you, see that it is read by the Laodiceans and that you read the letter from Laodicea." (For further parallels, see Schneemelcher 1965: 132.)

No motive for the composition of the apocryphal Laodiceans is apparent other than a desire to complete the Pauline corpus by supplying the letter of Col 4:16, thereby continuing the production of popular Christian texts in the pseudepigraphical tradition. Its persistence throughout the Middle Ages may be due to its incorporation of a number of doctrinal terms, concepts, and affirmations particularly important to the medieval Church, such as Paul's divinely appointed apostolate; the persons, though not the title itself, of the Trinity—God the Father, the Lord Jesus Christ, and the Holy Spirit; the day of judgment; salvation as eternal life; the mercy of Christ; rejoicing in suffering; the fear of God; standing firm in faith and resisting those who would lead astray; the truth of the Gospel; and intercessory prayer by a saint (Paul). With popular orthodoxy affirmed in so many ways in such a short writing, it is not surprising that literary and historical questions about it seemed unimportant to many medieval Christians. For them, Origen's words concerning Hebrews would have been appropriately applied to Laodiceans—its contents were worthy of Paul; therefore, it should continue to be treated as Paul's.

B. The Letter of Colossians 4:16

The apocryphal letter, therefore, proved to be a durable solution to the problem posed by Col 4:16, at least until the modern period. But other solutions have been proposed. A large portion of the early Gk discussion of Col 4:16 seems to have been aimed at strengthening the case against the apocryphal Laodiceans. As mentioned above, the argument was advanced that the wording of Col 4:16 (*tēn ek Laodikeias*—"the <letter> from Laodicea") indicates that the letter was not written to but from Laodicea. While this interpretation would allow Laodiceans to be written either by or to Paul (i.e., a letter which Paul wrote while at Laodicea or a letter from the Laodiceans to Paul), in either case it rules out a letter written by Paul to Laodicea (Lightfoot 1884: 273–74).

However, while it is grammatically possible to interpret Col 4:16 in this way, the immediate context requires a different interpretation. The letter is represented as exchangeable with Colossians. Two communities, only a three- or four-hour walk apart on a highway, receive two different letters. The author of Colossians urges its recipients to ensure that each community reads both letters. The word "from" indicates not place of writing but place of access to the letter.

Whether Marcion's renaming of Ephesians as Laodiceans was based on the close textual relationship between Ephesians and Colossians or nothing more than Col 4:16 is uncertain. Marcion's solution has also been urged in more recent times (Lightfoot 1884: 279). Another alternative was presented in its most extensive form by John Knox (1935), who argued that the letter of Col 4:16 is the Letter to Philemon. Both views rest on questionable though different assumptions and have little scholarly following today. Earlier suggestions that Galatians, 1 Timothy, one of the Thessalonian letters, or 1 John was the original Laodiceans are not worth serious consideration (Anger 1843: 16–21; Lightfoot 1884: 272–76).

The apocryphal Laodiceans of course was not written by Paul. But did Paul write the letter of Col 4:16? The issue has become more complicated in recent years by increasing skepticism concerning the Pauline authorship of Colossians itself. If Colossians was not written by Paul, then the only textual evidence in the canonical Pauline writings for a letter of his to Laodicea is removed. On the assumption of a Pauline Colossians, a case can be made that the letter of Col 4:16 was not written by Paul but by the member of the Laodicean-Colossian community highly recommended in Colossians, i.e., Epaphras (Anderson 1966). However, a non-Pauline Colossians makes the very existence of an epistle to the Laodiceans problematic. Indeed, it is possible that the Laodiceans mentioned in Col 4:14 never existed except in the mind of the Deutero-Paulinist who wrote Colossians. On the other hand, it could be argued that Col 4:16, even if part of a pseudepigraph, is intended to validate another writing. Otherwise, its presence in Colossians is difficult to explain.

The identity of Laodiceans has also been approached as a canonical question: how a companion epistle of Colossians could have been lost when its value and use should have been guaranteed by Col 4:16. The trail of this line of reasoning has led to the proposition that the Epistle to the Hebrews, an integral part of the Pauline corpus in the East from the 2d century on, and Laodiceans are one and the same (Anderson 1975).

However, the identity of the letter mentioned in Col 4:16 is so closely related to unresolved questions regarding the origin and purpose of Colossians that further progress on the first must await a more complete understanding of

Colossians as a whole. Pauline authorship of Colossians is less critical for this matter than its purpose and the call for an exchange of letters. Until a credible alternative emerges, it is best to assume that Col 4:16 refers to a real letter, whoever the author(s) of this letter and of Colossians may be. But whether that letter is extant under another name or was lost prior to the formation of the canon awaits a definitive statement.

Bibliography

Anderson, C. P. 1966. Who Wrote the Letter to Laodicea? *JBL* 85: 436–40.
———. 1975. Hebrews Among the Letters of Paul. *SR* 5: 258–66.
Anger, R. 1843. *Ueber den Laodicenerbrief. Eine biblisch-kritische Untersuchung.* Leipzig.
Blackman, E. C. 1948. *Marcion and his Influence.* London.
Ebied, R. Y. 1966. A Triglot Volume of the Epistle to the Laodiceans, Psalm 151 and other Biblical Materials. *Bib* 47: 243–54.
Harnack, A. von. 1924. *Marcion: Das Evangelium vom fremden Gott.* 2d ed. Leipzig.
James, M. R. 1924. *The Apocryphal New Testament.* Oxford.
Knox, J. 1935. *Philemon Among the Letters of Paul.* Chicago.
Lightfoot, J. B. 1884. *Saint Paul's Epistles to the Colossians and Philemon.* London.
Pink, K. 1925. Die Pseudo-paulinischen Briefe II. *Bib* 6: 179–92.
Quispel, G. 1950. De Brief aan de Laodicensen een Marcionitische Vervalsing. *NedTTs* 5: 43–46.
Schneemelcher, W. 1965. The Epistle to the Laodiceans. *NTApocr* 2: 128–32.
Sundberg, A. C., Jr. 1973. Canon Muratori: A Fourth-Century List. *HTR* 66: 1–41.

CHARLES P. ANDERSON

LAPPIDOTH (PERSON) [Heb *lappîdôt*]. Husband of Deborah the prophetess, living in the tribal hill country of Ephraim, between Ramah and Bethel (Judg 4:4). The derivation of his name is uncertain, but it probably is a feminine abstract form [Heb *-ôt*] of *lappîd,* meaning "torch" or "lightning" (*HALAT,* 506–7). The temptation to associate his name with Barak, also meaning "lightning," has been irresistible (Boling *Judges* AB, 95). The fact that the text identifies Barak as originating in the N part of Israel (Kadesh in Naphtali; Judg 4:6) makes this highly unlikely (cf. Soggin *Judges* AB, 64).

KIRK E. LOWERY

LARSA. An important Sumerian city that played a very active role in the beginning of the 2d millennium B.C. The city was built on the site of the present tell Senkéré about 20 km E of Uruk and about 40 km N of Ur. The Euphrates, which now runs more to the S, was able to irrigate the region then by means of a canal.

The tell was noticed by travelers as early as 1832, but the first excavation was undertaken by W. K. Loftus in 1854, when he took soundings from the high point of the tell. The inscribed bricks that were thus gathered allowed him to identify the Senkéré tell with ancient Larsa. Following Loftus, W. Andrae worked there for several days in 1903. But the attention of orientalists has mainly been attracted by the quality of the objects—the famous adorer of Larsa or the group of three standing ibexes, but also the large number of tablets—that came from clandestine excavations shortly after World War I. The exploration of the site was thus engaged under the direction of A. Parrot; the first excavation took place in the spring of 1933, but the second and the third did not occur until 1967. The fourth and fifth excavations were directed by J. Marqueron in 1969 and 1970. Since 1974, under the direction of J.-L. Huot, seven new excavations have taken place. In addition the region of Larsa was included in the survey done by R. McC. Adams and H. J. Nissen in order to study the organization of rivers and canals in S Babylonia.

The ovoid tell covers 2,000 m from N to S and 1,800 m from E to W. The average altitude is rather low, only 7 to 8 m in height, but the culminating point, which is the site of the temple of Shamash, the great sanctuary of the city called the Ebabbar, reaches 22 m.

Around this pole the village reaches down to a much lower level, with, in the region N of the Ebabbar, the domain of the palaces, including that of Nur-Adad. On the periphery, and more particularly on the E side, a rise in altitude could correspond to sectors occupied in earlier periods. The excavations are not advanced enough to provide any precise knowledge of the history of the city. It appears that its origins could go back to the Ubaid period, but nothing can be said about this period or the one following it. The oldest monument known to this day is the palace built by Nur-Adad (1865–1850 B.C.), and the texts are numerous for this period but practically absent for the 3d millennium. Larsa, in fact, only took on real importance after Gungunum defeated Isin (1932 B.C.), when he hoped to find there the heritage of the 3d Dynasty of Ur. From that time on, for a century and a half, Larsa was a dominant power; but it was never able to manipulate the existing equilibrium to its own advantage. When Hammurabi of Babylonia (1792–1750) took control of S Mesopotamia, he reduced Larsa to the rank of provincial capital. The city seems to have no longer played a major role in history, but it would remain important up until the Neo-Babylonian period and still knew activity even during the Hellenistic and Parthian periods.

One of the reasons for this long existence comes from the fact that the village sheltered one of the two large Mesopotamian sanctuaries dedicated to the solar cult. Larsa thus appears as the great center of the god Shamash (UTU in Sumerian), symbol of life, of light, and the expression of justice. It is understood that even after having to renounce all political pretensions, the city continued to exist thanks to its principal sanctuary, the Ebabbar. The excavations have not yet succeeded in pinpointing its origins, but its extreme antiquity is certain. It is apparently to the Old Babylonian period that one must credit the monumental form of the temple that is known, but the existence of certain rooms which are clearly unbalanced in their placement on the tell show an important transformation of the original plan, of which some vestiges have been found. The conception of the monument is grandiose: from tell Ebabbar, a succession of sanctuaries and paths join the ziggurat in a row of almost 300 m in length. The heart of the city is thus occupied by this unique complex that remained in this general form until the end of the 11th century B.C. In the 1st millennium, the temple seems to have been confined to the Ebabbar tell itself.

The second monument studied is the palace of Nur-Adad, which seems to be a very clear example, although incomplete, of palatial architecture from the beginning of the 2d millennium. Circumstances impeded Nur-Adad from finishing the palace and, for some unknown reason, none of his successors took it up again. The excavation has thus given us a building that has never been inhabited and that exactly reflects the thinking of the architect who conceived it. The official courtyard, the throne room, the administration sector, a small sector of stores, and the common areas appear very clearly in the parts that have been uncovered.

Despite the intensity of the clandestine pillaging, the regular digs have uncovered some very beautiful objects: a large statue (61 cm) of a seated person, of which the head is missing; an androcephalous bull of a Neo-Sumerian type; the kudurru of Kudur-Enlil with superimposed registers lined with divine symbols; and above all the kudurru of Nazi-Marutash, decorated with a superb dog of Gula, a real *chef-d'oeuvre* of animal sculpture. Finally, a very beautiful collection of gold objects consisting of tools and finished products of a rare quality came from a cache found under the floor of a room of the Ebabbar. For further discussion, see *RLA* sub "Larsa."

Bibliography

Heinrich, E. 1982. *Die Tempel und Heiligtümer im alten Mesopotamien.* Neukirchen-Vluyn.

Huot, J.-L. 1987. *Larsa, 10e campagne, 1983 et ʿOueli 4e campagne, 1983, rapport préliminaire.* Paris.

Margueron, J. C. 1982. *Recherches sur les palais mésopotamiens de l'âge du Bronze.* Paris.

JEAN-CL. MARGUERON
Trans. Stephen Rosoff

LASEA (PLACE) [Gk *Lasaia*]. A city located along the S coast of Crete about 5 miles E of Fair Havens or Kaloi Limenes. The ship carrying Paul, during his voyage to Italy, anchored at Fair Havens and supplies were probably obtained from nearby Lasea (Acts 27:8). The captain of the ship decided not to winter there, despite Paul's warnings, and sailed on to the W into a storm which wrecked the ship.

The textual variations in the spelling of the city's name may reflect an uncertainty of the location of the site. The relatively dense distribution of cities on Crete may have led to the confusion. Some scholars have equated Lasea with the Lasos mentioned by Pliny (*HN* 4.12.59). A Mediterranean survey team led by T. A. B. Spratt located ruins near Fair Havens which have been identified with Lasea. The ruins of the city have never been systematically explored, but several early tholos tombs in the vicinity have been documented.

Bibliography

Spratt, T. A. B. 1856. *Travels and Researches in Crete.* Vol. 2. London.

JOHN D. WINELAND

LASHA (PLACE) [Heb *lešaʿ*]. One of the places mentioned in Gen 10:19 which defined the limits of the territory of the Canaanites. Since the passage reads "in the direction of Sodom, Gomorrah, Admah, and Zeboiim, as far as Lasha," some scholars have assumed that Lasha represents the SE boundary of Canaanite land and have sought a location for it along the SE shore of the Dead Sea. Ancient and rabbinic tradition equated it with Kallirrhoe (modern Wadi Zerqa Maʿin), the hot springs and health resort of Herod the Great, but modern archaeological work in that area has provided no support for the identification. Others, by emendation of the name, have equated the place with Laish (Dan) and therefore have seen it as a N boundary of Canaan. Neither identification can be proved, and thus Lasha's location remains unknown.

Bibliography

Donner, H. 1963. Kallirrhoi, Das Sanatorium Herodes des Grossen. *ZDPV* 79: 59–89.

Westermann, C. 1984. *Genesis 1–11: A Commentary.* Trans. J. J. Scullion. Minneapolis.

GARY H. OLLER

LASHARON (PLACE) [Heb *laššārôn*]. The king of Lasharon is listed as one of the 31 Canaanite kings defeated by Joshua (Josh 12:18). Since the name Lasharon occurs nowhere else in either the OT or other ancient sources, and is accompanied in the same verse by Aphek (M.R. 143168), most scholars accept the LXX reading of the verse, "King of Aphek of/belonging to Sharon" (*LBHG,* 230). The Sharon is a geographical term used to describe the coastal plain located roughly between the Carmel and the Aphek region. Since there are Apheks in Asher and in Transjordan, it would not be unreasonable to specify in the text which Aphek was meant in this passage. See APHEK (PLACE).

Boling rejects this solution, suggesting that Lasharon could stand independently for the N coastal plain as a whole, which he notes would have been swampy and sparsely settled in antiquity (*Joshua* AB, 328). This does not explain why such a nonurban region would have a "king" like the towns in the rest of the list. If Lasharon is an independent location, it remains unidentified.

MELVIN HUNT

LAST SUPPER. According to the NT, Jesus of Nazareth was present at a final meal with his disciples on the night before his death (1 Cor 11:23–25; Mark 14:22–25; Matt 26:26–29; Luke 22:15–20; cf. John 61:51c). What actually happened at the Last Supper? Numerous analyses of the Last Supper have led to a remarkable variety of interpretations, many of which appear to have been influenced by the confessional stances of their proponents. In an effort to answer historical questions about the Last Supper, first some general observations will be made; then it will be asked whether the Last Supper was a Passover meal; and finally there will be an attempt to determine what Jesus said and did, and the significance of his words and actions.

A. General Observations
B. Was the Last Supper a Passover Meal?
C. The Words of Jesus
D. Questions of Meaning

A. General Observations

From the 3d century B.C. onward, there was a growing Hellenistic influence on Judaism, including Judaism in Palestine. This influence touched on most aspects of life, including table customs and feasts. The history of religions provides two analogies to the Last Supper: the significance of community meals in the OT and in contemporary Judaism (under the influence of Qumran) and the use of eschatological metaphors related to meals. C. Burchard (1987: 118–19; but see Lindars 1987: 193–96) suggests that perhaps *Joseph and Aseneth* can help explain why the central rite of Christianity was a solemn act of consuming bread and drinking from a cup, why gestures concerning these were remembered and attributed to Jesus, and why a narrative about these acts was formed at all. To be sure, the meals of the earthly Jesus can be compared to numerous noncultic friendship and family meals, and for the ancient oriental a common meal bound the table companions in fellowship. Jewish customs provide the background for understanding Jesus' actions at the Last Supper, whose framework was that of a Jewish festive meal, but not necessarily that of a Passover (Delling *TRE* 1: 49; Klauck 1982: 330–31; 369–70). According to von Meding (1975: 544–52), the historical background of the Last Supper is to be found in the ritual meal of Jeremiah (16:7), designed to console those who grieve. However, in this investigation one does well to recall Toynbee's caution that the uniformity of human nature sometimes produces similar results in similar situations where there can be no suspicion of any historical bridge by which the tradition could have been mediated from one culture to another. For instance, all human beings eat, and when they do most of them seek companionship with one another and with their god (Metzger 1968: 10–11). Moreover, some of the data postdates the NT evidence, and consequently should only with caution be used to explain it.

The NT texts themselves may well not lead us back to Jesus' own words but rather to an earlier report about those words. There is also the likelihood of an oral tradition in which there would be a considerable variability in the wording. Certainly, the texts that we now have do not postdate the actual event by many years, and the apostles who were present naturally functioned as a kind of check on what was said. However, we are not sure whether Jesus at the Last Supper used Hebrew or Aramaic or a combination of both. Jesus might have spoken in Aramaic; but as scholars (e.g., Fitzmyer 1979: 1–27, 38–43, 85–113; Hurst 1986: 72–73) stress, the mother tongue of Jesus is meagerly represented, so a skepticism toward older approaches used in reconstructing the language of Jesus is a healthy trend.

Most scholars now agree that Jesus' words and actions at the Last Supper should be understood in terms of his whole ministry. One fact of that ministry universally agreed on is that Jesus ate fellowship meals, at least some of which included sinners. This acceptance of sinners and outcasts into table fellowship implies forgiveness (e.g., Mark 2:15–17; Luke 5:29–32; 7:36–50; 15:1–2; 19:1–10; Reumann 1985: 4). Likewise, whatever the historical facts behind the feedings of the multitude (Mark 6:30–44; 8:1–10), they were fellowship meals. On the other hand, the first explicit references in the NT to an agape meal are in 2 Pet 2:13(?) and Jude 12.

In addition, granted the historical validity of Peter's identification of Jesus at Caesarea Philippi as "Messiah," what did the disciples think, thereafter, of meals they ate with Jesus? Did they view them as anticipations of the messianic banquet? The Last Supper would probably, at a minimum, have been Jesus' final act of fellowship with his disciples and an anticipation of the messianic banquet that he would share with them in the coming of the kingdom.

The vast majority of scholars recognize that Jesus ate a final meal with his disciples. Actually, the "breaking of bread" and "blessing" (thanksgiving) would have been typical of a Jewish meal, and there simply was not enough time for a cultic legend to develop (Marxsen 1952–53: 303). Also, it is the only one of Jesus' meals that can be dated, and the report about it could easily enough have been based on what those who were there remembered. Besides, some historical elements can be detected in the gospel account as a whole. For example, both Luke and Paul retain a reference to the meal between the liturgical actions over the bread and wine (Luke 22:20; 1 Cor 11:25), and there are two unprecedented actions of Jesus: he passed a single cup among his disciples, and, as a prophet, he explained his own symbolic gesture. Marxsen (1979: 102–8) is less sanguine about establishing the historical reality of the Last Supper.

Without yet entering into the question of literary genre, two reflections should be made about the Last Supper. It is questionable whether "parabolic" adequately explains Jesus' words and actions. Rather, Jesus performs an efficacious sign, a prophetic symbolic act. As Ezekiel (5:1–5) had identified his hair with Jerusalem, so Jesus has identified himself with the bread and wine (Beck 1970: 192–97). However, "symbolic" is not to be opposed to "real"; on the contrary, the symbolic is the depth dimension of the real (Léon-Dufour 1987: 10, 162–65). The Last Supper likewise resembles a farewell meal. This is the context in which it now appears in Luke 22:14–38, and John 13–17 supports such an understanding (cf. Gen 27:1–40; *Jub* 22:1–9; 31:22; *T. Napht.* 1:1–4; 9:2). The solemn nature of a farewell meal marks the significance of what is said by the one departing (Friedrich 1978: 310–14).

B. Was the Last Supper a Passover Meal?

Although a number of scholars identify the Last Supper as a Passover meal, a description of which is given in the Mishna (*Pesaḥ* 10; cf. Str-B 4/1: 41–76), the majority are still not convinced of this interpretation. However, many would concede that Jesus ate his final meal in a Passover atmosphere; there was, after all, the proximity of the feast. The cause of this scholarly disagreement is that, although the Synoptics identify the Last Supper as a Passover meal (Mark 14:12–16 parr.; Luke 22:15), John (13:1–2; cf. 19:14, 31, 36) does not. Jesus' Jewish opponents did not enter the praetorium so that they might not be defiled, but so that they could eat the Passover to be held after Jesus died (John 18:28).

The main proponent of the Last Supper as a Passover meal is Jeremias (1977: 15–88), and Leaney (1967: 51) provides a partial listing of scholars on both sides of this debate. The following are the weightier reasons for the claim that the Last Supper was a Passover meal. The Last Supper took place in the evening and extended into the night (1 Cor 11:23; cf. Mark 14:17; John 13:30), when it was obligatory that the Passover be eaten. Normally, the Jewish main meal was in the afternoon. Jews in the time of Jesus sat at ordinary meals, but the Passover ordinance was that they should recline as a symbol of liberty. In fact, Jesus and his disciples reclined at the Last Supper. A dish of hors d'oeuvres precedes the breaking of bread only at the Passover, and this dish is referred to in Mark 14:20; Matt 26:23, and John 13:26. It was customary on the Passover night to give alms to the poor (cf. John 13:29). Wine was drunk at the Last Supper, and the drinking of wine was obligatory at the Passover. The Last Supper concluded with the singing of a hymn (Mark 14:26; Matt 26:30), which would have been the second part (Psalms 114 or 115–118) of the *hallēl* which closed the Passover meal. After the meal, Jesus did not return to Bethany but went to the Mount of Olives, for after the Passover, one was supposed to stay within a certain distance of Jerusalem, which included Gethsemane but not Bethany. The Passover *haggadâ,* according to which the person presiding explained the various elements in the meal as it progressed, probably suggested Jesus' words over the bread and wine (Barclay 1967: 20–34; Ruckstuhl 1985: 41–44).

Opponents of this view have pointed out that a Jewish festive meal (cf. Str-B 4/2: 611–39) would satisfy most of these claims for the Last Supper as a Passover meal. Moreover, the mention of Jerusalem and of the *hallēl* belong to the redactional framework of the narratives. Further, in the days prior to his arrest, Jesus and his disciples would for reasons of security have met at night, so the meal at that time would not necessarily have been a Passover (Kahlefeld 1980: 42–43). More specifically, scholars raise the following objections to the claim that the Last Supper was a Passover meal. (1) Jesus shared his last meal with only the Twelve, a community of men, but a Passover was a family affair, with women and children present. Nor is Jesus portrayed as the paterfamilias, who would normally have left to an honored guest the closing blessing over the cup (Kuhn 1957: 83–4). (2) The Greek noun *azyma* is the proper designation of unleavened bread, but *artos,* "bread," occurs in the institution accounts (Mark 14:22; Matt 26:26; Luke 22:19; 1 Cor 11:23). (3) No mention is made of the paschal lamb or the bitter herbs (Bornkamm 1959: 149; see Mark 14:20; Matt 26:23; John 13:26). (4) The accounts speak of a common cup, whereas at the Passover, individual cups were used. (5) Mark 14:1–2 (= Matt 26:1–2; Luke 22:1) preserves the correct chronology, two days before the Passover and the feast of unleavened bread; the Synoptics mention the chief priests' and scribes' desire to arrest Jesus by stealth and to kill him, but "not during the feast, lest there be a tumult of the people" (Mark 14:2). This correct date is contradicted later in the text (Mark 14:43–50) when Jesus is arrested on the feast (i.e., the night of the 15th of Nisan). Likewise, Jeremias' translation of *Mē en tę̄ heortę̄* (RSV: "Not during the feast"; Matt 26:5; Mark 14:2) as "not in the presence of the festival crowd" is questionable. (6) On the festival day, the 15th of Nisan, some of the following events mentioned could not possibly have occurred: the carrying of arms (Mark 14:43 = Matt 26:47; Mark 14:47–49 = Matt 26:51–55; Luke 22:38), the session of the Sanhedrin and the condemnation of Jesus to death, the coming of Simon of Cyrene "from the country," Jesus' burial and the purchase of linen by Joseph of Arimathaea. (7) Jesus celebrated a different type of Jewish meal with his apostles, e.g., a *kîddûš,* a *ḥabûrâ* (Gamber 1987: 6–8, 31), or a solemn or festive Jewish meal. The most original tradition (Mark) has several features which correspond to the structure of the Essene cultic meal, and the daily meals of the Essenes were certainly analogous to those of the Jerusalem church (Kuhn 1957; 78–93). More likely, the Last Supper was a *tôdâ,* a liturgical meal accompanied by words of praise and proclamation, but not necessarily literally a sacrifice (Léon-Dufour 1987: 38–45; Giraudo 1981: 174–77; cf. 81–360). (8) Finally, the Jewish Passover meal was celebrated only once annually. How, in the early Church, did the custom develop that the Lord's Supper was regularly celebrated?

Proponents of the argument that the Last Supper was a Passover meal attempt to answer each of these objections. It is quite certain that the word *artos* can be used for unleavened bread, and the institution narratives are primarily cultic formulas of the early Church. Thus, the emphasis is on Jesus' words over the bread and wine, rather than on what was important at the ordinary Passover. Jeremias' translation of Mark 14:2 may be questionable, but pilgrims were already in Jerusalem several days before the feast, and the Jewish officials would have been concerned about their reaction to Jesus' arrest. Finally, the events indicated could have happened on the festival day. Soldiers and ordinary individuals, for defense, could bear arms on festival days or the Sabbath. Moreover, in spite of the prohibitions of executions on festival days, the rabbis held that in a few special cases (enumerated in Deuteronomy) the death penalty had to be carried out on the feast. Jesus, as a false prophet, would be one of these special cases (Deut 13:5). There is the additional technicality that the Romans, not the Jewish officials, were the ones who carried out the execution. The fact that Simon of Cyrene was "coming from the country" does not necessarily mean that he had been working in the fields on the festival day. It was too early in the day to be coming from the fields, and he may have been coming to the temple for morning service. Of course, he may not have been a Jew. Buying and selling were forbidden on the Sabbath and on feast days, but exceptions were made for real needs, like a death (Str-B 2: 812–34; b., *Šabb.* 151a; *t., Šabb.* 17.13; cf. John 13:29). Finally, the *qiddûš* was a prayer of sanctification said at the beginning of the Sabbath or of a festival meal by the head of the household over a cup of wine to be drunk by him and the others who were present. The Sabbath *qiddûš* always took place on Friday evening after sunset, when the Sabbath began, not earlier. A *ḥābûrâ* was a religious fellowship, and Pliny (*Ep.* 10.96.7) apparently viewed the Christian celebration in this way. But a *ḥăbûrâ* had particular concerns: observance of the Torah and performance of religious duties, including attendance at special ritual meals held in connection with circumcision, engagements, weddings, and funerals. Jesus and his disciples did not form such a fellowship (Higgins 1954: 13–23; Kilpatrick 1983: 67–68).

It is not possible to show that the Essene meal influenced the account of the Last Supper. The three definite texts (1QS 6.4–6; 1QSa 2.17–21; Josephus *JW* 2.130–31) about the Essene meal are laconic. This meal was celebrated twice daily, but not in the evening, and no women were present. Women may have been present at the Last Supper, and the order of blessings, instructions, and prayers at that meal differs from the order of the Essene meal. Moreover, at the Essene meal the benedictions were made by a priest who had precedence over everyone else present, and we are not sure that the Essenes drank wine at their meal (Jeremias 1977: 31–6, 46). However, that the Last Supper may have been a *tôdâ* meal appears to be a real possibility.

Other solutions have been proposed to explain why the Synoptics and John do not agree that the Last Supper was a Passover meal. There is, of course, the possibility that Jesus anticipated the Passover. Moreover, different calculations for the time of the Passover could have arisen, because Galileans, for various reasons, could have had trouble determining the exact time of the full moon. Finally, the Jews of Jerusalem may have postponed the Passover so as not to have two consecutive days of rest (Nolle 1948: 44–45).

Billerbeck proposes that two calendars were a day out of step with each other in the year of the Last Supper. These two calendars are alleged to have come into existence because of a dispute between the Sadducees and Pharisees, and were realized because extra days had to be inserted to keep the lunar calendar in harmony with the solar one, or because there had been a difficulty in determining the date of the new moon.

A. Jaubert (1957: 105–36) likewise argues that two calendars existed at the time. The official, priestly calendar was lunar, and that of Qumran, solar. John is correct by the official Jerusalem calendar, and the Synoptics are correct in terms of the calendar used at Qumran and, perhaps, in Galilee. According to the solar calendar, the Passover would have been on Wednesday. This would allow two whole days, from Tuesday evening to Friday afternoon, to account for the following gospel data: the paschal meal; the arrest at Gethsemane; the double trial before the Jewish officials; the trial before Pilate, with a visit to Herod followed by another session before Pilate; and finally the sentence, procession to Calvary, and death (Johnston 1957: 109–13; Vogt 1955: 403–13). However, Jaubert's theory has not commanded wide assent.

H. Hoehner assumes the existence of two different methods for calculating the hours of a day: sunset to sunset or sunrise to sunrise. The Galileans and the Pharisees would have used the latter method, and so celebrated their Passover one day earlier. But this theory would have Jesus celebrating the Passover on Nisan 14, which seems most unlikely. Billerbeck's theory appears to be the most reasonable of these three calendrical theories (Marshall 1981: 71–75).

Leaney (1967: 52–53, 62) contends that a considerable amount of weight has been given to the Fourth Gospel as a historical document, but that this is unwarranted. Certainly, all four gospels are strongly influenced by theological interests. Nonetheless, to suppose that the most obviously theological of them all can correct the others on details of history is extremely hazardous. According to John, Jesus is the lamb of God (John 1:29, 36) and was handed over to be crucified at the exact time when the Passover lambs were beginning to be sacrificed in the temple (John 19:14). Moreover, the anointing of Jesus at Bethany takes place six days before the Passover, when the lamb for the meal was chosen (John 12:1); and when Jesus' legs are not broken, this is understood as the fulfillment of the verse "Not a bone of him will be broken," part of the prescription for the treatment of the Passover lamb (John 19:36; cf. Exod 12:46; Num 9:12). This theological concern of John (cf. 1 Cor 5:7) would explain why he does not identify the Last Supper as a Passover meal. Furthermore, since a number of the indications that the Last Supper was a Passover meal are to be found in John's gospel, Ruckstuhl (1985: 43–44) claims that originally John's gospel saw the Last Supper as a Passover meal just as do the Synoptics. On the other hand, the earliest neutral Christian tradition and the evidence from astronomy support the chronology given in John's gospel (Ogg 1965: 96; Strobel 1977: 64–78, 450–56).

Were the Last Supper a Passover meal, the relationship between the old covenant and the new and between promise and fulfillment could be better clarified. But above all, at a Passover meal, Jesus' words of interpretation and the command of repetition would more easily be understood (Jeremias 1977: 88; cf. 1972: 201–3). However, none of the above theories about the Last Supper as a Passover meal has won the day.

C. The Words of Jesus

The NT texts (1 Cor 11:23–25; Mark 14:22–25; Matt 26:26–29; Luke 22:15–20; cf. John 6:51c) are the primary sources for determining what can be said historically about the Last Supper. Originally, these reports were handed on as units independent of the passion narrative (Schelkle 1976: 388), and their correct literary form is "etiology," which as such says nothing about the historical question, but only grounds and reflects the community's practice (Léon-Dufour 1987: 161; Neuenzeit 1960: 96–100). Since scholars regularly limit themselves to the "institution narratives" in their efforts to determine what happened at the Last Supper, this presentation will do likewise. But this is not to deny that Jesus at the Last Supper said and did more than is contained in these narratives; nor to accept the view that notices like the denials of Judas or of Peter are without historical basis. I will generally follow the lead of Merklein (1977: 88–101, 235–44) in the historical analysis of these texts.

Matthew follows Mark's account, but he does make some stylistic improvements. He adds "eat" to the words over the bread to parallel "drink" of the wine and makes the liturgical expansion, "for the forgiveness of sins." All of the other texts preserve some more primitive elements than does Mark (Hahn 1986: 247). For instance, we find "on the night" (1 Cor 11:23) and "after supper" (11:25) in Paul; in Luke (22:19–20), the double eschatological perspective and the omission of the copulative (*estin;* cf. v 19) with the word over the wine; and in John (6:51), the translation variant "flesh" (Jeremias 1977: 189).

Despite the fact that the shorter text of Luke 22:15–19a (omitting vv 19b–20) is claimed to be the more difficult reading, and that the normal tendency of its chief witness, Codex Bezae ("D"), is to expand a text, which it does not do in this case, nevertheless, most scholars follow Schürmann (1951: 364–92, 522–41; 1955: 15–132; Hook 1974: 624–30) and accept the longer text (Luke 22:15–20). The structure suggested by Petzer (1984: 249–52) for these verses gives support to this opinion. Actually, the longer text may be the more difficult reading, since one must now explain the presence of two cups and why one of them precedes Jesus' words over the bread. These difficulties probably explain why the Syriac versions have three different rearrangements of the texts (Barclay 1967: 38–39; see Metzger 1971: 173–77).

The Lukan and Pauline texts probably go back to the same traditional strand but are not dependent on one another. To be sure, Paul wrote first, but Luke (22:19–20) does not reproduce Paul's syntax in *touto mou estin,* "This is my," or *en tǭ emǭ haimati,* "(in) my blood," nor both commands of repetition (1 Cor 11:24–25). Moreover, the Lukan use of *didomenon,* "given," with the words over the bread, and the absence of *estin* from the words of the cup, may be explained by an Aramaic (Hebrew?) original. These points, plus a few characteristics noted below, lead to the conclusion that Luke is closer than Paul to the original form of their common traditions.

Mark's institution narrative is more consistently near the Semitic idiom. Jeremias (1972: 200) finds no fewer than 23 Semiticisms in Mark 14:22–25. Compared with 1 Cor 11:23–25, Mark relies more heavily on "and" and follows the Semitic syntax of genitives and verbs. The text in 1 Cor 11:24–25 does not show these clear traces of Semitic syntax; it also reduces the emphasis on blood (Kilpatrick 1983: 20–27).

There appear, then, to have been two traditional strands: Mark (Matthew) and Luke/Paul. Perhaps John 6:51c, ". . . and the bread which I shall give for the life of the world is my flesh," represents a third strand, although it bears a strong and developed resemblance to Luke 22:19 (cf. 1 Cor 11:24): "This is my body which is given for you."

The wording of these different strands provides a guide in reconstructing the phrasing of the oldest Aramaic or Hebrew tradition. The words "he took bread . . . broke . . . said/saying '. . . this is my body' " belong to the oldest tradition, because these words are common to both strands of tradition. Aramaic *gûp* may have been used for "body" (Dalman 1929: 130–31), but the implication would be the whole person, not the contrast "body (flesh) and blood." Mark's "blessed" (*eulogēsas* [14:22 = Matt 26:26]) is more likely to be original than the Lukan/Pauline "when he had given thanks" *(eucharistēsas),* because the verb *eulogein* translates Heb *bārak,* "bless," in LXX; in the tradition of prayer, *bārak* introduces Jewish festive meals. The Greek verb *eucharistein,* by contrast, never translates *bārak* in LXX; it is found only in apocryphal books for which no Semitic original is extant. "He gave" *(edōken)* could also belong to the original, for although Paul does not have it, it is logically presupposed. Moreover, the fact that Luke has it does not necessarily mean that he took it over from Mark. On the other hand, Mark does not mention the Lukan/Pauline "which is for you." Actually, Luke/Paul may well be the more original because the Markan reading could have been influenced by the liturgical unity of the words over the bread and wine. This unification allows the Markan tradition to place the phrasing after the cup and to apply it to both actions. In reality, a whole meal separated these events, and in such a case the Markan phrasing without further explanation would not have been understandable. Moreover, the Lukan/Pauline tradition finds support in John 6:51c, "for the life of the world." On the other hand, the Markan expression "for many" is to be preferred since it is more Semitic and corresponds better with the earthly Jesus' concern for all. The import of the phrase would be much like that of Mark 10:45: "For the Son of Man also came not to be served but to serve, and to give his life as a ransom for many."

Luke once has the command, "do this in remembrance of me"; Paul, twice (Luke 22:19c; 1 Cor 11:24c, 25c). If this command was original, the Markan tradition omitted it. Yet Paul's text leaves the impression of having expanded on the directive. Benoit (1939: 386) astutely observed, "A rubric is not stated, but executed," and if the Last Supper were a Passover meal, repetition of the injunction would follow naturally (cf. Exod 12:14, 26–27; 13:3, 7–9). The English translation which best renders all the nuances of the Greek is "Do this as my memorial" (Chenderlin 1982: 2). Jeremias' proposed paraphrase of the command (1972: 198), "Continue to bind yourself in table-fellowship to the messianic community that God may remember me," has not won wide acceptance. Certainly, the early Christians believed that they were to repeat the Last Supper event. Jesus did choose bread, a life-sustaining food, to express his lasting presence among his followers (Léon-Dufour 1987: 174–75).

The Lukan/Pauline "after supper" accords with the protocol of a Jewish meal, because the blessing of the cup was done after the meal (Kahlefeld 1980: 46–47). This wording was suppressed by the Markan tradition when it joined the cup with the bread.

The Markan "And he took a cup, and when he had given thanks he gave it to them" seems to be an effort to parallel the report about the cup with that about the bread. A similar effort is made by the Lukan/Pauline "likewise" or "in the same way" in "And likewise the cup." It is impossible to decide on the original wording, but there is no need to deny the fact that Jesus made reference to the cup.

The Lukan/Pauline words over the cup are older than those of Mark. Again, the Markan tradition, "This is my blood," parallels what is said about the bread. That the Lukan/Pauline "This cup (which is poured out for you is the new covenant) in my blood" would have been changed from such a parallel to its present phrasing is hard to imagine. Also, the Lukan text has no copulative verb and thus is closer to the Semitic original. The Markan tradition has placed the chief emphasis on the elements (i.e., bread and wine) and moves in the direction of a sacramental consideration. Moreover, the Markan wording, which draws a closer connection between Jesus and the blood, would be more repulsive to a Jewish audience. Finally, the Markan "and they all drank of it" is secondary. It somewhat parallels the "Take, (eat)" said of the bread and makes explicit an assumed action by the apostles.

A few scholars see the words over the cup to be a formula *ex eventu* (i.e., composed after the event). Thus, the Last Supper would have been a celebration *sub una* (under one species, bread), and the parallel actions and words related to the cup developed later as a counterpart to the bread narrative (see Beck 1970: 195–96). The Acts of the Apostles does speak only of "the breaking of bread," and the church in Syria during the first few centuries apparently knew of only one element at the Lord's Supper (Léon-Dufour 1987: 176). Also, the earthly Jesus' fellowship meals with his disciples may not have included wine. But the phrasing in Acts is an abbreviation and should not be taken to indicate only one element (Higgins 1954: 56–63). Very likely, the two kinds of meals that Jesus ate with his disciples only gradually were united, and the one viewed as more important prevailed (cf. Schürmann 1970: 68–70).

Both traditional strands relate the cup to a covenant motif. The Lukan/Pauline tradition sees an eschatological fulfillment of the prophetic promise of a "new covenant" (Jer 31:31), while the Markan one is typological and views Jesus' death as a repetition of the OT covenant sacrifice (Exod 24:8: "blood of the covenant"). To eliminate a covenant motif from the original tradition appears unjustified, given its presence in both traditions, but "covenant" does not occur in any of the sayings attributed to Jesus elsewhere in the gospel. Whether Jesus designated this covenant as "new" or in reference to Exod 24:8 is another question. Jeremias (1977: 194–95) earlier held on grammatical grounds that *tēs diathēkēs* (Mark 14:24: "of the covenant") was a later addition; in Aramaic a noun with a personal pronoun suffix cannot be followed by a genitive. But Jeremias has recognized that his linguistic objection was based on the false assumption that the sequence in Greek must have been that of the Semitic original. Besides, Emerton (1955: 238–40) has pointed out that in Syriac, a Semitic language akin to Aramaic, a suffix can stand for a noun in the genitive different from the one that follows it.

Significantly, the Qumran documents demonstrate that the idea of covenant was much alive at the time, and it should be noted that Exod 24:8 and Ezek 16:6 were used in the Haggadah to interpret the wine of the Passover as blood, making covenant between God and the people (Leaney 1967: 57). Lang (1975: 526–29) and Wagner (1975: 543–44) hold that "new covenant" is part of the oldest recoverable tradition. It could be argued that there was a reformulation of the cup-saying to give it a form parallel to the bread-saying. As a result of this process, the allusion to Exod 24:8 became all the clearer, and the word "new" was dropped, because a covenant established by Jesus' blood would ipso facto be to a different covenant from the Mosaic covenant and could only allude to the new covenant of Jeremiah (Marshall 1981: 45–46, 91–92). The original wording would have been "new covenant."

"Of my blood of the covenant," the Markan tradition writes, "which is poured out for many." Luke specifies the cup with the words "for you," while Paul does not. Were these words originally joined to the bread and only attached to the blood after the two actions were united, with reference to the intervening meal having been dropped? If "this is my body" and "this is my blood" are both left without explanation, there would be more confusion than communication. So either the redemptive theme and the covenant motif go back to Jesus, or at least one of them does; otherwise the words of Jesus are to be rejected in their entirety. This last position is difficult, if one accepts the eschatological statement of Jesus in Mark 14:25 (cf. Luke 22:15–18; 1 Cor 11:26), in which Jesus does give a positive interpretation of his death.

Mark 14:25 (Temple 1960–61: 77–85) and Luke 22:15–18 (cf. 1 Cor 11:26) introduce an eschatological aspect and provide a positive interpretation of Jesus' death. Mark 14:25 stands at the end of the account, while the passage in Luke 22:15–18 stands before it. Luke's placement may be more correct, and Schürmann (1953: 1–74, 123) has claimed that the Luke 22:15–18 text is an independent report and the oldest tradition of the Last Supper. Occasionally, Mark 14:25 is considered an abbreviation of these verses, but more probably Luke 22:15–18 is a further development of the former (Pesch 1978: 26–31). Luke 22:18 is less Semitic and so less original than Mark (Higgins 1954: 37). Merklein (1977: 236) contends that, since the authenticity of Mark 14:25 is hardly to be disputed (cf. Hahn 1986: 246–47; Léon-Dufour 1987: 165–68, 171), it can serve as a heuristic key in determining what Jesus did at the Last Supper. It allows us to conclude two things: Jesus reckoned with his proximate violent death (that of a prophet), yet he maintained the value of his message about the coming of the kingdom. In fact, a regular feature of Jewish thought is the messianic banquet God will prepare for his people (cf. Zeph 1:7; *1 Enoch* 62:14; *2 Enoch* 42:5). Jesus would not have needed tremendous prescience to realize his dangerous situation, and he did anticipate a resurrection of the dead. Moreover, the messianic banquet figures in his teachings (e.g., Luke 13:28–29; 22:30). It should be noted that a few scholars have proposed that Mark 14:25 is to be identified with the original words over the cup.

For Jeremias (1977: 207–18), the Luke 22:15–18 passage informs us of Jesus' avowal of abstinence on behalf of Israel. Jeremias sees the avowal confirmed by the practice of the Quartodecimans who, inspired by this example, fasted for the Jews during the night of the Passover and only ate their agape and Eucharist at 3 A.M.—the next morning. The Quartodecimans read and explained Exodus 12 and awaited Jesus' second coming at their Passover. Jeremias' student Lohse (1953: 62–89, 136–37) supports this position. However, G. Ogg (1965: 89–92) is less certain that the Quartodecimans fasted for the Jews; rather, he contends, it was a fast for the death of Jesus. In fact, Jeremias has not convinced many scholars of the historicity of such an avowal.

D. Questions of Meaning

Granted that we may not be able to get back to the original report about the Last Supper, what meaning is to be attributed to what we can recover? There is rather complete certainty about a number of items. Jesus did celebrate the Last Supper, and his words over the bread and wine were unique. The Last Supper was a fellowship meal like those he had celebrated any number of times with his disciples. These meals implied an acceptance of everyone, sinners included. But the Last Supper was also a thanksgiving or a blessing. Although thanksgiving was a part of every Jewish meal, nonetheless the Last Supper's joyful aspect was balanced by the sobering awareness that it was also a farewell meal. We simply cannot determine whether it was a Passover meal or not; however, a reasonable assumption is that it was celebrated in a Passover atmosphere. If it were not a Passover meal, it may well have been a *tôdâ* meal of praise and proclamation.

During the course of the meal, Jesus, in prophetic manner, identified himself with both the bread and the wine in the cup. At a meal people are fed, and Jesus did identify himself in some way with this nourishment.

There is no reason to deny that Jesus was aware of his forthcoming death and saw it as part of God's eschatological salvific activity (Schürmann 1973: 353–60). Almost everyone will agree that Jesus' death, as was his life, was for others. Such an understanding corresponds well with what we can determine about the earthly Jesus. Less enthusiasm has been shown for the contention that Jesus interpreted his death in terms of Isa 52:13–53:12 (but see Pesch 1978: 89–111). On the other hand, Jesus apparently spoke of a covenant; moreover, the evidence seems to favor his having spoken of a "new" covenant. The mention of covenant and blood implies sacrifice, and this, plus other actions of Jesus, may have led to the repetition of the meal. In fact, it was repeated. Finally, the vast majority of scholars accept the eschatological dimension of the Last Supper as a messianic banquet celebrated in anticipation of the coming kingdom (cf. Günther 1985: 41–64).

Bibliography

Barclay, W. 1967. *The Lord's Supper.* London.

Beck, N. A. 1970. The Last Supper as an Efficacious Symbolic Act. *JBL* 89: 192–98.

Benoit, P. 1939. Le récit de la Cène dans Lc 22,15–20: Étude de critique textuelle et littéraire. *RB* 48: 357–93.

Bornkamm, G. 1959. Herrenmahl und Kirche bei Paulus. Pp. 138–76 in *Studien zu Antike und Unchristentum: Gesammelte Aufsätze II.* BEvT 28. Munich.

Burchard, C. 1987. The Importance of Joseph and Aseneth for the Study of the New Testament: A General Survey and a Fresh Look at the Lord's Supper. *NTS* 33: 102–34.

Burkill, T. A. 1956. The Last Supper. *Numen* 3: 161–77.

Cavalletti, S. 1965. Le fonti del 'seder' pasquale. *BibOr* 7: 153–60.

Chenderlin, F. 1982. *"Do This as My Memorial": The Semantic and Conceptual Background and Value of "Anamnesis" in 1 Corinthians 11:24–25.* AnBib 99. Rome.

Dalman, G. 1929. *Jesus-Jeshua: Die Drei Sprachen Jesu, Jesus in der Synagogue, auf dem Berge beim Passahmahl, am Kreuz.* 2d ed. Leipzig.

Descamps, A. 1987. Les origines de l'Eucharistie. Repr. pp. 455–96 in *Jésus et l'Église.* BETL 77. Louvain.

Emerton, J. A. 1955. The Aramaic Underlying *To Haima Mou tēs Diathēkēs* in Mk 14, 24. *JTS* 6: 238–41.

Fitzmyer, J. 1979. *A Wandering Aramean.* SBLMS 25. Missoula, MT.

Friedrich, G. 1978. Ursprung, Urform und Urbedeutung des Abendmahls. Pp. 301–18 in *Auf das Wort komt es an,* ed. J. H. Friedrich. Göttingen.

Gamber, K. 1987. Die "Eucharistia" der Didache. *EphLit* 101: 3–32.

Giraudo, C. 1981. *La struttura letteraria della preghiera eucharistica.* AnBib 92. Rome.

Günther, H. 1985. Das Zeugnis vom Abendmahl im NT. *Lutherische Theologie und Kirche* 9: 41–64.

Hahn, F. 1986. *Exegetische Beiträge zum ökumenischen Gespräch.* Göttingen.

Higgins, A. J. B. 1954. *The Lord's Supper in the New Testament.* SBT 6. London.

Hook, N. 1974. The Dominical Cup Saying. *Theology* 77: 624–30.

Hurst, L. D. 1986. The Neglected Role of Semantics in the Search for the Aramaic Words of Jesus. *JSNT* 28: 63–80.

Jaubert, A. 1957. *La date de la Cène: Calendrier biblique et liturgie chrétienne.* EBib. Paris.

Jeremias, J. 1972. "This Is My Body . . ." *ExpTim* 83: 196–203.

———. 1977. *The Eucharist Words of Jesus.* Trans. N. Perrin. Philadelphia.

Johnston, L. 1957. The Date of the Last Supper. *Scr* 9: 108–15.

Kahlefeld, H. 1980. *Das Abschiedsmahl Jesu und die Eucharistie der Kirche.* Frankfurt am Main.

Kertelge, K. 1972. Die soteriologischen Aussagen in der urchristlichen Abendmahlsüberlieferung und ihre Beziehung zum geschichtlichen Jesus. *Trierer Theologische Zeitung* 81: 193–202.

Kilpatrick, G. D. 1983. *The Eucharist in Bible and Liturgy.* The Moorhouse Lectures 1975. Cambridge.

Klauck, H.-J. 1982. *Herrenmahl und hellenistischer Kult.* NTAbh N.F. 15. Münster.

Kuhn, K. G. 1950. Die Abendmahlsworte. *TLZ* 75: 399–407.

———. 1957. The Lord's Supper and the Communal Meal at Qumran. Pp. 65–93, 259–65, in *The Scrolls and the NT,* ed. K. Stendahl. New York.

Lang, F. 1975. Abendmahl und Bundesgedanke in Neuen Testament. *EvT* 35: 524–38.

Leaney, A. R. C. 1967. What Was the Lord's Supper? *Theology* 70: 51–62.

Léon-Dufour, X. 1987. *Sharing the Eucharistic Bread.* New York.

Lindars, B. 1987. "Joseph and Asenath" and the Eucharist. Pp. 181–99 in *Scripture: Meaning and Method,* ed. B. P. Thompson. North Yorkshire.

Lohse, B. 1953. *Das Passafest der Quartadecimaner.* BFCT 2/54. Gütersloh.

Marshall, I. H. 1981. *Last Supper and Lord's Supper.* Exeter.

Marxsen, W. 1952–53. Der Ursprung des Abendmahls. *EvT* 12: 293–303.

———. 1979. *The Beginning of Christology. Together with: The Lord's Supper as a Christological Problem.* The latter trans. L. Nietling. Philadelphia.

Meding, W. von. 1975. 1 Korinther 11,26: Vom geschichtlichen Grund des Abendsmahls. *EvT* 35: 544–52.

Merklein, H. 1977. Erwägungen zur Uberlieferungsgeschichte des neutestamentlichen Abendmahlstraditionen. *BZ* 21: 88–101, 235–44.

Metzger, B. M. 1968. *Historical and Literary Studies: Pagan, Jewish, and Christian.* NTTS 8. Leiden.

———. 1971. *A Textual Commentary on the Greek New Testament.* New York.

Neuenzeit, P. 1960. *Das Herrenmahl: Studien zur paulinischen Eucharistieauffasung.* SANT 1. Munich.

Nolle, L. 1948. Did Our Lord Eat the Pasch of the OT before His Passion? *Scr* 3: 43–45.

O'Flynn, J. A. 1958. The Date of the Last Supper. *ITQ* 25: 58–63.

Ogg, G. 1965. The Chronology of the Last Supper. Pp. 75–96 in

Historicity and Chronology in the New Testament. Theological Collections 6. London.
Patsch, H. 1972. *Abendmahl und historischer Jesus.* CThM A1. Stuttgart.
Pesch, R. 1977. *Wie Jesus das Abendmahl hielt: Der Grund der Eucharistie.* Freiburg.
———. 1978. *Das Abendmahl und Jesu Todesverständnis.* QD 80. Freiburg.
Petzer, J. H. 1984. Luke 22:19b–20 and the Structure of the Passage. *NovT* 26: 249–52.
Reumann, J. 1985. *The Supper of the Lord.* Philadelphia.
Ruckstuhl, E. 1985. Zur Chronologie der Leidensgeschichte Jesu. Pp. 27–61 in *Studien zum Neuen Testament und seiner Umwelt* A, 10, ed. A. Fuchs. Linz.
Schelkle, K. H. 1976. Das Herrenmahl. Pp. 385–402 in *Rechtfertigung: Festschrift für E Käsemann,* ed. J. Friedrich, W. Pöhlmann, and P. Stuhlmacher. Göttingen.
Schürmann, H. 1951. Lk 22:19b als ursprüngliche Textüberlieferung. *Bib* 32: 364–92; 522–41.
———. 1953. *Der Paschamahlsbericht Lk 22 (7–14) 15–18.* NTAbh 19/5. Münster.
———. 1955. *Der Einsetzungsbericht Lk 22,19–20.* NTAbh 20/4. Münster.
———. 1970. Das Weiterleben der Sache Jesu im nachösterlichen Herrenmahl. Pp. 63–101 in *Jesu Abendmahlshandlung als Zeichen für die Welt.* Die Botschaft Gottes: NT 27. Leipzig.
———. 1973. Wie hat Jesus seien Tod bestanden und verstanden? Pp. 325–63 in *Orientierung an Jesus,* ed. P. Hoffmann, N. Brox, and W. Pesch. Freiburg.
Schweizer, E. 1967. *The Lord's Supper according to the NT.* FBBS 18. Philadelphia.
Strobel, A. 1977. *Ursprung und Geschichte des frühchristlichen Osterkalenders.* TU 121. Berlin.
Stuhlmacher, P. 1987. Das neutestamentliche Zeugnis vom Herrenmahl. *ZTK* 84: 1–35.
Temple, S. 1960–61. The Two Traditions of the Last Supper, Betrayal, and Arrest. *NTS* 7: 77–85.
Vollert, C. 1960. The Eucharist: Quests for Insights from Scripture. *TS* 21: 404–43.
Vogt, E. 1955. Antiquum Kalendarium Sacerdotale. *Bib* 36: 403–13.
Wagner, V. 1975. Der Bedeutungswandel von *Bĕrît Hadāšâh* bei der Ausgestaltung der Abendmahlsworte. *EvT* 35: 538–44.

ROBERT F. O'TOOLE

LASTHENES (PERSON) [Gk *Lasthenēs*]. A native of Crete who became a high official under Demetrius II Nicator, a Seleucid king. Josephus informs us that Lasthenes served as this king's mercenary chief in Crete during the latter's accession (*Ant* 13.4.3.86), which he ultimately realized with a political victory over Alexander Balas (1 Macc 10:67). Lasthenes' main military contribution to Demetrius was assistance in aiding the latter's landing in Cilicia, ca. 147 B.C. Diodorus infers that Lasthenes later became the chief minister proper (Diodorus 33.4) of Demetrius, and possibly the governor of Coele Syria (1 Macc 10:69). Lasthenes' importance surfaces in a written exchange between Demetrius and Jonathan the Hasmonean, the high priest (1 Macc 11:20–37). The king, trying to flatter the Jews, recites his earlier letter sent to Lasthenes (1 Macc 10:22–26). Ironically, the first usage of the Demetrius-Lasthenes letter was to win support away from Jonathan, whereas the reference to the same letter (1 Macc 11:20–37) is now employed to flatter the same Jonathan. Lasthenes is referred to as "kinsman" and "father," which are court titles rather than indications of blood relationships. "Kinsmen of the King," who were much older than the king, such as Lasthenes was to Demetrius, probably received the title of "father" as well (Bickerman 1938: 42–43).

Bibliography

Bickerman, E. J. 1938. *Institutions de Séleucides.* Paris.

JERRY A. PATTENGALE

LATIN LANGUAGE. See LANGUAGES (LATIN).

LATIN VERSIONS. See VERSIONS, ANCIENT (LATIN).

LAVER [Heb *kiyyôr;* Gk *loutron*]. Bronze washbasin situated in both the tabernacle and temple courtyards. Although situated in the cultic precincts, the laver itself was not a ritual object. The tabernacle laver (Exod 30:18, 29; 31:9; 35:16; 38:8; 39:39; 40:7, 11, 30; Lev 8:11) was filled with water for the priests to use in washing their hands and feet (Exod 30:17–21). Made of the mirrors of the "women who ministered at the door of the tent of meeting" (Exod 38:8), it was placed on a bronze base between the altar and the entrance to the tabernacle.

The temple passages in 1 Kings contain a description of ten bronze lavers (1 Kgs 7:38), each supported by an elaborate stand (1 Kgs 7:27–37). The lavers themselves were bronze bowls, each with a capacity of forty baths (ca. 243 gallons). The stands were incredibly ornate. Each was 4 cubits square (ca. 6.5 ft square) and 3 cubits high (ca. 5 ft). The sides were set with framed panels decorated with animals—lions, oxen—and cherubim in relief. The frames themselves were decorated with "beveled work." Each stand rested on four bronze wheels, each 1.5 cubits high, with bronze axles, thus forming a sort of cart. Projecting 1 cubit upward from the stands at each corner were supports, decorated with wreaths, and holding a band or ring ("crown"), 0.5 cubit high, in which the laver itself was placed. The band was paneled, perhaps in metope divisions, and decorated with cherubim, lions, and palm trees.

Various archaeological discoveries contribute to an understanding of what lavers looked like (Paul and Dever 1973: 258–59). Metal lavers from Megiddo and Ras Shamra provide some information, as do some Cypriot bases. In particular, carriage bases from Larnaka have wheels, and one is decorated with a sphinx, a lion, a chariot, and two figures. Also, an 8th-century bowl from Salamis is made of bronze and rests on a tripod stand decorated with fanciful animals.

All of these artifacts feature some elements in common with the Solomonic lavers, but none can provide an exact parallel for these elaborate courtyard furnishings. If the biblical depiction is to be taken literally, the lavers would have been far taller than an average person. Thus, it is difficult to comprehend how they may have been used. Furthermore, it is unlikely that the relatively small wheels could have supported the stand, the laver, and nearly a ton of water.

Whatever the reality of the lavers was, they did not survive as long as the temple did. King Ahaz partially dismantled them (2 Kgs 16:17), removing the frames and the laver. But the stands themselves may have survived until the Babylonian conquest (2 Kgs 25:13, 16; Jer 52:17, 20).

The lavers were essential for priestly purification, and they may also have had symbolic value. The Hebrew word has been related to the Akkadian *kiuri,* or *ki-ùr,* meaning "copper caldron." This term may go back to a Sumerian term meaning "foundation of the earth" (*ARI,* 152–54). If so, the lavers participated in the cosmic terminology that characterizes many aspects of the vocabulary used for the Jerusalem temple.

The NT word *loutron* is translated "washing." It is the same as the LXX word for "lavers" and is used metaphorically in relation to baptism (Titus 3:5; Eph 5:26). See also SEA, MOLTEN.

Bibliography

Paul, S. M., and Dever, W. G., eds. 1973. *Biblical Archaeology.* Jerusalem.

CAROL MEYERS

LAW [Heb *tôrâ;* Gk *nomos*]. This entry consists of three articles, one surveying law as a cultural phenomenon in the ANE world in which the Hebrew Bible emerged, one examining the various forms of law present in the Hebrew Bible, and one surveying religious law in early Judaism of the NT period.

BIBLICAL AND ANE LAW

The considerable amount of evidence available from both the Bible and ANE sources makes a comparison of laws possible. The sources, social systems, types of cases, and principles behind juridical decisions require detailed treatment.

A. Sources Available for Study
B. Oral and Written Laws
  1. In the Ancient Near East
  2. In the Bible
C. Authority and Law
  1. In the Ancient Near East
  2. In the Bible
  3. Law and Ethics
  4. Covenant
  5. Apodictic Law
D. Shared Social Norms
E. Laws Protecting the Family
  1. Sexual Taboos
  2. Adultery
  3. Rape
F. Personal Injuries
  1. A Common Legal Tradition
  2. The Goring Ox
  3. Miscarriage
  4. Battery
  5. Talion and Compensation
G. Homicide
  1. In the Bible
  2. In the Ancient Near East
  3. Modern Perspectives on Ancient Values
  4. Unsolved Murder
H. Theft
  1. In the Bible
  2. In the Ancient Near East
I. Cultic Law
J. Law and Social Welfare
  1. Debts and Slavery
  2. Redemption and Release

A. Sources Available for Study

The Bible preserves several significant collections of laws: the Decalogue, the Covenant Code, the Holiness Code, and the Deuteronomic laws. These collections, although not labeled as such by the ancient writers, have been identified as literary units by modern scholars. Most, but not all of the formally stated biblical laws are found in these pentateuchal collections; and supplementary knowledge of biblical legal practices comes from narrative accounts and other, nonlegal books. But the Bible remains the single most important source for the study of Israelite society and culture. Modern archaeology, to be sure, has recovered meaningful data relating to some aspects of life in biblical times; however, the disappointingly small quantity of extrabiblical ancient Hebrew written records limits the ability of scholars to reconstruct and describe cultural features such as the nature and practices of biblical law beyond that which is recorded in the Bible itself.

Archaeology has been significantly more successful in providing knowledge about law in non-Israelite societies, particularly for those ancient communities of people who wrote their records on clay tablets in cuneiform scripts. These ancient cultures, namely the Sumerians, Babylonians, Assyrians, and Hittites, have yielded collections of their laws as well as of contemporary public and private documents describing a full range of legal and economic activities. The major law collections of the ANE are the Codes of Urnammu (CU, see *ANET,* 523–25), Lipit-Ishtar (LI, see *ANET,* 159–61), and Hammurapi (CH, see *ANET,* 163–80); the Laws of Eshnunna (LE, see *ANET,* 161–63); the Middle Assyrian Laws (AL, see *ANET,* 180–88); and the Hittite Laws (HL, see *ANET,* 188–97). They are supplemented by fragments recording additional Sumerian and Neo-Babylonian laws, as well as by scribal textbooks and other legal compositions such as royal edicts and treaties.

The contemporary ancient legal documents can be numbered in the thousands. They record the legal transactions from the everyday life of individuals and families. They come from many cities in western Asia and cover a span of over two thousand years. The sheer quantity of these ANE materials has created a discipline and discourse which are carried on separately from consideration of parallels or similarities to biblical laws and legal traditions. These nonbiblical materials need to be analyzed on several levels. One task or level is to sift through the documents of everyday life in an effort to describe the actual legal practices of the time. A second task is to compare the practices of everyday life with the provisions contained in the law collections in order to see if they are identical. A third task is to compare the legal practices of various periods and places. The comparative study of biblical and ANE law relates to this third level of analysis. Many legal practices and problems described in the Bible also appear in the nonbiblical ANE traditions. While there are, to be sure, cultural differences between these ancient societies, there are also similarities. The task of comparative study is to look at both differences and similarities in an effort to better understand the nature and scope of biblical laws and legal practices within their ancient setting.

B. Oral and Written Laws

1. In the Ancient Near East. It has become increasingly clear that the formal law collections, both in the OT and in the ANE, were not intended to be complete codes of law. The term "code" is still often applied and may be retained, provided that one realizes the term's noncomprehensive nature. A good illustration of the phenomenon can be seen in comparing the Eshnunna Laws (LE) with the Laws or "Code" of Hammurapi (CH). Both collections were written within a century of one another and emanate from virtually the same cultural milieu in Babylonia. Legal areas mentioned in both collections, for example, are the hire of wagons and boats (LE 3–5; CH 236–39, 275–77). The Laws of Hammurapi add a case (CH 240) dealing with losses due to collision and sinking of a craft, whereas the Eshnunna laws add another case, not covered at all in the Hammurapi laws, dealing with loss caused by someone using a vessel without the owner's permission (LE 6). Both additions seem to be valid cases that could have fairly been considered by either society in its respective law collection.

The collection of Eshnunna laws, which is about one fourth the size of the Hammurapi laws, includes additional provisions not found in the larger corpus. Thus, for example, one finds the hire of harvest workers (LE 7–9) and of a fuller (LE 14); a slave woman who covertly passed her child to a free family (LE 33–35); a bailee falsely claiming the theft of bailed goods in his possession (LE 36); the sale of an inheritance share by one of two heirs (LE 38); a biting by a mad dog whose owner was previously publicly admonished (LE 56–57); and a battery causing injury to a finger or collarbone (LE 43,46).

The Eshnunna laws, moreover, also contain cases which, while not found in the Hammurapi laws, do appear in other ANE legal compositions or in the Bible. For example, loan fraud (LE 20) is covered in the Edict of Ammiṣaduqa 5, 7 (Kraus 1984: 172–74); the rape of a slave woman (LE 31) is also dealt with in the "Code" of Urnammu (CU 8); the required payment for wet nurses (LE 32) is covered in the school composition *ana ittišu* III iii 45–50 (CAD L, p. 293 *lubuštu;* M pt. 2, p. 265–66 *mušēniqtu*); the redemption of a house sold for debt (LE 39) is dealt with in Lev 25:29–34; the case of an ox goring and killing another ox (LE 53) is discussed in Exod 21:35.

The incomplete nature of these Babylonian law collections is further demonstrated by other, significant omissions. There are important legal areas which were, clearly, fully operative in Babylonian society, since they are abundantly reflected in the contemporary documents. Some of these areas are even mentioned in the "codes" in a tangential or passing fashion, but the activities themselves do not appear as the primary subject of a law paragraph or provision. So, for example, one finds no cases directly dealing with arson, treason, theft of livestock, surety, barter, murder, manumission, or sale. The omission of such common cultural areas in the law collections can hardly be the result of any design or plan, particularly when one considers that, in the Hittite laws, some of these same areas are omitted while others like arson (HL 98–100), murder (HL 1–6), and livestock theft (HL 57–70) are included.

It is apparent, from all such omissions as described above, both of major concepts and of individual cases or provisions, that the validity of the Babylonian laws did not depend upon their being written down. The law collections themselves, moreover, appear as secondary inclusions within larger, nonlegal, literary frameworks: building inscriptions, monuments, and scribal textbooks and exercises. Even for royal edicts and treaties, there was likewise significant oral activity connected with their execution and promulgation. Writing functioned primarily as a means of disseminating and remembering information. The act of writing was not necessarily an inherent part of legal process; documents were not written for all transactions but, apparently, mainly for cases arising out of complicated, potentially contestable life situations. Thus, for example, real estate sales and manumissions, more often than not, were recorded inasmuch as the new owners or freed slaves needed proof of the change in status. But many other transactions, including marriage, division of property, adoption (without manumission), sale of immovables, and most criminal proceedings, typically do not appear to have required regular use of written records.

2. In the Bible. The biblical law collections, even when considered *in toto,* fall short of including all of the legal areas operative in ancient Israelite society. There are, first of all, categories which appear in the ANE laws but which are absent or unregulated in the OT law collections. Many of these categories are, however, alluded to in the Bible; thus, it is certain that they were operative in Israelite society. So, for example, robbery (tangentially mentioned in Lev 5:21–26; 19:13), hire of wet nurses, lease and rental of property, surety (cf. Gen 43:9; Prov 6:1; 20:16), hire of labor (cf. Lev 19:13; Job 7:2), bride-price and dowry (cf. Exod 22:16; 1 Sam 18:25), and sale (e.g., Isa 24:2; 2 Sam 24:24; etc.). In connection with sale, Jer 32:11 mentions the "sealed deed of purchase . . . and the open copy." This custom finds parallels in the Dead Sea Scrolls (*DJD* 2: 244–46), the Elephantine papyri (Porten 1968: 198–99), and the Mishnah (*B. Bat.* 10:1). This type of document is ultimately derived from the practice of using an inscribed and sealed clay envelope to contain and protect a cuneiform document; the text written on the inner tablet was duplicated on the outside envelope.

Some of the other "missing laws" also appear in the Mishnah. While one cannot assert that all regulations of the Mishnah go back to the biblical period, some laws apparently do, at least to the extent that they can be shown to have ANE parallels. For example, the Babylonian laws treat the case of how to dispose of marital gifts and property in a situation where either the bride or groom-to-be has died before the wedding. This case appears in LE 17 and CH 163–64. The case is not discussed in the Bible but does appear in the Mishnah (*B. Bat.* 9:5). Another such case is "assault" upon the dignity of an individual by slapping his face. This case is considered in LE 42 and CH 202–4, and in the Mishnah (*B. Qam.* 8:6); this offensive act is also addressed by the NT (Matt 5:39, Luke 6:29).

One can look again to the Mishnah for "preservation" of laws dealing with rental of houses and lease of fields (*B. Meṣ.* 8:6–9, 10:1–10). These activities are highly visible both in the Laws of Hammurapi (CH 42–47, E–G) and the contemporary cuneiform documents. An arrangement modeled after a field lease may be reflected in Lev 25:15–16. Another such example is the special class of dowry property (Akk *mulūgu;* Heb *mĕlōg*) and the type of property for which the user is responsible regardless of loss (Akk *ul imūtū,* "they shall not have died," said typically of livestock and thus described as *ṣōn barzel,* "iron sheep," in the Mishnah; cf. *Yebam.* 7:1, *B. Meṣ.* 5:6).

The paucity of ancient Hebrew records limits real knowledge about the use of writing in Israelite legal practice. Scholars have noted the absence of writing; for example, in the description of Abraham's purchase of the cave of Machpelah (Genesis 23) as well as in the redemption of Naomi's family property in Ruth 4:1–12. But documents were written for the redemption of family property by Jeremiah (Jer 32:6–14) and were prescribed for divorce in Deut 24:1–3, Isa 50:1, and Jer 3:8. Some scholars have seen the use of written documents as a late development, perhaps reflecting increased foreign influences and sophistications (cf. further Job 31:35). The biblical law collections, however, are all represented as part of orally delivered addresses or sermons. The renewal or rereading of the law is similarly depicted; the laws are read out to the populace in Deut 31:10–13, 2 Kgs 23:1–3, and Neh 8:1–9:3. So it would seem that in ancient Israel, as for her Near Eastern neighbors, writing was not an indispensable feature of the legal tradition and practice but functioned, rather, as an aid to memory (cf. Deut 31:22–26; Josh 24:26).

C. Authority and Law

1. In the Ancient Near East. The laws are upheld by the king as part of his duty of governance. The king is responsible for ruling the people in accordance with principles of justice and equity; the king functions as a judge for his subjects and from time to time also issues public decrees in order to afford redress to various groups of free citizens who have been disadvantaged due to debt. But the king is not the primary author or originator of the law. Even in their "codes," kings do not claim to have invented or discovered the laws they present.

The administration of justice, however, did not fall solely on the king. In addition, cases were heard by local courts of village elders, councils, or residential districts (Akk *šībūt alim, puḫrum, bābtum*); commercial affairs were regulated by the merchants of the city (Akk *kārum*). Cases also came before courts convened under the jurisdiction of provincial civil and military officials who, on some occasions, also functioned as judges. Temple priests were at times also judges, although more frequently they were involved in an ancillary way, administering an oath or ordeal for evidentiary purposes. All of these local courts, unlike the royal court of the king, were composed of three or more individuals who formed judicial collegia. The verdicts of judges were accorded great respect; in Mesopotamia, litigants who contested judgments were subject to heavy fines, mutilation, or death. In Ḫatti, one who rejected the verdict of the king had his house torn down; but one who rejected the verdict of the king's judge could suffer the death penalty (HL 173). This severe protection of authority is paralleled in Deut 17:8–13.

2. In the Bible. The royal court of the king appears in the OT (e.g., 2 Sam 15:2–6; 1 Kgs 3:28); a legend about Solomon portrays him as the ideal monarch and judge who sought and attained a quality of wisdom sufficient to judge (RSV "govern") his people in the most excellent fashion (1 Kgs 3:9–12). There were also local judiciaries consisting of village elders (e.g., Deut 21:2–3; 1 Kgs 21:8–11; Ruth 4:2, 9–11) or town councils (e.g., Deut 35:7–9; Ezek 16:40). The Bible speaks of specially appointed judges who presumably took their authority from the king or from the central government (2 Chr 19:5; Deut 16:18; Mic 3:9; 7:3).

Priests appear to play a noticeably larger role as judges in ancient Israel. They are pictured as functioning alongside of other royal appointees (2 Chr 19:8–11), alongside of the king himself (Deut 17:18–20), or even acting alone as if there were no other governmental structure (Deut 17:8–13; Ezek 44:23–24). Scholars have assigned this enhanced role for priests to the experiences of the Persian period, when Judea possessed only local government, led by the priestly elite in Jerusalem. Priests play only a cultic role during the early monarchy (2 Sam 20:26–27; 1 Kgs 4:4–5).

The ultimate authority of the laws was seen as coming from God. In this respect, Israelite society was very different from other ANE societies. Yet there are laws recorded in the Bible that do come from the reigning kings. There is, for example, the law of booty decreed by David (1 Sam 30:24–25); the terms used to describe this law, Heb *ḥōq, mišpāṭ,* are used also in the Pentateuch to describe divinely given laws (e.g., Lev 26:46; Deut 4:1, 5, 8; Ps 147:19). One thus cannot look to terminology as an indicator of divine origin since other terms used to denote law are likewise also operative in the human sphere. Thus, Heb *tôrâ* (Prov 1:8; 6:20; 13:14; 31:26) and *miṣwâ* (Prov 6:20; Jer 32:11; 35:16, 18; Isa 29:13; 2 Kgs 18:36) describe the instructions or commands of parents and monarchs. In a similar fashion, Heb *piqûd* and *ʿēdût* also arise, respectively, out of backgrounds that are taken from the sphere of human actions; namely, of assignment and of solemn stipulations accepted under oath (Tadmor 1982: 142–52). All of these terms relate to communications given by those in authority and imply the duty of the receiver or listener to obey. The authority could be parent, elder, government official, priest, king, or God.

Prophets do not appear to have functioned as judges, but were connected to the transmission of laws to Israel. The laws are pictured as coming to Israel through the agency of the prophets, especially Moses; and the term *tôrâ,* pl. *tôrôt,* eventually came to be used to describe any and all laws given by God to Israel via the prophets (Deut

4:8, 44; Jer 26:4–5; Lam 2:9; Neh 8:1, 8, 14). The laws in the Pentateuch are represented as spoken directly by God to Moses, who, not surprisingly therefore, is described as the prophet of highest rank (Num 12:6–8; Deut 34:10). Prophets otherwise do not appear to have played any role in the judiciary or in the everyday administration of justice, although there are a few attempts to create a link between the prophets and the judiciary. One case is the story of Jethro and Moses, where Moses is advised (Exod 18:21) to "choose able men from all the people such as fear God, men who are trustworthy and who hate a bribe." These men are then appointed to serve as judges of the "lower courts" under Moses. Another link appears in the hybrid career of Samuel who, in addition to serving as a priest under Eli (1 Sam 3:1), also was a "seer" (1 Sam 9:9), led his people to military victory (1 Sam 7:10–14), and together with his sons served as judge (1 Sam 7:15–8:3).

3. Law and Ethics. The linking of God to law added an important ethical dimension to the worldview of ancient Israel. Since God was the source of law, the failure to observe the law became an offense against the deity. This linking, however, also succeeded in placing ethics in the matrix of human history and fostered the concept of ethical standards to which God was also responsibly connected. One sees this, for example, in the protestations of Job and in the argument of Abraham (Exod 18:23–25); ". . . Shall not the Judge of all the earth do right?" This ethical idealism is very much present in the speeches of the prophets (cf., for example, 1 Kgs 21:17–19; Isa 1:15–17; Jer 22:13–17; Amos 5:12–15; 8:4–6; Mic 3:9–11, etc.). The other ANE cultures of course also believed in ethics, but they did not achieve this concept of an integrated moral universe.

4. Covenant. The laws in the Pentateuch are connected to the concept of the covenant, i.e., of bonds and agreements that were made between God, the sovereign Lord, and Israel, his subject people. The biblical covenants were modeled after the formal agreements or treaties that existed between monarchs and their vassals in the political sphere of the ancient world. Similarities in ceremony and detail have been noted; they include "the cutting of the covenant," which was accompanied by the slaughter of a sacrificial animal; public assembly; oaths of allegiance or agreement; invocation of the gods, and their curses upon those who violated the oaths or agreements (Weinfeld 1972: 59–146). However, the biblical covenants differ from the ANE treaties in that what were originally stipulations of allegiance or agreement (Josh 24:1–27) became much expanded and transformed into paragraphs of laws and commandments. Through their acceptance of the covenant, these were seen as becoming binding upon the Israelites (Exod 19:4–8; 24:3–8; Deut 5:1–5; 26:16–27:8).

Covenant is central to the presentation of the pentateuchal laws and commandments. The occasions of making and renewing the covenant became in fact settings for revealing and restating some or all of the laws (2 Kgs 23:1–3; Jer 34:8–22; Ezra 9–10; Nehemiah 9–13). The covenant also carried with it important theological ideas: the divine authority to command; the obligation of Israel to obey; the meting out of reward and punishment for keeping or disobeying the laws; the concept of an awesome but still intimate relationship between God and his people; authority for those individuals or groups who were seen as custodians or teachers of the law; and a continuing, eternal bond between God, the sovereign, and Israel, his vassal.

The ANE treaties were not used as vehicles for presentation of laws to the population in general. Their stipulations remained rooted in the actual political contexts in which they were written. They deal with political matters of loyalty, dealings with hostile powers, military activity and support, extradition of fugitives, and the like (McCarthy 1978: 82–83, 103, 107–121). There are, of course, also political covenants or treaties in the Bible (Gen 21:22–32; 31:44–54; 1 Kgs 20:34); and these are similar in character to their ANE counterparts. But the concept of a connection between divine covenant and divine law is solely a product of Israelite theology. See also COVENANT.

5. Apodictic Law. Some scholars, following Alt (1934: 134–71) have linked covenant with biblical laws or precepts formulated in "apodictic style." This term describes what Alt saw as categorical, unconditional formulations of laws, including those presented in the imperative form; that is, words and commandments spoken by God in direct address to the Israelites. The subject matter of these laws, more often than not, could be described as dealing with the "sacral realm of human relations with the divine"; i.e., moral pronouncements of general character rather than the illustrative situations of case law. The apodictically formulated laws relate to the religious as well as to the secular realm of life. Alt saw them as uniquely Israelite in origin, in contrast with the "casuistic" or case law which was part of a common heritage shared with the Canaanites and other Near Eastern peoples (see F.1. below).

Other scholars, however, have noted that second person imperative statements occasionally also appear in the Hittite vassal treaties alongside of the more common casuistically formulated ones (McCarthy 1978: 60–62, 82–83). There are noncasuistic formulations to be found even in the otherwise overwhelmingly casuistically styled ANE law collections. These also occur in the extensive nonlegal literature; e.g., in moral directives, wisdom compositions, or curse formulations (Paul 1970: 112–24). Second person address is frequently found in Hittite and Akkadian religious rituals (*ANET*, 207–10, 334–45). This usage offers a valid parallel to the frequent use of second person statements in the cultic commandments and procedures contained in the Pentateuch. Apodictic statements are therefore not unique to ancient Israel; they can be seen as deriving from contexts involving sermons, moral exhortations, and rituals.

D. Shared Social Norms

There are a number of striking parallels between some biblical and ANE laws; the similarities are so close that they invite comment and explanation. Certain similarities may derive from societal norms that were held in common by both ancient Israel and her neighbors. So, for example, one finds common attitudes and prohibitions against sorcery (Exod 22:17; Lev 20:27; Deut 18:10–14; CH 2; AL A47; HL 44, 170), kidnapping and sale of the abducted person (Exod 21:6; Deut 24:7; CH 14; and with less severe penalties, HL 19–20), and false witness (Exod 20:16; 23:1–3; Deut 5:20; 19:16–21; CU 25–26; CH 1, 3, 4). There is a call for honesty in dealing with others; e.g., a condemnation of judges who take bribes (Exod 23:8; Deut 16:19) and of merchants who sell with false weights and measures (Lev 19:36; Deut 25:13–15; CH 108). Since these offenses were often concealed from public knowledge, the ancient societies turned to their deity for appropriate punishments and rewards (Prov 20:23; Reiner 1958: 14, l. 46; Lambert 1960: 132–33, l. 97–102, 107–21). The ancient kings recognized, as their duty, the standardization of weights and measures (e.g., Yildiz 1981, the prologue; cf. Ezek 45:9–12).

There are common attitudes respecting property rights. Thus, one finds laws condemning the moving of boundary markers between properties (Deut 19:14; 27:17; AL B8–9; HL 168–69; Reiner 1958: 14, l. 46). The Bible and the Hittite laws, perhaps by coincidence, perhaps by tradition (see sec. F.1. below), juxtapose laws dealing with damage to a neighbor's property by trespassing animal or fire (Exod 22:4–5; HL 98–99, 105–7). There is recognition of a duty for property owners to protect others from the consequences of negligent acts of omission. In the Bible, one finds this duty expressed in the cases of the missing parapet (Deut 22:8) and the unfilled pit (Exod 21:33). In Babylonia, one finds this concept in the case of the farmer who failed to maintain or shut off irrigation channels shared with his neighbors (CH 53, 55). There are shared values relating to the return of lost property. Deut 21:2–11 and HL 71 are very similar cases dealing with the holding of a lost animal whose master cannot be identified. Both traditions include positive statements on the virtue of returning the lost animal or object to its owner (Deut 2:1; HL 45). There are also common laws about the responsibility for goods (Exod 22:7–9; CH 120; LE 36) and animals (Exod 22:12–13; CH 266–67; *ANET,* 525–26; Sumerian laws 9–10) left in safekeeping.

One finds common customs as well as common values. Many of these appear in the area of family; e.g., the giving of an extra share of inheritance to the first born. This right is vouchsafed even in the case of a second marriage (Deut 21:15–17; AL B1; *ANET,* 198, Neo-Babylonian laws par. 15; CAD E, p. 78, *elâtu* A). There are provisions dealing with obligations of the husband to both wives should he take a second wife (Exod 21:10–12; CL 24–28; CH 148–49, 170–71; Falkenstein 1956: 8–9; Schorr 1913: 316–17). Sons are usually the heirs, but daughters did inherit in the absence of sons (Numbers 27; 36; cf. Job 42:15; Thureau-Dangin 1907: 72, l. 44–45; CL 22; Civil 1965: 4–5; CH 180–81). Childlessness, i.e., having no heir at all, was a problem that could only be partly alleviated. For the widow left without children, there was levirate marriage (Gen 38:8–11, 26; Deut 25:5–10; Ruth 4; see also AL A30, 33, 43; HL 193). Adoption was another alternative; it was very common in Babylonia, Assyria, and N Syria in the 2d millennium (cf. CAD M pt. 1, pp. 319–21 *mārūtu,* 306 *mārtūtu*). Adoption is poorly attested in the Bible; but one finds awareness of the practice in 1 Chr 2:34–36, as well as fragments of formulas in 2 Sam 7:14 and Ps 2:7. Legitimation of children born of a slave concubine was another possibility (Gen 35:22–26; Prov 17:2; CH 170–71). A childless wife, at times, is even seen as providing her husband with a free (Frymer-Kensky 1981: 211–12; Greengus 1975: 13–24) or slave concubine (Genesis 16; 20:1–8; CH 144–46). There are common practices relating to divorce, e.g., in the recitation of oral formulas in Babylonia, the Elephantine papyri, and the Bible (Greengus 1969: 518–20), along with "stripping" the divorcée or widow who remarried of her husband's assets (Hos 2:4–5; Huehnergard 1985).

E. Laws Protecting the Family

1. Sexual Taboos. There are shared norms in the sphere of incest taboos. One thus finds common prohibitions against a man having sexual relations with his mother (Lev 18:7; CH 157; HL 189), daughter-in-law (Lev 18:15; 20:12; Deut 27:23; CH 155), daughter (Lev 18:10—actually for a granddaughter; there is no statement on a daughter, but the taboo can be inferred *a fortiori*—CH 154; HL 189 [and stepdaughter in 195]), or father's wife (Lev 18:8; 20:12; Deut 27:20; HL 190). For this last offense, a less severe penalty is given in CH 158; namely, being expelled as an heir. HL 190, moreover, does not consider relations with a father's wife to be a sin after the death of the father. These alternative views of this type of incest is echoed in the earlier history of Israel. Reuben, who had sexual relations with his father's concubine Bilhah (Gen 35:22), was likewise expelled from his position as chief heir by Jacob (Gen 49:34). The custom of taking one's father's wives after his death is also visible in the stories surrounding Absalom (2 Sam 16:22; 20:3) and Adonijah (1 Kgs 2:13–25).

Common sexual mores are visible again in the prohibition against a man having sexual relations with two related women, i.e., two sisters or a mother and daughter. The former situation is condemned in Lev 18:18 and HL 194, but was earlier permitted for the marriage of Jacob (Gen 29:21–30). The Hittites extended this prohibition even to half sisters or cousins of the woman in question; cf. the treaty of Šuppiluliumas I with Ḫuqqana of Ḫajaša (Haase 1984: 81–82). Sexual relations with a mother and daughter is prohibited in Lev 18:17; 20:14; HL 191. HL 194, 200, however, did not extend the full force of this taboo to two slave or captive women. There appears to have been a comparable prohibition against a woman having sexual relations with two men who were brothers or father and son. This latter situation is condemned in Amos 2:7; condemnation of both situations may be inferred, among the Hittites, from HL 194, which releases the taboo penalty for a slave woman. The situation of two brothers is condemned in the treaty with Ḫuqqana. The Bible does not discuss the situation of two brothers having sexual relations with an unmarried woman, but condemns it with the married wife of a brother (Lev 18:16; similarly, HL 195). One also finds commonly shared sexual taboos against bestiality (Lev 18:23; 20:15–16; Deut 27:21; HL 187–88, 200) and male homosexuality (Lev 18:22; 20:13; AL A19–20).

In Lev 18:3 and 27–29, it is implied that the Egyptians and the native peoples of Canaan did not observe the same taboos that were enjoined upon Israel. There is, unfortunately, no real data available for the sexual attitudes of the Canaanites, and the data for Egypt are likewise insufficient. But the cumulative evidence given above for the Hittites, Babylonians, and Assyrians suggests that the Israelites were neither the first nor only people to honor such taboos.

2. Adultery. The mores relating to adultery were similar but not uniform. In ancient Israel, if a married or betrothed woman committed adultery, both she and her paramour had to die (Lev 18:20; 20:10; Deut 22:20–24; Ezek 16:38–42); if the wife was a slave, then there was no penalty except that the paramour was required to provide a guilt offering (Lev 19:20–22). This case of adultery with a consenting slave wife has no ANE parallel. Babylonian and Assyrian laws also treat the case where a free married woman entrapped a man who did not know her status; in such cases, the wife dies but the man goes free (Yildiz 1981, law 7; AL A14, 22–23). The ANE laws also add another level of handling: if the husband wishes to spare his guilty wife, he may do so in Ḫatti and Assyria (he may also punish or mutilate her); but in every case, the same level of punishment meted out to the wife is also meted out to her lover (CH 129; AL A13, 15; HL 197–98). For these ANE societies, the wife and her lover shared the same penalty as long as they were both equally guilty of adultery. The biblical laws do not discuss any mitigating circumstances or variant handling; Prov 6:34–35 can be interpreted as depicting the rage of a betrayed husband who refused ransom or compensation from his wife's paramour. But one must recognize that ransom for adultery is so far not widely attested either in the Bible or in the ANE. There is a case of monetary compensation along with an exculpatory oath for near adultery in AL A22. This case has been compared with the mollifying gifts and the exculpatory declaration made by Abimelech to Abraham for the near adultery in Genesis 20. The case of a wife who is accused by a third party of adultery appears in the ANE law collections but not in the Bible (CU 11; CH 132; AL A17); the wife had to vindicate herself by submitting to an ordeal. The wife who was not accused but whose husband merely suspected her of adultery had to take an oath in CH 131. In such a case, Num 5:11–31 has an ordeal-like ceremony in addition to the oath.

The ANE laws, as pointed out above, do not have a parallel case to Lev 19:20–22 dealing with adultery with a consenting slave wife, but they do treat another situation, absent in the Bible, of the rape of a virgin slave girl (Yildiz 1981, laws 6–8). Finkelstein (1966: 360) has suggested that the slave's consent may have been meaningless; the penalty for rape may be seen as damage to property. The biblical law requiring a guilt offering may thus perhaps be a way of attaching some "guilt" to an otherwise unpunished or unpunishable act.

3. Rape. The laws on rape are similar in all of the ANE cultures. In the case of an unmarried virgin, the rapist pays a fine and must marry the woman and never divorce her; the Assyrian laws add talionic retaliation against the rapist's wife if he is already married (Deut 22:28; AL A55). The Sumerian laws 7–8 (*ANET,* 525–26) add mitigating factors: if the girl was in the street with her parents' knowledge, the rapist may or may not marry the girl. In the case of the betrothed or married woman, the penalty is death for the rapist and the woman goes free if one can presume that she struggled and was coerced. If the rape occurred in a remote spot, such as the fields or the mountains, the wife is presumed to have cried out and is thus innocent of wrongdoing. If the attack took place in the town, the woman is presumed guilty if she did not cry out (Deut 22:23–38; CH 130; LE 26; HL 197; AL A12, 16). The Assyrian laws (AL A23) add a further mitigation: in the case of the entrapped wife who was raped in town but who did not cry out when released, her paramour and procuress suffer the death penalty but the laws leave her punishment up to her husband.

F. Personal Injuries

1. A Common Legal Tradition. Certain laws which are found in the Bible and in the ANE collections not only deal with the same subject material but do so in a way that includes remarkably similar details. Prime examples are the personal injury laws of the goring ox and the pregnant woman who is struck and miscarries (described below). The repeated use of these specialized (some scholars say unusual and unlikely) life situations as the setting for illustrating what moderns might call principles of negligence and liability suggests that these laws might in fact be part of a literary or scholastic tradition, created for the purpose of teaching these principles. The law codes of the ANE, moreover, almost invariably present the laws in casuistic or case form. The casuistic style is very much the preferred mode of presentation in the scribal traditions of Mesopotamia and her neighbors. This mode occurs not only in law but also in the analytic literature of such things as omens, divination, and medical symptoms. In this vast, casuistically styled literature, the protasis states the problem while the remedy or interpretation appears in the apodosis. Then, too, there is the fact of the existence of ancient schools and the observed retention and transmission of such "classics" as the Code of Hammurapi in these schools over the centuries. See EDUCATION (MESOPOTAMIA). Because of these factors, scholars have looked for cultural sharing among ancient Israel, Babylon, Assyria, and Ḫatti. Some scholars, notably Alt (1934: 112–29), saw the Covenant Code, which contains the greatest number of parallels to the case laws of the other ANE law codes, as the oldest set of biblical laws. The basic materials of the Covenant Code, he suggested, might have been borrowed from the Canaanites, who held them in common with the other ANE peoples from whom law collections are known. Other scholars (Müller 1903: 210–44; Speiser 1963; Cardascia 1977; Westbrook 1988: 1–8) have visualized a continuing tradition of a Near Eastern common law in which ancient Israel more directly shared. At this stage of knowledge, however, the actual mechanisms of cultural contact and transmission still remain elusive (Finkelstein 1981: 17–20).

2. The Goring Ox. In the biblical version of the goring ox cases, the ox that gored a human must be stoned and its flesh not eaten. The Mesopotamian parallel cases say nothing at all about the fate of the ox (Exod 21:28–32, 35–36; CH 250–52; LE 53–54). Some scholars (Müller 1903: 165; Finkelstein 1981: 26–29) have explained the punishment of the ox as a religious value: the goring ox has "transgressed" the boundaries of the natural order by attacking a human being, whether free or slave. The idea of punishing animals is not confined to Israel; the Hittite laws (HL 199) present the case of an ox or a pig which leaped upon a man (apparently with sexual intent); the ox is to be killed but not the pig.

3. Miscarriage. In the case dealing with the pregnant

mother who dies when she is struck and miscarries, some of the ANE laws (CH 209–14; AL A21, 50–53) impose the death penalty, while others (Civil 1965: 4–6) require only compensation. The laws that impose the death penalty, moreover, also allow talionic reprisal against the pregnant wife or daughter of the man responsible. If the pregnant woman was a slave or a member of a lower social class, then the laws require only compensation.

A second case, which the above laws also present, is the situation in which the foetus dies but the mother survives. In all of the laws, the penalty is then only monetary. Sumerian laws 1–2 (*ANET,* 525–26), moreover, vary the penalty according to whether the blow was accidental or intentional. The Assyrian laws (AL A53) discuss one additional case, not treated by any other collection, dealing with the woman who induces her own abortion; the death penalty is given.

The biblical cases (Exod 21:22–24) have been subject to various interpretations, due to uncertainty about two Heb words: *ʾāsôn* and *pĕlīlîm* (RSV "harm, judges"). In the first case, where there is no *ʾāsôn,* the striker pays compensation in (accordance with the) *pĕlīlîm.* In the second case, where there is *ʾāsôn,* the consequence is talion, with the death penalty. The traditional interpretation of these verses follows the ANE parallel cases and takes *ʾāsôn* to denote the death of the mother. Accordingly, in the first case, where compensation is given, only the foetus dies; in the second case, which leads to talion, both mother and foetus are lost. Among modern scholars, Speiser (1963) has suggested interpreting *pĕlīlîm* in accordance with HL 17–18, where the compensation given for the foetus varies according to how close it was to birth. But other scholars have put forth other interpretations, claiming that *ʾāsôn* refers to the child rather than to the mother. For Jackson (1973), the first case deals with a premature but live child; the second deals with a stillborn child. For Westbrook (1986), the child in both cases dies; he interprets *ʾāsôn* as "unknown perpetrator"; the first case has an identified striker, but the second does not. He suggests that Exod 21:24 ("you shall give life for life") must be understood as compensation rather than as a death penalty. These alternative interpretations are defensible in view of the uncertainty about the meaning of the two words mentioned; however, they fail to explain the ANE parallel cases, as well as the fact that the traditional interpretation itself also has a long history, going back to rabbinic times.

4. Battery. The ancient personal injury laws dealing with battery exhibit remarkable parallels between ancient Israel and her neighbors. The catalogue of selected injuries listed in the Bible, i.e., eye, tooth, bone, hand, foot, etc., is very similar to what is found in other collections. These selections could simply be the product of shared human experience. But they could also be the product of a scholastic tradition, especially since one finds them associated with the rubric of talionic retribution.

The cases are numerous and varied. The Bible treats these injuries together as a group in several places (Exod 21:24–25; Lev 24:19–20, 22; Deut 19:21). In the other ancient codes the injuries are listed either separately or in smaller groups. Thus, eye (CH 196; LE 42; HL 7), tooth (CH 200; LE 42; CU 19; HL 7), foot (CU 15; HL 11), bone (CH 197; LE 45, CU 16), finger (LE 43), hand (LE 44; HL 11), nose (CU 17; LE 42; HL 13–14), ear (LE 42; HL 15), and collarbone (LE 46).

In general, the laws make the striking party subject to talion in all cases where the injury is permanent. The mitigating circumstances of intention are admitted in CH 206–7 in a case where the injury could have led to the death of the victim. In the same situation, Exod 21:18–19 omits consideration of intent. Both of these codes, however, make the striking party responsible for the victim's medical care and incapacitation. HL 10 also includes responsibility for medical costs and incapacitation in a case of a debilitating head injury.

There are two other cases of battery worthy of mention that involve talion. One is the case of the woman who in a fight assaults a man's genitals. The woman is punished by mutilation both in the Bible (Deut 25:11) and in the Assyrian laws (AL A8). The other case is the son who strikes his father or mother; he is punished by mutilation in CH 195 (this case mentions only the father) and by death in Exod 21:5.

5. Talion and Compensation. The presence of talion in the Bible and in the laws of Babylonia under Hammurapi and the absence of talion in the laws of Sumer, Eshnunna, and Ḫatti have stimulated scholarly discussion and debate. Previously, many scholars had argued that whereas earlier societies practiced talionic retribution, i.e., corporal punishments comparable to the injuries suffered, later and perhaps more enlightened societies renounced talion for monetary compensation. However, there were problems with this view after the ANE "codes" were discovered. For example, why in the Code of Hammurapi are personal injuries to freemen punished by talion but injuries suffered by lower social classes or slaves only punished by monetary compensation? Also, why do the codes in Eshnunna and Sumer, which are earlier in time than Hammurapi, know only compensation and no talion? A. S. Diamond (1957) has argued that this is the case because the simpler, less developed societies preferred to settle injuries through compensation; talion is not primitive but a later development, reflecting the advancing power of the state. Freemen are then protected by the more serious consequences of talion while slaves and lower classes are left with the older system of compensation. Talion is developed in order to give maximum protection to the rights of free citizens, both in the ANE and Israel. Diamond suggests that in societies where social stratification is present, talion also serves to remove the differences between rich and poor freemen; the wealthy person cannot then just "buy off" the damage caused by his offense.

Westbrook (1988: 41–47) argues that the division between talion and compensation has been overstated; in fact, both modes of settlement coexist at all times, in ancient Israel and in the ANE. The inclusion of either compensation or talion in a given law formulation is the product of didactic selection; the laws should not be read in contrastive but in complementary fashion. To sustain this view, however, one must address a number of problems. Among them are: (1) the need to reconstruct talionic reprisals into the laws where they are not absent, notably the law "codes" of Urnammu, Eshnunna, and Ḫatti; (2) the need to insert compensation into cases which state only talion; and (3) the need to take notice of the apparently simultaneous practices of applying talion to injuries sustained by the upper classes but requiring only compensation for injuries against lower social groups.

G. Homicide

1. In the Bible. The laws of all ancient societies uniformly condemn murder, but there are differences in the punishments meted out. Biblical law continued the tribalistic practice of allowing the kinfolk of the victim to take blood revenge against the slayer or his family members. Blood revenge was practiced during the early monarchy (2 Sam 14:7–11). The account of David's handing over the sons of Saul to the Gibeonites (2 Sam 21:1–15) shows that this talionic death penalty coexisted with the alternative of compensation. In Num 35:31–34, however, compensation for intentional homicide is strongly condemned. Additional reform came about through rejection of the earlier practice of extending responsibility to family members for crimes committed by an individual (2 Kgs 14:5–6; Deut 24:16; Ezekiel 18). In Num 35:9–28 and Josh 20:1–9, the concept of a city of refuge to protect accidental slayers from blood revenge is introduced; there is also an attempt to enforce some process of proof by two witnesses before vengeance could be taken against a murderer.

2. In the Ancient Near East. One finds the coexistence of compensation and blood revenge in Assyria in all periods (AL A10; B2; Roth 1987; CAD D, p. 79, *damu*). But among the Hittites one finds only compensation (HL 1–5); indeed, a letter of Ḫattusilis III to Kadašman-Enlil of Babylonia (ca. 1270 B.C.) explains that the slaying of Babylonian merchants in N Syria could only be redressed through compensation, and that it was not customary for the Hittites to give the death penalty for murder (Klengel 1980; Haase 1984: 86; *ANET,* 547). Murder of a member of the royal family, however, according to the edict of Telepinu, might be punished either by compensation or by the death of the murderer; the choice was left to the family (Haase 1984: 52–53). The situation in Babylonia was apparently different. While there is no case dealing directly with murder in the Code of Hammurapi, CH 153 metes out the death penalty to a wife who is an accessory to the murder of her husband. This same offense also led to the death penalty in an earlier, Sumerian record of a trial for homicide (*ANET,* 542).

3. Modern Perspectives on Ancient Values. The rejection of compensation for homicide in Num 35:31–34 has been taken by some scholars to reflect a deeply held principle; namely, that intentional homicide could never be assuaged except by the death of the murderer, as in Gen 9:5–6. These scholars see this rejection of compensation as marking an important cultural divergence between ancient Israel and her neighbors; it is a principle that reflects a high regard for the sanctity of human life (Müller 1903: 212; Greenberg 1960 and 1986).

Other scholars, however, have argued in almost the opposite fashion. They take the absence of the death penalty for murder, as well as its limited use overall in the Hittite laws, to be a mark of significant moral advancement in that society. They point to the stated abandonment of talionic penalties, e.g., in HL 92, 161–67, as further signs of this moral development (Haase 1987: 103).

4. Unsolved Murder. In the Bible (Deut 21:1–9), there is "guilt" attached to the magistrates (elders and judges) of the nearest neighboring community. They remove this guilt by an expiation ceremony which includes the killing of a heifer at a nearby stream, the washing of hands, and an exculpatory declaration by the magistrates. There is no compensation for the family of the victim, probably in keeping with the strong aversion to compensation discussed above.

The Hittite laws, which favor compensation, place the burden of the compensation on the property owners of the area where the murder took place (HL 6). The Hittite laws, further, include the case of the unsolved murder of a traveling merchant; here again, as in the letter of Ḫattusilis III cited above, there is compensation for the merchant and for any lost goods (HL 5).

The Babylonian laws (CH 23–24) address the case of the unsolved murder in connection with robbery. Here, too, the magistrates of the local community must give restitution for the goods and compensation for the victim. The same seems to have been true at Nuzi several centuries later (Gordon 1936).

H. Theft

1. In the Bible. Biblical responses to theft are varied: simple compensation is given to a keeper of livestock or shepherd from whom animals are stolen (Exod 22:10); the thief himself, however, if caught, must pay double if the stolen animals are recovered—and he must pay fourfold or fivefold (depending upon whether sheep or cattle are involved) for animals no longer recoverable. An impecunious thief could be sold into slavery (Exod 22:1). The theft of other personal property is covered in Exod 22:2. A thief breaking in during the day must not be killed, but a thief in the night could be slain without bloodguilt. One may also find readiness to apply capital punishment for theft in the statements made by David in 2 Sam 12:5–6, by Jacob in Gen 31:32, and by Joseph's brothers in Gen 44:9–10. Theft of property belonging to God (*ḥērem*) was punished by death (Josh 7:1, 18–25).

2. In the Ancient Near East. The Hittite laws treat theft in great detail. One finds penalties for the theft of certain domestic animals (ox, sheep, goat, horse, ass, mule) ranging from twice to fifteen times their value, depending upon the animal, its gender, age, etc. (HL 57–70). Theft of swine is punished by a lesser, monetary fine to the owner, ranging from six to twelve shekels, depending on the quality of the animal; theft of a piglet resulted in a smaller penalty (HL 81–85). Theft of other personal property was also punished by monetary fines along with restitution of the stolen objects. The penalties ranged from three to twelve shekels, depending on whether the thief was a freeman or a slave, the object stolen, the place, (i.e., whether in the barn or in the house), whether before or after the theft, etc. A slave might also be mutilated if he stole from a stranger's house (HL 91–97, 119–25, 127–43). Smaller monetary penalties were exacted from thieves who took produce from the garden or the orchard or stole timber (HL 101–4). The theft of bricks was to be repaid twofold (HL 128).

Theft of royal property could be punished by monetary fines; however, the theft of a bronze spear from the palace was punishable by death (HL 126). Theft or misappropriation of gold, silver, garments, or bronze implements belonging to a god's temple was also punished by death (*ANET,* 208).

In the laws of Babylonia, one finds parallels to the biblical cases of the housebreaking thief. The Eshnunna laws (LE 12–13) make the same distinction of whether the theft is by day or night: if by day, the penalty is compensation; if by night, the penalty is death. The penalty is the same whether the thief is found in the barn or in the house. The Hammurapi laws (CH 21) offer yet another parallel; a thief who is caught tunneling into a house shall be killed and hanged in front of his tunnel. The Laws of Hammurapi contain the most severe penalties for theft. Sellers and receivers of stolen goods belonging to a private person, a palace, or a temple receive the death penalty (CH 6, 9–13); looters and receivers of valuable property from minors or slaves are similarly punished (CH 7, 25). If a person, entrusted with a store of grain in order to look after farm activities (i.e., planting, feeding livestock) then steals the grain, the penalty is to cut off his hand if he is caught doing so; after the fact, the penalty is monetary. But the thief who cannot pay is subject to further physical violence: being dragged by oxen (CH 253–56).

Some scholars consider the death penalty for theft in the Laws of Hammurapi to represent an extreme point of view, one not in keeping with general Babylonian attitudes and practices. These scholars point to lesser penalties for theft even within the Laws of Hammurapi themselves and believe that the noncapital penalties are the earlier and more generally accepted laws of Babylonian society. Thus, for example, theft of timber was subject to monetary fine (CH 59) just as it is in the earlier Sumerian laws of Lipit-Ishtar (CL 10), in the Hittite laws (HL 128), and in the later, Neo-Babylonian laws (*ANET,* 197, par. 7—a case of a woman stealing brushwood). Monetary penalties are also given for theft of cattle (CH 8, 265), agricultural implements (CH 259–60), gold, silver, and other valuables consigned for transport or sale (CH 106–7, 112).

Further evidence for monetary penalties comes from four ancient documents of the kingdom of Eshnunna. In two trial proceedings for thieves (one free, one slave) caught while housebreaking, the civil magistrates bound the thieves over to the house owners for penal servitude (Greengus 1986: 157–59, 171–73; *ANET,* 545). This punishment finds its parallel in the sale of the thief in Exod 22:1, mentioned above. In the other two cases, thieves apprehended after the theft were likewise sentenced by the courts to monetary penalties (*RLA* 4: 249; Simmons 1960: 28–29).

The Assyrian laws (AL A3–4) contain a series of paragraphs dealing with restriction on a married woman's handling of domestic property; the stated penalty for taking and receiving these goods was death. However, theft of a stranger's property by a married woman was punished by compensation to the victim and mutilation of the woman by her husband (AL A5). If she stole temple property, the punishment was left up to the god's oracle (AL A1). AL C8 deals with the theft of animals and personal property; the penalties are monetary and a beating, plus a period of laboring for the king. If the thief is judged by the king himself, then the penalty would depend on the king's decision. However, just as in Babylonia, extant documents from the later Neo-Assyrian period repeatedly attest only to theft being punished by monetary penalties (CAD S, pp. 188–89, *sartu*).

I. Cultic Law

The ANE law collections have only infrequent references to cult or religious worship and practice. One may cite, for example, HL 166, which deals with a prohibition against mixed seeding that parallels Lev 19:19 and Deut 22:9; or CH 160, which, like Lev 19:23–25, suggests that new fruits were reckoned ready to be eaten in the fifth year of cultivation. The Hittite laws dealing with sexual taboos repeatedly use the term *ḫurkel,* "abomination," to describe these offenses (see sec. E.1. above). HL 25 levies penalties against one who fouls cisterns or vessels. But such examples are few in comparison to the biblical law collections which regulate many cultic and religious activities. The inclusion of such material in the Bible may be because the Bible received its final shaping during the latter half of the 1st millennium, during a time when ancient Israel became a small, theocratically governed province under Persian and Greek rule. The temple and its cult was one of the few areas that remained under indigenous, Israelite control. The exclusion of cultic laws in the ANE law collections may, correspondingly, have something to do with the subordinate roles of temples in autonomous, monarchal states.

Cultic regulations are by no means lacking in the ANE. In addition to the rituals cited above (sec. C.5.), one may also mention the Punic cult tariffs from Marseilles and Carthage (*ANET,* 656–57). Such regulations, however, do not appear as part of the royal law collections, which restrict themselves to situations of potential conflict arising out of person-to-person relationships. The biblical laws, which emanate from God, also include relationships between persons and deity. This extra or wider view may be considered another reason for the latitude of materials included in the pentateuchal laws.

J. Law and Social Welfare

1. Debts and Slavery. There was recognition, both in Israel and in the ANE, of social problems and dislocations caused by economic disparities and hardships. Especially severe was the problem of debt, which could force an individual to give up his property, home, fields, and eventually even his freedom. There is evidence in the laws of attempts to address these social and economic problems through relief-giving measures and regulations. The rights of a borrower with respect to items of his property pledged to his creditor are the subject of laws in the Bible (Exod 22:25–27; Deut 24:6, 10–13, 17; cf. Amos 2:8; 2 Kgs 4:1) and in the ANE (e.g., CH 49–52, 113, 241; AL C4, 9, G; CAD K, p. 308, *katû,* M pt. 1, pp. 372–73, *maškanu*). There is concern about persons who are distrained or enslaved because of their debts; such a person must be released after six years in the Bible (Exod 21:2–11; Deut 15:12–18) and after three years in Babylonia (CH 117). In the Assyrian laws (AL A39, 48) and in the Bible (Exod 21:7–11), one finds attempts to mitigate the consequences of debt slavery for unmarried women. There are laws aimed at preventing the ill-treatment of individuals, free or slave, who are left in pledge (e.g., LE 22–24;

CH 115–16, 118–19; CAD K, p. 460, *kiššatu*). The Bible, too, has laws bearing on the ill-treatment of distrained persons (Lev 25:39, 43, 53); and one may also look to Exod 21:20–21, 26–27, as a piece of a larger social policy protecting all types of slaves. Deut 23:15–16 departs from the other Near Eastern law collections by forbidding the return of a fugitive slave to his master. The Near Eastern laws consider return to be a duty (CU 14; CL 12–13; CH 15–20; HL 22–24).

2. Redemption and Release. Property and persons who passed out of the possession of debtors into the hands of creditors could often be redeemed (e.g., Lev 25:25–28, 47–55; Jer 32:6–15; Ruth 4:1–12; LE 39; CH 118–19; AL A48; CAD I/J, pp. 171–72, *ipṭirū*). Otherwise, the forfeiture or sale became final. But even in such cases, there was relief in the form of periodic "jubilees," or years of release, when properties might go back to the original owners. In the Bible, this event is termed *dĕrôr* or *yôbēl* (e.g., Lev 25:10–13, 23, 28, 31, 50, 54; Jer 34:8–16; Ezek 46:17). While the release for persons came after six years of servitude, the release for property was periodically set to occur every fifty years, irrespective of when the forfeiture or sale occurred (Lev 25:8–12).

In Mesopotamian sources, one finds an array of terms designating release; most importantly, Sumerian *ama.ar.gi$_4$*, *níg.si.sá*, and their Akkadian counterparts *andurāru mīšaru, kubussû* (cf. CAD A pt. 2, pp. 115–17; M pt. 2, pp. 116–17; K, pp. 489–90). These releases were most often associated with the accession of a new king or his "jubilee," celebrated some decades later. Typically, the release effected relief for various unpaid taxes on lands and harvests, cancellation of outstanding loans, discharge of debt hostages and slaves, annulment of property sales due to debts, or recompense for their loss.

The term *mīšaru,* often used in parallel with *kittu,* "truth," very early came to be a general term for "justice, equity." This development has been noted, especially in comparison with its Hebrew cognate *mêšārîm,* which is similarly translated. The question for biblical scholars, however, is to determine whether *mêšārîm,* like its cognate, also had a more specific meaning as a term denoting a royal release. There are frequent poetic images of God as king; and among these passages, one finds descriptions of his ruling the world *bĕmêšārîm,* "with equity" (e.g., Pss 9:9; 96:10; 98:9). One must also consider the fact that the social and economic factors which required relief were operative at all times, after the Exile as well as before. In Neh 5:1–13 is an episode similar to that of Jer 34:8–16; one finds persons and property being lost due to debt and a resolution to release secured by solemn oath. Nehemiah's release is not described by any specific term, but it may be seen as part of a continuing history of welfare actions in ancient Israel. Scholars have also pointed out that it is perhaps not accidental that the first laws of the Covenant Code are those dealing with debt slavery and release (Weinfeld 1982). The biblical laws prohibiting the taking of interest on loans may be seen as yet another attempt to alleviate the problems of debtors (e.g., Exod 22:24; Lev 25:35–38; Deut 23:20–21; Ezek 18:17; Amos 5:11). Elsewhere, usury was regulated but not forbidden, e.g., in Babylonia (CH L; LE 18; Greengus 1986: 194–96). The negative view of usury may reflect the experiences and attitudes of a largely agrarian Israelite society. This condition may likewise be the reason for the absence of biblical laws regulating the activities of merchants, professions, traders, and craftsmen.

Bibliography

Alt, A. 1934. *Die Ursprünge des israelitischen Rechts.* BSAW 86/1. Leipzig. = The Origins of Israelite Law. Pp. 101–71 in *Essays on Old Testament History and Religion.* Trans. R. A. Wilson. Garden City, NY, 1967.

Cardascia, G. 1977. Droits cunéiformes et Droit biblique. PWCJS 6: 63–70.

Civil, M. 1965. New Sumerian Law Fragments. Pp. 1–10 in *Studies in Honor of Benno Landsberger April 21, 1965.* AS 16. Chicago.

Diamond, A. S. 1957. An Eye for an Eye. *Iraq* 19: 151–55.

Falkenstein, A. 1956. *Die neusumerischen Gerichtsurkunden.* Vol. 2. ABAW 40. Munich.

Finkelstein, J. J. 1966. Sex Offenses in Sumerian Laws. *JAOS* 86: 355–72.

———. 1981. *The Ox That Gored. TAPhS* 71/2. Philadelphia.

Frymer-Kensky, T. 1981. Patriarchal Family Relationships and Near Eastern Law. *BA* 44: 209–14.

Gordon, C. 1936. An Akkadian Parallel to Deuteronomy 21:1ff. *RA* 33: 1–6.

Greenberg, M. 1960. Some Postulates of Biblical Criminal Law. Pp. 5–28 in *Yehezkiel Kaufmann Jubilee Volume,* ed. M. Haran. Jerusalem.

———. 1986. More Reflections on Biblical Criminal Law. Pp. 1–17 in *Studies in Bible,* ed. S. Japhet. *ScrHier* 31. Jerusalem.

Greengus, S. 1969. The Old Babylonian Marriage Contract. *JAOS* 89: 505–32.

———. 1975. Sisterhood Adoption at Nuzi and the "Wife-Sister" in Genesis. *HUCA* 46: 5–31.

———. 1986. *Studies in Ishchali Documents.* BiMes 19. Malibu, CA.

Haase, R. 1984. *Texte zum hethitischen Recht: Eine Auswahl.* Wiesbaden.

———. 1987. Kapitaldelikte im hethitischen Recht. *Hethitica* 7: 93–107.

Huehnergard, J. 1985. Biblical Notes on Some Akkadian Texts from Emar (Syria). *CBQ* 47: 428–34.

Jackson, B. S. 1973. Exodus XXI, 22–25. *VT* 23: 273–304.

Klengel, H. 1980. Mord und Bussleistung im spätbronzezeitlichen Syrien. Pp. 189–97 in *Death in Mesopotamia,* ed. B. Alster. Studies in Assyriology 8. Copenhagen.

Kraus, F. R. 1984. *Königliche Verfügungen in Altbabylonischer Zeit.* StDI 11. Leiden.

Lambert, W. G. 1960. *Babylonian Wisdom Literature.* Oxford.

McCarthy, D. J. 1978. *Treaty and Covenant.* AnBib 21A. Rome.

Müller, D. H. von. 1903. *Die Gesetze Hammurabis und ihr Verhältnis zur mosaischen Gesetzgebung sowie zu den XII Tafeln.* Amsterdam. Repr. 1975.

Paul, S. M. 1970. *Studies in the Book of the Covenant in the Light of Cuneiform and Biblical Law.* VTSup 18. Leiden.

Porten, B. 1968. *Archives from Elephantine.* Berkeley.

Reiner, E. 1958. *Šurpu: A Collection of Sumerian and Akkadian Incantations.* AfO Beiheft 11. Graz.

Roth, M. 1987. Homicide in the Neo-Assyrian Period. Pp. 351–65 in *Language, Literature, and History,* ed. F. Rochberg-Halton. AOS 67. New Haven.

Schorr, M. 1913. *Urkunden des altbabylonischen Zivil- und Prozessrechts. VAB* 5. Leipzig.

Simmons, J. D. 1960. Early Old Babylonian Tablets from Harmal and Elsewhere. *JCS* 14: 23–32.
Speiser, E. 1963. The Stem PLL in Hebrew. *JBL* 82: 301–6.
Tadmor, H. 1982. Treaty and Oath in the Ancient Near East. Pp. 127–52 in *Humanizing America's Iconic Book: Society of Biblical Literature Centennial Addresses 1980,* ed. G. M. Tucker, and D. A. Knight. Chico, CA.
Thureau-Dangin, F. 1907. *Die Sumerischen und Akkadischen Königsinschriften. VAB* 1. Leipzig.
Weinfeld, M. 1972. *Deuteronomy and the Deuteronomic School.* Oxford.
———. 1982. Justice and Righteousness in Ancient Israel Against the Background of Social Reforms in the Ancient Near East. Pp. 491–519 in *Mesopotamie und seine Nachbarn,* ed. H. J. Nissen and J. Renger. 25e Rencontre Assyriologique Internationale. Berlin.
Westbrook, R. 1986. Lex Talionis and Exodus 21, 22–25. *RB* 93: 52–69.
———. 1988. *Studies in Biblical and Cuneiform Law.* CahRB 26. Paris.
Yildiz, F. 1981. A Tablet of Codex Ur-Nammu from Sippar. *Or* 58: 87–97.

SAMUEL GREENGUS

FORMS OF BIBLICAL LAW

In addition to categorizing biblical texts according to content, scholars classify texts according to their literary form. In the case of those passages which clearly articulate laws, the form has not been so easy to classify.

A. Alt's Categories
B. Criticism of Alt's Categories
C. A Syntactical Categorization
  1. Laws in the Conditional Form
    a. "When/If" Form
    b. Relative Form
    c. Participial Form
  2. Laws in the Unconditional Form
    a. Direct Address
    b. Third Person Jussive
D. The Setting in Life of the Biblical Legal Forms

A. Alt's Categories

Biblical laws mostly follow the pattern of the ANE law collections. However, while legal forms in these corpora are relatively few, those found in the Bible vary greatly in number and composition. The forms of biblical laws have been studied by a number of scholars, including Jirku, Jepsen, and Mowinckel. But it is A. Alt's essay (1967), "Die Ursprünge des israelitischen Rechts," first published in 1934, that has dominated the field of biblical law for a long time.

Alt noted that a number of legal forms were juxtaposed in the book of the covenant and, using the tools of form criticism, set out to differentiate between them by identifying two major types: "casuistic" and "apodictic." A "casuistic" law, Alt pointed out, is one that is built on the sequence of a protasis and an apodosis of a conditional sentence. The main case is introduced by the Hebrew conjunction *kî* ("granted" or "supposing that") and subsidiary cases by the weaker Heb *ʾim* "if." In its pure form, Alt added, all parties in the law are referred to in the third person. As an example, he quoted Exod 21:18–19, "Supposing men quarrel and one strikes the other with a stone or with his . . . and the man [who was struck] does not die but keeps his bed . . . if then the man rises again and supported on his staff can walk in the street, he that struck him shall be clear, only he shall pay for the loss of his time, and shall have him thoroughly healed" (Alt 1967: 114).

Laws formulated in the "apodictic style," Alt stated, are generally rhythmic and terse; metrical in form; fundamental, categorical, and inclusive in character; they usually appear in series. He identified four groups: (1) laws introduced by an active participle and followed by the Heb formula *môt yûmāt* (e.g., Exod 21:12, 15–17); (2) a list of curses which begin with the Heb predicate *ʾarûr,* "cursed" (e.g., Deut 27:15–26); (3) three short series consisting of prohibitions in the second person singular (i.e., Lev 18:7–17; Exod 22:17, 20, 21, 27a–b [with interpolations], and Exod 23:1–3, 6–9 [with interpolations]; and (4) the Decalogue, where, as he put it, "the categorical negative is the strongest unifying element in the whole list" (Alt 1967: 153).

B. Criticism of Alt's Categories

Alt's distinction between "casuistic" and "apodictic" legal forms was accepted by many leading scholars, including W. F. Albright, U. Cassuto, W. J. Harrelson, R. A. F. Mackenzie, R. H. Pfeiffer, M. Noth, G. von Rad, and R. de Vaux. Even those who disagreed with some of his points continued to operate with his categories and terminology.

Naturally, Alt's classic division did not remain unchallenged, but further research showed a few shortcomings.

First, Alt did not recognize "mixed forms." Rather, he maintained that any deviation from the basic casuistic form was "a secondary variation in which stylistic elements of other forms have crept in" (Alt 1967: 114). This, however, led many scholars to contradictory conclusions. For instance, whereas O. Eissfeldt, who accepted Alt's division, considered the law in Exod 21:2 ("When you acquire . . .) as casuistic, J. van der Ploeg, another Alt follower, excluded it from this category.

Second, the participial forms presented a special problem. Alt had placed them among the apodictic laws, and in fact argued that they best exemplified the category itself; but other scholars, including M. Noth, J. J. Stamm, and M. E. Andrew, pointed to the description of the legal consequence as being reminiscent of the casuistic laws. Therefore, some followed Alt and placed the participial laws among apodictic (for example, H. J. Boecker, J. G. Williams, Pfeiffer, and Harrelson), while others (for instance, W. Kornfeld, R. Kilian) preferred to consider them casuistic.

Third, some scholars who have accepted Alt's two major divisions took a further step and provided subcategories based on content. For example, D. Patrick (1973) identified two different types of casuistic laws: (1) remedial law, where a penalty is prescribed in the apodosis (e.g., Exod 21:22); and (2) primary law which clarifies the rights and duties of the parties (e.g., Exod 21:2–6). Gilmer (1975) divided the casuistic "If-you" form into four subgroups: (1) the humanitarian If-you formulation; (2) the ceremonial If-you formulation; (3) the Holy War If-you formulation; and (4) the juridical If-you formulation.

Another group of scholars, however, went beyond Alt's

divisions and proposed different categories. For example, Cazelles (1946) offered four groups of laws: (1) casuistic; (2) participial; (3) direct style formula; (4) conditional formula in direct style. F. L. Horton (1971) outlined them as follows: (1) participial; (2) casuistic, including mixed and relative forms ("he who . . ."); (3) apodictic, including prohibitions (Heb *lōʾ* plus an imperfect verb form), wisdom prohibitives (Heb *ʾal* plus a jussive verb), and positive commandments. Lowenstamm (*EncMiqr* 5: 625–28) went even further and identified six different forms: (1) casuistic; (2) priestly ("he who . . ."); (3) commands or prohibitions in the third person; (4) commands and prohibitions in the second person; (5) participial; (6) mixed.

Fourth, beyond the issue of categories, some scholars raise questions about terminology. Boecker (1980), for example, replaces "apodictic" with the label "normative law." Gerstenberger (1965b) calls the second person prohibitions ("you shall not . . .") "prohibitives." W. Richter (1966) prefers to refer to the negative commands, Heb *ʾal* plus a jussive verb, as "vetitive." Even though Bright (1973) points out that there is a difference between the *"lōʾ* prohibitive" (mostly found in law) and the "*ʾal* prohibitive" (most suitable for wisdom), others argue that it is difficult to discern a distinction in force between the two. Sonsino (1980) argues that the term "apodictic/apodeictic," first proposed by Alt, is far from being adequate to refer to biblical law. This word actually means, "of clear demonstration, established on incontrovertible evidence" (*OED* 1: 387). It was used in Aristotelian logic to express certainty and absolute truth. As such, it is not appropriate to describe biblical laws which are considered products of divine revelation and not the result of logical conclusions.

C. A Syntactical Categorization

A study of legal forms in the Hebrew Bible shows that it is possible to group them in two categories based on their syntactical structure. Some biblical laws describe a case and then stipulate a legal consequence. Others present no case information. The first laws are retrospective and look back at a situation or a fact. The second type is prospective, absolute, and unconditional. On the basis of this distinction, the first type can be called "conditional," and the second "unconditional."

1. Laws in the Conditional Form. a. "When/If" Form. In this type, the protasis describing a case is introduced by the Heb particle *kî* ("when" or "in the case that"). The subordinate cases are introduced by Heb *ʾim* ("if"), *ʾô* ("or"), *ʾak ʾim* ("but if"), or *"wĕhāyâ ʾim* ("and if"). Three subgroups of this type can be identified:

(1) "When he." This is the predominant form in the ANE law collections. The protasis is introduced in Sum by TUKUM.BI, in Akk by *šumma* and, in Hit by *takku*. This form corresponds to Alt's casuistic laws. The verbs are usually in the third person imperfect, singular or plural. For example, "When a man steals an ox or a sheep, and slaughters it or sells it, he shall pay five oxen for the ox, and four sheep for the sheep" (Exod 21:37, JPSV). An important variation of this form is when the protasis is introduced by Heb *ʾîš kî* ("a man, when he . . ."), such as in Lev 24:17, "If a man kills any human being, he shall be put to death."

(2) "When you." In this form, both the protasis and apodosis contain verbs in the second person singular or plural. For example, "When you make a loan of any sort to your neighbor, you must not enter his house to seize his pledge: (Deut 24:10, JPSV).

(3) Mixed Forms. Here the protasis is in the third person and the apodosis in the second, such as in Deut 22:23–24, "When a virgin is pledged . . . , you shall bring . . ."; or conversely the protasis is in the second person and the apodosis is the third, as for example, "When you acquire a Hebrew slave, he shall serve . . ." (Exod 21:2).

b. Relative Form. The protasis here is introduced by the subject plus Heb *ʾăšer* ("who"), or simply by *ʾăšer* (Akk *awīlum ša,* or only *ša;* Hit *LÚ kuiš*). Two subgroups can be identified.

(1) Third Person Forms. See Lev 20:12, "A man who *(ʾîš ʾăšer)* lies with his daughter-in-law, both of them shall be put to death."

(2) Mixed Forms. There are a few examples of this form, found in cases where the verb in the protasis is in the third person imperfect, whereas the apodosis contains a verb in the first person perfect (e.g., "And whatsoever man there be of the house of Israel . . . that eateth any manner of blood, I will set My face against . . ." Lev 17:10, JPSV). The verb can also be in the second person perfect with *waw* consecutive, as in Lev 20:16, "A woman who approached any beast to mate with it, you shall kill *(wĕhāragtâ)* the woman and the beast . . ."

c. Participial Form. Here the protasis is introduced by a verb in the participial form and the apodosis, formulated in the third person, specifies the legal consequence, usually the death penalty. For example, "He who fatally strikes a man (lit. "the striker to death") shall be put to death" (Exod 21:12).

2. Laws in the Unconditional Form. a. Direct Address. (1) Positive Commands. (a) Second Person. For example, "You shall make an altar of earth . . ." (Exod 20:24).

(b) Imperative. For example, "Honor your father . . ." (Exod 20:12).

(c) Infinitive Absolute. For example, "Remember *(zākôr)* the sabbath day . . ." (Exod 20:8).

(2) Negative Commands. Either with Heb *lōʾ* plus a verb in the imperfect, such as "You shall not commit adultery" (Exod 20:14), or Heb *ʾal* and a verb in the jussive, such as "Do not degrade *(ʾal tĕḥallēl)* your daughter . . ." (Lev 19:29).

b. Third Person Jussive. (1) Positive Commands. For example, "The guilt offering shall be slaughtered . . ." (Lev 7:2).

(2) Negative Commands. For example, "They shall not shave smooth any part of their heads . . ." (Lev 7:2).

D. The Setting in Life of the Biblical Legal Forms

The origin and setting in life *(Sitz im leben)* of the biblical legal forms are obscure. One school of thought, represented by Alt, maintains that the so-called casuistic laws derive from a pre-Israelite period, perhaps the Canaanite legal system. On the other hand, as Alt argued, the so-called apodictic laws are Israelite in origin and emerged out of a cultic setting (see Deut 27:15–26; 31:9–13), namely, the "renewal of covenant" ceremony.

It is important to note, however, that there is a difference between the original setting in life which gave rise to a particular form, and the secondary setting in which the particular form became prevalent. Furthermore, as Gerstenberger (1965b) pointed out, it is highly problematic to place all the apodictic clauses within one cultic festival. Obviously, it is easier to identify secondary settings which employ specific forms by studying the different literary genres in the Bible. It is more difficult, if not impossible, to discover the original life setting which created the form.

Alt's assumption that the Israelites took over the casuistic form from the Canaanites has not been proved, inasmuch as no Canaanite law collection has yet been found. The dominant "when he" form was well known in the ANE law collections. See introductory article above. There is also no evidence, either biblical or extrabiblical, that the legal courts were the originators of the casuistic form, even though many scholars, including Alt, put forth a claim for this assumption. The original life setting of the "when he/you" form remains unknown.

The participial form was classified by Alt as part of the apodictic laws and he pointed to the curses in Deuteronomy 27 as its setting. However, it is highly doubtful whether curses are indeed laws. Some scholars (for example, F. Horton, R. H. Pfeiffer, S. Sandmel, H. Brichto, R. Sonsino) have argued that curses are basically part of liturgy or prayers, not of laws, although they are part of treaty formulas.

The contention that apodictic laws were purely an Israelite creation has already been disproved by many scholars who pointed out similar forms in ANE law collections, especially, the second person positive or negative commands. Also, there is little biblical evidence for a so-called covenant renewal ceremony, which presumably gave rise to the apodictic form. Nor is there proof that it ever took place periodically, in spite of Alt's contention.

Fohrer (1968) rightfully maintained that the directive "do this" or "do not do this" is as old as history itself. It is only when these commands or prohibitions form "series" that one can speak of patterns and look for a life setting. Gerstenberger (1965b), using the example of Jonadab ben Rechab's short prohibitions in Jer 35:6–7, argued that the original setting of the "prohibitives" is to be found in the instruction given within the tribe (i.e., Sippenethos). With regard to the "relative" form, Yaron (1962) observed that it is often used in proclamations and was most likely taken over by the legislators to express norms of conduct.

Bibliography

Alt, A. 1967. The Origins of Israelite Law. Pp. 101–71 in *Essays in Old Testament History and Religion.* New York.

Boecker, H. J. 1980. *Law and the Administration of Justice in the Old Testament and Ancient East.* Minneapolis.

Bright, J. 1973. The Apodictic Prohibition: Some Observations. *JBL* 92: 185–204.

Cazelles, H. 1946. *Etudes sur le Code de l'Alliance.* Paris.

Fohrer, G. 1968. *Introduction to the Old Testament.* Nashville.

Gerstenberger, E. 1965a. Covenant and Commandment. *JBL* 84: 38–51.

———. 1965b. *Wesen und Herkunft des "Apodiktischen Rechts."* WMANT 20. Neukirchen.

Gilmer, H. W. 1975. *The If-You Form in Israelite Law.* SBLDS 15. Missoula, MT.

Horton, F. L. 1971. A Reassessment of the Legal Forms in the Pentateuch and their Functions. *SBLSP* 2: 359–60.

Patrick, D. 1973. Casuistic Law Governing Primary Rights and Duties. *JBL* 92: 180–84.

Richter, W. 1966. *Recht und Ethos.* Munich.

Sonsino, R. 1980. *Motive Clauses in Hebrew Law.* SBLDS 45. Chico, CA.

Yaron, R. 1962. Forms in the Laws of Eshnunna. *RIDA* 9: 150–53.

RIFAT SONSINO

LAW IN JUDAISM OF THE NT PERIOD

Most generally, "law" meant "divine revelation." It could refer to the totality of revelation or to any part of it. It included commandments (do not murder), admonitions and advice (treasures gained by wickedness do not profit), theological affirmations (the Lord is one), stories (the Exodus), worship (the Psalms), and more. These examples are all taken from the Bible, the primary (although not the only) expression of the law or revelation of the God of Israel. A proper appreciation of Jewish "nomism" requires that this range of meaning be grasped. The Mosaic code was given after the Exodus from Egypt, and "law" embraces both the story of God's gracious deliverance of the Israelite people and the requirements that were laid upon them—as well as the subsequent stories of failure and forgiveness.

A. Range and Meaning
B. Sources
C. Character and Contents
D. Basic Distinctions
E. Interpretation
   1. Examples of Interpretation
   2. Interpretation of the Law in Common Judaism
   3. Pharisaic Interpretation and Traditions
   4. Essene Interpretation
   5. Authoritative Interpreters
F. Knowledge and Observance of the Law
G. Gentiles and the Jewish Law
H. Epitomes of the Law
I. Theological Context

A. Range and Meaning

Jews who knew other societies tended to identify the law of God with the values of the other cultures, with the result that the range of meaning embraced by the word "law" expanded still further. Thus Ben Sira equated universal Wisdom with the Jewish law (Sirach 24), and Philo attempted the much more difficult task of equating the law of Moses with cosmic order, the "law of nature" which governs the universe. The person who observes the Jewish law is thereby a loyal *kosmopolitēs,* citizen of the universe, observing the "sacred words of nature" (*Op* 3; *Spec Leg* 2.13). One who studies the "particular enactments" of the Mosaic law will find that they agree with "the principles of eternal nature" (*Vita Mos* 2.52; cf. 2.48–52). This is hard to show in detail, but Philo had allegory on his side.

Judaism is correctly called a religion of law, but this has not meant the reduction of philosophy, art, and science to the level of requirements which can be given in one sentence and either obeyed or not, but rather the expansion of the meaning of "law." It was once thought that the translation of Heb *tôrâ* by Gk *nomos* resulted in a narrowing of the conception of law from God's way in general to specific requirements. This has now been shown not to be correct. The semantic range of the words is approximately the same (Pasinya 1973; *IDBSup,* 909–11; when corrected by these and other studies, Dodd 1935: 25–41 still repays study).

In recent years scholars have rightly been concerned to correct the view that Judaism was "legalistic" in the pejorative sense, and this has led to the emphasis that *tôrâ* and *nomos* mean not only "law" but also "grace." When this emphasis is accepted, the characterization of 1st-century Jews as being "zealous for the law" (Rom 10:2) means not that they sought meritorious achievement and thereby became self-righteous, but rather that they lived faithfully within the covenant which was given by God's grace. The present author has argued that the context of grace is clear throughout Jewish literature of the period 200 B.C.E. to C.E. 200 and also that Paul, when criticizing "works of law," was not accusing his fellow Jews of legalistic self-righteousness (Sanders 1977; 1983). These points, however, should not prevent us from seeing that the words *tôrâ* and *nomos* usually mean "law" in our sense of the word.

While any part of revelation could be called part of God's law, both the Heb and Gk terms were especially used for commandments and prohibitions which are observable, or for the scrolls in which they are written down. When Josephus summarized "the laws and the constitution" (*Ant* 4.8.3 §194), he listed and explained commandments. In discussing the Greek translation of Hebrew Scripture, he spoke of the desire of Ptolemy II of Egypt to have a translation of "our law and the political constitution," but he added that the king had managed to obtain only the part containing "the law," not the entirety of sacred Scripture (*hoi hieroi grammatoi; Ant* 1.Proem.3 §11–13). Philo spoke of the Ten Commandments (*deka logoi,* "ten words") as "written laws" which had been "promulgated" by Moses. After discussing them he turned to the rest of the Mosaic legislation (*Dec* 1–2; *Spec Leg* I.1). The Ten Commandments are "general laws," while the others are "special" or "particular laws" (*Spec Leg* II.189). The "essentials of the law" in *Ḥag.* 1:8 are the commandments which are solidly based in Scripture, and the law which is read in *Roš. Haš.* 4:6 and *Meg.* 4:1–2 is distinguished from the Prophets.

Thus while a complete catalogue of occurrences of *tôrâ* and *nomos* would produce the range of meaning indicated in the first paragraph, the words usually mean "law." This discussion will take up law in this narrower sense, though we shall return to its place in Jewish thought more generally.

B. Sources

The sources potentially include all of Jewish literature over a range of some centuries. The Jewish literature which can be shown to have been written in the 1st century C.E. is this: the works of Philo and Josephus, several of the Dead Sea Scrolls, and a few works in the Apocrypha and Pseudepigrapha (e.g. *T. Mos., 4 Ezra, Ps.-Philo,* some of *Sib. Or.,* probably *T. Job*). The earliest layer of rabbinic literature reflects the first century but may not have been written until later. Both earlier and later sources, however, are relevant to understanding the conception of law in the NT period, e.g. Sirach, Wisdom of Solomon, 1 Maccabees, *Psalms of Solomon, Jubilees.* For one topic, oral law, it is necessary to consider the entire Mishnah and Tosefta. The sources which are employed most are Josephus, Philo, the DSS, and the earliest layer of the Mishnah. There are fairly short surveys of the Jewish law in Philo's *Hypothetica* and Josephus's *AgAp* 2.22–30 §190–219. (There is a relationship of literary dependence between these two texts, either because Josephus knew the *Hypothetica* or because of reliance on a common source, possibly also used by Pseudo-Phocylides. See e.g. van der Horst in *OTP* 2: 566.) More detailed accounts of the legislation are in Philo's *Dec* and *Spec Leg* and in Josephus's *Ant* 4.8.4–43 §196–301.

C. Character and Contents

The most striking characteristic of Jewish law is that the "religious" law covered everything. Moses "did not make religion [*eusebeia,* "piety"] a department of virtue, but the various virtues . . . departments of religion." Unlike other cultures, in Judaism "religion governs all . . . actions and occupations and speech" (Jos. *AgAp* 2.16 §170–71). They are not distributed among religious law, civil law, and philosophy.

Outsiders might speak of Jewish "ancestral laws" or "customs," and Josephus attributes these terms to gentiles (*Ant* 14.7.2 §116; 14.10.8 §213, 216; and frequently). He could use them himself (14.10.11 §223 and elsewhere), as could Philo (*Spec Leg* II.148). Josephus, Philo, and other Jews, however, regarded the "ancestral customs" as the will of God. The moral of Josephus's *Jewish Antiquities* was to teach that people prosper who "conform to the will of God," by which he meant the law (1. Proem 3 §14). Philo stated the case fully: While all people guard their own customs *(ethe),* this is especially true of the Jewish people. They hold "that the laws *(nomoi)* are oracles vouchsafed by God," a doctrine in which they are trained "from their earliest years" (*Gaium* 210). Moses is called by some the "legislator," but by others the "interpreter" of the sacred laws (*Vita Mos* I.1–2), which reflects Philo's view that they come from God. God himself spoke the Ten Commandments (*Spec Leg* II.189). The highest of God's powers is the legislative (*Sacr* 131). The Jews did not regard their "customs" as of human origin.

These two points, when combined, give the peculiar characteristic of Jewish law: all of life is to be governed by God's will. Scholars sometimes attribute this view to the Pharisees (Rhoads 1976: 34), but it springs from Scripture itself and was common to all forms of Judaism.

It was indicated above that "law" might go beyond "Scripture," and it has been customary to speak of the development of "oral law" in postbiblical Judaism. If all of life was to be lived in accordance with the will of God, the "will of God" had to be more comprehensive than what is found in Scripture. We shall understand better how the contents of the law could grow when we take up Interpretation (see E.).

D. Basic Distinctions

The Jewish law may be categorized in two ways: (1) Laws govern either (a) relations between humans and God or (b) relations among humans (with implications for the human-divine relationship). (2) Transgressions of the law are either (a) involuntary or (b) intentional. These categories are quite clear in Lev 5:21—Eng 5:15; 6:1. In these lines are seen the distinctions between unwitting and intentional transgression, and between sins against God (the holy things of the Lord) and those against both God and "the neighbor" (against the Lord by deceiving the neighbor).

Philo, with his eye on this passage, distinguished the categories in the same way and noted that they determined how atonement is made for transgression (*Spec Leg* I 234, based on Lev 15:14–19; 1.235–38, based on Lev 16:1–7). Atonement brings forgiveness (*Spec Leg* I 235; Lev 6:7), but in the case of transgression against a fellow human redress of the wrong was to precede the sacrifice (Philo ibid.; cf. Matt 5:23–24), a point not directly made in Leviticus. These passages do not cover all cases, but they exemplify the principles of categorizing the law and determining appropriate atonements. Knowledge of these basic categories seems to have been common in Judaism.

Modern scholars often try to divide the law into "ritual" and "ethical" categories, but this is an anachronistic and usually misleading division. (This was pointed out many years ago by Lake [1932: 207], but not often heeded.) In such analyses the "moral law" is often considered to be embodied in the Ten Commandments, but this puts the commandments governing use of the Lord's name, the Sabbath, and graven images into the "ethical" division, where they clearly do not belong. Similarly some say that the "Noachian" commandments—those thought to have been given to all the descendants of Noah, and therefore to be required of gentiles (see G. below)—are "moral" commandments. (See e.g., Simon 1986: 163–66.) But these, too, include idolatry and blasphemy. People often think of the early Church as accepting the "ethical" commandments; again this is seen to be the wrong categorization. According to Acts, the commandments which the Jerusalem church wished to impose on gentile converts included the prohibitions against idolatry and eating meat with the blood in it—neither one "moral" (Acts 15:20). The major laws which govern relations between humans and God—such as the prohibition of idolatry—were maintained in all branches of Judaism, and many were inherited by Christianity. The commandments "between human and human" have of course been deeply influential.

The anachronism of the moral/ritual distinction is seen in another way: "ritual" commandments not infrequently have an "ethical" aspect. Thus tithing (a "ritual" requirement) included charity (a "moral" duty), and the laws of the Sabbath provided rest for laborers and even for animals (Deut 5:14). There are certain overlaps between the ancient category of "commandments which govern relations with God" and the modern one of "ritual law," and between the ancient "commandments which govern relations with fellow humans" and the modern "ethical law," but no more than overlaps. First-century Jews did not see a difference between the commandment not to eat holy food when ritually impure and the requirement to pay part of the tithes to the poor—except for the difference in penalty. The same God gave both commandments, and loyalty to him required obedience of them equally.

Modern critics of ancient Judaism often think that it was overly preoccupied with "ritual" commandments. Besides the fact that this is an error in categorization, it is anachronistic in an even more profound way. In the context of the ancient world, what distinguished Judaism was that it included not only commandments between God and humans, but also commandments between human and human. It refused to separate religious cult from everyday behavior, thus drawing the latter into the realm of the former.

E. Interpretation

It belongs to the nature of law that it must be interpreted and applied. If, as in the case of Judaism, all of life is to be lived in accordance with God's will, the demands on interpretation are heavy. First-century Judaism did not call on individuals to decide in each encounter what it meant to love the Lord and the neighbor. Rather, certain ways of observing commandments grew over the years and became part of the law itself. Most observant Jews (and it will be argued below that most Jews were observant) were probably not conscious of living by interpretations of laws, but understood the law in light of the interpretation.

The biblical laws are by no means specific enough to cover all cases, and custom filled in the gaps. Further, biblical laws on the same topic sometimes disagree, and interpretations were required. Understanding biblical interpretation is fundamental to understanding Judaism, especially since in the NT period the various groups, parties, and sects presented their differences as being based on interpretation of Scripture (whatever the socio-politico-economic factors which are now thought to explain the groupings). To grapple with interpretation and tradition, and when these were included in "law" and not, and to understand how groups disagreed on interpretation, we may best take some examples.

1. Examples of Interpretation. a. Tithing. There are basically two different tithing laws in the Bible. Deuteronomy requires that one-tenth of agricultural crops and the firstlings of the flock and herd be taken to Jerusalem and eaten there, or converted into money which is spent in Jerusalem. Every third year, however (that is, the third and sixth years of each seven-year cycle), the tithe was not consumed in Jerusalem, but was given to the Levites and the poor (Deut 14:22–29; cf. 12:17–19). The second set of tithing laws, found in Numbers and Nehemiah, requires that one-tenth of crops and herds (counting adult animals as well as firstlings) be given to the Levites, who in turn tithe to the priests (Num 18:21–24; Neh 10:37–38). It is possible that Lev 27:30–33 preserves a third tithing law: one-tenth "to the Lord" could mean "directly to the priests," without making provision for the Levites. It is simplest, however, to read Leviticus in light of Numbers.

The 1st-century Jews, taking the entire Scripture to be the revealed will of God, naturally had to obey each set of laws. They were conflated in at least two different ways. Josephus (presumably reflecting the views of the priestly aristocracy) said that every year one-tenth was given to the Levites and one-tenth consumed in Jerusalem. In the third and sixth years there was a third tithe, to be given to the poor (*Ant* 4.4.3 §68; 4.8.8, 22 §205, 240; for three tithes cf. Tob 1:7–8). Rabbinic literature (possibly representing Pharisaic interpretation) requires only two tithes each year: the Deuteronomic, which is either "second tithe" (spent in Jerusalem in years one, two, four, and five) or the "poor tithe" (years three and six), and the Levitical, which is given each year except the seventh to the Levites (summarized in Danby 1933: 66 n. 9). If one assumes that all interpreters accepted that tithing laws did not apply in the sabbatical (seventh) year, these two opinions yield the following results: in each seven-year cycle there were, according to Josephus, fourteen tithes; according to the rabbis, twelve.

If these different opinions existed at the same time, which seems to have been the case, people must have been conscious of the difference. Presumably both the aristocratic priests and the Pharisees (assuming that rabbinic interpretation represents their views) saw their position as "interpretation" of the written law, the simple application of what it says, not as a supplement or "tradition" alongside it.

b. Sabbath. Biblical laws on the Sabbath are not numerous. Exodus 16 prohibits gathering food and cooking; the fourth commandment forbids "work" (Exod 20:8–11; Deut 5:12–15); Exod 34:21 explicitly includes plowing time and harvest as periods when the Sabbath must be observed, thus ruling out the appeal to "exceptional circumstances" as justifying nonobservance; Exod 35:3 prohibits making a fire; Num 15:32–36 shows that gathering firewood was forbidden and specifies the punishment for transgression as stoning; Num 28:9 *requires* sabbath offerings; Neh 10:31 forbids buying goods even from non-Jews; Neh 13:15–22 prohibits carrying burdens through the gates of Jerusalem and specifies several forms of agricultural labor as being forbidden; Jer 17:19–27 forbids bearing a burden through the gates of Jerusalem and even carrying it out of one's house.

Observance of the sabbath law depended on agreement with regard to the definition of "work." Even in the ancient world the conception of work varied a bit from time to time and group to group. The Bible does not explicitly include fighting as an activity forbidden on the Sabbath, and in the stories of warfare in the Bible the Sabbath does not figure; but sometime during the Persian or the Hellenistic period it came to be understood that fighting is "work." Warfare is included in a list of activities forbidden on the Sabbath in *Jubilees* (mid-2d century B.C.E.), but without the special stress that would indicate that the point was debated (*Jub.* 50:12). Some years earlier, at the beginning of the struggle which resulted in independence from Seleucid rule, a group of pietists was attacked on the Sabbath and destroyed because they would not fight. After this it was decided to fight in self-defense (1 Macc 2:29–42), and this was interpreted to mean only if directly attacked. The law as thus interpreted (fighting is work) and amended (fighting is permitted in case of direct attack) seems to have been accepted by all, not just the specially pious. This rule was observed in 63 B.C.E. by the followers of Aristobulus II, who was a friend of the "eminent" and an enemy of the Pharisees (*JW* 1.7.3 §145–47; cf. Dio Cass. *Hist.* 37.16.2–4; on party allegiance, see *Ant* 13.16.2 §411). In the parallel account in *Ant* 14.4.2–3 Josephus states that "the law" permits defense on the Sabbath only in the case of direct attack (§63). When, at the beginning of the war against Rome in C.E. 66, the Jews attacked on the Sabbath, Josephus, at least in retrospect, regarded them as forsaking religion (*eusebeia; JW* 2.19.2 §518). That Jewish refusal to fight on the Sabbath counted as an ancestral law is proved by the fact that Rome respected it, and Jews were excused from military service in the empire (e.g. *Ant* 14.10.12 §225–27).

The basic rule not to fight was apparently an unconscious interpretation of the sabbath law. The decision to fight if directly attacked was not, to our knowledge, justified by biblical interpretation, but was a rule of practice adopted by common agreement. It is noteworthy that Josephus calls them both "law": Custom and tradition, both unconscious and conscious, could become law. We may assume that in the 1st century there were many traditional practices which were accepted by everyone as being part of sabbath law.

2. Interpretation of the Law in Common Judaism. It is not possible to give a full list of interpreted laws as they were accepted by Jews generally, nor would it be feasible even if it were possible. We may, however, get some idea of the contents of law practiced by most Jews and the way in which it was interpreted if we consider (a) developments of the Ten Commandments, (b) the laws for which the Jews were famous (or infamous), and (c) commandments which are said to be in the law but which in fact are not (these were probably practiced quite widely). Some items are in more than one of the following categories.

a. Developments of the Ten Commandments. (1) The prohibition of idolatry in the first two commandments was interpreted to mean that Jews could participate in the common Greco-Roman culture to only a limited degree. Sacrifices were offered on *behalf* of the emperor, but the possible interpretation that they were offered to him was carefully avoided, even by Herod (Smallwood 1981: 83, 148). Jews were exempt from the requirement of participating in pagan rites or in the cult of the emperor (Smallwood 1981: 147, 345). Jews did not, however (with rare exceptions), attack pagan temples or idols, doubtless for practical reasons; but this restraint was justified exegetically by the Gk translation of Exod 22:28—Gk 22:27, "do not revile gods" (Philo, *Vita Mos* II.26 §205; *Spec Leg* I 7 §53; Josephus, *Ant* 4.8.10 §207; *AgAp* 2.33 §237).

Worship of the one God, which is assumed in the first two commandments, was meticulously kept. The sanctity of the Temple was observed by all until the final stages of the war against Rome (for example, Josephus was safe from Menahem when he took refuge in the priests' court: *Life* 5 §20–21); the Jews were allowed by Rome to execute gentiles who went beyond the Court of the Gentiles (*JW* 6.2.4 §126; pietist groups complained that the priesthood did not maintain strict enough standards (*Pss. Sol.* 8:11–12; CD 4. 18; 5.6–7); the ordinary people sometimes attacked or accused unworthy priests (*Ant* 13.13.5 §372; *JW* 2.1.2 §7); throngs came to the Temple, both from Palestine and abroad, especially at the pilgrimage festivals (e.g. *JW* 6.9.4 §423–28); money came from all over the known world into its coffers (see F.). In the Diaspora, besides sending money and gifts to the Temple and occasionally making a pilgrimage to Jerusalem, Jews came together locally for worship and study. The rights to assemble and to have a "place of their own"—allowed to few groups—seem to have been the most prized privileges in the Jewish Diaspora. In the series of decrees listed in *Ant* 14, these rights are mentioned most often (*Ant* 14.10.8 §213–16; 14.10.12 §227; 14.10.16 §234; 14.10.17 §235; 14.10.20 §242; 14.10.21 §245; 14.10.23 §257–58; 14.10.24 §260–61; on these, see F. below).

(2) Sexual Laws were elaborated, especially in the Diaspora, and Jewish condemnation of homosexual practice became more pronounced than the prohibition of adultery (*Let. Arist.* 152–53; *Spec Leg* III.37–42 and frequently in Philo *AgAp* 2.24 §199; *Sib. Or.* 2.73; 3.596; 5.430; probably Wis 14:26; *Ps-Phoc.* 3; Rom 1:26–27; 1 Cor 6:9.) Philo also condemned prostitution, claiming that the law requires the death penalty (*Jos* 43; cf. *Spec Leg* III.51; *Hypoth* 7.1). Both Philo and Josephus said that sex is only for procreation (*Jos* 43; *AgAp* 2.24 §199). Various forms of sexual transgression are condemned in Wis 14:24,26; *Sib. Or.* 5.430; Paul's vice lists; and many other places.

(3) "You shall not murder" was applied against the Greek practice of exposing infants (e.g. *Sib. Or.* 3.765). (In the pagan view it was not murder.)

(4) "You shall not steal" and other laws forbidding dishonesty were encapsulated in the epigram, "do not pick up what you do not lay down" (*AgAp* 2.27 §208; *Hypoth* 7:6, immediately after the epigrammatic version of Lev 19:18).

(5) The sabbath law, as we saw above, was further developed.

b. Laws for which Jews were Famous. Pagan comments reveal that in the Greco-Roman world Jews were famous (or infamous) for the laws governing circumcision, Sabbath, food, and the worship of a single, invisible God. The Jewish desire to maintain their own worship was recognized throughout the empire [E.2.a.(1)]. Jews were by no means alone in practicing circumcision, and all cultures have calendrical rites. Nevertheless, all four points brought criticism from pagans, which sometimes was thoughtful but which usually took the form of ridicule. (For Sabbath, food, and circumcision see the passages conveniently collected in Whittaker 1984: 63–85; see further the index in Stern 1976–84; for ridicule of the worship of an invisible God, see *AgAp* 2.7 §80–81.)

c. Laws Attributed to Moses which are not in the Pentateuch. (1) Fighting is forbidden on the Sabbath, except in case of direct attack (E.1.b. above).

(2) Prayer twice each day. The Bible requires that the commandments be recalled "when you lie down and when you rise" (Deut 6:7), and many people fulfilled this obligation by saying the passage in which it occurs (the *Shemaᶜ*, Deut 6:4–9 or only vv 4–5). Around this requirement grew the practice of praying twice a day as well, and Josephus regards this as part of the Mosaic law (*Ant* 4.8.13 §212–13). That Jews prayed every morning is implied by *Sib. Or.* 3:591–92. The rabbis expected prayer three times a day (*Ber.* 4:1), but in Qumran twice a day was the rule (1QS 9.26–10.1). The practice seems to have been widespread. The main thrust was probably thanksgiving (so Josephus).

(3) Attendance at synagogue and study of the Scripture on the Sabbath. This is regarded as part of the Mosaic law by both Philo (*Op* 128) and Josephus (*AgAp* 2.17 §175), and it is included in the Ten Commandments by Pseudo-Philo (*L.A.B.* 11:8).

(4) Education of children. Josephus attributes to Moses the requirement that children be taught to read and to learn the "laws and the deeds of their forefathers" (*AgAp* 2.25 §204).

(5) Purity laws. Jews throughout the world seem to have practiced extrabiblical purity laws, though not necessarily the same ones. In Palestine the use of standardized immersion pools was common (though more than one standard is attested) in order to facilitate the washings which are prescribed in the Bible. The pools themselves, however, are not biblical. In the Diaspora we learn of hand washing (*Let. Arist.* 305–6), and the construction of synagogues near natural water sources points to ablutions of some sort. The practice of building houses of prayer near the sea is said to be the Jews' "ancestral custom" in the decree of Halicarnassus (*Ant* 14.10.23 §258; cf. Acts 16:13). Philo considered it to be part of the Mosaic law that husband and wife should wash after intercourse before touching anything else (*Spec Leg* III.63). In *Sib. Or.* 3:592–93 there is a reference to morning ablutions. The extrabiblical purifications in the Diaspora may have arisen to compensate for the loss of those which the Bible requires for entering the Temple.

(6) The prohibition of abortion is attributed to Moses by Josephus (*AgAp* 2.24 §199–203).

(7) Burial rites were considered to be part of the law (*Hypoth* 7.7; *AgAp* 2.26 §205; cf. Tob 1:17).

(8) Animals were said to be protected by the law, especially if they take refuge in one's house (*Hypoth* 7.7,9; *AgAp* 2.29 §213).

(9) The binding force of vows was expanded by Philo (*Hypoth* 7.3–4; cf. the elaboration of oaths by the Pharisees according to Matt 23:16–22).

This is not a complete list of new "Mosaic" laws, but it indicates the way in which the law could grow to cover aspects of life not explicitly mentioned in the Bible. The points which were probably commonly accepted were the prohibition of fighting of the Sabbath; praying twice each day; attending synagogue on the Sabbath; teaching children the law (nos. 1–4). Most Jews probably extended the purity laws (5) in one or more ways. The other cases may not have been common, but they show the way in which the law naturally developed.

In some cases we can imagine the process of interpretation of the biblical law. Philo's new rule that nothing can be touched after intercourse may be compared to the biblical commandment not to touch holy things or enter the temple after intercourse and before purification (combining Lev 15:16–18,31; 22:3). The hallowing of other parts of life, especially in the Diaspora, is a natural development. Hand washing might be a partial imitation of the priesthood (cf. Exod 30:18–21), but more likely it is an application of Ps 24:4 ("clean hands and a pure heart"; cf. Deut 21:6 and the explanation in *Let. Arist.* 306). Hand washing in the Diaspora was probably influenced by pagan practice. (For ablutions in Greek religion see Ginouvès 1962: 309–10.) The instruction of children is required by Deut 6:7, and in the 1st century it was probably a self-evident interpretation to think that this included teaching them to read. Conceivably studying the law every seven days is derived from Deut 31:10, which requires that it be read in public every seven years. That prayer should accompany the recitation of the *Shema*ᶜ may have been self-evident. Whether or not these suggestions adequately explain the development of various laws, the principle in any case is clear: the law was lived, and this meant that it was interpreted, either unconsciously or self-consciously, and applied to cases which are not explicitly mentioned in it.

3. Pharisaic Interpretation and Traditions. a. Pharisaic Interpretation of the Law. Here we shall be concerned to illustrate, not canvass completely, Pharisaic interpretation of the law. We may take sabbath law as the main example. Pharisaic sabbath concerns can be at least partially reconstructed by studying the passages attributed to named Pharisees or to the Houses (Schools) of Hillel and Shammai. (The Houses discussions are for the most part one generation after the destruction of the temple in C.E. 70, but it is presumed that they maintain pre-70 Pharisaic traditions. The study of Pharisaic law is made possible by Neusner 1971 as modified by Sanders 1989.) The bulk of the surviving material consists of unresolved debates, so that often one cannot say what Pharisaic "law" was. An example is the question of giving work to gentiles which cannot be finished before the Sabbath begins, a practice which was prohibited by the House of Shammai but permitted by the House of Hillel (*Šabb.* 1:8). The topic may be regarded as a question of "interpretation": Does it matter who does the work? There were also debates between the houses over whether or not work which had been begun before the Sabbath could proceed if no further human effort was required: Could a bundle of flax finish drying in the warm oven (*Šabb.* 1:6)? This debate is part of the general interpretive question, what counts as work?

b. Pharisaic Traditions and the Question of Oral Law. All Pharisees, however, seem to have agreed on a very interesting development of sabbath rules. It is a conception indicated by the word *ᶜêrûb*, "the fusion of sabbath limits" (Danby). By the erection of cross-beams, for example, all the houses in a courtyard or along an alley could be "fused" into one house, and then vessels containing food could be carried from house to house, thus permitting communal dining on the Sabbath (despite Jer 17:19–27). Sadducees did not accept such traditions, and one who lived in the same group of houses could prevent this custom by taking possession of the walkway first (*ᶜErub.* 6:1).

The Pharisees did not pretend that the Bible allows the "fusion of sabbath limits," and this development is a "tradition" (Gk *paradosis,* Heb *qbl*). One of the chief characteristics of Pharisaism was the development of "traditions" which altered or supplemented the written law: "The Pharisees had handed down [*paredosan*] certain regulations [*nomima*] from [their] forebears [*ek paterōn diadochēs*], which are not recorded in the laws of Moses, and which on this account are rejected by the Sadducean group" (*Ant* 13.10.6 §297); "regulations [*nomina*] introduced by the Pharisees in accordance with the tradition [*paradosis*] of their fathers" (*Ant* 13.16.2 §408; see also Mark 7:3). The characteristic of "traditions" is that they are understood by neither proponents nor opponents to be interpretations of the Bible.

Did the Pharisees consider their "traditions" to be law? Until very recently the unanimous view has been that they did—that Pharisees held that they and their predecessors had inherited from the holy men of Israel, all the way back to Moses, traditions which were of equal standing with the written law. This view has been based on two foundations: In *ʾAbot* 1:1–2:8 there is a chain of transmission of *tôrâ* which runs from Moses to Hillel and Shammai; and which then branches, being continued both by Hillel's physical descendants and by his disciple Johanan b. Zakkai and his students. *Tôrâ* in this passage has been interpreted as including the Pharisaic traditions, which are then seen to be called "law." The second important piece of evidence is the statement which is ascribed to Hillel in *Šabb.* 31a (= *ARNA* 15) that there are two *tôrôt,* one the oral law *(tôrâ še-beᶜal peh).*

Before 1985 it could already be seen that this view is subject to challenge. Davies (*IDB* 3: 91) recognized that the term "oral law" is neither early nor widespread, and his discussion shows that he did not take the single ascription to Hillel to prove that Pharisees accepted a "two-fold law," written and oral. Other scholars also noted that the term for nonbiblical rules, according to Josephus, the NT, and early rabbinic literature, was not "oral law" but "tradition." Further, Rivkin (1984: 86–87) maintained that Pharisees held only other Pharisees responsible for observing their special rules. Observing them made one a Pharisee, but to be an obedient Jew one need only observe biblical law. Rivkin nevertheless used the term "two-fold law" to describe the Pharisaic legal corpus (Rivkin 1978).

Jacob Neusner, however, has argued that the entire theory of an oral law, coeval with the written law and equal in authority, is a late creation. The story about Hillel in *Šabb.* 31a, in which the term "oral law" occurs, is a retrojection from the time of the Babylonian Talmud (1985: 144–45). In the earliest rabbinic document, the Mishnah, no passage "demands the meaning 'not-written-down-Torah,' " and the implication of the regular distinction between "words of Torah" and "teachings of scribes" "precludes the conception of two Torahs of *equal* standing and authority, both deriving from God's revelation to Moses at Mount Sinai" (Neusner 1985: 26). The matter is actually not quite that clear, since Neusner considers *ʾAbot* not to be part of the Mishnah, but rather to date entirely from the time of the latest names in it, which puts it fifty years later than the Mishnah (1985: 6, 32). This principle, however, would take several other tractates out of the Mishnah. It is better to follow the usual practice of assuming that *ʾAbot* grew and that it contains late additions, rather than that it was written as a kind of pseudepigraphical work in the middle of the 3d century. When it is returned to the Mishnah, the matter changes a bit. The *tôrâ* in *ʾAbot* 1:1, which is said to have been handed down from generation to generation, cannot be the written law, since it is never maintained that the Pharisees and rabbis had a monopoly on that. It is, thus, nonwritten. But does it include the peculiarly Pharisaic *traditions* or only their *interpretations?* There is no answer within the tractate, which contains maxims but no legal discussions.

Neusner's challenge to the theory of "oral law" which goes back to Moses and was equal to the written law must be taken seriously, though when he excluded *ʾAbot* he made the case too easy. His second point is more persuasive: the Mishnah distinguishes between the words of the scribes and those of *tôrâ* in such a way as to "preclude" the view that the words of the scribes were *tôrâ.* Neusner's evidence (1985: 24–25) is not, however, complete. He intended to consider passages in which *tôrâ* and "words of the scribes" appear together, but some were omitted, and other passages on the words of the scribes were also relevant. Second, the meaning of the word *hălākâ* must be taken into account. Third, and most important of all, it is necessary to consider the passages which trace a rule to Moses.

A full study of the occurrences in the Mishnah and Tosefta of the three terms "words of the scribes," *hălākâ* and "Moses on Mount Sinai" is given in Sanders 1989. The results, which confirm Neusner's view, are these: (1) The words of the scribes are lower in importance than the words of the Bible *(tôrâ),* and transgression of scribal rulings is not considered to be real transgression. Thus, for example, according to *Para* 11:4–5 those who are impure only according to the words of the scribes may enter the temple. (2) The term *hălākâ* is often equivalent to "words of the scribes." In *ʿOr.* 3:9 *hălākâ* seems to be one grade closer to *tôrâ* than are the words of the scribes, but in other instances the meaning is the same: traditional rulings which do not need to be proved by argument in order to be accepted within the group (the rabbis and possibly the Pharisees before them). They are, however, lower in status than the *tôrâ* (e.g. *Ned.* 4:3). (3) In several passages *hălākâ* is used together with the phrase "received [as a tradition]" (usually *meqūbbāl ʾănî*). In these cases the traditional *hălākâ* is regarded as correct (e.g. *Yebam.* 8:3), but it is not equated with *tôrâ.* (4) *Hălākâ* is *tôrâ* only when it is interpretation of *miqrāʾ* ("what is written) or of *tôrâ.* Thus in *Ḥag.* 1:8 *hălākôt* are "the essentials of the law" only when they are based on scriptural law. (5) Rulings which are "received as tradition," even when not called *hălākâ,* are often authoritative (e.g. *Zebaḥ.* 1:3 = *Yad.* 4:2). (6) Tradition (by whatever name) *may be rejected.* This is the case if it is the opinion of an authority who was outvoted at the time (*ʿEd.* 1:6) or if there is a conflicting tradition (*Giṭ.* 6:7). A rabbi might also doubt that the report is true (*Ohol.* 16:1). Even after hearing a tradition the rabbis may debate the issue anyway (*Yebam.* 16:7). (7) Tradition may only supplement exegesis (*t. Pisha* 4:14 Lieberman; Zuckermandel 4:2), or a proof by exegesis may be appended (*t. Sukk.* 3:1). (8) A special subgroup of traditional *hălākôt* consists of rulings which go back to Moses on Mt. Sinai. These last are never said to be "oral law": they are rather *hălākôt,* and presumably like other *hălākôt* which are not *interpretations* of the written law, they are inferior to the *tôrâ.* (9) None of the major Pharisaic traditions (e.g. *ʿêrûb*) is proved by any of the terms included in this survey. (10) In every case of a rule which was "received as tradition," it was known to only one rabbi, and therefore it was not part of regular rabbinic instruction. This counts very strongly against the view that these terms indicate Mosaic law. We may consider two examples: One of the *hălākôt* which is said to be from Moses on Sinai was known only to R. Eliezer, and it is cited as a postscript after the story of a lengthy debate conducted in ignorance of it (*Yad.* 4:3 = *t. Yad.* 2:15–16). In another case R. Akiba hears a tradition, said to go back to Gamaliel I, when he is in Babylonia. On his return to Israel he asks the Pharisee's grandson, Gamaliel II, about it. The latter then remembers that his grandfather had made the ruling in question. There follows a debate on the topic which is not influenced by the tradition (*Yebam.* 16:7).

Since a study of the terminology for traditional rules in the Mishnah and Tosefta supports Neusner's study of the word *tôrâ* in the same two collections, we may conclude that the rabbis of the Mishnaic period did not hold the dogma of oral law which has been attributed to them. Presumably the same is true of the pre-70 Pharisees, on the assumption that the rabbis of the Mishnah and Tosefta would not have given their "traditions" a lower status than they had enjoyed among the pre-70 Pharisees.

We have not proved that the Pharisees did not observe common and widely known extrabiblical traditions. On the contrary, we can be sure that they did. "The fusion of sabbath limits" is the best example, but probably hand washing should be included here as well. This extrabiblical practice is probably attested in the Diaspora earlier than in Palestine (*Let. Arist.* 305–6; the date of this text is not certain). The Pharisees, however, do seem to have practiced it (*Ber.* 8:2). What is striking is that these traditions are not said to go back to Moses on Sinai.

It is equally important to note that rabbinic literature, which discusses them extensively, posits neither penalty nor atonement for transgression. We noted that *Para* 11:4–5 explicitly states that a person who is impure according to "the words of the scribes" may nevertheless enter the Temple without being considered to have profaned it. The Pharisees, if judged by early rabbinic literature, did not equate their extrabiblical traditions with the Mosaic law.

If Pharisees consciously kept their peculiar traditions separate from the law, they are to be seen, despite their willingness to introduce innovations, as deeply conservative. They intended not to change the biblical law. They regarded their *interpretations* of the law as correct, and it may be assumed that they tried to have them enforced in society as a whole. But their traditions were their own: they made them Pharisees. In this context it is significant that Josephus said of the Pharisees both that they were regarded as the most "precise" *(akribēs)* interpreters (*JW* 1.5.2 §110; 2.8.14 §162; *Life* 38 §191; cf. *Ant* 18.1.15 §15, "exegesis") and that they followed "traditions" *(paradosis, nomima)* which the Sadducees rejected because they are not part of the written law (*Ant* 13.10.6 §296–97; 13.16.2 §408; 18.1.3 §12). These two aspects, it appears, should be kept distinct.

This view of Pharisaic tradition places them in the mainstream of thought in the Hellenistic period, which venerated tradition but did not consider it the equivalent of law. In a passage which may be indebted to Aristotle (so Colson 1939: 8, 435), Philo distinguishes between "customs" *(ethē),* which are "unwritten laws," and the written laws. The one who obeys only the latter "acts under the admonition of restraint and the fear of punishment," while the one who obeys the customs displays voluntary virtue (*Spec Leg* 148–50; cf. *Gaium* 115). The Pharisees intentionally went beyond the letter of the law, and they seem to have considered themselves to be doing so voluntarily, rather than because they "knew" more laws than did others and thought that obedience to these further laws was strictly required.

4. Essene Interpretation. The Essenes had numerous

nonbiblical sabbath laws (staying with the same main example). According to Josephus they would not light a fire, remove a vessel "or even go to stool" on the Sabbath (*JW* 2.8.9 §147). The *Damascus Document* contains a long list of sabbath laws: the sectarian Sabbath began early, "when the sun's orb is distant by its own fullness from the gate" behind which it would set. Not only was the conduct of business forbidden, but so was speaking about work. One should not walk more than about 500 yards from home, edible fruit and other food could not be picked up, water could not be drawn or carried, perfume (or medicine) could not be worn—and so on (CD 10:14–11:18). Although most of the Sabbath regulations are not justified exegetically, one of them is: "Let no one offer on the altar on the Sabbath [any offering] except the burnt-offering of the Sabbath; for thus it is written: 'apart from your sabbath-offerings' " (CD 11.17–18, trans. Rabin 1958). The last phrase is taken from Lev 23:38. The context is ignored, as is common in ancient exegesis. According to Leviticus, on festival days special offerings were presented "besides" or "apart from"—that is, in addition to—the ordinary offerings of the day. According to CD, on the Sabbath one may bring no offerings "apart from sabbath offerings" rather than "in addition to them," thus reversing the plain meaning of the text. (Sabbath offerings had to be brought because of Num 23:9.)

The justification of the sabbath rules which are not supported exegetically is apparently given in CD 6.18–19: those who enter the covenant are "to keep the Sabbath day according to its exact rules and the appointed days and the fast day according to the finding of the members of the new covenant in the land of Damascus." "New covenant" here may be governed only by the appointed (festival) days and the fast (the Day of Atonement), but in principle the sect was willing to claim that its covenant was at least partially "new" and therefore different. This new covenant contained "hidden things" not previously known (CD 3:14). Similarly in one of the scrolls which represents the monastic community at Qumran a new member is required to take an oath to "return" to the "law of Moses" according to "all that was revealed of it to the sons of Zadok" (1QS 5:8–9). In this formulation the "law of Moses" includes the traditional Scriptures but also new revelations to the Zadokite priests, and the door is left open for there to be more: the partitive "of it" *(mimmennâ)* implies that more yet may be revealed.

The Temple Scroll (11QTemple) takes this position to its logical conclusion: it attributes a revision of substantial parts of the Hebrew Bible directly to God by use of the first person, and new laws are created. Thus, for example, a verse in Nehemiah is used in developing laws for a new festival, called by Yadin (1985: 102) the "Feast of the Wood Offering."

Thus both of the known branches of the Essenes (represented by CD and 1QS respectively) had it both ways: they accepted "the law of Moses" as their guide; they introduced new laws and claimed that they were new revelations from the same source. Their handling of and claims for the new sectarian rules contrast sharply with the Pharisees' position on their peculiar traditions.

5. Authoritative Interpreters. Once it is realized that law must be interpreted, the question of who the interpreters are becomes vital. Traditionally in Judaism the priests were the teachers and interpreters of the law, assisted by the Levites (Deut 31:9; Neh 8:3–9). During the Persian and Hellenistic periods, local government was headed by the high priest. According to Sir 45:17 the priests were the nations' teachers; and the Hasmoneans, originally ordinary priests, assumed the high priesthood and its authority before they took the title "king." In Herod's day no one else had much authority, but during the periods of direct Roman rule of Judaea (C.E. 6–41; 44–66) the prefects/procurators lived in Caesarea, and the chief priests were relied on to provide local government in Jerusalem (Sanders 1985: 194–98; 270; 312–17; cf. Goodman 1987).

Modern scholars have often denied that the priests still served as teachers and authoritative interpreters of the law in the NT period, proposing that the Pharisees had assumed that role. It is sometimes even said that the priests no longer cared to interpret the law, and one scholar has pushed this back to the time of Ezra, stating that he was a scribe and not a priest (despite Ezra 7:1–5; Neh 8:9) (Maccoby 1980: 61–62; Rajak 1983: 19). Appeal is made to Josephus' statement that the Sadducees (the dominant party among the priestly aristocracy) could accomplish nothing, since the masses preferred the Pharisees (*Ant* 18.1.4 §17). In other passages, however, Josephus states that the priests were the recognized authorities (especially *AgAp* 2.21 §184–89; *Ant* 14.3.2 §41; 20.10.5 §251). The second view is supported by the individual narratives in Josephus, the Gospels, and Acts of trials and of times of crisis, when the priests demonstrated their influence both with the crowds and with the Romans.

Even in the Diaspora, priests interpreted the law. In discussing the synagogue service Philo said that either a priest or an elder read and expounded the law (*Hypoth* 7.13), and other evidence indicates that priests retained their identity and influence in the Diaspora (*AgAp* 1.7 §32; Kraabel 1981: 84). We may conclude that in general the priests fulfilled their traditional office of interpreting the law (see also Neusner 1971: III, 230, 296).

There were also, however, lay teachers who often had considerable influence, as the story of Judas and Matthias (probably Pharisees) makes clear (*JW* 1.23.2–4 §648–55; 2.1.2–3 §4–13). The Pharisees, the Essenes and possibly other pietist groups had their own recognized authorities. Many Pharisaic regulations had to do with domestic arrangements with regard to work on the Sabbath and other holy days, avoiding corpse impurity, and other matters. There was also debate about public behavior which was in the control of the individual, such as whether or not to lay one's hands on the head of a sacrificial animal offered on a "festival day," when most forms of work were forbidden (*Ḥag.* 2:2–3). In only one instance is a Pharisee assigned a law which determined public policy: the *prosbûl,* a legal device for ensuring the collection of a loan during the sabbatical year, is attributed to Hillel (*Sipre Deut* 113; *Šeb.* 10:3–6). It is possible, however, that this regulation was not originated by him, since it is attested elsewhere (DJD 2 100–4 no. 18).

That Pharisees in particular were equipped, as were priests, with the education which allowed them to interpret the law is made clear by a story in Josephus. The council *(koinon)* in Jerusalem, at the behest of Simeon b. Gamaliel, decided to send a commission to investigate Josephus' conduct of the preparation for war in Galilee. The four commissioners were "of different classes of society but of equal standing in education," since those who were "of the lower ranks" *(dēmotikoi)* were Pharisees. The non-Pharisaic member was descended from high priests. The test was not knowledge of military tactics, but of the "laws" or "ancestral customs" (*Life* 39 §196–98).

Who followed which interpretation when there was a conflict is hard to know. We noted (E.1.a.) that the tithing laws were interpreted differently by the aristocratic priests and the Pharisees (if represented by the rabbis). Since priests and Levites collected the tithes in person (*Life* 12 §63; *t. Peah* 4:3), their interpretation doubtless often prevailed; but a group of farmers might band together and insist on separating tithes according to the more lenient Pharisaic interpretation.

The overall picture is this: (1) Many aspects of life were lived in accord with the law as commonly interpreted. (2) The priests retained their authority as interpreters of the law. During the Roman period the priestly aristocracy ruled Jerusalem, but priests were influential elsewhere. (3) Lay teachers of the law were also influential and at least sometimes had considerable followings. (4) Pietist groups could follow their own interpreters in many areas of life, especially private ones.

F. Knowledge and Observance of the Law

Josephus claimed that Jews differed from members of other societies because of their knowledge of and obedience to the law. "Should anyone of our nation be questioned about the laws, he would repeat them all more readily than his own name." He continued, "a transgressor is a rarity; evasion of punishment by excuses an impossibility" (*AgAp* 2.18 §178; cf. *Hypoth* 7.14). Both Philo (*Gaium* 192; *Hypoth* 6.9) and Josephus held that Jews were willing to die for the law, and Josephus especially used this statement to prove general Jewish loyalty to the law (*AgAp* 2.32 §234; see 30–32 §218–35; *Ant* 15.7.8 §248). Despite this claim, some—such as Josephus himself—preferred life to dying for the law. Nevertheless the history of the period shows that his claim was largely true. Again and again Jews faced death rather than transgress the law or allow profanation of the city and the temple (e.g., the Roman standards at the time of Pilate and the statue which Gaius ordered to be placed in the temple, *Ant* 18.3.1 §55–59; 18.8.2–5 §261–83). Gaius's threat led Philo to predict a worldwide revolt (*Gaium* 213–15; cf. 159, 192–215), and it is very likely that this would have been the consequence had the act been carried out. The cry, "no master but God" (*Ant* 18.1.6 §23), never ceased to rally people who were willing to die for the law. Hadrian's proscription of circumcision was probably a major cause of the second revolt (*HJP*[2] 1: 536–40).

The willingness to fight and die if need be might be said to have been motivated only by "nationalism," not by attachment to the observance of the law. Apart from the difficulty of distinguishing national identity from loyalty to the Mosaic code, there is further evidence of Jewish observance. Most generally, it should be borne in mind that true atheism was virtually unknown in the ancient world. Jews believed that God had given his law and that he took note of obedience and transgression. Popular indifference is less likely in that climate than in the modern one.

In giving more specific evidence, we begin with the Diaspora. Jews were famous throughout the empire for the persistence with which they maintained their "ancestral customs." We saw (E.2.b.) that they were ridiculed for their dietary laws and for keeping the Sabbath. In mixed cities gentiles exploited Jewish devotion to the Sabbath by bringing legal charges on the day of rest and in other ways (*Ant* 16.2.4 §45). Jews throughout the world paid the temple tax. Here the proof is simple: after the first revolt against Rome, the tax was directed to other purposes, and it was reimposed after the second revolt (Smallwood 1981: 345, 371–78, 480, 515–16). Several Jewish authors testify to the wealth which poured into the temple from the half-shekel tax, firstfruits and free-will offerings (*Let. Arist.* 40; *Gaium* 156; *Spec Leg* I.77–78; *Ant* 16.6.7 §172; 18.9.1 §312–13, all referring to offerings from the Diaspora), and these again may not be doubted. More than one avaricious gentile saw the temple as a source of wealth: it was plundered by Antiochus Epiphanes IV (1 Macc 1:21–24; *Ant* 12.5.4 §248–50), by Crassus (*Ant* 14.7.1 §105), and by Sabinus, procurator of Syria ca. 4 B.C.E. (*JW* 2.3.3 §50). Although Pilate confiscated sacred money to build an aquaduct, he did not plunder the temple treasury (*JW* 2.9.4 §175).

We can get a good idea of the publicly obvious laws which Jews in the Diaspora wished to observe by analyzing the proclamations and letters quoted in *Ant* 14. After Julius Caesar defeated Pompey and decided to bestow favor on the Jews, cities throughout the empire passed decrees either restoring Jewish rights or establishing them. Permission to assemble, to have common meals, to have a place of their own, and especially to keep the Sabbath heads the list. This complex of rights is followed by freedom from military service (sometimes connected with sabbath observance), permission to observe their rites and to give money for them, the right to have their "native food" supplied in the market, and permission to decide their own affairs (*Ant* 14.10.1–26 §185–268, esp. 214–64). Several of these items would not be at issue in Palestine, and other important observances would not have been mentioned because they were not subject to public observation or control. It is noteworthy that circumcision is not in the list. At that point in the history of the empire cultural homogeneity was not considered, and so circumcision was not an issue. When, almost 200 years later, Hadrian forbade circumcision, the consequences were disastrous, as we noted above. Circumcision was, however, known to be a distinguishing mark of Jews (E.2.b.). Despite the limitations of the evidence which these decrees provide, the list of practices, and in fact the existence of the decrees, support the view of general Jewish observance of the main laws.

This evidence from the Diaspora can be applied, *mutatis mutandis,* to Palestine, but more evidence can be cited. We may focus on the "common people." Modern scholars frequently say that the vast majority of Jews "neither knew nor followed the law," or that they were ignorant of it or "lukewarm" about obeying it (Lohse 1976: 80; Davies 1984: 17; Rhoads 1976: 33; Neusner 1986: 54). The only evidence from ancient sources which can be cited is John

7:49: "This crowd, who do not know the law, are accursed," which is taken to prove either that the generality of Jews did not know or keep the law, or that the Pharisees believed that they did not (the first view: Lohse 1976: 80; the second view: Jeremias 1969: 266). The same scholars would not take a single sentence in John as proving something about Jesus, and it can hardly be taken as satisfactory evidence for the common people of Palestine or the Pharisees. Against it stand all other sources.

No opinion could less-well reflect the overwhelming impression given by ancient literature, both Jewish and pagan, than the view that ordinary Jews neither knew nor observed the law. Even the Mishnah supports the opposite view. The rabbis, for example, thought that the ordinary people would protect items which belonged to a priest from contracting corpse impurity (*Ṭohar.* 8:2); they held them to be trustworthy about Second Tithe (*Ṭ. Yom* 4:5); and they regarded them as trustworthy with regard to the priests' portion of the Levitical tithe (*Dem.* 1:3). The rabbis, presumably following the Pharisees, had special tithing and purity laws which the common people did not keep, and these have given the wrong impression to scholars who have not distinguished the Pharisaic/rabbinic view of biblical law from their view of party "traditions." The learned and the pious did not think of the ordinary people as transgressing the major biblical laws.

Archaeology lends some support to the view that the laws were commonly observed. Numerous immersion pools have been found both in Jerusalem and elsewhere. With regard to the most difficult form of impurity to remove, corpse impurity, we may note Josephus's statements that Antipas had a hard time populating Tiberias, since it was built on a graveyard (*Ant* 18.2.3 §36–38). Philo regarded it as routine that pilgrims to the temple were kept outside for a week while they were purified of corpse impurity (*Spec Leg* I.261). During the brief reign of Archelaus there was a substantial riot which was caused, among other things, by his refusal to depose his high priest in favor of "a man of greater piety and purity" (*JW* 2.1.2 §7).

We may suppose that most Jews, both in Israel and in the Diaspora, observed most of the law. (For a slightly different but well-nuanced view of observance in Galilee, as judged by the 2d century rabbis, see Goodman 1983: 102–11.)

With regard to knowledge of the law, attendance at synagogue once a week was customary and was often regarded as a law, and so people heard the Bible read and expounded (E.2.c.(3); see further *Ant* 16.2.4 §43, "quoting" Nicolaus of Damascus; *Hypoth* 7.13; *Gaium* 156; *Hel. Syn. Pr.* 5:14–18). Synagogues (or houses of prayer) existed wherever there were Jews, and they fulfilled their function. Even without attending synagogues, Jews would learn the essentials of the religion and of the national way of life. The sabbath rest, the obligation of circumcision, the special dietary laws, and the reasons for the festivals would have been understood by all who lived within a Jewish community. Gentiles were widely acquainted with these practices (though sometimes imperfectly), and some found them attractive. The public importance of the feasts of pilgrimage (Passover, Booths, and Weeks), and of the fast day (the Day of Atonement), ensured that the relevant biblical passages were known.

Josephus, Philo, Pseudo-Aristeas, and others who waxed lyrical about Jewish knowledge and observance of the law of course engaged in idealization, and general education among the populace did not lead to universal obedience. But the fact of Jewish education in the biblical law and the rest of Scripture is undeniable, as is the overall loyalty of Jews throughout the world to the law.

Christian scholars have often supposed that Jewish law is extremely difficult: the laws were too numerous to know, let alone perform (in Bultmann's neat but ill-informed phrase, 1956: 66). This is not true. Josephus was correct when he wrote that the laws are "simple and familiar" (*AgAp* 2.22 §190). Rabbinic discussions of purity are involved and a bit difficult, but not many needed to follow them. In any case even these laws are easier than modern tax law—and they are less voluminous. Biblical law itself is simple and fairly small in volume. Most laws and semi-legal practices are obeyed by routine: waking, saying the morning prayers, blessing the bread, not killing or robbing anyone on the way to one's workplace, not cutting down one's enemy's fruit trees, listening quietly when lectured by one's parent—thus are fulfilled many laws each day.

G. Gentiles and the Jewish Law

Since the God who gave the law also created the universe, many Jews thought that his will should have been evident to all, at least to some degree. Philo equated the "law of nature" with the Jewish law (section A). This is an extreme position if one tries to harmonize Plato, Aristotle, and Moses. At another level of intellectual effort, however, many Jews would have agreed. Their God really had created the world, and his full will had been made known through Moses and the other prophets. In the new age there would be a common law for all (*Sib. Or.* 3.757–59). Gentiles had missed the revelation, but they should be able to discover some of it at least. This is put eloquently and gently in Wisdom 13 (Gentiles are "little to be blamed" for mistaking the creation for the creator, though they should have seen more clearly; praying to their own artifacts, however, is stupid and completely without excuse), with less nuance by Paul (Rom 1:18–23), and encouragingly by Philo (as did Abraham, others may study the world of sense perception and "come to find the likeness of the invisible world of mind," *Migr* 105; cf. 192–95 and often).

When it comes to particular laws, it is difficult to make good generalizations about Jewish expectations of gentiles. According to Pseudo-Philo, gentiles should know all the law and will be judged by it (*L.A.B.* 11:1–2). Few expected this much, and Noah was looked to as the source of laws which could be held to be universally binding. In *Jub.* 7:20 he is said to order his sons to do justice, "cover the shame of their flesh," bless the creator, honor father and mother, love the neighbor, and avoid sexual immorality and pollution. With great emphasis he warns that anyone who eats blood will be destroyed (7:28–33). This makes a total of seven commandments. In *t. ʿAbod. Zar.* 8:4 it is said that Noah gave his sons seven commandments, and six are then named: the establishment of courts and five prohibitions—idolatry, cursing the Name, incest, murder, and robbery. There are additions to this list in 8:6,8, based on Deut 18:10–11. Subsequently, rabbis would try both to employ the number seven and to take account of the commandments which appear in the Bible before the giving of the law on Mt. Sinai. (For these see *EncJud* 12: 1189–90; *EncJud* 12: 1190–91.) The list of prohibitions in Acts 15:29 ignores muder, incest, and robbery (forbidden throughout the world) and names only prohibitions which are peculiar to Judaism, but which many Jews seem to have thought gentiles should observe (avoiding meat with blood in it and meat offered to idols).

H. Epitomes of the Law

Epitomizing—often called summarizing—the law probably springs not from the feeling that the laws are too many and too burdensome, but from the desire to grasp the heart of the matter. The legal books of the Bible offer their own epitomes of the major categories of the law—commandments which govern relations between humans and God and those which govern relations among humans. The Deuteronomist seems to have intended the *Shema*ᶜ (Deut 6:4–9) to be a partial summary of the laws which had just been given (the Ten Commandments). "The Lord our God is one Lord" recalls the first two commandments. Similarly the author of Leviticus 19 grouped together several commandments which govern relations among humans and then concluded with summary statements: "you shall love your neighbor as yourself"; "you shall love [the stranger] as yourself" (Lev 19:18, 34). Jesus' statement that Deut 6:4–5 and Lev 19:18 are the greatest would not have surprised many (Mark 12:28–31). Philo singled out these same two commandments as giving the general burden of the law, though he put them in his own words: "God asks nothing . . . difficult, but only . . . just to love Him"; the law "stands preeminent in enjoining fellowship and humanity" (*Spec Leg* I.299,324). Similarly he noted that "two main heads" stand above all else in the law: "one of duty to God as shown by piety *(eusebeias)* and holiness *(hosiotētos)*, one of duty to fellow humans as shown by humanity *(philanthrōpia)* and justice *(dikaiosynē)*" (*Spec Leg* II.63).

Many Jews observed the commandment in the *Shema*ᶜ to place the laws on their doors and to wear them. According to Josephus, Jews posted on their doors and bound on their arms "the greatest of the benefits they have received from God" (*Ant* 4.8.13 §212–13). We cannot be sure what the passages were which he had in mind. One may assume that the Ten Commandments and part of the *Shema*ᶜ were included (as on the Nash Papyrus); possibly part of Deuteronomy beginning with 10:12, which is reminiscent of the *Shema*ᶜ (as on a *mezûzâ* parchment found in Qumran cave 8); possibly the Ten Commandments, the *Shema*ᶜ, Deut 11:13–21 and Num 15:37–41 (according to *Tam.* 5:1 the passages said twice daily by the priests). Traditional Jewish practice has been to put into the phylacteries (tephillîn) the four passages in which the wearing of "these words" on the hand and forehead are commanded: Exod 13:1–10; 13:11–16; Deut 6:4–9; 11:13–21. These passages singly or collectively summarize the main understanding of common-denominator Judaism: God chose the people, will preserve them, and requires obedience to the law.

There are also one-line summaries of the law, and these do not include the commandment to love God—perhaps because the passage was said every day and so was assumed. The best-known instance of a one-commandment summary of the law is a story told of Hillel, who said to a would-be proselyte, "What is hateful to you, do not to your neighbor: that is the whole Torah, while the rest is commentary thereof; go and learn it" (*Šabb.* 31a). Possibly this story is no more reliable than is the connected one about the oral law. In any case, the formula "what is hateful to you, do not to your neighbor" predates Hillel. It is found in Tob 4:15, written sometime in the 2d century B.C.E. There, however, it is one of a list of wise admonitions, not an epitome of the law. Philo gives a similar statement at the head of a list of laws and customs which exemplify it (*Hypoth* 7.6). The positive form of this principle is attributed to Jesus: "Whatever you wish that men would do to you, do so to them; for this is the law and the prophets" (Matt 7:12). These formulations, while all based on Lev 19:18, are cast in an epigrammatic mold. Finally, we note that Paul summarized the law by quoting Lev 19:18 (Gal 5:14; Rom 13:8–10). In the second instance he also cited the commandments not to commit adultery, not to kill, not to steal and not to covet. Interestingly, he then explained that since "love does no wrong to a neighbor" it "is the fulfilling of the law" (13:10). That is, Paul knew the negative form of the saying and found it useful.

One cannot determine the full contents of a teacher's ethics or theology from an epitome. Philo follows the negative love commandment with both negative and positive admonitions, such as, "If the poor or the cripple beg food of him he must give it as an offering of religion to God" (*Hypoth* 7.6). The epitomes of the law based on Lev 19:18 leave out of account the commandments which govern the human-divine relationship, but this does not mean that the person who employed the epitome would have tolerated idols (in the case of Paul, note Rom 1:23). Too much should not be expected of one-line statements of "the whole law," and we gather from them a basic thrust rather than a principle which truly encapsulates the entirety of the law. The rabbis subsequently offered numerous summaries or "cores" of the law, most of which are listed in Sanders 1977: 112–14.

I. Theological Context

Both theologically and chronologically election (or, more generally, grace) comes before the law, reward and punishment come afterward. All forms of Judaism of the period which are known to us regard the obligation to obey the law as the response to God's choice and deliverance of the Jewish people, and likewise they all regard him as reliable and just in giving recompense. Evidence from the main bodies of literature is given in Sanders 1977. The covenantal context of the Jewish law is clear throughout the rest of the literature (e.g. Ps.-Philo, *L.A.B.* 11:1–5; 13:10 and often; *Hel. Syn. Pr.* 4:38–40; 12:56–57), but it has been so often denied that we should add two representative statements by Josephus: at the sacrifices Jews (or possibly priests) do not ask God for blessings, "for He has given them spontaneously and put them at the disposal of all, but for capacity to receive, and, having received, to keep them" (*AgAp* 2.23 §197). Discussing the (supposed) requirement of the law to pray at dawn and bedtime, Josephus states that Jews should give thanks to God for the gifts which he has given them through the deliverance from Egypt, and they should post on their doors and their arms "the greatest of the benefits they have received from

God," thus showing to all "the loving care with which God surrounds them" (*Ant* 4.8.13 §212–13).

Bibliography

Bultmann, R. 1956. *Primitive Christianity in Its Contemporary Setting.* Trans. R. H. Fuller. London.
Colson, F. H. 1939. *Philo.* LCL 8. London.
Danby, H. 1933. *The Mishnah.* Oxford.
Davies, W. D. 1984. Law in First-Century Judaism. Pp. 3–26 in *Jewish and Pauline Studies.* Philadelphia.
Dodd, C. H. 1935. *The Bible and the Greeks.* London.
Ginouvès, R. 1962. *Balaneutikè: Recherches sur le bain dans l'antiquité grecque.* Bibliothèque des Écoles Françaises d'Athènes et de Rome 200. Paris.
Goodman, M. 1983. *State and Society in Roman Galilee, A.D. 132–212.* Totowa, NJ.
———. 1987. *The Ruling Class of Judaea: The Origins of the Jewish Revolt Against Rome A.D. 66–70.* Cambridge.
Jeremias, J. 1969. *Jerusalem in the Time of Jesus.* Trans. F. H. and C. H. Cave. London.
Kraabel, A. T. 1981. Social Systems of Six Diaspora Synagogues. Pp. 79–91 in *Ancient Synagogues.* Ed. J. Gutmann. Brown Judaic Studies 22. Chico, CA.
Lake, K. 1932. *Additional Notes to the Commentary,* vol. 5 of *The Beginnings of Christianity,* Part I: *The Acts of the Apostles,* 5 vols., ed. K. Lake and H. J. Cadbury. London. 1979.
Lohse, E. 1976. *The New Testament Environment.* Trans. John E. Steely. London.
Maccoby, H. 1980. *Revolution in Judaea,* 2d. ed. New York.
Neusner, J. 1971. *The Rabbinic Traditions about the Pharisees before 70.* 3 vols. Leiden.
———. 1985. *Torah. From Scroll to Symbol in Formative Judaism.* Philadelphia.
———. 1986. *Reading and Believing: Ancient Judaism and Contemporary Gullibility.* Brown Judaic Studies 113. Atlanta.
Pasinya, L. M. 1973. *La notion de nomos dans le Pentateuque grec.* Rome.
Rabin, C. 1958. *The Zadokite Documents.* 2d ed. Oxford.
Rajak, T. 1983. *Josephus.* London.
Rhoads, D. M. 1976. *Israel in Revolution 6–74 C.E.* Philadelphia.
Rivkin, E. 1978. *A Hidden Revolution.* Nashville.
———. 1984. *What Crucified Jesus?* Nashville.
Sanders, E. P. 1977. *Paul and Palestinian Judaism.* Philadelphia.
———. 1983. *Paul, the Law and the Jewish People.* Philadelphia.
———. 1985. *Jesus and Judaism.* Philadelphia.
———. 1989. *The Jewish Law from Jesus to the Mishnah.* London.
Simon, M. 1986. *Verus Israel.* Oxford.
Smallwood, E. M. 1981. *The Jews Under Roman Rule from Pompey to Diocletian.* SJLA. Leiden.
Stern, M. 1976–1984. *Greek and Latin Authors on Jews and Judaism.* 3 vols. Jerusalem.
Whittaker, M. 1984. *Jews & Christians: Graeco-Roman Views.* Cambridge Commentaries on Writings of the Jewish and Christian World 200 BC to AD 200. Vol. 6. Cambridge.
Yadin, Y. 1985. *The Temple Scroll.* London.

E. P. SANDERS

LAW, TABLETS OF THE. See TABLETS OF THE LAW.

LAYING ON OF HANDS. See HANDS, LAYING ON OF.

LAZARUS (PERSON) [Gk *Lazaros*]. The name of Lazarus, an abbreviated transcription of *El-azar* ("God helps"), appears in the NT only in the gospel of John and a short parable in Luke 16:19–31. It is the only proper name to appear in a NT parable attributed to Jesus. The Lazarus of the parable is a poor man who stands in contrast to a rich man, not only in life, but also after death, when their respective roles are reversed: Lazarus is in the bosom of Abraham, whereas the rich man is in Hades. The parable concludes with a significant logion, "If they do not hear Moses and the prophets, neither will they be convinced if some one should rise from the dead" (Luke 16:41), thereby suggesting a link between a man named Lazarus and teaching about the resurrection in early Christian tradition.

The Lazarus of the Fourth Gospel, an inhabitant of the town of Bethany and the brother of Martha and Mary, was raised from the dead by Jesus and was present at a meal six days before Jesus' final Passover, at which time his sister Mary anointed the feet of Jesus in preparation for Jesus' burial (John 11:1–12:11). This Lazarus, repeatedly described as loved by Jesus (John 11:3, 5, 36) and once as his friend (John 11:11), is one of the principal named disciples in the Fourth Gospel, even though his role is admittedly a passive one. He never makes an explicit profession of faith in Jesus, nor does he ever speak. The gospel shows no particular interest in his person or his personal history.

The literary form of the narrative in which he appears generally corresponds to that of the miracle story, but its dialogical structure and metaphorical character set it apart from the typical miracle stories of the Bible and the ancient world. Johannine style characteristics are found throughout the narrative in such a way as to impart a Johannine character to the entire account in its present form. Nonetheless scholars are convinced that the literary history of the narrative is quite complex. Its very complexity undermines attempts to determine precisely the earlier strata of tradition.

As to the origins of the Johannine story, scholarly opinion falls under three headings. Some scholars continue to hold that the raising of Lazarus was an historical event. Others hold that the Johannine story is a conflation of various material in Luke, particularly the parable of Luke 16:19–31 and the Martha and Mary story of Luke 10:38–42, along with the stories of the raising of Jairus' daughter (Luke 8:40–56; par., Matt 9:18–25; Mark 5:21–43) and the son of the widow of Nain (7:11–17). A third group holds that there is a common tradition behind the Lazarus story in John and the various other NT accounts of raisings from the dead.

Many scholars draw attention to the possible influence of popular legends and biblical motifs upon the Johannine narrative. Thus they eschew attempts to reconstitute factual events. The majority of scholars, in fact, consider that the search for facticity admits of no solution and that the argument over the historicity of the story is misguided. As a thoroughly Johannine story, the account is dramatic and largely symbolic; facts, as such, do not form its central theme.

The Johannine story is dramatically placed at the end of Jesus' public ministry, just before the Passion of Jesus, to which it directly leads (John 11:45–53; 12:10–11; cf. Mark 11:18; Luke 19:47–48). It is the last in the Fourth Gospel's series of signs, the import of which is principally christological. Although the traditions behind the story of the raising of Lazarus may have been influenced by an attempt to deal with the delay of the Parousia (John 11:6; cf. 1 Thess 4:13–17), the Johannine story is essentially a proclamation of Jesus' power over sickness and death. It is a portrayal of Jesus self-revelation as "the resurrection and the life" (John 11:25). As a narrative figure, Lazarus is the symbol of the authority, power, and significance of Jesus as the Resurrection and Life. He represents the disciple of Jesus who has died, and who will be raised because Jesus has been glorified (John 11:4, 40).

On the narrative level, Lazarus' four days in the tomb (John 11:6, 17, 39; cf. vv 13–14) point to the reality of his death. His death, though real, is not ultimate. Human death serves a divine purpose and is overcome through the resurrection effected through the power of Jesus. The gospel carefully distinguishes between the resurrection of the disciple (a resuscitation) and that of Jesus (a true resurrection). This is symbolized in the wrapping cloths: while Lazarus is unwrapped, Jesus leaves the wrappings behind (John 11:44; 20:4–7).

In the *Secret Gospel of Mark* Lazarus is cited, without specific mention of his name, as one blessed by Jesus and raised from the dead by Jesus at Bethany. Later tradition identified him as the bishop of Kition on Cyprus (Eastern tradition) or Marseilles (Western tradition). The British exegete J. N. Sanders held that Lazarus was the beloved disciple of the Fourth Gospel (John 13:21–26; 19:25–27; 20:2–10; cf. 18:15–16).

Bibliography

Collins, R. F. 1976. The Representative Figures of the Fourth Gospel. *DRev* 94: 26–46, 118–32.

Henneberry, B. H. 1984. *The Raising of Lazarus (John 11:10–44).* Ann Arbor.

Hock, R. F. 1987. Lazarus and Micyllus: Greco-Roman Backgrounds to Luke 16:19–31. *JBL* 106: 447–63.

Kopp, C. 1963. *The Holy Places of the Gospels.* Trans. R. Wells. New York.

Kremer, J. 1985a. *Lazarus: Die Geschichte einer Auferstehung.* Stuttgart.

———. 1985b. Die Lazarusgeschichte: Ein Beispiel urkirchliche Christusverkundigung. *GuL* 58: 244–58. Eng digest, The Awakening of Lazarus. *TD* 33 (1986): 135–38.

Pearce, K. 1985. The Lucan Origins of the Raising of Lazarus. *ExpTim* 96: 359–61.

Rochais, G. 1981. *Les récits de résurrection des morts dans le Nouveau Testament.* SNTSMS 40. Cambridge.

Schneiders, S. M. 1987. Death in the Community of Eternal Life. *Int* 41: 44–56.

Suggit, J. N. 1984. The Raising of Lazarus. *ExpTim* 95: 106–8.

Wagner, J. 1988. *Auferstehung und Leben: Joh 11, 1–12, 19 als Spiegel johanneïscher Redaktions- und Theologiegeschichte. Regensburg.*

RAYMOND F. COLLINS

LAZARUS AND DIVES. Only the Gospel of Luke has preserved a story that has come to be known as the Parable of the Rich Man and Lazarus (16:19–31). It tells of a rich man who, while alive, used to dress in purple and linen and to feast daily (v 19), and of Lazarus, a crippled, sick, and destitute man who used to lie at the rich man's gate in hopes of receiving leftovers from the latter's table (vv 20–21). After their deaths, however, Lazarus is secure in Abraham's bosom (v 22), whereas the rich man is in torment in Hades (v 23). He appeals to Abraham for mercy and specifically for Lazarus to come and relieve his thirst (v 23). Abraham, however, denies the request because an impassable chasm separates them (vv 24–26). The rich man then asks that Lazarus be sent to his five living brothers to warn them of a similar fate, but Abraham again denies the request, saying that they have Moses and the prophets (vv 27–29). When the rich man insists that only an appearance of one from the dead would cause them to repent, Abraham retorts that those who do not listen to Moses and the prophets are not likely to believe someone raised from the dead either (vv 30–31).

A. Distinctive Features

This parable is among the forty-odd parables of Jesus which are preserved in the canonical gospels. Indeed, the word "odd," now used in its more usual sense, may be the best way to describe this parable, at least initially, for interpreters have long noted its many unusual features. For example, when compared with the other parables, which focus on ordinary experiences, this one's depiction of life beyond the grave is immediately striking (Creed 1953: 209), and, on closer inspection, its surface and deep structures are likewise idiosyncratic (Funk 1982: 36, 40, 54). But what has most often drawn attention is the otherwise unprecedented use of a named character in a parable. Indeed, the surprising appearance of the poor man with the name Lazarus (who is not to be identified with the Lazarus of John 11) prompted some patristic commentators to classify this story as a "narrative" rather than as a "parable" (Plummer *Luke* ICC, 391). They were presumably thinking of a rhetorical definition of parable *(parabolē)* as a literary form which draws on ordinary or daily experiences and does not use specific or named individuals (John Doxapatres, *Hom. in Aphthon.* 3 [Walz 1835: 2.273]). In any case, the presence of a name for the poor man also prompted some copyists to name the rich man as well. Thus early on, the copyist of P^{75} names him Neues, whereas others over the centuries call him Nineve, Finaeus, or Phinees. In the late Middle Ages readers of the Latin Vulgate began to regard the adjective *dives* ("rich") as a proper name (*Rich*ard, as it were) (Cadbury 1962; cf. Grobel 1963–64: 381–82). Thus the title of this article: Lazarus *and Dives.*

B. History of Interpretation

For most of this century the view of Adolf Jülicher, Hugo Gressmann, and, to a lesser extent, Rudolf Bultmann have established the way that scholars approach and interpret this parable. Jülicher (1910: 2.634) divided the parable into two parts (vv 19–26 and 27–31) since he regarded the latter verses, which concern the fate of the five brothers, to be only loosely connected to the story about Lazarus and Dives. Gressman (1918) then proposed an Egyptian folktale of reversal as the source of the first part of the parable (vv 19–26) and claimed that the parable thereby had two points, one for each part, with Jesus' new conclusion to the folktale (vv 27–31) being the more important one (for the folktale itself: Griffith 1900: 42–43). This history of religions proposal seemingly confirmed Jülicher's literary analysis. Finally, Bultmann (1963: 203), approaching the parable as a form critic, asked whether one or both parts of the parable go back to Jesus himself, or are merely (as he thought) the product of the Church. How enduring and influential these literary, history of religions, and form critical studies have been is immediately apparent from a perusal of the articles, commentaries, and monographs on this parable since their time (Hock 1987: 448–51).

And yet, several recent studies of the parable hint at a new interpretation. For example, the parable's literary unity has received a sustained and sophisticated defense (Schnider and Stegner 1978–79). In addition, while some have pressed the parallels between the parable and Egyptian folktale (Grobel 1963–64), others have noted important differences (Fitzmyer *Luke X–XXIV* AB, 1127) or denied the relevance of the folktale altogether (Pax 1975: 267). In fact, the parallels are neither as close nor as explanatory as the constant citation of the folktale would suggest, and certainly not helpful precisely where the parable is most opaque, that is, in providing a rationale for the reversal in fortunes of Lazarus and Dives. Accordingly, some scholars have sought clarifying parallels in such Jewish sources as *1 Enoch* 92–105 (Nickelsburg 1978–79; Esler 1987: 189–91). But the closest parallel so far adduced comes from the mid-2d century sophist, Lucian of Samosata, whose highly Cynicized *Cataplus (Trip to Hades)* not only treats the theme of wealth and poverty, as does the Enoch literature, but also contains parallels in characters, plot, and dialogue which that literature does not (Hock 1987: 457–61). Indeed, the parallels are so close—the deaths of a rich man and poor man, their subsequent reversal in Hades, and the futile attempts of the rich man to change his new situation—that Lucian's and Luke's stories may ultimately go back to a common source: the Cynic Menippus' *Nekyia*, or *Trip to Hades* (cf. Diog. Laert. 6.101). In any case, the greater length of Lucian's *Cataplus* permits clarification of details in the parable—for example, the hedonistic and presumably immoral life-style implicit in Dives' characterization by reference to his fine clothing and sumptuous dining. More important, this greater length includes the plausible explanation for Lazarus' and Dives' reversal in fortune. Thus, in the light of Lucian's account, the reversal is not so much because of Dives' neglect of Lazarus outside his gate and Lazarus' faith in God, as so many interpreters have claimed (Hock 1987: 453 n. 28 and 454 n. 29); rather, it is because of Dives' wealth and the immoral hedonism which wealth allows and Lazarus' poverty which assures his purity and virtue (Hock 1987: 460–61).

Finally, Bultmann's denial of authenticity to this parable has met with some approval (Mealand 1980: 39–40; Horn 1983: 152, 181), though more often for vv 27–31 only (Crossan 1973: 66–67; Schottroff and Stegemann 1978: 38). But given the new views regarding the parable's literary unity and background, it seems appropriate to reopen this question and ask: Where should the origin of this parable be placed? To be sure, the parable is consistent with Lukan redaction with its emphasis on wealth and poverty (Esler 1987: 164–69), but pre-Lukan features in the parable already indicate that it is earlier than the redactor (Mealand 1980: 32). Indeed, similar views on wealth and poverty also appear earlier in Mark's gospel (4:19; 8:36; 10:17–27) and in Q (e.g., Matt 5:3 = Luke 6:20 and Matt 22:1–10 = Luke 14:15–24). Still, one might stop short of tracing the parable all the way back to Jesus, preferring instead to follow D. Mealand (1980: 48–49) in assigning the origins of the parable to the late 40s of the 1st century in Jerusalem when the Church faced a local famine. But such a sharp critique of wealth as that found in the parable hardly requires so specific an occasion, as the subject was a constant theme of Cynic philosophizing (see CYNICS) and was even a part of the sophists' repertoire (Russell 1983: 27–30). In addition, their repertoire also included the testimony of those from the dead, learned early on in the rhetorical exercise known as *eidolopoiia* (Aphth. *Rhetor.* 11 [Rabe 1926: 34]), which obviates the problem of Lazarus's return from the grave as presupposing the resurrection of Jesus (Mealand 1980: 48). And finally the Cynic tone to the parable need not cause a problem, given the Hellenization of Palestine in general and even the birthplace of Menippus in nearby Gadara (Strabo, 16.2.29). The parable of the Rich Man and Lazarus would therefore seem to have a good claim to authenticity.

Bibliography

Bultmann, R. 1963. *The History of the Synoptic Tradition.* New York.
Cadbury, H. J. 1962. A Proper Name for Dives. *JBL* 81: 399–402.
Creed, J. M. 1953. *The Gospel according to St. Luke.* London.
Crossan, J. D. 1973. *In Parables.* New York.
Esler, P. F. 1987. *Community and Gospel in Luke-Acts.* New York.
Funk, R. W. 1982. *Parables and Presence.* Philadelphia.
Gressman, H. 1918. *Vom reichen Mann und armen Lazarus.* Berlin.
Griffith, F. 1900. *Stories of the High Priest of Memphis.* Oxford.
Grobel, K. 1963–64. ". . . whose name was Neves." *NTS* 10: 373–82.
Hock, R. F. 1987. Lazarus and Micyllus: Greco-Roman Backgrounds to Luke 16:19–31. *JBL* 106: 447–63.
Horn, F. W. 1983. *Glaube und Handeln in der Theologie des Lukas.* Göttingen.
Jülicher, A. 1910. *Die Gleichnisreden Jesu.* 2 vols. Tübingen.
Mealand, D. L. 1980. *Poverty and Expectation in the Gospels.* London.
Nickelsburg, G. W. E. 1978–79. Riches, The Rich, and God's Judgment in 1 Enoch 95–105 and the Gospel according to Luke. *NTS* 25: 324–44.
Pax, E. 1975. Der Reiche und der arme Lazarus. *LASBF* 25: 254–68.
Rabe, H. 1926. *Aphthonii Progymnasmata.* Rhetores Graeci 10. Leipzig.
Russell, D. A. 1983. *Greek Declamation.* New York.
Schnider, F., and Stegner, W. 1978–79. Die offene Tür und die unüberschreitbare Kluft. *NTS* 25. 273–83.
Schottroff, L. and Stegemann, W. 1978. *Jesus von Nazareth: Hoffnung der Armen.* Stuttgart.
Walz, C. 1832–36. *Rhetores Graeci.* 9 vols. Tübingen.

RONALD F. HOCK

LEAH (PERSON) [Heb *lēʾâ*]. The elder daughter of Laban, sister of Rachel; Jacob's first wife and mother of six sons and a daughter. Leah's name probably means "cow"; her sister Rachel's, "ewe."

The stories of Genesis 12–50 focus on the threefold promise to the patriarch Abraham of land, descendants, and a great name (Gen 12:1–3), and how this promise is passed on from father to son. The narratives about the matriarchs, then, are not primarily about the women themselves as individuals, but rather about their roles as the legitimate or "correct" wife and mother of the male successor. The question of who is the correct wife, mother of the heir, should be seen in the context of marriage and kinship systems of the Israelite society. Marriage alliances here are endogamous, i.e., within one's own tribe or social group. Lines of descent are patrilineal, traced through the father instead of the mother.

Jacob's mother, Rebekah, expresses to Isaac her fear that Jacob would marry a Hittite woman, i.e., marry exogamously (Gen 27:46). Isaac then commands Jacob, "Arise and go to Paddan-aram to the house of Bethuel your mother's father; and take as wife from there one of the daughters of Laban your mother's brother" (Gen 28:2). Leah (and Rachel) are related endogamously to their husband Jacob as matrilateral cross-cousins: Jacob's mother's brother's daughters. See Wander (1981) and Donaldson (1981) regarding the complexities of such endogamous patrilineal relationships.

Several recent studies show that the biblical stories of the matriarchs follow a literary paradigm whereby the legitimate wife is paired with a rival co-wife who possesses certain characteristics that the other lacks (Brenner 1985; 1986; Cohen 1983). The competition and jealousy between the two are the destructive consequences of the patriarchal and polygamous society where the narratives are played out. Both sides represent incomplete womanhood, shadowy reflections of the other. Because of the asymmetry of both entities, the two women are locked in conflict until one can expel the other or the other dies. The person of Leah must therefore be studied along with her complement, Rachel.

Leah and Rachel are sisters married to the same man. Rachel is described as beautiful and lovely, and Leah's eyes are described as *rakkôt* (Gen 29:17). The word *rakkôt* is usually translated as "weak," but its more usual meaning is "tender" and "soft." In Deut 28:54, 56 and Isa 47:1, it denotes refinement and delicacy of breeding. Leah has often been maligned as unattractive, this focus on physical beauty sometimes interpreted as the reason Jacob loved Rachel more. However, it could be as Cohen (1983) suggests that while Rachel was more outwardly beautiful, her sister may have been more sensitive and kind—tender of spirit.

The identities of both women revolve around the common desire to bear sons for their husband. This is an expectation of the patriarchal society in which both live, of the women themselves, and also of the narrative structure of the text which concerns God's promise to the patriarchs of land, posterity, and a great name. The texts relate the bitter competition between the two sisters to realize their goal of sons for Jacob.

Leah, the older sister, the first wife, is unloved by her husband. But she is very fertile. She gives birth to six biological sons (Reuben, Simeon, Levi, Judah, Issachar, Zebulun; Gen 29:31–35; 30:14–20), two adoptive sons through her maid Zilpah (Gad and Asher; Gen 30:9–13), and a daughter named Dinah (Gen 30:21). Rachel is the younger sister, subordinate to Leah in the household as second wife, but cherishes her husband's love. Nevertheless, she is barren.

The climax of the two sisters' rivalry is over the mandrakes that Leah's son, Reuben, found for his mother (Gen 30:14–20). Mandrakes were considered an aphrodisiac and an aid to fertility. When Rachel asks for some from Leah, Leah bitterly reproaches her sister. Apparently, Jacob has been spending more time in Rachel's bed than in Leah's. Rachel agrees that for the mandrakes Jacob can spend the night with her. In an amusing episode, Jacob encounters Leah after a day's work in the field. Leah remarks that he must sleep with her, for she has "hired" him for the price of her son's mandrakes. Leah conceives in that union, but ostensibly the mandrakes worked for Rachel. She finally bears Joseph for her husband with the wish that she can bear another. Unfortunately, the next son born to Rachel, Benjamin, will result in her death due to a hard labor (Gen 35:16–19). The rivalry between the sisters ends, but at the price of one sister's death.

Bibliography

Brenner, A. 1985. *The Israelite Woman*. Sheffield.
———. 1986. Female Social Behaviour: Two Descriptive Patterns within the "Birth of the Hero" Paradigm. *VT* 36: 257–73.
Cohen, N. 1983. Sibling Rivalry in Genesis. *Judaism* 32: 331–42.
Donaldson, M. 1981. Kinship Theory in the Patriarchal Narratives: The Case of the Barren Wife. *JAAR* 49: 77–87.
Exum, J. C. 1985. "Mother in Israel": A Familiar Story Reconsidered. Pp. 73–85 in *Feminist Interpretation of the Bible*, ed. L. M. Russell. Philadelphia.
Wander, N. 1981. Structure, Contradiction, and "Resolution" in Mythology: Father's Brother's Daughter Marriage and the Treatment of Women in Genesis 11–50. *JANES* 13: 75–99.

GALE A. YEE

LEATHER. See DRESS AND ORNAMENTATION.

LEAVEN. See MEAL CUSTOMS (JEWISH DIETARY LAWS).

LEBANA (PERSON) [Heb *lĕbānâ*]. The name of a family of temple-servants who returned to Palestine with Zerubbabel shortly after 538 B.C.E., the end of the Babylonian exile. The name appears in Ezra 2:45 in the phrase "the sons of Lebanah" (Gk *labanō*), where the temple-servants are distinguished from the people of Israel, the priests, and the Levites. The parallel passage Neh 7:46–56 lists "the sons of Lebana" in Neh 7:48 (Gk *labana*), and the later parallel 1 Esdr 5:29 follows Ezra 2:45 with "the sons of Lebanah" (Gk *labana*). The word is found in some manuscripts as *lĕbānāʾ*, which has given rise to minor differences in transliteration. The Eng versions favor "Lebanah."

STEVEN R. SWANSON

LEBANON [Heb *lĕbānôn*]. The name of this region in the Levant (from the semitic root *lbn,* "to be white"), which in the historical books of the OT is generally preceded by the definite article, presumably alludes to the whiteness of the country's mountains when covered with snow (Jer 18:13). Lebanon's ancient boundaries are not sharply delineated in ancient sources, but probably were much like those of modern Lebanon except that the narrow strip of Phoenician territory on the Mediterranean coast where Tyre, Sidon, and other cities were located was not regarded as part of the region.

A. Geography and History

Lebanon's varied terrain consists of three major features. Parallel with the coastal plain, the Lebanon Mountains (referred to simply as "[the] Lebanon" or occasionally "Mt. Lebanon" in the OT [Judg 3:3]) rise to an elevation of more than 10,000 ft (3,300 m). Parts of the W slopes of this 100-mile (160-km) chain, benefiting from westerly Mediterranean winds, receive an average of 60 in (150 cm) of precipitation during the rainy winter season, which in higher elevations falls as snow. The E slopes descend to the fertile Beqa^{c}, a N extension of the Jordan Valley, which lies some 3,700 feet (1,100 m) above sea level. Although biblical writers were aware of its existence, the Beqa^{c} is seldom mentioned in the OT; it appears as the "valley of Lebanon" in Josh 11:17 and 12:7. The region's only major perennial river, the Litani, commences in the N-central part of the valley and flows SW until it debouches near Tyre on the S coast. East of the Beqa^{c} rise the more arid Anti-lebanon (i.e., "behind the Lebanon") Mountains, which, although somewhat lower than the W range, include at their S extremity Mt. Hermon, the summit of which has an elevation of some 9,200 ft (3,000 m). The Anti-lebanon is mentioned much less frequently in the OT than is the Lebanon range; it appears in Josh 13:5 as "Lebanon toward the rising sun." In several instances, however, the LXX appropriately translates the Heb "Lebanon" as "Anti-lebanon" (Deut 1:7, 3:25, 11–24; Josh 1:4, 9:1).

During the past hundred years archaeological excavations have been conducted at many sites in Lebanon, but much remains to be learned about the history of the region. Human habitation began in the Stone Age and can be followed through successive periods of Near Eastern history. Small and relatively defenseless, but occupying a strategic position in the Levant, the region was repeatedly invaded and conquered over the centuries. During the 2d and 1st millennia B.C., Lebanon participated in the broad cultural trends of the MB–LB, Iron Age, and Hellenistic Age, but the prosperity of the Beqa^{c} and the sparsely settled hill country was modest by comparison with that of the coastal Phoenician cities. In the Roman period a cult center at Baalbek in the Beqa^{c} became known throughout the empire for its magnificent complex of temples.

B. In the OT

Lebanon is mentioned nearly 70 times in the OT. The region was never part of the kingdom of Israel, although the book of Joshua asserts that Joshua conquered territory as far N as the town of Baal-gad at the S end of the Beqa^{c} (Josh 11:17, 12:7, 13:5–6), and represents God as declaring that he would give to Israel all of the territory "from the Negev to Lebanon" (Josh 1:4; cf. Deut 11:24). According to 1 Kgs 9:19 (= 2 Chr. 8:6), the S part of Lebanon was under Israelite hegemony for a brief time during the reign of Solomon, who is said to have carried out building projects "in Jerusalem, in the Lebanon, and throughout his whole dominion."

Although frequently harsh in their condemnation of Edom, Moab, Philistia, Syria, and other nations around Israel, the biblical writers almost always refer to Lebanon in a positive, or at least neutral, way, in part because it was a geographical region rather than a kingdom. Numerous passages allude to the richness of the country. The agricultural abundance of the Beqa^{c} is mentioned in Ps 72:16, where hope is expressed that the reign of a good king will cause crops to flourish like those of Lebanon. The region's wine is said to be famous (Hos 14:7). Lebanon is sometimes linked poetically with Sharon, Bashan, and Carmel, all of which were relatively fertile regions. In Isa 33:9 the prophet describes the desolation of Lebanon when God is not present (cf. Nah. 1:4), and two chapters later celebrates the restoration of Zion, when the wilderness will bloom and "the glory of Lebanon" will be given to the land (Isa 35.2; cf. 60:13).

So positive and compelling was the imagery of Lebanon for biblical writers that at times "Lebanon" was used almost as a poetic surrogate for "Israel." In contemplating the return of Jews from Egypt and Assyria in the postexilic period, Zechariah declares that God will gather the exiles "into Gilead and Lebanon, until there is no more room for them" (Zech 10:10–11). Although not among the tribes of Israel, Gilead had historically close connections with the N tribes. The terms "Gilead" and "Lebanon" are again linked in Jer. 22:6 (cf. v 23), where they appear as metaphors for Judah in her coming destruction; there are, however, no negative connotations regarding Gilead and Lebanon themselves, for God declares through the prophet that both Gilead and "the heights of Lebanon" are dear to him.

Particularly valued by the Israelites and other prophets of the E Mediterranean region were Lebanon's forests of pine, fir, cypress, cedar, and other trees (see Brown 1969: 140–212). The W slopes of the Lebanon range provided a superb climate for evergreen trees, whch were valued for the size and durability of their timber and even the fragrant odor of some of the wood (Hos 14:6; cf. Cant 4:11). The primeval forests, a few remnants of which survived into the 20th century in isolated places in the mountains, had been less depleted during the early biblical period than the oak forests of Palestine and Transjordan. The cutting of Lebanon's timber was initially a monopoly of the coastal cities, and later of the monarchs of conquering empires. Some of the wood was used regionally in the manufacture of ships (Ezek 27:5), and some was exported at considerable profit. As early as the 4th millennium B.C., Egypt was a purchaser of timber from Lebanon for use in the construction of buildings and boats. The OT contains numerous allusions to wood from Lebanon in connection with the Temple in Jerusalem (1 Kgs 5.6–14 – 2 Chr 2.7–16) and Solomon's "House of the Forest of Lebanon" (1 Kgs 10:21 = 2 Chr 9:20; cf. 1 Kgs 7:2 and 10:17). The Song of Solomon states—either factually or figuratively—that Solomon's palanquin was made of the wood of Lebanon (Cant 3:9). By the time of Hezekiah's rule in Judah in the late 8th century B.C., the forests of Lebanon had already suffered considerable depredation, most recently at the hands of Assyrian monarchs (2 Kgs 19:23 = Isa 37:24; Isa 10:34), who continued the royal monopoly. Around 520 B.C. Cyrus of Persia permitted timber to be brought from Lebanon for the reconstruction of the Temple in Jerusalem (Ezra 3:7).

Of all the evergreen trees of Lebanon, the cedar made the deepest impression upon the writers of the OT. Solomon is said to have delivered scholarly discourses on plants, "from the cedar that is in Lebanon to the hyssop that grows out of the wall" (1 Kgs 4:33). The cedars are cited a number of times as metaphors of loftiness and nobility (Isa 2:13, 10:34). Ps 104:16 declares that the trees of Yahweh are as green and leafy as the cedars of Lebanon. In Judg 9:15 Jotham's parable of the trees likens the people of the city of Shechem to the cedars of Lebanon. Ps 92:12 envisions the righteous person growing as tall as a cedar of Lebanon, while the Song of Solomon alludes to the bridegroom's legs being as sturdy and noble as the cedars of Lebanon (Cant 5:15). Not infrequently the cedars appear as a direct or implied metaphor for a ruler or an empire. Davidic kings of Judah are sometimes so designated, e.g., Isa 14:8 and Ezek 17:3. In Jer 22:6 the disobedience of Judah and her king is likened to the felling of the choicest timbers in Lebanon, and in v 20 of the same chapter Lebanon and Basham appear in poetic parallelism in a similar context. In 2 Kgs 14:9 (= 2 Chr 25:18) Jehoash, king of Israel, sends to Amaziah, king of Judah, a message in which he likens the two rulers to a thistle and a cedar on Lebanon, and immediately afterward likens himself to a wild beast of Lebanon. On occasion a non-Israelite ruler or empire is likened to a cedar of Lebanon (Isa 10:34; Ezek 31:3–18), but only as an opportunity for a prophet to point out how poorly the empire lived up to that noble image and how deserving it is of punishment. Habakkuk singles out the region as an instance of violence wrongly done to it—perhaps, it has been suggested, the felling of its trees (Hab 2:17).

Some allusions to Lebanon have overtones of myths about N Canaanite deities venerated in the mountains, e.g., Cant 4:8: "Come with me from Lebanon, descend from the top of Amana, from the peak of Senir and Hermon" (cf. 7:4). Although applied to Lebanon within the context of the OT, some of the more cosmological allusions to Lebanon or Hermon may, like ones pertaining to Zion as the "Mount of the Lord," perhaps have had their origins in the much older Canaanite religion.

C. In the NT. The NT does not mention Lebanon as such. There is no evidence that Jesus ever visited the region, although MT 16:13 records that he went into the district of Caesarea Philippi (Dan, or Panias) in the extreme N part of Palestine. Attempts to identify the "high mountain" of Jesus' transfiguration (Matt 17:1–11 and parallels) with Mt. Hermon in Lebanon must remain speculative, especially since Mt. Tabor in N Palestine is the traditional location of that episode. Tyre and Sidon appear in the NT, but, as in the OT period, the coastal region was regarded as part of Phoenicia rather than of Lebanon (cf. Mark 7:24–31).

Bibliography

Brown, J. P. 1969. *The Lebanon and Phoenicia.* Vol. I. Beirut.
Hitti, P. K. 1957. *Lebanon in History.* London.

ROBERT HOUSTON SMITH

LEBANON, HOUSE OF. See TEMPLE, JERUSALEM.

LEBAOTH (PLACE) [Heb *lĕbāʾôt*]. See BETH-LABAOTH (PLACE).

LEBBAEUS (PERSON). See THADDEUS (PERSON).

LEBONAH (PLACE) [Heb *lĕbônâ*]. A town in the hill country of Ephraim to the N of Shiloh (Judg 21:19). The exact location is disputed; both El-Lubban (M.R. 173164) and Lubban Sherqujeh have been suggested as possible sites. Though mentioned only once in the OT, it was apparently of sufficient importance to serve as a reference point for the location of Shiloh. See *HAB* and *GTTOT*.

ELMER DYCK

LECAH (PLACE) [Heb *lēkâ*]. A community founded by Er, son of Judah (1 Chr 4:21). The name is mentioned only this once; the location is unknown. The suggestion that the name might be a corruption of Lachish (as hinted by Aharoni, *LBHG,* 227) is untestable. The Chronicler adopts the genealogical formula "x the father of y" to describe the relationship between a community and its founder, so that the name is to be taken as that of a community rather than that of a person (so NEB).

ELMER DYCK

LECTIONARY. A lectionary is a collection of selected scriptural readings used in worship and arranged according to the liturgical year.

A. Early Jewish Lectionaries
B. Early Christian Lectionaries
   1. The Byzantine Lectionaries
   2. Construction and Text Sequence
   3. Origins and History of the Lection Systems
   4. Lectionaries of Other Regions of the Church
   5. Text-critical Value of the Lectionaries

A. Early Jewish Lectionaries

Evidence for the regular reading of the Law and the Prophets in worship during the 1st century C.E. is found in Josephus, Philo, and the NT. In *AgAp* 2.17.175, Josephus writes that Moses instituted the regular reading of the law. As the supreme form of instruction, the law was to be heard weekly in order that the assembled community should obtain a thorough and accurate knowledge of it. Philo (*Somn* II 18.127) also reflects an apparent sabbath practice of reading and expounding the holy books. In Acts 15:21, Luke states that Moses is ready every sabbath in the synagogues. Likewise, according to Acts 13:14–15 and Luke 4:16–17, the Law and the Prophets are read in the context of synagogue worship. Guilding (1960: 6) also cites the preface to Sirach as reflecting a 2d century B.C.E. practice in which the law was read publicly by Jews in Egypt. However, the precise meaning of this text is not clear. Even so, the evidence clearly points to regular readings from the Law and the Prophets in synagogue worship during the 1st century C.E. This practice certainly appears to derive from a much earlier date, but direct literary evidence is insufficient to document it.

It is less clear if these readings were conducted according to a fixed pattern or lectionary. By the time of the Mishnah, however, a regular pattern of readings is reflected (*m. Meg.* 3:4, 4:2–10). In *t. Meg.* 3:10 and *b. Meg.* 31b, the consecutive nature of the Torah readings for the sabbath afternoon, Monday, and Thursday services is indicated. Moreover, *m. Meg.* 4:10 and *t. Meg.* 3:4 imply that prophetic texts were also read according to a fixed pattern. *j. Meg.* 4:75a and *Sop.* 21:4 have been cited as evidence that Jewish tradition recognized stages in lectionary development (Guilding 1960: 8). In these texts, the lessons for the festivals and special sabbaths were thought to have been instituted by Moses, whereas the readings for the sabbath afternoons, Mondays, and Thursdays were considered to have been established by Ezra. From the beginning of the 3d century C.E., the evidence testifies to a regular pattern of readings from the Law and the Prophets in synagogue worship. However, the late date of this evidence makes its use, as witness to Jewish practice in the 1st century C.E. or earlier, methodologically problematic (Crockett 1966: 13–46; Heinemann 1968: 41–48; Morris 1964: 13–34).

Still unclear is the type of lectionary reflected in these Jewish texts. In *b. Meg.* 29b, it is written that the people of Palestine complete the reading of the Pentateuch in three years. Likewise, in *m. Meg.* 4:2–4, it states that the sabbath law is to be read by at least seven people, no one of whom may read fewer than three verses. Hence, the reading of the Law would consist of at least 21 verses. A lesson of this length read on each sabbath would correspond to a three-year cycle. It is indicated in *b. Meg.* 23a that the *Haftarah,* in order to correspond to the reading of the Law, should also consist of at least 21 verses. It may be that traces of a triennial lectionary can also be seen in the Masoretic divisions known as Sedarim, since these divisions accord roughly with a three-year cycle. It has also been argued that the Halakic Midrashim, *Mek., Sipra, Sipre,* reflect a Palestinian triennial lectionary (Guilding 1960: 9).

The starting date of this supposed lectionary (Nisan or Tishri) is also a matter of debate and conjecture (Büchler 1893: 420–68; 1894: 1–73; Guilding 1960: 11–20). Finally, Guilding argues that the hegemony of the Babylonian Gaonate eventually led to the replacement of the triennial lectionary by an annual lectionary in all but a few localities (1960: 8; cf. Crockett 1966: 23–24; Jacobs 1905: 254).

The arguments for a fixed triennial lectionary at an early date have been challenged. It has been noted that the NT does not mention a lectionary. Indeed, the evidence suggests that organized cycles of Sunday readings are not found in Christian circles until at least the 4th century (Dix 1945: 360–61). Furthermore, it is unclear whether the reference to three years in *b. Meg.* 29b is intended to be literal or approximate. There is no evidence that this cycle began at a fixed point or that it was used uniformly in all localities. If a lack of uniformity existed in the Amoraic period and perhaps later, it is argued that more could not be expected of an earlier period (Crockett 1966: 13–35; Heinemann 1968: 41–48; Morris 1964: 15–34). Hence, the topic of early Jewish lectionaries has provoked considerable debate.

Bibliography

Büchler, A. 1893. The Reading of the Law and Prophets in a Triennial Cycle. *JQR* 5: 420–68.

———. 1894. The Reading of the Law and Prophets in a Triennial Cycle. *JQR* 6: 1–73.

Crockett, L. 1966. Luke IV.16–30 and the Jewish Lectionary Cycle: A Word of Caution. *JJS* 17: 13–46.

Dix, G. 1945. *The Shape of the Liturgy.* London.

Guilding, A. 1960. *The Fourth Gospel and Jewish Worship.* Oxford.

Heinemann, J. 1968. The Triennial Lectionary Cycle. *JJS* 19: 41–48.

Jacobs, J. 1905. Triennial Cycle. *JEnc* 12: 254–57.

Morris, L. 1964. *The New Testament and the Jewish Lectionaries.* London.

JAMES W. AAGESON

B. Early Christian Lectionaries

1. The Byzantine Lectionaries. The liturgical books which the Greek Orthodox Church uses to this day include, along with the fixed and variable parts of liturgies and other offices, *to euaggelion* (in contrast to the *tetraeuaggelon,* the normal ms of the Gospels) and *ho apostolos,* occasionally combined into *to apostoloeuaggelon.* All of these books stand in a fixed tradition of content and form which reaches back to the early Middle Ages and thus well into the time of the tradition of manuscripts.

Thus it is that altogether almost 40 percent of all extant Gk mss of the NT also belong to these liturgical books. These liturgical mss with NT texts are collected under the designation *Lectionaries* and are listed independently. These represent an alternative to those mss (and accordingly to those text editions) which attach to consecutive offerings of verses in the NT information about the days on which the indicated Gospel or Epistle sections are to be read in worship. Whereas these latter editions always appear as an index, in which the sequence of the days of the church year and references to NT pericopes to be read are collected, the lectionaries offer, instead, exactly in the sequence according to which they are to be read, the actual text of NT passages.

A prerequisite for the emergence of such lectionaries is firm ecclesial organization which regulates the sequence of the celebrations of the church year, the liturgical arrangement of these celebrations, and the determination of Bible texts, prayers, hymns, etc. to be read. However, for historical reasons, such organization is nowhere imaginable before the 4th century. But since 95 percent of the 2,252 extant lectionary mss and fragments, i.e., over 2,000, show uniform arrangement in reference to the succession of days and celebrations and to the choice of pericopes, something more must stand behind these mss: a world church, such as it arose from the 5th to the 7th century in the Byzantine church with its center in Constantinople, dominant for Eastern Christianity.

2. Construction and Text Sequence. The succession of days in these Byzantine lectionaries conforms, of course, to the church year. Beginning with Easter Sunday and continuing for the holy season up to Pentecost, pericopes from Acts and John are offered for each day, including the weekdays. For the subsequent time lasting 16 or 17 weeks through September 14 (Holy Cross Day), the majority of lectionaries offer readings for Saturdays and Sundays *(sabbatokyriakar)* from Matthew and Pauline Epistles. Thereupon follows a similar 17-week period, up through the end of January or beginning of February and the pre-Lenten season, with readings for Saturdays and Sundays from Paul and Luke. It is otherwise in both of these latter periods with the mss intended for use in cloisters, for, since the liturgy is celebrated daily, the mss show readings for all days. In this case the Pauline Epistles as well as Matthew and Luke do not suffice, whereupon, in each period from the 12th or 13th week on are offered also readings mostly from Mark; and at the end of these periods are offered from the *Apostolos* readings from the Catholic Epistles.

During Lent *(tessarakostē)* the liturgy with the sacrifice of the mass is only celebrated on weekends; whereupon, for these days there are only NT texts, which come predominantly from Hebrews and Mark. On the weekdays, with the liturgy of previously consecrated elements *(prohēgiasmenōn),* the OT is read, which the rest of the time only finds use in other offices. During Holy Week, with its special, daily celebrations, up to Easter Eve, the Passion narratives of the Gospels are read.

Regularly following this cycle (the so-called *Synaxarion*), which is dependent upon the variable period of Easter, is a second cycle fixed on dates, beginning with the Byzantine new year on September 1. This series of days (known as *Menologion*) offers readings for a fixed calendar of celebrations of the Lord, Mary, and mainly the Apostles (e.g. Christmas, Epiphany, the Annunciation, Saints Peter and Paul). This cycle later expanded to include the many celebrations of the fathers, saints, and martyrs. Standard pericopes were predominantly read for these, which were then only notated, since they were, as a rule, already transcribed.

Combinations of readings and references for "special occasions" *(eis diaphorous mnēmas),* i.e. celebrations of explicitly local character or the pastoral offices (burial, etc), complete the Byzantine lectionaries.

3. Origins and History of the Lection Systems. The assignation of pericopes to reading cycles and individual celebrations is characteristic for the history of the origins of the lection systems and should be explained with reference to the development of Gospel pericopes in the Byzantine church. It is doubtless the case that for the central celebrations of Christendom, along with their preparatory celebrations and afterwards, germane pericopes were read: the baptism narrative for Epiphany (January 6—celebrated in the East into the fourth and fifth centuries with a function analogous to Christmas in the West), Luke 1:24ff for other high feasts such as the central celebration of Mary on March 25 *(annuntiatio, euaggelismos),* etc. Here one sees certainly the oldest stratum of the pericope system. The same obtains for the celebration of the Passion with its several modes of celebration in different regions of the Church.

Along with this basic situation with regard to pericopes, which is widely similar in all spheres of the Church, certain documents or groups of documents are read at certain times of the year in consonance with synagogue usage, as is evidenced in the homilies of the Church Fathers. Later, with the further evolution of the lection system, issues the determination of fixed reading sequences, first for Sundays, the weekly celebration of the resurrection of Christ. The Byzantine church affixed pericopes from John to the weeks after Easter, pericopes from Matthew to the weeks after Pentecost, and pericopes from Luke to the time from September on. These Sunday sequences offer in the unfolding of the Gospels the most important depictions from the life of Jesus or central addresses. Certainly for the Saturday celebrations of the liturgy during the same periods of time a series of pericopes from the same Gospels were chosen, a form of sequential reading of selected pericopes in the order of the book (so-called *Bahnlesung*), omitting texts already used.

The remainder of the text of the Gospels is used for pericopes which are read, principally in cloisters, in the liturgies on the rest of the weekdays, except during the weeks when the Gospel of John is read.

It can be demonstrated from the nature of pericope choices and from the bounded tradition in the lectionaries that the phases above are also a matter of successive historical developments which extend into the 7th and 8th centuries. Theologians have long falsely regarded the temporal order of these stages of development, setting it into premature times. C. R. Gregory identified temporal developments and maintained that he was able to place them from the beginning to the end of the 2d century. American lectionary scholars (who for a long time worked alone in the study of lectionaries, e.g., K. and S. Lake, E. C. Colwell, B. M. Metzger, A. Wikgren, and their students) modified this position and claimed to be able to date the Byzantine lectionary system from the 4th or 5th century. A. Ehrhard and the Hagiographies and, then, OT scholar A. Rahlfs proved that the concluding formation of the Byzantine lection system must have lasted into the early 8th century, an opinion which is fully substantiated by the age of extant manuscripts. That the book of Revelation was not used in the Byzantine lection system also is not contradictory. The book was recognized as canonical in the East from the 4th century, but it has its own tradition and history which make it quite independent of NT manuscripts.

The arrangement of pericopes in the lectionaries displays some peculiarities. After a standard introductory formula (*tō kairō ekeinō, eipen ho kyrios, adelphoi,* or the like), follow most often changes in the text's form. These are to acquaint the hearer with pertinent details of the reading which one otherwise could glean from the context. Occasionally at the end of the lection special key words are appended. Connectors of insertions or harmony-like combinations of the narratives of different Gospels also occur. Many of these details found their way into the mss of the continuous text.

4. Lectionaries of Other Regions of the Church. The

discovery in 1975 at the Sinai Cloister of ten new lectionaries has issued in new insights and points of view regarding the contruction of the lection system and of lectionaries. These Gk mss did not evidence the Byzantine system as was supposed, although they assumed the outward appearance of the Byzantine lectionaries. It was striking that these lectionaries offered only one cycle and that they inserted movable feasts, celebrations, and weeks of fasting between celebrations on fixed dates, using only Sunday readings. Between Easter and Pentecost, but with other demarcations, one reads from John; the following sixteen Sundays utilize pericopes from Matthew, the next fourteen Sundays readings from Mark, and the six Sundays in Lent the gospel of Luke.

It is further obvious that the readings for Easter and Eastertide are offered in connection with Holy Week. All told the sequence of pericopes, at the end of which stand pericopes for special occasions, proceeds one and a half times during the year. Because all witnesses are damaged at the beginning and at the end and differ in detail from one another, a uniform beginning (sometime in the spring) or end of the church year cannot be identified as is the case with the Byzantine lectionaries.

However, these new lectionaries, as well as others which were earlier already regarded as "outsider" mss, show some commonalities with the lection system from Jerusalem, which at that time was only extant in Armenian and Georgian manuscripts. This holds for the succession of celebrations as well as for the selection of pericopes. But as the Georgian lectionaries represent a later stage of development in relation to the Armenian lectionaries, so also the newfound Gk lectionaries in relation to the Georgian lectionaries. Their derivation from Jerusalem, however, is clear and can be shown with reference to the sequence of pericopes—their demarcations as well as rich arrangement for Holy Week. Indeed there is also a certain influence from Byzantium, especially in the externals such as introductory formulas and organization of the mss, which were written in the time from the late 8th century to the early 10th century.

A first publication of a sequence of pericopes from a comparable ms by G. Garitte in 1977 drew little notice. By virtue of the newfound lectionaries, this article has come into its own; however, a comprehensive discussion of the issues will be possible only after the publication of the Sinai lectionaries.

The Byzantine influence in these newfound lectionaries becomes ever more apparent, since one observes the following curiosities: in four of the new Sinai lectionaries there is a succession of days typical of the Jerusalem lection system, with its juxtaposition of fixed-date and movable feasts which continue beyond the bounds of Easter; and there are pericopes which display the specific delineation of the Byzantine lection system. The mss date from the time from the 11th to 13th centuries.

Besides the two groups there are in the list of lectionary mss witnesses that are not to be associated with the Byzantine lection system. Rather, these mss demonstrate an open relationship to Egypt—either they are bilingual Greek-Coptic or demonstrably discovered in Egypt. These display a prototype of the Coptic lection system, so also the few papyri (also from the sands of Egypt) with text that is not written progressively, offering only pericopes: P1 (papyrus Florence, 3d century), P3 (papyrus Vienna, 6th to 7th century), P6 (papyrus Strasbourg, 4th century), P34 (papyrus Vienna, 6th century), and P44 (papyrus New York, 6th to 7th century).

5. Text-critical Value of the Lectionaries. Miraculous text-critical worth has long been expected of the lectionaries, since their date of origin was at one time set too early, and also because it was maintained, on the basis of general experience and scanty examination, that all of the elements related to the liturgy, closely conditioned by tradition, must also preserve in the lectionaries the reading style of the earliest times. The systematic examination of the lectionaries in Chicago in the 1930's had a sobering effect. Certainly the early Byzantine reading styles determined the textual character of certain series of pericopes in the Byzantine lectionaries, which led some to maintain that the lectionaries were related to the so-called Caesarea text. The basic character of the text, however, is Byzantine. This obtains for the readings from the *Apostolos* as well. Therefore, the lectionaries have text-critical worth only for later tradition history, in specific, for the history of Byzantine texts.

The early Byzantine, and even pre-Byzantine, elements in the lectionaries with the late Jerusalem lection system support.this set of suppositions. More accurate details can be expected only after the publication of the new Sinai mss, a joint venture of the Hiera Synod of Sinai Monks and the Institut fuer neutestamentliche Wissenschaft, Muenster. See TEXTUAL CRITICISM (NT).

Bibliography

Aland, B., and Aland, K. 1989. *The Text of the New Testament.* Grand Rapids.

Aland, K. 1963. *Kurzgefasste Liste der griechischen Handschriften des Neuen Testaments.* ANTF 1. Berlin.

Garitte, G. 1977. Un évangéliaire grec-arabe du Xe siècle. Pp. 207–25 in *Studia codicologia,* ed. K. Treu. TU 124. Berlin.

Gregory, C. R. 1909. *Textkritik des Neuen Testamentes.* Leipzig.

Junack, K. 1972. Zu den griechischen Lektionare und ihrer Ueberlieferung der Katholischen Briefe. Pp. 498–591 in *Die alten Übersetzungen des Neuen Testaments, die Kirchenvaeterzitate und Lektionare,* ed. K. Aland. ANTF 5. Berlin.

Metzger, B. M. 1972. Greek Lectionaries and a Critical Edition of the New Testament. Pp. 479–97 in *Die alten Übersetzungen des Neuen Testaments, die Kirchenvaeterzitate und Lektionare,* ed. K. Aland. ANTF 5. Berlin.

Scriverner, F. H. 1894. *A Plain Introduction to the Criticism of the New Testament.* Vol. 1. 4th ed., ed. E. Miller. London.

Wikgren, A. 1963. Chicago Studies in the Greek Lectionary of the New Testament. Pp. 96–121 in *Biblical and Patristic Studies in Memory of R. P. Casey,* ed. J. N. Birdsall and R. W. Thompson. Freiburg.

KLAUS JUNACK
Trans. Ronald B. Thomas, Jr.

LEEKS. See FLORA.

LEFT, LEFT HAND. The Hebrew word *śĕmōʾl* indicates the left, the left side, or the left hand. It is used often with *yāmîn* to form a pair, left and right. When used as a general direction, left referred to north (Gen 14:15; Josh 19:27), the direction to one's left when one faced east.

There are a few instances where left has a negative connotation: "A wise man's heart inclines him toward the right, but a fool's heart toward the left" (Eccl 10:2). Likewise the separation of the sheep from the goats in Matthew 25, may suggest a negative connotation for the left: the goats who are to be condemned are placed on the left, while the sheep who are to be blessed are placed on the right. But most often neither right nor left is given a special connotation. In many cases, the path is a straight one from which one is not to depart, either to the right or to the left (Deut 5:32).

Left-handedness was unusual in ancient Israel, as in our culture. Few references are made to ones who were left-handed. In general, the right hand was primary, holding the major weapon, while the left hand held the defensive weapon. The right hand held the sword while the left held the shield. The right hand held the arrow and pulled the cord, while the left hand held the bow. Some specially skilled warriors were trained to use their left hand, thus giving them an advantage in combat situations. As such they were not natural left-handers, but had their right hands bound so that they were forced to become ambidextrous. Ehud was one such ambidextrous warrior. Because he could use the left hand as well as the right, he was able to hide his weapon and assassinate Eglon, king of Moab, striking him from the unexpected left side (Halpern 1988: 41; cf. EHUD). Among the warriors of Benjamin were 700 left-handed warriors (Judg 20:16), likewise ambidextrous.

Bibliography

Halpern, B. 1988. *The First Historians.* New York.

JOEL F. DRINKARD, JR.

LEGATE. See PALESTINE, ADMINISTRATION OF (ROMAN).

LEGION [Gk *legiōn*]. See ROMAN ARMY.

LEHABIM [Heb *lĕhābîm*]. Var. LUBIM. Descendants of Egypt according to the Table of Nations (Gen 10:13; cf. 1 Chr 1:11) who, according to the genealogies, is a son of Ham and grandson of Noah. While not direct, Semitic kinsmen of Israel, their association with Israel's powerful Egyptian neighbor make them a significant people to the writers of the genealogies. The Hebrew form of the name in the MT is not found outside these genealogies, so no further information is available. There is a widely held view that this is an alternate spelling of *lûbîm.* These are the Libyans, who are mentioned elsewhere in the OT (Nah 3:9; Dan 11:43; 2 Chr 12:3; 16:8). They lived in N Africa, immediately W of Egypt, so would geographically fit their position in the genealogies. The proposed reading is supported by the rendering of the name in the LXX.

DAVID W. BAKER

LEHEM (PLACE) [Heb *leḥem*]. A possible place name somewhere in the territory of the tribe of Judah, and is so rendered by the RSV (1 Chr 4:22). However, no such place has been identified. The name appears in a recorded event concerning two Judahites, Joash and Saraph, who had returned to Judah after a period of having ruled in Moab (or possibly having married Moabites). The Heb *wĕyāšubî lāḥem* presents some difficulty since various translations are possible.

1. It can be taken as a personal name, Jashubi Lehem, as done by the KJV, NKJV, NASB, and NIV. The verse would then read ". . . Joash and Saraph who ruled in Moab and Jashubi Lehem." Such a reading, however, does not simplify the identification and perhaps creates further ambiguity as to whether Jashubi Lehem is a place's or person's name.

2. As has been suggested, perhaps the phrase is not even a name but should be emended as evidenced in the Gk *apestrepsen autous.* The Hebrew would then read *wayyāšubû lāhem,* "but they returned" (lit. "returned to themselves"). Thus the verse would read ". . . Joash and Saraph, who ruled in Moab, but returned." Similar idioms or idiomatic forms are attested in Num 22:34; Deut 5:30; and 1 Sam 26:12.

3. Lehem in this verse could possibly be a shortened form of Bethlehem, as so rendered by the JB and TEV. If so, the verse would read ". . . Joash and Saraph, who ruled in Moab and returned to Bethlehem." This reading would appear to fit the Judahite context of the verse better.

4. Another possibility is to consider Lehem as a geographical name and to emend the reading to *wĕyōšbê leḥem,* "and the inhabitants of Lehem." The probability of this reading is enforced by the presence of *wĕyōšbê* and *yāšbû* in v 23 (cf. *ʾanšê rēkāh* of 1 Chr 4:12).

5. It is also possible to read *wĕyōšbê leḥem,* "and the inhabitants of bread," to parallel *weyōšbê nĕṭāʿîm,* "and the inhabitants of planters," in v 23. Both *leḥem* and *nĕṭāʿîm* should then be treated as names of agricultural districts for the royal workers.

WANN M. FANWAR

LEHI (PLACE) [Heb *leḥî*]. An unknown location, it appears in the Bible as a geographical designation in Judg 15:9, 14, 17, 19. (Otherwise *leḥî* appears in the Scriptures 21 times referring to the cheek, jawbone of a human being or an animal.) It is situated along the Philistine frontier and the lowland of the tribe of Judah, a site where the Judeans surrendered Samson to the Philistines. The place name also ties in with the description of Samson's exploits: slaying a thousand Philistines with the jawbone of a deadly donkey, and the miracle performed by God to quench Samson's thirst.

The Judeo-Aramaic variants *leḥî; lĕḥāyat; lihyāʾ; lĕḥāytāʾ;* and Arabic *laḥy(un)* are cognate with the biblical *leḥî.* Generally, the words are translated as "cheek," "jawbone." Yet, the connection of the biblical form and the variety of the Judeo-Aramaic forms with the Akk *lītu* or *lētu(m)* suggests a wider range of meanings. The Akkadian adds also the connotations of the "side" and metaphorically "side of an object," and "side of a topographical feature."

These meanings, while prevalent in the Targumim and Rabbinical sources, have never been utilized.

Scholars tended to view *leḥî* in Judges as a geographical place name. Among the prominent suggestions for a possible identification are Khirbet Lāqīya (M.R. 136081) close to Beer-sheba and Beit Jibrin (M.R. 140112). Both, however, are much too far from the place where Samson engaged the Philistines. Likewise, Abel's (*GP,* 369) proposal of Beit ᶜAṭāb is also farfetched. The most prevalent identification is with Kh. eṣ-Ṣiyyāgh (M.R. 149128) at the mouth of Wādi en-Najīl 2 km S of ᶜArtūf and 7 km E of Timnah. The meaning of the Arabic place name is "the Ruin of the Goldsmiths." The assumption is that the Arabic place name eṣ-Ṣiyyāgh represents the word *siagōn,* the Greek cognate of the Hebrew term *leḥî,* "cheek" "jaw," which appears in the Greek translations of Aquila, Symmachus, and in Jerome's Latin translation of Eusebius' *Onomasticon.* However, the resemblance of sound between the first two syllables even if possible to indicate relationship between the Greek word and the place name obviously represents a later tradition from post-OT times transmitted through Greek-speaking people and Christians. Further, there is no indication that the Greek translators perceived *siagōn* to mean a place name rather than a mere translation of the Hebrew word. Indeed Josephus (*Ant* 5 §300), who refers to *siagōn* as a place name, expressly says: "a spot which today is called *siagōn* = jawbone . . . but which of old was nameless." This leaves the above suggestion topographically valueless.

Taking another direction, Burney (*Judges* LBS, 371) suggests that *leḥî* is a geological formation reminiscent of a jawbone. He proposed the sawlike teeth appearance of Wādi Ismaᶜīn, a possible location since it may resemble a jawbone, but his evidence remains inconclusive.

The consensus among the scholars then is that *leḥî* denotes a specific place but there is no agreement as to its identification. Accordingly, it makes sense to seek the meaning of the word elsewhere. The neglected collateral evidence of the Akkadian sources is an essential clue for providing an alternative meaning for the term *leḥî.*

The Akkadian turns of speech in which the term *lītu* occurs show that metaphorically the cheek or the lower jawbone are employed for "border" or "limit" or "circumference." It is current in Akkadian literary sources and has been established as employing the metaphorical meanings by C. H. Gordon (1936: 81–2). It was the practice of the Nuzians to describe topographical features in terms of the lower facial part. Thus when they depict the beginning of the city limits they use the term "*le-et,*" "jawbone" of the city. In the same vein, a boundary of a parcel of real estate transfer is described as "along the "cheek" (i.e., "bank") of the PN canal." *Litu* therefore is an essential word in recording limits in the Nuzian legal documents. It seems that biblical *leḥî* follows its Akkadian forerunner. Accordingly, *leḥî* as a place is not a specific place name, but, as its Nuzian prototype, means any border—in this case the entire borderline between the Judeans and the Philistines.

Further, it is significant that in all passages where biblical *leḥî* connotes the physical cheek, jawbone, the Targumim substitute the biblical *leḥi* with a different Aramaic term.

Judeo-Aramaic variants of *leḥî,* however, are employed only in translating biblical terms associated with limits of districts or borders. It is only in Judges 15 and specifically in reference to *leḥî* (which according to the Targum designates a regional geographical description) that the Targum is meticulous in employing the biblical term *leḥî,* which resembles mostly its cognate *lētu* phonetically as well as semantically.

It also stands to reason that the deployment of Philistine troops is along the entire border rather than in a specific location. The proposal gains cogency from the use of the verb *wayyinnāṭēšû* (Judg 15:9) "they were deployed." The only other employment of the verb *nṭš* in the *Nipᶜal* in warfare occurs in 2 Sam 5:17;22 where the Philistines deploy troops over a wide geographical region to seize David, just as in the present case they spread out their soldiers to capture Samson. There and here *nṭš* is characteristic of army deployment for searching a specific foe (i.e., David and Samson) rather than for a siege of a particular location. Furthermore, the Masoretic pointing of the word *balleḥî* (Judg 15:9,19) definitely implies a common noun rather than a proper noun of a place. Thus enigmatic *leḥî* embraces an old meaning already embedded in its Akkadian precursor *lītu.*

Bibliography

Gordon, C. H. 1936. *Nouns In the Nuzi Tablets.* Paris.

Jastrow, M. 1943. *A Dictionary of the Targumim, the Talmud Babli and Yerushalmi, and the Midrashic Literature.* New York.

Schick, C. 1887. Artuf und seine Umgebung. *ZDPV* 10: 131–59.

MEIR LUBETSKI

LEHUN (M.R. 231097). A site located in the Madaba district (biblical Moab), on the N plateau of the Wadi Mojib (biblical Arnon), 7 km SE of Dhiban (biblical Dibon) and 3 km E of Ara'ir (biblical Aroer). The site, measuring 1100 m (N–S) by 600 m (E–W), has been excavated by a Belgian team directed by Dr. P. Naster (1977–84) and Dr. D. Homès-Fredericq (1977–88).

A chalcolithic settlement is attested by a number of surface flints and a few sherds. An EB I A-B tomb (ca. 3200–3100 B.C.) was found at the edge of the plateau in area B3. More than 130 ceramics, often undamaged, were discovered in a layer of 40 cm height. They can be compared with the pottery found in the cemetery of Bab edh-Dhra of the same period. An EB settlement in area C1 has still to be excavated (Homès-Fredericq 1986: 87–94).

At the end of the LB Age, an extensive village was located in area D: houses with ovens, silos, cooking pots, and storage jars, as well as a scarab of the 20th dynasty, were excavated. In the S part, chosen for its strategic position overlooking the Arnon valley toward the Dead Sea, the LB houses were levelled in the beginning of the Iron Age: their walls were used as foundations for a fortress (measuring 33–37 m [E–W] by 43 m [N–S]), built probably at the same period as the settlements of Balu'ah, Ader, and Medeniyeh. This fortification system may reflect the need of the Moabite kings to protect their possessions from the invasions mentioned in the Bible and from nomadic tribes.

The large amount of storage jars found in it suggests its use as a storage fortress, possibly built to supply the garrisons of Ara'ir. The breaks in the fortification walls and the filling in of the casemate rooms with stones attest different attacks of the building. A new year's bottle of the Saite period (7th–6th century B.C.) shows that Lehun was once more in contact with Egypt (Homès-Fredericq 1982).

The N part of the site seems to have been important in the Nabataean period both as an agricultural market and as a religious center: a square Nabataean temple (with sides measuring 6.25 m), built of local limestone, is decorated with the embossed technique popular in Palestine during the 1st century A.D. (Homès-Fredericq 1989). The pottery remains corroborate this date. An altar measuring 2 × 1.25 m, leaning to the E wall, shows a typical oriental pattern. In the 1988 season the temple was restored to a height of 3.4 m. A larger building in sector A1 (unexcavated) probably belongs to the same period.

A Byzantine or Early Islamic bell-shaped cistern has been discovered near an Islamic settlement in area A2, on the W slope of the wadi Lehun. A small road separates the presumed Islamic village from a late Mamluk mosque (15th century A.D.). A coin, discovered on the floor, gives a *post quem* dating for the mosque as after the late 14th century A.D.

Remains of Late Islamic walls and Ottoman houses and pipes show that the village of Lehun has been continuously occupied up until modern times.

Bibliography

Homès-Fredericq, D., and Hennessy, J. B. 1986–89. *Archaeology of Jordan.* Vols. 1–2. Louvain.

Homès-Fredericq, D. 1982. Un goulot de bouteille de Nouvel An trouvé à Lehun (Jordanie). Vol. 2, pp. 79–90 in *Studia Paulo Naster Oblata.* OLA 13. Louvain.

———. 1986. Lehun. In *Pottery and Potters: Past and Present,* ed. D. Homès-Fredericq and H. Franken. Tübingen.

———. 1989. Un temple nabatéen à Lehun (Jordanie). Vol. 2, pp. 575–80 in *Archaologia Iranica et Orientalis,* ed. L. de Meyer and E. Haerinck. Gent.

Denyse Homès-Fredericq

LEJJŪN (M.R. 228072). A site located in biblical Moab, ca. 40 km E of the Dead Sea at an elevation of ca. 700 m above sea level. A perennial spring feeds the Wadi Lejjūn, a tributary of the Wadi Mūjib. The site lies in a shallow valley surrounded by low hills on all sides but the E. Although situated near the edge of the desert, the site receives rainfall sufficient for dry farming of wheat in winter.

The earliest settlement now attested at Lejjūn is a substantial fortified city of the EB Age, as yet unexcavated. Kh. el-Fityān, a Roman *castellum* 1.5 km NW of the spring, seems to have been built over a Moabite fort. In the early Roman period, a Nabatean watchpost (Rujm Beni Yasser) was constructed on a hill 1.5 km E of the spring. Occupation resumed ca. A.D. 300 with the construction of a Roman legionary fortress for *legio IV Martia,* the smaller *castellum* of Fityān, and the reoccupation and reconstruction of Yasser. The site was then known as "Betthorus," if the commonly held identification is accepted, and was a key element in the Roman fortified frontier, the *Limes Arabicus.* The *limes* was intended to control the incursions of neighboring nomadic Arab tribes from the desert. The modern Arabic name, "Lejjūn," seems to be an Arabic corruption of the Latin *"legio."*

Excavations begun in 1980 by the Limes Arabicus Project have examined the legionary fortress, Fityān, Yasser, and the Roman forts of Qaṣr Bshīr, 15 km NE of Lejjūn, and Daʿjāniya, 75 km S of Lejjūn.

The rectangular legionary fortress (242 × 190 m, 4.6 hectares) is typical of Roman military architecture. The main building materials were limestone, chert, and basalt. The enclosure wall is pierced by four gates, one in the middle of each wall. Twenty U-shaped interval towers and four circular angle towers project from the wall. A major street *(via praetoria)* extends from the E gate to the center of the fortress; another major street *(via principalis)* runs from the N gate to the S and meets the *via praetoria* in the center of the fortress. Here is situated the headquarters building (*principia;* 63.5 × 52.5 m). This building consists of a large outer courtyard, a transverse inner courtyard, and a range of official rooms in the rear, including offices and the *aedes* or shrine of the legionary standards. The *aedes* is entered through a monumental entrance that once contained a barred iron gate, which permitted soldiers to view the sacred legionary standards, but insured the security of the shrine.

The E half of the fortress is devoted to long blocks of barracks. Their plan suggests an original legionary complement of 2,000 men. After an earthquake in 363, the original barracks were demolished and replaced by only half the former number, suggesting a reduction of 50 percent in the size of the legion in the late 4th century. The barracks have yielded evidence about the equipment, diet, and activities of the rank and file Roman legionaries.

A church is located within the fortress near the N gate. It appears to have been erected about 500 and was destroyed by the earthquake of 551. It is basilical in plan (24 × 13 m) with a narthex, apse, and sacristy. The church is small and rather shoddy, even by the modest standards of Transjordan. It lacks marble, mosaics, and frescoes. The date of the church and other evidence suggest that the bulk of the legion converted rather late to Christianity. Moreover, the pagan cult of the standards in the *principia* appears to have survived into the early 6th century.

Outside the fortress an extensive *vicus* or civilian settlement grew up. A large rectangular structure (35 × 28 m) excavated in the western *vicus* apparently served as a *mansio* or inn. It was built early in the 4th century, but was destroyed by the earthquake of 363. In the E *vicus* a Roman temple has been excavated; it also was built about A.D. 300 and testifies to the paganism of the original garrison.

A complex of hydrological installations is associated with the fortress, including a dam that conserved the outflow of the spring, two water channels that extended from the spring to the fortress, and a reservoir within the fortress.

Soundings at Kh. el-Fityān revealed a much smaller fort or *castellum* atop the steep N bank of the Wadi Lejjūn. The fort commands an excellent view in all directions and probably served as the hub of an observation and signaling system radiating from Lejjūn. The fort was erected contemporaneously with the legionary fortress about A.D. 300 and was occupied until the 5th century.

The watchpost of Rujm Beni Yasser, originally a Nabatean foundation of the 1st century B.C. or A.D., was reoccupied and enlarged by the Roman legionaries ca. 300. Like Fityān, it served as a component of the signaling system until abandoned during the 5th century.

The legionary fortress was built in the reign of Diocletian (284–305) as part of a massive military buildup in this sector of the frontier against nomadic Arab raids. There is as yet little direct evidence that the garrison evolved into *limitanei,* or hereditary peasant militia, as implied by the *Codex Theodosianus* in the early 5th century. Another earthquake in 502 damaged the barracks and the *principia.* The final occupation in the early 6th century suggests a reduced and rather rundown garrison. The ancillary posts, such as Fityān, Yasser, and Bshīr, were now abandoned. This may be associated with the demobilization of some *limitanei* by Justinian along the eastern frontier ca. 530. A final earthquake in 551 ended ancient occupation of the site.

Bibliography

Brünnow, R., and Domaszewski, A. von. 1905. *Die Provincia Arabia,* 2. Strasburg.
Glueck, N. 1934. Explorations in Eastern Palestine, I. Pp. 1–114 in AASOR 14. Philadelphia.
Parker, S. T. 1986. *Romans and Saracens.* ASORDS 6. Winona Lake, IN.
———. 1987. *The Roman Frontier in Central Jordan.* BARIS 340. Oxford.
———. 1990. Preliminary Report on the 1987 Season of the Limes Arabicus Project. *BASORSup* 26: 89–136.

S. THOMAS PARKER

LEMUEL (PERSON) [Heb *lĕmûʾēl*]. The king of Massa, whose words (received from his mother) are recorded in Proverbs 31. Virtually nothing is known of Lemuel except that his territory or tribe was Massa (31:1). Massa is listed among Ishmael's "descendants" (Gen 25:14), but its location remains uncertain. See AGUR; MASSA. Keil and Delitzsch identified it as either N Arabia or a region in the Hauran mountains (1873: 263). Some interpreters read the Heb *massāʾ* as "burden/oracle" rather than a place name. Keil and Delitzsch, however, pointed out that the designation "oracle" normally identifies a speech conveying God's judgment (261), and there is no hint of judgment in this passage. The name, "Lemuel" has been understood as a symbolic reference to Solomon (for the meaning of the name, see W. McKane *Proverbs* OTL, 408). Jewish rabbis translated it literally, "towards God" which was understood as a name for Solomon, according to Cohen (*Proverbs* SonB, 209). This could be related to the otherwise obscure LXX reading ("spoken *by God*"), where "Lemuel" has been translated rather than recognized as a proper name.

Bibliography

Keil, C. F., and Delitzsch, F. 1873. *Biblical Commentary on the Proverbs of Solomon.* Vol. 2. Grand Rapids. (ET 1950).

DONALD K. BERRY

LEND. See INTEREST AND USURY IN THE GRECO-ROMAN PERIOD.

LEOPARD. See ZOOLOGY.

LEPROSY. A disease in humans (also known as Hansen's disease) caused by the bacillus *Mycobacterium leprae.* This term "leprosy" is commonly used (more for convenience than medical accuracy) as a translation of Hebrew *ṣāraʿat* in the OT and Gk *lepra* in the NT. Scholars now generally agree that OT *ṣāraʿat* is not leprosy nor does it include it and that NT *lepra,* if it refers at all to leprosy, does so only as one among many skin conditions. See also SICKNESS AND DISEASE. This discussion will use the transliterations *ṣāraʿat* or *lepra* when speaking of the biblical condition and reserve the term leprosy for true leprosy. *ṣāraʿat* in the OT describes phenomenologically discrete lesions or defects which are found on human skin, in fabrics (cloth and leather), and on walls of houses. *lepra* in the NT is used of human skin diseases, following the OT tradition.

A. In the OT
  1. Scientific Diagnostic Suppositions
    a. In persons
    b. In fabrics and houses
  2. Sin and *ṣāraʿat*
  3. Pollution Effect
  4. Purification Rites
  5. Why is *ṣāraʿat* Impure?
B. In the NT

A. In the OT

The major discussion of *ṣāraʿat* is in Leviticus 13–14 of the Priestly legislation (= P) of the Pentateuch. Lev 13:1–46 treats the diagnosis of the condition in people; 13:47–59 treats its diagnosis in fabrics; 14:1–32 contains the prescriptions for the purification of people after recovering from the condition; and 14:33–53 discusses the diagnosis of the condition in houses and purification after their renovation. (Lev 14:54–57 is a titular subscript to both chapters.) P discusses *ṣāraʿat* elsewhere in Lev 22:4 and Num 5:2. Outside P, the condition is discussed in Exod 4:6–7; Num 12:10–15; Deut 24:8; 2 Sam 3:29; 2 Kgs 5:1–27; 7:3–10; 15:5 = 2 Chr 26:16–21. It is unclear if Job's ailment (Job 2:7–13) is to be considered *ṣāraʿat* (cf. 18:13).

1. Scientific Diagnostic Suppositions. a. In Persons. A major concern of scholars has been to describe what *ṣāraʿat* is scientifically. While they agree that in fabrics and houses it is a fungal growth, they have been slower in coming to a consensus about what the lesions or infections in humans are from a medical point of view. This situation is mainly due to problematic terminology in Leviticus 13–14 (such as *śĕʾēt, sappahat, baheret* [all types of inflammations, cf. 13:2, etc.]; *ʿāmōq/šāpāl* "deep" [what is meant by this is unclear; cf. 13:3, 4, 20, 21, etc.]; *kēhâ/kēhê* "fade (?); faint, dull (?)" [cf. 13:6, 21, 26, etc.]). This terminology can only be properly understood after a medical diagnosis of the conditions has been made; it cannot be a priori a major aid for determining what diseases the prescriptions intend.

Another problem in diagnosing *ṣāraʿat* is that the narratives and laws only give a very general description of the lesions. Even the detailed text of Leviticus 13 gives only enough description of the lesions that constitute *ṣāraʿat* so that a given condition may be determined to be pure or impure. They do not give full medical descriptions. This lack of description often allows for only broad, nonspecific, and consequently somewhat tentative conclusions (cf. Sussman 1967: 209–10). And finally, in some places P gives symptoms that are plainly undiagnosable according to modern medical knowledge.

Despite these problems, scholars have reached some agreement about the probable diagnosis of *ṣāraʿat* in humans. The most certain conclusion is that it is not leprosy and does not include it. The main argument for this is that the symptoms Leviticus describes do not suggest leprosy:

(1) The symptoms of leprosy progress very slowly over a period of several years. The swift development of *ṣāraʿat* required by quarantine periods of seven days (Lev 13:4, 5, 21, 26, 31, 33) does not fit leprosy.

(2) Leprosy is not curable without drug therapy; but Leviticus 13–14 indicate that a person may recover from *ṣāraʿat.*

(3) Leprosy is not primarily an exfoliative disease as is the case with *ṣāraʿat.*

(4) Though leprosy in darker skinned people could show hypopigmentation of the skin, the hair does not characteristically turn white or yellow as is required for some types of *ṣāraʿat* (Lev 13:3, 10, 20, 25, 30).

(5) Leprosy is not associated with boils or blisters (the meaning of *šĕḥîn* is uncertain) and burns as a secondary manifestation (Lev 13:18–23, 24–28).

(6) One symptom of advanced leprosy is the loss of feeling accompanying nerve destruction. Leviticus 13 does not discuss such a prominent symptom.

(7) And Leviticus 13 does not discuss the necrosis and destruction of the feet, hands, and facial bones associated with advanced leprosy.

If these considerations do not entirely rule out leprosy, at most it would be only one among many skin diseases that could be considered *ṣāraʿat.* But it is doubtful if leprosy existed at all in the ANE at the time of the OT so that it might be considered *ṣāraʿat.* No certain historical attestations of the disease exist (in documents or in material finds) in this area of the world before the time of Alexander the Great. Only about this time do Greek writers start talking about leprosy (mainly under the term *elephantiasis*). Human paleopathological specimens prior to the 6th century C.E. do not show skeletal changes that are characteristic of leprosy. Many passages from texts from the ANE and some archaeological data from before 300 B.C.E. which have been explained as indicating the existence of leprosy are extremely ambiguous and do not refer decisively to leprosy (Lowe 1947: 57–59; Moller-Christensen 1967; Hulse 1975: 87–90; Dols 1979: 314–18).

While it is easy to say what *ṣāraʿat* is not, it is more difficult to say what it is. Taking the non-P texts first, one finds a very general description of the symptoms. A frequently recurring description in these passages is that the lesion is "like snow" (Exod 4:6; Num 12:10; 2 Kgs 5:27). This may refer more to the flakiness of the lesion than to its color (the adjective "white" which appears in some translations of these passages is not in the Hebrew). Num 12:12, in which Aaron pleads Miriam's cause, gives a more vivid description of the condition: "Let her not be like a dead (fetus) which when it comes out of its mother's womb half of its flesh is eaten!" Though this is hyperbolic it nevertheless indicates that *ṣāraʿat* is to a certain extent exfoliative or desquamative. A fetus that has died in the womb takes on a reddish color which lasts for the first few days after death. After this period it becomes an odd brown-gray. As it continues to become macerated in utero before finally being expelled, the skin is shed in large sheets.

The evidence from the non-P texts does not allow for specific conclusions, but it is at least evident that *ṣāraʿat* is a disease or group of diseases in which there is flaking or exfoliation of the skin. Such symptoms are a prominent feature of skin diseases such as psoriasis, eczema, seborrhea, and certain mycotic infections.

The evidence from the P texts though more specific (yet to a certain extent unintelligible) does not contradict the picture gained from the non-P texts. Seven sections in Leviticus 13 discuss various conditions in human skin (vv 2–8, 9–17, 18–23, 24–28, 29–37, 38–39, 40–44; see D. Wright's chart summarizing the symptomatology in J. Milgrom *Leviticus* AB, on Leviticus 13). The diagnosis of 2 of these from a modern medical perspective is quite certain. Lev 13:40–41 clearly talk of normal balding of the head (alopecia; on Lev 13:42–44, see below). Lev 13:38–39 speak of multiple faint (or dull) white spots *(bĕhārōt)* on the skin, called *bōhaq.* This is probably one variety of leukoderma known as vitiligo in which patches of the skin and hair lose their pigmentation. Small to very large areas of the skin surface can be affected. It should be noted in vitiligo the skin does not flake. As we will see below, flaking is associated with possible unclean conditions. (Surprisingly, Lev 13:28–29 does not talk of the existence of depigmented hair common in vitiligo.) Both baldness and vitiligo are clean conditions (i.e., they are not *ṣāraʿat*).

The cases in the other sections of Leviticus 13 are more difficult to diagnose. Lev 13:2–8 can be subdivided into two cases: a general case in vv 2–3 and a dependent subcase in vv 4–8. The descriptions of the spots that can be called *ṣāraʿat* in Lev 13:4–8 are too general to allow specific medical identification. The symptoms are, summarily, a flaky patch of skin (presumably indicated by the color white, cf. the white and red-white spots or lesions with raw flesh in Lev 13:10, 14–16, 19, 24) without white hair or "deepness" which either spreads after one week or stays the same or spreads after two weeks. These symptoms fit many types of skin diseases such as psoriasis, seborrhoeic dermatitis, certain mycotic infections, patchy eczema and pityriasis rosea (cf. Hulse 1975: 96). This diagnosis correlates with the view of *ṣāraʿat* found outside P.

The diagnosis of the spots (a *śĕʾēt, sappaḥat,* or *baheret*) in Lev 13:2–3, on the other hand, is difficult, if not impossible. The main symptom here is whiteness of hair. It also has "deepness" which appears to require involvement of the skin, a visible subcutaneous lesion. And it is also may have flakiness: other cases of a *baheret* or *śĕʾēt* later in the chapter are described as white or red-white which suggests flakiness for these types of lesions (see the preceding paragraph). The condition is not vitiligo (which appears to be described in Lev 13:38–39), since it is generally not associated with flakiness or a subcutaneous lesion. While medical experts can suggest various rarer types of conditions which could fit the difficult and vague description of Lev 13:2–3 (e.g., some types of nevi), it is possible, knowing the systematic propensities of P, that this source has described a disease which does not reflect medical reality, perhaps by conflating symptoms of separate diseases thought to be impure.

The latter possibility is attractive since elsewhere in these regulations we find clear evidence of ideological systematization: (1) The term *ṣāraʿat* is applied to not only human skin diseases, but to phenomenologically discrete defects in fabrics and houses. (2) The literary and prescriptive structure of the *ṣāraʿat* rules for persons, fabrics, and houses is very similar. (3) Seven-day quarantine periods are prescribed for each of these three cases though the conditions are discrete. (4) The three cases focus on the color of the lesions as the main or initial criterion for diagnosis.

Other sections in Leviticus 13 describe what seem to be unreal conditions as well as symptoms that are roughly diagnosable, as in Lev 13:2–8. Lev 13:18–23 and 24–28 are parallel to each other and speak of secondary lesions arising from a boil or blister. The conditions that are initially judged to be *ṣāraʿat*—lesions with "deepness" and white hair—seem to be artificial like those in Lev 13:2–3. On the other hand, lesions developing from boils and burns that are quarantined because they lack white hair and "deepness" and then spread are *ṣāraʿat* and reflect the same real medical conditions as Lev 13:4–8.

Lev 13:9–17 is parallel to vv 2–8 (note the resumptive repetition of v 2 in v 9). The case of Lev 13:10–11 (a white *śĕʾēt* with white hair and ulcerated skin [*miḥyat bāśār ḥay;* cf. 1 Sam 2:15]; called a chronic or advanced *ṣāraʿat* lesion) seems to be an unreal condition. The ensuing verses discuss the case where the lesion expands so that it covers the entire skin. If it does this so that no ulcerated skin appears the lesion is pure (Lev 13:12–13; the lack of ulcerated skin is implicit from v 14). If ulcerated skin reappears, it is *ṣāraʿat* (Lev 13:14–15). If the ulcerated skin turns white again (i.e., flakiness without ulceration), it is pure (Lev 13:16–17). The point of Lev 13:12–17 is not to show a paradox (i.e., a small spot is unclean but a lesion that covers the whole body is clean), but to show that a lesion that does not have ulcerated skin is clean even though it may cover the whole body. This is a good case of how the symptomatology may be idealistic and not realistic. It is doubtful that in reality a lesion would cover the whole body. Such a description is a legal stratagem. In terms of a medical description, if the condition of white hair in Lev 13:9–11 is not to be carried through Lev 13:12–17, a condition such as psoriasis which may cover large parts of the body and develop broken or raw skin may be intended. If white hair is implicitly present in the cases in Lev 13:12–17, then it appears to be an unreal condition.

Lev 13:29–37 treats conditions of hair on the head or in the beard. The main case (Lev 13:30) speaks of a "plague" (*negaʿ*) which is "deep" and in which there is thin yellow (or copper colored, *ṣāhōb,* cf. Ezra 8:27) hair. This condition is a type of *ṣāraʿat* called *neteq.* Some have suggested that this may be diagnosed medically as favus, a mycotic infection with *Trichophyton schoenleinii* which can cause color changes in the hair, hair loss, and patches of scaling skin. In the ANE however, inadequate nutrition must always be considered a significant etiology for disease. For example, Kwashiorkor, a protein deficiency syndrome, which is still seen in Arab children, is associated with a copper-red to yellow colored fine hair and scaling of the skin (Wilkinson 1977: 166; Fitzpatrick et al. 1979: 1020–23).

Lev 13:31–37, a subcase of Lev 13:29–30, speaks of cases where "deepness" and black hair (and presumably yellow/copper-colored hair) do not initially appear in the suspected *negaʿ* spot. (This lack of black hair and presumably yellow/copper-colored hair may imply a hair loss has occurred at the spot.) If the spot spreads after one or two quarantine periods it is presumably *ṣāraʿat.* These symptoms are general enough to allow the same diagnosis as in Lev 13:4–8.

Finally, Lev 13:42–44 (which depends on the discussion of baldness in Lev 13:40–41) states that if a red-white *negaʿ* appears in the bald area of someone's head that looks like a *ṣāraʿat* condition, it is to be considered such.

To summarize the character of the human conditions, both non-P texts and parts of the P legislation consider *ṣāraʿat* to consist of several types of skin lesions which exhibit exfoliation or scaling of the skin and which persist and do not exhibit a course of healing within the prescribed quarantine periods. It seems that P has elaborated upon this basic symptomatology extrapolating other symptoms which are consistent with its system of purity and impurity but which do not reflect medical reality.

b. In Fabrics and Houses. In comparison to human lesions, the general diagnosis of *ṣāraʿat* in fabrics and walls of houses is relatively easy (see Lev 13:47–58 and 14:34–45). The condition basically consists of greenish or reddish spots that spread after a seven-day quarantine period. These defects appear to be different types of mycotic growths. *ṣāraʿat* in a house, for example, may be one of several types of wood-destroying or wood-staining fungi, which may have brown, pink, red, blue, and grayish-olive colors (Hunt and Garratt 1967: 23–43). Only greenish and reddish defects are considered *ṣāraʿat;* gray black or dark brown fungal spots are implicitly considered clean. Akkadian texts shows that fungal growths were portents of evil in Mesopotamia (see *CAD* 8: 133 and Caplice 1974).

2. Sin and *ṣāraʿat.* The OT often (though not always; cf. Exod 4:6) attributes the appearance of *ṣāraʿat* to God's punishment for sinful behavior. Naaman is cured from *ṣāraʿat* when he humbles himself, but scheming and deceitful Gehazi is cursed with it (2 Kgs 5). When King Uzziah acted arrogantly by illicitly offering incense in the temple, *ṣāraʿat* broke out in his forehead (2 Chr 26:16–21; cf. 2 Kgs 15:5). Miriam, complaining about Moses' marriage and leadership, was cursed with it (Num 12:10–15; cf. Deut 24:8–9). David curses Joab and his posterity with *ṣāraʿat* for the murder of Abner (2 Sam 3:29). P once attributes the condition to God's hand (Lev 14:34). (On skin diseases as punishment, see also Deut 28:27, 35). The OT is not alone in this explanation. Other cultures similarly attribute various skin diseases and real leprosy to sin (in Christianity and Islam, cf. Dols 1983; in China, cf. Skinsnes 1964: 23–24, 29; ancient Persia, cf. Herodotus

1.138; in ancient Mesopotamia, cf. Kinnier-Wilson 1966). This of course is just part of the larger tendency of premodern societies to attribute disease to supernatural causes. It must be noted, however, that though the OT may explain *ṣāraʿat* as arising from sin, having the disease itself with its concomitant impurity is not a sin. Particularly in P, having this type of impurity is not a sinful state; only mishandling it is. See UNCLEAN AND CLEAN.

3. Pollution Effect. The rules in Leviticus 13–14 are not just interested in diagnosing *ṣāraʿat* but have more as their goal the proper control of the condition since it is one of the more severe impurities in P. Not only can those persons and things suffering *ṣāraʿat* pollute holy items and therefore need to be kept separate from the sacred sphere (cf. Lev 22:4), affected persons and things are also able to communicate a level of impurity to profane (i.e., nonholy or common) persons and objects.

To be sure, P actually (and surprisingly) says little about the strength of the condition's impurity in regard to the profane. It only treats the effect of a suspected house (Lev 14:36, 46–47). The effect of unclean persons and fabrics, however, can be deduced. It is reasonable to suppose that persons and fabrics polluted at least like a suspected house. A suspected house pollutes anyone who enters it with a minor impurity lasting one day. Anyone who enters and tarries in this house has a slightly more severe impurity, requiring laundering, which lasts, according to the context of this rule and other purity laws, one day (cf. Wright 1987: 206–8). By analogy, being in the same enclosure with an affected person or fabric would pollute similarly. Another indication of the severity of the impurity is the extensive purification rites required (Lev 14:1–32, 48–53). As other impurities that need extensive purification rites communicate impurity to the profane sphere (e.g., those with abnormal genital discharges, Lev 15:1–15, 25–30; one corpse contaminated, Numbers 19), so would be the case with *ṣāraʿat.* The rabbis came to the conclusion that one who had *ṣāraʿat* polluted not only by being in the same enclosure with other persons and things (*m. Neg.* 8:8; 13:17, 11; *Kelim* 1:4), but like one with an abnormal genital discharge (*m. Zabim* 5:6; see DISCHARGE).

In addition to a person diagnosed as having *ṣāraʿat,* there is evidence to indicate that a person merely suspected of the disease could also pollute the profane sphere. A person who has been quarantined for two weeks but is in the end declared clean needs to launder (Lev 13:6, 34). After this prescription the text adds "and he shall be clean." Moreover, that a suspected house can pollute the profane sphere suggests that a suspected person should be able to pollute similarly. From the analogy with the house, one may conclude that a suspected person pollutes much like diagnosed persons which pollute like suspected houses (such is the conclusion of the Rabbis, *m. Meg.* 1:7; *Neg.* 8:8). This picture must be qualified slightly, for the person who is suspected for one week but who is afterwards declared clean is not required to launder (cf. Lev 13:23, 28). This hints that there may be a slight difference in the degree of impurity between one who is suspected for one week and one suspected for two weeks (cf. Wright 1987: 210–12).

Because of their ability to pollute the profane sphere, persons and things diagnosed or suspected of *ṣāraʿat* need to be restricted in or excluded from the area of human habitation or be otherwise destroyed. Lev 13:46 prescribes that those with *ṣāraʿat* must live outside the habitation (cf. Num 5:2–3). This restriction of *ṣāraʿat* affected persons is reflected outside P in Num 12:14–15; 2 Kgs 7:3–10 and perhaps 2 Kgs 15:5 = 2 Chr 26:21. Persons suspected of *ṣāraʿat* are to be shut up or quarantined (probably restricted in their homes) during the period of suspicion (Lev 13:4, 5, 21, 26, 31, 33). A suspected house is cleared out and shut up (indicating restricted access during this period; Lev 14:36–38). Suspected fabrics are quarantined as well (Lev 13:50, 54). *ṣāraʿat* infected building materials are to be disposed of outside the habitation in an unclean place (Lev 14:40, 41, 45) and fabrics incorrigibly infected are to be burned (Lev 13:52, 55, 57).

4. Purification Rites. The chapters from Leviticus prescribe purification rites for persons, houses, and fabrics that have recovered from the condition or that are declared clean after having been suspected.

The purification of persons is the most extensive (Lev 14:1–32). It consists of three parts: (a) 14:2–7: bird blood and water is sprinkled on the healed person by means of a live bird, cedar wood, crimson material, and hyssop. This sprinkling appears to remove impurity from the person. The live bird is sent away to remove the impurity from the person and locale (cf. the scapegoat in Lev 16:21–22). (b) 14:8–9: the person bathes, launders, and shaves at the beginning and end of a seven-day intermediate period. The requirement to wait a week before full impurity is achieved may be to make sure the lesion has really healed and would hence be similar to the seven-day quarantine periods in Leviticus 13. The healed person still can pollute to some degree and must dwell outside his tent (cf. Wright 1987: 212–13). And (c) 14:10–32: the person brings sacrifices and blood and oil is placed on his ear, thumb, and toe of the healed person (cf. Exod 29:19–21; Lev 8:22–30). By these rites, the person who was formerly excluded from society is readmitted to full communal and spiritual life.

A person suspected of *ṣāraʿat* for two weeks but declared clean purifies by laundering his or her clothing (Lev 13:6, 34). Bathing may be included since P often leaves this requirement unsaid (Wright 1987: 185 n. 38). In view of this, bathing may also be necessary for a suspected person after one week (Lev 13:23, 28).

The purification of a renovated house follows essentially the same rite as that used for the first part of a healed person's purification (Lev 14:49–53). A mixture of bird blood and water is sprinkled on the house by means of a live bird, cedar wood, crimson material, and hyssop. The live bird is sent outside the city into the open country, dispelling the impurity.

As for fabrics, the purification rite is so brief as to be almost missed: a fabric from which a suspected spot has disappeared is to be washed (Lev 13:58). The washing in v 54 (not the same as that in v 58) is for removing the spot, not purification.

The purification rites just discussed do not cure *ṣāraʿat* lesions; they only purify from residual impurity after the spot has been removed or disappeared, or has been determined not to be *ṣāraʿat.* Notably, though P prescribes means for removing *ṣāraʿat* spots from fabrics and houses (cf. the first washing in Lev 13:54 and the tearing out of the spot in v 56; also the removal of infected building materials and their replacement in Lev 14:40–42: note these are all very practical, not ritualistic, procedures), it does not prescribe any cure for *ṣāraᶜat* in persons. The only place where healing of human *ṣāraᶜat* is found is in 2 Kgs 5 where Elisha prescribes a ritual for Naaman. Significantly, it is a prophet who prescribes the healing rite, not a priest. This bifurcation of duties fits into the larger OT picture where prophets heal and priests diagnose (cf. 1 Kgs 17:17–24; 2 Kgs 4:17–37; 20:7 = Isa 38:2; Jesus follows the prophetic ideal in his healing of those with *lepra;* see below).

5. Why is *ṣāraᶜat* Impure? A question of much interest is why *ṣāraᶜat* is considered unclean. O. Skinsnes (1964) has shown in his study of leprosy in China that social reactions to skin diseases may be similar in unrelated cultures. That is, people have a common natural aversion toward skin diseases; fears of such arise naturally and independently. This natural fear can be explained by M. Douglas' theory of impurity (1966): what is considered impure is largely that which is irregular or out of place. Against the norm of whole, healthy skin, skin diseases are abnormal; hence they are shunned. J. Milgrom (*Leviticus* AB, on Leviticus 13–14) sheds light on this psychological aversion by arguing, as many biblical exegetes have in the past, that *ṣāraᶜat* is impure because it is connected with death. In the Bible, *ṣāraᶜat* was already connected with death (cf. Num 12:12; cf. Job 18:13) and later Jewish tradition looked on *ṣāraᶜat* as living death.

The foregoing helps to explain how aversion towards skin diseases may arise or be perpetuated in the biblical world, but it does not explain how or why a particular society, or part of that society (such as the P writers), formulated their view the ways they did. Social-anthropological and structuralist approaches are particularly helpful in explaining systems of purity rules. See UNCLEAN AND CLEAN (OT). Douglas argues (1966: 114–28) that purity rules that pertain to what leaves and enters the body reflect the society's larger concern for what happens at its social borders. The restrictions placed on the body mirror larger social concerns. J. Pilch (1981), building on Douglas, argues that *ṣāraᶜat* rules also reflect this concern about the integrity of social borders since the condition is one that affects the surfaces of bodies, houses (their walls), and fabrics. Correct control of these superficial impurities images the society's concern to control its social boundaries.

B. In the NT

References to *lepra* in the NT are found only in the Gospels. The context of most instances is Jesus' miraculous power to heal (Matt 8:1–4 = Mark 1:40 = Luke 5:12 = 16; Matt 11:5 = Luke 7:22; Luke 17:11–19). Jesus also charged his twelve disciples to do works similar to his including healing of those with *lepra* (Matt 10:8). Once Jesus makes reference to the healing of Naaman (Luke 4:27). Another story has Jesus staying at the house of Simon who was affected with *lepra* (Matt 26:6 = Mark 14:3). It is also possible that the disease of Lazarus in Luke 16:20 was *lepra.*

These references follow OT tradition. The LXX uses *lepra* to translate OT *ṣāraᶜat.* The use of *katharizō* "to purify" of Jesus' healing acts (Matt 8:2–3 = Mark 1:40–42 = Luke 5:12–13; Luke 4:27; Matt 10:8; Matt 11:5 = Luke 7:22; Luke 17:14, 17) also reveals dependence on OT tradition. This indicates that the same types of diseases termed *ṣāraᶜat* in the OT figure in the NT. That *lepra* has a connotation equivalent to OT *ṣāraᶜat* is also evident in Greek medical writers who most often use it to signify exfoliative skin diseases in general. These writers reserve the term *elephas* or *elephantiasis* for true leprosy.

There is some evidence, however, suggesting that though the NT term *lepra* followed OT tradition concerning *ṣāraᶜat,* true leprosy could have been included under the term *lepra.* The best historical reconstruction of the spread of leprosy argues that the disease appeared in the Near East about 300 B.C.E. (at this time the Greek physicians in Alexandria became familiar with the disease) and began to spread to Italy, for example, just two centuries later. This allows the possibility that the disease existed in Palestine shortly before the time of Jesus. Some Greek writers, too, confused the beginning stages of leprosy with other skin diseases called *lepra.* This shows that people at the time of the NT could have included leprosy under the term *lepra* (see Dols 1979: 314–18).

Bibliography

Caplice, R. 1974. An Apotropaion Against Fungus. *JNES* 33: 345–49.

Dols, M. W. 1979. Leprosy in Medieval Arabic Medicine. *Journal of the History of Medicine and Allied Sciences* 36: 314–33.

———. 1983. The Leper in Medieval Islamic Society. *Speculum* 58: 891–916.

Douglas, M. 1966. *Purity and Danger.* London.

Fitzpatrick, T. B. et al., eds. 1979. *Dermatology in General Medicine.* 2d ed. New York.

Görg, M. 1981. "Ausschlag" an Häusern: zu einem problematischen Lexem in Lev 14, 37. *BN* 14: 20–25.

Hulse, E. V. 1975. The Nature of Biblical "Leprosy" and the Use of Alternative Medical Terms in Modern Translations of the Bible. *PEQ* 107: 87–105.

Hunt, G. M., and Garrat, G. A. 1967. *Wood Preservation.* 3d ed. New York.

Kinnier-Wilson, J. V. 1966. Leprosy in Ancient Mesopotamia. *RA* 60: 47–58.

———. 1982. Medicine in the Land and Times of the Old Testament. Pp. 337–65 in *Studies in the Period of David and Solomon,* ed. T. Ishida. Winona Lake, IN.

Kraemer, J. L. 1966. *šĕqa ᶜărûrōt:* A Proposed Solution for an Unexplained *Hapax. JNES* 25: 125–29.

Lowe, J. 1947. Comments on the History of Leprosy. *Leprosy Review* 18: 54–64.

Meier, S. 1989. House Fungus: Mesopotamia and Israel. *RB* 96: 184–92.

Moller-Christensen, V. 1967. Evidence of Leprosy in Earlier People. Pp. 295–306 in *Diseases in Antiquity,* eds. D. Brothwell and A. T. Sandison. Springfield, IL.

Pilch, J. J. 1981. Biblical Leprosy and Body Symbolism. *BTB* 11: 108–13.

Seidl, T. 1982. *Tora für den "Aussatz"-Fall: literarische Schichten und syntaktische Strukturen in Levitikus 13 und 14.* Arbeiten zu Text und Sprache im Alten Testament 18. Ottilien.

Skinsnes, O. K. 1964. Leprosy in Society. *Leprosy Review* 35: 21–35, 106–122, 175–82.

Sussman, M. 1967. Diseases in the Bible and the Talmud. Pp. 209–21 in *Diseases in Antiquity,* eds. D. Brothwell and A. T. Sandison. Springfield, IL.

Wilkinson, J. 1977. Leprosy and Leviticus: The Problem of Description and Identification. *SJT* 30: 153–69.

———. 1978. Leprosy and Leviticus: A Problem of Semantics and Translation. *SJT* 31: 153–66.

Wright, D. P. 1987. *The Disposal of Impurity: Elimination Rites in the Bible and in Hittite and Mesopotamian Literature.* SBLDS 101. Atlanta.

David P. Wright
Richard N. Jones

LESBOS (PLACE). See MITYLENE (PLACE).

LESHEM (PLACE) [Heb *lešem*]. Var. LAISH. A city mentioned in Josh 19:47 which the Danites captured, but which is called LAISH in Judg 18:7, 27. The LXX of Joshua reads neither Leshem nor Laish, but Lachish (Gk *Lachis*). This shift probably indicates an effort on the part of the translators (or the source from which they worked) to correct what they perceived to be an error in the MT, which put the Danites so far N of their original inheritance. Both LXX texts of Judges (A and B), however, read Laish (Gk *Laisa*).

Dale W. Manor

LETHECH [Heb *letek*]. See WEIGHTS AND MEASURES.

LETTERS. This entry consists of three separate articles surveying epistolography in the biblical world. The first covers the many letters written in Hebrew that have been discovered as a result of archaeological work. The second examines Aramaic letters and letter types. The third examines Greco-Roman letter-writing conventions, providing an important backdrop to our understanding of NT literature.

HEBREW LETTERS

Archaeologists have discovered many letters written in the Hebrew language and dealing with a variety of different subjects.

A. The Study of Hebrew Letters
B. The Corpora
C. The Formulae
D. Transition to Body
E. Letter Types
F. Fragments of Letters Preserved in the Hebrew Bible

A. The Study of Hebrew Letters

The study of Hebrew epistolography in the biblical period only became genuinely possible with the discovery of letters from extrabiblical contexts. This is true because so few remnants of epistolary formulae are present in the letter fragments preserved in the Hebrew Bible and because of the historiographic problems of the Hebrew Bible. There were some early attempts at the study of the biblical Hebrew letters (especially Beer 1913; Marty 1939) but not until the publication of the Lachish ostraca was it possible, for example, to understand the phrase *wʿth,* which may be roughly translated "and now," (2 Kgs 5:6; 10:2) as an authentic remnant of the epistolographic style (*EncMiqr* 4: 972). The major groups of extrabiblical letters are those from Tell ed-Duweir (Tel Lachish in Hebrew), excavated in the 1930s and from Tel Arad, excavated in the 1960s. The *editiones principes* of these texts were primarily concerned with philological and historical questions (extensive bibliographies are to be found in Pardee 1982 and only the primary publications will be indicated here below). Loewenstamm's 1962 study (*EncMiqr* 4: 966–74) was pathbreaking, and since then Pardee has provided an overview (1978b) and a *Handbook* (1982). These studies were in many ways dependent on the study of Aramaic epistolography, for which documents were discovered earlier (see the following article).

In spite of the insights afforded by these extrabiblical documents, however, knowledge of Hebrew epistolography in the pre-Medieval periods is still extremely scanty because of the dearth of documents (there are a total of 48 epistolary documents between ca. 700 B.C. and 135 A.D.) and because of the concentration of these few witnesses into discrete groups, as defined both geographically (Lachish, Arad, Meṣad Ḥashavyahu, Dead Sea) and chronologically (ca. 700–586 B.C., A.D. 132–135). These two factors give relatively clear snapshots of certain letter-types from particular places and time periods but leave massive periods and areas totally unaccounted for. As a result the history and interrelationships of many epistolary features are at present untraceable.

B. The Corpora

The oldest Hebrew letters presently known are from the early or middle of the 7th century: Murabbaʿât 17, Arad 40, and Meṣad Ḥashavyahu (dates uncertain; see Pardee 1982: 117; 1978b: 323; and 1978a: 34 for bibliography). The first of these texts also has the distinction of being the only one of the pre-Christian Hebrew letters discovered to date to have been written on papyrus, all others being ostraca. Unfortunately, this document is the first stage of a palimpsest and only a few words are presently readable. The other two are in much better condition. Indeed, the Meṣad Ḥashavyahu ostracon is almost complete (Naveh 1960; 1962). This "letter" consists of a plea addressed by a reaper *(qṣr)* to his superior *(ʾdny hśr)* asking that a garment be returned to him that had been confiscated by a certain Hoshayahu ben Shabay, whose title is not given. Arad 40 is from 2 persons, addressed to the father of one of them ("Your son Gemar[yahu], as well as Neḥemyahu, (hereby) sen[d greetings to (you)] Malkiyahu").

Most of the *Arad letters (AI)* are convincingly dated to immediately before the final conquest of Judaea by Babylonian and Edomite forces in 597 B.C. (Lemaire 1977: 231–35) and most of them consist of orders from superior to inferior to release foodstuffs from the Arad storehouses. Three of them contain kinship terms in the address (16, 24, 40) and one is clearly from inferior to superior (18: *ʾl ʾdny ʾlyšb* "To my lord Elyashib"). One enigmatic Arad text (88) begins *ʾny mlkty* "I have become king"; it is not classified here as a letter because it contains no epistolary formula and because it is so lacunary as to preclude determining whether or not it was functioning to effect "communication between two or more persons who cannot communicate orally" (the working definition of a letter given in Pardee 1982: 2). See also ARAD OSTRACA.

The *Lachish letters* (Torczyner 1938) are dated to about ten years after the Arad texts, that is, shortly before the Babylonian invasion which resulted in the capture of Jerusalem in 586 B.C. The mention of Lachish by name in one of the texts without any indication that the writer was at Lachish (4:10) may imply either that Tell ed-Duweir does not represent the site of ancient Lachish or that Lachish 4 was brought there from another site (Pardee 1982: 94; cf. Ahlström 1983; Yadin 1981/1984). The remarkable correlations between the siege ramp at Lachish and the ramp illustrated in Sennacherib's reliefs (Ussishkin 1982) seem to constitute a strong argument in favor of the latter solution, while the fact that several of the texts from the site (but not including text 4) were written on sherds from a single pot found alongside uninscribed sherds from the same pot (Pardee 1982: 77; Yadin 1981/1984: 182) seems to constitute a strong argument in favor of the former solution. The majority view is that the formulation "we are watching for/over the Lachish signals" *(ʾl mśʾt lkš nḥnw šmrm)* does not constitute a problem for the identification of Tell ed-Duweir with Lachish (e.g., Yadin 1981/1984: 181–82), though those who make the assumption do not explain why Lachish is not identified as being the writer's location. Perhaps the best explanation is that the writer was physically at Lachish when writing but was responsible for a broader district and could, therefore, refer to all the towns within the district simply by name.

The Lachish letters are primarily military in nature, though the only unveiled reference to political and military activities speaks of an embassy to Egypt by a certain Konyahu ben Elnatan who is called śr hṣbʾ "General of the Army" (3:13–18). The apparent ease of movement at the time of this letter as well as references to the sending and receiving of letters (5, 6, 12, 16, 18) and to the harvesting and distribution of crops (5, 9) have led some commentators (Lemaire 1977: 139–43; Pardee 1982: 77–78) to date the documents prior to the Babylonian invasion of 588 B.C. rather than shortly before the termination of the invasion in 586, as has generally been thought. See also LACHISH LETTERS.

The letters found among the Dead Sea Scrolls have all come from sites other than the main caves associated with Qumran; that is, from caves in Wadi Murabbaʿât (Milik 1961), Naḥal Ḥever (Yadin 1961), and Naḥal Ṣeʾelim (Milik 1957: 21). They were found alongside letters (and other texts) in Aramaic and Greek; all the documents seem to have found their way to the caves at the time of the Bar Kokhba revolt. The epistolary documents originated in Bar Kokhba's own circles and were in some cases written by Shimon ben/bar Kosiba himself (e.g., Hebrew letters Murabbaʿât 43, Naḥal Ḥever 5/6 12).

These letters deal with provisioning the forces of the revolt and with various problems of discipline (Murabbaʿât 43 "I swear by the heavens: Should harm come to any one of the Galileans who are with you, I'll put your feet in fetters as I did to ben Aflul"; Naḥal Ḥever 4/6 12 "Well-off you are—eating and drinking from the goods of Beth-Israel and not giving a thought to your brothers"). One document (Murabbaʿât 42) is formally very distinctive in that it contains a list of witnesses; it functions as a letter of attestation regarding the proper ownership of a cow that had been purchased (or seized) by a member of the revolting forces (cf. the Aramaic letters which contain lists of witnesses). See also BAR KOKHBA (LETTERS).

C. The Formulae

The Hebrew letters are more limited in number and in type than the Aramaic letters. Because the number of formulae is thus correspondingly reduced our ability to interpret the proper usage and the function of each formula is severely limited. The most complete Hebrew letters of the biblical period consist of address, greetings, transition to body, and body. All of these elements are optional, including the body (though there are no Hebrew letters of the type, there are Ugaritic letters which consist entirely of formulae).

The letters of the Bar Kokhba period include these elements and closing formulae as well. The use of the epistolary formulae appears to have been much more rigidly prescribed in this period, for the address and the greeting formula *šlwm* are always present, where verifiable, in this corpus of texts.

The *address* may consist either of a simple prepositional phrase or of a complete verbal sentence. The simplest formula is *ʾl* + PN, "To PN . . ." (Arad 1–8, 10–12, 14, 17); this may be expanded by the insertion of a title, *ʾl ʾdny* + PN, "To my lord PN . . ." (Arad 18, Lachish 2, 6). The only address formula in the Bar Kokhba letters is prepositional, but includes reference to both the sender and the addressee: *mn* PN (+ title) *ʿl* PN (+ title), "From PN to PN. . . ." The verbal formula usually includes the verb *šlḥ*, "to send," as an epistolary perfect (Pardee 1983; Pardee and Whiting 1987) plus the phrase *lšlm* "to greet" (literally "for well-being"), e.g., *ʾḥk ḥnnyhw šlḥ lšlm ʾlyšb wlšlm bytk* "Your brother Ḥananyahu (hereby) sends greetings to (you) Elyashib and to your household" (Arad 16). This greeting formula thus contains an element of greeting but may itself be followed by another greeting formula (*brk* "to bless" [see below]).

Four of the Lachish letters (4, 5, 8, 9) and the judicial plea from Meṣad Ḥashavyahu contain no address formula. Because of similarities with other Lachish letters it is unlikely that this omission may be interpreted as indicative of a different origin for the letters in question. Either the address formula was not considered necessary because of a particular circumstance of transmission, as we have argued to be the case with the Meṣad Ḥashavyahu text (Pardee 1982: 23), or else all of these documents represent drafts, as Delekat (1970: 454) has suggested for the Meṣad Ḥashavyahu text and as Yadin (1981/1984) has surmised for the Lachish examples.

All of the Hebrew letters of which the relevant lines are preserved contain as part of the introductory formulae either the name, an epithet, or both of the recipient. The identification of the sender is much less frequent, however: seventeen of the Hebrew letters contain no marker whatever of the sender's identity. A clear chronological division may be seen here, for the sender is always identified in the Bar Kokhba letters.

Greeting formulae are always expressed verbally in the older corpora; there are five basic verbal expressions: (1) "to bless": *brktk lyhwh,* "I hereby bless you to YHWH" (Arad 16, 21, 40; compare the same formula in *Aramaic letters); (2) "to inquire": *yhwh yšʾl lšlmk,* "May YHWH inquire after your well-being" (Arad 18; also in Aramaic letters as well as in Ugaritic); (3) "to cause to hear": *yhwh yšmʿ ʾt ʾdny šmʿt šlm wṭb ʿt kym,* "May YHWH cause my lord to hear news of well-being and good (i.e., the best possible news) at this very time" (Lachish 5; with variants in Lachish 2–4, 8, 9); (4) "to cause to see": *yrʾ yhwh ʾt ʾdny ʾt hʿt hzh šlm,* "May YHWH cause my lord to see this time in well-being"; (5) "to send": *šlḥ šlḥt ʾt šlm bytk,* "I (hereby) send heartfelt greetings to your household" (Murabbaʿât 17). These greetings are always, where verifiable, from inferior to superior or between equals, never from superior to inferior.

All of the Bar Kokhba letters contain, where the relevant part of the text is extant, the one-word greeting formula *šlwm,* "Greetings."

D. Transition to Body

Most of the letters from the older corpora have an explicit marker of transition from the opening formulae to the body of the letter. This is the phrase *wʿt,* literally translated "and now," but the rhetorical function of which is to indicate a transition from a preamble of any sort to the purpose of the statement or from "topic to "comment" (Pardee 1985: 148). It is only omitted in five of the earlier Hebrew letters (Arad 4, 12; Lachish 2, 5, 6) and in the Lachish examples is in a sense replaced by the self-abasement formula *my ʿbdk klb ky,* "Who is your servant but a dog that. . . ." This formula of transition is the only epistolary formula that has been retained as such in the epistolary fragments preserved in the Hebrew Bible (2 Kgs 5:6; 10:2).

The Bar Kokhba letters contain a formulaically similar phrase, the particle *š* (paralleled in the Bar Kokhba Aramaic letters by the particle *d(y),* the equivalent of *š*). It is positioned between the greeting and the body and must be considered a vestigial formula, for it functions contextually neither as a conjunction nor as a relative pronoun. Unfortunately, the data for the history of this usage are missing and we cannot say for the present how the formula developed. It must have been sensed as awkward, for it is only present in half the letters for which the relevant section is extant and published (present in Murabbaʿât 42, 43; absent from Murabbaʿât 46; 5/6b Ḥever 12).

The body of the extant Hebrew letters differs considerably from that of the Aramaic letters, for while the latter contain extensive formulaic sections, such is not the case with the Hebrew letters. Indeed, one can only identify certain epistolary *topoi* of a very general character which have to do with the nature of things normally discussed in a letter (questions of sending, giving, returning an answer, etc.: Pardee 1982: 150). This important empirical difference is probably a result of the paucity of extant documents and of the nature of the documents themselves (brief texts on ostraca) rather than a reflection of a difference in manner of expression between Hebrew speakers and Aramaic speakers.

In the earlier period *closing greetings* were not used in letters written on ostraca—which is to say there are no examples of closing greetings from the earlier letters, for the end of Murabbaʿât 17, the only Hebrew letter on papyrus from this period, is not extant. In the letters from the time of Bar Kokhba, however, closing greetings were only omitted in one letter (Murabbaʿât 43), elsewhere consisting of a form of the verb *hwh* "to be" + *šlwm,* as in *ʾhwh šlwm wkl byt yšrʾl,* "May it be well with you and with all of Beth-Israel" (Murabbaʿât 42; see also Murabbaʿât 44, 46, 48; relevant section not extant in all other published documents).

The Bar Kokhba letters were also signed, which was not the case with earlier letters. There were four *signature formulae:* (1) that of the sender: PN *ktbh,* "PN has written (= dictated) it" (Murabbaʿât 42, [43], 46, 48); (2) that of the principal party in an agreement: PN *ʿl npšh,* "PN upon his 'life' " (Murabbaʿât 42); (3) that of a witness: PN *ʿd,* "PN: witness" (ibid.); and (4) that of a notary (?): PN *mʿyd,* "PN attests" (ibid.).

E. Letter Types

The limited corpus, made up of relatively brief texts that are often badly damaged, precludes an analysis of letter types such as is possible for the Aramaic letters. It is quite possible that the Hebrew letters fit more or less well into the same categories but on the basis of the present documentation this is not certain.

The most consistently different corpora are the ones defined chronologically: the early letters differ from those of the Bar Kokhba era both in actual formulae and in optionality of use of the formulae (for details, see above). The greeting formulae of the Lachish letters are different from those of the Arad group, a fact that is difficult to explain, for the two sites were only separated by a few kilometers and the two corpora are only separated in time by about a decade. Aside from these major and obvious differences, certain features overlap from one corpus to another and one cannot define a document or a corpus in terms of one criterion or set of criteria. Nor, because of the various limitations already mentioned, can we determine the origin or explain the preference for certain formulae (e.g., the difference between the Lachish and Arad greeting formulae). Not even content can be used as a criterion because virtually all of the letters come from military contexts and show a disconcerting sameness of interests and allusions. There are, of course, some exceptions to the sameness: the poor reaper begging to have his outer garment returned (Meṣad Ḥashavyahu); the subservient officer of the Lachish documents who insists that he can read the letters sent to him and that he has permitted no intelligence leaks; the personal touches of the Arad letters addressed to kin as opposed to the general terseness of the letters from superiors to inferiors; the wrangling over property that is typical of an army that has to live off the land (Murabbaʿât 42); the documents signed by Shimon ben/bar Kosiba himself, which have restored this figure from legendary status (Son of the Star) to that of a real revolutionary commander. These distinctive features are more easily perceivable because of epistolary considerations (e.g., we know that it is Bar Kosiba speaking because he has signed the letter; the list of witnesses in Murabbaʿât 42 is unique in the Hebrew corpus) or if the formulaic elements are defined in epistolary terms (e.g., the more effusive greetings in the letters between kin).

F. Fragments of Letters Preserved in the Hebrew Bible

There are eleven letter fragments in the Hebrew Bible that are reported in direct speech in contexts where a written missive is mentioned specifically (Pardee 1982: 169–82; for a broader study, where the mention of a written document is not placed as a limitation, see Knutson 1975): 2 Sam 11:15; 1 Kgs 21:9–10; 2 Kgs 5:6; 10:2–3, 6 (two letters); 19:10–13 = Isa 37:10–13; Jer 29:4–23, 26–28 (two letters); Neh 6:6–7; 2 Chr 2:11–15; 21:12–15. The contents of various letters and decrees are given in indirect speech in Esth 1:22; 3:13; 9:21; 2 Chr 30:1.

Because the epistolary formulae are not preserved (with the exception of *wʿth* in 2 Kgs 5:6; 10:2), not a great deal can be said about these texts in epistolary terms. The body of the extrabiblical letters has already been characterized as largely nonformulaic and the same can be said of the biblical documents. When dealing with the biblical texts one must contend with the additional problems of authorship and date, authenticity (in the present case, authenticity and/or exactness of the "quotation" from the "real" letter), and accuracy of transmission that are not present when dealing with the original epistolary documents.

It can be said in general that the epistolary fragments in the Hebrew Bible are of a brevity and sobriety that bespeaks authenticity of form if not necessarily of content. For example, *wʿth kbwʾ hspr hzh ʾlyk hnh šlḥty ʾlyk ʾt-nʿmn ʿbdy wʾsptw mṣrʿtw*, "And now, when this letter reaches you, I will have sent my servant Naaman to you for you to heal him of his leprosy (2 Kgs 5:6)." Whether or not the king of Syria ever sent one of his officials to the king of Israel in order that the latter have him healed of a skin disease, the letter, with the authentic touches in *wʿth* and in the epistolary *topos* of a reference to the present letter, is a perfectly plausible example of an ancient Hebrew letter. Other letter fragments, however, contain international professions of faith (2 Chr 2:10–15) and long discourses (Jer 29:4–23) that stand without parallel in the extrabiblical documents.

Bibliography

Ahlström, G. W. 1983. Tell ed-Duweir: Lachish or Libnah? *PEQ* 115: 103–4.

Beer, G. 1913. Zur israelitisch-jüdischen Briefliteratur. Pp. 20–41 in *Alttestamentliche Studien Rudolf Kittle zum 60. Geburtstag dargebracht*, ed. A. Alt. BWANT 13. Leipzig.

Delekat, L. 1970. Ein Bittschriftentwurf eines Sabbatschänders (*KAI* 200). *Bib* 51: 453–70.

Knutson, F. B. 1975. Literary Genres in *PRU IV*. Pp. 153–214 in *Ras Shamra Parallels* II, ed. L. R. Fisher. AnOr 50. Rome.

Lemaire, A. 1977. *Inscriptions hébraïques I: Les ostraca*. Littératures Anciennes du Proche-Orient 9. Paris.

Marty, J. 1939. Contribution à l'étude de fragments épistolaires antiques conservés principalement dans la Bible hébraïque: Les formules de salutation. Pp. 845–55 in vol. 2 of *Mélanges syriens offerts à Monsieur René Dussaud*. Bibliothèque Archéologique et Historique 30. Paris.

Milik, J. T. 1957. Le travail d'édition des manuscrits du Désert de Juda. VTSup 4: 17–26.

———. 1961. *Les grottes de Murabbaʿât*. DJD 2. Oxford.

Naveh, J. 1960. A Hebrew Letter from the Seventh Century B.C. *IEJ* 10: 129–39.

———. 1962. More Hebrew Inscriptions from Meṣad Ḥashavyahu. *IEJ* 12: 27–32.

Pardee, D. 1978a. The Judicial Plea from Meṣad Ḥashavyahu (Yavneh-Yam): A New Philological Study. *Maarav* 1/1: 33–66.

———. 1978b. An Overview of Ancient Hebrew Letters. *JBL* 97: 321–46.

———. 1982. *Handbook of Ancient Hebrew Letters*. SBLSBS 15. Chico, CA.

———. 1983. The 'Epistolary Perfect' in Hebrew Letters. *BN* 22: 34–40.

———. 1985. Review. *JNES* 44: 147–49.

Pardee, D., Whiting, R. M. 1987. Aspects of Epistolary Verbal Usage in Ugaritic and Akkadian. *BSOAS* 50: 1–31.

Torczyner, H. 1938. *The Lachish Letters*. Lachish 1. London.

Ussishkin, D. 1982. *The Conquest of Lachish by Sennacherib*. Tel Aviv.

Yadin, Y. 1961. Expedition D. *IEJ* 11: 36–51.

———. 1981/1984. The Lachish Letters—Originals or Copies and Drafts? Pp. 179–86 in *Recent Archaeology in the Land of Israel*. Washington, D.C. and Jerusalem.

D. Pardee

ARAMAIC LETTERS

Apart from a handful of texts in literary transmission (e.g., Dan 3:31–33; 6:26–28; Ezra 4:11–16, 17–22; 5:7b–17; 6:6–12; 7:12–26), published Aramaic letters from biblical times comprise some 70 examples written on papyrus or prepared skin, and some 46 brief messages written on ostraca. The vast majority of these letters are written in Imperial Aramaic. For a detailed listing see Fitzmyer's charts (1981: 40–46).

A. Terminology
B. The Modern Study of Aramaic Letters
C. The Corpus
D. Formulaic Features
   1. External Formulae
   2. Internal Formulae
E. The Main Aramaic Letter Types
   1. Egyptian-Style Family Correspondence
   2. Letter Types Sharing an All-Purpose Formulary
   3. The Style of the Persian Chanceries
   4. A Letter Type from the Beginning of the Christian Era

A. Terminology

The main Aramaic words used to designate letters (Dion 1981b) were *spr* and *ʾgrh*. The word *spr* can stand for many forms of the written word; curiously, this word only refers to letters in Egyptian family correspondence, where it is the term regularly used. As for *ʾgrh*/*ʾgrt*(*ʾ*) (Akk *egirtu*), this loanword too could originally receive other applications, but it soon became the general term for "letter," and it is widely used in our corpus. Other terms, many reflecting the cosmopolitan character of Imperial Aramaic, are either used sporadically (the Iranian words *ptgm,* "message," and *ništwn* "document," in Segal 1983: No. 125; Gk *qrtys* is not clearly a letter) or with specialized meanings (*ṭʿm,* "order," cf. Akk *ṭêmu; qbylh,* "complaint"; *zkrn,* "memorandum").

B. The Modern Study of Aramaic Letters

The study of Aramaic epistolography is a young discipline. The first Aramaic fascicule of the *Corpus Inscriptionum Semiticarum* (1889) contained only two fragmentary letters yielding any sense (nos. 144 and 152); the first one had been found in 1824. After the discoveries at Elephantine (1893–1909) and the basic philological work required for their publication, scholars focused their attention on the historical import of this find. In the 1970s a more literary approach to the letters emerged, stimulated by renewed interest in the form of NT epistles. In 1974 Fitzmyer (see now 1981) opened the way with a definitive description of the corpus and of the formal elements found in the letters. Alexander (1978) and Porten (1978; 1982) contributed many insights to the study of nonbiblical letters from the Persian era. Dion (1979; 1981a; 1982) extended to the other pre-Christian collections the analysis of formulary and *Sitz-im-Leben* exemplified by Whitehead's unpublished dissertation (1974) on the letters of Aršam. Any progress in the systematic study of ancient letter writing must rely on the efforts of philologists like B. Porten, excellently seconded by A. Yardeni, whose papyrological reconstructions deserve particular attention (see, above all, *TAD*).

C. The Corpus

The earliest example of an Aramaic letter is a 7th century ostracon from Assur (*KAI* 233), in a Mesopotamian form of Old Aramaic. This lengthy message deals with the business of high-placed servants of Assurbanipal, and is stylistically related to Neo-Assyrian royal correspondence (Dion 1979: 555–58). Next comes a document in Imperial Aramaic of the Neo-Babylonian period, the fragmentary papyrus letter of Adon, king of Ekron in Philistia (*TAD* A1.1). This is the first manifestation in Aramaic of an all-purpose letter type, best represented in the late 5th century by 15 papyri from Elephantine in Upper Egypt *(CAP).* These documents are largely centered on the crisis which came to a head in 410 B.C. with the destruction of the Yaho Temple of the Jewish garrison. Many ostraca, from the same community or nearby Aswan, show simplified forms of the same style (Dion 1982: 533–37).

A batch of 8 papyrus letters of another type (BK; see *TAD* A2.1–7), found at Hermopolis West and probably written in Memphis early in the 5th century, represent a different form of Egyptian Imperial Aramaic, with Western dialectical features. These letters embody the correspondence of fairly Egyptianized gentile families of Syrian origin; however, three other letters basically of this type and also from Lower Egypt (Bresciani 1960; see *TAD* A3.3–4), were apparently addressed to Jews of Elephantine.

More than 13 letters on skin in East Imperial Aramaic (Driver 1954; henceforth referred to as *AD*), found at an unknown Egyptian site, belong to the archive of the satrap Aršam; they were written ca. 410–407 B.C. and deal with the administration of Aršam's Egyptian estate. The same forms are observed in a letter on papyrus found at Elephantine (*CAP* 26), which conveys the satrap's detailed instructions for repairs to a ship.

In 1966–67 and 1971–73, British excavations at Saqqarah (Segal 1983) yielded 202 fragmentary papyri and a handful of ostraca carrying texts in Imperial Aramaic, largely from the 4th century B.C. Dozens could be letters of an official/financial character (Segal 1983: 8 n. 9); unfortunately, all seem to have lost their decisive introductory formulae. Most interesting is No. 26, dealing with sanctions against Ionians and Carians in "the harbor" (Memphis?).

The last important batch of papyri comes from what may be regarded as the very end of biblical times, the Second Jewish Revolt against Rome (A.D. 132–35). The eight letters of Simeon Bar Kosiba, Prince of Israel, are written in vernacular Palestinian Aramaic. They were found in the "Cave of Letters" in Nahal Hever, and are only available in preliminary publication (Yadin 1961; henceforth referred to as *Hev.*). These letters form part of a much larger collection of Aramaic, Hebrew, and Greek documents from this period, discovered in the Judean Desert in the vicinity of En-gedi. See BAR KOKHBA (LETTERS).

D. Formulaic Features

1. External Formulae. A certain set of stereotyped expressions regularly functions as an external frame around the message proper. These formulae are used to direct the letter to its recipient *(Address);* to establish contact (*Initial Greeting* plus *Introductory Particle* [Aram *wkʿt* or variants], "And now"); to end contact *(Closing Greeting);* and finally—in official letters—to record details useful to archives/chanceries (scribe's *Colophon; Docket* pointing out the letter's object). *Secondary Greetings* to or from third parties ("Greetings, So-and-so!"; "So-and-so asks how you are"), planted at random in and around the Body of letters to friends or family, marginally belong here; but our remarks will be limited to those formulae which occur through most of the documentation.

Two *Addresses* are always present (Porten 1983): an External Address, written on the back of the rolled-up papyrus; and an Internal one, placed at the beginning of the letter. Both formulae observe the same conventions in the crucial order of precedence between the names of sender and recipient; but the external address includes information (patronyms, etc.) omitted in the internal one. *Initial Greetings* also occur in several forms, important in distinguishing between the main letter types. Some are centered on the noun *šlm* (literally: "well-being"); one uses the verb *brk* ("to bless").

(In the following list of formulae and throughout the rest of this article, parentheses indicate the possibility of omission, and brackets indicate the possibility of variation; translations are rather stiffly literal, so as to reflect the Aramaic wording as clearly and consistently as possible.)

a. Well-being (šlm). A good example of this type of initial greeting is the following: *šlm [mrʾy] [ʾlhyʾ] (klʾ) yšʾlw (śgyʾ) bkl ʿdn* "May (all) [the gods] seek the well-being of [my Lord] [abundantly] at all times." This can be traced back to the LB Age through Hebrew, Neo-Assyrian/Neo-Babylonian, Ugaritic, and peripheral Middle Babylonian examples (Dion 1982: 541–46). Expanded forms occur, formulaic phrases of similar intent being appended to this one. A second example is this: *šlm wšrrt śgyʾ hwšrt lk* "I send you well-being and good health in abundance" (more greetings may be appended). A third example is the following: *šlm wḥyn šlḥt lk* "I send you well-being and life."

b. Blessing *(brk).* A good example of this type is the following: *brk[tk] l[Ptḥ] zy yḥzny* [or *yḥwny*] *ʾp[k] bšlm* "[I] bless you by [Ptah], that he may allow me to see [or show me] your face in well-being." The model is an Egyptian formula, documented in demotic since the 6th century B.C., with antecedents going back to the 19th Dynasty (Alexander 1978: 159; Couroyer 1978; Dion 1979: nn. 82 and 104).

2. Internal Formulae. Much of what is found within the body of an Aramaic letter is also formulaic in character, stereotyped expressions for ubiquitous needs and banal sentiments often being elicited by topics discussed in the letters. Many expressions, which occur only once in the small Aramaic corpus, are shown to be formulaic by parallels in other epistolographic traditions (Dion 1981a; 1982).

Some examples of such formulaic expressions appear in official letters and business letters: (1) *ʾyty [ly ʾlp ḥdh bydkm]* "There is [one boat of mine in your hands]" (this *ʾyty* + a noun is often used to introduce a topic); (2) *ʾp [qdmt znh] (ʾgrh) ʿl znh šlḥ[n]* "Even previously we have sent a letter about this;" (3) *ʾtʿst ʿl [ʾgwrʾ zk]* "Take thought for [that temple];" (4) *hn ʿl mrʾn [kwt] ṭb* "If it seems good to our lord;" (5) *kzy ʾgrtʾ [zʾ] tmṭʾ [ʿlyk]* "Whenever [this] letter reaches [you];" (6) *lʿbq* "Right away;" (7) *[ʿbdk ydnyh wknwth kn] ʾmrn* "Thus say [your servant Yedaniah and his colleagues]" (this is often used to introduce a statement); (8) *ʿl znh šlḥn hwdʿn* "This is why we send this information;" and (9) *śm ṭʿm* "Issue an order."

Other examples of formulaic expressions appear in letters written to friends and family: (1) *ʾl tṣpw ly* "Do not worry about me;" (2) *lkn ʾnh yṣp* "I am worrying about you" (this formula readily combines with the former one, as in Egyptian); (3) *ḥzy ʿl [ynqyʾ]* "Look after [the children];" (4) *mhy dh zy spr lh hwšrtn* "What is this, that you haven't sent me any letter?" (5) *mlʾ lbt* + pronoun: "to be full of anger against . . ."; and (6) *šlm (l)[nbwsh] tnh* "[Nabushah] is well here."

E. The Main Aramaic Letter Types

The external formulae used in Aramaic letters did not mix at random; their combinations formed a limited number of sets or *formularies,* which were deemed acceptable in various geographical areas and during various historical periods. The shape and permissibility of these formularies were conditioned by tradition and foreign influences as well as by the rank and identity of the correspondents and the nature of their business. Accordingly, more than one formulary was available to quite similar people setting out to discuss the same kind of topics. In Achaemenid Egypt for instance, Jews exchanging friendly letters could use either the strongly Egyptianized formulary best known from the pagan letters found at Hermopolis (see E.2 below), or an old West Semitic formulary which could apparently be plied to all sorts of purposes (see E.3 below). In the second case however, the intimate character of the communication is reflected in the addition of secondary greetings and/or a certain choice of internal formulae, which contribute to specify the *letter type* beyond the blank generic features of the formulary; the resulting form is described below.

In the following, only the best-known letter types will be described; a few examples of typological contamination will be noted where they belong. The large and early Assur ostracon remains isolated in our corpus; so also is a fragmentary complaint in letter form (*CAP* 16; discussed by Dion 1979: 577–78). The *zkrnʾ* recording a proposal for the rebuilding of the temple in Elephantine (*CAP* 32) is not really a letter, but a messenger's memorandum.

1. Egyptian-Style Family Correspondence. This type of letter is so designated because it has many features similar to Egyptian epistolography (Dion 1981a). Aside from ostraca, examples of this type of Aramaic epistolary are found in *TAD* A2 (all texts) and *TAD* A3.3. These date from the first half of the 5th century B.C., and reflect family members eager to keep in contact with one another, petty private concerns (such as purchases, wages, etc.). A good example of this type of letter is *TAD* A2.4:

> "Greetings, House of Banit in Assuan!
> To my lord Psami, your servant Makkibanit.
> I bless you by Ptaḥ, that he may allow me to see your face in well-being. Greetings, my mother Mama! Greetings, my brother Betay, with his household and his sons! Greetings, Raʿya!
> Do not worry about Harwas. As much as it's in my power, I am not leaving him alone; and now, I am exerting myself for him.
> To my brother Waḥpreʿ from his brother Makkibanit. I send you well-being and life. And now, if the (???) comes to you, send me a message through ʿAqba son of Waḥpreʿ. And now, whatever you may want, send me a message.
> Dispatch to me enough skins for a leather suit. Keep getting barley from Taši and giving it in payment for beams, and leave with Mama any beam you can find. I bought striped fabric and scented oil to bring to you folks, but I could not find anybody to bring it to you.
> And now, let them bring me castor oil: five handfuls.
> Do not worry about me; I am worrying about you.
> I am writing to ask how you are."
> *(On the back of the scroll:)*
> "To my father Psami, from Makkibanit son of Psami."

The elements associated with this type of formulary are the following (except for the date, elements in parenthesis are in fact used most of the time):

a. *(Temple Greeting),* exclusive to this letter type: "Greetings (= *šlm*), House of [Bethel] (and House of [the Queen of Heaven]) (in Assuan)!"

b. *Internal Address:* "To my [brother] So-and-so, (from) your [brother] So-and-so."

c. *Initial Greeting:* the writer seems free to choose between either (1) "[I] bless you by [Ptah], that he may allow me to see your face in well-being," or (2) "I send you well-being and life." The Padua letter (*TAD* A3.3) is exceptional in using "I send you well-being and good health . . . ," a formula best known from Aršam's archive.

d. *Secondary Greetings* (see D.1 above).

e. *Introductory Particle:* "And now."

f. *Arrangement of the Body:* this tends to be a random sequence of short paragraphs, often beginning "And now."

g. *(Date):* only *TAD* A3.3 is dated; the calendar is Egyptian.

h. *(Closing Greeting):* "I send this letter about your well-being *(lšlmk),*" i.e., "to ask how you are."

i. *External Address:* "To my ([brother]) So-and-so (son of So-and-so) from your ([brother]) So-and-so (son of So-and-so). (To be delivered to) [Assuan].

2. Letter Types Sharing an All-Purpose Formulary. The three important letter types discussed below (a-c) use the same basic set of external formulae; this formulary is also used in *CAP* 38, a unique letter of introduction (Dion 1982: 565–70). The four basic elements of the formulary include the following: *Internal Address:* "To [my lord] So-and-so, [thy servant] So-and-so;" *Initial Greeting:* "May (all) [the gods] seek the well-being of [my lord] (abundantly) at all times;" *Introductory Particle:* "And now;" *External Address:* "To [my lord] So-and-so (son of So-and-so), [thy servant] So-and-so (son of So-and-so). A business letter (*TAD* A3.10) provides a useful example:

"To my brothers Ḥuri and *pṭmḥw,* your brother Spentadata.

May all the gods seek the well-being of my brothers at all times.

And now, there is one boat of mine in your hands—I share ownership with its master. Look, as for my share, whatever Aramantidata tells you to load on it, and whatever he wishes, let it be done for him. Moreover, my share in the rent of the boat [ ] pay it out to him.

There is some silver, 8 shekels, which I gave to [ ] to pay for grain to deliver to my house; and there is silver, 1 karsh, which I gave you to buy grain for Yatma. Sum total of the silver: 1 karsh, 8 shekels. If you buy grain with it and deliver it to our houses, fine; if not, pay it out to Aramantidata, he will bring it to us. And if the grain . . . *(a line of ill-preserved text is omitted).*

As for *Pṭmḥw,* let him stay (?) with you in the boat; do not let him get away from you until he comes to me.

To my brothers Ḥuri son of [ ] and *Pṭmḥw,* your brother Spentadata son of Fravartipata."

a. Official Letters. There are several witnesses to this type of letter, all written on papyrus (*TAD* A1.1 [?]; *CAP* 17; 27 [?]; 30–31 [copies of the same letter]; 70 [?]. They all come from the last three decades of 5th century B.C., except *TAD* A1.1, which was written ca. 600. Such letters were for internal use by government administrators, and the recipients all seem to have been highly placed. Some of the phraseological details reflect Mesopotamian contacts, in contrast to the Egyptian contacts reflected in the family correspondence (E.1 above). The adjustments to the formulary include the following:

(1) *Internal Address:* these letters may add titles to recipient's and sender's names, and mention the latter's "colleagues."
(2) *Initial Greeting* tends to be expanded.
(3) *Body of the letter* tends to be basically twofold, containing (a) background information, and (b) the main thrust of the message (petition, etc.).
(4) *External Address* (missing on atypical *TAD* A1.1): precise titles are used; the external address can include a developed list of senders and colleagues (*CAP* 17; Porten 1983).
(5) *(Colophon):* see Porten 1983: 414.
(6) *(Date):* according to the Babylonian calendar; regnal years cited.

b. Friendly Letters. There are numerous witnesses to this type, all on papyrus (*CAP* 37; 39; 40; 41; 56 + 34; 57; *TAD* A3.9; it is not clear whether *CAP* 21 [the "Passover Papyrus"] should be included in this category, in spite of its lack of specifying features). Letters of this type tend to date from the late 5th century B.C. (although *TAD* A3.9 is from 399 B.C.). They were not addressed only to friends and family; this type was the regular medium used by the Jews of Elephantine to discuss community problems (*CAP* 37; 56 + 34; *TAD* A3.9; also *CAP* 21?). In such instances, a "brother" is not always a blood relation. Internal formulae similar to those in the letters from Hermopolis do not always predominate. The adjustments to formulary include the following:

(1) *Secondary Greeting:* "Greetings, (my lord) So-and-so!"
(2) *The Body:* more similar to "Egyptian Family Correspondence" (E.1 above) than to "Official Letters" (E.2.a above).
(3) *(Date):* only appears in *TAD* A3.9, where the Egyptian calendar is used.

c. Business Letters. The witnesses to this type of letter include *CAP* 42; 54 recto; 54 verso; *TAD* A3.10; A3.11. They all date from ca. 475–450 B.C. to ca. 375–350 B.C. The imperative tone, the lack of friendly phrases, and other indications (e.g. interracial character of the Berlin papyrus) show that "brother" in these letters amounts to a business partner. Note also the manner of dating and the fact that two examples were folded like contracts rather than letters. The adjustments to the formulary:

(1) *The Body* consists of short paragraphs focused on imperatives or volitional imperfects. Often, several alternatives are envisioned: "If . . .; but if . . ."
(2) *(Date):* when one is given (*CAP* 42), it uses both Egyptian and Babylonian month names and indicates the regnal year.

3. The Style of Persian Chanceries. All examples have to do with the satrap Aršam (412–407 B.C.), and most were sent to Egypt from Babylonia. All but *CAP* 26, which is a papyrus from Elephantine, were found together at an undisclosed location and are written on leather. *CAP* 26 letter exhibits a few formal peculiarities and differs from the other pieces in its direct relevance to public administration, whereas the texts on leather deal with the satrap's personal business. *TAD* 6 is also peculiar in that it is more a kind of passport than a real letter. Yet it is striking that the same basic formulary, the same dry and meticulous administrative style, should prevail everywhere, in Egypt as well as in the center of the Persian Empire. In fact, affinities for 5th century B.C. administrative documents in Elamite have been pointed out by Whitehead (1974: 176–78), and introductory formulae like those of the Aršam letters are still reflected in many documents of the 1st millennium A.D. (Harmatta 1957). As noted above, this unified and perduring chancery style was able to contaminate letters belonging to other types (*TAD* A3.1; *CAP* 42), and yet it did not prevent official letters from also being written according to the "all-purpose" formulary.

An example of the Persian chancery style is an order written in letter form (*TAD* 4):

"From Aršam to Armapiya.
And now, Psamšek, my superintendent, sent me a message and said thus: Armapiya and the troops under his command are not obeying me in my lord's business (about) which I am telling them.
And now, thus says Aršam: In the business of my estate, whatever Psamšek tells you and those troops under your command, obey him and do it.
Be sure of this: if Psamšek sends me any further complaint about you, you will be thoroughly interrogated, and a harsh sentence will be applied to you.
Bagasrava is cognizant of this order; Aḥpepi was the scribe."
(On the back of the scroll:)
"From Aršam to Armapiya.
Concerning the fact that Psamšek sent me a complaint."

The basic formulary is as follows:

(1) *Internal Address:* "From So-and-so to So-and-so." In every case the sender is at least equal in rank to the recipient; from available evidence it is not clear whether a subordinate could send a letter to a superior.
(2) *Introductory Particle:* "And now" (always *wkʿt*).
(3) *External Address:* resembles the Internal Address, but titles are used, and geographical information is provided ("who is in Egypt").
(4) *Docket:* a brief note about the content, beginning with *ʿl*,
"Concerning," is placed after the External Address.

Adjustments to the formulary as well as differences in the subject matter and the status of the correspondents make it possible to distinguish two letter types sharing the formulary described above:

a. Orders in Letter Form. The witnesses to this type include *TAD* 4; 7–11; cf. No. 6, and *CAP* 26 (with reservations, see above). The adjustments to the formulary include the following:

(1) *Arrangement of the Body:* background information is provided first, and then the order (*ṭʿm;* the Aram name of this letter type?).
(2) *Colophon:* twofold in texts of the main collection: "So-and-so is cognizant of this order; So-and-so was the scribe." On *CAP* 26 the formulation is somewhat different and suggests that the first official's title was *bʿl ṭʿm* (cf. Ezra 4:8–9, 17).
(3) *External Address:* includes the recipient's title, rather than sender's.
(4) *Docket: TAD* 8–9 and *CAP* 26 have a note in Demotic in addition to the Aramaic one (Whitehead 1978: 137–40).
(5) *(Date):* only on *CAP* 26 (using Babylonian month name and regnal year).

b. Letters to Equals. The witnesses include *TAD* 1–3; 5; and 12–13. The following adjustments to the formulary are noted:

(1) *(Initial Greeting):* "I send you well-being and good health in abundance" (such a greeting is omitted in *TAD* 12, which is a hostile letter). More wishes may be added, such as "Here things are fine with me; over there too, may things be fine with you!"
(2) *External Address:* usually lists the sender's title, not the recipient's.

4. A Letter Type from the Beginning of the Christian Era. There are several witness (*Hev* 1; 2; 4; 8; 10; 11; 14; 15 [all on papyrus]; and Yadin 1965: 111 [an ostracon from Masada]) to letter type dating ca. A.D. 66–135. An example of this type is *Hev* 15 (from the photo in Yadin 1971: 129):

"Shimʿôn to Yehudah bar Menasseh, to Qiryat ʿArabaya.
I have sent you two donkeys, in order that you send with them two men to Yehonathan Bar Baʿayan and to Masabalah, in order that they pack and send you palms and citrons at the camp. As for you, send away others, that they bring you myrtles and willows; then set those in order and send them to the camp. Large indeed is the army!
Be well."

Due partly to the preliminary nature of the publication, areas of uncertainty remain about some aspects of the formulary (e.g., was there any External Address?). Formal consistency does not seem as high as in letter types from earlier times (see esp. *Hev* 4). However, the following are noteworthy:

(1) *Internal Address:* Shimʿôn Bar Kôsibâ (the Prince over Israel), to So-and-so (+ geographical destination).
(2) *(Initial Greeting): šlm/slm* appended to the Address.
(3) *Introductory Particle: d(y).* In *Hev* 15, this is inserted within the first sentence.
(4) *Closing Greeting:* "Be well." The preliminary character of the publication often does not allow verification of its presence.
(5) *Sender's Signature:* "[Shimʿôn Bar Kôsibâ] has written this." (*Hev* 8). Same remark.

All the sufficiently clear examples carry commands of Bar Kôsibâ to his followers, not always of a military character, as shown by the example above. Letters in Hebrew from the same period (Pardee 1982: 122–44) use very similar formulae and cover an even greater variety of topics. Perhaps we are dealing with one more "all-purpose" formulary. Significantly, the most decisive phrases (Address, Initial Greeting, Closing Greeting) correspond to long-established features of Greek letters, documented in this same corpus from the Judean Desert: "So-and-so (+ title) to So-and-so, *Chareîn* ('Greetings') . . . , ʾʾErrōsō ('Be well!'). Here the multilingual character of epistolary forms appears more clearly than ever.

Bibliography

Alexander, P. S. 1978. Remarks on Aramaic Epistolography in the Persian Period. *JSS* 23: 155–70.

Bresciani, E. 1960. Papiri aramaici egiziani di epoca persiana presso il Museo Civico di Padova. *RSO* 35: 11–24.

Couroyer, B. 1978. BRK et les formules égyptiennes de salutation. *RB* 85: 575–85.

Dion, P. E. 1979. Les types épistolaires hébréo-araméens jusqu'au temps de Bar-Kokhbah. *RB* 86: 544–79.

———. 1981a. The Aramaic "Family Letter" and Related Epistolary Forms in Other Oriental Languages and in Hellenistic Greek. *Semeia* 22: 59–76.

———. 1981b. Aramaic Words for "Letter." *Semeia* 22: 77–88.

———. 1982. La lettre araméenne passe-partout et ses sous-espèces. *RB* 89: 528–75.

Driver, G. R. 1954. *Aramaic Documents of the Fifth Century* B.C. Oxford.

Fitzmyer, J. A. 1981. Aramaic Epistolography. *Semeia* 22: 25–57. (Revised from *JBL* 93 [1974] 201–25 = pp. 183–204 of *A Wandering Aramean* [Missoula, MT, 1979].)

Grelot, P. 1972. *Documents araméens d'Egypte*. LAPO 5. Paris.

Harmatta, J. 1957. The Parthian Parchment from Dura-Europos (Dura Parchment No. 12). *Acta Antiqua* 5: 261–308.

Kraeling, E. G. 1953. *Brooklyn Museum Aramaic Papyri*. New Haven.

Pardee, D. 1982. *Handbook of Ancient Hebrew Letters*. SBLSBS 15. Chico, CA.

Porten, B. 1968. *Archives from Elephantine*. Berkeley.

———. 1978. The Archive of Jedaniah Son of Gemariah of Elephantine—The Structure and Style of the Letters(1). *EI* 14: 165–77 (in Hebrew).

———. 1979. Aramaic Papyri and Parchments: A New Look. *BA* 42: 74–104.

———. 1980. Aramaic Letters: A Study in Papyrological Reconstruction. *JARCE* 17: 39–75.

———. 1982. The Archive of Yedaniah b. Gemariah of Elephantine: The Structure of the Letters and Their Style (2). Pp. 11–24 in *Irano-Judaica*, ed. S. Shaked. Jerusalem (in Hebrew).

———. 1983. The Address Formulae in Aramaic Letters: A New Collation of Cowley 17. *RB* 90: 396–415.

Segal, J. B. 1983. *Aramaic Texts from North Saqqâra with Some Fragments in Phoenician*. Texts from Excavations, 6th Memoir. London.

Whitehead, J. D. 1974. Early Aramaic Epistolography: The Arsames Correspondence. Ph.D. Diss., University of Chicago.

———. 1978. Some Distinctive Features of the Language of the Aramaic Arsames Correspondence. *JNES* 37: 119–40.

Yadin, Y. 1961. Camp D. *Yediot* 25: 49–64 (in Hebrew).

———. 1965. The Excavations of Masada, 1963/1964, Preliminary Report. *IEJ* 15: 1–120.

———. 1971. *Bar Kokhba*. London.

PAUL E. DION

GREEK AND LATIN LETTERS

The letter is one of the most common and socially significant kinds of written text from antiquity. Extant letters represent every level of Greco-Roman society from Egyptian peasants to Roman emperors. The letter served the most basic needs of day-to-day communication and the most highly developed art and ideology. The letter is also arguably the most important, and certainly the most prevalent type of literature in early Christianity.

A. Nature of the Letter
B. Sources
C. Letters and Education
D. Forms, Types, and Functions
E. Greek Epistolary Tradition
F. Latin Epistolary Tradition

A. Nature of the Letter

Three important characteristics of the letter are its occasionality, its fiction of personal presence, and its ability to absorb other genres. Letters more than other types of literature are obviously embedded in the social contexts and interactions of particular historical moments (for example, a nearly bankrupt shopowner sends a letter to a wealthy acquaintance begging for financial help). The times, places, social status, and historical contexts of sender and receiver are crucial components of a letter's meaning. The letter "fictionalizes" the personal presence of the sender and receiver. The authorial voice is constructed as if speaking directly to the audience. Letters also tend to be dialogical; the author in the text anticipates what the audience will say and how it will react. A letter may belong to an exchange of letters or other texts, and may incorporate portions of these texts into itself in the form of an imagined conversation. By its very nature the letter is able to assimilate texts belonging to other genres. Thus the letter has often served as the framework for essays, narratives, and poetry. In such cases the ostensible epistolary occasion and the audience may become purely fictional.

Some of these points are explicit in ancient epistolary theory, although both ancient and modern romantic notions about the letter's ability to convey unmediated personal presence has obscured the nature of epistolary rhetoric. Early in the 20th century, A. Deissmann contrasted the conventionality and artificiality of literary texts with the supposed spontaneous outpouring of personality in true letters. Today scholars are studying the highly conventional literary construction of the ancient letter's "outpouring of personality."

B. Sources

There are four different sources for our knowledge of ancient letters: letters preserved through literary transmission, letters discovered in modern times, letters preserved in inscriptions, and letters embedded in other kinds of literature. Many Greek and Latin letters were preserved and copied because they were valued as literature by certain communities. The Greek letters of Plato, Isocrates, Demosthenes, and Libanius and the Latin letters of Cicero, Pliny, Seneca, and Fronto fit into this category, as do the

Christian letters in the NT, of the Apostolic fathers, Basil, Gregory of Nazianzus, Augustine, and Jerome. Letters preserved in this way tend to be more consciously literary than letters from the other categories and are often highly shaped by Greek or Latin rhetoric. Some letters in this category were written and collected with an eye toward publication. They also reflect a higher social level than other sorts of letters.

If we had only letters preserved by literary transmission, we would know little about letter writing among the masses of common people in the Greco-Roman world. In the late 19th and early 20th centuries great quantities of texts were recovered during the excavations of towns and villages in the dryer parts of Egypt where papyrus could survive. These texts include many thousands of often fragmentary letters. A few show the influence of rhetorical and literary training, but most are simple communications involving business relations, legal appeals, friendship, and family matters. The papyrus letters together with those preserved by literary transmission provide a view of the whole world of letter writing from Hellenistic times to the Byzantine period. A number of letters, mostly from Hellenistic monarchs, were copied onto stone as inscriptions. Such letters served as royal propaganda. Some Epicurean letters were inscribed in stone by a certain Diogenes in the Lycian city of Oenoanda. Finally a fairly large number of letters are found embedded in literary works. These appear most frequently in historical, biographical, and fictional narratives (see Acts 15:23–29).

C. Letters and Education

Basic letter writing was probably taught to boys in the so-called secondary stage of education by a *grammaticus*. At least some teachers of rhetoric trained their students in epistolary style. Although epistolary style and theory belonged to the domain of rhetoric, they were never an integral part of the extant rhetorical systems. The earliest significant discussion is in the work *On Style (De Elocutione)*, wrongly attributed to Demetrius of Phalerum but actually written by someone else between the 3d century B.C. and the 1st century A.D. According to *On Style*, letters are to use the plain style or to employ a mixture of the plain and graceful styles. The letter is like one side of a dialogue. Letters also ought to be "real" communications between individuals and not technical treatises. Brevity is also desirable. Cicero in the 1st century B.C. and Seneca in the 1st century A.D. reflect a knowledge of Greek epistolary theory and probably of handbooks on letter writing. In the elementary rhetorical exercises of Theon (1st century A.D.), letter writing is an exercise in characterization *(prosopopoiia)*. In the early 3d century, the sophist Philostratus of Lemnos wrote a polemical work on proper epistolary style. The first rhetorician to include a full discussion of letters writing as part of a handbook comes only in the 4th century with Julius Victor who includes an appendix on the subject.

More important for the general practice of letter writing are epistolary handbooks. The apostle Paul and many other writers of Christian letters in the first three centuries reflect a handbook knowledge of letter writing style and theory. These handbooks fall into two types. The first kind are systematic treatises which show an interest in theory and a knowledge of rhetoric. The two extant representatives are the *Epistolary Types* also attributed to Demetrius of Phalerum and the *Epistolary Kinds* attributed in different manuscript traditions either to Libanius or Proclus. The first, in its original form, is probably from pre-Christian times and the latter is dated between the 4th and 6th centuries A.D. The handbook of "Demetrius" seems to have been written for professional letter writers in service to public officials. It discusses 21 types of letters. For each letter, "Demetrius" and "Libanius" provide a brief definition and a very brief sample letter often in the form of a rhetorical syllogism which captures the logic of the type. The handbook of Libanius discusses 41 types.

It is important to understand the interests of these handbooks and their approach to classifying letters. They show very little interest in style and structure. Rather each type represents a characteristic social occasion and shows how a certain social transaction could be effected by a letter. Thus, for instance, one writes a blaming letter when a social equal or inferior has failed properly to reciprocate benefits conferred by the writer. The letter informs the recipient that he or she has failed in this way and attempts to shame the recipient mildly, but not so as to destroy the basic relationship. The rhetorical tradition often used such stereotyped occasions for speech acts to classify speaking into genres. The broadest of these are the three divisions of rhetoric: The forensic speech of the lawcourt; the advising speech of the city council; the epideictic speech for praising good and criticizing evil. Most of the types of letters in the handbooks belong to the category of praise and blame and only a handful to the other divisions of rhetoric. Several letters in this category are types of exhortation and are so treated by the handbooks (e.g. letters of parenesis, consolation, admonition, rebuke, reproach).

A second kind of handbook is represented by the bilingual, Greek and Latin, Bologna Papyrus (3d or 4th century A.D.) and by model letters for students to copy (3d century B.C.–5th century A.D.). These show no interest in theory or rhetoric and often reflect only minimal literacy. The two kinds of letter-writing handbooks either aim at the beginning and advanced stages of education or were designed for people from different social-educational levels. The letters in the NT and among the writings of the Apostolic Fathers clearly reflect a knowledge of the more advanced level of handbook although not of advanced rhetorical training.

D. Forms, Types, and Functions

The thousands of papyrus letters discovered in Egypt largely represent common everyday kinds of letters produced by people with very modest levels of literacy. Frequently people who could not write had to dictate their messages either to a friend or a professional letter writer. Most common are family letters, letters of request, petitions, commanding letters, and letters of recommendation and introduction. The opening and closing conventions for Greco-Roman letters changed little over several centuries. This conservation is most clear among the common papyrus letters—by contrast most early Christian letters transmitted literarily seem quite creative. The ancient prescript typically contained three elements: the name of the sender, the addressee, and a salutation (for example, "Diogenes to Isias, greetings"). The prescript was often followed either by a wish for health or less frequently a thanksgiving or act or worship to a god. These basic elements could be amplified and elaborated in many ways. Usually letters closed with a formula of farewell and often with a list of greetings for others in addition to the addressee.

The letters of more educated people and literary letters are especially characterized by the ethos and conventions of Greek friendship. Classical Greek culture privileged friendship between male peers as the highest form of social relationship. The epistolary theorists assumed that the letter of friendship was both the most basic and highest form of letter writing. Consequently the ethos and language of Greek friendship shaped Greco-Roman letter writing as a whole although that of upperclass writers more than others. The ethos of friendship was largely expressed through a set of standard themes and commonplace expressions: The letter is a friendly conversation; friends reciprocate in all things; friends will sacrifice for one another; friends are frank with one another; through the letter friends are together though physically apart (1 Cor 5:3; 1 Thess 2:17; Col 2:5); the letter contains an image of the writer's character; the letter is a consolation for a friend's absence; expressions of joy upon receiving a friend's letter; expressions of longing for a friend (2 Cor 1:16; 1 Thess 3:6–10; Phil 22; 2 John 12; 3 John 14).

Early Christian letters most nearly resemble the letters of philosophers and moralists. The Hellenistic philosophies sought to guide people to the good and happy life. Some philosophical letters are instructional treatises in doctrines but most are letters of exhortation in which teachers seek to guide and mold the characters of disciples. The letters of Plato and Aristotle were influential models. Epicurus sent many letters to widely scattered communities of his disciples regulating community behavior and exhorting them to the life of friendship and tranquility. In the 1st century A.D., Seneca wrote 124 letters addressed to Lucilius. Whether the correspondence is real or fictitious is a matter of debate. Nevertheless, the letters realistically depict the way that philosophical guides employed letters to lead their friends toward the happy life. Such letters prominently adapt friendship to this relationship of guide and student and present the "author's" character as a model for imitation. The same kind of hortatory features characterize the letters of Paul and other early Christian letters. Numerous purely fictitious letters were also written in the names of famous philosophers such as Socrates, Diogenes, Crates, and Heraclitus. These are largely hortatory and show marked similarities to pseudonymous Christian letters such as the Pastoral Epistles (1 Timothy, 2 Timothy, Titus).

E. Greek Epistolary Tradition

Letters had a significant literary and ideological impact in the form of collections. These were usually made after the author's death, although sometimes a collection might be compiled by the writer himself. From the 5th and 4th centuries B.C., the letters of Demosthenes and Isocrates were important models of style in the rhetorical tradition. The philosophical schools, however, were the great collectors of letters in the Greek tradition of letter writing. From classical Athens only the letters of Plato are extant, and their authenticity has been a matter of debate since Richard Bently raised critical consciousness by showing that the collections attributed to Phalaris, Themistocles, Socrates, and Euripides were fictitious. The collections from the 4th through 2d centuries B.C. of Aristotle, Theophrastus, Crates, Arcesilaus, and Carneades were very influential but are now lost. Only a few letters of Epicurus (341–270 B.C.) are extant, but they were the most important models for hortatory philosophical letters in Hellenistic and Roman times. Unknown Cynic philosophers in the later Hellenistic period and early empire produced extensive collections of fictitious letters under the names of Anacharsis, Crates, Diogenes, Heraclitus, Socrates, and the Socratics. These served as models for the Cynic life and as propaganda for debates among various kinds of Cynics. Some of the 97 letters attributed to the neo-Pythagorean philosopher Apollonius of Tyana (d. ca. A.D. 97) are probably authentic.

The other important non-Christian group of letter collections in Greek are the erotic and fictional literary letters written between the 2d and 5th centuries. Aelian (170–235) wrote 20 rustic letters in atticizing style. Following the same archaizing nostalgia for classical Athens, Alciphron (2d century A.D.) tried to imagine the words and world of farmers, fishermen, prostitutes, and parasites from 5 centuries earlier in his 122 letters. The love letters of Philostratus (2d century A.D.) are addressed to women and boys. A similar collection from a contemporary, the sophist Lesbonox, is now lost. In the 5th century, Aristaenetus incorporated erotic themes and language from writers throughout antiquity in his love letters.

The end of the extant pagan Greek tradition comes in the 4th century with the 80 letters of the emperor Julian (the "Apostate") and the rhetorician Libanius' 1,600 letters. Both are important sources for the history and aristocratic culture of their century. Libanius' letters strictly follow the rules of epistolary theory with regard to brevity, subject matter, and form.

The Greek Christian tradition of letter writing is a marked modification of but not a departure from the non-Christian Greek tradition. Christianity emerged as a movement within Judaism, but distinctive Jewish traditions of letter writing had only a minor influence on early Christian letters. The letter does not seem to have had the cultural and ideological importance for ancient Judaism that it did for Christian and Greco-Roman culture in general. Though Jewish letter writing as such exerted only a little influence, the Jewish concepts, symbols, language, and ethos of earliest Christianity gave a distinctive stamp to Christian letter writing. The earliest extant Christian letters are from Paul the apostle to the Gentiles (ca. A.D. 10–ca. A.D. 62). His letters provided a formative shape for much of later Christian epistolography. Paul's letters are Christian adaptations of common Greco-Roman types: protrepsis (Romans); admonition, advice (1 Corinthians); rebuke, apologetic, advice (2 Corinthians); rebuke, advice, paraenesis (Galatians); friendship, paraenesis (Philippians); paraenesis (1 Thessalonians); admonition (2 Thessalonians); recommendation/mediation (Philemon). These are types of letters most commonly written by philosophers and moralists as they tried to guide their disciples toward the happy life.

Other NT letters (Colossians; Ephesians; 1, 2 Timothy; Titus; James; 1 Peter; 2, 3 John; James; Jude) can also be understood as adaptations of similar Greco-Roman types. This is also true of the letters of Ignatius and Polycarp (early 2d century) and the lost letters of Dionysius of Corinth (late 2d century). These earliest Christian letters differ most from the letters of the great age of Christian letter writing in the 4th and 5th centuries in two ways. First they make much less use of the rhetoric of the technical rhetorical handbooks and the traditions of sophistic rhetoric. Second the ethos of Greek male friendship is much less important for these early letters than is the familial ethos of the household. Greek Christian letter writing reaches its peak in the 4th century with Athanasius, Basil, Gregory of Nyssa, Gregory of Nazianzus, and John Chrysostom. These writers fully integrated Greek literary culture into the life of monastic and aristocratic friendship.

F. Latin Epistolary

Cicero (106–43 B.C.) is the fountainhead of the Latin epistolary tradition. His 931 letters were written between 68 and 43 B.C. and published after his death in four collections. Cicero was familiar with the themes and commonplaces of Greek friendship and epistolory theory. He may have been most responsible for naturalizing the Greek epistolary tradition in Latin. A collection of Augustus' letters was extant in the latter part of the 1st century A.D. but has perished. The poetic epistles of Horace and Ovid remain from the Augustan age (late 1st century B.C. and early 1st century A.D.). Seneca's letters to Lucilius are modeled after the letters of philosophical guides like Epicurus. Pliny the Younger (61–112 A.D.) published 358 literary letters which he arranged chronologically. The orator Fronto's (2d century A.D.) letters to Marcus Aurelius and others mix oratory and epistolary friendship.

This legacy of great collections of Latin letters is echoed in Christian form in the 4th and 5th centuries in the letters of Ambrose, Jerome, Augustine, Paulinus of Nola, Sidonius and the poetic and prose letters of Ausonius. In these, the Greek and the Latin, the pagan and the Christian, the philosophical and the sophistic epistolary traditions melded into a new synthesis which had an enormous effect on the literature and thought of the West.

Though Christian belief and thought has deep roots in Judaism, Christian letter writing was literarily an adaptation of the Greek and Roman epistolary traditions. Indeed the Christian tradition conformed itself more to the artistic and rhetorical standards of Greek and Roman letter writing in the last centuries of antiquity. The letters of Paul and the other NT letters struck educated people in late antiquity as strange products of a remote subculture. Nevertheless they are fundamentally Greco-Roman letters. Christian letters from Paul to the end of antiquity continued to function as types of Greco-Roman letters, as a tradition within a tradition.

Bibliography

Deissmann, A. 1910. *Light From the Ancient East.* Trans. 1910. Rev. 1927. Repr. Grand Rapids, 1978.

Doty, W. 1973. *Letters in Primitive Christianity.* Philadelphia.

Koskenniemi, H. 1956. *Studien zur Idee und Phraseologie des griechischen Briefes bis 400 n. Chr.* AASF B/102/2. Helsinki.

Malherbe, A. J. 1988. *Ancient Epistolary Theorists.* SBLSBS 19. Atlanta.

Stowers, S. K. 1986. *Letter Writing in Greco-Roman Antiquity.* Philadelphia.

Thraede, K. 1970. *Grundzüge Griechisch-römische Brieftopik.* Monographien zu Klassischen Altertumswissenschaft 48. Munich.

White, J. L. 1986. *Light From Ancient Letters.* Philadelphia.

STANLEY K. STOWERS

LETUSHIM [Heb *lĕṭûšîm*]. A clan name mentioned in the genealogy of Abraham by his wife Keturah in Gen 25:3. Letushim (the plural form may be compared to similar plurals for groups in Gen 10:4—Kittim and Dodanim) is listed as one of the three sons of Abraham's grandson Dedan, the son of Jokshan. These three sons are not found in the matching, but abbreviated, genealogical clan list in 1 Chr 1:32–33. This may reflect a shift in population or politics by the time of the Chronicler. Albright (1953: 9–11) suggested that Letushim be translated as "craftsmen" thereby designating them as part of the economy of the city of Dedan. Winnett (1970: 191) disputes this and the identification of Letushim with Syriac *latusa,* "one who sharpens the sword," arguing that based on Ezek 27:20 Dedan's sole manufactured export was "saddle blankets." Whether they received this title before or after they settled in Dedan the people of the Letushim clan represent one of several obscure Arabian tribal groups who inhabited the fringes of the Negeb and N Arabian regions. Their very obscurity added to the contrast the biblical writer(s) wished to make between Isaac and the other sons of Abraham.

Bibliography

Albright, W. F. 1953. Dedan. Pp. 1–12 in *Geschichte und Altes Testament.* Tübingen.

Winnett, F. V. 1970. The Arabian Genealogies in Genesis. Pp. 171–96 in *Translating and Understanding the Old Testament: Essays in Honor of Herbert Gordon May,* ed. H. T. Frank and W. L. Reed. Nashville.

VICTOR H. MATTHEWS

LEUCIUS (PERSON). See JOHN, ACTS OF.

LEUMMIM [Heb *lĕʾummîm*]. A clan name mentioned in the genealogy of Abraham by his wife Keturah in Gen 25:3. Leummim is listed as one of the three sons of Abraham's grandson Dedan, the son of Jokshan. These three sons are not found in the matching, but abbreviated, genealogical clan list in 1 Chr 1:32–33. This may be due to shifts in population or a change in the political situation by the time of the Chronicler. The plural form of the name may reflect its use by a particular population group in the city of Dedan (compare similar plural names in Gen 10:4, Kittim and Dodanim). Winnett (1970: 191) suggests that the name's more generic meaning of "tribesmen, clansmen" identifies the Leummim as "mixed elements" within the city. Their very obscurity was used by the biblical author(s) to starkly contrast the importance of the descendants of Issac, and even those of Ishmael, with the children of this secondary wife. They received no inheritance in Canaan and were sent away to live on the eastern fringes of the Negeb and N Arabian regions.

Bibliography

Winnett, F. V. 1970. The Arabian Genealogies in Genesis. Pp. 171–96 in *Translating and Understanding the Old Testament: Essays in Honor of Herbert Gordon May*, ed. H. T. Frank and W. L. Reed. Nashville.

Victor H. Matthews

LEVI (PERSON) [Heb *lēwî*]. The name of 4 people in the Bible. The meaning of the name is uncertain. Popular etymology in the Bible for the name is "to be joined" (Gen 29:34; Num 18:2, 4). More recent suggestions have included "to coil or twist" from Ar *lawa,* "to borrow" from Heb *lwy,* "priest" from Minaean *lwʾ*, and "to give oracles" from Ar *lawa.* None of these suggestions provides a satisfying or convincing solution to the problem of etymology. The name is also found in Amorite and Egyptian sources; the latter 2d millennium materials use the name as a geographical term for a region in SW Arabia. This, plus the early connection with Moses and his association with the region of Midian, may indicate a possible location for the origin of the tribe of Levi.

1. The third son of Jacob and Leah (Gen 29:34). He was the eponymous ancestor of the tribe of Levi, of the priestly Levites, and of all subsequent priestly factions. In some lists Levi is one of the twelve tribes, sons of Jacob (Gen 29:31–30:24; Deut 27:12–13; 1 Chron 2:1–2); however, in other lists Levi is replaced by Manasseh or Ephraim and thus not listed among the twelve (Num 1:5–15; 7:12–83; Josh 21:4–7).

The first descendants of Levi were Gershon (Gershom), Kohath and Merari (Gen 46:11; Num 3:17; 1 Chron 5:27—Eng 6:1), and all played a role in guarding (Heb *šmr*) and serving (*ʿbd*) the tabernacle (Num 3:21–37). Moses is said to have been a descendant of Levi (Exod 2:1–2) as were Aaron, Moses' brother (Exod 4:14; 1 Chron 5:27–29—Eng 6:1–3) and Zadok (1 Chron 5:27–34—Eng 6:1–8). Thus all three priestly groups, Levites, Aaronites, and Zadokites, traced their ancestry to Levi.

There are varying accounts of how Levi became a priestly group, the Levites. The first is in association with the golden calf story. After the "sons of Levi" killed the 3,000 men who were not on Yahweh's side (Exod 32:26, 28), Moses indicated that they had therefore entered the service of Yahweh (Exod 32:29). According to Numbers 3–4, the sons of Levi were taken by Yahweh instead of the firstborn (Num 3:45); and then following a census (Num 4:2), they were assigned various priestly duties (Num 4:1–49). If Aaron's descent from Levi is accepted, there is a third account in Exodus 28:1–4 where Moses is instructed by God to select Aaron from among the people to serve as priest.

Several stories demonstrate Levi's militaristic nature in Israelite society. In Genesis 34, Levi, along with Simeon, killed Hamor and Shechem in retaliation for the rape of their sister Dinah. Levi and Simeon guaranteed the success of their retaliation by attacking Hamor on the third day after he and the males of his city had been circumcised. A second account is that of the golden calf, mentioned above, where the sons of Levi killed 3,000 men for their apostasy (Exod 32:25–29). At numerous points the descendants of Levi (the Levites) were appointed "to guard" (rather than the usual translation of *šmr* as "to take charge of") the tabernacle or the ark (Num 1:53; 8:26; 1 Chron 23:4). The military nature of Levi is also noted in Jacob's blessing (Gen 49:5), and it became an explanation for the disappearance of Levi as a tribe (Gen 49:7) and the subsequent elimination of Levi from the list of twelve tribes. Finally, the intertestamental literature preserves the militaristic view of Levi (*T. Levi* 5: 3; *T. Sim.* 5: 4; *Jub.* 30: 18).

The militaristic activities of Levi have often posed a problem for scholars, as they attempt to relate the warlike Levi with the assumed irenic priests, the Levites. However, if one takes into consideration the fact that Levi's military actions are always in defense of Yahweh and the correct worship of Yahweh, the fact that the "sons of Levi," the priestly Levites, often performed militaristic activities such as guarding the tent of meeting, and the fact that Hittite parallels in the ancient world indicate that it is not unusual for priests to carry on martial activities, then it is no longer troublesome to connect Levi and the priestly Levites. Indeed, it is the fervent defense of Yahweh which is the consistent and characteristic role of Levi and his descendants.

Bibliography

Cody, A. 1969. *A History of Old Testament Priesthood.* Rome.
Gunneweg, A. H. J. 1965. *Leviten und Priester.* Göttingen.
Milgrom, J. 1970. *Studies in Levitical Terminology, I.* Berkeley.

John R. Spencer

2. The father of Matthat and son of Melchi, according to Luke's genealogy tying Joseph, the "supposed father" of Jesus, to descent from Adam and God (Luke 3:24). Gk *levi* may be an indeclinable form or a genitive form from Gk *levis,* although Blass/Debrunner are undecided (BDF pars. 53[1], 55[1e]). D omits Levi, substituting a genealogy adapted from Matt 1:6–15 for Luke 3:23–31. Apart from Luke 3:29, the name Levi falls within a list of 17 ancestors of Jesus who are otherwise unknown in the biblical documents, including Matthew's genealogy (Fitzmyer *Luke I–IX* AB, 500). Several problems revolve around the person holding this name, including the possibility that his son, Matthat, is the same person as Matthan in Matt 1:15, in which case the same person is given two different fathers. See MATTHAT #2. Kuhn (1923: 208–9) believes that the two Levi's of Luke 3:24 and 29 were originally identical, both derived from a common list that subsequently formed the basis for two parallel lists in Luke's genealogy: 3:26–29, Jesus to Mattathias, and 3:29–31, Joshua/Jesus to Mattatha. The first perhaps reflects a Hebrew context and the second, in an Aramaic context, tracing Mary's line of descent (since it does not mention Joseph as Jesus' father). Even though both Levi's are listed as fathers of a Matthat, this proposal has not proved convincing to most scholars.

3. The father of Matthat and son of Simeon, according to Luke's genealogy tying Joseph, the "supposed father" of Jesus, to descent from Adam and God (Luke 3:29). D omits Levi, substituting a genealogy adapted from Matt 1:6–15 for Luke 3:23–31. Apart from Luke 3:24, the name Levi is unknown as an ancestor of Jesus in any other biblical documents, including Matthew's genealogy, and falls within a list of eighteen otherwise unknown descendants of David's son Nathan (Fitzmyer *Luke I–IX* AB, 501). Jeremias (1969: 296) believes that it is anachronistic for Luke to include this name here, since there is no record of its use after the patriarchal period until the time of the Maccabees, although caution must be exercised in light of the limited nature of the available evidence. See above on Kuhn's proposal.

4. A tax collector who left his post to follow Jesus, throwing a big feast for him in his house (Luke 5:27, 29), known in Mark 2:14 as the son of Alphaeus. Because Levi is not mentioned in Luke's (6:13–16; Acts 1:13) or Mark's (3:14–19) lists of disciples, but a James the son of Alphaeus is mentioned at Mark 3:18, some texts list James at Mark 2:14 (see *NovTG*[26]), although a form of Levi is clearly the better reading, warranting an A from *UBSGNT* (see *TCGNT*, 78; cf. Taylor 1959: 202). "Levi the son of Alphaeus" is read in D at Luke 5:27 (for bibliography on textual problems see Lane *Mark* NICNT, 100–1). Levi is unknown in Matthew's Gospel, although a story is recounted of a disciple who was called to follow Jesus in the same manner (9:9) and who is mentioned as a tax collector in Matthew's list of disciples (10:2–4, esp. v 3). The question naturally arises whether this is the same man in all three gospel accounts (see Lamarche 1970: 127, for verbal parallels; Theobald [1978: 173] raises the possibility of Levi as a generic name in Mark's narrative). Several solutions have been proposed: They are two different people, a view held by several patristic fathers (e.g. Origen *Cel.* 1.62); they are the same person, since it is unlikely that the same event happened twice, and it was not unknown that a person could be known by two Semitic names, such as Levi Matthew (e.g., Joseph Barnabas [Acts 4:36]) (cf. Hervey 1853: 150–51, who speculates that Matthew was also related to Jesus); the account in one gospel has been transferred to the other gospel, probably as a Markan redactional creation (Pesch 1968: 43–45); and by the time of writing there was considerable confusion about the composition of the group of disciples (see Cranfield *Mark* CGTC, 102; Fitzmyer, 590; *TDNT* 4: 234–35).

Bibliography

Hervey, A. 1853. *The Genealogies of Our Lord and Saviour Jesus Christ, As Contained in the Gospels of St. Matthew and St. Luke.* Cambridge.

Jeremias, J. 1969. *Jerusalem in the Time of Jesus.* Philadelphia.

Kuhn, G. 1923. Die Geschlechtsregister Jesu bei Lukas und Matthäus, nach ihrer Herkunft untersucht. *ZNW* 22: 206–28.

Lamarche, P. 1970. L'appel à la conversion et à la foi: La vocation de Lévi (Mc 2:13–17). *LumVit* 25: 125–37.

Pesch, R. 1968. Levi-Matthäus (Mc 2:14/Mt 9:9; 10:3). *ZNW* 59: 40–56.

Taylor, V. 1959. *The Gospel According to St. Mark.* London.

Theobald, M. 1978. Der Primat der Synchronie vor der Diachronie als Grundaxiom der Literarkritik. *BZ* 22: 161–86.

STANLEY E. PORTER

LEVIATHAN [Heb *liwyātān*]. The name of a mythological sea serpent or dragon, personifying the chaos waters, mentioned in the Ugaritic texts, in the OT, and in later Jewish literature. Etymologically the name means "twisting one," as befits a serpent.

In the Ugaritic texts the name appears as *ltn* (*KTU* 1.5.I.1 = *CTA* 5.I.1), which has traditionally been vocalized as Lōtān, but it has been persuasively argued by J. A. Emerton (1982) that the correct rendering should be Lītān. In this Ugaritic passage (lines 1–4) Mot alludes to Baal's defeat of Lītān as follows, "Because you smote Lītān the twisting serpent, (and) made an end of the crooked serpent, the tyrant with seven heads, the skies will become hot (and) will shine." In the Baal epic we also find the goddess Anat (Baal's consort) claiming to have defeated Lītān (though he is not mentioned by name), amongst other mythological creatures: "Surely I lifted up the dragon, I . . . [and] smote the crooked serpent, the tyrant with the seven heads" (*KTU* 1.3.III.40–42 = *CTA* 3.III.D.37–39). This event seems to be described briefly in *KTU* 1.83.3–10 (= *UT* 1003.3–10) and *KTU* 1.82.1–3 (= *UT* 1001.1–3), the former passage ascribing the defeat of the dragon to Anat and the latter to Baal.

In view of a number of references in the OT to the defeat of the chaos monster at the time of creation (e.g., Leviathan in Psalm 74 and Rahab in Psalm 89), the question is raised whether the Canaanites likewise envisaged the dragon conflict as taking place at that time. Although the detailed description of the defeat by Baal of the sea god Yam (who is similar to, but not identical with Leviathan) does not appear to be associated with the creation of the world in *KTU* 1.2 (= *CTA* 2), it may be that the Canaanites did also envisage a primeval conflict with the powers of chaos prior to El's creation of the world. This would not only explain the creation context of such dragon passages as Psalms 74 and 89, and be consistent with the fact that the sea is a cosmic element; it might also account for the fact that at the very end of the Baal epic, perhaps corresponding to the time of new year's eve, the defeat of the dragon (*tnn* = Lītān) and Arš is looked forward to (*KTU* 1.6.VI.51–53 = *CTA* 6.VI.50–52). The Ugaritic allusions to the defeat of Lītān and other monsters, mentioned above, may therefore have had a creation context.

In the OT, Leviathan's defeat is attributed to Yahweh. In Ps 74:14 this is set in a creation context (vv 12–17), just as is the case with the defeat of Rahab, a similar or possibly identical sea monster, in Ps 89:11—Eng 89:10 (cf. vv 10–14—Eng 9–13). Attempts to claim that these two passages are really speaking of the Exodus are unconvincing. It is interesting that Ps 74:14 refers to the shattering by God of Leviathan's "heads" (pl.)—this is now illuminated by the Ugaritic texts, which reveal that he had seven of them.

In Isa 27:1 we read of an eschatological defeat of Leviathan by Yahweh. That a conflict originally associated with creation should become an element of eschatological imagery is explained by the principle *Urzeit wird Endzeit* (= the primeval time becomes the end time), which is attested elsewhere in apocalyptic literature, as in the notions of Paradise regained and a new heaven and a new earth. It is not possible to be certain which historical political power might be designated by Leviathan in Isa 27:1, though conceivably it is Egypt or alternatively the dominant world power of the time. What is striking is that the description of Leviathan as "the twisting serpent . . . the crooked serpent" in Isa 27:1 is remarkably close to the terminology used to describe Lītān in the Ugaritic text cited above.

In Job 40:25–41, 26 (—Eng 41:1–34) part of the second divine speech is a detailed description of Leviathan. Many commentators have believed, following the view of S. Bochart expressed in 1663, that Leviathan is here the crocodile, and similarly that Behemoth in Job 40:15–24 is the hippopotamus. However, good reasons can be put forward against Leviathan's equation here with the crocodile, or for that matter with any other actually existing beast. For example, Leviathan is said to breathe out fire and smoke (Job 41:11–13—Eng 19–21), which is suggestive of a mythological creature, and it is implicit in God's argument that no human is able to capture him. We probably have here the same mythological Leviathan who is attested elsewhere in the OT, and whom God overcame at the creation (though it is arguable that he now has only one head rather than seven). The point of God's argument seems to be that since Job cannot overcome Leviathan, how much less can he hope to overcome in argument the God who defeated him. Accordingly, Job repents in dust and ashes (Job 42:1–6). As part of the divine speech, Job is asked whether he can play with Leviathan (Job 40:29—Eng 41:5). This is clearly an allusion to Ps 104:26, where it is possible to render "There go the ships, and Leviathan whom you formed to play with." Whether this was what the author of Psalm 104 was intending to say, or whether we should prefer the translation, "There go the ships, and Leviathan whom you formed to play in it (*sc.* the sea)," the former interpretation is clearly what the author of the second divine speech presupposed. In Ps 104:26 Leviathan has sometimes been supposed to be the whale, but it is possible that here again it is rather a mythological creature which is in view.

Another reference to Leviathan occurs in Job 3:8, "Let those curse it who curse the day, who are skilled in rousing up Leviathan." These words form part of the passage in which the wretched Job laments the day of his birth, wishing it would be covered with darkness. That the rousing of Leviathan should betoken darkness is understandable if it implies the reversal of the process of creation; Gen 1:2 describes the pre-creation state of chaos as darkness. The popular emendation of "day" (Heb *yôm*) to "sea" (*yām*) in Job 3:8 is to be rejected: it would provide only a spurious parallelism, since the cursing of the sea would imply the opposite of the rousing of Leviathan.

Leviathan is also mentioned in later Jewish literature. For example, in 2 Esdr 6:49–52, *2 Bar.* 29:4, and *1 En.* 6:7–9, 24, Leviathan, along with Behemoth, is to be devoured at the Messianic banquet. Furthermore, there can be no doubt, in view of Leviathan's seven heads, that it is this mythological monster which underlies the seven-headed dragon (Satan) in Rev 12:3 and the seven-headed beast (Rome) in Rev 13:1, 17:3. Similarly, the seven-headed dragon in *Odes Sol.* 22:5, Pistis Sophia 66 and *Qidd.* 29b must also reflect Leviathan.

Bibliography

Day, J. 1985. *God's Conflict with the Dragon and the Sea.* Cambridge.

Emerton, J. A. 1982. Leviathan and *ltn:* The Vocalization of the Ugaritic word for the dragon. *VT* 32: 327–31.

John Day

LEVIRATE LAW

LEVIRATE LAW [Heb *yibûm*]. The Bible discusses levirate marriage in Genesis 38, Deut 25:5–10, and probably Ruth 4. According to Deuteronomy, when a man dies without leaving a son, his widow is forbidden to marry outside the family. Her husband's brother "takes her as his wife and performs the levir's duty. The first son that she bears shall be accounted to the dead brother." Should the levir refuse, the ceremony of *ḥălîṣâ* (removal of the sandal) is performed and the widow is free to marry outside the family.

Leviticus 18:16 and 20:21 totally prohibit marriage between a brother- and sister-in-law. The rabbis reconciled the contradiction between Deuteronomy and Leviticus by saying that Leviticus states the general principle and the law in Deuteronomy applies only when a married man dies without offspring (*y. Nĕd.* 3:5).

Most modern scholars agree that Ruth 4 describes a levirate marriage, although the descriptions in Genesis and Deuteronomy differ substantially (Ahroni 1984: 68). Scholars disagree as to whether Ruth reflects an early or late stage in the development of levirate law (Niditch 1985: 452–53).

Levirate marriage is one of the principle subjects of tractate *Yĕbāmôt* of the Mishnâ, Tôseptā, and the Palestinian and Babylonian Talmuds. Neusner (1980: 30–32; 1981: 137–43 and 194–97) reads Mishnâ *Yĕbāmôt* as a philosophical essay teaching that heaven's bond (levirate) and the earthly union (betrothal, marriage-contract, and consummation) correspond to each other, as do death at God's hands and divorce. Both God and man can sanctify woman and remove the sanctification. Neusner's conception of the Mishna as a philosophical essay has been criticized by Cohen (1983), Chernick (1984), and Maccoby (1984).

Rabbinic law tends to reduce the distinction between levirate marriage and other marriages. For example, the rabbis require a betrothal ceremony, *maʾămār* (declaration) (*t. Yebam.* 7:2; *b. Yebam.* 52a), similar to other betrothal ceremonies. The levir gives the widow an object of value in the presence of witnesses, or writes a document containing a betrothal formula, just as a man normally betrothes a woman.

Clear differences remain between levirate marriage and other marriages, however. The view that before betrothal a state of *ziqa* (prior attachment) exists between the levir and the widow has no counterpart in other marriages (*m. Yebam.* 3:9; *b. Yebam.* 26a). The widow in a state of *ziqâ* is forbidden to have sexual relations with an outsider, although the rabbis do not consider the children of such a union as illegitimate (Belkin 1970: 307–20).

Some scholars see a tendency to limit the application of the levirate rite in rabbinic law (Epstein 1942: 96; Gordis 1974: 248; Ahroni 1984: 70–73). On the basis of Deut 25:5 ("when brothers dwell together"), for example, the rabbis exclude maternal brothers and brothers born after the husband's death from the levirate obligation (*m. Yebam.* 2:1–2; *b. Yebam.* 17b). The rabbis interpret the phrase "and has no son" to mean offspring rather than son (*Sipre Dĕbārîm*, chapter 288; *b. B. Bat.* 109a), such that the marriage cannot be consummated if the child is illegitimate, female, or a grandchild (*m. Yebam.* 2:5; *b. Yebam.* 22b; *b. Nid.* 5:3).

Several facts belie this modern scholarly claim, however. First, there is no consensus among Talmudic rabbis as to whether levirate marriage or *halisa* are preferable (*m. Bek.* 1:7; *b. Yebam.* 39a–b and 106a). Second, according to rabbinic law the offspring of the levirate union are considered the levir's and the levir inherits his brother's estate (*m. Yebam.* 4:7). The rabbis contradict the plain meaning of scripture, which views the first child as the offspring, and perhaps the heir, of the deceased. Rabbinic law here works to promote levirate marriage, making it more attractive to the levir.

Belkin (1970: 293) thinks the rabbis valued the institution because it protected the widow and helped compensate the family for the loss it sustained. Niditch (1979: 149) thinks the rabbis shared the biblical view of levirate marriage as a socially constructive institution. Society allows a young woman only two proper roles. She is either an unmarried virgin in her father's house or a faithful, child-producing wife in her husband's or her husband's family's home. Through the levirate, society avoids a sociological misfit, the young childless widow. The levirate not only continues the line of the deceased, it reaffirms the young widow's place in the home of her husband's family.

Bibliography

Ahroni, R. 1984. The Levirate and Human Rights. Pp. 67–76 in *Jewish Law and Current Legal Problems,* ed. N. Rakover. Jerusalem.

Albeck, H. 1955. *Šišâ Sidrê Mishnâ: Našîm.* Tel Aviv.

Belkin, S. 1970. Levirate and Agnate Marriage in Rabbinic and Cognate Literature. *JQR* 60: 275–329.

Burrows, M. 1940. Levirate Marriage in Israel. *JBL* 59:23–33.

Chernick, M. 1984. Review of Neusner 1981. *Journal of Reform Judaism* 31: 111–14.

Cohen, S. 1983. Jacob Neusner, Mishnah, and Counter-Rabbinics. *Conservative Judaism* 37: 48–63.

Elon, M. 1977. *Hamišpāt Haᶜibrî.* 3 vols. Jerusalem.

Epstein, L. M. 1942. *Marriage Laws in the Bible and the Talmud.* Cambridge.

Gordis, R. 1974. Love, Marriage, and Business in the Book of Ruth. Pp. 241–64 in *A Light Unto My Path,* ed. H. N. Bream, R. D. Heim, and C. A. Moore. Philadelphia.

Halivni, D. 1968. *Mĕqôrôt Ûmĕsôrôt: Našîm.* Tel Aviv.

Katz, J. 1982. Yibûm Wĕḥălîṣâ Bitĕqûpat Habātar Talmûdît. *Tarbîz* 51: 59–106.

Lieberman, S. 1967. *Tôseptā Kipĕšûtâ.* Vol. 6. New York.

Lopez, M. 1979. Labĕᶜāyat Hayibûm Bizĕman Hazeh. *Šĕbîlîn* 31/32: 114–27.

Maccoby, H. 1984. Jacob Neusner's Mishnah. *Midstream* 30: 24–32.

Manor, D. W. 1982. A Brief History of Levirate Marriage as it Relates to the Bible. *Near East Archaeological Society Bulletin* 20:33–52.

Neufeld, E. 1944. *Ancient Hebrew Marriage Laws.* London.

Neusner, J. 1980. *A History of the Mishnaic Law of Women.* Pts. 1, 5. Leiden.

———. 1981. *The Evidence of the Mishna.* Chicago.

Niditch, S. 1979. The Wronged Woman Righted: An Analysis of Genesis 38. *HTR* 72: 143–49.

———. 1985. Legends of Wise Heroes and Heroines. Pp. 451–63 in *The Hebrew Bible and its Modern Literary Interpreters,* ed. D. A. Knight and G. M. Tucker. Chico, CA.

Thompson, D., and Thompson, T. 1968. Some Legal Problems in the Book of Ruth. *VT* 18: 79–99.

Wegner, J. R. 1986. Chattel or Person? The Status of Women in the System of the Mishnah. Doctoral Diss. Brown University.

Yaron, R. 1969. *Maqbîlôt Ladînê Šômeret Yābām Bamišpāt Harômî.* Pp. 263–79 in *Ad Secundas Nuptias Convolare. Symbolae Iuridicae et Historicae.*

RICHARD KALMIN

LEVITES AND PRIESTS. This article surveys the two main groups of cultic officials in the OT.

A. Introduction
B. The Desert Period
  1. Moses and Aaron in Old Narratives
  2. Moses and Aaron in the Genealogies
  3. Is Moses a Kohathite?
C. The Tribal Period
  1. Levi in the Tribal Lists
  2. Possible References to Levites in the Tribal Period
  3. Genealogy of Levites in the Tribal Period
  4. Levitic Groups
  5. Deuteronomy
  6. Summary
D. The Monarchical Period

A. Introduction

Since Wellhausen (*WPHI*) there has been wide acceptance of the view that the elaborate picture of the priests and Levites given in the "Priestly" sections of Exodus, Leviticus, and Numbers represents the last, not the earliest stage in the development of the Israelite priesthood. Wellhausen did not think that the Levites formed a special priestly class in Israel's early period, as an uncritical reading of the Pentateuch would indicate. Although he did not deny that there had been a tribe of Levi in remote antiquity, he believed that it had nothing to do with the priesthood, and further that it had already disappeared before the rise of the monarchy.

Therefore, according to Wellhausen, the priesthood did not play a significant role in Israel until the monarchical period, and those who functioned as priests were not Levites. Wellhausen saw priests come into prominence for the first time with Deuteronomy, which, following DeWette, he dated to the time of Josiah. Here priests were first called "Levites," but this new priestly class did not derive from the Levitic tribe of the premonarchical period. Rather, they simply assumed the name "Levite" as a patronymic in order to bind themselves together in a class.

Wellhausen stated that Deuteronomy's picture of the priesthood was never fully put into practice. He arrived at this conclusion by comparing Deut 18:6–7 (which invites the "Levite" to come to the central sanctuary to serve with the "fellow-Levites") with 2 Kgs 23:9 (which states that the priests of the high places did not actually come up to the altar of Yahweh in Jerusalem). From this, he believed, arose the distinction between priests and Levites made first by Ezekiel, then by P, and finally by the Chronicler.

Thus Wellhausen believed that he had "solved" the problem of the Levites by showing that they had never existed as a priestly class before the monarchical period; that is, not until the writing of Deuteronomy.

Wellhausen's reconstruction received a great deal of study, and in some cases revision, but the main aspects of his work were widely accepted. Once it was recognized, however, that OT traditions could have had a long oral history before they were written down, it became possible to reconstruct Israel's history, including that of the Levites, back into premonarchical times.

One of the most important of these post-Wellhausenian studies of the Levites that uses the history-of-traditions method is Kurt Möhlenbrink's article, "Die levitischen Ueberlieferungen des Alten Testaments" (The Levitical Traditions of the Old Testament), published in 1934. Möhlenbrink investigates four Levitic *Gattungen* (genres): *Listen* (lists), *Geschichten* (stories), *Satzungen* (regulations), and *poetische Stücken* (poems). In his discussion of the *Listen* he suggests how the Levitic genealogies may have come into their present form. One of his major contentions is that the Aaronite and Zadokite lines were secondarily added to earlier Levitic genealogies. The original form of the genealogy in Exod 6:16–25 (his *Schema* A) he dates sometime between David and Josiah, and Num 26:58 (his *Schema* E) he believes originated in the time "between Deborah and David."

Among the *Geschichten,* Möhlenbrink does not find any that can be dated as early as his *Schema* A, that is, preexilic times. He denies any original connection between Zadokites and Eleazarites and between Eleazarites and Aaronides. He does, however, believe that the Eleazarites were the priests of a Canaanite sanctuary at Gibeah already before the conquest of Palestine by Israel. Later they attached themselves to the Levites. In the *Geschichten* he also notes an original incongruity between Aaron and Moses.

On the basis of his investigation of the *Levitensatzungen,* of which he considers Deut 18:1–8 and Ezek 44:4–31 to be the oldest, Möhlenbrink again concludes that the Aaronite traditions are a late addition to the Levitic.

Möhlenbrink's study of the *poetische Stücke (Levitenlieder)* yields the following results: The "Levi" of Gen 49:5–7 (and of Genesis 34) had nothing to do with the Levitic priests. However, in Deuteronomy 33, Levi is a real eponym of levitical priests. It is a poem about the origins and privileges of the Mushites (Levites derived from or associated with Moses). It dates even earlier than *Schema* E, that is, shortly before or after the conquest.

An important work of recent years which takes seriously the early history of the Levites is a study by Frank Cross (*CMHE,* 195–215). Cross believes that various stories of conflict in the wilderness period contain much that bears upon the history of the early priestly houses of Israel. He finds such stories in Exodus 32; Numbers 12, 16, and 25; and Leviticus 10. He concludes that these stories of conflict can best be understood if one posits an ancient struggle between the Mushite priesthood centered at Shiloh and Dan (with allied Mushite-Kenite priesthoods at Arad and Kadesh) and the Aaronite priesthood of Bethel and Jerusalem.

Using the insights of Möhlenbrink and Cross, as well as a fresh study of the Levitic genealogies, one can now reconstruct the history of the Levites in three periods: desert, tribal, and monarchy.

B. The Desert Period

It is in the early traditions of the desert period where one first hears of Levites who served as priests. In fact, Moses, who not only served as Israel's leader during this period but also functioned as a priest (see, e.g., Exodus 24), was considered to be a Levite (Exod 2:11).

It appears that the Levites were divided into three main groups in the desert period, namely, Gershonites, Kohathites, and Merarites. This follows from a study of the Levitic genealogies, where Gershon-Kohath-Merari constitutes the oldest element, both stylistically and content-wise, and from such narratives as Num 3:21–37 and 10:17, 21, which state that the Levites encamped around the tabernacle and took charge of transporting it, setting it up, and taking it down.

According to the Levitic genealogies in Exod 6:16–25, Num 26:58b–60, 1 Chr 5:27–41—Eng 6:1–15, and 23:13, Moses and Aaron were brothers who descended from Kohath the son of Levi. In each case Aaron is listed first, which can mean that the genealogist considered Aaron to be older and/or more important than Moses.

1. Moses and Aaron in Old Narratives. According to Exod 2:16–22, Moses married Zipporah, the daughter of Reuel, a Midianite priest. That the priesthood of Moses was henceforth closely connected with Midian's is suggested by Exod 18:12, where in a cultic meeting of Israel and the Midianites the dominant partner was Jethro/Reuel (probably representing Moses, since Moses is not among Israel's representatives), while Aaron and the elders of Israel appeared as guests.

Although in Exod 4:14, Moses appears to be dependent upon Aaron when it calls Aaron Moses' brother (or "your fellow Levite"), in the old narratives Moses is usually the dominant figure. This is particularly clear in the plague stories, where Moses is constantly mentioned first. In the very first encounter with Pharaoh (Exod 5:1–4) Moses is first and Aaron second. In the fourth plague (8:16–28—Eng 8:20–32) Moses dominates the scene; in fact Aaron is mentioned only once in this connection (v 21—Eng v 25), and then he is in second place behind Moses. In the fifth plague (9:13–35) he is mentioned only once (v 27), again in second place; in plague eight (10:1–20) he is mentioned three times (vv 3, 8, 16), but always in second position; and in plagues nine (10:21–26) and ten (11:1–8) Moses acts alone.

At the time when Yahweh first sent manna to the people, Moses alone is mentioned (16:4–5). During the war with the Amalekites (chap. 17) Aaron is a military leader of the same stature as Hur (vv 10, 12), but he is not described as a priest, nor is he on a par with Moses. In chap. 18, where Jethro, Moses' father-in-law, acts as a priest by sacrificing, Aaron (v 12), together with the elders of Israel, apparently is involved only as a participant in the communal meal which followed.

In preparation for the giving of the covenant at Sinai (Exodus 19) Aaron is mentioned only once, and then in distinction to the "priests" (19:24; cf. v 22). Who these "priests" were is not indicated. Though Aaron was given the honor of being asked to go up the mountain with

Moses, in chap. 20 it is Moses alone (v 21) who drew near to speak to God. Then in the covenant proceedings recorded in chap. 24 Moses acts as a priest (vv 6, 8, 22), while Aaron, Nadab, and Abihu function on the same level as elders in two cases (vv 1, 9), and in another instance (v 14) Aaron and Hur stay with the elders.

In Exodus 32, Aaron attempted to act as a priest, but his actions were unorthodox, and he gained the condemnation of Moses. In addition, the Levites who sided with Aaron were punished, and the Levites who sided with Moses were formalized as priests (vv 25–29).

Deut 10:8 states that the Levites were set apart "to carry the ark . . . , to stand before Yahweh to minister to him." This may either refer to the events of Exod 32:25–29, or it may be an alternate tradition of a "setting apart" that took place at "Jotbathah" (10:7). Still another tradition mentions a constitutive act for Levi at Massah and Meribah (Deut 33:8–11).

The role of Aaron in the old narratives of Numbers is similar to that in Exodus. In 10:29–11:35 he does not appear at all, and Moses is the main figure. The same is true in chaps. 13–14; 21:4–35; and chap. 32.

In Numbers 12, Aaron, together with his sister Miriam, is actually opposed to Moses (cf. Exodus 32). They criticized Moses for his choice of a Cushite wife. This is perhaps a reference to Zipporah. For their action Aaron and Miriam were not only rebuked, but Miriam was punished with leprosy.

Cross (*CMHE,* 204) sees two themes in Numbers 12: (1) Moses' superiority over the house of Aaron as a mediator of the divine command; and (2) the legitimacy of the Mushite priesthood despite its "mixed" blood.

In summary, the old narratives present Aaron not as a priest but as an elder of the people who makes the life of Moses, the leader, difficult.

2. Moses and Aaron in the Genealogies. Exodus 6 contains a Levitic genealogy. Its basic form is *(w)bny X Y,* "(and) the sons of X are/were Y." The sons of Gershon, Kohath, and Merari are all listed according to this formula. This section is concluded with the statement (v 19b); "These are the families of the Levites according to their generations." This could mean that vv 16–19 once formed an independent genealogy.

Verse 20, however, uses a different formula from vv 17, 18, 19. On the basis of this variant wording, S. A. Cook (*EncBib* 1662) and others have concluded that the statement calling Aaron and Moses the sons of Amram is a secondary expansion of the earlier form of the genealogy (cf. also vv 23 and 25a). Accordingly, the inclusion of the family of Aaron in the final form of the genealogies would therefore be due to an "Aaronizing" *Tendenz* on the part of the genealogist.

In the genealogies where Aaron and Moses are called brothers (Exod 6:20, Num 26:59, and 1 Chr 5:29—Eng 6:3 and 23:13), according to a principle enunciated by A. Olrik (1909: 5), it is significant that each time the order is "Aaron and Moses," whereas in the narrative sections it is normally "Moses and Aaron." Secondly, Moses' sons are never mentioned in the genealogies (except 1 Chr 23:15). These two facts alone indicate that Aaron and Moses may not be as closely associated as is often thought, and that they are best studied separately.

3. Is Moses a Kohathite? This raises the question whether Moses is a Kohathite, as the genealogies indicate, or whether in keeping with the old narratives he is less closely associated with Aaron. There are certain indications that Moses was actually a Gershonite. According to Exod 2:22 and 18:3 Moses had a son called Gershom. This agrees with the genealogy in Judg 18:30. Could this Gershom be connected in some way with Gershon the son of Levi? Linguistically it is difficult to tell whether the name Gershon or Gershom is more original. Both *-ōn* and *-ōm* can be used as hypocoristic/diminutive endings in biblical Hebrew names (Noth *IPN,* 56). However, given the antiquity of the *ōn* hypocoristic ending in Northwest Semitic (Gordon 1955: 51) and its greater frequency in biblical Hebrew than *ōm,* it seems probable that Gershon is primary. Further evidence for the fluidity of the spelling of the name is found in Chronicles, where the son of Levi is called both Gershon and Gershom.

If Moses' son originally had the name Gershon, then, according to the principle of papponymy (Cross 1963: 120–21) which was widespread in the ANE, he may have been named after an ancestor by the same name. The ancestor after whom Moses named his son may therefore have been Gershon the son of Levi.

This reconstruction provides a possible explanation for the different pictures of Moses' family lineage that emerge from a comparison of the old narratives and the final form of the genealogies. It would also explain why several times in 1 Chronicles the old, no doubt original, order of Gershon-Kohath-Merari is changed to Kohath-Gershon-Merari. These indications can be taken to mean that in the late period both Moses and the Gershonites were being de-emphasized, at least insofar as their priestly role was concerned.

Another example of possible name confusion which may relate to the de-emphasis of Moses' priestly role is Eliezer the son of Moses/Eleazar the son of Aaron. If one allows for the possibility that in the Hebrew spelling of Eliezer the *mater lectionis* with the i-vowel is secondary, there was originally no difference in the consonantal spelling of these two names. Are Eliezer and Eleazar therefore one and the same? In view of the probable de-emphasis of Moses as a priest in post-Solomonic times, perhaps Eliezer the son of Moses became Eleazar the son of Aaron in the tradition.

In a similar way, Phinehas the son of Eleazar the son of Aaron (Num 25:7, 10) may originally have been associated with Moses. At any rate, one of the sons of Eli (who may have been a Mushite, 1 Sam 2:27) is named Phinehas (1 Sam 1:3). Phinehas the son of Eli could (again according to the principle of papponymy) have been named after a Phinehas of the line of Moses.

In certain of the Levitic genealogies (Exod 6:16–19; Num 3:17–21, 27, 33; and 1 Chr 6:1–4—Eng 6:16–19) the next generation after Gershon-Kohath-Merari associates the Mushites with Merari, and not with Gershon. This, however, is probably not to be construed as a biological relationship, but rather as reflecting some social function or status (Wilson 1979: 19). This seems to be supported by the fact that Exod 6:20–25 carries the genealogy forward in an inconsistent way (no descendants are listed for Libnei, Shimei, Hebron, Mahli, or Mushi), while Numbers 3 and 1 Chronicles 6 do not carry the genealogy foward at all. Furthermore, there are no narratives in the OT which would indicate that these linkages represent historical reality.

C. The Tribal Period

There has been much scholarly discussion as to whether "Levite" is an ethnic or functional appellative. The evidence presented so far seems to indicate that the Levites were mainly a group or groups related by blood. This does not necessarily mean that "Levite" is per se an ethnic term. It can be a designation for a group which, though related, had a common function, and who because of the common function received the name. This seems to be the case with the Levites, for according to Albright (*ARI* 109; 204–5, n. 42) the term *lawiyu,* from which he derived "Levite," means "a person pledged for a debt or vow (to Yahweh)." In other words, a Levite, etymologically speaking, was a priest.

It is therefore plausible that each of the major groups or clans of Levites (Gershon, Kohath, Merari) constituted a blood relationship within themselves but not necessarily between them. Thus also Moses and Aaron would not have to be related, even though they were both Levites in the sense that they were both priests. Or put differently, a clan constituted a blood relationship, and several such clans who had the common function of the priesthood joined together to form the tribe "Levi." Accordingly, the Levites comprised a group of clans who, taken together, could have been designated as a tribe.

1. Levi in the Tribal Lists. In his study of the twelve tribes, Martin Noth (1930) dealt with the various lists of the tribes. He found that they generally fall into three categories: (1) those in which Levi is included (always in third place); (2) those in which Levi is not present but in which Joseph has been divided into Manasseh and Ephraim to retain the total of twelve tribes; and (3) those in which Levi, Ephraim, and Manasseh are all included.

The third category Noth takes to be a late harmonizing of the first two categories. Concerning the second category, in which the lists do not include Levi, Noth plausibly shows that all are dependent on either Num 1:5–15 or Num 26:5–51. He believes that Num 1:5–15 originally had Gad in third place. Hence, the only difference between Num 1:5–15 and Num 26:5–51 is the different order of Ephraim and Manasseh. Noth takes Num 26:5–51, which puts Manasseh first, as the older of the two forms. Noth (1930: 30–31) believes that the oldest form of category one (with Levi, Joseph still being undivided) is found in Gen 49:1–27. Since the Song of Deborah in Judges 5 mentions Ephraim and Machir (Manasseh), Noth believes that Num 26:5–51 and 1:5–15 must postdate this Song. Therefore, he dates them in the second half of the period of the Judges. Gen 49:1–27, on the other hand, must antedate the Song of Deborah, since it still speaks of Joseph as undivided. This form of the list of the tribes Noth dates to the very beginning of the period of the Judges. Another reason why Noth feels that the original form of these lists must come from before the monarchy of David is his feeling that they would have come from a time when the tribes were still interested in maintaining their individual histories.

If, as Noth has plausibly shown, Gen 49:1–27 reflects the beginning of the period of the Judges, either Levi must have still existed as a tribe at that time, or Levi was still remembered as an integral member of an old six-tribe league (the Leah tribes) which now formed the basis for a new twelve-tribe league. According to Noth, this first or oldest list of the tribes retains the memory of a secular tribe Levi which by the time of the second list had declined to the point (cf. Genesis 34 and 49) where they were no longer mentioned.

Gunneweg (1965: 59–64) holds to the first alternative, namely, that Levi did exist as a tribe in the period of the Judges, and that one must explain the absence of Levi from the second category of tribal lists in some other way than by positing its nonexistence. Gunneweg seeks to explain the difference between category one (with Levi) and category two (without Levi) by seeing a difference in purpose between them. The first category he considers to be a *Mitgliederliste* (list of members) of the tribal league according to their eponymous ancestors; the second, since it substitutes Ephraim and Manasseh for Joseph, he takes as a geographical-political-oriented list. Accordingly, because Levi had no land, it was not included in the second list, but because it was a member of the tribal league it was listed in the first group.

Another way to understand the difference between categories one and two would be to consider the first category as a "religious" listing, that is to say, as the groups or tribes who were to appear before Yahweh at the central sanctuary three times yearly (cf. Exod 23:17; 34:23); whereas the second category could have been "political," meaning that from these groups men of war could be conscripted. Thus the Levites could be recognized as one of the member tribes of the tribal league, though they owned no land and their young men did not serve in war.

2. Possible References to Levites in the Tribal Period. **a. Joshua.** Joshua's terminology for priests is the same as in Deuteronomy. Therefore, when it speaks about "Levitical priests," it could be referring to Mushites (descendants/adherents of Moses).

Joshua 3:3 says that "Levitical priests" carried the ark as the Israelites crossed the Jordan. Therefore the priests who carried the ark around Jericho (Joshua 6) were probably also "Levitical priests," though it is not explicitly stated. At the time of the reading of the law of Moses on Mt. Ebal and Mt. Gerizim (Josh 8:30–35) it is again the "Levitical priests" who carry the ark of the covenant. (Cf. Deut 31:9–12, which says that "the priests the sons of Levi" who carried the ark were to read the law every seven years before "all Israel," perhaps meaning before the ark at the central sanctuary. See also Deut 27:9 and 27:14.)

Joshua 9:27 tells how the Gibeonites became "hewers of wood and drawers of water for the congregation, and for the altar of Yahweh." Though the altar they served is not mentioned, it could mean that they assisted the Levites at the central sanctuary.

Obviously these few references do not constitute a full history of the Levites/priests in the tribal league, but apparently by the time the book of Joshua was written, there was in Israel still the memory of a tradition that connected the Levites with the ark of the covenant and the public reading of the law in the very earliest period of the tribal league. And it should be noted that in the first twelve chapters of Joshua the term "sons of Aaron" does not occur.

The last half of the book of Joshua contains very little narrative material. The bulk of these chapters is usually considered to be later than chaps. 1–12. Briefly, however, the Levites are presented as priests who did not receive any land as their inheritance (13:14, 33; 14:3–4; 18:7). Instead, they are said to have received cities to dwell in (Joshua 21; cf. 1 Chronicles 6). There is general agreement among scholars that the account of the Levitical cities does not date to the tribal league; but that the Levites did not have any territory of their own and thus had to be given some special support by the rest of the Israelites is no doubt true. The book of Deuteronomy (18:1–5) suggests how the Levites at the central sanctuary were supported.

The book of Joshua mentions only one individual priest, namely, Eleazar. He is said to be involved in the distribution of the land (19:51) and of the Levitic cities (21:1). Both acts are said to have taken place at Shiloh. Eleazar's death is reported to have occurred in Ephraim (Josh 24:33).

Joshua 21 speaks of the three-fold division of the Levites, namely: Kohath, Gershon, and Merari. The order, with Kohath first, indicates that it is later than the traditional Gershon-Kohath-Merari sequence found in so many of the genealogies. The Kohathites are divided into two groups, the sons of Aaron and the rest of the Kohathites. Both in its order and in the division of the Kohathites Joshua 21 is identical with 1 Chr 6:39–45—Eng 6:54–60.

Joshua 24:33 states that Eleazar was the son of Aaron and that Phinehas was the son of Eleazar. This agrees with the genealogies in Exod 6:16–25; 1 Chr 6:27–41—Eng 6:1–15 and 6:35–38—Eng 6:50–53; and Ezra 7:1–5. However, see B.3 above.

Though the final editing of Joshua is placed into the 6th century B.C. by Noth and many other scholars, it is recognized today that the preliterary stage of many of the documents in the book go back to a time much earlier than the final editing of the book. Therefore, in general, it can be said that there is a priori no reason why at least some of the material concerning the Levites in Joshua cannot actually reflect the period that it purports to describe, i.e., the period of the Conquest. For further discussion see Noth (*Joshua* HAT) and Boling (*Joshua* AB).

b. Judges. Judg 1:16 states that the descendants of the Kenite (i.e., Hobab), Moses' father-in-law, went up from the city of the palms (Jericho) in Judah and settled in Arad.

Judges 4:11 states how Heber the Kenite left his kinsman in Arad and went and pitched his tent at the "oak" in Zaanannim, near Kedesh.

If Moses was a priest, then the Kenites, because of their relationship to Moses, may have also been priests. What is more, oaks were frequently considered sacred (cf. Josh 24:26; Gen 12:6); so 4:11, which mentions "oak," may mean that the Kenites built a sanctuary at Kedesh.

In their excavations at Tell Arad, Y. Aharoni and R. Amiran have found a sanctuary which B. Mazar (1964: 297–303) dates to "between the 10th century B.C. (Stratum XI) and a late stage in the history of the Kingdom of Judah (Stratum VIII)." Perhaps there was such a sanctuary at Arad also in earlier times, and, if so, it could have been the haven for Mosaic traditions, since the Kenites (who lived at Arad, 1:16) were connected with Moses by marriage. These traditions could have been transplanted to the North (Kedesh) by Heber the Kenite (cf. 4:11). According to the genealogy of Judg 18:30, Dan would have been another northern sanctuary where Mosaic, and consequently Levitic, traditions were preserved. According to 18:30 there was a Mushite priesthood in Dan "until the captivity of the land," that is, presumably until ca. 722 B.C.

Judges 17:7–13 speaks of a single Levite *(lwy)* of Bethlehem in Judah. This Levite is seen moving to Ephraim. There he was quickly taken in as the priest of the Ephraimite Micah, who up till then used his own son as a priest. This shows that from the beginning of the period of the Judges, Israelites looked upon the Levites as the appointed representatives of Yahwism and as specialists of the cult. Micah considered the presence of a Levite in his house as a pledge of the blessing of Yahweh (17:13). Perhaps the Levites enjoyed this position of prestige because they were the priests of the ark of the covenant.

Judges 18 continues the story of Micah's priest. Here it is reported how the Danites on their migration northward enticed him to join with them because in their new home they wished the services of a priestly technician who could declare to them the divine intentions (18:5) and who would be qualified to set up and care for a sanctuary. Thus whether in Ephraim where he sojourned, or in the tribe where he set up his final home, the role, importance, and benefits of Levitism were appreciated.

The name of the Levite is given in 18:30, namely, Jonathan ben Gershom ben Moses. Charles Hauret (1957: 108–9) does not feel the genealogy at the end of the story is an intrusion, as do many other scholars, but that it is an ancient tradition preserved in the priestly circles of the sanctuary of Dan. He also defends Jonathan against the charges by scholars who would make him "cunning," "greedy," "ungrateful," and "ambitious." Hauret maintains that, if Jonathan was not the most virtuous priest, he at least had the merit of ability. Hauret further believes that Jonathan may have been an actual grandson of Moses, because the migration of the Danites harmonizes well with the beginning of the period of the Judges.

If Judges 17–18 is any indication, Levites were scarce during the period of the tribal league. This is understandable if their major function was caring for the central sanctuary with the tent and ark. Only gradually, as their numbers grew, would some Levites be free to serve at local sanctuaries.

Judges 19–20 gives another story of a Levite. He was from Ephraim, and he took a concubine from Bethlehem-Judah. When the Benjaminites of Gibeah raped his concubine so that she died, the Levite "divided her, limb by limb, into twelve pieces" (19:29) and sent them throughout the land. As Polzin (1969: 239) has pointed out, this was probably a symbolic act which called on members of the tribal league to provide help which they had already pledged in a treaty. At any rate, the rest of the Israelites spontaneously rallied to the side of the Levite, and they gathered at Bethel to inquire of God (20:18, 26).

It is stated that the ark was at Bethel (20:27) and that it was served by Phinehas, the grandson of Aaron. Perhaps Phinehas was the chief priest of the central sanctuary in Ephraim, while his "cousin" Jonathan was the chief priest of the sanctuary of northern Dan. Assuming that this Phinehas was a Levite, this provides information which corroborates the picture given in Joshua, namely, that the most important Levites were in charge of the central sanctuary and its ark. Here we have the added information that the Levites at the central sanctuary are consulted before battle is joined against an enemy (Judg 20:18, 23, 26–28). To serve at the central sanctuary meant to stand before Yahweh *(lipnê yhwh)* and his ark (20:28). The phrase *lipnê yhwh* seems to be a technical term, for in 20:18 the Israelites consulted *bēʾlōhîm* (of God); in 20:23 they wept *lipnê yhwh* and consulted *byhwh* (of Yahweh); in 20:26 they wept and sacrificed *lipnê hywh;* and in 20:27 they consulted *byhwh* (of Yahweh) at the ark of the covenant when Phinehas (20:28) served as the priest *ʿōmēd lĕpānāyw* (i.e., standing before him = Yahweh, or it = the ark).

c. 1 Samuel. The priests at the beginning of the book are Eli and his two sons, Hophni and Phinehas (1:3). Some commentators try to guess who "the house of your father who belonged to the house of Pharoah when they were (slaves) in Egypt," taken from Yahweh's words to Eli (2:27), refers to. If one takes "house of Pharaoh" to be a synonym for Egypt, then a number of answers are possible.

Wellhausen considers it to mean Moses (*WPHI,* 142; cf. *CMHE,* 196). This view can be defended, if one takes "the house of Pharoah" literally, for of Israel's ancestors, only Moses lived in Pharoah's house.

The identification of the "faithful priest" (2:35) who is to replace Eli is also a problem. The immediate context suggests Samuel; but it could already be a reference to the fact that Zadok would eventually replace Abiathar as the main priest of the people (cf. 1 Kgs 2:26–27; 35).

The Levitic classification of Samuel is even more in doubt. Though he is included in the present form of the Levitic genealogies recorded in 1 Chr 6:7–13—Eng 6:22–28 and 1 Chr 6:18–23—Eng 6:32-38, these are simply secondary additions to what were originally schematic genealogies of seven and fourteen names respectively. These additions were taken from 1 Sam 1:1, where Samuel's forefather Zuph is said to be an Ephraimite. That Samuel functioned as a priest, at least on occasion (cf. 7:10, etc.), seems clear. Therefore one must either reckon with a non-Levitic priesthood during this time; or the term "Levite" was used more as an appellative meaning priest than as an ethnic title. According to the former view, anyone, including Samuel, could have been considered a "Levite," regardless of his tribal affiliation.

Yet there is another possibility concerning Samuel, namely, that despite certain priestly functions he was technically a "judge" (despite 2:11). At least Samuel's sons who succeeded him were called "judges" (8:1; cf. 12:2).

The sanctuary that Eli served was at Shiloh, when, according to 1 Samuel 4, Israel was defeated by the Philistines. Eli's sons died in battle, and the ark was captured. Eli himself died after hearing the news of the battle. Though there is no clear archaeological evidence, it is quite likely that Shiloh and its sanctuary were also destroyed (cf. Jer 7:12). This, plus the loss of the ark, would have affected the Levites drastically.

The only explicit mention of Levites is in 6:15, where it is stated that they took the ark of Yahweh after it was returned to Israel by the Philistines. The Levites put the ark on a great stone at Beth-shemesh. This description of the Levites' duties agrees with Deut 10:8; 31:9; Josh 3:3; 8:33. Beth-shemesh was, however, not the central sanctuary (6:15–7:2), and we hear no more of the ark until David became king. Accordingly, the Levites who had served at the central sanctuary now had to try to attach themselves to local sanctuaries. Ichabod (4:21; cf. 14:3a), the son of Phinehas, disappears from the scene.

Into this situation stepped Samuel who had been trained as a priest by Eli himself (1 Samuel 1–3), but who also can be reckoned as a prophet. He seems to have performed the duties of chief priest in Saul's time. However, he apparently made no effort to bring back the ark to a prominent place, nor did he work at a central sanctuary. Rather we find Samuel serving at various cities (Bethel, Gilgal, Mizpah, Ramah [7:15–17]). Therefore, Albright (1961: 18) may be right in concluding that Samuel diminished the role of priests and Levites and turned to ecstatic prophets and local sanctuaries.

In 1 Sam 8:1–5 and 12:2 it is indicated that Samuel's sons also served as priests or judges. But we hear no more of them.

Another priest at the time of Saul was Ahijah ben Ahitub ben Phinehas (1 Sam 14:3, 18). Hence, we may assume that the line of Eli had not died out, but it played an insignificant role compared to Samuel.

The Elides eventually established themselves at Nob (cf. 1 Sam 22:11) where Ahimelech is said to have been priest; but this is no doubt another name for Ahijah. Ahimelech/Ahijah's son was Abiathar. The Elides at Nob were murdered by Saul, and only Abiathar escaped. He took refuge with David (1 Sam 22:20–23) and became David's priest (1 Sam 30:7).

3. Genealogy of Levites in the Tribal Period. The narratives of Exodus indicate that Gershom is the son of Moses. This is put into genealogical form in Judg 18:30b which also adds the name of Jonathan. The descendants of Moses after Jonathan are not indicated by specific names. It is likely, however, that the name "Mushites" in the genealogy of Num 26:58a is a reference to them as a group. If Möhlenbrink (1934: 196) is correct, this dates from the period of the Judges.

4. Levitic Groups. According to a number of scholars, Num 26:58a preserves the memory of four Levitic groups in the tribal league period, namely, Mushites, Hebronites, Korahites, and Libnites.

The Mushites were the descendants of Moses. The Korahites would naturally represent the descendants of Korah and, like the Mushites, date to the tribal league.

The Hebronites were no doubt the inhabitants of the city of Hebron, mentioned in Josh 10:36 as having been taken by the Israelites during the conquest. By a process of elimination the Hebronites could be the descendants of either Kohath or Merari. However, since the Mushites probably were in control of the sanctuaries at Dan (Judges 17–18) and Kedesh (Judges 1 and 4), one would expect their rivals, the Aaronides, to be located in the South (although Arad in the South apparently remained Mushite). Hebron would therefore be the most likely place for their center. It is significant, accordingly, that in the account of the Levitical cities, Hebron is assigned to "the sons of Aaron, one of the families of the Kohathites who belonged to the Levites" (Josh 21:13 and 1 Chr 6:39–40, 42—Eng 6:54–55, 57). Thus the connection of the Hebronites with Aaron and vice versa seems very probable.

The Libnites are probably to be connected with the city Libnah conquered by Joshua in Josh 10:29–30. Hence, the Levitic Libnites probably date to the tribal period. Since we suggested the Mushites to be descendants of Gershon, the Hebronites of Aaron, and the Korahites of Korah, by a process of elimination the connection of the Libnites with Merari and/or Ithamar of the desert period suggests itself.

Of the four groups mentioned in Num 26:58, the Mushites and Libnites were probably the priests in charge of the central sanctuary with its tent and ark. The Hebronites and Korahites, on the other hand, had been discredited in the desert period. Therefore they probably served only at local sanctuaries during the tribal period.

5. Deuteronomy. This, however, does not exhaust the source material for the period of the tribal league. In recent years there has been a strong reaction against de Wette's and Wellhausen's dating of Deuteronomy to the 7th century B.C. (*WPHI,* 9).

In his *Studies in Deuteronomy,* Gerhard von Rad points out that Deuteronomy preserves traditions older than the final editing of the book. He goes on to suggest that the country Levites of the N kingdom were the bearers of these traditions. He makes the same conclusion about some material in the Holiness Code. G. E. Wright (*Deuteronomy* IB, 326) has accepted von Rad's conclusions, and he has emphasized even more strongly than von Rad that many of the Levites were teachers of the law rather than altar clergy.

J. A. Emerton (1962) has rejected Wright's view. He contends that Deuteronomy did regard all Levites as possessing priestly status and as being connected with sanctuaries. Emerton believes that there is no distinction in principle between altar priests and other Levites in Deuteronomy. While agreeing that the Levites were teachers of the law, he sees no basis for assuming that they could not also serve as altar priests.

This writer believes that Wright is correct in his belief that "Levitical priests" and "Levites" are not synonymous terms in Deuteronomy. However, he does not think that the distinction that Wright assumes, namely, that one group was altar clergy and the other teaching clergy is valid. Emerton is no doubt correct in his view that all Levites were in principle altar priests and that they could also serve as teachers. If there is nevertheless a distinction between "Levitical priests" and "Levites," what is it? We propose the theory that the two names do not represent two different groups living and working at the same time, but that they represent (essentially) the same group working at two different times. In order to test this theory we propose to take another look at the passages in Deuteronomy which speak to the matter.

First of all, the uniqueness of the terminology for priests in Deuteronomy needs to be noted. The terminology "sons of Aaron," used so frequently for priests in "P," is not mentioned at all in Deuteronomy. Aaron himself is mentioned only in the retelling of the apostasy with the molten bull (Deut 9:16–21) and with respect to his death (Deut 10:6 and 32:50). The dominant figure in the retelling of the exodus and wandering periods is Moses.

Moses does not identify himself as a Levite, nor does he mention them in his account of the molten bull incident. He does, however, say (10:8) that the tribe of Levi *(šbṭ hlwy)* was "set apart" as a special priestly tribe. This may have taken place at Jotbathah, one of the desert stations where Israel stopped, after Aaron's death. However, since vv 6–7 seem intrusive in the context, v 8 may also refer back to Exodus 32.

It is in the rest of the book where the two distinctive Deuteronomic types of terminology for priests occur.

The one is simply "the Levite" *(hlwy).* The Levite is said to live "in your gates = towns": 12:12; 12:18–19; 14:27–29; 16:11; 16:13–14; 18:6–7; 26:12. "Among you," found in 26:11, is an alternate expression. The name "the Levite" is used without the qualifying phrase "in your gates" only in 10:9. However, this perhaps is a reference to the "Levitical priests."

In all of these cases, except 10:9, the context is: The Israelite is to rejoice with the Levite (by providing food, etc., for him) when he goes to "the place which Yahweh your God will choose" (12:11, 18; 14:25; 16:11; 18:6; 26:2). The Levite is to be specially remembered, "because he has no portion or inheritance with his brothers/with you" (12:12; 14:27–29; cf. 10:9, 18:1).

The other main terminology is "Levitical priests," *hkhnym hlwym.* It is used in the following places: 17:9; 17:18; 18:1–2; 24:8; 27:9. The Levitical priests render legal decisions (17:8–9; cf. 21:5 and 24:8); and they are in charge of the Torah (17:18).

"The priests the sons of Levi" *(hkhnym bny lwy)* (21:5) is an alternate term for Levitical priests (cf. 17:8–9). It is also used in 31:9.

"Levi" in 10:8–9 seems to be equivalent to "Levitical priests" because it says he is to minister *(šrt)* to Yahweh, just as 18:7 and 21:5 describe the Levitical priests.

Similarly 33:8–11, where Levi is said to use Urim and Thummim, reminds one of the Levitical priests of 17:8–9 and 17:18.

"Priest" in 17:12 is surely also a synonym for "Levitical priests" in 17:9. In 19:17 "priests" is parallel with judges, as it was in 17:8–13. Hence, it again seems to be a reference to the Levitical priests. "Priest" in 26:3–4 is at the sanctuary that Yahweh chooses (v 2) and so must be a Levitical priest (cf. 18:6–7).

The plural "Levites" *(hlwym)* of 27:14 (cf. v 9) must be Levitical priests, since participating in a covenant ceremony agrees with the activities of Levitical priests as outlined in Josh 8:33 and Deut 31:9–11. For the same reason, "Levites" in 31:25–26 seems to refer to Levitical priests.

It is not absolutely clear who the "priest" of 20:2 is. But since preparing the people for holy war was a very important assignment, it would seem much more likely that this was the function of the Levitical priests, who throughout the book have the important assignments given to them.

Deut 18:1–8 is a disputed passage. First of all there is the question of the meaning of "the tribe of Levi" in v 1. Wright (1954: 326), in keeping with his theory of the Levites, concluded that the translation of the English Authorized Version was correct, in contradistinction to the RSV. AV reads: "The priests the Levites, *and* all the tribe of Levi, shall have no part nor inheritance with Israel." The RSV reads: "The Levitical priests, that is, all the tribe of Levi, shall have no portion or inheritance with Israel." The AV's use of *and* and the RSV's use of *that is* both represent attempts to interpret the Hebrew, which has no conjunction between the two phrases. Wright in following the AV understands "the tribe of Levi" to refer to the group entitled "Levites," which he describes in his article.

Emerton (1962: 133–34) has, perhaps, the better of the argument on this point. Following S. R. Driver (*Deuteronomy* ICC, 214), he contends that the second phrase in the Hebrew text is more naturally read as being in apposition to the first, as also the RSV has it.

There is, nevertheless, an element of truth in Wright's proposal, for while "the tribe of Levi" stands in apposition to "Levitical priests," it is an "explanatory" apposition which in effect corrects the first term as being inadequate as a statement of the one to whom the concept "no inheritance in Israel" applies, since this condition was shared by "Levites" as well as Levitical priests.

However, the expression, "the tribe of Levi," we see not just as being an explanatory "apposition" but as an explanatory "gloss." That is to say, it seems to come from the same hand as vv 6–8, which is probably an attempt (by a later hand) to give to the Levites of his own time what had (formerly?) applied only to the Levitical priests.

Basically, then, 18:1–8 is a description of the duties of the Levitical priests of the central sanctuary, but it also includes the thought that in principle "all the (rest of the) tribe of Levi" (v 1) and "the Levite" (v 6) had the right to perform these duties.

Though the country Levites *(hlwy)* therefore probably had the right to function as priests, they evidently did not do enough of this work to make a living at it. At any rate, Deuteronomy tells us clearly that they were poor and scattered. This gives a hint as to the time of the Levites. Their condition is reminiscent of the Levitic cities, since these cities were scattered throughout the land and could have served as a haven for the scattered Levites.

The account of the Levitic cities in 1 Chronicles 6 and Joshua 21, which Wellhausen called "historical fiction" (*WPHI,* 159–64), is now thought by many scholars to represent a certain reality. True, these cities were probably not reserved especially for the Levites already in the period of the Judges; but the list may represent an actual situation at the time of David (so Albright 1945: 49–73), or Solomon (Mazar 1960: 193–205), or Josiah (Alt *KlSchr* 2: 289–305), or at least some preexilic time (de Vaux *AncIsr,* 367; Haran 1961: 156). Accordingly, if the scattered Levites mentioned in Deuteronomy actually lived in the Levitic cities, the date for these Levites would be sometime in the monarchical period.

The other indication of the time referred to in the passages speaking about "the Levite" is the expression, "the place which Yahweh your God chooses." A prevailing view is that the law of centralization refers to Jerusalem in the time after 722 B.C. and before the time of Josiah.

The other main terminology, "Levitical priests" *(hkhnym hlwym),* seems to be used in Deuteronomy of the priests of the central sanctuary. In general these fell into four categories:

1. Using Urim and Thummim to obtain an oracle about various matters (17:9, 12; 19:17; 20:2; 21:5; 24:8).
2. Expounding the law of Moses (17:18; 27:9–10; 31:9–11, 24–26).
3. Serving before the ark (10:7–8; 31:9, 25).
4. Sacrificing and receiving offerings (18:1, 3; 26:4).

The key to dating the Levitical priests would seem to lie in determining the period when these activities were most likely carried on. It is generally acknowledged today that the use of Urim and Thummim was a very ancient priestly activity, which according to Deut 33:8 goes back to "Levi."

The idea of covenant renewal ceremonies in the tribal league has been widely held. At these ceremonies the law was recited and expounded (Josh 8:32–35 and 24:1–28). Therefore, there seems to be no reason not to accept Deuteronomy's statements (especially 31:9–11 and 27:14) that it was the Levitical priests who were engaged in the reading and exposition of this law at the central sanctuary.

Though the elaborate rules concerning sacrifice related in the Pentateuch no doubt correspond more to the practice of the later temple than to premonarchical times, there can be little doubt, based upon the study of ancient Canaanite cult practices, that Israel too had some sort of sacrificial system in its earliest period. That such sacrifice was the province of the priest goes almost without saying, and that the priests who engaged in this activity were Levites, as Deuteronomy claims, cannot be dismissed out of hand.

Finally, the ark, which according to Deuteronomy was carried by the Levites, is considered one of Israel's earliest cult objects, perhaps going back to Moses himself.

Deut 33:8–11, which in its content may reflect the tribal league period (Nielsen 1964: 18; Möhlenbrink 1934: 229), attributes to the tribe of Levi virtually the same activities that the rest of Deuteronomy attributes to the Levitical priests. For example, using the Urim and Thummim of 33:8 corresponds to category 1 above. Teaching the law of 33:10a corresponds to category 2. Putting burnt offerings on the altar of 33:10b is equivalent to category 4. Only category 3, serving the ark, is not mentioned specifically in Deuteronomy 33 as a duty of the Levitical priests, and that could well be implied, if the rest of the activities took place at the central sanctuary. It seems clear from such passages as Josh 8:30–35, Judg 20:26–27, and 1 Sam 4:3 that the ark was housed in the central sanctuary even before David brought it to Jerusalem (2 Samuel 6). Therefore, if Deuteronomy 33 (in its content) is as old as some scholars claim, this could be further evidence for placing the Levitical priests into the tribal league period.

Hence, the terminology "Levites" and "Levitical priests" seem to represent basically the same group of priests, but at 2 different times.

Accordingly, one can summarize the evidence of Deuteronomy as follows. The situation of the poor country Levite who is to be helped by the Israelites to come to the central sanctuary reflects the time between Jeroboam I and Josiah. It is very possible that this was part of a plan to tie the Levites to the central sanctuary in Jerusalem by giving them royal support. This support would have ended with Jeroboam I, who according to 1 Kgs 12:31 appointed "priests from among all the people who were not of the

Levites," and who of course attempted to cut off all ties with Jerusalem. The result, as far as the Levites in the north were concerned, would have been the poverty-ridden situation reflected in Deuteronomy.

The description of the Levitical priests seems to refer to priests of the central sanctuary. Though the dating is difficult, the connection with the ark (10:8; 31:9; 31:25; and also Josh 3:3 and 8:33) as well as with the covenant renewal festival at Shechem (27:9–14; 31:9–11; Josh 8:33) make it possible to conclude that in the statements about the Levitical priests of Deuteronomy one has a very ancient tradition reaching back to the tribal league.

6. Summary. Putting all the foregoing together, one obtains the following picture:

In the desert the Levites had been given the right to serve the ark. By virtue of this they became the keepers of the central sanctuary in the tribal league. It became their prerogative to expound the Mosaic law as well as sacrifice at the central sanctuary. As the Levites grew in number, not all of them could stay at the central sanctuary. This made some available for serving at local sanctuaries. Anyone could be a priest at a local sanctuary, but even there Levites were preferred. On the other hand, at the central sanctuary only the Levites could serve. These are the "Levitical priests" of Deuteronomy. All these Levites seem to be descendants of Moses and/or Ithamar. They were probably the Mushites and Libnites mentioned in Num 26:58a. The Aaronides (Hebronites) and Korahites were not influential during this time, and we have no record of their activities.

D. The Monarchical Period

The fall of Shiloh (see C.2.c above) would have had a profound effect upon the Levites who were in charge of the central sanctuary, that is, perhaps the Mushites. No longer were they able to support themselves by serving at the central sanctuary. Rather they had to seek employment at other sanctuaries. According to Judg 18:30, the priesthood of northern Dan had been Mushite since its inception. It is possible that some of the Shilonite Mushites resettled there when Shiloh fell. However, if the "molten image" of Dan was a bull icon (cf. Judg 17:3–4 and 18:17), as many scholars believe, it is doubtful if the Mushites of Shiloh, who were accustomed to the ark and cherubim as the symbol of Yahweh's presence, would have felt comfortable there.

Likewise, the Mushite Levites no doubt had difficulty attaching themselves to sanctuaries where Aaronides were in charge (e.g., Hebron). In Saul's day all of the descendants of Eli (Shilonite Mushites) who were in Nob, except Abiathar, were put to the sword for befriending David.

After David came to power he installed Abiathar as one of his two chief priests in Jerusalem. It is therefore likely that he would have invited other Mushite Levites to serve there as well. Thus in David's time Jerusalem probably not only became the haven of some refugees from Shiloh, but it also became the new home of the ark (2 Samuel 6), a sort of neo-Shiloh.

The installation of the ark in Jerusalem was the most important cultic event of David's reign. It is not entirely clear whether the Levites (= Mushites?) carried the ark alone, or whether they were assisted by priests (= Aaronides?). But we can be sure that David wanted to keep all elements of the population happy and that it was therefore his policy to invite representatives from as many sanctuaries as possible to Jerusalem.

David may have done even more for the Levites who found themselves scattered and without regular employment as a result of Shiloh's fall. Albright, as we have seen (C.5), suggested that the establishment of 48 Levitic cities (Joshua 21 and 1 Chronicles 6) is to be attributed to David. The Levites could have cared for the sanctuary in such cities and perhaps also taught the law, as they probably did in the tribal league, both at local sanctuaries and at the central sanctuary. No doubt by such an act as the establishment of the Levitic cities David not only would have wanted to help the Levites who were jobless and homeless to earn a living, but he would have also wished to create a group of influential people throughout his kingdom who would be loyal to him and the interests of Jerusalem.

Though David invited Abiathar (and other Mushite Levites?) to serve at the ark in Jerusalem, they did not have a monopoly on this service. David also brought another priest to Jerusalem who shared the office of chief priest with Abiathar. His name was Zadok. Zadok's origin has been much debated. In 2 Sam 8:17 he is introduced without explanation as one of David's two priests. He is called "the son of Ahitub," and the other priest, namely, Ahimelech, is called "the son of Abiathar" (cf. 1 Chr 18:16). Most commentators are agreed (on the basis of 1 Sam 22:20; 23:6; and 30:7) that Ahimelech was actually the father, not the son, of Abiathar. Furthermore, Ahitub is called the father of Ahijah/Ahimelech in 1 Sam 14:3 and 22:9, 11, 20, rather than the father of Zadok. Therefore, most scholars have concluded that 2 Sam 8:17 (in the MT) is out of order and that it originally read something like, "Zadok and Abiathar, son of Ahimelech, son of Ahitub, were priests." Thus Zadok would be left without genealogy, and his Aaronite ancestry as recorded in 1 Chr 5:27–34—Eng 6:1–8; 6:35–35—Eng 6:50–53; and Ezra 7:2–5 also becomes suspect. Instead, various theories have been proposed as to his real origin.

The hypotheses that Zadok stems from Gibeon or Kiriath-jearim do not have enough positive support to command many followers. However, the theory that Zadok was originally a priest at a Canaanite shrine of *ʾēl ʿelyôn* in Jebusite Jerusalem enjoys widespread acceptance. This theory is based on a supposed connection between the name "Zadok" and the figures of Melchizedek and Adonizedek of pre-Israelite Jerusalem. A variation on this theory considers Zadok to be a Jebusite priest who deserted to David already at Hebron.

More recently, the "Jebusite hypothesis" has come under attack, notably from F. M. Cross (*CMHE*, 209–15). Cross points out that one need not link Zadok with the tradition of Melchizedek or Adonizedek of Jerusalem simply because of the similarity in names, because *ṣdq* is a very common element in Northwest Semitic languages. Further, the texts (2 Sam 24:18–25 and 1 Chr 21:18–30) do not state that David pitched his tent at the Canaanite shrine of *ʾēl ʿelyôn* but on the threshing floor of Araunah. Next, it is difficult to believe that David, an orthodox Yahwist, would have asked a pagan priest to serve with Abiathar in the central shrine of his realm. Finally, if

Zadok in fact descended from Melchizedek, would not the later Zadokites have claimed him, rather than Aaron, as their ancestor?

After Cross' attack on the Jebusite hypothesis, he proposes a hypothesis of his own. This may be called the "Aaronite" or "Hebron" hypothesis. Cross begins by reevaluating the genealogies which claim that Zadok is the son of Ahitub (2 Sam 8:17) and a descendant of Aaron (1 Chr 5:27–41—Eng 6:1–15). Wellhausen thought that these texts had no historical value. Wellhausen based his skepticism about the genealogy of Zadok on the assumption that the Ahitub of 2 Sam 8:17 had to be the same man who is listed as the grandson of Eli in 1 Sam 14:3 and the grandfather of Abiathar in 1 Sam 22:20. Wellhausen therefore thought that the MT of 2 Sam 8:17, *wṣdwq bn ʾḥyṭwb wʾḥymlk bn ʾbytr khnym* ("and Zadok the son of Ahitub and Ahimelech the son of Abiathar were priests"), had been corrupted intentionally from an original: **ʾbytr bn ʾḥymlk bn ʾḥyṭwb wṣdwq khnym* ("Abiathar the son of Ahimelech the son of Ahitub and Zadok were priests").

Cross points out, however, that there is no textual evidence for Wellhausen's emendation, and it is difficult to understand why, if an ancient Zadokite wished to change the text, Zadok would be placed last. Furthermore, it is curious that Wellhausen's reconstruction provides no patronymic for Zadok, but two generations of ancestry for Abiathar. On the basis of 2 Sam 8:16 one would expect a single patronymic in each case.

Cross contends that there is no text-critical reason for removing Ahitub as Zadok's father. In terms of content, there is also no reason why there could not be two Ahitubs, one the grandfather of Abiathar and the other the father of Zadok, as the genealogies indicate (e.g., 1 Sam 14:3; 22:20; 1 Chr 5:27–34—Eng 6:1–8). That Zadok was not of the same line as Abiathar (who according to 1 Sam 14:3 and 22:20 is clearly a descendant of Eli) seems to be substantiated by 1 Sam 2:20–36, which according to most interpreters presents the line of Zadok as a replacement for the line of Eli.

Cross's reconstruction shows that the only element in the genealogy of 2 Sam 8:17 in the MT which is not authentic concerns the relation of Abiathar to Ahimelech. Cross traces the development of the MT by beginning with the Syriac version, which reads:

ṣdwq bn ʾḥyṭwb wʾbytr bn ʾḥymlk
(Zadok the son of Ahitub and Abiathar the son of Ahimelech)

On the basis of 1 Chr 18:16 it appears that originally Abimelech stood in the place of Ahimelech, thus:

ṣdwq bn ʾḥyṭwb wʾbytr bn ʾbymlk
(Zadok the son of Ahitub and Abiathar the son of Abimelech)

Cross proposes that *ʾbytr bn* (Abiathar the son of) dropped out by haplography, resulting in:

ṣdwq bn ʾḥyṭwb wʾbymlk
(Zadok the son of Ahitub and Abimelech)

Later, according to Cross, *ʾbytr* could have been inserted back into the text at the wrong place and filled out by *bn* (son of), resulting in:

ṣdwq bn ʾḥyṭwb wʾbymlk bn ʾbytr
(Zadok the son of Ahitub and Abimelech the son of Abiathar)

The final steps in the development of the MT would have been the adding of *w* (and) to *ṣdwq* (Zadok) and substituting *wʾḥymlk* (and Ahimelech) for *wʾbymlk* (and Abimelech).

Such a reconstruction of 2 Sam 8:17 agrees with the ancestry of Zadok as recorded in 1 Chr 5:34—Eng 6:8, and it would also mean that the Chronicler's genealogy (1 Chr 5:27–34—Eng 6:1–8, which makes Zadok an Aaronide, reflects historical reality. It would further explain how Abiathar could mistakenly have been reckoned as the father of Ahimelech.

Cross maintains on the basis of Josh 21:10, 13 and 1 Chr 6:42—Eng 6:57 that the Aaronides were tied to Hebron. Since the Hebronite clan played an important role in the crowning of David in Hebron (so Mazar) and no doubt throughout the seven and one-half years that David ruled Judah from Hebron (2 Sam 5:5), it is readily understandable that he should have made contact with Zadok. In fact, 1 Chr 12:27–29—Eng 12:26–28 speaks of Zadok as being over the priests (= Aaronides?) in Hebron. Though the numbers (4,600 Levites and 3,700 priests) are certainly too large, that there were Levites (under Abiathar) and priests (= Aaronides) under Zadok is probably true. At any rate, Zadok is placed at Hebron during David's reign there, and when David made his capital in Jerusalem, he no doubt invited Zadok to join him.

First Chronicles 15 says that there were six Levitic groups at David's time. We suggest that these groups may have related to the earlier groupings as follows: Gershom represents the Gershonites; Hebron, Uzziel, and Kohath represent the Kohathites/Aaronides; and Merari and Elizaphan the ancient Merarites.

According to 1 Chr 15:17–24; 16:4–7, 25 there were singers and gatekeepers among the Levites already in David's time. Albright has shown that, although the singers probably existed in the Chronicler's own time, it is highly likely that David had already originated musical guilds in his day (cf. 1 Chronicles 25), and that the names "Heman," "Asaph," and "Ethan" probably represent such ancient musical guilds. Regarding the gatekeepers, we are not sure whether they were all Levites in David's time, as 1 Chronicles 26 says. Probably not. David may also have been responsible for the organization of his priests, but it is doubtful that he had twenty-four divisions (cf. 1 Chronicles 24).

The most significant event for the Levites during the time of Solomon was his banishment of Abiathar and adoption of Zadok as chief priest (1 Kgs 2:26–27). It is possible that Solomon also installed an Aaronite priesthood at Bethel, replacing the Mushites. This would explain the expression in 1 Kgs 12:31 that Jeroboam appointed non-Levites there. These non-Levites could have been Aaronides who were not recognized by the Mushites. Halpern (1974: 519–20, n. 3) believes that Solomon allocated the Levitic cities and that the Gershonites/Mushites were assigned as far north as possible to keep them out of Jerusalem.

From this period on there is evidence that the Zadokites came to be referred to simply as "priests" (the Chronicler's term) or as the "sons of Aaron" (P's term), although according to our analysis they were probably Aaronite Levites. The term "Levites" would have henceforth referred mainly to the Mushites. This seems to be brought out in 1 Chr 15:4, where David called together "the sons of Aaron" and "the Levites."

The genealogy of 1 Chr 5:27–41—Eng 6:1–15 (cf. 1 Chr 9:11, Neh 11:11, Ezra 7:1–5), which begins with Levi, Kohath, and Aaron and ends with the exile, contains the following specific descendants of Zadok: Zadok (I), Ahimaaz, Azariah (I), Johanan, Azariah (II), Amariah (II), Ahitub (II), Zadok (II), Shallum, Hilkiah, Azariah (III), Seraiah, Jehozadak.

While it is obvious from a comparison with the priests mentioned in the books of Kings that there are historical gaps in the genealogy, some of the names are corroborated in the narratives of the OT. Ahimaaz is explicitly referred to as the son of Zadok who, together with Jonathan the son of Abiathar, served as a messenger between Jerusalem and the self-exiled King David (2 Sam 15:36; 18:19, 22, 27). Azariah (I) is referred to in 1 Kgs 4:2, albeit as a son rather than a grandson of Zadok. Amariah II is referred to in 2 Chr 19:11, Hilkiah in 2 Kgs 22:4, and Seraiah in 2 Kgs 25:18 = Jer 52:24). Other priests mentioned in 2 Kgs 11:9; 16:10; 2 Chr 24:20; 26:17; and 31:10 are evidently not to be identified with any in the list in 1 Chr 5:27–41—Eng 6:1–15, though one Azariah of Hezekiah's time is explicitly called a Zadokite in 2 Chr 31:10.

Because of the apparent discrepancies between the narratives of the books of Kings and Chronicles and the genealogy in 1 Chr 5:27–41—Eng 6:1–15, plus the repetition of the group "Amariah-Ahitub-Zadok" within the list, many scholars believe that 1 Chr 5:27–41—Eng 6:1–15 is an artistic creation of a priestly scribe. Thus, it is not surprising that, if one allows 300 years for the apparent 12 generations between Ahimaaz and Jehozadak (25 years per generation) and figures back from the destruction of Jerusalem in 587 B.C. (when Jehozadak lived, cf. 1 Chr 5:41—Eng 6:15), one falls considerably short of 959 B.C., the date when Solomon's temple was begun. This can, however, be explained by assuming that the genealogy represents a list which became stylized in Zadokite circles long before the Chronicler used it in his work. Hence, one would expect there to be historical gaps in the genealogy. Furthermore, the repetition of "Amariah-Ahitub-Zadok" within 1 Chr 5:27–41—Eng 6:1–15 should not be seen as necessarily an artistic creation, for it is now known from the Samaria Papyri (Cross 1963) and elsewhere that the practice of papponymy, as well as the repetition of similar names within a family line, was common in real life.

Some of the provisions concerning priestly duties contained in P are probably really a description of the cult during the time of David and Solomon, but it is difficult to recover this in detail. Accordingly, the material in Exodus relating to Aaron and his sons, the strands of Numbers which speak about "Levites under Aaron," "Aaron" and "sons of Aaron," and most of Leviticus may ultimately go back to Zadokite circles of monarchical as well as postexilic times.

As has already been indicated, at the time of the division of the kingdom the Levites in the levitical cities in the north were cut off from Jerusalem. Because of their background as priests of the central sanctuary in the tribal league, and because they had probably been closely tied to Jerusalem for their support since the creation of the Levitical cities by David, they were of course odious to Jeroboam I. Therefore, it is easy to comprehend why he appointed "non-Levites" as priests (1 Kgs 12:31). However, his action may not have extended beyond Bethel, since according to Judg 18:30b the Mushites = Levites were the priests of the Danites until the captivity (i.e., ca. 722 B.C.).

Second Chr 11:13–14 and 13:8–11 state that as a result of Jeroboam's action against the Levites some of them left their homes in the north and went to Jerusalem. But it is doubtful whether many went south, and those who did would not have received a very warm welcome from the Zadokites.

Therefore, the Levites may have been cut off from Jerusalem and other southern sanctuaries. In this situation they would have had limited opportunity to engage in sacrifices at any large sanctuary, and they would have become poor. Hence, G. E. Wright (1954), following von Rad, may be correct in stating that the "country Levites" were engaged mostly in teaching.

Accordingly, the Levites who did remain in the north could have preserved many traditions that eventually were published in the book of Deuteronomy found in Josiah's time. This included the tradition of how they, the Mushite Levites, had been the priests of the central sanctuary in the tribal league, even though Deuteronomy's term for the Mushite Levites of the tribal league is "Levitical priests." These Levites of the N kingdom expressed their hope of going up to Jerusalem again in Deut 18:6–7.

But the Levites who lived between the time of Jeroboam I and Josiah also wished to better their present situation as *personae miserae.* Therefore, they reminded the people of the obligations to care for the "Levite" when they went to "the place which Yahweh will choose" (Deut 12:12–13, 17–19; 14:23, 27–29; 16:11, 14–15; 18:6–7; 26:2, 11–13). There may have been such legislation already in the tribal league to provide support for those Levites who served at local sanctuaries rather than the central sanctuary, but now it took on new meaning and was promulgated with greater vigor.

Hosea, a northern prophet who worked ca. 750–725 B.C., condemns the priests for their wickedness in 4:4, 9; 5:1; and 6:9. H. W. Wolff (1956: 83–94) sees in 6:9 a reference to persecution of the Levites. He extrapolates from 8:5–6; 10:5; and 13:2 (where Hosea attacks the bull cultus, cf. 1 Kgs 12:28–29) and Exod 32:25–29 (where the Levites are opposed to the golden bull) the theory that Hosea had allied himself with the Levites in opposing the cult introduced by Jeroboam I (1 Kgs 12:25–33). According to Wolff's theory, the Levites were engaged in the preservation of early Mosaic traditions ever since Jeroboam I's appointment of non-Levitic priests (1 Kgs 12:31).

At the time of Abijah the Levites shared the priesthood of Jerusalem with the "sons of Aaron" (2 Chr 13:10). During Jehoshaphat's time the Levites were engaged in teaching (2 Chr 17:8). They were also arbiters in cultic and other disputes (19:8).

At the time of Joash there was a certain criticism of the Levites for their slowness in gathering funds for the renovation of the temple (2 Chr 24:5). But in Hezekiah's time they receive special praise (2 Chr 30:22), and various groups of Levites are mentioned (2 Chr 29:12–14).

The trend of upgrading the Levites, begun in Hezekiah's time, was seemingly continued by Josiah. He ordered the centralization of *all* sacrifice in Jerusalem, but he gave the Levites (of the countryside, including those still in the north) the opportunity to join their fellow Levites who were already in Jerusalem (cf. Deut 18:6–8). Thus Josiah sought to go back to conditions at the time of David. But according to 2 Kgs 23:9 the Jerusalem priests did not accept the country Levites.

Jeremiah also gives some information about priests. He in fact mentions the priests more often than any of the other writing prophets. He himself is said to be the son of Hilkiah (not the Hilkiah of 2 Kings 22–23) of the priests of Anathoth (1:1). This presumably means that he was of a priestly family; and, since he came from Anathoth, he may have been a descendant of Abiathar (cf. 1 Kgs 2:26–27). Yet we have no evidence that Jeremiah ever acted as a priest.

Jeremiah also calls attention to the sins of the priests, and he condemns them accordingly (1:18; 2:8, 26; 4:9; 5:31; 6:13; 8:1, 10; 13:13; 14:18; 23:11, 33–34; 32:32; 34:19).

Jeremiah tells us that it is the peculiar function of the priests to handle the Torah (2:8; 18:18). In 19:1 the "senior priests" *(zqny hkhnym)* are mentioned. It is unclear whether they are good or bad. Pashhur was an evil priest who opposed Jeremiah (20:1; cf. chap. 38). In chap. 26 the "priests and Prophets" opposed Jeremiah.

Priests are mentioned in 27:16 (Jeremiah speaks to them); in 28:1 (Hananiah the prophet spoke to Jeremiah in the presence of the priests); and in 29:1 (the priests in exile to whom Jeremiah writes).

Jer 29:24–32 informs us that Zephaniah the son of Maaseiah had replaced Jehoiada as the priest in Jerusalem (cf. 21:1; 37:3). Zephaniah refused to arrest Jeremiah.

Jeremiah foresees a time when the priests will again be good (33:17–22). The priests are called Levitical priests *(hkhnym hlwym),* which is Deuteronomic terminology. His hope is that these Levitical priests might occupy the priesthood forever.

If Abiathar was a Mushite, he would have kept Mushite traditions alive in Anathoth, the place of his exile. Accordingly, Jeremiah, coming from Anathoth, would have had northern theological training. Hence, when Jeremiah states that the priests of the future will be "Levitical priests," he may be using the term as it was understood in the north, and his words may in effect be a polemic against the Zadokite priesthood of Jerusalem.

Jer 52:24 says that the chief priest *(khn hrʾš)* at the fall of Jerusalem (587 B.C.) was Seraiah. This agrees with the genealogies in 1 Chr 5:27–41—Eng 6:1–15, Ezra 7:1–5, and Neh 11:11.

According to the view of Ezekiel, himself a priest, the only priests who will be eligible to perform all the priestly duties in the "new Jerusalem" are the Levites/Levitical priests who are descendants of Zadok. They are given this privilege because they remained faithful when the other Levites went astray (44:10–15; 48:11).

A question arises how Ezekiel can commend the sons of Zadok, whereas in the preexilic southern prophets they are harshly condemned. It is also necessary to ask what situation Ezekiel had in mind when he referred to the Zadokites' faithfulness and the Levites' sin. Wellhausen (*WPHI,* 122–27) answered by stating that Ezekiel was simply trying to legalize the consequences of Josiah's reformation of ca. 622 B.C. (2 Kings 22–23; 2 Chronicles 34–35). At that time the Jerusalem priesthood (i.e., Zadokites) participated in the reform, while the Levites who had formerly served at the high places were invited to come to Jerusalem but were not permitted to serve at the altar of the temple, presumably because they were rejected by the Zadokites (2 Kgs 23:9; cf. Deut 18:6–8). As a result, they were degraded. Most other scholars have followed Wellhausen's interpretation of Ezekiel's reasons for condemning the Levites (see Zimmerli *Ezechiel* BKAT).

As regards the question of the prophets' condemnation of the (Zadokite) priesthood of Jerusalem, Ezekiel evidently does not believe their aberrations were so great as to disqualify them as priests, although he too is critical of them in 7:6 and 22:26. However, Ezekiel's own criticism comes in the midst of a stylized condemnation of all the leaders of Israel and is therefore probably not to be taken as being specifically against the Zadokite priesthood. In fact, in chap. 8, which gives a picture of paganism in the temple, there is no explicit criticism of the priests. It must also not be forgotten that Ezekiel's references to the Zadokite priesthood after chap. 40 not only refer to it in the past, but they also deal with the idealized new Jerusalem, where the priesthood would as a matter of course be perfect.

The description of the duties of the "Levites" and "sons of Zadok" here corresponds well with the description of the "Levites" as hierodules of the "sons of Aaron" in P. Why, however, are the two groups referred to in two different ways? Scholars have made many guesses. Kennett (1904–5: 174) suggests that the Aaronides, who had previously been at home in Bethel, were invited to become the priests of Jerusalem during the time when the Zadokites were in exile in Babylon. F. S. North (1954: 194) holds that the Aaronides were in charge of Bethel, and that Bethel actually supplanted Jerusalem as the religious center of Palestine during the Exile. After the Exile the Zadokites returned to establish a new cult in Jerusalem, and now they claimed that they themselves were Aaronite in descent. T. J. Meek (1928–29: 155–56) assumes that the Aaronides took over the Jerusalemite priesthood during the Exile when the Zadokites were for the most part deported. After the Exile, Zadokites were again accepted into the higher priestly ranks, but there was a certain amount of friction until finally in NT times the Zadokites triumphed. George Berry (1923: 235) sees the "change" from the name "Zadokites" to "sons of Aaron" as the work of P who was seeking to enhance the glory of the Jerusalemite priesthood by giving it an ancient lineage. De Vaux (*AncIsr,* 394–97) rejects the contention that the sanctuary of Bethel took on new life after the reform of Josiah. Rather, he favors a view that the "sons of Aaron" constitutes a compromise between the descendants of Zadok and Abiathar, who, from the time of the Exile on, both traced their descent to Aaron, the Zadokites through Eleazar and the Abiatharites through Ithamar.

Our reconstruction shows that Zadok was a descendant of Aaron and Abiathar of Moses. The various links between Aaron and Zadok in the genealogy of 1 Chr 5:27–41—Eng 6:1–15, however, we have considered to be not genuine. This genealogy had no doubt been worked out by the Zadokite priesthood of Jerusalem to bolster its legitimacy. Though in itself, then, not entirely reliable, it nevertheless presented what we consider was a historical fact, namely, that Zadok was a descendant of Aaron.

Hence, we believe that the "sons of Aaron" and the "Zadokites" stood for one and the same thing, namely, the priesthood of Jerusalem. We also hold that one should not speak of a "change" from one terminology to the other. Rather they could be used interchangeably after the time of Solomon, depending on the context. Accordingly, when P spoke about the desert period he used the term "sons of Aaron," because Zadok would have been an anachronism for the time. On the other hand, Ezekiel, since he spoke about his own day and the future, was free to use the term "sons of Zadok."

Whether there was a high priesthood in preexilic times is still a moot point. De Vaux (*AncIsr*, 378) lists only four usages of "high priest" *(hakkōhēn haggādôl)* in preexilic texts (2 Kgs 12:11; 22:4, 8; 23:4). But in the parallels to these texts in Chronicles he finds other readings. Hence, he says that "all four references to the 'high priest' before the Exile seem to be later modifications." Nevertheless, the fact that the actual term "high priest" does not occur more often or seem more fixed in the tradition does not necessarily mean that the office did not exist.

It therefore appears most likely that the "chief priests" in Jerusalem from Solomon till the Exile were descendants of Zadok, and that the genealogy of 1 Chr 5:34–41; Eng 6:8–15 presents a reasonably accurate listing of its main members. The preexilic prophets, particularly Jeremiah, who was possibly a descendant of Abiathar, were generally critical of the Jerusalemite priesthood. Nevertheless, these priests were exalted in Ezekiel's plan for the new Jerusalem (40:46; 43:19; 44:15; 48:11) above the "Levites." The description of the duties of the "Levites" and "sons of Zadok" in Ezekiel corresponds quite clearly to the description of the "Levites" as hierodules of the "sons of Aaron" in P, and roughly to the terminology "priests and Levites" in the Chronicler. There are many theories concerning these differing terminologies. However, if the Aaronite ancestry of Zadok is sound, the terminology "sons of Aaron" for priests prior to Solomon (so in P) and "Zadokites" for those after his time would be precisely what one would expect. For further general discussion see Albright *FSAC* and Noth *ÜgS*.

Bibliography

Aharoni, Y. 1971. The Israelite Sanctuary at Arad. Pp. 28–44 *New Directions in Biblical Archaeology*, ed. D. N. Freedman and J. C. Greenfield. Garden City.

Albright, W. F. 1945. The List of Levitic Cities. Pp. 49–73 in *Louis Ginzberg Jubilee Volume*, ed. S. Lieberman et al. New York.

———. 1950. The Judicial Reform of Jehoshaphat. Pp. 61–82 in *Alexander Marx Jubilee Volume*. New York.

———. 1961. *Samuel and the Beginnings of the Prophetic Movement*. Cincinnati.

———. 1963. Jethro, Hobab and Reuel in Early Hebrew Tradition. *CBQ* 25: 1–11.

Auerbach, E. 1963. Der Aufstieg der Priesterschaft zur Macht im alten Israel. Pp. 236–49 in *Congress Volume Bonn 1962*. VTSup 9. Leiden.

———. 1969. Das Aharon-Problem. Pp. 37–63 in *Congress Volume Rome, 1968*. VTSup 17. Leiden.

———. 1975. *Moses*. Detroit.

Berry, G. 1923. Priests and Levites. *JBL* 42: 227–38.

Cody, A. 1969. *A History of Old Testament Priesthood*. AnBib 35. Rome.

Cohen, M. A. 1965. The Role of the Shilonite Priesthood in the United Monarchy of Ancient Israel. *HUCA* 36: 59–98.

Cross, F. M. Jr. 1963. The Discovery of the Samaria Papyri. *BA* 26: 110-21.

Emerton, J. A. 1962. Priests and Levites in Deuteronomy. *VT* 12: 129–38.

Gordon, C. 1955. *Ugaritic Manual*. AnOr 35. Rome.

Gunneweg, A. H. J. 1965. *Leviten und Priester*. FRLANT 89. Göttingen.

Haran, M. 1961. Studies in the Account of the Levitical Cities. *JBL* 80: 45–54 and 156–65.

———. 1978. *Temples and Temple Service in Ancient Israel*. Oxford.

Halpern, B. 1974. Sectionalism and the Schism. *JBL* 93: 519–32.

———. 1976. Levitic Participation in the Reform Cult of Jeroboam I. *JBL* 95: 31–42.

Hauer, C. E. Jr. 1963. Who Was Zadok? *JBL* 82: 89–94.

Hauret, C. 1957. Aux origines du sacerdoce danite, à propos de Jud., 18, 30–31. Pp. 105–13 in *Mélanges bibliques rédigés in l'honneur André Robert*. Paris.

Johnson, M. D. 1969. *The Purpose of the Biblical Genealogies*. SNTSMS 8. Cambridge.

Katzenstein, H. J. 1962. Some Remarks on the Lists of the Chief Priests of the Temple of Solomon. *JBL* 81: 377–84.

Kennett, R. H. 1904–5. Origin of the Aaronite Priesthood. *JTS* 6: 161–86.

Lefèvre, A. 1950. Note d'exégèse sur les généalogies des Qehatites. *RSR* 37: 287–92.

Malamat, A. 1968. King Lists of the Old Babylonian Period and Biblical Genealogies. *JAOS* 88: 163–73.

Mazar, B. 1960. The Cities of the Priests and the Levites. Pp. 193–205 in *Congress Volume Oxford, 1959*. VTSup 7. Leiden.

———. 1964. The Sanctuary of Arad and the Family of Hobab the Kenite. *EI* 7: 1–5. (In Hebrew). (ET *JNES* 24: 297–303).

Meek, T. J. 1928–29. Aaronites and Zadokites. *AJSL* 45: 149–66.

Milgrom, J. 1970. *The Encroacher and the Levite. The Term ᶜAboda*. Vol. 1 in *Studies in Levitical Terminology*. Berkeley.

———. 1975. The Priestly Doctrine of Repentance. *RB* 82: 186–205.

Möhlenbrink, K. 1934. Die levitischen überlieferungen des Alten Testaments. *ZAW* 52: 184–231.

Nicholson, E. W. 1967. *Deuteronomy and Tradition*. Philadelphia.

Nielsen, E. 1964. The Levites in Ancient Israel. *ASTI* 3: 16–27.

North, F. S. 1954. Aaron's Rise in Prestige. *ZAW* 66: 191–99.

Noth, M. 1930. *Das System der zwolf Stämme Israels*. BWANT 52. Stuttgart.

———. 1962. The Background of Judges 17–18. Pp. 68–85 in *Israel's Prophetic Heritage*. New York.

Olrik, A. 1909. Epische Gesetze der Volksdichtung. *Zeitschrift fur Deutsches Altertum und Deutsche Literatur* 51: 1–12.
Polzin, R. 1969. *HWQ*[c] and Covenantal Institutions in Early Israel. *HTR* 1969: 227–40.
Rad, G. von. 1956. *Studies in Deuteronomy.* SBT 9. London.
Strauss, H. 1960. *Untersuchungen zu den überlieferungen der vorexilischen Leviten.* Bonn.
Vaux, R. de. 1961. Lévites Minéens et Lévites Israélites. Pp. 265–73 in *Lex Tua Veritas,* ed. H. Gross and F. Mussner. Trier.
Waterman, L. 1937. Some Determining Factors in the Northward Progress of Levi. *JAOS* 57: 375–80.
———. 1941. Some Repercussions from Late Levitical Genealogical Accretions in P and the Chronicler. *AJSL* 58: 49–56.
Weinfeld, M. 1967. Deuteronomy—The Present State of Inquiry. *JBL* 86: 249–62.
———. 1972. *Deuteronomy and the Deuteronomic School.* Oxford.
Wellhausen, J. 1871. *Der Text der Bücher Samuelis.* Göttingen.
Wilson, R. R. 1975. The Old Testament Genealogies in Recent Research. *JBL* 94: 169–89.
———. 1977. *Genealogy and History in the Biblical World.* YNER 7. New Haven.
———. 1979. Between "Azel" and "Azel": Interpreting the Biblical Genealogies. *BA* 42: 11–22.
Wolff, H. W. 1956. Hoseas geistige Heimat. *TLZ* 81: 83–94. Repr. pp. 232–50 in H. W. Wolff, *Gesammelte Studien zum Alten Testament.* Munich. 1964.
Wright, G. E. 1954. The Levites in Deuteronomy. *VT* 4: 325–30.

MERLIN D. REHM

LEVITICAL CITIES. Unlike the other tribes (Josh 13–19), the Levites do not receive any allocation of land after the "conquest." Rather, the Levites are to inhabit 48 cities, called "Levitical cities," spread throughout the nation. These 48 cities, which include 6 "cities of refuge," are given to the Levites by the twelve tribes. The specific cities which are distributed to the Levites are found in lists of the cities in Josh 21:1–42 and 1 Chr 6:39–66—Eng 6:54–81. In addition, there is the "enabling legislation" of Num 35:1–8 which describes the cities and indicates that this distribution of cities to the Levites was ordered by God.

One of the questions which arises is why the Levites did not receive any land like the other tribes. One explanation is based on Gen 49:7, part of the Blessing of Jacob, in which Levi and Simeon are reported to have been "divided in Jacob and scattered in Israel" for their actions against the Shechemites (Genesis 34). Thus, they were no longer a tribe and received no land. A more plausible explanation is that because the Levites were set aside to be priests, they received no inheritance of land (Num 18:24; Deut 10:8–9; Josh 13:33; 18:7). Levi had no portion or inheritance with his brothers; Yahweh was his inheritance. This consecration to Yahweh is reflected in the Levites' redemption of the firstborn son (Num 3:11–12, 41, 44; 8:17–18).

In spite of this claim of "no inheritance," there are passages which suggest that the Levites did receive land (Num 35:1–8; Josh 14:4; 2 Chr 11:13–15; 13:2). What the Levites received, even mentioned in the "enabling legislation" for the Levitical cities (Num 35:1–8), was pasture land *(migraš).* This land is not residential or farm land, and thus it is not considered an inheritance.

Since the Levites had no inheritance, they needed some other means of sustenance or support. One suggestion is that their support came from the tithing given to them because of their priestly status (Num 18:21–24; Deut 18:1–4; Josh 13:14). Another suggestion is that since the Levites were landless, they were put in the same sociological category as the widow, orphan, and sojourner *(gēr)* and thus received support from the people (Deut 14:28–29; 16:11, 14; 26:11–13). The third possible means of support is from the cities and pasture land which the Levites were given (Josh 21:1–42; 1 Chr 6:39–66—Eng 6:54–81). Having pasture land meant they could raise herds, something priests in association with temples often did. Thus, it is through tithing, their functioning as priests, their status as landless, and their possession of cities, that the Levites are said to sustain themselves.

In understanding the lists of Levitical cities themselves, discussion has focused on three issues: the historicity of the lists, the date of the lists and the purpose of the cities. One of the early milestones in the discussion was an article by W. F. Albright (1945). In that article Albright dated the lists to 975–950 B.C.E., because he saw that as the only time in which all the cities were within the borders of the Israelite kingdom. However, the most significant element of Albright's article was his discussion of the textual history of Joshua 21 and 1 Chronicles 6. His comparison of the two texts and the LXX led him to conclude that LXX[B] of Joshua 21 was representative of the parent of both Hebrew versions. This argument remains the predominant view.

An alternate to Albright's dating came from A. Alt (*KlSchr* 1:306–15). Alt argued that there were two significant gaps in the lists of Levitical cities. There were virtually no Levitical cities in the area of Judah and in the hills of Ephraim. For Alt, these gaps were the very areas affected by Josiah's intervention into local sanctuaries during his reform. Thus, Alt dated the lists to a time after Josiah's reign (640–609 B.C.E.).

The supposition that Albright and Alt made, but did not articulate, was that the lists are realistic. Such an assumption results in a search for a point in history where the lists could reflect reality. M. Haran questioned this assumption and argued that the lists have both realistic and utopian features. Among the utopian features are the measurements of the land around the cities as 2,000 cubits, the identical dimensions for all 48 cities, the fact that the cities were the exclusive preserve of the Levites, and the distinction between priests and Levites. One might also add the selection of 48 cities as utopian since twelve tribes contributing 4 cities each is suspicious, especially since it is not even observed in the actual distribution (e.g., Naphtali gave only 3 cities—Josh 21:32). The realistic elements Haran lists include the dispersion of the tribe of Levi, the Levites in nonshrine cities, Levitical cities not within the ideal boundaries of Israel, the different social and economic position of the Levites relative to the priests, and the numerical superiority of the Levites over the priests. Haran concluded that the lists reflect a historical situation to which later utopian elements were added. Haran identified this later utopian hand as being that of the Priestly author. The historical situation he left unspecified.

This two-stage usage of the lists was expanded on by J. P. Ross (1973). He, and most scholars, argue that the current lists reflect the postexilic workings of the Priestly writer. However, Ross argued that the lists had an earlier context, unassociated with the priestly Levites. The lists were just plain town lists of the period of the monarchy which were resurrected in the time of Josiah to help deal with a controversy about the Levites. According to Ross, the presence of Levitical clans, the references to the Aaronites, and the division among twelve tribes were all added later, by the Priestly writer in the time after Nehemiah.

This perspective of Haran and Ross that the lists are a late construction and partially utopian is buttressed by a recent archaeological study. J. Peterson (1977) sought to identify the sites of the Levitical cities and, using archaeological evidence, to discover their time of occupation. Peterson was able to identify 45 of the Levitical cities. What was startling was that only 20 of the identified sites showed evidence of occupation in the 10th century. In contrast, only one site, Kishion, was not occupied in the 8th century. Therefore, Peterson concluded that the Levitical cities were from the 8th century.

The conclusion of Peterson affects the dating for the creation of the lists of Levitical cities, but the dating of the placement of the lists in their present context still needs attention. While the postexilic placement in 1 Chronicles is not questioned, the date of Joshua 21 is more difficult to establish. Joshua 21 is set within the Deuteronomic Historian's work which would normally suggest a late preexilic or exilic date (600–550 B.C.E.). However, several factors militate against such a date. There is a clear separation of priests and Levites (Josh 21:1–3, 13, 20). Aaron is seen as a priest in Joshua 21, which would be the only instance where Aaron appears as a priest in preexilic materials. There is linguistic evidence adduced by Auld (1979) and Ross (1973) which suggests that Joshua 21 is dependent on a tradition later than 1 Chronicles 6. Finally, there is the fact that the enabling legislation for the cities (Num 35:1–8) is Priestly material. All of these factors suggest a postexilic date for the list in Joshua 21, which comports with the argument that the Priestly "writers" were responsible for the insertion of the list of Levitical cities in Joshua 21. So the lists' present locations result from postexilic redacting.

In discussing the purpose of the Levitical cities, most reconstructions have been highly dependent on the dating of the lists. B. Mazar (1959) dated the lists to the time of the united monarchy. He argued that the placement and structure of the cities were influenced by Egyptian models and that the cities functioned as provincial administrative centers to serve the deity and king. In similar fashion, Mettinger (1971) saw a close connection between royal estates and fortresses and the Levitical cities placed near the borderlands. Thus, he saw the cities as integral to the construction of David's empire.

Unfortunately, the archaeological evidence refutes any claim that the Levitical cities date from the time of the united monarchy. So scholars have been forced to look elsewhere for an appropriate historical context. Both Peterson (1977) and Boling (1985) want to place the lists in the 8th century, based on the archaeological evidence. However, it is difficult to see any time in that period when all of these cities would have been part of the Israelite or Judean kingdoms or to see any clear rationale for the construction of the lists in that period.

The assumption that persists in the works of Mazar, Mettinger, Peterson, and Boling is that the lists are realistic. Given the archaeological evidence which rules out the time of the united monarchy and the geographical evidence which makes the 8th century doubtful, one is pushed to consider the possibility that the texts do not fit any preexilic historical situation. Rather, one must consider the possibility that they are creations from the postexilic period which sought to explain how the Levites fit into the early political, social, and theological structure of ancient Israel.

Bibliography

Albright, W. F. 1945. The List of Levitic Cities. Vol. 1, pp. 49–73 in *Louis Ginzberg Jubilee Volume.* New York.

Auld, A. G. 1979. The "Levitical Cities": Texts and History. *ZAW* 91: 194–207.

Boling, R. G. 1985. Levitical Cities: Archaeology and Texts. Pp. 23–32 in *Biblical and Related Studies Presented to Samuel Iwry,* ed. A. Kort and S. Morschauser. Winona Lake, IN.

Cody, A. 1969. *A History of Old Testament Priesthood.* AnBib 35. Rome.

———. 1975. Levitical Cities and the Israelite Settlement. Pp. 179–89 in *Homenaje a Juan Prado,* ed. L. A. Verdes and E. J. A. Hernandez. Madrid.

Gunneweg, A. H. J. 1965. *Leviten und Priester.* Gottingen.

Haran, M. 1961. Studies in the Account of the Levitical Cities. *JBL* 80: 45–54, 156–65.

Hauer, C., Jr. 1982. David and the Levites. *JSOT* 23: 33–54.

Mazar, B. 1959. The Cities of the Priests and the Levites. VTSup 7: 193–205.

Mettinger, T. N. D. 1971. *Solomonic State Officials.* Lund.

Milgrom, J. 1983. The Levitic Town: An Exercise in Realistic Planning. Pp. 185–88 in *Essays in Honour of Yigael Yadin,* ed. G. Vermes and J. Neusner. Totowa, NJ.

Mohlenbrink, K. 1934. Die Levitischen Uberlieferung des Alten Testaments. *ZAW* 52: 184–230.

Peterson, J. L. 1977. A Topographical Surface Survey of the Levitical "Cities" of Joshua 21 and 1 Chronicles 6. Th.D. diss. Chicago.

Ross, J. P. 1973. The "Cities of the Levites" in Joshua XXI and I Chron VI. Ph.D. diss. Edinburgh.

Spencer, J. R. 1980. The Levitical Cities: A Study of the Role and Function of the Levites in the History of Israel. Ph.D. diss. Chicago.

JOHN R. SPENCER

LEVITICUS, BOOK OF. Leviticus is the third of the five books of the Torah (Pentateuch).

A. Introduction
B. Contexts and Structure of Leviticus
  1. Cult and Purity (Chaps. 1–16)
    a. Officiation of Priests in the Sacrificial Cult (Chaps. 1–10)
    b. Purifications Conducted by the Priesthood (Chaps. 11–16)

2. Holiness of the Israelite People (Chaps. 17–27)
   a. Prologue and Epilogue to the Holiness Code (Chaps. 17; 26:3–46)
   b. Holiness Code and Addendum (Chaps. 18:1–26:2 and Chap. 27)
3. Text-Critical Considerations: The State of the Text of Leviticus

C. Historical Context of Leviticus: "Realistic Interpretation"
1. Issues of Interpretation
2. Comparative Method

A. Introduction

The name "Leviticus" represents the Latin form of the Greek name *Levitikon.* In Hebrew, the usual way of referring to this book is *wayyiqrāʾ* "He called," a mnemonic title which identifies the book by its first significant word. (Compare *Šĕmôt* "The names of—" for Exodus, etc.) As such, the name *wayyiqrāʾ* tells us virtually noting about the contents or significance of this biblical book. In contrast Greek *Levitikon* is a characterization, and the same is true of the rabbinic Hebrew name *tôrat kôhănîm,* an ambiguous name which is, however, highly instructive.

At first glance, Greek *Levitikon* is a puzzling name, because the Levites are mentioned only in passing; it is the book of Numbers which features the Levites. But to Greek-speaking Jews of antiquity, *Levitikon* probably connoted "priestly" in general. It may reflect Deuteronomic usage, since in Deut 17:9, 18; 18:1 the Israelite priests are referred to as *hakkôhănîm hallewîyîm,* "the Levitical priests." The postexilic prophet Malachi (2:6–7) speaks of Levi as the epigone of the Israelite priesthood and refers to "the covenant of Levi," the commission of the priesthood, which he sees as having been violated in his day. We can say, therefore, that the name *Levitikon* means "that which concerns the priests." This is close to the meaning of Hebrew *tôrat kôhănîm.* The component term *tôrâ* originated in priestly literature. It means "instruction, prescribed ritual, ruling." In chapters 6–7 of Leviticus we find manuals of practice addressed to the priests, and entitled *tôrâ.* For example: "This is the *tôrâ* for the burnt-offering" (Lev 6:2). This suggests that *tôrat kôhănîm* means "instructions *for* the priests." But, we could just as well render *tôrat kôhănîm* in other instances as "instructions *of* the priests," (or, "by the priests"). These are the rulings issued by the priests; their teachings transmitted to the people of Israel or to individual Israelites. This is the sense of *tôrâ* as priestly teaching in Jer 18:18; Hag 2:10–13; Mal 2:6–7; etc. The rabbinic term should be understood in both of its aspects.

B. Contexts and Structure of Leviticus

Leviticus consists almost entirely of law and ritual. In most instances, rituals are also formulated as laws and commandments. The book of Leviticus is organized according to a perceptible plan into two principal parts. Chapters 1–16 deal with the role of the priests as officiants in the sacrificial cult of worship, and as performers of rites of purification. Chapters 17–27 deal with the requirements of holiness; they preserve major priestly statements, addressed for the most part to the Israelite people. This, then, is how the book is organized. Part One (chaps. 1–16) is addressed to the priesthood and concerns cultic officiation and purity. This section represents *tôrâ for* priests. Part Two (chaps. 17–27) represents *tôrâ of,* or *by* the priests, addressed to the people of Israel, and commanding the pursuit of holiness as the collective goal of religious life.

1. Cult and Purity (Chaps. 1–16). a. Officiation of Priests in the Sacrificial Cult (Chaps. 1–10). (1) Types of Sacrifices (Chaps. 1–7). Chapters 1–7 of Leviticus prescribe the proper manner of preparing and offering the principal types of sacrifices which, separately and in various combinations, comprised the cultic regimen of biblical religion, as prescribed by the priestly school of biblical writers. These sacrifices answered the needs of both private and public worship. Each of the first three chapters of this section is devoted to one of the mainstays of the cult: the burnt offering *(ʿōlâ),* the grain offering *(minḥâ),* and the sacred gift of greeting *(šĕlāmîm).* Chapters 4–5 prescribe the sacrifices of expiation, the *ḥaṭṭāʾt* "sin-offering," and the *ʾāšām* "guilt offering." Chapters 6–7 deal with the allocation of portions of most sacrifices to the officiating priests, and in some cases, to donors of sacrifices as well. Most sacrificial offerings, with the exception of those offered in the manner of holocausts, contributed to the sustenance of the officiating priesthood. It was, in fact, essential to the efficacy of the sacrifices, especially with respect to sacrifices of expiation, that priests partake of them in the form of a sacred meal (Lev 10:12–19).

The prescriptions of chaps. 1–7 are followed (chaps. 8–10) by a description of the investiture of Aaron and his sons as the first legitimate Israelite priests, and the simultaneous consecration of the tabernacle and its altar. The sequence in chaps. 1–10 of Leviticus is: (1) rites at which priests were to officiate; (2) the authority or sanction of the Aaronide priesthood. This authority was granted by God and conferred by Moses in the formative period of Israel's history. There is little corroborative evidence for the ascendancy of the Aaronide priesthood in preexilic biblical literature, but there is ample evidence of a functioning priesthood from relatively early times.

Each of the principal types of sacrifices prescribed in Leviticus 1–7 had a distinctive character conveyed in part by the term used to designate it. The Hebrew term *ʿōlâ,* "holocaust," expresses the manner of offering that sacrifice. Its aromatic smoke "ascends" heavenward (the Hebrew verb *ʿālâ*) and is inhaled by the deity, in acceptance of the offering (Gen 8:21). In chap. 2, the term *minḥâ* likewise indicates the manner of disposing of the sacrifice. The Hebrew verb *nāḥâ* means "to bring forward, present," and *minḥâ* connotes, therefore, "that which is presented." As for the term *šĕlāmîm* of chap. 3, it is far more elusive, because it derives from the root *š-l-m,* which attests a wide range of meanings, from peace and well-being to sharing and covenant. The translation "sacred gift of greeting" is based on the evidence of Ugaritic and Akkadian, where nominal forms of the Semitic root *š-l-m* (*šlmm* in Ugaritic, and *šulmāmu* in Akkadian) designates gifts presented when one greets another or is welcomed into the presence of another. In cultic contexts, both Ugaritic *šlmm* and Akkadian *šulmāmu* designate sacrificial offerings. The *šĕlāmîm* are, therefore, the sacred gifts which accompany the word of greeting *šālôm.*

In practice, the *ʿōlâ* of chap. 1 could consist of large or small cattle, as well as certain birds. The *ʿôlâ* was sectioned, decapitated (almost always), skinned, and cleaned. The parts were burned to ashes on the altar of burnt offerings: it was a holocaust. The *minḥâ* of chap. 2 could be prepared in a number of ways. It was usually made of semolina (wheat flour) with olive oil and aromatic spices added. Usually, a fistful of the dough was burned on the altar, and the rest of the dough baked or fired. Some *minḥâ* offerings were offered as a holocaust. The meaning of the term *minḥâ* suggests that this type of sacrifice was originally set before the deity, rather than being burned on an altar. In fact, certain grain offerings continued to be presented in this way, with no part of them being placed on the altar (compare the provisions of Lev 7:10–14; 23:15, 17; 24:5–9, and Deut 26:1–11). These presented offerings were made of leavened dough *(ḥāmēṣ)* instead of unleavened dough *(maṣṣā)*, as is the rule in chap. 2. No leavened dough was allowed on the altar according to the priestly laws of the Torah. (Also note the *minḥâ*-holocaust of Lev 6:12–16.) As the importance of burnt offerings grew, the mode of presenting most types of *minḥâ* was adapted to the altar of burnt offerings, and a "token" (Hebrew *ʾazkārâ*) was burned on the altar.

The *ʿôlâ* and *minḥâ* of chaps. 1–2 are classified as "most-sacred offerings" *(qōdeš qodāšîm)*, which meant, practically speaking, that only consecrated priests could partake of them. Chapter 3 introduces a series of offerings of lesser sanctity, prepared in the manner of a *zebaḥ*, "sacred meal." Certain portions of such sacrifices, called *šĕlāmîm*, were burned on the altar, whereas most of the edible meat, of large or small cattle, was boiled in pots and allotted to both priests and donors. We learn something about the preparation and disposition of the *zebaḥ* from descriptions found in 1 Sam 2:13, 16; 9:22–24.

The *ʿôlâ* and *minḥâ* were often utilized in the public cult as well as for private worship, but the *šĕlāmîm* had only a very limited role in public worship, in the celebration of the Pentecost, according to Lev 23:19. In the public sphere, it seems to have been reserved largely for special dedications and historic convocations (Exodus 24, 1 Samuel 11, and 1 Kings 8).

Chapters 4–5 of Leviticus prescribe a regimen of expiatory sacrifices. The *ʾāšām* was a penalty, computed according to "valuations" (Heb *ʿērek*), and paid in the form of a sacrificial ram. It was ordained for inadvertent misappropriation of sacred property or the property of fellow Israelites, and for cases involving a false oath, a crime known as *maʿal*. The sacrificial ram was accompanied with a payment equivalent to 20 percent of the misappropriation, and was not efficacious unless full restitution had been made (Lev 5:14–16, 20–26). The phenomenology of the *ʾāšām* is best illustrated in the narrative of the expiatory gifts, called *ʾāšām*, which the Philistines dispatched to the Israelites so as to avert the wrath of the God of Israel (1 Samuel 6). A brief code governing the *ʾāšām* is also found in Num 5:5–10. The verb *ʾāšam* means "to be guilty, to incur blame."

As for the *ḥaṭṭāʾt*, there were two distinct types. Lev 4:1–21 ordains a *ḥaṭṭāʾt* consisting of a bull. Its purpose was to expiate for serious inadvertent offenses on the part of the chief priest, or the entire community. Sections of the bull were burned on the altar; what was not so disposed of was removed to a spot outside the encampment and, in a rite of riddance, was completely destroyed. The more usual type of *ḥaṭṭāʾt* most often consisted of small cattle, sections of which were offered on the altar; other parts were allocated to the priests. Such sin-offerings were required of individual Israelites, even tribal chieftains, who inadvertently transgressed the law. They served to square offenses with God and community and, at the same time, rewarded priests for their role in securing expiation on behalf of their fellow Israelites (Lev 4:22; 5:13, 17–19). There was provision for redressing the cost of this type of sin-offering by allowing it to consist of birds—even a grain offering—so as not to deprive any Israelite of expiation due to lack of means. The noun *ḥaṭṭāʾt* itself is based on the *Piʿel* stem of the verb *ḥ-ṭ-ʾ*, which means "to err, betray, offend." Quite often, the *Piʿel* stem connotes the undoing of what the simple stem conveys. On this basis, *ḥaṭṭāʾt* means "removal of sinfulness, purification."

It is important to emphasize that the expiatory system outlined in chaps. 4–5 of Leviticus did not apply to willful, flagrant violations of law. There was no way to expiate such acts ritually; authorized agencies imposed direct penalties on the guilty (Num 15:30).

Integral to the sacrificial procedures of Leviticus were various blood rites. In all cases of sacrifices of animal and fowl, it was required that the sacrificial blood be used in specified ways. Two functions are evident in these blood rites. One function was expiatory: Dashing or sprinkling of sacrificial blood on the side of the altar of burnt offerings, or pouring it onto the base of the altar as a blood libation (Lev 1:5; 3:2; 4:7; etc.). The original intent of such blood libations was to appease chthonic deities by offering them lifeblood, which increased their power. In the monotheistic cult of Israel, where blood also symbolized life, manipulation of sacrificial blood was conceptualized as a substitute for the lives of the worshippers, securing expiation for them, and protecting them when they were in God's immediate presence (Lev 17:11f.).

The second function was apotropaic. The application of sacrificial blood to the horns of the altar, and in rarer instances, to the horns of the altar of incense and other interior furnishings of the shrine represented the effort to ward off evil impurity—to protect the sacred appurtenances and sacred space from demonic penetration. This is why such utilization of sacrificial blood was restricted to expiatory offerings whose purpose it was to purify (see Lev 4:6–7, 17–18, 25, 30, etc. Also see the purificatory rites of Leviticus 16 for the Day of Atonement).

Chapters 6–7 of Leviticus specify in greater detail how priests were to officiate in the sacrificial cult. This involved keeping the altar fire burning continually and removing ashes regularly. Those portions of the sacrifices allotted to priests became their property. In the case of the *zebaḥ* "sacred meal," of which several types are stipulated in chap. 7, donors also received portions of the sacrifice. Chapter 7 enumerates three varieties of the *zebaḥ* called *šĕlāmîm*, first encountered in chap. 3: the votive *(neder)*; the voluntary contribution *(nĕdābâ)*; and the thanksgiving offering *(tôdâ)*, the last accompanied with two loaves of leavened bread.

(2) Ordination of the Priesthood in the Sanctuary (Chaps. 8–10). The last 3 chapters of the first major unit of Leviticus differ in their formulation from chaps. 1–7, which are *prescriptive,* commanding certain ritual performances. Chapters 8–10, on the other hand, are primarily *descriptive,* reporting on certain celebrations, set in the presettlement period of Israelite history. Chapter 8 describes how Aaron and his sons were installed in their priestly office by Moses, at God's command. Simultaneous with their investiture and consecration was the consecration of the tabernacle and its altar. Aaron, the chief priest, is the typological counterpart of the tabernacle; both were anointed with the same special oil. The commissioning of the priests is conveyed by the term *millûʾîm* "appointment." Chapter 8 concludes with specific instructions to Aaron and his sons regarding their participation in the sacred meal of their consecration, which lasted for seven days.

Chapter 9 describes the celebration of the eighth day, when the sacrificial cult was actually initiated, with the newly appointed priests officiating for the first time. This occasion held critical importance, because it was intended to verify that God had accepted the Aaronide priests and would receive their offerings favorably. A sequence of sacrifices celebrated this occasion. First, the tabernacle was purified by means of a *ḥaṭṭāʾt,* "sin-offering." Then, an *ʿôlâ,* "burnt-offering," was performed, to test God's readiness to accept the officiation of the Aaronide priesthood. This *ʿôlâ* was accompanied by a grain offering *(minḥâ).* Finally, the *šĕlāmîm,* "sacred gift of greeting," was offered and the priests joined with the deity in a "sacred meal."

A fire from within the tabernacle, God's fire, ignited the altar. Aaron blessed the people assembled. According to tradition, he did so in the words of the tripartite benediction preserved in Num 6:22–26. The "glorious presence" (Heb *kāḇôd*) of the God of Israel appeared to all the people, who prostrated themselves in adoration. God was present in the tabernacle and had indicated his favorable disposition.

Immediately, things began to go wrong. Nadab and Abihu, two of Aaron's sons, offered "hateful" incense in the tabernacle and the divine fire blasted them to death (Lev 10:1–2). Although the precise nature of their offense remains elusive, their dramatic death served to emphasize that extreme care was to be exercized by the priests in all aspects of officiation. A series of instructions on proper priestly conduct reinforces this message; Aaron and his two remaining sons are cautioned not to defile their consecration by mourning the dead of their family.

b. Purifications Conducted by the Priesthood (Chapters 11–16). (1) Dietary Code (Chap. 11). Now that procedures relevant to priestly officiation have been set forth, Leviticus addresses the purificatory functions of the priesthood. Chapter 11 presents a *tôrâ* of dietary purity, extending to the condition of vessels and to persons normally having contact with foodstuffs. These regulations are similar to those in Deuteronomy 14, and it is reasonable to conclude that Leviticus 11 is patterned after the Deuteronomic code. This is a logical assumption in view of the fact that Leviticus 11 goes further in dealing with the purity of foodstuffs.

One would have expected the dietary code to appear in the second part of Leviticus, since it is addressed to the Israelite people, in substance, and is dominated by the theme of holiness, as is Deuteronomy 14. It is possible, therefore, that chap. 11 was shifted from the so-called Holiness Code to the first part of the book, and reinterpreted as purity legislation. Prevention of impurity was a priestly function, as we read in a postscript to chap. 11 (vv 44–46). What had been priestly instruction addressed to the people was reoriented, and regarded as instruction for the priests, as well.

Leviticus 11 legislates the permissibility of animals for food on the basis of a classificatory scheme which distinguishes large land animals, aquatic creatures, flying animals, and social insects. Large land animals may be used as food only if they have fully cleft hooves and are ruminants. (The pig is prohibited because it does not chew the cud, although it has cleft hooves.) Only water creatures with fins and scales may be used as food. The long list of prohibited birds implies that all others were permitted. Winged swarming creatures are generally forbidden; four types of locusts are permitted because they have jointed legs. Also prohibited are land creatures that move without legs, four-legged beasts that walk on paws, and all many-legged creatures.

No physical purification (e.g., by means of water) is required of a person who has eaten forbidden foods. Nevertheless, according to Lev 5:2, one who mistakenly eats forbidden food is obliged to bring a sin-offering.

All attempts to formulate a consistent theory to explain why certain animals, fowl, and fish were permitted as food and others forbidden, or why certain physical criteria determined purity, have failed to account for certain anomalies. There are, nevertheless, some fairly prevalent correlations. Domestication is a pervasive factor. Animals raised and kept in proximity to human settlements were preferred as food; even deer, for instance, were permitted as food, probably because they shared certain features with domesticated animals. Herbivorous animals predominate in the approved diet. Digestion and locomotion are the two factors most important for determining acceptability. Ruminants meet the requirements of digestion. How living creatures obtain their own food is significant. Those creatures most "careful" in their own diet are fit sources of food for a holy, pure people. Animals with fully cleft hooves have "toes" of a sort, and meet the requirements of locomotion; those with paws do not. Fins and scales indicate proper locomotion for water creatures. It emerges that living creatures most resembling humans, and most familiar to them are acceptable as food sources.

A dominant theme in Leviticus 11, as in Deuteronomy 14, is Israel's distinctness as a pure and holy people. This distinctness was to be expressed in diet, as well as in sexual activity and religious worship. Israelites were to avoid *tôʿēbâ,* "abomination," in all three areas, and to avoid defilement (see Lev 18:24–30; 20:22–26; Deut 7; 14:3).

As chap. 11 proceeds, emphasis shifts from foodstuffs themselves to the problems of retaining the purity of foodstuffs and of vessels in which they are stored, prepared, and served. Seed and grains had to be kept dry, and impure persons and substances had to be kept away from food and vessels. Chapter 11 ordains a complex system of dietary restrictions and food care. The priests were trained to instruct the people on questions of purity, as regards proper diet.

(1) Other Purifications (Chaps. 12–15). Chapter 12 of

Leviticus deals with the ritual status of the new mother during the period following childbirth. She was declared impure for varying periods of time, depending on the sex of the newborn child, and was forbidden access to the sanctuary for that period of time. The fact that this period of restriction was doubled for a female child may be explained by the greater potential role of the female in human reproduction. By distancing childbirth from the cult it was intended that its celebration be kept within the family. In the polytheistic, mythological religions of the ANE, the life cycle was celebrated ritually and associated with the gods. This was incompatible with the Israelite monotheistic belief.

Various conditions were subsumed under the category of "impurity" (Heb *ṭûmʾâ*), both medical and otherwise. This classification did not imply that any offense had been committed, necessarily, only that danger threatened. Such was the case of the new mother. At the conclusion of the period of restriction, the new mother was required to offer an expiatory sacrifice, not because of any offense on her part, but because she was being readmitted to the sanctuary after a period of confinement, when she and her infant were vulnerable.

The second matter dealt with in this series of purifications is a complex of skin ailments, undoubtedly regarded as contagious. These, too, were classified as impure. The ailment called *ṣāraʿat* is sometimes translated "leprosy," although, from its given symptomology, it was more likely a type of psoriasis or other skin ailment. This condition could occur in acute or transient forms and resembled the blight and discoloration often evident in cloth and leather, and even in plastered building stones. These conditions are the subject of chaps. 13–14 of Leviticus. Intricate purificatory rituals are prescribed, including sin-offerings, so as to ward off the dangerous effects and the impurity of such affections. Some of these rites, such as the dispatching of a bird as a part of a riddance ritual, resemble the rites of purification of the sanctuary, as ordained in Leviticus 16. Quarantine and observation interacted with purification and sacrifice. Priests were instructed on how to diagnose acute *ṣāraʿat,* for which no cure was known. One suffering from acute *ṣāraʿat* was permanently banished as *ṭāmēʾ*, "impure" (Lev 13:45–46).

Chapter 15 concerns physiological phenomena, particularly abnormalities related to the human genitals. The normal menstrual cycle of the female was a matter for priestly regulation, and a woman was declared impure, a state termed *niddâ* "flow, menstruation" for seven days, during which time she could not have sexual intercourse with her husband. The menstruating woman was required to bathe at the conclusion of her period. There are also provisions for abnormal discharges from the genitals occurring outside the normal menstrual period.

The normal seminal emissions of the male were likewise classified as impure and required bathing for proper purification. Abnormal flux in the male produced even a greater degree of impurity. Taken as a whole, Leviticus 15 attests to the high degree of anxiety over human sexuality and reproduction. The category of *ṭûmʾâ,* "impurity," once again embraces both actual problems of a medical character and matters of ritual concern.

(2) Purification of the Sanctuary. The first part of Leviticus concludes with chap. 16, the elaborate ritual for purifying the Israelite sanctuary. Priestly tradition, as represented in vv 29–34 of this chapter, scheduled this purification as an annual event, to take place on the tenth day of the seventh month, only a few days before the major pilgrimage, the festival of booths (*ḥag hassukkôt;* see Lev 23: 26–44). Virtually all purification rites required sacrifice, and this in turn necessitated a pure sanctuary. After chaps. 11–15 had set forth the rites of purification to be conducted by the priests, chap. 16 instructed the priesthood on periodic measures necessary for maintaining the purity of the sanctuary itself.

The purification of the sanctuary was conducted by the chief priest; tradition identified Aaron as the one who had initiated these rites. The priest wore special vestments on this occasion and undertook to expiate, in turn, for his own offenses and those of his priestly family, and finally for those of all Israel. By "sins" (Heb *ʿăwônôt*) was meant those acts which defiled the sanctuary and its attending priesthood. At a certain point in the proceedings, the high priest, Aaron, entered the innermost shrine, the holy of holies, bringing with him sacrificial blood from the sin-offering. He stood directly in front of the *kappôret,* the sculptured lid covering the ark, the space from which divine forgiveness came. The God of Israel was envisioned as sitting astride the cherubs, which adorned the sculptured lid of the ark (1 Sam 4:4; 6:2; 2 Kgs 19:18; Isa 37:16). The priest applied sacrificial blood to objects and spaces inside the shrine, perhaps in order to seal up his route of egress and thus protect the shrine from defilement.

Alongside the offering of sacrifices, which effected riddance and removal, there was also the dispatching of the scapegoat, a riddance rite *par excellence,* with heavily magical overtones. Anthropologists and students of comparative religion have analyzed the scapegoat ritual extensively and have encountered similar practices in many parts of the world. The collected sins of the community were transferred to a kid goat, selected by lot, and carried off into the wilderness, to the domain of Azazel, the demonic ruler of the wasteland (see Lev 17:7). The scapegoat represents a vestige of pre-monotheistic religion, continued by the priests of Israel to dramatize expiation.

Appended to the principal rites of purification is the annual scheduling of the occasion called *yôm hakkippûrîm* "the Day of Atonement," (Lev 23:27). The basic objective of purifying the sanctuary and its attendant priesthood is extended to the people themselves. No actual rite of purification of the people of Israel was performed, but the ceremonial *identification* of the people with the actual purification of the sanctuary effected a purification of the populace. By fasting and other forms of abstinence, and by declaring this day a twenty-four-hour period of complete rest, the people were involved in the purification of the sanctuary in a meaningful way. The confession of sins by the officiating priest touched them as well.

2. Holiness of the Israelite People (Chaps. 17–27). In modern biblical scholarship, Leviticus 17–26 has come to be known as the Holiness Code. Admitting later interpolations, scholars have nevertheless been impressed by the unusual coherence of themes in this section of Leviticus, and by the consistent emphasis on holiness as the objective of collective existence. Chapter 27, which comes after the epilogue to the Holiness Code (Lev 26:3–46), belongs with chaps. 17–25, though it may be a later composition. In any event, it was clearly appended to the book of Leviticus, with no effort made to insert it before the epilogue.

Most of the contents of the Holiness Code are addressed to the entire people of Israel. Chapters 21–22 are exceptional in this respect since they deal with regulations governing the priesthood. The theme of holiness dominates chaps. 21–22. The sanctity of the priesthood was of concern to the whole people, and there is a symmetry between people and priesthood: both must be holy.

a. Prologue and Epilogue to the Holiness Code (Chaps. 17; 26:3–46). The Holiness Code opens with a prologue (chap. 17) and ends with an epilogue (26:3–46). This arrangement is characteristic of the other collections of laws preserved in the Torah. The subject of the prologue is proper worship. (Cf. Deuteronomy 12, which introduces the Deuteronomic laws, and Exod 20:19–23, which introduces the book of the Covenant. Both sources speak of proper worship.)

According to the prologue, which most likely expresses the Deuteronomic doctrine of cult centralization (Noth *Leviticus* OTL, 129–30) all sacrifices must be offered at the entrance of the Tent of Meeting (a way of referring to the sanctuary), on the one legitimate altar by a legitimate priest. No blood may be consumed, and sacrificial blood is reserved for ritual utilization on the altar to expiate sins. The earlier practice of offering sacrifice at various altars is outlawed.

The epilogue admonishes the Israelite people to obey God's laws and commandments, predicting the dire consequences of disobedience. A disobedient Israel will be exiled from its land and endure horrible punishments in foreign lands. Going beyond exile, and the threat of collective extinction, the epilogue holds forth the promise of restoration to the land, if only the people of Israel will show remorse for its past behavior and renounce its coldness toward God. In its thrust, the epilogue to the Holiness Code resembles the epilogue to the Deuteronomic laws (Deuteronomy 28–30), notwithstanding certain differences in the language and concepts characteristic of each composition.

b. Holiness Code and Addendum (Chaps. 18:1–26:2 and Chap. 27). (1) Family Law (Chaps. 18 and 20). Between prologue and epilogue, the Holiness Code presents important legal documents and commandments relevant to the life of the Israelite community. Chapters 18 and 20 present differing formulations of family law. It is not clear why such repetition was required. Chapter 18 is clearly the primary statement, and is formulated apodictically, whereas chap. 20 is casuistic in its formulation, specifying legal penalties. The introduction to chap. 18 speaks of avoiding the sins of the Egyptians of the land which the Israelites had just left, and the sins of the Canaanites of the land to which they would arrive. On the other hand, the introduction to chap. 20 (vv 2–5) focuses on the abominable cult of Molech, which appears to have involved child sacrifice, a practice for which death by stoning is legislated.

The chapter continues (20: 10–21) with restrictions on sexual congress between kin. A man was forbidden to marry his close relatives. Two factors combined to enhance the concern in ancient Israel with incestuous marriages. There was, first of all, a pattern of endogamy, epitomized in the narratives of the patriarchs. Marriages with Canaanites or Philistines were not acceptable. Then, too, there was concern for retaining ancestral lands within the larger family, or clan. Acting together, these two pressures created a situation in which marriages within the clan were subject to restriction so as to avoid incest. Chapters 18 and 20 place limits on sexual relations. These codes outlaw adultery, homosexuality, and bestiality. A holy community was one in which sexual energies were channeled according to divine will.

(2) "You must be holy, for I, the LORD your God, am holy!" (Chap. 19). Chapter 19 of Leviticus is a remarkable document of priestly *tôrâ,* showing the degree to which the priestly school of biblical times was sensitive to prophetic teachings, and laws governing human behavior. This composition emphasizes perhaps more than any other section of the Holiness Code what it truly meant to be a holy nation.

Chapter 19 stresses the interaction of social behavior and religious piety, two dimensions of life which were never meant to be regarded as separate. In tandem, chap. 19 commands observance of the Sabbath and respect for parents; it prohibits pagan funerary practices and commands respect for elders. It requires that sacrificial flesh be disposed of in certain ways, while condemning fraudulent economic dealings. The grafting and blending of vegetation separate in nature are prohibited, and Israelites are commanded to leave gleanings and corners of their fields for the indigent. Though idolatry is thoroughly condemned, Israelites are commanded to be kind to aliens, who may be idolators. By following the dictates of this mini-*tôrâ,* which echoes the commandments of the Decalogue, Israelites could hope to become a holy nation.

(3) Priestly Regulations (Chaps. 21–22 and 24). In symmetrical fashion, chaps. 21–22 deal with two factors relevant to purity: contact with the dead through funerary activity and restrictions on priestly marriage. An ordinary priest was generally forbidden to attend to the dead, except with respect to his close, consanguinal relatives. By declaring the human corpse the most impure object, a matter detailed in Numbers 19, priestly law effectively ruled out any funerary role for the priesthood. It is reasonable to conclude that the priesthood sought to prevent the spread of cults of the dead by distancing funerary activity from the public cult, or from private ministrations by the priesthood. This is further indicated by the fact that a Nazirite was also prohibited from contact with the dead (Num 6:1–21).

The second area of concern was marriage. Ordinary priests were prohibited from marrying a divorcée or a defiled harlot. An ordinary priest could marry a widow, however. In both areas, the high priest was subject to even severer restrictions. He was barred completely from contact with the dead, and could not even attend to the burial of his parents. He was restricted to marrying a virgin of a priestly family. He could not marry a widow.

The avoidance of divorcées reflects the laws of Deut 24:1f., which stipulate that the sole basis for divorce was serious sexual misconduct, such as adultery. A divorced woman was, therefore, stigmatized on the assumption that she had been guilty of such misconduct.

Chapters 21–22 of Leviticus deal also with the physical suitability of priests, and with defects and blemishes in sacrificial animals. The remarkable correspondence between the two categories suggests that the same concept underlies both classifications: what is offered to God must be of the best, sound and without defect.

Also included in chap. 22 are laws aimed at guaranteeing that sacred offerings *(qodāšîm)* be maintained in a pure state. Impure priests were to avoid contact with such materials. Sacred offerings were intended to sustain priests and those members of their families who shared the same domicile. Chapter 22 concludes with a brief code governing procedures of sacrifice. Mother animals and their offspring may not be sacrificed on the same day, and offspring could not be sacrificed until they were eight days old.

Chapter 24 of Leviticus is a brief and loosely organized collection of priestly laws, including the charge to Aaron to kindle the candelabra continually and to prepare the bread of display *(leḥem happānîm)*. The rest of the chapter deals with the crime of blasphemy, and an account of an actual instance of blasphemy in the days of Moses.

(4) Calendar of Festivals (Chap. 23). The sacred days of the year are significant aspects of any religious system. They constitute the *sancta* of the group, which lend to it a distinct identity. Leviticus 23 is the primary, priestly calendar of annual festivals, and is therefore a major source of information on biblical religion. Its precise position in the development of the Israelite festivals is not entirely certain. Here it will be the accepted view that this calendar reflects the rescheduling of the festivals which was legislated in Deuteronomy 16 and exhibits further indications of dependence on Deuteronomy. Its provisions represent therefore a stage in the development of the festivals subsequent to the Deuteronomic reforms, and of course, much later than the pre-Deuteronomic code of Exod 23:14–19, part of the Book of the Covenant.

According to Deuteronomy 12, all sacrifices, including those in celebration of the festivals, must be offered on a single altar, at a central "cult-place" (Heb *māqôm*). It has already been suggested in our discussion of the prologue to the Holiness Code (chap. 17) that this restriction underlies the law of Lev 17:1f.

Restriction of sacrifice to a single, central temple generated the most basic changes in the scheduling of the annual festivals and in other aspects of their celebration. The primary change was to defer the wheat harvest festival seven weeks, since it would be very difficult for Israelites to undertake two lengthy pilgrimages, the *maṣṣôt* pilgrimage and the pilgrimage of the wheat harvest, in close sequence to each other.

The content of Leviticus 23 gives evidence of considerable editing. Its requirements of sacrifice were subsequently elaborated in the provisions of Numbers 28–29. Chapter 23 is presented as a calendar of *môᶜădîm,* "set-times," a term used to designate annual occasions occurring at the same time each year. The calendar begins with the law of the Sabbath day, even though the Sabbath is not strictly speaking a *môᶜēd.*

The basic commandment of the Torah regarding the Sabbath is to cease all *mĕlā'kah* "assigned tasks." In priestly terminology, the Sabbath is *miqrā' qôdeš,* "a sacred convocation," and is to be celebrated as such in all Israelite habitations (23:1–3).

The order of the annual *môᶜădîm* is as follows:

(1) *Ḥag hammaṣṣôt,* "the pilgrimage festival of unleavened bread." This festival is to be celebrated for seven days, beginning on the fifteenth day of the first month, in the spring of the year. It is immediately preceded by the paschal sacrifice *(pesaḥ),* offered before evening on the fourteenth of the month. *Maṣṣôt* must be eaten for seven days, beginning as an accompaniment to the paschal sacrifice. The first and seventh days are proclaimed *miqrā' qôdeš,* days on which assigned tasks are forbidden. An offering by fire (Heb *'iššê*) of an unspecified character is to be offered on each of the seven days of the festival (23:8).

(2) Chapter 23 of Leviticus continues by ordaining certain religious activities for the period between the *maṣṣôt* festival and Pentecost, the wheat harvest festival, seven weeks later. The mere fact that the priestly calendar schedules this festival seven weeks after the *maṣṣôt* festival testifies to its acceptance of the Deuteronomic program, which called this occasion *ḥag šāḇûᶜôt* "a pilgrimage festival of weeks" (Deut 16:9–12). In our chapter, the laws governing the period between the *maṣṣôt* festival and the Pentecost highlight the importance of the Sabbath day as a point in time for calculating the passage of weeks. If consistent terminology were employed throughout, the *ḥag šāḇûᶜôt* of Deut 16:10 would have been called *šabbātôt* in Leviticus 23. The seven weeks are to be counted from Sabbath to Sabbath and not from any other day. This concept of marking time eventually led to the week which begins on Sunday and ends on the Sabbath. Lev 23:9–22 involves two desacralizations. At the beginning of the period of counting, on the day after the first Sabbath following the fifteenth day, the barley sheaf *(ᶜômer)* is presented, and on the morrow of the seventh Sabbath, at the end of the period of counting, the new wheat crop is desacralized with an offering of grain. The concept underlying desacralization is that God must be honored with the first fruits, because God grants humankind the blessings of the earth. Only then may humans have the benefit of the produce of the earth, and of the herds and flocks.

The Pentecost is not designated a *ḥag,* "pilgrimage festival," in the liturgical calendar of Leviticus. This is a significant departure from the law of Deuteronomy, which does use the term *ḥag* (Deut 16:10). The implicit change is endorsed subsequently by Num 28:26 (which does not use *ḥag*). The legislation in Leviticus 23 seems to implement a change in the method of celebrating the Pentecost. Whereas Deuteronomy envisions a pilgrimage festival at a central sanctuary, Leviticus describes a domestic festival during which offerings of first fruits are delivered to the sanctuary but no pilgrimage is undertaken (Lev 23:12–13, 18–20).

(3) *Ḥôdeš,* "the new moon" of the seventh month, is proclaimed as a day of rest, on which the ram's horn is sounded at the middle of the month to announce the forthcoming autumn pilgrimage. An offering by fire is presented (vv 23–25; cf. Ps 81:4).

(4) *Yôm hakkippûrîm,* "the Day of Atonement," falls on the tenth of the seventh month. The provisions relating to

this occasion have already been discussed above, in the summary of chap. 16. Here, we find the statement that any Israelite who fails to obey the regulations pertaining to this day shall be "cut off" from his clan. The Day of Atonement lasted a full twenty-four hours. There is no mention here of the main purification of the sanctuary (vv 26–32).

(5) *Ḥag hassukkôt,* "the pilgrimage festival of booths," is the name given to the festival in Deut 16:13f. It begins on the fifteenth day of the seventh month and lasts for seven days. The eighth day is declared a special day of assembly (*ʿăṣeret*). Assigned tasks are forbidden on the first and eighth days, and sacrifices ordained for each of the eight days (vv 33–36).

After a postscript summarizing the liturgical calendar (v 38) comes a second statement relative to the celebration of the festival of booths in the Israelite habitations. Greenery was utilized, symbols of fertility, and the Israelites dwelled in booths for seven days. The duty to dwell in booths is given an historical explanation: God provided temporary shelter for the Israelites on their way to the promised land, when they wandered in the wilderness. Realistically, it has been suggested that the throngs of Israelite pilgrims arriving in Jerusalem for the autumn celebration found it necessary to live in booths for the duration of the festival (cf. Nehemiah 8).

(5) Priestly Administration (Chaps. 25 and 27). Chapter 25 of Leviticus is the only explicit statement in Torah literature on the right of the Israelite people to the land of Canaan, usually referred to as "*the* land." This right imposed obligations. As stewards of God's land, the Israelites were obliged to obey God's commandments with respect to the land—its economic exploitation, its ownership, etc. Although chap. 25 never mentions a priestly or other agency which was to be in charge of land transfers, a major concern of this chapter, it may be assumed that the very inclusion of this legislation in Leviticus indicates that the priesthood was in charge of such business.

Essentially, this code of law prohibits the permanent alienation of any arable land in the land of Israel, and relegates sales of land to the status of long-term leases. On the Jubilee, or fiftieth year, all land sold or forfeited in payment of debts would revert to its original owner. The key term in chap. 25 is *ʾăḥuzzâ,* "land holding," a term which conveys the theory of stewardship. The land is truly possessed by God; its inhabitants are tenants, to whom has been transferred the right to live on the land.

After restating earlier laws on the Sabbatical, or seventh year, when the fields are allowed to lie fallow, chap. 25 introduces the Jubilee year. The Jubilee is an occasion of "release" (Heb *dĕrôr*), when all who are indentured will regain economic liberty. The land may never be sold beyond retrieval (*liṣmîtût*), and must be redeemed. But, as the laws of chap. 25 unfold, it becomes clear that the provisions for economic relief associated with the seventh year in Exodus 21 and 23 and in Deuteronomy 15 have been discontinued. The primary concern has shifted to guaranteeing the rights of Israelite landowners at the expense of those indebted or indentured. There is a concern to prevent acquisition of land by non-Israelites (Lev 25:47f.). Special legislation protected the property of the Levites, and urban dwellings could be acquired permanently if they had not been redeemed within one year. It was forbidden to hold Israelites as slaves, or to charge them interest, or mistreat them while indentured. See also JUBILEE.

In chap. 25, the concept of *gĕʾullâ,* "redemption," is fundamental. On the private level, redemption expressed itself in the efforts of clan relatives to come to the aid of those of their relations whose tenure over their land had been forfeited or threatened. Collectively, continued tenure of the land meant redemption for the people of Israel.

Finally, chap. 27 of Leviticus, which was appended to the book, deals with the financing of the sanctuary and its cult. Several sources of income are legislated. Traditionally, Israelites vowed donations to the sanctuary, by devoting weights of silver calculated as "equivalents" (Heb *ʿērek*) of their life-worth. This idiom of votive donations harks back to a time when persons were actually devoted to temple service. One would devote his life-worth to the sanctuary ("to the LORD"), and buy back his "life" by a donation—in other words, he would redeem himself. In a similar way, livestock and even real estate could be devoted and bought back in this way, with animals actually suitable for offerings remaining in the possession of the sanctuary. Chapter 27 also speaks of condemned land that became the property of the sanctuary. It concludes with reference to tithes of produce and livestock, which helped to support the clergy.

We have come, in this survey of the contents of Leviticus, all the way from sacrifice and purification, through family law and festival celebrations, to statements on land tenure and economic policy, as well as temple finances. These varied subjects addressed in the text of Leviticus actually reflect the multiple functions of the Israelite priesthood.

3. Text-Critical Considerations: The State of the Text of Leviticus. Before one can interpret an ancient book, it is necessary to be certain exactly what is written in it. Recently, parts of one or more scrolls of Leviticus, discovered at Qumran and written in a script imitative of earlier calligraphy (paleo-Hebrew) have been published by D. N. Freedman and K. A. Matthews (1985). These materials date to the last pre-Christian century. All instances where these ancient fragments differ from MT, LXX and the Samaritan version have been tabulated. The results of these comparisons indicate that the received text, the Masoretic version of Leviticus, was carefully copied, although a degree of fluidity is evident. The actual variations evident in the Qumran fragments are not what we would regard as "meaningful"; they do not reflect a different text having a different intent. Most are simply alternative ways of saying the same things, or conscious attempts at symmetry, the juxtaposition of syntax, etc. The LXX and the Samaritan versions are often interpretive, but seldom point to a different text as the basis of translation. Generally, the Torah books, with the exception of certain poetic sections, are in much better shape than other books of Scripture. This is probably because of the later importance of the Torah in the Jewish synagogue, and the basic role of Torah law in Jewish relation.

C. Historical Context of Leviticus: "Realistic Interpretation."

1. Issues of Interpretation. Thus far, the contents and structure of Leviticus have been discussed without specifying a historical context. No attempt has been made to place the laws and celebrations of this priestly composition in an historical setting, or to assess their degree of realism. Since late antiquity, traditional interpretation, both Jewish and Christian, has accepted the stated historiographic context of all Torah literature. The assumption was that the religious and social legislation of Leviticus, and of Torah literature generally, went into practice either in the time of Moses, or, as often stated, when the Israelites settled in Canaan.

Modern critical scholarship has demanded independent corroboration of traditional dates and attributions, and regards Leviticus as priestly literature. It is part of the *Priesterschrift* (abbreviated P), a documentary source which has a literary history of its own. In the absence of the types of indicators found in historical books of the Bible, determining the historical context of P requires special methods of analysis. The method which recommends itself is "realistic interpretation." By this we mean an approach to the study of the text which focuses on realistic indications, such as terminology and formulation, institutional makeup, precise legal provisions, and the relative chronology of the sources of Torah literature.

As regards the literary history of Leviticus, the major debate in modern scholarship has centered on the chronological relationship of P to Deuteronomy. Are the provisions of Leviticus predicated on the specific legislation of Deuteronomy, or do they generally precede the changes in religious worship legislated in Deuteronomy? Even before Wellhausen, modern biblical scholars had endorsed a late date for P, in the postexilic period. This view has been challenged most forcibly by Y. Kaufmann *(KRI),* who places P before Deuteronomy in the chronology of Torah sources. His realignment has, in turn, been challenged and has raised serious questions. Recently, H. L. Ginsberg (1982) has shown to what an extent the biblical festivals, as scheduled and prescribed in Leviticus and in the priestly sections of Exodus and Numbers, reflect and endorse the Deuteronomic doctrine of worship.

Ginsberg has advanced the hypothesis, on the basis of his original analysis, that the Deuteronomic doctrine of cult centralization originated in the N Israelite kingdom before its annexation by the Assyrians, toward the end of the 8th century, B.C.E. The Judean king Hezekiah had attempted to implement the Deuteronomic policy (2 Kgs 18:3–4, 22), but did not succeed at it. Since he was followed by the heterodox king Manasseh, who ruled Judah throughout most of the 7th century B.C.E., no progress was made in eliminating the *bāmôt,* the local and regional cult sites, until the reign of Josiah. In 622 B.C.E., Josiah, king of Judah, issued an edict endorsing the Deuteronomic policy, then interpreted to mean that sacrifice could be legitimately offered only in the Temple of Jerusalem (2 Kings 22–23). It is reasonable to suppose that most of the major changes in festival celebration and sacrificial worship emerged after the promulgation of Josiah's edicts. In turn, this suggests dating those priestly laws which show dependence on Deuteronomic doctrine to the period after 622 B.C.E., at the earliest, which brings us close to the Babylonian exile.

It was Wellhausen's keen insight (*WPHI,* 34–35) that the law of Leviticus 17, which requires that all sacrifices be offered at the entrance of the Tent of Meeting, is best understood as a priestly formulation of Deuteronomic doctrine on cult centralization, projected in a wilderness setting. It has already been noted that the seven-week deferral of the wheat harvest festival, adopted in Leviticus 23 and in Numbers 28, reflects the provisions of Deuteronomy 16. Ginsberg (1982) and Levine (1987) have shown that the epilogue to the Holiness Code (Lev 26:3–46) contains themes introduced by Ezekiel, and takes us well into the 6th century, B.C.E., the period of the Babylonian exile. Levine goes further, and sees in the epilogue, which evidences several internal strata, echoes of the end of the exile, and the early years of the return, at the end of the 6th century B.C.E. In Levine's view, Leviticus 25 is a document best understood as deriving from the early period of the Return.

Not only literary-historical analysis suggests that Leviticus in particular and P in general contain exilic and postexilic creativity, but also technical terminology and institutional structures. Such institutional structures are conveyed by terms of reference. It is important to differentiate between traditional terms and realistic, functional terms. We learn little about the precise historical setting of Leviticus from such terms as *hāʿām,* "the people," or even *bĕnê yiśrāʾel,* "the Israelite people," or even *bêt Yiśrāʾēl,* "the House of Israel," which is admittedly somewhat instructive. The truly functional terms for the Israelite collective are *ʿēdâ,* "community," and *qāhāl,* "congregation." The Aramaic cognate of Heb *ʿēdâ* is attested in documents from 5th-century-B.C.E. Elephantine, in upper Egypt. There the word refers to the garrison of Jewish mercenary troops residing there. Neither *ʿēdâ* nor *qāhāl* are kinship terms. It is interesting that the usual terms for "tribe" *šēbeṭ* and *maṭṭeh* are not used in Leviticus.

To refer to fellow Israelites, traditional terminology, such as *ʾāḥ,* "brother, kinsman," as well as somewhat distinctive, internal family terms, such as *šĕʾēr,* "flesh, relation," are used. Of greater historical and social significance is a term like *ʿămît,* "neighbor" (even *rēʿa,* "comrade") identifying a fellow member of the socioreligious community. A community whose members refer to each other as *ʿămît* (cf. Zech 13:7 where *ʿămît* is parallel to *rēʿa*) is not one defined by kinship and ancestry. It is rather a community composed of citizens, in our modern terminology. There are other subtle indications of this sort in Leviticus of a breakdown of the earlier clan system as the basis of overall social organization.

When we inquire as to where the community referred to in Leviticus (or the network of communities) lived, we again find it necessary to differentiate between traditional terms such as *maḥăneh,* "encampment," and functional terms such as *môšābôt,* "settlements"; *ʿîr, ʿārîm* "town(s)"; *ḥăṣērîm* "open settlements, villages"; and *migrāšîm,* "corrals" (but also "gardens") adjacent to the towns. Outside the area of the towns is the *śādeh,* "arable land."

We observe, therefore, realistic terms of reference which point to a network of communities, engaging in agriculture and pastoral pursuits, and settled in towns and villages. This is the realistic setting, whereas the traditional setting of Leviticus is cast in the wilderness, with the people living in encampments, having recourse to the Tent of Meeting (*ʾôhel môʿēd*) as their sanctuary.

The leadership of the Israelite community is also a matter for "realistic interpretation." There is only one reference in Leviticus to the *nāśîʾ*, "tribal chieftain," and it is hardly significant in our quest for ancient reality. In Lev 4:22–26 we are told that a *nāśîʾ* who transgresses is treated like any other individual Israelite. The *zĕqēnîm*, "elders," have only a ceremonial role, laying their hands on certain offerings, etc. The functional leaders are the priests. The high priest is mentioned in Lev 21:10, and designated "the anointed priest" in Lev 4:3. His offenses were to be expiated in the same manner as the collective transgressions of the entire people, because they affected the people as a whole (Lev 4:1–21). Administrative as well as religious functions are performed by priests, as appears from chap. 27, and most probably from chap. 25. In the traditional setting of Leviticus, Moses was, of course, the leader of the Israelites in every respect. But unless one accepts the historicity of this traditional setting, the only functional leadership resided with the priesthood.

In summary, a terminological analysis of the community structures expressed in Leviticus yields the following outline: we observe a socioreligious communal network, whose members are similar to citizens. The economy is agricultural and pastoral, and the people live in towns and open villages. The head of the communities is the chief priest, and the administration is composed of priests, who handle the affairs of the Temple (= sanctuary) and the society at large.

This profile would suit the life situation of the reconstructed Judean community in the period after the Return, in the late 6th century B.C.E. and thereafter. A hierocracy administered the Temple establishment and of Judea, as well, all under Persian imperial rule. The legislation of Leviticus 25, indicates an economically strained and somewhat stratified society, in which indenture was a frequent condition, and forfeiture of land a present threat. These conditions are very similar to what is described as the plight of the people in Nehemiah 5, which clearly reflects the conditions of life under Persian rule.

On the other hand, it is probable that some of the cultic praxis prescribed in Leviticus is of great antiquity and reflects preexilic patterns of worship. All of the contents of Leviticus need not be assigned to a single period of biblical history, and there are clear indications of internal documentary stratification in Leviticus. Nevertheless, the presence of early material, and even of some early language in Leviticus (and in P generally) does not lead to the conclusion that the overall regimen presented therein is as ancient as its oldest sources.

Much of the current debate centers around this very issue, namely, the relative valence given to older versus more recent materials, respectively. Those most heavily influenced by Y. Kaufmann (including Israeli scholars such as M. Haran, and American Jewish scholars like J. Milgrom) attach greater weight to evidence of antiquity in P. H. L. Ginsberg, B. A. Levine, and even the late E. A. Speiser as well as many Christian and humanist scholars conclude that P, in its final form, was compiled at a relatively late date, and contains some exilic and postexilic material.

2. Comparative Method. "Realistic interpretation" utilizes comparative evidence from the larger and smaller cultures of the ANE, contemporary with the biblical period, or having attested contact with Canaan, in earlier periods. Such comparative evidence sheds light on the derivation of social and legal institutions as well as on the phenomenology of sacrifice and purification. It is used by most contemporary specialists in the area of priestly literature, regardless of their views on dating with regard to the Deuteronomic question, etc.

To be brief, the legal institutions of Leviticus 25 include the moratorium known as *dĕrôr*, "release," and recall the *andurārum* of the Old Babylonian kings, Hebrew *liṣmītût*, "beyond retrieval," recalls the Akkadian documents from Ugarit, where the stative form *ṣamid/t* has essentially the same meaning. Penalties for cultic offenses recall similar punishments recorded in Mesopotamian and Hittite laws. Perhaps even more informative are the Mesopotamian magical texts, many of Neo-Assyrian and Babylonian provenance, which offer parallels to the rites of riddance and purification found in Leviticus 12–16.

On the level of terminology, we find both cognates and the semantic equivalents of specific biblical terms for sacrifice. These are mostly to be found in the Mesopotamian, Ugaritic and Phoenician-Punic vocabularies. As an example, the sacrificial offering *šĕlāmîm*, "sacred gift of greeting," is known both in Ugaritic documents of the LB Age, and in the Punic "tariffs" from Carthage, from the 4th–3d centuries B.C.E. (see Levine 1974). Even the formulation and composition of the biblical and extrabiblical ritual texts show remarkable affinity.

The phenomenology of sacrificial worship and ritual purification has also been clarified in comparative perspective, as has been the character of festival celebrations. All in all, the prescribed regimen of Leviticus now appears much less artificial, or simply programmatic, than it did in the early years of this century. Recent discoveries such as the Temple Scroll from Qumran have reinforced the conclusion that the sacred cult of biblical Israel remained of basic importance even after the period covered by the Hebrew Bible. However one determines the original life situations which produced the institutions and practices ordained in Leviticus, it is acknowledged that they were fully functional throughout most of the period of the Second Temple of Jerusalem.

Bibliography

Alt, A. 1966. The Origins of Israelite Law. Pp. 79–132 in *Essays in Old Testament History and Religion*. Oxford.

Daniel, S. 1966. *Recherches sur le vocabulaire du culte dans la Septante*. Paris.

Douglas, M. 1966. *Purity and Danger*. London.

Dussand, R. 1981. *Les origines Canaanéennes du sacrifice Israélite*. Paris.

Freedman, D. N., and Matthews, K. A. 1985. *The Paleo-Hebrew Leviticus Scroll (11QpaleoLev)*. Philadelphia.

Ginsberg, H. L. 1980. The Grain Harvest Laws of Lev. 23:9–22 and Num. 28:26–31. *PAAJR:* 141–54.

———. 1982. *The Israelian Heritage of Judaism*. New York.

Gray, G. B. 1971. *Sacrifice in the Old Testament*, with a Prolegomenon by B. A. Levine. New York.

Greenfield, J. C., and Shaffer, H. 1985. Notes on the Curse Formula of the Tell Fekherye Inscription. *RB* 92: 47–59.

Hallo, W. W. 1977. New Moons and Sabbaths: A Case Study in the Contrastive Approach. *HUCA* 48: 1–18.
Haran, M. 1960. The Uses of Incense in the Ancient Israelite Ritual. *VT* 10: 113–29.
———. 1978. *Temples and Temple Service in Ancient Israel.* Oxford.
Hurowitz, V. 1985. The Priestly Account of Building the Tabernacle. *JAOS* 105: 21–30.
Levine, B. A. 1965. The Descriptive Tabernacle Texts of the Pentateuch. *JAOS* 85: 307–18.
———. 1968. On the Presence of God in Biblical Religion. Pp. 71–87 in *Religions in Antiquity,* ed. J. Neusner. Leiden.
———. 1974. *In the Presence of the Lord.* Leiden.
———. 1981. Late Language in the Priestly Code: Literary and Historical Ramifications. *Proceedings, Eighth World Congress of Jewish Studies.* Jerusalem.
———. 1987. The Epilogue to the Holiness Code: A Priestly Statement on the Destiny of Israel. Pp. 9–34 in *Judaic Perspectives on Ancient Israel,* ed. J. Neusner et al. Philadelphia.
———. 1988. *Leviticus.* Philadelphia.
Milgrom, J. 1976. *Cult and Conscience.* Leiden.
Moor, J. C. de. 1970. The Peace-Offering in Ugarit and Israel. Pp. 112–17 in *Schrift en Vitteg . . . ,* ed. W. H. Gispen. Kampen.
Rainey, A. F. 1970. The Order of Sacrifices in Old Testament Rituals. *Bib* 51: 485–98.
Ritter, E. 1965. Magical Expert *(āšipu)* and Medical Expert *(asû). AS* 16: 299ff.
Sarna, N. H. 1962. The Psalm for the Sabbath Day. *JBL* 81: 155–68.
———. 1973. Zedekiah's Emancipation of Slaves and the Sabbatical Year. Pp. 143–49 in *Orient and Occident,* ed. H. A. Hoffner. Kevalear.
Speiser, E. A. 1960. Leviticus and the Critics. Pp. 29–45 in *Yehezekel Kaufmann Jubilee Volume,* ed. M. Haran. Jerusalem.
Tigay, J. 1978. Notes on the Development of the Jewish Week. *EI* 14: 111–21.
Vaux, R. de. 1964. *Studies in Old Testament Sacrifice.* Cardiff.
Wright, D. 1986. The Gesture of Hand Placement in the Hebrew Bible and in Hittite Literature. *JAOS* 106: 433–46.

BARUCH A. LEVINE

LEX TALIONIS. A law of retaliation by which the guilty party suffers the same harm as that experienced by the injured party. In biblical as in modern law the primary example of taliation is capital punishment for a judgment of murder (Gen 9:6, "Whoever sheds man's blood, by man shall his blood be shed"; Exod 21:12, "Whoever strikes a man so that he dies, he shall surely be put to death"; Lev 24:21, "Whoever kills a man shall be put to death"), although some commentators would restrict the term "talion" to nonfatal bodily injuries. The classic formulation of taliation in biblical law is "life for life, eye for eye, tooth for tooth, hand for hand, foot for foot, burning for burning, wound for wound, stripe for stripe" (Exod 21:23–25). This text is popularly quoted as "an eye for an eye (and a tooth for a tooth)," following Matt 5:38, and is popularly regarded as a summation of biblical law.

What occasions the detailed statement in Exodus 21 is the difficulty of appropriate punishment in the complex case of injury to a pregnant woman who gets caught up in a fight among men and suffers a miscarriage and possible further consequences, even death. (Exod 21:22–25, however, has several indications of complex redaction and scholars differ widely in reconstruction and interpretation.) A similar talionic statement occurs with reference to causing permanent bodily injury to a neighbor—"as he has done so it will be done to him: injury for injury, eye for eye, tooth for tooth; as he has injured a man, so shall it be done to him" (Lev 24:19–20). The principle of taliation is also invoked with reference to compensation for the death of a stock animal—the negligent owner of a dangerous ox gives "ox for ox" (Exod 21:36), and someone who kills another's animal gives restitution, "life for life" (Lev 24:18). In the case of false testimony, the penalty for the allegation is carried out on the perjuring party—"You shall do to him as he intended to do to his brother" (Deut 19:19). The added warning states, "You shall not show pity, but life for life, eye for eye, tooth for tooth, hand for hand, foot for foot" (Deut 19:21).

Biblical law does not know of the vicarious talion illustrated in the Laws of Hammurapi (## 116, 210, 230; cf. Middle Assyrian Laws ## A 50–52) in which someone responsible for the death of a citizen's son or daughter has his son or daughter put to death. The biblical emphasis is on punishment of the guilty person—"everyone will be put to death for his own sin," Deut 24:16; "so it will be done *to him,*" Lev 24:19—although vicarious punishment is known in extralegal situations. Also, unlike the Laws of Hammurapi (## 196–205), biblical law does not restrict the operation of talion to a specific class—talion among equals, but a fine if the injured person is of lower status.

Debate has also focused on whether the statement of talion was intended to govern actual practice—an actual tooth for a tooth—especially in earlier biblical times, or whether it articulated the principle that the punishment should fit the crime. As such, it would guard against excessive punishment for a wrong (contrast Lamech's boast, Gen 4:23–24) as well as the disparity of compensation assessed upon the wealthy malefactor whereas death is the penalty for the poor (contrast # 8 in the Laws of Hammurapi). In Exod 21:22–25, the expansive talion formula follows the reference to the woman and/or a fetus being injured and serves to adjust the punishment to the injury. (Immediately thereafter, Exod 21:26–27 illustrates the formula as a principle. A slave whose master destroys his/her eye or tooth gains freedom; the master loses a slave, not an eye or a tooth.) Likewise in Lev 24:19–20—bodily injury to another man—there is a catalog of possible injuries with corresponding punishments. Even in these texts, the talion formula might be taken to mean inflicting physical injury, yet in Deut 19:16–21 (false witness), the talion formula must be a statement of equivalent compensatory punishment. The penalty in the case involving perjury would be compensation or fine. (Mutilation is restricted in biblical law to the special circumstances of Deut 25:11–12.) Note also that in Leviticus 24 the talion formula is followed by another statement of principle: "There should be one law for you; as for the alien, so for the native, for I am the Lord your God" (Lev 24:22). In the historical traditions the principle of punishment paralleling the crime is recognized by king Adoni-bezek, who had his thumbs and big toes cut off as he had done to others; "as I have done, so has God requited me" (Judg 1:6–7).

A related debate concerns whether talion is more primitive than compensation—and therefore presumably morally inferior. Driver and Miles comment that "the whole system of punishments among the Semites was based on talion, which is itself nothing but a legalized limitation of the vengeance of the blood-feud" (Driver and Miles 1952: 60). But "blood-feud" is hardly the background of biblical or ANE law. Noteworthy also is that the oldest Near Eastern law provides for compensation, whereas the Laws of Hammurapi—possibly reflecting Amorite cultural influence—provide for vicarious talion as well as talion within classes. The principle of the punishment fitting the crime seems basic, complicated by the recognition of different legal classes.

At times, unimaginative societies have favored a policy of literal taliation—e.g., putting out the left eye of someone who injured another's left eye. But given the inherent difficulties in carrying out specifically equivalent punishment—someone with but one eye; parties of rather different ages, etc.—the famous "eye for an eye, tooth for a tooth" does not provide genuinely specific guidance any more than a literal interpretation of "If your right eye causes you to sin, pluck it out and throw it away" (Matt 5:29). In view of the Bible's interest in compensation to the injured party, as opposed to physical punishment of the guilty party, it seems likely that the reference to equivalency was intended even originally as a statement of principle. The injured party was probably seen as better served by compensation than by mere punishment.

The historical narratives mention instances of guards being responsible with their own life for a prisoner entrusted to them (1 Kgs 20:35–42; 2 Kgs 10:24), a variant of talion, but there are no sentences immediately carried out nor are the texts intended to reflect ordinary legal practice. In a parallel way, the prophet Ezekiel is responsible with his own life for the appropriate warning to sinners of the consequences of their wrongdoing. Also, the prophetic literature frequently points to a punishment of Israel or the nations corresponding to the wrong committed (Miller 1982). See also LAW.

Bibliography

Carmichael, C. 1985. Biblical Laws of Talion. *HAR* 9: 107–26.

Daube, D. 1947. *Studies in Biblical Law.* Cambridge.

Driver, G. R., and Miles, J. C. 1952. *The Babylonian Laws.* Vol. 1, *Legal Commentary.* Oxford.

Jackson, B. S. 1973. The Problem of Exod. XXI 22–25 (Ius talionis). *VT* 23: 273–304.

Loewenstamm, S. E. 1977. Exodus XXI 22–25. *VT* 27: 352–60.

Miller, P. D. 1982. *Sin and Judgment in the Prophets.* SBLMS 27. Chico, CA.

Paul, S. M. 1970. *Studies in the Book of the Covenant in the Light of Cuneiform and Biblical Law.* VTSup 18. Leiden.

Westbrook, R. 1986. Lex Talionis and Exodus 21,22–25. *RB* 93: 52–69.

H. B. Huffmon

LIBER DE INFANTIA.

See MATTHEW, GOSPEL OF PSEUDO-.

LIBNAH (PLACE) [Heb *libnâ*].

The second levitical city in the Judah/Simeon list. There are no Hebrew textual variations in either Josh 21:13 or in 1 Chr 6:42 [—Eng 6:57]. The first reference to Libnah in the biblical record is in the conquest narratives. Libnah was one of the towns in the S subjugated by Joshua. Following the conquest, Libnah was included in the allotment of Judah (Josh 15:42). During the reign of Jehoram, Edom revolted from the control of Judah and at the same time Libnah revolted (2 Kgs 8:22). The Chronicler justified Libnah's revolt against Jehoram "because he had forsaken the Lord, the God of his Fathers" (2 Chr 21:10). By the time of Hezekiah's reign and Sennacherib's campaign, Libnah had returned to Judah's control (2 Kgs 19:8; Isa 37:8). The final reference to the city describes it as the home of Hamutal, the mother of Jehoahaz and Zedekiah (2 Kgs 23:31; 24:18; Jer 52:1). There are no ancient nonbiblical references to Libnah. Three tells have been associated with biblical Libnah: Tell es-Safi, Tell Bornat and Tell Judeidah.

Albright (1921: 6) first suggested that Tell es-Safi (M.R. 135123) be identified with biblical Libnah. Up until 1921 it had been almost universally assumed that Tell es-Safi was the Philistine city of Gath. Albright, basing his argument on an assumption from 2 Kgs 8:22 that Libnah must have been situated on the border, concluded that Tell es-Safi is the only reasonable identification, because it is the only important tell on the border between Philistia and Judah which is in the district of Eleutheropolis (following Eusebius, *Onomast.* 120.23–25). Albright further substantiated his theory by discussing the name Libnah, "the white (city)" and Tell es-Safi, "the bright, shining tell." Tell es-Safi had received its name because of the white limestone scarps, a definite corroboration with Libnah. The final argument advanced by Albright was in relationship to Sennacherib's march to Jerusalem. He concluded that the route from Lachish to Jerusalem via Tell es-Safi was the most natural route for the Assyrian king to take. However, within two years Albright (1934: 9) had changed his mind about the identification of Tell es-Safi. Instead, he identified Tell es-Safi as Makkedah. Although Albright changed his mind, G. E. Wright (1971: 81) continued to identify Libnah with Tell es-Safi. Wright was convinced that Tell es-Safi's geographical location at the W opening of the Valley of Elah fit well the biblical descriptions of Libnah. Tell es-Safi is located at the W edge of the Shephelah as it enters the valley leading into the coastal plain. The Valley of Elah provided a good access into the hill country since the ascent was gradual and did not involve crossing many hills and valleys. As a result, Tell es-Safi stands as a fortress between the coastal plain and the Shephelah, protecting the entrance to the mountains and the valley.

The first and only major excavation conducted at Tell es-Safi was directed by F. J. Bliss and R. A. S. Macalister (1902). There have also been many surveys conducted at Tell es-Safi. The different periods of occupation which have been identified include EB, MB, LB, Iron I, Iron II, Hellenistic, Roman, Crusader, and Arab.

After Albright changed his mind about the identity of Libnah, he opted for Tell Bornat (M.R. 138115). Although Albright never detailed his reasons for choosing Tell Bornat, this identification has received wide acceptance among German and Israeli geographers and archaeologists. Aharoni (*LBHG,* 86) argued against the identification of Libnah with Tell es-Safi because Libnah is mentioned in Josh 15:42 alongside Mareshah, Keilah, and Nezib, towns in the SE Shephelah, and not with towns near Tell es-Safi. Tell Bornat is 9 km SE of Tell es-Safi, 3 km W of Tell Judeideh, and 8 km NE of Lachish. Near Tell Bornat is the Wadi Zeita, which is the shortest trade route to Hebron in the Shephelah. This means that Tell Bornat would have been a "junction city." Not only was there an E–W route near the city, but the *Via Maris* ran along the W edge of the Shephelah.

References to Tell Bornat by early geographers come rather late. The first geographer to mention the tell is Guerin (1869: 314). There have been no archaeological excavations at Tell Bornat, but many surveys. Historical periods which have been identified include EB, LB, Iron I, Iron II, Persian, and Arab.

The last site that has been associated with biblical Libnah is Tell Judeideh. Z. Kallai (1958: 153) first suggested this identification following the survey of Aharoni and Amiran for the Historical Geography Study Circle. Tell Judeideh (M.R. 141115) is located only 3 km due E of Tell Bornat and 10 km NE of Lachish. From the tell there are magnificent views of the coastal plain and the Judean hills. The site is also on a major E–W trade route to Hebron and to the Valley of Aijalon. Bliss (1900a: 94; 1900b: 200) directed the only archaeological excavation that has been conducted at Tell Judeideh. Since that excavation there have been many surveys. The pottery dates to the EB, Iron I, Iron II, Persian, Roman, and Byzantine periods.

The identification of biblical Libnah has remained somewhat of a question. Although the pottery found at Tell Judeideh could associate the site with Libnah, its traditional identification with Moresheth-Gath is probably correct. As all surveys and excavations at Tell es-Safi have shown, there was a large Philistine settlement at the site. It is only logical then to associate Tell es-Safi with the Philistine city, Gath. Although Tell Bornat is physically smaller than Tell es-Safi, the identification of Libnah with Tell Bornat does not minimize the importance of the city in ancient Israel. The size of the tell does not seriously affect the importance of city because "the pasture lands" were a significant part of each city's territory. Tell Bornat was on an important crossroads and its geographical location is strategically important. Although Tell Bornat cannot be absolutely identified with biblical Libnah, the evidence strongly supports this association.

Bibliography

Albright, W. F. 1921. Libnah and Gath. *BASOR* 4: 2–12.

———. 1923. Contributions to the Historical Geography of Palestine. Pp. 1–46 in *AASOR* 2–3, ed. W. J. Moulton. New Haven.

———. 1934. Researches of the School in Western Judaea. *BASOR* 15: 2–11.

Bliss, F. J. 1900a. First Report on the Excavations at Tell ej-Judeideh. *PEFQS,* 87–101.

———. 1900b. Second Report on the Excavations at Tell ej-Judeideh. *PEFQS,* 199–222.

Bliss, F. J., and Macalister, R. A. S. 1902. *Excavations in Palestine during the Years 1989–1900.* London.

Guerin, M. V. 1869. *Description Geographie Historique et Archeologique de la Palestine.* Vol. 2. Paris.

Kallai-Kleinmann, Z. 1958. The Town Lists of Judah, Simeon, Dan and Benjamin. *VT* 8: 134–60.

Wright, G. E. 1971. A Problem of Ancient Topography: Lachish and Eglon. *BA* 34: 76–86.

JOHN L. PETERSON

LIBNI (PERSON) [Heb *libnî*]. LIBNITE. **1.** All evidence indicates that the Libnites were a levitic family from the territory of Judah. Their name is probably derived from the name of the Judahite town Libnah (the expected form would be **libnātî,* but cf. *yĕhûdâ-yĕhûdî, ṣārĕʿâ-ṣārĕʿî*). A genealogical fragment of unknown origin quoted in the Priestly source lists the families of Levi as the Libnites, the Hebronites, the Mahlites, the Mushites, and the Korahites (Num 26:58). All these names have possible connections to Judah or its kindred Edom. Hebron, often used as the name of a levitic family (Exod 6:18; Num 3:19, 27; 1 Chr 5:28; 6:3; 15:9; 23:12, 19; 26:23, 30, 31) was the chief city of Judah and a Judean family name (1 Chr 2:43). Korah, ordinarily a levitic name, appears as a Judahite name in 1 Chr 2:43 and as an Edomite name in Gen 36:5, 14, 16, 18; 1 Chr 1:35, and the Korahites are said to be among David's early allies (1 Chr 12:7). Moreover, a fragment of a bowl discovered at Arad in Judah refers to "the sons of Korah" (Aharoni 1968, Miller 1970). It is probable that Mushi comes from *mōšeh* (Moses), and it is noteworthy that Jonathan, the son of Gershom, the son of Moses (Judg 18:30 [Greek version]; the MT reads "Manasseh" instead of "Moses") is called a Levite "from the family of Judah" (Judg 17:7). Mahli may not be specifically Judean, however, for the name is easiest to derive from Mahlah in Manasseh (Num 26:33; 27:1; 36:11; Josh 17:3; 1 Chr 7:18), but note the Judahite name Mahlon (Ruth 1:2, 5; 4:10), the Edomite name Mahalath (Gen 28:9), and the probable attestation of Mahli on a Persian period cosmetic burner from Lachish in Judah (Albright 1974). In short, Num 26:58 probably was not intended to be a comprehensive list of levitic clans, but was rather a catalog of the chief families native to or resident in Judah.

2. The Priestly genealogist considers Libni, along with Shimei, a subgroup of the Gershonites (Exod 6:17; Num 3:18, 21), and the Chronicler at times follows this scheme (1 Chr 6:2, 5—Eng vv 17, 20). Elsewhere, however, the Chronicler replaces Libni with Ladan (1 Chr 23:7, 8, 9; 26:21), a name unknown to P, which suggests that the name Libni was obsolete after the exile. Ladan, too, is a name with Judahite connections, for the similarly named Laadah is a grandson of Judah (1 Chr 4:21). That Libni is always the firstborn, whether of Levi (Num 26:58) or of Gershon, indicates the prominence of this family.

3. In the Chronicler's genealogy of Levi, Libni is also a subgroup, literally "son," of Mahli, the descendant of Merari (1 Chr 6:14—Eng v 29; cf. #2 above, 1 Chr 6:2, 5—Eng vv 17, 20).

Bibliography

Aharoni, Y. 1968. Arad: Its Inscriptions and Temple. *BA* 31: 2–33.

Albright, W. F. 1974. The Lachish Cosmetic Burner and Esther 2:12. Pp. 25–32 in *A Light unto My Path,* ed. H. N. Bream, R. D. Heim, and C. A. Moore. Gettysburg Theological Studies 4. Philadelphia.

Cody, A. 1969. *A History of the Old Testament Priesthood.* AnBib 35. Rome.

Gunneweg, A. H. J. 1965. *Leviten und Priester.* Göttingen.

Miller, J. M. 1970. The Korahites of Southern Judah. *CBQ* 32: 58–68.

Möhlenbrink, K. 1934. Die levitische überlieferungen des Alten Testaments. *ZAW* 52: 184–231.

WILLIAM H. PROPP

LIBYA (PLACE) [Heb *kûb*]. LIBYAN. A land and people in N Africa, immediately W of Egypt (Ezek 30:5). It seems that the oldest Egyptian terms for these W neighbors are *Tjehenu* and *Tjemehu* (from the 3d millennium B.C.), but from about the period of Rameses II (the 13th century B.C.) onward this group was called the *rbw* or *Libu* (Egyptians had no character for the *l* sound so *r* or *n* was substituted, therefore *rbw* was pronounced *Libu*). The Egyptian *Libu* probably was the source for the Gk *Libyēs* and the Heb *lûbîm* (1 Chr 12:3; 16:8). The Libyans and the Egyptians often were involved in skirmishes especially during the 12th–10th centuries B.C. Libyans figured prominently in the forces of Pharaoh Shishak (2 Chr 12:3) and it is probable that Shishak himself was of Libyan extraction. Pharaoh Shishak attacked Israel with 1200 chariots, 60,000 horsemen, and an army comprised of Egyptians, Libyans, Sukkiim, and Ethiopians (1 Kgs 14:25–28; 2 Chr 12:1–12). This invasion was interpreted as divine disciplinary action because Israel was ignoring the law. The Libyans also appear in the forces of Zerah (2 Chr 16:8) who may have been an Ethiopian officer who commanded an army comprised of Ethiopians and Libyans. Although the military strength of Zerah's forces was enormous, King Asa was able to rout them.

The relationship between the Libyans and the *lĕhābîm* is problematic (Gen 10:13; 1 Chr 1:11); *lĕhābîm* may be a variant form of *lûbîm.* Ham's third son was Put; Put was Egypt's brother (Gen 10:6). Moreover, Lehabim was Egypt's third son (Gen 10:13). Almost certainly the names Egypt and Lehabim are not individuals but peoples, therefore Put, Lehabim, and Egypt shared the same tradition which itself was linked to Ham. It is not surprising that parts of this tradition continuously reappear later in the prophets (Nah 3:9; Dan 22:43; cf. also Jer 46:9; Ezek 27:10; 30:5; 38:5) where some read *lûbîm* for *lûd.* The peoples of this tradition have often been called Hamitic peoples wherein "Hamitic" has designated the people, or perhaps only the languages, of Libya.

In the NT, while witnessing Jesus' trip to Golgotha, a Simon of Cyrene from Libya was pressed into service (Matt 27:32; Mark 15:21; Luke 23:26). Furthermore, people from "the parts of Libya about Cyrene" were in the crowd which witnessed Pentecost (Acts 2:10).

WARREN J. HEARD, JR.

LICE. See ZOOLOGY.

LICENTIOUSNESS. See VIRTUE/VICE LISTS.

LIFE, AUTHOR OF. See AUTHOR OF LIFE.

LIFE, TREE OF. See TREE OF KNOWLEDGE AND TREE OF LIFE.

LIKHI (PERSON) [Heb *liqḥî*]. The third son of Shemida (1 Chr 7:19) in the genealogy of Manasseh (7:14–19). His name appears only once in the Bible, and it is probably cognate with the Heb verb "take, grasp" *(lāqaḥ)*. Some have suggested, however, that "Likhi" is nothing more than a textual corruption of "Helek" (Heb *ḥēleq*), the name of one of Gilead's sons (Num 26:30; cf. Josh 17:2; see Noth *IPN*, 249).

1 Chr 7:19 is a genealogical fragment, and its relationship to the preceding collection of Manassite genealogical materials (7:14–18) is uncertain. The verse lists the names of Shemida and his four sons, but it does not specify the position of Shemida in the genealogy of Manasseh as a whole. Therefore, attempts have been made to find a logical relationship for the verse with the rest of the Manassite genealogy in 1 Chronicles 7. One proposal has been that Shemida was the fourth son of Hammolecheth (7:18), and so Likhi was her grandson (so Curtis and Madsen *Chronicles* ICC, 152). Another suggestion is that Gilead was the father of Shemida, just as Num 26:30–32 indicates (cf. Josh 17:1–3). Consequently, Likhi was the grandson of Gilead. Rudolph's formulation of this solution (*Chronikbücher* HAT, 69–71) has found wide acceptance, but it involves the wholesale emendation of the Manassite genealogy in 1 Chronicles 7 on the basis of Numbers 26:28–34.

M. PATRICK GRAHAM

LILITH (DEITY) [Heb *lîlît*]. Lilith is the Hebrew form of Akk *lilītu* (the feminine form of *lilû*), which was a species of lesser deities in Mesopotamia known for their diabolical activities (Farber *RLA* 7: 23; Porada *RLA* 7: 24–25; *CAD* s.v. *lilû*). Very little information has been found relating to the Akkadian and Babylonian view of these demons. Two sources of information previously used to define Lilith are both suspect. Kramer (1938: 5) translated *ki-sikil-líl-lá-ke₄* as "Lilith" in a Sumerian Gilgamesh fragment. The text relates an incident where this female being takes up lodging in a tree trunk which has a Zu-bird perched in the branches and a snake living among the roots. This text was used to interpret a sculpture of a woman with bird talons for feet as being a depiction of Lilith (Frankfort 1937: 130 fig 1, 134–35; Kraeling 1937: 18). From the beginning this interpretation was questioned (Opitz 1932: 330) so that after some debate neither the female in the story nor the figure are assumed to be Lilith (Ribichini 1978: 31–33; *RLA* 7: 25). The 1st millennium Syrian incantation from Arshlan-Tash, often cited as a Lilith reference also has been shown not to refer to this demon (Gaster 1942: 44, 50; Torczyner 1947: 29).

Amulets exist to ward off *lilītu* and the *lilû* family. Lilith was known to attack women in childbirth, a characteristic she may have adopted from Lamashtu (*EncJud* 11: 246–47; Farber 1989: 4, 103, 117, 142–43). The new infant was in more danger than the mother since Lilith could suck its blood, eat its marrow, and then consume its flesh (*RLA* 7: 23). To protect oneself from this demon one could write out incantations, wear amulets, or invoke gods or other demons, especially the king of the *lilû*, Pazuzu (Lambert 1968: 42, 46).

Two Jewish sources may be used to determine the activities of Lilith. The first of these are the four references to Lilith in the Talmud (*Nid.* 24b; *B. Bat.* 73a; *Šabb.* 151b; *ᶜErub.* 100b). From these texts it is clear that Lilith has the form of a woman with long hair and wings, who bears demonic offspring. There is a sexual aspect implied in the warning that men who sleep alone could be seized by her.

The other source of information on Lilith and her relatives is the series of Aramaic and Mandaic bowl inscriptions used to ward off demons. Most of these texts came from a Jewish community in Nippur, though they date from the 1st millennium C.E. (Montgomery 1913: 76–78, 117, 155–56, 209, 244, 259–60; Isbel 1975: 17, 44–45, 108, 120–21; Geller 1986: 108–9). These texts confirm Lilith's malevolent activities and they show her lurking around human habitations waiting for a chance to seize people. One incantation bowl bears a drawing of the shackled Lilith bound in chains around her neck, arms, and legs; she has been stripped bare and her hair loosed (Montgomery 1913: 154–55 no. 8 lines 2–3, pl. 8).

When only Jewish sources for the deity were known, it was assumed her name was a variant on *lylh* and thus she was understood to be the "night hag" (RSV Isa 34:14; *ERE* 4: 598). Once her Mesopotamian origins became clear the name was associated with Sum *líl*, "wind" (Meissner 1925: 201; Patai 1967: 207; *RLA* 7: 23).

Lilith was taken up by Jewish midrashic and cabalistic traditions and there is a rich literature which includes visions of her as a benign being as well as a demon (Patai 1967: 217–45). Currently Lilith is an inspiration for much creative writing and reinterpretation (Koltuv 1986: 126–27).

Bibliography

Farber, W. 1989. *Schlaf, Kindchen, Schlaf! Mesopotamische Baby-Beschwörungen und -Rituale.* Mesopotamian Civilizations 2. Winona Lake, IN.

Frankfort, H. 1937. The Burney Relief. *AfO* 12: 128–35.

Gaster, T. H. 1942. A Canaanite Magical Text. *Or* 11: 41–79.

Geller, M. J. 1986. Eight Incantation Bowls. *OLP* 17: 101–17.

Isbel, C. D. 1975. *Corpus of the Aramaic Incantation Bowls.* SBLDS 17. Missoula, MT.

Koltuv, B. B. 1986. *The Book of Lilith.* York Beach, ME.

Kraeling, E. G. 1937. A Unique Babylonian Relief. *BASOR* 67: 16–18.

Kramer, S. N. 1938. *Gilgamesh and the Ḫuluppu-Tree: A Reconstructed Sumerian Text.* Assyriological Studies 10. Chicago.

Lambert, W. L. 1968. Inscribed Pazuzu Heads from Babylon. *Forschungen und Berichte* 10: 41–47.

Meissner, B. 1925. *Babylonien und Assyrien,* vol. 2. Kulturgeschichtliche Bibliothek 1/4. Heidelberg.

Montgomery, J. A. 1913. *Aramaic Incantation Texts from Nippur.* Publications of the Babylonian Section 3. Philadelphia.

Opitz, D. 1932. Ausgrabungen und Forschungsreisen: Ur. *AfO* 8: 328–31.

Patai, R. 1967. *The Hebrew Goddess.* New York.

Ribichini, S. 1978. Lilith nell-albero Ḫuluppu. Pp. 25–33 in *Atti del 1° Convegno Italiano sul Vicino Oriente Antico (Roma, 22–24 Aprile 1976).* Orientis Antiqvi Collectio 13. Rome.

Torczyner, H. 1947. A Hebrew Incantation against Night-Demons from Biblical Times. *JNES* 6: 18–29.

LOWELL K. HANDY

LILY. See FLORA.

LILY-WORK. See CAPITAL.

LIMES, ROMAN (IN PALESTINE). Since Flavian days (69–96 C.E.), *limes* (pronounced: "lī′ mēz" according to Webster, but often pronounced "lē′ mis") has been the Roman term for the controlled and defended borders of the Roman Empire. Succeeding emperors gave major attention to the imperial borders, since maintenance of peace within the empire was considered not only vital for its prosperity, but a major inducement for the subjected nations to submit to Rome's domination. Furthermore, besides being the first line of defense, the *limes* was the zone of physical contact with the outside world, cultural as well as ethical, and a staging area for international trade, which was vital to Roman economy.

At first, Rome tried to base its border on natural obstacles, yet, when necessary, a network of fortifications, manned by more lightly armed troops (the *auxilia*) was established in front of the legionary bases. At times, these were connected by continuous obstacles (S.H.A., *Hadr.*, 12.6).

In an effort to ease the staggering financial burden, to free part of the armed forces from constant obligations to the frontier guard, and to repopulate the frontier zones, Diocletianus (284–305 C.E.) adopted earlier precedents and entrusted the frontier defense to a newly created corps of rural frontier militia *(limitanei),* which did part-time, and in emergencies, full-scale, hereditary service against the grant of border lands. The civil administration in the border areas was vested in the military commanders *(comites, duces)* and the privileged zones soon developed distinctive socio-ethical and agrarian settlement patterns, which in many ways influenced subsequent developments. These arrangements, with some modifications, remained in effect until the disruption of the empire in the W and the capture of its E parts during the Islamic conquest about 635 C.E. One cause of the territorial loss was the *limitanei*'s loss of military prowess which had become *de facto* farmers for all practical purposes.

The peculiar situation of the *limes* in Palestine was that the area was a border state, and it has always been essential to secure borders from incursions of outsiders. In years of drought, the threats posed by the incursions of desert fringe nomads (cf. Judg 4:3–5), could surpass the inherent antagonism between the sedentary farmer and the migrant husbandman. With apparently such a scenario in mind in the pre-Diocletian and probably pre-Severian period, there is a rabbinical ruling that permits the taking up of arms in border settlements, and issuing forth even on

Sabbath, not only to defend their lives, but also to prevent "loot of hay and straw" (*j. Talm. ʿErub.* 4, 21d).

The Romans were thus compelled to step into the Herodian border defenses (which seems also to have operated under the procurators) not only to ensure the Pax Romana, but to prevent anarchy in a country, where the borders with hostile raiders were not more than 80 km removed from Jerusalem. The Nabatean presence in the Negeb was no substitute, since it was confined largely to the major arteries of commerce, and with the means at their disposal, they could not prevent the swift desert raiders to cross over into Judea had they wished to do so. Even under less extreme conditions, such as in the Balkans, the Romans took care to fortify the borders, regardless of the existence of an allied *cordon sanitaire* all around them.

The various surface surveys (Gichon 1980), rabbinical literature, the excavations of stratum III at Arad and stratum I at Beer-sheba (Gichon 1980: 845), and the Flavian presence at Masada and En Gedi provide sufficient evidence for a Flavian establishment of the *limes.* After the Trajanic occupation of Nabatea, three forward lines were created by occupying the Nabatean installations along the three E–W routes: (1) En Tamar-Malatha; (2) Hatzeva (Eiseiba?)-Mampsis-Bersabee; and (3) Mojet Avad (Moa?)-Oboda-Elusa.

At the same time the Tranjordanian *limes* was established from Aila to the borders of Syria, together with the great military and commercial highway, to avert incursions from the Arabian desert. Following the Bar Kokhba Revolt (131/132–135), Hadrian seems to have evacuated the Flavian *limes* and entrusted the defense of Palestine mainly to the more forward *limes* and the *limes Arabicus,* E of the Jordan.

The insufficiency of this arrangement induced Diocletianus to create a united frontier command in S Transjordan and the Negeb, by attaching the former, S of Zoara, to the *provincia Palaestina.* While the increased threats from the tribes in the W and in the E were met as before, if these succeeded in breaking through, the other sector could be activated. To strengthen the W borders, the Flavian *limes* was reactivated, and in order to place the strategic reserve in the best possible position, the 10th Legion was moved from Jerusalem to Aila-Aqaba on the apex of the now fan-shaped network of defenses. In addition, a more permanent framework of confederate tribes beyond the borders was created.

In principle, these arrangements remained unchanged until the Islamic conquest (ca. 635 C.E.). However, the complications on the borders were such, that in addition to the shifts in tactics and individual strongholds, about 358 C.E., all of the *limes* area was made an independent province named *Palaestina Salutaris,* and after 429, renamed again *Palaestina Tertia.*

From the beginning, the *limes* fortifications comprised a network of forts, fortlets, and towers, strategically placed to deny the enemy of water resources, and to channel marauders into areas facilitating their interception by the mobile components of the *limes* garrisons. The disposition of the troops according to their headquarters has been preserved in the *Notitia-Dignitatum* (late 4th century?), which enumerates for the W front six elite cavalry units *(equites),* three infantry units *(cohortes),* and one unit of mixed composition *(cohortes equitatae)* against eighteen units in the Arava and in the E. The Beer-sheba edicts (Alt 1921) and the Nessana papyri (Kraemer 1958) record changes in the deployment of the troops in the course of the 5th and 6th centuries respectively.

The standard type of fortification was the courtyard fort, in which the flat-roofed internal buildings were built against the outer walls to provide maximum yard space, strengthen the walls, and enlarge the width of the battlements. Frequently, these rectangular structures had protruding corner towers (consequently named *tetrapyrgoi*). This form had been introduced into the Negeb not later than the Judean monarchy and was preserved during successive periods because of its suitability to local conditions.

Two further traits gave the *limes Palaestinae* primary importance in addition to its military significance: when overpopulation threatened the interior of W Palestine, the expansion into the arid Negeb and the development of sophisticated desert-fringe agriculture was the only recourse. Following the First Temple period and Nabatean precedents, the 4th to 7th C.E. Negeb attained an unsurpassed flourish of rural and urban colonization. While the military was thus able to base its upkeep and logistic support on the civilian infrastructure, it provided civilians with the protection necessary to survive in face of the "Saracens" (desert tribes).

In the Byzantine period, the frontier forces became more involved in agricultural activity after their structure converted to *limitanean* status. The Negeb may have been one of the frontiers on which the system was first tested as early as Alexander Severus (cf. S.H.A., *Alex. Sev.,* 18.4).

No less important than the land reserve was the Negeb's role as an overland bridge between the Mediterranean and the Red Sea, and as a link in the caravan trade with Arabia and beyond (e.g., *HN* 5.12.67; 6.32.144). In the 4th century, when political deterioration threatened commercial movement along the transasian "silkroad," the reviving Negeb roads were among the alternative routes. While in the agricultural belt, the ten *limes* towns profited from serving the transit trade, and in the more remote areas, the military outposts doubled as road stations *(mansiones)* for official travel *(cursus publicus)* and commercial traffic (Gichon 1974: 534–35).

Whereas the immediate rear of the Flavian *limes* remained Jewish until the Islamic conquest, Christianity began to spread in the 3d–4th centuries from the Philistine coast (St. Hilarion) and from the monastic establishments in the Judean desert and Sinai (St. Chariton, St. Catherina, etc.). By the 6th century, rich and impressive churches dominate the panorama of all *limes* towns.

The almost complete transformation of the *limitanei* into mere farmers (as shown in the Nessana papyri), and the friendly disposition of the Arab confederate tribesmen (on whom much of the *limes* defense was based after its hasty reconstruction following the Persian [Sassanian] occupation of Palestine in 614–28) toward the Moslem invaders, facilitated the piercing of the *limes* and the collapse of the Roman defense in 634–38 (Alt 1938). Deprived of the military shield, the civilian population withered away, and the *limes* zone was gradually reconquered by the desert.

Bibliography

Alt, A. 1921. *Inschriften der Palastina Tertia westlicher Araba.* Leipzig.
———. 1938. Das Ende des Limes Palaestina. *JPOS* 18: 149–60.

———. 1955. Neue Untersuchungen zum Limes Palaestinae. *ZDPV* 71: 83–94.
Colt, H. D., et al. 1962. *Excavations at Nessana I.* London.
Gichon, M. 1974. Towers on the Limes Palaestinae. Pp. 513–44 in *Actes IX Congress d'Etudes sur les Frontieres Romaines.* Bucharest-Cologne.
———. 1980. Research on the Limes Palaestinae—A Stocktaking. Pp. 843–64 in *Roman Frontier Studies 1979,* ed. W. S. Hanson and L. J. F. Keppie. British Archaeological Reports International Series 71. Oxford.
Kraemer, J. C. 1958. *Excavations at Nessana III—The Non-Literary Papyri.* London.
Parker, S. T. 1986. *Romans and Saracens.* Winona Lake, IN.
MORDECHAI GICHON

LINEAR B. See LANGUAGES (INTRODUCTORY SURVEY).

LINEN. See DRESS AND ORNAMENTATION; FLORA.

LINGUISTICS AND BIBLICAL STUDIES.

Linguistics is the study of language as language, in contrast to the study of any specific language. The term "general linguistics" comprehends all of the varied theoretical positions of linguists. There is no question that linguistics has much to offer students and teachers of the biblical languages (Hebrew, Aramaic, and Greek). A sizable number of scholars of biblical and other ancient languages have written of the potential contribution of linguistics to their research. A smaller number have written of the improvement that would come to the teaching of biblical languages through serious interaction with linguistics. Yet these contributions to research are still in their initial stages at the time of this writing, and the teaching of ancient languages is yet to be significantly affected by the insights of modern linguistics.

The beginning of linguistics as a field of study in its own right is variously dated from the historical/comparative study of the 19th century to the turn of the present century with the work of Saussure, or (for some) the approach pioneered by Chomsky in 1957. For the purposes of this article, however, it is necessary to survey earlier language study, in particular in the Greco–Roman period and in medieval times (especially medieval Jewish grammar), because of the influence of these periods on the study of the biblical languages up to the present.

A. The Study of Language Prior to the 19th Century

1. The Ancient East. The study of language in a general sense is as old as the oldest languages in which written texts are known, those of the ancient East. Akkadian grammatical texts from the mid-2d to the mid-1st millennium B.C. represent Sumerian according to certain paradigms, using grammatical terminology and morpheme analysis. Indian grammatical studies appear to have been indigenous from roughly the mid-1st millennium B.C. and forward. Because of their aim to preserve the correct pronunciation of the Vedic literature, they achieved such precision in phonetic analysis that ancient Sanskrit can still be pronounced with almost full accuracy, in marked contrast to Greek and Latin, not to speak of the biblical and other languages of the ANE. Sometime, probably during the second third of the 1st millennium B.C., Pāṇini produced an analytic and descriptive grammar which remains a definitive model for modern students of Sanskrit.

2. Greece. Most present-day linguists in the West trace the origins of their discipline to ancient Greece. The study of language among the Greeks arose in the 5th century B.C. within the larger context of philosophy and was primarily speculative. The Greeks debated whether the relationship between sound and meaning was necessary or arbitrary. While Plato (427–347 B.C.E.) was ambivalent on this issue, Aristotle (384–322 B.C.E.) believed that meaning was arbitrary and conventional. The Greeks also debated whether language was essentially regular (the analogist position), or irregular (the anomalist position). Sentence types were distinguished, as were parts of speech, although the basis for the latter was more logical than formal. The Stoics established the recognition of case and also discussed such features as number, gender, voice, mood, and tense. From the Alexandrian school, Dionysius Thrax (ca. 100 B.C.E.) wrote the first explicit description of the Greek language which became the prototype for subsequent descriptions of Greek and Latin.

3. Rome. In grammatical study as in other learning, the Romans venerated the Greeks and largely followed their lead. Because Latin was quite similar to Greek in overall structure, the work of the Greek grammarians could be applied to Latin without difficulty. The linguistic model was a word and paradigm type. Varro (116–27 B.C.E.) was perhaps the most original of Roman grammarians to write on the Latin language, though only slightly more than one-fifth of his twenty-five volumes on the subject survive. The two most influential Latin grammarians were Donatus (4th century C.E.) and Priscian (ca. 500 C.E.). Donatus' intentionally didactic grammar was used well into medieval times (and is said to have been the first book printed with wooden type). Priscian's grammar was quite long; it represents the culmination of late Latin grammatical study, and became the most widely used grammar of the medieval period.

4. Medieval Grammar. Under the influence of Donatus and Priscian, medieval grammatical study continued the Greco–Roman tradition. Aelfric wrote a Latin grammar (ca. 1000) and recommended it as an introduction to Anglo-Saxon, illustrating already the tendency to employ the Greco–Roman grammatical model in the study of other languages. The grammatical description of Latin was incorporated into the system of scholastic philosophy. While the speculative grammars of medieval modistae anticipated somewhat the recent interest in linguistic universals, their contribution would now be seen as quite limited because of their preoccupation with the Latin language and their commitment to a deductive approach based on Aristotelian logic. In Italy, Dante (1265–1321) remarkably anticipated diachronic linguistics and dialect research, but found no response to his ideas.

5. Arab Grammarians. From about the 8th to the 15th centuries of this era, Arab grammarians worked out an analysis of their language. Centers of grammatical study developed at Basra, Kufa, and Baghdad. The canons of classical Arabic grammar were established by Sībawayhi in the 8th century. His phonetic description is thorough, and his grammatical approach can be compared to the modern method of immediate constituent analysis. In the next three centuries Arabic grammar was systematized and placed on a par with other branches of learning. In the 12th through the 15th centuries the established system was condensed and refined.

6. Medieval Hebrew Grammarians. Jewish scholars of the medieval period also developed their own analysis of the Hebrew language. While the way was prepared by the Masoretes, this work actually began with Saadia Gaon (882–942 C.E.) in the late 9th and early 10th centuries. He produced the first vocabulary and the first grammar of biblical Hebrew. In the 10th century, the scholar ibn Quraysh produced the first systematic attempt to compare biblical Hebrew with Mishnaic Hebrew, Aramaic, and Arabic, an effort which was pursued by Jewish scholars throughout medieval times. The creative period of medieval Jewish grammar was from about 1000 to 1150, with Ḥayyūj, Janāḥ, and Samuel ha-Nagid representing the high point. Ḥayyūj expounded the principle of the triliteral root and distinguished the seven primary verbal conjugations which are still followed. After the Muslim persecution of Jews in Spain and their subsequent Jewish dispersal in 1148 came a period of adaptation. Joseph Qimḥi (ca. 1105–1170) introduced an analysis of the Masoretic vocalization system as consisting of five short and five long vowels, in contrast to the view of seven differences in quality (but not quantity) previously accepted among the Jews. His son David (ca. 1160–ca. 1235) brought this period of adaptation to its culmination with his grammar and lexicon, known as the *Miklol* (*Compendium;* the title was later applied only to the grammar). The main lines of approach to Hebrew set forth by the Qimḥis have continued to be followed in most Hebrew grammars. See also LANGUAGES (HEBREW).

7. The Renaissance. As the classical world was rediscovered in the Renaissance, language study was broadened to include contemporary national tongues as well as the Latin, Greek, and Hebrew which became the mark of the educated person. This brought the grammatical model that had endured from Greco–Roman times through the medieval period into contact with the fresh data of contemporary languages. The renewed study of Hebrew also brought about contact with the vastly different structure of a Semitic language and with the works of medieval Jewish grammarians. Yet the overall tendency was to study the European venaculars and even Hebrew and other non-Indo-European languages through the inherited model, which was not fundamentally modified.

8. The Enlightenment. During the 17th and 18th centuries, the study of languages reflected philosophical movements. The impact of empiricism can be observed in England in the study of spelling and its relation to pronunciation (under the terms "orthography" and "orthoepy") and in efforts to rework English grammar. By the 18th century, as a result of the effort to construct a universal grammatical theory, writers on language turned their attention to establishing correct norms in pronunciation and usage. As a result, grammars became largely prescriptive. At the same time, rationalism encouraged the production of philosophic grammars. The French Port-Royal school attempted to demonstrate a common logical and rational system behind the varieties of natural languages.

B. Modern General Linguistics

1. Historical/Comparative Linguistics. Linguistics, in its primary sense as the study of language itself, may be said to have been established in the 19th century. The field of historical and comparative linguistics emerged and became dominant during this time. It was pioneered for the African languages in 1783 by William Marsden, for the European languages in 1786 by Sir William Jones, and for the Finno-Ugric group in 1799 by S. Gyarmathi. Each of these scholars posited a genetic relationship among the languages within their respective language group, while Jones also spoke of a common ancestor language which no longer existed. This language, which was the parent of Sanskrit, Greek, Latin, and later European languages, came to be called Indo-European. A methodology was developed for reconstructing this common parent language; language change (especially in phonology) was studied; languages were classified by type; and major language families were delineated.

The actual founder of systematic comparative linguistics was Franz Bopp (1791–1867) with his treatise of 1816 on the inflectional endings of verbs in several Indo-European languages. He was followed by Jacob Grimm (1785–1863), generally regarded as the founder of Germanic linguistics, who studied the relationships between consonants in Germanic and other Indo-European languages and set these forth in what has come to be called *Grimm's law.* (In fact, his findings were anticipated by others and later extended by Karl Verner [1846–1896].)

In the last half of the 19th century, the views of mechanistic physics and especially of biological evolution were influential in linguistic theory. August Schleicher (1821–1868), first trained as a botanist, set out to treat language as a living organism under the analogy of evolution and to trace its development according to similar laws. From his work has come the concept of the descent of languages in a "genealogical tree" (the *Stammbaum* theory). A competing view, the wave theory, was that of Johannes Schmidt, who argued that linguistic innovations spread from a center (like waves on the surface of water) among speech communities.

In some ways the high point of the historical/comparative linguistics of the 19th century was achieved by the Neogrammarians. Originating in Leipzig, this group brought rigor to linguistic method and thereby put all succeeding linguists in their debt. On the other hand, they developed a position which could not be maintained in its extreme form. August Leskien (1840–1916) and especially Karl Brugmann (1849–1919) affirmed the thoroughgoing consistency of sound laws, and H. Paul called for an exclusively historical approach as the avenue to linguistic knowledge.

2. Structural Linguistics. The next major phase in the history of linguistics (and for many the beginning of modern linguistics) commenced with the work of Ferdinand de Saussure (1857–1913). His lectures on general linguistics at the University of Geneva (1907–13) were published after his death by colleagues and students (1959). These lectures laid the basis for much of the linguistic work that has followed.

Saussure pointed in a new direction (though he was anticipated in this by Humboldt in the 19th century) by distinguishing synchronic from diachronic analysis. Synchronic study investigates a language as it appears at a point in time; a diachronic approach analyzes the developments a language undergoes over a period of time. Whereas he recognized the need for both approaches, and spent a great deal of his life in diachronic study, his successors, especially in the United States, went on to emphasize the synchronic to the virtual exclusion of the diachronic. Saussure also distinguished language as a system *(langue)* from actual speech *(parole)*, the syntagmatic (linguistic elements that can be combined) from the associative (later called the paradigmatic, linguistic elements that can be interchanged), and the signified from the signifier. Perhaps most important, and in contrast to the piecemeal work of the 19th century, Saussure saw that a language is a system whose parts must be understood in relation to the whole; and for him this systematic character was present only in a language as it exists at a point in time, i.e., only in a language viewed synchronically.

3. American Descriptive Linguistics. The direction of American descriptive linguistics for roughly the first half of the 20th century was set by Franz Boas (1858–1942), Edward Sapir (1884–1939), and Leonard Bloomfield (1887–1949). Boas (1911) concentrated on American Indian languages and developed an inductive methodology for analyzing a language from its own structure, apart from any other language. He assumed that differences among languages were unlimited by any generally shared structures. Sapir (1921) gave classical expression to the concept of the phoneme, further emphasized the structural differences among languages, and examined the relationship of language to culture. In this last interest he was followed by Benjamin Lee Whorf (1897–1941), who drew a fundamental connection between language and world view. The dependence of a people on their language for their range of ideas about the world necessarily relates the two, Whorf argued. While a connection between language and culture has been generally acknowledged, the degree of dominance of the former over the latter argued by Whorf has not. In his book *Language* (1933), Bloomfield laid the foundation for the next quarter of a century by systematically articulating the principles of descriptive linguistics, though many of his ideas were already present in Boas.

Following Bloomfield, the subsequent influential American descriptivists, known as "Post-Bloomfieldians" (e.g., Bloch, Trager, Hockett, Hill, and Harris), in some cases took their heritage too far by pressing for mechanical operations ("discovery procedures" in this sense) and attempting to describe language without reference to meaning. A more productive direction within American descriptivism was set by Kenneth L. Pike with the theory of Tagmemics (1967, 1982). For Pike, language is to be understood in terms of discrete units, continuity and change, and relatedness (in his words: "particle, wave, and field"). He has insisted that any component of a language can only be analyzed in its relationship to the rest of the language and that form and meaning must not be separated in linguistic inquiry.

Not only was the impact of linguistics on language teaching in the United States essentially nil prior to World War II, the very teaching of foreign languages was at an extreme low. The war abruptly shattered such isolationism. In the postwar period, the armed forces led the way in instituting programs for efficient foreign language teaching, and they called on linguists for leadership. The traditional grammar and translation approach was put aside in a search for methods which would produce conversational fluency by the most direct route. However, as the biblical languages are no longer spoken and the goal of their teaching was translation and not fluency in speech, these fields were essentially bypassed by such developments.

4. Linguistics Outside the United States. Outside the United States, major developments in linguistics in this century have been diverse. Louis Hjelmslev (b. 1899) of Copenhagen pioneered the highly formal theory of glossematics (1961). Incorporating Saussure's emphasis on form over substance, glossematics sought to discover a system of categories from which could be derived the elements of a language. His work remained at the purely theoretical level, however, and was never applied to any actual language.

The Prague school is represented especially by Nikolay Trubetzkoy (1890–1938) and Roman Jakobson (b. 1896). Their linguistic theory is known as functionalism. Prague school theorists study language in terms of its distinctive function (out of which came Distinctive Feature Phonology), its demarcative function, and its expressive function. A productive result of the Prague school emphasis has been the recognition within languages of ranges of alternate "registers" or "styles" employed by speakers according to both their own background and the immediate social situation.

J. R. Firth (1957, 1968) was the first to hold a teaching position in general linguistics in England. He developed a contextual theory of language which called for analysis at the phonetic, lexical, grammatical, and situational levels in order to understand language in actual use. His attention went primarily to phonology and semantics. His view that phonetics has meaning led to an approach at the phonological level known as Prosodic Analysis. An explicit theory of language based on Firth's ideas and known as Neo-Firthian Linguistics, or, more recently, Systemics, has been developed by Halliday (1985).

5. Generative-Transformational Grammar. The most radical departure from earlier descriptive linguistics in the United States began in 1957 with the appearance of Noam Chomsky's *Syntactic Structures*. Numerous publications by Chomsky have followed. His thought has gone through several significant stages, and many other linguistic theories have developed under the influence of, or in reaction to, his views. His position has come to be known generally as Generative-Transformational (G-T) Grammar. American linguistics in particular has been fundamentally reshaped by his views. At issue is the very purpose of linguistic theory and the nature of the evidence upon which it rests.

Chomsky has grounded his views in philosophic rationalism. In breaking with structural, or descriptive, linguistics, he has resolutely turned from the empiricism that undergirded the work of his predecessors. He set out to achieve the sort of grammar that would explain a native speaker's internalized knowledge of his or her language, which is called competence, in contrast to the use to which this knowledge is put in actual speech, which is called performance. (Chomsky has not conceived of such a grammar as a replica of the human mind, but rather as a model that is comparable.) An acceptable grammar of a language, then, should produce the grammatical, or well-formed, strings (sentences) of that language (of which the potential number is infinite) and only those that are grammatical, and should capture the significant generalizations about them. The capacity to acquire this competence comes with being human and is akin to the notion of innate ideas associated with Descartes and the rationalist philosophical tradition. Another closely related goal is Chomsky's quest for universals in the explanation of linguistic phenomena.

From the beginning, Chomsky's central concern has been with syntax. In the second major phase of his theorizing, elaborated in his 1965 publication, *Aspects of the Theory of Syntax,* he set forth a model with a generative syntactic component and interpretive semantic and phonological components. Strings generated in the syntactic component are seen to be interpreted at the level of deep structure by the semantic component and transformed (by the application of rules) to the level of surface structure where they are interpreted by the phonological component.

Because of disagreement over the place of the semantic component, a division occurred after 1965 between adherents of Chomsky's view and others who espoused the theory of Generative Semantics (Katz and Fodor 1963). Chomsky modified his Aspects model (the Standard Theory) to produce the Extended Standard Theory (1970). He has since made further revisions resulting in the Revised Extended Standard Theory (Chomsky and Lasnik 1972) and still more recently in his position known as Government and Binding (1980, 1982). While the essential features of the Standard Theory have remained in Chomsky's later views, his emphases have changed; and he has attempted to constrain the power of the transformational component (which was almost unlimited in the Aspects model). Some of the competing theories which have emerged out of this process are Case Grammar (Fillmore 1968, 1977), Montague Grammar (Montague 1974), Relational Grammar (Perlmutter and Postal 1974, Johnson and Postal 1980), Daughter-dependency Grammar (Hudson 1976, Schachter 1980), and Context-free Grammar (Gadzar, Pullum and Sag 1980).

The influence of G-T Grammar is obvious. Models such as Chomsky's, Montague Grammar, and Relational Grammar have done the most to shape the current linguistic scene. Many linguists judge that the goals of linguistic theory have been established and that the domain of syntax has finally been conquered. At the same time, the future of these models is less than clear. Some linguists involved in fieldwork with languages never before analyzed are not content with any linguistic theory that has discarded the discovery procedures they require, although Chomsky's rejection of discovery procedures in the context of the search for mechanical procedures among Post-Bloomfieldians (later somewhat modified by him) is understandable. Again, the orientation of field linguists to the hard data of actual languages often steers them away from the extreme formalism of G-T Grammar. Many linguists question the existence of a deep structure or other aspects of the typically Chomskyan approach. It must be acknowledged, in any case, that prolific research has been spawned within this orientation, in particular by the work of Chomsky.

A sort of model-free linguistics is also developing in which those trained in the G-T paradigm rarely make explicit use of it as a frame of reference, e.g., Comrie (1981), Givon (1979, 1984), and S. Thompson. Such linguists are insisting on the freedom to make use of whatever model best explicates the issue at hand.

6. Stratificational Grammar. Another theory and a major development within general linguistics must be mentioned because of their promise for the present topic. Stratificational Grammar has been pioneered by Lamb (1966) and elaborated by Lockwood (1972) and others. It developed out of the glossematic theory of Hjelmslev. The work of Fleming (1979, 1988) is making the stratificational model more accessible to philologians and others interested in cross-disciplinary research. In stratificational theory, language is viewed as an integrated whole consisting of several strata (originally in Lamb the phonetic, phonemic, morphemic, lexemic, sememic, and semantic). Analysis is carried out both horizontally (in terms of the tactics of each stratum) and vertically (in terms of realization relationships among the strata). A primary appeal of Stratificational Grammar is its ability to trace the function of language in both directions, i.e., from speaker to hearer and conversely.

7. Discourse Analysis/Text Linguistics. While not a theory per se, Discourse Analysis is perhaps most important among recent methodological developments within general linguistics for the concerns of this article. Discourse Analysis extends the borders of linguistic investigation beyond the sentence to encompass entire sections of material viewed as communicable wholes. Although his teacher Zellig Harris had already pointed in this direction, Chomsky launched his endeavors with the sentence as the limit of analysis.

Impatience with this limitation led to the development of Text Linguistics in Europe during the late sixties and seventies, with leadership from de Beaugrande (1981), van Dijk (1972, 1977), Dressler (1972, 1981), and Petöfi (1983). In the United States, somewhat independently of Europe and known more often as Discourse Analysis, initial interest was stimulated by missionary translators who had learned the futility of sentence-by-sentence translation. Also prominent were such scholars as Chafe (1980), Hopper (1980), and Tannen (1984). The relevance of the entire context of a discourse to even the phonological level of analysis has been demonstrated by Mayers. Text Linguistics, or Discourse Analysis, has become a well-defined and important trend in world linguistics. It now provides one of the most fruitful avenues of rapprochement between linguists and biblical scholars. Among those leading the way in OT studies are Longacre (1979, 1983), Rabin (1982), Schneider (1974), Winther-Nielsen (1978), and (in the NT) Callow (1974), Funk (1975), Grimes (1975), and Louw (1973, 1981).

C. Biblical Studies vis-à-vis Linguistics

1. Hebrew Grammars. The biblical Hebrew grammars of Gesenius (edited by Kautzsch and translated by Cowley [GKC]); Bergsträsser; Bauer and Leander; and Joüon were written during the 19th century or early in the 20th, and generally reflect the philological approach which developed out of the Renaissance. This approach was based primarily on classical models (with attention to the work of the medieval Hebrew grammarians) and (in the grammar by Bauer and Leander especially) the historical/comparative approach of the 19th century. The classical models had been developed entirely on the basis of Greek and Latin, apart from the study of other languages. The historical/comparative approach had been formulated primarily by Indo-Europeanists at work on the data of the languages of their field, while Hebraists and other Semitists (as well as students of other language families) contributed little to this development. Thus, it was inevitable that these models would often not be suitable for the analysis of Semitic (or other non-Indo-European) languages.

While other Hebrew grammars have been produced, including those of Blau, Lambdin, Meyer, Richter, Sawyer, and Schneider, none has yet appeared on a scale comparable to GKC or Bauer and Leander. Sawyer (1976) has incorporated some insights from descriptive linguistics, and Andersen (1970, 1974) has utilized a tagmemic approach to study the Hebrew verbless clause and sentence. Richter (1978, 1979, 1980) is engaged in a serious effort to analyze biblical Hebrew linguistically, although he has largely bypassed the essential step of phonological analysis. Joseph Malone has studied many specific issues in Hebrew (and Semitic) from a G-T perspective. On the philological side, a considerably increased understanding of biblical Hebrew has been achieved through comparative data from other Semitic languages, especially of the NW Semitic group; but most of these results have yet to find their way into published grammars.

2. NT Greek Grammars. In the early 19th century Georg Benedikt Winer (1789–1858) brought a Port-Royal rationalist perspective to the study of NT Greek and also called for an internal analysis of the language. This latter impetus was profoundly vindicated when Gustav Adolf Deissmann (1866–1937) showed the close relation between the Greek of the NT and that of the Hellenistic papyri. The major grammars of Blass and Debrunner; Moulton, Howard, and Turner; and Robertson were, as in the case of Hebrew grammars, written in the late 19th and early 20th century (with the exception of Turner, who has written more recently). The German work of Friedrich Blass (1843–1907) emphasized a comparison with classical Greek, and Albert Debrunner (b. 1884) incorporated contemporary comparative material in his revision, as did Radermacher and Mayser in their grammars. The English contribution began with Moulton's strong insistence, following Deissmann, on the character of NT Greek as Hellenistic and as a reflection of spoken language. While Howard essentially published the work of Moulton in the second volume, he did indicate more openness to Semitic influence. This emphasis then came to the fore in the third and fourth volumes with Turner's conviction that biblical Greek is unique and that the influence of the Septuagint was determinative in its development. In America Robertson employed the historical/comparative approach. The descriptive linguistic paradigm of the first half of the 20th century is reflected in the Hellenistic grammar of Robert Funk and the introductory NT grammar of Goetchius. Probes in the application of G-T Grammar to the NT text have been made by Mueller (1978) and Schmidt (1981).

3. Synchronic and Diachronic Study. It may be that an unbalanced focus on synchronic analysis among linguists has been one of the significant impediments to interaction with students of biblical Hebrew. Aside from questions of the prehistory of the text and viable differences in the dating of various books and sections, the Hebrew Bible represents over a millennium of language development. The only synchronic reading which is possible (apart from multifaceted comparative reconstruction) is that of the Hebrew of the Masoretes, and their vocalization system was added about another millennium after the consonantal text finally reached its present shape and thus can scarcely represent precisely the Hebrew of any phase of the biblical period. In other words, a realistic linguistic analysis of biblical Hebrew cannot proceed on a purely synchronic basis. In NT studies this issue is not nearly so pressing because of the relatively short period of time during which all of the material was written.

4. Internal Analysis. In the study of biblical Hebrew, the insistence of Boas and Sapir that each language must be analyzed from within on its own terms instead of through categories derived from other languages cannot be overemphasized. This kind of analysis is still needed. An example of such a need is the frequent discussion of the biblical Hebrew noun in terms of cases, whereas case inflection had almost certainly been lost in Hebrew by the biblical period (though it was present in earlier NW Semitic). Another example is the ongoing effort to discover the categories which will best explicate the Hebrew verb, which categories need to be intrinsically derived from Hebrew itself (as well as from closely controlled cognate Semitic data).

In NT studies, Winer saw the need for internal analysis. The issue has focused thus far particularly on whether the language is simply the Hellenistic Greek of the time (Deissmann, Moulton), or a unique sort of Greek shaped by the influence of Semitic, especially through the Septuagint (Turner). Perhaps what is needed is a fresh approach, working from the vantage point of some model within general linguistics and grounding the study more broadly than only in the question of Hellenistic versus Hebraic (or Semitic) Greek.

5. Interdisciplinary Dialogue. Some of the barriers which have hindered students of the biblical languages in benefiting from general linguistics continue to constitute a challenge. One of these is the simple lack of contact between the fields. Another is the highly technical nature of so much of linguistic literature and the lack of effort on the part of many linguists to communicate to a wider audience, even to scholars in other disciplines. Perhaps even more important, the lack of theoretical consensus among linguists still leaves outsiders hard put to know where to begin in finding a point of entry.

Another serious concern arises from the assumption, continued among most linguists since the late 19th century, that only speech provides primary linguistic data.

Some linguists do argue, on the other hand, that writing also affords primary data for linguistic analysis, though of a different sort. Whether or not they are able to make their case, since all data from the ancient world are only written, it is essential for biblical studies that the discipline of graphemics (as the linguistic study of writing is often called) be developed so as to indicate how linguistic research may be applied to written data.

More encouraging signs may be found in the recently renewed attention among linguists to diachronic analysis and in the interest that is being expressed and demonstrated among scholars of biblical and other ancient languages in incorporating an understanding of linguistics into their work. In light of the good which will surely come as this happens, such interest must be encouraged. In light of the barriers which remain, the sights of biblical scholars must be set on a higher goal than merely that of finding another ready-made tool which can be added to their already overcrowded stock of methods for analysis. They must, rather, pursue a deeper insight into the nature of language and, thereby, into the meaning of texts, as they enter into dialogue with linguists. Linguistic theories and consequent methods of analysis can aid biblical scholars immensely. Conversely, as people who work with hard language data, biblical scholars can hope to contribute to the continuing effort of linguists to understand the phenomenon of language.

Those who wish to do further reading may find it helpful to begin with the introductions to general linguistics by Gleason (1961), Lyons (1968), and Robins (1980) and the histories of linguistics by Dineen (1967), Robins (1979), and Sampson (1980).

Bibliography

Andersen, F. I. 1970. *The Hebrew Verbless Clause in the Pentateuch.* JBL Monograph Series 14. Nashville.

———. 1974. *The Sentence in Biblical Hebrew.* Janua Linguarum Series Practica 231. The Hague.

Beaugrande, R. de, and Dressler, W. U. 1981. *Introduction to Text Linguistics.* Longman Linguistics Library 26. New York.

Bloomfield, L. 1933. *Language.* New York.

Boas, F. 1911. *Handbook of American Indian Languages.* Washington, D.C.

Callow, K. 1974. *Discourse Considerations in Translating the Word of God.* Grand Rapids.

Chafe, W. L., ed. 1980. *The Pear Stories, Cognitive, Cultural and Linguistic Aspects of Narrative Production.* Norwood.

Chomsky, N. 1957. *Syntactic Structures.* Janua Linguarum Series Minor 4. The Hague.

———. 1965. *Aspects of the Theory of Syntax.* Cambridge, MA.

———. 1970. Remarks on Nominalization. Pp. 184–221 in *Readings in English Transformational Grammar,* ed. R. A. Jacobs and P. S. Rosenbaum. Waltham, MA.

———. 1980. *Rules and Representations.* New York.

———. 1982. *Some Concepts and Consequences of the Theory of Government and Binding.* Linguistic Inquiry Monographs G. Cambridge, MA.

Chomsky, N., and Lasnik, H. 1972. Filters and Control. *Linguistic Inquiry* 8: 425–504.

Comrie, B. 1981. *Language Universals and Linguistic Typology.* Chicago.

Dijk, T. van. 1972. *Some Aspects of Text Grammars.* The Hague.

———. 1977. *Text and Context.* London.

Dineen, F. P. 1967. *An Introduction to General Linguistics.* Washington, D.C.

Dressler, W. 1972. *Einführung in die Textlinguistik.* Tübingen.

Fillmore, C. 1968. The Case for Case. Pp. 1–88 in *Universals in Linguistic Theory,* ed. E. Bach and R. Harms. New York.

———. 1977. The Case for Case Reopened. Pp. 59–81 in *Grammatical Relations,* ed. P. Cole and J. Sadock. Grammatical Relations 8. New York.

Firth, J. R. 1957. *Papers in Linguistics 1934–1951.* Oxford.

———. 1968. *Selected Papers of J. R. Firth, 1952–59,* ed. F. R. Palmer. Bloomington, IN.

Fleming, I. 1979. Discourse from the Perspective of Four Strata. Pp. 307–17 in *The Fifth Lacus Forum, 1986,* ed. W. Wölck and P. L. Garvin. Columbia, SC.

———. 1988. *Communication Analysis: A Stratificational Approach,* vol. 2. Dallas.

Funk, R. W. 1975. The Significance of Discourse Structure for the Study of the New Testament. Pp. 209–21 in *No Famine in the Land: Studies in Honor of John L. McKenzie,* eds. J. W. Flanagan and A. W. Robinson. Claremont, CA.

Gadzar, G.; Pullum, G.; and Sag, I. 1980. *A Phrase Structure Grammar of the English Anxilliary System.* Bloomington, IN.

Givon, T. 1979. *On Understanding Grammar.* New York.

———. 1984. *Syntax: A Functional-Typological Approach,* vol. 1. Amsterdam.

Gleason, H. A. 1961. *An Introduction to Descriptive Linguistics.* New York.

Grimes, J. E. 1975. *The Thread of Discourse.* Janua Linguarum Series Minor 207. The Hague.

Halliday, M. A. 1985. *Introduction to Functional Grammar.* Baltimore.

Hjelmslev, L. 1961. *Prolegomena to a Theory of Language.* Trans. F. J. Whitefield. Madison, WI.

Hopper, P. J., and Thompson, S. A. 1980. Transitivity in Grammar and Discourse. *Language* 56: 251–99.

Hudson, R. 1976. *Arguments for a Non-Transformational Grammar.* Chicago.

Johnson, D. E., and Postal, P. M. 1980. *Arc Pair Grammar.* Princeton.

Katz, J. J., and Fodor, J. 1963. The Structure of a Semantic Theory. *Language* 39: 170–210.

Lamb, S. 1966. *Outline of Stratificational Grammar.* Washington, D.C.

Lockwood, D. G. 1972. *Introduction to Stratificational Linguistics.* New York.

Longacre, R. E. 1979. The Discourse Structure of the Flood Narrative. *JAAR* Sup B, pp. 89–133.

———. 1983. *The Grammar of Discourse: Notional and Surface Structures.* New York.

Louw, J. P. 1973. Discourse Analysis and the Greek New Testament. *BTrans* 24: 101–18.

———. 1981. A Semiotic Approach to Discourse Analysis with Reference to Translation Theory. *BTrans* 36: 101–7.

Lyons, J. 1968. *Introduction to Theoretical Linguistics.* Cambridge.

Montague, R. 1974. The Proper Treatment of Quantification in Ordinary English. Pp. 221–42 in *Approaches to Natural Language,* ed. J. Hintikka et al. New Haven.

Mueller, T. 1978. Observations on Some New Testament Texts Based on Generative-Transformational Grammar. *BTrans* 29: 117–29.

Perlmutter, D. M., and Postal, P. M. 1974. *Lectures on Relational Grammar.* Amherst, MA.

Petöfi, J. S. 1983. Text, Signification, Models, and Correlates. Pp.

266–98 in *Psycholinguistic Studies in Language Processing,* ed. G. Rickheit and M. Bock. Research in Text Theory 7. Berlin.
Pike, K. L. 1967. *Language in Relation to a Unified Theory of the Structure of Human Behavior.* The Hague.
———. 1982. *Linguistic Concepts: An Introduction to Tagmemics.* Lincoln, NE.
Rabin, C. 1982. Discourse Analysis and the Dating of Deuteronomy. Pp. 171–77 in *Interpreting the Hebrew Bible: Essays in Honor of E. I. J. Rosenthal,* ed. J. A. Emerton and S. C. Reif. Cambridge.
Richter, W. 1978–80. *Grundlagen einer althebräischen Grammatik.* ATAT 8, 10, 13. Munich.
Robins, R. H. 1979. *A Short History of Linguistics.* New York.
———. 1980. *General Linguistics: An Introductory Survey.* New York.
Sampson, G. 1980. *Schools of Linguistics.* Stanford.
Sapir, E. 1921. *Language: An Introduction to the Study of Speech.* New York.
Saussure, F. de. 1959. *Course in General Linguistics,* ed. C. Bally and A. Sechehaye. Trans. W. Baskin. New York.
Sawyer, J. F. A. 1976. *A Modern Introduction to Biblical Hebrew.* Boston.
Schachter, P. 1980. Daughter-dependency Grammar. Pp. 267–99 in *Current Approaches to Syntax,* ed. E. A. Moravcsik and J. R. Wirth. Syntax and Semantics 13. New York.
Schmidt, D. 1981. *Hellenistic Greek Grammar and Noam Chomsky: Nominalizing Transformations.* SBLDS 62. Chico.
Schneider, W. 1974. *Grammatik des biblischen Hebräisch.* Munich.
Tannen, D. 1984. *Conversational Style: Analyzing Talk Among Friends.* Norwood.
Trubetzkoy, N. S. 1969. *Principles of Phonology.* Trans. C. A. M. Baltaxe. Berkeley.
Vachek, J. ed. 1964. *A Prague School Reader in Linguistics.* Bloomington, IN.
———. 1966. *The Linguistic School of Prague.* Bloomington, IN.
Winther-Nielsen, N. 1978. Poetik og Tekste Fortaellingen om Davids Hor og Mord (2 Samuel 11:1–12:25). *Haggamal* 1: 159–220.

WALTER R. BODINE

LINUS (PERSON) [Gk *Linos*]. A Christian mentioned after Pudens and before Claudia, who sent greetings along with them to Timothy (2 Tim 4:21). It has been speculated that Linus was the son of Pudens and Claudia, although it then becomes difficult to understand why he is mentioned between and not after them.

Because 2 Timothy is assumed to reflect an imprisonment of Paul in Rome (cf. 1:17)—although Caesarea has also been suggested—Linus is sometimes taken to be the Linus whom tradition identifies as the first bishop of Rome after the apostles. This linking goes back to Irenaeus (*haer.* 3.3.3) who stated that "the blessed Apostles having founded and built up the Church, committed into the hands of Linus the office of the episcopate. Of this Linus Paul makes mention in the Epistles to Timothy." This is then quoted by Eusebius (*Hist. Eccl.* 5.6) who also writes that "after the martyrdom of Paul and Peter, Linus was the first appointed to the bishopric of the church of Rome" (*Hist. Eccl.* 3.2). Eusebius notes that the episcopate of Linus lasted twelve years, after which he handed on his office to Anencletus (*Hist. Eccl.* 3.13). The *Apos. Con.* 7.46 likewise identify a person named Linus as the first bishop of Rome after the apostles and as ordained by Paul. The same text relates him to Claudia as Gk *linos ho klaudias,* i.e., as either her husband or brother. The question of historicity arises beginning with the earliest of these sources, the text from Irenaeus, which no doubt influenced the later sources. Hanson (*The Pastoral Epistles* NCBC, 164) has judged that Irenaeus' notation about Linus is unhistorical: "It assumes that the church in Rome had monepiscopacy in the 1st century, which it certainly had not." In addition, he points out that "it is also probably quite unhistorical to envisage either Paul or Peter or both as entrusting to anyone the leadership of a church which neither of them had founded." Nevertheless, Hanson (*The Pastoral Epistles* NCBC, 164) finds "a faint echo of history in the name [Linus]" for, as he remarks, "Are we to imagine the author of the Pastorals as freely inventing all these names [i.e., Eubulus, Pudens, Linus, Claudia]? It does not seem likely. They are probably part of his oral tradition."

Bibliography

Redlich, E. B. 1913. *S. Paul and His Companions.* London.

FLORENCE MORGAN GILLMAN

LION. See ZOOLOGY.

LITERACY. This entry consists of two articles, one covering literacy in the ANE (mainly Mesopotamia and Egypt), and one treating literacy in ancient Israel.

ANCIENT NEAR EAST

Although the ANE has been studied principally from written sources, discussion of the status of writing in its civilizations is only beginning. Many issues are involved. These range from the potentially factual, such as rates of literacy, through levels of literacy to the extent to which writing represents language, and the relation of writing to contemporaneous spoken language. More abstractly, effects of writing on social structure or on cognition are explored. This last problem has received particular attention, because it has been held, despite the counterexamples of Chinese and Japanese, that alphabetic writing which encodes vowels was a necessary precondition for such a phenomenon as the "cognitive revolution" of archaic and classical Greece (e.g., Havelock 1982), and may have similar consequences wherever it is introduced (Goody and Watt 1963; later modified, e.g., Goody 1987). Although few espouse a strong form of this hypothesis, it has stimulated discussion, serves as a point of reference, and is relevant for the world of the Hebrew Bible, with its alphabetical (though unvocalized) form of writing. Most studies that seek to test or replace the hypothesis examine the way in which writing is used and embedded in social structures, and place more explanatory weight on those structures.

A. Forms, Distribution and Use of Writing
  1. Mesopotamia and Surrounding Regions
  2. Egypt
B. Discussion

A. Forms, Distribution and Use of Writing

1. Mesopotamia and Surrounding Regions. From the 4th millennium B.C. Mesopotamia was linguistically and politically diverse. It strongly influenced areas as remote as Anatolia and Urartu in the 2d and 1st millennia B.C., and Iran in the days of the Persian Empire, while the cuneiform script and some of its languages survived into the Parthian period. All these regions wrote in cuneiform. In view of this enormous spread of time, space, and language, it is not meaningful to speak of one style of "Mesopotamian" literacy. There was a long initial development which created a script that could fully encode a language, with subsequent phases in which writing came to be both more and less widespread and important in social life. This complex picture has an analogy in successive political orders in the region (e.g., Yoffee 1988).

Writing was invented in S Mesopotamia, perhaps at Uruk (Nissen 1985), before the end of the 4th millennium B.C. (Michalowski 1990; Powell 1981). The separate system of Iranian writing, centered either on the Iranian plateau or in Susiana (Khuzestan), is as ancient, but it did not survive. The early tablets from Uruk, which are administrative and "lexical" (Green 1986: 465), have a repertory of about 1200 signs; they cannot be read in any particular language (Green 1981).

Only very gradually was the system modified to encode phonetic elements, perhaps starting from proper names. When a language becomes apparent, it is Sumerian, which has no known cognate. From earliest times, names of Semitic form are found, and there were probably always Semitic speakers in Mesopotamia. To this picture should be added the likely presence of the Elamite language in adjacent Susiana. This multilingualism is important both for the position of writing as a communicative system and for the later adaption of cuneiform for additional languages, a potential that was exploited many times.

The earliest Semitic texts, as against Semitic names, known in the Mesopotamian script are in Fara period tablets from Abu Salabikh (Biggs 1974: 42, 91); different Semitic dialects are attested slightly later from Ebla in Syria. There is controversy as to whether the principal dialect there was the language of Ebla itself ("Eblaite") or a Semitic language of N Mesopotamia—poorly known for this period—adopted with the script at Ebla (Michalowski 1987). From the succeeding Agade dynasty on, Akkadian became the dominant Semitic language written in cuneiform, and is known in many dialects from different areas. It traveled with the script to regions where cuneiform was adopted for different languages; those regions therefore also had multilingual written cultures. The two principal strands of Akkadian are Babylonian and Assyrian, which separated after 2000 B.C. By the time of the Agade dynasty, the isolated language Hurrian began to be written in cuneiform (Wilhelm 1982: 4–5, 11, 106–08). Although this survived for more than a millennium, it never became widespread, except perhaps around the capital of the Hurrian state of Mitanni (Waššukanni; site not identified).

From the mid-2d millennium B.C., the Indo-European Hittite language, together with its local forerunner Hattic (Kammenhuber 1969b) and the Indo-European Palaic and Luwian, were written in cuneiform (Kammenhuber 1969a). In Anatolia, the influence of cuneiform spread beyond the writing system itself with the invention of the hieroglyphic Luwian script, whose pictorial signs may have looked to Egyptian or Levantine models, but whose structure was patterned after cuneiform (Morpurgo Davies and Hawkins 1978). Cuneiform preserves traces of yet further languages, notably Amorite, the traditional language of an ethnic element in the Mesopotamian population of the late 3d and early 2d millennia B.C. (Gelb 1980). Comparable later phenomena are Kassite, which remains almost unknown, and Aramaic, used alongside Akkadian cuneiform in the 1st millennium B.C. and ultimately supplanting it.

Vast numbers of cuneiform tablets are preserved (cf. Veenhof 1986: 2–3), although their distribution is irregular; gaps were illustrated by the discovery of Ebla in the 1970s (Cagni 1987), of Tell Leilan (Eidem 1987), and of the Late Babylonian temple library at Sippar (Black and Ball 1987: 248–49) in the 1980s. Despite this abundance of material, the picture of the use of writing is limited. Most preserved tablets are bureaucratic or administrative.

Continuous language was not recorded until the ED period, and literary texts, narrowly defined, are not known before the Fara period (Biggs 1974: 28–42). The earliest of these are perhaps more sets of cues for oral performance than full texts (Michalowski 1990). Except on cylinder seals, writing was rare in public places and on works of art until the later 3d millennium B.C., and letters were uncommon. The most intense early administrative use of writing was during the Agade dynasty in Akkadian and the succeeding Ur III dynasty in Sumerian, by then probably a dead language (cf. Larsen 1988a: 188).

From the Isin-Larsa period on, Akkadian began to predominate over Sumerian in writing, but Sumerian was transmitted as long as Mesopotamian culture survived and spread to all areas where cuneiform was adopted. Whatever language was used in everyday writing, all known schooling was based on Sumerian, which was fundamental to many features of the cuneiform script and underlay sign lists and lexical lists. The main corpus of Sumerian literature is preserved only in Old Babylonian (OB) and later copies, and thus was in a dead language (e.g., Hallo 1975). The principal early Akkadian literary texts belong to the same period.

The only period during which there was widespread use of writing outside scribal classes was the OB/Old Assyrian (OA), from which large amounts of private correspondence are preserved, notably from the Assyrian trading colony of Kültepe/Kanish in Anatolia (e.g., Larsen 1976). This material uses a reduced range of signs that would have been relatively easy to learn (Larsen 1988b: 132–34; but see Morpurgo Davies 1986: 60–63). OB and OA are markedly different from the Old Akkadian (OAkk) of the Agade dynasty and may not derive directly from it (Reiner 1966: 21), so that they could at times have been relatively close to the current language of the Akkadian-speaking part of the population. The same can be said only of isolated other strands of the tradition, perhaps of Neo-Assyrian (NA) of the 8th–7th centuries B.C. and of subsequent Late Babylonian (LB). The Standard Babylonian (SB) of Akkadian literary texts was an artificial "dialect."

From the 1st millennium B.C. come major collections of literary material, especially the Library of Assurbanipal from Nineveh (Reade 1986; Parpola 1986); traditions of belles lettres, mathematics, and astronomy continued in Babylonia to the end of Mesopotamian culture. From the aftermath of the OB period on, the writing system became more complicated, in that it used an increasing number of signs, with more homophony. The same is true of the relatively short history of Hittite cuneiform, in the later stages of which more words were written in Sumerian and Akkadian (Morpurgo Davies 1986: 60–61). In some cases, these more complex practices could lead to greater "efficiency," because fewer signs were needed to write the same amount of text, but the general tendency is not popularizing. Rather, writing was kept within a scribal class, and there were sanctions, recorded in formal colophons on tablets and in one more explicit text (Beaulieu fc.), against transmitting knowledge of writing outside that class. The scribal group was exclusive also in that it did not include the leaders of states; but those people were as committed as the scribes to maintaining the cultural, as well as the administrative, tradition of writing.

In none of Mesopotamian history is there suitable evidence for assessing rates of literacy. Although in small social groups, such as the OA merchants, the rate may have been relatively high, the general impression is of very restricted literacy.

2. Egypt. Writing was invented in Egypt after the cultural and political unification of the country in late-predynastic times (ca. 3100 B.C.). The Egyptian script belongs to a unilingual culture and was hardly used to write other languages; even dialect forms are rare. There are two principal variants of the script, hieroglyphs, which have a pictorial form and are integrated with the system of pictorial representation, and cursive, the later hieratic, which was used for most writing on the artificial medium of papyrus. From about 650 B.C. a second cursive form, demotic, evolved. This was thenceforth the business script; from the 4th century B.C. or earlier, literary, and later religious, texts were also written in it.

The hieroglyphic script has a broader significance because of its integration with art; together these formed both the main medium of display and, in times before continuous language was written down, the central definition of the meaning of the Egyptian state and cosmos (Baines 1989). Most pictorial representation includes some writing. The presentation of the social order and cosmos on the monuments is strongly hierarchical, and positive values became attached to forms of writing that did not employ continuous language. Perhaps for this reason, it was some centuries before continuous language was written down, perhaps in the late 2d dynasty, even though the requisite sign repertory existed earlier.

Most preserved early writing is in ink or incised, on pottery, stone vases, or ivory tags, but papyrus was perfected by the middle of the 1st dynasty. Papyrus and wooden writing boards were the main writing media for administration. Because papyrus can be preserved only in dry conditions, the cursive written record is much less abundant than that on clay from the Near East (Veenhof 1986: 2–3); only for the New Kingdom village of Deir el-Medina (Valbelle 1985) and for the Roman period is the volume comparable, and most of the latter material is in Greek (Montevecchi 1973; Youtie 1981). Egypt has, however, preserved altogether more monumental writing than the Near East.

The earliest written materials are broadly administrative (Dreyer 1989), but it is uncertain whether writing was invented for administration and then adopted for display, invented for display, or devised for both at once. It is also an open question whether its invention was independent or was due to stimulus diffusion from Mesopotamia, whose influence was strong in the Delta (Von der Way and Schmidt 1987). Writing was used as the instrument of the unified nation state. In most periods, developments were introduced from the center.

The first major advance dates to the 2d–4th dynasties. Brief speeches of gods were recorded, and by the end of the 4th dynasty administrative documents including whole sentences were composed (Posener Kriéger 1979). The language of this period is termed Old Egyptian; it is not unitary. Most continuous Egyptian texts are in a simple form of meter (*LÄ* 4: 1127–54). The earliest form of "literary text" seems to have been the list, as in Mesopotamia; these are known from the 2d dynasty on (*AEL* 1: 3–5). In the 5th–6th dynasties, public and private uses of writing proliferated (Roccati 1982), and the Pyramid Texts in later pyramids provide indirect evidence for large corpora of religious texts, while medical and mathematical texts may also have been written. The design of documents became very elaborate (Helck 1974). Conventionalized representations in nonroyal tombs show scribes in almost every context of production and administration. The inner elite and kings were literate.

The central Old Kingdom is the period best suited for estimating the extent of literacy. If the size of the inner elite (a few hundred) and their supporting scribes (perhaps ten times that number) is related to the total population (perhaps a million), a rate of literacy of 0.3–1.0 percent emerges (Baines and Eyre 1983: 65–74). All these people will have been males in the service of the state or officials; there is no place for nonprofessional literate people and little evidence for female literacy.

During the 1st intermediate period, writing may have spread a little, while the succeeding Middle Kingdom saw a pervasive bureaucratization and the composition of much literature. The language of these periods is termed Middle Egyptian. Its orthography was regularized in the early 12th dynasty; it was probably an artificial idiom, for it is little different grammatically from Old Egyptian.

Middle Kingdom literature (*AEL* 1) focuses on the Instruction (or Wisdom) text, but includes other genres, notably narratives such as that of Sinuhe. Finds of groups of papyri from the 13th dynasty (Gardiner 1955) to the Roman period (Tait 1977) show that "literature" was the sum of transmitted old texts and could extend to copies of inscriptions. The chief context in which belles lettres were certainly used was in schools. Middle Kingdom literature is complex, serious, and focused on elite concerns; it was "classical" for later periods, and allusions to its phraseology show that it pervaded later written culture.

There was little essential change in the position of writing in the New Kingdom, but the culture of the period was more diverse, particularly in the 19th–20th dynasties, when Late Egyptian joined Middle Egyptian as a written form rather nearer to the spoken language. Monumental inscriptions of those dynasties stand linguistically between Middle and Late Egyptian. Later inscriptions reverted to Middle Egyptian, while documentary Late Egyptian continued to develop, being transformed ultimately into demotic (from the 7th century B.C.), which designates a form both of the script and of the language (Johnson 1986). From the later New Kingdom on, the chief repositories of traditional culture were the temples. The linguistic diversity of texts grew steadily, while in later times the spread of literacy may have declined. Here, the development of demotic is crucial, because the connection between hieroglyphs and the cursive was broken, and hieroglyphs developed from a repertory of a few hundred signs to one of several thousand, used in the most elaborate fashion in temple inscriptions of the Greco–Roman period (Kurth 1983). Literacy was probably less widespread in demotic than it had been in hieratic, while late hieroglyphic was the preserve of a small priestly group.

Ptolemaic and Roman rule did not bring an end to Egyptian writing, but the primary administrative language of the country was now Greek, and the rate of literacy in Greek was much higher than in Egyptian. Although there was considerable mixing of people over this long period, little Greek influence can be seen in Egyptian texts. Native written traditions survived and developed into the 3d century A.D., before disappearing in the face of changes in the Roman Empire and the spread of Christianity.

B. Discussion

The patterns of development and use of writing in the two principal cultural areas of the ANE are different in detail but share important features. Writing is part of the definition of these societies or civilizations and of their cultural awareness. This point is clearer for Egypt than for Mesopotamia, but is significant there too (Machinist 1986), despite the fact that writing was not used for high-cultural purposes for several centuries after its invention. Literacy was restricted in both cultures, being integral to administration and high culture in Egypt and subservient to those forces in Mesopotamia. In both, development toward encoding continuous language was slow. Even when written language arrived, it was restricted to particular dialects or standardized forms and subject to many conventions. In Mesopotamia and peripheral regions, the written language was a foreign one for many of its users. These restrictions of writing go together with limited access to written and artistic display. For Egypt this was chiefly in palaces, temples, and tombs; in Mesopotamia too, palaces (e.g. Winter 1981) and temples were central.

Thus, the position of writing in these societies could hardly have led to mass literacy; in Mesopotamia there were also formal barriers to learning to read and write. In neither region would acquiring literacy have brought obvious benefits for those outside the administration. If the question needs to be rehearsed, this position of writing might be sufficient explanation for the absence of some of the developments of Greece. But in Greece, the principal stimuli to development may have come from social forces other than writing (e.g., Murray 1980: 90–99), so that the argument would then be irrelevant, even if, as is likely, writing is necessary to sustain the complex and continued development of abstract modes of thought and argument.

If more appropriate criteria are used, the position and effects of writing in these civilizations remain crucial. The whole administrative apparatus was predicated on writing (cf. Gibson and Biggs 1987). Writing allowed historical transmission of cultural materials over vast spans of time with quite accurate knowledge of the periods from which it derived (more so in Egypt than in Mesopotamia; cf. Baines 1988; Michalowski 1983; see in general Assmann 1988). In Mesopotamia there were developments of mathematics and astronomy that would hardly have occurred in oral form (Machinist 1985). In Egypt, the religious controversy and development of the Amarna period belong in a high-cultural and written tradition (Assmann 1983: 96–143). These examples could be multiplied.

From an opposite perspective, it is important to see the effects of writing in the context of limited literacy. In societies where few are literate and writing is normally read aloud during composition and retrieval, the oral context dominates and envelops the written. That context is virtually lost, but it was all that most people experienced; no one was embarrassed not to be literate (Morpurgo Davies 1986: 55). Yet elite projects and elite display, which utilized and were organized through writing, consumed such a high proportion of resources that the written record gives a truer picture than it would of less unequal semi-oral communities. As well as recording that inequality, writing was a powerful aid to its existence.

Bibliography

Assmann, J. 1983. *Re und Amun: Die Krise des polytheistischen Weltbilds im Ägypten der 18.-20. Dynastie.* OBO 51. Fribourg.

———. 1988. Kollektives Gedächtnis und kulturelle Identität; and Stein und Zeit: Das "monumentale" Gedächtnis der altägyptischen Kultur. Pp. 9–19, 87–114 in *Kultur und Gedächtnis*, eds. J. Assmann and T. Hölscher. Frankfurt am Main.

Baines, J. 1988. Ancient Egyptian Concepts and Uses of the Past: 3rd to 2nd Millennium B.C. Evidence. Pp. 131–49 in *Who Needs the Past? Indigenous Values and Archaeology*, ed. R. Layton. London.

———. 1989. Communication and Display: the Integration of Early Egyptian Art and Writing. *Antiquity* 63: 471–82.

Baines, J., and Eyre, O. J. 1983. Four notes on literacy. *Göttinger Miszellen* 61: 65–96.

Beaulieu, P.-A. fc. New Evidence for the Existence of Secret Knowledge in First Millennium Babylonia.

Biggs, R. D. 1974. *Inscriptions from Tell Abu Ṣalābīkh.* OIP 99. Chicago.

Black, J. A., and Ball, W. 1987. Excavations in Iraq, 1985–6. *Iraq* 49: 231–51.

Cagni, L., ed. 1987. *Ebla 1975–1985. Dieci anni di studi linguistici e filologici: Atti del convegno internazionale (Napoli, 9–11 ottobre 1985).* Istituto Universitario Orientale, Seminario di Studi Asiatici, Series Minor 27. Naples.

Dreyer, G. 1989. Abydos: Umm el-Qaab. Deutsches Archäologisches Institut, Abteilung Kairo, *Rundbrief*, July 1989: 6–10.

Eidem, J. 1987. Note on Tell Leilan Tablets. *NABU* 1988: 123b.

Gardiner, A. 1955. *The Ramesseum Papyri.* Oxford.

Gelb, I. J. 1980. *Computer-aided Analysis of Amorite.* AS 21. Chicago.

Gibson, M., and Biggs, R. D., eds. 1987. *The Organization of Power: Aspects of Bureaucracy in the Ancient Near East.* SAOC 46. Chicago.

Goody, J. 1987. *The Interface between the Written and the Oral.* Cambridge.

Goody, J., and Watt, I. 1963. The Consequence of Literacy. *Comparative Studies in Society and History* 5: 304–45. Repr. 1968 in *Literacy in Traditional Societies,* ed. J. Goody. Cambridge.

Green, M. W. 1981. The Construction and Implementation of the Cuneiform Writing System. *Visible Language* 15: 345–72.

———. 1986. Archaic Uruk Cuneiform. *AJA* 90: 464–66.

Hallo, W. W. 1975. Toward a History of Sumerian Literature. Pp. 181–203 in *Sumerological Studies in Honor of Thorkild Jacobsen on His Seventieth Birthday, June 7, 1974,* ed. S. J. Lieberman. AS 20. Chicago.

Havelock, E. A. 1982. *The Literate Revolution in Greece and Its Cultural Consequences.* Princeton.

Helck, W. 1974. *Altägyptische Aktenkunde des 3. und 2. Jahrtausends v. Chr.,* MÄS 31. Berlin.

Johnson, J. H. 1986. *Thus Wrote ᶜOnkhsheshonqy: An Introductory Grammar of Demotic.* SAOC 45. Chicago.

Kammenhuber, A. 1969a. Hetitisch, Palaisch, Luwisch und Hieroglyphen-Luwisch. Pp. 119–357 in *Altkleinasiatische Sprachen.* HO 1/2/1-2/2. Leiden.

———. 1969b. Hattisch. Pp. 428–546 in *Altkleinasiatische Sprachen.* HO 1/2/1-2/2. Leiden.

Kurth, D. 1983. Die Lautwerte der Hieroglyphen in den Tempelinschriften der griechisch-römischen Zeit—Zur Systematik ihrer Herleitungsprinzipien. *Annales du Service des Antiquités de l'Égypte* 69: 287–309.

Larsen, M. T. 1976. *The Old Assyrian City-state and Its Colonies.* Mesopotamia: Copenhagen Studies in Assyriology 4. Copenhagen.

———. 1987. The Babylonian Lukewarm Mind: Reflections on Science, Divination and Literacy. Pp. 203–25 in *Language, Literature and History: Philological and Historical Studies Presented to Erica Reiner,* ed. F. Rochberg-Halton. AOS 67. New Haven.

———. 1988a. Literacy and Social Complexity. Pp. 173–91 in *State and Society: the Emergence and Development of Social Hierarchy and Political Centralization,* eds. B. Bender; J. Gledhill; and M. T. Larsen. London.

———. 1988b. What They Wrote on Clay. Pp. 121–48 in *Literacy and Society,* eds. K. Schousboe and M. T. Larsen. Copenhagen.

Machinist, P. B. 1986. On Self-consciousness in Mesopotamia. Pp. 193–202, 511–18 in *The Origins and Diversity of Axial Age Civilizations,* ed. S. N. Eisenstadt. N.p.

Michalowski, P. 1983. History as Charter: the Sumerian King List Revisited. *JAOS* 103: 237–48.

———. 1987. Language, Literature and Writing at Ebla. Pp. 165–76 in *Ebla 1975–1985. Dieci anni di studi linguistici e filologici,* ed. L. Cagni. Istituto Universitario Orientale, Seminario di Studi Asiatici, Series Minor 27. Naples.

———. 1990. Early Mesopotamian Communicative Systems: Art, Literature and Writing. In *Investigating Artistic Environments in the Ancient Near East,* ed. A. Gunter. Washington, D.C.

Montevecchi, O. 1973. *La papirologia.* Manuali universitari 1. Turin.

Morpurgo Davies, A. 1986. Forms of Writing in the Ancient Mediterranean World. Pp. 51–77 in *The Written Word: Literacy in Transition; Wolfson College Lectures 1985,* ed. G. Baumann. Oxford.

Morpurgo Davies, A., and Hawkins, J. D. 1978. Il sistema grafico del luvio geroglifico. *Annali della Scuola Normale di Pisa, Classe di Lettere* 3: 755–82.

Murray, O. 1980. *Early Greece.* Sussex.

Nissen, H. J. 1985. The Emergence of Writing in the Ancient Near East. *Interdisciplinary Science Reviews* 10: 349–60.

Parpola, S. 1986. The Royal Archives of Nineveh. Pp. 223–36 in *Cuneiform Archives and Libraries: Papers Read at the 30ᵉ Rencontre Assyriologique Internationale, Leiden, 4–8 July, 1983,* ed. K. R. Veenhof. Istanbul.

Posener Kriéger, P. 1979. Le prix des étoffes. Pp. 318–31 in *Festschrift Elmar Edel 12. März 1979,* ed. M. Görg and E. Pusch. ÄAT 1. Bamberg.

Powell, M. A. 1981. Three Problems in the History of Cuneiform Writing: Origins, Direction of Script, Literacy. *Visible Language* 15: 419–40.

Reade, J. 1986. Archaeology and the Kuyunjik Archive. Pp. 213–22 in *Cuneiform Archives and Libraries: Papers Read at the 30ᵉ Rencontre Assyriologique Internationale, Leiden, 4–8 July, 1983,* ed. K. R. Veenhof. Istanbul.

Reiner, E. 1966. *A Linguistic Analysis of Akkadian.* Janua Linguarum, Series Practica 21. The Hague.

Roccati, A. 1982. *La littérature historique sous l'Ancien Empire égyptien.* LAPO. Paris.

Tait, W. J. 1977. *Papyri from Tebtunis in Egyptian and in Greek (P. Tebt. Tait).* Texts from Excavations 3. London.

Valbelle, D. 1985. *"Les ouvriers de la tombe": Deir el-Médineh à l'époque ramesside.* Institut francais d'Archéologie Orientale, Bibliothèque d'Étude 96. Cairo.

Veenhof, K. R. 1986. Cuneiform Archives: An Introduction. Pp. 1–36 in *Cuneiform Archives and Libraries: Papers Read at the 30ᵉ Rencontre Assyriologique Internationale, Leiden, 4–8 July, 1983,* ed. K. R. Veenhof. Istanbul.

Von der Way, T., and Schmidt, K. 1987. Tell el-Faraᶜin—Buto 2. Bericht. *MDAIK* 43: 241–57.

Wilhelm, G. 1982. *Grundzüge der Geschichte und Kultur der Hurriter.* Grundzüge 45. Darmstadt.

Winter, I. J. 1981. Royal Rhetoric and the Development of Historical Narrative in Neo-Assyrian Reliefs. *Studies in Visual Communication* 7: 2–38.

Yoffee, N. 1988. The Collapse of Ancient Mesopotamian States and Civilization. Pp. 44–68 in *The Collapse of Ancient States and Civilizations,* eds. N. Yoffee and G. L. Cowgill. Tucson.

Youtie, H. C. 1981. *Hupographeus:* the Social Impact of Illiteracy in Graeco-Roman Egypt; and Because They Do Not Know Letters. In *Scriptiunculae Posteriores* 1: 179–99, 255–62. Bonn.

JOHN BAINES

ANCIENT ISRAEL

The Bible itself is a witness to Hebrew and Hellenistic literacy, the products of people who wrote in the expectation that others would read their works. Who could write and who could read in ancient Israel are questions which can be discussed from two independent sources of evidence: the information contained in the OT and the information from Hebrew and other ancient inscriptions.

A. The Biblical Evidence
B. The Epigraphic Evidence
C. Conclusions

A. The Biblical Evidence

From the book of Exodus onward, writing, books, and reading are mentioned frequently and without comment. Moses is portrayed writing the terms of God's covenant with Israel (Exod 24:4), the stages of Israel's journey from Egypt to Canaan (Num 33:2), his song (Deut 31:25), and the law (Deut 31:9), the last two being written to be taught and to be read in public respectively. The laws given in writing by God (Exod 32:16; 34:1, 4) were called "the book of the law" (Deut 28:58). Other leaders, secular and religious, read and wrote: Joshua from the book of the law (Josh 1:8; 24:26), Samuel the duties of the king (1 Sam 10:25), David letters to Joab (2 Sam 11:14), Jezebel letters in Ahab's name (1 Kgs 21:8f.), the king of Damascus to the king of Israel (2 Kings 5), Jehu to men of Samaria (2 Kings 10), Hezekiah read letters from Sennacherib and Merodach-Baladan (2 Kgs 19:14; 20:12). In all these cases the rulers may have read or written themselves but, equally, secretaries ("scribes") may have acted on their behalf, for there would be no need to mention the latter's role unless it was significant for the narrative, as when Jehudi read Jeremiah's oracles to Jehoiakim and the king cut up the scroll after a few columns had been read (Jer 36:20–26). However, Deut 17:18–19 does envisage Israelite kings copying and reading the law book for themselves. Kings had their official secretaries from David's reign (2 Sam 8:17; cf. 1 Kgs 4:3; 2 Kgs 12:10), and their control presumably extended over the clerks who operated Solomon's revenue-collecting system (1 Kings 4) and whatever administrative arrangements took its place in Israel and Judah. Local centers responsible to the capital would generate a certain amount of reading and writing in normal circumstances, enabling such levies as Menahem's to be raised (2 Kgs 15:19–20). Hezekiah's Passover proclamation assumed it could be read throughout the land (2 Chr 30:6).

While tax-collecting may have brought the ordinary farmer or citizen into contact with writing on occasion, as would any regular attempt to ensure all men paid the half-shekel tax to the sanctuary (Exod 30:13; 38:25ff.; cf. Matt 17:24–27), biblical laws expected a greater familiarity with those skills. A man divorcing his wife was to write a document of divorce for her (Deut 24:1–3; cf. Isa 50:1; Jer 3:8), and God's laws were to be written on the doors and doorframes of the houses (Deut 6:9; 11:20). Evidently, reading and writing were assumed to affect life at most levels; their existence was common knowledge, even if their practice was largely in the hands of specialists, the scribes. Isaiah could meet people able to read and people unable to read (Isa 29:11–12). The public reading of the Law, even if not carried out so regularly as prescribed by Deut 31:10–13, would emphasize the role of the book (cf. 2 Kings 22). Inscribed monuments visible to travelers, would also advertise the use of writing (cf. Josh 8:30–35).

If a man had a Scriptural text on his doorpost, did that bring an awareness of books and literature? The question is almost unanswerable from the biblical text. The ubiquity of references to writing and writing materials of several kinds, using terms which are seldom foreign to the Hebrew language (Heb *qeset* 'palette' came from Eg *gst,* since the art of writing in ink originated in Egypt), does seem to imply that books were not great rarities confined to temple or palace libraries. And although many of the references occur in texts from the latter part of the Monarchy, some are to be found in parts of the Pentateuch which standard literary analysis sets in the earlier part (e.g., Exod 17:14; 24:7 in E; Exod 32:32–33 in J).

B. The Epigraphic Evidence

Writing and reading were skills 2000 years old in Babylonia and Egypt by the time Israel became a kingdom. Although the scripts of both cultures had been current in Canaan, they gave place to the locally invented alphabet at the end of the 2d millennium B.C., and it was that script which the Israelites adopted.

Examples of ancient Hebrew writing are most plentiful from the 7th century B.C. and the early 6th, that is, from the last century of Judah's existence. Most are short notes or messages written in ink on potsherds, the scrap-paper of ancient times (see WRITING AND WRITING MATERIALS). They have been found in major towns such as Jerusalem and Lachish, in military settlements like Arad and Aroer, and in smaller places like Khirbet Qumran and Vered Yericho. Labels describing contents or naming the owner were scratched or pecked on wine jars at Gibeon and many other sites.

The most common inscribed objects are stone seals bearing the owner's name, often followed by the father's name, occasionally by a title. Hundreds are known either in the original stones or from their imprints on tiny lumps of clay. These clay bullae sealed papyrus documents. This is proved both by the impressions of papyrus fibers left on the backs of the bullae and by the recovery of similar bullae still attached to papyri in Egypt (e.g., at Elephantine; see *ArchEleph,* pl. 14a). Papyrus documents will not survive in the damp soil of most Palestinian sites, but in the dehydrated conditions of the caves near the Dead Sea one fragment has lasted from this period. Originally it carried a letter, then the ink had been partially washed away and an accountancy list written over it; papyrus was costly or hard to obtain. Bullae have been found in excavations at Jerusalem and Lachish, and by chance at other sites. A hoard of 255 obtained from antiquities dealers represents an archive of scores of papyrus documents (see Avigad 1986). Seal-stones are found in burials and in settlements, one coming from a remote farmstead in the Buqei'ah valley W of Qumran. Some seals were impressed into the fabric of jars, to indicate the place of origin or the capacity or for other purposes. Another class of inscribed stone from this period is weights. Fractions of the shekel had their value incised on them in words, obviously intended to be recognized, for some of the weights differ only a little in size. Besides these regular products of scribes and engravers, there are graffiti in tombs and other places, the spur-of-the-moment scribbles of mourners or visitors (e.g., Khirbet el-Qom, Khirbet Beit Lei, the caravanserai at Kuntillet Ajrud). Formal inscriptions are rare, a fact to be attributed to the constant occupation and rebuilding of major towns rather than to a disinclination to make such things. Small pieces of inscribed monuments have been found in Jerusalem and Samaria, and tombs of the very wealthy in Silwan had carefully cut notices declaring ownership and cursing plunderers. The outstanding piece of ancient Hebrew writing is the Siloam Tunnel Inscription (*ANET,* 321), engraved on the rock wall by lamplight in a position where few people would ever see it.

Its flowing script preserves the handwriting of a proficient scribe. See SILOAM INSCRIPTION.

All of these inscriptions date from the last 150 years of Judah's history. The Samaria Ostraca, consisting of over a hundred pieces, represent the work of clerks in the Israelite capital about 775 to 750 B.C. Apart from them, there are few ancient Hebrew texts which can be dated much before 700 B.C. This does not mean there was little writing in Israel earlier in the Monarchy. The Gezer Calendar is one piece of evidence from the 10th century B.C. for a knowledge of writing in Palestine, although the text is not certainly Hebrew. The monumental possibilities of the 9th century are demonstrated by the Moabite Stone, product of a culture so close to Judah's in nature that it would be hard to suppose Hebrew scribes incapable of preparing a similar memorial.

Epigraphic evidence fails to supply any Hebrew book earlier than the Dead Sea Scrolls. One discovery does illustrate the appearance of a book in the time of Isaiah (ca. 700 B.C.). Although not a Hebrew text, the inscribed plaster fragments from Tell Deir ᶜAlla cannot preserve a very different form. Written in black ink framed at the top and left side with red rulings and with initial and certain other words in red, the text, in Aramaic script, describes visions of Balaam son of Beor. No doubt this is an enlarged version of a column of a scroll, a book about Balaam. See also DEIR ᶜALLA (TEXTS). The form is seen more extensively in the oldest surviving W Semitic book scrolls, the Aramaic papyri containing the Wisdom of Ahiqar, and a translation of Darius the Great's Behistun inscription copied in the 5th century B.C. and found at Elephantine (see Millard 1982: 150).

C. Conclusions

Measuring literacy is a subjective exercise, dependent upon definition of the term and breadth of information on hand. For a dead culture the inquiry is almost wholly confined to assessing the products of the literate members of the culture. Israel provides the rare opportunity to set the evidence of a traditional literary text, the Bible, beside epigraphic remains. At once, some speculations arising from study of the former are extinguished by the testimony of the latter. Assertions that writing was confined to palace and temple to centers of administration and cult (e.g., Phillips 1968: 194) are now disproved. The wide distribution of ostraca and graffiti beyond major towns to military outposts and farms (see Millard 1985a: 302, 310–12) attests the presence of readers and writers in such places. Even if their presence was temporary, it disseminated awareness of the skills of literacy. Discovery of Hebrew ostraca in hoards has led to the supposition that potsherds were the Hebrew scribes' normal writing material, and that all their works were short (Warner 1980: 89). This is a misunderstanding of the situation. Ostraca survive because they are all but indestructible, while papyri perish. The nature of many Hebrew ostraca implies the production of more extensive documents collating and ordering their data. Where both ostraca and papyrus records survive side by side, as they do in Egypt, notably in the Aramean–Jewish colony at Elephantine, the ostraca carry ephemeral notes, messages and lists; the papyri contain legal deeds, longer or more important letters, memoranda and other documents that were to be kept for future consultation, and ledgers incorporating the details recorded on individual ostraca. In Egypt books were written on papyrus scrolls, and it is reasonable to suppose this was also true in Israel.

Protagonists of a major role for oral tradition in ancient Israel have developed the idea that an oral community's literature was only put into writing at moments of crisis (Nielsen 1954). In the face of an enemy threat, memories were tapped and the accumulated knowledge of the population written down. Apart from the inherent unlikelihood of this scenario, the epigraphic evidence tells against it. Documents from the closing stage of an occupation have a greater likelihood of surviving. Moreover, in Babylonia and Assyria where manuscripts of literary works may bear dates, the copying was clearly done over several years before the phases ended.

The distribution of Hebrew epigraphic material is one sign of a widespread awareness of writing; another is the large number of seals, the majority bearing the owners' names without any distinctive design, so that one could be distinguished from another only by the shapes of the letters. There are too many of these seals for them to have been only the insignia of government officers in the small state of Judah over the last hundred years of its life. Clearly they belonged to a wider group of landowners, merchants, and religious personnel. Either these owners or their secretaries had to read the tiny letters to identify the seals. Some expectation that seal legends might be read is also implicit in the impressions on jars. The fact that two common types carried the words "royal property" (*lmlk*) and the name of a place (Hebron, Soco, Ziph, or Mamshit) above and below a special emblem (Lemaire 1982) suggests some value was attached to the presence of the letters. Similarly, names scratched on pots imply ability to distinguish one from another on the part of the owners, at least.

The simplicity of the alphabet may be seen as an aid to literacy because it needed far less time and effort to memorize than the hundreds of Babylonian or Egyptian signs. Conservatism in scribal circles and the integration of writing systems in the national cultures helped Babylonian and Egyptian to continue into the Christian era. The invention of a cuneiform alphabet in Ugarit during the LB Age in imitation of the Canaanite alphabet is testimony to the scribes' realization of the advantages the new script brought. The effect is shown by the greater proportion of inscribed to uninscribed seals in Israel and Judah by comparison with Assyrian and Babylonian seals, and by the occurrence of casual graffiti in alphabetic scripts.

Whether in knowledge of the skills themselves or from observation of others using them, it is arguable that many Israelite and Judean citizens were aware of writing and its powers. Nevertheless, in normal daily business it was the professional scribes who did most of the reading and writing. Scribes were active in Canaan before Israel ruled there, already known by the term *sōpēr*. (This word appears as a W Semitic loanword in an Egyptian composition of the 13th century B.C., Papyrus Anastasi I [*ANET,* 476]; it is accompanied with the determinative indicating a scribe's palette, making its meaning clear, *contra* McKane [1965: 23ff.]). Some held high positions in court (e.g., Shaphan [2 Kings 22]), others worked as secretaries to individuals (as Baruch did for Jeremiah [Jeremiah 36, 45]), or presumably hired their services to anyone who had need of them. Some people who were literate did other work. The writer of one of the Lachish Ostraca protested indignantly, "My lord has as good as said, 'You don't know how to read a letter.' As the Lord lives, no one has ever had to read a letter to me! In fact, when I've read any letter that has come to me, I've been able to repeat its contents in detail!" (Lachish Letter 3; see Lemaire 1977: 100–1). The writer was commander of a military outpost. How such a man or any scribe learned to read and write is uncertain; there may have been schools with classes of pupils, or practicing scribes may have taken apprentices. Part of the training was probably the copying of works of Hebrew literature as a means to inculcate accuracy, grammar and style, and as a mental stimulus, as it was in Egypt and Babylonia. See EDUCATION (ANCIENT ISRAEL). The range of Hebrew literature in the Bible is comparable with surviving texts from those cultures, although not identical with them, and it would be strange if such works were preserved in writing in neighboring regions yet not in Israel and Judah. It is also noteworthy that many texts were written down at the time of composition in adjacent states, including such various genres as treaties or covenants (Aramaic from Sefire, *ANET,* 531–41), narratives of victory (like the Moabite Stone, *ANET,* 320), and prophetic oracles (*ANET,* 605–7; 623–26; 629–32; cf. Millard 1985b). Israel is unlikely to have had totally different literary habits.

The biblical evidence actually complements the epigraphic. The creation of a second copy of Jeremiah's oracles is not set out as an extraordinary event (Jer 36:28–32), nor is the writing of a deed of sale (Jeremiah 32). While the number of ancient Israelites who regularly read and wrote may have been very small and mostly professional scribes, the number who possessed marginal literacy was larger, and still more would likely have been able to recognize and write their names. (At Elephantine several legal documents bear signatures in the writing of people who were not used to using a pen; see Naveh 1970: 29–30). The majority of the people would have encountered writing on some occasion and would be aware of the power and possibilities it possessed, even in quasi-magical form (cf. Num 5:11–31 and the silver amulet plaques engraved with a form of Num 6:24–27 found in a late 7th century B.C. tomb in the valley of Hinnom).

In the light of the evidence from all sources it appears that literacy reached beyond the palaces and temples of Israel and Judah to quite small settlements. This means prophetic oracles, hymns, laws could have circulated in written form from an early time to offer an authority and a control on oral tradition. In discussion of the history of the books of the OT the role of Israelite literacy deserves to be given greater prominence.

Bibliography

Avigad, N. 1986. *Hebrew Bullae from the Time of Jeremiah.* Jerusalem.

Demsky, A. 1985. On the Extent of Literacy in Ancient Israel. Pp. 349–53 in *Biblical Archaeology Today,* ed. A. Biran. Jerusalem.

Driver, G. R. 1976. *Semitic Writing from Pictograph to Alphabet.* 3d ed. Oxford.

Lemaire, A. 1977. *Inscriptions Hebraiques.* Vol. 1, *Les Ostraca.* Paris.

———. 1982. Classification des estampilles royales judéenes. *EI* 15: 54*–60*.

McKane, W. 1965. *Prophets and Wise Men.* London.

Millard, A. R. 1972. The Practice of Writing in Ancient Israel. *BA* 35: 98–112. Repr. *BAR* 4: 181–95.

———. 1982. In Praise of Ancient Scribes. *BA* 45: 143–53.

———. 1985a. An Assessment of the Evidence for Writing in Ancient Israel. Pp. 301–12 in *Biblical Archaeology Today,* ed. A. Biran. Jerusalem.

———. 1985b. La prophétie et l'écriture: Israël, Aram, Assyrie. *RHR* 202: 125–44.

Naveh, J. 1970. *The Aramaic Scripts.* Jerusalem.

Nielsen, E. 1954. *Oral Tradition.* London.

Phillips, A. 1968. The Ecstatics' Father. Pp. 183–94 in *Words and Meanings: Essays Presented to David Winton Thomas,* ed. P. R. Ackroyd and B. Lindars. Cambridge.

Warner, S. 1980. The Alphabet: An Innovation and Its Diffusion. *VT* 30: 81–90.

A. R. MILLARD

LITERATURE. Articles pertaining to the literature of the biblical world may be found under EGYPTIAN LITERATURE; HITTITE TEXTS AND LITERATURE; LITERATURE, EARLY CHRISTIAN; SUMERIAN LITERATURE; and UGARIT (TEXTS AND LITERATURE).

LITERATURE, EARLY CHRISTIAN. Early Christian literature includes all the writings of the early Church. This body of literature is made up of many different genres such as letters, gospels, acts, and apocalypses which are related to the life and thought of the particular community.

A. Canonical and Uncanonical
  1. Gospels
  2. Acts
  3. Apocalypses
B. Apostolic Fathers
  1. Clement of Rome
  2. Ignatius and Polycarp
  3. Hermas
  4. Didache, Barnabas and Others
  5. Other Epistles
C. Apologists
  1. Quadratus and Aristides
  2. Justin Martyr
  3. Tatian and Athenagoras
  4. Latin Apologists
D. Heretics
  1. Marcion
  2. Gnostic Literature
  3. Manicheans
E. Christian Writers in the West
  1. Irenaeus
  2. Hippolytus
  3. Novatian
  4. Tertullian
  5. Cyprian
F. The Alexandrian Fathers
  1. Clement of Alexandria
  2. Origen
  3. Dionysius
G. Eusebius

A. Canonical and Uncanonical

In this article "literature" is used in a comprehensive sense: it is not restricted to works which were consciously composed for literary effect, but includes occasional compositions like personal letters. Moreover, no distinction is made between canonical and uncanonical literature. Such a distinction is important theologically and ecclesiastically, but not for the study of literary history. The earliest Christian literature is indeed found in the NT; that is to say, it comprises works which the Church eventually acknowledged as canonical. But canonical and uncanonical writings overlap chronologically: thus the letter of Clement of Rome to the Corinthians certainly, and the letters of Ignatius probably, antedate the latest NT documents (2 Peter, for example).

All the literary genres found in the NT are represented in uncanonical Christian literature of the earliest centuries A.D. Alongside the letters of Paul may be set the letters of Ignatius, half a century later. Alongside the four NT Gospels stand the "apocryphal" gospels, whether orthodox or heterodox—of a later date, it is true, but following the same literary pattern. Alongside the Acts of the Apostles stand the volumes of apocryphal Acts; alongside the Revelation of John stands the *Revelation of Peter.*

Of these genres only the first (letters or epistles) was familiar in the Greco–Roman world; the other three were distinctively Christian—or, so far as apocalypses are concerned, Jewish and Christian.

1. Gospels. All four of the canonical Gospels tell the story of Jesus' ministry, from his baptism to his death and resurrection. The first three (the Synoptic Gospels) share a considerable body of primitive Christian tradition, relating to both deeds and sayings of Jesus. The inclusion of so much common material, and the combination with this of material special to each evangelist, present us with what is commonly called the SYNOPTIC PROBLEM. The gospel of John has a core of narrative material, covering the same period but representing another line of tradition; this is set in the context of a body of teaching material, mainly in the form of discourse, showing a distinctive theology and style which are characteristically Johannine.

One of the earliest of the uncanonical gospels, the *Gospel of Thomas,* is a collection of 114 sayings ascribed to Jesus. About half of these have affinities with sayings recorded in the canonical Gospels. The *Gospel of Thomas* first became known from Greek papyrus fragments unearthed at Oxyrhynchus, Egypt, at the end of the 19th and beginning of the 20th century. Its complete text, in a Coptic version, was included in one of the thirteen papyrus codices discovered at Nag Hammadi, Upper Egypt, about 1945.

The later gospels were designed in part to supply information about Jesus beyond what is found in the NT Gospels. Most of them are attached to the name of an apostle or some other prominent figure in the primitive Christian story. While the NT gospels of Matthew and Luke give some account of Jesus' birth and infancy, others—the "infancy gospels"—undertake to give details of his parentage and early days which pious readers were anxious to know. The *Protevangelium of James,* for example, begins by relating the conception, birth, and upbringing of Mary, the mother of Jesus, and goes on to describe the birth of Jesus and its immediate sequel. The *Infancy Gospel of Thomas* contains stories of Jesus' boyhood, presenting him as an infant prodigy both at school and at play.

The *Gospel of Peter,* or all that is left of it, is a "passion narrative"; it was popular in some quarters of the early Church until a bishop of Antioch, at the end of the 2d century, exposed its docetic tendency: it represented Jesus' suffering on the cross as being apparent, not real.

The *Gospel according to the Hebrews* and the *Gospel according to the Egyptians* seem to have circulated in Alexandria among Jewish and gentile Christians respectively. The former bore some kind of relationship to the canonical gospel of Matthew, but includes some material not found there, such as the account of Jesus' appearance after his resurrection to Matthew's brother James (cf. 1 Cor 15:7). The *Gospel according to the Egyptians* has more of a gnostic tinge, as in Jesus' declaration to Salome, "I have come to destroy the works of the female." This implies an end to the cycle of conception, birth, parenthood, and death, with the reunion of male and female (or the reabsorption of the female in the male) in one person, as in the time before the formation of Eve.

The motif of Jesus' imparting further teaching to his disciples after his resurrection (cf. Acts 1:3) is found in a number of early Christian writings. About the middle of the 3d century, for example, an Egyptian gnostic wrote a Greek work known as *Pistis Sophia. Pistis Sophia* ("Faith Wisdom") probably represents the human soul, endeavoring to attain salvation. The work survives in a Coptic version. In it Jesus continues to live with his disciples for eleven or twelve years after his resurrection and tells them many things about salvation, especially in reply to questions, asked preeminently by Mary Magdalene (see PISTIS SOPHIA).

2. Acts. In the second half of the 2d century, there began to appear a body of "Acts" literature, of the same general character as the NT Acts of the Apostles, ascribed to Paul, Peter, Andrew, John, and Thomas.

The *Acts of Paul,* composed about 160 by a presbyter of one of the churches of Asia ("from love of Paul," as he said), is an early example of Christian fiction. It records various adventures of Paul; the most popular part of the work describes the activities of his female disciple Thecla. Unlike the Paul of the Pastoral Epistles, the Paul of this work deprecates marriage but promotes freedom of ministry for Christian women. The author's good intentions were not appreciated by his church leaders; he was deposed from the presbyterate (Tert. *De Bapt.* 17).

The *Acts of Peter* deal with Peter's residence in Rome, culminating with his crucifixion under Nero. The work includes an account of his encounter in Rome with Simon Magus. The *Acts of Andrew* (early 3d century) tell of Andrew's apostolic activity and his martyrdom at Patras. The *Acts of Thomas* and *Acts of John* are gnosticizing works. The former relates Thomas' evangelizing of India; it includes a beautiful poem called the *Hymn of the Soul,* about a prince who goes down to Egypt to recover a pearl of great price. The latter is said to have been composed by one Leucius, after whom all five of these *Acts* compositions are sometimes, but misleadingly, called the Leucian *Acts.* The *Acts of John* contains a poem, the *Hymn of Christ,* which has been set to music (as the *Hymn of Jesus*) by Gustav Holst; like the rest of the work, the hymn portrays a docetic Christ.

The works called the *Clementines,* claiming the authority

of Clement of Rome, share some of the characteristics of the apocryphal Acts. Two treatises deserve special notice: the *Clementine Homilies* and the *Clementine Recognitions.* These are to be dated in the 3d or early 4th century, but are based in part on earlier documents no longer extant, such as the *Acts of James* and the *Travels of Peter.*

The *Clementine Homilies,* which are introduced by an *Epistle of Peter to James,* comprise twenty discourses sent by Clement in Rome to James of Jerusalem; they give an account of Clement's travels in the East, where he met Peter and witnessed his contest with Simon Magus. The *Clementine Recognitions* record the adventures of Clement's parents and brothers, who lose touch with one another until they are "recognized" by Peter and reunited with one another and with Clement. Their theological tendency is Judaistic and Gnostic, but this probably belongs more to their sources than to their final authors.

3. Apocalypses. Apocalyptic literature originated in a Jewish milieu, although the work from which it is so called is the NT Revelation of John (the Apocalypse or "unveiling" par excellence). Apocalypses usually take the form of visions in which the seer, often a figure from earlier times (like Enoch), is shown things inaccessible to ordinary knowledge, such as the unexplored recesses of outer space or the mysteries of the divine purpose regarding future events.

The Revelation of John, firmly based in the contemporary situation in which the Church's prospects seemed hopeless, with the might of the Roman Empire deployed against it, looks forward to the triumph and universal sovereignty of Christ and his persecuted followers.

The *Revelation* (or *Apocalypse*) *of Peter,* which was read in some churches as an apostolic work from the late 2d to the 5th century, paints lurid word-pictures of the fate of the damned in the afterlife, and for long exercised an influence on Christian art, as in Dante's *Inferno* and Gustav Doré's illustrations of it.

A number of less important apocalyptic writings were current in the early Christian centuries. There was, for example, the *Apocalypse of Paul,* which undertook to divulge the "things that cannot be told" which the apostle heard on the occasion when he was "caught up to the third heaven" (2 Cor 12:2–4); it was evidently composed in the 4th century and had only a limited circulation.

B. Apostolic Fathers.

The Apostolic Fathers, so called since the 17th century, are a group of Christian writers of the first few generations after the apostolic age, from the end of the 1st century to about the middle of the 2d.

1. Clement of Rome. Clement, foreign secretary of the church in Rome, is credited with the authorship of a letter sent by that church to the church in Corinth, expostulating with it for its unruly behavior (commonly dated ca. A.D. 96). The so-called *Second Letter of Clement* is an anonymous homily of rather later date.

2. Ignatius and Polycarp. Of great importance are the seven letters which Ignatius, bishop of Antioch, sent to six churches and one individual when he was being taken through Asia Minor on his way to martyrdom in the Roman Colosseum (ca. A.D. 115). The one individual to whom he sent a letter was Polycarp, bishop of Smyrna. A letter of Polycarp has survived (possibly a combination of two letters) in which he replies to a request from the Christians of Philippi for copies of the letters of Ignatius which they thought he might be able to procure for them. Polycarp was a true "apostolic father" in the sense that he was believed to be a disciple of the apostles; he lived on to suffer martyrdom at the age of eighty-six (A.D. 155/6). An account of the *Martyrdom of Polycarp* has been preserved among the Apostolic Fathers.

3. Hermas. The *Shepherd of Hermas* is a work, partly allegorical and partly apocalyptic, composed by a Roman Christian early in the 2d century. It deals with moral problems which ordinary Christians were likely to encounter in daily life and attained great popularity in the West; at one time it almost made its way into the NT canon.

4. Didache, Barnabas and Others. The DIDACHE, or *Teaching of the Lord to the Gentiles through the Apostles* (a title based on Matt 28:18–20), is a primitive manual of church order, originating perhaps in Syria towards the end of the 1st century. (Later manuals of church order, such as the 3d-century *Didascalia* and the 4th-century *Apostolic Constitutions,* were modeled on the *Didache.*) Among the traditional material which the *Didache* contains is a body of ethical teaching, possibly of Jewish origin, called "The Two Ways"—the way of life and the way of death. This body of teaching appears also in the *Letter of Barnabas,* a document of approximately the same date, apparently of Alexandrian origin. The *Letter of Barnabas* is concerned to show that the Jews have misinterpreted the levitical ordinances of the OT by taking them literally; when they are understood allegorically, they are seen to impart moral lessons of permanent and universal validity.

5. Other Epistles. The anonymous *Letter to Diognatus* was sent by a Christian writer in the second half of the 2d century to an inquirer. It reveals a deep appreciation of the love of God displayed in the gospel and compares Christians' relation to the world with that of the soul to the body.

The *Epistle of the Apostles,* having come to light only in 1895, has not been conventionally included among the Apostolic Fathers. It purports to be a letter addressed to the churches by the apostles (including Nathanael, with Peter and Cephas named as two separate persons) and summarizes the main articles of Christian faith and hope. It was written in Greek, apparently in the province of Asia about the middle of the 2d century, but is known only from Latin, Coptic, and Ethiopic versions.

C. Apologists

One variety of Christian literature which flourished during the 2d century was apologetic. Christian apologists wrote to defend their faith against popular slander and official repression, and also against rival forms of belief and worship such as Judaism and Greek and Roman paganism.

1. Quadratus and Aristides. Some of the earliest works in this category, mentioned in ancient writings, are almost entirely lost, like the *Apology* of Quadratus, who about A.D. 124 addressed a defense of Christianity to the emperor Hadrian. Eusebius (*Hist. Eccl.* 4.3.2) preserves one sentence from it, in which Quadratus claims to have seen in his youth some people who had been healed, and even raised from the dead, by Jesus.

The *Apology* of Aristides, surviving complete in a Syriac version and partially in some other forms, was addressed to Antoninus Pius (138–161); it reviews other religions and concludes that Christians have a worthier appreciation of God than Greeks, barbarians, or Jews.

2. Justin Martyr. One of the greatest Greek apologists was the philosophically trained Justin, who addressed a lengthy defense of Christianity to Antoninus Pius and his two designated successors, and a shorter one, some time later, to the Roman senate. He argues that Christian faith is entirely harmonious with reason and defends Christians against current calumnies. These defenses brought Justin no advantage: he was executed, with a number of his fellow-Christians, about 165, by sentence of the Roman urban prefect (their trial is reported in the almost contemporary *Acts of Justin*). His Apology provides incidental information about Christian life and church practice in his day. Another of his works, his *Dialogue with Trypho the Jew* (ca. 140), undertakes to prove that the Church is the true Israel, in which the law and the prophets find their proper fulfillment.

3. Tatian and Athenagoras. Justin's pupil Tatian, an Assyrian by birth, wrote an *Address to the Greeks,* which defends the antiquity and purity of Christianity over against Greek paganism. Whereas Justin ascribed all that was good and true in Greek culture to the divine "word" (*logos*) which in due course became incarnate in Jesus, Tatian dismissed Greek culture and religion alike as wholly evil. Tatian is best known as compiler of the *Diatessaron,* a rearrangement of the four canonical gospels in which their component parts were unstitched and reassembled so as to form one continuous narrative (ca. 170).

Tatian's contemporary Athenagoras addressed a *Supplication* to Marcus Aurelius and his son Commodus (ca. 177), refuting defamatory reports about Christian morality. He also wrote a work on the resurrection of the dead.

4. Latin Apologists. Chief among the Latin apologists are Minucius Felix (early 3d century), whose *Octavius* reports a debate between a Christian and his pagan friend, which results in the pagan's conversion, and (most outstanding of all) Tertullian of Carthage, whose *Apology* (ca. 197), addressed to the governors of Roman provinces, exposes the absurdity of the accusations popularly leveled against Christians, and argues that those accusations can more properly be leveled against pagan deities.

It is not clear that the emperors and magistrates to whom these works were addressed ever saw them; there is certainly nothing to suggest that they had any effect on public policy toward Christians.

D. Heretics

The word "heretics" is used here in no pejorative sense: it denotes those Christian teachers who deviated from the line maintained by the leaders of churches which claimed to have been founded by apostles.

1. Marcion. Marcion, from Sinope on the Black Sea, produced (ca. 144) the first edition of the Greek NT of which anything is known. His edition, published at Rome, presented a text which reflected his dogmatic presuppositions. He was a wholehearted devotee of Paul, dedicated (like him) to the gospel of free grace; but he made a sharp cleavage between the Creator God of the OT, the God of Israel, and the previously unknown God whom Jesus revealed as the Father. The OT, he held, had nothing to do with the Christian revelation, and NT passages which seemed to recognize the authority of the OT were removed from the text, as being self-evidently corruptions introduced by judaizers.

Along with his edition of the NT Marcion issued a series of *Antitheses,* setting out the incompatibility of the two Gods and of the dispensations of law and gospel proceeding respectively from the one God and from the other. The *Antitheses* have not survived, apart from the lyrical celebration of divine grace which introduced them: "O wealth of riches! Ecstasy, power and amazement! Nothing can be said about it, nor even imagined about it, neither can it be compared with anything!"

2. Gnostic Literature. Gnosticism was a phenomenon of great diversity: it may be regarded as a general term for an alternative interpretation of Christianity to that handed down in the "apostolic tradition"—although it made its own claim to reproduce the apostles' teaching. The knowledge (*gnōsis*) which it cultivated was the knowledge of salvation. This in itself did not distinguish it from the apostolic tradition: much depended on the definitions of "knowledge" and "salvation." For the gnostics the essence of the primordial fall was the soul's loss of the true knowledge through contamination contracted from the material order; salvation lay in the recovery of the true knowledge. To aid human beings in its recovery was the function of the Savior. The descent of the Savior, his rescuing of those who, through loss of the true knowledge, found themselves astray in an unfriendly universe, and his raising them with him to the realm of light to which he and they originally belonged, was the story set forth in a variety of mythological forms.

Until 1945 knowledge of the tenets of Gnosticism was derived largely from the critiques of its opponents: since then the situation has been changed by the discovery of a gnostic library near Nag Hammadi in Upper Egypt—about fifty treatises in thirteen leather-bound codices. The treatises (copied in the 4th century A.D.) are preserved in Coptic; behind most of them lies a Greek original. Various gnostic schools are represented in the library: some of the most important emanated from the school of Valentinus (ca. A.D. 140), e.g., the *Gospel of Truth* (a meditation on the saving work of Jesus), the *Gospel of Philip,* and a treatise on the resurrection called the *Letter to Rheginus.*

Ptolemy, probably Valentinus' successor as head of his school, states his theological position in his *Letter to Flora* (preserved by the 4th-century writer Epiphanius); he undertakes to show (against Marcion) that the OT, properly understood—i.e., allegorically understood in accordance with Valentinian principles—retains its value for Christians.

An earlier gnostic writer, Basilides, wrote an exegetical work in twenty-four volumes, but only the merest fragments survive. He is credited with the composition of a *Gospel of Basilides,* but nothing certain is known of it.

3. Manicheans. One interesting gnostic development was Manicheism, originating with Mani (ca. 215–277), self-styled "Apostle of Jesus Christ," who resided for a good part of his life in Persia, and on March 20, 242, announced himself as a new prophet. Although Manicheism may have started as a Christian heresy, it developed into a new missionary religion, drawing in part on Zoroastrianism and Buddhism, which for a time rivaled Christianity. Its main feature was its thoroughgoing dualism, in which Light and Darkness were two equal and opposite principles. It was totally world-renouncing. Augustine was a Manichean for nine years (373–382) before his conversion to Christianity.

Manicheism gave rise to a rich literature, most of it surviving now in fragments in Central Asian languages, which, however, can scarcely be subsumed under Christian literature.

E. Christian Writers in the West

The teaching of the gnostics and others called forth replies and refutations from defenders of the apostolic tradition. Justin Martyr, for example, wrote a treatise *Against Marcion* which, unfortunately, has not survived.

1. Irenaeus. The greatest of the antiheretical writers of the late 2d century was Irenaeus (ca. 130–200), a native of the province of Asia who about A.D. 177 became bishop of Lyon in Gaul. He was able to view the contemporary state of Christian belief and life from a broad perspective. His work *Against Heresies,* in five volumes (surviving mainly in a Latin translation from the original Greek and partly in an Armenian translation), includes a critique of several gnostic schools. While his account of them is consistently hostile, it is shown to be reasonably accurate by the evidence of the gnostic library from Nag Hammadi. The positive element in his work is his establishment of the apostolic tradition: the rule of faith, handed down without change through a succession of bishops in those churches which were founded by apostles, provides a test by which everything that claims to be authentic Christianity can be assessed.

Another work of Irenaeus, *The Demonstration of the Apostolic Preaching,* presents an outline of the plan of salvation; it is extant only in an Armenian translation.

2. Hippolytus. In the following generation Hippolytus (died 235), a great scholar, bishop for a time of a schismatic Christian community in Rome, was the last significant Roman Christian to write in Greek. He wrote a number of exegetical works: His commentary on Daniel (ca. 204) seems to be the earliest orthodox commentary on any biblical book. His main work, in ten volumes, is entitled *The Refutation of All Heresies.*

3. Novatian. If Hippolytus was the last Roman Christian of significance to write in Greek, the first to write in Latin was Novatian (like Hippolytus, the leader of a dissident body, the Novatianists). A few treatises by him are extant; among them by far the most important is a well-constructed work *On the Trinity* (ca. 250).

4. Tertullian. Across the Mediterranean, in North Africa, Christian writings in Latin appeared in the last quarter of the 2d century. Tertullian of Carthage, whose *Apology* has been mentioned above, wrote voluminously on Christian doctrine and practice. In matters of Christian practice he took a uniformly puritan line, especially after his conversion (ca. 206) to Montanism, a charismatic movement which arose in Phrygia about the middle of the 2d century. He was a scathing controversialist, and wrote several antiheretical works: *Against Marcion, Against the Valentinians,* and others. Although his language in these works is hostile and abusive, his representation of the views which he attacks is generally reliable. It is to him, for example, that we owe much of what is known about Marcion's New Testament. Tertullian contributed weightily to the vocabulary of Latin Christianity. It is in his writings, for instance, that we first meet the word *trinitas* ("trinity").

5. Cyprian. Cyprian, bishop of Carthage (martyred 258), wrote a number of letters and treatises which, while they showed nothing of the intellectual power of Tertullian, expressed a pastoral concern which won them great popularity. His treatise *On the Unity of the Catholic Church* was specially influential in the early Church; even today its influence remains.

F. The Alexandrian Fathers

From 180 onward the church of Alexandria in Egypt was enriched by a succession of great teachers who were also prolific writers; many of their works have survived, though many more have been lost.

1. Clement of Alexandria. Clement, probably an Athenian by birth, lived in Alexandria between 180 and 202 and taught in the catechetical school which had been set up in that city by Pantaenus. Clement's surviving writings include the *Protrepticus* (an introduction to Christian ethics), a treatise on the gospel incident of the rich ruler (Mark 10:17–31), a collection of extracts from the OT prophets and another of extracts from the works of Theodotus (a disciple of Valentinus), and eight volumes of *Stromateis* or "miscellanies"—a wide-ranging and discursive work maintaining that Christian knowledge (*gnōsis*) is preferable to any other kind. Clement was a man of classical culture, and saw no reason why it should not be enlisted in the service of Christian truth: to his mind "the truth-loving Plato" speaks at times "as if divinely inspired" (*Strom.* 1.8).

2. Origen. Origen (185–254), a native of Alexandria, became head of the catechetical school soon after Clement's departure from the city, when he was barely out of his teens. In 231 he left Alexandria and lived from then on at Caesarea in Palestine. Most of his surviving works have unfortunately been preserved only in a Latin translation which does not always do justice to his thought: for one thing his translator, Rufinus of Aquileia (ca. 345–410), tries to make him conform to the orthodoxy of a later age. Origen has left a work *On First Principles,* in four volumes, containing a systematic exposition of the Christian faith, and an important defense of Christianity, in eight volumes, *Against Celsus* (a Platonic philosopher who about 178 had published an attack on Christianity in his *True Word*). Origen's *Hexapla* was an edition of the biblical text in six parallel columns (the OT comprised the Hebrew text and a transliteration into Greek characters, together with four different Greek versions). In its entirety it probably existed only in the original copy. Origen was an indefatigable commentator on the biblical writings, but most of his commentaries are lost. By the standards of later Christian generations he was judged to be in some respects heretical, but he was the eastern church's greatest scholar, and its greatest theologian before Athanasius (295–373).

3. Dionysius. Origen's pupil Dionysius, who became bishop of Alexandria in 247, was an able theologian with a rare sense of literary style. This appears, for example, in the course of his treatise *On the Promises,* in which he criticizes the literal millenarianism of Nepos, another Egyptian bishop. He points out that the Apocalypse, on which Nepos had based his arguments, has no apostolic authority, since stylistic criteria prove that the John who wrote it was not the author of the Fourth Gospel. This treatise, like the rest of his many works, has been preserved only in extracts quoted by later authors.

G. Eusebius

Our survey is designed to terminate at the end of the 3d century. One exception must be made—Eusebius (ca. 260–339), a native of Palestinian Caesarea, who became bishop of the church there in 314. The reason for including him is that he preserves quotations from so many earlier writings that are otherwise lost. It is he, for instance, who preserves the comment of Dionysius of Alexandria on the authorship of the Apocalypse. An older writer from whom he quotes is Papias, bishop of Hierapolis about A.D. 125, who in his five volumes of *Exegesis of the Lord's Oracles* recorded much primitive Christian oral tradition which he had assiduously collected. This compilation has been lost for centuries, apart from passages quoted by Eusebius and one or two other writers.

Eusebius' writings include his *Preparation for the Gospel,* his *Demonstration of the Gospels,* his *Martyrs of Palestine,* and—most important of all—his *Church History.* This work traces the advance of Christianity, especially in the E Mediterranean world, from NT times to his own day, to the eve of the Council of Nicaea (325). In spite of infelicities of construction and style, this is a work of inestimable value both in its own right and especially for its inclusion of extracts from many earlier Christian works which are no longer extant. Those works were accessible to him in the library of Caesarea accumulated by his mentor Pamphilus (martyred 309). Eusebius reproduced his extracts with remarkable accuracy: "in no instance where we can test does Eusebius give a doubtful testimony" (Lightfoot 1889: 49). He was highly esteemed by the emperor Constantine, and composed his panegyric at his death in 337. Despite its lavish flattery, this panegyric contains valuable historical material.

Bibliography

Altaner, B. 1960. *Patrology.* Trans. H. C. Graef. 1958. Freiburg and Edinburgh-London.
Aune, D. E. 1987. *The New Testament in its Literary Environment.* Philadelphia and Cambridge.
Bettenson, H., ed. and trans. 1969. *The Early Christian Fathers.* London.
Campenhausen, H. von. 1963. *The Fathers of the Greek Church.* Eng. trans rev by L. A. Garrard. London.
———. 1964. *The Fathers of the Latin Church.* Trans. M. Hoffmann. London.
Chadwick, H. 1966. *Early Christian Thought and the Classical Tradition.* Oxford.
Foerster, W. 1972. *Gnosis: A Selection of Gnostic Texts.* Vol. 1. Ed. and trans. R. McL. Wilson. Oxford.
———. 1974. *Gnosis: A Selection of Gnostic Texts.* Vol. 2. Ed. and trans. R. McL. Wilson. Oxford.
Goodspeed, E. J. 1937. *An Introduction to the New Testament.* Chicago.
———. 1950. *The Apostolic Fathers: An American Translation.* New York.
———. 1966. *A History of Early Christian Literature.* Rev. and enl. by R. M. Grant. Chicago.
Grant, R. M. 1961. *Gnosticism: An Anthology.* London.
———. 1988. *Greek Apologists of the Second Century.* London.
Hennecke, E. 1963–65. *New Testament Apocrypha.* 2 vols. Ed. W. Schneemelcher and R. McL. Wilson. London.
Koester, H. 1982. *Introduction to the New Testament.* 2 vols. Philadelphia.
Lightfoot, J. B. 1889. *Essays on the Work Entitled "Supernatural Religion."* London.
Pagels, E. 1979. *The Gnostic Gospels.* New York.
Robinson, J. M., ed. 1977. *The Nag Hammadi Library in English.* Leiden.
Schoeps, H.-J. 1949. *Theologie und Geschichte des Judenchristentums.* Tübingen.
Wallace-Hadrill, D. S. 1960. *Eusebius of Caesarea.* London.

F. F. BRUCE

LITTLE APOCALYPSE IN THE GOSPELS. See GOSPELS, LITTLE APOCALYPSE IN THE.

LITURGY, ANGELIC (4QShirShabb). See SONGS OF THE SABBATH SACRIFICE.

LIVES OF THE PROPHETS. See PROPHETS, LIVES OF THE.

LIVING CREATURES. See ZOOLOGY.

LIZARD. See ZOOLOGY.

LMLK JAR HANDLES. See STAMPS, ROYAL JAR HANDLE.

LO-AMMI (PERSON) [Heb *lōʾ ʿammî*]. See NOT MY PEOPLE (PERSON).

LO-DEBAR (PLACE) [Heb *lô dĕbār; lōʾ dĕbār*]. A non-Israelite city-state located in the Transjordan N of the Yarmuk River, near the watercourse. The name is variously spelled: Heb *lô dĕbār* in 2 Sam 9:4–5, and Heb *lōʾ dĕbār* in 2 Sam 17:27; Amos 6:13. In Amos 6:13, the name plays on its two Hebrew elements (*lōʾ* "no"; *dābār* "thing") meaning "nothing," which highlights the predicted punishment in v 14. Similar in spelling is Heb *lidĕbīr,* translated in RSV "to Debir," but possibly a variant spelling of the name "Lidebir." Though the etymology of the name is unclear, and quadraliteral roots are not characteristically Semitic, the single form *ldbr* is more likely to be a place name than the ambiguous word combination *lwʾdbr*; thus Lidebir is to be preferred.

In the days of Saul, either Ammiel or his son Machir ruled the city which appears to have become an ally of the new Israelite state. In view of the secret political asylum granted to Jonathan's infant son Meribaal after the death of Saul and his three eldest sons at Gilboa, some sort of preexisting political ties presumably existed between the two states. In the wake of the discovery that Machir was harboring Meribaal, it is likely that he was forced to become David's vassal. Machir performed vassal obligations to David along with Shobi ben Nahash of Ammon, and Barzillai of Rogelim in Gilead, by supplying troops and provisions to David during his conflict with Absalom.

In the Iron Age II period, Lidebir apparently became a satellite of Aram-Damascus. Jeroboam II, king of Israel (785–745 B.C.) is credited with restoring Israel's borders to their former limits under David, and with gaining control over Damascus and Hamath again (2 Kgs 14:23, 28). If the report is reliable, the states and their dependents probably were made vassals rather than being incorporated into Israel's boundaries as administrative districts (cf. David's policy to this effect mentioned above). Amos 6:13 seems to reflect the beginning of Jeroboam II's expansion into traditional Syrian territory in its allusion to the capture of Lidebir and its reference to the capture of Karnaim, often identified with mod. Tell Ashtarah (M.R. 243244), in the SE Golan heights.

The general site location can be determined from the boundary of Gad described in Josh 13:24–28. The phrase, "from Mahanaim to the border of Lidebir" (v 26b) is likely a secondary addition to the original Gadite description. The traditional homeland of Gad lay S of the River Jabbok, and Mahanaim was probably situated on the N bank of the river, and thus represented the southernmost boundary point for the territory of half-Manasseh. In light of the report in 1 Chr 5:16–17 that during the reign of Jotham, king of Judah, the Gadites dwelt "in Gilead, in Bashan and in its towns, and in all the pasture lands of Sharon to its limits," one can conclude that in the years preceding Jotham's reign the tribe of Gad expanded into the traditional territory of half-Manasseh. Verse 26b can be understood to reflect this expansion, and to represent the S and N boundary points, respectively, of the former territory of half-Manasseh.

Because the Gadites' expanded holdings in Gilead abutted, but did not encompass Lidebir, and the Yarmuk River represents the traditional N boundary of Gilead, it is logical to seek a site on the N bank of the Yarmuk for the city. Past suggestions of Tell Mghanne (Noth 1959: 45; Ottosson 1969: 128); Tell el Hamme (Metzger 1960: 101); Umm ed-Dabar (*GP*, 70; M.R. 207219); Khirbet Hamid (Mittmann 1970: 244); or Ibdar (*EncBib* 4: 2810), all of which lie S of the Yarmuk, are inconsistent with the biblical evidence. A possible candidate would be Tell Dober (M.R. 209232), strategically situated below the southwesternmost tip of the Golan, N of the Yarmuk, facing the Jordan Valley plain lying S and SE of the Sea of Galilee. The site has evidence of occupation in both Iron Age I and II (Kochavi 1972: 292), and lies along one of the proposed ancient routes by which one would have gained access to the international trade center of Damascus from Trans- and Cis-jordan (Mazar, Biran, and Dunayevsky 1964: 2). Saul's probable establishment of ties with Lidebir should be viewed in light of the city's proposed role as controller of access to the Golan from his state's territory.

Bibliography

Kochavi, M., ed. 1972. *Judaea, Samaria, and the Golan: Archaeological Survey 1967–1968*. Jerusalem.

Mazar, B.; Biran, A.; and Dunayevsky, I. 1964. ʿEin Gev Excavations in 1961. *IEJ* 14: 1–49.

Metzger, M. 1960. Lodebar und der *tell mghanne*. *ZDPV* 76: 97–102.

Mittmann, S. 1970. *Beiträge zur Siedlungs- und Territorialgeschichte des nördlichen Ostjordanlandes*. Wiesbaden.

Noth, M. 1959. Gilead und Gad. *ZDPV* 75: 14–73.

Ottosson, M. 1969. *Gilead: Tradition and History*. Lund.

Diana V. Edelman

LO-RUHAMAH (PERSON) [Heb *lōʾ rūḥamâ*]. See NOT PITIED (PERSON).

LOAN. See INTEREST AND USURY IN THE GRECO-ROMAN PERIOD.

LOCUST. See ZOOLOGY.

LOD (PLACE) [Heb *lōd*]. Var. LYDDA. A town in the N Shephelah whose founding was attributed to (one of) the sons of Elpaal, a Benjaminite (1 Chr 8:12). Its traditional location is modern Lod/el-Ludd (M.R. 140151), on the S bank of the wadi el-Kabir near the intersection of the main E–W road from Jerusalem to Joppa and the main N–S road from Damascus and Mesopotamia to Egypt. Although the Chronicler, perhaps influenced by the postexilic resettlement of Lod by Benjaminites (Ezra 2:23 = Neh 7:37; Neh 11:35), attributes the founding of Lod to a Benjaminite, the town's earliest tribal associations may have first been with Dan and then with Ephraim.

A. Historical Sources

While Aharoni and Avi-Yonah suggest that Lod may appear as #44 in the second group of Egyptian Execration texts (*MBA*, 26), its first definite mention is in the conquest list of Thutmose III (*ANET*, 263, #64). Lod is not mentioned again in ancient sources until the Persian period, so it may have been unoccupied during the latter part of the LB Age and the Iron Age. After its resettlement by Benjaminites in the early Persian period, Lod seems to have formed the westernmost extension of the territory of Judah, although several scholars have questioned whether the region of Lod actually formed part of the Jewish province (*GTTOT*, 392). Neh 11:35 suggests that Jews may have continued to live in Lod even during the Exile.

By the Hellenistic period the name of Lod had evolved into Lydda. During the reign of the Seleucid king Demetrius II (145 B.C.) Lydda, along with Apherima and Ramathea, was transferred from the control of Samaria to that of Judea (1 Macc 11:34; *Ant* 13.4.9 §127). Lydda subsequently became the capital of one of the eleven districts of Judea (*JW* 3.3.5 §54–55). During the time of the Roman civil war following the death of Julius Caesar, Cassius sold the people of Lydda into slavery for failure to pay the taxes needed to support his army (*Ant* 14.11.4 §275). After his victory over Cassius at Philippi in 42 B.C., Mark Antony restored the inhabitants of Lydda (*Ant* 14.12.2 §304–5).

The apostle Paul visited Lydda, where he healed Aneas, who had been bedridden for eight years (Acts 9:32–38). News of this miracle is said to have converted many people in Lydda and the Sharon, and to have prompted Peter's call to Joppa to raise Tabitha from the dead. Lydda was burned by Cestius and the 12th Legion early in the First Jewish Revolt, when all but fifty of its citizens were on a pilgrimage to Jerusalem for the Feast of Tabernacles (*JW* 2.19.1 §515). After Cestius' defeat, the Lydda region was placed under the command of John the Essene (*JW* 2.20.4 §567). When Vespasian marched against Jerusalem, his army resettled the ruins of Lydia with a population which included Jews loyal to Rome (*JW* 4.8.1 §445).

Around the time of Septimius Severus (A.D. 193–211), the city received the status of a Roman colony and was renamed Diospolis. Its Christian community was strong during the Byzantine period; Diospolis sent a bishop to the Council of Nicaea, and a Synod was convened there in 415. The town regained its traditional name after the Arab conquest. Lydda was believed to be the site of the martyrdom of St. George, and for a time the Crusaders referred to the town as St. George.

MELVIN HUNT

B. Archaeological Excavations

Today the ruins of ancient Lod are completely covered by modern buildings, thus preventing efforts to excavate the ruins of the historic town. However, on the N side there are a few houses and the edge of the mound was cut away, thus forming a section 2.5 m deep. In December 1951–January 1952 excavations were briefly conducted in three small areas at the site: (1) the N edge of the mound (area A); (2) the two sides of a small ravine (area B); and (3) a level area N of the cut mentioned above (area C). Neolithic and Chalcolithic remains were unearthed.

In area A, a trench was dug running from the base of the mound toward the summit, exposing part of a circular structure built of rubble. Beneath this structure was a mud-brick wall built on the sandy soil. Altogether, four phases of occupation could be distinguished in this section of the mound, all dating to EB I.

A dump of grey earth was discovered in area B, containing pottery resembling the Chalcolithic cultures of Wadi Rabah (stratum II), Jericho stratum VIII, and Ghassul. See RABAH, WADI; GHASSUL, TULEILAT EL-). The pottery of the first two types included sherds of jars with bow rims, splay-ended loop handles, and "black-burnished ware." Among the Ghassulian sherds were lug handles with triangular sections, cornets, and churns.

Shallow pits dug into the sand and containing Neolithic pottery were found in area C. Most of the pottery was characteristic of Jericho IX ware both in decoration and in form (see Kaplan 1969), providing a rare opportunity to examine such an assemblage this far from the Jordan rift.

Bibliography

Kaplan, J. 1957. Excavations at Lydda. *Bulletin of the Department of Antiquities of Israel* 5: 39–40 (in Hebrew).

———. 1969. A Suggested Correlation Between Stratum IX, Jericho, and Stratum XXIV, Mersin. *JNES* 28: 197–99.

———. 1977. Neolithic and Chalcolithic Remains at Lod. *EI* 13: 57–75 (in Hebrew).

JACOB KAPLAN

LOG [Heb *lōg*]. See WEIGHTS AND MEASURES.

LOGIA. Logia is a loan word from Greek (pl. of *logion,* a diminutive of *logos,* or "word") meaning "oracles" or "sayings." Among ancient Christian writers the term is employed in a variety of ways, referring to sayings of Jesus (e.g., Pol. *Phil.* 7:1; Eus., *Hist. Eccl.* 9.7.15), but also to accounts of things Jesus did (Eus., *Hist. Eccl.,* 3.39.15), to OT passages (Eus., *Hist. Eccl.,* 9.9.7; 10.1.4; etc.), or even to the OT as a whole (*1 Clem.* 19:1; 53:1; 62:3; Eus., *Hist. Eccl.,* 5.17.5; 6.23.2; 10.4.43). In the technical parlance of NT scholarship, however, it has come to refer specifically to *sayings* attributed to Jesus. This technical usage probably derives from R. Bultmann, who used its German equivalent as a formal category within which to consider the wisdom sayings attributed to Jesus in the synoptic tradition (73ff.). Taking the Greek term *logoi* ("words") as its virtual synonym, J. M. Robinson used Bultmann's formal category as a point of departure, and traced the use of *logia/logoi* by early Christian authors to designate collections of Jesus' sayings, such as the *Gospel of Thomas,* whose incipit reads: "These are the secret words (Coptic: *nshaje* = Greek: *logoi* or *logia*) which the Living Jesus spoke . . ." Other such early Christian sayings collections would have included the synoptic sayings source (Q) used by Matthew and Luke, the collection of sayings and parables in Mark 4:1–34, and the chain of sayings that occurs in *1 Clem.* 13:2. Robinson coined the term *logoi sophon* ("sayings of the wise") to serve as an appropriate name for this genre of early Christian writing, and duly noted the very close relationship of these collections to similar collections to be found in Jewish wisdom literature, as well as the wisdom literature of other Near Eastern cultures.

It is curious that, apart from the *Gospel of Thomas,* these early collections of Jesus' logia managed to survive antiquity only when they were incorporated into some other genre, such as the narrative gospel, from which they must now be reconstructed if they are to be studied at all. This may perhaps be taken as an indication that relatively early in its historical development, the Church lost interest in Jesus' sayings, or logia, as the focus of its theological reflection, preferring instead forms and genres that allowed for a wider range of christological imagining, going beyond the simple notion of Jesus as Wisdom's sage. It may also be that as the early Church moved gradually away from the socially radical lifestyle that Theissen and others have associated with the synoptic sayings tradition, it soon found the older collections of logia less appealing than narrative gospels, in which the radicalism of the itinerant sage could be softened, and stories depicting Jesus disputing with local figures such as the "Pharisees" could be introduced to better reflect and comment upon the conflicts these settled Christians were now having with their neighbors. Consequently, many of the logia the early Church attributed to Jesus are to be found today where the tradition has imbedded them artificially in an apophthegmatic context, in which the saying could be harnessed to address a particular *Sitz im Leben* of the early Church.

Bibliography

Bultmann, R. 1979. *Die Geschichte der synoptischen Tradition*. 9th ed. Gottingen.

Kloppenborg, J. 1987. *The Formation of Q: Trajectories in Ancient Wisdom Collections*. Studies in Antiquity and Christianity. Philadelphia.

Robinson, J. M. 1971. *LOGOI SOPHON:* On the *Gattung* of Q. Pp. 71–113 in *Trajectories Through Early Christianity*, ed. J. Robinson and H. Koester. Philadelphia.

Theissen, G. 1978. *Sociology of Early Palestinian Christianity*. Philadelphia.

STEPHEN J. PATTERSON

LOGOS. The ancient Greek word *"logos,"* usually translated "word," has a wide variety of meanings and is common to all periods of Greek literature, both prose and verse, with the exception of Epic literature where it is rarely used.

Logos is a verbal noun from the Greek verb *legō*. The two basic meanings of the verb are: (1) to count or recount, and (2) to say or speak. The various senses of *logos* cluster around the two meanings of that verb. Connected with the first meaning of *legō, logos* means "computation" or "reckoning." Depending on the context, the word can then mean "accounts," or "measure," or "esteem," that is, the value put on a person or thing. In mathematics, it means "ratio" or "proportion." Depending on the second meaning of *legō, logos* also has a wide variety of meanings: explanation, argument, theory, law or rule of conduct, hypothesis, formula or definition, narrative, oration, conversation, dialogue, oracle, proverb or saying. The specific meaning can be derived only from the context in which the word appears. Connected with both meanings of the verb, *logos* can mean the process by which both computations and explanations are produced. In this context, *logos* refers to the process of human reasoning, human rationality, and more broadly the rationality or the rational principle of the universe. These latter meanings are especially important in Greek philosophical literature. The word is rarely used in Greek to refer to a single word and never in grammar to refer to a vocable. In referring to a single word or a vocable, ancient Greek uses terms such as *lexis, epos, onoma,* or *rhēma* (LSJM, 1057–59; BAGD, 477–79).

A. *Logos* in Greek Philosophy
B. *Logos* in the Septuagint
C. *Logos* in Hellenistic Jewish Speculation
D. *Logos* in the New Testament in General
E. *Logos* in Johannine Literature
  1. *Logos* in the Prologue of the Gospel of John
  2. *Logos* in the First Epistle of John
F. *Logos* in Second-Century Christian Literature

A. *Logos* in Greek Philosophy

Logos had a long, distinguished, and very complex career in Greek philosophy. That career began with the pre-Socratic philosopher Heraclitus (ca. 500 B.C.E.). Most of the time Heraclitus employed the term *logos* in its more common meanings (proportion, account, explanation). Some scholars think that he always used the term in this way (Robinson 1987: 74–76, 114–15). But he may also have used it in the sense of an underlying cosmic principle of order, a principle that escaped the view of most people but which was grasped by the few who were wise (Diels and Kranz 1952: Fragments 1, 2, 50). This principle of order was related to the general meaning of measure, reckoning, or proportion (Kirk and Raven 1957: 188). It was the proportional arrangement of things that provided the ultimate order of all phenomena which on the surface appeared to be disparate in nature. This *logos* seems to have been material for Heraclitus and coextensive with the primary cosmic element of fire (Diels and Kranz 1952: Fragment 30).

Plato's (429–347 B.C.E.) use of *logos* in his dialogues was a very complex one. In its more philosophical sense, *logos* was associated with discourse or rational explanation rather than with the Heraclitean concept of an ordering principle of the material world. In contrast to myth *(mythos), logos* was a rational, true account (*Phd.* 61b; *Ti.* 26e). For Plato there was no greater misfortune than to become a hater of rational discourse *(logoi)* (*Phd.* 89d, 90d–e). Plato generally identified thinking *(dianoia)* and rational discourse *(logos); logos* was the inward dialogue of the mind as it flowed from the mind through the lips (*Soph.* 263e). Yet Plato also claimed that rational discourse *(logos),* even when it was in support of true belief, could not lead to real knowledge in the area of the sense perceptible (*Tht.* 201c–210d). Rational discourse or explanation, however, did play an important role at what Plato considered the higher levels of being, that is, at the level of the essence *(ousia)* or idea of things, and could lead to real knowledge (*Resp.* 534b–c).

Aristotle (384–322 B.C.E.) also used *logos* in several different ways. He often used the term *logos* in the sense of "definition." He also used it to mean "proportion" or "ratio" (*Metaph.* 991b). Aristotle, like Plato, often used the term *logos* to refer to rational speech and rationality. According to him, what distinguished human beings from lower animals was speech *(logos)* (*Pol.* 1253a). Later in *Pol.* 1332b, Aristotle used the same words but obviously meant that what distinguished human beings from lower animals was reason *(logos).* He also often introduced the concept of reason into ethical contexts. To live ethically, one must live according to reason or right reason *(orthos logos) (Eth. Nic.* 1144b); in this context right reason was identified with practical wisdom *(phronēsis).* Indeed, the specifically human function of human beings was an activity of soul which was in accord with reason *(kata logon) (Eth. Nic.* 1098a). This living in accordance with reason also involved overcoming the irrational elements of the soul and body (*Eth. Nic.* 1102a–1103b).

The concept of *logos* was central to Stoicism. In Stoicism, *logos* once again played a cosmological role. In this sense, Stoicism drew on Heraclitus (perhaps mistakenly) in a way that neither Plato nor Aristotle had (Long 1986: 145–47).

For the Stoics, *logos*, God, and nature were in reality one (Diog. Laert. 7.135; Plutarch, *De Stoic. repugn.* 34, 1050A). *Logos* was the rational element that pervades the controls all of the universe (*SVF* 1.87). *Logos* was the active element *(to poioun)* of reality while matter without quality was the passive element *(to paschon)* (Diog. Laert. 7.134). For the Stoics, however, both of these elements were ultimately material. *Logos* was identified by Zeno of Citium (335–263 B.C.E.), the founder of Stoicism, with fire and by Stoics from Chrysippus (ca. 280–207 B.C.E.) with a blend of fire and air, which they referred to as breath or spirit *(pneuma)* (Long 1986: 155). The passive element was identified with earth and water. The *logos* which permeated the universe was present in nature through seminal reasons *(logoi spermatikoi)* which served as the powers of order and growth in individual entities (*SVF* 2.1027).

While *logos* permeated and ordered all of nature, it was present in different parts of nature in different ways (Diog. Laert. 7.139). Only in human beings was *logos* present as part of their very nature. In other words, only human beings were rational (Cicero, *Nat. D.* 2.6.16). For the Stoics, human rationality *(logos)* was intimately connected with and reflected the rationality of the universe as a whole. While this view of human rationality at first looks very much like the views of Plato and Aristotle, human rationality for the Stoics, like the rationality of the universe as a whole, was material in character, while for both Plato and Aristotle human rationality was beyond the realm of the material. For the Stoics, the *logos* in human beings was part of the governing principle *(to hēgemonikon)* of the soul and for most of them was located in the heart (Long 1986: 171).

The concept of *logos* also played a crucial role in Stoic ethics. Human rationality was in tension with the passions *(ta pathē)* (Diog. Laert. 7.110). The goal of human life was to live a life in accord with *logos* or nature, that is, a life which was lived rationally and in which all of the other faculties of the soul were dominated by right reason *(orthos logos)* (Diog. Laert. 7.85–87). Such rationality united human beings with the rationality of the universe as a whole.

Given the fact that the *logos* of the universe always controlled the universe, the Stoics found it difficult to reconcile that control with an ethical theory, in the sense that, without some human capacity to choose one way or another, living in accordance with the *logos* of the universe was inevitable and so not a matter of virtue or vice. Yet the Stoics did maintain that there were good and bad human actions and that, through a long process of education and practice, human beings could reach the level of living in accord with the universal *logos* or nature (Diog. Laert. 7.86–87; Inwood 1985: 101–217). In the final analysis, however, the *logos* of the universe reconciled even human beings' evil actions into an ultimately perfect universe (Cleanthes, *Hymn to Zeus*, 11–21 in *SVF* 1.537).

As in the Greek philosophical tradition generally, *logos* was used in Middle Platonism (the Platonic tradition from ca. 80 B.C.E. to ca. 220 C.E.) in the sense of rational discourse and human rationality. At the level of cosmology, however, *logos* did not play quite the central role that it did in Stoicism. Nevertheless, it did play an important role in relation to other concepts in the Middle Platonic tradition.

Middle Platonism, in contrast to Stoicism and in keeping with its Platonic roots, emphasized the primary reality of the immaterial, intelligible realm. In keeping with this emphasis, one of the characteristics of Middle Platonism was its distinction between two aspects of the divinity. The first aspect of the divinity was essentially transcendent and basically inner-directed. The second aspect was an active, demiurgic power which was responsible for the ordering of everything else in the universe. The distinction was not simply metaphorical, but was meant as a metaphysical explanation which both preserved the transcendence of God and accounted for the relatively orderly character of the universe. Middle Platonists sometimes adopted the Stoic *logos* into their systems as the term for this active force of God in the world (Dillon 1977: 46). More often, however, they gave this demiurgic aspect of divinity a name other than *logos* (e.g., idea, mind). In contrast to Stoicism, both of these divine realities in Middle Platonism transcended the material level of reality and were part of the intelligible world. For example, one of the early Middle Platonists, Eudorus of Alexandria (fl. 25 B.C.E.), may have referred to the demiurgic combination of the Monad, which represented form, and the Dyad, which represented matter, as the thought *(logos)* of the essentially transcendent God, the First or Supreme One (Dillon 1977: 128; Tobin 1983: 14–15). A similar *logos* figure appears in Plutarch (ca. 50–120 C.E.) (*De Is. et Os.* 53–54, 372E–373C). The *logos,* which was identified with the Egyptian God Osiris, was the one who ordered and made manifest the material world and at the same time served as the intelligible paradigm for that world (Tobin 1983: 73–75). The same seems to have been the case for the 2d century C.E. Middle Platonist, Atticus (Dillon 1977: 252). This early Middle Platonic outlook influenced Hellenistic Judaism and particularly Philo of Alexandria.

B. *Logos* in the Septuagint

Logos was used frequently in the Septuagint. It was used to translate a number of Hebrew words (*ʾēmer* [word], 13 times; *millāh* [word], 30 times). Over 90 percent of the time, however, *logos* was a translation of the Hebrew word *dābār* (word). Both *logos* and another Greek word (*rhēma,* word) were used to translate *dābār. Rhēma* predominates in the Pentateuch (*logos,* 56; *rhēma,* 147); in Joshua, Judges, and Ruth they occur about equally (*logos,* 26; *rhēma,* 30). In the other biblical books, *logos* predominates (*logos,* 1065; *rhēma,* 352). This is especially true for the prophetic books (*logos,* 320; *rhēma,* 40) and wisdom literature (*logos,* 221; *rhēma,* 40) (*TDNT* 4: 92). One reason for the shift was due to differences in literary genre. In secular Greek *rhēma* carried less the meanings of "oracle" or "proverb" than did *logos,* meanings which were central to prophetic and wisdom literature respectively. Yet *rhēma* was sometimes used in the Septuagint with the meanings of "oracle" (Isa 16:13; 59:21; 66:5; Jer 1:1; 6:10; 16:10) and "proverb" (Prov 3:1; 7:24; 8:8; Eccl 1:1; 7:30; Sir 39:7). This suggests that there may also have been another reason for the shift from *rhēma* to *logos.* Because the prophetic and wisdom literatures were translated into Greek later than the Pentateuch, this shift from *rhēma* to *logos* and the preponderance of *logos* in prophetic and wisdom literature may reflect to some extent the growing influence on Hellenistic

Judaism of Hellenistic culture and philosophy with their emphasis on *logos.*

Logos in the Septuagint, like the Hebrew *dābār,* had a wide range of meanings. It meant narrative, speech, dialogue, oracle, or proverb. Because the Hebrew *dābār* and the Greek *logos,* however, did not have the identical range of meanings, the use of *logos* as a translation of the Hebrew *dābār* inevitably influenced the way in which *logos* was understood. In the Septuagint *logos* often took on a more dynamic meaning than it originally had in Greek (Isa 2:3: "And the word [*logos*] of the Lord [will go forth] from Jerusalem"; Isa 45:23: "My words [*logoi*] will not be frustrated; Ps 119:74: "For I have hoped in your words [*logous*]; Ps 147:15: "His word [*logos*] will run swiftly."). There is a sense of power and dynamism in this use of *logos* that was not part of its semantic range in secular Greek. In addition, *logos* and particularly the plural *logoi* were used to refer to the Mosaic Law (Exod 19:1; Deut 1:1).

In several Psalms (33:6) and in the Sirach (39:17, 31; 43:10, 26), *logos* was associated with God's act of creation and his maintenance of cosmic order.

> "By the *word* of the Lord the heavens were made,
> and all their host by the breath of his mouth." (Ps 33:6)
> "At his *word* the waters stood in a heap,
> and the reservoirs of water at the *word* of his mouth.
> At his command whatever pleases him is done,
> and none can limit his saving power." (Sir 39:17–18)
> "Because of him his messenger finds the way,
> and by his *word* all things hold together." (Sir 43:26)

While *logos* in each of these passages refers to God's command (see Gen 1:3, 6, 9, 11, 14, 20, 24, 26: "And God *said* . . .) and not directly to some cosmic principle of order, the association of God's *logos* with creation and cosmic order was an important influence on the use of *logos* in Hellenistic Jewish literature and speculation. In this way, *logos* also played a role similar to that played by wisdom in other biblical texts (Prov 8:22–31; Sir 24) although in a much less developed fashion.

C. *Logos* in Hellenistic Jewish Speculation

Logos became a much more important concept in Hellenistic Judaism and reached its climax in the writings of the Hellenistic Jewish exegete Philo of Alexandria (ca. 20 B.C.E.–50 C.E.). Although the beginnings of this process are lost to us, fragments from the Hellenistic Jewish writer Aristobulus (fl. 150 B.C.E.) indicate that this process had begun, although tentatively, by the middle of the second century B.C.E.

Aristobulus, who is mentioned in 2 Macc 1:10, was an Alexandrian Jewish exegete who sought to interpret the LXX in a way consistent with Greek philosophy, primarily Stoic philosophy but also including Platonic and Pythagorean elements (Walter 1964: 124–49). In one fragment (Eusebius, *Praep. Evang.* 13.12.3–4) in which he offered an interpretation of Gen 1:3, 6, 9 ("And God said . . .), Aristobulus claimed that Moses called the whole genesis of the world the words *(logoi)* of God. In another fragment (Eusebius, *Praep. Evang.* 13.12.10–11), Aristobulus connected wisdom *(sophia)* with a metaphorical interpretation of the seventh day of creation because, according to his interpretation, all things are contemplated in the light of wisdom just as all things are contemplated in the light of the seventh day mentioned in Gen 2:2. He then went on to connect the seventh day with the sevenfold *logos* which is the principle of order in the world (Eusebius, *Praep. Evang.* 13.12.13). For Aristobulus, then, both wisdom and *logos* served similar cosmological ordering functions (*OTP* 2: 834–35).

The connection between wisdom and *logos* was also made explicitly, although again in an inchoate way, in the Wisdom of Solomon, a Hellenistic Jewish text from perhaps first-century B.C.E. Egypt or Syria. God's word and God's wisdom were used in this text as two parallel ways of describing God's creation of the world and his creation of human beings (Wis 9:1–2).

It was, however, in the works of Philo of Alexandria that *logos* found its full flowering in Hellenistic Jewish literature. Philo of Alexandria came from a prominent Jewish family in Alexandria and, on the basis of his writings, obviously had a very good education in Greek philosophical literature. In his writings, which are primarily interpretations of the LXX of the Pentateuch (since he probably knew no Hebrew), he sought to interpret the Mosaic Law in the light of Greek, primarily Middle Platonic, philosophy. The concept of *logos* played a central role in these interpretations. Philo's use of *logos* must be seen within the tradition of Hellenistic Jewish wisdom speculation since Philo, in continuity with his predecessors, identified wisdom *(sophia)* with *logos* (*Leg All* 1.65; *Heres* 191; *Somn* 2.242–45) and gave both some of the same attributes (e.g., image of God [*Conf* 146]).

For Philo the *logos* was the intermediate reality between God, who was essentially transcendent, and the universe. While Philo could use the Stoic concept of the *logos* as the principle of rationality that pervades the universe (*Heres* 188; *Fuga* 110), Philo's *logos* primarily fits into the pattern of the intermediate figure found in most Middle Platonic systems. Philo depicted the *logos* in a variety of ways, and the figure had a number of different functions.

The first general function was cosmological. The *logos* was the image of God, the highest of all beings who were intellectually perceived, the one closest to God, the only truly existent (*Fuga* 101). This image, the *logos,* also served as the paradigm or model for the ordering of the rest of the universe (*Somn* 2.45). The *logos* was an image in a twofold way, a reflection of the truly existent God above and a model on the basis of which the rest of the universe below was ordered. The *logos* was the archetypal idea in which all of the other ideas were contained (*Op* 23–25). But the *logos* was not simply the image or paradigm according to which the universe was ordered, it was also the instrument *(organon)* through which the universe was ordered (*Cher* 127; *Spec Leg* 1:81). The *logos* was both the power through which the universe was originally ordered and the power by which the universe continued to be ordered. Philo called these two aspects of the *logos* the Creative Power and the Ruling Power, and he connected the first with the name Elohim (God) and the second with Lord *(kyrios),* the Greek word used to translate Yahweh in the LXX (*Vita Mos* 2.99–199). Other terms used by Philo to refer to the *logos* are the First-Begotten Son of the

Uncreated Father (*Conf* 146; *Somn* 1.215), the Chief of the Angels (*Heres* 205), the High Priest of the Cosmos (*Fuga* 108), and the Man of God (*Conf* 41, 63, 146). What was common to all of these designations of the *logos* was the intermediate role that the *logos* played between the transcendent God and the rest of the universe.

The second function of the philonic *logos* was anthropological. The *logos* was the paradigm according to which human beings were made, not the human being as a whole but only the human mind. In interpreting Gen 1:27, Philo noted that man was not created *as* the image of God but *according to* the image of God. He interpreted this to mean that man was created according to the *paradigm* which was the image of God (*Op* 24–25). For Philo this paradigm was the *logos,* and man was an expression at third hand (God-*logos*-human mind) of the Maker (*Heres* 231). In addition, a correspondence existed between the microcosm (human being) and the macrocosm (the universe). The human mind was to the rest of the human being (the irrational parts of the soul and the body) as the *logos* was to the cosmos as a whole (*Op* 69). The human mind not only had its paradigm in the *logos,* it was also in some fashion a fragment or an effulgence of the divine *logos* (*Op* 146, *Spec Leg* 4.123).

The third function of the philonic *logos* was anagogical, that is, the *logos* was meant to guide the human soul to the realm of the divine. For Philo the goal of the human soul was the knowledge and vision of God (*Quod Deus* 143), to become like God or to be assimilated to God *(homoiōsis tǭ theǭ)* (*Fuga* 63). The possibility of the human soul attaining the knowledge and vision of God was rooted in the soul's fundamental relationship to and participation in the divine *logos.* But the human soul must begin by recognizing its own nothingness in relationship to the divine and must realize that the divine is ultimately the author of everything that the human soul is capable of (*Somn* 1.60; *Leg All* 1.82). Once the human soul has realized this and turns to God (*Praem* 163), it can then detach itself from the body and the realm of sense perception (*Fuga* 91–92; *Heres* 69–74) and mystically rise above the material world and be free to contemplate the divine *logos* (*Somn* 1.71; 2.249) and in some very limited sense even God himself (*Migr* 170–75). In this process, the divine *logos* is the means and the guide of this mystical ascent (*Somn* 1.68–69, 86; *Leg All* 3.169–178) (Winston 1985: 43–55).

Because the *logos* functions in such a complex way in Philo's biblical interpretations, it is often difficult to understand precisely what he meant in those interpretations. Is the *logos* only a metaphor for God's power, a hypostatization of some aspect of God, or a reality distinct from if not independent of God? Is the *logos* personal or impersonal? The answers to these questions can never be altogether clear. One reason for this is that Philo was rooted in a larger tradition of interpretation, and some of his interpretations were derived from that tradition and were not completely integrated in his own thought (Tobin 1983: 1–35). But a basic sense of what Philo meant can be gained by paying attention to the kind of language he used and why he used it. Like other Middle Platonists, Philo thought that God in his essence could not be implicated in the material universe. At the same time, the relative order of the material universe had to derive at least indirectly from God. For Philo the *logos* served as the intermediate metaphysical reality through which the universe was originally ordered and by which it continued to be sustained in an orderly state. On the one hand, then, the *logos* was not simply a metaphor. It was meant to serve as a real explanation, one which safeguarded both the transcendence of God and the relative order of the universe. On the other hand, it was not a straightforward description of a being other than God. It was a real aspect of the divine reality through which God was related, although indirectly, to the universe (Runia 1986: 446–51). In much the same way, the *logos* cannot aptly be characterized as either personal or impersonal. It was rather the source of the intelligibility of the universe and so was itself intelligent in a way that transcended the universe and, in that sense, also went beyond the categories of either personal or impersonal. In this respect, Philo was very much like other Middle Platonists who also maintained both the transcendence of God and God's indirect relationship to the universe through the use of an intermediate metaphysical reality.

D. *Logos* in the New Testament in General

Logos is used 331 times in the NT and in most of the same ways in which it is used in the LXX and in Greek literature in general (BAGD, 477–79). It can mean a statement (Luke 20:20), an assertion (Matt 15:12), a command (Luke 4:36), a report or story (Matt 28:15), a proverb or saying (John 4:37), an oracle or prophecy (John 2:22), a speech (Matt 15:12), or the matter under discussion (Mark 9:10). In the plural *logoi* can refer to speeches of various sorts (Matt 7:24; 13:37; 26:1; Mark 10:24; 13:31; Luke 1:20; John 14:24). It can be used of *written* words and speeches, as well as of the separate books of a larger work (Acts 1:1; Heb 5:11). It can also be used, although not often, to mean "ground" (Acts 10:29) or "reason" (Acts 18:14) for something. With the exception of Johannine literature, however, *logos* is not used in the NT in the more philosophical senses of rationality or of the rational principle of the universe.

What characterizes the use of *logos* in the NT is not some new meaning for the word beyond what is found in the Septuagint but its reference to the divine revelation of God, specifically the divine revelation of God through Jesus Christ and his messengers. In many cases the "word of God" is simply the Christian message, the gospel. The apostles and preachers are said to "speak the word of God" (Acts 4:31), to "proclaim the word of God" (Acts 13:5), or to "teach the word of God" (Acts 18:11). Because it is the word of *God,* it is also efficacious (Heb 4:12; 1 Thess 2:13), to be received (1 Thess 1:16; Acts 8:14; 11:1) and to be acted on (Jas 1:21). Since this word of revelation is brought by Christ, the "word of the Lord," the "word of Christ," or the "words" of Jesus can be used in the same sense as the "word of God" (John 5:24; 12:48; 18:32; Acts 8:25; 12:24; 13:44, 48–49; Col 3:16). *Logos* is often qualified by other genitive phrases ("the word of the kingdom" [Matt 13:19]; "the word of salvation" [Acts 13:26]; "the word of reconciliation" [2 Cor 5:19]; "the word of the cross" [1 Cor 1:18]; "the word of righteousness" [Heb 5:13]). But *logos* is also often used with no qualifying genitive to refer simply to the Christian message as such (Matt 13:20–23; Mark 2:2; Luke 8:12–13; Acts 6:4; Gal 6:6; Jas 1:21).

E. *Logos* in Johannine Literature

The most striking use of the term *logos* in the NT is found in the Johannine literature, in John 1:1–18 and in 1 John 1:1–4. Both the interpretation of these texts and the religious and intellectual background against which they should be set are a matter of debate.

1. *Logos* in the Prologue of the Gospel of John. While some scholars think that the Prologue of John (John 1:1–18) is a unified whole and the work of the author of the Gospel of John (Barrett 1978; Borgen 1970), most think that there are literary stages in the Prologue (Becker 1979; Brown *John* AB; Bultmann *John* MeyerK; Haenchen *John* Hermeneia; Rochais 1985a; Schnackenburg *John* HTKNT; Schmithals 1979). Behind the present form of the Prologue lies a hymn which has been commented on and added to in order to be used as the beginning of the Gospel of John. There is a general consensus that vv 6–8 and v 15 (all of which are about John the Baptist) are later additions that serve to integrate the hymn into the present form of the Gospel of John, which originally began with the figure of John the Baptist. In addition, many scholars think that vv 12c–13 and vv 17–18 are explanatory comments which did not belong to the original hymn (Rochais 1985a: 7–9).

While the structure of the original hymn is a matter of debate, one can plausibly argue that it fell into three strophes (Rochais 1985b: 161–62). In the first strophe (1:1–5), the *logos* was with God at the beginning and was God and was the means through which the universe and life came to be. In the second strophe (1:10–12b) the *logos* came to its own, was not received by its own, but to those who received the *logos* gave the power of becoming children of God. In the third and final strophe (1:14, 16), the *logos* became flesh in Jesus of Nazareth and the glory of the *logos* was experienced by those who believed. John 1:10–12b originally referred to the presence of the *logos* prior to the incarnation, and only in John 1:14, 16 was the incarnate *logos* referred to. When the hymn, however, was later connected to the Gospel of John and John 1:6–9 (about John the Baptist) was inserted before John 1:10, everything after John 1:5 now came to be understood as referring to the incarnate *logos,* perhaps because the redactor of the gospel wanted to see everything from the point of view of the incarnate *logos* (Schnackenburg *John* HTKNT 1: 227–28).

How one understands the meaning of *logos* in the hymn depends to a great extent on what religious and intellectual background one thinks the Prologue should be set against. There are a variety of proposals in this area.

a. The *logos*, Targum, and Midrash. Some scholars understand the *logos* in the Prologue of John against the background of the targums (the Aramaic translations of the OT) and midrashim (certain kinds of Jewish interpretations of the OT). Renewed interest in this approach to the *logos* in the Prologue of the Gospel has been due especially to the discovery in 1955 of the Targum Neofiti I to the Pentateuch. The principal editor of Targum Neofiti I, A. Diez Macho (1968: 57–95) maintains that this targum is Palestinian in origin and should be dated in the late 1st century or the 2d century C.E. Some of the traditions found in it go back even farther.

M. McNamara (1968) has argued that the Prologue of John has been influenced by the liturgical traditions found in Palestinian Targums such as Neofiti I. As an example of this he offers the midrash of the Four Nights found in Targum Neofiti I to Exod 12:42. In this interpretation sacred history is summed up in four nights. The first of these nights is that of creation:

> "The first night: when the Lord was revealed over the world to create it. The world was without form and void and darkness was spread over the face of the abyss and the Word *(memrāʾ)* of the Lord was the light, and it shone; and he called it the First Night."

In this passage the Word (Aram *memrāʾ*) of the Lord seems to be identified with the primordial light which shone at creation. These same elements (the Word identified with light and the association of both with the creation of the world) are also found in John 1:1–18. McNamara maintains that the author of the Prologue would have heard a passage such as this read in the synagogue and would have been influenced by its viewpoint.

Another suggestion has been made by P. Borgen (1970) that the *structure* of the Prologue reflects a basic exposition (a. Word–God, 1:1–2; b. all things were made through him, 1:3; c. light, 1:4–5) and an elaboration in reverse order of the elements in 1:1–5 (c′. light, 1:6–9; b′. the world was made through him, 1:10–13; a′. Word–God, 1:14–18). He finds this same kind of structure involving basic exposition (a,b,c) followed by an elaboration in reverse order (c′,b′,a′) in the Targum Pseudo-Jonathan to Gen 3:24. Borgen (1972) has also tried to establish that *logos* and light were connected in learned Jewish exegesis. As an example he cites *Gen. Rab.* 3.3 which contains an interpretation of Prov 15:23: "A man has joy in the answer of His mouth; a word in season, how good it is." In the interpretation found in *Gen. Rab.* 3.3, the phrase in Prov 15:23, "the answer of His mouth," is understood as God's creative word and is connected with the phrase, "and God said, 'Let there be light' " in Gen 1:3. In Jewish exegesis, then, God's creative *word* is associated with the light, which was created in Gen 1:3, an association also found in John 1:1–5.

Attractive as this approach appears at first, there are significant problems with it. First, *memrāʾ* (word) as used in the targums is basically a buffer term to preserve the transcendence of God; it has no reality of its own (Hamp 1938; Muñoz León 1974: 106–15). This means that *memrāʾ* offers only a verbal parallel with the *logos* of the Prologue and not a conceptual parallel. Second, neither the targums nor Midrashic literature offer a *consistent* set of verbal or conceptual parallels which could plausibly serve as the background for the use of the term *logos* in the Prologue. Third, the dating of the targums, including the recently discovered Targum Neofiti I, is very much in dispute. While Diez Macho places Targum Neofiti I in the late 1st or 2d century C.E., other scholars (Fitzmyer 1979: 70–74) place it in the 3d century C.E. or later. Finally, one should not confuse the fixed literary form of targums such as Neofiti I with earlier, less formal and oral Aramaic translations (Golomb 1985: 2–8). One should use the targums, including Targum Neofiti I, for interpreting 1st century C.E. literature such as the Prologue only with great caution and only when the parallels are clear and consistent. Because of this one must look elsewhere for the basic background for the Prologue of John.

b. The *logos* and Gnosticism. R. Bultmann (*John* MeyerK) sought to locate the background for the *logos* of the Prologue in Gnosticism. According to him, the Prologue in its original form was a gnostic hymn to John the Baptist. The hymn was then Christianized and became a hymn to Jesus as the incarnate *logos.* At the same time it was interpreted as a Johannine polemic against followers of John the Baptist. According to Bultmann, behind this hymn stood a pre-Christian gnostic myth of a heavenly redeemer figure. On the basis of the analysis of later gnostic documents, Bultmann maintained that this redeemer myth presupposed an *Urmensch* (Original Man) who dwelt in the realm of light. This Original Man for various reasons became scattered about in the lower world of darkness in the form of human souls. God then sent a heavenly redeemer figure to awaken the human souls below and reveal to them their true identity and so bring them once more to the world of light above. In this form, Bultmann's view finds few supporters today. The main reason is that it is far from clear that the different elements that eventually went into forming the myth of the Original Man in later gnostic documents were already joined together in pre-Christian times (Brown *John* AB 1: lv).

The discovery of the gnostic documents at Nag Hammadi, however, has provided renewed interest in the relationship of the Gospel of John in general and the hymn from the Prologue in particular to Gnosticism. While the gnostic documents from Nag Hammadi are, in their present form, from the 2d and 3d centuries, some of the documents probably contain earlier material. This is particularly true for those documents which seem to have been only secondarily Christianized. Such documents point to at least an earlier non-Christian, if not a pre-Christian, Gnosticism. In their earlier non-Christian forms, many of these documents involve various sorts of interpretations of the early chapters of Genesis.

The document that has been most interesting for trying to understand the *logos* in the hymn from the Prologue of John is the *Trimorphic Protennoia* (NHC XIII.*1*) (*JAC* 17:110–25; Evans 1980; Janssens 1983; Schenke 1974). The *Trim. Prot.* probably has a very complex compositional history and reached its present form in the early 3d century C.E. (Turner 1988: 511). It seems to have undergone only secondary and, for the most part, superficial Christianization. The tractate proclaims three descents of a gnostic heavenly redeemer, Protennoia (the First Thought of the Father). The third of these descents is in the form of the Son or *logos* (*Trim. Prot.* 46.5–50.20). It is in this third section of the tractate that one finds the closest parallels to the *logos* in the hymn of the Prologue. In addition to the contrast of light and darkness found in both documents, terms such as *logos,* beginning, life, illumine, and glory appear both in the hymn and in the third part of the *Trim. Prot.* (Evans 1980: 397; Janssens 1983: 241–42).

The most striking parallel to the hymn from the Prologue is *Trim. Prot.* 47.14–18:

> "I revealed myself to them in their tents *(skēnē)* as Word and I revealed myself in the likeness of their shape. And I wore everyone's garment and hid myself within them."

As in John 1:14, the Protennoia has been revealed in human "likeness." In addition, there is the verbal connection of *skēnē* in the *Trim. Prot.* and *skēnoun* (to pitch one's tent, to dwell) in John 1:14. Yet the parallelism should not be pressed too far. Prior to its secondary Christianization, it is clear that this passage refers not to an "incarnation" in a specific individual but to the presence of the heavenly revealer figure among those who belong to the light (49.25–26). The reference to putting on Jesus (50.12) at the end of the tractate is clearly part of the secondary Christianization of the document.

While there are very important parallels between the hymn from the Prologue and this section of the *Trim. Prot.,* the *Trim. Prot.,* even without its secondary Christianization, is more developed in its viewpoint than is the hymn. This makes it improbable that the hymn in John's Prologue is dependent even on an earlier non-Christian form of the *Trim. Prot.* What is more likely is that both the *Trim. Prot.* and the hymn were distinct, dualistic developments of the traditions of Jewish wisdom speculation (Evans 1980: 399; Janssens 1983: 243; Turner 1988). Each of the texts, however, has developed those traditions and speculations in rather different directions.

c. The *logos* of the Prologue and Jewish Wisdom Speculation. The closest conceptual parallels to the use of *logos* in the hymn from the Prologue of John are to be found in Jewish wisdom literature (Proverbs, Sirach, Baruch, and the Wisdom of Solomon). The various attributes and activities ascribed to wisdom in Jewish wisdom literature are ascribed to the *logos* in the hymn in the Prologue. The following table lists the more important of those parallels (Rochais 1985b: 175–80):

In the beginning was the Word *(logos)* (1:1)	The Lord created me *(sophia)* at the beginning of his work, the first of his acts of old. Ages ago I was set up, at the first, before the beginnings of the earth. (Prov 8:22–23)
	From eternity, in the beginning he created me (wisdom), and for eternity I shall not cease to exist. (Sir 24:9)
And the Word was with God (1:1)	When he established the heavens, I (wisdom) was there. (Prov 8:27)
	When he marked out the foundations of the earth, then I (wisdom) was beside him. (Prov 8:29–30)
	With thee (God) is wisdom, who knows thy works and was present when thou didst make the world. (Wis 9:9)
All things were made through him (1:3)	For wisdom, the fashioner of all things, taught me (Solomon). (Wis 7:22)
	With thee (God) is wisdom, who knows thy works and

	was present when thou didst make the world. (Wis 9:9)
That which came to be in him was life (1:3–4)	For he who finds me (wisdom) finds life. (Prov 8:35) Because of her (wisdom) I shall have immortality. (Wis 8:13)
And the life was the light of men (1:4)	Wisdom is radiant and unfading. (Wis 6:12) For she (wisdom) is a revelation of eternal light, a spotless mirror of the working of God, and an image of his goodness. (Wis 8:26)
The light shines in the darkness, and the darkness has not overcome it (1:5)	Compared with the light she (wisdom) is found to be superior, for it (light) is succeeded by the night, but against wisdom evil does not prevail. (Wis 7:29–30)
He was in the world (1:10)	And I (wisdom) was his delight, rejoicing before him always, rejoicing in his inhabited world and delighting in the sons of men. (Prov 8:30–31) She (wisdom) made among men an eternal foundation, and among their descendants she will be trusted. (Sir 1:15) She (wisdom) reaches mightily from one end of the earth to the other, and she orders all things well. (Wis 8:1)
Yet the world knew him not (1:10)	No one knows the way to her (wisdom), or is concerned about the path to her. (Bar 3:31)
He came to his own (1:11)	Then the Creator of all things gave me (wisdom) a commandment, and the one who created me assigned a place for my tent. And he said, "Make your dwelling in Jacob, and in Israel your inheritance." (Sir 24:10) Afterward she (wisdom) appeared upon earth and lived among men. She is the book of the commandment of God and the law that endures forever. (Bar 3:37–4:1)
And his own received him not (1:11)	You (Israel) have forsaken the fountain of wisdom. (Bar 3:12; see also Prov 1:20–30)
But too all who receive him, . . . he gave power to become children of God (1:12)	Though she (wisdom) is but one, she can do all things, and while remaining in herself, she renews all things; in every generation she passes into holy souls and makes them friends of God, and prophets. (Wis 7:27)
And the Word became flesh and dwelt among us (1:14)	Then the Creator of all things gave me (wisdom) a commandment, and the one who created me assigned a place for my tent. (Sir 24:8) Afterward she (wisdom) appeared upon earth and lived among men. (Bar 3:38)

Both the *logos* of the hymn in the Prologue and wisdom in Jewish wisdom literature are with God in the beginning; both are involved in the creation of the world; both seek to find a place among humankind; both are within a Jewish tradition of speculation about the deeper meanings of the early chapters of Genesis. In addition, many of the parallels between the *logos* in the hymn and the figure of wisdom are found in passages which like the hymn are poetic in character (Prov 8:22–31; Sir 24). The parallels are not simply conceptual but also stylistic.

In Jewish wisdom literature, however, the figure of wisdom was never displaced by the *logos* as it was in the hymn in the Prologue. This striking difference indicates that the type of speculation found in the hymn has moved beyond the viewpoints found in Proverbs, Sirach, Baruch, and the Wisdom of Solomon. Such a displacement of wisdom by *logos,* however, is found in the works of the Alexandrian Jewish exegete Philo of Alexandria. As indicated above, Philo's conception of the *logos* is rooted in Middle Platonic philosophy. This conception of the *logos* has some striking parallels with the *logos* in the hymn in the Prologue (Argyle 1952: 385–86; Dodd 1953: 276–77).

Both Philo and the hymn use *logos* as the equivalent of *wisdom* in Jewish wisdom literature. In both cases, *logos* overshadows the figure of wisdom in importance. Both Philo (*Op.* 17, 24) and the hymn (John 1:1–2) understand the *logos* as a reality which existed with God before creation. Both Philo (*Somn* 1.228–30) and the hymn (John 1:1) use the anarthrous *theos* (God) to refer to the *logos.* Both Philo (*Conf.* 146) and the hymn (John 1:1–2) connect the *logos* with the "beginning" *(archē)* of Gen 1:1. Both Philo (*Cher.* 127) and the hymn (John 1:3) think of the *logos* as the instrument through which *(di' hou)* the universe was created. Like the hymn in the Prologue, Philo (*Somn* 1.75; *Op.* 33; *Conf.* 60–63) associates the *logos* with light. Finally, both Philo (*Conf.* 145–46) and the hymn (John 1:12) connect the *logos* with becoming sons or children of God.

While the parallels between Philo and the hymn of the Prologue are important, it is also clear that the concept of the *logos* in Philo is developed far more philosophically than it is in the hymn. Philo's concept of the *logos* is rooted in the metaphysics of Middle Platonism in a way that the concept of the *logos* in the hymn is not. Nor is the parallelism close enough verbally to assert that the author of the hymn was acquainted with the works of Philo. Nevertheless, the parallels between Philo and the hymn in the Prologue strongly suggest that the hymn cannot be seen simply against the background of Jewish wisdom literature. Rather, it must also be seen against the background of Jewish speculation about wisdom/*logos* which extended beyond Jewish wisdom literature and which included the kinds of speculative traditions about the *logos* which are reflected in the interpretations of a writer such as Philo (Rochais 1985b: 184–85). Both are part of the larger movement of Hellenistic Jewish wisdom/*logos* speculation.

The background of Jewish Hellenistic speculation on wisdom/*logos* also allows us to account for the similarities between the hymn in the Prologue and sections from the *Trim. Prot.* Both are rooted in similar Hellenistic Jewish speculative traditions about wisdom and the *logos.* The Christian circles from which the Prologue came were probably influenced by Hellenistic Jewish converts familiar with speculation about wisdom/*logos* found in Hellenistic Judaism (Schnackenburg *John* HTKNT 1:231).

The use of *logos,* however, in the hymn in the Prologue of John moves behind Hellenistic Jewish speculations about *logos*/wisdom in that it identifies this *logos* with Jesus of Nazareth. Neither Jewish wisdom literature nor the kind of Hellenistic Jewish speculation represented by Philo ever sought to identify either wisdom or *logos* with a specific human being. The hymn in the Prologue is the clearest example in first-century Christian literature of both an incarnational and a preexistence christology (Dunn 1980: 213–50). It affirms both that the *logos* has become flesh in the person of Jesus of Nazareth and that Jesus of Nazareth existed before the incarnation, indeed before the creation of the world, as God's divine *logos.* The development of this belief as it appears in the hymn and in the Gospel of John as a whole is the most characteristic development of the Johannine tradition.

The development of this belief, however, was not without a certain amount of ambiguity. This ambiguity is reflected in John 1:14 which affirms both that "the Word *(logos)* became flesh" and that "we have beheld his glory, glory as of the only Son from the Father." The first statement emphasizes the identification of the Word with the *human being* Jesus; the second the identification of Jesus with the *divine word.* There was an ambiguity between an incarnational christology and arguably a somewhat more docetic christology, at least a christology that did not value theologically the earthly life of Jesus including his crucifixion and death. Given the religious and intellectual background of the hymn in Hellenistic Jewish speculation, one can hardly be surprised at such an ambiguity.

2. *Logos* in the First Epistle of John. This ambiguity seems to have surfaced in the Johannine community shortly after the initial completion of the Gospel of John (ca. 90 C.E.) (Brown *The Epistles of John* AB, 73–79). Some members of the Johannine community wanted to emphasize the incarnational intent of the Prologue and the Gospel while others wanted to emphasize less the incarnational and more the divine aspect of Jesus as the *logos* (1 John 4:1–3; 2 John 7).

The ambiguity of the Prologue and the Gospel probably led to tensions between these two groups and finally to a schism. Specifically, disputes about the interpretation of *logos* emerge in the opening verses of the First Epistle of John (1 John 1:1–4). 1 John represented the views of that segment of the Johannine tradition which emphasized the incarnational side of the tradition, that is, the reality of the *logos'* earthly identification with Jesus of Nazareth.

In 1 John 1:1–4, the author emphasized that the Word of life (the *logos* of the Prologue of the Gospel) was the same one which was from the beginning and which the correct interpreters of the Johannine tradition had heard, seen with their own eyes, looked upon, and touched with their own hands, Jesus of Nazareth. Presumably this seeing, hearing, and touching was ultimately derived by this segment of the Johannine tradition from its relationship to the Beloved Disciple (John 13:23–26; 19:25–27; 20:2–10; 21:7; 21:20–23; 21:24) who was understood as the source of their tradition (Brown *John* AB 1: lxxxvii–cii; 1979: 33–34; Schnackenburg *John* HTKNT 3:375–88). In any case, over against his opponents, the author of 1 John wanted to emphasize that the correct interpretation of the Prologue and the rest of the Gospel of John involved affirming the theological significance of the earthly life of Jesus, the Word of life (Brown *The Epistles of John* AB, 151–88).

In the end, as Brown suggests (*The Epistles of John* AB, 103–130), the Johannine tradition represented by the author of 1 John was probably absorbed into the churches represented by the Pastoral Epistles, Acts, Matthew, and 1 Peter. The other more docetic Johannine group may have been absorbed into various 2d-century Christian gnostic groups. This would account for the fact that the first known commentary on the Gospel of John was by the Valentinian gnostic, Heracleon (ca. 160 C.E.).

F. *Logos* in Second-Century Christian Literature

The use of *logos* was widespread and played a diverse role in 2d-century Christian literature. It played only a minor role in the writings of Ignatius of Antioch who wrote of Jesus Christ as "the word which proceeded from silence" (*Magn.* 8.2). Given the context, *logos* was probably used in this passage metaphorically and with little or no mythological or metaphysical implications (Schoedel 1985: 120–22). The concept of *logos* was important, however, for the thought of the *Odes of Solomon.* In the *Odes* the *logos* was the mediation of creation (*Odes. Sol.* 16), of God's self-revelation (*Odes Sol.* 7.7, 12; 8.8; 12.10; 46.13–14), and of salvation (*Odes Sol.* 46.11, 15; 31.14) (Pollard 1970: 34). The *logos* also became incarnate, although it is not altogether clear whether the author was asserting the full humanity of Jesus (*Odes Sol.* 7.4, 6). The author of the *Odes of Solomon* may have been acquainted with the Gospel of John (Barrett 1978: 65).

The concept of *logos* was also important in various gnostic writings such as the *Gospel of Truth,* the *Tripartite Tractate* and in "orthodox" writers such as Justin Martyr, Theophilus of Antioch, and Irenaeus. There is, however, no clear reference to the *logos* from the Gospel of John in "orthodox" Christian writers until Theophilus of Antioch and Irenaeus of Lyons in the late 2d century. Justin Martyr, for whom the concept of the *logos* was of great importance, did not clearly refer to the Gospel of John. Justin's concept of the *logos* and its use in the interpretation of Jesus finds its religious and intellectual background in the continuation of Hellenistic Jewish speculation (*Dial.* 61–62) and in

Middle Platonism and Stoicism rather than in any direct dependence on the Gospel of John. The widespread use of *logos* in 2d-century Christian literature of various sorts and the fact that a good deal of this literature did not directly depend on the Gospel of John points to the continued influence of Hellenistic Jewish speculation on early Christian literature of various sorts.

Bibliography

Argyle, A. W. 1952. Philo and the Fourth Gospel. *ExpTim* 63: 385–86.
Barrett, C. K. 1978. *The Gospel According to St. John.* 2d ed. Philadelphia.
Becker, J. 1979. *Das Evangelium des Johannes.* 2 vols. Gütersloh.
Borgen, P. 1970. Observations on the Targumic Character of the Prologue of John. *NTS* 16: 288–95.
———. 1972. Logos Was the True Light. *NovT* 14: 115–30.
Brown, R. E. 1979. *The Community of the Beloved Disciple.* New York.
Diels, H., and W. Kranz. 1952. *Die Fragmente der Vorsokratiker.* 3 vols. Berlin.
Diez Macho, A. 1968. *Neophyti 1. Targum Palestinense.* Vol. 1, *Génesis,* 57*–95*. Textos y Estudios 7. Madrid.
Dillon, John. 1977. *The Middle Platonists.* Ithaca, New York.
Dodd, C. H. 1953. *The Interpretation of the Fourth Gospel.* Cambridge.
Dunn, J. D. G. 1980. *Christology in the Making.* Philadelphia.
Evans, C. A. 1980. On the Prologue of John and the *Trimorphic Protennoia. NTS* 27: 395–401.
Fitzmyer, J. A. 1979. The Phases of the Aramaic Language. Pp. 57–84 in *A Wandering Aramean.* SBLMS 25. Missoula, MT.
Golomb, D. M. 1985. *A Grammar of Targum Neofiti.* HSM 34. Chico, CA.
Hamp, V. 1938. *Der Begriff "Wort" in den aramäischen Bibelübersetzungen.* Munich.
Inwood, B. 1985. *Ethics and Human Action in Early Stoicism.* Oxford.
Janssens, Y. 1983. The Trimorphic Protennoia and the Fourth Gospel. Pp. 229–44 in *The New Testament and Gnosis: Essays in honour of Robert McL. Wilson,* ed. A. H. B. Logan and A. J. M. Wedderburn. Edinburgh.
Kirk, G. S., and J. E. Raven. 1957. *The Presocratic Philosophers.* Cambridge.
Le Deaut, R. 1974. Targumic Literature and New Testament Interpretation. *BTB* 4: 243–89.
Long, A. A. 1986. *Hellenistic Philosophy.* 2d ed. London.
Mack, B. L. 1973. *Logos und Sophia.* Göttingen.
McNamara, M. 1968. *Logos* of the Fourth Gospel and the *Memra* of the Palestinian Targum (Ex 12:42). *ExpTim* 79: 115–17.
———. 1983. *Palestinian Judaism and the New Testament.* Good News Studies 4. Wilmington, DE.
Muñoz León, D. 1974. *Dios-Palabra: Memra in los Targumim del Pentateuco.* Institución San Jeronimo 4. Granada.
Pollard, T. E. 1970. *Johannine Christology and the Early Church.* Cambridge.
Robinson, T. M. 1987. *Heraclitus: Fragments. Phoenix* Pre-Socratics 2. Toronto.
Rochais, G. 1985a. La formation du prologue (Jn 1, 1–18) (I). *Science et Esprit* 37: 5–44.
———. 1985b. La formation du prologue (Jn 1, 1–18) (II). *Science et Esprit* 37: 161–87.
Runia, D. T. 1986. *Philo of Alexandria and the Timaeus of Plato.* Philosophia Antiqua 44. Leiden.
Sabourin, L. 1976. The MEMRA of God in the Targums. *BTB* 6: 79–85.
Schenke, G. 1974. Die dreigestaltige Protennoia. *TLZ* 99: 731–46.
Schmithals, W. 1979. Der Prolog des Johannesevangeliums. *ZNW* 70: 16–43.
Schoedel, W. R. 1985. *Ignatius of Antioch.* Philadelphia.
Tobin, T. H. 1983. *The Creation of Man: Philo and the History of Interpretation.* Washington.
Turner, J. D. 1988. Trimorphic Protennoia (XIII.1). Pp. 461–79 in *NHL.*
Walter, N. 1964. *Der Thoraausleger Aristobulos.* Berlin.
Wilson, R. 1953. Philo and the Fourth Gospel. *ExpTim* 65: 47–49.
Winston, D. 1985. *Logos and Mystical Theology in Philo of Alexandria.* Cincinnati.

THOMAS H. TOBIN

LOIS (PERSON) [Gk *Lois*]. Lois, the mother of Eunice and grandmother of Timothy, was a Christian convert apparently at the hands of Paul and Barnabas in Lystra of Lycaonia (2 Tim 1:5; cf. Acts 16:1). 2 Timothy 1:5 indicates that she and her daughter Eunice were believers before Timothy. It is possible that the reference in 2 Tim 3:15 to Timothy's instruction from childhood in the sacred writings is an allusion to teaching he received from Lois and Eunice. Like her daughter, who is specifically identified as a Jewess (Acts 16:1), Lois was probably also Jewish. See the fuller discussion under EUNICE. See also TIMOTHY.

Bibliography

Gillman, F. M. 1989. *Women Who Knew Paul.* Wilmington, DE.

FLORENCE MORGAN GILLMAN

LOOPS [Heb *lulā*ʾ*ôt*]. Rings attached to the edges of the tabernacle's curtains so that they could be attached to each other (Exod 26:4, 5, 10, 11; 36:11, 12, 17). The loops were apparently made of wool, since the text states that they were "blue," which was one of the colors of the wool used to make many of the tabernacle's finest fabrics. Two sets of five curtains made of linen and colored wools were coupled to each other, with fifty golden clasps that attached together the fifty loops on the edge of each set. In this way the inner covering of the tabernacle's frame was formed. A similar procedure, using loops of unspecified material and bronze clasps, was used for the outer covering of goat's hair. See also TABERNACLE for a reconstruction of how the loop and clasp assembly coupled the tabernacle curtains.

CAROL MEYERS

LOOSING. See BINDING AND LOOSING.

LORD. See NAMES OF GOD (OT); YAHWEH (DEITY).

LORD'S PRAYER. The modern name for the prayer uttered by Jesus as recorded in Matt 6:9–13 and Luke 11:2–4. The Matthean form of the prayer is reproduced in the *Didache* (8:2), and faint echoes of its language can be detected in the prayer of Jesus in John 17.

A. Issues in Interpretation
1. Original Version
2. Relationship between the Versions
3. Various Documentary Attestations
B. Text
C. Origins
D. General Meaning
E. Points of Detail

A. Issues in Interpretation

Because of the complexity of the problems raised by the Lord's Prayer (LP), it is worth listing some of the chief "probes" which may be attempted. Not all the resulting perspectives are mutually consistent.

1. Original Version. Assuming the Gospels to be reporting and adapting a prayer spoken by Jesus, or a liturgical composition predating the writing of the Gospels, what was the form of that prayer, presumably in Aramaic, and how does it relate to the forms preserved in Matthew and Luke? This line of enquiry remains at the level of hypothesis insofar as it posits an original form of the LP which is independent of the Gospels themselves.

2. Relationship between the Versions. This immediately raises the question of the relationship between the gospels of Matthew and Luke, the question of John's use of one or both in his own distinctive manner, and of the *Didache*'s use of Matthew. This enquiry may still envisage the LP as an independent prayer in use in the early Church, but it may suggest a different perspective altogether.

3. Various Documentary Attestations. This redaction-critical or even "narrative" approach leaves aside the issue of putative original forms and concentrates instead on the subtle connections of the various versions of the LP with the Gospels and the *Didache* as writings with their own coherent identity. This perspective may in part be used alongside the two previous ones, but if taken in a thoroughgoing way it raises the possibility of a quite different kind of illumination. Questions of detail, such as the meaning of individual words, play their part within the major enquiries and are in turn affected by the various perspectives they suggest.

B. Text

The texts of the versions of the LP are given synoptically in Table 1. The versions of the LP in the gospels of Matthew and Luke, though distinct, are recognizably related, while that in the *Didache* is very close to the LP in Matthew. (This similarity of text is one of a number of close similarities between the *Didache* and Matthew, betokening the use of comparable traditions or the dependence of the former on the latter.) The Johannine material is less clearly involved in a study of the LP. What is at stake is a correct discernment of possible Johannine methods of using and elaborating material derived from or similar to that found in earlier Gospels. It is not implausible to see many elements and themes in the prayer of Jesus in John 17 as related to parts of the LP but developed in a Johannine manner.

Table 1: The Text of the Lord's Prayer

Line	Matt 6:9–13	Luke 11:2–4	*Didache* 8:2	John
1	Our Father who art in the heavens,	Father	Our Father who art in heaven,	17:1, 5 17:11, 21, 24–25
2	may thy name be hallowed.	may thy name be hallowed.	may thy name be hallowed.	17:11–12 17:26
3	May thy kingdom come.	May thy kingdom come.	May thy kingdom come.	17:1–2
4	May thy will come to pass as in heaven also on earth.		May thy will come to pass as in heaven also on earth.	17:4
5	Our bread for the morrow(?) give us today	Our bread for the morrow(?) give us each day	Our bread for the morrow(?) give us today	6:32–35
6	and forgive us our debts as we also have forgiven our debtors;	and forgive us our sins for we also forgive everyone indebted to us;	and forgive us our debt as we also forgive our debtors;	17:17
7	and do not lead us into test,	and do not lead us into test,	and do not lead us into test,	17:11–15
8	but rescue us from the evil one(?).		but rescue us from the evil one(?).	17:15

From the 4th or 5th century on, some mss of Matthew add a stereotyped doxology in scriptural style (see RSV marg.; cf. 1 Chr 29.11–13): "for thine is the kingdom and the power and the glory, for ever. Amen." There are minor variations, and the *Didache* omits "the kingdom."

Variations in the form of the LP did not cease with the writing of the Gospels and the *Didache*. Such variations are in no way surprising in the transmission of a text which was soon, and perhaps from the start, central in Christian liturgy and instruction. The operation of both liturgical and instructional use can be discerned. Thus, over a long period various mss have alterations, whether the addition of the liturgical doxology to Matthew or the harmonizing expansion of Luke's shorter version with Matthew's fuller and soon more widely used version. Both the gospel settings and that of the *Didache* reflect instructional needs, the provision of a guide for Christian prayer. Soon, this use widened and the LP became a basis for teaching. In Tertullian's *On the Prayer* (early 3d century), the version expounded is that of Matthew, but "our" is omitted before "Father," and lines 3 and 4 are reversed, perhaps so that in a catechetical context teaching on Christian life (doing God's will) might precede attention to the final End (the kingdom). Already in the 2d century, some Christians knew Luke's version with "may thy Holy Spirit come upon us and cleanse us" substituted for "may thy kingdom come," a wording still being copied in medieval times but probably originating in the LP's links with prebaptismal teaching, reflected as early as the *Didache*. The fluidity persists into more recent times. The doxology, long in abeyance in western Christian use, reappeared in 17th-century Anglican services and is included in recent Roman Catholic liturgical revisions. More recently some feminists have adapted the LP to begin "Our Mother" or "Our Parent."

Whatever the strength of liturgical and instructional pressures from early days to the present, these factors may not be the whole of the story. Other matters must come into play as we try to assess the origins and early development of the LP.

C. Origins

The oldest extant forms of the LP are those found in the gospels of Matthew and Luke. Any earlier history must remain obscure, but a number of hypotheses may be considered, each reflecting wider matters of NT studies and, as already indicated, sometimes compelling choices between methods of interpretation.

The most widely accepted view is that the LP goes back to the Aramaic teaching of Jesus. In due course, it was incorporated into a collection of his sayings (Q) and thence included in the gospels of Matthew and Luke, each of whom altered it in accordance with preferences of style, structure, or doctrine. Luke's version is considered to be closer to Q. Thus, Matthew added lines 2, 4, 8 (see Table 1), using typical language, and filling out the balance of the LP; while Luke altered the original "debts" to "sins" (line 6) and "today" to "each day" (line 5), a favorite phrase (9:23), and changed the tense of the verbs "give" (line 5) and "forgive" (line 6) to the present continuous, in order to turn the LP's application more usefully to everyday Christian living. This view is summed up in Jeremias' words: "in *length* the shorter text of Luke is to be regarded as original, and in general *wording* the text of Matthew is to be preferred" (Jeremias 1971: 196). On the basis of such a view, there have been various attempts to reconstruct an Aramaic text, which might then even be the very words *(ipsissima verba)* of Jesus.

Evidence for the existence of the LP before the writing of the Gospels is found in its intrusive appearance in Matthew 6, where the otherwise balanced treatment of the three aspects of piety (almsgiving, prayer, and fasting) is spoiled by its presence. The same point can be made about the *Didache*. The LP is less intrusive in Luke, though here too it may be read as a familiar formula which is given as *the* Christian prayer. On this view, though the two evangelists have each played a part in the wording of the LP, early Christian liturgical practice is the most likely milieu for the preservation of this piece of Jesus' teaching, even if it was included in a written collection of dominical sayings such as Q. Moreover, it may be that a reference to the LP is to be found in Rom 8:15 and Gal 4:6, and "Abba, Father" may even have been the name by which the LP was known (cf. *Paternoster* or "the Our Father" of later times).

The element of hypothesis may be reduced by taking a different approach. As they stand, the two early versions are part of the gospels of Matthew and Luke, and each version may be viewed in the context of its own gospel's structure and the flow of its narrative. Both versions respond interestingly to such treatment. Thus, Matthew's teaching on prayer centers on the avoidance of verbosity and prattling and on the necessity for single-minded attentiveness to God. By comparison with Jewish formulas (like the Eighteen Benedictions or the Shema), the LP, despite its strongly Jewish character as far as phraseology goes, is an admirable example of these qualities. It is resolutely theocentric, even though its structure involves an orderly shift from "thou" to "we" after line 4; it is simple in its wording; and it avoids concern with Jewish national restoration. Its petitions are, mostly, noticeably consistent with Matthean concerns and language. Its themes and style are at home in Matthew's Jewish Christian setting. The two verses that follow the LP further stress the matter of conditional forgiveness, a prominent concern of Matthew consistent with his general sense of strict rewards and punishments (16:27; 18:35; 25; and, also showing his feeling for reciprocity, 7:12). Luke's version also displays the characteristics of the particular evangelist, from the one-word address "Father" onwards (22:42; 23:34, 46). His brevity, by comparison with Matthew, finds a parallel in the Beatitudes (6:20; cf. Matt 5:3–12). Luke's everyday piety appears in his concern for God's constant provision of bread and for deliverance from sin and temptation. Most obviously, his placing of the LP in relation to Jesus' own praying accords wholy with his constant stress on Jesus' prayerfulness, noted by Luke alone at every major turn of his ministry (3:21; 5:16; 6:12; 9:18, 28; 22:32, 41), as does the gospel's shift from the LP to a major treatment of the various aspects of prayer, but with a continuing and realistic interest in "bread" (11:5–13).

The approach just outlined, which is compatible with a number of different opinions about the source from which the LP derives and the relationship among the Gospels, can receive a more definite outline. Such a definition is illustrated by M. D. Goulder's proposal (1963; 1974) that the phenomena of the Synoptic Gospels can be most economically explained by supposing that Matthew built up his gospel not only from direct assimilation of Mark but also from the midrashic development of "hints" in Mark. On this view, Matthew drew together the elements of the LP from the teaching and deeds of Jesus in Mark, seen in the light of his own interests and needs, in particular the desire to provide teaching for practical Christian living. The teaching in Mark 11:25–26 (which Matthew omits in its Marcan context) is then the basis for the LP, and its message is, as we have seen, emphasized not only in Matthew 6, where vv 14–15 use Mark's actual word "trespasses," moving away from Matthew's earlier "debts," but also elsewhere. It is possible that the Marcan passage also contributes the LP's opening in terms which became great favorites with Matthew (5:16, 45; 7:11, 21; 10:32–33; 12:50; 16:17; 18:10, 14, 19). Lines 4 and 8 both derive from the Gethsemane episode (Mark 14:32–42), with the former included also at 26:42. The petition for the coming of the kingdom is amply based in Jesus' preaching in Mark 1:14–15 and the parables of Mark 4. The Sinai model for the Sermon on the Mount as a whole brings manna to mind, as did Mark's feeding stories (6:35–44; 8:1–9), forming the basis for line 5 (cf. Mark 8:16–17). Other features confirm the Matthean nature of the LP. "Our Father" parallels Matthew's alteration of Mark's "Abba, Father" in 14:36 to "my Father" (26:39).

This proposal leaves no room for any hypothetical source, whether Q or an Aramaic original. The LP is Matthew's devout creation out of his knowledge of Jesus derived from Mark. In this view, it is best seen as from the start liturgical and instructional in purpose. (This would sufficiently account for its apparent intrusiveness in the pattern of Matthew 6, and accords with its role in *Didache* 8.) It was produced (like the gospel as a whole) to serve his church's needs, while being faithfully consistent with Jesus' teaching as he understood it. We may note that Matthew shows a sense of liturgical usefulness elsewhere, e.g., in his rubrical precision compared with Mark ("Take, eat," 26:26) and his reference to forgiveness of sins as a fruit of sharing the cup (26:28). From its beginning, then, the LP was what it has continued to be even in our day: a prayer of the Church adapted like all prayer to the perception of those who used it.

Luke's version may then be seen as the first such adaptation (with the *Didache* providing a much less innovative, roughly contemporary parallel). For if Q is redundant, Luke's use of Matthew as well as Mark becomes a live option, and attention focuses freely on the Lukan character of his version of the LP. The Lukan amendments to Q, as soon on the usual view of the matter, now appear as amendments to Matthew.

In this perspective, the subject of a possible Johannine version comes alive more convincingly. Just as Matthew is seen as having produced a model for Christian prayer in accordance with *his* understanding of Jesus' teaching, based on his perception of Mark, and Luke did the same consistent with *his* understanding, so John 17 may represent the Johannine way of carrying out the same task. Not surprisingly, its conceptuality is more sophisticated and its vocabulary typical of the writer (so that, for example, "hallow" becomes the Johannine "glorify"). In formal and intellectual terms, it departs much further from its models (whether those were earlier Gospels or traditions used by them) but all the same it is the result of an exercise which is recognizably of the same kind (Walker 1982). Moreover, it is a procedure of adaptation which is discernible in other parts of the gospel of John in relation to various elements in the tradition of Jesus' words and deeds (e.g., the discourse on the Bread of Life in chap. 6, especially v 51, in relation to the Synoptic story of the Last Supper).

It is evident that the origins and early development of the LP are far from clear, and a number of possibilities may be entertained. Each of them depends on the view taken of more general and fundamental questions of source, form, redaction, and narrative criticism; that is, on the manner in which the development of the Jesus tradition is understood, and in particular the degree of creativity which is attributed to the individual evangelists.

D. General Meaning

The LP, in its fuller form in Matthew and *Didache,* consists of an address (1), three second-person petitions relating to the fulfillment of God's purpose (2–4), and three or four first-person petitions relating to human needs (5–8: structurally, 8 may be meant as part of 7). The subject of all the petitions is arguably the same: the realization of God's ultimate purpose for the world and for his people. The thrust is firmly eschatological. In praying for "now" its eyes are towards the future.

However, the question of the LP's overall context of meaning is inseparable from the issues discussed above. If it is regarded as an independent form of words, derived from Jesus and merely incorporated (albeit with amendments) into the gospels of Matthew and Luke, and then also the *Didache* (and, though more inventively, perhaps too the gospel of John), then it is necessary to characterize its sense in its own right. The following points will then require consideration. LP is distinctly Jewish in character, with numerous parallels in Jewish forms of prayer, e.g., "Bring me not into the power of sin, iniquity, temptation or contempt; and let the good impulse have dominion over me but not the evil impulse" (*b. Ber.* 60b); Jewish piety is also reflected in the Matthean form of the LP's address (line 1). Its eschatological perspective, signifying the position of one for whom the decisive fulfillment is near and who longs for salvation, despite all hazards, is salient. The question of the relationship of the LP to other aspects of the tradition of Jesus' teachings immediately arises. The LP's sense of the imminence of the coming of the kingdom is in line with other sayings (e.g., Matt 12:28; Luke 11:20) that seem to speak vividly of its already realized presence. The prayer's eschatological concern comports with the detailed apocalyptic teaching found in Mark 13 and elsewhere, supposing that to be authentic in detail or general pattern.

If, however, each version of the LP is viewed as standing within the conceptual framework of the document in which it appears, then more detailed links with each of them can be presented and the LP can be tested for its Matthean or Lukan quality. General Jewish elements lead our attention to the specific relation to Jewish background discernible in each of those documents, with Matthew showing clear relations to forms characteristic of later rabbinic Judaism. General eschatological character is made more specific by being brought into relation with each evangelist's particular tendencies. We have already identified some of the links of the Matthean and Lukan versions of the LP with the rest of the Gospels concerned. We now mention some of their broader conceptual implications.

Matthew's version of the LP is wholly in line with his heightened awareness of the threatening nature of the approaching End, seen most plainly in the parables added to Mark in chap. 25, and his sense of the precarious nature of salvation in the light of the trials which will precede it (13:31–43, 47–50; 22:11–14). These features are echoed in lines 7 and 8. So, too, Matthew's sense of the balanced and reciprocal nature of forgiveness and responsibility for one's actions (6:14–15; 16:27; 18:23–35) is exemplified in line 6. Indeed, one might go further. In the light of 6:14–15, it looks as it forgiveness of sins is the sentiment uppermost in Matthew's mind in this passage, as indeed frequently in his gospel. On this ground, communal Christian life and relationship with God meet. Evidently it was in the light of this that Matthew understood the practical reality of the Kingdom's coming and the doing of God's will. For him the eschatological hope had concrete expression here. No wonder there is such stress on it in this gospel, no wonder that in the account of the supper, adding to Mark, he sees Jesus' blood as shed—and shared "for the forgiveness of sins" (26:28).

Luke's version also finds parallels in the character of Luke's understanding of Jesus' ministry and of Christian life. Prayer itself is accorded great importance in Luke's gospel. But the Lukan LP also has other features characteristic of Luke. Its content is probably best seen, as far as Luke's intention goes, as diverging from Matthew in the more practical and ethical way in which it sees the life of the kingdom. In this, too, as in its pithiness, it is parallel to his treatment of the Beatitudes (6:20–22). Line 5 in particular seems to substitute a concern with daily bread for Matthew's hope for the "bread of the kingdom" (see on line 5 below); just as his blessing (6:21) is for those who "hunger now" rather than Matthew's "hunger and thirst for righteousness" (5:6) and for the poor (6:21) rather than the "poor in spirit" (Matt 5:3). We recall, too, the strongly realistic picture of the new order Jesus brings depicted in the Nazareth sermon in Luke 4:16–20. It is possible that in line 7 Luke edges the sense of "temptation" toward a notion of everyday testing of faith in various moral predicaments and away from the ultimate (eschatological) test that will precede the End and that Matthew presumably has in mind. All the same, both evangelists see the present as already witnessing to the future, and the LP bears on both.

E. Points of Detail

As the foregoing discussion has made plain, the basic questions of gospel interpretation color the way in which the details are to be understood, but matters of detail also form the basis on which judgments of method and principle can reasonably be made.

1. Line 1. We have seen that both the Matthean and Lukan forms are typical of their writers. The idea of God as "Father" is well-established in Jewish usage (Isa 63:16; 1 Chr 29:10; Psalm 89:27; Sir 23:1, 4; 51:10), but it is more difficult to establish the spirit in which it is used. In particular, where does the LP stand in relation to a more personal style of piety in the period concerned? Certainly it lacks the national element often found in Jewish prayers, even though the eschatological tone involves the corporateness which the Matthean version makes explicit.

But the interesting issue concerns the background of "father" itself. Largely as a result of the work of Jeremias, the idea has become established that behind the term "father" lies the Aramaic *ʾabbāʾ*, and that this word, allegedly not found in Jewish addressing of God in prayer, expresses a peculiarly intimate, simple and even childlike relationship with God. Jesus both experienced and encouraged his followers to share this relationship. However, this view has been severely challenged, e.g., by Vermes (1973: 210), and Barr (1988), who affirm that *ʾabbāʾ* was used of God and carried no specific associations with child language. See also ABBA.

In any case, we should recognize that the relevance of this discussion of *ʾabbāʾ* to the LP rests on controvertible premises. It depends on the assumption that the LP's Lukan form is the more authentic, that it is an independent unit of tradition going back to Jesus, and that the inclusion of the Aramaic word in early Christian usage (Rom 8:15; Gal 4:6) above all on Jesus' lips (Mark 14:36), demonstrates its prominence in the self-understanding and piety of Jesus. On the other views of the LP's origin and development the issue is assessed differently. The simple address "father," appears as an established feature of Lukan usage, introduced as we have seen at numerous points, just as Matthew prefers "my/your/our father" (26:42; 5:16; 6:4, 9). Moreover, the connection of *ʾabbāʾ* with Jesus is only tenuously witnessed. Its use by Paul is not linked to Jews in any way. Its single gospel occurrence in the Gethsemane episode comes at a point where there is no one to overhear, and the idea that it is included for its known typicality is not supported by the rest of the gospel narrative; even in the Gethsemane story Matthew and Luke both replace it, with "my father" and "father" respectively, in line with their wording of the LP. As for its allegedly childlike resonances, the fact that in all three cases in both Paul and Mark, it is rendered simply by the ordinary, formal term *patēr* may be taken to show that the writers concerned were not aware of such associations; though a childlike deposition before God is certainly enjoined in passages like Mark 10:13–16 and Matt 11:25.

2. Line 2. The petition for the hallowing of God's name is the first which looks for the realizing of God's power plainly in the world, that is for the coming of the End (the use of the aorist tense, here and in lines 3 and 4, indicated event rather than process). The language is well-established in Judaism, with God's "name" signifying the reality and majesty of his presence, and "holiness" being his essential attribute (2 Sam 6:2; Jer 7:11; Lev 11:45). While the verb does not occur elsewhere in the Gospels in relation to God, Matthew makes much use of the idea of God's name or Jesus' name in this highly charged sense (Matt 1:23; 7:22; 10:22; 12:21; 18:5, 20; 19:29; 21:9; 23:39; 24:5, 9; 28:19). The last reference, concerning baptism, may come closest to shedding light on its use in the LP. Matthew's Church may well have seen initiation into the Christian community as an anticipatory realization of the "hallowing" of God's name which would soon take place on the grandest scale. In this sense, the LP's links with baptism, and the teaching which accompanied it, may go back to the earliest stage of its use that is visible to us, just as they are implied by its context in the *Didache* and, more formally, in a work like Tertullian's *On the Prayer*.

3. Line 3. The hope for the coming of God's kingdom is at the heart of the eschatological expectation, and this language pervades the tradition of Jesus' preaching in the first three Gospels, though not Jewish sources clearly belonging to this period. Mark 9:1 and 11:10 establish the idea of its "coming" in Matthew's primary source. He himself has several relevant uses of the verb (3:11; 11:2; 16:27–28; 21:9; 24:30, 42; 25:10; 26:64), but all speak of Jesus as the coming one; and 16:28 and 21:9 pointedly alter "kingdom" references in Mark to speak directly of him. However, the imminence of the kingdom is amply attested in both Matthew (3:2; 4:17) and Luke (9:27; 10:9), though in both Gospels there is a considerable range of concept and imagery implicit in the use of the term.

4. Line 4. The realization of God's will refers again to his ultimate purpose but specifically to his moral imperatives, in mind throughout Matthew's gospel with its ample ethical teaching. The idea of carrying out God's will occurs at 7:21; 12:50 and 18:14 (all reminiscent of the LP with the reference to "my father" or "your father"), as well as the crucial 26:42. This may be a conscious reproduction by Matthew of the language of the LP in a highly impressive context, by adaptation of Mark's different wording (14:36), using the noun rather than the verb, but in this added statement of his own. Luke has no reference to the idea of God's will apart from the Gethsemane saying (22:42), where he is close to Matthew's wording in 26:42 (but, as in lines 5 and 6 of the LP, substituting present for aorist), though see Acts 21:14 and 22:14.

The force of "as" in the final phrase is not wholly clear: does it mean "in the same way as" or "as much as," or simply "just as"? In heaven, God's will is already obeyed by angels (Matt 26:53) and that situation will be extended to earth where at present evil powers abound. So Jesus' exorcisms visibly presage the fulfillment of the LP. Then the remaining petitions of the LP shift the scene to earth and pray in effect for the working out of line 4.

It has long been suggested that this final phrase should be taken to accompany both of the preceding petitions. But though such a reading does not materially affect the sense, there is no good reason to suppose it was intended. If the prayer stood in Q or some other pregospel source in more or less its Lukan form, then the idea is gratuitous; and for Matthew any intended parallel with the ("as") clause in line 6 rules it out. If Luke knew and adapted Matthew's version, then he failed to understand his model in such a sense. In any case, the phrase bears all the marks of Matthew's style (e.g., 28:18), which suggests that Matthew sees the resurrection of Jesus as a decisive stage in the fulfillment of the LP (cf. also 16:28; 26:64).

5. Line 5. This most difficult (though apparently most straightforward) of the petitions raises two major questions: the meaning of Gk *epiousios,* usually translated "daily," and the bearing of the petition as a whole. The answer to the first affects the answer to the second, though not necessarily decisively.

The familiar English "daily" renders the Latin *quotidianus,* which established itself for lack of any better idea of how to render the Greek word and from a misunderstanding of its etymology. The fact is that, apart from its occurrence in the LP, *epiousios* has not yet been attested in literary or epigraphic sources (apart from one possible case, now unverifiable because the papyrus is not available; its text may have been inaccurately transcribed, the reference there being perhaps to daily rations; see Metzger 1957–58). This absence of parallels helps to create uncertainty about meaning as does obscurity of etymology. The word may arise from a compounding of the preposition *epi* with the verb "to be" *(eimi),* of which cognate examples are well established; or else from a compounding with the verb "to come" (also *eimi,* but differently accented and inflected). The former, more probable on semantic grounds, would yield a sense such as "essential," "necessary for subsistence." If it is thought that John has the LP in mind in the writing of chap. 6, then his reference to the "*true* bread from heaven" may represent an understandable "johannization" of such an interpretation with "bread" now allegorized. In the 3d century, Origen was already mystified by the word and took this interpretation further in a spiritualizing Platonist direction by rendering it "supernatural" heavenly bread as opposed to the mere earthly bread to which ordinary use of the LP refers.

The latter derivation of the word from "to come" pushes its chronological orientation into the future, though maybe with a backward look to the manna of the wilderness as a symbolic model (Exod 16:4). Manna is the morrow's bread, the bread of the coming day, the bread of the kingdom, now urgently longed for. This understanding, already found in some circles in the early Church, has the advantage of linking this petition with those that precede and follow it in the LP, thus giving it all its eschatological sense. It also confirms possible eucharistic associations of the LP, apparent in its context in the *Didache,* where the eschatological perception of the Christian meal is emphasized (*Did.* 9–10). Moreover, in Matthew's narrative the LP looks forward to the story of the Supper (26:26–29), mediated by the intervening feelings of the crowds (14:13–21; 15:32–39) if they were understood as foreshadowings of future messianic meals in the kingdom. The link with the Church's actual eucharistic observance may explain the uniquely "realized" quality of this petition ("today"), for it could be seen as answered in a measure by the rite itself. Though not ruled out, sense is less clear in Luke, where a plain request for food is probably in mind. For Luke the meeting of practical human need is the essence of the gift of the kingdom, to be sought "each day." Luke may still see the meaning as being "the morrow's bread," for a cognate word appears in this sense in Acts (7:26; 16:11; 20:15; 21:18; 23:11). It is not impossible that since the word is a rarity and possibly even a neologism, our different sources did not all take *epiousios* in the same sense.

Whatever Aramaic or other original there may have been, Luke's "each day" is generally agreed to be his own (9:23).

6. Line 6. There is uncertainty about the force of "as" in Matthew's version. In part at least, it may be stylistic, and thus parallel with line 4. But Matthew consistently sees forgiveness by God as bound up with the Christian's readiness to forgive others. As we saw, he may have been picking up and greatly extending in scope the statement in Mark 11:25. Luke sidestepped unclarity in this respect by means of a confident, perhaps semi-hortatory statement, "for we too forgive." For him, a spirit of mercy and generous forgiveness is basic to his understanding of Christian discipleship and its place can be simply accepted (1:77; 3:3; 4:18; 24:47; Acts 2:38; 5:31; 10:43). Luke's "sins" is also typical of his usage in these passages; while Matthew is inclined to see sin in terms of debt, and forgiveness as dispensation from debt, notably in the parable of the Two Debtors (Matt 18:23–35; a parable perhaps itself interacting with Matthew's wording of the LP) Luke retains the concept "sin" in the second half of the petition. In any underlying Aramaic version, this would not surprise, for "sin" and "debt" are attested as synonymous parallels in Jewish usage *(ḥṭʾh wḥwbtʾ).* However, this may not exactly explain the wording of Luke 11:4. On the view that Luke is close to Q, as the fount of the LP's Greek tradition, Matthew then took the hint of "is indebted to us" (probably originally meaning "does wrong to us") and let it pervade the petition as a whole. If, however, Luke was adapting Matthew's version, then here, in embarking on "sins" but failing to sustain it into the petition's second half, he has shown signs of imperfect control, slipping back to Matthew despite himself—and betraying his dependence on him. There is nothing unusual with Luke's open-armed "everyone" or in Matthew's relative caution.

7. Line 7. The Greek word *peirasmos* can refer to temptations to sin or to the testing of faith and obedience.

Sometimes, as in the *peirasmos* endured by Jesus in the wilderness, one sense merges into the other: the latter is uppermost in Mark 1:12–13, while the two coexist in the developed versions in Matt 4:1–11 and Luke 4:1–11. Here, given the dominant eschatological sense of the LP, the sense of "testing" is likely to be in view, for a period of suffering for God's elect was commonly seen as a preliminary to the coming of the End. It is well attested in apocalyptic literature, from Daniel onwards, where indeed it represented an interpretation of persecutions actually endured. It appears, then, in Christian apocalyptic expectation as expressed in the Gospels themselves (Mark 13; Matt 24; Luke 21). Closely germane to the LP, it appears in the Gethsemane story (Mark 14:38 and par.).

Given this sense of the word and so of the pattern, the difficulty often raised concerning the idea of God as a source of temptation to sin is a red herring; and the discussion in Jas 1:12–15, itself vacillating in its perception of the sense of *peirasmos,* is not relevant (though it is not impossible that it was prompted by the language of the LP). Nevertheless, once the original eschatological context of the LP faded and "temptation" came to be seen unequivocally as the subject of the petition, the difficulty inevitably arose. Hence the softening of the sense in some modern translations, and indeed in early interpretation, by shifting to the passive: as Tertullian said in comment, "that is, let us not be led." It is possible that Matthew is already sensitive to the point (see below on line 8). Given the early Christian perception of the conditions of the times of the End as already in existence in Jesus' ministry and their own lives, the risk of apostasy already colors this petition, perhaps especially in Luke (Acts 20:19; but see also Matt 13:21; and, once more, Gethsemane).

It may be felt that, all the same, there remains a problem of theodicy if God permits the undeserved suffering of his faithful ones, even if it be seen as a test of their faithfulness. The reply must be that the first Christians seem not to have experienced it as problem in this way. They were more conscious of the great prize beyond and indeed already present in the midst of their "light affliction." All the same, like Jesus on the eve of his death, and modeling themselves on him, they could pray for release or at least that the time be shortened (Mark 13:20; Matt 24:22).

8. Line 8. The final petition, in Matthew and the *Didache* along, at first sight does little more than repeat the sense of line 7. As earlier, it is Matthew who has the longer form and in all cases he exhibits the Jewish tendency to parallelism, as in the Psalms. The new element is the reference to the devil, if indeed *ho ponēros* is to be taken as personal (if impersonal, it refers to "evil" as a principle). If Matthew's usage is to guide us, the matter is open. The word is certainly a Matthean favorite, occurring 24 times, far more frequently than elsewhere. It is used of the devil in 13:19 and 38. If that is his sense here, it is possible that the clause was added as a way of easing the problem raised implicitly by its predecessor—it is the devil not God who is the real source of trials that Christians undergo. Whatever degree of formal dualism is involved, the petition seeks deliverance from all such sufferings, which, as just discussed with reference to line 7, may well have been thought to include temptations to sin. The different spheres of reference were scarcely distinguished, as in the "temptations" of Jesus in Matthew 4 and Luke 4, which were, in a sense, a rehearsal for his final and climactic Passion.

Bibliography

Barr, J. 1988. ʾAbbā Isn't 'Daddy.' *JTS* 39: 28–47.

Black, M. 1941. The Aramaic of *ton arton hēmōn ton epiousion. JTS* 42: 186–89.

Brown, R. E. 1961. The Pater Noster as an Eschatological Prayer. *TS* 22: 175–208. Repr. 1965.

Edmonds, P. 1979–80. The Lucan Our Father: A Summary of Luke's Teaching on Prayer? *ExpTim* 91: 140–43.

Evans, C. F. 1963. *The Lord's Prayer.* London.

Goulder, M. D. 1963. The Composition of the Lord's Prayer. *JTS* 14: 419–32.

———. 1974. Midrash and Lection in Matthew. London.

Harner, P. B. 1974. *Understanding the Lord's Prayer.* Philadelphia.

Jeremias, J. 1971. *New Testament Theology.* Vol. 1, *The Proclamation of Jesus.* Trans. J. Bowden. New York.

———. 1978. *The Prayers of Jesus.* Philadelphia.

Lohmeyer, E. 1965. *The Lord's Prayer.* London.

Manson, T. W. 1955–56. The Lord's Prayer. *BJRL* 38: 99–113.

Metzger, B. M. 1957–58. How Many Times Does "Epiousios" Occur Outside the Lord's Prayer? *ExpTim* 69: 52–54.

Smith, G. 1970. The Matthean "Additions" to the Lord's Prayer. *ExpTim* 82: 54–55.

Vermes, G. 1973. *Jesus the Jew.* London.

Walker, W. O. 1982. The Lord's Prayer in Matthew and John. *NTS* 28: 237–56.

J. L. Houlden

LORD'S SUPPER. The ritual meal celebrated in the early churches after the first Easter. As such, it should not be confused with the LAST SUPPER, to which it is nevertheless related.

A. Introduction
B. The NT Texts
  1. Paul
  2. Synoptics
  3. Acts
  4. Gospel of John
  5. Revelation
  6. Hebrews
  7. Jude and 2 Peter
C. Outside the NT
  1. *Didache*
  2. Ignatius
  3. Justin
D. Religious-Historical Backgrounds
  1. Jewish
  2. Pagan
E. Conclusion

A. Introduction

The designation "Lord's Supper" is derived from the Greek collocation *kyriakon deipnon* in 1 Cor 11:20. *Kyriakos* means something like "belonging to the *kyrios* (lord)" "owned by the *kyrios.*" In the papyri and inscriptions it designates Caesar's domain (in *OGIS* 669:18 [68 C.E.], *kyriakos logos* designates the imperial treasury). *Deipnon* was what the Greeks called the main meal of the day, eaten in the late afternoon or evening, in contrast to an early morning snack *(akratisma)* and to breakfast *(ariston),* eaten closer to noon (cf. Plut. *Quaest. conv.* 8.6.3–4). Moreover, *deipnon* also designated the festal meal or banquet (in the NT, e.g., Mark 6:21; Luke 14:16, 17, 24). Also, it was used quite frequently for cultic meals associated with sacrifices and the celebration of the Mysteries (cf. the Andania inscription [92 B.C.] *SIG*³ 736:96: *eis to hieron deipnon).*

In 1 Cor 11:17–34, Paul bases the Lord's Supper on the last supper Jesus ate with his disciples prior to his death (see also LAST SUPPER), and in that respect he is not alone. The Synoptic accounts of the institution of the Lord's Supper (Mark 14:22–26 = Matt 26:26–30 = Luke 22:15–20) also reflect the practice of communion in the church (Jeremias 1967: 100–102): on the one hand, they give the aetiological reason for the current practice of the church and lead it back to its sustaining foundation; on the other hand, they have received their shape and form from the liturgical practice of the church.

The situation is somewhat different in Acts 2:42, 46, where the expression "breaking bread," in summary fashion, is used for the celebration of the supper by the early church in Jerusalem. Whether that means that we are dealing with an essentially different kind of meal will have to be investigated. The search for the Lord's Supper in the text of the Johannine writings and in the Epistle to the Hebrews is problematic. The results of the research on these texts are equally controversial.

Among the early Christian writings outside of the NT the *Didache,* the letters of Ignatius of Antioch, and Justin Martyr's Apology deserve to be studied as witnesses to the Lord's Supper. In these writings the technical term for the Lord's Supper is *eucharistia* (cf. *Did.* 9:1; Ign. *Smyrn.* 8:1; Just. *Apol.* 66:1)—a word which took the lead in Christian tradition for a long time and which is still, as in the past, dominant in Catholic circles. At the same time *agape* becomes more independent as the Christian meal with its caritative and social characteristics. Aside from all this one needs to ask the history of religions question: Are there analogous phenomena in Judaism and in paganism, and to what extent have these influenced the development of the early Christian celebration of the Lord's Supper?

B. The NT Texts

1. Paul. a. 1 Cor 11:17–34. From a literary standpoint the oldest account of the institution of the Lord's Supper is found in 1 Cor 11:23–26. Paul reports the account essentially in the form in which he had learned to know it in Antioch in the 40's and as he had passed it on to the Corinthians when he established the church there. The traditional words "receive" and "deliver" *(paralambanein* and *paradidonai)* in v 23a are well known in the scholarly language of Rabbinism (cf. *Midr. Qoh.* 12:11) and of Hellenism (*Diod.* 5.2,3). They clearly indicate that the vv 23b–25 are a fragment of tradition (possibly with some Pauline touches). "From the *kyrios*" points to the earthly Jesus as the source of this catena of traditional elements. At the same time he is seen as the present exalted Lord who gives the sacrament its permanent validity. The rather scanty reference to the historic event of the passion in v 23b ("on the night when he was betrayed") sets the words of Institution off from the timeless, cyclic myths and formulae of the Mysteries.

The traditional text lays out another aspect of the meal in which the breaking of the bread at the beginning of the meal and the blessing of the cup at the end (cf. 11:25a "in the same way also the cup, after supper") surround the main meal. The words "for you," spoken at the breaking of the bread, are addressed to the participants of the Lord's Supper; they draw them into participation of the salvatory self-sacrifice of Jesus. The contents of the cup in v 25b are not directly identified as the blood. Rather, in the foreground stands the sealing of the eschatological new covenant in the death on the cross. Besides its vertical dimension (the God of the covenant creating a new people), this covenant has a horizontal aspect: the celebrants are brought together into covenant community.

Through the double *anamnesis* command the account of the Institution receives a special accent at the end of v 24 and v 25, which is missing from the Markan tradition. (Luke has one *anamnesis* command in connection with the saying about the bread.) The repeated command is aimed precisely at the partaking of the bread and cup, which suggests that this action was eventually separated from the main meal. From a theological viewpoint the *anamnesis* motif has certainly been influenced by the significant and broad meanings of the word "remembrance" *(zkr)* in the OT, in which the remembrance of the past is thought of as becoming actual in the present. The wording of the *anamnesis* command also resembles the commands in the institution of Hellenistic meals in memory of the dead (Chenderlin 1982: 143–45, 217), and in this way the Lord's Supper is brought into close association with this type of meal. Additionally, the doubling of the *anamnesis* command in v 25c possibly goes back to Paul and in any case he clearly expresses the relationship of the celebration to the Lord's death in v 26. The Lord's Supper, comprised of word and action, is a realistic proclamation of the past death of Christ on the cross. The celebrating church must not get lost in the present; the present Lord is the crucified and the coming one at the same time. Reminiscent of the eschatological outlook of Mark 14:25 ("until he comes"), Paul keeps the celebration of the Lord's Supper oriented to the longing expectation of the parousia.

In his quotation of the Words of Institution Paul has the Corinthian practice of the Lord's Supper in mind throughout. The members of the church presumably gathered in the home of a well-to-do Christian (e.g. in the house of Gaius, cf. Rom 16:23) on Saturday or Sunday night (cf. 1 Cor 16:2; Rev 1:10). They brought their provisions for the meal with them and these were then shared with others. The breaking of the bread and the blessing of the cup had already been combined as a special act at the end of the meal (Neuenzeit 1960: 69–76). At this occasion verbal acts of worship, such as the reading of the Scriptures, singing of Psalms, prophecy, and speaking in tongues, after the manner of 1 Cor 14:1–40, may have been added. At this point the Corinthian church clearly shows herself to be the *ekklesia,* the church of God (cf. 11:18, 22; 14:23).

The name "Lord's Supper" embraces the entire event, including the main meal, together with the concluding rite of the bread and wine. Besides the anamnetic component (looking back at the Lord's death) and the eschatological (looking forward to the parousia of the Lord; cf. the anticipation of "the day of the Lord" in the OT), the word *kyriakos* first and foremost takes on also the following meaning: one recognizes the presence of the Lord by his Spirit at the meal, both as host and Lord. And from his hands believers receive all the benefits of the meal. Even the provisions for the meal themselves have become the property of the Lord.

This ideal picture was rather badly disfigured by the misdemeanors occurring in Corinth. Poorer Christians and slaves, who could come only later, could participate in the rite of the bread and the cup, but were excluded from the main meal (Bornkamm 1970: 142–45). This social scandal, according to Paul, made it impossible for a true Lord's Supper to take place (11:20). Paul interprets such behavior as a violation of the very essence of the institution of the Lord's Supper (11:27). The intent of the salvatory Christ event—which is captured in the "for you" in the saying over the bread, and the notion of covenant in the saying over the cup—are thereby perverted.

According to Paul the consequences for the individual who sins in this way, as well as for the entire congregation, are disastrous (cf. 11:27–32). In his reference to the sick and the dead in 11:30 one cannot help but gain the impression that Paul ascribes the destructive powers of a tabu to the sacred food. One can readily document such thinking from the world of Paul (Klauck 1986: 327–28). On the other hand one should note carefully that Paul does not establish a direct relationship between sickness and personal guilt. Nor does he suggest that the worthy participation in the eucharist is a protection against one's own death. Rather, he has the church as a whole in mind; in the last analysis, it is the church that is sick. Moreover, those cases where death has occurred are seen in the light of the imminent parousia. Instead of hastening the parousia, the unworthy manner of celebrating the Lord's Supper permits the powers of destruction and death to carry on their activity in the present age.

Besides, Paul adds a few practical suggestions. In 11:33 he recommends that the Corinthians wait with the main meal until everyone has arrived and in that way the problems can be avoided. In 11:22, to be sure, another possibility emerges ("Do you not have houses to eat and drink in?"); namely, in an extreme situation, Paul would even entertain the possibility of separating the main meal from the bread/cup rite (in the terminology of a later period: the separation of Agape and Eucharist).

b. 1 Cor 10:14–22. In the context of his discourse on the participation in pagan sacrificial meals, Paul (1 Cor 10:1–13) first of all sets the example of the wilderness generation before the eyes of the Corinthians (cf. Willis 1985: 123–63). This generation allowed itself to be lulled into a false sense of security through "spiritual food" and "spiritual drink," i.e., through the manna and water from the rock. Paul sees prototypes of the Christian sacraments in the OT, but with unmistakable paraenetic intent.

In 1 Cor 10:16 he quotes a linguistically-polished fragment of tradition which he has taken from the eucharistic teaching of his Hellenistic churches (Käsemann 1970: 12). He himself puts it in question form to make it fit better with v 17, and mentions the cup before the bread. This unit of tradition expands and deepens the words of interpretation given at the institution of the Supper. When we read in v 16a, "The cup of blessing which we bless," Paul not only sets off the cup of the Christian Lord's Supper from the last cup of the Jewish festal meal, but he also points to the full development of eucharistic prayers, since blessing according to Jewish custom is bestowed by prayer (cf. the allusions to table grace in 1 Cor 10:30; Rom 14:6). Christian prayers of blessing at the Lord's Supper have not been handed down to us in the NT, but we do find them in the *Didache* (cf. *Did.* 9:2–4).

By contrast to the older saying over the cup (1 Cor 11:25), the cup in 1 Cor 10:16 is not equated with the new covenant but with the blood (cf. Mark 14:24)—an indication of more advanced reflection. What is new is the concept of *koinōnia,* which is derived not from Judaism but from the vocabulary for sacral meals in Hellenism. It signifies fellowship through participation (Hainz 1982: 18–35; cf. Willis 1985: 168–81). The eating of the bread and the drinking of the cup mediate personal fellowship with the crucified and glorified Christ through participation in his body and blood. At the same time there is a fellowship among those who jointly participate, as 10:17 makes more explicit. The twofold emphasis, that there is only one loaf was used at the Lord's Supper in Corinth (as Diog. Laert, *Vit. Phil.* 8:35 and Iambl. *VP.* 86 indicate for the Pythagorians). Through the communal participation in the one bread "the many" (Mark 14:24, "for many") become one body, i.e., one church, which is constituted by the Lord's Supper and understands itself as the body of Christ. "Body" is transmuted here as in 1 Cor 12:12–27 into an ecclesiological concept.

Whereas some Corinthian Christians apparently thought that baptism and the Lord's Supper would protect them in magical fashion from all dangers and permit them to participate in pagan cults, Paul argues in 10:18–22 that the sacramental components of the concept of *koinōnia* clearly demonstrate the incompatibility of the Christian Lord's Supper and pagan sacrificial meals. To be sure, for Paul there are neither gods (1 Cor 8:5) nor idols (cf. 1 Cor 8:4), but there are demons which stand behind pagan sacrifice as a fearsome reality. With this demonological interpretation of Gk polytheism Paul follows an OT-Jewish line of tradition (cf. Deut 32:17). We hear from non-Christian authors that demons establish a relationship between the gods and the people in sacrifices (Plut. *De def. or.* 13–14). Demons are said to feed on some parts of the sacrifice such as smoke and blood, and they try to enter the human body through the sacrificial meal (Iambl. *Myst.* 6:3; Porphr. acc. to Euseb. *Praep. Evang.* 4.23.3). Whether Paul, too, entertained the notion that sacrificial meals cause a demonic infection to take place can only be posed as a question. As far as the external rite is concerned, Paul in 10:21 singles out the cup of libation and the table in the hosting by the deity (cf. Isa 65:11). The cup of libation, with accompanying drink offerings, consists primarily of wine at a sacrifice and a symposium. Paul sets the "cup of the Lord," which is identical with the cup of blessing in 10:6, over against this pagan cup. The table has a different function in pagan cults than the altar. On the altar before the temple the sacrificial offerings are burned; on the table, often found inside the temple, one lays them down.

The table plays a significant role in *theoxenia* (where the gods act as hosts) and in the cult of the dead. In the OT, on which Paul leans linguistically (cf. Mal 1:7, 12), the "table of the Lord" means the table of showbread in the temple. The parallels in the celebration of the Christian Lord's Supper must be completely divorced from these contrasts. Paul, in fact, has the family table in mind around which a house-church would gather for the Lord's Supper.

One will not be able entirely to avoid the conclusion that Paul, by contrasting the Lord's Supper with pagan feasts, indirectly sets it into the category of sacrificial meals. However, one must then immediately ask for the basis of such an analogy. Paul first of all discovers parallels in the table fellowship which is established through the offering of a sacrificial gift. See SACRIFICE AND SACRIFICIAL OFFERINGS (NT).

c. Lord's Supper and Ministry in Paul. It seems strange that Paul, in the face of the disorders at the Lord's Supper mentioned in 1 Corinthians 11, and the confusion at the meetings of the church mentioned in 1 Corinthians 14, does not charge a single office bearer with the task of restoring order. Obviously presiding at the Lord's Table and at the meetings of the congregation was not yet restricted to one person. There are fellow-workers to whom people are to submit (1 Cor 16:16); there are administrative services (1 Cor 12:28); there are leaders (1 Thess 5:12; Rom 12:8). However, these are mentioned in so casual a manner and appear so late in the lists of gifts that one hesitates to give them a prominent place at the Lord's Supper or else the responsibility of presiding was not yet invested with great dignity. Different attempts have been made (among others the one based on *Did.* 10:7: "Permit the prophets to say thanks" [*eucharistein*], as often as they wish") to find the leader at the Lord's Supper in the ranks of the early Christian prophets. If one begins with the assumption that the early churches began as house churches, one has good reason to hold that the father of the household or the owner of the house in which the church met assumed the leadership at the Lord's Supper. When he was personally present, the apostle himself, as honored guest, very likely assumed this responsibility; but that need not have been so always and everywhere. At the ancient symposium, which may serve as a kind of analogy (see D.1 below), the symposiarch, the chairman of the event, was chosen at the occasion from among the guests. Women may also have presided at the Lord's Supper in early Christianity, like Junia the apostle (Rom 16:7), Phoebe the deaconness and leader (Rom 16:1, 2), Prisca the head of a house church (1 Cor 16:19; Rom 16:3–5), or Nympha (Col 4:15) as prophetess (cf. 1 Cor 11:5; Acts 21:9). Whether and in what capacity the bishops (note the plural) and the deacons (Phil 1:1) played a role at the Lord's Supper is hard to determine. The contours of the later monepiscopate become visible only in the post-Pauline Pastoral Epistles, but even here their duties are not restricted to the eucharist.

2. Synoptics. a. Mark. The Last Supper is here described as a Passover meal (Mark 14:12) and as Jesus' farewell banquet. The account of the Institution of the Lord's Supper in 14:22–25, however, shows no signs of a Passover. Everything that is typical of a Passover is missing: the paschal lamb, the stewed fruit, the bitter herbs, and the Passover haggadah. Various peculiarities of the text in fact seem to suggest that it served as aetiological cult-legend for the Lord's Supper. The breaking of the bread and the blessing of the cup have already been united into one act at the end of the meal—something that clearly emerges from Mark 14:26. The departure to the Mount of Olives follows immediately upon the interpretive words spoken over the bread and the wine (14:22–25). Moreover, this made possible the concentration of all interpretive additions, including the *hyper pollōn* ("on behalf of many") in connection with the saying over the cup (which seems to overload the text in its present form). Also, the extensive parallels in the saying over the bread and the cup in the first part ("this is my body"; "this is my blood . . .") is the result of liturgical practice. Hand in hand with that goes an increasing interest in the elements of the meal, the bread and the wine, interpreted as body and blood of Christ. The exhortation "take," at the beginning of the saying over the bread in 14:22, points in the same direction, and may express a certain reserve regarding the eucharistic gifts. The note, "and they all drank of it," in v 23b can be understood in the light of the custom of the use of one common cup by all the participants at the Lord's Supper, as long as the number of participants made this possible. Concerning the preferred OT paradigms, the new covenant of Jer 31:31 (cf. 1 Cor 11:25) is replaced by the covenant meal of Exod 24:6–11, which was accompanied by an unusual blood ritual. Thereby the writer introduces notions of sacrifice into the Synoptic tradition of the Lord's Supper. See also SACRIFICE AND SACRIFICIAL OFFERINGS (NT).

There can be little doubt that in the context of the present gospel text, the account of the Institution in Mark (as well as its side references) harkens back to the miracles of feeding (Mark 6:35–44; 8:1–10 par.), whatever its original source or form may have been. The Christian reader saw reflections of the Lord's Supper in the blessing and breaking of the bread by Jesus (as well as in the disciples' distribution of these to the crowds; 6:41: 8:6). At the same time the accounts reminded him of his social obligations to the hungry (6:37), which in the early church were closely connected with the practice of the Lord's Supper, and not only in Paul (Reicke 1951: 21–38).

b. Matthew. Matthew's version of the account of the Institution (26:26–29) can be understood as a further development of the Markan presentation. What is questionable, however, is whether it is sufficient to think of it simply as a literary recension or whether one should see reflections of church practice, which developed on the basis of the identical wording of Mark 14:22–25. The exhortation "take, eat" in Matt 26:26 and "drink of it, all of you" in 26:27 could be arguments for the latter (cf. Patsch 1972: 69–70, 103–4). The setting for the imperatives is most naturally to be found in the liturgical celebration in which bread and wine have already attained the aura of a numinous consecration. "For the forgiveness of sin" in 26:26 (cf. Matt 3:1–2 diff Mark 1:4) offers a theological explanation of "for the many" in the Markan tradition.

c. Luke. The account of the Last Supper in Luke 22:14–20 presents us first of all with a textual problem. In the so-called Western text vv 19b–20 are missing. A number of interpreters choose to cross off also v 19a as secondary, and draw some broad historical inferences on the basis of this shortened text, which suddenly looks altogether different from the traditional account of the Institution in Paul and Mark. However, in spite of opposing voices, the originality of the longer text, including vv 19b–20, can meanwhile be considered as secure (cf. Jeremias 1967: 133–53; Marshall 1980: 36–38).

In 22:14–20 Luke combines the Markan text-tradition with his own, which in his account of the Institution (22:19–20) is very similar to Paul's (Schürmann 1970: 17–31) and points to the account of the Passover meal in particular (22:14–18; called "account of the passover" here because of v 15: "I have earnestly desired to eat this passover with you before I suffer"). The obvious inclusion of the Last Supper within the framework of a Passover meal, which is thereby validated, certainly agrees with the historicizing tendencies of Luke. Somewhat attractive is the conjecture that vv 14–18 have their setting in an early Christian Passover celebration which took place once a year at Easter in connection with the celebration of the Lord's Supper (Schürmann 1968: 72–73; Kuhn 1957: 91–92), but convincing proof has not yet been given.

In Luke we discover a comment in the Easter narratives that the risen Christ breaks bread with his disciples (Luke 24:30), that he eats before their very eyes or with them (24:41–43; cf. John 21:9–13). Acts 10:41 also looks back: "To us . . . who ate and drank with him after he rose from the dead," as does the enigmatic expression *synhalizomenos* (possibly "eat together") in Acts 1:4. Cullmann (1966: 510–16) wanted to derive the practice of the Lord's Supper in the early church from these appearances of Christ at meals after Easter, but thereby he paid too little attention to the precarious historical basis for the corresponding traditions. Much more significant is the twofold observation from a hermeneutical standpoint: (a) Without the resurrection of Jesus and the experience of Easter on the part of the disciples, there would never have been a regular practice of the Lord's Supper, because it would have lacked the central theological presupposition; and (b) the Communal Lord's Supper was the place at which every believer, who was temporally removed from the first Easter, could gain the assurance of the presence of the risen Lord. Seen as a whole, the resurrection of Jesus is the real foundation for the shaping of the practice of the Lord's Supper and the conceptual development of sacramental categories. This entire process, to a large degree, runs parallel to the post-Easter unfolding of an explicit Christology.

3. Acts. a. The Breaking of the Bread. In the first big summary of the life of the early church of Jerusalem (Acts 2:42–47), Luke mentions the breaking of the bread twice, in Acts 2:42 and especially in 2:46: ". . . and breaking bread in their homes, they partook of food with glad and generous hearts." Here possibly a distinction between a regular meal ("partook of food") and eucharistic rite ("breaking bread") is suggested, even though originally both were integrated into one event. One gets the impression from Luke that a regular meal was held daily as a Lord's Supper in the various Christian homes in Jerusalem in the early church. This supper (according to Acts 6:1–2) also had caritative, that is, diaconic functions. However, that reflects an idealized view of the golden age of the beginning and cannot be accepted as historical reality. Household meals accompanied by eucharistic practices probably occurred only once a week, on the Sabbath (patterned after the Jewish Sabbath meal [*cena pura*?]) or on the Lord's day.

In Acts 2:7,11 the church at Troas gathers "on the first day of the week" (cf. Luke 24:1) to break bread, and Paul takes it in hand. Connected with that is the proclamation of the Word. The exact time seems to have been Sunday rather than Saturday night. The place is the upper room of a private house (20:8; cf. 1:13). That Luke at least has in mind the Lord's Supper, as he knows it from his church, could hardly be denied (cf. Wanke 1973: 19–24). Obviously he is connecting certain symbolic connotations with the meal. The place of the Lord's Supper is conspicuous ("upper room") as a place of fellowship (20:7) of light (20:8), and of life (20:12).

The same thing applies to Acts 27:35–36, in spite of the opinion of many exegetes to the contrary (cf. Wanke 1973: 25–30): on the ship that is in danger of shipwreck Paul takes bread (cf. Luke 9:16; 22:19; 24:30), gives thanks (*eucharistēsen,* cf. Luke 22:19), breaks the bread (cf. Luke 9:16; 22:19; 24:30; Acts 2:42, 46; 20:7,11) and eats it (Acts 27:35), as do the others until they have had enough (27:38). Here we come upon the same juxtaposition of the "breaking of bread" and "partaking of food" as in the summary in Acts 2:46. Luke knows how to distinguish these items. Paul's actions are distinguished from the main meal of his countrymen. There is hidden in it an unmistakable pointer to the Lord's Supper which lets all those in need experience the saving power of the risen Christ in the present.

b. Communion *sub una*? The fact that Luke mentions only the breaking of the bread has led variously to the assumption that the Lord's Supper was practiced *sub una,* i.e., with bread only, without wine or, as an alternative, water instead of wine. Among other things it has been suggested that wine would have been too expensive for the poor churches in the long run (Jeremias 1967: 108). A celebration of the Lord's Supper without wine can be documented from Jewish Christian tradition and apocryphal writings (Klauck 1986: 214–15, 225–32); however, it cannot have been the rule. Luke proceeds on the assumption that the breaking of the bread and the blessing of the cup has already been taken out of the context of the meal and has been isolated into a double act. On this assumption the breaking of the bread, a rite at the beginning of the meal only (as far as its origin goes), could include for him all the gestures and the words over the bread and the wine. They have become, in other words, names for the Lord's Supper. The absence of wine in Acts 2:46 would stand in contradiction to the strong emphasis on festal joy; for celebration and festivity at a meal were essentially determined by the availability of wine. For the Synoptic words of Institution it is important to note that the eschatological outlook (Mark 14:25 par.) which belongs to the earliest form of the text, explicitly speaks about "the fruit of the vine," and so a celebration without wine is no option.

c. A Dualistic Theory of Eucharistic Origins. Acts 2:46 plays a key role in Lietzmann's famous theory of a double origin of the Lord's Supper in the early church (Lietzmann 1979: 195–203)—an origin which had various forerunners and which to this day is given variegated forms (cf. Fuller 1963: 60–65). According to Lietzmann, the Jerusalem church celebrated its Lord's Supper with festive joy and as a continuation of the daily fellowship at meals with the earthly Jesus. This is contrasted by the Pauline example from 1 Cor 11:23–26, in which the Lord's Supper is tied to the sacrificial death of Jesus on the cross and which is consciously linked to Jesus' Last Supper. The texts of Acts 2:46, with its strong Lukan character, does not allow us to make such an historical conclusion (cf. the criticism, especially of Schweizer 1963: 344–47). The farewell banquet of Jesus stands in an unmistakable relationship to the fellowship meals Jesus provided for people during his earthly ministry. These two important facts must not be torn asunder. On the other hand, the celebration of the Lord's Supper experienced a rapid and stormy development which tended to go in various directions in the first few decades after Easter. But this process has not been sufficiently appreciated if one postulates a chronological sequence of distinct models or if one views them as mutually exclusive of each other. The reduction of two basic types means at the same time an illegitimate simplification of a very much more complex and differentiated situation.

4. Gospel of John. a. John 6 and John 13. John 13 reports in detail a farewell banquet which Jesus celebrated with his disciples in the face of his death (13:1–3). We discover that Jesus on that occasion washed the disciples' feet (13:4–11). Also we have the long farewell discourses in John 14–17, which find their setting within the framework of the Last Supper. Apparently the account of the Institution which the Synoptists and Paul focus on is lacking in John.

Instead, one finds the OT manna-typology assimilated into the discourse on the bread in John 6 (cf. Borgen 1965). Note particularly the verse at the end: "The bread which I shall give for the life of the world is my flesh" (6:51c). The wording is reminiscent of the saying over the bread from the Pauline-Lukan account of the Institution (1 Cor 11:24 = Luke 22:19), combined with the universalistic "for the many" from the Markan saying over the cup (Mark 14:24). The verse apparently assimilates the tradition of the Lord's Supper as found in the Johannine church, that celebrated the Lord's Supper. In John 6:52–58 we have the so-called eucharistic discourse which calls for the eating of the flesh and the drinking of the blood of Jesus in crassly vivid terms.

The structure and origin of John 6 is still being debated in scholarly research (cf. Léon-Dufour 1982: 290–300). A possible solution (for a somewhat different but related concept, cf. Wehr 1986) looks like this: In the light of the practice of the Lord's Supper in his church John, in the discourse on the bread (John 6:26–51), is concerned about a deeper symbolical-theological interpretation of the sacramental event. Its true content is faith and the personal encounter with Jesus in sign and word. The Evangelist thereby takes issue with the danger of a magical misunderstanding of the sacrament which threatens the loss of the practical meaning of the Supper for faith and life. For the same reason he leaves off the account of the Institution in John 13. The signal act of feet-washing brings into focus the loving self-giving of Jesus, which puts the believer under obligation in a much clearer manner.

The Evangelist lets us know his intention by adding the saying over the bread from the Lord's Supper in 6:51c. In the context of the saying over the bread one could read into the Supper two ideas, the sacramental and the personal-communative. The concept "flesh" (Gk *sarx*) is probably not to be understood as a translation variant of "body" (Gk *sōma*), but makes a bridge to John 1:14: "And the word became flesh." The materialization of the salvation experience which occurs principally by faith and is drawn into the sacrament is understood by the Evangelist as analogous to the incarnation of the heavenly Son of Man. Here as there, we have a scandalous event which calls forth the protest of the average consciousness. The opposition of the disciples in 6:60 against this "hard saying," which in 6:61–62 is applied to the descent of the heavenly Son of Man (cf. 6:50, 51), is clearly aligned with it. The problematic saying in 6:63: "It is the Spirit that gives life, the flesh is of no avail," does not annul 1:14 and 6:51, but adds a necessary expansion. The incarnation and embodiment, the descent, would remain ineffectual if it didn't also lead to the ascent of the Son of Man (6:62). The resurrection of Jesus truly sets the Spirit free; it embraces the meaning of the words concerning the earthly and makes possible faith, which is also at work in the Lord's Supper in the church.

The reaction of the disciples makes the saying about the bread in 6:51c the occasion to integrate the eucharistic discourse (6:52–58) at this point. This blocks the attempts to see in it a lecture on symbolism; much rather is it an attempt to underscore in dramatic fashion the reality of the sacramental. The occasion for this view was provided by the controversies concerning the right understanding of the Lord's Supper. Opponents who looked at 6:52–58 were either more docetically-gnostically influenced, or they were at home in Jewish-Christian circles in which the understanding of the real presence of Christ in the bread and the wine of the Lord's Supper was decisively rejected. In the eucharistic discourse the older church traditions are integrated with the sacramental orientation (cf. Wehr 1986), which the Evangelist himself, insofar as he knew them, opposed with rather strong reserve.

b. Further Texts. Some want to see eucharistic allusions, among other things, also in the following Johannine texts (cf. Johansson 1944: 263–68; Léon Defour 1982: 311–14): the wedding at Cana, with the changing of the water into wine (2:1–11); the discourse on the True Vine (15:1–5); the blood and water from the pierced side of Jesus (19:34); the meal with the risen Christ in the redactional addendum (21:9–13; see also under B 2c); and the witness of the water and the blood in 1 John 5:6–8.

In the light of the dominant symbolical strains of the Johannine language it is difficult to make a definite decision. One cannot, however, dismiss out of hand the possibility of eucharistic allusions in every case. Nevertheless, one should be slow to make quick identifications and should instead move with caution (Marshall 1980: 137). The hypothesis of an all pervasive theology of sacraments does not explain the real concern of the Johannine Evangelist.

5. Revelation. According to 1:3 and 22:18, the author of the Revelation of John wrote with the purpose of having his work read in the meetings of the church. For this reason one must ask how the liturgical language of the book, which has its origin in Jewish apocalypses, is to be understood in the context of early Christian worship (cf. Delling 1970: 449–50). Once again this raises the question of what part the Lord's Supper played in worship.

In Rev 3:20 we have the salvatory promise (harkening back to the metaphoric language of the parable in Luke 12:35–38?): "Behold, I stand at the door and knock, if any one hears my voice and opens the door, I will come in to him and eat with him, and he with me." The passage captures the expectation of the messianic meal at the end of the age which, however, can be anticipated also in the present, wherever there is a meeting with Jesus through faith. It seems possible that we have here, as in John 6, a deepened spiritual interpretation of the practice of the Lord's Supper. The same theme is struck in 19:7: "For the marriage of the Lamb has come, and his Bride has made herself ready" (cf. the beatitude addressed to those invited to this meal in 19:9). Here one can hardly see any connection with the Lord's Supper. Rather the emphasis is on the union between Christ and his church in the present and in the future (cf. 2 Cor 11:2) as a further development of the OT imagery of the marriage between God and Israel.

In Rev 11:17 a thanksgiving prayer is introduced with *eucharistoumen* (cf. *Did.* 9:2–3), but its contents rule out the notion of a eucharistic prayer. There remains, then, the conclusion of the book (22:6–21) in which some have discovered a variety of elements taken from the celebration of the Lord's Supper (cf. Prigent 1964: 37–45; Klauck 1986: 356–64). In this regard v 15 includes an excommunication clause which is to keep the unrepentant and the non-Christians away from the Lord's Supper (cf. 1 Cor 16:22; *Did.* 9:5). The words of invitation, "and let him who is thirsty come, let him who desires take the water of life without price" (v 17b), is then said to be an invitation to the Lord's Supper. "Amen. Come, Lord Jesus!" (v 20b) is the equivalent of the Aramaic *maranatha,* which clearly stands in the context of the Lord's Supper in *Did.* 10:6 and possibly in 1 Cor 16:22. However, even if certain liturgical elements should have been integrated into the conclusion of the book, one must consider that they take on a different function in a different literary context and cannot (nor do they wish to) reflect the complete sequence of events in an early Christian celebration of the Lord's Supper.

6. Hebrews. The author of the Epistle to the Hebrews develops his theology in large measure with the help of linguistic models taken from the OT and the Jewish sacrificial cult. Among them one finds also concepts that are known to us from the traditions concerning the Lord's Supper. In 9:20 he quotes the saying about "the blood of the covenant" from Exod 24:8, and not with the introductory "behold" *(idou)* as in the LXX, but rather with "this" *(touto),* a word that one tends to connect with the words of interpretation. "Blood of the covenant" occurs also in Heb 10:29. In 2:4 (connected with the verb "to share," *koinōneō;* cf. the *koinōnia* in 1 Cor 10:16), the author speaks of the blood and flesh (in this sequence and also in 10:19, 20; cf. also 9:12–14 in the matter of the blood of Christ). In Heb 8:8 (cf. 9:15) we encounter the "new covenant" of Jer 31:31 (cf. 1 Cor 11:24). Furthermore, there is mention of the tasting of the heavenly gift (Heb 6:4) and of an altar (*thysiastērion,* cf. 1 Cor 10:18), from which those who serve in the tent have no right to eat (Heb 13:10).

This has led researchers (cf. Williamson 1975: 300–1) in part to see in the eucharistic emphasis the hermeneutical key to the understanding of the Epistle to the Hebrews as a whole, going even to the extreme position in which "the bigger and more perfect tent" (9:11) is understood as the eucharistic body of Christ (cf. Williamson 1975: 304–5). On the other hand, the exact opposite conclusions have been drawn from the same texts, namely that the writer of the epistle rejects the Lord's Supper of the larger church and polemicizes against it. It is said that the author is anti-sacramentarian and that he does not feel comfortable with the concept of eating the body and drinking the blood of the Lord.

One should from the outset realize that the Epistle to the Hebrews has a strong emphasis on the verbal aspect of worship and sees the meetings of the church as non-cultic (cf. 10:25). The concepts such as "blood of the covenant," and "new covenant," have been taken over directly from the OT and not via the Lord's Supper tradition. "Blood" and "flesh" of Jesus Christ evoke memories of his bloody death on the cross. The cultic language is used by the author to explicate the non-cultic salvation events without creating new cultic forms. Whatever may be the reasons, the Lord's Supper appears to lie outside his theological interest (for further information and bibliography, see SACRIFICE AND SACRIFICIAL OFFERINGS (NT), and Williamson 1975: 302–12; Klauck 1982: 149–51).

7. Jude and 2 Peter. In Jude 12, in the context of the polemic against false teachers who are making their influence felt in the church, we read: "These are blemishes on your love feasts (*en tais agapais,* in the majority of manuscripts), as they boldly carouse together, looking after themselves." For the first time in the NT the communion meal of the church receives the name Agape (cf. Ign. *Smyrn.* 8:2), which in the 2d century C.E. develops a character quite distinct from the eucharist. See AGAPE MEAL. In Jude a single unified church meal is assumed, in which the main meal and the two-fold eucharistic rite still go together. As a whole, the meal underscores the significance of love as the life-principle of the church. From that position the caritative aspects of the meal are opened. Already the very fact that false teachers participate in the practices of the church are seen by the author of the epistle as scandalous. Very likely he also wants to suggest to the false teachers that they no longer take the Lord's Supper seriously, but that they have perverted it into a voluptuous feast and profaned it (cf. on this and the following point Völker 1927: 107–10; Reicke 1951: 352–67).

In similar fashion 2 Pet 2:13b takes a position against the false teachers: "They count it pleasure to revel in the day time. They are blots and blemishes, reveling in their dissipation *(en tais apatais),* carousing with you." The majority of the textual witnesses read *apatais,* not *agapais* as in Jude 12. Since one can assume that the author of 2 Peter is familiar with the Epistle of Jude, one will have to understand this change as a deliberate wordplay and as a bit of irony. The author does not want to give the honored name Agape to the meals which are being held with false teachers present. They have nothing in common with the Lord's

Supper but have already been perverted into revelry, as can be seen from the time in which they are held ("in the day time" instead of at evening). These love feasts *(agapai)* are actually a deception *(apatē)*.

C. Outside the NT

1. *Didache.* The *Didache* (cf. Wengst 1984: 43–57) in chaps. 9–10 offers prayers for a church meal which was held on the Lord's day, i.e. on Sunday (*Did.* 14:1), a meal consisting of the breaking of bread (ibid.) and which was called *eucharistia* (9:1,5). The procedure looks like this: A prayer is spoken, first over the cup of wine (9:2) and then over the bread (9:3–4). There follows, then, in reverse order, the consumption of the bread and wine (cf. 9:5; "eating . . . drinking"). In conclusion we have an afterdinner prayer (10:1–6), which gives the celebration the character of a regular meal (cf. 10:1: "After you have finished your meal, give thanks in this way"). The contents of these prayers closely resemble the Jewish-Hellenistic table prayers. They suggest that the elements of the meal are lifegiving spiritual food (10:3): "To us you have given spiritual food and drink and eternal life through Jesus, your servant." Bread in particular is seen as the symbol of the eschatological gathering of the people of God into one church (9:4: "As this piece of bread was scattered over the hills and then was brought together and made one, so let your church be brought together from the ends of the earth into your kingdom"). Finally, they stress also the eschatological orientation of the entire celebration (10:6 "Let Grace come and let this world pass away . . . Maranatha"). In 14:1–3 the sacrificial aspect is added which, however, cannot be related generally to prayer and lifestyle. Directly related to that are the church offices of bishops and deacons, mentioned in 15:1–2. They take over the functions of prophets and teachers and play a role also at the celebration of the Supper.

It could be that this meal has nothing to do with the Agape but rather with a celebration that represents the Lord's Supper functionally, even when the words of Institution and the interpretation seem to be missing. Instead we encounter an idea that leads to the development of independent eucharistic prayers. For that the contours of the account of the Institution of the Lord's Supper (". . . blessed it"; ". . . gave thanks") offered sufficient room for development (with reference to 1 Cor 10:16, see B.1 above; cf. Wehr 1986).

2. Ignatius. Ignatius repeatedly refers to the eucharist in his letters (cf. Schoedel 1985: 21–23, 97–99, 240–42; Wehr 1986). In *Eph.* 20:2 he mentions "the medicine of immortality" and "antidote against death" (cf. Christ as the "one physician" in *Eph.* 7:2). Thereby he introduces Hellenistic categories into the Lord's Supper. In *Smyrn.* 7:1 he formulates the confession for his theological opponents with their docetic Christology: "The eucharist is the flesh of our Savior Jesus Christ." The parallel between *eucharistia* and *thysiastērion* (altar of sacrifice in *Phld.* 4:1) suggests a strengthened consciousness with regard to the sacrificial character of the eucharist (Klauck 1982: 154–55).

What is particularly noteworthy is the fact that Ignatius ties the celebration of the eucharist closely to ecclesiastical office. In the absence of the bishop or one of his deputies there is to be no eucharist (*Smyrn.* 8:9). In retrospect that brings out our NT findings in bold relief. In the NT, presiding at the Lord's Supper is not closely connected with any specific office (see B.1.c above).

3. Justin. In Justin's *Apol.* 65–67, in which we have the most detailed description of the Lord's Supper in the early church, we encounter a situation that is similar to that of Ignatius. In his *Apol.* 65–67 the administration of the Supper is given over to a leader (*Apol.* 65:3,5; *prohestos*) who speaks the prayer of thanksgiving over the bread and the wine. Deacons distribute the eucharistic offering in the congregation (65:5). In a very difficult idiom Justin in 66:2 compares the efficacy of the prayer of blessing, which changes the bread and the wine into the flesh and blood of Jesus (the incarnation), and then he quotes the words of Institution. The words of interpretation have been reduced to the form: "This is my body," "This is my blood." Thereby the tendency to seek parallels which arise out of liturgical practice, and which in Mark distinguishes itself from Paul, arrives at its ultimate terminus (for bibliography, see Klauck 1986: 139 n. 324).

D. Religious-Historical Backgrounds

Religiously significant meals are a universal phenomenon in the history of religions (Bammel 1950), and not only in antiquity. In what follows we can sketch broadly the sociocultural context in which the development of the Christian Lord's Supper took place. Moreover, we need to inquire only about the post-Easter Lord's Supper, and not the Last Supper of Jesus, although they cannot be entirely divorced from each other. Thus, while the Pascha, Toda (Patsch 1972: 24–26, 39–40), the Kiddush and the Chabura (Jeremias 1967: 20–25) are possibly significant for the Last Supper, but are of no concern for our inquiry.

1. Jewish. Great significance must be attached to the daily Jewish meals and to Jewish banquets at which wine was used. The breaking of bread, the blessing of the cup, and the appropriate words of prayer have broken out of the framework of Jewish meals and have gradually been ritualized into a cultic rite. Of interest also is the fact that the breaking of the bread, seen terminologically, is found in the OT only in the context of funeral rites for the dead (Jer 16:7; cf. Lam 4:4; Ezek 24:17, 22). For the motif of festal joy (Acts 2:46) one might recall the joy-filled farewell meals of the patriarchs prior to their death (Johansson 1944: 29–38; Reicke 1951: 141–43).

A daily meal with bread and wine (or grape juice) over which a priest pronounces a blessing, is known also in the Qumran community (1QS 6:4–5): "And when a table has been prepared for eating or the new wine for drinking the priest shall be the first to stretch out his hand to bless the first-fruits of the bread and the new wine." In 1QSa 2:17–22 it is connected with the eschatological-messianic expectation. When the congregation gathers at the communal table and the new wine for drinking has been mixed, the priest shall first of all pronounce the blessing over the bread and then "the anointed one of Israel shall stretch out his hand for the bread" (1.20–21). Related are the meals of the Essenes (*JW* 2.8.5 §129–33) and in a broader sense also those of the Therapeutae in Philo *Vita Cont* 36–37 (on the sabbath), 73–74, 81–82 (at the weekly festival); cf. Kuhn 1957: 67–72, 76–77. One can tell from these examples how the anticipation of the end of the age and the separation from the Temple fundamentally enhanced the religious significance of private meals. Early Christian churches that came out of Judaism found themselves in a very similar situation.

It can be shown that as an interpretive model the OT-Jewish sacrificial meals had a pronounced influence on the tradition of the Lord's Supper, in particular the covenant meal in Exod 24:1–11. Nor should one underestimate the contribution of the wisdom literature, where Wisdom as hostess invites people to a meal (Prov 9:1–6) and in which one can consume wisdom as one does food. That language played into the metaphoric way in which Philo of Alexandria, for example, speaks of eating (cf. *Vita Cont* 35). The Therapeutae are "entertained by Wisdom, who richly and lavishly offers her precepts so that they . . . hardly partake of the necessary food every six days" (Klauck 1986: 168–72, 184–87).

The metaphorical language used for meals in wisdom literature, together with false views arising from current Hellenistic cults, have had an influence on the mysterious stylized meal settings in the Hellenistic-Jewish conversion novel *Joseph and Aseneth.* Particularly striking is *Jos. Asen.* 19:5: "And a man came to me from heaven and gave me the *bread of life* and I ate and I drank the *cup of blessing*" (cf. 8:11). At other places the "cup of immortality" is found as a kind of pendant (8:5; 15:5; 16:16). In the Psalm of Aseneth the cup is expressly called "the cup of wisdom" (21:21). A wisdom-interpretation of the OT manna tradition also forms the background for the honeycomb from which the angel of God breaks a piece and puts it into the mouth of Aseneth (16:13–15). As a negative counterpart we have the pagan sacrificial meals and the distribution of wine from which Aseneth sets herself off (10:13) and which she interprets as bread that strangles and as a deceptive cup from the table of death (21:14). The concept of a sacred meal in *Jos. Asen.* serves the purpose of portraying the conversion of a proselytess to Judaism, which occurs concurrently with the invitation into a mystery cult and is superior to it (cf. Klauck 1986: 187–96; the numbering of the text according to C. Burchard, *OTP* 2: 177–247).

2. Pagan. Religious rites and prayers in part also accompany the daily meals of pagan antiquity. Epictetus recommends that one speak a prayer of thanksgiving for nourishment (*Diss.* 2.23.5). Among the Greeks one finds a drink-offering at the conclusion of the meal for the Agathos Daimon (Athen. 15), whom one must imagine to be the embodiment of the good spirit of the home.

The symposium had a socially-prominent place. The social drinking party of free men, which might be connected with supper, had well-defined ritual forms. The sequence of the main meal, including a drink offering for the gods, philosophical discussions, musical-artistic presentations, speeches and songs at a symposium, could provide a structural equivalent to a church's celebration with a meal (1 Cor 11:20–21): eucharistic double action (1 Cor 10:16–17), worship in word with prophecy, glossolalia, the reading of scripture, interpretation, psalms, songs and prayers (1 Corinthians 14).

The regular form of a Greek sacrifice was the communal offering. It flowed into a festive meal on the part of participants and could, depending on circumstances, be interpreted as if one thought of the deity as host and participant. Meals eaten by the members of the many Hellenistic associations, which looked upon communal dining as their main purpose, and the meals in the cult of the dead, find their basis and foundation in the sacrificial meal. See ASSOCIATIONS, CLUBS, THIASOI. Among other things there was also the memorial meal at which the person of the deceased founder was central (for this entire subject cf. Klauck 1986: 40–91).

The meals in the mystery cults have always drawn special attention (Klauck 1986: 91–166). See MYSTERY RELIGIONS. They do not represent a unified type, however. Rather they integrate items taken from the sacrificial cult and from the societies in a variety of ways (Kane 1975: 321–43). However, one notices a tendency toward a stronger participation in the fortunes of the deity, which can go so far—as it does, for example in the Dionysios cult—to the consumption of the deity itself.

This Hellenistic context (which, incidentally, has left its marks on Diaspora Judaism) must at least be considered as the horizon for the understanding of the Lord's Supper in gentile-Christian churches. It may well be that the clarification of the meaning of sacrament was not left unaffected by this context.

E. Conclusion

The practice of the Lord's Supper in the early church and its rapid breakthrough on a broad front is best explained by the fact that it is based on an historical event in the life of Jesus. One needs to take into account the farewell banquet which Jesus celebrated with his disciples in the face of his death and which he used as the occasion to explain the sacrificial service of his life in word and action. At the same time this last meal constitutes the final point in the continuous practice of participation in meals throughout the public ministry of Jesus (cf. Mark 2:15–17 par.; 6:32–44 par.; 14:3 par.; Luke 7:36; 11:37–38; 14:1, 7, 15; 15:1–2; 19:1–10) and receives some of its significance from the numerous images and parables in which Jesus spoke of the coming banquet at the end of the age (Mark 2:19 par.; Matt 6:11; 8:11 par.; Luke 6:21 par.; 14:15–24 par.; 22:29–30). The determinitive theological impulse for the development of a new Christian meal, which is a kind of recapitulation of the communal eating with Jesus, comes first of all, from the Easter event. On the level of narrative one can detect such in the accounts of the meals which the risen Christ had with his disciples, meals at which he revealed himself. Related to that is the early tendency to tie the Lord's Supper to the Lord's day, to Sunday, as the day of the resurrection (cf. also *Ign. Magn.* 9:10).

Appropriately there may have been initially the dominant conviction that the exalted Lord was present as participant and host at the celebration of the meal in his church. This personal presence must be viewed as the sustaining basis for every form of the presence of the Lord in the sacrament. Besides that, the Lord's Supper was interpreted eschatologically above all in times of acute anticipation, as proleptic presence of the imminent end of the age which, in keeping with apocalyptic expectation, was to culminate in a festal meal. Through the deliberate step back to Jesus' Last Supper, and then, via the Easter event, an event that made the Supper possible, there is added another essential element: the commemoration of the death of Jesus on the cross in its saving power. This aspect of the presence of the death of Jesus was utilized above all by Paul within the framework of his *theologia crucis.*

All these forms of presence are naturally quite real. However, people have gotten into the habit of tying the real presence of the body and blood of Christ to the elements of the supper, i.e., the bread and wine. The words of interpretation in the account of the Institution are intended for this purpose. Within the NT such an understanding of the words of interpretation are to be found in John 6:52–58, possibly also in 1 Cor 10:16–22, certainly in Corinthians, and finally in the account of the Institution itself, if one reads it as cult-aetiology in the form in which Mark and Matthew give it. The significance of this model of interpretation for the ancient and medieval church's teaching on the eucharist is obvious. There is reason to suspect unmistakably the presence of a strong influence of Hellenistic thinking and Hellenistic cult-piety, both in the NT and in early Christian tradition.

Two factors are especially consequential for the external form of the celebration. First, the sacramental rite is separated from the main meal. The isolation of the cultic rite from the church's meal is certainly suggested in the NT, although there it is not yet complete. However, by the time of Justin, at the latest, this separation had become complete and permanent. From that time on eucharist and agape stand disconnected alongside one another. Second, the celebration of the eucharist was closely connected to a church office. In the NT we notice the gradual development of an abundance of official functions and services. These office bearers were certainly present at the Lord's Supper, but nowhere is their service explicitly related to the Supper. That, however, is exactly what happens in the 2d century C.E. in the three-tiered structure of church offices—a structure that is clearly visible from the standpoint of who is responsible to preside at the celebration of the eucharist.

The dialogue concerning the Lord's Supper that is going on today between Christian denominations is in many respects prejudiced by historical processes and decisions that have taken place outside the NT. It is, therefore, all the more necessary for a theological orientation that ecclesiastical tradition should be confronted critically with the witness of the NT. In the light of the NT one could legitimately conceive of several options within given limits.

Bibliography

Bammel, F. 1950. *Das heilige Mahl im Glauben der Völker.* Gütersloh.

Borgen, P. 1965. *Bread from Heaven.* NovTSup 10. Leiden.

Bornkamm, G. 1970. Herrenmahl und Kirche bei Paulus (1956). Pp. 138–76 in *Studien zu Antike und Urchristentum: Gesammelte Aufsätze II.* BEvT 28. 3d ed. Munich.

Chenderlin, F. 1982. *"Do This as My Memorial"; The Semantic and Conceptual Background and Value of Anamnēsis in 1 Corinthians 11:24–25.* AnBib 99. Rome.

Cullmann, O. 1966. Die Bedeutung des Abendmahls im Urchristentum (1936). Pp. 505–23 in *Vorträge und Aufsätze 1925–1962,* ed. K. Fröhlich. Tübingen.

Delling, G. 1970. Zum gottesdienstlichen Stil der Johannes-Apokalypse (1959). Pp. 425–450 in *Studien zum Neuen Testament und zum hellenistischen Judentum. Gesammelte Aufsätze 1950–1968,* ed. F. Hahn, T. Holtz, and N. Walter. Göttingen.

Fuller, R. H. 1963. The Double Origin of the Eucharist. *BR* 8: 60–72.

Hainz, J. 1982. *Koinonia. "Kirche" als Gemeinschaft bei Paulus.* Biblische Untersuchungen 16. Regensburg.

Jeremias, J. 1967. *Die Abendmahlsworte Jesu.* 4th ed. Göttingen.

Johansson, N. 1944. *Det urkristna nattvardsfirandet.* Lund.

Kane, J. P. 1975. The Mithraic Cult Meal in its Greek and Roman Environment. Pp. 313–51 in Vol. 2 of *Mithraic Studies: Proceedings of the First International Congress of Mithraic Studies,* ed. J. R. Hinnells. Manchester.

Käsemann, E. 1970. Anliegen und Eigenart der pualinischen Abendmahlslehre (1947/48). Pp. 11–34 in *Exegetische Versuche und Besinnungen I,* 6th ed. Göttingen.

Klauck, H. J. 1982. *Thysiastērion* in Hebr 13,10 und bei Ignatius von Antiochien. Pp. 147–58 in *Studia Hierosolymitana III,* ed. G. C. Bottini. Studium Biblicum Franciscanum. Collectio Maior 30. Jerusalem.

———. 1986. *Herrenmahl und hellenistischer Kult.* 2d ed. NTAbh Neue Folge 15. Münster.

Kuhn, K. G. 1957. The Lord's Supper and the Communal Meal at Qumran. Pp. 65–93 and 259–65 in *The Scrolls and the New Testament,* ed. K. Stendahl. New York.

Léon-Dufour, X. 1982. *Le partage du pain eucharistique selon le Nouveau Testament.* Paris.

Lietzmann, H. 1979. *Mass and Lord's Supper: A Study in the History of the Liturgy.* Trans. D. H. G. Reeve. Leiden.

Marshall, I. H. 1980. *Last Supper and Lord's Supper.* Exeter.

Neuenzeit, P. 1960. *Das Herrenmahl.* SANT 1. Munich.

Patsch, H. 1972. *Abendmahl und historischer Jesus.* CThM A1. Stuttgart.

Prigent, P. 1964. *Apocalypse et Liturgie.* Cahiers Theologiques 52. Neuchâtel.

Reicke, B. 1951. *Diakonie: Festfreude und Zelos in Verbindung mit der altchristlichen Agapenfeier.* Uppsala universitets arsskrift 5. Uppsala.

Schoedel, W. R. 1985. *A Commentary on the Letters of Ignatius of Antioch.* Hermeneia. Philadelphia.

Schürmann, H. 1968. *Der Paschamahlbericht Lk 22. (7–14.)15–18: I, Teil einer quellenkritischen Untersuchung des lukanischen Abendmahlsberichtes Lk 22.7–38.* NTAbh XIX/5. 2d ed. Münster.

———. 1970. *Der Einsetzungsbericht Lk 22.19–20; II. Teil einer quellenkritischen Untersuchung des lukanischen Abendmahlsberichtes Lk 22.7–38.* NTAbh XX/4. 2d ed. Münster.

Schweizer, E. 1963. Das Herrenmahl im Neuen Testament. Ein Forschungsbericht (1954). Pp. 344–70 in *Neotestamentica. Deutsche und englische Aufsätze 1951–1963.* Zürich.

Völker, K. 1927. *Mysterium und Agape.* Gotha.

Wanke, J. 1973. *Beobachtungen zum Eucharistieverständnis des Lukas auf Grund der lukanischen Mahlberichte.* Erfurter Theologische Schriften 8. Leipzig.

Wehr, L. 1986. *Arznei der Unsterblichkeit: Die Eucharistie bei Ignatius von Antiochien und im Johannesevangelium.* NTAbh Neue Folge 18. Münster.

Wengst, K. 1984. *Didache (Apostellehre). Barnabasbrief. Zweiter Cle-*

mensbrief. Schrift an Diognet. Schriften des Urchristentums 2. Darmstadt.
Williamson, R. 1975. The Eucharist and the Epistle to the Hebrews. *NTS* 21: 300–12.
Willis, W. L. 1985. *Idol Meat in Corinth: The Pauline Argument in 1 Corinthians 8 and 10.* SBLDS 68. Chico.

HANS-JOSEF KLAUCK
Trans. David Ewert

LORD, DAY OF THE. See DAY OF THE LORD.

LOST TRIBES, THE. The 3d century Christian Latin poet Commodian (in the *Carmen* and *Instructiones*) and the author of the *Acts of St. Matthew* may preserve an otherwise lost Jewish apocalyptic and apocryphal work that apparently described the living conditions of the lost ten (or nine and a half) tribes which were taken into exile by the king of Assyria. According to early rabbinics Rabbi Akiba claimed these tribes would not return, but Rabbi Eliezer disagreed, arguing that they shall move from darkness to light (*m. Sanh.* 10.3). We cannot yet be certain that an early Jewish apocryphon existed; but it is clear that the legend was widely known and influential. Did a Jew, perhaps in the late 1st century compose an exegetical expansion based on OT passages, especially 2 Kgs 17:23 (cf. 1 Chr 5:26, Isa 11:11, Jer 31:8, and Ezek 37:19–28)? Around 100 C.E. three Jewish works—namely *4 Ezra* (13: 34–51), *2 Baruch* (77: 17–26), and Josephus' *Antiquities* (11.5)—referred to this legend or document.

If Commodian excerpts this apocryphon in his *Instructiones,* and if the passage that refers to the destruction of Jerusalem in 70 C.E. is from this Jewish work, then the document must postdate 70, and was probably contemporaneous with *4 Ezra, 2 Baruch,* and the *Antiquities.* The parallels with the *History of the Rechabites* are numerous and significant. M. R. James suggested that "there evidently was a writing (presumably Jewish) which described the conditions under which the lost tribes lived."

The lost tribes live in a place (to the East; *4 Ezra* 13, *2 Bar* 77, *Ant* 11.5) which is not cold but pleasant (Ethiopic *Acts of St. Matthew*), and where a son does not die before his father (Ethiopic *Acts of St. Matthew,* Commodian), where the body suffers neither pain nor sores and dies after a long life and in a state of rest (Commodian). The people of the lost tribes fulfill the Law (*4 Ezra* 13: 42, Commodian), are hidden beyond a river (Commodian; it is called Sambatyon in some Jewish works, e.g. *Tg. Ps.-J.* on Exod 34:10), and shall return to the Land of Israel in order "to rescue their captured mother [= Jerusalem]" (*Hic tamen festinat matrem defendere captam.* Commodian). They desire neither gold nor silver, neither eat flesh (Commodian, Ethiopic *Acts of St. Matthew*) nor drink wine; they are nourished by honey and dew, and drink water flowing from paradise (Ethiopic *Acts of St. Matthew*). A man has one wife, and each is free from sexual lust; they offer their first born to God (Ethiopic *Acts of St. Matthew*). They do not lie (Commodian, Ethiopic *Acts of St. Matthew;* cf. *Hist. Rech.*); and youths do not speak in the presence of adults (Ethiopic *Acts of St. Matthew*). See *PMR,* 147–49.

Bibliography

Budge, E. A. W. 1889–1901. *The Contendings of the Apostles.* 2 vols. London.
James, M. R. 1920. The Lost Tribes. Pp. 103–106 in *The Lost Apocrypha of the Old Testament.* TED. London.
Martin, J. 1960. *Commodiani Carmina.* CCSL 128. Turin.
Salvatore, A. 1968. *Instructiones: Libro Secondo; Testo Critico, Traduzione, e Note Esegetiche.* Coll. di Stud. Lat. 17. Naples.

JAMES H. CHARLESWORTH

LOT (PERSON) [Heb *lôṭ*]. Lot, the nephew of the patriarch Abraham, plays a role in the story of Israel's ancestral origins (Gen 11:26–50:26). The son of Abraham's deceased brother Haran (Gen 11:27–31), he accompanies his uncle on the epic journey to Canaan (Gen 12:4–5). Once there the two eventually separate (Gen 13:1–18). The separation notwithstanding, Abraham later rescues his nephew, who had been captured by foreign kings (Gen 14:1–16). Lot has a more independent part in the account of Sodom and Gomorrah's destruction (Gen 19:1–29). But there is still a connection with Abraham in that Lot's exemption from judgment was due to his relationship to his uncle (Gen 19:29). After his escape from Sodom and the death of his wife (Gen 19:17, 26), his two daughters managed to insure their and his posterity through incestuous relations (Gen 19:30–38). The offspring were the ancestors of the Moabites and Ammonites, who were often enemies of later Israel.

Three times Lot is mentioned in non-narrative texts. Twice in Deuteronomy (2:9, 19) Israel is commanded not to engage Moab or Ammon in battle since the Lord promised them territory for being Lot's children. The other reference (Ps 83:8) lists Lot's children (i.e., Moabites and Ammonites) among Israel's adversaries. In the NT, Lot is viewed as a righteous inhabitant of Sodom and Gomorrah who was greatly vexed by the wickedness of the two cities (2 Pet 2:6–8). Deut 23:3–6 forbids Ammonites and Moabites entry to the assembly of the Lord. But Ruth, who was a Moabite, played a decisive role in the life of Israel (Ruth 4:13–22).

Source critics (*HPT* 263–64; von Rad *Genesis* OTL, 162–69, 210–20; Speiser *Genesis* AB, 77–81, 95–98, 135–46) have assigned most of the Lot material to the Yahwist or J source (Gen 11:28–30; 12:4a; 13:1–5, 7–11a, 13–18; 18:1–33; 19:1–28, 30–38) and a few verses to the Priestly (P) source (Gen 11:27, 31–32; 12:4b–5; 13:6; 13:11b–12; 19:29). Genesis 14 continues to elude classification. Some scholars hold that it is an ancient source (von Rad *Genesis* OTL, 170; Speiser *Genesis* AB, 106; *YGC,* 51), while others argue that it presupposes and therefore is more recent than the other narrative traditions (Kilian 1970: 24–25). In terms of the history of traditions, Lot is dependent on the Abraham-Sarah story everywhere except Genesis 19 (Westermann 1985: 127).

The essential historicity of the Lot pericopes, along with the ancestral narratives to which they belong, was accepted until recently (*BHI,* 103; Speiser *Genesis* AB, 108; Millard and Wiseman 1980). This assessment was based on claims that the names, customs, and socio-cultural background of the stories were parallel to and thus authenticated by actual 2d millennium documents from the ANE (*BHI,* 74–

96; *YGC,* 64–109; Dever and Clark *IJH,* 92–102; Selman 1980: 93–99). But the consensus has shifted (Thompson 1974: 315–16; Van Seters 1975; Dever andClark *IJH,* 102–48; Gottwald 1985: 161–78; Selman 1980: 99–103), in part because of the alleged lack of methodological rigor practiced by proponents, in part because of the emergence of new data and new interpretations of old data, and in part because of the growing awareness of the particular literary nature of the biblical traditions. It has also been common to view the patriarchal traditions as tribal histories told as individual histories (McKane 1979: 67–104). However, at best the question of the historicity of the traditions in which Lot appears is presently at an impasse.

For the last few years scholars have emphasized interpreting biblical narratives like those in which Lot appears along more literary and canonical lines. Without denying that there has been a long history of the various strands of the Lot traditions or that the story is composed of many separate sources and discrete units (Coats *Genesis* FOTL, 97–148), the final form is also a datum to be taken seriously (Alter 1981; Sternberg 1985; Clines 1978: 7–15; Miscall 1983: 1–10; *IOTS,* 1979). Whatever original purposes such traditions might have had—historical, etiological, legitimation of social, political or religious practices or ideas—they have now been put into a form of "poetics" (Sternberg 1985: 2) in which they function primarily as a work of literature with corresponding aesthetic, theological, and religious features.

From this perspective, Lot's importance in the story of Abraham and Sarah transcends the fact that he just happens to be a relative of the patriarch. In the narrative in its present form his role is strategic from the outset. Only a couple of verses after learning that Haran was Lot's father, we are informed that Abraham's wife Sarah was barren (Gen 11:27–30; Brueggemann *Genesis* IBC, 95–96). The couple's childlessness is highlighted by Lot's very presence. In a story which will soon turn on God's promise of a son and innumerable descendants (Gen 12:2, 7; 13:14–16; 15:1–6, 13, 18; 17:5–8, 16, 19–20; 18:10, 13–14; 21:1–7; 22:15–18), the fact that Sarah is barren while Abraham's brother already has a son (without any divine promise!) enriches the texture of the narrative. First the narrator subtly contrasts Abraham's childlessness with the fact of his brother's offspring. Later, Lot will be a nagging reminder that God's promise of progeny is yet to be fulfilled.

Abraham's allowing Lot to travel with him to Canaan cannot therefore be dismissed as an incidental detail (Alter 1981: 79–80) or merely as a preparation for chaps. 13 and 19 (von Rad *Genesis* OTL, 157; Speiser *Genesis* AB, 97; Westermann 1985: 152). God commanded Abraham to leave his country *(ʾereṣ),* kin *(môledet)* and father's house *(bêt ʾāb)* (Gen 12:1). Was Abraham then wrong to bring Lot along? Typically, interpreters have viewed this as an example of Abraham's sense of responsibility toward his brother's family (Speiser *Genesis* AB, 98). But it may perhaps more readily be seen as the first example of disobedience or weak faith on the part of Abraham. Abraham and Sarah certainly move back and forth constantly between faith and doubt, obedience and disobedience (cf. Gen 12:10–20; 16:1–16; 17:15–18; 18:9–15). Also, every episode in which Lot has a role is at best ambiguous and at worst negative relative to the future God has in mind for Israel's ancestors.

Once in Canaan, the first encounter between Abraham and Lot is problematic (Genesis 13). Their success in acquiring possessions (Gen 12:5, 16; 13:1–2, 5–6) leads their respective herdsmen to quarrel, thus obliging uncle and nephew to separate (Gen 13:5–7). When Abraham offered to allow his kinsman first choice of the land, taking whatever was left for himself, Lot opted for territory which the narrator distinguishes from Canaan (Gen 13:11–12; Helyer 1983: 79–80). What makes this significant is the possible if not probable intimation that Abraham brought Lot along with him in the first place not out of some sense of family responsibility (Westermann 1985: 176), but because he saw Lot initially as a security deposit toward God's promise of nationhood (Gen 12:2) and secondly as a potential heir for the land that was promised (Gen 12:7). It is instructive that immediately after Lot leaves, God appears and promises Abraham that Canaan will be given to *his* descendants, conspicuously excluding the nephew (Gen 13:14–17). It must be remembered that Abraham thought of the slave Eliezer (Gen 15:2) and later his son by Hagar (Gen 17:18) as potential heirs, even though this went against God's explicit statements. So Abraham gave Lot first choice not so much on the basis of a pious generosity which has the effect of emphasizing Lot's greed (von Rad *Genesis* OTL, 166–67) or because of his strong belief in the promise of land (Brueggemann *Genesis* IBC, 130). Rather, he was thinking in terms of Lot's proleptic inheritance of the land.

However, even after the separation Abraham is jeopardized by Lot's presence in the vicinity. When his nephew is captured by the alliance that attacked the cities of the plain (Gen 14:8–12), Abraham felt he had to intervene (Westermann 1985: 199). While his rescue attempt was successful, it involved a military venture which could have had disastrous results and in any case forced him to stray far from the land of promise (Gen 14:14–16). In the end Abraham (and God's plan) suffered no ill effects, but the episode would have been completely unnecessary had the patriarch left Lot home in the first instance.

Even in the story which focuses on Lot and his family almost exclusively, the ancestral saga remains in focus. There are two explicit connections. One is the similarity of the hospitality type-scenes (Alter 1981: 47–62) at the beginning of Genesis 18 and 19. Another is the notation that Lot was spared on account of his relationship to Abraham (Gen 19:29). In this light, Abraham's famous debate with God over the ethics of destroying the righteous with the guilty is telling (Gen 18:22–33). Why does Abraham argue in this vein? Is he simply making an abstract argument that God on principle should judge fairly (von Rad *Genesis* OTL, 207; Speiser *Genesis* AB, 135; Westermann 1985: 286)? Is he obliquely "instructing" God that there is another way to respond to sin than *quid pro quo* (Brueggemann *Genesis* IBC, 168–69)? The omniscient narrator (Sternberg 1985: 84 128; Alter 1981: 155–77) after all has long since informed us that Sodom and Gomorrah would in fact be destroyed (Gen 13:10), something which is also already in God's mind (Gen 18:17). God therefore broaches the subject with Abraham not simply because of the future greatness of the patriarch (Gen 18:17–19), but also to see how he responds, which explains why God puts the question to Abraham as though the decision were not yet made (Gen 18:20–21). To be sure, God's action here is based on Abraham's future role as a teacher of righteousness and justice in Israel. But the placement of the episode between another example of unfaithfulness (Gen 18:9–15) and a judgment potentially involving Abraham's nephew, links the matter of righteousness and justice to Abraham's concrete circumstances. In a sense, God is forcing Abraham to ponder justice and righteousness for intensely personal reasons, since there was apparently no possibility that destruction would be averted (Gen 13:10; 18:17; Westermann 1985: 292). How else could he become a teacher of righteousness and justice to his children?

Abraham responded positively and negatively to this "test." Positively, he deplores the possibility of destroying the innocent with the guilty—he does know something about justice and righteousness. Negatively, and doubtless more to the point, he is attempting to talk God out of indiscriminate destruction because he knew of Lot's presence there (Gen 13:10–12; 14:11–14). Abraham had to present his case abstractly, for were he more specific he would naturally have called attention to his awareness that Lot dwelt in one of the targeted cities. That in turn would underscore his initial disobedience to the very deity with whom he was bargaining. Only when Abraham is assured that God will not judge indiscriminately, does he stop debating and leave (Gen 18:33). Has Abraham concluded that he has succeeded in saving Lot by demonstrating a theoretical understanding of justice and righteousness, without the embarrassment of having had to mention his nephew by name? It seems so. But that God was only testing Abraham and not seeking his advice is shown by the fact that later Lot is removed from the city. Presumably, had Abraham's logic been the determinative factor, the whole city would have been saved by the presence of one or more righteous person(s) (Gen 18:26).

In the account of the destruction of the cities of the plain, Lot is the protagonist, not simply a supporting actor (Westermann 1985: 299). In this role he demonstrates a quality of character that measures up to his uncle's. His hospitality toward the divine visitors is equal to that which Abraham extended (Gen 18:1–8; 19:1–11); indeed, it may surpass it in that he goes to great lengths to protect his visitors from the wicked inhabitants of the city (cf. Judg 19:22–26). Though the visitors end up saving Lot rather than the other way around (19:9–11), his effort cannot be faulted. In spite of Lot's actions, however, he seems to be rescued only partially for his hospitality (19:19). The main accent falls on his relationship to Abraham (19:29), as though he would have been rescued no matter what his behavior (or Abraham's argument) had been. This is illustrated by his ineptitude, his reluctance to follow instructions precisely, and the fate of his wife (19:9, 14, 16–22, 26).

The story of Lot ends on an ironic note. Though he was rescued, there is still a final consequence to Abraham's having brought him to Canaan in the first place. After escaping to Zoar, Lot became frightened and repaired to a cave in the nearby hills to live with his daughters (Gen 19:30). The older daughter, apparently believing that they were the world's last survivors (Gen 19:31), suggested to her younger sister that they get their father drunk and sleep with him to preserve offspring. This the sisters do, resulting in two sons being born: Moab and Ben-ammi (Gen 19:33–38). Although the kinship ties with Abraham guaranteed a measure of future blessing to the offspring of these incestuous unions (Deut 2:9, 19), just as Abraham's offspring by Hagar also received a blessing (Gen 16:10; 21:17–18), that did not obviate the fact that in the future Israel's neighbors Moab and Ammon would be persistent enemies (Ps 83:8; Numbers 22–24; Judg 3:12–30; 1 Sam 11:1–11; Amos 1:13–15). This would serve as a poignant reminder of the first act of disobedience committed by their ancestral father Abraham. Whether Lot is to be seen as sinful in this story or not (von Rad *Genesis* OTL, 219; Brueggemann *Genesis* IBC, 176), the end result of his and his family's actions would not have been deleterious for Israel were it not for Abraham's initial failure. A further irony may be seen in the contrast between the way Lot's future was finally secured and the way Abraham's and Sarah's was (Genesis 21).

Bibliography

Alter, R. 1981. *The Art of Biblical Narrative.* New York.

Clines, D. J. A. 1978. *The Theme of the Pentateuch.* JSOTSup 10. Sheffield.

Gottwald, N. K. 1985. *The Hebrew Bible: A Socio-Literary Introduction.* Philadelphia.

Helyer, L. R. 1983. The Separation of Abram and Lot: Its Significance in the Patriarchal Narratives. *JSOT* 26: 77–88.

Kilian, R. 1970. Zur Uberlieferungsgeschichte Lots. *BZ* 14/1: 23–37.

McKane, W. 1979. *Studies in the Patriarchal Narratives.* Edinburgh.

Millard, A. R., and Wiseman, D. J., eds. 1980. *Essays on the Patriarchal Narratives.* Leicester.

Miscall, P. D. 1983. *The Workings of Old Testament Narrative.* Philadelphia.

Selman, M. J. 1980. Comparative Customs and the Patriarchal Age. Pp. 93–138 in A. R. Millard and D. J. Wiseman 1980. Leicester.

Sternberg, M. 1985. *The Poetics of Biblical Narrative.* Bloomington.

Thompson, T. L. 1974. *The Historicity of the Patriarchal Narratives.* BZAW 133. Berlin.

Van Seters, J. 1975. *Abraham in History and Tradition.* New Haven.

Westermann, C. 1980. *The Promises to the Fathers: Studies on the Patriarchal Narratives.* Trans. D. E. Green. Philadelphia.

———. 1985. *Genesis 12–36.* Trans. J. J. Scullion. Minneapolis.

FRANK ANTHONY SPINA

LOTAN (PERSON) [Heb *lôṭān*]. A son of Seir "the Horite" (Gen 36:20, 22, 29; 1 Chr 1:38–9), the father of Hori and Heman, and the brother of Timna (Gen 36:22). See also SEIR. As can be concluded from the tribal leader (Heb *ʾallûp*) mentioned for Lotan and his brothers in Gen 36:29–30, the "sons of Seir" were a group of tribes which formed a major segment of Edomite society in the 7th century B.C. See also HORITES. The tribal name may refer to a special garment worn by this particular tribe; cf. Heb *lôṭ*, "veil"; Akk *lîṭu* II, "some sort of cloth" (*AHW* 558); Eth *loṭä*, "change/put on clothes" (Leslau 1987: 321).

It is tempting to regard Abraham's nephew Lot (Genesis 13; 19) as the eponymous ancestor of this tribe. In this case, the Abraham people who may have come from the N (Knauf 1985: 46) came to an understanding with the indigenous Lot people after their arrival in the Hebron region (Gen 13: 5–13), and later witnessed the Lot people's retreat from the Wadi ʿArabah into the E mountain range (Gen 19:17–19, 30). As a pastoral group which lived on both sides of Wadi ʿArabah in the LB/early Iron Age and joined Edom in the later Iron Age, Lot/Lotan has a parallel in Reuel (Knauf 1988: 158–9; and cf. Ahlström 1986: 58–60).

Bibliography

Ahlström, G. W. 1986. *Who Were the Israelites?* Winona Lake, IN.

Knauf, E. A. 1985. Bwtrt and Batora. *Göttinger Miszellen* 87: 45–48.

———. 1988. *Midian.* ADPV. Wiesbaden.

Leslau, W. 1987. *Comparative Dictionary of Geez.* Wiesbaden.

Ernst Axel Knauf

LOTHASUBUS (PERSON) [Gk *Lōthasoubos*]. A leader of the people who participated in the assembly of the returned exiles when Ezra read the law of Moses (1 Esdr 9:44). His prominence in the community is suggested by his position on the platform with Ezra. In the parallel Neh 8:4, the name "Hashum" appears in place of "Lothasubus."

Michael David McGehee

LOTUS. See FLORA, BIBLICAL.

LOVE. This entry consists of two articles, one covering "love" as it is used in the Hebrew Bible, and the other covering "love" as it is used in the New Testament.

OLD TESTAMENT

The word love in English translations of the OT may represent any one of a variety of Hebrew terms. In translation, love appears with the wide range of meanings usually associated with this term in English usage: affection, friendship, loyalty, desire, liking, attachment. Yet each of the two commonly used Hebrew terms has a range of meanings that extends beyond the usual range of the English word love, and the range of meaning of the Hebrew terms overlaps but is not fully synonymous. The meaning of each Hebrew term is therefore best described separately.

The Hebrew terms translated by English love include the frequent noun *ḥesed,* the frequent verb *ʾāhēb* and its related nominal and adjectival forms, the less common nouns *dôd* and *raʿyâ,* the adjective *yādîd,* and the infrequent verb *ḥāšaq.*

A. *dôd* and *raʿyâ*
B. *yādîd*
C. *ḥāšaq*
D. *ʾāhēb*
  1. Secular Usage: Love Between Human Beings
  2. Love of Things and Qualities
  3. Religious Usage
  4. Theological Usage: God's Love
E. *ḥesed*
  1. Secular Usage: *ḥesed* Between Individuals
  2. Theological Usage: God's *ḥesed*
  3. Religious Usage: Human *ḥesed* to God and Neighbor

A. *dôd* and *raʿyâ*

Although in a number of occurrences *dôd* is the term for a paternal uncle (father's brother), its more frequent usage is for a man loved by a woman in a relationship anticipating marriage. Thus the term is most often translated "beloved" or "betrothed." The word in this meaning appears regularly in Canticles (e.g., 1:13, 14, 16; 2:3, 8, 9, etc.), a series of love poems celebrating the beauty of a betrothed couple in one another's eyes and the joys of their tender and intimate relationship. Connotations are personal, physical and sexual. Whatever literal or symbolic interpretation of these poems one adopts, these connotations of *dôd* remain constant. Outside of Canticles the meaning "beloved" for this term appears only in Isa 5:1.

The companion term for *dôd* in Canticles is *raʿyâ,* the term used for the woman as beloved in this intimate relationship (e.g., Cant 1:9, 15; 2:2, 10, 13). As with *dôd, raʿyâ* is peculiar to Canticles, with no clearly attested example outside this book.

B. *yādîd*

An adjective sometimes also used as a noun, *yâdîd* appears primarily in poetic passages in the Hebrew text. Most often the poet uses the word to refer to all or some part of the people of Israel as the beloved of God. Although the number of occurrences (less than 10 times) is not sufficient to draw a clear conclusion, the frequent association of this term with concern for the safety provided by divine protection is noteworthy. Ps 60:7—Eng 60:5 (= Ps 108:7—Eng 108:6) petitions God to come to the rescue of the beloved oppressed by military enemies; Deut 33:12 speaks of the tribe of Benjamin as beloved and therefore protected by God; Jer 11:15 challenges the false sense of security of God's beloved people who think that temple worship will avert God's judgment upon their unfaithfulness. Ps 127:2 refers primarily to individuals, but here too the theme of divine protection is present in the context.

C. *ḥāšaq*

This rare *Qal* verb has only five clear occurrences, but they span the range of secular, theological (God as subject), and religious usage. All the examples connote the desire of one party for permanent attachment to the other. Gen 34:8 speaks of Shechem's longing for Dinah, the young woman he hopes to marry. This longing includes a sexual component, since he has already "seized her" (RSV) and had sexual relations (v 2). Connotations of affection are possibly also included, since the text suggests that Shechem liked her more rather than less after he had forced himself upon her. In the other secular example of the term (Deut 21:11) appearance and physical desire are presumably primary factors, given the context of victorious warriors' selection of female prisoners as potential wives. The term is used of God's love for Israel in Deut 7:7 and 10:15; in both instances the more common term *ʾhb* (see below) also appears and the two should be understood synonymously. Finally, in Ps 91:14 deliverance is promised to the one who loves God.

D. *ʾāhēb*

This verb together with its cognate nouns occurs over 200 times in Hebrew Scripture. The pointing of the verb is generally *Qal,* with both stative and active forms. The *Qal* active participle is often translated "friend," while the root appears a number of times as a *Piʿel* participle with the meaning of "illicit lover." The verb can refer to love between human beings, to love of concrete things or behavioral qualities, to human love for God, or to God's love for individuals or groups. The frequent cognate noun *ʾahăbâ,* formed in the typical way for a Hebrew abstract noun, has the same range of usage. Positive or negative evaluation of love depends on the appropriateness of its object.

1. Secular Usage: Love Between Human Beings. The term is frequently used for the desire or attraction of one person to another of the opposite sex, with the end goal sometimes marriage, but sometimes primarily a sexual encounter. Examples resulting in marriage include Jacob's love for Rachel (Gen 29:18), and Michal's love for David (1 Sam 18:20). Focus on sexual desire is illustrated by Amnon's love for Tamar (2 Samuel 13) that results in rape. Often the balance between abiding attachment, romantic feeling, and sexual attraction cannot be clearly determined from a text; this ambiguity may well reflect the ambiguity of the situation such texts describe.

The word also refers to the positive feeling of attachment of one person for another in familial relationships, such as a husband's love for his wife (e.g., Elkanah and Hannah, 1 Sam 1:5), love of mother or father for child (Abraham and Isaac, Gen 22:2; Rebekah and Jacob, Gen 25:28), or love of a daughter-in-law for her mother-in-law (Ruth 4:15). These uses seem to focus on affection, care, and delight. A number of examples express explicit preference for one family member over another.

A specialized and important nuance of love between human beings, not normal to English usage, is its connotation of political loyalty. This usage is well illustrated in extra-biblical political texts of the 2d and 1st millennia from various parts of the ancient Near East outside of Israel (Moran 1963: 78–80), and is seen in the OT especially in the narratives concerning David, where we read that David is loved not only by Michal, but also by Saul (1 Sam 16:21), by Saul's servants (1 Sam 18:22), by all Israel and Judah (18:16), by all Israel (18:28, following the LXX), and by Jonathan (18:1, 3; 20:17; 2 Sam 1:26). This range of persons and groups who love David requires at least that the term be extended to include admiration of his special qualities, such as musical ability or military prowess. More than that, there are clear political overtones. Jonathan's love for David "as [Jonathan] loved himself" involves committing himself not just to David personally, but also to David's political cause (Fishbane 1970: 314); this love is the narrator's cue to the reader that even the potential blood heir to Saul's throne has cast his lot with God's anointed successor David. The references to the love of "all Israel" and of "all Israel and Judah" for David continue this nuance of political loyalty, and it is seen subsequently in the reference to Hiram of Tyre as David's *ʾōhēb* (*Qal* part., "friend"), his political ally.

2. Love of Things and Qualities. That which a person loves may classify the person as upright or wicked, wise or foolish. In such contexts the word carries the general connotation of setting one's heart and mind upon the object mentioned, giving it special attention or dedicating oneself to pursuing it. References to such things or qualities occur primarily in Psalms and Proverbs, but also in prophetic literature. Material goods are mentioned only infrequently as objects of love (e.g., wine and oil, Prov 21:17; silver, Eccl 5:9—Eng 5:10), and even these seem to function symbolically to indicate the person's attitude or focus in life. Much more common as objects of the verb are qualities or abstractions related to the life of the upright believer: righteousness (Ps 45:8—Eng 45:7), God's law (Ps 119:97) or commandments (Ps 119:47), pureness of heart (Prov 22:11), wisdom (Prov 29:3), good (Amos 5:15), truth and peace (Zech 8:19). By contrast there are other things it is obviously undesirable for people to love, such as evil (Ps 52:5—Eng 52:3), lying (Ps 119:163), strife (Prov 17:19).

3. Religious Usage: a. Human Love for God. A series of texts concentrated especially in Deuteronomy exhorts and indeed commands that Israel shall love God. The classic example comes in the commandment that concludes the *Shĕmaʿ* in Deut 6:4–5: "you shall love the LORD your God with all your heart, and with all your soul, and with all your might." This love that can be commanded by another has its conceptual roots, like the love of Jonathan, Israel, and Judah for David (see above), in the rhetoric of international relations in the ANE of the period, rather than from the sphere of conjugal intimacy. Rulers write to their equals with whom they are in treaty relationship concerning the importance of love; a ruler may command subject vassals to show love to the ruler as expression of their faithfulness to a treaty of protection provided by the ruler. Deuteronomy speaks of Israel's love for God in the context of the covenant established at Sinai, using terminology familiar from the political rhetoric of the culture. Here the love that God commands from Israel is not primarily a matter of intimate affection, but is to be expressed by obedience to God's commandments, serving God, showing reverence for God, and being loyal to God alone (10:12; 11:1, 22; 30:16). Despite the demand formulation, however, the inclusion of love in this series of requirements probably highlights the willingness with which Israel should walk with God.

Deuteronomy's usage of love as a duty owed to God in the covenant context probably had its roots not only in Near Eastern secular political terminology, but also in Israel's own early covenant vocabulary, since Deuteronomy 6 develops its emphasis by references to the Decalogue (Moran 1963: 84–87), generally taken to be much older than Deuteronomy. In the second commandment God offers "steadfast love (*ḥesed,* see below) to thousands of those who love *(ʾhb)* me and keep my commandments" (Exod 20:6 = Deut 5:10); Deut 6:5, 17 make allusion to this phrase.

b. Love of Neighbor and Stranger. Two important passages command the love of neighbor (Lev 19:18) and of stranger (Lev 19:34; Deut 10:19). Lev 19:34 seeks to bring "stranger" into the realm of "neighbor" by insisting that strangers be treated as native Israelites. Jesus cites the Leviticus 19 command to love the neighbor along with the Deuteronomy 6 command to love God in response to the question about the first or great commandment (Mark 12:29–31 [= Matt 22:37–39; Luke 10:27]). Despite the rarity of OT reference to love of neighbor, Israel's tradition strongly emphasized practical assistance as the right way of relating to others, especially the weak and underprivileged. As Rücker (1981: 14–15) suggests, this emphasis on practical action rather than on personal feeling may account for the rarity of formal reference to love of neighbor.

4. Theological Usage: God's Love. Love shown by God to an individual or to Israel is mentioned less than 25 times. Nevertheless, the concept of God's love is an important aspect of OT thought (especially when God's *ḥesed* is also considered: see below). Only Solomon is singled out as a named individual loved by God, and the early form of this claim (2 Sam 12:24) seems associated with an explanation of his alternate name "Beloved of the LORD" (from a different Hebrew root). References to Jacob as loved by God focus on the people as a whole, not the individual ancestor (Ps 47:5—Eng 47:4; Mal 1:2). In a number of examples God's love for the people is especially associated with the election of Israel and the ransom or redemption of Israel from its enemies. Deut 4:37, for example, joins God's love of Israel's ancestors with the choosing of their descendants; Isa 43:4 and 48:14 speak of God's love for Jacob/Israel in the context of redemption, ransom, and the defeat of Babylon. Although the Psalms make clear that God loves righteous persons (Ps 146:8) and righteousness and justice (Ps 33:5; 37:28), the persistence of God's love despite Israel's failings is highlighted in Jer 31:3: "I have loved you with an everlasting love."

A special play on the imagery of God's love for Israel appears in Hosea, who moves beyond general references (14:5—Eng 14:4) to root his usage explicitly in the nuances of familial relationships, especially the love of husband for wife (Hos 3:1) and parent for child (11:1). In both these texts the election/redemption theme is also prominent. The covenant between God and Israel, expounded in its fundamental political imagery in Deuteronomy (see above), is elaborated in Hosea using the imagery of a marriage relationship. The use of marriage imagery for the God-Israel relationship in Jeremiah 2–3 and Ezekiel 16 and 23 probably developed from Hosea's usage. A husband's authority over his wife, presupposed in Israel's culture, allows Hosea (and Ezekiel and Jeremiah) to maintain the political pattern of ruler (God) and subject (Israel) while at the same time highlighting caring and intimacy as appropriate aspects of the covenant relationship. Hosea focuses on the frustration of God with Israel's constant searching after other "lovers" (*mĕʾahăbîm* [*Piʿel* part.], 2:7, 9, 12, 14, 15—Eng 2:5, 7, 10, 12, 13) to provide material sustenance. These references to Israel's lovers generally point to other gods, and the imagery of adultery and harlotry underscores Hosea's stinging criticism of the cultic sexual activity he associates with the worship of Canaanite fertility deities. The mention of hired "lovers" (*ʾăhābîm* [noun], 8:9) focuses on other nations as a source of military aid alternative to reliance upon the LORD. Here the political connotation of love resurfaces, but the imagery of marital unfaithfulness may continue in the background. Beyond Israel's futile search for security apart from God and God's judgment of this infidelity, it is God's love rather than any achievement by Israel that makes possible restoration of the covenant/marriage relationship (Hos 3:1; Jer 31:3).

E. *ḥesed*

A frequent noun (approximately 250 times) in the OT, *ḥesed* has no verbal counterpart. The noun itself is frequently the object of the verb "to do" (*ʿśh*). Neither the cognate languages (Sakenfeld 1978: 16–21) nor the ancient versions (Goodman 1968) provide any significant help in interpreting the Hebrew term.

No one English term corresponds precisely to the Heb *ḥesed,* and the exact nuances of the term have been much debated. The King James Version (1611) sometimes used "kindness" or "loving kindness" (following the Coverdale Bible of 1535), but most frequently translated "mercy," as suggested by the regular rendering *eleos* in the LXX. The Revised Standard Version translators decided on four categories for translation: "kindness" in references to a particular act of one person toward another; "(deal) loyally" in reference to continuing behavior of one person toward another; "steadfast love" or "love" in reference to God's consistent behavior toward individuals or Israel; and "love," "devotion," "faithfulness," or "loyalty" (according to context) in reference to Israel or individuals in relation to God (Hyatt 1953: 20–21). Sakenfeld (1985) preferred the noun "loyalty," although she highlighted many discontinuities between the English and Hebrew words. Because of the inadequacies of all these English options, this article uses the transliterated Hebrew term rather than any one of the English words, each of which is misleading in a different direction.

Modern investigation of the meaning of the term began with the study by Nelson Glueck that quickly became a classic. Glueck (1927: 3) summarized the meaning of *ḥesed* in its secular usage as "conduct in accord with a mutual relationship of rights and duties"; he also emphasized the mutual or reciprocal and the obligatory character of the term in its religious usage for persons in relation to each other and to God (Glueck 1927: 34). Glueck did view God's *ḥesed* as a gift, rather than as a right, yet the mutuality of the relationship between God and the recipient of *ḥesed* remained central to his analysis (1927: 52). More recent scholarship has questioned and largely abandoned Glueck's emphasis on rights and duties as quasi-legal or traditional-cultural categories within which the term should be interpreted, and has greatly modified his understanding of mutuality by deemphasizing reciprocity. Nonetheless, Glueck's emphasis on the centrality of a relationship between the parties within which *ḥesed* is offered and received remains a basic and lasting contribution.

Elements contributing to a fresh understanding of the term include recognition of the importance of the existence of superior and inferior parties in a relationship when *ḥesed* is done (Masing 1954), an emphasis on unilateral assistance in a situation of special need (Sidney Hills, unpublished 1957 paper quoted in Sakenfeld 1978: 11–12), and greater attention to the specific types of relationships and circumstances in which *ḥesed* is done (Sakenfeld 1978 and 1985).

Three general aspects of the term may be noted before turning to subcategories of usage. First, *ḥesed* is not associated with inanimate objects or concepts (contrast love [*ʾhb*] of silver or righteousness; see above); it always involves persons. Second, *ḥesed* is requested of or done for another with whom one is already in relationship; the term does not appear in contexts where no relationship between the parties has been established. Third, *ḥesed* in its most basic form is a specific action, but from a series of such actions the term may also be abstracted to refer to an attitude that is given concrete shape in such actions.

1. Secular Usage: *ḥesed* Between Individuals. The secular meaning of *ḥesed* in stories of relationships between individuals remains reasonably constant across the various authors and periods of OT prose narrative. It is useful to distinguish between *ḥesed* in intimately personal relationships, usually familial, and in sociologically secondary relationships, usually political.

Intimate personal relationships in which an act of *ḥesed* is requested or done for another include Sarah and her husband Abraham (Gen 20:13), Abraham and his kinsmen Bethuel and Laban (Gen 24:49), Jacob and his son Joseph (Gen 47:29), and Ruth and her mother-in-law Naomi and Naomi's family (Ruth 3:10). Also to be considered in this category are ties between rulers and key court officials, notably Abner and Ishbaal (2 Sam 3:8) and David and Hushai (2 Sam 16:17). From such narratives a series of common features can be identified that together describe the character of an act of *ḥesed* and provide a baseline for assessment of other usage (Sakenfeld 1978: 44–45). First, the help of another is essential; the person in need cannot perform the action. Second, help itself is essential; the needy person's situation will turn drastically for the worse if help is not received. Third, the circumstances dictate that one person is uniquely able to provide the needed assistance; there is no ready alternative if help is not forthcoming from this source. Fourth, the person in need has no control over the decision of the person who is in a position to help, and there are no legal sanctions for failure to provide help; often no one else will even know of a negative decision. The potential helper must make a free moral decision, based essentially on commitment to the needy person within the relationship. While self-interest might occasionally encourage a positive response, the term *ḥesed* focuses the rationale for action on commitment to the other, not on advantage to the actor. Each of the English translational options—love, loyalty, kindness, and even the less viable mercy—highlights some of these characteristics of *ḥesed* while severely underplaying others of them; the possibilities and limitations of the English words are further heightened when the following examples of human *ḥesed* are considered.

An act of *ḥesed* may also be performed or requested in the context of secondary, non-intimate relationships. Examples include Joseph and the Pharaoh's Cup-bearer (Gen 40:14), Ahab and the Syrian ruler Ben-hadad (1 Kgs 20:31), Rahab and the spies sent by Joshua (Josh 2:12–14), Abraham and Abimelech of Gerar (Gen 21:23), David and the Ammonite king Hanun (2 Sam 10:1–2a = 1 Chr 19:1–2). In these narratives the person requesting *ḥesed* is careful to show that the relationship between the parties is in good repair, sometimes by pointing to an act of *ḥesed* done by the suppliant on a prior occasion when the relative circumstances of need of the parties were reversed. This overt emphasis on the quality of the relationship stands in contrast to the narratives featuring intimate personal ties, where requests for *ḥesed* are simply made and no reason for compliance is proposed; the requests in such cases are based on the very nature of the relationship, which need not be mentioned. In the secondary relationships there is more frequently a potential for self-interest in an actor's willingness to offer *ḥesed* (although the focus remains on commitment to the other); and in some of the examples the strength or even existence of a prior relationship between the parties has been disputed (Kellenberger 1982: 50–52, 118–20). The central features of critical situational need, unique opportunity to assist, and freedom of decision are common to *ḥesed* in both intimate and secondary relationships.

As with the term *ʾhb* (see above) there is a concentration of usage of the term *ḥesed* in the David narratives and especially in describing David's relationship with Jonathan (1 Sam 20:8, 14–15; 2 Sam 9:1, 3, 7); and as with *ʾhb* the narrator's use of *ḥesed* calls the reader's attention to both the personal and the political dimensions of the relationship between these two men. David and Jonathan enter into a covenant relationship (1 Samuel 18) which not only seals their personal friendship but also introduces the political complexities of their interaction as two potential successors to Saul's throne (Jonathan by blood descent, David by divine anointing). Jonathan does *ḥesed* for David by informing him of Saul's murderous plans; David does *ḥesed* for Jonathan after Jonathan's death by bringing Jonathan's son Meribaal back from exile to live at the royal court.

It is important to note that in all examples *ḥesed* is done by the circumstantially more powerful person in a particular situation and is requested or received by the circumstantially less powerful person. The giver and receiver of *ḥesed* within a relationship are always determined by the immediate circumstances, not necessarily by the established roles of the participants. Hence in circumstances of need conforming to their established cultural roles, the Jabesh Gileadites did *ḥesed* for their ruler Saul (2 Sam 2:5). But in circumstantial reversal of cultural roles, Abraham the husband requests *ḥesed* from his socially subordinate wife Sarah; David the king receives *ḥesed* from his politically subordinate adviser Hushai. The critical need of one of the parties, not the role, is always the criterion for identifying the recipient of *ḥesed*.

2. Theological Usage: God's *ḥesed*. The combination of factors involved in *ḥesed* in human interaction provides the basis for understanding its theological use and suggests why it became a central term for expressing God's relationship to Israel. Israel understood God to be committed to the community in covenant relationship as the One who provided for all needs, yet One also always free and uncoercible. The Hebrew term *ḥesed* compactly incorporates all three of these dimensions (commitment, provision for need, freedom) in a single word. This shorthand theological claim is given various emphases, however, in different streams of OT literature (Sakenfeld 1985: 39–82).

Within the theological stream of the Sinai or Mosaic covenant tradition, *ḥesed* highlights the freedom of God within the covenant relationship. Paradigmatic for this perspective is the decalogue's description of the LORD as One who brings judgment on those who "hate" God, but who shows *ḥesed* to those who "love" God (*ʾhb,* see above) and keep God's commandments (Exod. 20:5b–6 = Deut 5:9b–10). Here God's *ḥesed* is conditional, dependent upon the good repair of the covenant relationship that it is up to Israel to maintain. The need-providing content of this divine *ḥesed* receives some concreteness within this Mosaic covenant tradition in the deuteronomic picture of divine blessings: in fulfillment of the ancestral promises Israel will become a numerous people living in safety in the land given them by God. By contrast, Jer 16:5b speaks of the withdrawal of God's *ḥesed* in the face of Israel's disobedience; the consequences are life without gladness, decimation of the people by death with no time for burials or mourning, and exile to an unknown land.

But even the Mosaic covenant tradition does not make God's *ḥesed* completely dependent upon Israel's obedience; rather, it stretches the meaning of the term beyond its usual secular usage to incorporate the possibility of forgiveness as an act of divine *ḥesed.* (The term *ḥesed* is never related to forgiveness in secular examples.) Narratively this possibility is introduced immediately after the conditional statement of the decalogue, in the context of the apostasy of the Golden Calf (Exodus 32–34). As part of God's response to this apostasy, Moses hears the Lord's self-proclamation as One who is "merciful and gracious, slow to anger, and abounding in *ḥesed* and faithfulness, keeping *ḥesed* for thousands, forgiving iniquity and transgression and sin," even though sin will not be ignored and there will be punishment for iniquity (Exod 34:6b–7). Even in the face of the ultimate apostasy—worship of other gods—God does not end the relationship but offers the possibility of pardon. The phrasing of this proclamation was probably very ancient and was surely basic to Israel's liturgical life, as is apparent by its use in the Psalms (e.g., 86:15; 103:8), as well as in late texts such as Ezra's prayer (Neh 9:17b) or Jonah's protest to God (Jonah 4:2). The phrase "abounding in (Heb *rab*) *ḥesed*" is used only in reference to God and appears regularly in contexts involving divine forgiveness. Thus "abounding in *ḥesed*" conveys the essential way in which divine *ḥesed* moves beyond the normal parameters of *ḥesed* in human relationships. Forgiveness springs from God's radical commitment to the relationship with Israel (and indeed with all humankind, as the story of Jonah is meant to show). God's forgiveness fulfills a "need" that is basic to all other needs within the divine-human relationship—the very possibility of the continuation of the relationship. Forgiveness comes as a freely offered act and gift from God.

Yet in this Mosaic tradition, the emphasis on God's freedom means that continuation of the relationship never seemed fully assured. The interpretation of divine *ḥesed* by two other streams of Israelite covenant tradition, God's perpetual covenant with the Davidic line (so-called "royal" theology) and God's perpetual covenant with Abraham and his descendants as developed in the P strand of the Pentateuch, provides a theological counterpoint with greater emphasis on the commitment of God to Israel.

God's irrevocable commitment to David's line is described as God's *ḥesed* to David, especially in Psalm 89 and 2 Samuel 7. The underlying political imagery from ancient Near Eastern culture is that of a "royal grant," in which a royal figure gives to a faithful servant land and the right of his descendants to control it in perpetuity (Weinfeld 1970: 185–88). God by analogy grants to the faithful David and his descendants perpetual rule over the nation-state of Judah. Psalm 89 praises the incomparable Creator of the universe, whose throne is founded on justice and righteousness, before whom stand *ḥesed* and faithfulness almost as divine attendants (v 15—Eng v 14). Within this larger context of *ḥesed* as divine commitment to created order rather than chaos, God's perpetual and irrevocable commitment to the Davidic line is presented as divine *ḥesed* (vv 25, 29, 34—Eng vv 24, 28, 33). The relationship will be like that between father and first-born son, the covenant will stand firm, the line will be secure as the very heavens, and all enemies will be defeated. Even if disobedient rulers must be chastised, God swears that the relationship itself will endure: "I will not remove from him my *ḥesed,* or be false to my faithfulness. I will not violate my covenant, or alter the word that went forth from my lips" (vv 34–35—Eng vv 33–34).

In a similar vein, the deuteronomistic author of 2 Sam 7:11b–16 insists on the perpetual establishment of God's relationship with David. Here the word "covenant" is conspicuous by its absence; this author refers to covenant only in reference to the whole people, never to the king alone. Nevertheless, the passage describes a special relationship with the royal line, a relationship which will endure because divine *ḥesed* will never be removed (v 15). Since Israel's king is understood as "channel of blessing" through whom God provides for justice, peace, good crops, and long life for the whole people (Psalm 72), this tradition of God's *ḥesed* to the Davidic line indirectly insures blessing for all the people.

Probably developed in the context of Exile when both the Davidic and Mosaic theologies are in need of radical reinterpretation, the Priestly strand of the Pentateuch highlights the perpetual covenant with Abraham as ancestor of the community. While *ḥesed* is never explicitly mentioned in connection with the Abrahamic covenant, P's reuse of old traditions in Num 14:17–19 brings together the emphasis on the freedom of God from the Mosaic tradition with the emphasis on divine commitment from the royal theology (Sakenfeld 1985: 72–76). God's forgiveness is seen as an always surprising gift from One who is free to end the relationship with Israel. Yet at the same time, that forgiveness is ultimately grounded in the perpetual and unconditional commitment to Abraham that was made apart from and prior to commandment, land, nationhood, or kingship. As the refrain of Psalm 136 insists, God's *ḥesed* endures forever.

Key aspects of the concrete manifestations of God's *ḥesed* (ranging from maintaining the created order to provision of descendants, sustenance, land, leadership, and especially forgiveness) have already been mentioned. These are reinforced and supplemented by attention to the many references to divine *ḥesed* in the psalter (over 70 times scattered through over 45 psalms). Most frequently associated with *ḥesed* is a plea for deliverance from enemies (e.g., Ps 17:7; 143:12) or thanksgiving for such deliverance (e.g., Ps 138:2). This theme is echoed narratively by Jacob's appeal to God's *ḥesed* in his plea for deliverance from Esau (Gen 32:11–12—Eng 32:10–11). Related to petitions for deliverance are petitions for general divine protection so that trouble can be avoided (e.g., Ps 40:12—Eng 40:11), illustrated in narrative by God's protection of Joseph in prison (Gen 39:21). Finally, even as the covenant traditions associate God's forgiveness of the community with divine *ḥesed*, so also forgiveness of individual suppliants is closely associated with *ḥesed* (e.g., Ps 6:2, 5–6—Eng 6:1, 4–5; 25:6–7; 51:3—Eng 51:1). For individuals as much as for the community corporately, God's forgiveness as an act of *ḥesed* that continues the divine-human relationship is foundational to life itself and undergirds all other manifestations of *ḥesed*.

3. Religious Usage: Human *ḥesed* to God and Neighbor. Although religious usage is relatively infrequent (scarcely a dozen examples), it develops a special aspect of Israel's relation to God. In its secular usage, as outlined above, *ḥesed* involves aid for the circumstantially weaker and needy party in a relationship. When Micah declares the Lord's requirement to "do justice, love *(ʾhb) ḥesed*, and walk humbly with God" (6:8), he expands the sphere of relationship of each Israelite so that *ḥesed* involves active concern for the well-being of all the people of God, not just those known personally to each one, with particular concern for the poor or any others whose status lacks advocacy within Israelite society. This advocacy for the weak, through rescue or protection and especially through correct functioning of the courts, is to be taken on freely (as the content of *ḥesed*), even though it would be easy not to do so and there would be little or no consequence to the actors for failing to do so. In all these respects, this religious usage continues the emphases of secular usage, except that the sphere of relationship is enlarged.

There is, however, a distinctive nuancing of *ḥesed* in Hosea (as also with *ʾhb*, see above) that is carried forward in subsequent prophetic usage. In Hosea the word appears six times (2:21—Eng 2:19; 4:1; 6:4, 6; 10:12; 12:7). Although the subject of *ḥesed* in 10:12a (and in the related text in Jer 2:2–3) is disputed, it appears likely that in every instance *ḥesed* is something which Israel should do for God, rather than *vice versa*. Given the basic secular usage in which a circumstantially powerful party does *ḥesed* for a party in need, Hosea's use of the word must have been jarring, seemingly nonsensical, to his hearers. Yet by his seemingly illogical move in speaking of Israel's *ḥesed* to God, Hosea is able to convey a new dimension of the relationship between God and Israel (Sakenfeld 1985: 104–23).

In Hosea *ḥesed* is used as a summary term for Israel's carrying through on covenant commitment both to exclusive worship of the LORD and to communal justice; that is, *ḥesed* represents the entire decalogue in a single word. By using *ḥesed* for what Israel does for God, Hosea is able to emphasize that observance of the decalogue is not just something that God commands, but is more importantly what God desires or asks from Israel. Even though God is powerful and Israel dependent, *ḥesed* is nevertheless an attitude and action that Israel is somehow free to offer or to withhold. Divine judgment might "coerce" such behavior, but judgment by its nature cannot produce the *free* and *willing* behavior and commitment that is essential to *ḥesed*. Thus in speaking of Israel's *ḥesed* to God, Hosea is able to convey both the freedom of Israel within the covenant relationship and also the deep and urgent desire of God for Israel's free response.

Hosea's images of marriage and parent-child for the covenant relationship (see above) provide a context of intimacy in which the usual covenant usage of God's *ḥesed* offered to Israel can be reversed. God expresses frustration at the repeated failure of the people to live out their part of the relationship, and asks, even as a husband might ask a wife, that Israel show *ḥesed* by doing what is needed (namely, observing the decalogue) to save the relationship. Israel fails to respond, but Hosea declares that God will overcome this failure. Continuing the marriage image, God promises to remarry Israel and to provide Israel's *ḥesed* as a wedding gift, along with gifts of righteousness, justice, mercy and faithfulness (2:21–22—Eng 2:19–20). By this divine initiative a right relationship will be restored between God and Israel in the context of peace in the whole creation (v 20—Eng v 18), and Israel itself will finally reflect the qualities of its God.

Although Hosea speaks only of Israel's *ḥesed*, his climactic introduction of true human *ḥesed* as God's gift to Israel is connected to divine *ḥesed* as an expression of God's commitment to the human community. Even as God's *ḥesed* manifested in forgiveness makes relationship possible at all, so God's *ḥesed* manifested as care for the needy undergirds any human caring that makes for a just and peaceable world. From an OT point of view any human loyalty, kindness, love, or mercy (to refer again to the translation options for *ḥesed*), is rooted ultimately in the loyalty, kindness, love, and mercy of God.

Bibliography

Asensio, F. 1949. *Misericordia et Veritas, el Ḥesed y ʾEmet divinos, su influjo religioso-social en la historia de Israel.* Analecta Gregoriana 48/3/19. Rome.

DeRoche, M. 1983. Jeremiah 2:2–3 and Israel's Love for God during the Wilderness Wanderings. *CBQ* 45: 364–76.

Eissfeldt, O. 1962. The Promises of Grace to David in Isaiah 55:1–5. Pp. 196–207 in *Israel's Prophetic Heritage,* ed. B. W. Anderson and W. Harrelson. New York.

Fishbane, M. 1970. The Treaty Background of Amos 1:11 and Related Matters. *JBL* 89: 313–18.

Glueck, N. 1927. *Das Wort* ḥesed *im alttestamentlichen Sprachgebrauche als menschliche und göttliche gemeinschaftgemässe Verhaltungsweise.* Giessen. = *Ḥesed in the Bible,* trans. A. Gottschalk. Cincinnati. 1967.

Goodman, A. E. 1968. *Ḥsd* and *twdh* in the Linguistic Tradition of the Psalter. Pp. 105–15 in *Words and Meanings. Essays presented to David Winton Thomas,* ed. P. W. Ackroyd and B. Lindars. Cambridge.

Hyatt, J. P. 1953. The God of Love in the Old Testament. Pp. 15–26 in *To Do and To Teach,* ed. R. M. Pierson. Lexington, KY.

Jepsen, A. 1961. Gnade und Barmherzigkeit im Alten Testament. *KD* 7: 261–71.

Johnson, A. R. 1955. *Ḥeseḏ* and *Ḥāsîḏ*. Pp. 100–12 in *Interpretationes ad Vetus Testamentum Pertinentes Sigmundo Mowinckel.* Oslo.

Kellenberger, E. 1982. *ḥäsäd wäʾᵃmät als Ausdruck einer Glaubenserfahrung.* ATANT 69. Zurich.

Kuyper, L. J. 1962. Grace and Truth. *RefRev* 16: 1–16.

Masing, U. 1954. Der Begriff *Ḥesed* im Alttestamentlichen Sprachgebrauch. Pp. 27–63 in *Charisteria Iohanni Kõpp: Octogenario oblata.* Papers of the Estonian Theological Society in Exile, No. 7.

Moran, W. L. 1963. The Ancient Near Eastern Background of the Love of God in Deuteronomy. *CBQ* 25: 77–87.

Rücker, H. von. 1981. Warum wird *ʾāhab* (lieben) im Alten Testament selten zur Bezeichnung für Nächstenliebe gebraucht? Pp. 9–15 in *Dein Wort Beachten,* ed. J. Reindl and G. Hentschel. Leipzig.

Sakenfeld, K. D. 1978. *The Meaning of Ḥesed in the Hebrew Bible: A New Inquiry.* HSM 17. Missoula, MT.

———. 1985. *Faithfulness in Action: Loyalty in Biblical Perspective.* Philadelphia.

———. 1987. Loyalty and Love: The Language of Human Interconnections in the Hebrew Bible. Pp. 215–30 in *Backgrounds for the Bible,* ed. M. P. O'Connor and D. N. Freedman. Winona Lake, IN.

Snaith, N. H. 1944. *Distinctive Ideas of the Old Testament.* London.

Stoebe, H. J. 1952. Die Bedeutung des Wortes *Ḥäsäd* im Alten Testament. *VT* 2: 244–54.

Thompson, J. A. 1974. The Significance of the Verb *Love* in the David-Jonathan Narratives in 1 Samuel. *VT* 24: 334–38.

Weinfeld, M. 1970. The Covenant of Grant in the OT and in the Ancient Near East. *JAOS* 90: 184–203.

———. 1973. Covenant Terminology in the Ancient Near East. *JAOS* 93: 190–99.

Whitley, C. F. 1981. The Semantic Range of *Ḥesed. Bib* 62: 519–26.

KATHARINE DOOB SAKENFELD

NT AND EARLY JEWISH LITERATURE

One of the principal concepts of the NT, love is an important element of the teaching of Jesus, constitutive of much of Paul's theology, and fundamental to the doctrine of the Johannine writings. Love describes the nature of God, provides the basis of Christian ethics, and manifests the object of Christian faith and the culmination of Christian hope.

A. Love in the LXX
B. Love in the Writings from Qumran
C. Love in the Greco-Roman World
D. NT Terms and Meanings
   1. The *agapē* Family
   2. The *phileō* Family
   3. Agape and Eros
E. Love in the Synoptic Gospels
   1. The Double Command to Love
   2. Love of Enemies
   3. Love of Self
F. Love in the Johannine Community
   1. The Old and New Commandments
   2. God as Love
   3. The Scope of Love for the Other
G. Love in the Writings of Paul
   1. Love in 1 Corinthians 13
   2. Love of Enemies in Paul
H. Love in the Catholic Epistles
   1. Hebrews and James
   2. 1 Peter
   3. 2 Peter and Jude
I. Love in the Revelation of John
J. Conclusions

A. Love in the LXX

The LXX shows a decided preference for the Greek verb *agapaō* and the noun *agapē* in translating biblical Hebrew words for love. For the Hebrew terminology, see LOVE (OT). Greek *agapaō* predominates as a translation of Heb *ʾāhēb* in the Pentateuch and in 1–3 Kingdoms; the Greek noun *agapē* similarly serves to represent Heb *ʾahăbâ* in the majority of instances. Other words more common in non-biblical Greek as signifiers of love are used very little in LXX as equivalents of Hebrew terms to which they could be said to correspond. The Greek verb *eraō,* which can connote sexual love, is avoided altogether in the Pentateuch as a translation of Heb *ʾāhēb* (which can have the same connotations). (The cognate noun *erōs* could also serve as the name of the Greek god of love, whose veneration was widespread and popular.) *Phileō,* a milder term (though capable of indicating amorous interest: Tob 6:17), is restricted in the Pentateuch to Gen 27:9, 14 (both times translating Heb *ʾāhēb*) and Gen 37:4.

The range of meaning expressed by *agapaō* in Greek of the classical period and later includes affection, fondness, and simple contentedness. Its extensive use in the LXX as an equivalent of Heb *ʾāhēb* seems to indicate that the Hellenistic Jewish translators sought the least marked Greek term for expressions of love in their sacred texts, weighted as those scriptures had become with religious and theological importance. The lexical selectivity of the LXX probably brought the *agapē* word family into greater prominence as a vocabulary suitable for religious and theological discourse in early grecophone Judaism. To a considerable extent, the NT writers continued this preference for the *agapē* family in their vocabulary choices.

B. Love in the Writings from Qumran

The principal vocabulary of love in the Dead Sea Scrolls is associated with the Hebrew verb *ʾāhēb* "to love" and the cognate noun *ʾahăbâ* "love" (both of which were used in biblical Hebrew as well). Uses of *ʾāhēb* in the Qumran literature are all religious or theological (theological uses predicate acts of love on the part of God; religious use concerns human actors).

Love, and its opposite, hatred, are closely allied to the deterministic theology that informs the eschatological program evident at Qumran. In a passage of the Community Rule contrasting the divine creation of spirits of Light and spirits of Darkness, it is asserted that God "loves the one everlastingly . . . but the counsel of the other He loathes and for ever hates its ways" (1QS 3:26–4:1 [Vermes 1987: 65]). The prayer of a pious "servant" of God is that he may "[choose all] that Thou lovest and loathe all that Thou [hatest]" (1QH 14:10–11 [Vermes 1987: 200]), the rationale again being a predetermined division of spirits (and their "lots") between good and evil (1QH 14:12; cf. 17:24). Even the straightforward statement from the *Damascus Document* that "God loves knowledge" (CD 2:3 [Vermes

1987: 83]) emerges in a passage of instruction concerning the "ways of the wicked" that is explicit in declaring God's loathing for those predestined to wrath (CD 2:8–9).

The special love of God for the patriarchs is a theme of the *Damascus Document* that is elaborated with Torah citations and allusions (Deut 7:8–9, cited in CD 8:15; 19:2). It is love for these "first" fathers (CD 8:16) that guarantees God's love for "those who come after them" (CD 8:17 [Vermes 1987: 90]). The patriarchs Abraham, Isaac, and Jacob are honored with the designation *ʾwhbym lʾl* "friends of God" (CD 3:2–3 [Vermes 1987: 84]).

The predestination of spirits and the apportionment of divine love and hatred accordingly is taken as the model and guide of the Qumran community's ethic. The primary purpose of the saints who enter the community is "that they may love all that He has chosen and hate all that He has rejected" (1QS 1:3 [Vermes 1987: 62]). These categories correspond directly to the divinely predetermined "lots," a knowledge of which has been granted the Qumran community so that "they may love all the sons of light, . . . and hate all the sons of darkness. . . ." (1QS 1:9 [Vermes 1987: 62]).

In such a precarious situation, the community member must be ready to love and hate according to proper criteria (1QS 9:16, 21) and to give and accept reproof accordingly (1QH 2:14). Love is proportionate to a hierarchy of merit: "according to the greatness of his portion / so will I love him" (1QH 14:19 [Vermes 1987: 201]). Correction must be administered in humility and out of a mutual bond of *ʾhbt ḥsd* "loving kindness" (1QS 2:24; 5:4, 25; 8:2; 10:26; 13:18).

Yet even within this context of strict separation from the outside world, there is a concern for loving engagement between individuals: "They shall love each man his brother as himself; they shall succour the poor, the needy, and the stranger" (CD 6: 20–21 [Vermes 1987: 88]). The sectary's love for God is the fundament of membership in the community. "I have loved thee freely and with all my heart" (1QH 14: 26; cf. 15: 10), a hymn verse intones; the sentiment is striking amidst the strongly deterministic language of Qumran theology. Expressions of love for God are in fact confined to the hymns; the hymnist petitions to be granted the place "which [Thou hast] chosen for them that love Thee" (1QH 16:13 [Vermes 1987: 204]), in keeping with the allotted destinies of the righteous and the wicked.

C. Love in the Greco-Roman World

Love in the vocabulary of Greek philosophy is expressed by means of words from the *erōs* family and the *phileō* family. A primary question addressed in Plato's dialogues is the nature and end of *epithymia* "desire, longing" and the role of love in the fulfillment of desire. The answer spoken by Socrates in the *Symposium* (211b; 212b; 297d) is that mortality inspires the longing for immortality. Immortality is accessible to mortals by generation; the desire whose fulfillment results in reproduction of the self—in offspring and in education—communicates to us a higher mystery of an absolute, simple, and everlasting beauty towards which the individual soul aspires. Love *(erōs)* is both the aid and medium of the soul's ascent to immortality. (For an elegant analysis of sexual love in Plato, see Despland 1985: 157–62; on the *Symposium,* pp. 230–39.) The ultimate object of love in Plato's system is not the individual person but the transcendent Good. Human loves manifest the excellence of the ideal (Vlastos 1981: 107, 111).

In Aristotle, the *erōs* doctrine of Plato is the center of a metaphysics of the cosmos. Aristotle explains motion in the universe as the successive ascent of matter to form. The ultimate Pure Form from which all actual forms derive is itself unmoving, but moves all matter to receive form by means of the desire *(epithymia)* that *erōs* awakes in it. In Aristotle's famous formulation, the unmoved mover of the cosmos *kinei hōs erōmenon* "moves by being loved" (*Metaph.* 1072b3).

Aristotle's doctrine of human love (the *phileō* family) begins from self-love. The natural love of the soul for itself is the basis for the mutual love of souls that is friendship (wherein the other is a sort of second self; *Eth. Nic.* 1155a–72a).

It is not possible to describe adequately the views on love in the world in which Jesus lived and the NT was written. Nevertheless, it is useful to note some distinctives against which we can view the ways in which NT writers looked at love.

Some writers in the 1st century wrote primarily about love as sexual technique. Ovid's *Ars Amatoria* (written in Latin about the time of Jesus' birth) may be in this category, although he is concerned with more than merely technique. Ovid surely promotes the idea that the erotic is enjoyable and that sexual encounters are more pleasurable if they are illicit. Above all one gets the impression from Ovid that concerns of morality or responsibility can only tarnish sexual encounters. True love must not be encumbered by ethical questions. An element of parody is detectable in Ovid; nevertheless the main instructions (addressed to men) concern how to find, win, and keep a female lover.

There were also groups who advocated celibacy; how strictly, for how long, and for what reason is not always clear. We are baffled by the Qumranites on this score, for it seems difficult to imagine a Jewish sect dedicated to celibacy, even though Josephus (*JW* 2.8.2–13) and Philo (*Hypo* 11.14.18), portray the Essenes as misogynists. The question is not irrelevant, because one might think Jesus would have married, but those who have tried to convince us that he was married have not been successful. At the same time no shade of misogynism is found in Jesus; on the contrary, the evidence seems to suggest that Jesus was the only first century teacher who invited women to follow him and incorporated them fully into his group of disciples. Judaism certainly had a high view of marriage and spoke much of love, although public discussion of conjugal love was not in high favor, if the begrudging reception of the Song of Solomon among Second Temple Jewish leaders offers a reliable guide. The sources abundantly demonstrate that God's love formed the basis of Jewish existence, that God's command to love God and the neighbor was the highest demand affirmed in the recital of the *shemaʿ*.

Among Stoics and Cynics, Epictetus (ca. 60–120 C.E.) prefers to consider such matters of secondary importance; the ideal Cynic or wise man had more important things to do; he ought not to destroy the divine "messenger" that he is by the "distraction" of marriage or feeding babies in the middle of the night. There is no surer way to lose one's "kingship" (*Disc* 3.22.67–76). In respect to love, since the Stoics were down on loss of control and ecstasy, they had little use for sex, and the loss of autonomy inherent in marriage was abhorrent to them and "under the present circumstances not a matter of prime importance." The married state of Crates and Socrates is dismissed as having been consummated because of passion *(erōs)*; besides, the former's wife was herself another Crates (*Disc.* 3.22.76).

At the same time, Epictetus speaks of something very close to enemy love when he says that the true Cynic must "while he is being flogged . . . love *(phileō)* the men who flog him, as though he were the father or brother of them all" (*Disc* 3.22.54–55). Like Plato, he conceives of *erōs* as a disruption of peace of mind (3.13.10), and as robbing one of freedom (4.1.15–23).

Epictetus deals at length with the question "How then shall I become affectionate *(philostorgos)*?" (*Disc* 3.24.58). The answer is, "as a man of noble spirit, as one who is fortunate; for it is against all reason to be abject *(tapeinos)*, or broken in spirit, or to depend on something other than yourself or even to blame either God or man." He would have people become affectionate but maintain the rules. Natural affection profits nothing if you remain a slave or miserable. Why not love someone "as subject to death" (mortal) as one who may leave you, as Socrates loved his own children, in a free spirit as one whose first duty is to love the gods (*Disc* 3.24.58–60). Socrates succeeded in everything that becomes a good man because he remembered that his first obligation was to love the gods. It is becoming for us to be happy on any person's account and "to be happy because of all, and above all because of god, who has made us for this end."

A further model of love is the earlier Cynic philosopher Diogenes. "Come, was there anybody that Diogenes did not love, a man who was so gentle *(hemeros)* and kindhearted *(philanthropos)* that he gladly took upon himself all those troubles and physical hardships for the sake of the common weal?" (*Disc* 3.24.64). The manner of his loving *(phileō)* was such as becomes a servant of Zeus, caring *(kedemos)* for men indeed, but at the same time subject *(hypotasso)* to God. "That is why for him alone the whole world, and no special place, was his fatherland" (*Disc* 3.24.64).

It is a general rule that "every living thing is to nothing so devoted as to its own interest. Whatever, then, appears to it to stand in the way of this interest, be it a brother, or father, or child, or loved one *(eromenos)* or lover *(erastes)*, the being hates, accuses, and curses it. For its nature is to love *(phileō)* nothing so much as its own interest; this to it is father and brother and kinsmen and country and God" (*Disc* 2.22.15).

Does Epictetus teach that God loves? The question is addressed when he asks why God has sent him here, and "exhibits me to mankind in poverty, without office, in sickness, sends me away to Gyara, brings me into prison. Not because he hates me—perish the thought? And who hates the best of his servants?" (3.24.113–14). This statement is the closest Epictetus comes to affirming the love of the Deity. At the same time he affirms that humans serve "wholly intent upon God, his commands and ordinances" (3.24.113–14). That God is helpful *(ophelimos)* is about as far as he can go in his definition of God (*Disc.* 2.8.1) and he equates God with the Good. The true nature of God certainly is not flesh, land or fame. It is intelligence *(nous)*, knowledge *(episteme)* and right reason *(logos orthos)* (ibid.). Love is conspicuously absent.

His teacher, Gaius Musonius Rufus (ca. 30–101 C.E.) had stressed the "beneficence and kindly" nature of God *(Ep.)* 16.30; 17.15; Lutz 1947) and assumed that people could become like God. For Epictetus the chief element of piety is to have correct opinions about the gods: as existing and as administering the universe well *(kalos)* and justly *(dikaios)* and to resolve to obey them and to submit to everything that happens (*Enoch.* 31).

Musonius Rufus, who embodies the highest view of marriage in the 1st century, perhaps of any philosopher, is unique in forcefully suggesting that the highest form of love is that between two equal partners in marriage. To be sure, he suggests that coitus be restricted to procreation. One nevertheless suspects that the logic of his views on male-female roles is such that he and his wife lived higher than his own ideal. The purpose of marriage was not, however, to have children but, having been joined, to grow in common interest and build a unity (*koinonian mallon auxein pephyken hosper oud homonoian;* Lutz 1947: 91). Against the canard that marriage is a hindrance to philosophy Musonius cited Pythagoras, Socrates, and Crates, all of whom married, "and one could not mention better philosophers than these" (Lutz 1947: 92–93).

Human beings, Musonius holds, do not look only to their own interests but rather, like the bees, bend their energies to the common task, "and toil and work together with the neighbor *(plesion)*" (Lutz 1947: 93). "For humans evil consists in injustice and cruelty and indifference to a neighbor's trouble, while virtue *(aretè)* is benevolence *(philanthropia)* and goodness *(chréstotés)* and justice and beneficence and concern for the welfare of one's neighbor." In marriage this common life is nourished most fully; and because marriage contributes to the peace of the city, "he who destroys human marriage destroys the home, the city and the whole human race" (ibid.). But of most importance to Musonius is that "all consider first of all in rank the love *(philian)* of a man and woman." Even the gods, Eros, Hera and Aphrodite watch over it "when they bring together man and woman for the procreation of children" (Lutz 1947: 95).

Musonius brought together *agapaō* as a form of love present in the family between parent and child (Lutz 1947: 40, 104), between man and woman, *philia* (Lutz 1947: 94) and unlawful love between two people as *eran* and *aphrodisian* (86). His favorite word for love is *kedomia,* which combines the concept of care with that of affection and responsibility. While it lacks the warmth of the other words it has the virtue of stressing responsibility within a relationship. It is to Musonius' tribute that in marriage he (like Paul) saw that men and women are equal; "there is a common life, in which nothing private can be said to exist, not even the body" (Lutz 1947: 89; cf. 1 Cor 7:1–2). In the later history of the West Epictetus' view of love and marriage dominated, not that of his teacher, Musonius.

Musonius was an outspoken critic of pederasty, an institution embedded in Greco-Roman society for at least four hundred years, while Lucian and Plutarch in their dialogues seriously debate which is better, pederasty or heterosexual love.

Plutarch (ca. 45–120) also stresses brotherly love. In his treatise on that theme he remarks: "according to my observation brotherly love is as rare in our day as brotherly hatred was among the men of old" (*Moralia: On Brotherly Love,* [1] 478C). He notes the harmonious functioning of the body and concludes that nature has created from one seed and one source brothers "that for being separate they might the more readily co-operate with one another" (478 F). ". . . through the concord of brothers both family and household are sound and flourish, and friends and intimates, like an harmonious choir, neither do, say nor think anything discordant . . ." (479).

Most friendships are in reality shadows and imitations and images of that first friendship which nature implanted in children towards parents and in brothers towards brothers. The highest deed or favor one can render to parents is to love one's sibling; "to love one's brother is forthwith a proof of love for both father and mother" (480).

Perhaps the most intriguing evidence with respect to word usage is found in Plutarch's *Dialogue on Love.* Here in a way similar to Demosthenes' *Erotic Essay* (5–7; 4th century B.C.E.) all three words for love appear in the same sentence.

Plutarch traced how love moves as "Divine chaste love to be physician, savior and guide, coming to it through the medium of bodily forms from that "to the realm of truth" heavenly love contrives for us, as in a glass beautiful reflections of beautiful realities. Some because their parents have squelched this "fill themselves instead with the smoke of humbug and passion and slip away to dark and illicit pleasures and fall into a shameful decay" (765C).

Before long lovers *(erōmenoi)* learn to disregard the body of the beloved; "they move inward instead and attach themselves to his character." When they catch a trace of the Divine emanation or beguiling resemblance, they are intoxicated with joy and wonder and pay court to it, basking in the memory of ideal beauty and renewing their radiance in the presence of that genuine object of love *(era),* blessed *(makarion)* as it is, and beloved of all *(philion)* and worthy of all affection (*agapēton* 765D). Is it accidental that agapē comes as a climax of his discussion?

Popular ethical teachers discussed the relation of love to coitus. Plutarch's judgment that "love is a very complex emotion . . . one must know the right time *(kairos)*" (*Moralia: Table Talk* II 1.633F). Discussion on the matter (see Question 6, "Concerning the Suitable time for coition" *Moralia: Table Talk* III 5-6.653–55) belongs "among one's companions and friends, wine cup in hand." However in his *Advice to Bride and Groom* the topic of love does not figure prominently. At the same time he uses *agapao* to describe the love of a mother for her son and *phileō* for the love of a woman for her in-laws. If angry disagreements come the goddess Aphrodite is "the best physician for such disorders" (*Advice* 143). "The bed as a union of loving *(phileō)* enjoyment" will settle such quarrels.

Where does the NT community fit into this debate? Clearly "marriage is honorable among all and coitus is nondefiling [*amiantos*]" states Hebrews (13:4). One wonders why the point has to be made. It is noteworthy that Paul in all he says about love never joins it with sexual relations, and wherever he discusses sex or marriage, does not mention love. Marriage is a covenant; there are obligations and responsibilities, but erotic passion seems to be of no interest to Paul.

Paul freely advised married couples how to determine whether they should engage in sex in 1 Cor 7:3–5. His advice: Have it when one of you wants it. Either party can obviously take the initiative in making their wishes known. Even abstinence from one another must be done upon agreement (1 Cor 7:3–5). Paul does not, like Musonius, laud marriage as the highest form of love. What would he have said to such a notion?

Probably that marriage is an anodyne to sexual passion (1 Cor 7:2; 1 Thess 4:2–8). If Paul wrote Eph 5:25–33, then he pays marriage the highest compliment by using the analogy between marriage and Christ's love for the church. The center of that discussion is how a man loves his wife. Strangely he does not urge wives to love their husbands (a possible exception, Titus 2:4).

There is a vast field of discourse about love which has nothing to do with sex or marriage. The distinction is not easy to accept in our post-Freudian age, for love by definition has for moderns sexual dimensions and all human relationships have in them a sexual component. The acknowledgment of that fact makes it inevitable that the 20th century reader may detect an erotic dimension in the NT view of love even though the word *erōs* never appears on its pages.

D. NT Terms and Meanings

The English word "love" translates a group of Greek words in the NT, among which two word families, the *agapē* family and the *phileō* family, predominate.

1. The *agapē* Family. The Greek verb *agapaō* "to love" and the related nouns *agapē* "love," *agapēsis* "love," and the adjective *agapētos* "beloved, dear" are very frequent in the NT. The *agapē* family is critical to our perception of the nature and self-understanding of the early Christian communities. Words from the *agapē* family occur 341 times and are found in every book of the NT. Acts has only one occurrence of the adjective *agapētos,* but in Luke's Gospel both noun and verb appear. The *agapē* family is most frequent in some of the shortest books, e.g., 1 John (52x) and Ephesians (22x). It appears in the Pauline writings 96 times (excluding Ephesians and the Pastoral Epistles).

Agapan describes a life-enhancing action that flows from God to humans (Rom 8:37; 2 Cor 9:7) and vice versa (Matt 22:37). The commandment to love regulates human conduct within the church: "love one another" (John 13:34; 15:12, 17; 1 Thess 4:9; 1 Pet 1:22; 1 John 3:11; 2 John 5); and husbands are commanded to love their wives (Eph 5:25, 28; Col 3:19). But those outside also are to be loved: the neighbor (Rom 13:9), and enemies (Matt 5:44; Luke 6:28, 35). In particular love is directed towards fellow Christians (1 John 2:10; 3:10, 14; 4:20, 21) and within the family (1 Peter 3). It includes theology, for God is defined as love (1 John 4:9, 16), and ethics, for all of the Christian commands can be summed up in the command to love (Rom 13:8–10). The mandate for Christians to "love their enemies" stretches human capacity to its limits but is based on God's love for humans, "while we were his enemies" (Rom 5:10). Paul says that of the three things that last for ever, faith, hope and love, "the greatest of them all is love" (1 Cor 13:13).

2. The *phileō* Family. The Greek verb *phileō* "to love, fall in love" is used in the NT. This word family is also represented by a variety of compounds of more specific meaning: *philagathos* "loving goodness"; *philotheos* "lover of God"; *philostorgia* "natural love"; *philostorgos* "loving"; *philoteknos* "loving a child." Two other Greek words, *eran* and *stergeō*, were used in the 1st century. Of these *eran* does not appear in the NT, although it is debated whether the concept of *erōs* does. *Stergein* appears in the NT only in the compound word *philostorgos* (Rom 12:10).

3. Agape and Eros. The *agapē* family is most favored by the writers of the NT. Anders Nygren (1953: 48) described *agapē* as the "centre of Christianity, the Christian fundamental motif *par excellence*." He argued that sharp distinctions could be drawn between *agapē* and *erōs* and that Paul had given "the Christian idea of *agapē* its highest and . . . final expression" (143). By contrast the "Johannine idea of *agapē* . . . occupies a somewhat uncertain position between unmotivated and motivated love" (152).

In the last four decades Nygren's thesis has been all but discredited, in part because he sets such a sharp dichotomy between the Pauline and Johannine ideas of love. W. Thimme (1953: 108) proposed that in the NT there is a synthesis of *erōs* and *agapē* and that in particular *erōs* based on *agapē* plays a significant role. He saw *erōs* in the adoration of the miracle of the incarnation, in the love commandment itself, which assumes that love can be achieved, in the moral teaching based on union with Christ and in the longing of the earthly pilgrim to arrive in glory. If ecstasy is at the center of the idea of *erōs*, then surely there is no true *agapē* without it; a God who does not care whether people respond is hardly the God portrayed in Hosea or in the NT image of Jesus weeping over Jerusalem.

E. Love in the Synoptic Gospels

One of the striking features of the Synoptic Gospels is that they say nothing explicitly about God's love. Jesus himself never speaks about it, except to point out concretely in parables how gracious and accepting God is, especially of people who fail or who are marginalized in other ways.

The double commandment to love the Lord God with one's whole being and the neighbor as oneself appears in the triple tradition (Matt 22:37–40 = Mark 12:29–31 = Luke 10:26–28). The double command arises from a citation of Deut 6:5 and Lev 19:18, 34, both from LXX. There is, moreover, the commandment to "love your enemies" found in both Luke 6:27, 35 and Matt 5:44. Finally, there is the parable of the good Samaritan in Luke 10:29–37. This Lukan parable immediately follows the double command and has always been seen as in some way describing what love for the neighbor means. It is clearly one of the most difficult parables to interpret.

1. The Double Command to Love. Mark avoids the word "love" almost entirely, using it only to describe Jesus' affection for the rich young ruler (10:21), where neither Luke nor Matthew follows him. Only Lazarus, his sisters and the "beloved disciple" of the Fourth Gospel have a similar designation. When Mark describes the encounter with the lawyer (Mark 12:28–34) he shows little interest in it. Indeed "Mark's ethic is not articulated in terms of obedience to the love command . . ." (Furnish 1972: 74).

All but three of the eleven uses of the *agapē* family in Matthew derive from LXX. The verb *agapaō* in Matt 19:19 and 22:37, 39 occurs in citations of LXX. The adjective *agapētos* used in Matt 3:17 derives from Isa 42:1 (LXX), which is cited in full at Matt 12:18; the reiteration of 3:17 at Matt 17:5 is thus of the same derivation. The only use of the noun *agapē* (Matt 24:12) is a unique Matthean saying in the apocalyptic discourse; note that the verb *psychō* "grow cold" occurs nowhere else in the NT. The verb *agapaō* in Matt 5:43, 44, 46 (2x) (= Luke 6:27–28, 32–35) and 6:24 (= Luke 16:13) is the only member of the *agapē* family used in the "Q" tradition of sayings in Matthew. Its application in 6:24 is not theological or religious, but secular: divided loyalties produce conflicts of allegiance. The final statement "You cannot serve God and mammon" (note the shift to second person) relates the secular observation metaphorically to the theological realm.

For Matthew, the double commandment plays a formative role and has constitutive importance. Its importance is already seen in Matt 19:19, where in a recitation of the commandments Matthew alone adds: "and love your neighbor as yourself" as if it were one of the commandments.

Matthew also holds up the model of God's love when he urges the members of the kingdom to love their enemies: "only so can you be children of your heavenly father, who makes his sun to rise on the good and bad alike . . ." (Matt 5:45). Only in Matthew's gospel does Jesus predict that when false prophets will arise and lawlessness spreads, "the love (*agapē*) of many people will grow cold" (24:11). Although Matthew shows concern for the integrity of his community it is incorrect to see in the directive to admonish the fellow believer (Matt 18:15–22) a "certain tension" between this and teachings concerning love and forgiveness (Furnish 1972: 78, citing Bauer 1917: 39). Matthew sees such patterns of interaction as the true path to forgiveness and would follow Jewish belief that there is joy for those who rebuke in the name of peace (Prov 10:10; cf. 12:20; note the Qumran examples also). Genuine love is shown in Judaism by restoring the erring one, not by allowing that one to proceed as if no one cared (Klassen 1966: 192–200). For Matthew it is clear, however, that one obeys the great commandment as one shows love towards those one meets daily.

Scholars have devoted much research to the question whether Jesus was the first to combine the two commandments (Deut 6:5 and Lev 19:18b), and have come to conflicting conclusions. Burchard concluded that the double command was not created by Jesus and did not come into the Christian tradition through him (1970: 61). He was persuaded that those sections of the *T.12 P.* which presupposed the double commandment were pre-Christian, and thus gave evidence that Deut 6:5 and Lev 19:18, 34 were associated in pre-Christian Jewish ethical teaching. Jürgen Becker, on the other hand, considers it "beyond dispute that the love command came into Christianity through Jesus" (1981: 6). Despite Becker's confident assertion, however, the consensus of recent research is that the association of the two Pentateuchal passages that give rise to the double commandment did not originate with Jesus himself.

It is true that in the Synoptic Gospels Jesus speaks very seldom about the neighbor, and apart from the command to love enemies did not himself issue any command to love, or even use the word "love" with any frequency. Rather, the neighbor is described concretely: tax collector, prostitute, victim of a robbery, debtor, woman threatened with divorce. Likewise the deed of love is concretely viewed and described: table fellowship, emergency aid, release from debt, healing. Interpreters of Jesus are appropriately united in seeing the command to love one's enemy as a normative summary of the attitudes and action of Jesus, even though the words "neighbor" and "love" are not current terms of Jesus. He thinks in concrete terms. Nevertheless, the double commandment and the command to love the enemy are variations on the theme of going beyond set limits, a theme enunciated by Jesus (Becker 1981: 16).

The command to love the enemies is grounded ultimately in the patience and forgiveness of God and his compassion (Sir 18:8–14). Hebrew thought also affirmed that God had created both good and evil but could derive from that affirmation the sort of skepticism voiced by Qohelet: "one fate comes to all, to the righteous and the wicked" (Eccl 9:2). Jesus takes this typical experience and exalts it to the insight at a productive level that God is indiscriminately good. God guarantees to everyone without exception the constant provision of elementary essentials for life prior to their human self-actualization into good or evil. People are to imitate this aspect of God's character. If they do so they become children of God, a salvation predicated of the just (Wis 2:18; Sir 4:10).

The enemy is not the most distant neighbor—rather the enemy defines the basis for the love. The extreme case becomes the model for every social relationship. "Consequently a division into personal, social, vocational or political enmity is rejected, for love imitates God who, everywhere, constantly creates new possibilities for life." Love never asks, "Who is the other?" but only what the present possibilities might allow that one to become. Then it is also clear: "The imperative is no legal exaggeration, but rather an opening of a perspective, without exception, to meet everyone in a life-promoting or enhancing way, just as God the Creator does" (Becker 1981: 7). Any attempt to limit the scope of love of neighbor to the resolution of daily squabbles, or to interpret the love command as a call to "local cooperation" (Horsley 1987: 255–72), is out of touch with that social situation.

This grounding of the command to love enemies in the benevolence of the creator is integral to the dominant teachings of Jesus. First, in Jesus' proclamation of the Kingdom qualifications or determinations of the love object are meaningless. The goodness of God promised in this message on the human side presupposes a universal inclusion under the judgment of God (as seen in the preaching of John the Baptist [Luke 13:1–5]). If all are universally under judgment, then it is not their innate goodness which calls forth divine or human love. The radical quality of this starting point is clear when it is placed alongside the teaching of the Stoics, who based their doctrine of philanthropy on the belief that all people carry the same divine nobility. This demands reciprocally noble human relations—thus love. Love as Jesus defines it aims first of all at unconditionally overcoming lostness; it does not begin with nobility but with human misery (Becker 1981: 8). Moreover, love is a consequence of the rule of God; it arises out of the experience of salvation. Jesus tended toward a world-wide human horizon. The Samaritan did not ask whether the one he was helping was an Israelite (Luke 10:25–37; Mark 2:27; 7:15; 9:40).

A review of the references to the double command in Judaism indicates that *T. Iss.* 5:2 comes the closest: "Love the Lord and the neighbor," while 7:6 is a questionable reading. *T. Zeb.* 5:10 does not refer to love for God or neighbor. The oldest apparent appearance of the dual command is in *T. Dan.* 5:3, in the pithy formula, "Love God with your entire life and one another with an upright heart" (Becker 1974: 94). The other references often cited either stress the fear of the Lord and promise that those who keep the law will be loved by God (e.g., *T. Jos.* 11:1), or place so much stress on the fear of the Lord that the separate themes of love for God and love for neighbor are not kept discrete but run together. This blending of themes is evident in *T. Benj.* 3:3–4: "Whoever fears God and loves his neighbor cannot be plagued by the spirit of Belial because he is protected by the fear of God. Not even an attack of man or beast can coerce him because he is helped by the love of the Lord which he demonstrated to his neighbor" (*OTP* 1: 825–26). At the same time, since fear and love are not seen as polar opposites (Bamberger 1929: 50; Sander 1935: 52) it would appear that close ties exist between the *T. 12 P.* and the earliest Christian traditions. The direction of influence remains in dispute. Both the Jesus tradition and *T. 12 P.* bring together love for God and neighbor, on the one hand, and fear (where it is mentioned) and love, on the other, in an indissoluble way. The Gospels leave the impression that part of the point of Jesus' coming was to grant God's people "freedom from fear, to worship him . . ." (Luke 1:74) and that Jesus dropped the motif of fear entirely.

Great difficulties are created by this for scholars who are determined to treat Jesus as a Christian rather than as a Jew. For the argument goes that the coupling of these two commandments is an un-Jewish act, indeed that broadening the concept of neighbor to include the enemy is inimical to Judaism. Little wonder that Nissen (1974: 416) concludes with a question: "If indeed Jesus' double command of love was the sum and measure of God's Will, what does it then mean when it is said: Jesus was a Jew?" John Piper, however, saw the answer clearly: "The perceptive Jew must have viewed Jesus' love command as an attack on the Torah. . . . Jesus' command to love the enemy as well as the friend contained the seed for the dissolution of the Jewish distinctive" (1979: 91–92; 204, n. 83). The problem is one of Piper's own creation: to see Christianity as unique he must posit a Jesus who attacked the Torah. How can this be, since there is no evidence of such an attack in the NT sources themselves? The problem does not exist when the sources are carefully read.

Apparently the early church found the summary of covenant obligations in the double love commandment left by Jesus convenient and useful. Jesus and his followers in this respect built solidly on Jewish foundations and in continuity with Jewish teaching. To Simon the Just is attributed the statement that the fundamentals of life are summed up in Torah, worship and brotherly love (Herford 1971: 37–38); the saying brings together divine and human relations. There is abundant evidence that Judaism had over many years sought to isolate central affirmations and distill formulas which can be described as the summary of Torah (Nissen 1974: 389–415). That they did not seek to distill the law into "principles" is obvious; equally obvious is the fact that Jesus refused to treat love as a principle. There is no evidence that he sought to do away with Torah when he summarized it in the double love command. Jesus appears more interested in people and relationships than in principles.

Luke shares something of the polemical stance of Matthew. Polemic is evident in particular in the story of the woman who showed affection for Jesus at Simon's house (Luke 7:36–50). The contrast between her and the Pharisee is sharply drawn; three times Jesus points out that the host failed to perform his duties. In each case the woman went beyond what one would expect from a host. But the sharpest rebuke of all comes when Jesus says that he knows full well she is a sinner: "Her sins, which are many, are forgiven, for she loved much; where little is forgiven little love is shown" (Luke 7:47). The incident is unique in the early Christian records in its depiction of a woman's love for Jesus publicly displayed and highly commended. See KISS. Furthermore the measure of love (less/more) is seen again only in the narrative of the Fourth Gospel, where the Risen Lord presses Peter on whether he loves Him more "than these" (John 20:15–20).

Both Luke and Matthew have the statement "you will love the one and hate the other" (Matt 6:24; Luke 16:13), expressing in Hebrew idiom the sharp dichotomy between these two. Only Luke has retained the sharper word "hate" (14:26) where Matthew had chosen "to love *(philein)* more" (10:37) in the parallel saying. The same sharp antithesis between hate and love is seen also in 1 John. Within the context of family relations it is a convention seen in polygamous marriages (Deut 21:15), among the Levites (Deut 33:9), and, closer to Luke's time, as a theme in Epictetus, who uses similar language to describe how the wise man relates to his family (*Disc.* 3.3.5–10). Ernest Renan accused Jesus of insensitivity toward his immediate family. Overall the evidence does not support that accusation, but it does indicate that Jesus was able to devote himself to the larger family.

2. Love of Enemies. Although the command to love enemies is found only twice in the Gospels, seldom has its authenticity been questioned (Lührmann 1972; cf. Sauer 1985). Furthermore it is recognized that the idea is found in the epistles without the precise commandment. It was frequently cited, especially by the Apologists, as evidence that the early Christians were not haters of humankind (Osborn 1981). From the end of the 2d century to modern times, however, the idea has been either relegated to the personal realm or confined to a select group of Christians in religious communities; since the Reformation, Protestants advocating love of enemies have been dismissed as "enthusiasts."

This century has experienced a wave of interest in the teaching. Through the work of Michael Waldmann (1902) and Hans Haas (1927) the doctrine of disinterested love was demonstrated to be far from unique to Jesus. What had begun in this century as an attempt to show that enemy love was even found in the natural realm (Randlinger 1906; Bach 1914) soon became a deadly earnest pursuit during World War I, when scholars began seriously to study the idea of enemy love within Judaism (Fiebig 1918), and its uniquely Christian aspect was explored (Kattenbusch 1916). Moreover, the history of the idea and the extent to which it was practiced were analyzed (Bauer 1917).

It was not until the outbreak of World War II and the threat which international enmity now posed to human civilization, however, that scholars were drawn more deeply into the discussion and devoted much research to the theme. Nevertheless, the subject has so far brought forth only two book-length English contributions by biblical scholars. One (Klassen 1984) proposes that the source of the commandment can be traced to Judaism, from which Jesus took it, and that it has fundamental relevance for guidance on how to live today. The other (Piper 1979) derives the idea directly from Jesus and sees it as a radical departure from Judaism. Like Nissen's, Piper's understanding of Judaism makes it impossible for him to see enemy love arising within that religious framework. He is, however, able to follow his teacher Leonhard Goppelt and find in Jewish texts support for the practice of resisting wrong for the sake of one's neighbor. As long as this is done without hatred (from which faith will free) this will accord with the Sermon on the Mount. How this position is derived from a particular text itself is not clear; but the shades of Luther's two-kingdom view, now largely discredited, are obvious.

The argument for the genuineness of Matt 5:43–46 (= Luke 6:27–35), based by Bultmann and others on its alleged discontinuity with Judaism, must now be reopened. Indeed, the argument has been challenged recently by the theory that the gospel materials on enemy love are antedated by the materials in Paul (Sauer 1985). It seems to make the most historical sense to give full credit to Jesus himself as having first turned the idea of enemy love into a bold command for his community. The early Christian communities developed their traditions in response to what they considered Jesus to have said, but they did so selectively.

Luke and Matthew appear to be drawing from a common source which included at least the words: *agapate tous echthrous hymōn* "love your enemies" (Matt 5:44b = Luke 6:27b). Luke repeats the command (6:35a) after giving illustrations:

do good to those who hate you,
bless those who curse you
pray for those who abuse you (Luke 6:27c–28).

These three further imperatives spell out what it means to love enemies but they also spell out more fully the category "enemy":

LOVE	ENEMY
do good	those who hate you

bless	those who curse you
pray for	those who treat you spitefully

The first of these instructions is rooted in Greek thought, especially the maxim enunciated in many places that the goal of education to maturity (= *paideia*) is to learn to treat your friend properly and to take revenge on those who do evil to you (Klassen 1984). That same idea appears in Hebrew thought. Joab, for example, is astonished that King David inverts that pattern: "You love those who hate you and hate those who love you" (2 Sam 19:6).

Luke's second and third instructions are found throughout Jewish ethics in admonishments to return a soft answer for wrath, to return a blessing for a curse, and to pray for the abuser. Only in Judaism, which believed in the power of a blessing and in a sovereign God who answers prayer, could such an attitude emerge. But the power of prayer is here used not to curse but to invoke good. With this statement Jesus declared decisively that the curse no longer has a place. The Kingdom in which God rules has no room for curses.

Luke then offers four concrete examples of what the disciple is to do:

if hit on the cheek	offer the other one also
if your coat is taken	offer the shirt as well
to everyone who asks	give
from one robbing you	do not demand it back (6:29–30)

In sharp disjunction to this, Luke (6:31 = Matt 7:12) then introduces the so-called Golden Rule, a guideline which is based on reciprocity. "Treating others as you would like them to treat you" is to be understood here as putting oneself in the place of the other. This idea emerges first in Greek literature in Isocrates, but most likely originated in the Greek theater (Klassen 1984: 14). It is found in Jewish literature also. Both cultural traditions invite the actor to consider the effect of the action as if roles of agent and patient could be reversed. It is one of the wisest and most useful rules for human relations, even though it could be construed to contradict the non-reciprocal teaching on loving the enemy (Dihle 1962).

Luke follows the Golden Rule with three queries (6:32–34 = Matt 5:46–47), each one ending with the same question: "What credit is that to you?" What is in Matthew the expected reward of intensified righteousness is in Luke the "credit." The adversative *plēn* in verse 35 introduces the higher standard to which Jesus invites his hearers: "But you must love your enemies and do good and lend without expecting any return. Then you will have a rich reward: you will be children of the Most High, because that one is kind to the ungrateful and wicked. Be compassionate as your Father is compassionate" (Luke 6:35).

What is most important for Luke is that the disciple can become a child of God. The attribute of God which is most important is compassion towards the ungrateful and the wicked. Lacking is any utilitarian motive. This ethical guidance is fully and exclusively rooted in the nature and behavior of God. The only reward which is in sight is a relationship with God.

Can the enemy mentioned here be more closely defined? Some have argued that the illustrations point to personal life and that therefore the doctrine should not be applied to international or civic enmity. Others are persuaded that the term *echthros* is the standard NT term for "enemy" in its broadest sense and that the occurrence of the plural may indeed stress an inclusive usage. Of course between the time Jesus spoke those words and the gospel editors transmitted them the definition of enemy changed; few definitions change as quickly. Nevertheless an increasing number of scholars take this in its broadest sense even as they seek to find the sociological background of the original "Q" source as well as the Matthean and Lukan sources.

For Matthew the "love your enemies" teaching has a bit of an edge against the Jewish tradition, for it is found in the series of antitheses he presents in chap. 5. The first problem which presents itself here is the introduction: "You have heard . . . Love your neighbor, hate your enemy" (5:43). Much time has been spent trying to understand why Matthew added, "and hate your enemy." The answer seems to be quite simple. The formula "be good to your friends and hate your enemies" was very widespread in the ancient world and occurs in many layers of documentation. Rather than look in vain through Jewish sources, including Qumran, for these exact words, we should simply treat them as a part of general folk wisdom which Jesus' listeners had heard and which was well known to Matthew's audience as well.

The motivation for Matthew is the same as for Luke: becoming a child of God. "Only so can you be children of your heavenly Father" (Matt 5:45a). Instead of stressing the gentleness and compassion of God, Matthew stresses God's impartiality. The sun rises on good and bad alike, the rain is sent on the just and the unjust alike. An insight appearing in Jewish wisdom literature which there drives to cynicism—(so who cares?)—here is used to strike forth into a new ethical sphere. Both Luke and Matthew ask: "If you love only those who love you, what credit is that?" (Matt 5:46; Luke 6:32).

Matthew adds only one further point, the question of greeting (a topic not introduced by Luke). Johanan ben Zakkai, who escaped from Jerusalem when it was under siege to found the Academy at Javneh, had the reputation of greeting gentiles and others before they would greet him. In this way there could never be any doubt about his prayerful desire that the one he met should have God's *shalom*. Along the same lines Matthew invites his readers to exceed the friendliness of the heathen and to greet all whom they meet. It is a striking illustration, too often overlooked, bringing the entire discussion about enemy love into the concreteness of daily life.

Matthew's concluding statement, "Be you therefore mature even as your Father in heaven is mature (*teleios*)" (Matt 5:48), refers to the way in which enemies are treated. Don't play favorites. (The translation of Gk *teleios* by Eng "perfect" creates difficulties not found in the original text and suggests an impossible standard—hardly the intention of Jesus for his followers. Rather he provided them with permission and the empowering freedom to live as a child of God who loves even enemies.)

Both Matthew and Luke appeal to God's mercy, although they use different examples to demonstrate that mercy. In both God's example is to be followed; this becomes in Paul an *imitatio Christi* (Gerhardsson 1987).

The Gospel of Luke has one parable, the parable of the good Samaritan, which seeks to address the question posed by the lawyer: Who is my neighbor? (Luke 10:29). What is its point? A recent author (Monselewski 1967) listed a series of distinguished interpreters who see the parable as an illustration of how someone viewed traditionally as an enemy can love his enemy, the Jew, and help him in his distress. Thus to be a neighbor you love your enemy. The Samaritans were favored by Luke, to be sure, for he almost always portrayed them in a favorable light. From Josephus we learn that the Samaritans occasionally terrorized the Jews (*Ant* 20.6.1–3) and little love was lost between these two groups. Yet in the parable, it is the Samaritan who proves neighbor to his "enemy" and shows that categories, like enemies and friends, can change. The "enemy" may be the one assaulted, and the neighbor the one who assists the assaulted one.

Did Jesus himself love his enemies? Matthew 24 seems to suggest that he did not, and other events of his life are often cited in this way. If, however, he saw the injustices around him as capable of being righted only through the death of those who truly cared for their people, then his teaching and self-sacrifice do harmonize.

3. Love of Self. The question whether the text of the double commandment legitimates self-love in its directive to "love the neighbor *as yourself*" has been much debated. In our narcissistic culture inundated with popular psychology, many have taken this as a command for self-love. The text does not *command* self-love; possibly it recognizes its existence; at the very most it legitimates it.

The measuring rod is not "self-love." Certainly "as yourself" does not include the command to love oneself nor state that one should love oneself. The comparison was not intended to recognize the legitimacy of self-love but to point to the power of self-assertion (Michel 1947). In Nygren's scheme "*Agape* . . . excludes all self-love . . . [It] recognizes no kind of self-love as legitimate" (1953: 217).

The comparison appears quite frequently in Jewish sources beyond the Bible itself, e.g., *T. Sim.* 4:6: "In all his days [Joseph] did not reproach us for this deed, but he loved us as his own life . . ." It even appears in the context of enemy love: *T. Benj.* 4:3: "For a good man does not have a blind eye, but he is merciful to all, even though they may be sinners. And even if persons plot against such a one for evil ends, by doing good this man conquers evil, being watched over by God. He loves those who wrong him as he loves his own life" (*OTP* 1: 826; cf. *Jub.* 36:4; CD 6:20; *Arm* B 2:71; Sir 7:21; 31:14; Nissen 1974: 287–88). Could it be that what is meant in these texts is the same thing Epictetus means in his repeated references to "self-interest"?

F. Love in the Johannine Community

Love in the Johannine corpus merits a separate treatment. Not only does John use the term most often, which alone calls for some special attention, but his peculiar perspective also deserves analysis. The verb *agapan* appears 35 times in John and 28 times in 1 John. The noun *agapē* appears 7 times in the Gospel and 18 times in the epistle. In addition the adjective *agapētos* "beloved" appears 6 times in the epistle. The verb *philein* appears 13 times in the Fourth Gospel as well.

Fundamental to the message of the Fourth Gospel is that God loved (*ēgapēsen*) the world to the extent that he gave his Son to die for it (John 3:16). It also stands to reason that God loves the Son (3:35), but it is surprising to read that the reason God loves his Son is "I lay down my life" (10:19). This laying down of the Son's life is necessary so that the world "may know that I love the Father" (14:31). In the last prayer attributed to Jesus in John's gospel, he prays that the followers who come after him will all be one (*hen*), and that once they are "perfectly one" "the world will learn that you sent me, that you love them as you did me" (17:23). This interdigitation of the mission of the church and oneness is a very striking phenomenon; it is as if the world is kept from discovering the love of God by the brokenness of the church. The love which God has for the Son is not meant to stop with him. That love existed before the world began (17:24) and Jesus made it known to the disciples "so that the love God had for him might be in them, and I may be in them" (17:26). At times this love is viewed almost as an abstract entity, for Jesus says to his opponents, "the love of God is not in you" (5:42).

Jesus too is described as loving his own (13:1) even to the point of death. In preparing for that death, Jesus renders one last act of loving service to them when he washes their feet; in this act he provides them with an example of what they are to do for each other: "love one another so much that they are ready to lay down their life for their friend" (Sabbe 1982: 307). In particular Jesus loves Martha and Mary and Lazarus (11:5) and a special unnamed disciple who is described as the disciple whom Jesus loved (*agapaō*) (13:23; 21:7, 20) or the "beloved disciple" (19:26).

Of special interest is the discussion between Peter and Jesus after the Resurrection (John 21:15–23). Three times Jesus asks, "Simon Peter, do you love me?" It is not clear whether Jesus is asking whether Peter loves him more than the other disciples do, or whether he loves Jesus more than he loves his fishing nets, his crews, and family. Only in the first instance is the comparative question asked, and Peter never answers it directly. Both terms *philein* and *agapan* appear; the first two times Jesus asks Peter whether he loves him in the *agapan* sense; Peter answers with *philein*. There are no hidden meanings to be sought in the choice of words here (Brown *John XII–XXI* AB, 1102–3). Rather we must conclude that the terms were fluid for John and the context gave them their depth and their meaning.

What is most revealing in this pericope is that the love of the founding apostle is being tested by the Lord himself. This at once tells us something about the level of intimacy with which Jesus dealt with his disciples. It also indicates that the compassion of Jesus was extended even to the disciple who had most shabbily denied him. The purpose of the three questions was to reestablish the covenant in a threefold way, and above all to commission Peter to feed the lambs. Peter's love for Jesus is the only issue, which says a great deal about the type of Kingdom community Jesus wanted to build. The word "love" is probably equivalent to "be loyal to" here. The incident illustrates that Jesus loved Peter enough to renew his commission in spite of Peter's denial.

1. The Old and New Commandments. Greatest attention in this writing is given however to the love command. Introduced in 13:34 as a "new commandment," the standard is set: "As I have loved (*ēgapēsa*) you, so you are to love (*agapate*) one another." If that kind of love is present among them, then they will be recognized as his disciples. In a later discourse the test of this love is obeying Jesus' commands (14:15, 21, 23) and the result of such obedience is that the Father and Jesus will love such a one and come and disclose themselves to such a person (14:21), indeed make their dwelling with that one (14:23–24).

Furthermore much stress is laid on dwelling in Christ and in his love (15:10a). Doing so means to heed the Father's commands and to dwell in his love. The new commandment is repeated in John 15:12 and again at 15:17 the model of Christ's own love is cited. "There is no greater love (*agapē*) than this, that one should lay down one's life for one's friends (*philoi*)" (John 15:13).

In the Johannine epistles love is the dominant concept. And yet anyone expecting to find here a fuller development of the idea of loving the neighbor (Gk *plēsion*) or enemy (Gk *echthros*) finds nothing, for neither concept appears here. Instead we have the repeated exhortation to "love one another" (1 John 3:11, 23; 4:7, 11, 12; 2 John 5), or the criterion of "loving the brother" (1 John 2:10; 3:10, 14; 4:20, 21; 5:2 [= children of God]). There is not one reference to loving the neighbor.

Some observe a fundamental change here between the teaching of Jesus and the later church, including Paul. They find it most marked in the Johannine epistles. The intention of Jesus' view of love was "to disengage the idea of neighbor from every relation of 'proximity,' whether of family, friendship or nationality. . . . The neighbor in Christian language is, man" (Spicq 1963: 1.183). Since there is consensus on the belief that the early Church underwent a change on this issue, it is necessary to deal with it.

It is especially important to attempt to reconstruct the Johannine communities and try to ascertain the type of struggles going on in their midst (Rese 1985). Before rushing to judgment it may also be useful to remind ourselves that there is always a considerable gap between a leading pioneer and what comes after. There is especially a tendency to exalt what the leader said while bringing it in closer harmony with what the community themselves believe. To be sure Jesus taught love for the neighbor, and that teaching is retained in at least three epistles (Gal 5:14; Rom 13:9; Jas 2:8); but what Jesus taught is available to us primarily through the beliefs of established communities. Bultmann, while admitting that "John 13:34–36 refers not to love for humans in general, not to love for neighbor or enemy, but rather love within the circle of the believers" (*Johannes* MeyerK, 405–6) has not been able to persuade his colleagues that "it is obvious that" this love commandment does not render invalid but rather includes love of neighbor and enemy. What Bultmann considered obvious has been rejected by a consensus.

The three sections of 1 John dealing with the love command present an expanding circle of issues. The first instance pursues the question of "newness" and "oldness" of the command to love: it is old (2:7), a commandment which they had from the beginning. At the same time it is a "new" command, "which is true in him *and in you*" (2:8a). Evidence for this truth is that "the darkness is passing away and the true light already shining" (2:8b). The epistle considers three possible responses to this:

1. One says he is in the light and hates his brother—he is in the darkness still (2:9).
2. Another loves his brother and remains in the light, and there is no cause for stumbling in him [or it = the light] (2:10).
3. A third hates his brother; he is in darkness, walks in darkness and has no idea where he is going for the darkness has blinded his eyes (2:11).

The author's major concern is with those who hate the brother. While there may have been problems among the disciples when Jesus lived with them, a problem as serious as this is not reported. "God is light" the author has written at the beginning of the epistle (1:5) and when we walk in that light "we have *koinonia* with each other . . ." (1:7). The one who lives with integrity and keeps his word, truly in that one the "love of God has been fully realized" (2:5).

The difficulties within the Johannine fellowship have been indicated. To describe those who hate their fellow Christians as blinded and lacking in orientation and direction seems relatively mild. But the author of 1 John sees the problem as very urgent. This is not the time to talk about how to love an outside enemy when the love within the fellowship is degenerating into hatred.

The second section (1 John 3:10–18, 23) is on the one hand more condemning, but on the other also much more tender. The tenderness comes to expression in the form of address, "brothers" in 3:13 and "children" in 3:18 and "beloved" in 3:21. The tenderness is also manifest in the repeated use of the personal pronoun plural; thus the author identifies with his audience (1 John 3:11, 14b, 18, 23) when he refers to the love command. It is also more condemning because the lines are more sharply drawn: Cain killed his brother, thereby signifying that he was of the evil one. He hated Abel because Abel's works were righteous. The one who does not love (1 John 3:14) remains in death. So hatred and manslaughter are closely joined together. The writer of the epistle presumably had not only the story of Cain, but Jesus' own words of warning (Matt 5:22) against anyone who is angry with his brother, consigning to the fires of Gehenna anyone who called his brother a fool. So with all the discussion of hatred it is still clear that the author wants to stress Jesus, the positive model of love, and not the model of hatred, Cain.

"In this way we know love, that that one [Christ] laid down his life for us, and we ought also to lay down our lives for our brothers" (1 John 3:16). In a pronounced shift, the author turns from the prospect of martyrdom to the beggar on the street—"if anyone has the substance of this world and sees his brother having need and closes his heart of compassion, how can it be said that the love of God dwells in him?" (3:17). In this single illustration the act of love is stripped of all pomp and glory and placed within the reach of everyone. The deed of love may lead to laying down one's life for our fellow Christian. But in the meantime it can begin with concrete help to the needy on the street.

After one of the most penetrating treatments of how a guilty conscience can be stilled before God he moves to a short creedal statement: "This is his commandment, that we might believe in the name of his son Jesus Christ and love one another just as he gave us commandment" (1 John 3:23).

This section begins with an affirmation that love and doing justice reveal whether we have our origin in God or in the devil. Since our *angelia,* reason for existence, "which we have heard from the beginning" is "that we should love one another" one can only say that one who does not love his brother is not of God. This is not an eternal decree. One can change one's base of origin by doing justice and loving one's fellow Christian. To be transferred from death into life can be a state of certainty, and can be tested simply by the question, Do you love the brothers? (3:14). Jesus demonstrated that love by laying down his life on behalf of his community, and Christians should be willing to do the same for their brothers and sisters. This is not a theoretical test, nor one that has to wait for martyrdom; it can be undertaken the next time a person walks down the street and sees someone in need. Even if one closes the springs of compassion the author does not condemn, but merely asks, How can it be said that the love of God continues to remain in such a person? (1 John 3:17).

The author then appeals for love in deed and not just in verbal expression; therein alone lies true certainty and the great gift of boldness of expression, freedom of speech (Gk *parrēsia*) before God, and loss of the condemning heart. Ultimately our case, the author affirms, rests in the God who is greater than our hearts, knows all things, and is above all a God of love. The great commandment for this author is, Believe in the name of the son of God, Jesus Christ, and love one another.

The stress on "remaining," original with this author (Heise 1967: 171), is seen throughout this epistle (23x) and also in the Fourth Gospel (43x). "This is how we can make sure that he dwells within us: we know it from the Spirit he has given us" (1 John 3:24b). The ultimate test that they are remaining comes from beyond them but resides within. While "Greek philosophy contemplated that which is eternal [remains] the OT confesses the One who remains" (Heise 1967: 28).

2. God as Love. The third section which deals with love is 1 John 4:7–21. It begins with the call "Beloved (*agapētoi*), let us love one another" (1 John 4:7). The reason is that *agapē* has its origin in God and therefore anyone who continues to love signifies birth from God and knowledge of God. On the other hand, the person who remains in a state of not loving (so the pres. part) does not know God, because God's very nature is *agapē*. This famous and pithy definition of God has to do with ethics and not with essence. It is not to be turned into its converse, as if wherever there is love, there is also God. Again (as the plural pronouns indicate) the author identifies deeply with his readers and as he enters into the depths of the incarnation the readers (or listeners) are reminded that God's love was manifested among us (*en hēmin*) by this means: "he sent his only begotten son into the world in order that we might live through him" (4:9).

To anyone who accuses this author of stressing human love too much he answers directly: "In this is love, not that we loved God, but that he himself loved us and sent his son to undo and remove our sins" (1 John 4:10).

The obligation to love springs directly out of that Divine initiative. We ought to love one another, because God thus loved us (paraphrasing 1 John 4:11). The importance of this love for each other is stressed as a manifestation of God (1 John 2:5; 4:17–18).

The introduction of the formula, "By this we know" (4:13) signals the uppermost matter in the author's mind: How can one be certain? He returns to the presence of the Spirit; God's gift to the believers, first brought into the discussion in 3:24. The community is eyewitness and continues to bear witness to the Son as Savior of the world. Whatever may have been the content of the creed for this community, the essence of their faith is: "We know and have believed (both verbs in the perfect tense) the love which God has for (*en,* stressing internalized and personalized love) us" (4:16). More basic than that one cannot get!

With that the author comes to the second affirmation that God is love (1 John 4:16b). Here it serves to stress the abiding nature of God and the unchanging nature of God's way of dealing with the community. God remains in love. Love is made complete by its abiding presence in the community. Love banishes fear; for this author love and fear cannot exist side by side.

Two other appeals are made to the union between loving God and loving the brother. If someone says, "I love God" but hates his brother, "that person is a liar" (4:20a). Typical of this writer is a refusal to call people names. But similar to Paul certain conditions are outlined and if one places oneself under those conditions then one also must accept the title that goes with it. The judgment is reinforced by a strange bit of logic: "If he does not love the brother whom he has seen, how can he love God whom he has not seen?" (4:20b). It would seem that the power to love the brother who is visible should come from the invisible God. Indeed the author has previously established that God's love was prior to our loving him. Now, however, he is dealing with the conclusions to be drawn from evidence provided and removing from love that delightful trip into the general on which evasion thrives. He brings it down concretely into the reality of daily living. The liar must be exposed.

Finally, he makes an appeal to being born of God. Children act like their parents. If God the parent is loving, why should not the children be the same, unless, of course if they want to deny their parentage (5:1). "When we love God and obey his commands, we love his children too" (5:2).

3. The Scope of Love for the Other. This survey has shown that John's agenda is to restore love as the central reality of his community. Some modern writers accuse him of lacking the very love he espouses in his dealings with those who hate their brothers (e.g., Brown 1979: 131–35). But is this really true? He does not condemn them irrevocably to damnation or to separation from God. Those who have left are not told they cannot return. At the same time the community is to be one of love and not of hatred. To hate the brother is a serious offense, which if left unchecked will destroy the community as it may well destroy those who through hatred have lost their way and are wandering around in the dark. Hatred can lead to murder. Above all the community of Christ must begin within its own midst to nurture the tender plant of love. Paul likewise in his appeal to the Galatians urges that while working for the good of all, the "members of the household of faith" (Gal 6:10) are to receive priority. Jesus, when a woman brought an expensive gift of love and some criticized this as a waste which could have been used to help the poor, allowed the gift to stand; and Mark adds, "wherever in all the world the Gospel is proclaimed, what she has done will be told as her memorial" (Mark 14:3–9). In this way Mark and his community affirmed their belief that love begins with those closest to you. Love for enemies and for fellow Christians are not in conflict with each other—they nurture and nourish each other. Both are empowered by the divine initiative of love.

It has been stated that "where the command of brotherly love is understood as it is in 1 John, the command to love the neighbor is at least restricted, if not repealed" (Rese 1985: 54). Surely this does not stand. The NT author's writing addresses the topic which is the most pressing at the moment. It is incorrect to argue that because he does not mention it therefore he does not believe that husbands should love their wives! Nor is it clear that he has "a shrunken point of view in which there is room only for a conventicle of brothers who love each other and keep the world at a distance" (Rese, ibid.). He affirms that the whole world is redeemable (2:2) and indeed that God who is love sent his son *into the world* that we might live (4:9). There is clearly a sense of mission in this epistle, although at the same time it is written to restore the community to a correct sense of priorities. It is doubtful that we dishonor him by taking seriously his view of the world. Certainly his message that love within the brotherhood is essential is in harmony with Peter's admonition to his people, "love the brotherhood" (1 Pet 2:17).

G. Love in the Writings of Paul

From every aspect, however, it is Paul who makes the profoundest contribution to the Christian understanding of love. Paul sees himself profoundly loved by God/Christ, and his life depends upon that love; indeed, the life which he now lives is not his, but the life which Christ himself lives in Paul: "I live by faith in the Son of God, who loved me and gave himself for me" (Gal 2:20). Personal faith in divine personal love sustained Paul and had called him into service. This is so basic that God becomes for Paul "the God of Love" (2 Cor 13:11), probably his way of saying that God is love.

Striking as the personal reference in Galatians is, Paul seems most comfortable speaking about the love of God/Christ in the first person plural. He addresses the Christians in Thessalonica as the "brothers beloved of God" (1 Thessalonians 14; 2 Thess 2:13) and twenty-one times addressed fellow Christians, including one Persis, a woman, as *agapētoi* "beloved" (Rom 16:12). Paul repeatedly affirms that the life in Christ is what it is "through him who loved (*agapēsantos*) us" (Rom 8:37). He lives, furthermore, in the unshakable conviction that "nothing in all creation can separate us from the love of God in Christ Jesus our Lord" (Rom 8:39). Not only his personal history, but also the history of God's people is determined by God's love: "Jacob I loved, Esau I hated" (Rom 9:13); but even Jacob's people became a "no people," an "unloved nation" until God again called them, "My beloved" (Rom 9:25).

In the midst of the imponderables of history there is hope, and such "hope is no mockery, because God's love has flooded our inmost heart through the Holy Spirit he has given" (Rom 5:5). The proof of that love is that while we were still sinners, indeed God's enemies (Rom 5:10), Christ died for us (Rom 5:8). Consistent with Pauline theology the pre-Christian state of any individual is described as "under the dreadful judgment of God. But God, rich in mercy, for the great love he bore us, brought us to life . . ." (Eph 2:4).

Paul also speaks of the love of Christ as so commanding we have no choice (Gk *sunexō,* 2 Cor 5:14). "God's love 'sustains' us because it redeems and reconciles, and also because it draws believers into the realm of grace and places them under the command of their sovereign Lord" (Furnish 1972: 93). The whole of the Christian mission is a response to Christ's sacrifice. In a lofty prayer offered on behalf of the Ephesians the author's culminating request is that they "may be strong to grasp, with all God's people, what is the breadth and length and height and depth of the love (*agapē*) of Christ, and to know it, though it is beyond knowledge" (Eph 3:17–19). This is described as "the fulness of being."

Finally, Paul implores the Romans by the love of the Spirit (Rom 15:30) to be his allies in the fight. Possibly the author of Colossians was trying to relate the Spirit to love as well, but probably is speaking of the way in which love is demonstrated in the community of the spirit (Col 1:8). The central place which Paul attributes to love is seen most clearly in those passages where he attempts to define the essence of union with Christ. The letter to the Galatians forced that issue. In reviewing the alternatives Paul concludes: It is either freedom under Christ or trying to live under the law. Take it from me, he says: as for those who choose the latter alternative and receive circumcision, Christ will profit them nothing (Gal 5:2). He repeats, "anyone who undergoes circumcision obligates himself to keep the whole law" (5:3). The third statement moves to the one who seeks justification through the law; those people are "cut off from Christ and have fallen from the domain of God's grace" (5:4).

In contrast to those options Paul emphatically affirms, "But we await our hope of justification by the Spirit through faith. In Christ neither circumcision nor uncircumcision amounts to anything: all that matters is faith activated by love (*agapē*)" (5:6). This fundamental affirmation is supported throughout Pauline writings.

Love stands at the head of the list of the fruits of the Spirit Paul enumerates in Gal 5:22, and appears in a number of other series or lists (Eph 4:2; 4:32–5:2; Col 3:12; 2 Cor 6:6; 2 Pet 1:7).

1. Love in 1 Corinthians 13. This part of one of Paul's letters holds a special place as the highest tribute paid to love (*agapē*) in any Christian literature. The quality of its literary style and the problems in relating it to its context, but above all its lack of theology or Christology, have led interpreters to question whether it derives from Paul. The question of its relationship to the preceding and following portions of the letter is also vexing. Some have considered it an interpolation which seeks to bring Stoic values into Christianity; if written by Paul, it must have been written at a time when he was deeply influenced by Stoicism (Lehmann and Fridrichsen 1922: 56, 67). Others have pursued the Jewish background, either specifically in rabbinic thought (Gerhardsson 1978) or in the wider Jewish wisdom literature (von Rad 1953). Increasingly, interest is shown in seeing this treatment of love as part of the ongoing debate between Paul and the Corinthians, and above all in taking seriously the theological connections between 1 Corinthians 13 [where neither the word "God" nor "Christ" appear] and the rest of Pauline theology (Wischmeyer 1981; 1983; also Pedersen 1980).

When Paul promises to show a "better way" (Gk *kath'hyperbolēn hodon*) he is availing himself of a term much used in Judaism, but also commonly used by Epictetus (Weiss 1910). His better way is to reject the passion for charismatic gifts and concentrate instead on *agapē*, which he does not see as a charismatic gift.

The chapter (1 Corinthians 13) divides into three clearly distinguishable parts. Love is compared to tongues, to prophecy and to an act of charity.

1 Cor 13:1–3: (a) Speaking in tongues of men or angels without love is a clashing cymbal or noisy brass, perhaps reminiscent of the clashing cymbals of Cybele's procession conducted by priests who were, along with poets dubbed "drums and cymbals of self-advertisement" (DeWitt 1954: 146). (b) The gift of prophesy; knowing all mysteries and all knowledge; "Paul takes a specifically Christian factor—Spirit-inspired utterance in community—and transposes it into the universal style of wisdom teaching" (Conzelmann *1 Corinthians* Hermeneia, 220). If one has in addition to knowledge, faith sufficient to move a mountain, without love, "I am nothing." (c) If I give all I own, even deliver my body to be burned, without love, that profits nothing. This series moves from unusual speech to self-sacrifice. It highlights what can be done with the mind and what can be done by faith. By putting them all together in this way he covers all that is generally seen as religion: liturgy, articulate prophecy, and acts of charity. The case of self-immolation had numerous antecedents and was a standard illustration of the time (Weiss 1910: 315). Paul stresses that in the Christian community, one thing is essential: love.

1 Cor 13:4–7: The nature of love is here described in a single sentence comprising vv 4–7. The sentence is divided into four parts. First, verse 4a has two positive assertions: Love is patient, it is gentle. Then there follow seven negative affirmations about love (4b–5): love is not envious, boastful, conceited, rude, selfish, touchy, keeps no score of wrongs. The third part has a contrasting antithesis: Love does not gloat over other peoples' sins but rather delights in the truth (v 7). The fourth part consists of equal principle statements about the positive nature of love: love sustains everything, embraces everything, hopes everything and holds its own against everything.

The organization of the sentence is not logical but rather rhetorical, with an eye to the listener's response. There is general agreement that this paragraph has its closest connection with Jewish wisdom teaching (von Rad 1953); Wischmeyer (1981: 92–116) has isolated the connections with painstaking care. She concludes that although Conzelmann's observation is correct that the chapter contains no Christology, nevertheless "the Christian dimension is buried in the definition of the three concepts: faith, hope and love." Wischmeyer sees the Christology behind the way in which the attributes of love are put together here. In part, there is a literal copying of the traditional materials from Judaism, only what is in Judaism attributed to God and to the faithful sufferer is here attributed to *agapē*. Thus "*agapē* in Pauline theology is a theological and christological entity which at the same time constitutes the basic category of the life of faith. Consequently the forms of behavior belonging to *agapē* in Judaism, patience, hope and faith and being friendly towards one's neighbor can be taken over into the Pauline *agapē* concept" (Wischmeyer 1981: 115).

The difference from Jewish exemplars is also important. In Judaism it is the Torah which causes Job, Abraham and the martyrs of the Maccabean times to exhibit noble characteristics. Thus the new value placed upon *agapē* in the NT points to an implicit Christology without which the Pauline description of *agapē* seems inconceivable. The last verse of this section (1 Cor 13:13) points to the eschatological dimension of Paul's view of love, and with its stress on that which endures opens up the remaining part of the literary piece.

1 Cor 13:8–12: In a declaratory manner Paul describes the superiority of love in that it "never fails." It endures beyond the other three categories, tongues, prophesy, and knowledge, that he has already mentioned at the beginning of this chapter.

2. Love of Enemies in Paul. Because the specific command "love your enemies" does not appear in Pauline letters, it is sometimes argued that Paul does not know this command. A closer study of his writings makes it evident that the substance of the teaching is there (Huber 1982; Sauer 1985). The center of Pauline teaching on this matter is found in his grounding all of the Christian commands in the affirmation that "God loved us while we were his enemies" (Rom 5:10). In addition, Paul prescribes behavior towards those who persecute and those who curse along the same lines as Jesus does (Rom 12:9–21; 1 Cor 4:12–13). All vengeance is to be avoided and all retaliation in kind rejected. From the Jewish wisdom tradition he cites Prov 25:21 and urges that Christians feed a hungry enemy and give him something to drink. The victory he foresees of good over evil through this course of action is expressed in the image of coals of fire; the image employed in the Proverb derived ultimately from Egypt (Klassen 1963a) and has no direct connection with a desire to increase vengeance upon the enemies (contra Stendahl 1962). Paul uses Jewish and perhaps some Hellenistic wisdom concepts of battle and victory here and his concept of vengeance is related more to divine sovereignty than to personal satisfaction.

Paul did not himself consistently live up to this teaching if we take as historical Luke's account of his encounter with the High Priest Ananias (Acts 23:1–5). The pressures to omit this incident, given the Stoic age in which Luke wrote and the frequency with which his contemporaries discussed what a wise man does when hit in the face inclines one to treat the incident as genuine.

H. Love in the Catholic Epistles

1. Hebrews and James. The Epistle to the Hebrews has a total of five occurrences of words from the *agapē* family.

Heb 6:9 provides the only use of the vocative *agapētoi* "beloved." The part. appears in a catena of citations from LXX (1:9, citing Ps 45:7) describing the Son who "loved righteousness and hated lawlessness" and the verb in 12:6 (citing Prov 3:11–12 [LXX]) where God's discipline is based on God's love. The motivation of all the service and love (*agapē*) shown by the Christians addressed was "for [God's] sake (lit. name)" (6:10). One of the exhortations is to stir up one another to love (*agapē*) and good works" (10:24). Notable here is the combination of faith (10:22), hope (10:23) and love (10:24) although from a rhetorical point of view the stress is on the three verbs, "let us draw near" (10:22), "let us hold fast" (10:23) and "let us attend to arousing each other to love" (10:24), a threefold "mandate for the church in the world" (Glombitza 1967: 147). In Hebrews there is also an admonition for the continuance of *philadelphia* or brotherly affection (13:1).

James has three uses of the word "beloved" (1:16, 19; 2:5). At a more theological level the basic relationship to God is described as "those who love God" (1:12; 2:5) and the commandment to love the neighbor is described as "the royal [*basilikon*] law laid down in Scripture" (2:8). The meaning is that the law of love has its origin and derives its authority directly from God the King. Dibelius demonstrated the rich Jewish background for this expression and why it need not be attributed to Jesus. Its inspiration is more likely Lev 19:18 (LXX) and the warning not to despise the poor and favor the rich (Lev 19:15).

2. 1 Peter. The first chapter of 1 Peter includes love prominently among its themes (1:8). The love (*agapaō*) referred to is the love disciples have for Jesus Christ. But in the same context the writer urges his readers to love one another wholeheartedly with all their strength (1:22; note also 2:17; 3:8; 4:8). Given the frequency of this exhortation in the NT (14x) in the Pauline, Petrine and Johannine traditions, it has to be singled out as characteristic of the earliest Christian tradition. The occurrence of *agapaō* in 1 Pet 3:10 is traditional, deriving from Psalm 34 (LXX). In the gnomic saying "love covers a multitude of sins" (4:8), the verb *kalyptō* has generated considerable discussion. The context indicates that the writer is urging his audience to keep their love strong. A similarly worded statement appears in Jas 5:10. Both may allude to Prov 10:12. Finally, for this author the stress is on the way in which love comes into being through the power of regeneration, and his concern is that that love become an enduring state as indicated by his use of the term *ektenōs* (1:22; 4:8). This concern is also supported by his appeal at the end for Christians to greet each other with the "kiss of love" (5:14).

3. 2 Peter and Jude. Apart from the presence of both the word *philadelphia* and *agapē* at the close of the list of virtues in the first chapter (2 Pet 1:7) the author has little interest in love as an enabling and dynamic force to overcome the evils he sees in the church. He has the distinction of being the only NT writer to utter an unequivocal curse (2 Pet 2:14). The persons in mind may be the same as "those who live in the love of God" (v 1) and who are greeted: "Mercy to you and peace and love be multiplied" (v 2). The most unusual reference is found however in v 12 where reference is made to "men who are a blot on their love feasts, . . . drinking shamelessly and shepherding only themselves." This is the only reference to an *agapē* meal in the NT. Neither 2 Peter nor Jude contribute anything significant to our understanding of love in the NT.

I. Love in the Revelation of John

The writer of Revelation has been described as "living from a high pitch of hatred" (Bousset *Offenbarung* MeyerK, 271), as missing the "glow of enemy-love" and displaying instead a "virtuosity of hatred" (Preisker 1949: 205), and a "glowing hatred against all enemies" (Bauer 1917: 40). W. D. Davies saw in the book an "abortive hatred" towards the powers (*IDB* 2: 176) but the strongest indictments against the book have come from D. H. Lawrence (1931) and C. G. Jung, both of whom failed to see its rich symbolism as a carrier of truth. The latter saw the book as the hateful explosion of an old man at the end of his life who had spoken about love so much that he had repressed all feelings of hatred (Jung 1954: 125).

An examination of the text of Revelation reveals that the verb *agapaō* appears only four times, the noun *agapē* only twice and the verb *phileō* only three times. Of these usages, 1:6 joins with other NT witnesses in placing Christ's redemptive love (*agapē*) as the cornerstone of the Christian community. Love (*phileō*) is related to discipline leading to repentance (3:19, alluding to Prov 3:12; cf. Heb 12:5, which follows the LXX in using *agapaō*). The church at Ephesus is rebuked for having lost her first love (*agapē*) (2:4), the warm affirmation of affection for each other, and the translation of emotion into responsible moral action. Thyatira is praised for her "love (*agapē*) and faith, service and fortitude" (2:19).

At the core of our understanding of the Revelation is the symbol of the Lamb. Introduced in chap. 5 at a critical stage of the drama, it stands without modifier and from that point on is the main actor. Clearly the description of this Lamb epitomizes love as self-giving: "he was slain and by his blood persons of every tribe and language, people and nation" were purchased for God and made into a royal house (5:9). There is no direct love command in the book; nevertheless since the church is tested by its love and above all since the call to steadfastness revolves around remaining faithful in following the Lamb and at no place are readers urged to use violence or commanded to hate their persecutors, we may see the book as an example of leaving the execution of wrath in the hands of God and of the Lamb. There is, according to recent work on the book (Caird *Revelation* BHNTC), no need to see the book as a deviation from the NT ethic of love (which in any case is not incompatible with a deep commitment to the sovereignty of God). Indeed G. B. Caird states that the author had "learned from Christ that the omnipotence of God is not the power of unlimited coercion but the power of invincible love" (*Revelation* BHNTC, 19). Especially in chap. 22 Caird finds the image of Paradise restored to the nations "still bearing the wounds of those battles by which their hostility to the Lamb has been beaten down, smashed by the iron bar of his inexorable love" (Caird, 280). The message of the book would seem to be that those who follow the power of love rather than the love of power will conquer. But only those who follow the Lamb in serving others unto death will share in that victory. It may well be that in the

Apocalypse of John the symbol of sacrifice is taken over by a small beleaguered community and is transformed into a victory symbol.

J. Conclusions

Our survey has shown that as a whole the early Christian writings share the appreciation for love found in the Hebrew scriptures, especially in the wisdom tradition and later Jewish literature. We know of no Greek or Roman community in which love played such an important role, and it may be that Luke's reticence to use the word in Acts stems from his Hellenistic roots. For the early Christians, although there is little mention of love in the Gospels, the coming of the Kingdom in the person of Jesus was a sure sign of God's love for all people, indeed for the world. At the same time Paul's own strong sense of call was grounded in the love of God, and the church's constitution rested on that love. In turn a fruit of the spirit was love (Gal 6:22) and for Paul it was the greatest gift of all. Love was therefore freely commanded to Christians, first towards each other, then to all people, including the enemy. The NT documents show considerable tension between insider and outsider, no doubt stemming from an awareness that the boundaries of a community have to be established and maintained. The emergence of formulas like "the God of Love" (2 Cor 13:11) and the "love of Jesus Christ" (Rom 8:35) in early communities shows that they were able to develop both a theology and a Christology of love. This theology, built in the first instance on the Jewish experience, was given a strong impetus first by Jesus, who spoke little about love but practiced it in an exemplary fashion, and by Paul, who (like the Johannine community and the Petrine group) placed love into a central place. To understand the early Christians, one must give serious attention to the liberating and empowering view of love that they brought to the world.

Bibliography

Andolsen, B. H. 1981. Agape in Feminist Ethics. *JRE* 9: 69–83.

Bach, E. 1914. *Die Feindesliebe nach dem natürlichen und dem übernatürlichen Sittengesetz.* Kempten.

Bamberger, B. J. 1929. Fear and Love of God in the Old Testament. *HUCA* 6: 39–52.

Bauer, W. 1917. Das Gebot der Feindesliebe und die alten Christen. *ZTK* 27: 37–54.

Becker, J. 1974. *Die Testamente der zwölf Patriarchen.* JSHRZ 3. Gütersloh.

———. 1981. Feindesliebe-Nächstenliebe-Bruderliebe: Exegetische Betrachtungen als Anfrage an ein ethisches Problemfeld. *ZEE* 25: 5–18.

Bonnard, P. 1958. Love. Pp. 242–47 in *A Companion to the Bible,* ed. J.-J. von Allmen. New York.

Brown, R. E. 1979. *The Community of the Beloved Disciple.* New York.

Burchard, C. 1970. Das doppelte Liebesgebot in der frühen christlichen Überlieferung. Pp. 39–62 in *Der Ruf Jesu und die Antwort der Gemeinde.* Göttingen.

Clark, D. K. 1985. Philosophical Reflections on Self-worth and Self-love. *JPT* 13: 3–11.

Cohen, H. 1924. Der Nächste. Vol. 1, pp. 182–95 in *Jüdische Schriften.*

Das, S. 1985. Violence and Non-violence: Reappraising Gandhi's Understanding of the Sermon on the Mount. *BTF* 17: 41–64.

Davies, A. T. 1982. Law and Love in Judaism and Christianity. *ATR* 64: 454–66.

Despland, M. 1985. *The Education of Desire.* Toronto.

DeWitt, N. W. 1954. *St. Paul and Epicurus.* Minneapolis.

Dihle, A. 1962. *Die goldene Regel.* Göttingen.

Fiebig, P. 1918. Jesu Worte über die Feindesliebe im Zusammenhang mit den wichtigsten rabbinischen Parallelen erläutert. *TSK* 91: 30–64.

Fuchs, E. 1932. Was Heisst: 'Du sollst deinen Nächsten lieben wie dich selbst'? *TBl* 11: 129–40.

Furnish, V. 1972. *The Love Command in the New Testament.* Nashville.

Gerhardsson, B. 1978. I Kor. 13. Zur Frage von Paulus' rabbinischem Hintergrund. Pp. 185–209 in *Donum gentilicium.* Oxford.

———. 1987. Agape and Imitation of Christ. Pp. 163–76 in *Jesus, the Gospels, and the Church,* ed. E. P. Sanders. Macon, GA.

Glombitza, O. 1967. Erwägungen zum kunstvollen Ansatz der Paraenese . . . Heb X.19–25. *NT* 9: 132–50.

Haas, H. 1927. *Idee und Ideal der Feindesliebe in der ausserchristlichen Welt.* Leipzig.

Harnack, A. 1980. Der "Eros" in der alten christlichen Literatur. Pp. 81–94 in *Kleine Schriften zur alten Kirche.* Leipzig. Repr.

Heise, J. 1967. *Menein in den johanneischen Schriften.* Tübingen.

Herford, R. 1971. *Pirke Aboth: The Ethics of the Talmud.* New York.

Hochfeld, S. 1928. Das Gebot der Nächstenliebe. Vol. 1, pp. 328–89 in *Die Lehren des Judentums nach den Quellen.*

Hoffmann, E. 1926. Pauli Hymnus auf die Liebe. *Deutsche Vierteljahrsschrift für Literaturwissenschaft und Geistesgeschicte* 4: 58–73.

Horsley, R. 1987. *Jesus and the Spiral of Violence.* San Francisco.

Howe, R. L. 1969. *Herein is Love: A Study of the Biblical Doctrine of Love.* Valley Forge, PA.

Huber, W. 1982. Feindschaft und Feindesliebe: Notizen zum Problem des 'Feindes' in der Theologie. *ZEE* 26: 128–58.

Jung, C. G. 1954. *Answer to Job.* Trans. R. F. C. Hull. London.

Kattenbusch, F. 1916. Über die Feindesliebe im Sinne des Christentums *TSK* 89: 1–70.

Keating, J. F. 1901. *The Agape and the Eucharist in the Early Church.* London.

Klassen, W. 1963a. Coals of Fire: Symbol of Repentance or Revenge? *NTS* 9: 337–50.

———. 1963b. Love Your Enemy: A Study of New Testament Teaching on Coping with an Enemy. Pp. 153–83 in *Biblical Realism Confronts the Nation,* ed. Paul Peachey. Nyack, NY.

———. 1966. *The Forgiving Community.* Philadelphia.

———. 1980. The Novel Element in the Love Commandment of Jesus. Pp. 100–14 in *The New Way of Jesus,* ed. W. Klassen. Newton, KS.

———. 1984. *Love of Enemies: The Way to Peace.* Philadelphia.

Lapide, P. 1981. Es geht um Entfeindungsliebe. Realpolitik, wie sie die Bergpredigt eigentlich meint. *Lutherische Monatsschrift* 20: 505–8.

Lawrence, D. H. 1931. *Apocalypse.* New York.

Lehmann, E., and Fridrichsen, A. 1922. 1 Kor. 13: Eine christlich-stoische Diatribe. *TSK* 94: 55–95.

Lemcio, E. 1988. Pirke 'Abot 1: 2(3) and the Synoptic Reactions to the Commands to Love God and Neighbour. *Asbury Theological Journal* 43: 43–53.

Linton, O. 1964. Matthew 5:43. *ST* 18: 66–79.

Lohfink, G. 1982. Der ekklesiale Sitz im Leben der Aufforderung Jesu zum Gewaltverzicht (Mat. 5,39b–42/Lk 6,29f.). *TQ* 162: 236–53.

Lührmann, D. 1972. Liebet eure Feinde. *ZTK* 69: 412–38.

Lutz, C. 1947. Musonius Rufus: 'The Roman Socrates'. *Yale Classical Studies* 10: 3–147.
Luz, U. 1983. Feindesliebe und Frieden. *TE* 16: 3–13.
Michel, O. 1947. Das Gebot der Nächstenliebe in der Verkündigung Jesu. Pp. 53–101 in *Zur sozialen Entscheidung.*
Miller, P. C. 1986. 'Pleasure of the Text, Text of the Pleasure': Eros and Language in Origen's *Commentary on the Song of Songs. JAAR* 54: 241–53.
Minear, P. 1972. *Commands of Christ: Authority and Implications.* Edinburgh.
Moffat, J. 1929. *Love in the New Testament.* London.
Moltmann, J. 1982. Feindesliebe. *EvK* 15: 503–5.
Monselewski, W. 1967. *Der barmherzige Samaritaner.* Tübingen.
Montefiore, H. W. 1962. Thou Shalt Love the Neighbour as Thyself. *NovT* 5: 157–70.
Neugebauer, F. 1985. Die dargebotene Wange und Jesu Gebot der Feindesliebe: Erwägungen zu Lk 6,27–36; Matt 5,38–48. *TLZ* 110: 865–75.
Nikolaus, W. 1986. Eros und Agape: zum philosophischen Begriff der Liebe. *ZEE* 30: 399–420.
Nissen, A. 1974. *Gott und der Nächste im antiken Judentum.* WUNT. Tübingen.
Nygren, A. 1953. *Agape and Eros.* Trans. P. S. Watson. London.
Obayashi, H. 1981. Agape and the Dynamics of History. *ST* 35: 9–31.
Ortkemper, F.-J. 1980. *Leben aus dem Glauben.* NTAbh 14. Münster.
Osborn, E. 1981. The Love Commandment in Second Century Christian Writings. *SecondCent* 1: 223–43.
Outka, G. H. 1972. *Agape: An Ethical Analysis.* New Haven.
Pedersen, S. 1980. *Agape*—der eschatologische Hauptbegriff bei Paulus. Pp. 159–86 in *Die paulinische Literatur und Theologie.* Aarhus.
Perkins, P. 1982. *Love Commands in the New Testament.* New York.
Piper, J. 1979. *'Love your enemies': Jesus' Love Command in the Synoptic Gospels and in the Early Christian Paranesis.* SNTSMS 38. Cambridge.
Preisker, H. 1949. *Das Ethos des Neuen Testaments.* Gütersloh.
Quispel, G. 1979. God is Eros. Pp. 189–205 in *Early Christian Literature and the Classical Intellectual Tradition,* ed. W. R. Schoedel and R. L. Wilken. Paris.
Rad, G. von. 1953. The Early History of the Form Category of I Cor 13:4–7. Pp. 301–17 in *The Problem of the Hexateuch and Other Essays,* trans. E. W. T. Dicken. Edinburgh, 1966.
Randlinger, S. 1906. *Die Feindesliebe.* Paderborn.
Rausch, J. 1966. The Principle of Nonresistance and Love of Enemy in Mt. 5:38–48. *CBQ* 28: 31–41.
Reeder, J. P. 1980. Assenting to Agape. *JR* 60: 17–31.
Rese, M. 1985. Das Gebot der Bruderliebe in den Johannesbriefen. *TZ* 14: 44–58.
Reuter, H. R. 1982. Liebet eure Feinde! Zur Aufgabe einer politischen Ethik im Licht der Bergpredigt. *ZEE* 26: 159–87.
Rice, H. 1982. Love. *Theology* 85: 438–43.
Richardson, C. C. 1943. Love: Greek and Christian. *JR* 23: 173–85.
Romaniuk, K. 1964. Die vollkommene Liebe treibt die Furcht aus. *Bibel und Leben* 5/2: 80–84.
Ruiter, S. Tromp de. 1930. *Gebruik en beteekenis van Agapan in de Griekshe Litteratuur.* Groningen.
Sabbe, M. 1982. The Footwashing in Jn 13 and its relation to the Synoptic Gospels. *ETL* 58: 279–307.
Sander, R. 1935. *Furcht und Liebe im Palästinischen Judentum.* Stuttgart.
Sauer, J. 1985. Traditionsgeschichtliche Erwägungen zu den synoptischen und paulinischen Aussagen über Feindesliebe und Wiedervergeltungsverzicht. *ZNW* 76: 1–28.
Schneider, G. 1973. Die Neuheit der christlichen Nächstenliebe. *TTZ* 82: 257–75.
Schottroff, L. 1978. Nonviolence and the Love of One's Enemies. Pp. 9–39 in *Essays on the Love Commandment,* trans. R. and I. Fuller. Philadelphia.
Singer, I. 1966–87. *The Nature of Love.* 3 vols. Chicago.
Soble, A., ed. 1990. *Eros, Agape and Philia.* New York.
Spicq, C. 1963. *Agape in the New Testament.* 3 vols. St. Louis.
Stendahl, K. 1962. Hate, Non-Retaliation and Love: 1QS X 17–20 and Romans 12:19–21. *HTR* 55: 343–55.
Thimme, W. 1953. Eros im Neuen Testament. Pp. 103–16 in *Verbum Dei Manet in Aeternum,* ed. W. Foerster. Witten.
Vermes, G. 1987. *The Dead Sea Scrolls in English.* 3d ed. Sheffield.
Vlastos, G. 1973. *Platonic Studies.* Princeton. Repr. 1981.
Völkl, R. 1956. *Die Selbstliebe in der heiligen Schrift.* Munich.
Waldmann, M. 1902. *Die Feindesliebe in der antiken Welt und im Christenthum.* Vienna.
Warnach, V. 1951. *Agape.* Düsseldorf.
Weiss, J. 1910. *Der erste Korintherbrief.* Göttingen.
Wischmeyer, O. 1981. *Der höchste Weg.* SNT 13. Gütersloh.
———. 1983. Traditionsgeschichtliche Untersuchung der Paulinischen Aussagen über die Liebe (*Agape*). *ZNW* 74: 222–36.
———. 1986. Das Gebot der Nächstenliebe bei Paulus: eine traditionsgeschichtliche Untersuchung. *BZ* 30: 161–87.
Wolbert, W. 1982. Bergpredigt und Gewaltlosigkeit. *ThPh* 57: 498–525.

William Klassen

LOWER CRITICISM. See TEXTUAL CRITICISM.

LOZON (PERSON) [Gk *Lozōn*]. See DARKON (PERSON).

LUBIM. See LEHABIM; LIBYA (PLACE).

LUCIUS (PERSON) [Gk *Loukios*]. **1.** Lucius of Cyrene, a Jewish Christian prophet and teacher in the church at Antioch in Syria (Acts 13:1). He is listed in this text from Acts along with Barnabas, Simeon who was called Niger, Manaen, and Saul. Lucius is distinguished by his place of origin, Cyrene, which is the capital city of the Roman province of Cyrene in Northern Africa, a city famous for its Jewish inhabitants (see CYRENE). Thus, he probably was a Hellenistic Jew. Because of his Cyrenian origin, Lucius may well have been included among those from Cyrene who, along with those from Cyprus, traveled to Antioch after the persecution of Stephen to help found the church there (cf. Acts 11:20).

2. Lucius, a "kinsman" of Paul, who along with Jason and Sosipater, sent greetings from Corinth to the church in Rome (Rom 16:21). These three are identified by Paul as "my kinsmen," to be understood as Paul's fellow countrymen, that is, Jewish Christians. It is possible that Lucius 2 is identical with Lucius 1. If so, then at some point Lucius of Cyrene traveled from Antioch to Corinth.

The name Lucius is a Latin Praenomen common

throughout the Roman world. It is one of the Latin equivalents for the shortened Greek name *Loukas* (cf. *Loukanos*), "Luke," as is apparent from two inscriptions referring to a family who put up memorials in honor of the god Men Ascaenus at Antioch in Pisidia. The son's name is given as *Loukas* in one and as *Loukios* in the other (Cadbury 1920–33: 491). Some authors from patristic times to the present have identified Lucius of Cyrene with Luke the evangelist and companion of Paul (see Cadbury 1920–33: 494). For example, Ephraem of Syria adds "and Luke the Cyrenean" after "Mark" in Acts 12:25 (Armenian *Comm. on Acts* 12:25–13:3), thus suggesting such an identification (Fitzmyer *Luke I–IX* AB, 47). Also, the Western text (D) for Acts introduces the first "we" passage at Acts 11:28, implying that the author (Luke) was present in Antioch. This too has led to an identification of Luke with the Lucius present at Antioch in Acts 13:1.

The Lucius of Rom 16:21 has likewise been identified from the early Christian period to the present with Luke the evangelist. Origen was aware of some who made such an identification (*Comm. in Rom.* 10.39). If so, Luke would then be a kinsman of Paul, and thus a Jewish Christian. Though this is possible, the problem, as Fitzmyer (43) remarks, "is to explain why Paul would refer to Luke there as *Loukios,* when he elsewhere uses *Loukos* of him" (Philemon 24; Col 4:14; cf. 2 Tim 4:11).

While it is true that Lucius and Lukas can be used interchangeably, an identification of Lucius (of Cyrene) with Luke the evangelist and companion of Paul is unlikely because: (1) Lucius was a very common name; (2) the author of Acts, who does not identify himself elsewhere in the narrative, would be unlikely to present himself with the robust description of "teacher and prophet" in Acts 13:1; (3) Lucius of Cyrene was probably a Jewish Christian, and Luke the evangelist was probably a gentile Christian; and (4) a tradition from the end of the 2d century (Ancient Greek Prologue) is that Luke was a Syrian, native to Antioch.

Bibliography

Cadbury, H. J. 1920–33. "Lucius of Cyrene." Vol. 5, pp. 489–495, "The Beginnings of Christianity, ed. F. J. Foakes Jackson, K. Lake. London.

Deissmann, A. 1931. "Loukios–Lukas." Pp. 117–20 in *Festgabe von Fachgenossen und Freunden von A. von Harnack zum siebzigsten Geburtstagdargebracht,* ed. K. Hall. Tübingen.

JOHN GILLMAN

LUD (PERSON) [Heb *lûd*]. LUDIM. The Table of Nations (Gen 10:13) and the parallel genealogy in 1 Chr 1:11 identifies Ludim as one of the sons of Mizraim (Egypt), son of Ham, son of Noah. Further along in the same genealogy is a reference to Lud, a son of Shem and a grandson of Noah (Gen 10:22; 1 Chr 1:17). There appear, therefore, to be two peoples in the Israelite purview showing similar names. One of these is Semitic, the other not.

Several biblical texts associate Lud with Egypt. An oracle concerning Egypt in Jeremiah 46 affiliates Ludite warriors with those of Cush (Ethiopia) and Put (Libya; Jer 46:9). Egypt is warned that at the Day of the Lord, she and her allies, including the Arabs in addition to the three peoples just mentioned, will be destroyed (Ezek 30:5). These could all be allies, or possibly mercenary troops supporting Egypt. The latter is the case in an oracle to Tyre (Ezek 27:10), where these soldiers were drawn from Persia, Put and Lud. All of these references seem to point toward, or are amenable to, an interpretation placing the Ludim in N Africa. Neo-Babylonian texts place the *Ludu* in alliance with Egypt as well (see Parpola 1970: 227). The LXX and Syriac read Ezek 30:5 not as Ludim but Lubim. Some read this as a reference to Libya, strengthening an African connection for these people. The textual evidence for this alternate reading here or elsewhere is not compelling.

Another identification is made with the Lydians, inhabitants of west-central Asia Minor (Josephus, *Ant* 1.144). The origins of the Lydians are obscure (*CAH*³ 2: 438–9), so any possible Semitic origin is uncertain. So is the relationship between these Lydians and the previously mentioned Ludim. Perhaps these groups shared a common ancestry. The Sea Peoples who tried to settle on the Egyptian coast in the second half of the 2d millennium do seem to have roots in the Aegean region (see *CAH*³ 2: 374, 361). The reference to Ludim in Isa 66:19 places them among several witnesses to God's glory. These include groups associated with both Africa (Put, "Libya") and the Aegean (Javan, "Greece").

On the basis of these different points of evidence, a definite identification cannot be proposed. Groups from two different geographical areas sharing common ancestry, while not provable, would correspond to the available evidence.

Bibliography

Parpola, S. 1970. *Neo-Assyrian Toponyms.* AOAT 6. Neukirchen-Vluyn.

DAVID W. BAKER

LUHITH (PLACE) [Heb *lûḥît*]. A town in SW Moab, mentioned in the oracles of Isaiah (15:5) and Jeremiah (48:5). In both passages, Luhith (Heb *lûḥît* "terrace") is named as a prominent point on the slopes of Transjordan's escarpment, on or near the route that connected the plain of the Dead Sea with the tableland. On the "ascent of Luhith" the ancient Moabites sought to escape calamity in the Ghor (drought?), or they fled from the plateau in the face of war, depending on how the prophetic texts are understood. In either case, emphasis is placed upon laments that transcend topographical barriers. Modern Kaṯrabba is probably the site of ancient Luhith.

GERALD L. MATTINGLY

LUKE (PERSON) [Gk *Loukas*]. A physician and "fellow worker" with the apostle Paul (Philemon 24; cf. Col 4:14; 2 Tim 4:11). Luke apparently accompanied Paul on his journey to Rome, and is the reputed author of the gospel of Luke and the Acts of the Apostles. See LUKE-ACTS, BOOK OF. This entry consists of two articles assessing Luke's accomplishments as an historian and as a theologian.

LUKE AS HISTORIAN

The author of the two-part Lukan opus at no point comments on the literary character of his work, not even in the prologue. Only to the efforts of those who had earlier reported "of the things which have been accomplished among us" (Luke 1:1)—not to his own work—does he apply the technical terminology often used by contemporaries to describe historical or biographical writing (*diegēsis:* Luke 1:1; cf. Dion. Hal. *Ant. Rom.* I.7.4; Joseph, *JW* 7, 42; and Plut. *Lyc.* 1.7). With less sharply defined language Luke describes his own purpose as "to write down in proper sequence" (*kathexēs grapsai*; Luke 1:3). If indeed the author's purpose communicated at the beginning of Luke 1:3—to take up his pen in imitation of the precursors mentioned in Luke 1:1—was intended to refer not only to the fact of writing itself but also to the literary genre of the work, then the prologue would carry at least an indirect reference to the literary character of the twofold project: Luke would then also have undertaken to write a narrativation (*diegesis*).

Luke was more precise about his activity in preparation for the writing of his work than he was about its literary form. Before he wrote he had investigated everything carefully from the beginning (Luke 1:3). This is the same claim made centuries earlier by another author, the historian Thucydides: not writing down the events according to his whim but rather investigating the details with as much precision as possible (1.22.2). Such assurances became customary in the writings of later historians. Similarity in content and vocabulary between Luke's prologue and Thucydides' chapter on method clearly shows that Luke sought to be a historian. He need not necessarily have read Thucydides directly; rather he could have drawn on historiographical tradition or perhaps on rhetoric textbooks.

We find Luke's claim to be a historian recorded elsewhere in Luke-Acts, namely in the use of the first person plural or the so-called "we passages" in Acts 16:10–17; 20:5–8, 13–15; 21:1–18; 27:1 to 28:16. The reader can and should conclude from these passages that the reporter of these events was himself involved in them. Yet the "we" in these passages is intended to indicate merely a walk-on role. It implies and is intended to imply only that those involved (above all Luke himself) frequently traveled by ship and in the process endured all of the things that went with maritime travel in those days, e.g., storm and shipwreck. For it is only in conjunction with maritime travel that the "we" references occur. What initially appears to be an idiosyncrasy of the author has the deeper purpose of demonstrating his role as a historian. He wants to be taken for well-traveled, especially by ship, in order to prove that he has the experience necessary for him to be considered a pragmatic Hellenistic historian. Travels were an important part of the historian's expected range of experience (Polyb. 12 25h.1f; Diod. Sic., 1.4.1; cf. Lucian, *Hist. conscr.* 29). Thus Odysseus became an obligatory example for these historians—Polybius noted that writing history tests the mettle of a man (12.28.1; cf. 27.10). This led to the expectation that the true historian, like Odysseus, also have maritime experience. Lucian expresses this most clearly in his treatise on the writing of history. Because Lucian merely wants to give historians a few tips, rather than write history himself, unlike them he has no need to put up with the " 'spray and surf' (Hom. *Od.*, 12.219) and anxieties that afflict the historian" (*Hist. conscr.* 4). The assumption that the historian must undertake sea voyages is found already in Polybius (12.27.8–11), has been worked into the Homer-legend (*Vita Herodotea*, 6), and is even incorporated into comedy (Plaut., *Men.*, 234–238; 247f.). Since Lucian, who merely reflects widely transmitted assumptions, knew this rule, the presence of the "we passages" in Luke is not particularly surprising.

If Luke set out to be a Hellenistic historian then one could assume that his intentions would be apparent in the literary shaping of his work. To be sure, the Gospel of Luke reflects only a few characteristics of a historical account, but Acts makes up for this with a large number. The reasons for this discrepancy are obvious. As he wrote the first work (*prōtos logos*) (Acts 1:1), Luke had in front of him extensive source materials, Mark as well as the Sayings Source. The first of these already had a firmly established and apparently indispensable literary form, namely that of a gospel. In contrast Luke had a freer hand as he wrote Acts, since there were neither formal examples to follow nor large collections of source materials that might have limited his ability to give literary shape to his work. The source materials for Acts consisted largely of short discrete traditions which dominate what are normally referred to as the "itinerary" passages. Such brief units were much more easily melded into a narrative with its own character.

Luke reveals himself as a historian most visibly in the numerous speeches he placed in the mouths of the actors in the book of Acts. A total of about 24 speeches together makes up about one-third of the book (such speeches constitute approximately one-fourth of Thucydides's history and of Sallust's *coniuratio Catilinae*).

As with the speeches in the writings of Greek and Roman historians, those of Luke are not repetitions of addresses that were actually given; like those of secular historians, the speeches in Acts often do not fit the situation in which they are said to have been spoken or, if they do fit their context, they nonetheless extend far beyond that context. Thus, for example, the setting and speech in 17:16 and 17:22 contradict each other diametrically: 17:16 reports that Paul was extremely annoyed by the profusion of pagan statues in Athens; in his Areopagus speech (17:22–31), in contrast, the same profusion of idols led him to praise the piety of the Athenians in his captatio benevolentiae (17:22). Paul's self-defense (20:20–21, 27, 33–34) threads its way through his speech to the elders at Ephesus (20:18–35) yet no accusations are made by his listeners nor are such found elsewhere in Acts. In Acts 22:1–21 Paul is supposed to be defending himself (22:1) against allegations that he had defiled the temple (21:28), yet he devotes the speech itself solely to his Jewish upbringing and piety and to his conversion and commission to preach to the gentiles.

Problems of this sort can be resolved when the speeches are interpreted not in their immediate contexts but within the framework of the entire book, i.e., in light of the author's intention. Only then does it become apparent that Luke did not seek to report a particular historical event when he wrote up these speeches, rather, through the speeches he wanted to give his readers "insight into the suprahistorical meaning of the historical moment at hand," or insight into the "event's trajectory of meaning" (Dibelius 1951: 120–21). Thus he selected Athens, despite the fact that the actual results of evangelization there were rather meager (17:32ff.), to be the stage for Paul's speech. As the intellectual center of the world and a prime location for Hellenistic piety (thus the captatio's reference to the piety of the Athenians in 17:22), Athens had special meaning for Paul—it was the proper place for a programmatic confrontation between the Christian Paul and Greek thought. Luke's concern is with the "typicality of this confrontation, which in a larger sense is historical and which had perhaps more relevance in Luke's own day than it had at the time of Paul" (Dibelius 1951: 133), not unlike Thucydides' desire to illustrate an "ideal competition between two principles" in the speeches of the Melian dialogue (Thuc. 5.85–113; Jaeger 1936: 501). The address in Acts 20:18–35, which belongs to the genre of farewell speeches, must also be understood as the Acts-author's statement about the situation at hand. It is likewise directed solely at the readers of the book. Luke lets them know here that an epoch of the Church's history, the era of the apostles' disciples (second generation), was coming to an end with Paul's farewell to his mission field and that the Lukan "present" was beginning. Unlike the earlier period, which had been troubled by heresy (cf. 20:29–30), the present period possessed the complete and undiminished tradition that Paul had transmitted (20:27) and need not be made anxious by secret heretical teachings (20:30). The surprising irrelevance to its context of Paul's self-defense (22:1–21) also ceases to be unsettling if one does not see it in connection with the charge that Paul had profaned the temple, but instead applies Luke's historiographical intention as an interpretive key. It then becomes apparent that the author of Acts views the moment in which Paul reaches the end of his free activity as a moment of special historical significance, a moment that requires that the missionary to the gentiles look back and reflect on how he was led into a mission to the gentiles that was not bound by the Law. Ostensibly he does this in front of the crowd; actually he is addressing the readers' forum.

When Luke inserted speeches at the most important transitions in his narrative in order to illuminate the meaning of the particular moment and the trajectory of the events, he was basically doing nothing other than what Thucydides had done. For Thucydides "the ultimate aim of the speeches was to help the historian to interpret the events: they shed light on the inner interrelationships that otherwise . . . would be visible only indirectly in the structure and tone of the portrayal" (Gundert 1940: 98, cf. Luschnat 1942: 113ff. with reference to Thuc. 1.68–71, 73–78; 2.87, 89, and elsewhere). Luke was no Thucydidean in the style of Polybius. Yet the influence of the great Athenian is clearly perceptible in the speeches of the book of Acts, even if it most probably was transmitted over many stages of historiographical tradition rather than directly taken up by Luke.

In the case of one group of speeches, which have an obvious common pattern of organization, are all addressed to a Jewish audience, and are much better integrated into their context. Dibelius (1951: 142) sought to deny any connection with Greco-Roman historiographical tradition, suggesting instead that they reflect the pattern of Christian sermons of the time of Luke as can be seen in the so-called "mission speeches" (2:14–39; 3:12–26; 4:9–12; 5:29–32; 10:34–43; 13:16–41). Wilckens has shown (1961: 72ff.), however, that such a sermon pattern did not exist, and that these speeches must be interpreted as a peculiarly Lukan portrayal of what the author of the Acts wished to be understood as the essence of the apostolic proclamation. Thus they are examples not of preaching contemporary with Luke but of historical preaching characteristic of a particular epoch. Like the other speeches of Acts these invariably occur at decisive turning points in the Church's history. This is done, however, not by illuminating through the speeches the time-transcending meaning of the turning points, rather it is done in such a way that "in each decisive point of transition in mission history the verbally recounted sermon is offered as the dynamic factor that produces the events and directs their course" (Wilckens 1961: 96). A typical example is the sermon by Peter in 3:12–26, which produces the confrontation between the Jesus' gospel and Judaism that is so decisive for the future (cf. 4:1–3). Another example comes in Paul's speech in 13:16–41. Its conclusion takes the form of a final exhortation to repentance directed at the Jews. Out of Jewish unwillingness to respond to this call to repentance (13:44–45) comes Paul's shift from a Jewish to a gentile mission (13:46–47) that dominates the events described in Acts.

In this too Luke was dependent on Greco-Roman historiography. Speeches intended in a literary sense to set in motion decisive historical processes and thereby to make history are found in the great deliberation scenes of Livy's history. According to Livy the war between Rome and Antiochus III was sparked primarily by a speech delivered by Hannibal in the king's council, since "this speech not only impressed the king, but also reconciled him to Hannibal. Thus the result of this council-session was the decision to go to war" (35.19.7, cf. 5.49–55; 21.19.8ff.; 33.13.13). That this assumption about the history-making power of speeches was widely held among historians in the Greco-Roman world is most evident in the paradigmatic words of an otherwise not particularly original writer (E. Schwarz in PW, 5: 934), Dionysius of Halicarnassus. He tells us in his *Antiquitates Romanae* (7.66.3) that he was astonished at how many historians waste words on wars and the conditions that go with them yet, when recounting the political developments and crises, fail to transmit the speeches that brought forth such extraordinary and astonishing events. To recount words that shed light on the events that came to pass was the historiographical expectation Luke sought to fulfill in composing the "mission-speeches." Not for its own sake did he seek to meet this expectation, but in order to prove legitimate the historical process through which Jewish Christianity became the gentile Christian church of his day. He succeeded in this by showing how the proclamation of the Gospel by the apostles and by Paul, the ones chosen by the Lord himself to be witnesses "in Jerusalem and in all of Judaea and Samaria and even to the ends of the earth" (1:8; 13:47; 22:21), was, at each decisive turning point, the dynamic force responsible for the developments.

The narrative portions of Acts reveal their author as a Hellenistic historian almost to a greater degree than do the speeches (occasionally the narrative portions of Luke do the same, e.g., 4:16–30, cf. Busse, 1978: 55–67).

Luke offers no continuously advancing course of action. Instead he portrays the events as a sequence of individual episodes that normally lack any or have only minimal connection to the context, indeed, his episodes do not require the context in order to be understood. Examples of abrupt openings for new narrative episodes are found in Acts 10:1ff. and Acts 18:12, where the story begins in each case with the introduction of someone significant for the episode that follows. In other instances information that has already been given is retold in a new context (cf. Acts 10:5–6 with 9:43). Almost never does the action of one episode affect another event. For example, although the events of Pentecost in 2:1ff. fulfill a promise given at the Ascension (1:8) the Ascension is never mentioned in telling the Pentecost story. Even at their conclusions episodes are seldom linked factually with the context (cf. 14:18 and 14:19; 16:40 and 17:1; 19:40 and 20:1). The episodes of Acts were written above all as dramatic scenes, as living, vivid illustrations, concise and purposefully put together. Luke heightens the drama through climactic turning points (14:8–18; 16:16–40; 19:23–40) and dramatic effects (1:9; 10:44; 16:27–28; 18:12–17), both of which take the form of marvels (1:9; 10:44) or unusual acts of nature (16:26).

Luke employs the "dramatic episode" style (E. Haenchen *Acts* MeyerK) particularly effectively whenever he arranges specific assertions and their consequences into scenes. Stripped of their drab abstraction, such assertions are thus able to work upon the reader. For instance, nowhere does Luke say in the abstract that the state and its legal system are not suited to decide religious issues, or that such controversies are not adjudicable. Instead he demonstrates this thesis by way of concrete cases in scenes found in 18:12–17, 25:13–22, and 25:23–26, 32. Luke tells the reader the things he considers to be important doing so not in dry reports but in the action of vivid individual scenes, out of which the reader can draw all that is essential with his or her own eye.

Luke uses the style of a particular type of Hellenistic historiography here, the style of the tragedy/pathos-centered historiography. Its aim was "sub oculos subiecto" (Gellius 10.3.7 regarding Cicero's style), that is, the gripping shaping of graphic, true-to-life images that should lock in the reader's attention like a scene in the theater (Lucian, *Hist. conscr.* 51). Adherents of this school of historiography included Duris of Samos (cf. Diod. *Sic.* 19.108–9; 20.33–34), Phylarch (cf. Plut. *Cleom.* 19–20, 29, 38), Cleitarch, the historian of Alexander (cf. Diod. *Sic.* 17.26–27, 98–99), and Curtius Rufus (cf. 4.1.38–4.21), as well as the author of 2 Maccabees (cf. 3:1–40). All of them exhibit, more or less, those stylistic peculiarities that are characteristic of the Lukan episodes: frequent irrelevance to the context, a striving for vividness and a sensitivity to dramatic effects and climactic turning points. The individual stories of Livy are especially characteristic examples of this tragedy-pathos approach to history writing—they are "visually conceived, and their strength is found in their powerful imagery, in their vividness" (Burck 1964: 200–201; cf. Livy 2.40; 31.17; 45.12).

The inspiration and motivation for the tragedy-pathos approach was a portrayal of historical events that achieved complete reproduction of lived truth through imitation of reality, i.e., through *mimesis,* or *enargeia* (see the paradigmatic statement of Duris, *FGrH* 76 F 1). This did not mean that one aimed at historical facticity, indeed one viewed *mimesis* often as a suitable means to make history vivid even when historical facts were distorted through a recounting that aimed at a greater sense of "real life," or a portrayal that replaced facts with a "fictional or potential reality" (Strasburger 1975: 80; cf. Avenarius 1956: 130–40). Polybius' criticism of Phylarch is significant in this context: Phylarch makes use of the concerns of tragedy when he tried to "appeal to the emotions of the reader and to make the reader a fellow-sufferer in the events portrayed," but he neglects the concerns of the historian, namely, "to remember without distortion what had been truly done and said" (2.56.7–10). Tragedy-oriented historiography was concerned solely to lead the reader to enjoyment whether to mere entertainment (Cicero, *Fam.* 5.12.4), or also to *katharsis,* to "cleansing and/or freeing of the soul, which is the particular outcome of reliving the tragedy" (Strasburger 1975: 82). Livy once more offers the best illustration of this psychagogy, above all where his specific stories place before the reader "examples of the ancients" with their power for the present (e.g., 2.10; 2.12; 2.13.6–11), permitting the events portrayed to act as "salutary examples . . . for the human race" (5.27.13).

This style was perfectly suited to Luke's purposes. Given the delay of the *parousia,* Christians needed to find their place in the world. Yet this world was, even if not a priori (Acts 26:28, 31–32), certainly de facto becoming increasingly hostile towards Christianity (see Plin. *Ep.* 10: 96–97; Acts 20:25, 36–38, where Luke hints that he knew of Paul's death). Luke resisted some of the conclusions that might be drawn from this situation. On the one hand he opposed the sort of uncompromising Christian hostility toward the state and the society that is visible in the renewal of apocalyptic expectations shared by the Apocalypse of John. On the other hand he did not want to be content and not stand out (a later example of this stance is found in Tertullian, *de corona,* 1). Instead, the triumphal images in Acts 14:8–18, 16:16–40; 17:16–33; and 19:23–40 were intended to show that Christianity despite all resistance to it had always managed to succeed in the world. Such lively and therefore convincingly portrayed examples of successful actions in the past were supposed to arouse in the reader the hope that what was so clearly described in the past could become reality in the reader's present. Luke's psychagogic purpose is even clearer in those scenes in which he offers his political apologetic (18:12–17; 25:13–22; 25:23–26:32). These scenes reach their climax in the quasi-acquittal of Paul in 26:31 and the programmatic closing passage asserting that Paul worked for two years in Rome with no restrictions (28:31). Suffused with an aura of authenticity which seems fully credible because it is consistent, they place on the stage Luke's political argumentation.

Luke not only had to explain the problems resulting from the delay of the *parousia* and Christianity's consequent settling down in the world, but one of the most pressing questions had to do with the place in God's plan of salvation for a church made up solely of gentiles and lacking any outward continuity with Israel, to whom the gospel had originally been addressed (13:46). How Luke responded to this question is evident in the way he employed the "mission speeches" discussed above. Luke's answer to Christians' doubts is given in the narrative portion of his work, not in the form of an abstract exposition, but rather through incorporation into the action of dramatic scenes (8:26–39; 10:1–11, 18; 22:17–22). The historical information given is the fact that the shift from Jewish to gentile mission had taken place in earlier times not arbitrarily but under the stimulus of divine providence, that Paul was indeed explicitly commanded by the Lord to preach the gospel to the gentiles. This in turn offers the thesis that the gospel had been transferred from the hands of the Jews to those of the gentile church. Furthermore it is the history itself that gives the answer to pressing questions; once more the events described by Luke carry the marks of Livy's *salutaria exempla*—they do not merely tell history but in the telling offer help to resolve contemporary problems. This fits precisely the general purpose of Luke's historical writing as he himself tells us: to give the reader certainty about the traditions they had learned in the church's catechesis (Luke 1:4), i.e., to assure them that their Christianity was indeed in good shape.

Although Luke ought to be viewed as a Hellenistic historian, he clearly does not fit into a single type of Greco-Roman historiography. The expectation that a historian should have had personal experience (*empeiria* and *autopatheia*), the expectation that leads Luke to write his sea voyage passages in the first person plural, comes from pragmatic historiography. Luke is linked to this by the Thucydideisms of the prologue and his desire to emphasize the significance of historical events and to outline their trajectory through speeches. The dramatic episode approach, in contrast, was the narrative form of the tragedy-pathos historiography. He drew his method of imitating the Septuagint (Plümacher 1972: 38–72) from the Attic classicism that in his day was common not only to historians but to writers in other genres. Thus the author of Luke-Acts obviously chose his literary equipment with a view to expediency and not out of allegiance to a particular historiographical school.

It is just as difficult to locate the external form of Luke-Acts within the traditions of Hellenistic history-writing. On the basis of Acts's possessing the character of a historical monograph (corresponding to the pattern sketched by Cicero, *Fam.* 5.12, and similar to 2 Maccabees or Sallust's *coniuratio* and/or *bellum Iugurthinum*) and in view of the growing tendency to monographic classification in universal history (cf. Diod. *Sic.* 16.1), Luke-Acts could best be seen as an attempt to write a general history of Christianity (including the destiny of its founder, see Acts 1:1) in two loosely connected monographs.

Because Luke had no successors, Eusebius has received the title "Father of Church History." Yet the honor of having been the first Christian historian belongs to the unknown author of this twofold opus, a person later identified with the companion of Paul mentioned in Philemon 24, Col 4:41, and 2 Tim 4:11, even if he has only been (re)discovered as a historian in modern biblical studies.

Bibliography

Avenarius, G. 1956. *Lukans Schrift zur Geschichtsschreibung.* Meisenheim.

Barrett, C. K. 1962. *Luke the Historian in Recent Study.* London.

Boer, W. den. 1961. Some Remarks on the Beginnings of Christian Historiography. *StPatr* 4/2 = *TU* 79: 348–62.

Burck, E. 1964. *Die Erzahlungskunst des T. Livius.* Berlin and Zurich.

Busse, U. 1978. *Das Nazareth-Manifest Jesu.* SBS 91. Stuttgart.

Cadbury, H. J. 1927. *The Making of Luke-Acts.* London. Repr. 1958.

———. 1955. *The Book of Acts in History.* London.

Callan, T. 1985. The Preface of Luke-Acts and Historiography. *NTS* 31: 576–81.

Conzelmann, H. 1964. *Die Mitte der Zeit.* 5th ed. BHT 17. Tübingen.

———. 1972. *Die Apostelgeschichte.* 2d ed. HNT 7. Tübingen.

———. 1976. Luke's Place in the Development of Early Christianity: Studies in Luke-Acts. Pp. 298–316 in *Jesus in the Memory of the Early Church,* ed. N. A. Dahl. Minneapolis.

Dahl, N. A. 1976. The Purpose of Luke-Acts. Pp. 87–98 in *Jesus in the Memory of the Early Church,* ed. N. A. Dahl. Minneapolis.

Dibelius, M. 1951. *Aufsätze zur Apostelgeschichte.* 5th ed. 1968. FRLANT 60. Göttingen.

Dillon, R. J. 1981. Previewing Luke's Project from His Prologue (Luke 1:1–4). *CBQ* 43: 205–27.

Eltester, W. 1972. *Israel im lukanischen Werk und die Nazarethperikope.* Berlin.

Fusco, V. 1986. Progetto storiografico e progetto teologico nell'opera lucana. Pp. 123–52 in *La storiografia nella Bibbia: Atti della XXVIII settimana biblica.* Bologna.

Gasque, W. W. 1974. The Speeches of Acts: Dibelius Reconsidered. Pp. 232–50 in *New Dimensions in New Testament Study.* Grand Rapids.

George, A. 1968. Israel dans l'oeuvre de Luc. *RB* 77: 481–525.

Grässer, E. 1977. *Das Problem der Parusieverzögerung in den synoptischen Evangelien und in der Apostelgeschichte.* 3d ed. BZNW 22. Berlin.

Grech, P. 1982. Jewish Christianity and the Purpose of Acts. *SE* 7 = TU 126: 223–26.

Gundert, H. 1940. Athen und Sparta inen Reden des Thukydides. *Die Antike* 16: 98–114.

Hemer, C. J. 1977. Luke the Historian. *BJRL* 60: 28–51.

Hengel, M. 1984. *Zur urchristlichen Geschichtsschreibung.* 2d ed. Stuttgart.

Jaeger, W. 1936. *Paideia; die Formung des griechischen Menschen.* Vol. 1. 2d ed. Berlin.

Jervell, J. 1972. *Luke and the People of God.* Minneapolis.

Keck, L. E., and Martyn, J. L., eds. 1966. *Studies in Luke-Acts.* Nashville.

Kremer, J., ed. 1979. *Les Actes des Apôtres.* BETL 48. Louvain.

Kümmel, W. G. 1970. *Das Gesetz und die Propheten gehen bis Johannes.* Wuppertal.

Kurz, W. S. 1980. Luke-Acts and Historiography in the Greek Bible. *SBLSP* pp. 283–300.

Lohse, E. 1954. Lukas als Theologe der Heilsgeschichte. *EvT* 14: 256–75.

Löning, K. 1973. *Die Saulustradition in der Apostelgeschichte.* NTAbh 9. Münster.

Luschnat, O. 1942. *Die Feldherrnreden im Geschichtswerke des Thukydides.* Leipzig.

Maddox, R. 1982. *The Purpose of Luke-Acts.* FRLANT 126. Göttingen.

Marshall, I. H. 1979. *Luke: Historian and Theologian.* 2d ed. Exeter.

———. 1980. *The Acts of the Apostles*. Leicester.

Nuttall, G. F. 1978. *The Moment of Recognition: Luke as Story-Teller*. London.

Plümacher, E. 1972. *Lukas als hellenistischer Schriftsteller*. SUNT 9. Göttingen.

———. 1977. Wirklichkeitserfahrung und Geschichtsschreibung bei Lukas. *ZNW* 68: 2–22.

Reumann, J. 1968. Heilsgeschichte in Luke. *SE* 4 = TU 102: 86–115.

Robbins, V. K. 1975. The We-Passages in Acts and Ancient Sea Voyages. *BR* 20: 5–18.

———. 1978. Prefaces in Greco-Roman Biography and Luke-Acts. *SBLSP* pp. 193–207.

Roloff, J. 1979. Die Paulus-Darstellung des Lukas. *EvT* 39: 510–31.

Schneider, G. 1970. *Die zwölf Apostel als "Zeugen"*. Essen.

———. 1977. Der Zweck des lukanischen Doppelwerks. *BZ* n.s. 21: 45–66.

———. 1979. Apostelgeschichte und Kirchengeschichte. *IKZC* 8: 481–7.

Steichele, H. 1971. Vergleich der Apostelgeschichte mit der antiken Geschichtsschreibung. Diss. Munich.

Strasburger, H. 1975. *Die Wesensbestimmung der Geschichte durch die antike Geschichtsschreibung*. 3d ed. Wiesbaden.

Talbert, C. H., ed. 1978. *Perspectives on Luke-Acts*. Danville, VA.

Tiede, D. L. 1980. *Prophecy and History in Luke-Acts*. Philadelphia.

Trocmé, E. 1957. *Le "Livre des Actes" et l'histoire*. Paris.

———. 1983. The Beginnings of Christian Historiography and the History of Early Christianity. *ABR* 31: 1–14.

Unnik, W. C. van. 1960. The Confirmation of the Gospel. *NovT* 4: 26–59.

———. 1973. Once More St. Luke's Prologue. *Neot* 7: 7–26.

Wilckens, U. 1961. *Die Missionsreden der Apostelgeschichte*. 3d ed. 1974. WMANT 5. Neukirchen-Vluyn.

ECKHARD PLÜMACHER
Trans. Dennis Martin

LUKE AS THEOLOGIAN

Luke-Acts, occupying as it does one quarter of the text of the NT, is a major theological work, although some would question whether Luke should be called a theologian in the sense that this was his primary aim in his writings or that he was a deep theological thinker. Theological concerns and a theological outlook come to expression consciously and unconsciously in his work. Even those who emphasize that Luke was a historian agree that he uses history in the service of theology and that he intends his work to have a pastoral purpose.

Luke-Acts is later than Mark and Paul's Epistles, although it shows little if any use of the latter. Luke's work differs from that of Mark in that (a) he wrote a two-volume account which included the story of the continuation of the work of Jesus by his followers to the point where Paul reached Rome, and (b) he told the story of Jesus differently. The differences under the latter heading are not due simply to the use of material from other sources (including Q). Matthew shared much of the same resources, and yet he produced a different effect. The differences must, therefore, also reflect Luke's own approach. Yet the contrast between Luke and Mark should not be exaggerated. He incorporated Mark into his gospel without substantial change.

H. Conzelmann gave the decisive impulse towards recognition of Luke as a theologian with his thesis that Luke wrote under the influence of the delay of the parousia. He coped with this situation by abandoning the primitive belief that Christians were living in the last days and substituting a salvation-historical understanding of the Christ-event which made it the mid-point in a series of divine activities, preceded by the period of Israel and followed by the time of the Church (in which he and his readers now found themselves) which would last until the parousia at some indefinite point in the future. Before Luke developed this new understanding Christian existence was defined by the hope of the imminent parousia, but it was now seen to take place in the age of the Spirit which functioned as a kind of substitute for the hope.

Luke's framework of thought is salvation-historical, i.e., he operates with the concept of the saving acts of God taking place in historical sequence. But it is questionable whether he virtually created this framework. Mark was also under the same pressure of the time-factor which had already persuaded Christians that, even if the resurrection of Jesus was a sign that the last days were here, the parousia was not necessarily to follow immediately. It is still debated whether Luke envisaged salvation-history as falling into three periods with the time of Jesus (the middle of time) separated off from the parousia by the time of the Church (Fitzmyer *Luke* AB). More probably Luke saw a period of promise followed by an extended period of fulfilment. Yet even so for Luke, Christians were living in the last days and the parousia was still imminent and relevant though not immediate. Since then, Luke's theology is not decisively different from that of his predecessors at this point, it is dubious whether Conzelmann has correctly unearthed Luke's theological motivation and purpose.

A more satisfactory view starts from the recognition that Luke wrote an account of the origins of Christianity. He felt that the account of the ministry of Jesus had to be supplemented by the story of the founding of the church. The two parts of his work together were meant to enable Christians like Theophilus to know that their faith was not a matter of groundless speculation and credulity; rather the instruction which had led them to faith could be corroborated by the evidence of eyewitnesses and servants of the gospel which Luke had wrought into an orderly narrative. Luke's purpose was thus to create and strengthen faith by a narrative which showed how God was at work for human salvation. Luke's theme is accordingly salvation (O'Toole).

The fact that Luke found it necessary to tell the story of the Church as well as the story of Jesus indicates that the latter alone was insufficient for his purpose. The salvation-event includes both the ministry of Jesus and the proclamation of salvation by the Church. Jesus continues to be active by the Spirit and in the Church, so that the salvation which was manifested in his ministry is still effective for people separated from him geographically and temporally. It is not accidental that parallels can be traced between the gospel and Acts, between the activities of Jesus and his followers. Luke expresses the continuity between the message of Jesus and the proclamation of the Church and shows that what Jesus proclaimed has become a reality in the Church and in the time after Jesus.

Luke emphasizes the prophetic aspect of Jesus' ministry within the context of seeing him as Son of God and Son of man. Unlike the other Evangelists, he refers to Jesus as Lord in the gospel even before his exaltation.

The apostolic preaching in Acts pays little attention to the teaching and actions of Jesus in exactly the same way as the apostolic kerygma, as it can be reconstructed from the Epistles, concentrates on the death and resurrection of Jesus as the saving event. This further indicates why Luke was not satisfied merely to tell the story of the earthly ministry of Jesus. Luke takes over the church's doctrine of the death of Jesus reflected in Luke 22:19–23 and Acts 20:28, but he appears to incorporate it in a wider understanding of the work of Jesus. He is the Servant of God who has undergone suffering and has been exalted in order to continue his function of offering salvation to humankind.

An important element in Luke's theology is the universality of salvation and specifically the place of the gentiles among the people of God. The church is probably to be seen as the new Israel rather than as a renewed Israel incorporating the gentiles (Jervell). Both the coming of the Messiah and also the proclamation of salvation to the gentiles are constituent parts of God's plan revealed in prophecy. The gentiles are "saved" by faith, just like the Jews, and therefore they are not required to be circumcised or to keep the law, even though believing Jews may continue to observe the law. Yet Luke recognizes the problem of tensions over table-fellowship (Esler) and notes how gentiles were—at least in some churches—required to avoid unnecessary offense to Jews. Although the attempt has been made to see Luke as a passionate hater of Jews as such (Sanders), it is more likely that he simply expresses opposition to attempts to impose Jewish legalism upon gentiles.

The question of Luke's understanding of sin and salvation has been reopened by J.-W. Taeger who argues that for Luke the problem of humankind prior to faith is sins rather than sin as an alien force and that, consequently, humankind is in need of repentance and moral progress rather than a divine gift of salvation. But Luke's understanding does not differ significantly from that of Mark and Matthew. In any case, Acts is not a theological treatise and it contains doctrines largely in the form of evangelistic addresses, hardly the ideal medium for deep theological reflection on human sinfulness in the manner of Paul. What is important is that Luke sees a *praeparatio evangelica* in Judaism and perhaps even in the religious longings of paganism.

Luke appears to see the Spirit as especially the Spirit of prophecy which equips Jesus and the Church for their roles. He says little about the Spirit as the gift of salvation. The Spirit provides divine power for witness and salvation.

The new life associated with salvation is seen in terms of repentance and conversion. Particular stress is laid on self-denial, especially with regard to wealth. More than the other Evangelists Luke teaches the need for the rich to share with the poor and shows how this ideal found expression in the Jerusalem church.

Luke attaches great significance to the Twelve as the initial witnesses to the resurrection of Jesus who provide the continuity between Jesus and the Church and thus constitute its initial leaders. But he is aware that within a short time the leadership passed into the hands of James and a body of elders, although he says nothing about how this happened or about the details of church organization and structure. The position of Paul is ambiguous, the question of his apostleship and letter-writing being passed over in virtual silence, although clearly he is *the* missionary to the gentiles. Indeed, Luke shows little interest in the internal life and growth of the Church. He is primarily concerned with its missionary expansion from Jerusalem to Rome. This shows that we are not to expect from Luke a full, systematic account of his theology, if he possessed one, and should make us wary of drawing too far-reaching conclusions from the limited evidence which he provides.

Bibliography

Bovon, F. 1978. *Luc le Théologien.* Neûchatel.

Brown, S. 1969. *Apostasy and Perseverance in the Theology of Luke.* Rome.

Conzelmann, H. 1960. *The Theology of St. Luke.* London.

Esler, P. F. 1987. *Community and Gospel in Luke-Acts.* Cambridge.

Franklin, E. 1975. *Christ the Lord: A Study in the Purpose and Theology of Luke-Acts.* London.

George, A. 1978. *Etudes sur l'œuvre de Luc.* Paris.

Glöckner, R. 1975. *Die Verkündigung des Heils beim Evangelisten Lukas.* Mainz.

Horn, F. W. 1983. *Glaube und Handeln in der Theologie des Lukas.* Göttingen.

Jervell, J. 1972. *Luke and the People of God: A New Look at Acts.* Minneapolis.

Lohfink, G. 1975. *Die Sammlung Israels: eine Untersuchung zur lukanischen Ekklesiologie.* Munich.

Maddox, R. 1982. *The Purpose of Luke-Acts.* Edinburgh.

Marshall, I. H. 1984. *Luke: Historian and Theologian.* 2d ed. Exeter.

Minear, P. S. 1976. *To Heal and to Reveal: The Prophetic Vocation according to Luke.* New York.

Navone, J. 1970. *Themes of St Luke.* Rome.

O'Neill, J. C. 1970. *The Theology of Acts in its Historical Setting.* 2d ed. London.

O'Toole, R. F. 1984. *The Unity of Luke's Theology.* Wilmington.

Sanders, J. T. 1987. *The Jews in Luke-Acts.* London.

Seccombe, D. P. 1982. *Possessions and the Poor in Luke-Acts.* Linz.

Taeger, J.-W. 1982. *Der Mensch und sein Heil.* Gütersloh.

Tiede, D. L. 1980. *Prophecy and History in Luke-Acts.* Philadelphia.

Unnik, W. C. van. 1960. The "Book of Acts" the Confirmation of the Gospel. *NovT* 4: 26–59.

Wilson, S. G. 1973. *The Gentiles and the Gentile Mission in Luke-Acts.* Cambridge.

———. 1983. *Luke and the Law.* Cambridge.

I. HOWARD MARSHALL

LUKE-ACTS, BOOK OF. The conventional scholarly designation for the two volumes, the Gospel of Luke and the Acts of the Apostles, which are separated by the Gospel of John in the NT canon.

A. Introduction
B. Circumstances of Composition
C. Genre and Purpose

D. Literary Aspects of Luke-Acts
1. Style
2. Narrative Devices
3. Literary Structure
4. Prophetic Structure
E. The Prophet and the People
1. The Gospel Narrative
2. The Acts Narrative
F. Literary-Religious Themes in Luke-Acts
1. World Affirmation
2. The Great Reversal
3. Salvation
4. The Word of God
5. Conversion
6. The Response of Faith

A. Introduction

Ancient manuscripts do not place the Gospel of Luke and the Acts of the Apostles together, though canonical lists (e.g., the *Muratorian Canon*) attribute them both to Luke, who is regarded as a companion of Paul. The designation Luke-Acts reflects the conviction of virtually all contemporary scholars that the gospel and Acts were from the beginning a single literary work in both conception and execution (Cadbury 1927).

The writings invite this appraisal. Each volume is introduced by a prologue addressed to the same reader, Theophilus, possibly the patron who sponsored the composition (van Unnik 1973; Fitzmyer *Luke I–IX* AB, 299). The prologue to Acts provides a short summary of the first volume (Acts 1:1–2). The gospel prologue is more elaborate. It provides important clues to the nature and purpose of the two-volume work (Luke 1:1–4). In addition to the prologue, an intricate skein of sylistic, structural, and thematic elements binds the two writings together.

The decision to read these separate texts as a single literary work represents the triumph of a literary-critical approach to the NT writings, concerned less for the historical data contained in a writing, or the prehistory of its discrete parts, than with its distinctive voice. The method uses the discoveries of source and form criticism, but unlike them is concerned with a writing in its literary integrity (Beardslee 1970). To adopt the category "Luke-Acts," therefore, means to accept a contemporary literary designation in preference to the traditional perception of the texts or even their canonical placement.

Although the designation of Luke-Acts as a literary unity is now widely accepted, its implications have only begun to be developed. Commentaries, for example, continue to be written on each volume separately, with only minimal attention to the literary truncation involved. The Anchor Bible volumes devoted to these writings (Fitzmyer on Luke; Munck on Acts) do not entirely escape the problem.

Luke-Acts takes up fully a quarter of the NT canon. It is pivotal both for the history of earliest Christianity and for the development of its theology. See LUKE (PERSON). Although some overlapping is unavoidable, the specific topic of the present entry is Luke-Acts as a literary work. Attention must be given as well to some of its historical and religious claims, but only insofar as a connection can be drawn between them and the literary shape of the writing. The concern here is not only with what Luke-Acts says, but how it speaks.

B. Circumstances of Composition

Any discussion of the circumstances accompanying the production of Luke-Acts is inevitably circular. There are few external guideposts, so conclusions must be based on internal evidence, which can—notoriously—be construed in quite different ways. The issues of dating and authorship, for example, mutually impinge; and to a remarkable degree, each depends on a reader's overall conception of the writing.

The ancient manuscripts attribute the gospel to a certain Luke, whom patristic writers unanimously identify as the companion of Paul (Philemon 24; Col 4:14; 2 Tim 4:11), a supposition apparently supported by the so-called "we passages" of Acts (cf. 16:10–17; 20:5–15; 21:8–18; 27:1–28:16) in which the narrator suddenly shifts from third-person to first-person narration, suggesting the presence of an eyewitness (Fitzmyer *Luke I–IX* AB, 36). Critical scholarship has challenged the traditional attribution, arguing that the tone, perspective, and purposes of Luke-Acts better fit a later, "second-generation" composition (Loning 1981). A very late dating would obviously disqualify any companion of Paul as author. "Second-generation," however, is scarcely a precise designation. To place Luke-Acts as late as the 2d century (O'Neill 1961) is excessive. In fact, nothing in the writing prohibits composition by a companion of Paul and an eyewitness to some events. A thirty-year-old man who joined Paul ca. 50 C.E. would still only be sixty in the 80s, old enough and at sufficient distance to describe the beginnings of the movement with a certain nostalgia. Luke's failure to use Paul's letters or even to mention that Paul wrote letters argues in favor of an earlier rather than a later date. It is far more likely for Paul's letters to be ignored before the time of their collection and canonization than after. Some contemporary scholars argue the opposite way. They attribute some of Paul's letters to Luke's authorship, particularly the Pastoral Letters (Wilson 1979) perhaps even as the third volume of Luke-Acts (Quinn 1978). Such hypotheses fall short of proof and are less convincing than the traditional attributions for Luke-Acts and Paul's letters.

To state that Luke-Acts could have been composed by a companion of Paul by the end of the 1st century (probably between 80 and 85, though possibly earlier), does not by itself tell us anything about the nature of the writing or its historical accuracy. That the author is an admirer of Paul is obvious from the text in any case, and the number of events he could himself witness would have been small. For the rest, the author admittedly relied on other witnesses and written sources (Luke 1:1–2).

Nor does this attribution tell us anything about the author. Like the other gospel writers, Luke recedes modestly behind his narrative. Attempts to discover in his style the marks of a physician, for example, have been massively refuted (Cadbury 1920). The text does reveal more important characteristics of the author: his stylistic ability, which enables him to use various Greek dictions; his Hellenistic education, shown by his facile use of rhetorical conventions (Kurz 1980); his wide reading in Torah, manifested in his dense textual allusions and in the structure of his story;

his storytelling ability, demonstrated by his striking vignettes and parables. The text reveals most of all a synthetic narrative imagination, enabling him to make the story of Jesus (already current in the church) and the story of the church's beginnings into one coherent and interconnected story, showing in the process that it continued the still longer story of God and his people.

The provenience and audience of Luke-Acts are impossible to fix precisely. Ancient tradition wavers regarding the place of composition, and the text gives no firm clues (Fitzmyer *Luke I-IX* AB, 37–40). The circumstances of Luke's readers also escape easy detection, as the many suggestions concerning them suggest (Karris 1978; 1979). Certainly, his readers were Greek-speaking, and sufficiently acquainted with scriptural traditions to grasp at least the gist of his allusions. They were already Christian. They were almost certainly gentile; indeed, a great deal of Luke-Acts makes little sense if they were not gentile believers (Fitzmyer *Luke I–IX* AB, 57–59). Given the length, complexity, and literary sophistication of the work, it is far less likely that it responded to a specific or local crisis than that Luke intentionally addressed a much wider readership with magisterial ambition (Johnson 1979). If there is a crisis addressed by Luke-Acts—and there is—it is not one occasioned by momentary circumstance, but rather by the nature and development of the Christian movement itself.

C. Genre and Purpose

Luke is above all a gifted storyteller. His writing is filled with short vignettes, each of which imaginatively summons for the reader an entire world (Haenchen 1966: 259–60). In the gospel, Luke alone tells the parables of the Rich Fool (12:13–21), of Lazarus and Dives (16:19–31), of the Good Samaritan (10:30–35), and, most memorably, of the Prodigal Son (15:11–32). These parables are, of course, attributed to Jesus, although much of their shaping may be due to Luke himself (cf., e.g., Schweizer 1948). Luke weaves a delicate tapestry in his infancy stories (Luke 1–2) and in his resurrection accounts (Luke 24), which have an almost novelistic tone (Wanke 1973: 1–32). No less in Acts is his storytelling ability revealed: the death of Ananias and Sapphira (5:1–11), Peter's release from prison (12:6–17), and Paul's shipwreck (27:1–44) are small masterpieces of narration.

Luke is, however, considerably more than a miniaturist. His most impressive accomplishment is the forging of these short stories (many of them already circulating in some form) into one long, coherent narrative, which with masterful control brings the reader from the mists of antiquity all the way to a rented apartment in the empire's capital city, and within the space of 52 chapters creates out of sometimes unlikely material an uncanny sense of historical movement. Luke had at least one antecedent for the gospel narrative (Mark), which he used. But his unexampled contribution to Christian literature was the extension of that story to the time of his first readers, connecting them by narrative not only to the first days of the church and to Jesus' life and ministry, but as well to the whole story of God's people, reaching back even to Adam (Luke 3:38) (Kurz 1984).

Luke's choice of the narrative form is deliberate. He explicitly designates his work a *diegesis* "narrative" (1:1) and emphasizes that he tells events "in sequence" (*kathexes*, 1:3). It is clear from several other places that Luke regards the narration of events "in order" to have a peculiarly convincing quality (e.g., Acts 9:27; 11:4; 15:12–14). For him, the development of the plot itself, in sequence, has a persuasive force (Dillon 1981: 217–33). In this, Luke shares the conviction of Hellenistic rhetoric, which regards the *narratio* as critical to historical argument or personal defense, as he shows also in the construction of Paul's "defense speeches" (Acts 22:3–21; 24:10–21; 26:4–23) (Neyrey 1984). How this literary emphasis serves Luke's religious purposes will be discussed. But first, the implications of the narrative form for intepreting Luke-Acts should be mentioned.

To say that Luke-Acts is a story means, at the least, that it cannot be read as a systematic treatise filled with theological propositions. To use rhetorical terms as old as Aristotle (cf. *Poet.* 6: 19–22), for the reader to grasp Luke's *dianoia* ("theme" or "meaning"), it must be done in and through his *mythos* ("story line," "plot"), for it is found only there (cf. Frye 1969: 52–79). The meaning is fitted to the narrative form. Consequently, it is of the most obvious importance to locate where something occurs in Luke's story. The connections between individual vignettes are often as significant as their respective contents. The sequence itself provides the larger meaning.

To say that Luke-Acts is a single story also bears the implication that Acts not only continues but also provides Luke's own authoritative commentary on his gospel (van Unnik 1960). The determination of Luke's purposes or the understanding of a specific theme, therefore, must take the whole story into account, precisely in its narrative development. To discuss the "christology" of Acts mainly in terms of contrast to the gospel, for example (Moule 1966), betrays Luke's clear literary intention. Likewise, any discussion of "the poor" in Luke-Acts must take seriously the sudden disappearance of that terminology after chap. 16 of the gospel (cf. Karris 1978) and consider whether the theme might have had a limited literary function for the first part of Luke's story (Johnson 1977). The discussion of what Luke says on any subject is qualified by where he says it.

The category of story also points the reader to the importance of plot and characters, which are the constitutive elements of the *mythos*. The characters motivate and enact the plot; the plot reveals the characters in action. In Luke-Acts, the most important character is arguably the God who never appears but who in various ways directs the action, and with reference to whom all of the narrative unfolds. Special attention must be paid as well to Luke's stereotypical descriptions of his protagonists (Jesus and his successors). Finally, there are the interactions between Luke's heroes and those who respond to them, whether positively or negatively.

Does Luke's narrative match any conventional literary form of the ancient world? The question of genre is notoriously difficult in literary analysis, not least because the nature of genre itself is disputed. But it is certainly the case that Hellenistic culture, unlike our own, prized and employed conventional literary patterns. The question is of particular importance because if genre has a function, it is to create certain expectations in readers, and to program certain responses. When genre works, function truly follows form. If we can determine the generic character of Luke-Acts, therefore, we are given important clues to the way in which it would have been read and understood by its first readers—or at least the way Luke intended it to be understood.

The question of genre is here asked of Luke-Acts as a two-volume work, leaving aside whether a "gospel" is a separate genre (Talbert 1977) or "Acts" becomes one. In the 2d century "Acts" of various Apostles proliferated (e.g., *Acts Thom.* or *Acts Paul*). The suggestion that Luke-Acts resembles a Hellenistic Romance or Novel (Goodenough 1966: 57) will not be pursued here, however striking the similarities may be (Cadbury 1955: 57, and especially Pervo 1987). That classification is not only broad but it misses some of Luke-Acts' most important features. In Luke-Acts something more than aesthetic delight is operative, even in formal terms. The most common genres to which Luke-Acts is assigned are the Hellenistic History or Biography, and Jewish Apology. The decision requires a close consideration of the text.

The reasons for regarding Luke-Acts as a History are obvious and, to most scholars, compelling (Barrett 1961; Marshall 1970):

1. His gospel prologue not only looks like those prescribed for Greek historiography (cf. Lucian, *Hist. conscr.* 47–54), but also examples of such prologues (cf. Joseph. *Ant.*). He tells the reader that he is using earlier oral and written sources (Luke 1:1–2). But he has also done personal and accurate research (*akribos,* 1:3), implying that he can handle those sources critically. He is writing a "sustained and sequential" narrative *(kathexes),* the purpose of which is to give the reader certainty rather than surmise concerning the past and even present events (1:4).

2. Luke places the community traditions—the story of Jesus and the church—in the context of world history, connecting it not only to the story of Israel (cf. 1:5) but also to that of the *oikoumene.* Of the NT writers he alone provides chronological references for pivotal events (cf. Luke 1:5; 2:1–2; 3:1–2; Acts 18:12). He identifies power blocs and rulers in Palestine (Acts 12:20–22), Asia Minor (Acts 19:31), and Europe (Acts 18:12–17).

3. Above all, Luke shows the historian's instinct for causality. His narrative is essentially linear, moving the reader from one event to another. The term "in sequence" *(kathexes)* in the prologue is critical to understanding his composition (Schneider 1977). He draws connections between events, so that a thread of purpose is seen to run through his entire narrative.

The question of Luke's accuracy as a historian is discussed fully elsewhere—see LUKE (PERSON)—but some comments are appropriate here because the issue of genre demands consideration of what sort of historian Luke might be.

To a considerable extent, historians are dependent on their sources. Luke says that he had some reports from eyewitnesses (Luke 1:2). Perhaps his unusually good information on Herod's household came from such a source (Luke 8:3; 23:6–12; Acts 12:20–23) (Hastings 1958). The "we" source in Acts could also have come from an eyewitness, whether the author or another. But since the first-person plural was sometimes used conventionally in travel narratives, we cannot be certain (Robbins 1978). Luke also had written sources (Luke 1:1). For the gospel, he used Mark, materials from the source called Q, and other distinctive materials usually designated L. We can check his use of a source only in the case of Mark, since it alone remains independently intact. Q gives no real help, since the shape of this hypothetical source must be abstracted from both Matthean and Lukan versions.

Luke's use of Mark differs considerably from Matthew's use of the same source. When Luke follows Mark he does so more closely, though he tends to omit blatant doublets, such as the feeding stories, whereas Matthew increases them (Fitzmyer *Luke I–IX* AB, 62–82). Instead of inserting great blocks of discourse material into the narrative, Luke more subtly interweaves deeds and sayings. The sayings of Jesus in Luke's gospel consequently have a greater air of biographical plausibility (see esp. Luke 9–19). Luke uses Mark with reasonable fidelity. The larger problem is determining where Luke has a source. If Matthew and Mark were not available for comparison, it would be doubtful that we could detect where Luke is using Mark and where he is not.

The difficulty in detecting Luke's sources has two causes. The first is that Luke follows the respectable Hellenistic practice of rewriting his sources (cf., e.g., Joseph. *AgAp* 54). We can observe how he modifies the Greek of Mark's gospel, bringing it closer to his own liking. The second reason is Luke's capacity for writing convincingly in a variety of styles. If one were to excerpt and compare the Greek of Luke's prologue, the infancy accounts, Peter's Pentecost sermon, and Paul's defense speeches, one could reasonably think that they were from different writers. Luke follows the Hellenistic rhetorical ideal of "writing in character" *(prosopopoeia),* which fits style appropriately to character and occasion (Kurz 1980: 186). Paul in Athens, consequently, is much more "Greek" than Paul in the synagogue of Antioch. Similarly, the Greek of the infancy accounts has a semitic coloration. Some conclude that Luke was using Hebrew or Aramaic sources (Winter 1956). But when we observe elsewhere that Luke shows a flair and fascination for a biblical or—more accurately—septuagintal style, the determination becomes very difficult (Turner 1955–56).

The search for Luke's sources in Acts is even more frustrating, since there is no way to check his usage. It would appear that he had fewer sources and was able to exercise more literary control in Acts than in the gospel. Apart from the "we" sections—which are otherwise stylistically consistent with the material around them (Harnack 1907)—we can identify no certain sources. Attempts to find a "Jerusalem" or "Antioch" source in the first fifteen chapters of Acts have proved to be more complex than convincing (Dupont 1964).

How reliable—factually—is Luke the historian? Taking into consideration his use of the one source we can check, his general accuracy in matters we can otherwise confirm from archaeological or documentary sources, and the overall agreement between his account of Paul and that in the letters, we can conclude that Luke is accurate in what he tells us, certainly by the standards of Hellenistic historiography (Hengel 1979). The phrase "in what he tells us," however, is critical. Luke writes selectively. In the gospel, he omits portions of Mark (the so-called "great omission" of Mark 6:45–8:27), and he fails to mention any Galilean appearances of the risen Jesus. In Acts, Luke either does not know or chooses not to mention things otherwise known to us. He describes no Galilean mission of the church (notice the conspicuous silence in Acts 1:8 and 15:3). He tells us nothing of rural evangelization, since as a good Hellenist, his interest is exclusively urban. Of the first missionaries, he concentrates on Peter and Paul to the virtual neglect of all others. Although Paul's arrival in Rome is the climax of Acts, for example, he never bothers to inform the reader when the Christian movement itself reached the capital city (cf. Acts 28:14–16).

So much does Luke concentrate on Jesus and a few of his followers that he is considered by some to be less a historian than a biographer. It has been argued that the biographies of some Hellenistic philosophers (as in Diogenes Laertius' *Lives of the Philosophers*) provide the closest formal analogy to Luke-Acts: first the life of the Founder is considered, with a concentration on his wondrous birth and its portents, his deeds, and his teachings; then a succession narrative, which recounts the deeds and teachings of his disciples (Talbert 1974: 125–34). The suggestion is attractive and corresponds to some features of Luke's writing. The Lukan addition of infancy and appearance accounts certainly pushes the Markan gospel closer to a Hellenistic Biography, as does his placement of sayings material. The portrait of Jesus and the disciples, furthermore, is shaded to resemble the Hellenistic *Sophos* ("sage"). Thus, Luke emphasizes Jesus' innocence and courage during his passion (cf. below), and the disciples also show boldness *(parresia)* in their teaching (Acts 4:13); indeed, like Socrates, they choose to obey God rather than human authorities (Acts 4:19).

Careful analysis of extant Hellenistic biographies, however, does not adequately support the suggestion that Luke-Acts fits that genre (Barr and Wentling 1984: 72–76). The hypothesis must also leave out of account the clear clues of the prologue that Luke considers his work to be a history. He writes not simply of Jesus and his followers, but of the "matters *(pragmata)* accomplished among us." His narrative has a scope far wider than Jesus and his school. The people of Israel form one of the most important characters in his narrative, and much of Luke's concern is for the fate of this historic people. Because the story of Jesus and his disciples is placed within this broader story, his writing is more properly if roughly categoried as a form of History (Ehrhardt 1958: 45–46).

What sort of history, then, did Luke set out to compose? He was obviously a committed member of the movement he depicted. On the other hand, he was not attempting a comprehensive record of the Christian past. If, as the prologue suggests, Luke's composition was intended for publication, perhaps he meant to influence the wider world, and Luke-Acts is the first Christian *apologetic* literature.

Noting Luke's positive view of gentiles and in particular of Roman officials, some have suggested that Luke wrote an apology for the Christian movement as a whole (Cadbury 1927: 306–16; Easton 1936). By observing the political harmlessness of the movement magistrates might be convinced to grant Christians the same freedom enjoyed by "other Jews." In this light, Luke's portrayal of Christianity as rooted in Judaism makes a critical political point. The proconsul Gallio's decision in Acts 18:14–15 is therefore to be taken as exemplary: in matters of dispute among "Jews," magistrates need not meddle (Conzelmann 1961: 137–44). Luke's positive outlook on the empire has been interpreted in the other direction: Luke writes an apology for the empire, encouraging among the politically restive of his fellow Christians a non-apocalyptic, politically cooperative attitude (Walasky 1983).

Other scholars have noted the concentration on Paul in the latter half of Acts and have contended that Luke-Acts is an apology for Paul and his teaching (e.g., Goodenough 1966: 54). A variant of this theory has it that to appease a significant and theologically vocal minority of Jewish believers within the Christian movement (Jervell 1972: 153–207), Luke presents Paul not as one opposed to Torah and a renegade within Judaism, but as a true teacher of Israel, whose views are consonant with those of the Pharisees (cf. Acts 23:6; 28:17–20). Certainly Paul's dominant role demands explanation, but Luke's entire narrative ill fits such a narrow and specific function (cf. Maddox 1982: 20–21).

These suggestions are on the right track, but they define "apologetic" itself much too narrowly. They isolate one theme or emphasis in the narrative and make it determinative, directing it to specific inside or outside audiences. But Jewish apologetic literature of that period had a dual function. Ostensibly it defended Jews against misunderstanding and persecution. It also had an equally important function for Jewish readers, because it reinterpreted their traditions within a pluralistic context by bringing an outsider perspective to bear on them. Thus, in Philo, the symbols of Greek philosophy and history provided the categories for the interpretation of Moses (cf. *Vita Mos* I–II). Apologetic literature thus provided "security" to Jewish readers by demonstrating the antiquity and value of their traditions in a pluralistic context.

Luke-Acts has a similar double-edged function. To a hypothetical outside reader, it presents Christianity as enlightened, harmless, even beneficent. Its more immediate function is to interpret the gospel within the context of a pluralistic environment, composed of both Jews and gentiles (Tiede 1980: 1–18).

The gospel prologue (Luke 1:1–4) indicates that although Luke-Acts may have been published and thereby made available to a wider audience, it was addressed first of all to a Christian readership (Fitzmyer *Luke I–IX* AB, 299–300). Theophilus has already been "instructed" *(katecheo)* in the Christian story (1:4). Why, then, does Luke provide still another version for him? Luke writes, he says, to give his readers "security" *(asphaleia)* (1:4) in their knowledge of "the things brought to fulfillment among us" (1:1). Not only the distant past, therefore, but also present circumstances required interpretation: the "among us" reaches up to Luke's own day. The expression "brought to fulfillment" (or "accomplished") is in the passive voice. In the biblical idiom, this equals "realities which God has brought to fulfillment." The narrative, then, is about the fulfillment of God's promises, up to the present. But why is "security" required? And how will a narrative written "in sequence" provide it? Here we reach the key element in Luke's statement of purpose, and the single most important literary clue for the understanding of his narrative (Maddox 1982: 186).

The text of Luke-Acts overwhelmingly suggests that Luke's audience was made up predominantly of gentile believers. There may have been Jewish members among his readers, but the Jewish mission, which Acts shows up so repeatedly failing, appears to be if not completely over, less than vigorous. In contrast, the outlook regarding the gentile world is entirely positive. The closing statement concerning them is "They will listen" (Acts 28:28). Luke's readers are themselves evidence that Paul's prophecy came true. But precisely the two facts of gentile acceptance and Jewish rejection of the Good News create a severe "uncertainty" for thoughtful gentile Christians.

The problem is simple but profound. God's promises had been made to Israel, to the Jewish people, through Abraham (Gen 12:1–3). If that historical people was not now in possession of the promised blessings, but someone else was, what did that imply about God's faithfulness to his promises? Did God utterly betray his people and his word? This is a difficulty as much for gentiles as for Jews. Could they rely on the "things fulfilled among them" any more than the Jews could? If God failed the Jews, could he not betray the gentiles even more easily?

The problem addressed by Luke's narrative is precisely and properly one of theodicy. No less than does Paul in Romans 9–11, he defends the word and work of God in history. How does the literary shaping of his narrative accomplish this? By telling how events occurred "in order" *(kathexes),* Luke intends to show that God first fulfilled his promises to Israel, and only then extended the blessings to gentiles. Because God had shown himself faithful to the Jews, therefore, the word that reached the gentiles was also trustworthy. Here precisely is the importance of "order" or consecutiveness for Luke's narrative purposes. The saving of Israel was necessary for the security of gentile believers.

Luke is therefore an apologetic historian of a very special sort. He sets himself to write the continuation of the biblical story (Dahl 1966: 152–53), not to defend the Christian movement as such but to defend God's ways in history. By showing the story of Jesus to be rooted in that of Israel, and by demonstrating how God kept his promise by restoring Israel, Luke assured his gentile readers that they could have confidence in God's word to them. Luke's purposes are not determined by a momentary crisis or a doctrinal deviance (Talbert 1966). They are generated by the mystery of a messianic sect existing among gentiles. So successful was Luke in addressing the problem that his narrative has become the etiological myth of gentile Christianity (Johnson 1979: 94).

D. Literary Aspects of Luke-Acts

Luke's literary techniques serve his overall literary and religious purposes. We consider here aspects of Luke's style, his narrative techniques, and his structuring of the two volumes as a single narrative. These observations and examples are not exhaustive, but representative.

1. Style. Technical discussions of Luke's diction and syntax are readily available (Cadbury 1920; Fitzmyer *Luke I–IX* AB, 107–27). These sometimes fail, however, to touch on Luke's characteristic concerns, which can be illustrated by his use of Mark and of the OT.

a. Redaction of Mark. A careful comparison of Luke 8:26–39 (the healing of the Gerasene demoniac) with its source (Mark 5:1–20) shows that Luke follows Mark much more closely than does Matt 8:28–34 (which is virtually a different story). Nevertheless, he amends Mark carefully. His adjustments tend toward correctness, clarity, and consecutiveness.

First, Luke corrects Mark's infelicities. He considers the *horkizo,* "I adjure," of Mark 5:7 inappropriate as addressed to Jesus, so changes it to *deomai,* "I beg" (Luke 8:28). In Mark 5:9–10, he found a confusion of number, which he renders more consistent (Luke 8:30–31), as he does also the tense sequence of Mark 5:14 (in Luke 8:35).

Second, Luke clarifies the many small confusions Mark's narrative creates. Thus, he makes clear where the country of the Gerasenes was (8:26) and assures the reader that when Jesus stepped out of the boat, it was onto land, and not water (8:27). He takes note that the herdsmen saw the wondrous events before they fled (8:34) and supplies the appropriate motivation for the townspeople's request that Jesus leave (8:37). Mark's diffuse report in 5:16 Luke condenses into a succinct summary and interpretation (Luke 8:36).

Third, Luke arranges the narrative into a more logical order. He describes the demoniac's condition in 8:28 as an explanation of the statement in 8:29 rather than as an opening description, as in Mark 5:3–6. Luke's concern for consecutiveness is shown most of all in his avoidance of narrative surprises. He prepares the reader for later plot developments. Mark says that the herdsmen went into the city (5:14), without ever having stated that they or the demoniac were from there. In contrast, Luke prepares for the later statement by noting at the beginning that the man was from the city (Luke 8:27). He signals the restoration of the man by having him preach "in the city" (8:39), in contrast to Mark's "Decapolis" (Mark 5:20). Similarly, we read in Mark 5:15 that the exorcised man was "clothed," but have not been told he was naked. Luke supplies this deficiency by stating in the beginning that the man wore no clothes (8:27). Luke's concern for connections shows how consistently he thinks in terms of "in order" *(kathexes),* and also forms a narrative pattern: by preparing the way for every subsequent plot development, Luke in effect creates a literary pattern of "prophecy and fulfillment" within his narrative.

b. Biblical Imitation. Luke is a stylistic chameleon. His account of Paul's speech in the agora (Acts 17:16–31) could be from Dio Chrysostom, and the riot of the Ephesian silversmiths (Acts 19:23–41) from Lucian of Samosata. In these stories, Luke is the Hellenistic fabulist. He also shares the Greek literary fondness for archaizing (Plümacher 1972: 32–79). In apologetic literature, the claim to antiquity is enhanced by language derived from ancient scriptures. Luke is no less the Greek littérateur, then (Schubert 1954: 85), when in great stretches of his narrative he imitates the rhythms of the LXX. It is a diction wonderfully suited to his purposes. That Luke consciously adapts this "biblical mode" is shown by his facile use of other modes when the rhetorical ideal of prosopopoeia demands them. It is in fact one of the subtle pleasures of reading Luke-Acts to observe how his Greek becomes less "biblical" and more "Greek" as the gospel makes its way into the gentile world.

Beyond direct citations from Torah (discussed below), Luke uses biblical diction variously. In the Stephen speech (Acts 7:2–53) he excerpts and fits together pieces from a very long section of Torah (Richard 1978) so artfully that the result appears both as a seamless and spontaneous speech by Stephen, and as a straightforward recital of the biblical narrative, while it is neither. Similarly, the Magnificat (Luke 1:46–55) places in Mary's mouth words inspired by, and sentiments derived from, 1 Sam 2:1–10 (Hannah's song), yet with a remarkable freshness.

Luke also uses a range of allusions, which reveal a thorough knowledge of biblical cadences. The annunciation scene (Luke 1:28–38) not only builds on the "type-scenes" (Alter 1981) of previous bibilical annunciations (e.g., Judg 13:2–7) but overlays them with a dense texture of other allusions. The angel's greeting carries with it echoes of Zeph 3:14 and Zech 2:10 (Laurentin 1957); likewise the Transfiguration's conclusion. "Listen to him" (Luke 9:35) suggests that Jesus is the prophet, like Moses (Deut 18:15), to whom the people should listen (Schubert 1954: 181–82).

These examples also show the ways that Luke uses biblical prototypes to construct entire scenes. In both volumes, uniquely Lukan stories appear to depend on the imitation of biblical models, either for details of language or for the entire structure of the story. The death of Ananias and Sapphira (Acts 5:1–11), for example, is reminiscent of the stoning of Achan in Josh 7:1–26. Luke is particularly fond of stories involving the prophets Elijah and Elisha (Dubois 1973), both in smaller vignettes (cf. Luke 9:54 with 2 Kgs 1:9–16 and Luke 9:61 with 1 Kgs 19:20) and in more elaborate combinations. Luke 7:1–16 "fulfills" the allusion to Elijah and Elisha made earlier in Luke's narrative (4:25–27) by having Jesus do deeds which mirror theirs in 2 Kgs 5:1–14 and 1 Kgs 17:17–24 (Johnson 1977: 96–103). The use of the Elijah–Elisha cycle is most obvious in the distinctive Lukan rendering of the ascension and giving of the Spirit. The prophet Jesus departs and leaves his prophetic followers with a "double share" of the Holy Spirit so that they can do deeds as great as or greater than his own, just as Elijah did for Elisha when he departed in the fiery chariot (see Luke 24:51–53; Acts 1:9–11; 2:1–13, with 2 Kgs 2:1–14; cf. Lohfink 1971: 73). Luke's way of employing these biblical allusions is subtle and eludes the detection of his method, whether he worked directly from the text of Torah (Brodie 1984) or depended on reminiscence.

2. Narrative Devices. The impression of fullness given by Luke's narrative is due, particularly in Acts—where he had fewer traditional materials with which to work—to literary artistry. Out of disparate fragments he creates a sustained and coherent narrative by extending and amplifying the traditions available to him.

a. Summaries. He extends the narrative by means of summaries. These generalize details from specific stories, giving the impression of repeated or customary occurrence (Cadbury 1933; Zimmerman 1961). In the gospel, Luke took over from Mark (cf., e.g., Mark 1:39; 3:7–12) the use of such summaries, but he uses them far more extensively (Luke 1:80; 2:52; 4:14–15; 7:21–22; 8:1–3; 13:22; 19:47; 21:37). In Acts, the use of summaries is even more important. In the first chapters of Acts, there are three so-called "major summaries" (Acts 2:42–47; 4:32–35; and 5:12–16). They provide critical spacing for the narrative and provide the reader with the sense of time's passing. They also offer a "typical" glimpse into the life of the community in its earliest stages and are, as a result, highly idealized (Dupont 1969). Luke also uses smaller summary statements to advance his narrative in the later sections of Acts (cf. 5:42; 6:7; 9:31; 12:24; 19:20).

b. Speeches. Even more important is Luke's use of speeches. In the first eight chapters of Acts, there are nine speeches of greater or lesser length (Acts 1:4–8, 16–22; 2:14–40; 3:12–26; 4:8–12, 24–30; 5:35–39; 6:2–4; 7:2–53), which as a whole make up fully half of the narrative. Luke uses these speeches precisely the way a Hellenistic historian would (Dibelius 1956: 138–85). Whatever fragments of tradition or patterns of preaching they may retain (Dodd 1936), in their present form they are Luke's handiwork, reflecting his thought rather than that of the original speaker (Wilckens 1961). Luke provides what ought to have been said on a particular occasion. It is in the speeches above all that Luke observes prosopopoeia ("writing in character"). As a narrative device, the speeches interpret the story for the reader. Peter's Pentecost speech (Acts 2:14–36) interprets the wind and tongues far more directly for Luke's reader than for the diaspora Jews in Jerusalem. The interpretive function of speeches holds for the gospel as well. Luke arranges Jesus' sayings so that they both reflect and interpret the narrative progress surrounding them (e.g., Luke 4:16–30; 14:7–24; 15:1–32).

c. Journeys. Luke also uses journeys as a narrative device, as do other Hellenistic historians. Luke's narrative about Paul is dominated by a series of journeys, climaxing in his long sea voyage to Rome (Acts 27:1–44) (cf. Robbins 1978). And the central portion of Luke's gospel is taken up by the great "travel narrative" of chaps. 9–19 (Conzelmann 1952). Analysis of the chapters reveals that Luke created this dramatic stage of his story out of a variety of sayings material and a series of travel notices (9:51, 53, 56, 57; 10:1; 13:22, 31, 33; 14:25; 17:11; 18:31, 35; 19:1, 11, 28), which by careful editing he has made into a coherent and compelling whole.

d. Parallelism. Luke makes extensive use of parallelism in his narrative. His habit of matching events and characters throughout the two volumes has frequently been noted. As Mary is overshadowed by the Holy Spirit in Luke 1:34–35, for example, so are Mary and the disciples overshadowed by the Spirit at the beginning of Acts (1:13–14; 2:1–4). Peter and Paul work similar miracles (Acts 3:1–10 and 14:8–11; 9:36–40 and 20:7–12), which in turn mirror the miracles of Jesus (Luke 5:17–26; 8:40–56). Peter and Paul face similar threats (Acts 8:9–13 and 19:13–19) and enjoy similar miraculous escapes (Acts 12:6–17 and 16:25–34). The trial of Stephen in Acts 6:8–15 overlaps that of Jesus in Luke 22:66–71, and the connection between them is rendered unmistakable by Acts 7:56 (cf. Luke 22:69). The "passion" of Paul bears some resemblance to that of Jesus (see esp. Acts 21:1–14). By the device of parallelism, Luke accomplishes two things. First, he establishes connections among his main characters; second, he joins parts of his narrative together. Attempts to make parallelism (or chiasmus) the dominant architectonic element of his narrative, however, gain their plausibility by forcing the textual evidence (Morgenthaler 1949; Goulder 1964; Talbert 1974). They above all fail to reckon with the essentially linear character of Luke's narrative.

3. Literary Structure. Two structural components help Luke give shape to his overall narrative: geography and prophecy. They ultimately point in the same direction and serve his overall purposes.

a. Geography. Luke uses geography as a literary and theological instrument (Conzelmann 1961). The center of his story is the city of Jerusalem and the events which take place in it. The whole movement of the gospel is toward Jerusalem. The infancy account moves toward the presentation of Jesus in the Temple (2:22) and his discovery there as a young boy (2:41–51). The Lukan temptation account reverses the Matthean order of the last two temptations so that the climax is reached in Jerusalem (4:9). At the end of the Galilean ministry, the transfiguration account explicitly prepares for the journey to Jerusalem and Jesus' death (9:31). The journey itself begins with a solemn announcement (9:51) and continues with multiple references to Jesus' destination (13:22, 33–34; 17:11; 18:31; 19:11, 28). All of Jesus' resurrection appearances take place in the environs of Jerusalem. In the last of them Jesus instructs the disciples, "Stay in the city" (24:1–49).

The geographical movement in Acts is away from Jerusalem. The announcement of Jesus in Acts 1:8, "You shall be my witnesses in Jerusalem and in all Judea and Samaria and to the end of the earth," is carried out by the narrative (Menoud 1954–55): the ministry in Jerusalem (chaps. 1–7) is followed by the evangelization of Judea and Samaria (chaps. 8–12), then Asia Minor and Europe (chaps. 13–28). Each movement outward, however, also circles back to Jerusalem (see Acts 12:25; 15:2; 18:22; 19:21; 20:16; 21:13; 25:1).

Jersualem is therefore in spatial terms the center of Luke's narrative. The middle twelve chapters of the two-volume work narrate events there. Why does Luke make Jerusalem so central? The city and the Temple, which Luke treats as virtually identical (Bachmann 1980), were of obvious historical importance for Judaism and for the nascent Christian movement. But more than historical recollection is involved. For Luke, the city and Temple stand as symbols of the people of Israel. The death of Jesus and the beginning of the church there provide the paradigmatic expression of the Jewish people's acceptance or rejection of God's visitation. Jerusalem is the pivotal place in the story of the prophet and the people.

b. Prophecy. Proof from prophecy was a standard element in early Christian apologetic. In it, texts from Torah were said to be "fulfilled" by events in Jesus' life, death, and resurrection. Matthew uses a sophisticated form of this proof in his so-called "formula citations." Luke expands and refines the notion of prophetic fulfillment (Dahl 1966: 152). Not only do the events of Jesus' ministry fulfill Scripture, but stages of the church's life and mission do as well: they are among the things "fulfilled among us" (see Acts 3:24; 13:40; 15:15; 28:25–27). Unlike Matthew, Luke does not mechanically align texts and events. His references are more general and inclusive. He often uses the term "It must" *(dei)* of various situations, indicating how events were determined by prophecies: the suffering and glorification of the Messiah (Luke 9:22; 17:25; 24:7; Acts 3:21; 17:3), the apostasy of Judas and the election of Matthias (Acts 1:16–22), the sufferings of Paul (Acts 9:16), and of all Christians (Acts 14:22).

(1) Literary Prophecy. Specifically Lukan is the use of literary prophecy. Not texts from Torah, but utterances of characters in the narrative are explicitly shown to be later fulfilled. Only Luke has the three passion predictions (Luke 9:22, 44; 18:32–33) noted in the resurrection accounts as having been fulfilled (24:6–8, 44). Jesus' prediction of his witnesses' tribulations (Luke 21:12–15) is literally fulfilled in the narrative of Acts (4:3–5, 14; 5:17–42). His instruction about the proper response to unbelieving cities (Luke 9:5; 10:11) is carried out by the missionaries in Acts (13:51). Jesus says that the Twelve are to be judges over Israel (Luke 22:30), and they exercise such judgment among the people in Acts (5:1–11). The prophet Agabus predicts sufferings for Paul (Acts 21:10–14) that speedily come true (21:30–35).

(2) Programmatic Prophecy. Of particular importance for Luke's narrative are literary prophecies which serve a programmatic function. They are spoken by characters at critical junctures to interpret the narrative which follows. The reader understands the plot development as a fulfillment of the prophecy. The most obvious example is Jesus' statement in Acts 1:8, which serves as a guide to the rest of Acts (Dibelius 1956: 193–94). Similarly, at the end of Acts Paul's final statement, "the salvation of God has been sent to the gentiles, they will listen," is understood as having reached fulfillment among Luke's readers. Prophecies at the end and beginning of the gospel are also important. Jesus' promise of a "power from on high" (Luke 24:49) enables the reader to perceive the ascension (Luke 24:50–53; Acts 1:9–11) not as an absolute departure but as a transformed presence, and the gift of the Spirit (Acts 2:1–4) as fulfilling Jesus' saying, "I will send the promise of my Father upon you." The saying of Simeon, "This child is set for the fall and rising of many in Israel and for a sign that is spoken against" (Luke 2:34), prepares the reader to understand the entire gospel narrative as the story of a prophet whose ministry creates a division among God's people (Johnson 1977: 86–91).

(3) Speech-narrative Prophecy. Luke even arranges speech and narrative to form a "prophecy-fulfillment" pattern. He places speeches so that the narrative following them fulfills their point, often ironically. Jesus declares that a prophet is not acceptable in his own country, and his townspeople immediately reject him who is a prophet (Luke 4:16–30). Luke states that sinners accepted the prophet John, but the Pharisees rejected God's plan for them (7:29–30). Next he quotes the charge that Jesus was a friend of tax collectors and sinners (7:34), then shows Jesus in the following story to be accepted by a sinful woman and rejected by a Pharisee (7:36–50). Stephen, described as a prophet filled with the Holy Spirit, accuses the Jewish leadership of rejecting the prophets and of resisting the Holy Spirit; they respond by killing him (Acts 7:51–60). Paul warns the Jews of Antioch in Pisidia not to reject the good news lest it be given to others; they reject it, and the gospel goes to the gentiles (Acts 13:40–48). Speech and narrative are mutually interpretive.

4. Prophetic Structure. The prophetic structure of Luke's entire work is established by the relationship between the two volumes. First, the book of Acts both continues the story of the gospel and confirms it (van Unnik 1960). In Acts, Luke provides the first and authoritative interpretation of his own gospel. Acts' perspective is all the more important since Luke had much more freedom to shape it. Second, the two volumes are parts of a two-stage prophetic model. To demonstrate this, it is necessary to move from a consideration of the prophetic image of the main characters in Acts, to the implications of Luke's portrayal of Moses.

a. The Apostles as Prophets. Acts is appropriately called the Book of the Holy Spirit (Lampe 1955). The Spirit actively intervenes in the story, impelling and guiding it (8:29, 39; 10:19; 11:15; 13:2; 15:28; 16:6; 20:22). Indeed, Luke includes five separate accounts of the Spirit's manifest "outpouring" on believers (2:1–4; 4:28–31; 8:15–17; 10:44; 19:6). For Luke, all Christians "have" the Holy Spirit. But the most important of his characters are described as "men of the Spirit" in a special fashion. Luke does not call them "prophets," reserving that title for relatively minor actors (see 11:27; 13:1; 15:32; 21:10) (Ellis 1970). He does however, describe them in terms which mark them as prophets. The characters in Acts who fundamentally advance the plot (Peter, John, Philip, Stephen, Barnabas, and Paul) are described in stereotypical terms. They are "filled with the Holy Spirit" (4:8; 5:32; 6:3; 7:55; 11:24; 13:9). They are bold *(parresia)* in their proclamation (4:13; 13:46; 28:31). They proclaim "good news" (5:42; 8:4, 12, 25, 40; 11:20; 13:32; 14:7; 15:35), or the "Word of God" (4:29; 8:14; 13:5). They are witnesses (2:32; 10:41; 13:31; 22:20). They work signs and wonders (*semeia kai terata;* 4:30; 6:8; 8:6; 14:3; 15:12). They preach and perform these wonders "among the people" *(laos),* the Jewish population considered as God's people (3:12; 4:1; 6:8; 13:15). These characteristics suggest one image in the biblical tradition, that of the prophet.

b. Jesus the Prophet like Moses. When Peter interprets the outpouring of the Spirit at Pentecost for his hearers—and Luke's readers—he cites the prophecy of Joel 2:28–32 that the Spirit will be poured out on all flesh (Acts 2:17–21). Luke makes three small but significant changes in the Joel citation. He changes Joel's "after these things" to "in the last days," thereby defining Pentecost as an eschatological event. He adds the words "and they shall prophesy" in v 17, accentuating the prophetic character of the Spirit already suggested by the citation. He adds the words, "and signs on the earth below" in v 19, to form the combination "signs and wonders." By these changes, Luke brings together three elements—an eschatological Spirit of prophecy, manifested by signs and wonders—which in the biblical tradition suggest the specific image of Moses, the first and greatest of the prophets (cf., e.g., Ps 78:11–12, 32, 43). The text of Deut 34:10–12, in fact, had given rise to the messianic expectation of a "prophet like Moses":

> There has not arisen a prophet since in Israel like Moses, whom the Lord knew face to face, none like him for all the signs and wonders which the Lord sent him to do in the land of Egypt . . . and for all the mighty power and all the great and terrible deeds which Moses wrought in the sight of all Israel.

This expectation remained alive (cf. 4QTestim, 1–5) despite the statement of Deut 34:9 that "Joshua son of Nun was full of the spirit of wisdom, for Moses had laid his hands on him" (Teeple 1957).

The notion of a prophet whom "God raised up" had obvious potential for the proclamation of a resurrected messiah (Dupont 1967: 149). Immediately after the Joel citation, in fact, Peter refers to Jesus in this fashion:

> Jesus of Nazareth, a man attested to you by God with mighty works and wonders and signs which God did through him in your midst . . . this Jesus you crucified . . . but God raised him up.

Jesus is described in terms which in this connection unmistakably recall the prophet Moses.

In the narrative about the apostles, Luke emphasizes that the power active in their prophetic witness is the Spirit of Jesus (Acts 2:33; 3:13; 4:10; 13:30; 33). As Elijah gave a twofold portion of the Spirit to Elisha, so have the apostles received a manifest bestowal of Jesus' Spirit. The specific imagery is Mosaic, but so in fact was the biblical portrayal of Elijah and Elisha. The rejection of the apostles is foreshadowed by the passages recalling Jesus' rejection by humans and vindication by God (2:23, 36; 10:39). The longest of these statements relieves the people of responsibility because of their ignorance (3:17). And when he offers repentance to them, Peter draws an explicit connection between Jesus and Moses (Acts 3:22–23; Deut 18:15, 18–19):

> Moses said, "The Lord God will raise up a prophet among your brethren as he raised me up. You shall listen to him in whatever he tells you. And it shall be that every soul that does not listen to that prophet shall be destroyed from the people."

Both the apostles and Jesus, therefore, are described in terms reminiscent of Moses. The connection is made unmistakably in the description of Moses found in Stephen's speech (Acts 7:17–44). It appears to be a straightforward retelling of the biblical story. Closer analysis shows that Luke selected and structured the account of Moses so that it matches precisely the story of Jesus and his witnesses (Johnson 1977: 70–76).

c. The Mosaic Pattern. Moses' story falls into three stages: a first sending and rejection; an installation in power; a second sending and rejection. At the time when the promises to Abraham were about to be fulfilled (7:17), Moses is sent by God to "visit" the people and "save" them. They are "ignorant" of his identity and role, so they reject him a first time. Moses is forced into exile (7:23–29). While in exile, Moses encounters God and is empowered by him to return to the people a second time (7:30–34). Moses then leads the people out of Egypt with "signs and wonders." But the people reject him and his words a second time, preferring an idol made of their own hands. Those who reject him this second time are themselves to be rejected (7:39–43).

Moses is therefore sent twice, the first time in weakness, the second time in power. There are two offers of salvation to the people. The first is rejected out of ignorance, and leads to a second chance; when this is refused despite the experience of manifest signs and wonders, God rejects the people. These elements are striking enough, but Luke goes on to make the connection between Jesus and Moses absolutely clear. At the heart of Moses' story we find precisely the sort of statement concerning him made elsewhere about Jesus (Acts 7:35–37):

> This Moses, whom they refused, saying "Who made you ruler and judge?" God sent as both ruler and deliverer by the hand of the angel that appeared to him in the bush. He led them out, having performed wonders and signs in Egypt and at the Red Sea and in the wilderness for forty years. This is the Moses who said to the Israelites, "God will raise up for you a prophet from your brethren as he raised me up."

Did Luke's perception of Jesus' death and resurrection shape his portrayal of Moses? Or did the influence move in the opposite direction? We cannot know. It is clear, however, that this understanding of Moses shows the "necessity" of a prophet's suffering before glory and explains why Luke begins with "Moses and all the prophets" to demonstrate that necessity (Luke 13:33–34; 24:25–26, 44–46). The Mosaic pattern also establishes the typology and succession of spiritual authority important for Luke (Minear 1976: 81–147). Jesus is the prophet like Moses. Jesus had not, however, only been "raised up" in the sense of being "chosen"; he is "raised up" by the resurrection as Lord (Ps 110:1; Acts 2:34–36). As Moses "received the living words and gave them" to the people in the desert (Acts 7:38), so does the resurrected Jesus receive the Holy Spirit from God and pour it out on his followers (Acts 2:33). In the proclamation of these witnesses, the saving message of Jesus is filled with prophetic power and bears an equally powerful threat: those not listening to the voice of "this prophet" will be "cut off from the people" (3:23).

d. The Gospel in the Light of Acts. The pattern of the Moses story provides the basic structure for Luke's two-volume work. The gospel is the story of God's first sending of the prophet Jesus to "visit" his people for their "salvation" (Luke 1:68; 7:16; 19:44); of their initial rejection of this salvation, out of ignorance; and of Jesus being "raised up" out of death. Acts recounts Jesus' establishment in power, manifested by the gift of the Holy Spirit; the sending out of his witnesses empowered by that Spirit; and the second offer of salvation to Israel "in his name" (Acts 4:12; 5:31). This time, however, the cost of refusal is separation from God's people.

This pattern explains why Luke's geographic structure makes the Jerusalem narrative central. In Jerusalem the first rejection, the empowerment, the second offer, and the issue of the acceptance or rejection by the people are all played out. The geographic structure serves the story of the prophet and the people.

Luke was freer to shape this pattern in Acts than in the gospel. But if Acts provides Luke's understanding of the gospel story, we can expect to find within the gospel's tighter constraints intimations of this image of Jesus (Lampe 1955–56), and we do. When Jesus raises a widow's son (Luke 7:11–15), the story concludes (7:16):

> Fear seized them all, and they glorified God, saying, "A great prophet has arisen among us," And, "God has visited his people!"

The reader cannot but hear echoes of this earlier acclamation when later reading Acts 3 and 7. Likewise the voice at the transfiguration, saying "Listen to him" (Luke 9:35), anticipates Luke's development of the Mosaic image for Jesus in Acts 3:22. Finally, the disciples on the road to Emmaus (Luke 24:19) speak of "Jesus of Nazareth who was a prophet mighty in deed and word before God and all the people." The accuracy of their description is apparent only in the light of Acts (Gils 1957).

Stylistic tendencies, narrative devices, and literary structuring all help define the *mythos* of Luke-Acts as the story of the Prophet and the People. The next section will follow the plot through the gospel and Acts. The Markan framework is assumed, and particular attention is paid to specifically Lukan redaction. This reading will in turn make the *dianoia* of Luke-Acts clearer.

E. The Prophet and the People

1. The Gospel Narrative. a. The Infancy Account. Luke's infancy account (chaps. 1–2) is a form of haggadic midrash (cf. R. E. Brown 1977: 557–62), with language evoking both specific texts and the general atmosphere of the biblical world. After the elegant Greek period of the prologue (1:1–4), the reader is immediately transported to the world of Ruth and the Judges (1:5). The story of Jesus is thus rooted in the longer story of God's people. The infancy narrative also points forward, establishing by means of programmatic prophecies motifs that are later developed (Minear 1966).

The infancy account has a complex internal structure. It contains two sets of contrasting diptychs (Laurentin 1957). The annunciation to Zechariah (Luke 1:8–23) is contrasted to that made to Mary (1:26–38), and the birth of John (1:57–66) is placed against that of Jesus (2:1–21). The first diptych is followed by the visitation of Mary to Elizabeth (1:39–45) and the canticle of Mary (1:47–55). The second diptych is followed by the Purification, with its canticle and prophecy by Simeon, and praise by the prophetess Anna (2:22–38). A transition to the ministry is provided by the discovery of the young boy Jesus in the Temple (2:41–51). Short summaries describing the growth of Jesus and John also point to their future roles (1:80; 2:52). As always, the geographical center is in Jerusalem, with the narrative beginning (1:8) and ending (2:42) there.

The prophecies and canticles alert us to the significance of John and Jesus. They are both prophetic figures. John will "go before him in the spirit and power of Elijah . . . to prepare a people for the Lord" (1:16–17). Luke does not need to make a connection between John and Elijah later (cf. Luke 9:36 against Matt 17:11–13), for he has already made it here. Zechariah says of John, "You, child, will be called prophet of the most high" (1:76–77). John will be "great before the Lord" (1:15). But Jesus "will be great and will be called Son of the Most High" (1:32). They both stand in the line of the prophets, but whereas John remains precursor (cf. 7:24–35), Jesus is Messiah and Son and Lord (cf. 1:32–33).

Luke's characteristic preoccupation is the meaning of John and Jesus for Israel. John will "prepare a people for the Lord" (1:17), and in his canticle, Zechariah praises God for the "visitation" of his people to redeem them in fulfillment of his promises to Abraham (1:68–69; see Acts 7:17). The figure of Abraham and the fulfillment of God's promises to him play a more central role in Luke-Acts than in the other gospels (e.g., Luke 16:22–31; 19:9; Acts 3:25; 7:2–8; 13:26), precisely because Luke is concerned to connect the church's story to that of Israel (Dahl 1966). The language of "God's visitation" is echoed later (Luke 7:16; 19:44; Acts 7:23; 15:14) and signifies God's intervention to save his people (Comblin 1956).

Jesus' ambiguous relationship with the people is shown in the presentation scene. The "righteous and devout" Simeon had been awaiting the "consolation of Israel." When he takes the child in his arms, he praises God for allowing his eyes to "have seen thy salvation," which will be a "light of revelation unto the gentiles and for glory to thy people Israel" (2:29–32). The reader is here prepared for the spread of God's message to the gentile world (cf. Acts 13:47), but Luke's interest centers on the fate of Israel (cf. George 1968). The salvation brought by Jesus is to be its "glory." But then Simeon projects a harsher vision: Jesus will cause a division in the people (2:34). This programmatic prophecy is critical for understanding Luke's subsequent narrative. The pattern of the prophet like Moses would lead us to expect a complete rejection of the prophet sent by God, but Luke's alteration of that pattern shows the reader instead a *division* within the people of God (Jervell 1972: 41–72). Some accept God's prophet, and some do not. Whether they are part of God's authentic people depends on their choice.

b. The Prophetic Messiah. In the ministry narrative Luke continues to link John and Jesus. Luke makes clear that John is a prophet by stating, "the word of God came to John" (3:2). From this point, the "word of God" becomes thematic in Luke-Acts. It provides an explicit theological valuation of the speech of John, Jesus, and Jesus' followers and links them together in a succession of prophetic authority. In the parable of the sower, "the seed is the word of God" (Luke 8:11; see also 5:1, 8:21, 11:28), and in Acts, "the word of God" is synonymous with the Christian mission, "so the word of God grew and prevailed mightily" (Acts 19:20; see also 4:31; 6:2, 7). Jesus' baptism by John also suggests a prophetic anointing. Luke removes John from the scene to show that it is God who bestows the Holy Spirit on Jesus (Luke 3:21–22).

That Jesus is a prophetic Messiah is the point of Luke's version of the rejection in Nazareth (4:16–30). He moved the story from its later position in Mark to the beginning of Jesus' ministry, expanding it into a programmatic statement on the nature of that ministry (Tiede 1980: 19–63).

The reader has learned that Jesus received the Spirit bodily (3:22), was "full of the Spirit" when tempted (4:1), and began his preaching "in the power of the Spirit" (4:14). Now Jesus reads from Isaiah, "The Spirit of the Lord is upon me because he has anointed me to preach good news to the poor . . ." (4:18; cf. Isa 61:1–2; 58:6), and announces starkly, "Today this scripture has been fulfilled in your hearing" (4:21). Luke understands Jesus literally to be a prophet "anointed" by the Spirit, and therefore messianic (cf. also Acts 4:27; 10:38). His mission is to proclaim deliverance to the outcast and afflicted.

The other aspect of the prophetic ministry is that it causes a division in the people. The townspeople hear him gladly at first, but turn against him when he compares himself to Elijah and Elisha (4:25–27). They were prophets through whom God "visited" people outside the historical Israel. The townspeople represent those Jews who resist a visitation to any but themselves.

The next section of the gospel showing intensive Lukan redaction (chaps. 6–7) continues the prophetic pattern. Jesus proclaims blessings to the poor and woes to the rich in his Sermon on the Plain (6:20–26), thus fulfilling the programmatic prophecy of 4:18 (Schubert 1954: 180). Likewise, when Jesus sends a message to John (7:21–22), his list of wonders culminates in "the poor have the good news preached to them." The language of "rich and poor" in the first 16 chapters of the gospel is used in thematic statements and has the literary function of demonstrating that Jesus is the prophetic Messiah who proclaims Good News to the outcast, and as such is rejected by the rich and powerful. In the narrative itself, the role of "the poor" is played by the sinners and tax collectors, while the role of "the rich" is played by the Pharisees and teachers of law. Because God visits his people in Jesus' ministry, those who reject the prophet are themselves rejected from the people (Johnson 1977: 132–44).

The pattern is rounded out in chap. 7. Jesus compared himself to Elijah and Elisha in 4:25–27; now he works miracles that imitate theirs: as Elisha healed a foreigner through the intercession of a Jewish girl (2 Kgs 5:1–14), Jesus heals a gentile centurion through Jewish intercession (Luke 7:1–10). As Elijah raised a widow's son (1 Kgs 17:17–24), Jesus raises the widow of Nain's son (7:11–15). In the response Luke's thematic concern is explicit: Jesus is a "great prophet whom God raised up" and in his actions, God is "visiting his people" (7:16). Precisely at this point, Jesus sends word to John that "the poor have the good news preached to them" (7:22).

The conflict within the people generated by Jesus' prophetic ministry now emerges. Jesus praises John as a prophet and more than prophet (7:26). But John had been accepted as such only by "the people and the tax collectors"; in contrast, the "Pharisees and teachers of law" had rejected John, and therefore, "rejected God's plan for themselves" (7:29–30). They rejected John because he had a demon. They now reject Jesus because he is "friend of tax collectors and sinners" (7:34). Luke makes the following story "fulfill" the point of the sayings. Jesus is accepted by the sinful woman; he is rejected by the Pharisee who does not recognize in him a prophet sent by God (7:36–50).

The division in Israel is between the people of the land—in particular, those decreed outcast or marginal by ritual law—who by accepting this prophet are thereby being accepted into the people God is forming around him, and the leaders who already enjoyed "consolation"

(6:25; 16:25; cf. 2:25) and accepted neither John nor Jesus, seeking to "justify themselves" (see 16:15; 18:9).

c. Formation of the People. Luke shows a faithful people forming around Jesus from the beginning of his ministry, as sinners (5:1–11) and tax collectors (5:27) leave all (18:28–30) to follow him. From among them he chooses the twelve apostles who will be his prophetic successors (6:13; 9:10; 11:49; 17:5; 22:14; 24:10; Acts 1:2; 1:26; etc.). In 8:1–3, Luke shows us the small core of the restored people, the Twelve and a small group of women in Galilee.

Beginning in 9:1, Jesus prepares a new leadership for the people. Luke sends out the Twelve with authority and power like his (9:2, 11) and has them share in the distribution of food to the needy (9:10–17). Authority over the people and service at table are thereby linked. That these twelve will rule over Israel is suggested by the Lukan Parable of the Pounds (19:11–27) (Johnson 1982), and the parable of the Vineyard (20:9–18). It is made explicit in the bestowal of *basileia* (authority) on them at the last supper (22:30), which is fulfilled by their leadership over the Jerusalem community in Acts (S. Brown 1969: 164).

The formation of the people is sketched dramatically in the journey narrative (9:51–19:44). The transfiguration establishes that this journey is that of the prophet like Moses (Moessner 1983). Luke inserts into the travel framework the largest portion of his sayings material and surrounds Jesus with three groups: the crowd, the disciples (used more often here than in all the rest of the gospel), and his opponents (above all, in this section, the Pharisees). Luke notes editorially exactly what Jesus says to whom. To the opponents who test him, Jesus tells parables of rejection; to the crowds, he gives warnings of judgment and calls them to discipleship. To the disciples, he directs instructions on discipleship: prayer, hospitality, suffering, and the use of possessions (Reicke 1959). Luke arranges these materials, moreover, so that the audiences are alternated; Jesus appears to speak to each group in turn.

As Jesus journeys to Jerusalem to face his rejection and death at the hands of the leaders, Luke shows the prophet forming the true people of God around himself. When the Pharisees test him by asking when the kingdom of God will come (17:21), Jesus answers, "the kingdom of God is in the midst of you." In context, the statement is meant literally: the people obedient to God's rule is being formed by its positive reception of the prophet.

So effective is Luke's literary skill that the reader is not shocked to see a "whole multitude of disciples" (19:37) greet Jesus when he enters Jerusalem nor that the Pharisees typically respond by ordering him, "rebuke your disciples" (19:39). At the end of the journey, Jesus voices a lament over this city which does not recognize "the time of its visitation" (19:44).

d. The Passion Narrative. Luke deviates more substantially from Mark in the passion narrative than does Matthew. He deletes some incidents (like the anointing at Bethany), transposes others (like the charge against the temple, which is applied to Stephen in Acts), adds still others (like Satan entering Judas' heart). And he consistently edits Mark's account. Two emphases emerge from his redaction: the image of Jesus as a *sophos* (sage), and the diminished role of the populace in his death.

Luke shades the image of Jesus to resemble the ideal Hellenistic *sophos* whose self-control, freedom from fear, and courage are a model to his followers. At the supper, Jesus delivers a farewell address, handing over authority to his followers (22:29–30), instructing them and preparing them for the future (22:35–38) (Kurz 1985). In the garden, his followers are overcome with sorrow—a sign of cowardice—unlike Jesus (22:45) (Neyrey 1980). Jesus is still able to heal (22:51) and goes willingly to do his father's will (22:42). He shows his self-control and prophetic authority by his warning to the women of Jerusalem (23:28–31) (Neyrey 1985) and by his offer of paradise to the thief (23:39–43). The wise man is also a just man *(dikaios)*. Jesus' innocence, so emphasized by Acts 3:14, is here demonstrated by Pilate's threefold declaration of innocence (23:4, 14, 22), as given again by Herod as well (23:15). It is confirmed by the centurion's statement at the cross. Rather than identifying Jesus as God's Son (as in Mark and Matt), he declares, "Truly this man was righteous" (23:47). More than innocence is implied here, as Luke's other uses of the concept of "righteousness" indicate (cf. Luke 1:6, 17; 2:25; 16:15; 18:9, 14; 20:21; 23:50; Acts 3:14; 7:52; 22:14). Jesus is the "Just One" (Karris 1986).

Luke also minimizes the responsibility of the populace for the death of Jesus, in contrast to Matthew's heightening of it (cf. Matt 27:25). Luke knows and cites traditions blaming the whole people for Jesus' death (cf. Acts 3:14). But in his passion narrative he does all he can to exclude them from the action (Kodell 1969). The leaders of the people actively reject Jesus; the people are at most passive. The division is stated succinctly by the men on the road to Emmaus (Luke 24:20–21):

> . . . how our chief priests and rulers delivered him up to be condemned to death, and crucified him. But we had hoped that he was the one to redeem Israel.

With the anomalous exception of 23:13 (cf. Rau 1965), Luke makes some fifteen small alterations in Mark to remove the people as far as possible from the proceedings against Jesus (cf. 19:45–47; 20:1–2; 21:38; 22:2, 6, 47, 52; 23:1, 2, 27). Characteristically, Mark 15:29 and Matt 27:39 have all the passersby mock Jesus on the cross. In contrast, Luke has only the rulers mock him (23:35). Likewise Luke heightens the leaders' rejection of the prophet, portraying them as challenging Jesus to "prophesy" (22:64; cf. 22:52, 54). The common people, who had come to the death as to a spectacle, turn away "beating their breasts" (23:48). They show signs of repentance. Luke thus prepares for their conversion in Acts.

e. Resurrection and Ascension. As Moses was vindicated by God after his first rejection and sent back to the people with new power (Acts 7:34–38), so is Jesus vindicated by his resurrection, becoming the "prophet whom God raised up" in power (Acts 2:24; 3:13–15). Luke's presentation of Jesus' resurrection is particularly complex, spanning both volumes.

Unique to Luke-Acts is the ascension of Jesus (Luke 24:50–51; Acts 1:9–11; cf. Luke 9:31, 51). Although the ascension appears as a temporary departure, it is clear that Jesus is more present than ever, only in a new, more powerful mode. He is seen by Stephen (Acts 7:55–56) and by Paul (9:1–9; cf. 22:14). The presence of Jesus continues moreover in his spirit, which works through the deeds and words of his witnesses: they preach, teach, and heal "in the name of Jesus" (Acts 2:33; 3:6, 16; 4:10, 29–31; 5:32; 10:43; 16:18; 19:13).

The resurrection accounts of the gospel have several distinctive characteristics. They center in Jerusalem: the women at the tomb are not told to go to Galilee, but are told, "remember how he told you in Galilee" (Luke 24:6). This points to the second feature of Luke's accounts: he shows how Jesus' passion predictions came to fulfillment (Schubert 1954). Third, Luke has Jesus demonstrate "from Moses and all the prophets" how Jesus' sufferings were in fulfillment of the Scripture (Luke 24:25–26, 44). Fourth, the appearances combine matter-of-factness with mystery: on one hand, Jesus' bodily presence is stressed (24:30, 41–43; Acts 1:4; 10:41); on the other hand, he can be mistaken for a stranger (24:13–35), and his appearance can be met with incredulity (24:11, 24, 41). Fifth, the resurrection appearances provide a bridge to the second part of Luke's story: the risen Lord utters programmatic prophecies (24:47–49) which are fulfilled by the narrative of Acts (Dillon 1978).

2. The Acts Narrative. a. The Restored Israel in Jerusalem. The next part of Luke's story is most critical. In the Jerusalem narrative of Acts (chaps. 1–7), he must answer the fundamental question of God's fidelity to his promises, so that his readers will have security *(asphaleia).* To do this, he must demonstrate that in fact God did keep his promises to Israel, which can only be done by showing a restored Israel receiving the blessings God had promised to Abraham. Only then can gentile believers have confidence in the gift given them. Luke must show the identity of this restored people of God, the nature of its leadership, and the transfer of the Good News from Jew to gentile.

Luke's perception of the church as the restored Israel (Schmitt 1953) is signaled by Matthias' election (1:15–26). Luke has created an expectation for the outpouring of the Spirit (Luke 24:49; Acts 1:4, 8), and his natural tendency is to have fulfillment follow prophecy as rapidly as possible. The delay of this particular fulfillment shows how necessary Luke perceived the replacement of Judas in the apostolic circle to be. This can only be because the Twelve symbolize the twelve tribes of the restored Israel (Jervell 1972: 75–112). They are the nucleus of the people that is to be constituted and empowered by the Spirit. When the leadership of the people is in place, then the promised spirit could be given (S. Brown 1969: 94–97).

We have seen how Luke emphasizes the eschatological nature of Pentecost and the prophetic character of the Spirit. The conclusion of Peter's Pentecost speech is particularly important for revealing Luke's understanding of the first community in Jerusalem. After demonstrating that the messianic texts of Torah applied not to David but to Jesus, Peter declares, "Let all the house of Israel therefore know assuredly that God has made him both Christ and Lord, this Jesus whom you crucified" (Acts 2:36). The focus is on Israel. They had rejected the prophet and are now called to repentance. This is their second offer of salvation: "Save yourself from this crooked generation" (2:40).

If the people repent and are baptized, they will receive the Holy Spirit (2:38). But Luke defines this Spirit precisely as "the promise" (2:39). Here the visitation of God according to the promise made to Abraham is brought to fulfillment. For whom is the promise? "To you and to your children." First of all, then, for the Jewish population of Jerusalem, but not only for them: "And to all that are far off, every one whom the Lord God calls to him" (2:39). Those who respond make up the authentic people of God. In his idyllic portrait of the first community, Luke stresses its Jewish character (2:41–47). The community enjoys favor and steadily increases in size. In principle, therefore, the people of God have been restored within historic Israel, even having a universal character since it includes Jews from the Diaspora (2:12–13). Luke could have stopped here, for he has shown that God was faithful to Abraham and that part of the Jewish people enjoyed the blessings of the Spirit. But another issue remains: who are the leaders of this people?

b. Leadership over the People. Peter's speech following the healing of a lame man (Acts 3:11–26) interprets the next part of the narrative. He concludes with a promise and a warning. Those who repent will share in the "times of refreshment" (3:20) within the restored people of God:

> You are the sons of the prophets, sons of the covenant which God gave to our fathers, saying to Abraham, 'And in your posterity shall all the families of the earth be blessed.' God, having raised up his servant, sent him to you first. (3:25–26)

But Peter also warns that those who reject this offer will definitively be separated from the people (3:22–23).

The narrative following this programmatic prophecy focuses squarely on the apostolic witnesses. From the outside, their authority is threatened by the Sanhedrin, and they are twice brought to trial (4:1–22; 5:17–42). Within the people, however, they are established in power and "rule over Israel" (4:23–5:16).

The difference between the two trials is striking. In the first, the apostles are warned to cease preaching (4:21). But after they are newly empowered by the Spirit (4:23–31), they exercise even more authority: collecting and distributing possessions, boldly proclaiming, healing, and radically "cutting off from the people" those who do not acknowledge their prophetic authority (4:32–5:16). The second trial is occasioned by the Sanhedrin's "jealousy" of the apostles' success (5:17). The authorities cannot hold the apostles in prison; an angel frees them (5:19). Afraid of being stoned by the people, the Sanhedrin is reduced to requesting the apostles' presence at a hearing (5:26). And despite the beating they receive, the apostles continue to proclaim Jesus as Messiah (5:42).

The essential narrative point is clearly made. Whatever political machinations are still available to the Sanhedrin, religious authority over Israel—considered as God's people—has passed to the apostles. They rule over "the twelve tribes of Israel."

Once more, Luke could have stopped. But another question remained, which could only be answered by continuing the story "in order." How did the blessing of Abraham reach the gentile world? Was the community represented by Theophilus in essential continuity with Israel, or was it a new thing altogether, only artificially connected to the story of Abraham? Luke must now show how the gospel reached the gentiles. He first prepares a new leadership, using a fragmentary tradition concerning a dispute over the feeding of widows (6:1–6). The seven Hellenists were supposedly to serve at tables. Actually, they too are prophets who carry the mission beyond Jerusalem.

The Jerusalem narrative is effectively concluded with the trial, speech, and stoning of Stephen (6:8–7:60). With his death, the missionaries (except for the Twelve) are scattered and begin spreading the word beyond the city (8:1). We saw above how Stephen's speech offers an interpretation of Luke's entire narrative. It also contains a startling element of irony. Here is one described as a prophet attacking the leaders (cf. 6:12) for always resisting the Holy Spirit, killing the prophets, and murdering Jesus, the righteous One (7:51–52). They reject this prophetic attack and kill him who is full of the Spirit. And, at the moment of his death, he sees "the righteous one." Luke ends the Jerusalem narrative with a condemnation. It is a condemnation, however, not of the entire people of Israel, but of its leadership (contra Sanders 1984: 113–17). And the narrative's point is essentially positive: despite the hostility and rejection by the leaders, God's blessings were given to the Jewish people in Jerusalem and were accepted.

c. The Gentile Mission. God had always willed in principle that Israel's blessing should be extended to the gentiles (cf. Luke 2:32; 3:6; 4:25–27; 10:1–12; 24:47; Acts 1:8) (Dupont 1979; Wilson 1973). In the narrative of Acts, however, the gentile mission proceeds in a more haphazard fashion than the prophecies might suggest. Although gentiles are preached to because of Jewish rejection, that rejection is never portrayed by Luke as total. Some Jews, even in the Diaspora, convert to the Way. Believing Jews and gentiles together make up the authentic Israel, the people of God (Jervell 1972: 64–69).

As the Hellenist missionaries spread the message, the connection with Jerusalem is maintained. Representatives from Jerusalem confirm the work of Philip in Samaria (8:14–24). Barnabas, shown to be twice loyal to the apostles by receiving a name from them and laying his possessions at their feet (4:36–37), is sent to confirm the Antiochean foundation (11:22). Peter too works wonders beyond Jerusalem, in Lydda and Joppa (9:32–43), ending up in Caesarea. In his conversion of the centurion Cornelius, we are given the first narrative description of gentile conversion and its confirmation in Jerusalem (chaps. 10–11). The church grows organically from its roots in the restored Israel in Jerusalem.

From within this context Luke's hero, Paul, emerges. Glimpsed first as a collaborator at Stephen's death (8:1) and as a rabid persecutor of the Way, he encounters the risen Lord (9:1–9). After his baptism and instruction from Ananias, he preaches Jesus in Damascus and is persecuted, but is given access to the Jerusalem community through the intercession of Barnabas (9:27). He meets still more opposition and is sent to Tarsus (9:30). From there, Barnabas recruits him for the Antiochean church (11:25). Together they take a collection to Jerusalem (11:30) and, upon completing that task (12:25), are sent by the Antiochean church on mission (13:1–3). This summary is culled from a considerably more complex narrative, in which Paul's movements are intermixed with the mission of Philip, Peter, and John in Samaria and Judea, the conversion of Cornelius with its sequel and the imprisonment and release of Peter.

Literary art and theological purpose are here intertwined. Peter, Barnabas, and Paul appear and reappear as the central characters. The complexity of their interactions creates an impression of historical movement, and it also places Paul squarely within the overall missionary effort of the church. Luke thereby makes two points essential to his overall purpose. First, Paul's mission to the gentiles is not idiosyncratic but part of the Spirit-guided mission of the whole church. Second, his mission is intimately connected—and Barnabas' role is here critical—to the believing Jerusalem community and therefore to the restored Israel.

Luke's continuing concern for Israel is demonstrated as well by Barnabas and Paul's first missionary tour. Paul's sermon in Antioch of Pisidia emphasizes the fulfillment of the promises realized in Jesus: "We bring you the good news that what God promised the fathers, this he has fulfilled to us their children by raising Jesus" (13:32). And only when the Jews reject their message do the missionaries turn from them to gentiles. In Iconium and Lystra, the same pattern is repeated (Acts 14:1–21). Jewish rejection leads to a gentile mission. This is how God "opened a door of faith to the gentiles" (14:27), as Paul and Barnabas report on their return to Antioch.

Before Luke can describe Paul's far-ranging missionary work, however, he must first address the legitimacy of gentile inclusion within a messianic community. What were the implications for the church's identity as the people of God? The issue is joined by the Jerusalem Council (Acts 15:1–35). The council forms a watershed in the Acts narrative (Haenchen 1971: 461–62). Before it, all of the apostles were at least ostensibly in view. After it, Paul's work totally dominates. The council brings Peter back into the narrative for the last time. At the council, James is the chief spokesperson for the Jerusalem church, and he appears only once again to ratify its decision (21:18).

The story of the council itself forms the climax of a complex plot development that had quietly been providing the background for Paul's emergence. Acts 15 is intelligible only if read in conjunction with the conversion of Cornelius, for Luke shows in the narrative itself how the decision to recognize the full status of gentiles within the messianic people resulted from the interaction of divine guidance and human obedience (Johnson 1983).

The Jerusalem leaders had confirmed Peter's decision to baptize gentiles (11:18), but the issue of fellowship remained, an issue critical above all for Jewish believers, since they were already bound to Torah. Did gentiles belong to the people on an equal footing? Pharisaic believers attacked the foundations of gentile membership in the church, claiming that only full observance of Torah (including circumcision) could lead to salvation (15:1–2). The attack coincides with the arrival of Paul and Barnabas in Antioch, announcing the new mission to the gentiles (14:27–28). Luke effectively draws his main characters from their diverse missions to this one critical decision. The reader already knows God's will in the matter; will the church ratify God's action by its decision?

In the end, it does. No burden is placed on gentile

believers beyond the norms already familiar to them by their contact with Torah in the Diaspora (Wilson 1983). The regulations were not conditions of membership in the people, but observances which enabled fellowship with Jewish believers. The decision opened the way for a free gentile mission, for it recognized that gentile believers too were a part of the restoration of Israel (cf. James' citation of Amos 9:11–12 [LXX] in 15:16–17), and that God had "visited them to take from among the nations a people for his name" (Acts 15:14) (Dahl 1957–58). In the narrative of Acts, the council opens the way for a full concentration on the missionary work of Paul.

d. The Mission of Paul. The differences between the Paul of the letters and the Paul of Acts have been thoroughly cataloged; in apostolic style and in theological perspective Luke presents not a historical replica of Paul but one shaped by his own agenda (Vielhauer 1966; Müller 1981). The differences can also be overdrawn (Dupont 1962). More importantly, the divergences result from specifically Lukan literary and religious concerns that affect not only Luke's portrait of Paul but also of all his major characters: the connection to Jerusalem and Judaism; the powerful works and rhetoric; the stereotypical teaching.

Luke's treatment of Paul is decidedly positive. He designates him an apostle together with Barnabas (14:4), and—more tellingly—a witness (22:15; 26:16) (Rétif 1951). Like the other major figures of the church's mission, Paul is described in specifically prophetic terms (14:3), in his case sharpened by calling him a "chosen instrument" in 9:15 (cf. Jer 1:5 and Gal 1:15), and "light to the gentiles" in 13:47 (cf. Isa 49:6 and Luke 2:32). Paul is also the pastor of the church, as shown by his farewell discourse to the Ephesian elders. Luke here explicitly makes Paul a model for those succeeding him (Acts 20:17–35) (Prast 1979).

Paul was not alone or even the first in bringing good news to the gentiles. For Luke, however, he was preeminent in that mission. His ministry was in obedience to Jesus' command, a point emphasized in all three versions of Paul's apostolic call. The first is in direct narrative (9:1–9), the others in Paul's defense speeches (22:6–21; 26:12–23). The three versions tell the same story but with variations: his companions, for example, hear the voice but see nothing in 9:7, but in 22:9 they see the light but are deaf to the voice. The element of shining light is constant, and is connected to the commission to be a light to the gentiles. The climax of each version in fact is reached with the command to go to the gentiles (9:15; 22:21; 26:23). In the defense speeches, this causes an angry reaction (22:22; 26:24). As with the rejection of Jesus in Nazareth, the Jewish rejection of this prophet's message has something to do with its universal scope.

Yet Paul by no means preaches exclusively to gentiles. He turns to them only after repeated rejection in the synagogues. The first time it happens, Paul solemnly announces a redirection of his efforts to the gentiles (13:46). But we still see him preaching to Jews and even converting some, though he twice more declares a turn to the gentiles (18:6; 28:23–29). Even in the last and most somber of these pronouncements, made to the Jewish leaders of Rome, some Jews believe (28:24–25). Indeed, throughout Paul's ministry in the Diaspora, Luke shows a continuing division within the people. Some accept the gospel, others do not (see 17:4; 18:4; 19:9–10). The emphasis in Paul's ministry is definitely on those who do not, indicated by the distancing characterization "the Jews." It is used once in the gospel (Luke 7:3) and only nine times in Acts apart from Paul. But with reference to those who oppose Paul, Luke uses *Ioudaios* some seventy times.

Despite his rejection, Paul continues to define his mission in terms of God's care for Israel. In the defense speeches above all, Paul portrays himself and his work in terms of Jewish messianic expectation, specifically the Pharisaic hope in the resurrection, which he insists has come to fulfillment in the resurrection of Jesus (see 22:3–4; 23:6; 24:14–21; 26:4–11) (cf. O'Toole 1978). To the Jewish leaders of Rome, this "apostle to the gentiles" declares, "For this reason, therefore, I have asked to see you and speak to you, since it is because of the hope of Israel that I am bound with this chain" (28:20). However much Paul carried the gospel to the "end of the world" (Acts 1:8), he remained for Luke the "teacher of Israel" (Jervell 1972: 153–83).

F. Literary-Religious Themes in Luke-Acts

The *mythos* (story line) of Luke-Acts is the story of the prophet and the people. The *dianoia* (meaning) is God's fidelity to his promises giving gentiles security in their belief. Within this framework other literary and religious subthemes are developed.

1. World Affirmation. Luke-Acts has a positive view of the world. It is perhaps the least apocalyptic of the NT writings. Not only is Luke relatively unconcerned about the end time, but his historical enterprise bestows value on time itself. Luke approves as well those outside the Christian movement. Outsiders are generally regarded as reasonable and open-minded, the highest compliment paid by apologetic literature. The empire is not the instrument of Satan, but the condition for the safety and spread of the gospel itself. Luke-Acts recounts the conversion of gentiles and entirely lacks Matthew's xenophobia: gentiles can be "God-fearers," and even the uncoverted show kindness and intelligence (Acts 28:7–10). The portrayal of Christians corresponds to this perception of outsiders as enlightened. The apostles appear as self-controlled, courageous, just, law-abiding, reasonable men, the farthest thing from fanatics.

Luke-Acts affirms the value of human culture simply by the beauty of its fashioning. By shaping the Good News into literature, Luke implies the compatibility of Christianity and culture: human symbols are adequate vessels of the Good News.

2. The Great Reversal. The prophetic imagery of Luke-Acts is, however, joined to a prophetic critique of human religious expectations and values. In the "visitation of the people" by the prophet, there is effected a great reversal. Human security and complacency is challenged by the Good News. Those who are powerful, rich, and "consoled" within the people, who "seek to justify themselves," and who respond to the prophet only with "testing" and rejection, are themselves "cast down," or "lowered," or in the end, "cut off from the people." Those ordinarily deemed unworthy, lowly, marginal or even outcast are accepted by God and "raised up," becoming part of the restored people. This is the significance of the language of the "rich" and the "poor" (Luke 1:53; 4:18; 6:20–24; 7:22; 14:21; 16:19–31). The rich stand for those who have no need of consolation and who reject the prophet. The poor stand for all who have been rejected by human standards but are accepted by God, and who themselves accept God's visitation in the prophet. Among them are the crippled, lame, blind, and deaf, the sexually mutilated, and all those ritually excluded from full participation in the people. It includes the religiously unrighteous, the "sinners and tax collectors," and those who by virtue of their gender were denied full participation in the people. Luke's portrayal of Mary is emblematic of the way that God reverses the poverty and powerlessness of the human condition. Throughout his narrative, Luke gives positive attention to the role of women. The theme of reversal is emphatically expressed by the inclusion of gentiles (and Samaritans, whether Luke considers them gentiles or not) in the people of God.

3. Salvation. Human values are reversed by God not for the destruction of the wicked but for the saving of the lost. God's "visitation" is for their salvation (cf. Acts 7:25). Luke emphasizes the salvific aspect of the Good News more than any of the other gospels, first of all in the way he shapes the image of Jesus. The Prophet is also Savior (Luke 2:11), who brings salvation (1:69; 19:9) and works saving acts (7:50; 8:36; 8:50). He has "come to save the lost" (19:10). What is said of Jesus in the gospel applies to the apostles' mission in Acts as well. The message of God delivered by these prophets is above all one of salvation (Acts 15:11; 28:28). The theme of salvation is dominant in distinctively Lukan parables, above all in the parables of the lost sheep (13:3–7), the lost coin (15:8–10), and the lost son (15:11–32) (cf. Marshall 1970: 77–187).

4. The Word of God. The theme of God's word is obviously related to that of the Prophet and the People, for it is through the prophetic word that God addresses the people. Luke emphasizes the power of this word in Acts by showing it empowered by the Spirit and accompanied by signs and wonders. The mission itself can be described as the word of God growing and expanding (Acts 6:7; 8:14; 10:36; 11:1; 12:24; 19:20). In the parable of the sower, Luke interprets the seed explicitly as "the word of God" (Luke 8:11), and the human response of faith is defined in terms of hearing and obeying the "word of God" (Luke 5:1; 6:47; 8:13–15; 8:21; 11:28).

5. Conversion. The word of God, which reverses human expectations, demands a "turning" and acceptance of the prophetic word. Conversion is an important theme in Luke-Acts, intimately connected to the story of Prophet and People. Jesus' ministry is preceded by the word of God spoken through the prophet John, calling to repentance (Luke 3:7–14). Acts opens with the prophetic preaching of Peter, calling for repentance (Acts 2:37–40). Those who enter the people that God is restoring must "turn around" (Luke 5:32; 10:13; 11:32; 13:3–5; 24:47; Acts 3:19; 5:31; 8:22; 11:18; 17:30; 20:21; 26:20). The most impressive example of all, of course, is the "turning" of Paul from persecutor to apostle, and whose conversion/call is so paradigmatic that it is repeated three times (Acts 9:1–9; 22:6–11; 26:12–18).

6. The Response of Faith. God's restored people answer his visitation with "fruits worthy of repentance" (Luke 3:8; Acts 26:20). In the first place is faith. God requires faithfulness in return for his fidelity. In Luke-Acts, faith combines obedient hearing of the word and patient endurance (S. Brown 1969). It is not a momentary decision, but a response which grows and matures (Luke 8:15; 17:5–6). Essential to the response of faith is prayer, which is made thematic by Luke (Trites 1978). Jesus prays throughout his ministry (3:21; 5:16; 6:12; 9:28–29; 11:1; 22:41–44) and teaches his disciples to pray (11:2–4; 18:1; 22:46). Luke also provides splendid examples of prayer, showing that for this people, life is defined first of all by its relationship with God (1:46–56, 68–79; 2:29–32; 10:21–22; 22:42; Acts 1:24–25; 4:24–30).

Conversion demands that humans change their behavior in imitation of God. As God welcomes all into his people, so are Christians expected to show hospitality. The opening of the home and heart to the stranger is explicitly connected to the theme of accepting or rejecting the prophet (Luke 9:3–5; 10:2–16), and Luke provides explicit models for this response (Luke 10:38–42; Acts 16:11–15). Similarly, Luke's instructions on the use of possessions have their logic in the pattern of God's visitation. The prophet permits a place in the people for the poor and outcast. Those who accept the prophet are to share their possessions with the needy, whether through almsgiving (Luke 12:32–34; 16:1–13) or by the total donation of what they possess in a community of goods (Acts 4:32–37) (Johnson 1977). Finally, as God's visitation of the people for salvation is a revelation of his loving-kindness above all to the outcast (Luke 1:52–53, 58) so are his people to reach out in love to all (Luke 6:32–36; 10:27–37).

These are not all the literary and religious themes of Luke-Acts, but this listing demonstrates how the rich subthemes find their coherence in the story of the Prophet and the People by which Luke convinces his gentile readers that God's fidelity to his promise should give them confidence in their commitment to him.

Bibliography

Alter, R. 1981. *The Art of Biblical Narrative.* New York.

Bachmann, M. 1980. *Jerusalem und der Temple.* Stuttgart.

Barr, D. L., and Wentling, J. L. 1984. The Conventions of Classical Biography and the Genre of Luke-Acts. Pp. 63–88 in Talbert 1984.

Barrett, C. K. 1961. *Luke the Historian in Recent Study.* London.

Beardslee, W. A. 1970. *Literary Criticism of the New Testament.* Philadelphia.

Brodie, T. L. 1984. Greco-Roman Imitation of Texts as a Partial Guide to Luke's Use of Sources. Pp. 17–46 in Talbert 1984.

Brown, R. E. 1977. *The Birth of the Messiah.* Garden City, NY.

Brown, S. 1969. *Apostasy and Perseverance in the Theology of Luke.* AnBib 36. Rome.

Cadbury, H. J. 1920. *The Style and Literary Method of Luke.* HTS 6. Cambridge, MA.

———. 1927. *The Making of Luke-Acts.* New York.

———. 1933. The Summaries of Acts. Pp. 392–402 in *The Beginnings of Christianity.* Pt. 1: *The Acts of the Apostles.* Vol. 5. London.

———. 1955. *The Book of Acts in History.* New York.

Comblin, J. 1956. La Paix dans le Théologie de Saint Luc. *ETL* 32: 439–60.

Conzelmann, H. 1952. Zur Lukansanalyze. *ZTK* 49: 16–33.
———. 1961. *The Theology of St. Luke.* Trans. G. Buswell. New York.
Dahl, N. A. 1957–58. "A People for His Name" (Acts 15:14). *NTS* 4: 319–27.
———. 1966. The Story of Abraham in Luke-Acts. Pp. 139–58 in Keck and Martyn 1966.
Dibelius, M. 1956. The Speeches of Acts and Ancient Historiography. Pp. 138–85 in *Studies in the Acts of the Apostles.* Trans. M. Ling. London.
Dillon, R. J. 1978. *From Eyewitnesses to Ministers of the Word.* AnBib 82. Rome.
———. 1981. Previewing Luke's Project from his Prologue. *CBQ* 43: 205–27.
Dodd, C. H. 1936. *The Apostolic Preaching and Its Development.* London.
Dubois, J. D. 1973. "La Figure d'Elie dans la perspective lucanienne. *RHPR* 53: 155–76.
Dupont, J. 1962. *Le Discours de Milet: Testament pastoral de Saint Paul.* LD 32. Paris.
———. 1964. *The Sources of the Acts.* Trans. K. Pond. New York.
———. 1967. *Etudes sur les Actes des Apôtres.* LD 45. Paris.
———. 1969. L'Union entre les premières Chrétiens dans les Actes des Apôtres. *NRT* 91: 898–915.
———. 1979. *The Salvation of the Gentiles.* Trans. J. Keating. New York.
Easton, B. S. 1936. *The Purpose of Acts.* London.
Ehrhardt, E. 1958. The Construction and Purpose of the Acts of the Apostles. *ST* 12: 44–79.
Ellis, E. E. 1970. The Role of the Christian Prophet in Acts. Pp. 55–67 in *Apostolic History and the Gospel,* ed. W. Gasque and R. Martin. Exeter.
Frye, N. 1969. *Anatomy of Criticism.* New York.
George, A. 1968. Israel dans L'Oeuvre de Luc. *RB* 75: 481–525.
Gils, F. 1957. *Jesus Prophète d'après les Evangiles Synoptiques.* OrBibLov 2. Louvain.
Goodenough, E. 1966. The Perspective of Acts. Pp. 51–59 in Keck and Martyn 1966.
Goulder, M. D. 1964. *Type and History in Acts.* London.
Haenchen, E. 1966. The Book of Acts as Source Material for the History of Early Christianity. Pp. 258–78 in Keck and Martyn 1966.
———. 1971. *The Acts of the Apostles.* Trans. B. Noble et al. Philadelphia.
Harnack, A. 1907. *Luke the Physician.* Trans. J. R. Wilkinson, ed. W. D. Morrison. New York.
Hastings, A. 1958. *Prophet and Witness in Jerusalem: A Study of the Teaching of St. Luke.* Baltimore.
Hengel, M. 1979. *Acts and the History of Earliest Christianity.* Trans. J. Bowden. Philadelphia.
Jervell, J. 1972. *Luke and the People of God.* Minneapolis.
Johnson, L. T. 1977. *The Literary Function of Possessions in Luke-Acts.* SBLDS 39. Missoula, MT.
———. 1979. On Finding the Lukan Community. Pp. 87–100 in *SBLSP.*
———. 1982. The Lukan Kingship Parable (Luke 19:11–27). *NovT* 24: 139–59.
———. 1983. *Decision-Making in the Church: A Biblical Model.* Philadelphia.
Karris, R. J. 1978. Rich and Poor: the Lukan Sitz-im-leben. Pp. 112–25 in Talbert 1978.
———. 1979. Missionary Communities: A New Paradigm for the Study of Luke-Acts. *CBQ* 41: 80–97.
———. 1986. Luke 23:47 and the Lukan View of Jesus' Death. *JBL* 105: 65–74.
Keck, L., and Martyn, J. L., eds. 1966. *Studies in Luke-Acts.* Nashville.
Kodell, J. 1969. Luke's Use of *"laos,"* "People," Especially in the Jerusalem Narrative. *CBQ* 31: 327–43.
Kurz, W. S. 1980. Hellenistic Rhetoric in the Christological Proof of Luke-Acts. *CBQ* 42: 171–95.
———. 1984. Luke 3:23–38 and Greco-Roman and Biblical Genealogies. Pp. 169–87 in Talbert 1984.
———. 1985. Luke 22:14–38 and Greco-Roman and Biblical Farewell Addresses. *JBL* 104: 251–68.
Lampe, G. W. H. 1955. The Holy Spirit in the Writings of St. Luke. Pp. 159–200 in *Studies in the Gospels,* ed. D. E. Nineham. Oxford.
———. 1955–56. The Lukan Portrait of Christ. *NTS* 2: 160–75.
Laurentin, R. 1957. *Structure et Théologie de Luc.* 2 vols. EBib. Paris.
Lohfink, G. 1971. *Die Himmelfahrt Jesu.* SANT 26. Munich.
Loning, V. K. 1981. Paulinismus in der Apostelgeschichte. Pp. 202–32 in *Paulus in den neutestamentliche Spätschriften,* ed. K. Kertelge. Freiburg.
Maddox, R. 1982. *The Purpose of Luke-Acts,* ed. J. Riches. Edinburgh.
Marshall, I. H. 1970. *Luke: Historian and Theologian.* Exeter.
Menoud, P. H. 1954–55. Le Plan des Actes des Apôtres. *NTS* 1: 44–51.
Minear, P. 1966. Luke's Use of the Birth Stories. Pp. 111–30 in Keck and Martyn 1966.
———. 1976. *To Heal and to Reveal: The Prophetic Vocation according to Luke.* New York.
Moessner, D. P. 1983. Luke 9:1–50: Luke's Preview of the Journey of the Prophet like Moses of Deuteronomy. *JBL* 102: 575–605.
Morgenthaler, R. 1949. *Die lukanische Geschichtsschreibung als Zeugnis.* 2 vols. Zurich.
Moule, C. F. D. 1966. The Christology of Acts. Pp. 159–85 in Keck and Martyn 1966.
Müller, P. G. 1981. Der "Paulinismus" in der Apostelgeschichte. Pp. 157–201 in *Paulus in den neutestamentliche Spätschriften,* ed. K. Kertelge. Frieburg.
Neyrey, J. 1980. The Absence of Jesus' Emotions: The Lukan Redaction of Luke 22:39–46. *Bib* 61: 153–71.
———. 1984. The Forensic Defense Speech and Paul's Trial Speeches in Acts 22–26: Form and Function. Pp. 210–24 in Talbert 1984.
———. 1985. *The Passion according to Luke.* New York.
O'Neill, J. C. 1961. *The Theology of Acts in Its Historical Setting.* London.
O'Toole, R. F. 1978. *The Christological Climax of Paul's Defense.* AnBib 78. Rome.
Pervo, R. I. 1987. *Profit with Delight: The Literary Genre of the Acts of the Apostles.* Philadelphia.
Plümacher, E. 1972. *Lukas als hellenistischer Schriftsteller.* Göttingen.
Prast, F. 1979. *Presbyter und Evangelium in nachapostolischer Zeit.* Stuttgart.
Quinn, J. D. 1978. The Last Volume of Luke-Acts: The Relation of Luke-Acts to the Pastoral Epistles. Pp. 62–75 in Talbert 1978.
Rau, G. 1965. Das Volk in der lukanischen Passionsgeschichte: Eine Konjecture zur Luk. 23:13. *ZNW* 56: 41–51.
Reicke, B. 1959. Instruction and Discussion in the Travel Narrative. *SE* 1: 206–16.
Rétif, A. 1951. Témoignage et prédication missionaire dans les Actes des Apôtres. *NRT* 73: 152–65.

Richard, E. 1978. *Acts 6:1–8:4: The Author's Method of Composition.* SBLDS 41. Missoula, MT.
Robbins, V. K. 1978. By Land and by Sea: The We Passages and Ancient Sea Voyages. Pp. 215–42 in Talbert 1978.
Sanders, J. T. 1984. The Salvation of the Jews in Luke-Acts. Pp. 104–28 in Talbert 1984.
Schmitt, J. 1953. L'Eglise de Jerusalem, ou le "restauration" d'Israel. *RevScRel* 27: 209–18.
Schneider, G. 1977. Zur Bedeutung von *kathexes* im lukanischen Doppelwerk. *ZNW* 68: 128–31.
Schubert, P. 1954. The Structure and Significance of Luke 24. Pp. 165–86 in *Neutestamentliche Studien für Rudolf Bultmann.* BZNW 21. Berlin.
Schweizer, E. 1948. Zur Frage der Lukasquellen, Analyze von Luk. 15, 11–32. *TZ* 4: 460–71.
Talbert, C. H. 1966. *Luke and the Gnostics.* New York.
———. 1974. *Literary Patterns, Theological Themes, and the Genre of Luke-Acts.* Missoula, MT.
———. 1977. *What Is a Gospel?* Philadelphia.
———, ed. 1978. *Perspectives on Luke-Acts.* Danville, VA.
———, ed. 1984. *Luke-Acts: New Perspectives from the SBL Seminar.* New York.
Teeple, H. 1957. *The Mosaic Eschatological Prophet.* SBLMS 10. Philadelphia.
Tiede, D. 1980. *Prophecy and History in Luke-Acts.* Philadelphia.
Trites, A. 1978. The Prayer Motif in Luke-Acts. Pp. 168–86 in Talbert 1978.
Turner, N. 1955–56. The Relation of Luke I and II to Hebraic Sources and to the Rest of Luke-Acts. *NTS* 2: 100–109.
Unnik, W. C. van. 1960. The Book of Acts the Confirmation of Gospel. *NovT* 4: 26–59.
———. 1973. Once More, Luke's Prologue. P. 19 in *Essays on the Gospel of Luke and Acts.* Neot 7. Johannesburg.
Vielhauer, P. 1966. On the 'Paulinism' of Acts. Pp. 33–50 in Keck and Martyn 1966.
Walasky, P. W. 1983. *"And so we came to Rome": The Political Perspectives of St. Luke.* SNTSMS 49. Cambridge.
Wanke, J. 1973. *Die Emmauserzahlung.* ErfThSt 31. Leipzig.
Wilckens, U. 1961. *Die Missionsrede der Apostelgeschichte.* WMANT 5. Neukirchen.
Wilson, S. G. 1973. *The Gentiles and the Gentile Mission in Luke-Acts.* SNTSMS 23. Cambridge.
———. 1979. *Luke and the Pastoral Epistles.* London.
———. 1983. *Luke and the Law.* SNTSMS 50. Cambridge.
Winter, P. 1956. On Luke and Lukan Sources. *ZNW* 47: 217–42.
Zimmerman, H. 1961. Die Sammelberichte der Apostelgeschichte. *BZ* 5: 71–82.

LUKE TIMOTHY JOHNSON

LUMINARIES, WORDS OF THE. See WORDS OF THE LUMINARIES (4QDibHam).

LUNATIC. See SICKNESS AND DISEASE; DEMONS.

LUTE. See MUSIC AND MUSICAL INSTRUMENTS.

LUWIAN LANGUAGE. See LANGUAGES (INTRODUCTORY SURVEY).

LUZ (PLACE) [Heb *lûz*]. **1.** Formerly the place name for Bethel (Gen 28:19; 35:6; 48:3; Judg 1:23; *Jub.* 27:19, 26). According to Gen 28:10–22, it was Jacob who renamed the place Bethel after he encountered God in that place (M.R. 172148).

The tribal-boundary descriptions locate Luz on or near the common boundary between Joseph (Josh 16:1–3) and Benjamin (18:11–13). These two texts have occasioned some dispute regarding the actual geographical relationship between Luz and Bethel. One could interpret *wĕyāṣāʾ mibbêt-ʾēl lûzāh* "going from Bethel to Luz" (Josh 16:2) to mean that the border ran from Bethel to Luz and thus that the names indicated two distinct sites. Then the note that identifies Bethel with Luz in Josh 18:13 might be judged an interpolation, especially if one understood Beth-aven of 18:12 to be a distortion of Bethel. Having argued in this way, Noth located Luz at Beitîn, and he regarded Bethel as the name of a sanctuary in its immediate proximity which eventually gave its name to the town of Luz (Noth *Josua* HAT, ²1953: 101, 106, 109).

According to another interpretation, Luz and Bethel were successive names for one place. In favor of this position one may argue that the *āh* ending on *lûzāh* in Josh 16:2 is not necessarily locative (cf. the second *lûzāh* in Josh 18:13). Then one may interpret Bethel-Luzah as a compound name, as both LXX A (v 1) and LXX B (v 2) seem to have done (Kallai *HGB*, 129–31, 143).

2. A city built in the land of the Hittites by a former citizen of Bethel whom the conquering house of Joseph spared because he had shown them an entrance to Bethel (Judg 1:26). It has generally been understood that "the land of the Hittites" refers to the territory of Syria or Lebanon, which belonged to the Hittite empire before its collapse at the end of the LB Age. Another possibility, however, is that in Judg 1:26 the designation refers to the hill country of Palestine (as in Num 13:29; cf. Genesis 23 and 26:34) and that the new city of Luz was located W of Bethel, as suggested by the boundary description of Josh 16:2 (Gottwald 1979: 559–60).

Bibliography

Gottwald, N. K. 1979. *Tribes of Yahweh.* Maryknoll, NY.

WESLEY I. TOEWS

LXX. See SEPTUAGINT.

LYCAONIA (PLACE) [Gk *Lykaonia*]. The territory of the Lycaones was a region of Central Asia Minor N of the Taurus range, bordered on the W by Phrygia, on the E by Cappadocia, and on the N (after 232 B.C.) by ethnic Galatia.

A. General History

The name Lycaones is probably related to Lukka, an Anatolian people and territory mentioned in Hittite texts (Houwink ten Cate 1961: 195–56). One detached group of Lycaones, distinguished by W. M. Ramsay (1897: 664, 694; 1906: 366) as the "inner Lycaones," formed a western enclave in the heart of Phrygia; it is mentioned in inscriptions of the 3d century A.D.

In 401 B.C. Cyrus the Younger led his army through Lycaonia (a five days' march of ninety miles) on his way east to contest the succession to the Persian throne with his brother Artaxerxes II. Lycaonia evidently remained loyal to Artaxerxes, for Cyrus treated it as hostile territory and allowed his Greek followers to plunder it (Xen. *An.* 1.2.19).

In 333 B.C. Lycaonia became part of the empire of Alexander the Great and, after his death, of his Seleucid successors. In 188 B.C. the Romans transferred Lycaonia from the Seleucids to the kingdom of Pergamum. When the Romans accepted the bequest of the kingdom of Pergamum in 129 B.C., they bestowed its easternmost regions on neighboring rulers, Lycaonia going to the king of Cappadocia. Mark Antony gave western Lycaonia to Polemon of Laodicea in 39 B.C.; three years later he transferred the whole of Lycaonia to Rome's ally Amyntas, king of Galatia. Soon afterward Amyntas seized the eastern cities of Derbe and Laranda and added them to his realm. When Amyntas fell in battle against unruly tribesmen of the Taurus region in 25 B.C., his augmented kingdom was reconstituted by Augustus as the Roman province of Galatia. In 20 B.C. Augustus gave eastern Lycaonia to Archelaus, king of Cappadocia (Strab. 12.1.4; 12.2.7; 14.5.6; Dio Cass. 54.9.2). In western Lycaonia he planted two colonies of veteran soldiers—at Parlais and Lystra—and these were linked by a road system with Pisidian Antioch in Phrygia, another colony.

Eastern Lycaonia was bestowed by Emperor Gaius on Antiochus IV, king of Commagene, in A.D. 37. It was taken from him almost immediately afterward, but was restored to him by Claudius in 41 (Dio Cass. 59.8.2; 60.8.1). About that time Derbe, on the frontier between the province of Galatia and the kingdom of Commagene, received the honorific title Claudioderbe. Eastern Lycaonia now became known as Lycaonia Antiochiana (Ptol. Geog. 5.6.17; *CIL* 10.8660); Pliny the Elder calls it *Lycaonia ipsa* "Lycaonia itself" (*HN* 5.95). Western Lycaonia, which remained part of the province of Galatia, may have been distinguished as Lycaonia Galatica.

Under Vespasian (ca. 72) Lycaonia was reunited as a region of the amalgamated province of Galatia-Cappadocia; under Trajan (106) the two provinces were divided again; under Hadrian (137) a new province, the Triple Eparchy, combined Lycaonia, Cilicia, and Isauria.

The *koinon* or league of cities of Lycaonia comprised Laranda (its principal city for long periods), Barata, Ilistra, Derbe, Hyde, Dalisandos, and Savatra, but not Lystra, Axylon, or Iconium (which was a Phrygian city but sometimes, because of its proximity to the regional frontier, reckoned to Lycaonia, as in Cic. *Fam.* 15.4.2; Strab. 12.6.1; Pliny *HN* 5.25).

B. Lycaonia in the NT

Lycaonia first appears in the NT when Paul and Barnabas, forced to depart from Iconium because of a riot stirred up against them, "fled to Lystra and Derbe, cities of Lycaonia, and to the surrounding country" (Acts 14:6). This form of words implies that Iconium, which they had left, was not in Lycaonia. When they heard the Lycaonian language spoken in Lystra (Acts 14:11), they may have recognized that it was sufficiently unlike Phrygian for the difference to be obvious even to people who understood neither language. Whereas Phrygian was related to Thracian, the Lycaonian language was probably descended from Luwian, a language represented in Hittite texts.

Paul and Barnabas had an early opportunity of hearing Lycaonian when the people of Lystra, excited by Paul's healing a congenitally lame man, shouted that the gods had come down to them in human form. The two missionaries did not understand the words, but soon gathered their purport when preparations were set afoot to pay them divine honors. When Luke says that Barnabas and Paul were called Zeus and Hermes, respectively, we may infer that two corresponding Lycaonian gods were mentioned. On the other hand, there is evidence for the joint worship of Zeus and Hermes in that neighborhood: a 3d-century A.D. inscription from Sedasa (some 25 miles from Lystra) records the dedication to Zeus of a statue of Hermes by men with Lycaonian names (Calder 1910: 1–6), and an altar found near Lystra in 1926 is dedicated to the "hearer of prayer" (Gk *epēkoos*), i.e., Zeus, and Hermes (*MAMA* 8.1).

The Lystrans were naturally offended when their attempt to worship Paul and Barnabas as gods was repudiated, so they lent a willing ear to opponents of the missionaries who came from Iconium and fomented an attack on them. Paul in particular was fortunate to escape with his life after being stoned and left for dead at the roadside. On the next day the two set out for Derbe, some 60 miles distant. Here they reached the provincial frontier, if indeed they did not cross it: Derbe may have belonged to Lycaonia Antiochiana, as Ptolemy says (5.6.16; cf. Van Elderen 1970: 159–61). Derbe, in any case, was the farthest point they reached in their present journey; they retraced their steps. But they had made converts both in Lystra (notably Timothy, according to Acts 16:1–3) and in Derbe (among whom one Gaius is specially mentioned in Acts 20:4).

Paul passed through Lycaonia on at least one later occasion, and most probably two. On his way from Antioch to Troas with Silas, "he came also to Derbe and to Lystra" (Acts 16:1); at the latter place he persuaded Timothy to join him as his personal assistant. When, a few years later, on his way from Antioch to Ephesus "he went from place to place through the region of Galatia and Phrygia, strengthening all the disciples" (Acts 18:23), Galatic Lycaonia was almost certainly one of the areas visited. On the "south Galatian" view, the Christian communities of Lycaonia were among "the churches of Galatia" to which Paul's Letter to the Galatians is addressed (Gal 1:2; cf. 1 Cor 16:1).

Bibliography

Ballance, M. H. 1957. The Site of Derbe: A New Inscription. *Anatolian Studies* 7: 147–51.

———. 1964. Derbe and Faustinopolis. *AnSt* 14: 139–40.

Calder, W. M. 1910. Zeus and Hermes at Lystra. *Expositor,* ser. 7, 10: 1–6.

Houwink ten Cate, P. H. J. 1961. *The Luwian Population Groups of Lycia and Cilicia Aspera during the Hellenistic Age.* Leiden.

Jones, A. H. M. 1971. *Cities of the Eastern Roman Provinces.* 2d ed. Oxford.

Levick, B. 1967. *Roman Colonies in Southern Asia Minor.* Oxford.

Ramsay, W. M. 1896. The "Galatia" of St. Paul and the "Galatic territory" of Acts. Pp. 15–57 in *Studia Biblica et Ecclesiastica, IV,* by members of the University of Oxford. Oxford.

———. 1897. *The Cities and Bishoprics of Phrygia.* Vol. 1, pt. 2. Oxford.

———. 1904. Lycaonia. *Jahreshefte des k.-k. österreichischen Archäologischen Instituts* 7: 57–132.

———. 1906. The Tekmoreian Guest-Friends. Pp. 305–77 in *Studies in the History and Art of the Eastern Roman Empire,* ed. W. M. Ramsay. Aberdeen.

Van Elderen, B. 1970. Some Archaeological Observations on Paul's First Missionary Journey. Pp. 151–61 in *Apostolic History and the Gospel,* ed. W. W. Gasque and R. P. Martin. Grand Rapids.

F. F. BRUCE

LYCIA (PLACE) [Gk *Lysias*]. A rugged, mountainous district on the SW coast of Asia Minor. According to 1 Macc 15:23, Lycia was among the recipients of a letter from the Roman consul Lucius Calpurnius Piso in the 2d century B.C.E. concerning the Roman alliance with the Jews. Lycia is also mentioned twice in the context of Paul's missionary travels in the book of Acts. Paul changed ships at the Lycian port of Patara on his way to Jerusalem (Acts 21:1) and again at Myra on his journey to Rome (Acts 27:5–6).

The only level land of the district is on the alluvial plains formed by the Limyrus and Xanthus rivers. The elevations of five of the mountains in this W spur of the Taurus range are over 7,600 ft. with the highest reaching 10,125 ft. The mountainous topography accounts for the inhospitable coastline and the complete isolation of Lycia from Pamphylia to the E. The only suitable harbors were at Patara at the mouth of the Xanthus, Myra at the entrance to the Andriacus valley (both silted), Limyra at the mouth of the Limyrus river, and Telmessus on the Gulf of Fethiye (still in use). Pliny stated that Lycia had once had 70 towns, but by the time of his writing only 26 remained.

Little is known about the early history of Lycia, and much of what is known is of a legendary nature. According to Herodotus (1.73), the Lycians came from Crete under Serapedon (the exiled brother of Minos), perhaps via Miletus. The land was originally inhabited by a warlike people called the Solymi, who were driven out of the land by the followers of Serapedon (Homer *Il.* 6.180, 184; 10.430; 12.30). These followers were originally called Termilae, which may be attested in some 4th-century epichoric inscriptions. Lycia was named after the Athenian Lycus, son of Pandion, who was also exiled by his brother Aegeus and settled among the Termilae (Strabo 14.3.10).

The earliest Bronze Age inhabitants were related to the Hittites. Archaeological discoveries indicate that Elmali was inhabited in the EB Age. A tribe called the "Lukka" (or Eg *Lk*), which may have been Lycians, appears in Hittite, Ugaritic, and Egyptian records. In an Amarna letter (EA 38:11f.), the king of Alashiya complains of the aggressions of the Lukki people. In a letter from a Ugaritic king to the king of Alashiya, Lukka Land is mentioned in conjunction with a coastal region; the area is similarly described in Hittite sources as a turbulent region. The Lukka may have been allies of the Hittites at the battle of Qadesh between Rameses II and Mawatalis. Merneptah boasted that he won a victory in his 5th year against an alliance that included the *Lk* (Lukka?) in Libya.

Linguistic evidence indicates that a dialect of the Luwian language was spoken, and Luwian deities can be detected in personal names. The Lycian language and script, with an alphabet containing 29 letters (more than half of which appear to be Greek in form) were in use through the 4th century B.C.E. The language is only imperfectly understood, and some phonetic values are uncertain.

According to Homer (*Il.* 2.876–77), the Lycians allied with Priam and defended Troy against the Achaeans. Xanthus (modern Gunuk) was the principal city of Lycia, which headed a federation of cities and towns. Apollo and his mother, Ledo, and perhaps Hephaestus were the principal Lycian deities. A lyre on Lycian coins represented Apollo, who had a famous temple and oracle in the city of Patara, where he was fabled to spend his winters.

Lycia was the only power W of the Halys that was not subdued by Croesus (Hdt. 1.28). The Persians conquered the Lycians in 546 B.C.E. after a valiant resistance staged against Cyrus' general, Harpagus, who was stationed at Xanthus. The Lycians supplied Xerxes with 50 ships in his expedition against the Greek mainland (Hdt. 7.92). Lycia was temporarily liberated by Cimon and joined the Delian League for a short time before falling again under Persian control. Lycia was included in the Hecatomnid dominions, submitted to Alexander the Great and, after his death, passed into the hands of the Ptolemies. In 197 B.C.E., Antiochus III conquered the land. After his defeat at Magnesia in 189 B.C.E., the Romans placed Lycia under the control of Rhodes.

The Lycians were given their freedom in 169 B.C.E. The Roman generals Brutus and Cassius, however, sacked Xanthus for money in 42 B.C.E. The Lycians organized themselves into a confederation consisting of 23 cities with six cities (Xanthus, Patara, Pinara, Olympus, Myra, and Tlos) rising to predominant political positions (Polyb. 30.5; Strabo 14.3.2–10). The Lycian constitution was revoked in 43 C.E. by Claudius because of dissension between the cities, and in 74 C.E. Vespasian established the province of Lycia-Pamphylia under a praetorian prefect (Suetonius *Claud.* 25; idem. *Vit. Vespas.* 8; and Dio Cass. 60.17).

In the 4th century C.E., Myra was the seat of a Bishop Nikolas, who was martyred during the Diocletianic persecution of the Church. Saint Nikolas endeared himself to many by his generous habit of gift-giving. He became the patron saint of children and sailors, and through Dutch tradition became the Santa Claus of western Christendom.

SCOTT T. CARROLL

LYCIAN LANGUAGE. See LANGUAGES (INTRODUCTORY SURVEY).

LYDIA (PERSON) [Gk *Lydia*]. A devout Jew from Thyatira who was converted by Paul in the city of Philippi, as recorded in Acts 16:11–15. Lydia was a worshiper of (the one true) God, i.e., she was a practicing Jew. This may have been a lifelong commitment since there was a colony of Jews in Thyatira (Josephus *Ant* 12.119; Bruce 1951: 312–14). That she was meeting beside a stream on the Sabbath for prayer suggests that there were not enough Jewish men in Philippi to make up a quorum and establish a proper synagogue. Here we see a subtle but important point that Luke is trying to make—while Lydia could not be a founding member of a Jewish synagogue, she can be and is the first European convert to Christendom, and in fact is the founding member of the Christian community which begins to meet in her household (16:40). Jewish women in the Diaspora did participate in the Hellenistic renaissance and may have formed their own religious groups and held meetings for worship or prayer (as may be the case in this story). Nevertheless, there is no evidence of their being allowed to make up the quorum of a synagogue even in less restrictive environments like Macedonia. The evidence of women being financial patrons of Diaspora synagogues does not support another conclusion.

Note also that Lydia felt free, perhaps because of the liberating effect of the Gospel, to go against Jewish custom not only in speaking to Paul in public but also in inviting Paul and those with him, who were total strangers, to come and stay in her house (16:15). Herein we see a story of how the Gospel can free women from previous restraints, giving them new roles even as founding members of new Christian house churches.

It may be that, since the women of Macedonia were often noted for taking leading roles in society even before the time of Alexander the Great (Witherington 1988: 12–13), Lydia's new roles would have caused little or no surprise in the larger community. If, however, there were male Jews in Philippi her leadership role probably would have been surprising to them. Lydia, upon hearing the word of the Lord from Paul, was baptized, receiving the covenant sign of the new religion, something she could not do in Judaism. Thus Luke presents a story illustrating how the Gospel is for all sorts of people regardless of their gender, previous religious background, or economic status.

The name "Lydia" originally designated a person from the country called Lydia, i.e., the Lydian (Bruce 1951: 314). If this is the case in Acts 16, then we do not actually know this woman's name. However, at least as early as Horace (*Carm.* 1.8) Lydia had also become a personal name, and because the country of Lydia had been absorbed into the province of Asia when this story took place it is likely that Lydia is a personal name here (Conzelmann *Acts* Hermeneia, 130; Williams 1985: 273).

The city of Thyatira did exist in Paul's day and had long been a famous industrial center where purple dye was made. We are told that Lydia was associated with her hometown trade by being a seller of cloth colored with this royal purple dye (Acts 16:14). This means that Lydia was probably a financially independent woman, since material dyed royal purple was a luxury item that only royalty and the wealthy could normally afford, and since she has a house which will accommodate not only herself but also both her household (servants?) and guests. Homer (*Il.* 4 141–42) mentions two women who were famous for the art of purple dyeing in Lydia, so apparently the biblical Lydia was following a precedent of women being involved in this trade. It is likely she had come to Philippi, a Roman colony city, to sell her goods to some of the wealthy clientele there.

Bibliography

Bruce, F. F. 1951. *The Acts of the Apostles.* Grand Rapids.

Marshall, I. H. 1980. *The Acts of the Apostles.* Grand Rapids.

Thomas, W. D. 1971–72. The Place of Women in the Church at Philippi. *ET* 83: 117–20.

Williams, D. 1985. *Acts.* San Francisco.

Witherington, B. 1988. *Women in the Earliest Churches.* Cambridge.

BEN WITHERINGTON, III

LYDIA (PLACE) [Gk *Lydia*]. The region in W Asia Minor to which Paul and Silas proceed after their release from the Philippian jail in Acts 16:40.

A. Geography
B. History
  1. Prehistory
  2. Lydian Kingdom
  3. Persian Period
  4. Hellenistic and Roman Periods
C. Language
D. Religion
E. Material Culture

A. Geography

Ancient Lydia is located in western Asia Minor (modern Turkey). Its original territory included the Hermus (modern Gediz) and Cayster (modern Küçük Menderes) River valleys. The Meander (modern Büyük Menderes) River formed its southern boundary. Separating the Hermus and Cayster valleys is the Tmolus mountain range (modern Boz Dağ), where the once gold-bearing Pactolus stream rises and flows N to the Hermus plain. The Hermus valley provided a natural overland route from the Aegean coast to the Anatolian plateau. The modern Izmir–Ankara Highway follows this ancient road for much of its length. Under King Croesus in the 6th century B.C.E., the Lydian empire reached its greatest extent, from the Aegean to the Halys (modern Kızıl) River (Hdt. 1.28). Throughout its long history, the chief city of Lydia was Sardis, now the main source of archaeological evidence for Lydian material culture (Hanfmann 1983).

B. History

1. Prehistory. Little is known about Lydia in the prehistoric periods. Small settlements dating to the EB Age (3d millennium B.C.E.) were scattered on the shores of the Gygean lake (modern Göl Marmara) N of Sardis, and traces of LB Age (mid–late 2d millennium B.C.E.) activity have been found in the area of the ancient city. Hittite interest in western Asia Minor is attested by two 2d-millennium rock reliefs with Hittite hieroglyphic inscriptions, one a seated female on Mt. Sipylus (Manisa Dağ), the other a warrior figure in the Karabel pass, the latter attributed by Herodotus (2.106) to the Egyptian king Sesostris. Hittite records contain no reference to "Lydia" but "Assuwa" (as "Asia") may refer to Lydian territory in western Asia Minor. The Greek epic tradition concerning the Trojan War names as allies of the Trojans "Maeonians" who come from "Tarne," equated with Sardis by a scholiast (*Il.* 5.43–44). The *Iliad* also refers to "snowy Tmolus" (20.385), the Gygean lake, and the Hermus and Hyllus rivers (20.391–

92). Contact between Mycenaean Greeks and Lydians is indicated by mainland-type pottery and its local imitations at Sardis and other sites in Lydia. The Greek historical tradition tells of a dynasty born of Herakles and a Lydian slave woman, the Heraclidae, who ruled Lydia for twenty-two generations prior to the time of Candaules. The last Heraclid king, the uxorious Candaules, was supplanted by Gyges in ca. 685 B.C.E., the first Mermnad dynast (Hdt. 1.7–12).

2. Lydian Kingdom. Greek sources, especially Herodotus (1.6–95), and Near Eastern texts for Lydia during the Mermnad dynasty (ca. 685–547 B.C.E.) record the territorial ambitions and international contacts of the Mermnad kings. Gyges (ca. 685–652 B.C.E.) initiated expansion to the W by attacking Greek coastal settlements (Hdt. 1.14). His relationship with the Greeks, however, was not always hostile. Gyges was the first foreigner after Midas of Phrygia to place offerings in Apollo's sanctuary at Delphi (Hdt. 1.13–14). In response to Cimmerian raids in Asia Minor, Gyges sought an alliance with Ashurbanipal. In the Rassam Cylinder, Gyges is called Guggu of Ludu (perhaps the Gog of Ezek 39:1). Apparently the treaty with the Assyrians and his success against the Cimmerians were short-lived. In ca. 654 B.C.E., Gyges sent troops to help Psammetichus I of Egypt in his war of liberation against Lydia's former allies, the Assyrians (Luckenbill 1927: 297–98). And two years later Gyges himself was dead, the victim of another Cimmerian raid. Gyges' son and successor, Ardys (ca. 652–615 B.C.E.), and his successor, Sadyattes (ca. 615–605 B.C.E.), still had to contend with periodic Cimmerian incursions while pursuing their predecessor's policy of territorial expansion in Ionia. It was not until the reign of Alyattes (605–560 B.C.E.) that the Cimmerians were finally driven from Lydia. The appearance of the Scythians and Medes to the E, however, posed a new threat to Lydian security. After five years of indecisive battles between Alyattes and Cyaxares the Mede (during the sixth of which Thales of Miletos predicted the solar eclipse of May 28, 585 B.C.E.), peace was concluded under the auspices of the rulers of Cilicia and Babylon. To seal the pact, Alyattes' daughter was married to Astyages, son of Cyaxares (Hdt. 1.74). The offspring of this union, Mandane, became the mother of Cyrus the Great. Alyattes' son, Croesus (560–547 B.C.E.) ruled a vast empire, the downfall of which is well known to readers of Herodotus. Croesus' political connections extended from the Near East to the city-states of mainland Greece, Sparta and Athens chief among them. His extravagant dedications at Greek sanctuaries, from the quantities of precious metal at Delphi to the columns of the archaic Artemision at Ephesus, are attested in literary and archaeological sources. During his reign, he reduced all of the Greeks in Asia to tributary status (Hdt. 1.26). To the Greeks, Croesus' life followed a classically tragic pattern, a king whose great wealth and power so blinded him that he lost everything. Less than 50 years after his downfall, this last Mermnad king appears in all his Hellenized Oriental finery on a red-figure amphora painted by Myson, an Athenian (Louvre G 197), and, by the early 5th century, in the *Epinicia* of Bacchylides (3.23–62).

3. Persian Period. The agent of Croesus' fall from power was Mandane's son (and Croesus' nephew) Cyrus, the king of Persia. Under Cyrus and his successors, the former Lydian empire became a prized satrapy, Saparda, with its capital at Sardis. This city, third in importance after Persepolis and Susa, was the target of the unsuccessful Ionian revolt in 499 B.C.E. (Hdt. 5.100–102) and the mustering point for Cyrus the Younger's march to Cunaxa in 401 B.C.E. (Xen. *An.* 1.2.2–3). The satrapy itself was subject to the plundering raids of the Spartan king Agesilaus in the early 4th century B.C.E. (Xen. *Ages.* 1.33–34). Linked by the Royal Road to the Aegean coast and inland areas, Lydia continued to prosper under the influence of Ionian Greek and Achaemenid/Persian cultures.

4. Hellenistic and Roman Periods. In the course of liberating the Greeks from their Persian masters, Alexander the Great acquired Lydia in 334 B.C.E. (Diod. Sic. 17.21.7). Subsequently, the Seleucid kings ruled the region until 189 B.C.E., when Antiochus III was defeated by the Romans at Magnesia (Livy 37.44–45; 1 Macc 8:8). Lydia passed into the hands of the Pergamene kings, where it remained until the death of Attalus III in 133 B.C.E. This last Attalid king bequeathed his kingdom to Rome under the terms of his will, and Lydia soon became part of the proconsular province of Asia. The Mithridatic Wars (88–63 B.C.E.) and a disastrous earthquake in 17 C.E., which leveled twelve cities in western Asia Minor, Sardis foremost among them, contributed to the general decline of the region. Under the Roman emperors, however, Lydia regained some of its former glory. Diocletian created the "new" province of Lydia (ca. 300 C.E.), included in the diocese of Asiane. Three of the seven churches of Revelation were located in Lydian cities, a reflection of the importance of the province in early Christian times.

C. Language

Lydian is related to the Indo-European languages of Anatolia, such as Luvian and Hittite. Knowledge of the language is based on a relatively small corpus of inscriptions, around 100, including casual graffiti (Gusmani 1964: 1980). The alphabet makes use of modified Greek and Phrygian letter forms. The earliest inscriptions recovered so far date to ca. 650–600 B.C.E. Lydian persisted through the Persian period, to which the majority of inscriptions belong, including several Lydian-Aramaic bilingual funerary texts. Even when Greek became both the common and official language during the Hellenistic period, Lydian graffiti could still be found as late as the 2d century B.C.E.

D. Religion

Lydian gods emerge as an enigmatic mixture of native Anatolian, Near Eastern, and Greek elements (Hanfmann 1983: 90–96). To identify the uniquely Lydian elements is difficult. Artemis and Cybele (*Kuvava* in Lydian) were the most important goddesses, and Zeus (Lydian *Levs*) is chief among the gods. The Lydian god of wine, *Baki,* entered the Greek world as Bacchus/Dionysos. The major Persian contribution to the native tradition was the introduction of Anahita, the Persian Artemis. Hellenization appears to have changed the form but not the substance of native deities and their cults. Artemis, Cybele as Meter, and Zeus Lydios remain important. In the late 3d century B.C.E., Judaism entered W Asia Minor with the resettlement of Mesopotamian Jewish veteran families in Phrygia and

Lydia by Antiochus III (Joseph. *Ant.* 12.3.4). A large synagogue dating to the Roman period at Sardis reflects the enduring influence of Judaism in the region (Hanfmann 1983: 168–90). Christianization was a gradual process, completed in Lydia by the establishment of three of the seven churches of Asia at Sardis, Thyatira, and Philadelphia.

E. Material Culture

Long before the widespread hellenization of Lydia under the Seleucids, the influence of Greece, especially Ionia, is evident in painted pottery, terracotta revetments, and sculpture. Although native elements are observable in these forms of cultural expression, Greek traditions are the formative force. Lydian contributions mainly lie in the luxury arts, such as perfumes and scented ointments (Ath. 15.690b–d), carpets, textiles, and dyes (Pliny *HN* 7.196). According to Herodotus (1.94), the Lydians were the first to coin silver and gold, an attribution now supported by the discovery of a 6th-century B.C.E. gold refinery near the banks of the Pactolus stream at Sardis (Hanfmann 1983: 34–41). To Herodotus in the 5th century, the Lydians appeared close to the Greeks in their customs. The material evidence does not contradict this evaluation.

Bibliography

Burchner, L., Deeters, G., and Keil, J. 1927. Lydia. *PW* 12: 2122–2202.

Gusmani, R. 1964. *Lydisches Wörterbuch.* Heidelberg.

———. 1980. *Lydisches Wörterbuch: Ergänzungsband Lieferung 1.* Heidelberg.

Hanfmann, G. M. A. 1983. *Sardis from Prehistoric to Roman Times.* Cambridge, MA.

Luckenbill, D. D. 1927. *Ancient Records of Assyria and Babylonia II.* Chicago.

Barbara Kelley McLauchlin

LYRE. See MUSIC AND MUSICAL INSTRUMENTS.

LYSANIAS (PERSON) [Gk *Lysanias*]. According to Luke, Lysanias was the tetrarch of Abilene when John the Baptist began his ministry (Luke 3:1). Lysanias is not mentioned again in the NT, but the name appears several times in the works of Josephus. A ruler named Lysanias in Josephus died in 36 B.C.E. This has led some scholars to argue that Luke made a chronological blunder by depending on Josephus for the name Lysanias and thereby naming an individual long dead as the tetrarch in ca. 28 C.E. The apparent problem is heightened because Luke gives every indication that his gospel was written with critical care (Luke 1:3). The evidence seems to suggest that there were two individuals named Lysanias who ruled in the same general area but at different times, supporting the accuracy of Luke's account.

1. The earlier Lysanias mentioned by Josephus was the son of a certain Ptolemy (Joseph. *Ant.* 14.13.3; 15.4.1; *JW* 1.13.1). Lysanias, son of Ptolemy, ruled Chalcis in Lebanon (Joseph. *Ant.* 14.13.3). Later references to the name Lysanias in Josephus and Luke do not refer to the father, perhaps indicating a different individual. Because Chalcis was a larger territory than Abilene, it is likely that each was ruled by a separate person.

2. Thus it appears that another individual named Lysanias ruled over the district of Abilene. Josephus mentions that Gaius (Caligula) gave to Agrippa I all of the territory which had belonged to Herod the Great and added Abila to this territory (Joseph. *Ant.* 14.5.1; *JW* 2.11.5). Further inscriptional evidence may bear witness to a second Lysanias who ruled at a later date in the territory of Abilene. An inscription dated no later than 14 C.E., which states that it was the work of a certain Nymphaeus, a freedman of Lysanias, has been found near Abila. It appears that Josephus referred to two rulers named Lysanias but failed to distinguish one clearly from the other, whereas Luke mentioned only the later one.

Scott T. Carroll

LYSIAS (PERSON) [Gk *Lysias*]. **1.** See CLAUDIUS LYSIAS.

2. A Syrian of royal lineage appointed regent of the area from the Euphrates to the Egyptian border by Antiochus IV Epiphanes, when Antiochus raided Persia for money ca. 165 B.C.E. (1 Macc 3:33). He was also made guardian of the king's son, Antiochus V Eupator. Lysias was provided with half of Antiochus' army, including soldiers, cavalry, and elephants, and was instructed to defeat the Jews in Jerusalem. Lysias dispatched Ptolemy, the son of Dorymenes, Nicanor, and Gorgias to destroy Jerusalem (1 Macc 3:32–39), but Judas Maccabeus defeated them at Emmaus (1 Macc 3:40–4:25). 2 Maccabees (10:15–23) speaks of Gorgias waging war with mercenaries (presumably the same battle) and another battle between Judas and some Idumeans, but it is not clear whether the Idumeans acted with Gorgias or merely simultaneously.

The next year Lysias himself marched to Idumea and encamped at (or besieged) Beth-zur. Apparently Judas defeated Lysias, who retreated to Antioch for more mercenaries (1 Macc 4:27–35), though 2 Macc 11:6–15 says that the peace terms were negotiated, perhaps implying a standoff, and that Lysias returned to Antiochus V (in Antioch?). The retreat of Lysias gave Judas the opportunity to cleanse the temple in Jerusalem. Next, Judas waged his highly successful campaign in Transjordan (1 Macc 5:19–51 [= 2 Macc 12:2–28]). According to 2 Macc 12:27–28 Lysias was defeated at Ephron, but 1 Maccabees makes no such claim, and Lysias had been previously reported with the king (2 Macc 12:1). Judas meanwhile returned to Jerusalem (1 Macc 5:52–54 [= 2 Macc 12:31]) and next fought the Idumeans (1 Macc 5:65–68 [= 2 Macc 12:32–37]).

Antiochus IV Epiphanes, meanwhile, had been frustrated in his attempts to raise money in Persia (1 Macc 6:1–4). Learning that Lysias had failed in his attack upon Jerusalem and knowing himself to be near death, Antiochus appointed a new subordinate, Philip, to be regent and guardian over Antiochus V (1 Macc 6:14–15), thus setting up Lysias and Philip as competitors for his throne. Lysias heard of this action and set up young Antiochus V as king under his supervision. Seizing the moment of transition, Judas attacked the citadel built by Antiochus in Jerusalem in 167 (1 Macc 6:18–20; cf. 1:33). Lysias and

Antiochus marched again on Beth-zur, but 1 and 2 Maccabees disagree about the details. According to 1 Macc 6:32–49, Judas left the citadel for Beth-zur, camped opposite it at Beth-zechariah, engaged in battle, but lost when his troops saw the elephants of the Seleucids. According to 2 Macc 13:14–22, there was a previous skirmish at Modein, won by Judas through an attack on the elephants, followed by another victory by Judas at Beth-zur. A Jewish traitor revealed a secret to Lysias, who negotiated again with Beth-zur, presumably from a victorious posture.

One may surmise that the secret was that the city was out of food since the year was a Sabbatical year when no one could plant crops. So both sources ultimately agree that Lysias was victorious at Beth-zur. Next he besieged Jerusalem, which was facing the same food shortage. During the siege Lysias learned that Philip had set himself up as king in Antioch (1 Macc 6:48–56). Lysias made peace quickly with the Jews and took Antiochus back to Antioch, which he captured from Philip. In 161, however, Demetrius I Soter captured the city and had both Lysias and Antiochus V executed (1 Macc 7:1–4).

Bibliography

Harrington, D. J. 1988. *The Maccabean Revolt.* Old Testament Studies 1. Wilmington, DE.

Paul L. Redditt

LYSIMACHUS (PERSON) [Gk *Lysimachos*]. **1.** Lysimachus is reported to have composed the additions to the book of Esther (Add Esth 11:1), where he is identified as the son of Ptolemy and a Jerusalemite.

2. According to 2 Macc 4:39–42, Lysimachus appropriated sacred vessels from the temple after being made deputy by his brother, the high priest Menelaus (2 Macc 4:29). Lysimachus, with the apparent support of his brother Menelaus, armed some 3,000 men and attempted to enter the temple treasury. Inflamed by Lysimachus' sacrilege, the crowd attacked the would-be thieves, and Lysimachus was killed near the treasury. Menelaus was charged for the actions of his brother but he escaped punishment by winning the support of Antiochus IV through a substantial bribe to a confidant of the Seleucid king (2 Macc 4:43–50). Lysimachus, along with his brothers Menelaus the high priest and Simon the chief administrator of the temple, were leaders in the hellenizing party in Jerusalem. Although these three brothers were probably not Tobiads (a major family and political power among the pro-Seleucid hellenizers) they certainly would have been closely allied with these opponents of the Oniads, who favored the Egyptian Ptolemies (Tcherikover 1959: 153–54). The Oniad former high priest, Onias III, was murdered at the instigation of the Tobiad Menelaus (2 Macc 4:34). Josephus confuses the family relationships, making Menelaus (formerly known as Onias) the brother of Onias III and Jason (formerly Jesus), high priest and brother of Onias III (*Ant.* 12.5.1 §239; cf. 2 Macc 4:7–20). Lysimachus does not appear at all. (Josephus' confused account did not make use of 2 Maccabees, which chronicles the machinations of the hellenizers in detail, unlike 1 Maccabees, which Josephus did employ.) The illegitimate transfer of high-priestly power from the Oniads to Menelaus and the misdeeds of the hellenizers, including those of Lysimachus, would have embarrassed the priestly Josephus. Josephus would have sought to gloss over uncomfortable facts, including the attempted robbery of the temple treasury at the hand of the high priest's deputy and probably at his instigation. That Lysimachus' attempted robbery should have incited the crowd to murder indicates not merely the gravity of his offense but the growing outrage of the populace of Jerusalem at the activities of the hellenizers. Funds belonging to religious institutions were deemed inviolate by Hellenistic custom regardless of the religion, and Lysimachus' action was thus improper (Goldstein *II Maccabees* AB, 205). Later rabbinic literature would consider the theft of a sacred vessel a capital offense (*m. Sanh.* 9:6). It would, however, be in error to assume that this injunction was in force in the 2d century B.C.E. The reaction of the crowd to Lysimachus' attempted robbery reflected moral outrage at the behavior of the Hellenists, culminating in a sacrilegious act by the brother and deputy of the high priest.

Bibliography

Tcherikover, V. 1959. *Hellenistic Civilization and the Jews.* Trans. S. Applebaum. New York.

Michael E. Hardwick

LYSTRA (PLACE) [Gk *Lystra*]. A site located at Zoldera near Hatun Saray and lying about 24 miles S of Konya (37°36′N; 32°17′E); it was a moderately important, if somewhat rustic, market town in the relatively backward region of Lycaonia in south-central Turkey. In antiquity, Lycaonia was bounded on the W by Phrygia, by Galatia on the N, Cappadocia to the E, and the Taurus mountains on the S. The most important city in the area, then as now, is Iconium (Konya).

In the years of Roman rule over Asia Minor, Lycaonia owed its importance to its situation on the main road from the west-central coast through the Cilician Gates to the broad plain of Cilicia (Ruge PW 26: 2253–65). Lystra itself was about a day's journey from the main road, at the junction of two other roads which ran N from the northern Isaurian slopes of the Taurus, on the route that was known in antiquity as the *via Sebaste.* The city was a Roman colony, founded by Augustus in 26 B.C., and it was situated on a low hill rising out of the valley (Levick 1967: 51–52). The original settlers of the Augustan colony were veterans of the Roman army; and, despite the fact that they became thoroughly integrated with the local population within a generation or so, Lystra retained some vestiges of its Italian settlement for centuries (the predominance of the native Lycaonian element of the city, however, is illustrated in the story of Paul's visit in the A.D. 40s). One of these Italian features was the use of Latin rather than Greek for public inscriptions and on coin legends. Another was the town's constitution, which retained the traditional civic organization of a Roman colony. The chief magistrates were a pair of officials known as *duumviri,* the town council was referred to as the *ordo decurionum* instead of as the *boule,* as would have been the case in a Greek city, and the Latin word *populus* was used to describe the citizen body. Some

Italian cults came to be celebrated along with those of the native gods.

Augustus' choice of the site for this colony was dictated by military considerations. In the course of the civil wars after the murder of Julius Caesar in 44 B.C., Mark Antony had taken control over the E provinces of the Roman Empire—this by arrangement with Augustus after the defeat of Brutus and Cassius, two of Caesar's assassins, in 42 B.C. In the course of a thorough reorganization of the region, Antony had abolished the great province of Cilicia, of which Lycaonia had been a part, because it had not been economically practical for Rome to continue direct control over an area whose economy was seriously underdeveloped. He placed these areas under the control of various local dynasts who could keep better order than the Romans. Lycaonia had fallen to Amyntas of Galatia, and Augustus left him in power after his victory over Antony in 31 B.C. But when Amyntas died in 26 B.C., Augustus had no choice but to reinstate direct Roman government, and the kingdom of Amyntas became the Roman province of Galatia (Syme 1939: 325–32; cf. Levick 1967: 29–41, 195–97). To safeguard this territory, Augustus established a number of veteran colonies at strategic points. Lystra was the southernmost of these colonies, and its location suggests that Augustus intended it to be a base for the campaigns that his governors would wage against the tribes of the Taurus.

Lystra was founded as a military colony to protect Roman invasion routes into the Taurus and, conversely, to protect the main road in the N from raiders out of the mountains. Since the highlands were never brought completely under Roman control, Lystra probably retained its character as a frontier town throughout its history and, despite its Italian foundation, it became very much a Lycaonian town, rather than a Roman one. The nature of the place is best illustrated by Luke's account of the visit to Lystra that Paul and Barnabas made in the A.D. 40s. After Paul healed a cripple, according to the account in Acts (14:8–18), they were greeted by the local inhabitants who called out to them in Lycaonian. These people identified them as the local gods who, through a form of local syncretism, were identified with the Greek gods Zeus and Hermes. This is of some interest because the local Zeus, Zeus Ampelites, was portrayed on reliefs as an elderly bearded figure, and because he is sometimes depicted with a young male assistant. The identification by the people of Lystra of Barnabas as Zeus and Paul as Hermes "as he was the bringer of the word" suggests that they thought that the two men were functioning in the way that they envisaged their own gods as acting: the bearded Zeus was the initiator of the action and Hermes was his agent in carrying out the action. This further suggests that the people may have thought that Barnabas resembled their Zeus, while Paul resembled his helper. The passage is therefore of considerable importance as evidence for the physical appearance of Paul at this stage in his career, as well as for the nature of life at Lystra in this period (Robert 1987: 383; Lane Fox 1987: 99–100).

There is no description of any event at Lystra in literary works later than the Acts of the Apostles, but it is clear from inscriptions, coin finds, and administrative records that the community retained its urban identity until at least the 11th century. The latest finds are very close in time to the Seljuk conquest, and the toponym Zoldera, which preserves the memory of the name Lystra, suggests that it continued to exist for some time after the establishment of the Turkish kingdom at Iconium (Levick 1967: 183). Records of the church councils also make it clear that Lystra was substantial enough to have a bishop of its own and that its importance was not completely eclipsed by Iconium. The story of Paul's visit may have made it a place of some interest to people living in the Christian empire.

Bibliography

Lane Fox, R. J. 1987. *Pagans and Christians.* New York.

Levick, B. 1967. *Roman Colonies in Southern Asia Minor.* Oxford.

Robert, L. 1987. *Documents de l'Asie Mineure.* Paris.

Syme, R. 1939. Observations on the Province of Cilicia. Pp. 299–332 in *Anatolian Studies Presented to William Hepburn Buckler,* ed. W. M. Calder and J. Keil. Manchester.

D. S. POTTER

M

M. The abbreviation used in NT source criticism for the solely Matthean material found in the Synoptic Gospels. See SYNOPTIC PROBLEM; MATTHEW, GOSPEL OF.

MAʿIN (PLACE). See MEUNIM.

MAACAH (PERSON) [Heb *maʿăkâ*]. **1.** Son/daughter (?) of Nahor (Abraham's brother) and the concubine Reumah (Gen 22:24). Maacah's name appears in the genealogy of Nahor (Gen 22:20–24), where it is fourth and last in the list of Reumah's children (the others were Tebah, Gaham, and Tahash). Maacah is often considered to be the eponymous ancestor of the region S of Mt. Hermon (Josh 13:11; 2 Sam 10:6, 8). See also MAACAH (PLACE).

2. Wife of Machir; mother of Peresh and Sheresh (1 Chr 7:16). Maacah's name occurs twice in the genealogy of Manasseh's descendants found in 1 Chr 7:14–19. She is called first the "sister" (v 15) and then the "wife" (v 16) of Machir. Either there were two Maacahs, one Machir's sister and the other his wife, or more probably, vv 15–16 are textually corrupt, the identification of Maacah as Machir's wife (v 16) being preferred.

3. Concubine of Caleb, the son of Hezron; and mother of Sheber, Tirhanah, Shaaph, and Sheva (1 Chr 2:48–49). Maacah's name appears in the Calebite genealogy found in 1 Chr 2:42–55. She is the second of Caleb's two concubines, Ephah being the first (v 46).

4. Wife of Jeiel, father of Gibeon (1 Chr 8:29; 9:35). An ancestress of Saul, Maacah is named in the Benjaminite genealogy found in 1 Chr 8:29–40 and 1 Chr 9:35–44.

5. Wife of David; mother of Absalom (2 Sam 3:3 = 1 Chr 3:2). Maacah is the third wife/mother mentioned in two lists of David's sons born in Hebron (2 Sam 3:2–5 = 1 Chr 3:1–3). As the daughter of Talmai, king of Geshur, her marriage represented a diplomatic tie between David and Geshur and thus a threat to Ishbaal (Saul's son), who claimed sovereignty over Geshur (2 Sam 2:9). See also ABSALOM; QUEEN.

6. Father of Hanan (1 Chr 11:43). Maacah's name appears in the epithet of his son, who is third in a list of sixteen of David's "mighty men" (1 Chr 11:41b–47). This list is appended to the longer one found in 1 Chr 11:26–41a (= 2 Sam 23:24–39) and is found only in 1 Chronicles.

7. Father of Shephatiah, leader of the Simeonites (1 Chr 27:16). Maacah's name appears in the epithet of his son, who is second in a list of twelve tribal leaders reported living during David's reign (vv 16–22).

8. Father of Achish, king of Gath (1 Kgs 2:39). Maacah's name occurs in the epithet of his son, from whom Shimei's runaway slaves sought asylum during the early reign of Solomon.

9. Favorite wife of Rehoboam, king of Judah (1 Kgs 11:21); and mother (?) of Abijam/Abijah and Asa, both kings of Judah (1 Kgs 15:2, 10, 13; 2 Chr 11:20; 15:16); this Maacah was also the daughter (?) of Abishalom/Absalom. She is one of three mothers of kings accorded the title *gĕbîrâ* in the OT (see also 2 Kgs 10:13; Jer 13:18; 29:2). Asa removed Maacah from her position as queen-mother because she supported the worship of Asherah (1 Kgs 15:13; 2 Chr 15:16).

Maacah's relationship to Abijam/h and Asa is problematic. How can Maacah be the mother of them both when Abijam/h is said to be Asa's father (1 Kgs 15:8 = 2 Chr 13:23 [—Eng 14:1])? Various suggestions attempt to resolve this tension. Either (a) the mothers of Abijam/h and Asa had the same name but were different women; (b) Abijam/h and Asa were brothers, not father and son; or (c) Maacah was Asa's *grand*mother, not his mother. Each of these solutions, however, is speculative and not without its own problems. Understanding Maacah's relationship to Abijam/h is further complicated by 2 Chr 15:2, which states that Micaiah, the daughter of Uriel of Gibeah, was Abijam/h's mother. This contradicts the parallel passage found in 1 Kgs 15:10 and the tradition preserved in 2 Chr 11:20, which identify Maacah as his mother. Either (a) the tradition preserved in 2 Chr 15:2 is correct, and the presence of the name "Maacah" in 1 Kgs 15:10 and 2 Chr 11:20 is secondary; (b) the tradition in 1 Kgs 15:2 and 2 Chr 11:20 is correct and 2 Chr 15:2 represents an exegetical harmonization; or (c) there is no contradiction between the passages: "Micaiah" is simply a variant spelling of "Maacah." Moreover, if one reads "granddaughter" for "daughter," then the two epithets "daughter of Uriel" and "granddaughter of Abishalom" can be viewed as complementary, not contradictory (Uriel being understood as the husband of Tamar, Absalom's daughter).

If Maacah was the daughter/granddaughter of Abishalom/Absalom, the question still remains: Who was he? No place of origin is given for him in the regnal formulas. Was her father/grandfather the son of David, and was Maacah therefore of Davidic lineage? After all, (a) the only other Absalom mentioned in the OT besides Maacah's "father" is this son of David; (b) David's son would be well known and his place of origin unnecessary, and (c) Josephus records that Maacah was the daughter of Tamar and thus the granddaughter of Absalom, David's son (*Ant.* 8.9.1). However, while Absalom is not a common name in the OT, it does not necessarily follow that the two Absaloms are the same person. Moreover, the father's place of origin is missing for all but the last six queen-mothers. Does this mean that all of the other fathers were "well known"? Or does it simply indicate a gap in the writer's sources? Finally, while Josephus does identify the son of David as Maacah's grandfather, another early writer, Jerome *(Qu. Heb.)*, maintains that they are two separate people. See also MICAIAH; QUEEN.

LINDA S. SCHEARING

MAACAH (PLACE) [Heb *maᶜăkâ*]. Var. ARAM-MAACAH. MAACATHITE. A Syrian kingdom S of Mt. Hermon in the N Transjordan. Maacah was located E of the Jordan valley and N of the Yarmuk basin. Together with the kingdom of Geshur, Maacah formed the northern boundary of the (sometimes) Israelite territory of BASHAN, which belonged to the inheritance of the half-tribe of Manasseh in the upper Transjordan (Deut 3:14; Josh 13:11). The city of Abel Beth-Maacah (2 Sam 20:14; cf. *Abil-akka* in the annals of Tiglath-pileser III, KAT 265), where Sheba ben Bichri fled during his revolt against David, was probably located on Israel's northern border with Maacah.

When David began his historic expansion of Israelite power into the Transjordan, he was opposed by the Ammonites, whose capital lay opposite Jerusalem at the headwaters of the Jabbok. The Ammonites were joined in their opposition by several petty Syrian states (2 Sam 10:6–8), including Maacah, which probably had no difficulty in recognizing this threat. David's army, under the command of Joab, was trapped between the Syrians and Ammonites in open country. Joab, however, escaped disaster by dividing his forces into two wings, one under the command of Abishai, his brother, the other under himself, and attacking both sides simultaneously. When the Ammonites saw their Syrian allies driven back, they retreated into their stronghold, to which Joab then laid siege. According to 1 Chr 19:6–7, this battle took place before Medeba on the plateau N of the Wadi Mujib (the biblical Arnon) in the central Transjordan. The Ammonites are said to have "hired" the army of Maacah, along with other Syrian elements (in extremely exaggerated numbers) from as far away as Mesopotamia.

D. G. SCHLEY

MAADAI (PERSON) [Heb *maᶜăday*]. A descendant of Bani and one of the returned exiles who was required by Ezra to divorce his foreign wife (Ezra 10:34; 1 Esdr 9:34). According to Noth, the name Maadai is a short form of *maᶜadyâ,* whose meaning is unclear (*IPN,* 150). In the parallel text of 1 Esdr 9:34, the RSV lists Maadai among the descendants of Bani; however, the LXX reads *momdios,* and there is very limited correspondence between Ezra's list of Bani's descendants and that found in 1 Esdras. Maadai was a member of a family that returned from Babylon with Zerubbabel (Ezra 2:10; note that Binnui replaces Bani in Nehemiah's list [7:15]). For further discussion, see BEDEIAH.

JEFFREY A. FAGER

MAADIAH (PERSON) [Heb *maᶜadyâ*]. Var. MOADIAH. A priest who is listed in Neh 12:5 (MT) as having returned from exile to Jerusalem in the days of Zerubbabel. Later in the same chapter (v 17, MT), a certain Moadiah (Heb *môᶜadyâ*) is listed as the father of Piltai, the head of a priestly family. Inasmuch as even a quick overview will confirm the close correspondence between the names found in these two lists (i.e., vv 1–7 and 12–21), it is virtually certain that "Maadiah" and "Moadiah" represent two variant spellings of the name of the same individual (see, e.g., Bowman *IB* 3: 785, 788, who prefers the former as textually better attested). For the absence of Maadiah/Moadiah in the major LXX mss (as well as those of a majority of the other priestly households), see AMOK.

Recently Williamson (*Ezra, Nehemiah* WBC, 358–61) has argued persuasively for the relative primacy of the list of priestly families found in vv 12–21, from which a later editor has transcribed the list found in vv 1–7. As Williamson points out, it is less likely that someone invented the names of the added generation in vv 12–21, names which are not paralleled elsewhere, than that the names of the family heads were merely transferred from this list to the one found in vv 1–7. This reconstruction would tend to support the primacy of the spelling "Moadiah" (v 17) over "Maadiah" (v 5), a conclusion which, however, may be called into question on text-critical grounds. In particular, the secondary omission of a name after Miniamin (v 17b, MT) has apparently led to further textual disruption in the Versions. Such disruption, for example, is reflected in the reading *en kairois* attested in Codex Sinaiticus (supplied by a later hand inasmuch as there was a major lacuna, as noted above, in the major Greek witnesses); this reading probably presupposes the Heb *lĕmôᶜădêhā,* "at that time, in those days," for the MT *lĕmôᶜadyâ,* "of/to Moadiah." These two variants thus represent two possible vocalizations of the same consonantal text *(lmwᶜdyh),* with the former vocalization quite possibly the more original of the two (once a name dropped out after Miniamin, a scribe would not have expected two names in a row referring to the former generation). In any case, it is easier to explain an addition of the *waw* in v 17 (arising from prior textual corruption) than its deletion in v 5.

A third list of priests found in Neh 10:3–9—Eng 10:2–8—also evidences quite a number of similarities with the two lists of priests already cited from Nehemiah 12 (again, see AMOK). It is noteworthy that in Neh 10:9—Eng v 8—we read "Maaziah" (Heb *maᶜazyâ*), a relatively familiar priestly name, for the expected Maadiah/Moadiah (cf. Bowman *IB* 3: 785). Inasmuch as the list of priests in chap. 10 probably gathers its names from a variety of sources (Williamson *Ezra, Nehemiah* WBC, 362, cf. also pp. 325–31), not too much should be made of the apparent Maaziah/Maadiah correspondence, although such a correspondence does dovetail nicely with the other evidence favoring the spelling "Maadiah" (over "Moadiah") as the more accurate transcription of the priestly name found in Nehemiah 12.

WILLIAM H. BARNES

MAAI (PERSON) [Heb *māʿay*]. A kinsman of Zechariah and a musician who performed at the dedication of the Jerusalem wall (Neh 12:36). At the ceremony, he was part of the group which paraded to the right behind Ezra. His name is omitted in the LXX.

NORA A. WILLIAMS

MAARATH (PLACE) [Heb *maʿărāt*]. A town situated in the north-central hill country of Judah (Josh 15:59), within the same district as Beth-Zur. This settlement, whose name perhaps means "barren place" (from *ʿrh*, "lay bare"), is listed among the towns within the tribal allotment of Judah (Josh 15:21–62). It is perhaps the same place as Maroth (Mic 1:12). A very tentative identification (*IDB* 3: 196) places the ancient town at Khirbet Qufin, located approximately 11 km N of Hebron, just to the NE of modern Beit Ummar (M.R. 160114).

WADE R. KOTTER

MAASAI (PERSON) [Heb *maʿśay*]. One of the priests who, according to 1 Chr 9:12, was among the first to return from Babylonian exile and take residency in Jerusalem. There are two major points of confusion in this text, however. First, the sequence of names in 9:10–12 is itself confusing. The MT as it stands lists six such priests: Jedaiah, Jehoiarib, Jachin, Azariah, Adaiah, and Maasai, with only the last three being attributed genealogical information. The absence of such information for the first three has often led scholars to assume that the text or tradition has suffered in transmission, and that some of those first named were originally part of such genealogical information. In fact, Neh 11:10–14 preserves the list as only five: Jedaiah, Jachin, Seraiah, Adaiah, and Amashsai. It is generally assumed that the text of 1 Chronicles 9 is, in some way, dependent upon that of Nehemiah 11.

Second, although the names in the two lists are sufficiently close to assure a common tradition, there is considerable confusion in the specific details. Maasai in 1 Chr 9:12 corresponds to the Amashsai of Neh 11:13. This confusion, due to metathesis of the *mem* and *ʿayin*, leads to two different root-derivations of the name. The name Maasai means "work of Yahweh" and is attested in both the shorter form, as here, as well as in the longer form Maasyah(u). The name Amashsai, however, is more difficult. It seems to be a conflation of two forms of the same name, Amashai and Amasai. Both names mean "Yahweh has borne."

The identification of Maasai in 1 Chr 9:12 with Amashai in Neh 11:13 is supported by the similarities in their respective genealogies. Both are traced back through Adiel/Azarel, Jahzerah/Ahzai, and Meshillemith/Meshillemoth to Immer who, according to 1 Chr 24:14, held the sixteenth priestly course in the Davidic temple.

RODNEY R. HUTTON

MAASEIAH (PERSON) [Heb *maʿăśēyāh; maʿăśēyāhû*]. Var. BAALSAMUS; MOOSSIAS. A rather common Hebrew name attested both in the Bible and in a number of seals. In the Bible the name appears in the books of Jeremiah, Ezekiel, Nehemiah, and Chronicles, suggesting that it was especially common in the exilic period. Possible Hebrew variants of the name include Maasai (*maʿśay*, 1 Chr 9:12) and Baaseiah (*baʿăśēyâ*, 1 Chr 6:25—Eng 6:40).

1. One of the levitical musicians listed in the Chronicler's account of David's preparations for moving the ark (1 Chr 15:18, 20). Maaseiah was a lyre *(nēbel)* player and a member of the "second order" of Levites in charge of the music.

2. One of the military commanders ("commander of a hundred") who made a covenant with Jehoiada the priest in the palace coup that toppled Athaliah and replaced her with Josiah (2 Chr 23:1). This Maaseiah is called the son of Adaiah.

3. The officer *(šôṭēr)* who, according to 2 Chr 26:11, helped to prepare the divisions of Uzziah's army in the Chronicler's extensive account of Uzziah's prosperity and military might. LXX^B has the name Amaziah *(amasaiou)* here instead of Maaseiah.

4. The son of King Ahaz of Judah who was assassinated by a certain Ephraimite named Zichri, according to 2 Chr 28:7. The Chronicler gives this notice in the context of the account of Pekah's slaughter of Ahaz's warriors, which is explained as punishment for Ahaz's sins.

5. The commander *(śar)* of Jerusalem during the reign of Josiah (2 Chr 34:8). Maaseiah was a member of the party sent by Josiah specifically to repair the temple in the Chronicler's account of the king's reform.

6. The father of the prophet Zedekiah (Jer 29:21) whom Jeremiah accused of false prophecy in the context of his attack on prophets in 29:15, 21–23. The designation "son of Maaseiah" is lacking in the LXX version of the verse.

7. The father of Zephaniah the priest, according to Jer 21:1; 29:25; 37:3. Zephaniah was twice (21:1; 37:3) part of an envoy from King Zedekiah to Jeremiah inquiring about the safety of Jerusalem in view of the movements of the Babylonian and Egyptian armies. These visits afforded Jeremiah the opportunity to predict the fall of Jerusalem to Babylon. In 29:25 Zephaniah is the recipient of a letter from a certain Shemaiah, a prophet in Babylonian exile, upbraiding him for failing to control Jeremiah. This suggests both that the position held by Zephaniah was important (cf. Jer 52:24) and that the temple precincts were the location of much of Jeremiah's prophetic activity.

8. A doorkeeper of the temple in Jeremiah's day. Maaseiah is mentioned in Jer 35:4 in the context of the example of the obedient Rechabites and may be the same Maaseiah, father of Zephaniah, treated in #7.

9. The father of Azariah, a leader of the delegation which approached Jeremiah on behalf of the people asking him to intercede before God for them, according to LXX Jer 49:1. The MT version of the verse (42:1) reads "Jezaniah son of Hoshaiah" (cf. 40:8) instead of "Azariah son of Maaseiah." The LXX reading is probably correct at least as far as the occurrence of the name "Azariah," since 43:2 (= LXX 50:2) refers to Azariah in the company of those who were present when Jeremiah finished his oracle to the delegation.

10. One of the men of the tribe of Judah listed among the postexilic residents of Jerusalem in Neh 11:5. Maaseiah is called a Shelanite (amending MT's "Shilonite," which is corrupt). The Shelanites were the branch of the tribe of Judah which claimed descent from the patriarch's son Shelah (Gen 46:12; Num 26:19–20). The parallel list in 1 Chr 9:5 has the name Asaiah (*ʿăśāyâ)* instead of Maaseiah.

11. An ancestor of the only Benjaminite, Sallu, listed in Neh 11:7 among the postexilic residents of Jerusalem. Maaseiah is lacking in the parallel list in 1 Chr 9:7–8. The Benjaminite origin of the list is suspect since the names in it do not occur in other lists of Benjaminites (Gen 46:21; Num 26:38–41; 1 Chr 7:6–12; 8:1–40).

12. A priest at the time of Ezra who is mentioned among those who had foreign wives in Ezra 10:18 (= 1 Esdr 9:19). He was from the family of Jeshua, the high priest.

13. The same list from Ezra 10 also includes another priest named Maaseiah who had a foreign wife (Ezra 10:21 = 1 Esdr 9:21). In Ezra 10:21 he is called a descendant of Harim, while in 1 Esdr 9:21 he is a descendant of Immer, Harim not being mentioned.

14. A third priest in the list of those with foreign wives in Ezra's day. He is called a descendant of Pashhur in Ezra 10:22 = 1 Esdr 9:22.

15. One of the laymen ("of Israel") in the list of those with foreign wives (Ezra 10:30). He is listed as a descendant of Pahath-moab. In the parallel list in 1 Esdr 9:31 the name Moossias (Gk *moossias*) son of Addi occurs instead of Maaseiah.

16. The father of a certain Azariah, named among those who helped to repair the wall of Jerusalem (Neh 3:23). The corresponding LXX^{B} text (2 Esdr 13:23) has Madasel *(madasēl)* instead of Maaseiah. The list itself has probably been added to from the Nehemiah Memoirs (Blenkinsopp *Ezra-Nehemiah* OTL, 231).

17. One of the "chiefs of the people" *(roʾšê hāʿām)* in Neh 10:26—Eng 10:25—who affixed his seal to the covenant promulgated by Ezra. The list of those accepting the covenant is composite and widely agreed to be out of place. Indeed, the list precedes the covenant stipulations in vv 29–40—Eng vv 28–39—rather than following them as one would expect. Some of the entries in the list are tribal names rather than personal names (Williamson *Ezra, Nehemiah* WBC, 325–31). But this is not the case with Maaseiah. He may be the same individual discussed in #15 above or #18 below, since they were also laymen.

18. One of thirteen men who stood on either side of Ezra when he read the law to the people (Neh 8:4). These thirteen were apparently lay leaders who may have assisted somehow in the reading process. In the parallel to this verse (1 Esdr 9:43) the name Baalsamus (Gk *baalsamos*) is found in place of Maaseiah.

19. One of thirteen Levites mentioned in Neh 8:7 who assisted the people in understanding the law and who, according to 8:8, read the law clearly. Blenkinsopp (*Ezra-Nehemiah* OTL, 286–89) posits that vv 7–8 are part of a later strand of this account which incorporated the Levites within the episode, perhaps as a balance to the thirteen laymen mentioned in v 4 (see #18 above). The parallel to Neh 8:7 in 1 Esdr 9:48 has the name Maiannas (Gk *maiannas*) instead of Maaseiah (the RSV, however, reads Maaseiah).

20. One of seven priests with trumpets who participated with Nehemiah (Neh 12:41) in the dedication of the walls of Jerusalem. These seven priests are actually part of a chorus of sixteen, whose names are listed in 12:41–42. The names and activities of this chorus balance with those of an earlier chorus, listed in 12:32–36. The two choruses conducted simultaneous processions in the dedication ceremonies (see Blenkinsopp *Ezra-Nehemiah* OTL, 345). Both lists of names (vv 32–36 and vv 41–42) are probably insertions into Nehemiah's Memoirs (cf. Williamson *Ezra, Nehemiah* WBC, 369–70). The references to Ezra in vv 32 and 36 are likely glosses on the list of names. Hence, the passage cannot be used to argue for the contemporaneity of Ezra and Nehemiah. The Maaseiah in v 41 could be identified with #12, 13, or 14 above.

21. Another priest mentioned among the participants in the dedication ceremonies recounted in Neh 12:42 (see no. 20). This priest could also be identified with one of the Maaseiahs described above (#12, 13, or 14).

STEVEN L. MCKENZIE

MAASMAS (PERSON) [Gk *Maasmas*]. One of the leaders in the exilic community (1 Esdr 8:43). The RSV rendering Maasmas is from Codex Alexandrinus and Codex Vaticanus; the name appears as *semeia* in the Lucianic text. Furthermore, while Maasmas is not named in the parallel list in Ezra (8:16), Shemaiah (LXX *samaia*) is found in its place.

When Ezra learns that none of the sons of priests or of the Levites is among those who assembled at the river of Theras to return to Jerusalem, he sends ten leaders, including Maasmas, to Iddo to obtain the required number of priests and Levites.

JIN HEE HAN

MAATH (PERSON) [Gk *Maath*]. The father of Naggai and son of Mattathias, according to Luke's genealogy tying Joseph, the "supposed father" of Jesus, to descent from Adam and God (Luke 3:26). D omits Maath, substituting a genealogy adapted from Matt 1:6–15 for Luke 3:23–31. The name Maath falls within a list of seventeen ancestors of Jesus who are otherwise unknown in the biblical documents, including Matthew's genealogy (Fitzmyer *Luke I–IX* AB, 500), although Marshall (*Luke* NIGTC, 163) believes that Maath is equivalent to Heb *maḥat* (1 Chr 6:20—Eng 6:35 [LXX has *meth* in Rahlf's edition]; 2 Chr 29:12; 31:13 [both with *maath* in Rahlf's edition]). Kuhn (1923: 210–11) claims that in the original form of the genealogy Maath was not a name but a transliteration of Heb *mēʾēt,* "from," used as a sign of genealogical relation to link Naggia with Mattathias. He sees an analogous parallel with Menna (Luke 3:31), from Aramaic *minēh,* also meaning "from." Thus, according to Kuhn, the seemingly parallel lists of Luke 3:23–26 (Jesus to Mattathias) and Luke 3:29–31 (Joshua/Jesus to Mattatha) stem from the same original source, the first possibly preserved in a Hebrew context and the second in an Aramaic one. Kuhn's solution has not been accepted by commentators, although it is difficult to account for the significance of Maath's inclusion in the genealogy, since most theological explanations are improbable. For example, it has been suggested (e.g., Schürmann *Luke* HTKNT, 202–3) that Luke's genealogy consists of 11 times 7 names from Adam to Jesus, with the 12th period the messianic age. Thus Maath to Joseph would mark the 10th group, and Maath the initial name for the period. But this scheme is not clear from Luke's text (see Johnson 1969: 231–33).

Bibliography

Johnson, M. D. 1969. *The Purpose of the Biblical Genealogies.* SNTSMS 8. Cambridge.

Kuhn, G. 1923. Die Geschlechtsregister Jesu bei Lukas und Matthäus, nach ihrer Herkunft untersucht. *ZNW* 22: 206–28.

STANLEY E. PORTER

MAAZ (PERSON) [Heb *maʿaṣ*]. Eldest son of Ram, who in turn was the firstborn of Jerahmeel, the progenitor of an important clan of Judah. Maaz is noted once in the Chronicler's genealogies (1 Chr 2:27) and is a descendant from Jerahmeel's first wife. With his brothers, Jamin and Eker, this very brief genealogical record is concluded. The descendants of Atarah, another wife of Jerahmeel, are extensive.

Williamson (1979: 352) summarizes recent source criticism of the Chronicler's genealogies, concluding that 2:25–33 (of which Maaz is a part) and 42–50a form a related unit comprising an independent source used by the Chronicler and probably already containing the distinctive parallel opening and closing formulas. Elmslie (*Chronicles* CBC, 15) suggests that names such as Maaz may not reflect either specific individuals or places but rather preserve the idea that these formerly nomadic families now enjoyed a more settled life. More recent scholarship favors viewing all names in this genealogy as personal (Braun *1 Chronicles* WBC, 45).

The location of Maaz in a specific time period is difficult. Commentators maintaining the completeness of these genealogical records place Maaz somewhere near the middle of the period of the Egyptian sojourn; others, however, favoring the significance of the final line recorded (such as Maaz and his brothers), locate these men closer to the Chronicler's own day. Maaz is probably derived from the verb *mʿṣ* meaning "to be wrathful," and thus is often rendered "angry."

Bibliography

Williamson, H. G. M. 1979. Sources and Redaction in the Chronicler's Genealogy of Judah. *JBL* 98: 351–59.

W. P. STEEGER

MAAZIAH (PERSON) [Heb *maʿazyāhû*]. The name of the last of the twenty-four priestly courses or divisions listed in 1 Chronicles 24 (v 18), meaning "God is a refuge" or "stronghold" (*IPN,* 250; *IDB* 3: 197). It appears again as the name of a priestly family that served as a signatory to the covenant of Ezra, in what may well be an earlier listing preserved in Nehemiah 10 (v 8). One scholar conjectures that the name has been replaced in Neh 12:5 and 17 by the names Maadiah and Modiah (Brockington *Ezra, Nehemiah and Esther* Century Bible, 179), but there is no solid evidence to confirm this suspicion.

FREDERICK W. SCHMIDT

MACCABEAN REVOLT. The name commonly given to the revolt of Jews in Judea against Seleucid domination in the years 166–160 B.C.E. It is named after the surname of its leader, JUDAS MACCABEUS. It is also called the Hasmonean revolt, after the name of the family to which Judas, his father, and his brothers belonged. The duration of the revolt is sometimes considered to extend to the year 142 B.C.E., when Judea became independent. Yet here I will adopt the more narrow definition (166–160 B.C.E.). For the subsequent period, see JONATHAN and SIMON (PERSON) #5.

A. Sources
B. Course of Events
C. Causes
D. Military Aspects of the Revolt
E. The Revolt in Historical Perspective

A. Sources

The sources for the revolt pose various problems of interpretation and reliability. The principal sources are the books 1 Maccabees and 2 Maccabees. The first covers a short period preceding Antiochus' persecution, the persecution itself, the revolt, and the activity of Judas' brothers, Jonathan and Simon (roughly 169–139 B.C.E.). The author was an admirer of the Hasmoneans, and the book reflects the situation at the time of John Hyrcanus I. It probably embodies firsthand data either of the author himself or from eyewitnesses. The author also had access to some important documents.

The book of 2 Maccabees covers about 15 years before the persecution, the persecution itself, and the revolt up to the last victory of Judas Maccabeus at Adasa (161 B.C.E.) with which the book concludes. It is of a very different literary genre than 1 Maccabees, being an *epitome* (abridgment) in Greek of a lost book written by Jason of Cyrene. It concentrates on the temple, on miracles and piety, and on the didactic lesson to be drawn from the events. Judas is the hero of the book, which concludes with his last victory, not with his defeat and death soon afterward (160 B.C.E.). Nevertheless, 2 Maccabees serves as an important check on the 1 Maccabees account and is the sole source for the period of the Hellenizing movement (about 185–166 B.C.E.); and for some important documents (esp. chap. 11).

To these two principal sources we should add the book of Daniel, which is a contemporaneous apocalyptic work, and as such helps us to gauge the religious and political mood of that period.

Among the additional sources of secondary importance are Josephus' *Ant.* and *War,* which basically follow 1 Maccabees with some differences of doubtful value, and with a very important added document—the correspondence of the Samaritans and Antiochus Epiphanes (*Ant.* 12 §§258–64). Also of secondary importance are a propagandistic story preserved by Diodorus Siculus (books 34–35, 1.3–4), (probably) an apocalypse preserved in the *Book of Enoch,* and some Talmudic passages.

B. Course of Events

A concise summary of events leading to the Maccabean revolt must be given here in order to clarify its causes and the role of participants. About 200 B.C.E., after a century of Ptolemaic rule, Palestine fell into the hands of the Seleucids. Less than a decade later a most decisive event in the history of the Seleucid kingdom took place: Antiochus III (the Great) was defeated by Rome (battle of Magnesia, 190 B.C.E.). This defeat caused a considerable deterioration of both the Seleucids' international position and their internal affairs.

At the time of King Seleucus IV, son of Antiochus III, internal strife in Judea reached an unprecedented stage of violence. A coalition of nobles, which included members of the priestly tribe *(Mishmar)* of Bilga and of the house of Tobiah, strove to take away from the high priest Onias III some of his functions, or at least one of them because of its financial importance—the *Agoranomia* (supervision of the market). In the ensuing struggle not only was violence used, but the opponents of Onias III, headed by one Simon of the tribe of Bilga, called for the interference of the Seleucid government. Seleucus IV sent Heliodorus, his chief minister *(ho epi tōn pragmatōn),* to look into the finances of the temple and to confiscate whatever he might find necessary. For unknown reasons Heliodorus failed in his mission, but the internal strife continued and Onias felt compelled to go to Antioch to defend his position before the king.

Hardly had Onias arrived at Antioch, but Seleucus IV was murdered, and his brother, ANTIOCHUS IV, came to the throne (175 B.C.E.). Antiochus kept Onias in the capital and appointed in his stead his brother Jason *(Yoshua)* in return for a larger amount of money. Three years later Jason was replaced by Menelaus, a brother of Simon (the opponent of Onias III) of the priestly tribe of Bilga (172 B.C.E.).

In the course of these three years, two developments can be noticed. First was the usurpation of the high priesthood, which was transferred in contradiction to Jewish law from a high priest who was still alive and able to serve, to his brother and then to someone of a priestly line who had no right to the office. Second, a laxity toward Jewish law and practice is noticed under Jason and, even more, under Menelaus. This stronger Hellenization, or "Hellenistic reform" as it is called, stirred up opposition among the Jewish population. Violent confrontation even occurred between Menelaus' supporters, under his brother Lysimachus, and his opponents (2 Macc 4:29, 39–42). Already under Jason, Jerusalem was transformed into a Hellenistic city-state (2 Macc 4:9). It controlled the territory of Judea and was named after the king "Antioch in Jerusalem."

Antiochus' policy toward Ptolemaic Egypt also influenced the situation in Judea. Internal problems, combined with aggressive policy in the Alexandrian court, provoked Antiochus to invade Egypt, to try to settle affairs there according to his own interests, and later to crown himself king over Egypt. He went on two expeditions to Egypt and twice entered Jerusalem on his way back. On his second invasion to Egypt he was expelled by Roman order and took military measures against Jerusalem, which was occupied by enemies of Menelaus (who were probably anti-Seleucid).

Shortly afterward, Jerusalem was again taken by force, and a general persecution of the Jewish religion was ordered by the king. Cruel measures against Jewish Law were enforced in Judea. The study of the Law (Torah), observance of the Sabbath, and circumcision were forbidden. The daily sacrifice in the temple was canceled, and the altar was desecrated.

The Jewish population reacted in three ways to these measures: some reluctantly acquiesced; some preferred martyrdom rather than obey the king's orders; and some resorted to armed resistance. Among those who resorted to arms were Mattathias and his sons. When Mattathias killed the officer who came to his village, Modin, to force pagan rites on the inhabitants, a guerrilla warfare began (about 166 B.C.E.). Shortly afterward Mattathias died and the leadership of the rebels was given to his son Judas.

The Maccabean revolt is the armed resistance of this part of the Jewish nation, which was attached to its ancestral traditions and which fought against those who tried to impose the abandonment of the Torah and the adoption of pagan religion. Three main forces were involved in the resulting war: (1) the rebels under Mattathias and Judas, (2) the Seleucid military forces, and (3) the Hellenizers, i.e., Jews who supported the policy of annulment of Jewish religion. The Hellenizers were composed of an important part of the nobility, which had for some decades already adopted Greek manners and practices, including philosophical and religious concepts.

We know very little about Mattathias' fighting. His supporters were based outside the inhabited area and used guerrilla tactics, mainly attacking various places by surprise and reinforcing Jewish practices, especially circumcision. His main target was the Hellenizers as he tried to reverse the effects of the decrees that had been enforced on the people.

When Judas succeeded his father Mattathias, the course of events was changed. The increasing activity of the rebels now required the intervention of the Seleucid forces. From local skirmishes the war turned into a full-scale campaign. The first known battle the Jewish rebels fought was against Apollonius, who was probably governor of Samaria. We do not know why the governor of Judea did not himself take the field against Judas when the latter's activity grew more threatening to the Seleucid authorities. Probably he was either preoccupied and his forces were dispersed over the country, or he was shut in Jerusalem, or he simply needed reinforcements, which were recruited from neighboring Samaria. Be that as it may, Judas defeated Apollonius, probably by surprise, and by attacking his person he might have demoralized his forces already at an early stage of the battle.

Apollonius' defeat brought into the battlefield another commander: Seron. His precise place in the Seleucid military forces in Coele-Syria and Phoenicia is not clear. It looks as if Judas' forces were considered by Seron to be easy prey. Seron's overconfidence gave Judas and his highly motivated troops the opportunity once again to use surprise, and so to choose favorable terrain (Beth-horon) for battle and thus to defeat the enemy.

These two consecutive victories made Judas a real threat to Seleucid rule, and consequently a considerable army was sent against him by order of the king (1 Macc 3:27). The expedition was organized by Lysias, guardian of the king's son, who was in charge of the W part of the Seleucid empire, because Antiochus himself had gone E in an effort to reestablish Seleucid authority in Persia. Lysias entrusted the expedition to Ptolemy the son of Dorymenes, governor of Coele-Syria and Phoenicia, who appointed Nicanor son of Patroclus and Gorgias in charge of the army (2 Macc 8:9). It seems that Gorgias was the acting commander (1 Macc 4:1, 28).

The following details about the Seleucid command of this expedition follow the account in 2 Maccabees, which is preferable for historical information about the Seleucid activities to 1 Maccabees, which is much richer and more dependable for the battle of Emmaus itself. It should be mentioned that this is the first battle treated in 2 Maccabees that ignores Mattathias' role in the earlier stages of the revolt as well as Judas' victories over Apollonius and Seron, though 2 Maccabees gives a vivid description of the guerrilla warfare under Judas' (not Mattathias') command at the inception of the revolt (2 Macc 5:1–7).

The battle itself is a most important one in the course of the revolt and serves as an example of Judas' generalship. The Seleucid army encamped in Emmaus at the W entrance to the Judean hill country. From Emmaus an elite corps was sent to chase Judas in the mountains. We can detect here a battle plan of considerable sophistication, based on conclusions drawn from the former defeats of Seleucid forces at the hands of Judas. First, Gorgias did not invade Judea from the N, as was done by Apollonius and Seron, but preferred the western, less dangerous entrances. Second, Gorgias did not immediately enter the mountainous region, but prepared a base at a near but safe strategic location (Emmaus; see *MBA,* p. 119) and from there tried to infiltrate Judea. Third, by these tactics Gorgias did not permit Judas to choose the battlefield or to set an ambush for the invading army. He took the initiative and thereby achieved an initial advantage over the guerrillas.

Against this attack Judas showed his military skill at its best and got the upper hand in the face of an able Seleucid commander. On obtaining information about Gorgias' column, which entered the mountains to chase him down, Judas pretended to flee in panic with his followers. But he took his force at night in a flanking movement toward the Syrian camp at Emmaus and surprised it at dawn, taking advantage of the sun shining at the back of his men and in the faces of the astonished Syrian soldiers. Defeating the Seleucid garrison and burning down its camp, he halted his troops from plundering the spoils and put them into battle order to face the returning Seleucid column, which was frustrated by chasing him in vain all night.

These fatigued Syrian soldiers were not prepared for battle, and hence withdrew. Judas had won his most important victory. He was successful in repulsing not local second-rate troops under second-rate command, but a full-scale army led by a professional commander. He used a variety of means to overcome the enemy: efficient intelligence services, rapid mobility, motivation, discipline, and daring and imaginative leadership.

After Emmaus the Maccabean revolt became a major concern of the Seleucid government. Lysias felt obliged to take the field personally against the Jewish rebels (164 B.C.E.). He approached Judea from the S, through Idumea. Probably he considered this to be the safest way, since the S border passed near Jerusalem, where the garrison and the Hellenizers were hard-pressed by the rebels.

Getting to Jerusalem had also been the aim of the former Syrian expeditions, and it reflects the general military situation in the country. In the territory of Judea the rebels had the upper hand and were supported by the population. They concentrated their pressure now on the garrison at Jerusalem and on the Hellenizers, i.e., the citizen body of the *polis* Antiochus in Jerusalem, which was composed, more or less, of the Jewish aristocracy inclined toward Hellenism. The military expeditions mentioned above sought to relieve Antioch in Jerusalem from this pressure. They tried to pass across Judea to Jerusalem, but Judas was successful in stopping them either on their way (Apollonius and Seron) or at the entrance (Gorgias).

Lysias repeated this same effort, this time from the S. A battle took place at Beth-zur, and Lysias' army was repulsed by the rebels. The scarcity of information about this battle makes a worthwhile discussion about the tactics of the contenders impossible. What seems clear, however, is that the numbers assigned to Lysias' army, both in 1 Macc 4:28 (65,000) and in 2 Macc 11:2, 4 (more than 80,000) are not credible. The sizes of the Seleucid armies must have been less than this (1–2 Maccabees tend to give exaggerated numbers for the Seleucid armies so as to demonstrate the greatness of Judas' victories and of God's help to his people). It seems reasonable to assume that the opposing armies were more equal in military terms than our sources tend to admit. The Jewish potential was considerable and could reach about 20,000 fighters or more, whereas the Seleucid could not afford to send too many soldiers to Judea, considering the total size of the Seleucid army and its involvement at that time on the E front. At the early stages of the war they may have used mainly local troops and militia, and even later the regular army was numerically limited.

Lysias' failure to break through Judea and his consequent withdrawal opened the way for the rebels to regain the temple in Jerusalem (1 Macc 4:36–54). They took over the temple and its precincts, purified it, and renewed the worship. Their enemies were shut in the Akra citadel. One of the most repressive measures of the persecution was undone when the temple was rededicated, and a special holiday—Hanukkah—was declared to commemorate the event.

At this stage 1 Maccabees 5 introduces a series of battles outside Judea, in which Judas and his brother Simon went to rescue their Jewish brethren in Galilee and Transjordan, and also fought inimical neighbors. 2 Maccabees 12 puts these battles after the second expedition of Lysias, but this is the only expedition of Lysias mentioned in the narrative. It is probable that in both books the various battles have been grouped together thematically rather than chronologically.

Be that as it may, these battles show that the events in Judea had repercussions throughout Palestine. Conflicts of interests might have been acute between the Hellenistic *poleis* and the native population, including Jews. It is possible that the anti-Jewish policy of the Seleucid government also triggered ethnic conflicts between Jews and non-Jews. In any case, those events make it clear that the problems relevant to the persecution and to the Maccabean revolt were not confined to Judea alone, but to Palestine at large. In a way the battles of Judas and Simon in Galilee, Transjordan, Idumea, and the seacoast are precursors of the Hasmonean conquest in the decades to come.

The battles in Galilee were mainly against the *poleis* of Acco, Tyre, and Sidon, which attacked the Galilean Jews. In Transjordan they were against certain local commanders and various places where Jews were attacked. War also broke out in Joppa and Jabneh and on the Idumean boundary. We cannot enter into details here, but first it should be stressed that the Maccabees rescued Jews who were threatened, but did not occupy those territories. The most they did was to remove some of those people to Jerusalem for security. Second, those Maccabean forces under Judas and under Simon covered impressive distances on these expeditions, which indicates some degree of military proficiency. And third, we may wonder if those exploits would have been feasible had not the rebels enjoyed some sympathy among the local, native population, which had good reasons to hate the Hellenistic *poleis* and the Seleucid hegemony, and to support the rebellious Jews.

Without fixing too rigidly the chronology of these battles we come now to the second expedition of Lysias. This came about because of the pressure Judas continued to exert on the Akra after the rededication of the temple. The rededication of the temple was not the only achievement of the rebels. After Lysias' withdrawal, negotiations took place between the government and the Jews, and an annulment of the persecution was announced in the name of Antiochus IV (2 Macc 11:16–21, 27–33). Nevertheless, Judas and his supporters were not satisfied with these achievements. The Seleucid government had not recognized the rebels, had not removed Menelaus, and had not returned the temple to priests who were acceptable to the rebels.

Not satisfied with the bare annulment of the persecution and with being ignored by the government in favor of Menelaus, Judas (who had already taken the temple by force) now attacked the Akra. Under these circumstances Lysias and his young protégé (who, after the death of Antiochus IV in Persia at the end of 164, now became King Antiochus V) did not have much choice. They were obliged to come to the rescue of their own garrison and of the Hellenizers. A considerable army was assembled and Lysias, who took the king with him, led it to Judea. They again invaded Judea from the S and overcame the heroic Jewish opposition (1 Macc 6:31, 42–47). They took Beth-zur and at the battle of Bet-zachariah forced Judas to retreat. Then they came to Jerusalem and besieged Judas in the temple. It looked as if the war had been decided in favor of the Syrians.

But at this juncture Lysias was informed that a former general of Antiochus IV, Philip, had arrived from the E and claimed the regency (i.e., the guardianship of Antiochus V). He was forced to raise the siege and to rush back to Syria. So he came to an agreement with Judas and withdrew from Jerusalem. Some details of this agreement are known to us from another document, also preserved in 2 Macc 11:23–26. In this document Judas is not mentioned, but, in addition to the abolition of the persecution, which was already canceled by Antiochus IV, the temple was now given back to the Jews, an item which was missing from the former document of Antiochus IV. Of course, the temple had been taken and purified formerly by Judas, but this was a formal recognition of this fact.

This document was a decisive step by which Lysias tried to change the former policy of Antiochus IV, and he probably thought it feasible to return to the status quo ante in Judea. It seems that already on his first expedition Lysias was in favor of a more conciliatory policy toward the rebellious Jews. He was not the only Seleucid official who was against the policy of Antiochus IV toward the Jews and their religion (see Ptolemy Macron, in 2 Macc 10:12) and he was not perforce motivated by moral or ideological considerations. He might have thought pragmatically that support of the Hellenizers was unwise, since they proved themselves unable to keep peace and order and to provide support for the government, but were themselves in constant need of help. In other words, instead of being an asset they had become a burden. Lysias' attitude is clear in light of the fact that he executed Menelaus, who was "the cause of all the trouble" (2 Macc 13:4). The importance and the wide impact Lysias' decision had in the country is shown by the criticism of the citizens of Ptolemais and by the effort made by Lysias to explain his policy to them (2 Macc 12:25–26).

Had events gone otherwise, the revolt might have been ended at this stage. The conflict continued because the revolt changed the situation in Jewish society in Judea, as new social forces entered the arena, and because the feud between the Hellenized aristocracy and the rest of the people had not been settled (and probably became more bitter because of the persecution). Nevertheless, it should be remembered that although the struggle continued, religious persecution was not renewed. The struggle from now on was mainly national, social, and political, either within Jewish society or against Seleucid rule.

Soon after the execution of Menelaus a change took place on the Seleucid throne. Demetrius I, the son of Seleucus IV, escaped from Rome and successfully replaced Antiochus V. He appointed Alcimus to the high priesthood. With this appointment, under circumstances which are not completely clear to us, Judas did not acquiesce. Nevertheless, it seems that part of his supporters, the Hasideans, were ready to come to terms with Alcimus. Yet, for reasons unknown Alcimus had them murdered, which only strengthened Judas' activity and reprisals (1 Macc 7:8–25).

This time the new king, Demetrius I, took prompt action. He sent Nicanor to strengthen the position of his nominee Alcimus. After some negotiations between Nicanor and Judas, which failed (and which had been in bad faith on Nicanor's side, according to 1 Macc 7:27–32), the armies of Nicanor and Judas met on the battlefield at Adasa. Judas got the upper hand, the Syrians were defeated, and Nicanor was killed at the beginning of the battle. It may be that Judas intentionally directed an attack at the person of the commander with the aim of demoralizing the whole army: this had also been done in the first battle against Apollonius. Another element in this battle was the spontaneous attacks on the retreating Syrian army by the peasants in the surrounding areas. The 13th of Adar, the date of this victory, was declared a holiday, called the "Day of Nicanor."

At this stage Judas also initiated diplomacy to achieve his aims, and so he sent a delegation to Rome. This act was formerly encouraged by Roman emissaries who passed along the levantine coast on their way from Egypt to Syria. A letter on this matter, from the year 164 B.C.E., is preserved in 2 Macc 11:34–38. In addition, Judas could expect a warm welcome in Rome, because the enthronement of Demetrius I was against Roman wishes, and Roman policy toward him was inimical. Indeed, Judas' emissaries were kindly received at Rome, and a treaty was agreed upon between the Romans and the Jews (1 Macc 8:23–32).

The Jewish delegation to Rome did not deter Demetrius from taking strong action against Judas. He might not have been aware of the Roman–Jewish negotiations, and it seems that Judas' delegates returned too late to prevent Demetrius' attack on Judea. In addition, it does not seem that Demetrius would have acquiesced to Judas' activity, and in view of his policy in general he would have ignored the Roman intervention in favor of Judas. Yet Judas had nothing to lose by an appeal to Rome, and he might have considered a treaty with Rome to be an asset to Jewish policy, which indeed it was. This act shows that Judas had at this stage, if not earlier, definite political aims. For him, as for the government, the war for religious rights was over, and he envisaged now some kind of political independence for Judea.

Whatever plans Judas might have entertained, he had to face the army under the command of Bacchides sent against him by Demetrius I. On his way to Judea, Bacchides attacked and conquered a Jewish village or fortress named Mesaloth at Arbel, about whose location there is no consensus because of textual difficulties. Judas awaited Bacchides at Elasa with a relatively small force of 3,000 men. On the approach of Bacchides many abandoned Judas' camp until he was left with only 800 men. In spite of the advice of his friends, Judas decided to give battle to Bacchides, but the result was that he himself fell on the battlefield and his army dispersed (160 B.C.E.).

What was the reason for this dwindling of Judas' forces? One explanation is that since the religious persecution was over, many of his supporters lost their motivation and were reluctant to continue a war for political independence under the leadership of Judas (cf. the desertion of the Hasideans to Alcimus). Others explain Judas' weakening by some accidental event, like the season of the year or agricultural pressures on the peasants, or alternatively because of fatigue from the long war and fear of Bacchides' army (1 Macc 9:6). Others raise doubt about the authenticity of the information given in 1 Macc 9:5–9 and explain it as apologetic: the author of 1 Maccabees was looking for an excuse for Judas, the victorious hero, who this time had failed.

Be that as it may, with the death of Judas the Maccabean revolt as a historical process came to an end, defined by the persecution at the beginning and the defeat of Judas at the end. Indeed the Maccabean revolt activated a chain of events of a different nature, which went far beyond the battle of Elasa. It was focused on the Hasmonean dynasty, on national-territorial expansion, on mainly political, not military means, and on involvement in Seleucid affairs. Although some of these characteristics already existed in Judas' time, his death terminated the first stage of the process that led to an independent Jewish state. A new stage began some 8 years later with the rise to power of Jonathan, his brother.

C. Causes

What caused the Maccabean revolt? The answer is the religious persecution of Antiochus IV. But this answer touches only the surface of these events. First, one should inquire about the cause(s) of the persecution. Second, one must discover the various powers, groups, personalities, and ideas behind both the persecution and the revolt.

Antiochus' persecution poses a difficult problem for historians because of its uniqueness in antiquity. No real analogy can be brought forth, for religious persecution is contrary to the ideological, religious, social, and political code of the Hellenistic world and of the ANE and Roman civilizations as well. Under these circumstances scholars are looking for specific explanations for this phenomenon. Some postulate that the persecution was born in the mind of a crazy king, as supposedly confirmed by ancient sources. According to a more lenient judgment, Antiochus wished to unify his variegated empire under one religion or one culture, and on this issue he collided with the Jews. Some support for this view is derived from changes in Antiochus' coins and from some sentences in the book of Daniel (11:37). The common denominator of the various theories is that they explain very little, because they either have no answer to the question—why only the Jews were persecuted—or they do not fit with information from other quarters of Antiochus' realm, where various kinds of religion and worship were flourishing without interruption.

A breakthrough came with E. Bickerman's book *The God of the Maccabees* (1937). Bickerman transferred the initiative of the persecution from Antiochus to the Hellenizers under Menelaus. He explained their initiative on this matter as an effort to reform Jewish religion, and he explained the feasibility of such an idea by their background in Jewish culture, which supported such intolerant measures. Such measures cannot be adequately explained if one assumes they were initiated by Antiochus VI, who was raised in an atmosphere of religious pluralism, typical of Hellenistic culture.

V. Tcherikover (1961) refined Bickerman's suppositions. He repudiated Bickerman's idea of the Hellenizers as champions of "Reform Judaism" and as the initiators of the persecution (either they were Hellenized and tolerant, or Jewish and intolerant, as he put it). But he followed Bickerman in reading 2 Macc 4:9 as meaning that Jason bought a permit from the king to register inhabitants of Jerusalem as members of an organization called "Antioch in Jerusalem." On this Tcherikover agreed with Bickerman, with the improvement that this organization was a *polis* and not, as suggested by Bickerman, a *politeuma* (an ethnic organization, mainly for religious purposes, which could perform within a *polis*).

Tcherikover went on to define the persecution as a measure against Jewish resistance to the royal policy of supporting the Hellenizers. As he phrased it, "a revolt preceded the persecution," i.e., the persecution was decreed to crush a revolt, and the Maccabean revolt was not the only revolt in that period. It was preceded by at least the revolt against Lysimachus, Menelaus' brother (2 Macc 4:39–42). This he tried to show by a reconstruction of the course of events and their chronology.

But why was religious persecution used to crush a revolt? According to Tcherikover, it was because the opposition against the new "constitution" (the *polis* Antioch in Jerusalem and its Hellenized atmosphere) was led by the legal and spiritual leaders of the people, the Soferim (experts in the Law). To crush this opposition, the king thought he should eradicate the Law (Torah). By wiping out the Law and its guardians, the changes introduced into Judea would be accepted, so he thought.

No single isolated explanation seems satisfactory, and on some issues the various explanations are not contradictory. The sources support a comprehensive explanation, which may contain various causes and various components. It seems that the Hellenizers had a major part in the persecution, and Menelaus' group might have initiated or advocated its enactment. Antiochus' personality might also have contributed, and he might have been acting also under the strains of a recent defeat in Egypt. The suggestion that his long stay as a hostage in Rome influenced his deed cannot be substantiated.

In any case, the persecution was not a sudden decision, but an extreme measure after a long confrontation in which various groups were involved. The Jewish nobility was for some decades split into various groups, centered around some families, or parts of families torn within themselves. Such were the Tobiads and the Oniads. Other families were more unified, like the house of Bilga on the Hellenizers' side, or the Hasmonean family on the opposing side. The struggle was for political power, but the parties were also divided along political, social, and religious lines. Pro-Seleucids opposed the pro-Ptolemies; aristocracy was opposed by the common people and by the spiritual leadership and probably even by some sectarian groups; the attitude toward Hellenism divided the nobility itself. What we see is a mosaic of parties and interests, with Seleucid government involvement in all of it.

When the decree of the persecution was promulgated, the mosaic remained, but a clearer division of powers resulted. On the one hand there was Menelaus, supported by the Seleucid government (which, as we have seen, was not unanimous on this policy, but the decision lay with the king). On the other hand there were those who revolted, led by Mattathias and after him by Judas Maccabeus. In addition there were various groups: mild Hellenizers, who did not support the persecution or Menelaus (Jason; Alcimus); anti-Hellenizers within the nobility (the house of Hakoz); martyrs (1 Macc 2:31–38); Hasideans; Soferim; and also common people (probably "the many," *rabîm,* Dan 11:33–34).

The persecution caused a process which was contrary to the expectations of both Menelaus and Antiochus. Instead of the opposition being crushed by this drastic act, the majority supported the rebels, who became more and more powerful. Traditional Judaism as it had developed since the return to Zion proved too strong for its adversaries. The major political aim of the Seleucid government—to create a dependable power in a strategic region—proved wrong. Instead, the Seleucid government remained obliged to invest military power, so dear to it, in the project. Its supporters proved to be the weaker contender. Antiochus, on Lysias' advice, tried too late to disentangle himself from the trap. The Hellenizers estranged themselves from the people to such a degree that they lost any chance of regaining the people's confidence, and the rebels' achievements made it impossible to reverse the trend. So it came about that although the revolt was crushed militarily, the process created by it within Jewish society and throughout the region went on. The eventual result was an independent Jewish state.

There is no proof that there was a meaningful ideological component either in Menelaus' or in Antiochus' politics. Yet Bickerman's idea of some kind of religious reform cherished by the Hellenizers was further developed by M. Hengel (1974) and others. They suggest that the Hellenizers had an ideology to reform Judaism and to supplant traditional Judaism with the reformed version. However, it seems that the sources do not provide the evidence to substantiate this suggestion. Ideology played a minor role, if at all, on the Hellenizers' side in triggering these events. We tend to see the events as a career-oriented bid for power by the Hellenized nobility, which failed because of the strong intrinsic influence of Judaism on the majority of the people, a fact which was underestimated by both Menelaus and Antiochus.

D. Military Aspects of the Revolt

The Maccabean revolt was crushed but the process it began did not stop. There yet remains the question of the military confrontation between Judas and his supporters and the Seleucid military forces. The rebels got the upper hand in the countryside at the initial stages of the revolt, and they were striving to isolate, attack, and conquer Jerusalem. The Hellenizers under Menelaus' leadership (or simply the citizens of Antioch in Jerusalem) and the local troops were forced to evacuate the Judean hillsides and to defend themselves in Jerusalem. Their main stronghold was the Akra, from which they commanded the Temple Mount and its surroundings.

The Seleucid government was called to help its supporters and its forces in Jerusalem. At the beginning this was done with troops from the neighboring regions (Samaria, Coele-Syria, and Phoenicia) and afterward with royal armies sent by the central government. Judas' success was in intercepting these armies on their way to Jerusalem. His military success and the difficulty of the Seleucid government in relieving their allies in Jerusalem were major considerations in the annulment of the persecution.

Under what conditions was Judas able to achieve this success? What was the power ratio between his force and the Seleucids? According to the sources, the Seleucid army was much stronger in number and in arms. Generally speaking, the confrontation is portrayed as between a David and a Goliath, and the few overcame the many with the help of God. Yet this picture has been criticized by scholars on various grounds: the Seleucid military command at that time could not spare such incredible armies for Judea, the Jewish military potential was greater than we may gather from the sources, and those sources are not impartial on this matter. These points are true, and the most recent presentation of this matter, by Bar-Kochva (1988), seems most reasonable. We may conclude then that the Seleucid army was numerically limited and never exceeded 20,000 foot-soldiers and 2,000 horsemen, that Judas could master at the peak of his influence equal or somewhat greater numbers, and that military experience and expertise were also available in the rebels' camp.

Another argument concerns the tactics of the Maccabean army. Was it guerrilla warfare or an ordinary Hellenistic one, with the use of the phalanx and subsidiary units? Lack of clear evidence makes it difficult to arrive at a safe conclusion, and it may be argued that both guerrilla warfare and phalanx tactics were used in different stages of the revolt, depending on the situation.

Nevertheless, Jewish achievements (though not by the few against the many) were considerable. They were the result of the warriors' high motivation and the excellent command of Judas Maccabeus, who showed many of the outstanding qualities of a great commander: leadership, bravery, personal example, familiarity with the country and its physical layout, tactical versatility, and strategic understanding.

So, although the Syrians got the upper hand, the liberation movement continued. The Hasmonean leadership was a direct result of Judas' achievements. Yet the liberation movement itself should also be seen in the context of the disintegration of the entire Seleucid empire, as concisely phrased by the great Roman historian Tacitus: "Later on, since the power of Macedon had waned, the Parthians were not yet come to their strength, and the Romans were far away, the Jews selected their own kings" (*Hist.* 5.8.3).

E. The Revolt in Historical Perspective

The results of the Maccabean revolt were decisive in various aspects. Historically it created a process by which the Palestinian Jews founded an autonomous national state (different from many contemporaneous dynastic states) which encompassed most of the country. Not less important universally is that the survival of Jewish monotheism was achieved through the revolt, which overcame the religious persecution. The consequences of these events go far beyond the borders of Judea.

Bibliography

The literature on the Maccabean revolt is immense, and only a concise selection of more recent literature can be listed here. In many of the following books fuller bibliographic lists may be found.

Sources and Commentaries

Abel, F. M. 1949. *Les Livres des Maccabées.* Paris.

Dancy, J. C. 1954. *A Commentary on I Maccabees.* Oxford.

Goldstein, J. A. 1976. *I Maccabees.* AB. Garden City, NY.

———. 1983. *II Maccabees.* AB. Garden City, NY.

Habicht, C. 1976. *2 Makkabäerbuch.* JSHRZ 1/3. Gütersloh.

Lacocque, A. 1979. *The Book of Daniel.* Atlanta.

Montgomery, J. 1927. *The Book of Daniel.* ICC. Edinburgh.

Stern, M. 1974–84. *Greek and Latin Authors on Jews and Judaism.* Vols. 1–3. Jerusalem.

Zeitlin, S., and Tedesche, S. 1950. *The First Book of Maccabees.* New York.

———. 1954. *The Second Book of Maccabees.* New York.

Secondary Literature

Bar-Kochva, B. 1988. *Judas Maccabaeus.* Cambridge.

Bickerman, E. 1979. *The God of the Maccabees.* Trans. H. R. Moehring. Leiden. (Orig. ed. 1937.)

Bringmann, K. 1983. *Hellenistische Reform und Religionsverfolgung in Judäa.* Göttingen.

Fischer, T. 1980. *Seleukiden und Makkabäer.* Bochum.

Hengel, M. 1974. *Judaism and Hellenism.* Vols. 1–2. London and Philadelphia.

Millar, F. 1978. The Background of the Maccabean Revolution. (Rev. of Hengel 1974). *JJS* 29: 1–21.

Tcherikover, V. 1961. *Hellenistic Civilization and the Jews.* Philadelphia.

Will, E., and Orrieux, C. 1986. *Ioudaïsmos—Hellènismos.* Nancy.

URIEL RAPPAPORT

MACCABEE. A nickname given to Judas the son of Mattathias, the first general in the Jewish revolt against the Seleucids. See MACCABEUS.

MACCABEES, BOOKS OF.

This entry consists of three articles. The first covers the deuterocanonical books of 1 and 2 Maccabees, while the second and third cover the books of *3 Maccabees* and *4 Maccabees,* respectively.

FIRST AND SECOND MACCABEES

Two writings of the Christian apocrypha recounting the exploits of Judas Maccabeus, who forcefully opposed the efforts of Antiochus Epiphanes to suppress traditional worship and institutions in Jerusalem and Judea. "The Maccabee" has become an everlasting hero of world history thanks in part to the later works of Dante (*Divina Commedia, Paradiso* 18:40–42) and Handel (in his *oratorio* of 1747). Annually, during the festival of Hanukkah (Petuchowski 1984: 107–21, 137; see the bibliographies in *HJP*² 1: 163 n. 65; Fischer 1980: 91 n. 218), Jews in all countries commemorate the rededication of the Temple. It is noteworthy that the story of those events is recounted not so much in the rabbinical writings (Nodet 1986: 357–66) as in the apocrypha of the Christian tradition: the two books of Maccabees have not been preserved within the framework of the Hebrew Bible but within that of the Greek-language LXX, which the Christians adopted from the Jews of Egypt and Alexandria. Both 1 Maccabees and 2 Maccabees were regarded as more or less authoritative by the early Church (Abel and Starcky 1961: 8); St. Jerome, around A.D. 400, was the first who explicitly distinguished these *libri ecclesiastici* from the *libri canonici* of the Hebrew Bible. In 1534, Martin Luther relegated both books of Maccabees together with some other writings to the appendix of his translation of the Bible: *"the Apocrypha, that is, books which are not to be equated with Holy Scripture and yet which are useful and good to read."* In the Catholic Church both of these "apocryphal" works have been counted as "deutero-canonical" since the Council of Trent in 1546, whereas Protestants from the beginning (and the Russian Orthodox since the 19th century) have excluded them from their respective canons (Schunck, *1 Makkabaeerbuch* JSHRZ, 92–93; D. Kellermann 1987: 175). However, the present article emphasizes the historical issues without regard to the problems of canonicity.

A. The First Book of Maccabees
   1. Contents and Language
   2. Structure
   3. Date
   4. Theology and Tendency
B. The Second Book of Maccabees
   1. Structure and Sources
   2. Contents and Purpose
   3. Title and Transmission
   4. Scholarly Issues
   5. Theological Matters
C. Summary
   1. Recapitulation of the *Quellenkritik*
   2. Analysis of the Documents and Related Methodology
   3. Structures of the Histories of Events
   4. Aspects of Historical Inferences
   5. Conclusions

A. The First Book of Maccabees

1. Contents and Language. In the manner of the genuinely biblical historical works such as Judges, Samuel, and Kings, the so-called First Book of Maccabees in 16 chapters treats Judea's struggle for liberation from the Greco–Macedonian Seleucid kings. After a brief historical retrospect which looks back to Alexander the Great and the Diadochoi (1:1–10; Gafni 1984: 1), there subsequently follows, also by way of introduction, an account of Jason and Antiochus IV Epiphanes. It then deals with the "apostasy" in the country itself and with the "persecution," which culminated in the desecration of the temple in December of 167 B.C. (1:11–64). In the main section proper (2:1–16:22) we are told of the "breaking up" perpetrated by Mattathias, who came from the priestly family of Joarib and who dwelt in the countryside in Modein. We also hear of the deeds of his five sons: John, called Gaddi; Simon, called Thassi; Judas Maccabeus (the nickname may mean "the hammer-like"; see MACCABEUS); Eleazar Avaran; and Jonathan Apphus. The original title of the work may also have had something of this sense (Goldstein *1 Maccabees* AB, 16–21; Fischer 1980: 55–56 n. 141; Schunck, *1 Makkabaeerbuch* JSHRZ, 289; *HJP*² 3/1: 182–83). Historically, the book deals with events in Palestine from 166 to 135 B.C. It ends with the murder of Simon, high priest and prince of the land, who was the last surviving son of Mattathias. The brief conclusion (16:23–24) refers to a Chronicle of John Hyrcanus I, Simon's son and successor, which, however, is no longer extant.

1 Maccabees was originally composed in Hebrew, as both Origen and Jerome attest (Abel and Starcky 1961: 7 and n. a, 15; Goldstein *1 Maccabees* AB, 14–16; Schunck, JSHRZ, 289; Dommershausen 1985: 6; *HJP*² 3/1: 181–82 and n. 3; Enermalm-Ogawa 1987: 11–12; survey of research in Neuhaus 1974a: 47–49). The only surviving text is a Greek version containing many Hebraisms and translation errors (Neuhaus 1974a: 46), as, for example, in 10:1: "*Alexander . . . the Epiphanes.*" The Greek documents are retroversions, not the *verbatim* transmitted originals. The Old Latin version seems to have been based on an older, likewise Greek (and perhaps better) translation of the Hebrew original (Abel and Starcky 1961: 80; Momigliano 1975: 103; Goldstein *1 Maccabees* AB, 177–78; *2 Maccabees* AB, 126; Schunck, JSHRZ, 290). Already at the end of the 1st century A.D. Josephus utilized a partial (i.e., only extending to the burial of Jonathan in Modein [13:30]) Greek edition of the book (Fischer 1980: 110; Momigliano 1980: 561; Schunck, JSHRZ, 290–91; cf. Attridge 1984: 171, 214 and n. 51; *HJP*² 3/1: 183; otherwise Goldstein, *1 Maccabees* AB, 14 and n. 18, p. 56 and n. 8; cf. p. 176).

2. Structure. The structure of the work is chronological, with the provision that external events seem to have been first narrated when they became known or acknowledged in Jerusalem and Judea. It is only in the case of the report of the death of Antiochus IV that a distortion of the time-frame seems to have occurred, because the (probable) co-regency of his son Antiochus V is not considered there (Fischer 1980: 134–39; coins of Antiochus V, which bear what is probably Lysias' monogram, support the assumption of such a co-regency [Fischer 1986: 70]). Although 13:42 mentions its own chronology based on the regnal years of the high priest and prince of the land, the author of 1 Maccabees consistently adopts the dates of the Seleucid era, both thoroughly and reasonably according to the Babylonian–Jewish (not the Greco–Macedonian) reckoning (Fischer 1985b: 350–51; otherwise Neuhaus 1974b: 162–63; Goldstein, *1 Maccabees* AB, 21–25, 540–41, 544; *2 Maccabees* AB, 22–23, 32–33, 56–63, 71; *IJH*, 542; Bickerman 1979: 101–11; Schunck, JSHRZ, 291; Collins 1981: 150; Bringmann 1983: 15–28; Attridge 1984: 176 and n. 53; Will and Orrieux 1986: 160, 170 n. 5; cf. *HJP*² 1: 18–19; *HJP*² 3/1: 181).

The book itself recounts the acts of Mattathias and his five sons. It adheres to a markedly dynastic position and does not single out and relate the history of a class, a people, or a country as such. It appears to be homogeneous and well thought out, and is extremely stylized (Neuhaus 1974b: 171–75; otherwise Will and Orrieux 1986: 57). At the beginning of the work the poetic sections (Neuhaus 1974a; Enermalm-Ogawa 1987)—that is, the prayers (Flusser 1984: 572), speeches, addresses, laments, and songs of victory—serve to accentuate the course of the events. Later, as in Thucydides, it is the documents (Stern 1973: 184–89) which increasingly and by dynamically intensified turns interrupt the continuous narrative. To the extent that these documents derive from the 2d century B.C., they are presumably all authentic, even those pertaining to Sparta, and particularly the letters which, as such, also happen to represent only suggestions that were never in fact realized (e.g., 10:25–45; 15:2–9). Chap. 8 plays a key role in the middle of the book (Neuhaus 1974a: 113); there we find the introduction of the famous treaty (Momigliano 1980: 563) which Judas is said to have concluded with Rome, the (then) new and rising world power in the West (Gruen 1984: 16 n. 14, 42–46, 51 n. 189, 125, 316, 338–39, 428 n. 168, 668, 748). Such an accord was in fact only realized later, and then through Simon, the brother of Judas.

In stressing the reciprocal intention to conclude such a treaty, the author of 1 Maccabees cleverly compensates for the death of Judas, and, by the same token, he clarifies the most important element in Hasmonean foreign policy: its continuing reliance upon substantial diplomatic relations with Rome (Fischer 1981: 141–43). It must remain uncertain whether the contemporary historian Eupolemus, whom Judas had sent as his own Greek-language envoy to Rome (8:17), should be regarded as the source of this treaty. Nevertheless, the report itself is serendipitous both for the study of the sources and for interdisciplinary collaboration. The extrabiblical parallels clearly reveal how skillfully and ingeniously—in contradistinction to any Greco–Roman author, who would only have paraphrased the contents of such documents—the author of 1 Maccabees varied his diverse *Vorlagen* and presented them to his native Judean readership, especially a treaty which was reciprocally promulgated by Judas and the Romans, but not ratified (Fischer 1980: 105–21, 191; 1981: 141–42, 148, 150). An additional feature of the author's compositional method, tendency, and understanding is therefore secured, one which supplements the literary-critical analyses of Neuhaus 1974a and Enermalm-Ogawa 1987 (cf. also Dimant 1988: 392–95, 399 and n. 83 [on 2:49–64], 407 [on 5:48]).

The poetic pieces in the book contain both free and literal quotations of, as well as "plays" on, all three parts of the later canon (the Torah has no primacy; indeed, the most space is devoted to the writing prophets: Neuhaus 1974a: 177; Goldstein, *2 Maccabees* AB, 30–31 is imprecise). The biblical texts in question were brought into relation to the author's own time as "fulfilled prophecies," and hence they were actualized, as, e.g., Ps 79:2–3 in 1 Macc 7:16–17 (Dimant 1988: 390–91). However, this procedure is likewise not exact in the modern sense of historical criteria. In agreement with various scholars (Neuhaus 1974b: 163–75; Bringmann 1983: 13 and n. 8; cf. Schaefer *IJH*, 542), one should not accept the conclusions of the earlier German source-criticism about 1 Maccabees (for references, see Attridge 1984: 176 and n. 52; *HJP*² 3/1: 181 n. 2; Enermalm-Ogawa 1987: 11 n. 3). Further speculations on this topic are presented by Goldstein, *1 Maccabees* AB, 37–103; *2 Maccabees* AB, 28–54. For example, on the basis of 9:22 one can deduce neither a written *Vorlage* nor a *Vita* of Judas; rather the contrary.

3. Date. There is more agreement among researchers as to the question of the date of the book, which apparently appeared toward the close of the 2d century B.C. in Palestine (Abel and Starcky 1961: 17; Bickerman 1979: 94; Fischer 1980: 56 n. 141; Nickelsburg 1981: 117; Attridge 1984: 171; *HJP*² 3/1: 181; Momigliano's date of "between 146 and 129 B.C." [1980: 564–66] is certainly too early, while Goldstein's date of the time of Alexander Janneus around 90 B.C. [*1 Maccabees* AB, 62–63, 72; *2 Maccabees* AB, 71–83, 121] is possibly somewhat too late). At present, a less uncertain *terminus ante quem* for the composition of 1 Maccabees is not possible, although the thoroughgoing use of the Seleucid era (in spite of 13:42 and 14:43; cf. 2 Macc 1:9!), the harmonious relationship to Rome, and the untroubled dynastic concord of the Hasmoneans all suggest the early 1st century B.C., at the latest. At this time the "thieving" Hasmonean state (as the Greco–Roman authors, presumably following Poseidonius of Apamea and the official Seleucid terms, denoted it) strongly realized its *de facto* independence far beyond the borders of Judea and Samaria (Fischer 1985a).

4. Theology and Tendency. The theology of the book is biblical and conservative (Abel and Starcky 1961: 13–14; thoroughly now Neuhaus 1974a: 227–40). The authority of the oral tradition has receded into the background, which, however, did not rule out the "right" interpretation—as, e.g., in the case of self-defense on the Sabbath (on this problem, which was not ultimately solved at the time, see Habicht, *2 Makkabaeerbuch* JSHRZ, 187; Oppenheimer 1976: 34–38; Fischer 1980: 58–59 and n. 141; Nodet 1986: 325 and n. 9; Will and Orrieux 1986: 60, 158 and n. 109; D. Kellermann 1987: 174, 178). God, in place of whose name either "heaven" or the personal pronoun was used, appears as Israel's efficacious helper and as the Lord of the Covenant (Schunck, JSHRZ, 293; Enermalm-Ogawa 1987: 52; D. Kellermann 1987: 173); however, He figures less in personal prayer or accompanied by heavenly helpers or miracles, but rather through the Law, in action and universal trust: it was He himself who had called the Hasmoneans to be Israel's leaders! Prophecy was considered either fulfilled or ended, at least until "a new and reliable prophet should arise" (4:46; 9:27; 14:41; cf. Goldstein, *1 Maccabees* AB, 12–13). Any type of eschatology or ideology of martyrdom is absent (Neuhaus 1974a: 232; Goldstein, *1 Maccabees* AB, 12; U. Kellermann 1979: 88; Fischer 1980: 57 n. 142; Schunck, JSHRZ, 293; Will and Orrieux 1986: 58).

A thoroughgoing pro-Hasmonean (Habicht, *2 Makkabaeerbuch* JSHRZ, 188–89; Tcherikover, *WHJP* 1/6: 116; Schunck, JSHRZ, 292; Nickelsburg 1981: 114–17; Attridge 1984: 172–76; *HJP*² 3/1: 180–81), perhaps even Sadducean, tendency (most recently advocated by Fischer 1980: 56) interpenetrates the entire work, the unified structure of which has—in terms of speeches, concepts, and themes—been demonstrated by Neuhaus (1974b: 171–74). In spite of the "old-fashioned" colorization which manifests itself to some extent in the use of the Hebrew language and in the restoration of Israelite models (Rajak 1986: 141), the Maccabean revolt "according to the will of God," the attendant "liberation" of the Temple, the city, and the country, and finally the aggressive expansion so as to embrace the whole of Palestine and parts of Syria, all this legitimates the dominion of the Hasmoneans. Their rule was regarded as the fulfillment of prophecy and even as the re-establishment of the empires of David and Solomon (Fischer 1980: 182, following Neuhaus 1974a), although Jonathan and Simon had secured their power against the Judean establishment thanks in part to their position as Seleucid functionaries: they changed sides repeatedly and in this way "liberated their people from foreign rule" (Fischer 1985a). Since the Maccabees (or, as we read in 5:62, "those men, into whose hand the salvation of Israel was given") only derived from the low house of Joarib, there was neither a genuine biblical nor a priestly legitimation of the aspiring Hasmonean rule in reality but, in the Hellenistic sense, a very political and truly pragmatic foundation. This presupposition was, on the one hand, directed against the former high-priestly line of the Oniads, who were then resident in the Egyptian exile and in the Diaspora with the Ptolemaic kings. On the other hand, it was also opposed to the Pharisees, the apocalypticists, and the many sectarians in Judea itself (otherwise Efron 1987), who increasingly criticized the Hasmoneans because of their methods of rule and their susceptibility to Greek influence. Indeed, these groups disputed the legitimacy of the Maccabean line and the Hasmonean claim to the office of high priest; and these tensions reached a bloody culmination during the rule of Alexander Janneus (103–76 B.C.). However, the Sadducean conceptions of God, Law, and tradition in 1 Maccabees are not by themselves sufficient evidence to warrant the full ascription of the work to the Sadducees (cf. Bickerman 1979: 94; Efron 1987: 7–9, 14, 17).

In any case, such a Chronicle was not originally directed at foreigners or Greeks, but rather at the native Judean readership of ca. 100 B.C. These people may be characterized as intimately familiar with the writings of the fathers, conscious of the nation and its ideology, but at the same time practical (in a Hellenistic sense), that is, pragmatic and not eschatologically or apocalyptically oriented (although in general the last-mentioned viewpoint predominates in our extant tradition). The main military and political opponents (or scapegoats) were—as one would expect at the end of the 2d century B.C.—the Seleucid kings, rather than foreigners as such (like the Spartans and Romans). The inner-Judean opposition was either passed over in silence (like the "evil priest" Menelaus), or else they were indirectly dismissed, like the apocalypticists, who were relegated to their own sort of existence in the desert. The Hasmonean party proper identified itself with "the true Israel" (Neuhaus 1974a: 128; 1974b: 172), the identity and collective consciousness of which was accentuated by ahistoric terms (cf. Enermalm-Ogawa 1987: 50–51). Such characteristics suggest an author who was experienced in both politics and propaganda, perhaps a man who was schooled in Sadducean learning, who was in the immediate proximity of the Hasmonean princes and wrote, at their behest, as the "court chronicler" (on which position, see Neuhaus 1974a: 174–84, 215, 223–25).

On the basis of such presuppositions the figure of "the Maccabee" takes on, albeit *ex eventu,* the characteristics of a formidable individual, considered in a very Hellenistic sense, those of a *hērōs* or "savior" *(sōtēr)* on the Greek pattern. The effects of this figure survived his own lifetime and, like his father Mattathias, he bears the marks of the divine *ktistēs:* in spite of a superficial appearance of failure, Judas nevertheless established the rule of his house "according to the will of God," "in reality," decisively and permanently (Fischer 1980: 176–77; cf. Neuhaus 1974a: 115–17, 192–201; Will and Orrieux 1986: 57–58). Apart from the manifest Sadducean-Hasmonean elements, these sorts of disguised Hellenistic-messianic features may have contributed to the rejection of the work by the Pharisees and by later Judaism (Abel and Starcky 1961: 12–13; Fischer 1980: 57 n. 142).

In war either for or against the Seleucid kings whom they once served, in conflict with their own people, and in the service of the Sanctuary (which Hyrcanus I probably plundered; Fischer 1983), the Hasmoneans appear to have been colorful and discordant. Who is surprised, then, when the author of the work includes a *lament* on the occasion of the consecration of the Temple in 164 B.C. (Neuhaus 1974a: 81–82, 110, 112) and not, as one might have expected of the "liberator of Zion," a song of praise (Fischer 1980: 72–73)?

B. The Second Book of Maccabees

1. Structure and Sources. Whereas the "Sadducean (?) Chronicle" of the Maccabees (1 Maccabees) appears to have been written at one sitting (even though it is composed of a variety of materials it intensifies until the violent death of the last son of the "founder of the dynasty"), 2 Maccabees gives the obvious impression of being a *mixtum compositum* with a sort of introduction, two letters (1:1–10 and 1:10–2:18) and a foreword by the epitomizer himself (2:19–32), with an excerpt from the (assuredly originally Greek-composed) history by Jason of Cyrene, which is not elsewhere attested (3:1–15:36), and with the epitomizer's own epilogue (15:37–39).

The somewhat verbose epitomizer (or abridger), who modestly remained anonymous, abbreviated the five books of Jason (whose existence we are not to doubt with Nodet 1986: 330–31 n. 15; cf. Doran 1981: 81–83) into a single book (2:19–32; see Doran 1981: 77–81). This redactor organized and partially expanded the contents, as was then current practice (Habicht, *2 Makkabaeerbuch* JSHRZ, 171; Fischer 1980: 89, 139; Attridge 1984: 178 and n. 61; misunderstood by Goldstein *1 Maccabees* AB, 28). In 4:17 and 5:17–20 the epitomizer seems to comment on his *Vorlage;* in 12:43–45 (possibly following then-contemporary Egyptian practice) he further imputes to Judas the belief in resurrection (see Oppenheimer 1976: 39–40; U. Kellermann 1979: 87–88; cf. Bringmann 1983: 55 n. 17). In 6:12–17 it is apparently not Jason who speaks to us, but the didactic abridger (Habicht, JSHRZ, 171, 230 n. 12a; Momigliano 1980: 574; Nickelsburg 1981: 119 and n. 58; cf. Doran 1981: 53–55; Attridge 1984: 180 and n. 64), as is also the case in 7:42 (U. Kellermann 1979: 54, following Bunge). The martyr deeds of the aged Eleazar and of the Mother and her seven sons (6:18–7:42) might well also have been adopted from a different narrative (Habicht, JSHRZ, 171, 173; Fischer 1980: 28 n. 7; Collins 1981: 260–61, 310; Enermalm-Ogawa 1987: 89; otherwise U. Kellermann 1979: 55–58; Doran 1981: 21–22, 35–36). Later in *4 Maccabees* (*HJP*[2] 3/1: 588–93) we find that this passage—which was of such central importance for the epitomizer (U. Kellermann 1979: 54) and which was laden with emotion—has been expanded and elevated to the crown of biblical martyrology (U. Kellermann 1979: 35–38, following Surkau and Holl, speaks of it as *"the primeval martyr narrative of Judaism and the early church"*). Bickerman's analysis of the sources pertaining to Heliodorus' visit to the Temple (3:23–40) is doubtful (Habicht, JSHRZ, 172–73; Doran 1981: 19–21; Fischer fc.). The swashbuckling source theories of Goldstein (*1 Maccabees* and *2 Maccabees* AB) have been repudiated by Doran 1981: 17–19; see also the criticisms of Collins 1986: 73, 76.

It remains unclear whether the epitomizer arranged the two introductory letters (1:1–2:18)—which were probably originally in Aramaic rather than in Hebrew (but see Habicht, JSHRZ, 170 and n. 15; Alexander 1984: 594;

Enermalm-Ogawa 1987: 54, 56 and n. 2)—so as to preface the excerpt; Habicht (JSHRZ, 174–75) and Attridge (1984: 177–78) offer critical reviews of the research on this point. Although we must thank Habicht for a very penetrating source analysis of the entire book, his layer theory must remain hypothetical (Fischer 1980: 14–15). Earlier source theories have been surveyed by Schaefer (*IJH*, 543–44; *HJP*² 3/1: 531–34 is not useful on this issue).

In any case, the two letters form a sort of unity which distances itself formally, linguistically, and temporally from the rest of the book, the learned epitome (Fischer 1980: 86–89). Perhaps both letters derive from a Jewish archive in Alexandria (hardly in Leontopolis) or Judea (on which see Habicht, JSHRZ, 200 n. a). It appears that the first letter (1:1–10), from the year 124/3 B.C.—which is dated to the Seleucid era (on the Judeo-Babylonian reckoning)—is actually the second (!) injunction of the Judeans to their compatriots in Egypt to celebrate "the (eight-day) festival in the month of Chislev according to (!) the manner of booths [Sukkoth]" (on which see Oppenheimer 1976: 41–42; Doran 1981: 4–5). Then follows (1:10–2:18) the earlier communication of "those in Jerusalem and those in Judea and the council and Judas" to Aristobulus (on this well-known sage, tutor of princes at the Ptolemaic court, and probably also political leader of the Jewish Diaspora then dwelling in Egypt, see Fischer 1980: 89–90 n. 216; Conzelmann 1981: 153–55; Borgen 1984: 274–79; Collins 1986: 175–78; *HJP*² 3/1: 579–87). Apparently, this letter to Aristobulus is actually a companion-piece giving the deeper motivation of the first letter; of course, such an appendix is undated, following the archival custom of the time. However, the first (!) adhortatory letter from 143/2 B.C.—which is only mentioned in 1:7–8 (Fischer 1980: 88 and n. 213)—has not been preserved.

2. Contents and Purpose. The contents of the actual, strongly moralizing epitome, which is not precisely datable (otherwise, e.g., U. Kellermann 1979: 13, 59; Doran 1981: 111–13; Attridge 1984: 177), partially intersects with the account in 1 Maccabees. The epitome explicates the prehistory of the revolt from around 180 B.C. under Seleucus IV Philopater, describing the internal Judean rivalries, as well as the conflicts surrounding the office of high priest (*archiereus*), and the struggles for the "leadership of the people" (*prostasia tou laou*) under Antiochus IV Epiphanes, Antiochus V Eupator, and Demetrius I Soter. Aspects of the Seleucid government proper (and hence of the supraordinate imperial history) receive more attention here than in the more local-oriented "Chronicle of the Maccabees." At least, the epitome passes over Mattathias, who may have suffered a mortal wound in battle with government soldiers (Fischer 1980: 59 and n. 153). Because of the statement in 15:37, which is false by historical criteria (cf. C.3 below), it is probable that the five books of Jason, like the epitome, ended with the victory over Nicanor in 160 B.C. (on which see Habicht, JSHRZ, 171–72, 280 n. 37a; otherwise Goldstein *1 Maccabees* AB, 27, 33; *2 Maccabees* AB, 5, 12, 505). The epitome—or its *Vorlage(n)*—and 1 Maccabees seem to be independent of one another (on which see Doran 1981: 13–17; somewhat differently Nodet 1986: 330 n. 15), as already the thoroughly contradictory chronologies show (e.g., in connection with the death of Antiochus IV either before or after the restoration of the Temple; Fischer 1980: 133–39; 1985b: 351).

Although the epitome and the introductory letters are distinct from one another both linguistically and in source critical terms, their connection is probable as an intelligible, logical, literary, and above all propagandistic intensification, the purpose of which was to enable Hanukkah finally to establish itself among the Judeans of the Egyptian Diaspora after about 40 years. Such a concern explains why the first adhortatory letter of 143/2 B.C. was dropped; it was certainly in Aramaic and therefore somewhat antiquated; moreover, it was unsuccessful, so that the Greek epitome took its place. The Greek epitome was a work which, besides the extant letter to Aristobulus, provided the further, thorough, "historico-didactic" features so convincing to the ears of the Alexandrian Judeans. This also agrees well with the whole book, namely with the adoption of the festival at the Nile, which is certainly not attested prior to 124 B.C. Apparently, this same cultic intention served to attach the Ptolemaic Diaspora to the Hasmonean homeland; it may even have been directed against the Oniads, who lived in Egypt and fostered their own sanctuary in Leontopolis (Nickelsburg 1981: 121; Attridge 1984: 183; skeptically Doran 1981: 11–12 and Collins 1986: 78–80, who, however, mistakenly holds that such an "attempt to subordinate the Diaspora to Jerusalem" would have had to be both cleverly and tactfully presented). In other words, neither in an ancient nor in a modern sense is 2 Maccabees as a whole a work of history (otherwise Vermes 1984: 37–38); instead, it is a sort of "Festal Scroll," an aretalogy and didactic narrative of the wonder-working power of God, which both Jews and heathens of the time equally valued highly (Momigliano 1975: 104–5; 1980: 577–78; Attridge 1984: 183 and n. 68; Doran's objections [1981: 105–7] may perhaps apply to the epitome, but not to the whole of the book).

This common purpose of establishing the annual festival of Hanukkah (as it is called today) unifies the different parts of the writing, as was already seen by Bunge in his *Diss. phil.,* published in 1971. Accordingly, taken as a whole, 2 Maccabees in its present form displays the characteristics of a Judaism that was schooled in up-to-date Greek rhetoric and literary style (on the linguistic character of the book, see Abel and Starcky 1961: 26; Goldstein, *2 Maccabees* AB, 20 and n. 54; Dommershausen 1985: 9; esp. Doran 1981: 24–46; Enermalm-Ogawa 1987: 54–145). The ascription to Egypt seems certain (despite the hesitations of Vermes 1984: 30–31, 35–37; cf. Collins 1986: 11) because of the addresses of the two introductory letters, the origin of Jason in Cyrenaica, and the transmission of the writing within the framework of the LXX. The work probably became known there in the 1st century before or after the turn of our era (Habicht, JSHRZ, 169–70, 176; Fischer 1980: 14 n. 30; cf. Schaefer, *IJH,* 544; Dommershausen 1985: 9; Nickelsburg 1981: 121 thinks of an origin in Judea in the time of Alexander Janneus; cf. Will and Orrieux 1986: 62; Momigliano 1980: 571; [cf. 1975: 105] prefers the early date of 124 B.C.). Philo of Alexandria seems to have been familiar with the book (Habicht, JSHRZ, 177; *HJP*² 3/1: 534; otherwise Momigliano 1980: 577), as was the *Assumption of Moses* (U. Kellermann 1979: 94–95).

3. Title and Transmission. The title of the work is secondary or perhaps even tertiary; that is, it may have arisen in the course of the Christian use of the text. It was apparently the Christian tradition which united the "four" books of Maccabees and gave them their common designation which has lasted to the present (Habicht, JSHRZ, 169; Goldstein, *2 Maccabees* AB, 3–4 and n. 1). It was apparently also in this way that the original title of 1 Maccabees was lost, since it was only available to the Christians within the framework of the LXX. However, one ought not to exclude the possibility that already the Greek-speaking Jason had termed his book the "Maccabean History" *(Makkabaika)*. Later on, the title was more or less correctly transferred to the three other writings. The history and textual criticism of the text of 2 Maccabees are discussed by Abel and Starcky 1961: 79–82; Habicht, JSHRZ, 191–94; Goldstein, *2 Maccabees* AB, 124–27; *HJP*^{2} 3/1: 534–35.

4. Scholarly Issues. The two introductory letters present many problems. They were already composed in the 2d century B.C. No serious doubts as to the authenticity and unity of the first letter (1:1–10) have been raised since the fundamental investigation by Bickerman in 1933, although a few details remain controversial.

On the other hand, the second letter (1:10–2:18; bibliography in Fischer 1980: 87) is still generally considered to be a forgery (otherwise, e.g., Flusser 1984: 572 and n. 89). However, the allegedly historical argument against its authenticity (which derives ultimately from Holleaux) is unconvincing (Fischer 1980: 92–96): Antiochus III did in fact plunder the temple of Bel in Elam and was only subsequently *(tachy)* cut to pieces there in the sanctuary of Nanaia (1:13; cf. Dan 11:19!), where his son Antiochus IV was later to fail, dying shortly afterward in Tabai in Persia. Evidence is concealed in the Babylonian Talmud (*Šabb.* 21b) which expressly and independently confirms the date of the letter toward the end of 163 B.C. (cf. Fischer 1980: 90–92, 99–100, 216). Thus it appears that this document is really the sole authentic surviving record of Judas Maccabeus himself.

The contents may be paraphrased as follows: an introductory aretalogy of God simultaneously deprecates the "foreign king and rule" while "explaining" the "renewed Temple consecration" (on the varying designations for this festival see Fischer 1980: 90–91 and n. 218; Doran 1981: 4–5 and n. 9) by retrospect into the Israelite and pre-Hellenistic history. A second *Leitmotiv* emerges in the course of the letter: the "return of the Judeans" according to Isa 11:10, i.e., the ingathering of the Diaspora, as well as the "punishment of the oppressors of Israel." This *eschaton,* which is envisioned in the immediate future, is apocalyptically conceived on the basis of the "breakthrough of the kingship of God" which has so recently "revealed" itself in the "wonderful victory" over Antiochus IV and his son (1:11–17). In actual fact, Judas succeeded in bringing his threatened compatriots from Palestine back to the land of Israel. In staking his claim for complete freedom, the rebel formulated his own demand for leadership at the expense of the high priest, who had collaborated with the Greco–Macedonian kings. Ultimately, Judas' attitude was that of a statesman, politician, and military leader, and was not biblical and conservative but revolutionary and truly "Hellenistic" (Fischer 1980: 182–84).

Thus, the letter was intended to set in a new and deeper light the re-establishment of the "cult of the fathers" in which the Maccabee himself had participated together with Menelaus, the high priest and rightful representative of Judea, both under the authority of the "divine" king Antiochus V Eupator. The evidence for this is not only the date of the festival itself—that is, exactly three years to the very day after the desecration of the Temple (Nodet 1986: 327), probably on the same day of the month as the birth of Antiochus IV Epiphanes, who was revered as a god by his son and successor (Fischer 1980: 72–73 and *Add.*, p. 218)—but also a group of five documents which have been authentically transmitted to us outside the introduction, namely in the epitome. However, their correct sequence remains controversial.

These documents should be placed in the following order: 11:27–33; 11:34–38; 9:19–27; 11:22–26; and 11:17–21 (Fischer 1980: 64–80). The three last-mentioned letters together make up a single recording procedure which is completed by the writing of the Roman envoys (11:34–38). The chronological order emerges from simple reversal of the sequence in which the documents were archived; the two letters "of King Antiochus to the Judeans" (9:19–27; 11:27–33) have been exchanged and thus they represent the only real error in the epitome. The five documents (in Judas' archive?) were not originally intended for publication, which is evident from the lack of the relative order of the notification. This is important for the genuine evaluation and secondary application of these witnesses, in particular as regards what they suggest and offer as contemporary and later tendencies.

The two letters 11:22–26 and 17–21 expressly attest to the re-establishment of the earlier cult in Jerusalem, and thereby to the actual state of Seleucid sovereignty over Judea at the end of 164 B.C. Because of the Maccabean successes, as well as other reasons, Antiochus V changed his course with respect to the policies of his recently deceased father, Antiochus IV. It is possible that the third document, 9:19–27, represents an attempt to motivate and, propagandistically, to legitimize, this change of policy in order to secure the allegiance of all Judeans for the new and not yet come-of-age sovereign. However, the authenticity of this "hand-record," which so impressively bears witness to the "madness" of the "deathly ill" but nevertheless fairly pleasant "Epimanes," remains doubtful (Fischer 1980: 74–79, 87, 96; Doran 1981: 62; Alexander 1984: 586, 595 and nn. 61–62). However, in terms of contents, this writing forms a close counterpart to the "Judean" letter to Aristobulus (1:10–2:18), although the languages, presuppositions, motivations, thoughts, senders, and recipients of both records are very different, and have first been brought together by modern historical criticism.

Thus the question as to the historical intention, evaluation, and interpretation of the events in Jerusalem in December of 164 B.C. presents itself. It appears that Judas returned and submitted, at least externally and formally, to Seleucid authority. The Temple was restored and Menelaus was its first priest. Shortly afterward, however, Judas rebelled once more, only to be defeated in the summer (or autumn) of 163 by Lysias and the king, who, because of further dangers, withdrew from Jerusalem. Menelaus was sacrificed, and the Oniads escaped to Egypt (Fischer 1980: 80–85). In this seemingly paradoxical situation, in which the defeated Judas asserted himself, the rebels interpreted the "wonderful salvation" in their own sense, even though they had in fact returned to the Seleucid authority. Indeed, they remained peaceful for all of two years. In their own writings, however, they hailed God as "the true king," proclaimed the "return of the dispersed," and thus asserted on their own level the national state of Israel. Likewise, they celebrated the anniversary of the consecration of the Temple no longer out of loyalty to the hated Seleucid king but as the "true wonder of the in-breaking Lordship of God." With respect to their compatriots in Egypt, the letter to Aristobulus (1:10–2:18) testifies to this permanently rebellious, current-political, apologetical, and ideologized view of things, to which was opposed the pragmatic-positivistic understanding of matters held by Greeks such as Polybius.

In the epitome (or already in Jason's narrative) the restoration of the Temple in 164 seems likewise to have been "judaized." The death of the "archfiend" Antiochus corresponds to the "renewed Temple dedication" (Doran 1981: 61–63); Menelaus and the (new) king are passed over in silence, whereas Judas and his merits are emphasized (9:1–10:9). The reality of the events may be presented in 10:7 (Enermalm-Ogawa 1987: 92–93); the secondary evaluation of them in 10:4. The First Book of Maccabees is more instructive when, on the same occasion—apparently because of the restoration of Seleucid sovereignty—it intones a lament (see above). The varying designations of Hanukkah, the heathen elements in Judas' celebration, the anniversary date itself, and the noticeable reticence of the rabbis (Abel and Starcky 1961: 12), indeed the entire tendency both to excuse Judas (2 Macc 11:15) and even to present him as "the true high priest" (Fischer 1980: 212, 218, *Add.*, p. 75 n. 185; Nodet 1986) find an obvious and perhaps convincing explanation in this way. Rarely in the Hellenistic period do documents and literary accounts permit us direct insight into a then-current political controversy as well as into the contemporary Judean understanding of history.

It remains uncertain whether it was Jason, the epitomizer, or a later editor who first published these documents and/or organized them in their present sequence. In spite of Goldstein (*2 Maccabees* AB, 71, 81–83, 122 ["by 86 B.C.E."]), Attridge (1984: 177), and Collins (1981: 261–62; 1986: 72–73, 77 ["not long after the Maccabean revolt"]), it would be futile to speculate further over such questions as the place, time, person, activity, and character of this historian (?) in the manner of the earlier source criticism; in fact, we know nothing certain as to Jason of Cyrene (Abel and Starcky 1961: 26–27; Habicht, JSHRZ, 170, 173–74; Fischer 1980: 14 and n. 31; *HJP*[2] 3/1: 532).

As far as the epitome itself is concerned, the following organization may be discerned (Doran 1981: 93–94, 110; esp. Nickelsburg 1981: 118, here repeated):

1. Blessing: Jerusalem during the priesthood of Onias III (3:1–40);
2. Sin: Hellenization of Jerusalem under Jason and Menelaus (4:1–5:10);
3. Punishment: Reprisals of Antiochus IV (5:11–6:17);
4. Turning point: Deaths of the martyrs and prayers of the people (6:18–8:4);
5. Judgment and salvation: The victories of Judas (8:5–15:36).

This structure corresponds to the well-known Deuteronomistic scheme of sin and divine retribution (Nickelsburg 1981: 118–20; Rajak 1986: 141).

As far as the *Vorlage(n)* of the epitome is concerned, the following conclusion may perhaps be drawn: its depiction of the Seleucid administration and its *apparatus* is quite authentic and of historical value. This is occasionally confirmed by a primary epigraphic find (Habicht, JSHRZ, 178, 190). When Jason of Cyrene (writing from the point of view of the cosmopolitan Judean Diaspora) makes his judgments, his understanding of things is neither old-fashioned nor provincial (as is that in 1 Maccabees); rather, this Greek-speaking author is a valuable witness to the general literature, culture, and spirituality of Hellenistic times.

At least, the epitome is to be assigned to the "tragic" historiography of that period, as already Benedictus Niese emphasized in 1900 (Abel and Starcky 1961: 17; Goldstein, *1 Maccabees* AB, and 34 and n. 70, *2 Maccabees* AB, 20–21; Habicht, JSHRZ, 189–90; Bickerman 1979: 95–96; Enermalm-Ogawa 1987: 54; esp. Doran 1979: 107–10; 1981: 84–97; cf. *HJP*[2] 3/1: 533; the concept of "tragic historiography" is, however, just as problematic as are "Hellenism" and "ideology"; and yet it is well established today and is permissible from a scholarly point of view). Polybius, who represented the "pragmatic" direction in the 2d century B.C., concentrated on military and politics, that is, on the affairs of state *(ta pragmata)*. In contradistinction, the "tragic" historiography attempted to captivate its readers with a style which was rhetorical and dramatizing, which cascaded its effects, and which offered appealing entertainment and sensitive participation. It was in this sense that the epitome sought to shock its audience both psychically and physically through exaggeration and the broad depiction of horrific scenes and immeasurable passions, but also through praise for the heroic deeds of individuals and the terrible demise of the "archfiend." However, such moralistic and dramatizing applications often do damage to the truth of historical insight: Habicht (JSHRZ, 191 and n. 129–30) recognized the tendentious distortion of the "enemies," be they of foreign origin or from the author's own people. The use of intellectual concepts instead of moral categories which could have been appropriately applied is peculiar (13:23; 14:5 + 8; 15:33; cf. Habicht, JSHRZ, 190 and n. 122, following Abel). Among features which belong to the repertoire of the "tragic" or melodramatic account are such things as divine self-manifestations (*epiphaneiai:* Doran 1979: 113–14; 1981: 98–104; Momigliano 1980: 575), angels, heavenly riders, and dream-visions (*oneira* and *theōriai*) as in 2:21; 3:24–40; 5:2–4; 10:29–30; 11:6 + 8; 12:22; 15:11–16 + 22–23. Indeed, anything that was overwhelming, wonderful, and which escaped rational perception (2:21; 7:18; 12:15; 15:21) was prolixly presented. The style and vocabulary correspond to those of the Hellenistic environment, including the fact that it was possible to employ the term "barbarians" against the Greeks and Macedonians themselves (2:21; 10:4; 13:9; cf. 4:47). Expressions from the heathen religious sphere appear in 6:23 *(hadēs)* and 7:13–14 (*metallaxantos ton bion ap'* or *hyp'anthrōpōn;* Habicht, JSHRZ, 215 n. 7a, 235 n. 14a). At least linguistically, the terms *Hellēnismos* and *Ioudaismos* constituted no problem for Jason or the epitomizer, even though the author confused edifying didacticism with true rhetorical art. (On the conceptions of "Judaism" and "Hellenism," see Fischer 1980: viii and nn. b + c; Amir 1982; Gafni 1984: 1.1a; Bichler 1986: 12–19; Will and Orrieux 1986: 10–12.) Against this background, 1 Maccabees seems not merely to be more "Hebraic," but directly more sober, factual, political, and "pragmatic" (to use Polybius' term).

However, the epitome, or Jason, judaized the Greek and Hellenistic models (Doran 1981: 89–109; cf. Enermalm-Ogawa 1987: 118–19). The centerpiece is the Temple, its holiness, age, reputation, and place in the world. The "threat," "violation," "restoration," and "defense" of the Sanctuary are already sounded in the foreword of the epitome, 2:19–22 (Abel and Starcky 1961: 25; Habicht, JSHRZ, 186–87; now, thoroughly, Doran 1981: 47–76). Note, however, the remark in 5:19 *("the people were not chosen because of the place, but the place because of the people")*, which might seem to imply a sort of abstraction, i.e., a relation to the very biblical tradition and revelation which relativizes the visible cult, the (Greek!) language, and the "realistic reality" in the Hellenistic sense. We shall return to this point.

The epitome can hardly be called "Pharisaic" in a strict term (Habicht, JSHRZ, 189). It glorifies Judas and mentions Simon in such ways that we are unable to speak of a clearly pro- or anti-Hasmonean tendency; Goldstein (*1 Maccabees* AB, 33), Habicht (JSHRZ, 188), and Nickelsburg (1981: 121) are somewhat too reserved on this point (see also Collins 1986: 80; and Efron 1987: 19). Zion and the city, the land and the "Hebrews" remain as they are depicted: namely, as the sole, exclusive, and only rightful sites of the highest worship of God which all Judeans are obliged to accept. No claim for the right to an independent state, in the sense advocated by the Maccabees, is advanced (Habicht, JSHRZ, 188).

In actual fact, the problem of the Diaspora lay on another level. The question was not so much the politico-military or even the linguistic-cultural opposition; rather, it was defined by the religio-ideological competition between rigorous *Ioudaismos* (2:21; 8:1; 14:38; incorporated in the "Sanctuary," "city," "fatherland," "constitution," and especially in "the Law": 13:11 + 14; 15:17–8, etc.) and hedonistic-enlightened "Hellenism." Thus the more free and fashionable manners of the "foreigners"—Macedonians, Greeks, Egyptians, and Syrians—pursued a line that was *per definitionem* anti-Judaic. This conflict arose and persisted in the Diaspora; of course, it was less violent in the "Jewish" Judea of the Hasmoneans.

It is with sensibilities attuned to these nuances that we must understand the description in the epitome (or perhaps already in Jason's work) of the "time of persecution" in the homeland as the epoch of the most extreme "intermixture" *(epimixia)* according to 4:13; 14:3 + 38 (Fischer 1980: ix and n. d, 49 and n. 133; Habicht, JSHRZ, 271 n. 3b reads *amixia*). In this way the heathen cult in the Temple was the unheard summit of desecration (to Judean ears in the Diaspora!), in which it was possible for a genetic Greek (if there were any at all at this time!) to turn out to be a genuine "barbarian." Likewise, the "Hebrew," who was devoted to "the God of the fathers," was able to serve as a model of *hērōs* in the sense of the *ēthē kai pathē* of the Greek rhetorical and "affectionate" understanding. Such inversions are astonishing only to us. The Aristobulus letter (1:10–2:18) refers to the "victory" over the "sham-king" Antiochus and to the demand for an independent state; there is no question of any "persecution of the faithful" or "Hellenization," but only of "war" (2:14; Fischer 1980: 100). It is doubtful whether such a rivalry between "Judaism and Hellenism" in the Judean region itself during the Maccabean uprising is historically accurate (Fischer 1980: 174–88, 195; esp. 186–87; likewise, but for other reasons, Bringmann 1983: 12, 145–48; otherwise Habicht, JSHRZ, 185, who passes sentence *ex eventu*). Such considerations reinforce the ascription of the epitome (and of Jason?) to the Egyptian Diaspora, which was in fact persecuted (otherwise Doran 1981: 112–13; Rajak 1986: 132).

5. Theological Matters. In 2 Maccabees God is many-layered and many-sided, ambivalent and perhaps even discordant, as such self-contradictory (cf. Dommershausen 1985: 9–11; Enermalm-Ogawa 1987: 124–33, 138–41; the two introductory letters [1:1–2:18], which are more firmly anchored in Israelite tradition, deserve special study). He is the almighty God of Israel (8:15), the "Holy Lord of all Sanctification" (14:36) who concluded His Covenant with the fathers (8:15) and revealed Himself (3:24 + 30; 14:15; 15:34). Elsewhere, however, He is conceptually defined in good Hellenistic terms as "the Highest and Greatest" (3:31 + 36), although the superlatives do not simultaneously imply the existence or "real" power of other, lesser gods. God has need of nothing at all (14:35) and is Himself the One who created everything and man from nothing (7:11, 22–23, 28; 13:14; 14:46; on this *creatio ex nihilo* see Abel and Starcky 1961: 24–25; Habicht, JSHRZ, 187 and n. 101; U. Kellermann 1979: 73–77, with differentiations). He is the helper and comforter, but also the righteous judge who punishes stringently, not for revenge but for "improvement and for our warning," and who also permits the vicarious sacrifice of others. He allows Himself to be reconciled, and in spite of wrath and mutability He keeps faith with His Chosen People (Doran 1981: 53–55).

A theological foundation for the epitome (and the work of Jason?) is provided by the whole of the book of Isaiah and by Daniel 12 (U. Kellermann 1979: 81–85; Nickelsburg 1981: 121). The prophecies were believed to have been realized. Together with the Deuteronomistic understanding of the sin and the necessary (!) divine retribution (which was intensified by the collective responsibility), this conception led to an extreme tension and inversion: God's promise was held to realize itself even in the physical suffering of "the pious" (on this problem, see U. Kellermann 1979: 62, cf. 93). Such an assumption led to a specific martyrology, namely to the idea of the unusual hero who suffers in his innocence and dies; yet such a "child of heaven" is elevated by the righteous, compensating, and preserving God through a new creation and complete reversal of all things: to physical resurrection and eternal life (Abel and Starcky 1961: 18–21; Habicht,

JSHRZ, 187, 234 n. 9c; U. Kellermann 1979 *passim,* esp. 40; Fischer 1980: 165–68, 170, cf. 28–29, 151–54; Doran 1981: 110; Nickelsburg 1981: 120–21 and n. 60–62; Will and Orrieux 1986: 60–61). This "theologization" of human existence (Will and Orrieux 1986: 59–61) is entirely foreign to 1 Maccabees with its positivistic understanding of the world.

The question here is not whether resurrection as a projection of extreme retribution was intended to compensate ideologically and psychologically for a horrible reality; patterns of ancient Egypt (the Osiris cult), and of the Greek heroes who incarnated themselves vividly in permanent reverence, may be the antecedents of such conceptions. In any event, 2 Maccabees makes manifest the memory of the individual personality: after the "last judgment," resurrection of everybody was either supposed to be positive for "bliss" or negative for "eternal damnation." Nor will it be possible here to touch on the deeper theological problems as to why God surrendered to the most extreme tortures precisely those who were his most faithful, or why (to our limited human understanding) God appears to have "needed" reconciliation with and in Himself (which, according to Christians, was then effected by Jesus of Nazareth). The impression of divine discord remains, as in the last instance "evil" does not act of its own accord but rather as a divine tool.

Prayer (Flusser 1984: 572–73), mediation through didactic stories, as well as special intermediaries, including the dreams of Jeremiah and Onias III, won increasing influence at this time (Abel and Starcky 1961: 22–24; Habicht, JSHRZ, 187 and n. 104; U. Kellermann 1979: 12, 86–87; Fischer 1980: 103 and n. 253; Doran 1981: 71–74). Thus, the immediate access to God was seen as questionable and at least problematical. On the other hand, alongside of the "Covenant" and "honesty to the Law" (Collins 1986: 77), fear of God and personal reliance became new fundamentals of the faith (6:30; 8:18 + 23; 10:28; 15:7). Spirituality and "fidelity to the Law" appeared to be more important than sacrifice, cult, and other externals (2:22; 3:1 + 15; 4:11 + 17; 6:1 + 5–6 + 21 + 28; 7:2 + 9 + 11 + 23–24 + 30 + 37; 8:21 + 36; 13:11 + 14; 15:9). Such an individual attitude expressed itself in public "confession" and with emphasis, as when the "evil heathen" converted to the true faith and acknowledged God's efficaciousness to the entire world (Heliodorus in 3:35–39; Nicanor in 8:36; Antiochus Epiphanes in 9:11–27; Lysias in 11:13). A dynamic was founded in this spirit which developed further in Christianity and revolutionized the ancient world.

C. Summary

1. Recapitulation of the *Quellenkritik*. With the exceptions of the biblical citations and Judas' proposed treaty with Rome from 161 or 160 B.C., the sources of 1 Maccabees which date to the end of the 2d century B.C. remain uncertain. As far as 2 Maccabees is concerned, the following development in chronological sequence may be assumed (otherwise Nickelsburg 1981: 118). First was the alleged "Maccabean history" in Greek by Jason of Cyrene, now lost (which included a prehistory of the revolt, and which was written from the point of view of the Hellenistic imperial history). Later the epitome of this history was composed by a possibly Alexandrian Judean, with alterations and additions. It was strongly rhetorical, didactic, and emotionalizing; i.e., similar to the "pathetic" or "tragic" historiography according to the genuine Hellenistic tradition (as perhaps was already the case with Jason's work). The final stage was the entire book of 2 Maccabees, including the two introductory letters which were translated from Semitic-language originals. This final product was presented with the intention of introducing Hanukkah (or whatever it was then called) into the Judean Diaspora in Egypt. The *terminus post quem* of the final version of the book, as we now possess it, is the year 125 B.C.; at least it was apparently known to Philo of Alexandria in the beginning of our era.

2. Analysis of the Documents and Related Methodology. Without prejudice to the authenticity of Jewish-Hellenistic literature in general (e.g., Fischer 1980: 189–92; Alexander 1984: 585–88, 596; Schmidt 1986), the analysis of the documents which was introduced by Elias Bickerman proves to be a secure foundation for further study. Additionally, it is now possible to distinguish between suggestion and realization, primary and secondary publication, application, tendency, and audience(s). In this fashion it is permissible to reconstruct an original series of records (probably deriving from Judas' archive) within the epitome (see B.4 above) which was secondarily completed by the letter to Aristobulus (2 Macc 1:10–2:18). It is important to recognize the first recipients (cf. Vermes 1984: 33–39) in the late 60s of the 2d century B.C., as already the languages imply: Judas will have addressed himself to his compatriots in Egypt in Aramaic, while the Seleucid king must have written in Greek to his subjects (that is, to the local, more or less "Hellenistically" oriented elite of Judea!). There is no problem with the later target groups of the two books of Maccabees (which were then unified by the Christians according to their own points of view) around the end of the 2d and in the 1st centuries B.C.: namely, on the one hand, the native audience in Hasmonean Judea (1 Maccabees), and on the other, the "Hellenistic" Diaspora in Ptolemaic Egypt (2 Maccabees). Such a (partial) communicative reconstruction is a necessary presupposition of the true historical evaluation.

3. Structures of the Histories of Events. A history of events results from the unfolding of then-current political controversies and the peculiarities of the times. The outward quarrels in Judea which were conducted in "revolt" and with increasing "zeal" took place to attain freedom and self-determination, and were also concerned with the right of *asylia* (Fischer fc.), the office of high priest, and the "leadership of the people" (*JW* 1.31). However, already contemporaries recognized what may have been underlying reasons, namely the "battle for the Torah"—not only for its legitimacy as such (either in the pluralistic Diaspora or in confrontation with Antiochus IV in Judea), but also within the community itself as to the "right" understanding, the "authoritative" doctrine, and the practical embodiment in the context of a new time (on this, see Collins 1986: 12–15, 244–46; Will and Orrieux 1986: 60, 126–31, 134–36). The author of 1 Maccabees received the Israelite tradition immediately and as a matter of course; he passed it on straightforwardly in his own fashion and understood his time as "fulfilled prophecy" (Neuhaus 1974a: 180,

228–30). One aim of this writing was to establish strong identity in the Judean people (Enermalm-Ogawa 1987: 52–53). However, the more enlightened Diaspora, which was quite differently threatened both from within and from without, required argumentative and express commitment to the Law, a necessity which perhaps intensified the movement toward theology. In any case, the consequence of this development was the splintering of the biblical community into individuals and groups, reactionary or progressive, which ultimately combated one another, whether openly or covertly.

At the same time, the local process in Judea was intimately bound up with the events taking place on the broader field of the *Reichsgeschichte* (*grande histoire,* following Will and Orrieux). What the king needed was not so much a pious priest or financially sound Temple superintendent, but rather a capable vassal and military leader (Fischer 1985a). The struggle between the high priests, the Oniads, Jason, Menelaus, Alcimus, and Judas (and his brothers) was not merely a personal one; rather, it was a structural problem. The situation was complicated by the lasting claim that the Ptolemies, who had granted asylum to the Oniads, staked to Palestine. At the same time, in Judea the "orthodox" and the apocalypticists were increasingly reluctant to follow the Hasmoneans (otherwise Efron 1987), who deliberately expanded their "royal" authority according to the Greco-Macedonian conceptions.

For further details concerning the course of events see, most recently, Rappaport 1984, Fischer 1985a; fc. The increasing differentiation within the country itself is noteworthy, as is the political, cultural, and ideological emancipation of the Judeans (the "pariahs," in Max Weber's phrase) who, however, were not always accepted by their neighbors (which in turn produced and intensified Hasmonean self-awareness).

In spite of their biblical presuppositions, both books of Maccabees demonstrate the appropriation of such Hellenistic elements as an increasingly apologetic tendency, a "rhetoricalization," and evaluation of the individual. However, we must acknowledge some breaks which are quite manifest in 2 Maccabees. There the Greek-formulated *Ioudaismos* is contrasted with a "barbaric" *Hellēnismos,* a supreme example of a perverted propaganda. In spite of the allusions to its biblical antecedents, 1 Maccabees has abandoned the fundamental theological-biblical structure in favor of a secular historiography in the Greek tradition (Will and Orrieux 1986: 57). The transformation expresses itself also in the interpretive patterns. Judas led the Diaspora (whose members had, according to tradition, been "punished because of their own apostasy") back to their "home," whereas his brothers and successors (Mendels 1987: 47–51) undertook the expansion and even the enforced Judaization of Palestine. Thus, the racial identity of the Israelite people was imperiled without troubling the "Hellenistic" ruler and his colorfully assembled army. Instead of religious-cultural "separateness," the Hasmoneans now fostered the political enmity toward the rival Seleucids (Neuhaus 1974b: 172; Fischer 1980: 56 n. 142), as well as the "foreign-friendliness" toward Sparta and Rome (Will and Orrieux 1986: 58). The transience or actual devaluation and relativization of all concepts, norms, and behaviors became visible and, in terms of mentality, they created an atmosphere of doubt, ambiguity, and instability.

The superficially static Judean understanding of the world and of history (Rajak 1986) was dynamically, thoroughly, and fundamentally transformed through the Hellenistic influences. The loss of identity expressed itself particularly in the field of religion, notably the aggravation of the conflict over the Torah, its use, and the validity of both "written" and (steadily multiplying) "oral" authorities, beginning with the 2d century B.C. (Will and Orrieux 1986: 225–26). The translations and commentaries are the signposts of this development. Relativization expressed itself in a positivistic sense, as at the death of Antiochus IV before or after the restoration of the Temple, but also in the understanding of reality as such, of the effect and interpretation of events. We have already seen the cases of Judas' treaty with the Romans, of Hanukkah, and of the very odd concept of *Hellēnismos;* to this we may add the question of the constitution of Judea (monarchy or rule by priestly aristocrats), a theme which is connected with the problems surrounding the legitimation of the Hasmoneans. In 1 Maccabees Judas' death, the actual end of the revolt, was aptly compensated for by the everlasting "first treaty" with Rome. Indeed, this was in its origins the political tendency of a single party, i.e., the Maccabeans (in 2 Maccabees the same compensation for the failure of Judas is supplied by the Day of Nicanor, that is, the annual "victory-day" of the whole community). A similar observation applies to the book of Daniel, where the deceased Maccabee was elevated to the status of an eternal *hērōs,* the "Son of Man" (Fischer 1980: 152–54). In all these examples, the loss of a "pragmatic" understanding of history, as expressed likewise in the letter to Aristobulus (2 Macc 1:10–2:18), is remarkable (Fischer 1980: 171–73). Thus, the route leading to the rabbinical conceptions of history becomes more evident.

4. Aspects of Historical Inferences. Both books of Maccabees reveal Judean authors actively discussing the "sufferings" which had been inflicted by the heathen. In the course of this process the biblical faith increasingly assumed the linguistic, conceptual, and even aggressive forms of the "persecutors." Both writings were not originally missionary (in a Christian sense) works addressed to foreigners, but to a properly Judean audience. They were less apologetic than propagandistic. 1 Maccabees conservatively asserts the Sadducean position of the ruling Hasmonean against the "ultra-orthodox" opposition in their own country. 2 Maccabees, taken as a whole, seeks to establish in the Diaspora an annual festival along Greek lines; the work attempts this argumentatively and with psychological insight, while the epitome is especially didactic and rhetorical.

Both writings express the increasing degree of reflection upon the "self-apostasy" and the splitting of consciousness. In 2 Maccabees, it interpenetrates the whole of the epitome. Judas himself, however, was able to project the problem onto the Diaspora. In the letter to Aristobulus, if anywhere, it is only in 2:2–3 that we hear of such "apostasy." This corresponds to the genuine Maccabean ideology, which is probably present from 1 Macc 2:6 onward and in 2 Macc 8:1–4: the rebels regarded themselves as being persecuted, and thus as perfectly "righteous" (cf.

Enermalm-Ogawa 1987: 51), also as far as the question of fighting on the Sabbath was concerned. In 124/3 B.C., the first introductory letter of 2 Maccabees mentions the *"apostasy of Jason (the high priest) and his followers"* (1:7). This corresponds to the contemporary view of the Hasmoneans as in 1 Maccabees, namely that the internal political opponents are to be excluded from the "true (and allegedly positive) Israel."

In contradistinction to such *Realpolitik,* the earlier book of Daniel had asserted the idea of "self-apostasy among the people." Daniel also retained God's righteous punishment, the confidence in Him and His grace, as well as the deeper theological aspect of the "persecution" against which were counterpoised the optimistic Hasmonean concepts of the "fulfilled prophecy" and of the "renewal of the empires of David and Solomon" (cf. Fischer 1980: 182, following Neuhaus; Will and Orrieux 1986: 58). In the epitome, however, the equivocal and "theologically" intensified view (Will and Orrieux 1986: 59–61), which has traumatically influenced Jewish history until the present time (cf. Bickerman 1979: xii–xiii), became triumphant. Thus, a decisive transformation of the Judean mentality took place in the late Hellenistic period, the "breaking up" of the Maccabeans flared up and in time reached the "zeal" of the Zealots in A.D. 70. It was no longer the pragmatic attitude of a Polybius or of 1 Maccabees; rather, the religious emphasis and intensification established themselves on a permanent basis. From the Maccabeans' militant "confession" of God, the Law, and the faith of the fathers, the path ran to the Holy Maccabees, and to the Mother with her seven sons (2 Maccabees 7; *4 Maccabees* 8–17). For the first time in biblical religion, martyrdom had become a new type of divine worship (Conzelmann 1981: 16–18; further on this aspect and its historical consequences, see Abel and Starcky 1961: 30–34; U. Kellermann 1979: 12–13, 17–19, 94–142; cf. Efron 1987: 3, 54). Gradually, Jewish history took more and more the features of grief and pain.

The "Maccabees" were the first and only Saints to be reverenced by parts of both Judaism and Christianity up to the present time (Habicht, JSHRZ, 233 n. 7a; Fischer 1980: 28–29; Momigliano 1980: 575–77, 578 and n. 8). These champions were originally adored (in the Greek sense) at the site of their execution, at their grave in Antioch. In the course of history they developed into the prototypes of resistance to heathen and secular authority everywhere. Today the bones of these rebels, victims, heroes, or witnesses to Faith reside in Cologne, Germany. Their memorial day is August 1st.

5. Conclusions. 1 and 2 Maccabees testify to the diversity of the late-Hellenistic epoch in general and especially (in the sense of Baras *WHJP* 1/8: xxv–xxvii; Vermes 1984: 33–39) of the Judeans and the Diaspora in the age of the Second Temple. They emit echoes reminiscent of rifts in countries, sects, and individuals (otherwise Efron 1987: 20). We cannot claim that there was a "canonical unity" of the Judean nation and its Torah for the years of the protracted crisis (Tcherikover *WHJP* 1/6: 5–6). There were indeed Messianism and eschatology, as well as continual conflicts and doubts of oneself and the Law. Rather, we encounter different entities, languages, concepts, traditions, intentions, target-groups, varying and increasingly differentiated segments, and apologetically or polemically reacting identities and individuals. Both openly and in more covert form, intercultural connections become evident as, for example, when both the "Greek" Poseidonius from Syrian Apamea and the "Jewish" Pharisees, or the desert sectarians, characterized the active and "thieving" Hasmonean state as "degenerate" (Fischer 1985a).

This dynamic process of universalization and radicalization intensified the disintegration, the polarization and gowth of ideology, of which, finally, the Hasmoneans were the victims, and which, in Judaism, the rabbis were the first to pick up. In 2 Maccabees the characteristics of syncretism or *epimixia* (on the modern concept of syncretism see Will and Orrieux 1986: 147–48, 150) are openly displayed, whereas they are hidden in 1 Maccabees, even though man's own activity is much emphasized there (Neuhaus 1974a: 231–32, 240; Will and Orrieux 1986: 57–58). Resurrection and immortality in 2 Maccabees betray their proximity to Stoic philosophy; the belief in a life to come reminds us of the ancient Egyptians (U. Kellermann 1979: 28–29 n. d, e; 89–93; and cf. 46–53). The elevation of executed "champions" from among the "lower" echelons of the people is another characteristic of importance, as it prefigures the "King of the Jews" of the Christians. A feeling of inferiority (which simultaneously insisted on superiority), a sensitively concealed reaction to the perceived attractions of Hellenism, as well as the ruling Romans and the rise of the natives in the Ptolemaic Empire, the attendant dissemination of Egyptian religion throughout the world of Greek culture—amid such circumstances, contradictions, and changes, reality itself was stood on its head. Hanukkah turned out in the course of time to be, like Christmas, a heathen-biblical-Jewish-Christianizing festival (cf. Petuchowski 1984: 121; *"the same ceremony may express completely different ideologies"*). Historically it is hardly surprising that the Jews throughout the ages have always been celebrating the rededication of their Temple, which has long vanished, rather than the everlasting birthday of the "evil" King Antiochus, "the god manifest and bearing victory."

The rabbis have removed the two books of Maccabees from their writings; it was modern Zionism which rediscovered them for Jewish identity. The modern Maccabiade immortalizes precisely that Hellenism which Judas is supposed to have vanquished. The first Christians paid homage to the martyrdom and the most extreme witness of faith, the wonders and the visions, the angels and the Saints, the "Last Judgment," the "(physical) Resurrection," and other paradoxes (in the modern sense of the word), perhaps even to the innocent and vicarious sacrificial death of the righteous and suffering Son of Heaven for human atonement and reconciliation with God (on which see U. Kellermann 1979: 11–13). Both separately and together, the two books of Maccabees, and especially their prayers (Enermalm-Ogawa 1987: 142–45), have influenced the mentality of the Jews and Christians up to the present day. Out of the feeling of isolation, of being surrounded by enemies and persecuted until life and death hang in the balance, there arose an attitude which could not be counterbalanced by the claim of one's own superiority. Existential crisis and militant expansion were the psychological consequences for such a minority, and that irrespective of whether or not the threat was real or merely imagined.

Bickerman (1979: 92) recognized that the preservation of the faith in God was the best merit of the Maccabees. Behind the alternate powers of the world, their mutability as well as the deceptive meanings of writings in general, there is the nameless One who beams like Hanukkah from beyond History and Existence, self-contradictory and inconceivable to human sense: *Idem ipse fuit Deus triune puerorum, qui fuit Machabeorum. Illi de igne evaseruut, illi ignibus cruciati suut, utrique tamen in Deo sempiterno vicerunt* (St. Augustine).

Bibliography

Abel, F.-M., and Starcky, J. 1961. *Les Livres des Maccabées,* 3d ed. Paris.

Alexander, P. S. 1984. Epistolary Literature. Pp. 579–96 in Stone 1984.

Amir, Y. 1982. The Term Ioudaismos. *Immanuel* 14: 34–41.

Attridge, H. W. 1984. Historiography. Pp. 157–84 in Stone 1984.

Bichler, R. 1986. Die 'Hellenisten' im 9. Kapitel der Apostelgeschichte. *Tyche* 1: 12–29.

Bickerman, E. 1979. *The God of the Maccabees.* Trans. H. R. Moehring. Leiden.

Borgen, P. 1984. Philo of Alexandria. Pp. 233–82 in Stone 1984.

Bringmann, K. 1983. *Hellenistische Reform und Religionsverfolgung in Judaea.* Abh. Akademie der Wiss. Göttingen, Phil.-hist.Kl., 3d ser., 132. Göttingen.

Collins, J. J. 1981. *Daniel, First Maccabees, Second Maccabees.* Wilmington.

———. 1986. *Between Athens and Jerusalem.* New York.

Conzelmann, H. 1981. *Heiden-Juden-Christen.* Tübingen.

Dimant, D. 1988. Use and Interpretation of Mikra in the Apocrypha and Pseudepigrapha. Pp. 379–419 in Mulder 1988.

Dommershausen, W. 1985. *1 Makkabaeer 2 Makkabaeer.* Fasc. 12 in *Die Neue Echter Bibel,* ed. J. G. Plöger, et al. Würzburg.

Doran, R. 1979. 2 Maccabees and "Tragic History." *HUCA* 50: 107–14.

———. 1981. *Temple Propaganda: The Purpose and Character of 2 Maccabees.* Washington, DC.

Efron, J. 1987. *Studies on the Hasmonean Period.* Leiden.

Enermalm-Ogawa, A. 1987. *Un langage de prière juif en grec.* Stockholm.

Fischer, T. 1980. *Seleukiden und Makkabaeer.* Bochum.

———. 1981. Rom und die Hasmonaeer. *Gymnasium* 88: 139–50.

———. 1983. *Silber aus dem Grab Davids?* Bochum.

———. 1985a. Hasmoneans and Seleucids. Proceedings of the Conference *"Greece and Rome in Eretz Israel,"* Universities of Haifa and Tel Aviv (March 25–28, 1985). (forthcoming).

———. 1985b. Review of Bringmann 1983. *Klio* 67: 350–55.

———. 1986. Zur Auswertung seleukidischer Muenzen. *Schweizerische Numismatische Rundschau* 65: 65–72.

———. fc. Heliodor im Tempel zu Jerusalem—ein 'hellenistischer' Aspekt der 'frommen Legende'. *Festschrift Siegfried Herrmann,* ed. R. Liwak. Stuttgart.

Flusser, D. 1984. Psalms, Hymns and Prayers. Pp. 551–77 in Stone 1984.

Gafni, I. 1984. The Historical Background. Pp. 1–31 in Stone 1984.

Gruen, E. S. 1984. *The Hellenistic World and the Coming of Rome.* 2 vols. Berkeley.

Horst, P. W. van der. 1988. The Interpretation of the Bible by the Minor Hellenistic Jewish Authors. Pp. 519–46 in Mulder 1988.

Kellermann, D. 1987. Die Bücher der Makkabaeer. Pp. 167–82 in *Höre, Israel! Jahwe ist einzig,* ed. E. Sitarz. Stuttgart and Kevelaer.

Kellermann, U. 1979. *Auferstanden in den Himmel.* Stuttgart.

Mendels, D. 1987. *The Land of Israel as a Political Concept in Hasmonean Literature.* Tübingen.

Momigliano, A. 1975. *Alien Wisdom.* Cambridge.

———. 1980. *Sesto Contributo alla Storia degli studi classici e del mondo antico.* 2 Parts. Rome.

Mulder, M. J., ed. 1988. *Mikra: Text, Translation, Reading and Interpretation of the Hebrew Bible in Ancient Judaism and Early Christianity.* CRINT 2/1. Assen/Maastricht and Philadelphia.

Neuhaus, G. O. 1974a. *Studien zu den poetischen Stücken im 1. Makkabaeerbuch.* Würzburg.

———. 1974b. Quellen im 1. Makkabaeerbuch? *Journal for the Study of Judaism* 5: 162–75.

Nickelsburg, G. W. E. 1981. *Jewish Literature Between the Bible and the Mishnah.* Philadelphia.

Nodet, E. 1986. La Dédicace, Les Maccabées et le Messie. *RB* 93: 321–75.

Oppenheimer, A. 1976. Oral Law in the Books of Maccabees. *Immanuel* 6: 34–42.

Petuchowski, J. J. 1984. *Feiertage des Herrn.* Freiburg.

Rajak, T. 1986. The Sense of History in Jewish Intertestamental Writing. *OS* 24 (= *Crises and Perspectives*): 124–45.

Rappaport, U. 1984. The Birth of the Hasmonean State. Pp. 173–77 in *Recent Archaeology in the Land of Israel,* ed. H. Shanks and B. Mazar. Jerusalem and Washington, DC. Repr. 1985.

Schmidt, W. 1986. *Untersuchungen zur Faelschung historischer Dokumente bei Ps.-Aristaio.* Bonn.

Stern, M. 1973. Die Urkunden. Pp. 181–99, 448 in *Literatur und Religion des Frühjudentums,* ed. J. Maier and J. Schreiner. Würzburg.

Stone, M. E., ed. 1984. *Jewish Writings of the Second Temple Period.* CRINT 2/2. Assen and Philadelphia.

Vermes, G. [with Goodman, M.]. 1984. La littérature juive intertestamentaire à la lumière d'un siècle de recherches et de découvertes. Pp. 19–39 in *Études sur le judaïsme hellénistique.* Ed. R. Arnaldez et al. Paris.

Will, E., and Orrieux, C. 1986. *Ioudaïsmos-hellènismos.* Nancy.

THOMAS FISCHER
Trans. Frederick Cryer

THIRD MACCABEES

The document we know as "Third Maccabees" is not very aptly named. Whereas the work does contain echoes of several themes in 2 Maccabees, the historical events reflected in it antedate the Maccabean period proper by some 50 years, and there is nowhere any reference to the epic Maccabean struggle for freedom. Probably the title was used because the author's account of God's miraculous deliverance of the Jews from the destruction threatened by a foreign tyrant and oppressor was reminiscent of the Maccabean revolt and heroic Jewish resistance to the intervention of the Syrian emperor, Antiochus IV Epiphanes, in Palestinian territory and in Jewish affairs: in consequence of which *3 Maccabees* was placed alongside 1 and 2 Maccabees in the manuscripts.

There is little doubt that *3 Maccabees* originated in Alexandria, Egypt. Its style and literary flavor strongly resemble such other Alexandrian writings as 2 Maccabees and the *Letter of Aristeas.* Also the story is set mainly in Alexandria, and one of the author's chief concerns is the status of Egyptian Jews. There are certain similarities between *3 Maccabees* and the type of "historical romance" that flourished in the Hellenistic period. But on the whole it is best to think of his narrative as "pathetic" or "tragic" history. The writer seeks to play on his readers' emotions and to evoke their sympathy for his heroes and the cause they represent. He does so in the most flowery language, employing as many tricks of the rhetorician's trade as he can muster, adding purple passage to purple passage, and piling up epithet upon epithet.

The plot that unfolds in *3 Maccabees* is akin to that of the canonical book of Esther and the tales of divine aid for champions of the Jewish faith in Daniel 1–6. But it is unlikely that the author was directly influenced by any one canonical book. Instead, he draws freely on a variety of old biblical traditions, especially in the prayers offered by Simon and Eleazar in chaps. 2 and 6. His closest affinities, however, are with the Greek additions to Esther, which inserts a theological dimension the secular Hebrew Esther does not contain; in terminology, if not in thought, with the *Letter of Aristeas;* and in ideas, expression, and vocabulary with 2 Maccabees.

The first chapter of *3 Maccabees* begins abruptly and is somewhat disjointed throughout. Saved from a plot against his life, Ptolemy IV Philopator of Egypt proceeds forthwith to the defeat of Antiochus III the Great of Syria at the battle of Raphia (217 B.C.E.). In response to a courtesy visit from a delegation of Jewish elders, Ptolemy resolves to visit Jerusalem. The scene moves swiftly to the temple. Impressed by its magnificence, he insists, against the Law and despite all remonstrances and priestly prayers, on his right to enter. A mighty throng converges at once upon the temple: "The combined shouts of the crowd, ceaseless and vehement, caused an indescribable uproar. It seemed as if not only the people but the very walls and the whole pavement cried out, so much at that moment did they all prefer death to the profanation of the temple" (1:28–29). Simon the High Priest then offers a long prayer, rehearsing the mighty acts of God on behalf of his people Israel. God responds by imposing condign punishment upon Ptolemy, who suffers a seizure. The description of it is a good example of the bombastic language of *3 Maccabees:* "God scourged the one who was greatly exalted by his own insolence and effrontery, tossing him to and fro like a leaf on the wind until he fell impotent to the ground with his limbs paralyzed and unable to speak, completely overpowered by a righteous judgment" (2:21–22).

We next find Ptolemy back in Egypt, breathing vengeance against the Jews. He commands a census of all Jews in Alexandria in order that they might be reduced to slavery. Exemption is offered to those who agree to participate in the pagan mystery cult of Dionysus. Some do apostasize. But the great majority gallantly hold out for their ancestral faith. The angry Ptolemy then decrees that all Jews in his kingdom be transported in chains to Alexandria and there put to death. The account of their deportation (4:1–13) is a classic piece of "pathetic history" writing in the most florid style. Once arrived on the outskirts of the city, the vast multitude of Jews is herded into the racecourse (in this type of literature one does not ask how it could contain them). Ptolemy plans their destruction with Hermon, the captain of his five-hundred-strong elephant brigade. Three times Hermon, or finally Ptolemy himself, sets out on this nefarious exploit, and three times the scheme is thwarted by God's miraculous interference on behalf of the Jews (5:1–22, 23–25; 5:46–6:21). On the last occasion, by reason of the venerable Eleazar's prayer, by an amazing reversal, the elephants, previously intoxicated by doses of frankincense and wine, turn back on the king's own troops and trample them to death. In a fit of remorse Ptolemy undergoes a complete change of heart toward the Jews, orders their release and return home, and highly praises their God (6:22–29). The whole narrative of 5:1–6:29 is intended to illustrate both the power of prayer and the absolute sovereignty of the Jewish God.

At the close the Jews engage in joyous festival celebrations (6:30–41; 7:13–15, 17–18, 19–20), the first associated with their deliverance in Alexandria, the second with the assassination of three hundred of the apostate brethren, permission for which had been granted by Ptolemy (7:12); the third with their seven-day banquet at Ptolemais, their port of departure; and the fourth with their return home. The elaborate festival conclusion suggests that the story told in *3 Maccabees* may relate to the origination of the practice of an annual celebration among Egyptian Jews, possibly bearing some resemblance to the major feast of Purim.

Opinions differ regarding the extent to which *3 Maccabees* furnishes reliable historical information about the Jews in Egypt. The author does appear to have had access to some fairly trustworthy source for his report of the battle of Raphia (1:1–5), which accords with that of Polybius, and his portrayal of Ptolemy IV is consistent with what is known of him from elsewhere (e.g., Plutarch, Strabo, Diodorus Siculus): his love of banquets, his dependence on his courtiers, his efforts to unite Jews and Greeks in the cult of his ancestor Dionysus, his use of elephants for military purposes, and the format of his official decrees. Perhaps more importantly, certain key passages, difficult to interpret though they are (2:28–30; 3:1–10; 4:14–15), seem to point to *3 Maccabees* as a fair source of knowledge for the legal rights and status of the Jews in Alexandria. But it is stretching credulity too far to argue that the whole narrative is an accurate factual report of what happened, even down to the details—the supposition, for instance, that the administering of frankincense and wine to the elephants was a spectacular ceremonial-ritual preparation for the annihilation of the Jews as anti-Dionysian "heretics." Such a detail is better construed as a mark of the storyteller's art: it makes more feasible the miracle of the beasts' turning back by divine intervention and trampling Ptolemy's own forces to death (5:1–2, 10, 45; 6:18–21). For further discussion, see JUDAISM (IN EGYPT).

The author's purpose is not to provide a straightforward diary of events. Rather, he employs the medium of romantic historical narration, in an inflated and hyperbolic style (e.g., 2:17–29; 4:1–21; 5:45–51; 6:16–29), with strong apologetic intent, to demonstrate the goodwill of the Jews as loyal subjects of the king, to defend the unique quality of their life and religion, and to uphold the sovereign majesty of the God whose people they are. He is a strict conservative, in whom there is little or no trace of the more innovative type of thinking we find in apocalyptic or Wisdom literature, or in those treatises which seek a fusion of Hellenistic philosophy and Judaism (e.g., *4 Maccabees*). His theology and faith are completely orthodox. He accepts without question that God supports and blesses the righteous and punishes the wicked. He has the deepest reverence for the temple (1:9–29). His rigorous devotion to the Law is implicit in his report of the slaying of more than three hundred renegade Jews (7:14–15), in accordance with the injunctions of Deut 13:6–18.

It is hardly possible to trace the composition of *3 Maccabees* to any specific crisis in the history of Egyptian Jews, e.g., the threat imposed on them when Egypt was made a Roman province in 24 B.C.E. and the civic status of the Jews was endangered by the new Roman administration; or the persecution of Alexandrian Jews during the reign of Caligula, when he attempted to set up his effigy in the temple in 40 C.E. The book, with its emphasis on God's kindly providence toward his people and on their festival joy at the marvelous deliverances he wrought for them, does not have the flavor of a crisis document. In terms of its actual content it could have been produced at almost any time from ca. 200 B.C.E. to 50 C.E. The discussion concerning dating has focused largely on *3 Maccabees* 2:27–30, which records the census or registry *(laographia)* of the Jews in Egypt required by Ptolemy, and his command that those registered be "branded by fire on their bodies with an ivy leaf, the emblem of Dionysus." If the aim of the census were the levying of a poll tax, that would seem to indicate the location of *3 Maccabees* within the Roman period (the Roman *laographia*). If on the contrary the purpose of the census were deeply religious and had to do with the persecution of the Jews who rejected the divinity of Dionysus, that would tend to strengthen the impression that *3 Maccabees* belonged to the Ptolemaic period. Since it is by no means impossible to infer from *3 Maccabees* 2:27–30 that Ptolemy's motivation was in fact religious rather than fiscal, the passage can scarcely be taken as firm evidence for a date in the Roman period.

The literary connections of *3 Maccabees* are rather more promising for dating. The author is familiar (6:6) with the Greek addition to Daniel usually dated 165 B.C.E., and so his work can hardly be earlier than the latter part of the 2d century B.C.E. Also he shares with the *Letter of Aristeas*, normally assigned to ca. 100 B.C.E., a mode of salutation that was in popular use around that time (earlier and later papyri reveal different formulas), namely, *chairein kai errosthai*, "greetings and good health." In light of the striking correspondences of language and vocabulary between *3 Maccabees* and the *Letter of Aristeas* as well as 2 Maccabees, generally set not earlier than the last quarter of the 2d century B.C.E., a plausible conjecture for the date of *3 Maccabees* would be the latter part of that century or the early part of the 1st century B.C.E.

If, however, we assume that the *laographia* (*3 Macc.* 2:28) does relate to Roman census procedures, and specifically to the poll tax imposed on Jews by Augustus in 24–23 B.C.E., then *3 Maccabees* would have been written not too long afterward. Accordingly, on the ground that similarities are discernible between the Ptolemaic situation described in *3 Maccabees* and the circumstances of the Jews during the reign of Caligula (see above) in 38–41 C.E., when the Jerusalem temple was threatened and Alexandrian Jewry were suffering persecution, it is sometimes held that *3 Maccabees* belongs within that short period. But, as noted earlier, *3 Maccabees* is hardly a crisis document, and whether a writer of such fertile imagination and romantic tendency as *3 Maccabees* must have found the springboard to his Alexandrian–Ptolemaic novelette in so precise a moment of Roman imperial history remains open to question.

Bibliography

Anderson, H. 1985. The Third Book of Maccabees: A New Translation and Introduction. *OTP* 2: 509–29.

Collins, J. J. 1983. *Between Athens and Jerusalem.* New York.

Emmet, C. W. 1913. The Third Book of Maccabees. *APOT* 2: 156–173.

Hadas, M. 1953. *The Third and Fourth Books of Maccabees.* New York.

Kasher, A. 1985. *The Jews in Hellenistic and Roman Egypt.* Tübingen.

Rostovtzeff, M. 1964. Ptolemaic Egypt. *CAH* 7: 109–54.

Tarn, W. W. 1964. The Struggle of Egypt Against Syria and Macedonia. *CAH* 7: 699–713.

Tcherikover, V. 1959. *Hellenistic Civilization and the Jews.* Philadelphia.

HUGH ANDERSON

FOURTH MACCABEES

The document we know as *Fourth Maccabees* is not in any sense, unlike 1 Maccabees and to a lesser extent the more legendary 2 Maccabees, a historical or even quasi-historical record of the heroes, events, and circumstances of the Maccabean period. The name "Maccabees" is appropriate for *4 Maccabees* only insofar as its central theme is worked out at length in relation to the martyrdoms of the aged Jewish sage Eleazar and the mother and her seven sons. These martyrdoms belonged presumably to the early days of the Maccabean revolt, and stories about them were extensively developed in Jewish tradition (compare, e.g., *4 Maccabees* with 2 Maccabees). The author's own highly dramatic account of the last hours of each of the martyrs serves to confirm his thesis (in 1:1 he describes his essay as a "philosophical exposition") that "reason is absolute master of the passions" (1:7). Of the several titles given to *4 Maccabees* in the early centuries probably the most suitable is that of Eusebius and Jerome, "On the Supremacy of Reason."

Although a Syriac version of *4 Maccabees* appeared quite early, the text has come down to us principally in the great uncial manuscripts of the LXX, Sinaiticus and Vaticanus, and the later (possibly 9th century) Codex Venetus, which however lacks 5:11–12:1. The author of *4 Maccabees* undoubtedly wrote in Greek. He is sufficiently at home in the language to invent new and rather strange-sounding Greek words, like *allophyleō* "adopt the pagan way of life" or *misarētos* "enemy of virtue." His literary style clearly reveals the influence of the craft of the Greek rhetoricians. He is well versed in various aspects of Greek philosophy, or at least in Greek philosophical commonplaces. His chief aim is to show that the highest Greek virtues are subsumed under loyalty and devotion to the Law of Moses. The medium he employs is a somewhat repetitive series of theatrical descriptions of the horrendous tortures inflicted by their Syrian oppressors on Eleazar, the seven sons, and finally their mother, all of whom go down to the death clinging resolutely to their ancestral faith. In the speeches he places on the lips of his heroes in their very last moments, the author really expresses his own conviction that "devout reason" or "pious reason" alone enables men and women to control or suppress their natural feelings and desires. The phrase "pious or devout reason" *(eusebēs logismos)* occurs frequently in *4 Maccabees* (1:9, 13, 19, 30; 2:6, 24; 6:31; 7:16; 13:1; 16:1; 18:2) and is by no means easy to translate. It represents an odd admixture of Greek and Jewish elements, in which the faculty of human reason, so greatly valued in the Greco-Roman world, is identified with unflinching obedience to the Torah: "To the intellect God gave the Law, and if a man lives his life by the Law he shall reign over a kingdom that is temperate and just and good and brave" (2:23).

The date and place of origin of *4 Maccabees* are very difficult to determine. It is not necessary to posit a time of extreme crisis and threat for the Jews such as the reign of Caligula (37–41 C.E.) or the brief interval between the end of the Jewish War under the Trajan and the Hadrianic persecutions (117–18 C.E.). Whereas the major part of the work deals with the brave endurance unto death of the famous Maccabean martyrs, it is in fact a philosophical discourse on how and why such amazing courage was possible, and as such it could have been written almost any time in the last century B.C.E. until the reign of Hadrian in the early 2d century C.E. The likeliest hypothesis arises from a suggestion of E. Bickermann (1976): against the evidence of 2 Macc 3:5 our author describes Apollonius as governor of "Syria, Phoenicia, and Cilicia." Most probably he was alluding to Roman administrative practice in his own time. There are one or two indications (e.g., Gal 1:21) that Syria-Cilicia did once constitute one province, and we find in the *Annals* of the Roman historian Tacitus two passages that point to 19–54 C.E. as the era in which that usage was in effect for Roman provincial administration. We may think of *4 Maccabees* as roughly contemporaneous with the mission and letters of the Apostle Paul.

Numerous echoes of the thought and exegetical methods of Philo have led commentators to locate *4 Maccabees*'s composition in Alexandria. But the grandiose so-called "Asianic" literary style which is a feature of *4 Maccabees* flourished also in Asia Minor and the coastlands of the northeastern Mediterranean, and Antioch in Syria is a feasible alternative to Alexandria. Nevertheless it is very doubtful whether *4 Maccabees* was composed as a speech of commemoration to be delivered at the tomb of the Maccabean martyrs. Certain direct references have been taken to support the view that it was, e.g., (1) the epitaph on their tomb set out in 17:8–10; (2) 1:10, "I might indeed eulogize for their virtues those men who at this season of the year died together with their mother for goodness' sake"; (3) 3:19, "But the season now summons us to expound the theme of the temperate reason"; and (4) 18:20, "Ah! bitter was the day and yet not bitter." But rhetorical devices of this sort were often enough used in purely literary compositions to provide for the readers a sense of urgency, immediacy, and direct participation. In any case, in view of Jewish susceptibilities about anything like a cult of the dead, an annual festival commemoration of the Maccabean martyrs at the scene of their death is very questionable indeed.

Recent scholarship has made it plain that it is inappropriate to draw too rigid a dividing line between the Judaism of the Diaspora and that of Palestine, because the latter throughout the last three centuries B.C.E. was also subject to the infiltration of Greek ideas and practices. Nevertheless, *4 Maccabees* is patently a product of the Diaspora. The author is acquainted with neo-Platonic, neo-Pythagorean, Stoic, and Philonic philosophical principles. Especially does he share with Philo and the writer of the Wisdom of Solomon a firm belief in the Greek doctrine of the immortality of the soul (9:22; 14:5–6; 16:13; 17:12; 18:23). In fact, he purposely omits from his primary source, 2 Maccabees, those passages which attest the resurrection of the body (7:9, 11, 14, 22–23). Despite his orientation to Greek philosophy, he remains in every respect absolutely faithful to the Law of Moses. The first of the martyrs, Eleazar, speaks for the author when, under the taunts of Antiochus that the refusal to eat swine's flesh is an altogether silly scruple, he responds, "I am not so sorry for my old age as to become responsible for breaking the Law of my fathers. I will not play you false, O Law my teacher. I will not forswear you, beloved self-control" (5:32–34). What is at stake, in short, is the Law's integrity in the eyes of the world.

Eleazar is also the first spokesman for another very important aspect of the thought of *4 Maccabees*—"Be merciful to your people and let our punishment be a satisfaction on their behalf. Make my blood their purification and take my life as a ransom for theirs." Later on, in his own narration, the author writes, "The tyrant was punished and our land purified, since they became, as it were, a ransom for the sin of our nation. Through the blood of these righteous ones and through the propitiation of their death the divine providence rescued Israel, which had been shamefully treated" (17:21–23). Words like "satisfaction," "blood," "purification," "ransom," and "propitiation" clearly recapitulate longstanding OT traditions, e.g., the levitical regulations for the Day of Atonement (Lev 16; 17:11; etc.) and the very different portrayal in Deutero-Isaiah (e.g., Isa 53:5, 10, 11) of the servant of Yahweh who, whether a single individual or a group, would by suffering and sacrifice redeem God's people Israel. The notion of vicarious sacrifice and the saving efficacy of the death of the martyred righteous, however, naturally became specially prominent in the period after the Maccabean wars. Central and decisive for early Christianity of course was the message of the atoning or redeeming death of Jesus (see, e.g., Mark 10:45; Matt 20:28; Heb 9:12; Rom 5; 1 Tim 2:6). But there is no need to posit a direct literary dependence on any NT document for a work such as *4 Maccabees* or to suppose, as did A. Deissmann (1900), that Paul knew *4 Maccabees* as a contemporary bestseller.

There is no doubt at all that *4 Maccabees* did wield a direct influence on the development of Christian martyrology. A number of the great figures of the early church (e.g., Gregory Nazianzus, John Chrysostom, Ambrose, and Augustine) revered *4 Maccabees* as if it were a Christian text and "adopted" the Maccabean heroes as Christian protomartyrs. In later Jewish tradition, where the martyrs were a prototypical *kiddush hashem,* the stories told in *4 Maccabees* circulated in various forms, sometimes drawing on the account of Hannah in 1 Samuel 1–2 (see also 2:5). In a fateful moment of history when Luther nailed his theses to the door of the church at Wittenberg (1517), Erasmus made a Latin paraphrase of *4 Maccabees.*

The work stands as a unique memorial to an unknown loyalist Jew of the Diaspora, who was open to Greek philosophy and learning without for a moment compromising his Jewish faith, as well as to all who through the centuries have suffered and died for their religious convictions. See also *OTP* 2: 531–64; *EncJud* 11: 661–62.

Bibliography

Bickermann, E. J. 1976. The Date of Fourth Maccabees. P. 277 in *Studies in Jewish and Christian History.* AGJU 9. Leiden.

Breitenstein, U. 1978. *Beobachtungen zu Sprache, Stil und Gedankengut des Vierten Makkabäerbuches.* Basel.

Collins, J. J. 1983. *Between Athens and Jerusalem.* New York.

Deissmann, A. 1900. Das vierte Makkabäerbuch. Pp. 149–77 in *Die Apokryphen und Pseudepigraphen des Alten Testaments,* vol. 2, ed. E. Kautzsch. Tübingen.

Dupont-Sommer, A. 1939. *Le Quatrième Livre des Machabées.* Paris.

Emmet, C. W. 1918. *The Fourth Book of Maccabees.* London.

Hadas, M. 1953. *The Third and Fourth Books of Maccabees.* New York.

Lebram, J. H. C. 1974. Die literarische Form des vierten Makkabäerbuches. *VC* 28: 81–96.

Renehan, R. 1972. The Greek Philosophic Background of Fourth Maccabees. *Rheinisches Museum für Philologie* 115: 223–38.

Hugh Anderson

MACCABEUS [Gk *Makkabaios*]. The nickname given to JUDAS, the third son of Mattathias the first leader (ca. 166–160 B.C.E.) of the Jewish forces in the war of independence from the Seleucids (1 Macc 2:4; cf. 2 Macc 5:27 and Joseph. *Ant.* 12.266). In the course of time Judas' nickname (in the plural "Maccabees") was extended to include all of the heroes of this period, as well as other descendants of Judas' family, who were also called the Hasmoneans (see HASMONEAN DYNASTY). It was also applied to various books, three of which are set in the period of the revolt against the Seleucids (1–2 Maccabees, *4 Maccabees*), and one of which only very loosely relates to the heroic aspects of belief in God *(3 Maccabees).* The name never appears in rabbinic literature, and in fact it was the Christian church that preserved these books and cherished the memory of those heroes and martyrs.

The use of nicknames for Judas and other members of the family of Mattathias was perhaps necessitated because their given names (John, Simon, Judas, Eleazar, Jonathan) were so widely used, particularly among priestly families. The derivation of the nickname Maccabeus (as well as the nicknames of his brothers) is unclear, and the difficulties in explaining them are almost insurmountable. Nevertheless, many suggestions have been made. One fundamental thing that is not clear, however, is whether these nicknames were given at birth or in childhood, or later in adulthood as a consequence of certain great deeds.

In Jewish tradition the name occurs in Josippon (16:56 [Flusser ed.]), where it is written *mkby.* This spelling persisted in Jewish books, and was even deciphered (by way of notakiron) as *mî kāmōkâ bāʾēlīm YHWH* ("Who is like thee among the gods, O Lord?"; cf. Exod 15:11). It has thus been suggested that the name derives from *kābâ,* meaning "to extinguish or quench." In that case the name might underscore Judas as one who sought to eliminate Greek influence on Jewish life.

But the spelling *mkby* is not authentic, and *mqby* is preferred. This leads to the most popular explanation, that "Maccabeus" derives from the word "hammer" (Heb *mqbt*). This is very often compared to "Martel" (Lat for "hammer"), the nickname of Carl, conqueror of the Saracens in 732 C.E. In this case the name would signify the military victories of Judas, who hit his enemies like a hammer hitting a nail (see *HJP*², 30). However, if the name was given to Judas prior to the revolt against the Seleucids, and if indeed it was related to *mqbt,* "hammer," it could attest to some idiosyncratic physical anomaly, such as a head or skull that resembled a hammer (*ISBE* 3: 196). But whatever the correct derivation of "Maccabeus," Judas' exploits have always remained more important than his nickname.

Uriel Rappaport
Paul L. Redditt

MACEDONIA (PLACE) [Gk *Makedonia*]. MACEDONIANS. The land of the Makedones, a territory in the Balkan Peninsula, bordered on the W by Illyria, on the E by Thrace, and on the S by Thessaly. Its mountainous terrain is cut by the rivers Axios (modern Vardar) and Strymon (modern Struma), which flow into the Aegean from the N. It is covered today by northern Greece, southern Yugoslavia, and the southwestern corner of Bulgaria. The population was ethnically and linguistically mixed: the Macedonian language contained Thraco-Phrygian, Illyrian, and Greek elements.

A. The Macedonian Kingdom
B. Wars with Rome
C. The Province of Macedonia
D. The Churches of Macedonia
  1. Their Foundation
  2. Their Progress
  3. Their Involvement in Paul's Further Ministry
  4. In the Postapostolic Age

A. The Macedonian Kingdom

From ca. 1000 B.C. Macedonia was ruled by a monarchy and subordinate local princes. In the 7th century B.C. the Argead dynasty, with its capital at Aegae, was established by Perdiccas I and remained in power for three centuries, until the time of Alexander the Great.

During the Persian invasions of Europe from 514 to 479 B.C. the Macedonian kings collaborated with the invaders and so preserved their relative independence (Hdt. 5.17–18). Even so, Alexander I of Macedonia gave covert aid to the Greek city-states attacked by Xerxes in 480 B.C. (Hdt. 5.173; 9.45). Alexander extended his territory E to the Strymon, while on the W he annexed some areas on his Illyrian border. It was probably he who organized the citizen corps of foot guards *(pezetairoi)* who formed the backbone of the national army.

Alexander and his successors patronized Greek art and letters. The Macedonian royal house had already begun to be hellenized: at the beginning of the 5th century B.C. Alexander, while still crown prince, was allowed to compete in the foot race at the Olympian games (which were open to Greeks only), because he established his claim to be of Argive stock (Hdt. 5.22; 8.137). By the 4th century B.C. Macedonia was for most practical purposes part of the Greek world.

Philip II of Macedonia (359–336 B.C.) combined diplomatic with military skill. He enlarged his kingdom to the W and E at the expense of Illyria and Thrace; he subdued the independent Greek cities on the Aegean coast of Macedonia; he annexed Thessaly (353 B.C.) and intervened in central Greece, and at last, by defeating the forces of Athens and Thebes at Chaeronea in Boeotia in 338 B.C., he made himself master of the whole Greek mainland. Having thus united Macedonia and the Greek city-states, he planned to make war on Persia but was assassinated before he could begin to take action. His son and successor, Alexander III (the Great), made his united Greco-Macedonian inheritance the base for his conquest of W Asia and Egypt. It is with Alexander's penetration into Asia that the Macedonians make their first appearance in the biblical record.

Alexander figures repeatedly, although not by name, in the visions of the book of Daniel. His empire is the worldwide "kingdom of bronze" in Nebuchadnezzar's dream (Dan 2:39) and is represented probably by the leopard in Daniel's vision of judgment (Dan 7:6). He himself is the he-goat from the west in Dan 8:5–8 (or, more precisely, the "conspicuous horn" between the he-goat's eyes) and the "mighty king" of Dan 11:3. He is mentioned by name in the condensed summary of his career in 1 Macc 1:1–7; in the same book an incidental reference is made to a great treasure that he deposited in a temple of Elymais (1 Macc 6:2). In the Greek Esther (16:10) Haman is called a "Macedonian" (Heb *Agagite*).

With the division of Alexander's empire after his death (323 B.C.) Macedonia became a separate kingdom once more (under Cassander, one of Alexander's generals, and his successors); the city-states of Greece remained subject to it.

B. Wars with Rome

Macedonia clashed with the Romans when Philip V (221–179 B.C.) made a treaty with their enemy Hannibal during the Second Punic War (Polyb. 7.9). The First Macedonian War, as it is called by Roman historians, was inconclusive (214–207 B.C.). But when the Romans' hands were freed by their defeat of Hannibal (202 B.C.), they created an early opportunity of renewing war against Philip. The Second Macedonian War (200–197 B.C.) ended with Philip's defeat at Cynoscephalae (Polyb. 18.22–28). Philip's rule was thenceforth confined to Macedonia. Flamininus, the Roman commander, proclaimed the liberation of the city-states of Greece, over which Rome now established a protectorate (Plut. *Flam.* 10).

A generation later Philip's son and successor Perseus excited Rome's suspicions by his conduct; these suspicions were fomented by Eumenes II of Pergamum, Rome's ally. The Third Macedonian War (171–168 B.C.), which broke out in consequence, ended with Rome's victory at Pydna (Polyb. 31.29). The royal dynasty of Macedonia was abolished; the kingdom was divided into four republics (Livy 45.29.5–9). But in 149 B.C. one Andriscus, who claimed to be a son of Perseus, reunited Macedonia under his rule for a short time (Diod. Sic. 32.9b, 15). He was put down the following year, and the Romans annexed Macedonia as a province (Flor. *Epit.* 1.32.3).

The four republics lost their political significance but continued to be recognized as geographical divisions, numbered one to four: thus, according to the most probable reading of Acts 16:12, Philippi is called "a city of the first division (Gk *meris*) of Macedonia" (Haenchen 1971: 494; Conzelmann *Acts of the Apostles* Hermeneia, 130). Philippi was in no sense "the leading city of the district of Macedonia" (RSV); Thessalonica was the chief city and seat of government of the province of Macedonia, and Amphipolis was the chief city of the first district, to which Philippi belonged.

C. The Province of Macedonia

To strengthen their control of Macedonia, the Romans built a great military road, the Egnatian Way, across it from the Adriatic Sea to the Aegean.

The province of Macedonia became a base for the extension of Roman power into W Asia, on whose peoples the Roman overthrow of the Macedonian kingdom had made a deep impression (1 Macc 8:5). Some of the crucial battles of Roman history in the 1st century B.C. were fought on Macedonian soil. The brief engagement between Pompey and Julius Caesar at Dyrrhachium (at the western terminus of the Egnatian Way) early in 48 B.C. was followed by Caesar's victory over Pompey at Pharsalus later in the same year. (Pharsalus was in Thessaly, but Thessaly formed part of the province of Macedonia.) Six years later Antony and Octavian (the future Emperor Augustus) defeated Brutus and Cassius (Caesar's assassins) at the battle of Philippi (October 21, 42 B.C.).

Octavian (now Emperor Augustus) made Macedonia a senatorial province in 27 B.C. In A.D. 15 Macedonia and the senatorial province of Achaia to the south were combined by Tiberius, at their own request, with the imperial province of Moesia (north of Macedonia) to form one large imperial province (Tac. *Ann.* 1.76.4; 1.80.1). In A.D. 44, under Claudius, this united province was divided back into its component parts, and Macedonia became once more a senatorial province, governed by a proconsul (Dio Cass. 60.24; cf. Papazoglu *ANRW* 2/7/1: 302–69). But, by contrast with what happened in Cyprus (Acts 13:7, 12) and Achaia (Acts 18:12–17), no apostolic encounter is recorded with the proconsul of Macedonia.

D. The Churches of Macedonia

1. Their Foundation. Three of the NT epistles are addressed to Macedonian churches—two to the Thessalonians and one to the Philippians. In other parts of Paul's correspondence there are references to the churches of Macedonia (2 Cor 8:1–5; 11:9; Rom 15:26), in which the generosity of those churches is warmly commended.

Macedonia was evangelized quite early in the apostolic age: Paul, with some of his companions, first brought the gospel there. It has been inferred from Phil 4:15 ("in the beginning of the gospel, when I left Macedonia") that Paul evangelized Macedonia at a rather early stage in his apostolic career—in the early forties, according to M. J. Suggs (1960). But when Paul, writing to the Philippian Christians, says "in the beginning of the gospel," his meaning may be not "when I first preached the gospel" but "when you first heard the gospel."

The narrative of Acts suggests a date around A.D. 50 for the bringing of the gospel to Macedonia. Paul and two fellow travelers (Silas/Silvanus and Timothy) were on their westward way through Asia Minor in the direction of Ephesus when they were diverted by a divine monition and found themselves on the Aegean coast at Alexandria Troas in the northwestern part of the peninsula. There Paul dreamed that "a man of Macedonia" begged him to cross the sea to Macedonia and help the people there. "Immediately," says the narrator (who apparently joined the party at this point), "we sought to go on into Macedonia" (Acts 16:8–10). They therefore took ship for Neapolis (modern Kavalla), the eastern terminus of the Egnatian Way, and went inland to Philippi. A small group of disciples was formed there, but trouble broke out with the citizens and magistrates, and Paul, Silas, and Timothy had to take their departure. They went farther west along the Egnatian Way to Thessalonica, stopping briefly at Amphipolis and Apollonia. At Thessalonica they spent several weeks and planted a church, but when their presence provoked a riot and compromised them in the eyes of the city authorities, they had to leave hastily and stealthily. Paul had probably planned to push on farther west along the Egnatian Way, but had to turn off the main road and make for Beroea in Thessaly, 40 miles W-SW from Thessalonica. His opponents from Thessalonica followed him there and stirred up fresh trouble, which forced his Beroean friends to smuggle him out of the city and escort him to Athens, out of harm's way.

Paul was greatly disheartened by his first visit to Macedonia. He believed he had gone there under divine guidance, but had been virtually thrown out of one Macedonian city after another after being exposed to abuse and menace. His converts in those cities were bound to suffer because of their association with such subversive characters as he and his companions were made out to be. No wonder that when, shortly afterward, he arrived in Corinth it was, as he said, "in weakness and in much fear and trembling" (1 Cor 2:3). But the situation in Macedonia proved to be much more encouraging than he could have dared to hope: the newly planted churches in Philippi and Thessalonica gave him great cause for joy.

2. Their Progress. The churches of Macedonia, small as they were and powerless in worldly terms, showed that they were able to survive and grow in spite of their founder's abrupt departure. They not only maintained their faith against the pressure of opponents and well-meaning friends, but increased in strength by the boldness and persuasiveness of their witness. Even if an element of rhetorical hyperbole can be detected in the statement that, only a few weeks after the missionaries bade farewell to their Thessalonian converts, not only had the word of the Lord sounded forth from them in Macedonia and Achaia, but their faith was a matter of common report everywhere (1 Thess 1:8), it was a real state of affairs that was amplified thus.

In this activity the Christian women of Macedonia played an equal part with the men. The sources refer to the gospel ministry of Lydia, Euodia, and Syntyche (Acts 15:14–15; Phil 4:2–3), to the "leading women" who became foundation members of the church of Thessalonica, "not a few," says Luke (Acts 17:4), and to the "Greek women of high standing" who became believers at Beroea (Acts 17:12).

This prominence of women was in line with traditional Macedonian custom. The women of Macedonia enjoyed a degree of independence unknown in Greece proper. In the ruling circles women "played a large part in affairs, received envoys and obtained concessions for them from their husbands, built temples, founded cities, engaged mercenaries, commanded armies, held fortresses, and acted on occasion as regents or even co-rulers" (Tarn and Griffith 1961: 98–99; cf. Thomas 1972). The precedent they set was followed by freeborn women in lower social ranks.

3. Their Involvement in Paul's Further Ministry. Paul's converts in Macedonia were marked by quite outstanding generosity. They showed this in some degree by their personal gifts to him. The church of Philippi sent him a gift shortly after he left Philippi for Thessalonica, and did the same on later occasions (Phil 4:16). His needs in Corinth were supplied in part "by the brethren who came from Macedonia" (2 Cor 11:9). But in general Paul did not encourage his converts to make personal gifts to himself; he did encourage them to contribute to a cause which lay very close to his heart.

Paul did not visit Macedonia again for some five years after he left the newly planted churches there. After leaving them he spent eighteen months in Corinth, and from there he crossed the Aegean and embarked on his three-year Ephesian ministry. During his time in Ephesus he began to organize his relief fund for the Jerusalem church among his converts both west and east of the Aegean. He urged them to contribute as generously as possible to this good cause. When he sent two of his associates, Timothy and Erastus, from Ephesus to Macedonia (Acts 19:22), one of their commissions was no doubt to acquaint the Macedonian churches with his plans for this relief fund.

The Macedonian churches responded wholeheartedly to Paul's appeal. He later used their response as an incentive to the church of Corinth; he affirms, indeed, that they overstretched their resources, "for in a severe test of affliction, their abundance of joy and their extreme poverty have overflowed in a wealth of liberality on their part. For they gave according to their means, as I can testify, and beyond their means, of their own free will, begging us earnestly for the favor of taking part in the relief of the saints," i.e., the Jerusalem Christians (2 Cor 8:1–4).

At the end of his stay in Ephesus Paul visited the Macedonian churches (1 Cor 16:5; 2 Cor 1:16; 2:13; 7:5; Acts 20:1–3); it was from Philippi that he set out on his last journey to Jerusalem, accompanied by representatives of churches that contributed to the relief fund. Among these Sopater of Beroea and Aristarchus and Secundus of Thessalonica are named (Acts 20:4). But between his arrival in

Macedonia and his departure for Judea he probably spent more time in the former province than appears on the surface: it was almost certainly at this stage that he extended his area of apostolic service "as far round as Illyricum" (Rom 15:19). To reach Illyricum he presumably journeyed to the western terminus of the Egnatian Way and went north from there by the coastal road or by sea.

When the relief fund had been completed and the proceeds taken to Jerusalem, the Philippian Christians felt that they could once again express their concern for Paul by contributing to his personal needs. When his visit to Jerusalem ended in disaster and he was sent to Rome in pursuance of his appeal to Caesar, they sent him a gift, which he acknowledges in Phil 4:10–19. His acknowledgment shows both his deep gratitude for their loving care and the embarrassment which his independent spirit felt in accepting money from even such dear friends as these.

4. In the Postapostolic Age. The Macedonian churches do not play a prominent part in the surviving records of the period immediately succeeding the apostolic age, but what evidence there is bears witness to their fidelity to the apostolic teaching and example. Those of them which were situated on the Egnatian Way had repeated opportunities to provide hospitality and help of other kinds to fellow Christians traveling east and west.

A good example of such an opportunity is seen in the experience of Ignatius, bishop of Antioch, who was taken from Syria to Rome under armed guard about A.D. 115 to be exposed to wild beasts in the amphitheater. He and his guards traveled by road through Asia Minor to Troas, where they took ship for Neapolis and then followed the Egnatian Way to the Adriatic. They came first to Philippi, as Paul and his companions had done sixty-five years before.

We have no details about Ignatius' stopover in Philippi, but the Philippian Christians evidently did what they could for him and showed their interest in him after his departure by writing to Polycarp, bishop of Smyrna, to ask him for copies of any of Ignatius' letters that might be available to him. Polycarp's reply has survived. He expresses his joy that they "have followed the example of true love and have helped on their way, as opportunity offered, those who were bound in chains" (Ignatius is primarily in his mind). Then he adds, "I rejoice that your firmly rooted faith, renowned since early days, endures to the present time and produces fruit for our Lord Jesus Christ" (Polyc. *Ep.* 1.1, 2). Paul could have desired no better fruit from the tree which he and his associates planted.

Bibliography

Haenchen, E. 1971. *The Acts of the Apostles.* Trans. B. Noble and G. Shinn. Oxford.

Hammond, N. G. L.; Griffith, G. T.; and Walbank, F. W. 1972, 1978, 1988. *A History of Macedonia.* Vols. 1–3. Oxford.

Laourdas, B., and Makaronas, C., eds. 1977. *Ancient Macedonia.* Vols. 1 and 2. Thessaloniki.

Morgan, M. G. 1969. Metellus Macedonicus and the Province Macedonia. *Historia* 18: 422–46.

Suggs, M. J. 1960. Concerning the Date of Paul's Macedonian Ministry. *NovT* 4: 60–68.

Tarn, W. W., and Griffith, G. T. 1961. *Hellenistic Civilisation.* Rev. ed. New York.

Thomas, W. D. 1972. The Place of Women in the Church at Philippi. *ExpTim* 83: 117-120.

Walbank, F. W. 1940. *Philip V of Macedon.* Cambridge.

F. F. BRUCE

MACHAERUS

MACHAERUS (M.R. 209108). A site in Jordan that was fortified by several rulers and which is thought to have been the site of the beheading of John the Baptist.

A. Topography

The fortress of Machaerus is situated in Jordan between the Wadi Zerqa Maʾin to the N and the Arnon to the S, at a place where the high Moabite plateau begins to descend toward the depression of the Dead Sea. The rocky prominence with steep sides rises to an elevation of 700 m above sea level and is protected by deep ravines except on the SE and NW sides, where the mountain stretches out to form two saddles. Beyond the ravines, the terrain rises on three sides, with the exception of the W flank, to an average altitude of 720 m. There are no springs in the vicinity, and the vegetation is scarce or totally absent.

B. Identification

The mountain upon which the fortress was constructed is today known as Mishnaqa, from the Arabic verb *shanaqa,* which means "to hang." The ancient name, Machairous (Gk *Maxairous*), probably derives from *machaira* ("dagger" or "sword"), pronounced Makaveros by the Byzantines, and which is preserved in the small Arab village of Mekawer, a mile to the E of Mishnaqa. The identification of Mishnaqa with the ancient Machaerus, proposed by the German explorer U. Setzen in 1807, is accepted by everyone and has been confirmed by excavations.

C. Historical References

Pliny the Elder did not hesitate to classify Machaerus as "the most important Jewish stone fortress immediately after Jerusalem" (*HN* 5.15.72). According to Josephus, two successive fortresses were built at Machaerus. The first was constructed by Alexander Janneus (*JW* 7.171), probably about 90 B.C., and was destroyed by Gabinius in 57 B.C. The second was built by Herod the Great (*JW* 7.172) probably in 30 B.C. and surrendered to Lucinius Basso in A.D. 72 (*JW* 7.209). After the death of Herod the Great, Machaerus, in the S confines of Perea, was assigned to the tetrarch Herod Antipas (4 B.C.–A.D. 39), who imprisoned and killed John the Baptist there (Joseph. *Ant.* 18.116). At the death of Herod Agrippa (A.D. 44), the fortress passed into the direct control of the Romans and remained thus until 66, the outbreak of the first Jewish war. The rebels besieged by Lucinius Basso in 72 surrendered, delivering the stronghold to the Romans. Josephus, after an ample description of the strategic position of the mountain (*JW* 7.163–70), then described the Herodian fortress (*JW* 7.172–76).

D. Archaeological Investigation

Machaerus was extensively excavated in the years 1978–81 under the direction of P. Virgilio Corbo. E. J. Vardaman had made several soundings in 1968, while A. Strobel in 1974 published a study on the military camps and the encircling wall that the Romans had built for the siege of the fortress.

E. Results of Excavations

The four seasons of excavation from 1978 to 1981 have provided an almost complete plan of the Hasmonean-Herodian fortifications and a plan of the lower city.

The archaeological remains do not go beyond the chronological limits (90 B.C.–A.D. 72) suggested by the literary sources: the mountain was not occupied before the Hasmoneans and was no longer occupied after A.D. 72. The Hasmonean fortress was burned by Gabinius, but was not razed. Conversely, the royal Herodian fortress was systematically dismantled by the Romans who, in addition, threw down the hill a good part of the materials used for construction. A different fate was reserved for the lower city, which was subjected to Roman assault and burned.

Access to the royal fortress was across a viaduct whose foundation is preserved for 150 m along the SE saddle. The viaduct ended in the middle of the mountain near the No. 6 tower and also served as an aqueduct to carry rainwater to a series of huge cisterns hewn into the rock on the NE side of the mount. Between tower No. 6 halfway up the mount, and tower No. 1, at the summit, was the ascent path, protected to the S by defensive wall C and circumscribed to the N by the dwellings of the lower city.

The royal fortress covers an area of about 4,000 m^2 and is subdivided by a central corridor into two blocks. The E block consists of a paved central court bordered on the S by the thermal spring and on the N by a series of storerooms. The W block is constituted of a majestic peristyle, to the S of which rises the triclinium.

Of particular interest to the biblical scholar is the triclinium, which covers an area of 237.50 m^2 (25 by 9.50) and is formed by two adjacent but independent rooms, one for men and the other for women. The report of Josephus (*Ant.* 18.116–19) that John the Baptist was killed at Machaerus seems very reliable and is not easily explained as a Christian interpolation (cf. Mark 6:21–29).

Bibliography

Corbo, V. 1978. La Fortezza di Macheronte: Rapporto preliminare della prima campagna di scavo: 8 settembre–28 ottobre 1978. *LASBF* 28: 217–38.

———. 1979. Macheronte: La Reggia-Fortezza Erodiana. Rapporto preliminare alla seconda campagna di scavo: 3 settembre–20 ottobre 1979. *LASBF* 29: 315–26.

———. 1980. La Fortezza di Macheronte (Al Mishnaqa): Rapporto preliminare alla terza campagna di scavo: 8 settembre–11 ottobre 1980. *LASBF* 30: 365–76.

Corbo, V., and Loffreda, S. 1981. Nuove Scoperte alla Fortezza di Macheronte. Rapporto preliminare alla quarta campagna di scavo: 7 settembre–10 ottobre 1981. *LASBF* 31: 257–86.

Loffreda, S. 1981. Preliminary Report on the Second Season of Excavations at Qalʾat el-Mishnaqa: Machaerus. *ADAJ* 25: 85–94.

Piccirillo, M. 1979. First Excavation Campaign at Qalʾat el-Mishnaqa-Meqawer 1978. *ADAJ* 23: 177–83.

Strobel, A. 1974. Das römische Belagerungswerk um Macharus. Topographische Untersuchungen. *ZDPV* 90: 128–84.

STANISLAO LOFFREDA

MACHBANNAI (PERSON) [Heb *makbannay*].

One of the warriors from the tribe of Gad who joined David at his wilderness stronghold (1 Chr 12:14—Eng 12:13). The Gadites were from a Transjordan tribe to the N; by including them among those supporting David during the period of his fleeing from Saul, the Chronicler is demonstrating the extent of the support David enjoyed before he became king. Machbannai became one of David's commanders.

Bibliography

Williamson, H. G. M. 1981. We Are Yours, O David. *OTS* 21: 164–76.

RAYMOND B. DILLARD

MACHBENAH (PLACE) [Heb *makbēnâ*].

A name which appears in a genealogical list of Judah (1 Chr 2:49). Machbenah is generally taken to be a place name, and several identifications of its referent have been offered by scholars. According to Aharoni (*LBHG*, 227), Machbenah was a settlement of the sons of Caleb in the Judean hills south of Beth-Zur and Hebron. Some suggest that Machbenah should be linked with Cabbon (Josh 15:40) because of their apparent common root *kbn* (see, for example, *BDB*, 460). Others identify Machbenah with Meconah (Neh 11:28; see *IDB*, 3: 218). Simons (*GTTOT*, 155, 389) associated Machbenah, Meconah, and Madmannah (Josh 15:31).

DAVID SALTER WILLIAMS

MACHI (PERSON) [Heb *mākî*].

A man from the tribe of Gad, known only through association with his son Geuel (Num 13:15). Geuel was one of the twelve tribal representatives who left Kadesh to spy out the land of Canaan.

TERRY L. BRENSINGER

MACHIR (PERSON) [Heb *mākîr*].

1. The eldest of Manasseh's sons, whose name came to designate a large segment of the patriarch's tribe. Since his name derives from the Hebrew root *mkr,* it has been proposed that his name meant "bought," perhaps marking him as an orphan or waif (Hicks *IDB* 3: 218; *IPN,* 232).

According to Gen 50:23, Machir and his sons were born while his grandfather Joseph was still alive. Moreover, the text reports that Joseph adopted Machir's sons as his own (Richter 1979). Since Judg 5:14, however, mentions Machir as one of the tribes of Israel, alongside Benjamin and Ephraim, some scholars have concluded that Machir was not Manasseh's son and that Gen 50:23b must be regarded as an etiological addition, probably based on Gen 48:13–20 (Westermann 1986: 208). Genealogical material in Num 26:29; 27:1; and 36:1, however, reflects the same tradition of Machir's ancestry that is found in Genesis: Machir was the son of Manasseh but the father of Gilead. While the first text is a military census that includes Machir in the Manassite section (26:29–34), the second (27:1–11) and third (36:1–12), also genealogical texts, are concerned primarily with the matter of Zelophehad's daughters and whether they should receive an allotment of land.

Machir is also mentioned in texts that treat Israel's settlement in Palestine (Num 32:39–40; Deut 3:15; and

Josh 13:31; 17:1, 3). The verses in Numbers report that the descendants of Machir captured the land of Gilead and that Moses assigned the territory to them. Since the report is so general and is phrased in such a stereotypical fashion, it has often been regarded as a later insertion and without basis in any of the narrator's sources (Noth *Numbers* OTL, 240). Deuteronomy 3:15 makes similar claims for Machir; consequently, a number of scholars (e.g., Mayes *Deuteronomy* NCBC, 146) have concluded that it too is secondary, probably based on Numbers 32 and intended to correct Deut 3:12–13, which it contradicts. Joshua 13:31 assigns half of Gilead and part of Bashan to Machir, a report that is echoed in Josh 17:1–3. The latter passage, though, proceeds to explain that in addition to the territory given to Gilead, ten shares of land were allotted to other Manassite families—five to the clans of Hepher's brothers and five to the daughters of Zelophehad, son of Hepher (vv 1–6). The six families, called "sons of Manasseh," that are named are Abiezer, Helek, Asriel, Shechem, Hepher, and Shemida. It seems likely, therefore, that the writer believed that Manasseh had seven sons, the first of whom was Machir and the seventh Shemida.

Finally, two texts in 1 Chronicles mention Machir. In the first, it is noted that the daughter of Machir married Hezron of Judah and bore him a son, Segub (2:21–23). In the second passage, the Manassite genealogy of 1 Chr 7:14–19, there are a number of inconsistencies and confusing statements (Rudolf *Chronikbücher* HAT, 69–71; Braun *1 Chronicles* WBC, 110–11). The designation of Machir as son of Manasseh and father of Gilead is repeated, however, and additional bits of information are supplied: Machir's mother was Manasseh's Aramean concubine, and Machir's wife, Maacah, bore him Peresh (and possibly Sheresh).

2. The son of Ammiel, who lived at Lo-debar (2 Sam 9:4–5; 17:27). Machir may well have been a Manassite or Machirite, whose family had inherited land in Gilead with others in the clan of Machir. Although the precise location of Lo-debar is uncertain, it should probably be sought near the Jabbok and not far from Mahanaim. Aharoni and Rainey have proposed Umm ed-Dabar (M.R. 207219) as the most likely site (*LBHG*, 439).

Machir showed his loyalty to Saul by giving refuge in his home at Lo-debar to his crippled grandson, Meribaal/Mephibosheth, the son of Jonathan. This occurred after Saul and Jonathan were killed by the Philistines in battle at Mount Gilboa. After David consolidated his power over Judah and Israel, he sought a way to show kindness to one of Saul's descendants for the sake of his friend Jonathan. Therefore, when he learned of Meribaal's presence at Lodebar, he sent for him and provided him a place at court in Jerusalem (2 Sam 9:4–5).

Later, when David and his forces fled before the rebel army of Absalom, Machir joined others near Mahanaim to supply provisions for them (2 Sam 17:27). Therefore, it appears that David's kindness to the son of Jonathan won the loyalty of Machir. Langlamet (1976: 355), though, has suggested that the story in vv 27–29 is secondary and was added to prepare for the note in 2 Sam 19:32.

A number of scholars, however, have proposed other reconstructions for the history of Machir and his family. Zobel (1965: 112–15), for example, has argued that the tribe of Machir was unrelated to Manasseh and Ephraim and first dwelled near Dothan in W Palestine, where it grew to become a powerful entity alongside the surrounding Canaanite city-states. This is supported by three factors: (1) 1 Chr 7:14 claims that Machir's mother was an Aramean, which points to the tribe's non-Israelite origins; (2) Judg 5:14 suggests that Machir lay between Ephraim and Zebulun, near the battlefield on which Barak and Sisera's forces fought; and (3) Machir's entry into Palestine is mentioned in none of the biblical reports about Israel's settlement in the land. Moreover, Machir's name, which meant "sold," may be taken, along with the remark in Josh 17:1 that the family included many fighters, to indicate that the tribe sold its military services to the Canaanites, probably during the Amarna age. Pressure from Manasseh eventually forced Machir to become an unwilling dependent of Manasseh and to leave W Palestine for Transjordan. Machir's subservient status came to be reflected in the texts that traced the origin of the tribe to Manasseh, and since the descendants of Machir dwelled in Gilead, the patriarch Machir was called the father of Gilead.

Although he followed Zobel's historical reconstruction in several respects, de Vaux (*EHI*, 586–87, 651–52) diverged by arguing that initially Manasseh was a clan within Machir. It was only when the latter emigrated to Transjordan that Manasseh expanded to fill the void that was left. Later, Manasseh's name was extended to include Machir in Transjordan, and the biblical genealogies generally reflect this later state of affairs.

These reconstructions have not gone unchallenged, though. Mittmann (1970: 63–71, 213–16), for example, has far more confidence in the antiquity and historical accuracy of Num 26:29–30, which presents Machir as the son of Manasseh and father of Gilead. Furthermore, he argues that pressure from Canaanites, rather than Manassites, was more likely to have caused Machir to emigrate to Transjordan. In addition, Mittmann disputes Zobel's suggestion that Machir was a "mixed" tribe that included a strong non-Israelite element. Seebass (1982), in turn, has criticized Mittmann, arguing that Num 26:29–30 is derived from Num 36:1, 11, and so cannot be trusted as an ancient and reliable piece of tradition.

Finally, Lemaire (1981) has proposed that "Machir" was initially a geographic name that referred to a region in Transjordan on the plain that opens onto the Jabbok, near Deir ʿAlla. He denies that Judg 5:14 indicates that Machir was settled in W Palestine, since he finds no consistent pattern to the listing of the tribes in Judges 5. The population of this area was probably related to the Canaanites around Shechem and Beth-shan, and perhaps to the Arameans or Ammonites of the surrounding area as well. Therefore, there was no migration of Machir from W Palestine into Transjordan, but as 2 Sam 9:4–5 and 17:27 indicate, the tribe had lived in S Gilead long before Israelite tribes settled in the land.

Therefore, while scholars agree that, by the time of David, Machir was a tribal group in Transjordan, probably near the Jabbok, there is considerable disagreement about the tribe's ethnic composition and initial place of settlement in Palestine.

Bibliography

Langlamet, F. 1976. Pour ou contre Salomon? La redaction prosalomonienne de 1 Rois, I–II. *RB* 83: 321–79, 481–528.

Lemaire, A. 1981. Galaad et Makîr: Remarques sur la tribu de Manassé à l'est du Jourdain. *VT* 31: 39–61.
Mittmann, S. 1970. *Beiträge zur Siedlungs- und Territorialgeschichte des Nördlichen Ostjordanlandes.* ADPV. Wiesbaden.
Richter, H. W. 1979. "Auf den Knien eines anderen gebären"? (Zur Deutung von Gen. 30:3 und 50:23). *ZAW* 91: 436–37.
Seebass, H. 1982. Machir im Ostjordanland. *VT* 32: 496–503.
Westermann, C. 1986. *Genesis 37–50.* Minneapolis.
Wüst, M. 1975. *Untersuchungen zu den siedlungsgeographischen Texten des Alten Testaments. I. Ostjordanland.* BTAVO B/9. Wiesbaden.
Zobel, H.-J. 1965. *Stammesspruch und Geschichte.* BZAW 95. Berlin.

M. Patrick Graham

MACHNADEBAI (PERSON) [Heb *maknadĕbay*]. A descendant of Binnui and one of the returned exiles whom Ezra required to divorce his foreign wife (Ezra 10:40; 1 Esdr 9:34). According to Noth, this name is actually a corruption of Heb *mibbĕnê,* "from the sons of" (*IPN,* 249). If that is true, the phrase would introduce the next family from which offenders come. However, Shashai is not named as the head of a family in the lists in either Ezra 2 or Nehemiah 7. This is further indicated by the parallel text of 1 Esdr 9:34, where the phrase "of the sons of Ezora" replaces the name Machnadebai, perhaps preserving a name dropped from Ezra 10:40. Other scholars have argued that Zaccai (see Ezra 2:9) would be a better orthographic fit than Ezora (see Williamson, *Ezra, Nehemiah* WBC, 144). In 1 Esdr 9:34, the RSV also has Machnadebai, despite the LXX *Mamnitanaimos* eight names prior to Shashai, apparently in an attempt to harmonize the two lists. If we assume that Machnadebai is an individual, however, he was a member of a family who returned from Babylon with Zerubbabel (Neh 7:15; note that Bani replaces Binnui in Ezra's list [2:10]). See also BEDEIAH.

Jeffrey A. Fager

MACHPELAH (PLACE) [Heb *makpēlâ*]. A field with a cave purchased by Abraham as the burial site for family members (Gen 23). References to the site identify it as "the cave of Machpelah" (Gen 23:9) and "the field of Machpelah" (Gen 23:17). Originally purchased for the burial of Sarah (Gen 23), other family members were buried there, including Abraham (Gen 25:9), Isaac (Gen 39:29; 49:31), Rebekah, Leah, and Jacob (Gen 49:31; 50:13). Stephen's sermon implies that Jacob was buried at Shechem "in the tomb that Abraham had bought" (Acts 7:16); however, the OT identifies Shechem as the location at which Joseph was buried (Josh 24:32). Machpelah is located in Hebron, el-Khalil, and is labeled Haram el-Khalil, the Enclosure of Abraham. The OT simply locates it "east of Mamre" (Gen 23:19; 25:9).

A. The Purchase of Machpelah

The purchase of the cave of Machpelah and the transactions involved on the occasion of Sarah's death are the focal points of Genesis 23. The story relates how Abraham, "a stranger and a sojourner" (v 4), one who owned no property or family burial plot, went to the local Hittite inhabitants and landowners and negotiated the purchase of the field and the cave from Ephron the Hittite (see Van Seters 1975: 98–100).

Modern research has shed new light on ancient legal practices regarding the purchase of land; however, scholars disagree on the precise legal formula or custom that provides the background for the transaction in Genesis 23. M. Lehmann (1953) has suggested that the negotiations reflect land-purchase customs of the Hittite legal system. He based his conclusions on features of the account that seemed to parallel Hittite law. Abraham's attempt to buy property from the Hittites for a burial site was met with a counter offer to use but not buy the land (Gen 23:5–6). Abraham, then more specific, announced that he wanted to purchase the cave of Machpelah at the end of the field owned by Ephron (vv 7–9). Ephron, however, was not interested in selling a part of the property, the cave alone, but would sell the field and the cave together (v 11). Abraham then offered to buy the entire field (vv 12–13). Ephron announced a specific price (vv 14–15). Abraham agreed to the offer, and payment was made (v 16). According to this view, the major parallel between Hittite law and Genesis 23 is seen in Ephron's attempt to sell the entire plot. According to Hittite custom, the landowner who leased out or sold only a part of the property continued to be responsible for the feudal obligations of the plot. Therefore, Ephron attempted to sell the entire field in order to rid himself of these legal obligations.

Proposals other than Lehmann's have been set forth. More recently Gene Tucker proposed (1966) that while Genesis 23 reflects characteristics of ANE land transactions in general, the most prominent model for the account is found in the so-called "dialogue documents" of the Neo-Babylonian era. Here attention is called to the format of the formula, some features of which appear also in Genesis 23, such as the dialogue between buyer and seller, the payment formula, a statement about the transfer, and the presence of witnesses.

Raymond Westbrook (1971) suggests that after a review of ancient legal documents concerning the sale of property, the "double-transfer" model seems most plausible. This custom existed during the last half of the 2d millennium B.C.E. The double-transfer method includes two transfers: the first, the transfer of the land between the two parties involved, the second, a type of transfer in which the king made a gift of the land to the new property owner.

In addition to Genesis 23, the OT contains the accounts of other land purchases. Jacob bought land in Shechem from the sons of Hamor in order to build an altar (Gen 33:18–20), and David bought a threshing floor from Araunah on which to build an altar (2 Sam 24:18–25; 1 Chr 21:18–27). A comparison of the accounts shows certain similarities. At least the former is comparable in the local response to the buyer—"a prince among us" (23:6) and "will not their cattle, their property, and all their beasts be ours?" (34:23)—both of which suggest economic interests being enhanced by these new neighbors (this insight courtesy of Victor Matthews).

B. The History of Machpelah

Interest in the patriarchal burial site, Machpelah, has a lengthy history, which began during biblical times and continued throughout the postbiblical era to the present time. This interest is illustrated in the many accounts or traditions regarding pilgrimages to the site and descriptions or investigations of the site, many of which are reviewed by V. R. Gold (*IDB* 2: 218–20). These accounts demonstrate how the site has been reverenced by Jews, Christians, and Muslims. The major features of this history began with information from the *Testament of the Twelve Patriarchs* (20:6), which names Joseph among those buried at the site. A monumental building project during the Herodian period, probably the work of Herod the Great, included the construction of a large enclosure wall around the area and the erection of monuments or cenotaphs in honor of the patriarchal figures. A basilica-type church was built at the site inside the enclosure wall during the 5th or 6th century C.E. Arculf, who visited the site in 670, wrote not only about the monuments of the patriarchal figures but also mentioned the presence of a monument built for Adam. As control of the site went through a series of changes—Muslim, Crusader, Muslim—so the church was converted into a mosque, reconverted into a church, and again back to a mosque. During June 1119, the chambers below the surface of the site were investigated by removing stones from the floor of the church, and the bones of the patriarchs were reportedly found. (Gold *IDB* 4: 218–20).

C. Machpelah and Archaeological Research

The study of the site by L. H. Vincent and E. J. H. Mackey in the early 1920s helped stimulate interest in its architectural features and opened the way for debate concerning Herodian building techniques in the construction of the enclosure wall. Information from excavations at other sites has helped provide a better understanding of these features. This is demonstrated in recent articles by David Jacobson (1981) and Nancy Miller (1985). Miller refers not only to the ancient traditions associated with the site, but also to the excavations of Benjamin Mazar near the temple-enclosure wall in Jerusalem as well as the investigation of the chambers below the surface at Machpelah at Moshe Dayan. The excavations led by Mazar (1971) near the temple wall have provided new information that the Herodian masonry techniques used to construct the wall are similar to those used in the construction of the enclosure wall at Machpelah (Jacobson 1981: 73; Miller 1985: 30–32). Jacobson provides additional information for this conclusion by comparing the dimensions and noting the similarities of the enclosures at Jerusalem, Hebron, and Damascus (1981: 78–80).

The subterranean chambers where the remains of the patriarchal figures were supposedly entombed have received only limited investigation in recent times. In 1917 a British officer, Colonel R. Meinertzhagen, entered a subsurface chamber by means of a hidden entrance perhaps from the Crusader period. The date of the contents of the chamber is still debatable. The most recent investigation of the chambers came shortly after the Six-Day War of 1967 under the direction of Moshe Dayan (1978; 1976; cf. Miller 1985). The exploration of the subterranean area conducted one night was not done by Dayan himself, but rather by a 12-year-old girl who was lowered by rope through the small hole, 12 in. in diameter, in the floor of the mosque. The young girl, Michal, equipped with a torch, a camera, pencil and paper, and an instrument by which to secure measurements, took notes, photographs, and made sketches of what she found below. The area explored included a room, a long corridor, and a stairway. The room directly beneath the hole through which the girl was lowered was approximately 9.25 by 9.5 ft. At approximately 4.5 ft. from the floor, the four walls of the room arched inward toward the octagonal ceiling. The only contents of the room were three tombstones along one wall; the middle one, tallest of the three, bore an Arabic inscription from the Koran about Allah. Whether the tombstones covered entrances to other chambers has not been determined. An opening in one of the walls of the room connected the room to a corridor 57 ft. in length. The corridor, approximately 2 ft. wide and 3.5 ft. high, had walls made of ashlar stones and a ceiling of stone slabs. The corridor ended at a stairway with 16 steps leading upward. The upper end of the stairway was closed off by the stones that formed the floor of the enclosure. The room, the corridor, and the stairway were supposedly the same as some of the chambers investigated in 1119. Other than the tombstones or slabs in the square room and the inscription on the center slab, no other artifacts were found. While the account from 1119 reported the discovery of the bones of the patriarchs, no bones were found in the Dayan exploration (Miller 1985: 42–43).

Bibliography

Dayan, M. 1976. The Cave of Machpelah—The Cave Beneath the Mosque. *Qadmoniot* 9/4: 129.

———. 1978. The Little Girl in the Hebron Cave. Pp. 45–49 in *Living with the Bible*. New York.

Jacobson, D. M. 1981. The Plan of the Ancient Haram El-Khalil in Hebron. *PEQ* 113/2: 73–80.

Lehmann, M. 1953. Abraham's Purchase of Machpelah and Hittite Law. *BASOR* 129: 15–18.

Mazar, B. 1971. *The Excavation in the Old City of Jerusalem near the Temple Mount: Preliminary Report of the Second and Third Seasons, 1969–1970*. Jerusalem (in Hebrew).

Miller, N. 1985. Patriarchal Burial Site Explored for First Time in 700 Years. *BARev* 9/3: 26–43.

Tucker, G. M. 1966. The Legal Background of Genesis 23. *JBL* 85: 77–84.

Van Seters, J. 1975. *Abraham in History and Tradition*. New Haven.

Westbrook, R. 1971. Purchase of the Cave of Machpelah. *Israel Law Review* 6: 29–38.

LaMoine F. DeVries

MACRON (PERSON) [Gk *Makrōn*]. Var. PTOLEMY MACRON. In 2 Macc 10:12–13 the Seleucid official who "took the lead in showing justice to the Jews . . . and tried to settle matters peaceably." According to this account, the failure of his policy in some way is the explanation for the appointment of Lysias as "first-ranking" governor (cf. Goldstein *II Maccabees* AB, 387, who argues that there was a governor named Protarchus). This failure, coupled with mistrust because of his previous appointment as governor of Cyprus under Ptolemy VI Philometor (180–145 B.C.E.) and subsequent defection to Antiochus IV Epiphanes (175–164 B.C.E.) when he took over that island, led to his suicide by poison. There are a number of chronological problems arising from this account.

While the appointment by Antiochus V Eupator (164–162 B.C.E.) is his first mention in 2 Maccabees (10:11), Lysias plays a major role in the events of the reign of Antiochus IV Epiphanes (beginning with 3:32–35) in 1 Maccabees, the work usually considered to have a more reliable chronology of events. It is much more likely that 2 Macc 10:11 is actually referring to an enhancement of Lysias' role after the death of Antiochus IV Epiphanes, during whose eastern campaign he had been left in charge of the W portion of the kingdom as well as guardian for the child who would become Antiochus V Eupator.

Even though the period for the activity of Ptolemy Macron in Judea would seem in general to coincide with that of Ptolemy the son of Dorymenes (1 Macc 3:38–41; 2 Macc 4:45–46; 8:8–9), the efforts by the latter "to wipe out the whole race of Judea" is a very different response to matters concerning the Jews and precludes any identification between the two (cf. Abel 1949: 409–10). Chronological considerations based on inscriptional evidence also argue against that case (Goldstein, 388).

The inscriptional evidence, while somewhat ambiguous because of the many people who bore the name Ptolemy, points to Ptolemy Macron's presence in Cyprus until 168 B.C.E., when Antiochus IV Epiphanes took it over from Ptolemy VI Philometor (Levy 1950; Mitford 1957). Polybius mentions his prudent and cautious financial dealings as uncharacteristic of Egyptian governors (27.13). Macron was brought to Judea by Antiochus IV Epiphanes as governor. While it remains hypothetical, there seems to be merit to the argument that it was Ptolemy's policies which permitted the Jews to rededicate the temple in 164 B.C.E. If so, it was probably those same policies which made him unpopular with the king's friends.

While appealing, it is quite conjectural to hypothesize any connection between the policies of Ptolemy Macron and the letters in 2 Macc 11:16–21 and 27–38 (Bartlett 1973: 297).

Bibliography

Abel, F.-M. 1949. *Les Livres des Maccabées*. EBib. Paris.

Bartlett, J. R. 1973. *The First and Second Books of the Maccabees.* Cambridge.

Levy, I. 1950. Ptolemée fils de Makron. *AIPHOS*, 688–99.

Mitford, T. G. 1957. Ptolemy Macron. Pp. 163–87 in *Studi in onore de Aristide Calderini e Roberto Paribeni*, vol. 2. Milan.

Otto, W. 1934. *Zur Geschichte der Zeit des 6. Ptolemäers. Ein Beitrag.* ABAW Phil.-hist. Kl., n.s. 11. Berlin.

Plöger, O. 1958. Die Feldzüge der Seleukiden gegen den Makkabäer Judas. *ZDPV* 74: 158–88.

JOHN KAMPEN

MADABA (PLACE). See MEDEBA (PLACE).

MADAI (PERSON) [Heb *māday*]. The Table of Nations (Gen 10:2) and the parallel genealogy in 1 Chr 1:5 identify Madai as one of the seven sons of Japheth, who himself is a son of Noah. Descendants of Japheth are non-Semitic, Indo-European peoples situated mainly to the north of Israel. People called Madai appear in Akkadian texts from the time of Shalmaneser III (the mid-9th century B.C.). From these, and the texts of the people themselves, the area of occupation of the Madai or Medes is known to be Persia, or present-day Iran, immediately south of the Caspian Sea. Although their geographical origin is unknown, there they gained strength until they became a threat even to the powerful Babylonian empire (Isa 13:17; 21:2; Dan 5:28). The latter was finally brought to its end when Cyrus, king of the Persians, first conquered the Medes and then used his combined forces to defeat Babylon.

Bibliography

Cook, J. M. 1983. *The Persian Empire*. London.

DAVID W. BAKER

MADAʾIN SALIH. See ḤEGRA.

MADMANNAH (PLACE) [Heb *madmannâ*]. A village in the Negeb plains at the S end of the administrative districts of Judah (Josh 15:21). The founding of the place is attributed to Shaaph, a son of Maacah, the concubine of Caleb, and Jahdai, another son of Caleb (1 Chr 2:42–49). Therefore, Madmannah is in the "Negeb of Caleb" where David operated as an outlaw (1 Sam 30:14). It has been located in the vicinity of Khirbet Umm ed-Demineh, a place that apparently preserves the biblical name although the age of the remains at this ruin (primarily Roman-Byzantine) and its location in the Hebron hills, rather than on the Negeb plain, make it an unlikely choice. More probable is nearby Khirbet Tatrit (M.R. 143084), at a lower elevation and where Iron Age and later remains have been found. Some scholars believe Madmannah to be the same as Beth-markeboth because of its comparable position in the town lists in Josh 19:5 and 1 Chr 2:49. A similar problem surrounds the name Sansannah. However, the parallelism in these lists may be more apparent than real and may actually reflect differing usage. The lists, consequently, may refer to different places and may not necessarily be scribal errors. The name Madmannah is easily confused with a similar-sounding place, MADMENAH, mentioned in Isa 10:31. It has been suggested that *madmannâ* means "dung place," which perhaps more euphemistically may mean a village surrounded by agriculturally enriched, or manured, land.

HAROLD BRODSKY

MADMEN (PLACE) [Heb *madmēn*]. A town mentioned in Jeremiah's oracle against Moab (Jer 48:2). While sometimes thought to be identical with Dibon, it is more probably located at Khirbet Dimneh (M.R. 217077), approximately 2.5 miles NW of Rabbah (*IDB* 3: 220), which is along the King's Highway in central Moab (*LBHG,* 56, 439). Madmen means "dung hill," and Aharoni suggests that it is typical of place names derived from agricultural features (*LBHG,* 109). In Isa 25:10, "dung hill" *(madmēn)* is used as part of a simile indicating the destruction of Moab, though any connection between Isaiah 25 and Jeremiah 48 is uncertain (Carroll *Jeremiah* OTL, 779).

The oracles against Moab in Jeremiah 48 have long been noted for their length and prolific use of place names (cf. Carroll *Jeremiah* OTL, 781). Why the Jeremiah tradition has included reference to so many place names in chapter 48, including the otherwise obscure Madmen, can only be the subject of conjecture. Carroll (p. 779) proposes a word-play in Jer 48:2 between *mdmn* and *dmn* ("be silent"); this could suggest that the inclusion of this particular Moabite town in Jer 48:2 was in part determined by literary factors.

JOHN M. BRACKE

MADMENAH (PLACE) [Heb *madmēnâ*]. One of the places N of Jerusalem named by the prophet Isaiah in his vision of the Assyrian march against Jerusalem (Isa 10:31). Mentioned after Anathoth (2.5 miles NE of Jerusalem) and before Nob (1.5 miles N–NE of Jerusalem), Madmenah was close to the N limits of Jerusalem. It is sometimes identified with Shufat (M.R. 172135), about 2.5 miles N of the Old City of Jerusalem, but this is not certain. The name means "dung heap."

GARY A. HERION

MADNESS. See DEMONS; SICKNESS AND DISEASE.

MADON (PLACE) [Heb *mādōn*]. An important Canaanite city-state in the north, ruled by Jobab (Josh 11:1). Joining the alliance organized by Jabin, king of Hazor, it suffered defeat at the hands of the Israelites (Josh 12:19). The LXX does not mention Madon in any of its lists. It refers to Maron instead, in Josh 11:1. Where the MT has "the waters of Merom," the LXX reads "the waters of Maron." The list of the defeated kings in Joshua 12 makes no reference to either Madon or Maron. Judges 5:19 states that the battle of Deborah was fought by the waters of Megiddo. Obviously, the traditions are much confused about the names of these places. The place name *mdn* found in a list of Tuthmosis III is not thought to be a reference to the Madon of Josh 11:1. Its usual identification with the modern Khirbet Madin, purely based on the similarity of the names, cannot be supported by any other data. Because it is not mentioned anywhere else, this important city-state is likely to be identical with Merom, a place close to the waters of Merom, which is also mentioned in both Egyptian and Assyrian sources. The Deuteronomistic History mentions Merom because it was a powerful city-state and assigns it the function of illustrating how even such a mighty city was given into the hands of obedient Israelites.

PAUL BENJAMIN

MAGADAN (PLACE) [Gk *Magadan*]. After feeding the 4,000, Jesus navigated the Sea of Galilee and entered the region of Magadan (Matt 15:39). In the Markan parallel (8:10), Dalmanutha appears in the place of Magadan. Variant readings plague both of these texts; the uncertainty of the original text probably stems from the uncertainty of the location of both sites. Codex Koridethi (9th century) has changed both passages to read "Magdala," but the late date of the manuscript evidence and lack of corroborating support renders this reading doubtful. The reading "Magadan" is found in several late Markan manuscripts, but this reading, for the same reasons, also must be rejected. The motivation for the Markan change is almost certainly harmonistic. Some scholars have suggested Megiddo in place of Magadan, but this site is more than 20 miles from the Sea of Galilee and is therefore to be rejected, especially since no land travel is mentioned in the text. See Lohmeyer (1967) for discussion of proposed conjectural emendations of the text, but none of these suggestions is very convincing.

A few scholars have suggested that Magadan is to be located on the E shore of the Sea of Galilee, while others have placed it on the W shore. Neither context in Matthew or Mark is decisive. Matthew states that Jesus left the regions of Tyre and Sidon (cf. 15:29 with 15:21), but to which side of the Sea of Galilee did he go, east or west? Mark 7:31 records that Jesus left Tyre and Sidon headed N and then traveled S and E to the Decapolis on the SE side of the lake. The crossing, therefore, was apparently E to W. Mark 8:1, however, is punctuated with, "In those days," which perhaps means that 8:1–10 does not immediately follow 7:31–37. On balance, the W side of the lake is the probable site of Magadan because the language of Matt 15:29–31 suggests a Gentile province (15:31, "they praised the God of Israel," the "seven" baskets of leftover pieces, not the Jewish "twelve") and a remote place (15:33), which better fits the Gentile Decapolis on the E side of the Sea of Galilee, rather than the Jewish Galilee of the W side. Without evidence some scholars also identify Magadan as the hometown or birthplace of Mary Magdalene. Other writers also suggest that Magadan is to be identified with the modern Mejdel (M.R. 140105).

Bibliography

Lohmeyer, E. 1967. *Das Evangelium des Markus.* Göttingen.

WARREN J. HEARD, JR.

MAGBISH (PERSON) [Heb *magbîš*]. "Ancestor" of 156 people who returned from exile in the days of Zerubbabel (Ezra 2:30; LXX *Magebōs*). However, like so many other names in the Ezra 2 list, Magbish is more likely the name of a village; since the time of Abel (*GP* 2: 373) it has usually been identified with Khirbet el-Makhbiyeh (M.R. 145116), a site which has yielded Persian-period remains. Because Magbish is listed just before Elam in the Ezra 2 list, Simons (*GTTOT,* 380) prefers a slightly more southerly identification with Khirbet Qanan Mugheimis, 2 km W of Beit Alam (M.R. 145109).

There are also problems with the text. In the parallel Heb text of Neh 7:33, Magbish does not occur (although one LXX ms of this verse does refer to the "156 sons of *magebōs*"). Another parallel text, 1 Esdr 5:21, refers to the "156 sons of *Niphis,*" which the RSV renders as "Magbish" to harmonize with Ezra 2:30.

GARY A. HERION

MAGDALA (M.R. 198247) [Aram *magdalaʾ*]. MAGDALENE. Presumably the town of origin of Mary Magdalene

(*Magdalēnē,* Luke 8:2) generally identified with Migdal Nûnnaya of the Talmud ("Tower of Fish," *b. Pesaḥ.* 46b), which lies approximately one mile N of Tiberias. Magdala (meaning "tower") is usually identified with the city with the Greek name of Taricheae or Tarecheae in Josephus (*JW* 2.21.8; 3.9.7–3.10.5). Magdala-Taricheae would mean "Tower of [salted] fish." The difficulty in identifying Magdala with Taricheae is that Josephus seems to think Taricheae was 30 stadia from Tiberias, or 3.6 Roman miles (*Life* 32 §157), and Pliny places Taricheae S of Tiberias (*HN* 5.15). But as Pliny knows less detail about Palestine than Josephus, identification of Magdala with Taricheae seems relatively secure. Some scholars believe that Migdal Sebʾaiya (Tower of Dyers) of the Jerusalem Talmud is the same place (*y. Taʿan.* 69a).

The Greek name of this town gives it away as an important fishing center and fish export center in the Roman period. Many Roman fishing towns were named Taricheae. Strabo knows of Taricheae in Palestine and its salted-fish industry (16.2.45). Josephus noted that E Lower Galilee was divided into two toparchies, Tiberias and Taricheae (*JW* 2.13.2 §252). In this case Magdala-Taricheae was the administrative center of an area that extended eight miles W to the toparchy of Sepphoris and 10 miles N to the S boundary of Upper Galilee about 5 miles N of Capernaum. Magdala-Taricheae was important enough to have its own stadium (*JW* 2.21.3 §599). Its aqueduct extended to Ain el-Mudawwara 2.8 miles to the NW. After the founding of Tiberias in A.D. 20, Magdala-Taricheae lost its position as head of the toparchy in favor of Tiberias.

Magdala-Taricheae did not play any role in the ministry of Jesus. We know of no disciples other than Mary from this locality.

By A.D. 54, at the accession of Nero, Magdala-Taricheae and Tiberias passed to Herod Agrippa II, son of Agrippa I (*Ant.* 20.8.4 §159). Josephus claimed to have fortified Magdala-Taricheae in A.D. 66, though Vespasian took the city in the next year. Taricheae was the location of the only sea battle between the Romans and the Jewish rebels. It was a disaster for the Jews. Apparently the Jewish inhabitants of Taricheae did not believe they would ever regain the town, for they fled to Tiberias after this debacle. Vespasian ordered the slaughter of 12,000 refugees from Taricheae in the stadium of Tiberias, while 6,000 were sent to build Nero's canal at Corinth and 30,400 were sold as slaves (*JW* 3.10.10 §539–40). At the close of the First Revolt in 73, Taricheae seems to have been absorbed by Tiberias. Later, at the death of Herod Agrippa II, Taricheae passed directly to the new province of Palestine, ruled by a governor of senatorial rank who resided in Caesarea.

Magdala or Taricheae was not a place of pilgrimage from the 4th to the early 6th century. However, before A.D. 518, it was visited by a certain Theodosius, who added a note that "my Lady Mary was born" at Magdala, which city he knows only by that name (*Topography* 138). The nun Hugeburc recorded Willibald's visit to Magdala in A.D. 724 in a single sentence: "From there (Tiberias) they went along the sea and approached the village of Magdala" (*Life* 96.1).

Excavations at Magdala were conducted from 1971 through 1973. These excavations revealed a small building that is surely a small, undecorated synagogue, about 26.8 by 23.8 feet. It was provided with interior columnation around three sides and a set of five benches against the N wall. "Heart-shaped" or double columns stood at the corners of the lines of columnation. The excavators believe that the building was converted to a fish pond after A.D. 70, or after the First Revolt. This would suggest that the Jewish population that originally used it was gone. This small building with thick walls stood at the SE corner of two well-paved streets. The street passing in front of the synagogue is a bit more than 13 feet broad. Across the street to the W stood the base of a masonry and mortar tower about 29 × 32.5 feet with walls 7 feet thick. This tower still stands 21 feet high, but it is interpreted by the excavator as a water tower, not as a fish tower. On the S side of the Franciscan property of Magdala and extending outside the property lie the ruins of a monastery of the 5th and 6th centuries. It was furnished with fine mosaics in geometric designs.

JAMES F. STRANGE

MAGDALENE. See MARY (PERSON); MAGDALA (PLACE).

MAGDIEL (PERSON) [Heb *magdîʾēl*]. One of the Edomite "chiefs" (Heb *ʾallûpîm*) mentioned in Gen 36:40–43, an appendix which most likely ought to be attributed to the Priestly source. The name also occurs in the 1 Chr 1:51b–54 list, an abridged form of the Gen 36:40–43 appendix. This theophoric name means "God's/El's gift" (cf. Sabaean *ʾlmjd, mjdlt;* Safaitic *mjdʾl;* Arabic *mğed;* etc.). It is referred to by Eusebius (*Onomast.* 124.22–23) as the name of a site in the Gebalene. Thus, this Edomite "chief" may actually be a place name, analogous with Elah, Iram(?), Mibzar, and Pinon.

ULRICH HÜBNER

MAGGOT. See ZOOLOGY.

MAGI [Gk *Magos*]. See INFANCY NARRATIVES IN THE NT GOSPELS.

MAGIC. This entry consists of two articles, one survey of magical practices in the ANE, and another summarizing the references to magic in the OT.

ANCIENT NEAR EAST

In its broadest sense, "magic" is a form of communication involving the supernatural world in which an attempt is made to affect the course of present and/or future events by means of ritual actions (especially ones which involve the symbolic imitation of what the practitioner wants to happen), and/or by means of formulaic recitations which describe the desired outcome and/or invoke gods, demons, or the spirits believed to be resident in natural substances. For purposes of analysis, it is useful to make a distinction between problem-oriented rituals on the one hand and priestly activities such as the maintenance of the daily cult and the celebration of regularly scheduled festivals on the other, especially since this distinction corresponds to a native ANE division of labor among specialists in the supernatural (Engelhard 1970: 219–21). Since it is usual to classify priestly activities as "religion," "magic" is here confined to the problem-oriented rituals. It should be kept in mind, however, that these two types of activity were part of the same belief system and that there was none of the hostility between them to be seen in later times between "magic" and "religion." Exorcists and priests received the same education, served the same gods, and regarded each other as legitimate practitioners. The same can be said of the distinction between exorcists and physicians, both of whom practiced medicine in some sense of the word and who might even cooperate in dealing with complicated cases (Ritter 1965). See also DEMONS.

The magic of the pre-Hellenistic Near East, like the magic of peoples everywhere, utilized the procedures of apotropaion or exorcism (frightening a spirit away before or after it took up residence in a human being), propitiation (buying off a spirit), and transfer (giving an evil to someone or something else). What is striking about this tradition is the variety and the ingenuity of magical rites and formulaic recitations employed in it. Not only are there literally thousands of recipes for amulets, salves, and nostrums, but there is much manufacturing of figurines, which range in complexity from simple lumps of clay to elaborate representations of half-human monsters carrying real miniature weapons, with the details picked out in appropriately colored paint (Wiggerman 1986; cf. Borghouts 1978: no. 123). Egypt also generated a plethora of curious drawings on papyrus (Borghouts 1978: no. 40, for example). There was, moreover, a great variety of ways to transfer evil (*RLA* 7: 245–46, 248–49). Of particular interest to biblical scholars is the extensive use of "scapegoats," which might indeed be goats, but also figurines, pigs, mice, and even people (Lambert 1957–58; Kümmel 1967; *RLA* 7: 246–48). Especially emphasized in Hittite magic, but by no means absent from ancient Mesopotamia and Egypt, is the invocation of analogies to achieve desired ends (Ünal 1988: 74–85; *RLA* 7: 244–45).

A. Mesopotamia

For Mesopotamians, there was a clear distinction between black, or maliciously antisocial, magic (Akk *kišpū*) performed by a sorcerer/sorceress (Akk *kaššāpu/kaššāptu*) and white, or defensive, magic performed by legitimate practitioners, most notably the exorcist (Akk *āšipu/maš-māšu*). Sorcery was punishable by death (MAL A 47). White magic, conversely, was the gift of the gods (especially Asalluḫi and Marduk) to mankind (Reiner 1958: V–VI: 175; VII, VIII: 88–90) and could legitimately be used either to make sorcery turn against its human practitioner (Meier 1937; Lambert 1957–58) or to calm the gods themselves when they became angry by magically removing the moral or cultic offenses which had caused their anger (Reiner 1958) and/or by getting rid of the resulting illness and bad fortune (Ebeling 1915: 96–103; Farber 1977: 24–100). Magic was also an essential concomitant of the foundation of temples and other buildings (Ellis 1968; *ANET,* 339–42; Farber 1987: 241–44) or the consecration of a priest (Borger 1973) or the preparation of temple drums (*ANET,* 334–38; Farber 1987: 234–36). Apart from this, the Mesopotamians used magic to assist in childbirth (Lambert 1969; Cohen 1976: 133–40; Römer 1987: 204–7; Farber 1987: 274–77), to get cranky babies to go to sleep (Farber 1989), and to keep at bay such evils as plague (Reiner 1960), fever (Lambert 1970), toothache (*ANET,* 100–01; Farber 1987: 271), sties (Farber 1987: 272–73), the effects of dog bite (Römer 1987: 210–11; Farber 1987: 256), impotence (Biggs 1967), ghosts (Bottéro 1983: 174–96; Scurlock 1988), demons (Myhrman 1902; Lackenbacher 1971; Farber 1977; Geller 1985; Wiggerman 1986; Borger 1987), evil eye (Ebeling 1949: 203–11), slander (Gurney 1960), nightmares (Oppenheim 1956), and bad omens (Ebeling 1954–56; Laessøe 1955; Lambert 1957–58; Caplice 1965–71; 1973; 1974b). A further use of magic was to add extra deterrents to oath breaking and to give force to curses (*ANET,* 532–33, 538–41). More productive uses of magic were procedures designed to give success in war (Elat 1982; Römer 1987: 169–71; *RLA* 7: 224), in opening canals (von Weiher 1983: no. 5), in business enterprises such as taverns (Caplice 1974b: 23–24), or to force the return of runaway slaves (Ebeling 1954). Of less obvious social value were spells which could be used to win legal cases or to prevent other people from being angry with the practitioner (Ebeling 1931a: 16–44; 1949: 186–203; Whiting 1985; Römer 1987: 202–4; von Weiher 1983: nos. 23–24). Equally ambiguous was the category of love magic, which included such classic devices of love inducement as giving a woman an apple to eat and burying a figurine where she would have to walk over it (Biggs 1967: 71–78). In Mesopotamia, spirits of the dead (and of death) were contacted for purposes of necromancy by rubbing salves on the necromancer's face or by employing skulls or figurines as temporary houses for the spirit which was being summoned up (Finkel 1983–84; von Weiher 1983: no. 20). See also *RLA* 6: 439–46.

B. Hittite Anatolia

Hittite magic was very similar to Mesopotamian magic. Again, there was a careful differentiation between black magic (Hit *alwanzatar*) performed by a sorcerer *(alwanzinaš)* and white magic performed by legitimate practitioners, with the former strictly against the law (HL 44b, 111, 163, 170). An unusual feature of Hittite magic (as compared to Mesopotamian) is the prominence of "old women" among the legitimate practitioners and the lack of clear division of labor between diviners and exorcists (Engelhard 1970: 5–56). Also unusual is that the Hittite rituals usually give the name, profession, and/or homeland of the author of a magical ritual. Authors include not only "old women" and exorcist diviners, but priests, doctors, and ladies of the court (*RLA* 7: 242), whether Hittite or drawn from outlying territories such as Kizzuwatna (Cilicia), Mukiš (Tell Atchana in Syria), and Arzawa (Ephesus). As in Mesopotamia, white magic was a divine gift (*RLA* 7: 238) and could legitimately be used to placate angry gods; among the Hittites, this usually took the form of evocation rituals in which the divinity was lured from the place to which he had withdrawn back to Hatti where he could be pacified (Engelhard 1970: 105–13; Haas and Wilhelm 1974). Magic was also required at the foundation of temples and other buildings (Engelhard 1970: 86–95; Kellerman 1980). Apart from this, the Hittites also used magic to assist in childbirth (Sommer and Ehelolf 1924; Beckman 1983) or burial (Otten 1958), to avoid various evils including sorcery (Engelhard 1970: 61–71; Jakob-Rost 1972; Kühne 1973; Haas and Thiel 1978; Hutter 1988), impurity (Goetze 1938; Otten 1961; *ANET,* 346, 348–49; Engelhard 1970: 71–78; Hoffner 1973; Lebrun 1979), impotence (Hoffner 1987; Engelhard 1970: 78–86), quarreling (Jakob-Rost 1953; *ANET,* 350–51), slander (Szabó 1971), and illness (Kronasser 1961; Souček 1963; Kümmel 1967; *ANET,* 347; Kümmel 1987: 285–88, 289–92), and to keep ghosts (CHD 3/2: 176–79), demons (Carruba 1966), and bad omens (Kronasser 1962; Kümmel 1967) at a safe distance. A further use of magic was to make sure that those swearing oaths took these oaths seriously (Engelhard 1970: 95–105; Oettinger 1976). Success in warfare could be ensured, inter alia, by a special evocation ritual in which the enemy gods were lured away from their worshipers (*ANET,* 354–55; Haas and Wilhelm 1974) or anointing the troops, horses, and military matériel with a protective mixture (Laroche 1971: 162, nos. 8–14) or even by hexing the enemy's leader while protecting one's own (KUB VII 61). Even when unsuccessful in the field, morale could be restored by marching the defeated army between fires, thorn bushes, and halved animals and human prisoners (Kümmel 1967: 151). The Hittites, like the Mesopotamians, attempted to call up the spirits of the dead, although the details of the procedure are unfortunately lost to us (Laroche 1971: 154–55).

C. Egypt

In many ways, Egyptian magic was similar to Mesopotamian and Hittite magic. Here, too, gods were magicians (Borghouts 1978: no. 84), and the basic function of much of the magic was medical (Borghouts 1978: nos. 46–52, 55–58, 64, 71–81) and antidemonic (nos. 22–27, 33, 53–54, 65, 67–69), including remedies for such things as plague (nos. 13–18, 20–21), nightmares (nos. 6–7), headaches (nos. 37–45), bleeding (nos. 30–32), burns (nos. 34–36), swallowing a fly or getting a fishbone stuck in the throat (nos. 19, 28–29), difficult childbirth (nos. 60–63; cf. Lexa 1925: 27–33), hungry babies (Borghouts 1978: no. 70), and bothersome birds, reptiles, or wild animals (*ANET,* 326; Borghouts 1978, nos. 82–146; Sternberg-el-Hotabi et al. 1988: 358–80). There are also many examples of magic to be used on domestic or foreign enemies (Sethe 1926; *ANET,* 326–29; Borghouts 1978: nos. 5, 8–12, 59, 66) or to give success in love, legal cases, and the like (Borghouts 1978: nos. 1–4). However, there is one striking difference between this tradition and that of the Mesopotamians and Hittites, and that is that the Egyptians made no distinction in terminology between good magic and sorcery (both were referred to as *heka*). They tended also to treat their gods in a manner which Mesopotamians and Hittites usually reserved for demons—that is, by leveling blood-curdling threats at them at the first sign of insubordination (Borghouts 1978: no. 9, for example). Another unusual feature of Egyptian magic is the category of spells designed to get the soul safely to the underworld and to help it successfully to pass the native version of the Last Judgment (Faulkner 1969; 1973–78; Allen 1974; Sternberg-el-Hotabi et al. 1988: 405–31). Necromancy using corpses or scrying cups is attested in Hellenistic Egypt and may go back to earlier periods; moreover, it seems likely that letters to the dead (Gardiner and Sethe 1928) could have been used for this purpose. See also *LÄ* 1: 67–69, 864–70; 3: 1137–51.

D. Ugaritic, Aramaic, and Phoenician Texts

Relatively few magical texts have survived from these areas, and those which have come down to us are typically fragmentary and open to more than one interpretation. However, what we seem to have are texts designed to accompany marriage, childbirth, and burials (de Moor 1987: 141–45; Dietrich and Loretz 1988: 329–33) or to ward off ghosts and demons (de Moor 1987: 183–86; Dietrich and Loretz 1988: 333–39; Butterweck 1988), bad dreams (de Moor 1987: 181–82), infertility (Dietrich and Loretz 1988: 339–42), drunkenness (Dietrich and Loretz 1988: 342–45), and snakebite (Dietrich and Loretz 1988: 345–50). There is also one spell which could have been used to thwart a human adversary (Delsman 1988).

Bibliography

Allen, T. G. 1974. *The Book of the Dead.* SAOC 37. Chicago.

Beckman, G. 1983. *Hittite Birth Rituals.* StBT 29. Wiesbaden.

Biggs, R. D. 1967. *ŠÀ.ZI.GA: Ancient Mesopotamian Potency Incantations.* TCS 1. Locust Valley, NY.

Borger, R. 1967. Das dritte "Haus" der Serie *bīt rimki. JCS* 21: 1–17.

———. 1973. Die Weihe eines Enlil-Priesters. *BiOr* 30: 163–76.

———. 1974. Die Beschwörungsserie *bīt mēseri* und die Himmelfahrt Henochs. *JNES* 33: 183–96.

———. 1987. Pazuzu. Pp. 15–32 in *Language, Literature, and History: Philological and Historical Studies Presented to Erica Reiner,* ed. F. Rochberg-Halton. AOS 67. New Haven.

Borghouts, J. F. 1970. The Magical Texts of Papyrus Leiden I 348. *OMRO* 51: 1–248.

———. 1972. Magical Texts. Pp. 7–19 in *Textes et Langes de l'Égypte Pharaonique: Hommage à Jean François Champollion.* BE 64/3. Cairo.

———. 1978. *Ancient Egyptian Magical Texts.* NISABA 9. Leiden.

Bottéro, J. 1983. Les Morts et l'au-delà dans les rituels en accadien contre l'action des "revenants." *ZA* 73: 153–203.

Butterweck, C. 1988. Eine phönizische Beschwörung. Pp. 435–37 in *Religiöse Texte,* ed. C. Butterweck et al. TUAT 2/3. Gütersloh.

Caplice, R. I. 1965–71. Namburbi Texts in the British Museum I–V. *Or* n.s. 34: 105–31; 36: 1–38, 273–98; 39: 111–51; 40: 133–83.

———. 1973. Further Namburbi Notes. *Or* n.s. 42: 508–17.

———. 1974a. An Apotropaion against Fungus. *JNES* 33: 345–49.

———. 1974b. *The Akkadian Namburbi Texts: An Introduction.* SANE 1/1. Malibu, CA.

Carruba, O. 1966. *Das Beschwörungsritual für die Göttin Wišurijanza.* StBT 2. Wiesbaden.

Cohen, M. E. 1976. Literary Texts from the Andrews University Archaeological Museum. *RA* 70: 129–44.

Delsman, W. C. 1988. Eine aramäische Beschwörung. Pp. 432–34 in *Religiöse Texte,* ed. C. Butterweck et al. TUAT 2/3. Gütersloh.

Dietrich, M., and Loretz, O. 1988. Ugaritische Rituale und Beschwörungen. Pp. 299–357 in *Religiöse Texte,* ed. C. Butterweck et al. TUAT 2/3. Gütersloh.

Ebeling, E. 1915. Assyrische Beschwörungen. *ZDMG* 69: 89–103.

———. 1918–19. *Quellen zur Kenntnis der babylonischen Religion* I–II. MVAG 23. Leipzig.

———. 1931a. *Aus dem Tagewerk eines assyrischen Zauberpriesters.* MAOG 5/3. Leipzig.

———. 1931b. *Tod und Leben nach den Vorstellungen der Babylonier.* Berlin.

———. 1949. Beschwörungen gegen den Feind und den bösen Blick aus dem Zweistromlande. *ArOr* 17: 172–211.

———. 1953. Sammlungen von Beschwörungsformeln. *ArOr* 21: 357–423.

———. 1954. Eine assyrische Beschwörung um einen entflohenen Sklaven zurückzubringen. *Or* n.s. 23: 52–56.

———. 1954–56. Beiträge zur Kenntnis der Beschwörungsserie Namburbi. *RA* 48: 1–15, 76–85, 130–41, 178–91; 49: 32–41, 137–48, 178–92; 50: 22–33, 86–94.

Elat, M. 1982. Mesopotamische Kriegsrituale. *BiOr* 39: 5–25.

Ellis, R. 1968. *Foundation Deposits in Ancient Mesopotamia.* New Haven.

Engelhard, D. H. 1970. *Hittite Magical Practices: An Analysis.* Ph.D. diss., Brandeis.

Farber, W. 1977. *Beschwörungsrituale an Ištar und Dumuzi (attī Ištar ša harmaša Dumuzi).* Akademie der Wissenschaften und der Literatur, Veröffentlichungen der orientalischen Komission 30. Wiesbaden.

———. 1981. Zur ältern akkadischen Beschwörungsliteratur. *ZA* 71: 51–72.

———. 1987. Rituale und Beschwörungen in akkadischer Sprache. Pp. 212–81 in *Religiöse Texte,* ed. W. C. Delsman et al. TUAT 2/2. Gütersloh.

———. 1989. *Schlaf, Kindschen, schlaf!: Mesopotamische Baby-Beschwörungen und -Rituale.* Winona Lake, IN.

Faulkner, R. O. 1969. *The Ancient Egyptian Pyramid Texts.* 2 vols. Oxford.

———. 1973–78. *The Ancient Egyptian Coffin Texts.* 3 vols. Warminster.

Finkel, I. 1983–84. Necromancy in Ancient Mesopotamia. *AfO* 29/30: 1–17.

Gardiner, A., and Sethe, K. 1928. *Egyptian Letters to the Dead.* London.

Geller, M. 1985. *Forerunners to UDUG-HUL: Sumerian Exorcistic Incantations.* Freiburger Altorientalische Studien 12. Wiesbaden.

Goetze, A. 1938. *The Hittite Ritual of Tunnawi.* AOS 14. New Haven.

Gurney, O. R. 1960. A Tablet of Incantations against Slander. *Iraq* 22: 221–27.

Haas, V., and Thiel, H. J. 1978. *Die Beschwörungsrituale der Allaiturah(h)i und verwandte Texte.* AOAT 31. Kevelaer.

Haas, V., and Wilhelm, G. 1974. *Hurritische und luwische Riten aus Kizzuwatna.* AOATS 3. Kevelaer.

Hoffner, H. 1973. Incest, Sodomy and Bestiality in the Ancient Near East. Pp. 81–90 in *Orient and Occident: Essays Presented to Cyrus H. Gordon,* ed. H. Hoffner. AOAT 22. Kevelaer.

———. 1987. Paskuwatti's Ritual against Sexual Impotence. *AulaOr* 5: 271–87.

Hunger, H. 1976. *Spätbabylonische Texte aus Uruk* I. ADFU 9. Berlin.

Hutter, M. 1988. *Behexung, Entsühnung, und Heilung: Das Ritual der Tunnawiya für ein Königspaar.* OBO 82. Göttingen.

Jakob-Rost, L. 1953. Ein hethitisches Ritual gegen Familienzwist. *MIO* 1: 345–79.

———. 1972. *Das Ritual der Malli aus Arzawa gegen Behexung.* THeth 2. Heidelberg.

Kellerman, G. 1980. *Recherche sur les rituels de fondation hittites.* Ph.D. diss., Paris.

Kronasser, H. 1961. Fünf hethitische Rituale. *Die Sprache* 7: 140–67.

———. 1962. Das hethitische Ritual KBo IV 2. *Die Sprache* 8: 89–107.

———. 1963. *Die Umsiedelung der Schwarzen Gottheit: Das hethitische Ritual, KUB XXXIX 4 (des Ulippi).* SÖAW Phil.-hist. Kl. 241/3. Vienna.

Kühne, C. 1973. Das Ritualfragment KBo XVI 56 + KUB XXXIV 85. Pp. 161–67 in *Festschrift Heinrich Otten,* ed. E. Neu and C. Rüster. Wiesbaden.

Kümmel, H. M. 1967. *Ersatzrituale für den hethitischen König.* StBT 3. Wiesbaden.

———. 1987. Rituale in hethitischer Sprache. Pp. 282–92 in *Religiöse Texte,* ed. W. C. Delsman et al. TUAT 2/2. Gütersloh.

Lackenbacher, S. 1971. Note sur l'Ardat-lilî. *RA* 65: 119–54.

Laessøe, J. 1955. *Studies on the Assyrian Ritual and Series bît rimki.* Copenhagen.

Lambert, W. G. 1957–58a. A Part of the Ritual for the Substitute King. *AfO* 18: 109–12.

———. 1957–58b. An Incantation of the Maqlû Type. *AfO* 18: 288–99.

———. 1969. A Middle Assyrian Medical Text. *Iraq* 31: 28–39.

———. 1970. Fire Incantations. *AfO* 23: 39–45.

Laroche, E. 1971. *Catalogue des textes hittites.* Études et commentaires 75. Paris.

Lebrun, R. 1979. Lews Rituels d'Ammihatna, Tulbi et Mati contre une impureté. *Hethitica* 3: 139–64.

Lexa, F. 1925. *La Magie dans l'Égypte antique.* 3 vols. Paris.

Meier, G. 1937. *Die assyrische Beschwörungssammlung Maqlû.* AfO Beiheft 2. Berlin.

———. 1966. Studien zur Beschwörungssammlung Maqlû. *AfO* 21: 70–81.

Moor, J. C. de. 1987. *An Anthology of Religious Texts from Ugarit.* NISABA 16. Leiden.

Myhrman, D. W. 1902. Die "Labartu"-Texte. *ZA* 16: 141–200.

Oettinger, N. 1976. *Die militärischen Eide der Hethiter.* StBT 22. Wiesbaden.

Oppenheim, A. L. 1956. *The Interpretation of Dreams in the Ancient Near East.* TAPhS 46/3. Philadelphia.

Otten, H. 1958. *Hethitische Totenrituale.* VIO 37. Berlin.

———. 1961. Eine Beschwörung der Unterirdischen aus Boğazköy. *ZA* 54: 114–57.

Reiner, E. 1958. *Šurpu: A Collection of Sumerian and Akkadian Incantations.* AfO Beiheft 11. Graz.

———. 1960. Plague Amulets and House Blessings. *JNES* 19: 148–55.

Ritner, R. 1987. *The Mechanics of Ancient Egyptian Magical Practice.* Ph.D. diss., Chicago.

Ritter, E. K. 1965. Magical-Expert (*= āšipu*) and Physician (*=asû*). Pp. 299–321 in *Studies in Honor of Benno Landsberger.* AS 16. Chicago.

Roccati, A. 1970. *Papiro ieratico n. 54003.* Turin.

Römer, W. H. P. 1987. Rituale und Beschwörungen in sumerischer Sprache. Pp. 163–211 in *Religiöse Texte,* ed. W. C. Delsman et al. TUAT 2/2. Gütersloh.

Scurlock, J. A. 1988. *Magical Means of Dealing with Ghosts in Ancient Mesopotamia.* Ph.D. diss., Chicago.

Sethe, K. 1926. *Die Ächtung feindlicher Fürsten, Völker und Dinge auf altägyptischen Tongefässcherben des Mittleren Reiches.* ATAW 1926/5. Berlin.

Sommer, F., and Ehelolf, H. 1924. *Das hethitische Ritual des Pāpanikri von Komana.* BoSt 10. Leipzig.

Souček, V. 1963. Ein neues hethitisches Ritual gegen die Pest. *MIO* 9: 164–74.

Sternberg-el-Hotabi, H.; Gutekunst, W.; and Kausen, E. 1988. Ägyptische Rituale und Beschwörungen. Pp. 358–431 in *Religiöse Texte,* ed. C. Butterweck et al. TUAT 2/3. Gütersloh.

Szabó, G. 1971. *Ein hethitisches Entsühnungsritual für das Königspaar Tuthalija und Nikalmati.* THeth 1. Heidelberg.

Thomsen, M. L. 1987. *Zauberdiagnose und schwarze Magie in Mesopotamien.* Copenhagen.

Ünal, A. 1988. The Role of Magic in the Ancient Anatolian Religions according to the Cuneiform Texts from Boğazköy-Ḫattuša. Pp. 52–85 in *Essays on Anatolian Studies in the Second Millennium B.C.,* ed. H. I. H. Prince Takahito Mikasa. Wiesbaden.

Weiher, E. von. 1983. *Spätbabylonische Texte aus Uruk* II. ADFU 10. Berlin.

———. 1988. *Spätbabylonische Texte aus Uruk* III. ADFU 12. Berlin.

Whiting, R. M. 1985. An Old Babylonian Incantation from Tell Asmar. *ZA* 75: 179–87.

Wiggermann, F. A. M. 1986. *Babylonian Prophylactic Figures: The Ritual Texts.* Amsterdam.

J. A. Scurlock

OLD TESTAMENT

Interpretations of the nature, role, and content of magic and magical practices in the OT have varied greatly. Discussion has revolved around several issues: interpretation and translation of Hebrew terms referring to magical practices; evaluations of the significance of the different attestations of magic in the OT; and analysis of the relationship between magic and religion. Even the term "magic" (and that to which it refers) has proved very difficult to define. Recognizing the limitations and difficulties of any definition, the term "magic" will be used here to refer to methods associated with the gaining of suprahuman knowledge and power or with influencing suprahuman powers. Magic is often discussed in connection with divination (discerning the future). There is considerable overlap between magic and divination in both practice and use of terms.

A. Specialized Terminology
  1. Deut 18:10–11
  2. Other Terms
B. Place of Magic in the OT
C. Relation of Magic and Religion
  1. Social Sciences
  2. Comparative Near Eastern Studies
  3. Distinctive Nature of Israelite Religion

A. Specialized Terminology

Terms referring to magic and magical practices are found throughout the OT in a wide range of materials. However, specialized and technical vocabulary appears primarily in the legal materials (Deut 18:10–11; Lev 19:26, 31; 20:1–6, 27; Exod 22:18—Eng 22:17; see also 2 Kgs 21:6 = 2 Chr 33:6).

1. Deut 18:10–11. Interpreters generally agree that Deut 18:10–11 provides the most basic and inclusive list of magic terminology in the OT. However, understandings of these terms frequently differ since it is difficult to determine the precise practices to which the terms refer (e.g., the OT often sees divinatory practices as a subcategory of magic, and interpreters often appeal to different etymologies to explain the same Hebrew term). Further, translations frequently project back into biblical times practices seen as "magical" at the time of the translation.

a. *maᶜăbîr bĕnô ûbittô bāʾēš* ("one who makes his son or his daughter pass through the fire"). Interpreters debate the meaning of this phrase and its relationship to the other terms in Deut 18:10–11. This phrase has been taken to refer both to child sacrifice and to a type of "oracle ordeal." As a reference to child sacrifice, it is often interpreted as "propitiatory" and so divorced from the other magical/divinatory practices in the text. As a reference to a type of oracle ordeal, it is more frequently associated with either divination or magic.

b. *qōsēm qĕsāmîm* ("diviner, augurer"). Translations tend to equate *qsm* with divination. Commentaries, however, tend to view *qsm* as a more general term referring to the whole complex of magical and divinatory practices in ancient Israel. Arguments for understanding *qsm* as a very general term are based (1) on the Deuteronomistic tendency to list a general term first in a series with subsequent terms providing clarification and nuance, (2) on comparative etymology, and (3) on uses of *qsm* elsewhere in the OT (cf. Num 23:23; 1 Sam 15:23; 2 Kgs 17:17; Mic 3:6).

c. *mĕᶜônēn* ("soothsayer, observer of times, one who looks for omens, sorcerer, enchanter"). The term *mĕᶜônēn* is the first in the series of seemingly specialized terms for various types of magical and divinatory practices. The diversity in translation of this term reflects lack of scholarly consensus regarding the practice(s) to which it refers and its primary focus (magic or divination). Interpretations have relied strongly on etymological comparisons, variously equating *mĕᶜônēn* with divinatory practices such as observation of clouds, the "evil eye," "eyeing" or observing "the times," the humming sound associated with diviners, as well as with magic practices such as conjuring up spirits.

d. *mĕnaḥēš* ("augur, diviner, enchanter"). The precise meaning and focus of *mĕnaḥēš* are also difficult to determine because interpreters associate it with two different roots—*nḥš* and *lḥš*. Those emphasizing the connection with *nḥš* see it as a denominative from *nāḥāš* (snake) and associate it with some form of divination related to snakes. Those emphasizing the connection with *lḥš* tend to associate it more with magic—particularly with the use of charms and "enchantments" (cf. Isa 3:3; 3:20; 26:16; Jer 8:17; Eccl 10:11).

e. *mĕkaššēp* ("sorcerer"). There is general agreement regarding the meaning of the term *kešep,* usually translated "sorcery." However, there has been a tendency on the part of some interpreters and translations to use the negative and antisocial term "sorcery" for references to female practitioners of *kešep,* while employing the more neutral term "magic" for references to male practitioners. The unequal distinction between female and male practitioners seems present in the OT itself. The commandment in Exod 22:18—Eng 22:17 requires the community to put the *mĕkaššēpāh* (female) to death. However, in texts referring to the *mĕkaššēp* (male) either no precise penalty is given (Deut 18:10) or the judgment and punishment are left to God (Jer 27:9; Mal 3:5).

f. *ḥōbēr ḥāber* ("charmer, one who casts spells, one who uses charms"). Interpreters generally agree that the root *ḥbr* is related to the use of charms and spells. This connection arises from the widely recognized association of the root *ḥbr* with the idea of "uniting, joining, weaving." Many interpreters relate this concept to the practice of tying or wrapping magical knots or threads around people or objects, understood either to bind the gods to do one's will or to bind (disable) the object or person to be affected. Another interpretation relates the term to the idea that words are woven together in the spell itself. An alternative derivation of the term *ḥōbēr,* however, relates it to the Akk term *ḥabarum*—to be noisy, to make an indistinguishable clamor. Here, the *ḥōbēr* is seen as a "mutterer" (one who makes indistinguishable noises).

g. *šōʾēl ʾôb weyiddĕʿōnî* (literally, "an inquirer of an *ʾôb* or a *yiddĕʿōnî*"; "a medium or a wizard, one who traffics with ghosts and spirits, one who consults ghosts or spirits"). *ʾôb* and *yiddĕʿōnî* are two of three terms in Deut 18:11 seemingly related to the practice of necromancy (divination by inquiring of the dead).

Interpreters are uncertain about the precise understanding of the term *ʾôb* in the OT. This uncertainty arises from the variety of contexts in which the term appears, leading to its proposed connection with a wide range of different concepts—spirit, ancestral spirit, the person controlled by a spirit, a bag of skin, the pit from which spirits are called up, a ghost, a demon. Most interpreters simply admit the ambiguity of the term and acknowledge that it refers to several different but related objects—a ritual pit used by a necromancer, a spirit called up by a necromancer, and/or the necromancer himself or herself (cf. 1 Samuel 28).

The *yiddĕʿōnî* is closely associated in the OT with the *ʾôb.* While the term *ʾôb* appears independently, the term *yiddĕʿōnî* does not, raising the question of their relationship. Some interpreters see the two terms as a hendiadys (expressing a single idea by connecting two nouns with "and"), others (and most translations) see it as referring to separate people (e.g., medium and wizard). The difficulties in defining the term *yiddĕʿōnî* are similar to the difficulties with *ʾôb.* Most interpreters recognize the root *ydʿ* in *yiddĕʿōnî;* it is unclear, however, whether the "one who knows" is the entity being consulted or the practitioner doing the consulting. The frequent translation of *yiddĕʿōnî* as "familiar spirit" may be correct, but the close and problematic association of this term with medieval views of witchcraft should be kept in mind.

h. *dōrēš el-hammētîm* ("necromancer, one who calls up the dead"). This is the third term connected to necromancy in Deut 18:11. Interpreters generally agree that this is a straightforward reference to the practice of necromancy. However, the precise method by which this was done and its precise relationship to the *ʾôb* and *yiddĕʿōnî* is unclear.

2. Other Terms. In addition to the terms above, a number of other terms referring to magical practices appear in the OT.

a. *ḥăkam ḥărāšîm* ("skillful magician, magician, sorcerer"). This term occurs only in Isa 3:3. It is part of a list in Isa 3:2–3 listing the leaders in Jerusalem and Judah whom God will destroy. It is particularly notable that these verses classify three categories of diviners and magicians (*yônēn, ḥăkam ḥărāšîm,* and *nĕbôn lāḥaš*) as leaders in Judah along with the more traditional soldier, judge, prophet, and elder.

b. Terms Associated with Astrology. The OT uses three terms to refer to astrologers: *hōbĕrēw šāmayim,* "one who gazes at the heavens" (Isa 47:13); *hahōzîm bakkôkabîm,* "one who gazes at the stars" (Isa 47:13); and *gāzĕrîn,* "astrologer" (Dan 2:27; 47:7; 5:7, 11). The Aram term *gāzĕrîn* is used in the OT in connection with Chaldean "magicians" and "enchanters." It is related to the root *gzr,* "to determine or decree." Astrologers, then, read the signs in the heavens in order to determine and make known that which has been decreed.

c. Terms Associated with "Foreign" Magicians. The terms *ḥarṭōm,* "magician" and *ʾaššāp* (Aram *ʾāšap*), "enchanter" are associated particularly with foreign magicians. The term *ḥarṭōm* (Heb and Aram) is used to refer to the magicians of both Egypt (Gen 41:8, 24; Exod 7:11, 22; 8:3, 14, 15—Eng 8:7, 18, 19; 9:11) and Chaldea (Dan 1:20; 2:2, 10, 27; 4:7, 9; 5:11). The term *ʾaššāp/ʾāšap* appears paired with *ḥarṭōm* in almost every instance (Dan 1:20; 2:2, 10, 27; 4:7; 5:7, 11; alone in 5:15). OT evaluation of these foreign magicians seems to be mixed. In contests with Israel's God or God's representative they are always defeated; however, they are also frequently labeled *ḥākām,* "wise."

B. Place of Magic in the OT

The range of technical vocabulary, OT evidence for the knowledge and practice of a wide variety of magical and divinatory practices, and differing evaluations of magic in the OT itself leave interpreters divided regarding the general place of magic and magical practices in ancient Israel and the OT. Disagreement centers on two interrelated questions. First, should the OT prohibitions and negative evaluations of magic be viewed as the fundamental position of the OT, or should they be seen as simply reflecting the views of particular times or biblical writers? Second, does magic represent "primitive," foreign, or perverted influences on "true" Yahwism or does it represent an indigenous coterminous, or alternative form of Yahwism itself?

The OT prohibits the practice of magic or presents it negatively in a number of places (Deut 18:19–11; Lev 19:26, 31; 20:1–6, 27; Exod 22:17—Eng 22:18; 1 Samuel 28; Isa 8:19; 57:3; Ezek 22:28; Mal 3:5). However, neutral or positive references to a wide range of magical and divinatory practices—dreams, clairvoyance, hydromancy, belomancy, magic staffs, decisions by lots, juridical ordeals, blessings and curses, apotropaic measures, and so forth—are also scattered throughout the OT. The presence of both understandings in the OT raises the question of the relationship between positive and negative evaluations. Interpreters who take the prohibitive and negative statements as the primary response to magic in the OT and ancient Israel tend to devalue and ignore positive statements or view them as "violations" of the "normative" prohibitions referred to in other texts. Conversely, interpreters who see the prohibitive and negative statements as limited responses to magic at particular times or by particular interpreters (e.g., the Deuteronomistic tradition or individual prophets) tend to deemphasize the primary or normative role of the prohibitions in the OT overall.

Responses to the primacy of the prohibitions of magic in the OT are closely related to understandings of the religious history of ancient Israel. Those interpretations which maintain the primacy of the prohibition of magic also tend to emphasize magic as "primitive," or foreign, or as perverted Yahwism. In these cases, references to magic tend to be taken as evidence of early (pre-Yahwistic) practices, foreign impositions, or "survivals" of earlier practices into later times. On the other hand, interpretations which restrict the interest in prohibiting magic to particular time periods or interpreters are more willing to argue for magic as an indigenous and integral part of Israelite religion, or at least for differing evaluations of it in ancient Israel and the OT. Many of these interpretations include an acceptable role within the OT not only for particular magical practices, but also for a "magical world-view" in ancient Israel. Defining magic broadly and positively, these scholars see a "magical" underpinning for a variety of "religious" figures (prophets, "men of God," priests, kings) and "religious" practices (especially those associated with war, law, occupations, life events, illness, and death, and mourning).

C. Relation of Magic and Religion

Many of the differences referred to above arise from longstanding debates regarding the relationship between magic and religion. Many early understandings of magic in the OT were influenced by skepticism regarding the "reality" of "pagan" (irreligious) magic. Medieval interpretations were also strongly influenced by preconceptions regarding the sharp distinction between magic and religion. "Religion" was associated with the Church, "magic" and "witchcraft" with the devil.

Particularly influential for contemporary views of the relationship are three areas of study which became prominent in the late 1800s and early 1900s: early social sciences, comparative Near East studies, and apologetic interests regarding the distinctive nature of Israelite religious thought and practice.

1. Social Sciences. Aspects of several models proposed by the social sciences for the relationship between magic and religion still influence many discussions of magic in the OT.

a. Evolutionary. The evolutionary model understands magic as the first and most primitive stage in an increasingly sophisticated three-stage process (magic–religion–science). Interpretations of magic in the OT following an evolutionary model tend to view references to magic beliefs and practices as evidence of "primitive," "prereligious" elements (often associated with Canaanite influence) in ancient Israelite belief and practice. When such elements are present in a text, they represent evidence of either this primitive stage or later "survivals" of it.

b. Animistic. A variation of the evolutionary model is one which focuses more particularly on the developmental stages of religion and argues for the progress of religion from animism through polytheism to monotheism. The animistic model proposes that the earliest stages of religion reveal a strong belief in the presence and power of "spirits" and other supernatural forces in the world. Magic as an important part of this system is a method to control these spirits and supernatural forces. This understanding of magic as an instrument of control has affected many studies of magic in the OT; its most common use has been to argue for the distinction between practices concerned with *control,* "magic," and practices concerned with *worship,* "religion."

c. Psychological. Understandings of magic as a psychological "coping mechanism" are closely related to the view of magic as a method of control. Psychological theories emphasize the role of magic in enabling individuals to achieve control of their lives and world either by overcoming psychological fears or by creating additional confidence in practices already undertaken. Such theories have had variable influence on studies of magic in the OT. They have led some interpreters to treat magic sympathetically as an understandable practice in adverse circumstances; they have led others to interpret it as evidence for lack of trust in God.

d. Prelogical/Prescientific. Several scholars have argued for a distinction between earlier "prelogical" and "prescientific" worldviews and modern logical and scientific ones. According to these scholars, prelogical societies view the world "mystically"; that is, they explain events in supernatural rather than natural terms. Magic is a part of this prelogical and prescientific worldview in that it accepts the reality of supernatural forces and the efficacy of techniques to influence them, and it does not see the "modern" distinction between the material and the spiritual. This view often supports apologetics for magic in the OT. Further, it is often seen as a way to understand Israelite views of illness and oppression (particularly as they are reflected in the psalms), practices which have magical undertones such as ordeals, blessings and curses, and the workings of the cult.

e. Sociological. Early sociological theories of magic strongly emphasized the contrast between the social roles of religion and those of magic. In these theories, religion is understood as a group practice important for legitimating and sustaining the community as a whole. Magic, by contrast, is seen as individualistic and often antisocial, being frequently used to advance individual as opposed to community well-being. This dichotomy between religion as a social expression and magic as an individual expression can be seen in the work of many OT scholars.

f. Synthetic. Finally, later theories have synthesized various aspects of the theories above. An important trend in this synthesis has been the decreasing tendency to distinguish sharply between magic and religion. Instead, more recent models either emphasize the close interrelationship between magic and religion or see them as operating on a continuum.

2. Comparative Near Eastern Studies. Comparative material was used in developing the theories of the relationship between magic and religion outlined above. In addition, discussion of the nature, role, and content of specific details of magic in the OT has drawn heavily on ANE materials. As noted above, many terms and practices have been explained by parallels to Akkadian, Assyrian, Babylonian, Hittite, and Canaanite materials. Also, parallels to Arab, especially bedouin, terms, beliefs, and practices have been drawn, particularly in the early 1900s.

3. Distinctive Nature of Israelite Religion. Extensive use of comparative models and content, coupled with early tendencies to distinguish sharply between magic and religion, led to many studies arguing for the distinctive (unique) character of Israelite religion. This tendency had significant consequences for understandings of the role and significance of magic in ancient Israel and the OT, for it divorced magic and magical practices from the mainstream of Israelite religion and OT theology by being seen as "primitive," foreign, or "nonreligious." However, as noted above, not all interpreters accepted this view. At present, scholars remain divided.

In conclusion, the most recent work on magic in the OT is giving increased acknowledgment not only to the diversity of scholars' interpretations of magic in the OT, but also to the diversity of practices and positions represented in the OT itself. For further discussion see *EncJud* 6: 111–16; 11: 703–7; *IDB* 1: 856–58; 3: 223–25; *EncRel* 9: 82–89.

Bibliography

Neusner, J.; Frerichs, E. S.; and McCracken-Flesher, P. V., eds. 1989. *Religion, Science and Magic: In Concert and in Conflict.* New York.

Rogerson, J. 1988. Part One: The Old Testament. Pp. 3–150 in *The Study and Use of the Bible.* Vol. 2 in *The History of Christian Theology,* ed. P. Avis. Grand Rapids.

JOANNE K. KUEMMERLIN-MCLEAN

MAGISTRATE. See CITY AUTHORITIES.

MAGOG (PERSON) [Heb *māgôg*]. In the Table of Nations (Gen 10:2) and the parallel genealogy in 1 Chr 1:5, Magog is one of the six grandsons of Noah through his son Japheth. Others of this line are associated with Asia Minor (Javan, Tubal, Meshech), so a location for Magog also in this area is logical. It can also be supported by the reference in Ezek 38:1–6, where Gog, a king from Magog, is allied with Beth-togarmah, among others, which is described as coming "from the far north" (38:6). Not all of the listed allies are to the N of Israel, however, so the evidence is not compelling. Ezek 39:6 foretells judgment on Gog, which will include fire falling on Magog as well as upon "the island dwellers." The latter two passages portray these peoples as warriors from a distant land who will descend upon Israel in a cataclysmic battle. This eschatological motif is picked up in the NT, where Rev 20:8 pictures distant Gog and Magog allied with Satan in a final attempt to overthrow the people of God at the end of the age.

Scholars suggest several different locations for Magog. Skinner (*Genesis* ICC, 197) assumed the identity of Magog and *Gagā(ya),* which is mentioned in one of the Amarna letters from the mid-2d millennium B.C. (see *YGC,* 14 n. 40). They are identified there in a general way as people from the N. A more popular identification is that Gog is a Hebrew calque on the name of the Lydian king Gyges (ca. 680–ca. 648 B.C.E.; Akk *gugu*), and Magog is a derivation from Akk *mā(t) gugu* "land of Gyges." If this identification is correct, the etymological background of the term had been lost by the time of Ezekiel. He uses the Hebrew word for "land" alongside Magog, a redundancy if the word's etymological background were still well known. Another possible derivation involves the use of the Hebrew prefix *ma-* indicating "place of" (GKC, 236e). Therefore, Magog would be "Gog's place" (Wenham *Genesis 1–15* WBC, 217).

Josephus (*Ant.* 1.123) understood Magog to refer to the Scythians (Yamauchi 1982: 22; see 63–85), while the *Tg. Neof.* interpreted the name as *grmnyh (Germania).* This is possibly Germanica of Commagene in E Asia Minor. Jerome understood Magog to be the Goths (McNamara 1972: 194–95). The lack of any more specific geographical information makes any identification of Magog extremely uncertain.

Bibliography

McNamara, M. 1972. *Targum and Testament.* Grand Rapids.

Yamauchi, E. M. 1982. *Foes from the Northern Frontier.* Grand Rapids.

DAVID W. BAKER

MAGPIASH (PERSON) [Heb *magpîʿāš*]. A leader of the people in a signatory to the covenant established by Ezra (Neh 10:20). The meaning of the name is obscure, and at least one scholar has suggested that the place name Magbish (Ezra 2:30) has been mistaken for a personal name (Brockington *Ezra, Nehemiah and Esther* Century Bible, 180 and 181). It is more likely, however, that a family has assumed the name of the village in which they resided (Meyer 1896: 156; Williamson *Ezra, Nehemiah* WBC, 324).

Bibliography

Meyer, E. 1896. *Die Entstehung des Judenthums.* Halle.

FREDERICK W. SCHMIDT

MAGUS, SIMON. See SIMON (PERSON) #13.

MAHALAB (PLACE) [Heb *mēhebel*]. The RSV form of the name of a town listed before Achzib in connection with the tribal territory of Asher (Josh 19:29). The actual wording of the text is *mēhebel ʾakzîbâ.* In the AV the opening *mem* is regarded as a prefix ("from"), and MT *mhbl* is translated "from the coast" (to Achzib). Cooke (*Joshua* CBSC, 181) translates "by the region of" (Achzib). Most scholars, however, regard the *mem* as part of the word, and MT *mhbl* ("Mehebel") as a place name. The LXX^{B} of Josh 19:29 reads "from Leb and Achzib," which suggests that MT *mhbl* actually represents a metathesis of an original *mhlb.* This would then be supported by the data from Judg 1:31, which lists an "Ahlab" before Achzib (and a "Helbah" after it) as a town that Asher did not dispossess. Many scholars believe that all of these forms are corruptions of the same place name, "Mahalab," and that this should be identified with the Mahallibu mentioned in Sennacherib's third campaign (*ANET,* 287). This town would then be associated with Khırbet el-Mahalıb on the banks of the Litani River, 6 km NE of Tyre. See also AHLAB.

Naʾaman (1986: 57–60), however, who connects the Joshua town list to David's conquests, suggests that Khirbet el-Mahalib was almost certainly in the territory of Tyre and therefore could not have been captured by David. Therefore, he places the town mentioned in the Bible (MT *mhbl,* Helbah, Ahlab) farther S, tenatively at Ras al-Abyad. Kallai (*HGB,* 220–23) regards Ahlab and Helbah as two different places and does not connect the towns listed in Joshua with David's conquest. However, he believes that the list in Joshua appears in geographical order, so he also places MT *mhbl* (Josh 19:29) S of Tyre and identifies it with the Helbah of Judg 1:31 (but without locating it at a specific site). He identifies the Ahlab of Judg 1:31 with Mahallibu (Khirbet el-Mahalib).

The list of towns in Joshua that starts with MT *mhbl* (RSV Mahalab) is, however, almost certainly an addition to the text having a common origin with the Judges 1 list. The geographical order then does not necessarily coincide with that of the preceding section. The similarity of the place names "Mehebel," Ahlab, and Helbah to Mahallibu/Mahalib should be regarded as the deciding factor identifying RSV Mahalab (Mehebel)—as well as Ahlab and Helbah—with Khirbet el-Mahalib. The historical conclusion then must be that David indeed controlled this northern region and that the territory of Tyre was at the time very small.

Bibliography

Naʾaman, N. 1986. *Borders and Districts in Biblical Historiography.* Jerusalem.

RAFAEL FRANKEL

MAHALALEL (PERSON) [Heb *mahălalʾēl*]. Var. MAHALALEEL. **1.** Son of Kenan, born when Kenan was 70 years old (Gen 5:12–17; cf. Luke 3:37). At 65 years of age, Mahalalel sired Jared, and lived a total of 895 years. Comparisons with the genealogy of Cain in Genesis 4 have related this name with that of Mehujael (Wilson *GHBW,* 161–62). The initial *mem* and the final *ʾalep* and *lamed* are three consonants (half of the possible six) which the names share. The name Mahalalel is based upon two roots: *hll,* "to praise"; and *ʾl,* "god." The *mem* preformative on the *hll* may suggest an original participial form ("praising God") or a nominal form ("praise of God"). As with the *ʾl* root, names with the *hll* root appear throughout the OT period: in addition to the listing of Mahalalel in Nehemiah (see below), the name Jahallelel occurs twice (1 Chr 4:16; and 2 Chr 29:12; cf. Noth *IPN,* 205), and Hillel once (Judg 12:13, 15).

2. Judahite ancestor of Athaiah, of the clan of Perez (Neh 11:4).

RICHARD S. HESS

MAHALATH (PERSON) [Heb *māḥălat*]. **1.** Wife of Esau, daughter of Ishmael, sister of Nebaioth (Gen 28:9). Mahalath's name occurs in the P narrative of Jacob's departure (Gen 27:46–28:9). In response to Rebekah's complaints about Esau's Hittite wives (27:46), Isaac instructs Jacob to take a wife from the daughters of Laban (28:2). Seeing the command and blessing given Jacob (28:1–5), Esau realizes his father's displeasure (Gen 28:6–8) and marries Mahalath of the house of Ishmael (Gen 28:9). Thus, while Jacob departs to seek a wife from his mother's relative (Laban), Esau takes a wife from his father's house (Ishmael). While Gen 28:9 identifies Esau's Ishmaelite wife as Mahalath, the Edomite genealogy in Genesis 36 refers to her as Basemath. Moreover, 36:2 identifies Basemath as Ishmael's daughter, the sister of Nebaioth (cf. 28:9 for a similar description of Mahalath). This tradition, however, conflicts with Gen 26:34, which identifies Basemath as the daughter of Elon the Hittite. See also BASEMATH.

2. Wife of Rehoboam, king of Judah (2 Chr 11:18). Mahalath was the daughter of Jerimoth, an unknown son of David, and of Abihail, the daughter of Eliab, Jesse's eldest son. Her marriage to Rehoboam, her second cousin, is witness to a period of intermarriage within the Davidic house. Josephus attests to Mahalath's status by referring to her as Rehoboam's "kinswoman" (*Ant.* 8.10.1). One of eighteen wives of Rehoboam (2 Chr 11:21), Mahalath bore him three sons: Jeush, Shemariah, and Zaham (2 Chr 11:19).

LINDA S. SCHEARING

MAHANAIM (PLACE) [Heb *mahănayim*]. A city located in Gilead, along the Jabbok River, in the territory traditionally associated with half-Manasseh. The name appears to be a dual form (meaning "two camps" or "camp"), although the *-ayim* ending has alternatively been explained as an old locative ending (Mazar 1954: 230). Two popular etymologies are given for the site in Genesis 32. According to vv 2–3—Eng 32:1–2—it was where Jacob and his family encountered a troop of angels, while vv 8–11 (—Eng 32:7–10) explain that it was where Jacob divided his family and flocks into two companies to avert total annihilation in case Esau attacked him. According to vv 23–31 (—Eng 32:22–30), the site lay at a ford of the Jabbok, across stream from Penuel.

Mahanaim became the administrative seat of Gilead during Saul's reign and continued to serve in that capacity under Eshbaal (2 Sam 2:9). It was the site of Eshbaal's hasty coronation by Abner and the remaining Saulide troops who had regrouped there following Saul's defeat and death at Mt. Gilboa. See ABNER; ESHBAAL. David's use of the site as his temporary base of operations during Absalom's revolt (2 Sam 17:24–19:8) suggests its continued role as the administrative center of Gilead. Under Solomon, it served as the capital of District VII (1 Kgs 4:14). The city's characterization as a levitical city probably stems from its early role as an administrative center (Josh 21:36—Eng 21:38; 1 Chr 6:65—Eng 6:80).

Except for a possible allusion to the site in Cant 6:13, the latest reference to Mahanaim occurs in an Egyptian inscription on the S entrance to the temple of Amon at Karnak. It is included among the names of the cities that Pharaoh Shishak destroyed during his campaign in Palestine in the fifth year of the reigns of Rehoboam and Jeroboam. It is entry no. 22, and is written Ma-han-ma.

According to Josh 13:30, the city marked the S boundary of the territory of half-Manasseh in Gilead. A location on the N bank of the Jabbok is thereby indicated, which would be consistent with Solomon's appointment of Ahinadab ben Iddo, a Manassite, as head official in the city (1 Kgs 4:14; 1 Chr 27:21). The contradictory claim in Josh 13:26b that Mahanaim marked the S boundary of Gad appears to reflect the Gadites' later expansion into traditional Manassite territory. This situation is confirmed by the brief note in the Gadite genealogy in 1 Chr 5:16–17 that they occupied Gilead, Bashan and its towns, and all of the pasture land of Sharon during the reign of Jotham, king of Judah.

The site of Mahanaim can confidently be identified with Telul ed-Dhahab el-Garbi (M.R. 214177; Dalman 1913: 71–72; Noth, *Josua* HAT 1938, 55; Simons 1947: 37; Mazar 1957: 61; *LBHG,* 439), ruling out earlier proposed identifications with Khirbet Mahne (Oliphant 1881: 142–43); Tell Heggag (de Vaux 1941: 31); Tell er-Mrameh (Ubach, *EncBibBarc* 4: 1185–87); Tell er Reheil (Negenman 1969: 64); and Khirbet Suleiket (Merrill 1881: 437). Telul ed-Dhahab is located on the N side of the Zerqa, in an extension of land that projects S to form the W side of a sharp, *S*-shaped bend in the river. It has a smaller companion site, Telul ed-Dhahab es-Sharqia, located on the S bank of the river, which forms the E side of the *S*-curve. The latter is a strong candidate for PENUEL.

Mahanaim is built upon a natural outcropping of sandstone that lies at a natural ford of the river, which controls access to the adjoining iron-rich Ajlun region. Surface survey at the site has yielded extensive Iron I pottery, as well as Iron II ware, both of the periods required by the available biblical evidence. In addition, remains from the EB, Hellenistic, Roman, and Byzantine periods have been found. Bits of iron slag cover the upper terraces. A concentrated deposit, including slag, cinder, treated ore, and a furnace bottom, was discovered at the top of the E scarp, just SE of the main gate (Gordon and Villiers 1983: 283–84). No excavations have been completed at the tell to date. The site's strategic location as a gateway to the iron resources of the adjacent Ajlun probably led to its establishment as the administrative seat for Gilead in the early monarchy.

Bibliography

Dalman, G. 1913. Jahresberichte des Instituts für das Arbeitsjahr 1912/13. 8. Die Zeitreise. Auf den Suche nach Mahanaim. *PJ* 9: 66–73.

Gordon, R., and Villiers, L. 1983. Telul edh Dhahab and Its Environs. Surveys of 1980 and 1982, a Preliminary Report. *ADAJ* 27: 275–89.

Mazar, B. 1954. Gath and Gittaim. *IEJ* 4: 227–35.

———. 1957. The Campaign of Pharaoh Shishak to Palestine. VTSup 4: 57–66.

Merrill, S. 1881. *East of Jordan.* London.

Negenman, J. 1969. *New Atlas of the Bible.* Garden City, NY.

Oliphant, L. 1881. *The Land of Gilead.* New York.

Simons, J. 1947. Two Connected Problems relating to the Israelite Settlement in Transjordan. *PEQ* 79: 27–39.

Vaux, R. de. 1941. Notes d'histoire et de topographie transjordaniennes. *RB* 50: 16–47.

Diana V. Edelman

MAHANEH-DAN (PLACE) [Heb *maḥănēh dān*]. An area adjacent to Kiriath-jearim where 600 Danites camped during their migration N to LAISH (Judg 18:12); also, the place between Zorah and Eshtaol where the spirit of the Lord first began to stir Samson (Judg 13:25).

Scholars of the 19th century puzzled over how to reconcile Mahaneh-dan's location near Kiriath-jearim (Deir el-ʿAzar, M.R. 159135) with the location between Zorah and Eshtaol indicated by Judg 13:25. Groves (*SDB* 2: 1758) attempted a solution by identifying Eshtaol with Qasṭal (M.R. 164134), but this was rejected on the grounds that it required Eshtaol be located well within the territory of Judah (Porter 1866: 31).

By the end of the 19th century, most scholars posited the existence of two locations named Mahaneh-dan—one at Kiriath-jearim (Judg 18:12) as the camp occupied by the emigrating Danites, and the other (Judg 13:25) as a war camp from the days of the initial Danite campaigns in the Shephelah (Welch *HDB* 3: 214; cf. Porter 1866: 31). Alt (*KlSchr* 1: 126–75) modified this view by suggesting that the biblical references to Mahaneh-dan reflected a seasonal migration of the Danites in the days when they lived as nomads. According to Alt, the tribe wintered between Zorah and Eshtaol and in the summer moved to grazing areas near Kiriath-jearim. One wonders, however, if such an extensive migration would have taken place between areas as close to each other as Zorah-Eshtaol and Kiriath-jearim, or whether a Danite grazing camp would have been tolerated in the vicinity of a settled area like Kiriath-jearim.

Based on 1 Chr 2:52–54 and a presumed connection between the Manahathites/Menuhoth *(hammānaḥtî/hammĕnūḥôt)* and Kiriath-jearim and the Zorites *(haṣṣārʿî),* S. A. Cook (*EncBib* 3: 2904; 1907: 88) suggested that both references to Mahaneh-dan be emended to *mānaḥat-dān.* Though lately endorsed by Gray (*Joshua, Judges, Ruth* NCBC, 1967, 347, 368–69), Cook's suggestion may be faulted on the grounds that it requires that the etymology and context of Judg 18:12 be jettisoned in favor of an emendation for which there is no textual evidence. Other efforts toward a textual solution have explained the appearance of Mahaneh-dan in 13:25 as a gloss prompted by the existence in this passage and in 18:12 of the place names Zorah and Eshtaol (Burney 1918: 353; Simons *GTTOT,* 301).

There seems little reason to doubt the authenticity of Mahaneh-dan as it appears in Judg 18:12. Indeed, the name "camp of Dan" itself is more natural for a place in Judah than for a site in Danite territory (Moore *Judges* ICC, 326). Greater uncertainty, however, surrounds the use of Mahaneh-dan in Judg 13:25. A number of proposals may account for its appearance in this text. It is possible that there were two "camps of Dan." Alternatively, in this verse Mahaneh-dan may be a gloss brought on by the appearance here and in 18:12 of the names Zorah and Eshtaol. Error in transmission is also a possibility; perhaps Samson began his career as a judge not at the "camp of Dan" but at the "judge's camp" *(hammaḥănēh-dayyān).* Finally, Mahaneh-dan may be present in Judg 13:25 for literary or theological reasons. Perhaps the editor of Judges intended to contrast Samson's call to struggle at Mahaneh-dan with the 600 Danites' abandonment of that struggle at a place of the same name. Whichever explanation is accepted, any conclusion on Mahaneh-dan's occurrence in this passage must remain a matter of speculation.

Bibliography

Burney, C. F., ed. 1918. *Book of Judges with Introduction and Notes.* Oxford.

Cook, S. A. 1907. *Critical Notes on Old Testament History.* London.
Porter, J. L. 1866. Mahaneh-dan. Vol. 3, pp. 30–31 in *Cyclopaedia of Biblical Literature,* 3d ed., ed. W. L. Alexander. Edinburgh.

BRIAN P. IRWIN

MAHARAI (PERSON) [Heb *mahray*]. **1.** One of David's champions, a select class of warriors directly attached to the king for special assignments, named in the parallel lists of 2 Sam 23:8–39 (v 28) and 1 Chr 11:10–47 (v 30). Although of high repute, he is distinguished from the more elite warriors (vv 8–23 and 11–25) listed before his grouping. In both texts he, as well as the champion Heleb/Heled (2 Sam 23:29; 1 Chr 11:30), is said to be "of Netophah," a town in the hill country of Judah SW of Bethlehem (1 Chr 2:54; Ezra 2:21–22; Neh 7:26).

The same Maharai appears to be mentioned in a list of commanders found in 1 Chr 27:1–15 (v 13), since this list mentions eleven other mighty men found in 1 Chr 11:10–47. However, here Maharai of Netophah is further identified as "of the Zerahites," that is, one of the descendants in the lineage of Zerah, one of the twins born to Judah by Tamar (Gen 38:24–30; Num 26:20; Josh 7:17). These commanders were each in charge of a monthly course of 24,000 men, or possibly 24 "units," rather than "thousands" (Myers *Chronicles* AB, 183, 53, 98) in the armed service of the king, Maharai being in charge of the tenth month. This list of commanders and their functions is possibly a construct of its composer, since (a) no such monthly, conscripted, civilian army is mentioned elsewhere during David's reign; (b) the large number of 288,000 men, if the term is understood correctly, is improbable; and (c) one of the commanders, Asahel (v 7), was dead before David had rule over all Israel (Williamson *Chronicles* NCBC, 174–75). However, the author/redactor's thesis, that David made preparations for the proper ongoing cultic and national life of Israel, as illustrated throughout chaps. 23–27, draws on the fact that David took a census (vv 23–24; chap. 21) which could have been utilized for designing a monthly plan of conscription, a plan which would have been analogous to Solomon's monthly courses for his provision (1 Kgs 4:7–19).

RODNEY K. DUKE

MAHATH (PERSON) [Heb *maḥat*]. A Levite, the son of Amasai, and one of those who consecrated himself and went in to cleanse the house of the Lord according to King Hezekiah's command (2 Chr 29:12; cf. 31:13). At 1 Chr 6:5—Eng 6:20—Mahath appears in some versions (e.g., RSV, JB), although Jahath or Jehath is read in most versions (e.g., *BHS,* NEB, NIV, NKJV, NASB) and is probably the better reading. The two men, Mahath and Jahath, do not appear to be the same person, although they are distinctly related. Jahath of 1 Chr 6:20 is said to be a descendant of Gershom, the son of Libni, and whose son was Zimmah, while Mahath of 2 Chr 29:12 is said to be a descendant of Kohath, with both Gershom and Kohath being sons of Levi. The most detailed list of participants in the cleansing ritual is provided in 2 Chr 29:12, but a Mahath is also included in a different list of participants in 31:13. Several explanations are possible, although each is not equally probable: Mahath could be the only individual included in both lists, since the numbers appointed to the task were large and only representatively recorded; the two are different men who shared the same name, possibly appointed to different tasks, with Mahath of 29:12 a temple cleaner and Mahath of 31:13 an overseer of the now purified temple; and the second list in 31:13 is merely a stylistically characteristic list of names included by the Chronicler to emphasize the solemnity of the surrounding events (Coggins *1 and 2 Chronicles* CBC, 278), regardless of the status of Mahath in 29:12. Nevertheless, these are the only references to Mahath in the Bible, and nothing more is known of this individual or these individuals.

STANLEY E. PORTER

MAHAVITE, THE [Heb *hammaḥăwîm*]. A gentilic modifying Eliel, who is listed among David's "mighty men" (1 Chr 11:46). See ELIEL #4. This listing of David's military forces, beginning in 1 Chr 11:10, evidences the accumulating support that David received prior to his ascent of the throne. Several scholars have suggested emending the gentilic "the Mahavite" to read "the Mahanite," i.e., from Mahanaim (e.g., Williamson *1 and 2 Chronicles* NCBC, 104). This emendation would be consistent with the Transjordanian nature of the list in 1 Chr 11:42–47; this section is an expansion of 1 Chr 11:26–41, a list also found in 2 Sam 23:24–39. Several scholars, noting the expansion, suggest that 1 Chr 11:42–47 does not belong to the original list of David's supporters. Noth (*NCH,* 54–55), for example, considered the expansion a postexilic fiction of several families who wished to trace their lineage to the supporters of David. However, Myers (*1 Chronicles* AB, 90–91), points out that the Transjordanian nature of the expansion weighs against Noth's argument, suggesting that the list was available to the Chronicler and was added here to further enhance David's coterie of followers. Likewise, Ackroyd (*1 and 2 Chronicles, Ezra, Nehemiah* TBC, 54) sees the list as added by the Chronicler in order to emphasize names from Transjordan, because the main list was composed of names mostly from Judah and the hill country W of Jerusalem.

SIEGFRIED S. JOHNSON

MAHAZIOTH (PERSON) [Heb *maḥăzîʾôt*]. One of the fourteen sons of Heman who were appointed to prophesy with musical instruments under the direction of their father and the king (1 Chr 25:4). Mahazioth received the twenty-third lot cast to determine duties (1 Chr 25:30). Scholars have long suggested that the final nine names in 1 Chr 25:4 can be read as a liturgical prayer. For instance, Mahazioth can be treated as a nominal form of the root *ḥzh* and translated as "oracles, visions, clear signs." It would form part of the final line of the liturgical prayer as it is reconstructed by scholars. For a reconstruction and translation of the prayer, a summary of interpretive possibilities, and bibliography, see ELIATHAH.

J. CLINTON MCCANN, JR.

MAHER-SHALAL-HASH-BAZ

MAHER-SHALAL-HASH-BAZ (PERSON) [Heb *mahēr-šālāl-ḥāš-baz*]. Symbolic name given by Isaiah in Isa 8:1–4 to his newly born son. The name means "speedy spoil, hasty plunder" and is part of his strategy to discourage Judah (under King Ahaz) from submitting to Assyria as the price of safety. The occasion is the invasion of Judah by Syria and Israel (the so-called Syro-Ephraimite War, 735–732 B.C.E.). Isaiah had already assured Ahaz, who was apparently tempted to turn to Assyria for help (as in fact he did—cf. 2 Kgs 16:7–9), that the threat would quickly evaporate (Isa 7:3–9), and this prophetic act was intended to underline that message. The sequence described in 8:1–4 included writing out the name before witnesses, having relations with "the prophetess" (presumably Isaiah's wife), naming the child, and explaining the significance, namely, the demise of Syria and Israel within a limited time, i.e., the two or three years from the conception of a child to the speaking of its simplest words. By this Isaiah tells Ahaz (and the people—see v 6) that to seek help from Assyria is unnecessary because the present threat from Syria and Israel would quickly come to naught. (On Isaiah's use of symbolic names, see also 7:3, 14; 8:18; 9:5.)

JOSEPH JENSEN

MAHLAH

MAHLAH (PERSON) [Heb *maḥlâ*]. Two persons in the Hebrew Bible bear this name.

1. The first of Zelophehad's five daughters (Num 26:33; 27:1; 36:11; Josh 17:3). Although the etymology of the name is not certain, it has been suggested that it meant "the weak one" (Newman *IDB* 3: 227). Mahlah always occupies the first position in the listing of the five daughters of Zelophehad. The other four are Noah, Hoglah, Milcah, and Tirzah. In Num 36:11, the positions of Noah and Tirzah are exchanged.

Mahlah first appears in Num 26:28–34, the Manassite section of a military census. The focus of the passage is on the offspring of Hepher, whose son, Zelophehad, had five daughters. The next chapter reports that Mahlah and her sisters approached Moses and asked that an allotment of land be given to them (27:1–11), because Zelophehad had died in the wilderness and left no son to receive his inheritance of land and pass on his name (vv 1–4). When Moses brought the request before God, their wish was granted and a general decree issued that the same treatment should be shown to any daughter of Israel in similar circumstances (vv 5–11). Therefore, Mahlah and her sisters are remembered for the legal precedent that was established by their suit. Snaith (1966) has suggested that the story had no basis in fact but was composed in order to account for the presence of Manasseh in W Palestine, and other scholars are equally unsure of its historical accuracy (Butler *Joshua* WBC, 187).

Finally, the reader learns (Num 36:10–12) that an additional law was issued because of the situation that surrounded Zelophehad's daughters. Manassite tribal leaders were afraid that Mahlah and her sisters would marry men of another tribe and take their inheritance with them. This would have reduced Manasseh's territorial holdings (Num 36:1–4). Therefore, Moses commanded the daughters of Zelophehad to marry men within their tribe, and this decree was made law for any Israelite woman in similar circumstances (vv 5–9). Therefore, Mahlah and her sisters married their cousins from the tribe of Manasseh, so that their inheritance would remain within the tribe (vv 10–12). Fishbane (1985: 104–5) notes that vv 6–9 produce a legal fiction by subverting the decision in Numbers 27. Without the latter ruling, Zelophehad's property would have gone to the children of his brothers. With the ruling in Num 36:6–9, which requires Zelophehad's daughters to marry their paternal cousins, the result is the same.

Joshua 17:1–13 deals with the tribal allotment of Manasseh and continues the story of the inheritance of Zelophehad's daughters. The passage notes that Mahlah and her sisters petitioned Eleazar the priest, Joshua, and other tribal leaders to grant them the inheritance, as God had commanded Moses. The leaders complied with their request (vv 3–4). Therefore, in addition to the allotment that was given to Gilead (v 1), ten shares of land were given to other Manassite families—five to the clans of Hepher's brothers and five to the daughters of Zelophehad the son of Hepher (vv 2–6). Consequently, it appears that the families of Mahlah and her sisters assumed considerable significance within the tribe of Manasseh. See also MACHIR.

It has been proposed by Lemaire (1972: 13–15), who drew on earlier studies by Albright (1931) and Cross (1961), that biblical texts and the Samaria ostraca indicate that "Hepher" was the name of a geographical territory, rather than the name of a village. The names of the towns within it are given in the Bible as the names of the daughters of Zelophehad. Tirzah was its capital, and Mahlah, which Lemaire (1972: 16–17) identifies with the modern Abel Meholah, was another of its villages. Furthermore, Lemaire (1972: 18–20) suggests that the biblical report that the daughters of Zelophehad married their Manassite cousins does not in fact describe marriages of five Israelite women. On the contrary, the narratives reflect the establishment at Shechem (Joshua 24) of a tribal alliance between the non-Israelite villages in the "land of Hepher" and the Israelite clans of Manasseh. Although the details of Lemaire's reconstruction are open to serious question, it is clear from the Samaria ostraca that villages in Manassite lands of W Palestine bore some of the same names as the biblical "daughters of Zelophehad."

2. A Manassite, whose mother was Hammolecheth and whose brothers were Ishhod and Abiezer (1 Chr 7:18). It is unclear whether the name should be construed as a feminine form, since it occurs elsewhere as the name for one of Zelophehad's daughters (Num 26:33), or as a masculine form. Although Syriac mss omit Mahlah from the genealogy entirely, most interpreters do not regard this as sufficient reason to strike the name from the text of 1 Chr 7:18. It is puzzling that the name of Mahlah's mother is given, but her father is not identified. This is irregular, since the genealogies usually trace the lineage through fathers. Moreover, the relationship of Hammolecheth (and so Mahlah) to the rest of the tribe of Manasseh is uncertain. It appears most probable that she was the sister of Gilead (vv 17–18), although this is by no means sure. In this case, Mahlah's grandfather and great-grandfather would have been Gilead and Machir, respectively.

Bibliography

Albright, W. F. 1931. The Site of Tirzah and the Topography of Western Manasseh. *JPOS* 11: 249–51.

Ben-Barak, Z. 1980. Inheritance by Daughters in the Ancient Near East. *JSS* 25: 22–33.
Cross, F. M. 1961. Epigraphic Notes on Hebrew Documents of the Eighth–Sixth Centuries B.C.: I. A New Reading of a Place Name in the Samaria Ostraca. *BASOR* 193: 12–14.
Fishbane, M. 1985. *Biblical Interpretation in Ancient Israel.* Oxford.
Lemaire, A. 1972. Le "Pays de Hépher" et les "filles de Zelophehad" à la lumière des ostraca de Samarie. *Sem* 22: 13–20.
Sakenfeld, K. D. 1988. Zelophehad's Daughters. *PRS* 15: 37–47.
Snaith, R. N. 1966. The Daughters of Zelophehad. *VT* 16: 124–27.

M. Patrick Graham

MAHLI (PERSON) [Heb *maḥlî*]. A personal name whose suggested sources of derivation include Ar *miḥalun,* "cunning, cleverness" (*IPN,* 24), Heb *ḥlh,* "be weak, sick" (*HDB* 3: 214; KB, 513), Aram *ḥlʾ* (or maybe *ḥly*), "sweet, pleasant," and SW Ar *ḥlw,* "gift, spice" (both noted but not advocated by Loewenstamm *EncMiqr* 4: 800). Brockington (*Ezra, Nehemiah and Esther* Century Bible, 101) believes the meaning to be unknown. Not more than two individuals in the Hebrew Bible bear this name, and some have suggested, as genealogies are harmonized, that one person is represented in two different ways (*EncBib* 3: 2905; Cody 1969: 57 n. 65).

1. A Levite whose grandfather was Levi, whose father was Merari, and whose brother was Mushi. He is first mentioned (Exod 6:19, LXX = *Mooli*) in a genealogical text (vv 13–20) whose purpose seems to be to disclose the division between the sons of Aaron, i.e., the Aaronite priesthood, and the remaining Levite families (Galil 1985: 489). Cody (1969: 161 n. 40) believes that this personal name, along with three others (Libni, Hebron, and Mushi), derives from a levitical clan *(mišpāḥāh)* mentioned in Num 26:58 (see 3:33)—*hammaḥli,* "the Mahlites." Mahli is designated the head of a family *(mišpāḥāh)* (Num 3:20) in a levitical census (vv 14–39) wherein the "family of Mahlites" (v 33) are among the sons of Merari whose duties included care of the tabernacle's frames, bars, pillars, bases, and accessories (vv 36–37). These Mahlites are also listed, as mentioned above, in Num 26:58 (but not in the LXX) in the levitical section (vv 57–62) of a second census. Mahli is included by the Chronicler (1 Chr 6:4—Eng 6:19) in a genealogical listing of the sons of Levi (vv 1–5—Eng 16–30) where he is the first mentioned of Merari's two sons. In this list his family is traced for six generations (vv 14–15—Eng 29–30) through his son Libni; however, in the divisional organization of the Levites in 1 Chr 23:6–24, the sons of Mahli (v 21) are registered as Eleazar (who died without sons) and Kish (whose sons married Eleazar's daughters). In a later additional list of Levites (1 Chr 24:20–31)—Myers (*1 Chronicles* AB, 166) believes it to be a later addition to 1 Chr 23:6–24, Elmslie (*IB* 3: 425) sees it as a "very late" addition with no clear relation to 1 Chronicles 23, Braun (*1 Chronicles* WBC, 239) believes it was intended to supplement and update (241) the family list of Levites in 1 Chr 23:7–23—Mahli is mentioned as one of two sons of Merari (v 26) and as the father of Eleazar (who had no sons) and Ithamar (v 28). Concerning the insertion of vv 26b–27 and the person of Jaaziah opinions vary: Rothstein (*1 Chronikbuch* KAT, 440) believes that Jaaziah represents a later generation whose name is similar to that of Mahli's great-grandson Uzzah (1 Chr 6:14—Eng 6:29); Braun (*1 Chronicles* WBC, 240) admits to the possibility that he was an otherwise unknown son of Merari and therefore brother of Mahli; Curtis (*Chronicles* ICC, 274) believes him to represent, not a son of Merari, but the head of a family claiming such descent. Mahli is also mentioned as the head of the family to which the "man of discretion," who was brought to Ezra from Casiphia, belonged (Ezra 8:18; MT = "and Sherebiah"). 1 Esdras 8:46—Eng 8:47 identifies that man as *Asebēbias* (Sherebiah). In these last two texts Mahli is described as "the son of Levi" without mention of Merari. Möhlenbrink (1934: 209) discounts an attempt to understand this description that views Mahli as being conceived as Levi's son by referring to the wide range of meanings embraced by the Hebrew word for "son."

2. A Levite whose father was Mushi, son of Merari, and therefore was a nephew of the Mahli described above. He appears (1 Chr 6:32—Eng 6:47) in a list of levitical musicians (vv 16–32—Eng 31–47), schematically built around Levi's three sons (Myers *1 Chronicles* AB, 46), whose office as temple musicians resulted from Davidic appointment (v 16—Eng v 31). Elsewhere he is listed as having two brothers (1 Chr 23:23; 24:30).

Bibliography

Cody, A. 1969. *A History of Old Testament Priesthood.* Rome.
Galil, G. 1985. The Sons of Judah and the Sons of Aaron in Biblical Historiography. *VT* 35: 488–95.
Möhlenbrink, K. 1934. Die levitischen Überlieferungen des Alten Testaments. *ZAW* 52: 184–231.

Rodney H. Shearer

MAHLON (PERSON) [Heb *maḥlôn*]. Son of Elimelech and Naomi who married Ruth the Moabitess (Ruth 1:2, 5; 4:9). Mahlon and his brother Chilion left their home in Bethlehem and resided in Moab, where they married Moabite women. Mahlon is remembered as the deceased husband of Ruth, whose estate became the subject of Boaz's legal transaction at the city gate (4:5, 9–10). There is a legal problem with the transaction, however: in the narrative, Obed, the son of Ruth and Boaz, is the heir of all that belongs to Mahlon (4:10), but in the genealogy he is the son of Boaz (4:17b, 18–22). The Targum explains that the sons died as a result of their marriage to foreign women on polluted soil, but the narration does not condemn their marriage and is silent about the reason and circumstances of their deaths.

Since the Ruth story has commonly been taken as folklore, the names of the brothers have been assumed to be contrived in keeping with the story's genre. This suspicion is helped by the rhyming names of Mahlon and Chilion, which hint at an artificial construction. Midrashic authorities by an etymological interpretation attached significance to their names because of their untimely deaths. Mahlon meant "blotted out" *(mḥh)* and Chilion "perished" *(klh).* However, the etymologies of Mahlon and Chilion are uncertain. The root *mḥl,* except for some personal names, is not attested in the Hebrew Bible. Influenced by the parallel etymology of "Chilion," many (*IPN* 10) relate "Mahlon" to *mḥh* ("to be sick, ill"). Others have argued that the names are not necessarily fictitious since Elimelech and Chilion, for instance, are known from LB onomastica.

It is questionable whether parents would name their children "sickly" and "puny." But it may be that the characters are real and have been assigned these names as a result of their role in the story. A similar practice of ancient storytelling occurs in the book of Judges, where Cushan-risathaim is defeated by Israel (Judg 3:8–10); the name literally means "Cushan, double wickedness" and was probably a contemptuous title given to him by the Israelites.

Bibliography

Levine, E. 1973. *The Aramaic Version of Ruth.* Rome.

KENNETH A. MATHEWS

MAHOL (PERSON) [Heb *maḥôl*]. The father of Heman, Calcol, and Darda, who are mentioned in 1 Kgs 5:11—Eng 4:31. Solomon's wisdom is presented as superior to the wisdom of the sons of Mahol. The proper name "Mahol" occurs only in this passage. Neither his nationality nor the reputation for wisdom to which this verse alludes is provided in the OT. On the contrary, in the parallel passage in 1 Chr 2:6, *Zerah* is given as the father of Heman, Calcol, *Dara,* and others. Zerah's identification as the grandson of Judah (by Tamar, his daughter-in-law) ties the history of these sages to Israel. On the other hand, *bĕnê qedem* (1 Kgs 5:11—Eng 4:30) is the expected designation for easterners as opposed to Israelites.

Albright interpreted *maḥôl* as a technical designation rather than a proper name (*ARI,* 210). According to this reading the text would be rendered "sons of the dance" or "members of the musicians' guild." The verb *ḥûl* upon which the noun *maḥôl* is based literally means "to turn, dance." Mowinckel built upon Albright's thesis by suggesting a close relation between wisdom teachers and poetic prophecy in the temple. This association, according to Mowinckel, led to their identification as Levites with the term *maḥôl* (1962: 96–97). De Vaux claimed that the first choir was perhaps non-Israelite, that is, the original "choristers" were the eastern sons of *maḥôl* (see *AncIsr*). John Gray makes the broader claim that mention of the "sons of *maḥôl*" implies a Canaanite origin of psalms usage (*Kings* OTL, 147). The cultic origins of the term *maḥôl* are not as clear as such claims may lead the reader to believe.

Bibliography

Mowinckel, S. 1962. *The Psalms in Israel's Worship.* Vol. 2. Trans. D. R. Ap-Thomas. Nashville.

DONALD K. BERRY

MAHSEIAH (PERSON) [Heb *maḥsēyāh*]. The father of Neriah and the grandfather of Jeremiah's scribe, Baruch (Jer 32:12; Bar 1:1). He is also identified as the father of Neriah and the grandfather of Seraiah, a quartermaster who accompanied Zedekiah to Babylon in 594 B.C.E. (Jer 51:59). That both Baruch and Seraiah are described as sons of Neriah and grandsons of Mahseiah suggests that they were brothers. In Jer 51:59–64, however, Jeremiah instructs Seraiah to read a scroll regarding God's judgment against Babylon in much the same way Baruch had read Jeremiah's scroll regarding Judah (Jeremiah 36). So, while it is possible that Baruch and Seraiah were in fact brothers, the sons of Neriah and the grandsons of Mahseiah, the common lineage could also reflect an effort to connect the common function of these two in the Jeremiah tradition. Mahseiah is mentioned only in connection with Baruch and Seraiah. The name "Mahseiah" (Gk *Maasaias*) means "Yahweh is a refuge."

JOHN M. BRACKE

MAIL, COAT OF. See WEAPONS AND IMPLEMENTS OF WARFARE.

MAKAZ (PLACE) [Heb *māqaṣ*]. A city listed in Solomon's second administrative district, administered by Ben-geber. The other towns listed there (cf. also Josh 19:4–46) suggest that this district was in the Shephelah, probably between Nahal Ayyalon and Nahal Sorek. The LXX Machemas/Machmas suggests an original *mḥṣ,* and thus some would identify Makaz with Khirbet el-Mukheizin, about 4 miles S of Ekron. It has also been identified with a site (M.R. 144137) between Gezer and Timna (*RAB,* map on p. 85).

GARY A. HERION

MAKED (PLACE) [Gk *Maked*]. One of the five cities in Gilead in which Jews were being held captive by the gentile citizens (1 Macc 5:26). The city is perhaps the same as *m-q-t,* mentioned by Thutmose III in his list of Canaanite towns. The location of the site is open to question. Abel (1923: 518–19) and Aharoni and Avi-Yonah (*MBA,* map no. 189) identify it with Tell el-Jemid (M.R. 232237), while Grollenberg (1956: 156) and Simons (*GTTOT,* 425) identify it with Tell Miqdad. In either case the sequence of events recorded in 1 Macc 5:26–36 demands a location E of the Sea of Galilee, likely between Chaspho and Bosor, the cities defeated before and after it.

The early successes of the Maccabaean Revolt, including retaking the temple in 164 B.C., generated gentile reprisals. Many Jews in Gilead fled to a stronghold at the city of Dathema, from which they sent word to Judas for help. En route to rescue the refugees, Judas learned from a band of Nabateans that other Jews were under attack in Bozrah, Bosor-in-Alema, Chaspho, Maked, and Carnaim, as well as other cities (1 Macc 5:24–27). Judas defeated the gentiles in Bozrah, Dathema, and Chaspho before delivering the Jews in Maked.

Bibliography

Abel, F.-M. 1923. Topographie des campagnes machabéennes. *RB* 32: 495–521.

Grollenberg, L. H. 1956. *Atlas of the Bible.* Trans. J. M. H. Reid. London.

Tedesche, S., and Zeitlin, S. 1950. *The First Book of the Maccabees.* New York.

———. 1956. *The Second Book of the Maccabees.* New York.

PAUL L. REDDITT

MAKHELOTH (PLACE) [Heb *maqhelōt*]. The tenth encampment of the Israelites after leaving the wilderness of Sinai, as listed in Num 33:25–26, where it is placed between Haradah and Tahath. Many scholars suggest that Kehelathah in Num 33:22–23 is a duplicate for Makheloth in Num 33:25–26 since LXX preserves very similar names for both: Makellath in 33:22–23 and Makeloth in 33:25–26 (*GTTOT,* 256). Both names also have similar meanings, "assembly" or the like. If the equation is accepted, a possible location is Kuntillet ʿAjrud, also called Kuntillet Qraye (*GP,* 214; M.R. 094956). For a discussion of the location of any of the places associated with the journey of the Israelites from Egypt through Sinai see DOPHKAH.

Bibliography

Beit-Arieh, I. 1988. The Route through Sinai—Why the Israelites Fleeing Egypt Went South. *BARev* 15/3: 28–37.

JEFFREY R. ZORN

MAKKEDAH (PLACE) [*maqqēdâ*]. Amorite royal city in the Shephelah, or lowlands, of S Canaan, which after its conquest by Joshua (Josh 12:16) was incorporated into the tribal territory of Judah within the same district as Lachish (Josh 15:41). Following the defeat of the anti-Gibeonite coalition (Josh 15:10), the five Amorite kings who headed this coalition escaped to a cave near Makkedah, where they were caught and executed (Josh 10:16–27). Contrary to the attempt by Noth (1937) to discount these verses as merely an etiological story accounting for the heap of stones in front of Makkedah cave, this account most likely stems from historical events, the memory of which has been transformed and overlaid by editors whose primary interest appears to have been to demonstrate the overwhelming importance of Yahweh's role in the conquest of Canaan (Boling and Wright *Joshua* AB, 286–87). Following the account of the events at the cave, a description of the capture of the city of Makkedah, the execution of its king, and the utter destruction of its inhabitants (Josh 11:28) begins an independent unit consisting of a series of formulaic statements recounting the total conquest of S Canaan. Although some details are difficult to reconcile with events described earlier in the chapter, overall this unit makes considerable sense in both geographical and historical terms (Boling and Wright *Joshua* AB, 294–95). Presumably it was included because the editor wished to emphasize the totality of the conquest as well as the miraculous defeat of the anti-Gibeonite coalition. Despite considerable effort, no satisfactory candidate for the site of ancient Makkedah has been identified. All that we can say for certain is that the biblical passages support a location somewhere in the central or N Shephelah, in the vicinity of Azekah (Josh 15:10) and Lachish (Josh 15:41). Attempts to locate Makkedah farther to the S and E (Noth 1937) ignore these geographical hints and depend too heavily on the speculations of Eusebius (Wright 1946: 110).

Bibliography

Noth, M. 1937. Die funf Könige in der Hohle von Makkeda. *PJ* 33: 22–36.
Wright, G. E. 1946. The Literary and Historical Problem of Joshua 10 and Judges 1. *JNES* 5: 105–14.

WADE R. KOTTER

MALACHI, BOOK OF. The last book of the Hebrew and LXX canon (and thirty-ninth in the Protestant and forty-sixth in the Catholic English Bible).

A. Author
B. Historical Background
C. Literary Considerations
D. Text and Language
E. Date
F. Message and Theological Significance
G. Canonicity

A. Author

The name Malachi occurs in the OT only in the superscription of 1:1. In light of the introductory formula in Zech 9:1 and 12:1, "an oracle of the word of the Lord," Mal 1:1 may be an editorial preface marking the last of a series of three anonymous oracles appended to Zechariah 1–8. Further, some argue this name "Malachi" is an editor's title borrowed from the phraseology of 3:1, ultimately permitting its detachment from Zechariah and the completion of the sacred number of Twelve Prophets (see G below).

As a proper name Malachi may be translated "my messenger" or "my angel" (cf. Zech 1:9, 11), though context militates against the latter. Several commentators have espoused the view that Malachi is indeed a proper name (e.g., Childs, Kaiser, and Rudolph). Still others suggest that the name is a shortened form of Malachiah, meaning "Yah(weh) is my messenger" or "Yah(weh) is an angel." While highly irregular, this is not impossible given the unusual revelatory ministry of the angel of the Lord in the OT (cf. Judg 13:18; 1 Chr 21:18; Zech 1:11; 3:5; 12:8).

Despite the lack of attestation elsewhere, Malachi is similar to other OT names ending in *i*, such as Beeri ("my well," Gen 26:34; Hos 1:1), Ethni ("my gift," 1 Chr 6:41), Abi ("my father," 2 Kgs 18:2; 2 Chr 29:1), Uri ("my fire" or "my light," Exod 31:2; 1 Kgs 4:19), and Zichri ("my remembrance"(?), Exod 6:21; 1 Chr 8:19, 23, 27). Neither should this single occurrence of Malachi count as evidence against its use as a proper noun since both Jonah and Habakkuk are unique among the names of the Hebrew prophets.

The LXX understands Malachi as an appellative or official title when it translates "by the hand of his messenger." Here the first-person pronoun "my" has been changed to a third-person pronoun "his," despite the total lack of supporting textual evidence. This alteration made by the translators only serves to underscore the originality of the MT. By contrast, Jewish tradition remembered Malachi along with Haggai and Zechariah as men of the great synagogue. The Targum of Jonathan, Jerome, and Rashi (1040–1105) identified "my messenger" in 1:1 as a title for Ezra the scribe, the stance adopted by Calvin. Pseudo-Epiphanius, Dorotheus, Hesychius, and other church fathers accepted 4th century C.E. Jewish tradition collected in the *Lives of the Prophets* stating that Malachi was a Levite from the village of Sopha or Sophira of Zebulun. This tradition also claims that he was honored by the people for his piety and meekness and was given the name Malachi because he was "fair to look upon." Yet modern scholars usually dismiss these fanciful stories as valueless because of their late dates. While not ruling out the possibility of anonymity, it seems reasonable to conclude, whether for the sake of convenience or for the sake of logic, that the prophet's name or title was Malachi. This conclusion is strengthened by the absence of compelling evidence to the contrary.

Little else is known about the prophet Malachi. Like Obadiah, the superscription to his oracles traces no genealogical heritage. Malachi's prophecies do betray a strong interest in the temple, priesthood, and the sacrificial system (cf. 1:6–13; 2:1–4, 8–9; 3:3–4, 6–11). Yet he speaks as one observing that system from the outside (cf. 1:6; 2:2). He possessed a knowledge of both the Deuteronomic (1:8; cf. Deut 15:21) and Priestly (3:10; cf. Num 18:21) legal traditions. Malachi was clearly a man of considerable personal piety, grasping the import of God's holiness and the seriousness of personal sin before God (cf. 2:17–3:4; 3:6–7; 3:13–4:1). His staunch convictions against idolatry (2:10–12), easy divorce (2:13–16), and social injustice (3:5) bespeak a man of commitment and integrity, a throwback to the days of the preexilic prophets. Malachi was also a man of some courage, as seen in his bold upbraiding of the influential priestly class and the social elite (cf. 1:1–14; 2:1–4; 3:2–4).

Finally, Malachi demonstrates an important continuity with the covenantal message of earlier Hebrew prophets. He understood the priority of the internal attitude and motive over the external form (1:9–13; 2:2–3; 3:16–18; cf. Amos 5:12–15, 21–24; Mic 6:6–8). He also understood the blessing and curse of God to be rooted in personal and corporate obedience or disobedience to the stipulations of the divine covenant (3:16–4:3). He recognized that the demands of covenant included a righteous ethic, a code of behavior consistent with the nature of God, the covenant maker (3:5–7; cf. Isa 1:15–20).

B. Historical Background

The oracles of Malachi reflect conditions associated with the period of pre-Ezran decline (ca. 515–458 B.C., i.e., from the completion of the Second Temple to the ministry of Ezra in Jerusalem, assuming the traditional date for Ezra's journey to Jerusalem to be correct). While the Second Temple had been completed at the prompting of Haggai and Zechariah (Hag 1:1–6; Ezra 5:1–2; cf. Ezra 3:10–13; 6:13–15), the apathy and disillusionment within the restoration community, which permitted the temple precinct to lie in ruins for nearly twenty years, continued to permeate the group. The prophetic vision of a renewed Davidic state under Zerubbabel never materialized (Hag 2:20–23). The material prosperity predicted by Haggai (2:6–9) never came to pass, and the streaming migration of former Jewish captives foreseen by Zechariah (8:1–8) never occurred. Zerubbabel was likely deposed by order of Darius, who was attempting to control the upheaval in his newly acquired empire by ousting those in Persia and outlying provinces who were deemed political liabilities. The completion of the Second Temple ushered in no messianic age (Mal 3:6–12; cf. Zech 8:9–23). The ideal of Ezekiel's temple state quickly faded amid the stark reality of Persian domination and the problems of mere survival in a city surrounded by hostile foreigners. Zechariah's call to a deeper spiritual life went unheeded, and was even mocked by God's apparent failure to restore covenantal blessings (8:4–13; cf. 10:1–2; Mal 3:13–15). If the records of Ezra and Nehemiah are any indication, then the messianic oracles of Second Zechariah and Malachi had little impact on postexilic morale (cf. Ezra 9:1–4; Neh 5:1–8; 11:1–3). Given the testimony of scanty written documents to the contrary, even the prophetic voice soon ceased to be a factor in the Jewish restoration community (cf. Mal 4:5). Jerusalem, probably under a Persian governor, remained part of a small, struggling, and insignificant satrapy in the vast Persian empire—a social and political backwater. The Persians themselves were engaged in a titanic contest for control of the west against the Greeks.

It is against this background that Malachi prophesies in Jerusalem. The ongoing petty hostilities with the Samaritans and burdensome vassal status to Persia notwithstanding, the prophet's message focused on the quality of religious and social life with the restoration community. Skepticism and doubt characterized popular response to Yahweh as God (1:2). The priesthood was bored with formal religions (1:13) and showed only contempt and indifference to ceremonial and moral purity (1:6–12). The general populace had followed the lead of the priests (2:8–9). The people were cheating God out of his tithe (3:6–12) and the proper sacrifices sanctioned by covenant law (1:14). Even obedience to the stipulations of divine covenant was deemed useless because God was not acting in accordance with his nature (2:17; 3:13–15). This breakdown of functional Yahwism precipitated intermarriage with foreign women (2:10–12), attendant idolatry (2:11), scandalous divorce (2:13–16), as well as sorcery, adultery, perjury, and social injustice (3:5). The very elements of nature had compounded the misery and bleakness of the community with drought, blighted crops, and locust plagues (3:10–11). In the final analysis, it was a most dismal and sordid scenario to which Malachi came as God's spokesman.

C. Literary Considerations

The genre of Malachi remains a debated question. Past and present German scholarship (e.g., Rudolph) usually considers the oracles a type of poetry, while English scholars generally have regarded Malachi as prose (e.g., Torrey). This second view is corroborated by an analysis of the postexilic prophets utilizing the "prose-particle" counting method of Andersen and Freedman (*Hosea* AB, 57–66), in which the total occurrences of the Hebrew particles *ʾēt* and *ʾăšer* and the definite article *he* are apportioned to the total number of words per chapter of a given text (since in general these particles have long been recognized as typical elements of Hebrew prose and as atypical elements of Hebrew poetry). The frequency of these particles is high in prose (on a percentage basis 15 percent or more of all words), while the frequency of these particles in poetry is much lower (5 percent or less of all words). Analyzed from this perspective, Haggai, Zechariah 1–8, and Malachi demonstrate prose-particle frequencies very near to or above 15 percent, while Zechariah 9–14 exhibits almost equal ratios, having a prose-particle frequency of less than 1 percent in chap. 9. In a similar study, Hoftijzer (1965) traced the use of the particle *ʾēt* through most of the OT. Based upon his analysis of *ʾet syntagmemes* (i.e., the particle

ʾēt and the word or group of words following it), Hoftijzer (1965: 76–77) concluded that Haggai, Zechariah 1–8, and Malachi, at least in respect to their density of ʾet syntagmemes, were comparable to narrative material. He also concluded that Deutero-Zechariah was akin to Hebrew narrative, with the exception of chap. 9, where the ʾet syntagmeme density agreed with that in poetic material. Given this statistical evidence it seems safe to infer that Haggai, Zechariah 1–8, and Malachi are representative of Hebrew prose, while Zechariah 9–14 appears to be a mixture of prose and poetry. Following Andersen and Freedman (*Hosea* AB, 57–66, 313), the Hebrew of the postexilic prophets may be designated "oracular prose," so it may be distinguished as a genre somewhat different from the historical narratives (except for Haggai, which is "pure" prose).

Malachi's prophecy is simple, direct, and forceful. Indeed, 47 of the 55 verses in the book are first-person addresses to Israel, presenting a vivid encounter between God and his people. Unlike the "message formula" followed by "oracle" predominant in the earlier prophets, Malachi punctuates his message with a series of six questions and answers (1:2–5; 1:6–2:9; 2:10–16; 2:17–3:5; 3:7–8; 3:13–14). This catechetical or disputational format is characterized by the statement of a truth, hypothetical audience rebuttal in the form of a question, followed by the prophet's answer to the rebuttal through the restatement of his initial premise and the presentation of supporting evidence. This disputational form of prophetic speech occurs elsewhere in the OT (e.g., Isa 40:27–28; Jer 2:23–25, 29–32; 29:24–32; Ezek 12:21–28; Mic 2:6–11), but in Malachi it constitutes the focal point of the book's literary structure. Fischer (1972) has observed important connections between the form of Malachi's oracles and the content of his message, while acknowledging his mastery of the catechetical or disputational literary format. This dialectical development of the prophet's arguments becomes the precursor of the expositional method in the latter rabbinic schools.

It is possible that the terse sentences and point-blank style of Malachi attest to the original orality of the prophecies and probably indicate a minimal amount of editorial tampering with the text. This may help account for the scholarly consensus about the essential unity or integrity of the book. Other than the superscription of 1:1 (see G below), only three passages are consistently cited by the book's critics as additions by a later author or editor (1:11–14; 2:11b–13a; 4:4–6 [—MT 3:22–24]; see F below).

D. Text and Language

The Hebrew text of Malachi is quite well preserved. The two recent works of Kruse-Blinkenberg (1966, 1967) remain useful sources for the textual criticism of Malachi. He catalogs 111 divergences between the Peshitta and the MT and 96 variations between the LXX and the MT. However, the vast majority of these textual differences are inconsequential.

The LXX is a fairly literal translation of the MT and on occasion proves helpful in restoring words or phrases that may have dropped out of the MT text during the transmission process. For example, in 1:6 the LXX adds *phobēthēsetai,* "a servant 'fears' his master"; in 2:3 some LXX mss and the Vulgate read Heb *hazzĕrōʿa,* "arm, forearm," for the MT *hazzeraʿ,* "seed"; in 3:2 add *bāʾ,* " 'he comes' like a refiner's fire"; in 3:5 add Heb *mišpaṭ,* "those who turn aside 'judgment' for the stranger"; and in 3:19 read the LXX *kai phléxei aùtoús,* "burning like an oven, 'and it will consume them'." Yet the elliptical nature of Malachi's oracular prose necessitates the use of considerable caution in the reconstruction of the MT on the basis of the LXX's readings.

The Vulgate is also valuable for the textual criticism of Malachi because where it deviates from the LXX it retains readings that are even more closely related to the Hebrew. The published Qumran materials make no significant contribution to the Hebrew text of Malachi.

The text of Malachi contains a handful of expressions posing translation difficulties. For example, the JB, NEB, and commentators read the LXX *eʾis dómata* ("dwelling places of" or "pastures") for Heb *letannôṯ* ("jackals," 1:3); *nîbô* ("its fruit," 1:12; cf. Isa 57:19) is awkward; the active participles *ʿēr weʿōneh* (literally "awake and answering," 2:12) prompt a variety of interpretations (e.g., the Vulgate reads "the master and the scholar," the NEB translates "nomads" or "settlers" based on Arabic, and the RSV emends *ʿēḏ* "witness" for *ʿēr*); while the translation variations of 2:15 found in the Versions and commentaries mark this as the single most obscure verse in the book.

Lexical analysis of Malachi reveals a predilection for vocabulary outside that of the other postexilic writings. Malachi shares only 8 percent of its vocabulary with Haggai and Zechariah, while demonstrating a pronounced affinity for exilic and preexilic terminology (e.g., *ʾalmānāh, ʾărubbāh, ʾārār, beḵî, baʿal, beṣaʿ, gāʿar, ḥāmal, ḥinnām, kābas, môrāʾ, marpēʾ, segullāh, ʿānap̱, ʿāšaq,* etc.). In addition, Malachi shows a marked preference for poetic vocabulary usually restricted to the OT books of Job, select Psalms, Proverbs, and Lamentations (e.g., *ʾayyēh, ʾanāqāh, bāgaḏ, bāḥan, dimʿāh, zēd, zāqaq, ṭerep̱, lāhaṭ, nāʾap̱,* etc.). Finally, careful observation of the prophet's language shows that Malachi exhibits greater similarity to the vocabulary of Jeremiah and Ezekiel than any other OT corpora (cf. Hill 1983).

E. Date

Traditionally the date of Malachi's oracles has been related to fixed postexilic historical events, and hence to absolute chronological boundaries. These limits include a *terminus a quo* of 516/15 B.C. (the completion of the Second Temple) and a *terminus ad quem* of ca. 180 B.C. (i.e., the reference to the "Twelve Prophets" in Ben Sira 49:10). In addition, all previous investigations have focused on the thematic similarities, ritual practices, lexical parallels, and contiguous descriptions of the religious, social, and political conditions within the Jewish restoration community as recorded in the postexilic prophets and Ezra and Nehemiah. For example, Malachi attacks the very same abuses as do Ezra and Nehemiah (disrespect for the temple service, 1:7, 13; careless priests, 1:6–8; the cessation of tithes and offerings, 2:17 and 3:7–10; and intermarriage with foreigners, 2:10–16). Yet Malachi makes no appeal to the injunctions implemented by Ezra and Nehemiah to correct such abuses. Malachi prefers D over P in respect to religious and ceremonial law (since he makes no distinction between priests and Levites, cf. Deut 18:1 and Lev 1:5; Mal 1:4 mentions only the male sacrificial animal, and Mal 3:8–10 combines the heave offering with the tithe), suggesting a pre-Ezra date. In Malachi, Ezra, and Nehemiah the focus of attention is the deplorable state of affairs in Jerusalem (e.g., the degenerate priesthood, Mal 2:1–9 and Neh 13:1–30; intermarriage with idolatrous women, Mal 2:1–9; Ezra 9:1–2; Neh 1:1–3; rampant divorce, Mal 2:13–16; cf. Ezra 9–10; laxity in the payment of sacral dues, Mal 3:8; Neh 10:32–39; 13:10; and the oppression of the poor, Mal 3:5 and Neh 5:1–5).

Based on the strength of this sometimes conflicting and often ambiguous evidence, the overwhelming majority of biblical scholars past and present view Malachi as a contemporary of Ezra and Nehemiah and date his ministry to the mid or latter half of the 5th century B.C. (cf. Verhoef *Haggai and Malachi* NICOT, 156–60).

Recognizing the acute limitations of dating Malachi's oracles on the germane internal data, this study presupposes the validity of recent linguistic research in the typological categorization of biblical Hebrew. Rather than relating the book of Malachi to postexilic social conditions, religious practices, and historical events which assume an absolute chronology, this typological method, developed by Polzin (1976) relates Malachi to postexilic literature and therefore to a literary and relative chronological scale. The purely linguistic analysis employed by this approach to Malachi has the advantage of being far more objective than previous research, due to the statistical nature of the investigation. The systematic application of Polzin's nineteen grammatical and syntactic categories to the Hebrew text yields a typological continuum of biblical Hebrew demonstrating the relative chronological relationships of the selected corpora (for details see Hill 1983). A partial typological continuum and a summary of the typological analysis of the postexilic prophets is included in Fig. MAL.01 (A.1–13 and B.1–6 are the nineteen diagnostic categories).

Malachi shows remarkable typological affinity to Haggai, Zechariah 1–8 and 9–14, Joel and Jonah, as well as the P^g corpus. By contrast, Malachi demonstrates no typological affinity with Ezra, Nehemiah, Esther, or Chronicles and only minimal correspondence to the P^s corpus. Despite the probable changes taking place in the language spoken in Jerusalem and environs because of the immediate mixing with the language of the indigenous population, the written language of the postexilic prophets maintains a high degree of typological continuity with the written language of the exilic period. One can surmise that the prophets themselves were recently returned exiles, perhaps numbered among those who came to Jerusalem with Zerubbabel and Joshua (Ezra 2:1–2); hence the continuity with exilic language.

Based on the evidence from this typological analysis of the postexilic prophets, Malachi (and Zechariah 9–14) dates to the period of pre-Ezran decline (515–458 B.C.). Even though the temple had been rebuilt and the sacrificial system restored, the vision of Ezekiel's temple state quickly faded amid the stark reality of Persian domination and the problems of mere survival in a city surrounded by foreigners (cf. Hanson 1975: 280–86). Malachi's striking typological correspondence to Haggai and Zechariah 1–8 indicates that it was probably composed during the earliest years of the period of pre-Ezran decline.

	A													B						
	1	2	3	4	5	6	7	8	9	10	11	12	13	1	2	3	4	5	6	
JE	p	p	p	p	p	p	p	p	p		p	p	p							Polzin's classical BH
CH	p	p	p	p	p	p	p	p	p		p	p	p							
Dtr	p	p	p	p	p	p	p	p			p	p	p	p						
P^s	o	p	x	x	p	x	p	p	x		p	p	o	p						Polzin's LBH
P^s	o	x	x	x	p	o	x	p	x		x	x	o	x						
Chr	x	x	x	x	x	x	x	x	x		x	x	x	x						
Ezr			x	x	x	x	x	x	x		x	x		x						
N^2	x	x	x	x	x	x	x				x	x		x						
N^1	x̲	x̲	x	x̲	x	x	x̲	x	x		x̲	x	x	x						Polzin's "archaizing" LBH
Est	x			x̲	x	x̲	x	x	x̲		x̲	x	x̲	x̲	x					
Hag	p	p	p	x	p	x	x	p	p	*x*	p	p	x	p	*p*	*p*				Post-Exilic Prophets
Zech 1–8	p	p	p	p	p	p	x	p	p	*x*	p	p	x	p	*p*	*p*				
Zech 10–14	x	p	p	p	p	p	x	x	p	*p*	x	p	o	p	*p*	*p*				
Mal	p	p	p	p	p	x	x	p	p	*p*	x	p	o	p	*p*	*p*				
Joel	x	p	p	p	p	x	x	p	p		x		p		*p*	*p*				Additional Prophets
Jonah	x	p	x	p		x	x	p	p		p		x		*p*					

p = feature of classical BH
p = feature of classical BH in prophets, included for comparative purposes, not a part of Polzin's research or final typological tabulations
x = feature of LBH
x = feature of LBH in prophets, included for comparative purposes, not a part of Polzin's research or final typological tabulations
x̲ = Polzin's LBH "archaizing" feature
o = unique feature

MAL.01. Summary of the typological analysis of the postexilic prophets.

It is likely that exilic Hebrew was largely preserved (at least as the written language) in the official and religious circles of the restoration community by the first-generation returnees from Babylon. This would account for the linguistic similarities of the postexilic prophets to one another and to the P^g corpus examined by Polzin. Those original returnees probably influenced the restoration community for a maximum of fifty or sixty years; a *terminus ad quem* of ca. 475 B.C. for Malachi (and Zechariah 9–14) may be suggested. After 475 B.C. written works would and do reflect the language changes absorbed by the second-generation writers of the postexilic community (e.g., the P^s corpus).

The conclusions of von Bulmerincq (1921: 42–49), who dated the major portions of Malachi's oracle to ca. 480 B.C., and the conclusions of D. N. Freedman (IDBSup, 130–36), who places the composition of the postexilic prophets and their incorporation into the OT canon at ca. 500 B.C., prove to be consonant with this analysis (cf. Welch 1935: 113–25).

F. Message and Theological Significance

The book of Malachi consists of the superscription (1:1), six disputational oracles (1:2–5; 1:6–9; 2:10–16; 2:17–3:5; 3:6–12; and 3:13–4:3) and two appendixes (4:4 [3:22]; 4:5–6 [3:23–24]). The predominant theme of the prophecy is Israel's covenantal relationship with Yahweh and its attendant ramifications. In fact, the prophet specifically mentions the covenant of Levi (2:1–9). The covenant of the fathers, and the covenant of marriage (2:10–16), and the messenger of the covenant (3:1; cf. McKenzie and Wallace [1983] for a discussion of these covenantal themes). Other references containing identifiable covenantal terminology include God's love for and election of Israel (1:2–5), the use of the words *bgd* (cf. Ps 78:57; Jer 3:21) and *šmr* (cf. Deut 4:23; 8:11) in 2:10–16, and the blessings and curses formula in 3:6–12. For this reason some understand Malachi himself to be the "messenger of the covenant" (e.g., McKenzie and Wallace 1983: 553).

The covenantal themes of Malachi are so thoroughly integrated and logically presented within the prophet's discourse that any attempts at rearranging the material in the text prove most unconvincing (e.g., McKenzie and Wallace 1983: 562–63, who argue that 3:13–15 is out of place, and though its "style and perspective" match that of 3:1–12, they ultimately have no clue where it does belong). This unity of covenantal theme and the general context of the prophecy also precludes the deletion of the so-called nonoriginal passages in 1:11–14 and 2:11b–13a, despite the difficulties in translating and interpreting those verses. The issue is not one of "particularism versus universalism," but instead the nature of Malachi's audience, the "wicked" and the "faithful" in restoration Jerusalem. Too, the repetition of covenant violations and the development of arguments from the general to the specific is a consistent pattern in the book (cf. Mason *Haggai, Zechariah, Malachi* CBC, 144–45; Smith *Micah—Malachi* WBC, 321–25).

Malachi's initial oracle is a restatement of Yahweh's love for Jacob (1:2–5). Amid growing skepticism because the "Zion visions" of Second Isaiah, Haggai, and Zechariah never materialized, the prophet sought to assure the Jewish community that God still maintained covenant love for them (cf. Hosea 11). By recalling the patriarchal covenants Malachi reminds the people that an important part of the message of God's covenant love for Israel was the conditional nature of its consequent blessings (Gen 29:13–17; 35:1–4; Deut 28:1ff.).

Here Fischer (1972: 318–19) rightly observes that Malachi had to correct wrong thinking about the covenantal relationship with Yahweh. The vassal can place no demands on the suzerain. Loving God was not a cause for divine blessing but a condition, for God himself remains the only cause. This reminder of Israel's election by the sovereign Lord as a people for his possession also served to underscore the seriousness of the present situation (Deut 8:11–18; cf. Rom 9:13). The prophet reinforces his argument by pointing to the recent events in Edom (perhaps an invasion of Edom by Nabatean Arabs?), which served as a grim warning of impending divine judgment for those who despised the tokens of covenant like Esau (Gen 25:34; cf. Jer 49:7–22).

Further, as covenant maker Yahweh was Israel's father (Deut 32:6–12), and he was deserving of conduct appropriate to the bond (Exod 20:12; Deut 30:1–10). As Covenant maker Yahweh was also a covenant keeper (Exod 34:6–7; Ps 111:9), unchanging and faithful to his word (3:6; Deut 7:6–11). Malachi's five remaining disputations contrast Israel's faithlessness with Yahweh's faithfulness through the recitation of specific violations of the covenant's stipulations.

According to Fischer (1972: 317) the literary form of Malachi outlines the essence of the book. The prophet has shifted the locus of his message from the curse or blessing declarations to the introductory statements in which a question is proposed to Yahweh and he answers. Using this perspective in his analysis, Fischer summarizes the teaching of the disputations as follows: (1) Yahweh loves Jacob, (2) he is Israel's father and desires honest worship, (3) he is the father of all Israelites and expects true faithfulness, (4) God wants honesty, not words, because he is just, (5) God is faithful to his word and wants genuine worship, (6) a repetition of God's desire for honesty.

The second disputation (1:6–2:9) consists of two sections (1:6–14 and 2:1–9). Both censure the levitical priesthood, the first for their insolence in discharging the duties associated with the cultus, and the second for the double standard in their teaching and their lack of moral leadership (cf. Num 20:12; Deut 18:1–8; 33:8–11). The apathetic priests were permitting impure sacrifices in the temple in violation of the Covenant Code (Lev 22:20–22; Deut 15:21; 17:1). Malachi preferred the cessation of temple ritual to their religious indifference and even suggests that the gentiles are offering more appropriate worship to God (1:10–11). No doubt the priests are indicted first because their transgression of the holy covenant and disdain for the sacred office has polluted the worship of the people (2:8–9). According to the curse formula in predictable fashion, the priesthood will experience the same contempt and abasement they have shown to Yahweh (1:6; 2:9).

Lest the priests become scapegoats, the prophet rebukes the laity in the third oracle for their faithlessness to Yahweh (2:10–16). Even as the Levites had corrupted the covenant of Levi (2:4, 8), the people of Judah had transgressed the covenant of the fathers by marrying foreign women and divorcing their Jewish wives (2:10–11, 14). Marriage is a sacred covenant, blessed by God and honorable among godly people (Gen 2:24; Ezek 16:8; Hos 2:19). For Malachi the connections between covenant keeping with Yahweh and covenant keeping with a mate are obvious based on the familial nature of covenant elsewhere in the OT (cf. Jer 2:1–3; 31:32; Ezek 16:6ff.; Hos 2:1–19; 11:1–4). Here he not only condemns divorce generally among God's people, but also their remarriage to foreign women because of the consequent contamination of pure religion (cf. Num 25:1–9; 1 Kgs 11:1–4). God hates divorce (2:16), and these flagrant violations of Covenant law will not go unpunished (2:11; cf. Exod 19:5–6; Deut 7:3–4).

The fourth oracle (2:17–3:5) is a prophecy concerning the messenger of the covenant who prepares the day of God's vistation by judging Judah's sin and purifying their worship through the cleansing of the priesthood (3:1–4; cf. Zeph 1:14–18). The faithlessness of the Jews extends even to false speech about Yahweh, as they accused him of rewarding evil and being unjust (2:17; cf. Job 21:7–16; Mic 6:1–3; Hab 1:2–4, 13). This attitude toward God naturally spawned a variety of social and moral abuses in the restoration community (3:5). Ironically, the failure to authenticate the words of the covenant relationship with behavior of like kind had led to Judah's exile into Babylonia a century prior (Deut 11:22; 12:1; 30:1–4; cf. Isa 1:12–17; Jer 7:1–7; Hos 4:1–10; Amos 2:6–8; Mic 3:1–4).

Contrary to the popular perception, Malachi contends in the fifth oracle that Yahweh has been just and ever consistent with his own nature (3:6–7). The very fact that God has not consumed postexilic Jerusalem for covenant transgressions is testimony to his faithfulness and compassion (Pss 86:15; 111:4; Mic 7:18–20; Nah 1:1–3). The emphasis in this next-to-last disputation (3:6–12) is repentance, not tithing (3:7). The tithe was an important component of Israelite religion (cf. Lev 27:30; Num 18:26–28; Deut 12:18; 14:28–29), but given the list of covenantal offenses already cited by Malachi he can hardly be implying the mere reinstitution of the tithe would initiate divinely bestowed prosperity. The stinginess of the people was but a sign of their spiritual bankruptcy. By calling for the "full" tithe the prophet invites genuine repentance, a return to Yahweh with the whole heart (3:10; cf. Isa 29:13; Joel 2:12–13, 18–19). Only this kind of honest personal worship will open the windows of heaven, to the point that Malachi dares the people to exhaust the bounty of God's covenantal blessing (3:10–12; cf. Deut 15:5–6, 10).

The seeming triumph of wickedness over righteousness and God's apparent slackness in judging sin are the issues in the final pericope of Malachi (3:13–4:3). Here prophet outlines the specific charges of injustice the impudent complainers—not the "devout" as usually understood (since Heb *lûn,* commonly translated "murmuring," actually connotes open rebellion, cf. Exod 15:24; 16:2; Num 14:2; 16:11) in Jerusalem have lodged against Yahweh (3:13–15). They contend that it is futile to serve God because they have turned no profit (literally, the "cut" or percentage due them) from the observation of the commandments, fasting, and repentance. No advantage was gained from personal piety from their perspective; in fact evildoers were the ones who escaped the test of God. Continuing the distinction between the wicked and the righteous in his audience introduced at the outset of his prophecy, Malachi then contrasts the words of the believing God-fearers (3:16–17). Unlike the mercenary approach of their compatriots, they have responded to God with genuine reverence and worship. The disputation concludes with the prophet's answer to the alleged inequity of Yahweh's treatment of the restoration community (3:18–4:3). The coming day of the Lord will vindicate his justice, when the wicked are separated from the righteous by the fire of divine judgment (3:18). The righteous will escape the destructive wrath of God by virtue of their special covenantal relationship *(sĕgullâ)* with him and will experience the blessings of messianic restoration (4:2; cf. Num 6:22–27; Ps 107:20; Isa 63:1–6; Mic 2:13).

The closing verses of the book (4:4–6 [—MT 3:22–24]) are generally acknowledged to be editorial additions. The questions and answers are over, and the disputations have ceased. There is little to suggest that these verses are directly related to the previous section. Yet they represent more than the legalistic correctives of a disenchanted scribe since they do serve as guidelines for the righteousness central to the prophet's message. The Deuteronomic connections of 4:4 are numerous and well documented (e.g., Mitchell, Smith, and Bewer *Haggai, Zechariah, Malachi, and Jonah* ICC, 81; Mason *Haggai, Zechariah, Malachi* CBC, 159–60), and the verse may be an attempt to summarize the message of Malachi by reminding the people that they still stand under the tradition of Moses. The verse may also represent the work of the compiler of The Book of the Twelve, who sought to unite the Law and the Prophets as equally authoritative units of Scripture. Elijah functions as a prophetic archetype in 4:5–6, and the reference to him identifies the messenger of the covenant in 3:1. According to Childs (1979: 495–96), the effect of the second appendix is to balance the memory of the past with the anticipation of the future. While the verses seem an unduly harsh ending to Malachi and the Twelve, one must remember that the basic purpose of the prophetic ministry was to prepare the people of Yahweh for his day of visitation so that they might enter the rest of his salvation and escape the wrath of his judgment (cf. Isa 12:1–6; 33:2–6; Zeph 3:14–20; Zech 8:14–19).

The postexilic date for the book, the diminished stature of the restoration community in Jerusalem, and the dialectical nature of the prophet's oracles should not prompt an underestimation of Malachi's theological significance. Although the literary grandeur of Isaiah and the profound personal intensity of Jeremiah are lacking, these comparisons are questionable anyway since each prophet had to fulfill his specific commission in his own historical context. It remains more important to analyze how the prophet performed his task, examine his message within the scope of the broader prophetic movement, and seek to make appropriate contemporary application. In this respect Malachi proves a most fruitful and powerful study, and in many instances the prophecy is a throwback to the classical prophets of the postexilic era.

Foremost is Malachi's knowledge of and identification with the covenantal tradition of his prophetic heritage (3:1). Hence the book rests squarely in the midst of OT covenantal theology and in large measure embodies the essence of later NT thought. See COVENANT. For example, he recognized Yahweh as the maker and keeper of the covenant with Israel (1:2, cf. Exod 6:2–7; Jer 31:31–34; Heb 8:6–13) and acknowledged their "son" status as a consequence of this covenantal relationship (1:6; Hos 1:10; cf. Rom 8:14). Like his predecessors he understood the conditional nature of the covenantal relationship and the importance of the community's obligation to remain faithful and obedient to the stipulations of the divine treaty (3:16–4:3; cf. Ezek 16:59–63; 1 John 4:20–5:3), the seriousness of a breach of the covenant (2:1–8; cf. Isa 24:5; Jer 34:17–20; Heb 6:4–8), evincing a thorough acquaintance with the Deuteronomic blessing and curse formula (Deut 28:1ff.; cf. 1 Cor 11:27–32, i.e., the curse associated with abuse of the covenant-renewal meal of the NT), and the possibility for repentance and restoration (3:6–7; cf. Hos 14:1–9; Luke 3:1–14). The prophet was also keenly aware of the concept of individual and corporate responsibility within the covenant community (2:7–9, 13–16; cf. 2 Kgs 17:22, 34–39; 24:3–4; 1 Cor 5:1–8), and the attendant ethical duties those resident in that community had to one another and to the socially underprivileged (3:5; cf. Isa 1:16–17; Jas 1:26–27).

Malachi substantially affirms OT teaching about the nature and character of God. While God is father because of the covenantal relationship with Israel as sons and because he seeks a vital and intimate bond with them (1:6; 2:5–7; 3:17), he is also master and king (1:6, 14). Here the prophet is careful to present a balanced picture of Israel's Yahweh, lest the extremes of overfamiliarity or transcendent indifference distort the community's perception of their Lord. Unlike most other OT prophets, Malachi has little to say about the nations, yet it is clear that he acknowledges God's sovereignty in human history (1:3–5). Closely bound to this idea is Yahweh's love for and election of Israel as a special people (1:2; 3:17; cf. Deut 7:6–11). This choice on God's part and the subsequent covenantal bond serve as the platform for the prophet's entire discourse (cf. Rom 9:4–5). Since Yahweh is so linked to Israel he is faithful and unchanging (3:6), a covenant keeper extending mercy to his own, yet just (2:17), punishing those who trespass the covenant's stipulations (3:5, 18; 4:3). As God of the covenant he tests the faithful in order to purify them (3:1–4), and as the giver of good gifts he is not reluctant to bless and reward the obedience of his children (3:10–12).

Those who contend that Malachi only appreciates the cultic and legalistic aspects of Israelite religion have failed to consider fully his instruction on the nature of personal faith. It is clear from the prophet's handling of the objection that it is vain to serve God (3:14), that he espoused no merit system. Those who are spared divine judgment earned no special favor, they simply "feared the Lord and honored his name" (3:16). The prophet's insistence on true repentance for the renewal of genuine worship (3:2–4), honesty in giving (3:8–12), and personal piety (3:5–7) is an indication of an internal, not an external, religion. Naturally the recognition of Yahweh's holiness and righteousness led to the conviction that true service included rendering both liturgical and moral obedience to God (1:6–10; cf. Matt 23:23; Jas 1:27). Here Malachi penetrates the heart of OT faith when he appeals for a personal "walk" with the living God (2:6; cf. Deut 30:15–20; Mic 6:8).

Malachi's conception of the priesthood as the repository of the knowledge of God for the people (2:5–7) may be a result of his association with levitical circles, given the similarity of his oracles to the so-called "levitical sermons" of Haggai and the Chronicler (so Mason *Haggai, Zechariah, and Malachi* CBC, 137). The crucial role of the priesthood as righteous guideposts for the community is consistent with both OT and NT teaching regarding the responsibility of those in leadership positions (Num 20:12; 1 Sam 15:22–23; Isa 1:23–26; Jer 5:5; cf. Luke 12:48; Acts 6:3; Rom 13:4; 1 Tim 3:1–3; Jas 3:1).

The prophet's lofty doctrine of the institution of marriage as companionship with the wife of one's youth (2:14) and the shared responsibility of child rearing (2:15) is reminiscent of OT wisdom teaching (Prov 5:18; 10:1; 15:20; 31:26), while his censure of easy divorce anticipates the rigid instruction of Jesus and Paul in contrast to the Deuteronomist (2:16; cf. Matt 19:1–11; Mark 10:1–10; 1 Cor 7:1–16 versus Deut 24:1–4).

Malachi's eschatology shows no concern for a future temple; rather, he is interested in the reform of abuses in the cult here and now. While the prophet maintains a clear distinction between the fate of the wicked and the righteous in the community, he has little to say about the judgment of the nations or anything approaching universalism in the sense of the nations participating in the salvation of the Jews, as in Zechariah 9–14 (12:1–9; 14:1–3, 9–21). Malachi does not use the expression "day of Yahweh," but his understanding of that coming day (3:19) largely conforms to conventional OT patterns, with attention given to the judgment of Israel's sin for Covenant violations (3:5), and the preservation of a righteous remnant (3:3–4, 16–17). Malachi's picture of final judgment has a focus different from that of Zechariah, yet the two do emphasize the refining or purification of the faithful by fire (3:2; 4:1; cf. Zech 12:6; 13:9; cf. 2 Pet 3:10–12), and both recognize that God's ultimate purpose in judgment remains repentance (3:7; Zech 10:9–12; cf. Ezek 18:23, 30–32). Of special interest here is the striking contrast between the threatened "ban" or "curse" (Heb *ḥerem*) at the end of Malachi (4:6) and the repeal of the ban in Zech 14:11.

Malachi does make original contributions to Hebrew eschatology with the introduction of the "book of remembrance" in which are recorded the names of the righteous. The concept is probably the result of Persian influence on postexilic Judaism (cf. Esth 6:1; Dan 7:10; 12:1) and points to continued development in the Hebrew belief in afterlife. This book of remembrance may have inspired the notion of the "book of life" used to separate the wicked from the righteous at the final judgment in the Apocalypse (Rev 20:11–15). The unique OT expression "the sun of righteousness" in 3:20 (MT 4:2) is reminiscent of the winged solar disc representing the sun god in Mesopotamian and Egyptian iconography and is likely another indication of Zoroastrian influence on the Hebrew understanding of the fiery consummation (cf. Smith *Micah—Malachi* WBC, 339–40).

Finally, Malachi's obscure reference to the "forerunner" who prepares the way for the arrival of Yahweh (3:1) has proved difficult to interpret. Commentators are divided in their opinion over the identification of the messenger and his relationship to the "messenger of the covenant" mentioned later in the verse. It is unclear whether this "messenger" is a prophet, an angel, or a manifestation of God himself (cf. 1:1; see A above). The second appendix (4:5–6) connects the messenger with Elijah reincarnate. Elijah's role as a herald proclaiming the appointed time of Yahweh's fury and the inauguration of the messianic age was an important part of later Jewish tradition regarding the prophet (Sir 48:10–11; cf. Matt 17:3, 10; 27:47, 49; John 1:21; see Verheof *Haggai and Malachi* NICOT, 345–46). Jesus of Nazareth certainly understood the prophecy as prefiguring the ministry of John the Baptist (Matt 11:7–15), and the early church held the oracle to be fully realized in the relationship of John's mission with the initiation of the messianic kingdom of heaven by Jesus Christ (Mark 1:2–8; Luke 1:16–17; cf. Matt 11:1–6).

G. Canonicity

Malachi is the last of the short books constituting the collection of the Twelve Prophets. This collection follows the major prophets in the Hebrew canon; the grouping was known as early as Ben Sira (49:12), and it was also familiar to Josephus (*AgAp* 1.8.3). The canonicity of the

Twelve was never questioned, as rabbinic tradition held that the men of the Great Synagogue edited the corpus (*B. Bat.* 15a). Some LXX editions placed the Twelve before the major prophets and departed from the Hebrew sequence of placing Hosea first (whether for its length or for chronological considerations is unclear, cf. *B. Bat.* 14b).

Biblical scholarship has long assumed that the oracles contained in Zechariah 9–11, 12–14 and Malachi 1–4 (MT 1–3) are related, largely because of the use of Heb *maśśāʾ* in the superscriptions. In addition, these oracles have been considered to be anonymous documents. It is argued that these anonymous oracles were appended to Zechariah to round out the Twelve in order to complete the sacred number. Here Radday and Pollatschek (1980) concluded, based on computer-aided linguistic analysis of the postexilic prophets, that the editor of the Twelve Prophets had a collection of materials remaining from the compilation of Hosea to Zechariah 8. They suggest that this small library consisted of a few short but distinct manuscripts, which were attached to Zechariah 1–8 following the size principle. The two longer ones coalesced with Zechariah 1–8 to become chaps. 9–11 and 12–14. Two shorter pieces (Malachi 1–2 and 3) were then added to Zechariah with the superscription "by the hand of Malachi" inserted for the purpose of presenting a collection of prophetic books corresponding to the number of Israelite tribes. This clever editor turned a word found three times in the last chapters, *malʾāḵî,* into a name of a formerly unknown prophet.

Childs (1979), however, cogently counters that the superscriptions in Zech 9:1; 12:1 and Mal 1:1 demonstrate only superficial similarities. He notes that *maśśāʾ* is used in its absolute form in Mal 1:1 as a distinct superscription. In addition, Mal 1:1 reads *ʾel* ("to") rather than *ʿal* ("upon") and includes *bĕyad* ("by the hand of"). For Childs these and other expressions demonstrate both the integrity and the consistency of the title of Malachi with like features of postexilic literature. This leads him to conclude that these oracles had a history independent of one another. Thus, "the present independent status of Malachi did not arise from an arbitrary decision which separated it from the book of Zechariah. Rather its separate status is deeply rooted in the book's own tradition" (Childs 1979: 492).

Bibliography

Bulmerincq, A. von. 1921. Einleitung in das Buch des Propheten Maleachi. *Acta et Commentationes* B/1–3: 3–140.

———. 1922. Einleitung in das Buch des Propheten Maleachi. *Acta et Commentationes* B/1–3: 141–224.

Childs, B. 1979. *Introduction to the Old Testament as Scripture.* Philadelphia.

Fischer, J. A. 1972. Notes on the Literary Form and Message of Malachi. *CBQ* 34: 315–20.

Hanson, P. 1975. *The Dawn of Apocalyptic.* Philadelphia.

Hill, A. E. 1983. Dating the Book of Malachi: A Linguistic Reexamination. Pp. 77–89 in *The Word of the Lord Shall Go Forth,* ed. C. Meyers and M. O'Connor. Winona Lake, IN.

Hoftijzer, J. 1965. Remarks Concerning the Use of the Particle *ʾt* in Classical Hebrew. *OTS* 14: 1–99.

Kaiser, W. C. 1984. *Malachi: God's Unchanging Love.* Grand Rapids.

Kruse-Blinkenberg, L. 1966. The Peshitta of the Book of Malachi. *ST* 20: 95–119.

———. 1967. The Book of Malachi: According to Codex Syro-Hexaplaris Ambrosianus. *ST* 21: 62–82.

McKenzie, S. L., and Wallace, H. W. 1983. Covenant Times in Malachi. *CBQ* 45: 549–63.

Petersen, D. L. 1977. *Late Israelite Prophecy.* SBLMS 23. Missoula, MT.

Polzin, R. 1976. *Late Biblical Hebrew.* HSM 12. Missoula, MT.

Radday, Y. T., and Pollatschek, M. A. 1980. Vocabulary Richness in Post-Exilic Prophetic Books. *ZAW* 92: 333–46.

Rudolph, W. 1976. *Haggai—Zacharja 1–8—Zacharja 9–14—Malachi.* KAT. Neukirchen.

Welch, A. C. 1935. *Post-Exilic Judaism.* Edinburgh.

Andrew E. Hill

MALCAM (PERSON) [Heb *malkām*]. One of the sons of Shaharaim, a Benjaminite, by his wife Hodesh, appearing in 1 Chr 8:9 in an extended Benjaminite genealogy. The name appears elsewhere in the MT as that of an idol (Zeph 1:5, Molech), but the word also appears as the noun plus pronominal suffix (Amos 1:15) to be translated "their king" (Odelain and Ségineau 1981: 250; *ISBE*[1] 3:1971). Coggins (*Chronicles* CBC, 54) has acknowledged the scarcity of material concerning the Benjaminite names in vv 6–27. It is known, however, that Malcam was born to Hodesh and Shaharaim in Moab. This reference points to a relation between Israel and Moab that goes back to a time earlier than that reflected in 1 Chronicles 8. Ruth 1 and 1 Sam 22:3, 4 show the presence of Israelites in Moab; but it is apparent that this kind of sojourn would more likely have occurred before Moab regained its independence from Israel. Myers (*1 Chronicles* AB, 60) states that while Moab was under Israel's control, the Benjaminite association could have been accurate. Braun (*1 Chronicles* WBC, 128) states that most and probably all of the genealogies in this section have roots in the remote past but that their presence in 1 Chronicles reflects a great interest in the tribe of Benjamin during the exilic period and beyond. Malcam, like his brothers, is called a *roʾšê ʾābôt,* "head of a family." This designation has clear organizational implications in social, political, and military arenas (Harmon 1983: 150).

Bibliography

Harmon, G. E. 1983. *Floor Area and Population Determination.* Ph.D. diss., Southern Baptist Theological Seminary.

Odelain, O., and Séguineau, R. 1981. *Dictionary of Proper Names and Places in the Bible.* Trans. M. J. O'Connell. Garden City, NY.

G. Edwin Harmon

MALCHIAH (PERSON) [Heb *malkîyāhû*]. See MALCHIJAH.

MALCHIEL (PERSON) [Heb *malkîʾēl*]. MALCHIELITES. The second son of Beriah and grandson of Asher (Gen 46:17; 1 Chr 7:31). Asher was the second son of Jacob and Zilpah (Gen 30:12–13), the maid whom Laban gave to his daughter Leah (Gen 29:29). Malchiel was one of the sixteen persons among the sons and grandsons of Zilpah mentioned in the genealogy of Jacob who went with him to Egypt.

Malchiel was the leader of the clan of the Malchielites, one of the clans of Asher (Num 26:45). He is included among the men of Asher who were "heads of fathers' houses, approved, mighty warriors, chief of the princes" (1 Chr 7:40). He was the father of Birzaith (1 Chr 7:31). In the Hebrew text the name of Malchiel's son appears as Birzavith, but the Qere and the Ketib have a corrupt spelling of the name.

The name Milkil (Malchiel) appears in the correspondence of Amarna. In the letters of ᶜAbdu-Heba, the ruler of the city of Jerusalem, to the court of Egypt, Milkil appears as one of his most troublesome enemies. Jastrow (1892: 120) has identified the Asherites Malchiel (Milkil) and Heber with some of the groups that were included among the Habiru mentioned in the Amarna Letters.

Bibliography

Jastrow, M. 1892. Egypt and Palestine, 1400 B.C. *JBL* 11: 95–124.

CLAUDE F. MARIOTTINI

MALCHIJAH (PERSON) [Heb *malkîyāhû, malkîyāh*]. Var. MALCHIAH; MELCHIAS. Name of 13 persons in Hebrew Bible and Apocrypha.

1. A Gershonite Levite. According to the genealogy of 1 Chronicles 6, Malchijah is an ancestor of Asaph, the founder of a guild of temple musicians (v 25—Eng v 40).

2. Descendant of Aaron and head of a priestly family. When David divided the priests into twenty-four divisions (1 Chr 24:1–19), the fifth lot fell to Malchijah (v 9). In 1 Chr 9:12 and Neh 11:12, the genealogy of Adaiah, a priest in postexilic Jerusalem, is traced to Malchijah the father of Pashhur.

3. A Judean bearing the title "son of the king" (Heb *ben hammelek*) during the reign of Zedekiah (Jer 38:6). It is probable that this title (which occurs both in the OT and on a number of seals and bullae) refers to members of the royal family. It is apparent that some of these men held important administrative positions. According to Jer 38:6, the prophet Jeremiah was imprisoned in the cistern of Malchiah (Heb *malkîyāhû*). His duties, like those of Joash (1 Kgs 22:26; 2 Chr 18:25) and Jerahmeel (Jer 36:26), appear to have included the maintenance of state security. Possibly the same as #4 below.

4. Father of Pashhur (to be distinguished from the Pashhur mentioned in #2 above), a royal official during the reign of Zedekiah (Jer 21:1; 38:1). Possibly to be identified with #3 above.

5. Layman descended from Parosh. One of those required by Ezra to divorce their foreign wives (Ezra 10:25a; 1 Esdr 9:26).

6. In the Hebrew text, the name Malchijah occurs again in Ezra 10:25b. This reading is followed in a number of English translations of the Bible (e.g., JB, NEB, NAB). Both the LXX and 1 Esdr 9:26, however, support the reading "Hashabiah" (RSV).

7. Layman descended from Harim. One of those required by Ezra to put away their foreign wives (Ezra 10:31). Although it is possible that he is the same as #8 below, this is by no means certain (cf. Neh 7:35, 42). He is, however, probably to be identified with Melchias son of Annan, listed in 1 Esdr 9:32. This conclusion is supported by the order in which the families are listed in Ezra 10:25–44 and 1 Esdr 9:26–36 and by the fact that Malchijah (Gk Melchias) is the third name to appear in both Ezra 10:31 and 1 Esdr 9:32.

8. Son of Harim. One of those who repaired a section of the wall of Jerusalem in the time of Nehemiah (Neh 3:11). Possibly the same as #7 above.

9. Son of Rechab and ruler of Beth-haccherem. He was responsible for rebuilding the Dung Gate under the supervision of Nehemiah (Neh 3:14). It is unlikely that he was a member of the Rechabite community—Jonadab, the founder of this community, was another son of Rechab (cf. 2 Kgs 10:15, 23; Jer 35:1–19).

10. One of the goldsmiths who assisted Nehemiah in the rebuilding of the wall of Jerusalem (Neh 3:31).

11. A priest who participated in the dedication of the rebuilt walls of Jerusalem in the time of Nehemiah (Neh 12:42).

12. One of those who stood on either side of Ezra during the reading of the Law at a public assembly (Neh 8:4; cf. 1 Esdr 9:44). Although it is possible that these men were priests (the participation of the same number of Levites is mentioned in Neh 8:7 [cf. 1 Esdr 9:48]), the fact that this is not stated explicitly suggests that they were probably laymen.

13. One of the priests signatory to a legal document of reform associated with Ezra or Nehemiah (Neh 10:4—Eng 10:5). Although the term "covenant" is not used in Neh 10:1–40—Eng 9:38–10:39, the account probably relates to a covenant-making ceremony (cf. v 30—Eng v 29) that addressed itself to various concerns of the postexilic community. It would appear that the priests (unlike the Levites) are listed by their family names, and not as individuals. This Malchijah may thus be the same as #2 above.

Bibliography

Avigad, N. 1978. Baruch the Scribe and Jerahmeel the King's Son. *IEJ* 28: 52–56.

Herr, L. G. 1980. Paleography and the Identification of Seal Owners. *BASOR* 239: 67–70.

Rainey, A. F. 1975. The Prince and the Pauper. *UF* 7: 427–32.

JOHN M. BERRIDGE

MALCHIRAM (PERSON) [Heb *malkîrām*]. The second son of Jeconiah/Jehoiachin (1 Chr 3:18). The name means "my king is exalted."

RUSSELL FULLER

MALCHISHUA (PERSON) [Heb *malkî-šûaᶜ*]. The third-born son and fifth-born child of Saul son of Kish and his wife Ahinoam daughter of Ahimaaz (1 Sam 14:49; 1 Chr 8:33; 9:39). Nothing is known of his life except that he died alongside his father and two brothers, Jonathan and Abinadab, at the battle of Gilboa, where Saul unsuccessfully attempted to conquer the city-state of Beth-shan (1 Sam 31:2; 1 Chr 10:2). He apparently was at least 20 years of age (the legal age for military service: Num 16:2, 4) when he was killed. The biblical account does not indicate that he was survived by any children, which probably means that he was unmarried.

The name Malchishua means "the (divine) King is noble," or "the (divine) King is opulence" (BDB, 447); by a different etymology it could mean "help of the (divine) King" (Gray 1896: 146–47; see *IPN,* 154 and the discussion in *TPNAH,* pp. 114–15).

Bibliography

Gray, G. B. 1896. *Studies in Hebrew Proper Names.* London.

DIANA V. EDELMAN

MALCHUS (PERSON) [Gk *Malchos*]. **1.** See CLEODEMUS MALCHUS.

2. Malchus was a slave or servant of the high priest (probably Caiaphas—cf. John 18:13); Peter cut off his right ear when Jesus was arrested in Gethsemane (John 18:10). Only the gospel of John records Malchus' name. All four Gospels state that Malchus was the servant of the high priest, which distinguishes him from the officers sent by the chief priests and Pharisees to arrest Jesus (cf. John 18:18). Nabatean and Palmyrene inscriptions bearing the name Malchus indicate that it was a common Arab name and that Malchus may have been an Arab slave. A relative of Malchus was also a servant of the high priest and, while Peter was standing outside Jesus' trial, identified him as having been with Jesus (John 18:26). Peter may have struck Malchus because he was acting as the representative of the high priest in the arrest. The servants of the high priest were known to perform the underhanded dealings of the high priest (Joseph. *Ant.* 20.181, 206). Cutting off the right ear may have been Peter's impetuous response to the arrest of his friend (cf. John 13:37) or a calculated insult against the high priest through his servant. The latter is indicated by the indemnity laws of the time, which considered the right organs of the body to be more valuable. Only Luke 22:51 reports that Jesus healed the ear.

Bibliography

Jeremias, J. 1969. *Jerusalem in the Time of Jesus.* Trans. F. H. Cave and C. H. Cave. Philadelphia.

JOANN FORD WATSON

MALHATA, TEL (M.R. 152069). A town in the Negeb with remains from the Chalcolithic through the Early Arab periods.

A. The Site and Its Excavations

Tel Malhata (formerly Tell el-Milh) is a 1.5-acre mound located in the Negeb. It is situated at the confluence of the Malhata and the Beer-sheba rivers and is abundantly supplied with water by numerous wells. Extensive ruins from the Roman-Byzantine Period lie S of it in the plain and a smaller, lower mound, "Small Tel Malhata," is located N of it on the other bank of the river. The major mound was excavated by M. Kochavi in 1967 and 1971. The Roman-Byzantine site was excavated by M. Gichon, and the small mound was excavated by R. Amiran in 1979. Further salvage excavations were conducted at the Roman-Byzantine site in 1981.

Settlement began at Malhata in the Chalcolithic period and lasted until the Early Arab period. Occupational gaps occurred in the EB III—MB I, LB, Iron Age I, and Persian periods. All periods of occupation were attested on the major mound, but the small mound was inhabited in the early periods only and the Roman-Byzantine site only in the late.

Chalcolithic remains of the Beer-sheba culture and EB I–II layers were exposed in the lowest strata of the small mound. Finds of Egyptian imported ware (including three *serekhs,* i.e., conventions for inscribing the names of the earliest Pharaohs), lumps of bitumen from the Dead Sea, as well as various installations connected with crafts and small industries were found in the EB strata. The EB settlement was apparently an unwalled trading post on the Arad-to-Egypt commerce road.

The initial occupation of the major mound began in the MB II. Three MB II strata were distinguished, and date to the 17th–16th centuries B.C. The town was about one acre and was confined to the E part of the mound. It was surrounded by a massive earthen rampart, crowned with a wall 1 m wide. The rampart's outer surface was plastered and laid on a 30-degree incline to form a glacis.

An MB II occupation was detected also on the small mound. It was interpreted as remains of an unwalled suburb, where herds were kept and people could find shelter in the shadow of the fortified town. Malhata was the easternmost fortified town in a chain of sites forming the S border of Canaan in the MB Age. It was destroyed by fire and deserted in the mid-16th century B.C.

After about 500 years, settlement at the site resumed, but only on the major mound. In mid-10th century B.C., a new fortified city was erected on the mound. On the W side of the preexisting mound an earthen platform was built, enlarging the town's area by 50 percent. The slopes were stabilized by a cobblestone covering, forming a stepped glacis. A public building with thick plastered walls existed on the SW near the city wall. The first Iron Age city was destroyed at the end of the 10th century B.C., followed by a short-lived unwalled settlement.

The last phase of Iron Age Malhata was a densely built-up city, surrounded by a new wall which was reinforced with a new stone glacis. A tower projecting 8 m was preserved to a height of 10 m. The public house of the earlier phase was replaced with a series of storeroom houses, built and rebuilt on the same plan. The last Iron Age stratum was destroyed by an intense fire in the 6th century B.C. Among the many finds from this stratum were large amounts of Edomite pottery, an Aramaic ostracon, inscribed Hebrew stone-weights, and an imported archaic E Greek oeonoche. Iron Age Malhata was the most prominent town in the Negeb in the 10th century B.C., and it continued to be a major town in the region until the end of the kingdom of Judah.

The site was resettled in the Hellenistic period, as evidenced by surface finds from the Roman-Byzantine site. A large Late Roman cemetery and several buildings from the Byzantine period were excavated. The fort crowning the E spur of the major mound was still in use in the Early Arab period. Roman-Byzantine Malhata is thought to have been a garrison fort on the S borders of the Roman Empire, with a colony of *Limitanti* nearby.

B. The Problem of Identification

The identification of Malatha/Moleatha, a Roman-Byzantine fort, with Tel Malhata is generally accepted. The name of the earlier, biblical town, however, still eludes us. Many place names, taken mainly from the list of the inheritance of Simeon, have been suggested. Robinson (1856: 201–2), followed by Guerin (1869: 184–88) and others, proposed Moladah (Josh 15:26), relying on the resemblance between the Latin and the Hebrew names. Mazar (1965) and Garstang were impressed by the Bronze Age remains and identified it with Hormah (Num 14:45; Deut 1:44), where the Israelites were first involved in battle with a Canaanite city. Aharoni (*LBHG,* 201), from the same point of view, concluded that Malhata was Canaanite Arad. The absence of any LB remains on the site refutes the last two suggestions. Kochavi (*EAEHL* 3: 771) has suggested Baalath-Beer (Josh 19:8), while Naʾaman (1980) proposed Telaim, where King Saul summoned his army against the Amalekites (1 Sam 15:4).

Bibliography

Guerin, V. 1869. *Description de la Palestine,* vol. 3. Paris.
Kochavi, M. 1967. Notes and News: Tel Malḥata. *IEJ* 17: 272–73.
———. 1970. The First Season of Excavations at Tel Malḥata. *Qad* 3: 22–24 (in Hebrew).
———. 1972. Tel Malḥata. *RB* 79: 593–96.
———. 1980. Rescue in the Biblical Negev. *BARev* 6/1: 24–27.
Mazar, B. 1965. The Sanctuary of Arad and the Family of Hobab the Kenite. *JNES* 24: 297–303.
Naʾaman, N. 1980. The Inheritance of the Sons of Simeon. *ZDPV* 96: 136–52.
Robinson, E. 1856. *Biblical Researches in Palestine,* vol. 2. London.

Moshe Kochavi

MALLOTHI (PERSON) [Heb *mallôtî*]. One of the fourteen sons of Heman who were appointed to prophesy with musical instruments under the direction of their father and the king (1 Chr 25:4). Malloti received the nineteenth lot cast to determine duties (1 Chr 25:26). Scholars have long suggested that the final nine names in 1 Chr 25:4 can be read as a liturgical prayer. For instance, Malloti can be read as the first-person sing. *Piʿel* perf. form of the verb *mālal* "I said." It would form part of the fourth line of the liturgical prayer as reconstructed by scholars. For a reconstruction and translation of the prayer, a summary of interpretative possibilities, and bibliography, see ELIATHAH.

J. Clinton McCann, Jr.

MALLOW. See FLORA, BIBLICAL.

MALLUCH (PERSON) [Heb *mallûk*]. **1.** An ancestor of Ethan, who was a Levite and a singer in Solomon's Temple (1 Chr 6:44). Appearing in a schematic list that has the three sons of Levi as its focus, Malluch is described as a member of the Merari line (Möhlenbrink 1934: 202–3; Myers *Ezra-Nehemiah* AB, 46). The references to both Ethan and Malluch are at the center of debates over the list's nature and redaction, which has a parallel in 1 Chr 6:29–30 (Braun *1 Chronicles* WBC, 93–94).

2. One of twenty-two priests (Brockington *Ezra, Nehemiah and Esther* Century Bible, 197–98), or families of priests (Myers *Ezra-Nehemiah* AB, 196), who returned to Jerusalem with Zerubbabel (Neh 12:2).

3. The son of Bani or, if the text has been corrupted, perhaps Binnui (*bnwy*), or Bigvai (*bgwy*) (Ezra 10:29; cf. Williamson *Ezra, Nehemiah* WBC, 144). Malluch was one of the laity required by Ezra to abandon his foreign wife. The presence of his name in this list, which is absent from the parallel in Ezra 2, raises questions both about the nature of the documents that lie behind the lists, and about the way in which the writer has adapted those documents to suit his purposes (cf. Myers *Ezra-Nehemiah* AB, 87–88 and Williamson *Ezra, Nehemiah* WBC, 157–58).

4. A son of Harim and one of the laity required by Ezra to abandon his foreign wife (Ezra 10:32).

5. A priest and signatory to the covenant established by Ezra (Neh 10:4).

6. A leader of the people and a signatory to the covenant established by Ezra (Neh 10:27). At least one scholar conjectures that he may also be the Malluch of Ezra 10:32, mentioned in #4 above (*IDB* 3: 233).

Bibliography

Möhlenbrink, K. 1934. Die levitische Überlieferungen des Alten Testaments. *ZAW* 52: 184–231.

Frederick W. Schmidt

MALLUCHI (PERSON) [Heb *mallûkî,* Ketib; *mĕlîkû,* Qere]. Var. MALLUCH. A priestly family mentioned only in Neh 12:14 as one of some 20 such families serving in the days of Joiakim (vv 12–21). Previously in the same chapter (v 2), a certain Malluch (Heb *mallûk*) is listed as having returned from exile to Jerusalem in the days of Zerubbabel. Inasmuch as even a cursory overview will confirm the close correspondence between the names found in these two lists (i.e., vv 1–7 and 12–21), it is quite certain that the "Malluchi" of v 14 and the "Malluch" of v 2 represent two variant spellings of the same individual's (or family's) name. For arguments supporting the relative primacy of the list of priestly families in vv 12–21 over the corresponding list that precedes it in vv 1–7, see AMOK.

In regard to the variant spellings Malluch/Malluchi, most commentators prefer the former as the more likely original (note the LXX, which reads *malouch* in both verses). Bowman (*IB* 3: 788, following Rudolph) points out that the final *yod* of Malluchi in v 14 probably represents a dittograph of the *yod* in the following name, Jonathan (Heb *yônātān*). This, in turn, as Williamson (*Ezra, Nehemiah* WBC, 357 n. 14a) notes, presumably led to the Qere variant *mĕlîkû* (representing *waw*/*yod* confusion?). Further support for the primacy of the spelling "Malluch" is probably to be found in the analogous list of priests in Neh 10:3–9—Eng vv 2–8—where such a spelling is attested in v 5—Eng v 4. For a brief discussion of the origin and nature of this list, see MAADIAH.

William H. Barnes

MALLUS (PLACE) [Gk *Mallōs*]. A Cilician city located on the Pyramus river E of Tarsus on the S coast of Asia Minor. 2 Macc 4:30 recounts that the cities of Tarsus and Mallus were given by the Seleucid king Antiochus IV Epiphanes as a present to his concubine Antiochis. The transfer of the cities to Antiochis occasioned a revolt by the populace, which required Antiochus' personal attention. Mallus was under Ptolemaic rule from ca. 246 to 197 B.C.E., at which time it came under Seleucid control (Mørkholm 1966: 117 n. 6). That Antiochus should have given the city to his mistress as a source of income was not uncommon in antiquity. Thucydides (1.138.5) records that Themistocles was given the income of three cities by his king. Herodotus (2.98) points out an example of an Egyptian king who assigned a city to provide shoes for his mistress. Herodotus indicates that this was a common practice in Egypt under Persian domination. Cicero (*Verr.* 2.3.33) notes that this custom was common in Persia and Syria to provide for the needs of royal wives. There is no extant witness to this rebellion beyond 2 Maccabees and no evidence that would indicate why Mallus was so important that Antiochus IV should personally attend to the civic disturbance. Numismatic evidence indicates that Tarsus was an Antiochene city as late as 166 B.C.E. (Mørkholm 1966: 60 n. 32). Antiochene cities enjoyed a measure of self-government along with considerable prestige (Tcherikover 1977: 443–44 n. 12). It is apparent from 2 Maccabees that Tarsus, an Antiochene city, and its neighbor, Mallus, objected to being transferred from the authority of Antichus to his mistress and to bear a possibly increased financial burden. The rebellion of Antiochene Tarsus and Mallus could have embarrassed the king, prompting Antiochus to deal with the two cities personally. A successful revolt by these two cities on the edge of the Seleucid empire could also have threatened the security of the state (Abel 1949: 340).

Bibliography

Abel, F.-M. 1949. *Les Livres des Maccabées.* Paris.
Mørkholm, O. 1966. *Antiochus IV of Syria.* Copenhagen.
Tcherikover, V. 1977. *Hellenistic Civilization and the Jews.* Trans. S. Applebaum. New York.

MICHAEL E. HARDWICK

MALTA (PLACE) [Gk *Melitē*]. An island in the Mediterranean, about 60 mi. S of Cape Passero, Sicily and 220 mi. N of Tripoli, Libya; with 95 sq. mi., it is the largest of the five islands making up the modern country of Malta. Archaeological evidence exists for its occupation from about 3800 B.C., first by cave-dwelling farmers who produced a material culture similar to that found in Sicily and, later, elaborate tombs, temples, and a unique underground burial chamber, the Hypogeum, as it is called (2400–2000 B.C.). This was replaced by a culture of a southern Italian style. A Phoenician trading colony was established on the island before or during the 8th century B.C. The name of the island comes from a Semitic word (*meliṭa*) meaning "refuge," indicating a safe harbor. Diodorus (5.12.2–3; 1st cent B.C.), who himself came from nearby Sicily, says that the place was chosen as a stopping-off place to trade with the west (Spain).

The island came under control of Carthage, another Phoenician colony, in the 6th century B.C., when their homeland was taken by the Assyrians. In 218 B.C., the island came under Roman rule as part of the province of Sicily. Under the reorganization of the empire by Augustus, Malta was put under its own procurator. Although initially a prosperous island, it declined significantly as a result of frequent raids by pirates and the civil wars of the 1st century B.C. It had recovered by the mid-1st century A.D. and was (along with the neighboring island of Gozo [Gaulos]) granted municipal status (Lat *municipium*) in the early 2d century. Its citizens were granted Roman citizenship under Emperor Justinian (518–65). Even under Roman rule, however, the Maltese continued to maintain aspects of their Punic/Phoenician culture and language. In 870 Malta was taken by the Abbasid caliphs, but in 1090 it came under the control of a series of Christian crusader groups, culminating in the domination of the city by the Knights of St. John, who successfully defended the island against the Turkish forces of Suleiman I (1565). Its unique language in the present day is a mixture of N African Arabic and Silician Italian, and its culture reflects the rich diversity of its history.

Paul and his associates were shipwrecked here in the late autumn of A.D. 59 (Acts 27:27–28:11), having been driven helplessly for two weeks by the E–NE wind called "Euraquilo" ("Northeaster," NIV; Acts 27:14; its name is a Gk-Lat hybrid, Gk *euros* "east wind" + Lat *aquilo* "north wind"; today it would be called the *gregale*). The traditional site of the shipwreck is St. Paul's Bay, some 8 mi. NW of the modern capital of Valletta. In spite of recent attempts to suggest a location for the wreck on the island of Mijet or Melitene off the coast of Dalmatia (Acworth 1973, on the basis of the grammar of the narrative of Acts, historical data, and the name; Meinardus 1974, 1976, 1979, on the basis of ecclesiastical and local traditions), this is most likely the correct location (so Ramsay 1920; Finegan 1981; Kettenbach 1986; Bruce *Acts,* NICNT ^{2}1988; Hemer 1975; 1989; the latter has definitively answered the objections of Acworth), since it fits almost perfectly with the description given in Acts.

The local inhabitants are called "barbarians" (Gk *barbaroi*) by the author of Acts (28:2, 4), which indicates only that they did not speak Greek or Latin (hence the RSV's translation as "natives" and the NIV's "islanders"). Since their language was a Semitic tongue, Paul was probably able to converse with them by means of Aramaic. The leading local official, one Publius by name, is designated "first man" or "chief" (28:7, Gk *prōtos*), a title that is attested in inscriptions (*CIG* 14.60; *CIL* 10.7495). With reference to Paul's brush with the "viper" (Gk *echidna*; 28:3–4), it is worth noting that while there are no vipers or poisonous snakes on Malta today there is the *Coronella austriaca,* which resembles the viper. The native people's reaction to the snake's attaching itself to Paul—"No doubt this man is a murderer; for though he escaped from the sea, Justice [Gk *dikē*] has not allowed him to live" (28:4, NIV)—may refer to a hellenization of a Punic deity.

Some contemporary scholars have suggested that the travel narrative of Acts 27 and 28 is fictitious, patterned on the ancient novel. If that is so, it has been constructed with great skill, for it is, in fact, "one of our chief sources for ancient Greek language about seafaring" (Johnson 1987: 151) and is meticulously accurate in regard to its historical and geographical setting. As a result, few who are intimately familiar with the archaeological and historical data are inclined to doubt its essential historicity.

Among the more notable archaeological excavations of significance for the study of early Christianity are the remains of a large Roman villa at San Pawl Milqi, which has been identified with the home of Publius in which Paul and his associates would have been received; and a Punic sanctuary that fell into disuse toward the end of the 1st century and later was converted into a Christian church (Claridge 1976).

Bibliography

Acworth, A. 1973. Where Was St. Paul Shipwrecked? *JTS* 24: 190–93.

Bruce, F. F. 1977. *Paul: Apostle of the Heart Set Free.* Grand Rapids.

Claridge, A. 1976. Melita. Pp. 568–69 in *Princeton Encyclopedia of Classical Sites,* ed. R. Stillwell; W. L. MacDonald; and M. H. McAllister. Princeton.

Finegan, J. 1981. *Archaeology of the New Testament.* Boulder, CO.

Hemer, C. J. 1975. Euraquilo and Melita. *JTS* 26: 100–111.

———. 1989. *Historical Value of the Acts of the Apostles,* ed. C. Gempf. Tübingen.

Heutger, N. 1984. "Paulus auf Malta" im Licht der maltesischen Topographie. *BZ* 28: 86–88.

Kettenbach, G. 1986. *Das Logbuch des Lukas.* Frankfurt.

Johnson, S. E. 1987. *Paul the Apostle and His Cities.* Wilmington, DE.

Meinardus, O. F. A. 1974. Melita of Illyrica or Africana: An Examination of the Site of St. Paul's Shipwreck. *Ostkirchliche Studien* 23: 21–36.

———. 1976. St. Paul Shipwrecked in Dalmatia. *BA* 39: 145–47.

———. 1979. Dalmatian and Catalonian Traditions about St. Paul's Journeys. *Ekklesiastikos Pharos* 61: 221–30.

Ramsay, W. M. 1920. *St. Paul the Traveller and the Roman Citizen.* London.

Trump, D. H. 1972. *Malta: An Archaeological Guide.* London.

W. Ward Gasque

MAMDAI (PERSON) [Gk *Mamdai*]. An Israelite layperson and descendant of Bani who was forced to give up his foreign wife during Ezra's reform (1 Esdr 9:34).

MAMMON [Gk *mamōnas*]. Mammon (= Heb *mmwn,* Aram *mmwn*ʾ "wealth," "property") occurs in Matt 6:24 = Luke 16:13, "you cannot serve God and mammon" and in Luke 16:9, 11 in the phrase "unrighteous mammon." It is the normal word for "money," "wealth," in Mishnaic Hebrew, and is also attested in that sense several times in documents from Qumran (1QS 6:2; 1Q27 1,2,5 [probably], and CD 14:20), although the more usual word for "wealth" in Qumran literature is *hōn.* "Mammon" is not inherently evil, as may be seen from *m. Ber.* 9:5, commenting on Deut 6:5 (from the *Shema*): "[thou shalt love the LORD thy God . . .] with all thy strength" [that is], "with all thy wealth (mammon)." Its use then is broadly parallel to that of Qumran *hōn,* which often refers to the money or wealth which the prospective member is required to bring into the community when he joins it. In all gospel examples it occurs in words ascribed to Jesus. Here we may note: (a) Matt 6:24 and Luke 16:13c are verbally identical (not always the case in "Q" material); (b) Luke 16:1–13, apart from v 13, which acts as a call line for the whole passage, is material peculiar to Luke; yet within that material, in v 9, two well-known Semiticisms occur, namely, *ek* "from," meaning "by means of," and the "adjectival genitive": "[Make friends for yourselves] by means of the mammon of unrighteousness (= "unrighteous mammon," as given idiomatically in 16:11). All of this supports the view that Semitic material is to be found in the tradition preserved here by Luke. Because the Greek form of the word is *mamōnas,* it is on balance more probable that it reflects the Aram *mmwn*ʾ (pronounced "mammona") than the corresponding Hebrew.

Max Wilcox

MAMPSIS (M.R. 156048). A town established during the second wave of Nabatean settlement in the Negeb. It was originally founded as a station on a secondary road leading W from Petra and the Arabah. The site was completely rebuilt in the 2d century C.E. and became important with the establishment of Trajan's Via Nova, when it became the seat of a Roman garrison. The city was destroyed in one of the early pre-Islamic raids into the Negeb. The local economy was based on trade during the middle Nabatean period, on horse breeding in the late Nabatean period, and to some extent on agriculture in the Byzantine period.

A. Identification

Kurnub is ca. 40 km SE of Beer-sheba, at the junction of the N–S road extending from Jerusalem to Hebron to Aila, and the E–W road from Gaza to Beer-sheba to Aila. From the reference by Eusebius (*Onomast.* 8.8), and its position on the Medaba map, R. Hartman (1913) identified Kurnub as Mampsis, and this identification is now generally recognized.

B. History

Mampsis is mentioned first by Ptolemy (*Geog.* 5.16.10) in the form of "Maps," and, together with Elusa, is listed among the cities of Idumea W of the Jordan. Eusebius stated that "Mapsis" (emended by Jerome to Mampsis) was one day's march from Thamara, on the road from Hebron to Aila. In the 6th century, it was mentioned in the tax edict of Beer-sheba, and by Hierocles, who lists it among the cities of *Palaestina Tertia.* On the Medaba map, Mampsis is represented by an arched city gate with two towers, behind which rises a gabled building, apparently the cathedral. It was mentioned twice in a mid-6th century papyrus at Nessana.

C. History of Research

U. J. Seetzen marked "Karnupp" on his map in 1807 (Krause and Fleischer 1859: 403), describing the site as a fortress at the foot of a low hill with vineyards and gardens around it. Robinson (1841: 616, 622) in 1838 was satisfied to investigate it with binoculars from a nearby hill, mentioning churches or public buildings of another kind. The first plan of Mampsis was drawn by A. Musil in 1901 (1907:

25–28), who was the first to note a city wall with towers. He also identified two churches. His plan is invaluable, since the E part of the town has been destroyed by the construction of a British police station in that area during the 1930s. C. L. Woolley and T. E. Lawrence (1914–15: 121–28) drew another plan of the town, concentrating on the towers and the water system. They described the city wall as a mere fence to protect against incursion by the bedouin. The last and most detailed survey of Mampsis, until the recent excavations, was by P. L. O. Guy and G. E. Kirk in 1937 (Kirk 1938). They drew a more detailed plan of the town, and N of the city gate they discovered two large buildings covered by sand (Building VIII and apparently a fort), which had previously been undetected. They also located a "Hellenistic" cemetery about 1 km N of the town. In 1965–67 and 1970–72, large-scale excavations were conducted at Mampsis under the direction of A. Negev.

D. Excavations

1. Middle Nabatean period. The earliest ceramic, numismatic, and architectural remains are from the middle Nabatean period (ca. 25 B.C.E.–50/70 C.E.), when Mampsis was defended by a fort (Building XX) located on the high SE part of the site. A large portion of this building was covered by the British police station. It was rectangular with thick walls, inside of which was a courtyard surrounded by small rooms. The town also had strategically placed towers, one of which was 10 × 10 m and protected the descent into the wadi Nahal Mamshit to the spring. Near the N city wall was another large building (XIX) with a courtyard. A row of long storerooms flanked the courtyard on the SE side, and smaller rooms were on the NW side. The cemetery has also yielded ceramic and numismatic finds of the middle Nabatean period.

2. Late Nabatean period. Whether there was a break in occupation between the middle and late Nabatean periods at Mampsis is unclear, but the later period is represented by a different plan. A city wall, which underwent two phases of construction, encloses an area of ca. 10 acres. Four gates provide access to the town—two large gates and two postern gates. A natural gully forms the longest street, descending from the S northward, and separates the town into two unequal parts. The houses on the E are generally closely clustered with narrow streets; the W side of the town has generally wide streets.

Building I (ca. 35 × 20 m) in the W part of the town has been identified as a palace and is constructed to be essentially a self-contained fortress. It has a small entrance into a vestibule, which is protected by a guardroom. The entry provides access into an oblong courtyard (ca. 19 × 6 m), part of which was roofed. In the lower floor are an audience room along with an archive, servants' quarters, a "refrigerator" room, storerooms, and a niche, which appears to have been designed to cool water. The N end of the ground floor also has a residential section consisting of a bedroom, washroom, and two living rooms, which are separated from the rest of the floor through a vestibule.

To the SW of the palace stands Building II, which includes three elements—a tower (ca. 10 × 10 m), a courtyard, and buildings surrounding the courtyard. In the tower were three rooms in addition to the stairwell providing access to the upper stories. An unusual feature associated with this building was a series of steps which ascend to nothing—apparently a sort of loading dock to facilitate the loading and unloading of camels and donkeys.

Farther S (near the SW corner of the site) is Building XI (ca. 27 × 35 m), which appears to have been the house of a horse breeder. The N wing of the house had the living quarters, and in the SE corner were stables in which was a central area flanked by two aisles. Fodder was apparently stored in the central area, and the horses were tethered in the aisles. This house had a niche for cooling water, similar to that of Building I. There is evidence of a house shrine with a niche in the W wall to accommodate an image, and on the flat roof apparently libations were offered and incense was burned.

The E section of the town had what appears to have been a market area with several rows of rooms opening directly onto the street. Nearby was a large building (Building XII; ca. 40 × 40 m), with a vestibule giving access to a courtyard. A guardroom and "office" open into the vestibule. This building is decorated with Nabatean capitals and multicolored mosaics. One of its rooms may have been a vault with very thick walls; a hoard of some 10,500 Roman dinars and tetradrachmas was found in this area. An inner court is decorated with frescoes depicting mythological scenes, as well as floral and abstract designs. There are also quarters for the servants, workshops, a stable, and a lavatory with a flushing system.

To the N of Building XII was a roofed public reservoir (18 × 10 × 3 m). The reservoir had a settling tank which emptied into the rest of the reservoir. A conduit channeled water from the reservoir to a nearby Roman-Nabatean bath. The bath had a dressing room with stone benches along the walls. There were the traditional three baths—the cold bath (*frigidarium*), the tepid bath (*tepidarium*), and the hot bath (*cauldarium*).

Water was gathered by means of a series of dams built in the wadi to the S. The capacity was in excess of 10,000 m^3.

3. The Byzantine period. Several minor changes took place in the Byzantine period, although the changes were primarily on buildings from the Nabatean period—these consisted of different door placements and changes in building functions (e.g., Building XI with some modification became an apartment). The major changes were the construction of two churches.

The East Church (ca. 55 by 25 m) was built over the remains of a middle Nabatean fortress and several rooms of the marketplace. A symbolic burial of a piece of bone—apparently a martyr's bone—was discovered in the SE corner of the S room of the church. The church was decorated with mosaics of simple geometric designs and colored crosses.

The West Church (the Church of Nilus) is in the SW section of the town, next to the W wall. It was decorated with representations of birds and baskets of fruit against geometric backgrounds. A dedicatory inscription attributes the construction of the building to one named Nilus. The construction of the church is dated to the ca. 350–400 C.E.

4. Arab period. The only indications of an Arab presence at Mampsis are inscriptions engraved on the stones of the apse in the East Church. These contain verses from the Koran and various invocations. No coins or ceramics have been found from this period.

5. The Cemeteries. Three cemeteries have been found at Mampsis. A cemetery used by the Romans was located ca. 200 m NE of the site. Ten burials were excavated and consisted of monuments, either small stepped pyramids or heaps of boulders, over flat rocks covered with ash and incinerated bones. Two inscribed tombstones were found—one of a centurion who served in the Legio II Traiana Fortis and Legio III Cyrenaica, and another of a knight of Cohors I Augusta Thracum.

The Nabatean cemetery, 800–1,000 m N of town, consisted of pits 1–4 m deep in which the body was placed, either in a wooden coffin or directly on the soil. The body was then covered with several stones and then buried and the site marked with aboveground monuments.

Bibliography

Hartman, R. 1913. Materialien zur historischen Topographie der Palaestina Tertia. *ZDPV* 36: 110–13.

Kirk, G. E. 1938. Archaeological Exploration in the Southern Desert. *PEQ,* 211–35.

Krause, F., and Fleischer, H. L. 1859. *Kommentar zu Seetzen's Reisen.* Berlin.

Musil, A. 1907. *Arabia Petraea,* vol. 2. Vienna.

Negev, A. 1967. Oboda, Mampsis and the Provincia Arabia. *IEJ* 17: 46–55.

———. 1871. The Nabatean Necropolis of Mampsis (Kurnub). *IEJ* 21: 110–20.

———. 1974. The Churches of the Central Negev. An Archaeological Survey. *RB* 81: 397–420.

———. 1977. Kurnub. *EAEHL* 3: 722–34.

———. 1980. House and City Planning in the Ancient Negev and the Provincia Arabia. Pp. 3–31 in *Housing in Arid Lands,* ed. G. Golani. London.

———. 1988a. *The Architecture of Mampsis,* vol. 1. Qedem 26. Jerusalem.

———. 1988b. *The Architecture of Mampsis,* vol. 2. Qedem 27. Jerusalem.

Robinson, E. 1841. *Biblical Researches in Palestine,* vol. 2. London.

Woolley, C. L., and Lawrence, T. E. 1914–15. *The Wilderness of Zin.* PEFA 3. London.

Avraham Negev

MAMRE (PERSON/PLACE) [Heb *mamrēʾ*]. The name "Mamre" appears in several different contexts, all in the book of Genesis and all related to the patriarch Abram/Abraham. In only one passage (Gen 14:24) does the Bible unquestionably depict the name as belonging to a person, an Amorite who was one of Abram's allies in the battle against Chedorlaomer's coalition (on the problematic 14:13, see below). In a number of other passages the name is clearly portrayed as belonging to a place W of the cave of Machpelah, which Abraham bought from Ephron the Hittite (23:17; 25:9; 49:30; 50:13), a place identified with (a district of?) Hebron/Kiriath-arba (23:19; 35:27; cf. 23:2); see also HEBRON (PLACE); KIRIATH-ARBA; MACHPELAH. Two passages, in recounting the migrations of Abram/Abraham, note that the patriarch pitched his tent by "the oaks of Mamre" (Heb *ʾēlōnê mamrēʾ;* 13:18; 18:1), while a third passage (14:13) seems awkwardly to combine this toponymic reference to "the oaks of Mamre" with the personal name "Mamre the Amorite, 'brother' of Eshcol and of Aner." Thus, in two passages (14:13, 24) Mamre appears (along with Aner, Eshcol, and Abram) as one of four allies (covenant-partners) who joined forces on a specific occasion.

The nature of "Mamre" as a place name and as a personal name is inextricably tied to this reputed alliance, which seems closely linked to the place Hebron/Kiriath-arba. As his point of departure for treating the name "Mamre," Lipiński (1974: 48–51) turned to late, midrashic explications of the names Kiriath-arba and Hebron. There the former is understood as meaning "the City of Four [Quarters]," while the latter is understood as "Confederation" (cf. Heb *ḥeber*). Thus, for Lipiński, the four allies in Genesis 14 are actually literary personifications of the four clans of the area (and their respective sanctuaries), whose union gave rise to the municipality called Kiriath-arba or Hebron.

Lipiński reconstructed these four municipal clans/quarters/sanctuaries as follows. One, he suggested, was the Sanctuary of Eshcol (sacred to El and then Baal), site of the firstfruits of the vine (Heb *ʾeškôl,* "cluster [of grapes]") and the Dale of Eshcol. The second, associated with Aner, he believed to be a sanctuary of the goddess Anat, originally called **bêt ʿanāt rūm,* "temple of the Anat of the Above," the shortened form being **ʿanāt rūm* (indeed, *Anatram* is the goddess venerated by a Sidonian in Delos; Lipiński 1974: 53 and n. 2). Lipiński believed that vestiges of this shortened form are still retained not only in the Samaritan Pentateuch, which renders the name Aner as *ʿnrm,* but also in 1QapGen, in the metathesized form *ʿrnm.* But the MT tradition has intentionally deformed the sanctuary's name even further, reducing it simply to *ʿānēr.* For Lipiński, the third clan/quarter/sanctuary was the Cave of Machpelah, associated with the Hebrew patriarchs and matriarchs. The fourth (situated to the W of Machpelah) was associated with *ʾelōnê mamrēʾ,* "the oaks of Mamre." Many scholars, following the LXX and Syr, have long assumed that the original Heb text did not include the plural, but rather read simply *ʾēlōn* or *ʾēl-ōn,* "place of (the) god (Mamre)." Thus, Gen 14:13 (*whwʾ škn *bʾ ln mmrʾ hʾmry*) can easily be translated "he (i.e., Abram) was dwelling at the Amorite sanctuary of Mamre," and Mamre can be regarded as originally a divine name or epithet, "the (fatted) calf" (*mamrēʾ* being a toponymic form, **ma-mrīʾ,* derived from S Canaanite *mĕrīʾ* "fatted calf"; N Canaanite uses *ʿegel*). In Genesis 14, the author has personified the four districts of Hebron as four persons.

But within this same type of scheme, other linguistic explanations for the various sanctuaries are possible. For example, Eshcol could be translated "Place of Testiculus," derived from Heb *ʾešek* with a toponymic suffix (*− vowel + "l"*). Aner could readily be derived from Hitite *ani-ur* "ritual," an appropriate name for a sanctuary and its activities (the initial *ʿayin* phonetically effectuated by some form of Hess' Law; see Arbeitman 1981: 1011–15). The name *mamrēʾ,* however, is likely a Hebrew representation of Hittite *miu-mar,* "friendship, peaceful relations, alliance" (Arbeitman 1981: 959–1002; note also the traditional associations of "Hittites" with the Hebron area,

Genesis 23). Thus, Hit *miu-mar* is semantically identical to Hebron (Heb *ḥebr-ôn,* "place of the ally/confederate" (although the linguistic matters here may be further complicated by O'Connor's recognition of a Hurrian toponymic suffix *-mar/-mur,* such as in Tad-mor and Pal-myra [1988: 238 passim]). Again, the author of Genesis 14 later personified the name; but the original tradition behind 14:13 was that "(Abram) was dwelling at the Amorite sanctuary of Alliance."

Bibliography

Arbeitman, Y. L. 1981. The Hittite Is Thy Mother: An Anatolian Approach to Genesis 23. Pp. 889–1026 in *Bono Homini Donum: Essays in Historical Linguistics in Memory of J. Alexander Kerns,* ed. Y. Arbeitman and A. Bomhard. Amsterdam and Philadelphia.

———. 1988. Minōs, the Oaristēs of Great Zeus, *ha-, a-,* and *o-*Copulative, the Knossan Royal Titulary and the Hellenization of Crete. Pp. 411–62 in *A Linguistic Happening in Memory of Ben Schwartz,* ed. Y. Arbeitman. Louvain-la-Neuve.

Lipiński, E. 1974. ᶜAnaq-Kiryat ᵓArbaᶜ-Hebron et ses sanctuaires tribaux. *VT* 24: 41–55.

O'Connor, M. P. 1988. The Etymology of Tadmor and Palmyra. Pp. 235–54 in *A Linguistic Happening in Memory of Ben Schwartz,* ed. Y. Arbeitman. Louvain-la-Neuve.

Yoël L. Arbeitman

MANAEN (PERSON) [Gk *Manaēn*]. Mentioned in Acts 13:1 as one of the prophets and teachers in the church at Antioch who were present at the commissioning of Paul and Barnabas for missionary work. Manaen is called a *syntrophos* of Herod the Tetrarch, that is, Herod Antipas (4 B.C.E.–37 C.E.). *Syntrophos* means "nourished" or "brought up together with," "foster-brother," "companion (from one's youth), intimate friend" (BAGD, 793). The exact relation of Manaen to Antipas is not exactly known. It has been interpreted as "foster-brother," a boy of the same age as a royal prince who was brought up with him at court and retained the title in adulthood. It has been less restrictively interpreted as "courtier" or "intimate friend" (MM 615). In any case it was a very special relationship of honor. Manaen may have been Luke's source of information about Herod Antipas and his dynasty, information that is not found in the other Gospels. Manaen may have been related to an earlier Manaen, an Essene, who was a friend of Herod the Great, father of Herod Antipas, and predicted his ascension to the throne (Joseph. *Ant.* 15.373–79).

Bibliography

Deissmann, A. 1901. *Bible Studies.* Pp. 310–12. Trans. A. Grieve. Edinburgh.

JoAnn Ford Watson

MANAHATH (PERSON) [Heb *mānaḥat*]. A son of Shobal and grandson of "Seir, the Horite" (Gen 36:23; 1 Chr 1:40). This genealogy and its literary context suggest that Manahath was an Edomite tribe or clan of the 7th century B.C. See HORITES; SHOBAL. It is possible that elements of this Edomite clan at one time inhabited the Negeb. See MANAHATHITES.

The form of the name is difficult to explain. The vowel pattern of **mānaḥt* excludes a connection with Aram *nḥt* ("to descend") or with Heb *minḥâ* ("gift," also Phoen, Aram, and perhaps Ug). Possibly, **Mānaḥt* can be regarded as a "feminine" formation belonging to (Heb) *mānôaḥ,* "rest, resting place," which is also the name of Samson's father (1 Sam 13:2, etc.), further attested on a 7th-century B.C. Judean seal (Herr 1978: 130, no. 110). Because *Mānôaḥ* is derived from **Manāḥ, *Manāḥt* would lead to **Manaḥt,* hence *Mānaḥat* (the reduction of long vowels in double-closed syllables is a common Semitic feature).

Bibliography

Herr, L. G. 1978. *The Scripts of Ancient Northwest Semitic Seals.* Missoula, MT.

Ernst Axel Knauf

MANAHATH (PLACE) [Heb *mānaḥat*]. A place to which Benjaminite families from Geba, of the clan of Ehud, were "exiled" (1 Chr 8:6). Because it was a fellow Benjaminite, Gera (1 Chr 8:3), who "exiled" them (1 Chr 8:7, reading *hglm* as a verbal form, not as a PN "Heglam" [so RSV]), this "exile" may be understood within the context of Benjaminite colonization of the mountains of Gilead before the monarchy. Because the Benjaminite clan of Ehud (whose "father," incidentally, was Gera, Judg 3:15) settled in the vicinity of the modern town of ᶜAjlûn (Knauf fc.), Manahath should be sought in its environs; the place can be identified with Maḥnah (< **Maḥnat,* an easy corruption of **Manaḥt*), 7 km N of ᶜAjlûn (M.R. 221193). The area was occupied in the early Iron Age (Khirbet el-Hêdamûs at ᶜAin Maḥnah, Mittmann 1970: 68f.).

Manahath, meaning "resting place," is a genuine toponym that need not be connected with the Seirite clan or the tribe of Manahath, which belongs to an area where Benjaminites are never known to have settled. See MANAHATH (PERSON).

The place Manahath has previously been identified with the fortress *Manḫatu* (EA 292: 30; Moran 1987: 521), constructed in the Amarna period to defend the territory of Gezer against "the hostility from the mountains" (Schmitt 1980: 91–92). On both philological and historical grounds, however, this identification is not tenable (Niemann 1985: 156–58). Furthermore, Amarna-Akkadian *Manḫatu* may represent a Canaanite **manᶜat* ("Defense," a name that would suit a fortress well). (For ⟨ḫ⟩ representing Canaanite *ᶜayin* in Amarna-Akkadian, cf., e.g., *Ḫenianabi* EA 256: 26, which is an *ᶜAin ᶜAnab* "Spring of Grapes.") Not incidentally, there is a Sitt Manâᶜ and a Khirbet Mannâᶜ in the region where *Manḫatu* must be located (Schmitt 1980: 91).

Bibliography

Knauf, E. A. fc. Eglon and Ophra: Two Toponymic Notes on the Book of Judges. *JSOT.*

Mittmann, S. 1970. *Beiträge zur Siedlungs- und Territorialgeschichte des nördlichen Ostjordanlandes.* ADPV. Wiesbaden.

Moran, W. L. 1987. *Les Lettres d'el-Amarna.* LAPO. Paris.

Niemann, H. M. 1985. *Die Daniten.* FRLANT 135. Göttingen.

Schmitt, G. 1980. Gat, Gittaim und Gitta. Pp. 77–138 in *Drei Studien zur Archäologie und Topographie Altisraels*, ed. G. Schmitt and R. Cohen. BTAVO B 44. Wiesbaden.

ERNST AXEL KNAUF

MANAHATHITES [Heb *mānaḥtî*]. A clan of the Calebites (1 Chr 2:54), half of which was derived from SHOBAL and was called MENUHOTH (1 Chr 2:52). The other half of this clan, said to inhabit ZORAH, is also accounted among the sons of Shobal in 1 Chr 2:53, but among the descendants of Salma in 1 Chr 2:54.

It is impossible not to identify the Manahathites, sons of Shobal here in 1 Chronicles 2, with the Edomite (Horite) tribe or clan of Manahath, son of Shobal, mentioned in Gen 36:23; 1 Chr 1:40. See MANAHATH (PERSON). There are two historical situations that might have accommodated the appearance of an Edomite clan among the Calebites (i.e., the inhabitants of the Negeb): the premonarchic and the postexilic periods. In the premonarchic period, numerous tribes and/or clans lived on both sides of Wadi ʿArabah who later joined either Judah, or Edom, or both. See LOTAN. Because the ranked tribal system attested by Genesis 36 is, however, unlikely to have emerged in the LB or early Iron Age, a postexilic date for I Chr 2:52–54 is preferable. In this case, the presence of Shobalites at Kiriath-jearim (1 Chr 2:52) and Manahathites at Zora and Eshtaol (1 Chr 2:53–54) attests Idumean penetration into Judea proper, which is not unlikely given the fact that Judeans also settled, or Judean landlords also owned, territory within Idumea (cf. Neh 11:25–30). Judean presence within Idumea is evidenced by the Arad and Beer-sheba ostraca (de Geus 1980: 73; Ephʿal 1982: 200 n. 679).

A different view was advanced by W. Rudolph (*Chronicles* HAT, 27). He also dates 1 Chr 2:18–19, 50–55 to the postexilic period, but he assumed that Calebites left the Negeb under Idumean pressure and settled further N within Judea. There are, however, no indisputable references to the Calebites after the reign of David. After the Exile, the attribution of Idumean clans to the southern, albeit extinct and legendary, tribe of Caleb may have served to legitimize their abode in Judea.

Bibliography

Ephʿal, I. 1982. *The Ancient Arabs.* Jerusalem.
Geus, H. J. de. 1980. Idumaea. *JEOL* 26: 53–74.

ERNST AXEL KNAUF

MANASSEH (PERSON) [Heb *mĕnaššeh*]. Var. MANASSEAS. **1.** Son of Joseph, son of Jacob and, as such, the eponymous ancestor of one of the Israelite tribes. See MANASSEH (PLACE).

2. See MANASSEH, KING OF JUDAH.

3. Identified as a son of both Pahath-moab and Hashum, Manasseh is listed among the Israelites who dismissed the foreign wives with whom they were living in defiance of the law (Ezra 10:30, 33). In the parallel passage in 1 Esdr 9:31, he is called Manasseas (Gk *Manassēas*).

4. Identified as a son of both Hashum and Addi, this Manasseh is also listed among the Israelites who dismissed the foreign wives with whom they were living in defiance of the Law (1 Esdr 9:33).

5. The husband of Judith, Manasseh is described as having died from a sunstroke while overseeing a barley harvest (Jdt 8:2–3). A fictional character, the description of Manasseh's death may have been inspired by the story of the Shunamite woman's son (cf. 2 Kgs 4:18ff.; Enslin 1972: 110), but the similarities between the two stories are superficial at best (Craven 1983: 85 n. 41).

Bibliography

Craven, T. 1983. *Artistry and Faith in the Book of Judith.* SBLDS 70. Chico, CA.
Enslin, M. 1972. *The Book of Judith.* Leiden.

FREDERICK W. SCHMIDT

MANASSEH (PLACE) [Heb *mĕnaššeh*]. MANASSITE. Name of Israelite tribe in the hills of central Palestine; during the early monarchy it extended to include the inhabitants of central Transjordan (half-tribe of Manasseh).

A. Manasseh, Son of Joseph, Son of Jacob

The eponym of the tribe of Manasseh was the eldest son of Joseph and Asenath, the daughter of Potiphera the priest of On (Gen 46:20). *Mĕnaššeh* is a regular Hebrew personal name of a common type. It is a participle of the root *nšh* "he who makes forget," namely, the death of a prior child (cf. a popular name like Menahem). There is no doubt that this name was originally a personal name. It was probably the name of the ancestor of a clan, unlike such names as Judah or Ephraim, which originally had a geographical meaning.

B. The Place of Manasseh in the System of Twelve Tribes

There is not one system of twelve tribes in the OT, but two (see GAD). System A is mainly a list of patronyms and includes the tribes of Levi and Joseph. The second system, B, is geographical. It omits Levi, the priestly tribe without a territory, while Joseph is split up into Ephraim and Manasseh. Although it is repeatedly stated that Manasseh was Joseph's eldest son, the order is often reversed: Ephraim, then Manasseh. In some instances the biblical text as it now stands still shows "scars" indicating that in a former stage the text had the original order—Manasseh, then Ephraim—as is the case with Joshua 16 and 17 (de Geus 1976: 79–80). Indeed, it was apparently so well known that Manasseh was traditionally the eldest son/tribe that an explanation was needed to clarify the later situation, with Ephraim as the dominant tribe in the center of the country (Gen 48:13–14).

Two recent views with regard to the tribe of Manasseh are important. Until two decades ago it was generally assumed that the name "house of Joseph" was older than the separate tribes Ephraim and Manasseh. While expanding in the central hills after the period of settlement, Joseph split up into two separate tribes. Therefore system A was considered older than system B. Many historians, however, now accept the opinion that it was the other way around. The expression "house of Joseph" appears only at the beginning of the divided monarchy and denotes the core of the kingdom of Israel. In most cases "house of Joseph" has a polemic sound against "Judah" (de Geus 1976: 70–96; Lemche 1985: 284).

The second modern development is that Machir is no longer thought to be just another smaller splinter group of Joseph, but instead the name of an older tribal group. Neither was Machir simply an older name for Manasseh, as was often said in view of Judg 5:14. Machir was probably a small Israelite tribe that dwelled around Dothan during the LB Age and that later moved to Transjordan (de Geus 1976: 72). Only the rise of the Israelite state resolved the conflicts about land and power between the different Manassite clans and with the neighboring tribes.

C. Settlement

The process of sedentarization and reurbanization that is commonly known as the "settlement of the Israelite tribes" started at the beginning of the 12th century B.C.E. Archaeologically speaking this is the Iron Age I. It is significant that Finkelstein found that 70 percent of all Iron I sites in Palestine are located N of the modern town of Ramallah and S of the Jezreel valley. This is the territory of the tribes of Ephraim and Manasseh (*AIS*, 65–91, 352–56). In absolute numbers, 120 sites were located in Ephraim and 100 in Manasseh, by contrast to, for instance, only 12 for Judah. After a study of all of the newer material that has been published on early Iron Age sites in Transjordan, Finkelstein (*AIS*, 114–17) comes to the conclusion that a parallel process of sedentarization occurred there, rather than a migration with subsequent settlement from the W, as was assumed by Mittmann.

There is a remarkable difference between the settlement in Ephraim and that in Manasseh. The new Iron I sites in Ephraim are found far from the sparse LB towns. But in the land of Manasseh the Israelites settled among a population that had been sedentary for a long time. The tribal territory does not have the steep and forested slopes of Mount Ephraim. It consists of broad valleys and gentle slopes. The soils are fertile and easy to work. In the territory of Manasseh there were no less than 22 LB Age towns (cf. Ephraim, 5; Judah, 5). Some of these LB Age cities certainly continued well into the Iron Age and the Israelite period. A good example of this is the town of Shechem. The Bible also is very clear about the continuing Canaanite presence in the land of Manasseh (Judg 1:27; *AIS*, 90–91).

The oldest Iron Age I settlements of the country are found in the territory of Manasseh. Here the land was suitable for pastoralists who also raised some grain crops. These pastoralists had roamed around in the area already for some centuries (de Geus 1976: 164–71). What started in Manasseh—and probably parallel to it also in Transjordan—spread out from this nucleus: first to the S and the N, later also to the W.

D. History

Apart from the fertility of the land, four factors determined the history of the tribe of Manasseh: (1) the presence of so many Canaanite towns inside its territory; (2) the competition with the brother-tribe Ephraim; (3) the fact that all three successive capitals of the kingdom of Israel were situated inside its boundaries; and (4) the fact that the easiest passage to Transjordan and to the King's Highway is through the Wadi Farᶜah and along the Wadi Zerqa (Jabbok River).

Although the earliest Israelite population of Manasseh was rural, the tribal territory remained under the dominance of a number of towns in its heartland that only gradually became Israelite. Shechem, for instance, was already of importance to the oldest Israelites in the Bronze Age, but in the period of the Judges it still had a predominantly non-Israelite population (Judges 9). Like Tirzah and Hepher, Shechem was ultimately included in the tribal genealogy (Num 26:28–34; Josh 17:2–3). Other former Canaanite towns like Ibleam, Dothan, Beth-shan, Taanach, and Megiddo were more peripheral. Gradually all of these towns became Israelite. The example of Tappuah shows how slowly this development went. Tappuah, on the southern border of Manasseh, was a LB Canaanite town. Its surrounding lands became Manassite, but the town itself was Ephraimite. That is to say, the ruling family changed into an Ephraimite one at a time that the Ephraimites were already powerful enough to cause this change.

The OT shows several examples of an ancient rivalry against the rising tribe of Ephraim. The changed order, placing the elder brother behind the younger, has already been mentioned. Judges 6–8 tell us the story of Gideon's war against the Midianites. Gideon was a Manassite hero and judge. His allies, besides Manasseh, were Asher, Zebulun, Naphtali, and in a passive way the Israelite areas in Transjordan. The Ephraimites were purposely left out (Judg 8:1). The conflict between Gilead and Ephraim that is known as the *šibbōlet* incident (Judg 12:1–6) became very famous. This story also testifies to a linguistic distinction between the Gileadites from Transjordan and the Ephraimites. In the time of the monarchy this competition ended in favor of the Ephraimites. Not only was Joshua an Ephraimite, but also Jeroboam, the first king of the northern kingdom. In 1 Kgs 4:8 Solomon's first district is simply called the "mountain of Ephraim," although it is clear that Manasseh is meant.

The capitals Shechem, Tirzah, and Samaria are all situated inside Manasseh. During the dynasty of the Omrides Jezreel served as their private residency. Officially Jezreel belonged to Issachar. If Omri belonged to the same clan as Baasha, he was also an Issacharite. Geographically Jezreel belongs to Manasseh, so it is possible that the tribe of Issachar was a splinter group of Manasseh. This tribe is now missing in stories where it could hardly be missed, as in Judges 6–8, where the later territory of Issachar was the scene of the conflict. In 2 Sam 2:8–9 Jezreel stands for both Issachar and (West) Manasseh. In addition there are several Manassite enclaves inside Issachar, all former Canaanite towns (Josh 17:11; Judg 1:27).

It is evident that the last redactions of the traditions about the Israelite tribes in Transjordan were made when there was no longer an important Israelite population or military presence there. One feels in the texts the uncertainty of exactly how the situation had been (Wüst 1975: 59). It is clear that "half-tribe of Manasseh" is an artificial construction. The older traditions peak of Gilead and Machir. Both received a place in the Manassite genealogy of Numbers 26. In later traditions all Cisjordanian clans were regarded as the legal sons of Manasseh's first wife but the Transjordanian clans as sons of his Aramean concubine. It seems that all of these territories were lost after Tiglath-pileser III (but see GAD; perhaps Jerusalem kept in contact with former Israelite groups in Transjordan, which remained known in Judah as "Gad").

One should bear in mind that in the time of the early monarchy Transjordan was of great strategic importance. Transjordanian Israelites played a key role in many stories about Saul and his son Ish-bosheth. David also fell back on Gilead when his throne was threatened.

E. Territory

The territory of Manasseh, W of the Jordan River, consisted first of all of the northern part of the central Palestinian hills. The Jordan River was apparently the eastern border. The northern border should have been the valley of Jezreel. But as we have seen, here we find a number of Manassite enclaves in what became the territory of Issachar. The southern border seems to have been Wadi Qanah. Joshua 17 tells us that the western border was the sea. In reality it took a long time before Manassite/Israelite influence extended into the coastal plain. This remained at first firmly in the hands of Canaanites and Philistines. A Manassite town on the coast was Dor, while in the plain was situated "the land of Hepher" (if its identification with el-Ifshar is correct). Only at one place do we find a detailed border description: in the area of Tappuah. This city on the northern side of Wadi Qanah was Ephraimite. The text as it stands now, however, shows many "scars." The remark about Tappuah is undoubtedly a remnant of an older, more detailed border description. And it proves that such border descriptions did indeed exist and were old. Very probably they had once had an official function (de Geus 1976: 74–77). We do not have a town list of the tribe of Manasseh.

On the other hand, seven of the clans known from the genealogy of Numbers 26 appear as geographical districts in the Samaria ostraca. These ostraca date from the beginning of the 8th century B.C.E. They prove that these clan names at that time still functioned as names of districts. The seven are Shemida, Abiezer, Helek, Asriel, Shechem, Hoglah, and Noah. They are all situated around Samaria in central Manasseh.

Israelite settlement in Transjordan had two centers: a southern one and a northern one. The borders of the latter are roughly: to the N, the Yarmuk River; to the W, the Jordan River; to the S, the Jabbok River. It is as yet impossible to give a detailed description of the eastern border, which flanked the kingdom of Ammon. The list of Solomonic districts includes two districts in the half-tribe of Manasseh. A northern one on the plain of Irbid, S of the Yarmuk River, had its center at Ramoth-gilead (Tell er-Ramit). The other one was in the hills of the ʿAjlûn, its center being Mahanaim. This city is commonly identified with Tell Hajjaj, which should mean that the center of this district was situated in an enclave S of the Jabbok River. A very recent proposal is the identification of Mahanaim with Tell ed-Dhahab el-Gharbi, just N of the river.

Bibliography

Auld, A. G. 1975. Judges 1 and History: A Reconsideration. *VT* 25: 261–85.

Coote, R. B., and Whitelam, K. W. 1987. *The Emergence of Early Israel in Historical Perspective.* SWBA 4. Sheffield.

Coughenour, R. A. 1989. A Search for Mahanaim. *BASOR* 273: 57–66.

Demsky, A. 1982. The Genealogies of Manasseh and the Location of the Territory of Milcah, Daughter of Zelophehad. *EI* 16: 70–76.

Garsiel, M., and Finkelstein, I. 1978. The Westward Expansion of Joseph in the Light of the ʿIzbet Ṣarṭah Excavations. *TA* 5: 192–98.

Geus, C. H. J. de. 1976. *The Tribes of Israel.* Assen and Amsterdam.

———. 1983. Agrarian Communities in Biblical Times: 12th to 10th Centuries B.C.E. *Recueils de la Société Jean Bodin* 41: 207–38.

———. 1988. The New City in Ancient Israel. Two Questions concerning the Reurbanisation of ʾEreṣ Yiśraʾel in the Tenth Century B.C.E. Pp. 105–15 in *"Wünschet Jerusalem Frieden": IOSOT Congress 1986,* ed. M. Augustin and K. D. Schunck. BEATAAJ 13. Frankfurt.

Gottwald, N. K. 1979. *The Tribes of Yahweh.* Maryknoll, NY.

Kingsburg, E. C. 1967. He Set Ephraim before Manasseh. *HUCA* 38: 129–36.

Lemaire, A. 1981. Galaad et Makîr: Rémarques sur la tribu de Manassé à l'est du Jourdain. *VT* 31: 39–61.

Lemche, N. P. 1985. *Early Israel.* VTSup 37. Leiden.

Lindars, B. 1979. The Israelite Tribes in Judges. Pp. 95–112 in *Studies in the Historical Books of the Old Testament,* ed. J. A. Emerton. VTSup 30. Leiden.

Ottosson, M. 1969. *Gilead: Tradition and History.* ConBOT 3. Lund.

Rainey, A. F. 1988. Toward a Precise Date for the Samaria Ostraca. *BASOR* 272: 69–75.

Weippert, H. 1973. Das geographische System der Stämme Israels. *VT* 23: 76–89.

Weippert, M. 1971. *The Settlement of the Israelite Tribes in Palestine.* London.

Wüst, M. 1975. *Untersuchungen zu den siedlungsgeographischen Texten des Alten Testaments.* Vol. 1: *Ostjordanland.* BTAVO B/9. Wiesbaden.

Zobel, H. J. 1965. *Stammesspruch und Geschichte.* BZAW 95. Berlin.

C. H. J. DE GEUS

MANASSEH, KING OF JUDAH.

Manasseh, son of Hezekiah, was king of Judah ca. 687–642 B.C.E. According to 2 Kgs 21:1 and 2 Chr 33:1, Manasseh came to the throne at the age of 12 and ruled for 55 years. His mother was Hephzibah. A 55-year reign is difficult to reconcile with the chronologies of preceding and following kings and is perhaps exaggerated. Given Manasseh's youth at his accession, however, and especially in view of Hezekiah's illness, a ten-year coregency at the end of his father's reign is sometimes proposed as a way of reconciling the conflicting information (see, however, the new chronology proposed by Hayes and Hooker [1988: 71–83]).

A. Sources

The primary account of Manasseh's reign is given by the Deuteronomist in 2 Kgs 21:1–18, who claims that Manasseh's apostasy led Judah to ruin. The Chronicler follows suit and presents much the same picture for the earlier part of Manasseh's reign (2 Chr 33:1–10). But he adds in 2 Chr 33:11–17 an account of an invasion of Judah by

Assyrian forces, of the capture of Manasseh and his removal to Babylon (*sic!*), of Manasseh's repentance and return to Jerusalem, and of building and military activity in Judah, as well as of a religious reform to restore the worship of Yahweh. Not even a hint of these matters is given in the Deuteronomist's account, however, and scholars are divided on whether the Chronicler's added material is based on historical information.

Neither the Deuteronomist nor the Chronicler discusses Manasseh's reign in relation to the events of the time, so scholars are left with the problematic task of setting Manasseh's activities in a larger context. It is clear that Manasseh ruled when Assyrian power was unmatched in the Near East, but to what extent Manasseh's religious, building, and military activities can be correlated with Judah's situation under Assyria is a matter of conjecture.

The annals of Esarhaddon mention Manasseh among a group of twenty-two western kings who were compelled "under terrible difficulties" to transport building material to Nineveh for a project of the Assyrian king (*ANET,* 291). Manasseh is also named in an almost identical list in Ashurbanipal's account of rulers (only the "C" edition of the annals gives the full list of names) who presented gifts to him and then helped him conquer Egypt in 668/667 B.C.E. (*ANET,* 294). The striking similarity between Esarhaddon's vassal treaties (Wiseman 1958) and language in Deuteronomy, especially chap. 28, has led some scholars to conclude that the curses in that chapter were adapted from the maledictions in the treaties (Frankena 1965; Weinfeld 1965). Frankena has speculated that Manasseh, after swearing allegiance to the Assyrian king (in his view Manasseh was probably compelled to take a loyalty oath to support the succession of the crown prince Ashurbanipal), brought a copy of the vassal treaty back to Jerusalem, where it influenced the formulation of Deuteronomy (1965: 150). However one views the significance of the vassal treaties for the study of Manasseh, the Assyrian annals always refer to the Judean king as a loyal vassal.

B. Assessments of Manasseh

The Deuteronomist who gives us the account of Manasseh's reign in 2 Kgs 21:1–18 seeks to present the Judean king as a religious apostate. At the beginning of the account, the Deuteronomist states that Manasseh "did what was evil in the sight of Yahweh" (v 2), following the "abominable" practices (*tôʿăbōt*) of the nations who had lived in the land before the Israelites (v 3; cf. v 11). There follows a catalog of Manasseh's "sins," including the following: he rebuilt the shrines (*bāmôt*) that Hezekiah had destroyed; he set up altars for Baal and made a sacred pole, as Ahab had done; he worshipped all the host of heaven and built altars (for them?) in the temple; he built altars for all the host of heaven in the two courts of the temple; he caused his son to pass through the fire (child sacrifice?); he practiced soothsaying and divination, and consulted ghosts and spirits; he placed the image of Asherah in the temple; and he shed much innocent blood in Jerusalem. In sum, Manasseh committed great wickedness and in the process led Judah to sin.

Scholars have tended to accept uncritically the Deuteronomist's extremely negative evaluation of Manasseh, faulting the king for a "decline of traditional, national religion" (Greenberg, *WHJP* 4/2: 118), which brought with it "contempt for Yahweh's law and new incidents of violence and injustice" (*BHI,* 313). Kaufmann referred to Manasseh's reign as "the heyday of Judean idolatry" (*KRI,* 141). The tendency has been to see Manasseh as a bad king because the Deuteronomist presented him in that light.

Increasingly, however, the artificiality and tendentiousness of the Deuteronomist's account is recognized, and reassessments are appearing. Ahlström, for example, avers that "Manasseh cannot be called an 'apostate' " and insists that he must be considered a traditionalist who "came into conflict with those groups still advocating the religious ideas and the radical, utopian innovations of his 'unorthodox' father" (1982: 80). Such claims, obviously, proceed from a view of the religion of Judah radically different from the standard treatments.

In addition, the study of comparative materials has demonstrated that the pattern of alternating bad and good reigns before and after Manasseh—Ahaz (bad); Hezekiah (good); Manasseh and Amon (bad); Josiah (good)—follows a literary convention in ANE historiography which renders the neatness of the schema rather suspect from a strictly historical point of view (Evans 1983: 121–25). The Deuteronomist's contrasting depiction of Manasseh and Hezekiah, for example, is greatly overdrawn. Political and social conditions during the final years of Hezekiah's reign, following Judah's capitulation to Assyria in 701 B.C.E., continued into the period of Manasseh (Evans 1980: 166–67; cf., however, Soggin 1984: 238) and left the king with little room to maneuver. Nelson's study of Manasseh's "severely limited" options, at least before the 650s, leads to the conclusion, "There is no reason to condemn Manasseh for doing what he had to do" (1983: 181).

C. Manasseh and Assyria

The kingdom Manasseh inherited from Hezekiah was a small vassal state within the Assyrian imperial system. Assyrian records claim that when Sennacherib conquered Judah in 701 B.C.E. the territory beyond the immediate environs of Jerusalem was put under the control of Assyria's loyal Philistine kings in Ashdod, Ekron, and Gaza. Sometime during Manasseh's reign the territory was returned to Judah, presumably under conditions favorable to the Assyrians.

It has been commonplace to attribute many of Manasseh's religious practices to the powerful influence of the Assyrians over Judah in the early part of the 7th century. Hayes, for example, regards the biblical references to the worship of astral deities ("the host of heaven") during this time as an indication that "the imposition and encouragement of Assyrian religion was probably used as an important feature of Assyrian control" (*HAIJ,* 372). This view goes back to Oestreicher (1923) and has been adopted by many scholars who interpret the changing patterns of Judean religion from Ahaz to Josiah in close relationship to Judah's political stances vis-à-vis Assyria. Since the assumption was that Assyria imposed the worship of Assyrian gods on subject peoples, it followed that the non-Yahwistic religious practices during the reigns of Ahaz and Manasseh were due to the religious impositions of their imperial masters. The same line of reasoning led scholars to interpret the Yahwistic reforms of Hezekiah and Josiah as essentially political in nature, the goal being to assert political independence by eliminating Assyrian religious practices, which their predecessors had been obliged to institute.

On the basis of a thorough examination of the Assyrian evidence, McKay (1973) and Cogan (1974) have concluded that the Assyrians did not impose on vassal states the obligation to worship Assyrian gods (but see now Spieckermann 1982: 307–72). Vassal states, as distinct from provincial territories, were spared Assyrian interference in religious affairs, even though tribute payments and loyalty oaths were required to demonstrate allegiance to the Assyrian overlord. Furthermore, McKay and Cogan have shown that the non-Yahwistic religious practices in Judah during Assyrian domination display the characteristics of "popular Palestinian paganism" (McKay 1973: 67); they were "outgrowths of local traditions, popularly rooted" rather than coerced importations from Assyria (Cogan 1974: 86). This is not to claim, however, that there was no "Assyrianization" of Judah's religion. Both McKay (1973: 67–73) and Cogan (1974: 88–96) acknowledge a process of acculturation under the Assyrians which resulted in the popular resurgence and/or royal sponsorship of foreign cults under Ahaz and Manasseh (Cogan 1974: 88–96).

Beyond Manasseh's efforts to demonstrate his loyalty to Assyria, it is reasonable to assume that his religious policies were designed to win support within Judah by restoring the cultic practices which Hezekiah had taken away from the people. The connection between Hezekiah's reform and the subsequent national humiliation by the Assyrians would not have been lost on discerning Judeans. They would have welcomed Manasseh's reversal of Hezekiah's policies—policies which had cost Judah dearly in land and treasure. But others would have viewed matters differently. The Yahwistic priests in Jerusalem undoubtedly would have opposed Manasseh because of his sponsorship of non-Yahwistic practices. The levitical priests who served the local shrines may have opposed him also, for the same reason (Nielsen 1967: 105–6).

The circumstances prompting Hezekiah's reform, followed by Manasseh's reversal of the reform and then Josiah's restoration of many of the same reform measures, probably reflects a domestic conflict within Judah between rival social groups (Nielsen 1967: 104–6; Oded, *IJH*, 453–54). In 2 Kgs 21:16 it is mentioned that Manasseh shed much "innocent blood" in Jerusalem. Is this a reference to political murders? Some have suggested that it is, and in particular that it alludes to Manasseh's violent suppression of the prophets, whose voices were silent during his long reign. The legend of the martyrdom of Isaiah has inspired this view. Others maintain, however, that the absence of prophecy during Manasseh's reign was "in part because there were no major crises nor any real options in foreign policy for the prophets to preach about" (Nelson 1983: 181; cf. Nielsen 1967: 104–5).

D. 2 Chr 33:11–17

Scholars are sharply divided on whether the information supplied by the Chronicler in 2 Chr 33:11–17 is historically reliable. This account claims that Manasseh was taken as a bound captive to Babylon by the Assyrian forces, that he repented of his sins while there, and that he returned to Jerusalem and instituted a Yahwistic religious reform. (The apocryphal Prayer of Manasseh is a late attempt to construct the prayer of repentance to which 2 Chr 33:12–13 alludes. See MANASSEH, PRAYER OF.) The point at issue is which parts of the account, if any, can be given credence.

On the one hand, some claim that the crafting of the account was theologically motivated and is lacking in historical credibility. It has been referred to as an "edifying story" created by the biblical narrator to answer the perplexing question of why Yahweh would have allowed this most wicked king of all to rule longer than any other Davidic king (Soggin 1984: 239; cf. Myers *2 Chronicles* AB, 199). Ackroyd has stated that the Chronicler's portrayal of Manasseh was designed to speak theologically to the Judean exiles—"just as such a wicked king was taken captive, repented, and was restored, so the same was to happen to Judah" (Ackroyd, *1–2 Chronicles* TB, 198). Furthermore, the skepticism about Manasseh's repentance and reform has seemed justified in light of the reform measures undertaken by Josiah. Bright, for example, has dismissed the likelihood of a reform by Manasseh with the observation, "it is clear from II Kings, ch. 23, that the abuses for which he was responsible continued till Josiah removed them" (*BHI*, 313 n. 7; cf. *HAIJ*, 376).

On the other hand, the Chronicler's special material on Manasseh does not make major claims for the king's reforms. His actions were limited to the removal of a few objects from the temple, a few altars from within the city, the restoration of the altar of Yahweh in the temple, and the use of the restored altar for sacrificial functions. Thus the reform centered on the temple and little, if any, of it extended beyond Jerusalem. The Chronicler does claim that Manasseh commanded Judah to serve Yahweh, but it is unlikely that the king's command resulted in significant changes in the religious practices outside Jerusalem, despite the Chronicler's claim that the people thereafter sacrificed only to Yahweh.

Ahlström believes that the Chronicler's report "cannot be a complete invention," and he seeks to establish a plausible connection between Manasseh's cultic reorganization, on the one hand, and the king's building activities and changes in the defense system (2 Chr 33:14), on the other (1982: 76–81). According to Ahlström, such a connection can be found when one recognizes "the complex idea of religion as a national, territorial phenomenon" (1982: 77). He maintains that the restoration of the territory which had earlier been given by Sennacherib to loyal Philistine rulers called for the extension of Manasseh's administration "in order to re-incorporate these cities territorially and religiously into the kingdom of Judah" (1982: 78).

The Chronicler claims that Manasseh built an outer wall for Jerusalem and placed military commanders in the fortified cities of Judah (2 Chr 33:14) as indications of the king's loyalty to Assyria. According to some, Manasseh was allowed to strengthen his kingdom in order that Judah could serve as an effective buffer between Assyria and Egypt (Nielsen 1967: 104; cf. Nelson 1983: 181). The possibility that fortifications at Tell el-Ḥesi and Arad were also parts of Manasseh's defense system against Egypt has been hinted at by Ahlström (1982: 79).

Still another view is that Manasseh's building and military activities may be seen as a rebellion against Assyria, a possibility which would explain Manasseh's capture by Assyrian commanders and removal to Babylon (2 Chr 33:11). The most likely occasion for Manasseh's revolt, according to most scholars, would have been the civil war led by Shamash-shum-ukin against Ashurbanipal (*BHI*, 311, 341; Ehrlich 1965; Oded, *IJH*, 455–56; Reviv, *WHJP* 4/1: 200–201). Though centered in Babylon, the uprising stirred revolts elsewhere, and Manasseh could have been among those involved. If such a revolt occurred, however, it is difficult to fathom why the Deuteronomist would have suppressed this information, especially since Manasseh's capture could have been interpreted as divine punishment in a manner consistent with the Deuteronomist's ideology (Nielsen 1967: 104).

Another possible context for a revolt by Manasseh has been suggested on the basis of a fragmentary inscription of Esarhaddon. The text reports reprisals against Phoenician and Philistine cities which had apparently joined an anti-Assyrian conspiracy with the Egyptian king Tarqu (Tarhaqa). The inscription refers to twenty-two western kings who were subdued during Esarhaddon's campaign to Egypt (671 B.C.E.), but unfortunately the tablet is broken where the names of the rebellious rulers were probably listed. Manasseh may have joined this rebellion (Cogan 1974: 69).

E. Manasseh and the Fall of Judah

2 Kings blames Judah's fall on the sins of Manasseh (2 Kgs 21:11–15; 23:26–27; 24:3–4)—the hand in these passages is that of an exilic redactor—and in this fashion imitates the depiction of Jeroboam ben Nebat as the wicked ruler whose sins led the N kingdom of Israel to ruin. This portrayal of Manasseh as an *Unheilsherrscher* (interestingly, the Chronicler does not attribute the fall of Judah to Manasseh's sins) is a characteristic of the Deuteronomistic literature, which in this and other respects follows patterns in ANE historiography (Evans 1983).

F. Manasseh in Rabbinic Literature

The generally negative depiction of Manasseh reappears in rabbinic literature. Manasseh's idolatry, especially, is the subject of comment. The rabbis included Manasseh among those who have no share in the world to come, although Rabbi Judah disagreed because of the king's repentance (*m. Sanh.* 10:2). Rabbi Ashi, in a dream, learned of Manasseh's erudition and asked him why such a wise person worshipped idols. Manasseh responded, "Had you lived at my time, you would have caught hold of the hem of my garment and sped after me" (*b. Sanh.* 102b).

Bibliography

Ahlström, G. W. 1982. *Royal Administration and National Religion in Ancient Palestine.* Studies in the History of the Ancient Near East 1. Leiden.

Cogan, M. 1974. *Imperialism and Religion.* SBLMS 19. Missoula, MT.

Ehrlich, E. L. 1965. Der Aufenthalt des Königs Manasse in Babylon. *TZ* 21: 281–86.

Evans, C. D. 1980. Judah's Foreign Policy from Hezekiah to Josiah. Pp. 157–78 in *Scripture in Context: Essays on the Comparative Method,* ed. C. D. Evans et al. PTMS 34. Pittsburgh.

———. 1983. Naram-Sin and Jeroboam: The Archetypal *Unheilsherrscher* in Mesopotamian and Biblical Historiography. Pp. 97–125 in *Scripture in Context II: More Essays on the Comparative Method,* ed. W. W. Hallo, J. C. Moyer, and L. G. Perdue. Winona Lake, IN.

Frankena, R. 1965. The Vassal Treaties of Esarhaddon and the Dating of Deuteronomy. *OTS* 14: 122–54.

Hayes, J. H., and Hooker, P. K. 1988. *A New Chronology for the Kings of Israel and Judah.* Atlanta.

McKay, J. 1973. *Religion in Judah under the Assyrians.* SBT 2/26. Naperville.

Nelson, R. 1983. *Realpolitik* in Judah (687–609 B.C.E.). Pp. 177–89 in *Scripture in Context II: More Essays on the Comparative Method,* ed. W. W. Hallo, J. C. Moyer, and L. G. Perdue. Winona Lake, IN.

Nielsen, E. 1967. Political Conditions and Cultural Developments in Israel and Judah during the Reign of Manasseh. In *Fourth World Congress of Jewish Studies,* vol. 1. Jerusalem.

Oestreicher, T. 1923. *Das Deuteronomische Grundgesetz.* BFCT 27/4. Gütersloh.

Soggin, J. A. 1984. *A History of Ancient Israel.* Trans. J. Bowden. Philadelphia.

Spieckermann, H. 1982. *Juda unter Assur in der Sargonidenzeit.* FRLANT 129. Göttingen.

Weinfeld, M. 1965. Traces of Assyrian Treaty Formulae in Deuteronomy. *Bib* 46: 417–27.

Wiseman, D. J. 1958. The Vassal Treaties of Esarhaddon. *Iraq* 20: 1–99, plus 53 plates.

CARL D. EVANS

MANASSEH, PRAYER OF. This pseudepigraphal prayer, which is an individual lament of personal sin, is preserved primarily in Greek and Syriac. Many distinguished scholars consider that Greek is the original language; others conclude that it was composed in a Semitic language (see fuller discussion in *OTP* 2: 625–27). The prayer is too short and the history of transmission of both the Greek and Syriac texts is still too unclear to provide a firm conclusion regarding the original language.

Its penitential qualities, introspective and elevated perception of human need, as well as the denigration of Jewish prayer during the time of Jesus of Nazareth caused it to be labeled "Christian." Fabricius (1722: 1.1101) and Nestle (1899: 3: 18) claimed that it was written by a Christian. Migne (1856: 850) attributed the Greek text to the Christian author of the Apostolic Constitutions and tended to disparage the Prayer.

Now, thanks to a refined understanding of early Judaism and early Christianity, to an improved and more self-critical methodology, and to the discovery of numerous early Jewish hymns and prayers, it is certain that the Prayer of Manasseh was composed by a Jew, perhaps in or near Jerusalem, sometime before the destruction of the temple in 70 C.E. The author attempts to supply the prayer attributed by 2 Chronicles 33 to Manasseh (687–642 B.C.E.), the son of Hezekiah, supposedly the wickedest king of Judah.

For the Day of Atonement (Yom Kippur) the high priest would confess his own sins, as well as the sins of his family and the nation Israel. Confession of guilt and need for forgiveness were at the heart of early Judaism. As the Jewish expert Sandmel stated, the Prayer of Manasseh would "have fitted admirably" into the synagogue service for the Day of Atonement. For Goodspeed (1939: 56), the "simplicity, deep feeling, and power" of the Prayer of Manasseh "give it genuine religious worth, and remind us of the genuine religious feeling that welled up in Jewish hearts." Affirming that it is a Jewish prayer, B. M. Metzger (1957: 122) calls the Prayer of Manasseh "the little classic of penitential devotion," which "breathes throughout a deep and genuine religious feeling."

Two main themes run through the Prayer of Manasseh: God's infinite mercy and grace, and the conviction that contrition and repentance are effective. Similar to the canonical prayer of the penitent sinner, Psalm 51 (which the author undoubtedly had memorized), and parallel to *Joseph and Aseneth* (which he probably influenced), are these penetrating insights (translated from the Syriac):

And now behold I am bending the knees of my heart
before you;
and I am beseeching your kindness.
I have sinned, O Lord, I have sinned;
and certainly I know my sins.
I make supplication before you;
forgive me, O Lord, forgive me!

Bibliography

Baars, W., and Schneider, H. 1972. Prayer of Manasseh. Part 4, fasc. 6, pp. i–vii, 1–9 in *The Old Testament in Syriac according to the Peshitta Version.* Leiden.

Denis, A.-M. 1970a. Oratio Manassis. Pp. 115–17 in *Fragmenta pseudepigraphorum quae supersunt graeca.* PVTG 3. Leiden.

———. 1970b. La Prière de manassé. Pp. 177–81 in *Introduction aux pseudépigraphes grecs d'ancien testament.* SVTP 1. Leiden.

Diez Macho, A. 1984. Oración de Manasés. Pp. 209–10 in *Apocrifos del Antiguo Testamento,* vol. 1, ed. A. Diez Macho. Madrid.

Fabricius, J. A. 1722. *Codex pseudepigraphus veteris testamenti.* Hamburg.

Goodspeed, E. J. 1938. *The Apocrypha: An American Translation.* Chicago.

———. 1939. *The Story of the Apocrypha.* Chicago.

Metzger, B. M. 1957. *An Introduction to the Apocrypha.* New York.

Migne, J.-P. 1856. Manasses. Vol. 1, cols. 849–52 in *Dictionnaire des apocryphes* 1: 849–52.

Nestle, E. 1899. *Septuagintastudien.* Stuttgart.

Osswald, E. 1974. Das Gebet Manasses. Pp. 15–27 in *JSHRZ* 4/1. Gütersloh.

Rahlfs, A. 1931. Psalmi cum Odis. Pp. 361–63 in *Septuaginta: Societatis Scientiarum Göttingensis,* vol. 10. Göttingen.

JAMES H. CHARLESWORTH

MANDAEISM. The term "Mandaeism" is not an original self-designation of the religious community of the so-called "Mandaeans" (*mandayî*), which persists today in several settlements in S Iraq (Basra, Bagdad, Amārah, Naṣirīya, Sūq esh-Shuyukh) and in Iranian Khuzistān (Ahwāz, Disful, Shūshtār). It is thought that they now consist of ca. 15,000 members; the majority lives in Iraq (ca. 13,000). For centuries their main business seems to have been silver- and ironsmithing, boatbuilding and bridge construction. What they do not have in common with the surrounding people is their religious tradition and literature, which is written in a unique Semitic (east Aramaic) dialect and script (both are called by modern scholars "Mandaic").

A. Self-appellations

According to the Mandaean sources the earliest self-denominations are: "elect of righteousness" (*bhirē zidga*) and "guardians" or "possessors" (*naṣuraiyī*), i.e., of secret rites and knowledge. The word "Mandaeans" itself (*mandayī*) refers back to an ancient term for "knowledge," Gnosis (manda) and therefore means "Gnostics," but today it denotes the "laity" in distinction to "priests" (*tarmidī,* actually "disciples") and "initiates" (*naṣoraiyī*). Portuguese Catholic missionaries of the 17th century called them "disciples of John the Baptist," and they were known in European literature until the 19th century under this name or as "John-Christians" (actually, they only considered John the Baptist to be one of their prophets or "priests"). The Muslims gave them the name "Sabians" (in modern dialect: *Ṣubba*), known from the Quran and early Arabic literature; the designation enabled them to belong to the "people of the book" who are tolerated by Islam. Probably the original meaning of this word is "baptists, baptizers" (from the Aram root *ṣĕba,* "to immerse, baptize, wash").

B. Literature

It is noteworthy that the literature of this small community is quite extensive and diverse. It consists of ritual books (liturgies, prayers, hymns) and commentaries, theological-mythological tractates, illustrated scrolls, legends, and magical texts. Since we do not know the names and dates of the authors, redactors, or compilers, it is very difficult to give exact information about the origin and age of the literature. Very often the nature of the writings creates a problem for interpretation because early and late material is interwoven. Surely the collection of many writings into "books" had already started before the invasion of Islam into the Mandaean settlements in Mesopotamia. Apart from these, other texts have been transmitted in the earlier form of scrolls ("divans") rather than books, and they are illustrated in a peculiar artistic style. The oldest Mandaean magical texts (bowls and lead tablets) can be dated to the 4th and 5th centuries A.D.

Modern research in the scribal transmission of the texts, and comparisons of the special terminology, style, and phrases with non-Mandaean (Gnostic and Manichaean) literature have shown that the existence of the liturgical and poetic writings must be postulated already in the 3d century A.D. The script of texts was probably developed in the 2d century or earlier in order to preserve the more ancient religious tradition, which originated in Palestine and Syria and was brought orally to Mesopotamia.

The more important Mandaean works are the following: The "Treasure" (*Ginzā*) or "Great Book" (*sidra rabbā*) is the most complete collection of writings; it consists of two parts, the larger "Right Ginza" and the smaller "Left Ginza." The "Right Ginza" is a collection of eighteen tractates with predominantly cosmological (mythological), theological, and didactic content, while the "Left Ginza" deals only with the ascent of the soul to the realm of light; therefore it is also called "Book of Souls."

The "Book of John" (*draša dyahya*) of the "Books of the Kings" (i.e., Angels, *drašê d malkê*) is also a collection of mixed content. The main parts report on the "sermons" of John the Baptist, the "discourses" of Šum (Shem), the appearance of Anoš (Enosh) in Jerusalem, and the story of the conversion of Miryai (Mary the Mother of Jesus).

The liturgical hymns, prayers, and ritual instructions are collected in the "Canonical Prayerbook," in Mandaic called *Qolastā* ("praise" or generally "collection" of hymns). The first two books of the prayerbook contain the liturgy for the baptism and the mass for the dead; both are still used today by the modern Mandaean priests.

A series of other ritual texts or scrolls have been published only in recent times, e.g., the wedding ritual, a ritual for the ordination ("crowning") of priests, a ritual for the purification of a polluted priest. Similar texts are still unpublished. A large collection of writings only for priestly use is the so-called "1012 Questions" (*Alf Trisar Šuialê*).

Some of the scrolls are illlustrated, like the interesting "Diwan Abathur," which deals with the ascent of the soul through the heavenly purgatories, or the "Diwan of the Rivers," which gives an impression of the traditional world view of the Mandaeans. The only historical information is given by the (fragmentary) "Diwan of the great Revelation," called *Haran Gawaita.* Two scrolls contain speculative interpretations of rituals for the ascending soul ("Great First World," "Small First World"). The "Book of the Signs of the Zodiac" (*Sfar malwašê*) serves the priest for horoscopes and for giving names to the Mandaeans.

C. Doctrine

A real problem for research in Mandaeism is understanding the origin, growth, and development of Mandaean traditions. No scholarly consensus has yet been reached in regard to source analysis and redaction. Such analyses would undoubtedly enable scholars to isolate early traditions and thus to trace their development throughout the extensive and diverse Mandaean literature. Here only a brief summary of the main lines of Mandaean thought can be presented. The cosmology is marked by a strict (gnostic) dualism between a "world of light" (*alma dnhura*) and a "world of darkness" (*alma dhšuka*). The world of light is ruled by a sublime being who bears different names: "Life" (*haiyê*), "Great Life," "Lord of Greatness" (*mara drabuta*), "Great Spirit" (*mana rabba*), "King of Light" (*malka dnhura*). He is surrounded by a countless number of beings of light (*uthrê* or *malkê*), living in "dwellings" (*škinata*) or "worlds" (*almê*), performing cultic acts and praising the "Life." The world of light came into being from the "First Life" by way of descending emanations or creations, which are called "Second," "Third," and "Fourth" Life; they also bear personal names, such as Yošamin, Abāthur, and Ptahil. The last one is the later demiurge.

The "World of Darkness" is governed by the "Lord of Darkness" and arose from the "dark waters" (chaos). The main powers of the World of Darkness are a giant monster or dragon with the name "Ur" (probably a polemic transformation of Heb *ʾôr,* "light") and the evil (female) "spirit" (Ruha). Their offspring are demonic beings (*dēvs*) and "angels" (*malakê*). To them belong also the "Seven" (*šuba*) or the planets (*šibiahê*), and the "Twelve" (*trisar*) signs of the Zodiac.

The conflict between light and darkness, life and death, good and evil leads to the creation of the world (*tibil*) by the demiurge Ptahil with the help of the dark powers. In this process the body of the first man, Adam, is created by the same beings, but his "animating essence" is derived from the World of Light. This "substance of light" in Adam is called "inner (hidden) Adam" (*adam kasya, adakas*), and it represents the "soul" (*nišimta*) or "spirit" (*mana*) in humans, which has to be saved or rescued from the dark, evil body (= world) by heavenly beings of light. The salvation of these "souls" is the main concern of the Mandaean religion. One of its central creeds is the belief in several "messengers," "helpers," or "redeemers" sent by the "Life" in order to inform the pious of their "call" and to save their souls. The dominant figure of these "envoys of light" is the "knowledge of Life" *(Manda d Haiyê),* who is also called "Son of Life" *(Barhaiyê)* or "counterpart of Life" *(Dmuthaiyê).* Beside him stand the three heavenly Adamites, Hibil (Abel), Šitil (Seth), and Anoš (Enosh). Actually the Mandaeans know no "historical" redeemers but only "mythological" ones appearing throughout the ages of the history of the world as a repetition of the first revelation to Adam. Only after the confrontation with early Christianity did they develop the story that one of their messengers (Anoš or *Manda d Haiyê)* appeared in Jerusalem as an antagonist of Jesus Christ in order to expose him as a liar. In this connection John the Baptist played the role of a true Mandaean "disciple" or "priest" (*tarmida*). Whether reliable information about the early history of the Mandaeans in relation to the movement of the followers of John the Baptist can be derived from these tales is a problem that remains unsolved. For the Mandaeans John is not the founder of their religion but only one of their prominent representatives.

D. The Rituals

The center of the Mandaean religion is the cult. For centuries the traditional cultic locations (*mandi*) have been the principal points of the local communities. They consist—probably we have to say consisted—of a small hut (*maškna, bit manda, bimanda*) made of mud; in front of it lies the pool or "Jordan" (*yardna*) with "flowing water" (the sanctuaries are always situated next to rivers or channels). Elsewhere the rituals were performed on the banks of the rivers or creeks close to the residences of the community. Since the mid-1970s the Mandaeans have changed the tradition of their cultic areas in order to avoid polluted streams and rivers. Modern cultic structures (as in Baghdad and Basra) are built of bricks, and the ritual font is connected with the public water system.

The most important and oldest ceremonies are the "baptism" (*maṣbūtā*) and the "ascent of the soul" (*masiqta*). The baptism or "immersion" is performed every "Sunday" (the first day of the week, *habšabba*) in "flowing water" (*yardna*). It consists of two main parts: the first one is the actual baptismal rite including a threefold immersion (the participants dressed in the sacral white garments), a threefold "signing" of the forehead with water, a threefold gulp of water, the "crowning" with a small myrtle wreath (*klila*), and the laying on of hands by the priest. The second part takes place on the banks of the stream and consists of the anointing with oil (*sesam*), the communion of bread (*pihta*) and water (*mambuha*), and the "sealing" of the neophyte against evil spirits. Both parts are concluded by the ritual handclasp or *kušta* ("truth"). The purpose and meaning of the baptism is not only a "purification" of sins and trespasses but also a special kind of communion (*laufa*) with the world of light, because it is believed that all "Jordans" or "living waters" originate in the upper world of "Life." There is no doubt that the basic constituent features of the water ceremonies are derived from baptismal practices (lustrations) or early Judaism in the pre-Christian period. Apart from this "full baptism" ritual, there exist two lesser water rites.

The other chief ceremony is a kind of mass for the dead, or rather "for the soul" of the dead, called "ascent" (*masiqta*). It is performed at the death of a Mandaean and supports the "rise" of his soul to the world of Light and Life. It consists of lustrations with "flowing water" (*yardna*), anointing with oil, and crowning with a myrtle wreath. The main ceremony starts three days after death, when the soul is released from the body and beings its forty-five-day "ascent" through the heavenly Purgatories (*maṭarata*) until it reaches the "home of Life." Recitations from the "Left Ginza" and ceremonial meals serve the ascending soul (including its symbolic nourishment, rebirth, and creation of a spiritual body). The roots of these ceremonies and the idea of "meals in memory of the dead" probably go back to Iranian-Zoroastrian soil, but they are shaped by the gnostic background of the Mandaean religion.

The Mandaeans have many more rituals, such as the ordination of priests and bishops (*ganzibrê*), the end-of-the-year ceremony (Parwanaiya or Panǧa), the cleansing of the cult hut or temple, the marriage ceremony (which includes the baptism), and several kinds of funeral and commemorative meals (*lofani, zidqa brikha*).

Characteristic of the Mandaean religion is the close connection between rituals and gnostic ideas. It is not only "knowledge" (*manda, madihta, yada*) that brings salvation but the ceremonies, at first baptisms and "offices for the soul," which are indispensable means for the release. One may indeed say that here Gnosis has been implanted into the ancient stock of a cultic community of Jewish origin (cf. the so-called "baptismal sects"), but from this connection an authentic and even typical Mandaean-Nazoraean offspring has been created.

Bibliography

Drower, E. S. 1962. *The Mandaeans of Iraq and Iran.* 2d ed. Leiden.

Lidzbarski, M. 1915. *Das Johannesbuch der Mandäer.* 2 pts. Giessen. Repr. Berlin 1965.

———. 1925. *Ginzā: Der Schatz oder das grosse Buch der Mandäer.* Quellen der Religionsgeschichte 13. Göttingen. Repr. 1979.

Macuch, R., ed. 1976. *Zur Sprache und Literatur der Mandäer.* Studia Mandaica 1. Berlin.

Rudolph, K. 1965. *Theogonie, Kosmogonie und Anthropogonie in den mandäischen Schriften.* Göttingen.

———. 1969. Problems of a History of the Development of the Mandaean Religion. *HR* 8: 210–35.

———. 1970. Die Religion der Mandäer. Pp. 403–64 in *Die Religionen Altsyriens, Altarabiens und der Mandäer,* ed. H. Gese; M. Höfner; and K. Rudolph. Die Religionen der Menschheit 10. Stuttgart.

———. 1974. Mandaean Sources. Pp. 123–319 in *Gnosis,* ed. W. Foerster. Oxford.

———. 1975. Quellenprobleme zum Ursprung und Alter der Mandäer. Pp. 112–42 in *Christianity, Judaism and Other Greco-Roman Cults,* ed. J. Neusner. Leiden.

———. 1978a. *Mandaeism.* Iconography of Religions Section 21. Ed. T. P. van Baaren et al. Leiden.

———. 1978b. Der Mandäismus in der neueren Gnosisforschung. Pp. 244–77 in *Gnosis,* ed. B. Aland. Göttingen.

———. 1981. *Antike Baptisten.* Sitzungsberichte SAW Phil.-hist. Kl. 121–24. Berlin.

———. 1982. *Der mandäische "Diwan der Flüsse".* ASAW Phil.-hist. Kl. 70–71. Berlin.

Widengren, G., ed. 1982. *Der Mandäismus.* Wege der Forschung 167. Darmstadt.

Yamauchi, E. V. 1967. *Mandaic Incantation Texts.* AOS 49. New Haven.

KURT RUDOLPH

MANDRAKES. See PERFUMES AND SPICES; FLORA, BIBLICAL.

MANI (PERSON) [Gk *Mani*]. The Gk reading in 1 Esdr 9:30 for the person the RSV harmonizes as Bani, based on the parallel text in Ezra 10:29. See BANI.

MANICHAEANS AND MANICHAEISM.

Manichaeism was one of the major world religions and the only such religion to grow out of late antiquity's Near Eastern tradition of gnosis. See GNOSTICISM. Originally considered by Western scholars to be a Christian heresy, Manichaeism is now properly understood in the context of 3d-century Mesopotamian oriental religions. The religion was founded by the Iranian prophet Mani (216–77 C.E.) who deliberately created a universal and propagandistic religion in a context of diverse Christian, Zoroastrian, and Buddhist concepts. The religion moved E toward India and W into the Roman Empire already in Mani's lifetime, reaching as far W as Algiers and S Europe and as far E as central Asia and SE coastal China, where traces of the religion datable to the early 17th century can be identified.

A. Biography of Mani
   1. Birth and Early Life
   2. The Universal Religion and Its Propagation
   3. Mani's Sevenfold Canon
   4. Mani's Missionary Travels, Later Life, and Death
B. History of Research through the 19th Century
C. Great Discoveries of Manichaean Literature in the 20th Century
   1. Central Asian and Chinese Texts
   2. Greek and Latin Texts
   3. Coptic Texts
D. System of Belief and the Human Predicament
   1. The Past Time and the Two Principles
   2. The Present Time
   3. The Future Time

E. Structure of the Manichaean Church
F. History of Manichaeism after Mani's Death
  1. Missions to the West
  2. Missions to the East

A. Biography of Mani

1. Birth and Early Life. Mani was born on April 14, 216 C.E., to the southeast of the Mesopotamian city of Ctesiphon in the Parthian province of Asoristan. His parents were of Iranian descent. His mother, called Maryam in the Arabic, Syriac, and Greek sources, was related to the ruling Arsacid dynasty. His father, Patik, was a devotee in an Elchasaite Mughtasilist community, a Judeo-Christian baptismal sect with gnostic and ascetic features derived from the popular religious movement founded by the obscure figure Elchasai known from the Christian heresiologists (Merkelbach 1988a: 105–33).

Mani entered the baptismal sect at the age of four, but the most striking incident of his early life was a revelation he received at the age of twelve (April 1, 228) when an angel called "The Twin" (Arab *al-Twam;* Gk *suzugon*) appeared to him and ordered him to leave the baptismal sect at an unspecified later date. The crucial second revelation came at the age of twenty-four (April 19, 240) when the angel ordered him to begin his public ministry by openly preaching the newly revealed doctrine. This novel public teaching put Mani at odds with the traditional community and he was forced to leave with only the support of his father and two faithful followers. Although Mani's new doctrine contained many elements that were rejected by the baptismal community, the primary point of contention was probably his argument that ritual purity through baptism was of no avail and that true redemptive purity comes only from the physical and moral separation of light from darkness, spirit from matter, and good from evil.

2. The Universal Religion and Its Propagation. Mani proclaimed himself the apostle of light, the Paraclete incarnate (cf. John 14:16, 26), and the seal of the prophets who would bring the final revelation to the world. Mani viewed all previous religious traditions as contaminated versions of the originally true, though partial, teachings of the earlier prophets Buddha, Jesus, and Zoroaster (Zarathushtra). Mani, as the Seal of the Prophets, proclaimed instead the final revelation, the true universal religion which would unite all people through his teaching.

This grand plan required propagandistic methods designed to overcome the cultural and, especially, linguistic barriers which ultimately prevented the revelations of the earlier prophets from reaching the universal audience. Mani emphasized the need for the translation of Manichaean texts into all languages in order to propagate his teaching as effectively and quickly as possible. He even reformed the abstruse ideographic writing systems of the Iranian languages Parthian and Middle Persian by introducing the more comprehensive and phonetically oriented eastern Aramaic alphabet. He also produced in eastern Aramaic a corpus of seven canonical works, in direct contrast to the earlier prophets whose teachings were put into written form by their followers, who contaminated those teachings with their own interpretations. Perhaps Mani's most effective propagandistic tool was his ability to instill in his followers a sense of the absolute necessity for a lifestyle characterized by the propagation of the religion. Mani himself traveled extensively during his own lifetime and was influenced by the popular image of the traveling Christian apostle Thomas, who tradition holds traveled as far as India to spread the Christian faith.

3. Mani's Sevenfold Canon. Mani himself wrote and published a canon of seven works in the eastern Aramaic language: (1) *The Living Gospel,* (2) *The Treasure of Life,* (3) *The Pragmateia,* (4) *The Book of Mysteries,* (5) *The Book of the Giants,* (6) *The Letters,* and (7) *The Psalms and Prayers.* Mani also wrote the *Shaburagan* which replaces the *Psalms and Prayers* in some canonical lists, but in the Middle Persian language and specifically for the emperor Shapur I. None of these texts is known to survive today in a complete form. Much previous research in Manichaeism had been dependent on a considerable number of quotes and descriptions in the writings of Christian and pagan heresiologists and historians. The most important works were the *Acta Archelai* (Ries 1959: 395–98; Lieu 1988: 69–88), the writings of the former Manichaean Augustine (cf. F.1., below), and the works of the late-10th-century and early-11th-century Arab authors al-Biruni and Ibn al-Nadim.

4. Mani's Missionary Travels, Later Life, and Death. Mani's first mission was eastward, like that of Thomas before him, and he met an early success in what is now SE Iran with the conversion of Turan-shah, the Buddhist king of Turan, and his entourage (ca. 240–42). He continued to meet success during his return journey through Persia, Susiana, and Mesene (ca. 242–50). Mani returned to the Persian Sassanid Empire when the emperor Ardashir I died and his son Shapur I assumed the throne. He met with Shapur and was granted the freedom and protection to propagate the religion throughout the empire. Manichaeism was adopted by members of the emperor's family and by influential political figures (ca. 250–55). Mani wrote the *Shaburagan,* a summary of his teachings in the Middle Persian language, during this period of imperial favor and dedicated it to Shapur. Manichaeism then spread throughout Persia, beyond its borders, and even westward into the Roman Empire (ca. 255–56). It is noteworthy that Mani accompanied Shapur in the victorious Persian campaign against the Roman forces in which the emperor Valerian was captured at Edessa in 260.

Although Mani enjoyed imperial favor under Shapur, the Magian clergy of the official state religion Zoroastrianism grew intent on persecuting the prophet. When Shapur I died (ca. 272), his successors Hormizd (reigned 273) and Bahram I (reigned 273–77) both favored the traditional state religion. The Zoroastrian high priest Kerder, now strengthened by widespread nationalist aspirations, was successful in convincing Bahram to begin official persecution of the minority movement. By order of the emperor, Mani was arrested, brought to Gundeshahbur (Susiana), interrogated for one month under Kerder, and died in prison in about the year 277.

B. History of Research through the 19th Century

The success of the intense and almost universal heresiological polemic against Manichaeism resulted in the effective censorship and eventual elimination of Manichaean texts from the Western and Eastern manuscript traditions.

Heretics of all types throughout the medieval period were uncritically slandered as Manichaeans. Even Luther's Catholic detractors spoke of a revived Manichaeism. The Protestant response demanded a more objective understanding of Manichaeism, investigated known Manichaean evidences, and so initiated the modern study of the religion.

From the 16th through the 18th centuries, the works of Christian and pagan heresiologists were studied in depth, resulting in the interpretation of Manichaeism as primarily a Christian heresy, rather than as an independent religion in its own right (Ries 1988: 17–48). This position was challenged in 1734–39 by the Calvinist theologian Isaac de Beausobre who, apparently the first to reject the negative bias of the heresiological tradition, argued that Mani was a brilliant precursor of Luther and thus part of the history of reformed Christianity. Although this position was ultimately rejected, the great contribution of Beausobre's study was that it drew attention to the previously ignored Eastern sources, sources which a later generation was to take seriously (Ries 1988: 59–112).

About one hundred years later, F. C. Baur (1831) advanced Manichaean studies by explicating the significance of the Buddhist, Indo-Iranian, and Zoroastrian elements in Manichaeism, thus bringing the study of Manichaeism into its natural interpretive context: that of the history of oriental religions. G. Flügel (1862) was the first to discuss the significance of the newly discovered and less biased Arab authors, like the 10th-century historian Ibn al-Nadim, for a more objective understanding of Manichaeism. Flügel argued that Mani's eclectic oriental religion was primarily based on Zoroastrianism and Mughtasilism, which Mani then creatively reinterpreted using biblical models. K. Kessler's study (1889) pushed Manichaean origins even further back in time to the pre-Zoroastrian beliefs of Chaldeo-Babylonian religion. According to Kessler, Mani was concerned with recovering the original sources of Zoroaster's beliefs in an attempt to undercut his Magian opponents in the Sassanid court. To these ancient Babylonian beliefs Mani then added elements from Buddhism, Christianity, and Mithraism (a theory accepted by A. Harnack and W. Bousset).

C. Great Discoveries of Manichaean Literature in the 20th Century

The following survey of recently discovered Manichaean texts will cover only the most extensively studied and representative examples. Other texts are discussed by Lieu (1985: passim; cf. Ries 1988: 209–38).

1. Central Asian and Chinese Texts. German archaeological teams under the direction of A. von Le Coq and A. Grünwedel were engaged in four expeditions (1904–14) of ruined Manichaean monasteries at Turfan and Qoco in Sinkiang, China (north of Tibet; Lieu 1985: 199–201). The teams recovered thousands of fragments from heavily damaged Manichaean manuscripts. These Turfan fragments (many could not be conserved) are the disintegrated remains of what were once high-quality illuminated manuscripts which had suffered mutilation under Muslim conquerors in the 14th century. The texts are written in several Central Asian languages; the most common are Middle Persian, Parthian, Sogdian, and Uighur, but texts were also found in the rarely attested Tocharian B and Bactrian. They are now conserved in the collection of the Germany Academy of Sciences in Berlin.

Sir Aurel Stein discovered in 1905–7 the remains of a large hoard of Buddhist and Manichaean manuscripts in the Temple of the Thousand Buddhas at Tun-huang (500 km E-SE of Turfan). Stein recovered a long Manichaean confessional text in Uighur for Auditors entitled *Confessional for the Hearers,* and three Manichaean texts translated into Chinese from Iranian-language originals (Lieu 1985: 202–6; cf. the new text editions in Lin 1987: 168–265 and pls. 1–45): (1) the *Treatise,* a discussion on cosmogony and its implications for the everyday life of the Manichaean Elect and Auditors, now conserved in Beijing; (2) the *Hymnscroll,* now in London, and (3) *The Compendium of the Teaching of Mani, the Buddha of Light,* a summary of Manichaean teachings. This final manuscript's translation is dated in the text's preface to a date that can be assigned in the Western calendar to July 16, 731. The manuscript itself was physically divided into two parts before its acquisition by Stein in 1907 (London; Ms. Stein 3969) and Pelliot in 1908 (Paris; Coll. Pelliot No 3884; cf. Lin 1988: 89–92).

Western scholars are now informed of the numerous recent discoveries of Manichaean archaeological sites, artifacts, and texts in Central Asia and China through the works of S. N. C. Lieu (1985: 178–264, 322–25, 341–43) and Geng Shimin (1990). As an example of a most recent discovery of a Manichaean text in Chinese, Lin Wu-shu of Sun Yat Sen University (Guangzhou, China) published a fragmentary Manichaean inscription which was found in Fukien Province in 1988 (Lin 1989: 22–27, pls. I and II). The inscription on the large stele dates from 1315 to 1369, originally consisted of sixteen calligraphic Chinese characters (eight are fully extant and two are fragmentary), and is similar to another Manichaean inscription in Chinese in the famous Manichaean temple in Ch'üan-chou, also in Fukien Province. That temple was discovered in the 1950s and is today the only known intact Manichaean temple site (Lieu 1985: 212–13; Lin 1987: 145–58 and pls. 60a–b). The temple contains an intact low-relief statue of "Mani the Buddha of Light." Near the temple were found inscribed (ritual?) bowls and three Manichaean tombstones. The history of research on the temple site is surveyed with bibliographic data in a useful study by Geng Shimin (1990).

2. Greek and Latin Texts. Sensational discoveries of Manichaean manuscripts have also been made in the West. A. Henrichs and L. Koenen announced in 1970 the successful decipherment of a small parchment codex acquired by the University of Cologne (P. colon. inv. nr. 4780; all 192 pages were conserved by Anton Fackelmann in 1969). The *Codex Manichaeicus Coloniensis* (= *CMC;* from Lycopolis?) dates from the end of the 4th or the beginning of the 5th century and contains a Greek translation of a previously unknown Manichaean text originally written in Syriac with the title *On the Origin of His Body* (Koenen and Römer 1988). The text seems to be an anthology containing quotations from the works of several of Mani's early disciples edited by a final redactor around a core of Mani's own autobiographical statements. The traditions contained in the *CMC* concern Mani's latter days with the baptismal sect and his early missionary journeys after the age of twenty-four, and thus constitute some of the most important sources of information on the early period of Mani's life.

A fragmentary Manichaean parchment codex, the *Tebessa Codex,* written in Latin was discovered in a cave near Theveste (Algeria) in 1918 and placed in the National Library of Paris (*Nouvelles acquisitiones latines* 1114). Only twenty-five damaged leaves and the slight remains of four others are preserved from this codex with each page originally carrying two columns of Latin text (Merkelbach 1988b). The extant text contains two sections: (1) *cols. 1–20,* an apologetic discussion on the relationship between the two major groups in the Manichaean church, the Elect and the Auditors, with allusions to and quotations of relevant canonical gospel texts (like the relevant Mary and Martha story from Luke 10:38–42), and (2) *cols. 21–54,* a discussion in which the unknown Manichaean author defends the "nonwork ethic" of the Manichaean Elect (who had their practical needs met by the Auditors), apparently as an apologetic response to Christian charges that the apostle Paul had clearly condemned such dependent lifestyles in 2 Thess 3:10b ("If anyone will not work, let him not eat"). The Manichaean apologist begins with that Pauline text and then continues to defend the dependent lifestyles of the Manichaean Elect with allusions to and quotations of texts from nearly every letter in the Pauline (and Deutero-Pauline) canonical corpus (no reference to Romans or Galatians, or Hebrews, is found in the highly fragmented manuscript).

3. Coptic Texts. Any discussion on the sensational discovery of seven Manichaean books in the Coptic language from Medinet Madi, Egypt (ancient Terenouthis in the Fayyum), must begin with the famous "Mani-Fund" article of C. Schmidt and H. J. Polotsky (1933). The modern history of the manuscripts has been complex and tragic. Despite some early successes by British and German scholars, attempts to inventory, conserve, and edit the still unpublished and heavily deteriorated manuscripts have frustrated postwar researchers. However, a careful and detailed analysis of the manuscripts and the history of their research (up to mid-1989) has been produced by J. M. Robinson (1990). The present discussion is indebted to that study (and to unpublished files courtesy of J. M. Robinson and C. Colpe).

Seven papyrus codices with Manichaean texts in the Coptic language were discovered by local workers digging through the ruins of an ancient house in Medinet Madi probably sometime in 1929. An antiquities dealer showed at least one of the books, on November 29, 1929, in Cairo, to the Danish Egyptologist H. O. Lange, who did not purchase any of the books. They were all purchased in the next three years through a series of acquisitions by Sir Chester Beatty, an American businessman and art collector residing in England (two codices and parts of two others are now the property of the Chester Beatty Library, Dublin), and by the noted German papyrologist Carl Schmidt of Berlin (three codices and parts of two others are now the property of the State Museums of Berlin). A few leaves are in the national collections of Vienna and Warsaw.

The seven codices are listed and described below. The names for the books and their contents are mostly modern, based on extant titles or interpretations of the often obscure contents. A long awaited photographic facsimile edition of the Beatty codices is now available under the editorship of S. Giversen (1986–88; the Dublin manuscripts have been in Copenhagen since 1984). The peculiar Subachmimic Coptic dialect (L4) used in these texts has been discussed by W.-P. Funk (1985) and the date and morphology of the codices has been discussed by J. M. Robinson (1978: 33–43).

(i) The *Psalms* codex (Beatty Codex A) was divided into two parts before Beatty acquired it. The latter part of the codex was edited, translated into English, and published by C. R. C. Allberry (1938). The first part of the codex, estimated to contain about 155 leaves, awaits editing in the Beatty collection (Böhlig 1968a: 177–78). The *Psalms* codex appeared in Giversen's facsimile edition in 1988.

(ii) The *Synaxeis* codex (Beatty Codex B) was also divided into two parts before Beatty's acquisition. Before World War II Beatty had arranged for the codex to be conserved in Berlin. The bulk of Codex B is now in the Egyptian Museum in Berlin and has received much attention in recent years. The Berlin holdings include 125 leaves (= 250 pages) conserved under glass, five more glass frames with fragments of leaves, and the fragile remainder of the unconserved book block containing an estimated 70 to 120 leaves. The upper-facing page of the book block presents one more readable page, giving a total of 251 pages of exposed text in the Berlin collection (Mirecki 1988: 135–45). Thirteen unedited leaves from Codex B are in the Dublin collection and have appeared as unidentified "Varia" in Giversen's facsimile edition (1987: 101–26). Before the codex was purchased by Beatty, the antiquities dealer removed at least 31 damaged leaves so as to improve the appearance of the codex. These 31 leaves were later acquired by Schmidt (P. 15995), transcribed by G. Robinson, and are now in the State Museum of Berlin (Mirecki 1988: 140 n. 16). The single biggest problem concerning the editing of Codex B is the lost pagination of the 339 conserved pages and their positional relations to the leaves in the unconserved book block. The present author's work in Berlin has resulted in the first theoretical model for the codicological reconstruction of the entire codex (Mirecki 1988: 137 n. 13). That model suggests that the codex contains two texts; the first remains unidentified (a lengthy prooemium to the second text?) and the second is generally understood to be a series of homilies (Gk *synaxeis*) which reflect the structure and contents of the lost *Living Gospel* of Mani (Böhlig 1968b: 252–66). It is hoped that the model for codicological reconstruction will facilitate the production of facsimile and critical text editions within the present generation.

(iii–iv) Two related codices are the first and second volumes of the *Kephalaia* (Gk: "central principles") text. Volume I of the *Kephalaia* is conserved in the State Museum of Berlin (P. 15996). Pages 1–292 were published in a critical text edition with German translation by H. J. Polotsky and A. Böhlig (1940). There are a few unpublished leaves in Vienna (acquired by Grohmann), Warsaw (acquired as war spoils from Berlin), and the State Museum of Berlin totaling some 122 pages with assigned pagination and some 48 to 64 pages without assigned pagination, giving 170 to 186 unpublished pages of volume of the

Kephalaia was purchased by Beatty and is now part of the Dublin collection (Beatty Codex C). Volume II has been only partly transcribed. Giversen's facsimile edition appeared in 1986.

(v) The *Homilies* codex was also divided into two parts before its sale. The bulk of the codex was acquired by Schmidt (P. 15999) and a smaller portion by Beatty (Beatty Codex D). Beatty's part was conserved by H. Ibscher; a critical text edition with German translation was published by Polotsky (1934), and a facsimile edition was published by Giversen (1987). The bulk of Schmidt's unconserved codex was apparently taken from Berlin to Leningrad in 1946 and is now presumed a tragic loss.

(vi) The *Acts* codex was acquired by Schmidt (P. 15997) with its original wooden book covers still intact. A discussion and photograph of the intact codex was published by Schmidt and Polotsky (1933: 7–8, 27, pl. 2). Only a few leaves were conserved. One is now in the Beatty collection and its photograph was published in Giversen's facsimile edition (1987: viii–ix, pls. 99–100). Transcriptions by Schmidt and/or Polotsky of three pages, along with seven leaves transcribed by S. Patterson, and a possibly related eighth leaf transcribed by the present author, are in the State Museum of Berlin. A fragment of another possibly related leaf turned up in Warsaw after the war. The bulk of the *Acts* codex was never conserved, was apparently taken to Leningrad in 1946, and is presumed another tragic loss.

(vii) The *Letters* codex was also acquired by Schmidt (P. 15998). Confused museum records suggest that between 24 to 33 leaves (= 48 to 66 pages) are extant. Three leaves turned up in Warsaw after the war and the rest are in the State Museum of Berlin. As in the case of the *Homilies* and the *Acts* codices, the unconserved bulk of the *Letters* codex was apparently taken to Leningrad in 1946, and is presumed yet another tragic loss.

D. System of Belief and the Human Predicament

Mani's teaching embraced an elaborate historical drama of supracosmic proportions in which humanity's past origin, present predicament, and future possibilities are described. The drama centers its tacit theological concern on the existential question of the origin of evil in human experience. Mani employed a typical apocalyptic scheme in which cosmic history was divided into three time periods: the past, the present, and the future. The following discussion traces only the basic profile of Mani's system and refers the reader to the appropriate primary texts and the detailed discussions of Merkelbach (1986: 16–36) and especially of Lieu (1985: 5–21), to which it is largely indebted.

1. The Past Time and the Two Principles. In the *Past Time* there existed two eternal principles, one all good and the other all evil. The good principle exists exclusively within the Kingdom of Light and finds its focus in the Father of Greatness whose fourfold majesty embraces Divinity, Light, Power, and Goodness. His throne is surrounded by at least 156 peace-loving hypostases: twelve Aeons (in three groups of four each) and 144 Aeons of Aeons. The Kingdom of Light is constructed of five elements (*stoicheia:* air, wind, light, water, and fire) and contains five peaceful "dwellings" (intelligence, knowledge, reason, thought, and deliberation). The evil principle and the Kingdom of Darkness are the complete antitheses of the good principle and the Kingdom of Light. The many monstrous and agitated inhabitants of the Kingdom of Darkness are ruled by five evil archons (demon, lion, eagle, fish, and dragon) who are in constant opposition to each other and who, collectively, make up the hellish Prince of Darkness. They are sexually preoccupied, controlled by unreined passions, and dwell in an ominous netherworld of smoke, fire, wind, water, and darkness. The two kingdoms are completely distinct yet eternally coexistent.

2. The Present Time. The *Present Time* begins when the evil inhabitants of the Kingdom of Darkness drive a wedge into the Kingdom of Light in a lustful desire to mingle with the light. The Kingdom of Darkness is thoroughly aroused and its terrifyingly vicious inhabitants enter the light in a full-scale invasion. The Father of Greatness responds by evoking a series of hypostases which may need to be sacrificed to the invaders so as to satisfy them and stop the assault. The first evocation is the Mother of Life, who then evokes the Primal Man, who fights the incoming forces of darkness but loses his battle. The five evil archons (Prince of Darkness) then consume some of the light elements of the Primal Man's armor and, having unwittingly fallen into the trap of the Father of Greatness, are now dependent on the light for their continued existence. The Primal Man awakens from his sleep of forgetfulness, remembers his divine origins, and prays for his rescue. The Father of Greatness responds by evoking a series of beings who initiate the rescue of the Primal Man: the Friend of Lights evokes the Great Architect who then evokes the Living Spirit who evokes his five Sons (the Custodian of Splendor, the Great King of Honor, Adamas of Light, the King of Glory, and Atlas). The Living Spirit cries out from the Kingdom of Light into the darkness to the Primal Man, who answers. The Cry and Answer are hypostasized and ascend to the Kingdom of Light (representing the divine word of salvation and the positive human response). The Living Spirit then grasps the Primal Man by the hand and rescues him from the Kingdom of Darkness.

The rest of the drama in the *Present Time* focuses on the work of the Father of Greatness to regain all of the light particles swallowed by the five evil archons. The Living Spirit first creates ten heavens and eight earths out of the material corpses of the slain demons. He separates the swallowed light particles into three types: the first is undefiled and from it he creates the Sun and the Moon; the second is only partly defiled and from it he creates the Stars; the third is completely defiled and so he creates an elaborate cosmic mechanism (based on Persian alchemy?) to distill the light from the matter. The Living Spirit then evokes the Third Messenger, who evokes the zodiacal Twelve Maidens, collectively the Maiden of Light, who operate the cosmic Three Wheels created to distill the light particles out of the material universe. Another evocation is the Column of Glory (the Milky Way) which transports the recovered light particles from the distilling Three Wheels to the Moon and then the Sun, which function as ships transporting the light particles to their temporary haven (the New Earth created by the Great Architect). The Third Messenger and the Maiden of Light then excite the sexual nature of the male archons, causing them to ejaculate the light particles from within them. The Sun which excites the archons falls to the earth, becoming the source of all plant life. The female archons miscarry their light-bearing fetuses, which fall to the earth and copulate among themselves, becoming the source of all animal life. The sum total of all of these light particles trapped in matter, including plants and animals, is called the Living Self in Eastern Manichaeism but in the West is called the Suffering Jesus *(Jesus patibilis)* who is on the Light Cross *(crux luminus)*.

The Prince of Darkness, in an attempt to frustrate the cosmic distillation of light particles, gives birth to the two evil demons Saclas (Ashqulan) and Nebroel (Namrael) who eat the monstrous offspring of the miscarried fetuses in order to ingest their light particles. The two demons then copulate and Nebroel gives birth to exact miniature replicas (Gen 1:27) of the confused "light-matter" macrocosm: Adam and Eve. In a typically gnostic "inverted exegesis" of Genesis 1–5, the sexually oriented evil creator can only create by copulation and birth, and so can only create matter (which is inherently evil). He is completely unable to create in the manner of the Father of Greatness by *evoking* pure spiritual *hypostases*. Consequently, Adam (representing humanity) is specifically designed by the evil creator in his own image (Gen 1:26) to procreate sexually (Gen 1:27–28). Thus, Adam can only continue the evil cycle of birth, copulation, and rebirth and in so doing fulfills his natural inclination to be "fruitful and multiply" (Gen 1:28; 5:4b). Adam's nature (representing human sexuality) thus entangles the precious light particles, transmitted through male seed, in potentially endless generations of material bodies (representing human history). But Adam was ignorant of the light within him and the facts of his true origin in the Kingdom of Light. The evocations of the Father of Greatness then send Jesus of Light to awaken Adam (Gen 3:1), to inform him of his true nature (Gen 3:4–5), and to lead him to self-recognition (Gen 3:7, 11a, 22a). Jesus of Light helps Adam eat of the Tree of Life (Gen 3:22), warns him of the dangers of sexual procreation with Eve, and so encourages an ascetic lifestyle (central for Manichaean ethics). Then Eve and a male archon copulate and Eve gives birth to Cain (Gen 4:1), who then copulates with his mother Eve, who gives birth to Abel (Gen 4:2), and so begins the incestuous interaction of Cain (Gen 4:2a) and Abel with Eve and with each other's daughters borne by Eve (Gen 4:17). Eve then receives magical knowledge from an evil archon which would enable her to copulate with the ascetic Adam. She succeeds in her desire and bears Seth (Gen 4:25a), who, as the first true son of Adam (Gen 5:3, 4b), contains a significantly larger amount of light particles than the other offspring of Eve. The ascetic Adam and Seth, self-conscious particles of light entrapped in innately evil material bodies, become the exemplary human figures for Manichaean ethics (Gen 4:26b; 5:1–32; cf. Pearson 1988: 147–55).

3. The Future Time. The *Future Time* is the third and final act of the historical cosmic drama and provides for Manichaean ethics a preview into the system of rewards and punishments. The final and Great War will break out among the unenlightened powers of darkness when the distillation of light particles from the material cosmos has neared its completion. Jesus will return at a decisive eschatological moment as the Great King and will judge humanity and the infernal powers. The Elect will become angels, the Auditors will be judged righteous, and the sinners will be cast into hell with Eve and her hellish offspring. The cosmos will disintegrate and burn in a conflagration for 1,468 years. The remaining light particles will be gathered and finally return by ascent to the Kingdom of Light while the Prince of Darkness and his diabolical minions will be cast into a bottomless pit permanently sealed will a huge stone for all eternity. The two principles of Light and Darkness will again be two separate and distinct entities, but never again comingle.

E. Structure of the Manichaean Church

Just as Jesus of Light was the prime evocation of liberation for Adam, so the Great Nous (Great Mind) is the prime evocation from Jesus of Light for the liberation of Adam's descendants throughout human history, thus providing the unique Manichaean solution to the human predicament. The primary redemptive function of the Nous to reveal (1) the true knowledge of the origin and destination of the human soul (self-recognition) and (2) the two central precepts of Manichaean belief: the three periods of cosmic history and the existence of two eternally antithetic and supracosmic principles.

Individual human beings are replicant microcosms of the confused "light-matter" macrocosm. As such they endure an eternal struggle within their own souls for release from matter and return to their true home in the immaterial Kingdom of Light. After the individual human soul has been awakened by the Nous, that individual is conscious of the eternal dualistic realities which control its fate and can then hope to succeed against influences from the lower nature. This internal struggle was described by Mani in Pauline terms concerning the "New Man" (1 Cor 3:9–10) and "Old Man" (Eph 4:22–24) who are locked in mortal combat. The individual can succeed in this struggle through the continued protection of the Nous, which is accessible only in the teaching of Mani and the guidance of the Manichaean church. Strict adherence to the extreme ascetic requirements (sexual abstinence, poverty, vegetarianism) are impossible to enforce on the popular level and, were they to succeed, would result in the eventual extinction of the human race. Knowing that such commitment could be expected only from himself and a few choice believers, Mani divided his church into two basic classes, the Elect and the Auditors.

The Elect were required to keep the "Five Commandments" (to be pure and poor, not to lie, kill, or eat flesh) and to adhere to the "Three Seals." First, the "Seal of the Mouth" *(signacula oris)* included the avoidance of evil speech, the drinking of alcohol, and the eating of meat. The vegetarian requirement was imperative for the Elect since plants contained more light particles than flesh. The light particles were digested through the bodies of the vegetarian Elect, released through their belches into the atmosphere, distilled by the cosmic machine of the Three Wheels, and finally sent on their homeward journey along the Column of Glory (Milky Way) to the Kingdom of Light. Heresiologists thus ridiculed Manichaean Elect as "saviors of god" *(salvatores dei)*. Second, the "Seal of the Hands" *(signacula manuum)* forbade the Elect from any activity which might injure material objects containing light particles. Thus killing animals, planting, harvesting, or even walking over the smallest plants could prevent the liberation of the light particles (the divine Suffering Jesus). Since the procuring and preparation of vegetable foodstuffs often required the damaging or partial destruction of light-bearing plants, the Elect were not permitted to prepare their own meals, and instead were served by the Auditors, who were pardoned for the unavoidable destruction of plants. Even bathing was not allowed for the Elect since pure water could be defiled by contact with material bodily substances. Third, the "Seal of the Breast" *(signacula sinus)* focused especially on the avoidance of sexual intercourse since the process of birth, copulation, and rebirth was directly related to Adam's lower material nature and was meant by the evil creator to enslave light particles in material bodies. The "Three Seals" were required for all Manichaean Elect, while the Auditors were given lesser requirements allowing them to aquire wealth and to marry and/or maintain mistresses, but were urged to avoid sexual relations. Only the Elect would return to the Kingdom of Light directly after death, while the Auditors could only hope to enter into the bodies of vegetables after death and finally be freed through the digestive systems of the Elect. All humans who are not awakened by the Nous will be forever damned into an inescapable cycle of reincarnation in the bodies of animals, culminating in their permanent entrapment in the Kingdom of Darkness.

The leadership of the Manichaean church was comprised of the Elect. Extant Manichaean texts in Latin, Greek, Middle Persian, and Chinese are unanimous in documenting the four classes within the church hierarchy: (1) the central figurehead or pope (Gk *archegos;* Lat *princeps*) who is Mani's successor, (2) the Twelve Apostles, (3) the 72 bishops, and (4) the 360 elders. Only males could be enrolled in these four classes. Apart from this governmental hierarchy is the larger body of the Elect and the even larger group of Auditors.

F. The History of Manichaeism after Mani's Death

The history of Manichaeism after Mani's death is extremely complex due to its twelve-hundred-year development along a continuous geographical spectrum embracing western N Africa and S Europe on its western edge and coastal SE China on its eastern edge. The present study traces only the general profile of that geohistorical development and refers the readers throughout to the detailed study by Lieu, to which it is largely indebted, and the literature cited there (1985: 78–264).

1. Missions to the West. The intense heresiological polemic against Manichaeism resulted in a now only partially extant literary corpus reflecting the westward movement of the religion. One of the earliest influential anti-Manichaean texts was the *Acta Archelai* (ca. 340), first composed in Greek and then translated into Latin, Coptic, and probably Syriac. The *Acta* was a polemical biography of Mani, an antihagiography meant to call into question alleged divine influence on Mani's life and teachings. It may have been one cause for the creation of Manichaean hagiographies such as that exemplified in the *Cologne Mani Codex.* Cyril of Jerusalem (d. 386) found the *Acta* to be useful in a pastoral context, especially for the catechetical instruction of former Manichaeans. Ephraim of Syria (d. 373) composed a series of discourses and polemical hymns against Manichaean teaching and practice, which nevertheless continued into the next century in Ephraim's own Edessa. Titus of Bostra (d. 371) was in conflict with the Emperor Julian (reigned 360–63) during the latter's neopagan revival, but remained an effective polemicist against the Manichaeans, writing a polemical commentary on Luke and a four-volume refutation of Manichaean doctrine. Titus focused on the Manichaean solution to the problem of evil: the presupposition of an eternal evil principle. Epiphanius of Salamis (d. 403) wrote a lengthy refutation of Manichaeism in his well-known heresiology *Panarion* (ca. 376). John Chrysostom (Antioch) wrote vehemently against the religion in his polemical commentary on Mathew (ca. 390).

Manichaeans probably entered Egypt from Persia. C.H. Roberts (1938) published a manuscript containing the text of a pastoral letter against the Manichaeans by an unidentified late 3d-century bishop (Theonas?) of Alexandria. Serapion of Thmuis also wrote a lengthy refutation, *Against the Manichaeans* (ca. 339), and at about the same time the Neoplatonist and former Manichaean Alexander of Lycopolis rejected the naive literalism of Manichaean cosmology, as Augustine was to do several decades later. At the end of the 4th century, Didymus of Alexandria wrote a polemical commentary on biblical texts employed by the Manichaeans. The discovery of seven Manichaean codices at Medinet Madi in the Fayyum (see C.3 above) and the *Cologne Mani Codex,* probably in Lycopolis (see C.2 above), is further evidence of Egyptian Manichaeism.

Manichaeans probably entered N Africa (Africa Proconsularis) from Egypt. The *Tebessa Codex* and Augustine of Hippo's (354–430) nine-year association with the religion and later polemical responses against Manichaean doctrine and practice are the most famous examples of Manichaeism in N Africa. Augustine (Ries 1988: 125–93) was a Manichaean Auditor for nine years while keeping teaching posts in Tagaste and Carthage. His studies in rhetoric led him to the philosophical analysis of logical problems, which ultimately resulted in his gradual abandonment of Manichaean solutions. Augustine made a lateral move into Christianity under the influence of Christian intellectuals like Bishop Ambrose of Milan. He became an effective and vehement polemicist against Manichaean doctrine and practice until at least 399. Augustine's so-called "Anti-Manichaean Pentateuch" included five tractates written before his ordination in 391: *De moribus ecclesiae catholicae* (ca. 388–90), *De moribus Manichaeorum* (ca. 388–90), *De libero arbitrio* (ca. 388/391), *De genesi contra Manichaeos* (ca. 388–89), and *De vera religione* (390). After his ordination he continued his polemics against the Manichaeans with *De utilitate credendi* (391), *De duabus animabus* (392), *Disputatio contra Fortunatum Manichaeum* (August 28–29, 392), *Contra Adimantum Manichaeum* (394), *Contra epistulam, quam vocant Fundamenti* (396), *Contra Faustum Manichaeum* (ca. 397–98), *Disputatio contra Felicem Manichaeum* (ca. 397–98/404), *De natura boni contra Manichaeos* (399), and *Contra Secundinum Manichaeum* (399). Apart from these fourteen polemical tractates (and disputation records) dealing exclusively with Manichaeism, Augustine also produced writings which indirectly deal with the religion: *Confessionum* (397–401), *Epistulae* (nos. *79* and *236;* ca. 386–429), *Enarrationes in Psalmos* (*Ps. 140;* ca. 392–420), *Sermones 1, 2, 12, 50, 153, 182,* and *237* (ca. 391–430), *De agone christiano* (396), and *De continentia* (ca. 416–26).

Early evidence of Manichaeans in Spain is reflected in the anathematic abjuration text *Commonitorium* (= *Commonitorium sancti Augustini*) often attributed to Augustine but probably produced by Vincent or Lerins (ca. 434) on the basis of Augustine's anti-Manichaean works. An expanded version of this abjuration text was used by a certain Prosper of Lyons nearly a century later (526).

Imperial policies against the Manichaeans are clear evidence of the religion's presence in Rome itself, greater Italy, and throughout the empire. The emperors Diocletian (302), Valentinian I (372), Theodosius I (381), Theodosius II (408–50), Anastasius I (491–518), Justin I (518–527), and Justinian (529) all sought to control the spread of the religion. The fear of subversive political infiltration from Persia set the Roman authorities on guard against Manichaeans. Pope Leo I (ca. 444–45) delivered sermons meant to inform the faithful of the Manichaean threat, and even circulated a pastoral letter *(Ad episcopus per Italiam)* to the Italian bishops urging them to be aware of Manichaean infiltrations in the orthodox clergy. A 4th-century tombstone for a Manichaean Elect was found in 1906 in Salona on the Dalmatian (Yugoslavian) coast.

The dualistic teachings of various groups such as the Paulicians, Bogomils, Albigenses, and Cathars were misidentified as Manichaean, and these groups were consequently persecuted throughout the medieval period in W Asia and Europe. The early and influential anti-Manichaean tract *Acta Archelai* was an important heresiological weapon throughout much of this period and the history of its manuscript tradition reflects its usefulness in a wide variety of contexts.

2. Missions to the East. Manichaeism traveled eastward across Persia into Transoxania already in Mani's lifetime through the missionary work of Mar Ammo. In the 6th century the Eastern Manichaeans split from the authority of the Persian Manichaean *archegos* (under Mar Sad-Ohrmizd, d. 600) and established their own sect called "the True [Pure] Ones" or "Denawars," claiming authority from Mar Ammo. The Denawars moved eastward from Sogdiana and established in the Tarim Basin an ecclesiastical see in Qoco, the capital city of the Uighur Kingdom. The basin was a natural zone for cultural transmission between China and the West, so Manichaean missionaries in the basin followed the silk routes eastward and introduced the religion to China in the 7th century (T'ang Dynasty, 650–83). The common Buddhist culture shared by Turkestan and China facilitated this eastward expansion and accounts for many Buddhist features (technical terms) in eastern Manichaeism.

Manichaeans probably found their first converts in China among Turkish and Sogdian refugees who served as contacts for the native Chinese populace. Manichaean tradition in China maintained that the religion entered the Middle Kingdom through an unknown high-ranking Manichaean priest during the reign of Emperor Kao-tsung of the T'ang Dynasty. That priest's episcopal disciple Mihr-Ormuzd was later granted an audience with the reigning Empress Wu Tse-t'ien (684–704), herself a great patroness of Buddhism. Mihr-Ormuzd at this time initiated the translation of Manichaean works into Chinese. He presented the receptive empress with a Manichaean text entitled *The Sutra of the Two Principles* (*Erh-tsung ching*), destined to become the most popular Manichaean text in China. Her toleration of the religion alienated traditional Buddhists and Confucianists. The religion was subject to restrictive imperial legislation when her own ill-fated Chou Dynasty came to an end and the T'ang Dynasty was reestablished in 705.

Civil disturbances beginning in 721 caused the T'ang government to check foreign influence on local dissidents. A Manichaean priest was required in 731 to write a summary of Manichaean doctrine for official investigation (a copy of the text, now called the *Compendium,* was discovered by Aurel Stein at Tun-Huang in 1905–7; cf. C.1., above). This incident apparently resulted in the first Chinese imperial edict against Manichaeism in the following year (732), meant to limit the spread of the religion among Chinese nationals. It calls the religion a perverse belief masquerading as a school of Buddhism and intending to mislead the common people, and since it is the indigenous religion of the "Western barbarians," its followers will not be persecuted if they keep it to themselves and cease their propagandistic activities among the Chinese people.

The T'ang Dynasty encountered serious difficulties with the rebellion of the militarist An Lu-shan from 755 to 762. The dynasty had to abandon northern China to the rebellion and seek assistance from its western Uighur neighbors. The Uighur armies liberated the eastern T'ang capital city of Lo-yang in 762. It was in Lo-yang that Sogdian Manichaean missionaries converted the powerful Uighur Khagan, who then provided the religion with sorely needed political support in China. The T'ang government succumbed to political pressure from the Uighur Khagan to allow the propagation of Manichaeism in China. The religion spread through the Yangtze Basin, where four Manichaean temples were built in 768 and contacts with Chinese nationals were reinstated. The Chinese populace grew more intolerant against Uighur culture and the T'ang government began to legislate contacts between foreigners and the Chinese people. The government found itself relatively free of foreign influence when the Uighur Empire collapsed in 840. It closed Manichaean temples with an imperial letter of 843, resulting in a massacre of Manichaeans. Buddhism, Zoroastrianism, and Nestorian Christianity also fell out of imperial favor as Confucian influence now predominated at the imperial court and Western contacts declined.

Sogdian Manichaean missionaries who had worked among the Uighurs began with the collapse of the Uighur Empire to propagate the religion among the Kirghiz conquerors. Much of the Uighur nation moved to the southeast where they settled on the NW border of China. It was in Tun-huang that three Manichaean texts were discovered by Aurel Stein in 1905–07 (see C.1 above). Manichaeans remained influential in the Uighur court in the capital city of Qoco, the original site of the ecclesiastical see of the early Denawar Manichaeans. A. von Le Coq's second German expedition of 1904–05 discovered in Qoco thousands of high-quality illuminated Manichaean manuscripts (see

C.1 above). A Chinese expedition in 1930 discovered in Qoco a document detailing the economic and organizational issues related to Manichaean monasteries and their controlling house in Qoco, further evidencing the high economic and privileged social positions associated with the monasteries. Despite the political strength of the religion, the majority of people in the Uighur kingdom remained Buddhist or Nestorian. Evidence for Manichaeism in NW China cannot be found after the 10th century and the Tarim Basin itself came under Islamic rule in the late 11th century.

A fifty-three-year period of political chaos, commonly referred to as the Five Dynasties and Ten Nations (907–60), followed the fall of the T'ang Dynasty in 907 and provided Manichaean missionaries with the opportunity to propagate the religion in the coastal regions of SE China, notably in Fukien province. Buddhist historians of the following Sung Dynasty (960–1280) blamed the chaos of the Five Dynasties period, and other more current social problems, on Manichaeans who had by then integrated themselves into Chinese society. The Sinicization of Manichaeism, now called the Religion of Light (Ming-chiao), involved the establishment of Manichaean temples under the guise of Taoist temples. This resulted in one of the most significant early victories for Chinese Manichaeans: the inclusion of a major Chinese Manichaean text *(The Sutra of the Two Principles and the Three Moments)* into the official canon of Taoist scriptures compiled under Emperor Chen-tsung (reigned 998–1022). The text thus received imperial protection during the official confiscations of the early 1120s. The Fang La rebellion of 1120–22 set officials against unauthorized religious groups like Manichaeism, but focused especially on sectarian Buddhist and Taoist groups. Many such groups were called by the derogatory name "vegetarian demon worshippers" and were subject to blanket prosecution and harassment.

Invading Jurchens captured the N Sung capital in 1126, ending the Sung Dynasty's control over a unified N and S China. The Jurchens met difficult terrain and armed resistance as they attempted to conquer territories south of the Yangtze River. The remaining Sung government moved farther S, where it met established Manichaean communities. The government blamed five rebellions between 1130 and 1150 on "vegetarian demon worshippers" and issued twenty edicts against such groups between 1132 and 1209. Southern Sung Buddhist historiography was intensely polemical toward the memory of the Religion of Light. The Taoist historians, however, seem to be silent concerning the religion, perhaps as a result of their own syncretistic nature. Confucian scholars were often genuinely interested in Manichaean doctrine, but feared the social organization and potential political power of such groups.

The Sung government ended with the decisive invasion of the Mongols, under Kublai Khan, and a final battle south of Canton in 1280. China reopened its borders to foreign influence during the eighty-eight-year period of Mongol rule (1280–1368). The Silk Road was reactivated and the seas between the S China coast and the Persian Gulf were busy with trade ships. The Mongol policy of religious toleration, in contrast to that of the Sung, allowed Manichaean missionaries to continue their work without official harassment. Even Marco Polo seems to have encountered a group of Manichaeans he thought were Christians. The Mongol control of China began to erode with the death of Kublai Khan in 1294. A series of uncoordinated rebellions began in S China and increased to the point that one of the rebel leaders, the former Buddhist novice Chu Yüan-chang, recaptured Peking from the Mongols in 1368 and established his Dynasty of Light (Ming-chao). Several sects were proscribed by his edict of 1370, including the Religion of Light (Ming-chiao).

The rest of our knowledge of the Religion of Light in China concerns the Manichaean temple on Hua-piao Hill in Ch'üan-chou, Fukien province. An inscription on the temple's statue of Mani dates the statue to 1339. Historical references preserved in the writings of Ho Ch'iao-yüan (ca. 1600) suggest that the S Chinese Manichaeans in Ch'üan-chou were still considered a distinct social group at the beginning of the 17th century. But Chinese scholars of the Ch'ing Dynasty (1644–1912) had no exact knowledge of the identity and nature of the Religion of Light.

Bibliography

Allberry, C. R. C. 1938. *Manichaean Manuscripts in the Chester Beatty Collection.* Vol. 2, pt. 2. Stuttgart.

Baur, F. C. 1831. *Das manichäische Religionssystem.* Tübingen.

Beausobre, I. de. 1734. *Histoire de Manichée et du Manichéisme.* Amsterdam.

Böhlig. A. 1968a. Die Arbeit an den koptischen Manichaica. Pp. 177–78 in *Mysterion und Warheit: Gesammelte Beiträge zur spätantiken Religionsgeschichte.* Leiden.

———. 1968b. Zu den Synaxeis des Lebendigen Evangeliums. Pp. 252–66 in A. Böhlig, *Mysterion und Warheit.* Leiden.

Bryder, P., ed. 1988. *Manichaean Studies: Proceedings of the First International Conference on Manichaeism.* Lund.

Flügel, G. 1862. *Mani: Seine Lehre und seine Schriften.* Leipzig.

Funk, W.-P. 1985. How Closely Related Are the Subakhmimic Dialects? *ZÄS* 112: 124–39.

Geng Shimin. 1990. Recent Studies on Manichaeism in China. In Wiessner 1990.

Giversen, S. 1986–88. *The Manichaean Coptic Papyri in the Chester Beatty Library.* Vols. 1–4. Cahiers d'orientalisme 13, 15–17. Geneva.

Kessler, K. 1889. *Mani. Forschungen über die manichäische Religion.* Berlin.

Koenen, L., and Römer, C., ed. 1988. *Der Kölner Mani-Kodex.* Papyrologica Coloniensia Sonderreihe 14. Opladen.

Lieu, S. N. C. 1985. *Manichaeism in the Later Roman Empire and Medieval China: A Historical Survey.* Manchester.

———. 1988. Fact and Fiction in the Acta Archelai. Pp. 69–88 in Bryder 1988.

Lin Wu-shu. 1987. *Manichaeism and Its Spread to the East.* Beijing [In Chinese]. (1989 English review by P. Bryder in *Manichaean Studies Newsletter* 1 (1989): 15–19.)

———. 1988. On the Joining between the Two Fragments of "The Compendium of the Teachings of Mani, The Buddha of Light." Pp. 89–93 in Bryder 1988.

———. 1989. A New Find of [a] Manichaean Stone Carving in Fujian, China. *Manichaean Studies Newsletter* 1: 22–27.

Merkelbach, R. 1986. *Mani und sein Religionssystem.* Opladen.

———. 1988a. Die Täufer, bei denen Mani Aufwuchs. Pp. 105–33 in Bryder 1988.

———. 1988b. Der manichäische Codex von Tebessa. Pp. 229–64 in Bryder 1988.

Mirecki, P. A. 1988. The Coptic Manichaean Synaxeis Codex: Descriptive Catalogue of Synaxis Chapter Titles. Pp. 135–45 in Bryder 1988.
Pearson, B. 1988. The Figure of Seth in Manichaean Literature. Pp. 147–55 in Bryder 1988.
Polotsky, H. J. 1934. *Manichäische Handschriften der Sammlung A. Chester Beatty.* Vol. 1, *Manichäische Homilien.* Berlin.
Polotsky, H. J., and Böhlig, A. 1940. *Manichäische Handschriften der staatliche Museen Berlins: Kephalaia.* Berlin.
Ries, J. 1959. Introduction aux études manichéennes (2). *ETL* 35: 395–98.
———. 1988. *Les Études manichéenes. Des controverses de la Réforme aux découvertes du XXe siècle.* Louvain-la-Neuve.
Roberts, C. H. 1938. *Catalogue of Greek and Latin Papyri. 3.* Manchester.
Robinson, J. M. 1978. The Future of Papyrus Codicology. Pp. 33–43 in *The Future of Coptic Studies,* ed. R. M. Wilson. Leiden.
———. 1990. The Fate of the Manichaean Codices of Medinet Madi: 1929–1989. In Wiessner 1990.
Schmidt, C., and Polotsky, H. J. 1933. Ein Mani-Fund in Ägypten: Originalschriften des Mani und seiner Schüler. Pp. 4–90 in *SPAW* 1. Berlin.
Wiessner, G., ed. 1990. *The Proceedings of the Second International Conference on Manichaeism.* Bonn.

Paul Allan Mirecki

MANIUS, TITUS (PERSON) [Gk *Titos Manios*]. Var. MANLIUS; MANILIUS. One of two Roman envoys to the people of the Jews in 164 B.C.E. (2 Macc 11:34). There is no reference in any other source to an envoy named Titus Manius, and some believe the letter mentioned in this text to be fictitious. However, the content of the letter they sent to the Jews is plausible enough, for it accords with the policy of the Romans toward the area of Syria. The letter confirmed the privileges of Lysias to the Jews after his campaign of 163 B.C.E. against Judea. The Roman envoys offered to meet the Jews' own envoy in Antioch, and to present their proposals to the king.

In an effort to establish the identity of Titus Manius other ancient sources have been searched. Moffat points out that Polybius (31.9.6) mentions one Manius Sergius who was one of the envoys to Antiochus Epiphanes in 164 B.C.E., and Livy (43.2) speaks of a T. Manlius Torquatus who went on a mission to Egypt; but there is no record of Roman envoys to Syria with the names mentioned in this text. Moffat does not support Niese's emendation of "Manios Ernios" to "Manios Sergios"; nor does he accept "Titus" as a corruption of a name ending in "-tius" (*OTP* 1: 148). These positions and their implications have been discussed more recently in greater detail by Goldstein, who concludes that it is best to consider 2 Maccabees as the sole surviving evidence for the embassy of Quintus Memmius and Titus Manius (Goldstein *II Maccabees* AB, 422–425). See MEMMIUS, QUINTUS (PERSON).

Betty Jane Lillie

MANNA. The daily bread given by God to the Israelites during their forty years of wilderness wandering. Manna received its name reportedly from the question the Israelites asked when they first saw it, "What is it?" or "manna." Manna was given when Israel arrived in the wilderness of Sin and, along with occasional quail, was the only miraculous food supply the Israelites received during the forty years (Num 11:6). In fact, the supply did not cease until the Israelites arrived at the border of Canaan. The provision of manna was daily. The Lord promised to rain bread from heaven upon the ground. The people were instructed to gather it daily with the exception of the Sabbath. If they gathered too much, the remainder would spoil. Only on the sixth day were they permitted to gather a double portion (Exod 16:1–30).

Manna was described as a fine, flakelike frost. It was like a coriander seed, white, and had the taste of a wafer made with honey (Exod 16:14, 31; Num 11:8). Manna could be prepared in a variety of ways: ground into a meal, boiled in pots, or made into cakes. In other passages, manna is described as "heaven's grain" (Deut 8:3, 16; Neh 9:20; Pss 78:24, 105:40).

The provision was considered so miraculous that Moses commanded Aaron the high priest to gather an omer of manna and place it in the ark of the covenant that future generations might be reminded of the Lord's supply of bread to the great host of Israelites for forty years. In the NT, Paul called manna "spiritual" or "supernatural" food (1 Cor 10:3). Christ also compared himself with the bread that came down from heaven (John 6:31–65).

Manna has often been associated with natural phenomena. The most common natural explanation of manna proposes its connection with a gum resin produced by one or more varieties of flowering trees, such as *Alhagi maurorum* (Sinai manna), *Tamarisk gallica,* or *Fraxinus ornus* (flowering ash). The tamarisk bush annually produces a gum resin for three to six weeks. Recently, however, the natural production of manna has been associated with the excretions of two species of scale insects. In particular, manna-tamarisk is produced by the secretions and sting of a tree louse.

Bibliography

Bodenheimer, F. S. 1947. The Manna of Sinai. *BA* 10: 1–6.
Coppens, J. 1960. Les Traditions relatives a la manna dans Exode xvi. *EstEcl* 34: 473–89.
Haupt, P. 1922. Manna, Nectar, and Ambrosia. *AJP* 43: 247 ff.
Malina, B. J. 1968. *The Palestinian Manna Tradition.* Leiden.
Yamauchi, E. M. 1966. The "Daily Bread" Motif in Antiquity. *WTJ* 28: 145 ff.

Joel C. Slayton

MANNEANS. See MINNI (PLACE).

MANOAH (PERSON) [Heb *mānôaḥ*]. The father of the Danite hero Samson. Dan is described in Judg 13:2 as a "clan" (*mišpaḥâ*) rather than a tribe *(šēbeṭ),* perhaps an indication that it is in the process of settlement. The Danite camp is located at Zoran and Eshtaol in the Shephelah (13:25; 16:31; cf. 18:11–12) at a time (the late 12th century B.C.E.) when Philistine expansion had begun to put pressure on the Israelite tribes in this area (Judah and Dan). Scholars debate whether the Samson stories represent a time before or after the Danite migration to the north (see

Judges 18); clearly they reflect Dan's inability to settle in its assigned territory in the central hill country (Josh 19:40–48).

Manoah and his wife are the recipients of a birth announcement concerning Samson (Judges 13). Strikingly, in view of the fact that she has the central role, the woman's name is omitted. The story utilizes the typical motif of the promise to a barren woman of a son who will have a special destiny (cf. Sarah, Rachel, Hannah). The divine messenger appears to the woman alone with a birth announcement and instructions (13:3–5). She tells Manoah the essential facts (the injunctions placed upon her, the boy's destiny as a Nazirite) but omits certain key elements (that their son may not be shaved and that he will begin to deliver Israel from the Philistines). Manoah prays to be included in the events, "let the man of God whom you sent come again to us, and teach us what we are to do with the boy that will be born" (v 8), but in response to his prayer, the messenger again appears to the woman alone: "but Manoah her husband was not with her" (v 9). Manoah is brought to the messenger by his wife. When Manoah questions him, he receives even less information from the messenger than he had received from his wife (13:11–18).

Manoah and his wife offer a sacrifice to God (13:16–20). Only when the messenger disappears in the fire of the sacrifice does Manoah realize his divine identity (13:21); his wife had sensed it from the start (v 6). Manoah fears death, for he knows the tradition that one cannot see God and live (Exod 33:20; Judg 6:22–23; Gen 16:13–14; Exod 19:21; Gen 32:30). His wife, however, perceives a purpose behind the theophany and birth announcement and assures her husband that they will not die (in theophanies God usually gives this assurance). Not only does Manoah know less about the child's destiny than his wife, he also comprehends less well the divine plan.

Manoah and his wife play a small role in chap. 14, but do not appear in chaps. 15–16. In 14:1–4, they object to Samson's desire to marry a Philistine, for they are unaware that Samson's folly is part of God's plan (v 4). They are mentioned as accompanying Samson to Timnah in 14:5; and in 14:10, Samson's father goes with him to Timnah, presumably to arrange the marriage. Samson does not tell his father and his mother about killing the lion barehanded or about finding honey in its carcass sometime later; these events give rise to the riddle he puts to the Philistines at his wedding feast. When the Philistines answer the riddle, having deceitfully obtained the answer through Samson's wife, Samson pays off his wager and, in a rage, returns to his father's house (14:19). The final mention of Manoah's name appears in 16:31, where we are told that Samson was buried in his father's tomb.

Bibliography

Exum, J. C. 1980. Promise and Fulfillment: Narrative Art in Judges 13. *JBL* 99: 43–59.

J. Cheryl Exum

MANTELET.
See WEAPONS AND IMPLEMENTS OF WARFARE.

MANTLE.
See DRESS AND ORNAMENTATION.

MANUAL OF DISCIPLINE.
See COMMUNITY, RULE OF THE (1QS).

MAOCH

MAOCH (PERSON) [Heb *māᶜôk*]. The father of Achish, king of Gath (1 Sam 27:2). He is often identified with Maacah, father of Achish, king of Gath, of 2 Kgs 2:39. The names are similar (*māᶜôk* and *maᶜăkâ*), but over forty years separates the two incidents, making such an identification problematic. See also Klein *1 Samuel* WBC; and McCarter *1 Samuel* AB.

Pauline A. Viviano

MAON (PERSON)

MAON (PERSON) [Heb *māᶜôn*]. Son of Shammai, a descendant of Caleb (1 Chr 2:45). Whether Maon ("habitation") is the name of a person or the name of a town or region is not certain (compare Josh 15:55; 1 Sam 25:2); nor is it certain that this portion of the genealogy is in its original position. On the difficulties of the genealogy in 1 Chr 2:42–50a, see Williamson (Chronicles NCBC, 55) and Braun (*1 Chronicles* WBC, 40–41).

Craig A. Evans

MAON (PLACE)

MAON (PLACE) [Heb *māᶜôn*]. The name of two towns in S. Palestine.

1. A town in the hill country of Judah (Josh 15:55; Kallai *HGB*, 335, 347), together with other towns like Ziph and Carmel, located along the W edge of the Wilderness of Judah. Maon was approximately 8 miles S-SE of Hebron. Scholars identify the ancient site with Tell Ma'in (M.R. 162090; *HGB*, 290). Maon was in an area that provided pastureland for small cattle in the springtime (Aharoni *LBHG*, 30). The name "Maon" which means "abode" or "dwelling" suggests that the original settlement was named after the type of buildings characteristic of the town (Aharoni *LBHG*, 109), that is, dwellings, probably for herdsmen of that region. Reference to the "wilderness of Maon" (1 Sam 23:24–25; Maon in the LXX; Paran in the MT; Klein *1 Samuel* WBC, 245, see note 1.a) indicates that the name of the town was applied to the area around it (*LBHG*, 30). The "wilderness of Maon" was located in the Arabah S of Jeshimon (1 Sam 23:24).

In the OT, the wilderness of Maon and Maon the town are mentioned in the accounts of David's encounters during his flight from Saul. David sought refuge from Saul in the wilderness of Maon (1 Sam 23:24–25) following his escape from sites in the wilderness of Ziph (1 Sam 23:15–23). "The rock . . . in the wilderness of Maon" (v 25) probably refers to an area with rock formations, perhaps cliffs (see ROCK OF ESCAPE), that provided security for those seeking refuge. Maon was the hometown of Nabal, an influential citizen and wealthy herdsman in the area who operated a sheepshearing business in the nearby town of Carmel and with whom David had a serious clash (1 Sam 25:1–42).

While the history of Maon during the OT period has not been defined, it must have played an important role in the political and military matters in the hill country of Judah. David's marriage to Abigail, wife of the deceased Nabal, an influential citizen from Maon, seems to have had political overtones (1 Sam 25:39–42). Militarily, Maon was a valuable defense center since it and Ziph were fortified sites and formed a line of defense protecting Jerusalem from the SE (Har-El 1981: 14). A 7th-century-B.C.E. ostracon from Arad records the taxes the king of Judah received from Maon (*LBHG*, 399).

2. A site in SW Palestine about 11 miles S of Gaza, the modern Kh. Ma'in. Maon was one of the major synagogue site locations in Palestine (Meyers 1980: 98, see map and 105; *HAB*, 152, see map no. 2). See also MEUNIM.

Bibliography

Hal-El, M. 1981. Jerusalem and Judah: Roads and Fortifications. *BA* 44/1: 8–19.

Meyers, E. M. 1980. Ancient Synagogues in Galilee: Their Religious and Cultural Setting. *BA* 43/2: 97–108.

LAMOINE F. DEVRIES

MARA (PERSON) [Heb *mārāʾ*]. An appellative for Naomi, the mother-in-law of Ruth (Ruth 1:20). See NAOMI. Naomi and her family moved from Bethlehem-Judah to Moab where her husband Elimelech and their sons Mahlon and Chilion died (1:1–5). Upon her return to Bethlehem, the women of the city who had not seen her for ten years ask, "Is this Naomi?" (1:19). Naomi answers their question with a play on her name. "Naomi" means "pleasant," but because she had experienced bitterness in Moab she implores them to call her "Mara," meaning "bitter." By objecting to the name "Naomi," she is expressing the inappropriateness of her name since her condition has changed from joy to sorrow.

The name "Mara" has been commonly analyzed as an Aramaic form substituted for the Hebrew feminine noun *mrh,* which is the reading in several mss, derived from *mrr.* Others have explained the form as Hebrew rather than Aramaic, understanding the *ʾalep* as an orthographic difference or as a hypocoristicon.

The wordplay is completed by Naomi's explanation of her new name where the word *mar* is repeated: "for the Almighty has dealt very bitterly with me" (1:20b). This explanation was anticipated in 1:13 by the occurrence of the word *mar:* "it is more *bitter* for me than you." The use of wordplay and popular etymologies is a common feature of the Hebrew Bible. The story of Ruth is a storehouse of literary devices to inject subtle nuances of meaning, but Naomi/Mara is the only specific wordplay explained in the story itself.

KENNETH A. MATHEWS

MARAH (PLACE) [Heb *mārâ*]. After crossing the Red Sea and singing triumphantly over the demise of the Egyptians (Exod 15:1–21), Moses led the people into the Wilderness of Shur. They went three days without finding water and when they came to Marah (v 23), they found water but it was "bitter"; so they called the place Marah, which means "bitter" (BDB, 600). The usual interpretation is that the water was brackish, i.e., salty. The people complained and Moses cried to the Lord, who showed him a tree which he threw into the water and sweetened it.

After Marah, the Israelites traveled to Elim with its 12 springs and 70 palm trees (Exod 15:27). The summary of the wilderness wanderings in Numbers 33 says that after crossing through the sea, the people went three days into the Wilderness of Etham (v 6 gives Etham as the campsite after Succoth) and camped at Marah, and from there they went to Elim (vv 8–9).

Rylaarsdam (*IB* 1: 947) claims the Way of Shur is the familiar caravan route that approached Kadesh-barnea as it led to Beer-sheba. This is evidence that Mt. Sinai is in the Edom-Paran area and not at Jebel Musa in the S apex of the peninsula. It is impossible to definitely locate the site in his view. Brackish pools and wells are frequent in many desert areas. But a three-day journey by a caravan would perhaps cover 50 miles. The account in Exod 15:23 is in etiological form. Rylaarsdam notes a possible parallel story in Exod 17:7. It may be a different occasion of lack of water or it may be a different version of the same story. There was no water and people complained so Moses struck a rock and water came out. He called the place Massah ("proof" because they had "proved" the Lord) and Meribah ("contention" because of their complaints). This story is repeated without Massah in Num 20:1–12, at Kadesh-barnea after Sinai. In contrast to Rylaarsdam, Childs (*Exodus* OTL, 268) suggested the primary tradition is not etiological in form. If it had been, the new name would reflect the new state of the spring rather than the old.

Many locations have been proposed for Marah. While there is still some doubt, it was probably Ain Hawarah, 47 miles SE of Suez and ca. 7 miles from the Red Sea, separated from the sea by a range of hills. These are among the first springs on the ancient road to the Sinai mines which the Egyptians had exploited for centuries (Wright and Filson *WHAB*, 39). Keil and Delitzsch (n.d., 57) noted the first spot on the road through the Wilderness of Shur where water is found is Hawarah. Robinson described it as a basin 6–8 feet in diameter, with 2 feet of water in it. It was so bitter, so salty, Bedouins considered it the worst water in the whole neighborhood (1856: 66–67). Gehman (*NWDB*, 586) noted the well measures ca. 20 feet across but is much wider at the bottom and has a depth of perhaps 25 feet. The soil of the region abounds in soda and the water is salty and bitter.

Several other names have been compared to the Sinai exodus site. Maroth ("bitterness") is a town in Judah (Micah 1:12). "Merathaim," twofold bitterness or twofold rebellion, is a symbolic name for Babylon in Jer 50:21. The name may be a reference to Marratim, a lagoon or swamp in the region around the mouth of the Tigris and Euphrates rivers. The conclusion in any case is that though these are different places, they suggest the commonness of the place-name "bitter."

Bibliography

Keil, C. F., and Delitzsch, F. n.d. *The Pentateuch.* Vol. 1 of *Commentary on The Old Testament.* Trans. J. Martin. Grand Rapids. Repr. 1983.

Robinson, E. 1856. *Biblical Researches in Palestine.* Vol. 1. Boston.

HENRY O. THOMPSON

MARANATHA. The sentence *Maranatha* appears in 1 Cor 16:22 and *Didache* 10:6, in both cases with liturgical contexts. It is not a Greek word or phrase, and is not Hebrew, but rather a transliteration into Greek letters of an Aramaic phrase. Underlying the Greek text are the Aramaic words *mar,* "lord," and a form of the verb *ʾătāʾ*, "to come." The essential questions raised by the expression are the proper segmentation of the sentence (that is, as *maran atha* or as *marana tha*), its precise meaning, and the specific dialect of Aramaic that it represents.

The sentence *maran atha* would mean either "Our Lord/Master has come," or perhaps (if *atha* is interpreted as a participle) "Our Lord/Master is coming" (possibly, "will come"). The word division *marana tha* would give by contrast "Our Lord/Master, come!" (*tha* being the imperative). The proper segmentation of the expression is thus essential to its proper interpretation, and this in turn depends on a correct determination of the dialect of Aramaic it represents.

The context of the expression in both the NT and the *Didache* is formulaic. In Paul's usage it is linked to a curse: "If anyone has no love for the Lord, let him be accursed. *Maranatha*" (1 Cor 16:22). In the *Didache* the context is eucharistic: "Let grace come and this world pass away. Hosanna to the God of David. If anyone is holy let him come; if he is not, let him repent. *Maranatha.* Amen" (*Didache* 10:6). The outlook is clearly eschatological. The same type of outlook also appears in 1 Cor 11:23–26, a eucharistic section which includes the injunction, "For as often as you eat this bread and drink the cup, you proclaim the Lord's death *until he comes*" (1 Cor 11:26 [emphasis added]; see Kuhn *TDNT* 4: 471). This would point to the meaning "Our Lord, come!" Rev 22:20 indeed supplies such a sense: "Amen. Come, Lord Jesus!"

These examples of context and usage seem to indicate the segmentation *marana tha.* What, then, of the dialect? Presuming that the Aramaic noun *mār* ("Lord") carries a 1st-person plural pronominal suffix ("our"), is that suffix /-an/ (thus giving *maran*) or /-anā/ (giving *marana*)? (Both forms of the suffix are attested in different dialects of Aramaic.) Aramaic texts from Qumran and Wadi Murabbaʿat, along with the earliest known rabbinic text, the *Megillâ Taʿanit,* support the longer form /-anā/ (with a single possible exception) rather than the shorter /-an/. (The latter, shorter form is the usual form of the suffix in the Palestinian Talmud and the Midrash.) Evidence from Aramaic of the 1st century C.E. also suggests that the verb (spelled in Gk *tha*) could be in Aramaic either *tâ(ʾ)* or *ʾĕtâ.* Spelled in the Aramaic script, the underlying forms would then be written *mrnh th* or *mrnh ʾth.* The first of these probably lies behind *marana tha,* and the correct sense of the expression is probably "Our Lord/Master, come!"

MAX WILCOX

MARCHESHVAN [Heb *marḥešwān*]. The eighth month of the ancient Hebrew calendar, roughly corresponding to October–November. See CALENDARS (ANCIENT ISRAELITE AND EARLY JEWISH).

MARCION. To the heresiologists of later centuries, Marcion was the most formidable heretic of the 2d century C.E. His teaching sprang from a radical emphasis upon the discontinuity between Christianity and Judaism. The God of Jesus, he asserted, was not the same as the God of the Hebrew Scriptures. While this ditheism was an important element of Marcionism, theological innovation was not Marcion's hallmark. In fact, he was a radical Paulinist who rejected the OT writings and organized a church with strong ascetic tendencies. The scripture of his church comprised one gospel (a version of Luke), ten letters of Paul (not including the Pastorals and Hebrews), and his own work entitled "Antitheses"—a catalog of contradictions between the teaching of Jesus and that of the OT. Indeed, the first clearly delineated canon in early Christianity was that of Marcion.

A. Origin and Career
B. Marcion's Teaching
C. Marcion's Accomplishment
D. Marcion's Significance
   1. The Christian Canon
   2. NT Textual Criticism
   3. NT Literary Criticism
   4. The Earliest Pauline Reform

A. Origin and Career

Marcion was born in Sinope of Pontus in NE Asia Minor in the latter half of the 1st century C.E. While it is likely that he was raised a Christian, the report of Hippolytus that he was the son of a bishop of Sinope is suspect. Hippolytus contends that Marcion was excommunicated by his own father for seducing a virgin. The account has the flavor of heresiological polemic. Often enough in the writings of Church Fathers the greatest antagonists to Catholicism were accounted moral degenerates. More reliable is the reference made by Tertullian to Marcion's occupation—that of a *nauclerus* (shipowner). This does not seem to be polemically motivated and it accords with Marcion's later success as an organizer of a church that spread throughout the empire.

Biographical information on Marcion and his early work is scant and, as noted above, often of dubious reliability. Even the "one secure date" of Marcion's career, the year 144, in which he was excommunicated from Rome, has recently been called into question. It does not accord with the remark of Justin Martyr, who says in the year 150 that Marcion was alive "even until now." This and the fact that by Justin's time Marcionites could be found all over the empire suggest that he was active at least 10–20 years earlier (Hoffmann 1984: 44–47). The establishment of an earlier date for Marcion's activity is a matter of great significance for biblical studies, since it would strengthen the arguments of those who see the Pastoral Epistles or even the Acts of the Apostles as responses to Marcion's movement (Knox 1942: 139). At any rate, before his rejection in Rome he was active in western Asia Minor, specifically Ephesus. In Asia Minor he had encountered the Pauline corpus and was deeply affected by the struggles of the Apostle to the Nations. He began to teach the irreconcilability of the teaching of Paul and the prevailing Christian teaching, which was tightly bound to the OT.

B. Marcion's Teaching

To Marcion the only legitimate apostle was Paul. Other apostles, such as Peter, James, and John, had diluted and distorted the true teaching of Jesus. Marcion based this conclusion on his reading of Galatians 1 and 2. He saw in the letters of Paul dichotomies between faith and works of the Law—the way of Paul and the way of the Judaizers. He saw at the same time that Christianity was heavily reliant on the OT as a source of instruction and ethics. He noted that a great emphasis was placed on Christianity as the fulfillment of OT promises. One need only examine the patristic literature of the early 2d century (*1 Clement* and *Barnabas*) to realize that he was right. But Marcion noted, in addition, that the brilliant flame of the Apostle to the Nations had been reduced to a gentler glow. In many circles of Christianity Paul's basic teachings and writings were virtually ignored. Marcion surmised that Paul's gospel had been subverted, and so he set out to reconstruct that true gospel. This involved a summary dissolution of the tensions that characterized Pauline thought, namely, continuity with Judaism vis-à-vis discontinuity and freedom vis-à-vis obligation. The God from which Jesus was sent must have been other than the God of the Law (the Creator God). For the concept of another god, more precisely a lesser god—a Demiurge—Marcion was indebted to the gnostics. However, it is incorrect to label Marcion a gnostic. He did not engage in speculation about the creation of the cosmos. He did not interpret OT texts allegorically. He did not explain redemption in metaphysical terms nor insist on a secret, saving knowledge (Hoffmann 1984: 175–79). It seems, in fact, that he was not a deep or probing thinker. His theology was replete with discrepancies which Tertullian and others were only too happy to flaunt. But while his solution to the nettlesome features of Pauline theology lacked philosophical nuance, it provided a simple, graspable, and apparently consistent system—narrow in focus and easy to defend. His scriptures were selected and edited according to one overriding principle: the separation of Jesus from the OT God. He presented only one Gospel and one Apostle. To these he appended his own "Antitheses" in which he argued the principle of the opposition of the Gospel and the Law.

His christology has been characterized as modalist and docetic. It should be pointed out, however, that in his day neither of these had been officially condemned (Blackman 1948: 98). Jesus came from his Father, the Foreign God, and took on the appearance of flesh at that moment and maintained it until the crucifixion, at which point he left it. And so, for Marcion, what hung dead on the cross was not really Jesus. Yet this did not prevent Marcion from proclaiming that this apparent death had redemptive power. By it, Jesus saved the souls of those who would believe in him. Marcion even maintained the notion of the descent of Jesus among the dead. But for him this meant that Jesus freed those whom the Creator God had punished, e.g., Cain and the Sodomites. To Marcion the Creator God was not evil. He was only just. The Father of Jesus, in contrast, was loving.

When Marcion took his message to Rome he is said to have confronted Church leaders there with passages like Luke 5:36 (on sewing new patches on old garments). They found his solution to the difficulties posed by these passages—the total separation of the Gospel from the Law, the God of Jesus from the Creator—entirely unacceptable, and they rejected him.

Any number of people before and since Marcion received such a rejection and resolutely went on teaching to those who would listen. In most cases, once they died their following disappeared shortly thereafter. Marcion went much further than that. He set out to organize his own church, "the True Church," in his mind. Marcion's church taught from his own scriptures and required sexual abstinence (procreation being a command of the Creator God), but otherwise looked very much like the church which had rejected him. He took over the basic structures of worship and organization. Marcionites celebrated baptism and the Lord's Supper. They maintained the roles of catechumens, deacons and deaconesses, presbyters and bishops. In the Marcionite liturgy water was used instead of wine, wine thought to be the product of the Creator. But in most other respects it seems that Marcionite worship resembled that of non-Marcionites.

Marcion's modifications of church order may have involved a system of short terms of office for bishops, participation of women in significant leadership roles (since "in Christ there is neither male nor female"), and a reduction of the distinction between clergy and laity in general. It is difficult to ascertain just how far these reforms were actually instituted within Marcionism, as there is disagreement among the heresiologists on some of them. Adding to the confusion is the fact that Marcionite practices are in some cases polemicized along with those of Montanists and other sects. It is safe to say, however, that the overall tendency was toward a rather loosely organized church. We do not hear of Marcionite councils or synods. Marcion's clearly delineated canon and the limited scope of his teaching provided sufficient consistency for strong cohesiveness without superstructures.

C. Marcion's Accomplishment

Whatever the precise nature of Marcion's system of organization, there can be no doubt it was effective. The surest proof of this is the horror and vehemence awakened in Marcion's adversaries. Scholars conjecture that in numbers alone the Marcionites may have nearly surpassed non-Marcionites in the decades of the 160s and 170s. Justin contends that even in his time the Marcionites were spread throughout the empire. Marcionite teachings were challenged in the writings of nearly every major Church Father from Irenaeus, through Tertullian in the West and Bardesanes in the East, to Epiphanius and Ephrem Syrus. Theodoret of Cyprus speaks of winning over large numbers of Marcionites in the mid–5th century. Although Marcionism had begun to wane in the West in the 3d century, it remained vigorous in the East well into the 5th. Throughout that period Marcionite churches or chapels existed side by side with those of their opponents. In fact, Cyril of Jerusalem felt it necessary to warn his catechumens when not to be misled to a Marcionite church entering a city in search of a Christian place of worship.

In the eyes of the pagans the Marcionites were not distinct from non-Marcionites. During the persecutions many Marcionites suffered the martyr's death. The centuries-long endurance of Marcionism is even more amazing when one recalls that they recruited members through adult conversion alone.

D. Marcion's Significance

The real significance of Marcion and his movement for contemporary biblical studies is not limited to his impressive record as a church organizer. His significance may be considered in four areas:

1. The Christian Canon. While not all scholars agree that Marcion forced the creation of the Christian canon, we cannot deny that his was the first. His influence in this matter is manifest in the composition of the NT canon that was later to emerge. Marcion's basic framework of gospel and apostle is seen in the Gospels and "Apostles" (i.e., Acts and Letters) in the Christian NT. What is new is the addition of an apocalypse, yet even this takes the form of a corpus of letters by a representative of the apostolic age. It should be noted that the primary difference between Marcion's canon and the Christian canon is that the former is singular and the latter plural. A conscious step in the direction of diversity was taken by anti-Marcionite Christians of the 2d through 4th centuries.

The vociferous insistence of anti-Marcionite Christianity on the validity of the OT within the canon is a point which should not be missed in our time. Since rejection of the OT was an essential feature of Marcionism, it is straining the point only a little to say that among Christians today there are many virtual Marcionites.

2. NT Textual Criticism. Extensive quotations from Marcion's gospel and apostle have been preserved within the writings of his opponents. These provide the text critic with a reflection of the textual tradition of Luke and Paul in early 2d-century Asia Minor. The Marcionite text has been characterized as Western. Historically, the "Western Text" has been termed wild and loose, and relegated to a position of lesser importance in the assessment of text-critical problems. This situation is changing. The very term "Western Text" is considered by many to be misleading since it suggests reference to a single homogeneous text type. What has been called "Western Text" is in reality a number of non-Alexandrian text types. As text critics continue to analyze the "Western Text" and bring into sharper focus the disparate members within it, the testimony of Marcion, as one of the earliest reflections of a text in that group, will realize an even greater significance.

3. NT Literary Criticism. The shape of Marcion's gospel and Pauline corpus relates to questions about the composition of Luke and the Pauline corpus as a whole. It has been argued that Luke's gospel existed in an earlier form, without the infancy narratives and apart from Acts of the Apostles. Marcion's gospel begins with Luke 3:1. The question has been raised: Did Marcion actually remove chapters one and two from Luke, or did he receive that gospel in an earlier form which lacked them? The strength of this argument is diminished by the fact that in Marcion's gospel, Luke 4:31 seems to have followed directly on Luke 3:1. This increases the likelihood that Marcion was removing material. Nonetheless, the only known version of the Lukan gospel without the infancy narratives is Marcion's.

In terms of the Pauline corpus, Marcion attests a ten-letter corpus without the Pastorals. Was this an earlier form of the Pauline corpus than the fourteen-letter form which has come down to us? The earliest papyrus of the Pauline letters (P^{46}) does not include the Pastorals either. In addition, Marcion's order of the letters, once thought to be unique, has been found in some non-Marcionite Syrian catalogs. Thus the text of Marcion is an important piece in the puzzle of the development of the Pauline corpus. See MARCIONITE PROLOGUES TO PAUL.

4. The Earliest Pauline Reform. Perhaps the greatest significance of Marcion and his movement is the witness they provide of the earliest Pauline reform in the history of Christianity. Clearly, the success of Marcion's movement was not due to the depth or consistency of his theology. It has been explained here and elsewhere as a result of his skillful and energetic organizing, and the cohesiveness provided by his canon and sharply focused teaching. The powers of the letters of Paul as vehicles for reform must also be considered. The Pauline epistles have often triggered breakthrough insights. The examples of Augustine and Luther come immediately to mind. At several stages of the history of Christianity men and women have been inspired by Paul's willingness to challenge the recognized authorities on matters of principle. His passionate adherence to the truth of the gospel in the face of enormous personal risk is one with his incisive articulation of the central issues of the faith struggle.

It was an act of great courage for anti-Marcionite Christianity to accept into its canon the fuel for fiery reform—especially after they had seen the effects of its misuse by Marcion. Some have lamented that in the Christian canon the volatility of Paul and his teachings has been reduced by the inclusion of the Pastorals, Acts of the Apostles (in which Paul is subjugated to the Twelve), and other works in which anti-Paulinist references are made (2 Pet 3:15–17). But even if that be granted, history has shown that enough of the fire of Paul has remained in the Christian canon to trouble and to heal the Church.

Bibliography

Blackman, E. C. 1948. *Marcion and His Influence.* London.

Campenhausen, H. von 1972. *The Formation of the Christian Bible.* Trans. J. A. Baker. Philadelphia.

Clabeaux, J. J. 1989. *A Lost Edition of the Letters of Paul.* CBQMS 21. Wilmington, DE.

Harnack, A. von 1924. *Marcion: Das Evangelium vom fremden Gott.* TU 45. 2d ed. Leipzig.

Hoffmann, R. J. 1984. *Marcion: On the Restitution of Christianity.* AARAS 46. Chico, CA.

Knox, J. 1942. *Marcion and the New Testament.* Chicago.

Koester, H. 1982. *Introduction to the New Testament.* Vol. 2. Philadelphia.

JOHN J. CLABEAUX

MARCION, GOSPEL OF. One of the three major works, all now lost, from a famous dualist Christian of the mid-2d century: the other two were his *Apostle* and *Antitheses.* The basic theory of Marcion was that *the* gospel, known to Paul, was "interpolated by the defenders of Judaism," who corrupted it as they also corrupted Paul's letters. Marcion believed he could free the gospel from these interpolations, just as in his time scholars tried to reconstruct philosophies underlying Greek poetry or authentic ancient myths preceding current versions. In this way they "recovered" the authentic originals as Marcion recovered his *Gospel,* supposedly the original version of Luke. (Irenaeus says Marcion "circumcised the gospel.") Harnack and others tried to reconstruct Marcion's version but had to admit that the result was tentative because their reconstruction was based primarily on comments by his opponents. Tertullian (*Adv. Marc.* 4) wanted to show that even Marcion's Luke confirmed Christian doctrine: Epiphanius (*Haer.* 42) provided a similar discussion but cited 35 passages in which Marcion apparently altered the text. Inferences drawn from these witnesses are not fully reliable, though they are all we have, apart from a few details in the *Dialogue of Adamantius* and Syriac witnesses.

Harnack's reconstruction (1924) is based primarily on Epiphanius' supplemented from Tertullian. He rightly calls many passages in Luke "unattested" rather than "absent," noting how uncertain any reconstruction is, while Knox (1942: 86) lists "non-Marcionite passages": (cf. Hoffman 1984: 115–24).

A. The Gospel
B. Theological Modifications
C. Minor Verbal Changes or None
D. Uncertain Alterations
E. Principles for Discussing Marcion's Gospel

A. The Gospel

The *Antitheses* began with a Pauline exclamation about the gospel: "Oh wealth of riches! Folly, power, and ecstasy! seeing that there can be nothing to say about it, or to imagine about it, or to compare it to!" The *Gospel* was therefore a single, unique (and certainly not a four-part) work. Conceivably Marcion was protesting against the production of apocryphal gospels in his time.

The earliest witness to the *Gospel* is Irenaeus of Lyons (ca. 185), whose statements about Marcion's teaching are clearly based on it. "Jesus came into Judaea from that Father who is above the world-creating god, manifest in the form of a man, in the times of Pontius Pilate the governor, the procurator of Tiberius Caesar. He dissolved the prophets and the law (Luke 23:2 according to Marcion) and all the works of that god who made the world." Marcion "circumcised the gospel according to Luke and removed everything written about the birth of the Lord, and much of his teaching, in which he is plainly described as ackowledging the Creator of this universe as his Father."

Tertullian supplies more detail. Marcion "ascribed no author to the gospel" and held that "the title was adulterated" (4.3.5). The *Gospel* began thus: "In the 15th year of the principate of Tiberius he came down to Capernaum" (Luke 3:1; 4:31); compare 4:32, which Marcion reads as "They were astonished at his teaching, which was against the law and the prophets" (4.7.7). Compare Marcion's modification of Luke 23:2: "We found this man leading the nation astray" (Marcion adds "and destroying the law and the prophets") "and forbidding the payment of taxes" (adding "and leading women and children astray") "and calling himself Christ a king" (Tert *Adv. Marc.* 4.42.1).

B. Theological Modifications

Marcion thus did not preserve Luke's literary-historical prologue or relate stories about Jesus' family, his birth (rejecting the virginal conception with it), and his forerunner John (1–2; 3:1c–4:15; contrast 7:27). He said, however, that Luke 7:23, "Blessed is he who is not scandalized in me," refers to John the Baptist, as does "my messenger" in 7:27. (Harnack 1924: 197 claims that Luke 7:29–35 on John the Baptist was lacking but cites no evidence.) At Luke 16:16, "The law and the prophets until John," Marcion adds "from whom the kingdom of God is proclaimed," according to Tert *Adv. Marc.* 4.33.7: "and everyone forces [his way] into it." At Luke 8:19a, 20a, Marcion deletes mention of Jesus' mother and brothers but is willing for people to refer to them generally as "your mother and your brothers," thus probably omitting verse 19 (Knox 1942).

The passages discussed just below are the most important ones theologically, though the minor alterations considered later offer greater possibilities for trying to decide the priority of Luke to Marcion because most of them are theologically neutral.

Luke 5:14. "Go show yourself to the priest and offer the gift . . . as Moses commanded, as a testimony to them" (Marcion substituted "that this may be a testimony to you"). Marcion usually avoids mention of officers of the Jewish religion (cf. 9:22; 20:19; 22:4, 50; 23:50).

Luke 9:22. "Saying, the Son of Man must suffer many things" (omitting "and be rejected by the elders and chief priests and scribes": cf. note on 5:14) "and be killed and raised" (substituting "after three days" for "on the third day" with Mark and Codex Bezae and OL: Tert *Adv. Marc.* 4.21.7 reads "after the third day").

Luke 9:30–31. "And behold, two men were speaking (Marcion substitutes "standing," as in v 32) with him, Elijah and Moses [order reversed] in glory." Knox suggests he omits 9:31 where the two witnesses predict his death.

Luke 10:21. "I thank thee, Lord of heaven"—omitting both "Father" and "of earth," but continuing with "Yea, Father." This is attested by Tertullian (4.25.1). Similarly Marcion retains Luke 11:5–13 but has it end "how much more the Father?" (deleting "from heaven").

Luke 10:25. From Tert 4.25.14: Marcion deletes "eternal" and reads "What shall I do to inherit life?" (i.e., long life as in the OT). The Lord answered in accordance with the Law, "You shall love the Lord your God with all your heart and all your soul and all your strength"—since the inquiry was about life under the Law.

Luke 10:26, 28 from Epiphanius: "He said to the lawyer, 'What is written in the law?' And answering in accordance with the answer of the lawyer, he said, 'You said rightly; do this that you may live.' " This explains the canonical text (Harnack 1924: 206) and avoids having Jesus ask for observance of the Law.

Luke 11:2. From Tert 4.26.3–4: it is very likely that Marcion's version of the Lord's Prayer began, "Father, let thy Holy Spirit come upon us and cleanse us" (Harnack 1924: 207). Marcion seems to have held that "in the gospel Christ himself is the kingdom of God" (Tert 4.33.8, though Kroymann bracketed *Christus ipse;* compare Origen *Matthew* 14:7) and thus did not want to begin with "Thy kingdom come."

Luke 11:29–32. "This generation, a sign will not be given it" (11:29). Marcion "deletes the words about Jonah the prophet and Nineveh and the queen of the south and Solomon" (11:30–32: so Harnack 1924: 209 and Knox 1942 with reference to Tert 4.27.1): Jesus was not really foretold in the OT. Similarly Marcion deletes Luke 11:49–51 because of references to the wisdom of God and the prophets (Harnack 1924: 210).

Luke 12:6. Marcion omits the verse about God's care for sparrows and probably v 7 about the numbered hairs of the head (cf. 21:18): Tertullian mentions neither verse (Harnack 1924: 212). For Marcion God is a god of grace, not of nature. Thus at Luke 12:28 Marcion deletes "God clothes the chaff," and perhaps omits the whole verse (Harnack 1924: 214).

Luke 12:8. Instead of "He will confess before the angels of God" Marcion reads (with Sinaiticus and Matt) "before God" (Harnack 1924: 212).

Luke 13:1–9. Marcion deletes the section, which suggests that repentant Israel will be saved.

Luke 15:11–32. Marcion deletes the parable of the Prodigal Son (Harnack 1924: 219).

Luke 16:17. Marcion substitutes "my words" for "the law" (Tert 4.33.9). Cf. 18:18: 23:55: 24:25.

Luke 17:10b. Marcion deletes "Say that we are unprofitable slaves: we have done what we ought to do," presumably because it could point to the duty of observing the Law.

Luke 17:12, 14, and 4:27 (the ten lepers). Marcion deletes many items, changes "He said to them" to "He sent them," and makes many other changes, adding "There were many lepers in the days of Elisha the prophet and only Naaman the Syrian was cleansed" (deletion of "in Israel"): the same combination is mentioned by Tert 4.35.6 (Harnack 1924: 223; but including "in Israel").

Luke 18:18–20. Marcion deletes the title "ruler" and after the question alters Jesus' answer. Instead of "Why do you call me good?" he reads "Do not call me good" and changes the statement "No one is good but the one God" to "One is the good God the Father." Instead of "You know the commandments" Marcion reads "I know the commandments" (cf. note on 16:17).

Luke 18:31–33. Marcion omits the whole of this passion prediction as repetitious (Harnack 1924: 226). Knox (1942) claims Luke 18:34 was also omitted because it reiterates the disciples' ignorance.

Luke 19:9b. Marcion deletes "as he [Zacchaeus] is a son of Abraham," and Tertullian (4.37.1) calls him a gentile (Harnack 1924: 227).

Luke 19:29–46. Marcion deletes the section about the ass and Bethphage, the city, and the temples as a house of prayer not a den of thieves, presumably because the section involves fulfillment of OT prophecy.

Luke 20:9–17. Marcion deletes the story about the vineyard given to farmers and "What is the stone which the builders rejected?" presumably because of its close connection with Israel.

Luke 20:19. Marcion deletes references to "scribes," "chief priests," and "the people" because he does not refer to official groups within Jewish society (cf. note on 5:14).

Luke 20:37–38. Marcion deletes these verses, presumably because they praise Moses and the patriarchs.

Luke 21:18. Marcion deletes "A hair of your head will not perish" (Harnack 1924: 231; cf. 12:6–7).

Luke 21:21–22. Marcion deletes "Then those in Judaea should flee to the mountains," etc., because of the impending events in the expression "until everything written is fulfilled." (Tert 4.39.9 passes from v 20 to v 25 and therefore Harnack 1924: 231 deletes 21–24.)

Luke 22:4. "He spoke with [omitting "the high priests and"] the generals about how to betray him to them" (cf. note on 5:14).

Luke 22:16. Marcion deletes "For I say to you, I do not eat this from now on, until it is fulfilled in the kingdom of God," and probably vv 17–18 also (Harnack 1924: 233).

Luke 22:35–38. Marcion deletes "When I sent you did you lack anything?" and perhaps "And this that is written must be fulfilled. 'He was reckoned with the lawless ones' " (Harnack 1924: 234).

Luke 22:50–51. Marcion deletes Peter's smiting and cutting off the ear of the high priest's slave as well as the healing; perhaps also the question in v 49 (Harnack 1924: 234; cf. note on 5:14).

Luke 23:33a, 34b, 43, 44–45. "And coming to a place called Skull they crucified him [omitting "and the malefactors" and *perhaps* 34a, "Father, forgive them for they know not what they do," Harnack 1924: 236] and distributed his garments."

Luke 23:43. Marcion deletes "Today you will be with me in paradise" (Harnack 1924: 236 also includes vv 35–43 or [so Knox 1942] vv 39–43).

Luke 23:50, 53. "And behold, a man named Joseph [deleting his description as a councillor] taking the body, wrapped it in linen and placed it in a hewn tomb" (cf. note on 5:14).

Luke 23:55–56. "And the women came back and observed the Sabbath in accordance with the law (Marcion substitutes "law" for "commandment," Harnack 1924: 237; Codex Bezae omits; cf. note on 16:17).

Epiph (Adv. Haeres) *42. 9:* Marcion cut much out of the end of the gospel (Harnack 1924: 237) but we do not know what it was. Some examples include the following: *Luke 24:5–7:* "Those in bright clothing said, 'Why do you seek the living one with the dead?' [omitting "He is not here," for Christ is everywhere? Harnack 1924: 238] he has been raised: remember what he said while still with you [omitting "in Galilee"] that the Son of Man must suffer and be delivered' " (order reversed by Epiphanius not Marcion: Harnack 1924: 238). *Luke 24:25–31:* Marcion revised what was said to Cleopas (18) and the other disciple (13) when he met them: " 'O stupid ones and slow to believe all [deleting "that the prophets spoke" and substituting "that I" (or "he," Harnack 1924: 239 from Tert 4.43.4: cf. note on 16:17)] spoke to you; did he not have to suffer these things?' . . . When he broke the bread their eyes were opened and they knew him." *Luke 24:38a, 39:* "Why are you troubled? [Omitting the parallelism.] See my hands and my feet, for a spirit does not have [omitting "flesh and" according to Tert 4.43.6–7: Harnack 1924: 239] bones such as you see me having." But did the risen Lord have only a skeleton?

C. Minor Verbal Changes or None

In addition to Marcion's significant changes there are many passages with less important verbal changes. These may reflect contemporary textual variants or even Marcion's editing for literary purposes, such as to simplify stories.

Luke 5:24. Marcion changes the word order to indicate that the Son of Man's authority was not on earth but to forgive sins on earth. Epiphanius himself has the same reading. This kind of change was typical of the 2d century and later.

Luke 6:3. "Did you not read this, what David did? . . . He went into the house of God." The story is simplified. *Luke 6:16.* "Judas Iscariot, who became the betrayer": no change. *Luke 6:17.* Jesus came down "in them," not "with them"—this is more spiritual or merely a verbal variant? *Luke 6:19a, 20a.* "And the whole crowd sought to touch him [see below, 8:42–46] and he, raising his eyes," etc. Basically the same.

Luke 7:9b. "I say to you, I have found such faith not even in Israel." The word order is changed, not the meaning, which puts a centurion's faith above Israel's. *Luke 7:36b, 38, 44b.* The only change, perhaps stylistic, depicts the woman as anointing Jesus' feet before kissing them.

Luke 8:23a, 24b. Marcion seems to accept the text or make trivial verbal changes, substituting "rowing" for "sailing" and having Jesus rebuke not the "wave" but the "sea," with Matthew and Mark. *Luke 8:42b, 43a, 44, 45a, 46a.* "It happened that as they went the crowds crushed him. And a woman touching him was healed of her blood. And the Lord said, 'Who touched me? Someone touched me, for I knew power going out from me' " (cf. Tert 4.20.8: "Who touched me? Someone touched me, for I felt power going out from me"). The whole story is simplified.

Luke 9:1–2, 6. Marcion's only change is to add "cities" to the "villages" of v 9 (*Dial. Adamantii* 2.12). *Luke 9:16.* "Looking up to heaven he blessed [Marcion adds "upon"] them." The expression occurs in Codex Bezae and OL. *Luke 9:19–20.* Marcion modifies the scene of recognition by minor changes and by deleting "of God" from "the Christ of God" (cf. Mark). *Luke 9:40.* "I asked your disciples to cast it out" (omitting "and they were unable").

Luke 11:42. "You neglect the judgment [*krisin*] of God." Marcion substitutes "calling," *klesin,* probably rejecting a judgment by the good God. But he does not necessarily delete the rest of the verse (Harnack 1924: 210). *Luke 11:47.* "Woe to you, for you build the tombs [*mnemata*] of the prophets and your fathers killed them." Perhaps Marcion read *mnemeia* = *monimenta* (cf. Tert 4.27.8; Harnack 1924: 211).

Luke 12:4a, 5b. "I say to [deleting "you"] my friends" [or "you friends," Tert 4.28.3: Harnack 1924: 211], Do not fear those who kill the body [Marcion deletes further details according to Epiphanius, not Tertullian] but fear him who has authority to cast it into gehenna after killing it." *Luke 12:30b.* Same text as Epiphanius, perhaps "your" (Father) should be deleted as in 12:32 (Harnack 1924: 214). *Luke 12:31.* "Seek for the kingdom of God and all these will be added to you"; so Clement and Epiphanius *Luke 12:32.* Instead of "Your Father" Marcion (with Clement, *Quis div. salv.* 31.2) reads "Father" (Harnack 1924: 214). *Luke 12:38.* Instead of "second or third watch" Marcion reads "evening watch" with Codex Bezae, OL, and Irenaeus (Harnack 1924: 215). *Luke 12:46.* Same as "canonical" text (Harnack 1924: 215). *Luke 12:58b.* Same (Tert 4.29.16).

Luke 13:10–17. Marcion discusses a healing on the Sabbath (Tert 4.30.1). *Luke 13:15.* "Does not each one of you free his ass or his ox from a crib on the Sabbath and lead him to water?" (Harnack 1924: 217) *Luke 13:16.* "This daughter of Abraham, whom Satan bound." Acceptable because she was bound by Satan. *Luke 13:28.* Marcion changes the sentence to "When you see all the righteous in the kingdom of God, but yourselves held outside, there will be weeping and gnashing of teeth" (cf. A. Kroymann on Tert 4.30.5 [CChr 1: 1.629]; cf. Harnack 1924: 218) and deletes vv 29–35 because they suggest that Jesus' mission was to Israel.

Luke 16:22. Marcion retains the parable of Dives and Lazarus, and in 25b reads a reference to "this one" (Lazarus) rather than to "this place" (*Dial. Adamantii* 2.10 and a few NT mss agree: a trivial difference between *omicron* and *omega*). *Luke 16:29, 31.* He modifies Abraham's statement, "If someone from the dead came to them," to a more specific reference to the risen Jesus (so the author of *Dial. Adamantii* 2.10, though Harnack [1924: 222] claims that Epiphanius combined vv 29 and 31).

Luke 17:22. "The days will come when you desire to see one of the days of the Son of Man." Perhaps Marcion deletes "and you will not see it" (Harnack 1924: 224).

Luke 18:35, 38, 42. "It happened as they drew near to Jericho a blind man [Marcion may omit details] shouted, 'Jesus Son of David, have mercy on me' " (again, possibly omitting details, and adding 'And when he was healed" to "Jesus said, 'Your faith has saved you' ").

Luke 22:8. "And he sent [Marcion substitutes "said to"] Peter and the others, saying [Marcion deletes "saying"] 'Go and prepare that we may eat the Passover.' " These are stylistic changes. *Luke 22:14–15.* "And he reclined, and the [Marcion with many mss added "twelve"] apostles with him, and he said" [Marcion "to them"], 'With desire I have desired to eat this Passover with you before I suffer.' " Essentially the same. *Luke 22:41.* "He withdrew from them about a stone's throw and on his knees he prayed." There seems to be no change. *Luke 22:47–48.* "And Judas drew near to kiss him and [apparently deleting "Jesus"] said." *Luke 22:63–64.* Those present mocked him, beating and striking him saying, "Prophesy who it is [Marcion reads "was"] who struck you" (simply a grammatical correction).

Luke 23:44–45. "And the sun was darkened" (retained). *Luke 23:46.* "And crying out with a loud voice [including the quotation of Ps 31:6; Tert 4.42.6] he expired."

D. Uncertain Alterations

In several instances it is difficult to tell exactly what Marcion's reading was; the verses are: *Luke 5:39* (omitted, says Harnack 1924: 190, because lacking in Codex Bezae and OL manuscripts; unconvincing); *6:23c* (same as Luke); *9:35* ("beloved" with Matthew and Mark); *44b* (same as Luke); *22:44b* (did Marcion really omit the Bloody Sweat?).

E. Principles for Discussing Marcion's Gospel

In 4.43.7 Tertullian "explains" why Marcion's gospel contained passages favoring the Catholic position against Marcion's own views. He claims that Marcion left certain contradictory items in his gospel, so that from these he could argue both that he was not making deletions and that when he did so he was right. This psychological and theological claim is convincing only if Marcion was really editing the canonical Luke. If he used an earlier version the claim obviously fails. Unfortunately there is no reliable evidence for what Marcion's sources and procedure were, though it is reasonable to suppose, from what we know of his results, that Luke (or the version Marcion used) was not originally as full as it now is and that our text contains fewer interpolations than Marcion supposed. In other words, the book was not composed as systematically as either Marcion or his critics believed.

One might hope that early testimonies to Luke, canonical or not, could illuminate the situation, but Papias' comments on Luke, if any, are not preserved, and the "tradition" cited by Ignatius about the risen Lord may or may not echo Luke 24:36–43 (Koester 1957: 45–56).

As for studies of Luke's vocabulary and style, Knox claimed that they do not favor or oppose the traditional view, while Cadbury similarly argued that the presence or absence of non-Lukan words cannot be used to prove that Luke is or is not using a source. Such points, along with the failure of Tertullian's claim, suggest that details of Marcion's gospel can be recovered but not an overall picture. The argument that the "changes" correspond with Marcion's theology (Grant 1957: 115–19) is not convincing because conceivably Marcion may have relied on his "proto-Luke" instead of creating it.

Bibliography

Blackman, E. C. 1948. *Marcion and His Influence.* London.

Cadbury, H. J. 1943. Review of Knox 1942. *JBL* 62: 123–27.

Grant, R. M. 1957. *The Letter and the Spirit.* London.

Harnack, A. von. 1924 *Marcion: das Evangelium vom fremden Gott.* 2d ed. TU 45. Leipzig.

Hoffman, R. J. 1984. *Marcion: On the Restitution of Christianity.* AARAS 46. Chico, CA.

Holl, K. 1922. *Epiphanius: Ancoratus und Panarion II.* GCS 31. Leipzig.

Knox, J. 1942. *Marcion and the New Testament.* Chicago.

Koester, H. 1957. *Synoptische Ueberlieferung bei den apostolischen Vaetern.* TU 65. Berlin.

Rousseau, A., and Doutreleau, L. 1979. *Irénéé de Lyon, Contre Les Hérésies, Livre I.* SC 264. Paris.

Tertullian. 1954. *Tertulliani Opera.* Pars I. CChr 1/1. Turnhout.

Robert M. Grant

MARCIONITE PROLOGUES TO PAUL.

The Marcionite Prologues are brief introductions to all of the letters of the Pauline corpus (except Hebrews) which are found in all branches of the Vulgate (Vg) text. The shortest is a single sentence (13 words), the longest three sentences (43 words). The earliest and best Vg MSS include them. Among non-Vulgate Latin MSS they are most common in the OL: I-type. Their earliest attestation is in the commentary of Marius Victorinus on the Pauline letters (ca. 355–65). The date of their origin cannot be determined apart from a resolution of the controversy as to whether or not they were actually written by Marcionites. See MARCION.

A. Contents

The prologues to all of the community letters but 2 Corinthians and 2 Thessalonians follow a common pattern. Each begins with an ethnic or geographical identification of the recipients (e.g., "*Galati sunt Graeci*" and "*Romani sunt in partibus Italiae*"). Next noted or implied is that they received the gospel (some were, in addition, "overtaken by false apostles") and that they either held firm or betrayed the true gospel. Each prologue concludes with the remark that Paul commends the recipients, if they held firm, or calls them back, if they betrayed the gospel. In the same sentence reference is made to the city from which Paul wrote.

The prologues to 2 Corinthians, 2 Thessalonians, Philemon, and the Pastorals do not follow the pattern. These make no mention of the recipients maintaining or betraying the true gospel, but either identify the type of letter Paul wrote (2 Corinthians and Philemon) or summarize the contents (2 Thessalonians and the Pastorals). It is probable that these were composed at a time later than the prologues to the community letters.

B. Controversy over the Origin of the Prologues

The identification of these prologues as Marcionite derives from the argumentation advanced by de Bruyne (1907) and Corssen (1909), and has been held by Harnack, Knox, von Campenhausen, and Schäfer (1973). The prologues do not appear in any known Marcionite works nor are they mentioned by the heresiologists. But two facts would support a Marcionite origin. The first is the order of the letters that the prologues imply and the second is the emphasis they place on Paul as the apostle of the true gospel as opposed to other apostles. The first of these cannot be seriously contested. Connective words appear in some of the prologues which indicate that the prologue to 1 Corinthians ("these likewise heard the word of truth from the apostle") followed the prologue to Galatians ("these *first* heard the word of truth from the apostle"). Similarly, the prologue to Colossians probably came after the prologue to a letter to another city in Asia Minor such as Ephesus or Laodicea. In addition, the reference in the prologue to Philippians to that letter's origin in Rome would place Philippians near the end of a chronologically ordered Pauline corpus. The prologue to Romans makes sense only if one presumes it accompanied a 14-chapter form of that letter. All of this is explainable if the Pauline corpus for which the prologues were composed was the Marcionite one. Marcion's Pauline corpus as it can be reconstructed from the discussion of Tertullian throughout book 5 of *Adversus Marcionem* began with Galatians, had a shorter form of Romans, placed Colossians after Ephesians (which Marcion called Laodiceans), and placed Philippians near the end.

The emphasis within the prologues on Paul's opposition to false apostles has also been cited as evidence of Marcionite origin. It is especially significant that false apostles are mentioned in some of the prologues even though the letters they introduce do not dwell on that issue (Philippians and 1 Thessalonians). Many raise the question: Who but Marcionites would see the basic issue of almost every community letter in the light of Paul's opposition to false apostles?

The case is not unassailable. Objections were raised earlier in this century by Mundle, LaGrange and Bardy (*DBSup* 5: 877–79), and more recently by Schneemelcher, Frede (1964), Gamble (1977: 111–13), and Dahl (1978). Most of the proponents of the case for Marcionite origin must admit that the clearest expression of a Marcionite position—opposition to the Hebrew Scriptures—is found in the prologue to Titus, which most argue was composed by a "catholic" editor. A more serious objection is raised by the question with reference to all of the prologues: How did such tendentiously Marcionite material come to be incorporated into the text of "orthodoxy" in the first place? Were ancient editors insensitive to Marcionite inferences?

These initial shortcomings open the door to more serious objections. The argument based on the order of the Pauline letters that the prologue presume is not compelling. The Old Syriac attests a Pauline corpus with a similar order (Dahl 1978: 253–54). Galatians can be in the first position for chronological reasons rather than theological ones. Textual studies at the Vetus Latina Institute indicate that several orders of the Pauline letters existed (Beuron 1969: 290–303). The short form of Romans is attested in mss that show no connection to Marcion whatever (Gamble 1977: 15–29). Textual studies that sought to demonstrate a significant impact of the Marcionite text on the ms tradition at large have been soundly rejected (Frede 1964: 167–68). As for the recurrent theme in the prologues of the opposition of Paul to false apostles—many modern commentators see this as an overriding issue in Pauline interpretation. Therefore, one need not assume that the ancient editors who composed or included the prologues were insensitive to the Marcionite positions expressed in them. Rather, they, as Marcion, considered Paul their champion against false apostles—but the false apostles would be their own theological opponents. Further, the prologues themselves are not unequivocal in their characterization of the "false apostles." The prologue to 1 Corinthians refers to Judaizers and to philosophers of "wordy eloquence" and the latter is not a dominant Marcionite concern. Thus, present scholarship is divided over the origin of the prologues and those who oppose their Marcionite origin are gaining momentum.

C. Implications of the Prologues

If the prologues are of Marcionite origin they represent a great irony in the textual tradition of the Bible. The Marcionites would have succeeded in planting the seeds of their thoughts into the books and minds of Western Christians for 16 or 17 centuries, since relatively recent editions of the Vg contained them. But if this is so, what must be concluded about the critical acumen of ancient authors and editors who have accepted and transmitted the prologues? Even Marius Victorinus took no exception to them. The consistent transmission of the prologues in certain branches of the Latin textual tradition would bespeak the inviolability of a written tradition once it had been taken up, even though erroneously. One might ask what other influences the Marcionites or other sects may have had.

If one does not accept Marcionite origin of the prologues, the implications for their inclusion in the Latin mss are less dramatic but still substantial. If the prologues were created for a Pauline corpus not Marcionite but similar in order and content to Marcion's, then how are we to understand Marcion's role as an editor? Did he inherit rather than create his Pauline Corpus? Dahl and Frede argue that such a 10-letter Pauline corpus did exist from before Marcion's time and that it has had an effect on the Western textual tradition of the Pauline letters especially in the OL and Old Syriac which is yet to be analyzed and explained. The disappearance of that 10-letter Pauline corpus must be reckoned with when the development of the Pauline corpus is discussed.

However one decides the origin of the prologues, they attest that editors of the 3d century (possibly earlier) saw Paul's opposition to false apostles as a crucial theme for understanding his letters. This insight either comes from Marcion himself, or is merely congenial to his viewpoint. In other words, either the Marcionites infiltrated the Latin MS tradition with their ideas, or an idea of theirs was taken up in modified form by orthodoxy at a later time against other opponents. There is a caution in all of this against drawing too hastily, or too sharply, the lines between orthodoxy and heresy in the early centuries of Christianity.

Bibliography

Beuron, E., ed. 1969. *Vetus Latina: Die Reste der altlateinischen Bibel.* 24/2. Freiburg.

Bruyne, D. de. 1907. Prologues bibliques d'origin marcionite. *RBén* 24: 1–24.

Corssen, P. 1909. Zur Überlieferungsgeschichte des Römerbriefes. *ZNW* 10: 1–45, 97–102.

Dahl, N. A. 1978. The Origin of the Earliest Prologues to the Pauline Letters. *Semeia* 12: 233–77.

Frede, H. J. 1964. *Altlateinishe Paulus-Handschriften.* Aus der Geschichte der lateinischen Bibel 4. Freiburg.

Gamble, H. 1977. *The Textual History of the Letter to the Romans.* SD 42. Grand Rapids.

Schäfer, K. T. 1973. Marcion und die ältesten Prologe zu den Paulusbriefen. Pp. 135–50 in *Kyriakon,* ed. P. Granfeld and J. A. Jungmann. Münster.

John J. Clabeaux

MARCUS AURELIUS (EMPEROR).

Roman emperor (161–80) and Stoic philosopher who was born April 26, 121 as M. Annius Verus, son of a consular family of Spanish origin. His industry and seriousness were soon noticed by Hadrian, who arranged his education and betrothed him (136) to the daughter of L. Aelius Caesar, his adopted son and designated successor. When Aelius died (138), Hadrian took as his new heir Antoninus Pius. Pius in turn adopted Marcus, and Aelius' son Lucius.

After Hadrian's death (July 138), Marcus moved into the palace with Pius. He began higher studies, chiefly with the rhetorician Cornelius Fronto. A number of letters between them (the majority in Latin) survive in Fronto's correspondence, giving an insight into Marcus' nature at this time. It was only later (146–47) that his interests turned wholeheartedly to philosophy.

Quaestor in 139 and consul for the first time in 140 (with Pius), Marcus was betrothed (140) to Pius' daughter, his cousin Faustina the Younger. They married in 145, and in 146, on the birth of a daughter (first of thirteen offspring), he was granted the tribunician power and proconsular imperium. Succeeding Pius on March 7, 161, Marcus requested the same powers for Lucius, so making the principate truly collegiate for the first time. Marcus now took Pius' surname Antoninus, while Lucius took his surname Verus.

Although generally represented as a time of peace and prosperity, Marcus' reign had more than its share of natural disasters and military crises. An eastern war (162–66), in response to the Parthian seizure of Armenia, led to the importation of a plague which, combined with famine, seriously depopulated the empire. Then the northern provinces were invaded by migrating Germanic tribes (166–69), who were turned back only at Aquileia in northern Italy (169). On Verus' death (169), the need to stabilize the frontiers kept Marcus in the north (170–79) before he had to travel to Syria in response to the revolt (175) of Avidius Cassius. After the revolt fizzled out (176) Marcus journeyed northward again, leaving his son Commodus, now co-emperor (177), in charge in Rome. Successful against the Germanic tribes (177–79), Marcus was about to incorporate their territories into two new provinces when he fell ill and died at Vienna on March 17, 180.

It was during the northern campaigns that the *Meditations* (12 books, in Greek) were written. They contain few references to external events, but Marcus' preoccupation with the traditional Stoic principles of duty and self-sufficiency, and his obsession with life's transience and death as the common lot of humanity, clearly reflect the conditions under which they were written. Published posthumously with little editing, these personal, sometimes cryptic philosophical reflections rightly ensure for Marcus the fame on whose value and uncertainty he frequently ponders.

Like that of Epictetus, Marcus' Stoicism is more religious than philosophical in nature, emphasizing the need to love both God and one's fellow man. It is ironic, therefore, that Marcus should also be remembered as a persecutor of the Christians. Unjust too, for the anti-Christian hysteria of the 160s (Justin and his companions martyred at Rome, ca. 167, a date also given by Eusebius, perhaps wrongly, for Polycarp's martyrdom in Smyrna [Eusebius, *Hist. Eccl.* 4. 15; 16]) was a by-product of the plague, while the more extensive persecution at Lyons in 177 (*Hist. Eccl.* 5. pref; 1) was provoked by legislation allowing the use of condemned criminals as gladiators. The law was Marcus', not the use to which it was put.

Bibliography

Birley, A. 1988. *Marcus Aurelius.* Rev. ed. New Haven.

Brunt, P. A. 1979. Marcus Aurelius and the Christians. Vol. 1, pp. 483–520 in *Studies in Latin Literature and Roman History,* ed. C. Deroux. Collection Latomus 164. Brussels.

Farquharson, A. S. L. 1944. *The Meditations of the Emperor Marcus Aurelius.* Oxford.

———. 1951. *Marcus Aurelius: His Life and His World,* ed. D. A. Rees. Oxford.

Garzetti, A. 1974. *From Tiberius to the Antonines.* Rev. ed. Trans. J. R. Foster. London.

Grube, G. M. A. 1983. *The Meditations of Marcus Aurelius.* Indianapolis.

Haines, C. R. 1919–20. *The Correspondence of Marcus Cornelius Fronto.* 2 vols. LCL. London.

Klein, R. 1979. *Marc Aurel.* Wege der Forschung 550. Darmstadt.

JOHN WHITEHORNE

MARDUK (DEITY). Var. MERODACH. The patron deity of Babylon, Marduk first appeared in the 3d millennium B.C.E. as a minor Sumerian god. He was the son of Enki (Akk Ea) (Sommerfeld 1982: 9, 13). The status of the god rose with the fortunes of Hammurabi in the 18th century B.C.E.; yet throughout the Old Babylonian period Marduk's major concern remained the territory of Babylon (Hurowitz 1984: 191, 193–94). The Code of Hammurabi portrays Anu and Enlil proclaiming Marduk king over Sumer and Akkad, reflecting Babylon's rule over Mesopotamia (Ravn 1929: 88–90). In honor of their god the First Dynasty of Babylon appears to have built Esagila, the temple area dedicated to Marduk (Busink 1949: 54).

The decline of Kassite rule, in conjunction with a successful war against Elam (in which the statue of Marduk was recovered), sparked a theological glorification of the deity in the 12th century B.C.E. (Roberts 1977: 183–84; Lambert 1964: 10). At this time Marduk became viewed as the great cosmic ruler of the earth, taking on the deeds (and myths) of the major divinities of the Mesopotamian pantheon. The theology was embodied in the Enuma Elish in which Marduk appears as hero of gods and humans (Bottéro 1985: 115). See ENUMA ELISH. The creation of the universe by Marduk became the text for the New Year *akītu* celebration in Babylon (Black 1981: 40), where the recitation of the narrative and the names would recall Marduk's usurpation of the divine world (Bottéro 1977: 5–28; Lambert 1985: 60). By the 1st millennium B.C.E. Marduk was considered the supreme deity (Abusch 1984: 5), at least in Babylon.

The destruction of Babylon by Sennacherib's troops in 689 B.C.E. followed decades of turmoil in the city, which had been tolerated by the Assyrian rulers because of the veneration for Marduk and his city's culture; it is possible that the outpouring of Mardukian theology related to this event began with the turmoil itself (Diakonoff 1965: 346–47). The Esagila and its ziggurat, Etemenanki (first mentioned at this time in an historical text) were destroyed and the theological explanation was posited that Marduk, having grown furious over the corrupt behavior of his people, had, with all the other gods, abandoned the city to its enemies (Borger 1967: 12–19; *TCS* 5: 127). When the Assyrians left, they took the statue of Marduk with them. Esarhaddon reinterpreted Mardukian texts in order to rebuild the city and return the god, but not without checking the omens and not without trouble (Parpola 1983: 32–33; Lambert 1988: 158–59). The affair led to texts intended to show the relationship of Ashur and Marduk with respectful views of the latter (Soden 1955: 165; Frymer-Kensky 1983: 140).

The Neo-Babylonian Empire celebrated its independence with massive building projects, including the Esagila and Etemenanki. Marduk was glorified even to the point of being able to be seen as the *only* deity (Lambert 1975: 197–98). The divine family, Marduk, Ṣarpanitum, and Nabû, ruled the universe for half a century. When Nabonidus seized the throne in 555 B.C.E. he claimed that his right to rule and reform the cult came from Marduk (Beaulieu 1985: 83–86); then he abandoned the patron deity for the god Sin, leaving the *akītu* ceremonies to be improperly performed. This slight led Marduk's priests to seek Cyrus, the Persian, as a champion of their god. Cyrus claimed in an inscription that he was selected king and brought to the city by Marduk precisely to restore the lapsed cult (Beaulieu 1985: 354). The cult of Marduk survived into the Hellenistic period, though whether Marduk was worshiped to the time Babylon was finally abandoned late in the 1st century C.E. is unknown.

Bibliography

Abusch, T. 1984. The Form and Meaning of a Babylonian Prayer to Marduk. *JAOS* 103: 3–15.
Beaulieu, P. A. 1985. The Reign of Nabonidus, King of Babylon (556–539 B.C.). Diss. Yale.
Black, J. A. 1981. The New Year Ceremonies in Ancient Babylon: "Taking Bel by the Hand" and a Cultic Picnic. *Religion* 11: 39–59.
Borger, R. 1967. *Die Inschriften Asarhaddons Königs von Assyrien.* AfO 9. Osnabrück.
Bottéro, J. 1977. Les noms de Marduk, l'écriture et la "logique" en Mésopotamie ancienne. Pp. 5–28 in *Essays on the Ancient Near East in Memory of Jacob Joel Finkelstein,* ed. M. de J. Ellis. Memoirs of the Connecticut Academy of Arts and Sciences 19. Hamden, CT.
———. 1985. *Mythes et Rites de Babylone.* Bibliothèque de l'École des Hautes Études 4: Sciences Historiques et philologiques 328. Geneva.
Brinkman, J. A. 1983. Through a Glass Darkly: Esarhaddon's Retrospects on the Downfall of Babylon. *JAOS* 103: 35–42.
Busink, T. A. 1949. *De Babylonische Tempeltoren.* Lectiones Orientales 2. Leiden.
Diakonoff, I. M. 1965. A Babylonian Political Pamphlet from about 700 B.C. Pp. 343–49 in *Studies in Honor of Benno Landsberger on his Seventy-fifth Birthday April 21, 1965,* ed. H. G. Gütterbock, AS 16. Chicago.
Frymer-Kensky, T. 1983. The Tribulations of Marduk: The So-Called "Marduk Ordeal Text." *JAOS* 103: 131–41.
Hurowitz, V. 1984. Literary Structures in Samsuiluna A. *JCS* 36: 191–205.
Lambert, W. G. 1964. The Reign of Nebuchadnezzar I: A Turning Point in the History of Ancient Mesopotamian Religion. Pp. 3–13 in *The Seed of Wisdom: Essays in Honour of T. J. Meek,* ed. W. S. McCullough. Toronto.
———. 1975. The Historical Development of the Mesopotamian Pantheon: A Study in Sophisticated Polytheism. Pp. 191–99 in *Unity and Diversity,* ed. H. Goedicke and J. J. M. Roberts. Baltimore.
———. 1985. Ninurta Mythology in the Babylonian Epic of Creation. Pp. 55–60 in *Keilschriftliche Literaturen: Ausgewählte vorträge der XXXII. Recontre Assyriologique internationale Münster, 8.–12.7.1985,* ed. K. Hecker and W. Sommerfeld. Berlin.
———. 1988. Esarhaddon's Attempt to Return Marduk to Babylon. Pp. 157–74 in *Ad bene et fideliter seminandum: Fesgabe für Karlheinz Deller zum 21. Februar 1987,* ed. G. Mauer and U. Magen. AOAT 220. Neukirchen-Vluyn.
Oates, J. 1979. *Babylon.* London.
Parpola, S. 1983. *Letters from Assyrian Scholars to the Kings Esarhaddon and Assurbanipal, Pt. 2: Commentary and Appendices.* AOAT 5/2. Neukirchen-Vluyn.
Ravn, O. E. 1929. The Rise of Marduk. *AcOr* 7: 81–90.
Roberts, J. J. M. 1977. Nebuchadnezzar I's Elamite Crisis in Theological Perspective. Pp. 182–87 in *Essays on the Ancient Near East in Memory of Jacob Joel Finkelstein,* ed. M. de J. Ellis. Memoirs of the Connecticut Academy of Arts and Sciences 19. Hamden, CT.
Soden, W. von. 1955. Gibt es ein Zeugnis dafür, dass die Babylonier an die Wiederauferstehung Marduks geglaubt haben? *ZA* 51: 130–66.
———. 1971. Etemenanki vor Asarhaddon nach der Erzählung vom Turmbau zu Babel und dem Erra-Mythos. *UF* 3: 253–63.
Sommerfeld, W. 1982. *Der Aufstieg Marduks: Die Stellung Marduks in der babylonischen Religion des zweiten Jahrtausends v. Chr.* AOAT 213. Kevelaer and Neukirchen-Vluyn.

LOWELL K. HANDY

MAREAL (PLACE) [Heb *marᶜălâ*]. A place on the S border of the territory of the tribe of Zebulun (Josh 19:11) in the Jezreel Valley. Its precise location is unknown. Aharoni suggests (*LBHG,* 257) identifying it with Tell Thorah (M.R. 166228).

RAPHAEL GREENBERG

MARESHAH (PERSON) [Heb *mārēšâ*]. Two individuals of the tribe of Judah.

1. Firstborn of the family of Caleb and the father of Ziph and Hebron (1 Chr 2:42). The text is confused at this point, which is possibly due to dittography. The Hebrew has *mêšaᶜ*, "Mesha." However the RSV follows the LXX and reads "Mareshah."

2. Son of Laadah from the family of Shelah (1 Chr 4:21).

DAVID CHANNING SMITH

MARESHAH (PLACE) [Heb *mārēšâ*]. Var. MARISA. A town of Judah located in the S foothills.

A. Identification and History

Mareshah (Marisa, 1 Maccabees 5; 2 Maccabees 12) is identified with Tell Sandakhanna, located about 2 km S of Beit Govrin (M.R. 140111). This identification, first established by E. Robinson, is based on references from the Bible and Josephus. It is known as Marisa in the Apocryphal writings (1 Macc 5:66; 2 Macc 12:35) where it is only mentioned in passing.

Mareshah appears among the cities of Judah (Josh 15:44) and in the genealogies of the settlements (1 Chr 2:42) as belonging to the Calebites. The Bible gives no indication that it was a Canaanite city prior to the Israelite conquest. Following the division of the kingdom, Rehoboam fortified Mareshah as part of his SW defenses of Judah (2 Chr 11:5–10). Zerah the Ethiopian invaded the country about the time of Asa and reached Mareshah (about 900 B.C.E.), but was defeated in the major battle fought in the valley of Zephathah (N of Mareshah according to the LXX [2 Chr 14:8–9]). After the sack of Jerusalem by Nebuchadnezzar, Mareshah, together with all of S Judah, came under the influence of Edom.

In the Hellenistic period and perhaps even in the Persian period, a Sidonian community settled in Mareshah. Hyrcanus I captured Mareshah together with all of Idumea (*Ant* 14.364; *JW* 1.269). Afterward Beit Govrin replaced Mareshah as the district capital.

B. Excavations

An excavation was conducted at Tell Sandakhanna by F. J. Bliss and R. A. S. Macalister in 1900, as part of a series of excavations in the Shephelah in the years 1898–1900. Mareshah consists of a fortified upper city (ca. 150 m in diameter covering ca. 24 dunams), and a lower city, built around the upper city (covering ca. 300 dunams). The lower city included the subterranean complexes and the buildings above them. This area, together with the fortified tell, formed one of the largest Early Hellenistic towns in the country.

In 1902, Bliss and Macalister published the report of their excavation which concentrated on the upper city. Five years later, H. Thiersch published a detailed analysis of the report. A second analysis was published by Avi-Yonah 70 years after the excavation. The excavators identified three strata: two Hellenistic and one Israelite ("Jewish").

The Hellenistic city was almost square in plan (158 m E-W by 152 m N-S) and was surrounded by a wall defended with square and rectangular towers. The original plan of the city was organized according to the Hippodamian system, with 2 parallel main streets running E-W and 3 N-S streets intersecting the main streets at right angles. The streets varied from 2–6 m wide, most of which still had remains of paving. The street plan bounded 12 blocks of buildings, while the block located near the E wall was evidently the religious and administrative center. The three chambers in the center of the courtyard were used as a temple to honor a trinity of gods. A square structure with two courtyards, one a marketplace, the other a caravansary, also covered a city block.

Two types of buildings were identified: a large building consisting of rooms surrounding an enclosed court and a small building with rooms not arranged in a clear plan. Several buildings had remains of hearths, basins, shelves, and steps which led either to the roof or to the cellar.

Among the finds of the Hellenistic period were hundreds of vessels, Rhodian handles, 3 Greek dedicatory inscriptions, 16 small lead figurines which apparently served magical purposes, 51 limestone tablets, and 61 coins (including 13 Ptolemaic, 19 Seleucid, 25 from the time of John Hyrcanus, 1 Herodian, and 2 Greek coins of unclear provenance). Recent excavations directed by A. Kloner have found hundreds of vessels, Rhodian handles, figurines, and coins from the lower city and its caves.

The finds from the upper excavated tell and the underground systems indicate that at least three Hellenistic strata existed at Tell Maresha: Ptolemaic (3d century B.C.E.); Seleucid (2d century B.C.E.); and Hasmonean (late 2d–early 1st B.C.E.).

Beneath the Hasmonean layer, at a depth of 3.05 m, was an Israelite ("Jewish") stratum dated to the Iron Age 2C. The finds from this stratum include 17 *lmlk* seals—11 of the double-winged type and 6 of the four-winged type—from various cities: 3 from Hebron; 3 from *mmšt;* 6 from Socoh; 2 from Ziph; and 3 whose names are illegible.

C. Tombs

An extensive necropolis of the Hellenistic settlement surrounded the city. The E cemetery included 10 burial caves, 4 of which were investigated in 1902 by M. P. Peters and H. Thiersch. These caves, known as the "Sidonian tombs," contained many inscriptions, including the epitaph of Apollophanes, the son of Sesmaios, who died at 74 years old and who was the head of the Sidonian colony in Mareshah for 33 years. Two of these family tombs were richly decorated.

Tomb A, with the above-mentioned inscription, contained a painted frieze depicting someone playing a musical instrument, a rider, and many animals both wild and domesticated all arranged in a row above the gabled *kokhim* (loculi).

In Tomb B, among some of the paintings located on the inner wall of the cave and not recorded by the excavators, is a man crowned with a wreath, wearing a striped tunic, who walks while blowing a double flute. Behind him walks a woman playing a harp. Both these caves are dated, according to the dozens of inscriptions found there, to the 3d–2d centuries B.C.E.

The N cemetery contained 20 burial caves of the *kokhim* type. These *kokhim* were executed with gable-shaped facades and ceiling. Burial epitaphs were scratched above and between the *kokhim;* some were covered with later inscriptions written in mud. In all cemeteries, the entrances to the *kokhim* were built of small local blocks of soft limestone plastered over with mud. At least part of the population practiced secondary burial, with the bones of the deceased placed first in the *kokh* and later collected. Some of the caves of the N cemetery were reused in the 1st–4th centuries C.E. by the Jewish population of Beit Govrin.

D. Lower City and its Caves

Between the upper city and the groups of burial caves located 400–500 m away was the lower city. During the excavation of the upper mound, Macalister surveyed 63 subterranean complexes carved in the chalk. Most of these consisted of hall-like units, workshops, and storage rooms interconnected by passages and tunnels. Some complexes had more than 30 units. In recent reexaminations, additional rooms and halls were found which Macalister had not reached in his survey. Some new complexes were also found. Inside the systems were very rich finds from the 3d and 2d centuries B.C.E. In all, more than 100 cisterns, 40 columbaria used for underground pigeon raising, and 16 olive presses were found inside the halls of these complexes.

The well-known columbarium of A-Suk (Macalister no. 29) was a double cross in shape (28.36 m long) and had approximately 1900 niches. The majority of columbaria at Mareshah and other Hellenistic-Early Roman sites in the Judean Shephelah were carved in the same shape. The long walls enabled the carving of a maximum number of niches. In a columbarium unit in complex 21, four oil lamps were found in one of the niches and a small bowl containing unidentifiable material in another. These finds, contemporary with ceramic material found in the debris from the cave, date to the end of the 3d and the 2d centuries B.C.E.

Examination of the material recovered from the small bowls found *in situ* in the niches or in the central columbarium hall does not substantiate the theory that the columbaria were used for the ashes of human cremations. There were no remains of teeth or bone material. To this negative impression we may add the fact that there is no other evidence of Hellenistic columbaria in the country. The burials in Mareshah at the time were in *kokhim*-type burial caves. It is reasonable to assume that these small niches were dovecotes, which were familiar in the 3d century B.C.E. Later, in the 2d and 1st centuries B.C.E., the columbarium served a function unclear to us today.

Oil presses were installed in large underground rooms. The pressing was done by stone weights attached to the pressing beam. The beam was placed in a niche and held between two piers quarried from the living rock. The beam pressed the baskets of olive mash which were stacked in a deep circular shaft between the piers.

Mareshah was found to be an important economic center in the country during the Hellenistic period.

Bibliography

Avi Yonah, M. 1977. Maresha (Marisa). *EAEHL* 3: 782–91.

Bliss, F. J., and Macalister, R. A. S. 1902. *Excavations in Palestine 1898–1900.* London.

Kloner, A., and Hess, O. 1985. A Columbarium in Complex 21 at Maresha. *ʿAtiqot* 17: 122–33.

Oren, E. D., and Rappaport, U. 1984. The Necropolis of Maresha-Beit Govrin. *IEJ* 34: 114–53.

Peters, J. P., and Thiersch, H. 1905. *Painted Tombs in the Necropolis of Marissa.* London.

AMOS KLONER

MARI. The ancient name of Tell Ḥarīrī, a 54-ha. mound located in Syria on the middle Euphrates River (34°33′N; 40°53′E). This site has been extensively excavated, first by A. Parrot, and beginning in 1979, by J. Margueron. These excavations have yielded over 20,000 cuneiform texts, most of which are dated to the Old Babylonian period.

ARCHAEOLOGY

The city of Mari is found in the Syrian part of the Euphrates Valley 120 km S of the modern city of Deir-ez-Zor at the confluence of the river Ḫabur. It is also situated about 50 km N of the current border separating Syria and Iraq. The city was founded halfway up the side of the valley which distances it at more than 2 km from the right bank of the Euphrates River. Thus situated at the bottom of a valley, bordered by plateaus, where the steppe and desert predominate, but which connects the opulent Mesopotamian plain to the rich crossroads toward Syria in the north, Mari appears as a city ideally suited to control the traffic which travels down the river as well as over land between these two poles.

At the time of its discovery, the tell consisted of a principal hemispherical-shaped hill with a recto-linear facade facing NE; to the W and to the S a mound of earth formed a regular curve. The enclosure which surrounded the city was easily recognizable and it was assumed that the city had been constructed along the river, which determined its hemispherical form. However, from the excavations over the past years, it is now known that the original situation was very different: actually the city did not rely directly on the river and it was founded on a circular plan of which now only a part remains. See Fig. MAR.01. It is thus necessary to reconstruct the entire N and NE part of the city which disappeared due to erosion. Thus the *intra-muros* or diameter of the city seemed to have been a little under 2 km: the importance of the city from its very beginning can be understood from this one characteristic.

The most recent research conducted on the circular mound of earth has not uncovered the remainder of the enclosure; the arrangement that was brought to light seems to have been a dike to protect against floods rather than a defensive system. Therefore, it is not impossible that on this protective base a rampart had been built that would have subsequently disappeared. The major tell displays an asymmetry that is easily explained by the disappearance of part of the city: the culminating point juts out toward the NE and, while the inclines of the tell are slightly

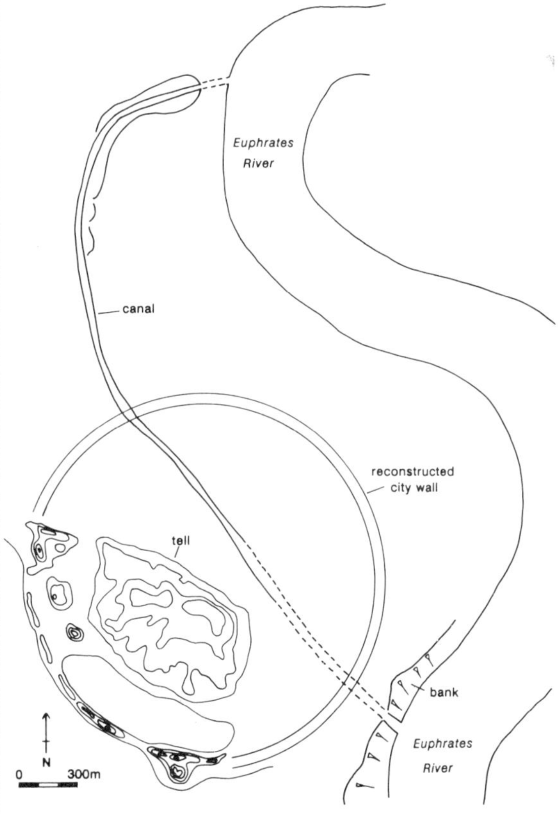

MAR.01. General site plan of Mari.

toward the W, S, and SE, there is a abrupt division to the N and NE where the most erosion has taken place. Finally it should be noted that the city was connected to the river by a canal which assured the continual supply of provisions and served as a link with the river traffic.

A. History of Exploration

Because it was situated off the path that descended into the Euphrates Valley, few travelers in the 19th and early 20th centuries had occasion to notice the desolate hills of Tell Hariri. But the accidental discovery of a statue fragment by bedouins who were burying one of their dead attracted the attention of Syrian archaeological authorities during the period of the French mandate in 1933. An exploratory mission was thus given to André Parrot, who examined the site beginning in December 1933. In January 1934 he found the Temple of Ishtar and its collection of statuettes, including the Lamgi-Mari statue that identified the site and the statue of Ebih-Il, perhaps the masterpiece of the Mari statuary. Thanks to this discovery it was decided that the site merited complete exploration. The following year, during the second dig, the discovery of the palace from the Old Babylonian (OB) period confirmed the exceptional value of the site. See Fig. MAR.02. Since then exploration has followed as regularly as the international situation has permitted.

During the first six seasons of excavation (1933–39) that he conducted before World War II, André Parrot concentrated his efforts on unearthing the different levels of the Temple of Ishtar, on unveiling the entire OB palace, sometimes called the Palace of Zimri-Lim (the name of the last sovereign who resided there), and on the study of the sacred precinct beginning with the excavation of the "ziggurat," of the Temple of Lions (still incorrectly called the Temple of Dagan), and of the Temple of Ninhursag.

From the resumption of the seventh season in 1951 to the tenth season in 1954 attention was given to the sacred precinct, followed by the unearthing of the Temple of Ninhursag, the uncovering of the different levels of the Temple of Shamash and of the *Massif Rouge,* and the discovery of the *Maison Rouge* and the temples of Ishtarat and Nin-zaza (that would provide the second collection of statuettes from the archaic period and make Mari the richest repository of 3d-millennium statuary). In addition, the Akkadian period was attested by a collection of bronzes inscribed with the names of the daughters of Naram-Sin.

The Suez crisis necessitated a new interruption in work. Thus the next period, from the 11th to the 21st seasons (1961–72) was a long period of regular research concerning the pre-Sargonic level which extends to the N of the ziggurat and above all several phases of the 3d-millennium palace rediscovered in 1964 under the ruins of the OB palace. The importance of Mari to the 3d millennium became immediately apparent.

A new interruption in the active excavation marked, from 1972 on, an interest in digging in order to preserve the notable ruins of the palace presumed to be pre-Sargonic. In 1974 a cover was put in place that slowed the destructive effects of erosion. A fourth period thus began in 1979 under the direction of Jean Margueron; five seasons of excavation were conducted until the fall of 1985. The research went on in the 3d-millennium palace since the layout of the palace was not yet understood, but the principal objective now was to obtain a better knowledge

MAR.02. Aerial view of excavations at Tell Hariri–Mari, showing OB palace (foreground) and pre-Sargonic quarters and temple of Ishtar (background). See also Fig. ART.05. *(Courtesy of Mission Archéologique de Mari)*

of the city itself. This permitted the unearthing of a palace from the Shakkanakku period (site A), the discovery of the oldest foundation of the city at the bottom of a stratigraphic boring (site B) and the defining of its original extension, and the study of the defensive system. The second objective—the study of the region and the integration of the city in the regional whole—was simultaneously taking place at the dig site and important results have already been obtained.

B. History of Mari

1. The Foundation of the City. The most recent research has thrown some light on the origins of the city, but important additions can still be hoped for. One must date the birth of Mari at the very beginning of Early Dynastic (ED) I. From this period on, the city had in all likelihood a circular configuration; from the original site only a third remains that can be explored. The essential characteristic that arises from this situation is that Mari was a new city founded under conditions of which we know nothing, but which probably accompanied the development of the valley, because in addition to the canal that links Mari to the river, a large canal on the left bank was discovered (already known in the beginning of its course under the name of Nahr Dawrin) whose beginning is found in the Ḫabur Valley more than 120 km upriver and which seems to have been principally destined to facilitate navigation. On the right bank, the remains of a large irrigation canal were found halfway up the hill, while a final canal was built at the foot of the W plateau to retain water which could rush down from the desert and to prevent it from flooding the fields and thus destroying the crops. The scale of this regional development is proof of the essential role played by Mari.

2. The First Centuries. We still know little about the city in these early periods; the base of the foundation was reached at only one point and if the ED II phase was found in several places one cannot really consider it known. The current documentation only permits one to say that the ED I period seems to have been quite long and that during the course of ED II, perhaps only at the end of this period, one notices vital improvements in living conditions and the introduction of collective improvements in the form of a sewage system. The great stone tombs from the Temple of Ishtar precinct—the oldest phases—belong to the beginning of this period.

3. ED III and the Beginning of the Akkadian Period. This is the 3d-millennium phase for which we have the most archaeological information and from which one can best see the organization of the city. In the palace, the P-1 phase gives us the image of a large-scale building whose dimensions remain unknown; the Sacred Enclosure, (i.e., the sanctuary itself) was still active, but the transformations affected the cultural structures; the altars constructed replace the slabs for libation from level P-2. The excavation permitted the unearthing of annexes and courtyards to the W and N of the sanctuary for which it is still difficult to define precise functions. A raging fire destroyed part of the building, which could have resulted in a reconstruction of certain sections (in particular the Sacred Enclosure and the building of the pillar room recently unearthed W of the annexes of Courtyard 4) and a simple redevelopment of the other sectors. It is, in any case, in this form that the use of the building extends into the Akkadian period. Undoubtedly tightly linked to this exceptional building was a section toward the E where André Parrot suggested that one could find the annexes of the 3d-millennium Dagan temple: however, the identification is not certain, even if a sanctuary can be discovered in the building that abuts the *Massif Rouge*, a high plateau in use during this period. Toward the S extends the sacred quarter, where some ruins belonging to the temples of Shamash and Ninhursag have been unearthed. However, from the other side of the line that divides this section, the temples of Ishtarat and Nini-zaza appear better preserved and present a comprehensible plan which allows one to place them in a category of sanctuaries belonging to Mari. One may add *La Maison Rouge* to the vestiges that are found SE of the sacred quarter, as well as the Temple of Ishtar to the W of the city and the abutting pre-Sargonic quarter. This period seems to have marked one of the great moments in Mari's history, as evidenced by the architecture, by its dimensions and its originality, and also by the splendid collection of statuettes found in the temples of Ishtar and Nini-zaza.

The king Lamgi-Mari, the intendant Ebih-Il, the great singer Ur-Nanshe, the head surveyor Shibum, and many others prove at the same time that Mari belonged to the civilization created by Sumer which covered a large part of Mesopotamia. To this remarkable group of artifacts one must add a large collection of characters destined to become part of the composition of mosaic panels, several decorated vases, two beautiful architectual models of a circular plan, and objects from everyday life. One should also note that about 40 tablets have been found in various spots on the site that allow us to place Mari with respect to Mesopotamian centers like Lagash or Abu Salabikh, or Syrian centers like Ebla.

4. The period of the Shakkanakkus. This phase begins in the middle of the Akkadian period, but we still do not know under what conditions. The title *šakkanakku* appears to designate the sovereigns of Mari for a period that extends from the second half of the 23d century to the beginning of the 20th century B.C., during which time the city was extensively renovated. The extent of these operations certainly suggests a period of great power. Several sections of the great royal palace excavated by André Parrot—in particular the W wing and the throne room—were built above the 3d-millennium palaces. It was at this time also that the upper terrace was built (often designated by the inadequate name "ziggurat"), closely associated with the Temple of Lions that abuts from the south, a temple that was mistakenly attributed to the god Dagan. To the S extend anonymous temples and the sanctuaries of Ninhursag and of Shamash. To the E of the sacred quarter, excavations since 1979 have unearthed a new palace, the construction of which is to be credited to the Shakkanakkus. It added to the other palace without subtracting from it for, of smaller dimension, it served either to house members of the royal family or as a place to withdraw when important construction was taking place in the main palace. Finally the last excavations have allowed the discovery of two royal tombs that were built under the throne room and beneath another great hall.

Few materials are characteristic of this period even though it lasted almost four centuries. One should note, however, the celebrated and severe Ishtup-Ilum, whose statue was found in the throne room of the great royal palace. One should also note the large pictoral composition that decorated room 132 of the same structure; this one revealed itself to be the sanctuary of Ishtar within the palace, and not an audience hall as had been previously assumed.

5. The Lim Dynasty. The last half century of Mari's history is also the best known as a result of written documents found during the excavations in the great palace before the Second World War. Nearly 15,000 archival documents concerning politics, the administration, and the economy were uncovered. This exceptional discovery furnished documentation that goes beyond the area of the city of Mari and casts new light on the entire Near East at the beginning of the 2d millennium. This richness should not make one forget that the connection is still poorly understood between the Shakkanakku period and the Amorite Dynasty (ca. 1800 B.C.), up to the time when Zimri-Lim succeeded in retaking power (ca. 1775) by banishing Yasmah-Addu, the son of Samsi-Addu.

Of the city of this period, we know of part of the sacred quarter with the upper terrace associated with the Temple of Lions which was equipped with a reworked esplanade, a new terrace of small dimensions that appears to function with the Temple of Shamash, and the Temple of Ninhursag that perpetuates the ancient tradition. The palace of the Shakkanakkus is still being unearthed and will continue to be, just like another building that has been found on the NW promontory of the tell during the 1985 excavation and of which one still does not know either the construction date or the exact use.

Only the richest structure remains, that which was the great royal palace. Although its construction began during the Shakkanakku period, it continued to be expanded and renovated during the reign of Zimri-Lim. See Fig. MAR.03. Already renowned in antiquity, it was found in such a state of preservation that it became the symbol of monumental Western architecture of the 2d millennium. Its remains allow one to understand with precision its architectural characteristics and to define the components of royal architecture of the period of the Amorite dynasties. It still possesses traits that directly link it to its 3d-millennium ancestor. The different quarters are orga-

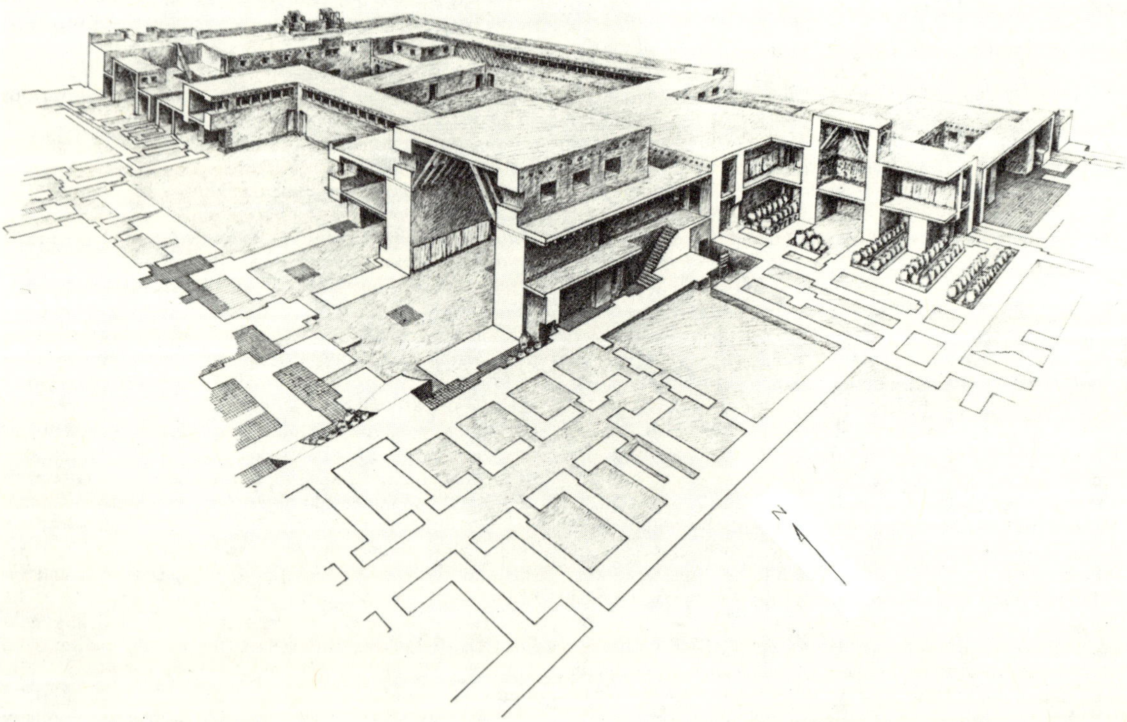

MAR.03. Isometric reconstruction of the E portion of the OB palace of Zimri-Lim. *(Courtesy of Mission Archéologique de Mari)*

nized around two large courtyards. See Fig. ART.05. The first (131) is part of the welcoming hall directing traffic either toward the temples situated on the former site of the ancient Sacred Enclosure, or toward the W half of the structure where the King's House and the House of the Women are. These latter houses are organized around the official grouping comprising the Palm Court (famous for the paintings that decorated its walls), the *Papahum,* and the throne room where important royal ceremonies and large banquets were held. The King's House encircled the throne room; toward the E, above a section of stores, the royal apartments were located on the second floor; to the S extended the servants' quarters; to the W one found the kitchens and the administrative offices. In this way the palace of Mari contains the different quarters which normally constitute a royal home from the beginning of the 2d millennium, but arranges them differently. Thanks to a unique preservation (walls more than 4 m high, murals still in place, intact daily conveniences such as the kitchen, bathrooms, etc.), a precise architectural study was carried out shedding new light on monumental architecture of this period.

6. The End of Mari. In a political context still somewhat obscure, it seems that Zimri-Lim, after a period of success, did not succeed in firmly implanting his control of the area. Hammurabi of Babylon, after having been his ally, turned against him in 1760 B.C. and defeated him; he then installed himself in the city, while Zimri-Lim disappears from our documentation. After having removed its riches (including probably most of the more important texts), Hammurabi decided to set the palace on fire, and then demolished it completely; the same end was reserved for other temples that were excavated, at the Shakkanakku palace, and at the building that was recently found on the NW promontory. Since then, Mari no longer existed as an important center, but only on occasion as a small town during the Assyrian period or as a village during the Seleucid period, as attested by the cemeteries that were found in various spots in the tell.

JEAN-CL. MARGUERON
Trans. Stephen Rosoff

TEXTS

It is commonly asserted that at Mari, A. Parrot was the "discoverer" of a library of 20,000 cuneiform tablets. Parrot himself was the source of these reports and he contributed greatly to their diffusion by writing a scientific contribution that he entitled: "Zimri-Lim of Mari, a literate prince." However, it must be noted that Mari, in spite of the considerable historical interest of the documents discovered there, has given us no intentionally gathered collection of literary or scholarly scientific works. There is nothing in common, in this sense, with the collections of Sumerian works of Nippur and Ur, which were gathered on private initiative, or especially that of Boghazköy (Hattusas) or Nineveh, which were collected on royal initiative. The importance of the Mari documents lies elsewhere.

A. Nature of the Documentation
  1. Palace Administrative Texts
  2. Other Types of Administrative Texts
  3. Letters
  4. Treaties
  5. Other Types of Texts
  6. Texts from Other Periods
B. Arrangement of the Texts in the Palace
C. Importance of the Mari Texts

A. Nature of the Documentation

Prior to 1972 nearly 20,000 complete tablets and fragments were found at Tell Hariri by A. Parrot. Since 1979 other fragments of a few thousand documents have been discovered during the excavations of J. Margueron. Moreover, the site has not ceased yielding all the documents hidden in its debris. Now that a general inventory has been done, it is possible to take account of that which is missing. The understanding of what we today possess of the Mari documents is much more subtle than the previous and crude distinction between "economic texts" and "letters" suggests. We are now able to provide a more detailed classification of the Mari texts.

1. Palace Administrative Texts. a. Expense Texts: Food and Drink. The major part of the administrative documents represents calculated expenses on reserves of raw materials gathered and stored in the royal palace. Moreover, since the management of these reserves was the main motivation for writing such texts, it seems that the absence of the king and his entourage from the palace brought a halt to this text writing. A spectacular example is given to us at the end of Zimri-Lim (ZL) year 8 and during the first four months of ZL year 9, when the entire court traveled W on a long trip that ended at Ugarit. All the texts from the palace that date from this time mark the royal periplus and point out the itinerary. The texts were brought back to the palace offices on the return journey, apparently no text having been written at Mari during the entire trip. Besides, one of the principal palace administrators, Dâriš-lîbûr, had left his offices in order to accompany the king.

It is not surprising that the text par excellence found in the royal palace is called "The King's Meal," which consists of monotonous listings *ne varietur* of meals served at the king's table and that of his follower (the *ṣâbum*), except for some wine and meat that were entered on other expense accounts because they probably originated from other departments independent from those that managed supplies of grains, oil, fruits, or sweets. These texts represent a total of more than 2,000 documents: good samples of them can be found in ARMT 9, 11, 12, and 21. A large number still remain unpublished. These documents are extremely important in determining when the king was present in his palace. Moreover, in addition to "normal" meals, they record, on recurrent dates, meals eaten in honor of the dead, either in honor of the souls of past kings *(kispum)* or of deceased members of the royal family *(mâlikum).*

b. Harem Texts. Distributions to the harem attest to the presence of a large number of women in the palace; daughters of the king (priestesses or princesses eligible to marry), women of the first rank *(kallâtum),* singers of first or second rank (most likely concubines), domestics of the two principal queens, and various female personnel maintaining the palace and its kitchens. This is well attested for at the end of the reign of Yasmah-Addu and for the beginning of Zimri-Lim's reign. Their presence, marked especially by texts showing expenses of oil or wool, is the sign of a retreat into the strongly walled palace of the female population that, in more secure and stable times, lived elsewhere (most likely in a less solemn and undoubtedly more comfortable place). If we are not informed as to what the royal harem was at the end of the reign of Zimri-Lim, we see by contrast Queen Shibtu and the royal children who, from the latter half of ZL year 10, came back to the capital, to the "little Eastern Palace," then took possession of the large palace itself. The small harem texts characteristic of the end of Yasmah-Addu's reign are studied in *MARI* 4, while good examples of the large harem lists dating from the first part of the reign of Zimri-Lim can be found in *ARMT* 22 and especially in *TEM* 4. The so-called *Archives of the Harem,* which represent fragments of administrative documents dealing with the management of the fortunes of the important women living in the palace, found in room 52, remain unpublished. At this point only the letters dealing with these women have been published (*ARMT* 10).

c. Audit Texts. The administrative activity in the palace periodically called for an audit. These audits are recorded by the writing of general inventories of expenses on raw materials. These texts are relatively isolated and they do not have the punctiliousness that one would imagine. They exist particularly in the first part of the reign, the time of the most intense occupation of the royal residence. It is likely that they were continued elsewhere from ZL year 5 and that they were filed and stored where the king was living. Upon reading them, one notices that they are not the simple recapitulative monotone of the small individual texts, written from one day to the next. It is possible that the scribes made some recording errors in writing the long summaries, because they were transcribing the different administrative actions from memory. In fact, one can also imagine that certain daily texts were written in a mechanical manner, and that the large summaries took account of performance slowdown or rectified certain views that were overly optimistic. Many of these large texts are published in *ARMT* 22.

d. Expense Texts: Metal and Fabrics. The major part of the expense texts is naturally made up of small tablets concerning the maintenance of the royal household. Aside from the table expenses (see above), one finds more than anything else some texts dealing with metal or fabric, which were put away in the storerooms of the royal palace itself. Anything that left the treasury was counted, i.e., complimentary shipments to other rulers of the time *(šûbultum),* presents to the women of high descent, to messengers, etc. These texts, when taken together, are extremely valuable in reconstructing the diplomatic life of the time. Thus, it is not by chance that one must wait until the end of ZL year 4 to see a jewel sent to the king of Eshnunna. In fact, it was only a few months earlier that the two kingdoms ended a long and bitter struggle. Likewise, thanks to the counting of presents, one has very valuable chronological information on the contemporary Elamite dynasty (Durand 1986: 118–22).

The majority of tablets dealing with metals provide information about the manufacturing of luxury objects. The king placed great emphasis on all working of gold, silver, and precious stones (especially lapis lazuli and rock crystal) because these materials were rare and frequently defective. Since the reserves apparently were not sufficient to provide everything that one wished, old jewelry was sometimes remelted in order to obtain material for creating new pieces. At the mercy of these manipulations, the metal waste multiplied and losses accumulated. At several stages in this work an inspection was made—particularly by the loss controllers *(ebbûtum)*—and these different acts generated some very useful texts concerning technical history.

e. Publication of the Palace Administrative Texts. All these aspects of the administrative texts from Mari are illustrated by different volumes that have been published: *ARM(T)* 7, 9, 18, 21–25. Most of these scholarly volumes were devoted to the fragments found in particular rooms in the hope that the use of the various palace rooms could be reconstructed. For the most part, this hope was defeated because the techniques used by A. Parrot to record the epigraphic discoveries in the palace was quite disorganized. Most likely, too many mixtures took place during the actual excavation for us to do precise studies. Also, the move toward publication was accelerated: *ARMT* 23 (= *AAM* 1), the work of a new team of editors, was the edition of all the administrative texts catalogued by G. Dossin, to which the texts of room 215 were added. Besides these, there were some attempts at an edition grouped thematically: *ARM* 18 treats some documents of the administration of Mukannishum; *ARMT* 25 should in theory give us the edition of all the documents treating metal. Another publication (*AAM* 2) should procure the complete catalog of all the administrative texts of the palace, arranged chronologically (as much as possible), summarizing briefly those that had already been published, editing those that were not yet published, and reconstructing those where additions and collations changed the interpretation drastically. The texts found by J. Margueron since the new excavations of the palace must be part of *AAM* 2; those found "outside the palace" will be the subject of a separate publication, together with those from their proper archaeological locations.

f. Evaluation of the Palace Archives. It appears that the archives that would allow us to discover the composition of the palace stores are totally missing. Most likely, that results from the large door cleared by A. Parrot and whether it served as a visitor's passageway, and not as the place where deliveries were received. This latter was probably called "Nergal's Door"; located to the E of the ceremonial entrance, this door represented the place where chariots, loaded with raw materials, passed through. See Fig. ART.05. If the "administrative offices" *(bît têrtim)* were found at the door of the palace residence *(bâbekallim),* another administration was found at "Nergal's Door." The area was never excavated and currently is covered by dumps from the palace excavation. In contrast, the inventory of the Mari tablets indicates that several lists of proper names as well as administrative texts (in poor shape for conservation purposes) were found "outside the palace, in the area of the ziggurat." In fact, the inventory is concerned not with the exterior of the palace, but with the area where the storehouses were located. An eventual expansion of the excavations will perhaps allow us to find the new administrative archives. However, even if the receiving department was found at this second door, it is possible that the archives themselves had been kept more to the S, in what is considered the "area of reserves," which was found leveled to its foundations.

2. Other Types of Administrative Texts. a. Gift Texts. At any rate, it is easy to establish that the only "entrances for goods" in the palace of Zimri-Lim are for those called *šûrubtum.* These consist of "countergifts," that is, in response to the *šûbultum* mentioned above. Thus one sees wine delivered, gifts coming from abroad (Carchemish, Aleppo, Kurdâ), olive oil sent from western regions (Alahtum), fine fabrics sent from the courts of Aleppo or Carchemish, etc. Such shipments are not only from neighboring kings, but also from great vassals and even great royal personages. Thus one can understand these taxes of grain (in relatively small quantities) on the "houses" of the great landowners in the surrounding areas of Mari, or shipments of one or two sheep to the palace from great dignitaries, sheikhs, governors, and even members of the royal family itself (including the queen and queen mother). All of these lists must be interpreted as "gifts" responding to a previous one, or expecting a "countergift" in return. These consist of personal, more or less spontaneous, contributions, never a general tax collection by the administrative authorities of the kingdom. Likewise, next to the small number of animals, one can see listed meat brought in (smoked?) from the S of Sinjar, or even farther. This consists of choice cuts which honor the king. Curiosities such as ostrich eggs and desert truffles *(kamʾatum)* also entered the palace. At certain times, the large courtyards of the palace were transformed into regular zoos by the number of animals sent by vassals and allies. All of these foodstuffs and animals so graciously given are meticulously recorded, probably because the king would take them into account in order to reciprocate at the appropriate time.

b. Texts Concerning Provincial Administration. It is not surprising that among the palace texts one finds nothing connected with the management of the provinces *(halṣum)* of the capital. These documents would have been found recorded in the palace of the governor *(šâpiṭum)*, which has not yet been discovered. It is only through the misunderstanding of a name that Bahdi-Lim, governor of the capital, was called "Prefect of the Palace." Even if the two great ministers who presided over the king's relations abroad or with his subjects actually resided "at the palace door" and kept watch to maintain a strict separation between the internal affairs of the palace and the outside world, the administrative leaders over the provinces or the royal workshops as well as the military authorities, police, or religious leaders—in effect, all persons who had nothing to do in the palace except by transitory title when the king summoned them there—kept their archives elsewhere; these archives are missing. From this point on, a study on the kingdom of Mari must take into account these missing parts of the documentation.

However, in spite of the archival separation, the king was informed regularly on all important administrative matters and, for further information, one sent to the palace, for temporary consultation or for safekeeping in the archives, tablets written outside the palace concerning events that took place outside its walls. This is the source of some very important documents informing us about the fundamental aspects of the administration, even if we cannot always gather from them as complete a reconstruction that we would wish.

Thus the king was also kept up to date on certain censuses taken of the people. About 30 large tablets represent the palace's copies of texts of the great census *(têbibtum)* that took place at the end of ZL year 4, after the reordering of the Benjaminites who rebelled and after the expulsion of the troops of Eshnunna who had come to support them. One sees listed here people taking oaths, coarsely gathered together by occupation, and enumerated place by place and district by district. It is possible that only the population that had to do with the palace was summoned and that the *têbibtum* was also a way of certifying, through oath-taking, the loyalty of a substantial part of the population. This census undoubtedly intended to take a count of the people after a period not filled with bloodshed but nevertheless marked by a change in the status of a great many people: many lost their freedom at the time of the razzias; others were brought back into the palace departments to which the conquering king assigned them. Besides the obvious onomastic interest, these lists also inform us as to the local regrouping of toponymies of the provinces of Mari, Terqa, Saggarâtum, etc., the major towns of the kingdom. These are the texts that best allow us to understand the geography of the heartland of the kingdom of Mari.

On sporadic occasions, a land occupation reform took place and long lists of fields were recorded. These did not concern the establishment of a plot of land, but rather a count of how many units of land were removed from one plot and added to another. Likewise, certain texts probably represent tax estimates and indicate the expected grain production. These two kinds of tablets are very valuable for distinguishing the toponymies of the region of Mari.

More than 20 or so large tablets represent the palace's copies of oaths taken at the end of ZL year 9 by a large number of women who were named according to their social status. These consist of wives, widows *(almattum)*, and single women of various backgrounds, the majority being women who had devoted themselves to a deity (usually *qaššatum)*, priestesses *(NIN-DINGIR-RA), or* "ecstatics" (clairvoyants—*muhhûtum*). We are not always informed as to what motivated these great oath-takings by such a substantial number of women. It is, however, a very important source for feminine onomastics of the time. Two good examples can be found in *ARMT* 9 and *ARMT* 23.

Censuses were established for some army corps at the time of departure for military expeditions. This was often useful in determining whether the number of Haneans or Benjaminites who should have been conscripted indeed were conscripted. These documents are known as "large tablets" and the inventories mention the men "nominally" *(tuppi lú ù šum-šu).* These documents are major sources for geography and onomastics. Examples can be found in *ARMT* 23 at the time when the troops from Mari went to help Hammurabi of Babylon in battle against Rîm-Sîn of Larsa. The publication of these large lists will entirely change the image that we have of the population of Amorite Syria and will enable a pioneering work like *Amorite*

Personal Names (Huffmon 1965) to be rewritten using an infinitely more vast basis of knowledge. However, one cannot claim to make a population count of the kingdom from these lists, nor to establish the rosters of the army.

The bills of sheikhs *(sugagûm)* that pay off a gift *(suggâgûtum)* consisting of gold, silver, or animals periodically informed the king of those who had sworn allegiance to him locally and who had thereby recognized his power. They are considered political texts, not texts of tax collections (as was initially believed).

The census listings, like those of the deported persons of Hurmiš (ZL year 11), had another motivation: that of informing the king of the increase of workers belonging to the royal residences following the conquests. These are specialized workers taken from their homeland along with their families. These lists inform us in an unexpected way about the population and the technologies of ancient Upper-Jezira and enable us to see more concretely the mobility of people torn from their native land, deported, redistributed, and diluted among other social groups into which they would eventually disappear. In capitals which were raided a short while later, one section of the population received special attention from the conqueror: the royal harems. These harems were brought back to Mari after an inventory noting the status of the various women (priestesses or wives) and the origin of royal captives. One finds the practice of combining the wives of the conqueror with those of the conquered to be rather systematic. For example, the texts show that the harem of Ashlakkâ, captured after the defeat of its king, was made up of the original princesses of other previously conquered capitals. This complexity of populations makes sense when one realizes that only two years later all the women of Zimri-Lim—girls, queens, concubines, and captives of diverse background—along with Zimri-Lim himself, either had to walk the road of victorious Babylon or be given in homage to other courts. All of these numerous texts allow us to understand better the incredible blend of populations, cultures, and languages that took place at that time in the Near East.

It is in these same categories of documents that the so-called censuses of teams of weavers must be included; this does not consist of inventories of "ergastulum" *(nêpârâtum)* but of counts of deported persons. One finds on these lists those redistributions of Benjaminite prisoners of war as well as the redemptions of slaves by their families throughout the Near East.

To these considerable administrative documents must be added some rare fragments of private archives of individual administrators, whose presence at the royal palace is still not understood. The legal texts must be considered, of which the partial edition in *ARM* 8 must be reconstructed after collations, additions, and adjunctions of unpublished material, in a later systematic study.

c. Expense Texts concerning the Palace Temples. Sacred expenses form another fragmentary group of tablets distinguished from the rest. The king of Mari and his court were not the only ones to inhabit the large palace. Since its very existence, the gods were believed to have resided there, because that which is called the Sacred Enclosure (considered by J. Margueron to be the avatar of the origin of the major temple of the city) established itself in the palace and represents the temple of the "Lady of the Palace" at the time of Yasmah-Addu and Zimri-Lim. See Fig. ART.05. Room 130, on the other hand, is the "Temple of Ishtar" or *bît birmî* ("The Temple with Paintings") mentioned in the texts. Quite often, it is to the gods present in these chapels and not to those of the urban temples that most of the sacred expenses (included in the costs of the palace) were dedicated. Their worship represents a "palace act" just like the great sacred ceremonies "The Ritual of Ishtar" or "The Ritual of *Kispum*" of the time of Yasmah-Addu. They are spoken of in the texts found at the palace because they describe intrapalatial activities, and are addressed to Ishtar or to the Lady of the Palace and to her consort the sun god, who is distinguished from the "Sun of the Skies." These texts are taken up again with other unpublished material in *ARMT* 26/3.

3. Letters. The large amount of epistolary documents, the "prestigious" documents among the group of Mari texts and those that have, until now, (unfairly) received most of the attention, deal mostly with diplomatic and administrative activities, but the abundance of anecdotes and subjects dealing with everyday life makes this documentation irreplaceable.

Now that the census of senders has been compiled and the large epistolary files reconstructed, it is possible to establish enormous gaps in our documentation, which a priori we should have been able to suspect. These gaps are first and foremost the result of human initiative. It has long been known that after the fall of Mari, an inventory of the palace archives was taken by the conquerors and that the texts had been regrouped chronologically (since the labels dating from one year of Hammurabi speak of the "Tablets of the servants of Shamshî-Adad" and of the "Tablets of the servants of Zimri-Lim"). One can deduce that the archives were in the process of removal and that for whatever reason, this undertaking was not completed by the Babylonians. In fact, what was Hammurabi supposed to do with this huge amount of texts dealing with local administration? He should have looked systematically for others of more immediate interest to him. As a matter of fact, it is easy to note that from this point on, almost all the letters from the chancelleries of the great international capitals of the ANE are now missing (Qaṭna, Aleppo, Carchemish, Ekallâtum, Susa, Babylon, Eshnunna, and Larsa). Even if we imagine that there were periods of strained relations between Mari and other kingdoms such as Ekallâtum, Eshnunna, or Susa, we know (through quotations in some letters) the gist of the royal missives from these palaces and also that there were intense diplomatic relations through epistolary interchanges.

The most flagrant loss is the absence of practically all the letters of Hammurabi. While the kings of Mari and of Babylonia, up until the final confrontation, held common politics and alliances, all that remains from the Babylonian chancellery are some insignificant missives written to governors Meptûm, Bahdi-Lim, or Buqâqum, which were certainly forwarded to the palace "for informational purposes."

Practically all the texts from Qaṭna are from Išhi-Addu, king at the time of Shamshî-Adad. Missing are most of the letters sent from Aleppo, each of whose kings was very close to Zimri-Lim, being his father-in-law or brother-in-law. There are only some fragments or erratic texts that escaped the inventory of the enemies.

One can certainly wonder whether in fact the texts had been destroyed by Zimri-Lim himself or if they had been removed for safekeeping when the Babylonian troops were threatening Mari. The second hypothesis is supported by the discovery that confiscated correspondence was put into archives in the royal palace of Mari by the scribes of Zimri-Lim himself; either they were intercepted on the roads, or more likely they were brought out from the chancelleries of conquered kings. If one puts aside the documents manifestly communicated to the king of Mari through loyalty (like the circulating letter that the Sukkalmah of Elam sent "to all the kings of Subartu" that he wanted to impress), we are aware of two particularly spectacular examples of this fact.

The letters exchanged between the diviners of Mišlân and Prince Sûmû-Dâbî at the time of the great rebellion of the Benjaminite kings were archived (published in *ARMT* 16). We also have several compromising letters sent to the kings W of Ida-Maraṣ. Thus there is one from the king of Ashnakkum, Ishme-Addu, at the time of the Elamite invasion in ZL year 9. One of these documents was published a long time ago as *ARM* 4: 20, but it was attributed to the correspondence of Yasmah-Addu of Mari and Ishme-Dagan of Ekallâtum. On the other hand, we have some missives addressed to the king Ibâl-Addu, around ZL year 11, which must have been confiscated in the chancellery of Ashlakkâ after his fall. It is possible that the correspondence of Ishme-Addu was found in the chancellery of Ashlakkâ.

One cannot consider that the correspondence with the principal kings was placed elsewhere than at the royal palace, in a temple, for example, because it is among the documents from the palace that the correspondence between Zimri-Lim and his vassals from Ida-Maraṣ was found—those kings who call him "Father" or "Lord" (i.e., the various kings of Ashlakkâ, Ashnakkum, Ilân-ṣurâ, Kahât, and Razamâ, to mention the most important ones)—as well as correspondence that comes from the great kingdoms of south Sinjar—those kings who address Zimri-Lim as "Brother" (i.e., the kings of Kurda, Andarik, Qatarâ, or Karanâ). Similarly, we have found letters at the palace from kings farther away, whose kingdoms were beyond the Tigris, like the princes of the Turukkians and of Habiru, or on this side of the river, like that of Mardamân. These documents date from the beginnings of the reign. We must thus resign ourselves to having no more than a partial vision of the external politics of Mari, and it is especially the governors and generals, those who are "on a mission," who inform us about the great events. The royal documents that would have been able to give us firsthand information are missing.

Similarly missing are the "duplicates" *(meher ṭuppim)* of letters sent by the royal chancellery (letters of which a copy was kept in order to be able to quote *verbatim* a proposition or stipulation, as was the custom at that time). Even though we still have several documents of this type for the reign of Yasmah-Addu, whose politics were not really of much concern to the Babylonians, these texts for the reign of Zimri-Lim (that we know once existed) are missing. It is likely that all these tablets were systematically removed by someone curious to know "the seamy side of life." The diplomatic life is indeed under the sign of strict respect to the sworn oath and the divine curse, going all the way to the annihilation of the perjurer. Undoubtedly the savage sacking of Mari after its fall, which was neither the custom of the time nor that of the victorious King Hammurabi, received justification following the scrutiny of the royal archives. Moreover, we know (even if we do not understand all the details) that at the final end of Mari, its king, breaking the ancient alliances with Babylon, had tried a rapprochement with that country's traditional (almost ancestral) enemy, Eshnunna. This city was destroyed at the same time as Mari, although it was, like Mari, one of the millennial powers of the ANE.

4. Treaties. It is not surprising that all of the international treaties that we know to have existed and that we should be able to find in great quantity (seeing the various attestations and quotations that we read from the correspondence) are missing from the roll. If we count the existing documents it is easy to see that only very little remains.

A treaty project between Mari and Babylon against Elam belonging to a genre called "small tablet" was reconstructed from two fragments (Durand 1986). This is a working document from which the "large tablet" must have been written, an official document with curses against the offender and perhaps with imprints of the royal seal.

A large treaty between Zimri-Lim and Ibâl-pî-el II of Eshnunna (established in ZL year 4) remains, but it is savagely mutilated; either the Babylonians broke it intentionally at the time of the pillage, or the people of Mari themselves did it at the time of the rupture between the two kingdoms in ZL year 2. This latter view is undoubtedly the best because a mutilation at the time of the destruction of the city should still allow us to find the missing fragments.

Another version remains of the same text, but it is shorter and very mutilated. A "small tablet" concerning Atamrum, king of Andarik, is also preserved, as is the text (in the Hanean language [Amorite]) of a *mišpaṭum* between two rival towns of Ida-Maraṣ, both subject to Zimri-Lim.

It is significant that one no longer finds a single treaty made with the vassals of Ida-Maraṣ, whose letters are abundant. It is possible that Hammurabi took away these texts that sanctioned everlasting obedience to Zimri-Lim by the princes that Hammurabi now wanted to attach to himself, or perhaps the royal administrators at the last minute had been able to hide these treaties for safekeeping.

5. Other Types of Texts. a. Literary Texts. There are a few other types of texts in the Mari palace, but what we would consider "literary texts" in the proper sense are totally absent. This is not to say that such texts did not exist at Mari. One letter tells us about the myth of the battle between the storm god and the sea, which is later recounted in texts from Ugarit. Two other letters make direct reference to the creation of man, or to a divine mission given to a human. Quotations from proverbs and wisdom literature are indeed plentiful. Thus it must be considered that the king's residence did not normally welcome this type of writing. The king did not intend to have a literary library. The tablets that contained such texts were at home among individuals whose trade was to read, write, and compose, perhaps in the private homes of the diviners (that we have not found). The few fragments of syllabaries found at Mari were in the small E palace, the temporary residence of the diviner Asqudum. The large palace has only yielded one syllabary of the TU-TA-TI type.

Two exceptional texts have been found at Mari which could possibly fall under the rubric of "literary." The first is the large "Epic Poem of Zimri-Lim," almost entirely preserved, of more than 100 lines, which sings the praise of the king and culminates in his entrance into the Temple of Dagan at Terqa at the end of the Benjaminite rebellion (cf. *AEM* 2). This is more a work by a lettered courtier than a gratuitous literary composition. It could have served as a composition destined to attract the good graces of the king. This work could also have served as a basis for a report on recent military events, made to the god Dagan of Terqa. The other text is a large bilingual letter, written in Sumerian and Akkadian and addressed to the king. It was written by a disgraced scribe who had his heart set on proving to his master his worth and abilities and thus seems to be a work of court flattery.

b. Ritual and Omen Texts. We have already seen above that the two great rituals which were found at Mari concerned palace events. Some fragments of bilingual psalms (Sumerian/phonetic Babylonian) must be added; maybe these were used, like several incantation tablets concerning the "dog bite," for prophylactic purposes. Perhaps, due to the dominant role that Asqudum played in the royal administration, we should have found among the documents from the palace a fragment of astrological omens and some pieces of hepatoscopic texts. These latter ones are attested to, however, by several quotations of primary clauses in the letters rather than through a library of textbooks.

Finally, all of these texts are more shreds of "utilitarian" and "technical" libraries (purification and divination) than proof that the king of Mari was a "clever scholar." However, it is permissible to wonder whether they were more numerous at a given moment and if what is missing was not made part of the booty of the conqueror. In fact, the hepatoscopic technique of Mari had its own specific characteristics and this practice supported those that were particular to Babylonia.

All of these texts are "royal" insofar as they concern the exercise of royal power in the highest degree. It is in this category, therefore, that the texts of "Protocols" will naturally fall; they represent oaths taken to the king by certain types of servants, and they also prefigure the "court edicts" several centuries before the Middle Assyrian or Hittite period, and the literature of the *adê,* more than a thousand years before the Neo-Assyrian Empire.

6. Texts from Other Periods. The texts that we have spoken about are those that compose the majority of tablets, dating from the 20 years covering the end of Yasmah-Addu and the reign of Zimri-Lim. Some texts from other periods exist, but in a much more limited number.

a. Earliest Texts. For example, some tablets come from the period prior to Sargon of Akkad (more or less contemporaneous with Ebla): about 50 such documents were published by Charpin (1987). The editor noticed that they were not all contemporary one with another and that they represented disparate archives. Judging from the great political importance of Mari at the time and from the state of preservation of the pre-Sargonic palace, it is likely that we will one day have, if not the ensemble of these archives, at least a most important census. At this time, the tablets should occupy only one extremely restricted zone: two or three rooms at the most, if they were not dispersed in antiquity at one time or another.

The actual time of Akkad is represented by only two or three documents, still unpublished. The UR III period is limited to two tablets, one of which may be a document from Tello, recently misplaced and confused with the exhumed tablets at Tell Hariri.

b. The *Šakkanakku* Texts. The documents called (by a misuse of the term) "šakkanakkus tablets" (*ARM* 19) in reality are documents immediately prior to the adoption of the writing method (phonetic values and paleography) known as "classic Babylonian" (see Durand 1985). The most recent of these texts does indeed date from the reign of Yahdun-Lim, who undoubtedly gave back to Mari its status as an international capital. Some of the documents from the period enable us to examine in detail the exceptional time that represents a change in the standard of written notation, a true "reformation of writing." One can establish that in agreement with Mesopotamian standards, this change bears a fourfold aspect, concerning not only the paleography of signs, but also their system of symbols, the format of documents, and the choice of written dialect. These documents are therefore naturally taken up again in comparison with the texts of Yahdun-Lim which give us the key in *AAM* 2.

B. Arrangement of the Texts in the Palace

How were the texts of the 2d millennium arranged in the palace? Above, we considered the disorder found in the archivage of the finds at the time of the hurried digging that exhumed the documents. These texts, roughly arranged by room numbers, only received an inventory number for a short time.

One point can be henceforth established: the scribes of Zimri-Lim considered the epistolary documents of the officials of Yasmah-Addu and those of the new king's servants to be archivable for the same reason. Moreover, in many cases, the administrators served these two masters with the same efficiency and devotion. By contrast, the administrative documents of the reign of Yasmah-Addu had been thrown out and were rediscovered, for the most part, in the berms or the foundations.

The entire documentation from the reigns of Yahdun-Lim and Sûmû-Yamam, by contrast, was considered to be "dead archives." When the excavations of A. Parrot unearthed some of them, it should be noted that the workers who were excavating had crossed (intentionally or not) the ground from the period of Yasmah-Addu or Zimri-Lim. That explains the rarity of these texts and the almost complete absence of the diplomatic correspondence of these kings, while the recent excavations, taking down the recent structures, are discovering some underground. This supports the conclusion that the royal palace was unoccupied for several years after Mari fell into the hands of the dynasty of Upper Mesopotamia. We know that following this there was important work done in the royal palace to put it back in order when Yasmah-Addu came to settle there, a little while before marrying a princess from Qaṭna. At this time, one should have systematically made a "clean sweep" of a past which was not at all to be reclaimed.

At present, in spite of everything, one can still have a general (if not a precise) idea of the ancient arrangement. The bulk of the (nonfeminine) correspondence was found at room 115; the major part of the administrative texts, at room 102. See Fig. ART.05. There were, in fact, several archivage areas of the administrative texts. It is possible to identify various "administrative reception areas" made up of rooms at the entrances of different areas of the palace (Durand 1987b).

C. Importance of the Mari Texts

All of these discoveries lead us to affirm the political value of writing in this period. We have proof of it thanks to the written documentation of Mari. Before this we only knew about the acquisitions or confiscations of tablets dealing with religion and magic in Babylonia or Assyria at the time of the assembling of the "library of Nineveh" or about the pillage of prestigious artistic documents, like the Code of Hammurabi or the Babylonian Kudurru brought by the Elamites to the acropolis of Susa. It is hoped that all of these missing Mari documents (which are so important) will someday be found in their probable places of exile. If they still exist, one must imagine them to be in the palace of Hammurabi of Babylon.

Therefore, the large amount of "letters" found at Mari consists of those sent by the king's servants. Several categories must be distinguished. Concerning the administrators, a distinction must be made between those that inform us about their local functions, exercising the duty assigned to them by the king (this is the majority, spanning quite a large period of time and often with vague internal chronology) and those administrators who are on an extraordinary mission (dealing with punctual transactions and serving as a basis for our relative chronology).

Among those who write from the place where they govern, the first rank is held by the members of the central administration, those who were among the top ministers. However, they are by far the least interesting. Their proximity to the king means that there is little information left from them; we only have letters written by them when they were on an outside mission or when the king was absent and they sent tablets to him to keep him up to date. Since these last letters were found at Mari and were obviously originals, we must deduce that the secretaries of the displaced king were carefully keeping these documents and were bringing them back with them to the palace when the king returned. Limiting ourselves to the time of Zimri-Lim, these high-ranking personages were Bannum, Asqudum, Sammêtar, Habdu-Malik, and Šunuhra-Halû. This last one held a special position: since it was he who apparently read the letters addressed to the king, letter writers often took care to send him a short personal note of explanation along with a gift so that the letter would be read to the king with goodwill. We have preserved almost all of these letters addressed to this important individual.

Several civil officials of high rank left important pieces of documentation: we refer to the *šandabakku* (accountant-archivist) Yasîm-Sûmû (*ARMT* 13) or Ṣidqi-Epuh. A special place is also held by the superintendent *(šatammum)* Mukannishum whose letters are an inexhaustible mine of information (*ARMT* 13 and *ARM* 18).

The correspondence from the governors, therefore, is the heart of our documentation. They had varying titles:

1. *šâpiṭum.* This title was used when the district was directly attached to the crown. Limiting ourselves only to the reign of Zimri-Lim and to the best-documented person, this applies to (a) the governors of Mari (Itûr-Asdû and Bahdi-Lim), which clearly demonstrates the separation of the district governor from the royal palace itself; (b) the governors of Terqa (Sammêtar and Kibri-Dagan); (c) the governors of Saggarâtum/Dûr-Yahdun-Lim (Sûmû-Hadum, Sumhu-rabi, and Yaqqim-Addu); and (d) the governors of Qaṭna (Zimri-Addu and Zakura-Hammu). This exceptional documentation understandably received the most immediate attention and gave rise to some fundamental publications: *ARM* 3, 6, 13 (in part), and 14. Others will soon be available, such as the one concerning the governors of Qaṭna (*ARMT* 20).

2. *hazzânnum.* This title applied to a military official of a district. The clearest example is that of Tuttul, Lânasûm, whose correspondence is published in *ARMT* 26/1 and *AEM* 2.

3. *merhûm.* This was an authority who supervised people engaged in transhumance. During the reign of Zimri-Lim, this was associated with Ibâl-pî-El and Ibêl-El, in charge of the Haneans in Ida-Maraṣ, and especially with the character Meptûm in the south. The correspondence of Ibal-El, which informs us firsthand about the NW border, must be dealt with ever since the publication of *AEM* 2; the correspondence of Meptûm, which talks about the SE border, concerns relations with Eshnunna and Babylon. It is in this correspondence that the most direct information on the end of Mari can be found.

For some of these officials, especially those whose power is military (like Yamṣûm of Ilan-ṣura or Itûr-Asdû of Ashlakkâ), it is difficult to know their title. They seem to have had a very important informative role and they have left us a large corpus of letters. The letters from Yamṣûm (*ARMT* 26/2) reveal more about the events of Ilan-surạ than those from the local king, Hâya-Sûmû, who evidently did not want to tell everything about his own deeds and actions, especially when he was pursuing interests different from those of his suzerain and father-in-law.

4. *sugâgum.* This title applied to the sheikhs who represented various local authorities officially recognized by the king. The vassals of the Mari king *(šaknum* or *šarrum)* are only particular examples of those whose power received more special recognition. They can sometimes take the appearance of a military governor, such as Hammân of Dêr (in part *ARMT* 26/1). Their correspondence is all the more intense as their problems increase in size. They are not bound to a duty of relaying such precise information as the so-called officials from Mari. In addition, they only write in a time of crisis, as when Hammân is threatened by the Benjaminites and the kings of Zalmaqqum (Harrân).

A special place is held by the correspondence of the Benjaminite kings. Two categories must be distinguished: the kings before the rebellion (Hardûm, Yaggîh-Addu, and especially Sûmû-Dâbî) and those who settled at the end of

ZL year 3 and at the beginning of ZL year 4 (Dâdî-Hadûn, Hammî-istamar, etc.). The Benjaminite kings practiced transhumance between the kingdom of Mari and the regions to the W, toward Yamhad to the N, going up the course of the Euphrates; toward Amurru to the S, and beyond the kingdom of Qaṭna to the shores of the Mediterranean. Certain letters are the fundamental documents for understanding the spirit of the time. Their letters, insofar as they deal with events between the accession of Zimri-Lim and the end of ZL year 4 are edited in part in *AEM* 2.

Some files of extreme importance are composed of fairly numerous letters from officials of Mari on various missions. Their interest lies in that they are regrouped according to time and give us concentrated information about a specific region at a particular time. There are various types of missions:

1. Military: ZL years 11–12 (Ibâl-pî-El in Babylonia [in part *ARMT* 26/1–2]); ZL year 10 (Zimri-Addu from Larsa [ARM 20]); ZL year 11 (Yasîm-El, Iddiyatum, or Habdu-Malik, from the NW border against Ishme-Dagan of Ekallâtum [*ARMT* 26/2]);
2. Civil: ZL years 1 and 2 (Asqudum and Rishiya, from Aleppo: matrimonial mission); ZL year *X* (contribution of the *âlum* to the god Adad of Aleppo [ARMT 26/1]);
3. Diplomatic: ZL year 2 (Dâriš-lîbûr, from Aleppo: at the time of the first rebellion of the Benjaminite chiefs [ARMT 26/3]); ZL year 4 (Sammêtar, at the end of the war with Eshnunna, when he is going to put the affairs of the east of the Jezira in order [AEM 2]);
4. Economic: ZL years 10 and 11 (Šunuhra-Halû, Dâriš-lîbûr, and Ṣidqi-Epuh, from Aleppo, at the time of the colonization of Alahtum [ARMT 26/3]).

A special place must be reserved for the numerous letters of Nûr-Sîn, from Alahtum, between ZL years 10 and 12, when the king of Mari bought a province in the kingdom of Aleppo in order to obtain certain products that he was lacking. This particularly spectacular file informs us not only about the economy, but also about the religion of the large western kingdom (ARMT 26/3).

Among the royal servants, the diviners hold an important position due to their "informant duty." Not only do they give us information concerning "live" hepatoscopy, as seen by practioners, but they are the source of a wealth of information concerning geography and military and political events, about which they questioned the deities (ARMT 26/1).

The harem archives had kept an important number of letters making up the feminine correspondence. This famous group of texts, the subject of countless studies since its publication (as *ARM* 10), talk especially about the administration of the palace or about religious subjects, the queens (for the same reason as the governors) themselves transcribing the substance of prophetic oracles that they had been informed of. The prophetic documents are taken up again in *ARMT* 26/1. Numerous texts emanating from the women still remain unpublished.

Until now, these documents were published by the name of their sender. However, the events are related by several people at once and often it is only through the juxtaposition of different stories or the restoration of a broken document by another in better form that it is possible to reconstruct the tangled thread of stories narrated during the course of many days. In addition, it has now been decided to publish complementary historical files. Some examples of this were given in *ARMT* 26/2 and this undertaking must be pursued in *AEM* 2 by editing all the documents relevant to the Benjaminite rebellions.

From the viewpoint of oral history and politics, the documentation from Mari brings us information about a vast portion of the Near East over a period of 20 years. This period covers the final 6 years of Yasmah-Addu and the 14 years during which Zimri-Lim reigned. The archives of Mari enable us to write about nearly all of the history of the intended period and there is no region that is not documented, apart from Egypt.

Beyond the Jezira to the NE, a region not otherwise documented until the discovery of the first texts of Tell-Leilân (Shubat-Enlil), all the important cities are more or less mentioned. We have firsthand knowledge about Hazor, the country of Canaan, Byblos, Alashiya, Ruhizzi, the region of Damascus, Kadesh, Qaṭna, Nazalâ, Palmyra, Ugarît, the region of Alalakh, Aleppo, Carchemish, Ursûm, Harrân, Burŭshkhanda, Kanish, Hattusas, Ashur, Nineveh, Kalhu, Ekallâtum, Arrapha, Qabra, Eshnunna, Ṣusa, Anshan, Dêr, Malgium, Babylon, Uruk, Maskan-Šapir, Larsa, even Dilmun. We learn of the succession of kings over several generations in many cities, the names of the deities, the order of worship, the formation of alliances, the manufacturing and production of local products; we also have an impressive onomastic and toponymic documentation. In particular, more than one place from the W regions of the Near East—in the past documented solely at the time of Alalakh IV, from El Amarna, or from Ugarît—is now attested in these texts.

Finally, the interest of the Mari texts also lies in that they provide us with a host of details on the extremely diverse and complex area of everyday life. We actually see people live, pray, do business, fight, and plot, either succeeding or perishing. Few human aspects escape us. In particular, the female population or individuals who do not belong to the world of the palace *(muškênum)* are more clearly revealed to us, better than in contemporary Babylonia, and more so than at any other time in Mesopotamia (with the exception of the end of the Neo-Assyrian Empire, whose archives offer many analogies to those of Mari).

JEAN-MARIE DURAND
Trans. Jennifer L. Davis

BIBLIOGRAPHY

The publication series for the Mari texts is the *Archives royale de Mari,* which originally fell under the general series *Textes cuneiformes du Louvre* (= *TCL*), but after 1976 was considered part of the series *Textes cuneiformes de Mari* (= *TCM*). The *Archives royale de Mari* consists of volumes of texts in autograph (= *ARM*) and corresponding volumes of texts in transliteration and French translation (= *ARMT*). For a list of the titles of the *ARM* and *ARMT* volumes up to 1983, see Pardee 1984. Recently two sub-series have been created which, although independent, also fall under the general rubric of *ARM(T)*. These are: *Archives administratives de Mari* (= *AAM*), and *Archives épis-*

tolaires de Mari (= AEM). These bear both their own volume numbers and *ARM(T)* series numbers.

Four studies by M. Birot on the economic texts found at Mari are commonly referred to in the Mari literature as TEM (= Textes économiques de Mari). These can be found in this bibliography under the following entries: TEM 1 = Birot 1953a; TEM 2 = Birot 1953b; TEM 3 = Birot 1955; and TEM 4 = Birot 1956. The journal entitled *Mari: Annales de recherches interdisciplinaires (= MARI)* is dedicated almost exclusively to Mari, and in it one can find many important studies not mentioned in this bibliography. Finally, two other recent summaries of the history and archaeology of Mari can be found in *RLA* 7: 382–90 (history), and *RLA* 7: 390–418 (archaeology, architecture, and art).

Archaeology

Al-Khalesi, Y. M. 1978. *The Court of the Palms: A Functional Interpretation of the Mari Palace.* BiMes B. Malibu.

Gates, M.-H. 1984. The Palace of Zimri-Lim at Mari. *BA* 47: 70–87.

Margueron, J. 1982a. Mari: Rapport préliminaire sur la campagne de 1979. *MARI* 1: 9–30; pls. 1–6.

———. 1982b. *Recherches sur les palais mésopotamiens de l'Age du Bronze.* 2 vols. Paris.

———. 1983. Mari: Rapport préliminaire sur la campagne de 1980. *MARI* 2: 9–35.

———. 1985. Quelques remarques sur les temples de Mari. *MARI* 4: 487–507.

———. 1986. Mari: principaux resultats des fouilles conduites depuis 1979. *CRAIBL* pp. 763–86.

———. 1987a. État présent des recherches sur l'urbanisme de Mari- 1. *MARI* 5: 483–98.

———. 1987b. Mari: capitale du Moyen Euphrates. *Dossiers histoire et archéologie* 122: 15–16.

———. 1987c. Mari: Rapport préliminaire sur la campagne de 1984. *MARI* 5: 5–26.

Parrot, A. 1935. Les fouilles de Mari. Première campagne (Hiver 1933–34). Rapport préliminaire. *Syria* 16: 1–28, 117–40.

———. 1956. *Le temple d'Ishtar.* Mission Archéologique de Mari 1. Paris.

———. 1958a. *Le palais: Architecture.* Mission Archéologique de Mari 2. Paris.

———. 1958b. *Le palais: Peintures murales.* Mission Archéologique de Mari 2. Paris.

———. 1959. *Le palais: Documents et monuments.* Mission archéologique de Mari 2. Paris.

———. 1965a. Les fouilles de Mari. Quatorzième campagne (Printemps 1964). *Syria* 42: 1–24.

———. 1965b. Les fouilles de Mari. Quinzième campagne (Printemps 1965). *Syria* 42: 197–225.

———. 1967. *Les temples d'Ishtarat et de Nini-Zaza.* Mission Archéologique de Mari 3. Paris.

———. 1968. *Le "trésor" d'Ur.* Mission Archéologique de Mari 4. Paris.

———. 1972. Les fouilles de Mari. Vingtième campagne de fouilles (Printemps 1972). *Syria* 49: 281–302.

———. 1974. *Mari, capitale fabuleuse.* Paris.

General Studies, History, and Texts

Batto, B. F. 1974. *Studies on Women at Mari.* Baltimore.

Birot, M. 1953a. Trois textes économiques de Mari (I). *RA* 47: 121–30.

———. 1953b. Textes économiques de Mari (II). *RA* 47: 161–74.

———. 1955. Textes économiques de Mari (III). *RA* 49: 15–31.

———. 1956. Textes économiques de Mari (IV). *RA* 50: 57–72.

———. 1973. Nouvelles découvertes épigraphiques au palais de Mari (Salle 115). *Syria* 50: 1–12.

———. 1980. Fragment du rituel de Mari relatif au kispum. Pp. 139–50 in *Death in Mesopotamia,* ed. B. Alster. Copenhagen.

———. 1985. Les chroniques "assyriennes" de Mari. *MARI* 4: 219–42.

Charpin, D. 1984. Nouveaux documents du bureau de l'huile a l'époque assyrienne. *MARI* 3: 83–126.

———. 1985a. Les archives du devin Asqudum dans la résidence du chantier A. *MARI* 4: 453–62.

———. 1985b. Les archives d'époque "assyrienne" dans le palais de Mari. *MARI* 4: 243–68.

———. 1987. Tablettes présargoniques de Mari. *MARI* 5: 65–127.

Charpin, D., and J.-M. Durand. 1985. La prise du pouvoir par Zimri-Lim. *MARI* 4: 293–343.

———. 1986. "Fils de Simʾal": Le origines tribales des rois de Mari. *RA* 80: 141–83.

Dalley, S. 1984. *Mari and Karana.* London.

Dossin, G. 1938. Un rituel du culte d'Istar provenant de Mari. *RA* 35: 1–13.

Durand, J.-M. 1985. La Situation historique des šakkanakku: Nouvelle approche. *MARI* 4: 147–72.

———. 1986. Fragments rejoints pour une histoire Elamite. Pp. 111–28 in *Fragmenta historiae Elamite,* ed. L. de Meyer; H. Gasche; and F. Vallet. Paris.

———. 1987a. Documents pour l'histoire du Royaume de Haute-Mesopotamie, 1. *MARI* 5: 155–98.

———. 1987b. L'organisation de l'espace dans le palais de Mari: Le témoiguage des textes. Pp. 39–110 in *Le systéme palatial en Orient, en Grèce et à Rome,* ed. E. Levy. Leiden.

Durand, J.-M., and Margueron, J. 1980. La question du Harem Royal dans, le palais de Mari. *Journal des Savants* (Octobre-Décembre): 253–80.

Finet, A. 1956. *L'Accadien des lettres de Mari.* Brussels.

———. 1965–66. La place du devin dans la societe de Mari. Pp. 87–93 in *La Divination en Mesopotamie ancienne et dans la regions voisines.* Vendomes.

Huffmon, H. B. 1965. *Amorite Personal Names in the Mari Texts.* Baltimore.

Kupper, J.-R. 1957. *Les nomades en Mesopotamie au temps des rois de Mari.* Paris.

———, ed. 1967. *La civilization de Mari.* Paris.

Kupper, J.-R. 1978. Les Hourrites a Mari. *RHA* 36: 117–28.

———. 1982. Mari entre la Mésopotamie et la Syrie du nord à l'époque Paléo-Babylonienne. Pp. 173–85 in *Mesopotamien und seine Nachbaren,* ed. H.-J. Nissen and J. Renger. Berliner Beitrage zum Vorderen Orient 1/1–2. Berlin.

Lafont, B. 1987. Les deux tablettes néo-sumériennes de Mari. *MARI* 5: 626–27.

Lambert, M. 1970. Textes de Mari—Dix-huitième campagne—1969. *Syria* 47: 245–60.

Lambert, W. G. 1967. The Language of Mari. Pp. 29–38 in Kupper 1967.

Lewy, H. 1967. The Chronology of the Mari Texts. Pp. 13–28 in Kupper 1967.

Limet, H. 1975. Observations sur la grammaire des anciennes tablettes de Mari. *Syria* 52: 37–52.

———. 1976. Le panthéon de Mari à l'époque des šakkanaku. *Or* 45: 87–93.

Malamat, A. 1971. Mari. *BA* 34: 2–22.
———. 1980. *Mari and the Bible, A Collection of Studies.* 2d ed. Jerusalem.
Marzel, A. 1971. The Provincial Governor at Mari: His Titles and Appointment. *JNES* 30: 186–217.
———. 1976. *Gleanings from the Wisdom of Mari.* Studia Pohl 11. Rome.
Matthews, V. H. 1978. *Pastoral Nomadism in the Mari Kingdom.* ASORDS 3. Cambridge, MA.
Muntingh, L. M. 1974. Amorite Married and Family Life according to the Mari Texts. *JNSL* 3: 50–70.
Noort, E. 1977. *Untersuchungen zum Gottesbescheid in Mari; Die "Marieprophetie" in der alttestamentlichen Forschung.* AOAT 202. Kevelaer.
Pardee, D. 1984. The Mari Archives. *BA* 47: 88–99. (Rev. J. Glass).
Römer, W. H. Ph. 1971. *Frauenbriefe über Religion, Politik, und Privatleben in Mari: Untersuchungen zu G. Dossin, Archives Royales de Mari 10 (Paris 1967).* AOAT 12. Kevelaer.
Rowton, M. B. 1967. The Physical Environment and the Problem of the Nomads. Pp. 109–21 in Kupper 1967.
Sasson, J. M. 1969. *The Military Establishment at Mari.* Studia Pohl 3. Rome.
———. 1972. Some Comments on Archive Keeping at Mari. *Iraq* 34: 55–67.
———. 1973. Biographical Notes on Some Royal Ladies from Mari. *JCS* 25: 59–78.
———. 1980. *Dated Texts from Mari—A Tabulation.* Malibu.
———. 1983. Mari Dreams. *JAOS* 103: 283–93.
Schmitt, A. 1982. *Prophetischer Gottesbescheid in Mari und Israel: Eine Strukturuntersuchung.* BWANT 6/14. Stuttgart.
Sollberger, E. 1967. Lost Inscriptions from Mari. Pp. 103–7 in Kupper 1967.
Westenholz, A. 1978. Some Notes on the Orthography and Grammar of the Recently Published Texts from Mari. *BiOr* 35: 160–69.

Brian E. Keck

MARIAMME (PERSON) [Gk *Mariammē*].

MARIAMME (PERSON) [Gk *Mariammē*]. This well-known name, important in Jewish eyes because of its connection with Moses' sister Miriam, designated no fewer than six queens or princesses in the house of Herod (see *HJP*², 287–329 for a summary history). Given the ramifications of the Herodian Dynasty, an attempt is made here to demonstrate the position of each queen within it.

1. Mariamme I. The second wife of Herod the Great. Despite the impressive career of his father, Antipater, Herod was regarded by the Jewish aristocracy as a "common man" *(idiotes).* As an Idumaean, he could be termed a "half-Jew" (*hemiioudaios,* Jos. *Ant* 14 §403). His second wife, Mariamme, brought him the Hasmonaean connection he required (Jos. *JW* 1 §241). Her father was Alexander, son of Aristobulus II, the last Maccabean ruler before the Roman conquest. Her mother, Alexandra, was the daughter of Hyrcanus II. That made her a great-granddaughter of Alexander Jannaeus and Alexandra Salome, and a great-great-granddaughter of John Hyrcanus.

Mariamme's father came into conflict with several Romans, from Pompey and Gabinius to Q. Metellus Scipio, who executed him in 49 B.C. (*Ant* 14 §125). Herod, on the other hand, achieved recognition by the Romans as king when he journeyed to Rome in 40 B.C. This did not yet give him possession of the land, and for three years he besieged Jerusalem, held by the Parthian protégé King Antigonus, Mariamme's uncle. In the spring of 37 B.C., Herod interrupted the siege to marry Mariamme, then returned with Roman assistance and took the city (*JW* 1 §§342–53). Conquest gave him possession, and the marriage lent "legitimacy" to his reign.

Mariamme bore him two daughters, Salampsio and Kypros, who married well and added six children to his growing line. One of them married King Agrippa I. Mariamme also bore two sons, Aristobulus and Alexander; the latter married the Cappadocian princess Glaphyra. Both sons sired important children, a total of seven, but both also later fell out with Herod and were executed by him.

Mariamme's brother and mother caused Herod some distress. The brother, Aristobulus III, became high priest upon Herod's nomination, even though this was unlawful since an incumbent had to be removed. Mariamme, supported by her mother, Alexandra, urged Herod to this action. He complied, but soon afterward arranged to have the lad "accidentally" drowned in a pool at Jericho (*Ant* 15 §§31–41; 51–56). Alexandra disliked Herod even before the murder of her son, and more than once invoked the aid of Cleopatra and Antony against him. She ultimately tried to seize the fortified places in Jerusalem, but was thwarted by the loyalty of Herod's lieutenants. Herod ordered her executed (*Ant* 15 §§23–80; 247–52).

Mariamme was noted for her beauty and "greatness of soul" *(megalopsychia).* But even Josephus, who admired her, considered her unreasonable, quarrelsome, and dangerously outspoken. Herod, always violently jealous regarding her, finally believed charges that she was unfaithful and was plotting his death. He had her executed, probably in 29 B.C., but afterward suffered from deep remorse for this (*Ant* 15 §§218–46).

2. Mariamme II. Herod married a second woman of this name. She also had the reputation of great beauty, but being the daughter of a priest of Alexandrian family named Simon, her family was "not distinguished enough for close relationship" with Herod, and so marriage seemed out of the question. However, even though his desire for her was great, he realized that it would be unseemly for him to take her by force. An expedient solved the dilemma: Herod appointed Simon as high priest, even though he had to remove an incumbent (as he had reluctantly done in the case of the brother of Mariamme I (see above; *Ant* 15 §§320–23). Herod seems to have named one of the impressive towers of his Jerusalem palace after her. See MARIAMME (PLACE).

Together they had a son, also named Herod, who was esteemed so highly that he was designated second successor, after Antipater (Herod's son by his first wife, Doris (*JW* 1 §§563; 573). Antipater resented this infringement on his right to choose his own successor (*JW* 1 §588).

Mariamme II was later implicated in a plot against Herod, but Herod punished her son instead of her, deleting young Herod from his will (*JW* 1 §599). The younger Herod carried on the line, marrying Herodias, granddaughter of Herod the Great. The couple produced Salome, who married Philip, tetrarch of Trachonitis (*Ant* 18 §136; *PW* 14: 158–61). Mariamme's fate seems not to be recorded.

3. Mariamme III. The wife of Herod's son Archelaus, who was set aside so that he could marry Glaphyra, the Cappodocian princess who previously had been married to Herod's son Alexander (*Ant* 17 §350; *JW* 2 §115). This created a scandal, since Jewish law forbade marriage to a brother's wife (*Ant* 17 §341). No progeny are recorded for her, on present evidence.

4. Mariamme IV. The daughter of Olympias (Herod's daughter by the Samaritan Malthace) and of Joseph (son of Herod's brother Joseph; *Ant* 18 §134). This distinguished lineage suited her for a marriage high in the Judean aristocracy, which she achieved. She is recorded as the first wife of Herod's grandson, Herod of Chalcis. They had a son, Aristobulus, who served as king of Armenia Minor under Nero (*JW* 2 §221; *ANRW* 2/8: 319–21).

5. Mariamme V. Herod's granddaughter. Josephus mentions her as one of the five children of Herod's son Aristobulus and of Bernice (daughter of Herod's sister Salome). When Herod executed Aristobulus about 7 B.C., his anger did not extend to the children. He was observed "caring for the orphans" in remorse over their father's execution. The orphans are described as "children" and this gives a rough idea of Mariamme's age at the time of her father's death (*Ant* 18 §134 refers to them "infants" [*nepious*]).

Herod betrothed Aristobulus' orphaned daughters to various members of the royal family. One daughter, the famous Herodias, married Herod's son by Mariamme II, and then subsequently married Herod Antipas. Another daughter went to an unnamed son of Antipater, Herod's son by Doris: presumably this daughter was Mariamme V. Her betrothal received an unexpected alteration. Antipater had grown alarmed at the preferential treatment accorded to his brothers' orphans, and requested that Herod give Mariamme not to his son but rather to *himself*. Herod agreed, and Mariamme married Antipater, but further traces of Mariamme are lacking (*JW* 1 §§552–567).

6. Mariamme VI. The daughter of Herod's grandson, King Agrippa I. Her mother was Kypros, daughter of Salampsio (Herod's daughter), and Phasael (Herod's nephew). These strong connections made her a desirable match. At the time of her father's death in A.D. 44, she was ten years old. He had already betrothed her to Julius Archelaus, and the marriage took place. They had a daughter, whom they named Bernice, possibly after Mariamme's sister, the famous Julia Bernice, whose career culminated in her charming the Roman emperor Vespasian and living for a time with the future emperor Titus "as if she were his wife" (Dio 66.15).

About A.D. 54, when she was twenty, Mariamme renounced her marriage with Archelaus and married an Alexandrian Jew, Demetrius. He held the office of alabarch there, probably connected with customs and taxation. Mariamme's sister Bernice married the son of another alabarch (*ANRW* 2/8: 299–305). As could be expected, Demetrius was "in the first rank for descent and wealth." The couple had a son to whom they gave the Roman name Agrippinus, a name that was not surprising given the increasingly close connections of Mariamme's family with Rome. Mariamme's brother, Agrippa II, in fact later joined Bernice in Rome. In the summer of A.D. 70, an attendant of Mariamme is mentioned taking part in the Jewish War. That appears to be the final mention of her (*JW* 2 §200; 5 §474; *Ant* 18 §§130–32; 19 §§354f.; 20 §§140 and 147).

Bibliography

Jones, A. H. M. 1967. *The Herods of Judaea.* 2d ed. Oxford.

Schalit, A. 1969. *König Herodes, der Mann und sein Werk.* Berlin.

Smallwood, E. M. 1976. *The Jews under Roman Rule, from Pompey to Diocletian.* Leiden.

RICHARD D. SULLIVAN

MARIAMME (PLACE) [Gk *Mariammē*]. The name of a tower in Herod's palace at Jerusalem, and several towns in ancient Syria-Palestine. The popularity of the name was heightened by the fact it was also the name of six women in the Herodian Dynasty. See MARIAMME (PERSON).

1. One of three "royal towers" built by Herod for his great palace in Jerusalem for members of his royal family. It was probably built to honor Mariamme II, since Josephus conjoins the building of the palace and his account of that marriage (*Ant* 15 §317–32). The other two towers were named Phasael and Hippicus (*JW* 2 §439).

These three towers are also described as "standing the highest of the towers" in the city. Since they were built on a hill, they commanded an even more spectacular view and were imposing to those standing below. The "Mariamme" tower reached some 90 feet high ("55 cubits"), with the bottom 33 feet or so ("20 cubits") built solid. The breadth was also about 33 feet. Its top stories were residential, and were by far more ornate than those in the other three towers (*JW* 5 §170).

Josephus mentions the "Mariamme" tower in connection with the Jewish War of ca. A.D. 66–70. After the war, when Jerusalem was being destroyed, the three towers were spared by Titus, who wished to leave them as a reminder to posterity of the former strength of Jerusalem (*JW* 7 §1–4). The "Tower of David," part of the "Jerusalem Citadel" still flanking the Jaffa Gate in Jerusalem, may incorporate in its lower courses portions of one of these three towers (Phasael?), although exact attributions vary. Portions of the other towers may be associated with the internal structure of the podium excavated in the courtyard of the citadel in 1968–69 (Amiran and Eitan 1975: 54; see also Höscher's contribution in *PW* 14: 1745–46).

2. Not surprisingly, given the building program of Herod and the prominence of the royal women named Mariamme, several places beyond Jerusalem bore that name. In Syria, S of Raphaneae (modern *Rafnije*), a Mariammia stood near the Eleutherus River, with settlement reaching back possibly to Alexander the Great. The local name Marjamin identifies the site even today. The location about halfway between the Mediterranean and the city of Emesa, perhaps in the territory of the Hylatae, would have made the city a strategic one for Herod. Its position just N of Lebanon led to its being described in antiquity both as "a city of Phoenicia" and as "a town of Syria" (*CIL* 12: 4899, calling it Mareammea). It belonged to the Roman province of Syria Secunda, and bishops from there are mentioned in A.D. 451, 458, 518, and 536. In this last year, one source mentions "the church in Mariamme."

In Phoenicia, a village of Mariamme is variously described as "one and one-half [Roman] miles outside Damascus" and as "outside Heliopolis." As Honigmann (*PW* 14: 1745–46) suggests, there may have been two such villages. Four other modern villages called *Marjamin,* one near Tyre (one on the Orontes, and two others more obscurely located) may bear witness to ancient foundations by the Herodian dynasty obsessed with the royal name Mariamme (Jones 1971: 267, 543 [Appendix IV, Table II]).

Bibliography

Amiran, R., and Eitan, A. 1975. Excavations in the Jerusalem Citadel. Pp. 52–54 in *Jerusalem Revealed: Archaeology in the Holy City 1968–1974.* Jerusalem.

Jones, A. H. M. 1971. *The Cities of the Eastern Roman Provinces.* 2d ed. Oxford.

RICHARD D. SULLIVAN

MARISA (PLACE) [Gk *Marisa*]. See MARESHAH (PLACE).

MARJAMAH, KHIRBET EL- (M.R. 181155). Albright (1923) suggested identifying Tell Marjamah with the town of Ephraim (2 Sam 13:23). However, the identification with Baal-shalisha (2 Kgs 4:42) in the land of Shalisha (1 Sam 9:3–4) seems to be more convincing (Kallai 1972b).

The tell encompasses 8.5 acres, 450 m above sea level, and is situated on one of the NE ridges of Mount Baal-hazor sloping down into the wilderness of Ephraim. It is bounded on the E by Wadi Sîʾah, on the S and SW by Wadi Sâmiyah, and on the NW by a small fault line separating the acropolis from the ridge ascending to the mountain. The junction of the two wadis forms a broad valley, Wadi ʿUssah (Nahal Yitav). This is the agricultural hinterland, watered by several strong springs of which ʿEin Sâmiyah is the strongest, and constitutes a part of the ancient road from Shiloh to the Jordan Valley. The steep slope forced the inhabitants of the site to build their town on terraces which can be seen clearly on the surface and gave the name to the tell (*rajama* = to heap up stones). Several ancient stone dressings cut into the exposed bedrock can be seen on the top of the tell. These include cup marks and steps leading to a small platform which could be a *bamah* (Albright 1923; Kallai 1972a). Nearby the remains of a massive apsidal tower were visible.

A. Mazar conducted excavations in 1975 and 1978 (Mazar 1977). On the northernmost edge of the tell overlooking ʿEin Sâmiyah, a section of the fortifications of the Iron Age II were exposed. (For an isometric drawing of the site, see Mazar 1982: 172.) They consisted of double walls leaning against each other, resulting in a total thickness of 4 m and built with large fieldstones. In several places a 3.5 m–thick retaining wall fit into the crevices of the slope to support this city wall from the outside. This wall continues southward. Inside the wall, parts of three small living quarters were exposed, which were built directly on the sloping bedrock and against the wall. The abundant jugs, bowls, sieves, lamps, and hole-mouth jars all date to the 9th–8th century B.C.E.

Some 15 m to the N of this area are the remains of the apsidal tower, protecting the natural moat against attacks from the ridge to the NW. The base of the tower was built with large boulders and is 14.4 m wide; the outside, facing the moat, was rounded. The overall length of the tower is ca. 20 m, preserved to a height of 6.5 m. On the top were remains of two rooms. Other smaller rooms were found farther inside.

In 1979 and 1980 another sounding farther toward the E was conducted by M. Zohar (1980). Five squares, extending from the edge of the tell up to the first terrace, yielded a dark earth mixed with ashes, bones, and a large amount of typical 8th-century pottery similar to Mazar's excavations on the top. The outlines of a casemate wall could be traced and one casemate room was cleared, which contained a variety of storage jars (but no bowls) and some clear indications of the final destruction—Assyrian bronze and iron arrowheads.

Beneath the floor of this casemate appeared the top of a massive stone wall which is dated tentatively to the EB Age. Farther up the slope remains of domestic architecture of the Iron Age were exposed. In one square, an attempt was made to reach earlier strata: below the floors of the Iron Age house was a fill containing a mixture of Iron Age I and LB IIB pottery, beneath which was a layer with typical LB pottery. 3.2 m farther down was a beaten-earth floor with MB III/early LB I pottery. Below this level was a soft brown-black earth mixed with ashes, bones, and characteristic EB sherds. On the E slope of the tell, facing Wadi Sîʾah, a substantial wall built of cyclopic masonry was visible on the surface. A sounding in the room of one of the towers associated with this wall revealed that these fortifications were constructed in the MB II and were reused in the Iron Age.

It is still unclear when the area around ʿEin Sâmiyah and Tell Marjamah was initially settled. It can safely be assumed that the site was one of the well-fortified cities of the EB II. The total absence of Khirbet-Kerak ware might imply that the site was abandoned during EB III. In the 2d half of the 3d millennium and the first centuries of the 2d, the area around ʿEin Sâmiyah was obviously an important tribal center for a pastoral population. This is evident from the rich cemeteries of the MB I in the vicinity and the still unexplored settlement on Dhahr Mirzbâneh across Wadi Sîʾah (Lapp 1966; Dever 1972; 1975; Yeivin 1971a, b, c).

Tell Marjamah resisted reurbanization until the MB, when a fortified settlement was erected over the EB remains, probably during the 17th century B.C.E. During the LB, the town grew beyond the walls spreading to the lower parts of the mound and was apparently unfortified. Base Ring II sherds indicate a continued occupation during the 14th (and probably also into the 13th) century B.C.E. There is so far no evidence for a destruction layer sealing the Canaanite town, and the ceramic remains of the early Iron Age are scanty, only some collared rim jars and a few typical cooking pots. During the 9th and 8th centuries, however, a well-fortified and prosperous Israelite town (Baal-shalisha?) developed on the site. It was destroyed by the incursions of the Assyrians under Shalmaneser V in 722 or slightly later under Sargon when the kingdom of Israel was conquered and its inhabitants led into the Exile.

The site of Tell Marjamah remained essentially deserted

thereafter, with only minimal evidence of occupation during the Hellenistic and Roman periods. In Byzantine times a small church (14 by 10.5 m) and a vaulted water reservoir were built on the S edge of the tell, and the settlement moved to Khirbet Sâmiyah some 400 m down the valley.

Bibliography

Albright, W. F. 1923. The "Ephraim" of the Old and New Testament. *JPOS* 3: 36–40.
Dever, W. G. 1972. Middle Bronze Age I Cemeteries at Mirzbâneh and 'Ain Sâmiya. *IEJ* 22: 95–112.
———. 1975. MB IIA Cemeteries at 'Ain Sâmiyeh and Sinjil. *BASOR* 217: 23–36.
Kallai, Z. 1972a. The Land of Benjamin and Mount Ephraim. Pp. 172–73 in *Judaea, Samaria and the Golan, Archaeological Survey in 1967–1968,* ed. M. Kochavi. Jerusalem (in Hebrew).
———. 1972b. Baal Shalisha and Ephraim. Pp. 191–204 in *Hamikra Vetoldot Israel: Essays in Memory of Ron Yishai,* ed. J. Liver. Jerusalem (in Hebrew).
Lapp, P. W. 1966. *The Dhahr Mirzbaneh Tombs.* New Haven.
Mazar, A. 1976. Khirbet Marjame ('Ain Sâmiya). *IEJ* 26: 138–39.
———. 1977. An Israelite Fortress-City near 'Ain Samiya. *Qad* 10: 111–13 (in Hebrew).
———. 1982. Three Israelite Sites in the Hills of Judah and Ephraim. *BA* 45: 167–78.
Shantur, B., and Labadi, Y. 1971. Tomb 204 at 'Ain Sâmiya. *IEJ* 21: 73–77.
Yeivin, Z. 1971a. 'Ain Samiyeh. *RB* 78: 424.
———. 1971b. A Silver Goblet from 'Ain Sâmiyah. *Qad* 4: 123–26 (in Hebrew).
———. 1971c. A Silver Cup from Tomb 204a at 'Ain Samiya. *IEJ* 21: 78–81.
Zohar, M. 1980. Notes and News. Tell Marjamah ('Ein Sâmiyah). *IEJ* 30: 219–20.

Amihay Mazar
Mattanyah Zohar

MARK ANTONY (PERSON). The principal ancient sources are Plutarch's *Life of Antony,* Books 2–5 of Appian's *Civil Wars,* and Books 41–53 of Cassius Dio's *History of Rome.* Antony was born about 83 B.C. and followed the usual "public" career for a well-connected young aristocrat with military service in various areas. This included service under Caesar in Gaul in the late 50's, following which he became one of Caesar's most ardent supporters. He was one of the tribunes in 49 who fled to Caesar's camp, providing him with the pretext to start the civil war with Pompey. During the period of Caesar's dictatorship, Antony was given various responsibilities, which culminated in the holding of a consulship with Caesar in 44. After Caesar's assassination, Antony assumed that he would succeed to Caesar's power, but he found a new and unexpected rival in Octavian, Caesar's grandnephew and adopted son, who secured senatorial support. Octavian soon turned against the senate and became reconciled with Antony, who had been joined by Lepidus, another of Caesar's adherents. These three men then took over the government, being named "triumvirs to reconstitute the state" *(triumviri reipublicae constituendae)* for five years. Enemies of each were proscribed, and a series of political executions followed. In 42 the triumvirs crushed the republican party led by Brutus and Cassius at the battle of Philippi; following this Antony went to Asia, which he had received as his share of the Roman Empire to control. It was now that he began his liaison with Cleopatra.

Problems for Octavian were stirred up in Italy by Antony's wife Fulvia and his brother, but the triumvirs were reconciled in 40 following Fulvia's death, the agreement being cemented by Antony's marriage to Octavian's sister Octavia. In 39 Antony returned to his provinces in the East and began preparations for a campaign against the Parthians, returning to Italy in 37 for the renewal of the triumviral powers for another five years. Back in the East, Antony now associated himself entirely with Cleopatra, assuming the style of an Eastern monarch and sending Octavia back to her brother. He invaded Parthia unsuccessfully in 36, but was more successful in Armenia in 34, capturing its king and taking him back to Alexandria. Taking advantage of the alienation of opinion which Antony's "oriental decadence" caused, Octavian now decided that it was time to move against his rival. The civil war culminated in a sea battle off Actium in western Greece on September 2, 31, in which Antony and Cleopatra were defeated. They fled to Alexandria, where Antony committed suicide in the following year when Octavian appeared before the city.

In his youth Antony had been violent and dissolute; later he proved to be a natural soldier, and his courage and generosity made him an acceptable leader to his troops. He was not without skill as a politician, but his temper and self-will sometimes led him into serious error.

Bruce A. Marshall

MARK, GOSPEL OF. Mark is, along with Matthew and Luke, one of the Synoptic Gospels. It is found as the second book in the NT canon.

A. Origin
   1. Author
   2. Date
   3. Occasion for Writing
B. Purpose
   1. Lack of Historical Interest
   2. Theological Purpose
C. Structure and Literary Patterns
   1. Intercalation
   2. Grouping of Similar Materials: Parables
   3. Public and Private Teaching
   4. Passion Predictions
D. Christology
   1. Son of God
   2. Christ
   3. Son of Man
   4. King
E. Literary Structure
   1. Jesus' Foreknowledge
   2. Jesus' "Mighty Acts"
   3. Irony
F. Form and Function

A. Origin

Little is known about the origin, date, and authorship of this gospel. The earliest record we have of such data is in material cited by the Church historian Eusebius. In that account, Eusebius (*Hist. Eccl.* 3.39.14–17) quotes Papias, who in his turn was quoting someone he, Papias, identified as "the elder." In that thirdhand account, we learn that Mark had been Peter's "interpreter," and that he had written down "accurately all that he remembered" although "not in order." Both phrases of that statement are important for an understanding of what Papias does, and does not, intend with his comments. In the first phrase, the Greek word translated as "interpreter" is *hermeneutes,* taken by some to imply that Peter spoke in another language than his hearers could understand. Yet in an earlier passage Mark had been identified in a similar context simply as Peter's "follower" (*Hist. Eccl.* 2.15.1), indicating that the word "interpreter" may be less technically intended than might first seem the case. Papias gives no hint that Mark needed to translate Peter's sermons from one language to another. The point seems to be that Mark was in a position to have accurate knowledge of Peter's understanding of the gospel. With respect to the second phrase, it is not clear what "order" is missing in Mark. Perhaps Papias (or the "Elder" he is quoting) meant Mark does not follow the order of another of the gospels, or that the order in Mark is not in accord with theological points the elder took to be important. In any case, "order" probably refers to some kind of arrangement of content, rather than to an accurate historical ordering of events. Papias may also imply here that Mark was following the order Peter gave in his preaching ("[Peter] used to give teaching as necessity demanded but not making, as it were, an arrangement of the Lord's oracles"; *Hist. Eccl.* 3.39.15), thus excusing Mark from any intentional errors of arrangement of whatever sort in his gospel.

While this tradition sounds straightforward enough, there are several reasons why one probably ought not take it at face value. Perhaps most important in this regard is what Papias has to say about the gospel of Matthew, namely that "Matthew collected the oracles in the Hebrew language, and each interpreted them as best he could." The problem here is that there is no evidence that the gospel of Matthew we have was composed in any language but its present Greek. If Papias was not speaking of our present Matthew, then how do we know he was speaking of our present Mark? If he was speaking of the gospel according to Matthew, then he may have been as inaccurate about Mark as he was about Matthew. The attempt to rescue the accuracy of this statement by suggesting Papias may have intended to describe "Q," a document thought by many scholars to underlie parts of Matthew (and Luke), does not save us from the dilemma of his inaccurate language; if Papias said "Matthew" but meant one of Matthew's sources (i.e., the conjectured document "Q"), how can we assume that when he said "Mark" he meant that gospel?

1. Author. Contrary to Papias' claims, intensive study of the materials of which Mark is composed has convinced critical scholars that much of that material as it currently appears must have had a period of oral circulation in the Greek language before it was included in the gospel, and that in addition it appears that some of the material in Mark was written down, perhaps even in rudimentary collections, before the writer incorporated it into his gospel. Perhaps most importantly, the gospel itself is anonymous; we receive no hint from its contents about its author. Had the author's identity been important for understanding the message, as was the case, for example, with the epistles of Paul, we would surely have been provided with the name in the gospel itself. Again, although tradition assigns the authorship to a man, there is no inherent reason why, given the gospel's own anonymity, it could not have been written by a woman, many of whom were prominent in the primitive Church (for the names of a few prominent women in only one of the churches Paul wrote to, see Romans 16:1, 3, 6, 12, 15). While we will follow the tradition, and will refer to the author in the masculine form, we will do so without prejudice to the real but unknown identity of the author.

With the falling away of any certainty that the author was someone named "Mark" there also fall away all attempts to identify him more closely by assuming any mention of a "Mark" in the NT must necessarily refer to the author of the gospel, and hence, by piecing together these references, to emerge with a portrait of the author. On that basis, many have conjectured that "Mark" was the son of the woman in whose house the disciples often met (Acts 12:12) and was a companion of both Paul (Acts 13:5; cf. 15:37) and Peter (1 Peter 5:13). Although his desertion of Paul and Barnabas on one of their missionary journeys (Acts 13:13) led to a low estimate of him by Paul (Acts 15:37–39), Paul's subsequent reference to him (Col 4:10) implies there was a later reconciliation between them. That gives us what appears to be a detailed picture of the author of the gospel according to Mark, yet most of that "information" about him has been secured in a rather speculative way. Add to that the fact that Mark was one of the most popular names in the Hellenistic age among both Greek-speaking people *(Markos)* and Latin-speaking people *(Marcus)*, and one can see how gratuitous it is to assume that the John Mark mentioned in Acts is necessarily the "Mark" to whom a later tradition assigned the authorship of the gospel.

If we cannot establish the identity of the author of Mark's gospel on the basis of such speculative combinations of disparate biblical references, however, we can determine some hints about him from the gospel itself. His confusion about Palestinian geography (the Greek of 7:31 shows the author assumes Sidon is south of Tyre, and that the Sea of Galilee is in the midst of the Decapolis, inaccurately in both cases) and his fluency in Greek make it likely he grew up in an area outside Palestine. His use of "Latinisms" (Greek words taken over from Latin, e.g., "centurion," [15:39], "legion" [5:9, 15], "denarius" [6:37; 12:15; 14:5]) was once thought to provide evidence which indicated that the origin of the gospel, or at least its author, was to be located in a Latin-speaking area of the Roman Empire, perhaps even Rome itself, but we now know that such Latinisms occur even in the Hebrew Talmud, indicating the prevalence of such "loan words" wherever Roman imperial power made itself felt.

Some have even found a covert self-reference to the author of the gospel in the account of the lad who fled naked during Jesus' arrest (14:51–52). Yet, even if it did refer to the author, it would still tell us relatively little about him. It is more likely, however, that this reference, like the one to Rufus and Alexander as the sons of the Simon of Cyrene who was pressed into service to carry Jesus' cross (15:21b), is to be understood as something Mark's congregation would have known about, but which would soon have been forgotten. (Matthew and Luke omit both items in their accounts, indicating that by the time they wrote, knowledge of both had been forgotten.)

The author's origin outside Aramaic-speaking Palestine is confirmed by the type of readers for whom he was writing. In the first place, the Aramaic words and phrases which Mark apparently found in his sources, and which he includes in his story, are without exception translated into Greek (*talitha cumi* in 5:41; *ephphatha* in 7:34; *eloi, eloi lama sabachthani* [this phrase seems to contain elements of Hebrew as well as Aramaic] in 15:34). In the second place, the Jewish customs to which Mark refers are explained (e.g., 7:2–4, although somewhat anachronistically). Both of these facts indicate that the intended readers of the gospel were also from an area outside the Aramaic-speaking regions of Palestine. Tradition has located that area in Rome, because of the traditional association with Peter, or in Alexandria, based on some remarks of Clement of Alexandria, a learned Christian of the 2d century, and either place is possible. Antioch, the place where the Christian gospel was first proclaimed to non-Jews (Greeks: Acts 11:20–21; cf. chaps. 10–11 for an account of the first gentile convert), would be another possible location. Given the present state of our evidence, however, it is very difficult to determine with any accuracy which site is most likely to have been the place where "Mark" wrote his gospel.

2. Date. The time of the composition of the gospel is also a matter of some speculation. To ask the question of the time of composition is, in the first instance, immediately to raise the question of the order in which the Gospels were written. Prior to the 19th century, it was generally believed that Matthew was the first gospel to be written, followed by Luke and then Mark. This position has found its most energetic proponent among current scholars in William R. Farmer, who has argued for the priority of Matthew, most notably in his book *The Synoptic Problem.* The theory of Matthean priority is called the "Griesbach hypothesis," named for the 19th-century German scholar who first gave it a detailed formulation. Although some scholars have supported Farmer's position, among them B. Orchard (1977) and H. H. Stoldt (1980), Farmer has failed for the most part to convince the majority of NT scholars, who continue to find that the evidence points to the priority of Mark. Although there are some apparent "conflations" (a combination of two phrases, both of which are presumed earlier than their combination) in the present text of Mark in such places as 1:32 ("that evening, at sundown"; cf. Matt 8:16 "that evening"; Luke 4:40, "at sundown") or 10:46 (cf. Matt 20:29 and Luke 18:35; for others, see Longstaff 1977), it is possible that such conflations resulted from a later revision of Mark after Luke and Matthew had appeared. The evidence for Markan priority remains convincing to the majority of modern scholars: for example, the tendency of both Luke and Matthew to shorten and polish Mark's stories (e.g., Luke 5:29 eliminates the ambiguity from the story in Mark 2:13–15 concerning in whose house the meal was held; Matt 17:13 eliminates a potential confusion about the subject of Jesus' conversation in Mark 9:11–13; Matt 8:28–34 and Luke 8:26–39 both condense and clarify Mark 5:1–20, but in different ways) and to eliminate many of the rough transitions in Mark's narrative. In addition, both Matthew and Luke possess two accounts of some sayings of Jesus, one of which is close to the form of the saying as found in Mark, and one of which is not, although its form in both Matthew and Luke is very close (e.g., Mark 4:25, Matt 13:12 and Luke 8:18 as one set; Matt 25:29 and Luke 19:26 as another). Such "doublets" look very much as though the authors of Matthew and Luke had a source of Jesus' sayings in addition to Mark which they used (scholars refer to it as the "Q" document); by including the similar saying from both sources, they produced the "doublets" we now find in Matthew and Luke, but not in Mark.

Scholars therefore find it easier to understand how the authors of Matthew and Luke, independently of one another, undertook to improve Mark's narrative, and supplement it on the basis of additional traditions (e.g., "Q," traditions about Jesus' birth and resurrection), than to understand why the author of Mark, possessing both Matthew and Luke, would rewrite some stories, making them less clear and less grammatically polished, and eliminate some other key materials from his own gospel which he would have found in the other two.

In determining the date of Mark, therefore, most modern scholars will assume that Mark was the first of the gospels to be written, and that hence it must obviously be dated earlier than either Luke or Matthew, who included among their sources (cf. Luke 1:1) a form of Mark very close to the one we have. References to the gospels in writings of the Church Fathers make it unlikely that any of the Synoptic Gospels could have been written much later than the middle of the 2d century; their evidence makes it more likely they were written at the latest near the turn of the 1st century. The destruction of the temple in Jerusalem in 70 C.E. would be useful in dating Mark if we could be certain there are direct references to it in any of the gospels. References to it in Matthew and Luke but not in Mark would be an indication Mark was composed prior to that date, and Matthew and Luke after it. Some have found references to the fall of Jerusalem in Matt 22:7 or Luke 19:43, neither of which has any parallel in Mark. Mark 13 does have references to the destruction of Jerusalem which some have seen as an indication Mark was writing around the time of its destruction in 70 C.E., but those references are cast in the future, and are indefinite in detail (e.g., 13:2; cf. 14:58; 15:29). Those who date it earlier, e.g., 64 C.E., do so on the basis of Papias' association of Mark with Peter, and the further assumption that Mark would have written his gospel shortly after Peter's death, in its turn assumed to have occurred during Nero's local persecution of Christians in that year. We have already found reason to question the data from Papias, so a date around 70 C.E. is probably as good a one as any.

3. Occasion for Writing. If more exact knowledge of the circumstances of the writing of the gospel remains elusive, several decades of intense study of the gospel of Mark allow us to draw a number of conclusions about the kind of problems the author sought to solve by composing this gospel, the kind of traditions he had from which to draw, and the methods he used in composing his story of the career of the adult Jesus of Nazareth.

It is evident from other NT materials that predate the gospels, notably the Pauline letters, that individual traditions about sayings and deeds of Jesus circulated apart from their present gospel contexts. Paul quoted a saying of Jesus about marriage and divorce (1 Cor 7:10, 11b) which, while close to the Markan saying in 10:11–12, differs enough to make it clear that it circulated independently of the form Mark gave it in his gospel (for further instances, cf. 1 Cor 9:14 with Matt 10:10b; Gal 5:14 [see also Rom 13:8–10] with Matt 22:37–39). Luke also preserves a saying of Jesus in Acts 20:35 unknown in any of the gospels. Paul further records appearances of the risen Jesus (1 Cor 15:3–7) which differ significantly from the accounts in the gospels, indicating their independent origin. Paul also preserves an account of the origin of the Eucharist (1 Cor 11:23–26) similar to but in small ways different from the accounts in the gospels. Such evidence makes it clear that Paul did not get his material from the gospels we know, and it also means that that material circulated as individual accounts of sayings and events before they were incorporated into a narrative framework.

If independent traditions provided early missionaries such as Paul with information about Jesus which they could use in their proclamation of the Christian faith, some events must have occurred which made it apparent that those individual traditions were no longer adequate for such tasks. Again, we have hints in Paul of some such events. For example, although the Corinthians had been told about the origin of the Eucharist (1 Cor 11:23), that obviously did not keep them from turning it into a travesty of what it was supposed to be (cf. 1 Cor 11:17–22). Knowledge of that isolated tradition proved less than adequate in that situation.

Similar problems relating to individual accounts of certain events and sayings of Jesus are reflected in other places in the NT as well. For example, as Mark makes clear in his gospel account, Jesus worked many mighty acts ("miracles"), of which Mark tells only a sample (cf. Mark 3:10; 6:56). As such accounts were told and retold, there was a danger that Jesus would be identified as a magician, whose own name could be used in conjuring spells (that happened, as Mark 9:38 makes clear; in the account in Acts 19:13–16 it backfired on those who tried it). There was the further danger that other magicians would try to purchase rights to such "tricks" from the followers of Jesus (for an example, see Acts 8:9–19). The problem was therefore not that people would not know how to identify Jesus as one who performed mighty acts, but that they would know only too well how to identify him, namely, as another of the many traveling magicians that roamed the Hellenistic world.

Again, preachers recounting the wise sayings of Jesus ran the risk that those who heard such reports would categorize Jesus as another of the philosophers who also roamed the Hellenistic world, dispensing wisdom in public and giving private instruction for a fee. Paul's preaching in Athens encountered such an attitude, where some Stoics and Epicurean philosophers thought they found in Paul a kindred spirit who was teaching the philosophical system of his master, Jesus (Acts 17:17–21). Again, the problem was not that people would not know what to make of Jesus on the basis of his teaching, but that they would know all too well what to make of him, namely, they would see him as another of the philosophers with whom they were so familiar.

Mark's solution to these problems was to incorporate the individual traditions of Jesus' mighty acts, his sayings, and the events of his life (e.g., the Eucharist) into a narrative that led inexorably to its climax on the cross. By devoting fully a third of his narrative to the last week of Jesus' life, spent in Jerusalem, Mark placed the whole account of Jesus under the rubric of his passion. In that way, Jesus' death and resurrection became the hermeneutical framework within which the sayings and deeds of Jesus were to be understood. Only if one understood that the Jesus who did the mighty acts and spoke wisdom was the one who died on the cross, Mark intends to say, would one truly understand Jesus. To show that it was the same Jesus to whom the individual traditions referred, Mark in his narrative reproduced those earlier traditions faithfully, so that the readers of the narrative would recognize the familiar forms of those earlier traditions they had known. It is that characteristic of Mark that makes his narrative seem less polished than that of Matthew and Luke, but it was necessary if people who read the narrative were to be assured that this was the story of the Jesus with whom they were familiar, not a new and different person with that name.

The emphasis on the suffering of Jesus, as well as of those who follow him (e.g., Mark 8:34–37) may also point to the fact that the readers for whom the gospel was written were now in danger of such persecution, and needed to be told that such persecution did not mean their faith in Jesus as God's Savior had been misplaced. The advent of persecution would have been discouraging for those who became Christian under the kind of glowing proclamation of which we find examples in the letters of Paul (e.g., 1 Thess 4:16–17; 1 Cor 15:51–55). Such a "theology of glory" would be called severely into question if persecutions were to arise. Such persecutions were of course possible at any time in the Hellenistic world for those who held to a religion other than that of the community in which they lived. Yet so long as Christians were identified with the Jews, as they were, since at first all were Jews, they could safely hide behind the concessions Jews had gotten from various Roman emperors. For example, Jews were excused from normal patriotic duties so long as daily prayers were said for the Roman emperor in the temple in Jerusalem.

When it became apparent, however, that Christians were different from Jews, they could no longer avoid confrontation when they avoided participation in the normal Roman festivals which, as a matter of course, included worship of pagan deities. At that point, they would be open to charges of social disruption and political disloyalty. Price (1984) has made a careful study of what the imperial cult meant in terms of participation for the average Roman citizen outside Rome itself in the period following the reign of Augustus, and shows how hard it would have been to avoid participation in such public festivals.

Mark's emphasis on the fact that no one could understand Jesus prior to his suffering and death on the cross, not even his own disciples (see 6:51–52; 8:17; 9:9–10), and the emphasis that if the master suffered so must his followers (e.g., 8:34) may well have been intended to meet just such a situation in which a theology of glory was called severely into question.

A third emphasis in Mark, namely the assurance that one cannot calculate by historic events when the risen Christ would return in glory, found again and again in chap. 13, may have been designed to head off discouragement when the destruction of the temple in Jerusalem was not immediately followed by that return. Mark preserves traditions that Jesus had predicted the destruction of the temple (e.g., 13:2), a charge his opponents had used against him at his trial (14:58; 15:29; for a thorough investigation of this matter, see Juel 1977). If, as 13:2 suggests, Jesus coupled such a prediction with statements about the coming kingdom of God (as he does in the rest of chap. 13), then it would not be surprising if many assumed that with that destruction, Jesus would return and bring in God's reign with power. The danger was that when that did not occur, many would assume the substance of the Christian faith had also been shown to be false. To prevent such a conclusion, Mark was careful to include traditions pointing out that not historic events (cf. 13:7–8, 12–13, 22–23) but cosmic signs (24–25) would herald Jesus' return. Indeed, the impossibility of such calculation is emphasized by Jesus' statement that not even he knows the time the kingdom will come into power (13:32).

If that is in fact what underlies the present shape of chap. 13, it helps us in solving a problem we mentioned earlier, namely the date of Mark. The understanding of Mark 13 proposed above would argue for a date of composition sometime around the destruction of the temple in 70 C.E., probably when that destruction seemed inevitable but had not yet occurred, e.g., between 68 when Jerusalem was invested, and 70, when the city fell.

In sum, the anonymous author of Mark, faced with the problems we have discussed, which seem implied by the particular emphases of Mark's gospel, resolved them by collecting and setting down a variety of traditions about Jesus which heretofore had circulated independently. The author of Mark put those traditions into a narrative controlled by the importance of Jesus' death and resurrection. It was the scholarly discipline called "form criticism" which made it possible to identify and isolate these originally independent units in Mark's narrative, and which therefore underlies the kind of solutions outlined above. The work of Bultmann (1963), Schmidt (1919), and Dibelius (1934) pioneered in this area.

B. Purpose

1. Lack of Historical Interest. Further careful study of the gospel of Mark confirmed the conclusion that when the author created his narrative in the way he did, he was more concerned to solve theological than historical problems, with the result that the gospel does not fit modern canons of historical accuracy. Study of the order of events as they occur in the gospel showed clearly enough that the author was not concerned with accuracy in the presentation of the itinerary of Jesus or in the chronology of his movements. For example, Mark uses an idiom *(eis to peran)* which means cross "from west to east" (cf. 10:1, where the force of *peran* is apparent from the context in which it is set) of two sea voyages in sequence with no intervening return, either by boat or on foot (4:35 and 5:1 for the first voyage; 5:21 for the second). Obviously, such a procedure is impossible. One simply cannot make two successive trips from west to east without returning, however that return be understood. Yet Mark has no mention of any return whatever. Again, in 6:45 he directs his disciples to take their boat to Bethsaida while he dismisses the crowds; in 6:53, with Jesus in the boat, they land at Gennesaret. Of course Jesus could have told the disciples of a change in plans when he got into the boat (v 51) or the wind could have blown them off course (v 48), but Mark's omission of such details indicates he was not interested in them when he composed his narrative.

The evidence for Mark's indifference to chronological accuracy is also attested in numerous places. If one limits oneself strictly to the chronological indications given in the narrative of Mark, for example, and does not supplement them from one's own imagination, one will note that all the events between 4:35 (evening) and 6:2 (a Sabbath, which began at sunset, i.e., 6 P.M.) will have taken place within a couple of hours, namely the time from late afternoon (the time indicated in 4:35) to the onset of the Sabbath with sunset (the next indication of time in 6:2), or at most within a 24-hour period, in either case a patent absurdity. Of course Mark did not mean that, but again, his lack of any specific notations of time which would make that clear shows this was not the kind of point about which he intended to be careful in constructing the narrative.

It was the dawning awareness of this fact that brought to an end the attempt to write lives of the "historical Jesus" based on the materials in the gospels purged of their supposedly later theological increments. The attempt to write such "lives" occupied gospel scholarship to a major extent both in Europe and American from the mid-19th to the early 20th century. It became clear that so much of the material necessary for such a "life" of the "historical Jesus" had to be provided by guesswork to fill in the gaps, however, that the course of such a "life" tended to reflect more the prejudices and presuppositions of the one making the guesses than it did the actual course of Jesus' life. Scholars have therefore concluded that based on the evidence we have, an accurate historical account of the life of Jesus cannot be reconstructed, whether on the basis of the material found in Mark alone, or on the basis of a combination of materials from all of the gospels.

Further study of the reasons for the order in which Mark placed his traditions, a study based on a method called "redaction history," led scholars to appreciate the theological subtlety with which this unknown author approached his task of constructing a narrative of the adult life of Jesus of Nazareth. The first redaction-historical work on Mark was published by Marxsen (1969). Norman Perrin (1969) gives a good account of this method of examining the gospel traditions, with a number of examples drawn from Mark's gospel, and Achtemeier (*Mark* Proclamation Commentary) gives a convenient summary of current methods of study and the conclusions about Mark such methods have made possible. An extensive bibliography of Markan studies has also been provided by Humphrey (1981).

2. Theological Purpose. The overall organization of the gospel of Mark, which indicates where Mark laid his priorities in his account of Jesus, must also be understood in theological terms. The following outline indicates how the structure of the narrative turns on points that bear such theological importance.

1. Jesus appears, preaching God's reign (1:1–3:6).
   - A. John the Baptist appears; the story begins (1:1–8).
   - B. Jesus introduced (1:9–15).
   - C. Jesus' ministry begins; he chooses disciples (1:16–20).
   - D. Jesus teaches and heals (1:21–45).
   - E. Jesus rejected; conflict with religious authorities (2:1–3:6).
2. Jesus ministers in Galilee (3:7–6:6).
   - A. Jesus designates 12 (3:7–19).
   - B. Jesus designates true followers (3:20–35).
   - C. Jesus teaches in parables (4:1–34).
   - D. Jesus performs mighty acts (4:35–5:43).
   - E. Jesus rejected; conflict with his own (6:1–6).
3. Jesus and the disciples under way (6:7–8:21).
   - A. Jesus sends out 12; John is killed (6:7–29).
   - B. Jesus feeds and heals (6:30–56).
   - C. Jesus teaches about the Law (7:1–23).
   - D. Jesus heals and feeds (7:24–8:10).
   - E. Jesus misunderstood by disciples and Pharisees (8:11–21).
4. Jesus heals blind eyes; teachings on the life of discipleship (8:22–10:52).
   - A. Jesus heals blind eyes (8:22–26).
   - B. First Passion prediction and attendant events (8:27–9:29).
   - C. Second Passion prediction and attendant events (9:30–10:31).
   - D. Third Passion prediction and attendant events (10:32–45).
   - E. Jesus heals blind eyes (10:46–52).
5. Jesus in Jerusalem (11:1–16:8).
   - A. Jesus appears in the Temple (11:1–12:44).
   - B. Jesus tells of final events (13:1–37).
   - C. Jesus' final acts—failure of disciples (14:1–42).
   - D. Jesus the king—failure of the authorities (14:43–15:47).
   - E. Jesus is risen—failure of the women (16:1–8).

The last verses in the text of Mark (16:9–20) are included in some translations, but they do not appear in the earliest manuscripts. These verses are clearly an amalgam of traditions from the other three gospels which was appended to the gospel of Mark to provide it, like the others, with resurrection appearances. In the opinion of most modern scholars, the gospel ended originally with 16:8. Boomershine and Bartholomew (1981) have done a careful literary and stylistic study of Mark which also supports that point.

Careful consideration of the outline given above will indicate the care with which Mark has constructed his gospel. Parts 1, 2, and 3, for example, each end with opposition to Jesus. Again, parts 2, 3, and 4 each begin with some action involving the twelve disciples. Or again, part 1 begins with John the Baptist as precursor of Jesus in preaching, while part 3 begins with John as precursor of Jesus in death at the hands of political authorities. One will note also that part 4 is artfully arranged to show that while Jesus can cure physical blindness, the disciples persist in their spiritual blindness, and that segments C, D, and E of part 5 each display the failure of some group around Jesus. It is clear from such examples that Mark did more than simply construct a random arrangement of traditions linked, if at all, by catchwords or catchphrases, as some form-critical scholars had once argued. Rather, Mark in fact exercised considerable care in the way he arranged and juxtaposed the various traditions available to him.

A careful examination of some of the points from the outline we noted above will show in more detail some of the points the author was making by the shape he gave to the gospel. It will also show how the author makes those points, namely more by the juxtaposition of the traditions with which he had to work than by extensive, or even minimal, editorial comments. Markan editorial activity is pretty much limited to occasional framing of an account from his traditions in order to fit it into his narrative (e.g., 4:1–2; 6:30–33), to various summaries of Jesus' activities (e.g., 3:7–12; 6:54–56), and to summary statements of points he wants to make (e.g., 8:19–21).

a. Opposition to Jesus. In pursuing that more detailed examination, we can gain some insight into how Mark arranged his traditions to show growing opposition to Jesus (the conclusions of parts 1, 2, and 3) by examining the collection of materials which concludes part 1, namely 2:1–3:6. Even a cursory reading will show that Mark has done little to integrate these stories into a smoothly flowing narrative unit. The almost accidental character of the arrangement is shown when one compares the way Matthew and Luke made use of this material. Neither evangelist felt compelled to reproduce either Mark's order (Matthew uses three of the stories in one place and two in another), or the method by which he connected the traditions (Luke, as we saw above, removes the ambiguity about whose house was the locus of the feast following Levi's becoming a follower of Jesus). Even though Mark did not rework his traditions, or put them in any necessary order, but simply placed them side by side, he nevertheless prepared the way for the point he makes in the concluding verse (3:6), where the authorities plot Jesus' death. Any one of the little stories in this collection made it clear enough that Jesus was coming into conflict with religious authorities, a conflict which would, if allowed to proceed, inevitably lead to Jesus' condemnation by them. It is just that point that Mark has emphasized by placing five such stories one after another, and placing at the conclusion the reference to the violence against him contemplated by the Pharisees and the Herodians. That Mark makes that point less by comment than by position of traditions is typical of his way of constructing his gospel, as is his intimation this early in the gospel of the final fate of Jesus. It is just that point, as we saw, that Mark emphasized about Jesus by making it the concluding point of each of the first three major segments of his gospel.

b. Role of the Disciples. The second point noted above

in relation to the structure of the gospel, namely the prominence of the disciples in the opening material of each of the first three major parts of the gospel, also shows the care with which Mark arranged his materials for the theological point he wished to make. The theme here considered, namely discipleship, is woven throughout the entire narrative, and a look at some of the ways that theme is dealt with will indicate the points Mark makes by his use of the traditions he had concerning the disciples.

The major theme in the treatment of the disciples is their inability to understand fully what Jesus intended by what he said and did during the period prior to his death and resurrection. This is displayed in exemplary fashion in the account of the transfiguration (9:2–8). The content of the event recorded here makes it unmistakable who Jesus is: he is to be associated in importance with Moses, the law-giver, and Elijah, who is by tradition the precursor of the Messiah (see 9:11–12). Indeed, God here identifies Jesus as his own son, with the additional command to the three disciples present (Peter, James, and John) to pay strict attention to what Jesus says. The further command that this event not be reported until after the resurrection (9:9) gives a clear indication that comprehension of the true nature and role of Jesus depends on that future rising of Jesus after his death on the cross.

Within that framework, Peter's confusion in v 6 is significant: in the midst of a visible display of Christ's heavenly glory, and in company with Moses and Elijah, Peter remains confused and fearful. That this is a Markan emphasis in this tradition is indicated by the fact that Luke's account of the same event omits Peter's fear (9:33), and Matthew in his account omits in addition Peter's confusion (17:4). The point here concerns less the character or mental acumen of Peter than it concerns Mark's understanding of the meaning of the career of Jesus. What is at issue is the point at which it becomes possible truly to understand who Jesus is and what he is about, and the answer implied here is that it is not possible prior to Jesus' death on the cross and his subsequent resurrection.

That same point appears in another episode involving Jesus and the disciples, namely the story of Jesus' appearing to the disciples in the midst of a stormy sea (6:45–52). The astonishment of the disciples is due less to their lack of mental acumen than to their sheer inability to understand at that point, as the final verse (52) makes clear: their incomprehension was due to the fact that "their hearts were hardened." Since in Semitic understanding, the heart was the seat of intellection, this statement concerns the disciples' inability to understand, not their inability to react emotionally. The passive form ("were hardened") is to be understood as the reverential passive, common among pious Jews who held that not only the name of the deity but even the word "God" was to be avoided where possible; the passive thus has the force here of "God hardened their hearts." This same point is made in an episode where Jesus again declares that comprehension has been withheld from them (8:17). In both cases, the disciples' incomprehension is something over which they have no control. For Mark, Jesus' fate is not determined by the mental acuity or its lack among his followers; rather his fate is in God's hands, and hence his suffering is inevitable.

The inevitability of that suffering is further emphasized in those passages where Jesus predicts to his disciples his impending fate in Jerusalem at the hands of the authorities (the Son of Man "must" suffer; 8:31). The repetition of that prediction (9:31; 10:33–34) emphasizes its certainty: Jesus' suffering in Jerusalem is not probable, it is inevitable. Yet even in the midst of such certainty, the incomprehension of the disciples remains uncompromised (9:32). The fourth major segment of the gospel (8:22–10:52) is shaped around the twin themes of the certainty of Jesus' impending suffering and the incomprehension of the disciples. The passage is bracketed by the two stories in Mark which concern the overcoming of blindness (8:22–26; 10:46–52), a device well known to ancient writers called an *inclusio,* whereby a part of a longer text was delimited through the repetition of some phrase or similar event. Taken in itself, the fact that the stories defining the unit deal with the healing of blindness implies the theme of the section: the blindness of the disciples.

The first passage about blindness overcome is followed by the confession of Peter that Jesus is the "Christ" (8:29). That confession, taken for itself, is in Mark's view correct; Mark shares the primitive Christian conception that Jesus is the one anointed by God ("Christ" is derived from Greek *chrio,* "anoint") to be his son and the savior of humankind. The problem lies not in the title as such, but in Peter's inability to include the dimension of suffering within his understanding of the task of God's anointed one, an inability which is identified as demonic (i.e., contrary to God's purposes; 8:32–33). This inability to understand the association of suffering with God's anointed one is not limited to Peter; it follows on each of the three predictions of the passion. In fact, it is part of a pattern that consists of a prediction by Jesus of his impending suffering (8:31; 9:31; 10:32–34); an account which reveals that one or more of the disciples have failed to comprehend that point (8:32–33; 9:32–34; 10:35–37); a further statement by Jesus on the nature of discipleship (8:34–38; 9:35–37; 10:38–45), and a tradition that indicates Jesus' exceptional nature (9:2–8; 9:38; 10:46–52). The remaining materials in this segment which fall outside that repeated pattern nevertheless also deal in one way or another with discipleship. Thus one of the five major segments of the gospel deals specifically with discipleship, and it is structured by a pattern of the disciples' lack of comprehension concerning what Jesus says about himself and about what following him, i.e., discipleship, means. Thus the point is reinforced that no one can understand, or follow, Jesus until after Jesus' suffering and resurrection.

The picture of failure on the part of the disciples is not limited to the early parts of the gospel, however. It continues in the account of Jesus' final hours with them. Here the inability of the disciples to comprehend takes the form of a vivid contrast between their expressed intentions and their actual deeds. In the setting of the final meal of Jesus with his disciples, for example, Jesus solemnly announces that one of them will betray him. Their response takes the form of each disciple individually asking Jesus "Is it I?" (14:17–19). Although the English can be ambiguous here—it could represent their dawning realization they were capable of such treachery—the Greek is expressed in such a way (*meti ego*) that the only answer the disciples will allow in response is "Of course not, don't be silly." Thus any hint of a self-probing on the part of the disciples is absent; each asserts that to think betrayal on his part is possible is to have a totally false view of him and his dedication. The same theme of the inability of the disciples to imagine they could abandon Jesus is represented in the scene that follows, which is set on the Mount of Olives (14:27–31). Jesus again has predicted his betrayal and abandonment by the disciples, and again, led by Peter, each denies himself capable of such an act.

The events which follow make clear the extent of the gulf between what the disciples imagined their situation to be, and what it in fact was. In Gethsemane, with Jesus in agonizing prayer, the disciples sleep (14:32–41). When Jesus is arrested, in stark contrast to the repeated asseverations of loyalty, they flee (14:50), even though there are some there willing to risk armed confrontation (14:47; it was not until later tradition that this act was attributed to Peter [John 18:10]). Peter, who led the group of disciples in their protestations of loyalty to the door of death, is singled out for special treatment. His threefold betrayal of his master, the third time accompanied by an oath (14:66–72), may reflect Jesus' threefold prediction of his passion.

In ways such as this, Mark illustrates that the resolve, even the dedication and asserted loyalty of the disciples comes to grief when it is tested. This is not for the sake of a psychological profile of the disciples, or to demonstrate their unalleviated perfidy (for a contrary view, see Weeden 1971). Jesus' promise to meet them in Galilee (14:28), repeated by the figure at the empty tomb (16:7) shows clearly enough, as does the very preservation of materials only the disciples could have known, that they did regain their loyalty and confidence in the risen Jesus. Rather, the point Mark makes by means of the way he deals with the traditions concerning the disciples relates to their inability, prior to Jesus' death and resurrection, to understand him, something that, upon his death, even so unexpected a person as a Roman centurion could do and publicly announce (15:39).

By means of such an arrangement of the traditions about the disciples, Mark makes his point that the passion of Jesus is the interpretative key to his career and its meaning. Despite all Jesus had told them, despite their association with him and their seeing what he did, despite their repeated oaths of loyalty to him, they could not understand him, or act upon such an understanding, until after the events of Jesus' passion and resurrection, which in Mark's view climaxed Jesus' career.

c. Role of John the Baptist. In addition to the order in which Mark placed the traditions he had which concerned opposition to Jesus (2:1–3:5, with the climax at 3:6), and those which concerned the disciples (esp. 8:22–10:52), Mark makes his theological point by the way he arranged the materials about John the Baptist, the first character mentioned in the gospel. A consideration of that arrangement will further illustrate how Mark achieved his theological points, namely more through the arrangement of traditions than through overt editorial comment.

The very first verse of the gospel shows the importance Mark attached to the figure of John. That opening verse may be paraphrased: "The beginning of the gospel of Jesus Christ was the appearance in the wilderness of John the Baptist, fulfilling the prophecy of Isaiah . . ." By beginning the story of Jesus in this way, Mark made it evident that one could not understand the significance of the total event of Jesus of Nazareth unless one also understood John the Baptist.

Part of that significance lay in the relationship of John's appearance to the tradition of the appearance of Elijah prior to the coming of the Messiah. John is described in 1:6, for example, in language that closely parallels a description of Elijah found in the LXX version of 2 Kings 1:8 (LXX 4 Kgdms 1:8). Again, according to another tradition, the hairy mantle was the sign of the true prophet (Zech 13:4; for a false prophet to wear such a mantle was a reprehensible attempt to deceive). Mark presents John as the long-awaited Elijah, a point that Jesus himself later affirms (Mark 9:13). By beginning the story of Jesus' Galilean ministry with John the Baptist, Mark announces his importance for understanding that mission, a point again confirmed by Jesus when he identifies the ability to understand the significance of John the Baptist with the ability to understand his own: to fail to understand the one necessarily leads to failure in understanding the other (11:27–33). Both Jesus and John share the same God-given authority.

Mark saw a further significance in John, however. Not only was John the precursor of Jesus in his preaching of repentance (cf. 1:4 with 1:15), he was also Jesus' precursor in his final fate. That point is made in the traditions that Mark assembled in 6:14–29. In one tradition (6:14–16), there is a discussion about the way in which Jesus was perceived by the public. Several possibilities are listed: Jesus is Elijah, he is another of the prophets. The major identification, however, is with John the Baptist. That is the official view, since that is also the identification Herod makes (6:16). Immediately following that identification, Mark appends the story of the death of John the Baptist, giving it all the more importance by telling it out of its natural sequence. This is one of the very few places Mark uses the literary device of the "flashback," withholding the narration of an event until a more appropriate time for its telling. The rarity of that device focuses all the more attention on it when it is used here. Clearly, John's death is very important for Mark in the story of Jesus of Nazareth.

The point to be made here is that just as John was Jesus' forerunner in his life and his preaching, so was he his precursor in his death. Thus John brackets the story of Jesus: just as John's appearance signaled the importance of the coming of Jesus of Nazareth, so the final fate of Jesus is announced by John's own death. As John preached, so did Jesus; as John died, so will Jesus: at the hands of ambivalent civil authorities (cf. esp. 6:20 with 15:10, 14). In this connection, it is interesting to note that contrary to other, non-Markan traditions, John did not die for political crimes. Such a tradition was current in 1st-century Palestine, and it can be read in Josephus' account of the people of Israel (*Ant* 18.5.2). There John was executed because Herod feared him as a potential political revolutionary. That is not the case in Mark, however. In Mark's narrative, it is clear, John died because of the religious content of his message (6:17–18). Like Jesus who was to follow in that fate, John ran afoul of the authorities because of his attacks on their observance of the religious law of Israel, or lack of it.

All of that shows the importance Mark placed on the figure of John the Baptist, both for Jesus' career and for his death. By using the traditions he had about John the Baptist in that way, and by reserving the story of John's death for a rare flashback in the narrative, Mark shows again how he makes his points by the arrangement of his traditions. In this instance, Mark made clear that Jesus' death was a necessary, indeed inevitable, climax to his career, just as it had been for his forerunner.

C. Structure and Literary Patterns

We have now seen some examples of the way in which Mark has created his narrative by a careful positioning of traditions which, for the most part, he reproduced in their familiar form, adding a minimum of material to give coherence to the story. In the course of such an arrangement of traditions, Mark put them into certain repeated patterns of organization. One such pattern is the collection of similar stories into one place. We have already seen one example of that (2:1–3:5), and the pattern is repeated in other places as well (e.g., parables, 4:1–34; discussions, 11:27–12:34).

1. Intercalation. There is another characteristic arrangement of traditions Mark used when he wished to indicate that two stories are to be linked, and are thus to interpret one another: that was to bracket one tradition with another. Thus, for example, into an account of the cursing of a fig tree (11:12–14, 20–21) Mark has inserted ("intercalated") the account of the cleansing of the Temple (11:15–19), indicating in that way that the "cleansing" in fact amounted to a "cursing" of temple worship which would bring it to an end as surely as the cursing of the fig tree brought it to an end. Again, Mark inserted the story of the healing of a woman with a flow of blood (5:25–34) into a story of the raising to life of the dead daughter of Jairus (5:22–24; 35–43), in that way bringing into the story of Jairus' daughter the emphasis on faith contained in the story of the woman cured of her blood flow.

To see the subtlety with which Mark created his narrative, it will be useful to examine a longer passage which illustrates how Mark made use of these devices of intercalating and collecting in his efforts to make his point by the juxtaposing of his traditions. To do that, we will examine the materials contained in 3:20–4:34, a passage which contains disputes, sayings, parables, and even references to mighty acts.

The first unit of the text, comprising 3:20–35, displays the common Markan technique of intercalating or bracketing one tradition within another in order to aid in the interpretation of the combination thus created. In this instance, an account of disbelief on the part of the scribes in the benevolent nature of Jesus' demon exorcisms and Jesus' reply (3:22–30) has been bracketed by an account of the judgment on Jesus by his own family as a result of a report that has reached them concerning his activities (3:21, 31–35; v 20 is Mark's introduction, emphasizing the crowds around Jesus). In this instance, it appears that the material within the bracketing traditions aids the interpretation of those placed around it.

There is no question about the negative evaluation put on Jesus by the scribes. They accuse him of being able to do his exorcisms because he is in league with Satan, the prince of the demons. Hence, they imply, demons obey Jesus as they would obey Satan, whom Jesus serves. Jesus' response indicates such an accusation is illogical, since, were Jesus working by Satan's power, it would mean Satan was in rebellion against himself, and therefore was destroying his own power (vv 23–26; the assumption is that Satan extends his power through the demonic possession of human beings). The statement is more than illogical, however; it is also blasphemous, since to say that about Jesus is to attribute to God's enemy what God himself is doing, something here identified as the one unforgivable sin (thus Mark in v 30 interprets the saying of Jesus in vv 28–29). To attribute to Satan the power of God which is able to overcome Satan (the point of v 27: Satan has been overcome by Jesus, who by God's power is the stronger) is to cut oneself off from the one who alone is able to rescue one, through the forgiveness of sin, from the power of Satan.

It is around that negative, and false, judgment of Jesus that Mark has set the tradition of Jesus' questioning relatives (as 3:31 makes clear, they are Jesus' immediate family). In this context, it is clear that we are not to interpret the desire of his family to draw him away as innocuous. The bracketed tradition makes it clear that the family shares, in one way or another, the negative viewpoint of the scribes toward Jesus. Mark thus guards against an interpretation of the coming of Jesus' immediate family to bring him away as motivated by incipient belief or sympathy toward what Jesus was doing or teaching, as Luke does in his gospel (see Luke 8:19–21, in its context there). Here the context (the scribes' negative judgment) reinforces an impression from the material itself (3:31–35, Jesus' physical family contrasted with his true family), namely that at this point, Jesus' family was completely unsympathetic to what he was doing. Typically for Mark, the traditions thus arranged confirm the point made by the collection of stories in 2:1–3:6: opposition to Jesus is growing, and it now includes not only the religious authorities, but even his own family.

Of significance within the bracketing tradition is the contrast between those who are "outside" and those who are "around Jesus" (his immediate family is outside, v 32; his followers are around him, v 34, and hence are his true family). The reader of Mark's narrative had learned earlier the names of some of those who are "around Jesus" (the Twelve, 3:13–19), and here the reader learns about some of those who are on the "outside" (scribes, representing the religious authorities in Jerusalem; his own immediate family). Two groups are thus identified, each characterized by its reaction to Jesus: those who reject him, and those who associate themselves with him. Of further interest is the fact that the groups who oppose him comprise, at this stage, those who ought to know Jesus best (his own family), and those who ought to know the most about the God by whom Jesus was sent (religious authorities). Those who ought to be most supportive of Jesus are therefore, in Mark's gospel, precisely those from whom he has the most to fear. These traditions thus imply what Mark will make explicit in 6:4: Jesus is without honor "in his own country, and among his own kin, and in his own house." The ultimate fate of Jesus—his death on a cross—is already inevitable, a point Mark surely intends to make by this arrangement of traditions.

2. Grouping of Similar Materials: Parables. The next unit of the narrative, 4:1–20, begins with the characteristic Markan notice that Jesus was surrounded by a crowd (4:1; remarks about crowds, along with remarks about Jesus being engaged in teaching, and being near the sea, occur most frequently in material that introduces and connects what by every evidence were once independent traditions, and hence show themselves to be written by Mark). That puts the reader on notice that again, Mark is responsible for joining the following material to what preceded it, just as he had combined the two earlier traditions by bracketing the one with the other. We are thus clearly involved here with material that Mark himself has combined.

It is further evident that Mark took the parable of the sower to be of central importance for understanding what Jesus was about. The double imperative relating to hearing in v 3 (the RSV omits one of them in its translation) indicates that while the parable itself began with such an imperative ("pay attention"), Mark has added a second ("listen"), thus pointing to its importance. He also added an injunction to listen after the parable's conclusion (v 9; the same saying is repeated in v 23), thus framing it with imperatives to pay close attention. In a later verse, Mark has Jesus identify this as his most important parable, and thus the key to understanding all others (v 13).

The parable tells about the ordinary actions a Galilean farmer would undertake in order to increase the harvest of his normal crop by some seven to ten fold. What is therefore striking about the parable is not the actions of the farmer, but the prodigious results of his activity (4:8). What on first observation seemed quite ordinary is, in the end, shown to have been quite extraordinary, yet no one could have realized that until the end, with its harvest, came along. That contrast between ordinary beginnings and extraordinary results dominates the parable, not, as some have suggested, the contrast between the seed wasted (vv 4, 5, and 7) and that which yielded grain (v 8). This latter interpretation is rendered unlikely by the fact that the word for "seed" in vv 4, 5, and 7 is in the singular, while in v 8 the word is found in the plural ("seeds").

The surprising contrast is in the way the parable ends after an ordinary beginning. Up to that time, it would have been possible, observing the sower, to assume he was nothing out of the ordinary, yet such an assumption would have been mistaken, as the harvest showed. Clearly something extraordinary was under way even as the sower began, but that was not clear from the beginning, only from the end. Applying normal criteria to the sower would have led one to miss this sower's significance. Hence the parable ends with a warning not always to trust normal judgments based on what seem at first normal phenomena. To judge Jesus that way means to miss his significance which will become evident at the end of his life (his resurrection) and at the end of his career (the Parousia).

In the context in which Mark has placed this parable, those who have performed such errors in judgment are the scribes and Jesus' family (3:20–35), who have judged Jesus by the normal criteria one would apply in such a situation. An ordinary person doing what Jesus was doing would have to be in his family's judgment "beside himself" (i.e., not in full control of his words and acts) just as any ordinary person performing the exorcisms Jesus did would stand under the judgment pronounced on him by the scribes. Those who judge Jesus on that basis have missed his connection to God's coming rule (cf. 1:15), and when that kingdom comes in power, they will be unprepared. Only those, apparently, who recognize that in Jesus God is doing something extraordinary will hold fast to the end, and be vindicated rather than surprised by his relationship to God's rule.

The following verses (14–20) provide an explanation of the parable, an explanation introduced with the observation (v 13) that this is the key to all of Jesus' parables. This explanation emphasizes to the virtual exclusion of all other points the need to listen carefully and hold fast to what Jesus says, regardless of subsequent difficulties one may encounter. The point Mark makes turns on how one listens, and responds, to Jesus, the point also of vv 10–12. Mark's Greek makes clear that what the disciples ask in v 10 is not *why* Jesus speaks in parables, but rather their question "concerns" the parables. It is a question therefore of the meaning of the parables, and Jesus answers in terms of the parable of the sower (v 13: "this parable"), thus pronouncing it the key to all the other parables as well. The answer is another formulation of the point that those who know what is going on with Jesus (the secret of v 11a, namely Jesus' connection to God's coming kingdom) do not err in their judgment of what he says and does, whereas those who judge him by usual criteria fail completely to understand anything about him at all (v 11b); to them all things are as obscure as the parables he tells. While they may see what he does, they do not really perceive its meaning; they may hear what he says, but they do not really understand its significance.

These verses (11–12) are introduced with the formulaic statement ("and he said [to them]") Mark regularly uses (see also 4:13, 21, 24) to incorporate independent sayings of Jesus, usually by adding them at the end of a tradition (cf. 2:27–28). The content of vv 10–11 shows the relation Mark saw between them and the traditions he placed prior to his collection of parables (i.e., 3:20–35). It was in those earlier verses that we found an example of those who could not perceive the meaning of what they had seen (the scribes and Jesus' exorcisms), just as it was there we found an example of those who could not understand what they had heard about Jesus (his family). Because they had thought they could judge Jesus the same way they judged others who might have done what he did (the ordinary sower!), they are fated to be no more than uncomprehending observers of just those events involving Jesus with their incredible import (4:12). Familiarity with religious matters, such as the meaning of exorcisms, or even familiarity with Jesus as a person, will not guarantee that one understands him. Those who fail to see his relation to the kingdom (the secret of 4:11) remain outside (the same word appears in vv 3:31, 33 and 4:11). Those who see in Jesus something worth following will one day possess that secret (the kingdom). It is they who are "around him" (the same phrase is used in 3:34 and 4:10).

The remaining verses (21–34) show, by the repeated use of the formulaic "and he said (to them)" in vv 21, 24, 26,

30 and the repetition of the injunction to careful listening in v 23 (see v 9), that this subsequent material about parables has also been assembled by Mark from independent traditions. The parable of the seed growing secretly (26–29) and of the mustard seed (30–32) again contrast beginnings and endings, the latter by contrasting an insignificant beginning (the small seed) with an unexpectedly great ending (the large bush), while the former points to the inevitability of the end (the harvest) once the beginning has been made (the sowing). The sayings (21–22, 24–25; 23 repeats 9) concern appropriate activities (putting lamp on lampstand [21b]; listening carefully [24–25a]) and inappropriate activities (putting lamp under bushel [21a]; not listening [25b]). Again, as in the parable of the sower, the need for the appropriate reaction is stressed.

The final two verses (33–34) represent the conclusion to the collection of parables and parabolic sayings. Since both verses presume the present context, and since v 34 employs yet another characteristic way Mark arranged his traditions, a characteristic we will examine in more detail below, both verses are probably to be assigned to Markan composition.

In that way Mark has taken a group of individual traditions (3:20 with 31–35; 3:22–27; perhaps 3:28–29; 4:3–8; 4:11–12, 14–20, 21–22, 24–25, 26–29, 30–32) and by arranging and connecting them (editorial work is probably to be found in 3:20, 30; 4:1–2, 9–10, 13, and 33–34) has created a coherent unit of his narrative which portrays both positive and negative reactions to Jesus. The rejection by those closest to him by blood (his family) and religious interests (the scribes as religious authorities) in its turn also points to that final abandonment of Jesus by all those who had been nearest to him.

3. Public and Private Teaching. There are additional patterns of traditions within the gospel of Mark that show some further characteristics of its author in the matter of creating his narrative. One such pattern which is to be found is displayed in those places where the public teaching of Jesus is followed by private instruction to his disciples (e.g., 4:1–12, 33–34; 7:14–23; 10:1–10) or public acts similarly followed by private explanation (9:14–29). Here the contrast between those "within" and those "without" appears to have determined this pattern of organization.

4. Passion Predictions. The pattern of the three predictions of Jesus' passion also display, as we have already seen, an arrangement of traditions which shows (a) the prediction, (b) failure to understand what Jesus has said, (c) instruction on discipleship, and (d) some indication of Jesus' exceptional nature (8:31–9:8; 9:30–41; 10:33–45). In addition to that, it also points to a certain predilection in Mark's gospel for events occurring in series of three: the three passion predictions and the three denials of Peter are perhaps the major examples of this tendency. A further pattern of which we have already seen examples and which is found throughout the gospel concerns the inability of anyone to understand who Jesus really is before his passion. Although the reader knows from the very first verse that Jesus is the Christ and the Son of God, that knowledge is shared prior to Jesus' death only by God (1:11; 9:7) and the supernatural demons (1:24, 34b; 5:7).

It was this inability of persons to recognize Jesus that caused Dibelius to characterize Mark as a book of "secret epiphanies" and William Wrede (1971) to speculate that the phenomenon of nonrecognition of Jesus as Messiah during his lifetime was due to the combination of later, messianic traditions with earlier traditions which were still nonmessianic in nature. Further study has indicated that it would probably be more accurate to speak of "messianic secrets" rather than to try to bring under one rubric all the material that points to a lack of recognition of who Jesus was prior to his passion. The phenomenon of "secrecy" probably has more to do with Mark's theological than with his historical strategy in his gospel, i.e., *no one* can understand Jesus prior to his death. (For a recent, careful discussion, see Raisanen 1976.)

The question of understanding or recognizing Jesus immediately raises the question of who the author of Mark thought Jesus to be, and what "understanding him" would entail. To raise that question in its turn is to be involved in the matter of the christology of Mark, and it is to that topic we must now turn.

D. Christology

That christology is an important question for Mark is clear from the very first sentence of the gospel, where Jesus is identified as "Christ" (unlike Matthew [1:21] Mark does not give the name "Jesus" an interpretation, and so it does not figure in Mark's christology), and as "Son of God" (although some early Greek manuscripts omit the phrase "Son of God" from 1:1, its importance for Mark is such that it must be considered in any discussion of christology, whether or not it was originally present in that first verse).

1. Son of God. While the title "Son of God" is known from contemporary Greek culture as a way of designating honor to outstanding individuals, the setting of the beginning of Mark's gospel, with its opening quotation from the OT (contrary to Mark's identification in v 2, that quotation given in that verse is from Mal 3:1, not Isaiah; v 3 is, however, taken from Isa 40:3), shows clearly enough that Mark's frame of reference is not contemporary Hellenistic culture, but the background of the Christian faith in the career of Israel as God's chosen people.

The first implied use of that title occurs in the story of Jesus' baptism, where a voice from heaven (following Jewish usage in which God's voice [Heb *bat qōl*] represents God himself) identifies Jesus as "my (i.e., God's) son." The language of 1:11 reflects Ps 2:7 and Isa 40:1. The point which appears to unite those two quotations is the kingly power associated with the title "Son of God" in the OT. While royal power is implied in the verse from Isaiah, where God's "chosen servant" (Isa 42:1) will establish "justice in the earth" (Isa 42:3b–4a), a task surely implying a king's power, the verse from Psalm 2 expresses the royal context outright. Originally an enthronement psalm, Psalm 2 was composed to celebrate the assumption of royal power by a king chosen by God to rule his chosen people and exercise vengeance over their foes who in opposing his people also opposed God. Verse 6 declares the enthronement; v 7 declares the enthroned king to be God's son, thus establishing the link between royal power and the title "Son of God" in the Psalm. That title is also used in the discussion of the establishment of a Davidic dynasty in 2 Sam 7:5–16. In that passage, Nathan announces God's will to David, and in describing David's eternal dynasty, cites God's promise that David's royal descendants will be "my son"—i.e., that "Son of God" will be a title for each succeeding king of Israel of the Davidic line.

Against that background, it appears one is to understand Jesus' baptism as his enthronement: at this point he receives the royal accolade "my son" directly from God. Yet in Mark the baptism is a private affair; the Greek of 1:10–11 makes clear that Jesus alone saw the heavens opened and the spirit descending, and the voice was directed to him alone ("*you* are my beloved son"; such privacy was eliminated by Luke, who described the opening of the heavens as an objective occurrence [3:21], and by Matthew, who also added that the voice was addressed to the bystanders ["*This* is my beloved son"; 3:17]). That raises the question about the point at which public acknowledgment will be made of the fact that Jesus is king. Since God himself has announced it, there can be little question of its truth, yet then why the secrecy? Why is the voice addressed only to Jesus? Even when the heavenly voice, in the Transfiguration (Mark 9:2–8), is directed not to Jesus but to the disciples with him there (v 7: "*This* is my beloved son"), the disciples are exhorted not to mention it until a specific future event (Jesus' resurrection; v 9). Indeed, the first public acknowledgment of Jesus as Son of God, made by supernatural demons who know about the divine sonship of Jesus, is met with the command to keep silent on that fact (1:25; see also 1:34; 3:12). When, then, will Jesus be enthroned? When will he be publicly acknowledged the king God has designated him to be? To read Mark's gospel is to be confronted with that question from the outset.

2. Christ. The second title applied to Jesus at the beginning of Mark's narrative, "Christ," simply intensifies that question. Derived from the Greek verb *chrio,* meaning "to anoint," the Greek adjective *christos* means "anointed (one)." The Hebrew equivalent also appears in Psalm 2, again to designate the king (v 2). It was with that act of anointing that one became king over God's people; that is the way both Saul (1 Sam 9:16; 10:1) and David (2 Sam 2:4; 22:51) were so designated. Thus the title "Christ" confirms the royal power declared in the title "Son of God" and that in turn raises the more insistently the question about when Jesus will be publicly acknowledged and ascend his God-appointed throne.

As was the case with the first public announcement of Jesus' close relationship to God ("Holy One of God," 1:24–25), so the first public utterance identifying Jesus as "Christ" is met with the command not to use the title publicly (8:29–30). Although Jesus does not deny the validity of the title "Christ" applied to him any more than he had denied the validity of the title "Son of God," Peter's reaction to Jesus' prediction of his own suffering indicates Peter had not used the title correctly (8:32–33). To assume that because Jesus was the Christ he would be immune from suffering is not only incorrect, it is in fact satanic (v 33b). The denial of Peter's understanding of the title "Christ" does not deny the appropriateness of applying the title to Jesus, including the royal implications it carries. Rather, the clarification Jesus gives to Peter's understanding of the title begins to clarify the kind of king Jesus is to be.

If the terms "Son of God" and "Christ" cannot yet be applied to Jesus, there is a term which can be appropriately applied to him, and that is the term "Son of Man." In fact, it is that phrase which Jesus substitutes for himself (8:31) immediately after he cautioned his disciples not to apply openly to him the term "Christ." Such substitution of the term "Son of Man" for other titles is in fact something Jesus regularly does in Mark (see esp. 14:61–62).

3. Son of Man. If therefore "Son of Man" is the designation Jesus applies to himself in Mark, we will have to assume it is a correct one as far as the evangelist is concerned, and investigation of its use will aid us in understanding how the author of this gospel wanted us to understand Jesus. Again, if, as we saw, the OT derivation of "Christ" and "Son of God" aided in understanding their meaning, the same approach ought to yield meaning in this case as well.

It is an interesting phenomenon that the phrase "Son of Man" is used only by Jesus in Mark (that is also the case, with one exception, in the other three gospels as well), and only to apply to himself. It is never used by Jesus of anyone else, and no one else ever calls Jesus by that term. That has led some scholars to theorize that the exclusive attribution of that term by Jesus to himself reflects an accurate historical reminiscence, and shows that the origin of the use of the term for Jesus goes back to Jesus himself. Again, while Jesus uses the term in Mark to designate himself in three general ways, namely in his current activity (e.g., 2:10), in his coming suffering (e.g., 8:31), and in his future return in glory (e.g., 14:62), no saying ever combines the latter two points. That led some scholars to postulate that the term was therefore used in two pre-Markan sources, one of which used the term to designate Jesus as the suffering one, the other to designate him (or another) as the one who would return in glory, but that those two traditions existed independently of one another; thus it was Mark's contribution to combine the two (e.g., Toedt 1965).

Despite intensive research, there is at present no scholarly agreement concerning this phrase. While there is at present a tendency to see it as a descriptive phrase, rather than as a messianic title current in Judaism in Jesus' time, scholars are currently in disagreement both about its origin and its meaning. Some have argued for an origin in the confession of the early Church, while others assign its origin to Jesus himself. Those who assign it to Jesus are in disagreement about whether its origin for Jesus was simply an Aramaic idiom used to refer to oneself and hence said nothing more about Jesus than it would say about anyone else who used the idiom, or whether Jesus himself derived it from Dan 7:13–14 and hence from the beginning intended it as an eschatological title.

Two carefully researched and well-documented books illustrate the problem. On the one hand, Kim (1983) has provided a cogent argument for the position that Jesus, deriving the term from Daniel 7 and combining it with insights drawn from the figure of the servant in Isaiah, intended it to be an eschatological description of his own function as one sent from God. On the other hand, Lindars (1983) has provided an equally cogent argument that the title cannot have originated in that way, but could only have been derived from an Aramaic idiom, and hence meant no more in Jesus' mouth that "this human being." Only later did Christian tradition provide the link to Daniel 7.

Whatever the origin of the term "Son of Man" may have been, however, by the time Mark was written, it had in fact come to be associated with Daniel 7, and was used as an eschatological title (for a different conclusion, see Kingsbury 1984). In that light it is interesting to examine the context of Dan 7:13–14, an examination which reveals that the phrase "Son of Man" is used to designate a royal figure. The Son of Man is to be given "dominion and glory and kingdoms, that all peoples, nations and languages should serve him; his dominion is an everlasting dominion, which shall not pass away, and his kingdom one that shall not be destroyed." Clearly the term "Son of Man" in this passage carries the same royal connotations that "Christ" and "Son of God" had carried: it points as they did to Jesus as God's king. Yet the way Jesus employs the term "Son of Man" in Mark's gospel provides the clue as to what kind of king Jesus is to be. He is to be a suffering king. The three times Jesus predicts his passion, he calls himself Son of Man (8:31; 9:31; 10:33). When Jesus faced the Jewish authorities at the time of his trial, and was asked whether he was "the Christ, the Son of the Blessed" (i.e., Son of God; 14:61), Jesus for the first time publicly admitted he was and immediately referred to himself as Son of Man (14:62).

The language of Jesus' reply to that key question is drawn from two sources which again prove instructive to examine. The first part of the answer, referring to being "seated at the right hand of power," is drawn from Ps 110:1, the content of which clearly marks it again as an enthronement Psalm (see esp. vv 1–3). The second part of the answer, referring to his return in divine glory (the meaning of "clouds of heaven") is drawn from Dan 7:13. Thus Jesus' public confession in Mark of who he is points to the equivalence of the three titles used, Christ, Son of God and Son of Man, with their one common element the reference to kingly power.

4. King. Jesus is thus, as his use of the phrase "Son of Man" makes clear, a suffering king. Yet the original question remains: when will he ascend his throne and be publicly acknowledged as king? The answer is provided in chap. 15 of Mark, where the term "king" is used of Jesus for the first time, but once it is introduced, it is thereafter used with great regularity. The use of the term "king" for the first time in chap. 15 has struck some as puzzling, since, they argue, Mark has to that point given no indication that that would be an appropriate designation for Jesus. Yet, as we have seen, the titles applied to Jesus in the preceding chapters in Mark have in fact not only prepared for its use, but have set the stage so that its use can be climactic for the narrative Mark has created.

The theme for this climactic chapter, namely the kingship of Jesus, is introduced in the opening scene with Pilate (v 2: "Are you the King of the Jews?"). The repetition by Pilate of that title in v 9 indicates it was not an accidental use or an aberration in Mark's narrative. Whether or not this title reflects the actual historical charge on the basis of which Jesus was crucified is not at issue here; as far as the gospel of Mark as narrative is concerned, it clearly reflects Pilate's opinion of Jesus. When the Praetorian guard also uses that title (15:18), it is clear that Jesus' public acknowledgment as king has begun a public acknowledgment that continues when he is openly identified as king by his enemies (15:32).

Still further confirmation that Jesus is now understood as king is furnished by the placard which was required at official Roman executions. That placard gave the reason for the execution, and had either to be affixed to the cross, or hung around the condemned criminal's neck. In the case of Jesus' execution, the placard read "The King of the Jews" (15:26).

It is only at this point that we find our answer to the question posed by the christological titles applied to Jesus in Mark, namely when he will be acknowledged as king and ascend his throne. Now the reader understands when Jesus is to be publicly acknowledged as king: in the moment of his suffering. Now the reader knows when Jesus will ascend his throne: when he is nailed to the cross. Now the reader has final confirmation of the kind of king Jesus is: a suffering king.

In addition to furnishing the climactic acknowledgment of Jesus as king, chap. 15 contains a further climax to Mark's narrative, namely the public acknowledgment by the centurion at the moment of Jesus' death that he, Jesus, is God's Son (v 39). As soon as Jesus died, the centurion—a soldier and hence hardly one learned in Jewish religious affairs—is able immediately to recognize Jesus as God's Son. Up to that point, no human being had been able correctly to identify Jesus in that way; at the moment of his death, an outsider is able at once to recognize who Jesus is. A key point in Markan christology is thus confirmed here: only after Jesus' death can he be recognized for who he truly is.

That is why the disciples were unable to recognize or acknowledge who Jesus was, simply because he could not be truly acknowledged as the king he is until he was enthroned—on the cross; he could not be confessed as king until he had been crowned—with death. That is also one reason why the demons were not permitted to acknowledge him: they knew him as a victorious, not a suffering, king (e.g., 1:24), and that could not be announced until after his passion. That is also why, in Mark's narrative, Jesus denied that he was David's son (12:25–37; cf. 11:10, where although in Matt 21:9 he is hailed as son of David, and in Luke 19:38 as king, in Mark only David's kingdom is mentioned, not his son), since the king of David's line was to be a victorious king who restored Israel's fortunes.

Yet kings are victorious; could God's anointed king be any different? Where are we to find Jesus' victory, particularly after his cry of dereliction from the cross (15:34)? Is Jesus finally a tragic rather than a triumphant king? To answer that question, another characteristic of Jesus in Mark's gospel must be considered, namely Jesus' wondrous foreknowledge. See also SON OF GOD; SON OF MAN.

E. Literary Structure

At this point in the investigation of Markan christology, we must follow a further step in the history of Markan research. Redaction-historical work led scholars to see that Mark had a theological purpose when he arranged his traditions in the order he did. That led to the further insight that such a careful ordering of material in order to make a particular kind of point was something Mark's gospel shared with other literary works. An outgrowth of the redactional-historical way of investigating Mark has thus been the attempt to investigate the gospel as a literary work, and to seek to determine its unity of plot and characterization without raising the question of whether a given passage comes from pre-Markan tradition or from the hand of Mark himself. An increasing number of scholars, borrowing from the insights of those who have analyzed literary narrative, have begun to investigate Mark in an effort to determine what results that kind of investigation would achieve. While some, like Kermode (1979) have concluded Mark's narrative is opaque (perhaps deliberately so), and hence finally unyielding to such efforts, and others, like Meagher (1979), have decided that the narrative is too confused to yield useful results to such investigation, still others, more numerous than those who have come to negative results, have found in Mark evidence of a carefully wrought narrative, with a coherent plot and consistent characterization. Among them are Kelber (1979); Petersen (1978; 1980); Rhodes and Michie (1982); and, from a slightly different perspective, but with the same result as far as the unity of Mark is concerned, Robbins (1984). McKnight has provided a good introduction to the method of literary criticism as practiced by these biblical, particularly NT, scholars (1985). It is within the framework of such an investigation of Mark's gospel as a unified literary work, particularly with respect to elements of plot contained within the narrative, that we must approach the question of Jesus' foreknowledge.

1. Jesus' Foreknowledge. It is evident that the Jesus who appears in Mark's gospel is able to know things that ordinary people cannot. There are reports that Jesus knew what other people were thinking (e.g., 2:8); he knew when a particular person had touched him even though crowds were pressing around him (e.g., 5:30); and the fact that in each case he remained uncontradicted when he revealed the thoughts of others shows that Mark understood Jesus to have been correct. More important for Mark's gospel is Jesus' knowledge of events yet to occur. Such prescience is displayed most clearly prior to the last week in Jerusalem in the three predictions of his passion. When those predictions turn out to have been correct, even in detail (cf. 10:33 with 14:63 and 15:1; 10:34 with 15:19), the reader's confidence in the accuracy of Jesus' foreknowledge is enhanced. Indeed, they are a way the author of Mark has used to heighten the reader's confidence that whatever Jesus predicts will happen, will in fact occur. It is just that confidence that will help answer the question about whether or not Jesus is a victorious king; we must now see how that works itself out.

While there are other instances of Jesus' ability to foreknow the future, we will limit ourselves to a discussion of those instances reported in chaps. 14–15. The first instance of Jesus' foreknowledge occurs in the account of the woman who anoints him with precious ointment (14:3–9). Jesus announces that by doing this she has prepared his body for burial. When we read later that Jesus was placed in the tomb without the usual preparation of the corpse (cf. 15:46 with 16:1), and that therefore his anointing at Bethany was his last anointing prior to burial, the striking nature of Jesus' foreknowledge is shown. It is probably not accidental that this prediction/fulfillment brackets the account of Jesus' final days in Jerusalem reported in chaps. 14–15.

Such prescience is again demonstrated when Jesus, in an earlier episode (13:2), tells his disciples that the temple in Jerusalem will be destroyed, a destruction already symbolically announced when Jesus temporarily brought worship in the temple precincts to an end (11:12–25). That predicted destruction then begins with Jesus' death, when the curtain that protects the holiest room in the temple (the "Holy of Holies") from profanation is torn from top to bottom (15:38); a profaned "Holy of Holies" is no longer a fit place for a holy God.

Jesus' foreknowledge is demonstrated a third time when he instructs his disciples about arrangements for their Passover meal together (14:12–15) and it occurs, even in detail, just as he had said it would (14:16). Mark gives no hint that Jesus had made these arrangements beforehand; that idea is a figment of modern historical imagination. During that Passover meal, Jesus predicts that his betrayer will be one of the Twelve with him at the meal (14:18–20), a prediction that proves tragically accurate with the betrayal by Judas (14:42). After the meal, Jesus foretells the desertion of all his disciples (14:27), and specifically the threefold betrayal by Peter (14:30), events that then occur, again in detail, as Jesus has said (14:50; 14:66–72).

In that way, Jesus' predictions are proved true, and the reader of Mark's narrative gains confidence in Jesus' ability to foreknow the future. That is important, since the events we have been discussing were not the only things Jesus predicted. Before the officials of Judaism, in answer to the question of Jesus' identity, he had said those questioning him would see him "sitting at the right hand of Power, and coming with the clouds of heaven" (14:62). That has yet to occur. Again at the Last Supper, Jesus had said he would drink wine anew in God's kingdom, and that has not happened. There is Jesus' statement to the disciples that he would go ahead of them to Galilee, after he was raised from the dead, and that isn't fulfilled in Mark's narrative either. Yet this very important promise is repeated and thus confirmed by the "young man" at the tomb (16:7), as though in that way the reader is assured that all other unfulfilled predictions of Jesus will also yet find their fulfillment.

In that way, Mark's narrative points beyond itself (its "narrative time") to a final fulfillment yet to occur. Perhaps for that very reason the gospel ends in so incomplete a fashion with 16:8, as though to emphasize that although Mark's narrative about Jesus is finished, the story of Jesus has yet to be completed. In that case, Mark will have called upon his readers to complete what remains of the story (e.g., 8:34–38; cf. 13:13b with 13:35–37; 14:9) in their own lives.

2. Jesus' "Mighty Acts." It is likely that Mark has devoted proportionately more space to stories about Jesus' mighty acts than has any other gospel author because they were a firm part of the tradition he was using, as Achtemeier (1970) has urged. Yet Mark has set those stories within a narrative framework that points attention away from the miraculous as such, and toward their significance for the ongoing importance of Jesus. The way Mark has used the first mighty act in his narrative illustrates that point.

The exorcism reported in 1:23–27a is interesting on two counts; the first because in it Jesus does not follow the normal course of an exorcist of that time in driving out the demon, and the second because of the framework Mark has put around it. First, the exorcism itself is unusual in that ordinarily an exorcist must first determine the name of the demon before he or she can command it to obey (e.g., 5:9). Again, in order to perform the exorcism, the exorcist must either delude the demon into thinking the exorcist is a supernatural being more powerful than the demon, or must convince the demon the exorcist is acting as a follower or "in the name of" some being more powerful than the demon (for the latter point see 9:38a). In this exorcism, Jesus does none of that. Indeed, since the demon already knows Jesus' name ("Jesus of Nazareth," 1:24), one would expect that the demon would therefore be in a position to control or at least resist Jesus. Yet none of that happens; Jesus simply commands the demon to depart, and it does. Little wonder the people are astonished (1:27a). Here is an exorcist who is so powerful he need not even follow the normal "rules of the game."

The second interesting point about this story is the kind of framework into which Mark has put it. 1:21–22 show the characteristics of Markan literary activity, and they present the exorcism in terms of teaching (vv 22, 27b) not of a mighty act. That is in fact characteristic of Mark: he associates Jesus as teacher with the mighty acts far more often than other evangelists do, often having him addressed as "teacher" in the midst of a mighty act in a way the other evangelists find inappropriate, and hence change (as just one example, cf. Mark 4:38 ["teacher"] with Luke 8:24 ["master"] and Matt 8:25 ["lord"], although English translations often misrepresent the Greek in these and similar verses). Thus, it is characteristic of Mark to associate Jesus as wonder-worker with Jesus as teacher. The point, made evident in what Mark must have meant as paradigmatic when he framed in that way the first mighty act of Jesus he reported—the point is that the power Jesus displayed in his mighty acts he also displayed in his teaching. As a consequence, even if the power displayed in his mighty acts is no longer available after his death, the power embodied in his teaching nevertheless is. Hence even those who follow Jesus in the period after his earthly life ended can still share in the power he displayed while he walked the land of Galilee. Thus mighty act and teaching both share in the same power at work in Jesus, and the combination of the two tells the reader that that power did not disappear with the death of Jesus.

3. Irony. A final characteristic of Mark's gospel to be mentioned is the irony that pervades the narrative. Perhaps because of the irony that lies at the heart of the story Mark tells—the Son of God who is rejected and killed by the very human race he had come to save—it is a characteristic appropriate to this kind of story. While the central core of that irony is surely the cross and resurrection—what God's enemies had meant as their victory and his defeat (the crucifixion of Jesus) he has turned into his victory and their defeat (the resurrection of Jesus)—there are other secondary ironies that abound in the narrative.

There is the irony contained in the story of the healing of a man with a paralyzed hand on the Sabbath (3:1–6). Some background is necessary to understand the story. The Jewish people regarded the Sabbath as a great treasure of their religious law, and its observance (no labor was permitted Jews on the Sabbath) had been officially acknowledged by Roman authorities since Julius Caesar decreed that the Jews had the right to observe it throughout the Roman Empire. Some rabbis affirmed it was the unique element of the Jewish law that set Israel apart from all other peoples: if other peoples had moral and sacrificial laws from their gods, they did not have the Sabbath. Obedience to Sabbath laws thus constituted Israel's primary religious responsibility. To be sure the Sabbath law to abstain from labor was not broken, the rabbis forbade any conduct that could contribute to labor: for example, one was not to carry anything, lest one carry tools; again, one was not to walk far from one's house, lest one go to one's fields. Establishing such rules to keep a law from being transgressed was called "building a fence around the law," and it was enjoined as one of a rabbi's chief endeavors (see Danby 1954, tractate *ʾAbot* 1.1). The point was clear: it was essential to protect the Sabbath law from transgression by all possible means. See SABBATH.

On such a Sabbath, Jesus was confronted in a synagogue by a man with a withered hand. The question was, would Jesus heal it on the Sabbath? It was not a question of whether mercy could be practiced on the Sabbath; the rabbis agreed that in an emergency help could be given on a Sabbath even if it did involve labor (see Matt 12:11). Rather, it was a question of timing: this was no emergency. The man had had the withered hand for some time, and could wait until the end of the Sabbath at sundown to be healed. In this situation Jesus posed a question about what was lawful on the Sabbath: "to do good or to do harm, to save life or to kill" (3:4). The question has an obvious answer; of course it is not lawful on the Sabbath, any more than on any other day, to do harm or to kill. Yet the reaction of the Pharisees, when Jesus healed the crippled hand, was to hold "counsel with the Herodians against (Jesus), how to destroy him" (3:6). What irony, when the Pharisees by their plotting demonstrate that they thought Jesus' good deed to the cripple was illegal while they, careful observers of God's law, on that same Sabbath tacitly affirmed the legality of doing harm by plotting to kill.

Again, there is the irony that scribes from the heart of Jewish religion, Jerusalem, who studied God's Torah to learn his will, were unable to recognize that the power by which Jesus worked was from that same God whose law they studied, and thought it came instead from God's enemy, Satan (3:22). Those who considered themselves most alert to God's ways with humanity were here unable to recognize what God was doing in Jesus.

There is the irony that those closest to Jesus, who responded to his call to accompany him with no question (1:16–20), would produce from among their number the one who was to betray Jesus, and that they themselves would not understand him (e.g., 8:17–18; 9:6) and in the end ignominiously desert him (14:50; 66–72).

There is the irony surrounding the parable Jesus told to the religious officials in the temple court, a parable about a vineyard and its owner, whom the tenants ignored and whose son they killed (12:1–12). By the very act of rejecting the content of the parable, they brought it to reality when they, too, rejected the owner of the "vineyard" (see Isa

5:1–7, where the vineyard is clearly Israel and its owner is God, a passage this parable clearly reflects) and killed his son, namely Jesus himself.

There is the irony of the treatment of Jesus before the Sanhedrin when, thinking to ridicule him by revealing the gap between what he had apparently claimed about himself (14:62) and what he was able to do, they called upon Jesus to "prophesy" (14:65), that very Jesus whose predictions, as Mark's narrative had shown, were so often and so remarkably proved to be true.

The trial of Jesus is, as one might suspect, shot through with irony. There is the irony of Pilate's action in the face of the charge of insurrection against Jesus, a charge presumed in his first question to Jesus (15:2; to claim to be king was to assert Caesar was not king, and hence was insurrection). Pilate's task as a Roman official was to maintain the *Pax Romana,* and to put down sternly any insurrection that threatened to breach the Roman rule so necessary for that peace to be maintained. Yet Pilate, in his attempt to temper justice with mercy, released Barabbas, who had been imprisoned precisely for his role in an insurrection and thus represented a threat to Roman rule, and condemned Jesus to death for the crime of insurrection he had not committed.

There is the irony of the action of the Roman soldiers at Jesus' trial who, thinking to mock Jesus by clothing and hailing him as king (15:17–18), in fact by those actions acknowledge him appropriately for what he was: God's chosen and anointed king.

There is the irony that Jesus' religious opponents were able neither to tell the truth nor lie when they intend to. Intending to tell the truth about Jesus when they accuse him of blasphemy in calling himself God's son (14:64), something God himself had twice acknowledged (1:11; 9:7), they pronounce a falsehood, only to be unable later to tell a falsehood when, intending to lie about Jesus by mockingly acknowledging him as Israel's king (15:32), they inadvertently announce the truth.

Perhaps the most striking irony of all is bound up with the strange ending of Mark's gospel (16:8). The women who had remained and watched the crucifixion of Jesus and who, coming to anoint his corpse, had instead been commissioned by the "young man" at the empty tomb to tell the disciples the good news of Jesus' resurrection and to remind them of his promise to meet them in Galilee failed to do so because of fear. These women had remained faithful to Jesus when the disciples, who could not come to terms with Jesus' impending death, had fled. It was that death that caused them to fear, and flee. Here, however, in a strange twist of irony, the women, hearing of Jesus' resurrection, similarly flee in fear. If the disciples were unfaithful because they could not come to terms with Jesus' death, the women proved unfaithful precisely because they had come to terms with it: it was the news he was no longer dead that proved unsettling to them. They in their turn were unable to come to terms with his life.

In the end, therefore, none proved faithful to Jesus. Yet the story of the career of the disciples with Jesus was eventually told, as was the story of the fear-filled disobedience of the women. Reconciliation with the risen Jesus thus did take place, allowing the story recorded in Mark's narrative to be told. Perhaps in that way Mark intended to point to the power of the risen Christ as alone able to reconcile to himself and to God a humanity given to treachery and desertion.

It is apparent, therefore, that even though the oldest manuscripts of Mark contain no accounts of the appearance of the risen Jesus, there can be no question that Mark knew Jesus rose from the dead. The promises of Jesus, which, as we saw, regularly turn out to be fulfilled, included his promise that he would meet his followers in Galilee (14:28), a promise repeated at the empty tomb (16:7). It was also repeated each time Jesus formally foretold the circumstances of his impending death (8:31; 9:31; 10:34). Another reason must therefore be found for the omission of accounts of resurrection appearances than that Mark somehow was embarrassed by them, or did not know about them. That reason is, as suggested above, likely to be theological, and has to do with Mark's strategy for the whole gospel.

It appears that one of Mark's theological goals with his gospel, therefore, was to move his readers from observers to participants, and thus to move them to share in the gospel whose beginnings he had narrated in his account of Jesus of Nazareth.

F. Form and Function

From all that has been discussed thus far concerning the gospel of Mark, it appears that the major problem with which Mark was working, namely the identity of Jesus, and the form of literature he chose to solve it, namely a narrative, were intimately related. That is to say, Mark's creation of his narrative structure embodied his solution to the problem of Jesus' identity (i.e., his christology), in that, as Mark understood it, Jesus' identity was a function of his destiny. Only when one knows what happened to Jesus (cross and resurrection) can one understand the meaning of what he said and did, and therefore who he was: God's son, the king of God's redeemed humanity.

It was to reinforce that point that Mark made all other christological titles subservient to the phrase "Son of Man." The superiority of that title over the others lies in the fact that for whatever reason, Mark saw it as the expression of Jesus' destiny, namely his death and resurrection. "Son of Man" in Mark therefore describes not so much identity as destiny. Yet in Mark, as we have seen, identity and destiny are inseparably bound up with one another. Thus when Jesus predicts his passion, he refers to himself as Son of Man, and whenever the question of his identity arises, whether implied or explicit, Jesus responds by referring to himself as Son of Man. Can Jesus, as one who employs God's prerogative of forgiving sins, be recognized as Son of God (2:5, 7)? No, he is Son of Man (2:10). Can he, when his actions reveal him to be Lord of the Sabbath, be recognized as son of David, who had acted in similar fashion (2:25)? No, he is Son of Man (2:28). Can he, as successor to John the Baptist and the prophets, be recognized as Christ (8:28–29)? No, he is Son of Man (8:31). Can he, in transfigured form, be recognized as Son of God (9:7)? No, he is Son of Man (9:9).

In similar fashion, when the question of Jesus' identity is finally answered, it is answered in terms of his destiny (14:61), that is, his identity as anointed Son of God is qualified by his destiny as Son of Man (14:62). Again, in a climactic statement defining the identity and purpose of Jesus, namely to atone for the sins of humankind, it is the title "Son of Man" that is used (10:45).

Again, because destiny and identity are so closely linked in Mark, the only ones who are able to identify Jesus as Son of God during his earthly career are those unaffected by that redemptive destiny: God himself (1:11, 9:7), and the demons (1:24; 3:11; 5:7). For all others, until Jesus' destiny is fulfilled on the cross, his identity as Son of God remains hidden. It was to make that point, it appears, that Mark gathered together the independent traditions circulating in the early Christian community of which he was a part, and assembled them into the narrative which he identified as "the beginning of the gospel of Jesus Christ, the Son of God."

Bibliography

Achtemeier, P. J. 1970. Toward the Isolation of Pre-Markan Miracle Catenae. *JBL* 89: 265–91.

Boomershine, T. E., and Bartholomew, G. L. 1981. The Narrative Technique of Mark 16:8. *JBL* 100: 213–23.

Bultmann, R. 1963. *The History of the Synoptic Tradition.* Trans. J. Marsh. 8th ed. Oxford.

Danby, H. 1954. *The Mishnah.* London.

Dibelius, M. 1934. *From Tradition to Gospel.* Trans. B. L. Woolf. Rev. 2d ed. London.

Farmer, W. R. 1964. *The Synoptic Problem.* New York.

Humphrey, H. M. 1981. *A Bibliography for the Gospel of Mark: 1954–1980.* New York.

Juel, D. 1977. *Messiah and Temple: The Trial of Jesus in the Gospel of Mark.* SBLDS 31. Missoula, MT.

Kelber, W. 1979. *Mark's Story of Jesus.* Philadelphia.

Kermode, F. 1979. *The Genesis of Secrecy: On the Interpretation of Mark.* Cambridge.

Kim, S. 1983. *The "Son of Man" as the Son of God.* WUNT 30. Tübingen.

Kingsbury, J. D. 1984. *The Christology of Mark.* Philadelphia.

Lindars, B. 1983. *Jesus Son of Man.* Grand Rapids.

Longstaff, T. R. W. 1977. *Evidence of Conflation in Mark? A Study in the Synoptic Problem.* SBLDS 28. Missoula, MT.

McKnight, E. V. 1985. *The Bible and the Reader: An Introduction to Literary Criticism.* Philadelphia.

Marxsen, W. 1969. *Mark the Evangelist.* Trans. J. Boyce et al. Nashville.

Meagher, J. C. 1979. *Clumsy Constructions in Mark's Gospel.* Toronto Studies in Theology 3. New York.

Orchard, B. 1977. *Matthew, Luke and Mark.* 2d ed. Manchester.

Perrin, N. 1969. *What is Redaction History?* Philadelphia.

Petersen, N. R. 1978. *Literary Criticism for New Testament Critics.* Philadelphia.

———. 1980. *Perspectives on Mark's Gospel.* Semeia 16. Missoula, MT.

Price, S. F. R. 1984. *Rituals and Power: The Roman Imperial Cult in Asia Minor.* Cambridge.

Raisanen, H. 1976. *Das "Messiasgeheimnis" im Markusevangelium.* Schriften der Finnischen Exegetischen Gesellschaft 28. Helsinki.

Rhodes, D., and Michie, D. 1982. *Mark as Story: An Introduction to the Narrative of a Gospel.* Philadelphia.

Robbins, V. K. 1984. *Jesus the Teacher.* Philadelphia.

Schmidt, K. L. 1919. *Der Rahmen der Geschichte Jesu.* Berlin.

Stoldt, H. H. 1980. *History and Criticism of the Markan Hypothesis.* Trans. and ed. D. L. Niewyk. Macon, GA.

Toedt, H. E. 1965. *The Son of Man in the Synoptic Tradition.* Trans. D. M. Barton. Philadelphia.

Weeden, T. J. 1971. *Mark—Traditions in Conflict.* Philadelphia.

Williamson, L. 1983. *Mark. Interpretation: A Commentary for Teachers and Preachers.* Atlanta.

Wrede, W. 1971. *The Messianic Secret.* Trans. J. C. G. Grieg. Cambridge.

PAUL J. ACHTEMEIER

MARK, JOHN (PERSON) [Gk *Ioan(n)es Markos*]. An early Jewish Christian who assisted with the 1st-century missionary activities of Paul, Peter, and Barnabas and who is associated by tradition with the gospel of Mark. The name is a combination of two appellations, the Heb *yōḥānān* ("Yahweh has shown grace"; cf. 2 Kgs 25:23) and the Latin "Marcus" (or the Greek *Markos*). Dual names commonly were employed during the period as a common custom within Hellenistic Judaism (see Acts 1:23, Joseph-Justus).

The NT provides scant information about the figure of John Mark. He initially is introduced at Acts 12:12, a scene in which Peter returns from prison to the home of Mary, "the mother of John whose other name was Mark." Both the house itself and the household of Mary probably were significant for the early Christian community in Jerusalem, since Peter seems to have known that Christians would be gathered there for prayer. Thus the role of John Mark in early Church tradition often is associated with the presumed wealth and prestige of Mary, who was a homeowner with a maidservant (Rhoda) and who could support gatherings of early Christians for worship. The common, though most likely errant, belief that John Mark was the "young man" who escaped capture by the Romans at the arrest of Jesus (Mark 14:51–52) rests upon the assumption that the Garden of Gethsemane was owned and tended by the family of Mary. According to this view, John Mark perhaps would have been stationed at the garden as a guard during the night watch. Another tradition, which maintains that the Last Supper (Mark 14) was held in the home of Mary, assumes that the household was familiar with the work of Jesus and was receptive to his activity. Papias of Hierapolis argues against a close relationship between Jesus and the family, however, since he notes specifically that Mark "had not heard the Lord, nor had he followed him" (Eus. *Hist. Eccl.* 3.39.15).

The only clear comment upon the activities of John Mark that is provided in the NT is the observation that he was one of numerous evangelistic missionaries who circulated during the 1st century (one of the 70 missionaries who are mentioned in Luke 10:1?). Accordingly, he is listed as an assistant to Paul and Barnabas during the first Pauline missionary journey (Acts 12:25; 13:5). Though the nature of that assistance is not specified, he may have served as a recorder, catechist, and travel attendant. Because of his status as the son of a prosperous Jewish-Christian family in Jerusalem and as the cousin of the wealthy landowner Barnabas (Col 4:10; Acts 4:36–37), John Mark would have been a natural selection for such a role. He later separated from Paul and Barnabas "in Pamphylia" (along the coast of S Anatolia), perhaps as the result of some unspecified disagreement. Paul thereafter refused to include him in subsequent travels (though Barnabas took him onward to Cyprus; Acts 15:37–39), and the account of Acts records his activities no further.

Apart from the testimony of Acts, his name (now listed only as Mark) reappears throughout the Pauline literary tradition as a reconciled missionary companion of Paul. Here he is remembered as one who labored faithfully for Christianity (2 Tim 4:11 and Philemon 24). The association of Barnabas with John "who is called Mark" in the record of Acts, on the one hand, and of Barnabas who was the "cousin" of Mark in the witness of Colossians, on the other hand, is an "undesigned coincidence" which suggests that the accounts of Acts and the Pauline Epistles in fact make reference to the same person (Taylor 1955: 29).

Though the figure of John Mark became a casualty of disputes within the Pauline missionary thrust, the Petrine tradition soon adopted an association with the name that has stood for centuries in ecclesial history. The initial evidence for this association appears in 1 Pet 5:13 where John Mark (again listed only as Mark) is mentioned by the author of the letter as "my son." While the name Mark in 1 Peter cannot be identified definitively with the figure of Mark who appears in the Acts narrative, a consistent picture of the role and activities of John Mark would result if such an association can be accepted (Martin *ISBE* 3: 260). From the testimony of Papias (Eus. *Hist. Eccl.* 3.39.16) we learn that common ecclesial tradition recognized Mark as the "interpreter" of Peter who recorded the words of the apostle as the foundation for a written gospel (cf. also Iren. *Haer.* 3.1.1). There is no question that Papias here refers to the gospel of Mark as we know it. And again, while the association of Mark (as recorded by Papias) with John Mark of Jerusalem is not above suspicion, this consistent caricature has been preserved by subsequent Christian tradition.

Numerous traditions about the person and activities of Mark soon arose among the Church Fathers. Hippolytus, for example, refers to Mark as "stump-fingered" or "shortened." The former translation may indicate that the historical figure of Mark possessed some peculiar physical characteristic (as is suggested by the *Anti-Marcionite Prologue* to the gospel from the 2d century). Modern scholars, however, often prefer to use the latter translation as a reference to the abbreviated nature of the gospel text itself (when compared to the other NT gospels) or in support of the manuscript tradition that concludes the gospel at Mark 16:8. Several early Christian traditions suggest that a close association existed between the figure of John Mark and the congregations of Alexandria, based upon the belief that he traveled to Egypt from Rome after the martyrdom of Peter (Eus. *Hist. Eccl.* 2.16.1). There is little information about the death of Mark. The claims for the martyrdom of Mark that appear in the *Paschal Chronicle* and in the *Acts of Mark* probably do not predate the 4th century (Swete 1909: xxvii–xxviii). For further discussion see Pesch *Mark* HTKNT.

Bibliography

Hendricksen, W. 1975. *New Testament Commentary: Exposition of the Gospel According to Mark.* Grand Rapids.

Holmes, B. T. 1935. Luke's Description of John Mark. *JBL* 44: 63–72.

Jones, E. D. 1921–22. Was Mark the Gardener of Gethsemane? *ExpTim* 33: 403–4.

Swete, H. B. 1909. *The Gospel according to St. Mark.* 3d ed. London.

Taylor, V. 1955. *The Gospel According to St. Mark.* London.

CLAYTON N. JEFFORD

MARK, SECRET GOSPEL OF.

An edition of the gospel of Mark known only from an incomplete letter of Clement of Alexandria discovered at the Greek Orthodox monastery of Mar Saba in the Judean desert. M. Smith has described how he found the hitherto unknown Clementine letter as he was studying and cataloging manuscripts in the monastery library in 1958. The letter was written in cursive Greek, dated to about 1750, on two and a half pages at the back of a printed volume of the letters of Ignatius of Antioch (Isaac Voss, editor, *Epistulae genuinae S. Ignatii Martyris* [Amsterdam: Blaeu, 1646]). In 1973 Smith published both his scholarly and his popular editions of the letter of Clement and the *Secret Gospel of Mark,* and almost at once controversy began to swirl around the text. The controversy has focused upon questions concerning the authenticity, contents, and interpretation of the Mar Saba text. To the present day Smith seems to be the only scholar who has seen the original manuscript, although at least one other scholar (T. Talley) made an unsuccessful attempt to view the text. Nonetheless, as Smith has summarized in his bibliographical essay (1982), most scholars he has reviewed now are willing to attribute the letter to Clement of Alexandria and the letter itself has been included in an addendum to the second edition of O. Stählin's *Clemens Alexandrinus.*

The Mar Saba manuscript opens with a titular phrase that indicates the source of the letter: "From the letters of the most holy Clement, (author) of the *Stromateis*" (lr:1). In the letter Clement commends and supports the recipient, a certain Theodore, for his opposition to the Carpocratians, who were libertine gnostics well known from ancient heresiological reports (Clement of Alexandria, *Strom.* 3.2–6; Iren. *haer.* I.25; Hippol. *haer.* 7.32; cf. Smith 1973b: 295–350). According to Clement's letter from Mar Saba, the Carpocratians employed an edition of the gospel of Mark which Carpocrates falsified by "mixing the most shameless lies with the undefiled and holy words" (lv:8–9). In contrast to the Carpocratian edition, Clement recognizes two authoritative editions of the gospel of Mark: (1) a public edition of the gospel, which Mark composed while Peter was in Rome and which seems to be identical or nearly identical with the canonical gospel of Mark; and (2) the *Secret Gospel of Mark,* "a more spiritual gospel for the use of those being perfected," which also included "the things appropriate for those progressing in knowledge" (lr:20–22). When Mark died, Clement writes, he left the *Secret Gospel* to the care of the Church at Alexandria, "where it even now is very carefully guarded, being read only to those being initiated into the great mysteries" (lv:1–2).

According to the letter of Clement, the *Secret Gospel* contained at least two passages not included in the public gospel of Mark, and Clement cites both of these two passages. The first passage (lv:23–2r:11), to be located immediately after Mark 10:34, recounts the story of the raising of a rich youth (*neaniskos*) of Bethany (cf. themes in Mark 10:17–22 par.). At the request of the sister of the youth, Jesus goes to the tomb, rolls the stone away from the door, and raises the youth from the dead. The youth looks upon Jesus and loves him, and after six days Jesus instructs him. In the evening the youth, "wearing a linen cloth on his naked body" (2r:8; cf. Mark 14:51–52, also perhaps 16:1–8), comes to Jesus, and Jesus teaches him "the mystery of the kingdom of God" (2r:10; cf. Mark 4:11). The second passage (2r:14–16), to be located within Mark 10:46, describes Jesus coming to Jericho and refusing to receive three women, including the sister and the mother of the youth.

Recent studies on the *Secret Gospel of Mark* suggest that the significance of the text may be realized through a redaction-critical study of the *Secret Gospel*. Several scholars (H. Koester, H.-M. Schenke, J. D. Crossan, M. W. Meyer) have proposed interpretations of the *Secret Gospel* that attempt to place the text within the redactional history of the Markan tradition, and in so doing they are unanimous in advocating the priority of *Secret Mark* to canonical Mark. "The basic difference between the two," Koester has stated, "seems to be that the redactor of canonical Mark eliminated the story of the raising of the youth and the reference to this story in Mark 10:46" (1983: 56). Scholars have also noted that this Markan account of the raising of the youth is remarkably similar to the story of Lazarus in John 11, except that the *Secret Gospel* account may well be more primitive than the Johannine account (the *Secret Gospel* lacks the details—personal names, descriptions of features of the miracle, etc.—and the theological themes of John 11). The presentation of the youth "whom Jesus loved" in *Secret Mark* (2r:15; cf. Mark 10:21) also bears striking resemblance to the BELOVED DISCIPLE in the gospel of John. These observations contribute to the discussion of the relationship between the Markan and Johannine traditions, and the roles of the Johannine Beloved Disciple and the Markan *neaniskos* as paradigms for discipleship.

Bibliography

Crossan, J. D. 1985. *Four Other Gospels: Shadows on the Contours of Canon.* Minneapolis.

Koester, H. 1983. History and Development of Mark's Gospel. Pp. 35–57 in *Colloquy on New Testament Studies,* ed. B. C. Corley. Macon, GA.

Meyer, M. W. fc. The Youth in the *Secret Gospel of Mark. Semeia.*

Schenke, H.-M. 1984. The Mystery of the Gospel of Mark. *SecondCent* 4: 65–82.

———. 1986. The Function and Background of the Beloved Disciple in the Gospel of John. Pp. 111–25 in *Nag Hammadi, Gnosticism, and Early Christianity,* ed. C. W. Hedrick and R. Hodgson, Jr. Peabody, MA.

Smith, M. 1960. Monasteries and Their Manuscripts. *Arch* 13: 172–77.

———. 1973a. *The Secret Gospel: The Discovery and Interpretation of the Secret Gospel According to Mark.* New York.

———. 1973b. *Clement of Alexandria and a Secret Gospel of Mark.* Cambridge.

———. 1982. Clement of Alexandria and Secret Mark. *HTR* 75: 449–61.

Stählin, O., ed. 1980. *Register.* Vol. 4/1 in *Clemens Alexandrinus.* 2d ed. GCS. Berlin.

Talley, T. 1982. Liturgical Time in the Ancient Church. *StLtg* 14: 34–51.

MARVIN W. MEYER

MARKETPLACE. See TRADE AND COMMERCE (ANE).

MAROTH (PLACE) [Heb *mārôt*]. A village in the Shephelah of Judah (Mic 1:12), otherwise unknown. LXX reads *odynas,* "sorrows." Identification with Maarath [Heb *ma*ᶜ*ărād*] in the hill country of Judah (Josh 15:59) is unlikely since it does not account for the LXX reading, explain the loss of ᶜ*ayin,* or match well with the other known towns in Mic 1:10–16, which are located W of the Judean hills in the Shephelah (cf. Josh 15:33–44). Similarly, the Galilean Meroth mentioned by Josephus (*JW* 3.3.1) is out of the question. Micah employs the feminine singular participle *yôšebet* (lit: "inhabitant of") within this dirge (vv 11, 12, 13, 15) to personify the population of these towns and villages which formed the defensive approach to "Mother Jerusalem" as her "daughters" (Heb *bānôt*; see 2 Chr 11:5–12; Judg 1:27; Haag *TDOT* 2: 336; cf. 2 Kgs 18:13–16). Maroth itself is a play on Hebrew *mārar,* "be bitter," and *mārâ,* "be rebellious." Hence, the paronomasia of 1:12 yields a sense akin to "Yes, Daughter Bitterbury longs for something sweet [Heb *tôb*], but no, something sour [Heb *rā*ᶜ] descends from YHWH to the very gate of [Mother] Jerusalem." See MORESHETH.

LAMONTTE M. LUKER

MARRIAGE. This entry consists of two articles. The first explores the subject of marriage and marriage customs in the ancient Near East and in the Old Testament. The second focuses on marriage as it is presented in the New Testament.

OLD TESTAMENT AND ANCIENT NEAR EAST

Like other features of religious communities, marriage and wedding customs tend to be traditional and time-honored. This is not an area where novelty reigns. Archaic language like "thereto I plight thee my troth" is quite acceptable at the ceremony of marriage, but very strange elsewhere. The OT covers a period of approximately 1400 years (Abraham to Ezra). It would seem, contrary to the statement made above, that marriage patterns in the patriarchal age differed, in some ways at least, from marriage patterns in the postexilic era (late 500 to 400 B.C.).

A. Introduction
B. In the Ancient Near East
C. In the Old Testament
   1. Parentally Arranged/Self-Initiated
   2. Endogamy/Exogamy
   3. Monogamy/Polygamy
   4. Among the Prophets
   5. In Wisdom Literature

6. Levirate Marriage
7. In the Creation Narratives

A. Introduction

Ancient Israel never produced a marriage manual for its citizenry. The creation story of Genesis 1 does indeed climax its narration with a wedding, an activity described by the narrator as "very good" in God's estimation. Similarly, the account of Genesis 2 concludes penultimately with the programmatic exhortation "a man shall leave his father and mother and cleave to his wife, and the two shall become one flesh" (2:24).

Even if this statement was first penned by later priestly writers, its placement near the beginning of Israel's canon of sacred literature may indicate its preeminence and foundational nature vis-à-vis marriage, at least in the judgment of those involved in the shaping of that canon. And yet the statement is primarily an idealistic one. It is surprising how few marriages in the OT, if any, conform to Gen 2:24. One would have to scour the pages of the OT to find instances of the man leaving his home, uniting with his wife, and forming a "one flesh" relationship.

The laws pertaining to marriage in the legal codes distributed throughout the OT are few and scattered. Most of these address issues such as whom one may not marry, how to determine virginity, the dissolution of marriage, remarriage, what is to become of a childless widow, etc. This is unlike ANE codes which tend to discuss matters of legal interest in *seriatim* fashion; thus the laws on marriage are for the most part all sequentially arranged in corpora like Hammurabi's Code (nos. 128–84; *ANET,* 171–174) or the Middle Assyrian Laws (nos. A.25–39; *ANET,* 182–183).

What we do have abundantly in the OT are stories about the marriages of men and women. On occasion the narration of these marriages is pivotal in the development of a major theme or motif. At other times their telling appears but peripheral. Some of these marriages appear, on surface, to be normal and predictable, while others border on the bizarre. Some of these marriages are marked by sanctity and integrity, while others are aberrant and profane. Taking all these marriage stories together, looking for common threads, and on that basis trying to construct an OT concept of marriage is like sitting beside our highways and parkways, observing the flow of traffic and the driving patterns of individuals, and on that basis composing a driver's manual. Both in driving and in marriage there is often a considerable difference between prescription and practice. For this reason, we will need to distinguish between the divine will in marriages and OT marriages as they are illustrated. The latter may reflect the former, but not necessarily so.

B. In the Ancient Near East

Most of what we know about marriage and wedding customs in the ANE is based on accounts of marriages involving people of power and influence in society, i.e., kings, pharaohs, potentates, nobility, even the gods themselves, or some epic hero whose legendary accomplishments raised him into the area of the divine. This is to be expected. The literature of antiquity highlights royalty more than it does the exploits of commoners. Thus, to read about the marriage of a pharaoh to his queen does not likely provide us any information on the marriage customs of the pharaoh's thousands of pyramid laborers, any more than the wedding of an Assyrian king served as a model for the wedding of one of his canal excavators. Likewise, one can't assume that the marriage of Prince Charles and Lady Diana was a typical late 20th-century wedding in England.

To begin our survey, we turn out attention to the Canaanites as revealed in the texts from Ugarit. Marriage is illustrated at three levels in Ugarit. First is marriage among (royal) mortals. In five of six cases the king was followed on the throne by his son. One king, Niqmad II, was succeeded by his son Arḫalba (ca. 1345–1336 B.C.). He in turn was followed not by a son, but by his brother, Niqmepa. Arḫalba was childless, and so he willed that his wife, Kubaba, should, after his death, be wed to her brother-in-law Niqmepa. Furthermore he added a solemn warning that no other man outside the family should seek the hand of Kubaba in marriage. Thus, in an Akkadian document from Ugarit (*PRU* 3: 16.144), Arḫalba warns: "Whoever, after my death, takes (in marriage) my wife, Kubaba daughter of Takan (?), from my brother—may Baal crush him . . ."

This text is of interest for two reasons. One, it illustrates the existence of levirate marriage (to be discussed below) at Ugarit. Two, Arḫalba's imprecation on anyone marrying his widow, excluding his brother, may reflect the desire to avoid loss of family property to outsiders; more likely, it illustrates the fact that Ugarit shared with Israel the concept that marriage to a former king's wife, or even his concubines, bestowed legitimacy on an aspirant who otherwise had no claim to the throne (see 2 Sam 3:7; 12:8; 16:21; 1 Kgs 2:13–25; Tsevat 1958).

The second level at which marriage is illustrated in Ugarit is in the marriage of the epic hero King Keret (named after the eponymous ancestor of the Cretans). As the epic opens, Keret's wife has been taken from him before she has given him an heir. The text reads (A.i.14; *ANET,* 143) that Keret "married the woman, and she departed." "Departed" here may be understood as a euphemism for "died" and thus Keret intends a second marriage (*ANET,* 143), or else his wife was kidnapped, and thus Keret intends the recovery of his abducted wife (Gordon 1964). In either case, the remainder of the epic details Keret's journey at El's direction to Udum, his eventual obtaining of his wife, Hurrai, their trip back to Keret's place, their marriage (or reuniting), and finally the divine promise of progeny. This text demonstrates, among other things, that real love and romance did play a vital part in marriage at Ugarit. Keret (Gordon 1966: 105) describes Hurrai in terms reminiscent of the Song of Songs: "Whose charm is like Anath's charm / Whose loveliness is like Astarte's loveliness / Whose brows are lapis lazuli / Eyes, bowls of alabaster!"

This concern with passionate devotion is a feature that Ugarit shares with pre-Solomonic historiography. By contrast, in the earlier literature of Egypt (e.g., Sinuhe) and Mesopotamia (e.g., Epic of Gilgamesh), and in post-Solomonic historiography, little interest is shown in romantic marriage. It is interesting to note even the structural parallels (Aitken 1984: 12) between the wooing of Rebekah (Genesis 24) and of Hurrai: (1) lack of a wife; (2) commission to secure a wife; (3) travel to land or city of the future bride; (4) rendering of divine aid; (5) beauty of bride remarked; (6) negotiations for the bride; (7) sending off of the bride; (8) marriage blessing; (9) travel back with the bride; and (10) the marriage.

The third level of marriage at Ugarit is marriage between gods and goddesses. Of particular interest is the marriage between the Canaanite moon god Yarih and the Mesopotamian moon goddess Nikkal. The purpose of the wedding is clearly fertility, symbolized in the child that Nikkal will bear to Yarih. Yarih is willing to pay her father a bride–price (*muhr*) of "a thousand (shekels) of silver / A myriad of gold" (beyond the range of normal human ability to pay) so that "she may enter his house." In return he will make her fertile: "I shall make her field into a vineyard / The field of her love into an orchard" (Gordon 1966: 99). The text is a *hieros gamos,* a wedding of the gods, whose fertility stimulates plentiful harvests for mankind. Although a mythological text, it demonstrates most of the major points of marriage at Ugarit: paying the bride–price by the groom to the bride's father, the dowry for the bride, a virilocal marriage in which the bride moves in with the groom, and a heavy concern with fertility. Thus, even the mythological narratives of Ugarit presumably reflect a common sociological province of marriage procedures and customs.

The marriage of the gods is certainly no innovation with Northwest Semites in the 2d millennium B.C. Well-known Sumerian inscriptions from the end of the 4th millennium B.C. describe in texts that are belletristic and ritual in nature the rite of sacred marriage of the bride Inanna (originally goddess of the communal storehouse), who meets her groom Dumuzi (the god of the date palm) at the gate and admits him and his servants who carry the bridal gifts. This scene is depicted on the Uruk Vase. Dumuzi is the personification of the power behind and in the annual date harvest, and Inanna is that storehouse in which Dumuzi deposits and stores his yield. Their mating is what Jacobson (1976: 47) calls "the sacred cosmic sexual act in which all nature is fertilized."

Akkadian myths might even portray the possibility of marriage between a goddess and a mortal. In the Gilgamesh Epic, Gilgamesh is proposed to by the goddess Ishtar (*ANET,* 83):

> Come Gilgamesh, be thou (my) lover!
> Do but grant me of your fruit.
> You shalt be my husband and I will be your wife.

Gilgamesh rejects her offer of marriage, primarily because of her past marital affairs (*ANET,* 84):

> Which lovers did you love forever?
> Which of your shepherds pleased you for all time?

After listing some of Ishtar's ex-lovers, Gilgamesh exclaims (*ANET,* 84),

> If you should love me, you would (treat me) like them.

As we indicated above, Mesopotamian legal documents deal with matters of matrimony. They do not deal abstractly, philosophically, or theologically with marriage. They are rules, plain and simple, defining the permissible and the nonpermissible with respect to items like divorce, dowry, marriage–price, and remarriage. A few samples from Hammurabi's Code will suffice. For example, a marriage contract is absolutely essential for a marriage (no. 128). If a man outlives his wife, her dowry belongs to her children, not to her husband (no. 162). If, however, the wife died without mothering any children, he is entitled to some of the dowry, but only if his father-in-law has returned the marriage–price (nos. 163, 164).

The Middle Assyrian laws provide legal justification for the institution of levirate marriage (discussed above in connection with Ugarit). Law no. 33 from Tablet A reads: "If, while a woman is still living in her father's house, her husband died and she has sons . . . If she has no sons, her father-in-law shall marry her to the son of his choice . . ." This law and others like it (nos. 25, 26, 27, 32) begin conspicuously with the phrase "if while a woman is still living in her father's house." Law no. 27 adds "and her husband has been coming in frequently." Assyriologists often call such a marriage whereby the husband lives with his wife in her father's house *erēbu* marriage (*erēbu* means "to come in, pay visits [to one's wife]"). The term is acceptable; however, the very next two laws (nos. 28, 29) indicate that *erēbu* was also used of normal marital arrangements in which a woman "went in/entered" her husband's house. The closest parallels to *erēbu* marriage in the Bible would be Jacob living with his wives in the home of Laban, Moses living with his wife Zipporah in the home of Jethro, and Samson who goes down to "visit" his wife at Timnah. An Egyptian example would be Sinuhe, a courtier in the entourage of Sesostris I, who in a time of crisis fled to Canaan, lived with a local family, and married the daughter. Of course, these examples are a bit different from the law cited in the code in that the husband is an outsider, a foreigner, while in the code the man initiated into the family is a native.

The 15th-century-B.C. cuneiform texts from Nuzi in NE Iraq have contributed significantly to our understanding of marriage in Mesopotamia. Since the majority of these texts are private documents, personal matters such as marriage are frequently mentioned. As in most of the Near Eastern cultures, heavy emphasis is placed on procreation as the main purpose of marriage. What is unique in the Nuzi texts is the inordinately heavy stress laid on the bride's fertility. In fact, a majority of the texts contain clauses concerned with the possibility of childlessness and the groom's right to acquire/be provided a new wife in case the first wife proves barren (Grosz 1981: 182).

Thus one marriage document (Grosz 1981: 166) reads:

> Zike, son of Akkuya, gave his son Shennima in adoption to Shuriḫa-ilu, and Shuriḫa-ilu gave Shennima all these fields. Should there be a son of Shuriḫa-ilu, he will be the chief heir, and Shennima will be secondary heir. . . . And he [Shuriḫa-ilu] gave Kelim-ninu as wife to Shennima. If Kelim-ninu bears children, Shennima will not take another wife, but if Kelim-ninu does not bear children, Kelim-ninu will take a slave-girl from the land of Nullu as wife for Shennima, and Kelim-ninu shall have authority over the child [of the slave girl].

This text not only parallels Sarah giving Hagar to Abraham (Gen 16:2) and Rachel giving Bilhah to Jacob (Gen 30:3), but the laws in Hammurabi's Code (nos. 144, 146, 147), all of which concern the (barren) wife who gave to her husband as surrogate for herself a female slave, and the female slave's ability or lack of ability to bear a child. It also illustrates an uxorilocally residing son-in-law who had to be adopted by his father-in-law lest the son-in-law's children belong to the father's lineage and not the father-in-law's lineage.

While this text has some affinities with the Jacob and Leah/Rachel marriages, the following text is even closer (Gordon 1964: 24–25):

> The adoption tablet of Nashwi son of Arshenni. He adopted Wullu son of Puhishenni. As long as Nashwi lives, Wullu shall be the heir. Should Nashwi beget a son, [this son] shall divide equally with Wullu, but [only] Nashwi's son shall take Nashwi's gods. But if there be no son of Nashwi, then Wullu shall take his daughter as wife to Wullu. And if Wullu takes another wife, he forfeits Nashwi's lands and buildings. Whoever breaks the contract shall pay one mina of silver [and] one mina of gold.

The Nuzi texts are, as one would expect, full of references to the bride–price (*terḫatu*) paid by the groom's family to the bride's family (i.e., her father or brother), and to the dowry (*mulūgu*), a gift received by the bride from her father at the time of her marriage. Such frequent emphasis on the bride–price (the references to *terḫatu* are more numerous than to *mulūgu*, and the *terḫatu* is always greater than the *mulūgu*) has the effect of role-casting the wife as the object of the marital agreement rather than as the subject.

In fact, there is some indication in the Nuzi texts that the payment of the bride–price could be postponed until the marriage was consummated, or until the bride had proven her fertility. Along possibly these same lines one text (Grosz 1981: 175) reads:

> Declaration with Kuni-ašu, daughter of Ḫut-tešup, made in front of these witnesses: "In the past, Akam-mušni married [me] off and took 40 shekels of silver for me from my husband, but now Akam-mušni and my husband are [both] dead, and now [as to] myself, Akkiya, son of Ḫut-tešup, seized me in the street as his sister and took the authority [of brother] over a sister for me. He will marry me off and taken 10 shekels of *šurampašḫu* silver from my [future] husband.

What is of special interest here is the reduction of the bride–price for Kuni-ašu from her first marriage (40 shekels) to her second marriage (10 shekels). This may be due to the fact that she is no longer a virgin, or that she has proved herself barren with her first husband (Grosz 1981: 175).

C. In the Old Testament

1. Parentally Arranged/Self-Initiated. The Hebrews shared with others of the ANE the practice of parentally arranged marriages. The basis for making this claim is scattered references in the OT narrative to such procedure. There is, however, no OT law that mandates this. Nowhere, for example, is there a law in the Deuteronomic code (Deuteronomy 12–26) to the effect that it is the responsibility of a father to select a bride for his son. There is a law that outlines procedures for dealing with a rebellious son (Deut 21:18–21), a recently married son (Deut 24:5), and a deceased son with no son of his own (Deut 25:5–10), but not one for an unmarried son. This is in contrast to the Laws of Eshnunna (ca. 2000 B.C.) one of which (no. 27) states (*ANET,* 162):

> If a man takes a(nother) man's daughter without asking the permission of her father and her mother and concludes no formal marriage contract with her father and her mother, even though she may live in his house for a year, she is not a housewife.

Similarly, the OT Wisdom Literature, while having much to say about healthy marital relationships, never classifies as wise one who chooses a wife for his son with prudence. Indeed Prov 19:14 affirms that a good wife is from the Lord, not from the husband's father.

The first instance of a parentally arranged marriage in the OT is Hagar selecting a wife for her son Ishmael from Egypt (Gen 21:21). If one attributes any credence to the year numbers of Genesis, which state that Abraham was eighty-six when he fathered Ishmael (16:16), and one hundred years old at Isaac's birth (21:5), and give a year or two for Isaac to be weaned (21:8), that would suggest that Ishmael was fifteen or sixteen when his mother arranged his marriage to a native-born Egyptian. This may reflect one of the justifications for parentally arranged marriages, namely, the relatively young age at which boys and girls reached marriageable age. It is unlikely, however, that Hagar's selection of a wife for her son may be sustained as an illustration of a parent's assuming the responsibility of spouse selection for a young child. Apart from the problems about the chapter's portrayal of Ishmael as still quite young (see 21:14–19), possibly still an infant in fact, Gen 21:20–21 indicates that Ishmael grew up, became an expert with the bow, and lived in the wilderness of Paran. Eventually Hagar chose a wife for him from Egypt (Gen 21:21). The interval between 21:14–19 and 21:21 is unknown. Even if Ishmael is cast out from Isaac at 15 or 16 years of age, he could be 17, 20, or 30 before his wife is chosen for him. On the other hand, those who were older when they married (Jacob, Esau, or Boaz) played a much larger role in the selection of their mate. But even advanced age did not itself guarantee autonomy in matrimonial matters. For example, Isaac is forty (Gen 25:20) when Rebekah is chosen for him, and Pharaoh gave Asenath, daughter of Potipherah priest of On, to Joseph as wife when Joseph was thirty years old (Gen 37: 45–46). The choice of Rebekah is the classic case of parentally arranged marriages (through Abraham's faithful servant [Genesis 24]). Isaac played no role, other than finding the choice to his satisfaction (24:67). Incidentally, the OT never mandates an ideal age range for marriage (cf., however, Buchanan 1956). In Egypt girls were married between the ages of twelve and fourteen, and young men between fourteen and twenty. In Greece girls were usually between fourteen and twenty, and men usually between twenty and thirty. In Rome, at the time of Augustus, the legal minimum age for girls was twelve, and for boys fourteen. The Talmud recommends marriage for girls at the age of puberty, which would be twelve or thirteen (*Yebam.* 62b). Males are encouraged to marry between fourteen and eighteen. A girl younger than twelve-and-a-half, according to Talmudic law (*Qidd.* 2b), could not refuse a marriage arranged by her father. Beyond that age her assent was essential (Yamauchi 1978: 241–43).

While Judah, son of Jacob, seems to have exercised considerable freedom in the selection of his wife (Gen 38:2), he did not extend that liberty to his son Er, but instead took Tamar as the wife for his firstborn (Gen 38:6). Subsequently he instructed another son, Onan, to "marry" his widowed daughter-in-law (Gen 38:8). Exod 2:21 implies that the Midianite priest Reuel selected Zipporah from his seven daughters and gave her to Moses, as Moses shifts from houseguest to helping hand to husband. Again in this latter case, Moses is no young immature adolescent who lacks the wisdom to select his own spouse. In the words of Exod 2:11 this happened sometime after Moses had "grown up," an age range that Stephen specifies with the proverbial "forty" (Acts 7:23).

Caleb, in an attempt to stimulate support for an invasion of the city Kiriath-sepher, offered his daughter Achsah as a trophy and wife to any man who would spearhead the attack. Othniel accepted the challenge, and in the process gained the hand of Achsah (Josh 15:16, 17 and Judg 1:12, 13). This particular story illustrates the fact that an esteemed bride could be obtained not by expensive gifts or a monumental bride–price, but by deeds of valor. It is comparable with David's marriage to Michal. Viewed from one perspective, David's marriage to Michal is parentally arranged (1 Sam 18:21), albeit for an ulterior motive. In the end, however, David won Michal not by paying a conventional bride–price, but by routing and slaughtering 200 Philistines and presenting their foreskins as evidence of his triumphs (1 Sam 18:27; 2 Sam 3:14). Even earlier than this, Saul tried to give his daughter Merab to David (1 Sam 18:17), again as a means of having David killed.

The pattern of parentally arranged marriages seems not to continue beyond Saul. Jesse, father of David, played no role in David's marriage to Abigail (1 Samuel 25), to Ahinnoam (2 Sam 2:2), to Maacah (2 Sam 2:3), to Haggith (2 Sam 2:4), to Abital (2 Sam 2:4), or to Eglah (2 Sam 2:5). And David did not select the Pharaoh's daughter for his son Solomon (1 Kgs 3:1), nor any women in his 700-member harem (1 Kgs 11:3).

Accordingly, we note a number of marriages in the OT in which the parents played an incidental, if not nonexistent, role in the marriage of their progeny. As we indicated above, where an older male was involved, the man, in several instances, took more responsibility in choosing a wife. We have already mentioned the marriages of Jacob (with, however, some guidance from the parents [27:46–28:2], even though Jacob must be older than 40 [cf. 26:34]), Esau, and Boaz. To these we might add Shechem's directive to his father about Jacob's daughter Dinah—"get me this young woman as a wife" (Gen 34:4), and similarly Samson's ultimatum to his parents—"I have seen a woman in Timnah of the daughter of the Philistines; now therefore, get her for me as a wife" (Judg 14:2). Samson's marriage is suspect on three grounds: (1) he marries a foreigner, (2) it is initiated by sexual attraction, and (3) it is against his parents' will (Bal 1987: 42). Both of these stories demonstrate that even when the initiative for spouse selection was with the husband-to-be, the formalities of parental arrangement were still followed. In such instances parental approval was assumed rather than solicited.

Abraham did not pick out a wife for Isaac. All that the father legislated was that the servant fetch a wife for Isaac from the country of Abraham's birth, and that she not be a daughter of the Canaanites (Gen 24:3, 4). If anything, the story highlights the role of divine providence in marriage. Parents supply only the most general guidelines. Furthermore, one reads in the story that Rebekah had the choice either to accept the servant's invitation to return to Canaan with him, or refuse that invitation (Gen 24:58). Her family fully honored her power of acceptance or veto. Interestingly, Abraham played no role in the story's climax. It was the servant and Rebekah, then Rebekah and Isaac alone in his late mother's tent. The text simply says (v 67), "and he loved her." Terrien (1985: 32) reminds us that the verb "to love" is susceptible of two different vocalizations: an "active" one ("and he made love to her"), which would emphasize the erotic aspect of their relationship, and a "stative" one ("and he was in love with her"), which expresses a lasting feeling rather than a temporary sensation. The Hebrew manuscripts clearly indicate the stative use.

Similarly, Isaac does not pick Jacob's wife. Like his father, his concern is that Jacob marry endogamously (Gen 28:1–5). Isaac and Rebekah are grieved by Esau's marriage to Judith and Basemath, who are Hittites (Gen 26:34, 35), but they cannot veto it. The same goes for Esau's subsequent marriage to Mahalath, the daughter of Ishmael (Gen 28:6–9).

To those who have lived all their lives in the West, parentally arranged marriages will seem strange, maybe even absurd, and at least an illegitimate extension of parental authority; however, much of the world still operates in this fashion. There is at least a double rationale for parental selection of marriage partners. For one thing, such an arrangement focuses attention upon the entire family unit, and not just on the couple alone. Secondly, it permits an understanding of love which has as much to do with the commitment of the will ("I love you because you are my wife") as it does with emotions, glands, and hormones ("you are my wife because I love you") [Baker 1984: 97].

2. Endogamy/Exogamy. Endogamy is the custom of marrying only within one's own group, such as a clan, tribe, etc. Exogamy is the custom of marrying outside one's own clan, tribe, etc. The OT reflects both systems in operation. Sometimes the two different types of marriage exist side by side, but more often than not, one exists to the virtual exclusion of the other.

Endogamous marriage is the norm in the patriarchal age. Thus we read that Abraham married his half-sister (Gen 20:12), Nahor married his niece Milcah (Gen 11:29). Isaac married his cousin Rebekah (Gen 24:15). Esau married his cousin Malhalath (Gen 28:9). Jacob also married his cousins Rachel and Leah (Gen 29:12). This latter case illustrates the common phenomenon of cross-cousin marriage, i.e., marriage between the offspring of siblings of opposite sex, one in which a man marries the daughter of his mother's brother, despite the close degree of consanguinity. It is a marital relationship that avoids "the extremes of too much endogamy on the one hand and too much exogamy on the other hand" [Oden 1983: 199]. Amram, father of Moses, married his aunt (Num 26:59). The unmarried daughters of the sonless Zelophehad raised the question of what would happen to inheritance in case of the marriage of female heirs (Num 27:1–11; 36:1–13). Would it be possible in such a situation for family inheritance to move outside the tribe? To prevent that, Moses informed the concerned parties that they could marry anybody they wish (note the latitude given here), but they could marry only within the family of their father's tribe (Num 36:6).

The justifications for endogamy are clear enough. It could be based on such a thing as unfriendly relations with a neighboring tribe. Or it may signal a need for separation from a majority group while living among or adjacent to foreigners. Thus, to give a contemporary example, a member of an Amish community could not marry somebody from a mainline Protestant denomination and remain in good graces with the Amish community. Where substantive religious issues are involved, endogamy reflects the practical need to preserve a certain norm of religious behavior, and also to maintain the ethnic purity of the tribe or family. The smaller the group, and the more entrenched its religious ethos, the greater the threat presented by exogamy to that group.

But the same biblical traditions also demonstrate that endogamy was not inviolable. Esau married two Hittites (Gen 26:34) and a Canaanite (Gen 28:6–9). Joseph married an Egyptian (Gen 41:45), Judah a Canaanite (Gen 38:2), Moses a Midianite/Cushite (Exod 2:21, Num 12:1), Samson a Philistine (Judges 14; 16:4–22), Boaz a Moabitess (Ruth 4:13), David a Calebite and Aramean (2 Sam 3:3), and Ahab a Phoenician (1 Kgs 16:31). Solomon pursued exogamy to the extreme (1 Kgs 3:1; 11:1; 14:21). There are also a few instances of an Israelite woman marrying a foreigner. Bathsheba married Uriah the Hittite (2 Sam 11:3); the Phoenician Hiram's mother was from the tribe of Naphtali (1 Kgs 7:13, 14), and Esther married the Persian King Ahasuerus. There is also the instance of Sheshan, who had only daughters, so he gave one of his daughters to his Egyptian slave (1 Chr 2:34–35). These exogamous marriages took place: (1) out of spite (Esau's); (2) when one was living in a foreign land for an unusually long period of time (Joseph's, Moses', Esther's); (3) with divine approval (but parental disapproval) as a means of moving against the enemy (Judg 13:3, 4); (4) for consolidation of political power (David's, as argued by Levenson and Halpern [1980: 507–18], Solomon's); (5) in blatant disregard for religious norms (Ahab's and Solomon's).

It is an overstatement to claim that the OT prohibits intermarriage with all gentiles. To be sure, Ezra and Nehemiah do make such a prohibition (Ezra 9–10; Neh 13:23–27) and probably were not the first to fulminate against exogamy, leading as it could to compromise or indifference. Judg 3:5, 6 makes the point in connection with its commentary on the apostasy of Israel that part of that downfall was due to Israel's intermarriage with the nations among whom she lived. Josh 23:12, 1 Kgs 11:4, and the priestly Exod 34:16 (in the context of a renewed covenant) emphasize the same.

It should be noted that one of the key passages on the subject in Deuteronomic literature, Deut 7:3, forbids intermarriage with the seven peoples to be dispossessed from the land, but does not name other foreigners. Interestingly, Leviticus 18 and 20 are replete with sexual taboos, but intermarriage is not among them (probably because the concern of these two chapters is with intrafamilial marriage). If all intermarriage is forbidden, then the law of Deut 21:10–14 would be odd, for it permits the Hebrew warrior to take a wife from female war prisoners. Furthermore, Deut 23:7, 8 seems to allow marriage with an Edomite or Egyptian after three generations (perhaps to provide sufficient time for the non-Israelite to acclimatize to Israelite practices). Amalekites, on the other hand, never qualify (Deut 25:17–19). It has been suggested that one interpretation for the Ammonite and Moabite "entering the congregation of the Lord" only after the tenth generation (Deut 23:2–6) is that intermarriage between Israelites and these two groups was postponed for ten generations. Contextually this interpretation is lent support by Deut 22:13–23:1, which deals with marriage laws. But in light of the book of Ruth, where intermarriage with Moabites did take place, it seems that "enter the congregation" is another way of saying "enter the temple of the Lord."

If the exogamous marriages of kings like David, Solomon, and Ahab are typical, then it is possible that "from the beginning of monarchy, the number of intermarriages increase, and exogamy is socially tolerated to the point where it inspires indifference rather than anxiety" (Brenner 1985: 116–17). If so, then perhaps the legal prohibitions against intermarriage were a Deuteronomic response to intentional deviation from the norm, a deviation made even more possible by the religious and political demoralization brought by the fall of N Israel in 722 B.C.

What was a minor entry in the Deuteronomic platform became a major component in the reforms of Ezra and Nehemiah. Two entire chapters in Ezra (9 and 10) are devoted to this subject (see also Neh 9:2; 10:30; 13:3, 23–27, 28). The guilty parties included members of the priests (Ezra 10:18–22), the Levites (Ezra 10:23–24), and the laity (Ezra 10:25–43). The postexilic prophet Malachi, and probably a contemporary of Ezra and Nehemiah, rebuked his people for marrying "the daughter of a foreign god" (Mal 2:11). Malachi's *bat-ʾēl nēkār* is the equivalent of *nāšîm nokriyyôt* in 1 Kgs 11:1, 8; Ezra 10:2; Neh 13:26. That Malachi uses the phrase "daughter of a foreign god" rather than "foreign women" suggests not only the evil of intermarriage per se, but the inevitable religious syncretism that accompanied such exogamous marriages. It is not difficult to see why such marriages might flourish in the postexilic era. For one thing, impoverished exiles, stripped of home and possessions, would opt to marry women from wealthy families (i.e., foreign) in order to advance their economic status. And again, the openness of the Persian administration fostered a more intimate give-and-take between its own populace and various displaced persons living within its borders (Glazier-McDonald 1987: 605).

Given this situation, Ezra's reform had as its goal a separation of Israel from everything that induced contamination. His goal, as argued by Bossman (1979: 36), was the purification of the people according to a priestly ideal of separation from all that is unclean. For Ezra it was impossible to make consonant with each other this penchant for intermarriage and God's call to his people to be holy. Anything that threatened to abort this movement of reformation in a community recently resettled, uncertain of its future, and searching for its identity had to be dealt with forthrightly, even if the measures seemed distasteful and counterproductive to the majority. Incidentally, there is no indication that Ezra's interdiction of marriage with foreign women extended to marriages of Judean Jews with Samaritan women. The latter do not fall into the category of *nāšîm nokriyyôt.*

It appears that postbiblical Judaism is closer to Ezra than it is to Moses on the question of endogamy/exogamy. For instance, *Jubilees* (mid-2d century B.C.) 30 states (incorrectly) that Moses outlawed intermarriage with all gentiles. However, *Jubilees* 30 (esp. vv 7–11) builds not on the locus classicus Deut 7:3–4, but on Lev 18:21.

Unlike the integrating Hellenizers of the 2d century B.C., the Maccabeans, of whom *Jubilees* is a product, pushed for stability through separation. Where could such separation be more manifest than in the avoidance of exogamous marriages? In agreement with *Jubilees,* the 1st-century-A.D. Jewish philosopher from Alexandria, Philo (*Spec Leg* 3.29), argued strenuously against intermarriage, using Moses for support, especially Deut 7:3–4, as did the Jewish historian in Rome, Josephus (*Ant* 8.190–96). For both of these authors exogamy was a violation of a Mosaic ordinance.

In contrast to *Jubilees,* Philo, and Josephus, rabbinic society seems not to have been disturbed by intermarriage. Both the Palestinian Talmud and the Babylonian Talmud are relatively quiet on the issue, and the prohibition of intermarriage does not even appear in the Mishnah (Cohen 1983: 27–28).

3. Monogamy/Polygamy. The ideal marraige in OT society was a monogamous one, one man for one woman, one woman for one man. The creation narrative (Gen 2:24) makes this point with its call to the man to forsake his mother and father and cleave unto his wife (not wives). In fact, there is only one illustration of the violation of that pattern in primeval history, and that is Lamech (Gen 4:23). A number of laws have been cited (*IDB* 3: 281) as support for monogamous marriage: Exod 20:17; 21:5; Lev 18:8, 11, 14, 15, 16, 20; 20:10; 21:13; Num 5:12; Deut 5:21; 22:22. Wisdom Literature also provides copious texts in support of monogamy: Prov 12:4; 18:22; 19:13; 21:9; Eccl 9:9; Job 31:1, 9–12; Sir 26:1–4. It would appear, however, that the main justification in using these verses to substantiate monogamy is the use of *ʾiššâ* in the singular. But a closer look at these verses raises serious questions about whether or not they provide credence for monogamy. For example, Exod 20:17 and Deut 5:21 list several things one is not to covet, and all the objects the individual is warned against coveting are in the singular. If it is possible for a man to have more than one manservant, maidservant, ox, or ass, he could have more than one wife. Or again, Lev 18:8, 11, 14, 15, 16, 20 all refer to uncovering the nakedness of somebody's wife, again always in the singular. However, one should not suppose, for example, that a person has only one sister (e.g., 18:9) since "sister" appears in the singular as well. In fact, Lev 18:9 warns against uncovering the nakedness of one's sister, who is further identified as "the daughter of your father or the daughter of your mother," indicating that a man could have multiple wives, providing sons and daughters from different mothers.

Indeed, the OT is replete with illustrations of polygamous marriages. To be more precise, it tells of instances of polygyny (one husband, more than one wife), but no instance of polyandry (one wife, more than one husband). Apart from the two wives of Lamech already noted, we recall (1) Abraham with Sarah and his concubines Hagar and Keturah (Genesis 16; 25:1–2); (2) Jacob with Leah and Rachel (Gen 29:15–30); (3) Esau with three wives (Gen 26:34; 36:2; 28:9); (4) Gideon with his "many wives" (Judg 8:30); (5) Elkanah with Hannah and Peninnah (1 Sam 1:2); (6) David with seven named wives (1 Sam 18:17–30; 25:38–43; 2 Sam 3:2–5) and additional unnamed ones (2 Sam 5:13); (7) Solomon and his royal harem (1 Kgs 3:1; 11:3; Cant 6:8); and (8) Rehoboam with his eighteen wives (2 Chr 11:21). There is one law in the Deuteronomic code (Deut 21:15–17) which does allow for one man to be married simultaneously to two wives. And the only individual who is admonished in the same code not to multiply wives is the king (Deut 17:17). No such prohibition is directed to the king's subjects.

Looking at these lists of polygamists, one is led to the conclusion that polygyny may have been limited to men who occupied leadership positions, who were well off, or who had some other claim to distinction. Indeed, de Vaux comments (*AncIsr,* 25): "it is noteworthy that the books of Samuel and Kings, which cover the entire period of the monarchy, do not record a single case of bigamy among commoners (except that of Samuel's father, 1 Sam 1:2, at the very beginning of the period)." However, the books of Samuel and Kings record little about any commoner, or the marriage of any commoner.

It is clear that in most of the above-cited instances polygyny was a major contributor to problems in the household. Witness the debacle between Hagar and Sarah, or Rachel's envying of Leah's fertility (Gen 30:1–2, 15), or the frustration of Esau's parents (Gen 26:35), or the liquidation of Gideon's seventy sons by Abimelech, his son by concubine (Judges 9), or Peninnah's provocation of Hannah (1 Sam 1:6), or David's in-house squabbling and treachery among half-brothers and half-sisters (2 Samuel 13, 1 Kings 1–2), or Solomon's forfeiture of his empire (1 Kings 11).

Wherever the emphasis of marriage is placed on procreation or the sexual satisfaction of the man, more than likely polygyny will flourish. But one should not attribute all instances of polygyny to lust. In a society that is overwhelmingly seminomadic and agricultural, the maintenance of several wives would supply an abundant work force to tend flocks and work fields.

4. Among the Prophets. It is the prophets whom we must credit with conceiving the idea of Yahweh as the husband of Israel in their attempt to graphically portray God's covenant election of Israel. The Torah, however, already hints of this kind of relationship between God and his people. For example, the commandment that urges aniconic worship of the deity finds its motivation in the affirmation that Yahweh is a "jealous" God (Exod 20:5). The Hebrew for the adjective "jealous" is *qannāʾ* (see also Exod 34:14). The related noun *qinʾâ* and verb *qinnēʾ* describe the agitation of a husband suspicious of his wife's infidelity (Num 5:14, 30; cf. Prov 6:34 for this noun *qinʾâ* used to describe the passionate feelings of a husband vis-à-vis his wife). The Torah also uses the verb *zānâ* ("go whoring") to express apostasy of Israel from Yahweh (Exod 34:15, 16), as well as the noun *zônîm* ("harlotry," Num 15:39).

The prophetic development of this figure built upon this tradition reflected in the Torah. Hosea was the first to advance the metaphor significantly. He was then followed by Jeremiah, Ezekiel, the exilic Isaiah, and Malachi. In Hosea's case his own marriage to Gomer was intricately connected with his meditation on Israel's marriage to Yahweh. It is still a moot point whether or not God instructed Hosea to marry a lady who was already a street harlot in order to illustrate God's choice of an already loose-living people, or whether Hosea married a lady who was potentially promiscuous, who subsequently abandoned the prophet, thus providing a poignant illustration to Hosea of Yahweh's hurting and grieving heart over the apostasy of his spouse.

Hosea 3 is the autobiographical account of Hosea's new marriage or remarriage. He "bought" (3:2) his spouse for fifteen shekels of silver. In between these two marriages of the prophet the second chap. expands on Hosea's experiences, justifying Hosea's divorce from Gomer (2:3–15—Eng 2:1–13), and addressing theologically Hosea's second marriage (2:16–25—Eng 2:1–23). Hosea is told by God to speak to the woman's children (i.e., the citizens of northern Israel) and urge them to "arraign your mother" (i.e., the kingdom of northern Israel), for of that Israel God will say: "she is not my wife [*ʾištî*] and I am not her husband [*ʾîšâ*]" (Hos 2:4—Eng 2:2). In the second half of this chapter, however, the emphasis is reversed, and Yahweh's marriage, or remarriage, with the people is depicted.

What is of special import here is the indication that because of God's (re)marriage to Israel, "In that day, says Yahweh, You will call me My husband / My man [*ʾîšî*], And no longer will you call me My master / My owner [*baʿlî*]" (Hos 2:18—Eng 2:16). To be sure, the use of *baʿlî* is directed against the false worship of the Canaanite baals of the fields, as the next verse makes clear: "And I will remove the name of the Baals from her mouth, and they shall no longer be mentioned by their name." But this is more than simply a broadside against Canaanite fertility concepts. What Hosea affirms is that in God's (re)marriage with his people, there will be more than a master-slave relationship. As Terrien (1985: 54) has stated, Hosea attacks the idea of "marriage as a contract of ownership through which a woman is nothing more than the property of a man. Israel . . . will not look at her God as if she were the slave of her master, but she will enjoy with him the status of partner and trusted friend."

It is of interest that it was Hosea, and not some of his contemporaries, such as Amos or Micah or Isaiah, who got the most mileage out of this daring marriage metaphor. There are hints of the concept in Amos, e.g., when he refers to "the virgin of Israel" (5:2), or when he uses a phrase like "you only have I known among all the families of the earth" (3:2), with its apparent conjugal symbolism. But there is nothing approaching Hosea's bold use of the metaphor. Nerved by his strong foundation in covenant theology with its emphasis on moral love, and caught in the trauma of his own marriage experience, Hosea may use the marriage metaphor as graphically as he does precisely because he is, unlike Amos or Isaiah, meeting head on a pagan cult that includes marriage themes in its mythology and sexual acts in its praxis (Hall 1982: 170).

Hosea's appropriation of Yahweh as husband and Israel as bride is the forerunner for similar emphasis in subsequent prophets. Jeremiah picks up this imagery in Jer 2:20–25 and 3:1–3. He even calls Judah's allies her "lovers" (22:20, 22; 30:14; see also Hos 8:9). Ezekiel 16 with its extended discussion of Judah as a nymphomaniacal adulteress is a classic passage. Two expressions, both in v 8, describe God's "marriage" to Judah before she sought other lovers. The first is "I spread my skirt/wing over you," which is another way of saying "I married you" (see also Deut 23:1—Eng 22:30; 27:20; Ruth 3:9; Mal 2:16). In marriage the man's garment covered the woman's nakedness, whereas adultery uncovered it. The second phrase is Ezek 16:8, "I entered into a covenant with you." This is one of only two places in the entire OT where marriage is spoken of as a covenant. The other is Mal 2:14. Finally, the later Isaiah used the same metaphor for God's attachment to Israel (Isa 61:10 and 62:5). In the latter God is compared to a bridegroom exulting over his bride. The prophets shared completely their Hebrew tradition that Yahweh is never conceived of as having sexuality. And yet they were not hesitant to speak of Israel as God's bride, an imagery that abounds in non-Israelite religions where the gods and goddesses were explicitly sexual. In exploiting the marriage metaphor even at the divine level, the prophets were in effect engaging in a demythologizing hermeneutic.

Apart from their symbolic use of the marriage metaphor, four of the prophets integrated their own marriage, or lack thereof, into their message. We have already mentioned Hosea's marriage to Gomer and the three children born of this marriage, to whom were given richly symbolic names. Isaiah fathered two children by his wife, who is simply styled "the prophetess" (Isa 8:3), and each of the children bore a symbolic name, ambiguous in their interpretation as either signs of hope or signs of judgment. The death of Ezekiel's wife, called "the desire of your eyes" (Ezek 24:16), is foretold to Ezekiel, and the prophet is instructed not to mourn for her, not even to shed a tear (Ezek 24:16–18). Similarly, mourning is to be withheld from those about to experience their own demise. Finally, Jeremiah provides the only illustration in the OT of a divine call to celibacy (Jer 16:2). The joy and fulfillment denied to him is a harbinger of days of judgment for Jeremiah's contemporaries. This particular prohibition for Jeremiah is not dated, but it must have come at a point in his ministry where all hope for the repentance and salvation of his peers became impossible. Jeremiah faced extinction on two fronts, one from his enemies, who wished to cut him off and blot out his name, the other from God, who denied him marriage, and thus progeny to perpetuate his name.

5. In Wisdom Literature. Ecclesiastes and Proverbs affirm repeatedly the happiness and delight in the reciprocal love of a man and woman in marriage. The writer of Ecclesiastes vetoes the solitary life with his famous "two are better than one" (5:9), then describes the life of mutuality these two may share (5:10–12). While these four verses may be describing simply the value of a friend, they suggest that marriage at its heart is a friendship, not a hierarchy between suzerain and servant. Thus there is a time for embracing (3:5b). Is it possible that the enigmatic "there is a time to cast away stones, and a time to gather stones" (3:5a) refers to times of sexual intimacy and euphoria and to times of sexual abstinence (Loader 1969: 242)? In both phrases the emphasis is on giving oneself to another, to intimacy. Eccl 9:9 admonishes one to live joyfully with the wife whom you love.

Proverbs reverberates with the same theme. See, for example, Prov 5:18–20; 6:29; 12:4; 18:22; 19:14; 30:19; 31:10–31. It is well known that Proverbs is written from the man's/husband's point of view. So Proverbs speaks of the husband who must live with a nagging wife who is like a dripping faucet (17:1, 14; 19:13; 21:9, 19; 25:24; 27:15–16; 30:23). Nowhere is there a proverb that counsels the wife on what she is to do when she has to share the home with an insensitive and obnoxious husband. To aid the male in finding the right wife, Proverbs lists a sample of commendable traits such a woman should exemplify (31:10–31). It does not provide a parallel list in order to assist the female to find a "virtuous husband." At the same time, the list of gifts possessed by this ideal wife are hardly the traditional cooking, cleaning, and conceiving. She is, in addition to a devoted mother and a loving wife, a business woman, a real estate agent, a farmer, a philanthropist, a craftsman, a seller, purchaser, and administrator.

We include the Song of Songs in this section even though it does not fall into the category of Wisdom Literature. One reason for utilizing the Song of Songs at this point is that, unlike Proverbs, it is written from a woman's point of view. It is a passionate love song in which a young bride and groom, now at the point of readiness for consummation of marriage, celebrate their reciprocal erotic love. Especially prominent in this rhapsody is the woman's passion for her lover. She is the one who seeks him, not vice versa (3:1–4; 5:6–8), and it is her recollections of his attractive features that are given prominence. It is important to observe that the Song extols not fertility but human love. For this reason, there is no allusion to any legal aspect of marriage, to procreation, or to the institution of the family. Here is further evidence, then, of the Bible's moving away from an exclusive focus on marriage as primarily the siring of progeny, i.e., marriage as a means to an end.

6. Levirate Marriage. Deut 25:5–10 provides legal sanction for a marriage between a widow whose husband died without offspring (the *yĕbāmâ*) and the brother of the deceased (the *yābām*). It is the responsibility of the latter "to perform the duty of a husband's brother" (*yābam*). When the brother-in-law chooses not to marry the *yĕbāmâ*, the ceremony of *ḥălîṣâ* (removal by the widow of the brother-in-law's sandal) takes place, and the widow spits in his face as well. This latter is a point of interest, for this law is the only one in the OT that includes in its statement of penalty an act of humiliation against the villain. The removal of the shoe by the woman is not an additional part of the insult. Rather, in removing the brother-in-law's shoe, with the town's elders as witnesses, the woman assumes the right to her freedom and full control of her destiny.

This type of marriage is known as levirate marriage, from the Latin *levir,* "brother-in-law." Its continuation into the NT era is demonstrated by the Sadducees' question to Jesus about the childless woman who was married in sequence to six of her late husband's brothers (Matt 22:23–33 = Mark 12:18–27 = Luke 20:27–40). We have seen that levirate marriage existed in Ugarit, in the Middle Assyrian (no. 33) and Hittite law codes (no. 193), and possibly in the Nuzi texts. In these texts the primary concern is with producing a (male) child to carry on the name of the deceased husband.

Two stories in the OT portray levirate marriage in operation: Genesis 38 and Ruth. However, when either one of these stories is aligned with the law in Deuteronomy, significant differences are apparent. For example, in Deuteronomy and Genesis 38 the levirate is compulsory; in Ruth it is not. Again, Deut 25:5–10 limits the levirate to brothers "who dwell together" (i.e., brothers who have not yet come into their inheritance and who have not yet established families of their own). On the other hand, Genesis 38 extends the levirate to the father-in-law and Ruth to a distant relative. Genesis 38 at least accords with Middle Assyrian Law no. 33 and Hittite Law no. 193, both of which mention first the brother as the normal partner, but allows his father this function as well. And thirdly, Deut 25:7 makes it clear that the levir's responsibilities are "to raise up a name for his brother." But note that it is Judah and Boaz, i.e., the real/biological fathers, who are mentioned in the genealogies of Perez and Obed, and not Er and Mahlon.

This latter point suggests that levirate marriage in the OT is not simply concerned with producing a male child nor with producing an heir to the dead man's property. It is concerned just as much, if not more, with the support and protection of the widow, and the perpetuation of family property within the immediate family (Thompson and Thompson 1968: 96). How close, one might ask, does the levirate marriage come to incest? At the end of the Genesis 38 story we read that the father-in-law Judah "did not lie with her [Tamar] again," for a marriage between father-in-law and daughter-in-law is not normal. By contrast, we do not read that Boaz ceased to "know" Ruth after he fathered Obed by her. His relationship to Ruth was distant enough for levirate marriage to evolve into normal marriage. In Lev 18:6–8; 20:11–12; and Deut 2:20, 22–23 appear kinds of sexual unions between kin that are illicit according to covenant morality. The various prohibitions include six relationships of consanguinity (based on blood), Lev 18:7, 9, 10, 11, 12, 13, and eight of affinity (based on marriage), Lev 18:8, 14, 15, 16, 17, 18. Presumably the list is selective rather than exhaustive, for how else would one account for the absence of both cousins and daughters from the above lists (Gottwald 1979: 302)? One of the sexual unions forbidden between relatives on the basis of affinity is sexual intercourse with one's sister-in-law (Lev 18:16). Now since the law of the levirate requires the brother-in-law to raise up a child to his deceased brother by way of marrying and having intercourse with his sister-in-law, then we have to assume that the legislation of Deut 25:5–10 is an exception to the legislation regarding marriage and/or sexual intercourse with one's sister-in-law.

7. In the Creation Narratives. The emphasis in Gen 1:1–2:3 in terms of human beings is first the creation of male and female with no differentiation between temporal priority and function, and second, the blessing of fertility and the mutual exercise of dominion given to these two. It should not go unnoticed that the two places where God "blesses" someone or something (1:22, 28) are followed immediately by the imperatives "be fruitful and multiply." Male and female in Genesis 1 are more of a biological pair than a social partnership. Little attention is paid to the relationship of male and female to each other, or to marriage per se. And yet the very fact that the power to reproduce is a blessing given to the male and female at their simultaneous creation, and therefore not dependent upon subsequent recitation of myth, is itself a refutation of the rationale of the fertility cult (Bird 1981: 147).

If Gen 1:1–2:3 says much about fertility and little about marriage, Gen 2:4–25 says much about marriage and nothing about fertility. In this portion, usually called the Yahwist (J) creation account, Yahweh-Elohim created the male first. Shortly thereafter Yahweh arrived at the conclusion that it is not good for man to be by himself. It was Yahweh, not the man, who made this determination, and he turned his attention to rectifying the situation of man's aloneness. Yahweh-Elohim proceeded to make for man a helper (v 18). The Hebrew word for "helper" (*ʿēzer*) has particularly rich nuances throughout the OT. For example, of the twenty-one times it is used, fifteen times it refers to divine help. Most of these refer to help in times of despair or distress. As his helper, woman rescues man from his loneliness and delivers him from his solitude. She is not somebody who supplies the necessary anatomical apparatus to allow the man to produce a second man.

This helper is to be "meet for him" (KJV) or "fit for him" (RSV), which are attempts to translate a Hebrew expression which reads literally "like what is in front of him," (*kĕnegdô*). A good translation would be "corresponding to," suggesting that both man and woman form a polarity. Neither is inferior/superior to the other, but one without the other is incomplete.

After extracting a "rib"(?) of Adam (the only time this Hebrew word [*ṣlʿ*] is so translated in the OT), Yahweh-Elohim "built" it into a woman (v 22). Upon seeing her, the man exclaimed: "this one is bone of my bones and flesh of my flesh" (v 23). This is more than simply an affirmation of blood ties. Both "flesh" and "bone" carry a double meaning. *Bāśār* means both "flesh/meat" and "weakness" (Isa 31:3). *ʿEṣem* means both "bone" and "strength" (cf. the verbal form *ʿāṣamtā* in Gen 26:16 ["you are stronger than we are"]). There is in both the man and the woman the inevitable presence of the strong and the weak, and the two are therefore necessary for each other "in sickness and in health" and "in plenty and in want" (Brueggemann 1970: 534). Marriage, then, is essentially a bond of covenant loyalty.

The penultimate verse in the Yahwist's account of the primal marriage is that a man is "to leave his father and mother and cleave unto his wife" (v 24). The verbs "leave/cleave" (*ʿāzab/dābaq*) are not chosen haphazardly. Both enforce the idea of marriage as covenant. For instance, *ʿāzab* is used to describe Israel's abandoning her covenant relationship with God, i.e., terminating one relationship only to start another (Jer 1:16; Hos 4:10). And *dābaq* is the verb used to encourage Israel to be faithful to her covenant relationship with her God (Deut 10:20; 11:22; 13:5; Josh 23:8; 1 Kgs 11:2). The result of such leaving/cleaving is that man and woman become "one flesh."

It is perhaps somewhat surprising to read that it is the man who abandons his parents and attaches himself to his wife. Would it not be more appropriate, especially in a patriarchal society, for a woman to leave her parents and attach herself to her husband? While this might possibly be a reflection of *erēbu* marriage, discussed above, it more likely reflects the revolutionary concept that a marriage between a man and a woman takes precedence over a man's duty to his parents. In Terrien's words (1985: 17) " 'maritality' displaces patriarchal filiality."

Bibliography

Ancient Near East

Gordon, C. H. 1964. Biblical Customs and the Nuzu Tablets. *BAR* 2: 21–31.

———. 1966 *Ugarit and Minoan Crete.* New York.

———. 1981. *Erebu* Marriage. Pp. 155–61 in *Studies on the Civilization and Culture of Nuzu and the Hurrians,* ed. M. Morrison and D. Owen. Winona Lake, IN.

———. 1987. The Marriage and Death of Sinuhe. Pp. 43–44 in *Love and Death in the Ancient Near East,* ed. J. H. Marks and R. M. Good. Guilford, CT.

Greengus, S. 1969. The Old Babylonian Marriage Contract. *JAOS* 89: 503–32.

Grosz, K. 1981. Dowry and Brideprice in Nuzi. Pp. 161–82 in *Studies on the Civilization and Culture of Nuzu,* ed. M. Morrison and D. Owen. Winona Lake, IN.

Jacobson, T. 1976. *The Treasures of Darkness.* New Haven.

Morrison, M. 1983. The Jacob and Laban Narratives in Light of Near Eastern Sources. *BA* 46: 155–64.

Parker, S. 1976. Marriage Blessing in Israelite and Ugaritic Literature. *JBL* 95: 23–30.

Roth, M. T. 1987. Age at Marriage and the Household: A Study in Neo-Babylonian and Neo-Assyrian Forms. *Comparative Studies in Society and History* 29: 715–47.

Selms, A. van. 1950. The Best Man and Bride—from Sumer to St. John. *JNES* 9: 65–75.

———. 1954. *Marriage and Family Life in Ugaritic Literature.* Pretoria Oriental Series 1. London.

Tsevat, M. 1958. Marriage and Monarchical Legitimacy in Ugarit and Israel. *JSS* 3: 237–43.

Van Seters, J. 1969. Jacob's Marriage and Ancient Near Eastern Customs: A Reexamination. *HTR* 62: 377–95.

Winter, U. 1983. *Frau und Göttin: Studien zum weiblichen Gottesbild im Alten Israel und in dessen Umwelt.* OBO 53. Freiburg.

Old Testament

Aitken, K. 1984. The Wooing of Rebekah. *JSOT* 30: 3–23.

Baker, J. P. 1984. Biblical Attitudes to Romantic Love. *TynBul* 35: 91–128.

Bal, M. 1987. *Lethal Love: Feminist Literary Readings of Biblical Love Stories.* Bloomington and Indianapolis.

Beeston, A. F. L. 1986. One Flesh. *VT* 36: 115–17.

Bird, P. A. 1981. "Male and Female He Created Them": Gen 1:27b in the Context of the Priestly Account of Creation. *HTR* 74: 129–59.

Bossman, D. 1979. Ezra's Marriage Reform: Israel Defined. *BTB* 9: 32–38.

Brenner, A. 1985. *The Israelite Woman.* Sheffield.

Brueggemann, W. 1970. Of the Same Flesh and Bone (Gn 2, 23a). *CBQ* 32: 532–42.

Buchanan, G. W. 1956. The Old Testament Meaning of the Knowledge of Good and Evil. *JBL* 75: 114–20.

Cohen, J. D. S. 1983. From the Bible to the Talmud: The Prohibition of Intermarriage. *HAR* 7: 23–29.

Davies, E. W. 1981. Inheritance Rights and the Hebrew Levirate Marriage. *VT* 31: 138–44, 257–68.

Friedman, M. 1980. Israel's Response to Hos 2:17b: "You are my Husband." *JBL* 99: 199–204.

Glazier-McDonald, B. 1987. Intermarriage, Divorce, and the *bat-ʾēl nēkār*. *JBL* 106: 603–11.

Gottwald, N. K. 1979. *The Tribes of Yahweh.* Maryknoll, NY.

Hall, G. 1982. Origin of the Marriage Metaphor. *HS* 23: 169–71.

Lawton, R. 1986. Gen. 2:24: Trite or Tragic? *JBL* 105: 97–98.

Levenson, J. D., and Halpern, B. 1980. The Political Import of David's Marriages. *JBL* 99: 507–18.

Lipiński, E. 1976. Le mariage de Ruth. *VT* 26: 124–27.

Loader, J. A. 1969. Qoh 3: 2–8—A "Sonnet" in the Old Testament. *ZAW* 81: 240–42.

Oden, R. 1983. Jacob as Father, Husband, and Nephew: Kinship Studies and the Patriarchal Narratives. *JBL* 102: 189–205.

Piper, O. 1960. *The Biblical View of Sex and Marriage.* New York.

Ringgren, H. 1987. The Marriage Motif in Israelite Religion. Pp. 421–28 in *AIR.*

Rowley, H. H. 1956–57. The Marriage of Hosea. *BJRL* 39: 200–33.

Terrien, S. 1985. *Till the Heart Sings. A Biblical Theology of Manhood and Womanhood.* Philadelphia.

Thompson, T., and Thompson, D. 1968. Some Legal Problems in the Book of Ruth. *VT* 18: 79–99.

Weiss, D. 1964. The Use of *qnh* in Connection with Marriage. *HTR* 57: 243–48.

Wilson, M. R. 1989. *Our Father Abraham: Jewish Roots of the Christian Faith.* Grand Rapids.

Yamauchi, E. M. 1978. Cultural Aspects of Marriage in the Ancient World. *BSac* 135: 241–52.

VICTOR P. HAMILTON

NEW TESTAMENT

It is frequently stated that the relatively few explicit statements on marriage in the NT make it impossible to identify either a specifically Christian marital ethos or a specifically Christian teaching on marriage, that Jesus' teaching on marriage is found primarily in the Synoptics' pericope on divorce (Mark 10:2–12), and that Paul was a misogynist who had a decidedly negative view of marriage. Each of these presuppositions relative to the NT authors' views on marriage stand in need of further nuance in the light of recent biblical scholarship.

A. Jesus
  1. Jesus and the Commandments
  2. Jesus and Divorce
  3. The Demands of Discipleship
  4. Marriage and the Resurrection
  5. The Marriage Banquet
B. Paul
  1. 1 Thess 4:3–8
  2. 1 Corinthians 7
C. The Post-Pauline Tradition
  1. Household Codes
  2. The Pastoral Epistles

A. Jesus

The relatively rare references to marriage in the canonical gospels is most probably due to the fact that the historical Jesus accepted marriage as a normal institution of his day, just as he accepted most other social institutions of his times. With his fellow Jews, Jesus regarded marriage as an integral and essential element in the fabric of Jewish life.

Although late in their origins, and permeated with significant theological motifs, the infancy narratives of both Matthew and Luke announce Jesus' birth within the context of the marital union of Mary and Joseph (Matt 1:18–25; Luke 2:4–6; cf. Matt 13:55). The Lukan infancy narrative significantly reflects the importance of offspring within marriage in its portrayal of the birth of John (Luke 1:5–25, 57–58). A history-of-traditions analysis of the first Cana pericope (John 2:1–12) suggests an early Sitz im Leben in the life of the historical Jesus, namely Jesus' attendance at a family wedding where his mother and other relatives were also present.

Jesus shared with his contemporary Jews a patriarchal view of marriage: a man marries and a woman is married (Luke 14:20; cf. 24:34–35; Mark 12:25; Matt 22:30). In accordance with typical Jewish mores, for which Gen 1:28 served as a scriptural warrant, many (probably most) of his disciples were married (Matt 8:14; 20:20; 27:56; Mark 1:30; 15:40; Luke 4:38; 8:3).

1. Jesus and the Commandments. Pre-Markan traditions, the nucleus of which may well go back to the historical Jesus, highlight Jesus' acceptance of the contemporary marital ethos. In a "rabbinic dialogue" (Mark 10:17–22; Matt 19:16–22; Luke 18:18–23), Jesus reiterates the importance of the commandments "do not commit adultery" and "honor your father and mother." An ancient tradition which most probably enjoyed an independent existence in the Palestinian church was used by Mark (Mark 7:9–13; Matt 15:3–6) to highlight the distinction between the commandments of God and human traditions. The pre-Markan tradition stressed the responsibility of children to provide for their parents.

The second antithesis of Matthew's Sermon on the Mount (Matt 5:27–28), which explains the commandment "you shall not commit adultery," in radical fashion so that it prohibits lust as well as adultery, reflects the catechetical tradition of Matthew's Hellenistic Jewish community. The Jesus who is presented as thus upholding the marital and familial *halakhah* is one who shares the views of his people. The logia attributed to Jesus in this regard are similar to statements attributed to various Jewish authorities.

2. Jesus and Divorce. Jewish authorities disagreed among themselves as to the interpretation of Deut 24:1. A well-known debate between the school of Hillel and the school of Shammai focused on the interpretation of the biblical phrase "something indecent." The disciples of Shammai interpreted the phrase strictly, that is, in terms of sexual immorality, while the disciples of Hillel interpreted the phrase more broadly so that divorce—a concession to the husband—was possible even if his wife spoiled a meal for him (*m. Giṭ.* 9:10). This debate provides the historical background (cf. Mark 6:17–18; Matt 14:30; Luke 3:19) for the controversy story in Mark 10:2–10 (Matt 19:3–12).

The core of Jesus' saying in Mark 10:11 (Matt 19:9) is certainly authentic since it is also found in the Q tradition (Luke 16:18; Matt 5:32) and as an independent word of the Lord in the Pauline tradition (1 Cor 7:10). Perhaps Matt 5:32 represents the oldest attainable version of the logion; it reflects a typically Jewish position in which only the man "who marries" may avail himself of Deut 24:1. Also, Mark 10:9 (Matt 19:6) can plausibly be attributed to Jesus.

As presently narrated, however, the entire dispute seems to reflect the kind of controversy in which the early Palestinian church was engaged. Moreover, both the Markan and the Matthean versions of the controversy give evidence of editorial modifications by the respective evangelists. Thus it is impossible to state just how much of the extant narrative reflects the historical ministry of Jesus. It is, nonetheless, quite probable that Jesus often spoke about marriage, most likely in a confrontational situation with some of the Pharisees. The extant narratives vividly proclaim that from a Jewish and a Christian perspective, the marital union is founded upon God's creative will.

Given the multiple attestation of Jesus' teaching on divorce within the NT, there is a virtual consensus among scholars that Jesus was unequivocally opposed to divorce. His teaching was a "hard saying," even for the NT authors. In order to accommodate the saying of Jesus' to his Hellenistic, and presumably Roman readership, Mark expands Jesus' saying so as to invoke Jesus' authority as also prohibiting a wife's divorce of her husband. His modification of the Jewish patriarchal tradition is also apparent in his addition of "against her" in Mark 10:11.

Matthew's redactional addition, "except for unchastity" (Matt 19:9; cf. Matt 5:32), is an obvious accommodation to his Hellenistic Jewish audience. The awkward phrasing of the exception in the original Greek shows that it relates to the interpretation of Deut 24:1. Scholars continue to debate about the meaning of the exception. The most common views are that it is a good-conscience clause directed to those who have availed themselves of the possibility provided by Deut 24:1, interpreted in a relatively strict sense, or that it reinforces the tradition of Jesus itself by exempting incestuous unions from the prohibition of divorce. Arguments for the latter opinion can be found in some parallel texts from Qumran (cf. CD 4:20–21; 11QTemple 57:17–19). In 1 Cor 7:12, Paul contrasts the traditional saying of Jesus with his own statement on the possibility of marital separation when a believer is married to an unbeliever. See also DIVORCE.

3. The Demands of Discipleship. In its present narrative context, Mark's version on the controversy over divorce is a story of the demands of discipleship relative to marriage. Mark also preserves the memory of earlier traditions which indicate that normal familial relationships are profoundly affected by discipleship and the announcement of the coming of the kingdom (Mark 10:29–30; par. Matt 19:29; Luke 18:29–30; cf. Mark 3:31–35, par.). Similar traditions are preserved in the Q material (Luke 12:53; Matt 10:35; Luke 14:26; Matt 10:37; cf. Luke 9:59–60; Matt 8:21–22; Matt 10:21), thus increasing the likelihood of their reflecting a situation in Jesus' own preaching. The early tradition does not suggest that discipleship entails the separation of husband and wife; however, Luke's editorial modification of the tradition indicates that discipleship could adversely affect even the marital relationship itself (Luke 14:26; 18:29).

4. Marriage and the Resurrection. Luke's redactional modifications of the earlier tradition may well reflect a tendency against marriage among some early Christians. The tendency was not only due to popular philosophical notions which viewed sex as evil and marriage as unwarranted, but also to common Jewish apocalyptic notions which hold that there is neither sexuality nor marriage in the age to come (cf. Rev 14:4). Such views, for which early Jewish Christians had some sympathy, are reflected in the dispute on levirate marriage (Mark 13:18–27; Matt 22:23–33; Luke 20:27–38). The controversy story reflects the polemics of the early Church, although some of its elements may go back to the historical Jesus. Not only does it contrast life in the age to come from life in the present, but it also proclaims that marriage for the sake of the name of a woman's first husband is inconsistent with a Christian view of marriage.

5. The Marriage Banquet. Early Jewish Christians capitalized on a biblical tradition (Isa 54:5; Jer 2:2; Hos 1:2–9; etc.) which found in marriage a symbolic expression of God's covenantal union with his people. Matthew, in traditions taken from Q (Matt 22:1–14) and his own sources (Matt 15:1–12) used wedding celebrations to symbolize the significance of Jesus' mission. The Johannine tradition spoke of Christ as the bridegroom (John 3:29; 2:9–10; Rev 19:7–9) and used the story of the wedding at Cana to symbolize the new relationship established by Jesus. Similar views were expressed in a much earlier period by the apostle Paul himself (2 Cor 11:2).

B. Paul

Paul's own views on marriage as it was to be lived among Christians were essentially expressed in 1 Thess 4:3–8 and 1 Cor 7:1–40. His letters nonetheless indicate that most Church leaders in his day were married (1 Cor 9:5) and there is substantial exegetical opinion to support the view that Paul himself may have been married, though he was apparently not married when he wrote 1 Corinthians (1 Cor 7:8). Certainly the marital team of Priscilla and Aquila were an important part of the gentile mission during Paul's time (Acts 18:18, 26; Rom 16:3–4; cf. 1 Cor 16:19; 2 Tim 4:19). Paul's espousal of some traditional (Jewish) views on marriage is reflected in 1 Cor 11:2–16, a passage which emphasizes that both men and women are to be properly attired when they make use of their prophetic gifts.

1. 1 Thess 4:3–8. Paul's earliest views on marriage are expressed in the earliest of his epistles. Paul shared the view of the Jewish paraenetic and polemical traditions in which sexual and marital mores distinguish God's people from the gentiles. He uses them to distinguish the behavior of the believer from the nonbeliever (v 5). Because Paul made use of a traditional *topos,* familiar to Hellenist and Jew alike, there is no real reason to think that the sexual and marital practices of the Thessalonian Christians were particularly lax. Paul was simply exhorting the neophyte Christians to a pattern of behavior consistent with their new situation. Specifically, he exhorted them to avoid immoral behavior, and positively encouraged them to marry (v 4, a verse that some authors, incorrectly, take to be an exhortation to sexual asceticism), while warning against adultery within the Christian community (v 6, a verse that some authors interpret as an exhortation to integrity in financial affairs). Paul urges that the marital relationship, lived as he encourages them to live it, be seen as a matter of their belonging to God ("their sanctification," v 3), a relationship in which the spirit is the empowering force (v 8). In typical fashion, Paul proposed fidelity to Jesus, the relationship with fellow Christians, and the fear of divine vengeance (see also Heb 13:4) as a triple motivation for the pattern of life which he had encouraged the Thessalonian neophytes to live.

2. 1 Corinthians 7. Paul's views on marriage and sexuality were reiterated and somewhat modified in 1 Corinthians 7. A letter from one of the Corinthian communities provided Paul with the occasion to offer his opinion. A popular slogan, "it is good for a man not to touch a woman," summed up the rigorously ascetical view entertained by some Corinthians. They rejected sexual intercourse and marriage. The slogan seems to reflect a rather dualistic understanding of the human being, most probably under the influence of some form of gnostic thought, and may well have represented the position of those elitists and enthusiasts whom Paul took to task in various other passages of his correspondence (cf. 1 Cor 8:1; 13:1).

Paul's response (1 Cor 7:2–5) to the Corinthians' query essentially reiterates the views which he had expounded in 1 Thess 4:3–8. In order that immorality be avoided (cf. 1 Thess 4:3), each person should have his or her own spouse (vv 3–4), a rather egalitarian view which distinguishes Paul's teaching in 1 Corinthians from the earlier expression of his teaching on marriage. This egalitarian view is consistent with Paul's exposition in the entire chapter (vv 10, 12–14, 16, 32–34).

The avoidance of immorality as a motivation for marriage (v 36) is entirely in keeping with the Jewish tradition. A novelty, however, is Paul's opinion that marriage is a charism, a special gift from God (v 7), a point of view that is in keeping with Paul's emphasis on the role of the spirit in 1 Thess 3:8. For Paul marriage is a sanctifying and salvific reality whose benefits redound not only to the believer but also to an unbelieving spouse and the children born of the marital union (vv 14–16).

In vv 5–6, Paul adds a brief thought on sexual abstinence to his response to the Corinthians' question. His thought patterns are in keeping with Jewish tradition. The schools of Shammai and Hillel disagreed among themselves as to how long a man might abstain from sexual intercourse with his wife, the former indicating two weeks as the permitted period, the later allowing only one week's abstinence (*m. Ketub.* 5:6), and then only under the condition that the wife's consent had been obtained. Among the rabbis an exception was made for the disciples of the sages who desired to study the Law, but even then the time of abstinence was limited to but thirty days. By way of concession (v 6), Paul allows for the possibility of sexual abstinence, but only under three conditions: that the abstinence be for the purpose of prayer, that there be mutual agreement, and that the period of abstinence be limited to a short time.

Despite Paul's rejection of the view that the moral good requires the avoidance of marriage and abstinence from sexual intercourse, Paul is disinclined to recommend marriage for all. Four times he expresses the view that it is preferable for Christians not to marry (vv 8, 25–35, 36–38, 39) and offers his current marital status as a desideratum. His dominant opinion, undoubtedly motivated by his eschatological views, is that one ought to remain in the state in which he or she was called: the married should remain married; the unmarried should remain unmarried (vv 12, 17, 24, 29).

Although Paul's opinion was undoubtedly formed in the light of his expectation of the proximate coming of the final times (v 26), he has also cited a pragmatic and functional thought as to why the unmarried should remain so. Just as some philosophers from within the Cynic-Stoic tradition had viewed marriage as necessarily burdensome and full of care, with the consequence, as expressed by some (e.g. Epict. *Discourses* 3.7 §19–22), that it is inappropriate for one with a divine mission, so Paul cited the normal cares and concerns of marriage as a reason why it might be preferable for the believer to remain unmarried. His stated advice was quite understandable within the Jewish and Hellenistic world in which he lived.

To which categories of Christians did Paul direct his advice that it was preferable for the unmarried to remain in an unmarried state? First of all, to the "unmarried (probably widowers) and widows" (v 8; cf. v 39). Paul had also been asked about virgins (v 25). Scholars debate as to what kind of "virgins" Paul had in mind as he responded to the inquiry. Were the virgins those who had never been married (with Paul's response then being ultimately directed to their fathers), those who were engaged (with the response then directed to the couple itself), or those involved in some sort of sexually abstinent "spiritual marriage"? Many scholars believe that having introduced the topic in v 25, Paul has first written rather generally about the marriage of the unmarried (with the practical result that the "virgins," *parthenōn,* of v 25 are simply the unmarried). Then, in v 36, Paul turned to the specific topic at hand and there, plausibly, "the virgin" is one who is engaged.

In sum, Paul's reflections are a mixture of tradition, theological reflection, popular wisdom, and pragmatism. He desires that both the married and unmarried remain in the state in which they are called and that they live accordingly.

C. The Post-Pauline Tradition

The dispute with groups influenced by various gnostic tendencies seems to have largely shaped the formulation of late first-century Christian views on marriage, particularly those that fall under the influence of the Pauline tradition. These views are most explicitly expressed in the household codes, whose presence is a characteristic feature of post-Pauline epistolary paraenesis.

1. Household Codes. The oldest Christian use of this motif appears to be in Col 3:18–4:1. Strikingly, the first pair of exhortations is addressed to wives and husbands. Wives are urged to be subject to their husbands, and husbands urged to love their wives. This paired exhortation introduces a series of two other relationships in which the socially inferior are exhorted to be obedient to the socially superior, while the socially superior are exhorted to be responsible toward those who are socially inferior. The exhortation addressed to wives (v 18) demands their obedience, but the middle voice of the Greek verb *(hupotassesthe)* appears to invite their voluntary submission while the imperative used in vv 20, 22 demands absolute obedience. While the use of the household code reflects the socially acceptable morality of the times, its insertion in a Christian "epistle" reflects the view that concrete social relationships are affected by one's relationship to the Lord.

The author of Ephesians has reformulated and considerably expanded (Eph 4:21–5:9) the paradigm which he found in Colossians. Significantly, he has provided the entire topos with a pertinent title, "Be subject to one another out of a fear of the Lord" (v 21). His reflections on the marital relationship continue to maintain a dominant patriarchal point of view, even to the point of apparently citing a supportive proverb (v 28b). In keeping with Jewish usage, wherein reflection on the household codes was enhanced by scriptural citations (the philosophical ethicists cited the ethical masters), the writer cites Gen 2:24 as the scriptural ground for marriage. While reflecting a contemporary view of how the marital relationship fits in with an ordered society, the writer uses marriage (both the relationship [vv 22–25, 29–32] and the wedding [vv 26–27]) as a metaphor for the relationship between Christ and the Church.

1 Peter also belongs to the body of post-Pauline epistolary literature. Its household code (1 Pet 3:1–7) continued the common Greco-Roman demand that wives be submissive to their husbands, but adds to it the injunction that husbands should live considerately with their wives. The exhortation which it addresses to wives is particularly significant in that it has an apologetic function insofar as Christians in an alien land were expected to live in such a way as to impress the gentiles by their socially acceptable conduct (1 Pet 2:11). Moreover, 1 Pet 3:17 provides additional motivation for marital submissiveness: there are biblical models to be followed (vv 5–6); the behavior of wives was also expected to lead to the conversion of their unbelieving husbands. When husbands were believers, their marital union could be considered as a union in the gift of life.

2. The Pastoral Epistles. While the household codes represent a Christian appropriation of dominant social standards, the Pastoral Epistles speak somewhat otherwise of marriage. Both overseers and servants are expected to be men of one wife (1 Tim 3:2, 12). The meaning of the expectation is uncertain. Are overseers and deacons expected to be chaste within marriage, monogamously married (i.e., one wife at a time), or married but once in their lifetimes? In context, the phrase "of one wife" expresses not only a moral qualification expected to be realized in the lives of Church leaders; it also expresses a necessary condition for their establishment of a personal household whose conduct provided an experience of household management for those called to management of a household church. Moreover, it espouses a view of marriage contrary to that held by those under the influence of Gnosticism, who avoided marriage and sexual relationships (1 Tim 4:3). To a large extent the anti-gnostic orientation of the Pastorals has also influenced the formulation of 1 Tim 2:15, on the relationship among marriage, salvation, and childbearing. Women are not to avoid marriage because of some sort of religious enthusiasm. For the pastor, marriage has its place in the real world in which Christians are called to live (1 Tim 5:14; Titus 2:4).

Bibliography

Balch, D. L. 1981. *Let Wives Be Submissive: The Domestic Code in 1 Peter.* SBLMS 26. Chico, CA.

———. 1983. 1 Cor 7:32–35 and Stoic Debates about Marriage, Anxiety, and Distraction. *JBL* 102: 429–39.

Baltensweiler, H. 1967. *Die Ehe im Neuen Testament: Exegetische Untersuchungen über Ehe, Ehelosigkeit und Ehescheidung.* ATANT 52. Zurich.

Collins, R. F. 1986. *Christian Morality: Biblical Foundations.* Notre Dame.

Descamps, A. 1978–80. Les textes évangeliques sur le mariage. Pp. 510–83 in *Jesus et l'Eglise: Etudes d'exégèse et de théologie.* BETL 77. Louvain.

Greeven, H. 1968–69. Ehe nach dem Neuen Testament. *NTS* 15: 365–88.

Miletic, S. F. 1988. *"One Flesh:" Eph. 5.22–24, 5.31: Marriage and the New Creation.* AnBib 115. Rome.

Sampley, J. P. 1971. *"And the Two Shall Become One Flesh": A Study of Traditions in Ephesians 5:21–33.* SNTSMS 16. Cambridge.

Verner, D. C. 1983. *The Household of God: The Social World of the Pastoral Epistles.* SBLDS 71. Chico, CA.

Yarbrough, O. L. 1985. *Not Like the Gentiles: Marriage Rules in the Letters of Paul.* SBLDS 80. Atlanta.

RAYMOND F. COLLINS

MARRIAGE, SACRED.

See SACRED MARRIAGE.

MARSANES

(NHC X,*1*). The gnostic tractate contained in Nag Hammadi Codex X. The codex, inscribed in the Lycopolitan (Sub-Akhmimic) dialect of Coptic, is poorly preserved, and considerably less than half of its text is recoverable. It is not absolutely certain that *Marsanes* was the only tractate in Codex X, but the extant material at the beginning and the end is coherent enough for that to be assumed. The subscript title is partially preserved on a small fragment of the last inscribed page (68).

"Marsanes" is the name of a gnostic prophet known from two other sources: the untitled text from the Bruce

Codex and Epiphanius' account of the "Archontic" gnostics (*Haer.* 40.7.6). According to these external testimonia Marsanes was a visionary who experienced an ascent into the heavens. An ascent experience and heavenly revelations are also features of the tractate *Marsanes.* In terms of literary genre, *Marsanes* is an "apocalypse" in which the author speaks in the first person to a group of initiates. The author is either someone named Marsanes, or, more likely, one who writes in the name of a prophet by that name. ("Marsanes" is probably a Syrian name; *mar* means "master" in Syriac.)

The first ten pages are relatively intact, and contain material relating to a gnostic ascent experience, or perhaps an ascent ritual. It includes a discussion of various levels of reality, symbolically referred to as "seals," ranging from the "worldly" and "material" (2,16–21) to the realms of the invisible "Three-Powered One," the "nonbeing Spirit," and the "unknown Silent One" (4,12–23).

Enough material is preserved in the middle of the codex to indicate that it contains speculations on the mystical meaning of the letters of the alphabet, and their relation both to the human soul and to the names of the gods and angels of the heavenly spheres.

The very fragmentary pages at the end contain material dealing with visionary experiences and a baptismal ritual. The tractate concludes with a word of encouragement to "those who will know him" (68,17, probably referring to the supreme Father mentioned at the beginning, 1,11–25).

Marsanes, a non-Christian gnostic text, belongs to those tractates whose features reflect a common "Sethian gnostic" system. The name "Seth" does not appear in the extant portion of the text, but it is possible that "Marsanes" is here considered an "avatar" of Seth, like "Zostrianos" in the tractate that bears his name (Pearson 1981a: 494–98). *Marsanes,* also like *Zostrianos,* is one of the tractates in the Nag Hammadi corpus that have been profoundly influenced by Platonist philosophy. The others are *The Three Steles of Seth* and *Allogenes. Allogenes* and *Zostrianos* were read in Plotinus' school in Rome, and it is possible that *Marsanes* was one of the "other," unnamed "apocalypses" referred to in Porphyry's account (Porp. *Vit. Plot.* 16).

The kind of Platonism reflected in *Marsanes* is one that coheres well, both in terms of its metaphysics and its ritual references, to that of the Syrian Neoplatonist philosopher, Iamblichus of Chalcis (ca. 250–325 C.E.). For *Marsanes,* as for Iamblichus, matter is not evil per se, and is even capable of salvation (5,14–26). The ritual material in *Marsanes* is comparable to "theurgy" as discussed by Iamblichus in his famous treatise, *On the Mysteries of Egypt* (Pearson fc.). The original Greek version of *Marsanes* was probably written sometime in the 3d century, perhaps in Syria.

Bibliography

Pearson, B. A. 1978. The Tractate Marsanes (NHC X) and the Platonic Tradition. Pp. 373–84 in *Gnosis,* ed. B. Aland. Göttingen.

———. 1981a. The Figure of Seth in Gnostic Literature. Pp. 472–504 in *The Rediscovery of Gnosticism.* Vol. 2 of *Sethian Gnosticism,* ed. B. Layton. SHR (Supplements to *Numen*) 41. Leiden.

———. 1981b. NHC X,*1: Marsanes,* introduction, transcription, translation, and notes. Pp. 229–352 in *Nag Hammadi Codices IX and X,* ed. B. A. Pearson. The Coptic Gnostic Library; NHS 15. Leiden.

———. 1984. Gnosticism as Platonism: With Special Reference to Marsanes (NHC 10,1). *HTR* 77: 55–72.

———. fc. Theurgic Tendencies in Gnosticism and Iamblichus' Conception of Theurgy. In *Neoplatonism and Gnosticism,* ed. R. T. Wallis and J. Bregman. Studies in Neoplatonism: Ancient and Modern, 6. Albany.

BIRGER A. PEARSON

MARSENA (PERSON) [Heb *marsĕnāʾ*]. One of the seven princes of Persia and Media who were the advisers of King Ahasuerus (Esth 1:14). See CARSHENA (PERSON). Although the presumption that the names of these counselors are Persian is reasonable (see the arguments of Millard 1977: 481–88, who counters the excessive caution of Moore [*Esther* AB, XLI–XLIV] regarding the reliability of the MT spellings), no name equivalent to this has thus far been found in the extant extrabiblical literature nor has a generally acceptable Persian etymology been suggested. The ending *-naʾ,* however, could well exhibit the same patrynomic suffix *-ina* that has been postulated for the name "Carshena," another of the seven advisers (Millard 1977: 485). For attempted etymologies see Paton *Esther* ICC, 68 and Gehman 1924: 324.

Bibliography

Gehman, H. S. 1924. Notes on the Persian Words in the Book of Esther. *JBL* 43: 321–28.

Millard, A. R. 1977. The Persian Names in Esther and the Reliability of the Hebrew Text. *JBL* 96: 481–88.

FREDERIC W. BUSH

MARSH. See GEOGRAPHY AND THE BIBLE (PALESTINE).

MARTHA (PERSON) [Gk *Martha*]. Martha (from the Aramaic meaning "lady" or "mistress") appears in the gospel of Luke as the sister of Mary (Luke 10:38–42). She reappears in the gospel of John as the sister of Mary and Lazarus (John 11:1–12:11). The family were inhabitants of Bethany, a town located about two miles (ca. 15 stadia; cf. John 11:18) from Jersualem. Luke does not mention that Martha had a brother named Lazarus nor that the sisters hailed from Bethany, but his placing of the story of Jesus' visit to their home immediately after the parable of the Good Samaritan which mentions the road from Jerusalem to Jericho (Luke 10:30–37, v 30) argues for a situs of their village near Jerusalem.

A. Luke

Scholars generally agree that the Lukan story has its basis in historical tradition. Martha was apparently the elder of the two sisters and the householder, since it was she who received Jesus into her house (Luke 10:38). For apparently unmarried women to have received a teacher into their home and engaged him in dialogue represents an unusual social situation in 1st-century Palestine.

A practical woman, Martha was distracted with the many

demands of hospitality during Jesus' visit and petitioned his assistance in obtaining her sister's help. Her request apparently merits a mild rebuke from Jesus (Luke 10:41–42, whose Gk text exists in several variant readings). Jesus' words do not denigrate Martha's household service, but imply that the female disciples of Jesus, as the male disciples, are first called to be hearers of the word (cf. Luke 11:27–28). Some commentators take the repeated "Martha, Martha" of v 41 as an indication that Jesus' seeming rebuke is, in fact, a call to discipleship (cf. Gen 46:2; 1 Sam 3:4; Acts 9:4; etc.).

B. John

In the Fourth Gospel, Martha and Mary, along with their brother Lazarus, are said to be loved by Jesus (John 11:5). In the canonical gospels they are the only persons so described. The Johannine story of the encounter between Jesus and the family at Bethlehem (John 11:1–12:11) is one of the longest in the NT. Scholars dispute among themselves as to the relationship between the Johannine narrative and various Lukan accounts (principally Luke 10:38–42, but also Luke 7:11–17, 36–50; 16:19–31; and 19:41–44), as well as the historical character of the Johannine story, but they stand in almost unanimous agreement in the affirmation that the Johannine characteristics of the account clearly mark it as a Johannine composition. The story has two principal parts, the story of Lazarus' resurrection (John 11:1–44), in which Martha enjoys a principal role, and the story of Jesus' anointing (John 12:1–11), where Martha's role is secondary to that of Mary.

In general the character portrayal of Martha in John 11–12 is similar to that of Luke 10:38–42, especially her initiative in dialogue and her service at table, but the central role accorded to the dialogue between Martha and Jesus in John 11:17–37 is proper to the Fourth Gospel. Martha has been inserted into the narrative by the evangelist as a mouthpiece for his own theology. The evangelist's composition of vv 20–27 and 39b–40 allows him to use Martha as a foil for Jesus' affirmation that he is the resurrection and the life (John 11:25).

Like the mother of Jesus (cf. John 2:3, 5), Martha sets the scene for Jesus' self-manifestation (John 11:21–22, 24, 39). Her belief is initially inadequate, not going beyond the future eschatology of the Bible and some contemporary Judaism (John 11:24). Later, in response to Jesus' question, "Do you believe?" Martha responds with the most fully developed confession of faith in the Fourth Gospel: "Yes, Lord, I believe that you are the Christ, the Son of God, he who is coming into the world" (John 11:27). Martha's profession is a model for the evangelist's own community. She sees in Jesus the Messiah, the Son of God, and the one sent by the Father.

That the evangelist considers Martha to be a model believer is evidenced not only in her confession of faith, but also in the fact that she is beloved by Jesus (11:5), is the recipient of a self-revelation by Jesus (11:25–26), and tells another about Jesus (11:28). Thus, despite her initial grief (11:19) and seeming incomprehension (11:39–40), she manifests the full pattern of discipleship.

C. Later Tradition

Many of the traits attributed to Martha by the evangelists correspond to those of deacons in early Church communities. Her portrait could be cited as a precedent for women deacons. An occasional feminist reading of the Lukan narrative suggests that the Lukan story, with its rebuke of Martha in 10:42, may have served to restrict women's leadership in the Church. The longer variant Greek readings of 10:42 may indicate that some Church circles found the shorter statement too radical. The short reading ("one thing is necessary") has often been used to contrast the active and contemplative lives, but this represents a use of the text beyond the exegetical warrants.

In the Coptic version of the early 2d century *Epistula Apostolorum,* Martha is portrayed as a witness to the risen Jesus and the first to tell the apostles about the resurrection, only to have her testimony rejected by them (see APOSTLES, EPISTLE OF). Her presence in this version is apparently in opposition to Mary Magdalene, the heroine of the gnostic tradition, whose presence in an analagous role is cited in the Ethiopian version of the manuscript.

Bibliography

Collins, R. F. 1976. The Representative Figures of the Fourth Gospel. *DRev* 94: 26–46.

Kopp, C. 1963. *The Holy Places of the Gospels.* Trans. R. Walls. New York.

Rochais, G. 1981. *Les récits de résurrection des morts dans le Nouveau Testament.* SNTSMS 40. Cambridge.

Schneiders, S. M. 1982. Women in the Fourth Gospel and the Role of Women in the Contemporary Church. *BTB* 12: 35–45.

———. 1987. Death in the Community of Eternal Life. *Int* 41: 44–56.

Schüssler Fiorenza, E. 1986. A Feminist Critical Interpretation for Liberation: Martha and Mary: Lk. 10:38–42. *Religion and Intellectual Life* 3:21–36.

Witherington, B., III. 1984. *Women in the Ministry of Jesus.* SNTSMS 51. Cambridge.

RAYMOND F. COLLINS

MARTYR, MARTYRDOM. In dealing with the phenomenon of martyrdom in the ancient Western world one immediately comes up against a complex of definitional problems (see also SUICIDE). Simply put, martyrdom refers to the act of choosing death rather than renouncing one's religious principles. Death then is voluntary, but not wholly so, since some element of compulsion exists, and some noble cause (in this case a *religious* one) is at stake. Is there a difference between taking one's life directly and allowing one's life to be taken? In some of the cases cited below the traditional "martyrs" seem eager to embrace death. Often there is a way of escape, some alternative to choosing death (as in the classic case of Socrates), so the degree and kind of compulsion can vary. It is particularly difficult to sort out the distinction between deaths motivated by religious principles, and others perhaps equally noble and morally motivated, but not directly associated with formal dogma. "Suicide," a comparatively recent word in English (Daube 1972), is often used to label cases of voluntary death which are viewed as less than noble, while "martyrdom" reflects a wholly positive evaluation. Yet it is clear, certainly in our ancient materials, that one person's suicide is another's martyr and vice versa. Here we enter the world of social and religious propaganda and polemic where the categories are loaded and the definitional lines are thin (Droge and Tabor 1992). Accordingly, in dealing with this topic, what is included, and perhaps more important, excluded, becomes crucial.

A. Hebrew Bible
B. Apocrypha and Pseudepigrapha
C. New Testament
D. Josephus
E. Rabbinic Materials
F. Later Christian Martyrs

A. Hebrew Bible

There are at least six cases of voluntary death recorded in the Hebrew Bible: Abimelech (Judg 9:54); Samson (Judg 16:30); Saul and his armor bearer (1 Sam 31:4–5 = 1 Chr 10:1–7); Ahithophel (2 Sam 17:23) and Zimri (1 Kgs 16:18–19). Based on the viewpoint of the authors and editors, are any of these understood as martyrs? Certainly not in the case of Abimelech. The deaths of Ahithophel and Zimri are recorded neutrally, with no evaluation either way. The death of Saul is seen as a fated punishment for his sins, and that of his armor bearer an accessory. Samson's case stands out in this regard. The account in Judg 16:31 is wholly positive. Samson's choice of death is his own, but he is supernaturally aided by Yahweh. Given his hopeless circumstances in the hands of the Philistines, his death becomes an act of self-sacrifice for the cause of Israel. This text might well be classed as a proto-martyrdom account.

The idea of choosing death as some type of a religiously motivated self-sacrifice occurs already in late portions of the Hebrew Bible. The so-called "suffering servant" texts in Second Isaiah (40–55) speak of a "servant of Yahweh" who willingly gives his life "like a lamb led to the slaughter" (53:7). He "makes himself an offering for sin" by "pouring out his soul to death" (53:10, 12). These texts became the source of much dispute and speculative interpretation among Jews and Christians (Williams 1975). Whether the author had in mind an actual or idealized individual, or the nation of Israel itself, the gripping language about choosing death captured the popular imagination (McKenzie *Second Isaiah* AB). Psalm 44, perhaps dating from the same period, appears to lament the death of those faithful to Yahweh in a time of persecution: "Nay, for thy sake we are slain all the day long, and accounted as sheep for the slaughter" (v 22).

There is a further reference to the idea of dying for religious faith in the book of Daniel, probably the latest document in the Hebrew Bible. Daniel tells of a time when a contemptible, blasphemous, gentile ruler will come to Jerusalem and profane the Temple, forcing Jews to violate the covenant (Dan 11:21, 29–32). During this time faithful Jews "shall fall by sword and flame, by captivity and plunder, for some days" in order to "refine and cleanse them" (vv 33–34). This terrible time of trouble will mark the end of the age, and lead to the resurrection of the dead and a final judgment (Dan 12:1–3).

Critical scholars are agreed that these thinly veiled references are to the Syrian successor of Alexander, Antiochus IV (Epiphanes), who in 167 B.C.E., according to Jewish legend, entered the Jerusalem Temple, instituted rites of idolatrous worship, and attempted to stamp out certain observances of Judaism. Interpretations of his motives and what actually transpired are disputed. The popular and legendary account is given in 1 and 2 Maccabees, though scholars dispute its historical accuracy (Bickerman 1937; Tcherikover 1959; Hengel 1974: 1.267–309). The author of Daniel sets his stories and visions in a much earlier time, during the 6th-century Judean captivity by the Babylonians, and the transition to their successors, the Persians. His well-known story of the three Hebrew youths, Shadrach, Meshach, and Abednego, who are thrown into a fiery furnace for their refusal to worship an image of gold, captures the essential spirit of an oft-repeated scenario (Daniel 3). They reply boldly to the Babylonian king Nebuchaddnezzar: "If it be so, our God whom we serve is able to deliver us from the burning fiery furnace; and he will deliver us out of your hand, O King. But if not, be it known to you, O king, that *we will not serve your gods or worship the golden image* which you have set up" (Dan 3:17–18). The key element here is the absolute and stubborn refusal to compromise, even if threatened with death.

In this story, written to build faith and encourage such resolution, the youths are delivered and the king himself becomes a convert to Yahweh. Yet Daniel is written to address those who had not experienced any such dramatic supernatural rescue. Is God unable or unwilling to intervene? Instead of immediate deliverance, Daniel holds out the imminence of the end of the age and the final judgment as incentive to those who so choose death. His message is clear—a heavenly reward is near, and the oppressors will soon be everlastingly punished (12:1–3). Clear and undisputed references to these ideas of final judgment, resurrection of both the righteous and wicked dead, and eternal life or everlasting punishment occur only here in the Hebrew Bible. Yet in the Hellenistic period they are found throughout our Jewish sources and become prime factors in the discussion of voluntary death. In all of the texts from this period on, beginning with Daniel, new answers are given to this old question—why do the righteous suffer and the wicked prosper? Vindication is promised, especially for those who choose to die, but only at the final judgment. Hand in hand with this expectation there is a full development in Jewish thought of notions about the afterlife, particularly the current state of these dead heroes who have offered up their lives and await vindication (Nickelsburg 1972; Collins 1974 and 1978). Also, as noted above, these terrible times come upon the people of Israel in order to "refine and cleanse" them before the end. Throughout these texts there is the notion of a faithful persecuted remnant, an "elect" group, who endure it all and will receive their reward.

B. Apocrypha and Pseudepigrapha

The *Testament of Moses,* parts of which come from this same period, also addresses this problem of the persecution of the righteous. Chaps. 8–10 appear to refer to the Antiochian "persecution." Chap. 8 describes the various tortures to be inflicted on Jews who will not give up their faith. In chap. 9 a Levite named Taxo exhorts his seven sons:

> Now, therefore, sons, heed me. If you investigate, you will surely know that never did our fathers nor their ancestors tempt God by transgressing his commandments. Yea, you will surely know that this is our strength. Here is what we shall do. We shall fast for a three-day period and on the fourth day we shall go into a cave, which is in the open country. There *let us die rather than transgress the commandments* of the lord of lords, the God of our fathers. For if we do this, and do die, our blood will be avenged before the Lord
>
> (9:4–7)

This is an extraordinary text. It seems to advocate a withdrawal from the world through fasting and retreat, ending in voluntary death of some type (perhaps through fasting?). This sacrificial death will bring about the intervention of God, and the manifestation of the kingdom described in chap. 10. Morton Smith (1971) has suggested on the basis of an earlier passage in 5:4–5 that the group behind this document, like other Jewish sectarians such as those at Qumran, rejected the sacrifices of the Jersusalem Temple as impure (1971: 120). If so, it might be that like the early Christians, these Jews saw the voluntary deaths of the righteous in sacrificial terms.

The books of the Apocrypha contain many such stories, often rivaling one another in their lurid accounts of heroism in the face of torture. 1 Maccabees reports that in the early stages of the revolt the Jewish rebels refused to fight, even if attacked, on the Sabbath day, choosing rather to die than to violate this commandment of God. They exhorted one another: "*Let us all die* in our innocence; heaven and earth testify for us that you are killing us unjustly" (1 Macc 2:37). On one occasion 1000 people, including women and children, chose to die in this manner. According to 1 Macc 2:39–41 this decision to allow oneself to be killed rather than resist on the Sabbath day was reversed by Mattathias and his men once they realized what a disaster the policy had brought about.

One of the more vivid stories in 1 Maccabees concerns one Eleazar, who fought against the Syrians under Antiochus V. The Syrians were using elephants in the battle. Eleazar, thinking that Antiochus himself was riding one particular beast, threw himself under the elephant, stabbed it from beneath, but was crushed to death when the animal fell. What might be seen as the foolish miscalculation of a would-be hero is transformed by the author into an act of salvific self-sacrifice. He comments: "So he *gave his life to save his people* and to win for himself an everlasting name" (1 Macc 6:44).

2 Maccabees, an epitome of a five-volume history by Jason of Cyrene, offers an extreme and exaggerated version of this period, roughly paralleling 1 Macc 1:10–7:50 (180–161 B.C.E.). Jason appears to be the first writer to celebrate the glorious deeds of these heroes who are willing to die for the faith. He fully accepts the developing idea of resurrection of the dead and final judgment and even endorses the notion of prayer and sacrifice for the dead (2 Macc 12:39–45).

According to this author the offenses of Antiochus were unconscionable. He dedicates the Yahweh Temple to Zeus, fills it with harlots and merchandise, and offers pigs and other abominable offerings on the altar. Jews are forbidden to circumcise their children and to practice the Torah, and were compelled to participate in the pagan sacrifices (2 Macc 6:1–7). He tells of two women who had dared to circumcise their children being paraded about the city "with their babies hung at their breasts, then hurled . . . down headlong from the wall" (2 Macc 6:10). Another group were burned alive when they gathered secretly to observe the Sabbath day (6:11). All this came about "not to destroy but to discipline our people," he declares (6:12). He recounts the dramatic story of Eleazar, an aged scribe of high position who chose the rack and death rather than eat swine's flesh (2 Macc 6:18–20). The author concludes the story noting that Eleazar's death left "an example of nobility and a memorial of courage" (v 31).

Two major themes in this account occur repeatedly in subsequent stories: the *willingness* of the individual to die, and the *nobility*, that such a death exemplifies. These are the very elements which complicate the questions of categorization and definition mentioned in the introduction above.

2 Maccabees contains an even more vivid version of the infamous story of the martyrdom of the mother and her seven sons. The "king" tries to force them one by one to eat swine flesh, and he falls into a rage as each in turn refuses. Echoing the determination of Daniel's three companions they declare, "We are ready to die rather than transgress the laws of our fathers" (2 Macc 7:2). They are subject to gruesome torture: scalping, amputation of hands, feet, and tongue, and being fried in a pan until dead. Each breathes his last with declarations of faith in the resurrection of the dead and warnings of future judgment for the torturers. The faith in justice and vindication in the afterlife (i.e., resurrection) is a dominant element of this story, and is repeated eight times.

The tales of Eleazar and the martyrdom of the seven brothers with their mother are picked up and elaborated in the 1st century book of *4 Maccabees*, which was never canonized but was treasured in the Eastern churches. The book is essentially an expansion of 2 Macc 6:12–7:42. In this later account Eleazar taunts his torturers: "I will not transgress the sacred oaths of my ancestors concerning the keeping of the law, not even if you gouge out my eyes and burn my entrails . . . get your torture wheels ready and fan the fire more vehemently!" (*4 Macc.* 5:29–32). In the case of the brothers and their mother, a new element is introduced. After denouncing his attackers the youngest brother "*flung himself* into the braziers and so ended his life" (*4 Macc.* 12:19). Similarly, his mother "when she, too was about to be seized and put to death, *she threw herself into the fire so that no one would touch her body*" (*4 Macc.* 17:1). This element of taking a hand in one's death comes up repeatedly in such stories and gives rise to obvious difficulties of interpretation and evaluation.

4 Maccabees also advocates the striking idea that these deaths bring *vicarious atonement* for the sins of the nation. The language used in this record is of particular importance. They become a "ransom for sin" and "through the blood of those devout ones and their death as an expiation" Israel is preserved (*4 Macc.* 17:21–22). They are those who "gave over their bodies in suffering for the sake of religion" and by them the nation gained peace (18:3–4; cf. 1:11).

The most gruesome story in the Apocrypha is that of Razis, an elder of Jerusalem in Maccabean times. His tale represents still another level of ambiguity in these accounts, for though under threat, he clearly takes his own life. He was denounced to Nicanor, the Syrian governor of Judea, as a strong and stubborn advocate of the Jewish faith. Nicanor sent 500 soldiers to arrest him. Razis took refuge in a tower and as the soldiers were about to break in he fell upon his own sword, "*preferring to die nobly* rather than fall into the hands of sinners and suffer outrages unworthy of his noble birth" (2 Macc 14:42). He only wounded himself and as the crowd burst through the door he ran upon the outside wall and jumped down into a courtyard below. The story ends with a vivid, indeed grisly, account of his death.

> Still alive and aflame with anger, he rose, and though his blood gushed forth and his wounds were severe he ran through the crowd; and standing upon a steep rock, with his blood now completely drained from him, he tore out his entrails, took them with both hands and hurled them at the crowd, calling upon the Lord of life and spirit to give them back to him again. Such was the manner of his death.
>
> (2 Macc 14:45–46)

C. New Testament

Seeley has related these martyrdom tales to the wider Greco-Roman concept of the "Noble Death," and shown how the NT materials build in various ways upon such an understanding (Seeley 1990: 84–112). What they lack is the kind of extended polemical defense and praise of voluntary death that one finds in these Jewish materials from Maccabean times. The early Christians simply begin with the presupposition that to die for the faith is thoroughly noble and good. The deaths of John the Baptist (Mark 6:14–29 = Matt 14:1–12; Luke 9:7–9), Stephen (Acts 7); and James (Acts 12:1–2) are all reported with this presupposition. The book of Acts reports numerous occasions when either mobs or authorities try to kill Paul (10:23–25; 14:5, 19; 17:6–10; 21:30–31; 22:22–23; 23:21) as well as Paul's own preconversion efforts to imprison and slaughter early Christian believers (8:3; 9:1). Paul confirms the essential points of Luke's account in his own letters (2 Cor 11:23–33; 1 Cor 15:9; cf. 1 Tim 1:12–15).

Of course Jesus himself is the preeminent model of the faithful martyr in the NT. He is directly called such twice in Revelation (1:5; 3:14). All four gospels stress that his death was voluntary. "No one takes it [my life] from me, but I lay it down of my own accord" declares the Jesus of the gospel of John (10:18). Mark places both the necessity of Jesus' death and his willingness on the lips of Jesus himself (Mark 8:31–33; 9:30–32; 10:33–34, 45; 14:36). Both Matthew and Luke follow Mark closely in this regard (e.g., Matt 16:21–23; Luke 9:51), while John makes the same point independently (12:27). Matthew and John place particular stress on Jesus' freedom to escape, and his willingness to die, at the time of his arrest (Matt 26:53–54; John 14:30; 18:4–8). This emphasis comes up repeatedly in various other ways in all four gospels (Droge and Tabor 1992). Paul's own understanding of Jesus' death appears to have close ties with the Maccabean materials surveyed above (Seeley 1990).

This willingness to choose death in the face of opposition is presented as a necessary and model behavior for the followers of Jesus as well (Mark 8:34–35 = Matt 16:24–25; Luke 9:23–24; John 15:18–20). Predictions that followers will be delivered up and killed, which may reflect social conditions of the post–70 C.E. period, run through all layers of the gospel materials (Mark 13:12–13 = Matt 24:9–10; Luke 21:12–17; Q Luke 12:4–5 = Matt 10:28; John 16:2).

Paul asserts not only his willingness to die, but even his preference for death over life (Phil 1:19–26). The way he poses his dilemma, and even the language he uses, reflects Greco-Roman philosophical disputes over the appropriateness of suicide (Droge 1988; Daube 1962; Palmer 1975). Such discussions are rooted in a long tradition of evaluations of the death of Socrates (Droge and Tabor 1992). How Paul actually died, whether by execution or by his own hand, or some combination of both, is unknown.

The book of Revelation refers to martyrs several times (5:9–11; 16:6; 17:6). They are singled out for special reward during the millennial reign of Christ (20:4–6). A specific individual at Pergamum, one Antipas, otherwise unknown, was apparently slain by authorities and is called "my witness [Gk *martys*] my faithful one" (3:13). Revelation also mentions the "two witnesses" or martyrs who are to appear at the very end of history, be slain, but then be resurrected from the dead after three days (11:4–13). The book of Hebrews exhorts its readers to be willing to die for the faith, like heroes of old, but the writer admits few if any have actually been faced with such choices (11:32–40; 12:3–4).

D. Josephus

Josephus is the richest source for examining the general phenomenon of voluntary death among Jews in Roman times. In his *Jewish Antiquities,* which covers Jewish history from Adam and Eve to the emperor Nero, he includes his own interpretation of the six standard examples of voluntary death in the Hebrew Bible. He also provides accounts of the Jews who chose to die around the time of the Maccabean revolt, all of which he views in a most positive way. His histories are full of a variety of other accounts of voluntary death; he reports as many as 25 separate incidents, with double accounts of several of them in the *Antiquities* and the *Jewish War.* Most of these took place during the war with Rome and more often than not he views them as heroic (Droge and Tabor 1992). He tells of his own narrow escape from a "death pact" at Jotapata while serving as commanding officer of the Galilean rebel forces during the Jewish revolt (*JW* 3.329–91). He is our main source for the infamous case of Masada, where, according to Josephus, 960 men, women, and children took their own lives rather than face Roman capture (*JW* 7.320–406). In the incidents at Jotapata and Masada he also provides us with extensive philosophical discussion of the general problem of voluntary death. Ironically, in the Jotapata situation, when his own life is at stake, he argues against suicide and counsels for surrender to the Romans.

On the other hand, in his long account of the Masada episode he presents the arguments of the Jewish leader Eleazar with some degree of sympathy. Even so, for Josephus these unfortunate victims of the revolt are still not the popular martyrs of subsequent imagination, whether ancient or modern (Ladouceur 1987).

E. Rabbinic Materials

The Mishnah, Talmud, and Midrash contain anecdotal accounts and technical discussions of the problems associated with voluntary death. The rabbis are interested in determining when, and under what conditions, one might endanger or take one's life, or allow one's life to be taken (see *Ber.* 3a, 8b; *Šabb.* 32a; *Pesaḥ.* 112a; *Taʿan.* 5b and the discussions by Goldstein 1989; Droge and Tabor 1992). The account of the death of Rabbi Hanina b. Teradion, who lived during the time of Hadrian, brings together some of the major interpretive difficulties (*b. Abod. Zar.* 18a–18b). He is taken by the Romans and burnt at the stake with a Torah scroll wrapped around him. At one point, seeking to lessen his suffering by hastening his death, his disciples cry out to him, "Open your mouth so that the fire enters into you." Haninah replies "Let Him who gave me [my soul] take it away, but *no one should injure himself.*" The text continues:

> The Executioner then said to him, "Rabbi, if I raise the flame and take away the tufts of wool from over your heart, will you cause me to enter into the life to come?" "Yes," he replied. "Then swear to me" [he urged]. He swore to him. He thereupon raised the flame and removed the tufts of wool from over his heart, and his soul departed speedily. The Executioner then jumped and *threw himself into the fire.* And a *bat-qôl* exclaimed: R. Hanina b. Teradion and the Executioner have been assigned to the world to come. When Rabbi heard it he wept and said: *One may acquire eternal life in a single hour,* another after many years.

Hanina's basic position is that one must not take a hand in even *hastening* one's death, God is the one who must take away life. Such a position might have been based on texts of the Bible (Job 1:21; 2:9–10; Eccl 3:2), or even the quotation from *ʾAbot* 4.22, "*without your will* you will die." In content it is reminiscent of the statements in Plato and Cicero that one is not to depart this life except at the bidding of the gods. And it closely echoes the argument of Josephus against suicide at Jotapata. But in this story, Hanina nonetheless agrees to have someone else, the Executioner, *act in his behalf,* immediately bringing about his death. Presumably this means he is not directly responsible. Yet *he* makes the choice, and accordingly, has an indirect part in the action. It is not clear in this story whether Hanina expects the Executioner to jump in the fire with him when he promises him eternal life for his assistance. Regardless, the act of the Executioner receives the highest approval, the voice from heaven declaring that he has obtained eternal life. If one can obtain life by a deliberate act of self-destruction, what happens to Hanina's original statement that one must not even hasten death, much less directly destroy oneself?

The text leaves all these elements in unresolved tension. The final declaration that "one may acquire eternal life in a single hour" is indeed a radical one. Here we have an outsider, a Roman official at that, who receives eternal life instantly *through voluntary death.*

F. Later Christian Martyrs

Christian accounts and discussions of martyrdom from the 2d and 3d centuries C.E. exhibit many of the same ambiguities and problems as these Rabbinic materials (Frend 1967; Fox 1986). It is seldom clear under what circumstances one is to offer up one's life, whether one can take a hand in one's own execution, and whether one should avail oneself of the opportunity of escape. The debate over martyrdom in early Christianity was extended and intense and often echoed the more general discussions about voluntary death and suicide in Greco-Roman culture (Droge and Tabor 1992). Ignatius, who died in 107 C.E., appears almost too willing to die. Like Paul, he sees his death as a means of joining Christ. "I long for the beasts that are prepared for me . . . I will force them to it . . . may I but attain to Jesus Christ" (*Ign. Rom.* 4–7). Like Razis and the Jews of Maccabean tradition, he views his death in sacrificial terms, but in this case following the model of Jesus. In the well-known *Acts of Perpetua and Felicitas,* a group of North African Christians are martyred during the reign of Septimius Severus. Perpetua, on trial, stresses her own free will in her death. She subsequently takes the hand of the young gladiator and guides it to her throat, showing that "she could not be killed unless she herself was willing" (21.8–10). This problem of "voluntary martyrdom" becomes a serious one. Eusebius preserves numerous accounts from the Great Persecution (303–312/3 C.E.) of individuals turning themselves in to be martyred or outright killing themselves (Droge and Tabor 1992). For example, he relates that a woman and her two daughters opted for "flight to the Lord" rather than be raped by their captors. They asked for privacy to relieve themselves and threw themselves into a nearby river.

Augustine, in response to the Donatist martyrs, and later in dealing with the chaos of the barbarian invasion of Rome in 410 C.E., sought to draw firm and dogmatic distinctions in his discussions of voluntary death and martyrdom. He argued that killing oneself, no matter what the circumstances, was a violation of the sixth commandment ("You shall not kill") and was, accordingly, murder (*City of God* 1. 19; see Droge and Tabor 1992 for a full discussion of the complexities of his position). Augustine's formulations dominated Western Christian thinking about all forms of voluntary death, whether understood as suicide or martyrdom, until modern times.

Bibliography

Bickerman, E. 1937. *Der Gott der Makkabaer.* Berlin.

Collins, J. J. 1974. Apocalyptic Eschatology as the Transcendence of Death. *CBQ* 36: 21–43.

———. 1978. The Root of Immortality: Death in the Context of Jewish Wisdom. HTR 71: 177–92.

Daube, D. 1962. Death as a Release in the Bible. *NovT* 5: 82–104.

———. 1972. The Linguistics of Suicide. *Philosophy and Public Affairs* 1: 387–437.

Droge, A. 1988. MORI LUCRUM: Paul and Ancient Theories of Suicide. *NovT* 30: 263–86.

Droge, A., and Tabor, J. 1992. *A Noble Death: Suicide and Martyrdom Among Greeks and Romans, Jews and Christians in the Ancient World.* New York.
Fox, R. L. 1986. *Pagans and Christians.* New York.
Frend, W. H. C. 1967. *Martyrdom and Persecution in the Early Church.* New York.
Goldstein, S. 1989. *Suicide in Rabbinic Literature.* Hoboken, NJ.
Hengel, M. 1974. *Judaism and Hellenism.* Philadelphia.
Ladouceur, D. 1987. Josephus and Masada. Pp. 95–113 in *Josephus, Judaism and Christianity,* ed. L. Feldman. Detroit.
Nickelsburg, W. E., Jr. 1972. *Resurrection, Immortality, and Eternal Life in Intertestamental Judaism.* Cambridge, MA.
Palmer, D. W. 1975. To Die Is Gain. *NovT* 17: 203–18.
Seeley, D. 1990. *The Noble Death: Graeco-Roman Martyrology and Paul's Concept of Salvation.* JSNTSup 28. Sheffield.
Smith, M. 1971. *Palestinian Parties and Politics that Shaped the Old Testament.* New York. Repr. 1987.
Tcherikover, V. 1959. *Hellenistic Civilization and the Jews.* Philadelphia.
Williams, S. 1975. *Jesus' Death as Saving Event.* HDR 2. Missoula, MT.

JAMES D. TABOR

MARY (PERSON) [Gk *Maria; Mariam*]. The name of six or seven women mentioned in the NT. The name derives from Heb *miryām.*

1. The mother of Jesus. See MARY, MOTHER OF JESUS.

2. Mary Magdalene. One of the most prominent of the Galilean women to have followed Jesus. Although none of the canonical gospels tells the story of the initial encounter between Mary Magdalene and Jesus, she appears in all four accounts, most significantly as a witness to the death, burial, and resurrection of Jesus.

a. The NT. The city from which Mary came is located at the S end of the Plain of Gennesaret, on the shore of the Sea of Galilee to the N of Tiberias. The Talmud situates a city known as "the Fish Tower" (Aram *Migdal nûnayyāʾ*) at a distance of 2000 cubits from Tiberias (*b. Pesaḥ.* 46a). The city is not mentioned by its proper name in the Bible, although a derived adjectival form *Magdalēnē* occurs in the NT (Matt 27:56, 61; 28:1; Mark 15:40, 47; 16:1, 9; Luke 8:2; 24:10; John 19:25; 20:1, 18), exclusively as a description of Mary. See MAGDALA (PLACE). Given its etymology, the city is probably to be identified with the Tarichaeae, known to Josephus (*JW* 2.21.3–4). The presence of a hippodrome in the city is an indication that its population of approximately 40,000 was predominantly gentile. Among the Jews the city enjoyed a poor reputation; later rabbis attributed the fall of the city to its licentiousness (*Midr. Lam.* 2:2).

(1) Luke. According to Luke, a Mary called Magdalene (*Maria hē kaloumenē Magdalēnē,* only in Luke 8:2) was one of a large group of women who provided for Jesus and the Twelve out of their means (Luke 8:2). The group included some women who had been healed of evil spirits and infirmities. One of these was Mary "from whom seven demons had gone out" (Luke 8:2; cf. Mark 16:9), an indication that because of her serious condition, an exorcism had been performed on her, most probably by Jesus himself. Mary was with the band of Galilean women who accompanied Jesus to Jerusalem, witnessed his crucifixion from a distance, observed the tomb with his body in position, went to the tomb with the burial spices which they had prepared, found the tomb empty, and experienced the startling appearance of two men in dazzling apparel (Luke 23:49, 55–56; 24:1–9). In the Lukan account, Mary is specifically identified as one of those who told the apostles about the Easter day events, only to have the report fall on deaf ears (Luke 24:10–11; cf. Mark 16:9–11).

(2) Mark. In the earlier, Markan narrative, the presence of Mary Magdalene at the crucifixion (Mark 15:40), the tomb (Mark 15:47), and the empty tomb (Mark 16:1) provides a link of continual witness to the death, burial, and resurrection of Jesus. In this role Mary is accompanied by Mary, the mother of James and Joses, and Salome (whose presence at the tomb is not specifically cited in 15:47), but the role of Mary is preeminent since she is always cited in the first instance. These three women are clearly identified as disciples of Jesus ("they followed him," Mark 15:41) who ministered to him. Their purpose in going to the tomb on the day after the Sabbath was to anoint Jesus' body. At the site, they discovered the open tomb and heard the paschal proclamation. Overcome with astonishment, they were afraid to tell anyone about the occurrence.

The so-called shorter ending of Mark, found in a few of the ancient versions, and some of the Greek manuscripts (but none earlier than the 7th century) corrects this image with a description of the women narrating the events to Peter and his companions.

(3) Matthew. Matthew's gospel closely follows the Markan account in identifying Mary Magdalene as one who observed the crucifixion (Matt 27:56), the burial (Matt 27:61), and the (empty) tomb which she had come out to see (Matt 28:1). Matthew, however, departs from the Markan story in citing the names and purpose of the women who accompanied Mary Magdalene. Matthew also significantly varies from Mark insofar as Matthew states that the women joyfully, albeit fearfully, ran from the empty tomb in order to tell the disciples the good news. Subsequently they encountered the risen Jesus who likewise entrusted to them the task of announcing the pascal proclamation (Matt 28:9–10). This pair of verses, which describe the women taking hold of Jesus' feet and worshiping him, is a literary doublet of the account of the appearance of the angel of the Lord.

(4) John. Mary is abruptly introduced into the Johannine narrative—similar, in many respects, to the Matthean—at John 19:25, where she is portrayed as being at the cross in the company of the mother of Jesus and Mary, the wife of Clopas. The Fourth Gospel does not portray her as an observer of the burial, but it does include a significant narrative account of Mary's presence at the empty tomb. In John 20:1–2, an unaccompanied Mary Magdalene goes to the tomb, which she finds empty, and thereupon runs to tell Peter that "they have taken the Lord out of the tomb."

Mary's solitary presence at the tomb is an example of Johannine dramatization, but the evangelist further exploits the tradition about her in an eight-verse narrative, where a scene is set at the tomb itself (John 20:11–18).

The narrative, without parallel in the Synoptic Gospels, contains the only two NT passages in which Mary Magdalene is simply called "Mary" (John 20:11, 16). Although an apologetic motif is present in the narrative insofar as Mary, representing the disciples (John 20:2, 13; cf. v 15), expresses the view that Jesus' body had been taken away by someone else, the dominant theme of the narrative is the development of Mary's faith.

Initially she had seen the empty tomb and had reacted in merely human fashion with tearful distress. Subsequently she saw Jesus, but did not understand who he was. The call of his voice allows her to recognize him but she believes him to be as he previously was, a teacher who could be physically embraced. Jesus then reveals that his resurrection implies his return to the Father. Commissioned to announce the meaning of the resurrection to the disciples, Mary makes the paschal proclamation: "I have seen the Lord." Thus Mary Magdalene typifies adequate faith in the resurrection of Jesus.

b. Other Traditions. From about the 6th century in the Western Church, but not in the Eastern, traditions developed which tended to identify Mary Magdalene with the sinful woman of Luke 7:36–50 and/or Mary of Bethany (John 11:1–12:8; Luke 10:38–42), but there is no historical evidence on which to base such identifications. Indeed, the weight of evidence of the canonical gospels would seem to militate against such identifications.

Undoubtedly the unsavory reputation of the city of Magdala contributed to the identification of Mary Magdalene and the woman of Luke 7:36–50. However, Mary Magdalene is formally introduced into the Lukan narrative at 8:2 (just two verses after 7:50), with no suggestion that she is a figure already known to the gospel's readership. Counterposed to the identification of Mary Magdalene with Mary of Bethany is the fact that Bethany is a Judean site while Magdala is a city of Galilee and Mary Magdalene is clearly portrayed as a Galilean woman in the Synoptic accounts.

Despite the unanimous witness of the fourfold gospel to Mary Magdalene's function in the resurrection narratives, she is not cited in the list of authoritative witnesses to the resurrection given by Paul in 1 Cor 15:5–6. Nonetheless, her role as an Easter figure and as the first resurrection witness is amply attested in later literature, most of it of gnostic origin.

One designedly anti-gnostic text which tells about Mary Magdalene is the 2d-century *Epistula Apostolorum.* The Ethiopic version (the role is played by Martha in the Coptic version) tells the story of Mary Magdalene, at Jesus' command, telling the disciples about the resurrection. According to the account, the disciples refused to accept both her testimony and that of a second woman. They did not come to believe until Jesus himself appeared to them.

c. Gnostic Literature. The 2d-century *Gospel of Peter,* of less than fully orthodox, but not yet fully gnostic, tendencies, specifically identifies Mary Magdalene as a "woman disciple of the Lord" who, for fear of the Jews, did not weep (as was customary) at the burial of Jesus. Determined nonetheless to weep at the sepulcher, she went to the tomb accompanied by other women. Having discovered the empty tomb and heard the paschal proclamation from a young man in shining robes, they fled the site in fear (*Gos. Pet.* 12–13).

The Coptic *Gospel of Thomas* (ca. 200 A.D.), attests to a competition between Mary Magdalene and Peter and the special relationship that bound Mary to Jesus. In the final logion (*Gos. Thom.* 114), Peter says to Jesus: "Let Mary leave us, for women are not worthy of Life." Jesus responds: "I myself shall lead her in order to make her male (a kind of androgynous reality), so that she too may become a living spirit resembling you males." In another logion, Mary (*Mariham*) is presented as asking Jesus, "Whom are your disciples like?" (*Gos. Thom.* 21).

The figure of Mary Magdalene appears in two other apocryphal gospels, preserved in fragmentary form, the 2d-century *Secret Gospel of Mark,* cited by Clement of Alexandria, and the *Gospel of Mary* (Magdalene). In the *Secret Gospel of Mark* an unnamed woman, identified as the sister of the one loved by Jesus and raised by him at Bethany, is rebuked by the disciples and, along with his mother and Salome, not received by Jesus. In the first part of the *Gospel of Mary,* Mark (Gk *Mariamme*) greets and consoles the sorrowing disciples. In the second fragment, Mary plays a dominant role. Her communication of the secret revelation made to her by the Lord, apparently in a vision (Gk *horama*) of the risen Lord, is met with unbelief by Andrew and with ridicule by Peter. She is, however, defended by a certain Levi who describes her as one made worthy by the Lord, known by him and one loved by him even more than the disciples.

The role of Mary (Coptic *Mariham*) as a questioner of Jesus is fully exploited in the early-3d-century *Pistis Sophia.* Thirty-nine of the sixty-four questions addressed to Jesus in that long text are attributed to Mary, who admits her persistence in questioning: "I will not tire of asking thee. Be not angry with me for questioning everything." Jesus replies: "Question what thou dost wish" (*Pistis Sophia* 139).

In the *Pistis Sophia* Mary is described as blessed, she whose heart is more directed to the kingdom of heaven than all her brothers, excellent, blessed beyond all women, beautiful in speech, the pleroma of all pleromas, the completion of all completions, superior to all the disciples (along with John the Virgin), and related hyperbole (*Pistis Sophia* 17, 19, 24, 34, 97, etc.). The *Pistis Sophia* also attests to Mary's role in the resurrection story (*Pistis Sophia* 138) and to the competition between Mary and Peter (*Pistis Sophia* 36).

In the *Sophia of Jesus Christ,* Mary twice appears as a questioner of Jesus, once with regard to the source of superhuman knowledge and once with regard to the disciples (NHC III,*4*). These are the only passages in the document where a woman is mentioned by name (*Mariamme* in Coptic), although the document makes reference to seven women.

In *The Dialogue of the Savior,* another Nag Hammadi text, Mary (Coptic *Mariam*) is portrayed as one of three disciples chosen to receive special teaching but she is more significant than the others, Matthew and Thomas, because "she spoke as a woman who knew the All" (NHC III, 139).

In the late-3d-century *Gospel of Philip,* Mary is called the companion of the Lord and described as one who always walked with him (*Gos. Phil.* 59, 63). She is portrayed as one whom Christ loved more than the other disciples and as one who was frequently kissed by Christ. The other disciples took umbrage at this and merited a rebuke from the Lord in the form of a parable (*Gos. Phil.* 63–64). In the 4th-century *Acts of Philip,* a woman named Mariamne appears as the sister of Philip. Her role is similar to that of Mary Magdalene in the gnostic tradition. She consoles Philip, is at the risen Christ's side when he divides the world into missionary sectors, and then accompanies Philip on his mission.

As a heroine in gnostic literature, Mary Magdalene appears as the first witness of the risen Jesus, as one particularly loved and praised by him, and as the recipient of secret revelations (many of the texts have the literary form of a dialogue with Jesus). This gnostic portrayal of Mary was apparently known to some of the Fathers, notably Hippolytus (*haer.* 5.7.1), Origen (*Cels.* 5.62.11), and Epiphanius (*Haer.* 1.2.26.41).

The developments of the portrait of Mary Magdalene depicted in gnostic literature are rooted in the tradition, attested in the canonical gospels, that the risen Jesus first appeared to Mary Magdalene and other women from Galilee. Many proponents of a revisionist version of early Christian history suggest that the role of Mary Magdalene was diminished in canonical literature because of the patriarchalism of early Church structures (Schüssler Fiorenza 1983: 50–51; 321–23; 332–33). The prominence accorded to Mary Magdalene in gnostic literature preserves and develops the earlier memory (Meyer 1985; Pagels 1979). The competition between Mary and Peter reflects the tension between heterodox Christianity and apostolic orthodoxy.

Bibliography

Bovon, F. 1984. Le privilège pascal de Marie-Madeleine. *NTS* 30: 50–62.

Collins, R. F. 1976. The Representative Figures of the Fourth Gospel. *DRev* 94: 26–46, 118–32.

Grassi, C. M., and Grassi, J. A. 1986. *Mary Magdalene and the Women in Jesus' Life.* Kansas City, MO.

Holzmeister, U. 1922. *Die Magdalenenfrage in der kirchlichen Überlieferung.* Innsbruck.

Kopp, C. 1963. *The Holy Places of the Gospels.* Trans. R. Wells. New York.

Meyer, M. W. 1985. Making Mary Male: The Categories "Male" and "Female" in the Gospel of Thomas. *NTS* 31: 554–70.

Pagels, E. 1979. *The Gnostic Gospels.* London.

Poterie, I. de la. 1984. Genèse de la foi pascale d'après Jn.20. *NTS* 30: 26–49.

Schneiders, S. M. 1982. Women in the Fourth Gospel and the Role of Women in the Contemporary Church. *BTB* 12: 35–45.

Schüssler Fiorenza, E. 1983. *In Memory of Her: A Feminist Theological Reconstruction of Christian Origins.* New York.

RAYMOND F. COLLINS

3. Mary of Bethany. Mary appears as the sister of Martha of Bethany in the gospels of Luke (Luke 10:38–42) and John (John 11:1–12:11). Luke does not identify her as having a brother named Lazarus nor as coming from Bethany, a town near Jerusalem (John 11:1, 18). The extant gospel accounts are colored by the language and theologies of the respective evangelists; nonetheless, given the remarkably similar character portrayal of Mary in both accounts, there is little reason to doubt that a single historical person lies behind both the Lukan and the Johannine narratives.

a. Luke. According to the Lukan account, "Mary sat at the Lord's feet and listened to his teaching" (Luke 10:39). Her demeanor, that is, her posture—indicated by a technical expression "to sit at the feet of" meaning "to be a disciple of"—and her listening clearly indicates that Luke considers her to be a disciple of Jesus. In the eyes of her sister, Mary is neglectful of the household responsibilities. Martha's criticism of Mary merits a mild rebuke from Jesus, who extols Mary's discipleship (Luke 10:42). In Luke's gospel Mary serves as a role model for female disciples.

b. John. In the Johannine narrative, although Mary is characteristically introduced as the one "who anointed the Lord with ointment and wiped his feet with her hair" and Lazarus is identified specifically as *her* brother (John 11:2; cf. v 32), Mary's role in the dialogue with Jesus prior to the resurrection of Lazarus is less significant than that of Martha (John 11:1–40). Mary quickly ran to Jesus (v 29) and fell at his feet (v 32), but she says only, "Lord, if you had been here, my brother would not have died" (v 32), a gentle reproach to Jesus, who had delayed his arrival (v 6). Mary's principal narrative role seems to have been to introduce the Jews, apparent sympathizers with her grief (vv 31, 33) who will later capitalize on the Lazarus incident in their plot against Jesus (John 11:45–53).

The Johannine technique of dramatization typically focuses upon one feature of the persons introduced into his narrative. In Mary's case, it is her anointing of Jesus, summarized in 11:2 and described at length in 12:1–12. Her gesture is characterized by its utter radicalness: (1) in the Jewish world it was scandalous for a woman to let down her hair in the presence of a man who was not her husband; (2) the anointing of feet was the task of slaves; and (3) the cost of the perfume (not mere oil) was extravagant (costing approximately 300 days' pay for the ordinary laborer).

Despite Judas' rejoinder, Mary's act was praised by Jesus and interpreted by him as a symbolic gesture. Since the anointing of feet was a typical funeral rite, Mary's anointing of Jesus' feet was a dramatic foreshadowing of his future burial. The evangelist does not, however, suggest that Mary had been aware of the symbolic nature of the dramatic expression of her devotion to Jesus.

The role accorded to Mary of Bethany in the gospels of John and Luke serves as a reminder of the role of female disciples in the communities of the respective evangelists. Jesus' praise of Mary makes her the only woman to be twice praised in the gospels for her devotion to Jesus (Luke 10:42; John 12:7). The mention of Jesus' love for her (John 11:5) singles her out as one of only two women (Martha is the other) cited in the canonical gospels as having been loved by Jesus.

c. Tradition. Scholars continue to study the relationship between the Johannine narrative of Jesus' anointing by Mary of Bethany and the Synoptic stories of the anointing of Jesus' head by an unnamed woman (Matt 26:6–13; Mark 14:3–9) and of the sinful woman forgiven by Jesus (Luke 7:36–50). The latter story was often later used as a link in the confusion between Mary Magdalene and Mary of Bethany, to which some Church Fathers (e.g., Augustine; Gregory the Great) and some gnostic texts (e.g., the *Secret Gospel of Mark*) attest. The majority of critical commentators refuse, however, to identify Mary of Bethany with Mary Magdalene. They consider the Johannine account (John 11:1–12:8) to be a radical reworking of ancient traditions by the author of the Fourth Gospel.

Bibliography

Collins, R. F. 1976. The Representative Figures of the Fourth Gospel. *DRev* 94: 26–46; 118–32.

Erb, P. C. 1985. The Contemplative Life as the *Unum Necessarium:* In Defense of a Traditional Reading of Luke 10:42. *Mystics Quarterly* 11: 161–64.

Feuillet, A. 1985. Le récit johannique de l'onction de Bethanie (Jn 12, 1–8). *EspVie* 95: 193–203.

Kopp, C. 1963. *The Holy Places of the Gospels.* Trans. R. Walls. New York.

Schneiders, S. M. 1982. Women in the Fourth Gospel and the Role of Women in the Contemporary Church. *BTB* 12: 35–45.

Schüssler Fiorenza, E. 1986. A Feminist Critical Interpretation for Liberation: Martha and Mary: Lk. 10:38–42. *Religion and Intellectual Life* 3: 21–36.

Witherington, B., III. 1984. *Women in the Ministry of Jesus.* SNTSMS 51. Cambridge.

Raymond F. Collins

4. The mother of James and Joses. This Mary was one of the women who followed Jesus during his Galilean ministry and who witnessed Jesus' crucifixion (Mark 15:40–41). Mark identifies her as the mother of James (the Little) and Joses (15:41), while Matthew calls her "the other Mary" (Matt 27:61), after first calling her the mother of James and Joses (Matt 27:56). Luke simply calls her the mother of James (24:10). It is difficult to know whether or not Mary the mother of James and Joses is to be identified with "Mary (the wife?) of Clopas" (see #5 below) mentioned as being at the cross in John 19:25, or even as the sister of Jesus' mother Mary. The former suggestion is probably overly harmonistic, since we are told at Mark 15:41 that there were many other female followers of Jesus present and watching his crucifixion. The latter suggestion is doubtful since it would require that two daughters in the same family be called Mary, though such a practice was not unprecedented in early Judaism.

Mary was a traveling companion of Jesus'; in fact, the comment that she "served him" probably means she provided financial support for Jesus' itinerant ministry. Mary accompanied Jesus on his last trip to Jerusalem (Mark 15:41), witnessed the burial of Jesus (Mark 15:47), and was involved with other women planning to wrap Jesus' body with spices on Easter morning (Mark 16:1). Thus, she was one of the first witnesses of the empty tomb and the angelic message about the resurrection (Mark 16:2–7 = Matt 28:8; Luke 24:9–11). Matt 28:9–10 may also suggest that she saw the risen Lord.

5. A follower or possibly a relative of Jesus mentioned by name only in John 19:25 where she is said to be "of Clopas." The Greek is elliptic and one can insert "the sister," or "the mother," or most likely "the wife" before "of Clopas." She may be the same Mary that the Synoptics identify as the mother of James and Joses, but we cannot be sure. It is possible, but not probable, that Clopas is to be identified with the Cleopas mentioned at Luke 24:18, since Cleopas is not a rendering of a Semitic name but a diminutive of Cleopatros, a Greek name. Thus, all we know about this Mary is that she was probably married to a man named Clopas, and she seems to have been a follower or relative of Jesus, since she is grouped with others who clearly fall into one or the other of these categories.

6. The mother of John (Mark), depicted only in Acts 12:12–16. This is probably the John who traveled with Paul and Barnabas doing missionary work in Cyprus (Acts 13:5), and who wrote the gospel bearing the name Mark. That Mary is a widow is indicated by the reference to the house belonging to her, rather than to her husband. That she is well-to-do is substantiated by the references to many people meeting at her home, and by her home having a courtyard with a gate and gatekeeping servant.

Mary's home is portrayed as a regular place for gathering and praying suggesting this Jerusalem home as one of the earliest house churches in all Christendom. Particularly in Jerusalem, having a house church took faith and courage in view of the precarious status of Christianity in its early years. Not only does Acts 12:1–7 tell of the arrest of Christian leaders such as Peter and the execution of James by Herod Agrippa I, but both Acts and the Pauline corpus indicate that at least some fellow Jews and some Jewish authorities did not accept Christianity merely as another Jewish sect (Acts 6:8; 8:3; 9:1–2; 1 Cor 15:9; Gal 1:13–14; 1 Thess 2:14–15). It is possible that the meeting discussed in Acts 12:12–16 was attended only by women since Peter's words suggest that James and the brethren are not present to hear his parting remarks.

In Acts 12, Luke stresses the importance of Mary and her contribution to early Christianity through her hospitality and her influence on her family. She is portrayed as a notable early Christian.

Bibliography

Bishop, E. F. F. 1954–55. Mary Clopas—Joh. xix.25, *ET* 65: 382–83.

Blinzler, J. 1967. *Die Bruder und Schwestern Jesu.* Stuttgart.

Burton, H. 1881. The House of Mary. *Expositor* 2d ser. 1: 313–18.

Riddle, D. W. 1938. Early Christian Hospitality: A Factor in the Gospel Transmission. *JBL* 57: 141–54.

Witherington, B. 1984. *Women in the Ministry of Jesus.* Cambridge.

———. 1988. *Women in the Earliest Churches.* Cambridge.

Ben Witherington, III

7. A Roman Christian who received greetings from Paul in Rom 16:6. Paul had been informed that she had "worked hard" in Rome (for a discussion of this phrase, see TRYPHAENA AND TRYPHOSA). There are two possibilities for identifying Mary (see the material in *StadtrChr* 66–67, 146–47, 152–53, 296). (1) "Maria" represents the Semitic *miryām,* in which case she was a Jewish Christian. But only nineteen Roman inscriptions show Jewish women bearing the Semitic name. (2) Five times more Roman inscriptions (ca. 108) suggest that "Maria" was the Latin name of the gens *Maria* (cf. "Marius"); women were often called by the name of their gens without cognomen. Two groups carried the name of the gens *Maria:* the noble members of the famous gens and the freed(wo)men of the gens with their descendants. The second group outnumbered the first. The chances therefore are that the Christian Mary was a freedwoman of the gens *Maria* or a descendant of a freed slave of this gens. Either way, she probably had Roman citizenship: slave masters with famous gens names like "Marius/is" possessed Roman citizenship and in most cases passed it on to their slaves on the occasion of their emancipation; the freed slaves then bequeathed the citizenship and the gens name to their freeborn children. Mary was probably a gentile Christian. See NEREUS.

PETER LAMPE

MARY, BIRTH OF. Title of the apocryphal text more formally called the *Genna Marias,* also variously known as the "Genealogy of Mary" or "Descent of Mary." One of the many books no longer extant that were popular among gnostic sectarians, *The Birth of Mary* is known only from an excerpt found in Epiphanius' *Panarion* (26.12.1–4). In the section cited by Epiphanius, the motivation for the execution of the prophet Zacharias on the Temple precincts (Matt 23:35; Luke 11:51) is elucidated by the identification of the prophet with the father of John the Baptist who sees a vision of God in the Temple while performing his priestly duties (Luke 1:22). In *The Birth of Mary,* Zacharias recounts his vision in the Temple as being an appearance of the God of the Jews as a man in the form of an ass. This anti-Judaic representation of the Jewish God is not unexpected, as the notion that the supposedly formless Yahweh of the Jews in truth had the head of an ass was common in pagan anti-Jewish polemic and also complies with various gnostic portrayals of the evil creator god often identified with the God of the Hebrew Scriptures. Although little can be determined concerning the provenance of *The Birth of Mary,* it is thought to have been composed sometime during the mid-2d century C.E.

Bibliography

Berendt, A. 1895. *Studien über Zacharias-Apokryphen und Zacharias-Legenden.* Leipzig.

James, M. R. 1924. Lost Heretical Books. Pp. 19–20 in *The Apocryphal New Testament.* Oxford.

Puech, H. 1963. Gospels under the Names of Holy Women. *NTApocr* 1: 344–45.

KATHLEEN E. CORLEY

MARY, DESCENT OF. See MARY, BIRTH OF.

MARY, GOSPEL OF. The first treatise in the Berlin Codex 8502. It represents a translation into Sahidic of a Greek original. The text is in poor condition, with several pages missing from the beginning and middle of the work (pp. 1–6 and 11–14). Greek fragments representing a variant of 17:5–12 and 18:5–19:5 were found in the Oxyrhynchus papyri of the Rylands library (Ryl 463). This Greek version is not identical with the Coptic. Greek words used in the latter do not always match what is found in the existing Greek fragments. The Coptic contains Mary Magdalene's reaction to Peter's rejection of her revelation (18:1–5), which is missing in the Greek. Thus there were at least two versions of this work in antiquity. The two writings which follow it in the Berlin Codex, *Apocryphon of John* (NHC II,*1;* III,*1;* IV,*1*) and *Sophia of Jesus Christ* (NHC III,*4*) survive in additional Coptic versions in the Nag Hammadi collection. The Greek papyrus has been assigned to the early 3d century C.E. This date would suggest that *Gos. Mary* was composed sometime in the late 2d century.

What remains of *Gos. Mary* consists of the ending of two separate revelations held together by a frame story about the gathering of the apostles after Jesus' ascent to the heavens. The first revelation is a dialogue between the risen Jesus and his disciples. The second is Mary's report of a private vision and its interpretation that the Lord had granted her.

The framework draws on a motif found in a number of Christian gnostic writings like *Ap. John* and *Soph. Jes. Chr.,* where the risen Lord instructs the disciples in the secret gnostic teaching which they are to spread in the world. The opening dialogue between Jesus and the disciples apparently provided the cosmological foundation for salvation in a teaching about the natures and their roots. Whatever has a material root is subject to passion, evil, sickness, and death. The gnostic possesses a different root and is enjoined not to participate in the passions of material nature (7:1–8:10). As he departs, the Lord commissions the disciples to preach the gospel of the kingdom. This commission alludes to several NT passages (8:7–9:4; Matt 28:10; John 14:27; 20:19–21; Luke 24:36; Matt 24:4; Luke 17:21; Matt 24:23; 7:7; 4:23).

Instead of fulfilling the commission, the disciples despair over the suffering that surely awaits them. At this point, Mary reminds them of the Lord's grace and protection. She alludes to their restoration to their true gnostic identity, "he has prepared us and made us into men" (cf. *Gos. Thom.* 114; and "put on the perfect man," *Gos. Phil.* 75: 20–35). Peter requests that Mary recount a revelation that she had had from the Lord which was unknown to the apostles. What survives of that section opens with a teaching about the mind as the intermediary between the soul and the spirit which makes the vision possible (10:10–22). It continued with an account of the soul's ascent past the cosmic powers to the triumphant announcement that it has overcome the world's bondage and will obtain rest (15:1–17:9). The objections to this teaching given by Andrew and Peter (17:10–22) may reflect those raised by orthodox Christians to gnostic teaching. They are silenced by Levi as contrary to the choice of the Savior. He has made Mary worthy of the revelation (18:2–16). Similar episodes in which Mary Magdalene's gnostic insight is defended can be found in *Pistis Sophia* and *Gos. Phil.* (II 63:34–37). In *Dial. Sav.* (NHC III,*5* 139,12–13) she is one of three disciples chosen by the Lord for a private revelation of the soul's destiny. They may indicate that the importance of women teachers in some gnostic circles survived the exclusion of women from teaching roles elsewhere in early Christianity. Finally, the apostles take up the Lord's commission to preach (18:17–19:2). A similar conviction that the apostolic preaching to the world was gnostic is found in *The Letter of Peter to Philip* (NHC VIII,*2*) where revelations are embedded in a frame story that alludes to Acts.

Bibliography

MacRae, G. W., and Wilson, R. McL. 1979. The Gospel According to Mary BG, *1*:7,1–19,5. Pp. 453–71 in *Nag Hammadi Codices V,2–5 and VI with Papyrus Berolinensis 8502,1 and 4*. NHS 11. Ed. D. Parrott. Leiden.

Pasquier, A. 1983. *L'Évangile selon Marie (BG 1)*. BCNHT. Quebec.

Till, W. C., ed. 1972. *Die gnostischen Schriften des koptischen Papyrus Berolinensis 8502*. TU 60. Rev. H.-M. Schenke. Berlin.

Wilson, R. M. 1957. The New Testament in the Gnostic Gospel of Mary. *NTS* 3: 236–43.

PHEME PERKINS

MARY, GOSPEL OF THE BIRTH OF. An abridged version of the Latin pseudo-Matthean infancy gospel, also known as the "Story of the Birth of Mary," which was composed sometime during the 8th–9th centuries C.E. Written as a corrective to the then widely popular tales which elevated Mary the Mother of God as the "queen of virgins," this narrative eliminated from the story the tradition of Joseph's first marriage which had been condemned as heretical, as well as omitted other particulars of the legend that were considered risqué. Although *The Gospel of the Birth of Mary* was often included among texts falsely attributed to Jerome, it gained its wide popularity after being included in James de Voragine's *Golden Legend* (1298). See also *NTApocr* 1: 406–7.

KATHLEEN E. CORLEY

MARY, MOTHER OF JESUS. Mentioned by name only in the Synoptic Gospels and Acts, the mother of Jesus is a character of some importance in the gospel of John as well (though her name is never given). She appears by implication elsewhere in the NT also, and becomes a figure of increasing attention in the noncanonical literature of early Christianity. The witness of the Christian Scriptures is the foundation of subsequent development of Mariological tradition in theology, doctrine, and devotion.

Genuine Pauline letters provide the earliest witness to the mother of Jesus. Although her name does not appear in any Pauline epistle, there are references to Jesus' birth in which his mother is implied. Among these are pre-Pauline formulas: "though he was in the form of God . . . he emptied himself . . . coming in human likeness; and found human in appearance" (Phil 2:6–7 NAB), in a context that stresses preexistence; "who was born of the seed of David according to the flesh" (Rom 1:3), part of the *praescriptio* (1:1–7) whose intent is to contrast Jesus' fleshly (i.e., Davidic) status with his spiritual (i.e., resurrected) status. The statement by Paul in Galatians that Jesus was "born of a woman" (4:4) may not carry any reference to his actual mother, because the expression is a commonplace designation of any human being (Job 14:1; 15:14; 25:4; cf. 1 Esdr 4:15; 1QH 13:14). The analogy between Jesus and Isaac, "born according to the Spirit" (4:29), does not necessarily indicate that Paul knew a doctrine of the virginal conception of Jesus, though the matter is problematic (see Brown et al. 1978: 45–49). There is no pervasive Isaac-Jesus typology in Paul. Pauline focus on the Jesus resurrection limits interest in his earthly life.

The two-source hypothesis of the Synoptic Gospels and the theological intentionality of the Matthean and Lukan infancy narratives together indicate Mark as the earliest witness to Marian tradition. Mark 3:31–35 (= Matt 12:46–50; Luke 8:19–21) describes Jesus' relationship to Mary and his family in a context of questions and controversy: Jesus' family sets out to seize him, apparently thinking him to be "beside himself" (3:20–21); Jesus, meanwhile, has spent his time with his chosen ones (3:13–19) and the crowd (v 20). Scribes from Jerusalem claim Jesus is possessed and casts out demons by Beelzebul's power, but Jesus replies in parables (3:22–27). When the "mother and brothers" of Jesus arrive, they stand outside and request to see him; but Jesus identifies those sitting around him as "my mother and brothers," the ones who do God's will (Mark 3:31–35). Thus the Markan context sets up a sharp distinction between "outsiders," i.e., Jesus' natural family and the scribes, and "insiders," i.e., his followers. Jesus declares his preference for an eschatological family (3:33–35). Membership in Jesus' family is not to be based on the relationships of kinship that are valued in society. The Matthean and Lukan parallels omit negative portrayals of Jesus' relatives, though they retain the saying that identifies his family as the ones who hear God's word and act on it (Matt 12:48–50; Luke 8:19–21). Matthew and Luke do not exclude Jesus' mother and brothers from the eschatological family, which later includes Mary and Jesus' brothers (Acts 1:14).

After Jesus' arrival in "his native place," i.e., Nazareth (NAB), family members are mentioned in a discussion about his teaching (Mark 6:1–6a = Matt 13:53–58; Luke 4:16–30). The epithet "Son of Mary" (Mark 6:3 = Matt 13:55; Luke 4:22) implies neither a doctrine of virginal conception nor Jesus' illegitimacy; the terms "brothers" and "sisters" in the same passage denote blood relations and extended family members (Brown et al. 1978: 65–72). Jesus' saying about a prophet's honor except among relatives (Mark 6:4; Matt 13:57; Luke 4:24) designates his family as "outsiders" unable to believe. Witnesses of the crucifixion are not identified with Jesus' family (Mark 15:40 = Matt 27:56; cf. Luke 23:49).

Christology is the primary focus of the Matthean and Lukan infancy narratives, which constitute the latest stage of gospel tradition (Brown 1977: 25–38). The narratives (Matthew 1–2; Luke 1–2) retroject the proclamation of Jesus' divinity at the resurrection and during the public ministry to his conception. Their historical value is open to question, including the portraits of Mary they give.

Matthew identifies Jesus as "Christ, the Son of David, the Son of Abraham" (1:1) in an unusual genealogy (1:1–17) which includes names of four women, Tamar (v 3), Rahab, Ruth (v 5), and Uriah's wife (Bathsheba, v 6), whose irregular conjugal unions nonetheless participate in God's plan. The story of Jesus' birth (vv 18–25) strengthens Mary's association with the women and Joseph's role (Brown 1977: 71–74). The extraordinary conception of Jesus is disclosed. Mary, "betrothed to Joseph," i.e., formally vowed to him but not sharing his home, is "with child of the Holy Spirit" (v 18). Joseph's predicament about the pregnancy and his resolution "to divorce her quietly" (v 19) is reversed through an angelic dream which also confirms the initial disclosure: Mary's conception is "of the Holy Spirit," i.e., the creative agency of God (v 20). A fulfillment formula (vv 22–23) associates Isa 7:14 with Mary's conception and birth of Jesus. The literary device is not recognized by some who read Isa 7:14 as a foreshadowing of Jesus' virginal conception and birth (Brown 1977: 143–53). Joseph, "son of David," obeys the dream directive in assuming legal paternity by taking Mary into his home and naming Jesus (vv 21, 25). Emphasis on Mary's virginity before Jesus' birth (v 25) neither affirms nor denies a sexual relationship with Joseph afterward. Joseph, directed by dreams (2:13, 19) provides lodging (2:11) and protection for the child and Mary (2:13–21), who functions stereotypically (2:11, 13–14, 21–22).

In the Lukan infancy narrative (Luke 1–2) Mary is featured in two pairs of scenes concerning the annunciation of Jesus' birth (Luke 1:26–38) and the birth itself (2:1–21). Surrounding these are stories that indicate the superiority of Jesus to John the Baptist (Luke 1:5–25, 39–56, 57–66, 67–80). The story of the annunication of John the Baptist's birth (Luke 1:5–25) to an elderly couple, Zechariah and his barren wife Elizabeth (1:7), stands in contrast to the annunciation of Jesus' birth to the virgin Mary (1:26–38), betrothed to Joseph (1:27; cf. Matt 1:18). A pattern of birth announcements familiar from the OT structures the scenes. An angel appears to Zechariah and Mary (vv 11, 28); they respond fearfully (vv 12, 29). Reassuring them, the messenger reveals God's agency in births from a barren, elderly womb and a betrothed virgin, and reveals the name of each child and his destined role in salvation (vv 13–17, 30–33). In both cases, the recipients of the message question the angel's revelation (vv 18, 34). The messenger responds and offers a sign (vv 19–22, 35–38). Some critics consider Mary's question in vv 34–35 an addition interrupting the sequence of the narrative. The question is best understood as a literary device to inform the reader, not an examination of Mary's personal psychology (Brown 1977: 303–9). The reply (v 35) describing God's creativity ("Holy Spirit . . . overshadow") is figurative language, excluding a sexual implication. It does not address Mary's biological virginity. Analysis of pre-Lukan and pre-Matthean tradition about the historicity of the virginal conception of Jesus is inconclusive (Fitzmyer *Luke I–IX* AB, 337–42). Mary's role as the "favored one" (Luke 1:28), i.e., mother of Jesus (Miriam of Nazareth), is the basis for her symbolic function as the disciple who hears and responds to God's word (v 38; cf. 8:19–21, 11:27–28; Acts 1:4).

The visitation episode (1:39–56) brings Mary to assist Elizabeth (1:36) in Zechariah's home. Elizabeth praises "the mother of my Lord" (vv 42–45) to which Mary's attributed Magnificat (vv 46–55) extols God who reverses the situations of the powerful and weak (Fitzmyer *Luke I–IX* AB, 357–71)

The diptych of the births (1:57–80; 2:1–20) presents additional parallels: birth, circumcision, naming, canticle. Joseph's lineage and relationship to Mary (1:27) is delineated in the enrollment in Bethlehem, Jesus' birth, shepherds' visitation, and Temple scenes (2:1–7, 16–38, 41–52). Mary's response to the shepherds' message (vv 17–19), Simeon's prophecy (v 34), and Jesus' words in the Temple (v 49) indicate her role as the believing disciple (vv 19, 50–51; cf. 1:38, 45) when the scenes are interpreted for their literary and theological intent rather than for their value as eyewitness testimony (Brown et al. 1978: 147–62).

The Fourth Gospel introduces the mother of Jesus at the wedding at Cana (2:1–11) and at the cross (19:25–27; cf. Mark 15:40–41 [= Matt 27:55–56]; Luke 23:49). The scenes are similar. There are no proper names: "mother of Jesus" (2:1, 2, 5, 19:25–26), "woman" (2:4, 19:26), "disciples" (2:2, 11), "Beloved Disciple" (19:26–27). Speech takes place in dialogue (2:3–5) or monologue (19:26–27). The scenes are linked to each other: Mary's misunderstanding (2:3) is a foil for her final role (19:26–27) just as the disciples' initial dependence on a sign (2:3, 12) is superfluous later (19:25–27). Historically improbable, the scenes symbolize the faith of Jesus' mother, who is dependent on familial ties (2:3–5). At Cana she and Jesus' "brothers" are distinguished from the disciples (2:12; see 7:3, 5, 10; cf. Mark 3:31–35 [= Matt 12:46–50]; Luke 8:19–21); at the cross, however, she is a model disciple (with the BELOVED DISCIPLE) who belongs to Jesus' true family. The portrait parallels the Lukan image.

Revelation 12 depicts two scenes which some associate with Mary. In "heaven" a "woman" who gives birth to a "male child" encounters opposition from a "dragon" (vv 1–6). On "earth" a "woman" with her "male child" escapes a "dragon/serpent" (vv 13–17). The author uses OT imagery as well as mythological sources to create the characters. The scenes depict God's protection of the "woman" and her "offspring." The "woman" symbolizes the OT people of God as well as the NT people of God, i.e., the Church. Some argue that Mary is the "woman" giving birth to the Messiah. Others point out that early Church writers like the author of Revelation did not identify the "woman" as Mary (cf. 12:9). The birth of the "male child" is different than Jesus' birth in Matthew 2 and Luke 2 (Brown et al. 1978: 223–39).

A few Apocryphal gospels expand the infancy narratives (Matthew 1–2; Luke 1–2). The *Protevangelium of James* presents Mary's parentage (Joachim and Anna), birth, childhood, virginity, marriage to Joseph, and the birth of Jesus. Mary's Davidic lineage supersedes the legal paternity of Joseph (Matthew 1–2). Allegations about Jesus' illegitimacy are refuted by Mary's miraculous birth and virgin birth. Joseph is a widower with children (who are the "brothers of Jesus" mentioned in the canonical gospels); by this means her perpetual virginity is protected (*NTApocr* 1: 366–67). Joseph's identification also occurs in the *Gospel of Peter* (*NTApocr* 1: 179). The *Infancy Gospel of Thomas* describes Jesus' boyhood activities of performing miracles and learning with Joseph as mentor. His mother plays a major role only in an expanded version of Luke 2:41–52, where the parents search for their child (*NTApocr* 1.391–92, 398–99). In contrast, the *Gospel of the Nazaraeans* situates her during Jesus' ministry, she requests to be cleansed from sin by John's baptism (*NTApocr* 1: 146–47).

Mariological studies developed historically within the context of Christian theology, doctrine (Borresen 1983; Maron 1983; Nissiotis 1983; Pelikan 1986; Tambasco 1984: 3–12, 38–53), and devotion (Tambasco 1984: 65–72). With biblical colleagues (Flanagan 1987; Reese 1977; Schineller 1987; van den Hengel 1985), contemporary scholars consider new paradigms for Mary (Bearsley 1980); interpretations of Mary vis-à-vis God (Boff 1987; Healy 1985; Johnson 1989), Christ (Johnson 1984), Church (Carr 1985), Christian feminism (Gordon 1982; Halkes 1983; Johnson 1985; Moltmann-Wendel 1983), and ecumenical dialogue (Ben-Chorin 1983; Brown 1975; Flusser 1988; Moltmann 1983).

Bibliography

Bearsley, P. J. 1980. Mary the Perfect Disciple: A Paradigm for Mariology. *TS* 41: 461–504.

Ben-Chorin, S. 1983. A Jewish View of the Mother of Jesus. Pp. 12–16 in Küng and Moltmann 1983.

Boff, L. 1987. *The Maternal Face of God: The Feminine and Its Religious Expressions.* Trans. R. Barr and J. Diercksmeier. New York.

Borresen, K. 1983. Mary in Catholic Theology. Pp. 48–58 in Küng and Moltmann 1983.

Brown, R. E. 1975. The Meaning of Modern New Testament Studies for an Ecumenical Understanding of Mary. Pp. 84–108 in *Crises Facing the Church.* New York.

———. 1977. *The Birth of the Messiah.* Garden City, NY.

———. 1981. Mary in Scripture. Pp. 23–37 in *Menlo Papers: Mary.* Hartford, CT.

Brown, R. E.; Donfried, K. P.; Fitzmyer, J. A.; and Reumann, J., eds. 1978. *Mary in the New Testament.* Philadelphia.

Carr, A. 1985. Mary in the Mystery of the Church: Vatican Council II. Pp. 5–32 in *Mary according to Women,* ed. C. Jegen. Kansas City.

Flanagan, N. M. 1987. Mary of Nazareth: Lady for All Seasons. *Listening* 22: 170–80.

Flusser, D. 1988. Mary and Israel. Pp. 7–16 in *Mary: Images of the Mother of Jesus in Jewish and Christian Perspective.* Philadelphia.

Gordon, M. 1982. Coming to Terms with Mary: Meditations on Innocence, Grief and Glory. *Commonweal* 109: 11–14.

Halkes, C. 1983. Mary and Women. Pp. 66–73 in Küng and Moltmann 1983.

Healy, M. 1985. Mary, Sea of Wisdom: Reflection on the Femininity of God. Pp. 33–50 in *Mary according to Women,* ed. C. Jegen. Kansas City.

Hengel, J. van den. 1985. Mary: Miriam of Nazareth or the Symbol of the "Eternal Feminine." *ScEs* 37: 319–33.

Johnson, E. A. 1984. Mary and Contemporary Christology: Rahner and Schillebeeckx. *EgT* 15: 155–82.

———. 1985. The Marian Tradition and the Reality of Women. *Horizons* 12: 116–35.

———. 1989. Mary and the Female Face of God. *TS* 50: 500–26.

Küng, H., and Moltmann, J., eds. 1983. *Mary in the Churches.* Concilium 168/8. New York.

Lonsdale, D. 1984. Theological Trends: Mary and the New Testament. *Way* 24: 133–45.

Maron, G. 1983. Mary in Protestant Theology. Pp. 40–47 in Küng and Moltmann 1983.

Moltmann, J. 1983. Editorial: Can There Be an Ecumenical Mariology? Pp. xii–xv in Küng and Moltmann 1983.

Moltmann-Wendel, E. 1983. Motherhood or Friendship. Pp. 17–24 in Küng and Moltmann 1983.

Nissiotis, N. 1983. Mary in Orthodox Theology. Pp. 25–39 in Küng and Moltmann 1983.

Pelikan, J. 1986. Mary: Exemplar of the Development of Christian Doctrine. Pp. 79–91. In *Mary: Images of the Mother of Jesus in Jewish and Christian Perspective.* Philadelphia.

Reese, J. M. 1977. The Historical Images of Mary in the New Testament. *MarSt* 28: 27–44.

Schineller, P. 1987. Mary: Model of Faith and Perfect Disciple. *Emmanuel* 93: 426–37.

Tambasco, A. J. 1984. *What Are They Saying About Mary?* New York.

Mary Margaret Pazdan

MASADA (M.R. 183080). A stronghold (which is a translation of the Hebrew) situated at the E Judean desert close to the Dead Sea, some 16.5 km S of En-gedi. It is along the famous Afro-Syrian geological break, and stands as a rocky mountain, separated from the cliff to form a natural fortress. The plateau on top of this unique mountain measures ca. 800 m (N–S) by ca. 300 m (E–W). The two main, and practically the sole, sources to study Masada are Josephus and the archaeological record.

The first to recognize the special virtues of Masada were the Hasmoneans. Masada was one of the first of their series of desert fortresses. They were the first to build roads to the mountain's top and to build houses and two or three water cisterns. Contrary to the belief after Yadin's excavations that all the buildings exposed on the mountain were built by Herod, it is now clear that some were earlier.

A. The Hasmonean Site

Josephus attributes the construction of Masada to Jonathan the High Priest, but practically all scholars agree that it was Alexander Jannaeus (103–76 B.C.) who first built on the site. To Hasmonean activity belongs a group of four small palaces at the mountain's center. The largest and most distinctive is the nucleus of the Western Palace. It was built around an inner courtyard with two reception rooms, one to the S of the court with access through a portico, and the other (the "throne room") adjacent to it. This palace also included a small bathhouse with a ritual immersion pool integrated into it. The three other palaces were much smaller, but no doubt were built according to the same architectural prototype, each with two similar triclinia (buildings Nos. 11, 12, and 13).

To the same period belongs also buildings Nos. 7 and 9 (?), a small bathhouse which was abandoned during the construction of Herod's storehouses, three columbaria towers (two square ones at the W and a round one at the center), two or three large cisterns, and a swimming pool (18 × 13 m) at the S edge of the mountain. Building No. 7 probably combined administrative, living, and storage facilities. It was built around a large courtyard with one or two rows of rooms around. Building No. 9, the so-called Caserna probably built by Herod, included 9 identical dwelling units, each comprised of a large room and two small ones. It had also a few more rooms, two of which may have served as stables.

At least twice Herod visited the site prior to his reign (37–4 B.C.). On the first occasion (42 B.C.), he was sent to recapture the site from a rebel and two years later returned to rescue his family and bodyguards following a long siege by Antigonus (during which they were nearly left without water, and only a sudden rain, which filled the few cisterns, saved their lives). Following his experiences, together with his general architectural interests, Herod decided to improve all of Masada's facilities. (See plan in *EAEHL* 3: 795.)

B. Herod's Masada

Herod gave special attention to the water supply. Twelve huge cisterns were carved into the NW side of the cliff. Four cisterns (each about 4000 m^3 in capacity), were placed in a row and were fed by the occasional floods which flowed in the wadi N of the mountain. The remaining eight cisterns (3000 m^3 each), were in a higher row and received floodwaters from a second wadi to the S.

These enormous cisterns were connected with the mountain's top by a system of paths. One pathway led from the lower cisterns first to the E main gangway (the "snake pass") and through it to the top. The other path, from the upper row, connected with the cisterns at the NW corner of the plateau (into the "water gate").

The largest concentration of buildings on top of Masada was along the plateau's N edge. It consisted of the Northern Palace, the large bathhouse, the storehouses, the earlier building No. 7, and the small palace building No. 9.

The Northern Palace was one of Herod's main architectural achievements. It was built on three natural terraces; about 30 m separate the elevations between the uppermost and the lowest levels of the palace. The entrance into the palace (from a large square situated to its S) passed through the upper terrace which served as the dormitory wing. In front of this wing was a large half-rounded courtyard surrounded by open colonnades.

Access to the lower terraces was by stairways and stairwells. The central terrace was a rounded structure with a few rooms attached to the cliff. Only the foundations of the rounded structure remain, but there are good reasons to believe that there was a *tholos*-shaped hall surrounded by a colonnade on these foundations.

The lowest and best preserved terrace was the square reception hall (9 × 10 m), surrounded by colonnades and a few adjacent rooms. A small bathhouse in the Roman style was in the basement floor. Colorful, well-preserved frescoes decorated this and probably the other terraces.

A large bathhouse was exposed S of the above-mentioned square. One entered it through a peristyled courtyard—a palaestra—and it included a large entrance room *(apoditerium),* a tepid room, a cold room *(frigidarium)* built as a ritual immersion pool, and a large hot room *(caldarium),* originally covered by a barrel-vaulted ceiling. Most of the heating installation (the *hypocaust*) was still preserved in the latter room. In the other rooms many of the wall and ceiling decorations have survived, such as wall frescoes and *opus sectile* floors.

A storehouse complex surrounded the large bathhouse on three of its sides. There were 11 long (27 m) storerooms and another group of 6 shorter (20 m) storerooms (all were 4 m wide). Additional storage and administrative rooms were exposed S of the main storage block and a watchtower stood at the S edge (on Masada's highest point to guard this important area). To the W of the main storage block was building No. 7. To its N was a large courtyard, which served as the W entrance to the N area. At a later stage, Herod placed the water gate at this point. At the same time, a few more storerooms were added at the S side of the N area, along with building No. 8, a small palace located outside the S entrance to the N area. Building No. 8 was similar (although with a slightly different plan) to the four Hasmonean palaces described above.

Major additions were added during Herod's life to the Western Palace and included large service wings, a few long storerooms, and a special wing built for the palace's guards. Eventually, it became the second largest complex on top of Masada.

With the later additions, Masada was fortified with a 1400-m long casemate wall, about 6.5 m wide. The wall included about 70 rooms, some short, but some more than 30 m long. The wall included more than 30 towers. Two gates provided access through the wall: the E gate, on top of the snake path and the W one, above the path from the W (now covered by the Roman siege ramp).

The defensive infrastructure, so well implemented by the Hasmoneans, but strengthened mainly by Herod, proved its viability about 100 years later, during the first Jewish revolt against the Romans.

Bibliography

Yadin, Y. 1965. The Excavation of Masada, 1963–64. *IEJ* 15: 1–120.

———. 1966. *Masada.* New York.

EHUD NETZER

MASH (PERSON) [Heb *maš*]. The Table of Nations presents Mash as a great-grandson of Noah through Shem and Aram, the ancestor of the Aramaeans or Syrians (Gen 10:23). There is no consensus of opinion as to the identity of Mash.

The LXX reads "Mosoch" ("Meshekh"). This corresponds with that name found in much the same position in the parallel genealogy in 1 Chr 1:17 (the preceding phrase "the sons of Aram," found in Genesis, has dropped out in Chronicles). LXX could reflect an older Hebrew tradition, before the loss of the final /k/ in Gen 10:23. It could also be a harmonization with the Chronicles genealogy. Against this proposal is the existence of the name Meshekh elsewhere in the Table of Nations (Gen 10:2), where duplicate names occur only rarely, if at all.

The Samaritan Pentateuch reads the name as Massa, which is the same as one of the sons of Ishmael in Gen 25:14. In the consonantal Hebrew script this would be the same as the geographical location Mesha in Gen 10:30. This site is apparently located in South Arabia. It would therefore fit with an Ishmaelite association, but not with the geographical location of the other identifiable descendants of Aram.

Three more northerly locales are possible in light of extrabiblical sources. Hittite texts refer to a Masa in west-central Anatolia (*CAH*³ 2: 253; *CAH*³ 2: 360). Gilgamesh visited the "mountain(s) of Mashu" which were in the direction of the setting sun in relation to his home in Uruk (tablet 9.2.2, 4.40). These are possibly in Lebanon (Wenham *Genesis* WBC, 230; cf. Masy, Smith 1915:17). There is also a Mount Masius (Tur Abdin) in northern Mesopotamia (Simons *GTTOT,* 8; Wenham *Genesis* WBC, 230), an area inhabited by Arameans (Roux 1964: 232). This would fit well with the biblical context. The relationship between these three northern locales is unclear. They could be completely different places, or they could be the identical location referred to in different sources.

Bibliography

Roux, G. 1964. *Ancient Iraq.* Cleveland.

Smith, G. A. 1915. *Atlas of the Historical Geography of the Holy Land.* London.

David W. Baker

MASHAL (PLACE). See MISHAL.

MASIAH (PERSON) [Gk *Masias*]. Forefather of a family included under the heading "the sons of Solomon's servants," who returned with Zerubabbel (1 Esdr 5:34). However, this family is not included in the parallel lists in Ezra 2 and Nehemiah 7.

Bibliography

Haran, M. 1961. The Gibeonites, the Nethinim and the Sons of Solomon's Servants. *VT* 11: 159–69.

Craig D. Bowman

MASKHUTA, TELL EL- (30°33′ N; 32°06′ E). A multicomponent stratified townsite in the Wadi Tumilat region of the E Nile delta, some 16 km W of modern Ismailia. It was first excavated in 1883 by E. Naville (1903). Subsequent investigations were conducted by J. Clédat (1910; 1914), and more recently by various members of the Egyptian Antiquities Organization. Beginning in 1977, multidisciplinary stratigraphic excavations of the "Wadi Tumilat Project" (1978, 1979, 1981, 1983, 1985) were undertaken by a team directed by J. S. Holladay (1982; 1987; 1988; MacDonald 1980; Paice 1987). The excavations were complemented by surveys of the site and its immediate region in 1977–78. A systematic stratified randomized transect survey of the entire length of the Wadi Tumilat, investigating all known antiquities sites, was conducted in 1983 under the codirectorship of C. A. Redmount and J. S. Holladay (Redmount 1989; 1990), in its turn complementing a systematic aligned 25-m gridded survey of the site itself by E. B. Banning in 1981.

A. Identification
B. Archaeological Findings
  1. 2d Millennium B.C.
  2. 1st Millennium B.C.
C. General Features
  1. Ramesside Monuments
  2. Canal and Commerce
D. Significance for Biblical Studies
  1. Exodus Traditions
  2. 7th-Century Socioeconomic Factors
  3. Tell el-Maskhuta Bowls

A. Identification

We do not know the site's name during the Egyptian Second Intermediate period (below). Based upon inscriptions found at the site by Naville (1903: 5–10; 14–24) and Holladay (fc.) and upon Egyptian literary references interpreted in the light of the site's chronology (Redford *LÄ* 4: 1056, especially n. 4), it is now certain that the Egyptian name of the site established by Necho II, ca. 610 B.C., was *Per-Atum Ṯukw* (*Pr-Itm Ṯkw:* the "Estate of Atum in *Ṯkw*"), which came into biblical Hebrew as *pitōm* (English "Pithom"; Exod 1:11), in the *region* of *Ṯkw,* biblical *sukkôt* (English "Succoth"; Exod 12:37; 13:20; Num 33:5–6). In literary contexts this may variously be shortened to *Pr, Ḥwt* ("Temple"), or *Ṯkw.* It is important not to confuse this *Pr-Itm* with other instances of the title, especially those relating to the much earlier "Estate of Atum" at Heliopolis and ʿAn (the region of Turah and the Red Mountain), of which the later cult installations are derivative (Redford 1963: 403–7; *LÄ* 4: 1056, n. 4; 1057, n. 20). Thus, the *Pr-Itm* mentioned on the 22nd-Dynasty statue of Ankh-renep-nefer (time of Osorkon II, ca. 875–850 B.C.), found by Naville at Tell el-Maskhuta (1903: 14–16, frontispiece and pl. 4), relates to the cult of Atum at Heliopolis and ʿAn, and not to the then unoccupied site of Tell el-Maskhuta, the statue only being relocated to the new *Pr-Itm* at some unknown time after 610 B.C. Studies of the literary occurrences of this name indicate that as the name of an E delta townsite, *Pr-Itm* does not antedate the Saite period (Redford 1963: 404, 416; *LÄ* 4: 1055–57, especially nn. 10–15). Combined with the archaeologically documented history of occupation at the site, these conclusions have obvious implications for the interpretation of the biblical text (below).

During classical times, the site was still known by its ancient name, as seen in the Pithom Stele (Naville 1903: 18–21) and by Herodotus' *Patoumos tēn Arabiēn polis:* "the Arabian town of Patumus" (2.158). Generally, however, it was known by its Hellenized translation-name of *Hērōōn polis* (Heroonpolis, Eroopolis, Heroon, Hero, etc.), as in the LXX of Gen 46.28, *kath Hērōōn polin eis gēn Ramessē,* "near Heroopolis in the land of Ramses." Under the Romans, this was shortened to *Ēro* (Ero, Hero, etc.) (Naville 1903: 8–9; 21–24; Redford, *LÄ* 4: 1054–56, cf. n. 2).

The site is mentioned (as "Heroonpolis" and "Hero") as late as A.D. 381 in the memoirs of the pilgrim Egeria (Wilkinson 1981: 101–2). By that time the location may have shifted somewhat from the present Tell el-Maskhuta.

B. Archaeological Findings

1. 2d Millennium B.C. Excavation and survey data agree in placing the first occupation of the site in the Egyptian Second Intermediate period. More exactly, in terms of agreement between the pottery analysis and a study of the scarab evidence (personal communication, J. Weinstein), the occupation could be specified as existing from the Syro-Palestinian MB II into the MB III period, perhaps ca. 1750 to ca. 1625 B.C., though neither the dates nor the time span should be treated as absolutes.

This occupation appears to represent an architecturally and culturally sophisticated seasonal (winter through wheat harvest) outpost of the pre-Hyksos and early Hyksos Asiatic occupation of the E delta, previously known from Tell el-Yehudiyeh (Petrie 1906: 3–15) and Tell el-Dabʿa (Bietak 1981). Although Egyptian elements are present, the architecture and material culture assemblage correspond most closely with those of the major center of Tell el-Dab^{c}a, of which the village at Tell el-Maskhuta may be a local outpost. Thus, the ethnic background of the inhabitants seems to derive from the Syro-Palestinian sphere, with some indications (e.g., the very distinctive forms of the thick-ware carinated bowls) suggesting at least partial derivation from N Syria rather than S Palestine.

The complex web of relationships obtaining between these E delta sites and the greater Syro-Palestinian culture sphere may be illustrated by two thumbnail sketches of the cooking pot series, an aspect of the material culture complex closely sensitive to intergroup (ethnic?) variation. First, the earliest occupational phases are characterized by the presence of large numbers of handmade flat-bottomed cooking pots, similar to the handmade vessels forming a minor constituent of the Palestinian MB I–II pottery repertoire (e.g., Cole 1984: 64–65), but generally lacking the latter's "rope molding" decoration. Identical cooking pots characterize MB (?) "Bedouin" encampments in the Sinai (E. Oren, personal communication), and yet others, not quite so closely similar, appear to be characteristic of some modern Bedouin encampments (Redmount 1990). The "Midianite," or "Negebite," pottery of the early S Palestinian Iron Age affords yet another set of similarities. This suggests that a minority of the early population—including elements closely related to food preparation—may have derived from local Bedouin elements. A possible corollary of this inference with respect to the Palestinian MB Age has to do with the identity of the (minority) bearers of similarly handmade cooking pot traditions in the predominantly urbanized MB culture which, as at Tell el-Maskhuta, is otherwise dominated by mass-produced pottery incorporating sophisticated fast wheel-forming techniques.

Later stages of the Tell el-Maskhuta Second Intermediate period occupation were dominated by "wheel made" hole-mouth cooking pots—already present at the stage of site formation, but in very low numbers. These vessels are most closely paralleled, as a group, by the wheel-made cooking pots of Middle Bronze II Shechem (Seger 1965: 236; fig. 111:s, t; Cole 1984: 63–65; fig. 18, subforms Ch. 11, Ch. 12). This is significant in that Shechem is one of the few truly "MB II" Palestinian stratigraphic sequences yet published. Similar vessels appear in limited numbers at Megiddo and Tell Beit Mirsim, and, to complicate the picture, they also characterize the Middle Bronze I stratification at Aphek, where they are termed "kraters" in Beck's analysis (1975: 48–50; figs. 2:7–8, 4:18–19, 6:15), the term "cooking pot" being reserved for a closely similar vessel form with an upright, rather than folded-back and pasted-down, rim (e.g., Beck 1975: figs. 2:11–14, 4:20–21, etc.). The vessel, with its distinctive "hole mouth" rim form, also seems to appear in limited numbers in stratification presently dated to the late 3d millennium in N Syria (Dornemann 1979: figs. 17:27; 18:51; and 19:1), but is already out of date there by the time of the later Middle Bronze Age (Dornemann 1979: figs. 20b–23).

After a short initial phase characterized by houses with thin walls only one brick wide, the inhabitants lived in well-built mudbrick houses, stored their grain harvests in above-ground circular (probably beehive-shaped) silos, and had well-defined property lines marked by curvilinear mudbrick walls. They buried their dead within the village itself, for the most part in underground mudbrick tombs (constructed in pits and subsequently backfilled), closely paralleling the simpler sorts of tombs from Tell el-Dab^{c}a (van den Brink 1982). Warriors' tombs—those characterized by the inclusion of weapons—were marked by external ass-burials (Holladay 1982: 44; pls. 40–41), a practice also known from Tell el-Dab^{c}a (van den Brink 1982: 46–47, 74–83) and Tell el-^{c}Ajjul in S Palestine (Petrie 1931: 3–5; pls. 8–9; 1932: 5; pl. 46; 1934: 16; pls. 50, 58; Petrie, MacKay, and Murray 1952: pp. 22–34; pl. 39). Infants were variously buried in miniature mudbrick tombs, in subcourtyard jar burials, or, in one case, in a mudbrick cist secondarily inserted into an outdoor mudbrick paving. The proportional rarity of such burials (as in Palestine), however, suggests that other practices—whether at the summer home site or at Tell el-Maskhuta—may have been the norm. Except for the jar burials (one of which had a red burnished juglet as an offering, the other had nothing), all these burials were marked by the presence of personal jewelry, including gold and silver earrings and headbands, silver torques and bracelets, scarabs (some gold- or silver-mounted), bronze and silver toggle pins, and, for the "warriors' " tombs, bronze weapons, in addition to food offerings and pottery. One of the latest burials yielded a scarab of Pharaoh Sebek-Hotep IV (13th Dynasty, ca. 1740–1730 B.C.). Other burials, whether simple inhumations or in disused silos, had either no grave goods or only very modest food and drink offerings, and may have been those of (Egyptian? Bedouin?) slaves or servants. Two burials in simple rectilinear mudbrick tombs appear slightly to postdate the period of occupation. Both individuals seem to have met a violent end, one by blows to the head from a typical chisel-shaped "Asiatic" battle-ax (Holladay 1982: 44–45; pls. 43–44—on the basis of further analysis now interpreted as a gracile male), the other possibly having suffered a broken neck.

These early inhabitants used standardized brick sizes, engaged in copper or bronze smelting, manufactured pottery on site, and used the vertical loom. They hunted gazelle, bubalis (a large antelope now extinct in Egypt), various smaller animals, and a variety of wading birds and waterfowl, and kept horses, donkeys, cattle, sheep, goats, pigs, dogs, and cats. Provisionally, camels seem to be present, possibly as a hunted wild species, though this finding must be subjected to further detailed stratigraphic analysis before it can be regarded as certain. The principal cultivated plants were barley and emmer wheat, harvested with composite sickles made from flint probably imported from the Sinai. Quartzite grinders, also imported either from the E desert or the Sinai, were used and reused even after initial breakage. The settlement went through some six architectural phases prior to its apparently peaceful abandonment at some time prior to the final phase of the developed Palestinian MB II tradition. The reason for the site's existence is still unclear, but may have had to do with border control and/or regulating or assisting overland trade during the winter months.

2. 1st Millennium B.C. Following a long abandonment, settlement was renewed early in the last decade of the 7th century B.C., in conjunction with Necho II's construction of a canal from the Pelusiac branch of the Nile River to the Red Sea by way of the Wadi Tumilat (Hdt. 2.158). Inaugurated by the sacrifice of a large number of young bulls buried in rectilinear graves (four were found in one limited excavation area), the new settlement witnessed, from its inception, a major linkage to the Mediterranean trade, attested by the presence of quantities of imported trade amphorae of Phoenician and Helladic origin. It was initially unfortified, but a heavy mudbrick fortification wall, enclosing an area of roughly 4 hectares, soon was erected, probably as an aftereffect of Necho's expulsion from Asia in 605 B.C. A massive destruction soon followed. This presumably, following the correlation of the pottery indicators with the historical data, marked Nebuchadnezzar's ill-fated campaign of 601 B.C., not hitherto known to have penetrated into Egypt. Successive destructions probably mark a second poorly documented campaign of Nebuchadnezzar in 568 B.C. and the Persian conquest of 525 B.C. Four great stelae erected by Darius the Great, one very close to the site, the rest arcing down toward the Red Sea, attest to Darius' "completion" (in his terms) of the canal. A burn layer and a blocked-up stone-lined well mark the 487 B.C. revolt against the Persians. There were traces of a minor Judean presence at the site (below), similar to those already witnessed from Daphnae and Eliezer Oren's N Sinai Survey Site T.21 (Migdol? Oren 1984: 24), after the 601 B.C. destruction, but prior to the 568 B.C. destruction. The site was continuously occupied until sometime during the 4th century B.C. (Monuments of the 30th Egyptian Dynasty, ca. 380–343 B.C., may, or may not, have been original to the site, below.) It was strongly reoccupied in conjunction with Ptolemy II's renewal of the Red Sea canal. There was a cultural hiatus during the 1st century B.C., with large-scale resettlement toward the end of the 1st century A.D. This phase appears to have been abandoned after a relatively short period, although the length of occupation has not yet been fully established, and is presently controverted.

C. General Features

1. Ramesside Monuments. Contrary to Naville's conclusions, which to a large extent are based upon inscribed Ramesside monuments found at the site, there is absolutely no evidence for a New Kingdom or 19th Dynasty occupation at the site, despite widespread excavation and intensive survey. The pottery evidence, which would be decisive, is entirely lacking. Thus, the site's numerous massive monuments obviously were imported following the building of the sea-level canal, which made relative child's play of the work of moving monuments weighing tons. Among these imports, items having to do with Atum are prominent, indicating a careful selection and purposive cult-related activity on the part of the royal patron—whether native Egyptian, Persian, or Greek. If the Ramesside monuments were already in place by the first part of the 6th century B.C., this would go a long way toward explaining certain aspects of the biblical account of the Exodus events (below). By whatever reckoning, their presence in later periods naturally contributed to the climate of understanding which led Naville to the interpretations voiced in his trailblazing work (1885; 4th rev. ed. in 1903).

2. Canal and Commerce. The site's later fortunes (ca. 610 B.C.–2d/3d [?] century A.D.) seem closely to parallel the fortunes of the sea-level Red Sea canal, and it would appear that the site was a major defense and control point, emporium, and entrepôt for this canal. It probably also served, during the Persian period (and later?), as a transfer point to and from Qedarite-controlled (and later Nabatean-controlled?) caravan routes in the Sinai, S Palestine, and the Transjordan (below). Massive storehouses, first found by Naville, and attributed to the building activities of the Israelites (Exod 1:11), may now be dated—in at least three major phases—to the later 3d and 2d centuries B.C., rather than to the Egyptian 19th Dynasty (Holladay 1982: 30–32). Smaller storehouses, differently sited than the very large Ptolemaic storehouses, are witnessed from the later Persian period and the reign of Ptolemy II. This suggests, but does not demonstrate, that the site's function as an entrepôt—which was demonstrably true for the later period—may have been part of a continuing site function from the early days of the settlement in the late 7th century B.C.; however, only moderately sized domestic (?) granaries widely distributed over the area of the fortified enclosure have so far been excavated from the Saite and early Persian periods.

Other socioeconomic activities witnessed for the site include a large temple of Atum, probably part of the site's foundation (Redford, *LÄ* 4: 1055), still functioning under the Persians (below), and apparently massively renewed under Ptolemy II. The economy was based upon architecture, herding, and a variety of craft-related industrial pursuits—probably only of local importance—such as bronze working, pottery making, large-scale commercial/temple-related (?) bread making, etc. Within this context, the Tell el-Maskhuta bowls (Rabinowitz 1956; Dumbrell 1971) become more comprehensible, appearing to be Qedarite state gifts to the temple in connection with caravan-related aspects of the S Arabian/Horn of Africa trade. This inference was given further substance, considering the archaeological "invisibility" of commodities like frankincense and myrrh, by the discovery of miniature incense altars (ultimately of S Arabian inspiration), and by the presence of Himyaritic (S Arabian) silver coinage, which are associated with overland aspects of the incense trade.

Heavy Phoenician involvement, possibly amounting to a monopoly of the canal-related Mediterranean trade entering the Pelusiac branch of the Nile, is attested not only by the presence of vast numbers of Phoenician amphorae, beginning with the earliest 7th-century levels, but also by a characteristically Phoenician terra-cotta figurine ("Seated Goddess," cf. Culican 1969) found in the remains of a small limestone shrine. This suggests the resident status of ethnic Phoenicians (cf. Hdt. 2.112 with respect to Memphis). Aside from the amphorae, however, Phoenician pottery (such as that typically marking Phoenician settlements along the Levantine coast) either does not appear or is extremely rare. In contrast to Naukratis or Daphnae, no great quantity of Greek ostraca or graffiti has yet been found at Tell el-Maskhuta. A few Phoenician ostraca, perhaps better termed "jar labels," do occur, however. The majority of the labels—on both Phoenician and Greek amphorae—are in demotic. Sizable quantities of Greek amphorae, second only to the Phoenician in their numbers, indicate that whoever the primary traders, the Greek islands—variously Thasos, Chios, Samos, and (rarely) Lesbos—were not excluded from the trading circle. (Under the Ptolemies, the custom shifted, as elsewhere in the Levant, to Rhodes, Cos, and Knidos.) Cyprus seems to be represented in the loop- or basket-handled jar series, and a few store-jars seem to come from the S coast of Palestine. Greek fine wares of the 7th–5th centuries were rare, particularly in comparison to Naukratis, or even to Daphnae. During the Hellenistic through Roman periods the local pottery was surprisingly similar to that common throughout greater Syria-Palestine, presumably witnessing to the Hellenistic through Roman *koine,* although many strongly Egyptian forms, now including domestic Egyptian amphorae, some copying earlier Phoenician types, continued at least as far as the later Ptolemaic period. Egyptian and Gallo-Roman amphorae, together with a few amphorae of Italian (Brindisi) origin and Palestinian vessels from the vicinity of Gaza, characterize the Roman period. Tombs of the Persian, Hellenistic (?), and Roman periods have been excavated at the site, mostly by the Egyptian Antiquities Organization (for the Roman period, see Holladay 1982: 38–43).

D. Significance for Biblical Studies

1. Exodus Traditions. The citation of Pithom and Raamses as store cities built by the children of Israel has long been held to be an important piece of evidence both for dating the Exodus and for validating the antiquity of Israel's traditions about the Exodus (Exod 1:11). These conclusions now seem viable only if the presently secure site identification is taken to be erroneous. With the determination of the actual settlement patterns at Tell el-Maskhuta, the burden of the evidence now shifts drastically to favor the late dating of this passage, as long argued by D. B. Redford (Redford 1963: 415–18). This raises questions about the actual origin and purpose of the citation. Citing the evidence for a minor post-601/pre-568 B.C. Judean presence, inferred from the presence of a characteristically Judean lamp (in this instance, handmade) and wine decanter, Holladay (1988) has suggested that the passage is an anachronistic gloss to the developing literature of the Passover Haggadah by Judean refugees. These refugees sought sanctuary in the E delta following the murder of the Babylonian governor Gedaliah ben Ahikam in 582 B.C. (Jer 41:1–45:1). In this analysis, the factual basis for the attribution is posited to be an incorrect "archaeological inference" arising from the Judean refugees' recent acquaintance with the evidence of earlier "Asiatic" remains at the site, particularly the rich and very un-Egyptian tombs, which would have been despoiled at every opportunity. If the Ramesside monuments were already in place (above), it is easy to see how the refugees' confusion could have been complete. In this connection, we should note the considerably later interest in Passover observance on the part of other Judeans resident in Egypt shown in the "Passover Papyrus" (*ANET,* 491). From this base, it would not be a far remove to the literary resources available to the later editors of the developing pentateuchal literature.

2. 7th-Century Socioeconomic Factors. With respect to the larger forces affecting the life of Judah, it can be argued that the advent of the sea-level canal in the reign of Necho signaled the end of the domination of the overland caravan routes of the immensely lucrative spice and incense trade. Not only do ship-borne goods travel at half the expense of camel caravans, despite the unfavorable sailing regime of the N Red Sea (Necho's fleet was based upon triremes; Hdt. 2.159) they also move more expeditiously and safely, with fewer revenues being extracted for safe passage. Monopoly of this trade (or tribute extracted from its profits) seems to have been the driving force behind much of the Neo-Assyrian and Neo-Babylonian effort in the W (Holladay fc.; Ephᶜal 1982). A good case can be made that much of Judah and the S Palestinian coast's material prosperity during the late 8th–7th centuries B.C. derived from revenues coming from the carefully controlled (e.g., the chariot city of Beer-sheba Strata III–II) overland transport route which followed the Beer-sheba-Zered Depression en route to Gaza and, probably, to Ashdod (Holladay fc.). From this perspective, there can be no question about the purpose of Necho's Red Sea canal: it was intended to capture, once and for all, the bulk of the spice and incense trade with the Mediterranean world. From this perspective, Nebuchadnezzar's two campaigns against Egypt become completely explicable. For Judah's part, it now seems extremely probable that the socioeconomic and political events, hitherto quite inexplicable, precipitating Josiah's death at Necho's hand are directly related to this ongoing struggle for control of this traffic.

3. Tell el-Maskhuta Bowls. Finally, the excavations at Tell el-Maskhuta offer a much fuller view of the site—and indirectly of the SE portion of the Levant—during the Persian period than has previously been available. From this perspective there can be no question of "Arabian" hegemony, e.g., that of Geshem, King of Qedar, over the Wadi Tumilat—however construed (above; Rabinowitz 1956; Dumbrell 1971). The site is culturally and economically "Egyptian," and canal-related, throughout. That leaves Ephᶜal's carefully researched historical conclusion—"[Geshem may be regarded as] a leader of the Qedar tribal league, whose [W] influence extended from the approaches to Egypt at least as far as southern Palestine, and who may have been 'king of the Arabs,' controller of Arabian trade in southern Palestine" (1982: 212–13)—as not only the simplest and most economical, but also the most fitting, interpretation. In this connection, state gifts to the sanctuary of a major trading partner, particularly at a primary point of contact, would not only have been wholly appropriate, but expected. The hoard of thousands of Athenian tetradrachms of approximately the same date (late 5th to early 4th centuries B.C., cf. Rabinowitz 1956: 4, n. 24), probably derives from similar gifts from the Mediterranean (i.e., Phoenician, or Phoenician and Helladic) end of the traffic. Once again, this highlights the great bearing of international commerce, in particular, the spice and incense trade, upon what otherwise might have been considered purely local concerns (Neh 2:19; 6:1–2, 6).

Bibliography

Beck, P. 1975. The Pottery of the Middle Bronze Age IIA at Tel Aphek. *TA* 2: 45–85.

Bietak, M. 1981. *Avaris and Piramesse.* London.

Brink, E. C. M. van den. 1982. *Tombs and Burial Customs at Tell el-Dabᶜa.* Beiträge zur Ägyptologie 4. Vienna.

Clédat, J. 1910. Deux monuments nouveaux de Tell El-Maskhouta. *RT* 32: 40–42.
———. 1914. Notes sur l'Isthme de Suez (monuments divers). *RT* 36: 103–12.
Cole, D. P. 1984. *Shechem I.* Winona Lake, IN.
Culican, W. 1969. Dea Tyria Gravida. *AJBA* 1/2: 35–50.
Dornemann, R. H. 1979. Tell Hadidi: A Millennium of Bronze Age City Occupation. Pp. 113–51 in *Archaeological Reports from the Tobqa Dam Project—Euphrates Valley, Syria,* ed. D. N. Freedman and J. M. Lundquist. AASOR 44. Cambridge, MA.
Dumbrell, W. J. 1971. The Tell el-Maskhuta Bowls and the "Kingdom" of Qedar in the Persian Period. *BASOR* 203: 33–44.
Ephᶜal, I. 1982. *Ancient Arabs.* Jerusalem.
Holladay, J. S., Jr. 1979. The Wadi Tumilat Project—1977 and 1978 Seasons. *Qadmoniot* 12: 85–90 (in Hebrew).
———. 1982. *Cities of the Delta, Part III. Tell el-Maskhuṭa, Preliminary Report on the Wadi Tumilat Project 1978–1979.* American Research Center in Egypt Reports 6. Malibu.
———. 1987. The Wadi Tumilat Project: Tell el-Maskhuta. Canadian Mediterranean Institute *Bulletin* 7/2: 1–7.
———. 1988. A Biblical/Archaeological Whodunit. Canadian Mediterranean Institute *Bulletin* 8/2: 6–8.
———. fc. Fit for the Gods: The Legacy of the Queen of Sheba. Canadian Society for Mesopotamian Studies *Bulletin.*
MacDonald, B. 1980. The Wadi Tumilat Project, a New ASOR Research Project in Egypt: Excavations at Tell el-Maskhuṭa, 1978. *BA* 43: 49–58.
Naville, E. 1903. *Store-City of Pithom and the Route of the Exodus.* Rev. and expanded 4th ed. Egypt Exploration Fund *Memoir* for 1983–84. London.
Oren, E. 1984. Migdol: A New Fortress on the Edge of the Eastern Nile Delta. *BASOR* 256: 7–44.
Paice, P. 1987. A Preliminary Analysis of Some Elements of the Saite and Persian Period Pottery at Tell el-Maskhuta. *BES* 8: 95–107.
Petrie, W. M. F. 1906. *Hyksos and Israelite Cities.* British School of Archaeology in Egypt 12. London.
———. 1931–34. *Ancient Gaza I–IV.* British School of Egyptian Archaeology 53–56. London.
Petrie, W. M. F.; MacKay, E. J. H.; and Murray, M. A. 1952. *City of Shepherd Kings and Ancient Gaza V.* British School of Egyptian Archaeology 64. London.
Rabinowitz, I. 1956. Aramaic Inscriptions of the Fifth Century B.C.E. from a North-Arab Shrine in Egypt. *JNES* 15: 1–9.
———. 1959. Another Aramaic Record of the North-Arabian Goddess han-ʾIlat. *JNES* 18: 154–55.
Redford, D. B. 1963. Exodus I 11. *VT* 13: 401–18.
Redmount, C. A. 1989. On an Egyptian/Asiatic Frontier: An Archaeological History of the Wadi Tumilat, Text and Plates. Ph.D. diss. Chicago.
———. 1990. New versus Old: Distinguishing Modern from Ancient Pottery in Surface Contexts. Paper read to the Pottery Symposium 1990. April 30–May 1, 1990. UC-Berkeley.
Seger, J. D. 1965. Two Pottery Groups of Middle Bronze Shechem. Pp. 235–37 in G. E. Wright, *Shechem.* New York.
Wilkinson, J. 1981. *Egeria's Travels to the Holy Land.* Rev. of 1971 ed. Jerusalem.

JOHN S. HOLLADAY, JR.

MASORAH. The term "Masorah" (tradition) refers, in its widest sense, to the traditional rules governing the production of a handwritten copy of the biblical text. This applies to a codex (book-form text) with vowel and accent signs, intended for the use of scholars, or a scroll without them, intended for use in the liturgy. These rules, which in their origin were concerned only with the latter type of text, cover all aspects of the production of such a manuscript, from the preparation of the materials to its completion. In the narrower sense, in which it is usually used, the term refers to the corpus of notes in copies of the Masoretic Text which were prepared for scholarly use.

A small circle *(circellus)* above a word in such a text (or between two or more words) indicates that a marginal note provides information on that word (or group of words). The basic information is given in the vertical margin beside the line of text. The most common information is represented by the letter *lamed* representing the Aramaic word for "none," indicating that the word (usually specifically that combination of letters) does not occur elsewhere. Where a word occurs more than once, other letters, representing numbers, are used to record the number of occurrences. One example is the first word in Genesis, *brʾšyt,* which, as the letter *he* signifies, occurs five times in the Leningrad Codex. In some cases, further highly abbreviated information is added. In Gen 1:1 the note adds "Three (of the five cases occur) at the beginning of a verse." A small proportion of these notes gives other sorts of information, such as the required pronunciation (Heb *qerê*) in cases where the form written in the text (Heb *kĕtîb*) suggests a different word. See KETHIB AND QERE. Collectively, these notes placed in the vertical margins of the text are known as the *masorah parva* or "lesser Masorah" (Mp), or Heb *masorâ qĕṭannâ.*

The details of the information summarized in the Mp are given in the lists of the *masorah magna* or "greater Masorah" (Mm), or Heb *masorâ gĕdōlâ.* The word in question, followed by the information given in the Mp, is typically used as a heading, and is followed by a list of the occurrences. Thus, "*brʾšyt* (occurs) five (times), three at the beginning of a verse: Gen 1:1; Jer 26:1; 27:1; and two within a verse: Jer 28:1; 49:34." The references are given in the form of key words quoted from the verse in question. One or two words usually sufficed for the scholars who used the earliest texts; later lists tend to use more. If blank leaves are left at the end of a codex, they may be filled with Masoretic lists known as the *masorah finalis.* Such material often gives other types of information, such as lists of words which occur once with and once without the conjunction, or lists of words written defectively (Heb *ḥāsēr,* lacking an expected vowel letter).

Manuscript codices differ in the Masoretic notes they provide. Moreover, in any particular codex, neither the lists of the Mm nor the notes of the Mp are necessarily given at every occurrence of the word(s) in question. Thus, the list of occurrences of the words *brʾšyt* is only given at Gen 1:1 in the Leningrad Codex. The note of the Mp is given in three different forms, and is altogether absent at Jer 26:1. The Hebrew University Bible Project edition reproduces the Masoretic notes and lists (as far as is possible) exactly as they occur in the Aleppo Codex. In the *BHS,* the Mp of the Leningrad Codex is harmonized, so that the fullest form of the note is given at each occurrence of the word in question. The lists of the Mm are published separately by G. E. Weil (1971).

The vast majority of the lists refer to the letters of the text. Some refer to pronunciation. The earliest of these are probably the *qĕrê* notes, since these, which give consonants representing the word to be read, would be largely superfluous after the introduction of vowel signs. A few notes, presumably from the latest period of the formation of the corpus, deal specifically with vowel or accent signs. Two categories of notes relate to the understanding of the text. The *tiqqûnê hasōpĕrîm,* eighteen cases in which the scribes are said to have "corrected" expressions which might seem disrespectful to God, are treated elsewhere. See EMENDATIONS, SCRIBAL. The *sĕbîrîn* notes are similar to the *qĕrê* notes in that they present a word other than that in the written text. For example, the text of Jer 48:45 presents a difficulty, because the feminine noun *ʾš* appears as subject of the masculine verb form *yṣʾ*. The *sĕbîrîn* note presents the expected feminine verb form. This is not done, as often used to be suggested, to correct the form written in the text, but to confirm it. The term *sĕbîrîn* means something like "they suppose," that is, "(people) suppose (that the verb should appear in the feminine form) *yṣʾh* (but in fact the text is correct as written)." The language of this note, and of the Masorah generally, is Aramaic, the language of scholarship for most oriental Jews throughout the first millennium C.E.

The available evidence suggests that the notes of the Masorah were built up over a long period, but largely before the general use of vowel and accent signs. The lists probably originally circulated independently, and were only later included in codices as a convenience to scholars. The total corpus of the notes and lists is very extensive; only a selection appears in most codices. Some collections of lists, such as those known as *Okhlah we-Okhlah* and *Diqdûqê ha-Teʿāmim,* were given titles as independent treatises, but this seems to have been a relatively late phenomenon.

The main purpose of the notes of the Masorah was undoubtedly the preservation of the traditional wording and spelling of the text. Their value for this purpose is proved by the fact that the variants found in medieval manuscripts, though numerous, are few and minor compared to those found in comparable bodies of traditional literature, as the Mishnah or the LXX. Many lists would have been of use for interpretation, however, and this was probably an important secondary purpose for their compilation. Other lists contain information of value for grammatical study, and are included in early grammatical works. The viewpoint of these lists is not that of the modern scholar, however, so they are now mainly of historical interest.

Bibliography

Weil, G. E. 1971. *Massorah Gedolah.* Vol. 1.

Yeivin, I. 1980. *Introduction to the Tiberian Masorah.* SBLMasS 5. Missoula, MT.

E. J. REVELL

MASORETES. The English equivalent of *baʿalê hammasorâ,* the name for the scholars whose work it was to maintain the tradition which governed the production of copies of the biblical text (the Masoretic Text) for liturgical or scholarly use. Earlier scholars engaged in this activity were known as "scribes" *(sōpĕrîm).* The work of the scribes was the establishment and preservation of the correct form of the consonantal text. A tradition recounts that they were called *sōpĕrîm* because they "counted" the letters, words, and verses of the text. (The verb [Heb *spr*] which gives rise to the word *sōpĕrîm* means both to write and to count.) This was one of the methods of ensuring that the spelling and wording of the text did not change.

The Masoretes continued this work, and extended it to individual words, recording, in numerous lists, the number of cases in which one spelling or another was used. Such lists provided a means of reference against which innumerable details of the spelling of the text could be checked. As the general populace, speaking first Aramaic, and later Arabic, found the ancient Hebrew of the text more and more difficult to read in the traditional way, systems of vowel and accent signs were developed to assist in the preservation and teaching of the traditional pronunciation and chant. In the last stage of Masoretic activity, these signs too were reduced to a fixed tradition, in which small details of sound change were precisely noted. This feature of the writing system, which gives such trouble to beginners in biblical Hebrew, derives from the desire to represent all significant features of the reading tradition. There would be no need to represent many of these details in a system intended for ordinary purposes. The vowel and accent signs have never been included in texts used in the liturgy, but, because they are so valuable for the understanding of the text, they are generally given in texts intended for scholarly and general use.

The "scribes" and the "Masoretes" thus differed in the type of work which they did, but not in their purpose. Both worked to ensure that the biblical tradition was passed on unchanged to succeeding generations. The beginning of activity of the "Masoretic" type may perhaps be dated as early as 500 C.E. The foundations of this work can be seen in the Talmudic literature. Many interpretations of biblical verses recorded in this material are based on the same details of spelling which were the concern of the Masoretes, such as the use or nonuse of vowel letters or of the conjunctive *waw.* Passages presenting these interpretations may even include a statement of the number of times the feature occurs, as do the Masoretic notes. However, most such passages are not formulated in the style typical of the Masoretes, and occasionally the information given conflicts with the later Masoretic tradition.

The treatise known as *Masseket Soferîm,* "The Tractate of the Scribes" (now associated with the Talmud as a "minor tractate") was probably composed in the 8th century C.E. In this tractate, the material found in the earlier Talmudic literature, with some additions, is presented in typical Masoretic style. The phenomena which are of interest are enumerated and are presented in lists similar to those of later Masoretic compilations.

The list which gives the differences between the *madinḥāʾê,* or "Easterners," and the *maʿărbāʾê,* or "Westerners," may contain some of the earlier material in these later Masoretic compilations. The differences listed are minor variations in the letters of the text. The identity of the two groups of scholars referred to is uncertain, and no text which can be classified as "Eastern" or "Western" in terms of these lists is now known.

A few Masoretic notes cite an authority for a particular reading. This may be a text, cited by a name, such as "Hilleli," or merely as "corrected" *(muggâ);* none of these texts have been preserved for us. The authority cited may be a scholar, a number of whom are referred to by name. Such scholars are cited as authorities for details of the vocalization or accentuation of individual words, and so must have been active during the final stages of the work leading to the completion of the Masoretic Text.

The only one of these names about which we have any significant information is that of ben Asher. Seven generations of Masoretic scholars are recorded, from the ancestor, R. Asher *ha-Zāqen,* down to Aharon ben Asher, the most famous of the Masoretic scholars. Aharon was evidently the ben Asher of the lists of variants *(ḥillûpîm)* between ben Asher and ben Naphtali. A few of these variants are minor matters of spelling; the majority are details of vowel painting and accentuation. No known text shows one of the sets of variants in these lists with complete consistency, but the Aleppo Codex, which was supplied with vowel and accent signs by Aharon ben Asher, corresponds with the ben Asher of the lists in 94 percent of the cases. (The Leningrad Codex, the next closest, corresponds in 92 percent.) Here, then, there is a real link between the texts which we have and one of the names in the Masoretic literature.

Even here, however, there is mystery. A number of the features in which ben Naphtali systematically differs from ben Asher (as the use of long *ḥireq,* as *lîśrāʾēl,* where ben Asher uses *šewa-yod-ḥireq,* as *lĕyiśrāʾēl*) are found in manuscripts, but neither the manuscripts which show them, nor any other known texts, show a high level of correspondence with the ben Naphtali of the lists overall. The highest level found (64 percent) is found in the Cairo Codex, which, according to its colophon, was written in 896 by Mosheh, the father of Aharon ben Asher. This is interesting evidence of the way the Masoretes worked. Despite his scholarly ancestry, Aharon evidently did not maintain a family tradition, but (presumably) promulgated the form of tradition formulated by the Masoretes of Tiberias as a group. This may add some plausibility to the suggestion that the name of ben Naphtali (of whom nothing is known beyond the divergence from ben Asher recorded in these lists) came to be used for any reading in known sources which was not accepted by Aharon ben Asher.

The work of the Masoretes can be said to have been crowned by the production of the Aleppo Codex, to which the vowel and accent signs and Masoretic notes were added by Aharon ben Asher. Of all currently known texts, this was evidently the first copy of the whole Bible which had been produced complete with these details. The tradition which it represented became the standard form of the text. This was due not only to the respect in which the name of ben Asher was held. His tradition represented the work of the Masoretes of Tiberias, who were renowned for their linguistic accuracy. More than this, their tradition was believed to be the authentic tradition of the Holy Land, passed on in unbroken line from the generation of Ezra.

Individual Masoretes such as Aharon ben Asher preserved and maintained individual traditions. In the finest codices, such as the Aleppo Codex, the Masoretic notes are consistent with the text of the codex in which they are written. Since each codex differs slightly from others, the Masorah of one codex is not fully consistent with the text of another. After the time of Aharon ben Asher, it became common to supplement the Masorah of one codex with further notes drawn from others, so that the individual traditions began to be mixed. The inconsistency between Masorah and text which resulted can already be seen to a slight extent in the Leningrad Codex, as in Isa 51:16, where the text reads *wʾśym,* but the Masorah requires *wʾśm,* the reading of the Aleppo Codex. Because of this, the chief concern of the Masoretic scholar came to be the selection of the best tradition in any given case from the manuscript variants available to him, as was the case with the work of Jacob ben Ḥayyim on his edition (Vienna 1524–25). This in turn has given way, in our own day, to the attempt to trace the different strands of the earlier traditions.

Bibliography

Lipschütz, L. 1962. *Kitāb al-Khilaf:* Mishael ben Uzziel's Treatise on the Differences between ben Asher and ben Naphtali. *Textus* 2: 1–58 (in Hebrew; the text); 1964.

Yeivin, I. 1980. *Introduction to the Tiberian Masorah.* SBLMasS 5. Missoula, MT.

E. J. REVELL

MASORETIC ACCENTS. The term "accent" (Heb *ṭaʿam*) refers to the signs marked on the words of the biblical text. These accents relate the words of the text to the music to which it is chanted in the liturgy. Accent signs do not represent individual notes, but groups of notes ("motifs" or "tropes") used in a particular form of chant. For this reason, the same accentuation has the capability to relate the words to the music of several different forms of chant.

The chant presents the text meaningfully to the congregation. The musical motifs mark off words, phrases, or larger units of meaning, and in combination show the relation of these units to each other. Consequently the accent signs in the text have something of the function of punctuation. Most accent signs are marked on the stress syllable of the word. In a few cases this indication of stress position is helpful in classifying the word.

In the standard Tiberian tradition, the accents used in the books of Psalms, Job, and Proverbs (known as the "Three Books") differ from those used in the rest of the Bible (known as the "Twenty-one Books"). The general principles governing the use of both sets of accents are the same. Thus both use accents of two types: (1) disjunctive accents (DA), which mark the last word in a semantic unit of one or more words; and (2) conjunctive accents (CA), which mark the words forming a semantic unit ending at the next disjunctive. Three other signs are also used, which are not considered as accents because they do not represent musical motifs. These are (1) *maqqēp,* which joins two or more words, all of which are chanted to the motif marked by the accent on the last word; (2) *gaʿyâ* (also known as *meteg*), marked on a syllable which is not accented to show that it receives slower pronunciation than it otherwise would (or, as some see it, that it has secondary stress. Conjunctives are sometimes marked as secondary accents with a word in a similar way); (3) *pāsēq,* which marks a slight pause after a word with a conjunctive accent.

The primary accent signs are listed in Fig. MAS.01. Names in parentheses identify an alternative form of the accent in question. The accent *paštā*ʾ (DA.3.b) is always marked on the last letter of the word. Where the last vowel is not stressed, it is marked on the letter before the stressed vowel as well. Other accents which are restricted to the first or last letter of the word (as *sĕgōltā*ʾ [DA.2.a]) are also regularly repeated to mark stress position in some manuscripts, but in the Aleppo and Leningrad codices, this is done only where the stress position is of particular significance.

The accentuation is based on the division of the text into verses (Heb *pāsûq*). This division appears to have been established in Talmudic times. (But the division into chapters, and so the numbering of verses, is medieval.) The verse division does not always coincide with the earlier division into *pisqōt* so that, occasionally, a paragraph division occurs within a verse (*pisqâ bĕʾemṣāʿ pāsûq,* as 1 Sam 14:12, 19, 37).

Disjunctive Accents (DA)

(1)	
a. *sillûq*	האֽרץ
b. ʾ*atnāḥ*	אלה֑ים
(2)	
a. *sĕgōltā*ʾ *(šalšelet)*	הרקיע֒ (ויאמ֓ר ׀)
b. *zāqēp (zāqēp gādôl)*	ובה֔ו (להבד֕יל)
c. *tipḥā*ʾ	בראש֖ית
(3)	
a. *zarqā*ʾ	אלהים֮
b. *paštā*ʾ	לאור֙ (ת֨הו֙)
c. *tĕbîr*	אלה֛ים
d. *rĕbîaʿ*	והא֗רץ
(4)	
a. *gereš (geršayim)*	המ֜ים (פר֞י)
b. *pāzēr (pāzēr gādôl)*	הרמ֡שת (באמ֟ה)
c. *tĕlîšā*ʾ	֠דשא
d. *lĕgarmēh*	וכ֣לי

Conjunctive Accents (CA)

mûnāḥ	בר֣א
mĕhûppāk	ב֤ין
*mêrkā*ʾ	א֥ת
*dargā*ʾ	ו֧ירא
ʾ*azlā*ʾ	ויקר֨א
*tĕlîšā*ʾ *qĕṭannâ*	אשר֩
galgal	אלפ֪ים
*mêrkā*ʾ *kĕpûllâ*	ל֦ו
*māʾyĕlā*ʾ	וי֖צא(־נ֑ח)

Other Signs

maqqēp	על־פני
gaʿyâ	וֽיהי(־אֽור)
pāsēq	אלהים׀ (֤)

MAS.01. The accents of the Twenty-one Books.

Each verse is an independent unit of accentuation, marked at the end with the accent *sillûq* (DA.1.a). (In most texts, two dots in vertical line, or some other sign, are also used to mark the divisions between the verses.) The other accents used in any verse depend on the number of words in the verse, and on their syntactic and semantic relationship. On a simple level, the accentuation can be described as marking "terminal" accent clauses (DA.1), ending with *sillûq* or ʾ*atnāḥ,* and "medial" accent clauses (DA.2), ending with *zāqēp* or *sĕgōltā*ʾ. The shortest verses contain only a terminal clause, such as Gen 2:1, "The heavens, and the earth and all their hosts were finished." A few verses such as Gen 23:12, consist of one medial and one terminal clause. However, where a verse contains more than one accent clause, it usually contains two terminal clauses, the first ending with ʾ*atnāḥ* (DA.1.b), the second with *sillûq.* A verse may be composed only of two terminal clauses, i.e., Gen 2:4, "These are the generations of the heaven and the earth in their creation [ʾ*atnāḥ*] on the day when God made earth and heaven [*sillûq*]." More often, one of the terminal clauses, or both, are preceded by medial clauses, i.e., Gen 2:3, "God blessed the seventh day [*zāqēp*] and sanctified in [ʾ*atnāḥ*] because on it he had ceased from all his work [*zāqēp*] which God had created by making." No verse contains more than two terminal clauses, but either may be preceded by several medial clauses. Where more than one medial clause is used before ʾ*atnāḥ,* the first may be marked by *sĕgōltā*ʾ, i.e., Gen 3:3, " 'From the fruit of the tree which is in the middle of the garden' [*sĕgōltā*ʾ] said God, 'You shall not eat of it [*zāqēp*] and you shall not touch it [ʾ*atnāḥ*] lest you die.' "

As these examples show, the accent clauses do not correspond to any particular syntactic structures, nor are they used to divide the verse into units more or less equal in length. They divide the verse into sense units related to the chant. The different possibilities of accentuation are used to indicate the relationship between these units, and (as a result) to highlight the significance of some. Thus, in Gen 3:3, the main division of the verse (marked by ʾ*atnāḥ*) comes almost at its end, showing the close relationship of the two prohibitions and emphasizing the warning of the penalty for transgression given in the last clause. The semantic analysis marked by the accentuation reflects, of course, the way the text was interpreted (on the basis of the tradition they had received) by the Masoretes who established the received accentuation.

The accent clauses are subdivided by the lesser disjunctive accents in much the same way as the verse is divided into clauses. The basic principle is generally described as "dichotomy." Each unit is divided in two (as is the verse by ʾ*atnāḥ*); each of those units may be divided in two again, and so on. The resultant analysis is similar to the analysis of speech into "immediate constituents." The accents can be classified in grades of disjunctive force (marked 1–4 in Fig. MAS.01) on the basis of their use in marking the dichotomy. Typically, a unit ending with an accent of one grade is divided by one of the grade below (as an ʾ*atnāḥ* unit by *zāqēp*).

A closer analysis of the use of accents must concern itself with the rules governing the sequence in which the accents can occur, and those governing the conjunctives which can be used before each disjunctive. The basis for these rules is the phonological structure of the words, and the music of the chant, rather than the syntactic or semantic relationship of the words. Musical requirements sometimes result in accentuation which seems illogical from the standpoint of syntax (i.e., a disjunctive accent used on a word which is closely related to the following). This is most striking with the (relatively high-grade) disjunctive *tiphā*ʾ (DA.2.C.). This accent must be used in any terminal clause which contains more than one accented word. As a result, *tiphā*ʾ may be used even on a preposition (*ʾt* in Gen 2:14), or a construct noun (*ydʿy* in Gen 3:5). In such cases, of course, the accent reflects a musical requirement, and does not imply any syntactic or semantic division.

The use of accents in the Three Books is more complex than in the Twenty-one, so only a superficial sketch can be given here. See Fig. MAS.02. Verses are commonly divided into two halves. In shorter verses, the first typically ends with *ʾatnāḥ* (DA.2) and is subdivided by *dĕḥî* (DA.8); the second ends with *sîllûq* (DA.1), and is subdivided by *rĕbîaʿ mûgrāš* (DA.5). Where the verse is longer, its main division is usually marked by *ʿôlēh wĕ-yôrēd* (DA.3), with *ʾatnāḥ* used to mark the main division of the second half. *Rĕbîaʿ* (DA.4) is also used as the main verse divider where neither *ʾatnāḥ* or *ʿôlēh wĕ-yôrēd* occurs (called "*rĕbîaʿ mûgrāš* without *gereš*"), and may act as a minor disjunctive (called *rĕbîaʿ qāṭan*) immediately before *ʿôlēh wĕ-yôrēd.*

As with the vowel signs, different systems of accent signs were developed. The "Palestinian" system appears to mark an accentuation the same as, or similar to, the standard Tiberian, but to mark it in less detail. In this system, as in the Tiberian, the accentuation of the Three Books differs from that of the Twenty-one. In manuscripts using the Babylonian system, the same signs are used in all books of the Bible. This system differs from the Tiberian in a number of details, the most striking of which is the fact that only one medial clause can be used before a terminal clause. The internal division of verses in Babylonian manuscripts quite often differs from the standard. In fact, differences may be found in all manuscripts, but in Palestinian and Tiberian manuscripts these typically affect only the subdivisions of the medial or terminal clauses.

Like the vowel signs, the accent signs were probably developed between 500 and 700 C.E. to mark an existing tradition of chant. The music of the chant is certainly very old. The close relationship between early Church music and traditional Jewish music suggests that both derive from music in use before Christians separated from Jews. Consequently the basis of the biblical chant was probably established before the turn of the era. Punctuation is marked (by dots or by spaces) in some manuscripts of the LXX which date from this period, and so must be Jewish. Greek literary texts typically do not use punctuation, so such marks may well reflect a Jewish tradition of division of the text, but their relationship to the later accentuation remains uncertain.

Disjunctive Accents (DA)		Conjunctive Accents (CA)	
1. *sîllûq*	ישב	1. *mûnāḥ*	בדרך
2. *ʾatnāḥ*	עמד	2. *mêrkāʾ*	א
3. *ʿôlēh wĕ-yôrēd*	רשעים	3. *ʿillûv*	תן
4. *rĕbîaʿ*	האיש	4. *ṭarḥāʾ*	כל
5. *rĕbîaʿ mûgrāš*	לצים	5. *galgal*	עצת
6. *šalšelet gĕdôlâ*	וכבודי	6. *mĕhûppāk*	כי
7. *ṣinnôr*	הלך	7. *ʾazlāʾ*	ייענני
8. *dĕḥî*	חטאים	8. *šalšelet qĕṭannâ*	ישועתה
9. *pāzēr*	בקראי	9. *ṣinnôrît*	קומה
10. *azla legarmeh*	פריו ׀ י		
11. *mĕhûppāk lĕgarmēh*	אשר ׀		

(Also *maqqēp*, *gaʿyâ*, and *pāsēq*, as in the Twenty-One Books)

MAS.02. The accents of the Three Books.

Bibliography

Dotan, A., ed. 1970. *Two Treatises on the Accentuation of the Old Testament by William Wickes.* New York.

Yeivin, I. 1980. *Introduction to the Tiberian Masorah.* SBLMasS 5. Missoula, MT.

E. J. REVELL

MASORETIC STUDIES. The work of the Masoretes in its most common form confines itself to listing the occurrences of some feature of the biblical text. Where opportunity arises, however, general descriptions are used to avoid the need for long lists, as in the note on *bzrwʿ* in Exod 6:6: "(This word is written) *plene* (with *waw*) three times in the Torah, and in all of the Prophets and Writings it is spelled this way (with *waw*) with three exceptions." In some cases the information recorded as a feature of spelling obviously has a purely linguistic basis, i.e., the note on *wmn kl* in Judg 7:23, "(This spelling—instead of the expected *wmkl*—occurs) twice (in the parts of the text written in Hebrew) but is regular in (the parts written in) Aramaic." That is, the *n* of the preposition *mn* typically assimilates to a following consonant in Hebrew, but not in Aramaic. General descriptions of this kind, with a list of exceptions, were an important part of the work of the latter Masoretes. The most famous medieval Masorete, Aharon ben Asher, himself made a short collection of such material, mostly concerned with the accents, which circulated under the title *Diqdûqê ha-Ṭeʿāmîm,* "Details of the Accentuation." Work of this sort continued after the Masoretic period, and resulted in a number of treatises which are still preserved. These typically include both material which we would consider purely linguistic, and so classify under "Grammar," and material which we would consider to be without linguistic relevance, and classify under "Masorah." Subsequently, it became usual to restrict works to one kind of material or the other, although the boundary between the two groups remains vague. In which category, for instance, should the unusual uses of *dageš* be placed?

At the same time, scholars still needed to work at the establishment of the correct text. As manuscripts were recopied in the 10th century and later, the traditions of individual Masoretes, each of which differed slightly from the others, became confused. The differences between the separate strands of tradition became variants in a single stream of tradition. Consequently there was a need to evaluate the variants, and to select from among them the correct reading of any given word. The problem was further complicated by differing pronouncements on particular questions by leading scholars of later eras. The considerable problems faced by an editor are described by Jacob ben Ḥayyim in the preface to his edition of the Bible (Venice 1524–25). The same problems would, of course, face any scholar who needed a correct text on which to base his studies.

As the Masoretic period grew more distant in time, there was a growing need to explain the aims and methods of the Masoretes to the many who were no longer familiar with them. Jacob ben Ḥayyim provides some information on this subject in his preface. A more famous attempt at explanation is found in the *Massoret ha-Massoret,* a book written in 1538 by Rabbi Eliyahu ha-Levi (whose name was latinized as Elias Levita.) This author was also interested in the place of the Masoretes in history, foreshadowing the interest in the history of the biblical text which became so great a concern for later scholars.

Many scholars worked in these three areas: (1) description of the features of the text; (2) determination of the best readings; and (3) the study of the methods of the Masoretes and their history, particularly between the time of Aharon ben Asher and the present century. The last major scholar in this phase of Masoretic study was C. D. Ginsburg. His introduction to his 1897 edition of the Bible is largely concerned with explaining Masoretic matters to the English-speaking world. He published a translation of Jacob ben Ḥayyim's preface, and of Eliyahu ha-Levi's *Massoret ha-Massoret* with the same purpose (1867). He also published a massive collection of Masoretic notes and lists (1880–1905). This material is taken from a wide range of sources, and contains much of great interest. However, treating the material from diverse sources as equally representative of "The Masorah," as if it were a single entity, reflected the approach of an earlier time. A more fruitful method was beginning to develop.

The present phase of Masoretic study was introduced by the German scholar P. E. Kahle. In his time, the discovery of manuscripts in the Cairo Geniza made Masoretic materials of all sorts, some from the 8th and 9th centuries, available to scholars. This included biblical texts with Palestinian and Babylonian vowel and accent signs, which clearly represented a tradition quite different from the standard, as well as other evidence of the work of the later generations of Masoretes. Some material of this sort had been known to and studied by scholars of the 19th century, but Kahle persuaded scholars generally of the importance of the nonstandard traditions. He also persuaded them of the importance of using the earliest form of the standard tradition available, an individual tradition produced by one of the leading Masoretes. As a result, the third edition of the text, edited by Rudolph Kittel *(BHK),* which was intended for critical study of the biblical text, was based on the best complete codex of the Bible available, the Leningrad Codex. Kahle was able to publish the *masorah parva* with this text; his plan to publish the *masorah magna* could only be realized by G. E. Weil in connection with the later (fourth) edition known as the *Biblia hebraica Stuttgartensia (BHS).* See MASORAH.

The availability of the early materials which Kahle did so much to publicize led scholars to concentrate on the study of the individual Masoretic traditions. Most recently, Israel Yeivin and many other scholars have made important contributions to Masoretic studies. Their work supplies scholars with a clear understanding of the aims and methods of the Masoretes, not previously available. It has also led to a better grasp of much of the variation in later Masoretic materials. For instance, 19th-century scholars typically approached the confusing use of *gaʿyâ (meteg)* in medieval manuscripts with the assumption that it represented corruption, through ignorance, of a single "correct" usage. It is now clear that this sign was used in different ways in different strands of tradition at the end of the Masoretic period. Confusion in later texts results from the fact that the use in these different strands have become confused. The effort to disentangle these strands, so that the usage characteristic of each can be described, has led to a much better understanding of the linguistic significance of *gaʿyâ,* and of its importance in accentuation. Close attention to the details of good representatives of individual traditions is similarly producing a much clearer picture of many other features of the text.

A final area of study is the different reading traditions still in use in the various Jewish communities. The possibility of making accurate recordings of living bearers of the different traditions, especially in Israel, has greatly stimulated the study of this material in recent years. Through the work of scholars such as S. Morag, it has already provided valuable data for understanding various features of the earlier manuscripts, in both standard and nonstandard forms of the tradition.

Masoretic studies today is thus not just concerned with the text of the Hebrew Bible in its many written forms, but extends to the oral presentation of the text. The main emphasis is not on the reconstruction of one "correct" form of the text and its supporting notes, but on the attempt to understand the variations in the sources in their original context. This will help scholars gain a greater knowledge of the history of the text, and of the written and oral presentation of it. In 1972, the International Organization for Masoretic Studies was founded by the American scholar H. M. Orlinsky to promote this work.

Bibliography

Ginsburg, C. D., ed. 1867. *Massoreth ha-Massoreth.* London. Repr. in *Jacob Ben Chajim Ibn Adonijah's Introduction to the Rabbinic Bible and the Massoreth ha-Massoreth of Elias Levita.* New York, 1968.

———. 1880–1905. *The Masorah Compiled from Manuscripts.* London.

———. 1897. *Introduction to the Massoretico-Critical Edition of the Hebrew Bible.* Repr. with prolegomenon by H. M. Orlinsky, New York, 1966.

Yeivin, I. 1980. *Introduction to the Tiberian Masorah.* SBLMasS 5. Missoula, MT.

E. J. Revell

MASORETIC TEXT. In its widest sense, the term "Masoretic Text" (MT) can be applied to any text of the Hebrew Bible produced under the care of scholars known as Masoretes, or any copy of such a text. In the narrower sense in which it is commonly used, it refers to the standard text of the Hebrew Bible, which is derived from the tradition of the Masoretes of Tiberias, the "Tiberian Tradition." This standard text has three main components:

the letters, the vowel signs, and the accents. In most manuscripts, a fourth component, the marginal notes of the Masorah, is represented at least to some extent.

The letters of the text form the oldest component, often called the "consonantal text." Where the biblical text is used in the Jewish liturgy, it is this "consonantal text" which is used, written by hand in a scroll. The text in such scrolls is written in rather narrow columns (each line typically contains 20–30 letters). The "songs" in the text, i.e., Exodus 15 and Deuteronomy 32, are spaced as poetry according to fixed conventions (which differ for these two chapters). The text is divided into sections (Heb *pisqōt*) by means of spaces (similar to those which divide the paragraphs of an English text) known as "open" *(pĕtûḥâ)* or "closed" *(sĕtûmâ)* according to the positioning of the space. These are often distinguished in later codices by the writing of *p* or *s* within the space.

The consonantal text as written in liturgical scrolls also includes the *puncta extraordinaria,* the dots (distinct from vowel and accent signs) found on some or all of the letters of one or more words in ten places in the Torah, four in the Prophets, and one in the Writings. The significance of these dots has been discussed by scholars from Talmudic times on, but no generally accepted conclusion has been reached.

Other features (with unknown origin and purpose) traditionally included as part of the consonantal text are the "inverted *nun*" signs found at Num 10:35–36, the four letters written above the line ("suspended," as *n* in *mnšh* in Judg 18:30), and letters written larger than usual (as at the end of the first and last word in Deut 6:4), or smaller (as *n* in *ʾrn* in Isa 44:14). Certain of these large and small letters appear in all mss, but texts vary widely in the number they use. The other features mentioned are the subject of a firm tradition, and appear in all carefully written scrolls. They also appear in the codices (manuscripts in book form) which typically include vowel and accent signs, and Masoretic notes. They are also usually included in printed texts. It must be noted that in the marking of *pisqōt* and the spacing of the "songs" of the text, the *Biblia Hebraica Stuttgartensia (BHS)* does not follow the traditional rules. In most passages where the *BHS* text is spaced as poetry, the editors are following modern scholarly opinion, not the Masoretic tradition.

The date of the "Synod of Jabneh" (90 C.E.) is conventionally given as that from which the form of the consonantal text can be regarded as fixed. Some parts of the text, such as the Pentateuch, were most probably fixed considerably earlier. However, the text as represented in the Dead Sea Scrolls from Qumran (ca. 300 B.C.E.–68 C.E.) is "fluid," that is, different copies of the same passage differ from each other in spelling and wording. The scrolls are written in broad columns, as are Samaritan texts, not in narrow ones, as is the later Jewish practice, and differ from the later tradition in other respects. On the other hand, the scrolls from Wadi Murabbaʿat (ca. 135 C.E.) show little variation from the later standard text. This is probably not simply because they were produced after 90 C.E., but because their owners were participants in Bar Kokhba's revolt against the Romans. Because this movement was supported by several prominent rabbis, it is likely that participants would use the text form which they favored.

There are indications that the text form which became standard in rabbinical Judaism had been preserved unchanged—at least to a large extent—from a considerably earlier period. Some archaic spellings are preserved (i.e., the 3d masc. sing. pronominal suffix written with *he,* not *waw*), and spellings characteristic of a late period, such as first-person *waw* consecutive imperfect forms with the "cohortative" affix, are common only in late books (i.e., Nehemiah); these are very rare in the Pentateuch as compared to the Samaritan Pentateuch, or to the Hebrew of the Qumran mss. Some Jewish mss of the LXX show features of format which are closely similar to those of the standard tradition (i.e., paragraph divisions corresponding to *pisqōt,* and the poetry format of Deuteronomy 32). The former, at least, is likely to reflect a tradition established in the Hebrew text.

Apart from the scrolls from Qumran and Wadi Murabbaʿat, the earliest known examples of the text of the Hebrew Bible come from the "Genizah" into which worn-out or unacceptable manuscripts of sacred (and other) texts were put in the synagogue of Old Cairo (Fustat). The building was brought into use as a synagogue in 882 C.E., so it is probable that the earliest material it contained dated from the 9th century. These texts provide evidence of great interest on the final stages of the development of the systems of vowel and accent signs. The consonantal text reflected therein differs little from the numerous manuscripts produced in medieval Europe. Each ms differs from the others in minor details, such as the use of vowel letters, conjunctive *waw,* and other prefixes, but substantial differences are very rare in the high-quality manuscripts known as "Masorah codices." Such manuscripts, carefully written, and provided with vowel and accent signs and Masoretic notes, were intended for the use of scholars. The great cost of producing a correct manuscript meant that many texts, intended for private use, were prepared without the expertise and safeguards used in the production of Masorah codices, and, as a result, contained many variants. Such "internal" variants, produced during the process of copying what was essentially a fixed text, are clearly of no interest for the earlier history of that text.

It has been argued that the texts from Wadi Murabbaʿat show that in 135 C.E., the Jewish text was essentially identical to the received standard text; therefore all variants in later texts are internal corruptions due to copyists' errors. However, the assumption that the texts owned by the revolutionaries of Wadi Murabbaʿat were typical of those in use throughout the Jewish world is difficult to accept. Most scholars maintain the older view that despite the scholarly promulgation of a particular text form, many manuscripts continued in use which contained variants such as those found at Qumran. These often correspond to the LXX where it differs from the standard Hebrew. During the process of transmission, these different text forms became confused (as later happened with Masoretic traditions from different sources). Consequently, some of these early variants deriving from nonstandard text forms, including the *Vorlage* of the Greek translation, eventually appeared in medieval mss. For this reason, the great collections of variant consonantal readings in medieval mss made in the late 18th century by Kennicott and by de Rossi are still valued.

The vowel signs and accent signs are generally regarded as representing a single integrated "reading tradition." However, the phrase and clause divisions marked in the text by the accent signs are not always consistent with those marked by features of the vowel pointing, such as "pausal forms." This may indicate that accentuation and vowel pointing derive from slightly different forms of the tradition. The stress position marked by the accents does appear to be that which gave rise to the vowel pointing. The vowel pointing is sometimes treated as the creation of the Masoretes. This is no doubt true for the signs, but the sounds which they represent certainly derive from an old tradition. The transliterations of the second column of Origen's "Hexapla" (ca. 200 C.E.) represent a tradition which differs from that of the standard voweling mainly in that some vowel changes completed in the later tradition are not completed in the earlier, and Origen's tradition is somewhat "vulgarized," namely, it replaces some archaic features with their equivalents in the language of the day. The reading tradition was probably essentially fixed before 500 C.E. possibly before 300.

The signs used to mark the vowels and accents were probably developed between 500 and 700 C.E., although an earlier date is possible. Other systems of signs were developed in addition to the "Tiberian" system used in the standard text. The most important of these other systems was the "Babylonian," which was widely used in the Eastern Jewish world. Manuscripts in which this system is used do not show consistent differences from the standard consonantal text. Their vowel signs reflect a different pronunciation (e.g., no equivalent to *segōl* is used), but many features shown in the standard text, such as pausal forms, are represented with little difference. The accent system also differs from the standard, but the verse divisions do not. Much the same could be said of the "Palestinian" vowel pointing, the other ancient system which has been studied in some depth; but this is much closer to the Tiberian system, and can be considered as representing a vulgarized form of the standard tradition.

The Standard Tiberian system of vowels and accents is represented in numerous manuscripts of the standard text (MT) dating from the 9th century on. Each differs from the other in many minor details, some of which reflect scribal carelessness. The majority (in Masorah codices) reflect the fact that the minor details of vowel pointing (such as the use of composite *šewa* signs) and of accentuation (such as the marking of *gaʿyâ* [*meteg*]) were never fully conventionalized. Variants in the use of accent and vowel signs in a large and diverse group of manuscripts in the British Museum were recorded in the 1897 edition of C. D. Ginsburg; those in a few of the most important codices are recorded in that of the Hebrew University Bible Project.

The "Aleppo Codex," which was supplied with vowels and accent signs and Masoretic notes by the famous medieval scholar Aharon ben Asher (ca. 915), is used as the base text for the Hebrew University edition. This codex, which is generally recognized as representing the Standard Tiberian tradition in its best available form, is unfortunately incomplete. The best complete manuscript is that known as the Leningrad Codex, dated 1009. This was copied and supplied with vowel and accent signs and Masorah according to a manuscript slightly different from the Aleppo codex, but as the colophon states, it was corrected "according to the most exact texts of ben Asher." Its text is printed in the *BHS*. In 1524–25, a complete edition of the MT (known as the "Bomberg," or "Second Rabbinic" Bible) was printed at Venice under the editorship of Jacob ben Hayyim, on the basis of the best manuscripts available in his day. This was the first edition resulting from a major effort of scholarship, and has been the basis of the traditional Jewish text ever since.

Scholars attempting to assess the relationship of the MT to its antecedents in the biblical period generally conclude, from the history outlined above, that the consonantal text has an ancient origin, while the vowel and accent signs do not. This is quite true when applied to the written signs, but to carry it much further is an oversimplification. The MT is a unity. Its letters were preserved and passed down through the same stream of Masoretic tradition which produced the vowel and accent signs. The Jewish rules governing the form of text suitable for liturgical use are not limited to the letters of the texts, but include their layout and other features mentioned above. The letters of the text cannot reasonably be regarded as an originally independent component onto which the Masoretic tradition has been grafted.

The biblical text inevitably functioned in the community in oral form: in the liturgy, in scholarly discussion, and in the teaching of the text to children. It is unlikely that the written text was much studied independent of such realization. Oral realizations probably varied between communities more than did written texts, but there is no reason to believe that the vowel pointing was considered to be outside the tradition, or to be an inferior part of it. The *ketib/qere* phenomenon shows the oral tradition dominating the written. See KETHIB AND QERE. The occasional references to pronunciation in rabbinic literature clearly assume a generally accepted vowel pointing, even though alternatives might be suggested for homiletic purposes. Vowel and accent signs are not a common subject for Masoretic notes, because the notes deal with the text in its written form, which did not include vowel and accent signs until near the end of the Masoretic period. The reading tradition did change in the process of transmission, but this is not an adequate reason to reject the form reflected in MT as "late."

Bibliography

Cross, F. M., and Talmon, S., eds. 1975. *Qumran and the History of the Biblical Text.* Cambridge, MA.

Ginsburg, C. D., ed. 1897. *Introduction to the Massoretico-Critical Edition of the Hebrew Bible.* London. Repr. with prolegomenon by H. M. Orlinsky. New York, 1966.

Goshen-Gottstein, M. H. 1963. The Rise of the Tiberian Bible Text. Pp. 79–122 in *Biblical and Other Studies,* ed. A. Altmann. Studies and Texts 1. Cambridge, MA.

Orlinsky, H. M. 1966. The Masoretic Text: A Critical Evaluation. Pp. I–XXXVII in *Introduction to the Massoretico-Critical Edition of the Hebrew Bible,* ed. C. O. Ginsburg.

Yeivin, I. 1980. *Introduction to the Tiberian Masorah.* SBLMasS 5. Missoula, MT.

E. J. Revell

MASREKAH (PLACE) [Heb *maśrēqâ*]. The hometown of the Edomite king Samlah (Gen 36:36; 1 Chr 1:47). See also SAMLAH. The place is unidentified; in addition, the toponym cannot be explained with certainty. If Lemaire's proposal (1988) that the "Edomite king list" (Gen 36:31–39) actually is a list of Aramaean kings from the 11th century B.C. proves correct, several Mishriqîyahs in Syria could be identified with Masrekah; otherwise, the place may be sought in S Transjordan and/or NW Arabia.

If the place-name is Canaanite, it could be explained by either Heb *śārōq,* "red" (cf. the name of Edom, "the red country"), or Heb *śōreq,* "grapes," *śĕrēqâ,* "grapevine" (cf. Isa 63:1–3, presupposing viticulture in N Edom which is also attested by medieval geographers). If the name is Arabic, it could be explained by *Mashriq,* "place of sunrise, east," a noun frequently attested in Arabic toponymy. If the name is Aramaic, it could be explained by *šĕraq,* "to split;" Aram *šĕraq* is the etymon of the modern place-name *Meshrâqâ,* 12 km S of Kerak.

Bibliography

Lemaire, A. 1988. Hadad l'Édomite ou Hadad l'Araméen? *BN* 43: 14–18.

Ernst Axel Knauf

MASSA (PERSON) [Heb *maśśâʾ*]. A son of Ishmael (Gen 25:14; 1 Chr 1:30). The "sons of Ishmael" were prominent Arab tribes of the 8th and 7th centuries B.C. See ISHMAELITES. As a tribe, Massa is attested both in the OT and in ANE texts.

According to Assyrian *Mašʾayya, "the Massaean" and Sabaic *msʾʾ* (personal name or tribal name), the name of the tribe was *Mašʾ; its etymology is unknown. The Masoretic vocalization *maśśāʾ* recalls "burden" (Albright 1956: 6) and may preserve contemporary evaluations of this tribe's behavior. Linguistically, there are no objections against the identification of Mesha, which deliminates the N border of the "sons of Jokshan" in Gen 10:30, with Massa (Meyer 1906: 244).

The admonitions Prov 31:1–9 are attributed to the mother of Lemuel, king of Massa. Both the prominent position of the queen mother and her advice against the consumption of wine recall an ancient Arabian cultural context (Knauf 1989: 72). These "Massaean proverbs" contain a number of Aramaisms which, orthographically, cannot have been composed before the Persian period (*pace* Albright 1956: 8–9). Whereas Prov 31:1–9 may serve, or may have been composed to serve, as an example for the "wisdom of the east," 1 Kgs 5:10 (see EAST, PEOPLE OF THE), the proverbs of Agur, son of Jakeh, of Massa (Prov 30:1–4) seem to ridicule the easterner's "wisdom."

It has been suggested that Meshech, mentioned together with Kedar in Ps 120:5, is a corruption of "Massa"; this assumption is, however, not necessary (Knauf 1989: 72, n. 363).

In Akkadian sources, the tribe is attested as early as 734 B.C., when the Massaeans paid tribute to Tiglath-pileser III after he had conquered Gaza. A cuneiform letter sent to Sargon II from Damascus may contain a note on a certain Asapi who went to the country of Massa (ABL 414 Rs. 13–14; Ephʿal 1982: 96–97); the reading *ma-sa-ʾ* is, however, not accepted by Parpola (1987: 139). According to CT 53, 289 Rs 8–9, Massa joined the "rebellion" of Yauṯaʿ against Ashurbanipal before 649 B.C. At approximately the same time, Massaeans raided a caravan of the Nebaioth on their way to the Assyrian king (ABL 260). At the end of the 5th century B.C., Massa and the Nebaioth are mentioned in Thamudic inscriptions as enemies of Tayma (Knauf 1989: 71–72 and n. 362). See also NEBAIOTH; TEMA. It is only by these inscriptions that the abode of Massa can be pinpointed to the vicinity of Tayma.

Bibliography

Albright, W. F. 1956. The Biblical Tribe of Massa' and Some Congeners. Vol. 1, pp. 1–14 in *Studi orientalisitci in onore di Giorgio Levi della Vida.* Rome.
Ephʿal, I. 1982. *The Ancient Arabs.* Leiden.
Knauf, E. A. 1989. *Ismael.* 2d ed. ADPV. Wiesbaden.
Meyer, E. 1906. *Die Israeliten und ihre Nachbarstämme.* Halle.
Parpola, S. 1987. *The Correspondence of Sargon II, Part I.* Helsinki.

Ernst Axel Knauf

MASSA (PLACE) [Heb *maśśaʾ*]. Apparently the name of the kingdom of Lemuel, whose mother taught him the proverbial wisdom preserved in Proverbs 31. If "Massa" is indeed a proper name, it probably refers to a prominent Arab tribe of the 8th–7th centuries B.C. See MASSA (PERSON). Others suggest that *maśśaʾ* here is a common noun, referring to the "oracle" taught to Lemuel the king.

MASSAH AND MERIBAH (PLACES) [Heb *massâ ûmĕrîbâ*]. Literally, "Testing and Strife," the site of an Israelite rebellion during the desert wandering (Exod 17:7). The precise location is unknown, since the Elohist places it at Horeb and near Rephidim (Exod 17:6, 8), both of equally unknown location, while P and Ezekiel place it at Kadesh, probably modern Ein el Qudeirat (M.R. 096006) in the Sinai. Possibly the place is imaginary. The names themselves are suitable for real springs, which were often the sites of contention or lawsuits (Gen 14:7; 21:25–32; 26:14–33; Exod 2:17). Some consider the two terms to derive from separate traditions (e.g., Cornill 1891: 20–34), but more likely they arose in poetic parallelism as in Deut 33:8. It is true, however, that some sources prefer one name over the other—Deuteronomy uses "Massah" (Deut 6:16; 9:22), and P uses "Meribah" or "Meribath-kadesh" (Num 20:13, 24; 27:14; Deut 32:51). Ezekiel, whose work is akin to the priestly source, refers to Meribath-kadesh in 47:19 (MT *mĕrîbôt*) and 48:28. Ps 81:8—Eng v 7 speaks of the waters of Meribah. Ps 95:8 also calls the place Meribah, but speaks of "the day of testing" *(massâ),* showing its acquaintance with the Massah–Meribah pairing.

Examination of the texts referring to Massah and Meribah shows that there was no unified tradition of what constituted the rebellion. Deut 33:8–11, though somewhat garbled in the MT, says that the Levites were tested and striven against at Massah and Meribah, where they were endowed with the priestly functions of divination, education, and sacrifice. Their test involved renunciation of kin.

On the other hand, Ps 81:8—Eng v 7 implies that all Israel was tested by the waters of Meribah. The trial in question seems to have been of their fidelity to Yahweh, the reward for which would have been sustenance (vv 11, 17). Vv 10–12 suggest, however, that the Israelites failed this test and were cast out. In other words, apostasy was committed at Meribah which bore the consequence of alienation or exile. Ps 95:8–11 specifies that Israel was punished with forty years of wandering in the desert for the sin of testing Yahweh at Meribah, but no details are supplied.

The pentateuchal prose traditions, Exod 17:1–7 and Num 20:1–13, vary markedly from these poetic texts. The former is basically Elohistic, though there have been many recent attempts to assign it to the J source (e.g., Noth *Exodus* ATD, 109–12). It is introduced by an itinerary note from the exilic stratum called P^2 by Friedman (1981: 77–81, 119–32), which tells how the Israelites arrived at Rephidim, but found no water (cf. Num 33:14); it is possible, however, that the end of v 1 goes with vv 2–7. Contrary to conventional analysis, however, there is no source break after v 1, for vv 2 and 3 are not doublets. The story runs as follows: The people quarrel with Moses and command him and Yahweh to give them water. Moses sees their grumbling as unjustified and refuses to help. The people grow thirsty and intensify their complaints. Finally Moses turns to Yahweh, who tells him to pass before the people on to Mount Horeb, where the deity will be standing. Moses is to strike the mountain (*ṣûr,* often translated "rock"), from which waters will flow. Moses does as he is commanded. The spring is named "Testing and Strife" because the Israelites strove with Moses and tested Yahweh, doubting his presence. According to E, Massah and Meribah are the springs of Horeb, while P^2 locates them at Rephidim, near Mount Sinai (Num 33:14–15).

The mention of Horeb is crucial to the proper interpretation of Exod 17:1–7. Older source critics believed (correctly) that while J and P call the mountain of Yahweh Sinai, E and D use the name "Horeb." See SINAI, MOUNT. More recent researchers have disparaged this criterion because, following Noth (*NDH,* 109 n. 10), they excise the name wherever it is found in Exodus. According to this view, the Israelites only reach the mountain of God in Exodus 19. The addition of "at Horeb" to the text is inexplicable, however, while retaining it makes several points more comprehensible. First, it explains how the Israelites can be at the mountain of God already in Exod 18:5 (E). Second, as Carmichael (1974: 244–45) has shown, it explains the connection of Exod 17:1–7 and 8–16—the Amalekites attack while Moses has left the people behind on his journey to Horeb. Third, the image of the mountain of God as a source of water or other beverages is found frequently in the Bible, though generally the mountain is Zion (Isa 33:21; Ezek 47:1–12; Amos 9:13; Joel 4:18; Zech 14:8; Ps 36:9–10—Eng vv 8–9; 46:5—Eng v 4; 65:10—Eng v 9). Finally, the waters of Horeb reappear in Exod 32:20 (also E, in my opinion), where they dissolve the ashes of the golden calf. Notice that in the latter story we have apostasy and levitical ordination through renunciation of kinship (Exod 32:26–29), themes that we saw above were associated with the Massah and Meribah tradition. These shared motifs derive from the prebiblical stage of Israelite tradition, whether written or oral, but they appear disjointed in the Elohistic source, as if the author had pulled apart the Massah-Meribah tradition to create Exod 17:1–7 and Exodus 32. Even if both Exod 17:1–7 and Exodus 32 are primarily J, as most commentators claim, the point is still valid, as long as they are of the same source.

The priestly writer tells the story of Meribah (also called Meribath-Kadesh) in a very different fashion, reworking the plot of the older Elohistic account to explain the deaths of Moses and Aaron in the desert (Num 20:1–3). His motivation for doing so is to exculpate Aaron, his primary hero, and denigrate Moses, about whom he is ambivalent. In this story Moses is commanded to take the rod and *speak* to the rock, but instead he hits the rock. For this act of disobedience, he and the apparently innocent Aaron are condemned to death. Note that in P Meribah is at Kadesh. To account for the two locations of Meribah, the Midrash postulates that the smitten rock followed the Israelites from Rephidim to Kadesh.

The gesture of striking the ground or a rock to produce a spring has many extrabiblical parallels. Bedouin have been observed to detect subterranean springs and break through to them with their staffs. Related stories within the Bible are the tale of Marah (Exod 15:23–26), where a stick is used to produce drinking water, and the incident at Beer (Num 21:16–18), where Yahweh provides the people with water through the leaders' use of their rods as digging implements (see Koenig 1963). Another good parallel to Massah and Meribah is the etiology of En-hakkore, where Samson thirsts and cries out to Yahweh, who causes a well to burst forth (Judg 15:18–19).

The story of Massah and Meribah is part of the murmuring tradition (see Coats 1968), which tells of Israel's repeated rebellions in the desert. Most of the murmuring accounts have an admonitory function, for they tell of Yahweh's punishment of Israel. Num 20:1–13 and Psalms 81 and 95 do speak of punishment at Massah/Meribah, but for the Elohist the story of the miraculous provision of water in the desert, like the traditions of the manna and the quail (Exodus 16; Numbers 11), is an example of divine beneficence in the most inhospitable of climes and expresses the Israelites' hope that such aid would ever be forthcoming. Many other biblical passages that refer to this miraculous water implicitly or explicitly connect the water with irrigation and natural fertility (Deut 8:15; 32:13–14; Isa 35:6–7; 41:17–20; 43:19–20; 48:21; 49:10; Jer 31:9; Pss 78:15–16, 20; 105:41; 107:35; 114:8; Neh 9:15, 20). Later exegetes, however, deconcretized the gift of water, seeing it as symbolic of the Torah or of the Holy Spirit (Bienamé 1984).

Bibliography

Bienamé, G. 1984. *Moïse et le don de l'eau dans la tradition juive ancienne: targum et midrash.* AnBib 98. Rome.

Carmichael, C. 1974. *The Laws of Deuteronomy.* Ithaca, NY.

Coats, G. W. 1968. *Rebellion in the Wilderness.* Nashville.

Cornill, C. H. 1891. Beiträge zur Pentateuchkritik. *ZAW* 11: 1–34.

Friedman, R. E. 1981. *The Exile and Biblical Narrative.* HSM 22. Chico, CA.

Koenig, J. 1963. Sourciers, thaumaturges et scribes. *RHR* 164: 17–38, 165–80.

Lehming, S. 1961. Massa und Meribah. *ZAW* 73: 71–77.

Propp, W. H. 1987. *Water in the Wilderness.* HSM 40. Atlanta.
Reymond, P. 1958. *L'eau, sa vie, et sa signification dans l'Ancien Testament.* VTSup 6. Leiden.

William H. Propp

MASSEBAH [Heb *maṣṣēbâ*]. The noun *maṣṣēbâ* derives from the Hebrew root *nṣb* which means "to take a stand" or "to stand" (BDB, 662–63). The RSV does not use the word "massebah," but substitutes "pillar," "stump," or "obelisk," depending on the context. The word "massebah" (pl. "masseboth"), however, is found frequently in archaeological reports and theological discussions.

The Hebrew word, *maṣṣēbâ,* is used in the Bible to refer to several different things, some of which are condoned, others of which are condemned. When YHWH appeared to Jacob in a theophany at Luz, Jacob commemorated the occasion by erecting a "pillar" and anointing it with oil and calling the place Bethel (Gen 28:18–22; which occurs again in Gen 35:9–15). Later in the narrative, when Jacob left Laban, YHWH reminded Jacob of the episode at Luz (Gen 31:13), apparently with no intended censure.

Pillars occasionally served as burial markers. Jacob erected a *maṣṣēbâ* to mark the grave of Rachel when she died on their way toward Ephrath (i.e., Bethlehem; Gen 35:19–21). Absalom later built a "pillar" in the King's Valley near Jerusalem as a memorial since he had no offspring to carry on his name (2 Sam 18:18).

The term *maṣṣēbâ* can also refer simply to the stump of a tree after it has been cut down (Isa 6:13), or to architectural features of buildings—i.e., structural weight-bearing pillars (Ezek 26:11; the context of this passage—the destruction of Tyre at the hands of Nebuchadnezzar—refers to the devastation of Tyre's fortifications and architecture, not to its religious practices).

A *maṣṣēbâ* might also be erected upon the completion of a ceremonial covenant agreement between either two individuals (e.g., when Jacob and Laban erect one to witness their pact; Gen 31:49–32) or between two larger parties (e.g., as part of the covenant ratification between YHWH and Israel, when Moses erected 12 *maṣṣēbôt* to represent each of the tribes; Exod 24:3–8). This probably was the purpose of the erection of the stone of witness at Shechem (Josh 24:25–27) at the covenant renewal between YHWH and Israel, although the stone is not called a *maṣṣēbâ* in the text.

Of course the most frequent use of the term places the standing stone in a religious context. Jeremiah refers to the destruction of the *maṣṣēbâ* in Hieropolis (Jer 43:13, i.e., Beth-shemesh; instead of "pillar" the RSV renders the word as "obelisk"). The religious pillars were often mentioned in conjunction with Asherim and/or altars and/or graven images (cf. Exod 34:13; Lev 26:1; Deut 7:5; 12:3; 1 Kgs 14:23; 2 Kgs 17:10). Several kings of the monarchies were condemned for introducing pillars into worship contexts (e.g., Rehoboam; 1 Kgs 14:23), and their use in the kingdom of Israel is described as a factor contributing to Israel's exile (2 Kgs 17:10). Two kings of Judah are described as having purged the country of pillars—Hezekiah (2 Kgs 18:4) and Josiah (2 Kgs 23:14).

In view of the range of application of *maṣṣēbâ* in the above survey, it would appear that the use of a pillar in itself was not condemned, but that the function of the artifact was what determined its legitimacy or illegitimacy. Of course, there is also a change in mood toward pillars since acceptable *maṣṣēbôt* were generally early and their condemnation occurs predominantly following the Deuteronomic legislation.

The identification of *maṣṣēbôt* in the archaeological record can be problematic. The above survey indicates that a number of items (including architectural structural features) could be identified as *maṣṣēbôt,* however, the term in modern literature has almost universally been restricted to religious contexts. While we may dismiss pillars that clearly are structural elements (i.e., the lines of pillars in the buildings at Megiddo, Hazor, and Beer-sheba), the identification of other pillars is more difficult because few stone pillars in ancient Palestine have writing on them to identify them as religious artifacts. The archaeologist must rely upon the context of the pillar to assist in interpreting its function (and then it must be approached cautiously).

R. A. S. Macalister's excavations at Gezer uncovered a series of 10 stone pillars which he interpreted as a high place. This interpretation was strengthened by the discovery of numerous infant burials in the area around the pillars. He assumed that the combination of these phenomena reflected the statements in the biblical texts which mentioned pillars and infant sacrifice in association with Canaanite worship practices. When W. G. Dever reexcavated Gezer in the 1960s, and after much more was known about the nature of MB Age burial practices, it became clear that the site was not the kind of worship area that Macalister had imagined. The burials were remains of typical infant burials of the MB I, and only later, in MB III, were the pillars erected. The pillars probably were cultic, but not in the sense of Macalister's interpretation—they probably were part of a covenant renewal ceremony between members of a city-state confederation similar to that described for Israel (Exod 24:3–8; *EAEHL* 2: 437–38).

Excavations at Hazor have revealed a series of small *maṣṣēbôt* in an LB IIB temple in Area C. One of these was engraved with the representation of the arms of a worshiper raised toward a disk (sun disk) and crescent carved on the top of the stela (Yadin 1956: 10).

Another clear example of a *maṣṣēbâ* was discovered by Aharoni in the Iron Age II shrine at Arad (1968). The carefully shaped stela stood in the back of a cubicle niche, which corresponded to the "Holy of Holies" of a tripartite temple. Preserved on the stela were traces of red paint; the *maṣṣēbâ* was found in association with two small incense altars. In the court of the building stood the remains of an altar of burnt offerings.

Bibliography

Aharoni, Y. 1968. Arad: Its Inscriptions and Temple. *BA* 31: 2–32.
Graesser, C. F. 1972. Standing Stones in Ancient Palestine. *BA* 35: 34–63.
Yadin, Y. 1956. Excavations at Hazor. *BA* 19: 2–12.

Dale W. Manor

MATHEMATICS, ALGEBRA, AND GEOMETRY. It is not possible to speak of any specific *biblical* mathematics. Neither the OT nor the NT was the product of cultures carrying a mathematical tradition of their own above a normal level of "folk mathematics." But both Testaments were products of cultures in contact with well-established and sophisticated mathematical traditions.

One of these is the Sumero-Babylonian tradition, known from a wealth of cuneiform tablets. Though probably less vigorous than in the early 2d millennium B.C., this tradition was still alive during the Babylonian Exile. Furthermore, it was apparently reflected in scribal education and in practitioners' ways throughout the Syrian area during the 2d and much of the 1st millennium B.C.

Another mathematical tradition of some importance for the OT is that of ancient Egypt. Already around the mid-2d millennium B.C. Syria was politically and commercially connected to Egypt; the Joseph story in Genesis displays an Israelite view on precisely the features of Egyptian economy which molded Egyptian mathematics; and in the centuries of the divided monarchy, the Egyptian hieratic numeral script was actually adopted by the Israelites.

The NT was written in the Hellenistic world and in Greek. In spite of this, the high "theoretical" level of Greek mathematics has left no traces in the NT text. Various quasi-philosophical currents dependent on Greek theoretical mathematics, however, are reflected both in the NT text and in ancient and medieval exegetical commentaries.

A. The "Folk" Substratum
B. Babylonian Mathematics
C. Syrian Descendants
D. Egyptian Mathematics
E. Greek and Hellenistic Mathematics and Its Aftermath

A. The "Folk" Substratum

Long before mathematical knowledge was borrowed from the neighboring high-level mathematical traditions, the early Hebrews were basically competent in numeration and metrology. This follows mainly from indirect arguments: evidence suggests that their cultural level and context were such that they needed mathematical concepts (especially in commercial intercourse with others), as did all Near Eastern populations in the 2d and 1st millennia B.C. Linguistic arguments support the conclusion and inform us at the same time of the probable limits of "folk" counting abilities: Heb *mēʾot,* "one hundred," is a common Semitic word. Heb *lĕʾōm,* "the people," on the other hand, corresponds to Akk *lim,* "one thousand," while Heb *ʾelep,* "one thousand," corresponds to Ethiopian "ten thousand." The common ancestors of the different Semitic groups will thus have counted into the hundreds before they split, no later than the 4th millennium B.C.; but they cannot have counted routinely into the thousands. When that became necessary, the different branches borrowed terms independently of each other.

A trace of "primitive" attitudes to numbers and counting can be found in 2 Samuel 24 (and 1 Chronicles 21), where David counts his people and is punished for his temerity. This fear (or taboo) of counting one's belongings is in fact widespread among populations who are either not familiar with or estranged from centralized states and administration.

Both because of the high numbers involved and because no traces of such estrangement from the ways of civilization are apparent, the many other censuses found in the OT cannot be connected to this ethnomathematical substratum. The occurrence of borrowed Babylonian metrology (the *šeqel*), used in the vicinity of the important censuses in the book of Numbers also speaks in favor of a possible borrowing of the habits and techniques of neighboring older civilizations.

B. Babylonian Mathematics

Babylonian mathematics was, in its origin, an offspring of early civilization, understood etymologically as incipient state formation. Basically, it was a scribal activity, performed by scribes and similar practitioners and used for practical purposes—and since almost all practical applications of mathematics before the classical era consisted in computation of something, the unorthodox label "Babylonian computation" would fit the endeavour better than the name "mathematics" (which shall nonetheless be used in the following).

This does not mean that Babylonian mathematics consisted in nothing but a set of practitioners' formulas. Firstly, as it shall be argued below, Babylonian calculators knew what they were doing and why they did so. Secondly, like many professional environments making heavy use of mathematics, the Babylonian scribal culture produced a level of particularly complex, theoretical (i.e., not practically relevant) problems with appurtenant techniques, especially in the field of algebra.

Traditionally, only the mathematics of the Old Babylonian and the Seleucid periods has been investigated and discussed in the literature. From the mid-1970s onward, however, a number of texts have been discovered which adumbrate the development of Babylonian mathematics from the Proto-Sumerian beginnings around 3000 B.C. to the Late Babylonian and Seleucid periods. Some of these texts and the conclusions drawn have been published; but others (as of February 1989) have only been presented at the Workshops on Concept Development in Mathematics (West Berlin, 1983, 1984, 1985, 1988), especially by Jöran Friberg, Peter Damerow, Robert Englund, and Marvin Powell, Jr.

Already long before the late 4th millennium, a system of arithmetical recording or accounting based on small clay tokens had been in use in the Near and Middle Eastern region (Schmandt-Besserat 1977). In the Uruk IV period (late 4th millennium, the period of state formation which also witnessed the development of writing), this system appears to have inspired both the development of writing and that of numerical and metrological notations. Insofar as mathematics is concerned, a trend toward harmonization of the various systems began. So the area unit SAR (apparently meaning a garden plot, the area to be irrigated from a single well, and in any case a "natural unit") came to be understood as the square of the basic length unit (the NINDAN, ≈ 6 m), and in general the whole system of area measures was keyed to the linear system (see Powell 1972). Moreover, subunit metrologies were developed, as far as one can judge, beyond the range of the traditional system. The whole system was interconnected in a way which soon permitted coherent calculations linking arithmetically linear extensions, areas, time, and other quantities which belonged together in technical or social practice (part of the background for these statements has only been presented in workshops and is as yet unpublished; but see, e.g., some examples presented by Friberg [1984] and the implicit overview in Damerow and Englund 1987).

No doubt Proto-Sumerian mathematics was created for the purposes of practical administration in what economic anthropology calls a "redistributive economy"; the replacement of natural but unconnected units by a complex of mathematically connected metrologies which correspond to the needs of the planning and accounting official rather than to those of the immediate producer. But the complexity of the system appears to go beyond even bureaucratic needs. Even though it is difficult to distinguish possible school tablets from indubitably administrative texts (only the latter contain officials' names), it is thus a fair assumption that the immediate root of the reorganization of a bundle of arithmetical techniques as coherent mathematics was the teaching in the temple school (this is argued more closely in Høyrup 1980: 14–17).

The early administration seems not to have distinguished bureaucratic from other priestly functions, and nothing in the mathematical substance distinguishes possible school exercises from other calculating texts. Only around the mid-3d millennium is the term for scribe (DUB-SAR) found in the sources; at this time we also encounter the nonbureaucratic use of the professional tools of the scribes: literary texts and mathematical exercises beyond the context of daily administration, the latter dealing, e.g., with the division of extremely large numbers by irregular divisors like 7 and 33 (a theme which dominates the small group of mid-3d-millennium mathematical exercises from Šuruppak and Ebla—see Friberg [1986: 16–22]; Høyrup [1982]). Even though such problems will have played no significant role in practical administration, they were evidently a central concern for a scribal profession testing its own intellectual abilities.

The trend toward increasing regularization continued throughout the 3d millennium and was brought to fruition in Ur III (21st century B.C.) (see Powell 1976). Early in the Ur III period an administrative reform was implemented which made extensive use of systematic and extremely meticulous bookkeeping. It seems probable that it was for use in this context that the sexagesimal-place-value system was created. See NUMBERS AND COUNTING. Mathematical school exercises pointing beyond the administrative domain have not been found, and from parallels in other cultural domains it seems to be a reasonable assumption that the centralized state had drained the sources for scribal autonomy and thus for further development of nonutilitarian mathematics.

Nonutilitarian mathematics was, on the other hand, central to OB mathematics, which is well documented in the sources (1900 to 1600 B.C., mainly the second part of this time span). In this period, which was characterized by a highly individualized economy (compared to other Bronze Age cultures) and by an ideology emphasizing the individual as a private person, the scribal school developed a curriculum which stressed virtuosity beyond what was practically necessary; the triumphs of Babylonian "pure" mathematics, not least the "algebra," appear to be a product of precisely this OB scribal school and scribal culture (see Høyrup 1985: 10–16).

Until Ur III all mathematical texts had been in Sumerian; even in Semitic-speaking Ebla, Sumerian mathematics was taken over in the original language. Old Babylonian mathematics, on the contrary, was written in Akkadian—supplementary evidence that it represents a new genre and a break with the (plausibly more purely utilitarian) Ur III tradition. Admittedly, quite a few texts are written predominantly by means of Sumerian logograms; but grammatical analysis shows that all but a handful of these word-signs are simply elliptic representations of Akkadian words and sentences.

Many mathematical tablets from the OB period onward are compilations, containing a variety of different problems. Often, utilitarian and theoretical problems are found together; but mathematical and nonmathematical matters are usually not treated in the same texts. Obviously, OB mathematics was not divided into fully distinct disciplines; on the other hand, mathematics as a whole was an autonomous concern—perhaps even (in the form of engineering, surveying, and accounting, or as a teacher's specialty) a distinct vocation.

In 1600 B.C. the Kassite conquest put an end to the OB social order, to the age-old scribal school, to the characteristic OB scribal ideology—and at the same time to the characteristic form of OB mathematics. Scribal training was from now on provided by scribal "families" as apprenticeship; and thus, to a certain degree, mathematics came to be mixed up with other subjects on the same tablets, having lost its disciplinary autonomy. The "mathematician" would from now on identify himself in the colophons of tablets, e.g., as "exorcist" (Akk *āšipu*) or "priest" (Akk *šangû*).

In the first centuries after the Kassite conquest, mathematical texts are virtually nonexistent, although a few Late Babylonian mathematical tablets have been discovered recently (one of them will appear in Friberg and Hunger, fc.). In the Seleucid era the development of computational astronomy (starting already under the Achaemenids) gave rise to a renaissance of numerical computation and, as a sequel, of some of the old theoretical problems.

As already stated, Babylonian mathematics really means "computation." In intermediate calculations it made use of the sexagesimal-place-value system. See NUMBERS AND COUNTING. The use of this system and the conversion of metrological values into "pure numbers" (and reversely, after a result was found) presupposed extensive use of mathematical, metrological, and technical tables. The first group encompasses tables of multiplication and of reciprocals (the division m/n was carried out as a multiplication $m \cdot 1/n$), tables of squares and square roots and of cubes and cube roots, tables of the root n of $n^3 + n^2$, and even quite a few tables of successive powers of a number. The second group contains tabulated conversions of metrological values into sexagesimal multiples of the basic unit and technical tables which contain "fixed factors" to be used in technical computation (the ratio between the squared diameter and the area of a circle; the quantity of bricks to be carried by one worker over a given distance in one day).

The basic contents of Babylonian utilitarian mathematics correspond to the following tables: multiplication tables, tables of reciprocals, metrological tables (which were aids for calculation), and the technical tables which constituted the nexus between mathematical computation and administrative and engineering reality. Mathematics was taught in school because the scribes should be able to calculate the areas of fields, the volume of canals to be dug out and of siege ramps to be built, and, not least, the manpower needed for these tasks. All these calculations were made pretty much as they would be made today, with one important exception: the Babylonians had no concept of quantifiable angle and hence nothing similar to trigonometry. In practical mensuration they would divide complicated fields into "practically right" triangles, "practically right" trapeziums, and "practically rectangular" quadrangles (distinguishing, we might say, a "right" from a "wrong" angle). They would then calculate as we do, knowing that their results were not absolute truth but apparently without having any definite idea about the nature and size of the errors. Presumably, they would see no decisive difference between the imprecision of manpower calculations and those of area determinations.

With these qualifications the Babylonians knew the area of a right triangle (in practical mensuration they would divide an obviously nonright triangle into two; in school exercises they might use the semiproduct of the two "best" sides). In a Late Babylonian text we also find the calculation of a height (by means of the Pythagorean theorem, known already in the OB period). Similarly, they would correctly find the area of a rectangle and of a "right" trapezium. The area of an irregular quadrangle might be found by means of the "surveyors' formula," as average length times average width. In practical mensuration this technique has probably only been used for fairly regular quadrangles, where it gives acceptable results. In school texts the technique is also used as a pretext for formulating algebraic problems in cases where it is extremely unrealistic. The area of the circle was normally found as $\frac{1}{12}$ times the square of the circumference (corresponding to $\pi = 3$), and the circumference as thrice the diameter. (One table of constants, however, has been assumed to contain a correction factor corresponding to $\pi = 3\frac{1}{8}$).

Prismatic and cylindrical volumes were calculated as base times "height" (viz., a side approximately perpendicular to the base). The volume of a truncated cone was found as that of a cylinder with the average diameter (which is correct for a cylinder, and only three-fourths of the true value in the extreme case where the cone is not truncated), and that of a truncated pyramid in one text as height times average base (in another text perhaps correctly). When in doubt, once again, the Babylonians would opt for a (rather arbitrary) compromise instead of giving up in the face of theoretical difficulties.

Prismatic and cylindrical volumes were probably derived from a "naive" consideration of proportionality. The basic unit of area was the SAR, and the basic unit of volume 1 SAR times 1 cubit, also called a SAR (to distinguish, modern historians speak of a "volume sar"). A prism with base A [SAR] and height 1 [cubit] would then have a volume of A [volume SAR]; if it were h cubits, thus h times as high, the volume would have to be $A \cdot h$. A corresponding argument of proportionality was apparently used when the height of a slope was found in similar cases. Certain terminological considerations suggest that even the area of rectangular figures was originally thought of in this way.

A specifically Babylonian geometric problem type is the partition of areas. Initially, this may have been a practical problem. No later than the 23d century B.C., however, it turns up as a theoretical problem: what is the length of the transversal if a trapezium is bisected by a parallel transversal? In the OB period even more complex problems of a similar kind are common, as are a number of other more or less complex and more or less artificial division problems.

Many practical computations, of course, were not concerned with geometric entities but with quantities of grain to be levied as dues, with commercial exchange, and with similar pragmatic concerns. The techniques used can be illustrated by paraphrasing an illustrative problem: two fields, 1 and 2, are given, from one of which 4 GUR (1 GUR = 300 QA, 1 QA $\approx$ 1 liter) of grain are to be levied per BUR (= 1800 SAR), while the other yields a rent of 3 GUR per BUR. The total yield and the difference between the two areas is given. First everything is converted into sexagesimal multiples of the fundamental units SAR and QA, in part through calculation, in part by means of a metrological table. The yield of that part of field 1 which exceeds field 2 is found. The remainder of the yield must then come from the remaining area, A, which is composed of equal portions from field 1 and field 2. The yield of one average SAR is found; this is divided into the remaining yield, giving the remaining area.

The idea behind the last step seems to be the "single false position" also known from other Babylonian texts: If the remaining area were 1 QA, it would consist of $\frac{1}{2}$ SAR from each field, which would permit that the yield be found as (say) p QA. In reality it is (say) $N \cdot p$ QA, and therefore the remaining area must be N SAR.

The procedure gives an impression (confirmed by many other texts) of ad hoc improvization, built on concrete thought, rather than standardized techniques when we get beyond the most basic methods (conversions, etc.). The same feature is also found in OB second-degree and higher "algebra," perhaps the most astonishing accomplishment of the Babylonian mathematical tradition. The term is put in quotes because it is not founded on symbols as is post-Renaissance algebra or on words for unknown numbers as are medieval Islamic and Italian algebra. Instead, it builds on "naive" geometry: where modern algebra presents us with a problem $x^2 + x = A$ (which may be transformed into $x \cdot (x+1) = A$), the Babylonians would consider a geometric rectangle the length of which is known to exceed the width by 1, and the area of which is known to be A; where we transform the equation in order to isolate x, the Babylonians would make corresponding cut-and-paste transformations of the rectangle. The way they did it would be intuitively obvious, and they would provide no Euclidean proof that the procedure was correct (hence the term "naive").

The basic transformations, e.g., the cutting up of rectangles, were made according to fixed schemes. But the OB scribes would also solve quite complex problems; and when transforming them into simple problems, they would make use of a stock of customary tricks but no standard formulas—precisely as they did in arithmetical problems. When used with intelligence (as it is in many texts), OB algebra is therefore highly flexible: as long as we stick to one or two variables and to the second degree, a set of operations almost as flexible as (and in its sequence of operations very similar to) modern symbolic algebra. Only in more complex cases do the disadvantages of the Babylonians' techniques become manifest.

Three qualifications should be given to the statement that OB algebra was geometric. First, the geometric entities involved were not abstract but concrete, measurable line segments and areas. Second, the geometric foundation did not prevent the technique from being applied to nongeometric quantities. We represent, e.g., an unknown weight, an unknown price by a pure number x; the Babylonian, however, would represent them by a line segment of unknown (but numerically knowable) length. Naive-geometric algebra was an all-around way to find unknown quantities involved in complex relations, truly, only artificial relations. (Babylonian scribal practice presented no problems of the second or higher degree; these had to be and were constructed in order to allow the display of scribal virtuosity).

Third, the statement is at cross-purposes with established beliefs. The interpretation which Neugebauer presented in the 1930s as a "first approximation" was at that time accepted at face value, and it has since then been conventional wisdom among historians of mathematics that Babylonian algebra was an algebra of numbers dealt with rhetorically as in the Arabic and Latin Middle Ages. Only recently has a detailed philological and comparative analysis of the text corpus and its terminology demonstrated that the numerical interpretation is in fact only a first approximation. (The reasons for this and the details of the reinterpretation are presented in Høyrup 1987.)

A final important problem type is made up by numerical investigations. Some of these are connected to the computation of reciprocals and hence to the needs of common computation. Others are inspired by the partition of the trapezium mentioned above and lead to indeterminate problems for pairs or sets of numbers. The most famous of all such texts is the tablet called Plimpton 322, a table making use of sets of Pythagorean numbers (i.e., numbers a, b, and c fulfilling the condition $a^2 + b^2 = c^2$).

Any mathematical corpus of knowledge is organized in a way which reflects its purposes, the ways of thought involved, and the underlying cognitive style. So was Babylonian mathematics as we know it. A general characteristic is its domination by methods, not problems. At the first, utilitarian level this reflects that we know Babylonian mathematics from school texts which served to train future scribes in the methods of their profession. For that purpose problems had to be constructed allowing the display of the methods to be learned. In practical life, on the other hand, the problems to be mastered were of course primary and the methods applied for that purpose secondary.

If we go to the "pure" level, however, we find the same primacy of methods, while Greek (and modern) pure mathematics take problems as their starting point and develop the concepts and methods needed to surmount them. In this case the training of practitioners explains nothing, since the particular methods belonging at this level had no practical application. Babylonian "pure" mathematics, however, had a purpose different from the scientific aim of Greek mathematics. As explained above, its rationale was the display of professional virtuosity, which also explains why it flourished in the OB era and disappeared from the archaeological horizon with the death of the scribal school.

Mathematical methods can be taught in two ways. One may present the methods in abstract terms, as theory, eventually to be illustrated by examples—or one may train exclusively through paradigmatic examples. Nowadays, the former way is supposed to be used at higher educational levels; and the latter is reserved for the early stages of school. The approach was different in Babylonian mathematics, where we know of no case of formulated theory and of only two or three where a paradigmatic example is used as the basis for a more general discussion of the method involved (though precisely these texts suggest that oral teaching would do so more often). The only cases where rules are formulated in the abstract, are found in a couple of texts from Greek-ruled Uruk (Friberg fc. in *RLA*).

This feature of Babylonian mathematics can be compared to the makeup of Babylonian legal texts like the Code of Hammurabi. "Hammurabi's Law" is no law book in the likeness of Roman Law. It is a collection of legal decisions made by the king, but of course only put together because the royal decisions were supposed to serve as paradigms for the judges of the realm. We may also draw a comparison with the listing of hundreds of separate cases in Babylonian omen texts.

One could say that Babylonian thought was more concrete and less inclined to abstraction than that of the modern mind. These terms, however, are used differently by a cognitive anthropologist like Levi-Strauss (1972) in his distinction between the "savage" and the modern mind. In other domains Babylonian thought may be concrete in a Levi-Straussian sense, with concrete entities acting as classifiers and imparting thereby some of their properties to the class which they embody (as a primitive society may suppose the members of an "arrow clan" to be swifter than others). But already in the systematization of the omen literature is an underlying implicit abstraction visible in spite of its origin in magic thought (Larsen 1987), and OB mathematics is still farther removed from Levi-Straussian concreteness. It was not their general mental makeup which prevented OB scribes from transforming their (already autonomous) mathematics into abstract science, but rather a lack of motivation for doing so: the "pure mathematics" which they created corresponded precisely to their socio-cultural needs, as the later development of Greek philosophy corresponded to that of the intellectually sophisticated stratum of the leisure class.

This is perhaps less true for the post-Kassite scribal priests, whose tablets might list togetherd metrological conversions and the sacred numbers of gods (Friberg, personal communication concerning an unpublished tablet). Since early times, indeed, the technical cunning of scribes had been surrounded by a sacred aura. In the 22d century B.C. King Gudea of Lagash claimed that he had designed the plan of the temple in the likeness of the scribal goddess Nisaba, "who knows the essence of counting." From the mid-3d millennium "sacred numbers" were also associated with the gods, and numbers were used in writing according to the rebus principle. In the early 1st millennium (before the development of mathematical astronomy), numbers were used cryptographically in a few astrological omen texts. In certain other texts numbers were used for "coding" in a way which may explain how the Assyrian king Sargon claimed the "number of his name" to be 16,283. All these phenomena are hardly to be considered ingredients of Babylonian mathematics, but they reflect the existence and importance of mathematical activities and do so most strongly in periods when mathematics was not an autonomous endeavor (they are significantly absent from the sources for OB scribal-school mathematics). Like marginal phenomena in general, they owe their existence to the core.

The main source collections for OB and Seleucid mathematics have been published by Neugebauer (1935). Thureau-Dangin (1938), Neugebauer and Sachs (1945), and Bruins and Rutten (1961). The best overviews of the contents of Babylonian mathematics are the ones by Vogel (1959, in German) and, especially, Vajman (1961, in Russian, but a German translation is underway). A more popular introduction is van der Waerden (1962: 37–45, 62–81). An overview of the various interpretations of the Pythagorean triples of Plimpton 322 has been given by Friberg (1981). The first survey of 3d-millennium mathematics was published by Powell in 1976; recent discoveries of importance are presented by Damerow and Englund (1987); Englund (1988); Friberg and Hunger fc.). A global overview including all recent discoveries is going to be published by Friberg (fc. in *RLA*), who has also written an excellent selective bibliography (in Dauben 1985: 37–51).

C. Syrian Descendants

The Israelites would have encountered Babylonian mathematics during the Exile but only in the late phase when it was mixed up with Babylonian religion and divination. Long before that they must have been confronted with its descendants "at home," in late 2d- and early 1st-millennium Syria.

After the mid-2d millennium the Canaanite city-states of Syria were politically dominated by Egypt. Characteristically, however, the Canaanite kinglets and pharaoh corresponded in Akkadian; Ugarit, the most prominent Canaanite state, developed its alphabetic script on the basis of cuneiform; and Ugaritic scribes were—just like their Hittite and Assyrian colleagues—taught according to the Sumero-Babylonian tradition (see Krecher 1969). The only traces of mathematics in their curriculum, however, consist in metrological lists. We may reasonably deduce that only the utilitarian stratum of Babylonian mathematics was adopted, while the theoretical superstructure was too much dependent on the particular OB socio-cultural situation to be interesting in the Canaanite cultural outposts. The same will in all probability have been the case in early Israel, whose vista of Babylonian culture was much more indirect, somewhat later, and (since it was largely mediated by the Canaanites) marked by distrust.

The closest point of contact will not have been the scribal, but rather the ill-documented master builders' or architects' tradition. We are told in 1 Kings 5–7 and 2 Chronicles 2–3 that Solomon called in Phoenician masters for the building of the temple, and it seems indeed that they also followed Canaanite models (*CAH* 2/2: 149). We have no direct testimony of the geometric lore of these masters, but an Islamic 9th-century mensuration text by one Abū Bakr shows an astonishing degree of continuity with the OB algebra, not only in mathematical substance and methods, but down to the rhetorical and grammatical structure. A story told by the late 10th-century mathematician Abū'l-Wafā᾿ suggests that the carriers of the continuous tradition were "artisans" *(ṣunnaᶜ)*, i.e., master builders and the like (see Høyrup 1986). There are even reasons to believe that the starting point for the OB algebraic tradition was a preexistent artisans' tradition, although the evidence is not compelling and the artisans may instead have been inspired by an originally scribal scheme.

Irrespective of its original relation to the OB scribal tradition, the same artisans' tradition seems to have permeated the whole Middle East; one biblical reflection is well-known: the "molten sea" set up by Solomon in the temple is claimed (1 Kgs 7:23–24; 2 Chr 4:2) to possess a diameter of 10 cubits and a circumference of 30 cubits, corresponding to the above-mentioned "Babylonian π" of 3.

D. Egyptian Mathematics

The other great Bronze Age mathematical tradition whose echoes can be traced in the Bible and, more distinctly, in the archaeological remains of the divided kingdom, is that of Egypt. Though the Egyptian tradition is in many ways parallel to the Babylonian tradition, the two were obviously independent.

Like its counterpart, Egyptian mathematics is a scribal endeavor which should also be labeled "computation." It arose in connection with administrative needs in the early state; Genesis 41 provides an Israelite perspective on that particularity of Egyptian social life (compared to that of pre-Solomonic Israel) which called for extensive computation. The Egyptian economy was, like that of the early Sumerian states, a redistributive system (the biblical descriptions of Solomon's temple building contain redistributive features, as well). Correspondingly, the calculation of rations and of provision for workers is a central topic in Egyptian mathematical texts, as is the calculation of areas and of the volumes of granaries.

It is not possible to distinguish a particular theoretical level in Egyptian mathematics. In that respect the two traditions differ. This is not to say, however, that Egyptian mathematics was a collection of formulas, nor (as we shall see below) that everything was always made in the way which suited practical applications best. There is, moreover, textual evidence that the scribes themselves saw their mathematical cunning as a high point of knowledge, as "rules for enquiring into nature, and for knowing all that exists, [every] mystery, . . . every secret"—as Peet (1923: 33) translates the introductory passage of the Rhind Mathematical Papyrus (RMP in the following).

There are fewer sources for the history of Egyptian mathematics than in the Babylonian case, and their chronological distribution is no less uneven. It is therefore only possible to give a very general overview of the historical development. The application of measures and the development of the metrological system began no later than the outgoing 4th millennium. Measures of capacity and of areas occur in texts from the 3d to 4th Dyn. (ca. 27th century B.C.). Already at the beginning of the 1st Dyn. (late 4th millennium B.C.) the system of linear measures was used in the canon governing the pictorial representation of human beings (Iversen 1975: 60–66), and from an early date it must also have been used in architectural design.

No direct evidence for 3d-millennium calculational techniques is available. From the way measurements and results are expressed, however, one can deduce that the later unit-fraction system (see below) was not yet existent as a coherent system but only as a way to express ad hoc expansions of the systems of metrological subdivisions. We also know that the scribal calculators were taught as apprentices, in immediate practice, and not in a school (see Brunner 1957: 11–15).

All this was to change in the Middle Kingdom, at the beginning of the 2d millennium. Scribal education from now on took place in a school, and many texts are known which reflect the way professional self-esteem was inculcated in the future scribes. The introduction to the RMP quoted above shows that even mathematics served this purpose, just as in the OB school.

A reorganization of the repertoire of fractions into a coherent system appears to have taken place at this time. The old metrological subdivisions were conserved, but they were now supplemented by a systematic notation for abstract numerical fractions. The basic elements of the system were the unit fractions $1/2$, $1/3$, $1/4$, . . . , $1/n$, together with the complement $2/3$. Any fraction had to be expressed as a sum of such unit fractions (none of them identical) in decreasing order. The Egyptian scribe would thus regard $2/5$ not as a number but as a problem, the solution of which was $1/3 + 1/15$. For practical uses these expressions were less handy than metrological subdivisions. For teaching purposes, however, they were better suited than subdivisions because everything could be expressed precisely; we may also assume that they played a role similar to that of OB higher algebra, because the manipulation of unit fractions required the same kind of mathematical virtuosity.

Once the unit-fraction system had been introduced into the school curriculum, the scribes began using it in practical life. At times the resulting contrast between gross, unnoticed errors and the meticulous precision of the notation may strike us as odd; it is understandable, however, if we see the use of the system as a sort of *art pour l'art,* as an expression of professional identity and not as a merely utilitarian device.

Our main sources for the overall contents and the techniques of Egyptian mathematics are two large papyri copied from Middle Kingdom originals, the Rhind Mathematical Papyrus (RMP) and the Moscow Mathematical Papyrus (MMP). The former is a fairly systematic handbook containing a wealth of intermediate calculations, while the latter is rather disorderly and apparently a students' workbook. The RMP is especially excellent as a survey of Middle Kingdom Egyptian mathematics. Very little is supplied by the MMP and other sources beyond confirmation and clarification of dubious issues found in the RMP.

Almost a third of the RMP is devoted to the computation of $2/n$ (n = 3, 5, . . . , 101) as a sum of unit fractions. This table is a prerequisite for all later calculations because of the distinctive way in which the Egyptians performed multiplication and division: *Multiplying* a number A by 29, the scribe would find by successive doublings $2A$, $4A$, $8A$, and then $10A$, and, by another doubling, $20A$, and finally add A, $8A$, and $20A$ to find the result. That is, the whole procedure was founded on successive doublings and decuplings. If A contained fractions with an odd denominator, the doublings would involve use of the $2/n$ table; so, if $A = 1/5$, $2A = 1/3 + 1/15$, $4A = 2/3 + 1/10 + 1/30$, . . . *Dividing* (as in RMP, problem 33) the number 37 by $B = 1 + 2/3 + 1/2 + 1/7$, the scribe would calculate successively $2B$, $4B$, $8B$, and $16B$, seeing that $16B$ fills out 37 apart from a remainder which is two times an implicit subunit $1/42$; since B is 97 times this same subunit, the remainder is twice $1/97 B$, and the full result of the division is $16 + 2/97$, i.e., in the required system, $16 + 1/56 + 1/679 + 1/776$.

Simple multiplications and divisions might give the impression that Egyptian mathematics was purely additive. As shown, however, by the latter part of the division, as well as by many solutions making use of "false positions" (cf. above) and of free manipulation of appropriate subunits, the Egyptian scribes had a perfect, though implicit, grasp of multiplicative relations and proportionality. Otherwise, indeed, they would have been unable to take care of their practical tasks.

A substantial part of the RMP focuses on problems arising through the use of the unit-fraction system, especially in connection with problems of division and proportionality. Some such problems deal with abstract numbers, others make the connection to daily practice clear, e.g., when loaves are distributed to workers and foremen (with double rations for the latter), when the connection between unit fractions and various metrological systems is dealt with, or when the quality of beer and the size of loaves are involved.

Another dominant interest is in geometric computation. As in Mesopotamia, area measures are mathematically connected to linear measures but are even more clearly conceptualized as the product of a fixed-standard width and a variable length. As in Babylonia, the concept of a quantifiable angle is absent; and triangular areas were found as the product of two sides containing a "practically right" angle. Trapeziums and trapezoids are absent from the sources; but the area of a circle is found as the square of $D - 1/9 D$ (D being the diameter), corresponding to $\pi = 256/81 = 3.16$ . . .—much better than the normal Babylonian rule.

Prismatic and cylindrical volumes were, of course, found without difficulty; it is more astonishing that the volume of a truncated pyramid was found correctly (MMP, problem 14). It is disputed whether a "basket" in MMP (problem 10) is meant to be a hemisphere. If it is, its surface is found accurately (given the above-mentioned "π"; but if a hemisphere is not meant, the computation suggests that the Egyptians would find the circular circumference (correctly) as the quadruple area of the circle divided by the diameter and the area of a semicylinder as the product of the curved and the straight side.

Geometry and geometric computations were also used in Egyptian architecture. Architectural and building problems, however, are not very conspicuous in the mathematical texts, which in fact contain only two types: first, the calculation of the slope of pyramids, according to the RMP, where it is dealt with five times; and second, the volume of a truncated pyramid, which is only known from MMP.

It is a recurrent claim that the Egyptians knew the Pythagorean theorem and used it in architectural construction. It should be observed, however, that the claim is not supported by any positive evidence. Many buildings, it is true, contain rectangles whose sides are to each other as 3 to 4, but nothing suggests that the Egyptians knew or were interested in the length of the diagonal.

Related to the use of geometry in architecture is the use in the pictorial arts of square grids and fixed proportions linked to the system of linear measures. This "canonical system" is one of the main factors creating the unique tenor of Egyptian art and which stabilized it for several millennia, until a metrological reform in the 7th century B.C. made it rather a factor of change.

Anything similar to Babylonian second-degree algebra was absent from Egyptian mathematics. The closest we come are two types of geometric problems. One is found repeatedly in the MMP: in a (practically) right triangle the area and the ratio between the sides containing the right angle are given; this is solved by means of a consideration of proportionality. The other comes from the Berlin Papyrus 6619 and can be translated into modern symbols as $x^2 + y^2 = 100$, $y = \frac{3}{4} \cdot x$; the solution is obtained by means of a false position ("always take a square of side 1; then the other is $\frac{1}{2} + \frac{1}{4}$").

These problems are atypical by being of the second degree. In fact, everything else related to algebra is of the first degree. But the techniques used are typical also of those first-degree problems which we would be tempted to solve algebraically. The "false position," in particular, may be regarded as a "poor man's *x*." The point in using an *x* is, in fact, that you can manipulate the unknown quantity as if it were a known number; taking preliminarily the unknown to be 1 (or any other convenient number) gives you the same possibility, as long as you stick to "homogeneous problems" (i.e., problems which can be reduced to the type $x^{11} = A$).

The above description does not exhaust the contents of Egyptian mathematics, but it covers the principal features as far as we know them and does so until the Assyrian domination. Then (modest) changes set in: a number of demotic mathematical papyri from the Hellenistic and Roman periods show, indeed, that material from the Babylonian or Middle Eastern practitioners' tradition had diffused into Egypt during the 1st millennium B.C. (perhaps carried by Persian military or fiscal surveyors?). Most conspicuous is an adoption of the Babylonian π.

Egyptian mathematical texts are problem collections, just like the Babylonian ones. The closest we come to a general description of methods is a phrase like the "always take a square of side 1" quoted above. But even in Egypt the problems were meant to be paradigmatic—as stated in the introduction to the RMP, they were regarded as "rules." In the texts, methods are thus primary and the problems secondary. In scribal professional practice, of course, the practical problems were primary; and since no clearly distinguishable level of nonutilitarian calculation developed in Egypt, the problems found in the texts are either real-life problems or structurally similar to problems encountered in "real life"—including problems arising from the idiosyncratic multiplication and division algorithms and the unit-fraction system. Globally regarded, the structure of Egyptian mathematics was thus determined by its practical duties and its characteristic methods and techniques, in mutual interaction and on an equal footing.

As in Babylonia, the mode of thought expressed in the mathematical texts is concrete. There is, however, one important difference. Babylonian mathematics, as we have seen, tended to represent other unknown entities by measurable geometric entities; the Egyptians, on the other hand, tended to represent everything by *pure numbers* (at least from the Middle Kingdom onward). Even though Babylonian mathematics is much more sophisticated in content than its Egyptian counterpart, the latter can thus be claimed to have gone farther in mathematical abstraction.

Old Babylonian mathematics, as we saw, appears to be purely secular. In later times the borderline between mathematics, divination, and religion seemed to have become somewhat blurred. In Egypt, as well, numeration and numbers played a religio-mystical role, as in the *Book of Dead,* where the deceased king is required to count his fingers (Neugebauer 1969: 9). But in spite of the "mysteries" and "secrets" spoken of in the introduction to the RMP, the mathematical texts themselves appear to be devoid of religious and occult connotations.

This is, of course, in disagreement with the widespread speculations on "pyramid mysticism." The pyramidological arguments build (at best) on a variety of numerical ratios purportedly found in the Cheops pyramid and claimed to reflect a precise knowledge of π and the "golden section." Two flaws, however, characterize these assertions (see Robins and Shute 1985). First, precise measurement of the (original!) dimensions of the worn-down pyramid is difficult; and in order to obtain their favorite ratios, the pyramidologists avoid using the best measurements. Second, nothing in the mathematical texts suggests the slightest interest in the numbers claimed to be embodied in the pyramids; so, e.g., the Egyptians did not use a number corresponding to π but instead an approximation (viz., $\frac{8}{9}$) to $\sqrt{(\pi/4)}$, which is quite another entity though of course just as mathematically serviceable. On the other hand, the best measurements of pyramidal slopes correspond precisely to the way pyramidal slopes are indicated in the RMP and come out mostly as 5 palms, 1 finger; or 5 palms, 2 fingers horizontally per vertical cubit (the former value being the favorite value in the RMP).

Both RMP and MMP exist in excellent editions. RMP was edited by Peet in 1923 with a hieroglyphic transcription (the original is hieratic) and English translation and commentary and again in 1927–29 by Chace et al. with free translation and commentary (vol. 1), and reproduction, hieroglyphic transcription, transliteration, and literal translation (vol 2). MMP was edited by Struve in 1930 with reproduction, hieroglyphic transcription, German translation, and commentary. A new edition of RMP intended for interested nonspecialists was published in 1987 by Robins and Shute. A collection of demotic mathematical papyri was published (with transliteration, and English translation, and discussion of terminological and technical continuity and change since the Middle Kingdom mathematics) by Parker in 1972.

Excellent surveys of Egyptian mathematics have been written by Vogel (1958, in German) and Gillings (1972). The latter work is inspiring but should be used with some caution, since the author often shows what imagined sources might have looked like and does so in the most exquisite and convincing hieratic hand. Both surveys include references to other works and to publications of minor sources. A comprehensive bibliography of works on Egyptian mathematics up to 1929 compiled by Archibald is included in Chace et al. 1927–29. A recent selective bibliography will be found in Dauben (1985: 29–37).

A fictional satirical letter much used in the school and reflecting the importance of mathematical computation in scribal occupations was published by Gardiner (1911).

The "canonical system" of the pictorial arts was described by Iversen (1975). Badawy's exposition of Egyptian architectural design (1965) should be used with circumspection.

The full range of Egyptian mathematics was probably never diffused to the Palestinian area. However, epigraphic evidence shows that from the time when the Israelite kingdoms began approaching a redistributive economy and the royal scribes came in need of computational tools, the scribes took over the Egyptian hieratic numbers (survey of the main evidence in Ifrah 1986: 271). These, however, are more complex than the hieroglyphic numbers which they represent in shorthand; and one can hardly imagine that they were adopted in isolation: they must have been imported together with at least part of that wider mathematical culture which they served. In all probability the administration in the divided kingdom will thus have been effected by means of Egyptian routines and techniques.

E. Greek and Hellenistic Mathematics and Its Aftermath

The third mathematical tradition of some importance in the biblical context was that of ancient Greece and of the Hellenistic world.

Early classical Greece was the cradle of "philosophy," i.e., of intellectual and scientific interest radically separated from direct social utility. While the nonutilitarian stratum of Babylonian (and, as far as it existed, Egyptian) mathematics had to look like a tool for scribal practice in order to serve the socio-psychological maintenance of scribal identity, Greek mathematics had to look "pure," i.e., unbound by social utility. Scribal work, indeed, had become a lowly occupation in classical antiquity, and had stopped being intellectually productive.

The starting point was apparently intellectual curiosity vis à vis the techniques of surveyors and accountants: why did these techniques work? At the end of the road we find Euclid's *Elements;* Archimedes' computations of circle, sphere, and paraboloid; and Apollonius' *Conics;* together with a number of minor astronomical works disguised as pure spherical geometry; and Ptolemy's monumental *Almagest.* All of this was fairly irrelevant to both Jewish and Christian culture until the High Middle Ages, and there is no reason to discuss it further here.

More important than the mathematical history as a whole in this period are several underlying traditions.

First there is the alphabetic number system. See NUMBERS AND COUNTING. It has been much disputed who first used the letters of the alphabet for numbers, and the question is not definitively settled. The Greeks did so at least from the late 3d century B.C. onward, but so did the Jews and other Semitic peoples. However, no evidence for Semitic usage can be dated before the 1st century A.D.; and until then another system seemed to be in use. For this reason (and various other reasons) it is the most reasonable assumption that the alphabetic number system was invented by the Greeks and then taken over by others in the Hellenistic world (see the discussion in Ifrah 1986: 286–302).

Originally, this was just a clever notation for numbers, soon, however, the possibility to read any alphabetic letter as a number was exploited in gematria, the substitution of the sum of constituent numbers for a word. An early and most famous example is found in Rev 13:18, the number of the beast being "the number of a man; and the number is 666." (This reminds one of the Assyrian king Sargon's claim concerning the "number of his name," but the resemblance is probably accidental.)

Of greater importance was the technique in medieval and Renaissance exegesis, viz., in the *Kabbalah,* where it was used extensively for symbolic identification of words with the same gematric number (see the description of both Jewish and Christian Kabbalah in Blau 1944).

Next there is the Pythagorean tradition. The Pythagorean brotherhood had formed in the late 6th century B.C. around Pythagoras, who was (*pace* an abundance of Neo-Pythagorean and modern authors) in all probability no "scientist" or "mathematician" but rather a shamanistic figure, as has been argued by Burkert (1972). Plausibly, however, numerology (on a traditional "folk" level) was a major ingredient in his doctrine. Over the 5th century, then, and concurrently with the development of scientific mathematics, the Pythagorean brotherhood (or one branch of it) appears to have extended the numerological interest, first by adopting an existing number-theoretical interest (the "doctrine of odd and even") and extending it and then by taking up theoretical geometry. (A satisfactory discussion of the relative chronology of "philosophical" and "Pythagorean" mathematical achievements would lead too far; but see Knorr [1975: passim]; Høyrup [1985: 19–21].)

In the 4th century B.C., the Pythagorean movement disappears as a scientific school, although throughout antiquity the basic Pythagorean arithmetical doctrine remained important. It is, in fact, a doctrine rather than a theory. The fundamental constituents are the canon of figurate numbers and the classification of numerical proportions. The doctrine was put forth through examples and without proofs. The discoveries made by late-ancient Neo-Pythagorean authors (if indeed they made them) were made empirically.

Figurate numbers are the numbers which arise when points are arranged in certain regular patterns. We still know the *square numbers,* $1 \cdot 1$, $2 \cdot 2$, $3 \cdot 3$, etc., and the *prime numbers,* which can only be arranged in a single row and in no other rectangular pattern. A third species are the *triangular numbers,* 1, 1 + 2, 1 + 2 + 3, 1 + 2 + 3 + 4, etc., and still others exist (*rectangular numbers* of the form $n \cdot (n + 1)$; *pentagonal numbers,* $1 + 2 + \ldots + (n-1) + n^2$, etc.). See Fig. MAT. 01.

The doctrine of proportions was coupled to the theory of musical harmony. An octave corresponds to a ratio 2:1 (in frequency, which the ancients did not know, and in string lengths on a monochord, which they did know); a fifth corresponds to the ratio 3:2, a fourth to 4:3, etc. All these are superparticular ratios, i.e., they have the form $(n + 1) : n$. Other classes are defined in similar ways.

Neo-Pythagorean arithmetic was considered indispensable for the understanding of (especially Platonic) philosophy and was hence a prolegomenon in the basic late ancient philosophical curriculum. In this way it spread to much wider circles than high-level mathematics. One place in general culture which was influenced by the Pythagorean doctrine was poetry. A number of texts (so Virgil's *Bucolica* and *Georgica*) are constructed around simple proportions (identity and superparticulars) and prime numbers. These mathematical relations turn up in the counting of lines, words, and letters—especially vowels.

Interestingly, this same technique appears to have been used in the gospel of Luke. As it is well-known, the Sermon on the Mount and the Lord's Prayer are rendered differently by Matthew and Luke. According to the linguist Jens Juhl Jensen (1986), who has compared the gospel text with the principles used in "Pythagorean" poetry from the same epoch, Luke's version (but not Matthew's) follows Pythagorean principles. It is of some exegetical interest that part of the difference between the two evangelists may be the necessary difference between translation into prose and into poetry governed by strict rules.

Neo-Pythagorean doctrines were also important in ancient and medieval exegesis, in particular the figurate numbers. An important character in this connection is Philo of Alexandria, and a good example is his discussion of the measures of Noah's Ark (edited by Paramelle [1984: 148–63] with a numerological commentary by Sesiano [205–9]). The length of 300 [cubits] represents the universe, because it is the 24th triangular number, 24 being the number of hours in a day and the number of letters in the Greek alphabet, $24 = 2^3 + 2^3 + 2^3$, and the triad 1 + 1 + 1 thus occurring doubly in 24 representing equality (identity of beginning, middle, and end). Furthermore, $300 = (1 + 3 + \ldots + 23) + (2 + 4 + \ldots + 24) = 144 + 156$, 144 being 12^2 and thus including (as dot patterns) the first 12 squares, while $156 = 12 \cdot 13$ "includes" (in the same sense) the first 12 rectangular numbers. So, 300 unites in itself equality and inequality, whereby it is similar to and represents the universe. Similar astute observations are made on the width and the height of the Ark.

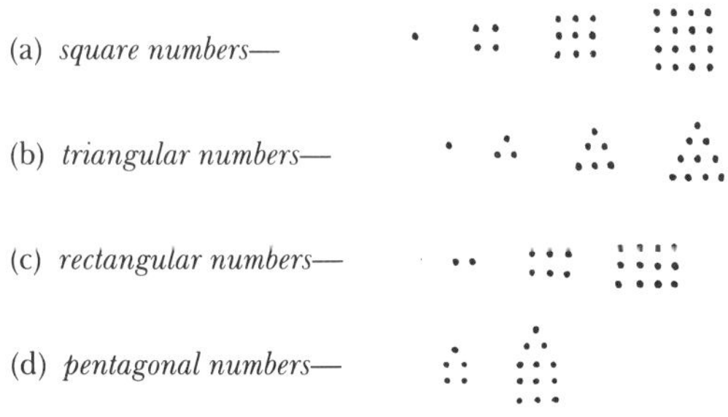

MAT.01. Patterns of figurate numbers.

Philo's numerology was taken over by both Ambrose and Augustine (who as a teacher had taught Neo-Pythagorean arithmetic in his own youth). But Christian authors until the early Renaissance would also make their own numerological exegesis. A late and beautiful example is Nicholas of Cusa's mathematical "proof" that trinity could not possibly have been quaternity (*De docta ignorantia* 1.20, ed. Wilpert 1967, 1: 59–60): maximal and minimal entities coincide (a fundamental principle in Cusanus' philosophy); in surveying, the necessary reduction to minimal entities leads to triangulation; ergo . . .

Scientific Greek mathematics only affected medieval exegesis on one point. As mentioned above, the "Babylonian π" is accepted in the Bible. This became a problem to medieval Jewish authors, who devised the explanation that the thread measuring the circumference of the molten sea ran around the inner surface (so explained in *Mišnat ha-Middot* 5. 3). This same idea was proposed not so long ago by the pyramidologist Berriman (1953: 97).

Summing up the influence of Greek and Hellenistic mathematics, we may conclude that it affected the biblical text itself in only a few unimportant aspects. As Judaism and (later) Christianity became integrated into general Hellenistic culture, however, Neo-Pythagoreanism and elementary Archimedean surveying had become an indisputable (and noncontroversial) part of the intellectual baggage of the Church Fathers and other commentators, and they would see no problem in using it as a tool for their exegetical efforts. This mathematical view was also inherited and promulgated by their disciples in the Middle Ages and the early Renaissance.

Bibliography

Badawy, A. 1965. *Ancient Egyptian Architectural Design: A Study of the Harmonic System.* UCPNES 4. Berkeley.

Berriman, A. E. 1953. *Historical Metrology.* London.

Blau, J. L. 1944. The Christian Interpretation of the Cabala in the Renaissance. Ph.D. diss., Columbia University.

Bruins, E. M., and Rutten, M. 1961. *Textes mathématiques de Suse.* Mémoires de la Mission Archéologique en Iran 34. Paris.

Brunner, H. 1957. *Altägyptische Erziehung.* Wiesbaden.

Burkert, W. 1972. *Lore and Science in Ancient Pythagoreanism.* Cambridge, MA.

Chace, A. B., et al. 1927–29. *The Rhind Mathematical Papyrus. British Museum 10057 and 10058.* 2 Vols. Oberlin, OH.

Damerow, P., and Englund, R. K. 1987. Die Zahlzeichenssysteme der Archaischen Texte aus Uruk. Vol. 2, pp. 117–66 in *Zeichenliste der Archaischen Texte aus Uruk,* ed. M. W. Green and H. J. Nissen. ATU 2. Berlin.

Dauben, J. W. 1985. *The History of Mathematics from Antiquity to the Present. A Selective Bibliography.* Bibliographies of the History of Science and Technology 6. New York.

Englund, R. K. 1988. Administrative Timekeeping in Ancient Mesopotamia. *JESHO* 31: 121–85.

Friberg, J. 1981. Methods and Traditions of Babylonian Mathematics: Plimpton 322, Pythagorean Triples, and the Babylonian

Triangle Parameter Equations. *Historia Mathematica* 8: 277–318.
———. 1984. Numbers and Measures in the Earliest Written Records. *Scientific American* (European Edition) 250/2 (February 1984): 78–85.
———. 1986. The Early Roots of Babylonian Mathematics. III: Three Remarkable Texts from Ancient Ebla. *Vicino Oriente* 6: 3–25.
Friberg, J., and Hunger H. fc. Seed and Reeds: A Metro-mathematical Topic Text from LB Uruk.
Gardiner, A. H. 1911. *Egyptian Hieratic Texts. Series I: Literary Texts from the New Kingdom. Part I: The Papyrus Anastasi I and the Papyrus Koller, together with Parallel Texts.* Leipzig.
Gillings. R. J. 1972. *Mathematics in the Time of the Pharaohs.* Cambridge, MA.
Høyrup, J. 1980. Influences of Institutionalized Mathematics Teaching on the Development and Organization of Mathematical Thought in the Pre-Modern Period. Investigations into an Aspect of the Anthropology of Mathematics. *Materialien und Studien: Institut für Didaktik der Mathematik der Universität Bielefeld* 20: 7–137.
———. 1982. Investigations of an Early Sumerian Division Problem, c. 2500 B.C. *Historia Mathematica* 9: 19–36.
———. 1985. *Babylonian Algebra from the View-Point of Geometrical Heuristics. An Investigation of Terminology, Methods, and Patterns of Thought.* Roskilde, Denmark.
———. 1986. Al-Khwârizmî, Ibn Turk, and the Liber Mensurationum: On the Origins of Islamic Algebra. *Erdem* 2: 445–84.
———. 1987. Algebra and Naive Geometry. An Investigation of Some Basic Aspects of Old Babylonian Mathematical Thought. *Filosofi og Videnskabsteori på Roskilde Universitetscenter. 3. Række: Preprints og Reprints 1987 Nr. 2.* In *AoF* 1990.
Ifrah, G. 1986. *Universalgeschichte der Zahlen.* Trans. A. von Platen. Frankfurt am Main.
Iversen, E. 1975. *Canon and Proportion in Egyptian Art.* 2d rev. ed. Warminster.
Jensen, J. J. 1986. *I begyndelsen var tallet: Pythagoræisk poesi gennem to årtusinder.* Copenhagen.
Knorr, W. R. 1975. *The Evolution of the Euclidean Elements.* Synthese Historical Library 15. Dordrecht.
Krecher, J. 1969. Schreiberschulung in Ugarit. Die Tradition von Listen und sumerischen Texten. *UF* 1: 131–58.
Larsen, M. T. 1987. The Mesopotamian Lukewarm Mind: Reflections on Science, Divination and Literacy. Pp. 203–25 in *Language, Literature, and History: Philological and Historical Studies Presented to Erica Reiner,* ed. F. Rochberg-Halton. AOS 67. New Haven.
Levi-Strauss, C. 1972. *The Savage Mind.* London.
Neugebauer, O. 1935. *Mathematische Keilschrift-texte.* 1–3. Quellen und Studien zur Geschichte der Mathematik, Astronomie und Physik 3/1–3. Berlin. Repr. 1973.
———. 1969. *The Exact Sciences in Antiquity.* New York.
Neugebauer, O., and Sachs, A. 1945. *Mathematical Cuneiform Texts.* AOS 29. New Haven.
Paramelle, J. 1984. *Philon d'Alexandrie, Questions sur la Genèse II 1–7.* Cahiers d'Orientalisme 3. Geneva.
Parker, R. A. 1972. *Demotic Mathematical Papyri.* Providence.
Peet, T. E. 1923. *The Rhind Mathematical Papyrus, British Museum 10057 and 10058.* London.
Powell, M. A., Jr. 1972. Sumerian Area Measures and the Alleged Decimal Substratum. *ZA* 62: 165–221.
———. 1976. The Antecedents of Old Babylonian Place Notation and the Early History of Babylonian Mathematics. *Historia Mathematica* 3: 417–39.
Robins, G., and Shute, Ch. C. D. 1985. Mathematical Bases of Ancient Egyptian Architecture and Graphic Art. *Historia Mathematica* 12: 107–22.
———. 1987. *The Rhind Mathematical Papyrus: An Ancient Egyptian Text.* London.
Schmandt-Besserat, D. 1977. *An Archaic Recording System and the Origin of Writing.* SMS 1/2. Malibu, CA.
Struve, W. W. 1930. *Mathematischer Papyrus des Staatlichen Museums der Schönen Künste in Moskau.* Quellen und Studien zur Geschichte der Mathematik 1. Berlin.
Thureau-Dangin, F. 1938. *Textes mathématiques babyloniens.* Ex Oriente Lux 1. Leiden.
Vajman, A. A. 1961. *Sumero-vavilonskaja matematika. III–I Tysjačeletija do n. e.* Moscow.
Vogel, K. 1958. *Vorgriechische Mathematik.* Vol. 1, *Vorgeschichte und Ägypten.* Mathematische Studienhefte 1. Hannover.
———. 1959. *Vorgriechische Mathematik.* Vol. 2, *Die Mathematik der Babylonier.* Mathematische Studienhefte 2. Hannover.
Waerden, B. L. van der. 1962. *Science Awakening.* 2d Ed. Groningen.
Wilpert, P. 1967. *Nikolaus von Kues, Werke. (Neuausgabe des Straßburger Drucks von 1488).* I–II. Quellen und Studien zur Geschichte der Philosophie 5–6. Berlin.

JENS HØYRUP

MATRED (PERSON) [Heb *maṭrēd*]. The mother—or father—of Mehetabel, wife of the "Edomite king" Hadad (II) (Gen 36:39; 1 Chr 1:50). See also HADAD (PERSON); MEHETABEL. Whereas the Hebrew Bible has "Matred, daughter of Mezahab" (see MEZAHAB), the LXX translates "Mathraeith, son of M." It is preferable to read *bn* instead of *bt* with the LXX, because Matred is a male rather than a female name.

The "Edomite King List" (Gen 36:31–39) is either a list of local rulers (some of which may have come from Arabia) in the country of Edom from the 5th century B.C. (Knauf 1985) or a list of Aramean kings from the 11th century B.C. (Lemaire 1988). The name "Matred" has parallels in (Classical and recent) Arabic (*Maṭrûd,* Caskel 1966: 404; *Maṭrûd* and *Mṭârid,* Hess 1912: 36). The root *ṭrd,* "to drive, drive off," is attested for both Aramaic and Arabic, whereas Heb *ṭārad,* "to flow continuously (water, speech)," provides an unlikely etymon for the personal name, as does Sabaic *mṭrd* "ritual hunt(?)" (Beeston et al. 1982: 154).

Bibliography

Beeston, A. F. L.; Ghul, M. A.; Müller, W. W.; and Ryckmans, J. 1982. *Sabaic Dictionary.* Louvain-la-Neuve and Beirut.
Caskel, W. 1966. *Gamharat an-nasab: Das genealogische Werk des Hisam ibn Muhammad al-Kalbi, II.* Leiden.
Hess, J. J. 1912. *Beduinennamen aus Zentralarabien.* Heidelberg.
Knauf, E. A. 1985. Alter und Herkunft der edomitischen Königsliste Gen 36, 31–39. *ZAW* 97: 245–53.
Lemaire, A. 1988. Hadad l'Édomite ou Hadad l'Araméen? *BN* 43: 14–18.

ERNST AXEL KNAUF

MATRED, RAMAT. See RAMAT MATRED (M.R. 118020).

MATRITES (PEOPLE) [Heb *maṭrî*]. A clan of the tribe of Benjamin. In a lot-casting procedure used to choose Israel's first king, the Matrites were chosen from the tribe of Benjamin, and Saul was chosen from the Matrites (1 Sam 10:21). Presumably the name is derived from the Hebrew word for rain and may mean "born during the rainy season" (Reymond 1958: 19–20). The name occurs once in Hebrew and twice in Greek in 1 Sam 10:21. The sentence "finally he brought the family of the Matrites near man by man" (RSV) is not found in the Masoretic Text but is based on the Greek translation of this verse. Some scholars think that these words were mistakenly omitted from the Hebrew text (McCarter *1 Samuel* AB, 190), while others argue that the shorter Hebrew text was later amplified by means of a similar text in Josh 7:17–18 (Barthélemy 1982: 165).

Bibliography

Barthélemy, D. 1982. *Critique textuelle de l'ancien testament.* OBO 50/1. Göttingen.

Koehler, L. 1940. Hebräische Etymologien. *JBL* 59: 37.

Reymond, P. 1958. *L'eau, sa vie, et sa signification dans l'ancien testament.* VTSup 6. Leiden.

STEPHEN A. REED

MATTAN (PERSON) [Heb *mattān*]. **1.** A priest of Baal who was killed before the altars of Baal, when Jehoiada the priest ordered the altars and images destroyed (2 Kgs 11:18; 2 Chr 23:17). Mattan is probably a truncated form of the common Semitic name *mttnyh* through loss of the divine-name suffix (see 2 Kgs 24:17; 1 Chr 25:4, 16; Neh 11:17, 22) and attested by a Lachish seal and several Phoenician and Punic inscriptions, although he himself was probably not a Phoenician (Rehm *2 Könige* EB, 119). Mattan was possibly Baal's chief priest (Keil n.d. 364), although he is one of only two recorded victims of Jehoiada's covenant with the people and king that they should be Yahweh's people (the other victim was Athaliah, who usurped the throne of her dead son, Ahaziah). The location of this temple of Baal is unknown; but it has been speculated that, on the basis of the limited success of Athaliah and her priest Mattan and of the fact that their deaths are the only ones mentioned, the worship was of a seasonal fertility cult, with altars or even a single altar, possibly in the temple of the royal palace (Gray *1 and 2 Kings* OTL, 580–81).

2. The father of Shephatiah, an official or prince in King Zedekiah's government, partially responsible for Jeremiah's being thrown into the cistern of Malchijah (Jer 38:1).

Bibliography

Keil, C. F. n.d. I and II Kings and I and II Chronicles, Ezra, Nehemiah, Esther. In vol. 3 of *Commentary on the Old Testament in Ten Volumes,* ed. C. F. Keil and F. Delitzsch. Grand Rapids. Repr. 1983–86.

STANLEY E. PORTER

MATTANAH (PLACE) [Heb *mattānâ*]. A camping place of the Israelites during the Exodus, located in Moab N of the river Arnon (Num 21:18–19).

In antiquity Eusebius and Jerome identified Mattanah with Maschana, said to have been situated on the Arnon river 12 miles E of Medeba (Lagarde 1887: 277, lines 82–83; 137, lines 30–31). Though the precise location of Mattanah is unknown, most scholars identify it with the site of modern Khirbet el-Medeiyineh (e.g., Glueck 1933–34: 13). Khirbet el-Medeiyineh (M.R. 236110) is a large tell situated on the left bank of the Wâdī eth-Themed in the upper regions of the Wâdī el-Wāle about 12 miles SE of Medeba. Glueck noted pottery sherds dated mostly to Early Iron I and traces of a wall surrounding the top of the tell. Halfway down the slope a wide ditch or dry moat encircles the mound.

Given (1) the apparent discontinuity in the sequence of place names between Num 21:16 and 19; (2) differences in readings between the LXX and the MT; and (3) the meaning of Mattanah ("gift," "donation,"), some commentators render the conclusion of Num 21:18 "a gift from the wilderness" (cf. Gray *Numbers* ICC, 290). This possible translation, however, creates difficulty with the following verse, where Mattanah clearly designates a location. Hence the majority of scholars retain the MT reading and treat Mattanah as a place name.

Bibliography

Glueck, N. 1933–34. *Explorations in Eastern Palestine, I.* AASOR 14. Philadelphia.

Lagarde, P. de. 1887. *Onomastica Sacra.* Göttingen. Repr. Hildesheim, 1966.

ARTHUR J. FERCH

MATTANIAH (PERSON) [Heb *mattanyāhû*]. Var. BESCASPASMYS. As many as 10 people in the OT bear this name. It is composed of the Hebrew word for "gift" *(mattan)* and the divine name, Yahweh. Such combinations of the divine name and some form of the verb *ntn* "to give" are called names of thanksgiving by Noth (*IPN,* 170). Other examples are Nathaniel, Elnathan, and Jonathan. This combination is also found in the W Semitic world outside the literature and culture of Israel (*IPN,* 170–71). Mattaniah, in its full form or in its abbreviated form, Mattan, is almost as common in nonbiblical Hebrew sources as in the Bible. The shorter form is seen in 2 Kgs 11:18 and Jer 38:1.

In the Lachish Letters 1:5 the full name "Mattaniah" appears with the patronymic Neriah (Heb *nryhw*), but no clue is offered as to his position or title (*TSSI* 1: 34). The almost-contemporary Arad correspondence contains no reference to the name, but the recently published collection of seal impressions (bullae) from Jerusalem (Avigad 1986) contains several. There are seven identifiable persons bearing the name Mattan (see bullae Nos. 113, 114, 115, 116a, 116b, 117, and 118) including three uses of the shortened name as a patronymic (bullae Nos. 21, 52, 74). Bulla No. 119 contains the name "Mattaniah son of Semachiah" (Heb *mttnyhw bn smkyhw*). The name is among the most popular in this collection of prominent civil servants in the late Monarchy of the 6th century B.C.E.

In the Bible all of the names apply to temple officials, priests, or prominent civil figures, reinforcing the general impression given by the nonbiblical material that the name was a favorite of such persons. While the name is found in stories dealing with the time of David (1 Chr 25:4, 16), Jehoshaphat (2 Chr 20:14), and Hezekiah (2 Chr 29:13), the references are found in the Deuteronomistic History, the book of Jeremiah, and the work of the Chronicler, including Ezra and Nehemiah, that is, in literature which reached its final form either during the Exile or in the postexilic period.

Of the ten men bearing the name Mattaniah, five were priests, one was a member of the royal family, and the other four were members of the postexilic Jerusalem elite. The shortened form of the name applies to members of similar classes of people, a priest (2 Kgs 11:18) and one of a group of "princes" (Heb *sārîm;* Jer 38:1, 4). The characters are listed below in their chronological order.

1. One of the fourteen "sons of Heman," a group of Levites which was appointed by David for temple service (1 Chr 25:4, 16). The duties of Mattaniah and his thirteen brothers were to "prophesy with lyres, with harps, and with cymbals" (1 Chr 25:4). They were accompanied by members of the sons of Asaph and Jeduthun. The reference is important because of its view of prophecy. A similar understanding is seen in the activity of the prophets whom Saul met (1 Sam 10:5–13) and the activity of Elisha (2 Kgs 3:15), in which prophecy is accompanied by instrumental music (Johnson 1962: 69–74). Ps 88:1 contains a dedication to "Heman the Ezrahite," thus continuing the tradition of the musical associations of this group. The reference in 1 Chronicles 25 is clearly anachronistic and reflects a later arrangement in the temple services.

2. The ancestor of Jahaziel, a member of the court of Jehoshaphat (ca. 877–853 B.C.E.) of Judah (2 Chr 20:14). The activity of Mattaniah's descendant is clearly a prophetic one and consisted of the giving of oracles of reassurance in time of national threat (Conrad 1985: 38–62). It appears that this became a regular function of "court prophets," but it had a long history (Blenkinsopp 1983: 61–68). In this case Judah was threatened with invasion by an alliance of Moabites, Ammonites, and Meunites, a S Transjordanian tribe from the region of modern Petra. As the oracle stated, the invasion was repulsed.

3. A Levite of the sons of Asaph who, together with his colleague Zechariah and representatives of the sons of Kohath, Merari, Gershon, Elizaphan, and Heman, was commissioned by Hezekiah (ca. 727–699 B.C.E.) to consecrate the temple during the king's reform of worship (2 Chr 29:13). As with the reform of Josiah, the Chronicler pays much more attention to the role of the temple Levites in the event.

4. The uncle (Heb *dôd*) of king Jehoiachin (ca. 597 B.C.E.) who was placed on the throne of Judah by Nebuchadnezzar of Babylon, after Jehoiachin had been taken into Exile (2 Kgs 24:17). It is assumed that the term *dôd* is to be translated as "uncle" in this context, but the term does have strong overtones of intimacy and closeness which go beyond matters of kinship (*TDOT* 3: 143–56). Mattaniah/Zedekiah reigned for a further eleven years (ca. 597–586 B.C.E.), rebelled against Nebuchadnezzar, and witnessed the invasion of Judah and the final destruction of Jerusalem. The name change was obviously a source of a prophetic pun by Jeremiah (Jer 23:6). The practice of renaming kings at the time of enthronement is not unknown in the ANE and is mentioned four times in the Bible. Solomon's pre-coronation name appears to have been Jedidiah (2 Sam 12:24–25); Jehoahaz, son of Josiah, was originally named Shallum (Jer 22:11); and Jehoiakim was originally called Eliakim (2 Kgs 23:13). The Babylonian account says nothing of a name change but does state that Nebuchadnezzar appointed "a king of his own choice" on the throne in Jerusalem (*TCS* 5: 102).

5. A non-Levite, one of the sons of Elam who had married foreign women after their return from Exile and for whom Ezra had insisted upon divorce (Ezra 10:26).

6. One of the sons of Zattu, a returnee, who divorced his wife, a foreigner, on the orders of Ezra (Ezra 10:27).

7. One of the eight sons of Pahath-moab who had married foreign women on their return from Exile and who were forced to divorce them on orders of Ezra (Ezra 10:30). It is possible that he is the same as Bescaspasmys (Gk *Beskaspasmus*) in 1 Esdr 9:31.

8. One of the twelve sons of Bani who was forced to divorce his foreign wife after the return from Exile (Ezra 10:37). Each of these family groups is mentioned among the returning exiles in Ezra 2:6–10 and Neh 7:11–13, and they are distinguished from the priests and Levites. The heads are called "chiefs of the people" (Neh 10:14), and those that married foreign women are listed as "from Israel" (Ezra 10:26) in contrast to the religious functionaries. All four of the family heads entered into the covenant with Nehemiah (Neh 10:14) to separate themselves from the "people of the land" in matters of worship, marriage, and other religious practices (Neh 10:28–31).

9. Mattaniah ben Micah, a member of the "sons of Asaph," was appointed by Nehemiah as "the leader to begin the thanksgiving in prayer" in the restored temple during the high priesthood of Eliashib (Neh 11:17). A descendant, Uzzi ben Bani, was "overseer of the Levites in Jerusalem" (Neh 11:22); and another descendant, Zechariah ben Jonathan, was a trumpeter in the restored cultus (Neh 12:35). The Mattaniah mentioned in Neh 12:8 as "in charge of the songs of thanksgiving," and the one mentioned in Neh 12:25 who was given guard duties at the storehouse of the gate are probably the same person. The absence of a patronymic would indicate that he would have been known and identified from the context. The general problems of this genealogy are discussed by Aufrecht (1988). Mattaniah, together with several other returnees, resettled in the region of Netophah in the hill country of Judah. This area is associated with modern Khirbet Bedd Faluh, a few miles SE of Bethlehem, near a spring bearing the name ʾAin en Natuf (1 Chr 9:15).

10. The grandfather of Hanan ben Zakkur, whom Nehemiah appointed as a faithful assistant to the new guardians of the storehouses (Neh 13:13). These men, Shelemiah the priest, Zadok the scribe, and the Levite Pedaiah, were appointed in the aftermath of the failure of the Levites to perform their duties. It is possible, though not certain, that Hanan was also a Levite.

Bibliography

Aufrecht, W. 1988. Genealogy and History in Ancient Israel. Pp. 205–35 in *Ascribe to the Lord: Biblical and Other Studies in Memory of Peter C. Craigie,* ed. L. E. Eslinger and G. Taylor. Sheffield.

Avigad, N. 1986. *Hebrew Bullae from the Time of Jeremiah.* Jerusalem.

Blenkinsopp, J. 1983. *A History of Prophecy in Israel From the Settlement in the Land to the Hellenistic Period.* Philadelphia.
Conrad, E. W. 1985. *Fear Not Warrior: A Study of the "al tira" Passages in the Hebrew Scriptures.* BJS 75. Chico, CA.
Johnson, A. R. 1962. *The Cultic Prophet in Ancient Israel.* 2d ed. Cardiff.

T. R. HOBBS

MATTATHA (PERSON) [Gk *Mattatha*]. The father of Menna and son of Nathan (and grandson of King David) according to Luke's genealogy tying Joseph, the "supposed father" of Jesus, to descent from Adam and God (Luke 3:31). D omits Mattatha, substituting a genealogy adapted from Matt 1:6–15 for Luke 3:23–31. The name Mattatha occurs nowhere else in the biblical documents, including Matthew's genealogy, and falls within a list of eighteen otherwise unknown descendants of David's son Nathan (Fitzmyer *Luke 1–9* AB, 501), although the name is similar to several others in the genealogies. Matthat (Luke 3:24, 29) and Mattathias (Luke 3:25, 26) in Luke's genealogy, and Matthan (Matt 1:15) in Matthew's. Kuhn (1923: 208–9) believes that Mattatha and Mattathias were originally identical, both derived from a common list that subsequently formed the basis for two parallel lists in Luke's genealogy: 3:26–29, Jesus to Mattathias; and 3:29–31, Joshua/Jesus to Mattatha. It is difficult to establish which was original, according to Kuhn, but Mattatha appears in the genealogy which does not mention Joseph as Jesus' father and thus may have traced Mary's line. Hervey (1853: 36–37, 88) explains the similar-sounding names as all derived from Heb *nātan* (Nathan), especially since Mattatha is listed in Luke as Nathan's son. Thus it confirms that Luke's genealogy traces David's line through Nathan. Johnson (1969: 240–52) goes further and sees an equation being made between Nathan in the genealogy and the OT prophet, thereby endorsing Jesus as prophet, although Abel (1974: 209) disputes this because of a lack of distinctly Lukan development of the prophetic motif. Establishing with certainty the basis for use of Mattatha is virtually impossible on the limited evidence.

Bibliography

Abel, E. L. 1974. The Genealogies of Jesus *HO CHRISTOS. NTS* 20: 203–10.
Hervey, A. 1853. *The Genealogies of Our Lord and Saviour Jesus Christ, as Contained in the Gospels of St. Matthew and St. Luke.* Cambridge.
Johnson, M. D. 1969. *The Purpose of the Biblical Genealogies.* SNTSMS 8. Cambridge.
Kuhn, G. 1923. Die Geschlechtsregister Jesu bei Lukas und Matthäus, nach ihrer Herkunft untersucht. *ZNW* 22: 206–28.

STANLEY E. PORTER

MATTATHIAH (PERSON) [Gk *Mattathias*]. During the public reading of the Law, Mattathiah was among the men who stood at Ezra's right side (1 Esdr 9:43). In the RSV, the same individual is called Mattithiah in the parallel account (Neh 8:4; see MATTITHIAH), though the Greek is identical for both (i.e., *Mattathias*). Furthermore, this Greek form of the name is the most common representation of the Heb *mattityâ/mattityāhû,* which is always rendered into English by the RSV as Mattithiah (see LXX in 1 Chr 9:31; 15:21; 16:5; 25:3, 21; cf. 1 Chr 15:18; Ezra 10:43). Therefore, it is unclear why *Mattathias* in 1 Esdr 9:43 is inconsistently translated by the RSV as Mattathias rather than Mattithias. For a similar example, compare Phineas in 1 Esdr 8:29 (Gk *Phinees*) with Phinehas in Ezra 8:2 (LXX *Phinees*).

JOHN KUTSKO

MATTATHIAS (PERSON) [Gk *Mattathias*]. **1.** Father of Judas Maccabeus and his four brothers (1 Macc 2:1–5), and son of John, and grandson of Simeon. Mattathias belonged to the priestly order Jehoiarib and is described as a Jerusalemite who settled in the village of Modein. It seems, despite the impression the author tries to create, that Modein was the ancestral residence of the family (cf. 1 Macc 2:17, 70; 9:19; 13:25–29), though it is quite possible that the family also had a domicile in Jerusalem (2 Macc 4:27 also gives the same impression). Mattathias' family might have been a prominent one, since it is so described in 1 Macc 2:17 and because it belonged to the order of Jehoiarib, which is the first in the priestly orders' list in 1 Chr 24:7. Yet we may suspect some effort on the part of our sources to promote the status of Mattathias' family according to the dynastic interests of the Hasmoneans. Some even suppose that Jehoiarib's prominent place as the first in the list of priestly orders in 1 Chronicles may be an interpolation of the Hasmonean period. Josephus and rabbinic sources call Mattathias Ḥashmonay, or add this nickname to him. The meaning of this word is unknown, though it may be compared to Mattathias' sons' nicknames. Some postulate a connection between Ḥashmonay and a village by the name Ḥeshmon (Josh 15:27), but this lacks any positive evidence.

Mattathias in his old age took the initiative to oppose by force of arms the imposition of the religious persecution of Antiochus IV (1 Macc 2:15ff.). In the year 166 B.C.E., when a Syrian military force arrived at Modein and convened the population for an ungodly sacrifice, Mattathias killed a Jew who was ready to perform the sacrilege; and then he killed the Syrian officer. After this act he fled to the mountains, where he was joined by supporters, among them a group of Hasidim. There Mattathias and his supporters decreed that it is permitted to fight in self-defense on the Sabbath (1 Macc 2:41).

The revolt under Mattathias, at this stage, was typical guerrilla warfare. It was aimed at the renegades (the Hellenizers), at destroying the pagan altars, and at enforcing the Jewish law whenever possible, especially the circumcision of children, which was prohibited by the Syrian king. In the year 146 of the Seleucid era (i.e., 166/165 B.C.E.), a short time after the beginning of the revolt, Mattathias died (2 Macc 2:69). A "Testament" (farewell address) is ascribed to him by the author of 1 Maccabees (2:49–68). His name is mentioned, among other rabbinic sources, in the prayer *ʿAl HaNissim.* Some have suggested identifying Mattathias with the figure of Taxo in the *Assumption of Moses.*

2. Third son of Simon, the founder of the Hasmonean dynasty, and grandson of Mattathias #1 (above). He was murdered with his father and brother by Ptolemy, son of Ḥabubos (1 Macc 16:14–16).

3. Son of Absalom and a commander under Jonathan the Hasmonean (1 Macc 11:70).

URIEL RAPPAPORT

4. The father of Maath and son of Semein according to Luke's genealogy tying Joseph, the "supposed father" of Jesus, to descent from Adam and God (Luke 3:26). D omits Mattathias, substituting a genealogy adapted from Matt 1:6–15 for Luke 3:23–31. The name Mattathias is unknown as an ancestor of Jesus in any other biblical documents, including Matthew's genealogy, although the name, with variants in spelling, is common in canonical and extracanonical texts (see elsewhere in this entry; Fitzmyer *Luke 1–9* AB, 500). Hervey (1853: 36–37, 135) claims that the similar sounding names in Luke's and Matthew's genealogies—Mattathias (Luke 3:25, 26), Mattatha (Luke 3:31), and Matthat (Luke 3:24, 29) in Luke and Matthan (Matt 1:15) in Matthew—are derived from Heb *nātan* (Nathan), especially since Mattatha is listed as Nathan's son in Luke 3:31, confirming that Luke's genealogy traces Joseph's line of David through David's son Nathan. See MATTATHA. Johnson (1969: 240–52) goes further and sees an equation being made between Nathan in the genealogy and the OT prophet, thereby endorsing Jesus as prophet, although Abel (1974: 209) disputes this because of a lack of distinctively Lukan development of the prophetic motif. If Kuhn (1923: 208–9) is correct that the two seemingly parallel lists of names in Luke 3:23–26 (Jesus to Mattathias) and Luke 3:29–31 (Joshua/Jesus to Mattatha) were originally one (see MAATH), then Mattathias may be a variant of Mattatha if the second list is early, possibly tracing Mary's line (since it does not mention Joseph as Jesus' father). Theological explanations for inclusion of Mattathias are improbable. For example, it has been suggested (e.g., Schürmann *Luke* HTKNT, 202–3) that Luke's genealogy consists of 11 × 7 names from Adam to Jesus, with the 12th period being the messianic age. Thus Zerubbabel to Mattathias would mark the 9th group, with Mattathias the terminal name for the period. But this scheme is not clear from Luke's text (see Johnson 1969: 231–33).

5. The father of Joseph (an earlier ancestor of Jesus) and son of Amos according to Luke's genealogy tying Joseph, the "supposed father" of Jesus, to descent from Adam and God (Luke 3:25). D omits Mattathias, substituting a genealogy adapted from Matt 1:6–15 in Luke 3:23–31. See Hervey (1853: 36–37, 135); Johnson (1969: 240–52). There is even less apparent theological motivation for inclusion of this name here than in Luke 3:26. Establishing with certainty the basis for use of Mattathias in Luke 3:25 or 26 is virtually impossible on the limited evidence.

Bibliography

Abel, E. L. 1974. The Genealogies of Jesus *HO CHRISTOS*. *NTS* 20: 203–10.

Hervey, A. 1853. *The Genealogies of Our Lord and Saviour Jesus Christ, as Contained in the Gospels of St. Matthew and St. Luke.* Cambridge.

Johnson, M. D. 1969. *The Purpose of the Biblical Genealogies.* SNTSMS 8. Cambridge.

Kuhn, G. 1923. Die Geschlechtsregister Jesu bei Lukas und Matthäus, nach ihrer Herkunft untersucht. *ZNW* 22: 206–28.

STANLEY E. PORTER

MATTATTAH (PERSON) [Heb *mattattâ*]. A son of Hashum and one of the sons of Israel who pledged to put away his foreign wife (Ezra 10:33). He is listed under the sons of Israel to distinguish his group of laymen from the sons of priests. It has been noted that the number of marital offenders is particularly small (cf. similar genealogical lists in Ezra 8:2–14 and one in inverted order in 2:2–61, where the family names can be found for many in the list in chap. 10), although it is far more likely that the list in Ezra 10:18–44 is only a partial list, since the problem of intermarriage with foreigners appears to have been a serious one (cf. Neh 13:23–29; Meyers *Ezra-Nehemiah* AB, 87).

STANLEY E. PORTER

MATTENAI (PERSON) [Heb *mattĕnay*]. **1.** A son of Hashum and one of the sons of Israel who pledged to put away his foreign wife (Ezra 10:33). He is listed under the sons of Israel to distinguish his group of laymen from the sons of priests. It has been noted that the number of marital offenders is particularly small (cf. similar genealogical lists in Ezra 8:2–14 and one in inverted order in 2:2–61, where the family names can be found for many in the list in chap. 10), although it is more likely that the list in Ezra 10:18–44 is only a partial list, since the problem of intermarriage with foreign women appears to have been a serious one (cf. Neh 13:23–29; Meyers *Ezra-Nehemiah* AB, 87).

2. A son of Bani and one of the sons of Israel who pledged to put away his foreign wife (Ezra 10:37). See #1 above.

3. A priest and head of the household of Joiarib, during the days of Joiakim the priest (Neh 12:19), a family name mentioned in Neh 12:6 for a priest or Levite who came up with Zerubbabel out of exile in Babylon. The use of "and" before Joiarib (1:6) indicates to some scholars that the list from this point on is an addition to an earlier list, perhaps reflecting the author's penchant for genealogies (Meyers, 196).

STANLEY E. PORTER

MATTHAN (PERSON) [Gk *Matthan*]. The son of Eleazar and father of Jacob according to Matthew's genealogy tying Joseph, the husband of Mary, to the house of David and Solomon (Matt 1:15). Codices B* and D read *Maththan.* The name Matthan appears as Mattan (Heb *matān*) in 2 Chr 23:17 (LXX *Matthan* in Rahlf's edition) and in Jer 38:1—LXX 45:1 (*Mathan* in Rahlf's edition), and it is found instead of *Maththanian* in 4 Kgdms 24:17 in Codices B and C (*Matthan* is read in B^{C}). It does not appear in the genealogy of 1 Chr 1:19–24 or in any other list of Jesus' ancestors, although Albright and Mann (*Matthew* AB, 4–5) believe the name is characteristic of names used in the last two centuries B.C. If there is no basis in history or tradition for the genealogies there is no need to harmonize this name with Luke's genealogy (*IDBSup* 354); but most scholars are not content with this solution, since there is an abundance of similar-sounding names in the two genealogies: Matthan (Matt 1:15), Mattathias (Luke 3:25, 26), Mattatha (Luke 3:31), and especially Matthat (Luke 3:24, 29—Codex D reads *Maththan* at Luke 3:24.). Hervey (1853: 36–37, 129–30, 134) claims that all of the above names are derived from Heb *nātan* (Nathan) and uses this to confirm that both Luke's and Matthew's genealogies are connected to the lineage of David's son Nathan. He concludes that Matthan (son of Eleazar) and Matthat (son of Levi) in Luke 3:24 refer to the same person on the basis of similar sound, common origin, and most important, similar placement in each genealogy. Gundry (1982: 18) accounts for their difference in this way: Matthew has changed the name of Joseph's grandfather, Matthat, to Matthan in order to conform exactly to the Hebrew, corroborated by Matt 9:9, where the author supposedly changed Levi (Mark 2:14; Luke 5:27) to Matthew, also supposedly based upon Heb *matān*. If the two names refer to the same person, however, a further problem is introduced: why is Matthan/Matthat given a different heir and a different father in the two gospel accounts? See MATTHAT #2 for a discussion of this problem.

Bibliography

Gundry, R. H. 1982. *Matthew: A Commentary on his Literary and Theological Art.* Grand Rapids.

Hervey, A. 1853. *The Genealogies of Our Lord and Saviour Jesus Christ, as Contained in the Gospels of St. Matthew and St. Luke.* Cambridge.

STANLEY E. PORTER

MATTHAT (PERSON) [Gk *Matthat*]. **1.** The father of Jorim and son of Levi according to Luke's genealogy tying Joseph, the "supposed father" of Jesus, to descent from Adam and God (Luke 3:29). (Codex B* reads *Maththat*, with several other variants in other texts, including D, which omits Matthat, substituting a genealogy adapted from Matt 1:6–15 for Luke 3:23–31). Apart from Luke 3:24 (see below), this name appears in a list of 18 ancestors otherwise unknown to the biblical documents, including Matthew's genealogy (Fitzmyer *Luke 1–9* AB, 501). Kuhn (1923: 208–9) argues that two seemingly parallel lists of names—Luke 3:23–26 (Jesus to Mattathias) and 3:29–31 (Joshua/Jesus to Mattatha)—were originally identical, the first perhaps reflecting a Hebrew context and the second, in an Aramaic context, tracing Mary's line of descent (since it does not mention Joseph as Jesus' father). Matthat is significant for Kuhn's analysis, since both lists have Levi as his father. Hervey (1853: 36–37, 129–30) believes that Matthat, like Mattathias (Luke 3:25, 26), Mattatha (Luke 3:31), and Matthan (Matt 1:15), is derived from Hebrew *nātan* (Nathan), providing evidence for Luke's genealogy tracing David's line of descent through his son Nathan (but see Marshall [*Luke* NIGTC, 162], who believes Matthat represents Heb *matat*). Johnson (1969: 240–52) goes further and sees an equation being made between the Nathan in the genealogy and the OT prophet, thereby endorsing Jesus as prophet, although Abel (1974: 209) disputes this because of a lack of distinctly Lukan development of the prophetic motif.

2. The father of Heli and son of Levi according to Luke's genealogy tying Joseph, the "supposed father" of Jesus, to descent from Adam and God (Luke 3:24). (Codex B* reads *Maththat*, and D reads *Maththan* in the substituted genealogy adapted from Matt 1:6–15). The name Matthat is in a list of 17 ancestors otherwise unknown to the biblical documents, including Matthew's genealogy (Fitzmyer *Luke 1–9* AB, 500). If there is no basis in history or tradition for the genealogies, there is no need to harmonize this name with Matthew's genealogy (*IDBSup*, 354); but most scholars are not content with this solution, since there is an abundance of similar sounding names in the two genealogies: Matthat (Luke 3:24, 29), Mattathias (Luke 3:25, 26), Mattatha (Luke 3:31), and especially Matthan (Matt 1:15). See Kuhn (1923: 208–9), Hervey (1853: 36–37, 129–30), Marshall (*Luke* NIGTC, 162), and Johnson (1969: 240–52). It is thought by many that Matthat the son of Levi (Luke 3:24) is identical with Matthan the son of Eleazar (Matt 1:15) on the basis of similar sound, common origin, and (most importantly) similar placement in each genealogy. See MATTHAN. If the two names refer to the same person, however, a further problem is introduced: why is Matthat/Matthan given a different heir and a different father in the two gospel accounts?

Ever since Julius Africanus' (3d-century-A.D.) letter to Aristides (Eus. *Hist. Eccl.* 1.7), levirate marriage has often been proposed as the solution to the problem of why Matthat's son in Luke is "Heli" and Matthan's son in Matthew is "Jacob," although Machen (1930: 208) supposes that Jacob, Matthan's son, died childless and that his nephew Joseph (son of his brother Heli) became his heir (a similar solution could be used if Matthat and Matthan are different people). If levirate marriage was still practiced (see Mark 12:18–27), then according to this analysis Heli and Jacob may have been full brothers, one of whom was without child and whose brother married the other's widow to produce an heir. Most scholars today propose Jacob in Matthew's account as the childless brother and Heli as the natural father of Joseph, although Julius Africanus suggested the reverse.

A similar solution would need to account for the fact that Matthat and Matthan are given different fathers, but appeal to levirate marriage again is highly improbable. Machen (1930: 208) suggests that "the kingly line became extinct with Eleazar (Matt 1:15), thus avoiding levirate marriage as the solution here. If Heli and Jacob were only half-brothers, i.e., with the same mother and different fathers, then it means that their mother married two different men with remarkably similar names—Matthat and Matthan—again highly improbable (see Brown 1977: 503–4). (Julius Africanus' Lukan genealogy omits Matthat and Levi, listing Melchi as the father of Eli by a woman, Estha, the widow of Matthan, rightly noted by Johnson as an artificial reconstruction [1969: 141–42].) It is more likely that the names Matthat and Matthan refer to two different men, since harmonization on the basis of the limited extratextual evidence is virtually impossible.

Bibliography

Abel, E. L. 1974. The Genealogies of Jesus *HO CHRISTOS. NTS* 20: 203–10.

Brown, R. E. 1977. *The Birth of the Messiah.* Garden City.
Hervey, A. 1853. *The Genealogies of Our Lord and Saviour Jesus Christ, as Contained in the Gospels of St. Matthew and St. Luke.* Cambridge.
Johnson, M. D. 1969. *The Purpose of the Biblical Genealogies.* SNTSMS 8. Cambridge.
Kuhn, G. 1923. Die Geschlechtsregister Jesu bei Lukas und Matthäus, nach ihrer Herkunft untersucht. *ZNW* 22: 206–28.
Machen, J. G. 1930. *The Virgin Birth of Christ.* New York.

STANLEY E. PORTER

MATTHEW (DISCIPLE). One of the twelve apostles of Jesus according to the four NT lists found in Mark 3:18; Matt 10:3; Luke 6:15; and Acts 1:13.

A. Etymology
B. Location of the Name "Matthew"
C. Gospel Parallels and Textual Variants
D. Solutions to the Variations
  1. Levi = Matthew
  2. "Matthew" was Changed to "Levi"
  3. "Levi" was Changed to "Matthew"
E. Textual Variants
  1. "James" in Place of "Levi"
  2. "Lebbaeus/Labbaeus" (= Levi) in Place of "Thaddaeus"
F. Redaction Criticism
G. The Name "Matthew"
H. "The Tax (Toll) Collector"
I. Church Tradition and the First Evangelist
J. Conclusions

A. Etymology

Greek *Maththaios* (mss Sinaiticus, B, D) or *Matthaios* is derived from Hebrew or Aramaic *Mattaʾi, Mattiyaʾ,* or *Mattiyah,* shortened forms of *Mattith-yah(u),* which is built on the Hebrew words *nātan,* "he gave," and *Yah(u),* a shortened form of "Yahweh"; an etymological meaning is "gift of Yahweh" or simply "gift of God."

B. Location of the Name "Matthew"

The name "Matthew" is found in two locations. The first location is in each of the four NT lists of the Twelve (eleven in Acts), close followers of Jesus (Matt 10:2–4; Mark 3:16–19; Luke 6:14–16; Acts 1:13). This group is usually called *mathētai,* "disciples" or "pupils," in the gospels of Matthew, Mark, and Luke; they are designated *apostoloi,* "apostles" or "missionaries," at the beginning of at least two, and probably three, of the four lists (Matt 10:2 [here only in Matthew]; Mark 3:14, mss Sinaiticus, B, etc. [cf. also 6:30]; Luke 6:13), in the gospel of Luke somewhat more frequently, and in Acts, where the term "disciples" designates a larger group of followers (contrast Paul, 1 Cor 15:5–7). In the lists, the name "Matthew" is seventh in Mark 3:18 and Luke 6:15 and eighth in Matt 10:3 and Acts 1:13. Thus the name is placed in a position of lesser status than the brothers Peter and Andrew or James and John, who always make up the first set of four names.

The second location of the name "Matthew" is in the Matthean version of the call of the man sitting at the "toll booth" (Matt 9:9; contrast Mark 2:14; Luke 5:27).

C. Gospel Parallels and Textual Variants

The problem concerning Matthew can be clarified by closely observing the most important gospel parallel variations and their ms variants.

According to the most reliable mss of the gospel parallels, the pertinent variations can be summarized like this.

1. The lists consistently refer to "James the son of Alphaeus," who is thereby distinguished in the same lists from "James the son of Zebedee" (Matt 10:3; Mark 3:18; Luke 6:15).

2. The lists do not refer to Levi, or to "Levi the son of Alphaeus" (see, however, the discussion of "Lebbaeus" below).

3. The lists refer to a certain Matthew (Matt 10:3; Mark 3:18; Luke 6:15; Acts 1:13).

4. Only in the list of the gospel of Matthew is this "Matthew" called "the tax collector" (Matt 10:3: *mathētēs*).

5. Only in the Matthean version of Jesus' call of the "man sitting at the toll booth" is the man named "Matthew" (Matt

Table 1
Gospel Parallels (with Textual Variants)

Disciple Lists:

Matt 10:3:	and	Thomas	and	Matthew the tax collector		James the son of Alphaeus, and Thaddaeus[2]	
Mark 3:18:	and			Matthew[1]	and Thomas and	James the son of Alphaeus, and Thaddaeus[3]	
Luke 6:15:	and			Matthew	and Thomas and	James the son of Alphaeus, and Simon who was called	the Zealot
Acts 1:13:		Bartholomew	and	Matthew,		James the son of Alphaeus and Simon	the Zealot

Man Sitting at the Toll Booth:

Matt 9:9:	a man . . .	called	Matthew	
Mark 2:14:			Levi[4]	the son of Alphaeus
Luke 5:27:	a tax collector	named	Levi	
Gos. Pet. 60:			Levi	the son of Alphaeus

[1]The tax collector: added in *thēta,* Ferrar Group, etc.
[2]Lebbaeus (Greek) or Labbaeus (Latin): D, the Old Latin "K," Latin versions; Lebbaeus who is called Thaddaeus: some later Greek texts.
[3]Lebbaeus (Greek) or Labbaeus (Latin): D and most Old Latin versions.
[4]James: D, *thēta,* Ferrar Group, 565, Old Latin, Diatessaron, Origen, Ephraem, Photius.

9:9), thus equating the Matthew in the call of chap. 9 with the Matthew in the list of chap. 10.

6. The one sitting at the toll booth in the gospels of Mark, Luke, and Peter (see PETER, GOSPEL OF) is not called "Matthew," but "Levi."

7. In Mark 2:14 and the *Gospel of Peter* 60, he is called "Levi the son of Alphaeus"; in Luke 5:27 he is called "a tax collector named Levi."

D. Solutions to the Variations

Some scholars conclude that the problem posed by the parallels and variants is insoluble. Three major solutions to the variations can be suggested.

1. Levi = Matthew. The first solution is that Levi and Matthew are the same person. One suggestion is that Levi was renamed "Matthew" by Jesus after he was called to be a disciple, a theory that sometimes attempts to build on the supposed changing of names by Jesus (e.g., Heb/Aram *Šimᶜōn* = Gk *Simōn;* Heb/Aram *Cephas* = Gk *Petros* [Eng "Peter"]). A second suggestion is that "Matthew" was the name given at baptism, "Levi" having arisen because Matthew was from the tribe of Levi. Both suggestions have been related to the traditional theory of authorship of the gospel of Matthew, that is, that the author Levi/Matthew is covertly referring to himself in the account of the call of Matt 9:9.

Both suggestions have difficulties. The first has to contend with that fact that no story about Levi renamed "Matthew" has survived and is therefore an argument from silence; that the names "Levi" and "Matthew" fall in different gospels; that the analogy with Cephas/Petros is not exact, that is, the latter is a special nickname built on a pun of great symbolic significance, namely, "rock" (Heb/Aram *kēphā*ʾ = Gk *petra*); and that that renaming story itself may have arisen in the early Church. The second suggestion is also an argument from silence about names in different gospels. Both are conjectures which attempt to harmonize the Matthean with the Markan and Lukan accounts of the call scene. As far as the author's covert allusion to himself is concerned, the call story does not mention authorship and viewpoint; moreover, one would have to accept Matthean authorship of the first gospel, which is contested (see below). However, denial of apostolic authorship does not at the same time answer the question about the identity of Matthew.

2. "Matthew" was Changed to "Levi." A second solution is that in the call scene "Matthew" (Matt 9:9) was changed to "Levi the son of Alphaeus" (Mark 2:14) or "a tax collector named Levi" (Luke 5:27). This solution can be related to any hypothesis which defends the gospel of Matthew as earlier than the gospel of Mark (the Traditional Hypothesis; the "Two-Gospel" or "Griesbach Hypothesis"). See SYNOPTIC PROBLEM. This solution runs up against a major problem: the name of a disciple, Matthew, which also occurs in Matthew's disciple list, where Matthew is called "the tax collector," has been replaced with an otherwise unknown disciple. A further problem for the view that Mark chose and then modified Luke ("Two-Gospel Hypothesis") is that one would need to explain why the Markan writer designates Levi, like James in the lists, "the son of Alphaeus." (Was there a tradition of two tax collectors, one named Matthew, the other Levi? Was Levi believed to be the brother of James, the son of Alphaeus?

3. "Levi" was Changed to "Matthew." A third solution is that the Lukan writer has accepted "Levi" from the gospel of Mark but removed the description "the son of Alphaeus" (Luke 5:27; cf. "James the son of Alphaeus" in his disciple list, Mark 3:18 = Luke 6:15), while the Matthean writer has changed "Levi" to "Matthew" (Matt 9:9) and subsequently correlated the name with one of the Twelve in his disciple list by describing this Matthew as "the tax collector" (Matt 10:3). In this solution only the Matthean writer would have removed the thirteenth disciple, Levi. Such a solution would correspond with 3d-century Origen's view that Levi was not one of the twelve disciples (Origen, *c. Cels.* 1.62). It also corresponds with the dominant modern view that the earliest gospel was Mark (the "Two-Source Theory"). This solution also has difficulties; before considering it further, however, it will be helpful to note some variants in the mss and some redaction-critical possibilities.

E. Textual Variants

1. "James" in Place of "Levi." In a few mss of the Markan call scene, "the son of Alphaeus" is James, as in the lists, rather than Levi (Mark 2:14 D, *thēta,* Ferrar Group, 565, Old Latin, Diatessaron, Origen, Ephraem, Photius). Should this be what the original Markan author wrote, there would be no thirteenth disciple; and the call scene would correlate with the list by means of the "James," not "Matthew," as in the gospel of Matthew. However, the ms evidence for this variant is considered to be relatively weak. Furthermore, the Lukan parallel to the Markan call scene still has "Levi the tax collector" and the Lukan reading has no ms variants (Luke 5:27). Therefore—the problem is related to synoptic relationships—the usual conclusion is that later scribes have changed "Levi the son of Alphaeus" in the call scene to "James the son of Alphaeus" (Mark 2:14) to make it conform to "James the son of Alphaeus" in the disciple list (Mark 3:16). This argument is all the more forceful if the Lukan writer, who has "Levi," found it in his Markan gospel (the "Two-Source Theory").

Oddly, a few of the same Markan mss that have James at the tax booth in Mark 2:14 persist in calling Matthew "the tax collector" in the disciple list in Mark 3:16 (*thēta,* Ferrar Group, etc.). However, these variants are considered so weak that many modern Greek editions of the NT do not even note them as alternatives; they undoubtedly show an influence from the Matthean gospel's designation of Matthew as "the tax collector" (Matt 10:3; cf. 9:9).

2. "Lebbaeus/Labbaeus" (= "Levi") in Place of "Thaddaeus." Still other ancient mss seem to make the correlation by the reverse maneuver, that is, by bringing an equivalent of "Levi" into the list, thus requiring removal of one of the Twelve. Thus, a few Western texts have Greek "Lebbaeus" or Latin "Labbaeus" for "Thaddaeus" in the disciple lists of the gospels of Mark (cf. Mark 3:18 D) and Matthew (cf. Matt 10:3 D, African Old Latin, "K," Latin versions; Latin of Origen); some later Caesarean and *koinē* Greek mss explain with the words "Lebbaeus who is called Thaddaeus." This is a correlation only if "Lebbaeus/Labbaeus" can be with certainty identified with "Levi." Not all modern scholars have accepted this identification. Nonetheless, 3d-century Origen, who knew the variant, explained it thus (Origen *c. Cels.* 1.62), and so do certain modern scholars. One suggestion is that the change from "Thaddaeus" to "Labbaeus" was first made in early Latin mss and subsequently to "Lebbaeus" in Greek mss (Ms D is bilingual Greek and Latin); if so, this change would have predated a variant in Greek texts which would have changed "Levi" to "James," since the latter would cancel the necessity for the former (Lindars 1958).

There are several implications of these ms variations: (a) Later copyists sought to align the person called at the tax booth with one of the twelve disciples in the lists. (b) The ms variants are best explained on the basis that Mark 2:14 of these mss (the call) contained "Levi" and that Mark 3:16 of these mss (the list) contained "Matthew." (c) The later copyists of the gospel of Mark may offer a clue about the original author of the gospel of Matthew, namely, the latter made a similar change from "Levi" to "Matthew" (Matt 9:9), and for the same reasons.

F. Redaction Criticism

Redaction criticism, which has usually been built on the view that canonical Matthew knows a gospel very close to canonical Mark, offers another perspective on the problem (Pesch 1968). Mark 2:14 contains typical Markan language and construction ("as he passed on," cf. 1:16; "and he says to him," cf. 1:44; 5:19; 7:18; cf. 1:41; 5:9; 7:34; 12:16; 14:30; "following" Jesus, esp. 1:18; 10:21; cf. 3:7; 6:1; 10:32; 10:52). Combined with Mark 2:13, a generally accepted Markan transition, it appears to have been constructed as an introduction to the following scene where Jesus is at table with tax collectors and sinners, perhaps in the house of Levi the son of Alphaeus (Mark 2:15: "In his house" is not clear; cf. Luke 5:29). The general point would be that Jesus "came not to call the righteous, but sinners" (2:17b), an important theme in Mark's first major section (1:2–34 + 2:1–3:6).

If Mark composed Mark 2:13–14 as an introduction to Jesus' meal at Levi's house and if the author of Matthew used the Markan gospel, then it would appear that the parallel to 2:14 in Matt 9:9 was not from Matthew's special tradition but an adaptation of the Markan text. First, the meal with the tax collectors and sinners seems to take place in Jesus' house in Capernaum (Matt 9:7, 10). Then, apart from the name change, there are some minor, but nonetheless, characteristic Matthean expressions vis à vis the gospels of Mark and Luke: the addition of the name "Jesus" (*ho Iēsous:* Matt 4:1, 17; 7:28; 8:14, 18; 9:9, 27; 11:1; 12:9, 15; 14:13; 15:29; 19:15) and "from there" (*ekeithen:* Matt 4:21; 9:9, 27; 11:1; 12:9, 15; 14:13; 15:29; 19:15), sometimes in combination (Matt 9:9, 27; 11:1); "a man" (Matt 13:31; 17:14; 19:3, 10; 26:72; esp. 27:32, 57); the Greek form of "called" (*anarthrous legomenos:* 2:23; 9:9; 26:36; 27:16, 33), which form the writer consistently uses simply to designate a name of a person or place. When persons have a second name or title, he employs "who is [also] called" (articular *ho legomenos:* 1:16; 4:18; 10:2; 26:3, 16; 27:17, 22). This fact excludes the first solution (4a above), that Levi and Matthew are different names for the same person.

Such tendencies can be reinforced by observing that the Matthean author is very particular about his use of the names, especially those of the twelve disciples (Pesch 1968). In contrast to Mark, he typically stresses the preeminence of Peter and seems to do so in the list (Matt 10:2: "first Simon . . ."; contrast Mark 3:16; Luke 6:13–14). Moreover, he aligns the list with the same sequence and language found in the original call scenes (cf. 4:18 with 10:2: "Simon who is called Peter and Andrew his brother"; 4:21 with 10:2: "James the son of Zebedee and John his brother"; cf. 17:1; contrast Mark 3:16–18: Simon . . . James . . . John . . . Andrew . . .). In general, he avoids superfluous and/or false names (e.g., persons: Mark 2:26; 3:16; 3:17 par.; Matt 10:2; Mark 5:22; 6:17; 10:46; 15:21; places: Mark 3:7; 5:20; 6:45; 7:31; 8:22); and, even more to the point, he omits the unknown Salome (Mark 15:40; 16:1; Matt 27:61; 28:1) and introduces a known woman, the mother of the sons of Zebedee (Matt 27:56; cf. 20:20; 26:37). All of these tendencies make plausible the Matthean change from "Levi" to "Matthew" in the call scene, thus bringing it into conformity with the list.

In short, redaction-critical arguments support the solution that the author of Matthew's gospel knew and changed the Markan "Levi" to "Matthew" in Matt 9:9 and then added "the tax collector" to that name in the list in 10:3, thus correlating the two passages. The basis for these changes would appear to be that the author of Matthew limits the disciples to the list of the Twelve, a limitation which can be further supported by a careful study of his use of the terms "disciples" *(mathētai)* and "twelve" *(dōdeka)* and their combination (Matt 10:1, 5; 11:1; 20:17; 26:14, 17, 18, 19, 26, 47) vis à vis Mark (Strecker 1966; Pesch 1968; Luz 1983). As noted above, the same motive can be traced in the copyists.

G. The Name "Matthew"

If the author of the first gospel, who was not the disciple Matthew, made the change from "Levi" to "Matthew" in the call scene and correspondingly added "the tax collector" to Matthew in his list, why did he choose the name "Matthew" and not another name from among the list of twelve disciples? Several answers have been given to this most difficult question, among which are the following (see Pesch 1968; Kiley 1984):

1. The author knew that *Matthias* was the only Levite in the list (1 Chr 25:3; 15:18, 21; 16:5; 25:21; 1 Esdr 9:43) and he associated this with "Levi" (Goulder 1974).
2. The author believed that Matthew had originally "compiled the sayings of the Lord in the Hebrew language" (Papias in Eus. *Hist. Eccl.* 3.39.16), sayings which he used in the composition of the gospel (a partial solution, says Kiley; cf. I below).
3. The author and/or his circles especially honored Matthew (Fenton *Matthew* PNTC).
4. The author saw "Matthew" = "gift of God" as representative of "tax collectors and sinners" of whom Jesus was a "friend" (Pesch 1968).
5. The author intended to underscore the idea that "disciples" (*mathētai:* Mark 2:15, 16 = Matt 9:9, 10) are those who should "learn" (*mathete:* Matt 9:13) the meaning of "I desire mercy, and not sacrifice" (Hos 6:6 in Matt 9:13; cf. 12:7); thus *mathētai* and *mathete* suggested *Matthias* as the true representative of "learning-discipleship" so

prevalent in the gospel (Kiley 1984). The last two suggestions are easiest to document on the basis of the text itself.

H. "The Tax (Toll) Collector"

The collectors of taxes and/or tolls in the NT are usually called *telōnai* ("tax collectors," Heb *qabbāʾîm,* or "toll collectors," Heb *môkĕsîn,* cf. Aram *mākĕsayyāʾ*). Zacchaeus is designated "chief tax collector" (Luke 19:2: *architelōnēs*).

By the 1st century in Roman Palestine, the traditional system of tax collection by a group of wealthy Roman officials, the so-called *societates publicanorum,* had been abolished (Donahue 1971; see TAX COLLECTOR). They were replaced by the *telōnai* mentioned in the NT. Direct taxes, that is, taxes on individuals and land, were handled directly by the local government, either the Romans or the tetrarchs, and their clients. Indirect taxes, primarily tolls related to transport of goods, appear to have been farmed out to the highest bidders who contracted to pay a certain sum to the government prior to collection; they and their subordinates then collected as much as they could, since any surplus beyond the contracted amount was profit. Such a system lent itself to corruption, dishonesty, and especially to repression of the poor peasantry who attempted to move their produce to market. Classical writers from antiquity, ostraca (cf. BAGD 812), nonliterary papyri (Lewis 1983), Josephus (*Ant* 17.204, *JW* 2.287), Philo (*Spec Leg* 3.30), the Talmud (e.g., *m. Ned.* 3.4), and the gospels (Matt 9:10–11; 11:19; Mark 2:13–17; Luke 3:12; 5:29–30; 7:34; 15:1; 18:13; 19:2) were united in their judgment that local officials responsible for the collection of taxes and tolls were especially despised in the Greco-Roman world. In the Talmud they are designated as "robbers"; in the gospel of Luke they are considered greedy (Luke 3:12–13); and elsewhere in the gospels they are usually linked with sinners (*hamartōloi:* Mark 2:15 = Matt 9:10–11 = Luke 5:29–30; Matt 11:19 = Luke 7:34; Luke 15:2; cf. Luke 18:10–14), prostitutes (Matt 21:31–32; cf. Luke 7:29; 18:11), and gentiles (Matt 5:46, 47; 18:17); perhaps, then, they were considered by pious Jews as ritually unclean.

In Matt 9:9, Matthew is described as "a man sitting at the tax office *(telōnion)*" and in 10:3 Matthew is designated a *telōnēs.* The location was probably a toll or customs office or booth normally found at ports of entry (Jos. *JW* 2.287), or on the boundaries between various districts, for example, Jericho (cf. Luke 19:2), or, in this case, Capernaum (Mark 2:1; Matt 8:5, 9:1). Presumably the first evangelist thinks of Matthew as one of the subordinate tax collecting officials who, working at his toll booth at Capernaum (Matt 8:5; 9:1, 10; cf. Mark 2:1), was the object of scorn (Matt 5:46), one to be associated with sinners, prostitutes, and gentiles (Matt 5:46, 47; 9:10–13; 11:19; 18:17; 21:31–32). Nonetheless, the Jesus who broke with social norms and purity regulations by eating with such persons (Matt 9:10; 11:19; cf. Mark 2:15–16; Luke 5:30; 7:34; 15:1) is represented as calling just such a person to be his disciple *(mathētēs),* a call to which this Matthew is reported to have responded.

I. Church Tradition and the First Evangelist

Titles to identify authors and distinguish them, that is, "According to X," were placed at the top of the first leaf of the mss of each of the canonical gospels sometime in the first half of the 2d century C.E. (cf. esp. the anti-Marcionite prologues to the gospels). "According to Matthew" became the title of the first gospel, an ascription that may in some way be related to the tax collector/disciple highlighted in Matthew's story (Pesch 1968). In any case the earliest Christian writer on the subject, Papias, wrote that Matthew "compiled *[synetaxato]* the sayings *[ta logia]* of the Lord in the Hebrew "dialect" *[dialectō]*; and each interpreted *[hermeneusen]* as he was able" (Papias in Eus. *Hist. Eccl.* 3.39.16).

There is much controversy about the Papias statement. First, there are the terms transliterated in Greek, most importantly, *ta logia,* which, if taken in its primary sense as "the sayings," does not easily describe the gospel of Matthew, though the description is not impossible. Second, even if Papias did mean the gospel of Matthew, the canonical Matthew that has survived was written in Greek, not in a Hebrew dialect (Aramaic?). Could Papias have meant one of Matthew's sources (see G.2 above)? Was there another, Semitic-language version of the gospel of Matthew? "Compiled" and "interpreted," or perhaps "translated," are also debated. Moreover, though the vast majority of modern critics date the Papias tradition about 135 C.E., it has been dated earlier than 110 C.E. (Gundry 1982, who dates the gospel itself before 63 C.E.). If the latter date is accepted, whoever wrote in the title possibly knew the Papias tradition, which would then have greater value for ascribing the gospel to Matthew (see D.1 above); if the former date is accepted, which has been an almost unanimous scholarly opinion, the situation is reversed, that is, Papias probably knew the title.

Most modern interpreters (contrast Gundry) have considered the Papias tradition, and therefore church tradition in the 2d century C.E. built upon Papias (Iren. *haer.* 3.1 in Eus. *Hist. Eccl.* 5.8.2; perhaps earlier is The Gospel of the Ebionites quoted in Epiphanius, *haer.* 30.13.2), to be inaccurate. The general view is that the gospel of Matthew was composed by an unknown Greek-speaking, Jewish-Christian author, probably about 85–90 C.E., probably in Syria (Antioch?), though somewhere in Palestine or the Transjordan has also been suggested. See MATTHEW, GOSPEL OF.

J. Conclusions

The above sketch tends to support the third solution noted at the outset, namely, that the writer of the gospel of Matthew has changed "Levi" (Mark 2:14) to "Matthew" (Matt 9:9) and then designated Matthew (Mark 3:18) as "the tax (i.e., toll) collector" in his list (Matt 10:3), thus removing the thirteenth disciple. This third solution is consistent with the position held by most, but certainly not all, scholars about the literary relationships between the first three gospels (the Two-Source Hypothesis). It can also be supported by redaction-critical arguments that Matthew reworked the Markan author's introduction into an account about Jesus' table fellowship with tax collectors and sinners (Pesch 1968). The author's attempt was to replace an unknown person in the call scene with a disciple known from the list, perhaps because the author and/or his circles especially honored Matthew, but as the text might more plausibly suggest, because the author saw Matthew ("gift of God") as representative of "toll collectors and sinners," of whom Jesus was a "friend" (Pesch 1968) and/or because *mathētēs* ("disciple") and *mathete* ("learn") suggested *Matthias* as the true representative of "learning-discipleship" so prevalent in the gospel (Kiley 1984). In any case, a similar motive for aligning the call of Matthew with the name "Matthew" in the disciple lists can be observed in the manuscript changes by later copyists.

Bibliography

Donahue, J. R. 1971. Tax Collectors and Sinners. *CBQ* 22: 39–61.
Goulder, M. D. 1974. *Midrash and Lection in Matthew.* London.
Gundry, R. 1982. The Authorship of Matthew. Pp. 609–22 in *Matthew: A Commentary on His Literary and Theological Art.* Grand Rapids.
Guthrie, D. 1970. *New Testament Introduction.* Downers Grove, IL.
Howard, G. 1987. The Place of Shem-Tob's Matthew within the Hebrew-Matthean Tradition. Pp. 155–80 in *The Gospel of Matthew according to a Primitive Hebrew Text.* Macon, GA.
Kiley, M. 1984. Why 'Matthew' in Matt 9,9–13? *Bib* 65: 347–51.
Kürzinger, J. 1983. *Papias von Hierapolis und die Evanglien des Neuen Testaments.* Regensburg.
Lewis, N. 1983. Census, Taxes, and Liturgies. Pp. 156–84 in *Life in Egypt Under Roman Rule.* Oxford.
Lindars, B. 1958. Matthew, Levi, Lebbaeus and the Value of the Western Text. *NTS* 4: 220–22.
Luz, U. 1983. The Disciples in the Gospel according to Matthew. Pp. 98–129 in *The Interpretation of Matthew,* ed. G. Stanton. Philadelphia.
Munck, J. 1962. Die Tradition über das Matthäusevangelium bei Papias. Pp. 249–60 in *Neotestamentica et Patristica.* NovTSup 6. Leiden.
Pesch, R. 1968. Levi—Matthäus (Mc 2:14/Mt 9:9, 10:3). Ein Beitrag zur Lösung eines alten Problems. *ZNW* 59: 40–56.
Strecker, G. 1966. *Der Weg der Gerechtigkeit.* FRLANT 82. Göttingen.
Wilkins, M. J. 1988. *The Concept of Disciple in Matthew's Gospel.* NovTSup 59. Leiden.

DENNIS C. DULING

MATTHEW, GOSPEL OF. The second longest of the four canonical gospels, traditionally placed first in the NT canon and hence referred to as "the first gospel" (without prejudice to the actual historical order in which the four Gospels were written). The ascription of this gospel to the apostle Matthew dates to at least from Irenaeus (ca. A.D. 185; cf. his *Adversus Haereses* 3.1.2; 3.11.8) and possibly from Papias (ca. 140), though it is not clear whether the collection of Jesus' *logia* by Matthew that Papias refers to is to be identified with our gospel of Matthew (cf. Eus. *Hist. Eccl.* 3.39.16).

A. Sources
B. Literary Genre
C. Time and Place of Composition
D. Occasion of the Gospel: a Church in Transition
E. Matthew's Church and the Synagogue
F. Author: Jew or Gentile?
G. Structure and Content of the Gospel
H. Major Theological Concerns
 1. Christology
 2. Kingdom of Heaven
 3. Salvation History
 4. Church
 5. Discipleship
 6. Morality

A. Sources

This article employs the two-source (or two-document) hypothesis as the most likely and most widely accepted Synoptic theory held today. It is presupposed therefore that Matthew used Mark's gospel and some form of the sayings source conventionally called Q. See Q (GOSPEL SOURCE); SYNOPTIC PROBLEM. Since, as the Qumran material makes clear, Judaism was acquainted with successive recensions of the same work, it is possible that Matthew employed slightly different forms of Mark and Q from those known to Luke or (in the case of Mark) to us. It is also possible that Q was already combined with Matthew's special traditions (M) before these two traditions were meshed with Mark in the gospel of Matthew; hence J. Brown speaks of Q^{mt} (Brown 1961).

It is questionable, however, whether we should think of M in terms of one fixed document in addition to Mark and Q, since M is simply an umbrella term used to designate any tradition in the gospel that cannot be traced to Mark, Q, or Matthean redaction. Thus M is isolated by a process of subtraction; it encompasses many different strata of tradition reflecting different theological positions. If M represents the traditions of the local church to which the author of the gospel belonged, then that church had a complicated history and was made up of a variety of contending groups.

A characteristic block of material within M is the group of fulfillment quotations or *Reflexionszitate;* these show how a particular OT prophecy is fulfilled in the life of Jesus. Soares Prabhu identifies fulfillment quotations by three characteristics: (1) an introductory fulfillment formula the key word of which is the passive form of the verb *plēroō* ("fulfill"); (2) a commentary function by which the quotation serves as an aside of the evangelist and does not form part of the narrative; (3) a mixed text form, at times closer to the MT, at times closer to the LXX (Soares Prabhu 1976: 19). Nevertheless, exegetes still debate exactly how many fulfillment quotations are to be counted in Matthew. Soares Prabhu accepts eleven: 1:22–23; 2:5–6; 2:15; 2:17–18; 2:23; 4:14–16; 8:17; 12:17–21; 13:35; 21:4–5; and 27:9–10. Other scholars would include 13:14–15 and 26:54, 56, while omitting 2:5–6. Also debated is the origin of the fulfillment quotations. Some see them as traditional (from testimony books or oral scribal traditions), while others view them as redactional creations of Matthew. In view of Matthew's tendency to seize upon and expand useful motifs in his tradition, both solutions may contain some truth. The use of the same Zech 9:9 quotation in both Matthew's and John's account of the triumphal entry into Jerusalem does seem to argue that fulfillment quotations (apart from the formulaic *plēroō*) were not simply creations of Matthew alone (cf. Matt 21:5; John 12:14–15).

The problem of the quotations' origin points up a basic difficulty in dealing with the M tradition: What is truly traditional and what stems from Matthew's redaction? The usual approach is to look for a heavy concentration of words, phrases, grammatical constructions, and theological concerns seen to be Matthean from the way Matthew handles texts that have a Markan or Q source. In the absence of such indicators, the passage can be declared traditional. This criterion must be used with caution, however.

If Matthew was a son of his local church and acted as a teacher in it for some time, it is only natural that the style of his tradition should be reflected in his own redactional activity. Hence the distinction between tradition and redaction in nonparalleled material is often difficult to make. The M material no doubt grew in liturgical and catechetical activity of the Church over decades and was the living Sitz im Leben in which Mark and Q were understood long before the sources were brought together by Matthew. M, therefore, should be viewed as a dynamic oral tradition rather than some sort of primitive document (contra, Kilpatrick 1946: 36).

To be sure, other theories on the origin of Matthew's gospel are defended today. In different ways Vaganay (1954) and Butler (1951) held to the priority of an Aramaic Matthew. Jeremias (1966) denied a written Q, and Wrege (1968) applied the theory to the Sermon on the Mount. Léon-Dufour (1962) preferred to speak of various blocks of tradition. The strongest opponent of the two-source theory today is Farmer (1964), who sustains a form of the Griesbach hypothesis: Matthew-Luke-Mark, Mark being the conflation of the first two. Nevertheless, the two-source theory still enjoys the widest acceptance and use on the international scene, has been tested exhaustively in lengthy monographs and commentaries on Matthew, and creates fewer difficulties over the long range than any of its competitors. For example, it explains the gospel relations in such Matthean texts as the temptation narrative, the prohibition of divorce, and the Passion Narrative better than does the Griesbach hypothesis.

B. Literary Genre

In 1915, Votaw (1970) stressed the similarities between the Gospels and popular Greco-Roman biographies of, e.g., Socrates. Largely forgotten in the heyday of dialectical theology, this proposal has been revived by Talbert (1977), who sees Matthew as a biography that presents the career of Jesus both as a legitimation of his teaching-legislation and as a hermeneutical clue to its meaning. Shuler (1982) has refined this suggestion for Matthew, seeing it as an "encomium" or laudatory biography. The most carefully worked out position is that of Aune, who sees the Gospels as a subtype of Greco-Roman biography, influenced as well by Jewish literary traditions and Christian content (Aune 1987: 46). While one cannot deny Matthew's similarities to these and other types of Greco-Roman literature (*praxeis, memorabilia* [Robbins 1984: 60–68], aretalogies, sayings of the wise), all these genres suit hypothetical sources better than the finished Gospels. A canonical gospel is best defined as a narrative of the words and deeds of Jesus of Nazareth, culminating inexorably in his death and resurrection, which narrative is meant to communicate to the believing audience the saving effects of what is narrated. The meshing of words and deeds, the inevitable thrust toward both death and resurrection, the quasi-sacramental intent of the narrative as saving proclamation, and a lack of any character sketch of the chief figure set our Gospels apart from the classical genres suggested. Indeed, attempts to find Greco-Roman genres and thought forms can produce strainted results that obscure rather than clarify (so in the case of Betz 1985). While drawing on extent forms, the evangelists, under the impact of the "good news" they had to convey, created a new literary genre that is best labeled simply "gospel." This comprehensive term seems preferable in the case of Matthew to one-sided designations like catechism (von Dobschütz 1928), manual of church order, the new Torah of Jesus (Bacon 1930), liturgical lectionary (Kilpatrick 1946), or book of kerygmatic history (Walker 1967). Each of these suggestions rests upon one Sitz im Leben reflected in the gospel. But the true Sitz im Leben of this huge gospel was the entire life of Matthew's church over decades (Trilling 1964: 220–21); initial instruction of both Jewish and gentile converts, the more advanced education of church leaders in faith and church order, liturgical reading, missionary appeal, and debates with Pharisaic Judaism.

This stress on the special Christian genre and Sitz im Leben of Matthew is not intended to deny the usefulness of the study of ancient Greco-Roman rhetoric for the NT (Beardslee 1970; Kennedy 1984). More problematic, however, is the application of modern literary or narrative criticism (Petersen 1978; Kingsbury 1986). Such narrative criticism was developed with a view to the 19th-century English novel; whether it totally fits a 1st-century-A.D. document of religious propaganda is questionable. Distinctions among real author, implied author, and narrator are made, only to find no useful application in the gospel text. Particularly problematic is the "implied reader": How much knowledge of 1st-century places, persons, and events is presumed by the critic in this hypothetical, ahistorical reader? Still, the inventory of events, characters, settings, points of view, and rhetorical techniques does help focus the reader's eye on particular phenomena in the text. Yet, while of some use, contemporary narrative criticism does not totally jibe with the genre of gospel and so cannot be the primary model for a critical approach to the text. Especially in Matthew's gospel, where the author consciously inserts large discourses into the Markan narrative structure and thus purposely halts the movement of the plot in favor of didactic blocks of sayings, the perspective of narrative criticism cannot encompass and explain the entire literary work.

C. Time and Place of Composition

For those who hold the two-source theory, dependence on Mark and Q makes a date after A.D. 70 almost inevitable. The variegated M material also seems to reflect a lengthy and convoluted history and necessitate a post-A.D. 70 date (contra, Robinson 1976: 86–117). The gospel in its final form bespeaks a mature theological development on such issues as salvation history, eschatology, and world mission. The gospel ends with a resounding affirmation of a mission to all nations; with baptism (with a triadic formula!) instead of circumcision as the initiation rite into the people of God; and the commandments of Jesus, not the Mosaic Torah, as the object of teaching (28:16–20). In some instances, the commands of Jesus involve not only a break with Pharisaic observances, but also the abrogation of laws in the Pentateuch (see, e.g., the rejection of both

Pharisaic hand washing and OT food laws in 15:1–20, esp. v 11). The very issues that were the battleground of Paul's day have become nonissues in Matthew's gospel. Matthew's additions to Mark's eschatological discourse emphasize three times the message of the delay of the Parousia (24:48; 25:5, 19). The center of gravity in Matthew's eschatology shifts toward the abiding presence of the risen Lord in his church (1:23; 18:20; 28:20). The Parousia remains important for paraenesis not because of its imminence but because of its severity, bringing about a final sharp separation in the mixed body of the Church (22:10–14). The obtrusive reference to the burning of a city in the parable of the great supper (not original, as the Lukan parallel, Luke 14:15–24, makes clear) does seem to be an allusion to the destruction of Jerusalem in A.D. 70 (Matt 22:1–14, esp. v 7). To speak of an OT theme here (Rengstorf 1960) does not explain why Matthew disrupts the flow of the parable to insert the theme where it does not seem to belong. The separation of Matthew's church from the synagogue (see E below) also argues for a post-A.D. 70 date. At the same time, the use of Matthew by Ignatius of Antioch (see below) necessitates a date of composition of the gospel before the early years of the 2d century (Brown and Meier 1983: 15–18).

Many places suggested fail to pass close scrutiny. A date after A.D. 70 makes composition in Judea, and especially a destroyed Jerusalem, hardly likely. The disruption of Jewish and Jewish-Christian life in Palestine because of the First Jewish War was immense; yet Matthew's gospel seems to reflect an organic development out of its Jewish matrix. The use of Greek in a gospel addressed to a whole church seems unlikely in Palestine, where the ordinary language of the common people was Aramaic and the sacred language was Hebrew. The disruption of a Jewish presence in Caesarea Maritima in A.D. 66 makes that city also a dubious candidate. What we do know of the origins of Christianity in Caesarea Maritima points to a liberal, Hellenist matrix with gentile sympathies rather than a conservative Jewish basis (Acts 8:40; 10:1–48). The N Syrian hinterland or the city of Edessa likewise runs into the problem of the common language of the ordinary people in those areas, namely, Aramaic. The cities along the Phoenician coast are possibilities, but we know next to nothing about them in the NT period. Moreover, the church of Matthew had to be prestigious and lively enough not only to support the production of this large gospel, but also to have it accepted in the churches at large in the 2d century. Such objections also hold true of Alexandria. The origin and state of Christianity in Alexandria in the 1st century are unknown to us.

Well-known, by contrast, is the most likely candidate, Antioch, the capital of Syria (Brown and Meier 1983: 18–26). A predominantly Greek-speaking metropolis with the largest Jewish population in Syria, it was the home of a Christian community founded in the late 30s by a Hellenist group of Jewish Christians who began a circumcision-free mission at Antioch (Acts 11:19–26). This mission was impeded for a while by the strict view of the James party from Jerusalem (Gal 2:11–14), but the gentile orientation of Ignatius of Antioch—something that is taken for granted—shows that the more liberal approach had won out before the beginning of the 2d century. This tangled history would help explain the different strata of tradition in Matthew. The struggles between Hellenists and the James party have left traces of both liberal and conservative views. The Jewish tone of the gospel would have been reinforced by the sizable Jewish population in Antioch. Dialogue and debate with the synagogue are reflected in the focus on Jewish customs and rites, on the Mosaic law, and on the fulfillment of prophecy. Yet the gospel stands on the borderline between the Jewish and gentile world. On the whole, Matthew's gospel employs better Greek than Mark's and uses Greek plays on words. Despite the strong Jewish tone, there are pointers throughout the gospel (2:1–12; 8:5–13; 15:21–28; 27:54) toward the climactic missionary charge in 28:16–20. Antioch supplies the perfect meeting place for the melting pot that is Matthew's gospel. Founded in the 30s, the Antiochene church enjoyed a lengthy, mostly undisturbed existence in a Jewish-gentile milieu, with time to develop a scribal tradition and perhaps a scribal school for the cultivation of OT texts and Christian traditions (Stendahl 1968). The composition of such a large gospel was no mean financial undertaking, and Kingsbury (*Matthew* Procl) claims to find hints in the gospel of a relatively affluent urban church. The special traditions about Peter in the gospel (e.g., 16:18) may reflect his influential role in Antioch in the first generation (see D below). Composition of the gospel at Antioch is also supported by the fact that Ignatius of Antioch is the first Church Father to use Matthew (Matt 3:15 in *Smyrneans* 1:1; Matt 10:16b in *Polycarp* 2:2; Matt 2:1–12 in *Ephesians* 19:2–3).

D. Occasion of the Gospel: a Church in Transition

The conclusion that Matthew's gospel was written at Antioch ca. A.D. 80–90 has important consequences for understanding the origin of the gospel as well as the history of the early Church. It enables us to plot the development of Christianity in one significant urban center in the first three Christian generations and thus to comprehend the problems and forces that led to Matthew's particular approach to the gospel traditions. From Acts and Galatians we know that the church at Antioch was founded by "leftist" Jewish-Christian Hellenists who were the first to begin a wide-ranging circumcision-free mission to the gentiles. Although this was opposed by the extreme right wing of Jewish Christians, the so-called Council of Jerusalem (A.D. 49) accepted the innovation. Soon afterward, however, because of pressure from the right-wing group around James, the brother of the Lord, Paul and Peter clashed at Antioch over table fellowship between Jewish and gentile Christians. Paul soon found it expedient to leave Antioch; he never mentioned it again in his letters and did not return for long sojourns. More to the point, Paul does not say in Gal 2:11–14 who won the argument at Antioch, although his victory in that debate would have been extremely helpful for his argumentation in Galatians 2. It thus seems likely that Peter won the debate and represented in Antioch an approach more conservative than Paul's, yet more open to the gentiles than the James group's. After the destruction of Jerusalem in A.D. 70, the second generation of Christians in Antioch was severed from the conservative umbilical cord of the mother church in Jerusalem. By this time the rejection of the Christian gospel by most Jews and its acceptance by many gentiles raised anew the question of how a church rooted in Judaism should relate to the larger gentile world. Matthew's gospel represents a conscious attempt at synthesis and compromise among the competing traditions inherited from the first generation. True to the Pauline thrust, it concludes with a clear legitimation of a universal mission, with no mention of circumcision; food laws are abrogated. Yet in the face of a flood of gentile converts with no heritage of Jewish morality, the gospel stresses the moral teaching of Jesus, affirming OT ethics even as it radicalizes or even transcends them at certain points. Matthew is pointedly trying to preserve both the new and the old wine (9:17c, a Matthean addition to the Markan statement of radical discontinuity). He is the scribe trained in the kingdom of heaven who brings forth from the storehouse of tradition things "new and old" (13:52; note the order of the adjectives: the newness of Jesus is the norm by which one properly interprets the OT tradition). It is no accident that the "liberal conservative" Matthew, seeking a moderate middle path from a Jewish past into a gentile future, exalts the figure of Peter as the "chief rabbi" of the Church (Matt 16:18–19). Historically, in a time of crisis, Peter did represent a centrist position between Paul on the left and James on the right. Faced with the remnant of a strong Jewish party and the problem of an influx of pagans, Matthew seeks the same sort of "balancing act" by meshing the various and not always harmonious traditions of Mark, Q, and M. Matthew's gospel thus has as its larger Sitz im Leben the crisis of a church in transition, seeking to preserve what is viable in its Jewish past as it moves into the uncharted waters of a predominantly gentile future in the Greco-Roman world. That this problem did not entirely disappear in the third Christian generation at Antioch is indicated by the seven authentic letters of Ignatius of Antioch. He, too, must fight a Judaizing group on the right (although by this time the Jewish influence is largely spent) and the new danger of a gnosticizing/docetic group on the left. His solution is typically Antiochene: a synthesis of major NT traditions, now involving Pauline, Matthean, and Johannine streams of thought (Brown and Meier 1983: 28–86).

E. Matthew's Church and the Synagogue

Many scholars, e.g., Barth (1963), Davies (1964), and Hummel (1966), maintain that Matthew's church is still tied to the synagogue, despite growing tensions. Highly "Jewish" material like the exhortation to accept the teaching authority of the scribes and Pharisees (23:2–3) is used as the basis for this position. However, an increasing number of exegetes, e.g., Strecker (1971), Trilling (1964), Frankemölle (1974), and especially Hare (1967), hold that Matthew's church had already broken with the synagogue by the time the gospel was written. Matthew's gospel has nine references to Jewish synagogues. Wherever the context fails to designate the synagogue as belonging to "the hypocrites," Matthew adds the qualifier "their" to indicate an institution that is now foreign to the Christians. Mark and Luke have no such consistent usage. Matthew thus creates a pointed linguistic opposition between "their synagogue" and "my [Jesus'] church" (Matt 16:18). This sense of break and distance is also seen in Matthew's addition to the end of the Markan parable of the evil tenants of the vineyard (Mark 12:1–12; Matt 21:33–43) in Matt 21:43: "Therefore I tell you that the kingdom of God will be taken from you and given to a people [*ethnos*] bearing its fruits." The kingdom is transferred from Israel to another people, non-Israel, the Church (Matthew never calls the Church the "new" or "true" Israel; for him there is too much of a break). Indeed, it is difficult to see how a group that pursued a universal mission without circumcision, rejected the food laws of the Pentateuch, abandoned the "teaching of the Pharisees and Sadducees" (Matt 16:11–12) in favor of the power to "bind and loose" invested in Peter (16:18–19) and the local church gathered around Jesus (18:18–20) could remain in union with the synagogue. It is sometimes suggested that the break was hastened by the insertion of the *birkat ha-mînîm,* the cursing of heretics and/or Christians, into the Eighteen Benedictions, a key prayer in the synagogue liturgy. But the date of the *birkat ha-mînîm* is disputed: some place it around A.D. 85; others, early in the 2d century. Moreover—as is often the case in juridical actions—such formal measures probably just finalized a process that had been going on for some time. The break with the synagogue need not be taken to mean that Matthew's church had given up all attempts to win over Jews; Jews are probably included, in undifferentiated fashion, in the mission to "*all* the nations" (*panta ta ethnē,* 28:19).

F. Author: Jew or Gentile?

Until the last few decades, the number of scholars who favored the view that Matthew, the redactor of the gospel, was a Jewish Christian was overwhelming. Yet, as R. E. Brown has pointed out (Brown and Meier 1983: 1–8), "Jewish Christian" is a category that admits of many nuances. Bacon thought of Matthew as a conservative Jewish Christian proposing a neolegalism (1928: 229). Von Dobschütz thought of a rabbi of the school of Johanan ben Zakkai who had ben converted to Christianity and had written a type of Jewish-Christian catechism (1928). Goulder has instead called Matthew a small-town scribe who applies midrashic techniques to Mark's gospel, which is Matthew's only extended written source (1974). Abel seeks to resolve the tensions in the gospel by positing two redactors: the first was an anti-gentile Jewish Christian, while the second was anti-Jewish and pro-gentile. More recently, scholars who see Matthew as Jewish view him as a moderate Hellenistic-Jewish Christian (Bornkamm: 1968) who was liberated from an earlier stringent Jewish Christianity which opposed the gentile mission and upheld the Pharisaic view of the Law. This position is maintained by scholars who hold that Matthew's church was still tied to the synagogue as well as by some who claim that the break had already taken place. The arguments for this position usually rest on the strikingly "Jewish" tone, language, and subject matter of the gospel. Rabbinic parallels are especially stressed.

In the last few decades, however, a vocal minority of exegetes has sustained the hypothesis that the final redactor of the gospel was a gentile (Clark 1947; Nepper-Christensen 1958; Strecker 1971; Trilling 1964; Walker 1967; van Tillborg 1972; Frankemölle 1974; Meier 1976). The fierce polemic against Pharisaism and Israel, the rejection of ritual observances and food laws, and openness to a gentile mission would of course be possible in a zealous Jew who had become a zealous Christian convert. We see something similar in Paul. Yet it is precisely the comparison with Paul that points up a striking difference. For all his polemics Paul affirms his great love for his own people (Romans 9), strives to gain their conversion, and affirms that on the last day "all Israel will be saved" (Rom 11:26). Matthew instead redacts the Markan Passion Narrative so that "all the people" (no longer just "the crowds") cry out to Pilate, as they request the crucifixion of Jesus, "His blood be upon us and upon our children!" Thus is a prophecy of Jesus (another Matthean redactional insertion into Mark) fulfilled: the kingdom of God is taken from Israel and given to another people. While Jews are probably included in the universal mission commanded at the end of the gospel, Matthew no longer speaks of Israel after the Passion Narrative; he speaks simply of "Jews" in 28:15. The extreme nature of the gospel's polemic, as compared with Paul's, does raise the question whether its author was Jewish.

More specifically, though, there seem to be places in the gospel where the author makes mistakes about the Hebrew Scriptures and about Jewish parties and beliefs—matters that an intelligent, well-educated, and highly articulate Jew would have known. One example is the mention of two animals in the entrance of Jesus into Jerusalem (21:2, 7). In this Markan narrative Matthew's major change is the insertion of a formula quotation (v 4) and the careful underlining of the literal fulfillment of the prophecy in Jesus' action (vv 2, 7). So literal must be the fulfillment that Matthew presents a scarcely imaginable description of Jesus riding on both animals. Matthew apparently understood the text of Zech 9:9 to be speaking of two separate animals, not the one animal that is in fact mentioned twice in Zech 9:9 because of the Hebraic parallelism. Such a misreading of the intent of the OT text is hardly understandable if the writer is an intelligent, well-educated Jew. There is no explanation for Matthew's doubling of the animals except a misunderstanding of the text. The rabbis would indeed at times ignore Hebraic parallelism when ignoring it served their theological purposes. But here in Matthew no special theological purpose is served except the theological purpose of literal fulfillment, a purpose that indicates that Matthew understood the text as literally meaning two animals.

Matthew seems involved in another slip concerning matters Jewish in his reference to the Sadducees in 22:23. Matthew, like Luke, is again dependent on Mark. In his description of the Sadducees, Mark in 12:18 says: "And there come to him Sadducees, who say there is no resurrection, and they asked him, saying . . ." Mark uses a relative clause to define the Sadducees as a group. Denial of the resurrection is a hallmark of the Sadducees as a party and not just a statement about what some particular Sadducees were saying to Jesus at one particular moment (a separate participle, "saying," indicates the words they address to Jesus). Luke makes the same point as Mark, employing an attributive participle with definite article to define the Sadducees' basic theology as a group (something Luke knows well; cf. Acts 4:1–2; 23:8). Josephus and the Talmud give similar descriptions. The fact that denial of the resurrection was basic to the Sadducean position can thus be presumed as common knowledge among Jews and even among some Christians of the 1st century A.D. and even later. Hence Matthew's change of Mark's description is especially strange (Matt 22:23): "There came to him Sadducees, saying there is no resurrection. . . ." Matthew has made the attributive clause or participle predicative. It no longer describes the basic position of the Sadducees, but simply reports what these particular Sadducees were saying or thinking as they came to Jesus. Once again, the only likely explanation of this garbling of the Markan tradition is ignorance of the Jewish situation before and after A.D. 70. Neither before nor after that date could any well-educated Jew make such a mistake in describing the Sadducees.

Moreover, this is not the only instance of Matthew's ignorance of the stance of the Sadducees. Matt 16:11–12 (clearly redactional) manifests the same lack of knowledge of the Jewish situation. While Mark 8:14–21 simply states that the disciples did not grasp what Jesus meant by avoiding the leaven of the Pharisees and the leaven of Herod, Matthew changes the reference to the leaven of the Pharisees and Sadducees (Matt 16:11). Then Matthew states that the disciples understood that Jesus was not talking about avoiding leaven in bread, but rather "the teaching of the Pharisees and Sadducees." Matthew uses the definite article with "teaching" and only one definite article for "the Pharisees and Sadducees." Thus, he thinks of the doctrine common to the Pharisees and Sadducees as one entity, set over against the teaching of Jesus. No Jew aware of the conflicts in Judaism before A.D. 70 and no Jew aware of the Pharisees' triumphant branding of the Sadducees' doctrine as heretical after A.D. 70 could have written such a sentence. Matthew must be considered to have been ignorant of the exact doctrine of the Sadducees. This is extremely difficult to reconcile with the theory of a Jewish-Christian redactor, while it jibes well with the theory of a gentile-Christian redactor. To all this, one might add the consideration that it is Mark, not Matthew, who displays the greatest number of Semitisms and outright Semitic words in his gospel. In fact, Aramaic words in Mark's text tend to be dropped by Matthew, with only the Greek equivalent retained. Matthew improves the highly Semitic Greek of Mark in the direction of more acceptable Greek usage, employing some Greek plays on words known from the classical period. Granted, no amount of argumentation in this question will generate absolute certitude. One could reconcile all these data with a picture of an enlightened, educated Hellenistic-Jewish Christian with universalistic views. Indeed, such a Jewish Christian could be thought of as having once shared the narrow views of his older tradition and as having developed slowly toward his present position. But as S. Schulz observes, such a "liberated" Hellenistic-Jewish Christian is hardly discernible from a gentile Christian (1967: 162). In the end, the theory of Matthew as a gentile Christian who had belonged to the Antiochene church (and perhaps its scribal school) for many years, who revered the Jewish-Christian traditions of his church, and who intended to preserve while interpreting them in his gospel seems to be able to explain all the data more easily.

In the light of all the data we have seen, it is extremely

difficult to hold that the gospel of Matthew was actually written by the apostle Matthew. But even the gospel narratives themselves create major difficulties for the attribution of Matthew's gospel to "Matthew-Levi" the tax collector. If we hold in the two-source theory, then this Matthew-Levi would have to be dependent on the evangelist Mark for much of his narrative material. Even the Church Fathers admitted that Mark was not an eyewitness of the earthly ministry of Jesus. Thus we would be left in the awkward position of claiming that the apostle Matthew, an eyewitness of the public ministry, copied a good amount of his account of the ministry from Mark, a noneyewitness. This relationship becomes incredible when we notice that the author of Matthew's gospel is dependent on Mark for the story of the call of Levi (or Matthew) the tax collector (Mark 2:13–17 = Matt 9:9–13). It is inconceivable that, in recounting the autobiographical story of his call by Jesus, Matthew the apostle would have to rely on the narrative of Mark, a non-eyewitness. Moreover, the very existence of one person called both Matthew and Levi is questionable. Mark 2:14 and Luke 5:27 know of a "Levi the tax collector," whom they do not identify with the Matthew (not called a tax collector) mentioned in the list of the Twelve. Only in Matthew's gospel is this tax collector, in the story of his call, named Matthew, not Levi (Matt 9:9). That one and the same Jew in the 1st century A.D. would bear two different Semitic first names is highly unlikely. Jews could certainly also bear a Greek first name in addition to their Semitic first name, or an indication of who their father was or where they came from, or some (serious or humorous) nickname. But to have two Semitic first names would naturally cause endless confusion. Hence it seems that it is the author of the First Gospel who has consciously changed Levi's name to Matthew and who has "cross-referenced" the change in the list of the Twelve by designating Matthew the apostle a tax collector, thus identifying two people who are distinguished in Mark and Luke. Why the first evangelist did this is not clear. It is possible that the first gospel does contain some special tradition originating from the apostle Matthew (Pesch 1968). Also possible, however, is a play on words in Greek (Kiley 1984). The evangelist may have noted the concentration of words for disciple and learning (*mathētēs* and *mathēteuō*) in the story and indicated that a prime example of the sinner called to be a *mathētēs* was Matthew.

G. Structure and Content of the Gospel

Under the rubric of structure we are considering the structure consciously intended by the author, and not the "deep structures" examined by contemporary structuralists (for the latter, see Patte 1986).

Scholarly opinions on the structure of Matthew's gospel vary widely. One reason for this is that Matthew is a superb "verbal architect," building his literary basilica with many finely fitted, interlocking stones. These interlocking literary structures include summaries of Jesus' activity (e.g., 15:29–31), summaries that form inclusions of whole sections (Jesus as teacher, proclaimer, and healer in 4:23 = 9:35), inclusions in individual pericopes (the first and eighth beatitudes in 5:3, 10), clear cross-references (two multiplications of loaves in 14:20 plus 15:37 = 16:9–10), subtle cross-references (monitory dreams given to gentiles to save Jesus: the Magi and Pilate's wife, 2:12; 27:19), numerical patterns, often in threes (9 beatitudes [5:3–12], 6 antitheses [5:21–48], 3 pious practices [6:1–18], 3 triplets of miracles stories [chaps. 9–10], 3 passion predictions on the way to Jerusalem [16:21; 17:22–23; 20:18–19]), repeated formulas (the concluding and transitional formula at the end of each of the five great discourses [see below]), blocks of similar material in similar forms (e.g., controversy stories in chaps. 12, 21–22), geographic patterns (Bethlehem in Judea ⟶ Egypt ⟶ Judea ⟶ Galilee ⟶ Nazareth ⟶ Capernaum ⟶ in and around Galilee ⟶ Judea ⟶ Jerusalem ⟶ Galilee). Faced with this wealth of structural elements, one must avoid subjective flights of fancy by concentrating on structural devices in the text that are clearly visible, occur repeatedly, and are spread throughout the body of the gospel. Of the many suggestions made in recent years, three are worthy of note.

A few critics in this century have held the view that the whole gospel is governed by one great chiasm or inverted (concentric) parallelism. That is, the gospel is divided into two halves, like the two halves of a parabola: pericopes at the outer limits of the halves correspond to each other (e.g., chaps. 1–2 and 26–28), pericopes a little further in correspond to each other (e.g., chaps. 3–4 and 24–25), and so on until one reaches the center of the chiasm at the center of the gospel. Green (1968) sees the center in chap. 11, while Fenton (1959) and Ellis (1974) see the center in chap. 13. The objective basis for this approach is the undisputed presence of inclusions at the beginning and end of the gospel. "Emmanuel, God with us" (1:23) and "Behold, I am with you all days" (28:10) provide the clearest example. Indeed, the whole of chaps. 1–2 and 26–28 forms a rough inclusion, with many of the themes and even rare phrases first seen in the Infancy Narrative (a "proleptic passion") returning in the Passion Narrative. Moreover, chaps. 11–13 do seem to witness a turning point in Jesus' relation with Israel. However, the attempt to extend these valid insights to the whole of the gospel, arranged as one grand chiasm, collapses of its own weight, improbability, and lack of objective criteria. The grand chiasm is basically the creation of the ingenious critic. Blocks of chapters at one end of the gospel are forced to correspond to relatively small sections at the other, corresponding themes are in the eye of the exegete rather than in the wording of the Greek text, and chiasm critics cannot agree on where the all-important center of the chiasm lies.

A second, more popular approach today is the one suggested by Krentz (1964) and championed by Kingsbury (1975: 1–39). Kingsbury postulates three main sections of the gospel, demarcated by "superscriptions" (1:1; 4:17; 16:21). Section One (1:1–4:16) sets forth the genesis and significance of the *person* of Jesus, emphasizing from the beginning the key title Son of God. Section Two (4:17–16:20) shows Jesus the Messiah offering salvation to Israel by his teaching, proclaiming, and healing, only to meet with rejection. Section Three (16:21–28:20) depicts the suffering, death, and resurrection of Jesus the Messiah, with its effect on Israel and all humanity. To support this division, Kingsbury places great weight on the phrase that occurs at 4:17 and 16:21: "From that time Jesus began . . ." He also claims that 3:1 ("Now in those days . . ." introducing the Baptist) belongs with chaps. 1–2 and that the prologue of the gospel extends to 4:16. More recently, Kingsbury has supported these insights of redaction criticism with arguments from modern narrative criticism (1986).

There are a number of problems with this approach. It is questionable whether five Greek words, occurring only twice in the gospel (4:17; 16:21), can be called a "fixed formula"; the concluding and transitional phrase at the end of each of the five great discourses deserves that label much more. It is also unlikely that *apo tote* ("from that time") indicates a major break from the preceding verses and a new beginning. In 26:16 *apo tote* begins the last sentence of the pericope of Judas' agreement to betray Jesus (26:14–16). In chap. 4, v 17 seems more natural as the last verse of 4:12–17; and in chap. 16, v 21 stands in the middle of the great Caesarea Philippi scene with its multiple interactions between Jesus and Peter (16:13–28), a scene which has its own christological inclusion (Son of Man in vv 13, 28). Moreover, precisely from a literary point of view, it is awkward to make 3:1–12 go with chaps. 1–2 when some thirty years have passed, the Baptist (a totally new figure, unlike his treatment in Luke's gospel) is introduced, and the phrase of 3:1 ("Now in those days . . .") sounds more like a clearing of the throat for the new beginning, the new eschatological event of the coming of the adult Jesus, rather than a mere link with the Infancy Narrative. The Baptist's proclamation is word for word the proclamation of Jesus in 4:17, supposedly in a different section of the gospel. In chap. 16 the expansion of the Markan Caesarea Philippi scene by Matthew explains the need for a caesura in 16:21. The more important literary datum is the Son of Man inclusion (16:13, 28) and the fact that a change in geography is signaled in 16:18 ("into the region of Caesarea Philippi"); no other change of place is indicated after that until 17:1 (going up the high mountain for the transfiguration). Literary signals thus indicate that the Caesarea Philippi scene in 16:13–28 is to be taken as a unit; to place a major division of the gospel at 16:21 tears apart the christological and ecclesiological synthesis that Matthew has carefully constructed.

The third division proposed is the most traditional and remains the most likely: The public ministry is made up of five major sections or "books," each with the pattern of narrative plus discourse, with the Infancy Narrative as prologue and the Passion Narrative as climax. This position enjoys the advantage of starting from clear, undisputed literary facts and slowly building up an argument with further literary data found in the text. The starting point of this position is that Matthew purposely builds large discourses out of disparate sayings of Jesus. As so often, Matthew has taken his cue from and expanded upon his sources: Mark had two discourses (parables [chap. 4] and eschatology [chap. 13]), while Q provided various blocks of sayings (e.g., the more primitive form of the Sermon on the Mount/Plain in Luke 6:20–49). Matthew enlarges these collections to monumental proportions, especially in the Sermon on the Mount and the eschatological discourse. Moreover, Matthew did not lump his discourses together in one section of the gospel; they are carefully spaced out over the length of the public ministry: Sermon on the Mount, chaps. 5–7; missionary discourse, chap. 10; parables, chap. 13; discourse on church life and order, chap. 18; eschatological discourse, chaps. 24–25. The result of this spacing out is that the body of the gospel naturally falls into large blocks of narrative then discourse, narrative then discourse. Matthew has thus significantly altered the configuration of Mark, where narrative loomed much larger over a few small discourses. Any literary analysis of Matthew must come to terms with this monumental remodeling of the gospel form in the direction of lengthy discourses.

Matthew's editorial hand is clear not only in this overall pattern of narrative plus discourse but also in the redactional formula he uses both to close the five major discourses and to provide a transition back to the narrative. The clause, "And it came to pass, when Jesus had finished these words [instructions, parables]," occurs at 7:28; 11:1; 13:53; 19:1; and 26:1. The precise wording and function of this clause are found nowhere else in Matthew or in the rest of the NT. That Matthew is carefully keeping count of his discourses and their structuring function is clear from his modification in the final occurrence of the formula, at the end of the eschatological discourse and of the whole public ministry, as the Passion Narrative begins: "Now it came to pass, when Jesus had finished all these words . . ." The collocation of the five sermons is thus anything but haphazard. This conclusion may also be supported by a consideration of the way Matthew introduces each of the discourses (Keegan 1982).

Thus, Matthew seems to demarcate precisely five major discourses as large structuring elements in his gospel. This is not to deny that the narrative sections have sayings material as well (e.g., the Beelzebul controversy in 12:22–45; the dispute over clean and unclean in 15:1–20). But these sections do not contain as lengthy a body of sayings of Jesus, uninterrupted by dialogue and directed solely or mainly to his disciples, as do the five discourses. Chapter 23 constitutes a special case. What is notable is the lack of unity in the audience addressed. Jesus begins (v 1) by addressing "the crowds and his disciples" (a unique phrase in the gospel; the five discourses are addressed primarily or solely to the disciples). In verse 13 Jesus begins the seven woes against the scribes and Pharisees, which employ the 2d person plural (vv 13–36); he concludes with an apostrophe to Jerusalem (vv 37–39). Although some would count chap. 23 as a separate discourse and others would see it as the first part of the eschatological discourse (chaps. 24–25), it seems best to consider it a bridge Matthew constructs between the controversy stories and parables of judgment on Israel, on the one hand, (chaps. 21–22) and the eschatological discourse, on the other. Before the sermon on the future judgment, Jesus pronounces judgment now on the leaders of Israel.

Another characteristic that marks off the five discourses is their careful positioning in the flow of the gospel, so that they take up a number of themes raised in the previous narrative, while also preparing for the narrative to come. The discourses thus act as pivots in the literary structure because of their Janus-like quality. The flow of each narrative section into its corresponding discourse can be sketched briefly as follows. Jesus, whose authority as Son of God has been validated by his baptism and temptation (which in turn pick up themes from the Infancy Narrative), leaves Nazareth for his "base of operations" in Capernaum; he calls his first disciples and attracts large crowds, who "follow" him (chaps. 3–4). The context is thus created for Jesus to teach authoritatively the basic requirements of true discipleship and following, viz., the Sermon on the Mount (chaps. 5–7; so ends Book One). Authority in teaching is matched by authority in deed in the three triplets of miracle stories (chaps. 8–9). What Jesus has been doing during his initial ministry in Galilee by way of proclamation and healing (summary in 9:35, looking back to 4:23) the Twelve are likewise commissioned to do (but without a mandate to teach) in the missionary discourse (chap. 10; so ends Book Two). The rumblings of opposition in Israel, heard faintly in Book Two, burst into the open in Book Three, abounding in controversy stories as well as in woes and rebukes by Jesus (chaps. 11–12). Jesus reacts to Israel's rejection by withdrawing verbally into the veiled speech of parables, just as he withdraws physically into a house with his disciples, who do understand him (13:1–52; so ends Book Three). As the breach with Israel widens, Jesus turns to concentrate on the formation of his disciples into the embryonic church; hence the prominence of Peter and the use of the word "church" *(ekklēsia)* in the narrative of Book Four (13:53–17:27). Naturally, the matching discourse focuses on church life and order, with "church" occurring twice (chap. 18; so ends Book Four). Amid increasing hostility, Jesus leads his embryonic church up the road to Jerusalem and to the cross, teaching the duties of the various states of life under the shadow of the cross (chaps. 19–20). Arriving in Jerusalem, he displays his authority by refuting the Jerusalem leaders in debate, by speaking parables of judgment on Israel, and by pronouncing woes against the scribes and the Pharisees (chaps. 21–23). Corresponding to this context of judgment is the sermon on the final judgment, the eschatological discourse (chaps. 24–25; so ends Book Five and the public ministry). All that remains is the great eschatological event of death-resurrection.

A number of misconceptions about this five-book division must be avoided. First, this division is not necessarily connected with the theory of Bacon (1930) and others who tried to see in the five books a reference to the Pentateuch, with Jesus as the new Moses teaching the new Torah. While the appearance of *biblos geneseōs* ("the book of origin," or possibly "the Book of Genesis") in Matt 1:1 make the allusion to the Pentateuch tempting, attempts to work out the correspondence in detail are forced, especially with regard to Leviticus and Numbers. Such strained explanations have brought the five-part division of the Matthean public ministry into disrepute, but unnecessarily. The five-book division rests on data internal to the gospel and has nothing to do with any Pentateuch hypothesis. Actually, five-part divisions of literary works were well-known in the Jewish and Greco-Roman world at the time. In Judaism, the Psalms, the Megilloth, and probably the original form of the *Pirqe ᵓAbot* all had fivefold divisions. Certainly no one has proposed that Irenaeus intended to write a new Pentateuch because his *Adversus Haereses* was divided into five books! Hence Matthew is simply taking up an honored literary convention, with no necessary connection with the Mosaic Torah.

A second misconception is that the five-book structure of the public ministry reduces the Infancy Narrative and the Passion Narrative to an unimportant prologue and epilogue respectively. It does not. One must be careful about terminology here. A prologue, especially in a biblical work, is not necessarily unimportant. John 1:1–18 is designated a prologue, without in any way reducing its significance for the meaning and structure of the Fourth Gospel. Actually, Matthew 1–2 is not unlike John 1:1–18 in that it answers questions about the nature, origin, and destiny of Jesus. It is a prologue that functions like the overture to an opera, sounding some key themes that will develop as the work progresses. In particular, Matthew's prologue introduces leitmotivs that return in the narratives of the passion and resurrection. Hence, instead of simply and solely providing an introduction to the public ministry, the Infancy Narrative acts also as a proleptic Passion Narrative. Indeed, the five books of the public ministry are basically intelligible apart from chaps. 1–2; in the ministry there is little by way of direct reference backward to the Infancy Narrative. Thus chaps. 1–2 are rightly set apart from chaps. 3–25. Similarly, the narratives of passion and resurrection are not relegated to the position of epilogue or appendix by the five-book division. They are rather the climax of the whole narrative. While up until chap. 26 individual events in Jesus' life fulfilled individual prophecies (the message of the formula quotations), starting in chap. 26 "all the writings of the prophets" are fulfilled (26:54, 56). This is why, with the exception of the apologetic use of the OT to explain the scandalous fate of Judas (27:3–10) no formula quotation is used in the Passion Narrative. The death-resurrection of Jesus constitutes the one world-turning, age-changing apocalyptic event that fulfills all prophecy and ushers in the age of the Church (28:16–20). Hence, like the Infancy Narrative, the Passion Narrative stands apart from the public ministry, not as epilogue but as all-encompassing climax. On this basis, the following structure may be proposed.

1. Prologue (Chaps. 1–2). Matthew is the only one of the four canonical Gospels that begins with the OT literary genre of genealogy (1:1–17). This underlines a major message of the whole work, echoed often in the fulfillment formulas: the prophecies of the OT are fulfilled in the life of Jesus. The 3 groups of 14 generations reflect an apocalyptic mind-set: all salvation history is divided into epochs that are guided by God to the consummation of his plan. Yet the appearance of the four strange women hints that the movement of the plan is not always in a straight line; the discontinuity of these four "holy irregularities" is woven around the main thread of continuity. The 3 groups of 14 may indicate that the time of Jesus is the period of perfection and fulfillment ($3 \times 14 = 6 \times 7$). The number 14 is also symbolic in Hebrew of the name David, and Jesus' status as Son of David is at the heart of chap. 1. The annunciation to Joseph (1:18–25) has as its main point the theme of continuity: by naming Mary's child and accepting him as his own, Joseph son of David inserts Jesus into the Davidic line. Yet the element of discontinuity is also present; the virginal conception is the supreme "holy irregularity," making this Son of David also Emmanuel, God with us. Chapter 1 thus explicates the first titles of 1:1, "Jesus Christ, son of David."

But Jesus is also "son of Abraham," the Abraham in whom all the nations were to be blessed (Gen 22:18). This promise is to be fulfilled at the end of the gospel, with the mission to all nations (28:16–20), but a foreshadowing of all the nations' coming to Christ is seen in the coming of the Magi. While the united front of Judaism (Herod, chief priests, scribes, all Jerusalem—Matthew is not concerned with historical probabilities) rejects Jesus, the gentiles follow the hints of natural religion and OT prophecy to reach and adore the King of the Jews. The Jerusalem rulers seek to kill Jesus, but amid the carnage God rescues his Son out of death (proleptic Passion Narrative). By his going down to Egypt and subsequent exodus, Jesus recapitulates the history of Israel, the son of God in the OT. The high point of the Infancy Narrative is reached in God's declaration through Hosea that Jesus is not only son of David, son of Abraham, son of Joseph, son of Mary, but preeminently "my Son" (Matt 2:15). The "salvation geography" of chap. 2 comes to rest at Nazareth in Galilee, which links up with the traditions of the public ministry (3:13; 4:13). Jesus shall be called a "Nazarean" (2:23) in the sense of the truly consecrated holy one who will save his people (cf. *nazîr* in the birth story of Samson, Judg 13:5, 7).

2. Book One (3:1–7:29). a. Narrative (3:1–4:25). The Baptist is introduced as the great preacher of repentance. Matthew tends to create parallels between John and Jesus; hence, Jesus' initial proclamation of the kingdom in Mark 1:15 is put into the mouth of the Baptist by Matthew (Matt 3:2). Thus John anticipates word for word the initial proclamation of Jesus in 4:17. The united front of Judaism, represented by the historically unlikely union of Pharisees and Sadducees, is opposed to John as it will be opposed to Jesus. John warns his adversaries of the fearful separation of good and evil and the fiery punishment to come; the theme of separation on the last day is dear to Matthew. The ability to remit sins is carefully withheld from John's baptism; it is accomplished only by the death of Jesus (26:28). John's subordination is also seen in the dialogue before Jesus' baptism. John should be baptized by Jesus, but Jesus explains the present order by a reference to fulfillment of God's saving plan, foretold in prophecy (3:15). The Father's voice in the theophany following the baptism is addressed not to Jesus (as in Mark, with his messianic secret), but to the bystanders. The Jesus-Spirit-Father concatenation at the Baptism of Jesus points forward to the triadic baptismal formula in the great commissioning (28:19). The sonship of Jesus, the true Israel, is then tested by the devil. Three times, like Israel in the desert, Jesus is tempted. But unlike Israel Jesus shows he is the true son by his obedience in the midst of affliction. He will not take the easy way to the kingdom that bypasses the cross. Returning to Galilee, Jesus takes up the fallen standard of the Baptist. He transfers his residence to Capernaum and begins a ministry that will ultimately bring light to the gentiles (Isa 8:23–9:1—Eng 9:1–2). With sovereign authority he calls his first four disciples and attracts large crowds from all four points of the compass. He has begun his triple ministry of teaching (note that the pedagogue Matthew puts that first; moral catechesis is a special concern for him), proclaiming, and healing (4:23). The highlighting of teaching is meant to introduce the first example of extensive teaching, the Sermon on the Mount. The core proclamation ("The kingdom of heaven is at hand") was already given in 4:17; the healings will be reported in chaps. 9–10.

b. Discourse (5:1–7:29). Structurally, the sermon can be divided into two parts. Up until 6:18 the sermon is dominated by groups of threes; after 6:18 it is a group of loosely associated commentaries on the petitions of the Our Father, which fittingly stands at the center of the sermon (Bornkamm 1978; Guelich 1982). The 9 (3 × 3) Beatitudes open the sermon with a two-edged message. The poor in spirit must wait confidently for God to bring salvation (apocalyptic type of beatitude), but in the meantime the disciples must imitate the saving action of God (mercy, peacemaking) in their own lives (wisdom beatitudes). They must hunger and thirst for justice (= God's salvation on the last day), but in the present they must suffer persecution because they do justice (= do God's will; Przybylski 1980; Broer 1986). Though persecuted by the world, they are to be the light of the world (triple parable of salt, light, and city).

As Jesus begins to interpret the Mosaic law for his disciples, he makes a basic statement of principle (5:17–20; Barth 1963; Meier 1976). He brings not dissolution of the Law but its fulfillment. Yet this fulfillment is prophetic, eschatological fulfillment, in which the fullness of the eschaton sometimes spills over and transcends the old vessel of the Law—as is seen in the antitheses. But that is not to lead any Christian teacher to laxity. Christian "justice" (= doing the will of the Father according to the teaching of Jesus) must outstrip the justice of the Jewish teachers in both quality and quantity. This principle is then illustrated in the 6 (3 × 2) antitheses (5:21–48). In the antitheses on murder, adultery, and love, Jesus radicalizes the Law by extending and interiorizing the obligation; in the antitheses on divorce, oaths, and retaliation Jesus radicalizes to the point of abrogating the letter of the Law. In each case it is the authoritative word of Jesus ("but I say to you") that decides the issue (cf. 7:28–29; 28:20). The overriding concern in all these commands is that the disciple be undivided in his love of God and neighbor (= being perfect, 5:48). The three pious practices of almsgiving, prayer, and fasting (6:1–18) show a similar contrast between Jewish and Christian approaches; stress is laid on avoiding ostentation, with a view to the eschatological reward. Eschatology is shown to be at the center of Jesus' moral exhortation by the placing of the eschatological prayer (the Our Father) at the center of the sermon. The disciple prays for the glorious manifestation of God (the hallowing of the name) on the last day in the coming of his kingdom, his definitive rule over humanity, when his will shall triumph (first half of prayer, the "thou" petitions). The second half of the prayer (the "we" petitions) probably refers to the banquet in the kingdom, final forgiveness at the judgment seat of God, and final deliverance from Satan; possibly, though, Matthew understood it in reference to daily needs in this world (though that fits Luke's wording better; cf. Luke 11:3). Beginning with 6:19, Matthew arranges various sayings of Jesus to comment on the petitions of the Our Father. In view of the coming kingdom, the disciples are not to worry about material needs, but are to put their future entirely in the hands of their provident Father (6:19–34). They should imitate the kindness of the Father in their own lives (7:1–

12). They must choose for or against acting on the words of Jesus right now; as they choose, so shall they be judged on the last day (7:13–29). The authoritative word of Jesus is the touchstone of salvation.

3. Book Two (8:1–11:1). a. Narrative (8:1–9:34). Matthew has already given examples of Jesus' proclaiming and teaching; he now presents 9 (3 × 3) stories of Jesus' miracles (Held 1963). Each triplet of miracles is demarcated by a buffer pericope dealing with discipleship. The streamlined miracle stories focus upon the encounter between the petitioner's word of faith and Jesus' all-powerful word of healing. Fulfilling OT prophecies, Jesus the servant shares his power with his community of disciples and points forward to the inclusion of gentiles in that community. The first triplet (8:1–17) shows Jesus' healing power directed to the marginalized: a leper, a gentile soldier and his servant, and a woman. In healing the leper, Jesus typically both breaks the letter of the Mosaic law and yet commands compliance with its ritual prescriptions. The healing of the centurion's servant foretells the entrance of the gentiles into the kingdom and the exclusion of Israel. The healing of Peter's mother-in-law and of many others shows Jesus to be the Isaian servant. The first buffer (8:18–22), stressing the cost of discipleship, looks forward to the second triplet (8:23–9:8). The stilling of the storm portrays the Church beset by the messianic woes and turning to its Lord in prayer. The theme of the disciples' "littleness of faith" overshadows the actual miracle (Bornkamm 1963b). In Gadara Jesus' power over chaos in nature is seen to extend to chaos in people, as he exorcises two demoniacs. The Church is to trust its Lord, because his triumph over evil is complete. This triumph is demonstrated also in the forgiveness of sins, empircally verified by making a paralytic walk. It is a power Jesus shares with human beings in his church (the *tois anthrōpois* of 9:8). The joyful triumph over sin is depicted in the second buffer (9:9–17) by Jesus' table fellowship with tax collectors and sinners. Against the Pharisees Jesus quotes Hosea 6:6 on the superiority of mercy to sacrifice (repeated in 12:7). The break with Pharisaic Judaism is sounded in Jesus' rejection of voluntary fasting, yet Matthew adds the moderating note that both new and old should be preserved (cf. 13:52). The third triplet (9:18–34) emphasizes the importance of faith, even in the face of death or blindness. The final healing, of a mute demoniac, points forward to the clash with Israel in Book Three, since it calls forth the charge that Jesus casts out demons by the prince of demons (9:34 = 12:24).

b. Discourse (9:35–11:1). The third buffer (9:35–38) is a bridge section. On the one hand, it forms an inclusion with 4:23 and rounds out the nine miracle stories. On the other hand, it introduces the missionary discourse: Jesus the good shepherd sends out his disciples to share in his mission. The "twelve disciples" (10:1) are introduced for the first time as Jesus confers his healing and exorcising powers on them (Matthew has no story of the choice of the Twelve). By calling them "the twelve apostles" (10:2)—the only time he does so in his gospel—Matthew already signals that the limited mission during the life of Jesus foreshadows the wider mission to come after the death-resurrection. Only vv 5–16 deal with missionary activity in the strict sense and remain within the initial limitation of the mission to "the lost sheep of [= who constitute] the house of Israel" (vv 5–6). Just as this restriction will be lifted after the death-resurrection, so too will the restriction on the disciples' power (the power to teach, not conferred here, is granted in 28:20). Verses 17–25 speak of all disciples faced with persecution, not just missionaries, and the horizon seems expanded to the gentiles (v 18). By inserting here material from Mark's eschatological discourse, Matthew stresses that the mission is not simply a matter of telling people about the eschatological event; it is part of the eschatological event. Three times the disciples are told not to fear earthly persecutors but only the final judge (vv 26–33). They must be ready to bear even the heavy cross of breaking family bonds. Jesus did the same; and, as goes the Master, so goes the disciple. The initial theme of mission returns in vv 40–42, along with Matthew's favorite theme of reward. The theme of opposition, persecution, and breach within the family of Israel prepares well for the narrative of Book Three.

4. Book Three (11:2–13:52). a. Narrative (11:2–12:50). The tension between Israel and Jesus heightens notably in Book Three. There is tension even with the Baptist, who is puzzled that the fiery judge he expected should turn out to be the healing servant of Isaiah's prophecies. Yet John, for all his limitations, does stand parallel to Jesus; for both, despite all the differences in their styles of preaching, have met with the same rejection of Israel (11:2–19). Jesus expresses the growing breach with his woes on the cities of Galilee that have rejected his call to repentance. In contrast he gives thanks to the Father for having revealed the secrets of the end times to the spiritual babes who have accepted Jesus. The Father and Jesus enjoy a mutual knowledge to which no one else has access, unless Jesus wills to mediate it through his revelation. For Jesus is the true wisdom teacher of the end time; indeed, he speaks like Wisdom itself in the OT as he invites the weary to learn from him (vv 20–30). The hostility of the leaders toward Jesus heightens in the two sabbath disputes, over plucking grain and healing. Jesus again demands mercy, not sacrifice; and for the first time we hear that the Pharisees seek to destroy him. Jesus, the gentle servant of Isaiah, responds not with vengeance but with peacable withdrawal; it is just such mercy that will give the gentiles hope (12:1–21). Jesus' merciful healing of a blind and mute demoniac leads only to renewed charges by the Pharisees of diabolic power. Jesus refutes the charge and goes on the offensive, warning that the condition of Israel after it rejects him will be worse than before he came. The break with the synagogue is graphically portrayed when the family of Jesus has to cool their heels outside, while inside Jesus teaches his true family, namely, those who do the will of his Father (12:22–50).

b. Discourse (13:1–52). The parable discourse is Jesus' verbal response to his rejection by Israel. Having given Israel an opportunity to accept his clear message (there is no thoroughgoing messianic secret in Matthew, as we find it in Mark), Jesus now responds to their refusal by withdrawing into the veiled speech of parables. The parables are a punishment because (v 13; contrast "in order that" in Mark 4:12) Israel has not seen the truth, while the disciples do (again, contrast the blind disciples of Mark). The split between synagogue and church shines through the presentation. The disciples will face the same sort of opposition, and a disappointingly large number will fall away (cf. 24:10–12). But as the allegorical explanation of the sower parable promises, the final triumph of the eschatological harvest is assured (13:1–23). The parables of the mustard seed and the leaven make the same point about the contrast between the unpromising beginnings of the kingdom and its future, universal victory (vv 31–35). Distinctly Matthean is the parable of the wheat and the weeds, with its allegorical explanation. While the parable (vv 24–30) stresses the need for the Church to exercise patience and restraint in this present world composed of good and bad, since no one is authorized to anticipate the final separation of good and bad at the last judgment, the explanation (vv 36–43) depicts in detail that fearful separation which will most certainly come. The certainty of strict judgment takes the place of the temporal imminence of judgment as the motivating force in Matthew's exhortations. (Indeed, the threat of eternal punishment stands near or at the end of each of the five discourses.) The theme of separation is dramatically acted out as Jesus leaves the crowds halfway through the discourse to speak to his disciples alone in the house (v 36). The break between Jesus and Israel, and between the Church and the synagogue, is thus visibly symbolized. Such stressful times of separation demand that one be willing to sacrifice everything joyfully for the one true value of the kingdom, as the parables of the treasure and the pearl point out (vv 44–46). The theme song of the separation of good and bad on the last day returns in the final parable of the fishnet (vv 47–50), which ends on the grim note of fiery punishment. Yet all is not lost; the Matthean disciples do understand how to combine properly the new teaching of Jesus with the ancient wisdom of Israel (v 52; note the order: "new and old"!). From now on, the chasm between these believing disciples and an unbelieving Israel will widen right up to the end of the gospel (28:15 versus 28:17a).

5. Book Four (13:53–18:35). a. Narrative (13:53–17:27). While Matthew formed Book Three largely from Q and M, the narrative of Book Four is mainly Markan. It is taken mostly from the great "bread section," Mark 6–8, where *artos, artoi* ("bread," "loaves") form a literary and theological leitmotiv, still visible in Matthew. In Book Four the great "ecclesiological book" of the gospel, Matthew highlights the role of Peter and references to the Church (*ekklēsia;* the word occurs in Matthew only in Book Four and nowhere else in the four gospels). Christology and ecclesiology are welded together as Jesus prepares for the founding of his church through the apocalyptic events of the death-resurrection. Hence this book is dominated by christological titles and passion predictions on the one hand and by teaching to and about the Church on the other.

The breach with Israel widens still further with Jesus' rejection at Nazareth and the martyrdom of the Baptist, who even in death is paralleled with Jesus. The Baptist's death is thus a prophecy that Jesus will meet a similar fate at the hands of Israel (13:53–14:12). Just as the arrest of the Baptist occasioned Jesus' coming into Galilee to begin the struggle (4:12), so now the Baptist's martyrdom occasions Jesus' temporary withdrawal (cf. 12:15), as he turns his attention more to the formation of his embryonic community. This community is nourished by the feeding of the 5,000, in which the eucharistic allusions are clear, and in which Matthew heightens the role of the disciples as go-betweens (14:13–21). The walking on the water reveals Jesus as the divine Savior of his imperiled church, that fittingly acknowledges him as Son of God (14:22–36; contrast Mark's blind disciples in 6:51–52; Heil 1981). The christological confession voiced here will be expanded by Peter in 16:16 and extended to the gentile centurion in 27:54. In 14:28–31, Peter is a prime example of a disciple who is "of little faith" *(oligopistos),* which for Matthew means having faith but panicking in a crisis and acting as though one did not have faith. Peter boldly begins walking on the water, trusting in the word of Jesus. But the forces of chaos cause him to sink into death, from which the saving hand of Jesus rescues him (an acting out of many of the Psalms of Lament in the OT). Jesus teaches his disciples to reject Pharisaic ritual concerns and even OT food laws (15:11, 17–18). The break with the Pharisees and the synagogue is expressed in the terse command: "Leave them; they are blind guides" (15:14). Having torn down these legal walls of separation, Jesus heals the daughter of the Canaanite woman, solely on the basis of the woman's faith. The stress that this case is exceptional and does not fit into the regular mission of Jesus (15:24) makes it all the more a pointer forward to the time of the Church (28:16–20). The time of the Church is again foreshadowed in the feeding of the 4,000 (15:29–39).

In chap. 16, Jesus transfers teaching authority from the Pharisees and Sadducees (again, the united front of Judaism; their teaching is corrupting leaven, vv 11–12) to Peter as "chief rabbi" in the church of Jesus. Typically, the disciples are not totally blind, as in Mark. But being of little faith, they fail initially to understand but do so after Jesus' instruction (vv 7, 12). Matthew expands Mark's Caesarea Philippi scene, which in Mark is a christological turning point in the messianic secret, into a grand christological synthesis of major titles. The union of Christ, church, and morality is clear. Jesus indicates he is Son of Man in the triple sense of earthly ministry (v 13), Suffering Servant (Son of Man is implied in v 21; cf. 17:22–23; 20:18–19; 26:2), and final judge (vv 27–28). By divine revelation, Peter recognizes Jesus as Messiah and Son of God (v 16). Jesus reciprocates in vv 17–19 by pronouncing a beatitude and conferring a title on Simon. Simon is the recipient of an apocalyptic revealation from the Father. Henceforth he will be called *petros,* the Rock (Peter was not a usual first name in Aramaic or Greek in the 1st century A.D.), for on this stable rock (cf. 7:24–25) Jesus will build his church (notice the future; the full founding of the Church takes place after the death-resurrection, in 28:16–20). Peter is made vicegerent over the new palace of Jesus, the royal Messiah (cf. Isa 22:15–25), with the power to decide what is permissible or not according to the teaching of Jesus ("bind and loose"). All this high christology and ecclesiology are then balanced by the first prediction of the passion. The ambiguous Peter revolts against the word of the cross; and Jesus tells him that he is playing the part of Satan, who sought to deflect Jesus from the cross with promises of easy triumph (4:1–11). Jesus tells all his disciples that they must follow the Son of Man on the way of his cross if they are to share in his kingdom (vv 24–28). As a continuation of the apocalyptic revelation to Peter, the transfiguration confirms that Jesus is the glorious Son of God (17:5); but the disciples must also listen when Jesus speaks of his death as Son of Man, following his forerunner, the Baptist (17:9–13). The disciples, though, still suffer from little faith, as is shown by their failure to cure the epileptic boy (17:14–20) and their sorrow at the second passion prediction (17:22–23). The question of whether Jesus should pay the temple tax (17:24–27) provides Matthew with an opportunity for the Lord to give practical instruction to his church through Peter and also to highlight Peter's unique relationship to Jesus (note that Jesus provides just enough money for himself and Peter; this apparent favoritism probably occasions the jealous question of the other disciples in 18:1).

b. Discourse (18:1–35). The narratives that focused on Peter, church, and the disciples naturally flow into the discourse on church life and order. The discourse has two major parts: (1) the need to care for children (vv 1–5) and for "the little ones," the lowly church members who are easily neglected (vv 6–14); (2) the need to apply church discipline to the recalcitrant sinful member of the church (vv 15–20) but always with a readiness to forgive (vv 21–35). Jesus tells the would-be leaders in the Church that they must be willing to assume the powerlessness and vulnerability of a little child; indeed, they must give special attention to such unprotected people. This includes not only literal children but all the spiritual little ones who are easily led astray by the bad example of others. All disciples (note the lack of any restriction to church leaders) must be good shepherds, leading the straying sheep back to the Father. But what of the arrogant sinner who remains in the Church and refuses private correction? Matthew provides a three-step procedure (based on Lev 19:17–18 and Deut 19:15 and seen also at Qumran), culminating in excommunication. Once again, we meet the phrases "church" and "bind and loose" (cf. 16:18–19), but here the church is the local community, and its action refers to expelling or admitting members. Such a serious decision is made in the presence and by the authority of Jesus (v 20). But the parable of the unforgiving servant (vv 21–35) reminds us that the final word on church discipline must be forgiveness within the family of God.

6. Book Five (19:1–25:46). a. Narrative (19:1–23:39). The narrative of the book divides into two parts: the journey to Jerusalem (chaps. 19–20) and the clash with the authorities in Jerusalem (chaps. 21–23). As Jesus leads his embryonic church up to Jerusalem and therefore to the cross, he instructs it on the obligations of various states of life; for Matthew, discipleship involves concrete moral imperatives. Appealing to the Creator's will in the beginning, Jesus, who restores in the end time the Creator's original order, forbids the intermediary expedient of divorce (19:1–9). The prohibition is formulated in a Jewish manner, from the male point of view (contrast Mark 10:11–12); as in Matt 5:31–32, "unchastity" (*porneia,* 19:9) probably refers to unions that the book of Leviticus considered incestuous. Voluntary celibates have a place in the kingdom, as do children (vv 10–15). On the other hand, the difficulty of the rich in entering the kingdom is demonstrated (vv 16–26); yet all things are possible with God. To the disciples, who have left all to follow him, Jesus promises a share in his final kingdom; but they are warned not to think they have a legal claim on God's gift and not to measure jealously their expected reward against that of others (the parable of the workers in the vineyard, 20:1–16). To blunt excessive concerns about reward, Jesus utters the third and longest prediction of the passion, the first one to specify his crucifixion and the role of the gentiles. The mother of James and John (introduced into the Markan story perhaps to spare the honor of two prominent members of the Twelve) ignores the message of the cross as she asks for the chief places at the heavenly banquet for her sons. Jesus promises a share in his cup of suffering, but leaves rewards in the kingdom to the Father. The other disciples prove just as ambitious, as their indignation shows. Jesus uses his own humble service unto death as Son of Man to show them what their ministry in the Church must be. Jesus describes his death as a ransom which buys back the whole group (the "many") from their bondage to sin (20:28). This text, along with 1:21 and 26:28, shows that Matthew does think of Jesus' death as a vicarious sacrifice (contra, Strecker 1971). The blind disciples need healing of their inner sight if they are to follow Jesus on the way to the cross; this is what is symbolized by the healing of the two blind men in 20:29–34. Again, the power of faith to heal is stressed—a faith expressed in the cry to the "Son of David," the messianic title that the leaders of Israel will not give Jesus but that the no-accounts and outsiders will.

The triumphal entry of the Son of David into his capital (21:1–11) brings together the themes of the literal fulfillment of prophecy (Zech 9:9), Jesus' foreknowledge (of the ass at Bethphage), and the disciples' prompt obedience to Jesus' command. Hailing Jesus with Ps 118:25–26, the crowds recognize the Son of David as a prophet; they fail to see him as Son of God and Son of Man. The "cleansing" of the temple (21:12–17) is actually a prophetic act symbolizing the rejection and destruction of the temple, to be replaced by the church. That full membership in the people of God is about to be widened is indicated by the healing of the blind and lame, i.e., marginalized members of the temple community, and the cries of the children, the little ones without rights or power. Protest comes from "the chief priests and the scribes." The mention of them is ominous. They first appeared in the gospel as advisors to King Herod in his plot to kill the infant Jesus (2:4–6); since then they have been mentioned together only in Jesus' prediction of his death. The cursing of the fig tree (21:18–22) is a prophetic parable in action. In the Matthean polemic it signifies that Pharisaic Judaism, covered though it be with the foliage of external piety, lacks that inner obedience to God which is the true fruit of religion. (One must remember that throughout Matthew's gospel references to Judaism reflect a fierce religious polemic, and not a sober, scientific analysis of religions.) This parable in action prepares for the verbal parables of judgment in chaps. 21–22. The initial dispute over Jesus' authority (21:23–27) sets the stage for the three parables of judgment and four dispute stories that follow. In the initial dispute, the Jewish leaders refuse to answer Jesus' counterquestion about the origin of John's baptism. The inability to teach on a matter of such importance reveals their lack of authority, and so Jesus feels no need to answer their question about his authority. The three parables of judgment that follow (21:28–22:14) have one central message: by rejecting the Father's will as revealed in the Son, Israel itself is rejected and another group (the gentiles) will receive the kingdom. (a) In the parable of the two sons (21:28–32), the leaders have said yes to God's will in the Law but have failed to act on their response; tax collectors and sinners (and, in Matthew's view, the gentiles) accepted the Baptist's (and later Jesus') call to repentance and so entered into the kingdom in the place of the leaders. (b) In the parable of the evil tenants of the vineyard (21:33–46), the Markan parable becomes for Matthew an allegory of salvation history. Before and after the Exile, God, the owner of the vineyard Israel, sent his people his servants the prophets; but they met ill treatment and martyrdom. Finally, he sends his Son, who is killed outside the vineyard (Jerusalem). God's response toward Israel will be the destruction of Jerusalem. Toward Jesus his response is the resurrection, which vindicates the rejected Son and makes him the cornerstone of a new people, who receive the kingdom that was taken away from Israel (v 43, a Matthean addition). Matthew thus pointedly adds an ecclesiological point to a christological parable. (c) Matthew again expands a parable of a dinner (cf. Luke 14:15–24) into an allegory of salvation history in the story of the royal wedding feast (22:1–14), with many motifs taken from the parable of the evil tenants. But now the two sets of servants are the OT prophets and the NT apostles; in both periods of history they meet with rejection, even murder. The king (God) destroys the city of the murderers (Jerusalem) and orders a universal mission. The result is the "mixed bag" of the Church, with "both bad and good" (v 10); hence, the extra parable in vv 11–14, in which the king enters (at the final judgment) to separate bad from good (cf. 13:24–30, 36–43, 47–50).

In 22:15–46 Matthew picks up the theme of the initial dispute story and gives four concrete examples of Jesus' superior teaching authority besting the Jewish leaders. Once again, the Pharisees and Sadducees together represent the united front of Judaism, hostile to Jesus. (a) Faced with the hypocritical question about the coin of tribute (22:15–22), Jesus first shows that his questioners, not he, carry and use the coin; then he enunciates a general rule—not a detailed solution to the problem—about rendering to Caesar and to God what is due to each. (b) Faced with the Sadducees' mocking question about the one woman married to seven brothers ("At the resurrection, whose wife will she be?"), Jesus replies that the Sadducees fail to understand both the Scriptures—in refusing to see intimations of resurrection in the Pentateuch, the only Scriptures they recognize as binding—and the power of God—in imagining that the resurrection would be a return to the conditions of earthly life (22:23–33). (c) The dispute over the greatest commandment (22:34–40) is not a dispute at all in Mark (12:28–34), where the scribe and Jesus agree. Reflecting the break with the synagogue, Matthew cannot conceive of a *Jewish* scribe sympathetic to Jesus. Jesus' reply is carefully balanced: love of God comes first, but it cannot subsist without a similar love, that of neighbor. Matthew adds that all the Law and the Prophets, the whole of sacred Scripture, stems from and are summed up in these two commands. Jesus both binds one to the Law as the expression of God's loving will and frees one from the Law when it is distorted by casuistry (cf. 5:17–48). (d) Having defeated his adversaries, Jesus now goes on the offensive by asking them whose son the Messiah will be (22:41–46). Their silence indicates that he alone, the true Son of David and Son of God (chaps. 1–2), is the legitimate interpreter—as well as fulfiller—of messianic prophecy. David's Son (by adoption) is David's Lord because he is also God's Son (by virginal conception).

Having demonstrated the bankruptcy of the "united front," Jesus pronounces judgment on them in chap. 23, which acts as a bridge to the discourse on universal judgment (chaps. 24–25). (a) The disciples are warned to avoid the titles and other trappings of power that have developed among Jewish teachers (vv 1–12). Actually, here and throughout chap. 23 Matthew may be excoriating tendencies he sees already present in the Christian community (Garland 1979). The fiery denunications are not to be taken as an objective description of 1st-century Judaism. Matthew aims at the teachers his two favorite charges: they say but do not do, or what they do is only for show; this is what Matthew means by "hypocrisy." (b) "Hypocrite" is the key word in the seven woes against the scribes and Pharisees, another Matthean tag for the united front of Judaism (vv 13–36). With increasing virulence, Jesus condemns the scribes and Pharisees for their split between saying and doing, between inward and outward reality. They mesh with their evil forebears as murderers of past and present prophets. (c) Jerusalem has been the center of such murders, and Jesus ends chap. 23 with a lament over the unholy city, soon to be left desolate. Jesus acts out that divine abandonment by leaving the temple for the last time in 24:1.

b. Discourse (24:1–25:46). The verbal battles with and condemnation of Judaism in the narrative of Book Five now flow into a discourse depicting worldwide upheavals and the universal judgment on the last day. The first half of the discourse (24:1–36) is basically from Mark and is more doctrinal, in that it teaches the order of events up to the coming of the Son of Man. After an initial prediction of the temple's destruction (vv 1–2), Jesus proceeds to the Mount of Olives, where the disciples' opening question carefully distinguishes between the destruction of the temple on the one hand and the coming of Jesus and the end of the age on the other (v 3). Writing after A.D. 70, Matthew is intent on not confusing the destruction of Jerusalem (which receives little attention in this discourse) with the still outstanding Parousia (the return of Jesus; only Matthew, among the evangelists, uses this word well-known in the epistles). A whole series of terrifying events must occur before the end; they are not the end, but only the "birth pangs." The Church will suffer persecution from without and, worse still, apostasy, hate, false prophets, wickedness, and lovelessness from within (vv 10–12). Matthew obviously writes from and for a church that has known deep divisions. Yet even this is not the end; the gospel must first be proclaimed throughout the whole world (v 14). Instead of speaking directly of the temple's destruction, as in v 1, Jesus now speaks of a desolating sacrilege in the holy place; the vague reference allows an application to future horrors that Christian apocalypticism expected before the Parousia. Included in such blasphemies are the false messiahs and prophets who will claim to fulfill the hope of the Parousia. But the real Parousia will be a public and cosmic event (vv 23–28). It will reveal the crucified Son of Man ("the pierced one" of Zech 12:10–14) to be the Son of Man of Daniel 7:13–14, coming to judge and save the world. The Markan half of the discourse ends with the parable of the fig tree, emphasizing that the end is certain and near, yet sudden and incalculable. The tone of imminence comes from the Markan material; Matthew now balances that with his emphasis on delay.

The second, a paraenetic half of the discourse (24:37–25:46) is more "Matthean" in that it comes to grips with the delay of the Parousia and the problem of flagging vigilance. The second half begins with three short parables from Q: the generation of Noah, the two pairs of workers, and the thief in the night (24:37–44). The parables stress the need to be vigilant in the face of the uncertain date of the Parousia. Then come the three great parables of vigilance during delay: the prudent or profligate servant (24:45–51), the prudent and thoughtless virgins (25:1–13), and the talents (25:14–30). Each parable sounds the theme of delay (24:48; 25:5, 19), thus balancing the note of imminence in the Markan part of the discourse (e.g., 24:34). The servant parable warns Christian leaders in particular not to become lax in the face of the Parousia's delay. The parable of the virgins warns that those who have not reckoned with the delay face the final separation from the elect that constitutes judgment for Matthew. The parable of the talents defines being vigilant during delay not as being inactive but as being faithful in doing God's will with all one's being. The conclusion (25:31–46) is not another parable, but the truth behind all the parables. The criterion for the final judgment and separation will be the deeds of mercy done to the poor and outcast and therefore to the Son of Man, who declares his solidarity with suffering humankind. The Son of Man then acts out this teaching in the climax of the gospel, the death-resurrection.

7. Climax: Death-Resurrection (Chaps. 26–28). Matthew binds together death and resurrection as one pivotal, earthshaking, apocalyptic event that puts an end to the old era of sin and death and brings in the new period of the Church. Even here the story reflects Matthew's weaving together of the themes of Christ, church, and morality. The dignity and foreknowledge of Jesus is heightened, especially with the use of the titles Son of Man (chap. 26) and Son of God (chap. 27). As the kingdom is transferred to the new people of God, the Church, the responsibility of Israel for the Messiah's death is stressed. The failure or courage of individual actors (e.g., Peter, Judas, the faithful women at the cross, Joseph of Arimathea) serves Matthew's moral exhortation. The narratives of death-resurrection are especially rich in cross-references, which make a neat structural outline difficult. The standard chapter divisions, which coincide with major time divisions, are used simply as a matter of convenience.

a. From Wednesday to Thursday Night (26:1–75). Matthew alone adds a fourth prediction of the passion of the Son of Man, thus emphasizing Jesus' knowledge and control of events. Jesus' mention of his death in the context of Passover intimates that his death will be the true Passover sacrifice (vv 1–2). His prophetic words actually set the events in motion; only after he speaks do his enemies gather to plot his death. The woman who anoints Jesus at Bethany provides both an inclusion with the women at the cross and tomb and a contrast with the Jewish leaders and with Judas. Her anointing is indeed the only one Jesus would receive, since in Matthew the women do not come to the tomb on Sunday morning with the intention of anointing the body. Just after Jesus shows contempt for money, Judas plans to betray him for money (the greed motif is not made explicit in Mark). The 30 pieces of silver (the payment of the rejected shepherd in Zech 11:12) echo the price of a slave's life in Exod 21:32—a paltry sum. The story of the preparation of the Last Supper (vv 17–19) demonstrates Jesus' sovereign command and the strict obedience of the true disciples (Mark emphasizes Jesus' miraculous knowledge). When Jesus predicts his betrayal at the supper, the innocent disciples address him as "Lord," the usual title used by believers, while Judas betrays himself by using "Rabbi," which, along with "Teacher," is the title used by unbelievers when they speak to Jesus. Fittingly, then, Jesus replies to Judas: "You have said it"—an ambiguous reposte that he will also use with Caiaphas and Pilate. In narrating the institution of the Eucharist, Matthew follows Mark but makes the two groups of words and actions more nearly parallel each other. He adds that the blood of Jesus—not John's baptism (cf. Mark 1:4)—is the means to the forgiveness of sins (cf. Matt 1:21; 20:28). Jesus promises that, despite the apparent failure of his mission, he will celebrate the messianic banquet with the disciples in the kingdom. From this point on, Matthew keeps stressing Jesus' desire to be with his disciples and their failure to be with him, despite Peter's boast that he will die with Jesus. In Gethsemane (vv 36–56), Jesus, the model of prayer, practices what he preached in the Sermon on the Mount by echoing phrases from the Our Father ("my Father . . . your will be done . . . enter into the test"). Ever in control, Jesus orders Judas to carry out what he has come to do, even as he commands his disciples not to use violence. By ordering that the sword be put away, Jesus once again teaches morality (echoing the Sermon on the Mount on nonresistance), proclaims his filial trust in the Father, and underlines his purpose of seeing prophecy fulfilled in the apocalyptic event of death-resurrection (with the exception of the formula quotation in 27:9–10, 26:54 and 56 take the place of individual formula quotations during the Passion Narrative). During the trial before the Sanhedrin (vv 57–75), and indeed throughout the passion, Matthew stresses the innocence of Jesus; he is the suffering just man of the Psalms. The power of Jesus is intimated in that the last two witnesses are not designated as "false," for they unwittingly speak the truth in claiming that Jesus can destroy the temple. Also unwitting and ironic is the way the high priest echoes Peter's confession at Caesarea Philippi when he asks Jesus "by the living God" whether he is the Messiah, the Son of God (26:63; cf. 16:16). While in Mark Jesus simply says, "I am," in Matthew the answer is the more indirect "you have said it." Immediately Jesus adds the corrective title Son of Man: "from now on" (i.e., from the turning point of death-resurrection) they will see Jesus as Son of Man exalted at God's right hand (Ps 110:1) and coming on the clouds of heaven (Dan 7:13–14)—a prophecy fulfilled proleptically in the final scene of the gospel (28:16–20). Peter's denial contrasts negatively with the Jesus who boldly proclaims the truth and positively with the Judas who despairs after his sin and commits suicide. Peter's bitter weeping betokens both the depth of his sin and the effectiveness of his repentance (he is obviously among the eleven rehabilitated disciples in 28:16).

b. From Friday Morning to Saturday (27:1–66). At the end of the night session, which concludes in early morning, the Sanhedrin sends Jesus to Pilate. In an interlude (the first separate story inserted into Mark's framework), Matthew depicts the fate of the betrayer, a different version of which is contained in Acts 1:15–20. The story sounds three Matthean motifs: Jesus' prophetic knowledge is confirmed (cf. 26:21–25); the Jewish leaders are responsible for the innocent blood of Jesus (cf. 27:25); even the tragedy of Judas' suicide was foreseen by God and fits into his saving plan (the formula quotation in vv 9–10; cf. 2:17). In the trial before Pilate (vv 11–26), the title Messiah is translated into the politically provocative title King of the Jews. The crowd must make the basic choice between Jesus, the true Son of the Father, and the prisoner Barabbas (= "Son of the Father"; some manuscripts sharpen the comparison/contrast by inserting "Jesus" before "Barabbas"). Like the gentile Magi (cf. 2:12), Pilate's wife also receives a monitory dream, urging noninvolvement in the plot of the Jewish leaders to kill Jesus. But the leaders persuade the crowds and thus coalesce with them into "all the people," who cry out for the death of Jesus and take the responsibility for his blood on themselves and their children (27:25, a Matthean insertion meant to explain the transfer of the kingdom from Israel to the Church; cf. 21:43, 23:35). For Matthew, the choice of Barabbas may also symbolize Israel's choice of armed political resistance to Rome, which led to the Jewish War and the destruction of Jerusalem. The mocking by the gentile soldiers (vv 27–31) likewise foreshadows the future faith of the gentile world, first expressed by these very soldiers after the death of Jesus (v 54).

At the crucifixion (27:32–44) the two titles stressed are King and Son of God (cf. chap. 2). The placard reading "King of the Jews" proclaims the ironic truth that Jesus is enthroned as King by his crucifixion. Twice into the mockery narrated by Mark, Matthew inserts the title Son of God (vv 40, 43). "If you are the Son of God . . ." echoes the challenge of Satan at the temptation (chap. 4). Like Satan and like Peter (16:22–23), the leaders tempt Jesus to understand the status of Son of God as a dispensation from suffering, as an easy, miraculous road to triumph. In this "last temptation of Christ," Jesus defines Son of God in terms of trustful obedience to the Father's will, even to the point of shameful death. The apocalyptic signs surrounding Jesus' death begin with the darkness, a symbol of God's wrath over a sinful world. For all his high christology, Matthew keeps the element of tension between divine and human by retaining from Mark the cry of abandonment (27:46). The cry fits in with the presentation of Jesus as the suffering just man of the Psalms (here, Ps 22:2). The drink of vinegar (v 48), like the drink mixed with gall (v 34), also echoes the Psalms of Lament (Ps 69:22—Eng 21). The death of Jesus unleashes a panoply of apocalyptic events (vv 51–54). The rending of the temple veil foretells the destruction of the temple and the cessation of its sacrificial cult in light of the sacrifice of Jesus (cf. 26:28). The earthquake, the shaking of the foundations of the old world as God brings in his kingdom, causes a chain reaction: the rocks split, the tombs of the holy Israelites of old are opened, and the dead come forth. The resurrection of the dead, prophesied by Ezek 37:12, is realized proleptically at the death of Jesus. Matthew thus proclaims that the death of Jesus is life-giving; it raises the dead to life. The theme of the earthquake, associated with resurrection from tombs and other apocalyptic imagery, serves to tie the death of Jesus together with his resurrection (v 53; cf. 28:1–10), creating one great apocalyptic event that ushers in the new period of the Church. This ecclesiological dimension is supplied by Matthew's redaction of the centurion's profession of faith in Mark. While the Markan centurion alone comes to faith because he sees how Jesus dies (15:39), in Matthew the centurion and the soldiers with him who had participated in the crucifixion (symbolizing the whole mass of sinful gentiles) see the apocalyptic events ushering in the kingdom and so repeat the confession of true disciples: "Truly this [omitting Mark's 'man'] was God's Son" (cf. 14:33). Both Jews and gentiles (the holy ones raised from their graves and the soldiers) are saved by the death of Jesus and brought into his community.

All that follows looks forward to the resurrection narratives. The connections create a "leap frog" effect: the women at the cross and tomb connect with the women at the tomb, the appearance to the women, and the appearance to the eleven; in between, the setting of the guard at the tomb connects with the guard struck down at the empty tomb and the guard's report to the Jewish leaders. Reflecting the split between church and synagogue, Matthew will not allow Joseph of Arimathea to have anything to do with the Sanhedrin, as in Mark 15:43; instead, he is a disciple of Jesus (27:57). The setting of the guard and the sealing of the tomb (vv 62–66), along with the false report of the guard (28:11–15), are unique to Matthew and reflect his apologetic against Jewish explanations of the resurrection; neither camp apparently claimed that the body was still in the tomb on the third day. The sealing of the tomb may echo Dan 6:17.

c. From Sunday to the End of the Age (28:1–20). One of the most significant aspects of the final chapter is the almost complete absence of christological titles. The one great title is "Jesus"; thus does Matthew emphasize the identity of the earthly Jesus with the Risen One (Bornkamm 1968). The two women who came to the tomb in v 1 correspond to the witnesses of the burial (27:61). They come simply "to see," since the seal on the tomb would prevent any anointing (the purpose of the visit in Mark). Since there was a tacit prohibition of depicting the resurrection itself, Matthew showers his apocalyptic themes on the empty tomb scene. Mark's young man becomes the dazzlingly bright angel of the Lord (not seen since the Infancy Narrative), descending from heaven amid an earthquake (cf. 27:51) and unsealing the tomb to announce God's triumph over death in the resurrection of Jesus. Like the guards at the cross, the guards at the tomb fear; but they become like dead men as the dead Jesus rises (cf. the contrast at the death of Jesus, 27:51–56). The angel's Easter proclamation is presented as the fulfillment of Jesus' prophecy; the women, unlike their Markan counterparts, run with both fear and joy to fulfill their commission. On the way Jesus appears to these women (28:9–10, unique to Matthew among the Synoptics). While at first glance superfluous, this appearance reaffirms the reality of the risen body (it can be touched); the restoration of the eleven to fellowship with Jesus, making possible the foundation of the Church (he calls them "brothers"; cf. 12:46–50); and—implicitly—the function of a resurrection appearance not as a return to an old relationship, but as the origin of a new mission (the women are not to cling to Jesus but are to deliver his message to the disciples). The good news of the resurrection is countered by the big lie of grave robbery (vv 11–15). As in the case of Judas, money is the problem solver. The soldiers do "as they were taught," the false teaching of the leaders competing with the true teaching of the disciples down to Matthew's day. This polemical stance may move Matthew to speak of "the Jews" (v 15; previously in the gospel only gentiles used that term); for him, Israel the chosen people is no more, its place being taken by the Church.

In the great commission that concludes the gospel (28:16–20), Matthew presents the risen Jesus as coming to his church; he is the Son of Man coming to believers in a proleptic Parousia. Contrary to Luke, Jesus does not go away from his church via ascension; hence, since Jesus stays with his church always, there is no need for a special sending of the Spirit to take his place. The regrouped eleven obey Jesus' command to go to Galilee, the very mention of which conjures up thoughts of the beginning of Jesus' ministry in Galilee of the gentiles (cf. 4:15). Throughout the gospel, the mountain has been a privileged symbol of Jesus the Son's eschatological authority and activity as he gathers his community and reveals the Father's will (4:8; 5:1; 8:1; 15:29; 17:1, 9; 24:3; 28:16). That the disciples worship Jesus yet doubt is a perfect paradigm of the littleness of faith that clings to all disciples up until the end of the age. The solemn declaration of Jesus falls into three parts. (a) Jesus proclaims that through the death-resurrection he has been exalted to the status of ruler of the cosmos, having all authority over heaven and earth (something never predicated of the earthly Jesus). The whole context reflects Dan 7:14, which describes the triumphant arrival of "one like a Son of Man" after the powers of evil have been defeated: "And power was given to him, and all nations . . . shall serve him" (cf. Dan 4:14). Jesus' prophecy in 26:64 is thus fulfilled. (b) Therefore, i.e., on the basis of his exaltation to universal rule, Jesus can now command a universal mission. This mission involves three things. First, the eleven are to make disciples of all the nations, an undertaking which means persuading people to do the will of the Father according to the teaching of Jesus and thus become Jesus' brothers and sisters in the family of God (cf. 12:46–50); in other words, it means following Jesus. Second, all the nations enter this family of God by being baptized. But this no longer entails John's baptism, but rather baptism into the divine reality revealed in the theophany after the baptism of Jesus: Father, Son, and Spirit (Schaberg 1982). To be baptized is to be plunged into the family life of God. Third, the object of teaching (which the eleven are empowered to do only now) is all and whatsoever Jesus taught during his earthly life; hence, the importance of the five great discourses. By this commission, Matthew concludes his gospel with a great reversal. The same person (Jesus) who formerly ordered the twelve disciples to undertake a mission *only* to Israel (10:5–6; cf. 15:24) now tells the same group to pursue a mission to all nations, with baptism instead of circumcision as the initiation rite and the commands of Jesus instead of the Mosaic law as the norm of morality. The death-resurrection has proved the watershed of salvation history. (c) The last word of the risen Jesus is a promise to remain with his church for all days, i.e., throughout the whole indefinite period of world history that extends from "proleptic" to "fully realized" Parousia, the end of the age, the hope of which is certainly not surrendered. But the emphasis on the in-between time, when Jesus Emmanuel (1:23; 18:20) abides with his church, empowering it to undertake the staggering task of a universal mission. Like Yahweh commissioning the great patriarchs and prophets of the OT, Jesus assures his wavering disciples that he will sustain them (Lange 1973). Michel was thus correct when he saw 28:16–20 as the key to the whole gospel (1950); it is a microcosm of Matthew's major theological concerns.

H. Major Theological Concerns

The structure and content of the gospel confirm the view that Matthew consciously introduces ecclesiological and moral concerns into traditional material that was mainly christological. Hence, the particular configuration "Christ-church-morality" captures what is specific to Matthew's thought. For purposes of clarity, however, these three themes can be further differentiated into six topics.

1. Christology. The discourses, especially the Sermon on the Mount, remind us that Matthew is capable of putting forth an evaluation of Jesus not dependent primarily on titles. The discourses obviously present Jesus as teaching authoritatively (7:29), and Jesus calls himself a teacher (23:8; 26:18). Yet, strange to say, to address Jesus as "Teacher" or "Rabbi" (in the vocative) is for Matthew the sign of an unbeliever, or at least of someone not yet a true disciple. Such an address indicates that the speaker sees Jesus merely as a human teacher and nothing more. True disciples, by contrast, address Jesus as "Lord" *(kyrie)*, expressing thereby their faith in his divine authority and his claim on them (cf. 26:22, 25). "Lord," however, occurs in Matthew mostly in the vocative; Matthew does not use it as a key title to explicate Jesus' transcendent status. Often behind the *kyrios* title stands the figure of Jesus as Son of Man.

There are a number of titles that Matthew uses positively and yet does not employ to develop the central mystery of Jesus. Among these lesser titles, "prophet" remains inadequate, since it can apply to others (e.g., the Baptist). Jesus, by contrast, is unique in that he fulfills the Law and the prophets, which all point to him (5:17; 11:13). Still, Jesus the Son is portrayed in a prophetic light as the last in the line of prophets rejected by Israel (23:34–39; Sand 1974). Likewise, the Infancy Narrative and temptation story present Jesus with Mosaic traits; but at best one can speak of Jesus not as the new Moses but as the one greater than Moses. In the Sermon on the Mount, e.g., Jesus takes the position of God, not Moses (cf. 5:27–28). Jesus is also called or alluded to as the (Isaian) servant (e.g., 3:17; 12:18), but the image is usually connected with Jesus as Son. Likewise, Emmanuel (1:23) lies within the orbit of Jesus as Son. Messiah *(christos)* and King stress that Jesus is the fulfillment of the ancient prophecies and promises made to Israel in general and David in particular. They also emphasize the royal authority of Jesus; but to receive its full weight, Messiah must be joined to Son of God (16:16; 26:63; cf. Nolan 1979). Son of David likewise emphasizes Jesus as the royal fulfiller of Israel's messianic hopes (1:1–17); it is precisely Joseph the Son of David who, by acknowledging the virginally conceived Jesus as his son, places him in the line of David (1:18–25). During the public ministry, Son of David is the address used especially by the marginalized and helpless who appeal to Jesus for healing (the Canaanite woman in 15:22; the blind men in 20:30). The Canaanite woman combines this title with Lord, indicating her true faith, while the Jerusalem crowds hail Jesus only as Son of David (21:9), without adding to it the title that shows true discipleship, "Lord." Hence the title Son of David reflects the paradox of Jesus the Jewish Messiah, who is accepted by the marginalized and even by pagans, while most Israelites reject him (Gerhardsson 1979).

For Matthew, the two key titles are Son of God and Son of Man, which combine a sense of Jesus' transcendent status with his central role in salvation history. Kingsbury (1975, 1986) emphasizes Son of God over Son of Man; Lange (1973) does just the opposite. Actually, neither title completely subsumes the other; yet the two share a certain amount of common ground. Instead of thinking of Matthew's christology as a circle with one central title, one should imagine an ellipse, with Son of God and Son of Man as the two foci. Hence it is best to speak of the Son christology of Matthew, with both titles included.

Matthew uses Son of God in the early chapters of his gospel to stress Jesus' direct origin from God and his filial relationship to God. Throughout the gospel, Matthew develops the title in terms of the obedient servant who recapitulates the history of Israel, the son of God in the OT, and who proves he is the true Son and Israel by withstanding temptation and doing the will of the Father (e.g., 2:15; 3:17; 4:1–11). By a grand inclusion, the same definition of sonship by obedient suffering returns at the mockery of the crucified Jesus (27:40, 43). Knowledge of Jesus as Son of God must come through divine revelation, but there is no Markan-style secret about this sonship in Matthew. At the baptism, God points out Jesus as his Son to others (note the "this is" in 3:17). After Jesus is revealed in divine majesty bestriding the waters of chaos, a whole group of disciples confesses him as Son of God (14:33). By the Father's revelation, Peter is able to say that Jesus is Messiah and Son of God halfway through the gospel (16:16)—a profession of faith confirmed by God at the transfiguration (17:5). At the trial before the Sanhedrin, Caiaphas unwittingly repeats Peter's profession of faith in his unbelieving question (26:63).

Still, both at Caesarea Philippi and at the trial, the limitations of Messiah and Son of God are seen in the fact that each time Jesus must supplement or correct these titles (note the "but I say to you" in 26:64) with the one title he constantly uses of himself, always in the third person: Son of Man. This unique and mysterious usage marks off Son of Man from all the other titles, whose meanings are much clearer from their OT usage. Son of Man is a title *sui generis.* It is more like one of Jesus' parables or riddles. Jesus can use it freely in public, people can understand that it refers to Jesus, yet no one seems to grasp the deep theological import Jesus gives it. From Mark and Q Matthew inherits three major meanings of Son of Man: (a) the lowly yet powerful servant of God during the earthly ministry (e.g., 8:20; 9:6); (b) the suffering, dying, and rising servant who gives his life as a ransom for the many (e.g., 17:22–23; 20:17–28; 26:2); and (c) the judge and/or deliverer on the last day (e.g., 10:23; 16:27–28; 24:30, 36 ["the Son" in v 36 is probably the Son of Man]; 25:31; 26:64). These various meanings are not hermetically sealed off from one another (cf., e.g., 16:13–28), but rather form a spectrum of meanings encompassing the whole of Jesus' earthly career, death and resurrection, and Parousia. The one stage of Jesus' career that was not explicitly covered by the Markan Son of Man was the present rule over the world by the risen Jesus. This gap is filled in by Matthew in his allegorical explanation of the parable of the wheat and the weeds (13:37). The use of "the Son" in the triadic formula of baptism (28:19) may also reflect Son of Man christology (Schaberg 1982). That not every reference to God as Father immediately implies the Son of God title is shown by 16:27, where the Son of Man at the last judgment is said to come "in the glory of his Father." This is hardly proof that Son of God absorbs Son of Man, since in Matthew the final judgment is a function proper to Jesus precisely as the Son of Man, not the Son of God. Nor can Son of Man be reduced to a circumlocution for "this man." That may or may not have been the meaning of the Aramaic phrase *bar ʾ(ĕ)našaʾ* in the mouth of the historical Jesus, but that usage must not be confused with the title in Matthew's redaction. Matthew writes in Greek, where *ho huios tou anthrōpou* (literally, "the Son of Man") has a peculiarly solemn and titular, yet puzzling ring. To translate it simply as "this man" would pass over the Matthean emphasis on the fulfillment of the prophecy of Dan 4:13–14, especially in 24:30.

2. Kingdom of Heaven. The theme of the kingdom of heaven mediates between Christ and church. In itself, the kingdom of heaven (or of God) indicates a transcendent and dynamic reality; it is an abstract way of saying that God is coming in power to exercise his rightful rule over his creation. Thus, the kingdom (or better, rule) of God is not first of all a place or space; yet, if God exercises his rule over concrete individuals and groups, spatial images naturally arise, as is the case in various sayings and parables of Jesus. Matthew alone among NT writers uses "kingdom of heaven," "heaven" being a respectful Semitic circumlocution for God. Matthew uses "kingdom of heaven" 32 times and "kingdom of God" 4 times (12:28; 19:24; 21:31, 43). The fact that the two forms can be used interchangeably even in a single pericope (19:23–24) shows there is no real difference in meaning. While its roots meaning in the preaching of the historical Jesus seems to have had a future-yet-imminent thrust, "kingdom of heaven" in Matthew has become a highly complex concept with a spectrum of meanings plotted out over the time line of salvation history. "Kingdom" becomes a process concept in Matthew. The kingdom existed already in the OT, for in some sense Israel possessed it (21:33–46, especially v 43). But the birth of Jesus, the King of the Jews (2:2), naturally entails a new, heightened presence of the kingdom. Yet both the Baptist and Jesus begin their ministries by proclaiming that the kingdom is drawing near (3:2; 4:17). The kingdom has already come in the exorcisms of Jesus (12:28); nevertheless, Jesus teaches his disciples to pray for its final coming (6:10) and to seek it (6:33). The apocalyptic events of death-resurrection mean a new stage in the coming of the kingdom, since for the first time Jesus is exalted to total power over the cosmos (28:16–20). He rules now as Son of Man in his kingdom (13:37–38, 41; cf. Kretzer 1971); but his visible coming as judge on the last day will mean the final and definitive coming of his kingdom (16:27–28), which will be the kingdom of his Father (13:43). The kingdom of heaven thus embraces the whole sweep of salvation history, as God's rule progressively breaks into and triumphs over the sinful human world. From its all-inclusive sweep, it is clear that the kingdom of heaven is not coterminous with the Church of Jesus, which begins to develop during the public ministry and is fully founded by the death-resurrection. The Church is that locus and instrument of the kingdom where Jesus is consciously confessed, worshipped, and obeyed. Making disciples of all the nations is the path the Church takes as it journeys through history toward the consummation of the kingdom. But with Matthew's tendency toward realized eschatology and high ecclesiology, kingdom and church are more closely associated in his gospel than anywhere else in the NT (cf. 16:18–19, and the ambiguity in the use of "kingdom" in 18:1, 4).

3. Salvation History. Implied in Matthew's process view of kingdom is a concept of salvation history. Matthew orders the many stages of the coming of the kingdom into three major periods: Law and prophets, earthly Jesus, and the Church. There is first of all the period of the OT, the Law and the prophets, which pointed forward to and prophesied the time of Jesus (11:13). The fact that all the formula quotations refer to and are fulfilled in the life and death of Jesus indicates that his earthly life is the second period, the midpoint of salvation history. It thus differs from the time of the Church, to which no formula quotation is applied. The distinction between the time of Jesus and the time of the Church, the third period, is reinforced by the different rules for mission. During his public ministry, Jesus was sent only to the land and people of Israel (15:24) and enjoined his twelve disciples to observe the same restriction (10:5–6). After the death-resurrection, the "turning of the ages," the exalted Jesus commands the same group to undertake a mission to all nations (28:16–20) until the Parousia (v 20). This outline of salvation history aids Matthew in resolving the tension between his more "conservative" Jewish-Christian and his more "liberal" gentile-Christian traditions. The more conservative material can be affirmed as true of the earthly ministry of Jesus, while the more open material can be referred to the time of the Church. Kingsbury, however, claims that Matthew divides history into two epochs according to the theme of prophecy and fulfillment: the time of Israel and the time of Jesus, the latter including the post-Easter period (1975: 31–37).

4. Church. Matthew alone among the evangelists uses the word "church" in his gospel. Although it occurs only three times (16:18; 18:17 [twice]), the whole of the public ministry aims at gathering disciples into the embryonic church that is then led up to Jerusalem for the death-resurrection, which makes possible the full founding of the Church in the last pericope of the gospel. At the death-resurrection, Israel disowns its Messiah (27:25) and the kingdom is transferred from Israel to the Church (21:43). Because of this note of rupture, Matthew never calls the Church the new or true Israel (contra, Trilling 1964); it is rather "another people," the Church of Jesus. All the discourses, but preeminently chap. 18, contain directions for the disciples living in the Church and spreading the Church up until the Parousia. Up until then the Church remains a mixed bag of "bad and good" (notice the word order in 22:10), and hence in need of authoritative direction (16:18–19) and disciplinary action (18:15–18; Bornkamm 1970). But the Church cannot presume to anticipate the final judgment (13:24–30), to which the Church and church leaders as well as nonbelievers will be subject (24:45–25:30).

Matthew gives no detailed description of church order and leaders. Christian prophets, just men (10:40–41), wise men, and scribes (13:52; 23:34) are all mentioned, with no indication of how they are ordered or whether they overlap. Peter is presented as the "chief rabbi" of "my church," i.e., the whole church of Jesus (16:18–19). He is depicted as the firm rock of stability, ensuring the Church against the powers of death and empowered to interpret the words of Jesus. The concentration on Peter, especially in Book Four, may reflect both the historical Peter's moderating role at Antioch between the Paul and James factions and Matthew's preference for such a middle path between extremists of left (amoral charismatics) and right (scrupulous legalists) in his own day. There is no indication that any single prominent figure presided over the Antiochus church in Matthew's day, though possibly the emphasis on Peter reflects a gradual movement from the loose college of prophets and teachers (Acts 13:1) in the first Christian generation to the one-bishop polity of Ignatius in the third Christian generation. The local assembly acts to excommunicate without any mention of church leaders (18:15–18), though this could be due to Matthew's desire to call all members to participation in church life in the face of a rising "clericalism" among leaders (cf. 23:1–12).

5. Discipleship. The theme of discipleship mediates between the themes of church and morality. As 4:18–22 graphically portrays, a disciple is one who heeds Jesus' call to follow him with total commitment. This following is not just a matter of physical movement. The ambivalent crowds, attracted to Jesus by his teaching and miracles, also follow him, but they lack the faith and understanding that mark true disciples. Unlike the Markan disciples, the Matthean disciples do believe (14:33) and understand (13:51); yet they are not idealized unrealistically. Faced with a crisis, the disciples panic and act as though they had no faith. This is the "little faith" (8:26; 14:31; 17:20) that characterizes disciples even during the time of the Church (28:17). Nevertheless, true disciples do accept the teaching of Jesus in the five great discourses; they are always the main or sole audience. The successes and failures of the disciples make them types of both Christians in general and of church leaders in particular; this holds true of Peter as well. That for Matthew discipleship need not always entail an itinerant life and literal abandonment of all possessions is intimated by such figures as Jairus (9:18–26), the host of the Last Supper (26:17–19), and Joseph of Arimathea (27:57–60). The decisive element of discipleship is rather hearing the word of Jesus and obeying it exactly (7:21–27; 21:6; 26:19). This is equivalent to doing the will of the Father (12:46–50); such obedient action makes disciples brothers and sisters of Jesus in the family of God—a good definition of the Matthean church. Hence the theme of discipleship naturally flows from the theme of church into the theme of morality.

6. Morality. Matthew has no single word corresponding to our "morality" or "ethics." The closest he comes to such a technical category is *dikaiosynē,* "justice" or "righteousness." While "justice" seems to mean God's saving activity or his gift of salvation in three cases (5:6; 6:33; probably 3:15), the other four occurrences have the ethical sense of good behavior, right conduct (5:10; 5:20; 6:1; probably 21:32). Significantly, this ethical sense of "justice" is never applied to Jesus' actions, since 3:15 probably refers to the fulfillment of God's saving plan, mapped out beforehand in prophecy. Justice in the moral sense is therefore the abstract form of Matthew's favorite phrase, "to do the will of the Father (or God)"—according, of course, to the teaching of Jesus. Jesus' teaching on the will of God is contained first of all in the five discourses, and preeminently in the Sermon on the Mount, the "Magna Carta of discipleship." The radical, demanding morality of the Sermon extends from general attitudes and actions (no anger, love of enemies) down to specific prohibitions affecting church life (no divorce, no oaths). This emphasis on stringent morality may come partly from Matthew's conservative Jewish-Christian tradition, which he finds useful in catechizing the increasing number of gentiles entering his church. This emphasis on moral endeavor does not, however, lead Matthew into Pelagianism. Forgiveness and salvation remain a free gift from God, received in faith (18:21–35; 20:1–16; 9:27–31; and 20:29–34) and made possible by the atoning death of Jesus (1:21; 20:28; 27:51–54). Radical demand flows from radical grace. It would be a mistake, though, to impose a Pauline approach to morality and the Law on Matthew; the key Pauline themes of the Law's multiplying transgressions and the Christian's freedom from the Law are foreign to the evangelist. Matthew's approach to the Law is more positive. Jesus basically affirms the Law (5:17–20), radicalizing and internalizing it (5:21–48), focusing upon its essential elements: love of God and neighbor (22:34–40; 19:18–19), the golden rule (7:12), mercy instead of ritual sacrifice (9:12; 12:7), and justice, mercy, and faithfulness (23:23). Disciples must first look within to the source of moral good and evil, i.e., the heart, and purify that; then whatever actions flow from the heart will be pure (15:1–20; cf. 5:21–30). Yet at times Jesus so radicalizes the Law that individual commandments are abrogated (e.g., his prohibition of divorce, oaths, and retaliation [5:31–39]; his rescinding of food laws [15:10–19]. From such instances, and from the general antithetical formula in 5:21–48, it becomes clear that it is the word of Jesus, not the words of the Law, that is the ultimate norm of morality for the disciple. Hence the gospel ends with the risen Jesus commanding the eleven to teach all nations to observe "all whatsoever I commanded you"—be it according to, contrary to, or simply apart from the Mosaic law. Finally, it should be noted that morality is taught not only in the discourses; the narrative likewise inculcates "doing the will of the Father" by example and counterexample. Jesus, of course, is the prime example of the obedient Son and servant of the Father (e.g., 4:1–12). In addition, from the "just" Joseph of the Infancy Narrative to the faithful women at the cross and empty tomb, various men and women exemplify in dramatic narrative the cost and reward of discipleship. Matthew has no difficulty in having Jesus speak about reward *(misthos);* it is an acceptable paraenetic motif. It is balanced, however, with the affirmation of God's sovereign freedom in rewarding (20:1–16) and with an emphasis on the disciples' attitude of trust in and abandonment to the care of their loving Father (6:25–34).

Bibliography

Abel, E. 1971. Who Wrote Matthew? *NTS* 17: 138–52.

Aune, D. 1987. *The New Testament in Its Literary Environment.* Philadelphia.

Bacon, B. 1928. Jesus and the Law. *JBL* 47: 203–31.

———. 1930. *Studies in Matthew.* New York.

Barth, G. 1963. Matthew's Understanding of the Law. Pp. 58–164 in *Tradition and Interpretation in Matthew.* Philadelphia.

Beardslee, W. 1970. *Literary Criticism of the New Testament.* Philadelphia.

Betz, H. D. 1985. *Essays on the Sermon on the Mount.* Philadelphia.

Bornkamm, G. 1963a. End-Expectation and Church in Matthew. Pp. 15–51 in *Tradition and Interpretation in Matthew.* Philadelphia.

———. 1963b. The Stilling of the Storm in Matthew. Pp. 52–57 in *Tradition and Interpretation in Matthew.* Philadelphia.

———. 1968. Der Auferstandene und der Irdische. Pp. 289–310 in *Überlieferung und Auslegung im Matthäusevangelium.* 5th ed. WMANT 1. Neukirchen-Vluyn.

———. 1970. The Authority to "Bind" and "Loose" in the Church in Matthew's Gospel. Vol. 1, pp. 37–50 in *Jesus and Man's Hope,* ed. D. Hadidian et al. Pittsburgh.

———. 1978. Der Aufbau der Bergpredigt. *NTS* 24: 419–32.

Broer, I. 1986. *Die Seligpreisungen der Bergpredigt.* BBB 61. Bonn.

Brown, J. 1961. The Form of "Q" Known to Matthew. *NTS* 8: 27–42.

Brown, R. E., and Meier, J. P. 1983. *Antioch and Rome.* New York.

Butler, B. C. 1951. *The Originality of St. Matthew.* Cambridge.

Clark, K. 1947. The Gentile Bias of Matthew. *JBL* 66: 165–72.

Davies, W. D. 1964. *The Setting of the Sermon on the Mount.* Cambridge. Repr. Atlanta, 1989.

Dobschütz, E. von. 1928. Matthäus als Rabbi und Katechet. *ZNW* 27: 338–48.

Ellis, P. 1974. *Matthew: His Mind and His Message.* Collegeville, MN.

Farmer, W. 1964. *The Synoptic Problem.* New York.

Fenton, J. 1959. Inclusio and Chiasmus in Mt. Pp. 174–79 in *Studia Evangelica I,* ed. F. Cross. Berlin.

Frankemölle, H. 1974. *Jahwebund und Kirche Christi.* NTAbh 10. Münster.

Garland, D. 1979. *The Intention of Matthew 23.* NovTSup 52. Leiden.

Gerhardsson, B. 1979. *The Mighty Acts of Jesus according to Matthew.* Scripta Minora 5. Lund.

Goulder, M. 1974. *Midrash and Lection in Matthew.* London.
Green, H. 1968. The Structure of St Matthew's Gospel. Pp. 47–59 in *Studia Evangelica IV,* ed. F. Cross. Berlin.
Guelich, R. 1982. *The Sermon on the Mount.* Waco, TX.
Hare, D. 1967. *The Theme of Jewish Persecution of Christians in the Gospel according to St Matthew.* SNTSMS 6. Cambridge.
Heil, J. P. 1981. *Jesus Walking on the Sea.* AnBib 87. Rome.
Held, H. J. 1963. Matthew as Interpreter of the Miracle Stories. Pp. 165–299 in *Tradition and Interpretation in Matthew.* Philadelphia.
Hummel, R. 1966. *Die Auseinandersetzung zwischen Kirche und Judentum im Matthäusevangelium.* BEvT 33. 2d ed. Munich.
Jeremias, J. 1966. Zur Hypothese einer schriftlichen Logienquelle Q. Pp. 90–92 in *Abba.* Göttingen.
Keegan, T. 1982. Introductory Formulae for Matthean Discourses. *CBQ* 44: 415–30.
Kennedy, G. 1984. *New Testament Interpretation through Rhetorical Criticism.* Chapel Hill, NC.
Kiley, M. 1984. Why 'Matthew' in Matt 9,9–13? *Bib* 65: 347–51.
Kilpatrick, G. 1946. *The Origins of the Gospel according to St. Matthew.* Oxford.
Kingsbury, J. D. 1975. *Matthew: Structure, Christology, Kingdom.* Philadelphia.
———. 1986. *Matthew as Story.* Philadelphia.
Krentz, E. 1964. The Extent of Matthew's Prologue. *JBL* 83: 409–14.
Kretzer, A. 1971. *Die Herrschaft der Himmel und die Söhne des Reiches.* SBM 10. Würzburg.
Lange, J. 1973. *Das Erscheinen des Auferstandenen im Evangelium nach Mattäus.* FB 11. Würzburg.
Léon-Dufour, X. 1962. Bulletin d'exégèse du Nouveau Testament. Théologie de Matthieu et paroles de Jésus. *RSR* 50: 90–111.
Meier, J. P. 1976. *Law and History in Matthew's Gospel.* AnBib 71. Rome.
———. 1979. *The Vision of Matthew.* New York.
Michel, O. 1950. Der Abschluss des Matthäusevangeliums. *EvT* 10: 16–26.
Nepper-Christensen, P. 1958. *Das Matthäusevangelium: Ein judenchristliches Evangelium?* Acta Theologica Danica 1. Aarhus.
Nolan, B. 1979. *The Royal Son of God.* OBO 23. Fribourg.
Patte, D. 1986. *The Gospel according to Matthew.* Philadelphia.
Pesch, R. 1968. Levi-Matthäus (Mc 2:14/Mt 9:9; 10:3), ein Beitrag zur Lösung eines alten Problems. *ZNW* 59: 40–56.
Petersen, N. 1978. *Literary Criticism for New Testament Critics.* Philadelphia.
Przybylski, B. 1980. *Righteousness in Matthew and His World of Thought.* SNTSMS 41. Cambridge.
Rengstorf, K. 1960. Die Stadt der Mörder (Mt 22,7). Pp. 106–29 in *Judentum, Urchristentum, Kirche,* ed. W. Eltester. BZNW 26. Berlin.
Robbins, V. 1984. *Jesus the Teacher.* Philadelphia.
Robinson, J. A. T. 1976. *Redating the New Testament.* Philadelphia.
Sand, A. 1974. *Das Gesetz und die Propheten.* BU 11. Regensburg.
Schaberg, J. 1982. *The Father, the Son and the Holy Spirit.* SBLDS 61. Chico, CA.
Schulz, S. 1967. *Die Stunde der Botschaft.* Hamburg.
Senior, D. 1975. *The Passion Narrative according to Matthew.* BETL 39. Leuven.
Shuler, P. 1982. *A Genre for the Gospels.* Philadelphia.
Soares Prabhu, G. M. 1976. *The Formula Quotations in the Infancy Narrative of Matthew.* AnBib 63. Rome.
Stendahl, K. 1968. *The School of St. Matthew and Its Use of the Old Testament.* 2d ed. ASNU 20. Lund.
Strecker, G. 1971. *Der Weg der Gerechtigkeit.* 3d ed. FRLANT 82. Göttingen.
Talbert, C. 1977. *What Is a Gospel?* Philadelphia.
Tillborg, S. van. 1972. *The Jewish Leaders in Matthew.* Leiden.
Trilling, W. 1964. *Das wahre Israel.* 3d ed. SANT 10. Munich.
Vaganay, L. 1954. *Le problème synoptique.* Bibliothèque de Théologie 3/1. Tournai.
Votaw, C. W. 1970. *The Gospels and Contemporary Biographies in the Greco-Roman World.* FBBS 27. Philadelphia.
Walker, R. 1967. *Die Heilsgeschichte im ersten Evangelium.* FRLANT 91. Göttingen.
Wrege, H. T. 1968. *Die Überlieferungsgeschichte der Bergpredigt.* WUNT 9. Tübingen.

JOHN P. MEIER

MATTHEW, GOSPEL OF PSEUDO-. The *Gospel of Pseudo-Matthew,* also known as the *Liber de Infantia* or the *Liber de Ortu Beatae Mariae et Infantia Salvatoris,* dates, most probably, to the 6th century although some scholars put it later. The gospel, which was compiled in Latin, is based upon two principal sources: the *Protevangelium* [*or Gospel*] *of James,* and the *Infancy Gospel of Thomas.* As the name of the work implies, the gospel became attributed to Matthew, though in some mss it is attributed to James. The real author of the work is unknown.

The gospel is introduced by three letters, one of which claims Jerome as its author. While there are some contradictions in these letters, in general they seek to confirm the authenticity and value of the gospel, stating that it was written by the apostle and in the Hebrew language.

The contents of the gospel may be summarized as follows.

A. The Birth of Mary and of Jesus

This first section of the gospel (chaps. 1–17) is based largely upon the *Protevangelium of James;* however, the author has felt free to add to and omit from his source.

Mary's parents, Joachim, a shepherd of Jerusalem, and Anna, daughter of Ysachar, have no child. Anna laments her childlessness and is visited by an angel who promises that she will have a daughter. Mary is born. At the age of fourteen, Mary refuses marriage on the grounds that she has taken a vow to virginity; however, an angel makes it clear that Joseph is to be her guardian. The section ends with the stories of the annunciation, the trip to Bethlehem, the birth of Jesus, the murder of the innocents, and the instruction to go to Egypt.

B. The Flight into Egypt

The origins of the traditions found in this section (chaps. 18–24) are unknown. Mary, Joseph, and Jesus set off for Egypt and come to rest outside a cave. Suddenly out of the cave come a number of dragons which proceed to worship Jesus. In this way the words of Ps 148:7 are fulfilled. Later other ferocious animals bow their heads to Jesus. Resting again, Mary wishes to have the fruit from a very high tree, while Joseph is more concerned with water. The tree bends down and allows Mary to take its fruit, and under its roots is found a spring. Arriving at a city called

Sotinen, they enter a temple in which reside 365 idols. At the sight of Jesus, the idols fall; and thus is fulfilled Isa 19:1.

C. The Boyhood of Jesus

With the exception of chaps. 25–26, the traditions found in this section (chaps. 24–41) come largely from the *Infancy Gospel of Thomas.* One sabbath day Jesus is playing by the Jordan when a boy spoils the pools he has made. The boy is struck dead; but seeing Mary's grief, Jesus restores the boy to life. Jesus next makes twelve clay sparrows, claps his hands; and they fly away. The son of Annas the priest breaks up the pools with a stick and is subsequently "withered up" by Jesus. On the way home Jesus slays another boy who is intent on injuring him, but later raises him again. Next follows a section on how Jesus astounded all with his wisdom. In chaps. 25–26 (not from the *Gospel of Thomas*) we hear again of Jesus' control over ferocious beasts. We hear also of how Jesus stretched a piece of wood that was too short, how he again astounded the teachers with his wisdom (and caused the death of one who struck him), and how he raised a rich man from the dead.

D. Conclusion

The final chapter (chap. 42) is not found in the *Gospel of Thomas* or the *Protevangelium of James.* It reports how Jesus blessed the members of his family and concludes by noting that whenever Jesus slept, the glory of God shone over him.

Clearly the gospel comes from the hand of one who held the persons of Mary and Joseph in high esteem. This is seen, for example, by the fact that whereas in the *Infancy Gospel of Thomas* the wood which Jesus stretched was accidentally cut too short by Joseph (13:1–2), in the *Gospel of Pseudo-Matthew* the wood is cut by one of Joseph's workers (chap. 37). So, too, in the *Infancy Gospel of Thomas,* Joseph takes Jesus by the ear to lead him home (5:2), a detail omitted by the *Gospel of Pseudo-Matthew.* Noticeable also is the desire to show that in the events of Jesus' life, certain OT prophecies are fulfilled.

As James (1924: 79) points out, the importance of the *Gospel of Pseudo-Matthew* does not center upon its contents, for most of the traditions are to be found elsewhere; rather, the gospel is important in that it was the means by which these traditions were communicated to the medieval Church. The *Gospel of Pseudo-Matthew* contributed significantly to the growth of the cult of the Virgin Mary and was a source of inspiration to later artists and poets (Warner 1976: 24–25, 30; James 1924: 79; *NTApocr* 1: 368). The *Gospel of Pseudo-Matthew* was in turn used as the basis for the *Gospel of the Birth of Mary.*

Bibliography

James, M. R. 1924. *The Apocryphal New Testament.* Oxford.

Santos Otero, A. de. 1956. *Los Evangelios Apocrifos.* Madrid.

Thilo, J. C. 1832. *Codex Apocryphus Novi Testamenti.* Leipzig.

Tischendorf, C. 1876. *Evangelica Apocrypha.* Leipzig.

Warner, M. 1976. *Alone of All Her Sex: The Myth and the Cult of the Virgin Mary.* London.

Kenneth G. C. Newport

MATTHEW, HEBREW VERSION OF.

Texts of Matthew in Hebrew first appeared in print in 1537 when Sebastian Münster published a manuscript of Matthew that he received from the Jews. In 1555 Jean du Tillet published another Hebrew Matthew (not radically different from Münster's) that also had been preserved by the Jews. Subsequently scholars incorrectly identified these texts as a translation of the Latin Vulgate. In 1690 Richard Simon mistakenly equated Münster and du Tillet with an earlier unpublished Hebrew Matthew preserved in the 14th-century Jewish polemical treatise, the *Even Bohan,* by the Spanish author, Shem-Tob ben-Isaac ben-Shaprut (= ibn Shaprut). The identification of Münster and du Tillet with the text of Shem-Tob discouraged subsequent scholars from investigating the latter until recently. Shem-Tob's Hebrew Matthew has now been published in full, accompanied by a critical apparatus, an English translation, and an analysis of the text (Howard 1987).

Apparently Shem-Tob's Hebrew Matthew is a Hebrew composition overlaid with scribal errors and layers of scribal modification. The modifications are (1) stylistic, consisting primarily of improvements in grammar and diction, and (2) revisions designed to make the Hebrew correspond more closely to the canonical Greek and Latin texts. Münster and du Tillet appear to be systematic revisions of the Shem-Tob type text designed to make it read even more closely to the Greek and Latin.

A pre-14th-century date for Shem-Tob's Hebrew Matthew is evidenced by its unique textual agreements with earlier Aramaic and Hebrew quotations of or allusions to Matthew in Jewish and anti-Christian writings. These include the Talmud (*b. Šabb.* 116^{b}), the *Tol'doth Yeshu* (6th–10th centuries), the *Book of Nestor Hakomer* (between the 6th and 9th centuries), the *Milhamot HaShem* by Jacob ben Reuben (1170), *Sepher Joseph Hamekane* by Rabbi Joseph ben-Nathan Official (13th century), and the *Nizzahon Vetus* (latter part of the 13th century).

The old substratum to Shem-Tob's Matthew is shown to be a Hebrew composition by a multiplicity of puns, word connections, and alliterations that are workable in Hebrew but not in Greek and Latin. The old substratum has textual affinities with some writings that vanished in antiquity but were rediscovered or recognized, in whole or in part, in modern times. These include the Old Syriac, the *Diatesseron* of Tatian, the *Gospel of Thomas,* and the hypothetical gospel source known as Q. On occasion the old substratum gives a Hebrew basis for variation between the Synoptic Gospels. Linguistically, it has characteristics that one would expect of a document written early in the common era and preserved by medieval Jewish scribes. It is written in biblical Hebrew with a healthy mixture of Mishnaic Hebrew and Aramaic forms overlaid with medieval scribal revisions designed to improve its grammar, diction, and general style.

Whether Shem-Tob's Hebrew Matthew is to be equated with the Hebrew Matthew referred to by Papias (ca. 60–130 C.E.) is unknown. (His reference is preserved in Eus. *Hist. Eccl.* 3.39.16). A comparison of Shem-Tob's text with quotations of a Hebrew Matthew or of a Hebrew apocryphal gospel cited by later writers (Epiphanius and Jerome) leads to the conclusion that Shem-Tob's Matthew was unknown by early gentile Christians.

Shem-Tob's Hebrew Matthew has a number of distinctive characteristics that place it into a different theological mode from that of the Greek text. Salient differences are the following:

First, in the Hebrew Matthew Jesus assumes a role somewhat different from his role in the Greek Matthew. Several times where the Greek reads "Son of Man," the Hebrew reads "Son of God" (16:27, 28; 26:64). Once where the Greek reads "Son of David," the Hebrew reads "Son of God" (21:15). Once where the Greek reads "Son of God," the Hebrew reads "God" (4:6). With one possible exception (16:16) Jesus is never seriously identified as the Messiah/Christ. In the Greek texts, for example, "Christ" appears at 1:1, 17, 18; 11:2, but not in the Hebrew. Primarily, the role Jesus assumes in the Hebrew Matthew is that of judge and avenger (Heb *gōʾēl haddām*). According to the Hebrew he will come with the "fire of the Holy Spirit" (3:11). This sets the stage for later references to his coming in judgment (13:41; 19:28; 24:37–41; 25:31ff.). Other matters of interest are: (1) Jesus adheres to the Law more strictly in the Hebrew text than in the Greek (5:17–48), and (2) his execution is depicted as a Jewish hanging in the Hebrew text rather than a Roman crucifixion (27:23, 26, 31, 38, 44; 28:5).

Second, in the Hebrew Matthew John the Baptist assumes a more salvific role than in the Greek text. In 11:11 the Hebrew reads that none has arisen greater than John the Baptist (without the additional words that appear in the Greek: "Yet he who is least in the kingdom of heaven is greater than he"). In 11:13 the Hebrew reads: "For all the prophets and the law spoke *concerning* (Gk reads "until") John." In 17:11 the Hebrew reads: "Indeed Elijah [= John the Baptist] will come and will *save* all the world."

Third, the Hebrew Matthew, in good Jewish fashion, envisions the inclusion of the gentiles to take place at the end of the present era rather than during it. In this respect it is anti-Pauline. The great commission (Matt 28:19–20) in the Hebrew text lacks mention of the gentiles and the trinitarian baptismal formula. This creates a new theological dimension for the First Gospel, which contains the limited commission at 10:5–6: "Go nowhere among the gentiles, and enter no town of the Samaritans, but go rather to the lost sheep of the house of Israel" (RSV), and the derogatory words regarding the gentiles at 15:26: "It is not fair to take the children's bread and throw it to the dogs" (RSV). The harshness of these words is unsoftened in the Hebrew by the final commission to all the nations (28:19–20) found in the Greek. According to the Hebrew the only hope for the gentiles in the present world is to be as dogs who eat the crumbs that fall from their master's table (15:27).

Even more decisive against the inclusion of the gentiles during the present era is the Hebrew text at 24:14–15. It reads: "And this gospel . . . will be preached in all the earth for a witness concerning me to all the nations and then the end will come. . . . This is the abomination which desolates which was spoken of by Daniel as standing in the holy place. Let the one who reads understand." Thus the Hebrew gospel interprets the "abomination which desolates" as the preaching of the gospel to the gentiles *before* the end.

It is not the case, however, that no hope of salvation is given to the gentiles by the Hebrew gospel. According to it the Son of Man will return in glory and gather all the gentiles before him. He will assign some to eternal life; others he will assign to eternal abhorrence (25:31–46). Salvation to some gentiles therefore will come at the end of the present era.

Bibliography

Herbst, A. 1879. *Des Schemtob ben Schaphrut hebräische Übersetzung des Evangeliums Matthaei nach den Drucken des S. Münster und J. du Tillet-Mercier.* Göttingen.

Horbury, W. 1983. The Revision of Shem Tob Ibn Shaprut's *Eben Bohan. Sef* 43: 221–37.

Howard, G. 1983. The Textual Nature of an Old Hebrew Version of Matthew. *JBL* 105: 49–63.

———. 1986a. Shem-Tov's Hebrew Matthew. In *Proceedings of the Ninth World Congress of Jewish Studies.* Jerusalem.

———. 1986b. Was the Gospel of Matthew Originally Written in Hebrew? *BRev* 2: 14–25.

———. 1987. *The Gospel of Matthew according to a Primitive Hebrew Text.* Macon, GA.

———. 1988a. A Note on the Short Ending of Matthew. *HTR* 81: 117–20.

———. 1988b. A Primitive Hebrew Gospel of Matthew and the Tol'doth Yeshu. *NTS* 34: 60–70.

Lapide, P. E. 1974. Der "Prüfstein" aus Spanien. *Sef* 34: 227–72.

———. 1984. *Hebrew in the Church.* Grand Rapids.

Marx, A. 1929. The Polemical Manuscripts in the Library of the Jewish Theological Seminary of America. Pp. 247–79 in *Studies in Jewish Bibliography and Related Subjects in Memory of Abraham Solomon Freidus (1867–1923).* New York.

Schonfield, H. 1927. *An Old Hebrew Text of St. Matthew's Gospel.* Edinburgh.

GEORGE HOWARD

MATTHEW, MARTYRDOM OF. How the apostle Matthew met his death is in some dispute. According to Heracleon (Clement *Strom.* 4.71.3) Matthew passed away naturally; this is a minority opinion, however; and Matthew has long been revered by the Christian Church as a martyr.

The traditions concerning the exact nature of Matthew's martyrdom are not unanimous regarding either the place or mode of Matthew's execution. The most influential tradition is that found in the official *Roman Martyrology* of the Catholic Church, according to which Matthew was martyred in Ethiopia (O'Connell 1962). This tradition is found also in *Foxe's Book of Martyrs,* where it is reported that Matthew was slain with a halberd in the city of Nabadar. The belief that Matthew was slain with a halberd, sword, or other sharp instrument is apparent in the depiction of Matthew in art, where the apostle often carries a spear.

According to the 5th-century *Hieronymian Martyrology* (*PL* 30: 433–86), on the other hand, Matthew was martyred in Persia, in the town of Tarrium; while according to the Greek *Martyrdom of the Holy Apostle Matthew* the apostle suffered execution by fire in the Roman province of Pontus, dying "around the sixth hour" (Lipsius and Bonnet 1898: 217–62). The Babylonian Talmud (*b. Sanh.* 43a) reports briefly that Matthai, one of the disciples of Yeshu, was executed (by the Sanhedrin) but gives no details. The relics of St. Matthew were reportedly found in Salerno in 1080.

Bibliography

Gaiffier, B. 1962. Hagiographie salernitaine: la translation de S. Matthieu. *Analecta Bollandiana* 80: 82–110.

Lipsius, R. A., and Bonnet, M., eds. 1898. *Acta Apostolorum Apocrypha.* Vol. 2. Leipzig.

O'Connell, J. B. 1962. *The Roman Martyrology.* London.

KENNETH G. C. NEWPORT

MATTHIAS (PERSON) [Gk *Maththias*]. The disciple chosen to fill the vacancy left by Judas among the Twelve (Acts 1:23, 26).

Matthias is a diminutive form of the common name Mattithiah, "gift of Yahweh." Apart from his election to the Twelve nothing else is known about him. Later legends numbered him among the Seventy disciples of Luke 10, identified him with Zacchaeus or Barnabas, and gave two different accounts of his death. An apocryphal gospel was written in his name.

Since there is no reliable information about him beyond these few verses in Acts, his importance lies in the ideas connected with the story of his election.

Luke, with two exceptions, limits the use of "apostle" to the Twelve. Paul seems to distinguish the Twelve from apostles (1 Cor 15:5–7). In unraveling the traditions behind the story of Matthias' election to the Twelve, it appears that Luke has imposed his own definition of the apostolate upon an earlier time. The Twelve were not originally apostles. They were eschatological representatives of messianic Israel. Symbolizing the twelve tribes, they stood as the foundation of the true Israel. It was essential that the vacancy left by Judas be filled in order to fulfill this function. With Matthias' election the early community stood ready for the eschatological gift of the Spirit at Pentecost and their anointing as the true Israel. It is doubtful that the Twelve functioned in this sense outside of Jerusalem or that they functioned for very long as a definite group within Jerusalem. This helps to explain the lack of knowledge about Matthias and others of the Twelve.

For Paul "apostle" refers to someone called to mission by a special appearance of the risen Lord. See APOSTLE. Luke gives Matthias' qualifications as having been with Jesus from his baptism by John until the ascension. This statement is the origin of speculation that he was one of the Seventy. The probable requirement for membership in the Twelve was simply being a witness of the resurrection. Luke has expanded this to include witnessing Jesus' life as a means of grounding the gospel tradition in eyewitness testimony. Luke's restriction of the term to the Twelve seems to reflect a later solution to the problem already felt in Paul's epistles as to how to distinguish true from false apostles. There are only twelve apostles, the foundation not only of the true Israel but also the Church (cf. Eph 2:20; Rev 21:14).

Luke tells us that Matthias was elected by lot. The exact meaning of the phrase in v 26 and the procedure it describes are uncertain. Some have thought that the verb *(didōmi)* implies that Luke may have meant by *klēpos* not "lot" but "vote." But it seems more likely that Luke, familiar with the LXX and the Hellenistic practice of selecting responsible officials by lot, understood the OT practice where stones with names on them were put in a vessel which was shaken until one fell out. It has also been argued that the word "lot" acquired a metaphoric usage in Judaism. In this view the story indicates that the community selected Matthias (the procedure left unspecified) and that they believed the decision was from God. It was his God given "lot" in life to be one of the Twelve. In this reconstruction Luke's source portrayed a metaphoric use of the word "lot" which he has objectified as a literal "casting of lots" (Beardslee 1960: 245–52). In any event the story makes it clear that God selected Matthias to fill Judas' vacancy. This causes speculations that Paul was meant to be the twelfth apostle and that Peter and the early community overstepped their authority in appointing Matthias to appear polemical.

Bibliography

Beardslee, W. A. 1960. The Casting of Lots at Qumran and in Book of Acts. *NovT* 4: 245–52.

THOMAS W. MARTIN

MATTHIAS, TRADITIONS OF. A work named and quoted by Clement of Alexandria, who attributes it to "Matthias the Apostle." This presumably refers to the Matthias who is named in Acts 1:23–26 as the man chosen to replace Judas among the Twelve. According to Eusebius (*Hist. Eccl.* 1.12.3) Matthias was one of the Seventy (Luke 10:1).

The extent and genre of the *Traditions of Matthias* is uncertain. Clement's citations from it are brief hortatory sentences (*Strom.* 2.9.45; 3.4.26; 7.13.82). But if *Strom.* 4.6.35 is derived from the same source, then the work may also have contained some narrative about Jesus. The quotations are not overtly gnostic, but according to Clement (*Strom.* 7.17.108) teachings of Matthias were used by Basilideans and perhaps other gnostic groups. According to Hippolytus (*Haer.* 7.20.1) Basilides and his son Isidore claimed to have learned from Matthias "secret words," which he had received in private teaching from the Savior.

Traditions of Matthias probably was composed in Egypt in the first half of the 2d century. It sometimes has been identified with a work called the *Gospel of Matthias,* but there is too little evidence to decide this question definitively (*NTApocr* 1: 312). The earliest author to mention a *Gospel of Matthias* is Origen (*hom.* I. *in Lc.*), whose information is repeated by Ambrose and Jerome. Eusebius (*Hist. Eccl.* 3.25.6) mentions it together with gospels of Thomas and Peter. He describes them as works which were composed by heretics, but which nonetheless were known to most writers in the early Church. The *Gospel of Matthias* is also named in lists of heretical works: the Decretum Gelasianum, the Catalogue of the Sixty Canonical Books, and a list in the Samaritan Chronicle No. II of false books allegedly used by Nazarene Christians.

JON B. DANIELS

MATTHIAS, ACTS OF. See ANDREW AND MATTHIAS, ACTS OF.

MATTITHIAH (PERSON) [Heb *mattityāh, mattityāhû*]. Var. MATTATHIAH. **1.** A Levite and son of Jeduthun (1 Chr 25:3) who played musical instruments before the ark during the time of David. Given the Chronicler's extreme interest in the installation of temple musicians (Braun *1 Chronicles* WBC, 186), further details are provided. Within a list that also includes a director, singers, and those who played harps, trumpets, and cymbals, Mattithiah played the lyre (1 Chr 15:18, 21; 16:5; 25:21). That this activity carried considerable religious significance is emphasized by the writer's describing it as "prophecy" (1 Chr 25:1).

2. A Korahite Levite and the first son of Shallum who served at the temple following the return from Exile (1 Chr 9:31). Mattithiah's specific responsibility was to bake the liturgical cakes for the temple service.

3. A son of Nebo who, persuaded by Ezra, agreed to renounce his foreign wife (Ezra 10:43 [LXX *Mathathia*]; 1 Esdr 9:35 [Gk *Mazitias*]). Not included within the lists referring to priests and Levites, Mattithiah was a member of the Israelite laity.

4. One of the men who stood on Ezra's right hand during the great public reading of the Law (Neh 8:4; 1 Esdr 9:43). Not designated as a Levite, Mattithiah's position at this event suggests that he was an influential or representative member of the Israelite laity. In 1 Esdr 9:43, Mattithiah appears as Mattathiah (RSV).

TERRY L. BRENSINGER

MAUL. See WEAPONS AND IMPLEMENTS OF WARFARE.

MAYOR. See PALESTINE, ADMINISTRATION OF (POSTEXILIC JUDEAN OFFICIALS).

MAZAR, TELL EL- (M.R. 207181). An Iron Age site nestled geographically and chronologically among its larger sister tells at Deir ᶜAlla and Saidiyeh. Though N. Glueck in the 1930s identified it from its surface pottery as an important Iron Age site (Glueck 1951: 302–3), Tell el-Mazar remained untouched until the University of Jordan excavated it during four seasons between 1977 and 1981.

Tell el-Mazar is located 3 km N of Tell DeirᶜAlla and about 3 km E of the Jordan river. It rises 24 m above the valley floor, at an altitude of 250 m below sea level. In antiquity the settlement at the site exploited the year-round waters of the Jabbok river and the rich agricultural lands around the tell. The ancient identification of the site remains unknown, but the modern name of Tell el-Mazar is thought to come from the nearby mosque and pilgrimage site of Mazar Abu 'Ubaidah, where the early Islamic general Abu 'Ubaidah was buried in A.D. 622.

Occupation of the site extends from the 11th century B.C. to the middle of the 4th century B.C., with signs of human occupation going back to the 13th century B.C. The site consists of the main tell and an associated sanctuary/cemetery area to the NW (Yassine 1983).

The earliest architectural remains on the tell are from the 8th/7th centuries B.C., when the Ammonite kingdom controlled the area from its capital at Rabbath-ammon (modern Amman). The formerly independent Ammonite kingdom came under the control of the Assyrians after the campaigns of Tiglath-pileser III in 732 B.C. While they paid tribute to the Assyrians, the Ammonites enjoyed a measure of local autonomy and prospered from the trade that flourished under the regional security provided by the Assyrian Empire (Bennett 1978, Lindsay 1976). Remains from this Iron Age II period include parts of a building with a square courtyard, whose floor was paved with flagstones. A storage jar in one room was still filled with wheat grain, while in another corner of the same room a bathtub was built on a brick platform. The rooms from this early settlement were destroyed by fire at the end of the 8th century B.C.—perhaps reflecting the destruction inflicted by the 701 B.C. campaign of Sennacherib (Yassine 1983: 512).

During the 7th century, the site was rebuilt and included a large, nonmilitary building that was used as a residence. It had a stone-paved open courtyard surrounded by rooms used for different purposes, including cooking and storage. A series of *tabuns*, or ovens, were found from this level. There is no evidence of destruction at the end of this phase (Yassine 1983: 510).

The next phase of occupation (the 7th/6th centuries B.C.) seems to have been during a period of prosperity and peace, to judge by the remains at the top of the mound of a large and impressive building. It commanded a fine view of the entire central Jordan valley and has been called a "palace fort." It was composed of rooms at two different levels, connected by a staircase. The utilitarian lower rooms included a kitchen and rooms for storage, weaving, and meat preparation. Because of the smaller size of the tell and the relatively more sophisticated mudbrick architecture compared to other Iron Age tells in the area, we speculate that this may have been the residence of a local governor or other official.

This settlement ended suddenly and violently, with great fires destroying the buildings. There were no human skeletons but many intact objects and full storage jars, suggesting that the inhabitants of the settlement escaped the final destruction by fire but were unable to take many belongings with them. This destruction may date from the Neo-Babylonian conquests during the reign of Nebuchadnezzer (Yassine 1983: 507–8).

During the 7th century B.C. the Ammonite, Moabite, and Edomite kingdoms in Jordan had prospered as self-governing vassals of the Assyrian Empire. This era of prosperity ended with the Neo-Babylonian conquests of Jordan and Palestine around 586 B.C., which may be recorded in the destruction levels at Tell el-Mazar. In the middle of the 6th century B.C., Neo-Babylonian rule in Jordan and the Ammonite kingdom ended when the Persians conquered the area and ruled for two centuries.

The tell was once again inhabited in the 5th century B.C., when intensive filling operations leveled the destroyed remains of the 6th-century-B.C. city. The quality of mudbrick construction seems inferior to that of the previous settlement, though the 5th-century-B.C. buildings are planned in a uniform and orderly manner, with a series of rooms around a central courtyard. These seem to have been "private industrial houses." The domestic utensils and industrial artifacts indicate that this settlement dates from the two centuries of Achaemenid Persian domination of Jordan/Palestine (from 538–332 B.C.). The Persian influence at Tell el-Mazar is reflected in stamp seals and impressions, metal products, bronze and silver jewelry, and ceramics (Yassine 1983: 503–7).

The latest occupation phase at Tell el-Mazar in antiquity was during the late Persian years of the 4th century B.C., a few decades before the armies of Alexander the Great conquered the area in 332 B.C. and ushered in the era of Hellenism. The most striking feature of the late Persian occupation was dozens of deep, rounded storage pits and silos. Some are over 2 m in diameter and 4 m deep. Usually, but not always, lined with bricks, stones, or mudbricks, these cylindrical or barrel-shaped pits were used to store chaff, charred grains, pottery, copper, stone vessels, or just rubbish. The excavators believe such grain silos were built on top of the Jordan valley tells because the dry climate of the valley and the steep slope and compact deposit of the tell combined to allow rainwater to run off quickly, producing ideal grain-storage conditions. The storage of grain on a large scale (also attested at Tell Deir ʿAlla and Tell Saidiyeh) may have been as security against famines, or may reflect a tax-gathering facility or support for a military force. The tell seems to have been abandoned in 333 B.C., when Alexander the Great's armies conquered the area.

The second part of the site is a low (1-m-high) mound located about 400 NW of the main tell, covering an area of some 1200 m². This area was first occupied in the 11th/10th centuries B.C., during the Iron Age IB–C. The excavations revealed the remains of a large, rectangular-plan building measuring 24 × 16 m. See Fig. MAZ.01. We called this an "open-Court Sanctuary," since it consists of an open courtyard flanked by rooms. The solid, 1.2-m-thick walls of the rooms and courtyard were made of mudbricks. The sanctuary seems to have been built toward the end of the 11th century B.C. and was destroyed late in the 10th century B.C. (Yassine 1984a: 115).

Three rooms on the N side of the courtyard yielded cult vessels (cylindrical incense burners and chalices), underground cisterns, storage jars, and a great deal of pottery. The large courtyard, with its main entrance in the S wall, facing Tell el-Mazar, was covered with a thick layer of ashy debris and burned materials, including pottery sherds, animal bones, grain, and fuel materials (brushwood and charcoal). There were three *tabuns*, or ovens, in the courtyard, a shaft tomb with three male burials, and, near the middle of the courtyard, a stone table that may have served as an altar. The sanctuary seems to have been the site of large-scale food processing, with refuse being disposed of in the courtyard.

It is believed that the sanctuary served a public purpose but was not a place of large-scale public worship.

After the sanctuary went out of use, the site NW of the tell was deserted for nearly 500 years. It was used again in the 5th century B.C., this time as a cemetery; and 84 graves were excavated in late 1979. The skeletal remains show the average life expectancy of the Ammonite people at that time was around 33 years (Yassine 1984b: 187).

Many of the warlike objects excavated from the tombs, such as arrowheads, swords, daggers, and spearheads, suggest the male burials were those of warriors (Yassine 1984b: 8). Five different kinds of burials were documented, including brick- and stone-lined pits, skeletons in shallow ceramic jars, and skeletons in bathtub-like clay boxes with handles. Some of the graves contained stamp or cylinder seals, which were placed on the deceased's chest or hung from the belt. A few had the name of the deceased (such as "Lhmyws son of Smṭ"; Yassine and Bordreuil 1982: 193; Yassine 1984b: 133). Most are important for their artistic and iconographic information, showing the cultural links between the Ammonite people and some of the nearby great civilizations in Persia, Egypt, and Assyria (Yassine 1982).

The seals, made of colored marble, agate, lapis lazuli, jasper, or limestone, had a variety of motifs. Among them were winged bulls and lions, a rider on a galloping horse aiming his bow and arrow at a gazelle whose foreleg is being bitten by a god, a Neo-Babylonian worshipper, a representation of two eyes around a nose, a cult scene of two worshippers flanking a stylus and a spade, two animals flanking a hero, two falcon-headed solar deities in human form flanking a stylistic tree, and walking bovine animals (Yassine 1982: 189–92).

A few ostraca from Tell el-Mazar were uncovered dated between the 6th century B.C. and the early Hellenistic period. Most of the personal names contained in the inscriptions have parallels in other sources. Of particular interest are the many personal names with the theophoric element *ʾl* (Yassine and Teixidor 1986).

Bibliography

Bennett, C.-M. 1978. Some Reflections on Neo-Assyrian Influence in Transjordan. Pp. 164–71 in *Archaeology in the Levant,* ed. P. R. S. Moorey and P. J. Parr. Warminster.

Glueck, N. 1951. *Explorations in Eastern Palestine, IV.* Pt. 1. AASOR 25–27. New Haven.

Lindsay, J. 1976. The Babylonian Kings in Edom 605–550 B.C. *PEQ* 108: 23–39.

Yassine, K. N. 1982. Ammonite Seals from Tell el Mazar. Pp. 189–92 in *Studies in the History and Archaeology of Jordan I,* ed. A. Hadidi. Amman.

———. 1983. Tell el Mazar, Field I. *ADAJ* 27: 495–513.

———. 1984a. The Open Court Sanctuary of the Iron Age I. *ZDPV* 100: 108–18.

———. 1984b. *Tell el Mazar.* Vol. 1. Amman.

Yassine, K. N., and Bordreuil, P. 1982. Deux Cachets ouest semitiques inscrits decouverts a Tell el Mazar. Pp. 192–94 in *Studies in the History and Archaeology of Jordan I,* ed. A. Hadidi. Amman.

Yassine, K. N., and Teixidor, J. 1986. Ammonite and Aramaic Inscriptions from Tell el Mazar in Jordan. *BASOR* 264: 45–60.

Khair N. Yassine

MAZOR, THE MAUSOLEUM

MAZOR, THE MAUSOLEUM (M.R. 145161). The site of a monument known as Makâm en-Nabi Yahyah, located on the road between the Tower of Aphek and Lod, near the abandoned village of el-Muzeiriah. This monument, which stands out noticeably on the landscape, measures 9.4 × 10.2 m, and in front it measures 4.8 m high; it is one of the few Roman period buildings in the country to be preserved virtually intact.

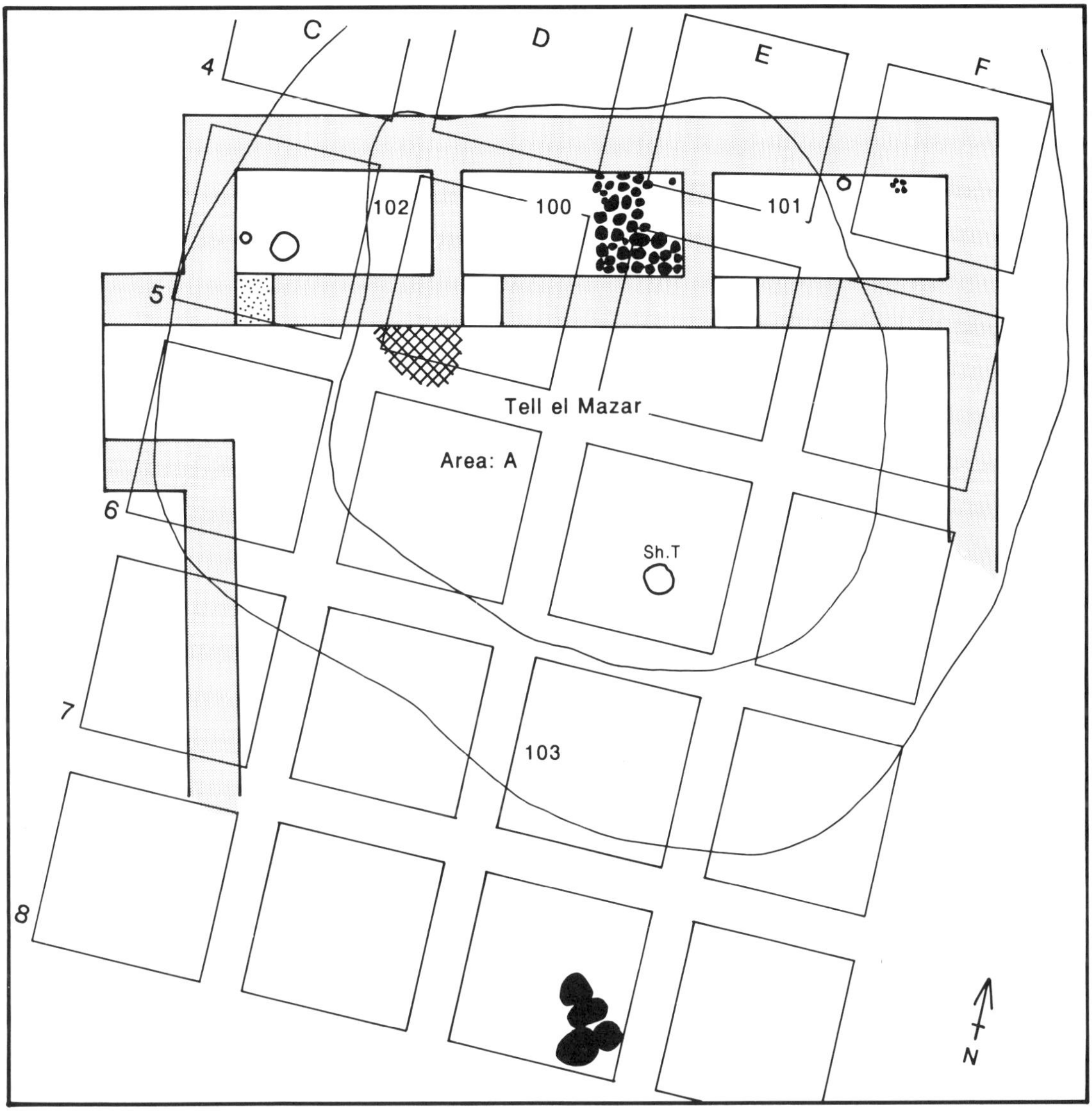

MAZ.01. Open court sanctuary at Tell el-Mazar—Iron Age I. *(Courtesy of K. Yassine)*

It was first investigated in 1872 and 1873; its ground plan was drawn; and the monument was dismissed as a "curiosity" (Condor and Kitchener *SWP* 2: 265–67). Initial trial excavations were carried out in 1964 and later in 1973 (Kaplan 1985). The interior of the building was discovered to have two rooms, with a portico in front. Room A is an ordinary burial chamber with two sarcophagi, in which were interred the bodies of a man and a woman. Presumably, the persons buried here were the owner of an agricultural estate (or a high government official) and his wife, since only such persons would have the wealth required to build such a mausoleum. Room B, which has niches or cells in its walls, is a "columbarium" room, evidently set aside for the master's slaves or freed slaves, whose cremated remains were placed in bags in the cells of the room.

The mausoleum also exhibits some unusual architectural elements, apparently related to some of humankind's earliest beliefs about death and resurrection. The "columbarium" contains certain features associated with doves, which characteristically served as emblems of Near Eastern goddesses (mother goddesses, fertility goddesses, Astarte,

Aphrodite, Atargatis, etc.). The dove is always depicted flying with outstretched wings, possibly symbolizing humankind's hope that the dead will yet return to the scene of life: the dove, taking off in flight from cemeteries and burial places, plucks the soul of the deceased from the netherworld and returns it to the world of the living.

The mausoleum has been dated to A.D. 300, the period of Emperor Diocletian, when the mystery cults (i.e., cults of the netherworld) still flourished and when Christianity had not yet become the state religion. It is possible, however, that the mausoleum was built during the brief reign of Julian the Apostate (A.D. 361–63), who wanted to reinstate the pagan cults.

Bibliography

Kaplan, J. 1985. The Mausoleum at Mazor. *EI* 18: 409–18.

JACOB KAPLAN

ME-JARKON

ME-JARKON (PLACE) [Heb *mê-hayyarqôn*]. A river or town mentioned in Josh 19:46 as part of the territory of Dan, prior to that tribe's northward migration to LESHEM (= LAISH [PLACE]). The boundary is described as going by way of Bene-berak, Gath-rimmon, "Me-jarkon, and Rakkon, with the territory over against Joppa."

There is general disagreement over whether Me-jarkon (lit. "waters of the Jarkon") refers to a perennial stream N of Tel Aviv called the Nahr el-Auja (= Yarkon river) or to a settlement. Scholars who believe that Me-jarkon was a town point out that it is not an impossible place name (cf. Me-jericho, Josh 16:1; Me-nephtoah, Josh 15:9). Thus Abel (*GP* 2: 53) identified Me-jarkon with Tell Jerîsheh (M.R. 132167), while Simons (*GTTOT*, 201) proposed Tell Qasile (M.R. 131168) a bit farther to the W. Those who say that Me-jarkon is a watercourse, indicate that the Nahr el-Auja is the most prominent geographic figure in the area and would readily serve to distinguish between tribal allotments (Lakkai *EncMiqr* 3: 888).

Any possibility of consensus, however, is complicated by textual problems. The MT in v 46a reads, *ûmê hayyarqôn wĕharāqqôn* ("and from the waters of Jarkon and the Rakkon"). The reference to *harāqqôn* is generally regarded to be a duplication of the preceding *mê-hayyarqôn* with some transposition, even though a suitable place name can be found for Rakkon in Tell er-Reqqeit (M.R. 129168). This conclusion is apparently confirmed by the LXX, which does not mention Rakkon: *kaí apó thalásses Ierakon* ("and on the west [seaward], the Jarkon"). The LXX also seems to indicate that the MT has lost the final *mem* of *ûmê,* reading "and the waters of" instead of "and on the west [seaward]." Following the LXX, the MT is thereby restored to read "and on the west [*wmym*], the Jarkon with the border opposite Joppa." Kallai (*EncMiqr* 3: 888) though, argues that the LXX is not reliable at this point, since the Syro-Hexapla, which is based on the LXX, reads the same as the MT. He therefore prefers to retain the original MT reading. He also believes that "the Rakkon" is a river and refers to the Nahr el-Barîdeh, the lowermost course of Wâdī Musrara (= N Ayyalon), which streams from S to N and parallel to the Mediterranean Sea, leaving Joppa W of the boundary line (*HGB,* 370). Naʾaman (1986: 112) prefers Noth's proposal and identifies this same stream bed with Me-jarkon. In either case the Nahr el-Barîdeh would denote a westward abutment of the border on the territory of Joppa, leaving it outside of the inheritance of Dan.

In the end most scholars prefer to identify the Me-jarkon with the Nahr el-Auja ("the tortuous river") which originates at the Rosh ha-ʿAin springs (M.R. 143168), the site of OT Aphek and NT Antipatris. From there it flows westward, where it is soon joined from the N by the Kanah stream (Josh 17:9–10), finally ending its winding 26-km course at the Mediterranean, about 6.5 km N of Jaffa. The name *yarqôn* is related to the Heb word *yarôq* ("green"), and probably refers to the large quantity of organic matter carried by the stream, giving it a pale green appearance. This same river was called Mê-Pîga during the Hellenistic period; it was named after the city of Pegae, which was located at Rosh ha-ʿAin before Herod built Antipatris.

Today the river is barred by sand banks; but in antiquity it was navigable for a certain length, explaining the existence of an anchorage at Tell Qasile, about 3 km inland on the N bank of the river. Maisler (1950–51: 62) and others have proposed identifying the Jarkon with the biblical Sea of Joppa. If so, then maybe the "cedar trees" cut down in Lebanon in Solomon's and Zerubbabel's days were floated up the Jarkon to Tell Qasile, where they were unloaded and forwarded to Jerusalem (1 Kgs 5:9 [= 2 Chr 2:16]; Ezra 3:7).

Bibliography

Maisler [Mazar], B. 1950–51. The Excavations at Tell Qasile. *IEJ* 1: 61–65.

Naʾaman, N. 1986. *Borders and Districts in Biblical Historiography.* Jerusalem.

R. A. MULLINS

MEAL CUSTOMS

MEAL CUSTOMS. This entry consists of three articles that discuss eating customs in the world of the Bible. The first deals mainly with the kosher dietary laws of Judaism that are rooted in the legislation of the Hebrew Bible. The second deals with eating customs in the Greco-Roman world, while the third focuses specifically on sacred meals in the Greco-Roman world.

JEWISH DIETARY LAWS

In its broadest sense the traditional designation *kašrût*—deriving from the Hebrew word the literal meaning of which is "correctness," "appropriateness"—can be applied to any matter of ritual acceptability or appropriateness, whether in reference to a written Torah scroll, to a temporary dwelling constructed for the pilgrimage Festival of Succoth, or to food. As it applies to food, kashruth covers the full range of biblical precept, rabbinic ordinance, evolving custom, and local practice within the Jewish community.

First, consideration will be given to those agricultural commandments that impinge on food consumption and that are relevant only to those residing in the land of Israel (as defined by its traditional biblical boundaries) including: the precepts of the Sabbatical and Jubilee Years, tithing and other priestly and levitical rights, the firstfruits, and the dues owing to the poor. Other agricultural restrictions—which may or may not apply to foods grown in the Diaspora (depending on which sources and authorities are consulted)—concern *ʿorlâ* (the fruit of young trees; see Lev 19:23) and new grain (Deut 16:9).

Apart from the matter of the fruit trees in the Garden of Eden, biblical references to dietary matters begin in Genesis with the observation that the "sinew of the thigh" is not eaten "until this very day" in commemoration of Jacob's nocturnal wrestling injury. This is the sole dietary matter mentioned in Genesis (Gen 32:33), with the exception of the Noachian prohibition on eating of a limb cut from a live animal (based on an interpretation of Gen 9:4).

The second restriction mentioned has to do with the way in which the original paschal sacrifice was to be eaten (Exod 12:8–14), followed by the ban on grain fermentation in connection with the Passover celebration, scattered throughout Exodus, Leviticus, Numbers, and Deuteronomy.

A third concern is the thrice-mentioned admonition dealing with "seething the kid in its mother's milk" (Exod 23:19; 34:26; and Deut 14:21). By far, the largest text is the listing of kosher animals in Leviticus 11.

In all areas of Jewish law, the biblical commandments are implemented in accordance with the interpretations and procedures recorded in rabbinic literature of late antiquity as expounded and elaborated in the commentaries and codes that begin appearing in the Gaonic period (ca. 9th century C.E. through the high Middle Ages). It is important to remember that—notwithstanding many wide areas of absolute conformity—evolving Jewish law, even within the normative Orthodox wing alone, has never been monolithic. As a result, it is usual for all popular guides to the practice of kashruth (including cookbooks) to contain strong disclaimers and exhortations to the reader to consult local competent rabbinic authority at all times.

The ban on the "sinew of the thigh" is accordingly implemented in the dissection of the entire sciatic complex as part of the ritual preparation of meat for consumption, while the restriction on "seething the kid in its mother's milk" is reflected not only in the practice of complete separation of meat and dairy foods and utensils in cooking, but also in prohibitions of eating these items together or benefiting from any other use of the combination.

Grain fermentation, while primarily concerned with the production and eating of leavened bread, also refers to other edible or potable commodities, including beer, food mixtures, food items such as sourdough that are not in themselves considered to be edible, and even nonfood items such as library paste.

But it is with meat and animal derivatives that the greatest bulk of legislation is concerned. The eleventh chapter of Leviticus details the division of animals into categories of permissible and forbidden. Biblical taxonomy, which is a system of classification unto itself, subdivides the animal kingdom into (a) land beasts, further divided into domesticated animals and wild beasts, (b) flying things, including birds and insects, (c) sea things, and (d) creeping things. See also ZOOLOGY.

Permitted land beasts include all warm-blooded animals, domesticated or wild, that are characterized as being both ruminants and ungulates. As examples of forbidden warm-blooded animals, the hare and the camel, which are not ungulates, and the pig, which is not a ruminant, are specifically mentioned.

By inference, pigeons and doves, which are included among possible sacrificial offerings, are permitted foods. Among the other permitted flying things are locusts, which have segmented legs, and those birds not specifically forbidden by list (Leviticus 11 and Deuteronomy 14). Thus, the chicken, duck, goose, and turkey, which are not specifically mentioned at all in biblical literature, are held to be permissible by common tradition.

Aquatic creatures that are permitted are restricted to fish which must have both fins and scales of a specified type; whales, eels, swordfish, shark, and sturgeon are, for various reasons, among the forbidden varieties.

Another parameter concerns the relationship between the sacrificial cultus and permissible food. While any animal that could be sacrificed was deemed fit for consumption, not all permissible food had a role in the various sacrifices. Fish, for example, were never offered on the altar; and the only birds that were sacrificed were the dove and the pigeon. Among the mammals, only cattle, sheep, and goats were offered. Furthermore, those animals which could be eaten, whether included in the sacrifices or not, are to be slaughtered in accordance with the specific procedures applicable to sacrificial mammals, which is to say that they are put to death by one sweep of an unblemished sharp knife that severs the jugular as well as the windpipe. In this manner, all meat that is consumed is in some way symbolically associated with the sacrificial cultus. Needless to say, an animal that dies of natural causes is forbidden. Fish and locusts are the only exceptions to the requirement of ritual slaughter.

But the symbols of sacrifice are not restricted to the manner of slaughtering the animal. A careful examination of the carcass is made, and any obvious organic oddity or malformation as well as any damaged organ that would render the animal unfit for sacrifice renders the animal unfit for consumption. These matters apply even to birds and mammals that never had a sacrificial role.

In addition, the animal's blood and tallow fat are never to be eaten, since the blood was drained and then dashed or sprinkled on the altar and the tallow fat (as distinct from suet) was always burned on the altar as the essentials of sacrifice. Kosher preparation, therefore, requires that the blood be drained as completely as possible and that the appropriate portions of fat be removed (although the tallow of wild animals, according to most authorities, is not banned). At the same time, the sciatic nerves are completely dissected out. (Because of the enormous labor involved in the dissection of the hind quarters, with respect to both the sciatic nerves and the removal of the tallow, meat beyond the twelfth rib is generally not prepared for commercial kosher consumption.)

The next step in the kashruth process is the effective removal of remaining surface and capillary blood by a process of salting, broiling, and rinsing of the meat or, except for the liver, by the alternative method of salting, soaking, and rinsing. This process of "kashering" is necessary for all animal protein, with the exception of locusts and fish.

Another parameter is the division of foods into categories of meat, dairy, and pareve (neutral), based on the biblical injunctions against "seething the kid in its mother's milk" that were cited above. This threefold biblical commandment is interpreted as a ban on the actual cooking together, as well as on the eating or other significant use of the product. It further affects the mere intermingling of meat and milk as well as the respective utensils or dishes used for cooking or eating.

Because the designation "kid" is interpreted to mean the young of any mammal (compare the English usage of "calf" to refer to elephants and whales), the prohibition is applicable to include the meat of one mammal and the milk of another. Rabbinic elaboration further applies the prohibition to the flesh of birds cooked in milk, possibly paralleling the reason for which birds require ritual slaughter. An interesting extension applies to the ban on cooking fish together with meat or fowl, as mentioned in passing in the Babylonian Talmud (*Ḥul.* 103-bff.), but not the consumption of fish and meat at the same meal. This stricture is perhaps the only area of kashruth where a ban is based on consideration that the combination may be toxic.

Other areas of kashruth concern the ban on wine (but not other fermented beverages derived from fruit or grain) pressed, processed, or handled by a non-Jew and less stringent restrictions on milk.

Because of the obvious complexity of all of the issues involved, the modern kosher food industry requires supervision by a cadre of professional personnel thoroughly versed in the disciplines of chemistry and food technology as well as rabbinic law. Since many ingredients may be derived from animal sources as opposed to vegetable sources, or by synthesis, the inclusion of stearates or other staple ingredients becomes and remains a problem unless the source of the product is determined. There is no guarantee that a well-known commercial product is universally kosher just because it is so certified at a specific manufacturing site.

The rationale behind kashruth, from the biblical and rabbinic standpoint, is simply a concern for sanctity. The eminent jurist Maimonides, for example, put forth the educated guess that the ban on cooking meat and milk together was related to an ancient pagan fertility sacrifice. Except for the matter of the supposed toxicity of fish cooked together with meat, all claims of a hygienic rationale are relegated to the status of additional benefit. And even here the medieval legal and philosophical sources disagree strongly.

The best indication that physical health is not at issue is perhaps to be seen in the principle of nullification, which is invoked in cases of the accidental commingling of foods, such as meat with dairy or kosher with nonkosher. If the problem involves solid masses—such as kosher and nonkosher cheese or kosher and nonkosher meat that have no distinguishing characteristics at all—which somehow get mixed together, then the principle of nullification by the majority takes hold. Essentially (although there are many variations on the implementation) if two of the three items are known to have been kosher, they all are kosher, and vice versa.

Nullification by the proportion of less than one part in sixty applies to situations which at least one of the commodities is a liquid. Most frequently, this involves the accidental mixture of meat and dairy, but the problem is by no means restricted to this illustration. If the one element is less than one-sixtieth of the total volume, the mixture is considered kosher.

Beyond this, specific instances adducing medical or hygienic reasons for kashruth are as different in nature as are the individuals who proposed them. Maimonides provided medical-philosophical arguments, while Nahmanides countered with medical-mystical ones. The former sought to justify his rationale by stressing the practice of kashruth as a depaganizing process, while for the latter the process was a humanizing one. In the 19th and 20th centuries, hygienic considerations were brought forward by both those who wished to perpetuate and continue with time-hallowed tradition and those who wished to do away with ritual law altogether in the process of religious reformation.

But the effects of practicing kashruth, from a socio-religious standpoint, are clear: the strictures of kashruth make social intercourse between the practicing Jew and the outside world possible only on the basis of a one-sided relationship, and that is on the terms of the one who observes kashruth. For further discussion see *EncJud* and *JEnc* articles on "Dietary Laws."

Bibliography

Dresner, S. H. 1966. *The Jewish Dietary Laws.* New York.

Grunfeld, I. 1972. *The Jewish Dietary Laws.* London.

GENE SCHRAMM

GRECO-ROMAN MEAL CUSTOMS

The NT and other Christian literature, as well as the religious literature of Judaism, have frequent references to meals of various kinds. The meal customs and rules of etiquette presupposed in such references are largely those of the surrounding Greco-Roman culture. Therefore a study of Greco-Roman meal customs provides the proper background for interpreting NT references to meals.

A. History and Development of Meal Customs
B. Main Features of Meal Customs
  1. Occasions For Meals
    a. Private Banquets
    b. Special Family Occasions
    c. Religious Festivals
    d. Club Meetings
    e. Religious Sects
  2. The Banquet
  3. The Symposium
C. Rules of Etiquette

A. History and Development of Meal Customs

Meal customs in the entire Mediterranean region seem to have become standardized in certain broad details during the Hellenistic and Roman periods (ca. 200 B.C.E. to 200 C.E.). Certainly the various ethnic groups maintained some practices unique to themselves such as the Jewish practices connected with the religious food laws or *kašrût.* Nevertheless, Greeks, Romans, Jews, and eventually Christians shared major components of the standard meal customs of this period.

The development of common dining customs is related to the adoption of the custom of reclining at formal meals by the various peoples of the Mediterranean world. Greeks, Romans, and Jews had traditions that their people once sat at meals before taking up the custom of reclining. This custom seemed to have originated in the Eastern Mediterranean world and was known to the Jewish people as early as the 8th century B.C.E. (Amos 6:4–7). The Greeks appear to have adopted the custom from the Assyrians and were practicing it as early as the 6th century B.C.E. (Dentzer 1971, 1982). The Romans soon followed suit. Since reclining tended to carry with it other meal conventions and since Greeks, Romans, and Jews were interacting culturally in many ways in this period, their meal customs also soon came to be standardized and shared in common.

B. Main Features of Meal Customs

1. Occasions for Meals. Generally speaking, our evidence attests to the common practice of eating three meals a day, although among certain groups, most notably the Jews of the Mishnah, two meals a day was more common. The major meal of the day in all cases was the evening meal (*deipnon* in Greek; *cena* in Latin). This was the meal that tended to have the most formalities connected with it. If a meal was to be used as a special occasion for a social gathering of friends or family or for a meeting of a club or religious group, it would normally be the evening meal. Thus the formal evening meal, or banquet, is the one to which the most elaborate traditions and rules of etiquette became attached.

a. Private Banquets. A householder might invite special friends to his home for a banquet. Such gatherings are referred to quite frequently in the literature (Pl. *Symp.* 174A; Plut. *Quaest. conv.* 615C–D, 626E, 628A, 635A; Petron. *Sat.* 26; Sir 13:9; 1 Cor 10:27). Customarily they were social occasions only for the free adult males of society. Meals of the *ḥăberîm* in Judaism seem to have been such a gathering of friends who took meals together; the meals of Jesus with his disciples have often been compared to this type of Jewish meal gathering. See also ASSOCIATIONS, CLUBS, THIASOI.

b. Special Family Occasions. Birthdays, weddings, funerals, and other special family occasions were regularly celebrated with a banquet (Plut. *Quaest. conv.* 717B; Lucian, *Symp.* 5; Matt 22:1–14; Luke 12:36; 14:8; John 2:1–11).

c. Religious Festivals. These were common in both pagan religion and in Judaism and were marked by sumptuous feasts. In the pagan world banquets would often be provided for the populace at large on the occasion of a religious festival.

d. Club Meetings. Formally organized clubs, whether trade guilds, funerary societies, religious associations, or even philosophical schools, usually centered their regular meetings around a communal meal.

e. Religious Sects. Religious sectarian groups, such as the Essenes and the Christians, had a formal organization similar to that of the clubs and also centered many of their meetings around meals (IQS 6:1–6; IQSa 2:11–22; Jos. *JW* 2.8.5; 1 Cor 11:20, 33; Pliny, *Ep.* 10.96).

2. The Banquet. The banquet was a social event of the first order, not just a time to eat. Invitations would be extended in advance either informally or in formal, written form (Pl. *Symp.* 174A; Xen. *Symp.* 3–4; Sen. *Ben.* 4.39.3; Pliny *Ep.* 1.15.1; Sir 13:9; Matt 22:1–10; Luke 14:16–24). Elaborate preparations were often made before the banquet. Standard customs included visiting the baths, dressing in special clothing, and otherwise preparing one's appearance (Pl. *Symp.*; *ILS* 7212.2.30). The Jewish Essenes seem to have elevated the custom of bathing before meals to the level of religious ritual (Jos. *JW* 2.129).

When each guest arrived, he was directed to the couches by a servant who removed the guest's sandals and washed his feet before he reclined (Pl. *Symp.* 175A; Luke 7:44–46). After the guests had reclined and before the meal began, water would be brought for them to wash their hands, a custom that became connected with religious ritual in Judaism (Ath. 14.641d; Mark 7:3; *m. Ḥag.* 2:5).

Banquets tended to take place in rooms especially designed for dining, although presumably any room large enough to hold the couches would suffice. Excavations have revealed certain standard features of dining rooms whether in private homes, sanctuaries, or public buildings. A "standard" dining room was designed to hold couches end-to-end along the walls in a configuration whereby the diners were all facing inward toward one another. The *triclinium*, or three-couch arrangement, which provided for nine diners or three per couch, was the most widely used, although there were many variations. The term *triclinium* eventually came to be used to refer to the dining room in general.

Positions around the table were customarily given a ranking. The location of the "highest" position might vary from place to place (Plut. *Quaest. conv.* 619B); but there was always some sense of ranking presupposed by the position of the diners, beginning with the "highest" position, which position could vary somewhat, and then proceeding in a descending order, usually to the right around the room, to the "lowest" ranking position. Thus the host had to decide where to place the guests according to their rank in society. Plutarch relates a situation whereby a distinguished guest arrived late to a banquet and, not finding an available position worthy of his rank, left angrily (*Quaest. conv.* 615D). Luke's Jesus plays on this same theme in the parable of the places at table (Luke 14:7–11).

Diners would all recline on the left elbow and eat with the right hand so that the placement of the recliners would be orderly. Couches were of varying designs and often were intended to hold more than one diner. Alcibiades, for example, joined Agathon and Socrates on their couch when he arrived late at the banquet of Agathon in Plato's famous *Symposium* (213B). Similarly, the NT references to "lying close to the breast of Jesus" or in the "bosom" of Abraham (John 13:23; Luke 16:22) are best understood as references to the position of a diner reclining in a normal position to the right of the person named and probably sharing the same couch; such a position to the right of the host is a position of honor.

There were two major courses in a banquet, the *deipnon*, or eating part, and the *symposion* (symposium) or drinking part. This form is reflected in the Lord's Supper traditions in the NT in which the wine is drunk "after supper [*deipnon*]" (Luke 22:20; 1 Cor 11:25). In some cases there was also an appetizer course at the beginning of the meal (Ath. 2.58b–60b). This custom is reflected in our earliest

Jewish Passover liturgy in which an appetizer course precedes the main course (*m. Pesaḥ.* 10:3).

The courses were marked off by special rituals. At the end of the *deipnon,* the servants removed the tables, swept the floor, brought water for washing the hands, and sometimes passed around garlands and perfumes (Ath. 11.462c–d). Then the bowl of wine was brought in and mixed with water for drinking. The proportion of water to wine varied, but common mixtures were five parts water to two parts wine or three parts water to one part wine (Ath. 10.426d). This was to be determined by the presider at the meal, either the host or the "symposiarch." The beginning of the symposium would then be marked by the offering of a libation to the gods and other religious ceremonies, such as the singing of a hymn (Pl. *Symp.* 176A; Xen. *Symp.* 2.1). These ceremonies are mirrored in the blessing over the wine in Judaism and the wine ceremony in the Christian Eucharist (*b. Ber.* 51a; 1 Cor 10:16).

3. The Symposium. Although wine could be drunk during the meal itself, the major part of the wine drinking took place after the meal proper during the second course known as the symposium. This was a period of extended leisurely drinking during which time the entertainment of the evening would also take place. The symposium entertainment took many forms. There were traditional games, such as kottabos, a popular party game in which the guests would compete for accuracy at flinging the last drops of wine from their cups at a target in the middle of the room. There were also various types of traditional performances—dramatic, musical, and dancing (Xen. *Symp.;* Pliny *Ep.* 1.15, 1.2; Sir 32:3–6). It was not uncommon among Greeks and Romans to indulge in sexual practices during the symposium, either with the female flute players, who were widely assumed to be prostitutes, or with their male companions. Jews and Christians, however, as well as the more moralistic of the Greeks and Romans, made a point of avoiding such activities at their banquets (Pliny *H.N.* 14:28; Philo *Cont.* 75–78).

Symposium entertainment might also take on a nobler or more serious purpose. In the philosophical schools, for example, the entertainment might consist of a philosophical discussion, a dialogue on a topic and in a form consistent with the meal occasion (Plato *Symp.* 176E; Ath. 5.185a; Plut. *Quaest. conv.* 7.7). In religious associations, such as Bacchic and other pagan religious societies, the symposium entertainment was a form of community worship or proclamation, as we know from inscriptions in which the rules for the meetings of these associations define such activities at their gatherings for communal meals (*SIG*^{3} 1109.111–17). Similarly, discussion of the Torah at meals was highly commended in Judaism (Sir 9:15–16; Philo *Cont.* 75–78; *m. ʾAbot* 3.3).

Literary descriptions of symposium dialogues led to the development of the literary form of the symposium, a form that is widely utilized in philosophical writings of this period and is influential in Hellenistic Jewish and early Christian literature as well (see e.g., the *Symposiums* of Plato, Xenophon, and other philosophical writers; compare the *Letter of Aristeas*). Both the Jewish Passover liturgy and the description of early Christian worship found in 1 Corinthians 11–14 contain formal elements that are related to the literary form of the symposium (Stein 1957; Smith 1980).

C. Rules of Etiquette

Etiquette to the ancients was a part of the theory of ethics and was therefore included in ethical discussions in philosophical literature. Various philosophers are said to have written treatises on meal ethics or "symposium laws" (Pl. *Leg.* 2.671C; Ath. 5.186b). In these treatises the emphasis is placed on proper behavior at a meal and the ethical grounding of that behavior. Some of the same types of concerns are also found in the statutes governing the banquets of clubs and associations. Many traditional elements of these ethical discussions come to be incorporated into the ritual and ideology of religious meals.

Aspects of social ranking in society were especially addressed in rules of etiquette. Besides the ranking of positions at table, the custom of reclining itself carried implications of social ranking. Thus only the upper echelon of society were to recline; women, children, and slaves were to sit at the meal. In the Roman period this custom in regard to women seems to have been relaxed somewhat since we find evidence of women reclining at meals (Val. Max. 2.1.2; Petron. *Sat.* 67–69; Lucian *Symp.* 8). Furthermore, these customs might be varied by various social groups. For example, some religious and funerary associations seem to have freely included slaves and women in their banquets. Similarly, Jews specified that even the poor were to recline at the Passover (*m. Pesaḥ.* 10:1). Another way in which social ranking was addressed was by providing a greater quantity or quality of food to those of the upper echelon; this custom has been suggested as a major reason for the problems at the Christian meal in Corinth (1 Cor 11:17–34; Theissen, 1982).

Since social ranking was so firmly a part of meal customs, rules of etiquette were often addressed to the proper ways in which the host was to place the guests (Plut. *Quaest. conv.* 1.2). Similarly, guests were urged to accept the position assigned to them and not try to usurp someone else's position (Association of Diana and Antinous [*ILS* 7212.2.25]; Sir 13:11; 32:1; Luke 14:7–11). Another characteristic ethical concern, found especially in the Jewish wisdom tradition but not uncommon in Greco-Roman moralism as well, is the call for moderation in food and wine (Pliny *H.N.* 14.28; Philo *Cont.* 74.81–82; Sir 19:1–3; 31:12–18, 22–30; cf. Prov 23:1–3).

Rules of etiquette tended to be especially concerned with maintaining good relations among the guests. The table was no place for argument, accusation, or loud and abusive language (*SIG*^{3} 1109.63–75; Sir 31:31). Indeed, "factions" of any kind at the meal were especially out of order (*ILS* 7212.2.26–28; 1 Cor 11:17–34). Entertainment should be planned so that all can enjoy it. Thus conversation at the meal should proceed in an orderly manner and on subjects in which all can participate (Plut. *Quaest. conv.* 614E, 675A; *SIG*^{3} 1109.63–67; Sir 13:8–13; 32:3–9; 1 Cor 14:26–33).

The philosophical discussions of ethics at a meal became rather standardized over the centuries and apparently penetrated into popular morality at all levels of society. The standard arguments of the philosophers describe meal ethics in terms of the virtues of friendship, pleasure, and love *(eros)*. Although this technical terminology is not used consistently in the nonphilosophical literature, the ideas are similar. Because the meal is a time of sharing food and companionship, one's behavior should be concerned with the welfare of the other or with the enjoyment or pleasure of the group as a whole (Pl. *Leg.* 671C–E; Plut. *Quaest. conv.* 618A, 660B; Sir 31:15; 41:19; 1 Cor 14:12, 26–33, 39–40).

Bibliography

Becker, W. A. 1891. *Gallus, or Roman Scenes of the Time of Augustus.* 10th ed. London.

Becker, W. A., and Göll, H. 1889. *Charikles.* 8th ed. London.

Dentzer, J.-M. 1971. Aux origines de l'iconographie du banquet couché. *RArch:* 215–58.

———. 1982. *Le motif du banquet couché dans le Proche-Orient et le monde grec du VIIe au IVe siecle avant J.-C.* BEFAR 246e. Rome.

Safrai, S. 1976. Home and Family and Religion in Everyday Life. Vol. 2, 728–833 in *The Jewish People in the First Century,* ed. S. Safrai and M. Stern. CRINT. Philadelphia.

Smith, D. E. 1980. Social Obligation in the Context of Communal Meals: A Study of the Christian Meal in 1 Corinthians in Comparison with Graeco-Roman Communal Meals. Th.D. diss., Harvard.

Stein, S. 1957. The Influence of Symposia Literature on the Literary Form of the Pesaḥ Haggadah. *JJS* 8: 13–44.

Theissen, G. 1982. Social Integration and Sacramental Activity: An Analysis of 1 Cor. 11:17–34. Pp. 145–74 in *The Social Setting of Pauline Christianity: Essays on Corinth,* ed. J. H. Schutz. Philadelphia.

DENNIS E. SMITH

GRECO-ROMAN SACRED MEALS

In scholarly discussion, the term "sacred meal" has often been equated with the idea of "sacramental meal," using the Christian Eucharist as a model. This rather narrow definition restricts the phenomenon in a way that does not do justice to the range of religious meals in the ancient world. Here the term is being defined more broadly, to refer to meals that function as religious ritual or that include or are a part of religious ritual. Such meals were quite common in all religious traditions in the ancient world. Furthermore, they often seemed to have common elements, as Paul states in 1 Cor 10:21 when he counsels against confusing the "table of the Lord" with the "table of demons." To understand properly Jewish and Christian religious meals of this period therefore one must understand the phenomenon of sacred meals in general.

A. Religious Ritual in Everyday Meals
B. The Religious Banquet
C. The Sacrificial Banquet
D. Eating Sacred Foods

A. Religious Ritual in Everyday Meals

Normal, everyday meals had customary religious components. Such formalities were especially pronounced at the formal evening meal, the *deipnon* or banquet. Here there were customary religious rituals, typified by the reference in Plato's *Symposium* to the ceremonies marking the transition from the supper to the symposium: ". . . they made libation and sang a chant to the god and so forth, as custom bids, till they betook them to drinking" (176A). The libation was a ceremony in which a special cup of wine, customarily the first of the course, was dedicated to a traditional deity, most often Zeus Sōtēr or some epithet of Dionysus such as "to the Good Deity" (Diod. Sic. 4.3; Ath. 11.486f–487b, 15.675b–c). Throughout the banquet there was a sense of connection to Dionysus, the god of wine. Thus dishes and dining rooms were lavishly decorated with his image and his presence at the gathering was equated with the presence of wine and was appealed to in discussions of the proprieties of the banquet (Plut. *Quaest. conv.* 615A).

Similar religious customs were found in Judaism; for example, here also there were specified prayers over various foods and especially over the wine (*m. Ber.* 6:1–8:8; see also 1 Sam 9:13; Jos. *JW* 2.131). In this case, of course, the prayers were directed to the one God of the Jews. Although not much is known about everyday meal practices among the early Christians, a Jewish version of the benediction over the eucharistic wine is evidently indicated by the terminology "cup of blessing" in 1 Cor 10:16 (compare e.g., *b. Ber.* 51a).

B. The Religious Banquet

Since the banquet was the formalized meal par excellence, it was the meal most often utilized in religious ritual. The meal itself would follow the same pattern as a normal banquet. It would take on a special religious nature, however, according to the setting, such as in a sanctuary; or according to the occasion, such as a sacrifice or religious festival; or according to the group gathered for the meal, such as a religious association. In such cases, the religious interpretation of the meal would most often involve a special elaboration of a traditional custom or motif already present in the meal. Thus the Jewish Passover meal, the Christian Eucharist and agape, the Greek and Roman meals of religious associations, as well as the ubiquitous sacrificial meal were all meals with special religious significance that also were structured as standard Greco-Roman banquets.

The primary banquet motif that was utilized in religious ritual was the idea of festivity. That is to say, a religious meal was not a solemn occasion, but rather was an occasion for joy and celebration. Thus in Greek the term *euphrosynē,* meaning "mirth" or "merriment," came to be used as a technical term for meals in general, and specifically sacrificial meals (*SEG* 1.248.19–20; Dio Chrys. *Or.* 3.97; Pl. *Resp.* 364B–C). The LXX utilizes the term and its verbal form with this same meaning in OT texts. Here one finds the command to "rejoice before the Lord" at Jewish festival meals (Lev 23:40; Deut 12:12; 14:26; 16:11; 16:15). In the NT, the joyful nature of the banquet is mentioned less frequently (but see Acts 2:46) and is most often connected with eschatological themes, as in Luke 14:15: "Blessed is he who shall eat bread in the kingdom of God" (see also MESSIANIC BANQUET). Other references to festive joy *(euphrosynē)* in early Christian worship most likely refer as well to the fellowship meal, especially the form of the meal known as the agape (*Barn.* 15.9; *Sib. Or.* 8.485; on the agape see Jude 12; Ign. *Smyrn.* 8.2; see also Reicke 1951: 201–22). In general therefore religious banquets retained the sense of pleasure and celebration inherent in the occasion of a meal and simply interpreted these as part of the religious experience.

C. The Sacrificial Banquet

Sacrifice was a primary form of religious worship in all of the major cultures of the ancient world, including those of the Greeks, Romans, and Jews. There were, of course, some forms of sacrifice in which the entire animal was burned or destroyed (e.g., *sphagia* in Greek religion; compare the *ʿōlâ* [RSV: "burnt offering"] in Judaism). However, a standard type of sacrifice was one in which a portion of the meat was used by the worshippers for food (e.g., *thysia* in Greek religion; compare the *šĕlāmîm* [RSV: "peace offering"] in Judaism). In the Greek form of this type of sacrifice, the animal was first slain at the altar by the priest, then it was cut up and portions divided among the deity (whose portion was burned on the altar), the priest or temple (for the ongoing support of the cult), and the worshippers (as a gift from the god; see classic descriptions of Greek sacrifice in Homer, e.g., *Od.* 3.439–63, 14.418–36; see also Burkert 1983: 3–7; on the inherent connection of the meal to the sacrifice, see Dio Chrys. *Or.* 3.97; for Jewish sacrificial ritual, see Leviticus 1–7; Sir 50:11–21; *m. Tamid*). Among the Greeks it was sometimes specified that sacrificial meat was to be eaten within the temple precinct (see the *ou phora* restrictions ["Do not carry away"] in various Greek sacred law inscriptions [e.g., Dow 1965]; compare Lev 7:15–18; 22:30); in most cases, however, it was apparently left up to the worshippers as to whether they would eat it at the sanctuary site, take it home to be eaten, or sell it to the public (on sacrificial meat's being sold at the marketplace, see 1 Cor 10:25–29). Dining rooms were commonly provided at sanctuary sites; the meals held there could presumably vary from highly religious to purely social.

The nature of the religious meaning to be attached to sacrificial meals in Greek religion has been the subject of much debate in scholarship. Paul, for example, is aware of meals at temples as being purely social (1 Cor 8:10); yet he can also contrast the "table of the Lord" with the "table of demons" (1 Cor 10:19–22), implying that they can also be similar in religious meaning. Apparently the meaning of the meal could vary from person to person and from place to place without the meal itself being significantly different in form.

The primary religious motifs connected with the sacrificial meal include the element of joy or festivity as mentioned above as well as some sense of what is often called "communion with the deity." Plato, for example, refers to festival meals as times when human beings may find "respite from their troubles" by "associating in their feasts with gods" such as "the Muses, and Apollo the master of music, and Dionysus," who are presumably present in the music and wine respectively (*Leg.* 653D).

The presence of the deity at the meal could be expressed in various ways. Often, the deity was regarded as presiding over the entire meal insofar as the sacrifice took place at the temple in the deity's presence. Similarly, in Jewish tradition, sacrificial meals and festival meals were to take place "before the Lord" (Deut 12:17–18; cf. 12:12; 14:26; 16:11; et al.). Other texts and rituals are more specific as to the role of the deity in the ceremony. In some cases the deity is specifically defined as host at the meal; see, for example, the invitations of the God Serapis to dine at his temple (Youtie 1948). To these one might compare the representations of Jesus as host at various meals in the Gospels, especially in the Last Supper accounts (Mark 14:22–25 = Matt 26:26–29 = Luke 22:15–20 = 1 Cor 11:23–25). In other cases the gods are pictured as guests at the meal, and sometimes a place at table is even provided for them. This type of ceremony is known as the *theoxenia* in the Greek world and the *lectisternium* in the Roman world (e.g., Pind. *Pyth.* 3.93–96; Livy 29.14.14). To this may be compared the OT story of Abraham and Lot entertaining divine guests (Gen 18:1–19:26) and the various ways in which dining with Jesus and with the risen Lord are depicted in the Gospels, with obvious ramifications for the interpretation of the Christian Eucharist and agape (Smith 1987).

The NT makes use of the imagery of sacrificial meals in its descriptions of the Lord's Supper, connecting the ceremony with a sacrificial interpretation of the death of Jesus ("This is my body which is for you," 1 Cor 11:24; "This is my blood of the covenant, which is poured out for many," Mark 14:24). Here there is no meat but rather bread which, along with wine, is connected symbolically with the "meat" and "blood" of the sacrificial victim. The presence of the Lord at the meal is referred to in various ways (besides the images of guest and host mentioned above) such as: memorial ("Do this in memory of me," 1 Cor 11:24); eschatological proclamation ("You proclaim the Lord's death until he comes," 1 Cor 11:26); symbolic representation ("The cup of blessing which we bless, is it not a participation in the blood of Christ? The bread which we break, is it not a participation in the body of Christ?" 1 Cor 10:16; "He who eats my flesh and drinks my blood has eternal life," John 6:54); and community identity ("Because there is one bread, we who are many are one body, for we all partake of the one bread," 1 Cor 10:17).

D. Eating Sacred Foods

Another way to define the concept of sacred meals is to place the emphasis on the eating of sacred foods rather than on the formal meal ceremony. This perspective is most closely related to the idea of sacramentalism in Christian eucharistic tradition. It is, of course, probable that sacrificial meat took on some sort of sacred quality, although the evidence for this is sketchy and much debated. Furthermore, wine tended to take on a numinous quality connected with the god Dionysus. But the idea of sacred foods is most often associated with rituals in the mystery religions. For example, during the initiation ceremony of the mysteries of Demeter at Eleusis a special potion concocted from grain, called the *kykeon*, was drunk; and this ceremony seemed somehow to be connected with the experience of the divine (Clem. Al. *Protr.* 2.21.2). In the mysteries of Mithras, there are references to a ritual meal with water and bread that was supposedly so close in meaning to the Christian Eucharist that Justin accused the Mithraists of copying the Christians (*Apol.* 1.66.4). Such "mystery meals" are often compared to the Christian Lord's Supper traditions since they seem to offer the nearest parallels to the idea of ritual food being somehow imbued with divine or "spiritual" power (as in 1 Cor 10:1–5; and Ign. *Eph.* 20.2).

A variation of this idea has the worshipper actually ingesting the deity, a practice referred to as "theophagy." This is the apparent sense of the Christian Lord's Supper in John 6:53–57 and in many liturgies outside the NT (Ign. *Smyrn.* 7.1). Some scholars have proposed finding a parallel to this idea in a ritual connected with Dionysus whereby worshippers acted out the actual ingestion of the deity by eating a raw animal. The evidence for this ritual is rather vague, however; and its interpretation is disputed in many recent studies, leading some to conclude that there is no evidence for the actual ritual practice of theophagy in the ancient world outside of Christianity (Henrichs 1980: 230). Indeed, there is still much debate over the form and meaning of sacred meals in the various mystery religions in general (Kane 1975). In most cases it would appear that where we have firm evidence of meals being eaten, it is simply another variation of the ordinary Greco-Roman banquet being utilized in a religious setting.

Bibliography

Burkert, W. 1983. *Homo Necans: The Anthropology of Ancient Greek Sacrificial Ritual and Myth.* Berkeley.

Casabona, J. 1966. *Récherches sur le vocabulaire des sacrifices en Grec, des origines à la fin de l'époque classique.* Paris.

Dow, S. 1965. The Greater Demarkhia of Erkhia. *BCH* 89: 180–213.

Henrichs, A. 1980. Human Sacrifice in Greek Religion: Three Case Studies. Pp. 195–235 in *Le sacrifice dans l'antiquité.* Fondation Hardt pour l'étude de l'antiquité classique, entretiens tome 27. Geneva.

Kane, J. P. 1975. The Mithraic Cult Meal in its Greek and Roman Environment. Vol. 2, pp. 313–51 in *Mithraic Studies: Proceedings of the First International Congress of Mithraic Studies,* ed. J. R. Hinnells. Manchester.

Klauck, H.-J. 1982. *Herrenmahl und hellenistischer Kult: Eine religionsgeschichtliche Untersuchung zum ersten Korintherbrief.* NTAbh n.s. 15. Muenster.

Nock, A. D. 1944. The Cult of Heroes. *HTR* 37: 141–74.

Reicke, B. 1951. *Diakonie, Festfreude und Zelos in verbindung mit der altchristlichen Agapenfeier.* UUÅ 5. Uppsala.

Smith, D. E. 1980. Social Obligation in the Context of Communal Meals: A Study of the Christian Meal in 1 Corinthians in Comparison with Graeco-Roman Communal Meals. Th.D. diss., Harvard.

———. 1987. Table Fellowship as a Literary Motif in the Gospel of Luke. *JBL* 106: 613–38.

Youtie, H. C. 1948. The Kline of Sarapis. *HTR* 41: 9–29.

Dennis E. Smith

MEARAH (PLACE) [Heb *mĕʿārâ*]. A place located between the ancient coastal cities of Tyre and Sidon, and identified among the numerous territories yet remaining for Israel to occupy (Josh 13:4). The exact identification and location of Mearah have been greatly disputed because of the difficulties of the text. The LXX reads *enantion* (or *apó*) *Gazēs,* "before [from] Gaza," which might suggest the reading *mēʿāzâ* (with *mem* representing the preposition and *zayin* replacing *reš*). But it can hardly be said that Gaza belonged to Sidon. A number of places have been suggested with reference to the nature and location of Mearah, including the caves of Mughar Jezzin E of Sidon; a location along the Wâdī Ara in the plain of Megiddo; and the reading of *mēʿārîm* as "from the cities." The place has also been identified by some scholars as Mogheiriyeh, 6 miles (ca. 9.5 km) NE of Sidon.

Ray L. Roth

MEASURE, MEASUREMENT. See WEIGHTS AND MEASURES.

MEAT. See MEAL CUSTOMS (JEWISH DIETARY LAWS); ZOOLOGY.

MEBUNNAI (PERSON) [Heb *mĕbunnay*]. Mentioned only in 2 Sam 23:27 as one of "the Thirty" (2 Sam 23:18–39), David's corps of military elite *(haggibbōrîm).* He was known as a native of Hushah *(ḥūšâ),* a village probably to be identified with modern Husan, 6 miles SW of Bethlehem. In spite of the possible kingdom period attestation of the name (Zeron 1979: 156), MT *mbny* (LXX *sabouchai*) should most likely be understood as a textual corruption (McCarter *2 Samuel* AB, 492) and the man himself identified with Sibbecai the Hushathite of 2 Sam 21:18 (= 1 Chr 20:4; see also 11:29; 27:11). See also DAVID'S CHAMPIONS.

Bibliography

Elliger, K. 1933. Die dreissig Helden Davids. *PJ* 31: 29–75.

Mazar, B. 1963. The Military Elite of King David. *VT* 13: 310–20.

Zeron, A. 1979. The Seal of "M-B-N" and the List of David's Heroes. *TA* 6: 156–57.

David L. Thompson

MECHERATHITE [Heb *mĕkērātî*]. The gentilic designation of Hepher, one of David's champions, a select class of warriors directly attached to the king for special assignments, named in the list of 1 Chr 11:10–47 (v 36), a list which, up to v 41a, parallels that of 2 Sam 23:8–39. If the designation is correct in this form, it refers to an unknown family group or place for the origin of Hepher. However, whereas 1 Chr 11:35b–36a reads, "Eliphal the son of Ur, Hepher the Mecherathite," the parallel text in 2 Sam 23:34 reads, "Eliphelet the son of Ahasbai of Maacah." Both texts appear to have suffered corruptions. If in Chronicles two names have been derived from the original name of Eliphelet's father (Driver *NHT,* 371; Rudolph *Chronikbücher* HAT, 102), then "the Mecherathite" is a variant of "son of the Maacathite" (RSV "of Maacah"), which might then be a reference to a Judahite clan associated with Eshtemoa the Maacathite (1 Chr 4:19), ancestor of a town S of Hebron (McCarter *2 Samuel* AB, 498–99).

Rodney K. Duke

MECONAH (PLACE) [Heb *mĕkōnâ*] 1. Settlement in S Judah listed among the villages occupied by those returning from Exile in Babylon (Neh 11:26). Its name may be derived from the root *kwn* ("be fixed"), perhaps meaning "resting-place" or "residence." There is general agreement that the list in Neh 11:25–36 is derived from an official document of the postexilic period (see Myers *Ezra, Nehemiah* AB, 187). If this list follows geographic order, Meconah should be found somewhere in the vicinity of Ziklag and En-Rimmon, both of which are located in the Negeb district of the tribal territory of Judah (Josh 15:31–32). Based on this geographic hint, Simons (*GTTOT,* 145) proposes an identification with Khirbet umm ed-Deimineh, on the NE outskirts of Beer-sheba. Unfortunately, we do not know whether this site was occupied during postexilic times.

WADE R. KOTTER

MEDAD (PERSON) [Heb *mêdād*]. According to Num 11:26 and 27, one of two elders of Israel (Eldad is the other) who received the spirit and prophesied inside the camp of Israel. Num 11:16–30 report God's distribution of a portion of the spirit given Moses to seventy elders of Israel. Moses and these seventy went outside the camp to the tent sanctuary. The elders received the spirit and prophesied there. Eldad and Medad had been "registered" (RSV), but did not go out of the camp, and so received the spirit there.

Gray (*Numbers* ICC, 114) points to the tension in the description of the relation between the seventy and Eldad and Medad (i.e., if "registered" means they were part of the seventy specified by God [Num 11:16], this conflicts with the report that seventy went out to the tent [Num 11:24]). Noth (*Numbers* OTL, 90) on this basis regards Num 11:26–29 as an addition to the story of the seventy elders and speculates that Eldad and Medad represent actual prophetic groups in Israel that used this story to claim Mosaic legitimation as part of their struggle for recognition.

The Sam. Pent. and LXX offer a variant spelling of the name "Modad" *(môdād)*—perhaps under the influence of the name Almodad *(ʾalmôdād)* in Gen 10:26. (Gray, 114) and Snaith (*Numbers* NCBC, 232) seem to favor this. However, in view of the support for the MT provided by the Vg and Peshitta, as well as the Targums, the spelling Medad should be retained.

The Palestinian Targums, by offering words for the prophecies Medad and Eldad were said to have delivered, exemplify some of the later exegetical interest these figures attracted. A like interest is attested in the Christian tradition by the lost *Book of Eldad and Modad.* See ELDAD AND MODAD.

RICHARD D. WEIS

MEDAN (PERSON) [Heb *mĕdān*]. A son of Abraham and Keturah and brother of Midian (Gen 25:2; 1 Chr 1:32). The "sons of Keturah" are a group of Arabian tribes and cities of the 8th through 5th centuries B.C. See also KETURAH. Medan could have been a tribe or a settlement in Wâdī Mudân (or Madân), which was situated in the basalt fields S of Midian. The wadi is mentioned by Islamic historians and geographers for the 7th century A.D. (Knauf 1985: 20–21). The name can be explained by either Arabic *dûn,* "low, inferior," or *madân,* a plant (*Ocymum hadiense*). Whereas Medan in Gen 25:2 and 1 Chr 1:32 is an independent geographic entry and not a variant for Midian mistakenly included, the reference to the "Medanites" in Gen 37:36 is an intentional misspelling for "Midianites" in order to mark this verse as a gloss (Knauf 1988: 27).

Bibliography

Knauf, E. A. 1985. Madiáma. *ZDMG* 135: 16–21.
———. 1988. *Midian.* ADPV. Wiesbaden.

ERNST AXEL KNAUF

MEDEBA (PLACE) [Heb *mêdĕbaʾ*]. One of the cities of the Moabite Mishor that was conquered and occupied by the Israelite tribes (Num 21:30; Josh 13:9, 16). The battle between the army of David and the coalition of Ammonites and Arameans (1 Chr 19:7) occurred in the vicinity of this city. Liberated by Mesha, the king of Moab (Mesha Stele, lines 7–9; *ANET,* 320), it is mentioned in the later biblical texts among the cities of Moab (Isa 15:2). During the Maccabean revolt "the Sons of Jambri" came out of the city and laid an ambush for a Jewish convoy led by John. They plundered the caravan and killed the brother of Judah. His death was avenged by Jonathan and Simon (1 Macc 9:36–42).

Josephus reveals that Medeba was subsequently conquered by John Hyrcanus after a long siege (*Ant* 13.9.1) and remained in the hands of the Jews at the time of Alexander Jannaeus (*Ant* 13.15.4). Hyrcanus II, in exchange for aid requested by him in the war against his brother Aristobulus II, promised to restore the city to King Aretas of Petra together with the other cities in the region (*Ant* 14.1.4).

The *Onomasticon* (128.20), and the geographers of the Roman-Byzantine period, Ptolemy (5.16), Hierocles (n. 721), and Giorgio Ciprio (n. 1062), record it as a city of the province of Arabia.

Christianity had spread by the end of the first two centuries to Arabia, and the region of Medeba had its martyrs during the persecutions of Diocletian. Only from the Acts of the Council of Chalcedon (A.D. 451) do we learn of the existence of a Christian community at Medeba headed by a bishop supported by Constantine, the Archbishop and Metropolitan of Bostra, who signed the conciliar decisions.

A. The Exploration of the City

The ruins of Medeba that preserve the name of the ancient city (M.R. 225124) are 30 km S of Amman on the King's Highway and were visited by U. Seetzen in 1807. Burckhardt passed by in 1812. The canon Tristram, who stopped among the ruins for four days in 1872, gives the first accurate description. In December of 1880 some bedouin Christian families, the Azizat of Kerak, pitched their tents among the ruins, which were given to them by the Turkish authorities, and soon they began to construct a provisional shelter with the squared stones from ancient buildings. Sensitized by their priests, among whom was don Giuseppe Manfredi, the new arrivals took care to conserve what they occasionally discovered. In 1881 the explorers of the survey brought to light the first significant evidence of the site's antiquity and history. In 1887 the missionary sent to Jerusalem the transcription of the first inscriptions of the mosaic floors of Medeba that turned out to belong to the Church of the Virgin. A guest of don Manfredi, G. Schumacher, stopped at Medeba in October 1891 and supplied the first general plan of the ruins and its monuments. The following year, P. Sejourne, after a stay at Medeba, wrote a brief summary about the discoveries that became ever more numerous. This was followed by Bliss in 1897, don Manfredi in 1898, Kluge and Pavlouskin in 1903, and Musil and Metaxakis in 1905. In 1897 the Medeba Map (see below) was discovered and published, which brought scholarly attention to Medeba. In the same year the mosaic of the crypt of Elisha and of the Church of the Prophet Elijah were brought to light with their inscriptions, along with other mosaics. In that year Medeba became "the city of the mosaics." Regular excavations were conducted in the city from 1965 to 1968 and again beginning in 1979.

B. Historical and Archaeological Synthesis

Medeba was built on a natural elevation of the Jordanian plateau with steep slopes to the W, S, and SE; the area to the N gradually slopes toward the surrounding plain. The tell has an easily recognizable acropolis and lower city. Until recently, the discoveries have been concentrated on the system of terraces of the acropolis slopes, and in the lower city where habitation developed in the Roman-Byzantine period. On the slopes of the heights that surround Medeba to the W and S was a necropolis which existed until the middle of the 2d millennium B.C. The chance discovery of two tombs in this area are until now the only witnesses of the occupation of the tell of Medeba from the 13th to the 10th centuries B.C. Otherwise, tombs go back to the 1st century B.C.

A great number of tombs from the 1st century A.D. were discovered and found to contain inscriptions attesting that Medeba and its surrounding territory belonged to the Nabatean kingdom of Petra. One inscription on basalt, in two exemplars, came from a funerary monument constructed in A.D. 37 (the time of Aretas IV) by the commander of the city of Abdobodat of the Amirat tribe for his father, Itaybel. A second bilingual inscription in Nabatean and Greek, dated to the third year of the province of Arabia (constituted by Trajan in A.D. 106), records the same tribe of the Amirat. A Greek inscription, from a tomb constructed by Abdallah the son of Anamos, is dated to the 43d year of the province (A.D. 148). With the exception of a centurion of the III Cyrenian legion, Gaius Domitius Alexander, who was honored by the city for his "worthy act," personal names in the inscriptions of Medeba are for the most part Semitic during both the Roman and Byzantine periods.

Coins minted in the city from the period of the Province of Arabia, with which Medeba was always associated, have been dated to the time of Septimius Severus, Caracalla, Geta, and Severus Alexander. There are essentially three types of scenes on the reverse of such coins: the Helios in four rows, the Tyche of the city, and a *betyl* in a four-columned temple. The Tyche is shown in two variants: standing and holding a cornucopia in her left hand, with a *betyl* in her right hand; or seated on a throne with a scepter in her right hand and an unidentified object in her left hand. From the Roman period is the colonnaded street oriented E-W that passed in front of the exedra (or nymphaeum) on which the Church of the Virgin was constructed, as are the capitals and pediments reused in the church of the 6th century.

Medeba's maximum urban extent, along with its most opulent lifestyle, occurred in the 6th and 7th centuries A.D. However, the inscriptions which accompany the mosaic floors of the churches are the primary sources of historical information available. Probably in the first decades of the 6th century, while Cyrus was bishop of Medeba, the baptistery of the cathedral and the church of the monastery of Kaiano on Mt. Nebo in the vicinity of the springs of Moses were decorated with mosaics. In 531 and 536 the bishop of the city was Elias, as recorded in the mosaics on Mt. Nebo. In 562, when the bishop of the diocese was John, a mosaic was completed in the chapel of Saint Theodore the Martyr in the atrium of the cathedral. During his episcopate John had a chapel built in the SE sector of the city in which was a mosaic. The Church of the Apostles was later built next to this chapel.

Two churches were built with mosaics in the city of Nebo. Probably in the same period a mosaic depicting iconographic motifs from the tragedy of Euripides was placed in the Room of Hippolytus to the N of the nymphaeum on the columned street. In the mosaic, the anonymous artist represented the Christianized Tyche of Medeba, seated with a cornucopia in her right hand and the cross in her left, beside the Tyche of Rome and of Gregoria-Constantinople, the two capitals of the empire of Justinian. At the same time the geographic map of the biblical lands (see C below) was placed in the church in the vicinity of the N gate of the city. An inscription on the plaster of a great cistern, on the N side of the church, attests the interest that the central authority had for Medeba, which lacked natural springs and therefore had to rely on aqueducts to supply water. In the valley SE of the acropolis was a great reservoir, 100 m square and 10 m deep.

The inscriptions record that from 576 until 602, Sergius, "the friend of God, the contemplative," was bishop. During his episcopate a mosaic was placed in the atrium of the cathedral (A.D. 576); the Church of the Apostles was built (578); the Basilica of Nebo was built in honor of Moses with the addition of the new baptistery, and the diaconicon was begun and brought to completion (587–98); the construction began of the ecclesiastical complex along the Roman road including the Church of the Virgin; and the Church of the Prophet Elijah which was finished, except for the crypt alleged to be Saint Elisha's (A.D. 602).

In 603 the bishop Leonizo, "sweetest and true friend of peace," succeeded Sergius. In that year a mosaic was placed in an empty space N of the church in the complex of the cathedral. In 608 the complex along the Roman road was completed with the funds set apart by Mena the son of Pamphylius. A chapel dedicated to the Virgin Theotokos was added to the baptistery on the S wall of the basilica.

Besides these dated monuments, several other churches and public areas had mosaics in them in the second half of the 6th century, when the activity of the mosaic artwork at Medeba was most intense.

After a period of silence in the historical sources and following the arrival of the Muslim forces, perhaps in 662, Bishop Theophanus led the Christian community. In February 662 the restoration of the mosaic of the Church of the Virgin on the Roman road was completed. The dedicatory inscription reveals that "the people—lovers of Christ of the humble city of Madaba" contributed to the completion of this work.

During the Umayyad period (A.D. 719/20), a mosaic was built in the church at Main, which was on the highest point of the acropolis. This building still stands and was the last-dated Christian monument of the region of Medeba. The mosaic is usually included in the school of Medeba.

C. The Madeba Map

The Madeba Map is the most famous of the antiquities of the site and is a mosaic map in the floor of one of the 6th-century churches. It is cartographically significant since it is the earliest extant map of Palestine. It apparently portrayed originally the area from Byblos, on the Mediterranean coast, to Thebes in Egypt. The inscriptions are written in Greek, and the layout generally follows the geographic orientations described in Eusebius' *Onomasticon.*

Taking into account the floor plan of the church and the position of the remaining fragments of the mosaic, the map must have decorated a panel 15.7 m long and 5.6 m wide. The approximately 150 remaining toponyms, which have for the most part been identified, refer to places located from the N extremity of Tyre and Sidon S to the delta of the Nile and from the Mediterranean Sea to the Arabian desert. The map is oriented towards the E, as are the cities and the buildings with their captions, which could be seen and read by whoever entered the church and faced the altar. In spite of the space limitations, which resulted in only approximate locations of the cities, it is clear that the intention was to provide the location of places along the highway networks of the region.

The places are indicated for the most part by vignettes and captions. The vignettes indicate the importance of the toponyms. The physical features of the Palestinian region are rendered with a pictorial realism that makes them easily identifiable: the central axis is formed by the course of the Jordan river and the Dead Sea; the Transjordanian plain with its steep wadis extends to the E; and to the W the mountains of Samaria and Judah are distinguished from the coastal plain. Along with the watercourses, the sea, and the mountains the mosaicist has added other easily comprehensible symbols, such as the palm trees that accompany the oases of Jericho and Zoar, the sources of the Jordan valley, the thickets along the course of the river, the ford with its characteristic hanging ferries, fish in the current, and two boats on the waters of the Dead Sea.

More important from a historical perspective are the peculiar indications of a place, like the twelve stones inserted into the wall of the Church of Golgotha, the well of Jacob at Shechem, the basin baptistery of the spring of Philip in the vicinity of Beth-zur, the terebinth or oak of Mamre, the basins in the springs of Calliroe, and the configuration of Kerak as a city-fortress in an isolated position on the mountain.

The mosaic reaches its figurative summit in the vignette of Jerusalem, which in some way is the central idea of the composition if not its exact physical center. The city, seen from a bird's-eye view, is represented with its walls, gates, streets, and principal buildings identifiable. The Cardo, which starts in the N with a central plaza in which is erected a memorial column, is dominated by the Constantinian complex of the Basilica of the Holy Sepulcher.

On the level of historical geography, the map's originality lies in these details. It depends on an ancient road map brought up to date for the needs of pilgrims of the 6th century who visited the Holy Land. On the artistic level, the map can be viewed as part of the renewed classicism of the Justinian era, of which the mosaics of Medeba provide numerous witnesses.

From the captions of the toponyms and principally by the direct references to the tribes of Israel (from the blessing of Jacob, which is cited in full), it is clear that the map is, above all, a document of biblical geography that had the *Onomasticon* of Eusebius as its primary source. The map encompasses the territory of the twelve biblical tribes and the surrounding regions, in such a way as to reflect the confines of Canaan as promised to Abraham (Gen 15:18). The addition of the localities of the NT and the preeminence given to Christian sanctuaries, to churches, and to the Basilica of the Holy Sepulcher make the map a contemporized Christian rereading of the story of salvation in its geographic aspect. At the center of the redeemed world is the holy city of Jerusalem that has as its primary building the Constantinian complex constructed on the Rock of Calvary and on the Tomb of Jesus.

Bibliography

Avi-Yonah, M. 1954. *The Madaba Map.* Jerusalem.

Donner, H., and Cuppers, H. 1977. *Die Mosaikarte von Madeba I.* Wiesbaden.

Gatier, P. L. fc. *Inscriptions Grecques et Latines: Philadelphia-Amman et Madaba.*

Harding, G. L. 1953. An Early Iron Age Tomb at Madaba. *PEFA* 6: 27–33.

Lux, U. 1968. Eine altchristliche-Kirche in Madeba. *ZDPV* 84: 106–58.

Paviloskij, A., and Kluge, N. 1903. Madaba. *Izvestija russkago archeologiskago Instituta w Constantinople* 8: 79–115.

Piccirillo, M. 1975. Una tomba del Ferro I a Madaba. *LASBF* 25: 199–224.

———. 1981. La cattedrale di Madaba. *LASBF* 31: 299–332.

———. 1982. La chiesa della Vergine a Madaba. *LASBF* 32: 373–408.

———. fc. *Chiese e mosaici di Giordania.* Vol. 2, Madaba.

Sejourne, P. M. 1982. Medaba. *RB* 1: 617–44.

Spijkerman, A. 1978. *The Coins of the Decapolis and Provincia Arabia.* Ed. M. Piccirillo. Jerusalem.

MICHELE PICCIRILLO

MEDIA (PLACE) [Heb *māday*]. An ancient Iranian kingdom which rose to power in the 7th century B.C., was allied with Babylon in the overthrow and destruction of the Neo-Assyrian Empire in 612 B.C., and was eventually absorbed into the Achaemenid Empire by Cyrus II. See CYRUS. Throughout Achaemenid history the Medes remained the second most important people in the empire after the Persians (see Esth 1:3).

Medes first appear in a Neo-Assyrian account of a military campaign in 835 B.C. in central W Iran. Continuing references to W Iran in Assyrian documents from the 9th to the 7th centuries B.C. show that the Medes were concentrated in central W Iran in the area of modern Kermanshah and along the High Road leading to modern Hamadan. To the S lay the kingdom of Ellipi; to the N the kingdom of Mannea.

It is clear that in the 9th and 8th centuries there was no unified kingdom of Media. The Assyrian texts speak of many small polities which are of either mixed ethnic composition or primarily Median, and which are ruled by "kings" or tribal chiefs. The Median language, documented in onomasticons, some place names, and loan words in Persian, is old NW Iranian (possibly the ancestor of modern Kurdish). There is, however, evidence in cuneiform texts for growing Median political unity during the 7th century; and Herodotus in his *Persian Wars* provides a detailed story of the creation and growth of that unity which is undoubtedly largely legendary.

According to Herodotus, Deioces was the founder of a centralized Median state in the 8th century B.C. Deioces was famous for his sense of justice, and the Medes invited him to be an adjudicator of their disputes. On condition that they make him king and build a great city at Ecbatana (Hamadan), he agreed. He is supposed to have reigned for 53 years. Deioces was succeeded by his son, Phraortes, who is reputed to have conquered the Persians. He lost his life in battle against the Assyrians after ruling 40 years. His son, Cyaxares, ruled 40 years and completely reorganized the Median army. Having done so, he allied himself with the Babylonians; and together they successfully effected the capture of Nineveh in 612 B.C. and the overthrow of the Neo-Assyrian Empire. Cyaxares was succeeded by his son, Astyages, who ruled for 35 years at Ecbatana, the capital of Media, until overthrown or conquered (the texts are not clear) by Cyrus the Great of Persia in 550 B.C.

Astyages and Cyaxares are well documented in contemporary cuneiform texts. From these sources it is clear that Cyaxares was the king of a united Media, which played a major role in the overthrow of the Neo-Assyrians. Following the fall of Nineveh, the Neo-Assyrian Empire was divided between the Medes and the Babylonians. Tradition has it that this expanded Media included territories as far E on the Iranian plateau as the area of modern Tehran, the whole of central-western and NW Iran, the mountainous areas of Anatolia as far W as the river Halys, and parts of N Syria (probably including the city of Harran). Thus when Cyrus the Great conquered Media, he fell heir to vast highland territories of the Near East. Astyages, and his war with Cyrus and the Persians, is also well documented in contemporary cuneiform texts. On the other hand, careful examination has failed to identify in contemporary texts the Phraortes and Deioces mentioned by Herodotus. Thus there remains no sound textual basis for the early history of a united kingdom of Media extending back through the early 7th and into the late 8th century. Nevertheless, a growing Median unity and power is historically documented for the latter half of the 7th century.

Depending on one's interpretation of the data, it can be argued that there is some evidence in the archaeological record of the 7th century B.C. which indicates increasing cultural unity in central-western and NW Iran and which might be associated with the political and military unification of Media. The three principal sites thus far excavated in W Iran which can with some certainty be described as Median are Baba Jan, Nush-i Jan, and Godin level II.

The geographic term "Media" is still used in Hellenistic times to refer to NW Iran, primarily to the regions now called Kurdistan and Azerbaijan. Clearly Media, and the Medes, played an important role in the early history of Iran.

T. CUYLER YOUNG, JR.

MEDICINE AND HEALING. Throughout the biblical tradition, healing is perceived as the work of Yahweh and his divinely empowered agents. In the Hellenistic period, these agents include physicians, although for the most part the biblical writers are hostile toward medicine, or they simply ignore it as having a potential for healing. How sickness is viewed, and therefore how healing is accomplished, are variously understood in the biblical writings. It is evident that changes in these perceptions correspond with changes in the cultural setting of the various biblical writers.

A. Yahweh as Healer

In all three sections of the Jewish Scriptures—the Pentateuch, the Prophets, and the Writings—the image of Yahweh as healer is present as a central aspect of God's relationship to the covenant people. In Genesis 20, where the story is told of Abraham's having deceived Abimelech by telling him that Sarah is his sister, Abraham intercedes with God to ward off punishment for Abimelech's unwitting sin. The result is that God heals Abimelech, his wife, and his slaves of the infertility which God had sent upon them (Gen 20:17). Following God's deliverance of Israel from slavery in Egypt by means of the plagues and the crossing of the Red Sea, Yahweh promises that if Israel obeys the commandments of God, the nation will escape all the diseases which beset the Egyptians, because "I am Yahweh, your healer" (Exod 15:26). Similarly in the Song of Moses (Deuteronomy 32), Yahweh declares, "There is no other god beside me; I kill and I make alive; I wound and I heal" (32:39).

Job celebrates the correctional role of God and "the chastening of the Almighty," and notes: "For he wounds, but he binds up; he smites, but his hands heal" (Job 5:17–18). The theme of God's restoring the faithful, following either human disobedience or divine chastening (which runs through the Psalms), is linked with healing (Pss 30:2; 41:4). At times healing is associated with forgiveness (Ps 103:3), with deliverance from imminent destruction (Ps 107:19–20), and with renewal of wounded human spirits (Ps 147:30).

It is in the Prophets, however, that Yahweh's role as healer is most fully represented. In Isaiah there are the repeated appeals to Israel to turn back to God and be healed (Isa 6:10; 19:22; 30:26), as well as the report of the ailing king Hezekiah's appeal to God to give him health and life (Isa 38:16). The dual roles of Yahweh as the one who both smites and heals are described with respect to the Egyptians (Isa 19:22) and Israel (Isa 57:18–19). In Isa 53:5, however, it is the suffering of the Servant of Yahweh that is to effect healing of God's people. Jeremiah appeals to the nation in God's behalf to return to God in order to find healing (Jer 3:22). Although he elsewhere laments the apparent absence of a physician to restore the health of the people (Jer 8:22), he also affirms in God's behalf the divine intention to restore and renew them (Jer 30:17; 33:6). The Exile of Israel to Babylon is a divine judgment from which there is no escape, since the sickness of the nation is beyond healing (Jer 8:15, 18, 22; 10:19; 14:19; 15:18; 17:9; 30:12–13; 46:11). The same note of the inescapable judgment, for which there is no healing, is sounded by Hosea and Nahum in connection with the captivity of the N tribes by the Assyrians (Hosea 5:13; Nahum 3:19). Analogously, God's vindication of Israel after her captivity in Babylon will result in judgment on that city, for which there is to be no healing (Jer 51:7–9). The image of Yahweh as healer in a more specific sense is offered by Ezekiel in his rebuke of Israel for its failure to care for the sick and the crippled (Ezek 34:4)—a role which Yahweh will fulfill for the benefit of the weak, the ailing, and the lost (Ezek 34:16). Zechariah offers a similar rebuke to those leaders of the people who fail to meet the needs of the maimed and the needy (Zech 11:15–17). Malachi announces the coming of an agent of God, "the Sun of Righteousness"—which means here, "the one who sets things right"—whose chief resource is "healing in its wings" (Mal 4:2).

B. Healing and Sickness as Signs of God's Favor and Punishment

Already implied in the roles of Yahweh and his agents, as sketched above, is the conviction that God gives or restores health to the faithful and sends sickness to the erring and disobedient. In addition to the previously mentioned punishment of Abimelech for taking Abraham's wife (Gen 20:1–18), there are reports of similar judgments on pharaoh (Gen 12:10–20) and again on Abimelech for taking Isaac's wife (Gen 28:1–14). The fact that these stories may be variants of a single tradition serves only to underscore the conviction evident in these materials that God brings sickness on those who violate the divine statutes, even unintentionally.

For members of the people, Israel, there is a direct link between sickness and ritual impurity, as is spelled out in great detail with respect to leprosy (Leviticus 13–14). That healing has taken place is to be confirmed by the priest (Lev 13:16; 18:37; 14:3), and atoning sacrifices are to be offered with the aim of attaining a cure of the disease (Lev 14:19–21, 29). Miriam is stricken with leprosy for her audacity in claiming a role equal with that of Moses as God's instrument (Numbers 12). Moses appeals to God for her healing, which takes place shortly (Num 12:13–15). Similarly, the bitter complaints of the people about the food supplied by God for them during the wilderness journey result in God's sending deadly serpents among them; when they become penitent, God provides through Moses a remedy from the deadly bite of the serpents (Num 21:4–9). When the Philistines captured the ark of the covenant and took it to their territory, the plague of tumors that broke out led their leaders to send the ark back to the land of Israel (1 Sam 4:10–6:18). Those who looked into the sacred ark out of curiosity (1 Sam 6:19) and even one who reached out to steady it as it was being transported on a wobbly cart (2 Sam 6:6–7) were struck dead for having violated the instrument of Yahweh's presence among his people. Similarly, Jeroboam's initial resistance to the unnamed "man of God" results in his arm's drying up, while the latter's failure to obey the word of Yahweh is punished by his being eaten by a lion (1 Kgs 13:1–25). On the other hand, Hezekiah's petition to Yahweh concerning his seemingly fatal illness is answered by the king's being restored to health. The assurance that this will take place is given by the backward movement of the sun on the sun dial (2 Kgs 20:1–11).

C. Physicians Offer Useless Advice

The relatively rare passages in the Hebrew Bible which mention physicians associate them with embalming or with unreliable claimants to healing powers. Joseph arranges with Egyptian "physicians" to prepare his father's body for transport to Israel and burial there (Gen 50:1–14). Asa, the king of Israel, is condemned because he did not seek healing from God for his lingering illness but turned instead to the physicians (2 Chr 16:12). The worthlessness of physicians is implied by Job in his rebuke of those who offer him useless advice (Job 13:4), as it is by Jeremiah's rhetorical question about the lack of a healing agent for God's people (Jer 8:22–9:6) and his sarcastic counsel to Egypt and Babylon to turn to physicians for help to escape the impending judgment of God (Jer 46:11; 51:8).

D. Prophets as Agents of Healing

Elijah, who took up residence at the home of a widow in Zarephath in the land of Sidon (1 Kgs 17:8–16), restores to life her son who was stricken with a fatal illness (17:17–23). This leads the widow to recognize the prophet as a man of God in whose mouth the word of Yahweh dwells (17:24). Similarly, the Syrian army commander, Naaman, seeks and receives a cure for his leprosy through Elisha, the prophet of Yahweh, who instructs him to bathe in the river Jordan, which he does and is cured (2 Kgs 5:1–14). This experience of a cure through obedience to the word of the man of God leads Naaman to declare that there is no God in all the earth except Yahweh, the God of Israel (5:15).

E. Physicians as Agents of God

In the midst of advice about seeking the way of truth from the Most High and living according to wisdom (Wisdom of Sirach 37), the author advises his reader to show due honor to the physician, whose ability to heal comes from God (38:1). The writer goes on to explain that it is God who created medicines out of the earth (38:4) and has granted human beings knowledge of these natural means of curing human ills. The druggist prepares the medicines, and the physician administers them. Both the patient and the physician are to pray to God for healing, but it is through the efficacy of these natural medicines that healing will take place, and God will give to the medical doctors the insights for effecting cures and restoring the ill to health (38:12–14). It is implied that sickness is the result of human sin, so that one is to pray that the sinner will fall into the hand of a physician—not because he is a charlatan, as implied in the older biblical sources, but because God has given him knowledge of the natural resources to bring about cures (38:15). It is noteworthy that this advice appears in a document written in the early 2d century B.C.E., which shows the influence of Greek culture at many points. With regard to medicine, it reflects the Stoic notion of natural law, which the physician can draw upon for effecting healing. It was in this period, and especially in Alexandria (where Sirach in its Greek version may well have originated), that the medical tradition linked with the 5th-century-B.C.E. figure of Hippocrates was flourishing, with its emphasis on the inherent healing capabilities of natural substances and the task of the physician to recognize and utilize these inherent powers. Sirach has taken over these basic insights and has adapted them within the framework of belief that the God of Israel is the ultimate power and wisdom guiding the universe and the affairs of the human race. Physicians are the divinely instructed instruments through which these powers which God has built into the created order may become available for human well-being. These insights and healing capabilities are not inherent in humanity, as might be the case with the Stoic view of natural law permeating the universe. Rather, they are part of the wisdom which God communicates for the welfare of earthly creatures.

Although Josephus credits some of human illness to the demons, as we shall note below, he shares with Sirach the belief that the inherent qualities of natural substances are potentially important for curing human ailments. Thus in his description of the Essenes (*JW* 2.136) he notes that they study ancient books and writings, especially those that seek to benefit the human body and soul through the cure of diseases, which are effected by medicinal roots and the properties of certain stones. Josephus also traces this kind of knowledge of natural healing substances back to Solomon (*Ant* 8:44–45), who studied all natural forms and substances and who knew their basic properties for effecting cures. On the other hand, Philo of Alexandria, in his treatise *On the Contemplative Life*, describes the Therapeutae as performing therapy in two ways: (1) The cures which they perform are superior to those performed by medical means, since the latter cure only the bodies, while the Therapeutae treat the human soul. Though the soul may be oppressed with seemingly incurable diseases, these are in fact caused by wicked pleasures; by desires, fears, and griefs; by covetous, foolish, and unjust acts; and by the forces of human passion and vice. (2) Through worship (which is a second meaning of *therapeuein*, from which the name of the group derives), the members of this sect are attuned to nature and its sacred laws, in accord with which they honor and obey the one true God. Like Stoic-oriented Greek medicine, Philo thought that the path to health—physical and psychic—lies through obedience to the God, whose laws are immanent in the created order of the world.

F. Sickness as Evidence of Demonic Powers

Written about the same time in the early 2d century B.C.E. as the Wisdom of Sirach is the book of Tobit, in which sickness is seen as the result of the work of demons in human life. When Tobit was blinded by sparrow droppings which fell in his eyes, physicians were unable to cure him (Tob 2:10). The entrails of a fish were the remedy to restore his sight (11:8) and at the same time were effective in expelling demons (Tob 6:7; 8:1–3). It is appropriate that the angel who assists in transmitting the information to make possible these cures and exorcisms is named Raphael: "God heals." But in the postexilic life of Israel, God works healing through intermediate agents, rather than directly as in the older layers of the biblical tradition. A similar role in the causing of human ailments is attributed in *1 Enoch* 6–11 to the fallen angels. They have disclosed to human beings the charms and enchantments and heavenly secrets (*1 En.* 7:1; 8:3; 9:6). It is Raphael once more who announces the doom of the fallen angels and the subsequent healing of the earth (10:4–14).

The book of *Jubilees* combines features of both Sirach and Enoch, in that the cures for human ailments are to be found among medicinal herbs, as well as through the direct action of the angelic powers in their cosmic struggle with the demons. The herbal remedies are ingredient in the creation; knowledge of their use has been granted to certain select ones among God's people (*Jub.* 10:10–14). Although God is ultimately in control over the fallen angels and the demons, he allows some of them to continue to exercise their malevolent power on earth as a part of the divine judgment of disobedient humanity (*Jub.* 10:7–8). The remedies for the evils that the demonic leader, Mastema, and the Egyptians work on earth are not given to them, however, but are vouchsafed to chosen human beings (*Jub.* 48:10). God permits human sickness and other disasters to occur, but in the end these powers will be overcome, and God's work of renewing the creation will be complete.

In his description of Solomon in *Ant* 8:44–46, Josephus portrays this archetypal wise man as possessing complete knowledge of the natural world, not merely for identification of all the birds and trees and animals, but also for the philosophical principles which underlie their existence. This, too, sounds like Stoic natural law; but Josephus then goes on to claim that Solomon was granted by God knowledge of the means for safeguarding humans from the power of the demons, so that the healing benefits might come to them. He composed the incantations for the relief of illnesses and passed on exorcistic formulas so that demons might be permanently expelled. Josephus attests that he has seen firsthand the efficacy of these exorcistic formulas attributed to Solomon, which had been invoked by one of his fellow Jews during the reign of the emperor Vespasian.

Direct evidence of the attribution of human ailments to demonic powers is available in the Dead Sea Scrolls. In the *Genesis Apocryphon* (1QapGen 20:12–29) there is a report of Abraham's healing action in behalf of the pharaoh. When Abraham lays his hands on the Egyptian monarch, the plague is expelled in the form of the demon that has been causing it. (The technical term *gʿr* is used here, conveying the sense that a hostile power has been brought under control, as does the Gk term *epitimao*, which in the gospels is often translated inadequately as "rebuke" [cf. Mark 1:25; 4:39; Luke 4:35; 8:24; Matt 8:18]). Because of pharaoh's unwitting violation of the law of Yahweh by taking Sarah as his wife, he has come under demonic control, from which he is released in response to his request to Abraham and that patriarch's action in expelling the demon. Similarly, in the Prayer of Nabonidus (4QPrNab) there is a report that the king has been struck by a severe sickness, just as in Daniel 4 Nebuchadnezzar had lost his mind and wandered like a wild animal. The term used in Nabonidus' prayer for deliverance is from the root *gzr*, which appears also in Dan 5:7, 11, and is to be linked with $g^{c}r$, and translated as "exorcist" rather than "astrologer." In all these cases what is at issue is the cure of an ailment and the pronouncement of the forgiveness of sins of a pagan ruler. Here again there is evidence that sickness is linked with subjection to demonic powers; and conversely, healing is achieved through exorcism of the hostile force. God is the ultimate source of healing in these documents, but the therapeutic power is administered through the medium of exorcism of the demonic agents.

G. NT Attitudes toward Physicians

In some strands of the tradition there are references to physicians as a given factor in the culture of the time, as when Jesus offers justification for his associations with tax collectors and sinners by a proverb-like utterance, "Those who are well have no need of a physician, but those who are sick" (Matt 9:12; Mark 2:17; Luke 5:31). At the same time there is a direct challenge to the adequacy of their methods of therapy, as when Mark 5:26 and Luke 8:43 report the inadequacy of the medical agents to cure the woman who in vain had spent all her wealth to procure their services. Luke also reports another proverbial saying of Jesus in response to his detractors who want evidence in Nazareth of his healing capabilities as reported to have occurred in Capernaum (Luke 4:23). The statement would seem to fit the context better if his detractors had said, "Physician, heal!," since what they are calling for is concrete local evidence of his reported healing activities elsewhere. It is the more striking, therefore, that one of the early Christian leaders, with whom the third gospel and Acts came to be associated in the traditions of the Church, was "Luke, the beloved physician" (Col 4:14).

H. Jesus as God's Healing Agent

In the gospel tradition three verbs are used to describe the healings performed by Jesus: (1) *hiaomai*, "cure," "deliver from illness"; (2) *therapeuo*, "wait upon," "care for," "heal"; (3) *sothesomai*, "make whole," "restore." Throughout the Synoptics there are summary statements about the healing activity of Jesus: examples may be found in Mark 1:32–34; 1:19; 6:56; Matt 4:23; 8:16; 14:15; 15:30; 21:14; Luke 6:5, 17; 7:20. The two features which appear in these are an emphasis on his role as healer, and the widespread interest that this activity evokes from his contemporaries.

In the healing stories, the response of faith is essential in order for the healing to occur, whether that faith is resident in the victim or in some person or persons who are hoping for a cure of a friend or relative. It is the faith of the friends of the paralytic who have lowered him through the roof that leads Jesus to pronounce forgiveness of the man's sins and to enable him to walk (Mark 2:4–12). It is Jairus' confidence in the ability of Jesus to heal his daughter that brings him to ask Jesus to do so (Mark 5:23), just as it is the faith of the woman with the bloody flow who reaches out in faith to touch Jesus and is thus healed (Mark 5:27–34). Similarly, in one of the summary accounts of Jesus' healing activity, there is mention of those who reach out in faith to touch the fringe of Jesus' garment (Mark 6:53–56; Matt 14:34–36). The father of the epileptic boy who comes to Jesus in behalf of his son declares his faith, and as a consequence Jesus expels the demon that causes the sickness (Mark 9:14–27; Matt 17:14–18; Luke 9:37–43). It is the faith of Bartimaeus that results in his sight's being restored by Jesus, as Jesus makes explicit (Mark 10:52). In the Q tradition, it is the faith of the centurion that brings about the restoration to health of his child (or servant) as is apparent from Jesus' contrast of this Roman officer's faith with the lack of it in Israel (Matt 8:7–8; Luke 7:9). Matthew has linked the rebuke of the disciples by Jesus for their lacking even minimal faith—"as a grain of mustard seed"—with their failure to be able to heal the epileptic boy (Matt 17:14–20).

At times the healing activity of Jesus is to be followed up by observance of ritual cleansing, as in the Markan and Lukan stories of the cure of lepers (Mark 1:40–45; Luke 5:12–16; Matt 8:1–4; cf. Luke 17:15). More frequently, however, his healing work is seen as a violation of the sabbath prohibition against work, as in his healing the man with the withered hand (Mark 3:1–6; Matt 12:9–14; Luke 6:6–11), the cure of the woman with the spirit of infirmity (Luke 13:14), and of the man with dropsy (Luke 14:1–6). Jesus is depicted as giving priority to the restoration of human health over the observance of even so central and venerable a law of Israel as the avoidance of work on the Sabbath. In addition, a share in the healing benefits of Jesus is extended to those outside the boundaries of the covenant people. This factor is explicit in the healing of the daughter of the Syro-Phoenician woman (Mark 7:24–30; Matt 15:21–28) and is at least implied in the summary reference to Jesus' restoration of a deaf mute whom he met as he passed through gentile territory (Mark 7:31–37; Matt 15:29–31). It is also pointed up in Luke's version of Jesus' sermon in Nazareth, where Jesus points to the precedent set by Elijah and Elisha in performing healings for the benefit of gentiles (Luke 4:25–27).

The source of Jesus' power to heal is God, as is made explicit in Luke 5:17. In the Q version of the controversy about the source of Jesus' power to perform exorcisms, he asserts that it is by the Spirit, or "the finger of God" that he expels demons (Matt 12:28; Luke 11:20), just as Israel had been delivered from slavery in Egypt by God's finger (Exod 8:19). In response to the question from John the Baptist as to who Jesus is, he depicts his role as enabling the blind to see, the lame to walk, lepers to be cleansed, the deaf to hear, and the dead to be raised. All these descriptions of the healing of humanity derive from the words of the prophet Isaiah (29:18–19; 35:5–6; 61:1), who announces what God will do in behalf of his faithful people in preparation for the new age. The claim that Jesus is indeed God's agent to accomplish these divine purposes by God's power is directly announced in Luke's account of the sermon of Jesus at Nazareth, where, having referred to this healing-and-renewing-activity promise by God (Isa 61:1–2), he adds, "Today this scripture has been fulfilled in your hearing" (4:18–21). Matthew has his own version of this claim in behalf of Jesus as healer (15:30–31), where he describes those afflicted with these same ailments, notes that Jesus healed them, and concludes that the crowd which saw these wonders "glorified the God of Israel." It is not surprising, therefore, that the gospel tradition also reports that certain persons try to exploit the power of healing and exorcism which God has given to Jesus by the use of his name to achieve similar wonders (Mark 9:38–41; Luke 9:49–50). Jesus is seen to recognize the efficacy of his name and does not deny its use to others. Chief among those who are not merely permitted but actually charged to carry forward work in his name are, of course, the disciples, who are commissioned by him to perform on the model of his exorcisms and healings and who do so (Mark 6:6–13; Matt 9:35–10:11; Luke 9:1–6). In Luke's gospel, seventy others are also sent out, presumably to a similar ministry of healing and preaching among the gentiles (10:1–12). They, too, are to engage in exorcisms and healings in the name of Jesus, their effectiveness in which is attested by them on their return (vv 17–20).

In the gospel of John there are no accounts of exorcisms, and the healing stories are told in such a way as to point up their symbolic significance for faith. That point is made explicit in the concluding remark of John about Jesus' signs in John 20:30, 31: these accounts of Jesus' activities have been written down in order to persuade the reader that he is the Son of God, thereby enabling the faithful hearer to gain eternal life. There may be symbolic significance in the Synoptic Gospels' reporting the recovery of sight by blind Bartimaeus at the end of the account of Jesus' public activity and prior to his rejection by the authorities in Jerusalem (Mark 10:46–52; Matt 20:29–34; Luke 18:35–43). Thus Bartimaeus symbolizes those who are able to discern who Jesus is, in contrast to those who think they can see but are blind to the purpose of God, as in Jesus' reference to the blind guides of the blind (Matt 15:14; Luke 6:39). This point is made explicitly in the story of Jesus' healing the man born blind (John 9:1–41), where Jesus notes the inability of the Pharisees to see who Jesus is (vv 40–41). The issue of insight into Jesus' role as the agent of God and that insight as a major point of division between the followers of Jesus and the Jewish leaders are described in John 9:22; there it is said that to confess Jesus as Messiah is the ground for expulsion of his followers from the synagogue. The inability of the leaders to see who Jesus is stands in sharp contrast with the discernment of the healed blind man—"Lord, I believe" (9:32)—and results in their subsequent rejection of his effort to explain to them Jesus' unique relationship with God as the one who brings the light of knowledge of God. Similarly, in John 4 the official's trust in the word of Jesus results not only in the healing of his son, but in the entry of the father and the entire household into the community of faith (4:53). John reminds his reader that this is "the second sign that Jesus did" and hence is of symbolic as well as of narrative importance. As a fitting climax to his account of the public career of Jesus, John describes in detail the circumstances of the death and restoration to life of Lazarus (11:1–44). In the course of the narration Jesus declares that he not only makes possible the resurrection, but that he *is* "the resurrection and the life" and that all who trust in him will never die (11:25–26). He invites his hearers to trust in him as God's agent, and later (12:37–50) he contrasts those who refuse to see in his "signs" the work of God in their midst (and who therefore do not share in the healing which God provides through him) with those who do trust and have therefore moved from darkness to light of the knowledge of God.

The passages quoted in John 9 from Isa 6:1, 10 also appear in a similar report of disbelief on the part of the Jewish leaders in Rome (Acts 28:27). Throughout the narratives of Acts there are reports much like those found in the Synoptic Gospels, only now it is the apostles through whom the healing power of God is manifest, as in the story of the lame man at the temple gate who was healed by Peter (Acts 3:1–10) and the account of Paul's healing the lame man at Lystra (Acts 14:8–10). As in the Synoptic tradition, an essential feature is that the man had sufficient faith to be healed (14:9). In the account of the healing of the father of Publius on the island of Malta, however, the only factor mentioned in the cure achieved is that Paul prayed and laid on his hands (Acts 28:7–8). The other cures which follow are noted with no details or accompanying features (Acts 28:9). In two crucial passages in Acts, there are explicit links between the healing activity of the apostles and that of Jesus: Acts 9:34 specifies that the healing of the paralytic Aeneas by Peter was the direct action of Jesus Christ; in Peter's description of the career of Jesus, he remarks that God's anointing of him with power and thus God's presence with him had been manifested in his good deeds and specifically in his "healing all that were oppressed of the devil" (Acts 10:38).

I. Healing Activity in the Pauline and Catholic Letters

In 1 Corinthians 12, where Paul is describing the charismatic gifts which the Spirit of God produces, he mentions the gifts of healing and the working of miracles (12:9–10, 29–30). He does not describe their occurring, nor does he indicate whether or not he shared in these gifts. They are, however, ranked by him in fourth place, after the roles of apostle, prophet, and teacher. Near the end of his hortatory treatise, the author of James asks his readers to confess their sins to one another and to pray for one another so "that you may be healed." Implicit in this exhortation is that sickness is related to sin, just as healing is linked with forgiveness, which as noted is also the case in the gospel tradition. What is wholly clear from this nonnarrative NT evidence is that healing continues to have a significant role in the lives of those who see themselves as the people of God.

J. Medicine in the NT?

Some scholars have sought to explain certain features of the gospel miracle stories as evidence of medical or magical technique. Two of the features of the miracle stories that have been linked with one or the other of these techniques are the laying on of hands and the application of spittle or mud made from it to the affected part. A story found only in Mark (8:22–26) describes Jesus's restoring the sight of a blind man of Beth-saida by spitting on the man's eyes and laying on his hands. In John 9:6, Jesus is described as making mud from spittle and placing it on the eyes of the man born blind, which mud, when washed away, results in his gaining sight. There is no hint of conscious or even implicit medical or magical technique here, however; and both stories lead directly into the question of Jesus' role as the anointed one of God. The implication seems to be rather the removal of the unclean or sinful element which has caused the blindness. Similarly, Jairus' request to Jesus is to come lay his hands on the ailing daughter (Mark 7:32–33; Matt 15:23–31); but there is no suggestion that the source of healing resides in the technique of touching. Rather, as Mark's version of the incident makes clear, the crucial factor is faith in the power transmitted through Jesus (Mark 7:36). In other gospel narratives Jesus is asked to lay hands on the sick (Mark 7:32–33; Matt 15:29–31), or he does so on his own initiative (Luke 13:13). Summary statements also note his healing through the laying on of hands (Matt 6:5; Luke 4:40). That this action is linked with the authority transmitted from God through Jesus is implied in the gospel accounts of the transfer of divine blessing to children through Jesus' laying on of hands (Mark 10:13; Matt 19:13–15; Luke 18:15). That the transmission of authority is the central factor in the laying on of hands is clearly the case in other NT writings, especially in Acts, where the imposition of hands by the apostles is essential for the assignment of responsibility (Acts 6:6), for conveying the Spirit to believers (Acts 8:17–19; 19:6), and for the assignment of Paul to the gentile mission (Acts 9:12–17; 13:3). A solemn warning in 1 Tim 5:22 concerns the hasty assigning of authority within the Church through the laying on of hands. In these accounts of the imposition of hands, there is neither magical nor medical technique but the symbolic transfer of power within the people of God.

K. Summary

The predominantly negative attitude toward physicians and medical technique in the Bible is, therefore, the reverse side of the conviction that it is God's intention and responsibility to care for the health of his people. This may be accomplished by direct action or through a human agent, whether through the prophets or Jesus or the apostles, and in a few texts, through physicians. In each case healing, which is essential to the fullness of human beings created in the image of God, is accomplished through God's action in behalf of members of the faithful community, communicated through a human agency or by direct performance. See also SICKNESS AND DISEASE.

Bibliography

Kee, H. C. 1986. *Medicine, Miracle and Magic in the NT.* Cambridge.
Palmer, B., ed. 1986. *Medicine and the Bible.* Exeter.
Preuss, J. 1978. *Biblical and Talmudic Medicine.* New York.

HOWARD CLARK KEE

MEDITERRANEAN SEA

[Heb *yām*]. An interior waterway linking together the continents Asia, Africa, and Europe. The term "Mediterranean" is derived from Latin *medius terra,* "midland," and in classical Roman literature was never associated with the sea. Biblical literature employs the NW Semitic term *yām* (Isa 24:15; Jer 46:18; Ezek 26:17–18; Jonah 1:11–13, 15; etc.). Akkadian probably borrowed the term as *yâmu* (Gordon *UT,* 19.1106), and the Egyptians definitely borrowed it as *ym* (Erman and Grapow, *WbÄS,* 78. The sense is still preserved in the place name al-Fayyum [Eg. *p3y(W)m*] = "the sea"). It entered Coptic vernaculars as s. EIOM; b. IOM a.f. IAM (Spiegelberg 1921: 25).

Yām is not only a term for the sea, but also represents the sea god. It is on the shores of the Mediterranean that the famous literary theme of the battle between Baal and the sea god *Yām* originated. The motif was exported to the Akkadians, who incorporated it into their language and literature (Jacobsen 1968: 107–8). The people of Ugarit embellished the theme (Gordon, *UT,* Text 68), and traces of it are found in the Bible (Isa 27:1; 51:10; Job 7:12; 26:12; Pss 74:16–20; 89:9–10; 93:3–4). In a Mari text (ca. the 18th century B.C.), the Mediterranean Sea is known both as a real sea and the personification of a sea god. The text relates that *Iaḫdum-Lim* reaches the shores of *ti-a-am-tu,* the Mediterranean Sea. His thanksgiving offerings, however, are presented to Sumerian *A-a-ab-ba* (elsewhere written A.AB.BA), the Mediterranean Sea personified as a sea deity (Dossin 1955: 5–6). The use of two different terms for the Mediterranean Sea suggests the dual aspects of this particular sea, so often portrayed in biblical literature.

The Near East is situated geographically between two major bodies of water: the Mediterranean Sea and branches of the Indian Ocean. Empires of the ancient world prided themselves on dominating the lands and peoples who lived in between the seas. A common expression of the Babylonians was *iš-tu ti-a-am-ti e-li-ti a-di ti-a-am-ti ša-ap-li-ti* "from the upper sea unto the lower sea," i.e., from the Mediterranean Sea to the Indian Ocean. While the Babylonians described the seas from their geographic vantage point, the biblical scribes, from their perspective, portrayed the ideal borders of Israel as extending *miyyām* *ʿad yām* i.e., from the Eastern to the Western Sea (Zech 9:11; Ps 72:8; cf. Amos 8:12). For Assyrian and Babylonian kings, the description was a reality, even if only for a short while; but for the biblical prophets it remained as a vision of the future.

The ancients were familiar with settlements all around the Mediterranean Sea. Thus an Assyrian king reports that tribute is paid by kings situated "in the midst of the sea." Ezekiel uses such a term when he prophesies calamity "in the midst of the seas" (Ezek 27:27). Sennacherib's annals record that the king of Sidon escaped into "the midst of the sea." This portends the beginning of the migration westward of Palestinians and Syrian natives afraid of the invading empires of the East. It also explains the biblical references to the return of the exiles from "the islands of the sea" (Isa 11:11). The aforementioned verse cites places designating East, North, and South. It is the islands of the sea which clearly refer to the west, thus indicating the islands in the Mediterranean.

The geographic map of the Mediterranean Sea is familiar to the biblical scribes. Even though not all the islands mentioned in the Bible are as yet definitively identified, the citations demonstrate acquaintance with locations both near and far. The Isle of Caphtor (Gen 10:14; Deut 2:23;

Jer 47:4; Amos 9:7) refers, according to the Aramaic translation, to Cappadocia, while others maintain that it designates the island of Crete (Simons, *GTTOT,* No. 46, No. 194, No. 295; Gardiner 1968: 201–4). Similarly, the prophet suggests to his audience to visit the Isles of Kittim (Jer 2:10). The *Tg. Neb.* equates it with "Appulia," the Vg with "Italy" (Ezek 27:7), and Donner and Röllig (*KAI* 1: 32) with the Gk *Kition.* Italy is also given as the identification of Isles of Elishah by the *Tg. Neb.* (Ezek 27:7). The Targum refers to the Isles of *gôyîm* as "the Islands of Peoples" (Gen 10:5; Zeph 2:11), possibly a general expression pertaining to inhabitants of the islands of the Mediterranean.

The familiarity of the Bible with locations beyond the immediate shores of Syria-Palestine indicates involvement with sea activities, both commercial and military. The 2d millennium B.C.E. witnessed the Canaanites of Syria-Palestine as the thalassocrats of maritime activities. The 1st millennium B.C.E. saw a change in the composition of the leading maritime forces in the Mediterranean. The Sea Peoples migrated to the shores of the E Mediterranean (Sasson 1966: 137–38), and the Hebrews gained a foothold along the shore (Gordon 1963: 22, 31). See GREAT SEA.

Intense competition along the E Mediterranean shores resulted in a search for new and profitable maritime ventures. This was accomplished for the Israelite monarchy when the innovative kings, David and Solomon, were able to conclude a series of agreements with sea traders of the Mediterranean par excellence, the Phoenicians. The peak was reached when Solomon's fleet, manned primarily by Israelites and assisted by Phoenicians, launched one of the most famous ventures to exotic lands.

During the period of the great prophets, maritime activity declined and reached its lowest ebb; yet it would be impossible to explain the sudden rise in Jewish naval and commercial affairs in the postbiblical era if one were to assume that Jewish seamanship ceased completely during the prophetic era. As a matter of fact, recent archaeological excavations along the coast of Israel show considerable maritime activity of Israelites and Judeans during the First Commonwealth (Maisler 1950: 67–76, 124–40, 198–218; Raban 1983: 229–51; Yeivin 1960: 193–228).

During the Greco-Persian wars Herodotus reports that the largest share of naval ships were supplied and manned jointly by Jews and Phoenicians, thus alluding to an old partnership which may never have been dissolved (Hdt. 2.104; 3.5; 7.89; Jos. *Ant* 8.262; *AgAp* 1.22, 168).

When the Maccabean kings captured Joppa, the Tower of Strato (later Caesarea), and the rest of the harbor cities along the Mediterranean, the sea-oriented activities once again flourished (1 Macc 8:11; 2 Macc 12:3). This interest is reflected by the maritime symbolism found on various archaeological artifacts of the period, notably, Jewish coins (Kindler 1966: 15–20).

The Roman hegemony did not put an end to Jewish naval and commercial interests. Joppa continued to thrive, and King Herod I built a seaport in Caesarea (*Ant* 16.9; *JW* 5.21). This was the largest in the region, and it played a principal role in trade from the E to the W. The maritime enterprises of the period have been demonstrated by the underwater archaeological excavations of the Palestinian coast (Raban 1983: 140–43), as well as by the marine symbols, ships, and anchors struck on contemporary coins (Meshorer 1967: 69, coins Nos. 56–60). The rebellion against the Romans (66–70 C.E.) eliminated the existence of a free Jewish fleet operating in the waters of the E Mediterranean (*JW* 3.419). The dimension of the calamity is not exaggerated by Josephus since it is suggested that three successive emperors celebrated the great victory by minting coins "Victoria Navalis" (Stieglitz 1975: 18–19; cf. Meshorer 1975: 38 No. 19).

During the NT era, the port cities were utilized not only for commercial purposes, but also for exporting the new religious concepts westward (Acts 9:36–49; 10:5–8). Preparation of Mediterranean society for Christianity depended heavily on the Jewish communities scattered around the Roman Empire (Acts 13:13–15, 14:1–2), the cosmopolitan seaport cities, and the well-traveled sea routes of the Mediterranean. The diffusion of Christianity, in large measure, can be attributed to the sailing of the apostles to various port cities of the Mediterranean, as described in the book of Acts.

Travel, however, was not possible throughout the year. The Rabbinic Sages recommended travel on the Mediterranean only from Pentecost until the Feast of Tabernacles. The hazardous period was known to be from the Feast of Tabernacles until Hanukkah, and even the large Alexandrian boats did not traverse the seas during this period (*Gen. Rab.* 6.5). Paul traveled the high seas during this dangerous time and nearly lost his life (Acts 27:7–44; 28:11).

The heritage of Western civilization along E Mediterranean shores was created not in a vacuum, but through the intermingling of the Mediterranean peoples, particularly the Greeks and Israelites. A catalyst for this interaction was the intense activity on the Mediterranean by the intrepid seafarers who took full advantage of its sea routes.

Bibliography

Day, J. 1985. *God's Conflict with the Dragon and the Sea.* Cambridge.

Dossin, G. 1955. L'Inscription de Fondation de Iaḫdun-lim, Roi de Mari. *Syria* 32: 1–28.

Elayi, J. 1984. Terminologie de la Mer Méditerranée dans les Annales assyriennes. *OrAnt* 23: 75–92.

Gardiner, A. H. 1968. *Onomastica.* Vol. 1. Oxford.

Gordon, C. H. 1963. The Mediterranean Factor in the OT. *VTSup* 9: 20–31.

Jacobsen, T. 1968. The Battle between Marduk and Tiamat. *JAOS* 88: 104–8.

Kindler, A. 1966. Maritime Emblems on Ancient Jewish Coins. *Sefunim* 1: 15–20.

Maisler [Mazar], B. 1950. The Excavations at Tell Qasile: Preliminary Report. *IEJ* 1: 67–76, 125–140, 194–218.

Mazar, A. 1986. Excavations at Tell Qasile 1982–1984; Preliminary Report. *IEJ* 36: 1–15.

Meshorer, Y. 1967. *Jewish Coins of the Second Temple Period.* Tel Aviv.

———. 1975. Catalog of Coins. Pp. 24–80 in *Ships and Parts of Ships on Ancient Coins,* vol. 1, ed. A. Ben-Eli. Haifa.

Raban, A. 1983. *Hannĕmālîm haqqĕdûmîm bayyām hattîkôn.* Pp. 121–46 in *ʾAqqan Hayyām Hattîkôn,* ed. Y. Karmon, A. Shmueli, and G. Horowitz. Tel Aviv.

Sasson, J. M. 1966. Caananite Maritime Involvement in the Second Millennium B.C. *JAOS* 86: 126–38.

Spiegelberg, W. 1921. *Koptisches Handwörterbuch.* Heidelberg.

Stieglitz, R. R. 1975. Maritime History on Jewish Coins. Pp. 18–19 in *Ships and Parts of Ships on Ancient Coins*, vol. 1, ed. A. Ben-Eli. Haifa.

Yeiven, S. 1960. Did the Kingdom of Israel Have a Maritime Policy? *JQR* 50: 193–228.

MEIR LUBETSKI

MEDIUM. See MAGIC.

MEGADIM, TEL (M.R. 145236). A site on the Levantine coast some 17 km S of Haifa and 2 km N of 'Atlit. The site was only occasionally occupied from the EB to the Byzantine periods. It is perhaps to be identified with Kartah, i.e., "town," a name mentioned in Josh 21:34 and a frequent component of Phoenician place names. Its principal remains were uncovered in the well-preserved town of the Persian period.

A. The Bronze Age

The EB and MB periods are known only through unstratified finds; however, it appears that the EB settlement was considerably larger than the later ones. EB I (gray-burnished ware and hole-mouth jars) and EB II (platters and a seal impression) remains are common. After a long period of abandonment, the site was reoccupied in the MB. Another period of abandonment appears to separate the MB from LB periods. The LB city had strong overseas commercial ties, as implied by the abundant Cypriot pottery.

B. The Persian Period

Three Persian period strata were identified in the excavations, but the dating of the earliest (stratum I) is uncertain. After a destruction level, the most substantial stratum (stratum II) was unearthed, representing a well-preserved and well-planned town which flourished in the 5th century B.C. The town was laid out in a quadrangle, foreshadowing a system that became popular in the later Hellenistic period. The casemate fortification wall probably served primarily as protection against pirates. Greek and Cypriot ware testify to an intensive overseas trade. In the beginning of the 4th century B.C., the town was destroyed, possibly as a result of the invasions of the 29th Egyptian Dyn. or during the Persian reconquest of the country (ca. 380 B.C.). Shortly afterward, the site was resettled for a brief period (stratum I) before being destroyed, perhaps at the time of the Tennes rebellion (351 B.C.) or, at the latest, during the campaign of Alexander the Great (332 B.C.).

After the Persian period, the site seems to have fallen into obscurity. A large public building on the peak of the mound is all that is known from later periods, and may be the horse-changing station and caravansary known as Mutation Certa mentioned by the Bordeaux Pilgrim (ca. A.D. 330).

Bibliography

Broshi, M. 1977. Megadim, Tel. *EAEHL* 3: 823–26.

M. BROSHI

MEGIDDO (PLACE) [Heb *mĕgiddô*]. A city in the valley of Jezreel. While the king of Megiddo is said to have been killed by the Israelites in their initial foray into Canaan (Josh 12:21) and Megiddo was allotted to the tribe of Manasseh (Josh 17:11), the Manassites were unable to accommodate the city (Judg 1:27). The site is mentioned in the Song of Deborah (Judg 5:19), but it is unclear whether the reference is as a geographic landmark or a statement implying occupation. Eventually the Israelites took control of the site, and it came under Solomon's administrative organization (1 Kgs 4:12). He later fortified it along with Jerusalem, Hazor, and Gezer (1 Kgs 9:15). Ahaziah was assassinated by Jehu and died at Megiddo (2 Kgs 9:27), and Josiah later was killed there when he met Neco (2 Kgs 23:29).

A. Site and Identification
B. History of Explorations
C. Excavation Results
  1. The Early Settlements
  2. The Canaanite City
  3. The Israelite City
  4. The Later Periods

A. Site and Identification

The ancient city is represented by a major mound, Tel Megiddo (Hebrew), known also as Tell el-Mutesellim (Arabic "the tell of the governor"; M.R. 167221). The mound rises ca. 30 m above the surrounding plain and measures ca. 300 × 230 m, covering an area of 50 dunams. Including the slopes, the mound covers an area of 74 dunams. A lower terrace extending to the NE of the mound was also inhabited during various periods. The settlement drew its water from two springs, Ain el-Kubbi to the NE of the site and another spring at the bottom of the W slope.

Megiddo is located in the W part of the Jezreel valley, nearly at the foot of Mt. Carmel. It is positioned not far from where the brook of Naḥal Iron (Wâdī Ara) enters into the Jezreel valley. Along this brook passed the main highway (Via Maris) from Egypt to Syria; and the narrow Naḥal Iron is the best point where the route can be controlled, hence the special strategic importance of Megiddo in ancient (and modern) times. Thus, having ample sources of water and a fertile valley nearby, located along an international commercial highway, and being of unique strategic importance, Megiddo became one of the most important centers in the country.

The identification of ancient Megiddo with Lejjun, ca. 1.5 km S of the mound, was first proposed in A.D. 1322 by the Jewish writer Eshtori Haparchi in his book *Caphtor Waperach* and independently in 1838 by E. Robinson during his first visit to Palestine.

B. History of Explorations

The excavation of Megiddo was initiated by the German Society for the Study of Palestine. It was the first major German excavation project in the Holy Land, and a large part of the costs were defrayed by Kaiser Wilhelm II. G. Schumacher, an architect who had previously conducted a survey in the Golan, directed the excavations, which took place between 1903 and 1905. Schumacher (1908) surveyed the site and its vicinity, cut a 20-m-wide trench across the mound from N to S, cut a number of 3-to-5-m-wide trenches across the summit and the slopes, dug two monumental Iron Age buildings on the summit (the *Tempelburg* and the *Palast*), and studied tombs and other remains in the vicinity of the site. The finds were later analyzed by Watzinger (1929).

In 1925 the Chicago Oriental Institute resumed the excavations under the direction of J. H. Breasted. From its inception the project was planned on a large scale, aiming at a horizontal exposure of one layer of habitation after the other across the entire mound. See Fig. MEG.01. The neglect of details and of vertical relationships which are essential to understand the stratigraphy, as well as the production of superficial excavation reports, characterized the work. Many of the difficulties which later arose in the interpretation of the finds stem from these deficiencies. No attempt was made to correlate the work with the German finds; and as a result, the Oriental Institute's plans and reports ignore crucial architectural data uncovered by Schumacher.

Fisher (1929) was director from 1925 to 1927. He built an expedition house on the lower terrace NE of the mound, prepared a chute on the E slope for removing debris, and excavated an area to the E of the site where the debris could be dumped. On the summit he excavated the area at the E side, where Schumacher had uncovered the *Tempelburg*.

Guy (1931) was director from 1927 to 1934. He cleared an area farther to the E of the mound, where early remains and tombs of many periods were discovered (Engberg and Shipton 1934; Guy 1938). He uncovered the remains of the Israelite strata across the entire summit (areas A–E), including the city gate and the stable compounds (Lamon and Shipton 1939), and cleared the water system (Lamon 1935). Guy introduced the use of a camera attached to a balloon for taking aerial photographs of the excavations.

Loud directed the work from 1935 to 1939, when the project ended because of World War II. He concentrated his efforts in selected areas (AA–DD), where he penetrated lower strata. In area BB, a wide trench at the E side of the site, he dug down to virgin soil. The results of his

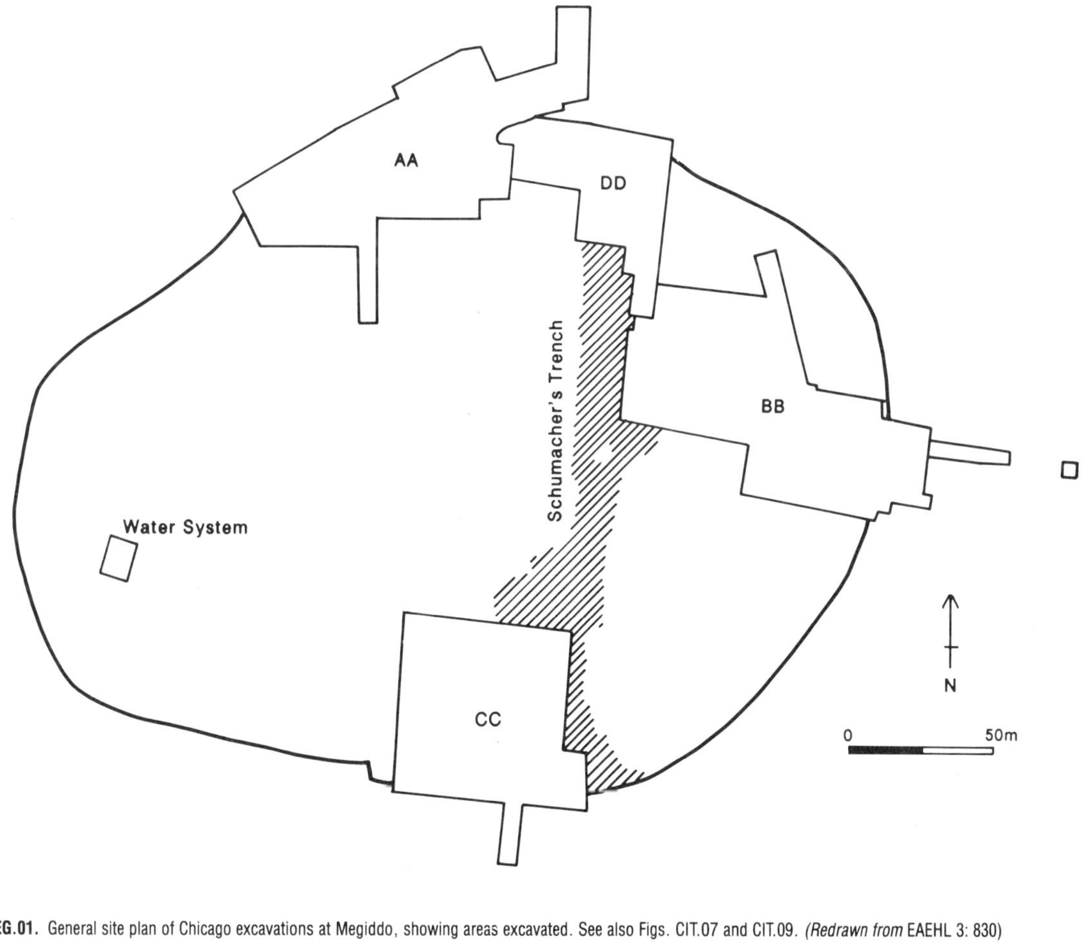

MEG.01. General site plan of Chicago excavations at Megiddo, showing areas excavated. See also Figs. CIT.07 and CIT.09. *(Redrawn from* EAEHL 3: 830)

work were inadequately published because of war conditions (Loud 1948; Shipton 1939).

Between 1960 and 1972, Yadin (1960, 1970, 1972) carried out small-scale excavations in the NE part of the site and near the "gallery" at the W side to clarify the stratigraphy of the earlier temples in area BB. In 1974 Eitan (1974) further studied Iron Age remains uncovered at the lower end of the E slope.

CHRONOLOGICAL TABLE
(Dates B.C. unless otherwise noted)

Periods and Dates	Strata	Special Data
PN B–EB I (6000–2950/2900)	XX–XIX	Stages VII–IV
EB II–IV (2950/2900–2200)	XVIII–XV	
EB IV (2200–2000)	XIV	Shaft Tombs
MB I (2000–1800)	XIII–XII	Egypt's Middle Kingdom
MB II–III (1800–1550)	XI–X	Egypt's Second Intermediate
LB I–III (1550–1130)	IX–VIIA	Egypt's New Kingdom
Iron IA–B (1130–1000)	VIB–VIA	
Iron IC (1000–930)	VB	David's Reign
	VA–IVB	Solomon's Reign
Iron IIA–B (930–734)	IVA	Divided Monarchy
Iron IIC (734–ca. 600)	III–II	Assyrian Rule
Babylonian–Persian (ca. 600–332)	I	Conquered by Alexander
Roman (31–A.D. 324)	New Settlement at Lejjun	

C. Excavation Results

1. The Early Settlements. a. Neolithic. Stratum XX represents the beginning of settlement on bedrock uncovered in area BB. Remains of stone and brick walls, floors, pits, and fireplaces cut in the surface of the rock were reported. Toothed-flint sickle blades and pottery fragments of the Yarmūkian culture date the settlement to the Pottery Neolithic B period. Loud considered one cave (labeled stratum -XX) to be earlier in date, assigning it to the Pre-Pottery Neolithic period.

b. Chalcolithic and Early Bronze I. Remains of EB I were uncovered in Stages VII–IV in the area excavated E of the mound (Engberg and Shipton 1934), indicating that the EB I unfortified settlement extended to a large area E of the site. Two "apsidal" buildings—rectangular buildings with one rounded end—which are typical to that period, were uncovered in Stage IV. The ceramic repertoire is characterized by gray-burnished "Esdraelon ware" and "grain-wash" pottery. A group of cylinder seal impressions stamped on pottery vessels found in Stage IV show connections to Syria, Mesopotamia, and Egypt (Beck 1975).

Stratum XIX in area BB is represented by a temple compound extending on the E slope of the site. The temple was the first of a number of sanctuaries built in this general area until the Iron Age (Epstein 1973; Dunayevsky and Kempinski 1973). The shrine was a rectangular room, its entrance located in one of the long walls facing the E slope. A number of stone slabs extending along the center of the room and adjacent to the walls must have been bases for pillars or other objects. A rectangular mudbrick platform, apparently an altar, which was enlarged in a later phase, was built opposite the entrance. It is possible that a badly preserved room to the N of the shrine served as a second, similar shrine. A sloping courtyard surrounded by a curving wall extended in front of the building. A round installation assigned to stratum XVIII (No. 4034), beside which a unique, ceremonial copper spear was found, probably formed a cultic basin in the courtyard. Remains of two layers of stone pavement were found in the courtyard. On some of the stone slabs were incised figures of men and animals in hunting scenes and decorative patterns.

The ground plan of the temple resembles that of the Chalcolithic, Ghassulian sanctuary at En-Gedi. Typical Ghassulian pottery, notably cornets, and other finds, were found here (and not elsewhere in Megiddo). Early Bronze I pottery is also reported from this area. This situation can be explained in two ways. One possibility is that the temple originates in the Chalcolithic period. Similar to the En-Gedi sanctuary, it may have been an isolated shrine located on the slope not far from a spring and facing the valley to the E; but it could have also been located in a Ghassulian settlement which extends in the unexcavated parts of the site. A second possibility is that the temple belongs to the EB I settlement, while its resemblance to the En-Gedi sanctuary and the presence of Ghassulian finds indicate the contemporaneity of the Ghassulian and EB I cultures (Kempinski 1989).

c. Early Bronze II–III. These periods are covered by strata XVIII–XV in area BB. Attempts to elucidate the stratigraphy and chronology were made by Kenyon (1958), Thompson (1970), Dunayevsky and Kempinski (1973), Kempinski (1989), and Brandfon (1977).

A massive city wall was built at stratum XVIII. Built of stone, it was ca. 4–5 m wide and preserved ca. 4 m high. In stratum XVII it was widened, becoming ca. 8 m thick. A turn inward at the edge of area BB shows that it did not surround the entire site. Kenyon's suggestion (1958: 52*) that in its initial stage the wall was merely a retaining wall supporting the adjoining edifice built up the slope is very attractive. The city wall indicates that Megiddo became a fortified, but smaller, settlement in EB II.

Altar 4017 was built in stratum XVII on the summit, near the edge of the E slope where the stratum XIX temple once stood. It is a circular, stone-built structure, ca. 8 m in diameter and 1.5 m high, with a flight of seven steps leading to its top. An enclosure wall surrounded it, and large amounts of bones and pottery were found within it. See Fig. MEG.02.

Three temples (4040, 5192, 5269) were added later near the altar. According to Loud they were all built in stratum XV dated to the EB–MB Intermediate period (= MB I or EB IV). However, it seems that Temple 4040 was built before the other two temples and that all of them date to the EB, when Megiddo was still a great urban center (Dunayevsky and Kempinski 1973).

All three temples have a uniform plan. Each temple consists of a rectangular cella entered through a porticoed porch. Two pillar bases were found in the center of each cella; and a platform, probably an altar, stood against the rear wall. A small side room was attached to each temple. The temples were probably dedicated to three different deities, and with the round altar they formed an impressive sacred area.

d. Early Bronze IV. During this period, settlement on the site continued but declined. Existence of a poor settlement is proven by contemporary pottery found in area

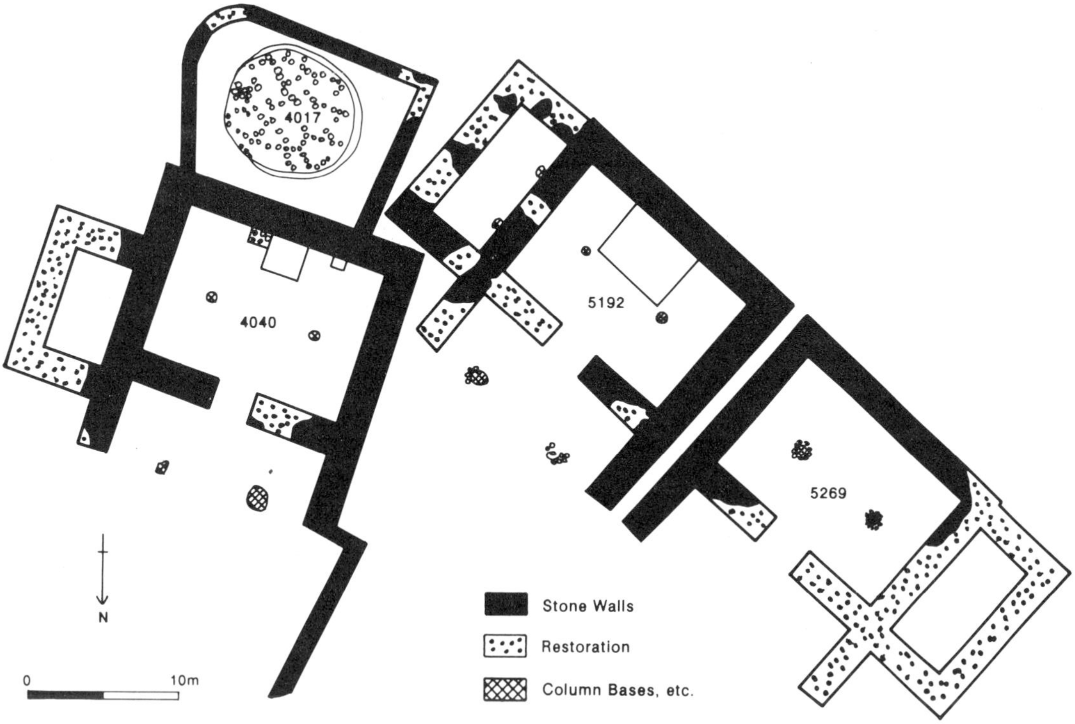

MEG.02. Sacred precinct in Area BB at Megiddo—EB Age. *4017*, round altar; *4040*, adjoining temple; *5192* and *5269*, later temples. *(Redrawn from* EAEHL 3: 833)

BB, and it probably includes many of the badly preserved structures assigned to strata XIV and XIIIB in that area. The earlier Temple 4040 was reused. The cella was filled with rubble and a small cell, measuring ca. 5.5 × 4 m, was prepared in its center. A cultic niche, located above the former altar, was built in the wall of the cell, opposite its entrance.

A number of rock-cut tombs were uncovered SE of the site (Schumacher 1908: 168–73; Guy 1938). Many of them, used for multiple burials, are characterized by their plan and pottery: a horizontal entrance cut at the bottom of a vertical shaft opens into a rectangular chamber which has entrances to three smaller side chambers cut at a slightly higher level. The pottery, which appears in a number of places in N Israel, includes wheel-made, gray vessels, decorated with wavy white bands, and is connected to the "caliciform" pottery of N Syria. Amiran (1960) defined it as Family C and Dever (1980) as Family NC in their classifications of the period's pottery.

2. The Canaanite City. The beginning of the MB in the 20th century B.C. marks the rebuilding of Megiddo in stratum XIII as an urban, fortified center—a Canaanite city-state which lasted without interruption until the destruction of the stratum VIIA city at the end of the LB Age in the 12th century B.C. The entire period is characterized by the presence and interests of Egypt in Canaan and Syria, and is affected by changes in the impact of Egyptian influence. Domination of Megiddo naturally was a prerequisite for Egyptian hegemony in Canaan.

Extensive remains of the city were uncovered in Schumacher's main trench and in Loud's areas AA–DD. The stratigraphic sequence is confused because of the custom of constructing tombs within the city limits (typical of the MB) and the difficulty in assigning them to city levels, the continuous occupation of the site, and the near absence of massive destructions by fire. Attempts at elucidating the stratigraphy and the history of the city were made by Epstein (1965), Kenyon (1969), Müller (1970), Dunayevsky and Kempinski (1973), Kempinski (1989), Kassis (1973), Gerstenblith (1983: 23–28, 114), and Gonen (1987).

a. Middle Bronze Age. The MB I parallels the Middle Kingdom in Egypt, i.e., the rule of the 12th Dyn. and renewal of Egyptian interests in Canaan and Syria. It is not clear how strong was the Egyptian influence at Megiddo. Significantly, the Execration Texts do not mention Megiddo; and this fact has been interpreted as an indication of Egyptian domination. A broken, black, stone statuette of Thuthotep, a high Egyptian official in the 19th century B.C., was found with two broken, black, stone Egyptian statuettes embedded in the raised platform of stratum

VIIB Temple 2048. The statues had probably stood in the earlier temple built on this spot; they were later broken when the temple was plundered, after which it was buried. The implications of this find for understanding the relationships with Egypt at the period of the Middle Kingdom are not clear (Wilson 1941). Strata XIII–XII are assigned to the MB I by some scholars (e.g., B. Mazar, Kempinski) but others (e.g., Dever, Gerstenblith, Davies) assign stratum XII to MB II.

During MB II–III, which parallel the Second Intermediate Period in Egypt, Egyptian impact on Megiddo weakened; and scarabs form the main expression of Egyptian influence (Tufnell 1973). Strata XI–X are usually assigned to this period.

The MB city is characterized by massive fortifications, uncovered in areas AA–CC in strata XIIIA–XI. In area AA the stratum XIII buttressed city wall and a city gate were uncovered. They were built of bricks on stone foundations. A stepped approach, supported by a retaining wall, led to the gate. The wall, gatehouse, and retaining wall were supported on the outside by a limestone glacis. The gate chamber included outer and inner doorways, ca. 2 m wide, oriented 90° to one another. The stepped approach, the narrow doorways, and the indirect passage indicate that the gate was planned for use by pedestrians. In stratum XII the city wall to the W of the gate was thickened by the addition of a new wall. The city wall also extended above the ruined stratum XIII gatehouse. In stratum XI a new city wall, with buttresses built along its inner face and a glacis leaning against its outer face, was built. On the E side the uncovered wall segment ended in a tower which may have formed part of the city gate.

In areas BB and CC the continued lines of the strata XIII–XII walls found in area AA were identified. In area BB a buttressed wall, 1.5 m thick, built of bricks on stone foundations, was assigned to stratum XIIIA. In stratum XII a similar wall, but of superior construction, and a tower adjoined the outer facade of the earlier wall, thus more than doubling its width. The city wall was preserved here to a height of more than 3 m. This system of walls was also uncovered in area CC, where it included an inner double wall and outer wall supported by a glacis. According to Loud the city walls in area BB were freestanding structures. However, the faces of these well-preserved brick walls were unplastered (Loud 1948: figs. 197, 199–200) and obviously were not meant to withstand rains. The data thus indicate that these walls were part of the fortifications' substructure and probably belong to a single fortifications system. The brick walls must have been supported by a glacis on the outside and a constructional fill on the inside, which were removed by Loud. Kenyon (1969: 44) observed that the wall is stratigraphically later than stratum XIIIA, and it probably dates to stratum XII or stratum XI in area BB.

The existence of a glacis on the slope and supporting massive brick walls, which must have formed part of the same fortification system, was manifested in seven narrow trenches cut by Schumacher around the site (1908: 23–36).

An impressive building with thick stone walls was uncovered in strata XI–X in area BB, to the NW of the sacred area. It is located near Schumacher's *Nordburg,* uncovered in his main trench (1908: 37–66; Loud 1948: fig. 415); and both apparently constitute parts of the MB II–III royal acropolis of Megiddo, which had been built in the central part of the site.

Schumacher (1908: 13–23, 66–77) uncovered a unique stone structure, the *Mittelburg,* which adjoined the S side of the *Nordburg.* This structure, in which Schumacher discerned a number of phases, contained three unique stone tombs, apparently for the burial of princes and nobles. "Burial chamber I," measuring ca. 2.6 by 2.15 m, was entered through a vertical shaft leading to a horizontal corridor. It contained a skeleton lying on a bench with a variety of adornments and scarabs mounted in gold. Four more skeletons, probably of his family or entourage, and many burial presents were found on the floor. The largest tomb was found empty and hence was not considered by Schumacher as a tomb ("chamber f"). This hypogeum is 5.6 m long, 3.7 m wide, and 3.1 m high and was entered through a shaft. It is beautifully built. All the chambers in the *Mittelburg,* and chamber f and its doorway in particular, are vaulted by fine-stone rudimentary corbeling—an early example of this building technique. Chamber f has been compared to the corbeled burial chambers from Ugarit.

The sacred area, i.e., the place where Altar 4017 and Temple 4040 were built in the EB Age, continued to function. Loud uncovered remains of buildings of strata XIII–IX on both sides of the sacred area, but he did not recognize any contemporary structure in the sacred area itself. He assigned an area above Altar 4017 covered with standing stone steles to stratum XII and a series of superimposed rubble pavements, as well as a heap of stones which could have been fallen steles, to stratum IX. He assigned the new temple built here (No. 2048) to stratum VIII, to the LB Age. However, it seems that Temple 2048 should be assigned to stratum X and dated to the MB Age (Epstein 1965; Dunayevsky and Kempinski 1973).

Temple 2048 has three superimposed phases. See Fig. MEG.03. The earlier one was preserved at foundation level and no floors, doorways, or finds could be associated with it. It is a massive rectangular structure measuring 21.5 by 16.5 m and containing a single room with a niche opposite the entrance. Two towers flanked the entrance. The thick, rubble foundation walls possibly indicate that the edifice rose to a considerable height. Part of the tower to the left of the entrance was constructed with ashlar stones, and it probably belongs to the superimposed LB structure. The temple resembles the large MB II temple at Shechem—both usually referred to as "tower temples" or "fortress temples."

Well-built domestic houses of this period were uncovered in areas AA and BB. The custom of intramural burial, inside and outside the houses, was common in Canaanite Megiddo. Many graves and stone-built tombs were found throughout the site and often it is not easy to assign them to the correct city level.

Typical to Megiddo at the end of MB III and the LB I is a fine group of decorated pottery known as "bichrome ware," thus named because its decoration, which consists of bands of red and black paint. Similar pottery is known from other sites in Canaan and Cyprus. Its origin was attributed at the time to Hurrian presence in Canaan

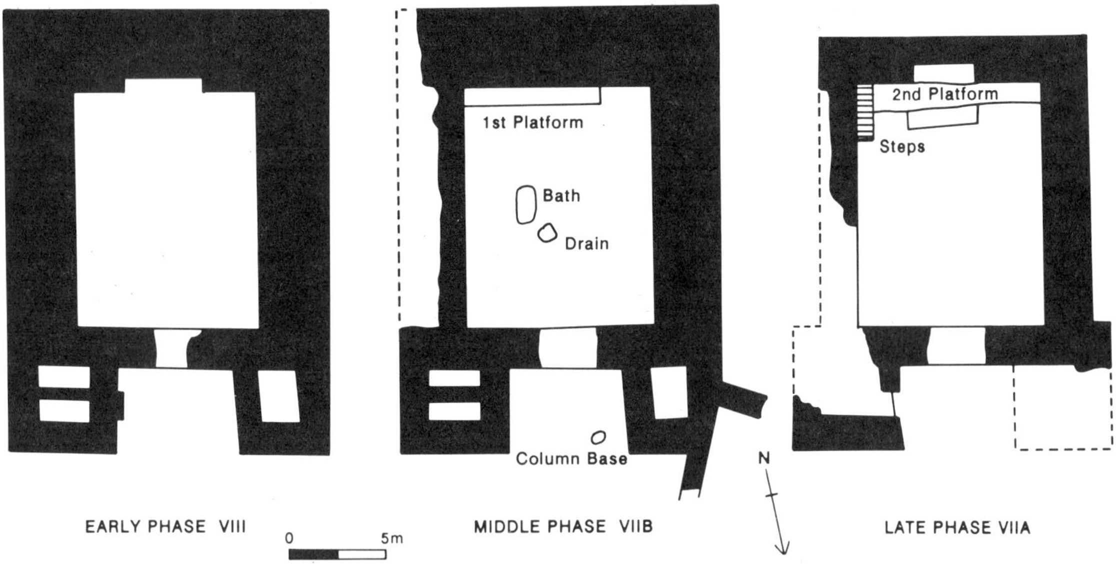

MEG.03. Three phases of the "Fortress Temple" in Area BB at Megiddo—MB Age and LB Age. *(Redrawn from* EAEHL 3: 838)

(Epstein 1966). Recent neutron-activation analyses (Artzy, Perlman, and Asaro 1978), however, indicated that one group of this pottery originated in Cyprus, while another, distinctive group originated at Megiddo. Both groups seem to have been contemporaneously used at Megiddo (Wood 1982).

b. Late Bronze Age. The expulsion of the Hyksos from Egypt and the campaign of Ahmose to Canaan ca. 1550 B.C. mark the renewal of Egyptian influence in the country. This event is usually adopted for the beginning of the LB Age. In general, it is very difficult to correlate the archaeological evidence from Canaan with the Egyptian inscriptional evidence. However, it seems quite possible that many cities in the S and inland regions of the country had been devastated, but not those in the coastal area and in particular not Megiddo, where no data indicating a destruction at that time have been found (Weinstein 1981).

The Egyptian conquest of Megiddo apparently occurred in 1479 B.C. during the first Asian campaign of Thutmose III. The events in Megiddo were recorded in detail and can be reconstructed (*ANET,* 234–38; Davies 1986: 51–56). While Thutmose III and his army progressed N along the coastal plain and the main highway, armies of the Canaanite kings led by the king of Kadesh on the Orontes concentrated near Megiddo. They decided to confront the Egyptian army at the place where the pass leading through the narrow Naḥal Iron opens to the Jezreel valley. Thutmose III learned in advance of his opponents' plan and held a conference, in which his commanders suggested taking alternative routes to the N or S of Naḥal Iron. Thutmose III, however, decided to take the direct route, crossed Naḥal Iron, and took the Canaanite armies by surprise. The Egyptians won the battle which followed, but the Canaanites managed to reach the city. Thutmose III laid siege and succeeded in conquering Megiddo after seven months. The annals give detailed lists of booty taken by the Egyptians after the battle and the siege.

The battle of Megiddo established the Egyptian domination in Canaan and Megiddo. The conquest of the city has been taken as an archaeological turning point between strata IX and VIII, but Shea (1979) is right that the annals do not mention a destruction of the city, and remains of such a destruction were not discerned in the excavations.

Megiddo is not mentioned in the annals describing the campaigns of Amenhotep II (1427–1401 B.C.), probably because it was dominated by Egypt (*ANET,* 245–48). This is manifested by two contemporary sources. One of the Taanach Letters orders the local ruler to send provisions and soldiers to the Egyptian commander at Megiddo. Papyrus Hermitage 1116A, dated to the 19th or 20th year of Amenhotep II, records presentations by Egyptian officials of grain and beer to envoys of various Canaanite cities, including Megiddo (Weinstein 1981: 13).

Eight of the cuneiform letters found in el-Amarna were sent from Megiddo (Mercer 1939: Nos. 242–48, 365) and testify to its importance. They apparently date to the later part of Amenhotep III's reign (1391–1353 B.C.) or to the earlier part of Amenhotep IV's reign (1353–1335 B.C.). Six of the letters were sent by Biridiya, the ruler of Megiddo, whose name is not Semitic. The letters express his loyalty to Egypt. Some of them discuss Biridiya's struggle with Labaya, the ruler of Shechem, who apparently attempted to take Megiddo by force but failed. In one letter (No. 244), Biridiya appealed for a garrison of 100 Egyptian troops to prevent the fall of the city. Two letters (Nos. 248, 365) discuss cultivation of estates in Shunem by forced labor.

During the reigns of Seti I (1306–1290 B.C.) and Rameses II (1290–1224 B.C.), Megiddo must have been firmly held by Egypt. The last Egyptian document of the New Kingdom which mentions Megiddo is papyrus Anastasi I, dating to the end of the 13th century B.C., in which Megiddo appears as a place name in a geographic description of Canaan.

By the beginning of the LB Age the palace was shifted from the center of the city to the N side; and four superimposed edifices built along the upper periphery of the site were uncovered in area AA in strata IX–VIIA. Particularly impressive is the stratum VIII palace. Its walls are ca. 2 m thick. A large court, 20 × 11 m, lay at its center, and another court to its W. Near them was found a large bathroom with a basin in its center and a floor covered with sea shells set in lime plaster. A hoard of ivory and gold objects was found beneath the floors in one of the rooms. The stratum VIIB palace, which uses the large court and bathroom of the previous palace, met its end by a severe destruction by fire.

A large city gate was built to the E of and near the palace in stratum IX (or even in stratum X) and was in use until the end of the stratum VIIA city. A wide roadway, paved with rubble and supported by a retaining wall, approached the gate. It was a monumental three-entry gatehouse, faced with ashlar stones. The floor of the gate passage was considerably raised in stratum VIIB. Significantly, the gatehouse does not have towers flanking the gate passage nor does it have deeply set foundations beneath the level of the floor as in other MB city gates around the country. This can be explained if it is assumed that the gate was constructed in a trench cut in the debris of the site or in the MB II glacis extending along its edge.

The absence of an LB city wall associated with the city gate, which is not even structurally connected to the back wall of the adjacent palace, has long puzzled scholars (Gonen 1987: 15–16). The above interpretation might help to furnish an explanation. It seems that the gate was incorporated in the MB fortifications surrounding the slopes of the site, which continued to function during the LB Age. These fortifications, crowned by the buildings located along the upper periphery of the site, probably formed the defense line of the city which faced Thutmose III's army in ca. 1479 B.C.

Another palatial complex was uncovered in strata VIII–VIIA in area DD to the E of the city gate. Excavation did not penetrate here beneath stratum VIII. Also, this edifice had a large rectangular court in its center.

Temple 2048 in area BB was rebuilt in stratum VIIB. It was based on the earlier foundations and had a similar plan. Only the back wall was thicker than that of the previous temple, and a raised platform replaced the cultic niche at the back of the cella. The temple was built of large ashlar stones. Two clay liver models and three bronze figurines of deities, one of them covered with gold, probably originated in the temple. The temple was destroyed by fire.

Many valuable objects were uncovered in the buildings and in the inter- and extramural burials. They include cylinder seals, bronze objects and figurines, faience vessels and amulets, alabaster vessels, gold objects, and gold jewelry. Of particular interest is a broken cuneiform tablet found by a shepherd after the termination of the excavations (Goetze and Levy 1959). It includes a section of the Epic of Gilgamesh and possibly derives from a scribal school at Megiddo.

c. End of the Canaanite City. Stratum VIIA represents a prosperous city. See Fig. CIT.04. The monumental structures in areas AA, BB, and DD indicate continuity of culture, although the palace and temple of stratum VIIB, and possibly larger parts of the city, were destroyed by fire. In area AA the three-entry city gate continued in use, and the palace was rebuilt. The palace was the largest of all the palaces successively constructed here. It was built around a central courtyard and was decorated with wall paintings, an indication of Egyptian influence. On its W side an annex, a three-chambered cellar, was added. Sealed by destruction debris in the cellar's back chamber, possibly the "treasury" of the palace, an assemblage of ivory objects and other precious items was found. In area BB the temple was rebuilt. Its walls were narrower than those in the earlier structures, and it now had a cultic niche built in its back wall as in the original building.

An ivory-model pen case bearing a cartouche of Rameses III found in the cache in the annex of the palace proves that stratum VIIA was not destroyed prior to the reign of that pharaoh (1182–1151 B.C.; low chronology of Wente and Van Siclen). A statue base of Rameses VI (1141–1133 B.C.; low chronology), was found buried in a pit in area CC. Originally the statue may have been placed in a temple, and it indicates the continuation of Egyptian rule in Megiddo during Rameses VI's reign (J. H. Breasted in Loud 1948: 135–38). The destruction of stratum VIIA probably occurred shortly afterward, ca. 1130 B.C.

The carved ivories found in the annexed cellar of the palace included 382 items (Loud 1939), the richest assemblage of Bronze Age ivories found in the Near East. The assemblage forms an assortment of objects of many types and various styles (Kantor 1956; Barnett 1982: 25–28; Liebowitz 1987). It includes locally produced ivories in Canaanite style and imported items in Egyptian, Aegean, Assyrian, and Hittite style. Of special interest is the Hittite plaque (No. 44) showing the Hittite king standing above rows of demons and beneath a winged sun disc. The stratigraphic context and the Rameses III cartouche date this assemblage to the 12th century B.C. But many scholars, notably Frankfort and Kantor (1956), believe that it represents a collection of ivories produced over a long period of time, mainly during the 14th and 13th centuries. Dothan (1982: 70–72) and Yadin (Aharoni and Yadin 1977: 848–49) believe that this collection was originally kept in a similar "treasury" in the stratum VIIB palace and then transferred to the new one. In any case, the assemblage indicates the prosperity of Canaanite art and culture in the later part of the LB Age.

d. Strata VIB–A. Following the destruction of the Canaanite metropolis, a poor settlement (VIB) was built; and it was soon replaced by a larger and richer settlement (VIA). The pattern of settlement radically differs from that of stratum VIIA; and the temple, palace, and city gate were not rebuilt. The settlement met its end by a destruction by fire. A city wall was not found; the excavators believe that the later city gate of stratum VA–IVB originated in stratum VIA; but this supposition seems doubtful. The buildings of stratum VIA, mostly of domestic nature, were built of bricks on stone foundations. The sole structure of a public nature is building 2072 in area AA. The building is located at the edge of the site, measuring ca. 32 by 37 m; it has thick walls and probably carried a second floor.

Sealed beneath the destruction debris of that level were a great number of pottery vessels. They include "collared-rim storage jars" and Philistine pottery. Of particular interest is a painted jug from Building 2072 which shows a procession of animals and a lyre player; it is known as the "Orpheus jug," as the scene is apparently associated with an early version of the Orpheus legend (Mazar 1976).

Typical to that city level are metal objects, mostly of bronze. A group of jugs, bowls, strainers, axheads, and spearheads was found in a single locus (No. 1739) in area CC. Schumacher (1908: 84–87) found in his "4th level" a number of metal objects, including five bronze stands and iron blades, which should probably be assigned to stratum VIA. The bronzework found in stratum VIA indicates a strong tradition of metalwork, which either continues the Canaanite tradition of bronzework (Negbi 1974) or was introduced into the country by the Sea Peoples (Tubb 1988).

e. Historical Correlations of Strata VII–VI. The archaeological data should be correlated with three historical aspects: (1) the decline of the Canaanite city-states and the end of Egyptian rule in Canaan; (2) the settlement of the Sea Peoples; and (3) the settlement of the Israelite tribes.

The destruction by fire of stratum VIIB in the later part of the 13th century B.C. indicates a forceful interruption in the Egyptian rule which is not documented. Stratum VIIA and the statue base of Rameses VI prove, however, that the Canaanite city was later rebuilt in the same tradition and even prospered and that it lived under Egyptian suzerainty until ca. 1130 B.C. It seems that the destruction of the stratum VIIA city coincides with the end of Egyptian rule in Canaan, and the two events may well have been connected. The history of Megiddo in the 12th century B.C. is very similar to that of Canaanite Beth-shan and Lachish during that period. According to Ussishkin (1985: 224–26) the decline of the Canaanite cities and the end of the Egyptian rule mark the end of the LB in Palestine.

The Philistine pottery found in Megiddo can be taken as an expression of Philistine presence. However, many of the items are sherds and were not found in a clear stratigraphic context. Dothan (1982: 70–80) argues that the appearance of Philistine pottery in stratum VIIA is proof of Sea Peoples' presence in that city level. But it seems that A. Mazar (1985: 96–97) is right that Philistine pottery appeared here in stratum VI and not earlier. Alt (1953), B. Mazar (1976), and Yadin (1970: 93–95) believe that Megiddo of stratum VIA, as manifested in its culture, was an 11th-century central Canaanite-Philistine city that was conquered and destroyed by David.

The king of Megiddo is mentioned in Josh 12:21 in the list of kings defeated by Joshua. Josh 17:11–12 and Judg 1:27 tell that the Canaanites continued to live in Megiddo until their subjection at a later period by the tribe of Manasseh (also 1 Chr 7:29). Albright (1936) believed that the expression "at Taanach, by Megiddo waters" (Judg. 5:19) in the Song of Deborah refers to a time when Megiddo was not settled, and he assigned the poem and the events described in it to the period immediately following the destruction of the stratum VIIA city. Aharoni (1982), following a suggestion of Albright, who later withdrew it, argued that stratum VIIA was destroyed by the Israelites and that stratum VIB was a small Israelite settlement. This view is supported by the use of stone pillars in buildings of stratum VI—a typical feature in Israelite buildings—and by the presence of "collared-rim storage jars" which are usually associated with the Israelite settlement in Canaan (also Kempinski 1989: 78–82).

3. The Israelite City. a. Stratum VB. This level includes remains of domestic structures in various parts of the site, probably the remains of a small, unfortified settlement. Remains of one larger building, probably a trapezoidal fort surrounded by a casemate wall, were uncovered at the NE edge of the site (Wightman 1984: 132–36). This settlement is usually considered to be Israelite, dating to the time of David.

b. The Solomonic City. Megiddo was included, together with Taanach and Beth-shan, in the fifth administrative district of Solomon (1 Kgs 4:12) and apparently here was the residence of the district governor, Baana son of Ahilud. In 1 Kgs 9:15 Megiddo is mentioned together with Jerusalem, Hazor, and Gezer as a central city built by Solomon. It is clear that the text refers to the building of monumental structures the construction of which was financed by the levies imposed by the king. The remains of the Solomonic city level have been uncovered since excavations at Tel Megiddo began in 1903. Of special importance is Yadin's work (1960, 1970), which resulted in redating City Wall 325 and "Solomon's stables" to the 9th century B.C. Scholars widely differ on the stratigraphic, chronological, and functional interpretation of the remains. The summary below is based on Ussishkin's views, but the different opinions will be stressed in the discussion of each aspect.

Stratigraphically, the Solomonic city level includes all the structures which are immediately beneath the city wall (No. 325) of stratum IVA and associated structures and above the building remains of stratum VB (which in turn was built above the burned brick debris of stratum VI structures). These remains were originally assigned by the American excavators to different strata, V (later VA), IVB, and IV. Albright (1943: 29–30 n. 10) observed that the remains assigned to strata VA and IVB are in fact contemporary and belong to one city level, which he labeled stratum VA–IVB, dated to the reign of Solomon. This concept was primarily followed by Wright (1950: 59–60) and Yadin (1970, 1972; Aharoni and Yadin 1977) and is generally accepted today (see Ussishkin 1980; Davies 1986). Kenyon (1964) differs on many stratigraphic details and adopts lower dates. Aharoni (1972, 1982), followed by Herzog (1986: 93–108), basically accepted the stratigraphy but labeled this city level stratum VA; assuming that the superimposed city level, stratum IVA (his IVB), represents the Solomonic city, he dated stratum VA–IVB to the reign of David. Wightman (1985) recently analyzed afresh the stratigraphy of strata VI–III and pointed out that the domestic and public structures had a different history.

Stratum VA–IVB includes three palatial edifices, Nos. 1723, 6000, and 338, built at the S, N, and E sides of the site respectively. See Fig. MEG.04. They were positioned

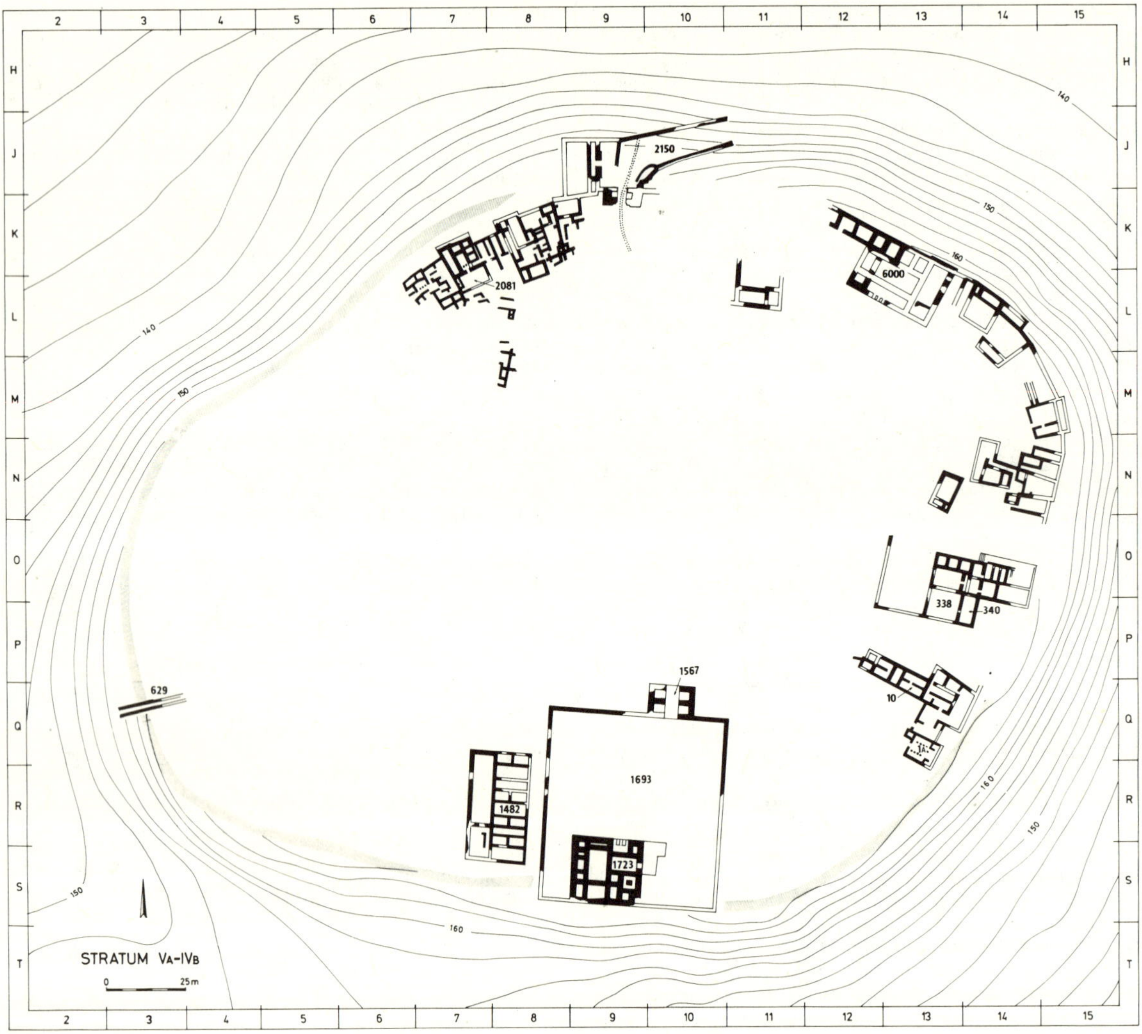

MEG.04. Plan of Stratum VA-IVB at Megiddo—Solomonic Period. *(Courtesy of D. Ussishkin)*

at the edge of the city, their facades facing its center; and their back walls reached the upper periphery of the site. All of them opened into spacious courtyards. A large building, No. 1482, believed to have had an administrative function, was built alongside the S palace compound, No. 1723. Large quarters of domestic buildings were uncovered along the E and N edges of the city. The N quarter also included a sanctuary (No. 2081).

The palatial buildings, the sanctuary, and the domestic structures built along the upper periphery of the site formed a line of defense around the city. According to Yadin this line of defense was a casemate city wall, best observed to the W of Palace 6000. The city gate was located, as in previous periods, in the N side of the city. It was the small, two-entry gatehouse, approached by a wide, lime-paved ramp (Loud 1948: 39–45). Stratigraphically it should be assigned to stratum VA–IVB as suggested by Loud (Ussishkin 1980; Herzog 1986: 93–108) rather than the so-called Solomonic four-entry gatehouse, which is later in date and belongs to stratum IVA. In addition, a postern (gallery 629) was built at the W side above the spring. It was excavated and dated by the American expedition to the 12th century (Lamon 1935) but correctly assigned by Yadin to stratum VA–IVB.

Ashlar masonry, possibly quarried SE of the site (Shiloh and Horowitz 1975), was lavishly used in the construction of the palatial buildings, in their massive foundations and their superstructure. Proto-Ionic stone capitals, which were mounted on stone pilasters or freestanding pillars, decorated monumental entrances in these buildings (Lamon and Shipton 1939: 55–57; Ussishkin 1970). Unfortunately, these edifices were largely destroyed when the ashlars were stolen for secondary use in stratum IVA. The construction with ashlar masonry, which originated in Egypt, appeared for the first time in Canaan in the LB temple and city gate at Megiddo and was introduced on a large scale during the reign of Solomon. Its appearance in Megiddo fits the description of ashlar masonry used in the construction of Solomon's palace in Jerusalem (1 Kgs 7:9–12). The wide use of ashlars was part of the Phoenician influence which dominated Solomon's building activities.

Palace 6000 was uncovered by Yadin (1970: 73–77). It was a rectangular building, measuring ca. 28 by 21 m; and following its destruction by fire, most of its stones were stolen. It seems to have been a ceremonial palace built as a *bit-hilani,* that is, a type of a ceremonial palace characterized by a monumental porticoed entrance and a large central hall which was commonly used in N Syria during that period. Palace 1723 (Lamon and Shipton 1939: 11–24) was built in a spacious, lime-paved, square courtyard. The entrance to the courtyard was through monumental gate 1567, which was largely uncovered by Schumacher (1908: 91–104), who labeled it *der Palast.* The palace was square in plan, measuring ca. 23 by 23 m. It was mostly preserved at foundation level, and hence its aboveground plan is open to conjecture. It seems probable that the edifice contained a residential as well as a ceremonial section, the latter built as a *bit-hilani* (Ussishkin 1966). Hence Solomonic Megiddo apparently contained at least two *bit-hilani* palaces, as, for instance, in the acropolises of Tell Tayanat and Zincirli (ancient Sam'al) in N Syria, which date to that general period. A number of scholars, however, believe that only Palace 6000 was a *bit-hilani,* while Palace 1723 had a different plan (Yadin 1970: 95; Fritz 1983: 22–25; Kempinski 1989).

The third palatial edifice, Building 338, was built at the highest place in the city. The building was constructed on an aboveground foundation podium. It was first uncovered by Schumacher (1908: 110–24), who identified it as a sanctuary; associating it with the stratum II fortress, he defined it as a *Tempelburg.* It was further uncovered by Fisher (1929: 68–74), who identified it as a "temple of Astarte," and by Guy (1931: 30–37), who identified it as the residence of the commander of the E sector of the city and assigned it to stratum IV (i.e., stratum IVA). Finally, it was studied by Lamon and Shipton (1939: 47–59), who accepted Guy's interpretation, which is generally accepted today. However, it seems that Schumacher rightly identified Unit 340 at the S part of the edifice as a shrine (Ussishkin 1989). Two large steles found inside hint at a dual cult performed here. Model shrines and stone altars found by Fisher to the S of Building 338 (May 1935) probably belonged to this shrine. While Unit 340 and its forecourt served as a sanctuary, other parts of the edifice may have had a secular function. A wing of the building uncovered by Schumacher but ignored by the American excavators antedates the stratum IVA city wall; hence the edifice dates to stratum IVB.

Sanctuary 2081 was built, like the palaces, with its back wall extending along the upper periphery of the site (Loud 1948: 45–46). Two monolithic stones found standing in its center were probably cultic steles. A cache of cultic equipment was uncovered here. Several stones carved in the shape of an eighth segment of a sphere found nearby (Lamon and Shipton 1939: 24) probably indicate that a large horned altar erected of ashlar stones of the type uncovered in Tel Beer-sheba stood in the courtyard of the sanctuary.

Much pottery was uncovered in stratum VA–IVB. Typical to it are red-slipped, irregularly burnished vessels which start to spread in Palestine at that time. Their appearance in Tel Megiddo is a chronological pivot for dating the appearance of this class of pottery.

The end of stratum VA–IVB is not clear. Megiddo is mentioned in the list of cities conquered by Sheshonk I in his campaign in ca. 925 B.C., and Albright proposed that the Solomonic city was destroyed by him. However, the data do not indicate an overall destruction of the stratum VA–IVB city. Only a number of structures, primarily Palace 6000 and Building 10, were destroyed by fire. The sporadic destruction could have been associated with the division of the united monarchy in ca. 930 B.C., or with Sheshonk I's campaign, or could have even occurred at a slightly later date.

However, it seems that the settlement continued to exist after 925 B.C. A fragment of a stone-carved stele of Sheshonk I was uncovered by Fisher (1929). It was estimated that the complete stele was ca. 3.3 m high and 1.5 m wide. It was probably erected not far from its find spot at the E side of the site, which was the highest point of the city at that time. Sheshonk I must have erected his stele in an existing, not in a desolate, city, with the intention of holding it in the future. The situation at Megiddo also indicates that Sheshonk I's campaign was meant to renew the Egyptian foothold in Canaan and to turn Megiddo into a major base for that purpose. But the Egyptian conquest was short-lived since a year later Sheshonk died and the new ambitious program was abandoned.

c. Stratum IVA. The stratum IVA city radically differs from that of the previous stratum VA–IVB city. See Fig. MEG.05. It seems that the change of character is an expression of a different function given to Megiddo as a result of the division of the monarchy. Once the kingdom had been divided, strategic needs must have changed; and thus Megiddo became a fortified stronghold instead of a civilian district center. The palatial compounds were no longer needed; and the walls of the edifices (except the shrine in Building 338 which was buried beforehand as an act of reverence) were dismantled, their stones taken for secondary use in the new buildings.

City Wall 325 surrounded the city. Because the wall was ca. 3.6 m thick, its two faces were built with insets and offsets. It was built of stone and did not have any foundations. The entrance to the city was through a complex city gate—the so called Solomonic gate (Lamon in Loud 1948: 46–57). A roadway led up to an outer, two-entry gatehouse. The latter opened to an open court; and behind it was built the inner, four-entry gatehouse which adjoined the city wall. The inner gatehouse rested on massive foundations, supported by a constructional fill, which were entirely exposed by the American excavators. The structure was built with ashlars removed from the stratum VA–

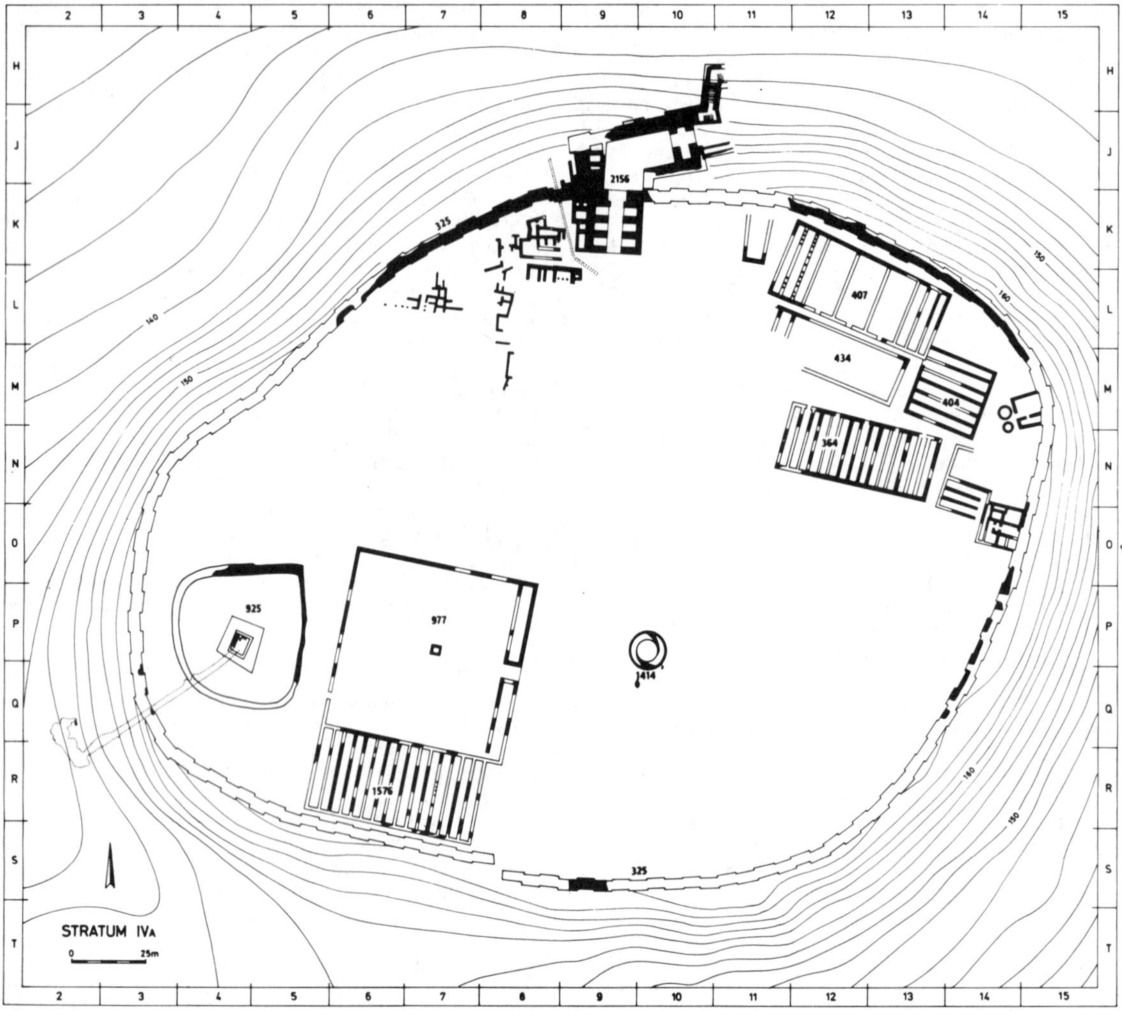

MEG.05. Plan of Stratum IVA at Megiddo—Divided Kingdom Period. *(Courtesy of D. Ussishkin)*

IVB buildings. The gate complex is similar to the 10th–9th centuries B.C. gate complexes at Gezer, Lachish, and probably Tel Batash (ancient Timnah), and the inner gatehouse also to the four-entry city gates in Hazor and Ashdod. All these gates are based on a similar foundations structure and ground plan.

The construction date of the city gate is a controversial issue. Stratigraphically, the city gate adjoins City Wall 325 and is contemporary with it, as concluded by the original excavators (cf. Aharoni 1972; Ussishkin 1980; Herzog 1986: 93–108). Hence, the city gate belongs to stratum IVA and dates to the period of the divided monarchy. Yadin (1958, 1970, 1972, 1980) believed that the four-entry gatehouse originated in stratum VA–IVB and dates to the reign of Solomon. This dating is primarily based on the similarity in plan between this gate and the four-entry gates in Hazor and Gezer—all three cities being mentioned together in 1 Kgs 9:15 as built by Solomon. Yadin offered a new interpretation of the stratigraphy to explain how the gate is earlier than City Wall 325; he based his explanation on the assumption (which seems utterly impossible) that the foundation structure of the gatehouse is in fact part of the gate's original superstructure. Yadin's dating is currently followed by most scholars (e.g., Davies [1986: 85–92], W. G. Dever, V. Fritz, P. R. S. Moorey, and Y. Shiloh [1980]). Aharoni and Herzog, who believe that the city gate belongs stratigraphically to stratum IVA (labeled IVB by them), however, date this stratum to the reign of Solomon; and hence they consider the city gate to be Solomonic in date.

A massive water system was built to enable easier approach to the spring located at the bottom of the W slope (Lamon 1935). It was dated by the American excavators to the 12th century B.C. but redated by Yadin. The stratum VA–IVB "gallery" was now blocked and so was the approach to the spring from outside. A vertical shaft was dug from the surface of the mound through the accumulated debris and the natural rock and had stairs prepared along its sides. It ended in a horizontal tunnel cut in the rock and leading to the spring. In a later stage the horizontal tunnel was deepened, enabling the water to flow to the bottom of the vertical shaft.

Two complexes of stables for horses were uncovered (Lamon and Shipton 1939: 32–47). This interpretation of the structures was first given by Guy (1931: 37–48), who associated them with Solomon's "cities for chariots and cities for horsemen" (1 Kgs 9:19). Pritchard (1970) suggested that these structures were storehouses or barracks; he based his opinion on analysis of structural characteristics and on the complete absence of equestrian accoutrements. Aharoni (1982) and Herzog (1973), who discovered a similar structure in Tel Beer-sheba, interpreted these buildings as storehouses. Fritz (1977) considered them to be barracks, and Herr (1988) suggested that they served as marketplaces. Yadin (1976) and Holladay (1986) further argued that these are stables for horses, and this interpretation forms the basis for the discussion below.

The S complex contains five units of stabling built in a row. Each unit was rectangular, measuring ca. 21 by 11 m, and contained a central, lime-paved passage and two side, stone-paved aisles. Each aisle was separated from the passageway by a row of stone pillars alternating with stone mangers—all of which are ashlar stones stolen from the Solomonic edifices. The side aisles served as stalls for the horses, and each pillar and the neighboring manger marked the position of one horse. Many of the pillars had holes cut in their corners for tethering the horses. Each aisle could accommodate 15 horses; hence each unit contained 30 horses, and the entire complex 150 horses. The stables opened into a spacious, lime-paved, square courtyard, measuring ca. 55 by 55 m. The courtyard, built on sloping ground, was based on a massive artificial fill laid here to level the floor. Lamon and Shipton suggested that a unit of chariots was stationed in the S complex and that the courtyard was used for their training. One can assume that the unit contained 100 chariots—3 horses per chariot.

The N complex contained similar stabling units, but they were not built according to a uniform plan and were not grouped around a large courtyard. Hence riding horses were probably garrisoned there. Lamon and Shipton calculated that this complex contained 300 or 330 horses; hence 450 or 480 horses were garrisoned at Megiddo.

Large amounts of water and supplies had to be daily provided for these horses. Water could have been easily brought from the water system; a square brick installation found in the courtyard of the S complex was interpreted as a tank for water. A large storage pit (No. 1414) was uncovered midway between the two stable complexes and assigned to stratum III (Lamon and Shipton 1939: 66–68). Stratigraphically, it could have belonged to stratum IVA, and it seems quite possible that it served as a central silo for keeping provisions for the horses. The pit was at least 7 m deep (its upper edge may not have been preserved), and its diameter at the bottom is 7 m. The entire construction was of rubble, and the rough surface had not been plastered. A pair of winding stairs were added. Its present capacity is ca. 450 m^3. Remains of chaff and grains were found inside, and the excavators estimated that the pit contained a certain amount of chaff when it fell into disuse. Assuming, as calculated by Holladay (1986: 118), that each horse consumed ca. 9.6 liters of supply per day, the pit could have held supplies sufficient for feeding 300–330 horses for 130–150 days.

The city of stratum IVA must have been a garrison city, and it is noteworthy that residential quarters were not uncovered. Here Ahaziah, king of Judah, died when he fled, riding wounded in his chariot, before Jehu's men (2 Kgs 9:27). The stable complexes prove that Megiddo was a center for Israelite chariotry and cavalry units at the time of the divided monarchy. The written sources indicate the weight of these units in the Israelite army. Thus the Assyrian annals indicate the strength of Ahab's chariotry and cavalry in the battle of Qarqar in N Syria in 853 B.C., as well as in the 8th century B.C. (Dalley 1985).

Three exceptionally fine seals apparently belong to this city level. Schumacher (1908: 99–101) uncovered two seals near the gate to the Palace 1723 compound. The first is a jasper seal portraying a roaring lion and inscribed "(belonging) to Shema, servant of Jeroboam," obviously Jeroboam II, king of Israel. The second, carved of lapis lazuli, portrays a griffin and is inscribed "(belonging) to Asaph." The third seal, uncovered by Guy on the surface of the site (W. E. Staples in Guy 1931: 49–68), is cut of serpentine. It depicts a griffin and a locust and is inscribed "Haman."

d. Stratum III. In 734 B.C. Tiglath-pileser III campaigned in Philistia and probably already held Megiddo. In 732 B.C. he conquered the N parts of the kingdom of Israel and annexed them to Assyria. Megiddo became the capital of the Assyrian province *Magiddu,* and stratum III probably dates to this period.

City Wall 325 continued in use in stratum III, but apparently a new city gate was constructed. See Fig. CIT.09. Remains of one or two gatehouses superimposed above the four-entry inner gatehouse were uncovered (Guy 1931: 24–27; Lamon and Shipton 1939: 74–83). The upper one was a two-entry gatehouse which belongs to stratum III. Beneath it were uncovered remains of a three-entry gatehouse. The excavators concluded that the three-entry gatehouse was never completed, as it was decided at the time of construction to alter the plans and erect a two-entry gatehouse instead. Yadin believed that the three-entry gatehouse was completed and used before being later replaced by the two entry gatehouse. The outer gate house was also rebuilt when the rebuilding of the inner gatehouse was carried out.

To the W of the city gate two public buildings (Nos. 1052, 1369) were uncovered (Lamon and Shipton 1939: 69–74). They portray several Assyrian architectural elements, notably a central, rectangular courtyard. It is clear that these buildings functioned as Assyrian government administrative or residential centers.

Large areas of the city were uncovered, revealing residential quarters which apparently covered the entire top of the mound. The houses were arranged in blocks which were separated by evenly spaced and parallel streets.

e. Stratum II. This stratum dates to the 7th century B.C. It is characterized by residential quarters similar to those of stratum III. New domestic houses were now built along the same pattern of streets. Remains of buildings uncovered near the upper periphery of the site indicate that City Wall 325 had fallen into disuse in stratum II or stratum I sometime before the settlement came to an end.

A large structure built at the E edge of the site was uncovered by Schumacher (1908: 110–21) as part of the *Tempelburg,* and by Fisher, who identified it as a fortress (Lamon and Shipton 1939: 83–86). It measures ca. 69 by 48 m and has a large, central court. The stone walls, preserved at foundation level, are ca. 2.5 m thick. According to Lamon and Shipton the fortress was built above the disused City Wall 325; hence the fortress functioned when Megiddo was no longer a fortified city. But stratigraphically this conclusion is not proven since nowhere do the walls of the structure reach the line of the city wall and both of them could have been contemporary. The buried shrine of Building 338 was located in the courtyard of the fortress and rose higher than the surrounding chambers. Hence the structure could have hardly served as a fortress; its function is unclear; and its ground plan seems to be related to the buried shrine (Ussishkin 1989).

In 609 B.C. Pharaoh Neco reached Megiddo on his way to Carchemish to aid Assyria against the Babylonians. Josiah, king of Judah, traveled to Megiddo and was executed there by Neco (2 Kgs 23:29–30; 2 Chr 35:20–24). This event is usually understood as an attempt that failed by Josiah to challenge militarily the Egyptian pharaoh. It was further concluded that Josiah's expanded kingdom included Megiddo and that the stratum II fortress was built by Josiah or by the Egyptians (Malamat 1973). However, Naʾaman (1989) is probably right that Josiah's kingdom was much smaller and that he was executed when he came to Megiddo to pay homage to the Egyptian overlord.

f. Stratum I. This stratum represents the last period of settlement on the mound, in the Babylonian and Persian periods, until the place was finally abandoned in the 4th century B.C. The abandonment of Megiddo could possibly be associated with Alexander the Great's conquest of Palestine in 322 B.C.

The remains of the Babylonian and Persian periods are relatively dull (Stern 1982: 5–8, 240). They include remains of many small houses, three long storerooms near the city gate, and a number of stone-built cist tombs.

The reference to Megiddo in Zech 12:11, mentioning "the mourning for Hadadrimmon in the plain of Megiddo," probably dates to the Persian or Hellenistic period. The mourning referred to could be a fertility ritual associated with the storm god Hadad-Rimmon. It indicates that Megiddo lay at that time in an area that was already little known to the Jews and regarded by them as alien and pagan (Davies 1986: 109).

4. The Later Periods. A Jewish village named Kefer ʾOtnay existed to the S of the site ca. A.D. 100. During the reign of Hadrian (A.D. 117–38), the Legio II Traiana was stationed here, and it was later replaced by the Legio VI Ferrata. Kefar ʾOtnay was renamed Legio, after the occupying force. Legio became the center of an administrative district; from this the Arab village of Lejjun in turn derived its name.

Schumacher (1908: 161–90) investigated extensive remains of the Roman and Muslim periods, including aqueducts, a theater, and tombs, as well as a possible site of a Roman camp, to the S of the site. Very interesting are two cremation burials, probably of soldiers of the VIth Legion, which were recently discovered (Tsuk 1988–89). Schumacher (1908: 151–53) also uncovered some late remains on the site, notably an Ottoman watchtower on the E side.

Bibliography

Aharoni, Y. 1972. The Stratification of Israelite Megiddo. *JNES* 31: 302–11.

———. 1982. *The Archaeology of the Land of Israel.* Philadelphia.

Aharoni, Y., and Yadin, Y. 1977. Megiddo. *EAEHL* 3: 830–56.

Albright, W. F. 1936. The Song of Deborah in the Light of Archaeology. *BASOR* 62: 26–31.

———. 1943. *The Excavation of Tell Beit Mirsim.* Vol. 3, *The Iron Age.* AASOR 21–22. New Haven.

Alt, A. 1953. Megiddo im Übergang vom Kanaanäischen zum israelitischen Zeitalter. *KlSchr* 1: 256–73.

Amiran, R. 1960. The Pottery of the Middle Bronze Age I in Palestine. *IEJ* 10: 204–25.

Artzy, M.; Perlman, I.; and Asaro, F. 1978. Imported and Local Bichrome Ware in Megiddo. *Levant* 10: 99–111.

Barnett, R. D. 1982. *Ancient Ivories in the Middle East.* Qedem 14. Jerusalem.

Beck, P. 1975. The Cylinder Seal Impressions from Megiddo, Stage V, and Related Problems. *Opuscula Atheniensia* 11/1: 1–16.

Brandfon, F. R. 1977. The Earliest City Wall at Megiddo. *TA* 4: 79–84.

Dalley, S. 1985. Foreign Chariotry and Cavalry in the Armies of Tiglath-Pileser III and Sargon II. *Iraq* 47: 31–48.

Davies, G. I. 1986. *Megiddo.* Cambridge.

Dever, W. G. 1980. New Vistas on the EB IV ("MB I") Horizon in Syria-Palestine. *BASOR* 237: 35–64.

Dothan, T. 1982. *The Philistines and Their Material Culture.* Jerusalem.

Dunayevsky, I., and Kempinski, A. 1973. The Megiddo Temples. *ZDPV* 89: 161–87.

Eitan, A. 1974. Megiddo: Notes and News. *IEJ* 24: 275–76.

Engberg, R. M., and Shipton, G. M. 1934. *Notes on the Chalcolithic and Early Bronze Age Pottery of Megiddo.* SAOC 10. Chicago.

Epstein, C. 1965. An Interpretation of the Megiddo Sacred Area during Middle Bronze II. *IEJ* 15: 204–21.

———. 1966. *Palestinian Bichrome Ware.* Leiden.

———. 1973. The Sacred Area at Megiddo in Stratum XIX. *EI* 11: 54–57 (in Hebrew).

Fisher, C. S. 1929. *The Excavation of Armageddon.* OIC 4. Chicago.

Fritz, V. 1977. Bestimmung und Herkunft des Pfeilerhauses in Israel. *ZDPV* 93: 30–45.

———. 1983. Paläste während der Bronze- und Eisenzeit in Palästina. *ZDPV* 99: 1–42.

Gerstenblith, P. 1983. *The Levant at the Beginning of the Middle Bronze Age.* ASORDS 5. Winona Lake, IN.

Goetze, A., and Levy, S. 1959. Fragment of the Gilgamesh Epic from Megiddo. *ʿAtiqot* (English Series) 2: 121–28.

Gonen, R. 1987. Megiddo in the Late Bronze Age—Another Reassessment. *Levant* 19: 1–18.
Guy, P. L. O. 1931. *New Light from Armageddon.* OIC 9. Chicago.
———. 1938. *Megiddo Tombs.* OIP 33. Chicago.
Herr, L. G. 1988. Tripartite Pillared Buildings and the Market Place in Iron Age Palestine. *BASOR* 272: 47–67.
Herzog, Z. 1973. The Storehouses. Pp. 23–30 in *Beer-Sheba I,* ed. Y. Aharoni. Tel Aviv.
———. 1986. *Das Stadttor in Israel und in den Nachbarländern.* Mainz am Rhein.
Holladay, J. S., Jr. 1986. The Stables of Ancient Israel. Pp. 103–66 in *The Archaeology of Jordan and Other Sites Presented to Siegfried H. Horn,* ed. L. T. Geraty and L. G. Herr. Berrien Springs, MI.
Kantor, H. J. 1956. Syro-Palestinian Ivories. *JNES* 15: 153–74.
Kassis, H. E. 1973. Beginning of the Late Bronze Age at Megiddo: A Re-Examination of Stratum X. *Berytus* 22: 5–22.
Kempinski, A. 1989. *Megiddo. A City-State and Royal Centre in North Israel.* Munich.
Kenyon, K. M. 1958. Some Notes on the Early and Middle Bronze Age Strata at Megiddo. *EI* 5: 51*–60*.
———. 1964. Megiddo, Hazor, Samaria and Chronology. *Bulletin of the Institute of Archaeology* 4: 143–55.
———. 1969. The Middle and Late Bronze Age Strata at Megiddo. *Levant* 1: 25–60.
Lamon, R. S. 1935. *The Megiddo Water System.* OIP 32. Chicago.
Lamon, R. S., and Shipton, G. M. 1939. *Megiddo I.* OIP 42. Chicago.
Liebowitz, H. 1987. Late Bronze II Ivory Work in Palestine: Evidence of a Cultural Highlight. *BASOR* 265: 3–24.
Loud, G. 1939. *The Megiddo Ivories.* OIP 52. Chicago.
———. 1948. *Megiddo II.* OIP 62. Chicago.
Malamat, A. 1973. Josiah's Bid for Armageddon. *JANES* 5: 267–78.
May, H. G. 1935. *Material Remains of the Megiddo Cult.* OIP 26. Chicago.
Mazar, A. 1985. The Emergence of the Philistine Material Culture. *IEJ* 35: 95–107.
Mazar, B. 1976. The "Orpheus" Jug from Megiddo. Pp. 187–92 in *Magnalia Dei: The Mighty Acts of God,* ed. F. M. Cross, W. E. Lemke, and P. D. Miller, Jr. Garden City.
Mercer, S. A. B. 1939. *The Tell el-Amarna Tablets.* Toronto.
Müller, U. 1970. Kritische Bemerkungen zu den Straten XIII bis IX in Megiddo. *ZDPV* 86: 50–86.
Naʾaman, N. 1989. The Town-Lists of Judah and Benjamin and the Kingdom of Judah in the Days of Josiah. *Zion* 54: 17–71 (in Hebrew).
Negbi, O. 1974. The Continuity of the Canaanite Bronzework of the Late Bronze Age into the Early Iron Age. *TA* 1: 159–72.
Pritchard, J. B. 1970. The Megiddo Stables: A Reassessment. Pp. 268–76 in *Near Eastern Archaeology in the Twentieth Century,* ed. J. A. Sanders. Garden City.
Schumacher, G. 1908. *Tell el-Mutesellim.* I. Leipzig.
Shea, W. H. 1979. The Conquests of Sharuhen and Megiddo Reconsidered. *IEJ* 29: 1–5.
Shiloh, Y. 1980. Solomon's Gate at Megiddo as Recorded by Its Excavator, R. Lamon, Chicago. *Levant* 12: 69–76.
Shiloh, Y., and Horowitz, A. 1975. Ashlar Quarries of the Iron Age in the Hill Country of Israel. *BASOR* 217: 37–48.
Shipton, G. M. 1939. *Notes on the Megiddo Pottery of Strata VI–XX.* SAOC 17. Chicago.
Stern, E. 1982. *Material Culture of the Land of the Bible in the Persian Period, 538–332 B.C.* Warminster.
Thompson, T. L. 1970. The Dating of the Megiddo Temples in Strata XV–XIV. *ZDPV* 86: 38–49.
Tsuk, T. 1988–89. The Aqueduct to Legio and the Location of the Camp of the 6th Roman Legion. *TA* 15–16: 92–97.
Tubb, J. N. 1988. The Role of the Sea Peoples in the Bronze Industry of Palestine/Transjordan in the Late Bronze-Early Iron Age Transition. Pp. 251–70 in *Bronze Working Centres of Western Asia,* ed. J. E. Curtis. London.
Tufnell, O. 1973. The Middle Bronze Age Scarab-Seals from Burials on the Mound at Megiddo. *Levant* 5: 69–82.
Ussishkin, D. 1966. King Solomon's Palace and Building 1723 in Megiddo. *IEJ* 16: 174–86.
———. 1970. On the Original Position of Two Proto-Ionic Capitals at Megiddo. *IEJ* 20: 213–15.
———. 1980. Was the "Solomonic" City Gate at Megiddo Built by King Solomon? *BASOR* 239: 1–18.
———. 1985. Levels VII and VI at Tel Lachish and the End of the Late Bronze Age in Canaan. Pp. 213–30 in *Palestine in the Bronze and Iron Ages,* ed. J. N. Tubb. London.
———. 1989. Schumacher's Shrine in Building 338 at Megiddo. *IEJ* 39: 149–72.
Watzinger, C. 1929. *Tell el-Mutesellim.* II. Leipzig.
Weinstein, J. M. 1981. The Egyptian Empire in Palestine: A Reassessment. *BASOR* 241: 1–28.
Wightman, G. J. 1984. Building 434 and Other Public Buildings in the Northeastern Sector of Megiddo. *TA* 11: 132–45.
———. 1985. Megiddo VIA–III: Associated Structures and Chronology. *Levant* 17: 117–29.
Wilson, J. A. 1941. The Egyptian Middle Kingdom at Megiddo. *AJSL* 58: 225–36.
Wood, B. 1982. The Stratigraphic Relationship of Local and Imported Bichrome Ware at Megiddo. *Levant* 14: 73–79.
Wright, G. E. 1950. A Review of *Megiddo II. JAOS* 70: 56–60.
Yadin, Y. 1958. Solomon's City Wall and Gate at Gezer. *IEJ* 8: 80–86.
———. 1960. New Light on Solomon's Megiddo. *BA* 23: 62–68.
———. 1970. Megiddo of the Kings of Israel. *BA* 33: 66–96.
———. 1972. *Hazor.* The Schweich Lectures of the British Academy, 1970. London.
———. 1976. The Megiddo Stables. Pp. 249–52 in *Magnalia Dei: The Mighty Acts of God,* ed. F. M. Cross, W. E. Lemke, and P. D. Miller, Jr. Garden City.
———. 1980. A Rejoinder. *BASOR* 239: 19–23.

DAVID USSISHKIN

MEGIDDO, PLAIN OF (PLACE) [Heb *biqʿat mĕgiddô(n)*]. The central portion of the Jezreel valley, nearby the city of Megiddo (M.R. 167221), mentioned only twice in the OT (2 Chr 35:22; Zech 12:11). Although it was the scene of many battles, the only one referred to in the OT occurred in 609 B.C. By that time, Josiah, the king of Judah, had completed many of his celebrated religious reforms, and Judah was again becoming a political power. On the international scene the Assyrians were succumbing to their foes, but Neco of Egypt wished to go to their aid. His line of march crossed the Jezreel valley at Megiddo, and there Josiah challenged him. Josiah was mortally wounded by an archer before the battle had barely begun. The sudden death of this reforming king led to deep mourning among religious circles in Judah (2 Chr 35:24–25). It may be that Zechariah's enigmatic reference to mourning for Hadadrimmon in the plain of Megiddo is also in some way connected with this incident.

Bibliography

Malamat, A. 1973. Josiah's Bid for Armageddon: The Background of the Judean-Egyptian Encounter in 609 B.C. *JANES* 5: 267–79.

MELVIN HUNT

MEGIDDO, WATERS OF (PLACE) [Heb *mê mêgiddô*]. This term occurs only in Judg 5:19, as part of the description of the place where the Israelites under Deborah and Barak fought with the chariot forces of Sisera. Scholars have noted that the verse does not specifically refer to the city of Megiddo (M.R. 167221), although Taanach (M.R. 171214) is mentioned. Precise identification of the waters is complicated by the inclusion of Taanach, since none of the wadis in the region flow by both sites.

Albright (1936: 27) believed that the Wâdī el-Lejjun, which flows from the hills behind Megiddo, was the "waters of Megiddo." He also held that the lack of a specific reference to Megiddo in the verse implied that Megiddo was uninhabited at the time of the battle. As a result, Albright dated the battle of Deborah and Barak to the period between Megiddo VII and Megiddo VI. However, Aharoni (*LBHG*, 28) uses the same information to derive a drastically reordered course of events.

Simons (*GTTOT*, 290) pointed out that the Wâdī el-Lejjun is both too small and too far from Taanach to be acceptable as the waters of Megiddo. He suggested the Naḥal Kishon, mentioned in Judg 5:21 and which drains the whole Jezreel valley, should be considered as an alternative identification.

While this interpretation is feasible, the term is yet to be satisfactorily identified, although it is clear its location should be sought in the region between Taanach and Megiddo.

Bibliography

Albright, W. F. 1936. The Song of Deborah in the Light of Archaeology. *BASOR* 62: 26–31.

MELVIN HUNT

MEGILLOTH [Heb *ḥamēš mĕgillôt*]. The term "megilloth" means scrolls and is used to refer to the "five scrolls," Song of Songs, Ruth, Lamentations, Ecclesiastes (or Qoheleth), and Esther, which are gathered together as a collection within the Writings (Heb *kĕtûbîm*) in modern printed editions of the Hebrew Bible. This sequence is meant to reflect the order of the feasts in which they are read: Song of Songs at Passover, Ruth at Pentecost (Heb *šābuʿōt*), Lamentations on the Ninth of Ab (commemorating the destruction of the temple), Ecclesiastes at the Feast of Booths (Heb *sukkôt*), and Esther at Purim. That this is a rather late grouping of books is evident from looking at the order in which these books were placed in various canon lists and manuscripts. The Babylonian Talmud in *B. Bat.* 14b places the order of the Writings as: Ruth, Psalms, Job, Proverbs, Ecclesiastes, Song of Songs, Lamentations, Daniel, Esther, Ezra (including Nehemiah), and Chronicles. This probably reflects the perceived chronological order of the books, with only Chronicles being out of sequence. The order in many Sephardic mss as well as Codex Leningradensus (A.D. 1008), the ms underlying the popular *Biblia Hebraica* (from the 3d ed. on), is: Chronicles, Psalms, Job, Proverbs, Ruth, Song of Songs, Ecclesiastes, Lamentations, Esther, Daniel, and Ezra-Nehemiah. This is interesting, because it shows that the five megilloth were already being grouped together as a separate collection within the Writings, albeit within a chronological order, from Ruth (in the period of the judges) to Song of Songs and Ecclesiastes, which were widely regarded as being Solomonic, to Daniel, the Jewish statesman who prophesied during the Exile, to Ezra-Nehemiah, postexilic Jewish reformers. When the megilloth became associated with the five festivals of Judaism, it is only natural that that would affect the order in which they would be placed in Jewish Bibles.

H. ELDON CLEM

MEHETABEL (PERSON) [Heb *mĕhêṭabʾēl*]. The name of two persons in the Hebrew Bible. The name means "God is bestowing good."

1. The wife of Hadad (II), king of Edom, and also the daughter of Matred, daughter of Mezahab (Gen 36:39; 1 Chr 1:50). This is most probably a genuine Edomite name. The participle of the H-stem *mĕhêṭab* < **muhayṭib* preserves the h-preformative. The same is the case in ancient Aramaic and ancient North Arabian (cf., e.g., *yhṯʿ*/ **yuhaiṯiʿ*, the name of an Arab tribal leader of the 7th century B.C.; Knauf 1985b: 6, n. 28). The root *yṭb*, however, is absent from Arabic. The name of Mehetabel's father, Maṭred, may also be Edomite. Names from *ṭrd* are attested for both Canaanite and Arabic (Knauf 1985a: 248). The second "daughter" need not to be changed into "son" if one assumes that Mezahab was the name of Mehetabel and Matred's town, village, or shire of origin, rather than the name of her grandfather (Weippert 1971: 436).

2. The grandfather or, more likely, the family of the prophet Shemaiah, son of Delaiah (Neh 6:10). Nehemiah rejected Shemaiah's oracle (Neh 6:12–14); Shemaiah had been paid to deliver this oracle by Tobiah, the Judean governor of the Persian province of Ammon and Nehemiah's adversary. Grammatically, the name Mehetabel suggests that his family may have been of Transjordanian origin. This could help to explain Tobiah's relationship to this particular prophet.

Bibliography

Knauf, E. A. 1985a. Alter und Herkunft der edomitischen Königsliste Gen 36, 31–39. *ZAW* 97: 245–53.
———. 1985b. *Ismael*. Wiesbaden.
Weippert, M. 1971. *Edom. Studien und Materialien zur Geschichte der Edomiter auf Grund schriftlicher und archäologischer Quellen*. Ph.D. diss., Tübingen.

ERNST AXEL KNAUF

MEHIDA (PERSON) [Heb *mĕḥîdāʾ*]. The name of a family of temple servants who returned to Palestine with

Zerubbabel shortly after 538 B.C.E., the end of the Babylonian Exile. The name appears in Ezra 2:52 in the phrase "the sons of Mehida," where the temple servants are distinguished from the people of Israel, the priests, and the Levites. The parallel passage Neh 7:46–56 also lists "the sons of Mehida" (Neh 7:54), as does the later parallel 1 Esdr 5:32. The Greek versions show three different transliterations of this word: *maouda* (Ezra 2:52), *meida* (Neh 7:54), and *meedda* (1 Esdr 5:32). It is, however, rendered consistently in the English versions.

STEVEN R. SWANSON

MEHIR (PERSON) [Heb *mĕḥîr*]. A descendant of Chelub in the genealogy of Judah (1 Chr 4:11). Nothing otherwise is known of him.

H. C. LO

MEHOLATHITE [Heb *mĕḥōlātî*]. A descriptive term indicating the place of origin of Adriel, the son-in-law of Saul son of Kish, and the first king of Israel (1 Sam 18:19; 2 Sam 21:8). According to the Masoretic vocalization, it is a gentilic form from the root *ḥwl,* meaning "to whirl," "dance." It is generally considered to be a reference to Adriel's association with the town of Abel-meholah in the W *ghor:* he is the one "from Meholah" (so Smith *Samuel* ICC, 172; Stoebe *Das erste Buch Samuelis* KAT, 345; Klein *1 Samuel* WBC, 189). However, an alternative explanation is possible based on a different vocalization of the consonantal text. The term could be a gentilic indicating Adriel's association with the Manassite clan of Mahlah: Adriel the Mahlathite. While the identification of a person by his town of origin or residence was a frequent biblical practice, other options included identification by patronymic, which would either be the name of one's father or one's clan affiliation (*PI* 1: 253), or by nationality. Examples of the last two options are conveniently provided by the list of David's mighty men in 2 Sam 23:8–39 and 1 Chr 11:20–47: Jeshbaal the Hachmonite; Ahiam the son of Sharar the Hararite; Helez the Paltite/Pelonite; Zalmon the Ahohite (cf. Eleazer son of Dodo son of Ahohi in 2 Sam 23:9); Bani the Gadite; Zelek the Ammonite; Gareb the Ithrite; and Uriah the Hittite. If the term is construed as a clan gentilic, it would no longer provide a firm association of Adriel with the town of Abel-meholah, since the clan could have occupied more than a single town.

DIANA V. EDELMAN

MEHRI LANGUAGE. See LANGUAGES (INTRODUCTORY SURVEY).

MEHUJAEL (PERSON) [Heb *mĕḥûyāʾēl, mĕḥîyyāʾēl*]. Son of Irad and father of Methushael in the line of Cain (Gen 4:18); however, the two appearances of the name are spelled with a slight difference in the consonantal Hebrew text (a distinction preserved in the Targums). The Peshitta and the Vulgate follow the first spelling (cf. also Targum Neofiti). The best attestations of the LXX seem to follow the second spelling *(maiēl).* The Samaritan Pentateuch avoids the issue by omitting the disputed syllable *(myḥʾl).* The fact that the Hebrew text was not harmonized attests to the care taken in preserving such differences, even when they exist side by side (Cassuto 1961: 232–33). Comparisons with the genealogy of Seth in Genesis 5 have related this name with that of Mahalalel (Wilson 1977: 161–62). The initial *mem* and the final *ʾalep* and *lamed* are three consonants (half of the possible six) which the names share. It is generally agreed that Mehujael is composed of two elements, the second of which is *ʾl,* "god;" but the first element is disputed (Westermann 1984: 328–29). On the one hand, Akk *maḫḫu,* "an ecstatic," has been suggested (Cassuto 1961: 232). On the other hand, West Semitic *mḥʾ*, "to smite," and a participial form of *ḥyh,* "to live," have also both been posited (Skinner *Genesis* ICC, 117, noting Philo and Jerome; Gabriel 1959: 414). These options would respectively render the names "ecstatic of God," "God has smitten," and "God gives life." The first two forms are unattested as bases of personal names; while the root, *ḥyh,* is attested in West Semitic names in virtually all periods (e.g., Eve, which may share a similar element).

Bibliography

Cassuto, U. 1961. *A Commentary on the Book of Genesis. Part I: From Adam to Noah.* Trans. I. Abrahams. Jerusalem.

Gabriel, J. 1959. Die Kainitengenealogie. Gn 4, 17–24. *Bib* 40: 409–27.

Westermann, C. 1984. *Genesis 1–11.* Trans. J. Scullion. Minneapolis.

Wilson, R. R. 1977. *Genealogy and History in the Biblical World.* YNER 7. New Haven and London.

RICHARD S. HESS

MEHUMAN (PERSON) [Heb *mĕhûmān*]. One of seven eunuchs, along with Biztha, Harbona, Bigtha, Abagtha, Zethar, and Carkas, of King Ahasuerus listed in Esth 1:10. The order of the names in this list may imply a ranking of importance among the seven. The specific office these eunuchs held is termed literally "the ones who minister before the king" (Heb *hamĕšārĕtîm ʾet pĕnê hammelek*) in Esth 1:10. It appears that they were chamberlains to the king and that their function was to wait upon Ahasuerus and to summon individuals before him when desired. They attempted to bring Queen Vashti from her banquet to the king's banquet (Esth 1:10–12), and perhaps they were also the ones sent to summon Haman to both of Esther's banquets with the king (Esth 5:5; 6:14). In addition, the episode in Esth 7:9–10, where Harbona informed the king of Haman's scheme to kill Mordecai, resulting in the king's ordering Haman's execution, may suggest that these particular eunuchs served also to look after the affairs of the king and to escort and execute condemned prisoners. Since they did not seem to have direct contact with the harem, most likely the term "eunuch" (Heb *sārîs*), with respect to their office, was only symbolic and should not be taken literally. Perhaps it would be better translated as "chamberlain," or "court official." It is known from ancient sources that the title "eunuch" could be applied to any number of court officials, from bureaucrats to military officers (Weidner 1956: 264–65). The fact that there were only seven who held this office may reflect Persian mythology, which saw the heavenly royal court of their high god as having seven ministers. Thus the earthly court of Ahasuerus was set up to imitate the divine model (Paton *Esther* ICC, 148).

The etymologies and ethnic origin of these seven names have been a topic of some debate. Some would like to view them as historical Persian names in order to affirm in part the historicity of the book of Esther. Others feel that the author of the book has invented them for his own purposes, and thus neither they nor the book should be considered historical (Moore *Esther* AB, 8–9). Most of these names do appear to be of Persian/Iranian origin; but their correct spelling is in doubt, making it difficult to determine their exact etymology. The various Versions of the OT exhibit a variety of forms for each one of these seven names. Thus, for instance, Abagtha (Heb *ʾăbagtāʾ*) is rendered as *abataza* by LXX^{bs}, as *zēbathatha* by LXX^{a}, as *achedes* by the OL, and as *ʾgbwtʾ* by the Syriac version. What is even more confusing is that the Lucianic recension of the LXX omits all of these names entirely in Esth 1:10. See Moore for a complete listing of the variants for all the names (*Esther* AB, XLI–XLIV). Because of the Versions' overwhelming lack of support of the MT readings, many scholars have doubted the accuracy of the spellings in the Hebrew text and have attempted to reconstruct the original names by other means. In the past some have used a so-called preferred reading of the LXX as a basis for reconstructing an original name because it fit the phonetic makeup of a likely Persian cognate. Thus the consonants of Biztha (Heb *bizzĕtāʾ*) were altered by some to read *mzdn* (= *mazdānā*?), following the reading of the LXX^{bs}, *mazan*, because it was phonetically equivalent to Pers *mazdānā*, "gift of (the god) Mazda." Likewise, Bigtha (Heb *bigtāʾ*) was read as *bgdtʾ* (= *bagedāta*?), supposedly following a misreading of LXX^{a}, *bazēthatha*, to agree with Pers *bagadāta*, "given by god." And finally, Abagtha (Heb *ʾăbagtāʾ*) as well suffered the same fate, being altered to *ʾbztʾ* (= *ʾabazatāʾ*?), following the LXX, *abataza* (Paton *Esther* ICC, 67–68). Others argued that several of these names were slightly misspelled variants of other personal names in the book of Esther. Mehuman was viewed as a variant for Memucan (Heb *mĕmûkān*) (Esth 1:14); Bigtha as a different spelling for Bigthan (Heb *bigtān*) (Esth 2:21; 6:2); and Abagtha some felt was a gloss of the previous name, Bigtha, in the list of Esth 1:10 (Paton *Esther* ICC, 67–68). In addition Duchesne-Guillemin saw the two lists of names in Esth 1:10 and 1:14 as duplicates but in reverse order of each other. Therefore Mehuman, the first name in Esth 1:10, was the same name as Memucan, the last name in Esth 1:14, and so on (Duchesne-Guillemin 1953).

Against these older views more recent scholarship has argued that the MT tradition tends to preserve the correct phonetic consonantal spelling of foreign names quite faithfully. Linguistic studies in the various Persian dialects have progressed greatly in the past generation, and now more precise phonetic correlations can be made between Persian words and the Hebrew spelling of them (Millard 1977: 482–87). Thus most of the seven names in Esth 1:10 have been found to be phonetically equivalent to attested Persian words or actual Persian proper names. The following correlations have been made:

Mehuman: From the Aramaic passive participle form, *mĕhaymân*, from the root *ʾmn*, meaning "trusty" or "eunuch"; or from O Pers *vahumanah*, "intelligent."
Biztha: Possibly from Pers *besteh*, "bound," or "eunuch."
Harbona: From N Pers *kherbân*, "donkey driver."
Bigtha: Possibly from O Pers *bagadâ*, "gift of god."
Abagtha: From M Iranian *gabata*, "fortunate one."
Zethar: From M Pers *zaitar*, "conqueror."
Carkas: From Avestan *kahrkâsa*, "vulture."

If these identifications are correct, then with one possible exception all of these eunuchs may have actual Persian names. If so, they themselves may have come from different cultural backgrounds judging from the fact that their names find their origins in so many diverse dialects of Persian. This is exactly the state of affairs one would have found at Ahasuerus' court. Aramaic records from Persepolis dating from his reign have shown that there were many different Aryan nationalities represented at court (Millard 1977: 482–84). Therefore one might use the above evidence to argue in part that the author of Esther derived the story from a historical account or at least had knowledge of some Persian names and customs.

Bibliography

Duchesne-Guillemin, J. 1953. Les Noms des Eunuques d'Assuerus. *Mus* 66: 105–8.
Gehman, H. S. 1924. Notes on the Persian Words in the Book of Esther. *JBL* 43: 321–28.
Mayrhofer, M. 1973. *Onomastica Persepolitana*. OAWPK. Vienna.
Millard, A. R. 1977. The Persian Names in Esther and the Reliability of the Hebrew Text. *JBL* 96: 481–88.
Weidner, E. 1956. Hof- und Harems-Erlase Assyrischer Konige aus dem 2 Jahrtausend v. Chr. *AfO* 27: 257–93.

JOHN M. WIEBE

MEINIM. Inhabitants of the city-state of Maʾin. See MEUNIM.

MEIRON (M.R. 191265). The site of ancient Meiron, also spelled "Meron," is located just N of the Wâdī Meiron, approximately 1 km N of the nearest site, Khirbet Shemaʿ, in the modern *moshav* of the same name. The site embraces some 200 dunams (ca. 50 acres) and is one of the largest ancient settlements of the Upper Galilee region. It is not to be confused with the "waters of Merom" of Joshua 11:5, 7 or Mero or Meroth of Josephus (*JW* 2.573; 3.39). The latter (M.R. 199270) has been recently identified by a new excavation team as Khirbet Marus, a site which the excavators maintain constitutes the northernmost border of the Galilee (Ilan and Damati 1985). Meiron is to be equated rather with the Talmudic village associated with Simeon bar Yochai and the priestly clan of Jehoiarib (1 Chr 24:7). By medieval times Meiron becomes an important Jewish pilgrimage place and is associated with the Feast of Lag B'Omer, celebrated 33 days after Passover.

The only excavations undertaken at ancient Meiron were conducted from 1971 to 1972, 1974 to 1975, and in 1977 and were directed by E. M. Meyers. The results of those campaigns are published in the Meiron final report (Meyers, Strange, and Meyers 1981). The excavations focused primarily on soundings in the town itself though it was also possible to do some limited soundings alongside the synagogue on the acropolis. The major recovery of material came from the insulae in the Lower City and is dated to the Middle-Late Roman period, the heyday of the ancient settlement.

The chronological span of materials recovered from the excavations ranges from the Hellenistic to medieval times. The following table summarizes the main cultural phases of the site:

Stratum	Dates	Description
I	200–50 B.C.E. (Hellenistic)	Scattered artifactual remains; only traces of structures.
II	50 B.C.E.–135 C.E. (Early Roman)	Limited architecture and related artifacts; small growing village.
III	135–250 C.E. (Middle Roman)	First major insula; village expanding.
IV	250–363 C.E. (Late Roman)	Peak of village life; synagogue built; gradual abandonment at end of stratum.
V	363–750 C.E. (Byzantine-Arab)	Village largely abandoned; occasional artifacts dropped by visitors or squatters.
VI	750–1000 C.E. (Early Arab)	Reestablishment of village life on a smaller scale.
VIIa	1000–1300 C.E. (Late Arab)	Continuation of stable village life; emergence as a pilgrimage center.
VIIb	1300–1400 C.E. (Late Arab)	Village in decline.

The typical basilican synagogue on the acropolis that had lain destroyed and bare since antiquity was dated by debris from within an annex to the late 3d century C.E. (stratum IV). It is the longest synagogue known from all ancient Palestine, 27.5 m long by 13.6 m wide. Three entrances mark the S end of the building, which is clearly oriented S toward Jerusalem. There are two rows of eight columns, each row running N-S. Heart-shaped columns are conjectured to have stood in the two N corners, and a gallery and clerestory roof are posited for the second story and above.

The Lower City excavations produced two large insulae preserved mainly in their stratum IV phase, one with a beautifully laid open courtyard of stone. A carpenter's shop and cooperage were among the major finds here. A ritual bathing complex was also identified in this area and dated to stratum III. It is quite clear that the first or ground floor of the complex was utilized for business or industry and that the second floor was reserved for living quarters.

On a terrace at a slightly higher elevation to the W, several large private dwellings were excavated. One was extremely well preserved. Because of their size and of the high quality of household goods discovered in them, they were called "patrician" homes by the excavators. A storage area (Room F) in one was found virtually undisturbed from antiquity, and its ceramic storage jars still contained quantities of wheat, beans, and walnuts. The foodstuffs were purposefully charred, however, and preserved for religious reasons, possibly as a symbolic gift for the destroyed temple which someday might be rebuilt; these were stored by the pious and priestly (?) owner of the house.

A series of cisterns was excavated, which produced a large quantity of whole or restorable pottery. Rainwater was readily available because of Meiron's location high on the mountain slopes; and because of the abundant water supply in the spring to the S, the town apparently shared with Khirbet Shemaᶜ its surplus.

Excavation of a small tomb complex produced quantities of restorable artifacts also. The mode of inhumation that was documented from the first century B.C.E. to the 4th century C.E. was secondary reburial or *ossilegium.* Although only fragments of stone ossuaries were found, many individuals were simply reinterred without a container for their skeletal remains. Study of the bones revealed a high degree of endogamy with a concomitant array of disease. Clearly the isolation of Upper Galilee is reflected in the study of human remains from Meiron.

The material culture recovered from ancient Meiron thus reveals a village that is both very much part of Roman life in ancient Palestine and at the same time separate from it. The coins show a special trade connection to the municipality of Tyre, but there are also connections with other major centers of trade and culture. The synagogue, which stands high on the slopes, clearly represents the crowning achievement of the members of the community, who achieved much of their financial success and independence from their cultivation of the olive tree and preparation of olive oil, the greatest natural resource of the upper Galilee.

Bibliography

Ilan, Z., and Damati, E. 1985. Excavation of the Synagogue at Meroth. *Qad* 18: 44–50 (in Hebrew).

Meyers, E. M. 1977. Meiron. *EAEHL* 3: 856–62.

Meyers, E. M., and Meyers, C. L. 1978. Digging the Talmud in Ancient Meiron. *BARev* 4: 32–42.

Meyers, E. M.; Strange, J. F.; and Meyers, C. L. 1981. *Excavations at Ancient Meiron, Upper Galilee, Israel 1971–72, 1974–75, 1977.* Cambridge, MA.

ERIC M. MEYERS

MELATIAH (PERSON) [Heb *mĕlaṭēyâ*]. One of those who worked on the wall of Jerusalem following the return from Babylonian exile (Neh 3:7). Melatiah worked along with Jadon the Meronothite and is identified as a "Gibeonite." His name means "Yahweh has delivered." The "men of Gibeon" to whom the verse refers were probably workmen under the leadership of Melatiah (Brockington *Ezra, Nehemiah and Esther* Century Bible, 136). He was probably an official in Gibeon (Clines *Ezra, Nehemiah, Esther* NCBC, 153). Because the Hebrew word *kissēʾ* can be translated either as "authority" or "seat of authority" (BDB, 490), one might follow the sense of the RSV translation of Neh 3:7 concerning the work of these men: "under the jurisdiction of the governor of the province Beyond the River"; or that of Fensham (*Ezra and Nehemiah* NICOT, 169): "up to the quarters of the governor of Trans-Euphrates," which would mean that the governor had a part-time residence in Jerusalem (Fensham, 174).

MICHAEL L. RUFFIN

MELCHI (PERSON) [Gk *Melchi*]. **1.** The father of Levi and son of Jannai according to Luke's genealogy tying Joseph, the "supposed father" of Jesus, to descent from Adam and God (Luke 3:24). D omits the name, substituting a genealogy adapted from Matt 1:6–15 for Luke 3:23–31. Apart from Luke 3:28, the name Melchi occurs nowhere else in the biblical documents, including Matthew's genealogy, and falls within a list of seventeen otherwise unknown descendants of David's son Nathan (Fitzmyer *Luke 1–9* AB, 500). Kuhn (1923: 208–9) argues that two seemingly parallel lists of names—Luke 3:23–26 (Jesus to Mattathias) and 3:29–31 (Joshua/Jesus to Mattatha)—were originally identical, the first perhaps reflecting a Hebrew context and the second, an Aramaic context, tracing Mary's line of descent (since it does not mention Joseph as Jesus' father). Melchi, in the first list, corresponds to Simeon, in the second list. With no major textual variants for Melchi and Simeon to support confusion of the two in the NT, Kuhn's theory has little plausibility. Kuhn further suggests (211) that Melchi, a name that rarely appears in Jewish literature, was a popular shortening of the more widely used Heb *mlkyh.* Julius Africanus lists Melchi as the father of Heli, omitting Levi and Matthat. On this see MATTHAT; Hervey (1853: 137).

2. The father of Neri and son of Addi according to Luke's genealogy tying Joseph, the "supposed father" of Jesus, to descent from Adam and God (Luke 3:28). D omits the name, substituting a genealogy adapted from Matt 1:6–15 for Luke 3:23–31. Apart from Luke 3:24, the name Melchi appears nowhere else in the biblical documents, including Matthew's genealogy, and falls within a list of eighteen otherwise unknown descendants of David's son Nathan (Fitzmyer *Luke 1–9* AB, 501). Kuhn (1923: 214; see also Hervey 1853: 38–39, 92, 148–49) argues that Melchi, as well as several other names in this section, is a corruption, in particular here of Heb *mlkyrm* found in 1 Chr 3:18, on the basis that Gk *Nēri* and *Melchi* are derived from a single name: Heb *nrymlky* (meaning "my king is my light"), possibly making it into 1 Chronicles through the corrupted intermediate form *mlkynry* (Kuhn believes he can prove the change from Heb *nry* to *rm*). This proposal has not won widespread acceptance, especially since there is serious question whether the genealogy at this point is based on 1 Chronicles (Marshall 1978: 164; cf. Jeremias 1969: 295–96).

Bibliography

Hervey, A. 1853. *The Genealogies of Our Lord and Saviour Jesus Christ, As Contained in the Gospels of St. Matthew and St. Luke* Cambridge.

Jeremias, J. 1969. *Jerusalem in the Time of Jesus.* Trans. F. H. Cave and C. H. Cave. Philadelphia.

Kuhn, G. 1923. Die Geschlechtsregister Jesu bei Lukas und Matthäus, nach ihrer Herkunft untersucht. *ZNW* 22: 206–28.

Marshall, I. H. 1978. *The Gospel of Luke: A Commentary on the Greek Text* NIGTC. Grand Rapids.

Stanley E. Porter

MELCHIAS (PERSON) [Gk *Melchias*]. See MALCHIJAH (PERSON).

MELCHIEL (PERSON) [Gk *Melchiēl*]. The father of Charmis, one of the elders of Bethuliah (Jdt 6:15). The name in Hebrew is Malkiel (Heb *malkîʾēl*). It occurs in the OT three times (Gen 46:17; Num 26:45; 1 Chr 7:31), where the person name is a member of the tribe of Asher. It is unlikely that the author of the book of Judith intended the reader to make an identification with this figure; the name is part of what Noth terms a "secondary genealogy," a genealogy having no independent existence apart from the narrative (see *HPT*). The name is probably given to lend the story verisimilitude.

Sidnie Ann White

MELCHIZEDEK (PERSON) [Heb *malkî-ṣedeq*]. The meaning of the name is "King of Righteousness," which is stressed by its being written in Gen 14:18–20 and in Ps 110:4 in two parts joined by a *maqqēp*, as if it were a title rather than a personal name. He is described as king of Salem and priest of God Most High *(ʾēl ʿelyôn).*

A. Gen 14:18–20
B. Ps 110:4
C. In Qumran Literature
D. The Letter to the Hebrews
E. In Mainstream Judaism

A. Gen 14:18–20

Melchizedek met Abram as he returned from his victory over Chedorlaomer and his allies, brought out bread and wine, and blessed Abram in the name of God Most High, maker of heaven and earth; "and he [Abram] gave him [Melchizedek] a tenth of everything." The intention of this passage, which forms the climax of the chapter, is transparent. It affirms that the priesthood of the supreme God, the creator of the world, had existed in Jerusalem not since Solomon but from before Abram's arrival in the promised land; that the priest of God Most High was at the same time the king of the city; and that Abram, who by his victory over Chedorlaomer, the former overlord of the country between Dan and Elath, had inherited his rights to it, paid a tithe to Melchizedek, thus acknowledging his superiority. This reflects and legitimizes the aspirations of the high priests of Jerusalem, who in the Persian period strove to be on a par with the secular governors of Judea, proclaimed the ideal of theocracy in the Priestly Code, and finally achieved secular power in the Hellenistic age.

Melchizedek's being the priest of God Most High *(ʾēl ʿelyôn)* does not necessarily point to the pre-Israelite, Canaanite character of both the priest and his cultus, as is often assumed (cf., e.g., *IDB* 2: 407–17; Speiser *Genesis* AB, 105, 109). It is true that in the late Phoenician theogony by Philo Herennius of Byblos the deity *Eliun* (explained in Greek as *Hypsistos,* "most high") appears as the oldest god, grandfather of Elos *(ʾēl)* and his brothers, and that in the much older Aramaic treaty from Sfire (mid-8th century B.C.), stele I:A:11, one finds *ʾl w ʿlyn* (*ʾēl* and *ʿelyōn*) among the divine witnesses of the treaty. But in both cases, El and Elyon are two distinct entities. The combined divine name *ʾēl ʿelyôn* is found in the OT (besides Gen 14:18–20; in Ps 78:35, cf. *ʾelōhîm ʿelyôn,* v 56); in 1 QapGen 21:20, where Abram built an altar in the oaks of Mamre and sacrificed on it to *ʾl ʿlywn;* and in 4 QPrNab, which uses *ʾl ʿlywn* throughout. In all of these passages God Most High is a synonym of Yahweh, as is the more common shorter epithet *ʿelyôn,* which is especially frequent in the Psalms. The assumption that the inclusion of *yhwh* before *ʾēl ʿelyôn* in Abram's reply to the king of Sodom, v 22, reflects a religious difference between the Hebrew Abram and the Canaanite Melchizedek (*IDB* 2: 412; Speiser *Genesis* AB, 109) is disproved by its absence from LXX, Syr, and the Genesis Apocryphon (which follows very closely the text of Genesis 14); it should be considered a late editorial gloss.

B. Ps 110:4

It is impossible to ascertain whether the image of the priest-king Melchizedek was created by the author of Genesis 14, or was already current in certain Jewish circles. Whatever the case, it had undergone a great sublimation by the time of the composition of Psalm 110, which contains the only other mention of Melchizedek in the OT. The psalm celebrates the elevation of a man to the dignity of priest, ruler, and warlord, a man whose identity is revealed by the acrostic formed by the speech of Yahweh in vv 1–4: *šmʿn,* "Simeon" (Pfeiffer 1948: 630). The warlike atmosphere of the psalm points to Simon Maccabeus, who became high priest, general, and ruler of the Jews in 141 B.C. The crucial v 3 has been poorly transmitted in the MT, and its rendering by the RSV is a paraphrase rather than a translation (but its emendation of *hadrê-qōdeš* to *harĕrê-qōdeš* should be retained). In the following quotation, the suggested restoration of v 3 has been done with the aid of LXX and the analogy with Ps 2:7 (in another Hasmonean enthronement hymn, cf. Pfeiffer 1948: 628):

(3) With thee is the dignity in the day of thy
power.
In the holy mountains, from the womb of Dawn,
like the Day Star I have begotten thee.
(4) Yahweh has sworn and will not repent:
"Thou art a priest forever
after the order of Melchizedek."

Thus Melchizedek is here not only the human archetype of the ideal priest-king of Jerusalem, but the eternal priest of Yahweh, a supernatural being engendered by Yahweh and comparable to the mythological figure of "Day Star, son of Dawn" *(hêlēl ben-šāḥar)* in Isa 14:12. Upon taking over the high priesthood and becoming a successor of Melchizedek, Simon Maccabeus is symbolically identified with him (cf. Ps 2:7: "Thou art my son, today I have begotten thee").

C. In Qumran Literature

Not only the official Hasmonean establishment, but also their bitter opponents, the Essenes of the Qumran community, gave Melchizedek a very high place in their heavenly hierarchy and eschatology. He is the central character in a fragmentary midrashic work (11QMelch) which interprets a number of verses from Isaiah, Leviticus, and other OT books dealing with remission of debts and liberation of slaves at the end of a jubilee cycle as referring to the last judgment and the final triumph of good over evil during the tenth jubilee of the Essene eschatological era. The faithful ones will be included in the lot of Melchizedek, and their transgressions will be forgiven. Melchizedek will be the judge both of the saints of God and of Belial and the wicked spirits of his lot. Assisted by all gods of righteousness, he will accomplish the utter destruction of Belial. In support of this, the interpreter adduces Ps 82:1–2: "God *(ʾelōhîm)* stands in the divine council *(ʿadat-ʾēl),* in the midst of gods *(ʾelōhîm)* he holds judgment. How long will you judge unjustly and show partiality to the wicked? *selah.*" Psalm 82 is one of the "Elohistic psalms," in which an editor has systematically replaced the divine name *yhwh* by *ʾelōhîm,* "God." For the author of Psalm 82, the god who holds judgment amidst his council of lesser celestial beings is Yahweh himself. He accuses his subordinates (to whom he had delegated the everyday administration of the world) of having neglected their duty of social justice; and he threatens them, despite their being gods and sons of the Most High *(ʾelyôn),* that they "shall die like men, and fall like one of the princes" (vv 6–7). Under "one of the princes" (*śārîm,* a title used for angels of the highest rank) the author of Psalm 82 understood the Day Star of Isa 14:12. The psalm ends with an appeal to God (Yahweh) to take over personally the judgment of the earth and all its nations. But for the Essene interpreter, the replacement of *Yahweh* by *ʾElōhîm* in v 1 made it possible to understand it not as "God" but as "a god," i.e., an angel, and to identify him as Melchizedek, and the gods whom he judges, as the spirits of the lot of Belial. Thus Melchizedek plays here the role of one of the two supreme spirits created by God—the spirit of light, opposed to the spirit of darkness. The latter, as one learns from the very fragmentary text, "The Vision of Amram" (4QʿAmram), has the epithet *mlky ršʿ* "King of Iniquity" as the last (and only extant) of his three names. This would represent an antithesis to the name of Melchizedek (cf. Milik 1972b: 126–39; 1972a: 77–86). But the three names of the spirit of light in 4QʿAmram have not been preserved; and in 11QMelch the evil adversary of Melchizedek is not called, symmetrically, *mlky ršʿ*, but Belial.

It has been assumed that the Qumran sect identified Melchizedek with the archangel Michael (van der Woude 1965: 301 n. 1, 367–73; Milik 1972b: 125). A certain similarity between the roles of Melchizedek in 11QMelch and Michael in 1QM 17:5–8, as well as in Daniel, does exist; but, as recognized by de Jonge and van der Woude 1966: 305, "Michael and Melchizedek are, however, not identified explicitly in the Qumran texts at our disposal. This identification is only found in certain medieval Jewish texts." In 1QM 9:14–16, Michael is only one of the four archangels, not one of the two antagonistic supreme spirits of the world. The image of Michael as the heavenly high priest appears in the midrashic literature, i.e., considerably later, and is probably of secondary derivation. See Fitzmyer's (1967: 32) cautious approach to the question of Melchizedek's identification with Michael. It is strange that 11QMelch contains no hint whatever to Melchizedek's priesthood; but in the light of the Letter to the Hebrews, it is highly probable that the view of Melchizedek as the eternal priest (cf. Ps 110:4) was shared by the Essenes. See also MELCHIZEDEK (11QMelch).

D. The Letter to the Hebrews

The Epistle to the Hebrews was addressed to a group of Judeo-Christians of Essene background and aimed at overcoming their lingering attachment to the idea of an exclusively levitical priesthood. It exhorted them to recognize that Jesus was a priest despite his non-levitical ancestry. It used as a precedent the image of Melchizedek, which it supposed was familiar to its audience. Heb 5:6; 6:20; 7:17 apply to Christ the words of Ps 110:4, "Thou art a priest forever, after the order of Melchizedek." Heb 7:1–2a refer to Gen 14:17–22, in which Abra[ha]m gave a tenth part of everything to Melchizedek. Verses 2b–3 explain that Melchizedek "is first, by translation of his name, king of righteousness, and then he is also king of Salem, that is, king of peace. He is without father or mother or genealogy, and has neither beginning of days nor end of life, but resembling the Son of God he continues a priest forever." The fact that Abraham gave a tithe of his spoils to Melchizedek, continues the Letter (7:4–10), proves that Melchizedek was superior to Abraham and, by implication, to Abraham's descendant Levi, who, as it were, paid tithes through Abraham, "for he was still in the loins of his ancestor when Melchizedek met him." Melchizedek blessed Abraham; now "it is beyond dispute that the inferior is blessed by the superior." Moreover, "here tithes are received by mortal men; there by one of whom it is testified that he lives." The choice (in Ps 110:4) of the phrase "after the order of Melchizedek" rather than "after the order of Aaron" confirms Melchizedek's precedence over levitical priests (Heb 7:14). The Letter's notion of Melchizedek as a primeval, immortal being, coeternal with the Son of God, gave rise to various heterodox opinions in the early Christian Church; and there even arose a sect of Melchizedekians who regarded Melchizedek as equal or superior to Christ; but by the 5th century A.D. the Church stopped such speculations and no longer occupied itself with the mysterious figure of Melchizedek.

E. In Mainstream Judaism

Philo Judaeus, in the earlier part of the 1st century A.D., and Josephus, in its latter part, were contemporaries of the last period of existence of the Qumran community. But their references to Melchizedek have nothing in common with the Essene view of him. According to Philo *Leg All* III 25–26 §§79–82, "Melchizedek, too, has God made both king of peace, for that is the meaning of *Salem,* and his own priest . . . a king peaceable and worthy of his [God's] own priesthood. For he is entitled "the righteous king," and a king is a thing at enmity with a despot [*tyrannos*], the one being the author of laws, the other of lawlessness." Josephus (*Ant* 1.10.2 §180) wrote that Abraham "was received by the king of Solyma, Melchizedek; the name means "righteous king," and such he was by common consent, inasmuch as for this reason he was moreover made priest of God; Solyma was in fact the place afterward called Hierosolyma." For both authors, Melchizedek was a righteous and worthy man, but only a man. Such was, apparently, the attitude of the Pharisees, who, being opposed to both the Hasmoneans and the Essenes, had no reason to share in their exaltation of Melchizedek. A late vestige of a higher status ascribed to Melchizedek is found in *b. Sukk.* 52b, in which R. Ḥānā bar Biznā, citing R. Simeon Ḥasidā, identified the "four craftsmen" of Zech 2:3 as the Messiah son of David, the Messiah son of Joseph, Elijah, and Melchizedek (thus in the Munich Codex; other manuscripts have *kōhēn ṣedeq,* "the Righteous Priest"). This seems to imply that Melchizedek was translated to heaven like Elijah and will reappear in the messianic era. In opposition to the Letter to the Hebrews, other rabbis identified Melchizedek with Shem, the son of Noah (who, according to the priestly chronology of Genesis, not only was still alive at the time of Abraham but even survived him by 25 years). This identification was taken up in *Tg. Neof.* and *Tg. Ps.-J.* According to R. Zechariah on the authority of R. Ishmael (*b. Ned.* 32b), God originally gave the priesthood to Shem-Melchizedek; but because the latter gave precedence in his blessing (Gen 14:19–20) to Abraham over God, the priesthood was withdrawn from him and given to the descendants of Abraham; and Ps 110:4 was interpreted "Thou [Abraham] art a priest forever because of the words of Melchizedek."

In the midrashic literature, Michael appears as the heavenly high priest who offers daily sacrifices. It is, however, questionable if this image goes back to the time of Qumran and reflects the identity of Michael with Melchizedek. It is rather another instance of transferring Melchizedek's functions to another character. Moreover, the whole idea may represent an elaboration of a passage in *b. Zebah.* 62a, concerning the rebuilding of the temple after the Babylonian exile: "But how did they know (the site of) the altar? Said R. Eleazar: They saw (in a vision) the altar built, and Michael the great prince offering upon it." Note that the archangel offered on an earthly, not a heavenly altar, and only in order to indicate its site to the restorers of the temple. As for the explicit identification of Michael with Melchizedek in two little known medieval esoteric works, outside the mainstream of kabbalistic literature (*Yalqūt ḥādāš* and *Midrāš hanneᶜlām*), we are probably dealing with independent constructions of their authors.

Bibliography

Bardy, G. 1926–27. Melchisédech dans la tradition patristique. *RB* 35: 496–509; 36: 25–45.

Carmignac, J. 1970. Le document de Qumran sur Melkisédeq. *RQ* 27: 343–78.

Delcor, M. 1971. Melchizedek from Genesis to the Qumran Texts and the Epistle to the Hebrews. *JSJ* 2: 115–35.

Fitzmyer, J. A. 1967. Further Light on Melchizedek from Qumran Cave 11. *JBL* 86: 25–41.

Jonge, M. de, and Woude, A. S. van der. 1966. 11Q Melchizedek and the *NT. NTS* 12: 301–26.

Milik, J. T. 1972a. 4Q Visions de ᶜAmram et une citation d'Origène. *RB* 79: 77–97.

———. 1972b. *Milkî-ṣedeq et Milkî-rešaᶜ* dans les anciens écrits juifs et chrétiens. *JJS* 23: 95–144.

Pfeiffer, R. H. 1948. *Introduction to the OT.* Rev. ed. New York.

Sanders, J. A. 1973. The OT in 11Q Melchizedek. *JANES* 5: 373–82.

Woude, A. S. van der. 1965. Melchisedek als himmlische Erlösergestalt in den neugefundenen eschatologischen Midraschim aus Qumran-Höhle XI. *OTS* 14: 354–73.

Yadin, Y. 1958. The Dead Sea Scrolls and the Epistle to the Hebrews. *ScrHier* 4: 36–53.

———. 1965. A Note on Melchizedek and Qumran. *IEJ* 15: 152–54.

Michael C. Astour

MELCHIZEDEK (11QMelch). In 1965 under the auspices of the Royal Dutch Academy of Sciences, A. S. van der Woude published 14 small fragments discovered in 1956 in Qumran Cave 11. That editio princeps of 11QMelch contained photographs, a transcription of the text, and a German translation. In 1966 van der Woude and M. de Jonge published a slightly altered transcription together with an English translation. The most significant improvements in the reading and restoration of the fragments have been published by Yadin (1965: 152–54), Fitzmyer (1967: 26–41), Carmignac (1970: 343–78), Milik (1972: 97–109), and especially Puech (1987: 488–507). Named initially after its chief character, Melchizedek, for its final edition in the series Discoveries in the Judaean Desert, 11QMelch has been provisionally designated as 11Q13.

On paleographic grounds van der Woude proposed (1965: 357) that the work should be dated to the first half of the 1st century C.E. Others have suggested the second half of the 1st century B.C.E. (Kobelski 1981: 3). 11QMelch is for the most part a single column of text of at least 25 lines; in its right-hand margin frag. 1 contains an insertion which belongs to the preceding column; frags. 2 and 7 provide the start of several lines of a third column. While Kobelski accepts Milik's placing of frag. 13, he argues (1981: 5, 23) that frags. 4, 5, 11, and 14 are not part of the main extant column; Puech (1987: 505–7) locates frags. 4, 5, 11, and 13 in col. 3. Milik (1972: 126) argues that while the manuscript itself is suitably dated at the turn of the era, because the "anointed one" (11QMelch 18–20) is probably the Teacher of Righteousness himself, the text was composed about 120 B.C.E. (also Puech 1987: 509–10).

Because the fragments include extracts from various biblical books, notably Lev 25:10–13; Ps 82:1–2; and Isa 52:7 and because in lines 12 and 17 the interpretation of the biblical texts is introduced with a formula including the word *pēšer,* 11QMelch is generically akin to the thematic exegetical documents from Qumran such as 4QFlorilegium and 4QCatena[a]: indeed 11QMelch 25 and 4QFlor 1:15–16 both cite Isa 8:11 as a supplementary text (cf. 1QSa 1:2–3; CD 8:16 = 19:29). It is better to understand 11QMelch as the interpretation of a series of biblical texts (Brooke 1985: 320–22), rather than as an elaborate exegesis based largely on one biblical text alone (Leviticus 25; cf. Fitzmyer 1967: 29; Isaiah 61; cf. Miller 1969: 467–69; and Sanders 1973: 374). It could be that this series of texts originally belonged together in some early Jewish liturgical setting, perhaps as readings for the Day of Atonement (11QMelch 7; Brooke 1985: 322–23). Within their present literary context it is likely that they belong to a much longer document of which 4Q180 and 181 are also copies (Milik 1972: 110–26).

This exegetical work is intricately constructed. The very piecing together of the fragments was facilitated by the systematic use of biblical texts in 11QMelch (van der Woude 1965: 355). On the basis of the various formulas used, it can be seen that the work offers interpretations for certain base texts (Lev 25:13; Ps 82:1–2; Isa 52:7); each interpretation includes supplementary texts (e.g., Deut 15:2; Isa 61:1) by allusion or direct citation. These supplementary texts are linked through catchword *(gĕzērâ šāwâ)* to the base text and sometimes to each other: e.g., Deut 15:2 (11QMelch 3–4) is linked to the base text of Lev 25:13 (11QMelch 2) through an analogous word use represented only in the LXX text type (Lev 25:13, *apheseōs;* Deut 15:2, *aphesis*); the allusions to Isa 61:1 are linked to the citation of Isa 52:7 through their common use of *bśr.* Also in the interpretations there are occasional short extracts from the base text.

The whole text is eschatological, concerning the "latter days" *(aḥarît hayyāmîm).* For the Sons of Light, Melchizedek will proclaim release and make expiation; for Belial and those of his lot, Melchizedek will exact the vengeance of the judgments of God. In this dualistic struggle, aspects of which reflect Iranian influence (Kobelski 1981: 84–98), Melchizedek acts as God's agent. All this will happen in the tenth and last jubilee period (11QMelch 7); this time scale for history echoes that of the Apocalypse of Weeks (*1 En.* 91:12–17; 93:1–10; 4QEn[g]) in which in the seventh part of the tenth week the eternal judgment is executed by the angels. This same judgment is declared to Michael by God in *1 En.* 10:12 (cf. Jude 6). This tradition justifies the conclusion of the majority of scholars that Melchizedek in 11QMelch is not a human but the archangel Michael in another guise with royal and high priestly characteristics (cf. Gen 14:18–20; Ps 110:4). In addition, Melchizedek is accompanied by the one who brings good news *(mbśr),* the anointed one *(hmšyḥ),* who may be the Teacher of Righteousness, or the eschatological prophet (Kobelski 1981: 61–62), or the Davidic Messiah (Fitzmyer 1967: 30).

Although the name Melchizedek appears in full only in this Qumran text, 11QMelch shares certain features with other texts. Its angelology is matched particularly in the *Songs of the Sabbath Sacrifice* (4Q400, 403, 405), in which the angels are often designed as *ʾēl* or *ʾelôhîm,* as in Ps 82:1 (11QMelch 10) and in 1QM. 4QʿAmram[b] and 4Q280 seem to refer to Melchizedek's chief opponent, Belial, under another name: *Melkirešaʿ.* The exegetical method and eschatological scheme are paralleled in other texts also.

The appearance of some key scriptural passages and the figure of Melchizedek himself have provoked an extensive scholarly literature on how 11QMelch may illuminate parts of the NT. Although some would deny any connection between this angelic Melchizedek and the priestly Melchizedek in Heb 5:5–10 and 7:1–7 (Horton 1976: 167–70), most scholars argue that the two texts preserve differing uses of the same Palestinian Jewish tradition. The debate in Heb 1:3–14 about the status of angels would seem to justify this; the same issue is also reflected in the use of Psalm 82 in John 10:34. The use of Isaiah 61 as a key text in Jesus' ministry (Luke 4:18–19; 6:20–21) implies that for Luke, Jesus was the eschatological liberator who fulfilled the role other Jewish traditions assigned to Michael or Melchizedek.

Bibliography

Brooke, G. J. 1985. *Exegesis at Qumran: 4QFlorilegium in Its Jewish Context.* JSOTSup 29. Sheffield.

Carmignac, J. 1970. Le document de Qumran sur Melkisedeq. *RevQ* 7: 343–378.

Delcor, M. 1971. Melchizedek from Genesis to the Qumran Texts and the Epistle to the Hebrews. *JSJ* 2: 115–35.

Fitzmyer, J. A. 1967. Further Light on Melchizedek from Qumran

Cave 11. *JBL* 86: 25–41. Repr. pp. 245–67 in *Essays on the Semitic Background of the NT.* 1974. Missoula, MT.
Horton, F. L., Jr. 1976. *The Melchizedek Tradition.* SNTSMS 30. Cambridge.
Jonge, M. de, and Woude, A. S. van der. 1966. 11QMelchizedek and the New Testament. *NTS* 12: 301–26.
Kobelski, P. J. 1981. *Melchizedek and Melchirešaᶜ.* CBQMS 10. Washington.
Milik, J. T. 1972. *Milkî-ṣedeq et Milkî-rešaᶜ* dans les anciens écrits juifs et chrétiens. *JJS* 23: 95–144.
Miller, M. P. 1969. The Function of Isa 61, 1–2 in 11QMelchizedek. *JBL* 88: 467–69.
Puech, É. 1987. Notes sur le manuscrit de XIQMelkîsédeq. *RevQ* 12: 483–513.
Richter, H.-P. 1987. Konkordanz zu XIQMelkîsédeq (éd. É. Puech). *RevQ* 12: 515–18.
Sanders, J. A. 1973. The Old Testament in 11QMelchizedek. *JANES* 5: 373–82.
Woude, A. S. van der. 1965. Melchisedek als himmlische Erlösergestalt in den neugefundenen eschatologischen Midraschim aus Qumran-Höhle XI. *OTS* 14: 354–73.
Yadin, Y. 1965. A Note on Melchizedek and Qumran. *IEJ* 15: 152–54.

GEORGE J. BROOKE

MELCHIZEDEK (NHC IX,*1*). The first of three gnostic tractates contained in Nag Hammadi Codex IX (1,1–27,10), inscribed in Sahidic Coptic. It is the only one of the Nag Hammadi tractates in which the figure of Melchizedek appears, though Melchizedek is treated in such other gnostic texts as *Pistis Sophia* and the *Books of Jeu.*

Owing to the fragmentary condition of the ms, less than 50 percent of the text is recoverable, but enough is preserved to allow for judgments to be made on such questions as literary genre, essential content, and religious character. Its superscript title is partially preserved.

Melchizedek is an apocalypse containing revelations given by heavenly intermediaries to Melchizedek, "priest of God Most High," who communicates the revelations to a spiritual elite. It is a Christian writing which reflects in its background the influence of sectarian Jewish speculations on the figure of Melchizedek, but whose chief preoccupation is the relationship between Melchizedek and Jesus Christ. The NT Epistle to the Hebrews supplies the key to the solution of that problem (Gianotto 1984: 187–275).

Melchizedek consists of three main parts: (1) first revelation, 1, 1–14, 15; (2) a liturgical interlude, 14, 15–18, 11(?); and (3) second revelation, 18, 11(?)–27, 10.

The first revelation contains prophecies of the ministry, death, and resurrection of Jesus Christ and predictions of the coming of heretics who will deny the reality of Jesus' incarnation, death, and resurrection. Melchizedek himself has a role to play as well, for he is not only the recipient of the revelation, but also a participant in it, as a future high priest.

The antidocetic polemic in this section is a surprising component to find in a gnostic text. This feature could indicate a connection, in the editorial history of the text, with the "Melchizedekian" sect described by Epiphanius (*Haer.* 55). The Melchizedekians had a low christology and insisted on the true humanity of Christ.

The interlude features certain ritual actions undertaken by Melchizedek and the offering up of prayers addressed to members of the heavenly world. The names of these various beings (Barbelo, Harmozel, Oroiael, Daveithe, Eleleth, et al.) belong to the "Sethian gnostic" tradition represented by the *Apocryphon of John* and related texts (Sevrin 1986: 222–46).

The second set of revelations transports Melchizedek into the future again, this time as the crucified, resurrected, and triumphant savior himself. If this interpretation of the fragmentary text is correct, *Melchizedek* teaches the identity of Jesus Christ with the ancient priest Melchizedek; i.e., Jesus is Melchizedek redivivus. Melchizedek's role as a returning high priest and eschatological holy warrior is to be understood against the background of such Jewish apocalyptic material as 11QMelch, *2 Enoch,* and the Similitudes of *1 Enoch* (chaps. 37–71: Enoch as the future "Son of Man"). The identification of Jesus Christ with Melchizedek is apparently derived from an interpretation of Heb 7:3.

A number of features in *Melchizedek* cohere with the aforementioned Melchizedekian heresy described by Epiphanius. The identification of Jesus Christ with Melchizedek is an idea that appeared in some early Christian circles, especially in Egypt.

The gnostic features of the text may be accounted for on the hypothesis that an earlier non-gnostic apocalypse has undergone Sethian gnostic redaction and revision. (For another view see Schenke 1980.)

The original language of *Melchizedek* was Greek. The final redaction was probably completed in Egypt sometime in the 3d century, though parts of the tractate are probably earlier.

Bibliography

Beltz, W. 1981. Melchisedek—eine gnostische Initiationsliturgie. *ZRGG* 33: 155–58.
Gianotto, C. 1984. *Melchisedek e la sua tipologia.* RBISup 12. Brescia.
Pearson, B. A. 1990. The Figure of Melchizedek in Gnostic Literature. Pp. 108–23 in *Gnosticism, Judaism, and Egyptian Christianity.* Minneapolis.
Pearson, B. A., and Giversen, S. 1981. NHC IX,*1: Melchizedek.* Pp. 19–85 in *Nag Hammadi Codices IX and X,* ed. B. A. Pearson. NHS 15. Leiden.
Schenke, H.-M. 1980. Die jüdische Melchisedek-Gestalt als Thema der Gnosis. Pp. 111–36 in *Altes Testament—Frühjudentum—Gnosis,* ed. K.-W. Tröger. Gütersloh and Berlin.
Sevrin, J.-M. 1986. *Le dossier baptismal séthien: Études sur la sacramentaire gnostique.* Bibliothèque copte de Nag Hammadi, "Études" 2. Québec.

BIRGER A. PEARSON

MELEA (PERSON) [Gk *Melea*]. The father of Eliakim and son of Menna, according to Luke's genealogy tying Joseph, the "supposed father" of Jesus, to descent from Adam and God (Luke 3:31). D omits Melea, substituting a genealogy adapted from Matt 1:6–15 for Luke 3:23–31. The name Melea occurs nowhere else in the biblical documents, including Matthew's genealogy, and falls within a list of eighteen otherwise unknown descendants of David's son Nathan (Fitzmyer *Luke 1–9* AB, 501). Kuhn (1923: 208–9) argues that two seemingly parallel lists of names—Luke 3:23–26 (Jesus to Mattathias) and 3:29–31 (Joshua/Jesus to Mattatha)—were originally identical, the first perhaps reflecting a Hebrew context and the second, an Aramaic context, tracing Mary's line of descent (since it does not mention Joseph as Jesus' father). Melea, in the second list, corresponds to Naggai, in the first list. With no major textual variants for Melea and Naggai to support confusion of the two, Kuhn's theory has little plausibility.

Bibliography

Kuhn, G. 1923. Die Geschlechtsregister Jesu bei Lukas und Matthäus, nach ihrer Herkunft untersucht. *ZNW* 22: 206–28.

STANLEY E. PORTER

MELECH (PERSON) [Heb *melek*]. Great-great-grandson of King Saul according to the genealogy in 1 Chr 8:35 and 9:41. The name is unique in the Hebrew Bible and in the epigraphic corpus; this probably motivated various translators of the LXX to level the MT in line with more common names, such as Malchiel (see Gen 46:17) or Malluch (e.g., Ezra 10:29). The name "Melech" is probably a shortened form of names such as Malchiah, "YH(WH) is king." The abbreviated form *mlky* is attested in a preexilic bulla (Shiloh 1986: 29), and the element *mlk* is very common in biblical and extrabiblical names (Avigad 1986: 73, 82, 87, 105, 106; Shiloh 1986: 29; Tigay 1986: 77–78; Fowler *TPNAH,* 350). Although theoretically the element *mlk* could be connected with the divinity called Molech in the Hebrew Bible, most scholars associate the Israelite names with YHWH and understand *mlk* as a divine epithet (Heider 1985: 229–32; Tigay 1986: 77–78; Fowler, 50–52). However, it might not be accidental that a descendant of King Saul was named Melech (Heb *melek*) "king." The ideology that Saul and his descendants were the legitimate kings over Israel continued to flourish after the ascent of David (Flanagan 1982; Brettler 1989: 423–25), and the name "Melech" for a member of Saul's family might indicate continued hope of recapturing the royal throne. Names compounded with *melech* were used with other people connected to human kingship. The judge who attempted to hold sway over all Israel is named Abimelech (Judges 9), and the indirect ancestor of King David according to Ruth, in which most names are symbolic, is Elimelech (Ruth 1:2). The symbolic use of names with the element *melech* elsewhere thus suggests that Melech in 1 Chr 8:35 and 9:41 is connected to human rather than divine kingship. On the repetition of Saul's genealogy in 1 Chronicles 8 and 9, see AHAZ (PERSON).

Bibliography

Avigad, N. 1986. *Hebrew Bullae from the Time of Jeremiah.* Jerusalem.
Brettler, M. 1989. The Book of Judges: Literature as Politics. *JBL* 108: 405–28.
Flanagan, J. 1982. Genealogy and Dynasty in the Early Monarchy of Israel and Judah. *PWCJS* 8: 23–28.
Heider, G. C. 1985. *The Cult of Molek: A Reassessment.* JSOTSup 43. Sheffield.
Shiloh, Y. 1986. A Group of Hebrew Bullae from the City of David. *IEJ* 36: 16–38.
Tigay, J. H. 1986. *You Shall Have No Other Gods.* HSS 31. Atlanta.

MARC Z. BRETTLER

MELONS. See FLORA.

MEM. The thirteenth letter of the Hebrew alphabet.

MEMMIUS, QUINTUS (PERSON) [Gk *Kointos Memmios*]. Quintus Memmius, one of two Roman envoys to the Jews in 164 B.C.E. (2 Macc 11:34). This envoy is mentioned along with his colleague Titus Manius, and the Vulgate designates them as *legati Romanorum,* "Roman legates." See MANIUS, TITUS. Efforts to establish the historicity of these envoys have produced no certainty. The content of the letter sent to the Jews by the Romans was possible enough, in view of the policies of the Romans toward the territory of Syria. However, dates and names within the passage do not fit the known events, so that some think that the letters and the embassy to the Jews are fictitious.

BETTY JANE LILLIE

MEMPHIS (PLACE) [Heb *nōp, mōp*]. Throughout most of Egyptian history, the principal residence and capital of the kings of Egypt, referred to in the oracles of several Hebrew prophets (Isa 19:13; Jer 2:16; 46:14, 19; Ezek 30:13; Hos 9:6). Apparently some of the Judeans who fled to Egypt during the Babylonian advance settled in Memphis (Jer 44:1). The site is identified with modern Mitrahineh, 13 miles S of Cairo on the W bank of the Nile.

The site was first settled by Menes, the traditional founder of the 1st Dyn. (Herodotus 2.99; see Kemp 1976), who ca. 3050 B.C. built a fortress there called the "White Fortress." Throughout the Old Kingdom (ca. 3050–2200 B.C.) the town was otherwise known as "the Residence" (Eg *ẖnw*), and here the ever-expanding bureaucracy and the administrative offices of the kingdom were centered. Because the early kings chose to build their pyramids in various sites within the area, a number of temporary "pyramid towns" sprang up to house the workers; these soon developed into faubourgs of Memphis, connected by a N-S canal (Goyon 1971). One of these, the pyramid town of Tety (ca. 2380–2350 B.C.), enjoyed continued prosperity during the 9th and the 10th dynasties (ca. 2180–2050 B.C.), when it became the metropolis of the entire district. Another town, built by Pepy I (ca. 2350–2315 B.C.), was called "Pepy is Firm and Fair" (Eg *pepy-mn-nfr*); and from Middle Kingdom times on the city was known by an abbreviated form of this name, *mn-nfr* (cf. Gk *Menophreōs, Memphis*; Akk *Mi-im-pi*; as well as the two Heb forms).

From the earliest times, Ptah appears as the principal god of the town, and his temple (originally on the S side of the "White Fortress") gradually became the focal point of the city. Its name, *Ḥwt-kȝ-ptḥ* ("*Ka* mansion of Ptah") was often used to designate the city itself and later, by extension, the entire country (cf. *Ai-ku-pi-ti-yo* in Linear B [Stieglitz 1976: 85]; *ḥkpt* in 2 Aqht V: 21, 31; and Gk *Aigyptos,* "Egypt"). Already in the Old Kingdom period copies of the royal annals were kept in Ptah's temple (Redford 1986). Ptah was essentially a creator god, celebrated for his creation by word of mouth (cf. *ANET,* 4–6), and, as a reflection of the political importance of his city, considered first divine king of Egypt (cf. Diod. 1.13.1–2). His consort was

Sakhmet, the lioness-headed plague bearer, and his offspring Nefertuia, the Lotus. He was also associated with the sacred bull APIS, who occupied an ancillary shrine adjacent to Ptah's temenos; and the chthonic god Tatenen, personification of the emergent alluvium. The principal and oldest goddess at the site was Hathor, Mistress of the Southern Sycamore, whose temple stood S of the Ptah enclosure (Mahmud 1978). Three km to the W of the city, on the edge of the desert cliffs, stood the ever-growing necropolis of the city, Sakkara, which took its name from the mortuary deity, Sokan (Lauer 1976, 1977). Here all of the first six dynasties of Egyptian history, except the 4th, are represented by mastaba and pyramid fields.

The collapse of the Old Kingdom after 2200 B.C. robbed Memphis temporarily of its status as royal residence, and primacy was ceded first to Herakleopolis (9th–10th Dyn.) and then to Thebes (11th Dyn.). Even when the center of the kingdom gravitated N in the 12th Dyn., it was not to Memphis, but to the new capital of Itj-towy (modern Lisht, 32 km S of Mitrahineh). Nevertheless, the city of Memphis revived somewhat during the Middle Kingdom, when part of the site was covered by tombs (Lilyquist 1974); and the cultic establishment experienced a renewal. Memphis was captured by the Hyksos ca. 1660 B.C. and, according to Manetho, was used by them as a residence (see HYKSOS). Its liberation is not recorded in any surviving text, but by the time of the final assault on Avaris, it was firmly in Egyptian hands.

From the reign of Thutmose I (ca. 1526–1515 B.C.) to the early years of Rameses II (after 1300 B.C.), Memphis regained its distinction of being the favored royal residence; and even after the construction of the new capital Pi-Ramesse (ca. 1290 B.C.), it maintained a central role in the administration (Badawy 1948). It was the seat of the N vizier and his council, responsible for Middle and Lower Egypt; and it became customary to appoint the heir apparent to the post of *sm*-priest of Ptah in the city. Thutmose III resided in the city and used it as a base of military operations (*Urk* IV: 1282). Amenophis II added a suburb called Peru-nefer, Thutmose IV a chapel, and Amenophis III a shrine and a large mortuary temple (Petrie 1909–10). Although Akhenaten probably never set foot in Memphis, he had a sun temple constructed at the site (Löhr 1975). In his third year, Tutankhamen took up residence in Memphis, and from that point until Ramesside times the town experienced a rebirth. The necropolis during this period displayed well-built mastabas of the highest magnates of the realm, such as the generalissimo Horemheb, the treasurer Maya, the princess Tia, the general Amenenioue, etc. (Martin 1977, 1982, 1983, 1984). Sety I built a temple at Memphis and resided at the site. Khamwese, son of Rameses II and priest of Ptah, undertook at Memphis a restoration of temples and ancient cults, an activity which is reflected in the noticeable "antiquarianism" of the period (Redford, 1986). Rameses II's own contribution to Memphis consisted of the refurbishing and expansion of numerous standing structures and the building of the present Ptah temple (Jeffreys 1984). He also transferred the place of burial of the Apis bulls from the aboveground cemetery to a subterranean serapeum. His son, Merneptah, built a palace and temple to Ptah at the SE corner of the city; and Rameses III of the 20th Dyn. also built a temple at the site.

During the Third Intermediate Period (ca. 1070–711 B.C.) the direct influence of Memphis on the politics of the realm declined somewhat. Although kings continued to lavish public buildings on the site—Siamun constructing a temple and Sheshonk I a mortuary temple and an embalming house for Apis—Memphis became little more than an appendage of princes of the reigning house. It resisted the invasion of the Nubian Pi'ankhy (ca. 717 B.C.) and was besieged and sacked. It suffered a similar fate at the hands of the Assyrians. Despite this decline, the tradition of Memphis' former importance survived in Palestine into the 8th century, judging from Isaiah's reference to it in a poetic parallelism that recognizes its princes (and those of Zoan) as "the cornerstones of (Egypt's) tribes" (19:13). At the same time, the tradition of its impressive necropolis seems to have been known to the prophet Hosea, who used that image to refer to the burial of the sinful Israelites (9:6).

The rulers of the 25th Dyn. restored Memphis to its former greatness and turned it into their residence, and the kings of the 26th Dyn. may also have resided there. Psamtek I (664–610 B.C.) enlarged the serapeum, HOPHRA contributed a palace on the N (Petrie 1909–10, II), and the Amasis Dynasty as a whole refurbished the Ptah Temple. Throughout the 7th and 6th centuries Memphis remained the political and cultic hub of Egypt, and as such it attracted the ire of Hebrew prophets in predictions which failed to materialize (cf. Jer 46:14–19; Ezek 30:13).

With the Egyptian Empire of the New Kingdom, Memphis had become the seat of a Canaanite community of merchants and mercenaries centered upon the temples of Baʿal and Astarte (Helck 1966). During the final days of Judah, Memphis received exiles fleeing the advance of the Babylonians (Jer 44:1). In Herodotus' time this enclave was dubbed "the Camp of the Tyrians" (Hdt. 2.111); and by that time the foreign community comprised Syrians, Carians, and Greeks as well.

During the first Persian occupation (525–406 B.C.), Memphis served as the headquarters of the governor and a garrison post. Cambyses ran afoul of the local priesthood (Hdt. 3.37), but Darius I underwent a coronation there. The 30th Dyn. (380–343 B.C.) contributed greatly to the embellishment of the city and the necropolis.

The priesthood of Ptah had always occupied a high rank in the Egyptian clergy (Freier 1976). Leadership of Memphis and its community gravitated in the Late Period into the hands of the high priests of Ptah who could trace their ancestry to a remote period. These reserved the right to crown the king, to officiate at the rites of Apis, and to keep the offering lists and king lists (see Redford 1986); and during Ptolemaic times, they were a major link between the Greek administration in Alexandria and the native population (Quaegebeur 1971, 1980). The priesthood of Ptah had, over the centuries, gained a reputation for wisdom and scientific knowledge, being the authors of the "deism" of the Memphite Theology, and accurate assessors of climatic conditions in central Africa and the cause of the annual Nile flood (Diod. 1.40.1–2; cf. Lucr. *De rerum natura* 6.738).

Memphis was chosen as capital by Ptolemy I in 321 B.C.

and initially received the burial of Alexander. Even after the transfer of the capital to Alexandria, Memphis remained the "royal city of the Egyptians" (Strabo 17.1.31), where kings were crowned and sometimes resided and where synods of the Egyptian priesthood were held (Crawford 1980).

Under Roman rule Memphis' decline was ensured. The governor visited it once a year on a circuit, to inspect the affairs of Upper Egypt. It might still attract royal visits (Suet. *Aug.*; Severus 18.1), but this was mainly due to the fame of Apis, whose worship outlived that of Ptah. With the edict of Theodosius (A.D. 395), its temples were shut and destroyed; and the site used as a quarry for later neighboring settlements.

Bibliography

Badawy, A. 1948. *Memphis als zweite Landeshauptstadt im neuen Reich.* Cairo.

Crawford, D. J. 1980. Ptolemy, Ptah and Apis in Hellenistic Memphis. Pp. 1–42 in *Studies on Ptolemaic Memphis,* ed. W. Peremans. Louvain.

Freier, E. 1976. Zu den sogenannten Hohenpriestern des Ptah von Memphis in Alten Reich. *Altorientalische Forschungen* 4: 5–34.

Goyon, G. 1971. Les ports des pyramides et le grand canal de Memphis. *RdÉ* 23: 137ff.

Helck, W. 1966. Zum Auftreten fremder Götter in Ägypten. *OrAnt* 5: 1–14.

Jeffreys, D. G., et al. 1984. The Survey of Memphis, 1982. *JEA* 70: 23–32.

Kemp, B. 1976. A Note on Stratigraphy at Memphis. *JARCE* 13: 25–28.

Lauer, J.-P. 1976. *Saqqara, the Royal Cemetery of Memphis.* London.

———. 1977. *Les pyramides de Saqqara.* Cairo.

Lilyquist, C. 1974. Early Middle Kingdom Tombs at Mitrahina. *JARCE* 11: 27ff.

Löhr, B. 1975. Aḥanjati in Memphis. *SAK* 2: 139–88.

Mahmud, A. el-Sayed. 1978. *A New Temple for Hathor at Memphis.* Warminster.

Martin, G. 1977. Excavations at the Memphite Tomb of Horemheb. *JEA* 63: 13–19.

———. 1982. A Facsimile Corpus of Decorated and Inscribed Tomb Reliefs of the New Kingdom. *GM* 57: 7ff.

———. 1983. Recent Discoveries of New Kingdom Date in the Memphite Necropolis. *JSSEA* 13: 44ff.

———. 1984. The Tomb of Tia and Tia. *JEA* 70: 5–12.

Petrie, W. M. F. 1909–10. *Memphis I–III.* London.

Quaegebeur, J. 1971. Documents concerning a Cult of Arsinoe Philadelphos at Memphis. *JNES* 30: 239ff.

———. 1980. The Genealogy of the Memphite High Priest Family in the Hellenistic Period. Pp. 43–82 in *Studies on Ptolemaic Memphis,* ed. W. Peremans. Louvain.

Redford, D. B. 1986. *Pharaonic King-lists, Annals and Day-books.* Toronto.

Smith, H. 1983. The Survey of Memphis, 1981. *JEA* 69: 69ff.

———. 1986. A Survey of Memphis. *Antiquity* 60: 88ff.

Stieglitz, R. 1976. The Eteocretan Inscription from Psychro. *Kadmos* 15: 84ff.

Donald B. Redford

MEMPHITE THEOLOGY. The name given to the text found on a stone dated to the reign of King Shabaka of the 25th Egyptian Dyn. (ca. 710 B.C.). The introduction of the text claims that it was a copy of a much earlier papyrus document which had been found partially destroyed; and because of its importance, Shabaka ordered that it be restored and inscribed on stone. This copy itself has also suffered badly over the centuries, with almost one-third of the text being obliterated as a result of the stone's having been used for milling.

The text has four main sections: the titles of King Shabaka, followed by a statement of the condition in which the original was found; the first part of the original document, which recounts Geb, the earth god's resolution of the conflict between Horus and Seth over the division of authority and territory after the death of Osiris; a long section which relates Ptah's creation of the cosmos, the gods, plants, crafts, towns, and "all good things"; and the final section, which contains a brief description of the rescue of Osiris' body by his sisters, Isis and Nephthys.

The text is of interest to Egyptologists because of its style, which has been interpreted either as a play (Sethe 1928) or as a treatise derived from dramatic performances of the myths which are alluded to in the text (Junker 1940, 1941). Although not mentioned in the Bible, this text has gained prominence because the method of Ptah's (Sandman-Holmberg 1946) creation has been compared to that ascribed to the god of Israel in the book of Genesis, that is, what has commonly been called "creation ex nihilo" (Finnestad 1976: 81).

The creation activities of Ptah are described as taking place through the agency of his heart and his tongue; the former being the seat of thought, while the latter represents the verbalization of the heart's thoughts. "Therefore, all work and all crafts are made, the activity of the hands, the motion of the legs and the movement of all limbs, according to this command which the heart developed and which comes forth on the tongue and creates the performance of everything" (Sethe 1928: ln. 58).

Analysis of the grammar and orthography of the text, along with studies of the religious and historical allusions made in the text, led early commentators to date the original document to the Old Kingdom (ca. 2500 B.C.), when the city of Memphis and its patron god, Ptah, held positions of critical importance in Egypt's geopolitical environment. No matter what chronological or dating systems are used, such a provenance would place the origin of this text at a period which is substantially pre-Mosaic and therefore a challenge to the supposed uniqueness of the Genesis account.

Recently, the veracity of the text's introduction has been called into question (Junge 1973: 195). This analysis concludes that there was a deliberate archaizing of the text and that it was actually a piece of political propaganda authored in the 25th Dyn. This thesis is not without its supporters (*AEL* 3: 5), while others, although unconvinced by the argumentation leading to a 25th Dyn. provenance, see the original text as dating to the high New Kingdom, perhaps to the reign of Rameses II (Schloegl 1980: 110).

While these technical matters remain topics of debate among Egyptologists, developments in other disciplines permit a better understanding of the salient feature of this text, creation through thought and word. This method was considered to be a highly sophisticated, almost metaphysical, description of creation which held a preeminent place within Western religious tradition because of its biblical roots.

Phenomenologists of religion have come to understand, however, that the actions of a creator god who uses thought and word are directly related to the incantations of a magician or the promulgations of a king. Indeed, specialists in comparative religion have found this type of creation story among many groups with strong magical or shamanistic traditions (Bergounioux and Goetz 1965: 69).

In this regard, one can cite hundreds of texts from the corpus of Egyptian mortuary literature as early as the Old Kingdom Pyramid Texts, where the creative power of the spoken word is a fundamental premise (Miosi 1982: 77). Far from being unique, then, Ptah's activities model a general and well-attested pattern of Egyptian thought which recognizes the creative power of the spoken word.

Bibliography

Bergounioux, F. M., and Goetz, J. 1965. *Prehistoric and Primitive Religions*. London.

Finnestad, R. B. 1976. Ptah, Creator of the Gods: Reconsideration of the Ptah Section of the Denkmal. *Numen* 23: 81–113.

Junge, F. 1973. Zur Fehldatierung des sogenannten Denkmals memphitischer Theologie oder Des Beitrag der aegyptischen Theologie zue Geistesgeschichte der Spätzeit. *MDAIK* 29: 195–204.

Junker, H. 1940. Die Gotterlehre von Memphis. *APAW* 23. Berlin.

———. 1941. Die politische Lehre von Memphis. *APAW* 6. Berlin.

Miosi, F. T. 1982. The Wsrt of Geb. *JSSEA* 12/2: 69–111.

Sandman-Holmberg, M. 1946. *The God Ptah*. Lund.

Schloegl, H. A. 1980. *Der Gott Tatenen*. Göttingen.

Sethe, K. 1928. Das "Denkmal memphitischer Theologie," der Schabakostien des Britischen Museum. *Untersuchingen zur Geschichte und Altertumskunde Aegyptens*. 10/1. Leipzig.

Frank T. Miosi

MEMUCAN (PERSON) [Heb *mĕmûkān*]. One of the seven chief counselors of Persian king Ahasuerus listed in Esth 1:14, 16, 21. These men are described as sages who held a prominent office next to the king which entailed advising him on matters of custom and law (Esth 1:13–14). Several classical authors make mention of such a group of seven chief judges or viziers who customarily decided questions affecting the conduct of Persian kings (Hdt. *Hist.* 1:107; 3:31, 34, 118; 7:19; Jos. *Ant* 11.31; X. *An.* 1.6.4; cf. Ezra 7:14; and 1 Chr 12:33; Paton *Esther* ICC, 153). In Esth 1:16–20 Memucan acts as the spokesman for this group when Ahasuerus seeks advice concerning what to do about his disobedient queen, Vashti. The seven sages advise that she is to be deposed and a successor sought, or else her example of disobedience will spread to every household in the realm resulting in great social upheaval when wives no longer obey their husbands. According to Clines this scene in the story should be seen as satire as the author describes the best minds of the kingdom formulating "a response which any self-respecting male chauvinist could easily dream up for himself" (*Ezra, Nehemiah, Esther* NCBC, 280). Memucan's name may be derived from Pers *memucāna*, "cloud," or *magavan*, meaning "a true member of the Magian tribe" (Paton *Esther* ICC 69; Gehman 1924: 325).

Bibliography

Gehman, H. S. 1924. Notes on the Persian Words in the Book of Esther. *JBL* 43: 321–28.

John M. Wiebe

MENAHEM (PERSON) [Heb *mĕnaḥēm*]. A king of the N kingdom of Israel in the latter half of the 8th century B.C.E. (ca. 746–737). The name "Menahem" is a nominal form of the verb *nḥm*, "to comfort," and is related to the name "Nehemiah" (Heb *nĕḥemyâ*). It is a common West Semitic name and is found in the Jerusalem bullae collection, where it appears on bullae Nos. 100–4 (Avigad 1986: 74–75). It is found once in the Arad Letters (No. 72; *AI*, 96). Apart from the name, Menahem, the participial form of the verb is used in the Bible mostly in late literature such as the Psalms (Ps 69:21), the Wisdom books (Eccl 4:1; Job 16:2), the Latter Prophets (Nah 3:7; Isa 51:12), and the Writings (Lam 1:2, 9, 16, 17, 21). Here the term means "comforter." In 2 Sam 10:3 (= 1 Chr 19:3) the term assumes a diplomatic status.

His activities are recorded in 2 Kgs 15:13–22 and have no parallel in Chronicles. He was the son of Gadi and probably originated from Tirzah. A brief outline of the account of his reign in 2 Kgs 15:13–22 is as follows. Menahem killed Shallum ben Jabesh, a usurper to the throne who had assassinated Zechariah, the last king of the Jehudite dynasty. Menahem's reaction was swift since Shallum had reigned for only one month in the capital city of Samaria. Menahem also had a role in the attack on Tiphsach, on the Euphrates river, and had shown the customary brutality of siege warfare of the time (v 16). At the invitation of Menahem, the Assyrian Tiglath-pileser III came to help Menahem retain his hold on his new kingdom; and the cost for this aid was one thousand talents of silver (vv 19–20). After payment Tiglath-pileser returned to Assyria; and sometime later Menahem died, presumably of natural causes, to be succeeded by his son, Pekahiah. Menahem reigned a total of 10 years in Samaria.

Although this outline appears to be straightforward, there are many critical historical and literary problems associated with this account, not all of which are capable of satisfactory solution.

The chronology of Israel and Judah in this period is extremely complicated; but although several adjustments have to be made in the reigns of kings before and after Menahem (Hobbs *2 Kings* WBC, 173–206), there is little reason to alter the length of Menahem's reign itself. Most historians allow it the 10 years allotted in the Bible, and its dates are usually given as 746–737 B.C.E.

Menahem's full name has generated some discussion. The reference to him as "son of Gadi" has led to speculation that he was originally from the E side of the Jordan, from the tribal area of Gad. It has been further suggested that there was political and military tension between the Transjordanians and Cisjordanians during the 8th century B.C.E. (Ishida 1977: 173–76). Shallum, it is to be noted, probably came from Jabesh in Gilead to lead an eastern revolt against the western king (Cogan and Tadmor *2 Kings*

AB, 170). Further, the assassination of Pekahiah, Menahem's son, was carried out by Pekah and 50 men from Gilead (2 Kgs 15:25). However, the geographic conflict is probably overrated; and there are ulterior motives for its creation, namely, the accommodation of the chronology of Pekah's reign. Menahem himself was responsible for the death of Shallum, an easterner; and Pekah was a close military associate (Heb *šālîš*) of Pekahiah. It is also unlikely that the patronymic of Menahem, Gadi, refers to his place of origin. It is a perfectly normal name for a person.

The reference to Menahem's military adventures in Tiphsach (2 Kgs 15:16) has caused considerable debate. Tiphsach is identified with Thapsachah, an important trade center on the banks of the Euphrates (*LBHG,* 16); and, according to many, it is unlikely that Menahem became involved so far away from Samaria during his reign (Cogan and Tadmor, *2 Kings* AB, 171). Many interpreters therefore suggest that the reference to Tiphsach is a mistake and seek to emend the text in accordance with one tradition of the LXX which suggests Tappuah, a site much closer to home. The town is mentioned as being on the border between Ephraim and Manasseh (Josh 16:8) and is usually identified with modern Tell Sheikh Abu Zarad (M.R. 172168). However, this emendation also has its problems since an attack on Tappuah, by now a small town of Manasseh, is just as difficult to understand. What would be the circumstances of such an attack? What would be the purpose of such an attack on a small, unimportant community? The difficulties with Tiphsach on the Euphrates arise if the text in 2 Kgs 15:16 is taken as another in a sequence of events in the reign of Menahem. But this is far from clear. The Hebrew begins with an unusual particle *ʾāz,* followed by an imperfect form *(yakkeh).* The style has been recognized as archival (Montgomery 1934) and offers not so much a sequence of events as a selection of events. Preceding years had seen the decline of Aram-Damascus, the temporary revival of Hamath, then the domination of the northern Levant by the Assyrians. It would therefore be difficult indeed to envisage Menahem, as king, invading Assyrian-held territory, but it would not be difficult to envisage an earlier Menahem in his capacity as a general in Jeroboam's army fighting on the northern border of the newly created Israelite empire. His capture of Tiphsach would inevitably become part of his military reputation. This tradition of the role of the early Menahem is, in fact, preserved in Josephus (*Ant* 9.228). If Menahem had been a general in Jeroboam's army, this position would also explain his loyalty to the house of Jehu and the speed with which he came to avenge the blood of Jeroboam's son.

A third problem with the reign of Menahem is the nature of the payment to Tiglath-pileser III mentioned in 2 Kgs 15:19–21. The data associated with this matter are as follows. It is known from the biblical account that Tiglath-pileser III, king of Assyria from 744 to 727 B.C.E., sent a military force to Israel during Menahem's reign (2 Kgs 15:19–20). It is also known from Tiglath-pileser's own accounts that he invaded Israel (Akk *sa-me-ri-na-a*) and exacted considerable tribute from the country (*ANET,* 283–84; *LAR* 1: 293; Cogan and Tadmor, *2 Kings* AB, 335–36). The problem consists of two issues. Are the two accounts reconcilable, i.e., does the biblical text speak of tribute payment? What is the date of Tiglath-pileser's invasion?

On the first matter it has been traditionally understood that Menahem paid Tiglath-pileser tribute and that he introduced a system of taxation of wealthy men (Heb *gibbôrêy haḥayīl*) to pay for the tribute. It is even suggested (*LBHG,* 370; McCarter *HDB*, 625) that the introduction of this taxation system was a major cause in the later downfall of Menahem, a suggestion, it must be noted, without historical foundation. The language of the account does not support this reading; and a better understanding is that Menahem paid Tiglath-pileser to send an army to help him firm up his hold on power in the north, presumably against those who might still support the aims of Shallum. The use of the term *gibbôr ḥayīl* (lit. "soldier") as a socio-economic designation is very unusual (Hobbs *2 Kings* WBC, 198–200). The payment was not a formal tribute, but payment for mercenary services. A parallel is found in Ahaz of Judah's appeal to the same king during the attack of Pekah and Rezin on Jerusalem (2 Kgs 16:5–9). Based on the payment, the expeditionary force sent should be calculated at approximately 75,000 men.

Three texts are cited from Assyrian sources in discussion of this incident. Two have long been known (*ANET,* 283–84; *LAR* 1: 293), and the third is a more recently discovered fragment (Levine 1972b). Unfortunately, the first text referring to Menahem (*ANET,* 283) is undated, although the reference to Hiram of Tyre would place it toward the end of Menahem's reign since Hiram succeeded to the throne of Tyre in ca. 738 B.C.E. But this text has the characteristics of a tribute payment from conquest, which is not the impression given in 2 Kgs 15:19–21. The reading of Menahem in the second text is not at all clear. That is unfortunate since the text is a comprehensive one and covers many years of the relationships between Assyria and Israel. The more recent text appears to be a reference to an exaction of tribute from Menahem at an earlier date since Hiram's predecessor, Tabal (Isa 7:6), is given as the king of Tyre. The order and dating of the annals of Tiglath-pileser III are extremely complicated problems with no sign of satisfactory resolution. What is certain is that Menahem's reign is to be seen against the background of the rapidly growing influence of Assyria in the west. Fifteen years after Menahem's death the northern nation of Israel had been destroyed. The literature referred to in the bibliography below will provide an entry into the subject of the complicated chronology of this period.

Bibliography

Alt, A. 1953. Tiglathpilesers III. erster Felzug nach Palästina. Pp. 150–62 in *KlSchr.* Munich.

Avigad, N. 1986. *Hebrew Bullae from the Time of Jeremiah: Remnants of a Burnt Archive.* Jerusalem.

Ishida, T. 1977. *Royal Dynasties in Ancient Israel.* Berlin.

Levine, L. D. 1972a. Menahem and Tiglath Pileser: A New Synchronism. *BASOR* 206: 40–42.

———. 1972b. *Two Neo-Assyrian Stelae from Iran.* Toronto.

Montgomery, J. A. 1934. Archival Data in the Book of Kings. *JBL* 53: 43–52.

T. R. Hobbs

MENANDER, SYRIAC. See SYRIAC MENANDER.

MENELAUS (PERSON) [Gk *Menelaos*]. One of three brothers who belonged to the priestly order of Bilgah at the time of Antiochus IV Epiphanes (as indicated by an improved reading of 2 Macc 3:4). Menelaus thus belonged to an important family which was striving to promote its status among the Jewish ruling circle, and which consequently came into conflict with the high priest Onias III. At first Menelaus was associated with Jason, who had replaced his brother Onias III as high priest in Jerusalem; then, while on a mission to Antiochus IV Epiphanes, Menelaus undermined Jason's position and, with Antiochus' support, won the high priesthood for himself (172 B.C.E.).

This was considered illegal in the eyes of many Jews (2 Macc 4:25, 26), since Menelaus was not of the legitimate priestly (i.e., Zadokite) family to which Onias belonged. Menelaus' (probably elder) brother Simon had previously been appointed provost (RSV "captain") of the temple (2 Macc 4:23; 3:4, 11) and had also used his position to undermine Onias. The appointments of both Jason and Menelaus to their respective offices were irregular, since they took place while the officiating high priest was still alive and not according to primogeniture. (This is on the assumption that at that time the king did not appoint—either de facto or de jure—the high priests to their offices.) After becoming high priest himself, Menelaus left his (probably younger) brother Lysimachus in charge in Jerusalem while he went to meet with Antiochus; there was a riot in Jerusalem, and Lysimachus was killed (2 Macc 4:29, 39–42). This accords well with a Talmudic reminiscence about a punishment inflicted on the order of Bilgah (*m. Sukkah* 8:8; *t. Sukkah* 4:28).

Jerusalem suffered many convulsions under Menelaus' tenure as high priest. The temple was robbed, a civil war broke out, and first Jason and then Antiochus IV invaded Jerusalem. Then came the infamous religious persecution (December 167 B.C.E.), the resulting Maccabean revolt, and about three years later the negotiations that brought an end to the persecutions. Menelaus is mentioned twice in those events. The first is in the letter of Antiochus IV to the Jews (2 Macc 11:27–33, vv 29 and 32). This letter seems to indicate that Menelaus left Jerusalem to meet the king (who was at that time in the upper satrapies, i.e., in Iran) and that it was Menelaus himself who negotiated the cancellation of the persecution, thereby maintaining his influence with the king, who lent support to his position in Judea. The second and last reference to Menelaus appears in conjunction with the beginning of Antiochus V's expedition to Judea (2 Macc 13:3–8). Since the temple compound itself at that time was under the control of Judas Maccabeus, Menelaus was eager to have Antiochus V return it to Menelaus' control. But when Lysias blamed Menelaus as "the cause of all the troubles," Menelaus was taken to Beroea and was executed according to the local custom: by suffocation in ashes.

Menelaus' career holds a central place in the various theories which propose explanations for the religious persecutions under Antiochus IV. Indeed, it seems that Menelaus had a crucial role in this event. The blame that Lysias casts on him as "the cause of all the troubles" cannot be dismissed, and his execution cannot be understood without it. The fact that 2 Maccabees treats this event from a highly theological perspective does not diminish the essential accuracy of the account.

If Lysias' accusation is correct, then Menelaus must have been involved in the religious persecution himself. Such accords well with the earlier career of Menelaus, especially his striving for power at all costs. Since his avenue to power included, among other things, the overthrow of the Jewish ancestral constitution, he was not deterred from its "logical" conclusion (the religious persecution) and its consequences. This policy was miscalculated and fell to pieces; because of the fierce "traditional Jewish" opposition under the leadership of the Maccabees, Menelaus attempted to change that policy. He seems to have been somewhat successful with Antiochus IV, but failed completely with Lysias, who rightly blamed him for his leading role in this political fiasco.

There was thus not necessarily any cultural religious ideology behind Menelaus' activities: he was mainly using "Hellenization" as a way to increase his own personal power and that of his supporters and probably to gain the support of Antiochus IV and key members of his entourage (especially Ptolemy son of Dorymenes?). For Menelaus, Hellenization was a means toward a personal end, not a cultural or ideological end in itself.

Josephus' accounts of Menelaus in *Antiquities* 12 (especially 239–40 and 383–85) and *Jewish War* (1.31ff.) contradict 2 Maccabees in various details. (Josephus tends to follow the account in 1 Maccabees, which does not mention Menelaus at all.) Most scholars consider Josephus an undependable source on this matter (Tcherikover 1959: 392–97).

Bibliography

Bickermann, E. 1979. *God of the Maccabees*. Leiden.
Hengel, M. 1974. *Judaism and Hellenism*. 2 vols. Philadelphia.
Millar, F. 1978. The Background of the Maccabean Revolution. *JJS* 29: 1–21.
Tcherikover, V. 1959. *Hellenistic Civilization and the Jews*. Philadelphia.

URIEL RAPPAPORT

MENESTHEUS (PERSON) [Gk *Menestheōs*]. 2 Macc 4:4 and 21 refer to Apollonius, the son of Menestheus, who was governor of Coele-Syria and Phoenicia in the reign of the Seleucid Antiochus IV Epiphanes. This Apollonius supported the Tobiad Simon in his intrigues against the high priest Onias. Polybius (31.13.2–3) describes a certain Apollonius as a favored official in the reign of Seleucus IV but who left the empire at the succession of Antiochus IV. This Apollonius had three sons, Apollonius, Meleager, and Menestheus, who supported the claim of Demetrius, the son of Seleucus IV, to the Syrian throne. Given the Greek custom of naming a son after the grandfather, it is possible that the Apollonius of Polybius is Apollonius, the son of Menestheus, of 2 Maccabees 4. Against this hypothesis is the opposition of the family to Antiochus IV and their preference for the line of Seleucus IV. However, the events in 2 Maccabees 4 could have preceded the sole rule of Antiochus IV after the murder of his co-regent Antiochus, the son of Seleucus (Mørkholm 1966: 41–50). The Apollonius and his family mentioned by Polybius need not have broken with Antiochus IV while he shared the throne with his nephew Antiochus from 175 to 170 B.C.E. (Goldstein *2 Maccabees* AB, 222). The identification of Apollonius as the son of Menestheus in 2 Maccabees 4 raises the question of the identity of the Syrian governor of Coele-Syria and Phoenicia of 2 Macc 3:5 who is described as Apollonius of Tarsus. If Apollonius, son of Menestheus, of 2 Maccabees 4 is the Apollonius in Polybius' narrative, the governor of 2 Macc 3:5 is a different Apollonius. If the son of Menestheus is not the Apollonius of Polybius, they could be the same person.

Bibliography

Mørkholm, O. 1966. *Antiochus IV of Syria.* Copenhagen.

MICHAEL E. HARDWICK

MENI (DEITY) [Heb *mĕnî*]. A god (or spirit) of destiny/fate; cf. the Heb verb *mānāh,* "number," "assign," "appoint." This deity is mentioned in Isa 65:11 as being worshipped, along with Gad (a god of fortune), by apostate Jews, probably in postexilic Judah. The RSV translates Heb *gad* as "Fortune" and *mĕnî* as "Destiny": "you . . . who set a table for Fortune and fill cups of mixed wine for Destiny." Most likely the setting of a table took place to venerate both deities, as also the filling of cups.

The name "Meni" has not been found with certainty in the pantheons of Assyria or Babylonia. Some scholars would identify Meni with Manu, apparently a deity worshipped in Asshur. On Achaemenid coins the name *ʿbdmnî* perhaps appears (it is a disputed reading), which may contain the name of the god: "Servant of Meni." A Greek-Latin inscription from an altar of Vaison in Provence (S France) reads in the Lat text *Belus Fortunae rector Menisque magister.* According to the Gk text *Belus* of the Lat text is Bel/Baal of Apamea (in Syria). Conceivably, then, *Fortunae* and *Menisque* also refer to Semitic divinities, respectively Gad and Meni.

Meni, (though) a male deity, probably is to be connected with the goddess *manât,* an idol (a large stone) worshipped by pre-Islamic Arabs. The Koran (Surah 53, 20) mentions her: "What think ye of Allat, and Al-Uzzah, and Manat, that other third goddess?" A word related to *manât,* the plural *mnwtw,* appears in the Nabatean inscriptions of Higr as a designation for a deity worshipped by the Nabateans; a corresponding word may be a divine name in South Arabian inscriptions.

There are various suggestions with regard to Meni in the scholarly literature, none of them proven. One is that the god, "Destiny"/"Fate," is a relatively late personification of the abstract "destiny," "fate." Evidence cited includes the Heb text of Isa 65:11, which provides *mĕnî* with the definite article (literally "for *the* Meni"; but note the lack of the *dāgeš forte* in the *mem*), possibly indicating that the Masoretes retained an awareness of an original "fate," "destiny." According to a second suggestion the worship of Meni in postexilic Judah is associated with the N migrations of the Nabatean Arabs and/or the Edomites. Another proposal sees Meni, paired with Gad ("Fortune," "Good Luck") in Isa 65:11, as a deity of bad fate/destiny. Very uncertain is the suggestion that, as Jewish tradition identified Gad with the planet Jupiter, and Arabic astrology regarded Jupiter as "the greater fortune," and Venus "the lesser fortune," Meni should be identified with Venus.

Isa 65:12 undoubtedly plays on the mention of Meni in v 11: the Lord (Yahweh) says that he will "destine" (Heb verb *mānāh*) the apostates "to the sword." The unfaithful, looking to Meni and not Yahweh as the controller of human destinies, will receive harsh judgment from the Lord. See GAD (DEITY).

Bibliography

Baudissin, W. 1902. Meni. Vol. 11, pp. 575–77 in *Realencyklopädie für protestantische Theologie und Kirche,* ed. D. Hauck. Leipzig.

WALTER A. MAIER III

MENNA (PERSON) [Gk *Menna*]. The father of Melea and son of Mattatha according to Luke's genealogy tying Joseph, the "supposed father" of Jesus, to descent from Adam and God (Luke 3:31). D omits Menna, substituting a genealogy adapted from Matt 1:6–15 for Luke 3:23–31. The name Menna occurs nowhere else in the biblical documents, including Matthew's genealogy, and falls within a list of eighteen otherwise unknown descendants of David's son Nathan (Fitzmyer *Luke 1–9* AB, 501). Kuhn (1923: 210–11) claims that in the original form of the genealogy Menna was not a name but a transliteration of Heb *mnnh,* meaning "from him," i.e., "descended from." Thus, according to Kuhn (208–9), the seemingly parallel lists of Luke 3:23–26 (Jesus to Mattathias) and 3:29–31 (Joshua/Jesus to Mattatha) stem from the same original source, the first possibly preserved in a Hebrew context and the second in an Aramaic one. Kuhn's solution has not been accepted by commentators. A second explanation has been proposed by Jeremias (1969: 296 n. 97), who argues that Menna is "evidently a dittography" for Melea, and this stands for a single name. Even though Menna is omitted in A, Marshall points out (*Luke* NIGTC, 164) that omission of Menna would disrupt Luke's "numerical scheme."

Bibliography

Jeremias, J. 1969. *Jerusalem in the Time of Jesus.* Philadelphia.

Kuhn, G. 1923. Die Geschlechtsregister Jesu bei Lukas und Matthäus, nach ihrer Herkunft untersucht. *ZNW* 22: 206–28.

STANLEY E. PORTER

MENORAH. See LAMPSTAND.

MENUHOTH [Heb *mĕnūḥôt*]. The name of half of the Manahathite tribe (1 Chr 2:52), which (according to 1 Chr 2:53 combined with v 54) inhabited Eshtaol. See MANAHATHITES. Most editors and commentators suggest correcting *ham-mĕnūhôt* (1 Chr 2:52) to **ham-mānaḥtî.* This correction is, however, unnecessary. Manahath/Manahathites can be derived from **manâḥ,* Heb *mānôaḥ.* See MANAHATH (PERSON). Menuhoth is a plural formation of the same name: **manâḥât* becomes **mĕnôḥôt* in Canaanite and finally, by dissimilation, *mĕnūḥôt* in Hebrew (as in *mĕgûrōt,* plural of *māgôr,* etc.). Tribal names ending in *-ât* (equals Canaanite *-ôt*) are very common among the recent Arab tribes; they are also attested in antiquity and usually occur with the definite article, as does Menuhoth. Among these names, feminine singular formations interchange freely with feminine plural formations (e.g., *jadarah* and *jadarât;* Knauf 1989: 65–66). The same linguistic mechanism holds true for Manahath and Menuhoth. Haroeh (Heb *ha-rōʾêh,* "the seer")—which 1 Chr 4:2 corrects to Reaiah (Heb *rĕʾāyāh* "YHWH saw")—is the proper name of the Menuhoth half of the Manahathites; it occurs as a personal name in Safaitic (with and without the definite article; Harding 1971: 263, 612).

Bibliography

Harding, G. L. 1971. *An Index and Concordance of Pre-Islamic Arabian Names and Inscriptions.* Near and Middle East Series 8. Toronto.

Knauf, E. A. 1989. *Ismael.* ADPV. Wiesbaden.

ERNST AXEL KNAUF

MEONOTHAI (PERSON) [Heb *mĕʿônōtay*]. According to the MT, Meonothai is the father of Ophrah (1 Chr 4:14). However, the Lucianic tradition of the Greek text of 1 Chr 4:13 indicates that Meonothai is also a son of Othniel, a brother of Hathath. Thus it is possible that the Hebrew text has suffered disturbance and the name "Meonothai" is lost by haplography from 1 Chr 4:13. The RSV translation follows the Lucianic reading.

H. C. LO

MEPHAATH (PLACE) [Heb *mêpaʿat*]. A levitical town which belonged to the territory of Reuben (Josh 13:18; 21:37; cf. 1 Chr 6:64—Eng 6:79). By the time of Jeremiah, it was part of the territory of Moab and an object of one of his oracles (48:21). The Hebrew Bible mentions only that the town was on the tableland of Moab (Josh 13:21; Jer 48:21). Eusebius later mentioned that a Roman military outpost was stationed there (*Onomast.* 128.21). The *Notitia Dignitatum* records that auxiliary local troops promoted to the Roman cavalry were stationed in the camp at Mefaa.

Three sites in Jordan have been identified with Mephaath—Tell Jawah, Khirbet Nefaʿah, and Umm er-Rasas. The first, Tell Jawah (M.R. 239140), is 10 km S of Amman. It was probably a fortress city during the Iron Age. There are vestiges of a city wall, and terracing on the sides of the mound, and many cisterns outside of the wall at the base of the hill. It is curious that the cisterns were outside of the wall, particularly at a fortress city when defense and security would be primary objectives of the inhabitants. Archaeological surveys at Tell Jawah have gathered pottery from Iron Ages I and II, although EB III and Arabic sherds have also been found (Glueck 1934: 4).

The second, Khirbet Nefaʿah, is located about 1.5 km N of Jawah; Alt (1933: 28–29) and Simons (*GTTOT,* 18) identify it as Mephaath because of the similarity of the names. Musil (1907: 352) visited the site and argued that it was a suburb of Tell Jawah, which was surrounded by a powerful, reinforced wall. Khirbet Nefaʿah overlooked the famous King's Highway a short distance S of Amman. The road passed within a few hundred meters of the site which made both it and Tell Jawah strategically important.

No serious archaeological survey has been conducted at Khirbet Nefaʿah. Musil (1907: 352–53) stated that the site was Roman, although he had no ceramic evidence for this conclusion; Alt (1933: 28) maintained that the ceramics pointed to the Bronze Age. Iron II sherds were identified by Peterson (1977: 693), although he refused to argue for Iron II occupation on such scanty evidence.

The third suggested identification is Umm er-Rasas (M.R. 237101). Mephaath was identified with the ruins of Umm er-Rasas in 1986 when M. Piccirillo discovered a mosaic in the floor of the 8th-century Church of St. Stephen which referred to the site as Kastron Mefaa.

These ruins were visited for the first time in 1816 by Buckingham and were then surveyed by Palmer in 1870, followed by Tristram in 1872, and by Brünnow-Domaszewski in 1897. In 1898 Clermont-Ganneau published a Nabatean inscription found at Umm er-Rasas (*CIS* II 19), and in 1933 Glueck (1934: 39–40) collected only Nabatean, Byzantine, and Arabic sherds from the site.

The ruins, located 30 km SE of Medeba, halfway between the King's Highway and the Desert Road at the height of Dhiban, consist of a walled area inside a fortified camp; an area of roughly the same dimensions extends outside the N wall of the camp. About 1.5 km toward the N is a tower which stands ca. 15 m high.

The military nature is reflected by the name Kastron Mefaa (i.e., "the camp of Mefaa"), which is recorded in the mosaic of the Church of St. Stephen. It was apparently to this site that Eusebius referred in his *Onomasticon.*

Bibliography

Alt, A. 1933. Die Ausfluge und Reisen. *PJ* 29: 7–29.

Brünnow, R. E., and Domaszewski, A. 1905. *Die Provincia Arabia.* Vol. 2. Strassburg.

Glueck, N. 1934. *Explorations in Eastern Palestine, I.* AASOR 14. Philadelphia.

Musil, A. 1907. *Arabia Petraea.* Vol. 1. Vienna.

Peterson, J. L. 1977. A Topographical Surface Survey of the Levitical "Cities" of Joshua 21 and I Chronicles 6. Th.D. diss., Seabury-Western Theological Seminary.

Piccirillo, M. 1986. The Complex of Saint Stephen at Umm er-Rasas—Kastron Mefaa. *ADAJ* 30: 341–52.

Saller, S., and Bagatti, B. 1949. *The Town of Nebo.* Jerusalem.

JOHN L. PETERSON
MICHELE PICCIRILLO

MEPHIBOSHETH (PERSON) [Heb *mĕpîbōšet*]. The purported name of two members of the house of Saul. The literal meaning of the name in Hebrew, "from the mouth of shame" or "from the mouth of (the deity) Boshet," is problematic and appears to result from a religiously motivated alteration of the name to avoid pronouncing the name of the Canaanite deity Baal. The original form of the name was probably Mephibaal (Heb **mĕpîbaʿal*), meaning "from the mouth of Baal" or "from the mouth of the Lord (Yhwh)." Although the standard LXX reading is *Memphibosthe,* the Lucianic recension and OL read *Memph(e)baal,* preserving the original form of the name. The element *bōšet* in the Masoretic form of the name means "shame," and was apparently substituted secondarily for the Yahwistic epithet *baʿal*, which fell into disfavor as it became the standard epithet for Yahweh's rival, the storm god. See ISH-BOSHETH.

1. A son of Saul by his concubine Rizpah (2 Sam 21:8). Together with his brother Armoni and five sons of Saul's daughter Merab, he was ritually executed in order to end a famine that persisted in the early years of David's joint reign over Israel and Judah.

2. Saul's grandson, the son of Jonathan (2 Sam 4:4). The name of Jonathan's son appears elsewhere (1 Chr 8:34; 9:40) as Merib-baal (LXX *Meribaal*). It is reasonable to suggest that the name of Jonathan's son Merib-baal became partly confused with the similar name of his relative Mephibaal, the son of Rizpah. The similar shape of the Hebrew letters *reš* and *pe* might have contributed to the substitution of the consonants of Mephibaal (**mpybʿl*) for an original Merib-baal (**mrybʿl*) in early mss of the biblical text. Tradition carefully distinguishes between the two individuals in 2 Sam 21:7, 8.

According to the biblical account (2 Sam 4:4) Mephibosheth, son of Jonathan, was crippled from an accident in infancy. After the deaths of Saul and Jonathan he placed himself under the protection of David (2 Sam 9:6) and enjoyed special status in the royal household (2 Sam 9:10–11). He was implicated in treachery during the rebellion of Absalom (2 Sam 16:1–4; 19:24–25, 30) but was spared by David when the rest of the house of Saul was exterminated (21:7).

Bibliography

Tsevat, M. 1975. Ishbosheth and Congeners: The Names and Their Study. *HUCA* 46: 71–88.

DIANA V. EDELMAN

MERAB (PERSON) [Heb *mērab*]. The eldest daughter of Saul, king of Israel (1 Sam 14:49) and wife of Adriel the Meholathite (1 Sam 18:19). Merab is introduced in a genealogical note concerning Saul (1 Sam 14:49–52). She is listed fourth in a series of five offspring (following her brothers—Jonathan, Ishvi, and Malchishua—and preceding her younger sister, Michal, v 49).

The account of Merab's marriage is found in 1 Sam 18:17–19. Saul promises Merab to David in exchange for David's support and military prowess. The narrator, however, interprets this as a ruse on Saul's part. Rather than risk raising his own hand against his rival, Saul plans to expose David to the hand of the Philistines (v 17). When this fails and the marriage date approaches, Saul instead arranges to have Merab marry Adriel the Meholathite (v 19).

Although 1 Sam 18:17–19 develops two previous ideas—the king's daughter given as a reward for bravery (17:25) and Saul's growing hostility toward David (18:6–16)—its position in the text is not without problem. The entire episode is missing from the LXX[B] and Josephus (*Ant* 6.10.2) and is thought by many commentators to be secondary. Moreover, the issue is further complicated by 2 Sam 21:8 (MT), which identifies the wife of Adriel as "Michal" not "Merab." In all probability, however, 2 Sam 21:8 contains a scribal error and "Merab" should be read instead of "Michal."

LINDA S. SCHEARING

MERAIAH (PERSON) [Heb *mĕrāyāh*]. The head of the priestly family of Seraiah in the time of the high priest Joiakim (Neh 12:12). Many have assumed that the name is a form related to Amariah (Heb *ʾămaryāh*, "Yahweh has said"). Whereas other LXX manuscripts have *Marea* or *Mar(a)ia* (equal to MT), the Lucianic recension reads *Amarias* for this name, reflecting Heb *ʾămaryāh* (Amariah). Amariah is a well-attested name in this period (Neh 10:4; 12:2, 13). The KB suggests that Meraiah is unrelated to Amariah and means "stubborn person" (cf. the Heb verb *mārāh* and the personal names *mĕrāyôt* and *miryām*; the proposed meaning of the name seems, however, somewhat improbable).

NORA A. WILLIAMS

MERAIOTH (PERSON) [Heb *mĕrāyôt*]. **1.** An Aaronite priest, ancestor of the high priest Zadok (1 Chr 5:32–33; 6:37—Eng 6:6–7, 52). Meraioth is also listed as an ancestor of Ezra in Ezra 7:3 and in 2 Esdr 1:2. The KJV, following Codex Alexandrinus, lists Meraioth as an ancestor of Ezra in 1 Esdr 8:1–2; the RSV, following Codex Vaticanus, omits Meraioth from the list. The list in Ezra 7 is probably the basis of the lists in 1 Esdras 8 and 2 Esdras 1.

2. The father of Zadok (1 Chr 9:11; Neh 11:11). The Chronicler twice represents Ahitub as the father of Meraioth, and Meraioth as the father of Zadok (1 Chr 9:11; Neh 11:11) in contradiction to the normal tradition of Ahitub as the father of Zadok (see, for example, 2 Sam 8:17; 1 Chr 5:34—Eng 6:8; 1 Chr 18:16). J. R. Bartlet (1968: 4) explained this anomaly by suggesting that Meraioth was added as "an explanatory marginal note on Ahitub" and subsequently was entered into the list in the wrong place.

3. A priestly house in the postexilic period (Neh 12:15). This occurrence of Meraioth probably should be read as Meremoth with the MT of Neh 12:3 and the Lucianic recension of the LXX.

Bibliography

Bartlet, J. R. 1968. Zadok and His Successors at Jerusalem. *JTS* 19: 1–18.

TOM WAYNE WILLETT

MERARI (PERSON) [Heb *mĕrārî*]. MERARITE. The etymology of Merari is uncertain. Evidently it is derived from a root *mrr*, which in Hebrew means "to be bitter." This would make a peculiar personal name; but it is probable (Kutler 1984; Ward 1980; Dietrich, Loretz, and Sanmartín 1973) that there is a particular usage, or even a distinct root, that refers to strength (for an opposing view see Pardee 1978). In Ugaritic the verb "to bless" is paralleled by a root containing *m* and *r* (*CTA* 15.2.14–20; 17.1.24–25, 35–37; 19.4.194–95), and there is a god named "Holy and *ʾAmrr*"; perhaps this is another usage of *mrr* referring to blessing or sanctification, which would also provide a suitable etymology for a personal name (cf. Loewenstamm *EncMiqr* 5: 475–77). If *ʾAmrr* is related to Merari, it is worth noting that the levitical name "Kohath" also appears in Ugaritic with a prosthetic *ʾalep* as *ʾAqht*.

Gordon (*UT,* 438) compares the Old South Arabic name *Mrr.*

1. Levi's third son or the clan claiming descent from him. Merari is listed after Gershon and Kohath by the Priestly (P) source and by the Chronicler as Levi's third son (Gen 46:11; Exod 6:16; Num 3:17; 1 Chr 5:27—Eng 6:1; 6:1—Eng 6:16; 23:6); therefore the Merarites are the third major levitical clan according to the genealogists. In turn, Merari has two sons, Mahli and Mushi (Exod 6:19; Num 3:20, 33; 1 Chr 6:4—Eng 6:19; 23:21; 24:26), implying that these were the principal Merarite families. According to 1 Chr 6:29–32—Eng 6:44–47; 23:21; and 24:30, however, Mushi is the father of Mahli; therefore at a later period, at least in some circles, Mushi had become the more important. In Ezra 8:18–19 Mahli and Merari are coordinate; conceivably the Mushites had co-opted the more venerable name Merari. Cross (*CMHE,* 195–215) has proposed that the Mushites claimed descent from Moses and had a formative influence in biblical tradition. If this is true, the lowly status of Mushi in the biblical genealogies indicates either its decline or an effort on the part of Zadokite rivals to deny its importance.

According to P, the Merarites of the desert period number 6,200 males over the age of one month (Num 3:33–34), or 3,200 men between thirty and fifty (Num 4:42–45). Their leader is Zuriel the son of Abihail, and they camp on the N side of the tabernacle (Num 3:35). The family of Merari is entrusted by Moses with carrying the solid structure of the tabernacle—the planks, pillars, stands, etc. (Num 3:36–37; 4:31–32)—while the Gershonites bear the textile components (Num 3:25–26; 4:24–26) and the Kohathites the holy vessels (Num 3:31; 4:9). The latter are expected to transport the sacra by hand, but the Gershonites are allotted two carts (Num 7:7) and the Merarites four (Num 7:8), in proportion to the weight of their burdens. The two lesser levitical orders are supervised by Ithamar, Aaron's youngest son (Num 4:28, 33).

The list of levitical cities (Joshua 21; 1 Chr 6:39–66—Eng 6:54–81) is probably based on 8th-century administrative records (Peterson 1977; Boling *Joshua* AB, 492–97). Assigned to Merari (Josh 21:34–40; 1 Chr 6:62–66—Eng 6:77–81) are the following cities: Jokneam, Karta, Dimna (Rimmono in Chronicles), Nahalal (Tabor in Chronicles) in Zebulon; Bezer, Jahza, Kedemoth, Mephaath in Reuben; Ramoth of Gilead, Mahanaim, Heshbon, and Jaazer in Gad.

The Chronicler enumerates Merarite personnel and clans of the reign of David (1 Chr 6:14, 29–32—Eng 6:44–47; 23:21–23; 24:27–30; 26:10–11), but these data cannot be taken at face value, for some names are also attributed to the reign of Hezekiah; compare 1 Chr 6:5–6, 20–21, 29—Eng 6:20–21, 35–36, 44 with 2 Chr 29:12. 1 Chr 15:17 makes Ethan the son of Kushaiah a contemporary of David; 1 Chr 6:29—Eng 6:44 tells of Ethan the son of Kishi (= Kushaiah?) the son of Abdi, also coeval with David; 1 Chr 23:21 lists Kish as the son or descendant of Mahli in the 10th century; 1 Chr 24:27, 29 makes Kish and Ibri (read Abdi?) individuals or clans of David's day. 2 Chr 29:12, however, has one Kish the son of Abdi as minister under Hezekiah. The latter source is perhaps more trustworthy, since the Chronicler was seemingly well-informed about Hezekiah's reign, while ideology compelled him to ascribe the organization of the levitical clans to David. Nevertheless, if the Davidic material is retrojected, so might the Hezekian be. The same is true of Josiah's building supervisors Jahath and Obadiah, both of Merari (2 Chr 34:12). In other words, all these figures might merely represent postexilic families. Some of the information about early Merarites is more plausible, however. It may be, for example, that the Asaiah of 1 Chr 6:14 is the same individual who assists in the installation of the ark in 1 Chr 15:6. 1 Chr 26:10–11 speaks of the sons of the Davidic Merarite Hosa: Shimri, Hilkiah, Tebaliah, Zechariah, and nine anonymous sons. We have no reason either to doubt or trust these reports.

The Chronicler's interest in levitical clans reflects their prominence after the Exile. When Ezra tries to assemble Levites to serve in the Second Temple (Ezra 8:15–19), only the Mahlites and Merarites of Casiphia, led by Sherebiah, Hashabiah, and Isaiah are available. 1 Chr 9:14 lists other Merarite returnees, but the parallel text Neh 11:15 lacks reference to Merari.

2. The father of Judith (Jdt 8:1; 16:6—Eng v 7).

Bibliography

Cody, A. 1969. *A History of the Old Testament Priesthood.* AnBib 35. Rome.

Dietrich, M.; Loretz, O.; and Sanmartín, J. 1973. Die ugaritischen Verben *MRR* I, *MRR* II und *MRR* III. *UF* 5: 119–22.

Gunneweg, A. H. J. 1965. *Leviten und Priester.* Göttingen.

Kutler, L. 1984. A "Strong" Case for Hebrew Mar. *UF* 16: 111–18.

Möhlenbrink, K. 1934. Die levitischen Überlieferungen des Alten Testaments. *ZAW* 52: 184–231.

Pardee, D. 1978. The Semitic Root *mrr* and the Etymology of Ugaritic *mr(r)* || *brk. UF* 10: 249–88.

Peterson, J. L. 1977. A Topographical Surface Survey of the Levitical "Cities" of Joshua 21 and 1 Chronicles 6. Th.D. diss., Seabury-Western Theological Seminary.

Ward, W. A. 1980. Egypto-Semitic MR, "Be Bitter, Strong." *UF* 12: 357–60.

William H. Propp

MERARITES [Heb *mĕrārî*]. A priestly family descended from Levi. The family is named after its ancestor Merari, who is listed as a son of Levi along with Gershom and Kohath. The family is further subdivided into two groups: Mahli and Mushi (Exod 6:19; Num 3:20). Generally the family is referred to as *bĕnê mĕrārî* "descendants of Merari." Etymologically the name Merari may mean something like "strength" or "power" (Noth *IPN,* 225).

Information about the Merarites is largely found in the work of the exilic Priestly writer and the postexilic Chronicler. Details about family members include their genealogical status and their cultic function as assistants for the priests throughout Israel's history from Mosaic to postexilic times.

During the wilderness period, the Merarites shared with the other Levites the responsibility for guard duty around the tabernacle both during encampment and travel (Num 1:53; Milgrom 1970: 8–16, 62–63). They were to encamp on the north side of the tabernacle. The Merarites were also specifically responsible for dismantling, transporting, and erecting the basic structural components for the tabernacle and court (Num 1:47–53; 3:33–37; 4:29–33). They were assigned four wagons and eight oxen to carry these materials (Num 7:8). According to census reports there were 6,200 Merarite males at least a month old (Num 3:34) and 3,200 of these were aged from 30 to 50 and thus suited for service (Num 4:43–44).

Since the Levites were not allotted a portion of land along with the other tribes, they were given cities with their common land (Joshua 21). The Merarites received twelve cities from the tribes of Reuben, Gad, and Zebulun (Josh 21:7, 34–40).

Along with Aaronites and other Levites, some 220 Merarites under the direction of Asaiah assisted David in carrying the ark of God to Jerusalem (1 Chr 15:1–15). Ethan represented the Merarites as a temple musician and singer (1 Chr 15:17). Other descendants such as Hosah (1 Chr 26:10) were gatekeepers of the temple.

Kish and Azariah from the Merarite family assisted Hezekiah in his cleansing of the temple (2 Chr 29:12). Likewise Jahath and Obadiah as Merarites provided leadership for repairing and restoring the temple under the direction of King Josiah (2 Chr 34:12).

When Ezra was preparing to return to Jerusalem, he was able to recruit some of the Merarites to serve as temple servants (Ezra 8:18–19).

Many scholars think that the history of the priesthood was more complex than these reports concerning the Merarites suggest and raise doubts about their historicity. One genealogical problem is found in Num 26:57–58, which juxtaposes two different genealogies for the descendants of Levi, one of which includes the Merarites. Scholars have argued that Levites carried out more priestly functions at certain times of Israel's history than these texts suggest (*AncIsr* 2: 358–71).

There were many struggles for power among different priestly groups throughout Israel's history (Cross *CMHE,* 195–215; Hanson 1979: 209–79). Each of these groups was interested in legitimizing its own rights and prerogatives and opposing those of other groups. Since the Chronicler and the Priestly source were either written by priests or supported a certain group of priests, they obviously presented a somewhat one-sided picture. These factors make the critical reconstruction of the history of the Israelite priesthood very difficult.

The information concerning the Merarites is meant to encourage them to be satisfied with their subsidiary role to the Aaronites because their role was assigned by God, meant to be hereditary, and a number of their ancestors enthusiastically helped the priests carry out their duties. While this legitimizes the Merarites in their subsidiary position, it also necessarily discourages them from seeking other more prestigious priestly functions.

Bibliography

Hanson, P. 1979. *The Dawn of Apocaylptic.* Rev. ed. Philadelphia.
Milgrom, J. 1970. *Studies in Levitical Terminology, I.* Berkeley.

STEPHEN A. REED

MERATHAIM (PLACE) [Heb *mĕrātayim*]. Derisive name for Babylon in Jer 50:21. It is presumed to be a wordplay on *marratum,* the Akkadian name for the marshy region in S Babylonia where the Tigris and Euphrates rivers converge at the Persian Gulf ("the sea of the Chaldeans," CAD M/1: 285 and Parpola 1970: 240–41). The Akkadian word is based on the meaning "bitter" as in salt water. The Hebrew base is *mārâ* "to be rebellious." Thus *mĕrātayim* is probably an artificial dual form suggesting "(land of) double rebellion" (Simons *GTTOT,* 451). This verse contains another wordplay in "Peqod" (Heb *pāqad* can mean "punish"). An important Aramean tribe in SE Babylonia was known as "Puqudu" in Akkadian texts. Together *mĕrātayim* and Peqod represent Babylonia in general.

Bibliography

Parpola, S. 1970. *Neo-Assyrian Toponyms.* AOAT 6. Kevelaer and Neukirchen-Vluyn.

BILL T. ARNOLD

MERCENARY. See MILITARY ORGANIZATION IN MESOPOTAMIA.

MERCHANT. See TRADE AND COMMERCE.

MERCY. See LOVE.

MERED (PERSON) [Heb *mered*]. Listed in the genealogy of Judah as son of Ezrah and the husband of Bithiah, the daughter of pharaoh (1 Chr 4:17).

H. C. LO

MEREMOTH (PERSON) [Heb *mĕrēmôt*]. A personal name whose meaning is unknown (Rudolph *Esra und Nehemia* HAT, 84; Brockington *Ezra, Nehemiah, and Esther* NCBC, 104) although several explanations have been suggested. Noth (*IPN,* 39) believes the *ôt* ending, found in other names, to be hypocoristic. Odelain and Séguineau (1981: 260) view it as having Ugaritic origin—"Moth has blessed." Yamauchi (*ISBE* 3: 324) suggests the meaning "heights," presumably from Heb *rwm.* The name appears on ostraca found at Arad (*EncMiqr* 4: 473; Myers *1 and 2 Esdras* AB, 93). Bratcher (*HBD,* 627) is correct in noting uncertainty as to whether the occurrences of the name in the Hebrew Bible designate different people or are several references to one individual and/or his family.

1. The eighth-listed of the twelve sons of Bani in Ezra 10:36 (but not listed among the sixteen in 1 Esdr 9:34). Since Bani is previously mentioned (Ezra 10:29) in the list of those who had married foreign women (vv 18–44), alternative readings have been suggested. This Meremoth (LXX Vaticanus, Sinaiticus *Ieramōth,* Alexandrinus *Marimōth*) is included with the laity, not the priests (vv 18–22) or Levites (v 23), who "sent them (i.e., their foreign wives) away, women and children alike" (see Blenkinsopp *Ezra-Nehemiah* OTL, 196, 197 for this translation and corresponding treatment of the corrupt MT of v 44b).

2. One of the priests listed in Neh 10:6—Eng 10:5 (LXX *Meramōth*) who were among those who sealed (LXX) the "firm covenant" (*ʾămānā*) made by the community (10:1—Eng 9:38). It is believed the name represents a patronym rather than an individual (Blenkinsopp *Ezra-Nehemiah* OTL, 313; Brockington *Ezra, Nehemiah, and Esther* Century Bible, 104; Rudolph *Esra und Nehemia* HAT, 17 n. 2) and that the list (vv 3–9—Eng 2–8), which was derived from the list in Neh 12:12–21, is a part of that larger name list (vv 3–29—Eng 2–28) secondarily inserted here to convey wide support for Nehemiah's reforms (Blenkinsopp, 313, 335; see Williamson *Ezra, Nehemiah* WBC, 325–31, for a discussion of Nehemiah 10).

Meremoth appears in Neh 12:3 (vv 3b–7a, which include the name *Marimōth,* are absent from all major LXX codices except the corrected Codex Sinaiticus) as the ninth of twenty-two "heads of the priests and of their brothers" during the days of the high priest Jeshua (v 7). He is said to have accompanied Zerubbabel and Jeshua in the return from captivity (v 1). Both Williamson (359–60) and Blenkinsopp (335) believe this list (vv 1–7) also derives from that in 12:12–21 the patronymics of which here serve as personal names (Blenkinsopp, 334; see Brockington, 104, who believes this is here a family name). It is possible, according to Williamson (362), that the Meraioth in 12:15 and Meremoth were the same, the former spelling resulting from reading *y* and *w* for *m* (*WDB,* 609).

3. The son of Uriah. In Ezra 8:33 (LXX *Merimōth*) and 1 Esdr 8:61—Eng 8:62 (*Marmōthi,* Alexandrinus *Marmathi*) he or his father (the appellative *hakōhēn* follows Uriah) is called "the priest." In Neh 3:4 (LXX *Ramōth* [Heb *(mĕ)rēmôt?*]) and 3:21 (LXX *Meramōth*) Uriah is referred to as "son of Hakkoz." This has led some, such as Jepsen (1954: 103), Kellermann (1968: 69), and Yamauchi (1980: 10), to conclude these are two different individuals. To the one was given the silver, gold, and vessels which those who returned with Ezra brought with them to Jerusalem (Ezra 8:31–34; 1 Esdr 8:60–63—Eng 8:61–64). Gunneweg (*Esra* HAT, 157) even suggests that these individual personal names are secondary additions for the purpose of creating "narrative color" and that the four who received the valuables were originally nameless in the tradition. The other Meremoth, the grandson of Hakkoz, is listed (Neh 3:4) among those who helped to repair the wall around Jerusalem, being assigned, along with three other "groups" (Myers *Ezra-Nehemiah* AB, 114), to the section between the Fish Gate and the Jeshana Gate. He also helped to repair a "second measured portion from the opening of the house of Eliashib to the end of the house of Eliashib" (Neh 3:21).

For those who conclude that these occurrences of Meremoth refer to the same individual, i.e., that the Uriah of Ezra 8:33 is identical to the Uriah of Neh 3:4 and 21, an intriguing situation emerges. The descendants of Hakkoz were among those unable to locate, upon their return from captivity, their proper genealogical registration. They were excluded from the priesthood as unclean by the governor (= Nehemiah 1; Esdr 5:40) until their status was determined by consulting Urim and Thummim (Ezra 2:59–63; Neh 7:61–65; 1 Esdr 5:36–40) or until the appearance of a high priest "clothed in manifestation and truth" (Gk 1 Esdr 5:40). Yet Meremoth, a descendant of Hakkoz, is functioning as a priest. Several attempts at solving this dilemma have been offered. Koch (1974: 191) believes Ezra, when he arrived in Jerusalem, recognized Meremoth as a priest but deposed him shortly afterward "by means of the Law he had brought with him." This argument tends to support the traditional order which has Ezra preceding Nehemiah. On the other hand, a "reverse order" is supported in other solutions. Bentzen (1931: 285) believed the high priest reinstated Meremoth as a priest, probably following the death of the governor Nehemiah, as a reward for his extra work on the high priest's house. Rudolph (HAT, 69) argued that Meremoth did not possess priestly legitimacy until Ezra's time. Rowley (1952: 159) believed the builder of a double portion of the wall during Nehemiah's time needed to be young and strong and therefore would precede the senior priestly official Ezra found as temple treasurer.

Bibliography

Bentzen, A. 1931. Priesterschaft und Laien in der jüdischen Gemeinde des fünften Jahrhunderts. *AfO* 6: 280–86.

Jepsen, Alfred. 1954. Nehemia 10. *ZAW* 66: 87–106.

Kellermann, U. 1968. Erwägungen zum Problem der Esradatierung. *ZAW* 80: 55–87.

Koch, K. 1974. Ezra and the Origins of Judaism. *JSS* 19: 173–97.

Odelain, O., and Séguineau, R. 1981. *Dictionary of Proper Names and Places in the Bible.* Trans. M. O'Connell. Garden City, NY.

Rowley, H. H. 1952. *The Servant of the Lord and Other Essays on the Old Testament.* London.

Yamauchi, E. 1980. The Reverse Order of Ezra/Nehemiah Reconsidered. *Themelios* 5: 7–13.

RODNEY H. SHEARER

MERENPTAH (PERSON). Twelfth son and successor of Rameses II. His name in Egyptian was "*Bȝ-n-rʿ*, beloved of Amun, *Mr-n-ptḥ,* pleased with Truth." Born to the queen Isit-nofret no later than his father's 20th year on the throne, and perhaps as early as his 5th (Harris and Wente 1980: 260–62), Merenptah (or Merneptah as he is commonly known) is earliest known as a king's scribe. Late in the second decade of his father's reign he may have participated in the attack on a N Syrian city, and later still in the war against Irem in Nubia. On the demise of his older brother Khamwese (whose daughter Isit-nofret he may have married), Merenptah became heir apparent and commander in chief of the army. Upon the death of his father in his 67th year of rule (June of either 1237 or 1223 B.C.), Merenptah succeeded to the throne as the fourth king of the 19th Dyn.

Merenptah continued to reside in the Pi-rameses residence his father had built in the delta (Gardiner 1918: 184, text no. 11), but he had other residences at Memphis and possibly Heliopolis. Sometime in his 2d year he went to Thebes "to see his father Amonrasonther"; and it was possibly at this time that he authorized the "great inventory" of all the temples of Egypt by the king's scribe and steward Yot. This assessment, intended to gauge the wealth of state and temple, issued in very little building, however; Merenptah was content to erect small monuments and to usurp others.

Merenptah preserved the N and S reaches of the empire intact (Redford 1986: 197 and n. 63), maintaining diplomatic ties with foreign principalities such as Ugarit; he even sent relief shipments of grain to his Hittite allies during a period of drought (Wainwright 1960). Sometime before the end of his 3d year a punitive campaign had taken place against the city of Gezer, which became the occasion for the king's epithet, "Subduer of Gezer," and was later to give rise to the "Fescennine" type verse which ends the famous "Israel" stele (*ANET,* 378). However, it remains a moot point whether Merenptah's forces actually came into contact with Israel on this occasion or whether Israel was simply included to round out a list of names representative of the inhabitants of the land (Engel 1979; Fecht 1983; Hornung 1983; Ahlström and Edelman 1985; Ahlström 1986: 37–40).

The major event in Merenptah's reign was the first Libyan invasion of Egypt, recorded in inscriptions from Karnak, Gurneh (*ANET,* 376–78), Kom el-Ahman, and Heliopolis. The Libyan tribes of the Labu and Meshwesh (Hdt. 4.191), long kept under surveillance during the reign of Rameses II (Habachi 1980), amalgamated their forces with certain sea-roving pirates from the Aegean—the Lukka (from Lycia), Shardanu (Sardonians from near Cyme), the Ekwesh (Koos?), the Teresh, and the Shekelesh—and descended on Egypt in Merenptah's 5th year. Merenptah received the news at the beginning of April and launched his forces about a month later, engaging the invaders at Per-Yeru in the NW delta. The Libyans were repulsed with a loss of over 9,000 dead.

Through most of his reign Merenptah was in poor health, and already in his 7th year burial goods were being moved into his tomb. He died sometime after his 10th year. His mummy shows a bald old man, rather obese, who suffered from degenerative arthritis and also from arteriosclerosis in the thigh. He had lost many teeth, and the heads of the femurs showed signs of fracture (Harris and Weeks 1973: 157). His name survives, curiously, in the place name Mereptoah mentioned by Josephus (Priebatsch 1975).

Bibliography

Ahlström, G. 1986. *Who Were the Israelites?* Winona Lake, IN.

Ahlström, G., and Edelman, D. 1985. Merneptah's Israel. *JNES* 44: 59–61.

Engel, H. 1979. Die Siegesstele des Merenptah. *Bib* 80: 373ff.

Fecht, G. 1983. Die Israelstele, Gestalt und Aussage. Pp. 106ff. in *Fontes atque Pontes.* Wiesbaden.

Gardiner, A. H. 1918. The Delta Residence of the Ramessides. *JEA* 5: 127–38, 179–200, 242–72.

Habachi, L. 1980. The Military Posts of Ramesses II on the Coastal Road and the Western Part of the Delta. *BIFAO* 80: 13–30.

Harris, J., and Weeks, K. 1973. *X-Raying the Pharaohs.* New York.

Harris, J., and Wente, E. 1980. *An X-Ray Atlas of the Royal Mummies.* Chicago.

Hornung, E. 1983. Die Israelstele des Merenptah. Pp. 224ff. in *Fontes atque Pontes.* Wiesbaden.

Priebatsch, H. 1975. Jerusalem und die Brunenstrasse Merneptahs. *ZDPV* 91: 18ff.

Redford, D. B. 1986. The Ashkelon Relief at Karnak and the Israel Stele. *IEJ* 36: 188–200.

Wainwright, G. 1960. Merneptah's Aid to the Hittites. *JEA* 46: 24ff.

DONALD B. REDFORD

MERES (PERSON) [Heb *meres*]. One of the seven princes of Persia and Media who were the advisers of King Ahasueros (Esth 1:14). See CARSHENA. Although the presumption that the names of these counselors are Persian is reasonable (see the arguments of Millard 1977: 481–88, who counters the excessive caution of Moore [*Esther* AB, XLI–XLIV] regarding the reliability of the MT spellings), no name equivalent to this has thus far been found in the extant extrabiblical literature nor has a generally acceptable Persian etymology been suggested. The name, however, would appear to be a variant of the name Marsena (another of the seven advisers) without the patronymic suffix, for which see the discussion of Carshena by Millard (1977: 485). For suggested etymologies see Paton *Esther* ICC, 68; Gehman 1924: 324.

Bibliography

Gehman, H. S. 1924. Notes on the Persian Words in the Book of Esther. *JBL* 43: 321–28.

Millard, A. R. 1977. The Persian Names in Esther and the Reliability of the Hebrew Text. *JBL* 96: 481–88.

FREDERIC W. BUSH

MERIB-BAAL (PERSON) [Heb *mĕrîb-baʿal; mĕrî-baʿal*]. The son of Jonathan, and grandson of Saul ben Kish. The Hebrew name is spelled *mĕrîb-baʿal* in 1 Chr 8:34 (2x), 9:40, but *mĕrî-baʿal* in its second occurrence in 9:40. The LXX reads *Meribaal* for both occurrences in 8:34 and *Maribaal* for both in 9:40; Syr reads *mrybʿl* in all cases. The rest of the references to this individual call him Mephibosheth. Unlike the other examples in which the epithet *baʿal,* "Lord," which originally was applied to Yahweh but later became associated primarily with his rival, the storm god, has been substituted with *bošet,* "shame," in this instance the first element of the name has also been altered. See ISH-BOSHETH. This unexpected development is best attributed to the partial confusion of Meribaal ben Jonathan with his relative Mephibaal ben Saul. See MEPHIBOSHETH.

The etymology of the name "Merib-baal" (or "Meribaal") is difficult to establish. Older opinions were noted by Noth (*IPN,* 143 n. 2); more recent speculation is discussed by Fowler (*TPNAH,* 61).

A. Meribaal from a Literary Perspective

Outside the genealogical notices, Meribaal is mentioned in five contexts in 2 Samuel. All are interrelated and are linked thematically with the sections in 1 Samuel involving Jonathan's covenant with David, further developing the motif of David's oath-bound love for Jonathan and his promise not to let the name of Jonathan be cut off from the house of David (1 Sam 20:16). In 2 Sam 4:4, after the report of the death of Eshbaal, the last direct heir to the Saulide throne, it is reported that Jonathan had a young, crippled son who was hidden by his wet nurse after the news of the death of Saul and Jonathan at Gilboa. The comment serves to alert the audience to the continuing issue of the legitimate succession to the throne of Israel and anticipates the Meribaal scene in 2 Samuel 9.

After intervening passages sketch David's establishment of his rule over Israel and Judah, 2 Samuel 9 tells of David's inquiry about any surviving Saulides to whom he can show kindness for Jonathan's sake. Ziba, a (former) servant of the royal family, is summoned and reveals Meribaal's existence in Lidebir. David has him brought to the Jerusalemite court, returns to him the Saulide patrimonial estates, which are to be worked by Ziba's family, and makes him and his son Mica regular members at the royal table.

Meribaal is next mentioned in 2 Sam 16:1–4, when, in preparation for David's retreat from Jerusalem during Absalom's revolt, Ziba provides the king with provisions and claims that Meribaal has declared his intention to be restored by Israel to his rightful throne as a descendant of Saul. In response to the allegation of treason, David is said to have confiscated Meribaal's estates and granted them to Ziba. The issue of treason is taken up again in 2 Samuel 19, after David's defeat of Absalom and his return to Jerusalem. Now Meribaal presents himself to the king as he returns, swears his innocence and Ziba's deceit, and is granted half of his former family estate by David.

The final reference to Meribaal occurs in 2 Sam 21:7, in the account of the ritual execution of seven Saulides to end a three-year famine. It is specified that David spared Jonathan's son from becoming a victim on this occasion because of the oath he had made with Jonathan. Verse 8 names Meribaal's secondary namesake Mephibosheth (Mephibaal), the son of Saul and Rizpah, as one of the victims.

B. The Historical Meribaal

Most of the details concerning Meribaal's life remain uncertain. His status as Jonathan's son has been challenged; it has been argued that he was Saul and Rizpah's son who was secondarily identified as Jonathan's son in order to develop further the theme of the covenant between David and Jonathan (Veijola 1978). This proposal is based primarily upon the references to Meribaal as the "son of Saul" and to Saul as Meribaal's "father" in 2 Sam 9:7, 9, 10; 16:3; 19:24. However, because Meribaal is explicitly identified as Jonathan's son and Saul's grandson in his first appearance in 2 Sam 4:4, and subsequently in 2 Sam 9:6 and 21:7, it seems best to construe the references to Saul as his "father" in the looser sense of "forefather" (cf. Gen 17:4; 28:13; Josh 24:3; Isa 51:2). Since Saul was the founder of the royal Saulide dynasty, it would have been appropriate to designate him as the founding forefather and to speak of the patrimonial estates handed down from Kish and his forefathers as the estates of Saul (2 Sam 9:8), even though he was only removed from Meribaal by two generations.

Meribaal's status as the eldest son of the heir to the Saulide throne explains his secret removal to Lidebir, where he could grow up in political asylum under the tutelage of Saul's ally, Machir ben Ammiel, and be able to reclaim the family throne in the event of future usurpations. The decision to spirit away the toddler probably would have been made in the wake of the crowning of the youngest surviving son of Saul and Ahimaaz, Eshbaal, who was himself a minor, in a time of severe political turmoil and threat to the fledgling state of Israel. If the notice that Meribaal had an infant son Mica when he was returned to the Davidic court is historically reliable, it would seem that the secret of his being and whereabouts was able to be kept for some two or three decades—well into David's reign. His return appears to have taken place before Absalom's revolt. It is likely that he escaped death during the ritual execution of his seven relatives during the three-year famine that occurred in the early years of David's accession to the Saulide throne (2 Sam 21:1–11) only because David was not aware of his existence. The reference to his sparing because of David's covenant with Jonathan in v 7 is a later literary reinterpretation of the incident.

Meribaal's lameness seems certain, although the report that it was caused by his nurse's accidentally dropping him during flight might be secondary literary embellishment. It generally is assumed that his physical handicap would have prevented him from being made king. Ritual laws prohibited the use of any physically blemished animal as a sacrificial offering (Lev 1:3, 10; 3:1, 6; 4:22, 27, 32) and prohibited a physically disfigured descendant of Aaron from serving as a priest (Lev 21:16–23). No law explicitly rejected a handicapped person from serving as God's earthly vice-regent, but by analogy, and because man was supposed to be made in God's image, it is likely that an heir-elect with a physical disability would have been passed over for another legitimate candidate for king. Even though Meribaal himself might not have posed a direct threat to David's claim to the throne because of his lameness, his son Mica would have been the next legitimate Saulide heir and a potential focus of rebellion. By making Meribaal and his young son mandatory members of the king's table at the Jerusalemite court, David could have kept them under constant surveillance and headed off any moves toward rebellion.

David's restoration of the Saulide estates to Meribaal has been interpreted against the background of the ANE practice of transferring patrimonial property without male heirs to the crown, or declaring it *bona vacantia.* Once Meribaal's existence was discovered and his repatriation accomplished, he had a legal right to the patrimonial estates of Saul and his forefathers. David was obligated by law to reconvert them from crown property to their former status as inalienable patrimonial land and return them to the family heir (Ben-Barak 1981). It seems that the characterization of David's return of the land as one of generosity stemming from his covenant with Jonathan is a later literary reinterpretation. David's subsequent confiscation and conversion of the Saulide patrimonial land to crown property in 2 Samuel 16 reflects the ancient punishment for treason (Ben-Barak 1981: 85).

Bibliography

Ben-Barak, Z. 1981. Meribaal and the System of Land Grants in Ancient Israel. *Bib* 62: 73–91.

Veijola, T. 1978. David und Meribaal. *RB* 85: 338–61.

Diana V. Edelman

MERIBAH (PLACE) [Heb *mĕrîbâ*]. Literally "Strife," an oasis in the Sinai and the site of an Israelite rebellion. Also called Meribath-Kadesh in the Priestly (P) source (Num 20:13, 24; 27:14; Deut 32:51), and Ezekiel (47:19; 48:28), and possibly in Deut 33:2, if one emends the difficult *mrbbt qdš* to **mmrbt qdš*. Exod 17:7 and Deut 33:8 explicitly, and Ps 95:8 implicitly, equate Meribah with Massah ("Testing"), a place also mentioned in Deut 6:16; 9:22. It seems the two names arose out of the Israelite practice of using synonymous terms in parallelistic poetry, though some scholars see independent traditions (e.g., Cornill 1891: 20–34). Such names for springs were not unusual, since water holes were often scenes of contention (Gen 21:25; 26:14–22; Exod 2:17), and arbitration (Gen 21:27–32; 26:28–33), or judgment; note that in Gen 14:7 En-mishpat, the "Well of Judgment," is identified with the oasis Kadesh. Nevertheless, tradition ties the names Massah and Meribah to a specific rebellion of the Israelites during their desert wanderings.

The location of Meribah is uncertain, and it is possible that the place is imaginary. The Elohist (E) locates it at Horeb (Exod 17:6) near Rephidim (Exod 17:8), both of which are of unknown location, while P and Ezekiel equate Meribah and Kadesh, probably modern ʿEin Qudeirat (M.R. 096006). See KADESH-BARNEA. The traditions are equally vague as to what transpired there. Deut 33:8–11 says that the Levites were striven against and tested there, earning the priestly office in return for their renunciation of kinship ties. It seems in Ps 81:8—Eng v 7, however, that all Israel was tested at Meribah and that they failed through apostasy (vv 10–12—Eng vv 9–11); and Ps 95:8–11 similarly records that for the sin of testing Yahweh at Meribah Israel was punished with forty years in the desert. Exod 17:1–7 says that at Massah and Meribah the Israelites rebelled against Moses and tested Yahweh by requesting water, which the deity granted at Horeb when Moses struck the mountainside with his rod. Finally, Num 20:1–13 tells the strange story of the sins of Moses and Aaron at Meribah.

According to the received text of Num 20:1–13, while the Israelites are camped at Kadesh they discover, after Miriam's death, that there is not enough water. The people rebel against Moses and Aaron, expressing their regret at having left Egypt. Moses and Aaron go into the tabernacle for advice, and Moses is told to take a rod from the tabernacle and to speak to a crag, which will gush at his command. Instead, Moses castigates the people and hits the crag twice with the rod, thus producing water. For his fault both he and his brother are condemned to die in the desert.

This story, part of the murmuring tradition (see Coats 1968), raises many questions. Firstly, why is this story so similar to Exod 17:1–7, and how can Meribah be both at Horeb and at Kadesh? Of course, the Documentary Hypothesis, especially in its formulation by Friedman (1981: 77–119), solves this problem. The earlier text is Elohistic, while our passage is a Priestly rewrite designed to replace the older account but ironically included with it in the redaction of the Torah. Secondly, why is Moses punished for such a trivial sin and Aaron for no sin at all? This, too, can be answered readily, provided we do not expect the Bible to conform to our morality. At least in Moses' case, one could argue that the slightest deviation from divine command deserves severe censure; and, after all, the penalty is deferred. But Aaron's condemnation remains inexplicable. It is more helpful to view the story as a fabrication of the Priestly writer or his sources, which faced the problem of a tradition of Moses' and Aaron's deaths in Transjordan (Num 20:23–29; Deuteronomy 34). Such an unexpected tragedy might naturally have been explained as the result of a sin, yet one could hardly imagine the brothers having committed a serious crime. The result of this tension is the divine overreaction in the text. The Deuteronomic (D) source solves the problem of Moses' death in a similar way by blaming it vaguely upon the people (Deut 1:37). Since in P Aaron is a spotless figure while Moses is ambiguous, the latter is chosen to be the culprit, while the former is punished in defiance of all logic and justice.

Of course, for centuries scholars have sought other explanations of Moses' sin, and these are discussed at length by Margaliot (1971) and Milgrom (1983). Besides the surface interpretation that Moses should have addressed the crag instead of hitting it, some have supposed that his sin lay in his words, "Listen you rebels—are we to produce water for you from this crag?" (Num 20:10; cf. Ps 106:33), either in that he lost his temper (Maimonides, Ibn Ezra), doubted Yahweh's power (Gressmann 1913: 150; Lohfink 1970: 55), or claimed the ability to work wonders himself (Bekor Shor; Arden 1957: 52; Margaliot 1971: 387–88; Milgrom 1983: 257–58). Milgrom suggests that speaking at all was a crime, since it created the impression of a magical incantation. Many modern exegetes have supposed that Moses' true crime has been censored (e.g., Gray *Numbers* ICC, 258). But all these explanations violate the plain sense of the text that Moses erred in striking the crag instead of addressing it as he had been commanded.

It is true that some details of the story remain strange, and this has been the cause of much of the reluctance to see Moses' hitting the rock as his basic crime. For instance, we elsewhere do not hear of a rod of Moses kept in the tabernacle. In fact, Num 20:8, 9, 11 are the only references to Moses' rod in P, which elsewhere speaks of *Aaron's* rod, kept in the tabernacle (Num 17:25–26). Moreover, why is Moses commanded to take the rod if he is not supposed to use it? The best solution to these problems is to emend Num 20:11 from "with his rod" (cf. vv 8–9) to "with the rod," as in vv 8–9 and in agreement with the LXX. In P "*the* rod" could only be Aaron's, but it is easy to imagine a scribe altering **bmṭh* to *bmṭhw,* since in the redacted Torah Moses' rod is more prominent than Aaron's and is featured in the similar story of Exod 17:1–7. If the rod is Aaron's rather than Moses', its function in the story becomes clear. According to P, Aaron's rod was preserved in the tabernacle so that it could be displayed as a warning in times of rebellion against aaronite and levitical authority. Accordingly, Yahweh's command to take out the rod is not a mandate to strike the crag with it. That Aaron's rod is the instrument of the sin implicates him in the offense by sympathetic magic.

In short, P has taken a story glorifying Moses and his miraculous rod (Exod 17:1–7) and rewritten it to condemn Moses and demonstrate the power of Aaron's rod, even when improperly used. But why did he move the spring from the mountain of lawgiving (Exod 17:6) to Kadesh? Most likely the intent was to harmonize conflicting traditions about Meribah and Kadesh. In Deut 1:19–46 the Israelites rebel against Moses and Yahweh at Kadesh, and both the people and their leader are punished there with forty years of wandering and death in the desert. On the other hand, Ps 95:8–11 preserves a tradition that the forty years were decreed at Meribah. By equating Meribah and

Kadesh, P reconciles these traditions. In P the death in the desert for the people is still associated with Kadesh (Num 13:26; 14:26–35), as is Moses' own death; but P accounts for the latter by rewriting Exod 17:1–7. P also brings his version of the Meribah story closer to that of Deut 33:8–11, which speaks of Yahweh's testing and striving against levitical priests, though in the older passage the test is passed. In Num 20:1–13 Moses fails the test of his faith in the power of the word, rather than of the physical act; and so he falls, taking his innocent brother down with him.

Bibliography

Arden, E. 1957. How Moses Failed God. *JBL* 76: 50–52.

Buis, P. 1974. Qadesh, un lieu maudit. *VT* 24: 268–85.

Coats, G. W. 1968. *Rebellion in the Wilderness.* Nashville.

Cornill, C. H. 1891. Beiträge zur Pentateuchkritik. *ZAW* 11: 1–34.

Friedman, R. E. 1981. *The Exile and Biblical Narrative.* HSM 22. Chico, CA.

Gressmann, H. 1913. *Mose und seine Zeit.* Göttingen.

Hölscher, G. 1927. Zu Num 20:1–13. *ZAW* 45: 239–40.

Kohata, F. 1977. Die priesterschriftliche Überlieferungsgeschichte von Numeri XX 1–13. *AJBI* 3: 3–34.

Lehming, S. 1961. Massa und Meribah. *ZAW* 73: 71–77.

Lohfink, N. 1970. Die Ursünden in der priesterlichen Geschichtserzählung. Pp. 38–57 in *Die Zeit Jesu,* ed. G. Bornkamm and K. Rahner. Freiburg.

Margaliot, M. 1971. Ḥēṭʾ Mōšeh wĕʾahărôn bĕmê Mĕrîbâ. *Beth Mikra* 19: 374–400 (in Hebrew).

Milgrom, J. 1983. Magic, Monotheism and the Sin of Moses. Pp. 251–65 in *The Quest for the Kingdom of God,* ed. H. B. Huffmon, F. A. Spina, and A. R. W. Green. Winona Lake, IN.

Propp, W. H. 1988. The Rod of Aaron and the Sin of Moses. *JBL* 107: 19–26.

William H. Propp

MERIBATH-KADESH (PLACE) [Heb *mĕrîbat qādēš*]. Var. MERIBAH; KADESH. The location of a source of water in the Wilderness of Zin, where the Israelites "broke faith" with Yahweh (Deut 32:51). The incident in question is almost certainly the same one reported prosaically in Numbers 20, where, at Kadesh in the Wilderness of Zin (v 1), the people are portrayed arguing with Moses over the lack of water (vv 2–5); an abundance of water is eventually procured after Moses improperly strikes a rock twice with his rod (vv 10–13). Ostensibly, traditions about this argument (Heb *mĕrîbâ*) at Kadesh led to the variant form Meribath-Kadesh. This form was retained as late as the time of Ezekiel, who used it to refer to the southernmost boundary of the promised land in his idealized vision of the restored Israel (Ezek 47:19; 48:28). See also KADESH-BARNEA; MASSAH AND MERIBAH; MERIBAH.

Gary A. Herion

MERKABAH MYSTICISM. See ENOCH, THIRD BOOK OF; JOB, TESTAMENT OF.

MERNEPTAH (PERSON). See MERENPTAH (PERSON).

MERODACH (DEITY) [Heb *mĕrōdāk*]. See MARDUK (DEITY).

MERODACH-BALADAN (PERSON) [Heb *mĕrodak balʾădān*]. A sheikh of the important Chaldean tribe of Bīt-Yakin and a contemporary of King Hezekiah (2 Kgs 20:12; Isa 39:1). During a career that spanned nearly 60 years, Merodach-baladan (Akk *Marduk-apla-iddina*) brought Chaldean and Aramean tribes together in opposition to Assyrian expansion in S Babylonia. Unfortunately, most of the surviving sources for Merodach-baladan's career are Assyrian. Like the Verse Account of Nabonidus, they paint a picture of an "outsider" who not only seized power by force, but also took prisoners and removed divine images from their temples. In his own accounts, he claims to have been a descendant of Eriba-Marduk, a king responsible for expansion and consolidation in Babylonia before 760 B.C. Brinkman's observation, that Merodach-baladan was Eriba-Marduk's grandson, is probably correct (Brinkman 1964: 9). During the reign of Tiglath-pileser III (745–727 B.C.), he sent tribute to the Assyrian capital. However, after the accession of Sargon II (722–705 B.C.) he attempted, with Elamite assistance, to thwart Assyrian intervention in S Babylonian affairs by seizing power himself. Under his leadership, after 721 B.C., both Chaldean and Aramean tribes constituted a formidable threat to the stability of the Assyrian Empire not only in Babylonia, but in Elam, Arabia, and Judah as well.

Merodach-baladan's own contemporary Babylonian sources portray him as a king who carried out important royal duties. Like earlier monarchs, he watched over irrigation canals, bridges, and temples, making sure they were kept in good repair. Furthermore, as Brinkman points out, there is no evidence that provincial administration was altered or impaired during his reign (Brinkman 1964: 17–18). While Assyrian inscriptions assert that the Babylonian economy suffered while he was in control, surviving contract tablets datable to the period 721–710 B.C. suggest a prosperity unequaled in virtually any previous period.

Merodach-baladan's name occurs in two places in the OT. In both instances (2 Kgs 20:12; Isa 39:1), he is said to have sent gifts to Hezekiah, king of Judah, upon hearing of his illness. Indeed, the annals of Sargon II and his successor, Sennacherib (705–681 B.C.) indicate that Merodach-baladan was quite active before and after Sennacherib attempted to take Jerusalem and force Judah to submit to his rule. During the period 710–705 B.C. the Chaldeans took advantage of both the marshy areas of S Babylonia, Assyrian preoccupation with other matters, and their opponent's military ineffectiveness to employ a defensive strategy. The result was that, while Sargon II was able to take several cities, including Dur-Yakin, Nippur, and Kish, Merodach-baladan was never captured, even though he sought and was denied protection in Elam. In 703 B.C. another revolt led to a certain Marduk-zakir-šumi's being elevated to kingship by the inhabitants of Babylonia. Merodach-baladan removed him within nine months while assembling support for himself from among Elamites and Arabs as well as Chaldeans and Arameans. Sennacherib subsequently marched on Babylon, captured Merodach-baladan's wife and his treasury, and attacked a number of towns associated with the Chaldeans in the S. In 700 B.C., despite yet another Chaldean uprising, Sennacherib drove his adversary out of Babylonia into Elam and placed his own son Assur-nadin-šumi on the Babylonian throne. Merodach-baladan did return briefly to his homeland of Bīt-Yakin before finding permanent refuge in Elam. He died in Elam a few years later.

Bibliography

Brinkman, J. A. 1964. Merodach Baladan II. Pp. 6–53 in *Studies Presented to A. Leo Oppenheim,* ed. R. D. Biggs and J. A. Brinkman. Chicago.

———. 1973. Sennacherib's Babylonian Problem. *JCS* 25: 89–95.

———. 1979. Babylonia under the Assyrian Empire. Pp. 223–50 in *Power and Propaganda,* ed. M. T. Larsen. Copenhagen.

———. 1984. *Prelude to Empire. Babylonian Society and Politics, 747–626 B.C.* Philadelphia.

RONALD H. SACK

MEROITIC LANGUAGE. See LANGUAGES (INTRODUCTORY SURVEY).

MEROM, WATERS OF (PLACE) [Heb *mê mērôm*]. The spring or water source associated with one of several Canaanite city-states. The area appears to have been the S Canaanite frontier of upper Galilee. It was at the "waters of Merom" that Jabin, the king of Hazor, assembled the combined Canaanite forces of N Palestine in an effort to stem the advance of the Israelites into Galilee (Josh 11:1–6). Joshua, always taking the offensive, apparently attacked the Canaanite forces at the "waters of Merom" from the relatively unoccupied forests (Aharoni *WHJP* 3: 118; and possibly the "forest of the gentiles" in Judg 4:16) of the southernmost highlands of upper Galilee. Apparently, the Israelites cut off the escape routes to the S from upper Galilee because the overthrown Canaanites escaped by the only available routes to the W (to Misrephoth, near Khirbet Musheirefeh [M.R. 161276] via Iqrit [H. Yoqrat; M.R. 176275] and Abdon [Tel ᶜAvdon; M.R. 165272]), N (toward Sidon via Yattir and Kanah), and NE (to the Mizpeh valley via Taphnith and Beth-anath [Safed el-battikh, M.R. 190289]), as indicated in Josh 11:6–9 (Rainey 1984: 192–93). Joshua then turned back from his pursuit of the Canaanites and secured his advance into Galilee by destroying Hazor and by occupying (if not subjecting to forced labor) the city-states of those kings who fled the battle at the "waters of Merom" (Judges 1).

Many have accepted the identification of Merom with the village of Meiron (M.R. 191265) on the E slopes of Jebel Jarmaq (Abel *GP* 2: 385). While there is a similarity in names, the historical geography of the "waters of Merom" of Joshua and early Egyptian and Assyrian sources does not coincide with Meiron. Several seasons of excavations at Meiron have prompted Meyers to suggest that "Meiron, [is] not to be confused with Meron of Joshua 11:5, 7" (*EAEHL* 3: 856) and that "the Spring of Meiron, possibly to be identified as ᶜEin Hatra, but surely not 'the waters of Merom' of Joshua 11:5, 7" (Meyers, Meyers, and Strange 1974: 3). Historical and geographic evidence (available archaeological evidence is inconclusive) tends to support Aharoni's (*LBHG,* 220–26) and Rainey's identification of the waters of Merom with Tell el-Khureibeh (M.R. 190275), just over 3 km S of Mârûn er-Râs (M.R. 192278).

Merom is first mentioned (*m-r-m-i-m,* No. 85) in the campaign annals of Thutmose III (1504–1450 B.C.E.) as having been taken during one of his 16 campaigns in the Levant to control rebellion. Rameses II, after a doubtful encounter with the Hittites in 1286 B.C.E., conducted several additional campaigns to bolster his authority in Palestine (ca. 1282 B.C.E.) and lists Merom (*m-r-m*) with Beth-anath (to the N of Tell el-Khirbeh) and Kanah (*q-n,* to the NW of Tell el-Khirbeh) as having been defeated. Tiglath-pileser III (733/732 B.C.E.) of Assyria also claimed to have taken Merom (*ma-ru-un, ANET,* 283), a claim which again suggests that Merom held a strategic place in the control of Canaanite upper Galilee.

Bibliography

Meyers, E. M.; Meyers, C. L.; and Strange, J. F. 1974. Excavations at Meiron, in Upper Galilee—1971, 1972. *BASOR* 214: 2–25.

Rainey, A. F. 1984. *Handbook of Historical Geography.* Jerusalem.

DALE C. LIID

MERONOTHITE [Heb *mērōnōtî*]. The gentilic identification of Jehdeiah, one of twelve stewards of royal property (specifically, the donkeys) appointed by David (1 Chr 27:30), and of Jadon who worked on the repair of the walls of Jerusalem in the time of Nehemiah. Nehemiah 3:7 states that one group of workers consisted of men of Gibeon and Mizpah, specifically mentioning Melatiah the Gibeonite and Jadon the Meronothite. This provides the only clue to the location of Meronoth, but its exact relationship to Mizpah is unclear (Williamson *Ezra, Nehemiah* WBC, 196–97).

RICHARD W. NYSSE

MEROZ (PLACE) [Heb *mērôz*]. A town mentioned only in Judg 5:23, in which the settlement and its inhabitants are cursed by an angel of the Lord for failing to aid the forces under Deborah and Barak in the fight against Sisera.

Several scholars have suggested locations for the town, despite the fact that the OT text gives few clues to the settlement's location. Abel (*GP* 2: 305) located Meroz at modern Kh. Marus (M.R. 199271), which is near Hazor. While Jabin of Hazor is mentioned in Judg 4:7 as the king whose army Sisera commanded, he is not mentioned in the Song of Deborah itself, and it is probable that the actual fighting took place in or near the Jezreel valley. For this reason, locating Meroz in the region of Hazor is questionable. There also seems to be no compelling reason to accept the suggestion that Meroz is a mistaken reading for either Merom (Josh 11.5) or Madon (Josh 12.19).

Alt (1940–41: 244) developed a theory that Meroz was a Canaanite settlement which had formed a treaty relationship with the new Israelite settlements. Alt suggested that the settlement remained neutral, unable either to fight with Sisera's forces or to break its pact with the Israelites. The curse was then necessary for the Israelites to abrogate the agreement, made in the name of the Lord, so the town could be punished. Yet in contrast to Jael the Kenite, who is praised in the next verse of the poem, and is clearly identified as a foreigner, Meroz and its people are not ethnically distinguished from the rest of the Israelites. Alt's interpretation of Meroz as a foreign ally of the Israelite towns, while imaginative, lacks support in the text.

Van Beek (*IDB* 3: 356) suggested that Meroz may be associated with the Shimron-meron (Josh 12:20), a large tell (M.R. 170234) on the NW edge of the Jezreel valley.

None of these identifications is convincing. Given the limited information provided by the verse, the exact location of Meroz has yet to be reliably determined.

Bibliography

Alt, A. 1940–41. Meros. *ZAW* 58: 244–47.

Melvin Hunt

MERRAN (PLACE) [Gk *Merran*]. This name (only in Bar 3:23, linked there with Teman) designates an area known for its wisdom. The word probably is a corruption of the name Midian. (In Heb, the similarity between the *reš* and *dalet* could cause a mistake in reading the middle letter of this word.) The verse in Baruch witnesses to the long-standing tradition that the area SE of Judah/Judea was famed for wisdom (cf. Jer 49:7; Obad 8; Job 1:3; 2:11). At the time of the writing (1st century C.E.), Arab peoples ("the sons of Hagar" in the same line) lived in the district. The passage exhorts Israel to seek wisdom, inasmuch as all neighboring peoples did not find it. The KJV has Meran, the RSV and the NEB have Merran, while the NAB has Midian.

John J. Schmitt

MEṢAD ḤASHAVYAHU (M.R. 120146). The modern name of an ancient fortress dating to the end of the Israelite period, discovered on the Mediterranean coast approximately 1.7 km S of Yavneh-Yam. In 1960 the fortress was excavated by J. Naveh (1962b), and in 1986 a rescue excavation was carried out by R. Reich (1986). During the 1960 excavation, a 14-line Hebrew ostracon was discovered inside one of the guardrooms (Naveh 1960; 1964; Amusin and Heltzer 1964; Talmon 1964). It is the letter of an agricultural worker who complains that his garment was confiscated (the reasons are not specified). Pleading innocence, he entreats the military governor to intervene and see that the garment is returned to him. This inscription is of special value because it sheds light on a practice attested in the Bible (Exod 22:26–27; Amos 2:8). In addition, five other ostraca and a stone weight (44.82 grams) were found in the vicinity of the gate (Naveh 1962a). One was inscribed "weighed four [shekels of] silver," and on two others the number "4" was indicated by four vertical strokes. One of the ostraca mentions a person named "Ḥashavyahu ben-Ya[. . .]," and consequently the site has been given his name.

The remains of the fortress itself cover an area of 6 dunams. It is composed of two rectangles forming an L shape conforming to the natural contours of the *kurkar* hill on which it stood. The larger rectangle (4 dunams) contains a courtyard and rooms adjacent to the wall, while the smaller one consists of three rows of houses flanking two streets. The 3.3-m-thick fortress wall was built of bricks on a stone foundation with buttresses along its facade (projecting about 0.7 m from the wall). The gate complex, including the guardrooms and towers, was built of dressed *kurkar* stone. The excavations uncovered the S wing of the gate and the building adjacent to it. Six test pits were also dug within the fortress area, all revealing the same information: a floor and, beneath it, either the natural *kurkar* bedrock or the sand fill used to level the area prior to the construction of the fortress. All evidence indicates that the fortress existed only for a very short period.

The pottery found on the floors included the local ware common in the 7th century B.C. However, coarsely made bowls and jars of a type previously considered to be of Persian date were also found, suggesting that the site must have been occupied during the final decades of the 7th century B.C. Among the finds was Greek pottery originating from the E islands of Greece and Asia Minor (so-called "East Greek pottery"), including amphorae, cooking pots, lamps, and cups. Much of it was decorated in the Middle Wild Goat style dated ca. 630–600 B.C. On the basis of this pottery, Naveh (1962: 98–99) concluded that the site had been occupied by settlers of Greek origin (probably mercenaries) who preferred to use the pottery to which they were accustomed. In this connection, it is noteworthy that Herodotus (2.152, 154) reports that Pharaoh Psamtik I (664–610 B.C.) hired Greek and Carian mercenaries. It seems likely that other contemporaneous rulers likewise used Greek mercenaries, and that the soldiers stationed at the Meṣad Ḥashavyahu fortress were employed by Josiah of Judah.

Judean control of the site is reinforced by the facts that the ostraca are written in biblical Hebrew, that they mention people with distinctively Judean names (Ḥoshayahu, Obadyahu), and that one seems to allude to a biblical custom regarding garments taken in pledge. Thus, Josiah seems to have expanded his control not only to the N and S but also to the W (2 Chr 34:6). The fortress was apparently abandoned in 609 B.C., the year that Pharaoh Necho defeated Josiah at Megiddo.

Bibliography

Amusin, J., and Heltzer, M. 1964. The Inscription from Meṣad Ḥashavyahu. *IEJ* 14: 148–57.

Naveh, J. 1960. A Hebrew Letter from the Seventh Century B.C. *IEJ* 10: 129–39.

———. 1962a. More Hebrew Inscriptions from Meṣad Ḥashavyahu. *IEJ* 12: 27–32.

———. 1962b. The Excavations at Meṣad Ḥashavyahu—Preliminary Report. *IEJ* 12: 89–113.

———. 1964. Some Notes on the Reading of the Meṣad Ḥashavyahu Letter. *IEJ* 14: 158–59.

Reich, R. 1986. Meṣad Ḥashavyahu. *Excavations and Surveys in Israel 1986* 5: 68–69.

Talmon, S. 1964. The New Hebrew Letter from the Seventh Century B.C. in Historical Perspective. *BASOR* 176: 29–38.

Ephraim Stern

MESALOTH (PLACE) [Gk *Messalōth*]. According to 1 Macc 9:2, the Syrian armies under Bacchides and Alcimus attacked Mesaloth in the Galilean town of Arbela located W of the Sea of Galilee (ca. 161 B.C.E.). The Gk *messalōth* (Codex Alexandrinus and the Latin; var. Gk *maisalōth* in Codices Sinaiticus and Vaticanus) appears to be derived from the Heb *mĕsillôt* ("roads" or "stairs"). The Heb *mĕsillôt* denotes an ascending road (LXX 2 Chr 9:11 translates the Heb *mĕsillôt* with the Gk *anabaseis*) or, as Abel suggested, caves (Abel 1961: 150). Indeed, Josephus' account of the events narrated in 1 Maccabees 9 notes that the besieged Jews of Arbela hid in caves (*Ant* 12.11.1 §421). Josephus also refers to the "village of the Cave of Arbela" located in the lower Galilee (*Life* 188). Josephus does not think Mesaloth is a place name but, rather, an ascent to a region with a number of caves. The translators of the LXX misunderstood the Hebrew original and treated Mesaloth as a place name rather than as caves or stairs ascending to the town of Arbela.

Bibliography

Abel, F.-M. 1961. *Les livres des Maccabées*. Paris.

MICHAEL E. HARDWICK

MESHA (PERSON) [Heb *mêšāʿ; mêšāʾ*]. **1.** A Moabite king who, in the 9th century B.C., led a successful revolt against his Israelite oppressors. To students of the Bible, Mesha is one of the best known non-Israelite kings, since he is the principal in a famous inscription, the Moabite Stone (or Mesha Inscription, hereafter MI), and he plays a leading role in an important biblical narrative, in 2 Kings 3. In fact, these two sources, the MI and 2 Kings 3, provide virtually all of the information that relates directly to Mesha. While these data are insufficient for the reconstruction of a detailed biography, the available evidence portrays a fascinating and capable character.

Mesha was the son of Kemosh-yat(ti), who "was king over Moab for thirty years" (MI, line 2) before Mesha succeeded him. It is probable that both father and son were Dibonites (line 2); Mesha gave much attention to the restoration of Dibon, his capital, after he liberated Moab from Israel (lines 3, 21–25).

While the Bible does not provide details concerning the subjugation of Moab to the Omride dynasty, the MI (lines 4–8) says that Omri and his son(s) held Moab in a tight grip for forty years. Indeed, the OT reports that Mesha, a "sheep breeder" (Heb *nōqēd;* cf. Amos 1:1 and the reference to sheep in the MI, line 31), "had to deliver annually to the king of Israel a hundred thousand lambs, and the wool of a hundred thousand rams" (2 Kgs 3:4). Given the importance of sheep in the region's modern economy, it can be assumed that such a tribute payment was well suited to ancient Moab, and there seems to be no compelling reason to attach a more exotic meaning to *nōqēd* in this instance (i.e., *nōqēd* is derived from the Akk verb, *naqādu,* "to probe," and indicates that Mesha was involved in augury). As king of Moab, Mesha was undoubtedly involved in animal husbandry, at an administrative level, and the exaction of heavy tribute—in the form of sheep and wool—was simply part of the Israelite overlordship.

After a generation-long period of oppression by Israel, Mesha launched an ambitious rebellion to reclaim the *mîšōr.* There are a number of historical-chronological problems associated with this revolt, but the apparent contradictions between the MI and the OT have been resolved to the satisfaction of many scholars (cf. MESHA STELE for more discussion of these problems). If it is assumed that Mesha launched his revolt after the death of Ahab (2 Kgs 1:1; 3:5), it is possible that the Israelites were preoccupied with the Assyrian threat that followed the conflict with Shalmaneser III at Qarqar in 853 B.C. and did not retaliate against Mesha immediately. Like other ancient rulers who were subject to the authority of more powerful kings, Mesha took advantage of the temporary lapse in strength that often accompanied the transition from one king to another.

Jehoram, the final king of the Omride dynasty, did respond to Mesha's uprising. The events recorded in 2 Kgs 3:6–27 are not narrated in the MI, but the genre of the Moabite stele makes such an omission normal. Mesha's victory at Kir-hareseth was explained by the intervention of the god Chemosh (or Kemosh), which was thought to have resulted from the king's sacrifice of his son (2 kgs 3:27).

Details of Mesha's revolt are provided in the MI. This dedicatory inscription was erected in Dibon ca. 830 B.C., after Israel's domination had been broken. The MI describes the political and military aspects of Mesha's most active years, an era that witnessed an extensive building program in the reclaimed towns of the Moabite tableland.

There is little doubt that Mesha's name meant something like "salvation" or "redeemer," though the exact etymology is uncertain. At least one scholar suggests that Mesha adopted the epithet "savior" only after he overthrew Israelite suzerainty. Such an explanation seems unnecessary, however, if the phenomenon of the *nomen-omen* is recalled: it is more likely that Mesha's parents gave their son a name that would befit the mission they hoped he could accomplish: liberate his people from Omride oppression. It is also possible that Mesha's name represented their belief in Chemosh as savior or basis of salvation. At any rate, the MI clearly emphasizes the salvific activities of Moab's chief deity (line 7). Thus, Mesha was appropriately named, and his political and military successes were attributed to the favor of Chemosh (lines 4–5, 9, etc.). Mesha's belief in divine intervention is reflected in the construction of a high place in Dibon (lines 3–4), the institution of *ḥerem* at Ataroth and Nebo (lines 10–18), and the existence of the MI itself.

GERALD L. MATTINGLY

2. One of the seven sons of Shaharaim, a Benjaminite, by his wife, Hodesh (1 Chr 8:9). Grohman (*IDB* 3: 418) points out that combination names, including Chemosh, the Moabite god, were common in Moab. Consequently, Corney (*IDB* 3: 357) has suggested that the name is an abbreviated form of "Chemosh is salvation." The name itself means "salvation" or "refuge." The Moabite connection of Mesha is highlighted in 1 Chr 8:8. Hodesh is said to have given birth to sons while living in Moab. This reference is clearly a hearkening back to earlier times when Moab was under Israelite control (Myers *1 Chronicles* AB, 60; Braun *1 Chronicles* WBC, 128). Mesha and his brothers are referred to as *roʾšê ʾābôt* or "heads of a family."

G. EDWIN HARMON

MESHA (PLACE) [Heb *mēšāʾ*]. One of the boundaries of the territory inhabited by the sons of Joktan (Gen 10:30), whose lands are described as extending "to Sephar, the hill country of the east." While most scholars have assumed a location somewhere in or near the Arabian peninsula, no firm identification has been made. Suggestions have included Mousa/Muza, a port mentioned by ancient authors (Ptolemy 8.22.6; Pliny *HN* 6.26) and probably located near Mokha on the E coast of the Red Sea about 100 miles N of Bab el-Mandeb, as well as Mesene, the Tigris delta area N of the Persian Gulf. Some scholars have equated the name with the Massa, a branch of the Ishmaelites (Gen 25:14) and posited a location somewhere in N Arabia. Employing additional evidence from Assyrian and Persian records, Cohen (*IDB* 3: 357) has proposed that Mesha, vocalized as Massa, be placed somewhere on a line between the head of the Gulf of Aqaba and the Persian Gulf. Because of the difficulty in locating Sephar, and without other evidence, all of these proposed identifications must remain conjecture.

Gary H. Oller

MESHA STELE. Discovered at Dhiban in 1868 by a Protestant missionary traveling in Transjordan, the 35-line Mesha Inscription (hereafter MI, sometimes called the Moabite Stone) remains the longest-known royal inscription from the Iron Age discovered in the area of greater Palestine. As such, it has been examined repeatedly by scholars and is available in a number of modern translations *(ANET, DOTT).*

Formally, the MI is like other royal inscriptions of a dedicatory nature from the period. Mesha, king of Moab, recounts the favor of Moab's chief deity, Chemosh (Kemosh), in delivering Moab from the control of its neighbor, Israel. While the MI contains considerable historical detail, formal parallels suggest the Moabite king was selective in arranging the sequence of events to serve his main purpose of honoring Chemosh. This purpose is indicated by lines 3–4 of the MI, where Mesha says that he erected the stele at the "high place" in Qarḥoh, which had been built to venerate Chemosh.

The date of the MI can be set with a 20–30-year variance. It must have been written either just before the Israelite king Ahab's death (ca. 853/852 B.C.) or a decade or so after his demise. The reference to Ahab is indicated by the reference in line 8 to Omri's "son," or perhaps "sons" (unfortunately, without some additional information, it is impossible to tell morphologically whether the word [*bnh*] is singular or plural). Ahab apparently died not long after the battle of Qarqar, in the spring of 853, when a coalition of states in S Syria/Palestine, of which Ahab was a leader, faced the encroaching Assyrians under Shalmaneser III. The date of the MI proposed here would agree with the consensus of paleography for a mid-9th century date, ca. 840–830 B.C.

There was little initially with which to compare the language of the MI other than classical Hebrew and some Phoenician texts. In the intervening years, however, a number of significant texts have been discovered which provide linguists with good comparative material (and tantalizing questions). The initial observation—that the Moabite language seemed similar to classical Hebrew—has been largely confirmed; nowadays, it appears Moabite had more similarities with Hebrew than with old Aramaic. It can be classified as a Northwest Semitic dialect close to Ammonite and Hebrew, though it does possess some Aramaic features (e.g., final *nun* [*n*] for the masculine plural absolute, final *hê* [*h*] for the third person pronominal suffixes). With the political and economic domination of Moab by Israel during parts of the 10th and 9th centuries, it is not surprising that Moabite would be similar to Hebrew or, since Ammonite would be Moabite's closest Transjordanian neighbor, that these two languages have a number of elements in common. At this stage of analysis several of the outstanding philological issues relate to the source of the remaining peculiarities of Moabite.

Although Israel is the only enemy of Moab and Chemosh mentioned in the MI, it seems likely that this results from the text's genre as a dedicatory inscription and its abbreviated style. Moabite relations with Israel were but a subset of the complicated and rapidly changing political landscape among states of this era and region. According to Assyrian annals, the Syro-Palestinian coalition that opposed Assyrian expansion was led by the kings of Israel, Damascus, and Hamath. Omri's son Ahab is specifically named in these extrabiblical texts. It is probable that these three states had worked out "parity" agreements among themselves, and the Phoenician ports and Arab caravans would have contributed to the strength of the coalition. Individually, these three would have had relations with smaller regional entities as their vassals, and Moab's subservience to Israel under the Omrides would fall under this latter category. Therefore, Moab's successful revolt is best understood as part of a breakdown of the larger coalition and the subsequent changing of certain vassal relationships.

The treatment of the Omride dynasty in 1–2 Kings concentrates on the kings' theological and moral failures, especially those of Ahab and his Phoenician queen, Jezebel. At best, the Assyrian threat is in the background of the biblical narrative. Warfare between Aram and Israel is noted during Ahab's last years (2 Kings 20, 22), however, a situation that would be repeated later (2 Kgs 10:32–33; 13:1–25). When one compares the biblical and Assyrian texts of the period, two problems stand out immediately. First, the Assyrian versions seem to presuppose that Israel and Aram were allies in the anti-Assyrian coalition. Second, there are different names given to the Aramean king in the two accounts. In the Assyrian version, he is called *Hadad-idri,* while the biblical account refers to him as Ben Hadad. 2 Kings refers to a revolt of Mesha after Ahab's death and to an abortive attempt by Ahab's son, Jehoram, with Judean and Edomite allies, to regain control of Moab by attacking the S Moabite plateau from the SW (2 Kgs 1:1; 3:1–27). In 2 Kings, therefore, nothing is said about the military campaigns in that part of Moab N of the Arnon, the subject matter of the MI.

Numerous historical analyses have been proffered to understand the MI in its context. Perhaps the best starting point for any reconstruction is the observation that the anti-Assyrian coalition fell apart and that the "ripple effects" of this dissolution are reflected vaiously in the MI and in 1–2 Kings. The MI recounts in selective fashion elements of the struggle in order to venerate Chemosh, while 1–2 Kings concentrates on Israelite (and particularly Omride) failures and the Israelites' struggles with their Aramean neighbors. Moab's freedom and Chemosh's faithfulness were paramount issues for Mesha. Those who compiled 1–2 Kings wanted to show Israel's failure with historical examples, and the account of Jehoram's failure to regain control of Moab was only an illustration of the larger pattern. It is possible, therefore, to provide a plausible historical setting for the MI with several different sequences when comparing it with the Assyrian texts and 1–2 Kings. A first option can fit the events of the MI into the sequence of 1–2 Kings by assuming that just after the 853 battle with Shalmaneser III, the Israelite/Aramean alliance fell apart, Ahab was killed, Mesha revolted and took control of the N plateau, and Jehoram failed to reinstitute Israelite control in his S assault. A variation would have Jehoram's assault coming first after an initial Moabite revolt, followed by Mesha's successful reconquest of the N plateau as narrated in the MI. A second option would begin with the assumption that the Israelite/Aramean alliance was strong as long as Ahab lived, with the Aramean wars attributed to him in 1 Kings really belonging to Jehoram or members of the Jehu dynasty. But by 841, about 13 years later, the alliance had been broken, new dynasties had been established in Samaria (Jehu) and Damascus (Hazael), and the former vassal relationship between Moab and Israel had been broken by Mesha's successful revolt. Thus, the Assyrian policy of divide and conquer had been at least partially successful. A third option simply begins with the MI, without a concern to coordinate events with those narrated in 1–2 Kings, and with the understanding that line 8 requires the start of Mesha's revolt before Ahab dies (i.e., reading the term *bnh* as "his [Omri's] son").

Chemosh, the god of Moab, was well known in the ANE long before the time of Mesha. For example, the name in cognate form appears in the Ebla and Ugaritic texts of N Syria. Line 17 of the MI refers to ᶜAshtar-Kemosh, a compound name that perhaps indicates a hypostatic union, with ᶜAshtar representing the feminine element (cf. Ishtar and Ashtarte) and Kemosh the masculine. Others have identified ᶜAshtar with the male deity, Aṯtar, in the Ugaritic texts and among certain early Arab tribes.

The MI attributes a previous Moabite decline to Chemosh's "humbling" (line 5) of his land, and Moab's recovery under Mesha was viewed as a sign of Chemosh's deliverance. Mesha states that Chemosh spoke to him (line 14), likely through a prophetic or priestly oracle. On at least two occasions, Mesha ritually slaughtered Israelites and dragged trophies of war before Chemosh as a sign of thanksgiving (lines 11–18). One verb *(ḥrm)* used to describe the assault on Nebo puts the city under a ban, terminology which is like that used several times in the Hebrew Bible. In fact, the MI as a whole reads almost like a narrative from the Hebrew Bible. (For bibliography, see EPIGRAPHY, TRANSJORDANIAN.)

J. ANDREW DEARMAN
GERALD L. MATTINGLY

MESHACH (PERSON) [Heb *mêšak*]. A Babylonian surname given to Mishael (Dan 1:7). See SHADRACH, MESHACH, ABEDNEGO.

MESHASH, KHIRBET EL- (M.R. 146069). A large, multiperiod site (also known as Tel Masos) located in the center of the Beersheba valley about 12 km E of Beersheba. The site was situated on the ancient intersection of the N–S route, between the Judean hills and the Arabah and Sinai, and the E–W route, between the coast and the Dead Sea and Moabite territory.

The site consists of three discrete settlement areas extending on both sides of the wadi Beersheba, built around a number of wells that even today serve as a major water supply for local bedouin (see EAEHL 3: 816). The small tell itelf, dating from the late Iron II period and including late Byzantine remains (see C. below), was already mapped by Conder and Kitchener in 1874, while Y. Aharoni, during intensive surveys in 1964 and 1967, discovered the other two nearby settlement areas: a MB enclosure across the wadi about 400 m S of the tell, and a large early Iron I village about 200 m NE of the tell (see A. and B. below). The site with its three settlement areas was excavated between 1972 and 1975 (Aharoni et al. 1975; Fritz and Kempinsky 1983).

A. The MB Enclosure

The salient feature of this settlement is a fortification rampart enclosing an area of over 4 acres. This rampart was only partly preserved, and a large part of the site had been washed away by the wadi; however, enough remained to indicate that this was the type of rampart typical of MB Palestinian cities. Two structures were exposed during the excavations, confirming that this was a two-phase settlement, the older structure being dismantled when the newer one was constructed. These two phases yielded homogeneous pottery dating to the 17th century B.C., and it is possible that this fortification represents an attempt by the MB coastal cities to control the route leading to the east.

B. The Early Iron Age Village

The most extensively excavated settlement was a large unfortified village extending about 200 m by 150 m. Covering approximately 15 acres, it constitutes the largest settlement of this period so far discovered. At several places beneath this early Iron Age settlement were found remnants of Chalcolithic cave occupation (subterranean dwellings). These dwellings are typical of the so-called Beer-sheba culture known throughout the Negeb. The collections of pottery and implements are meager, and the settlement seems to date sometime between 3600 and 3200 B.C.

The early Iron Age village was built above these Chalcolithic remains, and altogether three Iron I strata with a total of five phases can be distinguished:

stratum I —10th–11th centuries B.C.
stratum IIa —11th century B.C.
stratum IIb —11th–12th centuries B.C.
stratum IIIa—12th century B.C.
stratum IIIb—12th–13th centuries B.C.

The earliest phase (stratum IIIb) consists of floors, pits, and hearths, suggesting a "seminomadic" population dwelling temporarily in tents and huts. This population possibly may be identified with one of the waves of Israelite settlers who quietly penetrated into the Beersheba valley and took advantage of the occupation "gap" in the area at the time. Fritz (1981: 71) modifies this to suggest that these groups had already been living as seminomads within Canaan for several centuries, coexisting with the Canaanites until the disruptions of the LB/early Iron Age transition caused them to establish new settlements. Kempinsky (1978), however, sees the original nucleus of settlers as being composed of Canaanites who were joined by families from various N Negeb tribes (Simeonites, Kenites, Jerahmeelites, etc.); the two eventually integrated into one "ethnic" group (see also Ahlström 1984). The construction of actual permanent houses begins in stratum IIIa (mid-12th century B.C.).

In stratum II the site was more densely populated, with a large variety of different types of buildings. In addition to the dominant "four-room" house, there were "three-room" houses, broad-room houses, a courtyard house, and the so-called "Amarna house" (an Egyptian style of dwelling). Various other buildings had some sort of public function. Stratum I was badly eroded and seems to mark a certain decline. A large citadel structure in stratum I attests, perhaps, to the deteriorating security situation in the area around the time of David; the settlement was soon abandoned and its population transferred to other areas, perhaps to Tel Malḥata (M.R. 152069), 3.5 miles to the E.

The architectural diversity of this early Iron Age settlement (especially in stratum II) suggests that the population at that time (roughly the time of the Judges) was heterogeneous. Also militating against the usual tendency to regard this site as "Israelite" are both the notable absence of "collared rim" jars found at other early "Israelite" sites and the notable presence of pottery originating from the coastal areas of Canaan (Phoenician "bichrome ware," Philistine pottery, and also Midianite ware). A scarab that can be ascribed to the reign of Seti II (1204–1194 B.C.) was also found. This diverse assemblage shows the wide-ranging connections the village had in all directions, while the large quantity of bronze and copper implements indicate that copper processing played an important economic role.

C. The Iron II Tell

The third settlement area was the tell located about 200 m SW of the early Iron Age village. Dating to the 7th–6th centuries B.C., this settlement actually was little more than a small "fortress" (1.25 acres), probably connected in some way with the nearby population center at Tell Ira (M.R. 148071), 1.5 miles to the NE. Thus, the site of Khirbet el-Meshash had been abandoned for 300 years prior to the construction of this settlement. At the center of the tell stood a large building, which existed throughout all four phases associated with the settlement. Its function—whether administrative and/or military—was probably related to the abundant water resources located nearby; indeed, no fortifications were uncovered, and the size and arrangement of rooms in this central building suggest that it may possibly have served as a caravansery for the nearby trade routes, although no firm conclusions can be drawn since excavations here are incomplete. The pottery included typical Judahite ware as well as typical East Jordan ware. The settlement was probably destroyed during the Edomite conquests at the beginning of the 6th century B.C.

A group of Nestorian monks in the late Byzantine period (7th century A.D.) built a small monastery on the N part of this tell, using the S part as a large courtyard, which was surrounded by a wall. The entrance into the building led from this courtyard into a small hall, from which the central courtyard (with surrounding rooms) was accessible. A chapel was incorporated into the building; the apsis was rectangular, a unique feature among Nestorian churches, but characteristic of Syrian ones. The altar mensa (or table) was discovered out of place in a room next to the chapel. North of the chapel was found a crypt containing seven graves. Each grave contained two or three skeletons, all of which faced east. No furnishings were found, but the rubble inside the graves included pieces of plaster with fragments of inscriptions in the Syriac script written by Nestorians in the 8th century A.D., and other inscriptions incised in stone (also in Syriac) were found throughout the building. The monastery apparently did not last long, and it was destroyed violently and suddenly in the first half of the 8th century A.D.

D. Identification of the Site

Despite the long list of Negeb cities in Josh 15:21–32 and the lists of Shishak, the ancient name of Kh. el-Meshash has not yet been ascertained. Some scholars, following Aharoni (Aharoni et al. 1975), identify it with Hormah, mentioned in the inheritance of Simeon (Exod 21:4; Josh 19:4). But this inheritance list was probably compiled during the time of the monarchy, when (with the brief exception of the last few decades of the 7th century B.C.) Kh. el-Meshash was deserted. For the same reason, Crüsemann's identification of the site with Ziklag (1973: 222–24) is questionable. Naʾaman (1980: 146) suggested that the site should be identified with Baalath (Baalath-Beer in Josh 19:8), but this seems arbitrary. Fritz (Fritz and Kempinsky 1983: 235–38), noting that one would expect the name of the early Iron Age town to be mentioned in 1 Sam 30:27–31 (a passage dated by him to around the end of the 11th century B.C.), considers Siphmoth and Racal to be possible candidates, although at present the question of identification must remain open.

Bibliography

Aharoni, Y., et al. 1975. Excavations at Tel Masos. *TA* 2: 97–124.

Ahlström, G. W. 1984. The Early Iron Age Settlers at *Hirbet el-Mšāš* (Tel Masos). *ZDPV* 100: 35–52.

Crüsemann, F. 1973. Uberlegungen zur Identifikation der Hirbet el-Mšāš. *ZDPV* 89: 211–24.

Fritz, V. 1981. The Israelite "Conquest" in the Light of Recent Excavations at Khirbet el-Meshash. *BASOR* 241: 61–73.

———. 1983. Tel Masos: A Biblical Site in the Negev. *Arch* 36/5: 30–37.

Fritz, V., and Kempinsky, A. 1983. *Ergebnisse der Ausgrabungen auf der Hirbet el-Mšāš (Tel Masos) 1972–1975.* 3 vols. ADPV. Wiesbaden.

Kempinsky, A. 1978. Tel Masos: Its Importance in Relation to the Settlement of the Tribes of Israel in the Northern Negev. *Expedition* 20/4: 29–37.

Naʾaman, N. 1980. The Inheritance of the Sons of Simeon. *ZDPV* 96: 136–52.

V. F.

MESHECH (PERSON) [Heb *mešek*]. Meshech is one of the seven sons of Japheth, Noah's son, according to the Table of Nations in Gen 10:2 and the parallel genealogy in 1 Chr 1:5. The latter genealogy also lists another person with the same name as a son of Shem (1:17). In the Table of Nations (Gen 10:23) there is no second listing for Meshech, but there is a Mash, son of Aram, in the parallel position to 1 Chr 1:17. This could be a scribal error in which the last Hebrew letter of Meshech was dropped (so LXX). Mash could also be an entirely different entity. See MASH. Whatever the case regarding the name in Genesis, the Chronicles genealogy indicates two ethnically distinct groups, one of Semitic and one of non-Semitic descent.

Most references to Meshech in the OT are to the non-Semitic peoples. Five times in Ezekiel they are associated with Tubal. In Ezek 27:13, Meshech and Tubal, along with Javan (Greece), traded slaves and bronze with Tyre, the capital of Phoenicia. They must therefore have had some skill in metallurgy, since Tyre itself served as a source for metalworking skills (1 Kgs 7:13–14). In an oracle against Egypt (Ezek 32:17–32), numerous nations are to join destroyed Egypt in her entombment. Included among these northern nations are Assyria and Elam, northeast of Egypt; Edom and Sidon, nearer to hand on the north; and Meshech and Tubal farther north (32:26). The latter are characterized by this Israelite prophet of the Exile as uncircumcised (i.e., barbaric) terrorists.

In two eschatological passages, Meshech and Tubal are ruled by Gog of the land of Magog (Ezek 38:2, 3; 39:1). Gog opposes Israel, even going as far as staging a military assault on God's people (Ezek 38:14–16; 39:2). God, however, will oppose him and his armies in his power. Ultimately God will bring their destruction and death (Ezek 38:18–33; 39:3–6).

The last remaining biblical mention of Meshech is in the context of a lament. The psalmist bewails his habitation in Meshech and in the tents of Kedar (120:5). These people do not desire peace as the psalmist himself does. Kedar refers to a people in the Syro-Arabian desert area. The psalm text suggests a nomadic group, since they are associated with tents. This could be a reference to the descendants of the Semitic Meshech (1 Chr 1:17), since this locale is populated mostly by Semites. Another interpretation of the reference is to see both Kedar and Meshech as archetypical barbaric locations far removed from Yahweh and his land. Thus, it is not the location of the specific sites mentioned in the psalm which is of primary importance; rather, the writer is concerned about the great separation from Israel.

Akkadian sources from as early as Tiglath-pileser I (ca. 1100 B.C.; Parpola 1970: 252–53) mention Meshech, or the *muškaya* from the land of *mušku*. These people paid tribute to Assurnasirpal II (ca. 882 B.C.) from their capital in E Asia Minor (*GARI* 2: 123). This tribute included goods of bronze (see Ezek 27:13 noted earlier). At the end of the 8th century B.C., the king of Meshech was Mita, the famous Midas whose touch, according to legend, would turn everything to gold. In a letter to Sargon II dated ca. 709 B.C., Midas, ruler of the "land of Muski," seeks a peaceful relationship with the Assyrians.

Both Herodotus (7.78) and Josephus (*Ant* 1.124) place Meshech (Moschoi) in E Asia Minor. The latter locates these people in the area later known as Cappadocia (see *MBA* map no. 172). Herodotus (1.14) equates them with the Phrygians somewhat farther W in Asia Minor (see *MBA* map no. 172). These people migrated from E Europe into Asia during the 12th century B.C. (*CAH*³ 2: 417–18; Yamauchi 1982: 27). Some of the people of Meshech seem to have moved even farther east, around the Black Sea. There people referred to as Moschi and Tibarani were still found into the Persian period (*CAH*³ 2: 420–21). All of these references apparently relate to the non-Semitic Meshech. None clearly allude to a Meshech of Semitic stock.

Bibliography

Parpola, S. 1970. *Neo-Assyrian Toponyms.* AOAT 6. Kevelaer.
Yamauchi, E. M. 1982. *Foes from the Northern Frontier.* Grand Rapids.

DAVID W. BAKER

MESHELEMIAH (PERSON) [Heb *měšelemyāh; měšelemyāhû*]. A levitical gatekeeper, descendant of Kore (1 Chr 26:1), head of one of the major families of gatekeepers who served in the sanctuary in the days of David (cf. vv 2–3, 9). As Williamson (*1 and 2 Chronicles* NCBC, 169–70) points out, the present list in vv 1–11 divides the gatekeepers into three families: Meshelemiah, Obed-edom, and Hosah; but only two of these (Meshelemiah and Hosah) are firmly anchored with levitical genealogies. Thus, once again, the status of Obed-edom is somewhat uncertain in the traditions reflected in the Chronicler's work. (See the discussion in JEDUTHUN concerning the analogous situation found in 1 Chronicles 15–16.

Although vv 2–3 of 1 Chronicles 26 provide a list of seven sons of Meshelemiah in careful order (with the firstborn named Zechariah), we are later told in v 9 that the total of Meshelemiah's "sons and brethren" were some 18 "able men." Inasmuch as v 14 of the same chapter makes reference to a certain Shelemiah (Heb *šelemyāhû*), a gatekeeper also with a son named Zechariah (here described as a "shrewd counselor"), it seems quite certain that this Shelemiah is to be identified with the Meshelemiah of vv 1–9 ("Shelemiah" apparently representing a shortened form of the name). Williamson (1979: 253–54) is probably right to suggest that vv 12–18 of this chapter represent a later addition inasmuch as the reference to Obed-edom in v 15 is not intrusive here (in contrast to vv 4–8, as discussed above), and we would not expect two different spellings ("Meshelemiah" and "Shelemiah") for the name of one individual within the same passage.

The only other reference to Meshelemiah found in the Hebrew Bible is in 1 Chr 9:21. Here, his son Zechariah again is said to have played a prominent role among the gatekeepers established in office by David (the latter oddly linked to "Samuel the seer" in v 22; indeed, we are told in v 20 that Phinehas, son of Eleazar, had ruled over the ancestors of the same levitical gatekeepers in times past [cf. Williamson *1 and 2 Chronicles* NCBC, 90–91; Braun *1 Chronicles* WBC, 136–37]). The so-called "Chronicler" is far more concerned with emphasizing the levitical origins of the various cultic functionaries of the postexilic period than he is with chronological exactitude. See KORE. Curiously, in 1 Chr 9:17–19 (contrast v 31), levitical gatekeeper(s) named Shallum are described in terms very reminiscent of Meshelemiah (son of Kore son of [Ebi]asaph, chief of the gatekeepers, stationed on the east side; cf. 1 Chr 26:1–2, 12–14), leading to the conclusion that in 1 Chronicles 9 Meshelemiah and (at least) the Shallum of v 19 probably represent two variant names for the same individual (cf. Williamson 1979: 254; the Shallum of v 17 is probably postexilic).

In summary, Meshelemiah, Shelemiah, and Shallum seem to represent three different names for the same person; in each is to be found the Heb root *šlm,* "to be complete, sound." Dahlberg (*IDB* 3: 358) is probably correct in translating Meshelemiah as "Yah[weh] is recompense" or the like (also cf. *IPN,* 19, 31, 145, for pertinent Akkadian parallels).

Bibliography

Williamson, H. G. M. 1979. The Origins of the Twenty-Four Priestly Courses, A Study of 1 Chronicles xxiii–xxvii. Pp. 251–68 in *Studies in the Historical Books of the Old Testament,* ed. J. A. Emerton. VTSup 30. Leiden.

WILLIAM H. BARNES

MESHEZABEL (PERSON) [Heb *məšêzabʾēl*]. **1.** The grandfather of Meshullam, who was entrusted with the repair of more than one section of the walls of Jerusalem and its gates (Neh 3:4, 30; see Myers *Ezra-Nehemiah* AB, 114; Brockington *Ezra, Nehemiah and Esther* Century Bible, 135). Meaning "God is deliverer" or "God is delivering," the name is unusual in that it is based upon a participle that was introduced into Hebrew from Akkadian, through Aramaic. The presence of the participle is evidence of the impact of Aramaic upon Hebrew during the postexilic period (Brockington, 135).

2. A leader of the people and a signatory to the covenant established by Ezra (Neh 10:21).

3. The father of Pethahiah, an ambassador charged with representing Jewish concerns in the Persian court (Neh 11:24; see Myers, 189).

FREDERICK W. SCHMIDT

MESHILLEMOTH (PERSON) [Heb *məšillēmôt*]. **1.** An Ephraimite whose son, Berechiah, was a leader among the people. Along with several others, Berechiah protested the forced enslavement of captured Judahites and supported the prophet Oded in calling for amnesty for those Judahites captured in Pekah's war against Ahaz (2 Chr 28:12). This story supplements the information conveyed in 2 Kgs 16:5 and Isaiah 7–8, where we simply learn that, although Pekah and Rezin laid siege to Jerusalem, they could not defeat Ahaz. According to 2 Chr 28:5–15, however, the conquest could have been completed (esp. vv 5–6, 10) except for the last-minute intervention of the Assyrians. One or both of the stories may reflect a theological bias, and it is difficult to determine the exact extent of Judah's defeat at the hands of Israel and Syria.

2. A priest who is listed in the genealogy of Amashsai in Neh 11:13. He is likely to be identified with the Meshillemith of 1 Chr 9:12, who similarly is listed in the genealogy of Maasai. In both cases Meshillemoth/Meshillemith is reckoned as the son of Immer, the eponym of one of the major priestly phratries in the postexilic period who, according to 1 Chr 24:14, had been granted the sixteenth priestly course by David. The family of Immer and the families of Jedaiah (the family of the priest Jeshua), Pashhur, and Harim appear to have made up the major priestly phratries in the early postexilic period (Ezra 2:36–39; Neh 7:39–42). The lists suffer from general confusion, however, because the same name often appears in several places in such genealogies due to recurring preference for certain names within families. In addition, the lists were compiled as much for social and religious purposes as to provide historical information. Compare the similar names Meshulemeth, Meshelemiah, and especially Meshullam, all related to the notion that "God has/is paid back."

ROD R. HUTTON

MESHOBAB (PERSON) [Heb *məšôbāb*]. Descendant of Simeon (1 Chr 4:34), described as one of the "princes in their families" (1 Chr 4:38). The name probably means "returned" or "delivered." In the LXX the name appears as *Mosobab,* while in the Vg it appears as *Masobab.* Understanding neither Meshobab nor Jamlech (the name that immediately follows) as proper names, Lucian translates it as "having returned, he ruled." The name Meshobab, along with the names of the other Simeonite princes, is not found in any of the genealogies assigned to this patriarch. (Compare the Peshitta, where 1 Chr 4:34–41 contains no personal names.) Nevertheless, in view of 1 Chr 4:42, Meshobab and the others were probably part of the tribe of Simeon (Williamson *Chronicles* NCBC, 62).

CRAIG A. EVANS

MESHULLAM (PERSON) [Heb *məšullām*]. A personal name in the Hebrew Bible which grammatically corresponds to the *Puʿal* participle of the verbal root *šlm* and probably means "one recompensed (by Yahweh?)."

1. A son of Azaliah and the grandfather of Shaphan the scribe (2 Kgs 22:3), the latter having served in Josiah's bureaucracy around 621 B.C. Nothing is known of Meshullam's circumstances in life. Because his grandson served as a member of Josiah's bureaucracy, it is reasonable to speculate that Meshullam, too, might have served a previous king, perhaps Manasseh or conceivably even Hezekiah.

2. One of the sons of Zerubbabel (1 Chr 3:19). This fact situates Meshullam in the 6th century B.C. If he was born late in that century and if Ezra's mission to Jerusalem is dated to 458 B.C., it is conceivable that he could be the same Meshullam whose name occurs in Ezra 8:16 (see no. 10 below). If this is the case, he would have been in his 50s or 60s during Ezra's time.

3. A member of the tribe of Gad who settled in Bashan (1 Chr 5:13). The part of the list in which Meshullam's name occurs finds no parallel in other Gadite lists (cf. Gen 46:16; Num 26:15–18).

4. A son of Elpaal and a member of the tribe of Benjamin (1 Chr 8:17). His name occurs in a Benjaminite genealogical list that comprises all of chap. 8, which serves here to introduce the story of Saul's death in 1 Chronicles 9.

5. A Benjaminite and the father of Shallu (1 Chr 9:7). The latter's name appears in a list of the first exiles to return to Jerusalem. A variation of the list occurs in Neh 11:7, where again Meshullam is listed as the father of Sallu (= Shallu). The two lists do not contain the same names after the reference to Meshullam, which demonstrates that neither depends on the other. The two lists pose a problem of chronology: whereas 1 Chr 9:7 portrays Meshullam as the father of one of the first exiles to return to Jerusalem, Neh 11:7 portrays him as the father of one living in Jerusalem during the time of the rebuilding of the wall. The lists therefore deal with two different periods of time. The reference to Shallu/Sallu and to Jerusalem as his abode indicates that the Meshullam mentioned in both lists is the same. Yet, which of the lists is historically correct is difficult if not impossible to determine.

6. A Benjaminite and son of Shephatiah (1 Chr 9:8). The name here occurs in a list of the first of the exiles to return to Jerusalem. It is missing from the parallel list in Neh 9:7–11. In 1 Chr 9:9, Meshullam was the leader of his family.

7. The grandfather of Azariah and the son of Zadok (1 Chr 9:11). A parallel list occurs in Neh 11:1, 11 (see no. 5 above). Azariah was one of the first of the exiles to return to Jerusalem. Because Meshullam was the grandfather of a returning exile, it is highly likely that he lived in the late 7th century B.C. and witnessed the fall of Jerusalem in the early 6th century. This, of course, depends on whether or not the list in 1 Chronicles 9 is historically correct. The name Zadok here does not refer to the priest of the same name who was contemporaneous with Solomon.

8. The grandfather of Massai (1 Chr 9:12). Massai, a priest, was one of the first exiles to return to Jerusalem. As Massai's grandfather, Meshullam could have been a witness to the fall of Jerusalem in 587/586 B.C.

9. An overseer who served in the task of repairing the temple under Josiah in the 7th century B.C. (2 Chr 34:12). Meshullam is referred to as one of the sons of the Kohathites, a levitical family of some historic importance in the traditions of the Hebrew Bible. See KOHATH.

10. One of the leading men whom Ezra sent to Iddo of Casiphia to obtain Levite ministers for the temple (Ezra 8:16). A parallel version of this incident is found in 1 Esdr 8:41–46, where Meshullam is mentioned in v 43. On the one hand, it is conceivable that this Meshullam was the son of Zerubbabel (see no. 2 above); on the other hand, he might be identified with the Meshullam of Ezra 10:15, 29 (cf. 1 Esdr 9:14, 30). If the latter identification is upheld, we learn that he opposed the enforced divorcing of non-Israelite wives as mandated by Ezra.

11. A son of Berechiah and one who helped repair Jerusalem's fortifications (Neh 3:4, 30). Neh 6:18 relates that Johanan, son of Tobiah, took Meshullam's daughter as wife. Because Meshullam obviously supported Nehemiah's efforts to rebuild Jerusalem's walls, the notice of his daughter's marriage to the son of one who opposed Nehemiah is interesting. One possible effect intended by the notice of the union of Meshullam and Tobiah's families is to underscore the latter's failure to use his Judean relations to undermine the repairs.

12. A son of Besodeiah who helped repair a gate called Jeshanah in the Jerusalem wall (Neh 3:6). What Jeshanah (Heb *yĕšānâ*) means is not clear, and English translations do not agree on how to translate it ("old gate," RSV; "new city gate," NAB). Jeshanah was also a town toward which the gate faced; hence, perhaps, its name. See JESHANAH.

13. One of the men who stood next to Ezra as the latter read the Torah before the people (Neh 8:4). Such a position indicates one of important social rank, perhaps a priest (see no. 14 below). The parallel list in 1 Esdr 9:43–44 does not mention Meshullam. He is also missing from the Neh 8:4 passage in LXX^{B}. A patronym is not given here, which opens up the possibility of an identification with the Meshullam of Ezra 8:16 (see no. 10 above).

14. One of the priests who set his seal on a covenant to observe the Torah in Nehemiah's time (Neh 10:7). Because no patronym is given, it is conceivable that he is to be identified with one or more of the other occurrences of Meshullam in Nehemiah. If the date of Ezra's return to Jerusalem is 458 B.C. and not 398 B.C., an identification is possible with either no. 11, 12, or 13 above. In this case, persons who worked on the wall under Nehemiah could easily have been witnesses to Ezra's ministry.

15. One of the heads of the people who set his seal on the covenant ratified in Jerusalem after the Exile (Neh 10:20). As in no. 14 above, a patronym is not given. If the identifications suggested in no. 14 above are not valid, it is possible that they might be valid for this Meshullam.

16. One of the chiefs of a priestly family during the time of Joiakim (Neh 12:13). He is noted specifically as being a head of the house of Ezra, the latter not to be identified with the Ezra who returned to Jerusalem in the 7th year of Artaxerxes (Ezra 7:7; cf. Neh 12:1). The reference to Joiakim in Neh 12:12 likely locates Meshullam in the early 5th century B.C.

17. The chief of a priestly family of Ginnethon in the days of Joiakim (Neh 12:16). Ginnethon was one of the priests who returned to Jerusalem with Zerubbabel. As in no. 16 above, the reference to Joiakim locates Meshullam in the early 5th century B.C.

18. A gatekeeper during the days of the high priest Joiakim (Neh 12:25). Neh 12:26 also places him in the time of Nehemiah and Ezra. It is not clear whether the Chronicler intends the names Joiakim, Nehemiah, and Ezra to be read diachronically or synchronically. If the latter, the statement cannot be correct, because Eliashib was the high priest during the time of Nehemiah. If the former is intended, then one must consider that the span of time is quite considerable. Here Ezra's name follows Nehemiah's in contrast to the present order of the events as described in the books of Ezra-Nehemiah. It is possible, however, that the Chronicler intends the "days of Nehemiah the governor and of Ezra the scribe" to be seen in some degree as coincidental. In that case, the Chronicler views Ezra's mission to Jerusalem as preceding Nehemiah's in spite of the priority of Nehemiah's name in 12:26. This is the only way that Nehemiah and Ezra's ministries could have overlapped. Therefore, that Meshullam could have been a gatekeeper during the time of Joiakim as well as Nehemiah and Ezra is, if not probable, at least conceivable.

19. A participant who celebrated the rebuilding of Jerusalem's wall in a liturgical procession (Neh 12:33). He is designated as a prince of Judah. Conceivably, an identification is possible with no. 15 above. In neither case is a patronym given, and both cases indicate positions of leadership or influence in society. If Ezra's mission to Jerusalem is dated to 458 B.C., a possible identification with no. 13 above can be suggested. A prince of Judah might well be accorded the privilege of standing on the podium next to a reader of the Torah.

JAMES M. KENNEDY

MESHULLEMETH (PERSON) [Heb *měšullemet*]. Mother of Amon, king of Judah (2 Kgs 21:19). Meshullemeth's name appears in the regnal formula of her son in 2 Kings, but it is missing from the parellel account in 2 Chr 33:21. She is the daughter of Haruz of Jotbah and the first of five queen mothers for whom both the father's name and place of origin are given (cf. also JEDIDAH, HAMUTAL, ZEBIDAH, and NEHUSHTA).

The site of Meshullemeth's hometown, Jotbah, is uncertain. Usually identified as either *at-Taba* (M.R. 139878) N of Aqaba or Yodefat (M.R. 176248) in Galilee, its location is often interpreted as being politically significant. If Meshullemeth came from Galilee, then her marriage may reflect an attempt by Judah to secure N support (Cogan and Tadmor, *2 Kings* AB, 275). If Meshullemeth came from the far S, it is possible she was of Arab or Edomite origin (Montgomery, *Kings* ICC, 521; Gray, *1–2 Kings* OTL, 711). Her marriage might represent a strengthening of diplomatic ties between Judah and Arabia or Edom. In either case, Meshullemeth would be of non-Judean origin and her marriage diplomatically important. But who arranged her marriage, Hezekiah or Manasseh? Traditionally, it is assumed that Meshullemeth's marriage to Manasseh was part of Hezekiah's international policies. This assumption is challenged by Wilcoxen. Translating the term "son" as "grandson," Wildoxen suggests that Amon was the *grandson* of Manasseh. Meshullemeth would then be Manasseh's daughter-in-law instead of his wife (Wilcoxen 1977: 155–56). If this is so, then Meshullemeth's marriage (possibly to the son Manasseh sacrificed) was arranged by Manasseh and represents an intriguing glimpse into his diplomatic activities. See also QUEEN.

Bibliography

Wilcoxen, J. 1977. The Political Background of Jeremiah's Temple Sermon. Pp. 151–66 in *Scripture in History and Theology,* ed. A. Merrill and T. Overholt. Pittsburgh Theological Monograph Series 17. Pittsburgh.

LINDA S. SCHEARING

MESOPOTAMIA (PLACE). A Greek word which means "(land) in the midst of the river(s)" and in modern times has come to be interpreted as "the (land) between the (two) rivers," the two rivers being the Tigris and the Euphrates. In the English versions of the Bible the word "Mesopotamia" is used as a translation of words which are clearly different in meaning from the modern understanding of the word "Mesopotamia."

The word "Mesopotamia" in the English versions of the OT renders the Hebrew word *ʾăram nahărayim,* while in the NT passages it is the same word in Greek—Mesopotamia. The English renditions for the OT are based on the LXX translation, which also uses the Greek word Mesopotamia for the Hebrew. The Aramaic Targums, however, use the expression *Di al perat,* which literally means "that which is upon the Euphrates." Thus, the Targumic versions suggest a geographical location in the region of the Upper Euphrates.

The biblical passages where the English versions use the word "Mesopotamia" seem to confirm this geographical location. In Genesis 24, it is narrated that a servant of Abraham went to the city of Nahor in Mesopotamia to find a wife for Isaac. In Deut 23:5—Eng 23:4, there is reference to Balaam of Mesopotamia. In Judg 3:7–11, we read that the Lord delivered the Children of Israel into servitude under CUSHAN-RISHATHAIM, king of Mesopotamia. In 1 Chr 19:6–9, we are told that the Ammonites hired chariots from Aram-Maacah and from Zobah of Mesopotamia in their war with King David. The term Mesopotamia occurs twice in the book of Acts. In Acts 2, "residents of Mesopotamia" are included in the list of peoples of various lands who "were all filled with the Holy Spirit and began to speak in other tongues." Finally, in Acts 7:2, Stephen declares that God appeared to Abraham in Mesopotamia. From most of the above references it is clear that the geographical location of "Mesopotamia" was not the entire region between the Tigris and the Euphrates but only the area of the Upper Euphrates river in Syria.

There has been considerable debate among modern scholars as to the exact meaning of the Heb *ʾăram nahărayim.* The first element *(ʾăram)* designates what we call Syria and etymologically is related to the ethnic term Aramean. The meaning of the second element *(nahărayim)* is more difficult to determine, but it has been argued by many scholars that this is not a dual meaning, "two rivers," but rather a locative meaning, "riverine land"; that is, "land within the bend of the (Euphrates) river."

As stated at the beginning of this article, the word "Mesopotamia" is modern usage designates the region farther east than that in the Bible and includes all of the territory between the Tigris and Euphrates rivers right down to the Persian Gulf. Formal recognition of this meaning for the word came with British military presence in the region at the time of the breakup of the Ottoman Empire. For the history of ancient Mesopotamia in this larger sense, see MESOPOTAMIA, HISTORY OF.

A. KIRK GRAYSON

MESOPOTAMIA, HISTORY OF. In part because the Tigris and Euphrates rivers were homeland to some of the greatest political and military powers in antiquity, much of Mesopotamian history is linked with that of the Bible. This entry, which consists of five separate articles, surveys the history of ancient Mesopotamia. The first article covers the chronology of ancient Mesopotamia. The following two cover the prehistory of Mesopotamia and the 3d millennium B.C. The fourth and fifth articles, respectively, treat the history and culture of Assyria and Babylonia.

MESOPOTAMIAN CHRONOLOGY

The historical reconstruction of the past revolves around a comprehensive knowledge of absolute time and the sequence of known events. Unlike the situation in the modern world, wherein a reasonably accurate digital watch is worn on many a wrist, and where exactly datable events or reasonably precise schedules are commonplace, past processes and events cannot be dated so concisely. As a general rule, dating becomes progressively more complex the further back in time one goes. Whereas ancient historians certainly aspired to know the approximate date that a Babylonian king died or the exact years that an Egyptian pharaoh ruled, written records seldom preserved a king's name or described some "exactly" datable occurrence such as a coronation or a decisive battle. When such information does not exist, dating can only be *relative,* never *absolute* ("exact"). Relative dates are usually based on stratified, and thus sequential, archaeological materials: stone tools, metal tools and artifacts, pottery, figurines, and so on. The premise is that material found in the lowest part of an archaeological excavation, which is sequentially earlier than material accumulated above it, is also *relatively* earlier in time.

A. Prehistory
B. The Historical Era: 3d–1st Millennia B.C.
C. Sources for Mesopotamian Chronology and History
   1. Overview
   2. The 3d Millennium B.C.
   3. The 2d Millennium B.C.
   4. The 1st Millennium B.C.
D. Conclusion

A. Prehistory

Relative dating is the rule for much of the prehistoric era. Throughout most of the time span that human beings have roamed the earth, they lived as migrant bands that hunted and collected food and other necessities. Their tools were made primarily of stone, less often of other perishable materials such as wood. The long period of time in which rudimentary developments may be traced in stone tool technology is known as the Paleolithic ("Old Stone") Age (about 600,000–15,000 B.C.). The basic hunting-gathering economy—occasionally supplemented by selective use of certain plants and animals—prevailed in the Near East until about 10,000 B.C., when more sustained efforts at plant domestication and animal rearing significantly altered the course of human cultural history.

Changing human needs and the beginnings of food production required a different tool kit; the era from about 9000 to 3000 B.C. has thus been termed the Neolithic ("New Stone") Age. The first permanent settlements appear in the archaeological record at almost the same time. A sedentary way of life supported chiefly by food production, together with the changes it wrought—population growth, the accumulation of goods, loss of mobility—had major consequences for subsequent cultural stages in the ANE. The people who dwelt in those early sedentary communities did not depend exclusively on agriculture, but rather on a mixed-spectrum economy that included hunting and collecting, the herding of goats and sheep, fishing, and the cultivation of wheat and barley. Some sedentary villages were established prior to any sort of successful, sustained domestication: the walled community at Jericho between about 8000 and 7000 B.C., for example, subsisted chiefly on hunting and the intensive gathering of wild grains.

It is difficult to speak authoritatively on the reasons for sedentarization from our remote 10,000-year perspective: archaeologists have offered climatic, environmental, demographic, and technological explanations. Investigations of sedentarization, plant and animal domestication, urbanization, and other Near Eastern cultural developments before the historical period (before the advent of writing around 3000 B.C.) depend entirely on material evidence: bones, seeds, pottery, implements, weapons, art, and architecture.

Absolute dates from certain of these prehistoric materials are based on radiocarbon determinations—precise physical measurements of the decay state of carbon isotope ratios which allow determination of when a particular carbon-containing material (charcoal, bone, shell, etc.) stopped growing (i.e., died). It is thereby possible to assign to the specific archaeological level from which the radiocarbon-analyzed material was recovered an approximate absolute date (approximate because the computation must allow for a statistical counting error—plus or minus a number of years—that can be quite high). Dendrochronological ("tree-ring") calibration of radiocarbon-derived dates suggests that they deviate increasingly from actual calendar dates: from a 200-year error around 1000 B.C. up to a 900-year error around 5000 B.C. Although calibration curves are designed to transform a radiocarbon age or measurement into an actual calendar date, the limits of these curves currently do not extend earlier than the 6th millennium B.C.

B. The Historical Era: 3d–1st Millennia B.C.

By the end of the 4th millennium B.C., certain social elements in prehistoric Mesopotamia adopted writing (cuneiform), chiefly to keep records for their burgeoning economies. In nearby N Syria, by the mid-3d millennium B.C., scribes at Ebla had also begun to use Mesopotamia's cuneiform script to keep track of their wide-ranging economic affairs. With the advent of writing, the prehistoric period of the Near East increasingly becomes elucidated by an ethnohistoric, documentary record. The use of writing prompted remarkable, sociocultural innovations in 3d-millennium B.C. Mesopotamia and Syria. The scribal profession in Mesopotamia—where writing became something of an art—assumed unique importance by the teaching of the skills of communication in the cuneiform script, which served as the medium for the transmission and preservation of economic, legal, literary, and religious information, and for the maintenance of Mesopotamian culture.

For the historical era, there exist long lists of actual year names, king lists, historical chronicles, building inscriptions, and other written records—often based on or mentioning astronomical observations—that allow *absolute* dating. Yet it must be borne in mind that, for much of Mesopotamian history, accurate dates B.C. are hard to come by; sources often seem to contradict one another. More recent dates are almost always more accurate and have a lower margin of error.

C. Sources for Mesopotamian Chronology and History

1. Overview. Named after an annually appointed official, the Assyrian *limmu* ("eponym") lists make it possible to date events quite precisely back to 910 B.C. Earlier Assyrian *limmu* lists and Babylonian king lists allow us to date particular events or more general epochs during the 2d millennium B.C. within a margin of about ten years. Attempts at absolute dating in the surrounding regions (Syria-Palestine, Anatolia, Cyprus and the Aegean, Iran) require synchronization with episodes in Mesopotamia (or Egypt), where more secure chronologies have been established.

Observations of the planetary movements of Venus, possible only once in a 56- or 64-year cycle, have been recorded on the Babylonian "Venus Tablets." Although these tablets provide astronomical dates for the period prior to 1450 B.C., unfortunately they offer a series of possible dates rather than an agreed-upon single date: scholars still dispute which of three possible cycles these "Venus Tablets" refer to. Consequently, historians of the ANE must choose between three separate chronologies for 2d-millennium B.C. Babylonia: the high (the astronomical evidence presented by Huber is compelling), the middle, or the low (the low chronology finds few supporters). Although Babylonia's internal and relative chronology has been established reasonably well on the basis of year names, relative events are difficult to pinpoint in a secure, absolute dating system. Whereas the middle chronology is the most widely accepted and frequently used, in fact it provides only a compromise solution to a very complex problem. The relative sequence of events, nonetheless, offers a useful framework for the assessment of sociohistorical and sociocultural development and change.

Relative dating is well established from the 16th century B.C. back to the 24th century B.C. (the reign of Sargon and the Akkadian Dynasty). Two "historical" gaps of unknown duration occur during these 800 years, the earlier being about 2200 B.C., the latter about 1600 B.C. Although various cuneiform documents record the succession of kings and the length of their reigns, specific incidents and even entire eras remain unanchored in *absolute* time. Before 2400 B.C. in Mesopotamia, only approximate dates are possible: time estimations are derived from purely archaeological evidence, from paleographic data (the evolution of the cuneiform script in its earliest stages), and by all-too-few radiocarbon dates.

The chronology of Mesopotamia and that of much of the remainder of the ANE (especially Syria-Palestine) has been linked extensively to Egyptian *absolute* dating. During the historic period (post–3000 B.C.), written sources for dating in Egypt are similar to those found in Mesopotamia: king lists, royal annals, and biographic treatises. A "History of Egypt," written in Greek during the 3d century B.C. by an Egyptian priest (Manetho), was almost certainly compiled from some of the same lists that present-day historians use to reconstruct ancient Egyptian chronology. Although absolute dating in the earlier time periods, as in Mesopotamia, inspires less confidence, overall the period from about 330 B.C. back to 945 B.C. is reliably dated on the basis of astronomical observations, synchronisms, and the historically well dated reigns of certain pharaohs.

For the period from about 1550 to 1050 B.C., both a high and a low chronology have been postulated on the basis of astronomical observations of the Sothic star (Eg *Sepedet,* our Sirius). Noting the precise moment that this star appeared was critically important to the ancient Egyptians because it demarcated the start of their agricultural year: the annual rise of the river Nile (from melting snows in the Ethiopian and African highlands far to the south) more or less coincided with the heliacal (predawn) rising of Sothis on the horizon. Three chronologies result from the disagreement among Egyptologists over the location where these ancient observations took place. Either it occurred in the north, near Memphis (high chronology), in the south, near Thebes (middle chronology), or even farther south, at Elephantine (low chronology). Even if this dispute could be settled, the internal dating of some pharaohs' reigns is complicated by the possibility of coregencies (and thus overlaps in different reigns). Nonetheless, the margin of error for the period 1550–1050 B.C. is only a matter of 10–30 years, much less than the 120-year discrepancy in Mesopotamia.

Sesostris III, who ruled during the 19th century B.C., has a Sothic date recorded for his reign. Working backward from Sesostris, however, dating becomes increasingly uncertain because no further "fixed" points (like a Sothic date) are available to which one could attach a well-known, relatively dated sequence of events. As in Mesopotamia, archaeology, paleography, and artistic style provide at best a broad range of possibilities. Important refinements in radiocarbon-based dates for Egypt are limited chiefly to the 3d millennium B.C.

2. The 3d Millennium B.C. Mesopotamian history is divided into periods characterized by significant changes in society, economy, politics, and culture. The course of Mesopotamian history, although characterized by a recurrent trend toward local rule, was punctuated repeatedly by political systems of great organizational complexity that aimed for extensive dominion throughout the Near East. Local rule is best exemplified by Mesopotamia's most resilient sociopolitical institution: the city-state. Political control by individual city-states typified the Sumerian dynasties of the early 3d millennium B.C.

These first recorded dynasties were ruling families in various cities that passed political power from one generation to the next. As a result, the time span from about 2900 to 2350 B.C. is known as the Early Dynastic (ED) period. The chronology of this period is based primarily on archaeological data derived from excavations in the Diyala region, which can be employed only rarely to illuminate known political events. Although writing increasingly fulfilled economic, ideological, and administrative needs, archaeological excavation has provided only a limited corpus of textual evidence, and material data therefore remain central to historical interpretation. Nonetheless, such archaeological and documentary sources as exist portray ED Mesopotamian culture more clearly than that of any prehistoric period.

The main written sources for the Early Dynastic period are the following: (1) numerous cuneiform tablets from the cities of Ur, Lagash, Kish, and Shurrupak; (2) an important collection of literary tablets from Tell Abu Salabikh; and (3) detailed royal inscriptions from Lagash. The

Sumerian King List, composed early in the 2d millennium B.C., offers an important outline of the political history of Sumer and Akkad from prehistoric times; it becomes increasingly plausible as it approaches the period of its compilation. Despite its value for reconstructing Mesopotamian history, the King List is misleading in that it treats overlapping and contemporaneous city-state dynasties as successive. The remote past was difficult to render accurately, even for the conscientious chroniclers of the Sumerian King List.

With the advent of the Akkadian and Ur III dynasties during the latter half of the 3d millennium B.C., the Mesopotamian political structure shifted from localized city-state rule to territorial, nation-state rule. Dominance by the temple or city-state gave way to national monarchy, and territorial expansion became the operative goal. The task of controlling more extensive areas required administrative innovation, and here the Akkadian achievement was considerable. The Akkadians replaced the Sumerian system of diversified, local autonomy with a centralized state focused upon the king and his court at Akkad.

Different ideological and economic traditions governed the two peoples: the Sumerians' long tradition of temple and communal ownership was replaced by both royal and private ownership of land. Yet ethnic antagonism was purposefully minimized, and the Akkadians adopted the Sumerian cuneiform script to write their own Semitic language, newly dominant in Mesopotamia. Akkadians and Sumerians were two different peoples who spoke two different languages, but the prevailing culture was neither Sumerian nor Akkadian; it was overwhelmingly Mesopotamian.

In the style of most Sumerian kings, the dynastic rulers of Akkad commemorated their exploits in dedicatory inscriptions lodged at the temple of Enlil at Nippur. Although the originals still elude us, they were copied meticulously by devoted scribes: the tablets that survive are our main source for the history of the Akkadian era. These dedicatory inscriptions are supplemented by literary texts (e.g., "The Curse of Agade") and by later written documents, including the Sumerian King List. The epic tales of Sargon and his grandson Naram-Sin—the best known rulers of the Akkadian period—were written much later and mix fact with fiction. Archaeological evidence for this period is still sparse and leaves a decisive gap in our knowledge: the location of Agade—the capital city of Sargon and his successors—is still far from certain.

According to the Sumerian King List, after the fall of Akkad the city-state of Ur established dominion over Mesopotamia for the third time; consequently, its kings are known as the Ur III dynasty. Political stability returned to Mesopotamia, and in its wake followed the revival of Sumerian art, literature, and law (the so-called Sumerian Renaissance). Primary written sources for this period are abundant. Economic documents from administrative centers like Umma (near Lagash) and Puzrish-Dagan (near Nippur) number in the tens of thousands. In contrast to the scant archaeological evidence of the Akkadian period, the extensive construction projects of the Ur III rulers may be witnessed in most major Mesopotamian cities of the late 3d millennium B.C.

Although Sumerian again became the official language of the land, the concept of a Sumerian versus an Akkadian cultural identity is irrelevant. Traditional Sumerian literature was preserved, and hymns glorifying the ruler in the act of addressing the gods were composed. But the grandeur of the Sargonic state had become integrated into a broader Mesopotamian worldview, and Ur III kings adopted the titles of the Akkadian kings. Ur-Nammu, founder of the Ur III dynasty, claimed the title "King of Sumer and Akkad," and thus officially acknowledged Mesopotamia's composite origins: Sumerian and Akkadian culture were fused into one Mesopotamian civilization.

3. The 2d Millennium B.C. The term Mesopotamia refers not only to the culture of the Tigris-Euphrates region but also to the geographic region demarcated by the two rivers. During the 2d millennium B.C., Mesopotamia became divided into two historically important geopolitical regions: Babylonia and Assyria. Because the city of Babylon only became a significant political force early in the 2d millennium B.C., the geographic term Babylonia should not be used to refer to earlier time periods. For the 2d and 1st millennia B.C., the N and NE sectors of "Mesopotamia" may also be referred to as Assyria, the S sector as Babylonia. The two parts are divided by the Gebel Ḥamrīn ("Red Mountain"), a low-lying mountain ridge that extends southeastward from the Assyrian capital city of Ashur to the Diyala River basin.

Historical sources multiply greatly during the 2d millennium B.C. Thousands of cuneiform tablets have been excavated in Babylonia, N Syria, and Anatolia (Turkey). King lists from Isin, Larsa, Ashur, and Babylon, and lists of date formulae—whereupon each year of a king's reign was given a name—provide synchronisms as well as a useful chronological framework. From Babylon and Ashur in Mesopotamia, Mari and Alalakh in Syria, and Kanesh and Ḥattusha in Anatolia come international treaties, letters, accounts, contracts, and legal documents that illuminate the period between 1900 and 1600 B.C. like few others in ANE history. For the period of Kassite rule in Babylonia (about 1600–1200 B.C.), source materials become scarce; fewer than a thousand tablets have been published, although thousands more exist in museum collections.

The widespread, albeit insecure, political coalitions forged by Shamshi-Adad of Assyria (ca. 1813–1781) and Ḥammurapi of Babylonia (ca. 1792–1750) resulted in two extensive and partly contemporaneous territorial states. Emulating the Akkadian and Ur III dynasties, these two rulers sought to acquire territory and to secure the constant flow of vital raw materials into the bountiful but resource-barren alluvial plain of Mesopotamia. This reemergence of forcefully unified nation-states in Assyria and Babylonia may be attributed chiefly to the great military and administrative capabilities and the charismatic qualities of Shamshi-Adad and Ḥammurapi. Although both rulers failed to establish an enduring national state, the political power and cultural tradition in ancient Mesopotamia henceforth centered on these two polities. Even the later Kassites, who built their own fortress-city near Babylon, maintained the latter as their political, commercial, and religious center.

Historical and cultural developments in neighboring Syria-Palestine between 2000 and 1500 B.C. have been reconstructed largely through reference to Babylonian or

Egyptian documentary sources; cuneiform texts from Mari, Ugarit, or Alalakh illuminate events chiefly in N Syria. During these centuries, Amorite influence and domination expanded throughout the Levant and extended into the Egyptian Delta. Although other political crosscurrents dashed hopes of overall unity, individual Levantine city-states prospered as international trading contacts blossomed. The coastal position and port cities of the Levant (e.g., Ugarit, Byblos, Tyre) helped to make that area the commercial crossroads of the ANE by about 1500 B.C. Although the area also became a military battleground for its more powerful neighbors, local political control in Syria-Palestine was enriched by lucrative international trade. The most important cultural contribution of the area in the mid-2d millennium B.C. was the creation of an alphabet—a writing system that would replace the more complex and unwieldy Mesopotamian cuneiform and Egyptian hieroglyphic systems, and eventually be adopted the world over.

The fluctuating political fortunes of myriad Near Eastern states between about 1500 and 1200 B.C. can only be understood in an international context. Cuneiform letters found at Amarna in Egypt are international diplomatic documents, and similar texts sprang up at sites all over ancient W Asia. For the first time, and with lasting consequences, Egypt shared this international stage with the powerful states of Babylonia and Assyria and the Hittite kingdom in Anatolia. Whereas Cyprus and the Bronze Age cultures of the Aegean (the Minoans and Mycenaeans) played key roles in international trade within the E Mediterranean system, the scarcity of detailed and comprehensive written sources from those quarters means that their political and economic relationship to Near Eastern states can only be established archaeologically.

The complex interaction and shifting balance of power among all of these LB Age states and kingdoms impinged significantly upon the Levant. The positive impact of international trade and politics on the Levantine city-states, however, was balanced and ultimately offset by internal social change and population dynamics. These international and local events are highlighted by the above-mentioned Amarna Letters, one of the most significant finds of cuneiform tablets ever made. Discovered in 1887 at Akhenaten's capital in Middle Egypt, the Amarna Letters provide unparalleled insight into international diplomacy and commercial contact during the 14th century B.C. With few exceptions, the tablets may be dated to the reigns of Amenophis III or IV (Akhenaten). Forty-two of the approximately 380 tablets retrieved were letters exchanged between the pharaoh and the kings of Babylonia, Assyria, Mitanni (the Hurrians), Hittite Anatolia, Arzawa (a small state in Anatolia), and Cyprus.

Several Amarna documents list lavish gifts exchanged between royal courts. Envoys were entrusted with delicate political and diplomatic missions as well as the safe conduct of great riches. The immense variety and quantity of goods, and the frequency of such exchanges, suggest that what is described was not just the exchange of royal gifts but the basic mechanism of trade between Egypt and its neighbors: messengers were merchants as well as ambassadors. Despite strong foreign influence in the Levant at this time, the Amarna Letters and other cuneiform sources convey the impression that local dynasts effectively governed most Syro-Palestinian city-states. The Amarna Letters—the single most important source for interpreting internal politics during the mid-2d millennium B.C.—imply that the Syrian state of Amurru formed a successful, independent political movement based on popular support.

The Amarna archives also describe an omnipresent, socially restive group of people who spread throughout the Near East during the 2d millennium B.C.: the *Ḫapiru.* The fact that one could "become a Ḫapiru"—as the Amarna Letters state frequently—implies a lack of kinship or political ties; indeed, the *Ḫapiru* seem to include groups of differing ethnic composition, expatriate fugitives from various city-states and tribal communities. Some *Ḫapiru* served as mercenaries; others formed independent communal or semitribal organizations on the borders of settled areas, often in the hill and forest country of Syria-Palestine. Subject to no legal authority, the *Ḫapiru* endured on the outskirts of urban centers, where they maintained a fragile independence. The historical relationship between the social term *Ḫapiru* and the ethnic term "Hebrew" finds several defenders. Although the *Ḫapiru* were too broad and mixed a social group to be considered direct ancestors of the Hebrews, it is not improbable that some Hebrews were to be found among the *Ḫapiru.* Both were people without a homeland, members of an inferior class often feared and held in contempt by sedentary populations.

By the end of the LB Age (13th–12th centuries B.C.), a sequence of population movements, invasions, and destructions altered forever the essentially cooperative international relations that had been enjoyed by major and minor political states alike throughout much of the 2d millennium B.C. A combination of demographic, economic, climatic, and military factors accounts for the subsequent disorder throughout the Mediterranean.

4. The 1st Millennium B.C. Under the Assyrian kings of the first millennium B.C. and their Persian successors, the Mesopotamian trend toward organizational complexity and territorial expansion reached its peak. Local rule by city-states or more extensive rule by territorial states gave way to a highly centralized direct rule by empire. Starting around 1300 B.C. in Mesopotamia, the annals of the Assyrian kings—often regarded as proper historiographic documents—record basic geographic and tactical information about military campaigns. These annals also assign and criticize motives, appraise political events and individuals, and generalize about foreign peoples and lands.

Source materials for the 1st millennium B.C. are extensive; the annals of the Assyrian rulers and other royal inscriptions (Assyrian and Babylonian); hymns and paeans of praise (archives from Nineveh, Ashur, Kalhu, and Babylon); the *limmu* lists (already mentioned), which identify the regnal years of most Neo-Assyrian kings and occasionally refer to a campaign or a disaster that occurred during a particular year; dedicatory inscriptions of both Assyrian and Babylonian potentates, which praise the deeds and achievements of kings and gods alike; Babylonian chronicles that detail episodes (battles, treaties, deaths in the royal family) in a variation on the annalistic theme. Several Old Persian (cuneiform) inscriptions (some monumental in form) document selected events from the reigns of several Achaemenid rulers in Persia. The (mostly unpublished) astronomical diaries of Babylonia record—on a daily basis—death, plagues, and other calamities, exclusively as an appendix to the observation of planetary movements.

During the reign of the early Chaldean ("Neo-Babylonian") king Nabonassar (747–734 B.C.), certain events began to be recorded precisely and astronomical observations were noted accurately. The Greeks would later recognize Nabonassar's rule as pivotal in the development of science: the Gk word *Chaldean* came to mean "astronomer." An astronomical series of omens (entitled MUL.APIN—dated about 700 B.C. but based on earlier material) records the movements of the moon and planets. Although this series and other early efforts of Babylonian astronomy were somewhat superficial, after about 700 B.C. systematic stellar observations generated data that were calculated accurately enough to predict solstices, equinoxes, eclipses, and other planetary phenomena.

Chaldean astronomers also sorted out an elaborate, mathematical time-keeping system based on the number 60 (sexagesimal); ultimately this led to the division of hours and minutes still in use today. Because each Babylonian month began with the sighting of the new (crescent) moon, astronomers had to be able to predict this event accurately. Astronomers in the 3d and 2d centuries B.C., therefore, composed ephemerides that calculated and predicted new moons, eclipses, and other planetary and lunar movements. The rules for such calculations were outlined in accompanying documents called "procedure texts." Modern astronomers rank the methods developed by their Babylonian precursors to calculate the movements of the moon among the highest achievements of ancient science. It must be added that religious motives were predominant in Babylonian astronomy: the heavens were mapped and the ephemerides composed in order to elicit divine intentions.

The appearances of astrological omens based on astronomical observations date from the very beginning of the 2d millennium B.C., and were later grouped in series (e.g., *Enūma Anu Enlil*). The earliest-known systematic astronomical observations (of the planet Venus) date from the Old Babylonian (OB) period (18th–17th centuries B.C.). Intended to serve as a basis for omens, these "Venus Tablets" (discussed earlier) were not highly accurate but maintain a significant role in determining the chronology of the 2d millennium B.C. By the 7th century B.C., more accurate astronomical observations led to the development of a fairly precise calendar. Because the Babylonian month was lunar, each year comprised only 354 days; approximately every third year an extra month had to be inserted to bring the lunar calendar into line with the solar year. By the reign of the Chaldean king Nabu-Naṣir (757 B.C.), a regular, mathematically derived intercalation of seven months every nineteen years had been established. Known as the Metonic Cycle, this calendar served as the basis of the later Jewish and Christian religious calendars.

While the aims of the astronomers were religious, their methods were genuinely scientific, and their computations became instrumental in the invention of horoscopic astrology and the zodiac. At first, astrological omens were interpreted only with reference to the future of the country and its ruler. Horoscopic astrology, however, necessitated some technique whereby celestial phenomena could be related to individuals; that technique was the zodiac. By the 5th century B.C., the zodiacal belt had been divided into twelve zodiacal signs of 30 degrees each, a reformulation inspired by the schematic division of the year into twelve 30-day months (used in the 7th-century B.C. MUL.APIN text). Although Hellenistic Greeks were once credited with developing horoscopic astrology, the earliest-known Greek horoscope is dated 62 B.C.; the first-known Babylonian example was cast for a child born 29 April, 410 B.C., and at least four other examples are known from the 3d century B.C.

The division of the hour into minutes originated in Babylonia, but the division of the day into hours reflects both Babylonian and Egyptian influences. The Egyptians divided the period from sunrise to sunset into twelve parts, unequal because the length of the "hours" depended on the season of the year. Babylonian days consisted of twelve "double hours," each of which contained sixty "double minutes." Babylonian astronomers ultimately divided the entire day and night into six parts of equal and constant length for computational and observational purposes. Hellenistic astronomers adopted this subdivision of day and night into equal parts, and further divided the twelve double hours into twenty-four units. This division was comparable to that of the Egyptians, except that each unit now had equal length; and so the twenty-four-hour day came into being.

D. Conclusion

The science of astronomy directly influenced astrology, certain mathematical computations, and even the subdivision of the hour and day. Astronomy is Babylonia's most direct legacy and the only branch of ancient science to have survived the collapse of the Roman Empire.

The people of ancient Mesopotamia exhibited little sense of history as it is understood today. Royal annals and king lists served to glorify rulers or to legitimize their rule; year-dates were bureaucratic records, nothing more. Only by linking such "historical" records to more "neutral" events—e.g., the observance and registry of certain planets—is it possible to provide absolute B.C. calendar dates.

The attempt to synchronize specific happenings in diverse areas—especially in Syria-Palestine or Cyprus where finds of written records are quite limited—is a complex and arduous task that demands a high level of competence in diverse fields (archaeology, Assyriology, and astronomy, to mention but a few). Given such a situation, historians of the ANE can only offer what seems to be a plausible reconstruction of events, founded on detailed research into a variety of cultural materials. The resultant historical scenarios are tentative and will have to be readjusted and rewritten as more archaeological and documentary evidence accumulates.

Bibliography

Astour, M. C. 1989. *Hittite History and Absolute Chronology of the Bronze Age.* Studies in Mediterranean Archaeology and Literature 73. Partille.

Åström, P., ed. 1987. *High, Middle or Low?* 2 pts. Studies in Mediterranean Archaeology, Pocketbook 56–57. Göteborg.

Aurenche, O.; Evin, J.; and Hours, F., eds. 1987. *Chronologies du Proche Orient/Chronologies in the Near East. Relative Chronologies and Absolute Chronology 16,000–4,000 B.P.* BARIS 379. Oxford.

Carter, E., and Stolper, M. W. 1986. *Elam: Surveys of Political History and Archaeology.* UCPNES 25. Berkeley.

Gates, M.-H. 1987. Alalakh and Chronology Again. Pp. 60–86 in Åström 1987.

Harding, A. F., and Tait, W. J. 1989. "The Beginning of the End": Progress and Prospects in Old World Chronology. *Antiquity* 63/238: 147–52.

Hassan, F. A., and Robinson, S. W. 1987. High-precision Radiocarbon Chronometry of Ancient Egypt, and Comparisons with Nubia, Palestine and Mesopotamia. *Antiquity* 61/231: 119–35.

Hendrickson, R. C. 1985. The Chronology of Central Western Iran 2600–1400 B.C. *AJA* 89: 569–81.

Henige, D. 1986. Comparative Chronology and the Near East: A Case for Symbiosis. *BASOR* 261: 57–68.

Huber, P. J. 1987. Astronomical Evidence for the Long and Against the Middle and Short Chronologies. Pp. 5–17 in P. Åström 1987.

Huber, P. J., et al. 1982. *Astronomical Dating of Babylon I and Ur III.* Occasional Papers on the Near East 1/4. Malibu.

James, P. J., et al. 1987. *Studies in Ancient Chronology I: Bronze to Iron Age Chronology in the Old World: Time for a Reassessment?* London.

Knapp, A. B. 1988. *The History and Culture of Ancient Western Asia and Egypt.* Chicago.

Kuniholm, P. I., and Striker, C. L. 1987. Dendrochronological Investigations in the Aegean and Neighboring Regions. *JFA* 14: 385–98.

Leonard, A., Jr. 1988. Some Problems Inherent in Mycenaean/Syro-Palestinian Synchronisms. Pp. 319–31 in *Problems in Greek Prehistory,* ed., E. B. French and K. A. Wardle. Bristol.

Manning, S. 1988. The Bronze Age Eruption of Thera: Absolute Dating, Aegean Chronology, and Mediterranean Cultural Interrelations. *Journal of Mediterranean Archaeology* 1/1: 17–82.

Moore, A. M. T., et al. 1986. Radiocarbon Accelerator (AMS) Dates for the Epipaleolithic Settlement at Abu Hureyra, Syria. *Radiocarbon* 28/3: 1068–76.

Neugebauer, O. 1975. *A History of Ancient Mathematical Astronomy.* 3 vols. Studies in the History of Mathematics and Physical Sciences 1. Berlin.

Nissen, H. J. 1988. *The Early History of the Ancient Near East, 9000–2000 B.C.* Chicago.

Oppenheim, A. L. 1977. *Ancient Mesopotamia.* Chicago. Rev. ed. E. Reiner.

Redman, C. L. 1978. *The Rise of Civilization: From Early Farmers to Urban Society in the Near East.* San Francisco.

Reiner, E., and Pingree, D. 1975. *The Venus Tablet of Ammisaduqa.* BiMes 2/1. Malibu.

———. 1981. *Babylonian Planetary Omens.* Pt. 2, *Enuma Anu Enlil.* BiMes 2/2. Malibu.

Rochberg-Halton, F. 1987. *Aspects of Babylonian Celestial Divination: The Lunar Eclipse Tablets of Enuma Anu Enlil. AfO* Beiheft 22. Horn, Austria.

Saggs, H. W. F. 1989. *Civilization Before Greece and Rome.* New Haven.

Schmandt-Besserat, D. 1986. The Origins of Writing—An Archaeologist's Perspective. *Written Communication* 3/1: 33–45.

Shendge, M. J. 1985. The Inscribed Calculi and the Invention of Writing. *JESHO* 28: 50–80.

Weinstein, J. 1984. Radiocarbon Dating in the Southern Levant. *Radiocarbon* 26: 297–366.

Wilhelm, G., and Boese, J. 1987. Absolute Chronologie und die hethitische Geschichte des 15. und 14. Jahrhunderts v. Chr. Pp. 74–117 in Åström 1987.

A. BERNARD KNAPP

PREHISTORY OF MESOPOTAMIA

Southwest Asia must necessarily have been traversed by early people moving between Africa, Europe, and the Far East. To date, the earliest archaeological site with evidence of economic and social organization is that at ʿUbeidiyah in the valley of the Jordan river. When the site was occupied (about 800,000 years ago), the region was a humid steppe with a range of large herbivores. In the successive levels of this site were found varying proportions of chipped stone tools such as scrapers, utilized flakes, choppers, and rough bifaces, perhaps indicating variations in foraging activities (Bar-Yosef 1989). Occasional surface finds of such tools in the Tigris-Euphrates region indicate that such sites must also exist there (Smith 1986).

A. The First Mesopotamians: The Paleolithic Foragers
B. The First Villagers and the First Steps Toward Animal Domestication
C. Developed Village Societies of the 8th Millennium B.C.
D. The Impact of Irrigation on the Tigris-Euphrates Floodplain
E. The First Hierarchical Societies of the Early 6th Millennium B.C.
F. Developed Hierarchical Societies of the 5th Millennium B.C.
G. The First States of the 4th Millennium B.C.

A. The First Mesopotamians: The Paleolithic Foragers

It is only for the last glacial age, less than 100,000 years ago, that there is even a fragmentary archaeological record for foraging peoples in the valleys of the Zagros mountains bordering the Mesopotamian lowlands. The Middle Paleolithic Mousterian technologies, used until about 40,000 years ago, were based on amorphous stone flakes and produced expedient tools whose shape was apparently dictated by relatively simple handles and repeated resharpening. The people who used these technologies successfully hunted wild goats, cattle, and red deer (Hole and Flannery 1967).

Though the succeeding Upper Paleolithic peoples used a technology based on prismatic blades struck from carefully prepared cores and produced a range of standardized tools, there is no evidence that Upper Paleolithic peoples were more successful as hunters. Though we have bone tools from the earlier Baradostian assemblages (dating about 40,000 to 20,000 years ago) and both these and grinding stones from the later Zarzian assemblages (dating about 20,000 to 11,000 years ago), the Zagros sites have yielded no direct evidence of the more elaborated clothing or increased use of plant foods reported from other areas. Similarly, there is little evidence of social or ritual organization. This dearth is surely a result of the lack of recent fieldwork on Paleolithic sites in Mesopotamia (Smith 1986).

B. The First Villagers and the First Steps Toward Animal Domestication

By the end of the glacial period, the Zagros and Taurus foothills had not only the wild ancestors of goats, sheep, cattle, and pig but also stands of wild barley and einkorn wheat, which grew amidst the oak and pistachio forests as they proliferated in the warmer and more humid early postglacial climate (H. E. Wright 1976). It seems unlikely that the final Paleolithic peoples, those who used the microblade Zarzian technologies, would ignore such resources, but the evidence is slim. Our earliest evidence of extensive plant use is from village sites well south of the foothills along the Middle Euphrates of what is now Syria.

Here, at the sites of Mureybit and Abu Hureya, dating during the 10th millennium B.C. (Moore 1979), were seasonal settlements of perhaps 40 houses, at first oval but later with rectangular rooms, with associated grain-parching ovens and grain-storage facilities. The exploited grain was an einkorn wheat *(Triticum monococcum),* which retained the ability of wild plants to freely disperse seed (Flannery 1973); but the quantities of sickles present on the sites indicate that grain, whether wild or maintained by human cultivation, was systematically harvested. All animal bones discarded in these villages, however, were from hunted wild forms.

The first indications of the human manipulation of wild animals are sheep bones from the Zagros mountain cave of Shanidar. This site is outside of the normal range of sheep, and had been used for millennia by goat hunters. The herding of sheep in no way different from wild sheep *(Ovis aries)* at Shanidar is dated to the 10th millennium B.C. (Perkins 1964). Dating to the mid-9th millennium, and also located in the high Zagros, Ganj Darreh was a small hamlet of rectangular houses with evidence of the herding of goats little different from wild goats *(Capra hircus)* in the form of young goat bones (and even tracks imprinted in mud surfaces) and stocks of dung (Smith 1978).

We do not yet know exactly when and under what conditions the early experiments with grains and animals were combined to form a mutually reinforcing system of plant and animal domestication (Hole 1984), but there is evidence of this about 8500 B.C. (7500 b.c.) at sites such as Ali Kosh in the S Zagros foothills (Flannery 1969) and Cayonu in the Taurus foothills (Braidwood et al. 1981). All of these earliest villages in greater Mesopotamia are marked by small house complexes with a few rooms showing little variation from house to house. This pattern, coupled with the occurrence of burials in which only a few ornaments and personal items are found with some adults, implies that the first farmers had relatively egalitarian social patterns. The occasional occurrence of rare materials such as obsidian, turquoise, sea shells, and cold-hammered native copper in various sites far from their sources indicates that these scattered communitities were connected by reciprocal exchanges of gifts (Renfrew and Dixon 1976).

C. Developed Village Societies of the 8th Millennium B.C.

Whatever the social patterns of the first sedentary villages of the Near East, it has long been clear that by about 8000 B.C. (7000 b.c.), at least in the Levant and Anatolia, settlement systems indicate social differentiation. In contrast to the smaller village communities were larger communities such as Tell es-Sultan (Jericho) in the Jordan valley and Cayonu in the Taurus foothills near the Tigris' headwaters. By the end of the millennium, even larger sites such as ᶜAin Ghazal in the hills of Transjordan (Rollefson and Simmons 1987) and Çatal Hüyük in central Anatolia (Mellaart 1967; Todd 1976) had emerged. These larger settlements have evidence of community labor in public construction; diverse production activities, including indications that some people specialized in craft production; seemingly larger quantities of discarded exotic goods gained in exchange; and much evidence of shrines and social ritual activity. So far as one can tell, however, there was neither differentiation in household wealth beyond what is expected from personal achievement nor indications of the inheritance of social status in the mortuary evidence from these sites.

D. The Impact of Irrigation on the Tigris-Euphrates Floodplain

A transformation in food production is manifest in the middle reaches of the Tigris and Euphrates valleys shortly after 7000 B.C. (6000 b.c.). Dry farming—the cultivation of wheat (*Triticum* sp.), barley (*Hordeum* sp.), and pulses with the naturally available resources of rainfall and soils and the herding of goats (*Capra* sp.), sheep (*Ovis* sp.), and, in favored areas, pigs (*Sus* sp.) and cows (*Bos* sp.)—had been pushed beyond the limits of dependable rainfall, as indicated by the massive storage facilities of sites such as Umm Dabaghiyah in the Jazirah of Iraq, south of the 250-mm isohyet (Kirkbride 1973). In a few settlements east and south of the Jazirah along the middle reaches of the Euphrates and the Tigris, communities of the Samarran culture, we find direct evidence of irrigation farming. Forms of barley and bread wheat, which are better suited to the water-rich situation provided by irrigation, and larger seeded versions of oil-rich flax, thought to be produced only with irrigation, are attested at a number of sites. A small canal has been sectioned near the Samarran and post-Samarran village of Choga Mami (Oates and Oates 1976). Evidence of the keeping of cows regularly occurs with that of the still-predominant sheep and goats in Samarran faunal assemblages, a practice effective only in the harsh summer heat of Mesopotamia if the cows have shade trees, which must also be irrigated. Cows could have been used to plow soils, though this is not directly attested before 4500 B.C., and they could have been used to increase supplies of milk products, a change suggested by the diversification of large open bowls, but also not directly attested (Flannery 1969). Whether the use of bread wheat (*Triticum aestivum)* and milk products also implies the use of domesticated microorganisms to produce such foods as yogurt, cheeses, and beer is another possibility which has not yet been demonstrated. However, the documented changes alone indicate that food production had been fundamentally transformed, establishing patterns of diet which would predominate until rice, chickens, and water buffalo were introduced around the 1st millennium B.C.

Such changes in production might lead some to predict that the changes would result in the development of managerial roles and social inequality. There were definite changes in community organization, though not as many as one might expect. Most striking is the appearance of larger houses with a central hall, flanking which were a number of domestic apartments, workrooms, and storerooms (Roaf 1985). Certainly, the nuclear-family units of the early villages were being replaced by extended-family units, with a larger work force better suited to the tasks of small-scale irrigation (Flannery 1972). There is, however, no indication that any of these houses was significantly larger or more substantial than others in the community until the post-Samarran period. The one substantial mortuary series, that from Tell es-Sewwan, has almost exclusively the interments of children with marked variations in contributed objects (el-Wailly and Behnam 1965). However, this evidence can be interpreted in several ways. In sum, though the new food-production economy seems to have had an impact on family organization, there is no definite evidence that the egalitarian social patterns of early village society had been replaced by patterns of rank inequality.

Samarran agricultural and community patterns became established in both alluvial S Mesopotamia, an area where only irrigation agriculture and marsh or river collecting are possible, and SW Iran, where dry farming also can be practiced. Whether this was a result of the budding off and migration eastward of communities from the Samarran heartland or the diffusion of production practices to extant communities is still being debated. In contrast, in N Mesopotamia, though the Samarran communities had an impact on patterns of craft and style, there is no evidence of changes from early village patterns of plant and animal use or of small houses, and we have no reason to believe that farming or social organization changed greatly in the north.

E. The First Hierarchical Societies of the Early 6th Millennium B.C.

Societies which symbolized a modest degree of social inequality, with evidence of hierarchy at both the community and regional levels, are widely attested by about 5700 B.C. (5000 b.c.). Two distinct cultural spheres marked by different styles of display ceramics—broadly termed "Halaf" in N Mesopotamia and "Hajji Muhammed" in S Mesopotamia—can be characterized. If the delayed effects of irrigation on management, wealth, and social control were important in the emergence of hierarchy, we would expect such patterns of inequality to be more developed in S Mesopotamia. Though the evidence is poorer for the far south, we can assess this expectation.

Halaf ceramic styles had spread from the Mediterranean to the Diyala valley, at the edge of S Mesopotamia, by the early 6th millennium. Communities with these ceramics are also found in the Taurus and Zagros mountains, even on the shores of Lake Van. In the core region of the N Mesopotamian steppes, Halafian settlement systems are characterized by a few more elaborate centers and many undistinguished villages and camps. The documentation of modern fieldwork by British, Dutch, Iraqi, Soviet, and U.S. teams, when fully published, will enhance our knowledge of these systems. At present, the new work appears to reinforce the conclusions of Watson (1983) that the centers had shrines, differentiated residences, and associated workshops and that some families in these centers made greater use of both exotic materials, such as obsidian, and the products of Halafian specialists, such as finely crafted and decorated ceramics and stone ornaments. In contrast, the villages and camps had only modest residences and storage structures and limited access to display goods. Quantitative data on the by-products of food production have been published primarily for these smaller settlements, and thus it is difficult to assess questions of differential access to foodstuffs, though we do know that there was much variation in the basic patterns of dry farming, with hunting more important in some communities, pig husbandry more important in others, and so on. The evidence of funerals and other mortuary activity in the Halaf heartland remains limited, but at least some burials of adults and children appear to have had burial programs with redundant symbolic markers, suggesting that the more important families in the centers were ascribed their higher rank. Studies of settlement patterns indicate that the settlement clusters with their single level of emergent hierarchy were small (Oates 1980), with populations of 500 or more.

Hajji Muhammed styles mark display ceramics, typically the same larger open bowls important in Halaf assemblages, in several local systems in S Iraq and SW Iran, as well as in littorine settlements along the shores of the Persian Gulf. Though less well known than that of Halaf settlements, there is evidence of centers with both elaborate and modest architecture (Lloyd and Safar 1981) in contrast to smaller villages (Stronach 1961); and there is evidence that the elaborately decorated bowls were made in specialized shops and used more commonly by the occupants of the elaborate central buildings than by villagers (Wright 1981: 323–25). Limited faunal samples indicate that irrigation agriculture was complemented by cattle husbandry, hunting, and fishing, but quantitative information is limited. There is no mortuary information.

In brief, our present knowledge of the early 6th-millennium communities in lowland Mesopotamia suggests that similar social patterns were dependent upon very different patterns of food production. The social requisites for cooperation and the political potential for coercion inherent in irrigation were perhaps minor in the very small canal systems used in S Mesopotamia until after the rise of the first states. What, then, might explain the development of simple regional hierarchies and, perhaps, elementary ascriptive rank? One possibility, discussed years ago by Adams (1966: 48–50), is certainly conformable with such new evidence as is available from both the N and the S spheres. This is the differentiation in the bases of family wealth that arises from the stable productivity created even by small-scale irrigation, as well as from the reproductive potential of cattle herds and the bounty produced by organized marsh exploitation. Some families would thus have a heritable capacity to sustain dependents, give gifts, and acquire wives. Another possibility, regional rather than local in import, are the temptations for raiding raised by the increasing social differences between herders and cultivators that agricultural diversification would encourage (Lees and Bates 1974), and the related need for the formation of alliances between community leaders. This could, in turn, explain the broad distribution of ceramic styles associated with centers. Such propositions can only be evaluated with data from regional sequences that cover post-Samarran and early Halaf developments of the late 7th millennium, and such data are not yet available.

F. Developed Hierarchical Societies of the 5th Millennium B.C.

By 4600 B.C. (3800 b.c.), the lowlands of the Tigris-Euphrates drainage were occupied by communities participating in two new stylistic traditions, but within both of these spheres there were societies which appear to have differed in hierarchical complexity. Throughout the Tigris and Euphrates valleys, strictly speaking, and extending to the Syrian littoral of the Mediterranean, communities decorated their ceramics, and no doubt other goods, in the bold geometric style termed "ᶜUbaid." In the Karun drainage and throughout the S Zagros and adjacent Iranian plateau, communities utilized the finely drafted and more naturalistic late "Susiana" styles. Local styles were used in the N Zagros and adjacent Anatolian and Iranian plateaus.

In SE Mesopotamia—what is now S Iraq and SW Iran—communities participating in both ᶜUbaid and Susiana style spheres developed large centers, covering more than 10 hectares, with raised central areas or containing shrines, large residences, and storage facilities; modest residences are found around the raised areas. Surrounding these were smaller village- and hamlet-sized settlements whose access to the main center was mediated by smaller centers. Settlement sizes indicate that up to 12,000 people may have been united under a single center. In at least the latest of the Susiana societies (Wright 1986: 326–31), the evidence indicates that only one tenth of the seals, those with relatively complex designs, were used to authorize the closure of more than half of the stored goods. If the sealing and storage evidence argues for tribute collection by regional authorities, the occurrence of lesser quantities of centrally made fine ceramics at smaller settlements indicates the distribution of prestigious goods to local figures. Both these ceramics and some public architecture share some of the design iconography of the complex seals, probably a manifestation of an ideology of rank (ibid.), which would justify the collection of tribute for the benefit of a segregated elite. The evidence argues for something more than rank differences with local kin groups. These societies may have had emergent nobilities with two and sometimes three levels of control hierarchy. While the same kind of settlement differences occur among later ᶜUbaid communities in S Iraq (Wright 1981: 325–26), we lack the evidence of seals and sealings, there is no more complex elite iconography, and the extant mortuary evidence shows little differentiation. It is possible that hierarchy has a different ideational context along the lower Euphrates than on the plains of SW Iran. However, it is also possible that the disturbed conditions that preceded state emergence began earlier in the Mesopotamian heartland, and that formations comparable to those of the late Susiana chiefdoms will be documented when more is known about the earlier ᶜUbaid period.

In contrast to these complex social formations in the south, the N plains of Mesopotamia and the valleys of the Zagros show little evidence of large centers and elaborate settlement hierarchies. This may be a result of the masking of the major centers under the debris of later urban centers, since optimal settlement locations at river crossings and the like do not change on the steppes, as they do on the lower alluvium. At present, we have much evidence of small hamlets and villages with undifferentiated housing, some of larger rural residences with storage facilities, some of possible small centers with little differentiation of housing and burials and a single shrine group. If these represent relatively dispersed and simple social formations, how did they come to interact with S Mesopotamians and adopt nearly identical ᶜUbaid decorative styles? It would not be surprising if our understanding of N Mesopotamia during the 5th millennium were to radically alter with future regional studies.

G. The First States of the 4th Millennium B.C.

The record of cuneiform texts shows that petty dynasts, sustained in war by armies and in peace by scribes, ruled many of the cities of Mesopotamia by the middle of the 3d millennium B.C. (Nissen 1988: 125–58). However, the archaeological record indicates that societies of similar or even greater scale and complexity existed a millennium before, relatively early in the Uruk or Protoliterate period, even though recording systems rich enough to record the nuances of dynastic control did not yet exist. By about 3500 B.C., the city of Uruk on a branch of the lower Euphrates covered about 250 hectares, implying a population of 25,000 to 50,000 people (Nissen 1988). A regular distribution of large towns, small towns, and smaller rural settlements covered much of the irrigable southeastern alluvial plain (Adams 1981: 52–93; Johnson 1975; H. T. Wright 1986: 329–335) and the rain-watered NW steppes. Smaller towns were established in foothill valleys and along routes into the Taurus and Zagros mountains (Johnson 1987; H. T. Wright 1987). Throughout the Uruk cultural sphere, similar kinds of plain, standardized craft goods were produced, and buildings were built according to the same architectural standards. Administrators used similar kinds of tokens to record quantities of items (Schmandt-Bessarat 1979) and identical seals to authorize the storage of goods. Few scholars working on this period doubt that there were Uruk "states," that is, societies with specialized and internally differentiated political systems capable of forcing the obedience of citizens. However, changing governmental structures and the extent to which Mesopotamia was unified or divided up into regional or local polities at any point in time are not yet known.

Unfortunately, archaeologists can say very little about the transition from ᶜUbaid to Uruk societies. We do have evidence that the early 4th millennium was a period of conflict, population decline, and social movement, which conforms to various models of state development, but the evidence is very fragmentary. The end of the Uruk period, however, has been the object of much recent research (Finkbeiner and Röllig, eds. 1986). It is clear that post-Uruk inhabitants in the heartland of the lower alluvium carried on the technological, economic, and social patterns of Uruk times in a cultural phase termed "Jemdet Nasr," including a development of the protoliterate recording system to express not merely counts and lists but also words in a form of the Sumerian language. However, in S and SW Iran, the inhabitants participated in a different local cultural phase, termed "Banesh," developing a local urban economic and social formation using a very different "Proto-Elamite" writing system, perhaps expressing a form of the Elamite language (Sumner 1974; Alden 1982). Other culturally different groups appear in villages and towns in the N Zagros and the steppes of N Mesopotamia. The mythohistoric texts suggest that this period of cultural divergence was also one of interregional warfare, a prolegomenon to the complex political events of the 3d millennium B.C. (Adams 1966: 80–86, 122–30, 137–43; Nissen 1988: 127–97).

Bibliography

Adams, R. McC. 1966. *The Evolution of Urban Society.* Chicago.

———. 1981. *The Heartland of Cities.* Chicago.

Alden, J. R. 1982. Trade and Politics in Proto-Elamite Iran. *Current Anthropology* 23/6: 613–40.

Bar-Yosef, O. 1989. Excavations at ᶜUbeidiya in Retrospect: An Eclectic View. Pp. 101–112 in *Investigations in South Levantine Prehistory,* ed. O. Bar-Yosef and B. Vandermeersch. BARIS 497. Oxford.

Braidwood, R. J.; Cambel, H.; and Schimer, W. 1981. Beginnings of Village Farming Communities in Southeastern Turkey. *Journal of Field Archaeology* 8: 249–58.

Finkbeiner, U., and Röllig, W., eds. 1986. *Jemdet Nasr: Period or Regional Style?* BTAVO 62. Wiesbaden.

Flannery, K. V. 1969. Origins and Ecological Effects of Early Domestication in Iran and the Near East. Pp. 73–100 in *The Domestication and Exploitation of Plants and Animals,* ed. P. J. Ucko and G. W. Dimbleby. Chicago.

———. 1972. The Origins of the Village as a Settlement Type in Mesoamerica and Mesopotamia: A Comparative Study. In *Man, Settlement and Urbanism,* ed. P. J. Ucko, R. Tringham, and G. W. Dimbleby. Cambridge, MA.

———. 1973. The Origins of Agriculture. *Annual Review of Anthropology* 2: 271–310.

Hole, F. 1984. A Reassessment of the Neolithic Revolution. *Paleorient* 10/2: 49–60.

Hole, F., and Flannery, K. V. 1967. The Prehistory of Southwestern Iran: A Preliminary Report. *Proceedings of the Prehistoric Society* 33: 147–206.

Johnson, G. A. 1975. Locational Analysis and the Investigation of Uruk Local Exchange Systems. Pp. 285–331 in *Ancient Civilizations and Trade,* ed. C. C. Lamberg-Karlovsky and J. A. Sabloff. Albuquerque.

———. 1987. Changing Organization of Uruk Administration of the Susiana Plain. Pp. 107–39 in *Archaeological Perspectives on Western Iran,* ed. F. Hole. Washington, DC.

Kirkbride, D. 1973. Umm Dabaghiyyah 1972. *Iraq* 35: 1–8.

Lees, S., and Bates, D. 1974. The Origins of Specialized Nomadic Pastoralism. *American Antiquity* 39/2: 187–93.

Lloyd, S., and Safar, F. 1981. *Eridu.* Baghdad.

Mellaart, J. 1967. *Çatal Hüyük: A Neolithic Town in Anatolia.* New York.

Moore, A. 1979. A Pre-Neolithic Farmer's Village on the Euphrates. *Scientific American* 241 (August): 62–70.

Nissen, H. J. 1988. *The Early History of the Ancient Near East.* Chicago.

Oates, D., and Oates, J. 1976. Early Irrigation Agriculture in Mesopotamia. Pp. 109–35 in *Problems in Economic and Social Archaeology,* ed. G. Sieveking, I. H. Longworth, and K. E. Wilson. London.

Oates, J. 1980. Land Use and Population in Prehistoric Mesopotamia. Pp. 303–14 in *L'Archéologie de l'Iraq,* ed. M.-T. Barrelet. Paris.

———. 1983. ᶜUbaid Mesopotamia Reconsidered. Pp. 251–81 in *The Hilly Flanks and Beyond,* ed. T. C. Young Jr. Chicago.

Perkins, D. 1964. Prehistoric Fauna from Shanidar Cave. *Science* 144: 1565–66.

Renfrew, C., and Dixon, J. 1976. Obsidian in Western Asia: A Review. Pp 137–50 in *Problems in Economic and Social Archaeology,* ed. G. Sieveking, I. H. Longworth, and K. E. Wilson. London.

Roaf, M. 1985. ᶜUbaid Temples and Houses. *Sumer* 43: 89–92.

Rollefson, G., and Simmons, A. 1987. The Life and Death of ᶜAin Ghazal. *Archaeology* 40/6: 38–40.

Schmandt-Bessarat, D. 1979. An Archaic Recording System in the Uruk-Jemdet Nasr Period. *AJA* 83: 19–46.

Smith, P. 1978. An Interim Report on Ganj Darreh Tepe. *AJA* 82: 538–40.

———. 1986. *Paleolithic Archaeology in Iran.* Philadelphia.

Stronach, D. 1961. Ras al-ᶜAmiyah. *Iraq* 23: 195–237.

Sumner, W. A. 1974. Excavations at Tall-i Malyan 1971–72. *Iran* 12: 155–80.

Todd, I. A. 1976. *Çatal Hüyük in Perspective.* Menlo Park, CA.

Wailly, F. el-, and Behnam, A. S., 1965. Excavations at Tell es-Sewwan *Sumer* 21: 17–32.

Watson, P. J. 1983. The Halafian Culture: A Review and Synthesis. Pp. 231–50 in *The Hilly Flanks and Beyond,* ed. T. C. Young Jr. Chicago.

Wright, H. E. 1976. The Environmental Setting for Plant Domestication in the Near East. *Science* 194: 385–89.

Wright, H. T. 1981. The Southern Margins of Sumer. Pp. 295–346 in Adams 1981.

———. 1986. The Evolution of Civilizations. Pp. 323–65 in *American Archaeology Past and Future,* ed. D. J. Meltzer, D. Fowler, and J. A. Sabloff. Washington, DC.

———. 1987. The Susiana Hinterlands. Pp. 141–55 in *Archaeological Perspectives on Western Iran,* ed. F. Hole. Washington, DC.

H. T. WRIGHT

MESOPOTAMIA IN THE THIRD MILLENNIUM B.C.

An account of the early history of Mesopotamia must unavoidably begin with a reference, however brief, to the prehistoric age. By the middle of the 4th millennium B.C., the people known as Sumerians (probably indigenous to the area) developed a highly advanced and successful culture in the lower section of the Mesopotamian alluvium. This culture was dubbed "Uruk" after the name of their largest and most important city. Best known for such epoch-making achievements as urbanism and the invention of writing, the Uruk people also succeeded in establishing a network of commercial enclaves in the neighboring territories, including the upper section of the alluvium, the Susiana plain in Khustistan, the Diyala region, N Syria, most of Upper Mesopotamia, sections of Anatolia, and perhaps even the Nile Delta (Algaze 1986: 30–86; Postgate 1986; Sürenhagen 1986). The degree of influence these enclaves exercised over the periphery was uneven, ranging from outright colonization, as was clearly the case in the upper section of the alluvium, the Diyala region, and the Susiana, to cooperative ventures with the local population, as may have been the case in Upper Mesopotamia and

Anatolia. In terms of its impact, however, this expansion affected the periphery fairly uniformly, greatly accelerating the state-formation processes throughout the whole area.

The Uruk expansion came to an end during the last phase of the Uruk IV period or at the beginning of the Uruk III (= Jemdet Nasr) period, at the very latest (ca. 3100). At that time, the enclave network completely collapsed and the S influence waned in the periphery. Concomitant with this development was the reassertion of indigenous traditions throughout that area and the emergence there of local power structures.

As a result of these momentous changes, there developed, sometime during the Early Dynastic I period (ca. 2900–2750), a completely new power structure on the Mesopotamian alluvium. In this new picture, which was to remain largely unchanged for over a millennium, the Sumerian influence was confined primarily to the lower section of the alluvium—the historic land of Sumer or S Babylonia. The upper section of the alluvium—the land of Akkad or N Babylonia, extending N of Nippur as far as modern Baghdad—became the home of the Semitic Akkadians. Although the Semites (but not necessarily Akkadians) may already have lived in N Babylonia for centuries, coexisting peacefully with the Sumerian settlers, it was probably only in the Early Dynastic (ED) I period that this region, like other peripheral territories impacted by the Uruk expansion, saw the development of a native political and economic system. Significantly, this system was largely independent of and markedly different from the structures existing at that time in S Babylonia. The differences in the organization of the S and N proved very enduring, and it will not be an exaggeration to say that the subsequent history of Babylonia, down to at least 1500 B.C., was shaped to a large extent by the contrasting nature of the two systems. It is necessary, therefore, to draw at this point a brief sketch of both systems, with an implicit understanding that what is offered is a simplified, ideal model; the real picture involved much shading and overlapping, especially in the middle area of the alluvium where the S and N influences met.

The key characteristic feature of the S system was the institution of city-states. Although it is clear that the origin of the city-state must have been exceedingly ancient, certainly going back to the Uruk period, the lack of pertinent information makes it impossible to tell exactly how this institution came about.

In its classic form, the southern city-state was a clearly demarcated territorial unit, comprising a major city, the state's capital, and the surrounding countryside, with its towns and villages. The city-states bordered contiguously on one another, and there was little, if any, neutral space between them.

According to the official ideology, the city-state was the private property of an extended divine family. The main god, the head of the family, was the de facto proprietor of the whole state. At the same time, he—together with his spouse and children—owned as his exclusive domain the capital city and its surroundings. Junior deities owned smaller domains, centered upon towns and villages.

The divine families of all the city-states were united into one very large extended family, with Enlil, god of Nippur, occupying the position of the *paterfamilias*. Because of his rank, Enlil exercised lordship over the whole S. In this role, he served as an arbitrator in conflicts, especially border disputes, between individual city-states.

The single most important point about the city-state ideology is that the S was viewed as a closed political system, with the assumed existence of permanent, divinely sanctioned borders between the individual city-states. Obviously, this tenet made any form of territorial expansion within the system exceedingly difficult, rendering any notion of unification theoretically unthinkable.

The rule over the city-state was exercised by an official called an *énsi*, whose office combined both secular and religious duties. The *énsi* functioned as an earthly representative of the city-god, with their relationship being comparable to that existing between the steward of an estate and its absentee owner. In theory, the *énsi* was selected by the god from among the whole citizenry of the city-state, and he had to be divinely reappointed each year.

The society was envisaged as a single temple community, with all its members standing in the same subservient relationship toward the god. Class and social distinctions were comparatively unimportant, with the stratification being based on wealth rather than on origin. These features, and the fact that the level of social mobility was surprisingly high, gave the south a distinctly egalitarian character. Very significantly, chattel slavery was virtually unknown.

For its economy, the city-state depended on the decentralized system of self-sufficient temple households, which controlled most of the state's resources, most notably nearly all of its agricultural land. Private ownership of land was insignificant and seems to have been confined to orchards. In fact, the private sector as a whole was weak and poorly developed.

Turning now to the organization of N Babylonia, we note at the outset that until quite recently the growth of civilization in that region was viewed basically as a process of aculturation by which the seminomadic population of the north was brought into the orbit of the superior Sumerian civilization. Hence the view, still common in the literature, of the north as an extension, somewhat belated in its development, of the south. Today, however, owing primarily to the discovery of the Ebla archives, N Babylonia emerges as a phenomenon in its own right, whose development was contemporaneous with and largely independent of that of its S neighbor (Gelb 1981: 52–73). Moreover, it becomes clear that this development was part of a much larger picture which also involved N Syria, the Diyala region, and perhaps even Upper Mesopotamia. This dramatic change of perspective forces us to consider that, as far as its society and economy were concerned, N Babylonia gravitated primarily to the W, and that it was there, rather than in the S, that one should look for the origins of its institutions.

To begin with the question of the N government, the most striking fact is that the N seems never to have developed a system of independent city-states even remotely comparable to that of the S. On the contrary, there are strong reasons to believe that during the ED II and III periods (ca. 2750–2300) N Babylonia formed, for most of the time, a single territorial state, whose gravity point usually remained at Kish. The qualification "usually" that was just applied to the role of Kish is necessary, for we know that the political landscape of the N involved two other major powers, Mari and Akshak, which actively competed with Kish for the control of N Babylonia. And, if we can trust the testimony of the "Sumerian King List" (henceforth SKL), on at least two occasions first Mari and then Akshak actually achieved ascendancy over Kish (Jacobsen 1939: 103–7).

The reason why the N followed this particular path of development finds explanation in the distinctive character of its kingship, which was strong, authoritarian, and predominantly secular. As such, it sharply contrasted with the S kingship, which, as noted earlier, was generally weak and had an unmistakable religious character.

Although the N kingship may have had its ultimate roots in tribal reality (Moorey 1978: 165), its more immediate source probably was a city-based oligarchy, of the type known from Ebla and Mari. It is characteristic that, while extended families were a conspicuous feature of the N social landscape, tribes were not, thus attesting to the antiquity and strength of urbanism in that region.

As compared with the S society, the N one appears to have been more rigidly stratified. In particular, there is convincing linguistic evidence that the institutions of chattel slavery and villeinage had been part of the N reality long before they appeared in the S.

The contrast with the S continued in the sphere of economy, for there, too, the N displayed some marked differences. Most significant, the temple domain, so characteristic of the S economy, seems to have been of only marginal importance in the N, with the dominant economic institutions there being the palace and the private household. The considerable role of the private sector in the N is in fact striking, and must justly be considered one of the characteristic features of its economy.

The N system just described appears to have become operative sometime during the ED I period. To roughly this time one should also date the founding of the Kishite kingdom. Based on such evidence as the fact that SKL names Kish as the first dynasty after the flood (Jacobsen 1939: 77–85), and on the historical tradition describing the struggles of Uruk with the Kishite kings En-mebaragesi and Agga (Jacobsen 1957: 116–18), one can conclude that Kish exercised considerable influence in the S during the ED II period, and perhaps even during ED IIIb (ca. 2750–2600). The case of the Kishite king Mesilim, who, two or three generations before Ur-Nanshe of Lagash (ca. 2500), arbitrated a territorial dispute between Lagash and Umma (Cooper 1983b: 22), suggests that at times Kish even succeeded in establishing suzerainty over the S.

The immediate effect of this early Kishite domination apparently was that it brought the S into direct contact with N institutions, leading eventually to important systemic changes in the S society. As a result, S institutions, most notably the kingship, became stronger and thus better suited to compete with the N. Moreover, it was probably in response to the Kishite challenge that the concept of S unity acquired its full formulation. Whether or not this concept ever materialized in any formal arrangement, such as a league or an amphictyony (Jacobsen 1957: 106), it provided the S with a considerable measure of balance and internal security, thereby making it more resistant to outside threat.

However, while the short-term result of the N influence was to strengthen the original S structures, its long-term effect was destabilizing, for it familiarized the S with a model of kingship that was too attractive an alternative not to be tried at home. Thus, once the Kishite threat had been checked, there inevitably began attempts in the S at assuming ascendancy over neighboring states. First at Ur, then in Lagash, several rulers made important inroads toward accomplishing that objective. Some of them even assumed the prestigious title of *lugal Kiš,* "king of Kish." Much disputed by scholars (Maeda 1981), this title appears to have been, at least in the S, devoid of geographical connotations; if we are correct, in its S application *lugal Kiš* was a generic term which served to describe a particular form of kingship; namely, the autocratic and hegemonistic form of rule that the southerners associated with the Kishite kingdom.

The attempts at hegemony grew progressively bolder, by the ED IIIb period (ca. 2500–2300) crystallizing in the drive toward unification. By that time, the center of power had shifted to Uruk (under the Second Dynasty of Uruk), which assumed the ascendancy over Ur and was then able to claim a limited supremacy over the S (Cooper 1983b: 33–34). Such was apparently the intent of the title *lugal kalam-ma,* "king of the land," which was used by the Uruk ruler En-shakushana and, slightly later, by Lugal-zagesi. At the same time, however, these kings were careful to stress that their territorial claims were confined to the states of Uruk and Ur, and that, in that position, they held two separate kingships. This underscoring of the separate character of the kingships of Uruk and Ur is highly significant, for it attests to the enduring strength of the city-state ideology. In this light, Uruk's hegemony could not have amounted to much more than a position of primacy within the existing power picture.

Uruk's rise to supremacy culminated with the reign of Lugal-zagesi (ca. 2325–2300). Stemming, apparently, from Umma, Lugal-zagesi succeeded, either by force or through a dynastic arrangement, in establishing himself at Uruk and Ur (Cooper 1983b: 33–36). He then added Lagash to his possessions and, by securing for himself the recognition of the Nippur priesthood, became the first S ruler to achieve an effective hegemony over the whole S. Despite Lugal-zagesi's claim of having spread his influence all the way to the Mediterranean, his rule hardly extended beyond the strict confines of S Babylonia. It is also unlikely that he ever succeeded in turning his possessions into a uniform, centralized state, or that he even harbored such ambitions. Given the existing ideological constraints, such a step would clearly have been too radical for a southerner to contemplate. Psychologically, however, Lugal-zagesi's achievement constituted a dramatic break with the past and irrevocably changed the course of S history.

As it happened, the person who managed to capitalize on this achievement was, not surprisingly, a northerner. His name was Sargon, and he seems to have hailed from the obscure town of Akkade. If we can trust later semilegendary traditions, Sargon began his career very modestly, serving as a cupbearer at the court of Ur-Zababa, a ruler of Kish (Cooper and Heimpel 1983). Having found himself in control of N Babylonia, which he apparently achieved by deposing Ur-Zababa, Sargon could not have failed to recognize the unique opportunity that the precedent of Lugal-zagesi's state had created in the S. What followed is well known: Sargon marched S and, by defeating the S coalition led by Lugal-zagesi, brought about the unification of Babylonia (ca. 2300).

Momentous as this event had been, its immediate effects for Babylonia, at least in the areas of government and economy, were quite limited. During the reigns of Sargon and his two successors, Rimush and Man-ishtushu, the organization of the south remained virtually unchanged, with the city-states, now turned into provinces, retaining much of their former independence, both political and economic.

Rather than being devoted to administrative and economic reforms, the efforts of the early Sargonic rulers were primarily spent on the task of territorial expansion. The scale of that expansion was staggering, not to be duplicated until the times of the Neo-Assyrian Empire. Already under Sargon, Akkade's possessions included W Iran, N Syria, most of N Mesopotamia, and probably even Cappadocia. The reign of Rimush saw the extension of the Akkadian influence to SE Iran, while the campaigns of Man-ishtushu brought the might of Akkade even farther E, to the coast of Arabia. Though motivated primarily by economic reasons, these exploits had also an unmistakable heroic dimension, which suggests that less materialistic factors may have also been at work (Westenholz 1979: 108). In reading the inscriptions left by Sargon and his successors, one cannot fail to sense the pioneer spirit that accompanied the endeavors of these rulers: their elation over going where no one had gone before, the excitement of discovering the unknown.

Apart from the records of their military exploits and the accounts of their extensive building activities in and outside of Babylonia, information on the first three Sargonic rulers is scarce and mostly of an anecdotal nature. Sargon is credited with a reign of 56 years, but most of it probably belonged to the period before his conquest of S Babylonia. Among his domestic achievements, especially significant was the installation of his daughter En-heduana as the priestess of the moon-god Nanna at Ur (Hallo and Van Dijk 1968: 1–11), a tradition that was to be followed by Babylonian rulers down to Rim-Sin and revived by Nabonidus. The reigns of Sargon's sons, Rimush and Man-ishtushu, are reported to have lasted a total of 24 years. Since Rimush was allegedly the younger of the two, he may have been brought to power by a palace revolution. Rimush's reign was noted for the repeated uprisings in the S, which he crushed with unusual brutality (Foster 1982b: 47–50), and for his struggles with the E land of Marhashi for the control of Iran (Steinkeller 1982: 256–57). Rimush seems to have perished in another palace revolution, behind which there may have been the hand of his older brother Man-ishtushu. The events of Man-ishtushu's reign are even less well known, his chief claim to fame being the amphibious expedition he sent to the land of Makkan on the coast of Oman.

All in all, the reigns of Sargon and his two sons constituted the formative stage of the Sargonic empire. During that period, the empire acquired its physical shape, but little if any effort was made to turn it into an articulated system. These early Sargonic kings also failed to develop a comprehensive imperial policy. In this, they were largely prevented by the continuing opposition of the S city-states, which had only reluctantly accepted the rule of Akkade, revolting against it at every opportunity.

The task of creating such a policy and of consolidating the empire fell to Naram-Sin, Man-ishtushu's son. Naram-Sin's reign (36[?] years) began on an inauspicious note, for his accession was greeted by a general rebellion (Grayson and Sollberger 1976; Jacobsen 1978–79). The rebellion was originally confined to Kish, but it quickly spread to other N cities and then to the S, eventually enveloping the whole empire. Having fought "nine battles in one year," Naram-Sin, almost miraculously, emerged victorious from that ordeal, defeating the rebels and restoring the empire to its former borders.

It was, without doubt, this experience that convinced him of the pressing need to strengthen the fabric of the empire. This objective, however, was largely dependent on the prior resolution of the S question. Naram-Sin's response to that dilemma, suggested possibly by the Egyptian kingship, was to elevate himself to the divine plane (Al-Fouadi 1976; Farber 1983). By becoming a god, he placed himself above all the Sumerian *énsi*s, thereby providing some justification for the contradictory position of his kingship within the S ideological picture.

It is characteristic that the deification of Naram-Sin was carried out strictly within the framework of the city-state ideology. Since all gods possessed earthly domains, the divine Naram-Sin needed one too. And for Naram-Sin the choice of domain was obvious: he became the god of Akkade, by then the capital of the empire. As we learn from one of his inscriptions, this was accomplished by the unanimous decision of the great gods, in response to the request made by Akkade's population.

All that this solution accomplished, however, was to transfer the problem from the human to the divine level: in the new scheme, it was now the god of Akkade who had become a contradiction, for the importance he assumed far outstripped his standing in the pantheon.

Unavoidably, this put Naram-Sin in direct conflict with the head of the pantheon, Enlil, and his city, Nippur. Although it is most unlikely that Naram-Sin had deliberately challenged the authority of Enlil, as preserved in later tradition (Cooper 1983a), the very rise of Akkade to the status of an imperial capital could not but negatively affect Nippur's fortunes, hence giving rise there to anti-Sargonic feelings. While not presenting an immediate threat, these sentiments grew in strength during the reign of Naram-Sin's successor, eventually contributing to the demise of the Sargonic empire.

But the deification was only one element of Naram-Sin's reforms. Equally momentous was the introduction of a uniform administration for the whole empire. Its basis was an extensive system of provinces which were put under the care of royal appointees. Almost as a rule these were outsiders, either kinsmen of the king or members of his retinue. To strengthen the defenses of the empire, a chain of border garrisons was created, and an efficient system of communications, linking Akkade with all parts of the empire, was put in place. The operation of this new administration was greatly facilitated by the systematization of accounting procedures, with Akkadian replacing Sumerian as the language of government.

In the economic sphere, the greatest innovation of Naram-Sin's reign was the creation of a new category of land, the crown land, which was granted to the military and to other types of royal dependents in exchange for services (Foster 1982a: 109–13). Although this type of holding may have existed in the N even earlier, its appearance in the S was a complete novelty. Another N influence that made itself felt in the S during this period was the rapid spread of private property and of independent economic activity more generally. Though the S provinces were required to make regular contributions to the central government, there is little evidence of the state's direct involvement in the management of their economies.

During Naram-Sin's reign, the Sargonic empire reached the zenith of its power and influence, becoming a paradigmatic model that was to be emulated by future Mesopotamian rulers. It seemed that the sun would never set on Akkade, its quays overflowing with exotic products and materials, its streets teeming with foreigners. The arts and literature flourished, achieving unprecedented heights of artistic expression.

Under Shar-kali-sharri, Naram-Sin's son and successor, Akkade's fortunes began to decline, and by the time his reign of 25 years was over, the Sargonic empire was reduced to a small territory around the city of Akkade, perhaps extending into the Diyala region. Information on the events of Shar-kali-sharri's reign is exceedingly sketchy. In one of his year-formulas, Shar-kali-sharri claims a victory over the E lands of Elam and Zahara; since the battle was fought at Akshak, near the confluence of the Diyala with the Tigris, this probably was a defensive operation. Other year-formulas mention an expedition against the Amorites in the mountains of Basar (modern Jebel Bishri) and the capture of a Gutian king by the name of Sarlag, in all probability identical with Sarlagab, the 4th Gutian ruler according to SKL (Jacobsen 1939: 118–19). The mention of the Gutians is particularly ominous, since those foreign people were soon to profoundly affect the course of Mesopotamian history. The home of the Gutians was in the Zagros, roughly within the triangle marked by the modern cities of Kermanshah, Al Sulamaniyah, and Kirkuk that comprised the ancient lands of Harshi, Hu'urti, and Karhar. The Gutians themselves made their first appearance in Babylonia during the reign of Shar-kali-sharri or perhaps already under his predecessor, acting, as we learn from economic records, in the roles of mercenaries and seasonal workers. The correspondence of one Ishkun-Dagan, which dates to the time of Shar-kali-sharri, vividly depicts the bands of Gutians roaming the countryside and playing havoc with rural life (Oppenheim 1967: 71–72), and thus offers the earliest evidence of organized Gutian forays into Babylonia.

It appears that following Shar-kali-sharri's death there ensued a period of general anarchy, for at this point SKL asks dramatically: "Who was king? Who was not king?" It then listed four pretenders, with a combined reign of three years (Jacobsen 1939: 112–15). It was probably sometime during that period that the Gutians mounted what the later tradition wants us to believe was a full-scale invasion (more likely, a series of loosely coordinated excursions), succeeding eventually in establishing themselves as a dominant power in Babylonia.

The last nominal rulers of the Akkade dynasty were Dudu and his son Shu-Durul, whose combined reigns lasted 36 years. Although both Dudu and Shu-Durul are documented in historical records, practically nothing is known of their respective reigns. Since the name of the son invokes the river Diyala (ancient Durul), they probably had come from and possibly were in possession of the Diyala region. A dedication to the god Nergal of Apiʾak, made by the father, suggests that their influence may have extended to lower N Babylonia.

Following the Akkade dynasty, SKL lists in succession the Fourth Dynasty of Uruk (30 years) and the Gutian dynasty. It appears virtually certain that these two dynasties were contemporaneous, and that the reigns of the aforementioned Dudu and Shu-Durul likewise belonged to that same period. While the later historical tradition assigns to the Gutian dynasty a century or more, and identifies twenty-one or twenty-three Gutian rulers, modern research has shown that the period between the end of Shar-kali-sharri's reign and the accession of Ur-Namma, to which the Guti "domination" belongs, lasted no longer than 50 years (RLA 3: 713–14). Also to be revised is the traditional view which identifies the Guti as the sole cause of the collapse of the Sargonic empire. While the Guti invasions undoubtedly played a major, perhaps even the decisive role in that development, various other contributory factors, such as the systemic weaknesses of the empire and the pressures exerted by other foreign newcomers, especially the Hurrians and the Amorites, must have been equally important. Such a conclusion is consistent with the surviving archaeological record, which offers no evidence of a widespread destruction in Babylonia, particularly in the S, that could be attributed to the Gutian invasions.

As can be gleaned from the contemporary historical and economic records, the Gutian influence was limited primarily to N Babylonia and perhaps to some sections of the Diyala region. But, since these were precisely the territories where the realm of Dudu and Shu-Durul is to be sought, it is unlikely that even there the Gutian control could have been complete. With the exception of the northernmost states, such as Umma, Adab, and Uru-sag-rig, which seem to have recognized some degree of Gutian rule, the south enjoyed full independence. Thus Ur and Uruk were governed by a local dynasty (Fourth Dynasty of Uruk), while Lagash experienced a period of great prosperity under the dynasty of Ur-Bau. This shows that, in the S at least, the result of the Guti invasions was the return to the traditional decentralized pattern, with the concurrent revival of the institution of the city-state.

It was in the S that, some 30 years after Shar-kali-sharri's death, the concept of a united Babylonia was again revived. The impulse came from Uruk, at that time ruled by Utu-hegal (2119–2113), the founder and the sole ruler of the Fifth Dynasty of Uruk. By defeating and taking prisoner a Gutian king named Tiriqan, an accomplishment described in considerable detail in one of Utu-hegal's inscriptions (Römer 1985), Utu-hegal put an effective end to the Gutian presence in the S. This, in turn, enabled him to claim, and probably actually to achieve, a limited hegemony over

S Babylonia. In that role Utu-hegal arbitrated a border dispute between Ur and Lagash, settling it in favor of the Lagash ruler, possibly the famous Gudea. During his brief reign (seven years, six months, and fifteen days according to SKL), Utu-hegal also succeeded in putting Ur under his direct rule, installing there his own governor.

Although we can be certain that Utu-hegal had aspired to extend his influence over N Babylonia as well, those plans never materialized. Utu-hegal seems to have been prevented from doing this by the appearance on the scene of another ambitious individual, Puzur-Inshushinak, who, roughly around the time of Utu-hegal's accession, had come to power at Susa. Having consolidated his hold over the Susiana, Puzur-Inshushinak mounted a major campaign in the Zagros, conquering and sacking the lands of Kimash and Hu'urti (Scheil 1913: 7–16). Since these two lands almost certainly formed part of the Gutian homeland, their conquest at the hands of Puzur-Inshushinak could not but profoundly affect the political and military position of the Gutians in Babylonia. One cannot help but suspect that the Zagros conquests of Puzur-Inshushinak stood in some causal relationship with the aforementioned conflict between Utu-hegal and Tiriqan. Although the nature of that relationship and the underlying chronology remain unknown, it is clear that the combined effect of both events was the collapse of the Gutian power in N Babylonia.

The party to profit most directly from this development was Puzur-Inshushinak. As we can gather from the prologue to "Ur-Namma's Code" (Yildiz 1981) and from a recently published Isin inscription of Ur-Namma (Wilcke 1987: 108–11), sometime during the reign of Utu-hegal or shortly thereafter, Puzur-Inshushinak invaded the Diyala region. From there he moved into N Babylonia, capturing several major cities, among them Akshak, Marda, and Kazallu. In this way N Babylonia fell prey to another foreigner, sinking into a period of Elamite occupation or, as the ancient text puts it, "Anshanite slavery."

The task of reunification was continued by Ur-Namma (2112–2095 B.C.), the founder of the Third Dynasty of Ur. Ur-Namma, who possibly was a close relation (either a son or a brother) of Utu-hegal, began his career as Utu-hegal's governor of Ur. Following Utu-hegal's death, Ur-Namma took Uruk, either by force or simply through succession, eventually succeeding in imposing his rule over most of the S, most importantly, over Nippur, the religious capital of Sumer (Hallo 1966: 136–39). The notable exception here was Lagash, the largest and richest of the S city-states, which remained independent under the illustrious rulership of Gudea and his successors, well into the second half of Ur-Namma's reign (Steinkeller 1988b).

Shortly after assuming power and making Ur his capital, Ur-Namma embarked on an ambitious program of economic reconstruction. In an effort to revive the agriculture, Ur-Namma conducted extensive canal work in the area of Ur and farther S. This work improved and expanded the system of waterways, and thus also made possible the restoration of trade contacts with the gulf emporia of Tilmun and Makkan. Massive building projects were then carried out throughout the land, particularly at Ur and Nippur. The largest and most conspicuous of them was the temple complex of Nanna and Ningal at Ur, with its still-surviving ziggurat or monumental stepped tower. These architectural feats were paralleled by the equally outstanding achievements in the arts and literature. Ur-Namma may have also been responsible for the promulgation of the first "code" of laws, unless, as suggested recently (Kramer 1983; Steinkeller 1987: 21 n. 10), the author of that "code" was actually Shulgi, Ur-Namma's son.

The reign of Ur-Namma was notably peaceful and devoid of expansionist military activity. But this seems to have been due more to necessity than to design, for the simple reason that any attempt at territorial expansion, either toward the N or E, was impossible as long as the Elamites occupied N Babylonia. Eventually, however, Ur-Namma's position became sufficiently strong to enable him to challenge the Elamites (Wilcke 1987: 108–11). The result of that challenge was apparently a complete success: Puzur-Inshushinak had been soundly defeated, the trade routes had been reopened, and N Babylonia was free at last.

In spite of that victory, it remains uncertain whether Ur-Namma did in fact succeed in imposing his rule over N Babylonia. The evidence here is contradictory: on the one hand, we have the cadasters of Ur-Namma granting land rights to various N Babylonian cities, which implies his firm control over that region; on the other hand, there is a total absence of Ur-Namma's inscriptions from N Babylonia. The answer may be that Ur-Namma's success was only temporary, with the N again slipping away from his control, either back to the Elamites or perhaps even to the Gutians, for there are reasons to believe that, late in his reign, Ur-Namma fought the Gutians, perhaps even meeting death in that conflict (Kramer 1967).

While Ur-Namma should rightly be considered the founder of the Ur III state, its true builder was Shulgi, Ur-Namma's son and successor (2094–2047). The beginning of Shulgi's extremely long reign (48 years) seems to have been devoted to the task of reasserting and securing Ur's hold over N Babylonia. This objective was probably accomplished by Shulgi's fifth year as ruler, when he captured Der (modern Badrah), an immensely important strategic point controlling the main route to Elam. With this action any vestiges of Elamite influence that may have remained in the N were finally removed.

Roughly around his seventeenth regnal year, Shulgi launched a massive program of political, administrative, and economic reforms, which transformed Babylonia into a highly centralized bureaucratic state (Steinkeller 1987). Those reforms were carried out within a surprisingly short period of time, thus suggesting the existence of a single grand master plan, whose author, we have all reason to believe, was Shulgi himself.

One of Shulgi's first tasks was the creation of a unified administrative system for both the S and the N. This resulted in the division of Babylonia into over twenty provinces, which, in terms of their number and territorial extent, corresponded very closely to the former city-states. The provinces were administered by governors *(énsi),* who were royal appointees and could in theory be removed from office or transferred to other posts at the king's pleasure. In practice, however, the office of the governor tended to be hereditary, especially in the latter part of the period. As a rule, the governors were selected from among the local population, in an effort to placate the local elites and to win their support for the concept of a unified Babylonia.

Apart from the governor, each province also had a district military commander, or general *(šagina)*. Unlike the governors, the generals were predominantly outsiders, very often foreigners, who earned their positions through their service to the king. Many of them were related to the royal family, either by birth or through marriage.

In this dual mode of administration, the office of the general was clearly intended to counterbalance the position of the governor and to serve as a check on his powers, a type of institutional arrangement not unknown in the Orient, both in ancient and more recent times.

In the economic sphere, the most important of the Ur III innovations was the reorganization of the system of temple households. While preserving the fiction of divine domains, Shulgi put the temple households under the control of the provincial governors, thereby turning them and all their possessions into the de facto property of the crown. The surplus revenues of temple households, which in the past stayed in the provinces, were now sent to the king's coffers.

Reviving a policy first implemented by Naram-Sin, Shulgi also established throughout Babylonia a fund of royal land, which was distributed as allotments among various categories of royal dependents in exchange for services. This type of holding remained under the exclusive control of the provincial generals and other officials directly subordinate to the king.

Alongside these institutional changes, there came about various ideological transformations, the most momentous of which was the deification of Shulgi. In deifying himself, Shulgi undoubtedly drew on the example of Naram-Sin, but, learning from the latter's experience, he accomplished it in a much more politic and sophisticated way. First of all, in his new divine form he refrained from associating himself with any particular city-state, becoming instead a vague and inoffensive *dingir kalam-ma,* "god of the land," an echo of the pre-Sargonic title *lugal kalam-ma,* "king of the land." Moreover, he cleverly claimed familial links with the divine families of all the S city-states, thereby legitimizing his claim to their individual kingships. As a consequence, the successors of Shulgi were obliged to undergo separate investitures in each of the S capitals.

In contrast to the Sargonic period, whose dominant trend had been the spread of N influences to the S, the Ur III period witnessed a revival of S traditions and a conscious attempt to transplant the institution of the city-state to N Babylonia. This imposition of the S model on the N was clearly meant to create an ideological framework that would permit the king to claim the exclusive control over all the resources of the state, be they temple-owned or private. In that state, the entire population, from the royal family down to the serfs, was conceived of as a single pyramidal body of the king's dependents. Not surprisingly, the economic system thus obtained allowed virtually no room for any independent activity.

The revival of S traditions, apparent in the organization of the Ur III government and economy, manifested itself even more markedly in the cultural sphere. Thus, Sumerian was reinstated as the language of administration, and Babylonia saw an unprecedented flourishing of Sumerian letters. It was in consideration of these, as well as of similar developments in the fields of arts and architecture, that modern scholarship coined the term "Sumerian Renaissance" to describe, not without justification, the character of that period.

About the same time that Shulgi's program of domestic reforms began, the Ur III state entered into a period of rapid territorial expansion, mainly to the E of the Tigris and in SW Iran. The conquered territories, which formed a large belt extending southeastward from the left bank of the Tigris and running parallel to the Zagros range as far as the Persian Gulf, were incorporated into the Ur III state and organized into provinces (Steinkeller 1987: 30–37). These peripheral provinces, closely resembling the Roman *limes,* served primarily a defensive purpose, offering, in the W, a check against the Amorites, and securing, in the E, Ur's access to the Iranian plateau. The periphery was organized very much like the core provinces, with the difference being that all its land and other resources were apparently considered the property of the crown.

It is characteristic that, in marked contrast to the Sargonic dynasty, the Ur administration showed no apparent interest in a westward expansion. But this may have been due, at least partly, to the menacing presence of the Amorites in the Jezireh and along the middle course of the Euphrates.

This notwithstanding, the result of the Ur conquests was a virtual empire; though considerably smaller than the Sargonic one, it was better organized and showed a much higher level of internal cohesion.

Responding to the challenge presented by the possession of this vast and ecologically diversified area, Shulgi instituted a purposeful policy of regional specialization, with each major region concentrating on the production of different staples and goods. Such a policy, in turn, called for the presence of efficient redistributive mechanisms. In the core provinces, that need was met by the so-called *bala* institution, a central redistributive system which imposed on each province, depending on its size and economic capabilities, specific types of contributions and services (Hallo 1960; Steinkeller 1987: 27–30). The collection and redistribution of these contributions was done through the medium of centrally located establishments, the best known among them being Puzrish-Dagan near Nippur, devoted to livestock and animal products. The peripheral provinces were required to make similar contributions, such as the *gún ma-da* "tax of the (peripheral) territories," which was delivered to the same collecting centers (Steinkeller 1987: 30–36).

The operation of this highly intricate system was facilitated, and indeed made possible, by the creation of an enormous bureaucratic apparatus and by such technical changes as the normalization of accounting procedures and the reorganization of the mensural and calendric systems.

At the head of that bureaucratic edifice stood the chancellor *(sukal-maḫ),* the highest official of the land after the king, who possessed full authority in matters relating to civil administration, the army, foreign relations, and the conduct of law. Under him was a host of governors, generals, and innumerable other officials, a surprising number of whom were relatives of the king. In fact, it is not an exaggeration to say that virtually everyone who mattered in Ur III times (excluding the governors of the core provinces) was in one way or another related to the royal family; and because of this, the Ur III state was truly a family affair, very much like present-day Saudi Arabia with its House of Saud. Quite striking in this connection was the active role in government of the king's wives, sisters, and daughters, the best known example being the queen Abi-simti (Steinkeller 1981; Michałowski 1982).

In its contacts with the outside world the Ur III state retained a strikingly benevolent posture, its rulers displaying remarkably little of what may be called imperial ambition, so characteristic of their Sargonic predecessors. As noted before, their foreign conquests had a limited scope and were primarily motivated by defensive objectives. Foreign relations were regulated by an elaborate system of diplomatic arrangements, which involved dynastic marriages, vassal treaties, and frequent exchanges of ambassadors and goodwill gifts.

The political and economic system just described was put fully in place during Shulgi's reign. The reigns of his three successors—Amar-Sin (9 years), Shu-Sin (9 years), and Ibbi-Sin (24 or 25 years)—saw no substantial changes in that system, merely an effort to preserve it or, more to the truth, to save it from disintegration.

On the surface, the reign of Amar-Sin (2046–2038), Shulgi's son, was a period of peace and great prosperity, though there are indications that cracks were already beginning to appear in Shulgi's brilliant creation. In Babylonia, we can see particularistic aspirations reemerging for the first time, while in the periphery the loyalty of its inhabitants increasingly needed to be reinforced by punitive actions. Beyond the periphery, the vassal states of Ur remained in constant turmoil, seeking full independence. As a solution, these were eventually brought under the direct rule of Ur; but by so doing, the empire, partly against its own will, was drawn deeper and deeper into the foreign territory, only exchanging old enemies for new and more distant ones.

These processes greatly accelerated during the reign of Shu-Sin (2037–2029), Amar-Sin's brother. A major contributory factor was the growing power of the seminomadic Amorites, or Mardu as they were known to the Sumerians (Buccellati 1966; Wilcke 1969–70). Coming from their ancestral home in Syria, the Amorites began arriving in Babylonia during the Sargonic period or perhaps even much earlier. These early arrivals quickly adopted Babylonian ways and were already fully assimilated by the time Ur-Namma founded the Dynasty of Ur. They were followed by other Amorite tribes, which, descending from the amorphous "Land of the Mardu," situated somewhere in the Jezireh, continued to infiltrate Babylonia via the Diyala region and along the lower course of the Tigris, the same traditional route that had been used by their ancestors and probably by the early Akkadians before them. By the time of Shu-Sin, the punitive expeditions that had been periodically sent to the "Land of Mardu" and the system of defensive settlements created by Shulgi apparently proved insufficient to stem their progress, thus necessitating the building of a new line of fortifications, called the "Wall of Mardu," which ran from the Tigris, roughly in the area of Baghdad, deep into the Diyala region.

The main threat facing the empire, however, was in Iran. About that time, the previously disunited Iranian principalities, known collectively as the "Shimashkian lands," rejected their vassal status, forming a loose federation under the leadership of Zabshali (Stolper 1982: 45–54; Steinkeller 1988a). In response, Shu-Sin marched to Zabshali, a distant land in NW Iran, inflicting a defeat on the Shimashkian lands and pacifying them.

But this action had little effect; on the contrary, it probably only contributed to the intensification of unificatory processes in Iran, in turn destabilizing the periphery and demoralizing the core provinces of the Ur III state. During the last year of Shu-Sin's reign, the contributions of the periphery effectively stopped, ceasing completely during the second year of the reign of Ibbi-Sin, Shu-Sin's son and the last ruler of Ur (2028–2004). The loss of the periphery area and its contributions led to the total collapse of the redistributive system. This apparently happened during Ibbi-Sin's fifth year, when the collecting centers were dismantled and their vast officialdom was evacuated to the safety of Ur.

Even more ominously, in the Babylonian heartland the provinces of Umma and Lagash slipped away from the control of Ur (in the fifth and sixth years respectively, of Ibbi-Sin's reign), depriving the Ur III state of its main grain-producing area, and thereby spelling out disaster for its overspecialized economy.

Ibbi-Sin tried desperately to save the situation. In a last-ditch effort to reassert Ur's control over the periphery, he sent military expeditions against Simurrum in the N and against Huhnuri, the "lock of Anshan," in the E. Recognizing the threat presented by the growing power of the Shimashkian federation as well, he gave his daughter in marriage to the ruler of Zabshali.

Whatever tangible result these actions may have accomplished was nullified by the events taking place in Babylonia (Jacobsen 1953; Wilcke 1974). There, one province after another assumed independence, with their rulers, Ibbi-Sin's former underlings, taking Ibbi-Sin's titles and even claiming divinity. One of them, Ishbi-Erra, established himself in Isin, and when instructed by Ibbi-Sin to purchase grain for the starving capital at any price, he succeeded in obtaining for himself extraordinary powers which made him virtually independent. Not satisfied with this, he went on conquering the neighboring provinces. Once in control of Nippur, he raised claims to the Babylonian kingship, all this time retaining the pretense of being Ibbi-Sin's ally.

Ibbi-Sin was prevented from dealing effectively with Ishbi-Erra by the situation on the E front. By that time the leadership over the Shimashkian federation had passed from Zabshali to Anshan. Having consolidated his power in Iran, the ruler of Anshan, named Kindattu, made diplomatic overtures toward Ishbi-Erra, apparently in the hope of drawing him into an alliance against Ibbi-Sin (Stolper 1982: 47–48).

Although Ishbi-Erra may have lent a sympathetic ear to Kindattu's entreaties, perhaps even encouraging him in his plans, it is unlikely that he joined forces with the Elamites. Rather, he just sat and waited, still pretending to be on Ibbi-Sin's side. Finally, the armies of Kindattu descended on Ur, sacked it, and carried the hapless Ibbi-Sin off to Anshan. Their progress farther N was stopped by Ishbi-Erra, who was joined in that undertaking, as the sign of changing times, by an Amorite coalition. Two years later, Ishbi-Erra succeeded in expelling the Elamites from Ur. By bringing Ur under his control, he finally legitimized his claims to the Babylonian kingship. But Ur was never to be its seat again, that distinction having been conferred on the city of Isin, which was to enjoy it for the next century or so.

Bibliography

Al-Fouadi, A.-H. 1976. Bassetki Statue with an Old Akkadian Inscription of Narām-Sin of Agade. *Sumer* 32: 63–75.

Algaze, G. 1986. *Mesopotamian Expansion and Its Consequences: Informal Empire in the Late Fourth Millennium B.C.* Diss., Chicago.

Buccellati, G. 1966. *The Amorites of the Ur III Period.* Ricerche 1. Naples.

Cooper, J. S. 1983a. *The Curse of Agade.* Baltimore.

———. 1983b. *Reconstructing History from Ancient Inscriptions: The Lagash-Umma Border Conflict.* SANE 2/2. Malibu.

———. 1986. *Sumerian and Akkadian Royal Inscriptions.* Vol. 1, *Presargonic Inscriptions.* AOSTS 1. New Haven.

Cooper, J. S., and Heimpel, W. 1983. The Sumerian Sargon Legend. *JAOS* 103: 67–82.

Falkenstein, A. 1974. *The Sumerian Temple City.* SMS 1/1. Los Angeles.

Farber, W. 1983. Die Vergöttlichung Narām-Sîns. *Or* n.s. 52: 67–72.

Foster, B. R. 1982a. *Administration and Use of Institutional Land in Sargonic Sumer.* Copenhagen.

———. 1982b. *Umma in the Sargonic Period.* Hamden, CT.

Gelb, I. J. 1981. Ebla and the Kish Civilization. Pp. 9–73 in *La lingua di Ebla,* ed. L. Cagni. Naples.

Grayson, A. K., and Sollberger, E. 1976. L'insurrection générale contre Narām-Suen. *RA* 70: 103–28.

Hallo, W. W. 1960. The Sumerian Amphictyony. *JCS* 14: 88–114.

———. 1966. The Coronation of Ur-Nammu. *JCS* 20: 133–41.

Hallo, W. W., and Dijk, J. J. A. van. 1968. *The Exaltation of Inanna.* YNER 3. New Haven.

Jacobsen, T. 1939. *The Sumerian King List.* AS 11. Chicago.

———. 1943. Primitive Democracy in Ancient Mesopotamia. *JNES* 2: 159–72.

———. 1953. The Reign of Ibbī-Suen. *JCS* 7: 174–85.

———. 1957. Early Political Development in Mesopotamia. *ZA* 52: 91–140.

———. 1978–79. Iphur-Kīshi and His Times. *AfO* 26: 1–14.

Kramer, S. N. 1967. The Death of Ur-Nammu and His Descent to the Netherworld. *JCS* 21: 104–22.

———. 1983. The Ur-Nammu Law Code: Who Was Its Author? *Or* n.s. 52: 453–56.

Maeda, T. 1981. "King of Kish" in Pre-Sargonic Sumer. *Orient* 17: 1–17.

Michałowski, P. 1982. Royal Women of the Ur III Period—Part III. *AcSum* 4: 129–42.

———. 1987. Charisma and Control: On Continuity and Change in Early Mesopotamian Bureaucratic Systems. Pp. 55–68 in *The Organization of Power: Aspects of Bureaucracy in the Ancient Near East,* ed. McG. Gibson and R. D. Biggs. Chicago.

———. 1989. *The Lamentation over the Destruction of Sumer and Ur.* Mesopotamian Civilizations 1. Winona Lake, IN.

Moorey, P. R. S. 1978. *Kish Excavations 1923–1933.* Oxford.

Oppenheim, A. L. 1967. *Letters from Mesopotamia.* Chicago.

Postgate, J. N. 1986. The Transition from Uruk to Early Dynastic: Continuities and Discontinuities. Pp. 90–106 in *Ǧamadat Naṣr: Period or Regional Style?,* ed. U. Finkbeiner and W. Röllig. Wiesbaden.

Römer, W. 1985. Zur Siegeinschrift des Königs Utuhegal von Unug (± 2116–2100 v. Chr.). *Or* n.s. 54: 274–87.

Scheil, V. 1913. *Textes élamites-sémitiques.* MDP 14. Paris.

Steinkeller, P. 1981. More on the Ur III Royal Wives. *AcSum* 3: 77–92.

———. 1982. The Question of Marḫaši: A Contribution to the Historical Geography of Iran in the Third Millennium B.C. *ZA* 72: 237–65.

———. 1987. The Administrative and Economic Organization of the Ur III State: The Core and the Periphery. Pp. 19–41 in *The Organization of Power: Aspects of Bureaucracy in the Ancient Near East,* ed. McG. Gibson and R. D. Biggs. Chicago.

———. 1988a. On the Identification of the Toponym LÚ.SU(.A). *JAOS* 108: 197–202.

———. 1988b. The Date of Gudea and His Dynasty. *JCS* 40: 47–53.

Stolper, M. W. 1982. On the Dynasty of Šimaški and the Early Sukkalmaḫs. *ZA* 72: 42–67.

Sürenhagen, D. 1986. The Dry-Farming Belt: The Uruk Period and the Subsequent Developments. Pp. 7–43 in *The Origins of Cities in Dry-Farming Syria and Mesopotamia in the Third Millennium B.C.,* ed. H. Weiss. Guilford, CT.

Westenholz, A. 1979. The Old Akkadian Empire in Contemporary Opinion. Pp. 107–24 in *Power and Propaganda: A Symposium on Ancient Empires,* ed. M. T. Larsen. Copenhagen.

———. 1984. The Sargonic Period. *Incunabula Graeca* 82: 17–30.

Wilcke, C. 1969–70. Zur Geschichte der Amurriter in der Ur-III-Zeit. *WO* 5: 1–31.

———. 1974. Drei Phasen der Niedergangs des Reiches von Ur III. *ZA* 60: 54–69.

———. 1987. Die Inschriftenfunde der 7. und 8. Kampagnen (1983 und 1984). Pp. 84–120 in *Isin-Išān Baḥrīyāt III,* ed. B. Hrouda. Munich.

Yildiz, F. 1981. A Tablet of Codex Ur-Nammu from Sippar. *Or* n.s. 50: 87–97.

PIOTR STEINKELLER

HISTORY AND CULTURE OF ASSYRIA

The term Assyria is both a geographical and a political designation. Geographically speaking it is the N part of Mesopotamia. The geographic center of Assyria, commonly called the Assyrian heartland, is actually a triangle formed by the Kurdish mountains to the N, the Tigris river to the W, and the Upper Zab river to the E flowing into the Tigris at the southernmost tip. The four great cities of Assyria—Asshur, Nineveh, Arbela, and Calah—were all within this triangle or very near it. In historical times, the peoples residing in the Assyrian heartland expanded their influence well beyond this central region to include what one might call greater Assyria. The S extreme of this larger territory was the narrowest point between the Tigris and Euphrates rivers, approximately in the region of modern Baghdad. The E limit was the foothills of the Zagros mountains. The N limit was the Kurdish mountains, and the W limit was the Syrian desert.

In modern political terms the Assyrian heartland is entirely within the boundaries of the modern republic of Iraq, while greater Assyria expands into the S extreme of Turkey and the E extreme of Syria.

A. Geography
  1. Physical Features and Climate
  2. Natural Resources, Agriculture, and Animal Husbandry
  3. Trade, Communication, and Transportation
B. Sources
  1. Written Sources
  2. Archaeological Sources
C. Chronology
D. Political History
  1. Early Cities
  2. Old Assyrian Merchant Colony
  3. Shamshi-Adad I and His Time
  4. Hurrians and the Kingdom of Mitanni
  5. The Rise of Assyria (ca. 1741–1274 B.C.)
  6. The Middle Assyrian Empire 1 (ca. 1273–1207 B.C.)
  7. The Middle Assyrian Empire 2 (ca. 1132–1076 B.C.)
  8. The Arameans
  9. Assyria Revives (1075–884 B.C.)
  10. The Calah Kings (883–824 B.C.)
  11. Assyria and Urartu (823–745 B.C.)
  12. The Late Assyrian Empire (744–612 B.C.)
E. The Army
F. Hunting
G. Libraries
H. The State
I. Socioeconomic Structure
J. Legal Structure
K. Religion
L. Everyday Life
M. Legacy

A. Geography

1. Physical Features and Climate. The highest mountains in Assyria are the Kurdish and Zagros mountains, which have a maximum height of 3,600 m. The Assyrian heartland itself consists of gently undulating hills. West of the Tigris is a semidesert area called the Jezirah, stretching as far as the Euphrates river. The Tigris is the main river in Assyria, with its tributaries the Upper and Lower Zabs and the Shatt el-adheim. All of these rivers are swift-flowing and treacherous. Rafts and boats can be used on the Tigris S of Mosul, but even then the trip is quite dangerous.

It has been said that Assyria has one of the most pleasant climates in the world. The summers are warm but not excessively hot, the winters are cool but not excessively cold, and the springs and autumns are long and moderate. In contrast to Babylonia, rainfall in Assyria is regular and sufficient to produce luxuriant vegetation. In fact the E–W line separating the N area of regular rainfall from the S area of sporadic rainfall lies just S of the city of Asshur. There is evidence of a microclimatic change about 1200 B.C. in the central part of the Fertile Crescent, including Assyria; for some reason rainfall was reduced for several years, causing poorer crops and famine with severe economic and political results. It is also evident that extensive soil erosion took place over several millennia because of the cutting down of timber for burning and building. It is probable that in the 2d millennium B.C. there were still large forests teeming with vegetation and wild animals, and that in general the soil was richer and more productive than it is now

2. Natural Resources, Agriculture, and Animal Husbandry. The major natural resources of Assyria were soil and water, which supported agriculture and animal husbandry. It was possible for people to live almost anywhere in Assyria, thanks to the regular rainfall, and it was not necessary for them to cluster along the waterways as they did in Babylonia. Thus, in the historic period, much of the Assyrian heartland was populated by people carrying on agriculture and animal husbandry, and this soon spread to large parts of the Jezirah as the population of Assyria grew. The rivers produced abundant fish, while grape vines grew on the hillsides. Mosul marble, a relatively soft stone, was quarried for building and monumental sculptures, but the main building materials were clay bricks and bitumen found on the Euphrates in the vicinity of the modern city of Hit. There were and still are abundant salt flats in the Jezirah.

The bases of Assyrian economy were agriculture and animal husbandry. The two types of economy existed in a symbiotic relationship, with part of the land being used for pasture while the remainder was used for crop production. Barley was the staple grain, although other grains such as wheat were also grown. The barley was used to make bread and beer, while wine was produced from grapes. Sesame oil was used to flavor the bread. Green vegetables were not common, but spices such as mustard were known; and of course there was salt. The most popular vegetables were onions, garlic, and leeks. Fruits such as apples, grapes, and nuts were a normal part of the diet.

The most common animals bred were sheep and goats, which provided the material for textiles. Goat's milk was very popular and was used both for the milk itself and for cheesemaking. Pigs, cows, and various fowls such as ducks and chickens were commonly raised. None of these animals were slaughtered on a regular basis for their meat, the eating of meat being reserved for festive occasions. Oxen were used as draft animals, and donkeys and mules were used for transporting goods. The breeding of horses became common only in the middle of the 2d millennium, and the horse was a military animal used for drawing chariots and cavalry.

3. Trade, Communication, and Transportation. Trade was a vital part of the Assyrian economy from prehistoric times because of the lack of major natural resources. Moreover, Assyria was geographically located on the crossroads of extensive E–W and N–S trade routes. The city of Asshur was particularly important from this point of view, since it was the obvious crossing point for caravans traveling E–W in the foothills of the Zagros mountains. See ASSHUR (PLACE). In contrast to Babylonia, the rivers of Assyria were not particularly important for transportation since they were so treacherously swift. Thus, caravans and armies were forced to move by land, but on routes parallel to the rivers in order to have ready access to water for themselves and their beasts. Most roads were no doubt in terrible condition, full of ruts and potholes, but there were royal roads used by the king's messengers which were kept in a good state of repair. As to speed of travel, it is known that a caravan or military expedition could travel at the rate of approximately 25 km a day. This rate of course varied considerably, depending upon the terrain. For swift communication, the Assyrians established a system of relay posts where fresh horses were kept at the ready 24 hours a day. In this way the king could keep in touch with the most extreme parts of his empire and relay his orders with dispatch.

B. Sources

1. Written Sources. Assyrian royal inscriptions hold pride of place among the sources for Assyrian history, both because of the vast amount of information they supply and because they were the first cuneiform documents to be deciphered and studied in the 19th century of our era. (See *GARI; LAR*). This does not mean, however, that Assyrian royal inscriptions can be used uncritically; quite the contrary. They are royal boasts or propaganda, and the information they present was selected and arranged to enhance the image of the sovereign. The kind of information selected concerned the military, hunting, and building activities of the monarch which were considered to be the proper functions of an Assyrian king. The military narratives came to be lengthier as the centuries passed and also to be arranged more and more in an annalistic format, that is year by year with dates. The successes of the Assyrian armies were recorded in gory detail, but no mention was ever made of an Assyrian defeat or setback, despite the fact that it is well known from other documents that such humiliating events did take place. Thus, a historian using Assyrian royal inscriptions to reconstruct the events of a reign must be very careful and critical.

Fortunately, many letters from and to Assyrian kings have been recovered (see Parpola 1970; 1987). These letters provide considerable detail about what actually went on in the Assyrian court, in the provincial centers, and on the battlefield. Here we read of the king seeking and receiving advice from his senior administrators and debating major decisions. Numerous Assyrian contracts are preserved from almost all periods of Assyrian history (see Postgate, 1976). These consist of various kinds of legal records, such as marriage contracts, divorce contracts, adoption contracts, loans, and conveyances. The contracts provide considerable insight not only into the legal structure of Assyria but also into the socioeconomic situation. Large numbers of Assyrian administrative records have also been preserved from almost all periods of Assyrian history. These include such documents as lists of food and wine rations for court personnel, offerings given to temples, and wages paid to laborers.

There are other kinds of written sources from Assyria which appear from time to time. For example, there are a few treaties between Assyria and its neighbors, mainly from the 7th century B.C. There are also some prognostic texts from the same century which are records of the king's request for guidance from the diviners on major state decisions. These documents, which are unfortunately very badly preserved, provide some very interesting insights into the decision-making process in the Assyrian palace.

The later indigenous written sources for Assyrian history include a variety of documents written at various times for various reasons. Chief among these are the chronographic texts, king lists, and chronicles about Assyrian history (see TCS 5). We have several of these documents, and they are invaluable in that they provide the chronology and the coherent narrative of the political history of Assyria into which the numerous details from the other sources can be fitted. By far the most important document in this group is the Assyrian King List, which provides the filiation and length of reign of each king going back to the time when the kings were really no more than tribal chieftains. Among Assyrian chronicles, by far the most important is the Synchronistic History. This is a concise narration of relations between Assyria and Babylonia from the first half of the 15th century B.C. to about 800 B.C. Although it provides much useful information, it is unfortunately a very biased document since its purpose was to prove that whenever there had been conflict between Assyria and Babylonia, Babylonia was always in the wrong and lost. Speaking of Babylonia, the Babylonian Chronicle series (see the following article) is an important source of information on Assyrian history from the middle of the 8th century to the fall of the Assyrian empire at the end of the 7th century B.C. Miscellaneous texts such as laws, decrees, and epics also provide information on many facets of Assyrian civilization.

From the point of view of the historian it is unfortunate that beginning about 800 B.C. the Akkadian language, which had been spoken in Assyria since its beginning, was replaced gradually by the Aramaic language. It is unfortunate because while Akkadian was written on imperishable material such as clay and stone, Aramaic was written on papyrus and parchment, materials which are perishable in the Assyrian climate. From a variety of references, it is well known that Aramaic records were kept in Assyria beginning about 800 B.C., and that this recordkeeping in Aramaic became more common as time went on. This documentation is now entirely lost.

Until the middle of the 19th century of our era when cuneiform was deciphered, our only sources of information for Assyrian history were the Bible and classical authors. Since the decipherment of cuneiform documents, these sources now play a very minor role except for a few periods in Neo-Assyrian history when the Bible in particular provides insights unavailable from Assyrian documents. Among the classical sources, the chronology of Claudius Ptolemaeus is of interest in comparison with native Assyrian chronological lists. There are also legends preserved by such authors as Herodotus and Ktesias about Assyrian individuals such as Semiramis and Ahiqar.

2. Archaeological Sources. The ancient Assyrian cities of Nineveh, Calah, and Dur-Sharrukin were the earliest sites to be excavated by 19th-century archaeological pioneers. Among the finds were stone reliefs which lined the entrance and audience chambers of the Assyrian palaces. On these stone slabs were found inscribed cuneiform texts, together with scenes portraying the events narrated in the texts. The floor plans that have been uncovered are not by themselves very informative, but when they are related to the descriptions of buildings in texts one begins to understand the form and function of the various rooms in the palaces and temples. Archaeological excavation continues in Assyria to this day. Excavations are still being carried on at the major cities of Asshur, Calah, and Nineveh, as well as at provincial centers such as those along the Upper Habur river. These expeditions continue to add to our documentation on the history of Assyrian civilization and to fill in gaps.

C. Chronology

The chronology of Mesopotamia is structured on Assyrian chronology; in turn, the chronology of the entire Near East, including Anatolia, Syria-Palestine, and Egypt, is based upon synchronisms with Mesopotamian chronology. The reason for this is the fortunate fact that an astronomical observation provides a fixed date in Assyrian history. This date is the morning of June 15, 763 B.C., when an eclipse of the sun took place. This event is recorded in Assyrian documents which are dated according to a relative Assyrian chronology. Thus, working from the date 763 backward and forward one can establish absolute dates in Assyrian history for the entire 1st millennium. The sources which provide this reliable relative chronology in Assyrian history are the eponym lists and the king lists. The Assyrians named each calendar year after an official called an eponym or *limmu.* Lists of these eponyms were compiled in chronological order, and complete lists of them have been preserved for the entire 1st millennium. Legal documents, and frequently annals, were dated according to these eponyms. Thus, the astronomical observation which provided the absolute date of 763 for one of these eponyms automatically provided absolute dates for the entire list of eponyms and for every event dated by eponyms.

The second half of the 2d millennium B.C. (ca. 1500–1000 B.C.) is a rather different situation with regard to chronology. No complete list of eponym names has been preserved for this period. Thus, although we have the names of numerous eponyms, it is very difficult to establish their relative order; and this in turn makes it very difficult to establish an absolute chronology. The Assyrian King List is of little assistance in solving this problem other than establishing a general relative chronology. Thus, all the dates for the second half of the 2d millennium B.C. in Assyria may be out by approximately a decade either way. For example, a date of 1365 B.C. may in fact be as high as 1375 or as low as 1355 B.C.

Before 1500 B.C. the chronology of Assyria is even more confused. While there are some eponym lists they are very fragmentary, and the list of Assyrian kings is very suspect with regard to the accuracy of the numbers and the sequence of rulers. Synchronisms with Babylonian rulers and events are of little help here, since Babylonian chronology for this period is also very uncertain. What is desperately needed is (1) a fixed astronomical date and (2) a complete list of Assyrian eponyms for the entire period. Therefore, dates in Assyrian history before approximately 1500 B.C. may vary about sixty-four years either way.

In Assyria, the year in which a king died or vacated the throne was regarded as his last full regnal year by native historians. Although the new king took the throne immediately, this was regarded merely as his accession year, and for chronological purposes it was zero. The following year, his first full year on the throne, was recorded as his "first" year. Since the Assyrian year began in the spring (with the month Nisan), it spanned portions of two modern Western years, and to be absolutely precise one should normally cite Assyrian dates according to our calendar as overlapping, for example 759/758 B.C. Modern historians of Assyria, however, generally avoid doing this because it is rather pedantic.

D. Political History

1. Early Cities. The beginnings of Assyria go back to the 3d millennium B.C. and to a few autonomous city-states in the Assyrian heartland. Assyria as a political entity did not exist at this early stage; it was a development of the mid-2d millennium B.C. Instead, one finds by about 2500 B.C. a few independent city-states, chief among which were Asshur, Nineveh, and probably Arbela. Little is known of the history of any of these cities in this period, with the exception of Asshur. Arbela has never been excavated, since the modern city is right on top of the ancient tell. Nineveh, which has been excavated a number of times by various expeditions, has still not yielded very much documentary evidence for this early phase. Nevertheless, later allusions show that it probably was as old as the city of Asshur. For example, Shamshi-Adad I refers to the work of the Old Akkadian king Manishtushu (ca. 2300 B.C.) at Nineveh. This shows that the empire of the Old Akkadian monarchs extended as far N as Nineveh and, more importantly, that Nineveh was already a significant city in the region at that time.

Much more information is available on the history of the city of Asshur during the second half of the 3d millennium B.C. This city, like Nineveh, was also under the control of Manishtushu, since an inscription was found at Asshur of "a servant of" Manishtushu, presumably a governor under the Old Akkadian (OAkk) king. The lack of datable inscribed material before the OAkk period suggests that Asshur remained independent of S political and cultural influence until this time, but once this control was established it continued, or was at least renewed, in subsequent periods. Thus, we know that Asshur was under the political control of the Ur III dynasty, at least during the reign of Amar-Sin (ca. 2046–2038 B.C.), since we have from Asshur an inscription of that king's governor.

Asshur regained independence sometime after the reign of Amar-Sin. In fact, the rulers of Asshur soon turned the tables on the S culture of Babylonia. One such ruler, Ilushuma, carried out a raid on Babylonia, attacking such major cities as Ur and Nippur. It was simply a plundering expedition, and no attempt was made to establish continuous control. The subsequent rulers of the city Asshur during the remainder of this period concentrated upon construction work in the city itself. In particular, a great deal of effort and materials was devoted to the improvement of the temple of the god Asshur. It was a period of political stability and economic prosperity and a time when the Old Assyrian merchant colony flourished in Cappadocia.

2. Old Assyrian Merchant Colony. Thanks to an accidental discovery of a large archive of cuneiform documents in Anatolia, important information has come to light regarding the economy of the city-state of Asshur during its earliest history (Veenhof 1972; Larsen 1976). The archive was discovered at the modern site of Kültepe, which in ancient times was called Kanish. From this archive it has been learned that the city-state of Asshur had established a number of merchant colonies in Anatolia in order to promote trade. The archive from Kanish consists of thousands of cuneiform tablets, the vast majority of which are concerned with economic matters. There are contracts, administrative documents, and commercial letters. Unfortunately, the counterparts of this correspondence and related economic recording have not been found at Asshur itself. Possibly future discoveries will unveil this documentation. Since virtually no records are preserved from Asshur itself for this time, without the discovery of the archive it would have been assumed that the city was of very minor significance. Now we realize it was of major importance to international trade around the turn of the 2d millennium.

The Kanish colony was concerned mainly with trade in tin, which was an essential element, together with copper, to make bronze. Since this is the period commonly called the "Bronze Age," the significance of this trade need not be emphasized. The colony flourished for about 150 years (ca. 1900–1750 B.C.) and was a real colony, for the merchants were citizens of the city-state of Asshur living temporarily in Anatolia. They mixed with the natives in order to promote trade, but otherwise the colony remained an independent and relatively isolated establishment. The relationship was mutually beneficial, and thus little is heard of conflict between the Anatolian natives and the foreigners from Asshur. A rough modern analogy might be the European trading compounds in the Chinese city of Shanghai in the 19th century of our era.

3. Shamshi-Adad I and His Time. The early cities in the Assyrian heartland, and in particular the city-state of Asshur, were jolted out of their economic prosperity by the Amorite invasion. The Amorites were Semitic-speaking people from the Syro-Arabian desert who penetrated Mesopotamia about the beginning of the 2d millennium B.C. In the first two centuries of this millennium they established a number of dynasties at various city-states in Assyria, as well as in Syria and Babylonia. The invasions, which went on for many generations, caused considerable chaos and much fighting not only between the former inhabitants and the invaders but also between the various city-states.

The Amorite people were divided into many tribes, each led by a powerful chieftain. Among the most powerful was the tribe which produced Shamshi-Adad I (ca. 1813–1781 B.C.), one of the most colorful figures in early Assyrian history. Although clearly of nomadic ancestry, as one learns from scattered references in contemporary and later texts, Shamshi-Adad went to great pains, once he had gained control of the major part of Assyria, to have himself recognized as a legitimate ruler of the city-state of Asshur and in direct descent from the ancient rulers there. Thus, the Assyrian King List incorporates the Amorite ancestors of Shamshi-Adad as early rulers of Asshur, although obviously they were nomadic chieftains living in the desert. As to the early career of Shamshi-Adad himself, it is known that he traveled S into Babylonia, where he spent some time. He was obviously impressed by Babylonian culture and learned a great deal from it, since later in his career he encouraged the Babylonization of Assyrian culture, including Assyrian religion.

Eventually Shamshi-Adad went N up the Tigris, leading a group of warriors, and captured Ekallatum. After three years he then went farther N and attacked and captured the city-state of Asshur. He devoted himself to major construction work at the city. In particular, he concentrated upon the temple of Asshur, a god whom he regarded as equivalent to the Sumero-Babylonian deity Enlil. This is an indication of one of his attempts to encourage Babylonian culture.

If it were not for a chance discovery of a large archive of cuneiform documents at the city-state of Mari (see MARI) on the middle Euphrates, this is about all we would know about Shamshi-Adad I. But what a limited view this would be, for Shamshi-Adad, as we now know from the Mari archives, went on to greater things. When Yahdun-Lim, the king of Mari, was assassinated, possibly with the connivance of Shamshi-Adad's agents, Shamshi-Adad captured Mari and appointed his younger son, Yasmaḫ-Adad, as governor of Mari. At the same time, he appointed his eldest son, Ishme-Dagan, as governor of Ekallatum. Leaving these territories under his sons' control, Shamshi-Adad then proceeded farther W into Syria. He captured the city of Shubat-Enlil and made it his residence and capital. All this produced a N Mesopotamian power unprecedented in strength and extent. In effect, Shamshi-Adad controlled all of the region N of modern Baghdad, W of the upper Tigris, E of the middle Euphrates, and W into central Syria. The governing of such an extensive territory was by no means easy, not only because it had never been under central authority before but also because there were many Amorite tribes wandering about the region. Shamshi-Adad and his two sons had their work cut out for them trying to maintain stability and prosperity.

Despite Shamshi-Adad's own ability, one of his great frustrations was that his younger son, Yasmaḫ-Adad, was quite incapable. Yasmaḫ-Adad hated the battlefield as much as he hated the administrative office. He much preferred to spend his time in the harem, as we learn from letters of Shamshi-Adad rebuking him for not doing his job. Frequently in these letters Shamshi-Adad holds up his eldest son, Ishme-Dagan, as an example to be emulated. In one letter he says, "While your brother is victoriously campaigning you lie about down there among the women." Eventually Shamshi-Adad was forced to appoint advisers to his son who kept him informed separately of what was going on.

Despite the incompetence of Yasmaḫ-Adad, the remaining years of Shamshi-Adad were prosperous and relatively stable. When he died, however, about 1781 B.C., the fortunes of N Mesopotamia changed dramatically. Hammurapi of Babylon marched N and in the space of a few years captured first Mari and then Asshur. See History and Culture of Babylonia below. The history of the Assyrian region after Hammurapi's time is lost in obscurity. Barbarian tribes from the Zagros threatened Asshur and the other city-states, and a new people called the Hurrians invaded from the E and eventually controlled the region.

4. Hurrians and the Kingdom of Mitanni. After the death of Shamshi-Adad I in the 18th century, very little is known about the region of Assyria and about the city-states, such as Asshur and Nineveh, until the 14th century B.C. The reason for this lack of information was the chaos brought about by the mass migration of new peoples into N Mesopotamia. Chief among these were the peoples which founded the kingdom of Mitanni. This kingdom was centered on the Habur river, but in its heyday its influence spread as far W as the Taurus mountains and as far E as Assyria. Indeed, for a time it seems to have controlled the city-states of Nineveh and Asshur.

Unfortunately, very little information is available about the kingdom of Mitanni. Its capital, Washshukanni, has still not been located, and therefore the state archives of the kings of Mitanni have not been discovered. What little we know of this kingdom and its history we glean from foreign sources: Assyrian, Babylonian, Hittite, and Egyptian. As meager as this information is, it does allow us to realize that Mitanni was one of the greatest powers in the ancient world in the middle of the 2d millennium B.C. Its kings dealt as equals with the Egyptian pharaohs and Hittite monarchs.

Since Mitanni was such a great power, and controlled Assyria for a time, it is important to consider this kingdom and its civilization in any discussion of Assyrian history. Indeed, the two ethnic elements evident in the Mitanni kingdom, Hurrians and Indo-Europeans, also had a major impact on the region of Assyria and thus require detailed consideration. The term Indo-European refers basically to a large family of languages, among which are modern English, French, and German. Ancient languages included within this group are Latin, Greek, Hittite, and Sanskrit. The Hurrian language, on the other hand, has not been identified with any known family of languages. Certainly it is neither Indo-European nor Semitic. The Hurrians themselves entered Mesopotamia by way of the Caucasus from the steppes of central Asia. Evidence of their presence in Mesopotamia, which is supplied from personal names, goes back at least as far as the Third Dynasty of Ur (ca. 2000 B.C.). At this early date, they were in the east Tigris region, and for the next few centuries there is no evidence they spread beyond this area. Toward the middle of the 2d millennium, however, they began to move out, and eventually Hurrians were spread over most of the Fertile Crescent, their presence being evident in Assyria, Syria, Anatolia, and Palestine. In Assyria, the site which provides most of our evidence for a strong Hurrian presence is Nuzi.

As stated above, there are both Indo-European and Hurrian elements in the ethnic makeup of Mitanni, and the major and almost sole source of this information is personal names. The most common personal names of people of Mitanni are in the Hurrian language, but there are some names which are Indo-European. These latter names have one of two characteristics; either they are compounded with the name of an Indo-European deity known in Sanskrit (such as Indra, Vayu, Svar, Soma, etc.) or they are concerned with horses and horse racing, for it is a well-known phenomenon that early Indo-European culture was closely associated with horses and horse breeding. Thus, we find people of Mitanni with names in an Indo-European language with such meanings as "possessing great horses" and "he who had won seven prizes (at the horseraces)." A further piece of evidence for Indo-European presence in Mitanni is a horse-breeding manual, the original of which came from Mitanni but which is known only from a copy found at the Hittite capital of Hattusa. The text is written in the Hittite language, but some of the technical terms are in fact in an Indo-European language which is not Hittite. It is commonly assumed that this is the same language known at Mitanni. A final major piece of evidence is the name of a social class at Mitanni, which is "Maryannu." This is an Indo-European word meaning "young man, warrior." All of this evidence indicates not only that there were Hurrian and Indo-European elements in the kingdom of Mitanni but also that the Hurrian element was by far the most common. It is going too far, however, to conclude from this that the Indo-Europeans were the ruling class at Mitanni. Such a conclusion, which has been put forward by a few scholars, is unjustified by the present state of our evidence. Rather, we weem to be dealing with a society which is essentially Hurrian but which has at some time come into contact with Indo-Europeans and learned from them not only some of their language but also their horse-breeding techniques.

The people of Mitanni are responsible for introducing the use of the horse in warfare into the Fertile Crescent. They used it to draw a light two-wheeled chariot, which immediately gave them the upper hand in warfare. Soon, however, other peoples such as the Hittites and Assyrians learned how to use horses and light two-wheeled chariots in the same manner. But until they did so, Mitanni was one of the most powerful political and military forces in the Fertile Crescent.

5. The Rise of Assyria (ca. 1741–1274 B.C.). a. Eclipse (ca. 1741–1364 B.C.). Until the 14th century B.C., the term "Assyria" could be used only in a geographic sense, but in that period we see the first appearance of a state called Assyria. For a brief time under Shamshi-Adad I in the 18th century B.C., the various small city-states in the heartland of Assyria were linked together under one political authority, but the name Assyria was not applied to this entity. With the death of Shamshi-Adad I and the accession of his son Ishme-Dagan I (ca. 1780–1741), this very fragile unity disintegrated. For some centuries the various city-states continued to be independent of one another, and some at least eventually fell under the political control of the kingdom of Mitanni, as outlined in the previous section.

The eclipse in the history of the region called Assyria lasted for almost four centuries. As incredible as it may seem, virtually no documents and no information about the entire area are available for this long period of time. The only document which gives us any idea of the events of the period is the Assyrian King List, but for the period under discussion the succinct information in this list can only apply to the city-state of Asshur. Nothing is known of events at the other major cities of the region. The Assyrian King List assigns a reign of forty-one years to Ishme-Dagan I (ca. 1780–1741 B.C.), the son and successor of

Shamshi-Adad I. After the entry for this king, the list continues with a number of names and eventually informs us that a new royal line was founded by Adasi, who is referred to as "the son of a nobody" (i.e., he was a usurper). After Adasi and until the end of the period we are calling the eclipse, some contemporary inscriptions begin to appear at the city-state of Asshur, and gradually light is shed upon events there.

b. Ashur-uballiṭ I (ca. 1363–1328 B.C.). The long reign of Ashur-uballiṭ I marks the first appearance of Assyria as a political entity and the beginning of this nation's rise to become one of the great powers in the ANE. This is the period called the Amarna Age and Ashur-uballiṭ I played a significant role in this era, together with the leaders of the Hittites and of other major states in the Fertile Crescent—Egypt, Mitanni, and Babylonia. Ashur-uballiṭ I is the first Assyrian ruler to call himself "king of Assyria," previous rulers at the city-state of Asshur having called themselves only "vice-regent of the god Asshur." Native Assyrian tradition regarded the reign of Ashur-uballiṭ I as the beginning of Assyrian power.

Unfortunately, few details are known about the reign of Ashur-uballiṭ I. It is apparent that he controlled a unified and strong state, that he was recognized internationally as a great ruler, and that he actually controlled the Babylonian state for a significant period of his reign. On the international scene, two letters from Ashur-uballiṭ I were found at the Egyptian capital of Amarna. These letters were addressed to the Egyptian pharaoh, and in them the Assyrian addressed the Egyptian king as an equal and referred to establishing good relations, which obviously included trade and some kind of political cooperation.

Turning to his relations with Babylonia to the S, more details are available. According to our information, the daughter of Ashur-uballiṭ I was married to the Babylonian king, and their son, that is the grandson of Ashur-uballiṭ I, eventually came to rule over Babylonia. It is clear that Ashur-uballiṭ I supported and influenced his grandson on the Babylonian throne. When there was a rebellion in Babylonia, the grandson was killed and replaced by a native usurper. Ashur-uballiṭ I invaded Babylonia to avenge his kin, deposed the usurper, and put a king of his own choice on the Babylonian throne. Although no further information is available, it seems obvious that the Assyrian continued to exercise considerable control over Babylonian affairs during his lifetime.

c. Prelude to Greatness (ca. 1327–1274 B.C.). The stability that Ashur-uballiṭ I had brought about was to be an important foundation upon which his son, Enlil-narari, and his two grandsons, Arik-din-ili and Adad-narari I, could build the beginning of an empire. Altogether, these three reigns cover just over half a century. It was a period during which they struggled to maintain and expand the boundaries of Assyria, but it was also a period during which they finally lost control over Babylonia. In fact, the most significant achievement of the period on the part of Assyria was the expansion to the W into the territory controlled by the kingdom of Mitanni. The successes on this front brought wealth and confidence to the Assyrians and prepared the way for the establishment of a real empire.

Assyria's loss of Babylonia was due to the strength of that nation under its greatest king during the Kassite Period, Kurigalzu. On the other hand, the success of Assyria against Mitanni during this period was achieved, at least in part, because the Hittites were pressing very hard against the kingdom of Mitanni at the opposite end, on the W boundary of Mitanni. It was Adad-narari I who successfully carried out two major campaigns against Mitanni and began the process which would eventually incorporate half of Mitanni as part of the Assyrian empire.

6. The Middle Assyrian Empire 1 (ca. 1273–1207 B.C.). The continuing rise in the fortunes and power of the state of Assyria narrated in the previous section culminated in the establishment of the first Assyrian empire, commonly called the Middle Assyrian Empire to distinguish it from the Late Assyrian or Neo-Assyrian Empire. The Middle Assyrian Empire can be divided chronologically into two periods, and it is the first part which is our concern here. This covers the reigns of two kings, Shalmaneser I (ca. 1273–1244) and Tukulti-Ninurta I (ca. 1243–1207 B.C.). These two were the son and grandson, respectively, of Adad-narari I, and they built upon the stable and influential kingdom which they inherited to make of Assyria one of the most powerful nations in the ANE in the 2d millennium. Fortunately for us, a relatively large amount of documentation is available for the period so that we can see the evolution of this process in some detail.

The military campaigns of Shalmaneser I were conducted to the E, N, and W. He left Babylonia alone. The most important achievement of the campaigns of Shalmaneser I was the complete conquest of E Mitanni and the annexation of this region as an Assyrian territory. The way had already been cleared for these campaigns by Adad-narari I. Nevertheless, Adad-narari I had no real control over the region and the task was a formidable one, made more so because Mitanni was allied with the Hittites and the Arameans against Assyria. In his royal inscriptions, Shalmaneser I boasts that he defeated all three parties, namely the Hittites, the Arameans, and the army of Mitanni, and that ultimately he made E Mitanni a province in the Assyrian empire. Other sources for the period bear out the essential truth of his claims.

In the descriptions of the campaigns by Shalmaneser I, we first encounter the gory details of Assyrian conduct in warfare for which these people would become famous. For example, in a narrative regarding a campaign against the king of Mitanni, Shalmaneser I boasts that after slaughtering tens of thousands of the troops of Mitanni he blinded no less than 14,400 Mitannians whom he had taken alive as prisoners.

Tukulti-Ninurta I, the son and successor of Shalmaneser I, conducted campaigns similar to his father's. In addition, he campaigned against Babylonia and added this area to his kingdom for at least a short period of time. Indeed, the campaign against Babylonia by Tukulti-Ninurta I was the most momentous event of his time. By this period we have a little more information about Babylonia, and it is clear that the state was very weak. It had a tenuous alliance with the Hittites, one which was difficult to maintain because all communications had to pass through Assyria. There are three descriptions of the Babylonian campaign of Tukulti-Ninurta I: one in the royal inscriptions of Tukulti-Ninurta I, a second in a historical epic about Tukulti-

Ninurta I, and a third in a fragmentary account in a Babylonian chronicle. By far the most detailed version is found in the historical epic. This poetic narrative is, however, Assyrian and highly biased in favor of Tukulti-Ninurta I. Nevertheless, it is known from other sources that Kashtiliash, the Kassite king of Babylonia, was defeated and slain. The city of Babylon itself was plundered and its walls torn down as punishment. The statue of the god Marduk was carried off to Assyria. Certainly it is a fact that Tukulti-Ninurta I captured Babylon and controlled Babylonia for at least a brief period of time.

The significance of the other campaigns of Tukulti-Ninurta I which led him to the N, NE, and W of Assyria is eclipsed by the great victory over Babylonia. Nevertheless, these other campaigns were of importance. In particular, he was able to fend off an attempt by the Hittites to expand into E Mitanni, a region which had been incorporated into Assyria by Shalmaneser I. The narrative of the defeat of the Hittites by Tukulti-Ninurta I is of special interest to biblical students, since it contains the first recorded example of the deportation of peoples by the Assyrians. Such a procedure would be used much later against the Israelites, as narrated in the Bible. In the case of Tukulti-Ninurta I, a large group of the conquered Hittites were transported from Syria to labor camps in Assyria. By this practice, the Assyrians not only eliminated a troublesome element on their borders but also gained a significant increase in their labor force.

Tukulti-Ninurta I stands out as the most successful and ambitious Assyrian ruler for many centuries, but eventually he was surrounded and assassinated in his own palace. For many years after the assassination the fortunes of Assyria were in decline, and control over her territories slackened. Significantly, Babylonia took the opportunity during this weak period to break away and appoint its own king.

It is necessary to concentrate upon the military achievements of the Assyrian rulers, since these were the most important achievements of this militaristic state. Nevertheless, both Shalmaneser I and Tukulti-Ninurta I devoted much time and energy to building operations in the cities of Asshur and Nineveh. In addition, Tukulti-Ninurta I founded an entirely new city, Kar-Tukulti-Ninurta, which means "Quay of Tukulti-Ninurta." This new city was on the opposite bank of the Tigris from Asshur and a little N of that ancient city. At Kar-Tukulti-Ninurta, the king built a splendid palace, several temples, and a ziggurat, and he cut a channel for a canal to provide water for the gardens and the inhabitants. The entire city was surrounded by a wall. Here, Tukulti-Ninurta I took up residence, and it is in this palace that he was assassinated. In founding an entirely new capital, Tukulti-Ninurta I set an example for a few kings of the Late Assyrian Empire who would similarly found new cities.

As to other cultural activities of the period, there is some information. In particular the conquest of Babylonia, which involved carrying off Babylonian documents and people to Assyria, brought considerable cultural influence from Babylonia into Assyria. This is a process which had begun as early as the reign of Ashur-uballiṭ I, but the act of Tukulti-Ninurta I gave it great impetus. Thus, in literature and religion we now find significant Babylonian influence in Assyria.

7. The Middle Assyrian Empire 2 (ca. 1132–1076 B.C.). The assassination of Tukulti-Ninurta I began a temporary decline in the power of Assyria, a decline which lasted for about three quarters of a century and coincided with the fall of the Kassite dynasty in Babylonia. A major internal factor that contributed to this decline was dissatisfaction with the reign of Tukulti-Ninurta, which culminated in his assassination. External factors were the movements of new peoples into the Fertile Crescent that had a major impact not only upon Assyria but upon other important powers in the area as well. The most significant people involved were an ethnic group called by the Assyrians the Mushku and by classical authors the Phrygians. These people, among others, moved into Anatolia and brought about the collapse of the Hittite empire, and many Hittites fled to Syria for refuge. This brought them into direct conflict with Assyrian interests. With this, Assyrian expansion westward halted, but in fact Assyria now had to retreat in face of the pressure of various peoples on its W frontier. Another group of people who were beginning to apply pressure on Assyria's W flank were the Arameans, about whom more will be said later. During this brief period of decline, Assyria seems to have fallen briefly under Babylonian control.

Eventually Assyria, like a sleeping giant, reawakened under the leadership of Ashur-resha-ishi I. Before describing his reign, however, a major revolution in the art of warfare must be noted. It is about this time that iron became more common. The use of iron for weapons and armor marked a major change in the conduct of warfare. Its significance is at least as great as the introduction of the light horse-drawn chariot by the Indo-Europeans about the middle of the 2d millennium.

The accession of Ashur-resha-ishi I (ca. 1132–1115 B.C.) marks the beginning of the revival of Assyria's fortunes. By far the most important achievement of this king was the restoration of internal stability to the Assyrian state. He regained authority over all of the Assyrian heartland and restored peace and prosperity to the region. He newly defined or recaptured the borders and strengthened them by rebuilding old fortresses or erecting new ones.

It was the good fortune of Tiglath-pileser I (ca. 1114–1076 B.C.) to inherit a kingdom which was now internally stable, prosperous, and secure on its frontiers. See TIGLATH-PILESER (PERSON). Building upon this foundation this king, one of the greatest in Assyrian history, had the ambition and ability to create an empire. Under his leadership Assyria expanded in all possible directions, so that when he died Assyrian influence extended from the Mediterranean sea in the W to Babylon in the SE.

No sooner had Tiglath-pileser I ascended the throne than one of Assyria's most dangerous enemies, the Mushku, attacked. The Assyrian king responded immediately with a counterattack, and thus began many years of Assyrian campaigning to the W against the Mushku. The persistent campaigning not only stopped the Mushku but pushed them back westwards, and Tiglath-pileser I boasts of returning with rich booty from the plundered Mushku. These W campaigns also brought him into contact with the Arameans. Various Aramean tribes had formed coalitions in Syria, and in their own way they were as formidable an enemy to Assyria as the Mushku. A major confrontation between Assyria and the Aramean coalition took place at Jebel Bishri in central Syria. Assyria won the day, and for a time the tide of Aramean incursions was stemmed. The W campaigns of Tiglath-pileser I were by far the most important military activities of his reign, bringing under Assyrian influence all of Syria as far W as the Mediterranean sea and S Anatolia as far as the Taurus range.

Despite the major significance of the W frontier, however, one must not underestimate the importance of Tiglath-pileser I's campaign into Babylonia. The Assyrian and Babylonian armies fought on at least two occasions on the Lower Zab river, and eventually Assyria defeated the Babylonian army. The Assyrians then proceeded S into the Babylonian plain and captured major Babylonian cities, including Babylon and Sippar. No mention is made of S Babylonian cities in our Assyrian sources, however, and therefore we may assume that Tiglath-pileser I did not gain control there.

The benefit of these numerous and successful campaigns was that Assyria now enjoyed great prosperity, and this factor, together with the internal stability, fostered major cultural developments. Significant building operations were undertaken in the various cities of Assyria. In the legal sphere, scribes carefully compiled two sets of laws, one a collection of palace edicts of various kings as far back as Ashur-uballiṭ I and the second a collection of laws mainly concerned with the status of women in the Assyrian state (see *ANET,* 180–88). Babylonian influence is evident in a number of these cultural developments.

8. The Arameans. A discussion of the Arameans provides a suitable bridge between the 2d and 1st millennia in Assyrian history, for these people first appeared toward the end of the 2d millennium and played a major role in the ANE in the 1st millennium. The Arameans make up the third major invasion of the Fertile Crescent by Semitic-speaking nomads, the first being that by the Akkadians and the second that by the Amorites. A fourth invasion by the Arabs would come a little later. In highlighting these four major invasions, one must also note that gradual infiltration by Semitic-speaking nomads from the Syrian desert was going on all the time. Aramaic, the language of the Arameans, eventually became the language of the Assyrians and Babylonians, thus replacing Akkadian. Indeed, Aramaic by the middle of the 1st millennium was the international language of the entire ANE.

The name "Arameans" covers a large number of tribal groups, among which were a people called the Ahlamaeans. In fact, the Ahlamaeans are the earliest attested group of Arameans. The earliest datable reference to Arameans or Ahlamaeans appears in documents of the 14th century B.C. from Egypt (Amarna), Syria (Ugarit), Assyria, and Babylonia. In Amarna, the reference appears in a badly preserved letter, the context of which is not clear. At Ugarit, the name Aramean appears as a tribal identification for an individual, as a personal name, and as a topographical name. In Assyria, there is a statement in a royal inscription of Adad-narari I that his father, Arik-din-ili (ca. 1317–1306 B.C.), conquered the Ahlamaeans. In Babylonia, there is a letter of the late 14th century B.C. from Dur-Kurigalzu in which a tribe called Hirana, known from later sources to be an Aramean tribe, is mentioned.

After the 14th century B.C. references to Ahlamaeans and Arameans become more frequent, and it is evident that they were spreading widely throughout the Fertile Crescent. For example, in the 13th century B.C., a Babylonian king, Kadashman-Enlil II, complained to the Hittite king, Hattushilish III, that he had not been able to correspond with him because of the hostile Arameans. This statement indicates that large groups of Arameans were already well established in Syria along the upper Euphrates, a fact borne out by later historical evidence. It should also be remembered that the Arameans together with the Hittites fought on the side of Mitanni against Shalmaneser I.

It has already been noted that the decline in fortunes of Assyria after the death of Tukulti-Ninurta I was due in part to pressure from the Arameans on the W frontier of Assyria. Later, Ashur-resha-ishi I boasted that he had conquered them in the desert. As noted in the preceding section, Tiglath-pileser I defeated an Aramean coalition at Jebel-Bishri about 1100 B.C. The successor of Tiglath-pileser I, Ashur-bel-kala, recorded in the so-called Broken Obelisk a number of raids on Aramean groups in the 11th century B.C. in Syria. Further evidence from the late 11th century B.C. appears in the Bible, where we read of David's wars against the Aramean kingdom of Damascus. It was in fact the unified kingdom in Palestine established by Saul and continued by David that effectively prevented the Arameans from gaining control over Palestine. Similarly, the Mushku or Phrygians prevented the Arameans from pushing into Anatolia. These two factors then deflected the main thrust of the Aramean incursion so that it went SE into Mesopotamia.

Assyria lost considerable territory to this invading group, and there is some evidence that the Assyrians may have actually had to abandon their major cities for a brief period to the Arameans. The Babylonians suffered at least as much if not more from the Aramean attack. Our fragmentary sources indicate the confusion and chaos caused by the flood of Aramean warlike tribes into the Babylonian plain. In the 1st millennium, Arameans were present in two forms. First, there were a number of Aramean kingdoms in Syria that were the targets of Assyrian campaigns for centuries to come. Second, there were Arameans within Assyria itself, and their numbers gradually increased as time went by. This in turn had a major cultural impact upon Assyrian civilization.

By the 8th century B.C. the Aramaic language was widely written and understood in Assyria. Although only a few Aramaic documents have actually been recovered from this period because of the perishability of papyrus and parchment upon which they were written, there is ample evidence for the widespread use of the Aramaic language. There are Assyrian reliefs on which are portrayed scribes recording booty on scrolls, and these would only be used for the Aramaic language. There are references in Assyrian texts to the "Aramaic Scribe," and there is mention in Akkadian letters of correspondence being carried on in Aramaic between the Assyrian king and his officials. Even the Akkadian language itself was influenced by Aramaic both in the lexicon and in the syntax. By the 7th century

B.C., there were senior Assyrian officials bearing Aramaic names and speaking Aramaic. For example, the rabshakeh of Sennacherib at the siege of Jerusalem, as narrated in the Bible, could speak Aramaic as well as Hebrew (2 Kgs 18:19–35). See RABSHAKEH.

The reason for this major Aramaic presence was the increasing number of Arameans living in Assyria from the 9th century on. Many of these were brought by Assyrian kings as captives to work on building projects at Assyrian capitals, the most ambitious of which was that of Ashurnasirpal II at Calah. Even after the fall of Assyria in 612 B.C., Aramaic both as a language and as a culture continued to have a major presence in the Babylonian empire and later in the Persian empire.

9. Assyria Revives (1075–884 B.C.). The title "Assyria Revives" refers to the fact that after the death of Tiglath-pileser I in 1076 B.C. the fortunes and power of Assyria once again declined, and little is heard of this state until the accession of Ashur-dan II in 934 B.C., more than a hundred years later. The reasons for the decline were the lack of systematic administration for the vast territory which Tiglath-pileser I had conquered and the tremendous pressure applied by the Arameans during this period. By the turn of the millennium, Assyria was hard pressed on all fronts: to the S in Babylonia and to the W in Syria were the Arameans; to the N and E were the peoples of the Nairi lands. The situation improved, however, near the beginning of the 1st millennium when three successive kings brought about internal stability and launched military campaigns to regain lost Assyrian territory.

a. Ashur-dan II (934–912 B.C.). From this reign one may date the beginning of the Neo-Assyrian Empire. Ashur-dan II restored internal stability to the Assyrian state, and this enabled him to be the first king for over a century to conduct regular military campaigns abroad. The chief targets of these military expeditions were the Arameans and the recapture of territory which they had wrested from the Assyrians. In the tradition established by the MA monarchs, Ashur-dan II concerned himself with building activity. The city of Asshur had been neglected for over a century, and now the king commissioned construction work on the fortifications surrounding the city and palace.

b. Adad-narari II (911–891 B.C.). Adad-narari II continued the work of his father, Ashur-dan II, and campaigned even more extensively. In addition to pushing back the Arameans, Adad-narari II led expeditions against Babylonia and the Nairi lands. On these campaigns the Assyrian army marched as far W as the Balih river, as far S as the middle Euphrates, as far N as Lake Van, and as far E as the central Zagros mountains. The Arameans continued to be the central concern of the foreign policy of the Assyrians, however, as evidenced by the fact that no fewer than eight campaigns were conducted against them. The offensive against the Arameans was so successful that eventually Adad-narari II was able to lead his troops on an expedition through territory formerly controlled by them without meeting any opposition. On the contrary, as he traveled through the region, the local Aramean chieftains came to him voluntarily with tribute. This campaign was a "show of strength" campaign, a new feature of Assyrian strategy which would be imitated by subsequent kings. Another innovation is that in addition to building Assyrian garrisons on the frontier, Adad-narari also established storage depots at strategic points throughout his newly acquired territory for the supply of his army on campaign. In subsequent reigns, these storage depots would be developed into administrative centers, thus marking the beginning of a provincial system. Adad-narari continued the work of his father in reconstructing the fortifications and buildings at the city of Asshur.

c. Tukulti-Ninurta II (890–884 B.C.). With the reign of Tukulti-Ninurta II, a short period of consolidation began. Tukulti-Ninurta II set himself the task of organizing the nation and empire in a much more systematic manner. A good illustration of this new policy, and also of the extent of Assyrian control, is provided by a royal inscription of this king in which is described in detail a "show of strength" campaign conducted in approximately the same region in which Adad-narari II had led such a campaign. Like his father, he met no resistance on this campaign; as the Assyrian army approached, local rulers came to it and voluntarily offered provisions and tribute.

An innovation in the reports of Tukulti-Ninurta's campaigns is that reasons are given for these offensive actions, the reasons being reports of hostile acts on the part of the people who became the target of the campaigns. In other words, each offensive action by the Assyrians is justified by the claim that the people of the target area had initiated hostilities.

Tukulti-Ninurta II was more ambitious in his building projects, carrying out construction not only at Asshur but also at Nineveh. Little is known of his work at Nineveh, but at Asshur he continued to improve the fortifications and to restore the temples and palace.

10. The Calah Kings (883–824 B.C.). There are two peaks in the greatness of the Neo-Assyrian Empire, the first being the one which can be called that of the Calah kings, and the second being that of the Sargonid kings (see below). In between these peaks is a low point in Assyrian might. The name "Calah Kings" derives from the new capital created by the first of these kings, Ashurnasirpal II. This king, together with his son and successor, Shalmaneser III, not only created this new capital but also brought under Assyrian control an unprecedented extent of territory and wealth.

a. Ashurnasirpal II (883–859 B.C.). Ashurnasirpal II is the epitome of the ideal Assyrian king. As a fitting symbol of his exceptional might and accomplishments, he made a reality of the principle, which had been developing for some time, that the Assyrian king should campaign every year of his reign. It is known that he led at least fourteen major expeditions during his twenty-five years on the throne, and there were probably several other campaigns for which we have no information as yet.

To the east, in the area of the Upper Diyala in the Zagros mountains, Ashurnasirpal led three campaigns. The main target was a coalition of tribes headed by a certain Nur-Adad. In anticipation of the Assyrian invasion, Nur-Adad walled up a major pass in the mountains, but the Assyrian army broke through this wall and penetrated deep into Nur-Adad's territory, looting and destroying towns as they proceeded. When Ashurnasirpal was satisfied with the extent of his conquests and sated with the booty he had captured, he forced large numbers of conquered peoples to return to Calah to perform forced labor on the building projects there. To affirm his control over the Zagros area, he established a garrison and supply depot deep in the mountains.

In the N, NE, and NW, Ashurnasirpal launched a number of campaigns directed primarily against the lands of Nairu and Urartu. Toward the end of a series of campaigns in these areas which involved considerable looting and destruction, he appointed a governor over the district. The result of the extensive campaigning and of the administrative measures which Ashurnasirpal took in these areas was that for the remainder of his reign the people in these districts remained reasonably submissive and voluntarily sent tribute and workers to perform service in Assyria.

The campaigns stretched over most of the reign of Ashurnasirpal II and were interspersed by at least four campaigns to the W. The first major target was the tribe called Bit-Adini, which was settled in and around the city of that name on the Balih river. The city was captured and plundered and became a jumping-off point for Ashurnasirpal's campaigns further westward. Eventually the Assyrian army proceeded farther, and upon reaching the upper Euphrates received tribute without battle from the king of Carchemish. At a later date the Assyrians crossed the upper Euphrates and received tribute from various states W of the Euphrates. When Ashurnasirpal reached the Mediterranean sea, he performed the ancient ritual of washing his weapons in the water. The Phoenician cities of Tyre, Sidon, Byblos, and Arvad sent presents to the Assyrian conqueror. On his return he brought back cedar timber, for which Lebanon was famous, to use in his building projects at Calah.

The last direction of the campaigns was to the S along the Habur and middle Euphrates rivers. These areas had been carefully controlled by Assyria since the time of Adad-narari II, but the preoccupation of Ashurnasirpal II with campaigns in other directions inspired some peoples on the Habur and middle Euphrates to renounce vassalship. They were encouraged to do this by Bit-Adini to the W and Babylonia to the S. There were three separate attempts to throw off Assyrian control, and in each case Ashurnasirpal responded with lightning speed. As soon as word reached him of the rebellions, he reversed the march of his troops and fell upon the rebels unexpectedly. The guilty cities were plundered and burnt to the ground, and their leaders were horribly mutilated before being murdered. The result of these atrocities was that Ashurnasirpal had no further trouble along the Habur and middle Euphrates for the rest of his reign.

There were major innovations in administrative matters during this reign. In this period we find the first signs of a provincial administration. Ashurnasirpal II developed the idea of garrisons and supply depots in far-flung regions to the point that these became real administrative centers with governors. Moreover, it is clear from his inscriptions that he expected tribute to be contributed regularly and voluntarily. These are basic items in a properly organized provincial administration.

One of the most significant achievements of Ashurnasirpal was the construction of a new major Assyrian city, Calah. Until Ashurnasirpal chose Calah as his capital, it had only been a small village. At this modest site he erected enormous fortifications, a huge palace, and numerous temples, the chief of which together with its ziggurat was dedicated to the god Ninurta. This enormous task was carried out by the large numbers of captive peoples forced to come to Assyria for the purpose. At the completion of the erection of this magnificent city, Ashurnasirpal staged a banquet to which thousands of dignitaries, both native and foreign, were invited. This was a fitting tribute and conclusion to the reign of one of the mightiest Assyrian kings.

b. Shalmaneser III (858–824 B.C.). Shalmaneser III campaigned and constructed as vigorously and extensively as his father, Ashurnasirpal, and thereby added much territory and glory to Assyria. The most important areas in which he expanded were to the N and W, where his most formidable foes were, respectively, the kingdom of Urartu and the Damascus coalition.

Let us deal with the W campaigns and the Damascus coalition first. The resistance Assyria encountered centered around two coalitions, one in the N which included Carchemish and one in the S with its headquarters at Damascus. Shalmaneser III had considerable success in suppressing the N coalition and established a number of administrative centers in the region. But the S coalition was another story. This "Damascus coalition" included troops from a variety of nations, including Israel under its king Ahab. The major confrontation between the Assyrians and the Damascus coalition took place at the battle of Qarqar on the Orontes in 853 B.C. Unfortunately, the only detailed account we have of the battle is Assyrian, and according to this Shalmaneser won the day. This may have been true; however, the Damascus coalition was by no means destroyed at Qarqar. It continued to resist Assyrian advances in subsequent years. The Assyrians continued to pound away at these S states along the Mediterranean, and eventually the Damascus coalition disintegrated and the Assyrians laid siege to the city of Damascus itself. Shalmaneser was unable, as he tacitly admitted, to take Damascus, but he proceeded farther S and erected a stele on Mt. Carmel to mark the S extent of his expedition. He received tribute from Tyre and Sidon and from Jehu, the king of Israel.

Turning to the N and the kingdom of Urartu, Shalmaneser again campaigned much throughout his reign. The kingdom of Urartu was young and vigorous, and its territory spread like an umbrella over Assyria's N borders from Lake Urmia in the E to the source of the Euphrates in the W. By far the most important and impressive campaign against Urartu was that of 856 B.C., in which the Assyrian army swept right across Urartu from W to E. In the process the Urartian army was defeated, and numerous major cities were captured and destroyed. Urartian encroachment upon Assyrian frontiers was thereby checked, and a good deal of wealth and supplies, particularly horses, was won. In comparison to the W and N campaigns, Shalmaneser's two campaigns into Babylonia were relatively minor and were in response to an appeal for help by the legitimate king of Babylonia against his rebellious brother.

The construction activities of Shalmaneser were much more diversified than his father's, which had been concerned almost exclusively with Calah. At Calah, Shalmaneser completed, renovated, or expanded several buildings begun by his father. Most importantly he erected Fort Shalmaneser, the most extensive military emplacement ever excavated in W Asia, on the outskirts of Calah. At Asshur he restored the fortifications and some of the temples. He also did some work at Nineveh.

Toward the end of his life Shalmaneser let his control over the state loosen. In particular, he entrusted the leadership of military campaigns to one of his chief officers, Dayyan-Ashur, who was the tartan (field marshal) of the Assyrian army. The king no doubt did this because he was old and perhaps even ill, but the result was that a rebellion broke out when the monarch's control had relaxed; also, he had sons who were anxious to take over the state. Details of the rebellion are unknown, but out of the chaos emerged Shamshi-Adad V, one of his sons, as king. There is no information about the fate of Shalmaneser III; he may have died a natural death, or he may have been assassinated.

11. Assyria and Urartu (823–745 B.C.). For almost a century after the death of Shalmaneser III in 824 B.C., Assyrian history was dominated by the aggressive actions of the kingdom of Urartu, and for a time Urartu replaced Assyria as the dominant power in the area. While Assyria was preoccupied with defending itself against Urartu, peoples on its other frontiers, in particular the Babylonians, took advantage of Assyria's weakened position. Similarly, the Arameans and other peoples in the W renounced Assyrian vassalship and either declared themselves independent or allied themselves to Urartu. This period marks the low point in the history of the Neo-Assyrian Empire.

a. Shamshi-Adad V (823–811 B.C.). Shamshi-Adad V, although the son and successor of Shalmaneser III, was no match for his father. He gained the throne through mysterious circumstances resulting from the long rebellion at the end of the reign of Shalmaneser III, and instability and conflict continued to be characteristics of his reign.

First and foremost, Shamshi-Adad had to concern himself with the N frontier where it appears Urartu had encroached upon Assyrian holdings and was seriously threatening to invade Assyria itself. Shamshi-Adad boasted that he made three campaigns in this region. Despite his claim that these campaigns covered vast territories, the lack of precise details strongly suggest that these were little more than quick raids intended to intimidate Urartian aggression and at the same time to capture horses to build up the strength of the badly weakened Assyrian army. Once the internal troubles of Assyria had been settled and the N frontier reasonably secured, the Assyrian king launched four campaigns into Babylonia. Unfortunately, we have only Assyrian sources for these events, and they inevitably speak of the campaigns as major Assyrian successes. We are told that Shamshi-Adad gained control of all of Babylonia, that he imposed tribute upon the Babylonians, and that he forced upon them an agreement on the boundary between the two states.

Given the troubled nature of the times, it is not surprising that Shamshi-Adad had very little opportunity for building activity. He began the construction of a palace at Nineveh, which his son completed, and at the city of Asshur he did some repairs to the temple of Asshur. It is possible that he built a palace at Calah, but this is uncertain. Shamshi-Adad was buried at Asshur, and his inscribed sarcophagus was recovered by modern excavators.

b. Adad-narari III (810–783 B.C.). The empire which Adad-narari inherited from his father, Shamshi-Adad, was clearly in decline, and his entire reign was devoted to futile attempts to restore the fortunes of Assyria. A fascinating aspect of Adad-narari III's reign is that his mother, Semiramis, became a legendary figure, and tales about her have been preserved in later writings among the Arameans, Greeks, and Persians. Clearly she exercised considerable influence during her son's career, at least at the beginning, and this unusual fact of a woman playing a major role in Assyrian affairs of state caught the imagination of poets and writers.

Since Shamshi-Adad V had neglected the W frontier, it is not surprising that the first part of the reign of his son was concerned with military campaigns in that direction. Some states which had rebelled were once again brought under Assyrian authority, but the most significant achievement was the siege and capture of Damascus. Adad-narari's record of this event includes the statement that among the various cities which now paid tribute to Assyria was Samaria under King Joash.

Adad-narari continued Shamshi-Adad's policy of campaigning into Babylonia. The primary aim of these campaigns seems to have been the subjection of the Chaldeans, a group of West Semitic–speaking peoples settled in S Babylonia. At the same time, Adad-narari reasserted Assyrian authority over Babylonia, and he brought back captives to perform forced labor and imposed taxes and a boundary agreement upon the Babylonians.

The successes of the campaigns of Adad-narari III were superficial and when we look below the surface we see serious weaknesses. It is known from various steles discovered in scattered parts of Syria that a number of powerful individuals who paid lip service to the Assyrian king actually controlled extensive territories as virtually independent rulers. Adad-narari not only allowed this to occur but actually also encouraged it by granting land and privileges to these men.

Despite the weakness of the times, Adad-narari was able to carry out a number of building projects at Calah, Fort Shalmaneser, and Nineveh. Culturally, the most significant feature of the reign was the increasing influence of Babylonian religion on Assyria. The most important part of this phenomenon was the prominence given to the Babylonian god Nabu in Assyria during Adad-narari III's reign.

c. The Interval (782–745 B.C.). This period, which I have called the "Interval," is the lowest point in the power of Assyria during the time of the Neo-Assyrian Empire. Theoretically, there were three Assyrian kings during this time who had control, but practically the Assyrian empire was now totally fragmented into a number of virtually independent states ruled by former Assyrian governors. It is during this time that the kingdom of Urartu rose to its greatest power, and despite the attempts of the Assyrian kings as well as the independent governors to defend Assyrian territory, Urartu gradually expanded. At the end of the Interval, Urartu had complete control of all of the territory N of the Assyrian heartland stretching from the Iranian plateau in the E to N Syria and the Mediterranean in the W. Assyria was on the verge of extinction when Tiglath-pileser III came to the throne.

12. The Late Assyrian Empire (744–612 B.C.). The Late Assyrian Empire is frequently called the Sargonid Age, because all but the first two kings, Tiglath-pileser III and Shalmaneser V, were descendants of Sargon II. This age is the greatest and final flowering of Assyrian imperial power in the ANE.

a. Tiglath-pileser III (744–727 B.C.). Tiglath-pileser III was probably a usurper but a man of exceptional ability, since he quickly regained all the territory that Assyria had lost in the Interval. As we saw in the preceding section, Assyria was on the verge of losing its very independence to the kingdom of Urartu when Tiglath-pileser III came to the throne. But this king was able not only to drive Urartu out of territories previously claimed by Assyria but also to invade Urartu itself. Since Urartu had previously expanded into Syria in the W, Tiglath-pileser III in particular led a number of campaigns in that region against such states as Arpad. His defeat of these states, many of which had been allied against him, brought voluntary submission and tribute from the more S cities of Damascus, Hamath, Byblos, Tyre, and Samaria. After Tiglath-pileser had invaded Urartu and defeated its army, he was eventually able to concentrate more exclusively on the Mediterranean states. In 734 Tiglath-pileser led his army through Syria and Phoenicia to S Palestine, where he captured Gaza. He created an Assyrian trading center there and made Gaza a vassal of Assyria. This trading center was to facilitate economic communications between Assyria and Egypt. In the following years, various states in Syria and Palestine rebelled against Assyria, but they paid the penalty by being savagely attacked by the Assyrian army and incorporated as vassal states into the Assyrian empire. This was the fate of Damascus and Israel. See also TIGLATH-PILESER.

The other major military concern of Tiglath-pileser was Babylonia. By this time relations between Babylonia and Assyria had become very complicated. In contrast to the attitude of earlier Assyrian kings of the 8th century B.C., Tiglath-pileser's policy toward Babylonia initially had been to allow it to remain independent so long as it was friendly toward Assyria. To fulfill this aim he led a campaign early in his reign into Babylonia to secure the position of the Babylonian king, Nabu-nasir, with whom he seems to have had a treaty. The Assyrians then left Babylonia in peace until there was a rebellion against the son and successor of Nabu-nasir. The rebellion was led by a Chaldean called Mukin-zer, and the suppression of this rebellion caused Tiglath-pileser considerable time and energy. Once he had suppressed the rebellion, Tiglath-pileser, angry about the time he had wasted on this problem, ascended the Babylonian throne himself. Thus we have for the first time in Neo-Assyrian history a unified state of Assyria and Babylonia under one king. Not all residents of Babylonia were happy with this arrangement, however, and one dissident, a Chaldean called MERODACH-BALADAN, resisted Assyrian control during this and subsequent reigns.

Under Tiglath-pileser, a major reorganization and improvement of the army and the provincial administration was undertaken. Another feature of his reign was the massive deportation of peoples from rebellious areas, a policy which would be pursued regularly in subsequent times. Very few building projects were undertaken by this king, and that is not surprising given the time and energy he devoted to military and administrative measures. The main monument which he left was a new palace at Calah.

b. Shalmaneser V (726–722 B.C.) and Sargon II (721–705 B.C.). The reign of SHALMANESER V was very short and would hardly merit any mention except for the fact that it was almost certainly this king who conquered Samaria. Modern historians have debated for years whether Shalmaneser V or Sargon II actually achieved this, but the evidence is strongly in favor of Shalmaneser V. The exact dates of the siege, which lasted for two to three years according to the Bible, is uncertain, but the fall itself probably took place in 722 B.C. After the capture of Samaria, its inhabitants were transported to Assyria, and this operation took place mainly during the subsequent reign of Sargon II. Shalmaneser's reign was brought to an end by a revolution in which he was killed and a man called Sargon seized the throne by force.

This man, who became Sargon II, was probably not in the direct line of succession; in other words, he was a usurper. Be that as it may, he was a worthy successor of Tiglath-pileser III and emulated that sovereign by intensive campaigning during which he not only regained territory lost during the reign of Shalmaneser V but also added new regions to the empire. Sargon has actually left us an account of the events which led to his accession to the throne. The document, called the Asshur Charter, claims that Shalmaneser V wrongfully imposed corvée on the city of Asshur, with the result that the citizens of Asshur rebelled against him and put Sargon on the throne in his place. Sargon rewarded Asshur by eliminating the wrongful impositions and granting the citizens special privileges. The rebels on the other hand were punished, and 6,300 of them were deported to live in Hamath in Syria.

Assyria's internal difficulties during this time gave her vassal states in the W an excellent opportunity to rebel. Among the rebel states were Damascus, Arpad, and Samaria. As soon as Sargon had stabilized his control in Syria, he led an expedition to the W where he met the combined rebel forces at Qarqar in 720 B.C. Assyria's forces won a victory and then marched S to reconquer Gaza and defeat an Egyptian army on the border of Egypt. Sargon now carried out massive punitive operations, which included the deportation of large numbers of people to Assyria. He also established an Assyrian garrison on the Egyptian frontier. Philistia, in particular, received the attention of the Assyrian monarch, who, after a few years, was able to subdue completely the various Philistine cities, including Ashdod. Within the W territory claimed by Sargon was the island of Cyprus, a new addition to Assyrian influence.

To the NW, Sargon's campaigns were concerned with two major enemies, the Mushku or Phrygians led by Mita (the Midas of classical authors) and the Urartians under Rusa I and later Argisti II. The war between Sargon and Mita resulted in some slight territorial gain for Assyria, but the major achievement was eventual peace on this frontier. The Assyrian offensive against Urartu took place not only on the NW frontier but also on the N and NE frontiers. Frequently other peoples, including the Manneans and the Medes, allied themselves with Urartu against Assyria. To further complicate matters another people, the Cimmerians, were now well established in the area and actively hostile to both the Assyrians and the Urartians. As a result of Sargon's numerous campaigns, Urartian power gradually declined and Assyria gained the upper hand.

On the Babylonian frontier the most serious problem which Sargon had to deal with was Merodach-baladan, a Chaldean. Merodach-baladan seized the Babylonian throne during the confusion surrounding the accession of Sargon II in Assyria and remained there for the first twelve years of Sargon's rule in Assyria (721–710 B.C.). Eventually Sargon was able to dislodge Merodach-baladan in 710, and the Chaldean fled to hide in Elam. Sargon now entered Babylon in triumph and was crowned king of Babylonia.

Sargon II was one of those few Assyrian kings who built an entirely new capital. In this case the new city was Dur-Sharrukin, "Fort Sargon," just a few kilometers N of Nineveh. The central building of the new metropolis was the palace, but there was also a magnificent temple and ziggurat, and the entire complex was surrounded by an enormous wall. A beautiful park and numerous temples were also part of the city. People were transported from all regions to populate the new city.

c. Sennacherib (704–681 B.C.). With the reign of SENNACHERIB, the son and successor of Sargon II, the apogee of the Neo-Assyrian Empire was readied. Jerusalem, the capital of the kingdom of Judah under Hezekiah, became the focal point of Sennacherib's policy toward the W, for not only did Jerusalem refuse submission to the Assyrians but it also allied itself with the Egyptians and Ethiopians against Sennacherib. There is considerable controversy among modern scholars about the details of the military activities of Sennacherib in Palestine. The central question is whether there was more than one campaign against this region, and the biblical narratives are difficult to reconcile with what Sennacherib says in his royal inscriptions. Despite this controversy, some facts are clear. First, an Assyrian army defeated an allied Egypto-Ethiopian army at a place called Eltekeh in Palestine; this army had come to the aid of Hezekiah. Sennacherib then laid siege to Jerusalem. The city was not taken by force; instead, Hezekiah presented Sennacherib with rich tribute. However, other cities in Judah were not so fortunate. Many of them were captured, looted, and destroyed, chief among these being Lachish. An Ethiopian army moved into Palestine to deal with the Assyrian threat. The two armies—the Ethiopian and the Assyrian—camped opposite one another, and during the night before the battle was to take place, a mysterious event occurred. According to the Bible, the angel of the Lord descended upon the Assyrian camp and slaughtered all of the troops (2 Kgs 18:13–19:36). Varying versions of this strange tale are found in Josephus (*Ant* 10.1.4–5) and Herodotus (2.141), and probably the truth will never be known. The fact is, however, that the Assyrian army on this occasion withdrew in confusion and disgrace.

Turning to Babylonia, we are confronted with one of the most intriguing and enigmatic phenomena in Sennacherib's reign. Babylonian resistance to Assyria centered around the figure of the Chaldean Merodach-baladan, and when he died the resistance was continued by his son. Babylonian opposition to Assyrian rule found support among the Elamites, who provided troops. Merodach-baladan was very ambitious and wily in his endeavors to keep Babylonia independent of Assyria. He gained allies throughout the Assyrian empire, these allies including Hezekiah of Judah (2 Kgs 20:12–19). Sennacherib eventually drove Merodach-baladan out of Babylon and chased him into the S marshes, where Merodach-baladan found refuge by crossing over to the Elamite shore. Sennacherib then turned his attention to Babylon. After fierce fighting Babylon was captured by the Assyrians, and Sennacherib, according to his royal inscriptions, utterly destroyed the city, killing or driving out all of its inhabitants. This act, which took place in 689 B.C., marks the lowest point in Babylonian history for centuries.

A number of architectural and cultural projects are to be dated to this reign. Sennacherib chose Nineveh as his capital and set about a major urban renewal of this ancient city. He constructed a totally new palace complex, complete with park and artificial irrigation. He cut a swath right through the center of the city as a processional way leading from the bridge across the Tigris to his palace, and he erected enormous fortifications with gates and towers around the considerably larger city. His building projects at the city of Asshur were part of his attempt to reform Assyrian religion, the chief purpose being the subordination of the Babylonian god Marduk to the Assyrian god Asshur. This included the erection outside the city walls of a temple of the New Year (Akitu) which was decorated with images and inscriptions depicting the myth of Asshur (not Marduk) conquering the dragon Tiamat. Other evidence of the attempt to downgrade Marduk's position is provided by a fragmentary text which seems to describe a trial in which Marduk is judged to be inferior to Asshur.

The reign of Sennacherib ended in violence. There is much mystery and confusion about the actual events, but from native sources as well as from the Bible it is clear that Sennacherib was assassinated by one or more of his own sons. Out of the confusion arose Esarhaddon, a younger son of Sennacherib, to become king.

d. Esarhaddon (680–669 B.C.). ESARHADDON, a son of Sennacherib, is by far the most unusual of all Assyrian kings in that he was clearly more interested in cultural, and in particular religious, matters than in military achievements. Despite this predilection, however, it was during his short reign that Assyria first conquered Egypt. The view that Esarhaddon was less interested in military than in cultural matters is borne out by all of the written documents which have come down to us—royal inscriptions, letters, and oracle requests. These oracle requests were a fortunate discovery. They are records of inquiries by the king to the gods of divination, Shamash and Adad, through the diviners for guidance on state decisions.

By far the most important military aim of Esarhaddon was the conquest of Egypt, a goal which no doubt his father Sennacherib had fostered. This endeavor led the Assyrian armies down into Palestine and Phoenicia. While Egypt was penetrated more than once, the only really successful invasion took place in 671 B.C., when the Assyrian and Egyptian armies fought three separate pitched battles. The Assyrians were victorious and conquered the capital, Memphis. Governors were appointed and tribute collected for Assyria. But control over Egypt was very superficial, and on a subsequent campaign, aimed at trying to subdue the Egyptians more effectively, Esarhaddon died en route to Egypt. With the exception of two Phoenician states, Sidon and Tyre, the lands of Palestine and Phoenicia remained reasonably submissive to Assyria during the reign of Esarhaddon. Sidon was effectively subdued, but despite a lengthy siege Tyre was never taken; that achievement remained for Alexander the Great many centuries later.

In contrast to Sennacherib's policy toward Babylonia, Esarhaddon's policy was to appease the Babylonians through a rebuilding program and good government. The central portion of Esarhaddon's building program in Babylonia was the reconstruction of Babylon and in particular the rebuilding of the temple of Marduk.

All of Esarhaddon's building endeavors were quite diverse. At Nineveh he extended the large barracks originally built by his father, Sennacherib and built or restored a park and several temples. At Asshur he did considerable work on the temple of Asshur. Curiously, there are royal inscriptions in which the reconstruction of the Asshur temple at Asshur and of the Marduk temple at Babylon are described side by side. Calah and Arbela also were included in the major reconstruction programs of Esarhaddon.

Another interesting phenomenon was the role of Esarhaddon's mother, Naqiʾa (an Aramaic name; her Assyrian name was "Zakutu"). During the reign of her son, Naqiʾa exercised unprecedented authority and behaved like a sovereign in many ways, building a palace at Nineveh and even writing royal inscriptions. Reports on cultic and military matters were addressed to her, and a sculptor was commissioned to create a statue of her. At the death of her son, she continued to exercise authority during the early reign of her grandson, Ashurbanipal, before her own death.

Esarhaddon was very concerned over the succession, and he laid careful plans. In 672 B.C., the king assembled representatives from all parts of the empire and made them swear by the gods to respect his wishes with regard to the succession. The nature of the succession was totally new: Ashurbanipal was appointed heir to the throne in Assyria, while Shamash-shuma-ukin, his brother, was appointed heir to the throne in Babylonia. This was the first time the two states had been split between two Assyrian monarchs, and whatever good reasons Esarhaddon had for this decision, inevitably it led to civil war.

e. Ashurbanipal and the Fall of Assyria (668–612 B.C.). Superficially, Assyria seemed to be at the height of its power with the accession of Ashurbanipal, but in actuality decline had already set in. The first real military concern of Ashurbanipal was Egypt. Esarhaddon had begun the penetration of Egypt, but Ashurbanipal had to lead further campaigns there in an attempt to subdue that nation. In 667 B.C. he recaptured Memphis, which had thrown out the Assyrian garrison. The guilty Egyptians were punished and new governors appointed. A few years later, Memphis once again rebelled with the support of the Ethiopians. Ashurbanipal sent a second expedition to Egypt, which not only recaptured Memphis but gained the city of Thebes (ca. 663 B.C.) as well. This was the height of Assyria's penetration of Egypt. After this time, as Assyria's attention was distracted elsewhere, Egypt fell away from Assyrian control and eventually became independent.

The most serious military problem which Ashurbanipal had to face was Babylonia and its ally Elam. The unusual division of the succession between Assyria and Babylonia with Shamash-shuma-ukin, the brother of Ashurbanipal, being appointed king of Babylonia inevitably led to civil war. This broke out in 652 B.C. and came to an end four years later in 648. The struggle between the two brothers was bitter, and the sufferers were the Babylonians themselves, for most of the conflict took place on Babylonian territory. Despite the help of allies such as the Elamites and Arabs, Shamash-shuma-ukin finally lost. The ultimate disaster was a two-year siege of the city of Babylon during which the citizens suffered terrible hardship and famine.

The fall of Babylon meant that Ashurbanipal could concentrate on Babylon's ally, Elam. He led a series of successful and devastating raids into Elam, looting the countryside and sacking and destroying the cities. Finally, the capital of Elam, Susa, was captured and destroyed. Elam was by this deed effectively annihilated as a nation, but ironically for Assyria and Babylonia this made room for the influx of the Persians, who would eventually conquer Mesopotamia.

The building projects of Ashurbanipal were quite extensive. The untimely death of Esarhaddon had left a number of building enterprises unfinished, and these Ashurbanipal undertook to complete. Nineveh continued to be the place of the chief royal residence, and among the various works Ashurbanipal constructed there was the spectacular N palace, on the mound now called Kuyunjik. This, the last great Assyrian palace, was magnificent and included an extensive terrace, a large park with exotic trees, plants, and animals, and numerous rooms lined with enormous stone reliefs depicting the victories of Ashurbanipal. Many of these reliefs can be seen today in the British Museum in London. Ashurbanipal also carried out work on the barracks at Nineveh, as well as other palaces and temples. In addition, he did some work at Asshur, Arbela, and Calah and took upon himself the responsibility of finishing Esarhaddon's restoration program at Babylon.

The favorite recreation of an Assyrian king was hunting, and much information is available about the hunting activities of Ashurbanipal, both in written sources and in stone reliefs. In these, we find that the lion was the favorite prey of the king. The Assyrian hunted lions both in their habitats along the Balih river in Syria and in the marshes to the S of Babylonia. In addition, he had lions captured alive and brought to a large park in Assyria, where he could hunt them at his leisure. Such a hunt had a religious connotation and at the end of the chase, a ritual was performed, which ended with the king pouring a libation over the lions' corpses, as depicted in stone reliefs.

Ashurbanipal, unlike many of his predecessors, was intensely interested in cultural pursuits. This interest went back to his early education, for he boasted that he was not only taught how to ride horses, drive chariots, throw the spear, and shoot the arrow, but also how to read and write. No other Assyrian king has made this latter boast, and it is generally assumed that most Assyrian kings were illiterate. Ashurbanipal's ability in letters led him to be involved actively in the acquisition of large numbers of cuneiform tablets for his libraries at Nineveh. Much of this library has been recovered in modern times and is our major source for both Assyrian and Babylonian culture. For this, we owe Ashurbanipal a great debt.

The latter part of the reign of Ashurbanipal is shrouded in darkness, and he was succeeded by a series of insignificant kings. Assyria was already in decline by this time. The Babylonians, allied with the Medes, marched into Assyrian territory and eventually penetrated the Assyrian heartland itself. The city of Asshur fell in 614 B.C. Then, the Babylonians and Medes concentrated on the capital, Nineveh, which fell after a three-month siege in 612 B.C. Although a remnant of the Assyrian dynasty continued to attempt to rule from Harran for a few years after this disaster, the Assyrian empire had come to an end.

The reasons for the fall of Assyria are multiple and intertwined. One must date the beginning of the fall to the civil war between Assyria and Babylonia, which broke out in 652 B.C. Assyria never recovered from that conflict, although to all appearances it was the victor. Militarily, it was left weak and a prime target for major enemies on its horizons such as the Cimmerians, Medes, Manneans, and Babylonians. While these external factors were important reasons for the fall of Assyria, there were internal weaknesses as well. The Assyrian provincial administrative system was still a very primitive one. If chance had allowed the Assyrians more time, perhaps they would have developed a more effective system; the Achaemenid Persians did, and their provincial administrative system was based upon that of the Assyrians. Another internal factor was that Assyria had an absolute monarch. There are advantages and disadvantages to such a political system. As long as the character and personality of the absolute monarch was strong, the state was strong, but as soon as a weak man came to the throne disaster ensued. Ashurbanipal was clearly a very strong character, but he was succeeded by a series of weak individuals who lost control over the state.

In conclusion, one must observe that the "fall of Assyria" was really a transfer of power to the Babylonians, who under Nabopolassar and later Nebuchadnezzar II simply took over the Assyrian empire and continued to run it in the Assyrian manner. The Assyrians as a people continued to live in the region but had become subjects of the Babylonian monarchs. See the following article.

E. The Army

Assyria was a militaristic state, and the entire organization of the nation was centered around the army and warfare. It was this specialized concentration which over the centuries made Assyria the supreme political power in the ANE. Most of what we know of the Assyrian army comes from the Sargonid period; that is, the time of the Late Neo-Assyrian empire. Given the nature of our sources, there are no precise figures on the size of the Assyrian army, although by the Sargonid period it must have numbered several hundreds of thousands of troops. This vast resource of manpower would, however, be called up only for a major campaign. There was a very strict hierarchy in the organization of the army, and this hierarchy very closely paralleled the civil administration. The king was the supreme commander of the army, and immediately under him was the "field marshall" (Akk *tartan*). See TARTAN. The army was divided into units of various sizes and types, but the basic division was the "company" *(kiṣru),* which consisted of 50 men under a "captain" *(rab kiṣri* or *rab ḫanše).* The company, in turn, was broken down into files of 10 men. An officer carried a mace as the symbol of his authority.

The Assyrian army consisted mainly of infantrymen, but there were also smaller, more specialized units of chariotry, cavalry, and engineers. The infantrymen were equipped with spears, bows, slings, daggers, swords, maces, and battle-axes, and they defended themselves with various types of shields. The archers were a specialized group within the infantry. Each archer was equipped with his own quiver of arrows and a bow which was as tall as himself. Archers worked in groups of three, consisting of the archer himself, a spearman to protect him, and another man bearing an enormous shield to protect all three.

The light horse-drawn chariot was first introduced to the Fertile Crescent in the middle of the 2d millennium by the Indo-Europeans. It quickly became an integral part of the Assyrian army. Over the subsequent centuries, its form and efficiency was gradually improved, although the basic type of chariot remained the same, being a two-wheeled, open-backed vehicle drawn by one or more horses. In the 9th century B.C., each vehicle had a driver and an archer. Later, one or two shield bearers were added for the defense of the driver and archer. The bow used by the chariot's archer was much smaller than that used by the infantry archer.

Cavalries were not introduced in the Near East until the 1st millennium, but their introduction added considerable mobility to the Assyrian army. The cavalryman and the charioteer were the elite of the Assyrian army. Each cavalryman was equipped with a small bow and a short sword. In the 9th century B.C., he was usually accompanied by a second mounted man with a shield, who protected the archer and held his horse's reins when he was shooting. After the 9th century, this companion disappeared.

Apart from the standing army, which had been established by Tiglath-pileser III in the late 8th century B.C., all troops were raised under a special institution called the *ilku,* through which they were required to perform military service each year for a limited period of time. But as time went on, the *ilku* proved inadequate to provide the number of troops required, and toward the latter days of the Assyrian empire foreign troops and mercenaries were included in the ranks of the Assyrian army. Assyrians proper were spread around the empire as much as possible, since they were the most loyal, and they constituted the chariotry and cavalry divisions. The infantry consisted largely of foreigners and mercenaries, the foreigners being Arameans and at least some of the mercenaries being Greeks.

By the Sargonid period there were three basic kinds of soldiers: the permanent professional, the man fulfilling his *ilku* obligation, and the extraordinary soldier called up for a specific campaign. The raising of Assyrian troops was the primary responsibility of the captains, and each captain had a certain number of villages under his control.

The captain, in turn, was responsible to the provincial governor.

As for military strategy, there is little evidence of any major coherent system in the 2d millennium B.C. But by the 9th century with the reign of Ashurnasirpal II, the conduct of Assyrian warfare had become a relatively well organized matter. By this time it is clear that there was a grand plan behind the organization of the campaigns. Ashurnasirpal II, Shalmaneser III, and their successors carefully considered long-range policy before launching a series of campaigns. An Assyrian campaign normally started in the spring, as soon as the winter rains had stopped. The core of the army gathered at an appointed starting point, which was not necessarily the capital. Here, the monarch inspected the troops, and the priests and diviners performed the necessary religious rituals. As the army marched off it was preceded by the standards, accompanied by the priests, the diviners, and the king with his personal bodyguard. After these came, in the following order, the chariotry, the cavalry, the infantry, and the impedimenta. Further levies of troops would be picked up at gathering points in the regions of the empire through which the army marched on its way to the frontier. The army carried with it some food supplies when it started its march, and these supplies, mainly barley, were issued in daily rations. Essentially, however, the Assyrian army lived off the land through which it marched. At the successful conclusion of the campaign, the hostages and booty were paraded through the streets of the Assyrian capital. The king was driven in state in his ceremonial chariot, with the conquered princes and nobles plodding in chains behind him.

Assyrian military strategy involved pitched battles, siege warfare, and psychological warfare. In pitched battles, the fighting was usually performed hand to hand by the infantry under cover of the archers, chariotry, and cavalry. Special tactics used on occasion were midnight attacks, damming rivers to flood the enemy camp, and taking a position to cut the enemy off from its water supply. The main goal in all battles was the capture or death of the enemy leader, and the fulfillment of this was the immediate signal of victory.

The Assyrians were particularly adept at siege warfare, and they developed highly specialized siege techniques. These techniques were adopted by later imperial armies, including those of the Romans. But siege warfare was a prolonged and costly business, and even pitched battles consumed much time, manpower, and equipment. Thus, the Assyrians often tried psychological warfare first, using various methods to try and persuade the people of a target area to surrender without resistance. One such method was to surround a city and then send one or more high-ranking Assyrian officers to stand near the walls and harangue the inhabitants. These officers, who spoke the local language, presented arguments to the besieged people about why they should disobey their leaders and open the gates peacefully to the Assyrians. They were promised lenient treatment if they did so. A good example of this tactic is recorded in 2 Kgs 18:16–37, where it is narrated that Sennacherib sent his RABSHAKEH to the walls of Jerusalem to persuade the inhabitants to overthrow Hezekiah and surrender Jerusalem to the Assyrians.

If such psychological tactics failed, Assyria's methods changed dramatically. One or more groups or cities were singled out for a major onslaught, be it pitched battle or siege, and once they were defeated the people were horribly mutilated and slaughtered while their houses and towns were burnt to the ground. Victims were selected, their skins were flayed, and the mutilated corpses were hung on stakes surrounding the city. News of such horrible acts spread quickly throughout the region, and commonly the people submitted to the Assyrian army without further resistance. This "calculated frightfulness" or psychological warfare of the Assyrian army won it a notorious reputation in the Bible and in subsequent histories. Whatever moral judgement one might pronounce on such tactics, the practice was extremely effective; and one must remember that it was selective. Only strategic targets were singled out for this treatment, and there was a specific purpose behind it.

Another tactic which the Assyrians employed, and which also gave them a notorious reputation in ancient history, was the deportation of people. Populations of a given region were uprooted and moved to areas completely foreign to them, where they could no longer cause trouble. The reason for the deportation was to put down rebellious elements within the empire and at the same time to provide labor for major building projects or to develop uncultivated land in order to supply food for the increasing populations of the Assyrian cities.

The Assyrian army was the most successful army developed in the ancient world in pre-Persian times. One flaw did develop in the Assyrian fighting army, however, and that was the increasing use of foreign troops. But given the other major factors which led to the fall of Assyria, as outlined above, this flaw was probably a minor factor in the collapse of the Assyrian empire.

F. Hunting

The favorite recreation of the Assyrian monarch was hunting. This sport had the advantage of keeping him and his entourage in top physical condition during the lull between campaigns. Hunting as an Assyrian sport is attested already in the Middle Assyrian period. By the time of the Neo-Assyrian Empire, it had developed into a national institution similar in many respects to the annual campaign. Notable examples of this were the lion hunts of Ashurbanipal, which even had religious significance. They were attended by great ceremony and watched by the general populace. The gods Ninurta and Palil were the patron deities of the hunt.

The favorite hunting grounds of the Assyrian kings were the forests which once covered Syria between the Habur and upper Euphrates rivers. The larger the animal, the more valued it was as a prey. The Assyrians boasted most about killing or capturing such enormous beasts as elephants, lions, wild bulls, and panthers, which in antiquity were abundant in Syria. Lions were also found in the marshes in S Babylonia, where they were hunted by Ashurbanipal. Besides killing beasts, the Assyrians sometimes captured them alive and brought them back to populate game parks in Assyrian capitals. They hunted animals in a variety of ways. Sometimes they simply chased them with chariots, but at other times they stalked them on foot. It was a common tactic for the king and his entourage to lie in ambush in hollows in the ground while the king's men stampeded the animals toward them by battue. It is sad to record that the uncontrolled slaughter of animals in Syria, together with the uncontrolled cutting of timber in the region, led to the extinction of all large beasts and the destruction of the forests.

G. Libraries

Despite the fact that Assyria was a militaristic state and that the favorite recreation of Assyrian monarchs was hunting, the Assyrians had great respect for culture, and Assyrian libraries were major institutions in antiquity. These libraries were founded in Middle Assyrian times and contained largely Babylonian texts, for the Assyrians recognized that the Babylonians had special talent in literature and learning. The Assyrians themselves had scribes, of course, who occasionally wrote literary works, but such works were scarce and usually showed much Babylonian influence. The very idea of a library was in fact imported into Assyria from Babylonia. The assiduous collection of Babylonian written works probably began with the sack of Babylon by Tukulti-Ninurta I (ca. 1243–1207 B.C.).

In subsequent centuries, when Assyria was powerful, the kings set themselves the task of continuing and expanding such libraries. It eventually became a passion, and a good example of this is the last great Assyrian king, Ashurbanipal. This monarch sent out agents throughout Babylonia to collect, as he states in a letter:

> ". . . every last tablet in their establishments and all the tablets which are in Ezida. Gather together the entirety of . . . (a long list of text types) and send them to me. . . . If you see any tablet which I have not mentioned and it is appropriate for my palace . . . send it to me!"

By the Neo-Assyrian period, libraries existed in all major Assyrian cities and probably in many of the minor cities as well. Nabû was the patron deity of the libraries, since he was the god of the scribal craft. The libraries, at least in the temples, therefore were called Ezidas after the name of Nabû's shrine at Borsippa. The libraries consisted of collections of literary and related works inscribed in cuneiform on clay tablets. The tablets were arranged in several rows on clay shelves, as we know from a Babylonian library recently discovered at Sippar. Tablets containing catalogues of the works stored in the libraries were maintained, and some of these have been preserved. The library collections consisted of compositions of various types, including what we would call literary, learned, and religious works. In form, these library tablets are easily distinguishable from everyday documents by the extra care with which the scribes wrote them and the better quality of clay used.

As stated earlier, libraries existed in all major Assyrian cities as well as in most minor cities. In practice, archaeologists have so far recovered evidence of such libraries at Asshur, Nineveh, Calah, and the provincial city of Huzirina (= Sultantepe) on the Balih river. By far the most important and largest library so far recovered is that of Ashurbanipal at Nineveh. Because of the unscientific method by which these tablets were recovered, it is impossible to give an accurate estimate of the number of works this library once contained. It must have had at least 1,500 tablets, but how much higher one should push this figure is very uncertain.

While one generally thinks of the Assyrians as crude, military warriors, the Assyrian libraries are an example of the great cultural interest of the Assyrians. It is thanks to the Assyrian libraries that so much is known not only of Assyrian culture but also of Babylonian and Sumerian civilization.

H. The State

Politically, the Assyrian state was an absolute monarchy. The form of the Assyrian state and its kingship was essentially a native development, although there was some influence from Babylonia. By far the most important part of the concept of monarchy in Assyria was the link between the Assyrian king and the god Asshur. The Assyrian king was the representative of the god Asshur on earth and acted under his authority. In contrast to periods in Sumerian and Babylonian history when the king was regarded as a god, the Assyrian king was never deified. He was always regarded as a human being, albeit the supreme human being on earth.

The Assyrian king had absolute control over the state, but there were three checks to his absolute power: religion, legal precedent, and the attitude of his nobility. The monarch, as representative of the god Asshur on earth, had to respect religious practice, and this involved regular participation in religious rituals. With regard to legal precedent, the king had to respect the traditional rights of individuals, such as property ownership, and of groups or institutions, such as tax exemptions granted to privileged cities. As to the third check to his authority, the attitude of the nobility, the Assyrian king's position depended very much upon the support of the upper classes. On the few occasions in Assyrian history when the Assyrian king offended the nobility, the results were disastrous for the king. Apart from these three factors, the king had supreme power in Assyria.

The Assyrian king was the sole legislator in the state, and his "law-making" consisted of making royal decrees. There was not even an assembly in which his decrees might be discussed, although he did seek advice from his chief officials and sanction from the gods by means of omens. In the judicial sphere, the king was the supreme judge in the state, and legal disputes which could not be decided at a lower level eventually came to his attention. The Assyrian king was the commander in chief of the army and frequently led the army in person on campaign. As for religion, as already mentioned he was the representative of the god Asshur on earth. This involved his position as high priest of the god Asshur and required his presence frequently at major state religious festivals. In the economic sphere, in theory the Assyrian monarch owned all of the land in Assyria, and all commercial transactions, both domestic and foreign, were subject to his control and taxation.

In practice, the Assyrian king was isolated in his palace and harem from the Assyrian populace. Our sources allow us only glimpses of court life, but we can piece together from these a fuller picture by analogy with later oriental courts, in particular the Ottoman court at Istanbul, which was an indirect successor of the Assyrian court. A major institution in the Assyrian court was the harem, which consisted of a number of wives, concubines, serving maids, and eunuch guards. There was a strict order of precedence within the harem, with the queen mother at the top. Immediately under her in authority was the chief wife of the reigning king, her status being determined by the fact that she was the first wife to give the king a male offspring. Princes normally spent their early years in the harem. There was much rivalry and jealousy within the Assyrian harem, and since the heir to the throne spent his early years there, harem plots to overthrow the king were not uncommon.

Male primogeniture was the rule of succession in Assyria. As soon as the eldest son of the king had reached a certain age, he left the harem and was officially appointed crown prince in a special ceremony. At the end of the ceremony, he entered the "House of Succession" *(bīt redūti)*. Here, he was surrounded by a court similar to his father's, and he had his own personal bodyguard. In the "House of Succession," he received rigorous training and education as preparation for his eventual succession to the throne. Ashurbanipal gives us some information about this training, which may or may not have been typical. Ashurbanipal says that he learned to ride, to shoot, to read, and to write. At the end of this training, the crown prince was assigned an official position in the Assyrian administration. In the Sargonid period at least, this involved the prince becoming the king's representative at home, with full royal authority while his father was on military exercises. Since nothing is said about the crown prince being trained in administration while in the House of Succession, it is apparent that he learned this skill "on the job."

The Assyrian state was run by a bureaucracy which had a very rigid hierarchy. One might picture the hierarchy as a pyramid with the king at the pinnacle and under him several layers of officials, increasing in number down to the broad base which consisted of the labor force. Over the centuries, the hierarchial structure underwent changes, and numerous anomalies developed which were never fully resolved. The only major systematic reorganization of the administration took place during the reign of Tiglath-pileser III. Assyrian administration was essentially a military structure, since Assyria was a militaristic state. There was usually little if any distinction between military and civil service. Although the chain of command was generally rigidly restricted to the next layer in the administration, the king as absolute monarch had the right to intervene at any level in any affair.

Bureaucratic positions tended to be hereditary in practice, the son learning his father's job by working with him. Thus, we find that certain levels of the bureaucracy tended to be monopolized by a small group of families. Patronage was the rule in Assyria, and no one could get a position without influence.

Scribes were a special part of the Assyrian administrative system. The scribes were an elite group who had graduated from a demanding and lengthy educational system. There were scribes at every level of the bureaucracy, with the vice-chancellor at the top and the numerous lesser skilled scribes at the very bottom, who kept track of the unskilled laborers and their wages. Since the vast majority of Assyrian officials were illiterate, the scribes had considerable influence over the running of state affairs.

Assyrian officials derived their revenue from the resources under their jurisdiction, and the revenue was usually in kind. On occasion, the king would reward an official for special service with expensive clothing, jewelry, tax exemption, or residence for life at the palace. Officials, including scribes, constantly complained that they were underpaid, and the custom of bribery was universal. There is frequent reference in our sources to punishment for inefficiency and corruption, which is an indication that these were rampant. Nevertheless, the Assyrian officers seem to have been a relatively hard-working, conscientious lot, and the king generally set them a very good example in this regard.

For administrative purposes, the Assyrian empire was divided into two major units. The central and most important unit was the land of Asshur itself, the Assyrian heartland. This included the four major cities of Asshur, Arbela, Nineveh, and Calah, together with the surrounding agricultural land. Each of these cities had special privileges, including tax exemptions and military impositions.

Beyond the Assyrian heartland was "greater Assyria." The size and organization of this territory changed over the centuries. When it reached its greatest extent in the Sargonid period, two types of administration were used to control this vast territory. Some parts of the empire were directly controlled by the king through provincial governors, while other parts of the empire were controlled by treaty arrangements between the Assyrian king and the local ruler. Some of these rulers were regarded as equal partners in the treaty arrangements, while others were regarded as vassals. Treaty arrangements with vassals included keeping foreign princes and nobles as hostages at the Assyrian court.

Babylonia always had a special position in the Assyrian state, as observed already in the discussion of the political history. Assyria tried to deal with Babylonia by various means; for example, sometimes concluding treaties with Babylonian kings as equal partners, or at other times ruling Babylonia directly. The fact is that Assyria never was able to find a satisfactory solution for the administration of Babylonia.

The administrative center of the Assyrian state varied from time to time. Originally, it was at the city of Asshur, but in the 9th century Ashurnasirpal II made the center Calah. Finally, in the 7th century, Sennacherib chose Nineveh as the administrative center and this city remained the capital of the Assyrian state until its downfall. At each of these sites have been found remains of the state archives, including voluminous correspondence. These records and reports are in part a result of the king's standing order to all officials that they must report "whatever you see and hear." To ensure rapid communication between the capital and the outlying regions of the empire, there was a corps of messengers who were supported by a network of roads and posting stations. In an emergency, messages could be relayed even more quickly by a system of observation towers and fire signals. The Assyrian frontiers were carefully guarded by a series of fortresses manned by Assyrian troops.

I. Socioeconomic Structure

The socioeconomic structure of Assyria was very conservative and slow to change, a feature which it had in common with most preindustrial civilizations. Change in social structures and economic procedures was rare, the attitude being that if something had been good enough for previous generations it was certainly good enough for the present generation. Only when former ways of doing things were no longer possible did the Assyrians consider developing new approaches. This rarely happened, and so the socioeconomic structure of Assyrian civilization underwent only minor modification throughout its lengthy history.

The core of the Assyrian social structure was the tribe, and fundamental motives for every Assyrian's life were the protection and propagation of his family and tribe. This fact is well illustrated by the common personal-name type, whose use expressed the desire of the individual to preserve his tribe or family. This desire also found expression in the common practice of adoption, for adoption not only provided a childless couple with care for their old age, but also assured them of the continuation of their family. Even the dead were kept within the home, for they were buried under the floor.

Apart from this central position of the Assyrian family, there was a class structure which was closely linked to power, wealth, and social standing. The king was at the top, immediately succeeded by the nobility of varius levels. Under them came the lesser officials, then the skilled laborers, and finally, at the bottom, the unskilled laborers. The unskilled laborers consisted of two groups: freemen and slaves.

Slavery was not nearly so extensive in Assyria as it was in the Roman empire. Although slaves provided an important part of the labor force for Assyria, particularly for the major building projects of the kings, the Assyrian economy did not depend upon slavery as did the Roman economy. There were two types of slaves in Assyria; the debt slave and the prisoner of war. The debt slave was a native Assyrian, and his slavery lasted only so long as he was unable to pay off his debts. In other words, it was the Assyrian form of bankruptcy. A debt slave enjoyed a number of privileges; he could marry a free person, appear as a witness in a court case, conduct business transactions with other slaves or their masters, and even own property to which slaves were attached. In theory, it was always possible for a debt slave to pay off his debts and regain his freedom. In practice, however, manumission was rare in Assyria. The high interest rates, to be mentioned later, meant that it was not only easy to fall into debt slavery but that once in that situation it was very difficult to amass enough resources to buy one's way out of debt. The other type of slave, the foreign captive, was in an entirely different position. He had no real rights in Assyria, and he was given the most menial tasks to perform. His only hope of freedom was escape or death.

The status of women in Assyrian society was extremely low, even lower than in Babylonia. In Assyria, one rarely found a woman acting in a legal or business transaction on her own behalf, for she had virtually no legal rights as an individual. She was entirely dependent upon her male relations—father, husband, sons, and brothers—and their position in society. She was confined to separate quarters, the harem, and apart from her immediate male relatives her social intercourse was restricted entirely to other females. Marriage, the rearing of children, cooking, and the general care of the home were her established roles in life.

The vast majority of Assyrians lived in the large cities, the major centers being Asshur, Nineveh, Arbela, and Calah. There are no reliable statistics for population figures, but one estimate has concluded that Calah at its height contained about 63,000 inhabitants, while Nineveh probably had about 120,000 (Oates 1968: 43–44). The immediate surrounding countryside was insufficient to support such large numbers of nonproductive people, which is why, beginning in the 9th century B.C., the agricultural land cultivated by the Assyrians had to be extended. Ashurnasirpal began the program of deporting foreign peoples into the undeveloped regions of Assyria to create new farms in order to provide the growing city populations with the necessary food.

Within the cities, the streets were narrow and dark, being flanked by the blank walls of houses. An Assyrian house was centered around an inner courtyard, and apart from the street entrance there were no openings on the outside.

As has been observed, the socioeconomic structure of Assyria changed only when it was compelled to do so. Certainly, the economy was forced to alter as Assyria developed from a small cluster of autonomous city-states first into a nation and then into an empire. As the Assyrian empire evolved, in a sense two separate economic systems developed. In the Assyrian heartland itself, the economic structure which already existed continued with only slight alterations. Beyond the boundaries of the heartland, however, the economic organization of the territories now under Assyrian control inevitably changed.

In Assyria proper, the economic bases were agriculture, animal husbandry, and trade. The S border of Assyria coincided with the S limit of dependable, annual rainfall, so that Assyria's meadows could be cultivated with relative ease and profit. At the same time, the position of the city of Asshur at a strategic crossing point of the Tigris river meant that it straddled a major trade route between E and W. Thus, from earliest times the inhabitants of the Assyrian heartland were involved in foreign trade, a necessity since so many resources had to be imported into Assyria.

As to actual ownership of land, all land in theory belonged to the king as the representative of the god Asshur on earth. In practice, however, the crown had direct control over only a limited amount of territory. The rest was controlled by wealthy institutions such as temples or by large families. This still left much land in the control of private individuals. Frequently, land in Assyria was held under an arrangement called *ilku.* By this arrangement, the client had the use of the land in return for performing state service, which involved both civil and military works. Obviously land which had an *ilku* obligation was less valuable because the impositions involved were relatively onerous. In the Neo-Assyrian period, it was possible for the more important and wealthy Assyrian citizens to make payments in lieu of *ilku* service. This is significant for the history of the Assyrian army in the late period, since many wealthy landowners sent goods in payment of their *ilku* obligations rather than manpower. Thus, the state was forced to hire foreign mercenaries to fill the ranks of the army.

Crafts in Assyria were carried on in the palace and perhaps also in temples and on large estates. Originally the craftsmen actually worked in these buildings and were issued raw materials with which to make the finished products, but in Neo-Assyrian times craftsmen worked on a contract basis whereby they could repay their masters for the raw materials in a variety of forms and could keep back a certain amount for themselves as a commission.

Money was unknown in Assyria and seems to have been an invention of the Greeks. Business was carried on by trading in kind, although there was a standard of exchange in terms of precious metals, silver or copper. There was a standard for measurements, including weights. Some of these official weights have survived, being stone or metal carved in the shape of such animals as ducks or lions. These weights bear cuneiform inscriptions indicating their measurement. Careful accounts were kept of business transactions, and hundreds of administrative tablets, mainly from palaces, have been recovered. Prices fluctuated according to supply and demand, and there is no indication of state control over prices.

The economic organization of the Assyrian empire had one goal—the enrichment of the Assyrian heartland and in particular the Assyrian court. The Assyrian king had no interest in the economic development of the outlying regions. So long as these conquered territories contributed annual tribute to the state treasury and remained submissive to his control, he was happy. But as time went on, the nonproductive element of the population of the Assyrian heartland increased, and greater and greater demands were made on the outlying regions for supplies. This escalating oppressiveness increased economic hardship and engendered hatred of the Assyrian rule. It is no exaggeration to say that the economies of the outlying regions of the Assyrian empire were gradually destroyed in order to prop up an artificial economy in central Assyria. This economic circumstance was no small factor in the weakening and eventual fall of the Assyrian empire.

J. Legal Structure

The supreme legal authority in Assyria was the god Asshur, which meant in practice his representative on earth, the king, who was the chief justice in the land. The king rarely exercised his authority in this capacity, however, for most legal disputes were settled at a lower level. In ancient Assyria there was no specialized legal branch of the government comparable to what we are used to today in modern society. The vast majority of disputes were handled by the individuals involved, frequently with the intervention of a third party as an objective arbitrator. This third party was usually a neighbor. There were no courts as such, and there was no codified law. There was a document known now as the Middle Assyrian Laws (see *ANET,* 180–88), but this was more literary than legal. This is illustrated by the fact that in the few records of legal disputes from Assyria, no reference is ever made to the Middle Assyrian Laws. The real law of Assyria rested in custom and precedent. Disputes which could not be decided on this basis between the two parties, with the frequent help of a third objective individual, were referred to the official bureaucracy.

A number of Assyria's legal documents have come down to us. In Assyria, a legal document was the record of a transaction between two or more parties which included the names of witnesses to the transaction, the name of the scribe who recorded the transaction, and the date upon which it took place. A common feature of such texts was the inclusion of seal impressions of the major participants in the transaction. If an individual was too poor to own a seal, he pressed his fingernail into the moist clay, and this fact was duly noted on the tablet. Legal documents were frequently enclosed in envelopes of clay, and a brief version of the transaction was written on the outside of this envelope, which was then duly sealed. There were also legal documents in Aramaic on parchment or papyrus, but all of these have perished; only the bullae (lumps of clay with brief notes in Assyrian) which were squeezed over the cord binding these documents have been preserved.

In Assyria, there were four major kinds of legal documents: conveyances (sales), contracts, receipts, and court records. The word conveyance covers all texts which record the transfer of property, and most of these are therefore sale documents, although rentals, marriages, adoptions, and inheritances also come under this heading. Conveyances contained provision against future claims and penalties for making false claims, which included heavy fines and occasionally some bizarre provisions. For example, a guilty party might have been required to present a number of white horses to a god if he had been convicted of making a false claim about a sale. Or he might have been required to burn his eldest son or, even more curious, to swallow an enormous amount of wool, thus in effect committing suicide. These more bizarre penalty provisions seem to have been more theoretical than practical, and there is no evidence that they were ever enforced. In the case of the sale of slaves, the seller normally had to guarantee that the slave would remain free of illness for 100 days after the sale.

The second type of legal document, the contract, involved an obligation on the part of one party in favor of another, and this covered all kinds of loans and promissory notes. "True loans" were not common, since debts were incurred by the inability of an individual to pay the rent in the form of a portion of the harvest of land which he had contracted to cultivate. Interest rates were very high, the normal being in the range of 25–33 percent, but rates of 100 percent or more per annum are attested. For this reason, many people remained in debt for their entire lives, and frequently they went bankrupt, which means they fell into debt slavery. When a debt was paid, however, the tablet recording the debt was smashed, thus effectively destroying all evidence of the loan. Only occasionally, for special reasons, was it felt necessary to write out a receipt for the payment of a debt. Thus, this third type of legal document was relatively rare. The creditor always had the obligation to provide proof of a debt. If a creditor could not produce a contract with a record of the loan, he had no claim against an individual.

The fourth type of legal document, the court record, was uncommon. This reflects the fact already stated that most disputes were settled privately. On the rare occasions, however, when this proved impossible, the disputants would go to an official in the Assyrian administration for a decision. When this happened, an official record was made of the proceedings, and these are what we call court records. But it should be noted that no law court was involved here, since they did not exist in ancient Assyria. The disputants simply went to a high administrative official, who was often the mayor of their village or town. If this official could not come to a decision, the disputants were sent to the "ordeal." Unfortunately, little is known about the Assyrian ordeal. The presiding judge at the ordeal was the god, and after the litigants declared their respective claims before the god, the deity issued his verdict. How the god came to this decision and how it was announced are unknown, but the decision was final and binding upon both parties. It should be noted that no reference is made here to the king in this final appeal, although he was the supreme justice in the land. In administrative matters, it is known that an Assyrian subject could appeal directly to the monarch.

Murder and bodily injury were special cases. These again were normally settled by private agreement, and this is particularly so in the case of murder, for murder involved the blood feud, or vendetta. In Assyria, there was no such thing as a state crime apart from treason, which was punishable by death. Since there were no state crimes, prisons did not exist for the incarceration of criminals. However, the state might detain individuals for political reasons, and private individuals might forcibly restrain a person who had wronged them until the wrong had been redressed.

K. Religion

Religion is a complex subject in any civilization, and there is no exception to this for ancient Assyria. A primary consideration is the difference between the official or state religion and popular belief. This is true not only in ancient Assyria but also in modern society. What people actually believe, what they actually do in their religious observances, and what is actually recorded as official religious doctrine may be quite different matters. In dealing with an ancient society such as that of the Assyrians or Hebrews, our knowledge is inevitably limited to and conditioned by the written records. In the case of the Hebrews, this means the Bible; in the case of the Assyrians, this means the multitude of cuneiform writings concerning rituals, hymns, incantations, etc. Thus, most of what can be said here about Assyrian religion concerns the state religion.

Assyrian religion had two outstanding features: polytheism and the cult. The polytheistic nature of Assyria is comparable to that of Sumer or Babylonia, although the number of gods was more restricted. The chief gods in Assyria were Asshur, who was the king of the gods, followed by the goddess Ishtar and the gods Ninurta, Shamash, Adad, and Sin. Around each god there was centered a cult which included a large temple complex and a ziggurrat, as well as priests and a supporting staff. This cult involved the performance of regular religious rituals and the presentation of offerings.

The chief Assyrian god, Asshur, was almost characterless in comparison to the other gods of Assyria. Although he officially ruled and controlled all the land of Assyria and reigned supreme over all other gods, he really played no role in Assyrian mythology, and no personal characteristics are evident for him. This is in contrast to the other Assyrian deities.

Much more lifelike and vivid is the figure of the goddess Ishtar. She was responsible for two contrasting activities: battle and love. In both these spheres she played a leading role, and there is a major place for her in the mythology, which in origin at least is largely Babylonian. She was the patron deity of two major Assyrian cities, Nineveh and Arbela, which shows the high regard the Assyrians had for Ishtar. Part of her cult included female ecstatics; these were prophetesses who went into a trance and made pronouncements to the Assyrian king of future victories and prosperity. These pronouncements were duly recorded and sent to the king from Ishtar's cult at Arbela.

Another outstanding deity in Assyria was Ninurta, the god of warfare and hunting, who was the firstborn son of Asshur. Ashurnasirpal brought the cult of Ninurta to the fore with the dedication to Ninurta of the chief temple at his newly constructed capital of Calah. Adad, the god of storm and rain, was another distinctive Assyrian deity. He shared with Shamash the responsibility for divination. The god Shamash, the sun-god, was responsible for justice, a role he also played in Babylonian religion. It should be noted that all of these major deities were males with the exception of Ishtar. This is a reflection of the dominance of the male in Assyrian society, and the fact that Ishtar is an exception is because she was the patron deity of Nineveh in pre-Assyrian times.

Assyrian culture was greatly influenced by Babylonian culture, and this is particularly so in religion. Three distinctly Babylonian deities—Enlil, Marduk, and Nabû—became popular in Assyria at different periods. Enlil first appeared in Assyria during the reign of Shamshi-Adad I (1813–1781 B.C.). He was eventually identified with the god Asshur, who assumed his epithets and the cultic practices which surrounded him. The cult of Marduk appeared in Assyria by the 14th century B.C., and eventually Marduk became so popular there that Sennacherib, in the 7th century B.C., tried to suppress the Babylonian cult. Nabû, the son of Marduk, became popular in Assyria in the 9th century B.C. when great temples were built at Assyrian cities in his honor.

While the Assyrians may have had some religious rituals and practices of their own, by the time we reach the well-documented period in MA times, Babylonian influence is evident everywhere. Most religious ceremonies in Assyria, and in particular the New Year Festival, were greatly influenced by Babylonia.

So far only the major deities have been mentioned, but there were also many minor deities, all with their own temples and shrines. An Assyrian city had many temples in it devoted to these various gods and goddesses, and larger temples contained several shrines for different deities. A temple was a community unto itself, with its own hierarchy of personnel and its own economic resources, at least in origin. By the Neo-Assyrian period, however, Assyrian temples were no longer economically independent. They had become accustomed to receiving major benefits from royal campaigns. This brought them greater prosperity but at the same time meant they lost some control over their own affairs. Besides the priests, the temple personnel included artisans, scribes, kitchen staff, and domestic servants.

The king was the chief priest in the land since he was Asshur's representative on earth. His presence was frequently required at religious ceremonies, particularly at the celebration of the New Year, in which his right to reign for another year was confirmed by the god. Religion in the form of the temple rituals and divination had great influence on the Assyrian king. Not only was the king required to participate in religious rituals but he also felt compelled to consult the diviners regularly on major state decisions. Thus, the priests and diviners had a great deal of influence on state affairs.

By far the most important Assyrian ritual was the New Year ritual, called the *Akītu*. Most of the ceremony was performed in the *Akītu* temple, there being one outside the walls of each major Assyrian city. The ceremony involved an elaborate procession of the statues of the gods followed by a great feast. The *Akītu* festival included the coronation ritual in which the god Asshur confirmed the right of the king to rule for another year, and during which the princes and nobles renewed their loyalty oaths.

The Assyrians were tolerant of other religions and religious practices. They did not attempt to impose the worship of Asshur or any other Assyrian deity upon peoples they conquered. They did, however, carry off divine symbols of conquered peoples which they held as hostages in order to insure the loyalty of these suppressed populations. These symbols were returned once the Assyrians were assured that the people would be loyal. Indeed, far from suppressing foreign cults of conquered peoples, the Assyrian king sometimes presented offerings to them and sponsored building works on their temples.

Most of what we know, and therefore most of what has been said so far, concerns the official religion of Assyria. Very little is known of the religious beliefs and practices of the common people. The masses had little to do with the great state festivals other than to stand by the roadside watching the great processions go by. It is known that each Assyrian believed he had a personal god, and that this personal god would present his needs and desires to the higher gods. In return, each Assyrian was expected to present offerings to this individual god. Magic, both black and white, was widely practised among the common people, and we have many documents from Assyrian libraries recording incantations.

Divination, the prediction of the future, was closely related to Assyrian religion. Allusion to this practice has already been made in preceding paragraphs. In the Neo-Assyrian period, there were two major types of divination: astrology and extispicy. Astrology involved regular observation of the movements of the stars and planets and the recording of such movements and any events on earth which took place at the same time, for the Assyrians believed there was a link between what happened in the heavens and what would happen on earth. Extispicy meant the examination of the entrails of sacrificed animals, since the shape and color of these entrails, such as the liver and lungs, indicated what would happen in the future. Divination was carried out mainly by Babylonian diviners.

L. Everyday Life

Everyday life in Assyria was much the same throughout Assyria's history, the daily behavior of someone living in the Old Assyrian period being essentially the same as that of someone living in the Neo-Assyrian Empire. Of course there was a great deal of difference between the everyday life of a member of the upper classes in Assyria and a member of the lower classes. In the following discussion, such differences will be noted where appropriate.

The most outstanding characteristic of everyday life in Assyria was its spartanism. Assyria was a militaristic society, and everything revolved around the warrior. People who were not warriors were regarded simply as support staff for the fighting men. This, in particular, meant that the status of women was restricted entirely to that of supplying the needs of soldiers. Women were segregated from men and lived in a harem, and their role in society was to bear and raise children and to maintain the household. They were entirely dependent upon their male relatives and had few legal rights of their own. Men were the dominant sex, and in theory all men were soldiers and were subject to military conscription. In practice, certain types of workers, such as shepherds, were excluded from this service.

The standard of living in Assyria was relatively high for an ancient culture for two reasons. First, Assyria was naturally a highly productive region, and thus the inhabitants of the Assyrian heartland from prehistoric times enjoyed the fruits of the land and the products of animal husbandry. Second, in the Neo-Assyrian period, the residents of Assyria proper enjoyed the prosperity brought to their land by the hold their kings had over the surrounding economies. The food the average Assyrian ate consisted mainly of barley in the form of bread spread with sesame oil. The usual beverage was beer, although wine was not uncommon. For vegetables, they had onions, leeks, and garlic. In addition, they enjoyed eggs from chickens and ducks, and fish from the rivers. For sweets they had grapes and honey, and in the Neo-Assyrian period nuts became more common as exotic nut trees were introduced into Assyrian gardens. Goats produced milk, which was turned into ghee (clarified butter) and cheese. The meat of animals and fowls was rarely eaten, it being preserved for festive occasions since it was a luxury. Of course the upper classes and in particular royalty enjoyed meat and wine more regularly. In fact, royal banquets were far from uncommon.

Royal feasts are frequently mentioned in our sources, as they were used to celebrate a variety of occasions. Every new year in connection with the Akitu ritual, there was a ceremonial banquet called the *tākultu*. Other occasions for royal feasts were the conclusion of successful military campaigns and the end of major building projects. An example of the latter is the great banquet staged by Ashurnasirpal II to celebrate the completion of the building of his capital, Calah. The menu of this banquet, which was served to 70,000 guests invited from all parts of Assyria, the provinces, and the surrounding lands, was engraved on stone by royal scribes for posterity (cf. *ANET,* 558–60).

The basic material for constructing all buildings was mud brick, which was sometimes baked in the sun or, more rarely, in kilns for greater durability. Marble (the so-called "Mosul marble") was available in quarries in the vicinity of Nineveh, but given the difficulty of extracting, transporting, and working this relatively hard substance, its use was generally restricted to monumental buildings. Timber of various sorts, including the popular "cedars of Lebanon," was imported for these monumental buildings as well. The house of the middle-class Assyrian usually consisted of two stories built around an inner courtyard. There was a pool of water in the center of the courtyard and steps on the side that led up to a balcony surrounding the second story. Family life was centered on this courtyard, and all doors and windows opened onto it with the exception of the main doorway leading into the street. The houses of wealthier people and the palaces of the kings had extensive gardens. Assyria also had its homeless poor, who carved out sleeping quarters for themselves in the city walls or in the ruins of monumental buildings, while some simply slept in doorways. The streets were narrow, twisting, and filthy since they had open sewers in the center to carry off all waste from the houses.

A variety of textiles was woven from goat's hair and sheep's wool. The resulting cloth was dyed in various colors and cut into various shapes for clothing. In addition, both men and women wore some jewelry made from precious metals and stones, which had to be imported. Of course, the wealthier classes enjoyed more elaborate clothing and jewelry.

The favorite recreations of the Assyrians were military in character. They loved to hunt (on royal hunts, see above). Contests in archery, javelin-throwing, stone-slinging, and similar sports were other popular pastimes. The Assyrians also entertained themselves with more peaceful pursuits. The parades of the great religious festivals were eagerly watched by the common people lining the streets of the great Assyrian metropolises. In the squares and gates, scribes and poets recited epics and sang songs to the masses. Both the parades and the recitations were accompanied by vocal and instrumental music, the instruments including strings, winds, and percussions. Older and more sedentary people entertained themselves with board games, while children had toys such as clay models of chariots and soldiers.

M. Legacy

A major legacy of Assyrian civilization to the history of the world is the practical creation of an empire which embraced a large part of the civilized world. It was the Assyrian kings who first extended their authority well beyond the confines of national boundaries to rule over or effectively control a variety of far-flung peoples and territories. Subsequent conquerors—the Achaemenid Persians, Alexander the Great, and the Romans—would strive to emulate the Assyrian achievement.

A second legacy was the elaborate structure and formality of the Assyrian court, which survived in later, neighboring cultures such as Achaemenid and Safavid Persia and Ottoman Turkey. Similarly, Assyrian military organization, strategy, and tactics reappear in these and other later civilizations.

A more subtle legacy is the protective role which Assyria played in sheltering Babylonia from foreign conquest, thus allowing that land to devote so much energy to cultural pursuits. Indeed, Assyria took an active part in creating libraries in which Babylonian literary and scientific works predominated. The libraries of Ashurbanipal at Nineveh are still our most important source for Babylonian culture. See *CAH* 1–3; *GARI; TCS* 5; *LAR.*

Bibliography

Contenau, G. 1966. *Everyday Life in Babylonia and Assyria.* New York.

Frankfort, H., et al. 1954. *Before Philosophy.* Harmondsworth.

Grayson, A. K. 1987–90. *The Royal Inscriptions of Mesopotamia: The Assyrian Periods.* Vols. 1–2. Toronto.

Larsen, M. 1976. *The Old Assyrian City-State.* Mesopotamia 4. Copenhagen.

Oates, D. 1968. *Studies in the Ancient History of Northern Iraq.* London.

Olmstead, A. T. E. 1923. *History of Assyria.* Chicago.

Oppenheim, A. L. 1964. *Ancient Mesopotamia.* Chicago. Rev. ed. E. Reiner. 1977.

Parpola, S. 1970. *Letters from Assyrian Scholars to the Kings Esarhaddon and Ashurbanipal.* AOAT 5. Neukirchen-Vluyn.

———. 1987. *The Correspondence of Sargon II.* State Archives of Assyria 1. Helsinki.

Postgate, J. N. 1976. *Fifty Neo-Assyrian Legal Documents.* Warminster.

Roux, G. 1980. *Ancient Iraq.* 2d ed. Harmondsworth.

Saggs, H. W. F. 1965. *Everyday Life in Babylonia and Assyria.* London.

———. 1976. *The Encounter with the Divine in Mesopotamia and Israel.* London.

———. 1984. *The Might That Was Assyria.* London.

Smith, S. 1928. *The Early History of Assyria.* London.

Van Driel, G. 1969. *The Cult of Ashur.* Assen.

Veenhof, K. 1972. *Aspects of Old Assyrian Trade.* Leiden.

A. Kirk Grayson

HISTORY AND CULTURE OF BABYLONIA

The name "Babylonia" (see MESOPOTAMIA) can be used as both a geographical and a political term. As a geographical name it covers the S part of the modern Republic of Iraq, approximately from Baghdad in the N to Basra in the S. On the W it extends roughly to the border of Saudi Arabia and on the E to Iran. In ancient times this area was a unified political unit only in certain periods, including the latter years of Hammurapi (ca. 1792–1750 B.C.) and the time of the Neo-Babylonian Empire (627–539 B.C.). Before Hammurapi it was frequently divided politically into two areas, with Nippur at the center. The N was called Akkad and the S Sumer, and the phrase "the lands of Sumer and Akkad" was still in vogue long after the political division had any reality.

A. Geography
  1. Physical Features
  2. Climate
  3. Natural Resources
  4. Agriculture and Animal Husbandry
  5. Trade, Communication, and Transportation
  6. Settlement Patterns
B. Sources
  1. Written Sources
  2. Archaeological Sources
C. Chronology

D. Political History
   1. Akkadians, Amorites, and Sumerians
   2. Early Old Babylonian Period (ca. 2017–1793 B.C.)
   3. The Hammurapi Age (ca. 1792–1750 B.C.)
   4. The Fall of Babylon (ca. 1750–1595 B.C.)
   5. The Kassites
   6. Middle Babylonian Period (ca. 1595–1000 B.C.)
   7. Babylonia and Assyria (ca. 1000–627 B.C.)
   8. The Neo-Babylonian Empire (626–539 B.C.)
   9. Babylonia Under the Persians and Greeks
E. The State
   1. The King
   2. Administration
F. Socioeconomic Structure
G. Legal Structure
   1. Law Codes
   2. Law in Practice
   3. Status of Women
H. Literature, Learning, and Libraries
   1. Literature
   2. Learning
   3. Libraries
I. Religion
   1. State Religion
   2. Popular Religion
   3. Divination
J. Everyday Life
K. Legacy

A. Geography

1. Physical Features. Babylonia is the S part of Mesopotamia, the "Land Between the Rivers," a name which reflects the importance of the Tigris and Euphrates rivers. These join to form the Shatt-el-Arab, which drains into the Arabian/Persian Gulf in the S. A major tributary of the Tigris is the Diyala river. The rivers flood the flat plain in the springtime, bringing water sorely needed for plant growth. The S part of Babylonia consists of marshes, where, since prehistoric times, people have lived as much in boats as on land. The N extremity of the plain is determined by the narrowest point between the Tigris and the Euphrates, although culturally Babylonian civilization often stretched farther up the Euphrates to such ancient sites as Mari. To the W are the Syrian and Arabian deserts, and to the E are the Zagros mountains. From the point of view of physical geography, the Khuzistan plain to the SE is an integral part of Babylonia despite the presence between them of the Qarun river, which flows into the Shatt-el-Arab.

2. Climate. The climate of a region affects not only its flora and fauna but also the human inhabitants and their behavior. Thus, in prehistoric times, the dwellers of the Babylonian plain were prompted to invent artificial irrigation systems in order to regulate the erratic water supply from rainfall and flooding rivers so that crop production was possible. From late spring to late fall the weather is hot and dry, while in the winter and early spring it is cool, sometimes close to freezing, and rain falls in abundance. The sudden and frequent downpours turn dry gullies, known as *wadis,* into swift rivers in a matter of hours. In the dry weather, high winds from various directions blow up fierce sandstorms, and in late summer a scorching wind from the S arises which is important for the ripening of dates. As far as is known, there was no significant change in climate during the historic period.

3. Natural Resources. Babylonia was rich in only a limited number of natural resources: soil, salt, bitumen, reeds, water, fish, birds, animals, and plants. The soil was valuable not only for agriculture and animal husbandry but also as a source of clay for bricks (used for building) and for tablets (used for writing). Reeds from the marshes were used as writing styluses and in building, either as the main material in the construction of reed huts or, when coated with bitumen, for binding mats placed between layers of mud bricks. The rivers, marshes, and Arabian/Persian Gulf teemed with various types of fish and also provided useful communication routes by boat. Birds were abundant, especially in the marshes, for Babylonia was, and is, at the S end of a major flyway of birds migrating from Europe. Wild animals in antiquity ranged in size and type from mice and snakes to wolves, pigs, gazelles, onagers, and lions. Missing from the list of Babylonia's natural resources are important items such as stone, metals, and timber, which had to be imported through trade.

4. Agriculture and Animal Husbandry. Agriculture and animal husbandry were the mainstays of the economy of the Babylonian plain throughout ancient times. The chief crops cultivated were barley and sesame, the former to make bread and beer and the latter to make vegetable oil. Onions, garlic, leeks, and mustard were common, but green vegetables were rare. In S Babylonia the date tree was, and still is, grown in large plantations for its fruit.

The most popular domestic animals were mules, donkeys, cows, sheep, goats, pigs, dogs, and cats. Mules and donkeys were used as pack animals and for riding. Cows and goats provided milk and hides, while sheep produced wool. Only on special occasions would these animals be slaughtered for meat; chickens, ducks, geese, wild birds, and cheese were more economical sources of protein. Horses were not used extensively until the late 2d millennium B.C., when they began to be used for drawing chariots; the camel also became common at about that time.

5. Trade, Communication, and Transportation. Foreign trade flourished as early as prehistoric times, when the inhabitants of the Babylonian plain sought good timber (such as cedar from Lebanon) and stone (such as marble from Assyria) for building; metals (such as tin and copper) for weapons and utensils; and precious metals (such as gold and silver) and precious stones (such as lapis lazuli) for luxury items. Overland communication and transportation followed river courses, since these provided water and food for travelers. In particular, the Diyala valley was a conduit for goods traveling to and from the Iranian plateau. Water routes were intensively used, with rafts and boats plying up and down the Tigris and Euphrates and larger boats carrying cargo through the Arabian/Persian Gulf to the coast of Oman and beyond. The speed with which one could travel these routes varied according to many factors, such as weather, terrain, and means of travel. Under optimum conditions a caravan covered about 25 km a day, while a swift runner could cover about 160 km in the same time. This meant a trading caravan could ideally transport goods from the Gulf along the Tigris to the mouth of the Diyala, a distance of about 600 km, in about twenty-four days. A relay of fast runners could deliver a message over the same route in about four days, under ideal conditions.

6. Settlement Patterns. Inevitably, people settled in Babylonia by the water, for it provided their basic needs and was the easiest link for trade. Only as the inhabitants developed artificial irrigation were they able to spread beyond onto the plain. This required cooperation and organization, and thus urban communities developed. By the dawn of history (ca. 3000 B.C.), the Babylonian plain was dotted with a multitude of villages, towns, and cities. Along the Euphrates, on the periphery of the plain, were the seminomads, herders of sheep and goats, who wandered between the plain and the Syro-Arabian desert. They could not go far into the desert until they had the camel, in the 1st millennium B.C., and that is why they are called seminomads or donkey nomads. (Adams 1965; 1972; 1981).

B. Sources

Until the mid-19th century of our era, the only sources available for ancient Babylonian history were the scant remarks in the Bible and in the writings of classical authors. By A.D. 1850, this had all changed, thanks to the beginning of archaeological excavations at ancient sites and the decipherment of Babylonian inscriptions. Since that date, research on the archaeological and written remains of Babylonian civilization has added enormously to the sources for and knowledge of this ancient culture. This activity continues today; and as these words are being written, yet more sources are coming to light.

1. Written Sources. a. Indigenous. The contemporary, indigenous inscriptions of Babylonia, consisting of tens of thousands of texts, are by far the largest body of sources. These are written in the cuneiform writing system and in the Babylonian dialect of the Akkadian language. The vast majority of inscriptions are written on clay tablets, although some are on clay cylinders, bricks, stone slabs, and various objects made of precious stones and metals. These texts may be divided into a few groups; namely, royal inscriptions, letters, contracts, and administrative documents.

Royal inscriptions were originally written records commissioned by the king to report to the gods that he had fulfilled his duty on earth. Principally, this duty entailed building projects (such as a temple), so that royal inscriptions were normally building inscriptions. As to their pious purpose, very early they developed into boasts by the ruler of his achievements. As a source for reconstructing Babylonian history, they are useful because of the wealth of detail they provide about kings, gods, and buildings. But one must remember that they are "official statements," and therefore should be used carefully.

Fortunately, a significant number of letters, many of them to or from the king and his officials, have been recovered. These allow us to look behind the official facade presented by the royal inscriptions and snatch glimpses of what was really going on and how those in charge were reacting. Normally, letters can be used for historical research in a meaningful way only when there is a cohesive corpus. Thus, for example, we have scores of letters written by Hammurapi to his chief officer at the city of Larsa, and this permits us to study that king's treatment of a city which he had just conquered. Individual and broken letters are usually of minimal value.

Babylonian contracts and administrative documents number in the tens of thousands for certain periods, such as the NB Empire (627–539 B.C.). Like letters, they are normally only useful as sources when a cohesive corpus or archive has been recovered. A good example is the Murashû Archive, a corpus of documents left behind by a rich and influential family of businessmen of the Persian period (539–331 B.C.). See MURASHU, ARCHIVE OF.

Later indigenous written sources comprise chronicles, king lists, and literary texts. Fortunately for us, the Babylonians wrote a number of chronicles, mainly of the later period, which narrate concisely but precisely outstanding events year by year. These, together with lists of kings, are the backbone of our chronological reconstruction of Babylonian history. The chronicles are a reliable source in that they do not have a particular theory to prove, nor are they nationalistic in attitude. Literary texts of value to the historian are limited in number and very fragmentary. Nevertheless, they provide insights otherwise denied us; for example, a badly preserved historical epic of the late Kassite period (13th century B.C.) speaks of a religious rebellion against the reigning monarch, an event otherwise unknown from other sources. (Grayson 1975: 56–77).

b. Foreign. The earliest biblical reference to Babylonian history seems to appear in Genesis 14, in which an invasion of Palestine by eastern rulers is narrated. While the identity of these rulers and the events elude us, there can be little doubt that a kernel of historical fact lies here in obscurity and that the references to Amorites suggest the Old Babylonian (OB) period (ca. 2000–1595 B.C.). Much later in time, more concrete information appears in the biblical account (Isaiah 39) of the envoy sent to Hezekiah, king of Judah, by Merodach-baladan II, king of Babylonia (7th century B.C.). See MERODACH-BALADAN. This information is valuable in reconstructing the war waged by Merodach-baladan against Sennacherib, king of Assyria. See SENNACHERIB (PERSON). By far the most dramatic biblical source for Babylonian history (2 Kings 24–25; 2 Chronicles 36; Jeremiah passim) is about the invasion of Judah by Nebuchadnezzar II, king of Babylonia (604–562 B.C.). See NEBUCHADNEZZAR. The final capture of Jerusalem in 586 B.C. and the exile to Babylonia of many of its inhabitants is narrated in detail in the Bible, a welcome circumstance since the Babylonian chronicle for this period has not yet been found.

Among other foreign sources are the 1st-century writings of the Jewish historian Josephus, who wrote in Greek. Indeed, Babylonian history is touched upon by a number of classical authors, including Herodotus, Ctesias, Diodorus Siculus, Xenophon, and Claudius Ptolemaus. Legends these preserve about Babylonian personalities (such as Nitokris, "queen of Babylonia") may well have had a historical basis, but this is now difficult to document.

2. Archaeological Sources. The best-known Babylonian site, from an archaeological point of view, is the city of Babylon itself. Systematic excavation of this large tell was undertaken at the beginning of this century by a German expedition led by Koldewey. More recently, excavations have been resumed by the State Organization of

Antiquities of the Republic of Iraq. The monumental buildings, walls, and processional way of the Neo-Babylonian period (6th century B.C.) have been uncovered. Earlier levels are not so well preserved. At Dur-Kurigalzu, the capital of the Kassites (ca. 1595–1200 B.C.), digging has been done over some years, and both palaces and temples have been discovered. Other major archaeological sites are Nippur, Ur, Larsa, Isin, and Sippar, to name only a few.

C. Chronology

Babylonian chronology is well established for some periods but poorly known for others. The best period, from this viewpoint, is the time from the mid-8th century B.C. and later. There are three main reasons for this: the wealth of indigenous documents bearing dates; the Babylonian chronicles and king lists; and the link these have with voluminous Babylonian records of observations of the movements of stars and planets, which modern astronomers can date. Between ca. 1595 and 750 B.C., chronological evidence is much more sparse. There are relatively few dated documents and chronicles, and the king lists are so badly broken that sometimes even the names and order of the kings are unknown. For the oldest period, ca. 2000–1595 B.C., the relative chronology—the sequence of kings and events—is well known, but the absolute dates are very uncertain. There are, in fact, three schools of thought among modern scholars about these dates, giving rise to the terms "High Chronology," "Middle Chronology," and "Low Chronology." This article follows the Middle Chronology. For the High or Low chronologies, add or subtract, respectively, about sixty-four years.

D. Political History

If one could chart graphically the political history of Babylonia, it would appear like a rugged mountain landscape, the tall peaks symbolising the few periods of Babylonia's greatness and the deep valleys the long periods of weakness. For Babylonia, unlike Assyria, was rarely a great military or political power, the exceptions being the reigns of Hammurapi, Kurigalzu, Nebuchadnezzar I, and the Neo-Babylonian Empire. But even during the times of political eclipse, Babylonian culture flourished and left a legacy for Eastern and Western civilizations alike.

1. Akkadians, Amorites, and Sumerians. Babylonian civilization was a pastiche of cultures and peoples which blended together to create one of the world's great civilizations. The evolution of an outstanding culture from the fusion of different ethnic groups was an ongoing process in Babylonian history. It continued to operate as new peoples moved into the Babylonian plain in subsequent periods. Chief among the ethnic strains in the population of Babylonia ca. 2000 B.C. were the Akkadians, the Amorites, and the Sumerians. The Sumerians and Akkadians had been present in the area for a long time and had created a civilization in the 3d millennium, commonly called "Sumerian," of which Babylonian civilization was a direct heir. See above MESOPOTAMIA IN THE THIRD MILLENNIUM B.C. Some Amorites were also living in the plain with the Sumerians and Akkadians in the 3d millennium, but it was the massive immigration of Amorite tribes around 2000 B.C. that transformed the old order of things into Babylonian civilization.

The oldest of the three peoples were the Sumerians, who spoke a language which cannot be identified with any known family of languages. This is not unusual in the history of ancient SW Asia, where there were many such tongues. Both Akkadian and Amorite, on the other hand, belong to the Semitic language family, a group which also includes Hebrew and Arabic. The region from which Semitic speakers spread was the Syro-Arabian desert (as we shall see when discussing other such groups, the Arameans and Arabs). The origin of the Sumerians is still debated.

The Sumerian language was in decline by 2000 B.C., being gradually replaced by Akkadian. This latter language was now being influenced by Amorite, and out of this melting pot emerged the Babylonian dialect of Akkadian. The other major Akkadian dialect was Assyrian. A writing system called cuneiform, which had been invented for Sumerian a thousand years before, was borrowed by the Babylonians to write their own language. It is an indication of the influence of Sumerian culture in Babylonia, however, that the Babylonian scribes also continued to write literary and learned works in Sumerian, a language which was no longer widely spoken or understood. To the very end of Babylonian civilization, religious rituals, scientific compositions, and divinatory texts were written either in Sumerian or in a technical jargon which consisted largely of Sumerian logograms. But for affairs of state, business transactions, and everyday interchange, the Babylonian dialect of Akkadian prevailed from about 2000 B.C. until about 700 or 600 B.C., when another Semitic language, Aramaic, gradually gained popularity. This phenomenon was linked to Babylonian political and cultural history, as will be discussed later. Aramaic first became the everyday tongue and then slowly became more common in the domain of business and administration. At the same time, the Aramaic writing system, which utilized an alphabet, gained in favor. Nevertheless, Babylonian Akkadian and the cuneiform script continued to be used in some circles, essentially temples, until the beginning of the Christian era.

The borrowing of the cuneiform script and the continued, albeit restricted, use of the Sumerian language by the Babylonians were not the only spheres in which a Sumerian legacy is evident. In fact, Sumerian culture permeated Babylonian civilization, and it is no exaggeration to say that it is impossible to understand Babylonian history without a firm grounding in Sumerian history. Babylonian literature, law, religion, socioeconomic structure, and political structure all bear witness to a pervasive Sumerian presence. This influence was most evident in S Babylonia, the ancient center of Sumerian culture, although even in such a city as Sippar far to the N there was abundant testimony. Indeed, geography played a large role in this cultural continuum, for it was natural that later peoples, many of whom still had Sumerian blood, living in the same region, should carry on the same traditions. It is fortunate for us that the Babylonians were so influenced by and in awe of Sumerian culture, for it is primarily thanks to the Babylonians that so much of Sumerian literature and religion is known today. Most Sumerian literary and religious compositions were first written down in the early OB period (see 2. below) and deposited in libraries, the best of which was at Nippur. The discovery of the Nippur library in the last century opened to modern eyes the riches of ancient Sumerian civilization. Thus, in addition to Babylonia's own legacy (see K. below), her role in this respect has earned our gratitude.

2. Early Old Babylonian Period (ca. 2017–1793 B.C.). The fall of the city-state of Ur in S Babylonia ca. 2004 B.C. marked the end of Sumerian civilization, while the foundation of an Amorite dynasty at Isin, some distance N of Ur, in 2017 B.C., was the beginning of Babylonian civilization. There was some overlap, as evident from the dates, since the founder of the Isin I dynasty, Ishbi-Erra, was at first a vassal of Ibbi-Sin, the last king of Ur. But as Ur was more and more surrounded by enemies, primarily Amorite tribes and Elamites, Ishbi-Erra became increasingly independent. By the time Ur fell, Ishbi-Erra had already been acting as an independent ruler for some time.

The period of history which ensued is characterized by the emergence of various Amorite dynasties in various small city-states, each of which was autonomous if only for a brief time. Chaos and warfare between these city-states were rife, and frequently one or more of the city-states fell under the power of another. In the confusion two city-states, Isin and Larsa, often commanded center stage, however precariously, and thus the Early OB era is often called the Isin-Larsa period.

a. The Amorites. The Amorites were the moving force in this era, and it is this aspect of them which must be discussed here. The name Amorite embraces a number of Semitic-speaking tribes who came in large numbers from Syria-Arabia to Babylonia, and other parts of the Near East, toward the end of the 3d millennium. They were seminomads, or donkey nomads, despised by the residents of Babylonia because of their primitive ways but feared because of their fierce fighting qualities. Some actually entered Babylonia peacefully and took up menial tasks, such as digging ditches. Indeed this peaceful process had been going on long before 2000 B.C. But others entered with force and captured the key centers in Babylonia. Gradually they, like all immigrants to Babylonia, adopted the Babylonian language and customs, and even the later kings of the Amorite dynasties commonly bore Babylonian names. See also AMORITES.

b. Isin. The founder of the Isin dynasty, Ishbi-Erra, was an Amorite from Mari, a city on the middle Euphrates, and he was part of a whole group of immigrants to Isin from Mari. During his long reign (ca. 2017–1985 B.C.) he not only became the independent ruler of Isin but also gained control over Nippur and Larsa and even over Ur, to which he had formerly been subservient. It is apparent that he was struggling to hold sway over the territory which formerly had been the empire of Ur. It is not surprising, therefore, that he adopted the efficient if complex administrative system of the Ur bureaucracy. A new element appears in his administration, however. Officials in the state bureaucracy at Isin were extremely obsequious, as shown by the personal names which they adopted ("Ishbi-Erra-Is-the-Life-of-the-Land," "Ishbi-Erra-Is-the-God-of-His-Land," and "Ishbi-Erra-Is-my-God").

The history of Isin after Ishbi-Erra's death is a long tale of numerous rulers of limited political power constantly vying with the heads of other city-states for the upper hand. The first invasion of Babylonia by Assyria took place during this time. Of significance, though, is the fact that cultural activity was very much alive during this period and resulted, among other things, in the rebuilding of temples, the writing of literary compositions, and the compilation of "law codes." Moreover, a custom of the ruler issuing edicts to correct social and economic abuses now became well established. (Kraus, 1984.)

c. Larsa. The dynasty of Larsa was also Amorite and was founded about the same time as the dynasty of Isin, ca. 2025 B.C. Unlike the Isin rulers, however, the members of the Larsa dynasty were politically insignificant until a certain Kudur-Mabuk crashed into Larsa and made it his center of operations ca. 1834 B.C. Kudur-Mabuk was the colorful and energetic head of an Amorite tribe called Yamut-Bal. He and his tribe had been employed as mercenaries by the Elamites, but when he captured Larsa he regarded himself as independent, and nothing further is heard of Elam.

Kudur-Mabuk clearly had an ambitious and long-range policy. He seems to have treated the defeated people of Larsa well and appointed his son, Warad-Sin, as ruler of Larsa (ca. 1834–1823 B.C.) while he wandered forth once more to seek his fortune in war. Thus, the son looked after the administration of the state, and the father captured more territory for its domain. When Warad-Sin died, presumably at a relatively young age, Kudur-Mabuk was still alive and took over the administration for a time. But he had no liking for office work, and after a few months he appointed another of his sons, Rim-Sin, as king of Larsa.

Rim-Sin was destined to be the longest-living king in Babylonian history (ca. 1822–1763 B.C.). His reign marks the high point in Larsa's political fortunes. In the early years of his reign, Kudur-Mabuk paid careful attention to him, an indication of his youth and inexperience. Eventually, however, nothing more is heard of Kudur-Mabuk, for the old warrior had obviously died at last.

Between about 1820 and 1804 B.C., Rim-Sin was very active, undertaking numerous military campaigns. He gradually gained control of all Babylonia except the north. In his thirtieth year (ca. 1804 B.C.), he captured Isin. This was the high point of his career, and it was celebrated with due pomp and circumstance. It is of particular interest that he used this victory to date subsequent events in his reign. Thus, his thirty-first year was called "The first year after the king captured Isin"; his thirty-second year, "The second year after the king captured Isin," etc. This is the first known example in history of an era dating system. It was short-lived, however, for it did not survive Rim-Sin's death.

By the close of the Early OB period a number of phenomena had developed. Culturally, Babylonian civilization had passed through its formative years and was ready to blossom. Politically, socially, and economically, the scene was still confused, but the stage had been set for the entrance of one of Babylonia's greatest kings, Hammurapi.

3. The Hammurapi Age (ca. 1792–1750 B.C.). No king of Babylonia, with the exception of Nebuchadnezzar II, is so well known in modern times as Hammurapi. Although he is never mentioned in the Bible, the discovery of his famous "law code" in the last century has made his name a household word. Since then, industrious archaeological excavation and research over more than a century have presented a fuller picture of Hammurapi and his era. He was a giant among giants, his chief opponents being Rim-Sin of Larsa (discussed above), the kings of Mari, and Shamshi-Adad I.

a. Mari. The discovery in the 1930s of the Mari archives, consisting of about 20,000 cuneiform tablets, was the single most important event in reconstructing the history of the Hammurapi age. Most of the documents from Mari, located about 300 km upstream from Babylon, are letters and administrative texts, and from them we learn of the complex politics of the time in which international intrigues and coalitions were commonplace. Before the time of Hammurapi, Mari was one of several autonomous city-states in N Mesopotamia and Syria and was controlled by a dynasty of Amorite origin. An early important king of Mari was Yahdun-Lim, who claimed sovereignty over states as far W as the Mediterranean. He also concluded working agreements with the seminomadic tribes along the Euphrates that were perennial problems for Mari. But Mari soon fell under the sway of Shamshi-Adad I. See also MARI (ARCHAEOLOGY).

b. Shamshi-Adad I (ca. 1813–1781 B.C.). Shamshi-Adad I was also of Amorite extraction. During his successful military career he moved around a great deal but finally settled his capital at Shubat-Enlil in E Syria. At the height of his power he controlled the city-state of Asshur and the area of Assyria, and he, or at least his supporters at Asshur, went to some effort to promote the fiction that Shamshi-Adad was a rightful member of the ruling dynasty at Asshur. Thus, he was regarded in later tradition as a king of Assyria. It is relevant to our purpose that he captured Mari after Yahdun-Lim was assassinated and appointed his younger son, Yasmah-Adad, as governor of Mari. Ishme-Dagan, his elder son, was made governor of Ekallatum, just south of Asshur. Thus, Shamshi-Adad, with his two sons, ruled over most of N Mesopotamia. By this time, however, Hammurapi had ascended the throne at Babylon.

c. Hammurapi (ca. 1792–1750 B.C.). Hammurapi was the sixth member of the first dynasty of Babylon, another Amorite dynasty. When he ascended the throne, Babylon was only one of a few city-states of medium power. Earlier kings of Babylon had laid the foundations of political and military power firmly; nevertheless, with such foes as Rim-Sin to the S and Shamshi-Adad to the N, Babylon was not an obvious candidate for supremacy. But Hammurapi made it supreme, conquering the other states and inaugurating a cultural golden age in Babylonia. Indeed, this is the first time one can speak of "Babylonia" as a unified political entity.

The name Hammurapi is actually Amorite, and since his two immediate predecessors bore Akkadian names, this suggests a return to ancestral values. In this same vein, Hammurapi made extensive use of Amorite troops in his conquests. He was not merely a warrior, however. He frequently used international diplomacy to achieve his ends, as is apparent from the Mari archives. Peaceful measures were the salient features of the first half of his reign. He carried on friendly correspondence with Shamshi-Adad I, and there may actually have been a treaty between the two rulers. Similarly, there is some evidence of a treaty with Rim-Sin in those early years. This is suggested by Hammurapi's sending of his troops to defeat some nomads which had harassed Rim-Sin's territory.

But the scene changed when Shamshi-Adad died and Eshnunna, a city-state on the Diyala river, formed an alliance with Elam and marched against Mari. The death of Shamshi-Adad also led to a revolution at Mari, where Zimri-Lim, son of the assassinated Yahdun-Lim, gained control. In face of the dramatically changed political scene, Hammurapi allied himself with Zimri-Lim and thus forestalled the attempt of the Elamo-Eshnunna coalition to capture Mari.

Zimri-Lim and Hammurapi remained good allies for many years, exchanging friendly letters (of which many have survived) and helping each other in time of need. Nevertheless, they each had agents in the other's court who reported regularly on the other's movements. The king of Mari was wise to be on the alert, for eventually Hammurapi became more active militarily, his principal target now being Rim-Sin at Larsa. The campaign against Larsa lasted five years, at the end of which the city and its territory fell to Hammurapi and was absorbed into the Babylonian state.

Now that Hammurapi controlled all of S Mesopotamia, it is not surprising that he turned his attention northwards. He attacked Zimri-Lim at Mari and was immediately successful. Over the next few years he consolidated his hold over Mari and expanded his domain to embrace Asshur and the area in between. Now Hammurapi was king not only of the Babylonian plain but also of the area which would eventually be called Assyria.

The age of Hammurapi was not just one of military clashes. The "law code" for which Hammurapi has become so famous in modern times is an example of the concern the king had for justice. This is amply borne out by the royal correspondence found at Larsa, in which the king deals with individual complaints over land rights and related problems. It is very clear from this archive that the Babylonian monarch was accessible to any subject who had a just grievance. In fact, Hammurapi was, so far as one can tell, as good an administrator as he was a diplomat and soldier. In religion, the Sumerian beliefs and practices still prevailed, but there were some changes. Shamash, the sun-god and chief god of the N state of Sippar, now came to prominence. A curious institution at Sippar, consisting of celibate women being dedicated to Shamash, was favored by Hammurapi. In general, however, there was a tendency toward the economic weakening of the temple in favor of the palace. This process began in the 3d millennium as a result of the wealth that was brought back by the campaigning kings and deposited in the palaces. Finally, literature in the Akkadian language was flourishing by the age of Hammurapi, and many modern critics believe that this was the period of "classical Babylonian," just as 5th-century Athens was the time of "classical Greek."

4. The Fall of Babylon (ca. 1750–1595 B.C.). The decades after Hammurapi's death saw the leveling off of Babylonian power and then gradual decline. Samsu-iluna (ca. 1749–1712 B.C.), Hammurapi's son and successor, managed to maintain his hold over much of the territory he had inherited. But already in his time serious competition for supremacy, never really suppressed, came again to the fore. Chief among the competitors were the Kassites, the people of the Sea-Land, and Rim-Sin II of Larsa. It is these forces which gradually weakened Babylonian might, leading to its fall.

The Kassites were first mentioned by name in written documents from the reign of Samsu-iluna. In fact, there is a reference to a Kassite army. It is apparent from this, and from their subsequent seizure of power at Babylon (ca. 1595), that they continued to be troublesome to Babylonia throughout the two centuries under discussion, but few facts have so far been recovered to prove this.

More concrete information is available about the "Sea-Land," a literal translation of the Akkadian expression *māt tāmtim* used to describe the area of the marshes on the N periphery of the Arabian/Persian Gulf, part of the homeland of the Sumerians. About the time of the foundation of the first dynasty of Babylon, a dynasty of the Sea-Land emerged and eventually produced its most powerful king, Ilimaila, who was a contemporary of Samsu-iluna. Ilimaila chipped away at Babylon's S holdings and even gained control for a time over Nippur. The Sea-Land kings continued to wax in power until the end of the first dynasty of Babylon when the Sea-Land, like Babylon, was conquered by the Kassites.

During the reign of Samsu-iluna yet a third power, Rim-Sin II of Larsa, challenged Babylonian suzerainty. This Rim-Sin, a nephew of the great Rim-Sin, managed to gain independence for Larsa for perhaps as long as five years. From there he expanded his influence farther afield but eventually was defeated at Kish, near Babylon, and killed. This left Babylon, the Sea-Land, and the Kassites as the three major powers in the area until the fall of Babylon.

Very little information is available concerning the events leading up to the fall of Babylon. The dearth of documentation is in itself a testimony to the chaotic nature of affairs in the latter days of the first dynasty of Babylon. Only one fact is well documented: Babylon was actually captured ca. 1595 B.C. by a Hittite king, Murshili I, who looted the city and then withdrew. How it came about that a Hittite army was so far from home and that it retreated so quickly are mysteries, but the facts are attested to in both Babylonian and Hittite sources. The people who gained from this raid were the Kassites, who now entered Babylon and established there a dynasty which lasted for four centuries.

5. The Kassites. The Kassites, unlike other major migrants to Babylonia such as the Amorites or Arameans, remain very much of an enigma. There is doubt about their origin, their language belongs to no known family of languages, and they left little of their culture as a legacy to Babylonian civilization. Part of the reason for our lack of facts about them is, no doubt, that they were confined to Mesopotamia, whereas other large groups such as the Amorites and Arameans also had an impact on Syria-Palestine, and thus we learn about them from the Bible.

It is clear that the Kassites were illiterate nomads who probably came into Mesopotamia from the central Asian steppes either through the Caucasus mountains or the Iranian plateau. Virtually nothing of their language has survived, for they adopted the Babylonian language when they learned to write in cuneiform. They lived on the periphery of Mesopotamia for some time, possibly several centuries, before taking control at Babylon ca. 1595. As noted above, they are first mentioned by name in Babylonian documentation in the reign of Samsu-iluna, where they are in the form of an army; but, no doubt, peaceful Kassite penetration of Babylonia had gone on for some time before.

From Samsu-iluna's time onwards, there is evidence that Kassites were pressing into Babylonia both in armed bands and by peaceful means. The latter method is illustrated by Babylonian documents in which Kassites are listed as herdsmen and harvesters. More information about this early phase can be gleaned from a Babylonian king list, which gives the names in succession of the "Kassite Dynasty" in Babylonia. Although the list is in part badly broken, it is apparent from the large number of names and from synchronisms with later kings of Assyria that the earliest rulers in this list could not have been resident in Babylonia. In other words, the list seems to begin with the time when the Kassites had moved into the Mesopotamian periphery, long before they captured Babylon ca. 1595 B.C. In this early era the rulers could have been little more than tribal chiefs. The first such leader, Gandash, was probably a contemporary of Samsu-iluna and therefore the one who led the Kassite "army" against that king. Nothing is known about subsequent rulers, other than their names, until the accession of Agum II (the ninth in the list), who was probably the first Kassite to rule at Babylon.

6. Middle Babylonian Period (ca. 1595–1000 B.C.). The Middle Babylonian period covers two ruling dynasties at Babylon: the Kassite dynasty and the 2d dynasty of Isin. The two are divided by an invasion and capture of Babylonia by the Elamites ca. 1157 B.C. Each dynasty produced one outstanding monarch, Kurigalzu of the Kassite dynasty and Nebuchadnezzar I of the Isin dynasty. During the two dynasties, and particularly during the reigns of the two kings just mentioned, the culture and economy of Babylonia thrived. There were, nonetheless, long periods of depression caused largely by the inroads of Elamites and Assyrians.

a. Kassite Dynasty. Agum II seems to have been the Kassite king who first took control of Babylon after the Hittite raid ca. 1595 B.C. He ruled over Babylonia and the east Tigris region, the first area of Kassite presence. With one exception the events of his reign are virtually unknown: he won back from the Hittites the cult statue of Marduk, the tutelary god of Babylon, which had been part of the booty carried off in the Hittite raid. When the statue was returned, it was installed with much pomp and ceremony in the newly renovated temple of Esagil, symbolizing the return of Babylon's fortunes. In subsequent centuries Marduk's statue would again be seized as booty on no less than four occasions, each one marking a drastic decline in Babylon's morale.

In tracing the history of Babylonia we must now skip over more than two centuries, for lack of documentation, to the 14th century B.C. In this era letters found at Amarna, on the upper Nile in Egypt, suddenly illuminate the darkened stage, for many of these letters are from Babylonian kings to the pharaoh. See AMARNA LETTERS. The language of the letters is Babylonian and the script is cuneiform, evidence that Babylonian was the lingua franca of the Near East in the 14th century B.C. The Amarna Letters show that Babylonia was now accepted as a major power in the Near East and that its kings dealt as equals with the Egyptian monarchs. The main theme of the correspondence is an exchange of Egyptian gold for Babylonian princesses, who would enter the pharaoh's harem. It is reasonably obvious, then, that a treaty existed between the two nations. If written copies of such a treaty ever existed, they have not survived, and one can only surmise what the purpose was. But Egypt was very worried about the power of Mitanni in E Syria and also the Hittite invasion of W Syria. Egyptian interests would have been helped by a friendly ally on the other side of those two powers, and that consideration would lie behind any treaty.

The Amarna Letters provide a hint of the decline in Babylonia's importance, after a time, in Egyptian eyes. The Babylonian king began to complain that Assyrian ambassadors were being received at Amarna. This may have been shortly before Babylonia actually became a puppet state of Assyria under Ashur-uballiṭ I (ca. 1364–1329 B.C.), for letters of Ashur-uballiṭ to the pharaoh were also found at Amarna. Just how Assyria gained ascendancy over Babylonia is still to be explained by future discoveries. What is known is that the daughter of Ashur-uballiṭ was married to the Kassite king of Babylonia. The Babylonians rebelled against this king and put a usurper on the throne. Ashur-uballiṭ invaded Babylonia to avenge his son-in-law, put down the revolt, and installed another man as king. This information comes from two documents, the Synchronistic History and Chronicle P (see HISTORIOGRAPHY [MESOPOTAMIA] and *TCS* 5), which disagree in certain details although they both have the general outline presented here.

At some time after Ashur-uballiṭ's invasion, Babylonia regained independence and entered the greatest era of the Kassite period, the reign of Kurigalzu. This king not only held the Assyrians at bay, but he probably defeated their army on one occasion in a pitched battle at Sugaga, a place just south of the city of Asshur. He also launched successful campaigns against Elam, capturing the Elamite king, and possibly also the Sea-Land. Like most Babylonian rulers, he was a great builder. He erected temples and palaces at various cities, but his chief concern, and indeed creation, was the founding of Dur-Kurigalzu ("fortress of Kurigalzu"). At this city, virtually a suburb of modern Baghdad, he constructed a complex of temples and palaces which have been under excavation for the last four decades by Iraqi archaeologists. The temple tower (ziggurat) of Dur-Kurigalzu is still in large part standing today and dominates the surrounding landscape.

With the death of Kurigalzu, Babylonian history is again obscure, and apart from mention of occasional clashes with Assyria, little is known for a century or more. One of these encounters with Assyria, during the reign of Tukulti-Ninurta I (1244–1208 B.C.), led to an Assyrian invasion of Babylonia and to the death of its king, Kashtiliash IV. The Assyrians looted Babylon and carried off the Marduk statue. For a brief period afterward, Babylonia was ruled by Assyria. The death of Tukulti-Ninurta meant freedom again for the Babylonians, and during the next few decades Babylonia not only remained independent but may have exercised some authority over a temporarily weak Assyria as well. During this time the Marduk statue must have been returned, although no specific record has been preserved. Major changes were taking place within Babylonia in this period, these changes centering around a religious revolution which inevitably had a political and economic impact. The controversy, as we know from a recently published Babylonian epic, was instigated by the attempt to recognize officially the god Marduk as king of the gods. The nobles of Babylonia supported the cause and, after a struggle, forced the king Adad-shuma-uṣur (1218–1189 B.C.) to accede to certain demands. Precisely what these were is unknown, since the epic is badly broken (Grayson 1975: 56–77).

The end of the Kassite dynasty was rapidly approaching. During the one-year reign of Zababa-shuma-iddina (1160 B.C.), both the Elamites and the Assyrians invaded Babylonia from different sides. The Kassite dynasty was now tottering, although its last member, Enlil-nadin-ahhe, managed to hold onto power for three years before an Elamite attack in 1157 B.C. captured and carried him off to Elam. The statue of Marduk was also removed. The destruction of the Kassite dynasty by the Elamites was commemorated in various Babylonian literary works and won for the Elamites a notorious reputation, which would endure for centuries.

While the Kassites had little cultural impact upon Babylonian civilization, much happened in the cultural sphere during their four centuries of power. As noted already, the god Marduk was moving up in rank to become king of the gods, and Dur-Kurigalzu is a lasting monument to Kassite building endeavors. In literature there was much editing and organization going on, and most Babylonian literary works, such as the *Gilgamesh Epic,* were given their final form during this period. In addition, many original poetic works, mainly about such Kassite kings as Kurigalzu, were composed in this era. The cultural impact of Babylonia on the West, on the other hand, is apparent from the discovery of a cache of inscribed stone seals of the Kassite type at Thebes in Greece.

b. Second Dynasty of Isin. After the Kassite dynasty fell, there is obscurity in Babylonian history for a brief period. During this time a new dynasty, the "second Isin dynasty," was founded at Isin and eventually produced one of the most important kings of the Middle Babylonian period, Nebuchadnezzar I (1133–1116 B.C.; not to be confused with Nebuchadnezzar II of the Bible). By the time he ascended the throne the capital was once again Babylon rather than Isin or Dur-Kurigalzu.

Nebuchadnezzar I became famous in Babylonian history for two major reasons which are closely linked. The first reason is that he led one or more highly successful expeditions into Elam and severely battered this hated enemy. Dramatic details of part of this invasion are narrated in the text of a Babylonian boundary stone, wherein we read of the heat and thirst which afflicted the Babylonian soldiers who, nevertheless, conquered the Elamite army. We learn from the same source that the chariotry was particularly effective in winning the day. Elam was devastated and looted, and among the plunder brought back to Babylonia was the statue of Marduk. This, the return of Marduk's statue, was the second reason for Nebuchadnezzar's fame in Babylonian tradition. As remarked above, there is a pattern in Babylonian history revolving around the occasions when the statue was abducted by an enemy and later brought back. This, the third such time, was used by the Babylonian king to proclaim officially that Marduk was king of the gods. The movement in this direction, which must go back to the time of Hammurapi, gained momentum in late Kassite times, as observed when speaking of the rebellion against Adad-shuma-uṣur. Now the time was ripe to make the formal proclamation. The temple of Esagil was renovated for the occasion, and special hymns and poems were composed. The statue of Marduk was led down the great processional way, lined with Babylonians, and was accompanied by the statues of lesser deities. Once Marduk was installed upon his dais, and after the proper ceremonies and rituals had been performed, the other gods were returned to their shrines. Marduk now reigned supreme. His statue was not disturbed again until 689 B.C. (see D.8.c. below).

One final event known about the reign of Nebuchadnezzar I is that he made two attacks on Assyrian border towns. Our only source, the Assyrian *Synchronistic History*, says these attacks were unsuccessful. Even if this is true, the fact that Babylonia, not Assyria, was the aggressor is an indication of the relative strength of the two.

The subsequent kings of the second Isin dynasty are of minor importance, with the exception of Marduk-nadin-ahhe (1098–1081 B.C.), who raided the Assyrian border town of Ekallatu and carried off the statues of its gods. These statues remained in Babylonia for centuries, despite long periods of weakness, until Sennacherib recaptured them in the 7th century B.C. As the end of the 2d millennium approached, Babylonia once more entered a dark period. The Aramean invasions considerably constricted her ambitions and caused serious disruptions within Babylonia itself. In the wake of these incursions, a restored and even more vigorous Assyria pressed down upon Babylonia's N border.

7. Babylonia and Assyria (ca. 1000–627 B.C.). a. A Period of Weakness (ca. 1000–748 B.C.). During the 2d millennium Assyria increasingly became an important background presence in Babylonian history, and in the 1st half of the 1st millennium this was even more evident. Other peoples and powers, such as the Arameans and Elamites, had a significant impact upon Babylonia, but it was Assyria which gradually gained the leading control over Babylonia. At the beginning of the 1st millennium Babylonia was independent once again, for Assyria was struggling against the Arameans for its very survival. The Arameans penetrated Babylonia, too, winning land and wealth and causing much chaos.

There is more detailed information available for the 9th century B.C., which shows that Babylonia and Assyria, after some minor skirmishing, were on good terms. The first important Babylonian king of the millennium, Nabu-apla-iddina (ca. 887–885 B.C.), had a treaty with his Assyrian counterparts. His reign is a highlight in a bleak period of Babylonian history. The country's borders were secure, internal stability prevailed, and energy was devoted to reconstruction and restoration. For example, thanks to the discovery of a text of Nabu-apla-iddina's inscribed on a stone tablet, we know that the king sponsored the rebuilding of the temple of the sun-god (Shamash) at Sippar.

When Nabu-apla-iddina died, his successor, Marduk-zakir-shumi I (ca. 854–819 B.C.), renewed the old treaty with Assyria, which was now ruled by Shalmaneser III (858–824 B.C.). There is actually an Assyrian relief showing the two kings clasping hands to seal the agreement. The renewal of the treaty proved advantageous for Marduk-zakir-shumi; when his brother led a rebellion and seized some of Babylonia for himself, Marduk-zakir-shumi called upon Shalmaneser to intervene, invoking the treaty between them. The Assyrian responded by attacking and defeating the brother and restoring the kingdom intact to Marduk-zakir-shumi. After this incident, Babylonia continued to enjoy peace with Assyria and general prosperity. In fact, Babylonia subsequently was able to repay Shalmaneser's favor. When Shalmaneser was getting very old, a major rebellion broke out in Assyria and continued for some years. It appears that one of Shalmaneser's sons, Shamshi-Adad, sought and gained Babylonian support. A fragmentary copy of a treaty between Shamshi-Adad and Marduk-zakir-shumi I testifies to this, although the Babylonian king used the occasion to demote the Assyrian to a lower status so that in the treaty he appears as the lesser party. When the rebellion had been suppressed and Shamshi-Adad, the fifth king of that name, had been crowned, he invaded Babylonia, presumably out of revenge for the humiliating treaty imposed upon him. This is the first time for almost a century that there was open conflict between the two states. Shamshi-Adad V led three expeditions into Babylonia, capturing major Babylonian cities, including Babylon, and Babylonia was forced to pay tribute.

The Assyrian Adad-narari III (810–783 B.C.) continued the aggressive stance toward Babylonia, although it is unknown how many campaigns he sent there. A treaty favorable toward Assyria was imposed upon Babylonia, which again had to pay tribute. Fortunately for Babylonia, this reign marked the end of a troublesome time with Assyria. By the end of Adad-narari's reign, Assyria was once again hard pressed by another power, this time Urartu, and had no time to meddle in Babylonia. Thus for the first half of the 8th century B.C., Babylonia, free of foreign invasion, seemed to be in a position to enjoy peaceful pursuits. However, there is no clear evidence of economic prosperity or cultural development during this phase. Indeed, even the political history is obscure, which suggests that Babylonia was experiencing some difficulties. There is some indication of a major religious upheaval at the Ishtar temple in Uruk. Whether or not this was more widely spread is unknown.

b. Under Assyrian Control (ca. 747–627 B.C.). Babylonia's fate was closely linked to that of Assyria throughout this era, particularly so in the Sargonid age in Assyria. When Tiglath-pileser III (744–727 B.C.) took the Assyrian throne, Nabu-nasir (747–734 B.C.) had barely begun his rule at Babylon, a rule that held great promise for Babylonia: the borders were secure, the state was stable internally, the king encouraged literary and scientific projects (including astronomical observations and chronicle writing), and Tiglath-pileser III concluded a treaty with Nabu-nasir.

The death of Nabu-nasir brought an abrupt end to

Babylonia's fortunes. Mukin-zer, the leader of a tribe of Chaldeans in S Babylonia, attempted to seize the Babylonian throne, forcing Tiglath-pileser III to respond by invading Babylonia, pushing Mukin-zer and his forces back south, and having himself crowned as king of Babylonia. Thus, for the first time, Assyria and Babylonia were a united kingdom, ruled by an Assyrian monarch.

To understand subsequent events in Babylonian history, it is necessary to look briefly at the various groups now present in the Babylonian plain, for the Babylonian population was quite heterogeneous. Essentially there were four elements: "native" Babylonians, Elamites, Arameans, and Chaldeans. To this one must add a small group of Assyrians who came to Babylonia under the Sargonids as soldiers and administrators. Each of these groups had special interests and goals which frequently clashed with those of the others. Thus, throughout the Sargonid age Babylonia suffered from internecine unrest, and this caused Assyria to invade frequently, for Assyrian kings wanted both a subordinate and a stable neighbor to the south.

The most active of all anti-Assyrian agitators in Babylonia at this time was MERODACH-BALADAN II. He was the leader of a Chaldean tribe called Yakin and first took an active military role toward the end of Tiglath-pileser III's reign. When Sargon II (721–705 B.C.) ascended the Assyrian throne, Merodach-baladan had himself crowned king at Babylon. The Assyrian tried unsuccessfully to depose Merodach-baladan, who ruled Babylonia for the next decade. But in 710 B.C., Sargon finally defeated the Chaldeans, and Merodach-baladan took refuge in the S marshes.

Our sources for this period are primarily Assyrian, and their view is that Merodach-baladan and other active figures in Babylonia were "rebels" or "usurpers" who oppressed Babylonia, and it was only the Assyrians who restored peace and prosperity. This may, in part, be true, but the Assyrians were still making a profit out of Babylonia to the latter's disadvantage. This is evident from the increasing resistance to Assyrian rule, which came to a head in the reign of Sennacherib (704–681 B.C.).

Babylonia, as represented by Merodach-baladan and other leaders, staunchly resisted Sennacherib. Merodach-baladan actually regained the throne at Babylon briefly in 703 B.C., forcing the Assyrian to turn from other concerns (Palestine) and invade Babylonia. Merodach-baladan again fled south to the marshes, but over the next few years he stirred up opposition to the Assyrian occupation. Sennacherib attempted to rule Babylonia through puppet kings while he led the Assyrian army in an abortive attempt to capture Merodach-baladan. The critical point in this phase of Assyro-Babylonian affairs was the entry of Elam into the fray. The Elamites invaded Babylonia, captured Sennacherib's son and heir (who had been crowned king of Babylonia), and carried him off to exile and death.

Sennacherib was enraged by this, regarding it as Babylonian treachery. He launched vicious campaigns first against Elam and then against Babylonia, finally capturing Babylon itself in 689 B.C. He boasted that he had looted, burnt, and destroyed the city (*LAR* 2: 339–41). The statue of Marduk was taken away to Assyria. This was one of the lowest points in Babylonian history. Its capital city was in ruins, and its tutelary god was gone.

The next Assyrian king, Esarhaddon (680–669 B.C.), set himself the task of reconciliation with and reconstruction of Babylonia. This was a wise policy and won for him a reign untroubled on the S border. Esarhaddon ordered and had carried out the rebuilding of Babylon and in particular of Marduk's temple, Esagil. The god's statue was not actually returned until after Esarhaddon's death. For some unknown reason, Esarhaddon had decided that when he died his kingdom would be divided between two of his sons, and thus Ashurbanipal (668–627 B.C.) came to rule over Assyria and Shamash-shuma-ukin (667–648 B.C.) to rule over Babylonia. It was a major error, for it was only a matter of time before war broke out between the brothers. Shamash-shuma-ukin, although an Assyrian, had the support of Babylonia in his dispute with his brother. To this he added the aid of the Elamites and Arabs. Increasing unease broke into open battle in 652 B.C. and continued for four years, to 648 B.C. Assyria quickly gained the upper hand, and, after a long siege, Babylon fell and Shamash-shuma-ukin perished in his burning palace (*LAR* 2: 789–98). Ashurbanipal now ruled Babylonia through a puppet king, Kandalanu (647–627), but little is known of those years.

Given the tumultuous political scene in Babylonia during the Sargonid age, it is no surprise that cultural and economic pursuits did not flourish. There were brief periods when business could be conducted somewhat normally, of course, and there is slight evidence of literary activity, but taken as a whole it was a very bad time for Babylonia.

8. The Neo-Babylonian Empire (626–539 B.C.). a. Imperial Beginnings (626–605 B.C.). Out of the ashes of a Babylonia scorched by the Assyrians in 689 and 648 B.C. rose a new dynasty destined to establish both an independent Babylonia and Babylonian rule over the former Assyrian empire. The founder of this dynasty was Nabopolassar (625–605 B.C.), a Chaldean who was crowned king at Babylon after defeating an Assyrian army in Babylonia. No details of Nabopolassar's background are known; nor is there much firm evidence about the situation before the events leading up to his coronation. It is apparent, however, that the Babylonians were actively rebelling against the Assyrians and trying to expel them from their land. Nabopolassar became the champion of this freedom fight, and in 626 B.C. he led Babylonian troops to lay siege to Nippur, which contained an Assyrian garrison. The siege was lengthy and the people so impoverished that some of them, as we know from contracts discovered at Nippur, were forced to sell their children into slavery so that they could buy food. Eventually the siege was lifted when an Assyrian army arrived and pursued the Babylonian troops as far as Babylon. In a battle outside Babylon's walls, the Assyrians were defeated. This was the last attack Assyria ever made on Babylon. The Babylonians were so elated by this success that they crowned Nabopolassar as their king, thus founding a new dynasty. The new monarch's first act was to return to the Elamites statues of their gods which the Assyrians had abducted and brought to Babylonia many years earlier. This indicated a firm bond of friendship between the two states. Elam, however, had become very weak as a result of the raids of Ashurbanipal and in future years played no meaningful role in Babylonian affairs.

During the early years of Nabopolassar's reign, the Babylonian offensive went from success to success, and Assyria gradually withdrew to the north. When Nabopolassar pushed up to the Upper Euphrates region, Egypt became alarmed and sent aid to Assyria (616 B.C.). Such an alliance had never existed before and is a symbol of the momentous changes occurring in ancient Near Eastern politics. About the same time that Egypt aligned itself with Assyria, the Medes allied themselves with the Babylonians. The Medes had long been established in W Iran and more recently had spread their control westward into eastern and central Anatolia. For the next four years the Medes and Babylonians pounded away at Assyrian holdings and at the Assyrian heartland itself. In 614 Asshur was captured. Then, in 612 the allies laid siege to Nineveh. The siege lasted all summer before the city fell. A remnant of Assyrians escaped W to Harran, where a mini-Assyrian dynasty was established. Nabopolassar, supported by the Medes, attacked Harran in 610 and forced the combined armies of Assyria and Egypt to flee to Syria. In 609 this army returned and made a vain attempt to dislodge the Babylonians and Medes from Harran.

The decisive battle between the two sides came in 605 at Carchemish. Egypt now stood alone, for nothing is ever heard again of an Assyrian army. By this time the Babylonian army was being led in alternate years by the king Nabopolassar and his son and heir Nebuchadnezzar. In 605 the son was in charge of the expedition. Nebuchadnezzar led a surprise attack on the Egyptian army at Carchemish. The Egyptians were caught inside the walls but managed to break out and avoid being sealed in by a siege. The fighting was fierce, and the Egyptians eventually broke and ran with the Babylonians in hot pursuit, slaying every man they could catch. This was the ultimate victory for Babylonia. Assyria was destroyed, and Egypt had lost any credibility in Asia. Eventually the Babylonians would follow this up by campaigning to and claiming all of Syria-Palestine. But there was a slight delay. News arrived after the Battle of Carchemish that Nabopolossar had died. Nebuchadnezzar returned swiftly to Babylon, where he was crowned king.

b. The Empire (604–556 B.C.). Nebuchadnezzar II (604–562 B.C.) is widely known by readers of the Bible as the king responsible for the sack of Jerusalem and the exile of many of its inhabitants in 587 B.C. Be that as it may, Babylonia reached its greatest heights as a political power during his reign, and the Babylonian empire came to include essentially the same territory as the Assyrian empire. This extension of power was the result of vigorous campaigning by Nebuchadnezzar. No sooner were the coronation ceremonies over for Nebuchadnezzar, after the death of his father, then he hastened back to Syria to resume his campaigning. He had defeated the Egyptians at Carchemish in 605 B.C., but this did not automatically bring Syria-Palestine under Babylonian control. In the following years he led a series of expeditions W of the Euphrates. Sometimes local rulers acknowledged him as lord and paid tribute without question; at other times, they resisted and the Babylonian army laid siege to their cities.

By 601 Nebuchadnezzar felt his hold over Syria-Palestine was strong enough to permit a campaign against Egypt. This was a mistake. A pitched battle between the two forces in Egypt resulted in a stalemate, and Nebuchadnezzar, choosing discretion, led his army back to Babylon. After a year spent repairing the damage to his army and equipment, he resumed his Syrian campaigns. This was urgent, for the Babylonian humiliation in Egypt had encouraged W states to rebel. One such state was the kingdom of Judah and its capital, Jerusalem. Jerusalem during this period was torn between two factions, one pro-Egyptian and one pro-Babylonian. The king, Jehoiakim, and his supporters were in favor of siding with the Egyptians, but the prophet Jeremiah preferred the Babylonians. Although Jehoiakim had paid tribute to Babylonia after the Battle of Carchemish, Babylonia's ignominious withdrawal from Egypt in 601 led him to renounce his allegiance to Babylonia and throw in his lot with Egypt. Nebuchadnezzar could not let this key center fall away, and so in 597 he besieged and captured Jerusalem. He appointed a new king, Zedekiah, and imposed a heavy tribute. Jehoiakin, son of Jehoiakim who had died, his family, and many leading citizens were taken as captives to Babylon, and modern excavations have unearthed some of the lists of rations for these prisoners. This event was the first of two disasters for Jerusalem. Egypt, as Jeremiah had predicted, did not intervene.

In the years after 597, Zedekiah allowed himself gradually to be persuaded by those who favored Egypt. Eventually, with a promise of Egyptian support, he abandoned allegiance to Babylonia, refusing to pay tribute. In 587 Nebuchadnezzar again invaded Judah, capturing various cities as he marched on Jerusalem. These Judean cities were not plundered but were treated mercifully in a deliberate attempt to weaken the resolve of Jerusalem's defenders. Therefore, when Nebuchadnezzar laid siege to Jerusalem, Jeremiah and his supporters pointed to the lenient treatment of other cities and vainly urged capitulation. Meanwhile, the Egyptian army moved into Judah and tried, unsuccessfully, to lift the Babylonian siege. Then the Babylonians captured Jerusalem. The city was plundered and destroyed, its leaders were executed, and most of the remaining population were carried off in exile to Babylonia.

True to Babylonian tradition, Nebuchadnezzar was as much a builder and a patron of culture as he was a military leader. The wealth and political security which his campaigns produced enabled him to pursue these activities with unexcelled results. His building program at Babylon was extensive, involving major replanning and new construction. He built a new palace by the Euphrates at the N edge of the city. The walls also were rebuilt, and a bridge was constructed to facilitate communication between the two parts of Babylon that lay on opposite sides of the river. The temple tower (ziggurat), the legendary Tower of Babel, was completely restored, as was the temple of Esagil, Marduk's shrine, adjacent to it. The origin of the legendary idea of the "Hanging Gardens of Babylon" (one of the "Seven Wonders of the Ancient World") may have been the live vegetation growing at the top of the ziggurat that, from a distance, would have appeared to tower over the city walls.

While it is apparent that literary and artistic activity

must have flourished during this reign, it is difficult to document it since such creations are rarely dated. However, fragmentary remains of an epic about Nebuchadnezzar bear witness to the high regard which creative Babylonians had for him. Nebuchadnezzar's reign marks the apogee of the Neo-Babylonian empire. After his death he was succeeded by some relatively unimportant monarchs, including Evil-Merodach and Nergal-Sharezzer. If the kingdom was still strong, it was nevertheless no longer expanding.

c. Nabonidus and the Fall of Babylon (555–539 B.C.). Nabonidus, the last member of the Neo-Babylonian dynasty, is an intriguing figure. See NABONIDUS. While forces portending doom to Babylonia gathered on the horizons, he found time to promote a religious change, to undertake major building operations, and even to live in the desert for ten years. He did not, however, ignore the external dangers to Babylonia's security—far from it. When at last the Persian army invaded Babylonia, he fought valiantly but in vain to repel them.

Nabonidus' religious changes provide a key to his other actions. He was not in the direct line for the throne (one Babylonian text called him a "usurper"), and it is unknown how he became king. His mother, Adad-guppi, certainly played some part in this. She came from Harran, the city where the ruling Assyrian dynasty made its last abortive attempt to survive. There, she worshipped the tutelary deity, the god of the moon. When Nabonidus came to power, he promoted this cult of the moon and sought out similar cults in Babylonia. Thus he favored the Babylonian deity Sin, god of the moon and the city Ur. He had little interest in Babylon's god, Marduk. This brought down upon his head the wrath of the Marduk priests and supporters who, among other things, wrote literary works condemning Nabonidus for his sacrilege.

A second unique feature of this king's reign was his ten-year self-imposed exile in Tema, an oasis in the Arabian desert. While he lived there his son, BELSHAZZAR, managed affairs at Babylon. Many writers, ancient and modern, have suggested reasons why Nabonidus went to live there, but none of these reasons can be proved valid since no contemporary document gives details of the event. It is a fact that pre-Islamic Arabs in the Arabian peninsula revered the moon-god, and this may have been an important motivation for Nabonidus, given his intense interest in this cult. But this would not exclude one or more other reasons, such as an attempt to regain his health, for the long exile.

The third area of special interest in this reign was the manner in which Nabonidus conducted his building operations. It was, of course, usual for a Babylonian king to erect or restore monumental buildings, as Nabonidus did. What was unusual was the zeal with which he sought out ancient statues and inscriptions of his predecessors when digging in the foundations of old buildings. This characteristic has won for Nabonidus the epithet "the world's first archaeologist" among modern scholars.

Given these intriguing facets of the king's character, it is a pity he met such an ignominious fate. The Persians under Cyrus the Great had been gathering around the borders of the Babylonian empire, preparing for a major assault which took place in 539 B.C. The Persians came down the Diyala river, and Nabonidus, at the head of his army, met and fought with them at Opis near modern Baghdad. Nabonidus was defeated. The Persians then marched on Babylon where, according to a native source, the Babylonians opened the gates and with rejoicing welcomed Cyrus as a deliverer from the "tyrant" Nabonidus. This sounds like a biased account, and it is hard to believe that all Babylonians were glad to see the Persian invaders. Indeed, Herodotus says the city had to be taken by force. Whatever the truth, Babylon did fall to the Persians in 539 B.C., and so ended indigenous rule in Babylonia.

9. Babylonia Under the Persians and Greeks. Although the Babylonians ceased to be politically autonomous in 539 B.C., their civilization continued for several centuries under foreign rule. The conqueror of Babylon himself, Cyrus, ensured the preservation of Babylonian culture by avoiding any interference in domestic affairs so long as the Babylonians were loyal. This was a feature of Cyrus' rule, known from other areas he had conquered, notably Palestine. In the Bible, as in Babylonian works, Cyrus is enshrined as a savior who restored justice and good administration (cf. Isa 45:1–13). In Babylonia, this view of Cyrus is sometimes extreme and therefore suspicious, but the general picture is nonetheless valid.

Babylonia continued to be well treated under Cambyses II (529–522 B.C.) and remained docile. When revolt broke out in Persia at the death of Cambyses, however, Babylonia took the opportunity to appoint her own kings for a year or two. But Darius I (521–486 B.C.) successfully suppressed the rebellion and pacified the various parts of his empire, including Babylonia. He put the provincial administration in order, and Babylonia gained the doubtful honor of contributing more tribute to the Persians than any other province.

Only one further serious attempt at independence was made by Babylonia during the Persian era, and this was in the reign of Xerxes I (485–465 B.C.). The rebels put their own appointee on the throne and withheld tribute from Xerxes, thus bravely disowning any allegiance to Persia. Xerxes responded with devastating deliberation. He sent in an army which not only defeated the rebels but looted and destroyed Babylon as well. Marduk's temple, Esagil, was demolished and his statue carried off to Persia. It is not surprising, perhaps, that nothing further is heard of Babylonian rebellion for the remainder of Persian rule.

The incredible march of Alexander the Great through W Asia and his defeat of the last Persian monarch, Darius III (335–331 B.C.), is part and parcel of Babylonian history, for Alexander chose Babylon as the capital of his Asiatic-European empire. Tragically he died at Babylon at a young age, just as he had conquered the area from the Attic peninsula to the Ganges valley and was preparing to organize his empire. It would appear that the Babylonians liked Alexander, as well they might considering what he planned to do for them.

Because Alexander had not yet consolidated his empire, wars broke out among the Diadochi, Alexander's successors. From the conflicts emerged Seleucus I (305–281 B.C.) as king of Babylonia and W Asia. He founded both a new dynasty and a new dating system, the latter called the Seleucid Era and based on the date on which Seleucus marched into Babylon (312 B.C., a retroactive date). By this time the Greek language was widely spoken and written in Babylonia by the ruling and educated classes. Nevertheless, Aramaic and Akkadian continued to be used in some circles. In fact, Akkadian cuneiform was used for several centuries more in temples for religious, divinatory, and administrative texts, the last such text dating to A.D. 64.

There are no indications of major revolts by the Babylonians against their Seleucid masters. There was some dissatisfaction, however. This was in part due to the creation of a new city, Seleucia-on-the-Tigris, which drained off some population from Babylon. A more subtle reason for discontent is that the Babylonians felt themselves superior to the Greeks. This attitude is elusive to detect but there, nonetheless. There was a feeling that the Greeks were uncultured barbarians with no history or civilization to speak of. Thus, a Babylonian priest, Berossos, wrote a history of Babylonia in Greek, only fragments of which have survived, in order to teach his masters about a great civilization (i.e., the Babylonia civilization).

Eventually the Arsacids pushed into Babylonia in the 2d century B.C., forcing the Seleucids to withdraw to Syria. Our sources for the political history now rapidly dwindle, and little is known about the history of Babylonia in this time.

E. The State

The political structure of the Babylonian state was essentially that of the Sumerian state. Only gradually did changes take place to meet new conditions, particularly when Babylonia became a major imperial power in the 7th and 6th centuries B.C.

1. The King. The institution of monarchy in the Babylonian plain was Sumerian in origin. As in Sumer, the political philosophy was that monarchy came from the gods. The gods appointed a particular human being to rule and, in so doing, made him the supremely powerful human on earth. He had absolute power in every sphere—administration, courts, economy, army, society in general—except religion. In religion, he had to respect the position of the high priest, and this fact was made manifest once a year, in the New Year Festival. Part of the New Year's ritual called for the high priest to slap the king's face and pull him by the ears. The purpose of this was to remind the king that he was a humble servant of the gods. The king had certain duties to perform as a condition of his divine appointment. First, he was responsible for the nourishment of the gods, which meant that he had to contribute substantially from state resources toward the maintenance and building of the temples. Second, he was responsible for the "shepherding" of the people, which in fact meant maintaining an elaborate bureaucracy to carry out the administration. Third and finally, he had to administer justice to all, rich and poor, young and old; and thus, he was both a judge and a legislator.

In practice the monarchy was hereditary, with primogeniture (inheritance by the firstborn son) being the rule. The heir had to go through an elaborate coronation, which included both the gods and the Babylonian nobility approving his accession to the throne. There were numerous disruptions to the succession in Babylonian history, and there were many short-lived dynasties, particularly in the early centuries of the 1st millennium.

Along with the institution of monarchy came the idea that the king was divine, a concept also inherited from the Sumerians. This idea persisted in the early Old Babylonian period, during which many hymns were composed in praise of kings as gods and their names were preceded in writing by the cuneiform sign which indicated divinity. By the time of Hammurapi, however, the idea had died out and never reappeared. The image of the Babylonian king, as portrayed in literature and art, was of a pious ruler who fulfilled his divine commissions and had little to do with war and commerce. Of course in practice he had much to do in both spheres, particularly with regard to war during the Neo-Babylonian empire. This image is quite different from that of the Assyrian king, who is depicted as a vigorous, albeit pious, warrior.

2. Administration. While the king was an absolute monarch, he required an elaborately structured administration to run the state. It is a feature of Babylonian administration that any Babylonian who felt he had a grievance could appeal directly to the king. There are many examples of this happening and of a king, such as Hammurapi, taking direct charge and personally correcting the grievance.

Babylonian administration can be portrayed as a pyramid with the king at the pinnacle and the numerous unskilled laborers, including slaves, forming the foundation. In between were several layers of bureaucrats and workers. Directly under the king were the governors of provinces and city mayors. Under these were the superintendants of tradesmen and laborers, and under these, in turn, were the next lower classes. Among the general population, first came the freemen, who were economically well off, owning land and doing little or no actual labor themselves. Below them were the half-free, palace officials, tradesmen, and small tenant farmers who did much of the work. Then there were the slaves, who were either debt slaves or prisoners of war. On the periphery of this structure were the seminomads, who would perform public works, including fighting, in return for payment. A group outside of the system was the temple personnel, for the temple had its own administrative system.

At every level and in every segment of Babylonian administration there was the scribe, for meticulous records of administrative matters had to be kept. This was another legacy from the Sumerians. There were chief scribes attached to the court, scribes in the governors' palaces, and even scribes assigned to record the rations issued to gangs of workmen dredging out canals. It is fortunate for us that this was so, since most of what we know of Babylonian administration has been learned from the letters, lists, memoranda, etc., left by these scribes. Another ubiquitous occupation was that of tax collector. There were numerous tax collectors throughout the land to collect a share of every crop and custom duties on every item going through the cities' gates. Public works were performed by corvée, it being the responsibility of every Babylonian to contribute some of his time to the maintenance of roads and irrigation canals.

Over the long passage of time in Babylonian history, some fundamental changes in the monarchy and administration took place. In the Old Babylonian period, a change that had begun in Sumerian times came to fruition: the economic and political supremacy shifted from temple to palace, a change brought about by the increasing campaigns of the monarch which enriched his palace's treasury. By the time of Hammurapi, the palace was clearly more powerful and wealthy than the temple. During the 1st millennium, however, another shift developed: by the time of the Neo-Babylonian empire, the king had lost some authority and revenues to the provincial governors, the city mayors, and the temple. In fact, even under the Persians and Seleucids the temples were large and wealthy institutions.

F. Socioeconomic Structure

As in other aspects of Babylonian civilization, The Sumerian legacy in the socioeconomic structure is quite apparent. This is, in significant part, an inevitable condition imposed by Babylonian geography, which considerably limited the economic options open to the inhabitants of the plain. Thus both the Sumerian and Babylonian economic structures rested upon three foundations: agriculture, animal husbandry, and foreign trade (see A. 5–6 above).

The theory behind the economic structure was distinctively Sumerian and had been taken over by the Babylonians. According to this theory, the gods owned all the land and the king administered it for them. In practice, however, private ownership of land was common, and a Babylonian could buy and sell real estate at will. He need be careful only of two conditions, payment of taxes and provision of corvée labor, since ownership of any land entailed these two obligations. There were small and medium-sized plots of land as well as large estates, the latter sometimes consisting of land scattered over more than one province. Not only land transfer but virtually any economic transaction was carefully recorded in writing by the scribes, and tax collectors were at work everywhere, since virtually every transaction involved a payment to the palace.

Money did not exist in Babylonia—it seems to have been a Greek invention—and payment was in kind according to a standard exchange. Silver was the metal most commonly used as the standard, although in some periods use was made of other metals, such as gold, tin, or copper. This system was not so cumbrous as one might think, since credit was well known. Most transactions that were recorded, from small commissions to farm little plots of land to major property transfers, involved credit. The most important and wealthiest Babylonian businessmen, called the *tam kārum,* had extensive resources built on credit, and they dealt in both domestic and foreign trade. Interest rates varied a great deal, but 25 percent was common, rates of 33 percent to 50 percent were not unusual, and rates up to 100 percent were known. Because of such high interest rates, a large number of Babylonians were in debt all their lives, and many went bankrupt, which in Babylonian society meant they became debt slaves. They had the right to buy themselves out of slavery, and some did manage to do so. Despite these tragedies, credit and interest were the basis of an enormously successful economy, for as a Babylonian proverb stated: "Lending money is like making love and getting it back is like having a son."

There is some uncertainty about whether Babylonian business was uncontrolled (free market) or whether the state imposed some restrictions on it (state regulated). There is evidence on both sides of this question, and that is why there is uncertainty. On the one hand, it is clear from records of everyday transactions that prices fluctuated in relation to supply and demand. An extreme example is the exorbitant prices charged for food in 7th-century Nippur when it was under siege by Nabopolassar and food was very scarce. On the other hand, there are many references in Babylonian documents to royal decrees which state the cost of such diverse things as the purchase of grain and the rental of boats. The problem of these diverse facts remains to be resolved, but it is obvious that the Babylonian economic structure was neither entirely free nor entirely controlled.

The urban character of Babylonian society, another legacy from the Sumerians, is striking. The surrounding countryside merely served the needs of the city, which was the focal point of Babylonian economy and society—indeed the center of every aspect of Babylonian civilization. It was the city that fostered not only pragmatic pursuits but also intellectual and artistic endeavors. It is thanks to the urban centers that Babylonian civilization is noted for its art, literature, and science. There was much rivalry among the cities, and some of them, such as Babylon and Sippar, claimed ancient privileges which even the Assyrian conquerors had to respect. Those privileges involved such things as exemption from certain taxes, billeting of troops, and levying of troops.

The structure of Babylonian society was essentially the same as that of the administration, which has already been outlined (E. 2). Family and tribal affiliation was of fundamental importance to a Babylonian, and one usually remained in the social class into which one was born. It should be noted that slavery, although a basic element in Babylonian society, was not a major component either of the society or of the economy. The number of slaves was relatively small, and much of the menial labor was done by free or half-free individuals. This, of course, was in contrast to the situation in the Roman Empire.

Four observations can be made about the character of Babylonian society. First, Babylonians were a very religious people, and religion pervaded every aspect of life for everyone, from the king down to the slave (see I below). Second, they had a strong sense of morality, and there was strong disapproval when anyone broke the moral code. Gods could err morally as well, and there are examples of this in the mythology (see H below). Third, Babylonian society, like preindustrial societies in general, was very conservative. Change, if it occurred at all, was slow; for to their minds it was foolish to abandon a practice or theory that had existed since time immemorial. Fourth, and finally, it was a society very conscious of its past. Kings commonly referred to the achievements of their predecessors, and records of Babylonian history were kept in various forms for the use of the king and scribes. Epics about great heroes of the past were recited to the illiterate.

Over the many centuries that Babylonian civilization flourished, there were some gradual changes in the socioeconomic structure. By about 1000 B.C. some "large cities," such as Babylon, had emerged and become the focal points of Babylonian life. This process involved, in part, siphoning off population from other urban centers, particularly the old Sumerian cities in the south, which gradually shrank in size. During the 1st millennium, both domestic and foreign trade activity expanded as a result of imperial conquest first by the Assyrians and later by the Babylonians. Thus, by the time of the Neo-Babylonian empire, the Babylonian population and economy were concentrated in a few large cities and a few big temples.

G. Legal Structure

Since the discovery of the law code of Hammurapi in the 19th century, it has been well known how important the subject of law was in Babylonian civilization. The "Law Codes" (for several are now known) are, however, not really what the name suggests; to understand the legal structure of Babylonia, we must look as well at other documentation, contracts and court records. Only by combining these two different types of records can we achieve an understanding of the function and character of law in Babylonia. See LAW.

1. Law Codes. The law code of Hammurapi is now only one of several such documents known from ancient Mesopotamia. In chronological order there are the codes of Urukagina (ca. 2350 B.C.), Ur-Nammu (ca. 2112–2095 B.C.; *ANET,* 523–5), Lipit-Ishtar (ca. 1934–1924 B.C.; *ANET,* 159–60), Eshnunna (ca. 1900 B.C.; *ANET,* 161–3), and Hammurapi (ca. 1792–1750 B.C.; *ANET,* 163–80). Related to these are non-Babylonian codes, viz. the MA laws (*ANET,* 180–8), the Hittite laws (*ANET,* 188–97), and the Hebrew laws (Exodus 19–23). The languages of these documents vary, some being in Sumerian (Urukagina, Ur-Nammu, and Lipit-Ishtar), some in Akkadian (Eshnunna, Hammurapi, and MA), one in Hittite, and one in Hebrew; but they all share similarities in structure and content. A good illustration of the similarities is the group of laws concerning goring oxen:

Eshnunna	53. If an ox gored an(other) ox and killed (it), both ox owners shall divide the price of the live ox and also the equivalent of the dead ox.
	54. If an ox is known to gore habitually and the authorities have brought the fact to the knowledge of its owner but he has not had his ox dehorned; (if then) it gored a citizen and killed (him), the owner of the ox shall pay two thirds of a mina of silver.
	55. If it gored a slave and killed (him) he shall pay fifteen shekels of silver.
Hammurapi	250. If an ox, when it was going along the street, gored a citizen and killed (him), that case is not subject to claim.
	251. If a citizen's ox was an habitual gorer and his city-ward notified him that it was an habitual gorer, but he did not pad its horns (or) keep watch over his ox and that ox gored and killed a member of the citizen class, he shall pay one half mina of silver.
	252. If it was a citizen's slave, he shall pay one third of a mina of silver.
Exodus	21:28. If an ox gored a man or a woman and they died, the ox shall be stoned and its meat shall not be eaten but the owner of the ox shall be clear.
	21:29. If the ox habitually gored in the past and its owner was informed but did not keep watch over it and it killed a man or woman, the ox shall be stoned and its owner also shall be executed. 21:31. If it gored a man's son or daughter, he shall be dealt with according to this same law.
	21:32. If the ox gored a slave, male or female, the owner shall pay to their master thirty shekels of silver, and the ox shall be stoned.
	21:35. If one man's ox hurt another's and it died, then they shall sell the live ox and divide the price of it and the dead animal also they shall divide.

The similarities are striking and cannot be explained away simply by the fact that any society which used oxen would, from time to time, have trouble with renegade oxen (cf. Finkelstein 1981). There is a clear connection here. This is, of course, not surprising in the case of the Eshnunna and Hammurapi codes. They were close in time, culture, and geography.

But what about the Hebrew laws? To understand this connection one must look at the whole question of the relationship between Babylonian and biblical literature, since the Babylonian law codes were, as we shall see, as much literature as law (see H. 1 below). Just when these cultural similarities appeared is uncertain. It could have been in the Amorite period, when Amorites occupied both Babylonia and Palestine early in the 2d millennium; or it could have been in the Amarna age, when there was much international exchange throughout the Near East.

Other areas in which there is similarity are the prescribed punishments for bodily injury:

Eshnunna	42. If a man bit the nose of a(nother) man and severed it, he shall pay one mina of silver. (For) an eye (he shall pay) one mina of silver, (for) a tooth one half mina, (for) an ear one half mina, (for) a slap in the face ten shekels of silver.
Hammurapi	196. If a citizen destroyed the eye of a member of the citizen class his eye shall be destroyed.
	200. If a citizen knocked out the tooth of a citizen of his own rank, his tooth shall be knocked out.
Exodus	21:22–25. If men were fighting and hurt a pregnant woman so that she had a miscarriage and yet no harm followed, the one who hurt her shall be fined, according to what the woman's husband shall impose upon him; and he shall pay as the judges determine. If any harm follows, then you shall give life for life, eye for eye, tooth for tooth, hand for hand, foot for foot, burn for burn, wound for wound, stripe for stripe.

What is striking here is that the Eshnunna code prescribes financial restitution for bodily injury, but both the Hammurapi and Hebrew codes prescribe proportional physical retaliation against the guilty party. Thus, we see that the principle of reprisal (*lex talionis*), an eye for an eye and a tooth for a tooth, had a late appearance in Mesopotamia. Since Hammurapi was of Amorite origin, and the Amorites were also well entrenched in Palestine at about the same time, it seems that this custom may have been Amorite in origin.

The traditional modern term "law codes" implies a formal code such as the Romans had, or we have today, which is a comprehensive and cohesive collection of laws to be obeyed and used as the rule in legal disputes. Since the Babylonian documents were none of these things, it is really incorrect to use the term "law code."

Even a quick examination of Hammurapi's "law code" shows that it is not such a document. It is not comprehensive; it covers many legal situations but leaves many, including homicide, out. Nor is it cohesively consistent. In various sections of the code theft, for example, is dealt with but in different ways. In section 6 it is stated that the theft of any property from a temple is punishable by death, but in section 8 that theft of an animal from a temple means the thief must repay thirty times the animal's value. On the other hand, there is a total lack of evidence that anyone in Babylonia ever thought the code must be obeyed. In particular, among the large number of contracts and court records of Hammurapi's time, never once is the "code" referred to.

If these documents are not "law codes," what are they? To seek an answer to this question we must go back to the first document, that of Urukagina. This text is actually a royal inscription of Urukagina, last king of the first dynasty of Lagash. Within the royal inscriptions there was incorporated a record of numerous social and economic reforms which the king had decreed. Those reforms included reduction of taxes and what we would call "fair trade" enactments. Similarly, the very fragmentary text of Ur-Nammu is really a royal inscription, a record of reforms which he had carried out. The same is true of the Lipit-Ishtar "code." It is known that in late Sumerian times and the early Old Babylonian period, kings, when they first came to the throne, frequently issued numerous decrees to correct abuses which had been developing during previous reigns. Thus, for example, if too many people had been falling into debt slavery because of high interest rates, a new king might decree a reduction in the rate. Not only did this practice alleviate hardship, it also made the new ruler popular with the people. These decrees were written down in collections by the scribes, initially as archival records. But the collections proved useful to the scribes composing royal inscriptions, for they could and did copy them into the royal texts as proof that the king had ruled his people with justice. The Eshnunna "code" is actually such a collection of decrees, while the Hammurapi code, which has a lengthy prologue and epilogue, has the structure of a royal inscription. Thus, each article was, in theory, a decree originally intended to deal with a specific issue; but the scribes not only copied decrees from texts of previous rulers but also added some articles of their own to "round out" to their own satisfaction a particular theme.

The "law codes" then give us only part of the picture of the Babylonian legal structure. They reflect attitudes and mores peculiar to this civilization and, of course, give real indications of what Babylonians regarded as legally right and wrong; but we must go on to examine the everyday legal transactions in order to shed more light on this topic.

2. Law in Practice. There are two kinds of legal documents in Babylonia: contracts of various sorts and court records (cf. *ANET,* 217–22; 542–47). All legal documents had certain features in common. They were drawn up on clay tablets in the presence of witnesses whose names were written on the document, and the personal seal of each witness was impressed in the wet clay. Then a clay envelope was wrapped around the tablet and a précis of the contents inscribed over most of the surface. Thus, if anyone in the future tried to tamper with the document, it would immediately be obvious from the broken seals on the envelope.

Contracts included marriages, divorces, adoptions, conveyances (sales) of movable and immovable property, loans, and the hiring of human and animal labor. These were private transactions, and the state was not normally involved. The contracting parties, after an oral agreement, had a scribe draw up the necessary contract, as described above. Some types of contracts, such as marriage contracts, were for obvious reasons kept permanently. Tablets recording loans and debts, on the other hand, were destroyed when the debt was paid, thus eliminating the need for a receipt. If a creditor could not produce a written document proving a debt against someone, he had no legal claim against that person.

Court records are not nearly so common as contracts, since legal disputes were usually settled privately. But if the state legal machinery was put in motion, records of the proceedings had to be kept. Unfortunately, the court records are not very useful sources of information about how Babylonian courts worked. This is true where the customs had been well known to everyone involved, and so no need had ever been felt to write them down.

Judges did exist in Babylonia, and the king himself was the head of the whole judicial system, the supreme judge as it were. If all else failed, a Babylonian with a grievance could ultimately appeal to the king. More than one judge presided in a case, and they were assisted or advised by an assembly (*puhru*). Both claimant and defendant were called upon to state their respective cases and to produce witnesses to prove them. Oaths to the gods were taken by everyone. It is unknown how the judges came to a decision. However, when they could not reach a decision for some reason, they resorted to trial by ordeal. This meant the accused was thrown into the river. If he sank, he was guilty; if he survived, he was innocent. This was far more sensible than the water ordeal for witches in medieval Europe, where the survivor was judged to be a witch and burnt!

In Babylonian law there were no state cases. All disputes and all court cases were between private individuals. The state did not take anyone to court. Even in the case of homicide, it was the family of the victim which sought punishment and compensation. Here the vendetta, the blood feud, prevailed and led to terrible feuds between families. Imprisonment as a punishment was largely unknown, for there were no state prisons. The only reason anyone was ever incarcerated was for a political crime. Even this was rare, since execution was the common punishment for treason.

3. Status of Women. The status of women in Babylonian society is best discussed under the legal structure, since there is more information about the legal status of women than about other areas. In the Old Babylonian (OB) period, the status of women was relatively high, but as time went on, women's rights and prerogatives declined so that in later Babylonian history their status had greatly diminished.

Legally, a Babylonian woman in the OB period was equal with a Babylonian man in many respects. She could own, buy, and sell property as she liked. She could borrow and lend, she could adopt children, and she could serve as a witness to a contract. She could sue someone, and she could own her own seal. This leaves large areas, however, in which she had few or no legal rights. Most significant is that a woman was under the authority of either a man (a father or husband) or a temple. Most women, as most men, were expected to marry, and a man could have more than one wife. Until marriage a woman lived in her father and mother's house and was under the authority of her father. When she married, she moved to her husband's house, which meant the house of her father-in-law, and was under her husband's authority. Unmarried women entered the service of a temple. In the OB period, there are examples of women receiving a good education and even becoming scribes. Women living in a household were kept apart in a harem, and normally male visitors never saw them. The women were responsible for the cooking, cleaning, household chores in general, and care of the children. The amount of physical labor a woman actually did depended on the economic status of her family. A member of the court harem did no labor, since this was done by the palace staff. But even poorer families had servants of some kind to help with menial tasks.

There were various types of temple women, but one of the most important and interesting was the *nadītum,* which means "fallow woman"; that is, a woman who is not to bear children. The institution of the *nadītum* flourished during the OB period. While there were different kinds of *nadītums*, the best known were those who lived in a cloister. The largest cloister was at Sippar and was dedicated to the god Shamash. The women were regarded as brides of Shamash, and many bore names compounded with the divine name *Aya,* meaning the spouse of Shamash. The *nadītum* was not a priestess, for she neither performed rituals nor assisted in any. Exactly what her duties were and what went on inside the cloister are unknown. Clearly it was a religious institution, but there was an economic element as well. Most of the *nadītums* came from wealthy families, and when they entered the cloister, they were accompanied by a substantial dowry. This dowry was administered by the cloister but remained the private property of the *nadītum* and reverted to her family at her death. Thus, a family in dedicating a daughter to the cloister preserved some of its property intact. If the girl had married instead of becoming a *nadītum,* the dowry would have been lost to the family.

The rulers and officials of Babylonia were always men. Only rarely did a woman achieve any kind of political pwer; and when she did, she had no official status. To illustrate this point, let us look at two women, one from the Old Babylonian period and one from the Neo-Babylonian period. Shibtu was the wife of Zimri-Lim, king of Mari and contemporary of Hammurapi (ca. 1792–1750 B.C.). She took much interest in her husband's affairs, and Zimri-Lim soon learned that he could trust her to manage important state matters. This was particularly important when he was on campaign. A number of written reports from Shibtu to the king on various administrative matters have been preserved, and she was frequently entrusted with highly confidential matters. Yet her private side also emerges in the correspondence; in one brief but joyful letter, she announced to her husband the birth of twins. The other example of a stateswoman is Adad-guppi, mother of Nabonidus (555–539 B.C.). This remarkable woman lived to the age of ninety-five, having been born during the reign of Ashurbanipal (668–627 B.C.). She claimed to have served every king in the Neo-Babylonian dynasty and to have persuaded Nebuchadnezzar II to take her son Nabonidus into his service. Once established at the Babylonian court Adad-guppi no doubt continued to maneuver and manipulate affairs to her son's advantage. As a result, he eventually became king. Adad-guppi exercised so much authority that a legend evolved around her memory, portraying her as a queen in full control of Babylonia, a legend embedded in the histories of Herodotus (where she is given the name Nitokris).

H. Literature, Learning, and Libraries

One of the most significant legacies of Babylonian civilization is its extensive literature. The tradition of writing down legends and songs, which had been transmitted orally, for posterity began with the Sumerians, just at the beginning of the Old Babylonian period. Until that time very little Sumerian literature existed. But the scribes became worried that their civilization would die and so began an industrious and lengthy endeavor to preserve in writing their oral heritage. This impetus was passed on to the Babylonians.

In discussing the written records preserved in Babylonian libraries, an important distinction must be made. On the one hand, there is "literature" in the strict sense of the word (artistic and creative writings such as epics and myths); on the other hand, there are compositions of little or no literary merit, which, nonetheless, the Babylonians regarded as having lasting value (lexical texts, prognostic texts, etc.). In the following discussion we shall first speak of Babylonian "literature" in the strict sense; and then, we shall treat the other kinds of written works preserved in Babylonian libraries.

1. Literature. As stated above, the impetus to write literature in Babylonia goes back to the Sumerians. It is, therefore, not surprising to find Sumerian influence in the form, content, and style of Babylonian literary works. (A sample of Babylonian literature, in English translation, can be found in *ANET*).

One form of literature in which the Babylonians departed from the Sumerian inheritance was poetry. Babylonian poetry is a very distinctive art form, followed later in Hebrew and Arabic poetry. The chief characteristic of this poetry is parallelism. That is, there are two parallel parts to each phrase, line, or stanza. The parallels may be synonymous or antithetical, or yet some other variation. Apart from parallelism, there is nothing that can be called a universal characteristic of Babylonian poetry. It does not rhyme; while it may have meter, to date this has not been proved. A feature of Babylonian poetry is the frequent use of repetition. Long speeches are repeated verbatim in an epic, or the same motif will appear in the same words in different compositions. Thus, Ishtar's short lament over the destruction of the Flood appears in different epics.

While different genres are apparent in Babylonian literature, there is no evidence of how the Babylonians themselves divided up their literature or what names they gave for such English words as "epic," "myth," and "hymn." In modern terms, the following genres can be recognized: epic, myth, prayer, and hymn. Standing separate is a group of texts called "Wisdom," a name borrowed from a translation of the Hebrew term used to describe such book as Proverbs and Job.

Several Babylonian epics, which are in poetry, are known, and by far the most imporant is the GILGAMESH EPIC. There were Sumerian poems about Gilgamesh (*ANET,* 44–52), but the epic itself was a Babylonian creation (*ANET,* 72–99; 503–7). It is a lengthy poetic narrative of the life and adventures of Gilgamesh, ruler of Uruk, who sought in vain for eternal life. A version of the Flood story makes up part of this epic. The Flood story, of which there were several versions in Sumerian, is itself the major theme in the *Atram-hasis Epic.* Here, we read that when the gods decided to destroy humankind (because they made too much noise and disturbed the gods' rest), one man and his family were spared. This man's name was Atram-hasis.

Myths were very popular in Babylonia and were also written down in poetry. One myth is the *Descent of Ishtar Into Hell* (*ANET,* 106–9). This composition was originally in Sumerian, and the Babylonian version is essentially an edited translation. It describes the descent of Ishtar into hell in search of her lover, Dumuzi, who had been lured down there by the goddess of the underworld. An independent Babylonian myth is *Enuma Elish,* "When Above," sometimes called the *Creation Epic* (*ANET,* 60–72; 501–3). This is a kind of religious treatise, for it describes and justifies how Marduk, the god of Babylon, became king of the gods.

It is often difficult to tell the difference between Babylonian prayers and hymns, since there is usually no indication of whether the poem was accompanied by music. The number of such texts is in the hundreds, but only a small proportion, including a long hymn to Shamash, the sun-god, are of outstanding literary merit (cf. *ANET,* 383–92).

Within the general category of Wisdom Literature, there is a diversity of works. There are a few compositions sharing a common theme, the problem of evil, but each is unique in form. Such a work is one called *Ludlul Bēl Nēmēqi,* "I Will Praise the Lord of Wisdom" (*ANET,* 434–37; 596–600). In this lengthy and somber piece, the poet complains, like Job, that though he has been good all his life, his reward has been one long series of misfortunes. "Does the righteous man receive no just reward?" is his question. Another type of Wisdom Literature is represented by the "Disputes" and is Sumerian in origin. An example of a Babylonian Dispute is a work called *The Date Palm and the Tamarisk.* In this highly structured literary work a formal debate between the two kinds of trees takes place, each enumerating its merits to the disadvantage of the other. Finally, there were a number of Proverb collections, mainly in Sumerian but some in Babylonian (cf. *ANET,* 425–27).

Babylonian literary works such as these played a dual role in Babylonian civilization: entertainment and edification. Some of the Wisdom Literature, such as the *Wisdom of Shuruppak,* was intended to teach proper conduct to the young. On the other hand, the *Gilgamesh Epic* both edifies and entertains as the hero grapples with the reality of mortal existence. The vast majority of Babylonians were illiterate, which meant that they could not read this literature for themselves; it had to be recited to them in groups in formal or informal gatherings, sometimes with musical accompaniment. There is reason to believe that some compositions, such as the *Descent of Ishtar Into Hell,* was staged. The seven steps by which Ishtar entered hell, the actions of each step being precisely described, strongly suggest a dramatic performance.

2. Learning. Learning was the prerogative of the scribes, for only they were literate. In fact, learning in the academic sense was confined to a small number of scribes, since the majority were employed in everyday business, writing letters, contracts, and administrative texts. The privileged few who had free time to pursue knowledge were in the employ of the palace or temple. They were poorly lodged and not well paid, if we believe their frequent complaints. The daily activities of these scribes were diverse, depending on their training, talent, and experience. Some, such as the astrologers, were employed in divination, some in looking after the royal correspondence, some in preparing royal inscriptions for building works, and so on. The majority, however, spent much of their time making new copies of library and archival texts (similar to the occupation of monks in scriptoria in medieval Europe).

The scribal profession as a whole had a tremendous influence in Babylonian society, because most people could neither read nor write. Even the king and his chief officers were illiterate. This meant that all written communication with the king, as with anyone else, had to go through at least two scribes, one to write the letter and one to read it out upon arrival. Here, there was plenty of scope for slanted interpretation or misunderstanding. Occasionally, as in the Amarna Letters, the scribe writing a letter would add a note to the colleague who was to read the letter out, suggesting what the reader should emphasize.

As with all Babylonian occupations, the scribal profession was essentially hereditary. Of course one prerequisite was excellent eyesight, since magnification had not been invented. The course of study for the potential scribe lasted many years, probably until his late teens. The hours were long and the discipline, which included corporal punishment, strict. In the schoolhouse, learning was mainly acquired by rote, and the students copied and recopied set texts. Thousands of these copies, "school texts" as we call them, have been unearthed by modern excavations.

At least some, and possibly most, of the privileged scribes who gained senior positions in a palace or temple had a certain amount of time free from their formal duties to indulge in their own interests. These were the scholars and poets who produced Babylonian literature and scholarly texts. They were very conscious of their special status and proudly wrote down the name of the scribal school to which they belonged. The one place where they remained anonymous was in the authorship of literary texts. Thus, while we know the names of scribes who edited and copied such a famous text as the *Gilgamesh Epic,* we are never given the name of its author.

Babylonian learning included vast areas of knowledge which can be grouped together under the headings astrology and astronomy, extispicy and anatomy, medicine, mathematics, lexicography, theology, historiography, and commentaries. Some of this learning, mainly astronomy and mathematics, spread to Greece in the Hellenistic age. The Babylonian practice of divination (see I below) gave rise to extensive records of astronomical phenomena and calculations on future celestial movements, including eclipses. It also, in the case of extispicy (examination of animal entrails), led to the compilation of much material on anatomy and physiology.

Babylonian medicine had two sides, one practical and one theoretical. On the practical side, the Babylonians had a vast store of knowledge concerning herbs, medicines, and the symptoms for which they were efficacious. A Babylonian doctor could do certain kinds of surgery, such as an operation on the eye, probably to remove a cataract. On the theoretical side, the Babylonians had a vast store of incantations and rituals to exorcise the demons believed to cause a patient's illness. The incantation priests (*āšipu*) worked hand in hand with the practical doctors (*asû*) to cure a sufferer.

The heyday of Babylonian mathematics was the early Old Babylonian period (ca. 2000–1780 B.C.). During that time mathematicians went beyond the crude arithmetical necessities of everyday life to explore what we call algebra and geometry. They discovered Euclid's theorem and the Pythagorean triangle more than a thousand years before those Greek scholars lived. Scores of Babylonian "problem texts" have been discovered, and they include both practical problems (such as calculating the height of a ziggurat) and theoretical problems.

Lexicography, the science of words (the principles and practices of making dictionaries), was a highly important occupation. Next to prognostic texts, lexicographical texts were the most numerous in ancient Babylonian libraries. These included lists of names (plants, animals, professions, etc.), bilingual and multilingual dictionaries, and lists of cuneiform signs of various shapes and interpretations. Among this material were many lists of god names in which several divine names were frequently identified with one god, indicating a basic syncretistic theology.

As stated earlier, Babylonians were keenly interested in their past, and in academic circles this meant that scribes compiled works on the subject. These included king lists, chronicles, and poetic works about famous figures of the past. A few scribes went farther and wrote in a prophetic style about past events in an attempt to justify modern change or possibly even to make a real prediction seem credible. This literature (*ANET,* 451–52; 606–7), which has parallels in the biblical book of Daniel, may well be the beginning of apocalyptic literature. See APOCALYPSES AND APOCALYPTICISM.

As if this were not enough learning, the scribes occasionally indulged in highly esoteric composition. They wrote some commentaries to literary texts, which to our minds often seem abstruse and are difficult to read. From time to time they also wrote in numbers rather than in cuneiform signs, each number representing a syllable or word. Such passages are extremely hard to decipher. They were really learned games, such as difficult crossword puzzles.

3. Libraries. More is known about Assyrian libraries than Babylonian libraries. (The reader is referred to the discussion under Assyria [previous article] for fuller information than can be given here.) The reason is the chance of archaeology. Most libraries in Babylonia were unearthed in the 19th century before proper excavation techniques had been developed. At Asshur, on the other hand, scientific methods were employed with great benefit to modern knowledge.

Libraries no doubt existed in all major Babylonian cities; specifically, they have been discovered at Babylon, Borsippa, Sippar, and Nippur, to name the best known. The library discovered at Nippur is largely early Old Babylonian in date and Sumerian in content. Most of the tablets are now housed in Istanbul, Jena (East Germany), and Philadelphia. The libraries from Babylon, Borsippa, and Sippar are both Old and New Babylonian in date and the contents mainly in Akkadian. Most of these tablets are now in the British Museum.

Recently (1986), a whole new library was discovered at Sippar by archaeologists from the University of Baghdad. This is the most important find of the decade and when the tablets have been analyzed and published, they will supply much information on the subject. The texts seem to be Neo-Babylonian in date. The discovery also sheds light on the physical arrangements in a Babylonian library. The tablets were stored in deep cubicles made up of clay shelves and uprights. Brief markings on the tablet edges were notes ("call numbers") to assist the libraries in locating the texts they wanted.

I. Religion

Babylonian religion permeates Babylonian society, being present in every event, every action, every institution, every thought. This feature cannot be overemphasized, particularly in our modern secular society where such a phenomenon seems so strange. For this reason it has become fashionable in scholarly circles in recent years to be very negative about the possibility of our gaining an understanding of ancient religion. Some modern specialists in Babylonia claim that the very nature of the available sources excludes any comprehensive and profound knowledge of Babylonian religion (Oppenheim 1964); but this is overstating the case. Among the tens of thousands of artifacts and inscriptions which archaeologists have excavated, there is a wealth of information on the subject. This includes religious scenes in art, votive figurines from temples, mythological texts, rituals, hymns, prayers, and offering lists. We can never discover exactly what a given Babylonian thought about religion, of course, anymore than we can do this for a modern human being; but, as shall be seen in the following pages, we now have considerable information about this subject.

Babylonian religion was very heavily influenced by Sumerian religion, and all of the characteristics described here are characteristics of Sumerian religion. Babylonian religion had a number of outstanding characteristics. It was a polytheistic religion, the number of gods, goddesses, demons, etc., being in the hundreds. These were ranked in a hierarchy, but there were many overlaps and regional differences. To further complicate matters, each divinity had a spouse. The religion was animistic, for every animate and inanimate object was believed to have life and being. Cults were an important part of Babylonian religion, and every city had both major and minor cults, each with its temple, priests, offerings, and rituals. There was an official or state religion, and there was private religion. Morality was involved in Babylonian religion, and a very high ethical tone is evident in some writings. Divination and magic were important parts of the Babylonian way of life.

1. State Religion. The chief Babylonian gods, and the cities where their cults were centered, were Marduk at Babylon, Nabû at Borsippa, Enlil at Nippur, Ishtar at Uruk, Sin at Ur, Shamash at Sippar, and Nergal at Cuthah. When Babylonian history began, the Sumerian god An was still officially regarded as the king of the gods. In practice, Enlil, as in Sumerian times, played the chief role. See ENLIL. As time passed and the city of Babylon became the political and cultural center of the land, its god, Marduk, gradually moved into a more important position. Ultimately, he was officially recognized as king of the gods, during the reign of Nebuchadnezzar I (ca. 1125–1104 B.C.; see D. 6 above). Many of the attributes and much of the mythology attached to Enlil became his. In the late period, Marduk was often simply called *Bel,* "lord." Nabû was Marduk's son and was the god of scribes and learning. Libraries in temples were called "the shrines of Nabû." Ishtar was the mother goddess and the goddess of love. Sin was the moon-god, and his cult became unusually important during the reign of Nabonidus (see D. 8 above). Shamash was the sun-god and always had great prominence because he was in charge of justice and divination. Nergal, who was commonly associated with Erra, was the god of the netherworld, and death came under his jurisdiction.

Each cult not only had its own temple, personnel, and offerings but also its own festivals and rituals. The festivals of the major cults were, of course, more important than those of minor cults. The chief event of all was the *Akītu* or New Year Festival. This was celebrated every spring at Babylon for the first twelve days of Nisan, the first month of the year. The statues of gods from other cities, such as Nabû from Borsippa, were brought by boat with great ceremony to Babylon. Here, they greeted Marduk and accompanied his statue, placed on a ceremonial float, out of the temple. The magnificent procession progressed down the wide avenue from Marduk's temple through the Ishtar Gate to the *Akītu* house outside Babylon's walls. In this house rituals were performed and the *Enuma Elish* poem, describing how Marduk became king of the gods, was recited. Then Marduk was escorted back to his temple, and the gods returned to their own cities and temples. The Babylonian king had an essential role in state religion, and this was particularly apparent in the *Akītu* festival. At one point the chief priest would slap him in the face and drag him by the ears to Marduk's throne, where he forced the king to bow down and recite a confession. Another part of the *Akītu* festival was the sacred marriage between the king and the chief goddess, Zarpanitu. The marital act was actually carried out by the king with the chief priestess.

Babylonian mythology is quite colorful, and many of the myths, which are in poetry, are exciting to read (see H. 1 above). This is true in part because the Babylonians had a very anthropomorphic view of their gods. They believed that the gods looked, thought, and behaved just like human beings. The only difference was that the gods were immortal and normally invisible. In the mythology the gods loved, hated, fought, ate, drank, sinned, and repented just like mortals. Babylonian cosmology saw the world as divided into three parts, with heaven above, the netherworld below, and the earth in between. Shamash, the sun, traveled through the netherworld at night. The stars and planets were identified with specific gods, and their movements were carefully studied for astrological reasons. The earth itself was seen as a disk surrounded by salt water, with fresh water bubbling up from below the earth to form rivers and lakes. Babylonia and its two rivers, the Tigris and the Euphrates, were in the center of the world.

In Babylonian belief, the gods, heaven, and underworld had always existed. There are no stories of how the gods and their dwelling places evolved, as there are, for example, in Egypt. Humankind, however, was created by the gods, as was earth. There are various stories about the creation, but the central theme is basically the same: there was a major conflict between old gods and young gods. One story, *Enuma Elish,* says the reason for the war was that the young gods were making too much noise and disturbing the sleep of the old gods. Another story, *Atram-hasis,* says the young gods became tired of doing all the work to clothe and feed the old gods and went on strike. In *Enuma Elish,* Marduk is chosen champion of the young gods. He defeats the leader of the old gods, the dragon Tiamat, and creates earth out of her body. Then, with a lump of clay and some blood from the dead spouse of Tiamat, he creates man. Man is placed on earth to serve the gods.

The *Atram-hasis Epic* narrates the creation of man in somewhat the same fashion, but then goes on to describe the Flood. After humankind had been created and had relieved the young gods of menial toil, the humans multiplied rapidly. The noise this multitude made disturbed the gods, and after holding an assembly the gods decided to destroy their creations with a Flood. The Flood duly came and swept over the face of the earth. But one man, Atram-hasis (in other Flood stories he has other names), had been warned by the god Ea that the Flood was coming. He therefore built an enormous boat, loaded his family, livestock, and all his possessions into it, and thereby survived the deluge.

Death and its sequel were very gloomy subjects in Babylonian thought, for there was no concept of a happy afterlife. Slightly different views are given in different texts of what happened after death, but there is a pervading sense of misery. It was first and foremost important to bury a dead person, for otherwise his or her ghost (*eṭemmu*) would wander about homeless and might haunt relatives and friends. The body was buried under the floor of the family home, where antiquated family archives were also buried. After proper burial, the ghost went down to the netherworld. This is eloquently described in the *Gilgamesh Epic* (8: 34–39):

> To the dwelling where none may leave who have entered,
> On the way from which there is no return,
> To the dwelling where the occupants have no light,
> Where they eat dust and clay they consume.
> They are dressed like birds, wings are their clothes,
> They see no light but dwell in darkness.

Every human being went to this gloomy place upon death. There was no paradise for the good or hell for the bad. It is not surprising that Babylonians had a fatalistic view of life and that some of them practiced hedonism, getting as much pleasure from life as they could before they died.

The temples in which the cults had their homes were major economic and social institutions in Babylonia. To provide some impression of this, one might roughly compare it with the status of the Christian Church in Western Europe during the Middle Ages. Physically, the temple consisted of a large complex of buildings with shrines, kitchens, dormitories, workrooms, and storage rooms. Normally a temple tower, or ziggurat, was part of the temple complex. The size of a temple's staff depended on the temple's importance and wealth. The temple of Marduk at Babylon in the 1st millennium was an enormously large and rich institution. We have no indication of the numbers of people on its staff, but they were probably in the hundreds. At the top was the chief priest, and next to him were his chief advisers. There were several different kinds of priests who performed the various rituals and related sacred duties. Craftsmen and laborers, including kitchen staff and herdsmen, were employed by the temple both to provide for its own needs and to produce a surplus for trade and profit. A temple usually owned some land and also had a share ("offerings") in crops and herds from some property it did not own. The more important temples also received support from the palace, although the amount of this support varied from period to period. This support included building and repairs that were carried out by corvée at the order of the king. Containers were left at temple doors for worshippers to deposit voluntary offerings. Temple revenues were in kind, and the food provided for the gods was in practice consumed by the temple personnel.

2. Popular Religion. Little is known about popular religion in Babylonia, since most of our sources are artifacts and documents excavated at the large temples. It was believed that everyone, even the lowest slave, had a personal god and that the god's rank had a direct relation to the human's rank. The relationship between a human and his or her god was quite businesslike. The human provided food and clothing for the god, and the god, in turn, carried the human's requests—such as for good health—to a higher god who could perform the deed.

Magic, both black and white, was universal in Babylonia, but one suspects, although it cannot be proved, that it was particularly popular among poorer people. Incantations and rituals in the hundreds are known from the great libraries. These cover the whole gamut of life: love potions, illness, business affairs, a house infected with insects, childbirth, etc. Clay dolls with human hair were sometimes fashioned as part of a ritual, such as one designed to cast an evil spell on a person. Herbs and roots were the most common elements used in the rituals, and frequently the rituals describe how to use them to mix a poultice or medicine, particularly in the case of illness.

Babylonian texts occasionally refer to roadside shrines. Some of these were certainly part of the state religion, but others were probably manifestations of popular belief. Anyone who has traveled in the Near East must have been struck by the number of small shrines of virtually every religion in town and country alike, even today.

3. Divination. As religion permeated Babylonian civilization, so did divination. The theory and practice of prognostication—predicting the future—was endemic to this culture and affected every aspect of life. It was based on the belief that the gods, whenever they decided to do something, sent a message or messages to human beings through a variety of means. If humans wished to know what the gods intended, they had to learn how to read these signs.

Almost anything could be a medium for divine messages, such as the shape of smoke from a fire, the configurations of oil poured upon water, the flight of birds, or the sudden appearance of a snake. The Babylonians, building upon a Sumerian tradition, developed the science (if we can call it that) of reading these signs into a very complex and comprehensive system. This system was carefully recorded on clay tablets and filed away in libraries for reference. One gains some idea of the importance of divination to Babylonians from the fact that of all the documents stored in Babylonian libraries, prognostic texts were the most numerous.

The kinds of divination we know most about are those used by the king and his court. These were extispicy and astrology. Extispicy—the examination of the entrails of sacrificial animals for ominous signs—was popular in the Old and Middle Babylonian periods, but by the Neo-Babylonian period astrology had become more common. There were both active and passive approaches in divination. Thus, in the active approach the king would address a specific question to the diviners, asking if a certain proposal was approved by the gods. It might be a proposed campaign or the appointment of an official, or something else. The diviners would then sacrifice some animals or watch the heavens and, on the basis of their vast lore, report back to the king. It says much for the skill and common sense of the diviners that there is no case yet known in which any of them were later charged with a false prediction.

A passive approach to divination was also known. Thus, an astrologer might report to the king that his calculations showed that a solar eclipse would occur on such a date and that this meant the king would die. Necessary preventive action had, therefore, to be taken. In one such case, of which there are several examples, a substitute king was put on the throne and at the end of the ominous period was executed. Then the real king, who had been in hiding resumed his throne. Yet another type of passive divination is represented by dreams and prophecies. A king might receive a message from the gods in a dream, or it might be transmitted to him through a prophet. These prophets, or better, "ecstatics," were usually women who induced a trance upon themselves, probably by dancing. While the women were in the trance, the gods would send them messages for the king. Usually these messages were just good wishes for well-being and not at all like the powerful and often threatening messages of the Hebrew prophets.

J. Everyday Life

The everyday life of a Babylonian changed little over the centuries, for rapid change was unknown in preindustrial societies. Food, lodging, clothing, and general behavior patterns were essentially the same in Old Babylonian as in Neo-Babylonian times. This was true despite the frequent immigration of new peoples, since new population groups soon melted into Babylonian society, leaving little trace of their identity.

"A person is what he eats" is an old adage with much truth in it. One's diet affects one's thoughts and actions in a variety of ways. Thus, it is important to know what food Babylonians consumed. It was mainly cereal grains in the form of bread spread with oil pressed from sesame seed. The most common cereal was barley, which was also brewed for beer, the usual beverage. Wine was known but was reserved for festive occasions or for use by rich people. The people also ate leeks, onions, and garlic. Milk, usually from goats, was made into ghee (clarified butter) and cheese. Eggs from chickens and ducks were also part of the regular diet. Fish was commonly caught and eaten. For sweets, there were dates and honey. For most people, meat (fowl, sheep, or goat) was a rare luxury. Only the nobility could afford meat regularly; the lower classes were able to indulge in it only on festive occasions. Indeed, the upper classes had a great respect for good food, and many recipes for the preparation of a meal have been discovered. Not surprisingly, some of the recipes are similar to those for modern dishes found in the area.

There is a description of a banquet among the gods in the epic *Enuma Elish* (3: 133–37), and this may reflect human practice. The story does not tell us what they ate, except that they ate well, but it does say they drank enough to become quite cheerful:

> They chatted together as they sat down at the banquet,
> They ate festive bread and decanted the wine.
> They drank through straws the sweet liquor,
> As they drank the alcohol their bodies relaxed,
> They forgot their cares, their mood became expansive.

The universal building material for dwellings was mud brick, the only exception being in the marshes, where reeds were used. Stone and timber, which had to be imported and were therefore expensive, were used only for palaces and temples. The house of a family of modest means was usually of two stories surrounding a courtyard. There were no openings onto the street except for the door. All windows, which had no coverings, opened onto the courtyard, where there was a pool of water. The second floor had a balcony all around the courtyard. Wealthy families and certainly the king had gardens. There were poor people who were homeless, and many of them carved out niches for themselves in the city walls or in the ruins of old temples and palaces, while others simply slept in doorways. The streets were narrow, twisting, and filthy, since they had open sewers in the center to carry off all waste from the houses. The streets were also dark and dangerous at night because of robbers.

Clothing was a relatively simple matter for most people and consisted of one or two loose-fitting garments. The material came from goats' hair or sheeps' wool. Both men and women wore some jewelry. The upper classes and royalty had more elaborate garments and, of course, wore ornaments of precious stone, such as lapis lazuli, and of metal, such as gold and silver.

For recreation the Babylonians had a variety of options. There were the great religious festivals, which included parades which they could watch. Scribes and poets recited epics and stories to audiences in the squares and at the gates. Music, both vocal and instrumental, was sung or played universally from formal hymns in the great temples to popular folk tunes. A variety of instruments—strings, wind, and percussion—were used. Ball games and wrestling were favorite sports. The more sedentary could entertain themselves with board games, some of which have been recovered in modern excavations. For the children, there were toys such as clay model wagons and dolls.

K. Legacy

Babylonia left a legacy to civilization as a whole and to religion in particular. This is not surprising considering that Babylonia was one of the great civilizations of the Fertile Crescent, an area one could call the cradle of civilization and the cradle of three great religions: Judaism, Christianity, and Islam. A Babylonian legacy is also apparent in the modern region, southern Iraq, of the Babylonian plain and among its present inhabitants.

It is in the Bible that we find the most obvious Babylonian legacy, and since the Bible is sacred to Judaism, Christianity, and Islam, it is then a fact that all three religions have a legacy from the Babylonians. In the discussions above, a connection has been observed between Babylonian and Hebrew law and literature. It is possible that apocalyptic literature, such as one finds in the book of Daniel or the book of Revelation, has its origin in the Babylonian prophecies.

A legacy in the Bible unflattering to the Babylonians is interesting. Biblical writers had good cause to hate the Babylonians after the Exile, and this hatred took the form of regarding them as the archetypes of evil. The strongest expression is in the book of Revelation, where one reads of the iniquities of the "Great Whore of Babylon." Antagonism toward Babylonia went back much farther though, as we can see in the episode of the Tower of Babel in Genesis 11, where the writer is scornful of Babylon's wealth and pretensions, picturing its inhabitants as a godless and foolish bunch. These images of Babylon are still with us today, thanks to the Bible.

A final Babylonian legacy to religion is astrology. Astrology spread from Babylonia both east, to India and beyond, and west. In Western Europe, it gained a firm hold, thriving in the Middle Ages, and it still has a real presence in modern society.

Outside of religion, the most outstanding contribution which Babylonia has made to civilization is in science, a fact which has only come to light during the last few decades. As noted above, the Babylonians by about 1780 B.C. had made great strides in mathematics, algebra, and geometry. They had already made the discoveries which Euclid and Pythagoras would rediscover later. Before the middle of the 1st millennium they had such a wealth of astronomical data and expertise (compiled for the purposes of astrology) that they could measure the solar and lunar years very accurately. They could also predict eclipses of the sun and moon and many other celestial phenomena. This vast lore of learning and discovery spread throughout the Near East and Eastern Europe during the Hellenistic age and thus formed the basis for Greek science, which, in turn, is the basis of modern science. The Babylonians also knew a great deal about medicine and the structure of the human body, but whether much of this knowledge was passed on to the Greeks is unknown.

The influence of Babylonian literature on Greek literature has been shown to be a reality in recent years. There are, for example, reflections of Gilgamesh in the stories of Hercules, and some of the gods mentioned in the poetry of Hesiod reflect a Babylonian background. The Babylonians are famous in modern times for their law codes, and research during the last decade has shown a continuous chain in legal tradition from the Laws of Hammurapi through the Bible to modern law. (In fact there was a trial in the state of Michigan in the 1950s in which the goring-ox laws of Hammurapi's code were cited as bearing on the case! See Finkelstein 1981.)

The land where Babylonian civilization once flourished is now the S part of the modern republic of Iraq. Here, one can see a visible legacy of those ancient people in the minarets of the mosques. These towers remind one of the ancient ziggurats, or temple towers, the remains of which can still be seen at ancient sites throughout the land. In the early Middle Ages, when minarets were first being built, the ziggurats would have been even better preserved and apparent. Indeed, the famous medieval minaret at Samarra was consciously modeled after a ziggurat.

The Babylonian dialect of Akkadian is no longer spoken in the area, but there are still relics of it in the Arabic which is spoken in Iraq today. By this, it is not meant simply that Arabic, being a Semitic language like Akkadian, has words and grammatical structures related to those in Babylonian; this is certainly true. But beyond this, in isolated villages one often finds local words and expressions which are otherwise not known in Arabic but were current in Babylonian. An outstanding example of this is the technical terminology used by the date-palm cultivators in the extreme south. This terminology is actually Sumerian and therefore even older than Babylonian. But the Babylonians inherited it and passed it on to future generations.

Is there any trace of the Babylonian people themselves among the modern inhabitants of S Iraq? This is impossible to prove, but it seems highly probable. After all, when historians say a people "died out" or "disappeared," what they really mean (except in cases of genocide or mass migration) is that the old population intermarried and melted into the new immigrant populations. This was certainly the case with the Babylonians. One region which was isolated and therefore experienced little of this melting is the marshes in the extreme south (see B. above). Here the Marsh Arabs, as the people are called, live in much the same way as the ancient Sumerians and Babylonians. They are quite different in almost every respect from other Iraqis. Perhaps, then, they are the closest we can come to finding traces of Babylonians in the modern world.

Bibliography

Adams, R. M. 1965. *Land Behind Baghdad.* Chicago.
———. 1972. *The Uruk Countryside.* Chicago.
———. 1981. *Heartland of Cities.* Chicago.
Contenau, G. 1966. *Everyday Life in Babylonia and Assyria.* New York.
Finkelstein, J. J. 1981. *The Ox that Gored. TAPhS* 71/2. Philadelphia.
Frankfort, H., et al. 1954. *Before Philosophy.* Harmondsworth.
Grayson, A. K. 1975. *Babylonian Historical-Literary Texts.* Toronto.
Jacobsen, T. 1976. *The Treasures of Darkness.* New Haven.
Kraus, F. R. 1984. *Königliche Verfügungen in altbabylonischer Zeit.* Leiden.
Lambert, W. G. 1960. *Babylonian Wisdom Literature.* Oxford.
Lambert, W. G., and Millard, A. 1969. *Atra-hasis: The Babylonian Story of the Flood.* Oxford.
Neugebauer, O. 1957. *The Exact Sciences in Antiquity.* 2d ed. Providence.
Oppenheim, A. L. 1963. *Letters from Mesopotamia.* Chicago.
———. 1964. *Ancient Mesopotamia.* Chicago. (Rev. ed. E. Reiner. 1977.)
Roux, G. 1980. *Ancient Iraq.* 2d ed. Harmondsworth.
Saggs, H. W. F. 1962. *The Greatness That Was Babylon.* London.
———. 1965. *Everyday Life in Babylonia and Assyria.* London.
———. 1976. *The Encounter with the Divine in Mesopotamia and Israel.* London.

A. Kirk Grayson

MESSENGER. See TRAVEL AND COMMUNICATION.

MESSIAH. The term going back to *Messias,* a Gk form (John 1:41; 4:25) of the Heb *māšîah,* denoting an anointed person. Hebrew *hammāšîaḥ* (Aram *mĕšîḥā*ʾ), "the Messiah," is usually translated in Gk with *ho christos,* the Christ.

Because a central tenet of Christianity has always been the conviction that Jesus was the Christ (the Messiah expected by Israel), much attention has been paid to the study of Jewish expectations of the Messiah. The Christian focus upon the person of Jesus has led to an undue concentration on the *person* of the Messiah in Jewish thought, even in the works of recent scholars. One should realize that in the OT the term "anointed" is never used of a future savior/redeemer, and that in later Jewish writings of the period between 200 B.C. and A.D. 100 the term is used only infrequently in connection with agents of divine deliverance expected in the future.

The use of the term "Messiah" to denote any figure expected to introduce an era of eternal bliss, regardless of the terminology used in the source, leads to confusion. The words "messianic" and "messianism" have a still wider range of meanings; they are also used in connection with expectations of a definitive change in history which is not brought about by a particular future deliverer. (In fact, the expression "messianism without Messiah" has even been coined.) These terms also appear in studies by historians of religion and by social anthropologists, who use them in discussions of developments in later Western history and in other cultures (often under Western colonial, missionary, and modernizing influence).

In the analysis of the literature that concerns us here, we should employ the words "anointed" and "Messiah" only where the sources use the corresponding word in their own language. Similarly, "messianic expectation" should only denote the expectation of a redeemer who is actually called "Messiah." We should also be careful in employing the words "eschatology" and "eschatological." The basic element in the expectations which are commonly called "eschatological" is the conviction that God will complete and crown his dealings with his people and with the whole world by effecting a radical and lasting change, inaugurating a new era. God may use human or angelical intermediaries in bringing about this change, but quite often agents of divine deliverance are not found at all. The mythological imagery and the other expressions qualifying time and space used to describe this radical change are of secondary importance. Though it may be useful or even necessary to distinguish between the various images and concepts, we must be careful not to prejudice our analysis through inappropriate later terminology. We shall do well to use the words "eschatology" and "eschatological" without any modern connotations dependent on philosophical or theological theories concerning the relation between history and that which is "beyond history."

A. The Act of Anointing People
B. Anointed Persons
C. Anointed King(s) in the Psalms
D. OT Prophecies about Future Davidic Kings
E. "Anointed Ones" in Early Judaism (200 B.C.–A.D. 100)
F. Later Jewish Writings
G. Summary

A. The Act of Anointing People

The Heb verb *māšaḥ* is used to indicate the applying of oil to an object or person by either pouring, rubbing, or smearing. The usual Gk equivalent in the LXX is *chriein.* When the word is employed with persons, it denotes the conferring of a specific status (except Amos 6:6). Mostly kings are anointed (Saul, David, Absalom, Solomon, Jehu, Joash, Jehoahaz); however, in some instances (high) priests were anointed (so Aaron and his sons, and Zadok), as were prophets (in one OT case, Elisha).

1. Kings. In the Jotham fable (9:7–15) directed to those who had made Abimelech king at Shechem, the trees are portrayed as wanting to anoint one tree to be king over them. The initiative here is clearly with the king's (prospective) subjects. Likewise, the men of Judah anointed David king over the house of Judah (2 Sam 2:4–7), and they were followed by the men of Israel who made him king of Israel (2 Sam 5:4 = 1 Chr 11:3, cf. 2 Sam 5:17 = 1 Chr 14:8). The case of Absalom in 2 Sam 19:11 (—Eng 19:10) may be compared. During the dynastic conflicts preceding David's death Solomon was anointed, at David's instructions, by Zadok, the priest, and Nathan, the prophet (1 Kgs 1:34, 45; in v 39 only Zadok is mentioned as the one who "took the oil from the tent and anointed Solomon"). In 1 Chr 29:22 it is the assembly of Israel which makes Solomon king and anoints him as prince for the Lord (cf. 1 Kgs 5:15 [—Eng 5:1]). In 2 Kgs 11:12 a group of people proclaims Joash king and anoints him, against the wishes of Athaliah; the LXX attributes the actual anointing to Jehoiada, the priest (cf. 2 Chr 23:11; Jehoiada and his sons). In 2 Kgs 23:30 Jehoahaz is anointed by "the people of the land."

In 2 Sam 12:7 (cf. Ps 89:21—Eng 20), Nathan reminds David that it was YHWH who anointed him king over Israel, and this is also the message of the story in 1 Sam 16:1–13, where Samuel receives instructions from YHWH "to anoint for me him whom I name to you" (v 3), and where Samuel proceeds to anoint David in the midst of his brothers. We may compare here 11 QPs[a] 151:5–7 (cf. LXX Ps 151A). Anointing here indicates divine election (vv 7–12) and is accompanied by the gift of the Spirit (vv 13–14). Likewise, Samuel earlier had been instrumental in anointing Saul (1 Sam 9:16; 10:1); his action signified that YHWH had anointed him to be prince over his people Israel (10:1, 15:1, 17). In 10:5–6, 9–13, the Spirit of the Lord comes mightily upon Saul, and he prophesies (cf. 11:6, before an act of valor). This narrative is combined with the story of Saul's designation by lot (1 Sam 10:17–27) and the report that the people "made Saul king before the Lord in Gilgal" (1 Sam 11:15; cf. 12:1).

In 1 Kgs 19:15, 16, Elijah received YHWH's command to anoint Hazael to be king over Syria, Jehu to be king over Israel, and Elisha to be prophet in his place. In the case of Jehu this command was carried out by one of Elisha's assistants, who told the future king: "Thus says the Lord, I anoint you king over Israel" (2 Kgs 9:3, 6, 12; cf. 2 Chr 22:7); after Jehu reported this, his men proclaimed him king (v 13).

It is hazardous to use these stories in the books of Samuel and Kings for a reconstruction of the historical circumstances or of developments in ideas about kingship and the anointing of kings in various groups in Judah and Israel. For the purpose of the present inquiry, it is sufficient to note that in their final redaction these books show a clear emphasis on YHWH's initiative, election, and commission. This also comes out clearly in the term "anointed of the Lord" (discussed below).

2. Priests. In a number of passages generally considered to belong to the so-called "P Code," Moses receives the instructions to anoint Aaron (high) priest (Exod 29:7; Lev 8:12; cf. 6:13—Eng 6:20). Aaron is always mentioned together with his sons, however, and a number of times the sons also are supposed to have been anointed (Exod 28:41; 30:30; 40:13, 15; Num 3:3). In Lev 7:36 it is declared that it is YHWH who anointed Aaron and his sons. The idea is that the anointing/consecration guarantees an eternal priesthood for Aaron and his successors (Exod 40:15; cf. 29:29; Lev 6:15 [—Eng 6:22]; 16:32; Num 35:25). It should be added that in 1 Chr 29:22 the assembly of Israel anointed not only Solomon but also Zadok as priest.

3. Prophets. In 1 Kgs 19:16, Elijah is told to anoint Elisha to be his successor as prophet. The story of Elisha's call, however, does not mention any anointing; Elijah simply casts his mantle upon him (1 Kgs 19:19–21). When Elijah departs to heaven Elisha asks for and receives a double share of Elijah's spirit, and he takes up the latter's mantle (2 Kgs 2:1–14). We may compare Isa 61:1, where the prophetic author declares that the Spirit of God is upon him, because YHWH has anointed him. The emphasis is not on the rite of anointing but on the gift of the Spirit of God.

B. Anointed Persons

The Heb noun *māšîaḥ,* "anointed," is only used of persons, particularly of kings and (high) priests. In Ps 105:15, the term "my anointed one" occurs in parallelism with "my prophets" in a context that speaks about the patriarchs. In 2 Sam 1:21 it is found in connection with Saul's shield, but here a great number of manuscripts have the passive participle of the verb *māšaḥ.*

1. Anointed Kings. The emphasis on divine initiative in the stories about the anointing of kings is reflected in the popularity of the expression "the Lord's anointed" (*měšîaḥ YHWH*) and the corresponding expressions "my/your/his anointed." Saul is the Lord's anointed (1 Sam 12:3, 5), and therefore David spared his life: one should not raise his hand against the Lord's anointed (1 Sam 24:7, 11 [—Eng 10]; 26:9, 11, 16, 23). The Amalekite who claimed to have killed Saul at his request was put to death because he did not observe this rule (2 Sam 1:14, 16). We should compare here the warning in Ps 105:15: "Touch not my anointed ones, do my prophets no harm."

The expression "the Lord's anointed" is also used in connection with David's being anointed by Samuel (1 Sam 16:6) and as a reference to David in 2 Sam 19:22 (—Eng 21). In 2 Sam 23:1, David introduces himself as "the anointed of the God of Jacob"; the next verse continues: "The Spirit of the Lord speaks by me, his word is on my tongue."

In many so-called Royal Psalms the Davidic kings are regarded as "anointed by the Lord" (see D. below). We may add here 1 Sam 2:10 in the Song of Hannah (cf. 1 Sam 2:35, an oracle announcing a faithful priest . . . before "my anointed" for ever), Hab 3:13, and Lam 4:20 (bewailing the capture of "the breath of our nostrils, the Lord's anointed").

In all these texts YHWH's anointing of the king denotes the exclusive, intimate relationship between the God of Israel and the king whom he has appointed and given the power to reign in his name. The king is God's representative on earth and is thought to participate in God's sovereign rule. As ideas about this divine rule develop, the expectations also expand (see in particular the Royal Psalms). Quite exceptional is Deutero-Isaiah's application of the term "messiah" to the Persian king Cyrus: "Thus says the Lord to his anointed, to Cyrus" (Isa 45:1; cf., however, Hazael in 1 Kgs 19:15–17). For Israel's sake, YHWH calls this mighty king who does not even know YHWH by name. Cyrus gets the commission and the power to secure peace and freedom for God's chosen people (Isa 45:1–7); he is God's shepherd (44:28) where Davidic kings have failed.

2. Anointed (High) Priests. In Lev 4:3, 5, and 16, the (high) priest is called "the anointed priest"; in 6:14 (—Eng 6:22), "the priest from Aaron's sons who is anointed to succeed him." It is also probable that (high) priests are meant in Dan 9:25 (speaking about "the coming of an anointed one, a prince") and 9:26 (announcing that "an anointed one will be cut off"): Joshua, in the time of Zerubbabel, and Onias, in the time just before Antiochus IV Epiphanes' capture of Jerusalem, respectively. One should note that here *māšîaḥ* is used twice absolutely but without an article.

C. Anointed King(s) in the Psalms

In the Royal Psalms (see Psalms 2, 18, 20, 21, 45, 72, 89, 101, 110, 132, and 144), the theme "the king and his God" plays a significant role. These psalms belong to and contain different genres (intercessions for the king, prayers of the king himself, thanksgivings, laments, oracles, proclamations, etc.) and are difficult to date. Some will have had a place in the temple ritual and will have been recited at specific occasions or during regularly recurring celebrations while Davidic kings reigned in Jerusalem. Others may have been composed after the Exile. In any case, all psalms continued to be used long after there had been kings in Jerusalem, and this may have influenced their present wording. Referring to God's promises and his instructions to David and his dynasty, the psalmists make far-reaching assertions. These were related to the currently reigning king and his family, not to some future son of David. But because the ideal remained to a great extent unfulfilled in the present, and because these psalms were used for different kings in succession, it is not surprising that in later times these Royal Psalms were interpreted as referring to the future Davidic anointed of the Lord, whose arrival Israel hoped for.

There are a number of major theological ideas connected with the notion of the king as the Lord's anointed. In Psalm 45, a king's wedding song, the king is said to have been anointed with "the oil of gladness." He will reign in equity and righteousness, his throne is God's throne forever and ever (vv 6–7). Psalm 89 refers to God's anointing of his servant David (v 21—Eng 20). The king's (David's) relationship to God is one of a firstborn to his father. God has made a firm covenant with his offspring; he will punish them if they sin but continue to show them his steadfast love. They will reign forever, conquering their enemies (vv 20–38—Eng 19–37). The psalmist, clearly writing in a period of great distress, appeals to this covenant; he reproaches God for having forsaken his anointed and beseeches him to intervene: "Remember, O Lord, how thy servant is scorned . . . (the taunts) with which they [i.e., the enemies] mock the footsteps of thy anointed" (vv 39–53, esp. 51–52 [—Eng 38–52, esp. 50–51]). Psalm 89 should be connected with Nathan's prophecy to David in 2 Sam 7:14–17, partly referring to Solomon, but in its present form clearly speaking about David's dynasty (see esp. v 14: "I will be his father, and he shall be my son"; cf. also 1 Chr 17:3–15 and 1 Chr 22:8–10; 28:6–7, where Nathan's prophecy is applied to Solomon). In this context we should also mention Ps 132:10: "For thy servant David's sake do not turn away the face of thy anointed one"—a prayer put into the mouth of Solomon in 2 Chr 6:42. Next, there is Ps 132:17: "There I will make a horn to sprout for David; I have prepared a lamp for my anointed" (cf. 1 Sam 2:10). Also, Psalm 18 (a hymn of royal thanksgiving for God's help in obtaining a victory over his enemies) ends with a reference to God's "steadfast love to his anointed, to David and his descendants forever" (v 51 [—Eng v 50]; cf. 2 Sam 22:51; see also Ps 21:7; 144:10; and 2 Sam 23:5, which mentions an everlasting covenant between God and David).

Psalm 2 portrays the nations as plotting "against the Lord and his anointed" (v 2). The king will conquer and rule the earth, because he is God's king (v 6), even God's son: God decreed "You are my son, today I have begotten you (v 7). The king will be victorious over all God's opponents and his dominion will be worldwide, like that of God's. This idea is also found in Psalm 110, which in v 4 calls the king "priest forever after the order of Melchizedek," and in Psalm 72, which prays for fertility and peace, and extols the king's righteousness which has showed itself in his help for the poor and the oppressed (cf. the story of Solomon's dream at Gibeon in 1 Kgs 3:5–15).

In a number of other psalms the certainty of God's help for his anointed forms the basis of an appeal to God in days of trouble—see Pss 20:7 (—Eng 6); 28:8; and 84:10 (—Eng 9); cf. also Pss 61:7–8 (—Eng 6–7) and 63:12. When the king prospers, the people are secure in God's protection and individuals live in peace.

D. OT Prophecies about Future Davidic Kings

Except in Isa 45:1 and Hab 3:13 (already discussed above), the word "anointed" is not found in the books of Isaiah, Jeremiah, Ezekiel, or the Twelve Prophets. However, prophecies concerning future Davidic rulers found in these works contain elements that cannot be neglected in the present inquiry. They are mentioned here as they occur in the biblical books; as a rule, no attempt will be made to distinguish between genuine utterances of the prophet concerned and the additions to his work made later in the course of the formation of the present writings. The fact that certain ideas found expression is more important than their date; the analysis of the way in which they received their present form is bound to remain hypothetical in many cases.

In the much disputed prophecy of Isa 7:14, the name of the (royal?) child about to be born is Immanuel ("God is with us"), probably as a reminder of God's continuing care for the house of David and his people. In Isa 9:1–6 (—Eng 2–7), light in darkness, joy, deliverance from enemies, and peace are promised to be effected by a descendant of David who will reign forever with justice and righteousness (cf. 16:5; 32:1). His names are "Wonderful Counselor, Mighty God, Everlasting Father, Prince of Peace" (v 5 [—Eng 6]). In Isa 11:1–9, a situation is portrayed in which the tree representing the Davidic dynasty has been reduced to a mere stump. Yet a branch will grow out of its roots. The Spirit of the Lord will be on this descendant of David. His wisdom and knowledge are extolled, as are his righteousness and help for the meek of the earth. "He shall smite the earth with the rod of his mouth" (v 4; contrast Ps 2:7: "you shall break them with a rod of iron"). Verses 6–9 give a picture of a paradisiac situation on God's holy mountain; the earth will be full of the knowledge of the Lord. Verses 10–16 add that the nations will seek the root of Jesse, that Ephraim and Judah will be reunited, and that those in exile will be brought back.

The passage in Mic 5:1–3 (—Eng 2–4) announces the birth of a ruler from a renowned family of old (that of David) in Bethlehem. He will feed his flock and make them dwell securely, as would a good shepherd. He will be great to the ends of the earth, strengthened by the Lord and reflecting God's glory. Verse 2 (—Eng 3) mentions the return of the rest of the brethren to the people of Israel. Verses 5–6 add a prophecy concerning deliverance from the Assyrians.

In Jer 23:1–4, the shepherds are accused of neglecting their duty and scattering the flock. The Lord will bring his people back and appoint new and more responsible shepherds. In vv 5–6 the coming of a righteous "Branch" for David is announced. He will reign as king and execute justice and righteousness, and Judah and Israel will dwell together securely. His name will be "the Lord is our righteousness" (cf. the name of the last king, Zedekiah). This prophecy is repeated with some changes in 33:14–16. Verses 17–26, clearly reflecting a much later situation, interpret it collectively as referring to the eternal, unbreakable covenant between the Lord and David with his family, as well as with the levitical priests (cf. 1 Sam 2:35; 1 Chr 29:22; and Zech 4:14 and 6:9–15 below).

The verses in Ezek 17:22–24 portray how the Lord will take a young twig from the lofty cedar and plant it on a high mountain in Israel where birds of all sorts will gather in the shade of its branches. Comparison with 17:1–21 shows that the image refers to a future Davidic king, standing in clear contrast to Zedekiah, who has broken the covenant and is brought to Babylon. In Ezekiel 34 God accuses the bad shepherds who have neglected their flock and announces that he will gather together his flock and will himself care for his sheep. In this context he announces: "I will set over them one shepherd, my servant David, and he shall feed them . . . I, the Lord, will be their God and my servant David shall be prince (Heb *nāśîʾ*) among them" (vv 23–24). A period of peace and plenty will follow. Also in chapter 37 (the vision of the resurrection of Israel) "my servant David" is introduced as king and prince of the Israelite people, who have been brought together in their own land (vv 24–25). As in Hos 3:5 and Jer 30:9 (cf. Amos 9:11), "David" does not denote the name of the king expected to return, but a future ideal ruler from his family, a perfect servant of the Lord. It should be added that the blueprint of the new Israel found in Ezekiel 40–48 (in which everything centers around the new temple) pays much attention to the role of the Zadokite priests. The rights and duties of the prince in relation to the people and the temple are defined precisely.

In the time immediately after the Exile, Haggai, on God's behalf, commands the rebuilding of the temple. He directs his words to Zerubbabel, governor of Judah, and to Joshua, the high priest. In Hag 2:20–23 Zerubbabel is addressed as "my servant," and God assures him that "I have chosen you" (expressions recalling the status of Zerubbabel's ancestor David). In the upheaval and total renewal of the present world which the Lord will bring about, Zerubbabel will be the Lord's "signet ring" (cf. Jer 22:24); that is, he will be protected by God whose representative he is. Many exegetes think that Zerubbabel is intended in the references to "my servant the Branch" (Zech 3:8) and "the man whose name is Branch" (Zech 6:12). The fact that the crown is not given to him but to Joshua, the high priest (Zech 6:9–14), is problematic and should best be explained by a correction of the text at the time when high priests and not kings functioned as leaders in Jerusalem. According to another interpretation, "the Branch" (see Jer 33:14–26) really refers to an ideal Davidide of the future. We should note that he is expected to have a priest alongside his throne with whom he cooperates in good harmony (6:13; cf. Jer 33:14–26). In 4:14 there are two "sons of oil" (RSV "the two anointed") who stand by the Lord of the whole earth.

Among the prophecies which were later added to Zechariah 1–8 is an oracle (9:9–10) about a humble king riding on an ass, righteous and bringing salvation because God has shown his righteousness to him and given him protection. He is not said to belong to David's family, but allusions to Ps 45:4 (—Eng 4) and Ps 72:1, 8, are apparent. God will end war, and the king will command peace until the ends of the earth. In Zechariah 12, it is announced that God will protect Jerusalem from attack by all the nations of the earth. "The feeblest on that day will be like David, and the house of David shall be like God, like the angel of the Lord at their head" (v 8; cf. Exod 23:20). It is not clear (in v 10) who is meant by "the one whom they have pierced" and who will be the object of heavy mourning.

In summary, the prophecies listed in this section announce a decisive and lasting change in the plight of the people, brought about by God. War will end, peace and plenty will be restored, Israel and Judah will be reunited, people in Exile will return; salvation has worldwide dimensions. A new era is inaugurated that will never end; it is absolutely unthinkable that God would allow the earlier situation to return. In these prophecies, the central figure is a descendant of David who represents an ideal of kingship in the name of YHWH; this is also reflected in the books of Samuel and Kings and in the Royal Psalms. The complexity of this ideal allows for all sorts of nuances in the individual texts. The emphasis is not on the person of the future king but on the fact that, at last, the Davidic ideal, which no historical king (including David) ever fulfilled, will be realized. The importance that some of these texts attach to the future cooperation between king and high priest should also be noted.

E. "Anointed Ones" in Early Judaism (200 B.C.–A.D. 100)

1. Ben-Sirach. In Sir 36:1–17 a prayer is given for the deliverance and restoration of Israel in which God is expected to act himself, without any mediator. The verb "to anoint" occurs a few times in the Praise of the Fathers (chapters 44–50). Moses ordained and anointed Aaron with holy oil (45:15), Samuel established the kingdom and anointed rulers over his people (46:13), and Elijah is the one "who anointed kings . . . and prophets" (48:8; cf. 1 Kgs 19:15–16). In 46:19 we find the expression "the Lord and his anointed" in a reference to 1 Sam 12:5.

In chapters 44–50 we find a long eulogy of Aaron (45:6–22) who, with his descendants, is said to have received an eternal covenant (vv 7, 15). In 45:23–26, Phinehas is extolled as "the third in glory"; he and his descendants will have the dignity of the priesthood forever, in accordance with Num 25:10–13 (cf. Ps 106:30). Chapter 50 sings the praise of Simon, the high priest, son of Onias (who officiated around 200 B.C.); in the Heb version of 50:24 the wish is expressed that the covenant of Phinehas may remain for him and his descendants forever.

In 45:25 the covenant with Aaron is contrasted with that of David. The exact meaning of this verse remains uncertain. Enough is clear, however, to suggest that the author's attitude toward David and his family is ambivalent. David is praised (47:1–11), while Solomon receives praise and blame (47:12–22). God's care for the Davidic dynasty is mentioned regularly (47:11, 22; 48:15), but looking back on the history of the Davidic kings the author concludes: "Except David and Hezekiah and Josiah they all sinned greatly"—therefore the kings of Judah came to an end (49:4). In 49:11–12, Zerubbabel and Joshua are praised for their work on the temple. Above all, Sirach is clearly interested in God's promises concerning the (high) priesthood in the line of Aaron, Phinehas, and (implicitly, see 1 Chr 5:27–41 [—Eng 6:1–15]) Zadok (cf. Ezekiel 40–48). He does not neglect God's promises to David, but they do not seem to be relevant for his audience, neither in the present nor in the future.

An addition in the Heb version on 51:12 praises God "who makes a horn to sprout for the house of David" (cf. Ps 132:17) and "elects the sons of Zadok to be priests" (cf. Ps 132:16).

2. 1–2 Maccabees. The books of 1 and 2 Maccabees concentrate on the crisis caused by Antiochus IV Epiphanes' intervention in Jewish affairs leading to the capture of Jerusalem and the desecration of the temple, and on the role played by the sons of Mattathias in restoring the true worship in the temple and (relative) independence to Israel. For the present purpose it is relevant to note that Mattathias' resistance against the measures of the Syrian king is said to have been motivated by "zeal for the law" (1 Macc 2:26, 27). He follows the example of Phinehas (2:26), who in Mattathias' "testament" (2:49–70) is called "our father" (v 54). Again, it is stressed that he was deeply zealous and received the covenant of eternal priesthood. This statement prepares the reader for the appointment of Jonathan to the high priesthood by King Alexander (10:18–21) and for the solemn decree recorded in 1 Macc 14:25–48, according to which the Jews and their priests make Simon their leader (*hēgoumenos*) and high priest forever (vv 35, 41; vv 42, 47, add "commander" [*stratēgos*]; and v 47, "ethnarch"—cf. 15:1). In v 41 we read that the arrangement would last "until a trustworthy prophet should arise"—probably an arrangement to pacify those who believed that the true leaders of the people had to be designated by God through a prophet like Samuel or Nathan (cf. also 4:46).

The book of 1 Maccabees was written to legitimize the Hasmoneans' leadership in cultic and political matters, as high priests and princes (soon to be called "kings"). This leadership lasted until the days of Herod the Great, but it was not undisputed by those who questioned the legitimacy of the Hasmoneans and/or were opposed to the fact that they combined the two offices.

The book of 2 Maccabees covers a much shorter period than 1 Maccabees. One should note that the second of the two letters in chap. 1 is addressed to, among others, "Aristobulus who is of the family of the anointed priests" (1:10); i.e., the legitimate high-priestly family of the Zadokites to whom Onias, son of the Simon (Sirach 50), belonged. Onias' piety, the intrigues to replace him, and his murder receive much attention in chaps. 3 and 4 (cf. Dan 9:26 discussed above). In 15:12–16 he appears to Judas, together with Jeremiah, and intercedes for the oppressed Jews. He is clearly thought to be with God in heaven, like the martyrs whose suffering as pious servants of God and God's law has brought about a decisive turn in the fate of God's people (6:18–31; 7:12–42; also 14:37–46). The military activities of Judas Maccabeus and other pious Jews could only succeed after "the wrath of the Lord had turned to mercy" because of the martyrs' self-sacrifice (8:1–5). Although Judas' actions are important, he is portrayed throughout as one who continually expects his help to come from the Lord (e.g., 15:21–24).

3. The Book of *Jubilees*. *Jubilees* has to be mentioned here because of Isaac's blessing of Levi and Judah in 31:13–17 and 18–20, respectively. The emphasis is on the functions to be exercised by the two patriarchs and their descendants on behalf of Israel: Levi and his sons will minister in the sanctuary but will also be judges, teachers of the law, and rulers ("princes and chiefs"). In 30:18–20, the descendants of Levi are said to have been chosen for the priesthood because of Levi's zeal to execute righteousness, judgment, and vengeance in the Shechem case (Genesis 34). The parallel with Phinehas in Numbers 25 is clear.

Judah, on the other hand, will receive strength and power, and he will be Jacob's help; his righteousness will bring peace for all Israelites. Significantly, it is said to him: "A prince shall you be, you and one of your sons." Not only the patriarch or the tribe but also David and/or a future ideal Davidic king come into the picture. In *Jub.* 33:20, it is stressed that "Israel is a holy nation to the Lord . . . a priestly and royal nation for his possession."

4. The *Testaments of the Twelve Patriarchs*. In their present form, the *Testaments of the Twelve Patriarchs* are undoubtedly Christian, and this becomes particularly clear when the extremely varied passages dealing with the future are analyzed. Reconstructing earlier redactions of the Testaments or earlier traditions used in them, which might represent the ideas of *Jewish* groups handing down material connected with the twelve sons of Jacob, remains a hazardous undertaking. Many patriarchs speak about the position of Levi and Judah in the history of Israel. Levi will be priest, Judah will be king (*T. Iss.* 5:7), and the priesthood is superior to the kingship (*T. Jud.* 21:1–6a). A number of passages focus on Levi and depict him not only as a priest but also as ruler, teacher, judge, and/or warrior; in those passages Judah is often mentioned only in passing, or not at all (*T. Reu.* 6:5–7, 8, 10–12; *T. Sim.* 5:4–6; *T. Levi* 4:2–6; chaps. 5–6 [referring to the Shechem episode; cf. Genesis 34 and *Jub.* 30:18–20]; 8:2–17; chap. 13 *passim*).

Levi's descendants are, however, singled out as sinners against Jesus Christ in *T. Levi* 4:4, chaps. 10, 14–15, and 16; while in 5:2 it is expressly said that Levi's priesthood will be limited to the period before God's decisive intervention in the history of Israel. This corresponds with *T. Reu.* 6:8, which limits Levi's priestly activities to the period "until the consummation of times (the times) of the anointed high priest, of whom the Lord spoke." This is the only place where the word *christos* occurs (cf. *T. Levi* 17:2–3, where the passive participle *chriomenos* is used twice for persons anointed for the priesthood), and the reference here is to Jesus. This is clear in *Testament of Levi* 18, where the advent of a new priest is announced after a steady deterioration of the levitical priesthood. He is not said to be a descendant of Levi, and he is described with words and phrases which are partly parallel to those found in *Testament of Judah* 24, a chapter describing the advent of an ideal king from Judah, after a period of sin and exile for the sons of Judah. It has been assumed that these two Testaments originally closed with a description of an ideal levitical high priest and an ideal king from Judah. This has to remain a conjecture, however; in their present form both chapters refer to Jesus Christ.

Also, where "salvation" or "a savior" is predicted to come out of (one of) these tribes (*T. Sim.* 7:1–2; *T. Naph.* 8:2; *T. Gad* 8:1; *T. Jos.* 19:6 (11); cf. *T. Levi* 2:11; *T. Jud.* 22:2; *T. Dan.* 5:10), only one person is referred to—again it is Jesus, who is often connected with Judah in particular. The Testaments in their present form remain interested in the juxtaposition of Levi and Judah and of priesthood and kingship; but whenever they mention an agent of divine deliverance in connection with these two tribes or with one of them, they mean Jesus.

5. The Qumran Scrolls. The community which used the writings discovered in the caves at Qumran was a priestly sect led by Zadokite priests. Under the leadership of an influential teacher, the "Teacher of Righteousness," who was regarded as an authoritative interpreter of the Law and the Prophets, it separated from the Jerusalem temple and the Hasmonean priesthood officiating there. The group interpreted the events of the immediate past and present in the light of the Scriptures, and it also dreamed of a decisive turn brought about by God, when its views would be proved correct. The texts dealing with the future show a great variety in images and concepts. Attempts have been made to distinguish stages in the eschatology of the Qumran documents; yet a cautious, mainly descriptive approach seems advisable. Our evidence remains fragmentary, and it is probable that the members of the group, while adhering to some basic convictions, could differ in the description of details.

Restricting ourselves to those passages where the terms "to anoint" and "the anointed one" occur, we note first that in a number of cases the prophets of the OT are called "anointed ones" (CD 5:21–6:1; 1QM 11:7, 8; and especially CD 2:12, where we should read "the anointed ones of his Holy Spirit"). This corresponds to the designation "the anointed one of Spirit" used in 11QMelch 18 for the "one who brings good tidings" of Isa 52:7, clearly inspired by Isa 61:1. The good tidings are concerned with God's intervention in the future through Melchizedek, conceived as an angelic figure. Another future prophet is mentioned in 1QS 9:11: ". . . until there shall come the prophet and the anointed ones of Aaron and Israel," perhaps referring to Deut 18:18–19, a text mentioned in 4QTestim alongside Num 24:15–17 and Deut 33:8–11.

In 11QMelch 18 the word "anointed" is certainly not used as a technical term. With regard to the high priest and the prince expected in the future, the situation is not very different. The people at Qumran looked forward to the times when the meaning of the Law would be fully clear and when God's will would be obeyed completely. Then, a duly appointed high priest and a Davidic prince would discharge their respective functions properly. Then also, the final battle against demonic forces and human enemies would be won. In a number of texts—but by no means everywhere—the anointed status of high priest and prince is mentioned, so that it is advisable to avoid the translation "messiah," which suggests titular use.

In 1QS 9:11, "the anointed one of Aaron" figures beside "the anointed one of Israel." The latter designation returns in 1QSa 2:14, 20, a description of an eschatological banquet where he and the high priest and their subordinates are present. In lines 11–12, the priest is said to be "at the head of the whole congregation"; whether the expression "the anointed" mentioned here refers to the royal figure (and whether it is used absolutely) is not clear, due to the defects in the text. It is clear that the high priest is the leading figure; he is also the leading figure in the War Scroll, where "the prince of the congregation" is mentioned only in passing (1QM 5:1). God's directives for the war are transmitted by the high priest (1QM 2:1; 15:4; 16:13; 18:5; 19:11); victory is won through the help of the Holy Ones sent from heaven. The passage in 4QFlor mentions "the Branch of David" who shall arise with the Interpreter of the Law at the end of time (lines 11–12; cf. Jer 23:1–4; 33:14–16, etc.). Just before this, the *Florilegium* quotes from 2 Sam 7:11–14, and later it adds Ps 2:1. The "Interpreter of the Law" is also found in CD 7:18–21; he is said to come together with the "Prince of the whole congregation." He is a priestly figure. Also, in some other texts the king is portrayed as being dependent on the interpretation of the priests: see 11QTemple 56:21; 57:11–15 (cf. 58:18–21, where the king has to consult the high priest before going to war); and 4QpIsa[a] 8–10, which interprets Isa 11:1–3 as referring to "the Branch of David," and then makes the latter's judicial activity dependent on the teaching of the priests.

The meaning of the expression "anointed one of Aaron in Israel" in CD 12:23–24; 14:19; and 19:10–11 (cf. "anointed one from Aaron and Israel" in 20:1) remains disputed. The word *mĕšîaḥ* is found here in the singular, but many have argued that the expression nevertheless admits of a plural interpretation. Because CD 7:18–21 mentions two persons, the expectation of a priest and a king may also be assumed in the other passages. It is also possible that at some stage the prerogatives of the "anointed one of Israel" were absorbed into the concept of the anointed Aaronic priest.

The royal figure is often designated as prince (of the congregation) with a term taken from Ezekiel 40–48. He is also called "Branch of David" (to the texts just mentioned may be added 4QPBless 3–4), "anointed one of Israel," or (in 4QPBless 3) "the righteous anointed one" ("the anointed one of righteousness"), an expression close to the absolute "anointed one" which may be present in 1QSa 2:11. In 1QSb 5:20–29, a blessing for the prince of the future congregation has been preserved. It is concerned with his victory over the ungodly, his dominion over the earth, and his justice for the oppressed (it quotes Isa 11:4–5).

As may be expected from a priestly community, the future high priest is by far the most important figure, particularly as teacher of the law and mediator of God's will. His role may be compared to that of the Teacher of Righteousness in the past (CD 6:11). He is undoubtedly the primary leader of the people; he also plays an important role in 1QM, although he does not participate in the actual warfare (1QM 9:8), in contrast with the Davidic prince in 1QM 5 and elsewhere. To the texts already mentioned may be added 1QSb 3:1–7 and 18–21, a blessing for the future high priest, which is directly followed by a blessing for the sons of Zadok.

6. The *Psalms of Solomon*. The *Psalms of Solomon* were probably written around 50–40 B.C. by pious Jews propagating strict obedience to God's law. Psalms 2 and 8 react to Pompey's intervention in Judean affairs in 63 B.C., together with the events leading up to and following it. The authors are clearly opposed to the Hasmoneans, who had not discharged their priestly duties properly and had usurped the high priesthood (8:11) as well as royal authority (17:5–6). The authors also anticipate God's deliverance; in the case of *Psalms of Solomon* 17 and 18 (not in *Ps. Sol.* 11), this is expected from a Davidic king—e.g., *Ps. Sol.* 17:21: "Behold, O Lord, and raise up unto them their king, the son of David, at the time you have (fore)seen, O God, to rule over Israel your servant." This king will rule as the representative of God who himself is king of Israel forever and ever (vv 1, 46). In *Ps. Sol.* 17:21–45, the king's rule is described at great length with many references to the OT psalms and prophecies discussed above. Two features are dominant. First, the king will free Israel from its enemies, and the people in the dispersion will return and the nations will serve God. Second, the king will serve the Lord as the ideal pious, obedient, and wise man (these psalms, after all, are ascribed to Solomon), and unrighteousness will be banished from the country.

In 17:32 and 18:5, 7 (plus the superscription), the king is called "anointed." In view of 18:5 ("his anointed one"), the *christou kyriou* in 18:7 and the superscription to *Ps. Sol.* 18 are also translated "of the Anointed of the Lord." In 17:32 all Gk mss read *christos kyrios,* "an anointed Lord." The parallel expression in 18:5 would suggest that the Gk here is the result of careless copying or deliberate alteration on the part of a later Christian scribe in changing a genitive into a nominative (cf., e.g., Lam 4:20 LXX and Luke 2:11). Alternatively, we may assume that the king was designated by two honorifics following one another (cf. Dan 9:25 and the use of "Lord" in Ps 110:1). In any case, the expression is used in *Ps. Sol.* 17:32 as a qualification rather than a title; this is different in *Ps. Sol.* 18, a conventional composition made up when the psalms were put together into one collection. Here, "the anointed of the Lord" has become a fixed expression denoting the Davidic king appointed by God to bring about a turn in the fate of Israel.

7. Egyptian Jewish Sources. In the writings of Philo we find little that is relevant to our investigation. His description of the future happiness of the just and virtuous in his *On Rewards and Punishments—On Blessings and Curses* presupposes many elements of the common eschatological scenario; only in his interpretation of Num 24:17 LXX in *Praem.* 95 do we get a glimpse (and no more) of a savior figure.

In Book 3 of the *Sibylline Oracles* (very complex, and difficult to interpret), we see reference to "a holy prince" who "will come to gain sway over the scepters of the earth forever," introducing "the most great kingdom of the immortal king" (vv 46–50, to be dated after the battle of Actium in 31 B.C.). Verses 652–795 (a long eschatological passage to be dated around the middle of the 2d century B.C.) begin with a reference to "a king from the sun," sent by God, "who will stop the entire earth from evil war" and will act "in obedience to the noble teachings of the great God." Various traditional elements are found, including a reference to Isa 11:6–8 in vv 788–95.

The fifth book of the *Sibylline Oracles,* dating from the beginning of the 2d century A.D., refers to a savior figure who is depicted as coming from heaven. We read about a king sent from God to destroy all kings (5:108–9); a great star coming from heaven bringing destruction (155–61); an exceptional man from the sky (256–59; Christian interpolation in v 257); and a blessed man from the expanses of heaven who, with a scepter given by God, destroys the cities of the enemies and renews Jerusalem and the temple (414–33).

8. Pseudo-Philo. For the sake of completeness, we should mention here the *Liber Antiquitatum Biblicarum,* falsely ascribed to Philo and generally dated in the 1st century A.D. (before A.D. 70), which retells the story of Israel from Adam to the death of Saul. In a concluding note about Phinehas, it says that God anointed him in Shiloh when he appointed him priest (*L. A. B.* 48:2). Some scholars suppose that there is a textual mistake here and think that the original text spoke of Phinehas anointing Eli, his successor (50:3). The little boy Samuel is anointed (as priest?), hailed as prophet, and called "a light for this nation for a long time" (51:6–7). In 51:6, there is a clear reference to 1 Sam 2:10. Chapter 59 relates at great length David's anointing by Samuel. Verse 4 includes a hymn by David (cf. 11QPs^{a} 151:5–7; cf. Ps 151A LXX) in which he blames his brothers and parents for forgetting him "when the anointed of the Lord was to be designated." The descendant of David mentioned in 60:3 is probably Solomon, not a future ideal Davidic king.

9. Josephus. The Jewish historian Josephus is our most reliable source of information about the unrest in Palestine during the 1st century A.D., which found its climax in the war between the Jews and Romans in A.D. 66–70. At a critical moment in his life, Josephus had switched allegiances to the Romans, in his own view not for political reasons but guided by God, who granted him insight into his dealings with his people, in the past and in the present. Josephus' account of the events and the motives underlying people's actions is, therefore, biased. This comes out clearly in *JW* 6.311–13, where he speaks about an "ambiguous oracle" found in the Scriptures "to the effect that at that time one from their country would become ruler of the world." The ordinary people and the wisemen interpreted this as referring to a man from Israel. Josephus (who does not specify the scriptural passage) is convinced, however, that the oracle "signified the sovereignty of Vespasian, who was proclaimed emperor on Jewish soil."

Josephus records many incidents and rebellions from the death of Herod onward to the overall war in A.D. 66–70. In a number of cases these were led by men who were able to gather a substantial group of people around them. None of the men is called "anointed/messiah" by Josephus. Some of them were clearly brigands, leading groups of impoverished peasants, and at times resorting to guerrilla warfare against those in power. Others are described as prophetic figures resembling Moses (and Joshua)—see *Ant* 20.97–98; and *JW* 2.258–63 = *Ant* 20.167–71; *Ant* 20.188 (cf. the Samaritan Mosaic prophet in *Ant* 18.85–87, and the commotion in Cyrene recorded in *JW* 7.437–42). See also MESSIANIC MOVEMENTS IN JUDAISM.

Still others are reported to have had royal aspirations. Josephus mentions three such men in the time following the death of Herod the Great: Judas, Simon, and Athronges (*JW* 2.55–65; *Ant* 17.271–85). The extent to which these men and their followers fostered "messianic" hopes, inspired by popular memories of David as leader of a sizable band of brigands before being installed as king (1 Samuel 21–30), remains uncertain. It is said of two leaders in the Jewish War that they had royal aspirations. They were Menahem (see especially *JW* 2.433–34 and 441–48) and Simon bar-Giora (see especially *JW* 4.510 and 575; 7.29–31).

In two passages in the present text of the *Antiquities,* Josephus speaks about Jesus as the Christ. The first (18.63–64) includes the statement "He was the Messiah"; the second (20.200) introduces James as "the brother of Jesus who was called the Christ." Josephus may have included a notice or notices about Jesus (if only because at the end of the 1st century A.D. he was aware of the Christian claim that Jesus was the Messiah), but the present reports have certainly undergone Christian redaction. See also JOSEPHUS.

10. Early Christian Sources. The followers of Jesus of Nazareth regarded him as the Messiah expected by Israel. (For the typical Christian use of the term *(ho) christos,* see CHRIST.) In this section, Christian statements about Jewish beliefs in the Messiah are reviewed briefly, but they should be read against the background of discussions between Jews and Christians, like those mentioned in the book of Acts. There, Paul is portrayed as trying to convince members of synagogues in the Diaspora that Jesus is the expected Christ (Acts 9:22; 18:5; cf. 18:28 of Apollos). This included proving that the Christ had to suffer and to rise from the dead (17:3). In all instances, the designation *ho christos* is used, without any further addition.

In Mark 12:35, Jesus questions the obviously common conception of the scribes that "the Christ is the son of David"; in Mark 15:32, the chief priests and the scribes speak of "the Christ, the King of Israel." In the Markan passion story, much emphasis is placed on the fact that Jesus is the Christ and may be called King of the Jews, but without any political overtones that would justify his crucifixion. The apocalyptic discourse in Mark 13 anticipates false messiahs and false prophets (vv 21–22). The situation in the period leading up to the Jewish War is reflected here; the readers are reminded that Jesus the Christ, whose return to power is expected, differs completely from the popular leaders of the time.

In the discussions between Jesus (and in one case John the Baptist) and "the Jews" in the Fourth Gospel, the statements of the latter serve to highlight by contrast certain aspects of Johannine christology; yet they have some value in themselves. In 7:42, the Christ is said to be a descendant of David, and to be a native of Bethlehem; in 12:34, the Christ is said "to remain for ever"—reflecting the emphasis on David's everlasting kingdom (Ps 89:36–37; Ezek 37:25). In 7:27, the statement "when the Christ appears, no one will know where he comes from" may be connected with conceptions found in apocalyptic texts (see below). John the Baptist's declaration, "Among you stands one whom you do not know" (John 1:26), and his denial that he should be Elijah (1:21), may be explained by the conception of a savior living incognito on earth, to be revealed and to be anointed by Elijah (found as a Jewish notion in Justin's *Dialogue with Trypho* 8.4; 49.1; cf. 110.1).

The expectation that the Christ will do signs (John 7:31) is not found in Jewish sources; signs are usually connected with an expected prophet like Moses (also in John 6:14; 9:16–17). A similar leveling of different terminologies is found in 4:25, 29, where a Samaritan woman raises the question whether Jesus may be the Christ, and professes to believe in the Messiah who, "when he comes, will show us all things." The few indications we possess of a Samaritan expectation of a future agent of divine deliverance all point in the direction of a person like Moses, thought to be predicted by Deut 18:15–19. Sometimes this person is called *Taheb* ("the one who returns"), sometimes he is regarded as Moses redivivus (see a number of passages in the 4th century A.D. *Memar marqah*; three times it is said that the *Taheb* will reveal the truth). We may also compare the report about a Samaritan prophet in the days of Pilate (*Ant* 18.85–87).

11. Apocalyptic Texts. a. 1 Enoch. In this composite document, the book of Dreams (chaps. 83–90), to be dated just before 161 B.C., portrays the birth of a white bull (symbol of a good and pious man) after the final judgment (90:37). His relation to the wild ox in 90:38 is not clear. No special activities of the bull or the wild ox are recorded.

The dating of the Parables of Enoch (chaps. 37–71) remains disputed, since they are only found in the Ethiopic version, and no Aram or Gk fragments are extant. Most scholars now date this part of *1 Enoch* to the second half of the 1st century A.D. The central figure is a heavenly redeemer, often called "that (the) Son of man" (cf. Dan 7:9–14, referred to in *1 En.* 46:1–3), the Chosen One (cf. Isa 42:1; see *1 En.* 39:6; 40:5, etc.; and cf. 46:3), or the Righteous One (38:2; cf. 46:3, 56:3). The heavenly redeemer, who is thought to have been with God from the beginning (48:3, 6) and remains in God's presence, reveals all things to the elect and is the judge of the world and the champion of the righteous, destroying their enemies (who are God's enemies). See also SON OF MAN. So 48:8–10 speaks about the defeat of the kings of the earth by God's elect because "they have denied the Lord of Spirits and His Anointed." The phrase "his anointed" occurs here because of the reminiscence of Ps 2:2. In chapter 52, the visionary sees mountains of iron, copper, silver, gold, soft metal, and lead and is told by an accompanying angel that "these will serve the dominion of His Anointed that he may be potent and mighty" (52:4). In v 6, this is explained by their melting as wax before fire in the presence of the Chosen One. In the description of the complex redeemer figure in the Parables, elements from many Scriptural texts are used (e.g., Isa 11:2–4 in *1 En.* 49:3–4 and 62:2–3). This redeemer figure receives many names derived from Scripture, one of which is "His Anointed."

b. The *Syriac Apocalypse of Baruch*. Like *4 Ezra* (see below), *2 Baruch* was composed in the years following the destruction of the temple in A.D. 70. It has the expressions "My Anointed" (39:7; 40:1; 72:2), "my servant, the Anointed One" (70:9), and "the Anointed One" (29:3; 30:1). In all cases a royal figure is meant who reigns for a limited period, introducing a time of complete bliss and incorruptibility. In 70:9, it is said that "my servant, the Anointed One," will reign after wars and disasters on earth. The holy land will have peace (71:1); of the nations, only those who have not subjected Israel will be spared (72:2–6). Peace, joy, harmony, and health will abound (chaps. 73–74, with references to Isa 11:6–8 and Gen 3:16–18). Also, "For that time marks the end of what is corruptible and the beginning of what is incorruptible" (74:2).

In the interpretation of the vision of the vine and the cedar (chaps. 36–37), "the kingdom of my Anointed" is said to come after the end of the fourth kingdom (39:7). The enemies, including their last leader (represented by the cedar), will be destroyed. "My Anointed One" will charge him with all iniquities and destroy him on Mt. Zion (39:8–40:2). The Messiah will reign over the remnant of God's people in the place God has chosen (40:2). "His kingdom will stand forever, until this work of corruption comes to an end and the times appointed are fulfilled" (40:3).

In *2 Bar.* 29:2–30:1, the reign of "the Anointed One" in the holy land is described in paradisiac terms; the emphasis is on the slaughter of Leviathan and Behemoth for food, on abundant fertility, and on the return of the manna. When the Messiah's presence on earth has come to an end, he will return in glory, and a general resurrection will follow (30:2). The Messiah is clearly thought to have been in heaven before his revelation on earth (29:3; 39:7; cf. 73:1).

c. *4 Ezra* (= 2 Esdras). Four passages in this work mention an agent of divine deliverance. In 7:26–29, this agent appears (or "is revealed") with his companions when the now-invisible city and the now-concealed country become visible. He will bring 400 years (according to most versions) of happiness to all who survive. After that period everyone, including the divine agent, will die; there will then be a period of silence for seven days, as there had been at the beginning of creation; finally, the new aeon of incorruptibility will begin, bringing with it resurrection and judgment (7:30–44). The divine agent is called "my son, the Anointed One"; in this passage, "my son" must either be interpreted against the background of Ps 2:7 or be considered (as most scholars think) a translation of Gk *ho pais mou,* which should have been translated "my servant." As for the "companions" mentioned in 7:26, we may point to 6:26 and 13:52. Presumably, a select group of pious men are meant, including Enoch, Moses (?), and

Elijah. In 14:9 Ezra receives the promise that he will be taken away from the earth and "will remain with my son and with those like you, until the end of time." This translation is reported at the end of chapter 14 in the majority of the versions of the book.

In the interpretation of the vision of the Eagle and the Lion (11:1–12:3), the lion is explained as "the Anointed One whom the Most High has kept back to the end of days, who will spring from the seed of David" (according to all versions except the Latin; cf. Gen 49:9, 10). We note here the absolute use of the term (Lat *unctus*), the idea that the Messiah is already in existence (cf. *2 Baruch* and *1 Enoch*), coupled with the notion that he is a descendant of David. As in the vision itself (11:36–46), he charges his counterpart (the eagle = the Roman rulers) with certain crimes (12:32). The next verse adds that he will convict and destroy them; he will also give joy to the survivors in the land—until the day of the final judgment comes.

In chapter 13 the designation "anointed one" is not found. In a vision, a human figure comes from the depth of the sea and flies with the clouds of heaven (cf. Dan 7:2, 3, 13). He destroys a great host of adversaries with a stream of fire from his mouth (vv 3–11; cf. Isa 11:4 and Ps 18:9 [—Eng 8]). He does so after carving out a vast mountain and flying upon it (v 6; cf. Dan 2:34–35, 44–45). After the destruction of the enemies, he sends for a peaceful company that is joined by other people coming from captivity (Jews from the Diaspora) and still others (presumably converted Gentiles). The interpretation of the vision in vv 25–53 differs in many details from the vision itself. In vv 25–26 we hear that the man was held in readiness by the Most High through many ages; v 32 speaks of "my son/servant who will be revealed" (cf. also vv 37, 52). In vv 37–38, his main activity is (surprisingly) that he convicts the nations, reproaches them for their evil devices, and destroys them "without effort by means of the law." The man will stand on Mt. Zion—in fact, "Zion will come into sight before all men, completely and fully built" (v 36). He will deliver, order, and protect the survivors (vv 26–48) plus the returned ten tribes, which receive much attention (vv 39–47). In v 52, the companions of "my son/servant" are mentioned. No mention is made of a final judgment succeeding the days of this redeemer. The expectations concerning the end in general and the coming of an agent of divine deliverance in particular are clearly rather diverse in *4 Ezra*.

d. The *Apocalypse of Abraham*. This text, also usually dated some time after A.D. 70, mentions in 31:1 that God will sound the trumpet out of the air and will send his chosen one (Isa 42:1; cf. *1 Enoch* 37–71) who will summon God's people oppressed by the Gentiles.

F. Later Jewish Writings

The period from the destruction of the temple (A.D. 70) to the end of the 2d century is important because of the reactions to the events of A.D. 66–70 and the impact of the revolt of Simon bar-Kokhba in A.D. 132–135 leading to the expulsion of Jews from Jerusalem. In the present context, we shall restrict ourselves to some brief remarks.

1. The Eighteen Benedictions. This Jewish daily prayer is known to us in two later recensions, a longer Babylonian one and a shorter Palestinian one. We do not know exactly in what form(s) it was prayed in the 1st century A.D., before and after the fall of Jerusalem. Both versions pray for the gathering of the dispersed, for the reinstatement of the proper judges and counselors, for God's mercy on Jerusalem and the temple, and for the proper worship in the temple. The Babylonian recension speaks explicitly of God's return to Jerusalem and the rebuilding of the city. We find this in the fourteenth benediction that also prays: "raise up quickly in its midst the throne of David." The fifteenth benediction adds: "Make the Branch of David to sprout quickly, and let his horn be exalted by thy salvation. For we await thy salvation all the day. Blessed art thou, Lord, who makest the horn of salvation to sprout" (cf. Ps 132:17; Sir 51:12 [in Heb]; and the references to the "Branch of David" in Jeremiah, Zechariah, and the Qumran Scrolls). The fourteenth benediction of the Palestinian recension combines the prayer for Jerusalem with that for the house of David: "Be merciful . . . to the kingship of the house of David, thy (righteous) anointed. Blessed art thou, Lord, God of David, who buildest Jerusalem." The elements of the hope on God's intervention of the future found in these two recensions will certainly have formed part of the daily prayer in the period after A.D. 70 and, formulated differently, probably also in the years before.

2. Rabbinic Sources. It is notoriously difficult to use the data in the Mishnah, Tosephta, the two Talmuds, and the oldest Midrashim for historical purposes. One has to be extremely careful in establishing the original form of the many sayings of individual scholars, and the problems of ascription are many. The same holds true for the traditions about the various scholars.

No messianic sayings are recorded of Tannaitic scholars who died before A.D. 70. In sayings attributed to later Tannaim, we find a distinction between the days of the Messiah and the world/age to come, comparable to that found in *2 Baruch* and *4 Ezra* (though there are many differences of opinion as to the exact nature of the days of the Messiah). The Mishnah mentions the (Davidic) Messiah only in two places: *m. Ber.* 1:5 speaks about "this world" and "the days of the Messiah," while *m. Soṭa* 9:15 mentions further deterioration of the state of affairs "in the days of the advent (lit. the footprints) of the Messiah." It should be noted that the Mishnah speaks several times about "the anointed one," meaning "the anointed (high) priest" (in particular in tractate *Horayot*), and that it distinguishes him from "he who is dedicated by the many garments" (*m. Hor.* 3:4; *m. Meg.* 1:9; *m. Mak.* 2:6). If this contains a reminiscence of a time when (high) priests could not be anointed (later rabbinic sources mention that the oil of unction was hidden away in the days of Josiah), it may explain why the sect of Qumran, and probably other groups as well, anticipated the day when a properly anointed high priest would arise.

Very important is the tradition that Rabbi Akiba hailed the leader of the second revolt, Simon bar Kokhba, as the Messiah. On coins of the revolt, Simon is called prince (*nāśîʾ*; cf. Ezek 34:24 and the Qumran Scrolls) of Israel; sometimes he is mentioned together with Eleazar the Priest, who also appears singly. On some coins, a temple appears with a star above it. This may be a reference to Num 24:17, "a star shall come forth out of Jacob . . . ," the text that is central in the tradition concerning Rabbi Akiba, recorded in *y. Taᶜan.* 68d. In the variant sources there is a play of words on Simon's name. In newly discovered documents from the Judean desert, he is called "son of Kosiba"; the many who, like Akiba, hailed him as the Messiah called him "son of the star" (Aram *kôkbāʾ*). In rabbinic writings, the *s* in the name is usually changed to a *z* (bar-Koziba), implying that he was regarded as "the son of the lie" (i.e., a liar). The fact that Simon (not of Davidic descent, as far as we know) was regarded as Messiah by a great man like Rabbi Akiba shows the intensity of the longing for redemption and explains the great deception in the years after 135. The subtle change in the spelling of his father's name shows this, as does the saying of Rabbi Yoḥanan b. Torta, handed down together with that of Rabbi Akiba: "Akiba, grass will grow out of your cheekbones and the Son of David will still not have come." It is often thought that the notion of the death of a figure called Messiah, son of Joseph (or son of Ephraim), in the war against the final enemy, Gog, arose in the time after the defeat of Simon bar Kokhba (Kosiba). The notion of a Messiah from Joseph as a warrior is also found without the idea of defeat; according to some scholars, this must have existed earlier.

3. The Targums. It is difficult to assess the value of the messianic paragraphs in the various Aramaic translations of sections of the Hebrew Bible. We have to rely on manuscripts of a relatively late date, the texts of which are of a composite character; there are also many variations between related Targums, and the original wording and original date of the constitutive elements are difficult to establish. Yet much work is being done on these writings, especially with a view to investigating to what extent passages in them may shed light on discussions that are known to have taken place in the period from the 2d century B.C. to the 2d century A.D, in particular at the time early Christianity originated. One example may be given here. The star from Jacob in Num 24:17 was interpreted messianically by R. Akiba, as we have seen; in the Qumran Scrolls, Num 24:17 is connected with the prince of the congregation in 4QTestim 9–13 and 1QM 11:6–7. In CD 7:18–21, the "star" is interpreted as the Interpreter of the Law, while "the scepter" (mentioned immediately afterward in Num 24:17) is equated with the prince of the whole congregation (cf. 1QSb 5:27–28). The LXX version of the verse, which speaks about "a star" and "a man," is referred to in Philo, *Praem.* 95 (cf. *Vita Mos.* I 290). R. Akiba, therefore, was by no means the first to connect Num 24:17 with a future redeemer.

In *Tg. Onq.*, "the king" and "the Messiah" are spoken of; in *Tg. Ps.-J.*, "a king" and "the Messiah and a scepter"; in *Tg. Neof.*, with some variation, "a king" and "a redeemer and a chief" (so also *Frg. Tg.*). The Targums clearly represent an old traditional interpretation; their testimony supplements our evidence. On the other hand, it is only the evidence from older sources that enables us to determinate the date of the interpretation found in the Targums.

G. Summary

The term "Messiah"/"Anointed One" is not found very often in the Hebrew Bible and in the Jewish writings of the period between 200 B.C. and A.D. 100. In the Hebrew Bible, people are anointed to become kings, or (high) priests, or (in one case only) a prophet. In the great majority of cases, the term "anointed" is connected with a royal figure. In the Royal Psalms, God's promises and instructions to David and his dynasty are recalled. The psalmists make far-reaching assertions, but these are always connected with the reigning king (who, among other things, is called "the Lord's anointed") but not with a future son of David. Yet these psalms, which continued to be sung long after there were any kings in Jerusalem, will have helped to shape the hope for an ideal Davidic king. So did the prophecies concerning a future king from David's family, but in these texts the term "anointed" does not occur. It should be noted that in various texts importance is attached to cooperation between king and high priest.

An investigation of Jewish writings around the beginning of the common era reveals that the term "Messiah" was by no means generally used as a designation for God's representative or intermediary at the beginning of a new age of peace for Israel and the nations. The expectations of a radical and definitive change brought about by God did not necessarily include a task for (human or angelic) agents of divine deliverance, and the fact that God's agents were anointed need not be stressed. The expected future Davidic king in *Ps.Sol.* 17 is only called "anointed of the Lord" in passing; in *Ps.Sol.* 18, the term seems to have become a fixed expression in denoting the future ideal Davidic king appointed by God. The complex redeemer figure in the Parables of Enoch is only twice called "his (i.e., the Lord's) anointed," probably under the influence of Ps 2:2. A royal messiah is found in *2 Baruch* and *4 Ezra*; in these writings, his reign is a temporary one. In the documents of Qumran, we meet a future high priest who is once called "the anointed one of Aaron" and a future king called "the anointed one of Israel" or "the righteous anointed one." Whether the expression "anointed ones of Aaron and Israel" in the *Damascus Document* refers to two persons or to one remains unclear. In one fragment we meet a prophetic figure called "the anointed one of the Spirit" (cf. Isa 61:1).

Christian statements about Jewish beliefs and expectations found in the NT writings tend to put a relatively strong emphasis on the Jewish hope for the Messiah. They should be read against the background of discussions between Jews and Christians about Jesus, whom the Christians believed to be the Messiah (Christ).

Bibliography

Cazelles, H. 1978. *Le Messie de la Bible: Christologie de l'Ancien Testament.* "Jésus et Jésus-Christ" 7. Paris.

Cothenet, E. 1982. Onction. I. Dans l'Écriture. *Dictionnaire de la Spiritualité* 11: 788–801.

Dexinger, F. 1986. *Der Taheb: Ein "messianischer" Heilsbringer der Samaritaner.* Salzburg.

Grelot, P. 1962. Le Messie dans les Apocryphes de l'Ancien Testament. Pp. 19–50 in *La venue du Messie: Messianisme et eschatologie,* ed. E. Massaux et al. RechBib 6. Paris.

———. 1978. *L'Espérance juive à l'heure de Jésus.* "Jésus et Jésus-Christ" 6. Paris.

Horsley, R. A., and Hanson, J. S. 1985. *Bandits, Prophets and Messiahs.* Minneapolis.

Jonge, M. de. 1966. The Use of the Word "Anointed" in the Time of Jesus. *NovT* 8: 132–48.
———. 1969. The Role of Intermediaries in God's Final Intervention in the Future According to the Qumran Scrolls. Pp. 44–63 in *Studies on the Jewish Background of the New Testament,* ed. O. Michel et al. Assen.
———. 1972–73. Jewish Expectations about the "Messiah" According to the Fourth Gospel. *NTS* 19: 246–70.
———. 1974. Josephus und die Zukunftserwartungen seines Volkes. Pp. 205–19 in *Josephus-Studies,* ed. O. Betz, K. Haacker, and M. Hengel. Göttingen.
———. 1986. Two Messiahs in the Testaments of the Twelve Patriarchs? Pp. 150–62 in *Tradition and Reinterpretation in Jewish and Early Christian Literature,* ed. J. W. van Henten, H. J. de Jonge, P. T. van Rooden, and J. W. Wesselius. Leiden.
Jonge, M. de, and Woude, A. S. van der. 1973–74. Messianic Ideas in Late Judaism. *TDNT* 9: 509–27.
Klausner, J. 1955. *The Messianic Idea in Israel from Its Beginning to the Completion of the Mishnah.* Trans. W. F. Stinespring. New York.
Laperrousaz, E.-M. 1982. *L'Attente du Messie en Palestine à la veille et au début de l'ère chrétienne.* Paris.
Levey, S. H. 1974. *The Messiah: An Aramaic Interpretation.* Cincinnati.
Mettinger, T. N. D. 1976. *King and Messiah.* ConBOT 8. Lund.
Mowinckel, S. 1956. *He That Cometh.* Trans. G. W. Anderson. Oxford.
Neusner, J. 1984. *Messiah in Context.* Philadelphia.
Neusner, J.; Green, W. S.; and Frerichs, E., eds. 1987. *Judaisms and Their Messiahs at the Turn of the Christian Era.* Cambridge.
Pérez Fernández, M. 1981. *Tradiciones Mesiánicas en el Targum Palestinense. Estudios exegéticos.* Institución San Jerónimo 12. Valencia.
Schäfer, P. 1978. *Studien zur Geschichte des rabbinischen Judentums.* AGJU 15. Leiden.
Stone, M. E. 1968. The Concept of the Messiah in IV Ezra. Pp. 295–312 in *Religions in Antiquity,* ed. J. Neusner. Leiden.
Wacholder, B. Z. 1979. *Messianism and Mishnah: Time and Place in the Early Halakhah.* Jerusalem.
Woude, A. S. van der. 1957. *Die messianischen Vorstellungen der Gemeinde von Qumran.* Assen.

MARINUS DE JONGE

MESSIANIC BANQUET. The term refers to the use of the symbols of food and a festive meal to signify immortality and the joys of the end time or afterlife. The terms "eschatological banquet" and "apocalyptic banquet" are more correct for the general phenomenon, while the term "messianic banquet," technically speaking, refers primarily to traditions that make specific reference to the presence of the Messiah. However, because such distinctions are not always maintained in the scholarly literature, the concept as a whole will be discussed here. In our literature, it is primarily connected with the thought world of the apocalyptic, but aspects of the symbolism are widespread in the ancient world. Like other apocalyptic motifs, the messianic banquet has its origins in a complex mythological heritage from the ANE and is supplemented in the later periods by Hellenistic parallels.

A. Sacred Foods
B. The Divine Banquet
C. Actual Communal Meals

A. Sacred Foods

One motif connected with the messianic banquet theme places the emphasis on the numinous quality of certain symbolic foods. The characteristic theme here is that of the "food of the gods," which confers immortality on anyone who eats it. A prominent motif expressing this idea in ANE mythology is the "tree of life" whose fruit is deemed to have special life-giving qualities (Gen 2:9; Gaster 1969: 29–34, 336–38). There are echoes of this motif in the symbolism of the menorah in the biblical cult (Meyers 1976: 95–202). Apocalyptic literature utilizes it to represent the gift of eternal life to be given by God to the righteous at the end time (*1 En.* 24:4–25:7; *T. Levi* 18:11; *4 Ezra* 8:52; Rev 2:7, 22:2, 14, 19). For the Greeks, the "food of the gods" was ambrosia and the "drink of the gods" was nectar; these conferred immortality on all who partook of them (Hom. *Od.* 5.93; *Il.* 5.335–42; 19.38–39). In the Jewish work *Joseph and Aseneth,* a honeycomb is identified as the food of the angels that provides immortality to all who eat of it (16:14; also identified with "bread of life" and manna, Burchard OTP 2: 228 n.f).

The bestowal of "life" in the sense of immortality or eternal life at the end time is connected with other symbolic foods as well. Prominent images include basic foods such as water, wine, bread, and fish (Goodenough 1953–68: vols. 5 and 6; 12.94–131; Jeremias 1966: 233–34). In *Odes Sol.* 6:8–18, it is the "living water of eternity" that snatches the soul from death (cf. *Odes Sol.* 11:7–8, 30:1–7); so also in John 4:10–14 the "living water" of Jesus is "a spring of water welling up to eternal life." In Rev 22:1–2 and 17–19, the "water of life" is equated with the "tree of life" as a divine substance that imparts eternal life at the end time (see also 7:17; 21:6).

In the Greek tradition, wine is considered to be the gift of the god Dionysus to mortals, and its effects, ranging from pleasure to literary inspiration, are viewed as the blessings of the god (Henrichs 1982: 140–43), an idea that is echoed in some Jewish traditions as well (Smith 1975). One interpretation of Dionysiac wine-drinking was the idea that one thereby would consume the god; furthermore, Dionysiac beliefs also included the promise of a happy afterlife, although this was not necessarily specifically related to wine-drinking itself (Henrichs 1982: 159–60). In the Jewish text *Joseph and Aseneth,* however, the "cup of immortality" (8:5; 15:5) refers to a beverage that guarantees eternal life in heaven to those who drink it along with the "bread of life" and the "ointment of incorruptibility" (Burchard 1987: 109–17). The wine miracle of Jesus' in John 2:1–11 has similar overtones, since it is connected in this gospel with various references to symbolic life-giving substances ("bread of life," John 6:33; "water of life," John 4:14; "vine" as source of life, John 15:1–6). The strongest connection of wine with the "messianic banquet" theme, however, is to be found in the banquet motif as described in part B. below, since wine is a required component of any festive banquet.

Bread as a numinous food in biblical tradition is especially related to the miraculous bread from heaven or manna, where it is also associated with the miraculous water from the rock (Exod 16:1–17:7; Num 11:7–9; 20:2–13). These miraculous foods take on numinous qualities in a long and complex midrash tradition that is reflected throughout our literature. The bread becomes "bread of the angels," an apparent reference to the divine food eaten by angels (Ps 78:25; Wis 16:20; *4 Ezra* 1:19); and, as "bread of life," it is a food that confers eternal life on those who eat it (*Jos. Asen.* 16:8; 14–16; John 6:25–59). Philo interprets manna and rock to be types of the Logos, or word and wisdom of God, which nourish the soul (*Leg. All.* 2.86; 3.166–70). For Paul, manna and water from the rock are interpreted as "spiritual food" and "spiritual drink" and as symbolic of the Christian Lord's Supper (1 Cor 10:1–13).

Another creation theme that becomes a part of the messianic banquet tradition is the myth of Leviathan, one of the names given to the primordial sea monster representing the power of the sea whose defeat in a cosmic battle is a constituent part of the combat motif in many ANE creation myths. In the OT, the destruction of Leviathan by God represents God's power over chaos (Ps 104:26; Job 40–44; Rev 12:3–9; 21:1). The idea that Leviathan is not only destroyed but is also provided as food (Ps 74:13–14) becomes a symbol of the provision of divine food for the righteous in the new age (*2 Bar.* 29:1–4; *1 En.* 60:7–10, 24; *4 Ezra* 6:49–52; see also rabbinic references in Ginzburg 1909–38: 1.27–28; 5.41–46; and Str–B 4: 1156–65). The widespread fish symbolism that occurs in Jewish and Christian art (Goodenough 1953–68: 5.3–61; Snyder 1985: 24–26; 64:65) as well as in the NT (Matt 14:13–21 = Mark 6:32–44 = Luke 9:10–18 = John 6:1–15; Matt 15:32–39 = Mark 8:1–10; see also Luke 24:42–43; John 21:9–14) has been interpreted to signify fish as a numinous or eschatological food, an idea developed at least partially from the Leviathan myth (Goodenough 1953–68: 6.3–61).

B. The Divine Banquet

This is the primary messianic banquet motif since it places the emphasis on the banquet itself, a banquet at which the Messiah is deemed to be present. This theme has its apparent roots in another pattern found in certain ANE creation myths. These myths tell of a great battle being waged in the divine sphere. When the battle has been won, the gods assemble and celebrate the victory with a great banquet (*Enūma eliš* VI:69–94 [*ANET* 69]; Isa 34:5–7; Zech 9:15; Gaster 1961: 93–94; Hanson 1973: 46 n. 25; 53–55). Here the myth echoes the cultural tradition of the festive meal as the primary social institution for celebrating victory and deliverance (as in *3 Macc* 6:30–41; *Ps.-Philo* 27:9). Because apocalyptic literature takes up the combat and victory motifs, the banquet of celebration becomes a part of its repertoire as well (Hanson 1975: 300–22; Collins 1976: 207–9; 224–30).

This tradition is reflected in the description of the victory/coronation banquet of David in 1 Chr 12:38–40, a passage with strong messianic overtones. Here, the warriors gather and celebrate with their new king, the prototype of the Messiah. The nations come bearing gifts in tribute, and "there was joy in Israel" (v 40). This description reflects the form of the banquet of the end time, which is given a classic description in Isa 25:6–8:

> On this mountain the Lord of hosts will make for all peoples a feast of fat things, a feast of wine on the lees, of the lees well refined. And he will destroy on this mountain the covering that is cast over all peoples, the veil that is spread over all nations. He will swallow up death for ever, and the Lord God will wipe away tears from all faces, and the reproach of his people he will take away from all the earth; for the Lord has spoken.

These texts provide a summary of the basic motifs that come to be associated with the messianic banquet: victory over the primordial enemies (e.g., death), eternal joyous celebration, abundance of food, the presence of the Messiah, judgment, and the pilgrimage of the nations.

Thus, for example, in *1 Enoch,* "in that day" when the Lord shall triumph over the kings and other rulers of the earth, they will be judged and will become victims of God's wrath. Then a "sacrifice" (for the banquet) will be provided and "the righteous and elect ones . . . shall eat and rest and rise with that Son of Man forever and ever" (62:12–14). Here, judgment is expressed in terms of divine reversal; those who suffer now will rejoice "in that day"; those who hunger now will feast in the future. Others who may find a share at the table are those who give bread to the hungry in this life (*T. Isaac* 6:13). The table will be one with lavish provision of food and wine (as in Isa 25:6–8 quoted above; see also Joel 2:24–26; 3:18; cf. the "unfailing table" of *4 Ezra* 9:19). Indeed, it will be a table where, when the "Messiah is revealed," the primordial representatives of chaos, the monsters Behemoth and Leviathan, will be eaten (*2 Bar.* 29:1–4; see also the reference to death being swallowed in Isa 25:8 quoted above).

In the NT, the messianic banquet theme is especially prominent in the gospel tradition. Jesus' provisions for the hungry in his food miracles (Matt 14:13–21 = Mark 6:32–44 = Luke 9:10–17 = John 6:1–15; Matt 15:32–39 = Mark 8:1–10; John 2:1–11) are paralleled by the theme of the beatitudes: "Blessed are you that hunger now, for you shall be satisfied" (Luke 6:21 [= Matt 5:6 = *Gos. Thom.* 69b]). In one of the favorite images of the parables, the kingdom is compared to a great banquet (Matt 22:1–10 = Luke 14:16–24 = *Gos. Thom.* 64). Indeed, the themes of joyous banquet, judgment, pilgrimage of the nations, and presence of the Messiah are marvelously brought together in the early tradition: "The Son of Man came eating and drinking, and they say, 'Behold, a glutton and a drunkard, a friend of tax collectors and sinners' " (Matt 11:19 = Luke 7:34). This theme is then played upon by the gospel writers, especially Luke, with numerous references to table fellowship with Jesus (Matt 9:10–13 = Mark 2:15–17 = Luke 5:29–32; Smith 1987).

The theme of the pilgrimage of the nations to the table becomes the rallying cry for the emerging gentile church and, when combined with the divine reversal theme, is interpreted to mean that they will take the place of Israel at the table: "I tell you, many will come from east and west and sit at table with Abraham, Isaac, and Jacob in the Kingdom of heaven, while the sons of the kingdom will be thrown into the outer darkness; there men will weep and gnash their teeth" (Matt 8:11–12 [= Luke 13:28–29]; cf. Luke 16:19–31; 14:16–24 [= Matt 22:1–10]; 22:28–30; Jeremias 1958: 59–63). In a different context, this same theme is utilized in a Eucharistic passage in *Did.* 9.4 to represent the unity of the Church gathering at the table: "As this broken bread was scattered upon the mountains, but was brought together and became one, so let the Church be gathered together from the ends of the earth into thy kingdom."

The messianic banquet is sometimes represented as a wedding banquet, a motif that is closely related to the victory banquet in its mythological origins and connections with the themes of victory and kingship of the god (Collins 1976: 223–24). More specifically, this motif is related to the theme of the "sacred marriage," a concept with a rich heritage from ANE myth and ritual (Smith 1958: 32–71). This theme is especially prominent in biblical literature as a symbol for the relationship of God with the people of Israel (Hos 2:1–23; Isa 54:4–8; Ezek 16:7–8), or, in the NT, as a symbol for the relationship of Christ and the Church (John 3:39; 2 Cor 11:2; Eph 5:23–32). The wedding banquet as a reflection of the sacred marriage theme is found in Song of Songs (2:4; 5:1; Pope *Song of Songs* AB, 374–75; 504–10), but more important for apocalyptic thought is Isa 54:5–55:5, where the theme of a divine marriage (54:5) is combined with a joyful feast which is characterized by abundance of food (55:1–2), vindication for the righteous (54:6–17), and the pilgrimage of the nations (55:5). This theme is then taken up in the NT, where it becomes a prominent image for the joys of the kingdom in the gospel tradition, especially in the parables (Matt 9:15 = Mark 2:19–20 = Luke 5:34–35; Matt 22:1–14; 25:1–13; Luke 14:7–11; cf. John 3:29; *Gos. Thom.* 104) and the miracle at Cana (John 1:1–11). In Revelation it is the primary motif for the messianic banquet (19:7–9; 21:2, 9; 22:17; Collins 1976: 223–31).

Among the Greeks and Romans, the festive banquet was also utilized as a symbol for the joyous afterlife (Pl. *Resp.* 2.363.c–d; Lattimore 1962: 52), a theme especially associated with Orphic and Dionysiac beliefs (Henrichs 1982: 160). This idea is also associated with funerary reliefs that picture the deceased reclining at a festive meal, although there is some debate whether this motif is meant to refer to an eschatological banquet or whether it simply idealizes the past life of the deceased (Cumont 1942: 417–22; Nock 1946: 145 [= *Essays* 2.613]; Dentzer 1982: 530–32).

C. Actual Communal Meals

The examples mentioned to this point represent the symbolic use of meal motifs in literature and art which sometimes, but not always, have some connection to actual meals. Some texts, however, are more explicit in connecting the theme of the messianic banquet to actual meals of a community. The communal meals at Qumran, for example, seem clearly to have been defined as a proleptic messianic banquet, since the description of the meal is heavily liturgical in form and, furthermore, includes the presence of the Messiah (1QSa II.11–22; Cross 1961: 85–91). The interpretation of the Passover meal in Judaism also had eschatological overtones (Jeremias 1966: 59).

Other examples are less clear. Goodenough, for example, has proposed the existence of a "mystic meal" in Hellenistic Judaism, based especially on texts from Philo and meal symbolism found on Jewish monuments, but his conclusions are largely discredited today (Goodenough 1953–68: 12.94–105; 125–31; 190–98; Smith 1967: 57–59). The meal references in *Joseph and Aseneth* have suggested to many interpreters that actual ritual meals with cultic significance were being referred to, but the data are complex and subject to varying interpretations (Burchard *OTP* 2: 211–12 n. i; 1987: 113). From the world of the Greeks and Romans, the funerary banquet whereby the family and friends of the deceased would commemorate his death has been interpreted to signify in some sense the proleptic enjoyment of the eschatological banquet in the afterlife, but this interpretation is still much debated (Cumont 1922: 199–206; Kane 1975: 342–43). The ANE version of the funerary banquet, known as the *marzeaḥ*, has also been interpreted to have eschatological overtones (Porten 1968: 183) as well as connections with the sacred marriage theme (Pope *Song of Songs* AB, 210–29).

In the NT, most of the references to bread, wine, and meals in general have been interpreted to refer either primarily or secondarily to the Christian communal meals, either the LORD'S SUPPER or the AGAPE MEAL. This is true, for example, with many of the references to divine food. Thus, the "bread of life" in John 6 that provides "eternal life" to all who eat it, which is a christological reference in its primary sense, is specifically connected with the Eucharistic "flesh" and "blood" in vv 51c–57 (perhaps from a later redactor). So also the Eucharistic bread and wine are identified with "spiritual food" and "spiritual drink" (1 Cor 10:1–22) and deemed the "medicine of immortality" (Ign. *Eph.* 20:2).

The food miracles of Jesus are also related to Christian communal meals. For example, when Jesus provides miraculous bread, he does so with the same ritual actions as those mentioned in the Last Supper passages (Matt 14:19 = Mark 6:41 = Luke 9:16 = John 6:11; Matt 26:26 = Mark 14:22 = Luke 22:19 = 1 Cor 11:23–24; Luke 24:30). Thus, it is the "breaking of the bread" that signifies the presence of the Lord at the community meals (Luke 24:30–35; Acts 1:4).

When Jesus provides miraculous wine in abundance (John 2:1–11), it is at a wedding feast (= messianic banquet). Elsewhere Jesus' own wine drinking and the image of "new wine" are related to the theme of rejoicing in the presence of the bridegroom at the wedding feast (Matt 9:14–17 = Mark 2:18–22 = Luke 5:33–39; John 3:25–30; *Gos. Thom.* 47, 104; Jeremias 1963: 117–18). In the Last Supper tradition, the wine is given an eschatological interpretation: "Truly, I say to you, I shall not drink again of the fruit of the vine until that day when I drink it new in the kingdom of God" (Mark 14:25 [= Matt 26:29 = Luke 22:18]).

Thus, the various examples of food and banquet imagery in the NT, especially to be found in the Gospels and Revelation, clearly give prominence to the messianic banquet motif and, furthermore, connect that theme with the communal meals of the Church. This suggests that one of the ways in which early Christians interpreted their communal meals (both Eucharist and agape) was as a messianic banquet being celebrated proleptically in the presence of the risen Lord.

Bibliography

Burchard, C. 1987. The Importance of Joseph and Aseneth for the Study of the New Testament: A General Survey and a Fresh Look at the Lord's Supper. *NTS* 33: 102–34.

Collins, A. Y. 1976. *The Combat Myth in the Book of Revelation.* HDR 9. Missoula, MT.
Cross, F. M., Jr. 1961. *The Ancient Library of Qumran and Modern Biblical Studies.* Garden City.
Cumont, F. 1922. *After Life in Roman Paganism.* New Haven.
———. 1942. *Recherches sur le symbolisme funéraire des Romains.* Bibliothèque archéologique et historique 35. Paris.
Dentzer, J.-M. 1982. *Le motif du banquet couché dans le proche-orient et le monde grec du VIIe au IVe siècle avant J.-C.* BEFAR 246. Rome.
Gaster, T. H. 1961. *Thespis: Ritual, Myth, and Drama in the Ancient Near East.* Garden City.
———. 1969. *Myth, Legend, and Custom in the Old Testament.* New York.
Ginzburg, L. 1909–38. *The Legends of the Jews.* 7 vols. Philadelphia.
Goodenough, E. R. 1953–68. *Jewish Symbols in the Greco-Roman Period.* 13 vols. New York.
Hanson, P. D. 1973. Zechariah 9 and the Recapitulation of an Ancient Ritual Pattern. *JBL* 92: 37–59.
———. 1975. *The Dawn of Apocalyptic.* Philadelphia.
Henrichs, A. 1982. Changing Dionysiac Identities. Vol. 3, pp. 137–60 in *Jewish and Christian Self-Definition,* ed. B. F. Meyer and E. P. Sanders. Philadelphia.
Jeremias, J. 1958. *Jesus' Promise to the Nations.* London.
———. 1963. *The Parables of Jesus.* 6th ed. Rev. London.
———. 1966. *The Eucharistic Words of Jesus.* 3d ed. London.
Kane, J. P. 1975. The Mithraic Cult Meal in Its Greek and Roman Environment. Vol. 2, pp. 313–51 in *Mithraic Studies: Proceedings of the First International Congress of Mithraic Studies,* ed. J. R. Hinnells. Manchester.
Lattimore, R. 1962. *Themes in Greek and Latin Epitaphs.* Urbana.
Meyers, C. L. 1976. *The Tabernacle Menorah: A Synthetic Study of a Symbol from the Biblical Cult.* ASORDS 2. Missoula, MT.
Nock, A. D. 1946. Sarcophagi and Symbolism. *AJA* 50: 140–70 = Vol. 2, pp. 606–41 in *Essays on Religion and the Ancient World,* ed. Z. Stewart. Cambridge, MA.
Porten, B. 1968. *Archives from Elephantine.* Berkeley.
Russell, D. S. 1964. *The Method and Message of Jewish Apocalyptic.* Philadelphia.
Smith, D. E. 1987. Table Fellowship as a Literary Motif in the Gospel of Luke. *JBL* 106: 613–38.
Smith, M. 1967. Goodenough's *Jewish Symbols* in Retrospect. *JBL* 86: 53–68.
———. 1975. On the Wine God in Palestine (Gen. 18, Jn. 2, and Achilles Tatius). Pp. 815–29 in *Salo Wittmayer Baron Jubilee Volume,* ed. S. Lieberman. Jerusalem.
Smith, S. 1958. The Practice of Kingship in Early Semitic Kingdoms. Pp. 22–73 in *Myth, Ritual and Kingship,* ed. S. H. Hooke. Oxford.
Snyder, G. F. 1985. *Ante Pacem: Archaeological Evidence of Church Life Before Constantine.* Macon, GA.

DENNIS E. SMITH

MESSIANIC MOVEMENTS IN JUDAISM.

That Jews at the time of Jesus expected the coming of the messiah has been a central axiom of biblical studies. Recent critical analyses of Palestinian Jewish literature of late Second Temple times have indicated that there is little basis for that generalization (de Jonge 1966). The realization that "messianic" expectations were relatively unimportant in the literature of the time is also leading toward a more critical and confined use of the terms "messiah" and "messianic." Partly because of their supposed importance and centrality in the Jewish context of Jesus, and partly because of the Christian theological claim that Jesus constituted the fulfillment of the Jewish expectation, "messiah/messianic" came to be used as comprehensive terms for Jewish expectations of future salvation in general. Expectations of future deliverance and well-being are extremely diverse in biblical and other Jewish literature in postexilic times. Various (and often multiple) divinely chosen or sanctioned agents of salvation are mentioned, including angels, suffering righteous ones, and prophetic figures. Often the salvific action is taken directly by God, with no human agent involved. A "messiah" is mentioned infrequently in late Second Temple Jewish literature, and even then is not necessarily portrayed as engaging in redemptive action. Thus, there is increasing momentum in biblical studies to cease using "messiah/messianic" as synthetic terms covering any and all agents of salvation and expectations of future well-being. The current move is toward greater precision in the conceptual apparatus utilized in attempts to understand biblical literature and history. Use of the terms "messiah/messianic" would thus be confined to literary and historical phenomena (a) where the Hebrew term "messiah" or its equivalent occurs, (b) where another term that can be clearly established as closely associated occurs, or (c) where a particular social-historical form is evident that has previously been associated with the term. Because "messianic" has been used so generally and synthetically, however, we should take note of historical figures and movements that have previously been included under the term.

A. Popularly Anointed Kingship in Biblical History
B. Popularly Recognized Kings in Late Second Temple Times
C. Popular Prophets and Prophetic Movements

A. Popularly Anointed Kingship in Biblical History

Starting with the popular kingships of Saul and David, a tradition of "messianic" movements developed in Israel, as reflected in the books of Samuel and Kings. Partly because of their struggles to maintain independence of the Canaanite city-states, the early Israelites apparently resisted any form of kingship, the understanding having been, apparently, that Yahweh was their king. In crisis situations, leadership was provided by charismatic "liberators" such as Deborah (Judges 4–5) and Gideon (Judges 6–8). Gideon reportedly refused to accept the institutionalized rule of hereditary kingship on the principle that "the Lord will rule over you" (Judg 8:22–23). In response to the severity of the Philistine crisis, however, a popular form of kingship emerged first in the recognition of Saul and then especially of David as chieftains or kings of the coalition of Israelite tribes. The rise of David from his origins as a warrior and bandit chief to being "anointed" king by the assembled Israelites shows that popular kingship was a distinctive social-political form. Whatever the terminology used (*roš* or *nāśî*), popularly recognized or "anointed" kingship was a form quite different from either banditry or that of the charismatic "liberators." Whether known as "chieftain" or "king" (Num 31:8; Josh 13:21), the first popular kings of Israel, like the "chieftains" of the tribes, provided regularized, centralized political leadership (Bartlett 1969; Speiser 1967). David and his movement then provided the principal precedent and historical prototype for subsequent popular messianic movements.

Once the Davidic monarchy became established in its imperial domination of Palestine, it developed a self-legitimating royal ideology, with heavy borrowings of mythic motifs from Canaanite kingship. Much of the earlier scholarly discussion of messianic ideas and expectations drew heavily on this official royal ideology. That was understandable insofar as some of the texts that figured prominently in NT christology (e.g., Psalms 2 and 110) originated in the official royal Davidic theology. The imperial kingship, however, never completely replaced or suppressed the Israelite tradition of popular kingship in which David himself had begun. It lived on, particularly in the northern kingdom of Israel. Obviously its principal social location was not in the royal court but among the people, prophetic circles, and even the army. The tradition operated as a popular memory, capable of reappearance in concrete social movements (Tadmor 1968). It is an example of what anthropologists call a "little tradition," as opposed to the official "great tradition," although ironically our only evidence for it comes through the written narratives of the latter. Judging from their occasional appearances in biblical narratives, the popular messianic movements can be understood in terms of three principal characteristics: (1) kingship was constituted *by popular anointing* or election; (2) it was *conditional,* depending on the king's maintenance of a certain social policy; and (3) the anointing of a new king was usually a *revolutionary* action.

Physical strength and military prowess may have been prerequisites for recognition as king or chieftain (1 Sam 10:23; 16:18; cf. Judg 6:12; 8:22). The hero was made king, however, by popular acclamation, whether by the people as a whole, by a representative assembly of elders, or by the assembled peasant militia (Wolf 1947; Tadmor 1968).

First, "the men of Judah" and then "all the elders of Israel" "anointed David king" over Judah/Israel (2 Sam 2:4; 5:3; cf. 1 Sam 11:15 on Saul). Consistent with popular election, popular recognition could be withdrawn and another person acclaimed. Once David had established a more imperial monarchy over Israel, a large proportion of the people rejected him in favor of his son Absalom, whom they anointed to be (king) over them (2 Samuel 15–19; esp. 15:10–12; 19:10). When Rehoboam threatened to intensify Solomon's oppressive practices, Israel hailed Jeroboam "to the assembly and made him king" (1 Kgs 12:20; cf. 2 Kgs 23:30). It is a confirmation, not a contradiction, of the popular election of the king that Yahweh also "anointed" the kings through the hand of a prophet such as Samuel, Ahijah, or Elisha. Yahweh's anointing anticipated the people's action, and the popular election fulfilled the will of Yahweh (1 Kgs 11:26–40; 12:1–20; 1 Kgs 19:15–17; 2 Kgs 9:1–12; 9:13).

Secondly, as suggested in the abandonment of an alienated or oppressive king and the anointing of a new one, the popular kingship was conditional (*CMHE,* 221; 224; 233 n. 62). From their origins as a free people, the Israelites retained a sense of independence and a commitment to egalitarian social-economic ideals expressed in the Mosaic covenant. Their suspicions of established monarchy were rooted in earlier experiences of domination by Canaanite kings. Thus, when they experimented with a new political form in the Philistine crisis, they viewed kingship as subject to certain "covenantal" stipulations. Subsequent historical narratives portray the duties and responsibilities of kingship as "written up in a book and laid up before Yahweh" (1 Sam 10:25). The conditions of kingship were transmitted in covenantal traditions (Deut 17:14–20) and even found liturgical expression in the "great tradition" (Ps 132:12). Centuries later Jeremiah, in his prophecies against Davidic kings (Jer 22:1–9; 13–19), apparently gave voice to this same popular concern that kingship is properly conditional.

Thirdly, the people's or prophet's anointing of a king was a revolutionary act. In its very origins with Saul and David, popular kingship was a means of mobilizing centralized political-military power against the foreign domination threatened by the Philistines. Much of Israel, apparently including Judah, rose in rebellion against David in anointing Absalom over them. The revolutionary action of such messianic movements recurred in subsequent centuries. Like Ahijah's and the people's designation of Jeroboam as king, Elisha's and the Israelite army's anointing of Jehu brought a revolutionary overthrow of an established monarchy that had become intolerably oppressive. It would appear to be a manifestation of this same popular tradition when "the people of the land" anointed Jehoahaz in 609 following the fatal defeat of his father, Josiah, by the Egyptians, an action that was both resistance to foreign domination and, apparently, a rejection of the reactionary royal officials in Jerusalem. This last case shows how resilient the popular tradition of anointed kingship was, not just in the N kingdom of Israel but even in Judah, which had for centuries been dominated by the Davidic monarchy and its absolutist royal ideology.

B. Popularly Recognized Kings in Late Second Temple Times

Given the paucity of sources for Second Temple times, there is simply no way of telling whether, and how, this tradition of popular kingship may have remained alive among the common people. The fact that narratives of the popular anointing of kings such as Saul and David were included in the written documents of the great tradition makes it likely that the popular memory could have been reinformed through the continuing interaction of the official and popular traditions, particularly through the work of scribes and teachers whose responsibility it was to perpetuate the official tradition. There was certainly occasion for the memory of popularly elected kings to be revived in late Second Temple times when the Romans conquered Palestine and particularly when they imposed the tyrannical Herod as king. The Idumean strongman conquered the people with the aid of Roman legions, then taxed them heavily to support his lavish Hellenistic-style monarchy. As noted above, there is little by way of literary evidence for any longing for a messiah among the literate groups. But it would not be surprising if the ordinary people (who left no literary remains), suffering under an illegitimate and oppressive king installed by an alien imperial power, had been eager for an "anointed" king from their own ranks, like Saul or David of old.

Several movements, each headed by one who "claimed the kingship" or "was proclaimed king" by his followers, occurred around the time of Jesus. At the death of Herod in 4 B.C.E., revolts erupted in each of the principal Jewish districts of Herod's realm. These movements were led by Judas in Galilee, Simon in Perea, and Athronges in Judea. During the first great revolt against Rome in 66–70, there was a brief "messianic" incident among the group known as the Sicarii; and then there was a very powerful movement led by the popularly acclaimed king Simon bar Giora that became the largest force resisting the Roman reconquest in 69–70. Josephus, our principal source for these movements in 4 B.C.E. and 66–70 C.E., avoids any explicitly "messianic" language. Yet we cannot dismiss the social form in which he reports of these movements as due merely to his use of the typical Hellenistic terminology for kingship, such as "donning the diadem." The Israelite tradition of popular kingship had become embodied in biblical narratives and thus surely also in popular memory. Information to be gleaned from Josephus on certain aspects of these "kings" fits well with the interpretation of the biblical tradition concerning the popular "anointing" of kings (e.g., the great physical stature and military prowess of Simon, Athronges, and Simon bar Giora; *Ant* 17.10.6–7 §273, 278, likely reflects the tradition of the anointed king as a mighty warrior; 1 Sam 16:18; Michel 1967–68: 403). Furthermore, when we note that the prophetic figures and movements reported by Josephus were clearly informed by traditional biblical prototypes, the conclusion seems obvious that the groups led by the popularly proclaimed kings were "messianic" movements based upon the prototypical messianic movements of biblical history. In fact, Josephus' Hellenistic terminology of kingship points up the political authority seriously claimed or exercised by these kings and their movements.

The heads of the movements that arose at the death of Herod were all of humble origins. Athronges was a "mere shepherd" as David has been, according to the tradition; and Simon had been a royal servant, perhaps a tenant or lower-level official on one of the royal estates in Perea (*JW* 2.4.2–3 §57, 60; *Ant* 17.10.6–7 §273, 278). In Galilee the popular king was the son of a famous brigand chief; i.e., Judas was leading the revolt at the death of the tyrant who had killed his father a generation previously. (This Judas, the popular king in 4 B.C.E., was different from Judas of Galilee who led the "fourth philosophy" and its resistance to the Roman tribute in Judea in 6 C.E., a figure whom Josephus describes as a teacher, *sophistes*; *JW* 2.8.1 §118). All three movements were based in the countryside, and the followers of Simon, Athronges, and Judas were largely from the peasantry. A number of them may indeed have been "desperate men" (*Ant* 17.10.5 §271; cf. 1 Sam 22:2) because of the deteriorating economic situation of the peasants who were faced with the multiple demands of tithes, tribute, and taxes. "The brigands he collected," referring to Simon's movement, may be Josephus' pejorative phrase for the rebels, or it could be a reference to peasants who, having lost their land, had been drawn into bands of brigands who were hiding out in the mountainous terrain of Perea before joining Simon's movement (*JW* 2.4.2 §57).

The groups participating in these movements appear to have been somewhat organized, at least into "companies" for military purposes. Athronges' brothers served as heads of the divisions of the movement in Judea (*Ant* 17.10.7 §280–81). Josephus' report that the Pereans proclaimed Simon king in their "madness," and that they fought with "more recklessness than science," indicates the special inspiration underlying these movements (*Ant* 17.10.6 §274–76). The movements appear to have had a double goal: to liberate the people from Roman-Herodian domination and to restore the traditional ideals of a more egalitarian social-economic structure. According to Josephus, the groups stormed the royal palaces at Sepphoris and Jericho not merely because of the intolerable Herodian tyranny, and not simply to obtain weapons, but also in order to take back the goods that had been seized by Herod's officials (*Ant* 17.10.6 §274; *JW* 2.4.2 §57). They attacked the forces of both the Herodian and Roman rulers, and they raided the gentry's estates as well as royal residences. The long-suppressed resentment over prolonged political domination and economic exploitation poured out into an egalitarian anarchism typical among peasant uprisings.

The movements led by Athronges, Simon, and Judas were far more serious than marauding bands of raiders or extensive rural riots. They were genuinely political movements that resulted in effective control of considerable areas for a time. The very size of the army that Varus, legate of Syria, deemed necessary to reconquer Jewish Palestine (three legions and four regiments of cavalry, plus auxiliary troops) helps us appreciate the scope and importance of these movements. Even then, the movement in Judea continued for some time before the Roman and royalist troops could finally subdue the various companies of Athronges' peasant followers (*Ant* 17.10.7 §281–84). There is surely no direct connection between any of these movements and the later one focused on Jesus of Nazareth little more than a generation later. But the memory would have been fresh of the earlier movements of Jewish peasants, from villages near such towns as Bethlehem, Emmaus, and Sepphoris, who had taken action in common under a leader they recognized as king. As a reminder that we are dealing with actual people and places, it is worth noting that in 4 B.C.E., just a few miles N of the village of Nazareth, the town of Sepphoris was burned and its inhabitants sold into slavery by the Romans in retaliatory suppression of a popular messianic movement.

The brief appearance of Menahem as a royal pretender toward the beginning of the Jewish revolt in 66 C.E. was really more of a messianic incident among the group called Sicarii than a movement. This incident has been misinterpreted by those scholars who use Menahem as evidence for a supposedly violent "Zealot messianism" that can serve as a foil for portrayal of Jesus as a nonviolent messiah. It is even claimed that Menahem stood in a Zealot messianic dynasty. It is now becoming recognized, however, that the Zealots proper did not originate until the middle of the Jewish revolt, in the winter of 67–68, by which time the Sicarii, who had previously been mistakenly identified with the Zealots, had long since withdrawn to Masada, where they sat out the duration of the revolt. The Zealots were involved in a social-revolutionary movement like the messianic movements; but the social form taken by the Zealot movement was not popularly proclaimed kingship but popularly elected priestly leadership. The claim that they were part of a "messianic dynasty" is rooted in a mistaken identification of Judas, the popular king of 4 B.C.E., with Judas of Galilee, the scholarly leader of the "fourth philosophy" in 6 C.E., from whom Menahem was descended. It is clear that Menahem could not have been a "Zealot messiah."

The Sicarii had emerged in the 50s as an urban group engaged in terrorist activities, such as assassination—of high priests who were collaborating with Roman rule—and kidnappings—in order to extort the release of their members who had been taken prisoner (*Ant* 20.8.10 §186–87; 20.9.3 §208; *JW* 2.13.3 §254–57). Josephus does not even mention the Sicarii in his reports of the early stages of the revolt during the summer of 66. However, some of them had apparently joined the insurrection in Jerusalem in time to participate in the burning of the royal palaces, of the house of the high priest Ananias, and of the public archives (*JW* 2.17.6 §425–27).

Josephus finally reports three incidents involving Menahem, in rapid succession. First, Menahem obtained arms from Herod's arsenal at Masada, whereupon he "returned like a king to Jerusalem and, becoming a leader of the revolt, directed the siege of the royal palace" (*JW* 2.17.8 §433–34). Second, although there is no indication that he became the main leader of the rebellion, he clearly became a prominent leader, for Josephus describes the garrison besieged in the royal palace as negotiating "with Menahem and the leaders of the insurrection" (437). Third, Josephus reports that the "infatuated" Menahem having become an "insufferable tyrant," the followers of the temple captain Eleazar now "laid their plans to attack him in the Temple, where he had gone up in state to pay his devotions, arrayed in royal robes and attended by his suite of armed fanatics. Eleazar and his companions rushed upon him, and the rest of the citizens, to gratify their rage, took up stones and began pelting the arrogant doctor" (*JW* 2.17.9 §443–45). A few of the Sicarii managed to escape to Masada, where they sat out the remainder of the revolt. Menahem himself, having escaped temporarily, was soon caught, tortured, and killed (447–48).

This messianic incident among the Sicarii has some differences from, as well as similarities to, the popular messianic movements. While the Sicarii were attacked by the followers of the temple captain Eleazar, they apparently fought for the interests of the common people, having joined in the destruction of the public archives "to destroy the money-lenders' bonds and to prevent the recovery of debts" (427). In connection with the popular kings of 4 B.C.E. and Simon bar Giora later during the great revolt, Josephus describes social-economic, political, and military activities. In his portrayal of Menahem, he includes a dramatic religious feature as well: the ceremonial celebration of Menahem's claim to kingship in the temple. Finally, whereas the other figures who "claimed the kingship" were from the common people and were popularly acclaimed, Menahem was known as a scholar (*sophistes*, 445) like his (grand)father, Judas of Galilee, and he was also a leader of an urban-based group apparently without a broader base of popular support. In any case, having been cut short before it had a chance to build wider support, Menahem's posturing as king in the temple appears to have been more a messianic incident than a true movement.

Historically, the most important messianic movement at the end of the Second Temple period was that led by Simon bar Giora, who became the foremost political-military commander in Jerusalem during the great revolt and whom the Romans executed with pomp and ceremony as, in effect, the vanquished king of the Jews. Josephus reports far more extensively on Simon and his movement than he does on the popular kings in 4 B.C.E. In those reports, Simon appears as an active organizer of the movement he led.

Like those proclaimed kings following the death of Herod, Simon was of humble background; as his name indicates, he was a mere "son of a proselyte." He became the leader of a substantial force, as the insurrection erupted in the summer of 66, and was one of the heroes of the audacious Jewish victory over the Roman army that advanced on Jerusalem that fall (*JW* 2.19.2 §521). Once the high priestly aristocracy regained control of Jerusalem and organized a provisional government, however, the last thing they wanted was to have a popular military hero in command of a nascent peasant militia. Hence, they passed over Simon in making appointments of district commanders. With his great "physical strength and courage," however, Simon continued to foment rebellion in the toparchy of Acrabatene (*JW* 4.9.3 §503–4; 2.22.2 §652–53). When the junta in Jerusalem attempted to suppress his activities there, he simply moved elsewhere.

After the death of the high priest Ananus (summer of 68?), one of the principal leaders of the provisional government in Jerusalem, Simon began building a movement more systematically. A number of parallels between the rise of Simon and that of the popularly "anointed" prototype David emerge from Josephus' accounts. It is unlikely that this is due simply to the literary artifice of Josephus himself, who was especially hostile to Simon, probably because the "despot" had imprisoned his parents during the Roman siege of Jerusalem. Like David, Simon had begun as a leader of a guerilla band that posed a threat to the existing government, but then eventually he was followed by thousands of people as well as by a large army. The initial followers in both cases were the "worthless" and discontent (*JW* 4.9.3–4 §507–13; cf. 1 Sam 22:2); but with the people searching for effective leadership against impending foreign conquest, Simon, like David, came to be recognized as king by masses of people, including some of the notables. Moreover, when Simon moved first to consolidate control of S Judea before moving on Jerusalem, he may have had more than military strategy in mind. He may have been following the Davidic prototype, liberating Judea and establishing righteous rule there (Michel 1967–68). Establishing a firm base in Hebron, in particular, may have been especially symbolic; it was surely remembered as the place where David had first been anointed prince of Judah and from which, once he was recognized as king of all Israel, he went on to take Jerusalem and to liberate the whole country. Josephus' digression just at this point in his narrative to the great antiquity of Hebron and its association with Abraham may well have been an attempt to divert attention from the Davidic associations of Hebron (*JW* 4.9.7 §529–34).

The social-revolutionary aspects of Simon's movement come through far more explicitly in Josephus' reports than did those of the popular kings of 4 B.C.E. After decades of economic pressure on the peasantry under the exploitative rule of Herod and the double burden of having to pay tribute to Rome and dues to priests and temple, Simon and his followers were likely attempting to restore social justice. Simon's proclamation of "liberty for slaves and rewards for the free" (§508) has the ring of prophetic promises. Justice for the poor was to be a feature of the future king, the righteous branch of David, according to prophecies such as those in Isa 11:1–9 and Jer 23:5 (cf. Jer 34:8–9).

Simon's followers, however, were by no means simply an anarchic horde of peasants wildly plundering the estates of the wealthy and storming the barricades of the city. Judging from Josephus' account, Simon and his movement were well organized and disciplined. They even thought ahead about the support system that would be necessary for a prolonged war of liberation. Apparently Simon also maintained a rigorous social discipline once he became the foremost leader in Jerusalem. Acts by Simon that Josephus bitterly condemns, such as the execution of deserters, may have been evidence of the social-political discipline necessary to maintain order among a people subject to a prolonged siege (Michel 1967–68: 406). Simon's discipline can be understood in terms similar to those expressed in *Psalms of Solomon* 17. In the great "war" against the oppressive alien rulers, the anointed king would "thrust out sinners from the inheritance" and "not suffer unrighteousness to lodge anymore in their midst, thus purging Jerusalem, making it holy as of old" (*Ps. Sol.* 17:26, 29, 33, 36).

Two final symbolic events indicate unmistakably how Simon bar Giora had assumed the position of king of the Jews. Josephus reports that, as Jerusalem and the temple were being destroyed, Simon surrendered to the Romans in a highly dramatic act: dressed in a white tunic and a royal purple mantle, he arose out of the ground at the very spot on which the temple had formerly stood (*JW* 7.2.2 §29). The attire was that of a king, a symbolism that would have been clear to both Jews and Romans. This was the attire a king wore on formal state occasions, such as the funeral of Herod (*JW* 1.33.9 §671). Jesus of Nazareth was portrayed as being dressed in such garments when he was mockingly called "king of the Jews" (Mark 15:16–20). Not so clear, however, was the precise purpose Simon had in mind with this symbolic surrender. Was he, by this self-sacrificial surrender to the Romans as the unmistakable king and leader of the enemy, hoping to mitigate the Romans' punishment that would otherwise fall on his people with great severity? Whatever Simon's purpose in his dramatic surrender, the Romans indeed ceremoniously paraded him (appropriately robed), scourged him, and executed him as the enemy head of state and leader (was it explicitly as "king"?) of the Jews in one of the principal events of the triumphal celebration of the great Roman victory over the rebellious Jewish people (*JW* 7.5.3–7 §115–62). By contrast, Simon's rival for leadership, John of Gischala, was simply imprisoned.

The case most clearly recognized in scholarly literature as a messianic movement was the Bar Kokhba revolt of 132–35. Whereas there is very little occurrence of "messianic" ideas in Jewish literature prior to the messianic movements of 4 B.C.E., scholarly visionaries produced more explicit and elaborate pictures of a future messiah toward the end of the 1st century C.E., after Jerusalem and the temple had been destroyed (*4 Ezra* 13; *2 Baruch* 29; 36–40; 72–74). Thus, the Bar Kokhba movement may have been influenced by more clearly developed expectations of a messiah as well as by the biblical tradition of popular kingship. In any case, the revered elderly Rabbi Akiba, who had not forgotten his peasant roots, proclaimed that Simon bar Kosiba, the leader of the insurrection in 132, was the fulfillment of the oracle in Num 24:17: "a star shall go forth from Jacob"; hence the name *Bar Kokhba,* which means "son of the star" (*j. Taʿan.* 4.68d). Other rabbis, probably the majority, were not only skeptical but critical. The same rabbinic tradition has Yoḥanan ben Torta answer: "Akiba, grass will grow out of your cheekbones and the son of David will still not have come." Other rabbinic traditions denigrate the leader of the rebellion with a pun on his name; that is, bar Koziba, or "Son of the Lie." Akiba and the followers of Simon bar Kosiba, however, understood their leader in messianic terms. Coins from the first year of the revolt corroborate that Simon was regarded as the elect ruler, the "Prince (*nāśî*) of Israel."

Undeterred by rabbinic rejections, large numbers of Jewish people must have joined the movement. Simon and his followers established their own government in extensive areas of Judea while defending themselves against Roman attempts at reconquest. Their coins, inscribed "Year I of the Liberation of Israel" or "Year II of the Freedom of Israel," reveal that their assertion of independence from Roman domination had inaugurated a new era. Documents found at Muraba'at and Hever, moreover, indicate that Simon exercised a rigorous administrative and military discipline, and that he and the other leaders placed great emphasis on strict observance of traditional religious regulations. As in 69–70, the Romans sent a massive military force to reconquer the country, but Simon and his followers forced them into a prolonged war of attrition through skillful guerrilla operations based in caves and mountain strongholds. Only after extended campaigns and costly battles could the Romans finally "annihilate, exterminate, and eradicate" this messianic movement from the land (Dio Cass. 59.13.3).

That these popularly recognized kings and their "messianic movements" governed a limited area and were able to maintain the people's sovereignty for only a short time—ranging from a few weeks (Judas, son of Hezekiah) to a few years (Athronges, Simon bar Giora, and Simon bar Kosiba)—does not lessen their significance. That several of these movements occurred within a few generations at the end of the Second Temple period indicates not only that the Jewish peasantry was capable of producing its own leadership and of taking collective action in a politically conscious way, but also that the actions took a distinctive social form because of the peasants' memory of previous liberation and popular sovereignty.

C. Popular Prophets and Prophetic Movements

Certain prophetic figures who appeared in Judea in the mid-1st century C.E. have been labeled "messianic" prophets or "prophetic pretenders to messiahship" (*TDNT* 6: 812–28; Hill 1979). These labels, however, obscure both the distinctive character of the figures and the movements they led and their distinctive difference from the movements led by popular kings that can more appropriately be designated "messianic." Contrary to suggestions by some and the misleading label "messianic," there is no overlap or confusion between these two types of movements and their leaders. Our principal source, Josephus, writes explicitly that Theudas and "the Egyptian" appeared as *prophets,* and he mentions nothing to suggest that they also assumed some royal posture.

Prophets such as Theudas and "the Egyptian" must also be distinguished from other prophetic figures active in this same period. Reports about these figures in Josephus and the Gospels, when placed against the background of earlier (biblical) Israelite prophetic phenomena, indicate that these prophets were of two distinctive types, each reminiscent of or in continuity with a biblical tradition. Prophets of both types apparently arose from among the people, and not from one or another of the literate groups such as the Pharisees or Qumranites. But some of them, such as Jesus, son of Hananiah, and probably John the Baptist as well, were primarily individual spokespersons for God, delivering oracles of judgment related to their respective historical situations. Jesus is particularly reminiscent of Jeremiah in his lament over the doomed city of Jerusalem. During the Jewish revolt, other prophets (none of them named by Josephus) proclaimed oracles of deliverance. Judging from Josephus' reports, some of these may have been more apocalyptic in their inspiration and style, but the visionary imagery suggests that these prophecies concerned historical deliverance, not any "end of the world." These prophets, whether their oracles were of judgment or of liberation, were individual messengers, and none of them (including John the Baptist) appear to have organized or led a mass movement.

The prophets such as Theudas and "the Egyptian," on the other hand, inspired and led mass movements that were suppressed by Roman troops. On the basis of Josephus' general descriptions of several such movements along with his accounts of Theudas, "the Egyptian," and a Samaritan prophet, we are justified in discerning here a distinctive type of prophets and prophetic movements. That is, these prophets, while also messengers of God, did not simply announce the will of God but (1) led actions of deliverance (2) involving "revolutionary changes" (3) in accord with God's "design" and (4) corresponding to one of the great formative historical acts of deliverance led by Moses or Joshua.

According to Josephus' summary statements, there must have been several prophetic figures who at some point or another led their followers out into the wilderness in anticipation of new deliverance (*JW* 2.13.4 §259; *Ant* 20.8.6, 10 §168, 188). The most important, judging from their recollection in the NT as well, were those led by Theudas and "the Egyptian."

> During the period when Fadus was procurator of Judaea, a certain impostor named Theudas persuaded the majority of the masses to take up their possessions and to follow him to the Jordan River. He stated that he was a prophet and that at his command the river would be parted and would provide them an easy passage (*Ant* 20.5.1 §97).
>
> There came to Jerusalem from Egypt a man who declared that he was a prophet and advised the masses of the common people to go out with him to the Mount of Olives. . . . For he asserted . . . that at his command Jerusalem's walls would fall down, through which he promised to provide them an entrance into the city (*Ant* 20.8.6 §169–70; cf. *JW* 2.13.5 §261–62).

The placement of Theudas prior to Judas of Galilee (6 C.E.) in Acts 5:36 is merely either a result of chronological confusion or a lack of solid information by Luke. In Acts 21:38 Luke has simply confused "the Egyptian's" movement with the terrorism by the Sicarii during the same period under the governor Felix (52–60 C.E.). The fundamental reality of all of these movements appears to be that the prophets were leading their followers into some great anticipated liberating action by God.

Josephus says that these prophets were "fostering revolutionary changes" (*JW* 2.13.4 §259). From his explicit reference to "the masses" and "the common people," it is clear that the social base of these movements was the Judean peasantry. Their quest for "rest from troubles" and "freedom" or "liberation" suggests a rejection of the established order in hopes of attaining an independent life free of oppressive burdens. Some of these movements appear simply to be acts of withdrawing from an intolerable situation. The prophet from Egypt is more explicitly confrontational: he apparently led his followers out to participate in God's overthrow of the Roman-dominated established order in Jerusalem. There is no indication in our texts that any of these movements were violent, let alone armed, as has sometimes been suggested. But the brutal suppression of these movements by overwhelming military force indicates just how threatened the ruling groups were about the "revolutionary changes" that these prophets and their followers anticipated. At the very least, of course, if the participants abandoned their fields in anticipation of divine deliverance, then these movements posed a genuine threat to the productive base on which the ruling groups were economically dependent.

The report that the prophets would show their followers "marvels and signs that would be wrought in harmony with God's design" (*Ant* 20.168) should be read against the background of Jewish apocalyptic literature. "God's design" is apparently a reference to the "mystery" or plan of God for the resolution of the current crisis that figures so prominently in Daniel and the Qumran texts. The hostile Josephus writes that "deceivers and impostors, under the pretence of divine inspiration . . . persuaded the masses to act like madmen" (*JW* 2.13.4 §259). That is, stated in more positive, traditional biblical terms, these prophets, filled with the Spirit of God, inspired their followers with the conviction that they were called to participate in God's imminent liberating action.

A new action of deliverance anticipated by these prophets corresponded to one of the great historical acts of deliverance. The historical analogies according to which the new acts of salvation were imagined are clear, at least in general. The prophet from Egypt and his followers were clearly motivated by the great battle of Jericho; in similar fashion, God would now dramatically liberate Jerusalem from Roman domination. The "charlatan" who promised his followers "deliverance and rest from troubles if they chose to follow him into the wilderness" (*Ant* 20.8.10 §188) was surely attempting to realize a new exodus from bondage out into the wilderness, in imitation of Moses of old. The precise analogy in Theudas' case is less clear. Perhaps it should be seen as a new exodus and/or entry into the land: as Moses parted the waters for the deliverance from Egypt and/or as Joshua had parted the waters of the Jordan for the entry into the promised land, so Theudas was acting as God's agent in the new deliverance from Roman oppression and/or in reentry into the land of promise.

Israelite traditions had long since juxtaposed the Exodus from Egypt and entry into the land. And prophetic traditions such as that in Isa 51:9–11 had already conceived of new redemption along the lines of the original formative acts of redemption. Contrary to generalizations often found in scholarly literature, there is virtually no literary evidence for the currency of an expectation of an eschatological prophet like Moses in the 1st century (Horsley 1985a). In the cases of Theudas, the "Egyptian," and "the charlatan," however, there did occur concrete movements led by prophets in actions of liberation that correspond typologically to the great constitutive historical actions led by the prototypical prophets Moses and Joshua. Even though Josephus is careful to say only that Theudas and the "Egyptian" claimed to be prophets and that such leaders were really "deceivers and imposters," he nevertheless used for them the same distinctive language that he used in his accounts of Moses and his "signs and miracles" of deliverance (*Ant* 2.13.3 §286; 2.15.4 §327; cf. 20.8.6.10 §168, 188; *JW* 2.13.4 §259). Josephus' reports thus indicate that there must have been a distinctive social form of *prophetic movements* in 1st century Palestinian Jewish society, parallel to but different from the popular messianic movements.

Bibliography

Bartlett, J. R. 1969. The Use of the Word *rōʾš* as a Title in the Old Testament. *VT* 19: 1–10.

Fitzmyer, J. A. 1974. The Bar Cochba Period. *Essays on the Semitic Background of the New Testament.* Missoula, MT.

Hill, D. 1979. Jesus and Josephus' Messianic Prophets. Pp. 143–54 in *Text and Interpretation,* ed. E. Best and R. McL. Wilson. Cambridge.

Horsley, R. A. 1979. The Sicarii: Ancient Jewish "Terrorists." *JR* 59: 435–58.

———. 1984. Popular Messianic Movements Around the Time of Jesus. *CBQ* 46: 47–95.

———. 1985a. "Like One of the Prophets of Old": Two Types of Popular Prophets at the Time of Jesus. *CBQ* 47: 435–63.

———. 1985b. Menahem in Jerusalem: A Brief Messianic Episode Among the Sicarii—Not "Zealot Messianism." *NovT* 27: 334–48.

———. 1986. Popular Prophetic Movements at the Time of Jesus: Their Principal Features and Social Origins. *JSNT* 26: 3–27.

Horsley, R. A., and Hanson, J. S. 1985. *Bandits, Prophets, and Messiahs.* Minneapolis.

Isaac, B., and Oppenheimer, A. 1985. The Revolt of Bar Kokhba: Ideology and Modern Scholarship. *JJS* 36: 33–60.

Jonge, M. de. 1966. The Use of the Word "Anointed" in the Time of Jesus. *NovT* 8: 132–48.

Michel, O. 1967–68. Studien zu Josephus. *NTS* 14: 403–8.

Roth, C. 1960. Simon bar Giora, Ancient Jewish Hero. *Commentary* 29: 52–58.

Speiser, E. A. 1967. Background and Function of the Biblical NASI. *CBQ* 25: 111–17.

Tadmor, H. 1968. The People and the Kingship in Ancient Israel: The Role of Political Institutions in the Biblical Period. *Cahiers d'histoire mondiale* 11: 46–68.

Weisman, Z. 1976. Anointing as a Motif in the Making of the Charismatic King. *Bib* 57: 378–83.

Wolf, C. U. 1947. Traces of Primitive Democracy in Ancient Israel. *JNES* 6: 105–7.

RICHARD A. HORSLEY

MESSIANIC SECRET. Frequently in the Gospels, especially in Mark, Jesus is portrayed as trying to maintain an element of secrecy about himself and his work. Today, this feature is referred to as the "messianic secret," a term derived from the classic study of W. Wrede (1901; trans. 1971).

A. Wrede
B. Developments since Wrede
  1. The Historical Explanation
  2. The Apologetic Explanation
  3. The "Epiphanic" Explanation
  4. The "History of Revelation" Explanation
C. The Unity of the Secret
D. Conclusion

A. Wrede

Prior to Wrede's work, 19th-century scholars had read the Gospels, especially Mark, as almost exact transcripts of the life of Jesus. In particular, the secrecy texts in Mark were understood as evidence for the fact that Jesus wished to reveal his identity to the disciples only gradually so that they might come to a deeper understanding of him. Much of this was thrown into question by Wrede's work.

Wrede showed that no gradual development in the disciples' understanding can be traced in Mark. Instead, he argued that the theme of secrecy in Mark is all-pervasive. Wrede referred to a number of features in the gospel as evidence for this theme of secrecy: (1) Jesus explicitly commands the demons to be silent about his identity after exorcisms (1:25, 34; 3:11–12); (2) Jesus gives orders that his miracles are not to be publicized (1:43–44; 5:43; 7:36); (3) Jesus commands the disciples to be quiet about him (8:30; 9:9); (4) Jesus tries to keep his whereabouts a secret (7:24, 9:30); (5) Jesus gives private instruction only to a chosen few (7:17; 10:10); (6) the so-called "theory of parables" (4:11–12) shows that in Mark, Jesus teaches in parables in order deliberately to hide his intent from the crowds; and (7) despite their privileged position, the disciples in Mark regularly fail to understand Jesus (6:52; 8:17–21).

Wrede argued that all these features were unhistorical and were therefore secondary editorial additions to the tradition. For example, the secrecy charge at 5:43 was patently absurd, with a girl in a room just restored to life from death and the crowd clamoring just outside the door. Similarly, the theory of parables in 4:11–12 could not be traced back to Jesus, since Jesus used parables in order to make his message clear, not unintelligible (Wrede 1971: 62). Wrede found the key to the secrecy theme in 9:9. Here, a time limit is set so that the disciples are to remain silent about what they have seen until after the resurrection. Wrede argued that this time limit was intended to apply to all the elements of secrecy in Mark: the period prior to Easter was one of secrecy, but after the resurrection full revelation occurred.

Wrede also attempted to account for the origin of the secret. He argued that a primitive Christian belief was that Jesus had *become* Messiah at his resurrection (Acts 2:36; Rom 1:3–4); later Christian reflection led to the belief that Jesus' earthly life had also been messianic. The secret was the result of the coming together of these two views, so that Jesus' earthly life was now described as messianic but with the proviso that this could only be made public after the resurrection (Wrede 1971: 229).

One corollary which Wrede drew was that, if this reconstruction was right, the secret could only have arisen at a time when no explicit messianic claims by Jesus were known. Hence, "*Jesus actually did not give himself out as messiah*" (Wrede 1971: 230; Wrede's italics). This corollary by Wrede has often been criticized vehemently by many, and it has often been thought that Wrede's whole thesis could be refuted by pointing to messianic elements in the tradition which could be traced to Jesus. This probably misses the point of Wrede's analysis, which was an attempt to look at the gospel of Mark and to explain the actual secrecy motifs as they occur *in Mark.* Wrede's point about the lack of messianic claims by Jesus was only a corollary drawn from his theory about the origin of these secrecy motifs.

B. Developments since Wrede

Wrede's work has been extremely influential, even if his detailed theories are no longer accepted by many. Certainly he opened the way for later form and redaction criticism in seeing the gospel tradition as reflecting the beliefs of the first Christians quite as much as the life of Jesus.

1. The Historical Explanation. One of the most common reactions to Wrede, especially in English scholarship, has been to argue that much of the secrecy complex isolated by Wrede should be traced back to Jesus and attributed to a variety of reasons. Jesus may have wished to reinterpret the title "Messiah" (hence the secrecy charge in 8:30); he may have wished to avoid excessive publicity after the miracles; or he may have used the medium of parables in order to try to get people to think for themselves. Further, Jesus may have regarded his own role as Messiah as in some sense incomplete during his earthly ministry (Taylor 1948; Aune 1969; Dunn 1970; Moule 1975). However, it is still questionable whether Wrede's analysis has been met on its own terms; that is, as an analysis of Mark. How do the secrecy charges function within the gospel, and why do some of them appear in redactional, rather than traditional, strands of the gospel (e.g., 1:34; 3:11–12)?

Wrede's theories about the secondary nature of the secrecy elements have always received a more positive response in German scholarship. One modification of Wrede's theory which has gradually evolved, and is now generally accepted, concerns the stage at which the secrecy charges in Mark entered the tradition. Wrede argued that they were pre-Markan. Most today would argue that if they are secondary, they are due to Mark himself (Strecker 1983: 51–54). However, this necessitates a change in Wrede's explanation of the origin of the secret; for Mark provides no evidence that he is aware of a nonmessianic interpretation of the life of Jesus. Hence Wrede's corollary about the lack of any explicit messianic claims by Jesus must also be modified, since this corollary followed directly from Wrede's explanation of the origin of the secret in Mark (Strecker 1983: 54). Several alternative explanations have been proposed.

2. The Apologetic Explanation. According to this theory, the secrecy texts explain the failure of the majority of Jews to respond to Jesus (Dibelius 1934: 230; Burkill 1963), as well as, perhaps, the failure of the majority of Mark's contemporaries to respond to the Christian gospel (Watson 1985, who also stresses the social aspects of such a proposed Sitz im Leben for Mark). This theory encounters difficulties as an explanation for the whole secrecy complex in Mark. For example, it fails to explain the points in the gospel at which the secret is broken (1:45; 7:36–37, where Jesus' commands to silence are disobeyed). Also Jesus' final rejection by the Jewish authorities is not due to any secrecy about who Jesus is, since it is precisely at this point that the veil of secrecy is lifted (14:61–62).

3. The "Epiphanic" Explanation. Ebeling (1939) believes that the points at which the secret is broken form the basis for a very different explanation. According to this, the secrecy texts in Mark are simply literary devices which highlight Jesus' glory and the epiphanic nature of the events concerned. Thus, the accounts of the miracles show that Jesus' fame spread irresistibly despite all attempts, even by Jesus himself, to prevent it. Similarly, the theory of parables serves to highlight the transcendent nature of the revelation for the reader, who belongs with the disciples within the circle of initiates. This theory also runs into problems elsewhere in Mark as an explanation of the whole secrecy complex. Some secrecy charges are *not* broken (5:43), and the time limit in 9:9 is also not easily accommodated within the theory.

4. The "History of Revelation" Explanation. Perhaps the most popular theory today is that the secret represents Mark's understanding of the history of revelation (though within this broad explanation there are some significant variations). Wrede's explanation of the secret fails, since there is no evidence that Mark's material was ever understood non-messianically. Thus, many today would argue that the secret is not so much Mark's way of imposing messianic belief on non-messianic material as it is Mark's way of *controlling* his already messianic material to conform to his overriding theology of the cross. Thus, the secrecy elements form Mark's way of showing that Jesus' true identity can only be properly understood in the light of the cross. Prior to the crucifixion, Jesus' identity as "Son of God" might be misunderstood, and so confessions of this nature are regularly suppressed. Only as, and precisely as, the crucified one is Jesus' identity as "Son of God," not open to misunderstanding. Hence, only as Jesus dies can any human being come to the recognition that Jesus is the Son of God (Mark 15:39). The case for "Son of God" being the most important christological title in Mark, and for the secret being primarily concerned with Jesus' identity as "Son of God," is well set out by Kingsbury (1983).

The importance of the cross and resurrection is recognized by many as the key to understanding the messianic secret in Mark (Conzelmann 1968; Strecker 1983; Schweizer 1983). Within this overall explanation, there is scope for variation. Some have argued that the secret is a matter of past history alone, so that the present era of the Church is one of full and open proclamation (Strecker). Others would argue for a more "existentialist" explanation: the secret remains a secret for those outside the community; revelation after Easter is a possibility, but it only becomes an actuality for the person who is prepared to follow Jesus on the road to the cross, in the way of discipleship (Conzelman; the importance of the theme of discipleship is stressed by Schweizer). But in either case, the secret is to be interpreted as part of Mark's way of pointing to the cross as the essential clue to Jesus' true identity for the Christian disciple.

One development which has attracted some considerable support has been the attempt to specify in more detail the christology which Mark is seeking to control by the secret. Many have argued that Mark is opposing a specific christology, usually described as a *theios aner* christology; i.e., a view of Jesus as primarily the great miracle worker and bearer of supernatural power (Schweizer 1983; Luz 1983; Weeden 1971). Thus, Mark's use of the secrecy motif is to be seen as a conscious attempt to modify views about Jesus which were current in Mark's community. Criticisms can justly be brought against excessive use of the phrase *theios aner* itself (Kingsbury 1983: 25–45), but the idea represented by modern scholarship's use of the phrase may well have been current in Mark's day. Räisänen (1976; 1989) questions whether Mark was indeed opposed to such a view of Jesus, arguing that Mark's attitude to Jesus' miracles is wholly positive. Yet despite the importance of the miracles for Mark, there is still an element of reserve about them in the gospel: they can only occur in a context of faith (6:5; 9:23), and they are not to be had on demand (8:11–12). The theory that Mark is trying to modify such an alternative view of Jesus, whether by outright opposition (Weeden 1971) or by more gentle incorporation (Luz 1983), is thus a very attractive one.

C. The Unity of the Secret

In more recent studies, there has been a strong tendency to question very radically whether Wrede was justified in trying to explain all his evidence from Mark by a single theory. For example, the silencing of the demon in 1:25 was not originally part of Mark's messianic secret. Rather, it is a standard part of the exorcism itself. It is only in the later redactional summaries of 1:34; 3:11–12, that this motif is changed by Mark from a silencing—which is the actual act of overpowering the demon—to a silencing which prevents other people from learning the secret of Jesus' identity from the demons.

The "parable theory" text in Mark 4:11–12 should almost certainly be separated from the other themes (Räisänen 1989). These verses fit well with an "apologetic" type of explanation. They provide some reason for Jewish rejection of Jesus' message, and for a lack of positive response to the preaching of the Christian gospel by Mark's community, by claiming that such a lack of response is due to the divine will and has many precedents in the history of God's people (Mark 4:11–12 cites the classic "hardening" text of Isa 6:9–10). The verses thus provide encouragement and hope for a community that perhaps feels itself to be beleagured and unsuccessful in its mission. Such an explanation does not, however, adequately explain the other parts of the secrecy complex isolated by Wrede.

Within the rest of the secrecy complex, others have also questioned whether the evidence can all be explained by a single theory. Luz (1983) would distinguish between the secrecy charges concerning Jesus' identity (the "messianic secret" proper) and the secrecy charges after the miracles (the "miracle secret"). The latter are generally disobeyed and are to be interpreted as highlighting Jesus' glory as a miracle worker (the "epiphanic" explanation); the former are not disobeyed and show that Jesus' true identity is only to be seen in the light of the cross (the "history of revelation" explanation). While some of the details here may be questionable, this attempt to split up the various motifs referred to by Wrede is probably justified (Räisänen 1989).

One part of Wrede's evidence which is often considered separately today is the motif of the incomprehension of the disciples. This is certainly rather different from the other motifs in Wrede's complex. For example, in the other secrecy charges, those addressed have the right idea about Jesus and are told not to tell others; in the case of the disciples, they usually have the wrong idea, or even no idea at all about who Jesus is. One view which has aroused a lot of discussion is that the disciples represent a group within Mark's own community, and that Mark's unfavorable picture of the disciples represents a polemical attitude toward this group. Thus, many see the disciples in Mark as representative of the group which holds the christology which Mark is opposing; i.e., the *theios aner* christology (Weeden 1971).

Yet despite Mark's negative picture of the disciples, it is difficult to maintain that Mark's attitude to them is one of outright opposition. They do respond to Jesus' call (1:16–20; 3:13–19); they go out on mission (6:7–13); and they (probably) achieve their restoration with the risen Jesus (as 16:7 suggests). Thus, while Mark may well be trying to modify views of others within his own community, it is hard to see the *disciples* in the story as representative of these other people. It is more likely that the picture of the disciples in Mark is intended to enable the Christian reader to identify with them and to learn from their failings not only about the nature of discipleship but also about the forgiveness and grace of God which is available to those who fail (Best 1977; Tannehill 1977). A more positive role for the disciples is suggested by Räisänen (1989): they may function as the spokespersons for Mark's own views in a confrontation between Mark and the bearers of the Q tradition who have a defective understanding of Jesus and of the significance of his death and resurrection. Such a Sitz im Leben for Mark is, however, somewhat speculative and depends in part on the theory that Mark, unlike Q, is wholly positive about Jesus' miracles. Further, it must remain doubtful whether the disciples really do attain full understanding about Jesus in 8:27–29 (Räisänen): the sequel suggests that they still do not appreciate the full truth about Jesus and the nature of his task. Full insight about Jesus is only attained at the cross by human characters in the story.

D. Conclusion

Wrede's theories about the messianic secret have undergone many modifications since they were first published in 1901. Probably nobody today would give wholehearted support to all that Wrede said about the texts in Mark which he considered. Nevertheless, it is recognized that Wrede identified elements which occupy a key role in Mark's gospel. Many of these elements are due to Mark himself, and hence are not to be traced to Jesus, and their interpretation is vital for a proper understanding of Mark's gospel. Some parts of the whole complex of motifs considered by Wrede should probably be isolated from the rest and considered separately. Nevertheless, the remaining parts of the secrecy complex in Mark, whereby the secret of Jesus' identity is only fully revealed to human characters in the story when Jesus is seen as the crucified one, play a key role in the gospel. These secrecy texts are thus of vital importance in the understanding of Mark's christology and ecclesiology; i.e., in Mark's understanding of who Jesus was and of what it meant to be a disciple of Jesus.

Bibliography

Aune, D. E. 1969. The Problem of the Messianic Secret. *NovT* 11: 1–31.

Best, E. 1977. The Role of the Disciples in Mark. *NTS* 23: 377–401.

Burkill, T. A. 1963. *Mysterious Revelation.* Ithaca, NY.

Conzelmann, H. 1968. Present and Future in the Synoptic Tradition. *JTC* 5: 26–44.

Dibelius, M. 1934. *From Tradition to Gospel.* Trans. B. L. Woolf. New York.

Dunn, J. D. G. 1970. The Messianic Secret in Mark. *TynBul* 21: 92–117. Repr. as pp. 116–31 in Tuckett 1983.

Ebeling, H. J. 1939. *Das Messiasgeheimnis und die Botschaft des Marcusevangelisten.* BZNW 19. Berlin.

Kingsbury, J. D. 1983. *The Christology of Mark's Gospel.* Philadelphia.

Luz, U. 1983. The Secrecy Motif and the Marcan Christology. Pp. 75–96 in Tuckett 1983.

Minette de Tillesse, G. 1968. *Le secret messianique dans l'évangile de Marc.* Paris.

Moule, C. F. D. 1975. On Defining the Messianic Secret in Mark. Pp. 239–52 in *Jesus und Paulus. Festschrift für W. G. Kümmel zur 70. Geburtstag,* ed. E. E. Ellis and E. Grässer. Göttingen.

Räisänen, H. 1976. *Das "Messiasgeheimnis" im Markusevangelium.* Helsinki. Final chapter in Tuckett 1983: 132–40.

———. 1989. *The "Messianic Secret" in Mark.* Exp. ed. Trans. Edinburgh.

Robinson, W. C. 1973. The Quest for Wrede's Secret Messiah. *Int* 27: 10–30. Repr. as pp. 97–115 in Tuckett 1983.

Schweizer, E. 1983. The Question of the Messianic Secret in Mark. Pp. 65–74 in Tuckett 1983.

Strecker, G. 1983. The Theory of the Messianic Secret in Mark's Gospel. Pp. 49–64 in Tuckett 1983.

Tannehill, R. 1977. The Disciples in Mark: The Function of a Narrative Role. *JR* 57: 386–405.

Taylor, V. 1948. The Messianic Secret in Mark. *ExpTim* 59: 146–51.

Tuckett, C. M., ed. 1983. *The Messianic Secret.* London and Philadelphia.

Watson, F. B. 1985. The Social Function of Mark's Secrecy Theme. *JSNT* 24: 49–69.

Weeden, T. J. 1971. *Mark—Traditions in Conflict.* Philadelphia.

Wrede, W. 1971. *The Messianic Secret.* Trans. J. C. G. Greig. London.

C. M. Tuckett

METHEGH-AMMAH [Heb *meteg-hāʾammâ*]. Methegh-ammah is not known as a name of a place in the Bible, though some have interpreted it so (e.g., RSV). The Heb words *meteg-hāʾammâ,* which literally mean "the bridle of one cubit," appear only in 2 Sam 8:1: "David took (or received) the methegh-ammah from the hand of Philistines." According to *tg. Jon.* Gen 26:31, Isaac "took one cubit's length of the bridle of his ass, and gave it to him (Abimelech) as a sign of friendship." According to this explanation, the giving of the "bridle of one cubit" signified "friendship" or possibly surrender. This meaning fits well with the context of 2 Sam 8:1. Then the meaning becomes "David received the bridle of one cubit (as the token of surrender) from the hand of Philistines." This interpretation is not far from the translation of LXX: "David took the tribute from out of the hand of the Philistines." David might have received the bridle of one cubit as a token of surrender, together with the "tribute." The Vulgate translated it: "David got the bridle of gift from the hand of Philistines." Jerome considered the "bridle" itself a gift.

There is no biblical support to interpret Methegh-ammah figuratively as the "control of the mother city" because *methegh* ("bridle") is not used figuratively anywhere else in the Bible, and *ammah* as the word for *ʾēm,* "mother," is not used in the OT. It is a mere speculation based on a seemingly parallel text, "He took Gath and its towns from the hand of Philistines" (1 Chr 18:1), in which "Gath and its towns" corresponds to the methegh-ammah in 2 Sam 8:1. It is very difficult to consider that the Philistines had a capital or a centralized "mother city" because they had five cities under five rulers, but it is possible to consider Gath as the mother city for the surrounding towns. However, the question remains as to why the name of the mother city "Gath" was omitted in 2 Sam 8:1 even though there were four more mother cities besides Gath.

Yoshitaka Kobayashi

METHUSELAH (PERSON) [Heb *mĕtûšelaḥ; mĕtûšālaḥ*]. Son of Enoch when Enoch was 65 years old (Gen 5:21); and, at 187 years of age, father of Lamech (Gen 5:25). Methuselah lived 969 years (Gen 5:27), the longest life span of anyone mentioned in the Bible. The name Methuselah is composed of two elements. The first element reflects the West Semitic *mutu,* "man, husband." The second element, *šlḥ*, has been identified variously as a weapon, a canal, or a divine name (Skinner *Genesis* ICC, 131–32; Driver 1948: 77; 81). The association with a divine name is preferred on the basis of comparisons with early West Semitic names from Amarna (*mu-ut-ba-aḫ-l(ù)* EA 255, 3; *mu-ut*-dIM EA 256, 2, 5) and Ugarit (*mu-ut*-dU *PRU* 3: 205; RS 16.155.6; *PRU* 4: 234; RS 17.112.6; Sivan 1984: 250). The suggestion that the divine name be identified as Laḥ, with the antecedent relative pronoun *š* (Van Selms 1966: 318–26) is unlikely due to a lack of comparable structures (*mutu* + *ša* + divine name) attested elsewhere in personal names (see METHUSHAEL), and due to the name Shelah itself, which, if explained in the same way, would have no antecedent. On the other hand, a divine name based on the *šlḥ* root is plausible. Whether or not a Canaanite deity, Šalaḥ, was god of the infernal river (Tsevat 1954; Loretz 1975), and such a divine name may have formed part of the personal name Methuselah. The meaning of the name would then be, "man (i.e., devotee) of the deity Šalaḥ." However, a problem with this interpretation is that such a deity is not attested outside of personal names.

Outliving his son Lamech by five years, Methuselah died in the 600th year of his grandson Noah, in the year of the Flood according to the chronology of Genesis 5–6. Beyond the general recognition that the lengths of life spans decline as the genealogy of Genesis 5 progresses, the significance of Methuselah's long life is disputed. The relationship of Methuselah to Methushael, the corresponding name in the Cainite genealogical list of Genesis 4, is not clear. The LXX renders both names *mathousala*. However, it is unnecessary to posit one original name preserved in two separate traditions. Comparable ANE antediluvian genealogies preserve similar-sounding names which are contemporary but distinct and are intended to reflect distinctly different individuals (Finkelstein 1963: 50; *GHBW*, 150–51). There was also significant embellishment on Methuselah in late Second Temple writings, notably in *1 Enoch*.

Bibliography

Driver, S. R. 1948. *The Book of Genesis with Introduction and Notes.* 15th ed. London.

Finkelstein, J. J. 1963. The Antediluvian Kings: A University of California Tablet. *JCS* 17: 39–51.

Kraeling, E. G. 1922. Terach.—Methuselach. *ZAW* 40: 153–55.

Loretz, O. 1975. Der Gott *ŠALAḤ*, He. *ŠLḤ* I und *ŠLḤ* II. *UF* 7: 584–85.

Sivan, D. 1984. *Grammatical Analysis and Glossary of the Northwest Semitic Vocables in Akkadian Texts of the 15th–13th C.B.C. from Canaan and Syria.* AOAT 214. Kevelaer and Neukirchen-Vluyn.

Tsevat, M. 1954. The Canaanite God Šalaḥ. *VT* 4: 41–49.

Van Selms, A. 1966. A Forgotten God: *LAḤ*. Pp. 318–26 in *Studia Biblica et Semitica Theodoro Christiano Vriezen,* ed. W. C. van Unnik and A. S. van der Woude. Wageningen.

RICHARD S. HESS

METHUSHAEL (PERSON) [Heb *mĕtûšāʾēl*]. Son of Mehujael and father of Lamech in the line of Cain (Gen 4:18). Comparisons with the genealogy of Seth in Genesis 5 have related Methushael with Methuselah (*GHBW*, 161–62). The difference between the names is limited to the final two consonants: *mtwšʾl* vs. *mtwšlḥ*. The first element in the name Methushael reflects the West Semitic *mutu*, "man, husband." The remainder of the name may be composed either of the relative *š* followed by *ʾl*, "god"; or it may be made up of the single element, *šʾl*, which could either be a form of the verb "to ask" or the proper name "Sheol" (Gabriel 1959: 414–15).

Therefore, the name could mean either "man of God," "man of the request (i.e., prayer)," or "man of Sheol." If the name is West Semitic, the first option is less likely due to the absence of such relative pronouns in personal names (Gray 1896: 164–65; Moran 1961: 61; 70 n. 76; Huffmon *APNM*, 265; Gelb 1980: 33). As for the second option, the use of *šʾl* in a nominative form is also unusual in personal names. On the other hand, the use of a proper name in construct with a term such as "man" is paralleled in Methuselah and seems possible in this case, Sheol being understood as the name of a deity (Tsevat 1954: 45; *EncMiqr* 5: 643–44; *IDBSup*, 224; Gelb 1980: 26; 158–60). The name would then mean "man (i.e., devotee) of the god Sheol." Examples of *mutu* followed by a divine name occur in West Semitic personal names of the 2d millennium B.C. (Huffmon *APNM*, 234; Sivan 1984: 250), but not those of the 1st millennium. Although there are no other examples of personal names containing a divine name *šʾl;* there are examples of underworld deities, such as Nergal, Reshef, and Mot (Tigay 1986: 66–67 n. 12), appearing in West Semitic personal names.

Bibliography

Gabriel, J. 1959. Die Kainitengenealogie. Gn 4, 17–24. *Bib* 40: 409–27.

Gelb, I. J., et al. 1980. *Computer-Aided Analysis of Amorite.* AS 21. Chicago.

Gray, G. B. 1896. *Studies in Hebrew Proper Names.* London.

Moran, W. L. 1961. The Hebrew Language in Its Northwest Semitic Background. Pp. 54–72 in *The Bible and the Ancient Near East,* ed. G. E. Wright. London.

Sivan, D. 1984. *Grammatical Analysis and Glossary of the Northwest Semitic Vocables in Akkadian Texts of the 15th–13th C.B.C. from Canaan and Syria.* AOAT 214. Kevelaer and Neukirchen-Vluyn.

Tigay, J. H. 1986. *You Shall Have No Other Gods. Israelite Religion in the Light of Hebrew Inscriptions.* HSS 31. Atlanta.

Tsevat, M. 1954. The Canaanite God Šalaḥ. *VT* 4: 41–49.

RICHARD S. HESS

MEUNIM [Heb *mĕʿûnîm*]. MEUNITES. The Hebrew Bible gives the impression that these are a Transjordanian and/or Arabian people (1 Chr 4:41; 2 Chr 26:7; Ezra 2:50 = Neh 7:52). However, the actual spellings of the name(s) in Hebrew suggest that the Bible may actually be referring to *two* peoples: those from Maʿin and those from Maʿon. The Kethib of 1 Chr 4:41 and Ezra 2:50 reads *mʿynym*, "Meinim" (although in both passages the Qere to be read is *mĕʿûnîm*, "Meunim"). The Kethib of 2 Chr 26:7 and Neh 7:52, on the other hand, is *mʿwnym*, "Meunim." However, the problem is compounded by the fact that the LXX renders all four of these citations as *Minaioi*, "Minaeans." Furthermore, the LXX reads *Minaioi* also in 2 Chr 20:1 and 26:8, where the Heb reads *ʿammônîm*, "Ammonites." Since the word "Ammonites" does not make sense in either of these passages, it can be assumed that—prior to a metathesis of the *mem* and the *ᶜayin*—these passages also originally referred to *mᶜwnym*/*mᶜynym*. We cannot be certain how all of these biblical references should be distributed between these two peoples; however, on historical grounds (presented below) it is plausible to read *mĕᶜînîm* ("people from Maᶜin") in 1 Chr 4:41 and 2 Chr 26:7, 8; and to read *mĕᶜûnîm* ("people from Maᶜon") in Ezra 2:50 = Neh 7:52 and 2 Chr 20:1.

The **Meinim,** or Minaeans, were people associated with the S Arabian city-state *mᶜn* (*Maᶜîn, hence *mĕᶜînîm*). These people gained control of the incense road around 400 B.C. and established trading colonies in the major cities in W Arabia and Egypt and in Mediterranean port cities like Sidon. Gaza became their most important colony city. According to Diod. Sic. 3.42.5 (quoting a source from the 3d century B.C.), the Minaeans brought incense to Petra. Both at Gaza and at Petra, the Minaeans are attested epigraphically (Knauf 1985: 116–17). The Minaeans cannot have been present at Gaza in the 5th century (when the incense trade still was controlled by the Sabeans); nor were they "Arabs" or "nomads" (*pace* Katzenstein 1989: 79).

The Minaean presence at Gaza (which may have lasted beyond the city's destruction by Alexander in 332 B.C.) and at Petra forms the historical background of 1 Chr 4:39–41 and 2 Chr 26:7–8. In general, the historical material in Chronicles (unparalleled in Samuel and Kings) reflects the conditions of the Chronicler's own time; i.e., the 4th and/or 3d centuries B.C. (Welten 1973: 195–200). According to 1 Chr 4:39–41, Simeonites moved to "the valley" (Heb *haggay*); i.e., Gaia/al-Jîʾ, the ancient name of Wâdî Mûsâ at the entrance of Petra, and exterminated the Meinim (Kethib) whom they encountered there. The dating of this "event" to the time of Hezekiah (4:41)—a time when the tribe of Simeon had ceased to exist for several centuries—serves as a cross-reference to 2 Chr 26:7–8. This latter text (in the LXX) reports an action of Uzziah against the "Philistines, Arabs, and Meinim" resulting in a Minaean tribute to the Judean king which made his fame spread to Egypt. Demographically, this text actually presupposes the composition of Philistia's population in the *postexilic* period, and the Minaean trading network which included Egypt. The archaic terminology of the two biblical references conceals economic conflicts in late Persian and early Hellenistic Palestine expressed in the vocabulary of warfare and tribes looking for pasturage.

The **Meunim,** on the other hand, are the inhabitants of any one of several biblical places called Maon (Heb *māᶜôn;* the shift of *ô* in a stressed syllable to *ū* in a pretonic syllable is a frequent feature in Hebrew). The original tradition underlying 2 Chronicles 20 centers around a local conflict in the area between Tekoa (v 20) and Engedi (v 2). The "Maon" in this vicinity is probably the Moabite Beth-Baal-Meon, today Mâᶜîn (M.R. 219120). If its inhabitants were the Meunim (MT *mhᶜmwnym;* LXX *Minaioi*) of 2 Chr 20:1, the neighboring Moabites and Ammonites could easily have been incorporated in the tradition. In the next stage of the tradition's growth, another Maon, present-day Maᶜân (M.R. 220956), was regarded as the place of the Meunim's origin, leading to the incorporation of "Edom" (v 2) and "the inhabitants of Seir" (vv 10; 22–23) in 2 Chronicles 20. The temple slaves mentioned in Ezra 2:50 (= Neh 7:52) could have come from either of the two Maons mentioned, or even from the third Maon in Judah (Josh 15:55; 1 Sam 25:2; 1 Chr 2:45), which by that time was controlled by the Idumeans. See also MAON.

Ephᶜal (1982: 219–20) and Borger and Tadmor (1982) prefer to read "Meunim" (rather than "Meinim"/Minaeans) also in 1 Chr 4:41 and 2 Chr 26:7–8. They identify the Meunim with the Muʾnayya that Tiglath-pileser III mentions in connection with the border region between Palestine and Egypt. The Assyrian reference seems to match the two biblical references both geographically and chronologically. It is, however, impossible to identify the Akkadian tribal name "Muʾnaeans" (most probably from an ancient Arabic tribal name or personal name *Maᶜn) with Heb *mĕᶜūnîm* (from Maon/Māᶜân; Knauf 1985: 114–15). It is equally impossible to date the two biblical references to the time of Uzziah/Hezekiah on demographic grounds (see above). The reason that 2 Chr 26:7–8 was (erroneously) attributed to Uzziah was because of his action against three Philistine cities (2 Chr 26:6), a note which belongs to the small amount of reliable historical information in Chronicles (Welten 1973: 153–63). The dating of 1 Chr 4:41 to Uzziah's successor Hezekiah can be explained as a cross-reference from this account on the Meinim to the other one, 2 Chr 26:7–8.

Bibliography

Borger, R., and Tadmor, H. 1982. Zwei Beiträge zur alttestamentlichen Wissenschaft aufgrund der Inschriften Tiglatpilesers III. II. Die Meuniter. *ZAW* 94: 250–51.

Ephᶜal, I. 1982. *The Ancient Arabs.* Leiden.

Katzenstein, H. J. 1989. Gaza in the Persian Period. *Transeuphratène* 1: 67–86.

Knauf, E. A. 1985. Muᶜnäer und Mëuniter. *WO* 16: 114–22.

Welten, P. 1973. *Geschichte und Geschichtsdarstellung in den Chronikbüchern.* WMANT 42. Neukirchen-Vluyn.

ERNST AXEL KNAUF

MEVORAKH, TELL (M.R. 143215). A small mound (Ar: Tell Mubarak) in the Sharon plain, on the S bank of Nahal Taninim.

The Institute of Archaeology of Hebrew University conducted four seasons of excavations during 1973–76. In the first season, a trial trench was dug at the W end of the N slope. The excavation area was greatly enlarged during the second and third seasons and extended to the center of the mound and the E side. During the fourth season, the center of the mound was excavated to virgin soil. By the end of the fourth season, the stratigraphy of the mound was clearly established.

The first settlement (stratum XV) was a rectangular fortress built of mud bricks; founded on the low natural hill in the MB I. In the next stratum (XIV), also dating to the MB I, the fortress was surrounded by many residential houses which covered the entire hill. These settlements were unwalled.

During the MB II (stratum XIII), the inhabitants constructed a *terre pisée* rampart, about 30 m square, which buried the previous fortress and buildings to a height of 3 m. The rampart had a steep outer face, and from its ridge at the edge of the mound it sloped downward toward the inside, thus creating a crater. The rampart was constructed of a hard-packed core covered with rather loose layers of sand brought from the surrounding hills. Within this was an aggregate of stone implements from earlier periods which included a few obsidian tools dating from the Pre-Pottery Neolithic. The inner slope of the rampart was strengthened by a series of stone supporting walls. Some residential rooms and a large kitchen had been built inside the crater for the use of the settlers—probably soldiers of a small unit stationed there—and their families. Several burial jars of infants were discovered beneath the floors of the structures.

In the third season of excavations, the N section in the *terre pisée* was deepened to examine more closely the form of the natural hill. It became clear that both the slope of the hill and the *terre pisée* rampart were very steep. The footings of both descended into a layer of black soil peculiar to the beds of rivers or marshes. It seems, therefore, that the N end of the MB II fortress was bounded by water. The E side of the fortress may have been fortified differently—perhaps with a brick wall now eroded—but this assumption must await further excavations.

After the destruction of this settlement, another was built on the same location in the MB III (stratum XII). It appears that this was also fortified, since its walls and rooms were constructed within the rampart. The stone supporting walls of the inner slope were again strengthened. The main difference between the latter two MB settlements is the burial methods. The infant burial jars of stratum XII had not been buried under the floors as had been done in stratum XIII, but the outer slopes of the ramparts. On some of these jars are Hyksos stamp impressions.

Stratum XI, the first settlement of the LB, included the remains of a large building which occupied the entire excavation area. See Fig. MEV.01. Its form, interior installations, and especially the finds leave no doubt that it should be understood as a sanctuary. The N side of the building leans against the inner side of the MB rampart (as at Hazor, area C). Almost all of the sanctuary hall, measuring 10 m by 5 m and oriented E–W, was cleared. The floor and walls were all coated with beaten lime plaster. In the NW corner stood a rectangular (1 m by 1.5 m) plastered platform (ca. 0.6 m high) with five steps leading up to it from the E. On the lime floor near the

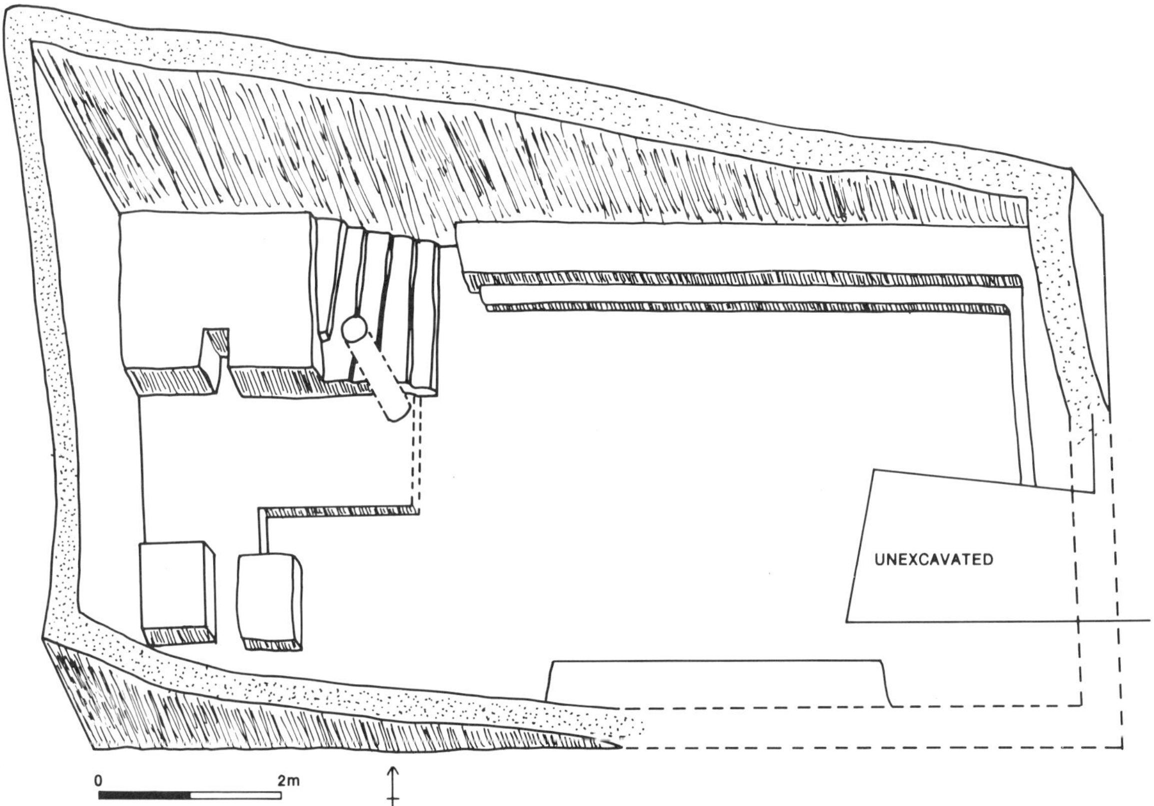

MEV.01. Isometric reconstruction of temple in Level XI at Tel Mevorakh—LB Age. *(Redrawn from Stern 1984: 5, fig. II)*

corner of the platform was the round imprint of a small (wooden?) column, which may have supported a canopy. A plastered bench ran along the W (short) end of the hall, and in front of it near the center of the room stood two plastered installations whose functions are still obscure. The long N wall was cleared along its whole length. Immediately to the E of the platform was a long, low plastered bench which reached the NE corner and then turned along the E wall. The bench thus extended more than 8 m. In the center of the hall stood a large round stone, which may have served as a column base. The floor of the sanctuary sloped toward the S where a drain running against another plastered bench was located. Because of the slope, the S wall was destroyed, except for a small section in the SW corner. The entrance to the sanctuary may have been in the S wall.

The sanctuary of stratum X consisted of the same building layout and orientation, but the platform and steps of the earlier period were enclosed and buried within two low walls which formed a new and higher platform (ca. 1 m high). The small finds preserved on this platform included two Mitannian-style cylinder seals, two faience disks, two cups (one of alabaster, the other of clay), a pair of bronze cymbals, a bronze knife, a javelin, and arrowheads. There were also many imported Cypriot vessels. Among the local ware of special interest were many jars, jugs, juglets, bowls, lamps, and, especially, decorated chalices and goblets. The only hint of the type of cult that practiced here was the discovery of a well-preserved bronze snake, about 20 cm long, which closely resembles the bronze snakes found in contemporary sanctuaries at Timna and Hazor.

The sanctuaries of both strata XI and X were bounded on the S and W by large stone-paved courtyards, the extent of which have not been determined. The sanctuary and its courtyards occupied almost the entire area of the LB site. The compound may therefore represent a wayside sanctuary, the first of its kind to be discovered in Israel.

Stratum IX, which consists of the remains of a large building with parts of two rooms and a stone pavement, stood over the remains of the earlier sanctuaries. The purpose and function of this LB building remain unclear.

The first stratum (VIII) of the Iron Age (IB) is represented by a rectangular platform which was filled to a height of about 1 m with homogeneous red-brick material. It was surrounded on the W, S, and E by a stone wall more than 1 m thick, while on the N it was set into the MB II rampart. This platform apparently served as the foundation of a building the remains of which are only scantily preserved on the N. The purpose of the Stratum VIII building is unknown, although from the foundation and few wall fragments that remain it appears to have been a large and important building. To the S of the platform, part of a courtyard was found with a floor of thick beaten lime.

Above the remains of the stratum VIII platform was a four-room house, also from the Iron Age IB (stratum VII), dated to the 10th century B.C. A large building was surrounded by a broad courtyard with a floor made of a thick layer of beaten lime, and the whole complex was encircled by a wall about 1-m thick. The pottery included local red hand-burnished ware and undecorated pottery, as well as imported Cypriot vessels, among them Cypro-Phoenician, Bichrome, and White Painted ware. This complex has been identified as either an administrative center or an official storehouse.

There are also three Persian phases. The lowest (stratum VI) is represented only by a series of deep pits filled with ashes, bones, and pottery, including Attic and Cypriot ware. On one of the local sherds found in a pit were rows of stamped rosettes much in the manner of the Judean stamps. In the second phase (stratum V), a building was found on the W part of the mound. In the upper phase of the Persian period (stratum IV), the entire mound was occupied by what seems to have been a single large building. Since the last two phases were encircled by a casemate wall, they may again be interpreted as an administrative center or large estate.

Above the Persians levels were some scattered walls, apparently belonging to the Hellenistic period (stratum III). Despite the many Roman and Byzantine finds collected on the mount (stratum II), it is clear that no structures from these periods were built on the summit. Instead, all building activity during these periods was limited to the surroundings, and a large wall, the purpose of which is not yet clear, was found at the base of the N side of the mound. Stratum I consisted of the entire surface of the site, which was densely covered by numerous graves of the Arab period. In one case, three superimposed graves were found. Most of them were normal cist graves, but two or three were unusual infant-jar burials.

Bibliography

Stern, E. 1977. The Excavations of Tell Mevorakh and the Late Phoenician Elements in the Architecture of Palestine. *BASOR* 225: 17–27.

———. 1978. *Excavations at Tel Mevorakh (1973–1976).* Pt. 1, *From the Iron Age to the Roman Period.* Qedem 9. Jerusalem.

———. 1984. *Excavations at Tel Mevorakh (1973–1976).* Pt. 2, *The Bronze Age.* Qedem 18. Jerusalem.

EPHRAIM STERN

MEZAHAB (PERSON) [Heb *mê zāhāb*]. The "father" (or "mother") of Matred, whose daughter Mehetabel married the "Edomite king" Hadad (II) (Gen 36:39; 1 Chr 1:50). See also MATRED; MEHETABEL; HADAD. *Mezahab,* which means "gold-water," is actually a place name rather than a personal name. As a personal name, Mezahab has a distant parallel in *Mâʾ as-Samâʾ*, a pre-Islamic Arab queen's name meaning "Water of Heaven" (Nöldeke 1879: 169, n. 4), which is, however, a *cognomen* rather than a personal name. In addition, the parallel would make Mezahab a female name, the mother of Matred, and the grandmother of Mehetabel. Such a genealogy appears to be unparalleled in the biblical world. However, women occupied more prominent positions among the ancient Arabs than they did among the Israelites (Knauf 1989: 24, n. 105), and the "Edomite kings" in Genesis 36 may have been Arab chieftains.

As a place name, Mezahab is Canaanite (or Ancient Aramaic). To call a native of Mezahab the "son" (preferable to the MT's "daughter"; see MATRED) of this place is in accordance with Hebrew usage (cf. the son of Jabesh, 1 Kgs 15:10). The place could have been situated anywhere in Edom, Palestine, or Arabia, even in Syria, if Lemaire's suggestion (1988) that the "Edomite king list" (Gen 36:31–39) actually is an Aramean king list of the 11th century B.C. holds true. Only Arabia is credited with having gold mines by ancient and medieval authors. The identification of Mezahab with DIZAHAB (Deut 1:1) can neither be substantiated nor rejected; in addition, Dizahab cannot be localized either.

Bibliography

Knauf, E. A. 1989. *Ismael.* 2d ed. ADPV. Wiesbaden.

Lemaire, A. 1988. Hadad l'Édomite ou Hadad l'Araméen? *BN* 43: 14–18.

Nöldeke, T. 1879. *Geschichte der Perser und Araber zur Zeit der Sasaniden.* Leiden.

ERNST AXEL KNAUF

MEZOBAITE [Heb *mĕṣōbāyâ*]. An adjective used to describe Jaasiel, one of David's champions; it describes a select class of warriors directly attached to the king for special assignments, named in the list of 1 Chr 11:10–47 (v 47), a list which, up to v 41a, parallels that of 2 Sam 23:8–39. Jaasiel, "the Mezobaite" (RSV), is found among the sixteen persons mentioned in the portion of the list which is unique to Chronicles (vv 41b–47). Because this adjective occurs with the definite article but without the gentilic ending *î*, and because no such place as Mezobayah is known, it seems probable that the term has been corrupted in transmission. It has been suggested (see Rudolph *Chronikbücher* HAT, 103) that two readings have been conflated: *miṣṣōbāh* ("from Zobah") and *haṣṣōbātî* ("the Zobaite"). Zobah was an Aramean kingdom located between the Lebanon and Anti-lebanon, against which Saul had fought (1 Sam 14:47). Since one characteristic of this portion of the warrior list (vv 41b–47) is that all of the identifiable places from which these champions came are in the Transjordan (Williamson *Chronicles* NCBC, 104), the suggested reading, "Jaasiel the Zobaite," seems appropriate.

RODNEY K. DUKE

MIBHAR (PERSON) [Heb *mibḥār*]. In 1 Chr 11:38, Mibhar, son of Hagri, is listed as one of David's mighty men. In what should be the parallel passage, 2 Sam 23:36, there is a variant in the Hebrew, and the entire verse is divided differently. The passage in 1 Chr 11:38 reads, "Joel brother of Nathan; Mibhar son of Hagri," while 2 Sam 23:36 identifies the warriors as "Igal son of Nathan from Zobah; Bani the Gadite."

There is such a variety of ways in which the warriors are referred to in these sections that it is not possible to decide definitely which is the more original form. It is worth noting, however, that in the extended list of "the Thirty" (2 Sam 23:24b–39; 1 Chr 11:26–47), it is only at 1 Chr 11:38 where the relationship of "brother" occurs; the normal way of identifying the warriors is "son of" when any family relationship is mentioned. The anomaly in the case of "Joel brother of Nathan" makes it probable that it is the original reading here; otherwise, it is hard to see why the text would have been changed. In the Gk mss we find "son of" in mss B S C_2, while the rest of them follow the Masoretic Text.

On the other hand, for "Mibhar son of Hagri" in 1 Chr 11:38, 2 Sam 23:36 has ". . . from Zobah; Bani the Gadite," reflecting the Heb *miṣṣōbâ bānî hagadî*. The OG for Samuel, however, reads *massaba uios agērei,* suggesting that its vorlage was in basic agreement with the Hebrew text of 1 Chr 11:38. This is an indication that the text of the Chronicler represents the more original form for "Hagri" (Heb *ḥgry*) in comparison to "the Gadite" (Heb *hgdy*), as found in 2 Samuel.

In the light of these preferences for the readings found in 1 Chronicles, it is likely that "Mibhar son of Hagri" should be maintained as the preferred reading for 1 Chr 11:38.

STEPHEN PISANO

MIBSAM (PERSON) [Heb *mibśām*]. **1.** A son of Ishmael (Gen 25:13; 1 Chr 1:29).

2. A son of Shallum, son of Shaul, son of Simeon (1 Chr 4:25).

Since all the sons of Ishmael were ancient N Arabian tribes (see ISHMAELITES), and since Mibsam is followed by Mishma both in Gen 25:13 and in 1 Chr 1:29 and 1 Chr 4:25, the two "persons" may be interpreted as representations of the same Arabian tribe or clan. It is conceivable that this "tribe," together with his "brother" Mishma, came to be included in the genealogy of the Israelite tribe of Simeon in 1 Chronicles 4. From Genesis 34, it can be inferred that the tribe of Simeon, living in the central hill country, had disappeared at an early stage of Israel's prehistory. All references to Simeon in the Negeb are ancient constructs trying to tie the name of this tribe into the geography of the authors' world centuries after the tribe had become extinct (Mittmann 1977: 217–19). The authors of 1 Chronicles 4 frequently took recourse to the names of tribes and clans inhabiting the Negeb in their own days, including Arabian and Edomite/Idumean population groups (Ephᶜal 1982: 199–200). See also EPHAH; MANAHATH (PERSON); MANAHATHITES.

The name is derived from Heb *bōśem,* Arabic *bašâm,* "balm." The tribe of Mibsam may well have been involved in the spice trade on the "incense road"; on the other hand, the name is attested as a personal name in Safaitic, and related names occur all over the Arabian peninsula (Knauf 1989: 68–69). See also BASEMATH.

Bibliography

Ephᶜal, I. 1982. *The Ancient Arabs.* Jerusalem and Leiden.

Knauf, E. A. 1989. *Ismael.* 2d ed. ADPV. Wiesbaden.

Mittmann, S. 1977. Ri. 1,16f und das Siedlungsgebiet der kenitischen Sippe Hobab. *ZDPV* 93: 213–35.

ERNST AXEL KNAUF

MIBZAR (PERSON) [Heb *mibṣar*]. One of the Edomite tribal chiefs (Gen 36:42; 1 Chr 1:53). The name means "fortified city, fortification," and MT *mibṣar* in Ps 108:11 [—Eng 108:10] should be emended to *māṣôr,* "entrenched, ramparted (city)," as in Ps 60:11 [—Eng 10:9]. Mibzar is one of the eleven names in the list of Edomite "tribal chiefs" (*ʾallûpîm)* in Gen 36:40–43, an addition probably originating with the P source. The name also recurs in 1 Chr 1:51b–54, an addition which represents a shortened version of Gen 36:40–43. Although some of the names cannot be classified with any certainty, Mibzar and Pinon are likely place names. See also PINON (PERSON). The original (?) place name of Mibzar was probably also used as an Edomite tribal name (and thereby worked its way into the OT genealogies of Edom as an eponymous ancestor). The place is attested in Greek *(Mazar/Mapsar/Mabsara)*, Latin *(Mabsar)*, Samaritan *(mābāṣer)*, and Syrian *(Mabẓer)* and could be identical with the settlement *(Mabsara/Mabsar)* which lay in the vicinity of Petra (*Onomast.* 134.20–21; Hieronymus 125.17–18). It is uncertain if the name is retained in the Arabic (Wadi) Ṣabra SW of Petra.

ULRICH HÜBNER

MICA (PERSON) [Heb *mîkāʾ*]. Var. MICAH. **1.** Also referred to as Micah *(mykh)*, the son of Mephibosheth and grandson of Jonathan (2 Sam 9:12). The name may be an abbreviation of the name *mykyh*, meaning "Who is like Yahweh?" (Brockington *Ezra, Nehemiah and Esther* Century Bible, 180). Born to Mephibosheth after David announced his intention to care for Jonathan's descendants, Mica presumably shared a place at the king's table with his father. He is said to have had four sons, one of whom seems to have been the father of a line which remained influential down to the time of the Exile (1 Chr 8:34–35; 9:40–41; cf. Myers *1 Chronicles* AB, 62). This seems to be in contradiction to 1 Chr 10:6, which states that Saul and his entire house perished at the hands of the Philistines. This apparent contradiction may be due to carelessness (Curtis and Madsen *Chronicles* ICC, 181), or it may be due to the use of archival material that has not been thoroughly integrated into the account (Myers *1 Chronicles* AB, 80; cf. Braun *1 Chronicles* WBC, 149–50). In any event, the Chronicler stresses not so much the extinction of the royal line as the influence of Saul's house as agents of divine rule (Coggins *Chronicles* CBC, 64; Braun *1 Chronicles* WBC, 149–50). Furthermore, scholars are widely agreed that chapter 10 is where the writer's real work begins (Myers *1 Chronicles* AB, 78–80).

2. A descendant of Asaph, the son of Zichri, a Levite and the father of Mattaniah, one of those who lived in postexilic Jerusalem (1 Chr 9:15). His name appears twice in parallels found in Nehemiah 11. In the first of these occurrences, he is again described as the father of Mattaniah (v 17), but in the second it is also noted that he was an ancestor of Uzzi, an overseer of the Levites in Jerusalem (v 22). In addition, the writer describes Mica as an ancestor of Zechariah, a trumpeter in the procession that celebrated the completion and dedication of the walls of Jerusalem (Neh 12:35).

3. A Levite and a signatory to the covenant established by Ezra (Neh 10:11).

FREDERICK W. SCHMIDT

MICAH (PERSON) [Heb *mîkâ; mîkāʾ*]. Var. MICA. The name of nine men in the Hebrew Bible. Micah is a shortened form of such names as Micaiah, "who is like YH(WH)," and Michael, "who is like God," which express the notion of God's incomparability (Labuschagne 1966). The longer form of the name is very common in extrabiblical sources (Avigad 1986: 70–73; Shiloh 1986: 29; Tigay 1986: 56–57). The short form *mîkâ* is found once on a preexilic bulla (Avigad 1986: 41).

1. A resident of the hill country of Ephraim who set up a local shrine, according to Judges 17–18. His name varies between Micah *(mîkâ)* and Micayhu *(mîkāyhû)*; such variation between the long and short forms of a single name is well attested (*TPNAH*, 150–53), though here it is possible that the variation in names reflects two sources that have been spliced together (Zevit 1983: 12). This Micah returns to his mother 1100 shekels of silver that he had stolen which his mother had sworn to make into a molten image; she uses 200 of them for that purpose (Judg 17:1–5). Originally, one of Micah's sons served as a priest at the shrine set up for the image; he is later replaced by an itinerant Judean Levite (17:7–13), a descendant of Moses (18:30), who is eventually kidnapped along with the cult statue by the Danites (Judges 18). The story is intended to be an illustration of the principle, "In those days there was no king in Israel; each person did as he or she pleased" (Judg 17:6; cf. 18:1). It is a strong polemic against Northern worship, and fits the anti-Northern pro-Davidic ideology of the editor of Judges (Brettler 1989: 418–20). Due to the story's strong ideological interest, it is impossible to use it for reconstructing the period of Judges. It is possible that the name Micah was chosen for ironic purposes; the person whose name glorifies God, by suggesting His incomparability, is a thief who helped establish illegitimate worship of God.

2. Great-grandson of Saul. In 2 Sam 9:12, his name is spelled *mîkāʾ*, and his father is listed as Mephibosheth; in 1 Chr 8:34, 35, and 9:40, 41, his name is spelled *mîkâ*, and his father is Merib-baal (see *TPNAH*, 59). The genealogy found in Chronicles was preserved because of a continued belief in the legitimacy of the line of Saul. The short notice in 1 Sam 9:12, that "Mephibosheth had a young child and his name was Micah," is given for similar reasons: Mephiboshet would later be killed (2 Sam 21:8), and the line of Saul would continue through Micah. See also MICA.

3. Son of Imlah, an Israelite prophet during the time of Ahab and Jehoshaphat according to 1 Kings 22 (= 2 Chronicles 18). In both Kings and Chronicles, his name always appears as Micayhu (*mîkāyhû;* RSV Micaiah), with the exception of 2 Chr 18:14, where he is called Micah. Variations between the long and short forms of a single name are well attested in biblical literature (*TPNAH*, 150–53).

4. The father of one of the members of the delegation sent by King Josiah to the prophetess Huldah. In 2 Kgs 22:12, the member is called Achbor son of Micaiah, while in 2 Chr 34:20 he is called Abdon son of Micah. It is possible that the family of this Micah had an important role in the Judean court (Cogan and Tadmor *2 Kings* AB, 282–83).

5. A prophet; see MICAH, BOOK OF.

6. A descendant of Reuben according to the genealogy in 1 Chr 5:5. This genealogy lists the descendants of Joel, whose exact relationship to Reuben is not known. According to 5:6, Micah's great-grandson Beerah was exiled to Assyria by Tiglath-pileser III in the second half of the 8th century B.C.E. However, "son" in these genealogies often indicates a linear descendant rather than a "son" of the next generation, so it is difficult to date when this Micah lived. The presence of the potentially problematic name Baal within this genealogy (1 Chr 5:5) probably attests to its antiquity (Williamson *1 and 2 Chronicles* NCBC, 85).

7. A Levite, father of one of the residents of Jerusalem, according to 1 Chr 9:15 and Neh 11:17. In 1 Chr 9:15, his name is spelled *mîkāʾ* (with final *ʾalep*), and in Neh 11:17 it is spelled *mîkâ* (with final *hê*). The development of the list in Nehemiah and the relationship between the similar lists in Nehemiah 11 and 1 Chronicles 9 are complex issues (Williamson *Ezra, Nehemiah* WBC, 344–50); however, the nonintegration of the temple functionaries into the Levites suggests a date for the section incorporating Micah of after the return to Zion and before the Chronicler (Williamson *Ezra, Nehemiah* WBC, 347; Blenkinsopp *Ezra-Nehemiah* OTL, 326). Neh 11:22 names Uzi, a great-great-grandson of Micah (spelled *mîkāʾ*); this section is within an appendix which postdates the earlier part of the chapter (Williamson, 349; Blenkinsopp, 326).

8. A Levite, eldest son of Uziel. This Micah *(mîkâ)* is mentioned in 1 Chr 23:20, in the list of Levites whom David organized; and in 1 Chr 24:24 and 25, a chapter introduced by a reviser of Chronicles (Williamson, 163), as being among the Levites who are not part of the twenty-four watches. Since Micah, living in the period of David, is listed as the "son" of Uziel, Levi's grandson, "son" is being used to indicate a linear descendant. The lack of father-son relationship is further indicated by Exod 6:22, where Micah is not mentioned among Uziel's children. This process of telescoping—skipping several intermediate generations within linear genealogies—is common in genealogical thinking (Wilson 1977: 197).

9. One of the signatories of the compact *(ʾămānâ)* in the postexilic period according to Neh 10:12 (—Eng 10:11), where his name is spelled *mîkāʾ*. The authenticity of this list has been debated (Williamson, 325–29), and it probably is not a list of actual signatories, but a schematic list of people who are known as important from other lists (Williamson, 330). In this case, this Micah might be identified with the Micah known from Neh 11:17 and 22 (= Micah 7). This might be supported by the appearance of the name Hashabiah as a signatory alongside of Micah, since Hashabiah's name appears in Neh 11:22 as Micah's grandfather.

Bibliography

Avigad, N. 1986. *Hebrew Bullae from the Time of Jeremiah.* Jerusalem.
Brettler, M. 1989. The Book of Judges: Literature as Politics. *JBL* 108: 405–28.
Labuschagne, C. J. 1966. *The Incomparability of Yahweh in the Old Testament.* Leiden.
Shiloh, Y. 1986. A Group of Hebrew Bullae from the City of David. *IEJ* 36: 16–38.
Tigay, J. H. 1986. *You Shall Have No Other Gods.* HSS 31. Atlanta, GA.
Wilson, R. R. 1977. *Genealogy and History in the Biblical World.* YNER 7. New Haven.
Zevit, Z. 1983. A Chapter in the History of Israelite Personal Names. *BASOR* 250: 1–16.

MARC Z. BRETTLER

MICAH, BOOK OF.

"Micah of Moresheth prophesied in the days of Hezekiah." These words of Jeremiah (26:18), confirmed by elements in the book of Micah itself, contain practically all that we know of the life of the prophet Micah. Moresheth (probably the same as Moresheth-Gath of 1:14) was a small town in SW Judah, not yet positively identified by archaeologists. Micah was active in Judah from before the fall of Samaria (1:2–7) in 722 B.C.E.; he lived under Ahaz (735–715) and Hezekiah (715–687) and was thus a contemporary of Isaiah, and he experienced (apparently) the devastation brought on by Sennacherib's invasion of Judah in 701 B.C.E. The heading of the book (1:1) adds the name of King Jotham (742–735) in dating the prophet's ministry, but nothing in the book confirms so early an appearance.

Micah is grouped with other relatively brief prophetic books in the collection called the Twelve or the Minor Prophets. Among this group, Micah is sixth in the Hebrew canon and third in the Greek ordering (after Hosea and Amos). Both of these orderings were apparently intended to place Micah with contemporary books.

A. The Contents and Outline of Micah
B. Modern Critical Study of Micah
  1. Literary Criticism of Micah
  2. Jeremiah 26 and Micah
  3. Micah 4 and Isaiah 2
  4. Redaction Criticism of Micah
  5. The Search for a Setting
C. The Text of Micah

A. The Contents and Outline of Micah

Like some other prophetic books, Micah is made up of short poems. Whether a given poem is clear and pungent, or obscure and puzzling, it tends to be self-contained. It does not necessarily follow from what goes before or lead into what comes after. There is little obvious architecture to the book. Some units seem to have been grouped together on a catchword principle (e.g., the repeated initial *ʾattâ* and *ʿattâ* in chaps. 4 and 5)—a most superficial organizing principle! Students may find profit in investigating works which discern a more evident plan in Micah (Renaud 1964; Willis 1969), but the following paragraphs are deliberately confined to a restatement of the content of the individual poems in sequence.

The Heading (1:1). In a form typical of prophetic books, an anonymous editor has supplied the name of the prophet, information about his time of activity, and an identification of his speech as the "word of Yahweh." It is noteworthy that "Samaria and Jerusalem" are given prominence as the foci of the prophet's attention, and that the editor knew at least a little about Micah independent of the words of the prophet, since the reference to Moresheth could not have been deduced from the book.

Punishment for Samaria (1:2–7). Drawing on ancient traditions for depicting a theophany, a striking self-manifestation of the deity (Jeremias 1965), the prophet depicts the impending coming of Yahweh to punish the idolatrous city. This is most likely an early (pre-722) poem, lightly contemporized at a later time by the addition of a reference to Judah and Jerusalem (1:5).

A Transitional Lament (1:8–9) depicting the prophet's own

excessive grief at the calamity and leading to a new subject: the doom to come on Judah and Jerusalem.

A Taunt or Lament over Judah (1:10–16)—of extraordinary obscurity—describes the destruction of the lesser towns of Judah, either as already suffered or as to come, evidently in the invasion of Judah by Sennacherib (701 B.C.E.). In most cases the lines of the poem are constructed on the principle that the name of the town is predictive, through punning, of its fate. The puns cannot, of course, be reproduced in translation; the effect is as though one said: "Ashdod shall be ashes."

Two Successive Doom-Speeches (2:1–5; 6–11) introduce themes characteristic of the prophet Micah as a champion of the oppressed small landholder. These speeches warn of the impending elimination of those who accumulate land from the sacred community, and illustrate the persistence of the prophet in the face of opposition from the land-grabbers.

The Divine Shepherd-King is pictured in 2:12–13 as gathering and leading a dispersed people ("Jacob"). Though all agree that this hopeful passage is not connected to its immediate context, it is difficult to assign it to a specific date or occasion, whether in the time of Micah or later. A venerable exegetical tour de force would take this optimistic fragment to be a word of the false prophets who were Micah's opponents; and other lines in the book that are at odds with the generally gloomy context are read in the same way (see, e.g., van der Woude, *Micah* POuT).

The general condemnatory tone of Micah 2 is resumed and sharpened in the three sections that follow, which focus on the corrupt leaders of Judah.

A Speech Against the Courts (3:1–4) depicts the judges of the people as cannibals, devouring every last scrap of their victims.

A Speech Against the Prophets (3:5–8) depicts them as both pettily venal and blind, in contrast to the real prophet, Micah, who is power-filled and implacable.

A Climactic Speech About Zion (3:9–12) resumes the indictment of judges and prophets, adds a line against the priests, and culminates in the famous saying, "Zion shall be plowed as a field," remembered in Judah a century after Micah's time (Jer 26:18).

The Coming Kingdom of God (4:1–5), centered at the sacred mountain, Zion, is the theme of a poem that the book of Micah shares with Isaiah (2:2–4). With its themes of universal justice, peace, and security, it may be thought of as beginning a new, more hopeful section of the book, but it also continues earlier themes by means of sharp contrast.

The remainder of the chapter is made up of brief, sometimes enigmatic poems on aspects of a glorious future:

The Kingdom of the Gathered Exiles (4:6–7).

Zion's Rule Restored (4:8).

Deliverance from Distress in Babylon (4:9–10).

The Threshing of the Enemies (4:11–13).

The Humiliation of the King (4:14). This seems to be a mere fragment, but it serves to introduce the theme of the royal Messiah, which is expanded in the following poem.

The Return of the Great Ruler from Bethlehem (5:1–4) is foretold in one of the book's most famous and influential passages, especially among Christian interpreters (cf. Matt 2:6; John 7:40–43). He is to reunite the people and bring peace.

Aspects of this promised peace are depicted in the next three oracles:

Assyria Eliminated (5:4–5).

The Irresistible Might of Jacob (5:6–8).

The Purified Nation (5:9–14). Alien elements that offend Yahweh—chariots, cities, divination, idols—will be removed, and the people's triumph over their enemies will follow.

A Covenant Lawsuit (6:1–8) follows, that is, a poem that represents God as indicting his people for breach of covenant. This suit is presented before the primordial witnesses to the agreement, the mountains, and includes a recital of the "saving acts of Yahweh," his actions in their early history. The extravagant offer of heightened sacrificial performance by the people is countered by a demand that they do justice, love kindness, and walk humbly with their God.

The two succeeding poems reintroduce the note of sharp social protest characteristic of earlier portions of Micah.

The City as a Cheat (6:9–16) announces appropriate curses on an unnamed city (Jerusalem? Samaria?) for its dishonest practices in trade.

A Disintegrated Society (7:17) gives a grim picture of where dishonesty and rapacity have gone so far that one cannot trust the most intimate of human relations: friend, lover, wife, father, child, master.

A Prophetic Liturgy (7:8–20) has been known by this designation since the influential study of H. Gunkel (1924). It is a "liturgy" because there is an alternation of speakers, a combination of themes, and a progression in mood. After the suffering people profess their continued confidence in God, a prophet announces that a great time is coming when the land will be enlarged and the people reunited. After a prayer by the people that God would "shepherd" them as in days of old, the liturgy closes with a pious acknowledgment of the greatness of God, manifested chiefly in his mercy and kindness.

B. Modern Critical Study of Micah

1. Literary Criticism of Micah. Like other prophetic books, Micah has been subjected to "literary criticism," that is, scholarly scrutiny concerned with the authorship and date of its various components. Ewald (1867) and especially Stade (1881; 1883; 1884; 1903) distinguished genuine from inauthentic and late elements in the book, using arguments that have seemed persuasive to most, and have remained decisive for much subsequent study.

Only chaps. 1–3 are the genuine words of Micah, and from these 2:12–13 must be subtracted as intrusive in its context. The hopeful material of the rest of the book contradicts chaps. 1–3 and must be discounted, especially in view of Jer 26:18, which knows Micah only as a prophet of doom. Some of the material, such as the liturgy of chap. 7, presupposes a different historical situation than that of the 8th-century prophet Micah. (Given the restricted compass of Micah, or the individual poems in the book, the study of vocabulary and style has had little place in these literary-critical arguments.)

2. Jeremiah 26 and Micah. The citation of Micah by the

elders of Judah, in Jeremiah's defense (Jer 26:18), is practically unique in OT literature and is rightly scrutinized for what it may tell of the nature of Micah's message and its effect. The context of Jeremiah 26, however, shows that the citation seems to be from a narrative, otherwise unknown to us, of a confrontation between Micah and King Hezekiah, and that in that context Micah's words about the destruction of Jerusalem were taken as a conditional prophecy, averted by the king's repentance. In literary criticism of Micah, then, it is illegitimate to use the Jeremiah passage to limit Micah's message to unrelieved doom.

3. Micah 4 and Isaiah 2. Micah 4:1–4 is the same as Isaiah 2:2–4, the only substantial difference being the addition in Micah of the line beginning: "But they shall sit every man under his vine." Every possible explanation for this circumstance has been defended by scholars at some time (see Wildberger 1972: 74–90), including arguments that the passage is really by Isaiah, or by Micah, or by neither. It seems unlikely that even further study and argument will produce a consensus. On the other hand, as a foil to Micah's bleak picture of the present, corrupt Zion (chap. 3), this picture of a purified, exalted holy city is not fundamentally out of harmony with the other elements in the book of Micah.

4. Redaction Criticism of Micah. Early literary criticism of Micah resulted in the identification of a small core of authentic material, and thereby raised the question of the origin and purpose of the rest of the material in the book, the "inauthentic" material being more abundant than the authentic. More recent 20th-century criticism has sought to restore a kind of unity to the book of Micah by picturing it as the result of a process of growth over time: the original core of the book was expanded in processes of comment or exegesis, and worship, as it was fitted for liturgical use by a community which both cherished and changed the original prophetic message. Examples of this kind of treatment of Micah may be studied in the works of Mays (*Micah* OTL), Willi-Plein (1971), van der Woude (*Micah* POuT), Renaud (1977), and Wolff (*Micah* BKAT). The sheer number of scholars who have attempted this kind of interpretation demonstrates its appeal, but the very pronounced lack of agreement among them shows how speculative it is.

5. The Search for a Setting. A different sort of attempt to rescue Micah from fragmentation and incoherence is presented in the commentary by Hillers (*Micah* Hermeneia). It proceeds from a comparison of the prophet's situation, and his reaction to it, to a recurring phenomenon in the history of religions: movements of revitalization, or "millennial" movements. Commonly, such movements arise when a people are deprived economically, and experience defection by those in temporal and spiritual authority. It is possible to see such factors present in Micah's Judah, following on the political and economic disruption caused by the fall of Samaria and the Assyrian pressure. Evidence of this is found both in extrabiblical records and in the book itself. Reactions to these depressing conditions, attested in the book of Micah and paralleled in movements of revitalization, include (aside from outbursts of protest) nativism, that is, a cutting off of foreign elements (5:10–15); belief in a "time of troubles" preceding a future reversal (5:3); belief in an impending reversal of social classes and the triumph of the pariahs (4:6–7); belief in a coming righteous ruler (5:1–6); and prediction of a new age (chaps, 4, 5). This hypothesis permits one to see many of the disparate elements in Micah as united by the common psychological or social situation from which they arise. Here and there, later ages have made changes or insertions (e.g., in the "Babylon" of 4:10), but more of the book may be thought to have originated in the 8th century than is commonly believed.

C. The Text of Micah

The Hebrew text of Micah is badly preserved, among the worst in the Bible in this respect. Although many passages present no textual difficulties or only trifling problems, others are badly, perhaps hopelessly, corrupt, a notorious case being the punning poem on Judean towns (1:10–16). Students of the book are compelled to turn for help to the ancient translations, such as the Greek (LXX) and Syriac, or to resort to conjecture to arrive at a text that makes sense.

New resources for reconstructing the text of Micah include several Hebrew manuscripts from among the "Dead Sea Scrolls." 1QpMi (IQ14) is a fragment of a commentary on Micah (Milik 1952; DJD 1: 77–80; cf. Horgan 1979; Carmignac 1962), and 4QpMi (4Q168) is an even shorter commentary or text of Micah (DJD 5: 36). Mur 88 (DJD 2: 181–205) is a long roll containing most of the Minor Prophets, but the text is so close to the traditional MT that it is of little if any use in correcting its deficiencies.

A notable addition to resources for reconstructing the history of the Greek version of the Minor Prophets is a text from the 1st century C.E. published by Barthelemy (1953; 1963). Evidence from this new source can now be used to supplement the LXX edition of Ziegler (1967).

Bibliography

Alt, A. 1955. Micha 2, 1–5 *Ges anadasmos* in Juda. *NTT* 56: 13–23.

Barthelemy, D. 1953. Redécouverte d'un chainon manquant de l'histoire de la Septante. *RB* 60: 18–29.

———. 1963. *Les devanciers d'Aquila.* VTSup 10. Leiden.

Carmignac, J. 1962. Notes sur les Pesharim. *RevQ* 3: 505–38.

Elliger, K. 1934. Die Heimat des Propheten Micha. *ZDPV* 57: 81–152.

Ewald, H. 1867. *Die Propheten des Alten Bundes.* 2d ed. Göttingen.

Gunkel, H. 1924. Der Micha-Schluss. *Zeitschrift für Semitistik* 2: 145–78.

Horgan, M. 1979. *Pesharim: Qumran Interpretations of Biblical Books.* CBQMS 8. Washington, DC.

Jeremias, J. 1965. *Theophanie: Die Geschichte einer alttestamentlichen Gattung.* WMANT 10. Neukirchen-Vluyn.

Lindblom, J. 1929. *Micha literarisch untersucht.* Acta Academiae Aboensis, Humaniora 6.2. Helsingør.

Milik, J. 1952. Fragments d'un Midrash de Michée dans les manuscripts de Qumran. *RB* 59: 412–18.

Renaud, B. 1964. *Structure et attaches littéraires de Michée IV–V.* CahRB 2. Paris.

Renaud, B. 1977. *La formation du livre de Michée.* EBib. Paris.

Ryssel, V. 1887. *Untersuchungen über die Textgestalt und die Echtheit des Buches Micha.* Leipzig.

Stade, B. 1881. Bemerkungen über das Buch Micha. *ZAW* 1: 161–72.

———. 1883. Weitere Bemerkungen zu Micha 4.5. *ZAW* 3: 1–16.
———. 1884. Bemerkungen zu vorstehendem Aufsatze. *ZAW* 4: 291–97.
———. 1903. Streiflichter auf die Entstehung der jetzigen Gestalt der alttestamentlichen Prophetenschriften. *ZAW* 23: 153–71.
Wellhausen, J. 1892. *Die zwölf kleinen Propheten übersetzt, mit Noten.* Berlin.
Wildberger, H. 1972. *Jesaja.* BKAT. Neukirchen-Vluyn.
Willi-Plein, I. 1971. *Vorformen der Schriftexegese innerhalb des Alten Testaments.* BZAW 123. Berlin.
Willis, J. 1969. The Structure of the Book of Micah. *SEÅ* 34: 5–42.
Ziegler, J. 1967. *Duodecim Prophetae.* Septuaginta: Vetus Testamentum auctoritate Academiae Litterarum Gottingensis editum 13. 2d ed. Göttingen.
Ziegler, J. 1943. Beiträge zum griechischen Dodekapropheton. *NAWG,* 345–412.

DELBERT R. HILLERS

MICAIAH (PERSON) [Heb *mîkāyāh; mikayhû*]. **1.** Mother of Abijah, king of Judah (2 Chr 13:2). Micaiah's name appears solely in the Chronicler's regnal formula for Abijah, where she is identified as the "daughter of Uriel of Gibeah." Her name and parentage are problematic. In the parallel passage in 1 Kgs 15:2, the king's mother is "Maacah, daughter of Abishalom." Furthermore, in 2 Chr 11:20 (a list of Rehoboam's wives and offspring) she is referred to as "Maacah, the daughter of Absalom." Thus, while 2 Chr 11:2 refers to her as "Micaiah, daughter of Uriel," both 1 Kgs 15:2 and 2 Chr 11:20 identify Abijah's mother as "Maacah daughter of Abishalom/Absalom." For a complete discussion of this problem, see MAACAH (PERSON); see also QUEEN.

2. Prince during the reign of Jehoshaphat (2 Chr 17:7). Micaiah is the fifth and last prince mentioned in a list of princes, Levites, and priests sent by Jehoshaphat on a teaching mission throughout Judah (17:7–9). This incident is unique to the Chronicler's treatment of Jehoshaphat and is sometimes viewed as a doublet of 2 Chr 19:4–11.

3. Son of Imlah, and the Israelite prophet who appears in the narrative describing oracular inquiries made by the kings of Israel and Judah (1 Kgs 22:4–28 = 2 Chr 18:3–27). Ahab suggests an alliance with Jehoshaphat aimed at recapturing Ramoth-gilead from the Syrians (1 Kgs 22:3–4). Jehoshaphat agrees but insists Ahab first seek oracular guidance from the prophets of the Lord (v 5). Gathering about 400 prophets. Ahab inquires whether or not to engage the Syrians in battle (v 6). Their advice is unanimous—the Lord will deliver Syria into their hands. Jehoshaphat, however, asks if there are any other prophets Ahab can consult (v 7). Ahab admits there is one prophet left—Micaiah—but grudgingly insists Micaiah never prophecies anything good where Ahab is concerned (v 8). At Jehoshaphat's insistence, Ahab sends for Micaiah (v 9). While Micaiah is being summoned, Zedekiah, son of Chenaanah, appears before the kings. By symbolic action and oracle, Zedekiah predicts Syria's defeat (vv 11–12). When Micaiah is brought before Ahab and Jehoshaphat, he initially agrees with Zedekiah. When pressed, however, Micaiah relates visions which predict the death of Ahab (v 17) and explain why the other prophets promise victory. He says that Yahweh, seeking to entice Ahab into battling the Syrians, sent a lying spirit to the prophets (vv 19–23). Upon revealing this vision, Micaiah is struck by Zedekiah (v 24) and imprisoned by Ahab (vv 26–28).

Questions have been raised concerning the historical scenario presented in 1 Kings 22. See AHAB. De Vries (*1 Kings* WBC, 265–66) separates the story into two narratives, one reflecting the conditions found in the reigns of Joram and Ahaziah (Narrative A) and the other dating 100 years later in the reign of Hezekiah (Narrative B). Miller suggests that the account originally consisted of a battle report reflecting the reign of Jehoahaz. Later, it was expanded to include the prophets and was associated with Ahab and Jehoshaphat (*HAIJ,* 253; 299–302). Both scholars assume extensive literary activity behind 1 Kings 22, which makes the chapter difficult to use for historical reconstruction.

4. A Levite (Neh 11:17, 22; 12:35). His father's name is problematic, being either Zabdi (Neh 11:17) or Zaccur (12:35). Micaiah's name occurs solely in the genealogies of his descendants, where he is identified as (1) the father of Mattaniah, a Levite living in Jerusalem (11:27); (2) the great-great-grandfather of Uzzi, overseer of the Levites in Jerusalem (11:22); and (3) the great-great-grandfather of Zachariah, a trumpeter (12:35).

5. Priest during the time of Nehemiah (Neh 12:41). Micaiah's name appears fourth in a list of seven priests with trumpets. They formed part of the crowd that, along with Nehemiah, was present at the rededication of Jerusalem's walls.

Bibliography

De Vries, S. J. 1978. *Prophet against Prophet.* Grand Rapids.
Miller, J. M. 1966. The Elisha Cycle and the Accounts of the Omride Wars. *JBL* 85: 276–88.

LINDA S. SHEARING

6. The father of Achbor (2 Kgs 22:12) and probably the grandfather of Elnathan ben Achbor. Achbor was one of the men sent by Josiah (ca. 621 B.C.E.) to consult Huldah, the prophetess, about the newly discovered book of the law. The Chronicler's parallel account mentions "Abdon the son of Micah" instead of "Achbor the son of Micaiah" (2 Chr 34:20). See ACHBOR. Elnathan ben Achbor was the royal official sent by Jehoiakim (ca. 609 B.C.E.) to extradite Uriah, the prophet, from Egypt (Jer 26:22). See ELNATHAN. This Micaiah would have been at least 50 years of age at the time his son Achbor was sent to Huldah, and at least in his late 60s when (his grandson?) Elnathan was sent to Egypt. Thus, there is some question about whether this Micaiah (Heb *mîkayāh*), whose father is not named, is the same as Micaiah (Heb *mikayhû*), the son of Gemariah, who was politically active as late as 605 B.C.E. (see #7 below).

7. The son of Gemariah and grandson of Shaphan, and a (older?) contemporary of the prophet Jeremiah (Jer 36:11–13). It was this Micaiah (Heb *mikayhû*) who in 605 B.C.E. first reported to the Judean princes the words that Baruch read from Jeremiah's scroll.

Can this Micaiah be equated with the father of Achbor (see #6 above)? The difference in the spelling of the names can be explained simply as an alternate usage of long and short forms of the theophoric element Heb *-yāh* or *-yahû*. Some scholars suggest that the narratives mentioning the two Micaiahs (2 Kgs 22:3–23:24 and Jeremiah 36) are related and must be read as a unit (Carroll, *Jeremiah* OTL, 663; Thompson, *Jeremiah* NICOT, 628). Assuming that 2 Kings was available to the writer of Jeremiah 36, the name "Achbor" provides a literary link which helps to contrast the responses of the two kings when presented with a scroll (Isbell 1978; Nicholson 1970: 43). Similarly, Jeremiah 26 and 36 share key words and are also sequentially linked, like a short story (see Kessler 1966; Lohfink 1978).

When considered together, however, these three texts present problematic genealogical data. In 2 Kings 22 and its parallel in 1 Chronicles 34 (set in 621 B.C.E.), Shaphan the secretary and Ahikam ben Shaphan are listed as contemporaries of Micaiah's son Achbor. In Jeremiah 26 and 36 (set 13 and 17 years later, respectively), the contemporaries of Achbor's son Elnathan are listed as the familiar Ahikam ben Shaphan and also Micaiah ben Gemariah ben Shaphan and Gemariah ben Shaphan. If this Micaiah ben Gemariah is the same as the father of Achbor (see #6 above), then four generations of Micaiah's family could simultaneously have been politically involved when Jeremiah's scroll was read and later presented to King Jehoiakim: his grandson Elnathan, his son Achbor (not mentioned as being present in Jeremiah 36), Micaiah himself, and his father Gemariah. The absence of Achbor and the listing of Elnathan before his supposed great-grandfather in Jer 36:11 and 25 represent political and genealogical problems which are compounded even more if this Elnathan is identified as the father-in-law of Jehoiachim (2 Kgs 24:8). See ELNATHAN. This Elnathan would have been at least in his late 40s when Jeremiah's scroll was read, Micaiah would have been in his late 80s, and Gemariah would have been politically active at over 100 years of age. Overall, these genealogical data support the conclusion that Micaiah, the son of Gemariah, and Micaiah, the father of Achbor, were two distinct individuals.

Bibliography

Isbell, C. D 1978. 2 Kings 22:3–23:24 and Jeremiah 36: A Stylistic Comparison. *JSOT* 8: 33–45.

Kessler, M. 1966. Form-Critical Suggestions on Jeremiah 36. *CBQ* 28: 389–401.

Lohfink, N. 1978. Die Gattung der "Historischen Kurzgeschichte" in den letzten Jahren von Juda und in der Zeit des Babylonischen Exils. *ZAW* 90: 319–47.

Nicholson, E. W. 1970. *Preaching to the Exiles*. Oxford.

MARK J. FRETZ

MICHAEL (ANGEL) [Heb *mîkāʾēl*]. In the elaborate angelology that emerged in Judaism during the Hellenistic period, Michael is a prince (*śar;* Dan 10:13, 21) or archangel (*archangelos;* Jude 9; *1 En.* 20:1–7; 71:3; *2 En.* 22:6 [A]; *4 Bar.* 9:5). His name means "Who is like God?" He frequently plays a role in late Jewish and Christian literature, but is mentioned in Scripture only in Dan 10:13, 21; 12:1; Jude 9; and Rev 12:7 (cf. 1 Thess 4:16).

Michael, along with Raphael, Gabriel, and Phanuel, is one of the four archangels present before the throne of God (*1 En.* 9:1; 40; 54:6; 71:8–9, 13; cf. *1 En.* 87:2; 88:1; 1QM 9:14–15) and of a larger group of archangels numbering seven (*1 En.* 20:1–7; Tob 12:15; cf. *1 En.* 81:5; 90:21–22; Rev 8:2). He is often represented as the leader of the archangels (*Ascen. Isa.* 3:16).

In his capacity as archangel, Michael has several roles. He is first of all the patron angel of Israel (Dan 10:23; 12:1; *1 En.* 20:5; 1QM 17:6–8; cf. *T. Mos.* 10:2). In this capacity he fights for Israel against the rival angels of the Persians (Dan 10:13–14, 20–21) and will deliver Israel from the tribulation of its enemies in the last days (Dan 12:1; cf. Rev 12:7–9; *T. Levi* 5:5–6). He is the champion of Israel against the forces of Edom (i.e., Rome; *Exod. Rab.* 18:5), and his name is emblazoned on one of the four towers used in the holy war against the Kittim (i.e., Romans; 1QM 9:14–15). In this bellicose capacity, Michael is called an archistratig or chief captain (*2 En.* 22:6 [J]; 33:10).

Michael is also an intercessor for Israel before God (Tob 12:15; cf. *T. Dan* 6:2; *T. Levi* 5:5–6) as well as for the entire world (*1 Enoch* 9; *Ascen. Isa.* 9:23 [Latin]). In relation to this role, he is described as merciful (*1 En.* 20:5; 40:9; 68; cf. 71:3) and righteous (*4 Bar.* 9:5; cf. *1 En.* 71:3), and as opening the gates of heaven for the righteous (*4 Bar.* 9:5). He is the guardian of the soul of Abraham (*T. Abr.* 19:4) and contended with Satan for the body of Moses (Jude 9). This latter story is probably derived from the lost ending of the *T. Mos.* (so Origen *princ.* 3.2.1) and dealt with Satan's claim that Moses did not deserve an honorable burial because he had murdered the Egyptian (Exod 2:12). In tradition, Michael does bury Moses (*Tg. Ps.-J.* on Deut 34:6).

Keeping the heavenly books is also attributed to Michael. The reference in Dan 12:1 to Michael defending those of Israel whose names are found "written in a book" led to the notion that Michael himself was the recording angel (cf. *Ascen. Isa.* 9:19–23 [Latin]). He was the intermediary between God and Moses when the Law was delivered to Moses (Gk *Apoc. Mos.* 1; cf. *Jub.* 1:27–2:1; Acts 7:38, 53) and puts the Law in the hearts of believers (*Herm. Sim.* 8.3.3). He is also the guardian of the secrets by which heaven and earth are established (cf. *1 En.* 60:11–25).

Michael is the leader of the angels that cause Satan to fall from heaven (Rev 12:7–9), and he will be one of the four archangels who bind the armies of Satan and throw them into the furnace (*1 En.* 54:6). He may be the archangel that announces the Parousia (1 Thess 4:16).

Bibliography

Berger, K. 1973. Der Streit des guten und des bösen Engels um die Seele. Beobachtungen zu 4QAmrb und Judas 9. *JSJ* 4: 1–18.

Bishop, E. F. F. 1964. Angelology in Judaism, Islam, and Christianity. *ATR* 46: 142–54.

Horodetzky, S. A. 1928. Michael und Gabriel. *MGWJ* 73: 499–506.

Lueken, W. 1898. *Der Erzengel Michael*. Göttingen.

DUANE F. WATSON

MICHAEL (PERSON) [Heb *mîkāʾēl*]. "Michael" appears to be a popular Judean name in the Persian period. The name possibly originated during the Exile in Babylon (see #1 and 10 below), and the Chronicler drew upon it to complete artificial genealogies, particularly those related to the tribe of Issachar (see #5 and 8 below). Interestingly, the name became less prominent once it was associated with a heavenly being in the Hellenistic period (see MICHAEL [ANGEL]) and only returned to prominence after the rise of Christianity.

1. The father of Sethur, the Asherite representative sent by Moses into Canaan to spy out the land (Num 13:13). This Michael appears in a list (Num 13:4–15) commonly ascribed to the Priestly writer. The historical provenance of the list is difficult to discern, as it contains both early and late onomastic evidence. Michael, however, seems to represent a later strand of onomastic development within the list, as the name arises in conjunction with other names with the theophoric *ʾēl* (see Gray *Numbers* ICC, 135–36). Michael may then represent a name generated from the Priestly writer's own era that was used to supplement an earlier list.

2. According to the Chronicler, a member of the Transjordanian tribe of Gad during the reigns of Jotham and Jeroboam II (1 Chr 5:13). The nature of the list in which Michael appears remains unclear. While some data indicate that the Chronicler used a nonbiblical source in 1 Chr 5:11–17 (see Williamson *1 and 2 Chronicles* NCBC, 64–65), the presence of the Chronicler's style and of the name "Meshullam," a prominent postexilic name, suggests that the Chronicler composed the genealogy artificially or at least supplemented an earlier list with names from his own era.

3. A Gadite, the son of Jeshishai and the father of Gilead (1 Chr 5:14). Michael here appears as a forefather of the Gadite of the same name mentioned in 1 Chr 5:13. Textual problems in 1 Chr 5:14–15 complicate further the obscure origin of the section (see also #2 above).

4. According to the Chronicler, the great-grandfather of Asaph, the levitical singer (1 Chr 6:25—Eng 6:40). The only context in which Michael appears within a levitical genealogy is in 1 Chronicles 6, a fact made conspicuous by his absence in the related levitical genealogy of 1 Chr 6:1–15—Eng 6:16–30). Curtis and Madsen (*Chronicles* ICC, 134–36) have plausibly conjectured that the Chronicler expanded the genealogy of 1 Chr 6:1–15—Eng 6:16–30 with common names from his era, such as Michael, in order to make Asaph contemporaneous with David. The Chronicler thereby harmonized his genealogical records with his historical narrative.

5. According to the Chronicler, a military leader, the son of Izrahiah, from the tribe of Issachar during the reign of David (1 Chr 7:3). The dependence of 1 Chr 7:1 upon Numbers 26 and Judg 10:1 (see Curtis and Madsen *Chronicles* ICC, 144–45), its style, and the lateness of the names of Michael's immediate kin suggest that the Chronicler has artificially constructed this genealogy from common names from his own era. Rudolph (*Chronikbücher* HAT, 64) plausibly conjectured that "sons of Izrahiah" (v 3a) may have appeared in the text as a result of dittography. If so, the text originally portrayed Michael as one of the five sons of Uzzi, the brother of Izrahiah, rather than his son.

6. A Benjaminite inhabitant of Jerusalem, the son of Beriah (1 Chr 8:16). For further discussion, see JAKIM.

7. A military leader of the Mannassites who deserted to David at Ziklag (1 Chr 12:20). For further discussion, see JERIMOTH #4.

8. The father of Omri, the administrator of the tribe of Issachar during the reign of David (1 Chr 27:18). The inclusion of both the sons of Levi and the sons of Aaron in the twelve-tribe structure of Israel reveals the late, artificial nature of the list of the princes of Israel in 1 Chr 27:16–22. The Chronicler has utilized the name "Michael," already identified with the tribe of Issachar (see #5 above), to create anachronistically an administrative structure during the reign of David. It may even be possible that the Chronicler meant for the reader to equate "Michael, the son of Izrahiah" of 1 Chr 7:3 with "Michael, the father of Omri" of 1 Chr 27:18.

9. According to 2 Chronicles, a son of Jehoshaphat and a brother of Jehoram (2 Chr 21:2). 2 Chr 21:2–4 alone describes the misfortune of Michael, along with his brothers Azariah, Jehiel, Zechariah, and Shephatiah. Michael and his brothers receive wealth and their own fortified cities from their father (2 Chr 21:3a). Their fortune, however, is short-lived. Following Jehoshaphat's death, firstborn son and heir designate Jehoram purges his kingdom of all potential rivals to the throne, including Michael and his brothers. While some commentators believe that the Chronicler here preserves an authentic preexilic source (see Myers *2 Chronicles* AB, 120), the style, themes, and commonality of names in Chronicles and the postexilic period suggest that the Chronicler has created the passage for his narrative purpose. The Chronicler most likely anachronistically retrojected the postexilic name "Michael" into the time of the divided kingdom for this purpose.

10. A 5th-century B.C.E. Diaspora Judean in Babylon whose son, Zebadiah, led eighty kinsmen back to Judea from Babylon with Ezra (Ezra 8:8). However, the parallel account in 1 Esdr 8:34 identifies Michael as the father of Zeraiah, the leader of seventy men. Michael was from the family of Shephatiah, a family involved in the first repatriation of Judah under Zerubbabel (Ezra 2:4). For further discussion, see GERSHOM. The family does not appear again in the reforms of Ezra or Nehemiah.

JOHN W. WRIGHT

MICHAL (PERSON) [Heb *mîkal*]. The younger daughter of Saul, king of Israel (1 Sam 14:49), and the wife, first of David (1 Sam 18:27), then of Palti/Paltiel (1 Sam 25:44; 2 Sam 3:15–17), and then finally again of David (1 Sam 3:15–17). Michal is introduced in a genealogical note concerning Saul (1 Sam 14:49–52). Appearing fifth and last in a list of Saul's offspring (v 49), she is preceded by her three brothers (Jonathan, Ishvi, and Malchishua) and an older sister (Merab). In the narrative, Michal loves David, a fact which pleases her father Saul (1 Sam 18:20). Once again (cf. 1 Sam 18:17–19) Saul promises his daughter to David. For the bride-price of a hundred Philistine foreskins, David can become son-in-law to the king (vv 21–27). Although Saul explains the bride-price in terms of revenge against his enemies (v 25), the narrator imputes a more nefarious reason for Saul's request: by sending David against the Philistines, Saul hopes he will be killed (vv 21; 25). Saul's plan fails, however, and David returns with the foreskins to claim his promised wife, Michal (v 27). The narrative concludes with a David whom Saul fears and hates (v 29), but whom both Yahweh and Michal (or Israel, Gk) love (v 28).

Saul's hatred of David is the backdrop to 1 Sam 19:11–17. Knowing her father's plan to kill David, Michal warns him and helps him escape. She lowers David through the window (v 12), makes the bed look as if he is still in it (v 13), and twice lies to Saul—first saying David is sick (v 14) and then insisting that David threatened her into helping him (v 17). Nothing more is heard of Michal until the brief note in 1 Sam 25:44: following David's marriage to Abigail (v 42) and Ahinoam (v 43), the narrator notes that Saul gave Michal, "his daughter" and "David's wife," to Palti, son of Laish from Gallim.

Saul's reported actions in 1 Sam 25:44 are the source of David's request in 2 Sam 3:12–16. Approached by Abner concerning an alliance, David stipulates that Michal must be returned before negotiations can commence (vv 12–13). This request is formalized by a message to Ishbosheth, Saul's son, demanding her return (v 14). In a highly dramatic scene, Ishbosheth takes Michal from her new husband and returns her to David (vv 15–16).

The final narrative concerning Michal is found in 2 Sam 6:16–23, the entry of the Ark into Jerusalem. Looking out the window, Michal, "the daughter of Saul," sees David dancing before the incoming Ark and despises him (v 16). After criticizing David for his behavior, Michal herself is rebuked (vv 20–22). Following this harsh interchange, the narrator notes that Michal, "the daughter of Saul," remained childless until her death (v 23).

(The reference to Michal, wife of Adriel, and her five sons in 2 Sam 21:8 is probably a scribal error and should read "Merab" [cf. RSV].)

Historians have puzzled over why Saul would offer one of his daughters to David, a supposed rival. Either Saul, as the text suggests, never intended the marriage to take place (assuming David would be killed by the Philistines) or else the time frame in 1 Sam 18:20–28 must be questioned. Two suggestions are to place the marriage before David's relationship to Saul deteriorated (Ishida 1977: 22) or to place it after Saul's death—cf. 1 Sam 3:12–13 (*NHI*, 184–86).

What was the political significance of David's marriage to Michal? Morgenstern (1929) identifies the marriage as a "*beena*-marriage," by which succession to the throne passed through the distaff side of the family. If this were so, then David's marriage to Michal constituted a legal right to Saul's throne. Morgenstern's argument, however, assumes a matriarchate in Israel—an assumption for which there is little evidence. It is more likely that David married Michal to gain a toehold in Saul's house. Since David's power base was in the south, he needed Michal to attract the pro-Saulide population and establish a claim to Saul's throne.

More recent treatments of Michal's marriage to David focus on the literary artistry of the story (see especially Alter 1981: 118–26; Fokkelman 1986: 209–47). See also QUEEN.

Bibliography

Alter, R. 1981. *The Art of Biblical Narrative.* New York.
Fokkelman, J. P. 1986. *Narrative Art and Poetry in the Books of Samuel.* Vol. 2. Assen.
Ishida, T. 1977. *The Royal Dynasties in Ancient Israel.* New York.
Morgenstern, J. 1929. Beena Marriage [Matriarchate] in Ancient Israel and Its Historical Implications. *ZAW* 47: 93ff.

LINDA S. SCHEARING

MICHAL, TEL (M.R. 131174). A site located on a *kurkar* (sandstone) cliff overlooking the Mediterranean about 6.5 km N of the Yarkon River estuary. Ancient remains are spread over five separate locations: the high tell (0.3 hectares), rising 30 m above sea level, the slightly lower N hill (about 4 hectares), and three hillocks 200 m to the E. The region was never suitable for dry farming because of the infertility of the sandy soil and poor drainage conditions. Some sustenance was certainly afforded by fishing, horticulture (grapes and figs), and hunting, but the main economic basis was apparently outside support by central political authorities and a coastal maritime trade. An underwater *kurkar* ridge at the foot of the tell may have provided a safe channel for the anchoring of small ships.

The ancient name of the site is unknown, although in the 1920s the local inhabitants referred to the immediate vicinity as "Dahrat Makmish." The official name is now Tel Michal (or Tel Mikhal).

Between 1958 and 1960, N. Avigad excavated the NE hillock, where he uncovered three superimposed cultic structures dating to the Iron Age, Persian, and Hellenistic periods. Large-scale excavations, directed by Z. Herzog, J. D. Muhly, and G. Rapp, Jr., were conducted between 1977 and 1980.

The first settlement at Tel Michal was erected on the high tell in the MB III (Stratum XVII, late 17th century B.C.), at the time that the Fifteenth (Hyksos) Dynasty was expanding from Lower Egypt along the coastal plain of S Canaan. The newcomers constructed an earthen platform, 4 m high, on which to erect their buildings. Little of this phase survived, since most of the W, seaward side of the original mound was destroyed either by wave abrasion or tectonic shocks. A second such catastrophe occurred at the end of LB I (Stratum XVI, mid-15th century). To compensate for the missing portion of the mound, huge earthworks were constructed against the E slope after each disaster, thereby increasing its width by about 30 m. A thick wall of Stratum XVI at the N end of the mound may have been part of a fort guarding the coastal approach.

The third phase, LB IIA (Stratum XV, 14th–13th centuries), left few remains, since the Iron Age builders leveled off the old ruins and dumped the debris down the slopes. A great amount of LB pottery, including a rare assemblage of decorated kraters, was found scattered on the S slope.

The tell remained abandoned for about 300 years and was resettled only in the 10th century B.C., when the three E hillocks were occupied for the first time. There were two phases of private dwellings (Strata XIV–XIII) on the high tell. An open high place was built on the NE hillock, a chapel with a stone-built altar, surrounded by *favissae,* on the E hillock, and two bench-lined structures on the SE hillock. Two winepresses were found nearby. This phase corresponds with Phoenician colonization of the central coast of Israel during the period of prosperous commercial relations between Tyre and the United Kingdom (1 Kings 9). A few meager remains in Stratum XII hint at limited occupation in the 8th century B.C.

Toward the end of the 6th century, Tel Michal entered into a long period of prosperity. Six phases of Persian-period settlement were recorded on the high tell (Strata XI–VI, ca. 525–300 B.C.). A large fort or administrative building stood at its N end, and several dwellings stood to its S. A storeroom for wine containing more than twenty storage jars was excavated, as well as a deep circular silo for grain storage.

A domestic quarter covering at least half a hectare grew up on the N hill. Pottery kilns were found on its W and N slopes. One of these collapsed with five recently fired storage jars still inside. These may have been containers for the wine processed in the nearby contemporary winepresses, two of which were excavated. A huge cemetery covered most of the E slope. Although only about 10 percent of it was exposed, it contained more than 120 burial sites of various types: cist tombs, pit graves, and infant storage jar burials. The grave goods included bead jewelry, bowls, necklaces, anklets, bronze fibulae, tools of iron, and even nails of wooden coffins.

From the temple on the NE hillock, dozens of clay and stone figurines with Phoenician affinities were recovered. There was another, smaller chapel on the E hillock, surrounded by *favissae,* one containing intact, unused oil lamps.

Following the conquest of the area by Alexander the Great, occupation continued uninterruptedly into the Hellenistic period, as testified by coins dating to the end of the 4th century B.C. The beginning of the 3d century saw an upsurge in building activity (Stratum V). A central fortress covered most of the high tell, and a large, community winepress was sunk into the debris on the N hill. A new shrine was constructed over the former chapel on the NE hillock. The monumental architecture points toward control by central economic and political powers; Ptolemaic (Stratum V) and Seleucid (Stratum IV). A hoard of 47 tetradachmas of Ptolemy I–III was found buried in the E hillock.

In the 1st century B.C., Tel Michal was incorporated into the Hasmonean kingdom. The discovery of several coins of Alexander Jannaeus and the presence of a small fort on the high tell (Stratum III) indicate that it may have been one of the fortified points on the "Jannaeus line."

In the Early Roman period (first half of the 1st century A.D.), a citadel (about 40 m by 40 m) with a watchtower in its courtyard was erected on the high tell (Stratum II). The site was then deserted for some 700 years, except for a small lookout tower of the Early Arab period (Stratum I). Afterward, Tel Michal was completely abandoned.

Bibliography

Herzog, Z.; Negbi, O.; and Moshkovitz, S. 1978. Excavations at Tell Michal 1977. *TA* 5/3–4: 99–130.

Herzog, Z., et al. 1980. Excavations at Tel Michal 1978–1979. *TA* 7/3–4: 111–51.

ZE'EV HERZOG

MICHMASH (PLACE) [Heb *mikmāś; mikmās*]. An OT town located near the boundary between the tribes of Benjamin and Ephraim. The first Heb spelling is found mainly in preexilic narratives: 1 Sam 13:2, 5, 12, 16, 23; 14:5, 31; Isa 10:28; and Neh 11:31, while the second spelling is only used in postexilic narrative accounts: Ezra 2:27; Neh 7:31 (but note the reversion to the alternative spelling in Neh 11:31). The site is mentioned also in 1 Macc 9:73.

Modern scholars have consistently identified Michmash with the Arab village of Mukhmas (M.R. 176142), 11 km NE of Jerusalem. Recent archaeological surface surveyors, however, found only scattered late Iron Age sherds at Mukhmas, and therefore have proposed that biblical Michmash existed 1 km to the N, at Khirbet el-Hara el-Fawqa, where Iron Age I and II sherds were found (Kochavi 1972: 180).

Michmash nestled among the hills forming the N side of the deep Wadi es-Swenit, which extends from the central Palestinian hill country into the Jordan valley. Since this canyon becomes an impassable gorge immediately E of Michmash, the most easterly ancient road in the vicinity linked Michmash with Benjaminite Gibeah/Geba (Jaba), 2 km to the S on the opposite rim of the canyon, by way of the "Michmash Pass" (1 Sam 13:23; also called the "Geba Pass"; cf. Isa 10:29; Judg 20:33?). On each side of this pass reportedly stood two rock columns nicknamed Bozez ("slippery"?) and Seneh ("tooth"?), cf. 1 Sam 14:4–5; these probably correspond to rock formations currently found in the wadi nearly 200 m below and 1 km SE of Mukhmas.

Michmash figures prominently in the story of the Hebrew uprising against the Philistines early in Israel's history (1 Sam 13–14). Saul is reported to have struck down a Philistine *nĕṣib* ("governor"? "garrison"?), which caused the Philistines to fortify Michmash with chariots and infantry (13:4–6); the figures mentioned in the report (e.g., 30,000 chariots) are clearly exaggerated. Saul is associated closely throughout the story with Gibeah (probably an ancient toponym for Jaba), across the valley from Michmash.

Another source (13:23–14:23) seems to focus on Jonathan's role in the battle of Michmash (Blenkinsopp 1964; Arnold 1987: 184–218). Leaving Geba (Jaba) where he had struck down the Philistine *nĕṣib* (13:3), Jonathan and his squire made their way down through the Michmash pass and climbed up the steep hill, where they surprised the Philistine soldiers at Michmash. After having been joined by Saul's men, the Israelites then reportedly chased the Philistines past Beth-aven (Tell Maryam?) toward Aijalon (14:31). The notice that Saul stationed 2,000 troops to be with him in Michmash (13:2), which now prefaces the entire account, probably originally referred to the outcome of the battle of Michmash (Miller 1974: 161).

After the division of the kingdom, Asa fortified Mizpah and Geba as N fortresses of Judah (1 Kgs 15:22); the Wadi es-Swenit became the border between Judah and Israel, and Michmash probably thus lay within Israelite territory. In Isa 10:27c–32, there is a report of the advance of an invading army over this border as it progressed toward Jerusalem. This force reportedly crossed the Geba pass after having left its support equipment in Michmash (10:29) before resuming its march the next day.

In postexilic times, the village was one of the Jewish towns under Persian rule. In Neh 11:31, Michmash is listed among the cities inhabited by Benjaminites, while Ezra 2:27 (= Neh 7:31) reports a population there of 122.

In the Maccabean era, Jonathan resided at Michmash, from which he ruled his loyal Jewish followers (1 Macc 9:73) before moving to Jerusalem.

Bibliography

Arnold, P. 1987. *Gibeah in Israelite History and Tradition.* Ph.D. diss., Emory.

Blenkinsopp, J. 1964. Jonathan's Sacrilege: 1 Sam 14:1–46. A Study in Literary History. *CBQ* 26: 423–49.

Dalman, G. 1904. Der Pass von Michmas. *ZDPV* 27: 161–73.

Kochavi, M. 1972. *Judea, Samaria, and the Golan: Archaeological Survey 1967–68.* Jerusalem (in Hebrew).

Miller, J. M. 1974. Saul's Rise to Power: Some Observations Concerning 1 Sam 9:1–10:16; 10:26–11:15; and 13:2–14:46. *CBQ* 36: 157–74.

PATRICK M. ARNOLD

MICHMETHATH (PLACE) [Heb *mikmĕtāt*]. The northern point of the boundary separating Ephraim from Manasseh (Josh 16:6; 17:7). The site is said to be east of Shechem, though most scholars agree that the direction is more accurately to the SE. The text does not indicate whether the site is an actual settlement or simply a striking geographical feature. Kallai (*HGB*, 400–401) summarizes the possibilities: the Gebel ʾel-Kabir range (that would place the site to the NE of Shechem, well into Manasseh); a valley, specifically the Wadi Bedan, which descends southeastward toward the Jordan valley. If it were a settlement, the site would most likely be Khirbit ʾIbn Naser. Evidence favoring one site over another is inconclusive.

ELMER H. DYCK

MICHRI (PERSON) [Heb *mikrî*]. A Benjaminite mentioned only in 1 Chr 9:8 (MT) as an ancestor of the clan of Elah, one of four such clans listed in vv 7–9 as having returned from the Babylonian Exile. The corresponding Benjaminite section in the parallel list found in Nehemiah 11, however, omits any mention of the clan of Elah (indeed, only one clan, that of Sallu, is seemingly to be found in vv 7–9 [but cf. Curtis and Madsen *Chronicles* ICC, 171 concerning Ibneiah]). This curious anomaly led Williamson (*1 and 2 Chronicles* NCBC, 89) to suggest that the Chronicler's inclusion of four Benjaminite clans is the more plausible of the two extant traditions, and that something more than scribal error must be posited to explain the differences between the two lists.

In regard to the meaning of the name "Michri," Noth (*IPN,* 189, n. 3) pointed to the root *mkr,* "purchase," or the like. He suggested that Michri's parents perhaps meant to convey by such a name that their child represented some sort of just "recompense" or "compensation" on the part of the deity.

In place of the unique form *mikrî* found in the MT of 1 Chr 9:8, both the LXX and the Syriac attest the relatively familiar name MACHIR (Heb *mākîr*); this probably represents a metathesis of the *reš* and the *yod.* Less likely is the suggestion that the MT form resulted from a dittograph of the subsequent *waw,* later read as *yod* (the two letters are virtually indistinguishable in the later Judean scripts).

WILLIAM H. BARNES

MIDDIN (PLACE) [Heb *middîn*]. Town situated in the wilderness of Judah (Josh 15:61), within the same district as En-gedi. This settlement is listed among the towns within the tribal allotment of Judah (Josh 15:21–62). Recent archaeological work in the Buqeiah valley has uncovered three Iron Age fortress-farms which may be associated with the towns of this district (Stager 1976). If the list in Josh 15:61–62 runs N to S, then ancient Middin is probably to be located at Khirbet Abu Tabaq (Boling and Wright *Joshua* AB, 392; M.R. 188126).

Bibliography

Stager, L. E. 1976. Farming in the Judean Desert During the Iron Age. *BASOR* 221: 145–58.

WADE R. KOTTER

MIDIAN (PERSON) [Heb *midyan*]. MIDIANITES. The son of Abraham and Keturah in the genealogy of Genesis 25:2. It is also the name of an ethnic or political population group especially associated with S Transjordan that played a very important role in the earliest history of ancient Israel, and is probably the earliest identifiable Arabic-speaking social group.

A. The Name

The origin of the name *midyan* is unknown, though it has been suggested (Mendenhall 1973: 163ff.) that the root *mady-* is non-Semitic, and possibly cognate to the designation of Medes of much later times. The biblical genealogy (Gen 25:2) includes two variants, *midyan* and *medan,* cognates of both of which appear in Greek sources of the Hellenistic period as names of towns E of the Gulf of Aqaba (Knauf 1985).

B. Midianites in Early Biblical Tradition

Biblical tradition listed the eponymous ancestor, Midian, as one of six sons born to the patriarch Abraham by his second wife, Keturah (Gen 25:1–6). According to this account Abraham sent these sons away from Canaan to the E country, a tradition that implies an origin in Canaan proper for these proto-Arabic tribal designations. This tradition is now powerfully reinforced by linguistic evidence that derives the pre-Islamic Arabic language and writing system from the Bronze Age Mediterranean coastal region (Mendenhall 1985: chap. 10).

The Midianites as a historically existent society are represented in the Joseph stories (Gen 37:25–36) as traders traveling by camel caravan between Gilead (N Transjordan) and Egypt, and in this case dealing in slaves as well as "gum, balm, and myrrh." The term Midianite alternates with the term Ishmaelite, probably to be explained by the fact that at the time the narrative reached its present form, the Midianites had ceased to exist as a distinct social group but were identified with an ethnic group later called Ishmaelites. The narrative certainly is not earlier than the monarchy, and there is no reason to believe that it is based upon any historical event. However, the narrative does evidently make use of historical memory concerning the Midianites, and the picture it yields is plausible in view of present information concerning the society and its culture.

In contrast, the connections between Moses and the Midianites are manifold, detailed, and remarkable (Exod 2–4, 18; Numbers 25, 31) and can hardly be explained on any basis other than historical fact. Upon fleeing from Egypt to somewhere in the Sinai Peninsula after killing the Egyptian overseer, Moses joined and then married the daughter (Zipporah) of a Midianite sheepherder, variously named Reuel, Jethro, or Hobab. This Midianite shepherd was in later tradition promoted to the Midianite priesthood, doubtless because of the tradition in Exod 18:12, where we are told that Jethro offered a burnt offering and sacrifice, followed by a common meal with "all the elders of Israel." Clearly the later tradition was unaware of the significance and social context of a typical *menseff,* which at that time may very well have been an implied covenant of peace between the two groups.

By his wife, Moses had two sons named Gershom (or Gershon) and Eliezer (Exod 18:3–4). In Exod 4:18–20, his wife and sons were taken with him to Egypt, but in Exodus 18:2 they are still with Jethro—a fact that is explained by the statement that Moses had "sent her away," i.e., divorced her. Exodus 18 is the original and correct version, for the sons are repeatedly called "her sons." This corresponds to the ancient customary law by which children born to a *ger* (i.e., a resident alien) normally remain with their maternal grandfather, as in the law of Exod 21:4, and implied also in the Jacob-Laban narrative. All of these Midianite names except Eliezer actually occur in pre-Islamic Arabic inscriptions, together with most of the other names cited in biblical sources as those of Midianite or Moabite persons (Mendenhall 1984).

Later, the band of escapees from Egypt was guided in the desert by Moses' father-in-law (Num 10:29–32), though later pious tradition evidently entirely forgot this feature of the period of Wanderings and substituted the miraculous (and drastically misunderstood) pillar of cloud and pillar of fire as desert guides (Exod 13:21–22; Num 9:15–23).

The organization of the small band was carried out according to the recommendations of Moses' father-in-law (Exod 18:13–27). The system of "rulers" of thousands, hundreds, fifties, and tens is essentially the ANE military organization, and the rudiments of the system may be identified in the census lists of Numbers 1 and 26 (Mendenhall 1958) and in the story of Gideon, where there are contrasts between "thousands" and hundreds. Whatever the social organization may have been, it is remarkable that Israelite tradition attributed it to the Midianites. Even more significant is the fact that the narrative implies that Moses' band did *not* have a preexistent social organization. This is, of course, quite in contrast to later orthodox dogma expressed in the narratives that the ancestors of all the twelve tribes went down into Egypt, and of course their descendants, complete with tribal organization, emerged from Egypt with Moses. The "mixed multitude" (Exod 12:38; Num 11:4) was the original band of Moses' followers, and the twelve tribes were added to the traditions after the formation of the Federation in Palestine proper.

Moses invited his hosts to join them in the quest for the promised land (Num 10:29), but the Midianites declined the offer. This tradition is especially important since it indicates that Moses and his band of followers were willing and eager to obtain adherents and followers of the new ideology: like all other religious movements in their formative period, the survival and success of the religious society depended upon its attractiveness to potential new adherents.

The next connection with the Midianites was tragic (Numbers 25). The festivities at Baal-Peor, somewhere near the foot of Mt. Nebo, induced one of Moses' band to join in the pagan (fertility?) rite, and a zealot for Yahweh killed both the Israelite and the Midianite princes involved (Mendenhall 1973: chap. 4). The result was lasting hostility between the two groups, and in Numbers 31 the last act of Moses' life is to order the extermination of the Midianites, in a narrative that reflects little historical reality other than a reflection of certain practices of the monarchy, and the late ideology of the priestly author of the narrative. It is probable, however, that there had been an armed conflict between the two groups, reflected in the brief notice of Josh 13:21. A nucleus of historical fact probably is involved in the names of the five kings of the Midianites who were killed in the battle, for one of the names, Rekem, is recorded by Josephus as being the original native name of Petra. Another of the names, Evi, occurs on an Ammonite seal of the 8th to 7th centuries B.C. (Hammond 1960), and the other names also occur in pre-Islamic Arabic inscriptions.

The last episode concerning the Midianites took place in Canaan proper with action concluding in Transjordan, and is recorded in considerable detail (Judges 6–8). The defeat of the Midianites by Gideon and his small band evidently had a considerable impact, for it is cited by Isaiah (9:4) centuries later as a precedent for later anticipated acts of God. The Midianites are again represented as camel riders, but this time as warriors, not as caravan traders. For various reasons, the periodic incursions of the Midianite camel riders are almost certainly to be interpreted as regular tax-collecting expeditions. In spite of the agriculture engaged in around the Midianite heartland, there is little doubt that the production of foodstuffs there was inadequate for the population, and thus the more highly productive regions of Palestine proper were called upon regularly for contributions, especially at harvest time. It is tempting, in view of all the evidence, to conclude that the Midianites may well have exercised a temporary imperial domination of Palestine and Transjordan at the very beginning of early Israel's history. Again, the parallel to the Philistine domination is striking, including the fact that, according to the biblical tradition, the Midianite policy consisted of a coalition of five kings.

The last reference to Midian as an existent political entity is the laconic notice in Genesis 36:35 that states that Hadad, son of Bedad, the fourth king of the Edomites, defeated the Midianites in the land of Moab. This event may reasonably be placed shortly after 1100 B.C. All subsequent references to Midian seem clearly to be geographical or genealogical in nature. The name remained in use as a place name, and local traditions concerning Midian and the Midianites continued until the rise of Islam. According to the Quran, the father-in-law of Moses was sent as a prophet to the Midianites to warn them of the coming destruction.

C. Midian in Later Biblical Tradition

In the narrative of the rebellion of the Edomite prince Hadad in 1 Kgs 11:18, the term Midian has already become a geographical designation—presumably referring to some section of S Transjordan. From "Midian," Hadad set out for Egypt to escape the wholesale slaughter of Edomite males that was carried out by David and Joab.

In later biblical tradition dealing with the "conquest" period, Midian is very closely associated with Moab: in the Balaam story, elders of Midian are mentioned together with elders of Moab (Num 22:4, 7) as being sent to N Syria to fetch Balaam. Similarly, in Josh 13:21, the Midianite kings of Num 31:8 are listed, but designated as *nesîkê* of Sihon, king of the Amorites who ruled in Heshbon. The term *nesîkê* is obscure and relatively late (cf. Mic 5:4 [—Eng 5:5]; Ezek 32:21), but is probably intended to indicate that they were chieftains who derived their authority from Sihon and thus were client chieftains.

Later biblical references to the conflict with Midian, however, seem to refer only to the Gideon narrative of Judges 6–8, for it was, of course, the victory that had special significance for the mainstream of the biblical tribes in Palestine proper. Psalm 83:9–12 refers to the Midianite personages by the names they have in Judges, and it refers to their destruction as a precedent for the coming destruction of surrounding enemies. In Isaiah 9:3 and the late prose addition of 10:26, the victory over Midian also is cited as a precedent for the coming defeat of the enemies of the kingdom of Judah. Finally, in Hab 3:7 and Isa 60:6, the prophecies reflect the usage of the word "Midian" as a purely geographical designation.

D. The Midianite People and Culture

Though older scholarship saw the Midianites as typical bedouin nomads because of their possession of camels, it is now clear that they had a complex and highly sophisticated society at a time when there is no reason to believe that the bedouin culture even existed (Knauf 1985). The biblical account twice gives us the names of their five kings (Num 31:8; Josh 13:21), which strongly suggests that their political organization consisted of a federation of five city-states, much like the well-known federation of the Philistines, and similar federations of the Etruscans in Italy, who were also of Anatolian origin.

Archaeological evidence strongly indicates that Midian was an important political entity that came into existence rather suddenly in the N Hejaz region, E of the Gulf of Aqaba, sometime in the 13th century B.C. Recent surveys have revealed evidence of numerous town and village sites in that region from the end of the LB into the early Iron ages (Parr et al. 1970; Ingraham et al. 1981). The people certainly spoke a language that was an archaic ancestor of Arabic, and they possessed a highly sophisticated culture that had connections from Anatolia to Egypt.

Recent archaeological surveys in the Hejaz have revealed massive walled cities, sophisticated irrigation installations, evidence of mining and smelting operations, and, most important, a unique type of painted pottery that has since been recognized as occurring in sites in the Jordan valley and Palestine proper. The painted pottery is of particular importance since the painted motifs are very closely akin to the Mycenaean pottery of Anatolia and the Aegean, while the technology of pottery manufacture is most closely related to that of Egypt (Parr 1982). See also QURRAYAH. The Midianites, therefore, constitute another example of a society that was familiar with, and created a demand for, Mycenaean types of ceramics that had to be locally manufactured in the early Iron Age. This is entirely parallel to the similar taste for Mycenaean types of pottery that brought about the local production of the well-known Philistine wares. Similar cultural processes can be observed also at Ras Ibn Hani, on the coast just N of Ugarit. This aspect of Midianite culture justifies the conclusion that there was some element in the society that had roots in the Anatolian/Aegean region, however remote they may have been.

Recent archaeological investigations have thus completely changed dominant views concerning the Midianites, and as usual new questions are raised which are not so easily answered as the old ones. One of the most basic is, What is or was meant by the term "Midianite"? In this case (as in many, if not most, other cases of terms that we regard as "ethnic" designations), the term most probably arose from some small grass-roots social organization; then, as the society grew in size and developed into a political power structure or federation, the term became increasingly remote from its original context (both social and geographical). The consequences of a failure to recognize contrasts in the meaning of such designations of social groups have often been unfortunate.

Because the homeland of the Midianite archaeological culture is clearly in the region to the E of the Gulf of Aqaba, there has been a naive tendency to assume that all references to Midianites must either come from that region or be fictitious. In turn, this has long led to the entirely gratuitous assumption that Mt. Sinai must be somewhere in the deep S of Transjordan or in the NW region of the Arabian peninsula. The latter theory was based on the erroneous assumption that the description in Exod 19:16–25 of the theophany at Mt. Sinai derived from a volcanic eruption, which could only have taken place in the Hejaz during historical times. The narrative of the event at Mt. Sinai is a very typical description of a theophany in a thunderstorm, and is closely paralleled even in Homer's *Iliad.*

The presence of Midianite shepherd bands in the Sinai should not be a problem since the discovery of the Mari documents. Large-scale sheepherding requires considerable travel between summer and winter pasturages, often involving tens or hundreds of kilometers. There is no plausible objection to the presence of shepherd bands in the Sinai who were identified or identified themselves as adherents of the political/cultural system of the Midianites. The same is true of populations in the Jordan valley just N of the Dead Sea. The Midianites can no longer be regarded naively as primitive nomadic barbarians; they were a complex and cosmopolitan civilization with a highly diverse economy and, in all probability, an extensive control system for a few decades that included parts of Palestine and Transjordan. It is not surprising that this early society impressed itself upon the memories of populations of the region even until the rise of Islam.

Bibliography

Bawden, G., and Edens, C. 1988. Tayma Painted Ware and the Hejaz Iron Age Ceramic Tradition. *Levant* 20: 197–213.

Hammond, P. 1960. An Ammonite Stamp Seal from Amman. *BASOR* 160: 38–41.

Ingraham, M., et al. 1981. Preliminary Report on a Reconnaissance Survey of the Northwestern Province. *Atlal* 5: 59–84.

Knauf, E. 1985. *Madiama. ZDMG* 135: 16–21.

———. 1988. *Midian.* ADPV. Wiesbaden.

Mendenhall, G. 1958. The Census Lists of Numbers 1 and 26. *JBL* 77: 52–66.

———. 1973. *The Tenth Generation: The Origins of the Biblical Tradition.* Baltimore.

———. 1984. Qurayya and the Midianites. Vol. 3, pp. 137–45 in *Studies in the History of Arabia.* Riyadh.

———. 1985. *The Syllabic Inscriptions from Byblos.* Beirut.

Parr, P. 1982. Contacts between Northwest Arabia and Jordan in the Late Bronze and Iron Ages. Pp. 127–33 in *Studies in the History and Archaeology of Jordan, I,* ed. A. Hadidi. Amman.

Parr, P.; Harding, G.; and Dayton, J. 1970. Preliminary Survey in N.W. Arabia, 1968. *Bulletin of the Institute of Archaeology* 8–9: 193–242.

Sawyer, J., and Clines, D., eds. 1983. *Midian, Moab, and Edom.* JSOTSup 24. Sheffield.

George E. Mendenhall

MIDRASH. The rabbinic term for biblical exegesis, a noun derived from the Heb root *drš,* which in the Bible means "to inquire, investigate," generally with God or a human king as the object of the verb.

A. Appearance of *mdrš*
B. Definitions
C. Midrashic Activity within the Hebrew Bible
D. Translation as Midrash
E. Rewriting the Bible
F. Midrash at Qumran
G. Rabbinic Midrash
  1. Classification of Rabbinic Midrashim
  2. Characteristics of Rabbinic Midrash

A. Appearance of *mdrš*

Ezra 7:10 is the first place in which a written text appears as the object of *drš* (Gertner 1962a: 5). Heinemann (1946: 182–85) has argued that by the end of the OT period the verb *drš* had acquired the sense of "inquiring in order to do." In the documents from Qumran, *drš* has a variety of meanings, such as searching, inquiring, seeking, visiting, caring for, desiring, wishing, studying, investigating, and interpreting (Gertner 1962a: 11). Beginning in the Tannaitic period, the root *drš* signifies some type of logical deduction (Heinemann 1946: 185), but in the rabbinic corpus *drš* is used primarily as a term for investigating the Torah (Gertner 1962a: 6–8).

The noun *mdrš* appears twice in the Bible. The passage in 2 Chr 13:22 mentions "the midrash of the prophet Iddo," and 2 Chr 24:27 refers to "the midrash of the book of kings." Driver (1963: 529) and Bloch (*DBSup* 5: 1264) suggest that the term means virtually the same in Chronicles as it later means in the rabbinic texts; the latter refers to these books as "historical works which gloss Scripture with the goal of instruction and edification." Bacher (1965: 104) thought that in Chronicles *mdrš* referred to a book, an essay, or a study. Gertner (1962a: 10–11) stated that it referred to a narrative or account, and Zeitlin (1953: 24–25) claimed that in Chronicles the term *midraš* referred to a book in which were recorded the inquiries of the kings and the answers and explanations of the prophets. Lieberman (1950: 48) argued that *mdrš* did not have a technical meaning in Chronicles, while Finkelstein (1930: 56) suggested that the *mdrš* of the prophet Iddo was a collection of oracles and that the *mdrš* of the book of kings was "probably our book of Kings." We must conclude that the meaning of *mdrš* in Chronicles is simply lost to us at present (Wright 1967: 37).

Mdrš conveys a variety of meanings in the literature from Qumran. It refers to judicial investigation, study of law, and interpretation. Although *mdrš* alone does not necessarily refer to biblical interpretation when it appears by itself in the Qumran texts, when it is used in connection with a verse from Scripture it does seem to have a more comprehensive meaning than either *pyrwš* or *pšr* (Wright 1967: 40–41).

Although in the rabbinic corpus *mdrš* may mean study or inquiry in a general sense, its main use in these documents is to designate Scriptural interpretation. In the rabbinic collections the term signifies both the process whereby Scripture is expounded and the product of that exegesis (Gertner 1962a: 9).

B. Definitions

It has been common to define midrash in terms of its function or purpose. Slonimsky (1956: 235) found the essence of midrash in its "feeding of the life-impulse when harassed and threatened by tragic circumstances." Sanders (1972: xiv) wrote that "when one studies how an ancient tradition functions in relation to the needs of the community, he is studying midrash." Bloch (*DBSup* 5/29: 1263–80; cf. Wright 1967: 19–20) has offered several functional definitions of midrash; the major characteristic she attributes to midrash is its attempt to make a biblical text contemporary and relevant. Wright (1967: 67) has stressed the literary form of midrash and wrote, "the basic midrashic structure . . . is merely that one begins with a text of Scripture and proceeds to comment on it in some way." However, Gertner (1962b: 268–69) drew a distinction between covert midrash—in which neither the text, nor the midrashic idea, nor the midrashic technique is defined or mentioned—and overt midrash—in which the verse, idea, and most often the technique are explicitly stated. Finally, Sanders (1972: xiv) argued that "any definition of midrash which limits its scope to the citation and use of an actual biblical passage is deficient."

Given the varieties of functions attributed to midrash, the fact that many have ignored the possibility of midrash's being a scholarly, holy game (Heineman 1954: 2; Frankel 1956: 29; Porton 1979: 131), and the possibility that anything might be midrash if we do not require a clear connection between the comment and the verse, midrash is best defined as follows:

"Midrash is a type of literature, oral or written, which has its starting point in a fixed canonical text, considered the revealed word of God by the midrashist and his audience, and in which this original verse is explicitly cited or clearly alluded to" (Porton 1979: 112; 1981: 62; cf. Childs 1972: 49).

C. Midrashic Activity within the Hebrew Bible

Robert (1934: 42–68, 172–204, 374–84; 1935: 344–65, 502–25; 1944: 192–213) was one of the first to place the roots of the genre of midrash in the postexilic biblical texts by noting that phrases reappear in the later books of the Bible with different meanings from those they had in earlier biblical texts. They carry a new significance in their new contexts (Vermes 1961: 4). Modern scholars have pointed to a variety of biblical books as examples of midrashic activity (Seeligman 1953: 150–81; Willi-Plein 1971). Although not employing the term midrash, Sandmel (1961: 105–22) drew attention to some "haggadic" passages in Genesis, and Vermes (*CHB* 1: 199) has claimed that Deuteronomy is partly the result of the midrashic enterprise. Zunz (1966: 45) claimed that Ezekiel was a type of midrash, for it contains the oldest examples of modification of Pentateuchal law. Halperin (1976: 129–41) has argued that Ezek 10:9–17 is an example of midrash, Bloch (*DBSup* 5: 1271–72) has pointed to sections of Ezekiel as midrashic, and Bruce (1972: 38–40) has claimed that expressions in Ezekiel and Habakkuk "call to mind" phrases in earlier prophetic books and should be considered midrashic passages. Both Childs (1971: 137–50) and Bruce (1972: 42–52) have pointed to some of the titles of the biblical Psalms as reflecting midrashic activity. In addition, Zunz (1966: 38), Schurer (*HJP*[1], 340), Weingreen (1951–52: 186–87), and most recently Willi (1972) have spoken of Chronicles in terms of midrash. It seems clear that several scholars have found the origin of midrash in the Hebrew Bible itself; however, Towner's claim (1973: 1) that the Bible does not comment upon itself in the same manner as nonbiblical texts do should be examined carefully.

D. Translation as Midrash

Translation involves interpretation. As Ben Sira's grandson states, "things once written in Hebrew do not have the same force in them when put into another language . . . [and books] differ not a little in translation from the original" (Goodspeed 1959: 223). Therefore, it is legitimate to consider the LXX and the Targums as types of midrash. In addition, there is little doubt that both the LXX (Rabin 1968; Bickerman 1959) and the Targums contain midrashic elements. Recent scholarship has argued that some of the LXX's midrashic passages were created by the original translators, while others are the result of editorial revisions (Gooding 1974: 1–11). There are several Targums, and they are of different types (*HJP*[2] 1: 99–114; Grossfeld 1972–77). *Targum Onkelos* is more or less a literal translation of the text, and most of its paraphrases occur in the poetic passages. *Pseudo-Jonathan* covers most of the Pentateuch and contains a number of unique paraphrases and some interpolations from midrash. *Neofiti I* is the Palestinian Targum par excellence (Porton 1979: 119–22). Because each of these Targums contains paraphrases, interpretations, and the like, each is a type of midrash.

E. Rewriting the Bible

The *Liber Antiquitatum Biblicarum* (James 1971), the *Genesis Apocryphon* (Fitzmyer 1966), Philo's *Life of Moses*, Josephus' *Antiquities* (Attridge 1976), and *Jubilees* (VanderKam 1977) represent another type of postbiblical midrash: the rewriting of the biblical account. This genre of midrash retells the biblical story by adding details, explaining difficult passages, rearranging material, and the like (Porton 1979: 122–25; 1981: 72–74).

F. Midrash at Qumran

There is a close relationship between many of the documents from Qumran and the Hebrew Bible. Some scholars have even suggested that the Bible was the focal point of the religious life of the Qumran community (Stendahl 1968: 61; Brownlee 1951: 56). The most important type of midrashic activity which occurred among the sectarians at Qumran was the pesher (see PESHARIM, QUMRAN). While there has been some debate over whether or not one can properly call the pesharim "midrashim" (Vermes 1955: 96–97; Roth 1960: 51–52; Slomovic 1969: 1–15; Porton 1979: 125–27; 1981: 75–77), according to our definition they are midrashim, albeit of a special type. The most important idea behind the pesharim is that the sectarians at Qumran believed that the biblical prophecies were being fulfilled in the history and life of the Qumran community (Allegro 1964: 130; Bruce 1961: 70; 77; Stendahl 1968: 190; Roth 1960: 52). Thus, the pesharim are eschatological, or even apocalyptic (Cross 1961: 76–78; 112–13; Slomovic 1969: 9).

Although Slomovic (1969: 5–15) has argued that some of the same exegetical techniques were used in the pesharim and in the rabbinic midrashim, there exist some important stylistic differences between the pesharim and the rabbinic texts: (1) the pesher quotes an entire passage of Scripture and follows it with an interpretation that has a tenuous relationship to the biblical passage, while the rabbinic texts often cite single words and phrases and present directly their interpretation; (2) the midrashim sometimes quote scholars, while the pesharim are always anonymous; (3) the several pesharim appear in only one copy, while there are a multiplicity of versions of the rabbinic midrashim; (4) the rabbinic texts are collections of statements, some of whose original contexts are unknown and some of whose original contexts were probably in nonmidrashic settings, while the comments in the pesharim make sense only as commentaries to the biblical text; (5) the presuppositions behind the pesharim and the midrashim are different, for the single purpose of the author(s) of the pesharim was to demonstrate that the biblical prophecies were coming into being in their community, while the rabbis had a variety of purposes for creating their midrashim and midrashic collections (Porton 1979: 126–27; Brownlee 1951: 75).

G. Rabbinic Midrash

Rabbinic midrash is the creation of a subsection of the ancient Jewish community, the rabbis, whose defining characteristic was their knowledge of the Torah, both oral and written; therefore, their engaging in the creation of midrash was one manifestation of their focusing their individual lives on the Torah (Porton 1985: 1–3).

1. Classification of Rabbinic Midrashim. It is common to distinguish between legal midrashim (midrash Halakah, e.g., *Mekhilta, Sipra, Sipre*) and nonlegal midrashim (midrash Haggadah, e.g., Genesis and Leviticus Rabbah). However, this distinction is misleading. First, the so-called halakic midrashim contain a good deal of nonlegal material, and the so-called haggadic midrashim contain a significant number of legal statements. Second, it is simplistic to draw a sharp difference between legal passages and nonlegal passages, for both served as interpretations of revelation and as guides to one's actions. Third, as Bacher (1892: 416–19) has shown, the word *agadah* originally meant "exegesis"; therefore, the term "midrash Haggadah" is a tautology. Fifth, the so-called "halakic midrashim" contain exegeses on the legal and nonlegal portions of the biblical text upon which they comment.

It is also common to distinguish between Tannaitic and Amoraic midrashim. However, the exact reasons behind these designations is unclear. If they refer to the sages cited in the collections, they are inappropriate, for the Amoraic midrashim contain interpretations attributed to Tannaim, and the Tannaitic collections contain comments attributed to persons who may be considered early Amoraim. If the terms are meant to indicate the periods in which the collections were edited, this also presents a difficulty, for we simply do not know when the collections came into their present form or a form similar to the one in which they now exist.

On the basis of literary characteristics, we can define two types of rabbinic midrashim: the expositional and the homiletical. Expositional collections present a running commentary to consecutive verses of the biblical text; homiletical collections do not offer a running commentary on a single biblical book. The latter midrashim often deal with only a few opening verses of a biblical section, such as *Leviticus Rabbah,* or seem to be organized around verses read on holy days, such as the *Pesiqta de Rab Kahana* and the *Pesiqta Rabbati.* The expositional collections seldom cover an entire book. And despite the claims of many scholars, the homiletical midrashim should not be viewed as sermons delivered by rabbis in the ancient synagogues (Sarason 1981: 62–67). We simply do not know enough about the rabbis' activities to claim that they ever delivered sermons to the general public. Also, exactly how these sermons came to be written down and transmitted to us presents a problem (J. Heinemann 1970; 1971a: 141–50; 1971b: 100–22; 1971c: 808–34).

2. Characteristics of Rabbinic Midrash. Rabbinic midrash exhibits certain traits which differentiate it from other forms of biblical exegesis of our period. First, rabbinic texts are collections of independent units. Unlike the case with the pesharim, the translations, and the rewriting of the biblical narratives, the sequential arrangement of the passages of the midrash is most probably the work of the editor(s). It is likely that many of the comments that now appear in the midrashim were not originally created for a running commentary and that much of the homiletical material is literary creation from smaller units (Sarason 1982). In fact, we have many examples of midrashic comments appearing in other contexts as nonmidrashic passages (Porton 1985; Fraade 1983: 245–301). Second, we often find more than one comment per biblical unit: several synonymous, complementary, or contradictory remarks may appear in connection with a single verse, word, or letter. In the other examples, we find only one comment for a given biblical unit. Third, a large number of the rabbinic statements are assigned to named sages. However, the editors and authors of the rabbinic collections remain a mystery just as the creators of the majority of the other forms of Jewish exegesis from this period are also unknown to us. Fourth, the rabbinic comment may be directly connected to the biblical unit or it may be part of a dialogue, a story, or an extended soliloquy. The comment may answer a question which refers to the text but which need not be connected with the biblical passage to be comprehensible. Also, one interpretation may be the result of another explanation of the text given in the same context. Fifth, rabbinic midrash atomizes the text to a greater degree than any of the other forms of midrashic activity with the exception of the LXX and the Targums, which must, because they are translations, treat every element of the biblical passage. Each word or letter may serve as the basis for an exegetical remark of the rabbis. Sixth, often the specific method which forms the basis of the comment is explicitly mentioned by the rabbis.

Rabbinic midrash must be seen as an essential element in the rabbinic worldview. For the rabbis, the Torah was their link between this world and God. A rabbi was a rabbi because he alone knew the totality of revelation, and the written and oral versions of the Torah, and it was his task, as a rabbi, to study and to actualize the Torah's content. For the rabbis, midrash was, above all, a religious, God-centered, activity. The Bible contained all the secrets of the universe, and it was the source of all knowledge and wisdom; the Torah was the complete public revelation of the One, Only, and Perfect God to His people. The Bible was the ultimate guide for human action, the final arbiter between right and wrong, true and false. Every element of the text—every letter, every verse, every phrase—was written as it was for a specific reason and purpose, and it was the rabbis' task to discover the reason and to explicate the purpose. Furthermore, the Bible formed an integrated and interrelated whole, and it was one of the major rabbinic goals to demonstrate the unity of purpose and the singleness of intent of the Bible. However, the rabbis realized that the Bible spoke to different people, even to different rabbis, in different ways; therefore, the rabbinic masters accepted the possibility of multiple interpretations of biblical passages. As long as a rabbi approached the text as a legitimate member of the rabbinic class, his explanation of the Bible had to be taken seriously, and the comment itself became part of the ongoing process of the rabbinic explication of revelation (Neusner 1972: 44–128; Porton 1985: 1–3).

Modern scholarship divides early rabbinic exegesis into two major schools: that of Ishmael and that of Akiba (Heschel 1962: xxxvii–lix; Porton 1982: 205–11; Chernick 1979; Grabbe 1982: 527–32). Ishmael's school is pictured as the more logical, while Akiba's exegesis is seen as more mystical and imaginative. However, recent work has demonstrated that it is difficult to distinguish between the exegetical techniques used by Ishmael and those used by Akiba (Porton 1982: 205–11). While there may have been two or more schools of rabbinic exegesis, there is no evidence that they began with these two sages.

Scholars have also pointed out that there are lists of exegetical principles attributed to various sages, such as Hillel's seven principles, Ishmael's thirteen, and Eliezer's thirty-two (Strack 1959: 93–98); however, again, recent inquiries have shown that the authenticity of these lists is open to serious question (Porton fc.). Furthermore, there is no evidence that the sages mentioned actually preferred to use the principles attributed to them in the lists. Finally, as Lieberman (1950: 47–82) and Daube (1949: 234–64) have shown, the exegetical techniques assigned to the rabbis were those commonly used by the Hellenistic rhetoricians. Thus, the most we can say is that our texts leave the impression that the exegetical techniques of at least some of the early rabbis were similar to the exegetical practices of their non-Jewish neighbors.

Bibliography

Allegro, J. 1964. *The Dead Sea Scrolls: A Reappraisal.* Harmondsworth.

Attridge, H. 1976. *The Interpretation of Biblical History in the* Antiquitates Judaicae *of Flavius Josephus.* Missoula, MT.

Bacher, W. 1892. The Origin of the Word Haggadah (agada). *JQR* 4: 406–29.

———. 1965. *Die exegetische Terminologie der judischen Traditionsliterature.* Hildesheim.

Bickerman, E. 1959. The LXX as a Translation. *PAAJR* 28: 1–40.

Brownlee, W. 1951. Biblical Interpretation Among the Sectarians of the Dead Sea Scrolls. *BA* 16: 54–76.

Bruce, F. F. 1961. *Second Thoughts on the Dead Sea Scrolls,* 2d ed. Grand Rapids.

———. 1972. The Earliest Old Testament Interpretation. *OTS* 17: 37–52.

Chernick, M. 1979. The Use of Ribbuyim and Miᶜiutim in the Halakhic Midrash of Ishmael. *JQR* n.s. 70: 96–116.

Childs, B. 1971. Psalm Titles and Midrashic Exegesis. *JSS* 16: 137–50.

———. 1972. Midrash and the Old Testament. Pp. 45–60 in *Understanding the Sacred Text,* ed. J. Reumann. Valley Forge.

Cross, F. 1961. *The Ancient Library of Qumran.* Garden City.

Daube, D. 1949. Rabbinic Methods of Interpretation and Hellenistic Rhetoric. *HUCA* 22: 234–64.

Driver, S. R. 1963. *An Introduction to the Literature of the Old Testament.* New York.

Finkelstein, L. 1930. The Origin of the Synagogue. *PAAJR* 3: 49–59.

Fitzmyer, J. 1966. *The Genesis Apocryphon of Qumran Cave 1.* Rome.

Fraade, S. 1983. Sifre Deuteronomy 26 (ad Deut. 3:23): How Conscious the Composition? *HUCA* 54: 245–301.

Frankel, I. 1956. *Peshat in Talmudic and Midrashic Literature.* Toronto.

Gertner, M. 1962a. Terms of Scriptural Interpretation: A Study in Hebrew Semantics. *BSOAS* 25: 1–27.

———. 1962b. Midrashim in the New Testament. *JSS* 7: 267–92.

Gooding, D. W. 1974. On the Use of the LXX for Dating Midrashic Elements in the Targums. *JTS* 25: 1–11.

Goodspeed, E. J. 1959. *The Apocrypha: An American Translation.* New York.

Grabbe, L. 1982. Aquila's Translation and Rabbinic Exegesis. Pp. 527–36 in *Essays in Honour of Yigael Yadin,* ed. G. Vermes and J. Neusner. *JJS* 33.

Grossfeld, B. 1972–77. *A Bibliography of Targum Literature.* 2 vols. Cincinnati.

Halperin, J. 1976. The Exegetical Character of Ezek. X 9–17. *VT* 26: 129–41.

Heinemann, I. 1946. The Development of Technical Terms for the Exegesis of Scripture: I: DRS. *Leš* 14: 3–4; 182–89.

———. 1954. *The Paths of the Agadah.* 2d ed. Jerusalem.

Heinemann, J. 1970. *Sermons within the Community in the Talmudic Period.* Jerusalem.

———. 1971a. Profile of a Midrash: The Art of Composition in Leviticus Rabba. *JAAR* 39: 141–50.

———. 1971b. The Proem in the Aggadic Midrash: A Form-Critical Study. *ScrHier* 22: 100–122.

———. 1971c. ᵓÔmānût haqqompoziiah bammidraš wayyiqrāᵓ rabba. *Hasifrût* 2: 808–34.

Heschel, A. 1962. *Theology of Ancient Judaism.* New York.

James, M. 1971. *The Biblical Antiquities of Philo.* New York.

Lieberman, S. 1950. *Hellenism in Jewish Palestine.* New York.

Neusner, J. 1972. *There We Sat Down: Talmudic Judaism in the Making.* Nashville.

Porton, G. 1979. Midrash: Palestinian Jews and the Hebrew Bible in the Greco-Roman Period. *ANRW* 2/19/2: 103–38.

———. 1981. Defining Midrash. Pp. 55–92 in *The Study of Ancient Judaism I: Mishnah, Midrash, Siddur,* ed. J. Neusner. New York.

———. 1982. *The Traditions of Rabbi Ishmael.* Pt. 4. Leiden.

———. 1985. *Understanding Rabbinic Midrash.* New York.

———. fc. Ishmael as Exegete. In *Texts and Contexts of Ancient Judaism and Christianity,* ed. G. Porton.

Rabin, C. 1968. The Translation Process and the Character of the Septuagint. *Textus* 6: 1–26.

Robert, A. 1934. Les attaches littéraires bibliques de Prov. I-IX. *RB* 42: 42–68; 172–204; 374–84.

———. 1935. Les attaches littéraires biblîques de Prov. I–IX. *RB* 43: 344–65, 502–25.

———. 1944. Le genre littéraire du Cantique des cantiques. *Vivre et Penser* 3: 192–213 [= *RB* 52: 192–213].

Roth, C. 1960. The Subject Matter of Qumran Exegesis. *VT* 10: 51–69.

Sanders, J. 1972. *Torah and Canon.* Philadelphia.

Sandmel, S. 1961. The Haggada Within Scripture. *JBL* 80: 105–22.

Sarason, R. 1981. Toward a New Agendum for the Study of Rabbinic Midrashic Literature. Pp. 53–73 in *Studies in Aggadah, Targum and Jewish Liturgy in Memory of Joseph Heinemann,* ed. J. Petuchowski and E. Fleischer. Jerusalem.

———. 1982. The Petihot in Leviticus Rabba: "Oral Homilies" or Redactional Constructions? Pp. 557–67 in *Essays in Honour of Yigael Yadin,* ed. G. Vermes and J. Neusner. *JJS* 33.

Seeligman, I. 1953. Voraussetzungen der Midraschexeges. VTSup 1: 150–81.

Slomovic, E. 1969. Exegesis in the Dead Sea Scrolls. *RevQ* 25/7/1: 1–15.

Slonimsky, H. 1956. The Philosophy Implicit in the Midrash. *HUCA* 27: 235–90.

Stendahl, K. 1968. *The School of St. Matthew and Its Use of the Old Testament.* Philadelphia.

Strack, H. 1959. *Introduction to the Talmud and Midrash.* New York.

Towner, W. S. 1973. *The Rabbinic "Enumeration of Scriptural Examples."* Leiden.

VanderKam, J. 1977. *Textual and Historical Studies in the Book of Jubilees.* Missoula, MT.
Vermes, G. 1955. À propos des Commentaires bibliques découverts à Qumran. *RHPR* 35: 95–102.
———. 1961. *Scripture and Tradition in Judaism.* Leiden.
Weingreen, J. 1951–52. The Rabbinic Approach to the Study of the Old Testament. *BJRL* 24: 166–90.
Willi, T. 1972. *Die Chronik als Auslegung.* Göttingen.
Willi-Plein, I. 1971. *Vorformen der Schriftexegeses innerhalb des Alten Testaments.* Berlin.
Wright, A. 1967. *The Literary Genre Midrash.* New York.
Zeitlin, S. 1953. Midrash: A Historical Study. *JQR* n.s. 44: 21–36.
Zunz, L. 1966. *Die gottesdienstlichen Vorträge der Juden.* Hildesheim.

GARY G. PORTON

MIGDAL-EL (PLACE) [Heb *migdal-ʾēl*]. Town in the allotment of Naphtali (Josh 19:38). Most scholars feel that since Migdal-el is mentioned together with Yiron, it must have been in Upper Galilee, though its exact location is unknown. Woudstra (1981: 293), however, does mention a possible identification of Migdal-el with Mejdel-Islim, about 16 miles E–SE of Tyre.

Bibliography

Woudstra, M. H. 1981. *The Book of Joshua.* Grand Rapids.

DAVID SALTER WILLIAMS

MIGDAL-GAD (PLACE) [Heb *migdal-gād*]. Town situated in the Shephelah, or low country, of Judah (Josh 15:37), within the same district as Lachish. This settlement, whose name perhaps means "tower" of Gad (from *gdl,* "be great") is listed among the towns within the tribal allotment of Judah (Josh 15:21–62). Based on its geographical location and the similarity in sound and meaning, most scholars (e.g., Boling and Wright *Joshua* AB, 385) have suggested a tentative identification with Khirbet el-Mejdeleh, which is located approximately 6 km SE of Lachish (M.R. 140105). However, archaeological evidence for occupation during the Iron Age is lacking.

WADE R. KOTTER

MIGDOL (PLACE) [Heb *migdôl*]. A town or city thought to be located in Lower Egypt. It is cited in three different situations. In Exod 14:2 and Num 33:7, Migdol is mentioned as a place near the spot where the Israelites had camped before crossing the Red Sea. It is described as being situated near Pi-ha-hiroth, Baal-zephon, and the sea. It is definitely thought to be located in the E Delta region, but the exact site is unknown. Suggested sites include Tell el-Her and Tell el-Maskhuta. See also PI-HAHIROTH; BAAL-ZEPHON; RED SEA.

In Jer 44:1 and 46:14, Migdol, with Tahpanhes and Memphis, is designated as a main residential location for Jews in Lower Egypt. Ezekiel uses Migdol and Syene, in Ezek 29:10, as geographical extremes of the boundaries of Egypt. Migdol is used for the N designation and Syene for the opposite S point.

The name "Migdol" used in these various contexts may not belong to the same location, but there is not enough evidence to rule out this possibility. The word is of W Semitic origin (most likely Canaanite). It is found as an Egyptian loanword that is used commonly to mean "tower" or "fortress" and as a place name for various military stations that are found in the outer boundaries of Egypt. It appears in the Tell el-Amarna Letters (EA 234: 29), but no reference to its precise location is given.

JEFFREY K. LOTT

MIGHTY MEN. See DAVID'S CHAMPIONS.

MIGHTY ONE. See NAMES OF GOD IN THE OT.

MIGRON (PLACE) [Heb *migrôn*]. A locality in Benjamin (1 Sam 14:2; Isa 10:28). Commentators have assumed that the Hebrew toponym refers to a small town or village; unfortunately, the two biblical texts referring to Migron appear to give contradictory information regarding its location. In 1 Sam 14:2, the site is associated closely with Gibeah (= Geba, or modern Jaba, 9 km NE of Jerusalem on the S flank of the Wadi es-Swenit). In Isa 10:28, however, Migron seems to be placed between Aiath (et-Tell) and Michmash (Mukhmas) on the N side of the Swenit. A. Alt (1927: 17–20) identified Migron with Tell Maryam (M.R. 175141), 1 km SW of Mukhmas, on the grounds that the invading army of the Isaian oracle passed through Migron, while its baggage was left nearby at Michmash. If Migron were a biblical village, Tell Maryam is certainly a candidate, along with a number of Iron Age sites in the vicinity of Mukhmas, e.g., Tell el-Askar (M.R. 176143) or Khirbet el-Qubbe (M.R. 176141; Kochavi 1972: 180–82).

Quite possibly, however, the toponym does not refer to a village at all, but to the impressive Wadi es-Swenit. This canyon extends from the central Palestinian watershed through the Jaba/Mukhmas area, where it deepens dramatically as it joins the Wadi el-Qelt and issues into the Jordan valley near Jericho (Dalman 1905: 161–75). See Fig. MIG.01. The ancient name *migrôn* (from the root *ngr,* "to gush forth") is similar in form to that of other Canaanite valleys (e.g., Arnon, Kishon, Kidron) and would refer to the occasional floods which sweep the wadi in winter and spring.

The reference in 1 Sam 14:2 ought then be translated, "Saul camped on the outskirts of Gibeah under 'the Pomegranate' in the Migron." The "Pomegranate" is probably identical with the "Pomegranate Rock" of Judg 20:45–47, to which 600 Gibeahite soldiers fled for refuge after an ambush by Ephraimite warriors. See RIMMON. This rock is likely the large pockmarked cave called el-Jaia in the S wall of the Wadi es-Swenit, less than 2 km E of Jaba (Gibeah/Geba). Saul and his 600 men seem to have sought refuge in this cave while the Philistines occupied nearby Michmash above the valley (cf. 1 Sam 14:11).

Isaiah's description of the invading army (10:28–29) ought not be read as a consecutive itinerary; rather, the point of the passage is that the invader "passed over the Migron" after having left military equipment in Michmash. The thought is paralleled by the following comment, that the army "passed over the Geba Pass, and spent the night." The ancient Migron apparently formed the international boundary between the kingdoms of Israel

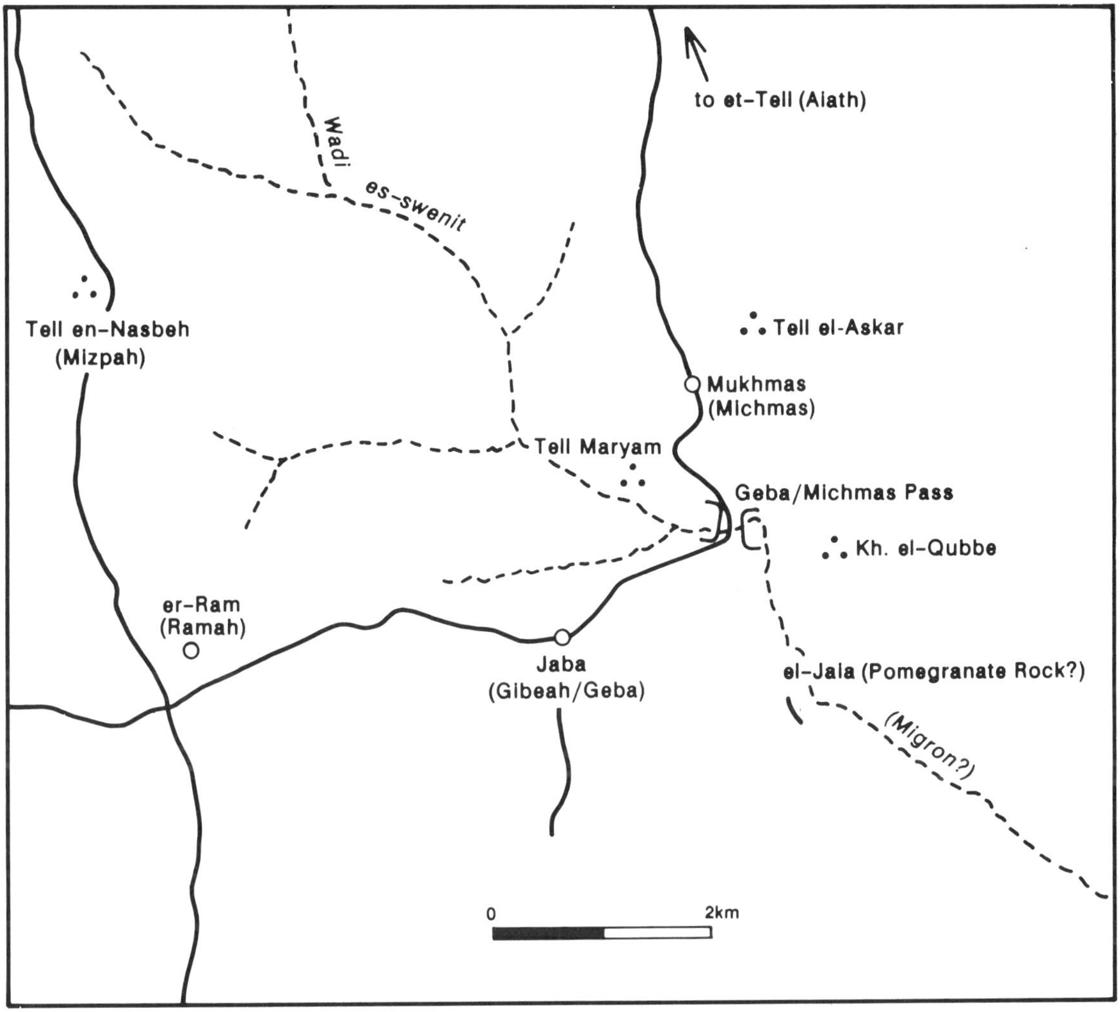

MIG.01. Regional map of Migron. *(Map by P. M. Arnold)*

and Judah in the late 8th century B.C., and the Geba Pass marked the highway crossing over this border. Isaiah's parallelism seems to draw dramatic attention to this military violation of Judah's N boundary.

Bibliography

Alt, A. 1927. *PJ* 23. Berlin.

Dalman, G. 1905. Das wādi eṣ ṣwēnīt. *ZDPV* 28: 161–75.

Kochavi, M. 1972. *Judea, Samaria, and the Golan: Archaeological Survey 1967–68*. Jerusalem (in Hebrew).

PATRICK M. ARNOLD

MIJAMIN (PERSON) [Heb *miyyāmîn*]. Four individuals in the Hebrew Bible bear this name. **1.** A priest who appears in an organizational list associated with David (1 Chr 24:9). According to the genealogical information in 1 Chronicles 24, Mijamin was a descendant of Aaron through the family of either Eleazar or Ithanar. When lots were cast in order to organize the various officers of the temple, he was assigned to the sixth of twenty-four divisions. Given the postexilic perspective of Chronicles, Mijamin is further seen as an ancestor of a later priestly family (Braun *1 Chronicles* WBC, 228).

2. A son of Parosh and a member of the Israelite community whose members agreed to renounce their foreign wives and children (Ezra 10:25; 1 Esdr 9:26). Following more specialized lists referring to priests and Levites, Mijamin is included among the laity.

3. A priest who joined in with officials and laity alike in "sealing" the covenant with Nehemiah (Neh 10:8—Eng 10:7). Given Israel's disappointing record of obeying the

Lord in the past (Neh 9:1–37), a public confession of sin resulted in the establishment of a new covenant and a new determination within the postexilic community (Neh 9:38).

4. A priest who returned to Jerusalem with Zerubbabel following the Exile (Neh 12:5). Appended in the book of Nehemiah, the list in which Mijamin appears can be chronologically associated with Ezra 2:36–40.

The name Mijamin is actually a contracted form of MINIAMIN (Heb *minyāmîn,* "from the right hand," i.e., "a favored one"), which appears in 2 Chr 31:15. The fact that the Syriac of Ezra 10:25 reads Benjamin rather than Mijamin might suggest a possible equation. However, such an equation seems doubtful insofar as the name Mijamin itself occurs in various Neo-Babylonian and Persian documents.

TERRY L. BRENSINGER

MIKLOTH (PERSON) [Heb *miqlôt*]. The etymology of this name, which is not attested outside of the Bible, is problematic. The ending *-oth (ôt)* is very rare in personal names (e.g., Naboth), and Noth's claim (*IPN,* 39) that it is used in hypocoristic names has little basis. The remaining element *mql* is used in Hebrew of a "rod" or a "staff," but this element is not found in other Hebrew names, though the name *mql*ʾ is known from Phoenician (Benz 1972: 353). Perhaps Mikloth should be connected to names, such as Koliah (Jer 29:21; cf. Benz 1972: 353 and Fowler *TPNAH,* 358), which contain the element *qôl,* "voice." Despite the difficulty in finding a likely etymology for Mikloth, no obvious emendation presents itself; and the name is supported by the versions.

1. A Benjaminite, the son of Avi-Gibeon or Jeiel according to 1 Chr 8:32 and 9:37, 38. Mikloth's name is missing in the MT of 8:31; but context, most of the versions, and the parallel 9:37 suggest that it must be restored there (Rudolph *Chronikbücher* HAT, 78). It is unclear if Mikloth is related to Saul; this depends on whether the Kish of 1 Chr 8:30 is to be identified with the Kish of v 33 (Demsky 1971: 16–20) and whether we assume (with Curtis and Madsen *Chronicles* ICC, 164) that the Chronicler has intentionally substituted Gibeon for Gibeah, Saul's birthplace. In 1 Chr 8:32, it is implied that some part of Mikloth's family moved to Jerusalem, but it is unclear exactly who moved (Williamson *1 and 2 Chronicles* NCBC, 86). On the repetition of this genealogy in chaps. 8 and 9, see AHAZ.

2. An official (Heb *nāgîd*) of Dodai the Ahohite, one of David's twelve monthly officials, according to the MT of 1 Chr 27:4. This institution is not authentic and is probably based on a similar list of Solomon's in 1 Kgs 4:7–19; it suggests that the period of David was a time of total order (Williamson, 174–75). The text of 1 Chr 27:4 is highly problematic and requires emendation. The two words which follow "the Ahohite" are *ûmāḥăluqtô ûmiqlôt,* "and his division and Mikloth." These words are graphically very similar to and are probably a corrupted dittography of the name of Dodai's tribe (Levi?), which became corrupted to *ûmāḥăluqtô,* "and his division," which is commonly used throughout the chapter. The verse would then have originally read ". . . Dodai the Ahohite, from the tribe of X, the officer"; this would be similar in structure to v 14, ". . . Benaiah of Pirathon, of the sons of Ephraim." Others (e.g., Rudolph *Chronikbücher* HAT, 178) follow the LXX and omit the three words *ûmāḥăluqtô ûmiqlôt hannāgîd,* "and his division and Mikloth, the officer."

Bibliography

Benz, F. L. 1972. *Personal Names in the Phoenician and Punic Inscriptions.* Studia Pohl 8. Rome.

Demsky, A. 1971. The Genealogy of Gibeon (I Chronicles 9:35–44): Biblical and Epigraphic Considerations. *BASOR* 202: 16–23.

MARC Z. BRETTLER

MIKNEIAH (PERSON) [Heb *miqnēyāhû*]. One of the Levites of second rank appointed to provide music during David's second effort to move the ark to Jerusalem (1 Chr 15:18, 21). For further discussion, see ELIPHELEHU.

RAYMOND B. DILLARD

MILALAI (PERSON) [Heb *milălay*]. A kinsman of Zechariah and a musician who performed at the dedication of the Jerusalem wall (Neh 12:36). At the ceremony, he was part of the group which paraded to the right. His name is omitted in the LXX. KB suggests that the name is either a short form of *millalyāh* ("Yahweh has spoken"; cf. Aram *mallēl*) or the result of a dittographic error (note the similarity of the following word: *gilălay*).

NORA A. WILLIAMS

MILCAH (PERSON) [Heb *milkāh*]. **1.** Daughter of Haran, and therefore also sister of Lot, who married her uncle Nahor (Gen 11:29). Because she was the mother of Bethuel, Milcah also became the grandmother of Rebekah (Gen 22:20–33; 24:15). Whatever was the text is to be understood in terms of original sources, the present text relates Milcah to Abraham through both of his brothers, Haran and Nahor (Noth *ÜgS* 235, n. 579).

Milcah's unusual relationship with Nahor (as both niece and wife) has led to comparisons with "marriage adoption" contracts from Nuzi involving the legal status of "daughter," "daughter-in-law," and "sister" (Speiser 1963: 25; following the ANE legal customs identified by Koschaker 1933). However, there are problems with these comparisons. Nuzi contracts are not necessarily concerned with marriage between the contracted parties (Greengus 1975: 22); instead, they provide the woman with the support of an additional family, a relationship which has been described as similar to "godparents" (Grosz 1987: 140). Some contracts at Nuzi do deal with the transference of rights in terms of who has the legal right to arrange the marriage of the person being "adopted." The biblical narrative does not discuss any transfer in the rights of giving Milcah in marriage (Thompson 1974: 233; Eichler 1977: 48–59).

The name "Milcah" is a feminine form of the root *mlk,* "ruler." Its meaning is similar to that of Sarah, and has been interpreted as an honorific description of the individual's position within the family group (Stamm 1967: 326).

2. Daughter of Zelophehad, who, along with her sisters, was responsible for eliciting Mosaic legislation regarding the daughter's right to inheritance where the father had no son (Num 27:1–11). This may be similar to practices at Nuzi and elsewhere in the ANE where daughters became recipients of inheritance property, and as such could legally be designated "sons" with provisions to keep the inheritance within the father's family, even after the marriage of the daughter (Ben-Barak 1980; Paradise 1980; 1987; Huehnergard 1985: 429–30). For hypotheses about the location of Milcah's inheritance, see HEPHER (PLACE).

Attempts have been made to associate the names of Milcah's sisters with the names of towns or of Aramean tribes, but so far a geographical identification for Milcah has not been established (Gray 1896: 116; Noth *ÜgS* 164–65; Budd *Numbers* WBC, 300). However, an association of Milcah with Hammolecheth of 1 Chron 7:18 has led to identifying territory near Tell el-Farah North as that belonging to Milcah (Demsky 1982: 70–75).

Bibliography

Ben-Barak, Z. 1980. Inheritance by Daughters in the Ancient Near East. *JSS* 25: 22–33.

Demsky, A. 1982. The Genealogies of Manasseh and the Location of the Territory of Milcah Daughter of Zelophehad. *EI* 16: 70–75. (Hebrew, English summary, p. 254*).

Eichler, B. L. 1977. Another Look at the Nuzi Sistership Contracts. Pp. 45–59 in *Essays on the Ancient Near East in Memory of J. J. Finkelstein,* ed. M. de Jong Ellis. Memoirs of the Connecticut Academy of Arts and Sciences 19. Hamden, CT.

Gray, G. B. 1896. *Studies in Hebrew Proper Names.* London.

Greengus, S. 1975. Sisterhood Adoption at Nuzi and the "Wife-Sister" in Genesis. *HUCA* 46: 5–31.

Grosz, K. 1987. Some Aspects of the Adoption of Women at Nuzi. Vol. 2, pp. 131–52 in *Studies on the Civilization and Culture of Nuzi and the Hurrians,* ed. D. I. Owen and M. A. Morrison. Winona Lake, IN.

Huehnergard, J. 1985. Biblical Notes on Some New Akkadian Texts from Emar (Syria). *CBQ* 47: 428–34.

Koschaker, P. 1933. Fratriarchat, Hausgemeinschaft und Mutterrecht in Keilschriftrechten. *ZA* 41: 1–89.

Lemaire, A. 1972. Le "pays de Hepher" et les "filles de Zelophehad" à la lumière des ostraca de Samarie. *Sem* 22: 13–20.

Paradise, J. 1980. A Daughter and Her Father's Property at Nuzi. *JCS* 32: 189–207.

———. 1987. Daughters as "Sons" at Nuzi. Vol. 2, pp. 203–13 in *Studies on the Civilization and Culture of Nuzi and the Hurrians,* ed. D. I. Owen and M. A. Morrison. Winona Lake, IN.

Speiser, E. A. 1963. The Wife-Sister Motif in the Patriarchal Narratives. Pp. 15–28 in *Biblical and Other Studies,* ed. A. Altmann.

Stamm, J. J. 1967. Hebräische Frauennamen. Pp. 301–39 in *Hebräische Wortforschung: Festschrift zum 80. Geburtstag von Walter Baumgartner,* ed. B. Hartmann et al. VTSup 16. Leiden.

Thompson, T. L. 1974. *The Historicity of the Patriarchal Narratives.* BZAW 133. Berlin.

Richard S. Hess

MILCOM (DEITY) [Heb *milkōm*]. See MOLECH (DEITY).

MILDEW. See LEPROSY.

MILE. See WEIGHTS AND MEASURES.

MILESTONES. See ROADS AND HIGHWAYS.

MILETUS (PLACE) [Gk *Milētos*]. A city on the SW coast of Turkey where Paul stopped and sent for the elders of Ephesus (Acts 20:15, 17), and where Paul had to leave Trophimus, who was ill (2 Tim 4:20).

The city is near the mouth of the Meander River on the SW coast of Turkey, 30 miles due S of Ephesus. Miletus was originally a coastal city, built on a peninsula with four natural harbors, but because of the silting of the area and the shifting of the course of the Meander (modern Menderes or Maiandros) River, it now lies more than 5 miles from the sea. In 1980, prehistoric potsherds were discovered in stratigraphic levels immediately above bedrock, which indicates that a settlement of some kind existed here at that time (Müller-Wiener 31:1981: 201).

According to Strabo (14.1.6), the city was founded by Cretans of the Minoan period, after which it was occupied by Mycenaeans from Achaia who used it as a fortress outpost in the 14th century B.C. Homer implies that the men of Miletus joined the Carians against the Greeks in the Trojan War about 1250 B.C. (*Il.* 2.868ff.). The city was destroyed about 1200 and repopulated by Ionians, according to Strabo, although the Greeks may never have abandoned it. It soon became the most important of the twelve cities of Ionia, probably because of its great harbor facilities and its navy, which enabled the city to establish prosperous new colonies in Egypt and on the shores of the Black Sea. Several offshore islands were under the control of Miletus during this time, including Patmos.

By the 6th century B.C., Miletus became the most prosperous Greek city, not only of Ionia, but of all Asia Minor. Its necropolis was discovered in 1987 in the village of Yeni Balat (Mellink 1989: 122–23), from which fine examples of pottery, sculpture, and dedicatory reliefs testify to the artistic and commercial prominence of the city. Miletus was one of the first cities of the ancient world to mint coins. Around the end of the 5th century B.C., the Milesian alphabet was adopted by Athens and became the standard writing system of the Greeks.

The city came under Persian influence in 546 B.C. and led the Ionian cities in the revolt against Persia in 499 B.C. This resulted in the destruction of the city by the Persians in 494, after a fierce battle was fought nearby on both land and sea. Herodotus records that "Miletus was reduced to slavery" (6.18ff.). The temple of Apollo in Didyma, about 10 miles S of Miletus, was also destroyed, but it was soon rebuilt and processions were resumed each spring between the sanctuary of Apollo Delphinios in Miletus and the temple in Didyma. The Sacred Way, connecting these two sanctuaries of Apollo, was eventually paved with large limestone slabs during the reign of Trajan in the 2d century A.D. This splendid street has been found in excavation, and work is being conducted to study its surroundings, which include colonnaded halls, fountains, a nymphaeum, and a two-story gate. Four levels of the roadway were identified in 1987 (Müller-Wiener 1988: 194).

After the Persian destruction, Ephesus surpassed Miletus as the largest city in Ionia, and it never regained its former status. However, even though the city waned in prominence during the classical period which followed, it was still an important center of commerce and art in Ionia. Its estimated 60,000 inhabitants rebuilt the city on a grid that originated in the 6th century and became widely used throughout the Mediterranean world for the next several centuries. This grid, later called the "Hippodamian Grid," was popularized by a citizen of Miletus named Hippodamus, who, in 479 B.C., used it in laying out the city. The grid somewhat resembled a checkerboard, but having rectangles rather than squares in the pattern. The city walls were not completed until the time of Alexander the Great, who captured Miletus in 334 B.C. In the Roman period, it was one of the principal metropolitan areas of Asia Minor.

The central part of the city lay on the S shore of the Bay of Lions, between hills of the peninsulas on the E and W. Eumenes II, an Attalid ruler of Pergamum in the 2d century B.C., was one of the great builders of the later city. He built the gymnasium, preserved only in Roman reconstruction, the W gate, and probably the stadium as well. Another period of intense building activity was experienced under Trajan, who erected the majestic nymphaeum and paved the Sacred Way. However, the greatest builder of Miletus was Faustina, the wife of Marcus Aurelius. She had spent some time there in A.D. 164 and was so impressed that she made a considerable donation toward the construction of the baths, which were named for her. The bathhouse is the largest and best preserved building on the site. Faustina also participated in the erection of the Roman theatre, one of the best preserved and most impressive structures in Turkey. The baths stood S of the hill on the W peninsula, SE of the market area. The theatre, which could seat 15,000, was built into the S side of this hill, as a reconstruction of an earlier Hellenistic theatre.

When the apostle Paul visited the city, it already had three impressive marketplaces, testimony to the abundance of trade stimulated by its four harbors. The South Market, situated SE of the theatre hill, is the largest Greek agora known to have existed in the ancient Greek world, covering more than 108,000 square feet. It was also used as a place for formal occasions, such as dedications by the Roman emperors. The beautiful North Gate, or Market Gate, leading into the South Market, was not built until the 2d century A.D. It was removed from its site by the German excavator and taken piece by piece to the Pergamon Museum in Berlin, where it now can be seen in a magnificent state of reconstruction.

Several temples stood in Miletus when Paul was there: the Athena Temple, S of the theater and the West Market; the sanctuary of Apollo (the Delphinion), by the harbor of the Bay of Lions; and the temple of Apollo in Didyma. There was also a bouleuterion, or senate house, in the form of a small odeion, which was built between the North and South markets. A sixteen-columned harbor gateway had been set up near the Delphinion in the first half of the 1st century A.D., just before Paul's arrival. The central of its three entrances opened toward the S onto a magnificent processional road, which measured 92 ft wide and extended southward for more than 300 ft. Vergilius Capito, a friend of the Roman emperor Claudius, built, with the emperor's aid, a colonnaded Ionic porch (stoa) along the E side of this road, as well as a small bathhouse further E. Claudius died about the time Paul first visited Miletus (Acts 20:15, 17). There was also a gymnasium in the city, as well as a stadium whose arena was 95 ft wide and 630 ft long.

Paul's first visit was at the conclusion of his third missionary journey, on which he bypassed Ephesus, traveling S from Troas, and stopped at the larger harbor facilities at Miletus. There, he summoned the elders from the church in Ephesus and spoke to them. He had bypassed Ephesus and landed in Miletus because he was in a hurry to get to Jerusalem by Pentecost (Acts 20:16) and did not want to spend time in the Ephesian area where he had worked for almost three years (Acts 20:31).

A second visit by Paul to Miletus, probably several years later, is indicated in 2 Tim 4:20, when he left Trophimus, the Ephesian, there due to the latter's illness.

Bibliography

Akurgal, E. 1970. *Ancient Civilizations and Ruins of Turkey.* Istanbul.

Kleiner, G. 1976. Miletos. Pp. 578–82 in *Princeton Encyclopedia of Classical Sites,* ed. R. Stillwell. Princeton.

Mellink, M. J. 1989. Archaeology in Anatolia. *AJA* 93: 122–25.

Mitchell, S. 1985. Archaeology in Asia Minor, 1979–84. *Archaeological Reports (for 1984–85)* 31: 85–86.

Mitchell, S., and McNicoll, A. W. 1979. Archaeology in Western and Southern Asia Minor, 1971–78. *Archaeological Reports (for 1978–79)* 25: 63; 73–75.

Müller-Wiener, W. 1978. Recent Archaeological Research in Turkey; Miletus, 1977. *AnSt* 28: 28.

———. 1981. Recent Archaeological Research in Turkey; Miletus, 1980. *AnSt* 31: 200–201.

———. 1983. Recent Archaeological Research in Turkey; Miletus, 1982. *AnSt* 33: 256.

———. 1984. Recent Archaeological Research in Turkey; Miletus, 1983. *AnSt* 34: 229–30.

———. 1986. Recent Archaeological Research in Turkey; Miletus, 1985. *AnSt* 36: 206.

———. 1987. Recent Archaeological Research in Turkey; Miletus, 1986. *AnSt* 37: 185–86; 209.

———. 1988. Recent Archaeological Research in Turkey; Miletus, 1987. *AnSt* 38: 201–202.

JOHN MCRAY

MILH, TELL EL.

See MALHATA, TEL.

MILITARY ORGANIZATION IN MESOPOTAMIA.

The Mesopotamian army (Akk *ummānu, emūqu,* and *illatu* [rare]) is made known to us through representative monuments and texts from the period of the Sumerian city-states in the 3d millennium B.C., up until the fall of the Assyrian empire, and then again during the Babylonian empire under the attack of the Persians at the end of the first half of the 1st millennium B.C. The army served as an instrument of rivalries among Sumerian states, between Assyria and Babylonia, and among these countries and their powerful neighbors (most notably Elam, Egypt, the Hittites, the Mitannians, the Urartu, and Syrian principalities). The army was also confronted with waves of invaders who, over the course of time, attacked the rich Fertile Crescent, peoples such as the Guti, Sea Peoples, and Suteans. These confrontations brought about an evolution of military techniques adapted to the equipment and techniques of their enemies.

It is with the appearance of the royal military around 2700 B.C. and the struggle for hegemony among the Sumerian city-states that the cities began to surround themselves with thick walls: the excavations of Uruk uncovered a thick, 9.5-km-long wall defended by some 900 semicircular towers.

The "Stele of the Vultures" (*ANEP,* pp. 94–96) gives us a good example of the army of this period: it was organized into powerful units of six ranks, each one composed of ten men and one "officer." The primary weapon was the lance, but the mace and the encased ax, with a long, narrow blade with cutting edges, also made up part of the Sumerian soldier's equipment. The sword was also used after the mastering of metallurgy made possible the attainment of a shock-resistant blade. The protective gear of the fighter consisted of a pointed helmet, covering the ears and the back of the neck, and a small sleeveless cape, reinforced with metal and a large rectangular buckle made of wood covered with fur and studded with metal plates.

Chariots supported the infantry. Attested as far back as the middle of the 4th millennium by the archaic tablets from Uruk, their military usage, adopted by the different Sumerian city-states, represented an innovation that transformed the technique of combat. The chariot was composed of a large box, protected by a high frontal platform raised up on four wheels. According to the remains found at Kish and the decorations of the Standard of Ur (*ANEP,* p. 97), it was constructed of reed and wood, and was reinforced with metal and leather. Although it was strong and stable, it was too heavy for tactical maneuvers, and the traction of its four harnessed onagers was reduced by the position of the yoke which rested between the shoulder blades of the animal. The chariot was ridden by two men, the driver and a fighter armed with a lance, javelins, and an ax. This chariot was used to transport warriors and equipment and, once the enemy ranks were broken, to pursue the fleeing enemies. Another lighter two-wheeled chariot is also attested; it doubtless was used to ensure communications. The Fara texts, which furnish bills for repairs to the chariots and lists of troops in the garrison or sent into battle, show that the maintenance of the equipment rested with the administration of the Palace. See also CHARIOT.

The size of these Sumerian armies was low: around 600–700 men. One text itemizes the "conscripts" of Sumer: 182 men from Uruk, 192 from Adab, 94 from Nippur, 60 from Lagaš, 56 from Šuruppak, and 86 from Umma—670 in total. When conflicts arose, the regular army was reinforced by country militias levied from among the beneficiaries of arable land grants, to which nomad contingents could also be added.

The rise of Sargon around 2370 B.C. marked the triumph of a new army—one more technologically advanced and armed with the composite bow. Strength was also increasing: King Sargon was said to have attacked Syria with 5,400 men and his son Rimuš to have taken 5,700 prisoners from the Sumerian coalitionists who rebelled against him.

When the Sumerian rulers of the Ur III empire reorganized their army after the destruction of the Guti, they continued to equip it with a body of archers, based on the Akkadian model.

Throughout Mesopotamian history, the "private" (ERÉN) belonged to the staff of the palace, for whom he carried out civil as well as military tasks according to the circumstances. An unskilled laborer, he took care of agriculture and security operations, or waged battle. The army was reinforced by the incorporation of prisoners, notably Elamites, all the more so in order to fight against the incessant infiltration of nomads; some garrisons were stationed permanently in different points of the empire, especially along the borders.

During the entire period from the end of the 3d millennium to the beginning of the 2d, when the Mesopotamians were in contact with new populations, transformations progressively took place which became apparent in the 18th century and lasted up until the 1st millennium. These transformations mainly concerned the use of the horse and chariot, the improvement of siege equipment (assault towers and battering rams), the appearance of the supply services, and a developed intelligence service.

Decorated images from this period are rare, but the written documents, the Mari letters for example, describe the techniques used at the time of the sieges: the assailants filled in the moat that protected the town with a "mountain" of earth; this access ramp allowed the attack of the walls, while the archers, stationed on wooden towers, covered the soldiers who were maneuvering the battering ram. The chariots blocked the access and prevented the approach of any external help. In response to these techniques, deeper moats, advanced walls, and glacis were developed to protect the walls from siege engines.

Moreover, this period is marked by a general development of military strength and a strengthening of the military formation of garrisons which were stationed permanently in numerous towns. The armies, whose size was still increasing, were often heterogeneous: the Babylonian forces included Elamites, Kassites, Chaldeans, Arameans, people from Mari, Hanaeans, and Yaminites. The integration of these contingents often presented a difficult problem for the central authority, notably for the nomad elements who were prone to desert at the slightest opportunity. At Mari, a *sugāgum,* in charge of the relationship between the royal administration and each of its communities, was responsible for the recruitment and the overseeing of units.

These armies included some mercenary troops, but only the sums of money and the gifts received by the high-ranking officers appeared in the "pay rosters"; for the professional soldiers (*rēdûm, bāʾirum*), the military service obligation was clearly linked to the usufruct of a piece of land, which was granted by the king in exchange for military service (cf. Hammurabi Code, §26–41).

In the first half of the 2d millennium, the assembled strength for large operations could be important: at the time of the siege of Nurrugum, Shamshi-Adad (1814–1782 B.C.) raised 60,000 men.

However, from the 17th century onward, another innovation improved the art of war: the appearance of a new type of war chariot. Light, equipped with two spoked wheels (four, six, or eight spokes), it was capable of quick and decisive maneuvers on the battlefield. In fact, if the horse and chariot were familiar for a long time, it was the Mitannians and the Kassites, great horsebreeders, who gave to the cavalry and chariotry their importance in the army and in society.

Some technical modifications, most often with Kassite names (the circle of the wheel, *allak,* the spoke, *anakandaš/akkandaš,* etc.) improved the chariot: the box was made lighter and placed on two wheels of a larger diameter. The wheels were situated more in the rear in order to lighten the load.

The "aristocracy" of the Mitannian cavalrymen generalized the use of the chariot in Mesopotamia by extending it to this particular form of chase known as "war." The commanders of the chariot squadrons, the *maryannu,* formed an elevated status in Mitannian society, and one finds officers occupying such a position also in the western regions of the Near East, which probably did not include Mitanni but who were influenced by that state.

The men that formed the crew of the chariots (*rākib narkabti*) had at their command a type of stableman (*kizû*); the units, probably of 10 chariots since a "dizainier" (*emantuhlu*) commanded them, were grouped in companies of 50 chariots under the orders of a "commander-of-50" (*rab hanša*).

Even though, at Nuzi and at Alalakh, one knows of some cases where the chariot masters sold their chariot, it seems that the chariotry belonged to the palace. Towns and villages, by way of an obligatory allowance, had to donate chariots, or parts of chariots, that were then collected by the officials and redistributed according to need. In the meantime, the chariots were stocked in warehouses and arsenals with the equipment, labeled as belonging to companies of the right or the left. A senior officer of the royal house (*šākin bīti*) was in charge of all this.

The chariots, whose manufacture called for local raw materials (wool and leather) but also imported materials (wood and bronze), represented an important investment and were an element of prestige and wealth. The period from the 16th to the 9th century B.C. is known as the age of chariotry in all of Mesopotamia.

The perfected chariot was adopted by the Hittites, who also applied the progress made in using horses: a Hittite work, although signed with a Hurrite name (*kikkuli*), reveals the technique of training a team of horses.

At the time of the battle of Kadesh, the Hittite army numbered more than 35,000 men and 3,500 chariots, and the Egyptians came close to being conquered by an outflanking movement by the Hittite chariotry that took them off guard.

The development of chariotry and the number of horses created the acute problem of replenishment of stores. During operations, it became necessary to live off the land: summer, harvesting time, was thus the season when war was waged, despite the heat, all the more so since the dry terrain avoided the risk of the chariots getting bogged down in mud.

Until the reign of Tiglath-pileser III (744–727 B.C.), the army did not undergo any other important transformations, except perhaps the introduction of an army of slingers. The evolution of tactics, at least in Assyria, was more definite than that of technique. In fact, with Tukulti-Ninurta I (1244–1208 B.C.), the army became the tool of a policy of terror: towns were reduced to ashes, bodies of enemies piled up into heaps, and prisoners were mutilated. The objective of the war was not to annex new territory but to drain the riches and raw materials, and the consequences thereof must have dissuaded eventual resistance. This was the time of great raids across the whole country; thus, for example, Tiglath-pileser I (1115–1077 B.C.) pursued the Ahlamū-Arameans at the front of their chariots over hundreds of kilometers.

At the same time, the role of the warrior was exalted, as the poem of Erra shows. The army was the instrument of the god Ashur, destined to universal domination; warfare ideology thus found a juridical and religious basis.

During the 10th and 9th centuries, the army's strength was still increasing—Shalmaneser (858–824 B.C.) raised 120,000 men in one expedition across Syria—but two characteristics should be emphasized: on one hand, the growing importance of cavalry; on the other hand, a change of tactics. The army abandoned the great raids—(they allowed deep breakthroughs but let the nomads group themselves in the rear)—in favor of adopting a method of harassing the enemy in a defined space in order to assure lasting control of the terrain, even at the price of prolonged sieges.

With the country in submission, the army took part in economic exploitation. Loaded with booty and tribute-money—replenishment of stores, chariots, horses, oxen, precious objects, and cedar beams—it advanced no more than 20 or so miles on its daily marches.

On the other hand, the cavalry continued to grow in importance, still remaining tied to the chariotry with which it fought. The bas-reliefs of the palace of Nimrod show how the cavalrymen (most often barefoot and without a saddle or stirrup) operated in pairs: one held the reins of two mounts, the other fought with a powerful composite bow, wearing the cross-belt on his back, and a long, straight sword at his side. This was the system of modified chariotry; the bronze doors of Balawat illustrate the fundamental role that it played in battles and sieges.

It is with the reforms of Tiglath-pileser III, in the 8th century B.C., that the army of the last Assyrio-Babylonian empire was constituted. The Sargonids indeed continued his policy and his imperialistic aims using the methods by which it was equipped.

This powerful army belonged to a strongly centralized empire, which determined a certain number of its characteristics: the establishment of points of appui; increase in the number of liaison agents assuring the collection and transmission of information as well as the dispatching of orders; the organization of troops into permanent and provincial units. Numerous foreign contingents were integrated and were kept at a distance from their native land in order to break all "national" cohesion.

The strongholds assured in all of Assyria not only the surveillance of the surrounding countryside, the settling of nomadic populations, and exchanges with the natives, but also the collection of tribute money and free passage on main routes. They were the departure points of expeditions and the storehouses and warehouses for the replenishment of arms. There, like elsewhere in the country, these soldiers (*ṣābu*) carried out the service of the king (*dullu ša šarri*) which consisted of military as well as civil tasks for the economic well-being of the country.

These strongholds were connected to the central authority by a complex organization of messengers: ordinary messengers (*mār šipri*), mounted messengers (*rakbu*), emissaries (*kallap šipirti* or *kallû*). These couriers were responsible for a specific portion on the strategic itineraries.

The intelligence service, in which the crowned prince played an important role, was an essential piece of the military formation: the *dayyālu* were specially trained scouts to go and look for information, sometimes far in front of the lines. Trustworthy men (*ša qurbuti*) were in charge of verifying the authenticity of the information and assuring good transmission and coordination of orders.

Chariotry and cavalry remained the shock weapons par excellence but their respective importance changed in favor of cavalry. From now on, chariots together with the infantry played the role of light artillery from which volleys of arrows were shot. There were three men per chariot: the driver, an archer, and a third charioteer (*tašlīšu*), a shield bearer. Under Ashurbanipal a heavier chariot appeared with larger wheels which carried four men.

The "lists of horses," which included the names of superior officers of the cavalry and chariotry, show that there was an appeal to experts and specialized foreign contingents. For the chariots, the Syrian town of Samaria, the only non-Assyrian town whose unit was incorporated with its officers (*rab urâte*) in the royal army without losing its national identity, occupied a privileged position. The extreme skillfulness of its charioteers rested without a doubt on a clear technological advance (already evident under Shalmaneser) and the fact that they were professional soldiers; this professionalism gave the Assyrian king enough confidence to integrate these mercenaries into units composing his own permanent army.

As for the cavalry, it was the Urartians who furnished specialized units to the Assyrian army: their expertise was famous if one believes the account of the 8th campaign of Sargon II. However, they were integrated into the Assyrian army in various units, subordinate to an Assyrian command, perhaps because the absence of the mercenary tradition rendered their loyalty less certain.

This cavalry (*sisû ša pēthalli*) presented, from the time of Sargon on, contingents who could attain 1,000 cavalrymen; from then on they evolved independently, and a new type of reins allowed their hands to be free to fight.

The important place held by chariotry, and even more so by cavalry, brought about the need for an abundant supply of remounts: some officers had the specific task of assuring the dispatching of horses, which was done more or less by lots, from one or several towns. The horses from the country of Kuš (Nubia), which were equipped with a proper harness, were considered the best for pulling chariots, while those from Mesu (in Iran) were the best for riding.

If a large part of this remount was furnished by tribute money from the eastern countries, one nonnegligible part was bought notably in Egypt and in Mannean country; an active and lucrative trade was led by specialized merchants (*tamkār sisê*).

Hanas (stud farms) were introduced in various places in the empire, especially in Syria and in the Assyrian capitals, Kalhu, Dur-Šarrukin, and Nineveh, whose arsenal (*ekal māšarti*) had been reconstructed on a larger scale in order to "make the horses gallop exhaustively."

As the name of an officer shows ("commander-of-50") and the composition of the cavalry units (approximately 50, 100, 150, 200, 300, and even 500 men) the tactical base unit (*kitullu, pirra*) must have been 50 cavalrymen.

The infantry (*zūku*) constituted the essential part of the army and was particularly efficient in sieges and in operations on the mountainous periphery of Mesopotamia. The populations there most often waged partisan wars which limited the usefulness of chariots.

The footmen included the heavy infantry (spear carriers) and the lighter infantry (slingers and archers). These archers could have been Assyrians but were more often raised by seminomadic populations, notably the S Babylonians, where the men, hunters and shepherds, personally possessed a bow and were skilled in using it.

To that were added the sappers; the *ṣab hupši*, the *kallāpu*, as well as the *kitkittû* who were in charge of destroying the enemy's defenses with spears and axes.

This army was composed of numerous foreign contingents who were often specialized. These contingents could be integrated in the existing units, which was the case of the conquered troops enrolled in the victorious army (for example, 10,000 Syrian archers and shieldbearers, 30,000 archers and 20,000 shieldbearers from Tabal, 30,500 Elamite archers and 30,500 Elamite shieldbearers incorporated by Sennacherib) or they even formed their own units like those levied on certain seminomadic tribes, particularly the Itueans and Gurreans who formed a sort of permanent "foreign legion" often used in military operations or as police throughout the empire.

Without coming back to the specialized Syrian troops in chariotry and those from Urartu for cavalry, it is necessary also to point out the presence in the Assyrian army of Arab contingents, on camels, pictured on the reliefs of the palaces of Tiglath-pileser III and of Ashurbanipal. Sidonians are likewise attested as specializing in the construction of boats. The role of the naval fleet in the army is very rarely mentioned in the Akkadian texts.

If the royal requests for oracles suggest there was a fear of rebellions, the contemporary documents hardly ever state acts of desertion or of disciplinary action; only the semi-nomads appear to have tried to take advantage of their mobility and of their knowledge of the country in order to escape from levies decreed by the central authority.

Whatever branch of the service the soldier belonged to, he was often enriched from pillaging and the gathering of booty, but nevertheless, throughout Mesopotamian history the soldier was locked into a situation that often approached that of a slave, deprived of any juridical status.

The hierarchy clearly distinguished the low-ranking staff (proper and specialized military) and the high-ranking staff, composed of the full ranks whose duties were both civil and military. The military titles were based either (1) on the number of men commanded by them: commander-of-50 (*rab hanšu*), leader-of-1000 (*rab 1 lim*), or (2) on the nature of the troop: *rab kalle,* "leader of dispatchers"; *rab raksu,* "leader of mounted messengers"; *rab kallāpāni,* "leader of sappers"; *rab dayyali,* "leader of scouts"; *rab urâte,* "leader of harnessing"; *rēš narkabti,* "master of the chariot"; *rab mugi ša pethalli,* "cavalry commander"; *rab mugi ša narkabti,* "chariot commander." The *mušarkisu* was in charge of all of the above.

The grades did not have the same importance in the different branches of service. The officers of cavalry and of chariotry were often rich, powerful, and important persons. The guard (*kiṣir šarruti*) constituted an elite army whose captains (*rab kiṣir*) were directly appointed by the king. The Assyrian army made up the provincial army units relieving the officers (*šaknu, bēl pāhati*) and the royal army (in the restricted sense of the term), itself constituted troops directly dependent on the king (*ša qurbuti*) and of troops "of the palace" under the command of the "great eunuch" (*rab ša rēši*).

The staff was composed of the great ones from the empire: from the second half of the 8th century this constituted two "generals-in-chef" (*turtānu*), that "of the right" and that "of the left." The "herald of the palace" (*nāgir ekalli*), the "great butler" (*rab šāqê*), and the "great senior officer" (*abarakku (rabû)*), as well as the other commanding officers, had military responsibilities. The king was the head of the army and actually directed the majority of campaigns; however, sometimes a general acted in his name, according to his orders.

This army, as powerful and well organized as it was, could not prevent the fall of the Assyrian empire (610 B.C.), then that of the Babylonian empire (539 B.C.) at the hands of the Persians. Everything had been centralized in the hands of the king; with the disappearance of the central authority, the army lost all cohesion and effectiveness.

Bibliography

Barnett, R. D. 1958. Early Shipping in the Near East. *Antiquity* 32: 220–30.

Bonnet, H. 1926. *Die Waffen der Völker des alten Orients.* Leipzig.

Brenjes, B. 1986. Kriegswesen im alten Orient. *Altertum* 32: 133–42.

Cassin, E. 1965. Tecniche della guerra e strutture sociali in Mesopotamia nella meta del II milenio. *Revista storica italiana* 77: 1–11.

———. 1968. A propos du char de guerre en Mésopotamie. Pp. 297–308 in *Problèmes de la guerre en Grèce ancienne,* ed. J. P. Vernant. Paris and The Hague.

Cavaignac, E. 1924. Le code assyrien et le recrutement. *RA* 21: 59–64.

Dalley, S. 1985. Foreign Chariotry and Cavalry in the Armies of Tiglat-Pileser III and Sargon II. *Iraq* 47: 31–48.

Dalley, S., and Postgate, J. N. 1984. *The Tablets from Fort Shalmaneser.* Cuneiform Texts from Nineveh 3. Oxford.

Dossin, G. 1938. Signaux lumineux au pays de Mari. *RA* 35: 174–86.

Eichler, B. L. 1983. Of Slings and Shields, Throw-sticks and Javelins. *JAOS* 103: 95–102.

Eph'al, I. 1983. On Warfare and Military Control in the Ancient Near Eastern Empire: a Research Outline. Pp. 88–106 in *History, Historiography and Interpretation,* ed. H. Tadmor and M. Weinfeld. Jerusalem.

———. 1984. The Assyrian Siege Ramp at Lachish: Military and Linguistic Aspects. *TA* 11: 60–70.

Evans, G. 1960. An Old Babylonian Soldier. *JCS* 14: 34–36.

Follet, R. 1957. "Deuxième bureau" et information diplomatique dans l'Assyrie des Sargonides. Pp. 61–83 in *Scritti in onore di Giuseppe Furlani.* RSO 32. Rome.

Garelli, P. 1968. Note sur l'évolution du char de guerre en Mésopotamie jusqu'à la fin de l'Empire assyrien. Pp. 291–295 in *Problèmes de la guerre en Grèce ancienne,* ed. J. P. Vernant. Paris and The Hague.

———. 1972. Problèmes de stratification sociale dans l'Empire assyrien. Pp. 73–79 *Gesellschaftsklassen im alten Zweistromland in den angrenzenden Gebieten,* ed. D. O. Edzard. Munich.

Gelb, I. J. 1973. Prisoners of War in Early Mesopotamia. *JNES* 24: 70–98.

Goetze, A. 1963. Warfare in Asia Minor. *Iraq* 25: 124–30.

Graeve, M. C. de. 1981. *The Ships of the Ancient Near East (2000–500 B.C.).* OLA 7. Louvain.

Harmand, J. 1973. *La guerre antique de Sumer à Rome.* Coll. Sup., l'historien, 16. Paris.

Herzog, C., and Gichon, M. 1978. *Battles of the Bible.* New York.

Houwink ten Cate, P. H. J. 1983. The History of Warfare according to Hittite Sources: The Annals of Hattusilis I. *Anatolica* 10: 91–109.

Hrouda, B. 1963. Der assyrische Streitwagen. *Iraq* 25: 155–58.

Jean, C. F. 1942. L'armée du royaume de Mari. *RA* 42: 135–48.

Klengel, H. 1981. Krieg, Kriegsgefangene. Pp. 241–46 in *RLA* 6: 3–4.

Landsberger, B. 1957–58. *Aspu* "Schleuder," *assukku* "Schleuderstein." *AfO* 18: 379–80.

———. 1959–60. Nachtrag zu *aspu* "Schleuder." *AfO* 19: 66.

Littauer, M. A. 1976. New Light on The Assyrian Chariot. *Or* n.s. 45: 217–26.

Littauer, M. A., and Crouwel, J. H. 1979. *Wheeled Vehicles and Ridden Animals in the Ancient Near East.* Leiden.

Madhloum, T. 1965. Assyrian Siege-engines. *Sumer* 21: 9–15.

Malbran-Labat, F. 1982. *L'armée et l'organisation militaire de l'Assyrie à l'époque des Sargonides.* Genèva.

Manitius, W. 1910. Das stehende Heer der Assyrerkönige und seine Organization. *ZA* 24.

Matthews, V. H. 1981. Legal Aspects of Military Service in Ancient Mesopotamia. *Military Law Review* 94: 135–51.

Mierzejewski, A. 1973. La technique de siège assyrienne aux IX–VII siècles avant notre ère. *Etudes et Travaux* 7 (Varsovie): 11–20.

Miller, R.; McEwen, E.; and Bergman, C. 1986. Experimental Approaches to Ancient Near Eastern Archery. *World Archaeology* 18: 178–95.

Moorey, R. S. 1970. Pictorial Evidence for the History of Horse-riding in Iraq before the Kassite Period. *Iraq* 32: 36–50.

Moortgat, A. 1930. Der Kampf zu Wagen in der Kunst des alten Orients. *OLZ* 33: 841–54.

Munn-Rankin, J. J. 1956. Diplomacy in Western Asia in the Early Second Millennium B.C. *Iraq* 18: 68–110.

Nagel, W. 1966. *Der mesopotamische Streitwagen und seine Entwicklung im ostmediterranen Bereich.* Berlin.

Nougayrol, J. 1963. Guerre et paix à Ugarit. *Iraq* 25: 110–23.

Oded, B. 1979. *Mass Deportation and Deportees in the Neo-Assyrian Empire.* Wiesbaden.

Özgen, E. 1983. The Urartian Chariot Reconsidered, I. Representational Evidence 9–7th Centuries B.C. *Anatolica* 10: 111–31.
———. 1984. The Urartian Chariot Reconsidered, II. Archaeological Evidence 9–7th Centuries B.C. *Anatolica* 11: 91–154.
Parpola, S. 1981. Assyrian Royal Inscriptions and Neo-assyrian Letters. Pp. 117–34 in *Assyrian Royal Inscriptions: New Horizons*. Ed. F. M. Fales. Rome.
Parr, P. J. 1968. The Origin of the Rampart Fortifications of Middle Bronze Age Palestine and Syria. *ZDPV* 84: 18–45.
Postgate, J. N. 1974. *Taxation and Conscription in the Assyrian Empire*. St. Pohl, Series maj. 3. Rome.
———. 1979. The Economic Structure of the Assyrian Empire. Pp. 193–221 in *Power and Propaganda: a Symposium on Ancient Empires*. Mesopotamia 7, ed. M. T. Larsen. Copenhagen.
Quesada Sanz, F. 1985. El mundo sumerio-acadio y la aparicion de la guerra organizada. *BAEO*: 61–92.
Rainey, A. F. 1965. The military personnel of Ugarit. *JNES* 24: 17–27.
Reade, J. E. 1972. The Neo-Assyrian Court and Army: Evidence from the Sculptures. *Iraq* 34: 87–112.
Rowton, M. B. 1982. War, Trade and the Emerging Power Center in *Mesopotamien und seine Nachbarn*. BZVO 1. Berlin.
Saggs, H. W. 1963. Assyrian warfare in the Sargonid period. *Iraq* 25: 145–54.
Salonen, A. 1942. *Nautica Babylonica*. SO 11. Helsinki.
———. 1950. Notes on Wagon and Chariots in Ancient Mesopotamia. *StOr* 14.
———. 1951. *Landfahrzeuge des alten Mesopotamia*. AASF B72. Helsinki.
———. 1956. *Hippologica Accadica*. AASF B100. Helsinki.
Salonen, E. 1965. *Die Waffen der alten Mesopotamier*. SO 33. Helsinki.
———. 1968. Zum altbabylonischen Kriegswesen. *BiOr* 25: 160–62.
Sasson, J. M. 1969. *The Military Establishments at Mari*. Studia Pohl 3. Rome.
Schaeffer, C. F. A. 1938. Contribution à l'étude de l'attelage sumérien et syrien aux IIIème et IIème mill. *Préhistoire* 6: 49–63.
Schroeder, O. 1920. Dokumente des assyrischen Militarismus. *OLZ* 23: 155–58.
Soden, W. von. 1963. Die Assyrer und der Krieg. *Iraq* 25: 131–44.
Sollberger, E. 1972. Ur-III Society: Some unanswered Questions. Pp. 185–89 in *Gesellschaftsklassen im alten Zweistromland und in den angrenzenden Gebieten*. Munich.
Watkins, T. 1983. Sumerian Weapons, Warfare and Warriors. *Sumer* 39: 100–2.
Yadin, Y. 1963. *The Art of Warfare in Biblical Lands*. London.
———. 1972. The Earliest Representation of Siege Scene and a "Scythian Bow" from Mari. *IEJ* 22: 90.
Young, T. C. 1983. The Assyrian Army on the Middle Euphrates: Evidence from Current Excavations. *Bibliotheca Syro-Mesopotamica* 56: 19–32.

F. Malbran-Labat
Trans. Jennifer L. Davis

MILK. See ZOOLOGY.

MILL, MILLSTONE.

MILL, MILLSTONE. Throughout the ANE the grinding of flour was considered a dull and onerous job, performed by slaves in the larger households, by housewives in the smaller ones (Exod 11:5; Isa 47:2; Job 31:10; Eccl 12:3). Because of the necessity of reducing grain to groats, meal, or flour, however, milling was very much part of domestic life. The scraping sound of grinding stones was as characteristic of a habited home as the light of the lamp (Jer 25:10; cf. Rev 18:22). For most women, grinding was a daily recurring task. To dispossess a family of its hand mill (*rēḥayim*) would amount to taking away its means of sustenance (Deut 24:6; cf. *Ant* 4.8.26). Alongside the small-scale grinding done in the homes of ordinary citizens, there is ample evidence for the existence in the ANE of larger "milling houses," often run by the state. As a rule, working conditions here were bad; most of the employees had come under the pressure of poverty and famine. Because of the semipermanent need for more grinders, the authorities were often led to use prisoners of war as millers. The Mesopotamian "mill house" (*bīt ararri*) did in fact serve as a prison, a usage obliquely referred to in the LXX text of Jer 52:11 (*oikia mylōnos*). Judean prisoners of war in Babylonia ended up in such milling plants (Isa 42:7; Ps 107:10–16; Lam 5:13), experiencing a fate similar to that of Samson (Judg 16:21).

While the most simple way of crushing grain was to pound it in a mortar (cf. Num 11:8), the more efficient hand mill (called *rēḥayim, ṭaḥănâ* [Eccl 12:4] or *ṭĕḥôn* [Lam 5:13]) was widely used in OT times. Although currently used in the handbooks, the term "hand mill" can easily give rise to misleading associations. The *rēḥayim* was in fact a "saddle-quern," consisting of two complementary stone slabs: the *pelaḥ taḥtît*, the slightly concave "nether stone" (Job 41:16), and the smaller, loaf-shaped, upper stone called *(pelaḥ) rekeb* (cf. Akk *narkabum*), "rider (stone)" (LXX *epimylion*, Deut 24:6; Judg 9:53; 2 Sam 11:21). The lower millstone was proverbial for its hardness (Job 41:16); basalt, imported from the Hauran, was a common material, yet limestone was frequently used as well. The upper millstone, made of basalt or sandstone, was quite heavy. Used as a missile, it could prove detrimental to the human skull (Judg 9:53; 2 Sam 11:21). Kneeling in front of the quern, the miller moved the "rider" up and down the lower stone, thus grinding the grain between the two. This characteristic working position, the upper part of the body exercising additional pressure on the upper stone, is represented by a number of Egyptian statuettes. In the later Iron Age the technique was slightly improved by the introduction of two new features. The upper slab was provided with a funnel-shaped hole through which the grain could be poured, and with an edge sufficiently deep to hold a wooden bar by which the stone could be brought into motion. Also places of enforced labor like the one in which Samson spent the last months of his life were equipped with hand mills; we have to picture a room like the one discovered by archaeologists in the Western Palace at Ebla, where sixteen grindstones were found in their original places.

By the Hellenistic period the rotary mill found its way into Palestine. Based on a Gallo-Roman model, it was made of a large convex nether stone (the *ʾisṭrôbil*, from Gk *strobilos*, "pinecone") surmounted by a concave upper stone named *qelet*, a term derived from Gk *kalathos*, "basket." The Babylonian Talmud informs us that an upper class housewife might possibly do the grinding herself with the small hand mill, but that she had her servant girls work with the larger rotary one (*b. Ketub.* 59b). This rotary mill was commonly driven by a donkey or a mule. In rabbinical writings it is therefore called the *rēḥayim šel ḥămôr,* "donkey mill," as opposed to the *rēḥayim šel ʾādām,* "man-operated mill." The NT passages which speak of drowning a man by fastening a *mylos onikos* round his neck and throwing him into the depth of the sea (Matt 18:6; Mark 9:42; Luke 17:2 has *lithos mylikos*; cf. Rev 18:21) refer to the heavy upper stone from the rotary mill.

Contrary to what is often asserted, there is no evidence of the use in biblical times of small rotary hand mills equipped with a peg by which the "rider" was made to turn around a small plug of hardwood fixed in the center of the lower stone. It is true that the Gk term *onos,* "donkey," can refer to the upper grinding slab, and that the Heb word *ḥămôr,* also meaning "donkey," is sometimes used in the Mishna and in later writings as a metaphorical designation of a load carrier, such as the bed-base (e.g., *m. Kelim* 18:3). Yet to conclude from these data that the *rēḥayim šel ḥămôr* was in fact a small rotary hand mill fixed upon an undercarriage is unwarranted speculation. The Jerusalem Talmud refers to the practice of putting a horse to treading the mill (*rêḥayim*), which supposes the presence of animal-driven rotary mills in Palestine (*y. Pesah.* 4.31a). It is, furthermore, not accidental that in the Greek text of the Gospels the millstone is no longer called "donkey" (*onos*) but "donkey-driven" (*mylos onikos*). The archaeological evidence adduced in support of the small rotary mill is based on erroneous interpretation. What modern scholars have considered to be Iron Age milling implements are in fact potter's wheels, as the smooth surfaces of the objects in question show. In order to serve their purpose, grinding stones needed to have a rough surface. The rotary hand mills used by Palestinian Arabs and described by ethnographers of the 19th and 20th century did not come into use until the Middle Ages.

Bibliography

Amiran, R. 1956. The Millstones and the Potter's Wheel. *EI* 4: 46–49 (in Hebrew).

Lieberman, S. 1980/81. [Grain] Mills and Those who work them. *Tarbiz* 50: 126–35 (in Hebrew).

Moritz, L. A. 1958. *Grain-mills and Flour in Classical Antiquity.* Oxford.

Toorn, K. van der. 1986. Judges XVI 21 in the Light of the Akkadian Sources. *VT* 36: 248–53.

KAREL VAN DER TOORN

MILLENNIUM. Millenarianism is a variant of Jewish and Christian eschatology. The literal meaning of millennium (from Lat *mille*) is a "thousand," but the term is used of the expectation of a span of years which may be more or less than a thousand. This usually follows the destruction of evil and precedes the creation of a new heaven and a new earth and the enjoyment of eternal bliss. In some traditions the Messiah and the faithful reign in this earthly kingdom.

A. The Pseudepigrapha

The concept of this temporary reign is found in Jewish literature although it is not present in the Hebrew Scriptures. It does, however, occur in the Pseudepigrapha. In the Apocalypse of Weeks, *1 En.* 93 intimates the government of "his flock" or "all creation" (B and C) by the elect in the eighth week. No mention is made of the Messiah. *2 En.* 32:3–33:1 has a similar chronology. The eighth day (i.e., the year 8000) begins a time "not reckoned and unending." *2 Bar.* 29–30 describes a time of great earthly fertility for the righteous when the Anointed One is revealed. After this period those who sleep will arise and "the multitudes of the souls will appear together, in one assemblage, of one mind." We may compare *2 Bar.* 39:3–40:4 "he (the Anointed One) will . . . protect the rest of my people who will be found in the place that I have chosen. And his dominion will last forever until the world of corruption has ended." *4 Ezra* 7:26–31 gives a more detailed picture. The city and the land will appear again, the Messiah and the elect will be revealed, and they will rejoice for 400 years. This passage shows obvious Christian redaction. Then the Messiah and all human beings will die and the earth will go back to its primeval silence. After this the general resurrection and judgment occur.

4 Ezra 7:53–55 (23–26) implies an earthly paradise for the righteous. *4 Ezra* 20:25–27, 38–59 speaks of the restored Jerusalem (cf. 13:36). *Pss.Sol.* 17:26f. expects the Messiah, the gathering together of the people and tribes, the purification of Jerusalem (17:30), and the coming of the nations to bring gifts to Jerusalem (17:31). The *Sibylline Oracles* (5:414–30) anticipates the Messiah, the new city, and the new temple. We may also compare the Jewish-Christian *Apoc. El.* 5:36–39 which mentions a 1000-year reign.

B. Rabbinic Sources

Rabbinic references to the temporal messianic reign are as follows: *Pes.* 68a refers to the Messianic age and states that the "righteous are destined to resurrect the dead." *Ber.* 34b makes a distinction between this world and the days of the Messiah: in the latter there is no subjugation to foreign powers. A similar thought is expressed in *Sanh.* 91b. In *Sanh.* 99a three opinions are cited: "R. Eliezer said: The days of the Messiah will last forty years . . . R. Eleazar b. Azariah said: Seventy years . . . Rabbi said: Three generations . . . R. Dosa said: Four hundred years . . . Rabbi said: Three hundred and sixty-five years, even as the days of the solar year . . . Abimi the son of R. Abbahu learned: The days of Israel's Messiah shall be seven thousand years . . . Rab Judah said in Samuel's name: The days of the Messiah shall endure as long as from the Creation until now . . . R. Nahman b. Isaac said: As long as from Noah's day, which are mine . . ." For further distinction between the days of the Messiah and the world to come see *Šabb.* 63a; 113b. In *Sanh.* 97a Tanna debe Eliyyahu teaches that the Messianic era will last 2000 years (cf. *ʿAbod. Zar.* 9a). *Sanh.* 97b states that the son of David will come after not less than 85 jubilees, he will come in the last one. R. Hanan b. Tahlifa says after 7000 years and R. Abba the son of Raba (Babylonian Amora) after 5000 years. R. Jahocachua predicted 2000 years; Barakhja and R. Dosa, 600 years; Jose the Galilean 60 years or three generations; R. Akiba 40 years and Rabbi three generations (also 365 years).

C. Christian Idea of the Millennium

The idea of a messianic interregnum was adopted by Christians. In the NT we find an implicit reference to an interregnum in 1 Cor 15:23–28 where Christ will rule until the cosmic powers, including death, have been conquered and then he will hand over the kingdom of God (cf. Col 1:12–13). However, the only explicit reference to a messianic interregnum in the NT occurs in Rev 20:4–6, a text which has often taken on a fascination and extravagant importance for Christians. This pericope comprises the final acts of the mythic drama of the Divine Warrior portrayed in Revelation. It is the establishment of a temporary kingdom on the purified earth which appears to be refertilized by the blood of the slain (Rev 19:12–18). The saints, perhaps only the martyrs, experience "the first resurrection" and reign for a thousand years with the Messiah. Then comes the general resurrection, the judgment, and the creation of a new heaven and a new earth. Christians have traditionally interpreted this text allegorically and see it as a symbolic reference to the "death" and "resurrection" of Christians through baptism. They understand this to be the first resurrection. The thousand year span is the time from the birth of Christ until his parousia. Rev 20:4–6 is also used as one of the key texts which indicate that all baptized Christians share in the sovereignty and priesthood of Christ.

A similar concept of the interregnum occurs in the *Ascen. Is.* 4:1–18. Here Christ with his angelic forces destroys Beliar and his armies and takes them to Gehenna. Then he gives rest to the faithful who survive on earth with the saints who descend from heaven. No definite time span is mentioned. After this interim reign the faithful leave their bodies and ascend to heaven.

D. Patristic Evidence

1. Papias. Our first evidence of patristic belief in the millennium is from Papias as cited by Irenaeus (*Haer.* 5.33.4) and Eusebius (ca. 260–ca. 340 *Hist. Eccl.* 3.39). Papias is an enigmatic but important figure in the history of early Christianity. He was born about 70 C.E. and appears to have written about 125–130 C.E. He was a "hearer" of John, a companion of Polycarp, and later the bishop of Hierapolis. Irenaeus (ca. 130–ca. 200 C.E.) judges Papias to be an important witness to the eschatological tradition of the early Christian communities. Papias seems to have had a fairly representative group of apostolic traditions at hand, from both Palestine and Asia Minor. Irenaeus says that Papias wrote about the millennium in his Fourth Book and described it as a period of prodigious fertility and of profound peace. There will also be harmony among the animals (cf. Isa 40:6) who will no longer be carnivorous. Papias states that this is not to be taken in an allegorical sense, that is, it does not mean merely that the various nations will dwell in the peace of one faith. Our next reference to Papias is Eusebius (*Hist. Eccl.* 3.39), he says: "Among these (things of a fabulous nature) he (Papias) says that there will be a millennium after the resurrection of the dead, when the personal reign of Christ will be established on this earth." The witness of Papias is not to be taken lightly because he intimates that his eschatological tenets came through the "elders" who saw and heard John the disciple of the Lord.

2. Justin Martyr. Justin Martyr (100–165 C.E.), the most significant apologist in the 2d century, also bears witness to the belief in the millennium. The relevant text is found in *Dial.* 80–81. The main features of interest are as follows. Trypho, the Jew with whom he debates, challenges Justin on the purported Christian belief that "this place, Jerusalem, shall be rebuilt; and . . . your people . . . gathered together, and made joyful with Christ and the patriarchs, and the prophets, both the men of our nation, and other proselytes who joined them before your Christ came." Justin assures him that many Christians do hold this belief but other sincere Christians are not of this mind. He adds "but I and others who are right-minded Christians on all points, are assured that there will be a resurrection of the dead, and a thousand years in Jerusalem, which will then be built, adorned, and enlarged, [as] the prophets Ezekiel and Isaiah and others declare." Justin bases his belief on the Hebrew Scriptures and obtains his idea of a thousand, as do Jewish writers, from Ps 90:4 "the day of the Lord being a thousand years" (cf. 2 Pet 3:8). We may summarize Justin's views as follows: the millennial belief is held by many Christians but not by all; the center of the kingdom will be the renewed Jerusalem; people will live lengthy lives; there will be physical begetting; the animals will live at peace with one another and with human beings; there will be a wondrous fertility of the earth.

3. Irenaeus. The next important writer to witness to millennial belief among Christians is Irenaeus (130–ca. 200). He was one of the most important Christian theologians and heresiologists of the 2d century. Irenaeus (*Haer.* 5:32–39) elaborates the millenarian theory which he inherited through Papias and Justin. He inserts his eschatological (apocalyptic) beliefs into his recapitulation theory. He states that, as the world was made in six days, so it will end in 6,000 years. The Antichrist, symbolized by the number 666, will reign for three and a half years and will then be destroyed by Christ and sent into the lake of fire. The righteous, however, will be brought to the times of the kingdom, that is, "the rest, the hallowed seventh day." God's promise to Abraham will be fulfilled and he will receive the promised inheritance of the land (Genesis 15). Irenaeus supports this tenet from Matt 8:11 "many from the east and the west shall sit down with Abraham and Isaac and Jacob."

The last part of the text under discussion (*Haer.* 5:37–39) is not found in all manuscripts and may have been precluded because of Irenaeus' millenarian belief. (However, some fragments of the Syriac and Armenian versions were found in the early part of this century.) Irenaeus conceives of an earthly kingdom as the beginning of incorruption "by means of which kingdom those who shall be worthy are accustomed gradually to partake of the divine nature (*capere Deum*)." The righteous receive the land which was promised to Abraham and reign in it. Irenaeus argues that Abraham and his seed will receive the promised land at the resurrection of the just because God's promise cannot fail and he did not inherit the land during his earthly life (cf. Acts 7:5). The just will comprise both Jews and Gentiles. He also asserts that Christ referred to the millennium (earthly kingdom) when he said that he would not drink of the fruit of the vine until he drank it anew in the kingdom of the Father (Matt 26:29).

4. The Montanists. The millennial belief was received enthusiastically by the Montanists (ca. 156–200 or later), but they expected the heavenly Jerusalem to descend at Pepuza in Phrygia, not Jerusalem (Epiph. *Anac.* 48:1). From Phrygia, Montanism spread to Africa, Gaul, and Rome.

5. Tertullian. Tertullian (ca. 160–ca. 220), the foremost Western theologian, championed both the cause of millenarianism and the Montanists. In *Adv. Marc.* 3:24–25, he states that the Jews will be restored to Palestine and that the city of Jerusalem will come down from heaven. The faithful will reign for 1,000 years. He adds that in one city in Asia Minor, the new Jerusalem had been seen hovering in the sky for 40 days. Tertullian repudiates an allegorical interpretation of these things (*Adv. Marc.* 4:31).

6. Commodianus. Commodianus (3d century or later) followed the schema of 7,000 years (*Carmen* 791–96). He adopted chiliastic views and expected marriage, the begetting of children, a clement climate, universal peace, and the return of the ten tribes.

7. Victorinus of Pettau. Victorinus of Pettau (d. ca. 304), author of the oldest extant Latin commentary on the Apocalypse, takes a more modest approach but keeps quite close to a literal interpretation of Rev 20:4–6 except that he sees the millennium as the fulfillment of God's promise to Abraham. Jerome (342–420 C.E.) thoroughly redacted this commentary of Victorinus and interpreted the millennium allegorically.

8. Lactantius. A more fervent adherent to the chiliastic approach is later found in Lactantius (ca. 240–ca. 320). He draws upon the *Sibylline Oracles* and describes the righteous as begetting children and being served by the heathen (Div. Inst. 7:24). He states that the cosmic bodies will be radiant and the earth prodigiously fertile. Among other sources Lactantius was influenced by the *Fourth Eclogue* of Vergil (70–19 B.C.E.).

The millennial belief in the early church was a tradition that was both vigorous and persistent and one which obtains in many persuasions today. Many Christians who opposed the belief accused Christian millenarianists of "Judaizing." Millenarianism was entertained by the *docti (-ae)* and the *indocti (-ae)* alike. It was the subject of serious debate in the major centers of Christian theology in Rome, Alexandria, Asia Minor, and perhaps Gaul.

The Gnostic, Cerinthus (ca. 100 C.E.), as reported by Eusebius (*Hist. Eccl.* 3.28) taught not only millenarianism but a crass chiliasm. During the thousand years people would dine sumptuously and celebrate nuptial joys.

Nepos of Arsinoe (cited by Eusebius, *Hist. Eccl.* 7.24) espoused a millenarianial theology characterized by a crude chiliasm. Apollinaris of Laodicea (ca. 310–ca. 390 C.E.) also taught a millennial theology but we only know this from Epiphanius (ca. 315–403) who said that the faithful would have the same bodies as they have now and they would keep the OT law, including circumcision (*Panarion* 77:36–38). According to Basil (ca. 330–79 C.E.), Apollinaris' views were more mythical but he did expect the observance of the Sabbath, circumcision, and the dietary laws (*Ep.* 263:4).

Similar ideas appear in Methodius of Olympus (d. ca. 311 C.E.). He scorned the Jewish interpretation of the Feast of Tabernacles. Combining a biblical realism with allegorization, he understood it as a type of the resurrection and the setting up of the tabernacle in the 7,000th year in the new creation. He speaks about celebrating with Christ "the millennium of rest" and that after the thousand years the body will be changed "from a human and corruptible form into angelic size and beauty" (*Symp.* 9:5).

The early theology of Augustine of Hippo (354–430) also shows millenarian tendencies but his later eschatology is influenced by Tyconius and he abandons millenarianism (*De civ. D.* 20:6–7).

E. Opponents of Millenarianism

Origen (ca. 185–ca. 254) made the first attempt to discredit a millennial interpretation of Rev 20:4–6 and replaced it with a spiritual interpretation by applying it instead to the spiritual growth of the soul which begins in this life and continues in the next. Tyconius, the Donatist theologian (d. ca. 400) taught that the thousand years of Rev 20:4–6 refer to the present age and to those who are reborn through baptism: the physical resurrection is in the future. The millennial rule of Christ extends from his passion to his second coming. It was Tyconius who influenced Augustine to move from his millennial position to a spiritualization of the thousand years (*De civ. D.* 20:7; cf. Maiers 1981, 108ff.; 130; 161ff.; 174ff. and 294ff.). In his later teachings on eschatology, Augustine spiritualized the millennium which he taught began with the incarnation of Christ and was fully realized in the earthly church.

The millennial hope lived on in some of the Protestant reformers, e.g., the Anabaptists of the 16th century. It obtains today in various forms among the Mormons, the Seventh Day Adventists, and the Jehovah Witnesses.

It is especially noteworthy that Christopher Columbus and other pioneers in the New World were influenced by Joachism, a development of the ideas of the "millennium" as taught by Joachim of Fiore (1135–1202). Adherents to this eschatological tradition anticipated a new age which would be ushered in by spiritual persons, thus supplying a powerful incentive to colonize the New World. Many identified these with the Franciscans and the Dominicans in their work in Latin America: they saw the New World as the new earthly Paradise.

Bibliography

Beegle, D. 1978. *Prophecy and Prediction.* Ann Arbor, MI.
Bietenhard, H. 1953. The Millennial Hope in the Early Church. *SJT* 6: 12–30.
Cohn, N. 1970. *The Pursuit of the Millenium.* New York.
Maier, G. 1981. *Die Johannesoffenbarung und die Kirche.* Tübingen.
Phelan, J. L. 1970. *The Millennial Kingdom of the Franciscans in the New World.* 2d ed. Berkeley.
Williams, A., ed. 1980. *Prophecy and Millenarianism.*

J. MASSYNGBAERDE FORD

MILLO (PLACE) [Heb *millôʾ*]. An unspecified place associated with the City of David. It is mentioned in this connection in six OT passages (2 Sam 5:9; 1 Kgs 9:15, 24; 11:27; 1 Chr 11:8; 2 Chr 32:5), and once (spelled defectively) in the construction *bêt millōʾ* "house of Millo" (2 Kgs 12:20 [RSV]; cf. LXX [v 21] *oikou Mallō* "house of Mallo"). The word *millôʾ* is frequently analyzed as a noun associated with the Heb verb *mālēʾ* "to be full." The Millo at the City of David has been interpreted as referring to the filling of a breach in a wall, the filling of a space in the Tyropoeon Valley between the western and eastern ridges, the filling of a gap between the City of David and the temple mound, a filled stone tower, or the rebuilding of (damaged) supporting terraces. The archaeological evidence uncovered in recent years at the City of David points to the meaning "repair of supporting terraces" along the precipitous steep eastern ridge of the City of David.

After conquering the city from the Jebusites, David would have needed to repair these terraces to support his residence and other structures built on them (2 Sam 5:9; 1 Chr 11:8). Later Solomon has to rebuild these terraces again (1 Kgs 9:15, 24; 11:27); another interpretation suggests that in 1 Kgs 9:24 the text means that Solomon filled up the gap between the City of David and the temple platform where the king may have built a palace for his wife, Pharaoh's daughter. Still later Hezekiah again repaired these City of David terraces, at least on the eastern slope if not elsewhere in the city (2 Chr 32:5).

The etymological explanation of Millo is not entirely secure. It is not reflected in LXX's rendering *akra* "citadel." An Egyptian etymology has also been proposed. See BETH-MILLO. It is possible that during the divided monarchy the term Millo was replaced by the term Ophel (from a Heb word meaning "to rise"), signifying a raised fortress or citadel such as the Ophel at Jerusalem (2 Chr 27:3; 3:14), and the ones at Samaria and at Dibon (Mare 1987: 65–66; Mazar 1975: 173). See OPHEL.

The phrase *bêt millōʾ* (2 Kgs 12:20) recalls the similar (but differently spelled) expression referring to a stronghold called Beth-millo, located near Shechem (Judg 9:6, 20 [2x]; 2 Kgs 12:20).

Bibliography

Kenyon, K. 1974. *Digging Up Jerusalem.* London.
Mare, W. H. 1987. *The Archaeology of the Jerusalem Area.* Grand Rapids.
Mazar, B. 1975. *The Mountain of the Lord.* Garden City, NY.
Simons, J. 1952. *Jerusalem in the Old Testament.* Leiden.

W. Harold Mare

MINAEAN LANGUAGE.
See LANGUAGES (INTRODUCTORY SURVEY).

MINAH
[Heb *māneh*]. See COINAGE; WEIGHTS AND MEASURES.

MINIAMIN
(PERSON) [Heb *minyāmîn*]. **1.** The eponymous ancestor of a priestly family at the time of the high priest Joiakim (Neh 12:17).

2. A priest present at the dedication of the Jerusalem wall (Neh 12:41).

3. An assistant to Kore, the overseer of freewill offerings for the temple, in the time of Hezekiah (2 Chr 31:15). Miniamin was one of those who distributed portions in the priestly cities. The LXX, Vg and the Syr have Benjamin (Heb *binyāmîn*) here.

Only the assimilation of the *n* distinguishes Miniamin from Heb *mîyāmîn,* which the RSV renders Miamin (Ezra 10:25; Neh 12:5) and Mijamin (1 Chr 24:9; Neh 10:8). While the literal meaning of the name ("from the right") is clear, there has been dispute over the significance of the name. KB suggests that it may be related in meaning to Benjamin, hence denoting "southern." Noth *(IPN)* suggests that the name denotes "lucky person." The name is also attested in cuneiform business documents dated in the reigns of the Persian emperors Artaxerxes I and Darius II.

Nora A. Williams

MINIM.
See EBIONITES.

MINISTRY IN THE EARLY CHURCH.
When discussing the early Christian understanding of ministry, one must be prepared to distinguish the extent to which the NT conceives of ministry in terms of particular functions performed by titled persons associated with institutionalized offices and exercising some formal authority, and the extent to which it conceives of ministry in the more nonofficial terms of general service performed by any Christian believer.

A. Terms for "Ministry"
B. Jesus' Ministry as Model
C. Ministry in the Early Church
D. Ministry in Matthew's Gospel
E. Ministry According to Paul
   1. Spiritual Gifts and Ministry
   2. The Apostle
F. Ministry in the Pastoral Epistles
   1. Elders, Bishops, and Apostles
   2. Ordination
G. Ministry in the Johannine Corpus
   1. The Gospel of John
   2. The Epistles and Revelation
H. Conclusion

A. Terms for "Ministry"

In the time of the NT writers there were four possible Greek terms for "(official) ministry": (1) *telos:* "office" or "free service," as rendered by a citizen, emphasizing its perfect fulfillment; (2) *timē:* "office," sometimes generally "task," stressing the dignity that is combined with its practice; (3) *archē:* "office" or "magistracy" in its character of leadership, of leading those who will follow; and (4) *leitourgia:* "public service," performed by citizens at their own expense to the community or to the gods (e.g., organizing and financing a temple festival; and the "ministry" of the priests in the LXX).

With the exception of *telos,* these words appear also in the NT in the sense of "official ministry." As such, however, they describe only the ministry either of Jewish priests (*timē;* Heb 5:4, cf. 3:3 of Moses; *leitourgia;* Luke 1:23; Heb 8:6), of pagan civil officers (*timē;* cf. Rom 13:7; *archē;* Luke 12:11; 20:20; Tit 3:1; *leitourgia;* cf. Rom 13:6), of (good or bad) angels (*archē;* Rom 8:38; 1 Cor 15:24; Eph 1:21; 3:10; 6:12; Col 1:16; 2:10, 15; Jude 6; *leitourgia;*

cf. Heb 1:7), or, finally, of Jesus himself (*timē;* cf. Heb 3:3; *archē;* cf. Col 2:10; *leitourgia;* cf. Heb 8:2; 10:11–12). Similarly, the terms *hierateia* ("priesthood") or *hierateuein* ("to serve as a priest") are used of Jewish priests (Luke 1:9; Heb 7:5), while *(arc)hiereus,* ("high)priest," is used of Jewish or pagan priests (Acts 14:13) and of Jesus himself (Heb 2:17; 5:6 etc.), and *hierateuma* ("body of priests") is used of the Church as a whole (1 Pet 2:5, 9).

In Rom 15:16, Paul speaks of himself as a "minister *(leitourgos)* of Christ, who performs a priestly service *(hierourgein)* to the gospel" by bringing all nations as an offering to God, as Isa 66:20 has foretold. Here Paul may also have been influenced by the prophecy of Isa 61:6 that, in the time of fulfillment, all Israelites will become the "ministers" (*leitourgoi,* the only place in which this term and all its derivatives appear in Isaiah). Otherwise, none of the words listed above distinguishing an "official" ministry from a service freely rendered by any citizen or member of a religious group are ever used in the NT for the ministry of one or several believers (as distinguished from the whole body). In Acts 13:2 the subject of *leitourgein* is, probably, "prophets and teachers," however, what they are doing is certainly not different from what all members of the Church are doing time and again; in Phil 2:17, 25, 30 *leitourgia (leitourgos)* designates charitable help.

This is significant due to the fact that this particular usage is characteristic of all the different NT writers and that it cannot be attributed to any literary interdependencies. It does not say that there were no ministries of single persons or of groups of persons within the church; rather it indicates that the NT writers consistently refused to make any distinction between an official ministry of a selected person or group and that of any believer. Despite the fact that the Greek-speaking world offered to the early Church a rather rich vocabulary for the notion of "ministry," most NT writers instead utilized a comparatively rare Greek word that hardly ever appears in the LXX: *diakonia,* "service" (especially of a place at table). Even the personal form of *diakonos* ("servant, slave, waiter") is to be found only in Esther (1:10; 2:2; 6:1–5), in an additional verse in Prov 10:4 (not found in the MT), and once in the very late book of *4 Maccabees* (9:17). Thus, strangely enough, a secular term is used to describe any ministry in the Church, be it a special one or one done by all the members.

This spontaneous usage in all the different layers of NT literature shows what an impression the challenge of Jesus' way of life and teaching made on all his followers. The total (eschatological) newness of a service without institutional hierarchies or resort to force was so striking that it became impossible to speak of the honor or the exemplary model of an "official" ministry apart from that of any other person in the church. Wherever somebody was serving Christ, it was exactly what a slave would do for his lord, i.e., a simple, worldly service, not a domination of others.

B. Jesus' Ministry as Model

Jesus held no official title or responsibility. He was neither an elder nor a member of the central council; neither a scribe nor a priest. When people called him "rabbi," it meant nothing more than "sir"; we never hear of any rabbinic sage who taught Jesus, or of Jesus' adherence to any rabbinic school. His parables were totally different from those of the rabbis, not illustrating some ethical or dogmatic statement, but self-contained stories, in the telling of which the kingdom of God became reality for the hearer. He was not even a teacher in the strict sense of the word. There was neither theology, nor christology, nor pneumatology one could learn from him and transmit to others; yet theology, and christology, and pneumatology came to life implicitly in his whole ministry, in his healing, in his fellowship with tax collectors, and in his parables and ethical commandments.

In contrast to the Jewish student who asks a rabbi for permission to follow (and study with) him, Jesus called his own followers. When someone would ask to follow him, he was either sent back (Mark 5:19) or the affiliation proved unsuccessful. Jesus' authority apparently was such that, with the exception of the rich ruler (who, primarily approached Jesus on his own initiative!, Mark 10:17–22), it never failed to inspire a following (see Luke 9:59 = Matt 8:21). Jesus did not even ask his future disciples whether they could read, for he did not intend to introduce them to a rabbinic course in exegesis, but into his own communion with God. Though a call of women into discipleship is not reported, it is clear that women followed him (Luke 8:1–3; Mark 15:41). "Serving" seems to be their specific form of discipleship (Mark 1:31; 15:41; Luke 8:3; John 12:2), and in so doing they perform the ministry of the angels (Mark 1:13) and of Jesus himself (Mark 10:45; Luke 22:27; 12:37, cf. John 13:1–11), the ministry that the male disciples should have performed (Mark 10:43–44; Luke 22:26, cf. John 12:26; 13:12–17).

Jesus likely called a group of twelve disciples to participate in his whole ministry. It is true that 1 Cor 15:5 speaks of "the Twelve," not of the "eleven." This, however, was a fixed phrase and does not prove its origin in an appearance of the Risen Lord to a group that had not existed previously. Thus, the historicity of the twelve disciples around Jesus is very probable, since it is difficult to imagine that the experience of a post-Easter group would be projected back into the earthly life of Jesus in such a way that one name was substituted by that of Judas Iscariot. There is, with the exception of a Qumranian body of fifteen (consisting of three priests and twelve laymen; 1QS 8:1), no evidence of a Jewish office of twelve persons apart from that of the twelve tribal princes and/or chief priests (see also 1QM 2:1–3; 11QTemple 57:11–15; 4QOrd 2:4; 3:4). This means that the twelve disciples of Jesus represented the twelve tribes and manifested Jesus' desire to call back to God the whole people of Israel, not merely a penitent part of it. Hence, their role was regarded as an eschatological one (Matt 19:28; Luke 22:30; cf. Rev 21:12, 14), not an office in an earthly institution. Whether Jesus ever considered what their function might be among his followers after his death is disputed. The Last Supper was, at least, directed towards some kind of continuation, and few doubt that Peter indeed received some kind of a specific commission (Mark 16:7; Luke 22:32; John 21:15–18), though not in the form of Matt 16:18–19 (see D below).

Before the mission of the Twelve (Mark 6:7–13) or the seventy [two] (Luke 10:1–12) Jesus bestowed upon them the authority of both proclaiming the kingdom of God and healing/exorcising. This double authority is typical of all apostolic authority, whether reported by Mark (6:12–

13), Matthew (10:8), Luke (10:9), John (14:12; 15:27), Paul (Rom 15:18–19), or in Acts (2:42–43). It is the power of his words and deeds that makes the authority of an apostle manifest.

C. Ministry in the Early Church

Jesus' impact on the early Church was considerable. Some followed his example literally as itinerant prophets (*Did.* 11:8), giving up their permanent domicile, probably also family (*Did.* 11:11?) and possessions (Matt 23:34; 10:41).

Also in the more or less institutionalized parish the newness of its life, inaugurated by Jesus, was manifested. Its real center, however, was not something like a temple cult or a synagogue service, but a meal. The scriptures were no longer interpreted by the trained scribe, who knew all the parallels, but simply by reading them in the light of what had happened in the life, death, and resurrection of Jesus. The old rule of a minimum of ten persons for a prayer service no longer obtained, since wherever two or three were gathered in his name, he would be present (Matt 18:20). This did not exclude a kind of leadership of the Twelve (1 Cor 15:5; for Luke these were identical with the apostles; Acts 1:26; 2:42; 6:2). Historically, we are not sure what their function really was. Clearly some functional leadership was exercised by the three "pillars" (Gal 2:9), Peter, John, and James (a former unbeliever). This shows both God's faithfulness to his previous call during the earthly ministry of Jesus and his freedom to choose new vessels of his gifts (which becomes even more striking in the subsequent call of Paul). The Spirit, of course, could lead former Pharisees (Paul), scribes (Matt 13:52), or priests (Acts 6:7) into the new fellowship, provided that this did not lead to a new hierarchy of trained or ordained officers over against laypersons (Matt 23:8–10; Mark 10:43–44). Consequently, there were no specifically "holy" persons or places; all church members were holy and all the earth was the Lord's (Acts 9:13, 32, 41; 1 Cor 10:26).

"The seven" were chosen "to serve tables" (Acts 6:2). However, one of them was also preaching and doing wonders (6:8, 10), while another was an evangelist (21:8; 8:5, 35, 40). Since, according to Acts 8:1, the persecution following Stephen's martyrdom spared the apostles, it seems that it targeted only the party of the Hellenists within the Jerusalem church and that the seven were its leaders (perhaps already within the social-welfare system of the Jewish synagogue prior to the split between Christian and non-Christian Jews; Walter 1983). If Stephen and Philip are typical examples, the Hellenists were a group under charismatic leadership and were clearly distinguished from the leadership under the Twelve.

Paul was called to his ministry by the risen Christ himself. Since this happened after the ascension, he was, in the strict understanding of Luke, not an apostle (Acts 1:21–22). He belonged to the "prophets and teachers" in Antioch, i.e., to the preachers of the local church. He, together with Barnabas, was called "apostle" in the sense of "missionary" (Acts 14:4, 14), probably in traditional Antiochean language. No apostle ordained or installed him to this service (13:1–3).

In Acts 15:6 and 21:18 we suddenly read of "elders" (or "presbyters"), apparently led by James. He appears unexpectedly in 12:17, singled out from the Church as a whole (cf. also 15:13). This fits into the picture of Gal 2:9, where he is mentioned first among the three "pillars," before Peter (see also 1:18–19). All this suggests that he succeeded Peter as the central leadership figure after Peter's imprisonment and departure from Jerusalem. We are never told how and when elders were introduced. It might have been assumed that the Church would simply adopt the familiar order of the Jewish synagogue as long as it still considered itself part of such a group. Acts 14:23 states that Paul appointed elders in Asia Minor. Historically, this may be questioned, since Paul never mentions elders in his undisputed letters (nor in those to the Colossians or Ephesians). According to Acts 20:28 they should rather be "overseers" *(episkopoi)* of the Church. While later this word would become an official title ("bishops"), here it still indicates function (and "elder" remains the name of the office).

James 5:14; 1 Pet 5:1, 5 and the Pastoral Epistles are witnesses of this order, though it is not always clear where "elder" means an (official) minister and where it simply refers to an older man (1 Tim 5:1–2; 1 Pet 5:5) or even one of the first generation of the Church, who had seen one or several of the original apostles (thus, probably, the author of 2 and 3 John, and Papias [Eus. *Hist. Eccl.* 3.39.4]). Doubtless, there were men "of repute" in the church of Jerusalem (Gal 2:2), and Paul acknowledges their authority (which he believed was equivalent to his own). These included James the brother of Jesus; Peter, and John; and in a wider sense "all the apostles," who seem to be a larger group than the Twelve (1 Cor 15:5, 7, cf. 5:6). But since Paul is silent on this point we do not know how early elders became officers in this church and what their status and rights actually were.

D. Ministry in Matthew's Gospel

Most NT scholars believe that the author of the gospel of Matthew lived within a Jewish-Christian Judaism, and that his intended audience was a group of Jewish Christians living in Syria, and especially in Antioch and its surroundings. Matthew's understanding of ministry therefore must be viewed in that light.

Only Matthew reports Jesus' admonition that his disciples should never let themselves be called "rabbi," "father," or "master" (23:8–10). This indicates both the presences of teachers within the Church, and the concern not to elevate them above others, since all of them are but "servants" (v 11) of one another. The task of the rabbi "to bind" and "to loose" is given explicitly to Peter, though these verses (16:17–19) are almost certainly not authentic word of Jesus; otherwise the mere warning to the disciples and Peter in Mark 8:30–33 would be unimaginable. A Semitic background is not to be doubted, however. The words may mirror the situation of an early stage of a Jewish-Christian church, for which the Jesus tradition handed down by Peter was of crucial importance. It might even be that 1 Cor 3:11 already corrects such a claim by a Petrine church. It is also in the gospel of Matthew that we read about a similar authority being given to every member of the Church (18:18 and 19), and it is very difficult to decide which saying is older. In the context of Judaism "binding" and "loosing" means to declare which commandment is still binding and which is not, and by so declaring to bind or release a person from guilt. (For instance, the ban on any work on a sabbath does not bind the priest who has to bring offerings; thus he is released from any guilt when doing his prescribed work.) Basically this has been done for the whole Church in the teaching of Peter, and is going on continually, on this basis, in detailed decisions of the Church. In practice, they will be given by ecclesiastical scribes (13:52). It is possible that 16:19 emphasizes more ethical decisions, while 18:18 focuses on declarations of guilt or forgiveness, but the distinction is questionable since the same verbs are used in both passages.

This "teaching to observe all that I have commanded you" (28:20) is so important because this "last commission" of Jesus is associated with the sending of the disciples to all the nations. Thus, teaching and observing is expected first from the Twelve (especially from Peter) and then from all believers. The tension between the Mosaic law (still valid) and the mission to the gentiles (who are now accepted into the Church) is resolved by Matthew in the highest commandment to love God and one's neighbor. This is the "constitution" of the Church, which defines all the single commandments. This "golden rule" also forms the inclusion of the main body of the Sermon on the Mount in 5:17 and 7:12; it is added by Matthew in 19:19 (and, in its OT wording, in 9:13; 12:7) and emphasized specifically in 22:39–40.

The warning against pseudo-prophets (7:15–23) proves that there were also faithful prophets working in the Church in Matthew's day. It is not their prophecies, exorcisms, and mighty deeds that go wrong, but their "lawlessness," which leads to their neglect of love (24:11–12). The existence of prophets in Matthew's church is buttressed by the promise of Jesus to send prophets (and wise men and scribes, 23:34). Matthew 10:41 suggests that they are rather itinerant prophets. The most astonishing fact is the total lack of any reference to elders or to any fixed ecclesiastical organization. The sinner, in danger of getting lost, is to be dealt with by any member of the Church as a whole, not by some leading authority (18:10–20). The ministry is seen in its OT and Jewish context as that of prophets (perhaps already receding into the background) and rabbis or scribes (responsible both for ethical decisions and for the interpretation of the scriptures in the new light of Jesus Christ). But none of them held an institutional office or rendered a service that could not be rendered by any other gifted member. Therefore, the Church is ruled by love, which does not allow a minister to be exalted over non-ministers on the basis of their respective functions, since all of them are but servants.

E. Ministry According to Paul

1. Spiritual Gifts and Ministry. The freedom of God is manifested in the call of Paul (an early persecutor of the Church who had never been a disciple of the earthly Jesus) to be his decisive witness before all nations. Though Luke (on the basis of Acts 1:21–22) might not include him among the apostles, Paul himself saw the "apostle" as the witness whom the risen Christ had installed for the proclamation of the gospel, and he insisted that his apostleship was equal to that of the Twelve and any apostles called before him (1 Cor 9:1; 15:5–8). Neither he nor Acts tell of any formal authority held by the originally chosen apostles, and even Gal 1:11–17 excludes such. (Paul did not even meet Peter and James until three years after his call (Gal 1:18–19).

There were certainly leaders in the churches founded by Paul ("those who are over you," or "who care for you," 1 Thess 5:12), as well as "first converts" who "devoted themselves to the service of the saints" and should, therefore, "be given recognition" (1 Cor 16:15, 18). Phil 1:1 mentions "overseers and servants," using the same terms that later designate "bishops and deacons," but apparently these are used here to qualify their functions, not as titles. No installation or legitimation either by the apostle or by the Church is mentioned; they have dedicated themselves to serving the Church. Rom 12:8 considers "those who are over (you)" to possess a special gift of the Spirit, in the same way as others may be prophets, or teachers, or healers. This shows that the Spirit is not opposing, but rather creating legal order. Being an overseer (bishop) or servant (deacon) is due to one gift among many, not qualitatively different from other gifts.

In 1 Cor 12:28, Paul initially enumerates persons ("first apostles, second prophets, third teachers"), followed by other gifts, to which he refers impersonally: "then miracles, healing charisms, helping, administration, various kinds of tongues" (RSV personalizes all of them). But in Rom 12:6–8 this is reversed; personal terms are used for "teachers, exhortors, contributors, helpers, and merciful people," whereas "prophecy" and "deacony" are spoken of impersonally. Thus, apostles, prophets and teachers are, as a rule, certainly of first importance in the Church, and Paul naturally thinks of them first. They belong to the "higher gifts" of 1 Cor 12:31, in other words, to those gifts that are normally needed most urgently. Yet, this does not lead to any fixed hierarchy which would distinguish members of a special quality (officers or priests) from other members without it, and it may be that in another situation different gifts would become preeminent.

Nor does Paul qualify male ministers differently from female ones. In Christ, "there is neither male nor female" (Gal 3:28), and this basic truth should manifest itself in the order of the Church, if only she covers her head, as it was customary in Paul's time (1 Cor 11:5–6, 13). The passage 14:34–35 prohibiting any speaking by a woman in the church service must, therefore, be a very early—but non-Pauline—marginal remark. While it is found in all manuscripts, it is variously placed either after v 33 or after v 40. This suggests that subsequent copyists inserted a marginal note, some at the place where it started (after v 33), others where it ended (after v 40). It may have been first written under the influence of 1 Tim 2:11–12 (cf. below). According to Rom 16:7, there was even a woman among the apostles (see TEV; RSV translates "men of note"): "Junia" is a well-known female name, whereas there is no evidence whatsoever for a male name "Junias" (since the name appears in the genitive case, both forms are equally possible). This woman might have been the wife of Andronicus (Brooten). In a similar way Phil 4:2–3 speaks of two women that are co-workers of Paul "in the gospel" (meaning "in the proclamation of the gospel"). It is uncertain whether

Paul would have regarded them as "apostles" (in the full sense of the word, not in the sense of "messengers of the churches" as in 2 Cor 9:23) although such is possible.

There is only one standard for evaluating the gifts of the Spirit: "love" (1 Corinthians 13), which expresses itself "for the common good" (1 Cor 12:7) in "building up the church" (14:3, 5) and, thus, actually proclaiming "Jesus as lord," not just one's own ideas (12:3). Love demands a way of speaking to which the Church as a whole or even an outsider is able to respond (14:16, 23–25). 1 Corinthians 14:29 is, unfortunately, ambiguous so that it does not become clear whether those who "weigh what is said" by the prophets are, in Paul's understanding, all the church members or just other prophets. For pragmatic reasons, some gifts must be known to and recognized by the Church. For example, people must know the "administrator" to arrange for a meeting place, but it is not necessary to know who exercises the gift of intercession for the Church, even though this ministry may be much more important than administration. Such a service recognized by the Church, in a more or less formal way, may be called an "office." This would not give it a different or special character, but would simply indicate that it has (for practical purposes) been given a recognized place within the order of the (local) parish.

2. The Apostle. For Paul, only apostleship is unique because the apostle is the witness of the risen Christ, the one foundation of the Church (1 Cor 3:11). That the apostle has seen him in a way clearly distinguished from all later experiences in visions and auditions (2 Cor 11:16–17; 12:1–4) makes his ministry unique (Gal 1:12; 1 Cor 9:1; 15:8). See also APOSTLE. The apostle is certainly more than an eyewitness to an event that happened at a certain point of history. He also conveys salvation to his hearers. This is done by the authority of his proclamation of the gospel. Even though the gospel of the crucified and risen Christ can be expressed in a credal formula which Paul "has received (from the church tradition in Jerusalem or Antioch) and handed down" to the Corinthians (1 Cor 15:1–5), the authority of Paul's preaching is not derived from that of other apostles (Gal 1:11–12); he could legitimately oppose Peter just as he could the "superlative apostles" in Corinth (Gal 2:11–20; 2 Cor 12:11–12).

The pivotal question for the Church is whether this ministry of the apostle (certainly set apart from others by Christ himself) was to be continued after the death of all the early apostles and, if so, in what way. In the authentic letters of Paul we see only that he often sent fellow workers to churches that he himself was unable to visit. Occasionally, he pointed to the fact that they were "appointed" (not by himself, though, but by the churches; (2 Cor 8:19, 23). No special rite of installation is mentioned; Paul seems to be referring either to an informal recognition of his messengers by the churches or to their decision to send some of their members to him. Without any doubt, his proclamation of the gospel must go on. Thus, there are some services without which the Church cannot live, whereas others (like speaking in tongues, mentioned in 1 Cor 12:10, 28–30; (also 1 Thess 5:19?; but not in Romans 12) may not be found in all the churches. One might include in the lists of indispensable services the administration of baptism and eucharist, though the apostles did not usually baptize (1 Cor 1:14–17, cf. Acts 10:48; 2:41–42; 19:5–6, etc.) and Paul never mentioned anyone presiding over the eucharist (instead, he addressed himself to the whole church when speaking of it; (1 Cor 10:15–17; 11:23–34). Thus, preaching the word, baptizing, and gathering for the eucharist must continue, and a church cannot be "Christian" without being responsible for these; but Paul seems unconcerned whether these are to be administered by persons specifically appointed or by any member appointed time and again by the Spirit.

F. Ministry in the Pastoral Epistles

1. Elders, Bishops, and Apostles. The Pastoral Epistles certainly presuppose "elders" and "deacons" in the churches they address (1 Tim 3:8–13; 4:14; 5:17–19; Tit 1:5). The term "the women" in 1 Tim 3:11 refers either to the wives of the deacons (but why would they not be mentioned in vv 1–7 with regard to the "bishop"?) or perhaps to deaconesses. Pivotal is the relation of the "bishop" (1 Tim 3:1–2; Tit 1:7, both times in the singular) to the "elders." Is there one bishop, chosen out of and presiding over the group of elders as described in the letters of Ignatius? Or are there, in each local church, several bishops, identical with the "elders who rule well" (as opposed to other elders who do not rule; 1 Tim 5:17; though this phrase may also simply mean that some are excelling in the task of ruling common to all elders)? However, the transition in Tit 1:5–6 is abrupt without any hint that a new ministry should be introduced, and what that text demands of elders, 1 Tim 3:2, 5 similarly demands of the bishop. "Bishop" here still seems to be a term qualifying the function of a person whose official title is "elder," as in Acts 20:28. That means that the singular is generic and due to traditional exhortations or ways of speaking, as we might say: "Appoint good ministers in your church, for the servant of the lord must be . . ." Strikingly different from Paul is the fact that here there is no place for female elders or bishops (1 Tim 2:11–15). However, the ministry of intercession by "enrolled" widows (1 Tim 5:5, 9) is taken seriously.

No name or title is given to the ministry of the addressees, Timothy and Titus, yet it is clear that they were formally installed by the laying on of the hands of the apostle (2 Tim 1:6) and/or the elders (1 Tim 4:14). Were these persons considered successors of the apostle and, if so, in what way? They were appointed to a local church (Ephesus and Crete, where several towns with churches existed), and it seems that Timothy was called back to the apostle either permanently or for a longer period, whereas Tychicus was sent to Ephesus (2 Tim 4:9–12, 21). Succession to the ministry of the dying Paul may be the issue implicitly dealt with in 2 Timothy, even though this is not explicitly mentioned. The text does not offer any doctrine of apostolic succession, though it would soon prompt a long development in this direction.

2. Ordination. Unfortunately, we know very little about Jewish ordination. Rabbinic ordination seems to have been practiced at least by the time of the Pastorals epistles (beginning of the 2d century?), in accordance with Num 27:18–23. Some late rabbinic sources (*Sipre Num.*, Tanchuma: Str.B 2: 648) imply that the Spirit is transferred to the ordinand, but earlier rabbinic ordination seems simply to have recognized the wisdom acquired through disciplined study. We do not know in what way such studies were a binding condition (prescribed length of time, exams) nor how early ordination authorized a person to make autonomous decisions in legal matters. It is clear, however, that the central role of the "charisma" in 1 Tim 4:14 and 2 Tim 1:6 definitely differs from what we know of Jewish ordinations, the more so since it is given "by prophecy" or "because of prophecies." The charismatic element still played a considerable role, and it was the free utterance of the Spirit that enabled the church to ordain a person to a special ministry.

What the Pastorals suggest as a good "apostolic" order is, indeed, ordination, conveying the gift of the Spirit to Timothy (not merely an installation to a specific ministry, locally and temporally limited). It is focused on a leading position within a local church (Ephesus) or a region like Crete, where Titus should "appoint elders in every town" (Tit 1:5; cf. 2 Tim 2:2). Thus, this position seems to be superior to that of a bishop or elder (see H below). There is no doubt that this is the model that will become historically fruitful for the development of the institutional church.

G. Ministry in The Johannine Corpus

1. The Gospel of John. A totally different concept of ministry is found in the Johannine writings. Except for the traditional phrase "one of the Twelve" (John 6:71; 20:21), the Fourth Gospel only once speaks of the Twelve (6:67–70), though at the crucial place where Peter confesses Jesus as "the holy one of God." Otherwise, the evangelist always speaks of "the disciples." Since, according to 11:48, almost everyone (except the authorities) seems to have believed in Jesus, and since the farewell discourse with its "new commandment to love one another" is obviously not limited to a special group within a wider body of disciples (13:34; 15:12–17), we cannot be sure how many "disciples" John believed were present at the last meal and at the commission by the risen Christ. According to 21:2, Nathanael (who is not found in any list of the Twelve) belonged to the group of disciples in the first days after Easter, and the very important figure of "the disciple whom Jesus loved" is never named nor given a special status like "one of the Twelve." He might be John (whose name is never mentioned in the Fourth Gospel) or a Jerusalemite "known to the high priest" (18:15), or an Essene, or even a merely symbolic representative of the true believer (Bultmann). The term "apostle" is lacking in the Johannine writings, except in the general sense of "messenger" (13:16), which suggests that it was still used in its functional meaning, not as a title (Klauck).

The gospel of John seems to imply no specific ministry different from that generally given to every disciple. Whereas among nonbelievers there is mention of Roman and Jewish officers, a captain of a band of soldiers (18:12), Pilate (18:29, etc.), and the high priest (11:49, etc.), among the disciples only Judas is mentioned apparently holding an office (13:29). According to John 21 (probably added to the original gospel by the evangelist himself or by one of his followers) Peter is given the commission "to tend the sheep" of Jesus (vv 15–17). The literary function of the pericope is to present this commission as the Risen Lord's forgiving response to Peter's threefold denial, which shows that service in the Church is a matter of mere grace, not of human merit.

Otherwise, there is no apparent institutional structure of the group of disciples. There are no mediators between Christ and his believers; everyone is in direct contact with the Lord. This manifests itself, probably unconsciously, in the choice of images. Whereas Paul's simile of "the body" stresses the interdependence of all members, the Johannine "vine" (15:1), "shepherd" (10:11–18), and even "grain of wheat" (12:24) emphasizes the sole importance of Christ himself and the immediacy of every disciple to him. No sheep, no branch, no grain is "helping" the other one; they all receive their lives directly from the one vine, the one shepherd, the one root and stem. The commandment to love is certainly central, but it is not structured or institutionalized in any way. It is limited to the brothers and sisters, and 1 John 2:15 explicitly warns against loving the world. Nonetheless, "loving one another" in a totally united church is directed by Jesus himself towards winning the world to faith (17:21–23). God has loved the world when he gave his son (3:16) to save the world (6:33, 51; 12:47). Whereas Paul becomes "everything to everybody in order to save people everywhere" (1 Cor 9:22), reaching out to the world in a centrifugal way, the Johannine church concentrates, in a centripetal way, on full association in itself, on a loving brotherhood and sisterhood secluded from the world outside, in order to become contagious and to win the world for a life in faith and love. If there is a missionary activity it consists of leading the unbeliever to Jesus himself (1:36–51; 9:27; 11:28; 12:21–22 etc.), and here, female disciples are equivalent to male ones (4:39–42; 11:28; 20:18; the first witness of the risen Lord being a woman, cf. Matt 28:9–10).

2. The Epistles and Revelation. More important are the epistles. Some power was evidently exercised in the Church by Diotrephes, who refused to accept the messengers of the author and even banned "from the church" those who did (3 John 9–10). Unfortunately, we are not sure whether the author saw in him a representative of the institutional church or simply a wealthy church member skeptical of itinerant prophets. Nor do we know whether the author himself belonged to a group of such prophets, to a conventicle (Käsemann), or a "school" (Schürmann, also Klauck) within or outside of the Church in his country or region. However, 1 John states that all the believers "have been anointed by the Holy One and are all knowing" and that, therefore, they have no need that anyone should teach them; on the contrary, since the anointment teaches them about everything, it is true and no lie (2:20, 27). Yet, it is made quite clear that this anointment (the Spirit) can never speak anything that would differ basically from "what they have heard from the beginning" (2:24).

The picture of the Church in Revelation is not extensive enough to define its structure. The "angels" of the communities addressed in chaps. 2–3 are certainly no (monarchical) bishops, but a kind of heavenly counterpart to the earthly congregation (cf. the Jewish guardian angels of the nations). The astounding fact is that these congregations are living in Asia Minor, not that much earlier than those of the Pastorals and of Ignatius. And yet, only prophets play a role, and no other ministry seems to be existent.

One could even ask whether not all members of these churches were themselves at least potentially prophets.

Thus, the Johannine literature, perhaps even including Revelation, witnesses to a form of a church in which the Spirit itself is the one leader. (On the use of "elder" in 2–3 John, see C above.) Any ministry is given by the Spirit (or by the risen Lord in the exceptional case of Peter, John 21), and it is the spirit that represents Jesus in the time after Easter (John 14:16–17, 26; 15:26–27; 16:7–14). The authority of any ministry is the power of the Spirit, and it lasts as long as this power manifests itself.

H. Conclusion

Thus, at the end of the NT period, the Church was confronted with 2 options. On the one hand, it could have developed along the lines of the Pastoral Epistles, ordaining bishops (eventually one in each local parish; Ignatius) and installing elders and deacons. No group, not even a group of believers, could hope to exist over an extended period of time without some such institutional order, and the order of bishop(s)-elder(s)-deacon(s) was a workable arrangement. It would remain legitimate, according to NT standards as long as (1) it would not remain compulsory for all times and places but would flexibly yield to the will of God pertaining to new and different challenges and circumstances that might arise; (2) no ministry would impart to its bearer a qualitatively different status from that of all other believers (like that of the OT priest over against the laity); and (3) the free prophetic utterance of the Spirit is taken seriously, especially in the selection of people to be ordained. (According to the Pastoral epistles, this should be restricted to men only, but according to Paul and John, women could be included.) The danger associated with this line of development is that it could yield a church in which the institutional structure of offices and the proper performance of liturgical rites dominate and strangle the life of the Spirit.

On the other hand, the Church could have developed along the lines of the Johannine literature, responding to the movement of the Spirit, which is not limited to the mediation of any ministry. The authority of its prophets and prophetesses would be paramount (as is the case in charismatic movements from the ancient Montanists to some of the modern period). This again is legitimate according to NT standards as long as (1) such a church would not exclude any kind of order to prevent it from dissolving into disorganized chaos; (2) the "charismatics" would not elevate themselves (and their gift) above other members; and (3) the authority of the basic gospel as preached from the beginning would not be disputed either by new religiously experienced revelations or by any adaptations to modern trends popular in the contemporary world. The danger of this development is a church dominated by some strong "charismatic" individuals who may confuse their own wishes and visions with those of the Lord.

The ecumenical church of today confronts a related twofold problem. On the one hand, is the special status of the apostle, whose authority is qualitatively different from that of other believers, due merely to his status as an eyewitness to the appearance of the risen Lord, or does that special status continue (though not in the role of eyewitness) to apply to the office of priests, whose authority would, in some ways similarly differ from that of other believers? And on the other hand, does a church body without any institutional ministry still constitute a Christian church? Whatever the decision is, there is no doubt that any ministry in the Church should comply with Jesus' rule that those in positions of authority must be the servant of all (Mark 9:35; 10:43; Luke 22:26, cf. John 13:13–17).

Bibliography

Aune, D. E. 1983. *Prophecy in Early Christianity and the Ancient Mediterranean World.* Grand Rapids.

Banks, R. 1980. *Paul's Idea of Community.* Exeter.

Barret, C. K. 1985. *Church, Ministry and Sacraments in the New Testament.* Grand Rapids.

Bittlinger, A. 1967. *Charisma und Amt.* Calwer Hefte zur Forderung biblischen Glaubens und Christlichen Lebens. 85. Stuttgart.

Blank, J. 1982. *Vom Urchristentum zur Kirche.* Munich.

Bonnard, P. 1980. Normativite du Nouveau Testament et exemplarité de l'église primitive. In *Anamnesis,* ed. P. Bonnard. RTP. Lausanne.

Bovon, F. 1983. Israel, die Kirche und die Volker im lukanischen Doppelwerk. *TLZ* 108: 403–14.

Bronx, N. 1969. Historische und theologische Probleme der Pastoralbriefe des Neuen Testaments. *Kairos* 11: 77–94.

Brooten, B. 1982. *Women Leaders in the Ancient Synagogue.* Chico, CA.

Brosch, P. 1951. *Charismen und Aempter in der Urkirche.* Bonn.

Bultmann, R. 1985. *Das Evangelium nach Johannes.* 20th ed. (ET 1959).

Campenhausen, H. von. 1953. *Kirchliches Amt und geistliche Vollmacht in den ersten drei Jahrhunderten.* BHT 14. Tübingen.

Cothenet, E. 1987. Temoignage de l'Espirit et interpretation de l'écriture dans le corpus johannique. In *La vie de la Parole.* Paris.

Domalgalski, B. 1982. Waren die Sieben (Apg 6.1–7) Diakonen? *BZ* 26: 21–23.

Dunn, J. D. G. 1975. *Jesus and the Spirit.* London.

Ellis, E. E. 1973–74. Spiritual Gifts in the Pauline Community. *NTS* 20:128–44.

Gnilka, J. 1969. Geistliches Amt und Gemeinde nach Paulus. *Kairos* 11: 95–104.

Hahn, F. 1970. *Der urchristliche Gottesdienst.* SBS 41. Stuttgart.

———. 1986. *Exegetische Beitrage zum ökumenischen Gesprach.* Göttingen.

Hainz, J. 1972. *Ekklesia, Strukturen paulinischer Gemeindetheologie und Gemeindeordnung.* BU 9. Regensburg.

———. 1982. *Koinonia.* BU 16. Regensburg.

Haug, M. 1984. *Die Kirche des Neuen Testamentes.* Stuttgart.

Hengel, M. 1968. *Nachfolge und Charisma.* BZNW 34. Berlin.

Käsemann, E. 1960–64. *Exegetische Versuche und Besinnungen.* 2 vols. Göttingen.

———. 1982. *Kirchliche Konflikte.* Göttingen.

Kertelge, K. 1982. *Gemeinde und Amt im Neuen Testament.* Biblische Handbibliothek 10.

Kertelge K., and Schnackenburg, R. 1979. *Einheit der Kirche.* QD 84.

Klauck, H. J. 1985. Gemeinde ohne Amt. *BZ* 29: 193–220.

Kümmel, W. 1987. Das Urchristentum, d Aemter und Aemtsverstandnis. *TRu* 52: 111–54.

Lohfink, G. 1984. *Wie hat Jesus Gemeinde gewollt?* 4th ed. Freiburg.

Lohse, E. 1951. *Die Ordination im Spätjudentum und im Neuen Testament.* Göttingen.
Martin, R. P. 1964. *Worship in the Early Church.* London.
Michel, O. 1983. *Das Zeugnis des Neuen Testaments von der Gemeinde.* Basel.
Ollrog, W. H. 1979. *Paulus und seine Mitarbeiter.* WMANT 50. Neukirchen-Vluyn.
Rendtorff, T. 1983. *Charisma und Institution.* Gütersloh.
Rohde, J. 1976. *Urchristliche und frühkatholische Aemter.* Theologische Arbeiten 33.
Roloff, J. 1980. Die ökumenische Diskussion um das Amt im Licht des Neuen Testaments. Pp. 139–64 in *Das Amt im ökumenischen Kontext.* Stuttgart.
Satake, A. 1966. *Die Gemeindeordnung in der Johannesapokalypse.* WMANT 21. Neukirchen-Vluyn.
Schmithals, W. 1961. *Das kirchliche Apostleamt.* FRLANT 81. Göttingen.
Schnackenburg, R. 1961. *Die Kirche im Neuen Testament.* QD 14. Freiburg.
Schulz, S. 1976. Die Charismenlehre des Paulus. Pp. 443–60 in *Rechtfertigung.* Tübingen and Göttingen.
Schürmann, H. 1970. Die geistlichen Gnadengaben in den paulinischen Gemeinden. Pp. 236–67 in *Ursprung und Gestalt.* ed. by H. Schürmann. Düsseldorf.
Schüssler Fiorenza, E. 1972. *Priester fur Gott.* NTAbh 7.
Smith, D. M. 1974. Glossolalia and Other Spiritual Gifts in New Testament Perspective. *Int* 28: 307–20.
Stalder, K. 1984. *Die Wirklichkeit Christi erfahren.* Zurich.
Theissen, G. 1983. *Studien zur Soziologie des Urchristentums.* 2d ed. Tübingen.
Vogtle, A. 1985. Exegetische Reflectionen zur Apostoliztat des Amtssukzession. Pp. 221–79 in *Offenbarungsgeschehen und Wirkunsgeschichle.* ed. by A. Vogtle. Freiburg.
Walter, N. 1983. Apostelgeschichte 6.1 und die Anfange der Urgemeinde in Jerusalem. *NTS* 29: 370–93.
Zimmermann, F. 1984. *Die urchristlichen Lehrer.* WUNT 2/12. Tübingen.

R. EDUARD SCHWEIZER

MINNI (PLACE) [Heb *minnî*]. One of three nations summoned by Yahweh to attack Babylon (Jer 51:27). It seems certain that Minni is to be identified with the Manneans, a group located in a small but politically significant area S of Lake Urmia (Yamauchi 1982: 41). This connection is supported by the identity of the other two nations mentioned with Minni in Jer 51:27, Ararat and Ashkenaz. These peoples were little-known groups living in the N regions of W Asia. Ararat ("Urartu" in Assyrian sources) extended from modern Soviet Armenia and Iran into SE Turkey, but its geographical center was Lake Van. Ashkenaz is believed to be equivalent to "Ishkuza," the Assyrian name for the Scythians. The equation of Minni and Mannea is also in accordance with phonetic principles common to cuneiform sources and Heb (see *hatti* becoming Hittite, Gelb *IDB* 3: 392).

The history of Mannea may be traced from the time it is first mentioned in the inscriptions of Shalmaneser III (858–824 B.C.). Early in its history, Mannea was caught between two powerful neighbors at war with each other, Urartu and Assyria. Mannea continued to be mentioned in the Assyrian records over the next two centuries, sometimes as allies, sometimes as enemies (for a list of references to the *mannai,* see Parpola 1970: 236–37). The unfortunate Manneans were aligned with the Assyrians when the empire fell to the coalition of the Medes and Chaldeans. Their territory was allocated to the Medes and incorporated eventually into the Persian Empire. A Mannean contingent may have served in Cyrus' army when he took Babylon in 539 B.C. (Yamauchi 1982: 43).

It is impossible to be certain about the ethnic makeup of the Manneans. Many assume they were descended from the Indo-European Hurrians, but others have suggested a native population of long standing (Yamauchi 1982: 41).

Bibliography

Parpola, S. 1970. *Neo-Assyrian Toponyms.* AOAT 6. Kevelaer and Neukirchen-Vluyn.
Yamauchi, E. 1982. *Foes from the Northern Frontier.* Grand Rapids, MI.

BILL T. ARNOLD

MINNITH (PLACE) [Heb *minnît*]. One of the twenty Ammonite cities which were captured by Jephthah according to Judg 11:33. Although there is some question about the text, several translators believe Ezek 27:17 names Minnith as the source of the wheat Judah traded with Tyre. Others have preferred to amend the text to read "olives" instead of Minnith (e.g., AV; RV; RSV).

In *Onomastica* (140.3), Eusebius identified biblical Minnith with a village, known to him in Greek as *Maanith,* some 4 Roman miles from Esbus (modern Hesban) on the way to Philadelphia (modern Amman). This statement, combined with the fact that Judg 11:33 couples it with the S city of Aroer as an opposing boundary, has led scholars to locate the site somewhere between Hesban and Amman.

The most likely candidate at present is Umm el-Basatin (Umm el-Hanafish; M.R. 232137). A modern village covers much of the tell, but a large amount of ancient architecture is still visible. Although the site has not been extensively excavated, a recent survey recovered sherds from Ayyubid/Mamluk, Ottoman, Byzantine, Late Roman, Early Roman, Iron 2/Persian, and Iron 1 periods.

Bibliography

Alt, A. 1933. Die Ausflüge und Reise (Strassen um Philadelphia). *PJ* 29: 27–28.
Ibach, R. 1987. *Hesban 5: Archaeological Survey of the Hesban Region.* Berrien Springs, MI.

RANDALL W. YOUNKER

MINT. See FLORA.

MINUCIUS FELIX. Only one work, the *Octavius,* survives from this late-2d- or early-3d-century Christian apologist. Many readers regard it as the jewel of Christian Latin in the first three centuries. When contrasted with the other early apologies, its immediacy, intimacy, and informality call to mind the tone of Xenophon's *Symposium,* not Plato's. Refreshingly undogmatic, it contains not a single reference to scripture, nor does it broach a single item of doctrine. Although mentioned by ancient writers (Lactant. *Div. Inst.* 1.11.55 (*PL* 6.180); Jerome, *De vir. ill.* 58 (PL 23.706)), the *Octavius* fell into obscurity in the 5th century, and remained undiscovered until 1560 C.E. In that year, the French scholar F. Baudouin discerned that the eighth book of Arnobius's *Adversus nationes* was, in fact, Minucius Felix's lost *Octavius.* The only other work attributed to Minucius Felix is one named by Jerome, *De fato (vel contra mathematicos),* but he regards it as spurious; it has not been transmitted.

Jerome *(idem.)* describes Marcus Minucius Felix as a Roman lawyer of note. Certain references in the *Octavius* suggest its author possessed detailed knowledge of African affairs (e.g., 14.1; 30.3; 31.2). This has led some scholars to claim that the author was, at least originally, an African. While African authorship is argued by some (Beaujeu 1964: xxii–xxv; xliv–xlvi), other scholars reject the proposal.

In composing the *Octavius,* Minucius Felix drew on sources, both in form and in letter. His principal debt is to Cicero's *De natura deorum.* Not only is the form analogous at many points (e.g., introductory prologue, which sets the topic, and introduces the characters in the dialogue), but there is textual dependence as well (various passages in *Oct.* 19 = *Nat. D.* 1.25–42). Additionally, there are numerous quotations from or allusions to other classical and Christian writers (among the many: Plato, Zeno, and Thales; Justin and Tatian). Certain interesting descriptions of Christian religious practice in Minucius Felix's locale are mentioned: they followed Jewish dietary law, abstaining from meat sacrificed to idols (12.5; 38.1), and from meat with blood in it, i.e., not slaughtered in accordance with kosher regulations (30.6). This is remarkable evidence of the influence of Judaic-Christianity, whose interpretation of the Apostolic Decree (Acts 15:19–21) was at variance with the "liberal" Pauline interpretation (Gal 2:7–10), in the Latin West.

The *Octavius* itself is a dialogue between two friends of Minucius Felix (who calls himself Marcus in the dialogue), a fellow Christian, Octavius, for whom it is named, and a pagan fellow barrister, Caecilius. Written after Octavius's death, it recalls a pleasant day the three spent at Ostia, walking and debating the virtues of Christianity. Caecilius asks Marcus to judge the debate. He then proceeds to make a case for adhering to the traditional Roman religion and attacks Christianity with the usual charges of cannibalism, atheism, incest and superstitious beliefs (e.g., end of the world). Octavius responds with what is—for a 2d- or 3d-century apologist—remarkable restraint. Appealing largely to reason and philosophy, Octavius rebuts the charges, capping his argument by claiming that Christians "do not preach great things, but live them" (38.6). The dialogue is a purely intellectual exercise; it ends with Caecilius' conversion.

Dating the *Octavius* is the key to dating Minucius Felix, and although the efforts have been maximal, the results have been minimal. A first difficulty is to decide the authenticity of the events: did the three friends actually have such a talk, or did Minucius Felix create a fictive encounter as a vehicle for his ideas? Scholars have usually assumed that the participants are real, and that some such encounter occurred, although the actual conversation is largely the invention of Minucius Felix. Internal evidence for dating is virtually nonexistent, save for a reference to Fronto (fl. ca. 140–175 C.E.), who appears to have recently attacked Christians (31.2). However, one must then decide whether the reference to Fronto is genuinely from the time of the encounter, or whether, given that Minucius Felix states he is writing after Octavius' death, Fronto's attack came later and has been retrojected into the dialogue. A final complicating problem are the parallels between the *Octavius* and Tertullian's *Apologeticum* and *Ad nationes* which indicate literary dependence. Scholarship has been divided on the order of priority. The priority of Minucius Felix, the use of a common source, and the dependence of Minucius Felix have all been suggested. Current scholarly fashion gives priority to Tertullian. If one accepts that sequence and dates the *Apologeticum* and *Ad nationes* ca. 197 C.E. (so Barnes 1985: 55), then the *Octavius* must be later, presumably from the first half of the 3d century. Such a dating, while generally accepted today, is at odds, however, with the reference to Fronto.

Bibliography

Altaner, B., and A. Stuiber. 1980. Minucius Felix. Pp. 146–48 in *Patrologie.* 9th ed. Freiburg.
Bardenhewer, O. 1913. *Geschichte der altkirchlichen Literatur.* Vol. 1. 2d ed. Freiburg.
Barnes, T. D. 1985. *Tertullian.* 2d ed. Oxford.
Baylis, H. J. 1928. *Minucius Felix and His Place among the Early Fathers of the Latin Church.* London.
Beaujeu, J. 1964. *Minucius Felix: Octavius.* Paris.
Clarke, G. W. 1974. *The Octavius of Marcus Minucius Felix.* New York.
Kytzler, B. 1982. *Minvcivs Felix Octavivs.* Leipzig.
Quasten, J. 1950. Minucius Felix. Pp. 155–63 in *Patrology.* Vol. 2. Utrecht. Repr. Westminster, MD, 1983, 1984.
Quispel, G. 1949. A Jewish Source of Minucius Felix. *VigChrist* 3: 113–22.

William L. Petersen

MIQṢAT MAᶜASE HATORAH (4QMMT). A sectarian polemical document, six incomplete manuscripts of which (4Q394–99) were discovered in Qumran cave 4. Taken together, they provide a composite text of about 120 lines. The preserved text, which apparently covers about two-thirds of the original scroll, derives from the middle and the end of the document. The beginning is completely lost.

The document is in the form of a letter (having a sender and an addressee) and is unique in language, style, and contents. The title *miqṣat maᶜasê hattorâ,* meaning "some of the precepts of the Torah," has been taken from the concluding passage, reading: "we are sending you some of the precepts of the Torah."

A. Contents, Structure, and Historical Setting

It appears that MMT consisted originally of four sections: (1) an opening formula, now completely lost; (2) a calendar of the sect (with a 364-day year); (3) a list of more than 20 *halakhot* (= precepts), all of which are peculiar to this group; and (4) an epilogue which discusses the separation of the group from normative Pharisaic Judaism and attempts to persuade the addressee to adopt their *halakhic* views. The *halakhot* represent the heart of the letter, with the other sections as their framework (the calendar, although a separate section, belongs to the *halakhic* domain). Most of these *halakhot* concern the Temple, dealing with its purity, sacrifices, and festivals. The author states that disagreement over these *halakhot* is what caused the sect to secede (Heb *pāraš*) from the rest of the people (the verb *paraš* relates to the same root as the name of the Pharisees).

There are three parties in MMT, referred to as *we, you* (sometimes singular, sometimes plural), and *they*. Who were these parties? Clearly the *we*-party is the author, who generally uses the expression "we maintain" (Heb *ʾnḥnw hwšbym*) expressing the sect's *halakhic* views. The *you*-party is the addressee; the prevailing second person expression in this case is "and you know." The addressee may be the leader of Israel, being compared to David and addressed as follows: "for the welfare of you and your people," and "for the welfare of you and Israel." The *they*-party is a group about whom it is said that "they do such-and-such," where the reference in each case is to some specific *halakhic* practice. A study of the *halakhic* views of this group shows that they should be identified with the Pharisees.

It appears that MMT, which discusses the invalidity of the *halakhot* of the *they*-party (i.e., the Pharisees), was written by the Teacher of Righteousness and addressed to the Wicked Priest and his colleagues. This is inferred both from the contents of MMT and from Pesher Psalms 37 (= 4Q171 3–10 iv 7–9) which states that the Wicked Priest tried to kill the Teacher of Righteousness "because of the precepts and the law which he [= the teacher] had sent him." (Note the similar passage from MMT quoted above.) Assuming that the Wicked Priest is Jonathan the Prince, MMT was composed at about 150 B.C. It stands to reason that the schism mentioned in MMT occurred a short time before the composition of the document. The paleography may also imply such an early date, as does the contrast of MMT with the prohibition of disputes with opponents found in 1QS 9:16–17.

B. The Halakhot

The *halakhot* of MMT concern the Temple cult, and most are related to biblical laws as understood by the sect. The following *halakhot* are extant (in the order of their appearance in the text):

1. Gentile grain should not be brought into the Temple.
2. A fragmentary *halakha* about the cooking of offerings.
3. A fragmentary *halakha* about sacrifices by gentiles.
4. Cereal offerings should not be left overnight.
5. The purity of those preparing the red heifer.
6. Several *halakhot* concerning the purity of skins.
7. The place of slaughtering and offering sacrifices.
8. Slaughtering pregnant animals.
9. Forbidden sexual unions.
10. Banning the blind and deaf from the "purity of the Temple."
11. The purity of the streams of liquids poured from a pure vessel into an impure one.
12. Dogs should not enter into Jerusalem.
13. The fruit of the fourth year is to be given to the priests.
14. The cattle-tithe is to be given to the priest.
15. Several regulations about the impurity of the leper during the period of purification until final purification.
16. The impurity of human bones.
17. Marriages between priests and Israelites are forbidden.

Some of the *halakhot* are already known from the Temple Scroll (11QTemple, nos. 4, 18, 13, 16). Some others have no parallel either in the Temple Scroll or in any other text from Qumran. Of special interest are two *halakhot* that parallel *halakhic* views explicitly ascribed to the Sadducees (nos. 5, 11; cf. *m. Yad.* 4:7, *Para* 3:7). In both cases the *halakhic* views attributed to the Sadducees are identical to those of MMT. It is significant to note the similarity in terminology between MMT and the Mishna in these parallel *halakhot.* This similarity implies the existence of a polemic between the Dead Sea sect and the ancestors of the rabbis. Thus, other disputed *halakhot* in rabbinic literature and in the Dead Sea Scrolls may have their origins in this polemic—e.g., the *halakha* about the deaf (no. 10) throws light on the evidence in *t. Ter.* 1:1 that all the purities of Jerusalem were prepared by the deaf son of R. Yohanan ben Godgeda.

The *halakhic* attitude of MMT is much stricter than that of the rabbis. For example, MMT identifies Jerusalem with the Camp mentioned in the Torah and asserts that all purity laws which were to be observed in the Camp should be observed in Jerusalem (contrast the more lenient rabbinic attitude in *t. Kelim, B. Qam.* 1:12).

C. The Language

The Hebrew of MMT is peculiar. Its grammar is basically that of the other Dead Sea Scrolls. However, the relative particle is *š-* (*ʾšr* occurs only once), and the participle is extensively used. An especially large number of Mishnaic words occur in the *halakhic* part of MMT; some of these are *halakhic* terms. There are also words unattested in any other Hebrew source. The following are of special interest: *hʿrybwt hšmš,* "sunset"; *bšl š-*, "so that"; *bgll š-*, "because"; *prt hḥṭʾt,* "the red heifer"; *mʿśym,* "precepts"; *ʿbrh,* "pregnant," *swmym,* "blind," *mwṣqwt,* "uninterrupted streams of liquid"; and *mśktwb,* "as is written."

D. The Contribution of MMT to the Study of Judaism

At this early stage of research, the contribution of MMT can not be fully evaluated. The following are a few preliminary remarks.

1. As has been noted, MMT consists of controversial *halakhot* and thus provides evidence not only for the *halakha* of the sect, but also for that of its opponents. Examining the *halakhic* view of the latter, we learn that they are nearly always identical with those of the rabbis. This is also the case in additional polemical passages in other Dead Sea Scrolls. This identity proves that the opponents of the sect were the predecessors of the rabbis, most probably the Pharisees. It further demonstrates that the corresponding rabbinic *halakha* (to *halakhot* discussed in the Dead Sea Scrolls) was established at a very early date. This contra-

dicts the view of those scholars who believe that the Pharisaic *halakha* was a "new" *halakha*. The halakhic correspondence with the Mishna serves to authenticate those historical sections in the rabbinic sources as truly reflecting the reality of the Second Temple period, even though they were put in written form much later (contra some recent scholarly trends).

2. MMT contributes much to our knowledge of the history of sectarianism in that period. For example, until now there was no explicit evidence concerning the reasons for the schism. Josephus gives the impression that the sects were primarily divided over theological questions, for instance those relating to the resurrection of the dead or the role of Divine providence. MMT proves that the real reason was the controversy over ritual laws. Josephus' description should be understood as an attempt to produce an explanation that would make sense to his Greek (and Roman) readers.

3. Of special interest to biblical scholars are the interpretations given in MMT to certain juridical passages in the Torah in particular, and its methods of interpretation in general.

4. The contribution of MMT to the history of the Hebrew language is also significant, but requires a more detailed discussion than can be undertaken here.

Bibliography

Baumgarten, J. M. 1980. The Pharisaic-Sadducean Controversies about Purity and the Qumran Texts. *JSS* 31: 157–70.

Milik, J. T. 1962. Le rouleau de cuivre provenant de la grotte 3Q (3Q15): orthographe et langue. *DJD* 3 (Texte): 221–27.

Qimron, E. 1986. *The Hebrew of the Dead Sea Scrolls*. HSS 29. Atlanta.

———. 1988. The Holiness of the Holy Land in the Light of a New Document from Qumran. Pp. 9–13 in *Pillars of Smoke and Fire*, ed. M. Sharon. Johannesburg.

Qimron, E., and Strugnell, J. 1985. An Unpublished Halakhic Letter from Qumran. *BibAT* Pp. 400–7.

Strugnell, J., and Qimron, E. fc. *Miqṣat Maʿase HaTorah. 4Q394–399*. HSS. Atlanta.

Elisha Qimron

MIRACLE.

This entry consists of two articles, one covering signs and wonders in the OT, and the other treating signs and wonders recounted in the NT.

OLD TESTAMENT

A. Terminology
 1. *nēs*
 2. *gĕdālôt*
 3. *niplāʾôt*
 4. *peleʾ*
 5. The verb *plʾ*
 6. *ʾōt* and *môpēt*
B. Miracle and Creation
C. Precisely the Right Moment
D. Definition of Miracle
E. Control Mechanisms
 1. Repetition
 2. Restoration of Prior Conditions
 3. Prayer
 4. Prior Announcement
 5. Paradox
 6. Miracle within a Miracle
 7. Limitation
 8. Foreigners Acknowledge a Miracle
 9. Multiple Test Criteria
F. Miracle and History
G. Miracle and Myth
H. Miracle and Magic
I. Implements for Performing a Miracle
J. The Performer of the Miracle
K. The Initiative for the Performance of a Miracle
L. Miracles of Life, Death, and Healing
M. Purpose of the Miracle
 1. Trial
 2. Reward and Punishment
 3. Grace
 4. Faith in God and in His Messenger
 5. The Remembrance of Miracles
N. The Rationalization of Miracles

A. Terminology

1. *nēs*. The study of "miracles" in the Hebrew Bible may be, in fact, an illegitimate pursuit. Hebrew has no equivalent term for the English concept "miracle." It is only in rabbinic Hebrew that the word *nēs* is found with this meaning: "Ten wonders were wrought for our fathers in Egypt, and ten at the [Red] Sea" (*ʾAbot* 5:4); "If one sees a place where miracles have been wrought for Israel, he should say, blessed be He who wrought miracles for our ancestors in this place" (*m. Ber.* 9:1). In the Bible, however, the word indicates a long pole enabling something set upon it to be seen at a great distance (Num 21:8–9; Isa 30:17), or a pole for a banner (Isa 33:23; Ezek 27:7). Only in one verse does *nēs* mean a sign or wonder (in the wake of a miraculous event): "And the earth opened its mouth and swallowed them up together with Korah when that company died, when the fire devoured two hundred and fifty men; and they became a sign" (Num 26:10). In the wake of another miracle (the victory over Amalek), Moses erects an altar and calls it *"YHWH nisî,"* but the meaning of *nēs* here is not clear.

2. *gĕdōlôt* (only in the plural). This term is used once in reference to human action, the "man of God" who performs miracles, as in the words of the "king of Israel" to Gehazi, Elisha's servant: "Tell me, please, all the great things *(gĕdōlôt)* Elisha has done" (2 Kgs 8:4). "Great things" in general indicates something beyond one's power or unattainable: "Neither do I concern myself with *great matters*" (Ps 131:1; cf. also Jer 45:5). The word *gĕdōlôt* thus mostly indicates God's actions, which at times have the character of a miracle: "Who had done *great things* in Egypt/Wondrous works in the land of Ham/Awesome things by the Red Sea" (Ps 106:21–22). Job 9:10: "He does *great things* past finding out, Yes, wonders without number," refers both to the upheaval of the order of creation (vv 5–7) and to the greatest miracle of all—the creation (vv 8–9). The word *gĕdōlôt* can simultaneously refer to both creation and God's righteousness in managing worldly affairs (Job 9:9ff.; and as to God's righteousness in judgment, cf. Ps 71:19). *Gĕdōlôt,* therefore, belongs to actions done within the overall sphere of God's power and sovereignty.

3. *nipla*ʾ*ôt* (only in plural). The term *nipla*ʾ*ôt,* as the parallel term to *gĕdōlôt,* also refers to the expression of God's sovereignty, of which miracles are only one aspect. In prose *nipla*ʾ*ôt* indicates God's salvation of his people in the Exodus from Egypt and the conquest of the land (Exod 34:10; Judg 6:13). These saving acts are at times bound up with miracles (Exod 3:20; Josh 3:5; Neh 9:17). Poetry also contains references to the act of redemption and the miracle of the Exodus (Mic 7:15; Pss 78:4, 11, 32; 106:7, 22).

In psalmic literature *nipla*ʾ*ôt* can refer to other saving acts as well. The refrain "Oh, that men would give thanks to the Lord for his goodness, and for his wonderful works to the children of men" (Ps 107:8, 15, 21, 31), refers to the deliverance of individuals from trouble (wanderers in the wilderness, prisoners, the infirm, and sailors). The rescue of an individual from his enemies is expressly conceived as a revelation of God's righteous judgment; the declaration: "I will praise you, O Lord, with my whole heart; I will tell of all your *marvelous works*" (Ps 9:2) relates to acquittal in judgment (cf. e.g., vv 8, 20; cf. Psalms 71; 86). God's reign of justice is bound up with his being the creator of the universe. In Psalm 96, which invites all the earth to "declare his glory among the nations, his *wonders* among all peoples" (v 3), the Lord is praised both for his act of creation (v 4) and his righteous judgment of the earth and its peoples (v 13; cf. also Pss 75:2–5; 145:5–8). God's righteousness is enjoyed not only by man, but also by the entire creation (145:15–16). The word *nipla*ʾ*ôt* is found in connection with the creation also in Job 37:5–12.

4. *pele*ʾ. The noun *pele*ʾ appears exclusively in poetry. It is usually found as the object of the verb ʾ*śh,* "to do," and refers to God's saving acts: "Will you work *wonders* for the dead? Shall the dead arise and praise you?" (Ps 88:11); and on the national level: "O Lord, you are my God. I will exalt you, I will praise your name, for you have done *wonderful things* . . . For you have made a city a ruin, a fortified city a ruin" (Isa 25:1–2). The wonder/saving act may be connected with miracles (such as Exod 15:11; Pss 77:12, 15; 78:11–13). Occasionally, like the other terms discussed here, *pele*ʾ indicates God's work in creation and sovereignty over its order (Ps 89:6; cf. also vv 10–13).

5. The Verb *pl*ʾ. This root, from which the nouns *nipla*ʾ*ôt* and *pele*ʾ are derived, indicates in its verbal usage that which is beyond man's understanding. The intensity of Jonathan's love is beyond David's understanding: "your love towards me was more marvelous than the love of women" (2 Sam 1:26). The inability to come to a decision in judgment is also described by means of this verb: "If a judgment proves to be beyond your ability (to decide) . . ." (Deut 17:8). Man cannot comprehend the Lord and his ways (Judg 13:18 [should be translated "unfathomable"]); is incapable of understanding the ways of creation (Prov 30:18–19); man cannot hide from God, who governs all creation: "Indeed, the darkness shall not hide from you . . . for you have formed my inward parts . . . *marvelous* are your works" (Ps 139:12–14). The root *pl*ʾ is sometimes parallel to the root *gdl* (from which the noun *gĕdōlôt* is derived) and both indicate God's actions in different spheres of existence (Isa 28:29; Joel 2:26; Ps 31:22).

6. ʾ*ōt* (and *môpēt*). The semantic field of the word ʾ*ōt* is similar to that of the word *nēs,* though whereas *nēs* received the meaning of a miraculous deed only in postbiblical literature, such a meaning is found for ʾ*ōt* already in the Bible itself. The basic meaning of ʾ*ōt* is "mark, sign" (Gen 4:16; Exod 12:13), as well as "banner, standard" (Num 2:2). The "lights" in the heavens also have the function of "signs" (Gen 1:14), that is, indications of the transitions between different units of time.

In the Priestly source of the Pentateuch the "signs" are tangible and concrete, as in the series of 4 covenants made with a certain select body of people, each more limited than the preceding: the sign of the rainbow in the cloud for the covenant with the renewed humanity (Gen 9:13); the sign of circumcision for the covenant with Abraham (Gen 17:11); and the sign of the Sabbath for the covenant with the Israelites (Exod 31:17). The fourth covenant—with the priesthood (Num 25:10–13)—needs no sign: The existence of the priesthood is itself the sign of the covenant. Additional signs in the priestly source are equally concrete and are connected with ritual/worship. These signs testify to a miraculous event whose lesson must be remembered: the altar covered over with the metal of the censers of the 250 men who sided with Korah (Num 17:1–15 [—Eng 16:36–40]); Aaron's rod, kept as a sign before the ark (Num 17:25–26 [—Eng 10–11]); compare also the sign of the 12 stones after the crossing of the Jordan (Josh 4:5–7).

In the book of Deuteronomy, in contrast, the "signs" (or the frequent expression "signs and wonders," ʾ*ōtôt ûmōptîm*) are the miraculous events of the past that the people are obliged to remember (7:19; 11:3; 26:8; 29:2; 34:11). As a rendering of this Hebrew expression, Biblical Aramaic employs the phrase ʾ*atayā*ʾ *wĕtimhayā*ʾ, "signs and wonders"; see the words of the kings who witnessed the miracles performed for those who honor God's name (Dan 3:32–33 [—Eng 4:2–3]; 6:28). The term *môpēt* means a miraculous sign also when it appears by itself (Exod 7:9; the LXX, however, reads "sign or wonder"), and in 1 Kgs 13:3: "And he gave a sign *(môpēt)* the same day, saying, 'This is the sign *(môpēt)* which the Lord has spoken: Surely the altar shall split apart, and the ashes on it shall be poured out." In place of the word ʾ*ōt* in 2 Kgs 20:8–9, the word *môpēt* appears in the parallel passage in 2 Chr 32:24, demonstrating the interchangeability of these two words. A phrase which sometimes accompanies the giving of a divine sign to someone is "And this shall be to you (sing. or pl.)/us (a sign)" (Exod 3:12; 1 Sam 2:34; 14:9–10; 2 Kgs 19:30; 20:9; Jer 44:29).

B. Miracle and Creation

The distinctiveness of the phenomenon of miracles cannot, then, be understood on the basis of the various terms employed to express the notion. It is equally impossible to grasp the essence of the biblical miracle by viewing it simply as a violation of the rules of natural order, since the concept of nature and natural laws is foreign to the religious literature of the Bible. Instead of this concept, the Bible speaks rather of the creation. Philo of Alexandria sees the creation as the miracle par excellence: "these extraordinary and seemingly incredible events are but child's play to God in comparison with that which is really great and worthy of contemplation—the creation") (*Vita Mos* 212–13), and the understanding of the rabbis is close to this; in their view the biblical miracles were predetermined during the six days of creation (*ʾAbot* 5:6). Since the miracle is a continuation of the creation, the author of the Korah story is obliged to describe the miraculous opening of the mouth of the earth in terms of creation (Num 16:30). In the miracle, God indeed demonstrates his rule over that created by him: he can halt the course of the heavenly bodies (Josh 10:12–13) or temporarily remove the boundary fixed between sea and dry land (Exodus 14).

The creator may temporarily alter the order of creation, but miracles do not bring any new creatures into the world nor do any new elements become added to it (the manna is perhaps an exception to this rule, but here also there is a clear effort to make things sound more rational—Exod 16:31; see N below). The elements of the miraculous deed are derived from creation, from the already existing and familiar; the miracle, at times, simply brings about a change in the organization of these elements. Such a reordering makes for a surrealistic environment in which natural boundaries are obscured: Sea becomes dry land; a man (Elijah) ascends to the heavens; rain pours down in the middle of the summer harvest; heavenly bodies deviate from their fixed courses; the dead become alive, etc.

C. Precisely the Right Moment

Not all miracles disturb the order of creation. When events appear to take place at just the right moment—when a person or object materializes on the scene at the precise instant to meet the critical need (a kind of deus ex machina)—this also can be regarded as a miracle. After the angel's poetic announcement to Hagar that Ishmael will not perish from thirst we read: "And God opened her eyes, and she saw a well of water. Then she went and filled the skin with water, and gave the lad a drink" (Gen 21:19). The end of Saul's journey in search of the lost donkeys precisely upon arriving at Samuel's town is no mere coincidence, and Saul does not attain to the kingship by chance; Saul finds himself there in accordance with a divine plan to cause the anointer to meet up with the anointee (1 Sam 9:15–16). In some cases God's intervention to cause things to take place at the right moment is not explicitly mentioned in connection with the "miraculous coincidence," even though the divine activity in the story surrounding the event is quite clear: "Then Abraham lifted his eyes and looked, and there behind him was a ram caught in a thicket by its horns" (Gen 22:13). God's intervention is not mentioned also in the two incidents which take place at the beginning of the story of Moses: Moses' being found by Pharaoh's daughter (Exod 2:5ff.) and his coming to sit down by a well in Midian (vv 15ff.), both of which appear later to have been divinely arranged.

The disrupting of the order of creation and events taking place at just the right moment are sometimes mixed together, as in the prologue to the book of Job: the first and third disasters are events—robberies—taking place at the precise moment, in line with the story's theme (1:15, 17). The second and fourth, on the other hand, are the result of an upsurge of the forces of creation, fire, and wind (vv 16, 19). The rabbis also viewed these incidents as miracles: "It once happened that a fire broke out in the courtyard of Joseph b. Simai . . . and a miracle happened on his behalf, rain descended and extinguished [it]" (*b. Šab.* 121a).

D. Definition of Miracle

Since God's intervention in earthly events without disrupting the order of creation can be considered a miracle, one may question whether every divine intervention should be considered a miracle as well. Thus, for example, God's intervention on behalf of his people in war: several of Israel's victories are accompanied by supernatural events. In the conquest of the first Canaanite city, Jericho, for instance, the city walls collapse after seven circumambulations of the city by the ark, and the priests' blowing of the trumpets (Joshua 6; see also 2 Kgs 19:35; 2 Chr 20:24–25). In other passages a military maneuver is mingled with a divine miracle, such as in the war against Amalek (Exod 17:8–16). Where the text is elliptical and only indicates that the Lord dumbfounded the enemy and struck them, it is questionable if this should be considered a miracle. The different literary formulations of the victory over Sisera provide a good indication of how the text itself can present an event in both miraculous and non-miraculous ways: the prose narrative—"And the Lord routed Sisera and all his chariots and all his army with the edge of the sword before Barak" (Judg 4:15)—is very different from the poetic expression of the same event (which recalls the defeat of the Egyptians at the Red Sea), whose miraculous nature is much clearer: "They fought from the heavens; the stars from their courses fought against Sisera. The torrent of Kishon swept them away" (Judg 5:20–21). Similarly, the coming of the Spirit of the Lord upon a hero is accompanied at times by a miraculous feat, such as the slaying of a thousand Philistines with a donkey's jawbone (Judg 15:14–17). It is less clear if cases should be termed miracles where the narrator chooses only to relate that the deliverer overcomes his foes by the power of the Spirit (such as Judg 3:10). The same uncertainty applies to stories which do not mention the Spirit at all, reporting only that the Lord gave the enemy into the hand of Israel (e.g. Num 21:34–35; Deut 2:31).

A similar observation can be made regarding divine punishment by means of a catastrophe. Occasionally, such a punishment is accompanied by a disturbance in the order of creation, as in the ten plagues of Egypt and the drowning of the Egyptians in the Red Sea (Exodus 7–14), the divine fire which incinerates Aaron's sons when they offered strange fire to the Lord (Lev 10:1–3), or the punishment of the 250 people who offer incense in the Korah rebellion (Num 16:31). Sometimes the miraculous character is less conspicuous, as in the death of Uzzah, who touched the divine ark (2 Sam 6:8–9) or the plague which broke out in the incident of Baal Peor (Num 25:9). Nothing remains, however, of any miraculous element in the story of the death of Er and Onan (Gen 38:7, 10), or the striking of Nabal (1 Sam 25:38), or the death of Bathsheba's firstborn son (2 Sam 12:14).

Is there, then, any line of demarcation between a divine-miraculous punishment and one that is not miraculous? Furthermore, can divine revelation, the appearance of God or of his angel to man, be considered a miracle? If revelation was a commonplace occurrence it could not be considered miraculous, and, to be sure, there are traditions which accept such appearances nonchalantly, such as God's conversation with Abraham (Gen 18:35) or a revelation to Isaac (Gen 26:2). Nevertheless, the notion prevails in the Bible that "for no man shall see Me, and live" (Exod 33:20), and certain mortals who attained to divine revelation express their surprise at remaining alive (Gen 16:13; 32:31) or fear for their lives (Judg 6:22; 13:22; Isa 6:5). Many times the divine appearance is not met with indifference, but the visited person responds passionately, as when Joshua falls upon his face before the Commander of the Lord's army (Josh 5:13–15; cf. Lev 9:24; Num 17:10; 20:6). The revelation is sometimes accompanied by an additional miracle, as in the case of the bush that burns but is not consumed (Exod 3:2). It is, then, difficult to set a standard for distinguishing between miraculous and non-miraculous divine appearances.

One must finally ask if events which are intuitively considered miracles are to be included as miracles, even though the narrator relates them in practically incidental terms. Examples here include (1) the plagues God brought upon Pharaoh for taking Sarai Abram's wife (Gen 12:17), which are, in fact, a parallel in miniature of the clearly miraculous series of the plagues of Egypt, and (2) the foreshortened description of the collapse of the walls of Aphek in the wake of the victory over Aram (1 Kgs 20:30)—a weak parallel to the miraculous fall of the walls of Jericho (Josh 6). Further, one may ask if the visitation of Ruth—"the Lord gave her conception" (Ruth 4:13)—is a miraculous act; the same consideration applies to the many visitations of barren wives found in the Pentateuch and Former Prophets.

The key in determining whether an event is miraculous or not lies in the degree of power and magnitude of the event as it is expressed in the text; it is not the quality of the phenomenon which decides the question but rather the manner of its formulation. The decisive factor is a literary one: the expression of excitement and wonder in the face of an incident and the amount of words devoted to its description. The definition of miracle in the Bible, then, is a literary definition: an extraordinary occurrence, attributable to God's hand (which at times disrupts the order of creation), and which leaves a marked impression in the text; the criteria for determining what is to be considered a miracle are literary in character.

E. Control Mechanisms

The literary formulation of an extraordinary event, together with certain control mechanisms, can reveal whether or not a narrator intended to draft his account of an event as a miracle. The criteria which help to determine the character of a given story consist in details that an author may incorporate into the narrative in order to come to terms with the doubts of both the characters in the narrative and of his reader, as well as to inspire belief in the miracle. The following are the most conclusive tests:

1. Repetition. The ability to repeat an action or perform a miracle whenever needed refutes the assumption that the event occurred simply by chance: the healing of those bitten by the snakes (Num 21:4–9) is not a once-only deed. Each and every bitten one is healed only upon gazing at the brass serpent (v 9). When the Philistine god Dagon falls before the ark of the Lord (1 Sam 5:2–5), the Philistines put him back in his place, failing to understand that it was God who caused the image to fall. It is the second fall which proves that God's hand is at work. Here, however, the repetition is combined with graded intensification—God's second blow to Dagon is graver than the first (v 4).

2. Restoration of Prior Conditions. The miracle-doer's ability to restore conditions to their former state after a supernatural event proves that a guiding hand is in control: Jeroboam's hand withers as a result of his attempt to harm the man of God (1 Kgs 13:4), but it is restored after the man of God's prayer (v 6). So, too, in the stories of the signs performed by Moses: the rod becomes a serpent and then changes back to a rod (Exod 4:2–4); his leprous hand "was restored like his other flesh" (vv 6–7).

3. Prayer. A miracle taking place after prayer cannot be taken as coincidence: the waters of Marah are cured after Moses' prayer (Exod 15:26), and the thirsty Samson's prayer brings about the splitting of the hollow place at Lehi, permitting water to come forth (Judg 15:18–19).

4. Prior Announcement. The prior announcement, similar to the prayer, testifies to the fact that the miracle is the result of divine intervention. Before the crossing of the Jordan, for example, Joshua announces: "Sanctify yourselves, for tomorrow the Lord will do wonders among you" (Josh 3:5), and further on (vv 10–13) he details what will happen when they cross.

5. Paradox. The words of Tertullian: "It is to be believed absolutely because it is absurd . . . it is certain because it is impossible" (*On the Body of Christ,* 75), are relevant for many miracle stories: the narrator or one of his characters emphasizes the "absurdity" of a miraculous event. At times the aspect of absurdity precedes the execution of the miracle and underlines the difficulty inherent in conditions at the beginning of things. Before the waters of the Jordan are divided to enable the Israelites to cross it is stated that "the Jordan overflows all its banks during the whole time of harvest" (Josh 3:15). Before it begins to rain, Samuel declares: "Is today not the wheat harvest?" (1 Sam 12:17). A character may express the paradox incidental to his doubt that a promise will be fulfilled: "Shall a child be born to a man who is one hundred years old? And shall Sarah, who is ninety years old, bear a child?" (Gen 17:17; cf. also 18:12). Sometimes the paradox is formulated by means of a negative particle or expression (Exod 3:2, 3; 1 Kgs 13:28; 2 Kgs 3:17; 20:10; Dan 3:27).

6. Miracle within a Miracle. This phenomenon, so termed in rabbinic literature, is similar to the paradox: in order to allow no room for denying the miraculousness of an event, the miracle is executed by means which appear to make its success more difficult. This Elisha cures the waters of Jericho with salt (2 Kgs 2:21); Elijah, seeking God's response in sending fire on the altar, makes things even more difficult by pouring water over it (1 Kgs 18:34).

7. Limitation. When a miracle encompasses only a certain well-defined group and bypasses another, there is clearly a deliberate intention at work. In the story of the plagues of Egypt the differentiation between the Israelites and Egyptians is pointed out in the cases of the plague of flies (Exod 8:18 [—Eng 8:22]), the pestilence (9:4, 6), hail (v 26), darkness (10:23), and the firstborn (12:21–23). A spatial limitation is perceptible in the signs of Gideon's fleece (Judg 6:35–40): First, the fleece is wet and the surrounding ground is dry; afterward the ground is wet while the fleece is dry. A temporal limitation is found in the case of the manna, when the Israelites are given a two-day portion on the sixth day (Exod 16:29), while on the seventh day there is no manna at all (v 27).

8. Foreigners Acknowledge a Miracle. Four of the plagues of Egypt are formulated as a competition between Moses and Aaron and the Egyptian magicians. In the first two, blood and frogs, the magicians manage to effect the same results as Aaron (Exod 7:25; 8:3), but are unable to undo it. A turn takes place in the third plague: the magicians are unable to produce lice (8:14 [—Eng 18]) and confess, "This is the finger of God" (v 15 [—Eng 19]). The plague of boils is the climax of the competition: this time, the magicians themselves become victims of the plague (9:11). Another competition takes place between Elijah and the prophets of Baal (1 Kgs 18). Even though Elijah allows his opponents to go first, allots them plenty of time, and even handicaps himself by pouring water on the altar, it is he who succeeds. The foreigner's admission of a miracle is an excellent proof of its miraculous nature. In the two parallel stories of martyrdom in the book of Daniel (chaps. 3, 6), both Nebuchadnezzar and Darius praise the God of Israel (3:28–29; 6:27–28) after Daniel's friends are saved from the fire and Daniel is saved from the den of lions.

9. Multiple Test-Criteria. In the plague narrative, for example, one finds the combination of the competition of the magicians, prayer, differentiation between the Israelites and the Egyptians, and repetition, i.e., a series of ten plagues. Elijah's miracle on Mt. Carmel integrates competition, a "miracle within a miracle," and Elijah's prayer to the Lord.

F. Miracle and History

The miraculous deeds of the Bible are an organic part of biblical historiography. Since God is the God of history who actively intervenes in its development, he deliberately chooses on occasion to work miracles in order to accomplish his will—and, as mentioned, the miraculous is not significantly different from other ways of divine intervention. History opens with the miracle par excellence, the creation, and from then on miracles are interwoven in a greater or lesser concentration over the length of Israelite history: from barren women giving birth to the fathers of the nation; through the Exodus, accompanied by signs and wonders; the wanderings in the wilderness under divine protection and sustenance, though God also judges their disobedience; the wars of conquest, some of which are accompanied by miracles; the exploits of the judges (Gideon, Samson); the miraculous deeds of the prophets of the monarchic period; and even the miracles worked for Daniel and his friends in exile, demonstrating that God's sovereignty is over the entire earth. The historical psalms also frequently mention miracles in order to stress God's gracious acts (105; 136), and Israel's ingratitude (78; 106). The historical surveys given by certain leading biblical figures (and which express highly developed historiographical concepts) also give voice to the role of miracles in history (cf. Nehemiah 9: the miracles, according to this chapter, are a sign of God's protection and grace towards Israel, a background against which the people's ingratitude is emphasized.

G. Miracle and Myth

The connection between the miracles of the Bible and the world of myth arises from a comparison between the miracles the Bible attributes to God's angels (or to God's appearance in the guise of an angel) and parallels attributed to the gods (in the plural) in classical literature. The miracle story of the visitation of the elderly Abraham and Sarah with a son, and the announcement given them by their three guests, is strikingly paralleled in the story of the birth of Orion as told by Ovid (*Fast.* 5: 493–540). The story recounts that one day, when the gods Zeus, Hermes, and Poseidon were touring the earth, they were well received by the farmer Hyrieus who was not aware of his guests' identity until he had finished preparing them a meal. The gods sought to reward him and promised to answer whatever wish he desired. The farmer asked for a son and the gods carried out his wish. The work of Ovid is parallel also to the story of the miraculous destruction of Sodom, which continues the whole story in the book of Genesis. Two of the three men who visited Abraham make their way to Sodom (Gen 19:1) in order to destroy it (v 13). Lot shows the visitors the proper hospitality, but the men of the city try to harm them. The city is destroyed, and only Lot and his household escape. *Metamorphoses* (book 8: 611–724) tells of the two gods, Jupiter and Mercury, who visit a Phrygian village. Whereas the villagers do not offer the gods (in human guise) any hospitality, the elderly Baucis and Philemon make every effort to do so. Ultimately, the gods reveal their true identity and their intention to destroy the inhospitable village and its inhabitants. The gods take the elderly couple up to the mountains (see also Gen 19:17); when they look back they see their village's destruction. The Bible takes pains, however, to obliterate the mythical character by attributing the main miracle, the destruction of Sodom and Gomorrah, to God: "Then the Lord rained brimstone and fire on Sodom and Gomorrah, from the Lord out of the heavens. So He overthrew those cities" (vv 24–25).

Miracles ascribed in the Bible to prophets are attributed in their parallels in classical literature also to the gods. A miraculous feat similar to that performed by Elisha when he made the ax head float (2 Kgs 6:1–7) is performed also by Hermes (Aesop's Fables, ed. Chambry, Fable 253). In both stories the ax's owners are poor; in both the ax, meant for chopping wood, falls into a river. But whereas in the biblical story the miracle concerns retrieving the ax head for its owner—causing it to float by casting a piece of wood into the water—in the Aesopic parallel the miracle consists in taking out of the water axes of gold and silver that did not fall in the river, but are miraculously brought forth. Moreover, while the biblical miracle is intended to enhance the prophet's reputation, its parallel in classical literature is generically a wisdom fable which concerns speaking the truth and its reward.

The Bible also transforms mythological figures into human ones, while attributing their wondrous deeds to God. The Samson stories, for example, reveal much similarity to the traditions of Hercules. In the ancient oral tradition

Samson was a mythological figure, a sun-hero (which accounts for his name, composed of the Hebrew word for "sun"), whose power lay in his hair. The Bible, however, is careful to obscure the mythological character of the traditions, and even uproot them altogether. According to the Bible, Samson's long hair is simply part of his Nazirite vow. When he transgresses the terms of this vow and Delilah shaves his locks, his strength is gone because God punishes him by abandoning him. When Samson thinks, for example, that he killed 1,000 men with the jawbone of a donkey by his own prowess (Judg 15:14), the reality confronts him, and in his thirst he prays and confesses: "You have given this great deliverance by the hand of Your servant" (v 18). The miracle performed is not of his own doing but by the hand of the Lord. For an additional affinity between the biblical miracle and the world of myth, see I below (on the "rod").

H. Miracle and Magic

In contrast to miracle, magic is performed by people, namely by professional practitioners of the art who are capable of forcing their will upon creation and creatures alike. While miracles are expressions of God's righteous governance of the world, the use of magic is governed only by the magician's inclination and is not always activated by moral considerations. The Bible admits, albeit in a very small voice, the existence of magic and attributes to it only limited power. After Aaron casts his rod on the ground, which becomes a serpent in the sight of Pharoah and his servants, the Egyptian magicians do the same thing, even though Aaron's feat comes out ahead: "But Aaron's rod swallowed up their rods" (Exod 7:10–12). The competition between Aaron and Moses and the Egyptian magicians which concludes with the former's victory over the latter is described above (see E.8.). The Bible portrays further encounters with magicians-sorcerers which end in the victory of God's messenger, namely the failure of the court magicians to solve Pharoah's dreams (Gen 41:8) as opposed to Joseph's divinely assisted success (v 16), and the failure of Nebuchadnezzar's wise men to interpret his dream in contrast to Daniel's success (Dan 2:47).

The Bible can apparently allow the limited power of magic due to its acceptance and practice in neighboring societies. A complete denial of its effectiveness might have brought about much more dangerous conclusions: that the magicians perform their feats by the power of other gods (cf. Deut 13:2–3). The recognition of magic's power, however, does not imply any agreement or acceptance; the Bible denounces magic thoroughly and forcefully (cf., e.g., Exod 22:17; Deut 18:10; Mic 5:11; Mal 3:5). A genuine magical character nevertheless underlies the last meeting between King Joash and Elisha (2 Kgs 13:14–19). The king's shooting of arrows while the prophet lays his hands upon him, determines the fate of the war against Aram (vv 15–17). An additional and equally clear example of a magical act is Jacob's manner of recovering the salary of which Laban had robbed him (Gen 30:35–43). Since the Bible cannot tolerate the notion that a man, at his own initiative and ability, could change the order of creation, Jacob testifies in the next chapter that it was God who is responsible for the deed: "but God did not allow him to hurt me. 'If he said thus: "the speckled shall be your wages,' " then all the flocks bore speckled" (31:7–12).

Further relics of a belief in magic can be found concerning the various implements employed by the miracle workers, as well as in the attribution of certain miracles to a man and not to God (see below). The significance of the relation between magic and miracle lies in the fact that what appears now to be a miracle in its literary formulation, may, in certain cases, have been originally an act of magic, later adapted to the world of biblical thought.

I. Implements for Performing a Miracle

Many miracles are performed simply by speaking. Usually, the prophet proclaims the word of the Lord, such as: "This is the sign which the Lord has spoken: Surely the altar shall split apart. . . . And the altar was split apart . . . according to the sign which the man of God had given by the word of the Lord" (1 Kgs 13:3–5; see also 1 Kgs 17:14–16; 2 Kgs 3:15–17; 4:43–44). Occasionally, however, the speaking is accompanied by the employment of a miraculous instrument. Elisha, for example, cures the water of Jericho with salt that he casts into it (2 Kgs 2:20–21), adding the words, "Thus says the Lord: 'I have healed this water.'"

The miracle instrument par excellence is the rod. The rod in Moses' hand is sometimes called "the rod of God" (Exod 4:20; cf. 7:17; Isa 10:26). The Lord's angel also performs a miracle with the aid of a rod (Judg 6:20–21). The notion that the deity holds a rod is very much in line with prevailing beliefs of the ANE. The attribution of ownership of the rod to man is thus an expression of the polemic against myth. The rod is said to belong to Aaron in several of the plague accounts (Exod 7:19; 8:1–2; 12–13), while in other miracles it is said to belong to Moses (Exod 10:12–13; 14:16; 17:5). The demythologization of the rod, however, does not solve the problem of its magical character; on the contrary, if the story of Massah and Meribah sees the rod as a legitimate miracle-producing implement (Exod 17:5–6), the parallel story of the water of Meribah (Num 20:1–13) tries to create the impression that the use of the rod was not indispensable. God commands, "Take the rod; you and your brother Aaron gather the assembly together. *Speak* to the rock before their eyes" (v 8), but Moses sinned by striking the rock with the rod (v 11).

A similar polemic against the rod's power is recognizable in the story of the resuscitation of the Shunamite's son. Gehazi, Elisha's servant, does not succeed in bringing the boy back to life by means of his master's staff (2 Kgs 4:31). Only the prophet's own action, together with prayer, is efficacious. The polemic takes on a different form in Exod 4:2: the miracles are performed with the rod simply because it happens to be in Moses' hands at the time.

The brass serpent was prescribed by God as the remedy for the venomous snake bites due to the image's similarity to the cause of the problem (Num 21:4–9). Since, according to the story, it is God himself who instructs Moses to construct the brass serpent, it cannot be seen as a magical implement with any powers in and of itself. Nevertheless, it was taken by the people as precisely that—if not really as a divine entity—as seen from the mention of its later destruction by Hezekiah (2 Kgs 18:4).

The representation of the ark of the Lord as a miracle-performing implement transfers the weight of attention from prophecy to priesthood, closely connected with the ark. The ark, even if it is not exactly an implement, represents the presence of God (e.g., see 1 Sam 4:7–8). The miraculous collapse of the god of the Philistines, Dagon, before the ark of the God of Israel (1 Sam 5:1–5) in the former's own sanctuary, demonstrates that the ark signifies God's presence, before whom all idols are nothing. The deaths of the men of Beth-shemesh who had looked at the ark of the Lord (1 Sam 6:19–20) also supports the notion that the ark represents God, the sight of whom can be fatal. The death of Uzzah, who actually touched the Ark, should be similarly understood (2 Sam 6:1–10).

The replacement of the prophetic rod with the priestly Ark is found in the stories concerning the miraculous happenings it brings about, stories similar to those about the miracles of the rod. The crossing of the Jordan by means of the presence of the Ark (Joshua 3–4) is parallel to the crossing of the Red Sea with the help of the rod (Exod 14:16). The plague engendered by the ark against the Philistines (1 Samuel 5–6) recalls in many details the plagues of Egypt in which the rod played a part (cf. the overt allusions to the plague narrative in 1 Sam 4:8; 6:6). The ark takes an important role in the story of the fall of the walls of Jericho (Joshua 6) and serves to actualize the notion that "the Lord will fight for you, and you shall hold your peace" (Exod 14:14).

J. The Performer of the Miracle

The persons active in the performance of miracles are the prophets, especially Moses, Elijah, and Elisha. More than once, clear similarities can be seen between their respective deeds, such as crossing the sea (Exodus 14) or the Jordan (2 Kgs 2:8, 14); multiplying food and oil (1 Kgs 17:8–16; 2 Kgs 4:1–7, 42–44); and resuscitating a dead child (1 Kgs 17:17–24; 2 Kgs 4:18–37). Other miracles are attributed to priests. Aaron, for example, is party to some of the miracles performed by his brother Moses, as in the story of the signs performed before Pharaoh (Exod 7:8–13), the plague narratives (Exod 7:19; 8:1–2, 12–13; 9:8–9), and in halting the plague in the wake of Korah's rebellion (Num 17:11–13). In the miracles in which the ark plays a central role the priests are also counted partners, namely the story of the crossing of the Jordan on dry land (Joshua 3–4) and the collapse of the walls of Jericho (Joshua 6).

The performance of miracles by human beings alone was liable to cause the event to break the bounds of miracle and be viewed instead as magic (see H above). In the story of the resurrection of the dead man whose corpse touched the bones of Elisha (2 Kgs 13:20–21), the narrator does not involve God in the deed because of the abhorrent nature of the subject at hand: burying the dead. However, it is precisely this story which preserves something of the original character of the Elisha stories, in which the miracle is attributed to the prophet and not to God (cf. 2 Kgs 8:4). In several of the Elisha stories the part played by God is rather small (2 Kgs 4:1–7, 38–41; 6:1–7). Only Elisha's title, "man of God," makes any reference to his dispatcher.

The uniqueness of portraying Elisha as a miracle worker, whose stories are told to his own credit, can be seen by a comparison of his stories to their parallels elsewhere in the Bible: in the story of the sweetening of the waters of Marah (Exod 15:22–26), Moses expresses his helplessness in his cry to God, who then shows him the solution (v 25). In the parallel story of the curing of the waters of Jericho, Elisha solves the problem quite easily (2 Kgs 2:20–21a), and only afterwards attributes the miracle to God: "Thus says the Lord: 'I have healed this water" (v 21b). Note that when the narrator refers to the execution of this announcement he reverts and says: "So the water remains healed to this day, according to the saying of Elisha [and not of the Lord!] which he spoke" (v 22).

In the story of the reviving of the Shunamite's son it is the prophet's act which lies at the center (2 Kgs 4:33a, 34–35). Only a few words, "and he prayed to the Lord" (v 33b) refer to God's part. The proportions are reversed in the parallel story of the resurrection of the widow's son by Elijah. Here it is prayer which stands at the center of things (1 Kgs 17:20–22), and between one prayer and the next appear a few words revealing that the prayer was in fact accompanied by an act: "And he stretched himself out on the child three times" (v 21a). In most miracles, then, both man and God take part in the performance of the miracle, such as in the plagues of Egypt (Exodus 7–11), or in bringing forth water from a rock (Exod 17:1–7). To treat one example in more detail, we take the crossing of the Red Sea: The Israelites cry to the Lord (14:10), and complain to Moses (vv 11–12). Moses promises the salvation of the Lord (vv 13–14), and God then instructs him as to what he should do (v 16). Moses stretches forth his hand, but it is the Lord who causes the sea to go back by a strong east wind and makes the sea into dry land (v 21). Also when God commands Moses again to stretch forth his hand in order to cause the waters to return and drown the Egyptians (v 26), it is God who routs the Egyptians in the midst of the sea (v 27). The narrator finally indicates the impression of the act on the people: "Thus Israel saw the great work which the Lord had done against Egypt" (v 31a). But Moses' part is not discounted: "and believed the Lord and his servant Moses" (v 31b).

Some miracles are formulated in one tradition (the main one) as a cooperation of God and man, but reappear in another which attributes the feat to God alone. In the Song of the Sea, Moses is not at all mentioned, let alone given credit for the miracle (cf. especially Exod 15:1, 8, 10); it is not Moses who stretched forth his hand, but rather the Lord: "You stretched out Your right hand; the earth swallowed them" (v 12). In other references to this miracle as well, no mention of Moses' role is to be found (Josh 2:10; 4:23; Ps 66:5–6; 78:13; 106:9–11; 114:1–3; 136:13–15). An exception to the rule is Psalm 77, which unexpectedly incorporates into its conclusion reference to Moses and Aaron in an apparently secondary passage (v 21).

The activity of God exclusively in the performance of miracles is particularly conspicuous in events in which the miracle is of heavenly origin, such as fire coming down from the heavens in order to punish (e.g. Gen 19:24), or on the altar in order to express God's choice and will that he be worshipped on that same altar (Lev 9:24; 1 Kgs 18:38–39; 1 Chr 21:26; 2 Chr 7:1–3; in the last two of these stories the Chronicler adds this miraculous motif where it is not present in the Former Prophets.

Natural phenomena which come down from the heavens, though not at their normal time or in the normal way, are also attributed only to God (even if the initiative is at times taken by man), as in bringing down rain at the time of the summer harvest at Samuel's request (1 Sam 12:10–12) or the hailstones that the Lord casts down on the Amorites (Josh 10:11). God alone also alters the course of the heavenly bodies (while man is party only in expressing the request; cf. Josh 10:12–14; 2 Kgs 20:10–11).

Alongside the Lord, one also finds his angels active at times. Occasionally, great plagues are attributed to an angel, such as the plague which struck the Assyrian camp (2 Kgs 19:35). In the plague of pestilence in the wake of David's census, God is the initiator but it is the angel who carries it out (2 Sam 24:15–16). The reason for the separation is apparently the desire to prevent the attribution of calamity to God. The separation between the entity responsible for executing the calamity and the Lord is observable in the introductory story of the book of Job: it is Satan who exercises control over Job's property, family, and person (1:12; 2:6) in order to test him. However, the angels also have a positive function: to deliver those worthy of deliverance (1 Kgs 19:11; Dan 3:25; 6:23), or to perform a miracle as a sign of the fulfillment of promises (Judg 6:17–21; 13:20).

K. The Initiative for the Performance of a Miracle

Human initiative for the performance of a miracle derives from man's needs or problems. He does not seek to have his problem solved particularly by a miracle, but prays to God out of recognition that he is incapable of coping with the difficulty. The problem which incites to prayer may be an expression of trial (see M.1 below) such as thirst (Exod 15:25) or hunger (Exod 16:4), or punishment of sin, such as the plagues of Egypt, Miriam's leprosy (Num 12:9–10), the plague of the snakes (Num 21:6), or Jeroboam's withered hand (1 Kgs 13:4). In all of these examples the one praying is the prophet, the intercessor between God and those suffering a miraculous punishment initiated by God. The notion of the interceding prophet is so deeply rooted in biblical literature that even in a story revealing a direct connection between God and the wrongdoer, such as God's revelation to Abimelech in a dream in the night, God commands the king to ask the intercessor, Abraham, to pray on his behalf (Gen 20:7, 17).

When man's suffering is not directly due to sin, he can still turn to God in prayer (which leads to a miracle), such as Hannah's prayer for a son (1 Sam 1:11–12), or Hezekiah's turning to the Lord in the time of his illness (2 Kgs 20:2–3). Similarly, the seekers of signs initiate miracles and prays. Gideon, for example, seeks a sign to strengthen him in his mission (Judg 6:17, 36–40). Likewise, prophets can desire a sign for the people, as with Samuel who asks for rain on a summer harvest day (1 Sam 12:17), or Elijah who wants an answer from God in the form of fire on the altar (1 Kgs 18:36–37). Prophets may initiate a miracle in order to salvage their injured honor (1 Kgs 20:35–36; 2 Kgs 2:24). Occasionally, man's initiative gains particular attention, such as in the halting of the heavenly bodies at Joshua's request: "And there has been no day like that before it or after it, that the Lord heeded the voice of a man; for the Lord fought for Israel" (Josh 10:14), as well as in the resuscitation of the son of the widow from Zarephath: "Then the Lord heard the voice of Elijah; and the soul of the child came back to him, and he revived" (1 Kgs 17:22).

God initiates miracles in order to give man his just retribution—either reward or punishment—and even to bestow grace upon them (see M.2 below), or to teach them a lesson, as in the opening of the mouth of Balaam's donkey (Num 22:28), or the series of miracles performed for Jonah. A miraculous revelation is generally solely God's initiative, such as the appearance of an angel in the fire of the altar (Judg 6:20), or the burning bush that is not consumed (Exod 3:2).

L. Miracles of Life, Death, and Healing

The majority of biblical miracles are directly or indirectly connected with life and death, the exceptions to this rule being primarily the signs (*ʾôtôt*). Among life-miracles are counted the attainment of immortality (Enoch, Gen 5:24; Elijah, 2 Kgs 2:11–12), and the revivification of the dead (1 Kgs 17:17–24; 2 Kgs 4:32–37; 13:20–21). The miracle is capable of bringing forth new life: to make barren wives bear children (Gen 21:1–2; 25:21–26; 30:22–24; Judg 13:2–24; 1 Sam 1:11–20; 2 Kgs 4:14–17).

Healing from severe illness is also likened to revival of the dead. When Aaron intercedes on Miriam's behalf he says: "Please do not let her be as one dead" (Num 12:12); Hezekiah, who is cured from the boil, is said to have "lived" (2 Kgs 20:7), and those bitten by the serpents, when they look at the brass serpent, "shall live" (Num 21:8). The words "shall live" are used also for one saved from thirst (Judg 15:19).

A considerable part of the interest in life and death issues are centered in the area of healing. The reason for this concentration lies in the biblical concept that God is the Healer par excellence (see Hos 6:1: Jer 17:14; Ps 41:5). The book of Chronicles also expresses the idea that turning to earthly physicians is a sin (2 Chr 16:12; note the midrashic treatment of King Asa's name, which means "physician" in Aramaic).

This notion is given clear expression in those miracle stories which employ the root *rpʾ*, "heal," in reference to God's action (cf., for example, Gen 20:17–18; 1 Sam 6:3; 2 Kgs 2:22; 20:5), and particularly in the story of the healing of the waters of Marah: "If you diligently heed the voice of the Lord your God and do what is right in His sight . . . I will put none of the diseases on you which I have brought on the Egyptians. For I am the Lord who heals you" (Exod 15:26). Sickness and healing are two sides of the same coin. At the end of the story of the waters of Marah, God promises not to bring sickness on Israel if they will keep his commandments; yet in the conditional curse of Deuteronomy 28, God threatens with sickness any transgressors (vv 22, 27–28). In several miracle stories one finds illness (punishment) and healing (grace) one alongside the other (see Gen 20:17–18; Num 21:6–9; 1 Kgs 13:4–6). Miriam is punished with leprosy for not acknowledging Moses' authority and for her rebellious speech to him, and she is healed after Moses' prayer (Num 12:13). The order of events is just the opposite in the story of

Naaman's leprosy (2 Kings 5). Naaman, who acknowledges God and his servant Elisha, is cured first, whereupon his leprosy falls upon Gehazi, the prophet's servant, who did not acknowledge the authority of his master and even lied to him boldfacedly (v 27).

M. Purpose of the Miracle

1. Trial. The performance of a miracle is closely connected with putting to trial, either through a miracle by which God tests man, or a situation in which man tests God. The words which reveal the theological basis of the story of the waters of Marah, namely, "There He made a statute and an ordinance for them. And there He tested them" (Exod 15:25b), translate the miracle from its momentary importance into something atemporal. The main purpose of the miracle was not to quench the Israelites' thirst; it is no coincidence that a succeeding verse describes the bountiful supply of water in their next station in the wilderness (v 27), illustrating that if the Lord had wanted to give them water, he need not necessarily do so miraculously. The sweetening of the waters is thus a trial, intended to test the Israelites' faith in their deliverer: after God brought them out of Egypt with signs and wonders, and performed the great miracle of the parting of the sea, the people complain about the first difficulty that confronts them (v 24). The Israelites failed the test, but were not punished; the miracle at Marah is a fitting opportunity to give a sermon on obeying the Lord and observing his commandments (v 26).

From the trial by thirst the text moves on to a trial by hunger: "that I may test them, whether they will walk in My law or not" (Exod 16:4). In the continuation of the chapter it becomes clear that God was testing Israel in the matter of observing the Sabbath, in particular the prohibition to go out and gather manna on the Sabbath day (v 29). And, to be sure, even though they received a double portion on the sixth day, and this did not rot (v 24), some people could not withstand the trial (v 27). This deed provokes a strong response from God (v 28).

The progressive deterioration expressed in the portrayal of the people's behavior continues when they change from being the tested into the testers. The issue of thirst again arises. This time, immediately upon arriving at the place of encampment, and with no indication of the gravity of the thirst, the Israelites complain: " 'Give us water, that we may drink.' And Moses said to them, 'Why do you contend with me? Why do you test the Lord?' " (17:2). The miracles of the wilderness wanderings are understood, then, as a series of trials which the people and their God undergo. This representation of the period as one in which the Israelites tested God is also presented in Num 14:22–24 (cf. also Ps 78:40–43, 56–58).

The issue of miracles and trials is not limited to the period of wilderness wanderings. The book of Deuteronomy is aware of the possibility that a prophet propogating idolatry might seek to convince his hearers by performing a sign or wonder (13:1–3). The legislated solution of this difficulty is as follows: "You shall not listen to the words of that prophet . . . for the Lord your God is testing you to know whether you love the Lord your God . . ." (vv 4–5 [—Eng 3]).

An individual may, at times, test God by requesting a sign. Gideon asks for two signs from God in order to confirm that God will fulfill his promise to deliver Israel through him. When Gideon makes the request for the first sign he showed no fear (Judg 6:36–37), and God answers his request as if this testing of God is appropriate (v 38). In his second request, on the other hand, Gideon already fears that he may have stretched things a bit too far: "Do not be angry with me, and let me speak just once more" (v 39; cf. Gen 18:32; Judg 16:28). This time Gideon is aware that he is testing God: "Let me test, I pray, just once more with the fleece" (v 39). Gideon's language is cautious: "Let me test," and not "let me test you."

Unlike the Gideon story, in the story of Hezekiah's request for a sign, God offers the king the choice of two opposite possibilities: "Shall the shadow go forward ten degrees or go backward ten degrees?" (2 Kgs 20:9). The king chooses the more difficult of the two. Also when God allows Ahaz to ask for a sign he gives him a choice between two contraries: "Ask it either in the depth or in the height above" (Isa 7:11).

Like Gideon, Jonathan, son of Saul, also tests God's readiness to give his enemies into his hands before going out to battle. But whereas Gideon asked for a sign despite God's announcement that he would deliver him, God's intention is not made clear to Jonathan. Jonathan does not turn directly to God asking for a sign. He describes two possible situations, the actualization of one of which would indicate God's intention to grant victory (1 Sam 14:9–10). The character of the sign requested is also somewhat different: while Gideon expected a sign involving the disrupting of the order of creation, Jonathan expects a human response perfectly within the range of possibility. Avoiding a direct request for a sign is observable also in the story of the Philistine's return of the Ark of the Lord (1 Sam 6:6–9), though their avoidance derives from their being foreigners, non-Israelites.

In the story of the competition between Elijah and the prophets of Baal, the request for the sign is not solely at the initiative of the prophet. Elijah only determines the "stage directions"—the place, time, and manner. Elijah's request is not made because of his own lack of faith in God; just the opposite is true (cf. his confident lack of concern demonstrated in his giving advantage to his opponents). The test is meant to prove to his rivals who the real God is, and that Elijah is the real God's emissary (1 Kgs 18:36–37).

A clear example of the decline in the legitimacy of asking for a sign from God is found in the three versions of the story of Hezekiah's request for a sign. In the primary version (2 Kings 20) the king asks for a sign confirming his promised healing (v 8), and even chooses, as mentioned, the more difficult option (v 10). In Isaiah 38, however, one finds an obvious change: Hezekiah does not ask for a sign (the request at the end of the chapter, v 22, is a secondary edition based on the version in the book of Kings). It is the prophet who suggests a sign as a direct continuation of the promise of healing: "And this is the sign to you from the Lord . . ." (v 7). In the version of Chronicles, the whole matter of the sign shrinks to an incidental remark: "and he prayed to the Lord; and He spoke to him and gave him a sign" (2 Chr 32:24). The Chronicler does not reveal why the "sign" was given or what the sign was. The sign is again mentioned in Chronicles as part of the reason for the visit of the Babylonian embassy. Whereas according to the books of Kings and Isaiah the Babylonians came, "for he (Merodach-baladan) heard that Hezekiah had been sick" (2 Kgs 20:12; Isa 39:1), in 2 Chronicles 32 they came because of their interest in the miracle, namely, "to inquire about the wonder that was done in the land," for which reason "God withdrew from him, in order to test him, that He might know all that was in his heart" (v 31). Again, note the careful language: according to Chronicles it is God who tests Hezekiah and not vice versa. The notion that one should not request a sign from God because God should not be tempted is expressed in Ahaz's words (Isaiah 7). The Lord suggests that he ask for whatever sign he wants (v 11), but Ahaz answers: "I will not ask, nor will I test the Lord" (v 12). However, it is precisely this answer with its denigrating attitude toward sign seeking that provokes the prophet's anger (v 13). Isaiah's indignation can be understood in light of the fact that the initiative for requesting the sign came from God. Man must not shrink from asking for a sign when it is God himself who instructs him to do so.

2. Reward and Punishment. Stories in which a miracle is performed as a reward for one person (and never for a group) are few. It happens on occasion that a person's extraordinary piety is rewarded: the ascension of Enoch in Gen 5:23–24 (the only miracle of reward in the entire Pentateuch); the widow whose creditors come to take her children as slaves asks Elisha to rescue her on the basis of her husband's piety: "and you know that your servant feared the Lord" (2 Kgs 4:1); Hezekiah is healed after his prayer: "Remember now, O Lord, I pray, how I have walked before You in truth and with a loyal heart" (2 Kgs 20:3 = Isa 38:3). Later literature describes the reward of those willing to be martyred for their faith, as seen in the deliverance of Daniel's three friends from the fiery furnace (Daniel 3), and Daniel himself from the lion's den (chap. 6). Three additional stories depict the miraculous reward of people who gave hospitality to God's messengers: the provision of the widow who takes Elijah into her home (1 Kings 17:8–16) and the resuscitation of her son (vv 17–24); a son born to the Shunamite woman who received Elisha and his revival after his death (2 Kgs 4:8–37). Finally, note how Genesis 18, which describes at some length the generous hospitality Abraham and Sarah bestowed upon the three men, is very similar to the story of the Shunamite woman and constitutes a clear parallel to the birth of Orion in reward of hospitality given to the gods in Greek classical literature (see G above). Nevertheless, Genesis 18 is not formulated as a story of reward—this to prevent the impression that God's intention is in any way influenced by the quality of the hospitality shown by Abraham toward his guests.

Miraculous punishments are several times more frequent than those of reward and, unlike the latter, are not limited to individuals. Punishment miracles come as recompense for an attitude towards God or his messengers (and not for harming one's fellow). Both the individual and the group may be punished for an improper cultic act (Lev 10:1–2; 2 Chr 26:16–26; 2 Kgs 17:26); for unintentional violations of sanctity (1 Sam 6:19–21; 2 Sam 6:6–9); impugning a prophet's honor (Num 12:1–16; 16; 1 Kgs 13:4, 6; 20:35–36; 2 Kgs 1:1–17; 2:19–22; 5:20–27). An individual who transgresses God's word is punished (Gen 19:26; 1 Kgs 13:24–25, 28), as well as a group complaining against God (Num 11:1–3, 4–34). On occasion, the group is punished for the sin of the individual, as seen, for example, in the closing of all the wombs of Abimelech's house for taking Abraham's wife (Genesis 20), and the punishment of the Egyptians by plagues for the sin of their king (Exodus 7–12). King David chooses collective rather than personal punishment for his census of Israel (2 Sam 24:14–15, though he later reneges [v 17], apparently a later addition; cf. the smooth transition from v 16 to v 18).

3. Grace. The miracles of grace include several of Elisha's miraculous feats (such as 2 Kgs 2:19–22; 4:38–44; 6:1–7). The visitation of barren women, like Hannah (1 Samuel 1), is also an act of grace, even though it is part of the divine plan of Israel's history. Such an integration of miracles of grace and the divine will is even more prominent in the visitation of Samson's mother: the angel brings tidings of his birth because of the role already reserved for him in delivering his people (Judg 13:5). Similarly, in the patriarchal narratives the births of Isaac and Jacob fulfill God's promise to Abraham concerning offspring and land. Many national miracles combine God's grace with the accomplishment of his promises, such as the dividing of the Red Sea, the provision of the Israelites in the wilderness, and the miracles performed for them during the conquest of Canaan. The cessation of punishment after the wrongdoer shows regret is also an act of grace (as in Num 12:14; 21:8; 1 Kgs 13:6).

4. Faith in God and in his Messenger. A clear and frequent purpose of the miracle is to inspire faith in God: thus Elijah asks, "Hear me, O Lord, hear me, that this people may know that You are the Lord God" (1 Kgs 18:37); the people in their reaction to the falling fire exclaim, "The Lord, He is God . . ." (v 39). Lack of faith in God in spite of his miracles stirs up God's anger; in his words to Moses, God states, "How long will these people reject Me? And how long will they not believe Me, with all the signs which I have performed among them?" (Num 14:11). Faith in God leads to fear of God: ". . . that all the peoples of the earth may know the hand of the Lord, that it is mighty, that you may fear the Lord your God forever" (Josh 4:24; note also the nations' fear in the wake of God's miraculous deeds in Exod 15:14–16; Josh 2:19; 5:1). Non-Israelites express their faith in God in a positive manner: After hearing Moses recount the miraculous deliverance from Egypt, Jethro says "Now I know that the Lord is greater than all the gods" (Exod 18:11). Similarly, Naaman declares after being healed from leprosy, "Indeed, now I know that there is no God in all the earth, except in Israel" (2 Kgs 5:15). Likewise, Nebuchadnezzar and Darius are overwhelmed after seeing the miracles done to deliver those willing to be martyred (for their faith in God), namely Daniel and his three friends (Dan 3:28–29; 6:27–28).

The fear of God which results from observing a miracle has, in Israel, its practical implementation and expression in a renewed commitment to observe God's commandments. See, for example Exod 15:26; cf. M.5 below. A strengthened faith in God is frequently combined with a strengthened trust in God's messenger. After the miracle of the crossing of the Red Sea it is said: "Thus Israel saw the great work which the Lord had done in Egypt; so the people feared the Lord, and believed the Lord and His servant Moses" (Exod 14:31). The crossing of the Jordan also serves to enhance the image of Joshua, Moses' successor: "On that day the Lord magnified Joshua in the sight of all Israel; and they feared him, as they had feared Moses, all the days of his life" (Josh 4:14). So also, in the story of the competition between Elijah and the prophets of Baal, Elijah asks that the miracle be done in order that the people might come also to acknowledge God: "Let it be known this day that You are God in Israel, and that I am Your servant, and that I have done all these things at Your word" (1 Kgs 18:36).

Prominent in the Elisha narratives are miracles designed to increase respect for a prophet. Elisha's servant, for example, tells the king the *gĕdōlôt* of his master (2 Kgs 8:4), a term otherwise reserved exclusively for God's *"great things"* (cf. A.2). Moreover, the aim of the introduction to the Elisha stories (2 Kgs 2:1–18), a story which demonstrates Elisha's miraculous ability, is to announce that "the spirit of Elijah rests on Elisha" (v 15). The story of the healing of the waters of Jericho enhances the prophet's reputation by ending with the words: "So the water remains healed to this day, according to the saying of Elisha which he spoke" (2 Kgs 2:22; cf. further 4:38–41).

Miracles function at times as a kind of "commission paper" for God's messengers, as seen in the signs to be performed by Moses when he returns to Egypt; the miracles are performed so "that they may believe that the Lord God of their fathers . . . has appeared to you" (Exod 4:5; cf. vv 8–9). God may give a sign in order to make known whom he has chosen, as in the budding of Aaron's rod (Num 17:16–20).

5. The Remembrance of Miracles. A miracle must be observed by someone. Seeing a miracle has a decisive effect on those who witness it: "Then the fire of the Lord fell and consumed the burnt sacrifice . . . and when all the people saw it, they fell on their faces; and they said, 'The Lord, He is God! The Lord, He is God!' " (1 Kgs 18:38–39; cf. Exod 4:30–31; 14:31; Lev 9:24; 1 Sam 12:16–18). The emphasis on having seen miracles as a major basis for faith characterizes the book of Deuteronomy: "did God ever try to go and take for Himself a nation from the midst of another nation, by trials, by signs, by wonders . . . according to all that the Lord your God did for you in Egypt before your eyes?" (Deut 4:34; cf. also 1:30; 7:19; 29:1). Other passages in Deuteronomy even identify seeing with knowing: "Know today that I do not speak with your children, who have not known and who have not seen the chastening of the Lord your God. . . . His signs and His acts which He did in the midst of Egypt" (11:2–3); "but your eyes have seen every great act of the Lord which He did" (v 7; for the identification of seeing and knowing cf. also Josh 24:31 with Judg 2:7). Such an identification emphasizes the importance of the direct effects of seeing a miracle for faith in God.

A story may substitute the recounting of miracles for the actual observation of them. Someone who has obtained God's salvation tells of his wonders: "I will praise You, O Lord, with my whole heart; I will tell of all Your marvelous works" (Ps 9:2; cf. also 71:14–17; 96:3–4). In the story of the plagues God announces: "But indeed for this purpose I have raised you up, that I may show My power in you, and that My name may be declared in all the earth" (Exod 9:16; cf. also Josh 2:10; 9:9–10). When Gehazi tells the king of Elisha's miraculous feats (2 Kgs 8:4), this inspires the king to rescue the woman from her distress.

In several cases, the text testifies that the story of God's salvation was transmitted from generation to generation. Gideon reveals this awareness in his complaint over Midianite subjection: "O my lord, if the Lord is with us, why then has all this happened to us? And where are all His miracles which our fathers told us about, saying, 'Did not the Lord bring us up from Egypt" (Judg 6:13; cf. Pss 79:13; 145:4–5). The purpose of retelling the story to succeeding generations is to inspire faith: "that you may tell in the hearing of your son and your son's son the mighty things I have done in Egypt, and My signs which I have done among them, that you may know that I am the Lord" (Exod 10:2). Compare also the opening of the historical Psalm 78 meant to encourage observance of God's commandments: "I will open my mouth in a parable; I will utter dark sayings of old, which we have heard and known, and our fathers have told us. We will not hide them from their children, telling to the generation to come the praises of the Lord, and His strength and His wonderful works that He has done. . . . That the generation to come might know them, the children who would be born, that they may arise and declare them to their children, that they may set their hope in God, and not forget the works of God, but keep His commandments; and may not be like their fathers, a stubborn and rebellious generation" (vv 2–8).

A miracle story by itself, without any obligatory features, may fall short of its mark. To avoid this possibility, the people are obliged to make the yearly Passover sacrifice, which is meant to arouse the next generation to ask: "what do you mean by this service" (Exod 12:26), whereupon the parents are to respond: "It is the Passover sacrifice of the Lord, who passed over the houses of the children of Israel in Egypt when He struck the Egyptians and delivered our households" (v 27; cf. also 13:8–10). The book of Deuteronomy expands this question of the sons to cover all God's commandments: "When your son asks you in time to come, saying, 'What is the meaning of the testimonies, the statutes, and the judgments which the Lord our God has commanded you?' then you shall say to your son: 'We were slaves of Pharaoh in Egypt, and the Lord brought us out of Egypt with a mighty hand; and the Lord showed signs and wonders before our eyes, great and severe, against Egypt, Pharaoh, and all his household" (6:20–22).

A solid testimony of a miracle's occurrence (more so than the commandment bound up with its commemoration) is a tangible object taken from the site of the event. Joshua commands, at the time of the crossing of the Jordan, to take 12 stones from the Jordan "that this may be a sign among you when your children ask in time to come, saying, 'What do these stones mean to you?' " (Josh 4:6; cf. vv 20–23). In the wake of the miracle of the manna, Moses, in the name of the Lord, commands the people to put some of the manna into a vessel to keep as a remembrance (Exod 16:32–34), and Aaron's budding rod is similarly set "to be kept as a sign against the rebels" (Num 17:25 [—Eng 17:10]). Here also (as in previous examples), the object *(reliquae)* is intended to provide a lesson for the people, and not to be venerated as some kind of sacred object. It may be that the trespass offering returned by the Philistines with the ark of the Lord after they were visited with plagues (1 Sam 6:4) also functioned as a *reliquae* of the miracle. The dangers inherent in such *reliquae* can be seen in the echo of the brass serpent in 2 Kgs 18:4.

Now and then a place name commemorates a miraculous event that took place there, such as Taberah (Num 11:3); Kibroth-hattaavah (v 34); Perez-uzzah (2 Sam 6:8). Thus the name of a certain place functions as a kind of monument to the miracle wrought at that very place.

N. The Rationalization of Miracles

Biblical literature sometimes reveals a tendency to make the miraculous seem more rational. This is the case, for example, in the formulation of the miracle of the quail in Num 11:31: "Now a wind went out from the Lord, and it brought quail from the sea." It is the wind, a natural phenomenon, that brings the quail to the camp at the right moment (cf. the more "miraculous" version in Exod 16:13). In a similar manner the book of Deuteronomy removes the element of wonder from the story of the cluster of grapes brought back by the spies from Canaan. It is no longer a grape cluster of fantastic size that must be carried on a pole between two men (Num 13:23–24), but Deuteronomy simply states, "And they departed and went up into the mountains, and came to the Valley of Eshcol, and spied it out. They also took some of the fruit of the land in their hands and brought it down to us" (Deut 1:24–25). Note that Deuteronomy preserves the place name "Valley of Eshcol" (i.e., "valley of the grape cluster"), but obscures the character of the event by simply stating that they brought back "some of the fruit of the land."

The miraculous element at times disappears when a story is transferred from one figure to another, and is replaced by a rationalistic parallel. When God promises Joshua that he will give the city of Ai into his hands, God commands Joshua: "Stretch out the spear that is in your hand toward Ai, for I will give it into your hand," and Joshua hastens to carry out the order (Josh 8:18). According to these verses Joshua's action was meant to signal those waiting in ambush to attack (v 12). The act of stretching out the spear recalls the story in which Moses is the hero in the battle against the Amalekites (Exod 17:8–16). Moses' action, however, is no mere signal but a miraculous implementation of victory: "And so it was, when Moses held up his hand, that Israel prevailed" (v 11). Moreover, the instrument which serves Moses is not a weapon like the spear, but rather "the rod of God" (v 9), the miraculous implement par excellence. Nevertheless, to the Joshua story a secondary verse was added (v 26) which disrupts the continuity between the counting of the victims and the mention of the spoil, an addition lacking in the LXX, and intended to bestow upon the story a miraculous character and assimilate it to Moses' deed: "For Joshua did not draw back his hand, with which he stretched out the spear, until he had utterly destroyed all the inhabitants of Ai."

The account of the war of the three kings against Moab (2 Kgs 3) tells of an optical illusion: the sun shining on the water "paints" it the color of blood. This sight causes the Moabites to think that their enemies had killed one another, and on the basis of this mistaken assumption they confidently advance to take the spoil and are routed (vv 22–23). The blood/water element in this rationalistic story calls to mind two miraculous stories dealing with the transformation of water into blood at the hand of Moses, namely, one of the signs performed before Pharaoh (Exod 4:9), as well as the plague of blood (Exod 7:17ff.).

Bibliography

Fishbane, M. 1975. The Biblical OT. *Shnaton* 1: 213–34 (in Hebrew).

Gehman, H. S. 1960. Natural Law and the Old Testament. Pp. 109–22 in *Festschrift H. C. Alleman,* ed. J. M. Myers, et al. Locust Valley, NY.

Groot, A. de. 1965. *Das Wunder im Zeugnis der Bibel.* Salzburg.

Keller, C. A. 1946. *Das Wort OTH als "Offenbarungszeichen Gottes."* Basel.

Lewis, C. S. 1947. *Miracles.* London.

McCasland, S. V. 1957. Signs and Wonders. *JBL* 76: 149–52.

McKenzie, J. L. 1952. God and Nature in the Old Testament. *CBQ* 14: 18–39; 124–45.

Polhill, J. B. 1977. Perspectives on the Miracle Stories. *RevExp* 74: 389–400.

Pritchard, J. B. 1950. Motifs of Old Testament Miracles. *Crozer Quarterly* 27: 97–109.

Quell, G. 1961. Das Phanomen des Wunders im Alten Testament. Pp. 253–300 in *Verbannung und Heimkehr,* ed. A. Kuschke. Tubingen.

Stoebe, H. J. 1972. Anmerkungen zur Wurzel PLʾ im Alten Testament. *TZ* 28: 13–23.

Stolz, F. 1972. Zeichen un Wunder. *ZTK* 69: 125–44.

Weir, M. C. J. 1958–9. Some Thoughts on Old Testament Miracles. *ALUOS* 1: 25–42.

Wilms, F. E. 1978. *Das Wunder im Alten Testament.* Regensburg.

Zakovitch, Y. 1983–4. Control Mechanisms in Biblical Miracle-Narratives. *Shnaton* 7–8: 61–73 (in Hebrew).

YAIR ZAKOVITCH

NEW TESTAMENT

A. Definition and Terminology
B. Demarcation of the Extraordinary
C. Conflicts Over Miracle
D. Form and Rationale of Miracle Accounts
E. Setting of NT Miracle Accounts
F. Paul
G. Mark
H. Matthew
I. Luke–Acts
J. John
K. The Letter of James
L. The Book of Revelation
M. Trajectories

A. Definition and Terminology

The word "miracle" derives from the Latin *mirari,* "to wonder at." Thaumaturge ("miracle worker") and thaumaturgy ("miracle-working") derive from Gk *thauma,* "wonder," "marvel" (cf. Rev 17:6). That which causes wonder—the extraordinary—is one essential element in miracle. The other is that the extraordinary phenomenon is inexplicable in terms of familiar, everyday causation and so is ascribed to a superhuman force or agency.

Several terms, variously translated, denote this phenomenon in the NT: *dunamis,* "mighty work," "miracle," "wonder" (in the singular, Mark 6:5; usually in the plural, *dunameis,* e.g., Matt 7:22; Acts 2:22); *teras,* "wonder," "portent" (in the NT, only in the plural, *terata,* e.g., Acts 2:22; 2 Cor 12:12); *sēmeion,* "sign," i.e., extraordinary sign, i.e., "miracle" (especially in John, usually in the plural, *sēmeia,* e.g., 2:11, 23; 20:30); *paradoxon,* "strange thing" (in the NT, only in Luke 5:26; plural, *paradoxa*). These words sometimes occur in combination, e.g., *sēmeia* and *dunameis* (Acts 8:13); *sēmeia* and *terata* (Mark 13:22 = Matt 24:24; John 4:48; Acts 2:43; Heb 2:4; cf. Deut 13:1, 2; 34:11; Ps 135:9); *dunamis (-meis), sēmeia,* and *terata* (Acts 2:22; Rom 15:19; 2 Cor 12:12).

Some interpreters have sought to establish distinctions between these terms or between Christian and pagan terms for extraordinary phenomena. *Sēmeia* or *dunameis,* it is said, or especially *sēmeia,* are distinctive Christian terms, denoting God's extraordinary acts performed to effect his purposes and not simply to arouse wonder and awe, for which *teras/terata* is the customary (and pagan) word (see *TDNT* 7:200–269; 8:113–26; Moule 1965). Such distinctions are untenable: early Christian writers, as well as the translators of the OT into Greek and Jewish writers of the 1st century C.E. (like Philo and Josephus) frequently use *teras/terata* in a positive sense, often coupled, or interchangeably, with *sēmeion/sēmeia,* which, when used to designate extraordinary phenomena, functions very similarly to *teras/terata* (e.g., Acts 2:22, 43; 4:30; 5:12; 6:8; Rom 15:9; 2 Cor 12:12; Heb 2:4; see Remus 1982b).

Certain terms are commonly used to describe the reaction to extraordinary phenomena. Those who hear the account of Jesus' healing of the Gerasene demoniac by driving the possessing demons into a herd of swine are "amazed" (Mark 5:20, *ethaumazon;* other examples of *thaumazein:* Matt 8:27 = Luke 8:25; Matt 15:31; John 7:21; Acts 2:7). Those who observe the healing of a deaf man are "astonished" (Mark 7:31, *exeplēssonta;* another example of *ekplēssesthai:* Luke 9:43). After Jesus raises a girl from the dead, people are "amazed" (Mark 5:42 = Luke 8:56, *exestēsan;* other examples of *existanein:* Matt 12:23; Acts 2:7, 12; 10:45; 12:16) or struck with "amazement" (*ekstasis,* Luke 5:26; Acts 3:10). These terms certify to those hearing or reading a miracle account that something extraordinary has occurred. Other terms that indicate the impression made by an extraordinary phenomenon include "fear" or "awe" or "wonder" (*phobos,* Mark 4:41; Luke 7:16; Acts 5:11) or to be "afraid" (*phobeisthai,* Mark 4:41; 5:15 = Luke 8:35; Matt 9:8; 17:6), "astonishment" (*thambos,* Luke 4:36; 5:9; Acts 3:10) or to be "astonished" (*thambeisthai,* Mark 1:27). These terms sometimes occur in combination: "amazement *[ekstasis]* seized them all, and they . . . were filled with awe *[eplēsthesan phobou]*" (Luke 5:26); "and they were filled with wonder *[thambous]* and amazement *[ekstaseōs]*" (Acts 3:10); "they feared great fear *[ephobēthēsan phobon megan]*" (Mark 4:41); "they were afraid *[phobēthentes],* and they marveled *[ethaumasan]*" (Luke 8:25). All these terms certify to those hearing or reading a miracle account that something extraordinary has occurred.

In early Christian literature outside the NT and in pagan and Jewish literature of the period certain formulas of acclamation identify or name the superhuman agency that works the extraordinary phenomenon, e.g., "God is Great!" or "God is One!" (e.g., *Acts of Paul and Thecla* 38; in *NTApocr.* 2: 363; other examples and discussion of the acclamations *Heis Theos* ["God is One!"], *Megas ho theos* ["God is great!"], *Mega to onoma* ["Great is the name" of the deity So-and-So!] in Peterson 1926: 183–222).

In the NT these formulas do not occur; instead, one finds the identification or naming of the agent or power responsible for the extraordinary phenomenon expressed in phrases such as "to praise God" (*doxazein ton theon,* e.g., Mark 2:12 = Matt 9:8; Luke 5:26; 7:16; 13:13; 17:15; *ainein ton theon,* Acts 3:8–9; *doxazein* in combination with *ainein,* Luke 2:20), "to give praise to God" (*didonai ainon tō theō,* Luke 18:43), or "to rejoice" (*chairein,* i.e., at the wondrous deeds of Jesus, Luke 13:17).

B. Demarcation of the Extraordinary

Miracle accounts presuppose that those who are reported as participating in or observing the deed or event, as well as those who hear or read the account, will agree that something extraordinary has occurred. The canons of the ordinary—that by which something is demarcated as extraordinary—vary from people to people, culture to culture, age to age; and within peoples, cultures, and ages. That which is adjudged extraordinary in one age, e.g., human flight, may be considered commonplace—ordinary—in another. The NT miracle accounts are not unique in the Greco-Roman world; they share with it common canons of the ordinary. What distinguishes them is the divine reference: they attribute the extraordinary phenomenon reported, not to deities of pagan polytheism, but to the one God of the Jewish tradition and/or his agents, Jesus or Jesus' apostles.

Canons of the ordinary in the Greco-Roman world fall into several basic categories corresponding to various areas of human experience. Some of the canons pertinent to NT miracle accounts will serve to illustrate (for further examples, especially from contemporary pagan sources, see Remus 1983, chaps. 2 and 3).

The life stages of the ordinary human being provided a number of such canons. Human reproduction (and animal reproduction generally) had received considerable attention in scientific treatises by Greek philosophers such as Aristotle and in agricultural treatises by Roman essayists such as Cato the Censor and Varro. Widely circulated stories of virgin births—i.e., departures from the ordinary— show it was common knowledge that humans ordinarily come into the world, after gestation of about 9 months, through intercourse of man and woman. Hence, Mary asks how she can bear a child when she has had no sexual relations with a man (Luke 1:34); Joseph, learning of Mary's pregnancy, resolves to divorce her quietly because he assumes she has had sexual relations with another man (Matt 1:18–19).

Normally, humans attain their mental powers slowly and grow to a more or less limited height. Such knowledge is implicit in the story of Jesus' precociousness (Luke 2:41–

52), which astonishes (*eksistanto,* 2:47) those who witness it, and in the accounts of Jesus as enormously tall, either before his resurrection (*Acts of John* 90; in *NTApocr* 2: 226) or after (*Gospel of Peter* 40; in Cartlidge and Dungan 1980: 85).

Ordinary human bodies are subject to the limitations imposed by specific gravity, tangibleness or visibility, space, and mortality. It is this canon that gives point to NT accounts of Jesus walking on the sea (Mark 6:45–52 = Matt 14:22–33; John 6:15–21) and rising through the air (Acts 1:9); wondrously eluding enemies (Luke 4:30; John 8:59; 10:39) and transporting himself and others through space (John 6:21); rising from the dead and then materializing and dematerializing (Luke 24:31, 36).

The awe and astonishment, noted above, which greet wondrous healings and resurrections show that implicit in accounts of such deeds is a consensus that they are beyond ordinary human capacities. As a man whose sight Jesus has restored says, "Never since the world began has it been heard that any one opened the eyes of a person born blind" (John 9:32). When the townspeople of Lystra respond to Paul's healing of a lame man by proclaiming Paul and Barnabas divine, Paul counters by asserting that he and Barnabas are but human, constituted as the Lystrans themselves are (Acts 14:15); that is, incapable of wondrous deeds apart from divine assistance.

Ordinary flora and fauna also constituted canons by which people in the Greco-Roman world demarcated the extraordinary. Balaam's second-sighted, talking ass (Num 22:23–30) is familiar to readers of the Bible. Early Christian literature contains accounts of animals that worship the infant Jesus (*Gos. Ps-Matt.* 14, 18–19; in Cartlidge and Dungan 1980: 100–1) and an ass that performs an exorcism and preaches a sermon (*Acts of Thomas* 74, 78–79). In the NT the only accounts of extraordinary events involving animals and plants are those in which Jesus exercises control over them (wondrous catches of fish, Luke 5:1–11; John 21:1–11; the fish with a coin in its mouth, Matt 17:24–27; the withering of a fig tree cursed by Jesus, Mark 11:12–14, 20–21 = Matt 21:18–19). Absent from the NT are accounts of genetic malformations (e.g., two-headed animals) and reproduction of a species by a different species, which were often interpreted as portents from deity.

Regularity in the cosmic order gives point to certain hyperbolic statements in the NT and to accounts of wondrous irregularities. These hyperbolic statements—faith can move mountains (Mark 11:23 = Matt 21:21; Matt 17:20; 1 Cor 13:1) or transplant trees into the sea (Luke 17:6)—are akin to a common poetic device known as *adynaton,* "the impossible," e.g., rivers flowing upstream, night not following day, the sun changing its course, trees in the sea (see further in Grant 1952: 57–58; on NT hyperbole, see Stein 1985). The subsiding of a storm in obedience to Jesus' command (Mark 4:35–41 = Matt 8:23–27; Luke 8:22–25) and the darkness at noon during his crucifixion (Mark 15:33 = Matt 27:45, Luke 23:44–45) represent wondrous departures from everyday experience of cosmic order. In Greek and Latin literature that order is designated as "nature" (Gk *physis;* Lat *natura;* see further Remus 1984). In the NT this usage is found in Rom 11:21, 24 and 1 Cor 11:14, but not, as it often is in Greek and Latin literature or in much of Western thought generally, in connection with miracle.

C. Conflicts over Miracle

Since canons of the ordinary are social and cultural judgments, conflicts may arise over what is considered extraordinary and whether or not an extraordinary phenomenon is a "miracle," that is, is attributable to deity. Extraordinary phenomena reported among distant peoples and in remote geographical areas, for example, were often not referred to deity by Greek and Latin writers; the exoticness of such phenomena was sufficient explanation of their extraordinariness. The philosophical, historical, and medical traditions of knowledge, much of which was the common stock of educated persons in the Greco-Roman world, frequently offered explanations of extraordinary phenomena that made reference to deity unnecessary. For example, in explaining epilepsy as like other diseases and therefore treatable by medical means, physicians in the Hippocratic tradition of medicine came in conflict with persons who used rituals and incantations to overpower the deities whose indewelling they viewed as the cause of "the sacred disease." Rival traditions of healing are seen also when early Christian claims for Jesus as a healer come in conflict with pagan claims for the deity Asclepius as a healer (see Rengstorff 1953; Dölger 1950; Edelstein 1945, 2:132–38; Remus 1983: 105–16).

In the NT itself, the accounts of the Beelzebul controversy (Mark 3:22–30 = Matt 12:22–32; Luke 11:14–23; 12:10) illustrate both a common means of denying divine reference to an extraordinary phenomenon, namely, stigmatization, and how group loyalties enter into such denials and counterassertions. Opponents of Jesus charge that he casts out demons by Beelzebul, the prince of demons. The wonders worked by "the lawless one" of 2 Thess 2:9 are associated with Satan. This kind of stigmatization—denying divine reference to an extraordinary phenomenon by attributing it to malevolent powers rather than to benevolent deity—was employed by early Christians such as Justin Martyr (*1 Apol.* 54.6, 8, 10; *Dial.* 69.1–3; 70.5) to discredit pagan miracle claims; it drew on Jewish and Christian traditions that associated pagan piety with demons (e.g., 1 Cor 10:20; Rev 9:20). Jesus' defense in the Beelzebul accounts, stating that those who are not for him are against him and implying that those who attribute his exorcisms to Beelzebul are guilty of sinning against the Holy Spirit, would serve as a warrant for early Christians in defending their own thaumaturgy and exorcisms in the name of Jesus.

Another way of stigmatizing an extraordinary phenomenon and denying it divine reference was to characterize the agent of the phenomenon or the phenomenon itself as "false." "False prophets," it is said, will work signs and wonders (Mark 13:22 = Matt 24:24). In 2 Thess 2:9 the signs and wonders worked by "the lawless one" are said to be false. Falsity is often associated with deceit. The "false prophets" of Mark 13:22 = Matt 24:24 work their signs and wonders in an attempt to deceive the elect, and "the lawless one" deceives those who are perishing (2 Thess 2:10). In the last days, the world deceiver will appear as a son of God and will work signs and wonders (*Did.* 16:4).

Another means of stigmatization—and every effective in

view of the dire social and legal consequences (Remus 1982a: 153)—was to charge that a wonder worker was in fact a magician. The Simon who attempts to buy the gift of the Holy Spirit (Acts 8:19–20), and who came to be regarded by mainstream Christianity as the archheretic, was stigmatized in post-NT writings by the epithet *magus,* "magician," and in the NT by the report that he practiced magic (*mageia,* Acts 8:11), in contrast with the apostles, who perform signs and miracles by the power of Jesus (8:13). Similarly, Bar-Jesus, the opponent of the Christian message on the island of Cyprus, is labeled a false prophet and a magician (*magos,* Acts 13:6, 8).

Whether persons in the Greco-Roman world who were accused of practicing magic actually did so may be difficult to determine: "magic" was an elastic term, not least because it was commonly used in polemic. In Robert Grant's dictum, "in polemical writing, your magic is my miracle, and vice versa" (1966: 93). The "wise men" (RSV) who come from the east at Jesus' birth (Matt 2:1–16) are in fact *magoi,* upper caste Persian priests versed in astral lore, figures familiar to the Greco-Roman world through the writings of the Greek historian Herodotus and others. However, Christian writers in the 2d century generally viewed these *magoi* as "magicians" and/or interpreters of the stars whose coming to Jesus signified his greater power, which freed the *magoi* from servitude to magic and astrology and, indeed, had put an end to the power of magic and placed such knowledge of the stars in the service of Christ (Ign. *Eph.* 19:3; Justin, *Dial.* 77.4; 78.1, 7, 9; 88.1; 102.2–4; Iren. *haer.* 3.9.2 [Harvey ed., 3.10.1]; Tertullian, *De idololatria* 9). Early Christians go to great lengths to refute charges that Jesus was a magician or that the miracles they claimed or proclaimed were worked by magic (Just. *1 Apol.* 30; *Dial.* 69.7; Tert. *Apol.* 21, 23).

Another way of denying that an extraordinary phenomenon was a miracle was to assert, as Celsus the 2d century philosopher and critic of Christianity did against Christian miracle claims, that it was an illusion (reported in Origen, *Cels.* 1.41), an hallucination (7.35), or simple fabrication (1.68), even while he affirms pagan miracle claims of a similar nature (3.24, 26).

These various disputes about miracle claims show that the Beelzebul controversy and other disputes about miracle claims in the NT are not unique: they were common in the Greco-Roman world, especially between competing social and religious groups such as Christianity and paganism or between one variety of Christianity and another. The disputes also illustrate how social and cultural factors were operative when persons in the Greco-Roman world, Christians included, observed an unusual phenomenon or heard reports of such and then decided whether or not it was indeed authentically extraordinary, inexplicable in terms of familiar causation, and worked by divine power; that is, was a miracle.

D. Form and Rationale of Miracle Accounts

Certain basic elements are essential to a miracle account, whether in the NT or elsewhere: the deed or event must be perceived to be extraordinary and beyond human capability; it must be inexplicable except by attributing it to or associating it in some way with superhuman agency. These elements are evident in the typical form of miracle stories that involve a thaumaturge: a situation beyond human control is described; the thaumaturge becomes aware of or involved in the situation, and then works a wondrous change in it; proof of the change is adduced; the spectators are astonished. In the NT miracle accounts, other elements often considered essential to stories or to historical accounts are commonly missing or left vague and in the background. The characters are few or described en masse ("a great crowd," Mark 7:34 = Matt 14:14; "all" the spectators, Mark 1:27; 2:12; Acts 9:35; "all the people," Luke 18:43; Acts 3:9) and except for the thaumaturge are usually identified only in a general way ("a paralyzed man," Mark 2:3 = Matt 9:2; Luke 5:18; "a woman with a hemorrhage," Mark 5:25 = Matt 9:20; Luke 8:43; "a deaf man with an impediment in his speech," Mark 7:32; "a man blind from birth," John 9:1; "a certain man lame from birth," Acts 3:2). In the NT gospels, designations of the time of a miracle are either very general ("on the Sabbath," Mark 1:21 = Luke 4:31) or omitted entirely; the geographical locations are occasionally identified explicitly (Capernaum, on the sabbath, Mark 1:21 = Luke 4:31; Bethsaida, time unspecified, Mark 8:22; Jericho, time unspecified, Mark 10:46 = Matt 20:29; Luke 18:35; Bethany, time unspecified, John 11:18), but more commonly they are either very general ("the country of the Gerasenes" or "Gadarenes," Mark 5:1 = Matt 8:28; Luke 8:26; "the region of Tyre and Sidon," Mark 7:24 = Matt 15:21; "the region of the Decapolis," Mark 7:31) or quite vague ("beside the sea," Mark 5:21; "a lonely place," Mark 6:32 = Matt 14:13; cf. Luke 9:12; "in villages, cities, or country" in Gennesaret, Mark 6:56). The effect of this lack of detail and specificity is a focus on the thaumaturge and the miracle itself.

An account of a nature miracle that clearly demonstrates this form is Jesus' stilling of the storm (Mark 4:35–41 = Matt 8:23–27; Luke 8:22–25): A storm threatens to swamp the boat in which Jesus and the disciples are crossing the Lake of Galilee; in their peril the disciples appeal to Jesus, who is asleep (this detail, omitted in Luke, heightens the drama as well as foreshadows Jesus' sovereignty over the wind and water); he rebukes the wind and commands the waves to be silent; there is a great calm; the disciples are afraid (Mark, Luke) and marvel at Jesus' power over wind and water. Other NT accounts of nature miracles that display this form are the wondrous catches of fish (Luke 5:1–11; John 21:1–14), Jesus' walking on the sea (Mark 6:45–52 = Matt 14:23–33; John 6:16–21), the feeding of the multitudes (Mark 6:35–44 = Matt 14:15–21; Luke 9:12–17; John 6:1–14; Mark 8:1–9 = Matt 15:32–39), and the changing of water into wine (John 2:1–11). In the OT the form is evident in such accounts of nature miracles as the crossing of the Red Sea (Exod 14:10–31) and some of those associated with Elisha (2 Kgs 4:38–41; 4:42–44; 6:1–7).

Much more numerous in the NT are accounts of healing miracles. The typical form is as follows: the sickness is described (e.g., its duration, the debilitating or life-threatening symptoms, the failure of physicians and medicines to effect a cure); the sick person and the healer encounter one another; the healer, through word or manipulations and use of substances (but sometimes with none of these), works a cure, which usually is sudden; proof of the healing is supplied; the spectators (if any) are amazed.

This form is evident in both ancient and modern healing accounts. Vespasian, the 1st century A.D. Roman general and future emperor, is approached by a blind man, with the request that Vespasian apply spit to his cheeks and eyeballs, and by a man with a crippled hand, with the request that Vespasian step on the hand. After some hesitation, and after consulting physicians, Vespasian complies with the requests, and both men are healed immediately, as is attested by witnesses (Tac. *Hist.* 4.81; Suet. *Ves.* 7; Dio Cass. *Hist.* 65.8; ET in Cartlidge and Dungan 1980: 156). In the 3d century account by Philostratus of a 1st century thaumaturge named Apollonius, a boy bitten by a hydrophobic dog barks, howls, and goes about on all fours, an affliction that has already lasted for thirty days (*VA* 6.43). Apollonius encounters the boy and, knowing what dog it is and where he is to be found, has him summoned and commands him to lick the boy's wound, whereupon the boy returns to normal and, as final proof of his healing, drinks water (i.e., he is no longer hydrophobic). In a 20th century account, a deacon in Oral Roberts' church who has dropped a heavy motor on his foot sits screaming with blood running out of his shoe. Roberts is summoned, kneels, prays, straightens up. The deacon, his pain gone, stops screaming, takes off his shoe, and finds the foot again normal (see Jacobs 1962: 39).

A NT example is the healing of a hemorrhaging woman (Mark 5:25–34 = Luke 8:43–48; less fully, and with significant variations, in Matt 9:20–22): the woman has been afflicted for twelve years; she has consulted physicians and spent all her money seeking a cure, but her condition has only worsened; she touches Jesus' garment, and the flow of blood stops immediately; Jesus asks who touched him, since he has felt power flow from him; the disciples (Luke: Peter) protest that there is a crowd, and many people are touching him; Jesus insists, however, and the woman—fearful and trembling—comes forward and confesses what has happened; Jesus bids her go in peace.

Here and in other accounts the mere touch of the healer or of something that touches him (the fringe of Jesus' garment, Mark 6:56 = Matt 14:36) or has touched him (handkerchiefs or aprons that have touched Paul, Acts 19:12), or even his shadow (Peter, Acts 5:15), is regarded as able to effect a cure. Hence the numerous accounts of Jesus touching the sick or wounded (Mark 1:41 = Matt 8:3; Luke 5:13; Mark 7:33; Matt 8:15; 9:29; Luke 22:51), or being asked to do so (Mark 3:10 = Luke 6:19; Mark 8:22), or of Jesus or his apostle laying hands on them (Mark 1:41 = Matt 8:3; Luke 5:13; Mark 6:5; 8:23, 25; Luke 4:40; 13:13; Acts 28:8) or requested to do so (Mark 5:23 = Matt 9:18; Mark 7:32).

Underlying these and other healing accounts is the idea, common in the Greco-Roman world, that power resides in or emanates from certain persons, objects, and words (see, e.g., Plutarch, *Causes of Natural Phenomena [Quaestiones naturales]* 916D; *Philosophers and Men in Power [Maxime cum principibus]* 777F). "All the crowd was seeking to touch Jesus, because power was going forth from him and was healing them all" (Luke 6:19; cf. 5:17). "Jesus perceived in himself that power had gone forth from him" when the hemorrhaging woman touched his garment (Mark 5:30). According to Eunapius (4th century C.E.; *VS* 148), after an impressive speech by the famous Christian orator Prohairesios, people kissed his hands and feet and licked his chest as they would a statue of a god, because they thought him possessed of divine potency. Hence, objects associated with potent persons were seen as having power (see above), as were even certain kinds of objects, either in themselves (magnets, stones) or when inscribed (amulets) or sculpted (statues) (see Nilsson 1948a: 103–9). Likewise, the words of a potent person have power; when Jesus identifies himself to those who come to take him in the garden by saying, "I am he" (a revelatory formula), they draw back and fall to the ground (John 18:5–6); when he addresses an illness (Luke 4:39) or a dead person (Mark 5:41 = Luke 8:54) or a demon (see below), these obey.

Consequently the invoking of Jesus' name by his followers has power to heal (Acts 3:6; 4:10, 30) and to exorcize demons (Luke 10:17; Acts 16:18; cf. 19:13). The author of Acts reports that some itinerant Jewish exorcists attempted (unsuccessfully) to appropriate the name of Jesus for exorcistic purposes (19:13–17). According to Origen, the name of Jesus for exorcistic purposes (19:13–17). According to Origen, the name of Jesus has such power against demons that it is sometimes effective even when bad men utter it (*Cels.* 1.6). Jesus' name, along with other Jewish names, is attested in the Greek and Coptic magical papyri from Egypt (see Nilsson 1948b: 5–8; Gager 1972, chap. 4) and accords with common thaumaturgical use of the name of a deity or some other powerful figure, often from a foreign culture and in a foreign tongue (for a parody that illustrates the stereotype, see Lucian of Samosata *Am.* 12; also his *Men.* 6–10).

As in OT healing and resurrection accounts, so also in those in the NT the causes of sickness and death are often not named (Mark 1:30; 5:25; cf. 1 Kgs 17:17; 2 Kgs 5:1). In other such accounts, however, disease and death are associated with or ascribed to sin (John 9:1–3; cf. Num 12:9–12; 16:41–50; 2 Kgs 5:20–27) or Satan (Luke 13:16) or demons (Mark 9:17–18 = Luke 9:39). Where there is no explicit reference to demonic cause of illness, the terminology may suggest it. Thus Jesus, asked to heal a deaf mute, "sighs" or "groans" (*estenaxen*, Mark 7:34), as though struggling with the power that binds (7:35) the man's tongue; or Jesus may "threaten" *(epitimān)* a disease as though an evil power inhabits it (Luke 4:39). In exorcism accounts, where demonic possession is made explicit, such terminology is also employed (e.g., Mark 1:25 = Luke 4:35; Mark 9:25 = Matt 17:18; Luke 9:42). Implicit in such terminology is the concept of power, already noted in healing accounts: a greater power (the thaumaturge) compels a lesser (the demon[s]) to leave a possessed person. Asceticism was seen as a means to such power (see, e.g., *Apoc. El.* 1:21 [*OTP* 1: 738]: fasting "releases sin . . . heals diseases . . . casts out demons"), which suggests why at Mark 9:29 some NT manuscripts add "fasting" to "prayer" as necessary in order to be able to cast out a certain kind of demon. The form of exorcism accounts conforms to that of healing accounts generally (see, e.g., Mark 1:21–28 = Luke 4:33–37; Mark 5:1–20 = Matt 8:28–34; Luke 8:26–39; *Ant* 8.46–48; Lucian of Samosata, *Am.* 16; 31; Philostr. *VA* 4.20).

A number of miracle accounts follow the basic form

outlined above but are embedded in narrative frameworks that lead up to or focus on a pronouncement by Jesus and have therefore been aptly titled by Vincent Taylor (1935: 30) "pronouncement stories" (Bultmann 1963: 11, 209, calls them "apophthegms"; Dibelius 1935: 26, "paradigms"). An example is the healing of a crippled woman on the sabbath (Luke 13:10–13), followed by a pronouncement (in the form of a rhetorical question) by Jesus. Other examples are Mark 2:1–12 = Matt 9:1–8 = Luke 5:17–26; Mark 7:24–30 = Matt 15:21–28; Mark 11:12–14, 20–26 = Matt 21:18–22; Matt 8:5–13 = Luke 17:1–10; 17:11–19. See also APOPHTHEGM.

Examination of the setting of these various miracle accounts in the life of early Christian communities provides clues to why early Christians transmitted and recorded the accounts and offers important insights into the life of these communities.

E. Setting of NT Miracle Accounts

A number of passages in the NT and other early Christian literature indicate that miracle accounts figured prominently in a number of settings in the life of early Christian communities. One such setting was the defense of Christian practices and beliefs. Over against Jewish criticisms or in intramural Christian disputes, some of the pronouncement stories cited above for their inclusion of miracle accounts would justify Christian practices regarding the sabbath (e.g., Luke 13:10–13) or Christian attitudes to non-Jews (e.g., Mark 7:24–30 = Matt 15:21–28). A pronouncement story like Mark 2:1–12 = Matt 9:1–18 = Luke 5:17–26 would justify Christians' claims that Jesus had authority to forgive sin and would provide a warrant for their own forgiving of sins by his authority (cf. Matt 16:19; 18:18; John 20:23).

Christian practice of thaumaturgy, especially healing rituals, was another context in which accounts of miracles worked by Jesus played a role, both before and after their collection and recording in the Gospels. That Christians practiced such rituals is evident from a number of texts. Paul cites healing and working of miracles *(dynameis)* as gifts of the Spirit (1 Cor 12:9, 10), and the letter of James (5:14) outlines a procedure for healing that employs prayer and anointing with oil "in the name of the Lord" (cf. Mark 6:13). Outside the NT, Irenaeus (*haer.* 2.32.5 [Harvey ed., 2.49.3]), Justin Martyr (*2 Apol.* 6.6; *Dial.* 30.3; 76.7; 85.2–3), Tertullian (*Apol.* 23.6), Origen (*Cels.* 1.6; 3.24; 7.4, 67), the Acts literature (*Acts Pet. Paul* 77, *Acts John* 79; *Acts Thom.* 47–48; 141), and Christian magical papyri (in Preisendanz 1974, papyri 5b, 18, 19) describe healings and exorcisms by Christians or in Christian communities. A number of these texts invoke the name of Jesus, or recite brief credos about him or "formulas from the holy scriptures" (Origen, *Cels.* 7.67), or refer to healings by him recorded in the Gospels. The stories of healings by Jesus provided precedent and warrant for Christians' practice of healing rituals. The fact that the transmitters and recorders of these stories included certain details of how Jesus healed suggests that early Christians also looked to these accounts for techniques to be used in their healing rituals (cf. the dialogue in Mark 9:28–29, and Dibelius 1935: 84, 86–87).

These techniques were not peculiar to Christians. The use of foreign words (*talitha koum,* Mark 5:41; *ephphatha,* Mark 7:34) is common in pagan healing accounts (e.g., Lucian *Am.* 9, 12, 31; *Men.* 6–10; Philostr. *VA* 4.45) and in the magical papyri (see Nilsson 1948b: 5–8; Gager 1972, chap. 4). There are also parallels to Jesus' use of saliva (Mark 7:33; 8:23; John 9:6; cf. Vespasian's healing of a blind man, cited above), to his sighing (Mark 7:34; cf. the magical papyri cited in Dibelius 1935: 85–86), and to his touching of the afflicted person or taking hold of the person's hand (Mark 1:31 = Matt 8:15; Mark 1:41 = Matt 8:3 = Luke 5:13; Mark 5:41 = Matt 9:25 = Luke 8:54; Mark 7:33; 8:22–23, 25; Matt 9:29; 20:34; Luke 7:14; 13:13; 22:51; cf. Philostr. *VA* 3.39; 4:45).

The similarity between these techniques and those used by pagan healers and persons regarded as magicians was one reason some pagans and Jews in the 2d century charged that the healings attributed to Jesus and his followers were worked through magic (Celsus, in Origen, *Cels.* 1.6, 71; Tert. *Apol.* 21.17; 23.7), which Christians vigorously denied (Just. *1 Apol.* 30; Tert. *Apol.* 23.12–19). Similarly, some modern scholars see a sharp discontinuity between these accounts and pagan healing accounts, claiming that Jesus healed simply by a word and dismissing as insignificant the materials and gestures he employs in some of the healing stories. This position is difficult to maintain: some of the healings include words, materials, and gestures, or simply happen (Mark 5:28–29 = Luke 8:43–44). To say that Jesus healed simply with a word does not in fact distinguish his healings from pagan healings or from magic: words themselves could be construed as magic manipulations, as Origen states explicitly (*Cels.* 1.24–25; 5.45) and as is clear from the magical papyri, amulets, cursing tablets, and literary texts concerning magic, with their abundant formulas for incantations and their special words and syllables for apotropaic and other uses.

Indeed, one reason Christians were successful in winning converts was that as part of their missionary proclamation they told stories of miracles worked by their savior which had affinities with those circulating among pagans. Such stories, pagan or Christian, were winsome because they raised the hope that as the healer had once acted in the past, so now he might do so again. Sick persons who journeyed to the Asclepius temples at Epidaurus in Greece or on the island of Cos came in the hope that they would be wondrously healed as were the persons described in the inscriptions on votive tablets at the temples there (examples in Edelstein 1945, 1: Testimonies 423, 794; Cartlidge and Dungan 1980: 151–53). For pagans accustomed to such stories about their deities and thaumaturgists, Christians' proclamation of miracles worked by Jesus would serve as a counterpoise to Christian proclamation of a savior apparently so powerless that he was unable to escape the ignominy of death on a cross. The connection of Christian thaumaturgy and Christian mission is made explicit in several NT texts. According to Matt 11:20–21 = Luke 10:13, the working of miracles is expected to lead to repentance (cf. also Mark 6:12–13), and thaumaturgy—healing of the sick, raising the dead, cleansing of lepers, exorcisms—is seen as part of mission in Matt 10:7–8 = Luke 9:2 and Luke 10:8–9. In defense of his apostolic mission and ministry, Paul cites as "signs" *(sēmeia)* of his apostleship his working of "signs" *(sēmeia),* "wonders" *(ter-*

ata), and "mighty works" *(dynameis)* (2 Cor 12:12; similarly Rom 15:19). The purpose of his thaumaturgy, says Paul, is "obedience of the gentiles," i.e., their coming to faith in Christ (Rom 15:18).

When Paul's letters were then read in Christian assemblies, his declaration of his thaumaturgical powers would serve to strengthen the authority of Paul and his message. Such proclamation—of wonders worked by Paul as well as by Peter—is explicit in a number of passages in Acts (see below) and would also serve to strengthen the faith of believers. The same would be true of the recounting of the stories of miracles worked by Jesus.

In the life of early Christian communities miracle stories and thaumaturgy thus played important roles. But, as has already been indicated, they also stood in tension with the Christian proclamation of the crucified Christ, as is evident in the writings discussed next.

F. Paul

Paul, as was indicated above, in several passages refers to his thaumaturgical powers as evidence of his apostleship. Far outweighing these passages, however, are others in which he cites his sufferings as demonstrations of his apostleship (1 Cor 4:11–13; 2 Cor 6:3–10; 11:23–27) and insists on his weakness as a condition of the manifestation of Christ's strength in him (1 Cor 4:9–10; 2 Cor 4:7–12; 11:30; 12:1–10). This interpretation of his apostleship he relates to his sickness (2 Cor 12:7–10) but especially to the weakness of a crucified savior in whom he sees the strength and wisdom of God revealed (1 Cor 1:18–25), a view deriving from a wondrous event: the appearance of the risen Christ to him (1 Cor 15:8) and his call to be an apostle (Gal 1:15–16). Paul makes these paradoxical assertions of God's power and strength over against persons who stress thaumaturgy as proof of divine mission. A similar antithesis is found in the gospel of Mark.

G. Mark

Miracle accounts play an important role in the gospel of Mark, constituting a substantial portion of the narratives of the first nine chapters. The description of John the Baptist's work that opens the gospel culminates in his proclamation that one mightier than he is yet to come (1:7). That one is Jesus, whose miracles are the first steps in establishing the reign of God that Jesus, at the beginning of his ministry, announces is near at hand (1:15). With the power of the Spirit that descended on him at his baptism (1:10), Jesus demonstrates, through displays of power, that God's reign is beginning: he heals illnesses (1:29–34, 40–42; 2:1–12; 3:1–6; 5:21–43; 6:53; 7:31–35; 8:22–26; 10:46–52), wondrously feeds multitudes of hungry people (6:30–44; 8:1–9), walks on water and stills wind and wave (6:45–51), and withers a fig tree to its roots (11:14, 20–21; on this difficult passage see Cotter 1986; Achtemeier, *Mark* Proclamation, 23–25). Like one who binds a strong man in order to plunder his house (3:27), so Jesus, having overcome Satan in the wilderness (1:12–13), compels Satan's forces to obey him, driving them out of the humans they afflict (1:23–26, 34; 3:11; 5:1–20; 7:24–30; 9:14–26).

Why Jesus should command the demons not to reveal his true identity can be explained in some cases as a common element in an exorcism story (Jesus commands the demon to be still, 1:25, even as he commands the raging storm to be still, 4:39). In other passages, however, the commands to demons not to reveal who he is (1:34, 3:12), and to persons he heals (1:43, 7:36) or raises from the dead (5:43) to tell no one of it, can be attributed to the evangelist's concern that Jesus not be viewed simply as a miracle worker. Rather, Jesus must suffer and die; this is his "messianic secret," and to deny that necessity is viewed in 8:31–33 as Satanic; these verses provide readers with the key to unlock the Markan "messianic secret" and thus to see the miracles worked by Jesus in relation to his suffering and death. To perform the miracle of descending from the cross, as some of the bystanders mockingly exhort Jesus to do in order that they may "see and believe" (15:32), would be to attempt to achieve by wondrous display and main force what can only be accomplished through service unto death (10:45). The taunt "He saved others, himself he cannot save" (15:31) expresses ironically the same view of messiahship. Thus it is that Jesus acknowledges publicly that he is the Christ (14:61–62) only *after* it has become clear that the Christ must suffer and die. For the same reason he commands his followers not to reveal he is the Christ until after his suffering, death, and resurrection (8:29–33; 9:9, 31–32; 10:31–32); and the only public confession of Jesus as Son of God that does not meet with a rebuke or a command to silence comes after Jesus' death is accomplished (15:39).

The miracle at the baptism of Jesus through which God designates Jesus as his chosen one (1:11) is followed by the miracles which demonstrate that God's reign draws near, but it is the baptism of his death (10:38), where Jesus is powerless, which the evangelist sees as the decisive victory over the forces that oppose God's reign. (On the preceding, see further Perrin 1971; Kelber 1976; Rhoads and Michie 1982.)

H. Matthew

The basic outline of the gospel of Matthew is close to that of the gospel of Mark, which means that here, too, Jesus is depicted as the Christ who suffers and dies and not simply as a miracle worker, even though Matthew includes virtually all the miracle stories recorded in Mark (missing are Mark 1:23–28; 7:32–37; 8:22–26) but also others not found in any of the other NT Gospels (Matt 9:27–31, 32–34 [cf. 12:22–24]; 14:28–31; 27:52–53; 28:2–4, 9–10, 16–20).

One distinctive characteristic of the Matthean miracle stories is their tautness; many of the colorful details found in the other gospels are lacking (cf., e.g., Matt 8:28–34 with Mark 5:1–20; Matt 9:18–26 with Mark 5:21–43; Matt 20:29–34 with Mark 10:46–52). On the other hand, some of the narratives include material not found in the other gospels (cf., e.g., Matt 14:22–33 with Mark 6:45–52; Matt 15:21–28 with Mark 7:24–30). Also noteworthy is the evangelist's artful grouping of miracle accounts (e.g., Matthew 8–9). These Matthean usages bring to the fore several distinctively Matthean themes that interpret the miracles, and Jesus as miracle-worker, for readers (see especially Bornkamm 1963; Held 1963).

Jesus' miracles are sometimes presented in Matthew as the fulfillment of scripture (1:22–23; 8:17; 12:17), a prominent Matthean theme (on the fulfillment theme in general and its application to the Matthean birth narratives and the miracles they recount, see Brown 1977). These formulaic citations attached by Matthew to miracle accounts served several purposes: instruction in how the miracles fulfilled the scriptures (didactic) as well as defenses of them based on scripture and proof that Jesus is God's promised Messiah (apologetic and theological). He is thus set apart from other thaumaturgists, who do not have such prophetic testimony.

Jesus is Messiah not only in word—in the Matthean discourses—but also in deed (Schniewind *Matthew* NTD, 8, 106), as made clear in Matthew's introduction (4:25) and conclusion (9:35) to the Sermon on the Mount (chaps. 5–7) and miracle stories grouped in Matthew 8–9. In their stark Matthean versions they focus on Jesus the Christ. Thus, in the healing of Peter's mother-in-law, Jesus appears alone with her (8:14–15), in contrast with the other accounts (Mark 1:29–31; Luke 4:38–39). The Matthean version of the Gadarene/Gerasene demoniac(s) (8:28–34) lacks many details of the Markan (5:1–20) and Lukan (8:26–39) accounts, and, in contrast to them, presents the demons' response to Jesus neither as apotropaic ("I adjure you by God," Mark 5:7) nor as supplicatory (Luke 8:28) but as an implicit confession of Jesus' messiahship: He is the one who has "come" to demonstrate God's sovereignty over evil by subjecting demons to torment, even "before the time" of their final judgment that will establish God's reign (Matt 8:29); accordingly, it is not pigs who "drown" in the lake (Mark 5:13 = Luke 8:33) but demons who "die" there (Matt 8:32).

Matthean abridgement and expansion of some of the synoptic miracle accounts bring to the fore two other important Matthean themes: faith (and the negative "little faith") and discipleship. Compared with the Markan (5:21–43) and Lukan (8:40–56) versions of the healing of the hemorrhaging woman, Matthew's is reduced to a scene involving only Jesus and the woman in which her faith in Jesus' power to heal, and Jesus' rewarding of her faith, stand out sharply (9:18–26; the same focus on faith and its reward in the succeeding account, 9:27–31). In contrast with the Lukan version (7:1–10) of the healing of the centurion's son/slave, Matthew's (8:5–13) is shorter, and the faith of the centurion, which is the heart of the story in both gospels, is accentuated by a distinctively Matthean conclusion: "As you have believed, so be it done for you" (8:13; cf. 9:29; 15:28). On the other hand, the Matthean account of Jesus' healing of the daughter of the Syro-Phoenician woman (15:21–28) is longer than the Markan parallel (7:24–30) by virtue of the inclusion of a dialogue between Jesus and the woman which raises the question of relations between Jews and non-Jews and answers it by reference to her faith, which surmounts the barrier (8:28).

Jesus and his disciples figure in the synoptic stories of Jesus stilling the storm (Mark 4:35–41; Matt 8:23–27; Luke 8:22–25) and of Jesus and Peter walking on water (Mark 6:45–52; Matt 14:22–33). Matthew's versions, however, point to the nature of discipleship and contrast with it "little faith." Immediately preceding the account of the stilling of the storm Matthew has placed sayings on the cost of discipleship: a scribe who wishes to follow *(akolouthein)* Jesus, i.e., be his disciple, is told that he can expect none of the comforts of home (8:19–20); and a disciple who wishes to return home to bury his father is told to let the dead bury their dead and to follow *(akolouthein)* Jesus (8:21–22). Only in Matthew's gospel do Jesus' disciples then *follow (akolouthein)* him into the boat, where the storm breaks upon them and they in their distress cry out to him to save them (8:23–25). Jesus asks why they are afraid, "you of little faith *[oligopistoi]*" (8:26); he then threatens *(epitimēsen)* the storm as one would an evil power (see D above) and it subsides. Similarly, Peter, walking on the water toward Jesus at Jesus' command, grows fearful and begins to sink, but Jesus takes his hand and asks why he doubted, "you of little faith *[oligopiste]*" (14:31). Those who follow Jesus and become his disciples could conclude from these passages that they would know peril because of the evil forces that oppose God's reign, but they should not be of "little faith" because he is their living and present Lord (18:20; 28:20) and would deliver them.

Moreover, as he once worked miracles, so now his disciples, at his command and empowered by him, will do the same. In the discourse commissioning his disciples to go forth to proclaim the kingdom (chap. 10), Jesus empowers them not only to cast out unclean spirits (thus also Mark 6:7; Luke 9:11, "demons") but also to "heal every disease and every sickness" (Matt 10:1), indeed, to perform virtually every miracle ascribed to Jesus in Matthew 8–9 (10:8). The passages that follow, depicting the trials and persecution that await such thaumaturgical missionaries (10:17–39), are addressed to the Risen Lord's disciples, i.e., the evangelist's contemporaries, for that is their situation (Vielhauer 1965: 64–67; Higgins 1964: 100–4; Kingsbury, *Matthew* Proclamation, 74, 90–91). Receiving them is the same as receiving him and the one who sent him (10:40). Accordingly, in the pericope that immediately follows the commissioning discourse, Jesus' recital of miracles, in response to John the Baptist's question whether he is the messiah (11:2–6), would apply to his disciples as well as himself: the miracles of both proclaim he is indeed "the one who is to come" (11:3).

That his disciples are expected, both by themselves and by others, to perform miracles is indicated in Matt 17:14–20, a sharply abridged version of the story of a demon-possessed boy (contrast Mark 9:14–29 and Luke 9:37–43). The father has brought him to the disciples for healing; when they are unable to comply he turns to Jesus for help, and the disciples ask Jesus the reason for their inability to perform the healing (the verb "unable" *[adunatein]*, 17:16, 19, 20, ties the Matthean narrative together). He, as their teacher and the teacher of the church (28:20), then instructs them: it is because of their "little faith" *(oligopistian)*. Nonetheless, for a person with "faith like a grain of mustard seed . . . nothing will be impossible" (17:20). Their failures, whether walking on water or attempting a healing, make clear that Jesus' disciples possess no miraculous power in themselves; only by faith in him and by his command can they work miracles such as he did and thus proclaim God's reign and him as God's messiah.

I. Luke–Acts

Six of the miracle stories in the gospel of Mark are not included in the gospel of Luke; five of these (Mark 6:45–52; 7:24–30; 7:31–37; 8:1–10; 8:22–26) occur in Mark 6:45–8:26, the "Great Omission." Whether the evangelist did not include the cursing of the fig tree (Mark 11:12–14, 20) so as not to cast doubt on Jesus' rationality or his ethical character is unclear (see Cotter 1986; Achtemeier 1975: 548). Common to Luke and Matthew ("Q") are Luke 7:1–10 = Matt 8:5–13 and probably Luke 11:14 = Matt 12:22. Peculiar to Luke are 5:1–11; 7:11–17; 13:10–17; 14:1–6; 17:11–19; 22:50–51, and the resurrection and ascension accounts (24:13–35, 36–49, 50–53).

Among the NT gospels only the gospel of Luke has a sequel by the same author—the Acts of the Apostles—and the two writings illuminate one another, also in the miracle accounts (see Achtemeier 1975; Conzelmann 1960: 177–83; Held 1963: 277, n. 2). The characterization of Jesus in Peter's missionary sermon in Acts 2 as "a man attested to you by God in mighty works and wonders and signs" (2:22; cf. Acts 10:38) is an apt summary of the evangelist's treatment of the synoptic miracle traditions. Unlike the gospel of Mark, which has proportionately more miracle stories than either Matthew or Luke but carefully subordinates them to the passion and death, and unlike Matthew, which uses miracle accounts as vehicles for themes central to that gospel, in the gospel of Luke the focus of the miracle stories is on their evidentiary and missionary function: more than in the other gospels the miracles demonstrate that Jesus is the one anointed by God's Spirit to carry out a divine mission in fulfillment of God's promises (Luke 4:18, a quotation from Isa 61:1–2 and 58:6) both through teaching and miracles, which thus serve as the basis of faith and discipleship.

The evangelist's careful balancing of teaching and miracles, and indeed the prominence he accords miracles, are seen already in the programmatic sermon in the synagogue in Nazareth. Much longer than the parallels in Mark (6:1–6) and Matthew (13:54–58), the sermon, after announcing that Jesus will both teach and work miracles (Luke 4:18–22), refers to miracles he has already performed; the account then concludes with a miracle (4:23–30). Whereas the Markan account of the healing of a leper closes with a summary statement of Jesus' popularity (1:45), Luke explains that people come "to *hear* and to be *healed*" (5:16); similarly, Luke 6:18, "to *hear* him and to be *healed*" (Mark 3:8, people come only because they heard what Jesus "did," i.e., worked miracles); 9:11, Jesus *teaches* and *heals* (Mark 6:34, Jesus only teaches).

Luke's customarily careful treatment of synoptic traditions is evident also in the miracle stories. In the Markan account of the healing of a blind man at Jericho the man hears Jesus is coming and, though blind, comes (how?) to Jesus on his own (10:47, 50); in the Lukan version Jesus commands the blind men to be *brought* to him (18:40). In Mark 1:45 it is unclear whether it is the healed leper or Jesus who goes out and begins to "proclaim much" and "to spread the word" (of the healing? the gospel?) and is therefore unable to enter openly into a city; all of these difficulties are avoided in Luke's account (5:15). Moreover, while the Markan account may be taken to mean that the leper disobeyed Jesus' command to tell no one of his healing (1:44), Luke states that the report of the healing simply "spread" (Luke 5:15), with no indication of any involvement by the leper and thus no disobedience on his part. Similarly, in Luke 4:33–34 the demon does not speak again after Jesus has commanded it to be silent, in contrast to Mark 1:24–26; Luke is also careful to report obedience to Jesus' commands by sick persons, details lacking in Mark (contrast Luke 5:24–25, the man "went home," with Mark 2:12, no such mention; Luke 6:8, the man "stood up," with Mark 3:3, no such mention).

Prominent in the Lukan miracle accounts is a concluding acclamation: people praise God (5:26; 7:16; 9:43; 13:13; 18:43) or rejoice (13:17). This typical characteristic of miracle stories confirmed to hearers or readers of a story that a miracle had indeed occurred and commonly identified the power(s) responsible. In the gospel of Luke the acclamations affirm that God is working through Jesus, who by performing miracles is carrying out his divine mission (4:18–30). That miracles perform this evidentiary function in Luke is suggested already by the attention the author devotes to them but is also indicated further in various ways.

In contrast with the Matthean version of John the Baptist's questioning of Jesus (11:2–6), which might be seen as occasioned by miracles worked by Jesus' disciples (Matthew 10), Luke's account is preceded directly by two miracle stories (7:17), so that "all the things" John has heard about Jesus are specifically miracles. Moreover, before Jesus replies he performs many healings (7:21), thus anticipating and substantiating the reply; and he instructs John's disciples to report what they have "*seen* [i.e., miracles] and heard" (7:22), in contrast to Matthew's Jesus, who places hearing before seeing (11:4; Achtemeier 1975: 552). While the author of Luke may not have shared Philo of Alexandria's view of sight as the most superior and least deceptive of the senses (*Abr* 57, 60, 150, 153, 156, 158–62, 166; cf. his invidious comparison of Ishmael, meaning "hearing God," and Israel, "seeing God," *Fuga* 208), in this passage as well as in others in his gospel "seeing" is conspicuous. At Jesus' entry into Jerusalem his followers praise God for "all the mighty works *[dunameōn]* that they had seen" (19:37). "Blessed are the eyes that see what you see," says the Lukan Jesus (10:23), in contrast to the version of the saying recorded in Matthew, which concludes, "and your ears, for they hear" (13:16). When the risen Jesus eats a piece of fish in the presence of the disciples to demonstrate that it is indeed he, they see him do so, though Luke does not state that in so many words (24:41–43).

As was indicated above, trust in the miracle worker and/or the power(s) responsible for a miracle is the expected response to thaumaturgy. This expectation is especially evident in both Luke and Acts, where faith and discipleship often follow a miracle (Achtemeier 1975: 553–56). Whereas in Mark (1:16–20) and Matthew (4:18–22) the first disciples respond to a simple summons of Jesus, in Luke the call comes after the miraculous catch of fish (5:1–11) and after Jesus' miraculous power has been demonstrated to Peter (healing of his mother-in-law, 4:38–39, which *follows* the call in Mark and Matthew) and to readers (4:31–41). The call of Levi (5:27–28) follows immediately upon a miracle (5:17–26) whereas in Mark teaching intervenes (2:13). Only Luke states that Jesus' women disciples were persons who had been healed by him (8:2).

That Jesus is a thaumaturge in the tradition of Moses, Elijah, and Elisha—that is, that he stands in the tradition of those great Hebrew prophets, thus setting him apart from other thaumaturges of the Greco-Roman world—is suggested by the evangelist in various passages in Luke-Acts that recall or imitate traditions in the Scriptures (on such *imitatio* in Luke-Acts, see Brodie 1984). As Moses worked "signs and wonders *[terata kai semeia]*" (Acts 7:36; cf. Exod 7:9 LXX, *semeion ē teras*) and predicted that "God will raise up for you, from among your compatriots, a prophet like me" (Acts 7:37; see Deut 18:15; similarly, Acts 3:22), so Jesus was "a man attested to you by God through mighty works and wonders and signs *[dunamesi kai terasi kai sēmeiois]*" (Acts 2:22)—indeed, a man "whom God raised" (2:24). After Jesus, like Elijah, resuscitated a dead son and "gave him to his mother" (Luke 17:15 = 1 Kgs 17:32 LXX), the people exclaim that "a great prophet has been raised up among us" (Luke 17:16; cf. a similar story told of Elisha, 2 Kgs 4:18–37; on pagan parallels to the Lukan account, especially Philostratus, *VA* 4.45, see Fitzmyer *Luke 1–9* AB, 656–57). When Jesus' fellow townspeople expect him to work miracles in Nazareth such as those he had performed in Capernaum, he replies that "no prophet is accepted in his home country" (Luke 4:23–24), and by citing the examples of Elijah and Elisha and their miracles among non-Jews he implicitly compares himself to them (4:25–27). Elijah's miraculous assumption *(analēmphthē)* into heaven (2 Kgs 2:11) is echoed in the announcement at the beginning of the Lukan travel narrative, of Jesus' assumption *(analēmpsis)* (9:51; cf. Acts 1:11, Jesus "was assumed *[analēmphtheis]* into heaven"). Sometimes, however, the Lukan Jesus is dissociated from Elijah and indeed appears as his anti-type (Talbert 1984: 93–94); unlike him, Jesus refuses to call down avenging fire from heaven (Luke 9:54–55; cf. 2 Kgs 1:10, 12; contrast also Luke 9:62 and 1 Kgs 19:21), in accord with the general Lukan stress on Jesus' compassion, also present in miracle accounts (Luke 7:13; 8:52).

When Jesus summarizes his ministry in a message to Herod Antipas, it is as a prophet who works miracles and perishes as a result (13:31–33), and in mourning his death his disciples remember him as "a prophet mighty in deed and word" (24:19) who was handed over to be crucified (24:20).

It is as one empowered by the Spirit which inaugurates the various phases of his ministry in Luke (Fitzmyer *Luke 1–9* AB 227–28) that Jesus performs his miracles (4:18; Acts 10:38, "how God anointed Jesus of Nazareth with the Holy Spirit and with power, how he went about doing good and healing all who were oppressed by the devil, because God was with him"). His final words to his disciples in the gospel are a promise that he will send them what the Father has promised, namely, "power from on high" (24:49). This promise is repeated at the beginning of Acts (1:4) and fulfilled on Pentecost, when in fulfillment of prophecy (2:17, citing Joel 3:1) God's spirit is poured out upon the disciples (Acts 2:4, 33). In Luke's characteristic sequence, the bystanders "*see* [the wondrous giving of the Spirit and of tongues, 2:3–4] and hear" (2:34), and thousands come to faith (2:41). In the next chapter, Peter, calling on the name of Jesus, heals a lame man (3:1–11); Peter then addresses the astonished witnesses of the miracle, attributing it not to any power or piety of his own (3:12) but to God, who glorified his servant Jesus by raising him from the dead (3:13–15) and through faith in his name worked "what you see and hear" (3:16); then follow both hostile reaction and faith (4:1–4).

This pattern is characteristic of the miracle accounts in Acts: empowered by the Spirit (mentioned 57 times), and often in Jesus' name (see D. above, and Conzelmann 1960: 178, n. 3), his followers work miracles that continue Jesus' ministry and, alongside missionary preaching, win many times more followers than he did (e.g., 2:41; 4:4) while at the same time arousing opposition.

In addition to various summary statements of "signs" *(sēmeia)*, "wonders" *(terata)*, and "mighty works" *(dunameis)* wrought by Jesus' followers (2:43; 4:30; 5:12; 6:8; 8:6; 14:3; 15:12), Acts contains accounts or summary statements of healings and exorcisms (3:1–16; 5:16; 8:7–8, 13; 9:17–18, 33–35; 14:8–10; 16:16–18; 28:7–9; by remote means, whether through Peter's shadow [5:15] 19:11–12 or through handkerchiefs and aprons that have touched Paul [19:11–12]), as well as accounts of resurrections (9:36–42; 20:9–12), of punitive miracles (5:1–11; 9:1–9; 12:20–23; 13:6–11; 19:13–16), of miraculous liberations (5:17–25; 12:5–11; 16:23–30), of nature miracles (2:2–3; 4:31; 8:39), and of dispensations of gifts or powers exceeding normal human capabilities (2:4–6; 28:3–6).

As Peter is featured as the leading apostle in the first half of Acts, and Paul in the second half, so also the miracles attributed to each correspond closely in number and kind (Hardon 1954: 308–9); cf. Acts 2:43 and 14:3; 3:1–16 and 14:8–10; 5:1–11 and 13:6–11; 4:31 and 16:25–26; cf. also 5:15 with 19:11–12; 9:33–35 with 28:7–9; 9:36–42 with 20:9–12; 5:17–25 and 12:5–11 with 16:23–30.

The miracles cited by Jesus in reply to John the Baptist's question (Luke 7:22 = Matt 11:5) are in Acts worked by his followers as well, thus attesting that he is indeed "the one who is to come" (Luke 7:19 = Matt 11:3). Each time the Christian movement is established in a new location, moving from Jerusalem to Judea, Samaria, and "the end of the earth" (Acts 1:8), miracles are an essential element in the process, so that, finally, all opposition overcome, the reign of God and teaching about Jesus Christ are proclaimed and taught "openly and unhindered" (28:31).

J. John

The 7 miracle accounts in the Fourth Gospel are all found in chapters 1–12: (1) water into wine (2:1–11); (2) healing of an official's son (4:46–54); (3) healing of a paralytic at Bethesda (5:1–15); (4) feeding of a multitude (6:1–14); (5) walking on water (6:16–21); (6) healing of a blind man (9:1–41); and (7) resurrection of Lazarus (11:1–44). Number (1) is peculiar to John. Three are reported also in the Synoptic Gospels: numbers (2) (Matt 8:5–13 = Luke 7:1–10), (4) (Mark 6:32–44 = Matt 14:13–21 = Luke 9:10–17), and (5) (Mark 6:45–52 = Matt 14:22–33). Three are parallel in type to miracles reported in the Synoptics: numbers (3) (Mark 2:1–12 = Matt 9:1–8 = Luke 5:17–26), (6) (Mark 10:46–52 = Matt 20:29–34 = Luke 18:35–43; Matt 9:27–31), and (7) (Luke 7:11–17). That there are 7 such accounts is regarded as significant by some, but whether the evangelist did is doubtful (see, e.g., Bultmann *John* MeyerK, 112, n. 3). In addition to these longer accounts, there are (8) the brief report of the boat suddenly at land (6:21) and (9) the falling back and falling to the ground of Jesus' captors when he says, "I am he" (18:4–6), as well as summary statements that Jesus performed miracles (2:23; 3:2) and possessed praeternatural knowledge (2:25; 4:16–19, 29).

Though the number of miracles in John is fewer than in any of the Synoptic Gospels, their importance has long been recognized by scholars, even while their meaning, function, and source have been much discussed and disputed, beginning with the distinctively Johannine terminology for miracle. Aside from the word *terata,* "wonders," in the stock phrase *sēmeia kai terata* (4:48; see A.), miracles are called either *sēmeion,* "sign" (2:18; 4:54; 6:14, 30; 10:41; 12:18) and in the plural *sēmeia,* "signs" (2:11, 23; 3:2; 6:2, 26; 7:31; 9:16; 11:47; 12:37; 20:30) or, consistently in the mouth of Jesus and as a more inclusive term that can embrace Jesus' words (14:10)—or, indeed, his whole mission (17:4) as well as his miracles—*ergon,* "work" (e.g., 7:21; 10:32) and in the plural *erga,* "works" (e.g., 7:3; 9:3–4; 10:25, 32, 37–38; 14:10–12; 15:24).

The use of the distinctive term *semeion/-a* for miracle in the Fourth Gospel as well as certain clues in the narrative point to the evangelist's use of traditions, or even a collection ("signs source"), containing accounts of *semeia* (for a discussion of a "signs source" and a survey of the scholarly literature, see Fortna 1970; Nicol 1972; Martyn 1979: 164–68). See also SIGNS/SEMEIA SOURCE. Thus, the statement in 4:54 that Jesus' healing of the official's son (4:46–54) was "the *second* sign that Jesus did when he came from Judea to Galilee" (4:54)—even though 2:23 and 3:2 state that he performed many signs between the first sign (2:11), turning water into wine, and this second one—and the fact that the account of the healing begins by referring back to the water-into-wine account (4:46) and that the geographical location and the pattern of both accounts are very similar (see Brown *John 1–12* AB, 194) suggest that the healing account followed the account of the wine miracle directly in a source employed by the evangelist. The conclusion of chap. 20, that "Jesus did many other signs [. . .] that are not recorded in this book" (20:30), is inappropriate insofar as much material intervenes between this passage and the last of the signs in chap. 11; such a conclusion would be appropriate to a collection of signs, however.

As to the meaning of *semeion/-a,* the view, held by some, that because the miracles in John are designated as "signs" they are therefore somehow distinct from "miracles" (Trench 1953: 343–44; *TDNT* 7: 240, 249) is untenable (Remus 1982b: 548–50). The basic sense of *semeion* is "identifying mark" or "sign," with no necessary divine reference. Thus social convention could designate the ringing of a gong, a beacon fire, or the shadow of the pointer on a sundial as *semeia* that signify—have meaning—beyond themselves in the ordinary affairs of life; if a *semeion* was extraordinary, however, it could point to the divine as cause, i.e., be considered a miracle (both uses in Plut. *Vita Per.* 6.2–4). In the gospel of John the *semeia,* measured by common canons of the ordinary current then, are extraordinary and point beyond themselves to the divine. The identity and nature of the divine to which they point, however, is even more extraordinary: They identify Jesus as the light (8:12; 9:5; 12:46) and life (11:25; 14:6) of the world, the bread of life from heaven (6:35, 41, 48, 50, 51), and the Logos who, through the signs, reveals his glory (1:14; 2:11; 11:4), which is also the glory of God his Father (11:4; 11:40), since he and the Father are one (10:30, 38; 14:3, 10, 11, 20; 16:15, 32; 17:21) and since he does the Father's will (4:34; 5:30; 6:38) and works (*erga:* 4:34; 5:36; 9:4; 10:25, 32, 37; 14:10; 17:4).

Not surprisingly, then, the miracles evoke a variety of responses (cf. Haenchen 1962–63; Brown *John 1–12* AB, 531–32) which may reflect the evangelist's milieu as well. The responses can be listed as follows.

1. For some, Jesus' wonderworking certifies him as prophet or thaumaturge sent by God (2:11, 23; 3:2; 4:39, 45–47, 49, 53; 6:2, 14; 7:31; 11:45–48; 12:11, 18). If the gospel, even while providing an account of Jesus' earthly ministry, does so in light of the evangelist's own situation (Haenchen 1962–63: 212–14; Nicol 1972: 145–49; Martyn 1979: 29, 82–89, 129–51; Brown 1979), so that he is at the same time reflecting on reactions in his own day to proclamation of Jesus' *semeia,* then these passages point to a time in the history of the Johannine community, represented in the *sēmeia* traditions, when Jews responded positively to such proclamations and without risk of exclusion from the synagogue. Such exclusion developed later, leading to fear and secret discipleship on the part of some of the Jews who believed in Jesus because of his *semeia* (3:1–2; 9:22, 34; 12:42; 16:2–4; cf. 7:13 and 19:38; see Nicol 1972: 143–45; Martyn 1979: 37–62).

2. Whereas in category 1 the term "the Jews" is used in a neutral sense (3:1; 11:36–37, 45; 12:9), in the gospel generally "the Jews" is more often a negative term designating those Jews who are skeptical toward or reject the *sēmeia* and/or the claims Jesus makes in connection with them (2:18, 20; 5:10, 16; 6:41, 52; 9:18; 10:24–25, 31–33; 12:11). Sometimes the Jews who reject the *sēmeia* are specified further as "the Pharisees" (7:31–32, 47–48; 9:13, 15–16, 40–41; 11:46–47; 12:18–19) or "the rulers" (7:48), though the latter term more often designates persons in category 1 (3:1; 7:26, 50; 12:42). The hostility between Jesus and Jewish authorities in his day is reflected in these passages; but equally, if not more, important, they reflect antagonism between the evangelist's community and the Jews of his day (see Martyn 1979: 84–89; Brown 1979: 40–43).

3. The fact that the gospel of John includes the *sēmeia* traditions noted in category 1 indicates that the evangelist placed some value on them. Nonetheless, the Johannine Jesus is critical of response to his *sēmeia* of the kind indicated in category one. It is untrustworthy (2:24) and wrongly motivated (6:26); ultimately, it fails (12:37). But there are those who see Jesus' miracles for what they are, signs identifying him as the life and light of the world, the bread from heaven, the one sent by the Father (2:11; 6:69; 9:38; 11:41–42) to do his works (5:36; 10:25). Jesus can therefore invite belief in his works as a way to perceiving that he and the Father are one (10:38; 14:11). Jesus' miracles interpreted in this way would evoke from "the Jews" the quite understandable charge of blasphemy (10:33; cf. 5:18; 8:58–59; 19:7). Even his disciples fail to comprehend his relation to the Father (14:8), eliciting an astonished reaction from Jesus (14:9) and, later, the prediction that the faith they profess (16:30) will not stand the test (16:32)—not surprisingly, for to believe such claims requires a resocialization (Meeks 1972: 70–71); or,

in the words of the evangelist, the Spirit/Paraclete must come and bestow true understanding of Jesus and his *sēmeia* (14:16, 26; 15:26; 16:13–14). That will occur only after Jesus is no longer with his disciples (16:7; cf. 7:39).

4. Once Jesus departs to the Father, his working of signs is at an end. Except for 20:31, they are not mentioned after chap. 12. The subsequent chapters prepare for his departure and glorification on the cross, for which the *sēmeia* and the glory they revealed were a prelude. For readers of the gospel, the faith that is required and is pronounced blessed is that which does not need visible verification before believing (20:29). The account of the healing of the official's son (4:46–54), which seems to belong in part to this category (the official simply accepts Jesus' *word* that his son lives, 4:49) and in part to category 1 (he and his household believe *after* the son is healed, 4:53), points to editing of *sēmeia* traditions by the evangelist: 4:48 ("Unless you [plural] see signs and wonders you [plural] will not believe") is inappropriately addressed to the official, who believes without seeing, while the second-person plural suggests that this is a critical comment on the Galileans who welcome Jesus because they have seen all the things (i.e., the *sēmeia*) he has done in Jerusalem (4:45; see Bultmann *John* MeyerK, 204–207; Fortna 1970: 41; Nicol 1972: 28–29). At this point in the gospel, 4:48 anticipates 20:29 and a time when believing without seeing will be a necessity.

For the evangelist and his readers that time is the present, and in his gospel Jesus speaks both as the earthly ("the hour is coming") and the exalted one ("and now *is*") (4:23; 5:25). Even as the disciples after the resurrection "remember" and believe what Jesus said about the temple-body *sēmeion* (2:18–22; cf. 14:26: the Paraclete will "remind you of all that I said to you"), so in the evangelist's "now" the Spirit/Paraclete has disclosed to him what was only hinted in the words and works of the earthly Jesus and what his disciples were incapable of receiving before his exaltation (16:12).

The Johannine Jesus therefore unfolds the full, symbolic import of his *sēmeia*—their *sign*ificance. The turning of water into wine (2:1–11) symbolizes what happens in Jesus' entire ministry: the revealing of his, and his Father's, glory (2:11; 1:14). Just as no one, even his mother (2:4), can demand a *sēmeion* from him (6:30), so no one can take Jesus' life without his willing it (10:17–18)—at the proper "hour," namely, his glorification on the cross (2:4; 12:23; 17:1)—as he demonstrates through miraculous invulnerability until that hour (7:30; 8:20; 18:6).

John 6 contrasts two understandings of the *sēmion* of the loaves and fish (6:1–14; see Borgen 1965; Meeks 1972: 58–59). The literalists in the narrative desire a steady supply of food from Jesus (6:15, 26) or demand from him a *sēmeion* like the wondrous manna from heaven (6:30–31)—something not to be expected from this man of ordinary, familiar parentage (6:42). The evangelist, however, intepretes the miraculously multiplied loaves as symbolic of Jesus as the true bread from heaven, given by the Father even as the manna was (6:32–33, 41); unlike ordinary bread, which perishes (6:27), and manna, which sustained life only for a time (6:49), Jesus is the life-giving (6:33, 51) bread of life (6:35, 48), and those who eat of it will neither hunger nor thirst (6:35) and, indeed, will live forever (6:51). Work *(ergazesthe)* for such bread, says Jesus (6:27); but, in fact, one receives it—i.e., believes in Jesus as the one sent by God—as gift, i.e., a work *(ergon)* that *God* does (6:29; cf. 6:36–40, 44–45).

To the blind man who receives the gift of sight (9:17) Jesus, as a further gift, reveals his true identity. The blind man believes, and thus truly sees (9:35–38), whereas, ironically, those who have sight do not in fact see because they reject the *sēmeion* which points to Jesus as the light of the world (9:5; cf. 1:5, 9; 12:35–36, 46) and which thus brings judgment: the sightless see; whereas the seeing are sightless (9:39; cf. 12:40) and, abiding in sin (9:40–41; cf. 12:46), have incurred judgment (3:18, 36). Even as Jesus sought out the blind man after he has been put out of the synagogue (9:35), so he will find those in the evangelist's day who are expelled from the synagogue for confessing Jesus as the Christ (9:22; cf. Martyn 1979: 37–62).

The raising of Lazarus (John 11) is anticipated by the two *sēmeia* in chaps. 4 and 5, both of which demonstrate Jesus' power to give life (5:21). This final *sēmeion* abounds in typical Johannine irony that, again, plays off literal versus symbolic meaning (see Brown *John 1–12* AB, 431, 434; on Johannine irony, see Duke 1985). Jesus' delay in going to Lazarus' aid demonstrates greater love than if he had gone immediately, since Lazarus' sickness, which results in his death, is yet "not unto death" (11:1–6), for, though he will die, yet he will live when he hears Jesus' voice (11:43), even as those who, though they die (cf. 16:2) but believe in Jesus, will live (11:25). Martha takes Jesus' assertion that Lazarus will rise as a commonplace statement of Jewish belief in resurrection of the dead on the last day (11:24), not realizing he means in the present. Indeed, because Jesus is the resurrection and the life, those who live and believe in him will, unlike Lazarus, never die (11:26). Jesus' gift of life to Lazarus glorifies Jesus as a miracle-worker (11:4) but, ironically, leads to his own death (11:46–53), the "exaltation" (3:14; 8:28; 12:32–33) which is, ironically, his ultimate glorification (see Meeks 1972: 62–64). As a result, readers of the gospel, without seeing *sēmeia,* pass even now from life to life when they hear his word (5:24; cf. 3:36) or from death to life in response to his voice (5:25). Such life-giving power characterizes the "greater works *[erga]*" which the Father will show the Son (5:20–21) and which those who believe in the Son will themselves do (14:12).

K. The Letter of James

James 5:14–15 outlines a procedure for healing: the sick person calls the elders of the church who pray over the person after anointing him/her "with oil in the name of the Lord." Oil was commonly regarded as a healing and refreshing agent (Isa 1:6; Luke 10:34; Plato, *Menex.* 238A; Philo, *Somn* 2.58; Jos. *Ant* 17.172 = *JW* 1.657; Pliny, *HN* 15.19; 23.34–50; Seneca, *Ep.* 53.5; for subsequent references and the development of rites of anointing in the orthodox and Roman Catholic churches, see Mayor 1913: 170–73). However, other elements in the procedure, as well as the procedure itself, indicate that (as in Mark 6:13) more than the common medicinal powers of oil are involved here. This is a wondrous healing, and the oil is one of the means employed (on the use of material means in thaumaturgy, see D above). The praying mentioned in vv

14 and 15 stands in the tradition of prayer connected with wondrous healings (1 Kgs 17:21; 2 Kgs 4:33; Sir 38.9) or with miracles generally, examples of which are cited in 5:17–18. Whether the invocation of the name of the Lord occurs in the prayer or apart from it is unclear, but it functions to bring the power of that name to bear on the sickness (see D above); 5:15 states therefore that the *Lord* will raise up the sick person. Sin is not given as the cause of sickness here, but the long association of the two (see D above) may underlie the statement that if the sick person has sinned, it will be forgiven (5:15)—another reason for invoking the name of the Lord, for only the Lord has the authority to forgive sin and the power to overcome any demonic power associated with it.

The faith that prays for healing (5:15) is the faith of the community, including that of the sick person who has called the elders (Schlatter 1932: 280–81). The next verse specifies further the involvement of the entire community in prayer for healing (5:16a). The role played in health and healing by community belief is attested in modern anthropological and sociological studies (Cannon 1942; Lévi-Strauss 1967: 169–73; Kiev 1964: 8–11, 15, 26, etc.). In the healing ritual in James 5:14–15, the community is represented by the elders, i.e., authorities who, by reason of age or other qualifications, have been designated as leaders. They, rather than charismatics (as in 1 Cor 12:9, 28, 30), are entrusted with healing. Verses 5:14–15 represent an institutionalization of caring for the sick and healing that developed in early Christianity (in addition to the early Christian sources cited in E above, note the role of church leaders in caring for "the weak" or "the sick" *[asthenountōn]* in Acts 20:35; Polycarp, *Phil.* 6).

L. The Book of Revelation

In the Jewish apocalyptic tradition taken over by early Christians, the appearance of signs and wonders (*sēmeia kai terata;* see A above) or the working of wondrous signs *(sēmeia)* by deceivers presage the last days and the great eschatological reversal that will deliver the elect from their tribulations and punish their oppressors. In the NT this tradition of apocalyptic miracles is represented in passages such as Mark 13:22 (= Matt 24:24), 2 Thess 2:9, and several passages in the book of Revelation (Gk *apokalypsis*). The visions revealed to the seer (Revelation 1) disclose the future and proclaim that, despite appearances to the contrary, the Lord reigns supreme over all opposing forces (19:6, 15–16; 21:22). The readers and hearers of the book (1:3), who are suffering persecution (probably late in the 1st century), can take comfort in this, and, because they have been forewarned, can recognize the revelatory signs *(sēmeia)* that will precede their deliverance.

In 12:1–3 two *sēmeia* appear in the sky, one a woman in the throes of childbirth (i.e., the birth pangs of the messianic age), the other a many-headed and many-horned dragon. The woman represents light (12:1: sun, moon, stars); the dragon, i.e., Satan (12:9), representing the forces of darkness, attempts to destroy her and her child, but is prevented from doing so and departs to war on her other offspring, i.e., the followers of Jesus (12:4–17). The next chapter, veiling its references to the Roman empire and emperor worship in apocalyptic imagery, forewarns these followers that the dragon's authority will pass to certain beasts (13:2, 12), one of which will work miraculous *sēmeia* (fire from heaven and power of speech to an image) that will deceive people into worshiping the first beast (13:13–15). In 19:20 this second beast is identified as a false prophet; from its mouth, and the mouths of the dragon and the first beast (the Roman Empire), issue demonic spirits that work *sēmeia* and assemble the kings of the earth for the day of the great eschatological battle against God (16:13–14).

Prior to that day the Lord, too, has prophets endowed with miraculous powers (11:3–6) that recall miracles worked by Moses (Exod 7:17, 19) and Elijah (1 Kgs 17:1; 2 Kgs 1:10). The prophets are killed; but then, miraculously sufflated (Rev 11:11; cf. Ezek 37:5–10), they rise and are taken up into heaven (Rev 11:12; cf. 2 Kgs 2:11). Their fellow sufferers on earth can take comfort in this and await the end when the dragon, the first beast, and the false prophet will be cast into the lake of everlasting fire (Rev 19:20; 20:10) and those faithful to the Lord will worship the Lord in a new earth and heaven (Rev 21:1–22:5).

M. Trajectories

The importance of miracle in the NT writings is evident from this overview. In subsequent Christianity miracle continued to be equally if not more important.

Were the miracle accounts in the scriptures to be taken literally or nonliterally? The resurrection of Jesus and of believers, e.g., might be viewed in stark physical terms, after the pattern of John 11:1–44 or Luke 24:36–43 (cf. Celsus in Or. *Cels.* 5:14); or, following Paul's comparison of resurrection to the difference between seed and resulting plant (1 Cor 15:35ff.) or the symbolic interpretation of resurrection in John or the view that resurrection is in the present (John 5:25; 2 Tim 2:18), resurrection might be intepreted in various non-literal ways (gnostics, e.g., Basilides in Hippol. *Her.* 7.27.10; Origen, see Chadwick 1948). Literal interpretation of miracles (e.g., Marcion in the 2d century; see Harnack 1924: 66–67, 259*–60*) is outweighed by typological or allegorical intepretations (Smalley 1964) until the Reformation era, when literal interpretation is reaffirmed, posing problems that the Enlightenment struggled with, and problems that are the subject of continuing study (see Grant and Tracy 1984; Harvey 1966; Keller 1969).

At a number of places in this article reference has been made to the important place of miracles in post-NT Christianity—in mission, apologetic, and healing rituals (see D. and E.). Such activities, and the differing ways in which miracle accounts in scripture were interpreted, involved Christians in conflict with one another and with non-Christians (see C.). In the persecutions suffered by Christians, miracles came to be attributed to or associated with martyrs or their remains ("relics"), similarly, with the Christian ascetics, whose rigorous life became a new form of martyrdom. The cult of the saints, in which miracle has played such a key role, is a legacy of those periods (see P. Brown 1981; Ward 1982; Weinstein and Bell 1982). The powerful presence of Christ in sacraments, only hinted at in the NT (1 Cor 11:30; John 6:52–58), becomes evident in miracles associated not only with water or baptism (e.g., *Acts Thom.* 52; Jerome, *Life of St. Hilarion* 20; Augustine,

City of God 22.8; Gregory the Great, *Dialogues* 1.10) but also with the eucharist (e.g., *Acts Thom.* 5; Gregory, *Dialogues* 2.24).

For Christianity, as for so much of religion generally, "Miracle is faith's dearest child" (Goethe). Much of that legacy in the West is nurtured by the NT.

Bibliography

Achtemeier, P. J. 1975. The Lukan Perspective on the Miracles of Jesus. *JBL* 94: 547–62.
Betz, H. D., ed. 1985. *The Greek Magical Papyri in Translation, Including Demotic Spells.* Chicago.
Borgen, P. 1965. *Bread from Heaven.* NovTSup. Leiden.
Bornkamm, G. 1963. The Stilling of the Storm in Matthew. Pp. 52–57 in *Tradition and Interpretation in Matthew,* ed. G. Bornkamm et al. Trans. P. Scott. Philadelphia.
Brodie, T. L. 1984. Greco-Roman Imitation as a Partial Guide to Luke's Use of Sources. Pp. 17–46 in *Luke-Acts: New Perspectives from the SBL Seminar,* ed. C. H. Talbert. New York.
Brown, P. 1981. *The Cult of the Saints.* Chicago.
Brown, R. 1977. *The Birth of the Messiah.* Garden City, NY.
———. 1979. *The Community of the Beloved Disciple.* New York.
Bultmann, R. 1963. *History of the Synoptic Tradition.* Trans. J. Marsh. New York.
Cannon, W. B. 1942. Voodoo Death. *American Anthropologist* 44: 169–81.
Cartlidge, D. R., and Dungan, D. L. 1980. *Documents for the Study of the Gospels.* Cleveland.
Chadwick, H. 1948. Origen, Celsus, and the Resurrection of the Body. *HTR* 41: 83–102.
Cotter, W. 1986. "For It Was Not the Season for Figs." *CBQ* 48: 62–66.
Conzelmann, H. 1960. *The Theology of St. Luke.* Trans. G. Buswell. London.
Dibelius, M. 1935. *From Tradition to Gospel.* Trans. B. L. Woolf. New York.
Dölger, F. J. 1950. Der Heiland. Pp. 241–72 in *Antike und Christentum.* Ed. F. Dölger. Münster.
Duke, P. D. 1985. *Irony in the Fourth Gospel.* Atlanta.
Edelstein, E. J., and L. 1945. *Asclepius.* 2 vols. Baltimore.
Fortna, R. T. 1970. *The Gospel of Signs.* Cambridge.
Gager, J. G. 1972. *Moses in Greco-Roman Paganism.* SBLMS 16. Nashville.
Grant, R. M. 1952. *Miracle and Natural Law in Graeco-Roman and Early Christian Thought.* Amsterdam.
———. 1966. *Gnosticism and Early Christianity.* 2d ed. New York.
Grant, R. M. and Tracy, D. 1984. *A Short History of the Interpretation of the Bible.* 2d ed. Philadelphia.
Haenchen, E. 1962–63. "Der Vater, der mich gesandt hat." *NTS* 9: 208–16.
Hardon, J. A. 1954. The Miracle Narratives in the Acts of the Apostles. *CBQ* 16: 303–19.
Harnack, A. von. 1924. *Marcion: Das Evangelium vom fremden Gott.* Leipzig.
Harvey, V. A. 1966. *The Historian and the Believer.* New York.
Held, J. H. 1963. Matthew as Interpreter of the Miracle Stories. Pp. 165–299 in *Tradition and Interpretation in Matthew,* ed. G. Bornkamm et al. Trans. P. Scott. Philadelphia.
Higgins, A. J. B. 1964. *Jesus and the Son of Man.* Philadelphia.
Jacobs, H. B. 1962. Oral Roberts: High Priest of Faith Healing. *Harper's Magazine* 224 (February): 37–43.
Kelber, W. H., ed. 1976. *The Passion in Mark: Studies in Mark 14–16.* Philadelphia.
Keller, E., and M.-L. 1969. *Miracles in Dispute.* Trans. M. Kohl. Philadelphia.
Kiev, A. ed. 1964. *Magic, Faith, and Healing.* New York.
Lévi-Strauss, C. 1967. *Structural Anthropology.* Trans. C. Jacobsen and B. G. Schoepf. Garden City, NY.
Martyn, J. L. 1979. *History and Theology in the Fourth Gospel.* 2d ed. rev. and enl. Nashville.
Mayor, J. B. 1913. *The Epistle of St. James.* London.
Meeks, W. A. 1972. The Man from Heaven in Johannine Sectarianism. *JBL* 19: 44–72.
Moule, C. F. D. 1965. The Vocabulary of Miracle. Pp. 235–38 in *Miracles: Cambridge Studies in Their Philosophy and History,* ed. C. F. D. Moule. London.
Nicol, W. 1972. *The Sēmeia in the Fourth Gospel.* NovTSup 32. Leiden.
Nilsson, M. P. 1948a. *Greek Piety.* Trans. H. J. Rose. Oxford.
———. 1948b. *Die Religion in den griechischen Zauberpapyri.* Bulletin de la Société Royale des Lettres de Lund 2. Lund.
Perrin, N. 1971. Towards An Interpretation of the Gospel of Mark. Pp. 1–78 in *Christology and a Modern Pilgrimage,* ed. H. D. Betz. Claremont.
Peterson, E. 1926. *Eis Theos: Epigraphische, formgeschichtliche und religionsgeschichtliche Untersuchungen.* FRLANT n.s. 24. Göttingen.
Preisendanz, K., ed. and trans. 1974. *Papyri Graecae Magicae.* 2d rev. ed. by A. Henrichs, K. Preisendanz, and E. Heitsch. Stuttgart.
Remus, H. 1982a. "Magic or Miracle"? Some Second-Century Instances. *Second Cent* 2: 127–56.
———. 1982b. Does Terminology Distinguish Early Christian from Pagan Miracles? *JBL* 101: 531–51.
———. 1983. *Pagan-Christian Conflict Over Miracle in the Second Century.* Patristic Monograph Series 10. Cambridge, MA.
———. 1984. Authority, Consent, Law: *Nomos, Physis,* and the Striving for a "Given." *SR* 13: 5–18.
Rengstorf, K. H. 1953. *Die Anfänge der Auseinandersetzung zwischen Christusglaube und Asklepiosfrömmigkeit.* Münster.
Rhoads, D., and Michie, D. 1982. *Mark as Story.* Philadelphia.
Schlatter, A. 1932. *Der Brief des Jakobus.* Stuttgart.
Smalley, B. 1964. *The Study of the Bible in the Middle Ages.* Notre Dame.
Stein, R. H. 1985. *Difficult Sayings in the Gospels.* Grand Rapids.
Talbert, C. H. 1984. Promise and Fulfillment in Lucan Theology. Pp. 91–103 in *Luke-Acts: New Perspectives from the SBL Seminar,* ed. C. H. Talbert. New York.
Taylor, V. 1935. *The Formation of the Gospel Tradition.* 2d ed. London.
Trench, R. C. 1953. *Synonyms of the New Testament.* Grand Rapids.
Vielhauer, P. 1965. Gottesreich und Menschensohn in der Verkündigung Jesu. Pp. 55–91 in Vielhauer. *Aufsätze zum Neuen Testament.* Munich.
Ward, B. 1982. *Miracles and the Medieval Mind.* Philadelphia.
Weinstein, D. and Bell, R. M. 1982. *Saints and Society.* Chicago.

HAROLD E. REMUS

MIRIAM (PERSON) [Heb *miryām*]. **1.** A woman in Israel's wilderness community who exercised religious leadership alongside Moses and Aaron (Mic 6:4). Introduced as prophetess and Aaron's sister, Miriam led the women in the celebration at the Sea (Exod 15:20–21) and joined Aaron in a rebellion against Moses, for which she was punished with leprosy (Num 12:1–15; cf. Deut 24:9). The Levitical genealogies of Num 26:59 and 1 Chr 5:29—Eng 6:3 list her as sister of Aaron and Moses. According to Num 20:1, she died and was buried at Kadesh. The prophet Micah (6:4) regards her as a divinely commissioned leader alongside Moses and Aaron during the wilderness journey.

The seven texts which mention Miriam by name (cf. Exod 2:1–10) bear repeated testimony to her leadership role in the wilderness community. Exod 15:20–21 is generally regarded as the earliest account of the Israelites' celebration of the event at the sea. It is striking that the earliest tradition portrays Miriam, not Moses, as the first to articulate, through ritual song and dance, the religious dimension of Israel's foundational event.

In Num 12:1–15 different layers of tradition present Miriam and Aaron raising controversies with Moses regarding his Cushite wife and his authority in rendering God's word. The latter controversy clearly reflects a crisis of religious leadership. The account seeks to establish the primacy of Moses as God's spokesperson, but in doing so it does not negate the authenticity of Miriam and Aaron as mediators of God's word. Although the background of the Cushite wife controversy is unknown, the use of the feminine singular Hebrew verb in 12:1 suggests that some level of tradition viewed Miriam alone as confronting Moses on the matter. Comparison with other controversy stories in the wilderness narratives suggests that Moses' leadership is at the heart of the Cushite issue and that in presenting the problem, Miriam voiced a matter of community concern (see Burns 1987: 68–71).

While several scholars cite the prophetess designation in Exod 15:20 as a basis for interpreting Miriam's role in the dispute over oracular authority in Num 12:2–9 as a prophetic one, Burns (1987: 48–67) has argued that the controversy of Num 12:2–9 reflects struggles between priestly, not prophetic groups. If that view is correct, Numbers 12 does not contribute to the portrait of Miriam as prophetess. Unlike Deborah and Huldah, no characteristic prophetic activity is attributed to Miriam in the biblical texts. Thus, the prophetess designation in Exod 15:20 may well be an anachronism.

There is little doubt that the view of Miriam as sister of Moses and Aaron is the product of a long history of tradition. The three leaders are presented together without kinship terminology in Numbers 12 and Mic 6:4. The designation of Miriam as Aaron's sister in Exod 15:20 may be an attempt by a late priestly writer/editor to relate this early cult leader to Aaron. From there it was a small step to include her in the Levitical genealogies of Num 26:59 and 1 Chr 5:29—Eng 6:3. Contemporary scholarship suggests that biblical genealogies reflect much more about functional relationships than actual biological ties (see especially Wilson *GHBW*). Thus, in linking Miriam with Moses and Aaron, late priestly genealogists offer much the same view of Miriam as do Numbers 12 and Mic 6:4, that is, as a religious leader alongside Aaron and Moses. The record of Miriam's death and burial at Kadesh has a similar function insofar as the deaths of the three wilderness leaders are artificially constructed in such a way as to coincide with the last three stops on the wilderness journey.

In presenting Miriam, biblical writers from earliest to latest periods of composition offer only glimpses of a woman in the wilderness community who exercised leadership in the cultic sphere and who claimed authority as a spokesperson for the Divinity. Martin Noth (*HPT,* 182) was undoubtedly correct in saying that "at one time much more was told about her which is now completely lost."

2. A Calebite relative of Ezrah (1 Chr 4:17). The writer of 1 Chr 4:15–23 includes Miriam in an early list of Calebites. The text of v 17, in which the name appears, is difficult. In the MT the verse begins with a list of the four children of Ezrah and then continues, "and she conceived Miriam" and two others. The RSV (following the LXX in part) transposes Mered and Bithiah, the pharaoh's daughter, from v 18 of the MT to v 17, thus presenting them as Miriam's parents.

Bibliography

Burns, R. J. 1987. *Has the Lord Indeed Spoken Only through Moses?* SBLDS 84. Atlanta.

Görg, M. 1979. Mirjam: ein weiter Versuch. *BZ* 23: 285–89.

Trible, P. 1989. Bringing Miriam Out of the Shadows. *BRev* 5: 14–24, 34.

RITA J. BURNS

MIRMAH (PERSON) [Heb *mirmâ*]. Benjaminite who appears in an extended genealogy of Benjamin (1 Chr 8:1–40). Mirmah is one of the seven sons of Shaharaim by his wife, Hodesh (1 Chr 8:10). The name means "deceit" and is found nowhere else in the MT nor in the Apocrypha and deuterocanonical literature. 1 Chr 8:8 indicates that Shararaim had already divorced Hushim and Baara and was living in Moab. Rudolph (*Chronikbücher* HAT, 77) sees the structure of this extended genealogy lying in the geographical breaks showing parallel lists of Benjaminite families and their dwelling locations at a given time, probably either Josiah's reign or the postexilic period. Williamson (*Chronicles* NCBC, 82) sees no structure whatever in the genealogy. However, there is an obvious connection between the family of Mirmah and Moab. This connection seems to hearken back to a time when Moab had not yet achieved independence from Israel (Myers *1 Chronicles* AB, 60; Braun *1 Chronicles* WBC, 128). Mirmah is referred to as one of the *roʾšê ʾābôt* or "heads of a family."

G. EDWIN HARMON

MISHAEL (PERSON) [Heb *mîšāʾēl*]. Var. MESHACH. Three individuals in the Hebrew Bible bear this name.

1. A Levite in the line of Kohath, son of Uzziel, and cousin of Aaron (Exod 6:22). When Nadab and Abihu, Aaron's sons, were killed for presenting unauthorized offerings, Moses instructed Mishael and his brother Elzaphan to remove their bodies from the camp (Lev 10:4).

2. One of the men who stood on Ezra's left hand during the great public reading of the law (Neh 8:4; 1 Esdr 9:44). Not designated as a Levite, Mishael's position on this occasion suggests that he was possibly an influential or representative member of the Israelite community.

3. One of Daniel's three companions who were among those selected by Nebuchadnezzar to receive special training (Dan 1:6). Surnamed Meshach by the Babylonians (Dan 1:7), Mishael joined Daniel and his friends in rejecting the king's rich food in favor of a simple Hebrew diet (Dan 1:8–21). He also provided prayer support when Daniel faced the challenge of recounting and interpreting Nebuchadnezzar's dream (Dan 2:17). As a result of the accurate narrative and his friendship with Daniel, Mishael ("Meshach") was promoted to a leadership position over the province of Babylon (Dan 2:49).

In a separate story, Mishael ("Meshach") and his companions were thrown into a fiery furnace because of their refusal to bow down to a statue erected by Nebuchadnezzar (Dan 3:8–30). In light of this remarkable stand of faith, Mishael came to serve as an example to the threatened Palestinian Jewish community during the first two centuries B.C.E. of trust in God and subsequent deliverance (1 Macc 2:59; Pr Azar 66; *4 Macc.* 16:3, 21; 18:12).

The Hebrew name "Mishael" *(mîšāʾēl)* possibly means "Who is what God is?" Similarly, the Babylonian surname Meshach *(mêšak)* has been arguably associated with the Akk *Mišaaku,* meaning "Who is what (the god) Aku is?" (*IDB* 4: 302). Some have suggested that the etymological difficulties surrounding *mêšak* may indicate an intentional alteration of the original form in order to blur an undesirable connection with a foreign god (Montgomery *Daniel* ICC, 129–30).

TERRY L. BRENSINGER

MISHAL (PLACE) [Heb *mišʾāl*]. Var. MASHAL. One of the cities assigned to the tribe of Asher (Josh 19:25–26). Mishal is also designated as one of the four cities in Asher's territory which are to be set aside for the Levitical tribe of Gershom (Josh 21:30; 1 Chr 6:59 [—Eng 6:74] where the variant Mashal is found).

Mishal is mentioned in Egyptian literature as *m-s-i-r,* "r" being an Egyptian equivalent for the "l" which did not occur in that language. The name is found in the Execration Texts from the 19th century B.C. (Aharoni *LBHG* [1967 ed.], 133) as well as in the accounts of the military campaigns of Thutmose III (ca. 1490–1436 B.C.; *ANET,* 243). Mishal is listed there with other sites from the plain of Acco, suggesting that it is the same as the city of Asher (M.R. 164253; Aharoni *LBHG* [1967 ed.], 381; Kallai *HGB,* 207, 429).

DAVID W. BAKER

MISHAM (PERSON) [Heb *mišʿām*]. A Benjaminite, son of Elpaal, one of those who helped build Ono and Lod (1 Chr 8:12). The origin and provenance of "Misham" is unknown. Noth *(IPN,* 251) compared it to the Ar *misʿāmun,* meaning "rapidly flowing (from a river)." Curtis and Madsen (*Chronicles* ICC, 160), noting the uniqueness of the name, suggested that v 12a, which lists the sons of Elpaal, is a transcriber's blunder since Elpaal's sons are also listed in vv 17–18. If the sons of Elpaal—Eber, Misham, and Shemed—were deleted from v 12a this would make Elpaal the *one* who built the towns of Ono and Lod. Misham could then be identified with the more common Meshullam (v 17).

TOM WAYNE WILLETT

MISHMA (PERSON) [Heb *mišmāʿ*]. **1.** A son of Ishmael, and brother of Mibsam (Gen 25:13; 1 Chr 1:29). **2.** A son of Mibsam son of Shallum, son of Shaul, son of Simeon (1 Chr 4:25). One may conclude from the fact that Mishma and Mibsam occur together both in Genesis 25 and 1 Chronicles 4 that 1 Chr 4:25 testifies to the settlement of these 2 Ishmaelite tribes or clans, wholly or in part, in the Negeb during the exilic and/or postexilic period. See also MIBSAM.

Heb *mišmāʿ* means "hearing"; a verbal noun like this does not easily form a tribal name. If one disregards the Masoretic vowel pattern (which may be borrowed from Mibsam, since both names seem to occur as a fixed formula), the name can be explained as **Mušāmiʿ,* derived from **Šamaʿīl* and denoting "those who have joined (the tribe of) *Šamaʿīl*". Similarly, in the recent past the Âl Nebhân were also called Menâbhe, and the tribe of Amīr in pre-Islamic Nagran were joined by the people of Muhaʾmir (Knauf 1989: 69, and n. 342). In this case, the tribe Mishma can be identified with the *Isammeʿ* (*I-sa-am-me-ʾ,* i.e. *y(ĕ)šamiʿ* for ancient Ar *yušāmiʿ,* the imperfect form corresponding to *Mušāmiʿ*), an Arab group encountered by Ashurbanipal (Knauf 1989: 9, n. 40).

Bibliography

Knauf, E. A. 1989. *Ismael.* 2d ed. ADPV. Wiesbaden.

ERNST AXEL KNAUF

MISHMANNAH (PERSON) [Heb *mišmannâ*]. One of the eleven warriors from the tribe of Gad who joined David at his wilderness stronghold (1 Chr 12:14—Eng 12:13). For further discussion, see MACHBANNAI.

RAYMOND B. DILLARD

MISHNAH. An early 3d-century C.E. compendium, largely legal, containing regulations and beliefs foundational of rabbinic Judaism and thus of all later Jewish thought.

A. Language and Date
B. Origin and Redaction
C. The Mishnaic System
D. Content
E. Context

A. Language and Date

Written in terse Hebrew, the Mishnah builds upon the Hebrew Bible in its attention to the latter's legal materials and language (lexicon and morphology) (Segal 1958: 5–12; 150). Nonetheless, the text stands quite independent of biblical antecedents, developing autonomous areas of interest that it expresses through very few, tightly controlled rhetorical patterns (Neusner 1981: 243–48).

The Mishnah attributes its materials to about 150 authorities, who flourished in the three-century period from ca. 50 B.C.E. to 200 C.E. (fewer than 80 authorities are cited with any frequency). These teachers, usually given the title "rabbi," appear in the Mishnah regularly grouped into roughly three consistories: (1) teachers who flourished before Rome's destruction of the Second Temple in 70 C.E.

(the Pharisaic period), (2) those who taught after that first war against Rome but before the Bar Kokhba revolt in 132–35 C.E. (the Yavnean period), and (3) authorities living in the period from the Bar Kokhba revolt to the Mishnah's reduction to writing *ca.* 200 C.E. (the Ushan period) (see Danby 1977: 799–800).

B. Origin and Redaction

Jewish theology, especially from the Babylonian Talmud (5th–6th centuries C.E.) on, accords the Mishnah the status of *Oral Torah.* Deemed part of the dual revelation to Moses on Sinai, the Mishnah is thought to contain authoritative and binding explanations of the Hebrew Bible. The Mishnah thus serves as complement and supplement to the *Written Torah's* otherwise sketchy legal materials, found in the Covenant, Holiness, and Deuteronomic Codes.

This theological viewpoint, that the Mishnah has the full status of Sinaitic revelation, has sharply influenced subsequent historical judgments about the text. Until recently, scholars held that early rabbinic teaching contained a more or less accurate record of oral judgments handed down over many centuries (see e.g., Albeck 1979: 24–39). These particular statements of the oral law were collected into many and varied editions (scholars termed such supposed collections "Rabbi So-and-so's Mishnah"), each a partial legal record of actual Judaic practice near the turn of the millennium (Epstein 1979: 96–199).

In line with a new literary theory (Neusner 1981: 281–83) scholars now view the Mishnah not as a mere legal register. Rather, the Mishnah comprises a set of extended essays that frame critical topics (the nature of sacred time and space, for example) in particular formulary patterns, so as to argue in behalf of the rabbinic world view (Neusner 1981: 122–26). The Mishnah—and the rabbinic movement for which it serves as constitution—constitute the direct *literary* response to nearly 3 centuries of Roman occupation of the Jews' homeland. This theory allows readers to understand how the text speaks far beyond the mere details of its sometimes picayune rules, addressing directly the imperial context.

Jewish reaction to Roman rule is first evident in several messianic movements, including earliest Christianity and the Essene community at Qumran, but especially in renewed nationalism surrounding the appointment of Bar Kokhba as messianic general. But after two unsuccessful wars against Rome, including the defeat of Messiah Bar Kokhba's army, a communal sense of failure, powerlessness, and disappointment took hold, especially in the mid-2d century. In response, the rabbis composed a holy book, the Mishnah, that reflects upon—and overcomes—Israel's current oppressed situation (Neusner 1981: 282–83).

C. The Mishnaic System

In adducing various topics, the Mishnah divides life into its component parts as the rabbis themselves saw things. These parts constitute a theological network representing three major interests: *priestly* attention to holiness, *scribal* concerns for the correspondence of word and act, and ordinary *householders'* regard for daily conduct.

The Mishnaic system built of these parts is comprehensive, in that virtually any part of early rabbinism fits within; the system is thoroughly interconnected, for to understand any single paragraph or chapter, one needs to know a myriad of others; and the system is elegantly rigorous, because the Mishnah carefully combines formulaic patterns and themes to emphasize the detailed rules under discussion. This book, which constituted Judaism's primary first-order systematics, thus may be described as a sustained, rational discourse on a set of intellectual categories and problems, which establishes a comprehensive framework for the religion.

It should now be clear that the Mishnah's topics do not merely represent everything in Scripture; the Mishnah often reads the Hebrew Bible in quite unpredictable ways, sometimes even ignoring basic scriptural conceptions. For example, one of the Mishnah's crucial concerns is to establish the correspondence of a householder's actions and intentions. Earlier biblical materials ruled that anything placed upon the altar immediately became sanctified (e.g., Exod 29:37). The Mishnah, for its part, held that only items offered with the priest's proper intention take on consecrated status (Eilberg-Schwartz 1986: 149–63). In like fashion throughout the Mishnah, the major ideas expressed, building upon but not limited to the scriptural account, are those of the rabbinic movement. So too the Mishnah's interests do not reflect real legislative settings alone. At least two-thirds of the Mishnaic law addressed the Temple and its regular maintenance—a full 130 years after the Temple had been destroyed.

D. Content

The rabbis' theological program—neither wholly fundamentalistic nor solely determined by legislative needs—emerges clearly from an analysis of the categories utilized by the Mishnah's composers and redactors. The Mishnah comprises six major sections, subdivided into sixty-three individual tractates ranging from three to twenty-four chapters and raising the following questions.

1. The Divison of Agriculture *(zĕrāʿîm).* How does God's ownership of the Land of Israel affect Israelites' use of that Land and its produce?

2. The Division of Appointed Times *(môʿēd).* How does God's interaction with Israel in history serve to orient the calendar, marking out special times requiring special actions by Israelites?

3. The Division of Women *(nāšîm).* How does the special sanctity demanded of Israelites by God affect their relationships within the family unit, and especially with women?

4. The Division of Damages *(nĕzîqîn).* How does the unity and equality of God's holy people Israel demand special action in business, government, and day-to-day dealings?

5. The Division of Holy Things *(qodāšîm).* How does the worship of God demand special action in the Temple, God's holy locus?

6. The Division of Purities *(ṭohărôt).* How does extending the holiness required in God's Temple to everyday life demand special attention to all aspects of life vis à vis cultic purity?

Although compiled after the Temple's destruction, the Mishnah's clear aim is to establish continuity with that institution and its rite. The consequent need for holiness expressed within each division stems from the particularity of God's relationship with Israel. The Mishnah as a whole thus puts forward larger questions: What must a Jew do to reflect the special relationship between self and God? How does one cooperate in God's overall scheme? The answers lead us to the details of rabbinic law, expressed in the individual rulings and disputes that make up the Mishnah's bulk.

More central to understanding the Mishnah's importance as a cultural artifact are the basic assumptions of the system, not only as a whole, but in each of its parts as well: (1) God owns the Holy Land [*Division of Agriculture*] and (2) gives it to the people with whom he has had a long-standing historical relationship [*Division of Appointed Times*], namely Israel (hence the appropriate Judaic idiom, the Land of Israel). (3) The Israelites owe God and his appointed representatives payment for their use of the Land [*Divisions of Agriculture and Holy Things*], in addition to (4) special actions in response to history [*Division of Appointed Times*]. (5) The holiness required in God's worship must also inform mundane activity [*Division of Purities*], extending to both levels of the Israelite clan: (6) one's own immediate family [*Division of Women*] and (7) the larger family of the Children of Israel [*Division of Damages*].

E. Context

In its details and emphases, then, the Mishnah attended to recent history. Long-standing Roman domination over the Land of Israel conditioned the Mishnah's assertion that God alone rules sovereign over the Land and history. Under Roman imperial rule, the rabbis erected a framework of thought and practice on which to build Judaism's future.

So it is that the early rabbinic cultural system, embedded in the details of the Mishnah's rules, set the agenda for later rabbinic thought. It was complemented by other works, notably the Tosefta (a one-generation-later supplement of similar type), as well as Midrashic literature, much of which aims at connecting the legal traditions explicitly with the Hebrew Bible and its concerns. In even closer fashion, the Mishnah provided the starting point for the two Talmuds, which at least formally constitute paragraph-by-paragraph commentaries on it. Similarly, Jewish literature up to our own day deals largely with the topical program first introduced by the Mishnah.

Bibliography

Albeck, Ḥ. 1978. *The Six Divisions of the Mishnah.* 6 vols. 4th ed. Jerusalem (in Hebrew).
———. 1979. *Introduction to the Mishnah.* 5th ed. Jerusalem.
Cohen, S. J. D. 1987. *From the Maccabees to the Mishnah.* Library of Early Christianity 7. Philadelphia.
Danby, H. 1977. *The Mishnah: Translated from the Hebrew with Introduction and Brief Explanatory Notes.* Oxford.
Eilberg-Schwartz, H. 1986. *The Human Will in Judaism.* BJS 103. Atlanta.
Epstein, J. N. 1979. *Introduction to Tannaitic Literature.* Ed. E. Z. Melamed. Jerusalem.
Neusner, J. 1981. *Judaism: The Evidence of the Mishnah.* Chicago.
———. 1988. *The Mishnah: A New Translation.* New Haven.
Segal, M. H. 1958. *A Grammar of Mishnaic Hebrew.* London.
Strack, H. L. 1982. *Einleitung in Talmud und Midrasch.* Rev. and ed. by G. Stemberger. Munich.

Roger Brooks

MISHRAITES [Heb *mišrāʿî*]. Members of one of the clans from Kiriath-jearim on the N border of Judah (1 Chr 2:53). This family of Judahites was one of the groups from which the Zorathites and Eshtaolites came. (Zorah and Eshtaol are listed together in Josh 19:41 among the first cities of the Danites before their migration to the N.) The Mishraites apparently descended from Shobal, the grandson of Caleb, who in turn was the great-grandson of Judah, son of Jacob. This, however, is not clear since, instead of being the physical ancestor of the inhabitants of Kiriath-jearim, Shobal may have been the founder of the city. All the clans in 1 Chr 2:50–55 originated in the S, and all were in close relation to Judah. It is widely held that these lists in their geographical arrangement reflect ancient sources (Coggins *Chronicles* CBC, 22). The form *mišrāʿî* is an adjective from *mišrāʿ*, the name of an unknown person. In the Babylonian vocalization the first vowel shows up as *a* and not as *i*, which is the case in the Tiberian system (Kahle 1902: 70).

Bibliography

Kahle, P. 1902. *Der masoretische Text des Alten Testaments.* Leipzig.

Edwin C. Hostetter

MISPAR (PERSON) [Heb *mispār*]. Var. MISPERETH. One of the leaders of the group of returnees from Babylonian exile who is listed along with Zerubbabel in Ezra 2:2 [= Neh 7:7 = 1 Esdr 5:8]. Nehemiah, supported by 1 Esdras, gives the name as Mispereth. One name has apparently been dropped from the Ezra list, for those in Nehemiah and 1 Esdras include twelve leaders in what is probably a symbolic representation of all Israel. For further discussion concerning the list in Ezra 2, see AKKUB.

Chaney R. Bergdall

MISREPHOTH-MAIM (PLACE) [Heb *miśrep̄ot māyim*]. A place in the S border of Sidon. It is also used as a parallelism for the S boundary of Sidon (Josh 11:8). Being located on the border, there is a tradition of regarding it as a frontier city. Though its exact location is disputed, it is thought to be at the N end of the Plain of Acco on the Israel-Lebanon border, and generally identified with Khirbet Musheirefeh. In view of a lack of sufficient archaeological evidence, either from the LB Age or early Iron Age, some have doubted the above identification. It should be noted that Mahalab reckoned to Asher (Josh 19:29) in the northernmost area is located S of the Litani river and the land that remained to be possessed began at Misrephoth-maim (Josh 13:1–6), which must have been a natural border. The fact that the Litani river is mentioned nowhere in the Bible makes one wonder if by Misrephoth-maim the Litani is actually meant. Another feature of this place-name is that the second part of the name can be vocalized *miyyam* to mean "on the west." It is probable that *mym* is intended to express both meanings. Misrephoth-maim is referred to in the book of Joshua as the border of the territory of the Sidonians (Josh 13:6) and as the S border of the hill country of Lebanon, the inhabitants of which the Lord undertakes to drive out. Hence, it has a significant function in the Deuteronomistic History (see Judg 3:3f; 10:6; and 1 Kings 5:6).

Paul Benjamin

MITANNI. A confederation of HURRIAN states located in N Mesopotamia and Syria in the second half of the 2d millennium B.C. Its capital was Wašukanni, perhaps near the head of the Habur River at Tell Fakhariyah. The circumstances surrounding the formation of Mitanni and its early history are unknown. However, Mitanni became the most powerful state in Mesopotamia and Syria during the Amarna period and survived in substantially reduced form into the reign of Shalmaneser I of Assyria (1274–1245 B.C.).

Like much concerning the Hurrians and their history, Mitanni is known primarily from sources stemming from Egypt, Syria, the Hittites, and Mesopotamia. Furthermore, the chronology of Mitanni is fraught with difficulties. The fragmentary information about Mitanni's history must be correlated with the chronologies of a number of nations, some of which are themselves imprecise.

One important issue encountered in discussing Mitanni is that a number of terms was used to describe it. The term "Mitanni" was essentially a political term used to define the confederation of Hurrian states and their vassal states. Hanigalbat was an Assyrian geographical term applied to the lands of northern Mesopotamia in which Mitanni was located. Hurruhe was a Hurrian term referring to the "Hurrian land," apparently located in the northern part of Mitanni. It also seems to have described a separate kingdom within Mitanni, perhaps the earliest Hurrian state. Nahrina/Nahrima/ Aram Naharaim were Canaanite, Egyptian, and Aramaean terms meaning "Land of the two rivers," also describing generally the region in which Mitanni was located. Khor/Khurri were the terms used by the Egyptians for Syria-Palestine because of the Hurrian population they encountered primarily in Syria (Gelb 1944).

At certain times in Mitannian history, all of these terms designated the same entity. Mitanni, the political body, was constantly changing, though, as vassals changed allegiances or were conquered. Hurruhe became an independent state in the later period of Mitannian history. The geographical terminology employed by the Assyrians and western groups remained in use after Mitanni fell, and the ethnic terminology of the Egyptians (Khor/Khurri) rapidly came to mean simply "The North." Thus, the sources must be approached cautiously where these designations are employed.

A. Ethnic Identity of Mitanni

Mitanni was essentially Hurrian, though there is evidence for a small Indo-Aryan element among the population. This group has been credited with the transformation of the scattered Hurrian states before c. 1550 B.C. into Mitanni, but this remains an open question. The language of Mitanni was Hurrian, not "Mitannian" as was initially believed (Gelb 1944). Moreover, the dialect of Hurrian in use in Mitanni is grouped with that of Kizzuwadna (Cilicia) and Ugarit (Diakonoff *SCCNH* 1: 77–90).

As Mitanni expanded, West Semitic–speaking peoples in the Syrian city-states and Assyrians came under Mitannian sway. In the vassal states in the west there were certainly people knowledgeable in Egyptian if not Egyptians, and in the east people with Babylonian names are attested within Mitannian territory. In Mitanni's later years, Hittites also were present in states that were under Mitannian control at times.

B. History of Mitanni

The first known ruler of Mitanni was one Kirta, father of Šuttarna I. These names appear on a seal at Alalakh belonging to Saustatar, a later Mitannian ruler (Goetze 1957; Wiseman 1953; Albright *YGC*). It may have been Šuttarna I who launched Mitanni on its period of expansion (Drower *CAH* 10: 417–525), for the next king, Parattarna, is attested at both Alalakh and Kizzuwadna (Wiseman 1953; Goetze 1957), to the west of Mitanni proper. Moreover, the next king, Saustatar, ruled not only Alalakh and Kizzuwadna, but also Assyria and Nuzi in the land of Arraphe (Smith 1940; Goetze 1957; Wiseman 1953; Starr 1937–39; Gelb 1944). This Saustatar is called "son of Parsatatar" on his seal inscription at Nuzi (*HSS* 9.1). Possibly Parsatatar and Paratarna are the same individual (Starr 1937–39).

At this juncture in Mitannian history the chronology is most unclear. The major question is: How did Mitanni's expansion relate to the campaigns of Tutmosis I (1525–c.1512 B.C.), Tutmosis III (1504–1450 B.C.), and Amonhotep II (1450–1425 B.C.) of Egypt, all of whom are known to have operated up to the Euphrates and taken *mariyannu* as prisoners? At present, it appears that Paratarna and Saustatar predate Tutmosis III and that it was the confederation they created that opposed Egypt during that pharaoh's reign (Redford 1979).

Traditionally, a major source used for reconstructing the chronology of this period is the Inscription of Idrimi of Alalakh, an "autobiographical" account of his exploits to gain the throne of Alalakh and his reign. This inscription provides names of his contemporaries and the length of his reign. However, the validity of this text as a true autobiography has been called into question. Instead, it may have been a "pseudo-autobiography" written at a later date and containing more legend than fact (Sasson *SCCNH* 1: 309–24). Therefore, the entire issue of the dates of Paratarna and Saustatar must remain open.

Another issue to be considered is the nature of Mitannian rule. Each of the states known to have been vassal to Mitanni had its own king bound to Mitanni by a vassal treaty sworn by oath and sanctified by sacrifice. The kings governed the internal matters of their realms and could make treaties with other states vassal to Mitanni, as Alalakh and Kizzuwadna did. There is evidence from NUZI, however, that the Mitannian king had some control over the distribution of real estate within the vassal states (*HSS* 9.1). In disputes between vassal states the king of Mitanni was the arbiter as he was in any cross-jurisdictional matter (Drower *CAH* 10: 417–525). In part because they were so loosely organized, these vassal states shifted allegiance readily in the face of danger. Thus, even the notion of a monumental Mitannian empire may be simply an impression created by the surviving documents.

After Saustatar, the Mitannian kings are known primarily through Egyptian sources. Relations were tense between the two nations until the time of Tutmosis IV (1425–1417 B.C.) when Artatarma I sent his daughter to Egypt to be the wife of the Egyptian pharaoh. This is the first instance of diplomatic marriage between the two states, a certain sign of warming relations. At the same time, Mitanni was smaller than it had been. Assyria became independent in the east, and some of Mitanni's Syrian territory had been lost to Egypt. Presumably, the change in the two nations' relationship reflects the desire of both to have peace in Syria. Šuttarna II of Mitanni also sent a daughter, Gilu-Hepa, in a diplomatic marriage, perhaps to Amonhotep III. She was accompanied by 317 Mitannian handmaidens.

The institutions of diplomatic marriage, attested in the Near East from the 3d millennium B.C. on, served a number of purposes during the late 2d millennium. First, it signaled the sincere desire of the nations involved to have peace and was a serious goodwill gesture. Second, the bride's household, composed at least in part of personnel from home, served as a kind of listening post on activities in the host country. Valuable information might be passed on in the normal course of communication between the bride and her family. Third, the bride's father endowed her with an enormous dowry including semi-precious gems, textiles, furniture, elaborate vessels, objects of art, and the like. These dowries, therefore, were a means of transmission of valuable luxury goods among the courts of the time and helped in the spread of artistic styles and motifs throughout the Near East. In return, the bride's father received a substantial "bride price." When Egypt was involved, the price was gold, for which all of the nations of the time were hungry. The "dowry" and "bride price" arrangement, was, in fact, a sort of high-level luxury trade.

When Tušratta came to the throne of Mitanni, he wrote in very friendly terms to Amonhotep III assuring the pharaoh that the excellent relations their two nations had enjoyed would be reinstated. Apparently there had been some difficulties, possibly connected with a usurper who had murdered Tušratta's brother. In addition, with Tušratta's ascent to the kingship, the kingdom of Hurri under Artatama I broke away from Mitanni declaring himself rightful king. This matter was placed before the gods in a kind of divine court to adjudicate between Tušratta and Artatama I. Though weakened by the loss of Hurri, Tušratta was able to defeat a Hittite army and send some of the booty to Egypt as a sign of his good faith with the pharaoh. Tušratta also sent his daughter Tadu-Hepa to Egypt to marry Amonhotep III. Tadu-Hepa seems to have been married to the next pharaoh, Amonhotep IV, as well.

Tušratta and Amonhotep III and IV communicated frequently. Aside from the usual Amarna letter bickerings about the exchange of gold, an interesting topic of correspondence was the statue of Ištar of Nineveh that Tušratta sent twice to Egypt to help heal the pharaoh.

Tušratta's reign was beset with difficulties. The Hurri lands broke away and coveted his throne. The Hittites emerged under their King Suppiluliumas as a formidable political and military power, Egypt lost interest in its Near Eastern territories during the reign of Amonhotep IV, and the Assyrians were a growing threat.

First, the Hittites made Kizzuwadna a vassal state. Then, they allied themselves with the Hurri-lands. The First Syrian Wars of Suppiluliumas destroyed Mitannian control of Syria, but Tušratta continued to support revolts against the Hittites in the formerly Mitannian vassal states. These became the reason for Suppiluliumas' Second Syrian Wars, those that took him to the heart of Mitanni. Before embarking on this campaign, Suppiluliumas entered into a diplomatic marriage with Babylon and a peace treaty with Ugarit. With the south of Mesopotamia and the Syrian coast secure, Suppiluliumas marched to Wašukanni taking Mitannian cities and garrisons along the way. Tušratta was murdered in a coup that included his son Sat-tiwaza (perhaps spelled Kur-tiwaza or Mat-tiwaza) who became king of Mitanni. Meanwhile, Mitannian territory was shared by a state called Alše and Assyria (Goetze *CAH* 17: 1–20).

Tušratta's defeat and death were understood as the decision of the gods in favor of Hurri. Thus, Šuttarna son of Artatarma of the Hurri-lands claimed the throne of Mitanni and Sat-tiwaza fled. He attempted to enter Babylonia but was refused on the grounds that Babylon was neutral. Finally, he was taken in by Suppiluliumas, who married him to his daughter (Goetze *CAH* 17: 1–20).

Artatarma and Šutarna, the kings of Hurri who occupied the throne of Mitanni, lavished attention on Assyria and Alše whom they must have seen as potential protectors. They gave riches from the treasuries of Mitanni to both nations. Tušratta's palace was demolished and a silver and gold door that Saustatar had taken from Assyria was returned. They confiscated the personal property of private individuals, and certain high officials were handed over for punishment (Gadd *CAH* 18: 21–48).

To counter the growing strength of Assyria, Suppiluliumas began yet another great campaign, the goal of which was to reestablish Sat-tiwaza on the throne of Mitanni. Meeting relatively little resistance from the Assyrians and the Hurri-lands, the prince became king of Mitanni and vassal of Suppiluliumas. The events of his reign are unknown, but he may have been defeated by the Assyrians at some point, perhaps during the reign of Ashur-uballit I (1365–1330; Goetze *CAH* 17: 1–20; Gadd *CAH* 18: 21–48).

From the time of Sat-tiwaza until the reign of Shalmaneser I of Assyria (1274–1245 B.C.) the Assyrian sources record a series of encounters with and rebellions in Mitanni. Mitanni was an ally of the Hittites at the Battle of Kadesh (1285 B.C.) and the Hittite hand is apparent in the revolts that plagued Assyria in the region. Thus, Suppiluliumas' vision of a Mitanni that would be a buffer between Assyria and the Hittites was fulfilled. Finally, Shalmaneser I conquered Mitanni and ended the political life of that Hurrian state.

C. The Role of Mitanni in Near Eastern Culture

The culture of the Mitannian state was basically Hurrian. Of special interest are the Nuzi-ware pottery and the "Mitanni style" in glyptic art, a fine example of which is the seal of Saustatar on *HSS* 9.1 (Smith 1965). What is associated with Mitanni demonstrates the syncretism of elements from Syria, Mesopotamia, Egypt, and the Aegean—all attesting to the internationalism of the era.

It must be noted that there is far more information concerning Hurrian culture in general than for Mitannian in particular. Evidence for the Hurrians derives from a number of sites, some of which were controlled by Mitanni, but all of which were influenced by earlier and contemporaneous cultures. The center of Mitanni, its capital Wašukanni, has not yet been excavated, nor have other significant Mitannian cities. The true character of Mitannian, and therefore indigenous Hurrian, art, architecture, literature, and religion must await such research.

At this point in time, Mitanni's major contribution to the Near East is found in its role as the N Mesopotamiaan—N Syrian transmitter in the diffusion of culture in the late 2d millennium B.C. Because of its military and political power it was able to weld a fractious and diverse array of small states into a reasonably unified body which enabled communication across a wide area in the Near East. Through its diplomacy with Egypt and its subsequent relations with Egypt, the Hittites, and Assyria, it was a cultural crossroads. Moreover, Mitanni's friendship with Egypt brought peace to the Near East for a time. Commerce, industry, and the arts flourished during the Amarna period. The city-states that straddled the trade routes of Syria and N Mesopotamia reaped enormous profits from local business and the taxes levied on merchants. In this period of prosperity, Mitanni was an economic power whose vassals shared in the wealth generated by international trade and internal stability. Thus, Mitanni enriched the Near East both economically and culturally.

D. Mitanni and the Old Testament

Mitanni does not appear in the OT. Even if the references to Hurrians in Palestine reflect a Hurrian presence there in the late 2d millennium B.C., the territories they would have been in were well within the Egyptian sphere of influence and not that of Mitanni. These areas figured only in the campaigns of the pharaohs as they marched to meet Mitanni or the Hittites. Otherwise, they were immersed in the politics and military actions involving Egypt and local Canaanite groups.

It was long asserted that the MB Age, before the birth of Mitanni, was the "date" for the patriarchal era. The seminomadic lifestyle of the patriarchs suited the social milieu of that era, and the political situation in Palestine (a sparse population lacking the semi-independent and feuding city-states of later times) would appear to be hospitable to the movements of the Patriarchs (see *BHI*).

On the other hand, some have dated the events of the patriarchal narratives to the Mitannian era (Gordon 1964 and 1965). According to this system, on the grounds of biblical chronology, Abraham would be dated to the Amarna period, hence to the time of Tušratta. The travels of Abraham and his family from N Syria to Egypt and back and their regular interaction with urban centers are to be understood in the context of the mercantile activities of the late 2d millennium B.C. rather than as the wanderings of the nomads of the earlier era. The importance of trade and the well-documented interaction between Syria and Egypt during the late 2d millennium B.C. are cited in support of this theory. Furthermore, the encounter of Abraham with the coalition of kings from the Mesopotamian sphere in Genesis 14 suggests that Abraham's sphere was not entirely peaceful. This incident is seen as reminiscent of the accounts of hostilities in the Amarna Letters.

Placing the patriarchs in the LB Age makes them participants in and beneficiaries of the cross-cultural interaction of the time because few in the Near East were unaffected by the broad and deep changes that occurred during this era. The numerous parallels between the Nuzi texts and the patriarchal narratives and the Ugaritic materials and the OT would therefore be understood in light of contemporaneity and cultural diffusion at the beginning of Hebrew history.

Recently, however, both the MB and LB Age dates for the patriarchal era have been discarded by those who favor a 1st millennium date for the composition of the narratives. In any case, the late 2d millennium B.C. in which Mitanni figured so prominently was a cultural "watershed." During this time, the various cultures of the Near East mingled their religious, artistic, literary, and technical ideas and skills. The nations that arose at the dawn of the 1st millennium B.C. were the heirs and perpetuators of this legacy.

Bibliography

Gelb, I. 1944. *Hurrians and Subarians.* SAOC 22. Chicago.

Goetze, A. 1957. On the Chronology of the Second Millennium B.C. *JCS* 11: 53–73.

Gordon, C. H. 1964. Biblical Customs and the Nuzi Tablets. *BAR* 2: 21–33.

———. 1965. *The Ancient Near East.* 3d ed. New York.

Redford, D. 1979. A Gate Inscription from Karnak and Egyptian Involvement in Western Asia During the Early 18th Dynasty. *JAOS* 99: 270–87.

Smith, S. 1940. *Alalakh and Chronology.* London.

Smith, W. S. 1965. *Interconnections in the Ancient Near East.* New Haven.

Starr, R. F. S. 1937–39. *Nuzi. Report on the Excavations at Yorghan Tepa near Kirkuk.* 2 vol. Cambridge, MA.

Wiseman, D. J. 1953. *The Alalakh Tablets.* London.

MARTHA A. MORRISON

MITE. See COINAGE.

MITHKAH (PLACE) [Heb *mitqâ*]. The thirteenth encampment of the Israelites, after leaving the wilderness of Sinai, as listed in Num 33:28–29, where it is placed between Terah and Hashmonah. Its name, "Sweetness," may be based on the existence of a good spring, as is the case with Jothbatha in Num 33:33–34 and Deut 10:7 where the name of the site, "Pleasantness," is definitely connected with a water source. Most scholars are unwilling even to suggest a possible location for this site, though it must lie between the wilderness of Sinai and Kadesh-barnea. For a discussion of the location of any of the places associated with the journey of the Israelites from Egypt through Sinai see DOPHKAH.

Bibliography

Beit-Arieh, I. 1988. The Route through Sinai—Why the Israelites Fleeing Egypt went South. *BARev* 15/3: 28–37.

JEFFREY R. ZORN

MITHNITE (PERSON) [Heb *mitnî*]. A descriptive adjective of Joshaphat, one of David's champions, a select class of warriors directly attached to the king for special assignments, named in the list of 1 Chr 11:10–47 (v 43), a list which, up to v 41a, parallels that of 2 Sam 23:8–39. Joshaphat, "the Mithnite," is found among the sixteen persona mentioned in the portion of the list which is unique to Chronicles (vv 41b–47). Because no such place or family is known, it seems possible that the term has become corrupt in transmission. The Greek translation reads a *b* for the *m,* but such a confusion of the Hebrew consonants is not uncommon (Allen 1974: 109). If the text could be restored and/or the place identified, it is probable that it would be in the Transjordan area, since in this portion of the warrior list (vv 41b–47) all of the identifiable places from which these champions came are in this area (Williamson *Chronicles* NCBC, 104).

Bibliography

Allen, L. C. 1974. *The Greek Chronicles: The Relation of the Septuagint of I and II Chronicles to the Massoretic Text.* Part II: Textual Criticism. VTSup 27. Leiden.

RODNEY K. DUKE

MITHRAS, MITHRAISM. In Old Persian, the word "mithra" means "contract." Mithra was regarded as a god who stood for a societal structure based purely on relationships ("contracts") between persons. Thus, among the Persians, Mithra was above all the god of the king and his warriors. He was also honored by nations connected with the Persians, for example the Armenians and the peoples who lived around the Black Sea. In the Hellenistic period the cult of Mithra is especially well attested for the Cilician and Pamphylian pirates and the large sanctuaries at Commagene, i.e., in the S and SE of modern Turkey.

From about 80 A.D. onwards there is evidence for a Mithraic mystery cult in Rome. One can only hypothesize as to how this cult arose. M. P. Nilsson supposed that it was not a process which developed gradually over time, but rather a single accomplishment on the part of one religious genius. There is much which recommends this view. About a dozen of the evidences for the mysteries of Mithra can be dated to between 90 and 140 A.D. From the period after 140 until the year 313, we have hundreds of Mithras monuments, above all from the capital, Rome, and from the military borders (the Danube, the Rhine, and the Wall of Hadrian in Britanny). The cult was exclusively for men and was especially popular among soldiers and the imperial personnel (slave and freedmen). Some persons of the equestrian order who rose to high military positions were adherents of the Mithras cult. For the aristocracy of the Roman empire, the senatorial class, Mithras remained an alien god for a long time. Nor was he admitted among the Roman national deities. Whereas the adherents of Mithras made loyalty to the emperor a part of their religion, the emperors for their part generally displayed reserve towards the mystery cult.

The cult of Mithras was observed in artificial caves which were regarded as an image of the cosmos. The caves were 15–20 meters long and 8–10 meters broad; a religious community, then, will not have exceeded 30–50 persons. The caves were illuminated by means of artificial light. At the far end was always an image of the god about to sacrifice the divine bull. The image represents the creation of the world from that primal sacrifice which is the holy myth of the Mithras initiates.

In the middle of the picture one sees the god who has leapt onto the back of the bull; he is about to sacrifice him by thrusting the knife into the carotid artery. In the upper left corner of the picture is the sun-god; often a sunbeam descends down from him to Mithras, and on this sunbeam a raven flies down to the god to announce that it is time to sacrifice to the bull. In the upper right corner of the picture is Luna. To the left and right of Mithra and the bull stand two Persian shepherds (Cautopates and Cautes). They represent the setting and rising sun. Under the bull are representations of three animals: a scorpion, a snake, and a dog. They are hurrying in order to drink the sperm and blood of the sacrificed bull. A lion often joins this group of animals.

This cultic representation existed as a fresco or a relief. In the latter case, the image could sometimes be turned on a peg. The back of the relief then showed Mithra and Helios consuming the bull in a sacramental meal. Mithras and Helios here represent the two supreme grades in the hierarchy of the seven Mithraic grades, the Pater and the Heliodromus, and the meal was the archetype of the communal meals of the Mithras initiates. Every Mithraeum was at the same time a dining room.

Whether or not the bull was actually sacrificed in the cult is a point of debate. A consideration which suggests that this was not the case is that the Mithraea appear to have been too small for this practice. There are no positive testimonia about a sacrifice.

Ancient Persian religious conceptions live on in Roman Mithraism, but in many respects this was an entirely new religion. It is pervaded by conceptions about the divinity of the stars, conceptions which were developed by philosophers and astronomers in the Hellenistic and Roman periods. Mithraic initiates were divided into seven ranks, each of which corresponded to one of the seven planetary gods. These are the same gods after whom the days of the week are still named today. On the representations of Mithras sacrificing the bull, each of these ranks is represented by a figure. The system is as follows:

Rank	Name	Symbol	Planet	Day of the Week
1	Corax (raven)	raven	Mercury	French mercredi
2	Nymphus (chrysalis of the bee)	snake	Venus	vendredi
3	Miles (soldier)	scorpion	Mars	mardi
4	Leo	dog, lion	Jupiter	jeudi
5	Perses	Cautopates	Luna	lundi, Monday

6	Heliodromus (courier of the sun)	Cautes	Sol (sun)	Sunday
7	Pater	Mithras	Saturn	Saturday

A mosaic pavement of a Mithraeum in Ostia represents this sequence of ranks by the image of a ladder with eight rungs. In each of the seven fields between the rungs are the symbols for the seven ranks. Adherents of the religion of Mithras were continually reinitiated as they ascended this symbolic ladder. Expectations concerning the afterlife were connected with these ceremonies. The initiates hoped that after death their souls would ascend through seven planetary spheres to that of the fixed stars, the true home of the human soul. Platonism influenced this astral piety; it has nothing to do with astrology. Central to astrology is the concept of a fate that cannot be altered, whereas the initiates of the cult of Mithras hoped to return to the soul's original home by leading a righteous and pious life.

In addition to the cosmogonic sacrifice of the bull, there were other Mithraic myths: the birth of Mithras from a rock; Mithras's journey in a carriage together with the sun-god; Helios riding on horseback through heaven; Mithras throwing a spear against the rock (a fount of water then sprung forth from this rock; the mythologem thus has been compared to Moses striking the rock with his staff).

In the 2d and 3d centuries this mystery cult competed with its slightly older rival, Christianity. Polemical passages against the mysteries of Mithras are found in the writings of Christian authors (Just. *Apol.* 66, *Dia.* 70 and 78; Or. *Cels.* 6.22; Tert. *Ad Marc.* 1.13; *De bapt.* 5; *De corona militis* 15; *De praescr. haeret.* 40).

When Constantine lent his support to Christianity, the Mithras initiates who were frequently imperial employees and soldiers, apparently abandoned their cult with almost no opposition. Evidences for the cult of Mithras appear again in Rome in the period 357–87. This time they come from the Roman aristocracy, which opposed the new Christian capital of Constantinople. In doing so they incorporated the cult of Mithras in their religious syncretism. The victorious Christians destroyed most of the Mithraea, and they erected their churches above the Mithraic caves as a sign of the victory of Light over Darkness. Archaeologists have discovered and excavated in Rome many Mithraea under the churches.

Bibliography

Cumont, F. 1896–99. *Texts et monuments figurés relatifs aux mystères de Mithra.* 2 vols. Brussels.

———. 1903. *The Mysteries of Mithra.* Trans. T. M. McCormack. Repr. 1956.

Merkelbach, R. 1984. *Mithras.* Königstein.

Turcan, R. -A. 1981. *Mithra et le mithriacisme.* Paris.

Vermaseren, M. 1956–60. *Corpus inscriptionum et monumentorum religionis Mithriacae.* 2 vols. The Hague.

———. 1963. *Mithras, The Secret God.* London.

R. Merkelbach

MITHREDATH (PERSON) [Heb *mitrĕdāt*]. Var. MITHRIDATES. **1.** Persian official identified as the treasurer (Heb *gizbār,* possibly derived from Old Persian *ganzabara;* see Bowman 1970: 28) of Cyrus (ruled 539–530 B.C.E.); he was charged with the responsibility of counting out the temple vessels to be returned to Jerusalem (Ezra 1:8 = 1 Esdr 2:11). The temple vessels given to Sheshbazzar (ca. 538 B.C.E.) to carry to Jerusalem are specifically identified as those which Nebuchadnezzar had taken from the Jerusalem temple in 587/6 B.C.E. (Ezra 1:7 = 1 Esdr 2:11). The parallel version of the event in 1 Esdr 2:11 identifies the treasurer as Mithridates (Gk *mithridatēs;* note the LXX *mithradatēs*), a Greek rendering of the Persian name (see also v 16). However, the LXX differs from Ezra 1:8 and 1 Esdr 2:11 by taking the Hebrew *gizbār,* "treasurer," for a second name, calling him Mithradates Gasbarenos. 1 Esdras, not dependent upon the LXX, correctly translates the Hebrew *gizbār,* "treasurer," with the Greek *gazophylax.*

2. Persian official named along with Bishlam and Tabeel as co-senders of correspondence to the Persian king Artaxerxes (ruled from 465–425 B.C.E.) (Ezra 4:7 = 1 Esdr 2:16). The content of the actual correspondence is not specified, but the redactor's context suggests that it was unfavorable to the Jews in Judea and Jerusalem. The LXX version translates Bishlam into a prepositional modifier, saying that the letter was written "in peace" (Heb *bišlām* is translated into Gk *en eirēnē*), from Tabeel to Mithradates. Olmstead (1948: 314), following the LXX reading, presents Tabeel as working on behalf of the Jews; he sought to establish legal precedent (hence the collection of Aramaic documents) for Jewish rights to rebuild by corresponding with Mithredath, a Persian official. The parallel account of this correspondence in 1 Esdr 2:16 locates this episode just after the return under Sheshbazzar and conflates the correspondents in Ezra 4:7 and Ezra 4:8, making one group of correspondents to Artaxerxes comprised of Bishlam, Mithridates, Tabeel, Rehum, Beltethmus, and Shimshai the scribe.

Bibliography

Bowman, R. A. 1970. *Aramaic Ritual Texts from Persepolis.* Chicago.

Olmstead, A. T. 1948. *History of the Persian Empire.* Chicago.

David E. Suiter

MITRE. See DRESS AND ORNAMENTATION.

MITYLENE (PLACE) [Gk *Mitylēnē*]. The chief city of the island of Lesbos, the largest of the Aegean islands located near the shore of Asia Minor (modern Turkey). Paul briefly visited this city during his third missionary journey (Acts 20:14). Paul, after visiting Macedonia, traveled to Troas and then went cross-country to Assos. Paul joined his companions on the ship at Assos and then sailed to Mitylene. They spent the night at Mitylene (39°06′N; 26°34′E) before sailing S to Chios and Samos, eventually traveling on to Jerusalem. It was common for ships to overnight in convenient harbors and set sail early in the morning to take advantage of the favorable morning winds.

The city is built upon an extension of land that was originally a small island, but which later was connected to the larger island by a causeway. The city, therefore had two excellent harbors, one on either side of this promontory. This area was colonized by the Aeolians prior to 1000 B.C., who provided the dialect for the poetry of Alcaeus and Sappho who wrote in the early 6th century B.C. These poems hint at the internal strife which plagued the city leading to the overthrow of several tyrants.

Mitylene became an important naval power and founded colonies on the coast of Mysia and Thrace. Disputes over some of these colonies brought the city into conflict with Athens. After playing an important role in the Ionian revolt, Mitylene was captured by the Persians. Later the city became an important member of the Athenian alliance. At first, Mitylene joined Athens in the Peloponnesian War, but it revolted twice (428 and 419 B.C.) from this agreement. This action was met with severe punishment which nearly brought annihilation to the city and marked the end of its military power.

Mitylene made an alliance with Alexander the Great and later came under Roman control. The status of "free city" was conferred upon the city by Pompey the Great and it became a popular resort for aristocratic Romans. In A.D. 151, an earthquake destroyed the city. In the Middle Ages the term "Mitylene" was applied to the entire island.

JOHN D. WINELAND

MIZAR (PLACE) [Heb *miṣʿār*]. Mt. Mizar, a peak whose precise location is unknown, is mentioned in Ps 42:7 (—Eng 42:6). The phrase *mēhar miṣʿār* ("from Mt. Mizar") is usually understood to refer to the location of the psalmist. The geographic references of the verse move from the general to the specific locality, an example of focusing that is common in Hebrew poetry, "I remember you (God) from the land of Jordan, the Hermon range (literally "the Hermons"—*ḥermônîm*), from Mt. Mizar." Apparently, the geographical area specified is the headwaters of the Jordan in the Hermon range. "Mt. Mizar" then would specify a peak in that area. Its name has been related to three names in this area with the same or similar radicals (Zaʿura, Wadi Zaʿârah, Kh. Mezâra), which may preserve the hill's name (Smith 1932: 477). On the basis of the meaning of the name *har miṣʿār*, "the little hill," some suggest that it functions to contrast this "little hill" (maybe even Mt. Hermon itself) with the grand hill of God's sanctuary to which the psalmist longs to go, "your holy hill" (Ps 43:3; cf. Ps 68:17–19 [—Eng 68:16–18]). Others suggest that the phrase designates the destination to which the psalmist wishes to go (i.e., Zion "the little hill") rather than the psalmist's present location, "I remember you . . . far away from the little hill" (i.e., Zion). Goulder (1982: 23–27) interprets it as a reference to Tel Dan at whose sanctuary the psalmist wishes to worship.

Bibliography

Goulder, M. D. 1982. *The Psalms of the Sons of Korah.* Winona Lake, IN.

Kruse, H. 1960. Two Hidden Comparatives: Observations on Hebrew Style. *JSS* 5: 333–47.

Smith, G. A. 1932. *Historical Geography of the Holy Land.* London.

PAUL R. RAABE

MIZMOR. See PSALMS, BOOK OF.

MIZPAH (PLACE) [Heb *hamiṣpâ*]. Var. MIZPEH. A place-name connected with several biblical sites in and around Palestine. The toponym, deriving from the root *ṣph* meaning "to guard," or "to watch," suggests the location at a site of a military outpost, observatory, or "watchtower" (see the usage of the word in Isa 21:8).

1. Mizpah of Benjamin. The most significant "Mizpah" in the OT was a city of political, military, and cultic significance located in Benjaminite territory. It frequently appears in stories set in the premonarchical period and is associated with a motif whereby all the Israelite tribes gather in solemn cultic assembly to pray before undertaking Holy War against an enemy.

Mizpah is first mentioned (Josh 18:26) in the Benjaminite town-list when Joshua reportedly allotted cities captured in the Conquest to the various tribes. Most scholars now regard this list as a monarchical-era administrative record which has been literarily projected into Israelite antiquity by late editors. The document nevertheless suggests that Mizpah existed in Iron Age II, and that it was located, like the other cities in the second half of the list (Joshua 25–28), in Benjaminite territory astride or W of the Palestinian watershed.

In the account of the outrage at Gibeah and its aftermath (Judges 19–21), Mizpah reportedly served as the base camp where all Israel rallied before the YHWH to hear the victimized Levite's grievance against Gibeah (20:1, 3). All the Israelites except Jabesh-gilead, allegedly swore an oath not to marry their daughters to a Benjaminite (21:1); Jabesh-gilead missed the solemn assembly (21:5, 8) and was accordingly punished. Literary evidence suggests that this information belongs to a postexilic Priestly redaction of the Gibeah Outrage tradition, and should not be regarded as historical (Arnold 1990: 159–65). These passages reflect, instead, the cultic significance of Mizpah in the exilic and postexilic period when it possessed a "house of the Lord" (Jer 41:5); Priestly editors evidently wished to project this importance back into Israel's past.

Mizpah's relation to Samuel is a considerably more complicated question. On the one hand, many scholars consider as ancient and historical the report (1 Sam 7:16) that Samuel judged Israel on a yearly circuit involving Bethel, Gilgal, and Mizpah (Miller and Hayes, *HAIJ*, 96). Moreover, the notice (7:12) locating Eben-ezer between Mizpah and Jeshanah ("the tooth"—cf. 14:4–5) is possibly an old etiology. However, the claim that Samuel summoned "all Israel" to a cultic assembly with him before the Lord at Mizpah (7:5–7), where God responded to their prayers and fasting with a miraculous rout of the Philistines (7:7, 11), evinces motifs and interests so similar to the Gibeah account that one may doubt its historicity. No less dubious is the report that Samuel chose Saul as the first king over Israel in a lottery held in Mizpah (10:17). Once again, late editors have apparently transferred Mizpah's postexilic cultic importance into Israel's early days.

Less historically questionable and more significant for understanding Mizpah's importance is the report in 1 Kgs 15:16–22 that King Asa repulsed the Israelite Baasha's incursion into Judean territory and his attempt to cut off safe access to Jerusalem (ca. 900 B.C.E.). After dismantling the offending Israelite fort at Ramah (er-Ram, 7 km N of Jerusalem), Asa's corvée reportedly used its stones and timbers to fortify two new Judean fortresses presumably farther N: Mizpah and Geba (1 Kgs 15:22 = 2 Chr 16:6). Since Geba guarded one important highway across the Judean-Israelite border at the Geba Pass (see GEBA), it is only logical to assume that Mizpah "watched" over the other major route, the watershed highway, at the frontier between the two countries.

Recent research (e.g., Aharoni 1968: 30) suggests that such border fortresses not only controlled military and economic access to Judah, but served an important cultic function as well. Sites like Mizpah may have contained sanctuaries where travelers could offer proper sacrifices to the national lord on entering or leaving the land. This role may explain the origins of Mizpah's subsequent cultic importance in Judah, and Hosea's vague condemnation against the priests, who "have been a snare at Mizpah" (Hos 5:1).

The Bible does not mention Mizpah in relation to events in the three centuries after its foundation as a border fortress. In the chaotic period after the destruction of the Temple in Jerusalem (586 B.C.E.), however, Mizpah achieved its greatest significance. The Babylonian invasion probably devastated most of the cities of S and W Judah, including Jerusalem, but seemingly left the remote N redoubt of Mizpah intact. At this fortress, the newly appointed, pro-Babylonian, governor Gedaliah set up his motley government and established a new capital (2 Kgs 25:23); there the nationalistic Ishmael assassinated the quisling and most of his puppet government as well (2 Kgs 25:25; but see the extended account of these events in Jer 40:1–41:16).

That Mizpah achieved premier sanctuary status in Judah in this period is indirectly proved by Jer 41:4–6, which reports that eighty Israelites made a pilgrimage in order to offer grain and frankincense at the "house of the Lord"—apparently in Mizpah itself. It is likely that Mizpah retained its status as capital of Judah and primary temple for many decades, until the reestablishment of Jerusalem late in the 6th century B.C.E. It is also possible that postexilic literary circles were active in the city during this period, which may account for its inclusion and legitimation in premonarchical stories such as Judges 20, 1 Samuel 7, and possibly Judges 11.

When the returned exiles rebuilt Jerusalem, artisans from Mizpah contributed their services to various architectural repairs on the city (Neh 3:7, 15, 19). Otherwise, little is known about Mizpah during the Dark Ages of Persian and Hellenistic colonialization of Judah. During the Maccabean Revolt in the 2d century B.C.E., Jewish fundamentalist forces under Judas assembled for a religious service in Mizpah in memory of its former preeminence as a holy place (1 Macc 3:46).

Modern debate as to the location of Mizpah began over a century ago when E. Robinson proposed that Nebi Samwil, a formidable mount 8 km NW of Jerusalem, best fit the topographical requirements for Mizpah (1856: 575); a long succession of scholars through W. F. Albright concurred in this opinion. Such an identification is unlikely, however, in view of Nebi Samwil's location (i.e. farther S than er-Ram), its high elevation, and its distance from any militarily strategic point (e.g., the watershed highway). Archaeological investigation, moreover, has not produced findings which would corroborate a Mizpah identification for Nebi Samwil (Kochavi 1972: 185).

The most likely site proposal was first advanced by A. Raboisson (1897), who suggested that a mound 12 km N of Jerusalem named Tell en-Naṣbeh (M.R. 170143) not only fit Mizpah's topographical requirements, but retained an Arabic version of the original Hebrew place name. A series of scholars concurred, and W. F. Bade finally excavated the tell from 1926 to 1935. While this expedition found no incontrovertible proof linking Mizpah to Tell en-Nasbeh, its findings are strongly suggestive of such an identification (McCown: 1947). See NASBEH, TELL EN-.

Tell en-Nasbeh was occupied in the Iron, Persian, and Hellenistic ages, fitting Mizpah's chronological requirements. Moreover, its massive Iron Age walls, glacis, and towers correspond to the type of fortress construction one would expect on the basis of 2 Kgs 15:22. its N-facing gate was well positioned to receive travelers *en route* to Jerusalem. Some sixty-eight *lmlk* seals confirm Tell en-Nasbeh's Judean setting, and a seal inscribed to "Jaazaniah servant of the king" may relate to an official of Gedaliah named ion 2 Kgs 25:23. The site lay astride the watershed highway just a few km S of the probable Judean-Israelite border, which extended some 8 km SE toward Mizpah's twin fortress, Geba. Together, these strongholds guarded Judah's N border for most of its 300-year history.

2. Mizpeh of Moab *(miṣpēh).* David reportedly brought his Bethlehemite parents to the court of the king of Moab in this city while Saul pursued his renegade rival (1 Sam 22:3). Its location is purely a matter of conjecture; both Kerak and Rujm el-Meshrefeh SW of Madaba in Jordan have been proposed.

3. Mizpeh of Judah *(hamiṣpeh).* This town was purportedly assigned to the tribe of Judah by Joshua after the Conquest (Josh 15:38). It is specifically listed among towns in the Shephelah (15:33), and is therefore often identified with a site bearing a linguistically similar modern place-name: Tell es-Safiyeh (M.R. 135123), 13 km NE of Kiryat Gat (however, others identify Tell es-Safiyeh with ancient Philistine Gath; Aharoni *LBHG,* 434).

4. The land of Mizpah *(hamiṣpâ).* A coalition of kings representing N Palestinian peoples including the Hivites near Hermon "in the land of Mizpah" (Josh 11:3) supposedly gathered at the waters of Merom to fight Joshua's Israelite forces, which defeated and pursued them as far as "the valley of Mizpah" *(miṣpeh)* on the E (11:8). These references are vague, and the area difficult to locate. If the "Mizpah" so named represents a city, it might lie in the extreme N of Palestine; some have proposed modern Qalat es-Subeibeh, 3 km NE of Banias, on the basis of the rough linguistic similarity of its name to Mizpah.

5. Mizpah of Gilead *(hamiṣpâ).* As a symbol of a covenant of friendship ending his bitter dispute with Jacob, Laban erected a sacred cairn *(maṣṣēbâ)* at a place called "Gal-ed" or "Mizpah" (v 49) somewhere in the land of Gilead (Gen 31:43–55). This pericope is surely an etiological account explaining why a local site somewhere in N Transjordan was called "Mizpah." The reason for the name stated in the text is that the Lord was to "watch" the performance of the covenant makers. It is possible that a ruined watchtower named Mizpah gave rise to a local folktale relating how the ancient patriarchs had built a cairn (note the similar Hebrew term *maṣṣebâ*) to seal their peace agreement. Whatever the origins of this tale, the extremely vague topographical references in the piece do not allow a reasonable location of the place.

The tragic story of Jephthah's vow (Judg 10:17–11:40) might involve this same village in Gilead. The assembled Israelites swore a solemn oath of witness (see Gen 31:44–52!) in Mizpah with the bastard Jephthah of Gilead agreeing to follow him in battle against the attacking Ammonites. Possessed by the spirit of the Lord, Jephthah made the rash vow, which would later lead to the death of his daughter at Mizpah, in exchange for divine help in crushing Ammon.

The possibility that two "Mizpahs" are involved in this story cannot be excluded, and that the site of the cultic Israelite assembly (10:17; 11:11) is none other than Mizpah of Benjamin (cf. Judg 20, 1 Sam 7). In any case, Mizpah of Gilead (called *miṣpēh* in Judg 11:29) was a distinct site, possibly that mentioned in Gen 31:49 (see also Josh 13:26, where a "Ramoth-mizpeh" is named). Proposals for the modern location of this village are simply based on phonetics: Suf near Jerash, and Kh. Jelᶜad, some 24 km NW of Amman.

Bibliography

Aharoni, Y. 1968. Arad: Its Inscriptions and Temple. *BA* 31: 2–32.
Albright, W. F. 1924. Mizpah and Beeroth. Pp. 90–112 in *Excavations and Results at Tell el-Ful (Gibeah of Saul).* AASOR 4. New Haven.
Alt, A. 1910. Mizpa in Benjamin. *PJ* 6: 46.
Arnold, P. 1990. *Gibeah: The Search for a Biblical City.* Sheffield.
Baumann, E. 1911. Die Lage von Mizpa in Benjamin. *ZDPV* 34: 119–37.
Kochavi, M. 1972. *Judea, Samaria, and the Golan: Archaeological Survey 1967–68.* Jerusalem (in Hebrew).
McCown, C. C. 1947. *Tell en-Nasbeh.* New Haven.
Muilenberg, J. 1955. Mizpah of Benjamin. *Studia Theologica Scandinavicorum* 8: 25–42.
Raboisson, A. 1897. *Les Maspeh.* Paris.
Robinson, E. 1856. *Biblical Researches in Palestine.* 3 vols. Boston.

PATRICK M. ARNOLD

MIZZAH (PERSON) [Heb *mizzâ*]. The fourth son of Reuel and the grandson of Esau (Gen 36:13, 17; 1 Chr 1:37). In Gen 36:17 he is listed as one of the "tribal chiefs" (Heb *ʾallûpîm*) of Edom, and as such the name probably represents a clan within the Esauite-Edomite tribe of Reuel. There is no clear explanation for the meaning of the name.

ULRICH HÜBNER

MMŠT. One of the 4 place-names found in stamp impressions on the handles of Judean storage jars, which are known as the "royal-stamp jar handles." See STAMPS, ROYAL JAR HANDLE. Since the name does not appear in the Bible, the pronunciation is unknown. By convention, the hypothetical pronunciation "Memshat" is generally used.

Since the other place-names found in the stamps—Hebron, Soco, and Ziph—are major Judean cities, the appearance of the otherwise unknown *mmšt* is puzzling. Some have proposed that the word is an abbreviation or dialectical variant of *memšelet,* "government" or "administration," and that the fourth city is therefore Jerusalem. Strong objections have been raised against this solution, and it retains only a few adherents.

Royal stamps bearing the name *mmšt* have been found predominantly in N Judah. This fact plus the lack of a suitable Iron Age sites in the far S seems to rule out various proposals for a locale in the Negeb. Most commentators therefore look to the area around Bethlehem or in the NW of the kingdom in the Aijalon-Zorah region for possibilities: ᶜAmwas near Latrun has been proposed. A definitive solution, however, awaits further investigation.

Bibliography

Lemaire, A. 1975. *Mmšt* = Amwas, vers la solution d'une énigme de l'épigraphie hébraïque. *RB* 82: 15–32.
Rainey, A. F. 1982. Wine from the Royal Vineyards. *BASOR* 245: 57–62.
Welten, P. 1969. *Die Königs-Stempel: Ein Beitrag zur Militärpolitik Judas unter Hiskia und Josia.* Wiesbaden.

H. DARRELL LANCE

MNASON (PERSON) [Gk *Mnasōn*]. The name Mnason, possibly a Hellenized form of Manasseh (Bruce 1985: 99), may be derived from *mnasion* a word used in ancient Cyprus for a measure of grain. Sinaiticus replaces Mnason with Jason, a rather common name among Hellenized Jews. Mentioned only in Acts 21:16, Mnason provided lodging for Paul and his gentile companions.

Mnason was a native of Cyprus like Barnabas (Acts 4:36). Munck (*Acts* AB, 209) suggests that he may have been among the Cypriots who left Jerusalem after the stoning of Stephen and preached the gospel directly to the Greeks at Antioch (Acts 11:19, 20).

The fact that Mnason is called an "early disciple" has engendered considerable discussion. Rengstorf (*TDNT* 4: 458, n280) considers Mnason a personal disciple of Jesus. Hughes (*ISBE* 3: 388) suggests that he was one of the 120 in Acts 1:15. Knowling (1912: 448) proposes that he was a convert of Barnabas from among the Hellenized Jews in Jerusalem. The matter is not easily resolved. Luke did not consider Jesus' circle of disciples to be small (Luke 6:17; 19:37), therefore Mnason's discipleship could go back to the days of Jesus' ministry. However, in Acts 15:7 Peter uses the term "early" *(archaiô)* to refer to the time when Cornelius was converted (Acts 10:1–11:18). Thus, Mnason's conversion may have occurred at any time from early in Jesus' ministry through the early years of the Jerusalem church.

A textual problem in Acts 21:15–17 betrays some uncertainty as to where Mnason lived. According to D and a handful of Syriac manuscripts, Mnason's house was in a village between Caesarea and Jerusalem. The arrival of Paul and his companions in Jerusalem is then described in v 17 where "the brethren" (presumably the whole Christian church) received them gladly. But the most natural reading of the vast majority of manuscripts (contra Knowling 1912: 447) suggests that "the brethren" were limited to Mnason and his associates in Jerusalem and that Paul was received "gladly" by only a few. It was not until the next day that Paul met James and the elders (Acts 21:18). Verse 22 implies that the bulk of Jewish Christians were still unaware that Paul had arrived. While Delebecque (1983: 446–55) considers D Luke's own clarification of an earlier text, it is more likely D's copyist attempted to smooth over the Jerusalem church's apparent snub of Paul.

If Mnason was living in Jerusalem at that time, it is likely, as Haenchen (1965: 607) and Stählin (*Apostelgeschichte* NTD, 275) suggest, that he identified himself with the Hellenists of Acts 6 and the theology of Stephen (Acts 6:14). Most of Paul's eight gentile companions were uncircumcised (cf. Acts 20:4). The typical Christian in Jerusalem would find hospitality problematic under such circumstances. But as a Hellenist, Mnason would be open to such hospitality. As an "early disciple" he was known and respected by the church at Jerusalem. As a Cypriot he had connections with people Paul knew and trusted. Thus, the "disciples of Caesarea" (Acts 21:16) considered Mnason the logical choice to host Paul and his companions in Jerusalem.

The mention of Mnason's name and the reference to his being an "early disciple" suggest that he may have been a source of information about events in Caesarea and Jerusalem that are reported in Acts (see Bruce *Acts* NICNT, 402–3; Foakes Jackson and Lake 1933: 270 and Ramsay 1911: 309n).

Bibliography

Bruce, F. F. 1985. *The Pauline Circle.* Grand Rapids.

Cadbury, H. J. 1926. Lexical Notes on Luke-Acts. III. Luke's Interest in Lodging. *JBL* 45: 305–25.

Delebecque, E. 1983. La dernière étape du troisème voyage missionnaire de saint Paul selon les deux versions des Actes des Apôtres (21, 16–17). *RTL* 14: 446–55.

Foakes Jackson, F. J., and Lake, K. 1933. *The Beginnings of Christianity.* Pt 1, vol. 4. London.

Haenchen, E. 1965. *The Acts of the Apostles.* Trans. B. Noble and G. Shinn. Rev. R. McL. Wilson 1971. Philadelphia.

Knowling, R. J. 1912. *The Acts of the Apostles.* The Expositor's Greek Testament. Vol. 2. Ed. W. R. Nicoll. London.

Ramsay, W. M. 1911. *The Bearing of Recent discovery on the Trustworthiness of the New Testament.* Grand Rapids. Repr. 1953.

JON PAULIEN

MOAB (PLACE) [Heb *mo*ʾ*āb; mô*ʾ*āb*]. MOABITES. In ancient times, the region immediately east of the Dead Sea and the people who occupied that region. Most of the ancient references to Moab are provided by the Hebrew Bible which seems to use the term primarily in reference to the people (Num 22:4).

A. The Name
B. The Land
C. Archaeological Explorations in Moab
  1. Nineteenth-Century Explorers
  2. Developments in the 1930s
  3. Archaeological Investigations Since the 1930s
  4. Some Implications of the Archaeological Evidence
D. Moab and Moabites in Ancient Texts
  1. Moab in Egyptian Sources
  2. The Mesha Inscription and Other Moabite Fragments
  3. Moab in the Assyrian Texts
  4. Moab and Moabites in the Hebrew Bible
E. Moabite History
  1. Moabite Origins
  2. Early Moabite Monarchy?
  3. Mesha's Kingdom
  4. Moab under the Assyrians, Babylonians, and Persians
  5. Moab during Classical Times
F. Moabite Place Names
  1. Northern Moab
  2. Plains of Moab
  3. The Southern Plateau
G. Moabite Religion

A. The Name

None of the various etymologies that have been proposed for this name is entirely convincing. Gen 19:37 attributes it to the unusual circumstances of the birth of two brothers, Moab and Ben-ammi, who are said to have become the ancestors of the Moabites and Ammonites respectively. The narrative records that Lot's two daughters conceived through their father and that the elder daughter named her son "Moab" saying he is "from my father" (Heb *mē*ʾ*ābî*). G. A. Smith connected the name Moab with the Hebrew verb *ya*ʾ*ab* ("to desire"); this *mô*ʾ*bî* would be the participial form of the verb meaning "the desirable" land or people (1914: col. 3166). Others have attempted to explain the name on the basis of Arabic cognates; e.g., *ma*ʾ*âb* which can mean "(the land of) the sunset." In this case, the name Moab would have been coined by Bedouin tribes of the desert for whom the land of Moab would have been the land of the sunset (Vollers). A recent proposal connects the name Moab with that of a prince of "Upper Shûtu," *Shemu*ʾ*abu(m),* known from the Egyptian Execration Texts. The Egyptians knew the Shûtu as a nomadic people who inhabited parts of Palestine, so "Upper Shûtu" may have included the region of ancient Moab. Note also in this regard that Num 24:17–18 identifies the Moabites as "the sons of Sheth." Except for the initial *šîn,* on the other hand, the consononts of *Shemu-*ʾ*abu(m)* correspond to those of Moab. According to the proposal, therefore, *Shemu-*ʾ*abu(m)* was a dynastic name which came to be applied to the region east of the Dead Sea and the people who inhabited the region. The *šîn* would have been dropped along the way for some reason or other (Grohman 1958: 39–48).

B. The Land

The settled population of ancient Moab was concentrated on the narrow strip of cultivable land sandwiched between the ragged and steep Dead Sea escarpment and the Arabian desert (approximately 90 km/60 miles N–S by 25 kms/15 miles E–W). For the most part this is rolling plateau about 1,000 m (3,000 feet) in elevation or 1,300 m (4,300 feet) above the Dead Sea. It is bisected by the steep

Wādî el-Mūjib river canyon (the River Arnon of biblical times), and is bounded on the S by another major canyon, Wādî el-Ḥesā (the River Zered of biblical times). Both the Mūjib and the Ḥesā emerge from the desert side of the Moabite plateau and drain W to the Dead Sea. Less prominent wadis along the entire length of the Dead Sea escarpment create the ragged effect mentioned above.

The soils of the Moabite plateau tend to be thin; there are relatively few springs; and the waters of the Mūjib and the Ḥesā are virtually inaccessible due to their steep canyon walls. The plateau is, however, well watered by winter rains, and the soil is porous enough to hold this moisture for cereal crops and pasturage for sheep and goats. Places where the soil is deeper and springs are available (especially along the wadis which cut into the plateau from the Dead Sea escarpment) support fruit trees and vineyards. Thus, despite its deficiencies, Moab is reasonably good agricultural land and accordingly is strewn with ruins of settlements from ancient times. Moab's favorable agricultural situation is presupposed by the biblical story of Ruth, which has as its setting a time of famine of Judah. According to the story, Naomi and her family emigrated temporarily to Moab where food was still available (Ruth 1:1, 6).

It is useful to distinguish between the main Moabite plateau (the region between the Mūjib and the Ḥesā) and N Moab (the region N of the Mūjib). The main plateau is somewhat isolated by the geographical barriers mentioned above—Wādî el-Mūjib on the N, Wādî el-Ḥesā on the S, the Dead Sea escarpment on the W, and the Arabian desert on the E. Northern Moab is more open to the outside world, on the other hand, and was much better known to the biblical writers. It corresponds roughly to what they called the "tableland" (Heb *mîšor*), or the "tableland of Medeba" after the chief city in N Moab (Deut 3:10; 4:43; Josh 13:9, 16–17, 21; 20:8). Among other towns in N Moab were Heshbon, Elealeh, and those mentioned in Jer 48:21–24.

The openness of N Moab made it more vulnerable to encroachment also, especially by the Israelites and the Ammonites. It often changed hands, and the local population very likely had mixed loyalties. This situation is well illustrated by an inscription from the reign of King Mesha who ruled Moab in the 9th century B.C. (see below). While the inscription assumes that the region N of the Mūjib belonged historically to Moab and credits Mesha with recovering it from Israelite control, it also mentions Israelite elements in the local population, elements which had been there as long as anyone could remember: "And the men of Gad had dwelt in the land of Ataroth always and the king of Israel built Ataroth for them, . . ." (lines 10–11).

Several biblical passages seek to establish an Israelite claim to this valuable tableland (Num 21:21–31; 32; Deut 2:26–37; Judg 11:12–28). It is maintained in these passages that the Arnon/Mūjib was the true N boundary of Moab, that Moses conquered all of the region N of the Arnon from an Amorite king named Sihon, and that Moses then assigned all of the conquered tableland to the tribes of Gad and Reuben. These passages contrast with others, however, and with the general terminology of the Hebrew Bible, which assume that Moab extended as far N as Heshbon and Elealeh (see Num 21:20, for example, and the oracles concerning Moab in Isaiah 15–16 and Jeremiah 48). In fact, even part of the Jordan Valley—the area immediately NE of the Dead Sea, between the Jordan River and the W slopes of the "tableland"—is occasionally referred to in the Bible as the "Plains (Heb *ʿarbôt*) of Moab" (Num 22:1).

C. Archaeological Explorations in Moab

1. Nineteenth-Century Explorers. During the 19th century, local Bedouin tribes dominated the area between the Mūjib and the Ḥesā, and outsiders who entered this region did so essentially at their own risk. Among the few daring travellers who traversed the whole Moabite plateau prior to 1870 and whose published observations deserve special mention were Ulrich Seetzen, who passed through the Moabite region in 1806, Ludwig Burckhardt in 1812, Charles Irby and James Mangles in 1818, and F. de Saulcy in 1851. Typically the travellers of this period commented on the numerous ruins from ancient times scattered throughout the Moabite plateau, but the circumstances rarely allowed them to investigate.

De Saulcy's 1851 discovery of the so-called Shīḥān Stele at Rujm el-ʿAbd was an exception. Rujm el-ʿAbd, a stone heap long since dismantled, was located at the site of the village school of present-day Faqūʿ. The stele is a basalt stone (1.03 × .58 m) which presents in bas-relief a male figure in helmet and short skirt holding a spear. At his left is an animal, possibly a lion. Comparative study indicates close parallels with the monumental art of the "neo-Hittite" cities of N Syria and suggests an Iron Age date (Warmabol 1983). Whether the figure represents a warrior or a god (perhaps Chemosh) cannot be determined.

An even more important development was the discovery of the famous MESHA STELE (sometimes called the "Moabite Stone"). Discovered by F. A. Klein among the ruins of ancient Dibon (present-day Dhībān) in 1868, the Mesha Stele is a basalt slab, approximately one meter high and engraved with a legible text of more than 34 lines in the ancient Canaanite language and script. One learns from the inscription that it was commissioned by king Mesha of Moab in connection with the building of a sanctuary dedicated to Chemosh. The inscription itself reports the major accomplishments of Mesha's reign and thus provides a brief glimpse of Moabite affairs during the mid-9th century (see below).

In 1870 the American Palestine Exploration Society was founded and undertook to map E Palestine. Two expeditions were sent, the first led by J. A. Paine and Lieut. E. Z. Steever in 1872, the second by Selah Merrill in 1875–77. Both expeditions involved explorations in N Moab, but the results were not very satisfactory in either case. Thus C. R. Conder undertook in 1881 to map the Transjordan and began in N Moab where the Americans had left off. Unfortunately, Conder had to withdraw from the project after only ten weeks in the field because of the limitations of his permit. During that time, however, he surveyed approximately 500 square miles. Specifically, he covered from Wādî Zarqā Maʿīn (which reaches the Dead Sea SW of Mādabā) northward to Wādî Nimrīn/Shuʿeib (which reaches the Jordan opposite Jericho) and northeastward from the upper branches of these two wadis to Amman (Conder 1889a; 1889b).

In 1894 the Ottoman government reasserted its authority between the Mūjib and the Ḥesā, and for approximately a decade thereafter the region was reasonably well policed. Several scholars seized the opportunity. F. J. Bliss, for example, in an 1895 excursion, cleared up the confusion evident in earlier maps regarding the relative positions of the upper branches of the Mūjib. R. Brünnow, assisted by A. von Domaszewski, made three excursions (1895, 1897, 1898) in connection with his monumental study of the Roman road system and fortifications in the Transjordan. Alois Musil, primarily a geographer, explored extensively in S Transjordan and NW Arabia between 1896 and 1902; he devoted the first volume of his *Arabia Petraea* to the region E of the Dead Sea and prepared a 1:300,000-scale map which indicates the approximate locations of numerous ruins in that region.

2. Developments in the 1930s. Political circumstances (the Kerak rebellion in 1910 followed by World War I) prevented significant developments relative to the archaeology of Moab for the next twenty-five years (from 1905 to 1930). The discovery of a third monumental stele in 1930 initiated another flurry of archaeological exploration in the area of ancient Moab. This was the so-called Bālūᶜ Stele, discovered by R. Head among the extensive ruins at Bālūᶜ. A conical-shaped basalt stone (1.70 m high × .70 m wide at the base) it bears both an inscription and a raised relief. Unfortunately the inscription is so poorly preserved that even the language cannot be identified. The relief is quite clear, however, and consists of three figures, probably a king (center) flanked by a god (left) and a goddess (right). The composition of the relief as well as its details are derived almost entirely from Egyptian prototypes. Clearly the sculptor was acquainted with Egyptian art, although certain details suggest that the artist was a non-Egyptian who adapted the Egyptian style to some purpose as yet unclear (Ward and Martin 1964: 68). The headdresses of the three figures are particularly interesting. The god wears the double crown of upper and lower Egypt. The goddess wears a crown similar to that of Osiris. The king's headdress is similar to that worn by the "Shâsu" in Egyptian reliefs from Dynasties 19 and 20 (see below). Thus it seems reasonable to date the Bālūᶜ stele to approximately the end of the LB Age and to see it as evidence (along with references in Egyptian texts to be discussed below) that Egyptian influence extended to the S Transjordan at that time.

Beginning in the spring of 1933, Nelson Glueck conducted surveys in the Transjordan. Not surprisingly, in view of the Bālūᶜ discovery three years earlier, he concentrated that first season on the Moabite plateau. He spent about three weeks in the area E of the Dead Sea and visited more than a hundred sites. In 1936 he returned to the Moabite region and examined more sites in N Moab and in the southern half of the S plateau—i.e., S of the Kerak-Qaṭrāna road. The importance of Glueck's work in Moab had less to do with the discovery of new sites or with the thoroughness of coverage (since most of the ruins which Glueck visited had been reported already by Musil), than with the fact that he was the first to examine the surface pottery of a large sampling of sites throughout the Transjordan. Glueck's reports published in the *AASOR* became the standard authority on the S Transjordan in general and the Moabite region in particular until the late 1970s.

Three of Glueck's observations were very influential on subsequent treatments of Moabite history. (1) He concluded that there was a virtual gap in the sedentary occupation of S Transjordan between the end of the EB Age and the end of the LB Age—i.e., from approximately 1900 to the 13th century B.C. This was followed, he contended, by a surge of village settlements during the 13th century. These new villages represented new settlers, he believed, namely the Moabites and Edomites. (2) He reported that the borders of the Iron Age kingdoms in the Transjordan, including Moab, were protected by a system of strategically located forts. (3) He reported a concentration of Iron Age sites along the traditional N–S route through the lands of ancient Moab and Edom, the route of the old Roman road and essentially that of the modern paved road, and argued that this would have been the "Kings Highway" mentioned in Num 20:17 and 21:22.

In November of 1933, W. F. Albright and J. W. Crowfoot made soundings at Adir and Bālūᶜ respectively. Albright's probe at Adir produced remains primarily from EB through what he called MB I and dated 2000–1800 B.C., although at one spot he also uncovered some Iron II sherds. Crowfoot found Iron Age remains at Bālūᶜ, including a small section of casemate wall which he dated to Iron I. However, neither Albright nor Crowfoot uncovered materials from the time of the supposed occupational gap, which seemed to confirm Glueck's position.

3. Archaeological Investigations Since the 1930s. Archaeologists have given only sporadic attention to the Moabite plateau since Glueck's survey and, until 1976, have confined their efforts almost entirely to N Moab. Excavations at six sites have produced remains relevant to this discussion of the ancient Moabites: Dhī bān (excavated 1950–56 and 1965), Khirbet el-ᶜĀl (1962), ᶜArāᶜir (1964), Tell Ḥesbān (1968–76), Khirbet Medeinet el-Muᶜarradieh (1976, 1982) and Khirbet Bālūᶜ (1986). Dhībān produced remains from primarily Iron II and later periods. The small amount of Iron I material apparently was not located stratigraphically. The excavators of el-ᶜĀl reported EB, MB, Iron I, and Iron II pottery, but again none of it in clear stratigraphical context. ᶜArāᶜir proved to be a prominent Iron Age fortress on the ruins of earlier buildings. The pottery is mainly from the 11th through the 9th centuries B.C. At Tell Ḥesbān, the only one of these sites which has been both excavated and published with reasonable thoroughness, the evidence indicates an Iron Age I–II settlement with nothing earlier than the 12th century. Khirbet Medeinet el-Muᶜarradieh and Khirbet Bālūᶜ are the only sites in this group located S of the Mūjib. The former turned out to be another Iron Age fort. Constructed near the end of the 13th century at the earliest, the fort was destroyed at the end of the 12th or early 11th century. Excavations at Khirbet Bālūᶜ (the same site probed by Crowfoot in 1933) are still underway and are producing primarily Iron II remains.

Three archaeological surveys conducted recently add to the information derived from these excavated sites. The team that excavated Tell Ḥesbān conducted a survey of other archaeological features in the immediate vicinity (approximately a ten-mile radius) and reported sites from all phases of the Bronze and Iron Ages. A survey team directed by the author during 1978–82 and concentrating on the S plateau between the Mūjib and the Ḥesā registered over 400 sites, again representing all phases of the Bronze and Iron Ages. The third survey, conducted in 1983–86 by Udo Worschech and called the "Northwest Ar el-Kerak Survey," concentrated on the NW quadrant of the southern plateau and Wādî Ibn Hammād.

Mention should be made finally of two tombs cleared at Mādabā which produced artifacts dating from the end of the LB Age and the beginning of Iron I, and of occasional excursions into Moab by members of the Deutsches Evangelisches Institut für Altertumswissenschaft des Heiligen Landes during 1956–64 and 1984–85. Primarily interested in historical geography, the participants in the Evangelisches Institut excursions have sherded a number of sites and made useful observations regarding Moabite toponymy (see especially Kuschke 1962; Donner 1964; Schottroff 1966).

4. Some Implications of the Archaeological Evidence. Although the above is not a comprehensive overview of all archaeological activities on the Moabite plateau, it does cover the items which have relevance for reconstructing the history and material culture of the Moabites. Obviously, the land of ancient Moab still is not very well known archaeologically. Only one Iron Age site, Tell Ḥesbān, has been excavated with any degree of thoroughness, and most of the excavated sites are located N of the Mūjib. Yet the following observations are in order.

By 1970, when Glueck published a revised edition of his *The Other Side of the Jordan,* evidence had begun to emerge which indicated that there was not a total gap during the MB and LB Ages. Recognizing this, he softened his position considerably. The trend has continued, and the recent evidence suggests that the hypothesis probably should be dropped altogether. Obviously the MB and LB Ages were not a high point of urban life in Moab; but people were living on the plateau at that time, and living at some of the same city/village sites which have been occupied off and on throughout the ages. Moreover, while the number of settlements (as represented by surface pottery) increased dramatically during the Iron Age, the artifactual evidence recovered thus far is insufficient to determine whether there was a sudden increase in the number of villages at the beginning of Iron I. In short, rather than an occupational gap during the MB and LB Ages concluded by a sudden surge of Iron I settlements, it may be more accurate to project a gradual increase in the number of settlements from a low point in the MB Age to a high point in Iron II.

The question of border forts surrounding ancient Moab requires further investigation. Clearly there were some Iron I border forts, such as Khirbet Medeinet el-Muᶜarradieh excavated by Olávarri. Yet several of the ruins which Glueck proposed as Moabite border forts show predominantly Nabatean and Roman pottery. Without excavating, therefore, it is difficult to know whether these sites were actually fortified during the Iron Age. Glueck's claim that a pattern of Iron Age settlements marked the route of the "Kings Highway" mentioned in Num 20:17 and 21:22 must be qualified as well. It is not at all clear that *derek hāmmelek* should be read as a proper name or that the road(s) to which the Num 20:17 and 21:22 refer passed through the Transjordan. While there are Iron Age sites situated along the route of the later Via Nova, the most recent archaeological evidence does not indicate a particular concentration of Iron Age sites along this route.

There is some conflict between the archaeological findings at Dhībān and Tell Ḥesbān (the sites of ancient Dibon and Heshbon respectively) and evidence pertaining to these two cities supplied by the ancient written records. If *Tipun* in the so-called "Palestinian List" from the reign of Tuthmosis III and *Tbniw* in the inscription from the reign of Ramesses II are to be identified with Dibon (see below), then one would expect Dhībān to show archaeological evidence of occupation during the LB Age. Yet excavators reported nothing from either the MB or LB Ages at Dhībān and only a small amount of Iron I material. Late Bronze remains were to be expected at Tell Ḥesbān also, since the Israelites are reported to have defeated King Sihon of Heshbon at the time of their Exodus from Egypt (Num 21:21–35; Deut 2:30–37; Judg 11:19–22), and the Exodus is usually dated during the LB Age. Yet the earliest significant remains uncovered at Tell Ḥesbān date from the 12th century B.C., well after the close of the LB Age. Moreover, even the 12th century remains at Tell Ḥesbān are meager.

Finally, while certain features of the material culture of the Moabites suggest influence from the direction of Egypt (Bālūᶜ Stele relief) and N Syria (Shīḥān Stele), there is even more abundant evidence of close continuity between the material culture of the Moabites and that of their immediate neighbors, including Israel (pottery styles including the collared rim jars and a "pillared building" at Khirbet Medeinet el-Muᶜarradieh, language and script of the Mesha Inscription, etc.). This duality of cultural connections is illustrated by a proto-aeolic capital first reported by Glueck at Meḍiebiᶜ, an Iron Age ruin situated on the desert frontier of the S plateau. Although the nearest parallels are from W Palestine (Megiddo, Samaria, Ramat Raḥel), the motif is best known from the coast of Asia Minor.

D. Moab and Moabites in Ancient Texts

Ancient Egyptian, Moabite, and Assyrian inscriptions provide occasional bits of information about ancient Moab and the Moabites. Also Moab figures prominently in the Hebrew Bible.

1. Moab in Egyptian Sources. The so-called Execration Texts from the 19th or 18th centuries B.C. (MB Age) contain possible references to places in Moab. Also these texts mention "rulers of the Shûtu" among Egypt's Asiatic enemies. We have already referred to one of these Shûtu rulers, Shemuʾ-abu(m), and suggested the possibility that "Shûtu" is the Egyptian equivalent of "Sheth" which in turn is paralleled with Moab in Num 24:17–18. It does not follow, of course, that the Shûtu of the MB Age were specifically Moabites, but only that the biblical poet, composing at a much later time, regarded the Moabites as belonging to Shûtu stock.

Egypt maintained a strong presence in Syria-Palestine during the LB Age, beginning especially with the reign of Thutmosis III (ca. 1482–1450 B.C.). The texts indicate contact primarily with the towns and villages along the main roads, but the Egyptians also encountered non-sedentary folk throughout Syria-Palestine whom they referred to generally as "Shâsu." None of the Shâsu references in the Egyptian texts point specifically to the region E of the Dead Sea. Yet the Egyptians no doubt would have considered this region, at least its desert frontier, as Shâsu territory. It has been observed, moreover, that the central figure depicted on the Bālūᶜ Stele wears a headdress of exactly the sort worn by Shâsu in Egyptian reliefs from Dynasties 19 and 20. It is tempting to conclude, therefore, that Bālūᶜ figure was a Shâsu king. This may, however, be a hasty conclusion. While Shâsu clearly are depicted with this sort of headdress in the Egyptian reliefs, it is less clear that all of those so depicted were Shâsu.

One of the topographical lists from the reign of Thutmosis III, the so-called "Palestinian List" (also called the "Megiddo List"), may indicate that he passed through the Moabite plateau on one of his Asiatic campaigns. This depends, however, on a somewhat tenuous identification of the places mentioned in the list with places in Moab. Two other inscriptions suggest that Ramesses II (ca. 1304–1237) may have campaigned in the region two centuries later. The first of these, a brief topographical list inscribed on a statue of Ramesses II, includes what appears to be the name "Moab." Unfortunately, the list is brief and largely destroyed. The second is actually a grouping of three texts, two of them original lines of palimpsests, from the inscriptions on the outer face of the E wall of the Court of Ramesses II of the Luxor temple. K. A. Kitchen reconstructed the three texts and identified one of the places mentioned, *tbniw,* as Dibon. As indicated above, however, this identification encounters some archaeological difficulties and has been challenged on other grounds as well.

The conclusion that the region E of the Dead Sea was well within the range of Egyptian influence during the Middle and Late Bronze Ages seems certain, even when allowance is made for the various uncertainties mentioned above. Moreover, this conclusion is confirmed by the Bālūᶜ Stele which, as indicated above, probably dates near the end of the LB Age.

2. The Mesha Inscription and Other Moabite Fragments. The Mesha Inscription appears on a memorial stele erected by King Mesha who ruled Moab during the 9th century B.C. Mesha seems to have taken the throne roughly midway through the reign of Ahab of Israel (ca. 873–851 B.C.) and lived to see the collapse of the Omride dynasty which occurred soon before 841 B.C. As was typical of royal memorial inscriptions of the day, the Mesha Inscription begins by introducing Mesha and then proceeds to describe the major achievements of his reign. Two items stand out, both mentioned in the opening lines: the recovery of the land of Medeba from Israelite control, and the building at Qarḥoh of a sanctuary dedicated to the Moabite god Kemosh (Chemosh). Apparently, the stele was established on the occasion of the completion of the sanctuary. (See the English translation in *ANET,* pp. 320–21.) After a lengthy prologue, the text recounts Mesha's actions in connection with the recovery of the land of Medeba and what apparently was a fairly extensive building program at Qarḥoh. Recovery of the land of Medeba involved the taking of at least three Israelite cities: Ataroth, Nebo, and Jahaz. Against Ataroth and Nebo, Mesha launched campaigns that concluded with massacres of their respective populations. Less clear are the circumstances of the taking of Jahaz, which had been fortified by the Israelites and possibly served as an administrative center while N Moab was under Israelite control. The Israelites may have abandoned Jahaz without a fight since Mesha claims to have taken it without any mention of military action or massacre. Moabite loyalists resettled Ataroth, Jahaz, and probably Nebo (although this is not stated specifically).

The sanctuary was only part of a much more extensive building program at Qarḥoh, which in turn probably was the royal (acropolis) district of Dibon, Mesha's capital city.

Mesha's building activities elsewhere in the land included work at Baal-meon (a reservoir), Qaryaten, Aroer, and Bezer. He also built several Moabite sanctuaries (Beth-bamoth, Beth-diblathain, Beth-baal-meon) and improved the road crossing the Arnon. As the inscription draws to a close, Mesha claims that "all Dibon" was loyal to him and that he ruled over a hundred towns which he had brought under Dibonite control. The last lines, which are badly damaged, report a campaign against Hauronen.

The name of Mesha's father may be provided by a small inscription fragment discovered at Kerak in 1958 (or soon before). This basalt fragment, only 14 × 12.5 cm, seems to have a close parallel in a funerary stele discovered near Aleppo in 1891. If so, then the inscription was written in horizontal lines across the garment of a standing figure. Parts of only four lines survive and have been reconstructed by W. L. Reed and F. V. Winnett to read as follows:

. . . K]*mšyt,* king of Moab, the . . .
. . . of Kemosh (to serve) as an altar (?) because he . . .
. . . his . . . And behold I made . . .

The script resembles that of the Mesha Inscription. Moreover, the first part of the king's name is missing in the Kerak fragment, while the last part of the name of Mesha's father is missing in the Mesha Inscription (*Kmš*[. .]). The translation proposed above reconstructs them as the same name, Kemoshyatti.

Two more fragments with bits of Canaanite (Moabite) script have been discovered, one at Dhībān and one at Khirbet Bālūᶜ. In neither case can a full word be reconstructed with some degree of certainty. Also an ostracon with a possible *mem* and *waw* has been discovered at Khirbet Bālūᶜ.

3. Moab in the Assyrian Texts. The 734–732 B.C. campaigns of Tiglath-pileser III brought all of Syria-Palestine, including the Moabite region, under Assyrian domination. Thus the royal Assyrian documents provide occasional glimpses of Moabite affairs. The first such glimpse is provided by a fragment of a clay tablet discovered at Nimrud. This fragment provides a long list of kings who paid tribute to Tiglath-pileser shortly after 734 B.C. Among the kings listed is one Salamanu of Moab (*ANET,* 282). Another text, a prism fragment dating from the reign of Sargon II (721–705 B.C.), mentions Moab among certain Palestinian kingdoms implicated in an anti-Assyrian revolt led by Ashdod in 713 (*ANET,* 287). The revolt, signalled by Ashdod's refusal to pay the required annual tribute to Assyria, was quickly crushed. Presumably Moab paid off Sargon and escaped punishment.

Two letters, which cannot be dated specifically but belong approximately to the period of Tiglath-pileser and

Sargon, also mention Moab. One records the delivery of horses, presumably as tribute, to Calah by officials from Egypt, Judah, Moab, and Ammon. The other, from an Assyrian official and delivered to Nineveh by a messenger named Ezazu, reports a raid on Moabite territory by men of Gidir-land (Saggs 1955).

A certain Kammusunadbi from Moab is mentioned among the local Palestinian kings who rushed with presents to assure Sennacherib of their loyalty when he marched against Philistia and Judah in 701 B.C. (*ANET,* 287). A much shorter text from the reign of either Sennacherib or his successor Esarhaddon reports further tribute from the Ammonites, Moabites, Judeans, and possibly Edomites (*ANET,* 301). A King Musuri of Moab is listed among others (including Manasseh of Judah and Qaushgabri of Edom) who transported building materials to Nineveh during the reign of Esarhaddon (*ANET,* 291). Musuri, Manasseh, and Qaushgabri are listed again among local Palestinian rulers who delivered presents to Ashurbanipal and provided military service for the latter's wars against Egypt (*ANET,* 294).

Finally, two texts from the reign of Ashurbanipal are instructive in that (a) they presume that the kingdoms of the Transjordan are loyal Assyrian vassals and thus due Assyrian protection, and (b) they witness to the fact that protection was needed from the direction of Arabia. The threat seems to have been primarily from the Qedarites, a largely nomadic people who roamed the desert region E and SE of Damascus. One of these texts reports a campaign conducted by Ashurbanipal against Uateʾ, identified in the text as king of Arabia but elsewhere as son of Hazaʾil, king of Qedar (*ANET,* 297–98). In the other text Ashurbanipal claims credit for a victory over Ammuladi, king of Qedar, although one Kamashaltu king of Moab seems to have been the actual victor (*ANET,* 298).

4. Moab and Moabites in the Hebrew Bible. The biblical books Genesis through Joshua present an essentially continuous narrative which begins with creation and presents a highly theologized account of Israelite affairs until they are securely settled in "the Land of Canaan." Moab and the Moabites play a fairly prominent, although secondary, role in that story.

The Moabites appear first in Gen 19:30–38, the story of Lot's seduction by his two daughters and the resulting births of the two sons, Moab and Ben-ammi. Gen 36:31–39 (= 1 Chr 1:43–50) may be a Moab-related text as well. These verses purport to present a list of "kings who reigned in the land of Edom before there reigned any king over the children of Israel," but it has been observed (a) that the list seems to have been derived from two different sources, and (b) that one of the sources probably pertained to early Moabite, rather than Edomite, rulers. Specifically, three of the names in the list may have Moabite connections: Bela the son of Beor whose city was Dinhabah; Hadad the son of Bedad, who smote Midian in the field of Moab; and Hadar (or Hadad) whose city was Pau (Bartlett 1965).

According to the biblical narrative which continues through the books of Exodus and Leviticus to Numbers 21, the Israelites escaped from Egypt under the leadership of Moses, wandered for forty years in the wilderness, and arrived finally at the plains "across the Jordan from Jericho." There they remained encamped, we are told, until Moses died (Deuteronomy 34) and Joshua led the Israelites across the Jordan into the land of Canaan (Joshua 1–3). The plains of Moab provide the setting for a considerable portion of the Genesis–Joshua narrative, therefore, from Numbers 21 through Joshua 3. The events reported in these chapters may be summarized as follows.

The Israelites reached N Moab and defeated Sihon, an Amorite king who had taken this region from the Moabites and ruled it from Heshbon. They also defeated Og, another Amorite king who ruled still further N, and thus gained possession of virtually all the Transjordan (Num 21:10–35). Balak, a Moabite king, called on the prophet Balaam to curse the Israelites who now were encamped in the plains of Moab. Balaam, insisting that he could speak only what God gave him to speak, blessed Israel instead of cursing them (Numbers 22–24). Some of the Israelites began to worship Baal of Peor, and one even cohabited with a Midianite woman. Phinehas, son of Eleazer the priest, killed the couple. God commanded Moses and Eleazer to harass and smite the Midianites (Numbers 25). Moses and Eleazer conducted a census of the congregation, after which Yahweh provided further legal and cultic instructions (Numbers 26–30). Israel avenged the Midianites; the Reubenites and Gadites were assigned territory in N Moab; Manassehite clans received territory still further N, and Yahweh provided further instructions (Numbers 31–36). Moses reviewed key events which had occurred while the Israelites wandered in the wilderness and camped in the plains of Moab, reviewed the law which God had handed down to him, viewed the promised land from Pisgah, and died (Deuteronomy 1–34). Leadership was transferred to Joshua at that point, who began preparations for the conquest of Canaan (Joshua 1–3).

Events of the "Plains of Moab" stage in the Israelite journey from Egypt also are mentioned from time to time later on in the biblical narrative as it continues through 2 Kings (see, for example, the summary of conquests in Joshua 12–13 and the exchange of messages between Jephthah and the Ammonite king in Judg 11:12–28).

One must take into account that Genesis–2 Kings is a composite narrative composed long after the described circumstances and events would have occurred. Its composite character becomes especially obvious when one examines the "plains of Moab" segment summarized above. In addition to abrupt shifts in vocabulary and literary style which sometimes are noticeable even in translation, there is corresponding disunity in the content of the story. For example, the Israelite defeat of Sihon and seizure of his kingdom is reported in Num 21:21–30 as if there were no Moabite king with conflicting territorial claims. Then the Balak/Balaam episode which follows (and which has Balak much concerned about Israelite presence in the plains of Moab) is narrated without any apparent awareness of Sihon's role in political affairs or that the Israelites had already taken from Sihon all of the territory N of the Arnon.

Traditio-historical considerations also caution against an uncritical acceptance of the testimony of the narrative. The story about Lot and his daughters has all the appearances of a folk story, for example. And the claim that Sihon took from Moab the region N of the Arnon and then lost it to the Israelites has obvious propagandistic overtones; it seeks to legitimize Israelite possession of territory which even other parts of the Hebrew Bible recognize as belonging historically to Moab. Moreover, as indicated above, the Sihon tradition is contradicted by archaeological evidence. Heshbon, identified as the capital of Sihon's Amorite kingdom, apparently was not even occupied at the time when these events supposedly occurred.

Nevertheless, even if the Genesis–Joshua account cannot be taken at face value for purposes of historical reconstruction, matters of historical interest pertaining to Moab can be gleaned from the traditions embedded in it. The story of Lot's daughters, for example, in spite of its folkloristic character and derogatory slant, shows that the Israelites regarded the Moabites and Ammonites as relatives. The common heritage of these peoples is suggested also, as we have seen, by their shared material culture. Other passages in the Hebrew Bible indicate that there was constant interchange between the Israelites and Moabites including intermarriage. The genealogical record at the end of the book of Ruth is especially noteworthy in this regard. It claims, namely, that King David himself was descended from the Moabitess Ruth. Among the numerous obscure notations in the genealogies of 1 Chronicles 1–8, on the other hand, is mention of a Moabite ruler of Judaean descent (1 Chr 4:22). 1 Chr 8:8–10 speaks of one Shaharaim (presumably a descendant of Benjamin, although the context is unclear) who ". . . had sons in the country of Moab after he had sent away Hushim and Baara his wives. He had sons by Hodesh his wife: Jobab, Zibia, Mesha, Malcam, Jeuz, Sachia, and Mirmah. There were his sons, heads of fathers' houses."

The Sihon passages bear witness to the political conflicts between the Israelites, Moabites, and Ammonites during biblical times, indicate that competition for control of N Moab was a central issue in much of this conflict, and remind us that international disputes always involve some degree of propaganda warfare. No doubt the Moabites and Ammonites also had their own versions of earlier history which supported their respective claims to N Moab.

Similarly, the traditions that report religious apostasy and violence at Beth-peor, although projected back to the Mosaic era when all Israel supposedly was camped in the Plains of Moab, probably had more to do with the ongoing experiences of Israelite clans who lived permanently among the Moabites (and Midianites!) in the disputed region. While many will have married non-Israelite wives and worshiped local gods at Moabite shrines, there will have been counter efforts to maintain ethnic and religious distinctiveness; and this distinctiveness will have added a local dynamic to the violence which inevitably occurred each time the disputed territory changed hands (e.g., David's selective massacre of Moabites; Mesha's massacre of Gadites).

The cultic center at Beth-peor on the NW edge of the Moabite plateau apparently played a central role in much of this struggle, and the conflicting attitudes which Israelites would have held concerning this shrine are reflected in the conflicting biblical traditions regarding Baalam. Numbers 22–24 reflects an essentially positive attitude toward Beth-peor and Baalam. It was from Beth-peor, we are told, that Balaam uttered his third oracle of blessing upon the Israelites. Numbers 25 and 32 depict Beth-peor as an evil place, on the other hand, symbolic of the evils of religious apostasy. Balaam, correspondingly, is an evil prophet who encouraged Moabite and Midianite women to draw Israelite men into their foreign cult (see also Deut 23:4; Josh 22:17; Neh 13:2; 2 Pet 2:15).

The ambivalent cultic situation in which the Israelites who settled E of the Jordan found themselves is reflected further in Joshua 22.

The Genesis–Joshua narrative continues in the books of Judges–2 Kings (excluding Ruth). The next reported event in Israelite-Moabite relations is an episode associated with the time of the Israelite judges when "Eglon the king of Moab" allied himself with the Ammonites and Amalekites, defeated Israel, and took possession of "the city of Palms." Thus the people of Israel served Eglon for eighteen years, according to the story, until Yahweh raised up a deliverer. This deliverer was Ehud, a Benjaminite, who assassinated Eglon, mustered an army, and seized the fords of the Jordan so that about 10,000 Moabites were killed (Judg 3:12–30).

After the Eglon/Ehud episode, the Judges–2 Kings corpus contains only brief references and one extended narrative (2 Kgs 3:4–27) pertaining to Israelite-Moabite relations. Saul is reported to have "fought against all his enemies on every side, against Moab, against the Ammonites, against Edom, against the kings of Zobah, and against the Philistines; wherever he turned he put them to the worse" (1 Sam 14:47). David, while a fugitive from Saul, left his parents with the king of Moab (1 Sam 22:3–4). Yet we read later in the account of his reign that David ". . . defeated Moab, and measured them with a line, making them lie down on the ground; two lines he measured to be put to death, and one full line to be spared. And the Moabites became servants to David and brought tribute" (2 Sam 8:2). Unfortunately the text of 2 Sam 24:5–7, which reports a census undertaken by David, is difficult to follow. It seems clear, however, that the census officials began at Aroer on the N bank of the Arnon and worked northward from there. Thus David apparently exercised direct control only over N Moab. Solomon is reported to have indulged the worship of foreign gods in Jerusalem, and Josiah to have reversed this policy two centuries later. In both instances Chemosh, the Moabite god, is mentioned (1 Kgs 11:7, 33; 2 Kgs 23:13).

2 Kings 1:1 and 3:4–5 report that king Mesha of Moab, who had been required to deliver annual tribute to Ahab, rebelled against Israel following Ahab's death. 2 Kgs 3:6–27 recounts then Jehoram's unsuccessful attempt to restore Israelite authority over Moab. After the Omride-Mesha conflict, the Moabites are mentioned only twice more in the Judges–2 Kings narrative. Both instances have to do with Moabite raids W of the Jordan (2 Kgs 13:20–21; 24:2). Apparently, the latter half of the 9th century was a bleak time for the peoples of Palestine, as illustrated by the Elisha stories. None dared challenge the Syrians who exploited the land without providing security. 2 Kgs 13:20–21, intended to illustrate the power of Elisha even after his death, mentions Moabite raids which presumably occurred under the shadow of Syrian oppression. Moabite raids would continue to be a problem in still later years. 2

Kgs 24:2 reports that, when Jehoiakim rebelled against Nebuchadnezzar, Yahweh "sent against him bands of the Chaldeans, and bands of the Syrians, and bands of the Moabites, and bands of the Ammonites."

References to Moab and Moabites in the prose sections of the Hebrew Bible appear outside the Genesis–2 Kings corpus also. The book of Ruth has been mentioned already. Regardless of the historicity of the story, one must consider the underlying assumption of the storyteller that Moab would have been a reasonable place to go in search of grain when famine struck Judah. The Chronicler provides a not entirely convincing story of how Yahweh saved Jerusalem during Jehoshaphat's reign from a combined attack by Moabites, Ammonites, and Meunites (2 Chr 20:1–30). The city was saved, according to the story, without its defenders so much as raising a spear. Mention should be made also of two Moab references in the prose sections of Jeremiah. Near the beginning of Zedekiah's reign, when Jeremiah warned the king against challenging the Babylonian hold on Judah, he apparently attempted to send the same message to neighboring kings by way of their envoys who had come to Jerusalem to confer with Zedekiah. The kings of Edom, Moab, Ammon, Tyre, and Sidon are mentioned in particular (Jeremiah 27, see esp. v.3). Jeremiah 40:11–12, on the other hand, describes circumstances after the Babylonians had captured Jerusalem for a second time and placed the government in the hands of Gedaliah. At that time Jews who had fled to the Transjordan began to return to their homes, and Moab, Ammon, and Edom are specified as the lands to which they had fled.

In the poetical sections of the Hebrew Bible, references to Moab and the Moabites are usually in very generalized contexts which treat Moab as an enemy along with other neighboring nations. Thus in Exodus 15, the so-called "Song of the Sea," the Moabites figure among those terrified by Yahweh's mighty deeds in Israel's behalf (Exod 15:14–15). Moab appears also in Psalm 60 and 108, which partially duplicate each other. These communal laments appear to Yahweh to show his strength and express confidence that he will do so. The salvation oracle is given as divine proclamation: "Moab is my washbasin; upon Edom I cast my shoe; over Philistia I shout in triumph" (Ps 60:8; 108:9). Similarly, Psalm 83, which probably dates from the waning years of the Judean monarchy before the collapse of the Assyrian empire, calls upon God to take vengeance on various enemies including Moab.

The books of Amos, Isaiah, and Jeremiah include collections of oracles directed against individual foreign nations (Amos 1–2; Isaiah 13–23; Jeremiah 46–51). The oracles in Amos introduce the book, and all of them follow a similar format. They address in turn Damascus, Philistia, Tyre, Edom, the Ammonites, and Moab (2:1–3). The collection of Moab oracles in Isaiah 15–16 and Jeremiah 48 partially duplicate each other. Jeremiah additionally includes a variant version of the Num 21:27–30 oracle pertaining to Sihon and Heshbon. Very little specific information about Moabite history can be derived from any of these prophetical texts. The one cited above from Amos leaves us completely in the dark, for example, as to the identity of the Moabite king who burned the bones of the Edomite king or the circumstances of his deed. The oracles do, however, have some implications for the historical geography of Moab, even if the evidence they provide is difficult to interpret.

In addition to these oracles which focus specifically on Moab, several other poetical texts mention Moab in anticipation of a restoration of Israel and downfall of her neighbors (Isa 11:12–16; 25:10–12; Jer 9:25–26; 25:15–29; Ezek 25:8–11; Zeph 2:8–11; see also Balaam's oracle in Num 24:15–24, esp. v 17). Finally, some mention should be made of the occasional references to Moab in postexilic biblical texts, most of which also mention the Moabites along with Judah's other neighbors in derogatory fashion (Ezra 9:1; Dan 11:41; Jdt 1:12; 5:2; 5:22; 7:8). Neh 13:1 notes that the books of Moses denied Moabites and Ammonites admission to the assembly of God because of their behavior toward Israel at the time of the exodus. The Hebrew text of Sir 36:10, reminiscent of Num 24:17 and Jer 48:45, specifies "Moabite" princes as the object of divine wrath.

E. Moabite History

Moab was one of several relatively small kingdoms that emerged in the Levant during the early centuries of the Iron Age, existed for a time alongside each other, and then fell under the domination of the Assyrians. Those kingdoms which survived the Assyrians with their national identity intact would not survive the Babylonians, Persians, Greeks, and Romans, who dominated the Levant each in turn after the Assyrians. Among these Iron Age kingdoms was Moab. Unfortunately very little is known about the origin of the Moabites or the details of their history.

1. Moabite Origins. According to the Genesis-Joshua narrative reviewed above, the Moabites descended from an ancestor named Moab, Lot's son/grandson (Gen 19:37), and their land was inhabited in earliest times by a race of giants known as the Emim (Deut 2:10). One would suppose also, from an uncritical reading of the narrative, that the Moabites already were organized into a monarchy when the Israelites passed through the Transjordan on their exodus from Egypt (Num 21:10–20; Deut 2:9–19); that the Moabite king on the throne at the time was named Balak (Num 22–24); that a large section of Moabite territory (N Moab) had been lost to an Amorite king named Sihon soon before the Israelites arrived on the scene (Num 21:26–30), and that the Israelites took this Moabite territory from Sihon (Num 21:21–25). As observed above, however, the Genesis-Joshua narrative is not a reliable source of information regarding Moabite origins. For one thing, it was compiled several centuries after Balak and Sihon supposedly lived.

We know now that, contrary to Glueck's findings, the Moabite plateau was occupied to some degree throughout the Bronze Age. Neither does the archaeological evidence suggest a major cultural break in the S Transjordan between the Bronze Age and the Iron Age. There is no reason to suppose, accordingly, that the Moabite kingdom emerged from newcomers to the region. In other words, the Moabites of biblical times may have been, for the most part, descendants of the general population which had inhabited the region E of the Dead Sea from earliest times.

2. Early Moabite Monarchy? All of our information about the Moabite kingdom(s) prior to King Mesha also comes from the Hebrew Bible, beginning with the references indicated above to an early Moabite king named Balak. Judg 3:12–30 mentions another Moabite king named Eglon who ruled "the city of palms" (probably Jericho) during the time of the Judges. The biblical narratives pertaining to Balak and Eglon have very obvious legendary overtones. But even if they are to be taken as historically trustworthy, one cannot assume that Balak and Eglon ruled over a united Moabite state which included all of the region E of the Dead Sea. More likely, the political situation in S Transjordan during the opening centuries of the Iron Age will have been characterized by political disunity and diversity. There will have been a few modest cities, each with its king who also controlled some of the surrounding countryside. However tribal elders also will have played a role in the political structure, especially among the villages scattered throughout the land. Also from time to time there will have arisen local chieftains who carved out local kingdoms. Eglon may have been a king of this sort. Even Mesha's realm, as we shall see below, may not have encompassed all of Moab.

By the same measure, the biblical claim that David defeated Moab (2 Sam 8:2) does not necessarily mean, as often presupposed by Bible atlases, that he conquered and annexed to Israel all the land of Moab from the Dead Sea to the desert and from Heshbon to the River Zered. More likely, he subjugated only the region N of the Arnon.

3. Mesha's Kingdom. The only Moabite king that we know much about and, correspondingly, the only period of Moabite history for which we have any substantial details, is king Mesha who ruled from Dibon during the mid-9th century B.C. He was a contemporary of the strong Omride dynasty of Israel (Omri, Ahab, Ahaziah, Jehoram) and is reported in the Hebrew Bible to have rebelled against Israelite domination after Ahab's death (2 Kgs 1:1; 3:4–27). The main reason that Mesha and his period is so well known, however, is that he left his own record of his major deeds—the Mesha Inscription. Unfortunately the information provided by the Mesha Inscription does not correlate easily with the related materials in the Hebrew Bible (esp. 2 Kgs 1:1 and 3:4–27). Thus the following proposed reconstruction of events is somewhat hypothetical.

Mesha followed his father to the throne in Dibon roughly midway during Ahab's reign. Most of N Moab was under Israelite domination at the time and Mesha, as his father before him, had to pay annual tribute to the Omrides. The political situation in Israel took a turn for the worse after Ahab died, and Mesha seized the opportunity to rebell. At first the "rebellion" would have consisted of Mesha's refusal to pay the annual tribute, along with preparations for defense in case Israel took military action. When it was apparent that Ahaziah, who followed Ahab to the throne, could not take action because of a personal accident and other difficulties in Samaria (2 Kings 1), Mesha proceeded with military moves of his own intended to restore Moabite control over N Moab. Probably it was necessary only to settle affairs with a few pro-Israelite cities, perhaps only Ataroth and Nebo, since most of the population of the disputed region was Moabite and would have welcomed the change. When Ahaziah died, Jehoram ascended the throne in Samaria and organized a military campaign against Mesha. The account of the campaign in 2 Kgs 3:4–27 is beset with literary problems and its details should not be pressed too far (Miller 1967; Bartlett 1983). The essence of the account is that the attacking army approached Moab from around the S end of the Dead Sea, devastated fields and cisterns throughout the land, laid siege to Kir-hareseth where Mesha had retreated, but then withdrew from the city when Mesha sacrificed his oldest son on the city wall.

Mesha seems to have had a long reign and claims in his inscription to have been an active builder. Near the end of the inscription, where it is badly damaged and concluding lines are broken off entirely, Mesha claims to have undertaken a victorious military campaign against Horonaim. It is noteworthy that, with the possible exception of the Horonaim campaign, all of Mesha's activities reported in the inscription were confined to N Moab, the region N of the Arnon. Whether the Horonaim campaign would have taken him into the main Moabite plateau depends on the location of Horonaim (see below). Even allowing for the possibility that Horonaim was located S of the Arnon, however, the pattern of his recorded deeds strongly suggests that Mesha's effective rule was confined to N Moab.

4. Moab under the Assyrians, Babylonians, and Persians. The Assyrian texts imply that Moab fell under Assyrian domination during the 8th century B.C. as did the remainder of the Levant. Also the Assyrian texts provide the names of four additional Moabite kings: Salamanu, who paid tribute to Tiglath-pileser; Kammusunadbi, who pledged loyalty to Sennacherib; Musuri, a contemporary of Manasseh of Judah, Esarhaddon, and Ashurbanipal; and Kamashaltu, who defeated the Qedarites later on in Ashurbanipal's reign. Precise dates are unavailable for any of these four kings.

According to Josephus, the Ammonites and Moabites were brought under Babylonian subjection five years after the destruction of Jerusalem (*Ant* 10.9.7). Presumably the peoples of the Transjordan, including the Moabite, submitted to Persian occupation as well, although there is no specific evidence available in this regard.

5. Moab during Hellenistic-Roman Times. We are dependent almost entirely on Josephus for information about circumstances in the Transjordan during Hellenistic and Roman times. That the whole Transjordan was regarded as part of Arabia (i.e., Nabatean realm) by the beginning of the 1st century B.C. is presupposed by Josephus' account of the warfare between Alexander Jannaeus (103–76 B.C.) and the latter's Nabatean contemporary, Obodas I. Josephus reports, namely, that Alexander overcame "the Arabians, such as the Moabites and Gileadites, and made them bring tribute" (*Ant* 13.13.5 §374). Later on, according to Josephus, Alexander "was forced to deliver back to the king of Arabia the land of Moab and Gilead, which he had subdued, and places that were in them" (*Ant* 13.14.2 §382). This leaves the reader somewhat unprepared for Josephus' account of the negotiations between Hyrcanus II and Aretas III after Alexander's death, at which time Hyrcanus supposedly offered to return the Moabite cities if Aretas would support his bid for the Judean throne (*Ant* 14.1.4§18). Pompey's eastern campaign in 64–63 B.C. brought all of Syria-Palestine under the shadow of Rome. Nabatea, including the Moabite region, became a client kingdom. No doubt the bulk of the population consisted of descendants of the ancient Moabites, and the name would survive for a long time—e.g., in that of the two chief cities, Rabbath Moab and Karak Moab. For all practical purposes, however, the history of ancient Moab had come to an end.

F. Moabite Place Names

Since most of the written information about ancient Moab must be gleaned from non-Moabite sources, it is not surprising that the towns and villages of the more accessible region N of the Arnon/Mūjib are much better documented than those of the S plateau. Most of the Moabite towns and villages mentioned in the Hebrew Bible, for example, and virtually all of those which can be located today with any degree of confidence, were situated in N Moab. Noteworthy also is the fact that Mesha's capital city, Dibon, and all of the other places mentioned in his inscription with the possible exception of Hauronen, were located N of the Arnon/Mūjib.

1. Northern Moab. As indicated above, the following site identifications have been proposed for places mentioned in Egyptian sources: *tipun/tbniw* (equated with Moabite Dibon which is identical in turn with present-day Dhībān; M.R. 224101); *kurmin* (present-day ʾUmeiri); and *betaʾe* (present-day Jelūl). While these identifications are plausible, only the Dibon/Dhībān equation can be regarded as reasonably certain. In addition to Dibon, the following towns and villages in N Moab known from the Hebrew Bible and/or the Mesha Inscription can also be located with reasonable confidence: Elealeh (present-day el-ʿĀl; M.R. 228136), Heshbon (Tell Hesbān; M.R. 226134), Nebo (possibly Khirbet el-Mukhaiyat [M.R. 220128] near Jebel en-Nebā), Medeba (Mādabā; M.R. 225124), Baal-Meon = Beth-meon = Beth-baal-meon = Beon (Maʿīn; M.R. 219120), Ataroth (Aṭārūs; M.R. 213109), Mephaath (Umm er-Riṣāṣ), and Aroer (ʿArāʿir; M.R. 228097). Beth-Peor would have been situated on the NW edge of the Moabite plateau, on the spur W of Tell Ḥesbān and overlooking Wādī ʿAyūn Musa. The name of ancient Kerioth probably is preserved in that of present-day el-Quraiyāt M.R. 215105), and the name of ancient Kiriathaim in that of Kirbet el-Qureiye near ʿAyūn ed-Dib.

Bezer and Jahaz seem to have been prominent towns in N Moab and should be represented by equally prominent archaeological sites. Thus Bezer, which is listed in Josh 20:8; 21:36 and 1 Chr 6:63 as a Refuge/Levitical city and described in Deut 4:43 as "Bezer in the wilderness on the tableland" often is associated with Umm el-ʿAmad (M.R. 235132) on the desert side of N Moab. Jahaz, mentioned as the scene of Israel's defeat of King Sihon of Heshbon (Num 21:23; Deut 2:32; Judg 11:20) and depicted as a place of some military importance near Dibon in the Mesha Inscription, possibly is to be associated with present-day Libb (M.R. 222112). Some scholars, however, contending that the Israelites would have approached Sihon's realm from the desert side, search for Jahaz nearer to the desert frontier (e.g., Khirbet el-Medeineh [M.R. 236110] on Wādī el-Themed).

2. Plains of Moab. Situated in the Plains of Moab were Nimrah, Beth-Jeshimoth and Abel-shittim. Nimrah probably is to be associated with present-day Tell Nimrīn. Eusebius and Jerome identify Beth-Jeshimoth with a place called Ismuth (*Onomast.* 266.27; 233.81; 103.9), the ancient name of which probably is preserved in that of present-day Khirbet es-Suweimeh (M.R. 206131). However, contemporary scholars usually accept Glueck's view that Tell ʿAẓeimeh (M.R. 208132) nearby is the actual site of Beth-Jeshimoth. Earlier scholars generally identified Shittim with Tell Kefrein; but the more recent tendency, again following Glueck, has been to associate it with Tell el-Ḥammām (M.R. 214138).

3. The Southern Plateau. Although the name Rabbath-Moab does not appear in any extant pre-Roman sources, it is by etymology an early Moabite name and is to be equated with present-day er-Rabbah (M.R. 220075). Rabbath Moab/er-Rabbah, which came to be called Areopolis during Late Roman and Byzantime times, has also been equated with Ar Moab. However there is very little to recommend this Rabbath Moab/Ar equation. A more likely site for Ar is probably Khirbet Bālūʿ. Ar seems to have been a city of some importance (the name "Ar" is derived from the word for "city") closely associated with Arnon. The ancient city represented by Khirbet Bālūʿ would have been the gateway to the S plateau from N Moab, on the other hand, since the ancient N–S route through the Transjordan will have descended into the Arnon/Mūjib canyon at Aroer, followed the canyon bed into the Wādī el-Bālūʿ tributary, and then ascended the plateau of the S plateau at Khirbet Bālūʿ.

Kir-hereseth (Kir-heres, Kir-hares) usually is equated with present-day Kerak (M.R. 217066) on the basis of the Targumic rendering of "Kir" as *kerak* (Isa 15:1; 16:7, 11) and the geographical implications of the narrative of 2 Kgs 3:4–27. But neither of these lines of evidence can be regarded as very secure. "Kir" is a common element in Moabite place names, and the Targum rendering may be a simple translation meaning "fortified city" rather than the proper name of a city. Literary critics have raised serious questions about the unity and historicity of 2 Kings 3, and even if taken at face value this narrative does not necessarily support the Kir-hereseth/Kerak identification.

The "ascent of Luhith" mentioned in Isa 15:5b–6 generally is associated with an ancient roadway which ascended the Moabite plateau along the N slopes of Wādī en-Numera. Thus Luhith and Horonaim, which are mentioned together in the Isaiah passage, would have been located along this roadway (but see Worschech and Knauf 1986). Present-day Kathrabbā seems the best candidate for the Luhith.

G. Moabite Religion

The Moabites of the Iron Age will have inherited religious concepts and practices from their Bronze Age predecessors, whose religious practices will have been similar in turn to those of their Canaanite neighbors W of the Jordan (see Mattingly, *EncRel* 10:1–3). Place names such as Beth-baal-peor, Beth-baal-meon, and Bemoth-baal indicate the existance of local Baal shrines, for example. The Bālūʿ Stele indicates strong Egyptian influence near the end of the LB Age, which no doubt will have extended to religion. As indicated above, the god and goddess depicted on opposite sides of the central figure may be Egyptian deities. The place name Horonaim is also suggestive in this regard. A deity named *Horôn* apparently was worshipped in both Egypt and Canaan (e.g., at Beth-horon). The place name Nebo may pertain in some way to the god Nabû worshipped in Babylon (Isa 46:1–2).

Chemosh emerged as the national god of the Moabites, however, and was understood to have the same special relationship with them that Yahweh had with the Israelites. Jeremiah refers to the Moabites as "the people of Chemosh" (48:46; see also Num 21:29). Chemosh appears as an element in royal names (*Kammus*unadbi, *Kamas*haltu); and the flowering of the Moabite kingdom under Mesha prompted the building of a royal compound in the capital city which featured a Chemosh sanctuary.

The Moabites believed that their military successes and failures depended upon Chemosh's favor or disfavor, so that the Mesha Inscription reads very much like some parts of the Hebrew Bible. Moab had fallen into difficult times because Chemosh was angry with his land, according to the inscription. But then it was Chemosh who enabled Mesha to recover the lost territories, commanded him to attack Hauronen, and presumably gave him victory there as well. Thus, Mesha dedicated the sanctuary to Chemosh "because he saved me from all the kings and caused me to triumph over all my adversaries" and the conquered territories were incorporated into Chemosh's domain. As Joshua is said to have devoted the city of Jericho with all its spoils and inhabitants to Yahweh for destruction (Josh 6:17–21), so also Mesha consecrated the people of Ataroth and Nebo to destruction (*ḥērem*) in gratitude to Chemosh. The narrative in 2 Kings 3 has Mesha resorting to child sacrifice, which also was not unknown in Israel (see, e.g., 2 Kgs 16:3). Jer 48:7 refers to the priests of Chemosh, and the terminology of the Mesha Inscription suggests some system of divination—"Chemosh said to me, 'Go down, fight against Hauronen." Several animal and human figurines have been found on Moabite sites, some of which may have had religious significance.

Chemosh apparently was not just a local Moabite deity. A god named Kamish may appear in lists of deities from the EB archives at Ebla. Gods with similar names appear in a Babylonian list dating from the MB Age and in a LB Age tablet from Ugarit. Possibly Kemosh was the chief deity of the famous city of Carchemish in N Syria. Providing further evidence of the international scope of Chemosh worship (or evidence of the presence of Moabites in Egypt) are theophoric personal names based on Kemosh (*Kemoshyhi, Kemoshzdk, Kemoshplt*) known from ostraca, graffiti, and papyrus fragments discovered at Sakkar.

The reference to *ʿštr-kmš* in line 17 of the Mesha Inscription has been interpreted two different ways. Possibly it has to do with Chemosh's consort, a female deity presumably associated in some way with the goddess Ishtar or Astarte. Alternatively, it may be a compound name for Chemosh himself—i.e., he would be associated in some way with ʿAshtar, a male Canaanite deity, firstborn of the supreme god El, known from the Ugaritic texts. John Gray, a proponent of this latter view, has collected data which suggests that this Canaanite ʿAshtar (*ʿAttr*) was identical with a S Arabian god *ʿAttar* who was associated in turn with the morning and evening star (1949b). According to Gray, Chemosh, Milcom (the god of the Ammonites), and *Šlm* (apparently worshipped in Jerusalem as indicated by the names Jeru*salem Solom*on, and Ab*salom*) were all epithets or hypostases of this same astral deity. Thus the royal Moabite name *Shalam*anu (no less so than *Kammus*unadbi and *Kamash*altu) would be theophoric names pertaining to ʿAshtar = Chemosh = Milcom = Šlm. Likewise, Judg 11:24 would not be mistaken when it identifies Chemosh as the god of the Ammonites, since Chemosh and Milcom would have been alternate designations for the same god.

Bibliography

Albright, W. F. 1924. The Archaeological Results of an Expedition to Moab and the Dead Sea. *BASOR* 14: 1–12.

———. 1934. Soundings at Ader, A Bronze Age City in Moab. *BASOR* 53: 13–18.

———. 1936. The Canaanite God Ḥaurôn (Ḥôrôn). *AJSL* 53: 1–12.

Bartlett, J. R. 1965. The Edomite King-List of Genesis xxxvi.31–39 and II Chron.i.43–50. *JTS* 10: 301–14

———. 1973. The Moabites and Edomites. Pp. 229–58 in *POTT.*

———. 1983. The "United" Campaign against Moab in 2 Kings 3:4–27. Pp. 135–46 in *Midian, Moab and Edom,* ed. J.F.A. Sawyer and D.J.A. Clines. JSOTSup 24. Sheffield.

Boraas, R. S., and Geraty, L. T. 1976. *Heshbon 1974: The Fourth Campaign at Tell Heshbân.* Berrien Springs, MI.

———. 1978. *Heshbon 1976: The Fifth Campaign at Tell Heshbân.* Berrien Springs, MI.

Boraas, R. S., and Horn, S. H. 1975. *Heshbon 1973: The Third Campaign at Tell Heshbân.* Berrien Springs, MI.

Brünnow, R. E., and Domaszewski, A. von. 1904–9. *Die Provincia Arabia.* 3 vols. Strassburg.

Conder, C. R. 1889a. *Heth and Moab.* London.

———. 1889b. *The Survey of Eastern Palestine.* London.

Crowfoot, J. W. 1934. An Expedition to Bālûʿah. *PEFQS,* 76–84.

Donner, H. 1957. Neue Quellen zur Geschichte des Staates Moab in der zweiten Hälfte des 8. Jahrh. v. Chr. *MIO* 5: 155–84.

———. 1964. Remarks and Observations on the Historical Topography of Jordan. *ADAJ* 8–9: 88–92.

Glueck, N. 1934. Explorations in Eastern Palestine I. PP. 1–113 in AASOR 14. New Haven.

———. 1939. *Explorations in Eastern Palestine III.* AASOR 18–19: 60–138.

———. 1940. *The Other Side of the Jordan.* New Haven.

———. 1943. Some Ancient Towns in the Plains of Moab. *BASOR* 91: 7–26.

Gray, J. 1949a. The Canaanite God Horon. *JNES* 8: 27–34.

———. 1949b. The Desert God ʿAṯtr in the Literature and Religion of Canaan. *JNES* 8: 72–73.

Grohman, E. D. 1958. A History of Moab. Diss. Johns Hopkins.

Hadidi, A. ed. 1982. *Studies in the History and Archaeology of Jordan.* London and Amman.

Horsfield, G., and Vincent, L. H. 1932. Chronique und Stèle Égypto-Moabite au Balouʿa. *RB* 41: 417–44.

Ibach, R. D. 1987. *Archaeological Survey of the Hesban Region. Hesban 5.* Berrien Springs, MI.

Kautz, J. 1981. Tracking the Ancient Moabites. *BA* 44: 27–35.

Kitchen, K. 1964. Some New Light on the Asaitic Wars of Ramesses II. *JEA* 50: 47–70.

Kuschke, A. 1962. New Contributions to the Historical Topography of Jordan. *ADAJ* 6–7: 90–95.

———. 1967. Horonaim and Qiryathaim. Remarks on a Recent Contribution to the Topography of Moab. *PEQ* 99: 104–5.
Menéndez, M. 1983. The Iron I Structures in the Area Surrounding Medeineh Al Maᶜarradjeh (Smakieh). *ADAJ* 27: 179–84.
Miller, J. M. 1967. The Fall of the House of Ahab. *VT* 17: 307–24.
———. 1974. The Moabite Stone as a Memorial Stele. *PEQ* 106: 9–18.
———. 1979a. Archaeological Survey of Central Moab:1978. *BASOR* 234: 43–52.
———. 1979b. Archaeological Survey South of Wadi Mūjib: Glueck's Sites Revisited. *ADAJ* 23: 79–92.
———. 1982. Recent Archaeological Developments Relevant to Ancient Moab. PP. 169–73 in Hadidi 1982.
Mittmann, S. 1973. Das südliche Ostjordanland im Lichte eines neuassyrischen Keilschriftbriefes aus Nimrūd. *ZDPV* 93: 15–25.
———. 1982. The Ascent of Luhith. Pp. 175–80 in Hadadi 1982.
Murphy, R. E. 1952. A Fragment of an Early Moabite Inscription from Dibon. *BASOR* 125: 20–23.
Musil, A. 1907–8. *Arabia Petraea.* 2 vols. Vienna.
Olávarri, E. 1965. Sondages a ᶜArôᶜer sur l'Arnon. *RB* 72: 77–94.
———. 1969. Fouilles a ᶜArôᶜer sur l'Arnon. *RB* 76: 230–59.
———. 1977–8. Sondeo Arquelogico en Khirbet Medeineh junto a Smakieh (Jordania). *ADAJ* 22: 136–49.
———. 1983. La Campagne de fouilles 1982 à Khirbet Medeinet al-Muᶜarradjeh Prés de Smakieh (Kerak). *ADAJ* 27: 165–78.
Piccirillo, M. 1975. Una tomba del Ferro I a Madeba. *Liber Annuus* 25: 199–224.
Redford, D. B. 1982. Contacts Between Egypt and Jordan in the New Kingdom: Some Comments on Sources. Pp. 115–20 in Hadadi 1982.
Reed, W. L. 1972. The Archaeological History of Elealeh in Moab. Pp. 18–28 in *Studies on the Ancient Palestinian World,* ed. J. W. Wevers and D. B. Redford. Toronto.
Saggs, W. F. 1955. The Nimrud Letters—II Relations with the West. *Iraq* 17: 126–60.
Saller, S. J., and Bagatti, B. 1949. *The Town of Nebo (Khirbet el-Mekhayyat).* Jerusalem.
Schottroff, W. 1966. Horonaim, Nimrim, Luhlith und der Westrand des Landes Ataroth. *ZDPV* 82: 163–208.
Smith, G. A. 1904–5. The Roman Road between Kerak and Madeba. *PEFQS* 1904: 367–77; 1905: 39–48.
———. 1914. Moab. Col. 3166–3179 in *EncBib.*
Tristram, H. B. 1873. *The Land of Moab.* New York.
Tushingham, A. D. 1972. *The Excavations at Dibon (Dhībān) in Moab: The Third Campaign 1952–53.* AASOR 40. Cambridge, MA.
Van Seters, J. 1972. The Conquest of Sihon's Kingdom. A Literary Examination. *JBL* 91: 182–97.
Vollers, K. 1908. Der Name Moab. *ZA* 21: 237–40.
Ward, W. A., and Martin, M. F. 1964. The Bālūᶜa Stele: A New Transcription with Palaeographical and Historical Notes. *ADAJ* 8–9: 5–35.
Warmanbol, E. 1983. La stèle de Ruğm el-ᶜAbd (Louvre AO 5055). *Levant* 15: 63–75.
Winnett, F. V., and Reed, W. L. 1964. *The Excavations at Dibon (Dhībān) in Moab.* AASOR 36–37. New Haven.
Worschech, U. F. 1985a. *Northwest Ard el-Kerak 1983 and 1984: A Preliminary Report.* Munich.
———. 1985b. Preliminary Report on the Third Survey Season in the Northwest Arḍ el-Kerak, 1985. *ADAJ* 29: 161–73.
Worschech, U. F. and Knauf, E. A. 1986. Diamon und Horonaim. *BN* 31: 70–94.
Worschech, U. F., Rosenthal, U., and Zayadine, F. 1986. The Fourth Survey Season in the North-west Arḍ el-Kerak, and Soundings at Baluᶜ 1986. *ADAJ* 30: 285–309.

J. Maxwell Miller

MOAB, CITY OF (PLACE). The place where Balak went to meet Balaam, a site located "on the boundary formed by the Arnon, at the extremity of the boundary" (Num 22:36). "City of Moab" is the translated equivalent of "Ar of Moab" (Num 21:28); the two designations probably refer to the same town. Ancient Ar's exact location remains unknown, though several proposals have been made. Neither Rabbah (ancient Areopolis) nor el-Misnaᶜ fulfill the basic requirement of the text, i.e., location on or near the Arnon gorge. Ar, the city of Moab, may have been located at el-Baluᶜa, ca. 7 miles NE of Rabba.

Gerald L. Mattingly

MOABITE LANGUAGE. See LANGUAGES (INTRODUCTORY SURVEY).

MOABITE STONE. See MESHAᶜ STELE.

MOADIAH (PERSON) [Heb *môᶜadyāh*]. The eponymous ancestor of a priestly family headed by Pittai at the time of the high priest Joiakim (Neh 12:17). Some have suggested that this name is to be identified with the name Maadiah (Neh 12:5), the etymology of which is also uncertain. If the name Moadiah is a distinct and separate entity, however, the question remains whether it derives from *yᶜd* (Yahweh summons) or *mᶜd.* The biblically attested meaning of the latter verbal root is "to slip, totter," forming the unlikely construction "Yahweh totters." A more likely meaning, "to promise," is attested in Old S Arabic (KB) which, when connected with the theophoric element, would result in "Yahweh promises."

Nora A. Williams

MOCHMUR (PLACE) [Gk *Mochmour*]. A wadi mentioned as a geographical locator in the book of Judith (Jdt 7:18). Otherwise unknown under the name "Mochmur" (the name is missing in the Vulgate), but it has been identified with the Wadi Qana, a tributary of the Jarkon river located 15 miles from Ekrebel (see *MBA*). The wadi forms the boundary between the territories of Manasseh and Ephraim (Josh 16:8; 17:9), and is SE of Dothan, the correct geographical location according to the book of Judith. However, it is quite far from the location of Bethuliah given in the book of Judith; if the purpose of the men of Esau and Ammon was to blockade the water supply of the city, it seems pointless to journey so far to the SE. Enslin (1972) has given as a possibility the Wadi Makhfurlyeh, S of Nablus. This identification is not as precise as that of the Wadi Qana. It is, however, closer to the purported location of Bethuliah. Of course, given the genre of the book of Judith, it is entirely possible that the name is fictitious. See also JUDITH.

Bibliography

Enslin, M. S. 1972. *Book of Judith.* Leiden.

SIDNIE ANN WHITE

MODAD. See ELDAD AND MODAD.

MODEIN (PLACE) [Gk *Modein*]. An ancient village located ca. 20 miles NW of Jerusalem in the region of Lydda (Lod). Modein is only mentioned briefly in 1 and 2 Maccabees (cf. Goldstein, *I Maccabees* and *II Maccabees* AB) where its importance is chiefly due to its association with Mattathias and other leaders of the Maccabean revolt (see especially 1 Maccabees 2 and Josephus, *Ant* 12–13). Although Robinson reports that "Sôba has now for centuries been regarded in monastic tradition as the site of the ancient Modin" (Robinson 1841: 328–30), the town is confidently to be identified with modern Ras Medieh (M.R. 150148), a typical tell of the Shephelah of Judah. This site may be more fully described by referring to three facets of its history: the Maccabean rebellion, the monumental tombs erected to the Hasmoneans, and Rabbi Eleazar, another famous inhabitant of this town.

A. The Maccabean Rebellion

Modein is first mentioned in 1 Maccabees 2. In 168 B.C.E., the Hellenistic Seleucid ruler Antiochus Epiphanes captured Jerusalem and desecrated the temple. At this time an attempt was made to force the Jews to abandon their traditional religion and unite with the rest of the Seleucid kingdom in worshiping Hellenistic deities. In the midst of the turmoil in Jerusalem, Mattathias and his five sons (John, Simon, Judas, Eleazar, and Jonathan) escaped to Modein. Soon, however, Syrian officers came to Modein to enforce the policies of Antiochus. Mattathias, because he was both a priest and leading citizen, was chosen to make the required sacrifices with the expectation that once he did so the rest of the town would follow suit. He refused, and when a Jew who *was* willing to make the sacrifice stepped forward, Mattathias, in a righteous rage, killed him at the altar. He then killed the Syrian officer and tore down the altar upon which the sacrifice was to have been made. Following this, Mattathias and his five sons fled into the hills, calling upon those who would defy the Syrian policies to join them in guerrilla resistance. Thus began the Maccabean rebellion which three years later resulted in the recapture of Jerusalem and the rededication of the temple.

References to Modein (Modiith) in the Mishnah indicate that this town came to mark the boundary of Judah. Thus, *Pesah.* 9.2 reads, "What counts as a *journey afar off?* Beyond Modiith, or a like distance in any direction." *Ḥag.* 3.5 reads, "From Modiith and inwards men may be deemed trustworthy in what concerns earthenware vessels; from Modiith and outwards they may not be deemed trustworthy." The two further references to Modein in connection with the Maccabean rebellion reflect this use of the term.

1 Macc 16:4–10 relates the story of an important battle in the Maccabean rebellion which took place in the vicinity of Modein. The aging ruler Simon entrusted command of the armies to his two sons Judas and John without relinquishing his own authority or position. The battle against Kendebaios is launched from an encampment at Modein and serves to mark the first stage of the transition in leadership from Simon to his son John.

The final, although problematic, reference to Modein is found in 2 Maccabees 13. The narrative describes a massive expedition of Seleucid forces under Antiochus V against the Jews. Judas Maccabaeus, after a period of prayer and preparation, decided not to wait for the town to be attacked but instead to march out and confront the Syrian troops at the border of Judea. Making camp near Modein, Judas attacked the Syrians by night, killed some 2,000 men in the encampment, and stabbed the lead elephant to death, producing such havoc that the Syrians were thereafter unable to mount a successful attack against Judea. This narrative has been extensively discussed in commentaries on 2 Maccabees. The discussion reveals that there are a number of important points which are difficult to reconcile with other historical information about this period. For example, such an attack would have represented a drastic shift in Seleucid policies toward the Jews and been at variance with the agreements just described in 2 Maccabees 11. Rather than seeking to perpetuate violence upon them, Antiochus V seems to have adopted a more conciliatory attitude toward the Jews of Judea. Likewise, the statement that the Syrians came equipped with elephants and chariots armed with scythes is hard to reconcile with a military campaign to be launched in the hill country of Judea. The historicity of these details is, therefore, to be doubted although the possibility remains that the narrative incorporates information from the oral traditions about Maccabean victories which circulated soon after they were accomplished (see the more complete discussion in Goldstein, *II Maccabees* AB, 454–58).

B. The Hasmonean Tombs

The references in 1 Maccabees to members of the Hasmonean family being buried in the tomb of their fathers at Modein (2:70; 9:18–21) are explained by the narrative in 1 Maccabees 13:25–30 (cf. Josephus, *Ant* 12.210–12). The reader is told that Simon constructed an impressive tomb with an accompanying monument of polished stone to mark the resting place of his parents and brothers. He also erected seven pyramids, columns, carvings of ships' prows, and other architectural features which could be seen from a considerable distance. Both Eusebius and Jerome are among the later authors who express knowledge of these structures, indicating that for some centuries they remained impressive monuments to the achievements of the Hasmonean family and were undoubtedly visited by pilgrims. Today scant remains at a site awaiting excavation mark the spot near Ras Medieh taken to be the location of these tombs (M.R. 149148).

C. Rabbi Eleazar of Modein

Little is known about one other distinguished resident of Modein, Rabbi Eleazar. Known simply as "the man from Modein," a teaching of his is preserved in *ʾAbot* 3.12: "R.

Eleazar of Modiim said: 'If a man profanes the Hallowed Things and despises the set feasts and puts his fellow to shame publicly and makes void the covenant of Abraham our father, and discloses meanings in the Law which are not according to the halakah, even though a knowledge of the Law and good works are his, he has no share in the world to come.' " Although he was associated with the famous Rabbi Gamaliel II at Jamnia, Eleazar's biography ends in tragedy for he was executed on a false charge of treason in 135 C.E., apparently at the order of Bar Kokhba himself (Willoughby, *IDB* 3: 421).

Bibliography

Robinson, E., and Smith, E. 1841. *Biblical Researches in Palestine, Mount Sinai and Arabia Petraea.* Boston.

THOMAS R. W. LONGSTAFF

MODERN VERSIONS OF THE BIBLE. See VERSIONS (MODERN ERA).

MOETH (PERSON) [Gk *Mōeth*]. An alternate form of the name NOADIAH.

MOLADAH (PLACE) [Heb *môlādâ*]. Settlement within the tribal territory of Simeon (Josh 19:2; 1 Chr 4:32), later incorporated into the Negeb district of Judah (Josh 15:26). The differences between the list in 1 Chronicles 4 and that of Josh 19:1–9 seem to be merely editorial in nature, suggesting that both are derived from a single document describing the territory of Simeon sometime early in the period of the monarchy, presumably before Simeon was consolidated with the tribe of Judah (Myers *1 Chronicles* AB, 25–31). The differences between these lists and that of Joshua 15 are more difficult to explain unless they reflect the political and demographic adjustments made necessary by the consolidation process (Boling and Wright *Joshua* AB, 436–37). Moladah is also listed among the towns occupied by those returning from exile in Babylon (Neh 11:26, with a defectively written *holem*). There is general agreement that this list is derived from an official document of the postexilic period (Myers *Ezra, Nehemiah* AB, 187). The name of this settlement, whose meaning is clearly related to the verb *yld* "to give birth," has led to the very speculative conclusion that this was the site of a shrine for barren women (*IDB* 3:421–22). The fact that Khirbet el-Waten, a group of ruins 12 km E of Beer-sheba (M.R. 142074), bears a name that also deals with kinship and childbearing, combined with its location within the appropriate region, provides sufficient evidence for a tentative identification (Boling and Wright *Joshua* AB, 382).

WADE R. KOTTER

MOLDING [Heb *zēr*]. A band used to encircle the interior cultic appurtenances of the tabernacle. The molding was made of gold and was placed around the ark (Exod 25:11; 37:2), the table for the bread of the Presence (Exod 25:24, 25; 37:11, 12), and the incense altar (Exod 30:3, 4; 37:26, 27). Since these three holy objects were meant to be portable, they were all fitted with rings through which poles were inserted. The molding may thus have been a decorative element and also a strengthening band.

CAROL MEYERS

MOLECH (DEITY) [Heb *mōlek*]. Var. MOLOCH. Traditionally rendered Molech (or Moloch, representing LXX *moloch*) the term is of disputed meaning; it occurs eight times in the OT text (Lev 18:21; 20:2, 3, 4, 5; 1 Kgs 11:7; 2 Kgs 23:10; Jer 32:35) and one time in the NT (Acts 7:43). Molech is found generally in contexts of cultic child sacrifice and particularly in phrases containing some or all of the words *hʿbyr ʾt-bnw wʾt-btw bʾš lmlk* ("to cause one's son or one's daughter to pass over by the fire to Molek").

A. Theories Regarding the Meaning of "Molech"
  1. Traditional Interpretation
  2. Eissfeldt's Reinterpretation
  3. Weinfeld's Theory
B. Philological Evidence
C. Biblical Evidence
D. Summary

A. Theories Regarding the Meaning of "Molech"

1. Traditional Interpretation. Traditionally, Molech has been understood as the name of a deity to whom children were burned in sacrifice, first by the Canaanites and then by the Israelites, particularly in a cultic installation known as the "Tophet" in the Valley of the Son of Hinnom, immediately south of Jerusalem. In favor of this understanding there is now a broad range of ANE literary evidence which suggests the worship of a god known as Malik or Milku/i from as early as the 3d millennium B.C. through the OT era. Malik was an extremely popular element in personal names at Ebla, although contexts are presently too scanty to permit firm conclusions regarding the god's nature in the Eblaite cultus. The same god is also evidenced in personal names from the next (i.e., second) millennium at Mari, and in addition, we find in the Mari texts references to recipients of funeral offerings called *maliku,* apparently the shades of the dead or underworld deities. This netherworld connection is reinforced by the evidence from Akkadian texts, in which Malik appears in god lists, from the Old Babylonian period on, equated with Nergal and in which the *mal(i)kū* appear in connection with the Igigi and Anunnaki as chthonic beings involved in the cult of the dead ancestors. Finally, the comparative literary evidence moves closer to home for OT studies, as the Ugaritic texts list a god *Mlk* resident at *ʿṯtrt* (*Ugaritica V* 7:41; 8:17), the same "address" as that assigned elsewhere to the netherworld deity *Rpu* (Rapiu), and testify to the inclusion of beings known as *mlkm* in the cult of the dead in contexts which suggest their similarity to (if not identity with) the *rpum,* the shades of the dead royal ancestors (known later in the Bible as the Rephaim, where the term has been broadened to include all the dead, e.g., Ps 88:11). From this evidence there emerges the picture of a netherworld deity involved in the cult of the dead ancestors (perhaps even their king, given the apparent associations with the West Semitic root *mlk,* "to rule, be king").

2. Eissfeldt's Reinterpretation. Since 1935 the discussion of Molek has been dominated by the thesis of O. Eissfeldt, that the term is cognate with the Punic *mlk* (or "*molc*[*h*]" in Latin transcriptions) and is thus not a divine name or title but a technical term for a type of sacrifice. *Mlk*/*molc(h)* is found on several stelae excavated from Punic colonies in North Africa (such as Carthage) and the western Mediterranean islands, almost always compounded with another phonemic element (e.g., *ʾmr*/Lat *omor*), and dating from the 7th or 6th century B.C. to the 3d century A.D. Because the inscriptions regularly name Baal-Hammon (Latin Saturn) or Tanit as the recipient of the sacrifice, while the *mlk* + expression appears in a variety of syntactical positions within the inscriptions, Eissfeldt was persuaded that the latter were not references to a divinity, but terms for the sacrifice or its victim. Given the associations of the OT term "Molek" with child sacrifice and the depiction of lambs about to be slain on stelae inscribed *molchomor,* Eissfeldt proposed that the Punic *mlkʾmr* was testimony to the development of a practice of substitutionary sacrifice of a lamb (*ʾmr*; cf. Heb *ʾimmēr*) for the human child, while the other elements compounded with *mlk* had to do with other variants of the original practice of child sacrifice, the *mlk* per se. The latter was most provocatively attested in a single inscription (Constantine Neopunic 30) as *lmlk,* which Eissfeldt read, "as a *molk*-sacrifice," and compared to OT *lammōlek,* the form in which Molek occurs in seven of the eight OT attestations.

Two independent sources of data have lent substantial force to Eissfeldt's proposal. First, a long series of classical authors, from Sophocles in the 5th century B.C. to Dracontius in the 5th century A.D., write of the Phoenician and Punic practice of cultic child sacrifice by fire (see especially Mosca for texts and discussion). Second, archaeologists digging at Carthage and other Punic colonies in the western Mediterranean have located sacred precincts (or "tophets," using the OT term) containing urns with ashes and bone remains of children and animals (see TOPHETH). Although such precincts have not always been discovered at the locales of the stelae bearing *mlk*-inscriptions, the evidence from Carthage, where the proportion of animal bones mixed with human appears to *decrease* over time, establishes the Punic practice of cultic child sacrifice under the term *molk* for most scholars, regardless of their views on OT Molech.

3. Weinfeld's Theory. A third theory also requires mention, although it has to do not so much with the meaning of "Molech" as with the nature of the associated cult: Moshe Weinfeld's (1972) proposal (following many medieval rabbis) that the cult of Molech was indeed directed to a pagan deity, Baal-Hadad (under the title of "king"), but that historically it never entailed actual sacrifice or burning of children, only their dedication to the deity in a fire ceremony. Weinfeld stresses the use of verbs which need not mean to sacrifice (*ntn,* "to give"; *hʿbyr,* "to cause to pass over") in the descriptions of the cult in the OT legal and historical material, while explicit "death" verbs (such as *śrp,* "to burn"; *zbḥ,* "to sacrifice"; and *šḥṭ,* "to slaughter") are found only in the references of the latter prophets and writings, which Weinfeld terms "moralizing" and "tendentious." Although many scholars are sympathetic with Weinfeld's qualms about the historical value of the prophetic and hagiographic references, most concur that he has overstated his case regarding the legal material, especially. The verbs *ntn* and *hʿbyr* may or may not of themselves entail sacrifice, but Num 31:23 suggests that *hʿbyr bʾš* (the phrase used of the cult in Deut 18:10 and elsewhere) does indeed entail burning in the fire.

B. Philological Evidence

The adjudication of the issue of the meaning of "Molech" is partially dependent on how one understands the word philologically. Scholars since A. Geiger (1857) have proposed that the form represents a "dysphemism," or tendentious distortion, of the Heb *melek* (king) by substitution of the vowels of *bōšet* (shame); this was apparently done on occasion with *baʿal* (e.g., Ishbosheth). Thus, the term might have referred originally to a "king" god (or even Yhwh himself under that title). If this hypothesis is correct, the Punic cognate proposed by Eissfeldt would be lost and some understanding as a divine name or title necessitated. However, Eissfeldt and his defenders have raised cogent objections to the dysphemism theory, particularly as they have inquired why the simple substitution of the vowels *ō-e* should have suggested *bōšet* to the ancient reader, rather than any other word with the same vowels. For their part, they prefer to see in Molek an o/u-class "segolate" noun, cognate with the Punic *molk.* On the other hand, it is equally possible to see in "Molek" a form of the Qal active participle of *mlk,* meaning "ruler" (as would be suggested by the LXX's translation *archōn,* in the Leviticus passages), or a derivative from an a-class segolate noun, like the Akk *malku*/*maliku* ("king"), so that the traditional explanation of Molek also remains viable.

C. Biblical Evidence

Inevitably, then, one must attempt a close reading of the biblical texts containing Molech and other related texts to attempt to settle the matter. Within the legal texts, Lev 18:21 and 20:2–5 are crucial because they contain five of the eight attestations of Molech in the MT. On the one hand, Eissfeldt and his supporters have shown that the MT vocalization of *lmlk* as *lammōlek* in 18:21 and 20:2–4 is quite likely in error: the LXX translates without the article, so that the original probably read **lĕmōlek,* permitting comparison with sacrificial terms such as *lĕʿōlâ* ("as a burnt offering") in Gen 22:2, so as to yield the rendering, "as a *molk*-sacrifice." On the other hand, the removal of the article does not eliminate the traditional interpretation, and the juxtaposition of 20:5b ("I shall cut off him and all who whore after him, to whore after [the] Molech") with v 6, which condemns "anyone who turns to the ghosts and the 'knowers' to whore after them," is congruent with the portrait of the chthonic deity and denizens connected with the cult of the dead ancestors, as was seen above in the comparative literary evidence. Further support for the latter perspective appears in Deut 18:10, where "one who causes his son or his daughter to pass over by the fire" is condemned at the head of a roster of diviners and mediums.

The historical material compels us to ask after the provenance, duration and status of the cult of Molech in Israel (in addition to our questions about the meaning of the term). Of the two occurrences of "Molech" in the historical books, one (1 Kgs 11:7) is generally eliminated as a confusion of Molech with Milcom, god of the Ammonites (cf. 1 Kgs 11:5, 33). (It may be noted, for example, that the two deities have separate cult places defiled by Josiah in 2 Kgs 23:10, 13.) Otherwise, the cult is repeatedly attributed to the Canaanites as source (indeed, as the very archetype of their depravity [Deut 12:31; cf. passages cited below]), but it is not specifically mentioned in Israel until the reigns of Ahaz (2 Kgs 16:3) and Manasseh (2 Kgs 21:6), the villains of the Deuteronomic History. (Because of Ahaz's religious impressionability on his trip to Damascus [2 Kgs 16:10–16], some scholars have argued for a Syrian or Assyrian source for the cult.) Outside of a general accusation against the N kingdom (2 Kgs 17:17) and a specific indictment of the Sepharvites exiled by the Assyrians to the province of Samaria for "burn[ing] their children in the fire to Adrammelech and Anammelech" (2 Kgs 17:31;), see SEPHARVAIM the cult is attested solely in the "tophet" of Jerusalem's Valley of the Son of Hinnom, which Josiah then defiled as part of his elimination of Canaanite influences on Judah's worship (2 Kgs 23:10). Whether the cult was later revived is disputed: it is not again mentioned in the history, but Jeremiah (7:31–32; 19:5–6, 11; 32:35; and probably 2:23 and 3:24) and Ezekiel (16:20–21; 20:25–26,30–31; 23:36–39) indict their contemporaries for the practice, while Isa 57:5,9 may indicate some survival of the cult after the exile (particularly if *melek* in v 9 is to be read as *mōlek*; cf. *RSV*).

Thus, given the relative paucity of clear references to the cult of Molech, it is decidedly difficult to reconstruct its history with confidence; it is equally difficult to comment with authority on its legal or social status during that history. Eissfeldt contended that the sacrifices had been directed to Yhwh as part of the licit, state religion of Judah until Josiah's reform, after which they faded from memory until the original significance of "Molech" was forgotten and the deity born of desperation to interpret the OT references. In fact, the licit status of the cult may be proposed, even if one holds for the traditional understanding of the term, and particularly on the basis of Isa 30:33, in which the prophet, presumably during Hezekiah's reign, depicts the Tophet as prepared to receive the Assyrian king in sacrifice (on this reading the Canaanite cult of Molech would have been subordinated at Jerusalem to that of Yhwh). As for the sociological nature of the cult, many scholars (including Eissfeldt) have argued that the practitioners were parents offering their firstborn sons in (mis-)obedience of the "Law of the Firstborn" in Exod 13:2,11–15; 22:28b–29—Eng 29b–30; and 34:19–20 (cf. Ezek 20:26). However, this seems unlikely, given the references to sons and daughters as victims (2 Kgs 23:10 and elsewhere) and perhaps even to multiple victims within a family (2 Chr 28:3; 33:6).

It is not surprising, given the aforementioned shortage of evidence, that scholars have struggled to find additional references to the cult of Molech. Often the search entails revocalizing MT *melek* in a provocative context. It might be noted that in this activity such scholars are but following the lead of the LXX, which reads *Moloch* in Amos 5:26 (followed by the NT in Acts 7:43) and Zeph 1:5 (but *archōn* in Lev 18:21; 20:2–5 and *basileus* in 3 Kgs 11:5 [MT 1 Kgs 11:7]!). Other verses commonly included in the discussion by this means include 2 Sam 12:30 (=1 Chr 20:2); Isa 30:33; 57:9; Jer 49:1,3 and the Milcom references in Kings, listed above. Since *melek* is an extremely common noun (with over 2,500 occurrences), there is much fodder for speculation, but, with few exceptions, such proposals have commanded little assent.

Other attempts to expand our understanding of the cult have involved appeals to passages concerning child sacrifice or, more broadly, human sacrifice. In addition to the "Law of the Firstborn," discussed above, special stress has been placed on the "Akedah" account (Genesis 22), the vow of Jepthah (Judges 11), King Meša's sacrifice of his son (2 Kgs 3:27) and such prophetic allusions as Hos 13:2; Mic 6:7; and Isa 66:3. While none of these clearly has to do with the cult of Molech (particularly if one concedes that the cult was not necessarily of the firstborn son), they can, to a greater or lesser degree, all assist in illuminating the worldview of those who engaged in the sacrifice of their children.

D. Summary

The "Molech question" remains a good candidate for what Adolf von Harnack once called it: "the greatest question, without a doubt, of the comparative history of religion." We can say what it was apparently not: neither a regular cult (such as one of firstborn sons) nor an occasional one based on military emergency (such as is exampled in 2 Kgs 3:27) seems congruent with the clear biblical references. The repeated occurrence of references to the Molech cult in contexts suggesting divination, along with the chthonic connections of the god Malik (Milku/i) in the comparative literary material, suggest that the sacrifices played a role in the cult of the dead ancestors (so explicitly in Ps 106:37–38), while the OT historical references suggest that the cult was adopted from the Canaanites and practiced mostly (if not exclusively) by the residents of Judah (especially the kings) in the Valley of the Son of Hinnom. See DEAD, CULT OF THE.

As for the meaning of "Molech," the Punic inscriptional and archaeological evidence adduced by Eissfeldt and his supporters presents a strong case for their contention that a cult similar in many respects to that found in Israel was practiced in the Punic colonies. However, the connection of the biblical cult with the Punic practice and the term used to describe it remains loose: no secure archaeological or inscriptional evidence for the presumed Punic/Israelite "missing link" in Phoenicia has been unearthed to date. Indeed, the use of non-inscribed stelae in the earliest layers of the Punic "tophets" leaves open the possibility that the Punic usage of *molk* was an intra Punic development, rather than a feature common to Israel, Phoenicia, and the Punic colonies. On the other hand, those favoring the traditional interpretation must concede that the portrait of a god Molek remains frustratingly difficult to draw with precision, and that the ultimate "why" of the cult occasions much speculation, but little certainty.

Bibliography

Eissfeldt, O. 1935. *Molk als Opferbegriff im Punischen und Hebräischen und das Ende des Gottes Moloch.* Beiträge zur Religionsgeschichte des Altertums 3. Halle.

Heider, G. C. 1985. *The Cult of Molek: A Reassessment.* JSOTSup 43. Sheffield.

Mosca, P. G. 1975. Child Sacrifice in Canaanite and Israelite Religion: A Study in *Mulk* and *mlk*. Ph.D. diss. Harvard.
Weinfeld, M. 1972. The Worship of Molech and of the Queen of Heaven and its Background. *UF* 4: 133–54.

GEORGE C. HEIDER

MOLID (PERSON) [Heb *môlîd*]. Son of Abishur and Abihail (1 Chr 2:29) and a descendant of the important line of Jerahmeel (by his wife Atarah) of the tribe of Judah. Molid and his brother Ahban conclude this brief genealogical record. Variant spellings are found in the LXX (Vaticanus and Alexandrinus) and many scholars consider those genealogies corrupt suggesting the nature of apparent scribal errors. The genealogies of Jerahmeel in the MT are viewed by most contemporary scholars as being in good order. For further discussion of the provenance and authenticity of the genealogies in 1 Chronicles 2, see MAAZ.

Locating Molid in time is difficult. Some commentators view these genealogical records as complete and place Molid in the latter years of the Egyptian sojourn; others, however, consider such names as reflecting a concern closer to the date of the authorship of the book. Molid is probably derived from the verb *yld* meaning "to bear," "bring forth," or "beget" and is often rendered "begetter."

W. P. STEEGER

MOLLUSKS. See ZOOLOGY.

MOLOCH (DEITY) [Gk *moloch*]. See MOLECH.

MOLTEN IMAGE. See IDOL, IDOLATRY.

MOLTEN SEA. See TEMPLE, JERUSALEM.

MONEY. See COINAGE.

MONKEY. See ZOOLOGY.

MONTANUS, MONTANISM. A Christian sect arising in the late 2d century and stressing apocalyptic expectations, the continuing prophetic gifts of the Spirit, and strict ascetic discipline.

A. Origin of Montanism
  1. Titles Given the Movement
  2. Sources of Information
  3. Locations of the Early Montanists
B. Montanism in Phrygia
  1. The Question of Ecstasy
  2. Montanist Doctrines
C. Montanism in Rome
  1. Sources
  2. Tertullian's Account of Praxeas
  3. Hippolytus and the Question of New Revelation
  4. The Muratorian Canon
  5. Pseudo-Tertullian and the Paraclete
  6. The Debate Between Gaius and Proclus
  7. Irenaeus and Those Who Rejected the Gospel of John
  8. Summary of the Debate at Rome
D. Montanism in North Africa
  1. Relation to Montanism in Rome
  2. Differences between Tertullian and Earlier Montanists
  3. The Question of New Revelation
  4. The Point of Contention between the Montanists and the Orthodox

---

A. Origin of Montanism

Montanus, a Phrygian Christian, began to prophesy in the small village of Ardabav in Phrgyian Mysia about A.D. 172. Two women, Priscilla and Maximilla, who also prophesied, became his devoted followers and were influential in the dissemination of his teachings.

1. Titles Given the Movement. The followers of Montanus and the prophetesses were usually referred to as Cataphrygians by the Fathers, the title indicating the Phrygian provenance of the movement. They seem to have used the title "the New Prophecy" of themselves. They were later called Montanists after the name of their founder.

2. Sources of Information. The Fathers indicate that the Montanists produced numerous treatises. These have all perished, however, except the treatises written by Tertullian (A.D. 155–220) after he had adopted Montanism. Our knowledge of Montanism depends, therefore, on those few Montanist fragments preserved in the Fathers, on the descriptions of Montanist beliefs and practices the Fathers give in their attempts to refute them, and on certain treatises of Tertullian.

The writings of Eusebius (A.D. 263–340) and Epiphanius (A.D. 315–403) are most important for our knowledge of the earliest period of Montanism in Phrygia because of earlier sources they have preserved. Eusebius preserves quotations from two sources concerning Montanism in Phrygia. The first, and most extensive, is from an unnamed author who claims to have participated in oral debate with Montanists in Galatia and to have written his account of them thirteen years after Maximilla died (*Hist. Eccl.* 5.16–17). Apollonius, the author of Eusebius' second source, claims to have written his treatise against Montanism forty years after Montanus began prophesying (*Hist. Eccl.* 5.18).

Epiphanius claims to have used both oral and written sources in his section on the Montanists, but he does not identify his sources (*Haer.* 48.15). It has been established that he used a source dating from the late 2d or early 3d century as the basis for his account in *Haer.* 48.1.4–13.8. The debate that he describes in this section has the same general contours as that described in Eusebius' sources, which suggests a Phrygian provenance.

Tertullian's writings from his Montanist period (A.D. 207–20) are also important. There is a general consensus today, however, that they should not be used to reconstruct earlier Phrygian Montanism. He appears to have introduced his own modifications to their teachings. His statements, therefore, can only be used with confidence in reference to earlier Phrygian Montanism when they find confirmation in the material in the sources preserved by Eusebius and Epiphanius.

3. Locations of the Early Montanists. Early Montanism was centered in three major geographical areas. Phrygia, where it arose, continued to be the most prominent. Sozomen said in the mid-5th century that there were still multitudes of Montanists in Phrygia (*Hist. Eccl.* 2.32.6). Montanism also appeared quite early in Rome. The third area was N Africa, where Tertullian became its most prominent spokesman. Because the sources related to each region show differences in the Montanist teachings, we must focus on Montanism in each area in order to see what was peculiar to the debate in each place, as well as what belonged to the movement in general.

B. Montanism in Phrygia

We begin with Montanism as it appeared among its founders in Phrygia. All that can be learned about Montanist teachings from the few words preserved from Montanus himself is that he claimed to be the mouthpiece of God (Epiph. *Haer.* 48.4, 10, 11). While this claim was attacked and defended in different ways in the different locales, it nevertheless formed the center of the controversy between the Montanists and the Church. Epiphanius asserts that the Montanists held the same view of the Father, Son, and Holy Spirit as the Church, but erred in the matter of spiritual gifts (*Haer.* 48.1.4). The anonymous source of Eusebius concurs that the point of contention was the prophetic activity (*Hist. Eccl.* 5.16.6–10; 17.4).

1. The Question of Ecstasy. The debate about the Montanist prophecy in Phrygia centered on the manner in which it was done. The possibility of prophecy did not enter the debate. Eusebius asserts that the many divine charisma still in existence throughout the Churches then caused many to accept the Montanist prophets (*Hist. Eccl.* 5.3.4). The opponents in Phrygia attempted to prove that Montanus was a false prophet because he prophesied in a state of ecstasy. Epiphanius sets this as the major topic. "Let us examine," he says, "what constitutes prophecy and what constitutes false prophecy" (*Haer.* 48.3.3). He argues that true prophets in both the OT and NT were always in possession of their understanding when they uttered their prophecies. The Montanists had appealed to Gen 2:21 which, in the Septuagint, reads: "And God cast a state of ecstasy on Adam, and he slept." They juxtaposed Eph 5:31–32 to prove that Adam prophesied on this occasion (Epiph. *Haer.* 48.6; Tert. *An* 11.4), and consequently, that he prophesied in ecstasy. Epiphanius' source can answer this argument only by arguing that ecstasy has many meanings in the Scriptures, and that in Gen 2:21 it refers to sleep. The Montanists had appealed also to Psalm 115:2 and Acts 10:10–14 to support ecstatic prophecy and had cited Abraham, Moses, Agabus, Judas, Silas, the daughters of Philip, Ammia, and Quadratus as prophets of whom they were the successors (Epiph. *Haer.* 48.7ff.; Eus. *Hist. Eccl.* 5.17.2–4). It is noteworthy that none of the earliest sources describing the debate with Montanism in Phrygia indicate that either Montanus or the two prophetesses ever appealed to the Paraclete passages in John 14–16 in support of their prophecy.

2. Montanist Doctrines. Other points of Montanist doctrine also appear in subordinate roles in the sources descriptive of the debate in Phrygia. They did not permit a second marriage after the death of a spouse (Epiph. *Haer.* 48.9). This, along with most of the points which follow, appears to have belonged to the movement universal, for it is also attested in Tertullian (*Marc.* 1.29; *Monog.* 1.1–6; 14.3–5). They also instituted new and more frequent fasts (Eus. *Hist. Eccl.* 5.18.2; cf. Epiph. *Haer.* 48.8.7–8; Tert. *Ieiun.*1; Hippol. *Haer.* 8.19; 10.25).

It is also obvious that all Montanists held martyrdom in high esteem. They appealed to the large number of their martyrs as proof of the power of the Spirit in their midst (Eus. *Hist. Eccl.* 5.16.20; cf. 5.18.5–6). It is apparently in opposition to some boast about martyrs that Gaius asserts in his debate with Proclus that he can point out "the trophies of the apostles" (Eus. *Hist. Eccl.* 2.25.5–7). It was his way, perhaps, of trumping the Montanist claim to have a superior number of martyrs. Tertullian asserts that the Spirit exhorts to martyrdom, never to flight or bribery to avoid it (*Fuga* 9.4; 11.3; 14.3). This esteem has caused some to argue that the Montanists advocated voluntary martyrdom. There are some funerary inscriptions in Phrygia dated from A.D. 248 which contain the enigmatic phrase: "Christians for Christians." This epitaph has been used to argue that the Montanists flaunted their faith. Most references to Christianity on tombs from this period of escalated persecution are in cryptic language. It has been argued that these inscriptions from Phrygia which make open reference to Christian faith must come from Montanists. E. Gibson, however, who has most recently examined these inscriptions concludes that there is no necessary connection between them and Montanism. W. Tabbernee has argued convincingly from the literary sources that, apart from Tertullian, the early Montanists' attitude to martyrdom was not substantially different from that of the Catholics.

The Montanists were also noted for their eschatological views. They anticipated an imminent end to the present order. Maximilla declared: "After me there will no longer be a prophet, but the end" (Epiph. *Haer.* 48.2.4). The assertion that Maximilla predicted wars and anarchy (Eus. *Hist. Eccl.* 5.16.8) should be connected with this oracle, for such were viewed as precursors of the end in the primitive Christian eschatology (Matt 24:6–8). The assertion by Apollonius (ca. A.D. 212) that Montanus renamed Pepuza and Tymion, small villages in Phrygia, "Jerusalem," and "wanted people to gather there from everywhere" is also an allusion to their view that the end was imminent (Eus. *Hist. Eccl.* 5.18.2), for Epiphanius quotes an oracle, outside his early source, which he attributes to either Quintilla or Priscilla in which the prophetess asserts that Christ revealed to her that Jerusalem would descend from heaven at Pepuza (*Haer.* 49.1). Tertullian, however, whose chiliast eschatology did not change much from his Catholic to his Montanist period, speaks only of Jerusalem being brought down from heaven for a thousand years (*Marc.* 3.24), and never mentions Pepuza. Apart from locating the new Jerusalem at Pepuza and connecting the date of the end with Maximilla's death, the Montanists' eschatology did not differ in any considerable way from that of the earliest Christians (Matt 24:34, 42–44; 1 Cor 7:29; 1 Thess 5:2–3; Rev 21:2).

This brief survey of Montanist doctrine confirms that prophecy was the primary point of contention between the Montanists and the Catholics. The other doctrines represent only minor differences from Catholic belief and practice, differences that would have been irritating, but hardly heretical. The Churches of Asia appear even to have been willing to acknowledging prophecy, providing it was not accompanied by ecstasy.

C. Montanism in Rome

The focal point of the debate shifts when we move from Phrgyia to Rome. The issue no longer is ecstasy but new revelation.

1. Sources. The sources for our knowledge of Montanism in Rome are minimal and difficult to interpret. They consist of a section of Tertullian's *Against Praxeas;* a paragraph in Irenaeus' *Against Heresies*; some fragments preserved by Eusebius of a dialogue between Gaius, a Roman presbyter, and Proclus, a Montanist; some statements in Hippolytus' *Refutation of All Heresies* and in his *Commentary on Daniel*; Pseudo-Tertullian's *Against All Heresies,* in that it appears to be an epitome of Hippolytus' lost *Syntagma*; and the Muratorian Canon.

We shall begin with the later material in Tertullian and Hippolytus and work backwards to the earlier, more fragmentary material so that we have a tentative framework for the earlier pieces of the puzzle.

2. Tertullian's Account of Praxeas. Tertullian provides one of our clearest statements about Montanism in Rome, yet even it has major ambiguities. He says that when Praxeas visited Rome the bishop of Rome at that time "had already acknowledged the prophecies of Montanus, Prisca, and Maximilla" and, consequently, "had brought peace to the churches of Asia and Phrygia." Praxeas, who had come to Rome from Asia, by denigrating the Montanist prophets and their churches, and by citing the negative views of earlier bishops of Rome, forced him to "recall the letter of peace he had already sent and to desist from his intention of admitting the gifts" (*Prax.* 1). This openness to the Montanist prophecy by a bishop at Rome is contrary to all other evidence. Unfortunately, we can only speculate about the bishop's identity. The most widely accepted conjecture is that it was Zephyrinus, bishop from 198–217. This conjecture best fits both the statement that earlier bishops of Rome had viewed Montanism negatively, and the assumed time of Praxeas' activities in the city.

3. Hippolytus and the Question of New Revelation. Hippolytus, (ca. A.D. 170–236) a presbyter at Rome during the episcopacy of Zephyrinus and later, took a radically different view of the Montanist prophecy. While he does not mention the Montanists in his *Commentary on Daniel,* many of his statements appear to have them in view (Klawiter 1975). He relates, for example, the story of a leader of a church in Pontus who, instead of paying careful attention to the Scriptures, began to believe in visions which he himself had seen. His congregation was decimated because he prophesied that the judgment would occur in a year. Many neglected their fields and sold their possessions and, when the end did not occur, were reduced to begging (*Dan.* 4.19). Hippolytus comments: "These things happen to uneducated and simple people who do not give careful attention to the Scriptures" (*Dan.* 4.20). That he had the Montanists in view is further suggested when he adds that some were even then experiencing the same things by paying attention to visions and by appointing additional fasts (*Dan.* 4.20). These were charges commonly leveled at the Montanists, some repeated by Hippolytus himself when he attacked them in his *Refutation of All Heresies* (8.19).

This story provides a clue to Hippolytus' approach to the question of Montanist prophecy. He stressed the importance of basing everything on the authority of Scripture in opposition to believing in visions and dreams. He considered prophecy to have ended. The words of the prophets and apostles contained in the Scriptures should guide the Church. He asserted that the Montanists, however, claimed to have learned more through their prophets "than from the law, the prophets, and the Gospels" (*Haer.* 8.19; 10.25). The crux of the question for Hippolytus was the issue of additional revelation.

4. The Muratorian Canon. The Muratorian Canon, which is usually dated at approximately this same time (ca. A.D. 200) and located at Rome, rejected the *Shepherd of Hermas* for what appears to have been the same reason. It had only recently been written, and could be published "neither among the Prophets, whose number was complete, nor among the apostles." This appears to be a statement about the completion of revelation. Joined with Hippolytus' views, it suggests that there was little sympathy for contemporary prophecy at Rome in the late 2d and early 3d centuries.

5. Pseudo-Tertullian and the Paraclete. Hippolytus also indicates that the Montanists differentiated the Holy Spirit as he appeared in the apostles and as he appeared in the Montanist prophets, and that they considered the latter to have had the greater gift (*Haer.* 8.19). Pseudo-Tertullian offers a clearer statement. He notes that there were two groups of Montanists, the followers of Proclus and the followers of Aeschinus. We know Proclus was in Rome (Eus. *Hist. Eccl.* 6.20.3). Both groups said that the apostles had the Holy Spirit but the Montanist prophets had the Paraclete. They also agreed that the Paraclete revealed more in Montanus than Christ revealed in the gospel, a claim for additional revelation, and that the things revealed in Montanus by the Paraclete were also better and greater, a claim that the new revelation superceded the old (*Haer.* 7). It should also be noted that here and in Hippolytus' *Refutation of All Heresies* we have the first explicit statements that the Montanists used the term "Paraclete" to describe the source of their prophecies. The Montanists at Rome had begun to interpret the experience of their prophets in light of the Paraclete passages in John 14–16. The debate between Gaius and Proclus takes us deeper into this aspect of their teachings.

6. The Debate Between Gaius and Proclus. Eusebius locates the debate between Gaius and Proclus at Rome in the time of Zephyrinus (*Hist. Eccl.* 6.20.3). He tells us only that Gaius asserted that he could point to the trophies of the apostles (*Hist. Eccl.* 2.25.7) which, as we noted previously, probably countered the Montanists' boast about their martyrs, and that he curbed their rashness "in composing new scriptures" (*Hist. Eccl.* 6.20.3). The latter suggests that Gaius had the same attitude toward new revelation that we have seen in Hippolytus and the Muratorian Canon. Bar Salibi, a 12th-century Syrian exegete, says that Hippolytus defended the Johannine authorship of the gospel against Gaius, who credited both the gospel of John and the Apocalypse to the heretic Cerenthus. Eusebius also notes that Gaius attributed the Apocalypse to Cerenthus (*Hist. Eccl.* 3.28.1–2). Gaius' rejection of the gospel of John may have been prompted partially by the Montanists' use of it at Rome to validate new and superior revelation through the Paraclete (John 16:7, 12–13).

7. Irenaeus and Those Who Rejected the Gospel of John. Irenaeus refers to some who reject both the gospel of John and the prophetic Spirit (*Haer.* 3.11.12; *Dem.* 99). The people referred to appear to have been anti-Montanists, but Irenaeus gives no indication of their location. We have already seen that the latter view was present in Rome around the end of the 2d century in Hippolytus, the Muratorian Canon, and Gaius, and that Gaius also rejected the gospel of John. Irenaeus had visited Rome in 177 during the episcopacy of Eleutherus (174–89) to deliver a letter concerning Montanism in Asia and Phrygia. Praedestinatus' statement that Soter, Eleutherus' predecessor at Rome (166–74), wrote a treatise against the Montanists, indicates that Rome was wrestling with the Montanist question prior to Irenaeus' visit (1.26). It is quite possible that the views held by Hippolytus and Gaius were already present at Rome when Irenaeus visited Eleutherus and that he became aware of these views there. It is sometimes argued that the views Irenaeus refers to were those of the *Alogoi,* discussed by Epiphanius (*Haer.* 51), who rejected the gospel of John and the Apocalypse, and that their provenance was Asia. There is no evidence, however, for locating the *Alogoi* in Asia. Epiphanius gives no indication of their location. Labriolle (1913) argued that Epiphanius' discussion of the *Alogoi* was dependent on Hippolytus' attack on Gaius' rejection of John. If this is true, the *Alogoi* were most likely a Roman group. Rome is, in fact, the only place where views similar to those Epiphanius attributes to them are attested in the early Church.

8. Summary of the Debate at Rome. If this reconstruction is correct, we may sum up the Montanist debate at Rome as follows. There was, in general, an attitude at Rome at the end of the 2d century which was hostile to new revelation. To gain a hearing in this environment the Montanists had to justify the validity of post-apostolic prophecy. To do this they appealed to the Paraclete passages in the gospel of John. On the basis of these same passages, primarily John 16:12–13, they could also, as Pseudo-Tertullian points out, claim that what was revealed by the Paraclete through their prophets superceded what Christ had revealed in the gospel. To refute these claims some of their opponents, including the presbyter Gaius, rejected the authority of the gospel of John.

If the bishop of Rome to whom Tertullian refers in *Against Praxeas* was indeed Zephyrinus, and if Tertullian has not exaggerated the extent of his openness to acknowledge the Phrygian prophets, then his brief recognition of the new prophecy before yielding to Praxeas' pressure was an anomaly in the Roman attitude toward prophecy at the end of the 2d century.

D. Montanism in North Africa

Our earliest sources for Montanism in N Africa are *The Passion of Perpetua and Felicitas,* which some attribute to Tertullian, and the treatises of Tertullian composed after he became a Montanist.

1. Relation to Montanism in Rome. Montanism in N Africa shows the influence of the innovations introduced at Rome. Tertullian knows the distinction between the activity of the Holy Spirit in the apostolic age and in the age of the new prophecy, although he does not accept the view that the Montanists had a fuller participation in the Holy Spirit than did the apostles. He argues that the Paraclete reveals the fuller intention of the apostles (*Monog.* 3). He also interprets the new prophecy in terms of the Paraclete passages in John (*Virg.* 1; *Monog.* 1.1–6; 2.1–4).

2. Differences between Tertullian and Earlier Montanists. We have already noted where Tertullian either agreed with or differed from the Phrygians in their views on marriage, fasting, martyrdom, and eschatology. Two other points of difference need to be noted. The Phrygians, with their two famous prophetesses, allowed women great freedom for ministry in the Church. Origen asserted that the disciples of Priscilla and Maximilla were not obedient to the biblical command to let the women be silent in the churches (*Cat. ad Cor* 14.36). Tertullian, however, would not permit a woman "to speak in the church," or to perform any other function which belonged to a man (*Virg.* 9; *An.* 9.4). Tertullian also argued that the power to forgive sins belonged to the spiritual man, not to the bishop. The position of the earliest Phrygian Montanists on this issue is not clear. Tertullian quotes an oracle in his argument, but ascribes it only to the Paraclete, without identifying the human agent (*Pud.* 21).

3. The Question of New Revelation. The center of the debate in N Africa, as in Rome, was about the possibility of new revelation. The author of *The Passion of Perpetua and Felicitas* asserts that they recognize both new prophecies and new visions. The view of the Catholics comes out obliquely in the exhortation not to think "that the divine grace dwelt only with the ancients, whether in the grandeur of martyrdoms or of revelations" (1.4). Tertullian advances a similar argument about the continuation of the operation of divine grace in the Church, and accuses the Catholics of fixing "boundaries for God" (*Ieiun.* 11; cf. *Virg.* 1.5).

The new revelations which have come through the Montanist prophecies do not, Tertullian argues, relate to the rule of faith. This continues one, unalterable, and incapable of reformation. The prophecies concern discipline. The Paraclete was sent, he argues, because the mediocrity of man could not grasp everything at once. Christian discipline, therefore, is being brought to perfection gradually through the continued activity of the Paraclete. He defines the Paraclete's task as follows: "To direct discipline, to reveal the Scriptures, to reform the understanding, to advance the understanding to better things" (*Virg.* 1.6–8).

4. The Point of Contention between the Montanists and the Orthodox. This passage brings us to the heart of the Montanist issue. The new prophecies do not appear to have involved any basic doctrines of the Church. Epiphanius agrees with Tertullian when he asserts that the Montanists held the same view of the Father, Son, and Holy Spirit as the Catholics. He adds that they accepted the OT and NT, and believed in the resurrection of the dead (*Haer.* 48.1.3–4). Hippolytus does note that some Montanists held a modalist view of God (*Haer.* 8.19), and Pseudo-Tertullian ascribes this view to the Montanists who followed Aeschinus (*Haer.* 7). After the Trinitarian and Christological controversies this charge is brought indiscriminately against all Montanists. Didymus of Alexandria, for example, repeatedly accuses them of believing "the same one is Father, Son, and Holy Spirit (*Trin.* 2.15; 3.18; 3.23; Jerome, 41.3), even attributing this view to Montanus himself (*Trin.* 3.38; 3.41), something for which there is no evidence in the early sources.

The teachings of the new prophets concerned such things as how many times one might marry, when and how long one should fast, and how one should behave when threatened with martyrdom. These were not inconsequential questions, but they all lay outside matters of the creed. They were issues for which one might have expected to be disciplined, but not pronounced heretical. The issue, of course, concerned these matters only indirectly. The battle raged around the right of the Montanists to propagate their teachings by appealing to the authority of the Spirit. Tertullian brings this out clearly in the following passage: "Let consideration of the Paraclete as some authority belonging to us pass into the background for the present. Let us unroll and read the instruments of the ancient Scriptures which we have in common" (*Monog.* 4.1).

Montanism arose when the Church was consolidating its authority in its bishops, creed, and canon. Whether it arose because of this trend and was an effort to revive a more primitive form of the Church, or whether its appearance was simply coincidental to this trend cannot be determined conclusively. It was, nevertheless, the issue of authority which made Montanism a heresy.

Bibliography

Aland, K. 1960. Bemerkungen zum Montanismus und zur fruehchristlichen Eschatologie. Pp. 105–48 in *Kirchengeschichtliche Entwuerfe*. Gütersloh.

Barnes, T. D. 1970. The Chronology of Montanism. *JTS* n.s. 21: 403–8.

Gibson, E. 1978. *The "Christians for Christians" Inscriptions of Phrygia.* HTS 32. Missoula, MT.

Heine, R. E. 1987–88. The Role of the Gospel of John in the Montanist Controversy. *SecondCent* 6: 1–19.

———. 1989. *The Montanist Oracles and Testimonia.* Patristic Monograph Series 14. Macon, GA.

Klawiter, F. C. 1975. The New Prophecy in Early Christianity: The Origin, Nature, and Development of Montanism, A.D. 165–220. Diss. Chicago.

Labriolle, P. de. 1913a. *La crise montaniste.* Paris.

———. 1913b. *Les sources de l'histoire du Montanisme.* Collectanea Friburgensia 24. Paris.

Powel, D. 1975. Tertullianists and Cataphrygians. *VC* 29: 33–54.

Schepelern, W. 1929. *Der Montanismus und die phrygischen Kulte.* Tübingen.

Tabbernee, W. 1985. Early Montanism and Voluntary Martyrdom. *Colloquim* 17: 33–43.

RONALD E. HEINE

MONTH. See CALENDARS.

MONUMENTS, CHRISTIAN (ROME). See ROME, CHRISTIAN MONUMENTS AT.

MOOSSIAS (PERSON) [Gk *Moossias*]. See MAASEIAH.

MORDECAI (PERSON) [Heb *mōrdĕkay; mōrdŏkay*]. **1.** A character in the book of Esther.

a. Mordecai in the Hebrew Book of Esther. Mordecai is a central character of the book of Esther, second in importance only to Esther herself. While the credit for effecting the deliverance of the Jewish people from the massacre designed by their enemy Haman and authorized by the Persian king Ahasuerus belongs largely to her, Mordecai also has a significant part to play in the development of the plot.

He is first introduced into the narrative as a Jew living in the acropolis of Susa, the Persian capital (Esth 2:5). He is said to belong to a Benjaminite family which had been exiled from Judea along with the king Jehoiachin in 597 B.C.E. The wording of 2:5–6 may suggest that Mordecai himself had been deported from Jerusalem at that time, though that would make him at least 115 years old in the third year of Ahasuerus (Xerxes), which is when the story of Esther is set (483 B.C.E.). The storyteller may of course be suffering from some chronological confusion, but it is more likely that it is Mordecai's grandfather Kish that is said to have been exiled then.

The name Mordecai is almost certainly derived from Marduk, the name of the chief god of Babylon (though R. Lemosín has recently suggested it was Hurrian or Elamite, meaning "the man *par excellence*" [1983: 209–13]). It was evidently an acceptable Jewish name (cf. the Mordecai 2 mentioned in Ezra 2:2); it is perhaps a "gentile" name roughly equivalent to some Jewish name (Esther herself has both a Jewish name, Hadassah, and a "gentile" one, Esther).

When we first hear of Mordecai, he is Esther's guardian and adoptive father following her parents' death; he is her cousin and she is the daughter of his uncle Abihail (2:7, 15). Adoption is not a practice known to Hebrew law, though it is well attested in Babylonian legal documents; this reference is perhaps a hint of how well integrated Mordecai is into non-Jewish society.

It has often been thought that Mordecai is presented as some kind of Persian official. He lives in "the acropolis of Susa" (1:1), rather than simply in the city of Susa, and he is several times depicted as sitting "at the king's gate" (2:19, 21; 3:2; 5:9; 6:10, 12; cf. 2:11)—which sounds like technical terminology for the administrative headquarters of the Persian court (so Wehr 1964: 247–60; Loretz 1967: 104–8; Gordis 1981: 384). Perhaps some official position in the palace also explains best how Mordecai comes to gain news of a plot to assassinate the king. Nevertheless, the story makes excellent sense if Mordecai has no status at the court and is no more than one of the countless loungers about the palace gates.

After Esther has been taken into the harem, Mordecai

passes on to her his knowledge of the plot against the king's life which he has discovered (2:22). In chap. 3 Mordecai makes his most important contribution to the progress of the story when he jeopardizes the security of the Jewish people by refusing to do obeisance to the newly elevated Haman; it is this inadequately justified stubbornness that proves the root cause of Haman's plot to destroy all the Jews of the Persian Empire. In chap. 4 Mordecai redeems himself somewhat by making a positive intervention on behalf of the Jews and insisting that Esther enter the king's presence uninvited and beg for the life of her people.

His further appearances in the narrative cast him in a rather passive role. Quite by chance he next comes to the king's attention when his loyalty is remembered and rewarded (6:1–11). Thereafter, once Esther has successfully unmasked Haman, Mordecai is promoted to his place as vizier (8:1–2), but simply because of his relation to Esther. His final act is to record the events in which he participated and to add his imprimatur to the observances of Purim, which the Jews had already instituted (9:20–22, 31). Nothing but generalities are reported of his achievements in the Persian government (10:3).

b. Mordecai in the Greek Book of Esther. Mordecai takes on greater importance in the longer and later Greek version of the book of Esther (Clines, *HBC,* 815–19). Here narratives of a dream of Mordecai and its interpretation have been added to form the framework of the entire book (Addition A 1–11 = 11:2–12; F1–10 = 10:4–11:1); in the dream Mordecai and Haman are portrayed as two dragons locked in cosmic and apocalyptic conflict over the fate of the Jewish people. The effect of the insertion of the dream, as a divine revelation of what is foreordained, is to establish Mordecai rather than Esther as the primary hero of the story.

A secondary element in Addition A is an elaboration of the narrative of Mordecai's discovery of the plot against the king's life (A12–17 = 12:1–6), foregrounding even more the significance of Mordecai's courage. In Addition C the inclusion of the Prayer of Mordecai (C1–10 = 13:8–17) serves from a narrative point of view to explain Mordecai's reckless and largely unmotivated refusal to do obeisance to Haman: it was solely to avoid "setting the glory of a human above the glory of God" (C7 = 13:14). At the same time the addition conforms the character of Mordecai more closely to the ideal of the pious Jew.

In line with the increased prominence given to Mordecai in the Greek book is the assurance in its opening sentences that, even before his elevation to the viziership, Mordecai is "a great man, serving in the court of the king" (A2 = 11:3); in the Hebrew story, as we have noted, it is far from certain that Mordecai holds any office in the Persian bureaucracy when the story opens. A final stage in the development of the tradition about Mordecai has come about by the time of 2 Maccabees, when the day of festival (Purim) in commemoration of the victory of the Jews over their enemies has become known as "Mordecai's Day" (2 Macc 15:36). Mordecai's usurpation of Esther's role is almost complete.

c. Mordecai in History. The question of whether or not there was a historical Mordecai depends entirely upon a judgment on the historicity of the book of Esther in general. While there is perhaps no element in the narrative that is plainly impossible historically, most scholars find in the accumulation of narrative coincidences a sign that the story is essentially fictional.

Some have indeed believed that Mordecai is identical with the official Marduka known from a Babylonian tablet discovered probably at Borsippa near Babylon and deriving in all likelihood from the earliest years of Xerxes. The Assyriologist A. Ungnad, who published the tablet, believed that the official in question was in Borsippa on a mission from Susa, and that it is unlikely that there should have been two high-ranking Persian officials in Susa with the same name; consequently he claimed that this text thus provides the sole extrabiblical attestation of Mordecai (1940–41: 244). Others argue that the existence of this Marduka at least prevents us from regarding the biblical Mordecai as a purely fictional character (Moore 1975: 74). But there is nothing in the cuneiform document to show that the persons mentioned came from Susa, and since Marduka in fact is called the "scribe" (or possibly "accountant") of Ushtannu, who is known to be the satrap of the province of Babylon and Beyond the River, Marduka was in all probability resident in Babylon or its region, not in Susa.

Since Ungnad's discovery, the name Mordecai has also been found in Aramaic papyri of the 5th century B.C.E., in the form *mrdk,* as the name of an official probably located in N Mesopotamia (Driver 1957: 27–28). Other attestations of names compounded with Marduk also exist (Driver 1957: 56). The evidence, it should be noted, shows only that the name was borne by officials (whether they were Jewish or not) in the Persian Empire (see further, Clines fc.).

No credence is now given to the older theories that the names Mordecai and Esther are rare forms of the names of the Babylonian deities Marduk and Ishtar and so reflect some myth about them (Jensen 1892: 47–70, 209–26; cf. also Zimmern 1903: 514–20). It is equally improbable that Mordecai signifies "worshiper(s) of Marduk" and that the book of Esther represents a conflict between the devotees of Marduk and Ishtar and those of Anahita and Mithra (Lewy 1939: 127–51).

2. A family head who returned to the land with Zerubbabel and is listed as settled in the province of Judah (Ezra 2:2; Neh 7:7).

Bibliography

Clines, D. J. A. 1984. *The Esther Scroll.* JSOTSup 30, Sheffield.
———. fc. In Quest of the Historical Mordecai.
Driver, G. R. 1957. *Aramaic Documents of the Fifth Century B.C.* Abridged and rev. ed. Oxford.
Gordis, R. 1981. Religion, Wisdom and History in the Book of Esther—A New Solution to an Ancient Crux. *JBL* 100: 359–88.
Horn, S. H. 1964. Mordecai, A Historical Problem. *BR* 9: 14–25.
Jensen, P. 1892. Elamitische Eignennamen: Ein Beitrag zum Erklärung der elamitischen Inschriften. *WZKM* 6: 47–70; 209–26.
Lemosín, R. 1983. Estudios filológicos-derásicos acerca de Ester y el Iran antiguo (II). El nombre *Mŏrdeḵay. AulaOr* 1: 209–13.
Lewy, J. 1939. The Feast of the 14th Day of Adar. *HUCA* 14: 17–51.

Loretz, O. 1967. *Šʿr hmlk*—"Das Tor des Königs" (Est 2,19), *WO* 4: 104–8.
Moore, C. A. 1975. Archaeology and the Book of Esther. *BA* 38: 62–79.
Ungnad, A. 1940–41. Keilinschriftliche Beiträge zum Buch Esra und Ester. *ZAW* 58: 240–44.
———. 1942–43. Mitteilungen. 4. Zu Zaw 1940/1 S. 240ff. *ZAW* 59: 219.
———. 1959–60. Neubabylonische Privaturkunden aus der Sammlung Amherst. AfO 19: 74–82.
Wehr, H. 1964. Das "Tor des Königs" im Buche Esther und verwandte Ausdrücke, *Der Islam* 39: 247–60.
Yamauchi, E. M. 1980. The Archaeological Background of Esther. *BSac* 127: 99–117.
Zimmern, H. 1891. Zur Frage nach dem Ursprunge des Purimfestes. *ZAW* 11: 157–69.

David J. A. Clines

MOREH (PLACE) [Heb *môreh*]. The word Moreh has a range of meanings including teacher, diviner, and archer.

A. Oak of Moreh [Heb *ʾēlôn môreh*]

The word *ʾēlôn* is traditionally translated as oak, although it may refer to the terebinth tree. The KJV translation of "Plain of Moreh" is incorrect. The reference to *ʾēlôn môreh* occurs twice in the OT. When Abraham enters Canaan (Gen 12:6), he sets up an altar to the Lord before a tree near Shechem (M.R. 176179). There the Lord promises Abraham that the land will be given to his descendants. An Oak of Moreh is also mentioned in Deut 11:30 as part of a description of the location of Mt. Ebal (M.R. 176182) and Mt. Gerizim (M.R. 176178), mountains which overlook Shechem.

In several other instances, the OT text refers to trees in the Shechem area. In Gen 35:4, Jacob buries idols and jewelry under a tree at Shechem. In a later episode, Joshua sets up a stone under a tree at Shechem as a witness to the pact between the Israelites and the Lord (Josh 24:26). It would seem reasonable to associate these events with a tradition connected to the cult place Abraham was believed to have used.

Two passages in the Abimelech saga also mention trees at Shechem. In Judg 9:6, Abimelech is crowned king at the oak of the "pillar" in Shechem, a tree found by the Beth-millo, within the town. In Judg 9:37, forces attacking Shechem come upon the city from the direction of the Diviner's Oak, which should not then be located within the city. Clearly, it is not possible that both of the trees could be associated with the Oak of Moreh.

Wright (1964: 129–37) discussed the relationship of a cult site excavated at Shechem and the tradition of the Oak of Moreh. He believed that since the MB temenos at Shechem was outside the city wall but included within the city during the time of Abimelech, it was possible to link directly the sacred areas of Abraham, Joshua, and Abimelech. Such a reconstruction is possible, given the persistence of cult sites through time. The evidence, however, is far from conclusive, since numerous sacred sites can cluster in the same area. The exact location of the Oak of Moreh cannot be determined, although a place outside the city walls of Shechem seems the most reasonable.

B. Hill of Moreh [Heb *gibʿat hammôreh*]

Judg 7:1 mentions a hill below which the Midianites camped on the night Gideon attacked them. Moore (*Judges* ICC, 200) attempted to locate the battle in the region of Shechem, because he associated the hill with the Oak of Moreh at Shechem. However, references to the Spring of Harod (M.R. 184217) in Judg 7:1, to the Valley of Jezreel in Judg 6:3, and to Tabor (M.R. 187223) in Judg 8:18, all point to a N location for the conflict. Nebi Dahi (M.R. 183225) is generally accepted as the location of the ancient Hill of Moreh. As Malamat (1953: 65) has noted, the topography of that region fits the geographical requirements of the OT passage quite well.

Bibliography

Malamat, A. 1953. The War of Gideon and Midian—A Military Approach. *PEQ*, 61–65.
Wright, G. E. 1964. *Shechem.* London.

Melvin Hunt

MORESHETH (PLACE) [Heb *môrešet*]. Var. MORESHETH-GATH. A satellite village of Gath in the Shephelah (Mic 1:1, 14; Jer 26:18). The *nomen proprium loci* actually occurs only once in Mic 1:14 as Moresheth-gath, "Possession of Gath." In the other two cases the gentilic form, *môraštî* is employed to describe the prophet Micah. The city is in the vicinity of, but probably distinct from, both Mareshah and the Philistine Gath. Micah certainly implies such distinction as does the spelling. Mareshah is well attested elsewhere, and 2 Chr 11:8 is not a serious problem since Gath was at times under Israelite control. Another suggestion is that "gath" is used literally to mean "wine press," but this does not help with the location: "possession of wine press" (if this is the correct etymology) makes little sense, and the rest of Micah's poem (1:10–16) is centered around Gath. Therefore, the consensus is that Moresheth-gath was a satellite village near the city of Gath, what we might refer to as a "suburb" (cf. 1 Sam 6:17–18).

If this is the modern Tell ej-Judeideh (M.R. 141115) as most believe, about 10 km NE of Lachish, it is significant that in both these locations copious jar handles with the stamp *lmlk*, "to/for the king," have been found. David had a provincial palace at Lachish; and Adullam, Gath, Mareshah, and Lachish, all mentioned by Micah, were fortified by Rehoboam (2 Chr 11:8). The contention of Micah's dirge is that the cardinal sin of Judah was her militarism (1:13); so the wrath of God would destroy the militarized Shephelah as it approaches Jerusalem (1:12). The oracle reflects the campaigns of Sargon against the Philistia in 720 or 714–11 and Sennacherib's destruction of the Shephelah fortifications as he advanced upon Jerusalem in 701 (2 Kgs 18:13–16) laying "siege to 46 of [Hezekiah's] strong cities, walled forts and to the countless small villages in their vicinity" (*ANET,* 288). Moresheth-gath was surely among the villages.

Micah's pun depends on the similarity between "possession of" and "bride of" [Heb *mĕʾōrešet*]. In the wheeling and dealing of international politics, towns and villages might be given up as royal dowry (1 Kgs 9:16). Such, symbolically at least, was the fate of Moresheth-gath who had pledged herself to the military establishment of Lachish, Gath, and Mareshah. Micah's paronomasia can be translated: "Wherefore pay the dowry for Bride-of-Gath!" (1:14). Her sister cities met a similar fate (vv 13 and 15). See MAROTH.

LAMONTTE M. LUKER

MORIAH (PLACE) [Heb *mōriyyâ*]. **1.** "The land of Moriah," mentioned in Gen 22:2, where God sent Abraham to sacrifice his son, Isaac, on one of the hills in the region. The passage in which the name occurs (Gen 22:1–19) is known as the Aqedah in Jewish tradition (the "binding" of Isaac). It derives mainly from the E source.

The MT also calls the place *yahweh yirʾeh,* "Yahweh will see" in v 14. This seems to be a corruption of an original *ʾelohîm yirʾeh.* "God will see" (found in the Sahidic Coptic version and the unpublished Qumran manuscript 4QGen Ex[a]; see Davila, fc.). The corruption arose through a folk etymology that associated Moriah with the Hebrew root *rʾh,* "to see," and the divine name *Yah,* short for Yahweh; thus "vision of Yahweh" or the like. This etymology is incorrect; it does not explain the *o* vowel in the name. The actual meaning is unknown.

This Moriah is described as being in a hilly region, about 3 days' journey from Beer-sheba (Gen 22:4). However, this information is not helpful in establishing where Moriah was found since "the third day" may simply be an epic convention for a short journey. The location of the place is disputed (see below).

2. "The hill of Moriah," according to 2 Chr 3:1, the site in Jerusalem where Solomon built the Temple of Yahweh. It is also identified in the same verse with the threshing floor of Ornan (Araunah) the Jebusite (cf. 2 Sam 24; 2 Chr 21). See ARAUNAH. The text of the rest of the verse is corrupt. It appears to refer to the story in the passages just cited, in which David carries out a census and is punished by Yahweh with three days of plague over the whole country, delivered by Yahweh's angel. 2 Chr 3:1 seems to say that this location is where Yahweh (reading with the LXX) appeared to David, and that David appointed the threshing floor as the site for the future temple.

The obvious question at this point is how the two Moriahs are related. It is generally agreed that the location in Gen 22:2 cannot be the same as the one in 2 Chr 3:1. Jerusalem is in a wooded area, to which it would not be necessary to carry firewood (Gen 22:6). Also, it does not make sense that the whole land should be called Moriah if the word is a name for the Temple Mount, nor that the hill bearing the name should be called merely "one of the hills" in the area (Skinner *Genesis* ICC, 1910: 328–29).

Two possibilities have been suggested. First, it may be that Moriah was originally associated with the binding of Isaac, and that the Chronicler or his source erroneously identified the site of the Temple Mount with Moriah in order to give the temple and Jerusalem a more ancient sanctity (Gold *IDB* 2: 438–34).

A more likely explanation is that Moriah was originally the name of the Temple Mount, and that the actual location given in Genesis 22 was suppressed and replaced by Moriah in order to associate the patriarch with the site of the future temple in Jerusalem. There is no indication that the writer of 1 Chr 3:1 was aware of any connection between Abraham and Mt. Moriah; he only mentions its association with David and Solomon. Surely he would have referred to the binding of Isaac if Moriah had appeared in Genesis 22 in his time (von Rad *Genesis* OTL, rev. ed. 1972: 240). Instead, it is probable that the name that originally stood in Gen 22:2 was replaced by Moriah sometime after the time of the Chronicler, but before the translation of the LXX. Various possibilities have been advanced for the original name. One is the land of the Amorite [*haʾemōrî*], reading with the Syriac Peshitta (Skinner *Genesis* ICC, 1910: 328–29). This name looks somewhat like Moriah, and the similarity could have suggested the change to a scribe. Another possibility is the land of Jeruel [*yerūʾēl*], from 2 Chr 20:16 (Gunkel *Genesis*[2] HAT, 169–71). It seems to be derived from *ʾēl,* "God" and the root *rʾh,* so its meaning is similar to the false etymology for Moriah. Such a similarity could have led to the substitution of the latter for the former.

Today the site of Mt. Moriah, the temple platform, is located in the SE corner of the Old City of Jerusalem and is occupied by the Muslim shrines known as the El-Aqsa Mosque and the Dome of the Rock. The latter is the third most holy place for Islam, after Mecca and Medina. According to Muslim tradition it was from the Temple Mount that Muhammad ascended into heaven (the vision is described in Sura 17 of the Quran). The W side of the platform includes the Western Wall or Wailing Wall, where Jews have traditionally come to mourn the loss of the temple.

Bibliography

Davila, J. R. fc. The Name of God at Moriah. An unpublished fragment from 4QGenEx[a].

JAMES R. DAVILA

MORTAR, THE (PLACE) [Heb *maktēš*]. A neighborhood in Jerusalem, which, at the time of Josiah, may have also been the center of some commercial activity (Zeph 1:11). Three things are noteworthy about the reference to this neighborhood. First, it existed toward the end of the 7th century B.C. (time of Josiah; Zeph 1:1), and second, it is mentioned in connection with the "Second Quarter," which was a W neighborhood incorporated into Jerusalem around the time of Hezekiah (late 8th-early 7th century B.C.). See SECOND QUARTER. Third, the Heb *maktēš* normally refers to a hollow place, or a bowl-shaped depression (hence "mortar"; cf. Prov 27:22), which could easily serve as a geomorphological description of a sunken valley (cf. Judg 15:19?). Given these three items, it is possible that this neighborhood was part of the W annex to the City of David, and only came to be regarded as a "mortar" after neighborhoods were established on the eastern slopes of the W hill. In this case, the "mortar" would likely be associated with (some portion of) the Tyropoeon valley, which lay outside the city until the 8th century B.C. (*EAEHL* 2: 597).

GARY A. HERION

MOSAIC COVENANT. After the mixed band of Hebrews (Exod 12:38; Num 11:4) fled Egypt and were delivered at the sea by Yahweh, they came to Mt. Sinai where they recognized and affirmed a special relationship: Yahweh was their God, they were Yahweh's people (Exodus 19–24). This relationship was described using the sociopolitical analogy of covenant; since it took place at Sinai under the leadership and mediation of Moses, it is known (though neither expression, as such, occurs in the Bible) as the Sinai covenant or the Mosaic covenant.

A. Historical Questions
  1. Exodus and Sinai
  2. Covenant Analogy
B. Covenant in Exodus
  1. Yahweh's Action
  2. Israel's Response
  3. Obligation
C. Covenant in Deuteronomy
D. Covenant Morality
E. Covenant in the Prophets
F. Covenant in New Testament

A. Historical Questions

The historical reconstruction of Israel's Exodus from Egypt and covenant making at Sinai bristles with difficulties: exactly when? where? who? etc. Some scholars regard these as nearly insoluble (*HAIJ,* 54–79), while others are more optimistic (Bright *BHI,* 120–43; de Vaux *EHI,* 359–452). Here we need mention only two issues.

1. Exodus and Sinai. While source critics of the 19th century had already raised the issue that the Sinai complex was originally historically distinct from that of Exodus-Kadesh (Nicholson 1973: 4–5), the publication of G. von Rad's programmatic essay (originally published 1938, Eng trans. 1965) began a new phase. In it he isolated form critically what he called "the short historical creed," (e.g., Deut 26:5b–9; 6:20–24; Josh 26:2b–13). These give a summary of God's actions on behalf of Israel but contain no mention of the events at Sinai with its theophany, covenant, and law. The historical summary and the Sinai material were originally two distinct traditions; the former was passed on and celebrated at the Feast of Weeks in Gilgal; the latter, at the Feast of Tabernacles at Shechem. The Yahwist, writing at the time of David and Solomon, was the first to combine these two complexes of traditions into one continuous story (Nicholson 1973: 1–11). Ten years later, M. Noth *(HPT)* extended the discussion to include also those themes contained in the historical credo, arguing that they were all originally independent traditions. Differing from von Rad, he saw the combination of themes, particularly that of Sinai, as occurring before the monarchy in the tribal period (Nicholson 1973: 11–20). These opinions were strongly challenged by a number of scholars (Nicholson 1973: 32–52) and, while discussion continues, a large number of scholars would see Exodus and Sinai as being part of *one* tradition from the beginning (*EHI,* 401–19).

2. Covenant Analogy. Scholarly understanding of covenant in the OT has gone through various phases (Oden 1987: 429–47; Nicholson 1986: 3–117); particularly important is the recognition and study of covenant as an analogy borrowed from the sociopolitical realm. We do not have anything in our modern societies exactly like the covenant. Ancient social organization was largely one of clans and tribes; in some areas small city-states existed. From time to time a city-state (e.g., Ashur, Babylon) would extend its power and become virtually an empire. The relationships between these various groups had to be regulated for the stability of social and political life. The covenant served this function. See also COVENANT.

A covenant was an agreement or promise between two parties solemnly professed before witnesses (usually the respective gods) and made binding by an oath expressed verbally or by some symbolic action. As a result of covenant, a new relationship was established (Kalluveettil 1982: 15,211–13), a relationship often expressed in kinship terminology. The goal of covenant was *šālôm,* peace, wholeness of relationship. Covenant is not, however, a univocal term always referring to the same kind of agreement in exactly the same way. A variety of forms occur: family kinship, royal grant, international treaty (parity type or suzereignty type), etc.

Particularly influential has been the theory (connected especially with G. Mendenhall 1954b) that the Mosaic covenant, from its beginning, was understood on the model of the suzereignty treaty (Nicholson 1986: 56–82). This in turn has come in for some telling criticism; the treaty pattern is clearest in the later deuteronomic literature (McCarthy 1978; M. Weinfeld 1972).

B. Covenant in Exodus

The basic description of the making of the Mosaic covenant is found in Exodus 19–24. The account contains three elements: (1) Yahweh's action; (2) Israel's response; and (3) Israel's obligation.

1. Yahweh's Action. Facing certain death at the sea at the hands of the Egyptians, the fleeing Israelites were gifted by Yahweh with new and unexpected life. Guided by Yahweh through the wilderness, they came to Sinai where they had another experience of Yahweh. This awesome appearance (theophany) of God is described in the classic language of the appearance of the storm god, with dark clouds, thunder, and lightning (*CMHE,* 147–69).

2. Israel's Response. God had delivered Israel at the sea, led them through the wilderness, and appeared to them at Sinai. Israel recognized Yahweh's special care on their behalf and sealed a covenant which expressed this realization. The sealing ceremonies are described in Exodus 24 where two ritual actions are significant: (a) a blood ritual (Exod 24:6–8); and (b) a meal ritual (Exod 24:11, 5).

In the larger biblical context, a special relationship existed between the blood and life; one's life was envisaged as inherent in the blood itself (Lev 17:11; McCarthy 1978: 95,255). To share the same blood was to share the same life, to belong in some way to the same family. Moses sprinkled blood on the altar (representing God) and then on the people. They had the same blood "in their veins." The meal ritual is also rich in symbolism. In the ancient world, sharing a meal expressed likewise belonging to one family and sharing one life. To harm someone with whom table-community had been shared was a serious offense (Ps 41:10). Sharing a meal was a common form of covenant sealing (e.g., Gen 26:30; 31:46, 54). The reference to eating and drinking (Exod 24:11) suggests a covenant meal, while a further reference may be found in v 5 which tells us that bulls were sacrificed as *šělāmîm.* Variously translated as "peace offerings" or "communion sacrifices," these were characterized by the fact that the victim was shared. After part was burned for God, part went to the priest, and the rest belonged to the offerer who ate it at a joyful meal with family and friends (Lev 3:1–17; 7:11–21). Both rituals express the meaning of covenant: a relationship of life and *šālôm* between Israel and God.

3. Obligation. These rituals are preceded in the text by a recitation of the words and ordinances of the Lord to which the people promise obedience. Covenant involved obligation (E. Kutsch [1972] has proposed that the word *běrît,* usually translated "covenant," should in fact be translated "obligation," but this is problematic [McCarthy 1978: 16–18; Nicholson 1986: 89–109]). Covenant obligation, however, should not be viewed as imposed from the outside. It flows from the very nature of covenant. Because of the new relationship, behavior should change. Israel was gifted with life by Yahweh; the covenant expressed that shared life. New behavior flowed from new covenant life.

This new behavior of Israel was manifested in two areas. The first is the vertical relationship with Yahweh. Freed from the slavery of Egypt, Israel now belonged to Yahweh; they must live as Yahweh's people and special possession (Exod 19:4–6). Their deliverance from Egypt was not just a freedom *from,* but also a freedom *for.* The goal of the liberation from Egypt is Israel's service of Yahweh (Exod 4:23; 5:1,3; 7:16, 26; 8:16; 9:1, 13; 10:3). Israel's first obligation is to worship only Yahweh (Exod 20:2–3); the first and basic sin, therefore, against covenant is idolatry. The second area of new covenant life involves the horizontal relationship with others. In saving Israel from the Egyptians, Yahweh was involved in social behavior; the covenant at Sinai revealed an intrinsic connection between the nature of Yahweh and the demands of social justice. How Israel treated each other would be a sign of how seriously they were devoted to Yahweh. A special area of concern here is the treatment of the poor, the oppressed, the alien. A motive frequently found in covenant law (e.g., Exod 22:21; 23:9; Lev 19:34; Deut 15:1–11) for not oppressing the weak is "because you were once strangers (aliens) in the land of Egypt." It would be a contradiction for Israel, freed from oppression by Yahweh, to become themselves oppressors of the weak. These two aspects of covenant living should not be viewed as separable and distinct; they are flip sides of one coin which are intrinsically connected and stand or fall together. If Israel fails to live out its commitment, the existence of the covenant itself is in jeopardy.

The Pentateuch now presents a large number of laws as having been given to Moses at Sinai (e.g., the Ten Commandments and the Covenant Code [Exodus 20–23]; the Holiness Code [Leviticus 17–26]), but it is very difficult to say how much, if any, of this formed part of the original Sinai experience. All of the laws, deriving mostly from later periods in Israel's history can easily be grouped under the heading of either right worship of God or of correct social behavior. These are all only further specifications of the basic covenant obligations. As later generations of Israel retold and renewed their basic covenant story, they included new laws and regulations which made their covenant real for them in the new situations of their lives. All of these developments were attributed to Moses at Sinai because this was where their covenant began.

C. Covenant in Deuteronomy

Presented as three discourses of Moses, the book of Deuteronomy is addressed to all the people in the plains of Moab and focuses on the covenant at Sinai (Horeb). The covenant themes are so much in evidence that it has been considered a covenant document par excellence.

The initiative is with God who has chosen Israel, a choice based not on Israel's greatness or moral status (Deut 7:4; 9:4–6) but simply on Yahweh's gracious love (Deut 7:6–8). Israel is repeatedly called on to "hear" and "remember" this covenant (Deut 5:1; 6:4; 4:9, 23; 5:15) because it was made not only with their ancestors but is also with all of them "today" (Deut 5:1–3; 26:16–18; etc.). If they truly do this, they will faithfully and loyally obey the covenant with its commands and statutes. The most basic of these is the call to worship only Yahweh (Deut 6:4–5); this then overflows into all areas of life, e.g., concern for the poor (Deut 15:1–18), and justice in the legal system (Deut 16:18–20) as well as in the economic sphere (Deut 25:13–16). It extends even to caring for the natural environment (Deut 20:19–20). All of this is part of Israel's response of love to the gracious love of God (Achtemeier 1987). Israel's very life and existence depend on this; covenant fidelity will lead to blessing; infidelity, to curse (Deuteronomy 28).

Whether the Mosaic covenant was modeled from the beginning on the analogy of the ancient suzereignty-vassal treaties is the subject of some dispute. While not agreeing with the extreme position of L. Perlitt (1969) that covenant thinking appeared in Israel only at this time (Cazelles 1972; McCarthy 1972b; Nicholson 1986: 109–17), most scholars would agree that the treaty analogy is most clearly present in Deuteronomy and deuteronomic material (McCarthy 1978: 157–208; Weinfeld 1972: 57–157). The elements of the structural form are present, as well as characteristic vocabulary and phrases (McCarthy 1978: 288–89). While the beginnings of Israel's use of the treaty analogy may be older, its form in Deuteronomy seems to have been influenced by the fact that for over a century Israel had been a vassal subjected to the suzereignty of Assyria. The development of the treaty analogy would thus be a creative response to and polemic against the crisis of Assyrian domination (Lohfink *IDBSup,* 229–32; 1977).

D. Covenant Morality

Too often in the past, the Mosaic covenant morality has been caricatured as an extrinsic legalism or minimalism. While it is true that this can and, in fact, has happened, it is also true that authentic covenant morality is of a totally different kind. The morality embodied in the covenant is (1) one of response, and (2) one of dialogue. (1) Israel is called to respond to the blessings and gifts—most basically the gift of salvation—received from God. This response is specified in several ways: to listen to (obey) the word of God; to fear the Lord; to worship (serve) the Lord (e.g., Deut 10:12). Mosaic covenant morality is, however, also (2) one of dialogue. Just as God loved Israel, so Israel is to love God; just as God is faithful to the covenant, so Israel is to be faithful; just as God is righteous, so Israel is to be righteous; just as God freed from injustice and oppression, so Israel is to free from injustice and oppression. The goal of covenant can be summed up in three words: life, peace, justice. These are all terms of relationship. The covenant expresses that God and Israel are one family, sharing one life. It is approached best, not in legal terms, but in interpersonal ones.

A further question might be asked: why the Mosaic covenant at all? Could God not have led Israel from Egypt directly into the land of Canaan, the land of the promise? The entry into the land may have been the ultimate goal, but the more proximate goal of the deliverance from Egypt was "that they might serve me" (Exod 4:23). In Egypt, Israel was the oppressed, Egypt, the oppressor. As history attests, what often happens when the oppressed are freed is that they eventually become oppressors in turn. The slave becomes the taskmaster. The root problem is that they both share a basic set of values; they disagree only on the present arrangement of things. If Israel, newly freed from Egypt, went directly into Canaan and assumed power there, why would they be any different? They went first to Sinai and to covenant. Covenant with Yahweh, a God who frees from oppression, called them to a whole different view of reality, a new set of values, and a totally different style of life. To live the covenant truly is to worship this God and to be concerned for the rights and social needs of others. When Israel failed to do this, the covenant provided the framework and categories for evaluating and critiquing their lives and behavior. Prominent in this regard were the prophets.

E. Covenant in the Prophets

While the prophets are certainly related to covenant, the exact way of describing this relationship is less clear. Some scholars have proposed that the prophets consciously saw themselves as continuing the role of Moses as covenant mediator. Others viewed the prophets in the light of the treaty covenant analogy. Two dimensions in particular were stressed: the prophets indict Israel for covenant failure using the form of a covenant lawsuit (the *rîb*); the punishments they threaten derive from treaty curses which follow on infidelity (Hillers 1969: 120–42). All these suggestions have come in for criticism and modification (McCarthy 1972a: 35–40, 78–79; Clements 1975: 8–23).

The prophets were rooted in Israel's tradition of covenant and covenant obligation (whether or not this was understood as a treaty). When Israel failed to be faithful to its covenant, the prophets appealed to this common memory as the basis of their critique (Tucker 1985: 328–35; Kapelrud 1984). Thus, Israel yielded to the temptations of the culture around them and fell into false worship; Elijah (1 Kgs 18:21), Isaiah (1:12–16), Jeremiah (7:6,9), Ezekiel (18:5–6), for example, challenge the people to cease following Baal and to adhere only to Yahweh. If they do not do this, their sacrifices and feasts are empty and worthless. Idolatry is the fundamental sin against covenant. In the same way, the Israelites violate the covenant in their dealings with each other. Instead of fidelity, justice, and mercy, lying, stealing, adultery, and murder are found (e.g., Hos 4:2; Jer 7:5–6, 9; Ezek 18:6–8). Amos, Micah, and Isaiah are particularly eloquent in their denouncing violations of the legal and economic systems, so essential to just community living (e.g., Amos 2:6–7; 5:1; 8:4–6; Mic 2:1–3; 3:11; Isa 3:14; 5:11–12). Once again we see that the twofold obligation of correct worship and correct social behavior are two sides of one coin. Attempts of scholars to separate them (e.g., the prophets rejected cult and promoted social justice [Napier *IDB* 3: 901–3]; the prophets taught "do justice first, then worship" [Miranda 1974: 58]) are inadequate.

In evaluating the behavior of the people in the present, the prophets looked to their past covenant tradition. The covenant has been broken and no longer exists. "I am not your God; you are not my people" (Hos 1:9; Jer 11:10; 31:32). Punishment will follow; the people will be exiled out of the land. But this is not the last word. Looking beyond the judgment, the prophets see a new future. God will bring the people through the desert in a new Exodus (e.g., Isa 41:17–20; 51:9–11); they will receive a new heart to enable them to be faithful to the covenant (Jer 31:33; 32:39–40; Ezek 36:26). The Lord will make a new covenant with them; once again, "I will be their God, and they shall be my people," (Jer 31:33; Ezek 34:25; 37:26–27). In depicting their new future, the prophets drew on the images of the old Mosaic covenant.

F. Covenant in New Testament

The early Christians, whose writings are preserved in the NT, were convinced that in Jesus of Nazareth, the hope of a new covenant had been fulfilled (Heb 8:7–9:22). Paul, in the spirit of controversy, draws sharp distinctions between the old covenant and the new (e.g., 2 Cor 3:4–18), but the lines of continuity are clear in the gospels. At the Last Supper, Jesus gives his disciples a cup to drink, "This cup is the new covenant in my blood" (Luke 22:20; 1 Cor 11:25) which will be poured out for the forgiveness of sins (Matt 26:28; see Jer 31:34). Like the old covenant at Sinai, the new one is sealed with a meal and blood ritual. Christians are one family with God, sharing one life. And like the old, this new covenant manifests itself in the new life the Christian should lead. Like Moses on Mt. Sinai, Jesus, on a mountain, gives a new covenant law (Matthew 5–7). Jesus' teachings, example, and life are the commandments of the new covenant (John 15:12; 13:14–15, 34). For Christians, the promise of the Mosaic covenant has become a reality in Christ.

Bibliography

Achtemeier, E. 1987. Plumbing the Depths. *Int* 41: 269–81.

Cazelles, H. 1972. L. Perlitt et la théologie de l'Alliance. *BibOr* 29: 323–26.

Clements, R. E. 1975. *Prophecy and Tradition.* Atlanta.

Hillers, D. R. 1969. *Covenant: The History of a Biblical Idea.* Baltimore.

Kalluveettil, P. 1982. *Declaration and Covenant: A Comprehensive Review of Covenant Formulae from the Old Testament and the Ancient Near East.* AnBib 88. Rome.

Kapelrud, A. S. 1984. The Prophets and the Covenant. Pp. 175–83 in *In The Shelter of Elyon,* ed. W. B. Barrick and J. R. Spencer. JSOTSup 31. Sheffield.

Kutsch, E. 1972. *Verheissung und Gesetz.* BZAW 131. Berlin.

Levenson, J. D. 1985. *Sinai and Zion.* Minneapolis.

Lohfink, N. 1977. Culture Shock and Theology. *BTB* 7: 12–22.

McCarthy, D. J. 1972a. *Old Testament Covenant: A Survey of Current Opinions.* Atlanta.
———. 1972b. *bĕrît* in Old Testament History and Theology. Review of *Bundestheologie im Alten Testament* by L. Perlitt. *Bib* 53: 110–21.
———. 1978. *Treaty and Covenant.* 2d ed. AnBib 21a. Rome.
Mendenhall, G. E. 1954a. Ancient Oriental and Biblical Law. *BA* 17: 26–46.
———. 1954b. Covenant Forms in Israelite Tradition. *BA* 17: 50–76.
Miranda, J. 1974. *Marx and the Bible.* Maryknoll, NY.
Nicholson, E. W. 1973. *Exodus and Sinai in History and Tradition.* Richmond.
———. 1986. *God and His People: Covenant and Theology in the Old Testament.* Oxford.
Oden, R. A. 1987. The Place of Covenant in the Religion of Israel. Pp. 429–47 in *AIR.*
Perlitt, L. 1969. *Bundestheologie im Alten Testament.* WMANT 36. Neukirchen-Vluyn.
Rad, G. von. 1965. The Form-Critical Problem of the Hexateuch. Pp. 1–78 in *PHOE.*
Tucker, G. M. 1985. Prophecy and the Prophetic Literature. Pp. 325–68 in *The Hebrew Bible and Its Modern Interpreters,* ed. D. A. Knight and G. M. Tucker. Philadelphia.
Weinfeld, M. 1972. *Deuteronomy and the Deuteronomic School.* Oxford.

MICHAEL D. GUINAN

MOSERAH (PLACE) [Heb *môsērâ*]. Var. MOSEROTH. A campsite of the Israelites, the 26th of the 40 stages during their wandering in the wilderness (Deut 10:6), called "Moseroth" (Heb *mōsērôt*) in Num 33:30–31. These are the only references to the name, and its location is unknown.

The name is commonly derived from the verb *ʾsr,* "to bind" (BDB, 558, 564), so this may be the "place of binding" or the place of the covenant. The verb also means imprison, and Payne (1980: 1026) suggests the name means "chastisement" for the trespass at Meribah (Num 20:24; Deut 32:51).

In Deuteronomy, the Israelites left Beeroth ("wells") Bene-jaakan and arrived in Moserah on their way to Gudgodah. In Num 33:30, they left Hashmonah and camped at Moseroth and from there went to Bene-jaakan.

In Deuteronomy, Moses' brother Aaron, the high priest, died and was buried at Moserah, and his son Eleazar was installed as high priest. But in Num 20:22–29 and 33:38, Aaron died at Mount Hor. The latter is traditionally identified with Jebel Nebi Harun at Petra but it is also in the region of Kadesh (Num 20:22; 33:37). Moserah is in the line of march from Sinai (Num 33:16) to Ezion-geber (v 35). But Marsh (*IDB* 2: 296) notes that 13 places on the line of travel are mentioned only here so it is impossible to know the exact route. The reversal of the names, Moserah/oth and Bene-jaakan, suggests two different sources in Numbers and Deuteronomy.

Wright (*IB* 2: 398; *WHAB,* 66, map X) suggests Beeroth may be Birein N of Kadesh-barnea, about halfway to Rehoboth. Pfeiffer and Vos (1967, map 2) place it there. This would presumably put Moserah/oth in the same general area. This is in line with a N route for the Exodus with Sinai at Jebel Helal, i.e., the Israelites stopped at Kadesh-barnea, Bene-jaakan, and Moserah/oth, on the way from Sinai to Ezion-geber. If Sinai is Jebel Musa in S Sinai, the Israelites went from Sinai up the E coast of the Sinai peninsula to Ezion-geber and then went to Kadesh-barnea. i.e., Moserah/oth is on the E edge of the Sinai peninsula, not in N Sinai in the wilderness of Zin. But for the time being, its location cannot be known for certain.

Bibliography

Payne, D. F. 1980. Moserah. *The Illustrated Bible Dictionary* 2: 1026.
Pfeiffer, C. F., and Vos, H. F. 1967. *The Wycliffe Historical Geography of Bible Lands.* Chicago.

HENRY O. THOMPSON

MOSES (PERSON) [Heb *mōšeh*]. The man chosen by God to lead the Hebrew people out of Egyptian bondage, to preside over the Sinai ceremony constituting those people as the people of God, and to lead the Hebrew people to the promised land. As such, Moses is arguably the most prominent person in the Hebrew Bible, and he looms large in early Jewish and Christian writings. This entry consists of two articles. The first surveys primarily Moses as a figure in the OT and in early Judaism. The second concentrates specifically on the portrayal and role of Moses in the NT.

OLD TESTAMENT

A. Historicity of Moses
 1. Critical Analysis
 2. Historical Analogy
 3. Possibilities and Probabilities
 4. More Probable Probabilities
B. Biblical Portraits of Moses
 1. Yahwist-Elohist Traditions
 2. Deuteronomic Tradition
 3. Priestly Tradition
C. Post-biblical Portraits of Moses
 1. Hellenistic Judaism
 2. Palestinian Judaism
 3. Rabbinic Judaism

A. Historicity of Moses

No portion of the Bible is more complex and vigorously debated than the story of Moses, and few persons have evoked such disparate views. No extant non-biblical records make reference to Moses or the Exodus, therefore the question of historicity depends solely on the evaluation of the biblical accounts.

One interpretation is the assumption of early Jewish and Christian traditions that the Pentateuch is an accurate historical record written by Moses himself. This conservative view persists in both traditions today along with a rejection of all the claims of critical scholarship. Apparently there is no inclination to ask, "How is it possible for 200 years of critical research to be completely wrong?" K. A. Kitchen declares, "Now, nowhere in the Ancient Orient is there anything which is definitely known to parallel the elaborate history of fragmentary composition and conflation of Hebrew literature (or marked by just such criteria) as the documentary hypothesis would postulate" (1966: 115). Following the suggestion of W. W. Hallo

(1962: 26), J. H. Tigay traces several stages of the *Gilgamesh Epic* over a period of 1,500 years and concludes, "The stages and processes through which this epic *demonstrably* passed are similar to some of those through which the Pentateuchal narratives are *presumed* to have passed. What is known about the evolution of the *Gilgamesh Epic* shows that some of the results of biblical criticism are at least realistic" (1985: 27).

The opposite extreme is J. Van Seters' declaration: "The quest for the historical Moses is a futile exercise. He now belongs only to legend" (*EncRel* 10: 116). The basis for this radical claim is his conviction that the Deuteronomistic History (Dtr) and the three histories based on it (J, P, and Chronicles) have *no* accurate, authentic material earlier than the last preexilic period (1983: 361–62).

While Van Seters is correct in claiming that some units are collections of disparate data by later editors attempting to make a complete story, his basic theory goes too far. Ancient sources have *linguistic fingerprints* and in reworking the texts the editor-authors did *not* smudge or erase all the fingerprints. Z. Zevit affirms that Dtr's sources "contained high-quality intelligence of a type that a later creative author would have been unable to concoct on his own." To assume, moreover, that these fingerprints "are due to the conscious archaizing of late exilic authors who had no pre-exilic literary models . . . is to attribute a linguistic sophistication to the ancient historians unparalleled elsewhere" (1985: 77).

1. Critical Analysis. In between the two extreme positions is a whole spectrum of views combining historical and critical concerns.

Early scholars, using mainly *source analysis* (J, E, D, and P), were critical of the Moses narratives, but they believed that behind the biblical text was a historical core with Moses as Israel's leader during the Exodus, Sinai covenant, and desert wanderings. Polarization of scholars began in the 20th century with H. Gunkel's *form-critical* approach, and the gap widened with the *tradition-history* studies of G. von Rad and M. Noth.

This change, according to von Rad, was "the result of the investigation of the history of traditions; and this has only been brought into full play in our own time." Thus, for him, the attempt to isolate an "actual historical course of events . . . has turned out to be mistaken" (*ROTT* 1: 3). Behind the Hexateuch, von Rad sees, ". . . only certain interpretations and conceptions of older traditions which originate in milieux very different from one another and which must also be judged, from the point of view of form-criticism, as completely diverse" (*ROTT* 1: 4). Consequently, in von Rad's opinion, "We can no longer look on it as possible to write a history of the tradition attaching to Moses, and of where it was at home" (*ROTT* 1: 291). If we try to date the Moses traditions "we are seldom able to advance beyond very general datings, if we are not in fact altogether in the dark" (*ROTT* 1: vi).

Because the cultic recitals in Deut 26:5–9; 6:20–24; and Josh 24:2–13 make no reference to the revelation of Yahweh at Mt. Ṣinai, von Rad concludes that the Sinai story was a very late insertion into the redemptive story of the Exodus and settlement in Canaan (*PHOE*, 3–8, 13). He claims that these traditions, joined first by the Yahwist (*PHOE*, 54), had canonical patterns and became cult-legends at separate sanctuaries: *Sinai* with the Feast of Booths at the Shechem covenant festival, and *Exodus/settlement* with the Feast of Weeks at Gilgal (*PHOE*, 43, 45). While the cult had some later influence on the formation of these legends, it did *not* produce them (*PHOE*, 22).

M. Noth, expanding on von Rad's work, determines to penetrate into the preliterary phase of the traditions in order to ascertain the origins and first stages of growth in the development leading to the Pentateuch (*HPT*, 1–2). He isolates five themes, fixed during oral transmission, which were essential for the faith of the separate Israelite tribes: patriarchs, exodus, wanderings, revelation at Sinai, and Conquest/occupation. Since he considers all material connecting these themes as secondary, and observes that the name "Moses" occurs "with striking infrequency" outside of the Pentateuch (*HPT*, 156), he comes to the radical conclusion that Moses is an editorial bracket binding all the themes together (*HPT*, 160–61). For Noth, the most historical reality of the person Moses is his death and burial in Transjordan (*HPT*, 173).

However, this pessimistic view hinges on some very subjective interpretations. In fact, Noth states explicitly that his conclusions about the Sinai tradition are "not conclusive arguments" because one could speak only "in terms of a certain probability" (*HPT*, 62).

A number of younger scholars, using Noth's tradition-history approach, reject his conclusion that all the themes are independent and the binding material secondary. W. Beyerlin, on the basis of Exod 20:2, claims that "the Decalogue originated somewhere where we can count on the presence of those who experienced *both* the Exodus *and* the meeting with God on Sinai" (1965: 145).

In his *Moses: Heroic Man, Man of God*, G. W. Coats claims that the Moses narratives "constitute a body of tradition with valid form-critical character" (1988: 38). Working with the whole range of literary methods, Coats takes issue with Noth's claim that Moses is a secondary redactional bracket: "Moses cannot be eliminated so readily from the various themes of tradition, and, as a consequence, the assumption of independence collapses" (1988: 37).

B. Childs is concerned to highlight the fundamental dialectic of the canonical process within Israel whereby "the literature formed the identity of the religious community which in turn shaped the literature" (*IOTS*, 41). He favors a sociological understanding of Moses' role:

> Especially in such passages as Ex.20.18–20 and Deut.19.15ff., that which is being described is not simply a historical event, but rather an etiology for the establishment of something institutional and ongoing. Moses' role as covenantal mediator in the Sinai tradition has a decided cultic stamp which seems to point to an office within an institution (*Exodus* OTL, 355).

In this connection, Coats' comments are also instructive:

> The issue at stake . . . is whether a standing office has influenced the shape of the Moses traditions. Is the cultic office of covenant mediator the proper *Sitz im Leben* for this facet of the Moses tradition? Or was the tradition shaped basically by a popular literary process as a nar-

rative convention for depicting the leader with at best only tangential contacts with the cult? (1988: 138).

The most thoroughgoing sociological approach is N. K. Gottwald's *The Tribes of Yahweh.* He acknowledges his debt to Noth and observes (1979: 72) that Noth (*HPT,* 259) leaves unanswered "the problem of what brought about the unity 'Israel' and the common Israelite consciousness." The purpose of Gottwald's study is "to *begin* with the tantalizing enigmatic questions with which Noth's provocative analysis of the Pentateuchal traditions *ends*" (1979: 72). Gottwald believes that biblical scholars, given to "hyperspecialization" of detailed studies with limited scope, have not adequately addressed this historical-sociological problem, and insofar as it has been treated "it has been 'answered' by theological fiat" (1979: 5–7, 73). Thus he contends that "the valid intention of biblical theology can only be fulfilled by 'biblical sociology' " (1979: 911). In following up on this approach, Gottwald (1979: 78) declares:

> The proclamation of the themes in the cult was a communal speech-act, . . . of a special kind, which we have called cultic-ideological. . . . It was meaning-charged speech elucidating the identity of Israel, . . . speech that proclaimed the divine power in which the community was grounded, . . . speech that addressed the community with its most fundamental obligations and reminded it of its most fundamental resources. . . . even speech which allowed for the direct declamation of the divine word to the community.

Then he adds the caveat, "We must necessarily view the finished product of these early historical traditions . . . as 'unplanned' by any one person or group of persons within any single context" (1979: 78).

2. Historical Analogy. In opposition to tradition-history proponents, a number of mediating scholars maintain that *historical analogy* should play a role in the literary-sociological study of Scripture, especially in connection with the Moses story. Human experience shows that observation and understanding of key events varies with the personality, training, and insight of the participants. This was undoubtedly true of those who followed Moses; therefore, it is highly probable that two or three variant traditions developed fairly soon after the Exodus and Sinai events. From this viewpoint, the variant biblical traditions need not be understood as originating in "completely diverse milieux." Moreover, while culture has influence on gifted persons, it does not initiate their innovative ideas and movements. Rather, the initial impact toward change is made by creative individuals, not culture. Furthermore, all great leaders of people and movements have had to play a number of roles, consequently it is not feasible to squeeze highly talented people into any single mold.

In addition to *source criticism,* the use of *stylistic criteria* (poetic form, syntax, and spelling) for dating texts (*YGC,* 1–52), and data from *archaeology and inscriptions* for portraying the background of the biblical narratives, W. F. Albright employs *historical analogy* because it "plays a particularly important role" for the study of the Bible (1966: 11). He recognizes that it "does not constitute proof when taken alone" (1965: 268), but he concludes that the biblical tradition about Moses "is strongly supported by historical analogy, and is now being confirmed by a rapidly increasing mass of evidence uncovered by archaeologists and philologians" (1976: 120).

Similarly, J. Bright, a student of Albright, reacting to the reductionist views of von Rad and Noth, claims:

> Over all these events there towers the figure of Moses. Though we know nothing of his career save what the Bible tells us, the details of which we have no means of testing, there can be no doubt that he was, as the Bible portrays him, the great founder of Israel's faith. Attempts to reduce him are extremely unconvincing. The events of exodus and Sinai require a great personality behind them. And a faith as unique as Israel's demands a founder as surely as does Christianity—or Islam, for that matter. To deny that role of Moses would force us to posit another person of the same name! (*BHI,* 126–27).

W. Eichrodt comes to a similar conclusion, "*At the very beginning of Israelite religion we find the charisma,* the special individual endowment of a person; and to such an extent is the whole structure based on it, that without it it would be inconceivable" (*ETOT,* 292).

3. Possibilities and Probabilities. Because of the complexities of the biblical text and the lack of certain data, conclusions about a historical Moses are narrowed to possibilities and probabilities.

For some scholars the question of historicity begins with the name "Moses." The biblical writer apparently did not know that it was a shortened Egyptian name, but assuming that Pharaoh's daughter knew Hebrew, he had her use popular etymology to base the name on the verb *māšâ* ("to draw out"): "Because I drew him out of the water" (Exod 2:10). The name actually stems from the Egyptian verb *msy* "to give birth" and appears as "Mose" with the name of a god: e.g., Tuthmosis "Toth is born" and Rameses "Re is born." Since the Egyptians often shortened such names to "Mose," it is implicit that "Moses" was longer at first, but there is no indication as to the deity involved (e.g., no "Yamses"). While the name is proper for the circumstances of the Exodus story, it *alone* does not prove that Moses was a historical figure.

R. de Vaux, holding more to probabilities, affirms that traditions (myth or history) "were not created by cult—cultic practices simply helped to recall traditions" (*EHI* 1: 185). He realizes that oral tradition can be forgetful and at times invents a great deal, yet "it is faithful in some ways" (*EHI* 1: 184). The tradition of Moses in Midian is early and has a historical basis (*EHI* 1: 330). Moreover, Moses was involved with the Exodus and Sinai: "There is . . . no impelling reason for eliminating Moses from any of these traditions; on the contrary, there is positive evidence for believing that they are closely interconnected" (*EHI* 1: 453).

The "quest for the historical Moses" presents more of a difficulty for Childs (*IOTS,* 178), and very little of his commentary on Exodus attempts to wrestle with historical problems and data. Yet, notwithstanding some expansion of the text in Exodus 3, due to the later prophetic office, Childs affirms that the call of Moses was authentic:

> It (tradition) recognized correctly that a new element entered with Moses which set it apart from the patriarchal period. . . . Moses' call recounts the deep disruptive seizure of a man for whom neither previous faith nor personal endowment play a role in preparing him for his vocation (*Exodus* OTL, 56).

Coats does not attempt a reconstruction of an original Moses tradition because his goal "is to describe the various images used by various texts in the Old Testament for depicting the characteristics of this giant" (1988: 36). It is implicit, however, that he gives credence to Moses as lawgiver: "The earliest picture of Moses available, perhaps the only picture of Moses from the period before the monarchy, depicts Moses as lawgiver (Deut 33:4)" (1988: 199). As another indication, Coats observes, "There is no law tradition without Moses" (1988: 169). It is also implicit that the mediation of Moses in giving the law to the people has its counterpart in his heroic representation of the people before Yahweh with respects to their concerns and intercession for their sins (1988: 159, 165–66).

Gottwald recognizes some historical traces in the text, "Moses is recalled as an actual person who was of Levitical kinship, who intermarried with Midianite 'semi-nomads,' who led a slave revolt, who was reportedly buried in Transjordan" (1979: 35). On the contrary, he contends that "we are not in a position to calculate the part that the historical Moses played in introducing Yahweh, in explicating him as a deliverer from opposition, as one with whom to covenant, and as a law-giver" (1979: 37). Then he comments, "Possibly the later tradition is correct in believing that Moses had the decisive part to play in all these respects. But only possibly" (1979: 37).

Since Gottwald is more confident about a proto-Israelite "Moses group" than the specific person Moses, he makes some additional suggestions:

> . . . it is highly probable that the notion of Yahweh as a god who delivers from oppression was introduced first among a group of proto-Israelites for whom Moses was one, although not necessarily the only, leader. . . . it is at least possible, conceivably probable, that notions of covenanting between god and people and of divine lawgiving were introduced in some form among that same group of proto-Israelites in which Moses was a leader (1979: 36).

Gottwald thinks that covenanting and law giving in this group "were relatively undeveloped," and even if they did occur at Sinai, we do not know how they were understood and practiced (1979: 36–37). See also COVENANT; MOSAIC COVENANT.

4. More Probable Probabilities. It is evident from this survey that all critical theories and reconstructions involve probabilities, and so the issue of Moses' historicity must attempt to ascertain which probabilities are more probable.

For Noth, the first *historical fact* about Israel is that the twelve-tribe confederation settled in Canaan after the occupation and worshipped as a community. There the various tribes told their own unique stories and in time "all Israel" came to feel that it had shared in all of these experiences (*HPT,* 43–45). Gottwald attempts to solve Noth's problem of accounting for "the unity 'Israel' and the common Israelite consciousness" by attributing to the cultic gatherings a special kind of speech-act filled with the charisma of Israel's identity, obligations, resources, and even a divine word. There is no doubt that such issues were discussed in the development of Israel, but can its *origin* be explained by ecumenical-like worship services and consultations without the primary input of a Yahwistic, covenant group inspired by the Exodus and Sinai experiences under the leadership of Moses? In spite of lapses from some members, the Song of Deborah (Judges 5, ca. 1150–1125 B.C.) indicates that fairly early the Israelite tribal league was a functioning unity motivated by the Yahwistic faith. Bright comments:

> Indeed, had not the nucleus of Israel, already in covenant with Yahweh, appeared in Palestine and, banding with disaffected elements there with whom it made common cause, won notable victories, it is difficult to see why groups of such mixed origin, and geographically so scattered, would have come together in confederation under Yahweh's rule at all (*BHI,* 168).

For von Rad, the fusion of the exodus-settlement and Sinai traditions occurred *first* by the Yahwist, thus blending "the two fundamental propositions of the whole message of the Bible: Law and Gospel" (*PHOE,* 54). Whether articulated or not, human existence (individual, familial, and cultural) has had to deal with the issues of justice and mercy. Is it feasible to separate this reality into monolithic strands and claim that for 200 years separate traditions consistently preserved a half of the dialectic truth without recognition of or concern for the other half? Accordingly, mediating scholars wonder why it is impossible for these two facets to be involved in the difficult experience of the Yahwistic group in the desert after deliverance from Egypt. As R. F. Johnson notes, "But it is easily possible to consider the biblical account of Mosaic leadership a more credible explanation of Israel's early period in Palestine than any other available thesis (*IDB* 3: 442).

In summary, the evaluation of the evidence and counterclaims in the scholarly debate about Moses seems to favor, as the most probable conclusion, a modified form of the Moses story. In response to Yahweh's call in Midian, Moses—the Hebrew with the Egyptian name—led his people out of Egypt, constituted them as a people of God by mediating the covenant at Mt. Sinai, interceded for them during the desert wanderings, and brought them to Moab where he died.

B. Biblical Portraits of Moses

The issue of various portraits of Moses, like the question of historicity, depends on one's interpretation of the biblical text, and again there is great diversity.

The conservative tradition holds that the interchange of divine names is the intention of the author, not the result of separate sources. "We may assume," U. Cassuto claims, "that in each case the Torah chose one of the two Names according to the context and intention" (1961: 31). While "Yahweh" reflects Israelite theology and traditions about God and his people, "Elohim" is appropriate for non-Israelites, universal tradition, and those who think of Deity in abstract terms (1961: 31–32). "However," as Childs observes, "both the extreme artificiality by which meaning is assigned to the use of the names, as well as the constant need to adjust the theory in every succeeding section, does not evoke great confidence in this approach" (*Exodus* OTL, 53). Cassuto is nearer the truth when he comments:

> The stream of this tradition may be compared to a great and wide-spreading river that traverses vast distances; although in the course of its journey the river loses part of its water, . . . and it is also increasingly augmented by waters of the tributaries that pour into it, yet it carries with it, . . . some of the waters that it held at the beginning when it first started to flow from its original source (1961: 102–3).

Thus, while Cassuto denies the sources of the critics, he affirms that numerous traditions have come together.

Years of research concerning the source and tributaries of the text resulted in the classical view of source criticism: J and P (southern), E and D (northern) as separate traditions or recensions of Israel's history. Yet these accounts tend to be *one-sided,* like a portrait featuring the most attractive profile. An example is von Rad's separate portraits of Moses in J and E. While recognizing that Moses appears throughout the Yahwist account, he claims: (1) Moses' call "was only for the purpose of informing Israel in Egypt" about Yahweh's intentions, and so it would be "utterly wrong if we were to understand Moses' call as an appointment to be Israel's leader, for in this source document the leadership of Israel is Jahweh's alone"; (2) Yahweh effects the miracles "without any assistance from Moses;" (3) "Moses retires right into the background;" and (4) for the narrator no "particular theological stress" is made of "Moses' function in the various conflicts and crises" (*ROTT* 1: 291–92).

On the other hand, according to von Rad, "There is a noticeable difference in the picture of Moses given by the Elohist:" (1) the idea of Moses' office has changed, "E has pushed Moses much more into the foreground as the instrument of God in effecting the deliverance;" (2) moreover, "Moses is now the miracle-worker, in fact almost to the point of being a magician;" (3) Moses' importance is enhanced "by setting Aaron over against him. . . . Moses is God for Aaron, and Aaron the mouth for Moses—Moses is the creative initiator and Aaron only the executive speaker (Ex. iv. 16);" and (4) Moses is a prophet in E, but "of a special type—he is much more the prophet of action, taking an active hand in the events" (*ROTT* 1: 292–93).

In reaction to the atomizing of the text by radical source-critics, a number of scholars have observed wider frameworks and patterns for understanding the text. These are helpful, and, as Childs notes, "to show a larger pattern which cuts across the sources does not disprove their existence" (*Exodus* OTL, 150). Yet there has been increasing question about E because of its fragmentary nature and the difficulty in determining where it begins and ends. The problem involves the complex history of J and E. In some places, like Exodus 19, it is impossible to untangle them completely. Evidently the two were mixed at times in oral transmission and this condition carried over into the groundwork source behind J and E. In any case, in the growth of these traditions various literate persons, whether working as compilers, redactors, or authors, were prompted by new historical situations to make relevant theological notes about the events described. Thus, after the division of the kingdom, E became the northern counterpart of southern J and such crucial passages as Exod 3:9–15; 20:1–17; and 24:3–8 indicate its distinctive perspective. Some time after the fall of the northern kingdom, the E tradition, even with some of its divergent views, was subsumed within J, and so from the point of view of the JE redactor(s), most certainly in Judah, the E material was understood in the light of J.

Coats affirms that "the classical definition of order in the relationships of the sources holds even in the face of challenges," thus J is the oldest, D next, and finally P. He deviates by claiming that "in those places where E appears, the source is an expansion of J, thus dependent on J" (1988: 36). Nevertheless, G. Fohrer, building on Wellhausen's analysis, makes a definitive defense of the E source stratum (1968: 152–58).

A new approach to Exodus-Deuteronomy is the hypothesis of Coats: *"The Moses narratives, structured as heroic saga, merge with the narrative tradition about Yahweh's mighty acts, structured around confessional themes"* (1988: 37). *"This heroic tradition,"* according to Coats, *"binds the hero with his people. Either by military might, or by skillful intercession, or by familiarity with surroundings and conditions, he defends and aids his own. He brings 'boons' to his people"* (1988: 40). Coats recognizes that the two models are narrative opposites, at times complementary, at times contradictory, but his concern is to define "the relationship between these two structural patterns. Moses is the heroic man and the man of God" (1988: 42). The series of praises to Yahweh for the mighty acts in behalf of his people came from the ritual of Israel's sanctuaries. Yet this tradition was only half of the historical reality. The other half was preserved by common folk who transmitted orally the narratives about Moses. This heroic man was also the man of God because he was the human agent facilitating the acts of God.

Childs, like Coats, values the sources, yet finds great insight in the *composite portraits,* "The final literary production has an integrity of its own which must not only be recognized, but studied with the same intensity as one devotes to the earlier stages" (*Exodus* OTL, 224).

1. Yahwist-Elohist Traditions. In highlighting the JE portrait of Moses it will be helpful at times to note how the stories about Moses complement the confessional themes in the Exodus, desert, and Sinai episodes.

Although the folkloristic narratives of Exod 1:15–2:22 lack specific historical references, they declare that Moses, born during the oppression of a Pharaoh and reared in his court, was a Hebrew from the house of Levi who cared for his own people. After his flight to Midian he showed similar concern for the daughters of the priest Reuel (Jethro), then married one of them.

Exod 3:1–12 relates the essence of the actual call and commission of Moses. The burning bush, however understood, is the means of initiating a dialogue with Moses. In vv 7–9 Yahweh sees, hears, knows his people's plight, and determines to free them and bring them to a good land. In v 10 Moses is commissioned to be his agent, but he demurs and is given a sign to reassure him. When Moses inquires about God's name he is told, "Yahweh . . . is my name for ever" (3:15). This new name is an authentic claim of E, in contrast to J where the worship of Yahweh begins with Seth and Enosh (Gen 4:26). The crucial point of the combined JE text is that Yahweh authorizes Moses to confront Pharaoh and free the Hebrews.

According to JE in Exod 5:1–15:21, Moses requests Pharaoh, in Yahweh's name, to let the Hebrews go into the desert to hold a feast. He refuses and when nine plagues do not change his mind, Yahweh kills the Egyptian firstborn. With a cry of anguish, Pharaoh and the Egyptians urge Moses and his people to leave. Pharaoh changes his mind, however, and pursues them. Yahweh's miracle at the Reed Sea provides escape for the people and death for Pharaoh's army.

Behind this composite picture some scholars find two separate accounts. R. de Vaux, for example, holds to an *Exodus flight,* led by Moses, and an *Exodus expulsion,* with the death of the firstborn (*EHI* 1: 373). According to Coats, when the negotiations during the nine plagues fail, Moses has the people acquire silver and gold jewelry from the Egyptians. This spoliation, the beginning of the Exodus, is possible because Yahweh gives the people favor with the Egyptians and Moses is very great in the land (Exod 11:3). Then Moses calls his people to leave in haste under his leadership without the permission or even the knowledge of Pharaoh (1988: 97–98, 108). On the other hand, Childs holds to one exodus after ten plagues, because he shifts Exod 11:4–8 to follow 10:29 so that Moses announces to Pharaoh the death of the firstborn before leaving "in hot anger" (*Exodus* OTL, 161).

Divine and human participation are combined again in the victory at the Reed Sea. Praises to Yahweh, both in poetry and narrative (probably from the cult), attribute "natural" causes to God: the strong east wind; the clogging of the chariot wheels; and the routing of the army. Moses, on the contrary, performs the "wondrous" events: stretching out his hand (rod) to divide the sea and cause its return. Both aspects appear in J's summary: "Israel saw the great work which Yahweh did against the Egyptians, . . . and they believed in Yahweh and his servant Moses" (14:31). Since belief is rooted in trust and willingness to obey, this affirmation goes beyond a cognitive recognition of Moses: they are ready to obey him.

The dominant feature of the desert wanderings is the sojourn at Mt. Sinai. The essential narrative (Exodus 19–24; 32–34) is a very complex conflation of J and E, with only a few verses from P. A crucial fact is that vv 19:4 and 20:2 bind the Sinai event with the Exodus: the appeal for Israel's covenant obedience is based on God's gracious act of freeing them from Egypt.

In line with the sources, critics tend to see two different traditions in the Sinai pericope. The dominant theme is from E: when God declares the commandments to the people (20:1–17) they are fearful and urge Moses to mediate God's word (20:18–20), which he does, functioning as a *priest,* in the blood ritual ratifying the covenant (24:3–8). The subordinate theme is from J: Yahweh speaks with Moses in the presence of the people so that they will believe him (19:9, 19), then instead of a covenant with the people, Yahweh makes a covenant with Moses in their behalf (34:27). For Childs, the two themes, fused in the preliterary stage, are rooted in different settings: E in the covenant renewal ceremony, and J in the tent of meeting (*Exodus* OTL, 358). Coats, on the other hand, considers the two traditions complementary, stemming from the storytelling of the people (1988: 133).

In addition to its cruciality in Israel's history, the version of the covenant in E has important clues related to the historicity of Moses. The covenant ceremony opens with a comment that Moses "told the people all the words of Yahweh and all the ordinances" (24:3), yet in the rest of the ceremony only the "words" are involved. It is apparent that originally 24:3–8 followed the "words" (commandments) in 20:1–17. Later, an editor inserted the collection of regulations in 20:22–23:33, considering it a further revelation to Moses at the mountain. While the first part consists largely of conditional "ordinances" (If [when] . . . then . . .) related to agricultural, village life, 22:18–23:19 has a number of regulations which, like the commandments, are in the imperative form, "You shall (not)." Childs considers them as premonarchic and notes that "some of the material stems from a very early period which may reach back into the wilderness period" (*Exodus* OTL, 456). A still later editor, working with the expanded text, added "and all the ordinances" (24:3), to make clear that the whole collection was included in the "Book of the Covenant" (24:7) used by Moses at the ceremony.

Although there are different expansions within the commandments of Exod 20:2–17 (E) and Deut 5:6–21 (D), the two collections come from a common northern tradition. There is no indication how to separate them, nor does it state there were *ten.* The designation "Ten Words" (Decalogue) comes from Exod 34:28. Each commandment appears elsewhere in the Bible, but in time tradition determined that these were unique and reflected the essence of God's will. The first three pertain to God and the rest refer to human relations. The eight negative commands set the boundary of covenant life with God. To step beyond these restrictions is rebellion leading to death. The two positive words are instruction for living within God's will. See TEN COMMANDMENTS.

There is a timeless, transcultural quality about them, and Noth himself acknowledges that "the Decalogue is the only legal entity in the OT which indicates no certain reference to the conditions of life in an agricultural community." Furthermore, since the writings of the prophets "appear to presuppose the commandments," Noth comments that "for the pre-prophetic period all possibilities of dating are open," yet because of his tradition-history presuppositions he rules out any date "before the conquest" (*Exodus* OTL, 167). If not all, at least some of these stipulations were involved in the desert covenant. Human experience indicates that the guidelines for any religious or political agreement require continual interpretation and additional specifications. Accordingly, it is quite probable *analogically* that Moses began the process of interpreting the commands, regardless of how many there were. Evidently Joshua continued the process after entering Canaan (Josh 24:25–26). It is possible that this updating, not described explicitly, appears in the collection (20:22–23:33) attributed to Moses.

In any event, after the apostasy concerning the golden calf, Yahweh determines to destroy the people and make Moses a great nation (32:1–10). Moses intercedes for them (vv 11–14), even offering to be blotted out of God's book if Yahweh does not forgive their sin (v 32). Thus again, the complementary facets of Moses' role as *mediator* are highlighted: Moses is both God's representative to the people—man of God as *lawgiver*—and the people's representative to God—heroic man as *intercessor.* A special feature of Moses' role as lawgiver is that during the revelation of the law Moses, unknowingly, attains a "shining face." Since the people draw back from him on his return, he puts on a "veil" (Heb *masweh*). The only occurrences of this term in the entire Bible are the three uses in this passage (34:29–35). The practice was also probably associated with the Yahweh-Moses conversations at the tent of meeting outside the camp (33:7–13). That tradition was superseded by the priestly tabernacle inside the camp, therefore the veil as a special symbol of Moses is an early feature. As Coats observes, "The heroic man transfigured by the presence of God, . . . is uniquely the man of God" (1988: 138).

In JE the Sinai narratives separate the desert journeys into two units: Exodus 15–18 and Numbers 10–36. While the rigors of desert life before Sinai evoke murmurings, Yahweh listens to the complaints and supplies the people's needs. On the other hand, after Sinai the murmurings against Yahweh and Moses provoke God's anger. Moral responsibility was fixed at the covenant with Yahweh, therefore rebellion results in censure and punishment (Numbers 11–14, 16).

When Moses' unique authority is challenged by Miriam, an editor comments, "Moses was very meek, more than all the men that were on the face of the earth" (Num 12:3). This meekness (humility) implies that Moses was not overbearing in his role as leader. Yahweh had commissioned him, therefore Yahweh defends him, "With him I speak mouth to mouth, clearly, and not in dark speech" (Num 12:8). Although Moses intercedes for Miriam's healing, she must spend seven days outside the camp before being restored. When the people believe the majority report of the spies and refuse to leave Kadesh to begin the conquest of Canaan, Yahweh appears at the tent of meeting and threatens again to disinherit his people. Moses makes such an eloquent, rational appeal, Yahweh pardons them, but the adults will pay a price: they will never enter the promised land (Num 13:25–14:23). Even though the designation is not used, Moses functions as the *shepherd* of his people. He is human, however, and because the load of the murmuring people is too heavy, he objects to Yahweh's command to carry them "as a nurse carries a sucking child" (Num 11:10–15).

2. Deuteronomic Tradition. While the portrait of Moses in Deuteronomy (D) retains much of the composite picture in JE, there are some distinctive features and emphases. In the summary of the experiences after Horeb (1:6–3:29) Moses is the *leader,* yet he is no wonder-worker. The reference in 34:11 to signs and wonders is a late addition to D. At the request of the people, Moses continues to be their *mediator* (5:5, 27), yet a new feature appears in the preface to the book: Moses purposes *to explain* what Yahweh has commanded (1:5). Thus Moses is not only a *lawgiver:* he becomes the law's *interpreter.* This claim is basic to the structure of the book. After the commandments are given, the text is largely a series of homilies by Moses. The topic in chap. 6 is the *commandment,* a restatement of the negative first commandment in a positive form (6:4–5), and chaps. 6–11 spell out its meaning and implications. The same is true in chaps. 12–26 for the *statutes and ordinances.* Thirty-six times in chaps. 4–30 Moses states "I command you," therefore these interpretations, while rooted in the Torah of Yahweh, tend to become the Torah of Moses.

The purpose of the instructions is more than didactic, however. Moses strives to elicit obedience from his stubborn people. His persuasive pleas are laced with enticements: "that it may go well with you" or "that you may prolong your days in the land." To ensure that future generations have his teachings, Moses commands the people to keep them foremost in their consciousness and to use every occasion to teach them to their children (6:6–9).

In JE the call of Moses and the communication of God's words to his people indicate that he is a prophet, but in D this role is specifically stressed. To counter the anticipated temptations of pagan divination in Canaan, Moses promises that Yahweh "will raise up for you a prophet like me, . . . him you shall heed" (18:15). It is implicit in Moses' promise of another prophet and his command to teach the next generation that his task is nearing completion.

As Moses reminds the people of their rebellious history, he reviews, in a paraphrase of Exod 32:11–14, his traumatic intercession with Yahweh, pleading for forty days and nights to disregard the stubbornness, wickedness, and sin of the people (9:25–29). Yahweh spares the people, but he prohibits Moses from entering the promised land: "Yahweh was angry with me also on your account, and said, 'You shall not go in there' " (1:37). Thus the *intercessor* becomes the *suffering mediator.* Moses does not complain, but he intercedes for himself: "Let me go over, I pray, and see the good land beyond the Jordan" (3:25). Although D never explains why Moses has to pay the price, Yahweh rebuffs him, "Speak no more to me of this matter" (3:26).

Thus, Moses vicariously bears Yahweh's wrath against his people. His death alone in Moab takes on a vicarious quality as well. Yahweh buries him and "no one knows the place of his burial to this day" (34:6). There can be no sacred monument where pilgrims can share in a memorial ceremony for Moses. He must live in the hearts of the people as the greatest prophet of all, the one with whom Yahweh spoke "face to face" (34:10).

3. Priestly Tradition. The last source to be incorporated into the Hebrew Bible was P. Features in common with JE and D point to a tradition shared during oral transmission and indicate that P has some early material. Its distinctive differences stem from a long history of separate development in Jerusalem. During the Babylonian exile, the priests had no temple in which to serve, so they turned their attention to preserving and authenticating the priestly traditions and way of life. The JE and D traditions were subsumed within the P framework to form a new composite story of Israel's early history. Still later, probably after the exile, more additions were made by priestly redactors. We know nothing of the various priests involved in this process, but it is clear that they had the last word in forming the Pentateuch. Consequently, the P portrait of Moses will highlight some different features.

The first major change in the picture is Exod 6:2–7:7, originally a doublet of Exod 3:1–4:17 (JE). P is more explicit than E (Exod 3:15) that *Yahweh* is a new name for the God known to the patriarchs as *El Shaddai* (6:3). The E version of Aaron's commissioning (Exod 4:14–16) is shortened and given a prophetic nuance: "See, I make you as God to Pharaoh; and Aaron your brother shall be your prophet" (7:1). In P, moreover, Moses is relieved of the physical aspects in confronting Pharaoh and his magicians: Moses gives the orders, but Aaron, with his rod, effects some of the plagues (7:19). Furthermore, Pharaoh is hardened so that Yahweh can multiply the signs (11:9–10).

The most radical shift in perspective occurs in the Sinai narratives. In Exod 24:16–18, P notes that Moses enters the cloud of Yahweh's glory on Mount Sinai and stays there forty days and nights. When Yahweh finishes speaking with Moses he hands him "the two tablets of the testimony . . . written with the finger of God" (Exod 31:18). Between the two passages P inserts the lengthy instructions for making the tabernacle and its equipment. It is P's method of declaring that the blueprints for the tabernacle came from Yahweh himself. When Moses, on seeing the golden calf and the dancing people, shatters the two tablets (Exod 32:19) he is doing more than symbolizing the broken covenant. For P this is a traumatic loss of the blueprints. It is imperative that they be written again. When Moses returns with the second set of tablets (Exod 34:29), the tabernacle, designed by God, can be constructed (Exod 35:1–40:33).

In the tabernacle instructions, Yahweh requests, "And let them make me a sanctuary, that I may dwell in their midst" (Exod 25:9). Therefore, when the cloud of Yahweh's glory fills *the priestly tabernacle, the new tent of meeting,* it is a confirmation that Yahweh is moving from Mount Sinai to his new residence. Another clue for understanding P's claim is Yahweh's statement in connection with the instructions for the tabernacle furniture: "There I will meet with you, and . . . from between the two cherubim . . . I will speak with you of all that I will give you in commandment for the people of Israel" (Exod 25:22). Accordingly, Lev 1:1 and Num 1:1 claim that Yahweh reveals the priestly insights and regulations to Moses at the tent of meeting. R. Knierim notes incisively:

> From now on, Yahweh would meet Moses from the sanctuary in Israel's midst, and no longer on Sinai. The mountain belonged to the past. The presence belonged to the sanctuary. Its legitimacy and identity were secured by the continuity of the revelation of God from the mountain. And now, Yahweh could give the ultimately decisive instructions concerning the ongoing life of Israel. These instructions have two foci: the provision of the atonement institution for the continuous liberation from the destructive burden of guilt and pollution (Leviticus 1–16), and the regulations for Israel's societal life as a "holy" community (Leviticus 17–27). The Sinai-pericope aims at the book of Leviticus. This book is the center of the Pentateuch (1985: 405).

In short, Exodus-Numbers is dominated by the P portrait of Moses as Yahweh's unique mediator communicating *all of God's Torah* (commandments, statutes, and ordinances) to the people.

Whereas JE and D recognize the humanity of Moses, P goes on to portray him and Aaron as sinners: ". . . you did not believe in me, to sanctify me in the eyes of the people of Israel" (Num 20:12). The fault seems to be based on the rash statement in 20:10: "Hear now, you rebels; shall we bring forth water for you out of the rock?" When Moses strikes the rock twice he seems to do so with an assurance he has the power to produce water. In this act he does not really believe in Yahweh, nor does he honor God in the people's presence, therefore he will never enter the promised land.

Because the priests understood Israel's history as Yahweh's divine plan, P was more concerned than JE or D with genealogies and chronological data. Its dates are relative, however, and provide no accurate pegs for setting the dates of Moses. Archaeological surveys of the Sinai peninsula indicate that the only habitation in the Late Bronze and Iron I periods (1500–1000 B.C.) was along the Mediterranean coast and at the mining operations of Serabit el-Khadem. If accurate, the report that Moses did not take the coastal route (Exod 13:17–18) poses a problem for 14th, 13th, and 12th-century dates for the Exodus/Conquest. The scholarly consensus of a 13th-century date for Moses is eroding, but ambiguous data make any alternatives equally tenuous.

C. Post-biblical Portraits of Moses

Since the Torah has a number of intriguing, ambiguous, and even troublesome statements, it was inevitable that thoughtful persons, both common folk and scholars, would feel compelled to expand the portraits of Moses more in line with their own theological and philosophical views.

1. Hellenistic Judaism. Since some Hellenistic and Roman writers were critical of Moses and his laws, scholarly Jews in these cultures countered the false charges and tried to enlighten their opponents.

A prime example is Philo of Alexandria, Egypt (1st century A.D.). He weaves together what he has read and heard in the conviction that he has a better knowledge of Moses than any others. Since Philo believes that Greek philosophy is a development from the God-given teaching of Moses, he uses Greek reasoning and ideas to ensure that his Hellenistic audience will have an accurate understanding of Moses. As a "divine man," Moses is superhuman. His physical, mental, psychological, and spiritual gifts are supreme, and his experiences in the royal court and in Midian prepare him to be the ideal king for leading the Hebrews. Moreover, as the perfect ruler, Moses has the faculty of legislation, to command and to forbid; the role of high priest, to care for things divine; and the function of inspired prophet, to declare what cannot be understood by reason (*Vita Mos* II.2.3.187).

The Jewish historian Josephus Flavius writing for a gentile audience, portrays Moses as the "divine man" of Greek culture as well as the Israelite "man of God." As Israel's lawgiver he becomes the legislator and founder of a "theocracy," the ideal society (*AgAp* 2.16. §165). Josephus claims that Moses' gifts were so evident to the Egyptians he was made the general of the Egyptian army during a campaign against the Ethiopians. Not only was he victorious; he married an Ethiopian princess (*Ant* 2.10.2). This tale is one of a cluster of stories expanding on the intriguing claim that Moses had taken a Cushite wife (Num 12:1).

Moses "surpassed in understanding all men that ever lived and put to noblest use the fruit of his reflections." He found favor "chiefly through his thorough command of his passions, which was such that he seemed to have no place for them in his soul" (*Ant* 4.8.49). In concluding his eulogy Josephus declares, "As general he had few to equal him, and as prophet none, insomuch that in all his utterances one seemed to hear the speech of God Himself" (*Ant* 4.8.49).

2. Palestinian Judaism. Since tradition held that the time of prophecy had ceased, Moses became the mouthpiece for some Jews who felt compelled to share their insights. In the *Testament of Moses,* which reinterprets Deuteronomy 31–34, Moses informs Joshua that God created the world on behalf of his people Israel (*T. Mos.* 1:12). Moreover, from the beginning of the world God designed him to be the mediator of the covenant (1:14). In Deut 34:5, Moses apparently dies alone, but in alerting Joshua of his impending death, Moses states that he is going to sleep with his fathers "in the presence of the entire community" (1:15). Joshua is upset at the news and grieves at the loss of "that sacred spirit, worthy of the Lord, manifold and incomprehensible, master of leaders, faithful in all things, the divine prophet for the whole world, the perfect teacher in the world" (11:16). No place will be appropriate for his burial because "the whole world is his sepulcher" (11:8). The text in 12:6 is broken, but it seems that Moses is assuring Joshua that even in death he will make intercessions for their sins.

The mystery surrounding Moses' death perplexed Judaism, and so various expansions of the text appeared. A fragment of one explanation is preserved in Jude 9: "But when the archangel Michael, contending with the devil, disputed about the body of Moses, he did not presume to pronounce a reviling judgment upon him, but said, 'The Lord rebuke you.' " Origen (ca. A.D. 185–254) claimed that the passage was from the *Assumption of Moses,* but unfortunately the text has been lost. Since the end of the *Testament of Moses* has been lost as well, it is difficult to determine whether the two were separate books, or the *Assumption* was the concluding part of the *Testament.*

Jubilees, an expanded commentary on Genesis 1–Exodus 12, purports to be God's word to Moses on Mount Sinai in addition to the Pentateuch, "the first law" (*Jub.* 6:22). It is a revelation from God and the angel of the presence, with the sacred time from Adam to Sinai divided into 49 Jubilees of 49 years (seven weeks of years). Moses is addressed by "you" and told his own story (chaps. 47–48). The basic message is the necessity of faithful obedience to the Torah. Moses is informed that the Patriarchs set the standard by rigorously keeping his law.

The Essenes considered themselves the "true Israel" and went into the Judean desert at Qumran as a community "to prepare the way of Yahweh" (Isa 40:3) by devoting itself to the study of the Torah. Their "Teacher of Righteousness," convinced that end times were near, claimed to have the key for unlocking all the truths hidden in the revelations of Moses and the prophets. The solar calendar, set forth in *Jubilees,* became the standard for the liturgical year at Qumran because it was based on God's creation and the authority of Moses. Moreover, the age of Moses becomes the model for the messianic age. The "prophet to come" (Deut 18:15, 18) is an eschatological figure associated with the priestly and Davidic messiahs.

While P claimed that all the laws of Exodus-Numbers were revealed to Moses, later tradition concluded that all of the Pentateuch came from Moses, including the statement of his death and burial. This conviction evoked a probing study *(midrash)* of the whole Torah. The results of this devotion were classified as: *halakah,* interpretation of a religious or civil law as a guideline for life; and *haggadah,* explanation of non-halakic material (genealogies, narratives, poems, parables, and proverbs) as homiletical, edifying, and entertaining narrative. While *halakah* was mainly under the jurisdiction of the scholars, *haggadah* was expanded and carried on largely by the common people. Their creativity and ingenuity resulted in some excessive embellishments with which the scholars took issue at times.

An excellent compendium of these Jewish tales is *Legends of the Bible* by Louis Ginzberg. The birth of Moses is an example of the free rein imagination of *haggadah:* "At the moment of the child's appearance, the whole house was filled with radiance equal to the splendor of the sun and the moon. A still greater miracle followed. The infant was not yet a day old when he began to walk and speak with his parents, and as though he were an adult, he refused to drink milk from his mother's breast" (1956: 288–89). A variant of Josephus' story about the Cushite wife has Moses fleeing from Pharaoh and coming across Kikanos, king of Ethiopia, and his army besieging a city. He finds favor with them, and when Kikanos dies Moses is made king and given Adoniah, the Ethiopian queen, widow of Kikanos, as his wife. He reigns for forty years then goes on to Midian because he still fears Pharaoh (1956: 299–302).

Moses ascends into heaven three times: (1) from the Burning Bush as an assurance about his call and the promise that he will be given the Torah (1956: 311–12); (2) from Mt. Sinai for forty days and nights to receive and study the Torah (392–98); and (3) from Mt. Nebo to see the reward awaiting him and to visit the Messiah (492–93). By kissing Moses on the mouth, God takes his soul to heaven where he continues as a servant of the Lord. God buries his body in a place, unknown to Moses and Israel, at the end of a passage leading to the graves of the Patriarchs (502).

3. Rabbinic Judaism. It became increasingly evident within the more complex cultures of Persia, Greece, and Rome that Moses' law needed updating. The problem was to authenticate the growing corpus of new regulations. The rabbis solved the problem by claiming that this oral tradition was revealed to Moses on Mt. Sinai along with the written law: "Moses received Torah from Sinai and passed it on to Joshua, and Joshua to the Elders, and the Elders to the Prophets, and the Prophets passed it on to the men of the Great Assembly" (*m. ʾAbot* 1:1).

The rabbis accepted the biblical portrayal of Moses, but their preoccupation with the Torah and its implications highlighted Moses' role as *teacher.* Although they disagreed among themselves over the centuries, they considered themselves disciples of the "great teacher."

The *haggadah* has some amusing tales about the revelation of the Torah. On reaching heaven, Moses finds God ornamenting some letters of the text with crown-like decorations. On inquiring about their meaning he is told: "Hereafter there shall be a man called Akiba, son of Joseph, who will base in interpretation a gigantic mountain of Halakot upon every dot of these letters." Moses requests to see this man and is permitted to hear Akiba instruct his students. He is grieved, however, because he cannot understand the discussion. Moses is contented when, in answer to a question, Akiba states, "This is a Halakah given to Moses on Mt. Sinai" (Ginzberg 1956: 395). In general, the rabbis recognized the distinctiveness of their interpretations, but to show their loyalty to the written law, they described their conclusions as a mountain of truth suspended by a hair from the Torah.

Bibliography

Albright, W. F. 1965. *History, Archaeology, and Christian Humanism.* London.

———. 1966. *Archaeology, Historical Analogy, and Early Biblical Tradition.* Baton Rouge.

———. 1976. Moses in Historical and Theological Perspective. Pp. 120–31 in *Magnalia Dei: the Mighty Acts of God.* Garden City.

Auerbach, E. 1975. *Moses.* Trans. and ed. R. A. Barclay, and I. O. Lehman. Detroit.

Beyerlin, W. 1965. *Origins and History of the Oldest Sinaitic Traditions.* Trans. S. Rudman. Oxford.

Buber, M. 1958. *Moses: The Revelation and the Covenant.* New York.

Cassuto, U. 1961. *The Documentary Hypothesis and the Composition of the Pentateuch.* Trans. I. Abrahams. Jerusalem.

Coats, G. W. 1988. *Moses: Heroic Man, Man of God.* JSOTSup 57. Sheffield.

Fohrer, G. 1968. *Introduction to the Old Testament.* Trans. D. E. Green. Nashville.

Ginzberg, L. 1956. *Legends of the Bible.* Philadelphia.

Gottwald, N. K. 1979. *The Tribes of Yahweh.* Maryknoll, NY.

Gressmann, H. 1913. *Mose und seine Zeit.* Göttingen.

Hallo, W. W. 1962. New Viewpoints on Cuneiform Literature. *IEJ* 12: 13–26.

Kitchen, K. A. 1966. *Ancient Orient and Old Testament.* Downers Grove, IL.

Knierim, R. P. 1985. The Composition of the Pentateuch. *SBLSP* 24: 393–415.

Rowley, H. H. 1950. *From Joseph to Joshua.* London.

Schmid, H. 1968. *Mose: Überlieferung und Geschichte.* Berlin.

Tigay, J. H. 1985. *Empirical Models for Biblical Criticism.* Philadelphia.

Van Seters, J. 1983. *In Search of History.* New Haven.

Zevit, Z. 1985. Clio, I Presume. *BASOR* 260: 71–82.

DEWEY M. BEEGLE

NEW TESTAMENT

References to Moses are found throughout the NT literature. Most often he is mentioned in connection with the law or in respect to his leadership role. As will be evident below, Moses is cited notably in comparisons drawn between Judaism and Christianity, usually to express the superceding of Judaism or its fulfillment by Christianity.

A. Pauline Epistles

Paul makes explicit reference to Moses only in Romans and 1–2 Corinthians. In one instance he speaks of death having reigned "from Adam to Moses" (Rom 5:14) using Moses to express the end of the time period before the law was revealed. Elsewhere Paul refers to Moses as the one to whom God spoke the law (Rom 9:15), and in turn the one who himself authored the law (Rom 10:5, 19; 1 Cor 9:9).

In 1 Cor 10:2 Paul expresses the unusual idea that all those who passed through the Exodus were "baptized into Moses *(eis Mōysēn)* in the cloud and in the sea." He is evidently referring to incorporation into the leadership of Moses. While the phrase *eis Mōysēn* is modeled on the baptismal formula *eis Christon* (Rom 6:3; Gal 3:27 cf. 1 Cor 12:13), it can hardly bear a similar sense of immersion in water since the Israelites passed through the sea as on dry land.

In 2 Cor 3:7–18 are found Paul's most sustained remarks about Moses (see Lambrecht 1983b: 368; Theissen 1987: 115–75). Moses is used in sketching two comparisons. With Exod 34:29–35 evidently in mind, Paul opposes "the dispensation of condemnation" and "the dispensation of righteousness" (2 Cor 3:9). The former came with such splendor that Moses had to veil his face because of the brightness it reflected (3:7), a splendor that nevertheless was not lasting. In contrast, for Paul the dispensation of righteousness, i.e., the dispensation of the Spirit (3:8), far exceeds in splendor and is a permanent dispensation (3:11). Paul is thus enabled by hope to be "very bold, not like Moses, who put a veil over his face so that the Israelites might not see the end of the fading splendor" (3:13).

Within the same passage the veil image is also applied to the Jews (see Wong 1985: 54–59). In Paul's view "to this day whenever Moses [i.e., the law] is read a veil lies over their minds" (3:15). But the Christians, however, "with unveiled face" behold as in a mirror (see Lambrecht 1983a: 246–51) "the glory of the Lord" and are "being changed into his likeness" (3:18). This latter comparison suggests a shift in Paul's use of Moses. While he represents that dispensation which has been superseded in the first instance, in the second he is that revelation which the Jews failed to perceive but which becomes comprehensible for one who "turns to the Lord" (3:16).

B. Mark, Matthew, Luke-Acts

The Synoptics and Acts frequently refer to Moses in citing prescriptions of the law. Phrases are used such as "Moses commanded," "Moses said," "Moses wrote," "Moses allowed," and similar constructions (Mark 1:44 = Matt 8:4 = Luke 5:14; Mark 7:10; 10:3–4; Mark 12:19 = Matt 22:24 = Luke 20:28; Matt 19:7–8; Acts 3:22; 26:22). The Pentateuch itself is designated as "the book of Moses" (Mark 12:26), "the law of Moses" (Luke 2:22; 24:44; Acts 13:39; 15:5; 28:23) or just "Moses" (Luke 16:29, 31; 20:37; 24:27; Acts 15:21).

In the Transfiguration scene Moses appears along with Elijah (see Pamment 1981: 338–89; Moiser 1985: 216–17) and both talk with Jesus (Mark 9:4–5 = Matt 17:3–4 = Luke 9:30, 33). While in Mark and Matthew the topic of their conversation with Jesus is not disclosed, in Luke they are depicted as talking about Jesus' *exodos* (9:31). Moses and Elijah function in the Transfiguration episode as foils to Jesus. As representatives of the Israel of old they disappear, leaving Jesus alone. The instruction by the heavenly voice to listen to Jesus (Mark 9:7; Matt 17:5; Luke 9:35) "relates him intimately to the reshaping of Israel as God's people" (Fitzmyer *Luke I–IX* AB, 795).

Among the Synoptics only Matthew refers to "Moses' seat" (23:2). This is an image used to express the teaching authority of the scribes, for teachers and judges of Jesus' time normally sat to perform their functions. In a similar vein, some have seen in Matthew's description of Jesus' teaching (in a sitting position) from the mountainside (5:1–2) as deliberate analogy with Moses' actions on Sinai (e.g., Allison 1987: 203–5). Jesus then would be presented as the second or new Moses, the better lawgiver. However, it is not certain that such a comparison was intended (Donaldson 1985, *passim*). It can be noted, for example, that Moses ascended Mt. Sinai for reasons other than teaching and that he descended the mountain in order to instruct the people (Exodus 19). Nonetheless, elsewhere (chaps. 1–2) Matthew constructs a parallelism between various events surrounding the births of Moses and Jesus which is quite apparent. This seems to be intentional (Brown 1977: 110–19) although Moses is not mentioned by name.

In Acts, Moses is referred to twice as the embodiment of Judaism, such that Stephen could be accused of having spoken "blasphemous words against Moses and God" (6:11) and Paul of having taught the gentiles "to forsake Moses" (21:21). Acts also refers to Moses as the deliverer of the "customs" of Judaism (6:14; 15:1).

Ironically, while Moses was cited in accusation against Stephen, it is Moses who functions in the speech of Stephen as an indictment against those Jews who rejected Jesus (7:2–53). This passage, which contains numerous details about the life of Moses (7:20–24, 30–38, 44), stresses the rejection of Moses by his own people (7:25–29, 39–40, 52), clearly reminiscent of the treatment accorded Jesus by Stephen's listeners (7:52). It thus appears the author of Acts intends Moses to be viewed as the type of Jesus, i.e., Jesus is the prophet who like Moses was rejected by his people (Johnson 1977: 70–76).

C. John

The Fourth Gospel also establishes a parallelism between Moses and Jesus in various respects, yet also proclaims that Jesus surpasses Moses (see Meeks 1967: 319; *IDBSup*, 606). For example, in 1:17 the law "given through Moses" is analogous to, yet fulfilled by, the "grace and truth [which] came through Jesus Christ." Further comparisons where Jesus transcends Moses are made between Moses who "lifted up the serpent in the wilderness" (3:14) and "the Son of man [who himself must] be lifted up" (3:14); also, as Moses "gave . . . bread from heaven" (6:32), Jesus' Father gives "the true bread from heaven" (6:32).

The Johannine author affirms that God spoke to Moses (9:29) and that Moses gave not only the law (7:19; cf. 7:23; cf. also 8:5 within the interpolation 7:53–8:11) and circumcision (7:22), but also wrote of Jesus in the law (1:45; 5:46). From the author's perspective, those who truly believed the writings of Moses (5:46) would thereby believe Jesus. Thus, rejection of Jesus in fact leads to accusation by Moses (5:45). At the same time there is an ambivalence toward Moses on the author's part (*IDBSup*, 606), for being a disciple of Moses is incompatible with being a follower of Jesus (9:28).

D. Hebrews

The author of Hebrews, concerned primarily to prove the preeminence of Christianity over Judaism, characterizes Moses as similar to Jesus, yet inferior to him. Moses is portrayed as having been "faithful in all God's house as a servant, to testify to the things that were to be spoken later" (3:5; cf. 3:2; Num 12:7), while Christ is described as "faithful over God's house as a son (3:6). Building on the metaphor of God's house as being the community of believers, the author describes Jesus as being worthy of "more glory than Moses as the builder of a house has more honor than the house" (3:3).

Numerous references are also made to Moses in respect to his leadership of those who left Egypt (3:16, 18), the Hebrew priesthood (7:14), the tabernacle he erected (8:5), the law he delivered (9:19; 10:28), and his trembling with fear on the mountain (12:21). With each of these instances aspects of Judaism are contrasted with Christianity, the former in each case superseded by the latter. Only in 11:23–24 is Moses cited in a context where he is to be emulated, not supplanted. In this passage Moses is held forth as an exemplar of faith; he is one of that great "cloud of witnesses" (12:1) who surround believers in Jesus and who urge the believers to "run with perseverance" (12:1) the race set before them.

E. Revelation

The only explicit reference to Moses in Revelation occurs in 15:3 where those who had conquered the beast are depicted as standing beside the sea of glass with harps of God in their hands while "they sing the song of Moses, the servant of God, and the song of the Lamb." The text of the song is then quoted in 15:3–4.

The phrase "the song of Moses, the servant of God" is reminiscent of Exod 14:31–15:21 where Moses and the people of Israel sing a song to the Lord extolling God's power and exulting in the destruction of their enemies. As that song in Exodus 15 was sung on the shore of the Red Sea, so in Rev 15:3 will the victorious martyrs sing beside the sea of glass. However, there are serious difficulties in interpreting this passage since the song in Rev 15:3–4 is not one of triumph over enemies as in the Exodus text, but rather of glorifying the Lord. Furthermore, it is hard to understand why the author of Revelation would have envisioned Christian saints before the throne of God singing the song of Moses as given in Exodus 15. Consequently some have viewed the phrase concerning Moses in 15:3 as an interpolation.

F. Others

In two texts, Jude 1:9 and 2 Tim 3:8, it is noteworthy that both sources derive their data about Moses from legendary material.

In the letter of Jude, which is concerned with warnings against false teachers in the church, the presumptive attitudes of those teachers toward angels is contrasted with the restraint exhibited by the archangel Michael toward another angel. Michael in "contending with the devil, disputed about the body of Moses," yet "did not presume to pronounce a reviling judgment upon him, but said, 'The Lord rebuke you' " (Jude 9). According to several early Christian writers (e.g., Clement of Alexandria, Origen) this episode refers to the burial of Moses and was recounted in the *Assumption of Moses,* a Jewish apocalyptic work now known only fragmentarily, and without the relevant section.

In a similar context concerned with heretics, the author of 2 Timothy states that "as Jannes and Jambres opposed Moses, so these men [heretics] also oppose the truth" (3:8). While in Exod 7:11 magicians argue against Moses before Pharaoh, their names are not given. Later Jewish tradition, however, supplied their names and histories (see the overview of sources in Dibelius-Conzelmann *Pastoral Epistles* Hermeneia, 117).

Bibliography

Allison, D. 1987. Jesus and Moses. *ExpTim* 98: 203–5.

Badke, W. B. 1988. Baptised into Moses-Baptised into Christ. *EvQ* 10: 23–29.

Brown, R. E. 1977. *The Birth of the Messiah.* Garden City, NY.

Donaldson, T. 1985. *Jesus on the Mountain: A Study in Matthean Theology.* JSNTSup 8. Sheffield.

Johnson, L. T. 1977. *The Literary Function of Possessions in Luke-Acts.* SBLDS 39. Missoula, MT.

Lambrecht, J. L. 1983a. Transformation in 2 Cor 3:18. *Bib* 64: 243–54.

———. 1983b. Structure and Line of Thought in 2 Cor 2, 14–4, 6. *Bib* 64: 344–80.

Meeks, W. A. 1967. *The Prophet-King: Moses Traditions and the Johannine Christology.* NovTSup 14. Leiden.

Moiser, J. 1985. Moses and Elijah. *ExpTim* 96: 216–17.

Pamment, M. 1981. Moses and Elijah in the Story of the Transfiguration. *ExpTim* 92: 338–39.

Theissen, G. 1987. *Psychological Aspects of Pauline Theology.* Trans. by J. Galvin. Philadelphia.

Wong, E. 1985. The Lord is the Spirit (2 Cor 3, 17a). *ETL* 61: 48–72.

Florence Morgan Gillman

MOSES, ASSUMPTION OF. See MOSES, TESTAMENT OF.

MOSES, TESTAMENT OF. A pseudepigraph extant in a single, poorly preserved, incomplete, and at times illegible Latin palimpsest discovered in the Ambrosian library of Milan and published by Ceriani in 1861. The manuscript dates from the 6th century C.E., but orthography and style indicate that it is a copy of an early 5th century writing. The Latin text is clearly a translation from a Greek document which may be as early as the late 1st or early 2d century C.E. Most early editors assumed that Greek was the original language, but it is now universally agreed that the Greek text available to the Latin translator is itself a translation of a Semitic writing. Whether the Semitic text was Aramaic or Hebrew remains a matter of dispute, but the latter is more probable.

Ceriani, on the basis of quotations in the Acts of the Council of Nicea and scattered patristic references, entitled the manuscript "The Assumption of Moses," an account of Moses' being taken directly to heaven rather than dying a natural death. This story is well known in many Jewish writings and is probably referred to in Jude 9. The present text, however, knows nothing of an assumption and clearly indicates that Moses died a natural death (1:15; 3:13; 10:14). Some ancient quotations and stichometries (lists of books and number of lines contained in each) refer to both and *Assumption of Moses* and a *Testament of Moses.* The relationship between them is not clear. It has been proposed that they were either two distinct works, a single work consisting of two sections, or two separate works which were subsequently joined together. It is more prudent, lacking manuscript evidence, to refer to the present work as the *Testament of Moses* and leave open the question whether an account of Moses' assumption followed the mutilated ending of 12:13.

A. Contents

Couched in the well-known testament genre—deathbed words of an ancient worthy to his people, his family, or his successor—the *Testament of Moses* purports to be the final statement of Moses to Joshua. In summary fashion, Moses outlines the Conquest (2:1–2), the time of the Judges and the united kingdom (2:3–4), and the period of the divided kingdoms (2:5–9). Chapter 3 relates the fall of Jerusalem to the Babylonians (vv 1–3) and the reunion of all the tribes in the lands of their exile (vv 4–14). Moses then foretells the return from captivity (4:1–6) and the rebuilding of Jerusalem. Chronological referents in chaps. 5–8 are confusing (see below on date and provenance), but the general sense is clear. Moses predicts the apostasy which will arise among the Hellenizing Jews in the times of Antiochus, the Hasmoneans, and Herod, and the consequent severe persecutions including the partial destruction of the Temple (6:9).

Chapter 9 recounts an episode of the resolve of a faithful Levite, Taxo, and his seven sons to die rather than desert their faith. This story is followed by an apocalyptic hymn which portrays the destruction of the evil one at the hands of Israel's guardian angel (10:1–2), cataclysmic cosmic events, and the exaltation of Israel at the end of days (10:3–10). The manuscript concludes with a dialogue between Joshua and Moses in which Joshua expresses his fear that after Moses' death the enemies of Israel will overwhelm them. Moses assures him that God's purpose will not fail and that the covenant promises will abide (10:11–12:13). At this point, in the middle of a sentence, there is a break in the text and the remaining contents are lost.

B. Date and Provenance

Proposed dates for the *T. Mos.* range from the time of Antiochus Epiphanes to the middle of the 2d century C.E. Internal evidence and external attestation rule out serious consideration of a date later than the end of the 1st century C.E., and probably a date later than the middle of that century. R. H. Charles' careful analysis which limited the period of composition to 7–30 C.E. was regnant in scholarly circles from the time of his proposal in 1897 until the past two decades (see *APOT* 2: 407–24). Considerable recent scholarship, on both theological and form critical grounds, has revived the proposal of an Antiochan date. The crux of the issue is the apparent disruption of the chronological order of chaps. 6–8. Chapter 6 clearly refers to the reign of Herod the Great, and the particularity of details in chap. 8 seems to point to the persecutions of Antiochus. Charles proposed that chaps. 6–7 had been erroneously inserted between chaps. 5 and 8 in the process of transmission, while the newer thesis (championed especially by Licht and Nickelsburg) contends that the chapters are a post-Herodian interpolation into a document of the Maccabean era. Both proposals have considerable merit. Dislocation in the transmission of an ancient text is well attested, as are reworkings of an older text by subsequent generations. Both proposals perhaps attribute a logic to an apocalyptic author which is not altogether necessary. The most that present research can affirm is that the extant text of the *T. Mos.* should be dated after 4 B.C.E., and probably before 30 C.E. There is also a strong possibility that some sources incorporated in the text had a considerable prehistory, either oral or written.

Attempts to identify the religious community to which the author of the *T. Mos.* belonged are inconclusive. Almost every well-known religious group of the general period, from the Samaritans to the Sadducees, has been suggested. Three proposals warrant serious consideration: (1) the Hasidim of the Maccabean period; (2) a branch of the Pharisees; and (3) the Essenes. The date assigned to the composition of the *T. Mos.* is a significant though not totally decisive factor. An Antiochan dating would rule out the Pharisees and the Essenes, while a post-Herodian dating militates against the Hasidim.

Increasing awareness of the complexity of Judaism in this period cautions against attempting to identify every document of the era with a specific *known* group. The *T. Mos.* clearly reflects the milieu of movements, including the Pharisees and Essenes, which developed from the circles of the Hasidim, but a more precise identification goes beyond the evidence presently available.

C. Theological Emphases

The theological framework of the *T. Mos.* combines, somewhat awkwardly, the traditional view that the fortunes of the community results from its obedience or disobedience with the conviction that all that has come to pass or will come to pass has been predetermined by God and revealed to Moses. Determinism, however, is the overriding element which undergirds the book's fundamental message. Since God has determined all things in the past and future (3:11–12; 12:4–5), the reader may accept with assurance the assertion that the hour of God's intervention on behalf of his people is at hand (10:1–10). However great the vicissitudes of the past and the travails of the present, God's covenant promises, confirmed by his oath, will not fail (cf. 1:8–9; 3:9; 4:2–6; and especially 12:7–13). The pragmatic purpose of apocalyptic thought, to provide a living hope in a dying age, is the fundamental emphasis.

Claims that the idea of God's creating the world for his people (1:12) and the allusion to Moses' preexistence and role as a mediator (1:14) appear first in the *T. Mos.* are inconclusive. Similarly, the view that the *T. Mos.* is the first writing to speak of an extramundane eschatological triumph for Israel is based on a questionable reading of 10:10. Matters of priority and dependence among the documents of the period are elusive, but these do not detract from the contributions of the *T. Mos.* to an understanding of the ideological milieu of the era.

Recent scholarship has focused on the role of Taxo (9:1–7) and his vow of martyrdom as precipitating the divine vengeance depicted in the eschatological hymn of chap. 10 (vv 1–10). It is proposed that this act is to provoke God to intervene on behalf of his people and thus inaugurate the eschatological age. This proposal is persuasive, on both theological and form critical grounds, but remains moot. It can also be argued that the story is rather a singular example of the woes which will precede the divine intervention rather than an act which precipitates it. Divine vengeance is clearly present. The connection between Taxo's vow of martyrdom and its onset is problematic, possible but not proven.

D. Relation with Other Writings

The *T. Mos.,* like most writings of the period, is replete with allusions to books in the Hebrew canon. Deuteronomy 31–34 is the fundamental base and, in a loose sense, the *T. Mos.* can be read as a midrash on those chapters. Possible relationships with other noncanonical books, e.g., *1 En.* and *2 Bar.* and a number of Qumran writings, have been suggested and carry varying weights of possibility. Questions of the interdependence of writings of this period, as noted earlier, remain unresolved. Such interdependence is certainly possible, but a common ideological setting may also account for the alleged parallels.

Special attention has been called to possible allusions to the *T. Mos.* in the NT. The most often cited passages are Jude 9, 12–13, 16; 2 Pet 2:13; Acts 7:36–43; and Matt 24:19–21 (with parallels). Acts and Jude are the most probable, though the clearest reference in the latter (v 9) properly belongs to the Assumption of Moses and not to the extant Testament. If the author of Jude does cite either as Scripture, interesting questions are raised about the nature of canon.

Although, as one recent commentator has concluded, the *T. Mos.* may not be very original in its theological bases, it does provide valuable confirmation of, indeed the extension of, information about the thought world of early Judaism and early Christianity, a matter of increasing interest among biblical scholars.

Bibliography

Brandenburger, E. 1976. Die Himmelfahrt des Moses. Pp. 57–84 in JSHRZ 2. Guttersloh.

Charles, R. H. 1897. *The Assumption of Moses.* London.

Denis, A. M. 1970a. *Introduction aux pseudepigraphes grecs d'Ancient Testament.* SVTP 1. Leiden.

———. 1970b. *Fragmenta pseudepigraphorum quae supersunt graeca.* PVTG 3. Leiden.

Laperrousaz, E. M. 1970. *Le Testament de Moïse (generalment appelé "Assomption de Moïse"): Traduction avec introduction et notes.* Sem 19. Paris.

Licht, J. 1961. Taxo, or the Apocalyptic Doctrine of Vengeance. *JJS* 12: 95–103.

Nickelsburg, G. E. W. ed. 1973. *Studies on the Testament of Moses.* Cambridge.
Rowley, H. H. 1963. *The Relevance of Apocalyptic.* New York.
Sweet, J. P. M. 1984. The Assumption of Moses. Pp. 600–16 in *Old Testament Apocrypha,* ed. H. F. D. Sparks. Oxford.
Wallace, D. H. 1955. The Semitic Origin of the Testament of Moses. *TZ* 11: 321–28.

JOHN F. PRIEST

MOST HIGH [Heb *ʿelyôn*]. Meaning "the Exalted One," *ʿelyôn* is the title given to the highest of the gods in the Canaanite pantheon and was appropriated by the Hebrews as a title for Yahweh at various intervals in the life of the nation (e.g., Deut 32:8–9; 2 Sam 22:14; Pss 7:17; 97:9). Used frequently in Gen 14:18–22, *ʿelyôn* appears in combination with the title *ʾēl.* This combination is susceptible of more than one interpretation and can be taken as a divine name with its modifier (Cross 1962: 241; *TDOT* 1: 255–56), or as the name of another deity and, therefore, as an intrusive element (Della Vida 1944: 3–9). Scholars also disagree on the extent to which this title has been assimilated with the Mosaic religion. Some scholars believe that the term has been thoroughly assimilated, the title equated fully with Yahweh and his worship (Anderson *IDB* 2: 412). Others argue, however, that decisive differences existed between the Jerusalem cultus of pre-Israelite times and the Mosaic religion (Cross *TDOT* 1: 256). Later in the nation's history the term fell into neglect, preserved only in poetry and liturgies. But in the late postexilic period it enjoyed new popularity, lending itself easily to an emphasis upon the transcendence of God in, for example, Daniel, 1 Esdras, the Wisdom of Sirach, *Enoch, Jubilees,* and *4 Ezra* (*IDB* 2: 412). The term (Gk *hypsistos*) is also used to a limited degree in the NT (Mark 5:7 [= Luke 8:28]; Acts 7:48; 16:17; Heb 7:1).

Bibliography

Cross, F. 1962. Yahweh and the God of the Patriarchs. *HTR* 55: 225–59.
Della Vida, G. 1944. El Elyon in Genesis 14:18–20. *JBL* 63: 1–9.
Fisher, L. 1962. Abraham and His Priest-King. *JBL* 81: 264–70.

FREDERICK W. SCHMIDT

MOT (DEITY) [Heb *māwet, môt*]. The word *māwet/môt* is often used in the Hebrew Bible to refer to the realm of death and occasionally it is personified as the chthonic power behind sterility, drought, disease, wickedness, and death itself. We knew of a Canaanite deity bearing the name "Muth" from the account of Sanchuniathon's *Phoenician History* by Philo of Byblos (see Eus. *PE* 1.10.34; Attridge and Oden 1981: 57, 76–77) which tells us that "the Phoenicians call him Death and Pluto." Yet it has been the publication of the Ugaritic texts which have provided us with the most abundant and accurate literature on the Canaanite deity Mot (*mt* vocalized *môtu*), the god of death and the netherworld, who plays an adversarial role to Baal, the god of life.

A. In the Ugaritic Texts
B. In the Hebrew Bible
C. Conclusion

A. In the Ugaritic Texts

Mot bears the epithet "son of El" *(bn lm)* as well as the epithet "Beloved of El, the Warrior" *(ydd/mdd il ǵzr).* In *CTA* 6.6.24–29 Šapšu, the sun goddess, speaks of El as the father of Mot in a context which illustrates Mot's subservience to and dependence on El, the head of the pantheon. It is easy to see why such a potent combatant as Mot was called "warrior" or "hero," but why was he called the "beloved" of El? Pope (*IDBSup,* 607), noting that the normal response to Mot by both gods and humans was fear and dread, suggests that "beloved" is an intentional euphemism for the opposite sense (cf. Cassuto 1971: 64). Others (e.g., Oldenburg 1969: 132–34) take a different approach implying that Mot was El's beloved precisely because he did battle with Baal who was a rival to El's power. Thus Mot and Yamm, who also bears the epithet *ydd il,* are allies of El and thus called his "beloved." Neither of these interpretations are entirely convincing. Rather than celebrating Mot's victory, El mourns the death of Baal. El rejoices at the news of Baal's revival, and his threatened intervention in the battle scene between Baal and Mot in *CTA* 6.6.16–35 gives the victory to Baal.

In the past scholars have attempted to equate Mot with various other gods of the Ugaritic pantheon including Resheph (C. F. Pfeiffer), Yamm (S. Mowinckel), Horon (W. F. Albright), and Dagan (F. Løkkegaard) as well as the alter ego of Baal (R. deLanghe and I. Engnell). None of these attempts has proven successful (see Watson 1970: 139–41, 162–63 which includes bibliography on above scholars). Mot was a powerful deity in his own right, reflecting one of the most primary forces of nature. There are, however, clear parallels between the Baal-versus-Mot narrative and the Baal-versus-Yamm narrative suggesting that the former may have been modeled at least in part on the latter (Smith 1986b: 327–28; 1987: 292–93).

In the Baal Cycle (*CTA* 4–6), the major texts describing Mot's activities, it is his battle with Baal which takes center stage. We find Mot described as dwelling in the underworld (*arṣ;* for "land" = "underworld" see Tromp 1969: 23–46 and *CAD* E s.v. *erṣetu*) at the base of 2 mountains which seem to stop up the underworld (*CTA* 4.8.1ff.). The description which follows describes his abode as "watery pit/ooze" *(hmry),* "decay" *(mk)* and "slime" *(ḫḫ).* Yet in addition to this watery place Mot also rules over *dbr // šd šḫlmmt.* These terms are difficult to interpret, but they seem to refer to the desert steppe illustrating the forces of drought (Clifford 1972: 79–86; Smith 1986a: 311–14).

When Baal sends messengers to Mot he instructs them of the danger of getting too close to Mot "lest he put you in his mouth like a lamb, crush you like a kid in his jaws" (*CTA* 4.8.17–20). Later in the story we find a description of Baal's descent into the very throat of Death whose insatiable appetite is described in graphic detail:

[špt lʾa]rṣ špt lšmm	One lip to the earth, one lip to heaven,
[yʾrk l]šn lkbkbm	(Mot) stretched out his tongue to the stars.

yʿrb bʿl bkbdh	Baal entered his innards,
bph yrd	He descended into his mouth. (*CTA* 5.2.2–4)

Elsewhere we have the description of Mot eating with both hands when he is hungry (*bkl<ʾa>t ydy ʾilḥm; CTA* 5.1.19–20; cf. Job 18:13).

Thus Baal declared himself to be the eternal slave of Mot (*ʿbdk ʾan wdʿlmk CTA* 5.2.12). Eventually Baal is rescued by the capable goddess Anat who annihilates Mot in the following fashion:

tʾiḫd bn ʾilm mt	She seized El's son Mot
bḥrb tbqʿnn	With a sword she split him,
bḫṯr tdrynn	With a sieve she winnowed him,
bʾiš̄t tšrpnn	With fire she burned him,
brḥm tṭḥnn	With millstones she grounded him,
bšd tdrʿnn	In the field she scattered him (*CTA* 6.2.30–35)

Most scholars have seen a fertility ritual behind these lines involving some type of imitative magic. The piling up of agricultural metaphors has led most scholars to assert that what happens to Mot is a reflex of the harvesting of grain (e.g., de Moor 1971: 212–15; 1987: 88–89). Others (e.g., Watson 1972: 60–64) disagree arguing that what we have is simply the ritual destruction of a hostile deity.

With the death of Mot, Baal is revived and fertility returned to Ugarit with the heavens raining oil, the wadis running with honey. Due to the cyclical orientation of the agriculturally based religion (cf. de Moor 1971: 9–28), it is not surprising that later on in the story (seven years having elapsed) we once again find Mot engaged in a fierce battle, this time with Baal himself.

ytʿn kgmrm	They butted each other (?) like beasts (?)
mt ʿz bʿl ʿz	Mot was strong, Baal was strong;
ynghn krʾumm	They gored each other like wild oxen,
mt ʿz bʿl ʿz	Mot was strong, Baal was strong;
ynṯkn kbṯnm	They bit each other like serpents
mt ʿz bʿl ʿz	Mot was strong, Baal was strong;
ymṣḫn klsmm	They kicked (?) each other like stallions (?)
mt ql bʿl ql	Mot fell, Baal fell. . . . (*CTA* 6.6.16–22)

The stalemate is brought to an end when suddenly we hear Šapšu declaring to Mot that he will not prevail over Baal. She threatens the intervention of El who has decreed that Mot must submit. Mot becomes afraid and withdraws from the picture leaving Baal once more enthroned.

In addition to the Baal Cycle we have mention of Mot in a text which scholars have called "Shaḥar and Shalim: The Birth of the Two Gracious Gods" (*CTA* 23). At the beginning of this text we read about a deity known as *mt-w-šr.* On analogy to Kothar-wa-ḫasis, the craftsman of the gods, most scholars see a singular deity here with a double name. Most scholars see *mt* as a reference to Mot yet there is considerable difference of opinion with regard to the translation of *šr* with suggestions including "death and dissolution," "death and evil," "Mot and prince," "radiant Mot," etc. What is clear is that this deity wields two scepters which bear fitting descriptions for the God of death:

bdh ḫṭ tkl	In one hand a scepter of bereavement,
bdh ḫṭ ʾulmn	In the other hand a scepter of widowhood.

Tsumura (1974: 407–13) compares an Aramaic incantation bowl picturing the angel of death with a sword in one hand and a spear in the other.

We find little evidence of a cult of Mot. As of yet we have found no temple dedicated to him, no mention of him in any of the pantheon lists and no sacrificial or offering texts addressed to him (de Moor 1970: 222). On the other hand, there was a vibrant cult of the dead at Ugarit (Lewis 1989: 5–98).

B. In the Hebrew Bible

In the Hebrew Bible *māwet/môt* often refers to the realm of death and occasionally refers to death personified. There is a fluidity in the biblical texts between Mot (and Sheol for that matter) as a person and a locality. Scholars vary as to how prevalent Mot was in the Hebrew Bible. On one extreme some scholars (e.g., Smick 1980: 497) argue that Mot "was not mentioned in the OT" (cf. Kaufmann 1960: 311–16), while on the other extreme Mot has been read into almost every mention of death.

There are several passages where it is hard to ignore the presence of a personified Death. The description of insatiable Death in Hab 2:5 (cf. also Isa 5:14; Prov 1:12; 27:20; 30:15b–16; Ps 141:7) is remarkably reminiscent of Mot's insatiable appetite in *CTA* 5.2.2–4 (see above; Lewis 1989: 152–53). Ravenous Death is also depicted in Job 18:13–14 where he is described eating greedily as in *CTA* 5.1.19–20 mentioned above. In light of the descriptions of Mot's (and Sheol's) voracious appetite which includes imagery of Mot swallowing his victims whole, it is not only ironic but also quite significant to find Yahweh swallowing Mot in Isaiah 25:8 (for other swallowing imagery used of Yahweh cf. Lam 2:5; Ps 21:10—Eng 21:9; 55:10—Eng 55:9; Isa 19:3). Likewise, the "covenant with Death and Sheol" in Isa 28:15, 18 is best understood against the backdrop of the Canaanite god Mot.

Death is personified twice in Hos 13:14, a passage describing Yahweh's ransoming Ephraim from the grasp and plagues of Death and Sheol (Andersen and Freedman *Hosea* AB, 639–40). In Psalm 49:15, Death is described as a shepherd of those who descend into the underworld. Cant 8:6 refers to love being "as strong as Death" which Pope (*Song of Songs* AB, 668–69; cf. Pardee 1987) argues as an allusion to Mot rather than the superlative usage suggested earlier by Thomas (1953: 221; cf. Waltke and O'Connor 1990: 269). For additional occurrences of personified Death which have been suggested by scholars see Cooper (1981: 392–400).

Some attempts at seeing Mot in the Hebrew Bible have not been successful. Albright (1950: 11, 13, 17) emended Hab 3:13 to describe a direct conflict between Yahweh and Mot yet his emendation has not generally been followed (Heibert 1986: 37; Tsumura 1989: 40–45). Jeremiah 9:20—Eng 9:21 is frequently quoted as illustrating parallels between the worlds of Ugarit and the Bible. Death (*māwet*) is described as entering through windows in Jer 9:20 and this has been compared on numerous occasions with *CTA* 4.6.12 which describes Baal's refusal at first to have windows in his palace due to the threat of Mot (e.g.,

Cassuto 1975: 35, 133–35; 174). Yet, as noted by many scholars, it is Yamm and not Mot who is the enemy Baal fears. More fruitful background material for Death entering the window in Jer 9:20 may be drawn from the Mesopotamian sphere (see Paul 1968; Smith 1987).

C. Conclusion

At Ugarit, Mot is a decidedly more personal being portrayed as the archenemy of Baal. The degree to which Ugaritic Mot is seen behind biblical texts will continue to be debated. Yet the personification of Death in the Hebrew Bible is too prevalent and enduring to be regarded merely as a poetic metaphor or literary device. In ancient Israel, Death was considered to be a real person. At the same time, however, in the religion which becomes normative Yahweh must absorb all aspects of divinity. Just as he takes on the attributes of other Canaanite deities such as El and Baal, so too he takes on the attributes of Mot, although he is never called by this name. Yahweh, by definition, must absorb any divine powers usually ascribed in the ANE to other deities (cf. Miller 1986: 242–44 who points out similarities with supreme national deities in Mesopotamia such as Marduk and Ashur). Thus the God of the Hebrew Bible has "terrors" (*biʿûtîm,* Job 6:4) corresponding to those of Mot, who is called in Job 18:13 "the king of terrors" (*melek ballāhôt;* Pope *Job* AB, 135–36; Habel *Job* OTL, 287–88). Compare also the "breakers" of Yahweh in Ps 42:8—Eng 42:7 with the "breakers" of Death in 2 Sam 22:5—Eng 22:4 (cf. Ps 35:5; 50:22). Yahweh also has a chthonian entourage which makes up his cosmic army: "Before him marched Plague (Deber), Pestilence (Rešep) followed close behind" (Hab 3:5; cf. Deut 32:24; Ps 78:48). Yet in the final analysis, in the eschatological battle described in Isa 25:8, Yahweh swallows up Mot forever *(neṣaḥ).* As Gropp has aptly noted, this once-and-for-all victory "contrasts strikingly with the periodic struggle between Baal and Mot, growing out of an agriculturally based religion. Further, Baal's dominion never extends completely to the realm of Mot. Yahweh's dominion, on the other hand, is quite absolute."

Bibliography

Albright, W. F. A. 1950. The Psalm of Habakkuk. Pp. 1–18 in *Studies in Old Testament Prophecy,* ed. H. H. Rowley. Edinburgh.

Attridge, H. W., and Oden, R. A. 1981. *Philo of Byblos: The Phoenician History.* Washington, DC.

Cassuto, U. 1971. *The Goddess Anath.* Trans. I. Abrahams. Jerusalem.

———. 1975. *Biblical and Oriental Studies.* Vol. 2. *Bible and Ancient Oriental Texts.* Trans. I. Abrahams et al. Jerusalem.

Clifford, R. J. 1972. *The Cosmic Mountain in Canaan and the Old Testament.* HSM 4. Cambridge.

Cooper, A. 1981. Divine Names and Epithets in the Ugaritic Texts. Pp. 392–400 in *Ras Shamra Parallels,* vol. 3, ed. S. Rummel. Rome.

Cunchillos, J. L. 1985. Le dieu Mut, guerrier de El. *Syria* 62: 205–18.

Hermann, W. 1979. Jahwes Triumph über Mot. *UF* 11: 371–77.

Hiebert, T. 1986. *God of My Victory. The Ancient Hymn in Habakkuk 3.* HSM 38. Atlanta.

Kaufmann, Y. 1960. *The Religion of Israel.* Trans. M. Greenberg. New York.

Lewis, T. 1989. *Cults of the Dead in Ancient Israel and Ugarit.* HSM 39. Atlanta.

Miller, P. D. 1986. The Absence of the Goddess in Israelite Religion. *HAR* 10: 239–48.

Moor, J. C. de. 1970. The Semitic Pantheon of Ugarit. *UF* 2: 187–228.

———. 1971. *The Seasonal Pattern in the Ugaritic Myth of Baʿlu according to the Version of Ilimilku.* AOAT 16. Neukirchen-Vluyn.

———. 1987. *An Anthology of Religious Texts from Ugarit.* Leiden.

Oldenburg, U. 1969. *The Conflict Between El and Baʿal in Canaanite Religion.* Leiden.

Pardee, D. 1987. As Strong as Death. Pp. 65–69 in *Love and Death in the Ancient Near East,* ed. J. H. Marks and R. M. Good. Guilford, CT.

Paul, S. M. 1968. Cuneiform Light on Jer 9, 20. *Biblica* 49: 373–76.

Pope, M. H. 1965. Mot. *WbMyth* 1/1: 300–2.

Smick, E. 1980. *mût.* Pp. 496–97 in *Theological Wordbook of the Old Testament,* ed. R. L. Harris et al. Chicago.

Smith, M. S. 1986a. Baal in the Land of Death. *UF* 17: 311–14.

———. 1986b. Interpreting the Baal Cycle. *UF* 18: 313–39.

———. 1987. Death in Jeremiah, IX, 20. *UF* 19: 289–93.

Thomas, D. W. 1953. A Consideration of Some Unusual Ways of Expressing the Superlative in Hebrew. *VT* 3: 209–24.

Tromp, N. 1969. *Primitive Conceptions of Death and the Nether World in the Old Testament.* BibOr 21. Rome.

Tsumura, D. T. 1974. A Ugaritic God, Mt-w-šr, and His Two Weapons (UT 52:8–11). *UF* 6: 407–13.

———. 1989. Ugaritic Poetry and Habakkuk 3. *TynBul* 40: 24–48.

Waltke, B. K., and O'Connor, M. 1990. *An Introduction to Biblical Hebrew Syntax.* Winona Lake, IN.

Watson, P. L. 1970. *Mot, The God of Death, at Ugarit and in the Old Testament.* Diss. Yale.

———. 1972. The Death of "Death" in the Ugaritic Texts. *JAOS* 92: 60–64.

THEODORE J. LEWIS

MOTH. See ZOOLOGY.

MOTHER. See FAMILY.

MOUND, SIEGE. See WEAPONS AND IMPLEMENTS OF WARFARE.

MOUNT OF OLIVES (PLACE). See OLIVES, MOUNT OF.

MOUNT, SERMON ON THE. See SERMON ON THE MOUNT/PLAIN.

MOUSE. See ZOOLOGY.

MOZA (PERSON) [Heb *môṣāʾ*]. **1.** Son of Caleb born to his concubine Ephah according to 1 Chr 2:46. The name Moza does not follow the usual patterns of Hebrew personal names, and should be seen as a place name which has been construed as a personal name in order to explain the relationship between Calebite clans in different geographical locations. Many other of the personal names in this list reflect geographical locations (Rudolph *Chronikbücher* HAT, 21–22). Perhaps Moza should be identified with the city Mozah *(hammōṣâ)* mentioned within the tribal boundaries of Benjamin in Josh 18:26 or should be related etymologically to *mṣh,* "to drain out," and was named after a prominent wine or oil press that was located there (Rudolph, 21, n. 2). This section of the Judah genealogy in Chronicles has no extant preexilic parallel, but is probably based on earlier sources. That genealogy contains two sections dealing with the descendants of Caleb (2:18–24 and 2:42–55); this structure was created by the Chronicler who ordered a symmetrical genealogy of Judah which emphasized the prominence of David (Williamson 1979).

2. A Benjaminite, a 7th generation descendant of King Saul according to the genealogy of 1 Chr 8:36, 37 and 9:42, 43. His descendants continue the main line of the Saulide genealogy. The genealogy of Saul preserved in the Chronicler's sources reflects the notion of Saul's continued legitimacy, even after the ascent of David. See MELECH. There is some variation of the vocalization of this name in the LXX, but this probably reflects the translators' attempt to grapple with Moza as a personal name. Indeed, in this genealogy, Moza reflects the Benjaminite city Mozah, since this section of the genealogy uses place names as personal names to define a relationship between various Benjaminite cities by positing an ancient kinship relationship between ancestors with the city names. This genealogy contains the geographical names Alemeth, Azmaveth, and possibly Jarah *(yᶜrh),* which might be identified with the city Kiriath-jearim *(qryt yᶜrym)* (Demsky 1971: 19). The construal of geographical names as personal names is typical of genealogical thinking (Wilson *GHBW*), and is found elsewhere in biblical genealogies (Demsky 1982). On the doubling of the Benjamin genealogy in 1 Chronicles 8 and 9, see AHAZ.

Bibliography

Demsky, A. 1971. The Genealogy of Gibeon (1 Chronicles 9:35–44): Biblical and Epigraphic Considerations. *BASOR* 202: 16–23.

———. 1982. The Genealogy of Menasseh and the Placement of the Inheritance of Milcah Daughter of Zelophehad. *EI* 16: 70–75 (in Hebrew).

Williamson, H. G. M. 1979. Sources and Redaction in the Chronicler's Genealogy of Judah. *JBL* 98: 351–59.

Marc Z. Brettler

MOZAH (PLACE) [Heb *mōṣâ*]. A town of Benjamin mentioned after Mizpeh and Chephirah (Josh 18:26). The location is uncertain, but it was probably in the vicinity of modern Mevasseret Yerushalayim (M.R. 165135), 7.5 km W of Jerusalem. A derivative of its name seems to have been preserved in the nearby ruin of Kh. Beit Mizza, the heavy *ṣ* of Hebrew passing into the light *z* of Arabic. Suitable Iron Age pottery (including a *lmlk* jar handle), building remains, and burial caves of the 8th–7th centuries B.C.E. have been found there.

The name of Moza [Heb *môṣāʾ*] appears in the genealogy of Benjamin (1 Chr 8:36–37), suggesting to some scholars that the settlement may have been founded by an Israelite tribesman (Aharoni *LBHG,* 246). One of Caleb's sons is also called Moza (1 Chr 2:46), but it is doubtful whether there is any connection between him and the Benjaminite site (Avi-Yonah *EncJud* 12: 494). It is also possible that the town's name was derived from a water source, since numerous springs exist nearby (Kallai *EncMiqr* 5:229). A third suggestion is that *mōṣâ* (= Heb "source" or "origin") refers to a nearby clay source that modern geologists call the Moza Formation. Neutron activation analysis (NAA) studies have confirmed that many vessels made in the Jerusalem area during OT and NT times were manufactured from these clays (Gunneweg et al. 1985: 272).

Although Mozah is not mentioned in any written sources of the Persian period, the name of this town was stamped on the handles of storage jars from the 5th–4th centuries B.C.E. found in excavations at Jericho, Gibeon, and Tell en-Nasbeh—an indication that Mozah was an administrative and/or pottery manufacturing center.

Sometime during the Second Temple period, Mozah moved from its more defensible location on a hill to a nearby spot in Wadi Beit Nahina (= N. Shmuel), about 2 km S of Kh. Beit Mizza. The Babylonian Talmud (*Sukk.* 45a) states that Mozah was a place below Jerusalem where willows were gathered for Sukkoth, and that it was the same as Colonia. This description fits very well the location of modern-day Moza (M.R. 166134), a small settlement built adjacent to the Arab village of Qālûnya which preserves the Latin name of "Colonia."

The circumstances surrounding the renaming of Moza is given by Josephus (*JW* 7.6.6 §217). Following the Jewish Revolt of 70 C.E., Vespasian settled 800 demobilized Roman soldiers in a town Josephus calls Emmaus (Gk *Ammaous*). The village name was then changed to Colonia-Emmaus, or Colonia, for short. A "source of Colonia" (perhaps Ain Moza) is mentioned by Cyrillus Scythopolitanus (*v. Sab* 67).

Early surveys in the vicinity of Qalûnyah uncovered the remains of a Roman road which once linked Jerusalem with Jaffa, a road station, a bath, Jewish and Roman tombs, and a Byzantine monestary (Press 1952: 559). In 1973, I. Eisenberg carried out a salvage dig at Moza where he discovered remains of the Roman period and apparently part of the colony established there by Vespasian. Among the finds were a *prutah* from the days of Pontius Pilate and a silver coin from the time of Vespasian (1974: 64).

Some have suggested that the Colonia-Emmaus mentioned by Josephus should be identified with the Emmaus of Luke 24:13. However, rather than the 30 stadia (ca. 6 km) figure given by Josephus, Luke records the distance at 60 stadia. Either Luke meant it as a round-trip numeral, or another location is intended (cf. 24:33). Some Gk mss give a 160 stadia figure for Emmaus.

Bibliography

Eisenberg, I. 1974. *Hadashot Archaeologiyot* 48–49: 64–65 (in Hebrew).

Gunneweg, J.; Perlman, I.; and Meshel, Z. 1985. Origin of the Pottery of Kuntillet ᶜAjrud. *IEJ* 35/4: 270–83.

Press, I. 1952. *môṣāʾ*. Pp. 558–59 in vol. 3 of *A Topographical-Historical Encyclopedia of Palestine.* Jerusalem (in Hebrew).

R. A. Mullins

MU. The twelfth letter of the Greek alphabet.

MUGHAYYIR, TELL EL- (M.R. 238225). A site about 12 km NE of Irbid, on an agricultural plateau cut out of the fertile agricultural plain S of Wadi el-Yarmouk by two valleys, the Wadi eš-Sellale and the Wadi Rahub. The region S of the village has a concentration of springs and archaeological sites.

Tell el-Mughayyir lies at the S edge of the modern village of el-Mughayyir, and is situated on the edge of an 80 m escarpment of the Wadi Rahub. Its position affords a panoramic view of the surrounding area. The tell is relatively small, ca. 150 m × 150 m, and has a maximum height of 7 m. The summit of the tell covers an area of ca. 40 m × 30 m.

The region has not been previously well documented despite the richness of its material. N. Glueck surveyed the region from 1939–47, and from 1963–65. S. Mittmann conducted an intensive survey which led to the conception of the joint excavation project in 1974 and 1975. A second project began in 1984 and continued in 1985 with simultaneous excavations at both Tell el-Mughayyir and Khirbet Zeiraqoun under the direction of S. Mittmann and M. Ibrahim. As well as continuing excavation on both these sites the joint project aims to conduct a detailed survey of the area and investigate tombs within the region including an Epipaleolithic site at the edge of the Wadi Rahub.

Tell el-Mughayyir has a long, though discontinuous, history of settlement from the pottery Neolithic to the earliest phase of the EB Age, the EB IV, and then from the Iron Age I until the Hellenistic period. This density of occupation in such a relatively small area makes stratigraphy complicated. Within 3 m were five main strata, each with different construction plans. The architectural phases span the Iron Age II to the Hellenistic period. It seems clear that the walls belong to a closed complex, almost square, which occupied the summit of the mound in each phase.

The findings of the lower layers were the least complicated because an area of packed clay sealed the Iron Age pottery. The upper layers were more complicated, and the architecture of the Persian period, for which there is a ceramic evidence, remains undefined. Further complicating the stratigraphy is the intensive construction of later phases, and the installation of silos, which disturbed lower levels. The function of later building phases is not clear: perhaps the presence of silos suggests an important farm estate.

These storage pits are the most salient feature of all phases. The uppermost phase is represented by two cistern-shaped storage pits about 3 m deep. In phase four were five pits, whose stone-lined openings were covered in every case and marked by vertical stones. Within phase five was a stone circle of a silo opening. Phase three exhibited entirely different types of pits—they consisted of two box-shaped structures made of undressed stones about 1 m high and separated from each other by a 1 m wide corridor.

The dominant ceramic wares were from the Iron Age and Hellenistic periods, though Hellenistic fine wares were notably few. Several of the forms, however, were unique to this region.

Bibliography

Glueck, N. 1951. *Explorations in Eastern Palestine, IV.* Vol. 1. AASOR 25–28: 105–24. New Haven.

Ibrahim, M., and Mittmann, S. fc. The Excavations at Tell el-Mughayyir and Khirbet Zeiraqoun, 1984. In *Studies in the History and Archaeology of Jordan, vol. 3,* ed. A. Hadidi. Amman.

Mittmann, S. 1970. *Beiträge zur Siedlungs und Territorialgeschichte des nördlichen Ostjordanlandes.* ADPV. Wiesbaden.

SIEGFRIED MITTMANN
MOAWIYAH M. IBRAHIM

MULBERRIES. See FLORA.

MULE. See ZOOLOGY.

MUPPIM (PERSON) [Heb *muppîm*]. A son of Benjamin (Gen 46:21) included among the seventy people who traveled with Jacob to Egypt. The genealogy of Benjamin presents numerous problems which do not contribute to a positive identification of Muppim.

According to the genealogical list of Gen 46:21, Benjamin had ten sons and Muppim was his eighth son. The sons of Benjamin were: Bela, Becher, Ashbel, Gera, Naaman, Ehi, Rosh, Muppim, Huppim, and Ard. However, in the LXX translation of this verse, only the first three persons are his sons. The next five are the sons of Bela, and Ard is Benjamin's great-grandson and a grandson of Bela.

The genealogy of Benjamin in Num 26:38–40 gives Benjamin five sons: Bela, Ashbel, Ahiram, Shephupham, and Hupham. Ard and Naaman, who appeared in Genesis as sons of Benjamin, appear in Numbers as the sons of Bela. The genealogy of Benjamin in 1 Chr 7:6 gives him three sons: Bela, Becher, and Jediazel. Another chronology, found in 1 Chr 8:1–2, gives Benjamin five sons: Bela, Ashbel, Aharah, Nohah, and Rapha.

Confronted with the fact that Muppim appears as a son of Benjamin only in the genealogical list of Genesis, scholars have proposed different solutions. Gray (*Numbers* ICC, 393) believed that Muppim was not a genuine name but that it came about as a faulty reading of the consonantal text. Several scholars (Williamson 1973: 377; *1 and 2 Chronicles* NCBC, 78; Braun *1 Chronicles* WBC, 106–7), accepting the corrupt text of 1 Chr 7:12 as a broken genealogy of Benjamin, identify Muppim with Shuppim and with Shephupham (Num 26:39). But this identification is not universally accepted. The New Jerusalem Bible, without any comment, places Shuppim among the sons of Naphatali while the RSV, following the MT, identifies Shuppim as one of the sons of Ir, a Benjaminite.

Bibliography

Williamson, H. G. M. 1973. A Note on I Chronicles VII 12. *VT* 12: 375–79.

CLAUDE F. MARIOTTINI

MURASHÛ, ARCHIVE OF. The modern name given to a group of Babylonian legal documents compiled at Nippur during the last half of the 5th century B.C. The archive records business operations conducted by members of a single family or by their agents. It is named for the family's ancestor. In its original form, it included a few Aramaic documents written on leather, no longer preserved. The greater part was drafted in cuneiform, and about two-thirds of the 879 known tablets and fragments are published (Hilprecht and Clay 1898; Clay 1904; 1908; 1912; Lutz 1928; Krückmann 1933; Stolper 1985). They are the largest coherent source of documentary evidence for conditions in Babylonia at the midpoint of Achaemenid Persian rule (for general expositions see Cardascia 1951; Stolper 1985; and van Driel 1989; for appraisals of contemporary Babylonian documentation see especially Oelsner 1976; Joannès 1982, and van Driel 1987).

A. The Nature of the Business

The firm was active in a region of about 100 km^2 around Nippur (Zadok 1978), though members of the family paid occasional visits to Susa or Babylon. The texts were written in the reigns of Artaxerxes I and Darius II and in the first regnal year of Artaxerxes II (454–404 B.C., with most of the texts dated 440–416 B.C.).

Among the many kinds of transactions recorded, two general areas of concern predominate. In one, agricultural contracting, members of the Murashû firm acquired real properties by lease, pledge, or mandate, receiving land from proprietors in the vicinity of Nippur and irrigation rights from government agencies. They combined these items with resources of their own, chiefly movable inputs—draft animals, plows, harness, seed, and perhaps agricultural labor—in subleases to tenants of their own, some of whom issued subsubleases in turn. In this way, the firm transformed a juridically determined pattern of land tenure into an economically determined pattern of exploitation; enabled landholders to transform fixed allotments into sources of cash income; assured the regular exploitation of allotted lands and the regular production of cash taxes for the Achaemenid government; and presumably turned a handsome profit. In the second area of concern, the supply of short-term credit, the firm issued loans secured by pledges of smallholdings: that is, state allotments of farmland granted to soldiers and workmen on condition of tax and service obligations. When such loans went unpaid, the firm obtained use (though not titular ownership) of the pledged lands; it continued to discharge the tax encumbrances, and the smallholders became the firm's indebted tenants. The records of these pledges and debts—all representing unpaid obligations—form the largest single category of texts in the archive. There was, therefore, some tension between the convenience of the firm's services and its dilatory effect on the position of small-scale landholders.

Since most of the Murashûs' discernible income was in the form of produce (chiefly dates and cereals) and most of their discernible outlay was in the form of silver (chiefly paid in rents and taxes), the firm had a third major area of operation that has left no surviving record: it transformed crops into cash, possibly through sales of crops to supply the urban populations of the region.

The Murashûs were therefore commercial contractors who dealt in different ways with diverse beneficiaries of crown grants and appointments. Some of the firm's customers were officials or contractors who oversaw the use of crown lands proper, of temple holdings managed in the crown's interest, and of the irrigation facilities that were crucial to all Babylonian agriculture (Stolper 1985: 36–51). Others were the smallholders who occupied "fiefs" called in Babylonian "bow land," "horse land," or "chariot land," that is, allotments intended to support archers, cavalrymen, and chariot crews. The families to whom the government granted such smallholdings were organized in corporate groups called *ḫaṭrus* (a term of uncertain etymology, perhaps borrowed from Aramaic or an Iranian language; see Cardascia *RLA* 4: 150–51), whose overseers were responsible for extracting the taxes and services incumbent on the holdings. The groups were named for military, administrative, craft, or agricultural occupations of their members, for the estates or administrative organizations to which their members were attached, or for the geographic or ethnic origins of their members (Cardascia 1958; 1977; Stolper 1985: 70–100).

Still other customers were the bailiffs of larger, complex estates, including manors called by the names of proprietors characterized as royal officials or as princes, manors named for anonymous social ranks ("estate of the crown prince," or "estate of the queen"), or for the administrative offices of which the holdings were the perquisite and support ("estate of the equerry," "fields of the treasury"). The staffs of many such estates controlled *ḫaṭrus* of attached workers, and therefore administered the smallholders' taxes and services (Stolper 1985: 52–69). The proprietors of such estates included some of the leading figures of imperial politics. The Murashû texts accordingly document the Babylonian interests of some surprisingly eminent persons: Parysatis, Darius II's queen; Arsames, the satrap of Egypt and Darius' uncle; Menostanes, the son of the governor of Babylonia, a cousin of Artaxerxes I, and an ally of the pretender Sogdianus; Artoxares, a courtier who fell from favor under Artaxerxes I but returned as one of Darius II's early allies; and others known from classical accounts of Achaemenid court politics.

Although the archive is chiefly a legal record of the obligations created or discharged by local transactions in agricultural resources, it discloses hierarchies of claims to rents, taxes, and services that also reveal some of the political and administrative structures through which the Achaemenid empire controlled the province of Babylonia and extracted its wealth, and it shows some of the effects that imperial politics produced on local economic conditions (see Lewis 1977: 70–82; Stolper 1985: 122–24, 150–56).

B. The Personal Names

Non-Babylonian groups and individuals with non-Babylonian names are common in the Murashû texts, a conspicuous result of Babylonia's incorporation into the vast and polymorphous Achaemenid empire. Some of the *ḫaṭru* names in particular indicate that the members traced their descent from distant regions of the empire: groups of Phrygians and Sardians, Carians, Melitenians and Urartians, Cimmerians, Tyrians, Arabs, and Indians. Some may have been descended from the victims of earlier deportations; others were imperial troops settled on subsistence allotments in Babylonia. Some members of these groups kept non-Babylonian personal names, but acculturation is clear in the frequency of routine Babylonian and Aramaic names among them. In fact, of about 2,200 personal names in the Murashû texts, about two-thirds are Babylonian and about one-quarter are Aramaic; the residue are Iranian, Anatolian, Egyptian or are drawn from various West Semitic languages.

Since the earliest publications of the Murashû texts, special attention has been given to the Jewish personal names—that is, names compounded with the divine name Yahweh and other West Semitic names considered typically Jewish (Šabbātai, Haggai, Minyāmîn)—on the assumption that the bearers of these names and their families exemplified the descendants of the Jewish exiles in Babylonia in the days of Ezra and Nehemiah. Little can be said of them, however, that distinguishes them from other inhabitants of the region. The term "Jew" never appears in the Murashû texts, whether to characterize an individual or a group. The bearers of the eighty or so attested Jewish names lived in many villages around Nippur, not in a distinct local enclave. They have no special role in the texts, but figure as smallholders, as petty officials, or as witnesses. They rarely did business on sabbaths or feast days, but they were assimilated to the extent of giving some of their children Babylonian names. In short, as portrayed in the medium of Babylonian legal recording, they seem no less Babylonian than any other parties to the texts. (See Bickerman 1978; Coogan 1976; Zadok 1977b; 1977c; all citing earlier literature.)

Similar comments apply to the bearers of Iranian names, another conspicuous minority in the Murashû texts. While Iranians always dominated the highest political offices of the Achaemenid empire, they were also to be found at all ranks of Babylonian society, from noble proprietors of large estates through more or less petty officials to chattel slaves. They did not have exclusive control over any of the modest juridical and administrative offices that occur in the Murashû text, but generally shared these functions with indigenous Babylonians. A few bearers of Babylonian names gave their children Iranian names, as if to emulate the empire's rulers. Far more bearers of Iranian names gave their children Babylonian names, undergoing the same acculturation as other immigrant populations in Babylonia (see Zadok 1977a).

The Murashûs were not "bankers" in any conventional sense, but they generated cash and credit in the local economy. They were certainly not tax-farmers under direct contract to the provincial government or the crown (see especially Cardascia 1951: 189–98, with critique of earlier portrayals), but their successful operations depended on the patronage of some government agencies and prominent aristocrats. The archive's detail and specificity are extraordinary, but most of the relationships and conditions that it portrays were not special to Nippur. Other contemporary texts assure that other firms conducted similar operations, under similar conditions and on a similar scale in other parts of Babylonia, sometimes also dealing with exalted figures of imperial politics (van Driel 1987; Stolper fc.).

Bibliography

Bickerman, E. J. 1978. The Generation of Ezra and Nehemiah. *PAAJR* 45: 1–28.

Cardascia, G. 1951. *Les archives des Murašû.* Paris.

———. 1958. Le fief dans la Babylonie achéménide. Pp. 57–88 in *Les liens de vassalité et les immunités,* 2d ed. Recueils de la Societé Jean Bodin 1. Brussels.

———. 1977. Armée et fiscalité dans la Babylonie achéménide. Pp. 1–10 in *Armées et fiscalités dans le monde antique.* Paris.

Clay, A. T. 1904. *Business Documents of Murashû Sons of Nippur.* The Babylonian Expedition of the University of Pennsylvania, Series A: Cuneiform Texts, 10. Philadelphia.

———. 1908. *Legal and Commercial Transactions Dated in the Assyrian, Neo-Babylonian and Persian Periods.* The Babylonian Expedition of the University of Pennsylvania, Series A: Cuneiform Texts, 8, Part 1. Philadelphia.

———. 1912. *Business Documents of Murashu Sons of Nippur.* PBS 2/1. Philadelphia.

Coogan, M. D. 1976. *West Semitic Personal Names in the Murašû Documents.* HSM 7. Missoula, MT.

Driel, G. van. 1987. Continuity or Decay in the Late Achaemenid Period: Evidence from Southern Mesopotamia. Vol. 1, pp. 159–81 in *Achaemenid History: Sources, Structures and Synthesis,* ed. H. Sancisi-Weerdenberg. Leiden.

———. 1989. The Murašûs in Context. *JESHO* 32: 203–29.

Hilprecht, H. V. and Clay, A. T. 1898. *Business Documents of the Murashû Sons of Nippur.* The Babylonian Expedition of the University of Pennsylvania, Series A: Cuneiform Texts, 9. Philadelphia.

Joannès, F. 1982. *Textes économiques de la Babylonie récente.* Études assyriologiques 5. Paris.

Krückmann, O. 1933. *Neubabylonische Rechts- und Verwaltungs-Texte.* Texte und Materialien der Frau Professor Hilprecht Collection of Babylonian Antiquities im Eigentum der Universität Jena, 2–3. Leipzig.

Lewis, D. M. 1977. *Sparta and Persia.* Cincinnati Classical Studies n.s. 1. Leiden.

Lutz, H. F. 1928. An Agreement between a Babylonian Feudal Lord and his Retainer in the Reign of Darius II. UCPSP 9/3: 267–77.

Oelsner, J. 1976. Zwischen Xerxes und Alexander. *WO* 8: 310–18.

Stolper, M. W. 1985. *Entrepreneurs and Empire: the Murašû Archive, the Murašû Firm, and Persian Rule in Babylonia.* Uitgaven van het Nederlands Historisch-Archaeologisch Instituut te Istanbul 54. Leiden.

———. fc. Mesopotamia: 482–330 B.C. In *CAH* 6/11/b. 3d rev. ed.

Zadok, R. 1977a. Iranians and Individuals Bearing Iranian Names in Achaemenian Babylonia. *IOS* 7: 89–138.

———. 1977b. *The Jews in Babylonia in the Chaldean and Achaemenian Periods in the Light of the Babylonian Sources.* Tel-Aviv.

———. 1977c. *On West Semites in Babylonia during the Chaldean and Achaemenian Periods, an Onomastic Study.* Jerusalem.

———. 1978. The Nippur Region during the Late Assyrian, Chaldaean and Achaemenian Periods. *IOS* 8: 266–332.

MATTHEW W. STOLPER

MURATORIAN FRAGMENT. An early, incomplete listing of NT books, the Muratorian Fragment occupies a prominent place in any discussion of the history of the Christian canon of scripture. Its relative importance in such discussions depends, in large part, on the date and provenance assigned to the Fragment. Until quite recently, Roman provenance and a late 2d or early 3d century date (180–200 C.E.) were taken for granted. It was assumed that the Fragment represented the earliest datable canon list. Those assumptions have now largely eroded, and a new consensus appears to be emerging, one which sees the Muratorian Fragment as a 4th-century, Eastern (either Syria or Palestine) list. If that is the case, the earliest datable NT list would be that of Eusebius in *Ecclesiastical History* 3.25, and the Muratorian Fragment should be read in relation to it, as another, albeit important, witness to canonization process in its final stage.

Discovered by Lodovico Antonio Muratori (1672–1750) in Milan's Ambrosian Library in 1740, the Fragment is preserved in a codex dating to the 7th or 8th century. Small portions of the same list were also found in four Latin mss (11th or 12th century) at Monte Cassino. Muratori himself suggested that the Latin text was a clumsy translation of a Greek original, a suggestion that has received almost universal support.

Beginning in mid-sentence, the Fragment consists of 85 lines. Its abrupt ending has suggested to some that it is defective there as well. NT books which the list accepts as authoritative include: The Four Gospels (Matthew and Mark are not mentioned explicitly but are presumed in the now lost lines 2 and 9); the Acts of the Apostles; 13 letters of Paul (excluding Hebrews); Jude; 1 and 2 John; the Wisdom of Solomon; the *Apocalypse of John;* and the *Apocalypse of Peter.* The list admits that not everyone in the Church accepts the last two works cited. James, 1 and 2 Peter and 3 John are passed over in silence. The *Shepherd of Hermas* is rejected because it is late. Writings emanating from Gnostic, Marcionite, or Montanist (Cataphyrgian) circles are rejected outright.

Adolf von Harnack has been called the "last great apologist" for the importance of the Muratorian Fragment in canon history. He was confident that the provenance and date of the Muratorian Fragment had been firmly established yet felt, however, that its character had been misrepresented. He thought the list, with its authoritarian tone, to be an official document, published in Rome, defining the content of the NT for the whole Church. He was convinced the author must have been the Bishop himself, or less likely someone writing at the Bishop's behest. Harnack suggested Victor, Bishop of Rome (189–199) or less probably, Zephyrinus (199–217), or someone under his authorization, as the author.

But Harnack was not the last great apologist for the Muratorian Fragment. It has found a latter-day advocate in Hans von Campenhausen. While agreeing with his predecessors that the list is Western and must date to the end of the 2d or, at the very latest, the beginning of the 3d century, Campenhausen finds in the Muratorian Fragment a parade example of the synthesis which obtained as a result of the dialectical forces he believed shaped the Christian canon of Scripture: the thesis of Marcionism with its reductionist "canon" and the antithesis of Montanism with its expansionist "canon."

All future defenders of the Muratorian Fragment as a Western, late 2d or early 3d century canon list must come to terms with the challenges leveled at that position by Albert C. Sundberg, Jr. It is Sundberg who initially made the case for the 4th century date and Eastern provenance of the Fragment. The linguistic arguments for Roman provenance based on explicit references to Rome (lines 74–76), the presence of the word *urbs* (standing alone) in line 38, the use of *catholica ecclesia* in line 66, are shown by Sundberg to be inconclusive. Similar arguments for a late 2d or early 3d century date based on the phrase *nuperrime temporibus nostris* in lines 73–77 are also dismissed by Sundberg.

Sundberg believes that linguistic arguments must be supplemented by careful analysis of the internal evidence of the Fragment. His primary attention is directed to the anomolies of this list which cannot be paralleled within the 2d century Church Fathers and which find parallels only in substantially later materials. For example, the *Shepherd* was universally accepted in both the East and the West, but was first called into question in the East by Eusebius. The presence of the Wisdom of Solomon in a list of NT writings has precedents in the East (Eusebius, Epiphanius, *Codex Alexandrinus*), but not the West. The equivocal status of the *Apocalypse of John* and the *Apocalypse of Peter* accords better with a later, Eastern setting than a Western (Revelation was subject to question in the East only after Dionysius [265]. The *Apoc. Pet.* was relatively unknown in the West and a contender for a place in the NT only in the East).

Although Sundberg's thesis is not without its detractors, it has won considerable acceptance and further confirmation. Robbins grants that the Fragment is preoccupied with the Johannine literature—Gospel, Apocalypse and Epistles, but notes that debates about the latter, the Epistles, did not arise until after Epiphanius. Methodius, observes Robbins, also made a case for the acceptance of the *Apocalypses of John* and *Peter,* and favored the Wisdom of Solomon. Robbins also shows that questions about the number of the Catholic Epistles find their earliest parallel in Eusebius. Indeed, one of the most important consequences of Sundberg's work on the Muratorian Fragment is the reassessment of Eusebius' role in the formation of the Christian canon of Scripture.

Bibliography

Campenhausen, H. von. 1972. *The Formation of the Christian Bible.* Philadelphia.

Collins, R. F. 1983. *Introduction to the New Testament.* Garden City.

Ferguson, E. 1982. Canon Muratori: Date and Provenance. *StPatr* 17/2: 677–83.

Gamble, H. Y. 1985. *The New Testament Canon.* Philadelphia.

Hahneman, G. M. 1988. More on Redating the Muratorian Fragment. *Studia Patristica* 19–23. Louvain.

Robbins, G. A. 1986. *PERI TON ENDIATHEKON GRAPHON: Eusebius and the Formation of the Christian Bible.* Ann Arbor.

Sundberg, A. C., Jr. 1968. Toward a Revised History of the New Testament Canon. *SE* 4: 452–61.

———. 1973. Canon Muratori: A Fourth-Century List. *HTR* 66: 1–41.

Gregory Allen Robbins

MUREX. See PURPLE; ZOOLOGY.

MUSHI (PERSON) [Heb *mûšî*]. MUSHITES. Son of Merari, grandson of Levi (Exod 6:19; Num 3:20; 1 Chr 6:4—Eng 6:19; 6:32—Eng 6:47; 23:21, 23; 24:26, 30); also a designation of a levitical family or clan descendant from him (Num 3:33; 26:58). There are discrepancies between the various levitical genealogies of Exodus, Numbers, and 1 Chronicles. Three priestly families—the Gershonites, the Kohathites, and the Merarites—derive from Levi in Exod 6:19, Num 3:20, 26:57, 1 Chr 23:6, but five levitical families—the Libnites, the Hebronites, the Mahlites, the Mushites, and the Korahites—are found in Num 26:58 (only four in the LXX which omits the Mahlites). It is argued that Num 26:58 represents an older tradition wherein priestly families were associated with geographical location (Libni, Hebron, and Korah which is thought to be the name of a city in 1 Chr 2:43). Mushi, however, is not a city, but is generally thought to be a tribal name derived from Moses. In spite of many variations in the levitical genealogies of the Chronicler, consistently Mahli and Mushi are said to be the sons of Merari (1 Chr 6:4—Eng 6:19; 23:21; 24:26).

The association of the terms "Mushi" and "Moses," the conflicts between Aaron and Moses (Exodus 32; Numbers 12), and several incidents occurring in the wilderness concerning priests (Lev 10:1–7; Num 16; 25:6–15) have led F. M. Cross *(CMHE)* to argue for the existence of a preexilic Mushite priesthood attached to the Shiloh shrine that rivaled the Aaronid priesthood which later came to dominate in Jerusalem. The paucity of evidence makes it difficult to argue for a Mushite priesthood and its place in the origin of ancient Israelite priesthood, but Cross' reconstruction has a certain plausibility to it. See also Budd *Numbers* WBC; Braun *1 Chronicles* WBC; and *AncIsr.*

Bibliography

Möhlenbrink, K. 1934. Die levitischen Überlieferungen des Alten Testaments. *ZAW* 52: 184–231.

PAULINE A. VIVIANO

MUSIC AND MUSICAL INSTRUMENTS.

This entry contains two articles. The first surveys the subject of music in the broad sense, as it is depicted in the biblical text. The second focuses specifically on musical instruments mentioned in the Bible.

MUSIC IN THE BIBLE

Evidence of music and dance is found throughout the biblical text. This investigation will survey the use of music in the Hebrew Bible and NT, as well as evidence of its social and religious setting in the ancient world.

A. Introduction
B. Purposes: Secular
C. Purposes: Religious
D. Musical Terminology
E. Music in the NT

A. Introduction

The myth of "the origin of skills" found in Gen 4:20–22, which records the "first" smith (Tubal-cain), the "first" cattle-breeder (Jabal), and the "first" musician (Jubal), portrays the three occupations most necessary (at least in the mind of the later biblical writer) to the earliest periods of human history. The fact that the musician is placed in the company of the more practical occupations suggests the antiquity of music and the regard in which it was held by Israelite culture.

Certainly Israel's neighbors provided a host of examples of musical expression. Mesopotamia and Egypt have long histories of both popular and religious music, which must have been known to the Israelites. Professional musicians, like the *kalû* harp-player so well attested in ancient texts from Mari and Uruk (Foxvog and Kilmer *ISBE* 3: 437), may well have been models for the levitical musicians in the Jerusalem temple. The types of instruments, liturgical chants, penitential prayers and laments, and hymns of praise created by these ancient civilizations set a standard of style and composition which was undoubtedly relied upon by the Israelites.

Archaeological discoveries have also added to our knowledge of ancient forms of music, the methods used to play them, as well as the postures of dancers captured in midstep in ancient Egyptian tomb paintings (see figs. 72–84 in Sendrey 1974, and 11–12 in Polin 1954). A wide variety of instruments are depicted in these scenes, showing their development through time, and a few have survived, attesting to their manufacture and providing clues to the musical intervals favored and possible reconstructions of notation by modern musicologists (Shanks 1980: 20–22).

As one might expect, music changed and became more complex and institutionalized as ancient Israel's society evolved from a pastoral nomadic tribal society to a village and later to an urban culture. Tracing these developments can provide an excellent sense of the cultural history of this ancient civilization. By examining each of the situations in which the biblical narrative describes the use of music and/or dance, a pattern of behavior and performance emerges.

However, before there were words there was music. From their earliest origins, humans have imitated the sounds around them and experimented with creating new ones (Madge 1977: 60). Once they had exhausted all the possibilities of their own voices, artificial noisemakers began to be invented. (See following article.) First among these were percussive sounds, caused by hitting sticks together or drumming on a log, tapping on a stretched animal skin, slapping one's thigh or stomach with the flat of one's hand. The movement of wind through the trees would have suggested additional sound possibilities: noises made with the mouth and lips, the sound of a leaf as air is blown across it, the blat produced by blowing through an animal horn (Polin 1954: xx). The range of sounds thus created was eventually augmented by the invention of stringed instruments. This would have been a somewhat later development since it required more than materials readily at hand and further experimentation to develop a sense of range and style. Once animal gut was strung on a bow for hunting, however, the twang as the arrow took flight would have announced the tonal possibilities that led to the invention of the harp and lyre.

B. Purposes: Secular

Even in its most primitive forms, music would have been employed by human communities for a variety of purposes. For instance, it could be used to soothe a child (see the Sumerian lullaby in *ANET,* pp. 651–52) or restive flocks of sheep. While engaging in strenuous or monotonous work (e.g., treading grapes—Jer 25:30 and 48:33—or digging irrigation canals or wells—Num 21:17–18—or raising a new house or barn), musical chants could be used to help maintain the rhythm of the workers and speed completion of the day's toil.

Yet another common use for music and dance would have been in celebrations, both large and small. They were used to mark the major events in the life of the people or just to express their joy and contentment with life. Thus, in Eccl 3:4, in the litany of the events of life, dancing is contrasted with mourning (see also Lam 5:15 and Ps 30:12—Eng v 11). Not all frivolity was acceptable to the biblical writers, however. For example, a mocking drunkard's song is mentioned in Ps 69:13—Eng v 12, and in Job the sufferer observes with incomprehension that the children of the wicked dance while the wicked themselves sing to the rhythm of the tambourine, lyre, and pipe (21:11–12).

The diversions provided by entertainment were essential to their lives, amid so many concerns over hostile environmental conditions and unfriendly neighbors. That could well explain, at least in part, the sanctity of the hospitality code which required that visitors (both relatives and strangers) be housed, fed, and sent away with good feelings. Hosting visitors also afforded a measure of entertainment for both householder and guest, which, as suggested by Laban in his chiding of Jacob, may have included songs and instrumental music (Gen 31:47).

Since the economic base for most of the population, even during the monarchic period, was primarily a mixture of pastoral and agricultural activity, planting, harvesting, and sheepshearing would have been occasions for mass get-togethers and religious celebrations. Thus the maidens of Shiloh danced each year beside their vineyards (Judg 21:19–21), and the sons of David made merry at a feast following the shearing of Absalom's sheep (2 Sam 14:28). In the case of the Shiloh festival and the maiden's dance in Cant 6:13, dancing provided an opportunity for eventual matchmaking, serving both a religious purpose and aiding in the perpetuation of the community (Eaton 1975: 137).

Weddings were also occasions in which music and other merriment took place. Samson's riddle, so filled with alliteration and wordplay (Nel 1985: 542–43), suggests a chant or plainsong style that would fit into the festivities of his marriage feast (Judg 14:14). The ritual of the marriage feast also included a staged meeting between the bride and the groom's party, who were accompanied by musicians playing tambourines (1 Macc 9:37–39; Sendrey 1969: 461). They and the whole company then joined in songs as the feasting and other activities commenced (Jer 16:9). Curiously, the wedding feasts described in the NT (Matt 22:1–13 and John 2:1–11) do not include any mention of musicians or songs. However, these may have been such common aspects of the feast that they were simply to be assumed by the audience.

Births, with their promise of new life and continuity of inheritance, were also marked by ceremony and ritualized singing. Even before the infant was born, chants and incantations were used to guard it and effect a speedy and safe birth (van Dijk 1975: 55). In preparation for the birth, midwives were called in, and in some cases singers were also summoned to celebrate the birth and guard the child (e.g., see the Ugaritic legend of Aqhat, *KTU* 1.17 II: 10–42; *ANET,* pp. 150–51). The use of the "Fear not" formula by the midwives in Gen 35:17 and 1 Sam 4:20, followed by the mother naming the newborn child, suggests a traditional litany to be sung or chanted at the birth of sons. This is at least partially echoed in the Lucan account of Jesus' birth, in which angels tell the shepherds not to fear, then name the child and sing in chorus (Luke 2:9–14).

With the establishment of a royal court, new applications for music and dance were introduced. The coronation of kings was announced by the blaring of trumpets (2 Sam 15:10; 1 Kgs 1:39), and in Solomon's case a procession marching to the tune of pipes (1 Kgs 1:40). The latter marks an intentional paralleling of his father's career. David had also entered Jerusalem in procession as the ark of the covenant was brought to the new capital city. On that occasion the people sang as they marched to the sound of lyres, harps, tambourines, castanets, and cymbals (2 Sam 6:5). Upon reaching the city, David both worshiped and demonstrated his right to rule through the power of Yahweh and the ark by dancing "with all his might" as horns played (vv 14–15). It is quite likely that David's dance and procession were subsequently reenacted by his successors to the throne, thereby legitimizing their rule and invoking the covenant Yahweh made with David (see Psalm 132; Eaton 1975: 138).

There are in fact a whole group of "enthronement psalms" (among them Psalms 2; 20; 72; 89; 101; 110; 144) which reiterate the Davidic dynasty's right to rule and which were probably used in an autumnal festival to commemorate its founding (Johnson 1967: 68–72; Mowinckel 1962: 152).

Among the events that would have taken place in this annual festival is a grand procession, perhaps using Psalm 68, which exhorts the people: "Sing to God, sing praises to his name" (v 5—Eng v 4), in its opening chant. Priests and nobles, advisers and representatives of designated tribes, would march through the streets of Jerusalem to the temple with "the singers in front, the minstrels last, between them maidens playing timbrels" (v 26—Eng v 25). There sacrifices and speeches would be made, which, as in this psalm, would include in condensed form the triumphant acts of Yahweh (Weiser *Psalms* OTL, 487). Both Yahweh, "who rides upon the clouds" (v 5—a title also used for Baal in the Ugaritic epics, e.g., *KTU* 1.2 IV:8) and his chosen king were thus exalted.

Once enthroned in their palaces, kings and their wealthy nobles would have wanted to add all the luxuries found at other royal courts. Thus, as described in Eccl 2:8, they "gathered . . . silver and gold and the treasure of kings and provinces . . . singers, both men and women, and many concubines, man's delight." Singers and musicians became one of the trappings of power (2 Sam 19:35), both for entertainment and ostentation (Isa 5:12). Such extravagance led to social criticism by the prophets. Among these voices of dissent was that of Amos, who chastised the wealthy who "stretch themselves upon their couches, and eat lambs from the flock . . . , who sing idle songs to the sound of the harp. . . ." (6:4–5).

The military also made use of music, but this was principally to rally their forces (Judg 3:27; 6:34), to guide disparate groups of men on the battlefield, or to signal troops to advance (Num 10:9) or retreat. Sendrey (1969: 469–70) suggests there may have been preparatory "war dances" prior to battles. He cites Ezek 6:11, "Smite with your hand, and stamp with your foot," as an allusion to such a dance. Isa 13:3, which enjoins the soldiers to "consecrate themselves" before the coming battle, may also be an indication of ritual activity, including dance.

The trumpets used by Gideon (Judg 7:15–24) served the additional function of startling the Midianites and aiding in the Israelites' surprise attack. Similarly, the blasting of rams' horns by the Israelite priests in the siege of Jericho added to the psychological effect after the people had marched in silence before the city for six days (Josh 6:3–16).

Victories, of course, sparked spontaneous celebration and joy (Judg 11:34). To commemorate these occasions heroic ballads and songs of praise to Yahweh were composed. Among the best examples of these hymns of thanksgiving are the "Song of the Sea" (Exod 15:1–18), the ballad of victory over Sihon and the Amorites (Num 21:27–30), and the "Song of Deborah" (Judges 5). Each of these epic poems, as well as the shorter boastful chants of Lamech (Gen 4:23) and Samson (Judg 15:16), have a rhythmic style. The instrumental accompaniment, while subordinate to the reciting of the verses, would have helped to create mood, heighten tension, and add to the symmetry of the composition (Polin 1954: 14). Dance, too, would have been a part of these celebrations, as processions of women with hand-drums performed a "round-dance" *(māḥôl)* as they joined the victorious soldiers or priests on their way to the sanctuary of Yahweh (Eaton 1975: 137).

Less elaborate chants, designed to accompany rhythmic dancing, were also composed. The progressive phrase sung by village women to welcome Saul and David—"Saul has slain his thousands, and David his ten thousands" (1 Sam 18:7)—must have haunted King Saul. These women would have stamped their feet as they sang and whirled to the sound of the timbrel just as modern bedouin women still do today (Sendrey 1969: 466). Just how pervasive this phrase became can be seen in its repetition among the Philistines two separate times in the narrative (1 Sam 21:11; 29:5). There was probably at one time an entire body of heroic epics and chants which is no longer in existence. They may have been included in either of the lost resources of the biblical writers: the Book of the Wars of the Lord (Num 21:14) or the Book of Jashar (Josh 10:13; 2 Sam 1:18).

C. Purposes: Religious

The use of music for religious purposes can be seen in both popular as well as institutionalized settings. For peasant and king alike, music served as part of the process of mourning or lamentation (2 Sam 3:32–34; Judg 11:40). Funeral processions throughout the ANE included professional mourners, beating their foreheads, moaning, and shuffling to the sound of wailing flutes (Sendrey 1969: 471; Eaton 1975: 137). Sickness and premature death were basic facts of life for these ancient peoples and thus they created songs, musical noisemakers (such as the bells on the robe of the high priest—Exod 28:33–35), and dances with an apotropaic purpose. The hope was that by soothing the sick (1 Sam 16:16) or frightening away the demons who caused the illness, a cure could be effected.

The apotropaic character of religious ritual, including song and dance, is clearly seen in the case of the frightened Israelites who asked Aaron to create a golden calf for them when it appeared that Moses was lost and they needed a tangible object to worship in order to placate their fears. Their worship included loud, frenzied singing and dancing (Exod 32:19), which may be a polemic used by the writer to differentiate between Canaanite worship of idols (as well as the golden calves at Dan and Bethel) and proper Israelite (Jerusalem's) rituals (see Childs *Exodus* OTL, 559–60 for a discussion of this passage). One indication of this is the similarity between their actions and those of the prophets of Baal in 1 Kgs 18:26–29. These prophets chanted an invocation, "O Baal, answer us!," and danced a limping stutter-step. Then, in their frenzy to be answered, they cut themselves and shouted. Elijah mocks them and their ineffectual actions, ultimately ordering their deaths just as Moses orders the deaths of the unfaithful Israelites.

Eventually apotropaic chants and dances became more complex and served as the basis for much of Israelite religious drama and ritual. For instance, the psalms associated with the recitation of the creation story—Psalms 8; 19; 104; 139—contain both the literary as well as musical elements (based on the superscription rubrics, choral markers, and assonances in the text) needed for a proper performance. Similarly, in the narrative sections of the biblical text are found stories which include both apotropaic and celebratory musical expressions. For example, the "Song of the Sea" and the "Song of Miriam" in Exodus 15 suggest relief as well as fear of the elements which had been unleashed to destroy the pharaoh's chariots.

Several examples in the prophetic narratives suggest that music and dance were an intrinsic part of religious expression. For instance, the prophets whom Saul encountered as they processed down from the high place, playing harp, tambourine, flute, and lyre, were prophesying as the music put them into an ecstatic state (1 Sam 10:5). Elisha employed the use of a musician to bring on a prophetic trance in 2 Kgs 3:15.

Pantomime, so common among the prophets who enacted prophecy, could in some cases be identified as a sacred dance. An example of this is found in 1 Kgs 22:11, where the court prophet Zedekiah used stylized iron horns to portray the vigor with which Jehoshaphat and Ahab would defeat their enemies. Undoubtedly, he stomped about like a bull (a common symbol for the Canaanite god Baal) during his performance, which was probably not spontaneous but rather a traditional dance designed to invoke the aid of the gods in this military endeavor (Eaton 1975: 139).

Another occasion for religious singing would have been during pilgrimages to sacred shrines and temples. This was a common activity among the Israelites, starting in the settlement period. For instance, Elkanah and his family annually made the trek to Shiloh to worship before the ark of the covenant (1 Sam 1:3). Following the construction of the temple in Jerusalem and the emphasis placed on annual festivals and sacrifice by the kings (especially Hezekiah and Josiah), annual events like the Passover would have brought many people to the city. Along the way, entertainment would have included the singing of pilgrim songs, such as the "Songs of Ascent"—Psalms 120–134—which extol the opportunity to "go up" to Jerusalem and worship in the sanctuary at Zion, and are probably associated with the three great agricultural festivals (Exod 23:17; Deut 16:16).

As music became more formal, professional guilds of musicians were employed to form choirs and orchestras which served at the various temples and shrines and in the palace. One sign of this is found in the book of Amos. During his stay at Bethel, Amos harangued against the emptiness of the worship in the temple there, declaring that Yahweh would no longer listen to the worshippers' songs and harps (5:23). Yet another indication of these musician guilds is found in the Assyrian Annals. Following the siege of Jerusalem by the Assyrian king Sennacherib, King Hezekiah was forced to pay a huge ransom for the city which included male and female musicians (*ANET,* p. 288).

The Israelite musician guilds have many parallels throughout the ANE. They in essence represent the movement of music into a formal liturgical setting with a set religious calendar of performances. Sarna (*EncJud* 13: 1317) suggests that the levitical singers, said to have been appointed by David to the task of performing the music in the Jerusalem temple (1 Chronicles 6; 15; 16; 25; 29; 2 Chr 35:15), were actually in place within the cultic community not long after this traditional date. Whenever they were appointed, it would have been their responsibility to make constant praise to Yahweh, and "prophesy with lyres, with harps, and with cymbals" (1 Chr 25:1). Among the themes of their music was the call for Yahweh to have mercy and to care for the people (Psalms 23; 46) and curse the wicked (Psalm 58). They also recited the epic history of Yahweh's past victories at the major festivals and the coronation of kings (Psalms 78; 81; 105).

These levitical singers, whose original leaders are said to be Asaph, Jeduthun, and Heman (1 Chr 25:1) were probably even more prominent in temple worship during the Second Temple period following the Exile. They were joined in the organization and performance of all liturgical music by several other groups, including those associated with Chenaniah, "leader of the music of the singers" (1 Chr 5:27), and Mattithiah and five other men, who were "to lead with lyres" (1 Chr 15:21). Still another group, the Korahites (1 Chr 6:7), were also apparently members of the musical community, since their name appears in the superscription of a number of psalms (42; 44–49; 84–85; 87–88).

Each guild would have ultimately created and become associated with a particular repertoire of songs—thereby aiding in the transmission and survival of this sacred music (Sarna *EncJud* 13: 1317). Their survival during the Babylonian Exile and their importance to the establishment of the Second Temple community can be seen in the list of the exiles who returned with Zerubbabel to Jerusalem. Here it states that 200 male and female singers (Ezra 2:65) as well as 128 "sons of Asaph" (2:41) were a part of the company of returnees.

In light of the later prominence of the guilds, it is interesting to note that the "sons of Asaph" are showcased in the ceremony dedicating the laying of the foundation of the restored temple in Ezra 3:10–11, playing trumpets and cymbals and singing responsively a hymn of praise to Yahweh. However, no musicians or choirs at all are mentioned in Solomon's formal dedication of the temple in 1 Kings 8. It seems likely, however, that such events demanded music and ritual dancing and in fact several times reference is made to "prayer and supplication" (8:28, 30, 33). The absence of performers in the text probably reflects a more focused intent on the part of the writer, who did not choose to crowd his scene with obvious details.

D. Musical Terminology

Despite the fact that the music of ancient Israel is, for the most part, lost to us, there is ample evidence which indicates just how organized music and musical performance actually was. This includes the technical terms found in the Psalms. These consist of rubrics, formal instructions to the choirmasters (*laměnaṣṣēaḥ*—a term that appears 55 times in the Psalms and in Hab 3:19). They deal with style, tone (*ʿal-haššěmînît*—"on the eighth"—Psalms 6; 12, but not an octave, which was unknown to the Israelite musicians), instrumentation (*něgînôt*—stringed instruments—Psalms 4; 6; 54; 55; 67; 76), and even the tune to employ (*ʾal-tašḥēt*—"Do not destroy"—Psalms 57–59; 75; and *ʿal-ʾayyelet haššaḥar*—"According to the Hind of the Dawn"—Psalm 22). A few were used to signal the genre type. Among these is *šiggāyôn* (Psalm 7), which is related to the Akk word *šegu,* "to lament," and therefore may serve as the label for a song of lamentation.

Cues are also given. For example, *ʿal mût labbēn* (Psalm 9) may indicate the use of a male soprano voice, *ʾel hanneḥîlôt* (Psalm 5) may be a cue for the entrance of wind instruments. Most of these terms appear in the superscriptions of the psalms, but a few, like *selâ,* appear in the body of individual psalms. This presently untranslatable word, which occurs 71 times in 39 psalms and three times in Habakkuk (3:3, 9, 13), may have served as a breath marker, an indicator to musicians to enter, or simply as an affirmation of what had just been said.

More general terms also appear in the superscriptions. Some of these are labels, like *těhillâ* ("song of praise"—Psalm 145) and *těpillâ* ("prayer"—Psalms 17; 86; 90; 102; 142; Hab 3:1), which apply to nearly all the psalms. Others are more explicit in designating the type of psalm and in some case the repertoire or guild to which it belongs. Among those most commonly used are the following.

1. *maśkîl.* This term is found in the headings of thirteen psalms (32; 42; 44; 45; 52–55; 74; 78; 88; 89; 142). Its root origin is probably *śākal,* "to comprehend," and thus it has been interpreted by many scholars to designate a didactic poem. This is such a general label; however, the term must have some more particular meaning—perhaps, as Sendrey (1969: 104) suggests, it is the indicator of a penitential song.

2. *mizmôr.* Appearing only in the Psalms, this term is found 57 times, always in association with a personal name; it probably is a label indicating music associated with liturgy and the guilds.

3. *šîr.* While this is a generic term, simply meaning "sing," it also has technical qualities, appearing 30 times in the Psalms as well as elsewhere (Exod 15:1; Num 21:17; Deut 31:19, among others). It is found in the heading as well as in the body of the psalm, and is sometimes accompanied by *mizmôr.* In certain contexts, therefore, it seems to indicate a body or a particular type of religious music. A sign of this is in the title *šîr hammaᶜălôt,* "Songs of Ascent," found in Psalms 120–134.

E. Music in the NT

The destruction of the temple in Jerusalem in 70 C.E. set the stage for new forms of musical expression among the Jews. Public music and dance had already been restricted on the Sabbath (*m. Besa* V:2) and it became even more restrained in response to Greek and Roman rule and culture (Sendrey 1969: 468–69). Only Luke 7:32 and Matt 11:7 specifically mention fluting and dance in the NT and in the former this involves the play of children.

It was in the synagogue, however, that music continued to flourish and serve as an emotional and didactic aid to the maintenance of Judaism. The levitical guilds were now gone and instrumental music was forbidden in the synagogue, leaving vocal music to evolve in a new way. Thus the writers of the NT and the founders of the new Christian movement very likely adopted what they knew of synagogue music to their own worship. That would explain why Paul, who is familiar with musical instruments, considered them "lifeless" (1 Cor 14:7–8) and promoted worship in the form of "psalms and hymns and spiritual songs, singing and making melody to the Lord" (Eph 5:19).

The borrowing from synagogue worship of both hymn and chorus singing added the emotional, communal feeling needed to help build the new movement. Instruction without the freedom to express joy and praise would have quickly become dull. In any case, many of these early Christian groups met in the local synagogue and they would have been familiar with the form of worship conducted there. It would have been only natural to employ the same hymns they already knew while adding new ones to reflect their new theological understanding. Among these may be the "Worthy art thou" hymnic fragments in Rev 4:11; 5:9–10, and the songs of victory and assurance in Rev 7:15–17; 11:17–18. Eventually, as the Christian movement became more international, Hellenistic musical influences were introduced, but antagonism to instrumental music, so closely associated with pagan religions and the spectacles of the Roman colosseum, continued for several centuries (Werner *IDB* 3: 469).

Bibliography

Dijk, J. J. van. 1975. Incantations accompagnant la naissance de l'homme. *Or* 44: 52–79.

Eaton, J. H. 1975. Dancing in the Old Testament. *ExpTim* 86: 136–40.

Johnson, A. R. 1967. *Sacral Kingship in Ancient Israel.* Cardiff.

Madge, W. 1977. *Bible Music and its Development.* London.

Mowinckel, S. 1962. *The Psalms in Israel's Worship.* Nashville.

Nel, P. 1985. The Riddle of Samson. *Bib* 66: 534–45.

Polin, C. C. J. 1954. *Music of the Ancient Near East.* New York.

Sendrey, A. 1969. *Music in Ancient Israel.* New York.

———. 1974. *Music in the Social and Religious Life of Antiquity.* Rutherford, N.J.

Seow, C. L. 1989. *Myth, Drama, and the Politics of David's Dance.* HSM. Atlanta.

Shanks, H. 1980. World's Oldest Musical Notation Deciphered on Cuneiform Tablet. *BARev* 6/5: 14–25.

VICTOR H. MATTHEWS

MUSICAL INSTRUMENTS

The evidence concerning musical instruments in the Bible includes scriptural references and archaeological discoveries. The latter provide a context for the scriptural references in the musical usage of the ANE and in the range and character of musical instruments known there. Recent developments in this field include the reconstruction of such musical instruments on the basis of archaeological finds and consequent discoveries concerning the tonal range, timbre, and techniques involved in the playing of such instruments. The limited range of the archaeological finds in Palestine which relate to musical practice during the biblical period raises important questions as to how the scriptural references should be interpreted: Should the translation of biblical terms apparently referring to musical instruments be restricted by the limitations of those finds, and should the limited character of those finds be taken as a general indication of the nature of the biblical musical tradition? Was it primarily vocal, and only instrumental to a secondary extent?

The scriptural references themselves require attention at several different levels. As we have indicated, one of these levels is the relation of the terms used to actual instruments known from archaeological finds. Another level is concerned with the role of those terms within the development of the scriptural material: How do they fit into the various literary and oral contexts to be assumed as part of the history of the present scriptural and intertestamental texts? Since in many cases that history stretches over several centuries, do those terms refer to changing practices and patterns of musical activity? Or even if it is granted that musical traditions are slow to change, do the changes in cultural and religious patterns implied by the history of the scriptural tradition require us to exercise care in assuming that a particular musical term can always be taken to refer to a specific, identifiable piece of musical practice? At the very least these questions caution against the acceptance without further inquiry of the translations used for musical instruments in modern versions of the Bible.

A. Idiophones
1. *mĕnaᶜanᶜîm*
2. *mĕṣiltayīm*
3. *ṣelṣĕlîm*
4. *kymbala*
5. *šālīš*
6. *paᶜămōn*
B. Membranophones *(tōp)*

C. Aerophones
  1. Group 1
    a. *ḥālîl*
    b. *nĕḥīlôt*
  2. Group 2
    a. *šôpār*
    b. *ḥăṣoṣĕrâ*
    c. *qeren*
    d. *yōbēl*
D. Chordophones
  1. *kinnôr*
  2. *nēbāl*
  3. *ᶜûgāb*
E. Daniel 3
  1. *qarnāᵓ*
  2. *mašrôqîtāᵓ*
  3. *qaytrôs*
  4. *sabbĕkāᵓ*
  5. *pĕsanterîn*
  6. *sûmpōnyâ*
F. *salpinx* in the NT

A. Idiophones

Idiophones are musical instruments of resonant material which emit sounds when they are shaken, struck, flexed, or rubbed.

1. *mĕnaᶜanᶜîm.* Possible translations at 2 Sam 6:5 include "shakers" (probably preferable), "rattles," "castanets," "sistrums." The context is a joyful, whirling dance as part of a procession to Jerusalem. David and the Israelites are "making merry" to the accompaniment of various percussion and string instruments. "Shakers" (i.e., gourds, or clay and pottery shapes, filled with seeds, shaken by the dancer) are an ancient and widespread form of accompaniment to dance. "Shakers" and "rattles" (perhaps distinguishable from shakers only by the way in which they are held) are well attested archaeologically as early as the 2d millennium B.C.E. in Babylonia, and have been found in several Palestinian sites datable to the 14th–10th centuries B.C.E. They have parallels in modern African cultures. Castanets are also known in the ancient world; for example, in the form of Egyptian clappers and Mesopotamian clackers. The "sistrum," (the Vg translation at 2 Kgdms 6:5), which is a rattle within a frame, is best known from Egyptian sources, and may well have been known in Davidic times.

2. *mĕṣiltayīm.* The Heb word *mĕṣiltayīm* may refer to twin cymbals, saucerlike plates with pierced centers for wire finger-holds and reflexed rims. They were capable of producing a high-pitched tinkling when struck together or when one was dashed against the rim of the other (Yadin 1972: 69 for a pair of these inside a bronze bowl in a 14th century B.C.E. stelae temple). Alternatively the reference may be to small bronze cones, sometimes for striking against each other vertically, which produced a resonating or dull clash according to the way in which they were held or struck.

The word *mĕṣiltayīm* appears only in Ezra, Nehemiah, and 1 and 2 Chronicles. Its uses may be grouped as follows: (a) in apparently stereotyped lists (as in Neh 12:27; 2 Chr 5:12; 29:25); (b) as expansions of musical references in 2 Samuel (as in 1 Chr 13:8—an expansion of 2 Sam 5:6—and 1 Chr 15:28, both in connection with the ark's procession to Jerusalem); (c) in other levitical material (e.g., 1 Chr 15:16; 16:5c; and 25:6). Together these present the ritual associations of the use of the twin cymbals by the musicians of the Second Temple. They hint at the varying levels of the tradition and varying emphases on priestly and levitical responsibilities in those different levels. The twin cymbals were used to accompany singing alongside strings and trumpets, to provide other percussion effects, or possibly to lead or begin choral singing. The number of the musicians involved has been understood symbolically. The Psalms use a different form of the word (cf. *ṣelṣĕlîm*).

3. *ṣelṣĕlîm.* The Heb word *ṣelṣĕlîm* appears in 2 Sam 6:5 and Ps 150:5. These are distinct contexts: the former has already been described as a dance-procession, the second is a hymn of praise involving most of the instruments known in Israelite music. In Psalm 150 the cymbals are described as *ṣilṣĕlê tĕrûᶜâ* and *ṣilṣĕlê šāmaᶜ*. These are generally understood as musical terms, either indicating the kind of cymbal used (high-pitched or low-pitched), or the musical use made of the cymbals (clashed or allowed to ring). It is possible, however, that the additional terms indicate primarily how they were employed in the temple worship and only secondarily what kind of cymbals they were or how they were played. The *ṣilṣĕlê tĕrûᶜâ* would then be "cymbals of acclamation," introducing the acclamation of praise by the singers or the assembled crowd, and the *ṣilṣĕlê šāmaᶜ*, a calling for attention, although whether this was human attention or divine attention is not clear. The relation of this to the temple worship is dealt with below.

4. *kymbala.* The word *kymbala* frequently indicates the use of cymbals in Gk translations of the OT. It does so also in 1 Cor 13:1. This Pauline verse is open to a number of interpretations. It may be a comparison of "speaking with tongues of men and of angels" with bombastic musical instruments (*chalkos* = a bronze gong, *kymbala* = bronze cymbals), contrasting these with the way of Christian love. Alternatively it may compare glossolalia and visionary voices with inessentials such as the bronze jars used as theatrical acoustic amplifiers and *kymbala alalazonta,* the cymbals used in the temple ritual, contrasting both with the one essential quality of love.

Following the first interpretation, *kymbala alalazonta* in the context of 1 Cor 13:1 provides difficulties, *kymbala alalazonta,* "wailing cymbals," could have the orgiastic associations of a bacchantic rite, reminding the reader of associations between such orgies and "speaking with tongues." That would be a critical reference to "speaking with tongues," and also, from the literary point of view, a harsh association of ideas. Following the second interpretation, *"alalazonta"* makes better sense, since the root of that word is associated, not least in the Gk translations of the OT, with Jewish "acclamations of praise." As compared with love, glossolalia and the cultic cymbals leading the temple acclamations of praise are both dispensable.

5. *šālīš.* The Vg translates Heb *šālīš* at 1 Sam 18:6 as "sistrum." It is by no means certain that *šālīš* is a musical instrument. The context is the singing and dancing of the Israelite women welcoming Saul and David, so a reference to a musical instrument here would be appropriate. But even if it is a musical instrument, its exact character remains uncertain. The sibilant character of the word *šālīš,* and a possible association with the Hebrew root for "three," makes "sistrum" as likely a translation as any (Sendrey 1969: 381). The sistrum was a common iconographic element in the Egyptian cult of Isis in all periods.

6. *paʿămōn.* In Exod 39:24–26 and 28:35, Heb *paʿămōn* is often translated "bell." It is quite possible that the word originally referred to platelets or bell-shaped objects hung as decoration around the high priest's robe and as a means of deflecting destructive powers. By the 1st century C.E. and perhaps even earlier, these were understood to be "bells" in a modern sense, i.e., bells with a ringing clapper inside each cavity (cf. Philo *Vita Mos* II. 110[23]).

B. Membranophones *(tōp)*

These are musical instruments from which sound is produced by movement of a stretched membrane, often of skin. The Hebrew word associated with this type of instrument is *tōp*. Possible translations include "drum," "frame drum," "tambourine," and "timbrel." In some cases the generic term "drum" may be an appropriate translation (cf. Gen 31:27, where the drum and lyre accompany songs; and Isa 5:12; 30:32; Ps 81:3, where the drum is made to "sound out"). In other cases, a "frame drum" may be indicated, i.e., a hand drum with a skin stretched over a circular (cf. Jer 31:4) or triangular frame, gripped by the left hand, with the fingers of the left hand tightening or releasing the tension on the skin, which is then struck with the palm of the right hand. 1 Sam 10:5 (and possibly Exod 15:20) includes such a frame drum as part of the so-called "Canaanite orchestra" (or "band" in the RSV; on this see C.1.a. below; on the evidence for this, cf. the 10th century B.C.E. Ashdod pottery stand, probably of Philistine origin). Some prefer the translation "tambourine" or "timbrel," but that suggests additional jingling circlets of metal. The evidence for such instruments is late, and the main uses of *tōp* are early. The Heb *tōp* is thus associated with singing, festivals, processions, and bands.

C. Aerophones

Aerophones are musical instruments which produce sound through vibration of air in, through, or around them. They can be subdivided into two main groups.

1. Group 1. In this group of aerophones, sound is produced at the point where air enters the instrument.

a. *ḥālîl.* (1) A double-pipe. A "double-pipe" is composed of two pipes, cones, or cylinders, in a V-shape with a reed or reeds at the point of the V. The two pipes may be the same length, one having several holes and the other one hole only, so that the latter acts as a kind of drone. An example of this may be 1 Sam 10:5, where the *ḥālîl* is another part of the "Canaanite band." Reed-pipes were also associated with funeral songs (cf. Jer 48:36 and Matt 9:23). Reed instruments may have been used to express great pathos.

(2) A single-pipe. This was particularly popular at feasts (cf. Isa 5:12; 30:29).

(3) Pipes or flutes. Extant from the 1st century C.E. is an example of a bone-flute with a blocked top and a narrow entrance into the instrument's vertical cavity. There are other kinds of flutes, some vertical, with the player blowing over the top rim, others transverse, with the opening on the upper side of the instrument. In a context such as 1 Kgs 1:40, the reference may be to several different kinds of pipes or flutes, although perhaps not including reed pipes. In 1 Cor 14:7 an instrument of the flute family may be intended (*aulos* Gk).

b. *nĕḥīlôt.* The Heb *nĕḥīlôt* (cf. Psalm 5) are probably the lamentation-pipes for which monuments and reliefs give impressive evidence.

There are other Hebrew terms sometimes associated with this class of aerophones, but the evidence concerning them is not strong, e.g., *ʿal ʿălāmôt* (cf. Psalm 46). 1 Chr 15:20 suggests that an instrumental interpretation of this word is inappropriate. It could perhaps refer to vocal instructions (cf. Exod 15:20; Judg 11:34).

2. Group 2. In this group of aerophones the lips of the player produce the vibration of air.

a. *šôpār.* Since the ancient distinction between the Heb *šôpār* and the trumpet does not correspond to the modern distinction between "horn" and "trumpet," the simple transliteration "shophar" (rather than "ram's horn," as a translation of the Heb) has much to commend it. The *šôpār* has two interrelated areas of association.

(1) War. The *šôpār* has sacred associations, even in battle (Josh 6:4–20; Judg 3:27; 6:34). It was used for signaling (1 Sam 13:3; Isa 18:3; 27:13; 58:1; Jer 51:27; 4:5, 19, 21); it was used by the watchman (Jer 6:1, 17; Ezek 33:3–6), and as a warning to repent (Amos 2:2; 3:6; Hos 5:8; Joel 2:1, 15; Zeph 1:16; Hos 8:1). 1QM illustrates these uses of the *šôpār,* except that the trumpet is given greater precision in signaling detailed instructions to the army. The Chronicler has a distinctive view of the relative positions of *šôpār* and *ḥăṣōṣĕrâ.*

(2) Worship. the *šôpār* was sounded throughout the land on the Day of Atonement (Lev 25:9). Zeph 1:16 provides a parallel for this, with clear military links. The *šôpār* is linked with the *tĕrûʿâ;* this has a rich series of associations—warnings concerning holiness and judgment (Lev 26:16ff.), and celebration of victory and blessing for the land. 1 Kgs 1:34, 39, 41 and 2 Kgs 9:13 refer to the use of the *šôpār* in connection with royal coronations.

b. *ḥăṣoṣĕrâ.* In connection with this Hebrew word, a passage in Josephus (*Ant* 3 §291) is particularly relevant:

> Moses further invented a kind of clarion which he had made for him in silver, on this wise. In length a little short of a cubit, it is a narrow tube, slightly thicker than a flute, with a mouthpiece wide enough to admit the breath and a bell-shaped extremity such as trumpets have. It is called asosra in the Hebrew language.

Where *šôpār* and *ḥăṣōṣĕrôt* occur together (Hos 5:8 and Ps 98:6) it is convenient simply to transliterate the former as "shophar" and to translate the latter as "trumpet." But whether or not this is an accurate rendering depends on two factors: to what date should a text such as Ps 98:6 be assigned? And, at what date did the instrument described by Josephus first appear in Israelite-Jewish culture?

The silver trumpets made of hammered metal (Num 10:1) had a specific liturgical function at the end of the OT period (cf. Sir 50:16–19). 2 Kgs 12:13 suggests that they also had a role in the temple at an earlier period. In Numbers, as in Ecclesiasticus, they are signs of divine favor.

The *ḥăṣōṣĕrôt* are played by the priests rather than by the

Levites in the later strands of the tradition in Chronicles (2 Chr 5:12). In the earlier strands that distinction is missing or blurred (1 Chr 16:42; cf. 2 Chr 29:25, where the Levites play "the instruments of David"). The Targumic evidence in 1 Chr 13:8 supports the translation of *ḥăṣōṣĕrôt* as "trumpets."

c. *qeren.* The Heb word *qeren* is parallel to *šôpār* in Josh 6:5. Some suggest that *qeren* refers to "horn" without any metal attachment, whether as mouthpiece or as bell. But that should not be taken to suggest that *šôpār* did not also carry the same possible sense. (For the use of *qeren* in Aramaic, see below).

d. *yōbēl.* The Heb *yōbēl* is parallel to *šôpār* in Exodus 19 and Joshua 6. Again, like *qeren,* it is probably an alternative designation for (rather than a subcategory of) the *šôpār.* In Exod 19:13 God gives notice that the *yōbēl* is to be blown as permission for the people to approach the mountain (cf. the use of *salpinx* in Heb 12:19); in v 16 the *šôpār* sounds, and in v 19 it becomes an accompaniment to the divine voice. Read as a consecutive narrative the passage gives the impression that the *yōbēl* and the *šôpār* are the same instrument. The word *yōbēl* may, of course, betray the presence of different strata in the text; the word marks the start of the sacred festival in Lev 25:34. In Joshua 6 the narrative appears to use different words for the same instruments. Some argue that the verb used in Exod 19:16 and Josh 6:5 with *yōbēl* indicates a louder kind of *šôpār,* but the verb could simply mean a particular way of sounding the *šôpār.* Since the narrative in both places depends on the sacred quality of the instrument rather than on decibels, the verb may not possess a decisively musical significance in either place.

D. Chordophones

These instruments produce sound from the plucking or bowing of strings stretched over or into a sounding box. The Mesopotamian and Egyptian instruments identifiable from depictions and descriptions include three main types: (1) the harp (akin to the warrior's bow with up to twelve strings), with the soundbox on the horizontal or the vertical part of the bow; (2) the lyre (Eg. *knnwr*), with two arms (symmetrical or asymmetrical) raised from ends of the soundbox, supporting a yoke from which the strings (three to eleven in number) descend into or over the soundbox; and (3) the lute, whose strings stretch along a narrow neck and then over a bulging soundbox. Details concerning the length of string, tuning, playing, and damping in the use of these instruments have been partly clarified from three interrelated areas of research: the study of ancient notations, the study of the depictions of players, and modern reconstructions and recordings (Wulstan; Kilmer). The lyre is well represented in Israelite archaeological finds (e.g., the 12th century B.C.E. Megiddo ivory plaque, the 7th century B.C.E. Jasper Seal, and the Bar Kokhba coins ca. 132 C.E.). The lute is less well attested (cf. the 16th century pottery figurine from Tell el-Ajul, and the 15th–13th century Beth-shean bronze statuette). The harp is not found at all.

1. *kinnôr.* The identification of Heb *kinnôr* with the lyre is very probable (cf. *Ant* 7.306, the various versions of the OT which understand *kinnôr* as a *kithara,* and Abraham ben Meir ibn Ezra's description; by contrast, the links of the harp with Syria are insufficient to explain the forty-two uses of the word *kinnôr* in the OT [cf. Juv. *Sat.* 3.63–4 "obliquas chordas"]).

The associations of the *kinnôr* with singing are ancient (Gen 31:27; 2 Sam 6:5; Isa 23:16) and highly significant in the Psalm material (cf. Pss 57:9; 98:5; 147:7; 149:3; 150:3; 1QH 5:30; 11:22f. [*TDOT* 4: 91–98; *RGG* 4: 1201]—cf. also the Wisdom context in Ps 49:5). A feature of David's selection as a *kinnôr*-player by Saul (1 Sam 16:16) was that he should "play [Heb *ngn*] *with the hand*"—as distinct, perhaps, from "with the plectrum"? The "Canaanite prophetic band" seems to have included the *kinnôr* (1 Sam 10:5). The exact nature of the wood used in its construction is unfortunately unclear (1 Kgs 10:12; 2 Chr 9:11), nor can we be sure of the character and associations of its sound, except that considerable variation was possible. It can sound "sweet" (Ps 81:2) or "soft" (Ps 92:4); but does the Heb *hmh* mean "groaning" (cf. Ps 55:17) or "sounding"? Does *šĕʾôn* mean "din" in Isa 24:8, and is this the sound of the instrument, or a tumult of singers? Is it or is it not an appropriate instrument for a lament (cf. Psalms 43 and 137)? The rhythmic character of the *kinnôr* was proverbial (Isa 30:32), especially when played with the plectrum. It remained a cultic instrument in the developed pattern of Second Temple worship and was seen in continuity with the prophecy of preexilic times (1 Chr 25:4).

2. *nĕbāl.* With this Heb term we enter a far more difficult area, as the variant translations in the OT versions show. The term appears parallel to *kinnôr* in 2 Sam 6:5, 1 Sam 10:5, Pss 57:9; 71:22; 81:3; 108:3; 150:3 and in the Chronicler; in Pss 33:2; 92:4; 144:9 it is parallel to *kinnôr* but is itself linked with the term *ʿaśôr* ("ten stringed"?). It appears to have cultic associations in Amos, especially in 5:23 and 6:5, of which some suggest that the language evokes dissolute, noisy improvisation indicating careless self-confidence. Amos seems to imply that the instrument is plucked with the fingers. Josephus (*Ant* 7.306) agrees, describing it as having twelve notes (*phthongous* cf. 1 Cor 14:7). The rabbis regarded it as a larger, lower-pitched *kinnôr,* and modern writers sometimes affirm the use of different sizes of instrument, unwisely using as a basis the evidence from 1 Chr 15:20f. (cf. above on *ʿal ʿălāmôt;* the difficulties in interpreting *ʿal ʿălāmôt* make it doubly difficult to reach a conclusion regarding *šĕmînît,* especially the conclusion that *šĕmînît* refers to an instrument capable of playing an octave lower). Attempts to derive the character of the instrument etymologically can be misleading, as we shall see below; but it is possible that in this case the word *nĕbāl* evokes the picture of a bulging bottle (cf. LXX 1 Kgdms 10:3; Jer 13:12). The lute is the most appropriate stringed instrument known from archaeological work to correspond to such a picture. It would not, however, be wise to assume that *nĕbāl* should always be translated "lute" (it could refer in some contexts to a different size of lyre).

3. *ʿûgāb.* The Heb *ʿûgāb* is usually considered a wind instrument. The arguments for this involve an etymological association with the flute family, the role of Gen 4:21, the weight of discussion among modern commentators (Sendrey), and *Tg. Onq.* on Gen 4:21. But there are arguments against this view: Josephus regarded Jubal as creating two string instruments; the LXX and Peshitta at Gen 4:21 suggest that *ʿûgāb* was a stringed instrument; and

Symmachus has *kithara* at Job 21:12 and Ps 150:4. An important new piece of evidence is the discovery of the Hebrew version of Psalm 151 in the Qumran Psalm Scroll. Ps 151:2 (Heb) reads:

> My hands have made a *ʿûgāb*
> and my fingers a *kinnôr.*

The parallelism between *ʿûgāb* and *kinnôr* suggests either that *ʿûgāb* was a general word (e.g., "instrument") or a particular string instrument. The harp is a possibility (Bayer). In that case *minnîm* in Ps 150:4b may be a general reference to strings, and *ʿûgāb* a particular example of a stringed instrument. The presence in this psalm of an instrument which otherwise found little place in Canaanite or Israelite instrumentation is not an insuperable problem. In Job 21:12 and 30:31 *ʿûgāb* is an instrument expressive of joy and contentment.

E. Daniel 3

From the Hellenistic period there is pictorial evidence of an increased use of mixed groups of musicians (Fleischhauer 1982: 150). Recent discussions of the "orchestra" of Nebuchadrezzar in Daniel 3 (Mitchell), in attempting to place individual instruments mentioned there as early as the 6th century B.C.E., have neglected this factor. There are undoubtedly early traditions in the book of Daniel and the "orchestra" could be one of these, but the depicting of an Eastern potentate as possessing a mixed orchestra would have constituted a significant barbaric motif in the eyes of an early 2d century B.C.E. reader. According to Daniel 3, this mixed orchestra included the following instruments:

1. *qarnāʾ*. The translation "horn" (Aram *qarnāʾ;* Heb *qeren*) is often favored here, on the grounds of language and because of the assumed rarity of *trumpets* within the depictions of musical instruments from the 6th century B.C.E. "Horn" would then be understood as an instrument formed from the horn of an animal. If, however, the book of Daniel is read as addressed in its final form to Hellenistic times, then the possibilities of translation are much greater. "Pagan" bands included brass instruments. In such a context *qarnaʾ/qeren* could be understood as the equivalent of the *cornu* (Latin) or the *buccina* (Latin), although the distinction between these two names is a matter of debate. The *tuba* (Latin) and *lituus* (Latin, see below) might also to be considered. Perhaps an appropriate translation of *qeren* here might be "bugle-horn."

2. *mašrôqîtāʾ*. The LXX translates *mašrôqîtāʾ* as *"syrinx,"* and the Vg translates it as *fistula,* either of which might point to panpipes, a row of pipes of different lengths bound together, which produce a piccolo-type sound capable of birdlike twittering and running scales. Some scholars relate the Aramaic name to a Semitic root, "to hiss or whistle." The humble "whistle" is also a possible contender for an orchestral place.

3. *qaytrôs*. The LXX translates this Aramaic word as *kithara,* and *qaytrôs* itself may actually be a loanword from the Gk *kithara* or *kitharis.* In a 6th century B.C.E. Babylonian setting this would be the lyre; in a Hellenistic setting the Aramaic name would evoke the Greek style of instrument and of performance depicted on Greek amphora from the 5th century B.C.E. (Michaelides 1978, cf. Rev 14:2; 18:22).

4. *sabběkāʾ*. The LXX and Vg translate this Aramaic word as *"sambyke,"* which probably was a stringed instrument of the harp family with a large sounding-board of proverbially barbaric and immoral character (Michaelides). It was employed in Hellenistic times as part of instrumental bands (Fleischhauer 1982: 187). Those who argue for Daniel 3 as representing an actual 6th-century B.C.E. orchestra suggest that it is a loanword indicating an Assyrian-type horizontal harp.

5. *pěsanterîn*. The LXX and Vg translate this Aramaic word as *"psalterion,"* a member of the harp family and well-known in Greek circles from the 4th century B.C.E.

6. *sûmpōnyâ*. The discussion of this word is complicated by the presence in Luke 15:2 of the Gk word *symphonia,* which is often confused with the Aram *sûmpōnyâ.* In all probability the two are unconnected. *Symphonia,* from which English has the derivation "symphony," can indicate either sound made by voices singing together (Peshitta and Harclean at Luke 15:2 understood *symphonia* in this sense), or voices together with instruments, or simply "a band." Some argue for the translation "bagpipe," others "double pipe," but NEB's preference for "music" is probably correct. *Sûmpōnyâ,* by contrast, is probably a transliteration of a dialect form of the Gk *tympanon,* a kettledrum. This would provide the orchestra in Daniel 3 with a much-needed percussion instrument (one which had been in use from Mesopotamian times; Mitchell).

The impression given by these individual discussions reinforces the view that to the 2d century B.C.E. reader the band of Nebuchadrezzar described in Daniel 3 would have sounded bizarre and absurd, and so would have underscored the book's contempt for idolatry.

F. *salpinx* in the NT

Already several aspects of NT usage have been considered, insofar as the NT reflects traditional folk music practiced over many centuries. There remains, however, one distinctively NT usage which deserves separate attention: the references to *salpinx.*

The Gk word *salpinx* can refer to a wide range of musical instruments. We have seen already that it has a LXX usage covering *qeren, šôpār,* and *ḥăṣōṣěrôt.* The Gk *salpinx* functioned in military and cultural contexts. It heralded the opening of competitions and the verdict of the judges. It played an important part in Etruscan and Roman military circles. Other instruments referred to by the word *salpinx* were the *cornu* and *buccina,* which were also military instruments, and which, despite their raucous character, were used in various instrumental combinations (Fleischhauer 1982: 16). With the *lituus,* they are depicted in representations of solemn funeral processions, civic ceremonies (cf. perhaps Matt 6:2 with irony or sarcasm), and military triumphs. The *lituus* has been reconstructed from archaeological finds, and its haunting alpine-horn call must have been familiar wherever Roman soldiers made their camps and wherever gladiatorial combat took place. The *tuba* (as the relief on Trajan's Column indicates) accompanied military marching and marked the strategic movements of troops in war (cf. 1QM; 1 Cor 14:8), and with the *buccina* and *cornu* it was intended to create panic among the enemy.

In intertestamental literature the sounding of a *salpinx* was understood to initiate messianic times (1 Thess 4:16; cf. also the holy war tradition in *L. A. B.* 36:3), the gathering of God's people who had been humiliated by the heathen (*Apoc. Ab.* 31.1), or the resurrection of God's people (*Ques. Ezra* B 12; 1 Cor 15:52). The golden trumpet pointed heavenward heralds a series of scenes: it puts heart into the seer, splits the heavens wide open, calls the saints to intercession as they do daily when the trumpets answer each other between heaven and earth, and warns of the coming wrath of God's judgment (*Apoc. Zeph.* 9–12; Matt 24:31). The association of the trumpet with the fire is particularly strong in judgment scenes (*T. Ab.* 12:10; cf. Heb 12:19), and the Feast of Trumpets no doubt lent strength to this tradition (*L. A. B.* 13:6). Proclamation of both the mercies and majesty of God is another function of the trumpet (*L. A. E.* 47:1). Sometimes this is associated with cosmic motifs (*L. A. B.* 32:18).

The use of *salpinx* in the NT is therefore distinctive not only because of its extremely rich group of associations, the trumpet being part of a series of interlocking motifs—musical, ritual, secular, and cosmic—but also because it focuses these motifs in a single Greek word. This is all the more interesting in the case of Revelation because the imagery there is based on what is heard (Rev 1:10). It also explains the construction of the trumpet scenes, since these bring together the devastation of the earth with its plague and its cosmic associations (Rev 8:6–9:13), the call to penitence (Amos 3:6; Joel 2:1, 15; Rev 9:20), the prophetic associations of judgment (cf. Rev 18:22, where the songs to the *"cithara,"* musicians, players of the *"aulos"* and the *"salpinx"* are heard no more), and the announcement of the Day of the Lord (Revelation 14). The holiness of the divine presence is also evoked by the trumpet references (4:1), as they reflect the interplay of heavenly and earthly liturgies (8:1ff.).

Bibliography

Bayer, B. 1967. *Material Relics of Music in Ancient Palestine and its Environs.* Tel Aviv.

Fleischhauer, G. 1982. *Musikgeschichte in Bildern* II.

Gelb, I. J. 1975. Homo Ludens in Early Mesopotamia. *StOr:* 43–75.

Haifa Museum. 1972. *Music in Ancient Israel.* Haifa.

Michaelides, S. 1978. *The Music of Ancient Greece: an Encyclopaedia.* London.

Mitchell, T., and Joyce, R. 1965. The Musical Instruments in Nebuchadrezzar's Orchestra. In *Notes on Some Problems in the Book of Daniel.* London.

Rimmer, J. 1969. *Ancient Musical Instruments in the British Museum.* London.

Sendrey, A. 1969. *Music in Ancient Israel.* London.

Spycket, A. 1972. La Musique Instrumentale Mesopotamienne, *Journal des Savants:* 153–209.

Wulstan, D. 1968. The Tuning of the Babylonian Harp. *Iraq* 30: 215–43.

Yadin, Y. 1972. *Hazor.* Oxford.

IVOR H. JONES

MUSTARD SEED. See FLORA.

MUSTER GATE (PLACE) [Heb *šaʿar hammipqād*]. One of two inner gates (the Water Gate [Neh 3:26] and the Mifqad, or Muster Gate [Neh 3:31]) of Jerusalem on the E side of an enclosure that surrounded the sacred temple precincts and the royal compounds. To the W was the sacred temple enclosure and its E gate kept by Shemaiah (Neh 3:29). Opposite the Muster Gate to the E was the outer defensive wall of the city and the house of the Nethinim (temple servants) and the merchants (Neh 3:31).

Outside the temple precincts and its E gate was the "open place" or "plaza" of the House of God (Ezra 10:9) where Ezra gathered the people of Judah and Benjamin. It was here that Ezekiel described (Ezek 43:21) a sin offering that was to be burnt in the *mipqād habayit* (or "Mifqad of the House" [of God]). This plaza was also referred to (2 Chr 29:4–5) when Hezekiah assembled the priests and the Levites in the "open place" or "plaza" on the E (of the temple precincts).

Bibliography

Avi-Yonah, M. 1954. The Wall of Nehemiah—A Minimalist View. *IEJ* 4: 239–48.

Vincent, L.-H., and Steve, M.-A. 1954. *Jerusalem de l'Ancien Testament.* Paris.

DALE C. LIID

MUTILATION. See PUNISHMENTS AND CRIMES.

MYCENAEAN LANGUAGE. See LANGUAGES (INTRODUCTORY SURVEY).

MYNDOS (PLACE) [Gk *Myndos*]. A city on the coast of Caria in SW Asia Minor to which the Roman consul Lucius addressed a letter (ca. 139 B.C.) proclaiming the renewed alliance between Rome and the Jews (1 Macc 15:23; see 15:16–21 for general text of the letter). It has been suggested that the account of this letter (15:15–24) should be placed immediately after 14:24 (Goldstein, *1 Maccabees* AB, 492–94). Myndos is associated with modern Gumushli, near Halicarnassus.

GARY A. HERION

MYRA (PLACE) [Gk *Myra*]. An important city on the Lycian coast in SW Anatolia. Its name was later associated with myrrh, but there is no evidence that this spice was ever traded there. For example, Constantine Porphrogenitus declared: "Thrice blessed, myrrh-breathing city of the Lycians, . . . spouts forth myrrh in accordance with the city's name."

The city of Myra was located on the plateau about 3.5 miles from the coast (36°17′ N; 29°58′ E), but its name also included its port of Andriace (now Andraki). The Myrus or Andracus River flowed past the city to the coast in a narrow valley. Its estuary is now submerged in sand dunes. The ruins of the city of Myra are now located 1 mile N of the village of Demre.

It was at Myra (i.e., Andriace) according to Acts 27:5–6 that Paul and his fellow travelers transferred from a ship from Adramyttium to an Alexandrian grain ship bound for Italy, which had probably sailed directly N from Egypt to Lycia. In Acts 21:1, Codex D and some other mss add the words "and Myra" after "Patara." The apocryphal *Acts of Paul and Thecla* recount the preaching of Paul at Myra (James 1924: 281–84; Schneelmecher *NTApocr* 2: 363–67).

Though literary texts do not mention Myra until the 1st century B.C. (Bean 1978: 120), many Lycian inscriptions of the Persian period have been recovered from Myra (Jones 1971: 98). In the Hellenistic era, Myra was one of the six largest cities of the 23-member Lycian League (Magie 1950: 532; Stark 1956: 130). In Roman times, it became more important than its rival city Patara, 40 miles to the W. See PATARA.

In 197 B.C., Antiochus the Great conquered Lycia, including Myra. After his defeat by the Romans at Magnesia in 189 B.C., Lycia was granted to Rhodes. Then in 169 B.C. the Romans declared the Lycians free. In 88 B.C. Ptolemy IX of Egypt, fleeing from his mutinous army, took refuge at Myra. Lentulus Spinther, Brutus' lieutenant, coerced the city into donating money for the republican cause in 42 B.C. In A.D. 18 Germanicus, who visited Myra, was honored with a statue, proclaiming him "Savior and Benefactor." Augustus and Tiberius were both hailed as the "Benefactor and Savior of the whole universe" by Myra (Magie 1950: 498, 529; Vermeule 1968: 225). A colossal head of Augustus was recovered at Myra (Vermeule 1968: 175, fig. 107).

Vermeule (1968: 153) comments: "The Lycians were proud, independent, and poor in the Roman period, a fact which is reflected in their lack of major coins." One exception is a fine coin of Gordianus III from Myra. Coins and inscriptions indicate that the chief deity of Myra was Artemis Eleuthera, a mammiferous goddess like Artemis of Ephesus (Kirsten 1978).

The monuments of Lycia, including those of Myra, were first brought to light by the journal and drawings of the celebrated British traveler Charles Fellows (1841). The cliffs near Myra are honeycombed with elaborately carved tombs, some with painted reliefs. These date from the 4th century B.C. Akurgal (1970: 263) declares: "The rock-cut Lykian tombs of Myra are among the most fascinating historical remains of Turkey."

The theater, which originally held about 11,000, had a podium eight feet high (Stark 1956: 152). Of the Roman type, it was one of the finest theaters built in Asia Minor (Fellows 1841: 115). The road between Myra and Andriace is lined with numerous sarcophagi. At some distance from the sea is the granary of Hadrian, "one of the best-preserved monuments of imperial efficiency in Asia Minor" (Vermeule 1968: 225). It has seven long store rooms behind a 200-foot facade.

Though no excavations have been conducted, careful studies of the visible remains, mainly of Byzantine date, were conducted between 1965 and 1968 (Borchhardt 1975). Harrison has identified the remains of five churches at Andriace (1963: 142–43).

The most famous church is that of the legendary St. Nicholas at Myra. Nicholas was born at Patara ca. 300 B.C. and served as the bishop of Myra. Late sources, uncorroborated by contemporary evidence, allege that Nicholas was imprisoned during Diocletian's persecution, that he was present at the Council of Nicaea in 325, and that he died ca. 350 (Anrich 1913 and 1917; Bean 1978: 125–26).

His church, which had fallen into ruins, was not rediscovered until 1841 (Borchhardt 1975: 303). It appears that Nicholas' remains were at first buried outside the city walls with only a small monument. By the mid-5th century inscriptions and literary references attest to his heightened popularity. It was probably in the 6th century that a basilica was erected over his tomb, a time when the legendary tales of his generosity and miracles developed (Kirsten 1978: 468). The first reference to his grave as a martyrium is dated to 565.

Myra became a popular center for pilgrims in the Middle Ages, as oil seeping from St. Nicholas' tomb was regarded to have healing powers. In 1087 men from Bari, in S Italy, carried off the saint's relics to their home as an act of *sacra furta,* "sacred theft" (Stark 1956: 150; Bean 1978: 125; Geary 1978). Nicholas eventually became the patron saint of children, sailors, and merchants, of Greece and of Russia, and was finally transformed in America as "Santa Claus."

Bibliography

Akurgal, E. 1970. *Ancient Civilizations and Ruins of Turkey.* 2d ed. Trans. J. Whybrow and M. Emre. Istanbul.

Anrich, G. 1913, 1917. *Hagios Nikolaus.* 2 vols. Leipzig.

Bean, G. E. 1978. *Lycian Turkey.* London.

Borchhardt, J. 1975. *Myra: Eine lykische Metropole in antiker und byzantinischer Zeit.* Istanbuler Forschungen 30. Berlin.

Fellows, C. 1841. *An Account of Discoveries in Lycia.* London.

Geary, P. J. 1978. *Furta Sacra: Thefts of Relics in the Central Middle Ages.* Princeton.

Harrison, R. M. 1963. Churches and Chapels of Central Lycia. *AnSt* 13: 117–51.

James, M. R. 1924. *Apocryphal New Testament.* Oxford.

Jones, A. H. M. 1971. *Cities of the Eastern Roman Provinces.* 2d. ed. Oxford.

Kirsten, E. 1978. Artemis von Ephesos und Eleuthera von Myra. Pp. 457–87 in *Studien zur Religion und Kultur Kleinasiens* 2. Ed. S. Sahin; E. Schwertheim; and J. Wagner. Leiden.

Magie, D. 1950. *Roman Rule in Asia Minor.* Princeton.

Stark, F. 1956. *Lycian Shore.* New York.

Vermeule, C. C. 1968. *Roman Imperial Art in Greece and Asia Minor.* Cambridge.

EDWIN M. YAMAUCHI

MYRRH. See PERFUMES AND SPICES; FLORA; INCENSE; and FRANKINCENSE.

MYRTLE. See FLORA.

MYSIA (PLACE) [Gk *Mysia*]. A region of NW Asia Minor along the Hellespont and the Aegean Sea. The ancient geographers disagree on the exact boundaries of the region of Mysia and it appears to have varied continually from the time of Homer (Strabo 12.4.5–6; and 12.8.1–3). Mysia was divided into Mysia Major and Minor by Strabo and Ptolemy. Mysia Major probably corresponded to the region around Mt. Olympus, which the Mysians occupied through the time of Croesus (see Strabo 12.4.10; 12.8.3; and Hdt 1.36), and Mysia Minor corresponded to the region adjacent to Lydia on the banks of the Caicus River and Pergamum (Strabo 12.8.1).

The Mycians were not indigenous to Asia Minor, but migrated from Thrace (perhaps along with the Lydians) and were originally known as the Moesians (Strabo 12.3.4; 12.4.8; 12.8.3). According to Herodotus, the Mysians were a numerous and powerful people prior to the Trojan War, subjugating regions of Thrace and Macedonia (Hdt 7.20.75). Homer listed the Mysians among the allies of Priam, but assigned them to the regions of Thrace (*Il.* 13.5). The people who are called the "Musoi" (or "Musa") in Hittite and Egyptian documents (14th and 13th centuries) may be the Mysians. After the fall of Priam's Troy, the Mysians controlled the Troad for a short time (Strabo 12.4.6).

Mysia came under the control of the Lydians by the reign of King Alyattes, the father of Croesus. When the Lydian Empire fell to the Persians, Mysia was consolidated into part of Darius' second satrapy (Hdt 3.90). Orontes, the satrap of Mysia, revolted against Artaxerxes in 349 B.C.E. and ruled NW Asia Minor.

After Alexander the Great conquered Asia Minor, the Mysians were controlled successively by Antigonus, until 301 B.C.E. (battle of Ipsus), Lysimachus, until 281 B.C.E. (battle of Corupedium), and the Seleucids. In 283 B.C.E., Philetaerus, Lysimachus' treasurer, established the Pergamene Dynasty of the Attalids with Ptolemaic aid. When Antiochus III was defeated at the battle of Magnesia in 190 B.C.E., the Romans rewarded Eumenes II, the king of Pergamum, with the region of Mysia (Livy 38.39). The Pergamenes, however, had to conquer the region of Mysia Olympene in 184/3 B.C.E. from Prusias (Polyb. 4.50; 4.52; 21.48). When Attalus III bequeathed his kingdom to the Romans in 133 B.C.E., Mysia was annexed to the Roman proconsular province (Cicero *QFr* 1.8), but during the Empire it formed a separate district and was governed by a procurator.

Although the Mysians were stereotyped as lazy cowards (Demosthenes *De Cor.;* Aristotle *Rh.* 1.12.20; and Cicero *Pro Flac.* 27; see also ibid. *Orat.* 8), they proved to be dependable mercenaries. After the defeat of Antiochus III, the peace of Apameia in 188 B.C.E. forbade the Seleucid Empire from recruiting soldiers in Roman domains (Polyb. 21.42; and Livy 27.38.10) and forced the Seleucids to find an increased number of volunteers from Greek free states like Pergamum. Antiochus IV had a unit of 5,000 Mysian mercenaries in his army, under the charge of an individual called a Mysarch. The most infamous Mysarch was Apollonius, who in 167 B.C.E. led his mercenaries in an expedition against the city of Jerusalem (see 1 Macc 1:29–35; 2 Macc 5:23–26; and Josephus *Ant* 13.5.3–4 §246–56). The title "Commander of Mysians" (*sar musim* or *sar misim*) was distorted in 1 Macc 1:29 to "taskmaster" or "tax-gathering official" *(sar missim).*

The two principal cities in Mysia, Adramytium and Pergamum, were major Jewish centers by the 1st century B.C.E. (Cicero *Flac.* 68; Josephus *Ant* 14.247–55). Paul passed through two towns in Mysia: Troas (Acts 16:8, 11) and Assos (Acts 20:13). The church at the city of Pergamum was also addressed by John in Revelation (Rev 1:11; and 2:12–17).

SCOTT T. CARROLL

MYSTERY RELIGIONS. The mystery religions were secret religious cults that flourished during the Greco-Roman period. These religions, involving the worship of deities from Greece, Anatolia, Egypt, Persia, and Syria, manifested diversity in their points of geographical origin, and heterogeneity in their patterns of historical development and theological orientation. Yet, in spite of their differences, the mystery religions warrant being discussed together because they all represent a particular form of religion. Commonly originating in ancient tribal and even fertility rituals, these religions emphasized salvation for individuals who decided, through personal choice, to be initiated into the mysteries, and thereby to feel close to each other and to the divine.

Unlike official, public religions, in which people were expected to show outward allegiance to the gods and goddesses of the *polis,* or state, the mystery religions stressed an inwardness and privacy of worship within groups that were frequently close-knit and egalitarian. The devotees of the mysteries ordinarily shared in celebrations that were public in nature (e.g., parades and processions, with music and dance, and preliminary rituals of purification and sacrifice), as well as in secret ceremonies that remain largely unknown. In descriptions of the Eleusinian mysteries it is said that the secret observances included "things recited" (Gk *legomena*), "things shown" (Gk *deiknymena*), and "things performed" (Gk *drōmena*), and such observances may have been typical of the mystery religions in general. Usually a sacred meal was shared by those initiated into the mysteries. At least some of those who participated in the secret ceremonies underwent an extraordinary experience that could be described as death and rebirth. That some such emotionally gripping experience was of fundamental significance in the mystery religions is confirmed by Aristotle, who concluded, in a fragment preserved in Synesius (*Dio* 10), that initiates into the mysteries did not learn anything *(ou mathein ti),* but rather had an experience *(pathein)* and were put into a certain state of mind *(diatethēnai).*

A. "Mystery" and the Mysteries
B. Greek Mystery Religions
   1. Eleusinian Mysteries
   2. Andanian Mysteries
   3. Mysteries of Dionysos
C. Mystery Religions of Middle Eastern Origin
   1. Mysteries of the Great Mother and Attis
   2. Mysteries of Isis and Osiris
   3. Mysteries of Mithras
D. Relationship to Early Christianity

A. "Mystery" and the Mysteries

The word "mystery" (Gk *mystērion*) derives from the Gk verb *myein,* "to close," referring to the closing of the lips or the eyes. The "closed" nature of the mystery religions may be interpreted in two ways.

A person (Gk *mystēs*, pl. *mystai*) who had experienced the *mystērion* was required to maintain closed lips in order not to divulge the secret revealed at the private ceremony. Pledges of silence were intended to ensure that the holy secret would not be disclosed to profane outsiders. Most *mystai* observed their vows of silence, and as a result comparatively little is known of the secret ceremonies of the mystery religions. However, Christian converts who had once been initiated into the mysteries and Christian authors who claimed to possess knowledge about the mysteries sometimes were eager to expose what they believed to be godless secrets of these religions (cf. Arnobius of Sicca, *Adversus Nationes;* Clement of Alexandria, *Protrepticus;* Eusebius of Caesarea, *Praeparatio Evangelica;* Firmicus Maternus, *De errore profanarum religionum;* Hippolytus of Rome, *Refutatio Omnium Haeresium*). Further, the Greek general Alcibiades may well have been accused of betraying the pledge of silence by engaging in a parody of the Eleusinian mysteries of Demeter and Kore during a drinking party (cf. Plutarch *Alc.* 19.1–2).

An initiate into the mysteries also participated in the closing (and the subsequent opening) of the eyes. As people with closed eyes remain in darkness until they open their eyes to see the light, so the *mystai* whose eyes were opened moved from darkness to enlightenment, both literally and metaphorically. The contrast between closed and open eyes, between darkness and light, was accentuated within the initiatory ceremonies, which often took place at night and which employed the light of torches (at times with reference to the light of the sun; cf. Apuleius of Madaura, *Met.* 11.23–24). The significance of the closing and opening of the eyes is also maintained by Greek terms used to designate priests and initiates. For example, one of the priests in the mystery religions was termed "one who shows sacred things" (Gk *hierophantēs*); in the Eleusinian mysteries the highest stage of initiation was designated that of "beholding" (Gk *epopteia*), and one who attained such an initiatory status was called "beholder" (Gk *epoptēs*). Pindar, in a fragment preserved in Clement of Alexandria (*Strom.* 3.3.17), likewise used visual imagery in his blessing upon one initiated with the Eleusinian mysteries: "Blessed is one who goes under the earth after seeing these things. That person knows the end of life, and knows its Zeus-given beginning."

The word "mystery" (Heb *sôd;* Heb and Aram *raz;* Gk *mystērion*) is also used in the OT, NT, and Dead Sea Scrolls (see Brown 1968). On *mystērion* in 1 Cor 15:51 see D below.

B. Greek Mystery Religions

Within the world of ancient Greece the mysteries that were celebrated included the Eleusinian mysteries, the Andanian mysteries, the mysteries of Dionysos, the mysteries of the Kabeiroi (or, Cabiri, the great gods) at Samothrace, and the lesser known mysteries at Phlya. Mention may also be made of the mysteries founded by Alexander of Abonoteichos in honor of the serpent Glykon, an incarnation of the god Asclepius, since these mysteries were satirized by Lucian of Samosata (*Alex.* 38–43) with images and terms familiar from the Eleusinian mysteries.

1. Eleusinian Mysteries. The most influential and popular of the Greek mysteries were the Eleusinian mysteries. Celebrated at Eleusis (modern Elefsis) near Athens, these mysteries focused upon Demeter, the "Grain Mother," and Kore, the "Maiden." From early times an agricultural cult at Eleusis observed rituals commemorating the fertility and life of grain; the later Eleusinian mysteries employed similar rituals, but directed particular attention at the transformed life of people. Hence Hippolytus could observe (*Haer.* 5.8.39) that among the "things shown" in certain Eleusinian mysteries was a single head of grain that was beheld in silence, apparently as a manifestation of the life in grain and in all. Likewise, Cicero could have Marcus comment (*Leg.* 2.14.36) concerning the Eleusinian mysteries that "we have learned from them the fundamentals of life *(principia vitae)* and have grasped the basis not only for living with joy but also for dying with a better hope." The dramatic story of Demeter and her dying and rising daughter Kore, as told in the *Homeric Hymn to Demeter,* narrates a mythic tale of the rape of Kore by Hades (or Plouton, "Wealthy One"), the grief of Demeter and her quest for Kore, and the subsequent founding of the Eleusinian mysteries by Demeter herself. That tale may well have functioned as the "sacred account" (Gk *hieros logos*) of the mysteries of Demeter and Kore. Just before 600 B.C.E., it would appear Athens took control of Eleusis, and thereafter Athens assumed jurisdiction of the Eleusinian mysteries. Later mysteries of Demeter and Kore were celebrated at a site in Alexandria, Egypt, that was also called Eleusis.

2. Andanian Mysteries. The Andanian mysteries are known from references in Pausanias and from the Rule of the Andanian mysteries, an inscription that may be dated to 92/91 B.C.E. Celebrated at Andania in the southwestern Peloponnesus, these mysteries were dedicated to several deities: Demeter, Hermes, Apollo Karneios, Hagna (Hagnē), and the great gods. According to the Andanian Rule, the epithet Hagna ("Holy One," "Pure One") designated a goddess (as well as a fountain) in the Andanian mysteries; later Pausanias understood Hagnē to be a title of Kore. The Rule of the Andanian mysteries is a public record of the regulations to be followed in the celebration of the mysteries. The Rule outlines in detail what must be attended to by participants in the mysteries (e.g., the oaths, the clothing, the processions, the tents, the funds, the sacrifices, the musicians, the sacred meal) and what penalties must be assessed for transgressions, but nothing forbidden is divulged by the Rule. Rather, the Rule discusses only the outward trappings of the mysteries, and employs deliberately cryptic phrases (e.g., "the things pertaining to the initiation") to refer to what must be kept secret.

3. Mysteries of Dionysos. The mysteries of Dionysos (or Bacchos) were remarkably diverse in character. Dionysos was the Greek god of fertility, animal maleness, wine, drama, and ecstasy, and his worshipers acknowledged his presence in the phallus set in the *liknon* (a winnowing basket sometimes used as a cradle), in the raw flesh of wild beasts, in the goblet of wine, in performance in the theater, and in spiritual bliss. As portrayed in Euripides' *Bacchae,* the archaic mysteries of Dionysos involved the female devotees of the god (i.e., Bacchae, also known as maenads, or women in a Dionysian frenzy) participating in the raw power of Dionysos by tenderly nursing wild animals or savagely tearing animals (and eventually the impious Pentheus himself) to pieces. According to Livy (39.8–19), the Roman Bacchanalia included sexual irregularities that prompted the Senate to adopt a decree, *Senatus Consultum de Bacchanalibus*. The famous frescoes in the Villa of the Mysteries at Pompeii employ a variety of Dionysian motifs in order to present what also may be interpreted as mysteries of sexuality, but here Dionysian sexuality takes on a more domesticated character. The Rule of the Iobacchoi records the regulations of an Athenian Bacchic club that enjoyed the Dionysian pleasures of eating, drinking, and dramatic performances. Among the Orphics the Dionysian practice of tearing flesh (Gk *sparagmos*) and devouring it raw (Gk *ōmophagia*) became the original transgression for those who wished to live a life of purity and thus to allow the soul to realize Dionysian bliss. An Orphic lamella from Thessaly presents the soul of a dead person professing the twofold nature of a person (i.e., earth, or Titanic flesh, and heaven, or the divine nature of Dionysos—cf. the view of Plato) but stressing the primacy of the divine: "I am a child of earth and of starry heaven, but my race is of heaven (alone)." Similar expressions are occasionally to be found in the highly syncretistic Orphic hymns (cf. hymn 13, "To Kronos").

C. Mystery Religions of Middle Eastern Origin

During the Hellenistic and Roman periods mystery religions originating in the Middle East became increasingly attractive to people of the Mediterranean world. Oftentimes colorful and exotic in their manifestations, these mystery religions derived, directly or indirectly, from Anatolia, Egypt, Persia, and Syria, and encouraged the worship of the Great Mother Kybele and her lover Attis, the Egyptian deities Isis and Osiris (or Sarapis), the Persian deity Mithras, and the Syrian goddess (cf. the Great Mother) and the slain youth Adonis.

1. Mysteries of the Great Mother and Attis. The Anatolian mysteries of the Great Mother (Magna Mater), often named Kybele (or Kybebe; in Latin, Cybele), are rooted in the fierce religious traditions of ancient Phrygia. In 204 B.C.E. the Anatolian goddess was formally welcomed into Rome, and thereafter the worship of the Great Mother was prominent in the Roman world. The mysteries of the Great Mother and her young paramour Attis were renowned for unusual festivals and flamboyant followers. The Christian poet Prudentius describes, with horror and disgust, the gory *taurobolium* (ritual slaughter of a bull), in which a person descended into a pit in order to be drenched with the blood of the sacrificed bull. An inscription dated to 376 C.E. states that a person who thus bathed in the bull's blood was "reborn for eternity" (Lat *in aeternum renatus*). The most spectacular followers of the Great Mother and Attis were the Galli, who imitated the mythological actions of Attis by castrating themselves, and then adopted transvestite practices appropriate for those who voluntarily had become eunuchs devoted to the Great Mother. According to rather late sources, during the springtime, a Roman festival in honor of the Great Mother and Attis commemorated the death of Attis in a dramatic fashion, and reaffirmed life and joy in a portion of the festival aptly named the Hilaria. The actual ceremonies of the mysteries of these Anatolian deities remain unknown, but a formula (termed a *symbolon* in Gk) cited by Clement of Alexandria (*Protr.* 2.15) provides enigmatic hints: "I have eaten from the drum (or, tambourine); I have drunk from the cymbal; I have carried the sacred dish; I have stolen into the inner chamber." Variant readings for this *symbolon* may be found in Firmicus Maternus (*Err. prof. rel.* 18.1).

2. Mysteries of Isis and Osiris. Although Egyptian "mysteries" of Isis and Osiris were celebrated in ancient Egypt at Abydos and other locales as mystery plays of succession and funerary rituals of mummification and burial, the Egyptian mystery religions themselves became established during Greco-Roman times. The goddess Isis was venerated throughout the Greco-Roman world, and those who revered her produced temples, statues, and paintings, and aretalogies on her behalf. Among the shrines of Isis is the well-preserved temple of Isis at Pompeii, with its sacred utensils, works of art, and adjacent shelter with Nile water for lustrations. The god Osiris, brother and lover of Isis and lord of the realm of death, also attracted many devotees, who sometimes worshiped him as Sarapis or Osiris-Apis (Osiris joined to the Apis bull). In book 11 of his *Metamorphoses* Apuleius portrayed his protagonist Lucius being saved and humanized by Isis, and initiated into her holy mysteries. The portrayal of the initiation of Lucius includes an account of the preliminary rituals as well as a guarded description of the secret ceremonies: "I approached the border of death. I trod the threshold of Proserpine and, borne through all the elements, I returned. At midnight I saw the sun shining brightly. I approached the gods below and the gods above, and in their presence I worshiped them." While the language Apuleius employs is deliberately vague, he does depict the experience of initiation as an experience of darkness, death, and perhaps also rebirth (cf. his use, elsewhere, of the Lat *renatus*, "reborn" or "born again").

3. Mysteries of Mithras. The Greco-Roman worship of Mithras derived from Persian sources, and retained certain Persian motifs, but the mysteries of Mithras are best understood as a Roman phenomenon that thrived in the Roman Empire from the 2d century C.E. on. (The earliest references to the Mithraic mysteries are to be found in Plutarch's account [*Pomp.* 24.1–8] of the Cilician raiders who celebrated secret rites of Mithras.) Men attracted to Mithras, particularly soldiers, sailors, and imperial officers, entered the Mithraea (sanctuaries of Mithras) in order to participate in initiatory rituals and other ceremonies. Tertullian enumerates lustrations, ordeals, and tests of valor in which initiates participated, and Justin Martyr refers to holy Mithraic meals in which initiates took bread and a cup of water (or a mixed cup of water and wine) and uttered certain formulae. Initiation into the mysteries of Mithras took place in progressive stages, and ordinarily seven stages are specified: raven (Lat *corax*), bridegroom (*nymphus;* alternately, occult, *cryphius*), soldier *(miles)*, lion *(leo)*, Persian *(Perses)*, courier of the sun *(heliodromus)*, and father *(pater)*. These seven stages may correspond with seven stations that decorate several Mithraea at Ostia Antica, and perhaps also with the seven gates of heaven (associated with the seven planets and seven metals) designated for the Mithraic ascent of the soul according to Celsus (in Origen, *c. Cels.* 6.22), as well as with the seven stages of ascent in the "Mithras Liturgy." Often richly decorated with works of art, Mithraea exhibited mythological, astronomical, and astrological imagery, and featured, in the apse of a typical Mithraeum, the figure of Mithras *tauroktonos,* Mithras slaying the bull. (On the possible astrological understanding of the figure of Mithras *tauroktonos,* see Ulansey 1989.) A brief inscription from the Mithraeum of Santa Prisca in Rome may provide a soteriological interpretation of the slaying of the bull: "And you [i.e., Mithras] have saved us, having shed eternal blood." Another inscription from the same Mithraeum describes Mithraic salvation as rebirth and creation, brought about through a sacred and perhaps sacramental repast: "one that is piously reborn (Lat *renatum*) and created *(creatum)* by sweet things."

D. Relationship to Early Christianity

Early Christianity emerged and developed within a religious context that included the mystery religions, and the early Church showed obvious similarities to the mysteries. Like the Greco-Roman mysteries, early Christianity was a religion of salvation and personal choice, and, like the devotees of the mysteries, Christian initiates underwent such ceremonial rituals as purification, fasting, and baptism in order to be admitted to the group. The Christian group itself was understood to be a new community of believers in which, ideally at least, "there is neither Jew nor Greek, there is neither slave nor free person, there is not male and female" (Gal 3:28). For Paul and many after Paul, Christian baptism was interpreted as a death experience (cf. Rom 6:3–4) that was linked to the experience of new life (understood apocalyptically by Paul). Entry into the Christian community allowed believers to share in a sacred meal, the Eucharist, which commemorated the death of Christ. By eating of the bread and drinking of the wine in the Eucharist, Christians participated in the passion of Christ, and assimilated the saving power of the Cross into their lives. Many early Christians claimed to realize their salvation through a transforming encounter with a dying and rising Christ, so that Paul could speak of living "in Christ" (Gk *en Christō*) and John could refer to being "born again" or "born from above" (Gk *gennēthē anōthen;* cf. John 3:3). Paul compared the mystery (cf. *mystērion,* 1 Cor 15:51) of the death and resurrection of people to the planting and sprouting of a seed (1 Cor 15:36–38) in a manner reminiscent of the Eleusinian mysteries. John incorporated a similar theme into the Fourth Gospel as a saying of Jesus (John 12:24). Further, John narrated the story of Jesus performing the "sign" of changing water to wine (John 2:1–11), a miracle commonly associated with Dionysos (e.g., see Pausanias, book 6: Elis 2, 26.1–2). Finally, the adoration of the Virgin Mary paralleled the forms of veneration traditionally reserved for the Egyptian goddess Isis. Like Isis, Mary was presented as a blessed mother who was acclaimed queen of heaven (Lat *regina caeli*) and was often portrayed with her son Jesus sitting formally on her lap just as Horus sits on the lap of Isis.

Ancient and modern interpreters have tried to account for these similarities between the mystery religions and early Christianity by proposing theories of dependence. Early Christian authors like Justin Martyr (*1 Apol.* 66.4; *Dial.* 70.1) and Tertullian (*De praescr. haeret.* 40) explained that similarities between Christianity and Mithraism were due to demonic imitation of true Christianity. Some modern scholars have tried to argue that the mystery religions and early Christianity were dependent upon each other, and that Christianity in particular borrowed substantially from the mysteries. Even in the early Church, Clement of Alexandria (*Protr.* 12.120) posited, in a somewhat similar vein, that Christianity is indeed a mystery religion with "truly sacred mysteries" that offer pure light and a vision of the only true God, but Clement sharply contrasted the Christian mysteries with what he judged to be shameless and corrupt Greco-Roman mystery religions.

The most balanced and judicious interpretation of the relationship between the mystery religions and early Christianity avoids simplistic conclusions about dependence, and acknowledges the parallel development of the mysteries and Christianity. To be sure, religions may appropriate themes from each other, and, given the syncretistic milieu of the Mediterranean world during late antiquity, it is quite possible that such a relationship may have existed between the mystery religions and early Christianity. It seems clear that from the 4th century C.E. on, Christianity adopted a significant number of non-Christian practices. Yet many of the points of resemblance between the mysteries and Christianity may be attributed to the fact that they responded in a similar fashion to the religious challenges of the Greco-Roman world. As Greco-Roman religions, the mysteries and early Christianity often addressed similar social and religious needs, and offered to devotees similar experiences, rituals, and ways of salvation and transformation.

Bibliography

General

Burkert, W. 1987. *Ancient Mystery Cults.* Cambridge, MA.

Campbell, J., ed. 1955. *The Mysteries.* Bollingen Series 30, Papers from the Eranos Yearbooks. Princeton.

Meyer, M. W., ed. 1987. *The Ancient Mysteries: A Sourcebook.* San Francisco.

Nock, A. D. 1963. *Conversion.* London.

———. 1972. *Essays on Religion and the Ancient World,* ed. Z. Stewart. 2 vols. Cambridge, MA.

Reitzenstein, R. 1978. *Hellenistic Mystery-Religions.* Pittsburgh Theological Monograph Series 18. Pittsburgh.

Greek Mystery Religions

Bianchi, U. 1976. *The Greek Mysteries.* Iconography of Religions: Greece and Rome 3. Leiden.

Dodds, E. R. 1951. *The Greeks and the Irrational.* Berkeley.

Guthrie, W. K. C. 1952. *Orpheus and Greek Religion.* 2d ed. London.

———. 1955. *The Greeks and their Gods.* Boston.

Kerényi, C. 1977. *Eleusis: Archetypal Image of Mother and Daughter.* New York.

Lehmann, K., ed. 1958. *Samothrace.* Bollingen Series 60. New York.

Mylonas, G. E. 1961. *Eleusis and the Eleusinian Mysteries.* Princeton.

Nilsson, M. P. 1961. *Geschichte der griechischen Religion.* HAW. Munich.

———. 1972. *Greek Folk Religion.* Philadelphia.

———. 1975. *The Dionysiac Mysteries of the Hellenistic and Roman Age.* New York.

Otto, W. F. 1965. *Dionysus: Myth and Cult.* Bloomington, IN.

Mystery Religions of Middle Eastern Origin
Bell, H. I. 1975. *Cults and Creeds in Graeco-Roman Egypt.* Chicago.
Cumont, F. 1896–99. *Textes et monuments figurés relatifs aux mystères de Mithra.* 2 vols. Brussels.
———. 1956. *The Oriental Religions in Roman Paganism.* New York.
Frazer, J. G. 1961. *Adonis, Attis, Osiris: Studies in the History of Oriental Religion.* Part 4 of *The Golden Bough.* New York.
Hinnells, J. R., ed. 1975. *Mithraic Studies.* 2 vols. Manchester.
Merkelbach, R. 1984. *Mithras.* Königstein/Ts.
Solmsen, F. 1979. *Isis Among the Greeks and Romans.* Martin Classical Lectures 25. Cambridge, MA.
Ulansey, D. 1989. *The Origins of the Mithraic Mysteries.* New York.
Vermaseren, M. J. 1956–60. *Corpus Inscriptionum et Monumentorum religionis Mithriacae.* 2 vols. The Hague.
———. 1977. *Cybele and Attis.* London.
Witt, R. E. 1971. *Isis in the Graeco-Roman World.* Ithaca, NY.

Relationship to Early Christianity
Anrich, G. 1894. *Das antike Mysterienwesen in seinem Einfluss auf das Christentum.* Göttingen.
Bousset, W. 1970. *Kyrios Christos.* Nashville.
Brown, R. E. 1968. *The Semitic Background of the Term "Mystery" in the New Testament.* Facet Books, Biblical Series 21. Philadelphia.
Hatch, E. 1957. *The Influence of Greek Ideas on Christianity.* New York.
Metzger, B. M. 1968. Methodology in the Study of the Mystery Religions and Early Christianity. Pp. 1–24 in *Historical and Literary Studies: Pagan, Jewish, and Christian.* NTTS 8. Leiden.
Nock, A. D. 1964. *Early Gentile Christianity and Its Hellenistic Background.* New York.
Smith, J. Z. 1990. *Drudgery Divine: On the Comparison of Early Christianities and the Religions of Late Antiquity.* Chicago Studies in the History of Judaism. Chicago.

Bibliographic Surveys
Epp, E. J. 1974. Mystery Religions of the Greco-Roman World. Pp. 355–74 in *Sourcebook of Texts for the Comparative Study of the Gospels,* ed. D. L. Dungan and D. R. Cartlidge. SBLSBS 1. Missoula, MT.
Metzger, B. M. 1984. A Classified Bibliography of the Graeco-Roman Mystery Religions 1924–1973 with a Supplement 1974–77. *ANRW* 2/17/3: 1259–1423.

MARVIN W. MEYER

MYSTICISM. Defined as "piety in so far as primary importance is attached to inner religious experience, to religion as occurring in the soul" (T. Andrae), or as "the sense of the presence of a being or reality through other means than the ordinary perceptive processes or the reason" (J. B. Pratt). W. James lists four characteristics of the mystical experience: ineffability, a noetic quality, transience, and passivity. In some cases the mystical experience leads to a sense of unification with the divine *(unio mystica)* or of loosing oneself into "the void" or "the infinite." In others there is an experience of intimate fellowship with God that leaves personality intact. Accompanying phenomena include visions, auditions, trances, and states of ecstasy.

Whether or not there is mysticism in the Bible is mainly a matter of definition. The personal concept of God in biblical religion does not allow for a sense of unification, which is more characteristic of pantheistic religions. There may, however, be indications of "milder" forms of mysticism in the Bible, even if we do not accept the wider definition of mysticism as "true personal religion."

Visions and auditions are reported by the OT prophets (Isaiah 6; Ezekiel 1–3; Micah ben Imlah 1 Kgs 22:19–23) though the question of prophetic ecstasy is debated. When the prophets speak in Yahweh's name, there is no identification with God on the part of the prophet, for the formula "Thus says Yahweh" is clearly a messenger's formula (Gen 32:4). Ezekiel's frequent use of "like" or "the likeness of" (esp. chap. 1) in the descriptions of his visions could be an indication of the ineffability of his experience (cf. Daniel 7, in which the use of "like" is a literary device). As far as the noetic aspect is concerned, the prophetic experience is certainly thought to mediate a specific kind of knowledge, though evidence does not permit a definite conclusion as to the exact character of the inspirational experience. In some cases the prophets may remain passive, while God speaks to them, but there are also cases when ecstasy is prompted by music (1 Sam 10:5) or when the prophet waits for a message (Hab 2:1; Isa 21:6). Mystics are often reported to quiver; there are also examples of anesthesia or paralysis. One can note Ezekiel's lying immovable for a considerable time (Ezek 4:4) or of passages such as Jer 4:19, which speaks of pain and anguish, but the reaction could just as well refer to the contents of his vision rather than being the result of a mystic experience (cf. Isa 21:3–4). On the whole, the prophets are never described as introspective, and they are always aware of the distance between them and Yahweh. Moreover, the biblical texts do not provide us with adequate information concerning the mental state of the prophets.

Franken (1954) finds examples of a mystical attitude in many of the Psalms. The psalmist stands silent, waiting for his God (Pss 37:7; 62:6), he "clings" to God (Ps 63:9), he cleaves to him in love (Ps 91:14). Many of the expressions referred to are connected with worship in the temple: the psalmist takes refuge in God (Pss 57:2; 61:5), he has sweet communion with him in his house (Ps 55:14). This is intense religious emotion, but there is no question of loosing oneself in God. There is "communion" but no mystical union with God. Medieval Christian mystics (e.g., Bernard of Clairvaux) used the love lyrics of the Song of Songs to describe the mystic's loving communion with God, but this represents an allegorical interpretation of texts that were likely meant to be taken literally and contain no mystical allusions.

In the NT Paul reports that he knows a man who had been caught up to paradise in the third heaven and heard unspeakable words that a man is not allowed to utter (2 Cor 12:2, 4). It is likely that this refers to some kind of mystical experience and possible that the unspeakable words allude to the ineffability of that experience (however, it could refer to the name of Yahweh, which should not be pronounced). Since Paul is markedly reticent about the details of his experience, even to the point of speaking about himself in the third person, it is impossible to draw any further conclusions.

Visions are mentioned several times in the NT, but nowhere do we get information that would enable us to describe them as mystical. Revelation seems to come closest to a mystical experience (1:10—"I was in the Spirit on the Lord's day"), but it is hard to ascertain how much of the text is based on literary convention. In any case it shows, as do some passages in Daniel, that such visionary experiences were regarded as possible and "normal" in such situations.

When Paul says, "it is no longer I who live, but Christ who lives in me" (Gal 2:20), this is not a description of a transient mystical experience of unification with Christ, but rather a statement of a sense of continuous communion. When the church is said to be the body of Christ and the Christians its limbs (1 Cor 12:27), the point is the various functions of those limbs, and not just a description of mystical unity (cf. Rom 12:4–5). Nor does Jesus' parable of the vine and the branches (John 15:1–8) contain any allusion to the individual's mystical unity with him.

Bibliography

Franken, H. H. 1954. *The Mystical Communion with JHWH in the Book of Psalms.* Leiden.

Lindblom, J. 1962. *Prophecy in Ancient Israel.* Oxford. Repr. 1978.

HELMER RINGGREN

MYTH AND MYTHOLOGY. This entry consists of three separate articles. The first addresses the question of what is meant by the term "mythology," and how scholars have come to apply this term to certain portions of biblical literature. The second entry focuses more specifically on an examination of the "mythic" elements of the OT. The third entry surveys mythology in the Greco-Roman world.

MYTHOLOGY

Parts of the Bible have been classified by many scholars as "mythology." There has been a great deal of debate among scholars concerning the definition of mythology and its role in ancient society and literature.

A. Mythology and Biblical Study
  1. 19th Century Beginnings
  2. David Friedrich Strauss
  3. The Century after Strauss
B. The Problem of Defining Myth
  1. Myths as Stories about the Gods
  2. Toward a More Adequate Definition
C. The Meanings and Functions of Myths
  1. Forerunners of Modern Explanations of Myth
  2. Myths, Like Science, are Attempts to Explain
  3. Myths are Expressions of the Mythopoeic Mind
  4. The Myth-Ritual Theory
  5. Myths and Society
  6. Myths and the Unconscious
  7. Structural Analysis
  8. Conclusions

A. Mythology and Biblical Study

1. 19th Century Beginnings. The critical study of myths, and the application of the fruits of this study to materials in both the Hebrew Bible and the NT, began long before the modern period. As early as the initial Christian centuries, the Church Fathers began both to denigrate other religions' myths as the result of the deification of ancient cultural heroes (see C.1 below) and to allegorize what might be seen as myths in the Bible. However, scholarly interest in mythology burgeoned dramatically during the course of the 19th century in Germany and then in Great Britain and elsewhere. Thus the scientific study of myths, including the possible presence of mythical materials in the Bible, is normally said to have begun in the 19th century.

There are several reasons for the notable increase in the attention paid to mythology in the 19th century, among scholars generally and among biblical scholars in particular. First, the Romantic movement's emphasis upon the imagination carried with it a resurgent interest in the earliest sources of humanity's poetic expressions, including above all early myths. Second, some initial results became available from the intense historical investigation of the Bible, which had begun in earnest in the 18th century and which would so dominate the 19th century that these hundred years are often called "the historical century." These results suggested that many of the stories we find in the Hebrew Bible and the NT are a result not of anything like eye-witness testimony but rather of a long process of community tradition. Since this same process is that which is responsible for the creation and preservation of myths, an obvious conclusion was that myths and biblical traditions might fruitfully be studied together. Finally, this same century witnessed the discovery of an increasing number of extrabiblical myths which were very similar to many biblical incidents. For example, by the final third of the 19th century scholars could read a Mesopotamian account of the Flood (now known to be a part of the composite Gilgamesh epic) which in its broad outlines was identical to the account related in Genesis 6–9. These discoveries would eventually force scholars to reconsider the relationship between mythology and biblical tradition.

2. David Friedrich Strauss. In 1835 D. F. Strauss (1808–74) published the first edition of his *Life of Jesus.* Identifying the mythical chiefly with the miraculous, Strauss undertook a comprehensive investigation into the origin of mythic materials in the gospel accounts of Jesus. He argued that the growth of traditions about Jesus was much like the growth of stories about any remarkable man: soon after the death of such a man, the historical gives way to the development of the legendary. Strauss concluded that a great many of the gospel stories—including not just the accounts of Jesus' birth, but also the stories about Jesus' baptism, about the call of the disciples, about various feeding and healing miracles—were mythical rather than historical.

For many readers, especially those unacquainted with the growing body of historical-critical inquiries into the Bible, Strauss' publication was their first introduction to the view that many biblical incidents were not historically "true," at least in the ordinary sense of the word. These readers were naturally shocked, indeed outraged, by the suggestion that the Bible rested upon myth rather than upon historical reality. The crisis which ensued had effects which lasted long after the early end of Strauss' own career as a scholar. These effects included an abiding hesitancy on the behalf of many biblical scholars to speak of the Bible and myth in the same breath, except to deny the presence of the latter in the former.

3. The Century after Strauss. For more than a hundred years after the furor which accompanied the publication of Strauss' *Life of Jesus,* the problem of mythology and the Bible ceased to exist in any significant way. This remained true despite the mounting number of extrabiblical myths with close or remote analogies to stories within the Hebrew Bible and the NT. Though the reasons for the cessation of sustained inquiry into the issue of mythology and the Bible are complex and include the memory of the fate of Strauss and his publication, the chief reason which was offered was simple and direct: there were no myths, at least complete myths, in the Bible. The refusal to label any significant biblical story as a myth was based upon the definition of myth which was accepted and repeated by most biblical scholars throughout this long period (see B below). This definition, made popular by the folklorists Jacob and Wilhelm Grimm in the first half of the 19th century, was that myths were stories about the gods. The key to this definition, upon which most students of biblical religion seized, is that the final word ("gods") is plural. Almost all scholars in the years following Strauss' explosive volume agreed that in order to qualify as a myth, a story had to recount the deeds of more than one deity. Since both the Hebrew Bible and the NT are testimonies to an evolving or an achieved monotheism, the conclusion reached was that there could be no stories about gods, and therefore no myths, in the Bible.

Although this general argument was repeated by almost every major biblical scholar throughout these years, an especially noteworthy and influential proponent was Hermann Gunkel (1862–1932). Gunkel, a member of the important History-of-Religions group of German biblical scholars and among the founders of form-criticism, shaped the study of the Hebrew Bible in the present century as fundamentally as any other single scholar. Fairly early in his career, Gunkel wrote a volume (1895) which utilized fully many of the recently discovered Near Eastern texts, from ancient Mesopotamia especially, and which demonstrated how much mythology lay behind the biblical view of the beginning and end of the world. Despite this demonstration, however, Gunkel continued to maintain, though not always with consistency (Rogerson 1974: 59–63), that the Hebrew Bible was essentially monotheistic and hence contained no complete myths. What we do find in the Hebrew Bible, he claimed, were "original myths" that have come into the Bible only "in comparatively faded colors"; for example, we have in Gen 6:1–4 (the story of the mating of divine beings with women) "nothing but a torso" of a once more elaborate myth (Gunkel 1964: 14–15). Since the religion of Israel "from its beginning tended toward monotheism," Gunkel continued, Israel preserved no myths because "for a story of the gods at least two gods are essential" (1964: 15).

Despite the great changes in the understanding of myth which obtained in such fields as anthropology, sociology, and psychology in the first half of the 20th century, the simple definition of myth as a story about the gods, and with this the denial of the presence of myths in the religion of Israel or in Christianity, continued to dominate biblical scholarship. This is easily documented by brief glances at the most widely utilized introductions to and theologies of the Hebrew Bible. Biblical introductions repeated until quite recently both the statements that myths assume a polytheistic background, hence that no complete myth plays a role in Israel's religion, and that what appear to be myths in the Hebrew Bible are only the fragments of myths borrowed from other Near Eastern cultures (Weiser 1961: 57–59; Eissfeldt 1965: 35–37; Fohrer 1968: 87). The authors of influential biblical theologies similarly relied upon this line of reasoning and then frequently went on to contrast the supposed cyclical, naturalistic, and mythical thinking of Egypt, Mesopotamia, and Canaan with the reputed linear, historical, and anti-mythical thinking of Israel (Wright 1952: 38–48, 125; von Rad *ROTT* 1: 27–28; 136–41; 2: 110–11, 349).

A signal that the century-long pause in addressing squarely the issue of mythology and the Bible was drawing to a close came with the demythologization program begun in the 1940s by the NT scholar Rudolf Bultmann (1884–1976). Bultmann began with an understanding of myth which was at once much broader than the definition used by other biblical scholars (myths are stories about the gods) and much more consistent with the definitions of myth utilized by anthropologists, historians of religion, and others. Myths, for Bultmann, are the ways in which a culture symbolizes and objectivizes its entire world view. The way in which almost all NT stories come to us is thus mythical: "the whole conception of the world which is presupposed in the preaching of Jesus as in the NT generally is mythological"; this conception includes that of a three-storied universe of heaven, hell, and earth, of the intervention of supernatural beings, and of miracles (Bultmann 1958: 15). The task of the 20th-century human seeking to appropriate the message of Jesus, then, becomes one not of dispensing with biblical mythology but rather of translating this mythology, which represents a worldview different from our own.

Bultmann, of course, created with his demythologizing program a controversy among scholars not unlike that prompted by Strauss a century before. Among the criticisms often voiced was that Bultmann simply substituted his own particular philosophical mythology for that of the NT. Still, the evidence is clear that however much many scholars wished to disagree with Bultmann, he had raised again an issue which had long been too easily side-stepped. That the issue of mythology and the Bible was ripe for more thorough investigation is indicated by the appearance of several studies in the 1950s which began to question the wisdom of the long dominant claim that there are no myths in the Bible. Thus, Davies followed Bultmann's lead in looking about at the understanding of myths in other academic disciplines. He concluded that "mythology is a way of thinking and of imagining about the divine rather than thinking and imagining about a number of gods" and thus that "the content of the myth, whether polytheistic or otherwise is accidental to the nature of myth" (Davies 1956: 88). This conclusion means, of course, that any definition of myth which limits myths to stories about gods is radically inadequate. At about the same time, McKenzie noted (1959: 267) that the definitions of myth utilized by contemporary students of this phenomenon meant that the old view that there were no myths in the Bible was simply untenable.

How far biblical scholarship was moving is plain in B. S.

Childs' important volume *Myth and Reality in the Old Testament* (1960). Although some of the statements in his study are not at great variance with those that had been made repeatedly during the previous century, Childs' understanding of myth is throughout informed by developments in other fields of inquiry. Noting the inadequacy of the long-regnant, narrow definition of myths as stories about the gods, Childs was among the first to observe that the real damage done by the continued reliance upon this definition, with its easy elimination of myth from the Bible, was the "tendency among those using this definition to fail to see the essential problem of myth in the Old Testament" (1960:15). Childs' study is largely devoted to the investigation of a number of biblical passages with identifiably mythical origins. In some of these passages (Gen 1:1–2), Childs finds the myth is still present, though in tension with an alternate view, while in other passages (Gen 6:1–4), he concludes that the original material has been demythologized. On the issue of mythical time, Childs rejects the cliché that Israel's neighbors thought cyclically while Israel thought linearly and concludes rather "the evidence of an *Urzeit-Endzeit* [Primeval Time–End Time] pattern within Israel is overwhelming" (1960: 76).

More conclusive proof yet of biblical scholarship's entrance into the wider realm of discussion about the origins and meanings of myth is F. M. Cross' *Canaanite Myth and Hebrew Epic* (1973). This study reflects a mature assessment of the importance of the Canaanite mythical materials unearthed at Ras Shamra in Syria in the late 1920s. These Ugaritic myths, as they are standardly called, demonstrate for Cross the bankruptcy of the position that Israel's religion is completely novel and discontinuous with Canaanite culture. Rather, the common pattern of Canaanite cosmogonic myths shows up repeatedly in biblical literature. This pattern is one of (1) a battle between a divine warrior and a chaotic sea god; (2) the victory of the divine warrior; and (3) the proclamation of this warrior as king with the completion of his sanctuary. The pattern corresponds to the structure of many biblical texts, sometimes in purely mythical form (Psalms 29, 89, and 93), sometimes in the form of a mixture of mythical and historical traditions (Psalm 77; Isa 51:9–11). The conclusion is thus that "in Israel, myth and history always stood in strong tension, myth serving primarily to give a cosmic dimension and transcendent meaning to the historical, rarely functioning to dissolve history" (*CMHE,* 90). Cross thus rejects the notion that we see in the Hebrew Bible either a gradual historicizing of myth or a mythologizing of history. Instead, both myth and history are present throughout. These conclusions mean, of course, that such issues as the relationship of myth to history or the origins, meaning, and functions of myth in general can return to the center of attention within biblical study.

B. The Problem of Defining Myth

In spite of the great attention devoted to mythology in the past two hundred years, nearly every student of this phenomenon laments the difficulty of formulating a truly adequate definition of myth. For example, Mircea Eliade, perhaps the 20th century's leading historian of religion, begins a volume devoted to myth with the admission that "it would be hard to find a definition of myth that would be acceptable to all scholars and at the same time intelligible to nonspecialists" (1963: 5). Closer still to desperation is J. Rogerson's statement that "finding an adequate and all-purpose definition of myth" remains an "impossible task" (1974: 173). This admitted difficulty has not prevented the appeareance of many studies, especially recently, attempting to formulate an adequate definition (Barr 1959; Bascom 1965; Rogerson 1978; Honko 1984; Kirk 1984).

1. Myths as Stories about the Gods. The Greek word from which comes our word "myth" originally meant simply "something said" or "something told," i.e., a story. Later in Greek tradition, the word came to mean a false story or a fabrication, a meaning our word "myth" still has in some contexts. When modern folklorists began to study myth, they utilized that definition made generally known by the Grimm brothers: a myth is a story about the gods.

This definition proved inadequate because it implied at once too much and too little. It implied too much in its suggestion that myths are limited to a polytheistic setting, thus removing from consideration any traditional stories told outside of such a setting. As the classicist G. S. Kirk observes, while some myths do treat the gods, others "are not primarily about gods at all, and have no ancillary implications of sanctity or tabu" (1984: 57). On the other hand, the definition implied too little. It was not sufficiently specific; some criteria were wanted beyond simply "a story" and "about the gods."

2. Toward a More Adequate Definition. Following upon the birth of both anthropology and the study of comparative religion at the end of the 19th century, a long series of definitions for myth were proposed as alternatives to the admittedly inadequate "myths are stories about the gods." A complete list of these definitions would be neither useful nor possible in the present context. But a selection of those proposed by some of the more influential students of myth might prove helpful in demonstrating both variety and continuity in the achievement of this important task of definition. The British anthropologist Sir James George Frazer (1854–1941), perhaps best known as the author of *The Golden Bough,* toward the end of his scholarly career defined myths as "mistaken explanations of phenomena, whether of human life or of external nature" (1921: xxvii). To Bronislaw Malinowski (1884–1942), who was among the first anthropologists to demand extensive field work as a prerequisite to reaching any conclusions about a given culture, a myth is "a pragmatic charter of primitive faith and moral wisdom" (1954b: 101). The definition in a standard dictionary of mythology published after World War II is as follows: a myth is "a story, presented as having actually occurred in a previous age, explaining the cosmological and supernatural traditions of a people, their gods, heroes, cultural traits, religious beliefs, etc." (*FWSDFML,* 778). Eliade, who admitted the problems inherent in any definition of myth, proposes that "myth narrates a sacred history; it relates an event that took place in primordial Time, the fabled time of 'beginnings'. . . . The actors in myths are Supernatural Beings" (1963: 5–6). The American biblical scholar T. H. Gaster suggests that a myth "may be defined as any presentation of the actual in terms of the ideal" (1954: 185). For the theologian P. Ricoeur myths are "traditional narratives which tell of events which happened at the origin of time and which furnish the support of language to ritual actions" (1969: 101). And W. Burkert, a prolific German scholar whose analyses of myths have found a wide audience of late, concludes that "myth is a traditional tale with secondary, partial reference to something of collective importance" (1979: 23).

Even though an initial reading of these selected definitions might suggest something like complete disagreement and hence chaos, there are in fact a number of elements which most of the definitions share. These elements are three, or perhaps four, in number. To qualify as a myth, scholars are beginning to agree, the material has to be (1) a story, and (2) traditional—that is, transmitted, usually orally, within a communal setting; further, these traditional stories must (3) deal with a character or characters who are more than merely human. In light of the apologetic use to which the older, 19th-century definition of myth was put (to deny the presence of myths in biblical text), note that this third criterion can be met by the presence of a single superhuman being in a tale. In addition, several of the above definitions suggest the addition of a final criterion, that myths (4) treat events in remote antiquity. That these three or four elements are the key criteria is indicated by the current definitions upon which many folklorists rely. A sample of two of these will demonstrate this: (1) "myths are prose narratives which, in the society in which they are told, are considered to be truthful accounts of what happened in the remote past. . . . their main characters are not usually human beings" (Bascom 1965: 4); and (2) myths are "the traditional tales of the deeds of *daimones:* gods, spirits, and all sorts of supernatural or superhuman beings" (Fontenrose 1966: 54–55). Because of its brevity and yet its conclusion of three of the criteria listed above, Fontenrose's definition is perhaps the most adequate and stands the greatest chance of commanding wide assent.

Under the heading of the definitional problems here, one additional issue requires treatment. This is the issue of the possible distinction between myths on the one hand and legends and folktales on the other. This has long been a matter of great interest to biblical scholarship; many scholars have argued, for example, that it is vital to see a particular story in the Bible as a legend or a saga rather than a myth. Regrettably, there is nothing like a consensus among current students of myth on this issue. Some folklorists find a clear distinction between myths, folktales (identified by folklorists with *Märchen* in German, *contes populaires* in French), and legends (German *Sagen,* French *traditions populaires*). The distinctions most often proposed are that folktales are regarded less seriously than are myths, and that legends are both set in a less remote era than are myths and deal solely with human characters (Bascom: 1965: 4, 16). Other scholars doubt that any such distinctions are at all useful or legitimate (Kirk 1970: 31–41; 1981: 55). Burkert, for example, argues that the distinction between myths and legends or sagas so favored by biblical scholars is purely a part of an apologetic tradition and will not stand up to the available evidence (1979: 24).

C. The Meanings and Functions of Myths

For a long time, the material in the Bible which scholars suggested might qualify as mythic and hence might correctly be subjected to mythical analysis was limited to those passages obviously borrowed from the collections of myths among Israel's Canaanite, Mesopotamian, and Egyptian neighbors. Hence, passages like Gen 6:1–4 (the mating of divine beings with humans), Gen 6:5–9:17 (the Flood Story), various references to cosmic mountains in Ezekiel and the Psalms, portraits of Yahweh in a divine-council setting (Psalm 82; 2 Kings 22), or allusions to a battle between Yahweh and a cosmic monster (Job) were identified as mythical in origin and then studied as myths.

The definition of myth utilized at present by the widest array of scholarly disciplines (see B above) suggests rather that a great deal of the material, not just selected borrowings, in both the Hebrew Bible and the NT qualifies as mythic. Of course, not all biblical scholars will agree with this. Some will want to continue to defend the traditional distinctions between myths, on the one hand, and legends or folktales, on the other. In any case, it is clear that much biblical material (1) is in story form, (2) shows the signs of traditional transmission in a communal setting, and (3) refers to a deity and/or supernatural beings. It thus satisfies the three criteria implicit in an adequate definition of myth.

The inclusion of many of the stories in the Bible within the category of myth means that a subject of great interest becomes that of the origins, meanings, and functions of myths. Several recent surveys of this subject are available (Cohen 1969; Kirk 1970; Rogerson 1974: 175–78; Burkert 1979; Segal 1980). The number of different categories of myths' meanings and functions is to some extent arbitrary. Here, six distinct categories are covered, following a brief account of older attempts to account for the meanings and functions of myths. Each of these six categories of mythic explanation will be briefly described, then followed with some account of the advantages and disadvantages of each.

1. Forerunners of Modern Explanations of Myth. From antiquity through the second third of the 19th century, a number of traditional accounts of the rise and meaning of myth were available. Probably the most popular of these was that which saw myths as originating in stories told about human heroes and kings. As these stories circulated among wider groups down through the years, the heroes and kings responsible for their origin became gradually deified. This account of myth is often labeled "Euhemerism." The label comes from the name of a 4th century B.C. geographer and novelist, Euhemerus of Messene. Euhemerus wrote, in Greek, a travel tale called *Sacred Scripture,* in which he told of a fanciful trip to an Indian Ocean island where he discovered that the gods worshiped in various religions were originally human heroes. Euhemerus' account was translated early into Latin and became an important source for early Christian writers who saw all pagan deities originating in this way. This Euhemeristic tradition certainly continues to flourish and many popular accounts of myth still rely upon it implicitly.

An immediate forerunner to those theories of myth still seen as of great value is the thesis of a German linguist who spent most of his career at Oxford, Friedrich Max Müller (1823–1900). His thesis began from the hypothesis that all European languages are the descendants of the language spoken by the Aryan invaders of India. This Aryan language was notable for its polyonymy (a single object designated by several names) and its homonymy (several objects designated by a single name). These characteristics, along with others such as gender endings, led to confusion at a later era when the language was no longer spoken and was replaced by the early versions of modern European languages. This confusion meant that common nouns were taken to be the names of deities and that originally straightforward descriptions of phenomena, especially the phenomena of nature, were wrongly taken to be stories about deities. These stories are, then, the original myths in Müller's view. Most of the stories are about nature, particularly about dawn and sunset; hence Müller's theory is often called that of "solar mythology."

Euhemerism and Müller's solar mythology are hardly the only models for the origin of myths prevalent before the end of the 19th century. They are, however, typical of many such models in that they attribute the origin of myth to some elementary confusion. In the case of Euhemerism, early people confused human heroes with deities. In the case of solar mythology, early people confused clear accounts of the workings of nature with dramatic narratives about the dealings of gods and goddesses. Few of the theories about myth which still find advocates today ascribe this sort of confusion to the makers of myth.

2. Myths, Like Science, are Attempts to Explain. A view of the origin of myth which still commands wide assent is that which compares myth with science and finds in both an expression of the human desire to explain puzzling phenomena. The only significant difference between the two is that myths come from an early stage in human development, while science comes from an advanced stage. Myths are thus immature science. Myths, in this view, thus meet an intellectual need, the need for explanation. For this reason, this theory is sometimes labeled the "intellectualist" theory.

One of the founders of modern anthropology, E. B. Tylor (1832–1917), was responsible for the fullest statement on behalf of the intellectualist theory (1871). Tylor was a cultural evolutionist who thought that the characteristics of primitive thought were evident in various "survivals" among modern humans. Tylor was also the chief architect of the notion that religion begins as "animism," the ascription of living souls *(anima)* to everything in nature. He thus felt himself able to construct a comprehensive history of human religious development. Though he argued that humans have developed, that we have abandoned the myth-making stage for the scientific stage, he also maintained that the human desire to know the causes of all phenomena has not changed. Hence, myths reflect both a particular stage in human development and the universal and continuing need for humans to explain things. An important implication of Tylor's theory is that, since myths are like science, myths are neither irrational nor illogical, though they may be wrong.

Tylor was not alone in holding this view in his era, nor has this view ceased to find advocates. Among Tylor's near contemporaries, Frazer held most centrally to this basic theory, though he also participated somewhat in the myth-ritual circle (C.4 below). It will be remembered that Frazer defined myths as "mistaken explanations of phenomena, whether of human life or of external nature" (1921: xxvii), a definition in complete accord with the Tylor intellectualist tradition. Though this tradition has never disappeared from the scholarly scene, it has been revived with enthusiasm of late by several anthropologists. R. Horton, for example, argues (1967) that traditional thought in Africa uses the same theoretical models, if different language, as does modern science.

The chief advantage of the Tylorean intellectualist theory is that it does give so-called "primitives" credit for thinking. Unlike other theories according to which early humans cannot and/or do not think logically and rationally, according to this theory early humans are driven by the same intellectual needs and possess the same intellectual equipment as moderns. Secondly, the theory does accord with the literal, narrative level of many myths. Perhaps the majority of myths, and certainly the etiological aspects of all myths, claim to explain things. Tylor's intellectualist view takes these claims seriously.

This theory also seems to possess some disadvantages. Even though it credits primitives with thinking, it is based upon an evolutionary model which sees primitives as ignorant and wrong. Much anthropological field work in the present century disputes this view. Malinowski, for example, found so-called "savages" fully as scientific as 20th-century Europeans "if by science be understood a body of rules and conceptions, embodied in material achievements and in a fixed form of tradition and carried on by some sort of social organization" (1954a: 34). Secondly, the theory of Tylor seems unable to account for the demonstrable fact that myths are a social phenomenon. If myths are purely a result of the innate human desire to seek explanations, then why should they not remain individual and private?

3. Myths are Expressions of the Mythopoeic Mind. Another explanation of the meaning and function of myths is that which sees them as primarily expressive, rather than explanatory, and as a product of a kind of thinking called "mythopoeic." Mythopoeic thought, according to those who find this concept accurate and useful, is not so much an earlier stage of modern thought, as mythical thinking was for Tylor. It is instead a different kind of thought altogether. Mythopoeic thought works expressively, mystically, and poetically. Such thought seeks to participate with phenomena, not explain them.

For much of his career, the French anthropologist Lucien Lévy-Bruhl (1857–1939) defended the concept of mythopoeic thought and ascribed to it the origin of myths (1923; 1925). Lévy-Bruhl sometimes used the adjective "pre-logical" to describe this mode of thought. By "prelogical," he did not mean that primitive peoples were incapable of thinking logically but that they did not do so (Segal 1980: 24–25). Rather than thinking logically, such peoples, argued Lévy-Bruhl, thought mystically and made no distinctions between the physical or the material and all other realms of experience. They thus did not explain with reference to natural causation. They rather expressed themselves in myths, which reflected their urge to participate in everything around them.

Even though anthropologists, especially those with some field work experience, have been most reluctant to adopt this theory, which does not seem to describe the thought of the peoples they have studied, and even though Lévy-Bruhl himself renounced his view toward the end of his life, this theory has found a wide hearing among many literary critics, philosophers, and biblical scholars. Biblical scholars appear to rely chiefly upon the work of E. Cassirer for their notion of mythopoeic thought. Cassirer, like the early Lévy-Bruhl, sought the key to understanding myths in the distinctive sort of thinking which he found to produce myths (1923–31). This sort of thinking was antiempirical, and quite different from scientific thought. The influence of both Lévy-Bruhl and Cassirer is particularly evident in an often cited article by H. and H. A. Frankfort, written as the first chapter in a volume about ancient Near Eastern thought (1946). For the Frankforts, ancient mythical thought does not distinguish between subject and object, as does scientific thought. Instead, mythopoeic thought addresses the world as "thou," and participates with this world rather than seeking to analyze it (Frankfort 1946: 4–6). "Primitive thought," the Frankforts maintain, "cannot recognize our view of an impersonal, mechanical, and lawlike functioning of causality" (1946: 15).

An advantage of the theory that myths stem from mythopoeic thought is that it recognizes the special and distinctive character of myths. Unfortunately, this view has seemed to have little more to recommend it. Most scholars who have lived among "primitive" communities have found little evidence there for wholesale thinking of a different sort from that which typifies modern groups. The evidence rather suggests that both some primitives and some moderns think more emotionally, expressively, poetically, and illogically than do other primitives and other moderns. The division, that is, is one within each group, not between primitive peoples on the one hand and modern groups on the other. Early in his study of Greek mythology, Burkert suggests we dispose of "the nostalgic idea of a golden age when a race of poetically minded primitives uttered myths instead of plain speech" (1979: 24). Kirk's summary critique of the theory of mythopoeic thought is similarly harsh but reflects fairly the general assessment today: "the polarization between fully rational thought (which is usually held to begin, in the Western tradition, at some time after Thales) and non-rational or 'mythopoeic' thought is logically indefensible and historically absurd" (1984: 58–59).

4. The Myth-Ritual Theory. According to this theory, myths are always to be studied together with the rituals which accompany them. This is so because myth and ritual are two parts of a single phenomenon: myths are the spoken counterpart to that which is being performed. This theory is also sometimes called "patternism" because several of its advocates have claimed to have discerned a pattern, in many Greek and Near Eastern myths and rituals, of (1) conflict, (2) death or disaster, (3) lamentation, and (4) rebirth.

The myth-ritual view stems most directly from the statements of the great Scottish scholar William Robertson Smith (1846–94). Smith began his career as a biblical scholar, but then was removed from his position as a professor at the Free Church College, Aberdeen, largely for making popularly available the conclusions of German biblical scholarship. In his lectures on Semitic religion, Smith said, "It may be affirmed with confidence that in almost every case the myth was derived from the ritual, and not the ritual from the myth" (1927: 18). This statement represents what has been called the "boldest" of the myth-ritual positions: the statement asserts not just that myths ought to be studied together with rituals; rather, all myths originate as rituals. Many other myth-ritualists hold a more moderate position, arguing not that all myths started their lives as rituals, but rather that myths and rituals generally belong together in religious life and hence are to be discussed as one.

Taking their lead from Robertson Smith, a group of classicists and anthropologists, chiefly at Cambridge University, offered a total view of myth based upon the presupposition that myths belong with rituals. These included Jane Harrison (1850–1920), Frazer in part (Ackerman 1975), F. M. Cornford (1874–1943), A. B. Cook (1868–1952), G. Murray (1866–1957) and others, a group sometimes called the Cambridge school of myth-ritualists. Their study of myth persuaded them that a basic myth-ritual pattern was very widespread in Mediterranean antiquity and lay behind the structure of Greek drama. They also went further afield, to ancient Mesopotamia, where they read the Babylonian creation myth *(Enuma Elish)* as the "libretto" to the spring New Year "Akitu Festival." This group of scholars thought they had found in Enuma Elish and the festival to which they argued it was attached a pattern: (1) A king, acting the part of a deity, fights with a chaotic monster, (2) is defeated, (3) is mourned, but then (4) rises again.

In either its bolder (all myths originate as rituals) or more modified (myths usually accompany rituals) forms, the myth-ritual theory was long of great importance in biblical scholarship. The list of major scholars influenced by myth-ritualism is long and includes such names as S. Mowinckel, I. Engnell, A. R. Johnson, and many others. But the two most ardent advocates of the position are perhaps S. H. Hooke and T. H. Gaster. Hooke edited several volumes, for which he also wrote introductory essays, outlining the myth-ritual pattern and then applying it to a variety of biblical texts (1933). Gaster found particularly supportive evidence for a myth-ritual position in the Ugaritic texts from ancient Syria. The thesis of several of his publications is that ancient Near Eastern myths reflect "a pattern and a sequence of ritual acts which, from time immemorial, have characterized major seasonal festivals in most parts of the world" (1977: 12). This pattern Gaster detected in several Psalms (Psalms 29, 89, 93, 97, 99), as well as elsewhere in the Hebrew Bible. Though Gaster insistently claimed that he was defending only the more moderate myth-ritual position (that we view myth and ritual together as one thing), both his definition of myth as something which parallels a ritual, and his scheme according to which myths begin as accompaniments to rituals but are later separated from this context (1954: 185–203), suggest perhaps the strongest of the myth-ritual positions.

Unlike the theory which anchors myths in a hypothesized sort of mythopoeic thinking, the myth-ritual position has several advantages and continues to find ready support. Initially, it is undeniable that many myths do accompany rituals. This seems especially true of several Canaanite or Ugaritic myths, which formed a part of the culture out of which early Israel emerged. Secondly, this position possesses the advantage of placing myths in an authentic, "lived" religious setting. As such, it is a good counter to any theories which abstract myths out of the group experiences in which myths are formed and continue to survive.

Still, the myth-ritual theory, like all those offered by students of myth over the past century, runs into several problems (Fontenrose 1966; Kirk 1970: 12–31; *CMHE,* 82–83). If it is undeniable that many myths do accompany rituals, it is also the case that some do not. In some cultures, it appears that no myths are connected with rituals. Frazer himself, who sometimes spoke as a myth-ritualist, noted late in his career that the number of myths directly tied to rituals is "almost infinitesimally small, by comparison with myths which deal with other subjects and have had another origin" (1921: xxviii, n. 1). Moreover, the key examples so favored by the early myth-ritualists and their followers among biblical scholars—the Babylonian Akitu Festival and *Enuma Elish,* and the tales of Attis, Osiris, and Adonis—all turn out to be examples supportive of myth-ritual conclusions only if one utilizes very late and unreliable evidence (Burkert 1979: 100–1). Finally, to explain myths by asserting that they originate as rituals can be seen as a failure to offer any explanation at all (Kirk 1970: 17–19). If myths do originate as rituals, then we require an ensuing explanation of the meanings and functions of ritual; and this has not always been forthcoming.

5. Myths and Society. Another theory of continuing persuasiveness looks first and foremost to the social setting of myths. All of the most adequate definitions of myth offered in the 20th century stress that myths are *traditional* stories, that is, that they originate and are transmitted in a communal context. The theory under consideration here argues that the function of myth is precisely to cement social bonds, to bring together disparate people as a group, and then to support these peoples' group identity.

Once again, this theory can be traced most directly to Robertson Smith. That which Smith found absent from previous discussions of religion was the awareness of religion's social dimension. He then argued, for example, that sacrifices were originally meals shared between a religious community and its deity or deities; these sacrifices thus functioned to cement social bonds. What was true of sacrifice was true generally. Hence, Smith's famous and enormously influential statement that early "religions did not exist for the saving of souls but for the preservation and welfare of society" (1927: 29). The French sociologist Emile Durkheim (1858–1917) acknowledged his debt to Robertson Smith in shaping this idea into a general account of religion. Durkheim thus viewed myths as a means by which "the group periodically renews the sentiment which it has of itself and of its unity; at the same time, individuals are strengthened in their social natures" (1915: 420).

Though many scholars could be cited as among those who developed the implications of what Robertson Smith and Durkheim had concluded about the social function of myths, none did so more powerfully than Malinowski. It will be recalled that Malinowski devoted several years of his life to field work in the southwest Pacific and saw such experience as crucial preparation for any generalizations about culture. His own experience convinced Malinowski that myths are not speculative or symbolic abstractions. Myths rather perform emphatically practical functions. "Myth," Malinowski determined, "performs in primitive culture an indispensable function: it expresses, enhances, and codifies belief; it safeguards and enforces morality." A myth is therefore "not an intellectual explanation or an artistic imagery, but a pragmatic charter of primitive faith and moral wisdom" (Malinowski 1954b: 101).

Given Malinowski's frequent appeal to the practical function of myths as charters for social behaviour, this theory of myth is often called "functionalism" or "the charter theory." Although biblical scholarship rarely refers explicitly to either Malinowski or to the concept of functionalism in mythic interpretation, this particular theory of myth has been widely utilized in the study of the religion of Israel. Whenever we read that a particular biblical story is a model for Israelite behavior or that another story serves to give the nation a sense of identity over against other groups, standing implicitly and perhaps unconsciously behind such statements is a functional theory of mythology. Similarly, the recent return to an interest in the social background of the religion of Israel—the social context of those responsible for the creation of the Israelite nation, the social setting of the Israelite prophets, etc.—assumes that most biblical texts yield an accurate, mirror reflection of group identities. This assumption stands or falls with the critical assessment of the social model for myths.

Like the myth-ritual theory, the social context theory has the advantage of taking into consideration the actual, empirical conditions under which myths are transmitted. The theory has thus had a great deal of appeal to ethnologists, who have repeatedly argued that only "armchair" anthropologists like Tylor or Frazer could fail to see the centrality of myths' social functions. Secondly, at least on the literal, surface level, many myths are most economically interpreted as charters for socially beneficial behavior. The social context theory proposes that we take this literal level seriously.

Despite this theory's obvious strengths and its continued usefulness in many areas of inquiry, it is not without disadvantages as well. First, the theory has difficulty accounting for the presence of the unusual, the bizarre, or the fantastic in myths (e.g., humans transforming themselves into plants or animals; heroes dismembered and then reassembled; nonhuman beings who speak; people transported vast distances in a flash; etc.). What possible purpose in the interest of group identity and unity can such elements perform? Related to this objection is that which observes that there is much in many myths which appears socially disruptive. Any list of the chief themes in world mythology would have to include incest, murder, cheating, and other similar themes; and these acts are frequently performed by the hero of the myth. How can we see such themes serving as charters for socially beneficial behavior? Thirdly, and most importantly, the functionalist theory of myth has to assume throughout a one-for-one correspondence between empirical social conditions and those social conditions which appear in myths. Though ethnographic research sometimes demonstrates that there is such a correspondence, this research also shows that often many aspects of the society in which the myth lives are nothing like the society depicted in the myth and never have been (Oden 1979–80). It seems particularly important for biblical scholars interested in the social context of Israelite religion as reconstructed from biblical narratives to take into account this objection.

6. Myths and the Unconscious. In several ways, this theory of the origin and meaning of myths is the psychological equivalent to the social theory described immediately above. As the latter theory posits that myths function to fulfill social needs, this theory posits that myths function to fulfill individual, psychological needs. In its various forms, this view begins by presupposing the existence of an unconscious. The human unconscious then needs expression; and the origin and meaning of any myth is to be sought in this need.

There are two chief versions of this psychological theory. The first is that of Sigmund Freud (1856–1939), whose name is synonymous with the birth and impact of modern psychology. For Freud, the human unconscious is a repository of various instinctive drives. These drives include especially sexuality, but also various agressive urges. These drives need expression. However, for anyone to act directly in response to these drives would be enormously disruptive, indeed chaotic. Hence, myths function to express imaginatively what normal humans cannot express in conduct. Myths are thus very much like dreams: both myths and dreams function to release the tension created by the impossibility of acting continually and directly in response to unconscious drives.

A second version of the psychological theory is that associated above all with Carl Jung (1875–1961), who was for some time an associate of Freud. Jung, too, begins by presupposing the existence of an unconscious. However, for Jung this unconscious is also collective, not solely individual, and the unconscious yields not so much aggressive drives as it does a kind of spiritual drive for meaning (Segal 1980: 12). Like Freud's, Jung's research is partly based upon the study of dreams. But Jung's research into dreams and myths convinced him that the same symbolic representations appear in both, and hence "that we must be dealing with 'autochthonous' revivals independent of all tradition." These " 'myth-forming' structural elements" Jung labeled "archetypes" (1969: 71–72). Given that myths come from the unconscious, which is not fully rational, Jung is not willing to endorse a rational or logical investigation into the meaning of myths. Myths simply express the collective unconscious; no more needs to be or can be said about their meaning.

An initial strength of the psychological theory of myth is that it offers one explanation for the universality of myths. Why is it that in every culture, at least in some stage of that culture's development and perhaps at every stage, we find myths? And why is the shape of many of these myths from disparate areas of the world quite similar? Freud and Jung have a ready answer to such questions: myths appear everywhere and mythic themes are similar precisely because all humans have an unconscious. Secondly, this theory offers a powerful account for the strength of myths. People often feel very strongly about their myths and are willing to defend them at great length. The psychological theory accounts for this strength by locating the drive behind myth in human instinct.

This theory, too, possesses its share of problems. First, the theory is difficult either to prove or to falsify. The evidence for its correctness is the human unconscious; and this remains a posited realm, one not open to the kinds of empirical investigation upon which scholarship depends. Secondly, Jung especially, along with some of his followers, makes a great deal of the universal nature of the dream- and myth-symbols he discusses. Further research has indicated that many of these symbols are nothing like universal. They are rather limited to a quite narrow stratum of Western thought; and even within this stratum, the symbols prove to be less widespread than Jung and his followers believed. Thirdly, and related to the second objection, the psychological theory leaves little room for the kind of cultural relativism that much 20th-century ethnographic research has claimed to discover (Dundes 1984: 270). Psychological theories tend to deal in "universals"; many historians, anthropologists, and others dispute the existence or usefulness of universals when dealing with the great variety of human cultures.

7. Structural Analysis. A final theory for the meaning and function of myth is structural analysis. It is almost wholly the result of the investigations of a single scholar, the French anthropologist Claude Lévi-Strauss. Structural analysis as practiced by Lévi-Strauss "contains the one important new idea in this field since Freud" (Kirk 1970: v–vi). Precisely because of its novelty, this theory is also controversial, and requires somewhat more elaborate description. Some scholars find the theory difficult to understand or to put into practice. Others claim to understand Lévi-Strauss but disagree vehemently with his presuppositions and results. Still others find it the single soundest approach to myth available.

The two phenomena to which Lévi-Strauss most often compares myth are language itself and music. The first of these comparisons suggests to him that linguistics might provide the key to understanding myth. What modern linguistics has demonstrated, according to Lévi-Strauss, is that meaning is produced by relationships, not by essences. That is, phonemes (the basic sound units in language) mean nothing in and of themselves. Phonemes only produce meaning in their interrelationships with one another. The same is true, Lévi-Strauss suggests, of the elements in myths. These mythic elements, "mythemes," mean nothing in and of themselves. They rather produce meaning by the structure of their relationships with one another—hence the reason for calling this theory "structuralism." For example, one cannot ask: "What does the moon or a freshwater deity mean in this myth?" One can only ask: "How are the various elements in the myth related to one another, and where else do we find the same or opposite relationships in the culture that produced this myth?"

This means, of course, that the plot-line of a myth is something to be little heeded. The narrative flow of a myth is rather an instance of the deceptive nature of appearances. Lévi-Strauss compares the study of myth with the study of geology, because in both apparent reality is not true reality. The surface appearance of geological phenomena is deceptive; and the truth is often the contrary of what appears. The same is true, Lévi-Strauss maintains, of myths' surface structure or narrative level.

Hence, myths require "decoding" and this process of decoding requires that the student of a culture's myths read and analyze *all* of that culture's myths. Just as a single mythical element means nothing by itself, so too a single myth acquires meaning only when compared with many additional myths. This aspect of structural analysis is particularly well illustrated by Lévi-Strauss' analysis of the Tsimshian Indian (from British Columbia) myth of "Asdiwal" (1976: 146–97), an analysis which many scholars agree is the most successful and persuasive single study by Lévi-Strauss. About halfway through this study, Lévi-Strauss states "having separated out the codes, we have analyzed the structure of the message. It now remains to decipher the meaning" (1976: 165). In order to "decipher the meaning," Lévi-Strauss turns to a summary of a number of additional myths from the same Tsimshian culture.

If these procedures describe how we ought to study myths, what is it that myths do for humans? Lévi-Strauss' most often cited answer to this question is the following: "the purpose of myth is to provide a logical model capable of over-coming a contradiction (an impossible achievement if, as it happens, the contradiction is real)" (1963: 229). What is particularly noteworthy in this answer is the phrase "logical model." This means that for the first time since Tylor, a theorist has suggested that the chief function of myth is an intellectual or logical, rather than an emotional, psychological, or social, task. At the same time, however, Lévi-Strauss refers constantly to ethnographic information about a culture's social structure, because he finds here other instances of the same structural relationships which appear in myths.

The contradiction which myth seeks to surmount is very often in Lévi-Strauss' investigations that between nature and culture—i.e., the fact that humans perceive that they are of nature like all other animals and yet they speak and create their own worlds in a way that animals do not. This basic contradiction is often played out in a group of myths through a series of binary, symbolic pairs. Thus, a myth which speaks of north and south, women and men, upriver and downriver, etc., may actually be using these terms as codes for a more universal contradiction.

There have been a number of biblical studies in the past decade which label themselves "structural" studies. The great majority of these follow a mode of literary structuralism which is far removed from the structural study of myth inaugurated by Lévi-Strauss. Only studies which refer to some series of structures in a culture, like the structure of kinship relationships, in addition to those discovered in a body of myths really fall into the category of the structural analysis suggested as a means to study myths. Though there are a few instances of this kind of analysis applied to biblical and other Near Eastern myths (Oden 1979; 1983), most scholars have provisionally concluded that too little ethnographic data is available from either ancient Israel or the social world of early Christianity to allow for a meaningful structural analysis.

One strength of structural analysis as practiced by Lévi-Strauss is that it represents such a departure from the various theories utilized previously. Its novelty has created a great interest in both the theoretical and the practical aspects of the study of myth, an interest unparalleled since the turn from the 19th to the 20th century. Second, for the first time since Tylor, this theory regards seriously the thinking of so-called "primitives" or "savages." Lévi-Strauss repeatedly tries to demonstrate that these groups possess intellects every bit as advanced and logical as do modern societies. In this sense, structural analysis is the precise contrary to the theory of mythopoeic thought. Third, Lévi-Strauss has affirmed the necessity of studying all of a culture's myths. This has meant that he and others have begun to read and think about myths long neglected as of peripheral significance. And finally, structural analysis has appeared to produce significant results for some mythical collections. Many of the South American myths studied by Lévi-Strauss, for example, no longer seem as chaotic and nonsensical as they once did.

This final theory is again heir to a number of potential weaknesses. Like the psychological theory, structural analysis has seemed to many scholars difficult either to falsify or to prove true. Since many of the myths refer to other myths, and since Lévi-Strauss has said that myths in the end "signify the mind that evolves them" (1975: 341), we are left, as with the psychological theory, with reference to something beyond empirical testing. Secondly, it may be the case that the linguistic analogies Lévi-Strauss utilizes are at fault, that linguistics does not prove that all meaning is produced by relationships as he has argued. Thirdly, Lévi-Strauss proposes to bypass the narrative level of myths. Yet an element common to almost every single definition of myth is the element of narrative. If the narrative level is so vital that it serves partially to define myth, then how can one ignore it in mythical analysis? Finally, a number of scholars, including especially biblical scholars, have found structural analysis dangerously ahistorical. Lévi-Strauss takes little account of the differences introduced into myths by their historical transmission. It is possible that an answer to this objection may result from the work of Burkert, who combines structural analysis with an awareness that any myth "bears the marks of its history, of multiple levels of application and crystallization" (1979: 27).

8. Conclusions. In 1921, Frazer (xxvi) condemned a particular theory of myth on the ground that it suffered "from the vice inherent in all systems which would explain the infinite multiplicity and diversity of phenomena by a single principle, as if a single clue, like Ariadne's thread, could guide us to the heart of this labyrinthine universe." Frazer's objection is a particularly effective, even poetic, statement of what many students of the myths in the Hebrew Bible and the NT might say about the various theories of myth now available. Not all these theories can be utilized at once, simply because some flatly contradict others. And new evidence has yielded the conclusion that some theories are beyond repair (a good example is that based on the supposition of a special sort of mythopoeic thinking). Still, central elements in several of the theories summarized above have stood up remarkably well to repeated critical inquiry and can easily be combined with elements from quite different theories to produce a rich synthesis. It is precisely such a synthesis which intrigues the student of mythology with the promise of reaching important new conclusions.

For example, though the evolutionary aspects of the intellectualist model associated in origin with the name of Tylor must be jettisoned, Tylor's insistent emphasis upon the human need for intellectually satisfying explanations is very much in accord both with recent ethnographic investigation and with the foundations of structuralism. The tellers of ancient myths appear to have been as reluctant to allow apparent contradictions to go unexplored as is any modern scientist. Any who propose to explain a body of myths while ignoring this human need for logically satisfying explanation do so at their own peril. So too, though the generalizing excesses of myth-ritualism are patent, the discovery that some myths are related to rituals remains an important one. Certainly, myth-ritualism can be applied only to those myths whose relationship to rituals is beyond reasonable dispute; and, as certainly, the myth-ritual mode of analysis must be founded upon a coherent and sustainable theory of the meanings and functions of ritual. But if these two criteria are met, there is no reason why this theory, too, cannot be combined in a controlled fashion with elements from other theories.

Those students of myth who urged that attention be paid to the social role of myths represent another instance of a significant discovery which has been modified but hardly discarded by more recent investigators. Myths' communal origin and transmission demand that any analysis of them heed their relationship to their social setting. The chief caution here is that future work cannot ignore the evidence that demonstrates that there is very often nothing like a one-for-one relationship between social structures as portrayed in myths and the empirical social structures of the society which produced and repeated the myths. A highly structured and hierarchical society, for example, can produce myths portraying a quite unhierarchical, egalitarian social background; and the opposite (an egalitarian society whose myths portray a hierarchical social setting) can also be true. There is surely a relationship between myths and society; but this relationship is nothing if not complex.

Finally, structuralism, too, has encountered heated objections but none which demands that we ignore all of the results which Lévi-Strauss claims to have attained. Investigators today are much less willing to select a few myths and grant to these selected few a kind of privileged status than was possible before the advent of structuralism. Structural analysis asks that we ignore no myth in a given culture and no element in a given corpus of myths, however bizarre or opaque such myths or mythical elements may appear. The results of such renewed attention to previously side-stepped materials cannot help but produce new insights, even if these insights demand some reformulation of structuralism's own foundations. This will be especially true in the realm of history, where the effects of the transmission of myths through time will have to be compared with the alleged stability of basic mythic structures.

In all these areas, then, a century's reflection and discovery have refined the basic insights of a number of originally quite separate models for the meaning and function of myth. The careful utilization of aspects of each of these theories, in their present refined state, is that upon which future work will build.

Bibliography

Ackerman, R. 1975. Frazer on Myth and Ritual. *Journal of the History of Ideas.* 36: 115–34.

Barr, J. 1959. The Meaning of 'Mythology' in Relation to the Old Testament. *VT* 9: 1–10.

Bascom, W. 1965. The Forms of Folklore: Prose Narratives. *Journal of American Folklore* 78: 3–20.

Bultmann, R. 1958. *Jesus Christ and Mythology.* New York.

Burkert, W. 1979. *Structure and History in Greek Mythology.* Berkeley.

Cassirer, E. 1923–31. *Philosophie der symbolischen Formen.* 2 vols. Berlin.

Childs, B. S. 1960. *Myth and Reality in the Old Testament.* SBT 27. Naperville, Il.

Cohen, P. S. 1969. Theories of Myth. *Man* n.s. 4: 337–53.

Davies, G. H. 1956. An Approach to the Problem of Old Testament Mythology. *PEQ* 88: 83–91.

Dundes, A. 1984. *Sacred Narrative, Readings in the Theory of Myth.* Berkeley.

Durkheim, E. 1915. *The Elementary Forms of the Religious Life.* Trans. J. W. Swain. London.

Eissfeldt, O. 1965. *The Old Testament: An Introduction.* Trans. P. R. Ackroyd. New York.

Eliade, M. 1963. *Myth and Reality.* Trans. W. R. Trask. New York.

———. 1969. *The Quest: History and Meaning in Religion.* Chicago.

Fohrer, G. 1968. *Introduction to the Old Testament.* Trans. D. E. Green. Nashville.

Fontenrose, J. 1966. *The Ritual Theory of Myth.* University of California Folklore Studies 18. Berkeley.

Frankfort, H., and Frankfort, H. A. 1946. Myth and Reality. Pp. 3–27 in *The Intellectual Adventure of Ancient Man,* ed. H. Frankfort et al. Chicago.

Frazer, J. G. 1911–15. *The Golden Bough: A Study in Magic and Religion.* 3d ed. 12 vols. London.

———. 1921. *Apollodorus: The Library.* LCL. London.

Gaster, T. H. 1954. Myth and Story. *Numen* 1: 184–212.

———. 1977. *Thespis: Ritual, Myth, and Drama in the Ancient Near East.* New York.

Gunkel, H. 1895. *Schöpfung und Chaos in Urzeit und Endzeit: Eine religionsgeschichtliche Untersuchung über Gen 1 und Ap Joh 12.* Göttingen.

———. 1964. *The Legends of Genesis: The Biblical Saga and History.* Trans. W. H. Carruth. New York.

Honko, L. 1984. The Problem of Defining Myth. Pp. 41–52 in Dundes 1984.

Hooke, S. H. 1933. The Myth and Ritual Pattern of the Ancient East. Pp. 1–14 in *Myth and Ritual: Essays on the Myth and Ritual of the Hebrews in Relation to the Culture Pattern of the Ancient East,* ed. S. H. Hooke. London.

Horton, R. 1967. African Traditional Thought and Western Science. *Africa* 37: 50–71, 155–87.

Jung, C. G. 1969. The Psychology of the Child Archetype. Pp. 70–100 in *Essays on a Science of Mythology,* by C. G. Jung and C. Kerényi. Trans. R. F. C. Hull. Bollingen Series 22. Princeton.

Kirk, G. S. 1970. *Myth: Its Meaning and Functions in Ancient and Other Cultures.* Cambridge.

———. 1984. On Defining Myths. Pp. 53–61 in Dundes 1984.

Lévi-Strauss, C. 1963. *Structural Anthropology.* Trans. C. Jacobson and B. G. Schoepf. New York.

———. 1975. *The Raw and the Cooked: Introduction to a Science of Mythology.* Trans J. and D. Weightman. New York.

———. 1976. *Structural Anthropology.* Vol. 2. Trans. M. Layton. New York.

Lévy-Bruhl, L. 1923. *Primitive Mentality.* Trans. L. A. Clare. London.
———. 1925. *How Natives Think.* Trans. L. A. Clare. New York.
Malinowski, B. 1954a. Magic, Science and Religion. Pp. 17–92 in *Magic, Science and Religion, and Other Essays By Bronislaw Malinowski,* ed. R. Redfield. Garden City, NY.
———. 1954b. Myth in Primitive Psychology. Pp. 93–148 in Malinowski 1954a.
McKenzie, J. L. 1959. Myth and the Old Testament. *CBQ* 21: 265–82.
Oden, R. A. 1979. "The Contendings of Horus and Seth" (Chester Beatty Papyrus No. 1): A Structural Interpretation. *HR* 18: 352–69.
———. 1979–80. Theoretical Assumptions in the Study of Ugaritic Myths. *Maarav:* 2: 43–63.
———. 1983. Jacob as Father, Husband, and Nephew: Kinship Studies and the Patriarchal Narratives. *JBL* 102: 189–205.
Ricoeur, P. 1969. Guilt, Ethics and Religion. Pp. 100–17 in *Talk of God: Royal Institute of Philosophy Lectures, Volume Two: 1967–68.* London.
Rogerson, J. W. 1974. *Myth in Old Testament Interpretation.* BZAW 134. New York.
———. 1978. Slippery Words: V. Myth. *ExpTim* 90: 10–14.
Segal, R. A. 1980. In Defense of Mythology: The History of Modern Theories of Myth. *Annals of Scholarship* 1: 3–49.
Smith, W. R. 1927. *Lectures on the Religion of the Semites.* 3d ed. London.
Strauss, D. F. 1835. *Das Leben Jesu.* Tübingen.
Tylor, E. B. 1871. *Primitive Culture.* 2 vols. London.
Weiser, A. 1961. *The Old Testament: Its Formation and Development.* Trans. D. M. Barton. New York.
Wright, G. E. 1952. *God Who Acts.* SBT 8. Chicago.

ROBERT A. ODEN, JR.

MYTH IN THE OT

The scholarly debate regarding the presence of myth in the OT is relatively recent, having only begun late in the 18th century. Since its inception, the use of this category in biblical studies has met with varying degrees of acceptance and rejection. A concensus on the definition of myth is still wanting (see previous article); hence, the identification of mythic elements—and their significance—in the OT text is much debated. This article will trace the development of this discussion in OT research.

A. Early Attempts to Study Biblical Stories as Myth
B. Hermann Gunkel and the "History of Religions" School
C. Myth and the OT in the First Half of the 20th Century
   1. Continuations of the 19th-Century Tradition
   2. New Directions: OT Myths and the Cult
D. Myth and OT in Recent Study

A. Early Attempts to Study Biblical Stories as Myth

As with many areas of biblical scholarship, the origins of the modern encounter between OT study and the category of myth are to be sought in the 18th and early 19th centuries (Kraus 1969: 147–51). This is not to say that no notice whatsoever was taken prior to the Enlightenment of the possibility that OT material could be looked at as myth. Still, it was the era of the Enlightenment and the ensuing Romantic period which first gave broad and lasting impetus to this possibility. These movements are known above all for their stress upon historical inquiry as the most fruitful way in which to grasp the full significance of all human phenomena. As such, scholars, from the end of the 18th century onward, placed special emphasis upon the remotest origins of all literary and religious texts. Against this background, writers from the Romantic period argued that the human heart first spoke in poetry and in myth. Hence, there arose a desire to recover and to appreciate anew these ancient, mythic expressions of humanity.

Exemplary of the blossoming interest in myth is the work of the brothers Jacob (1785–1863) and Wilhelm (1786–1859) Grimm. Their collections of myths were in the service of the increasingly regnant model that humanity's earliest literary productions began as myths. Against this background, it began to seem possible that OT stories, too, had such an inception, and thus might usefully be studied as myths.

Among those who pursued this possibility with the greatest vigor was the German scholar David Friedrich Strauss (1808–74). Strauss' published work dealt primarily with the NT rather than with the OT. However, the questions he raised and the answers he proposed in his *Life of Jesus,* first published in 1835 (see Schweitzer 1961: 68–71; and Frei 1974: 233–44) were at least as applicable to OT traditions as Strauss had suggested for the NT. Strauss presented in carefully documented detail the argument that many, perhaps most, biblical stories were nothing like the eye-witness testimony they had long been assumed to be. These stories were instead the products of long processes of community tradition. And stories behind which lay such a process were prime candidates to be labeled myths.

Strauss equated the "mythical" with the "miraculous," and on the basis of this equation subjected to analysis all of the miraculous material in the Gospel accounts of Jesus. His argument was in many ways founded on the ancient theory of Euhemerism, according to which all myths began as tales about historical heroes whose actions were exaggerated and who became superhuman in the course of their further development. Stories about Jesus, Strauss suggested, developed in much the way that stories about any remarkable person did. Whenever such a person dies, his memory is preserved such that the historical quickly becomes the superhuman and the mythical. That which is particularly notable about Strauss' *Life of Jesus* is the breadth to which he was willing to extend his basic thesis (Frei 1974: 233–44). Strauss made bold to argue that the mythical was present not just in the accounts of Jesus' conception and birth, but also in the many details in the Gospel narratives—in the stories of Jesus' baptism, for example, or of the various healing and feeding miracles.

Though Strauss was not the first to label biblical stories as myths, he was made to bear a burden which more properly belonged to the entire historical-critical approach to the Bible. For many pious readers, a first acquaintance with the shocking conclusions of this approach coincided with their acquaintance, often at second- or third-hand, with Strauss' volume. For such people, what was shocking was the most basic conclusion of both Strauss and his predecessors: that the bulk of OT and NT narratives were not historically true, even if mythical materials did offer a deeper kind of human truth. Thus, the initial stage of the inquiry into the Bible and myth reached conclusions which conflicted with many peoples' deeply held views about the reliability of the Bible. As Albert Schweitzer wrote, Strauss' *Life of Jesus,* "into which he had poured his youthful enthusiasm, rendered him famous in a moment—and utterly destroyed his prospects" (Schweitzer 1961: 71). The public indignation directed against Strauss led to his dismissal from his academic post at Tübingen, destroyed his academic career, and led him to withdraw for most of his life from the world of biblical scholarship.

B. Hermann Gunkel and the "History of Religions" School

The lead that Strauss' work might have given to 19th-century OT scholarship was not pursued, even though the OT provided at least as much potential for mythological study as did the NT. For example, the stories of the endangering of an ancestress (Genesis 12, 20, 26), of a young man falsely accused of attempting to rape the wife of a powerful official (Genesis 37–50), or of a national saga which includes a dramatic crossing of a body of water (Exodus 15) were all stories known in nonbiblical, mythological traditions. The negative reaction to Strauss' *Life of Jesus* resulted in long reluctance by scholars to label biblical stories as myths, a pause that persisted in some respects for a full century following the appearance of Strauss' study in 1835. The "problem" of the Bible and mythology had ceased to be a problem, argued a variety of biblical scholars, because there were no myths, at least no complete myths, in either the OT or the NT.

The insistent claims that the OT contains no myths seem notably odd because the very years in which scholars were voicing such claims coincided with a striking increase in the number and the awareness of myths from Mesopotamia, Syria, Egypt and elsewhere similar to biblical tales in many regards. By the final quarter of the 19th century, scholars in a variety of academic disciplines knew of a flood hero more ancient than Noah in a Mesopotamian version of Genesis 6–9, or of a first human called Adapa who was prevented by a Mesopotamian deity from attaining immortality (see *ANET,* 72–99 for the Epic of Gilgamesh, whose 11th Tablet portrays the deluge; Oden 1981: 197–216, for the more recently discovered Epic of Atrahasis; and *ANET,* 101–3 for Adapa).

In the face of such evidence, how could scholars exile the genre of myth from the OT? The answer is quite simple: the strategy of exiling myth from OT studies was to do so *by definition.* Almost without exception, biblical scholars in the decades following Strauss relied upon a single and most convenient definition for myth. This was the definition first popularized by the Grimm brothers, which labeled a myth as "a story about the gods." The key to this definition for biblical scholars in the period here under discussion was that the final noun, "gods," is in the plural. Both the OT and the NT, scholars agreed, were of the highest significance in the development of human religions for their witness to the evolving truth of monotheism. If the lasting contribution of biblical religion was monotheism, there could be no talk of gods in the Bible. And if there was no talk of gods in the Bible, then there are in the Bible no myths. (For a discussion of an adequate definition of myth, see previous article.)

So cleanly did this utilization of the Grimm brothers' definition of myth sever mythology from the Bible that virtually every discussion which touched upon myth within the world of late 19th- and early 20th-century biblical study rehearsed this definition with the predictable conclusion which ensued. Both Julius Wellhausen (1844–1918) and William Robertson Smith (1846–94), to whom we owe major and lasting advances in OT study, used the conventional Grimm brothers' definition of myth. So too, at greater length, did Hermann Gunkel (1862–1932), whose work shaped 20th-century biblical inquiry as did perhaps no other single scholar.

Gunkel provides a striking instance of the tension that began to mount at the conclusion of the 19th century between increasing archaeological evidence for mythical material in the Bible on the one hand and the repeated denial of the presence of myths in the Bible on the other. In 1895, Gunkel published a volume entitled *Schöpfung und Chaos,* which inaugurated the "History of Religions School" in the eyes of those scholars who belonged to this group. This school, which numbered among its illustrious members Albert Eichhorn, W. Wrede, Wilhelm Bousset, W. Heitmüller, Hugo Gressmann, and others (see Kraus 1969: 327–40), relied fundamentally upon extrabiblical texts which archaeology was making increasingly available in the years just before the turn of the century. Indeed, the larger program of the "History of Religions School" was most basically founded on the project of fully utilizing texts from outside the OT to explain the development of the OT, in opposition to previous scholars, such as Wellhausen, who were accused of failing to utilize such extrabiblical texts.

Gunkel's central thesis in *Schöpfung und Chaos* is that a single myth—a broadly defined myth of the defeat of a chaos dragon—lies behind several OT and NT stories concerning the beginning and end of the world. However, despite the skill with which Gunkel developed this thesis, he, too, continued throughout his life to stand within the main camp of those who denied that mythical thinking played any major role in the development of the OT. Though his statements on myth in his voluminous publications are not entirely consistent, Gunkel *was* consistent in defining myths as stories about the gods and in demanding that "for a story of the gods at least two gods are essential" (Gunkel 1964: 15; see also Rogerson 1974: 59–63). Since the OT, Gunkel went on to say, "from its beginning tended toward monotheism," the Bible contains no complete myths. What the Bible does contain, which Gunkel's own research forced him to admit, is "original myths" from other lands, myths that now appear in the Bible only "in comparatively faded colors." The story of the mating of divine beings with women in Genesis 6:1–4, for example, was originally an elaborate myth but is now "nothing but a torso" of a complete myth (Gunkel 1964: 14–15).

C. Myth and the OT in the First Half of the 20th Century

1. Continuations of the 19th-Century Tradition. The simple but powerful maneuver of denying that the OT offers any evidence of complete myths by relying upon the

Grimm brothers' definition continued to play the lead role in discussions by biblical scholars about myth and the OT for a surprisingly long period in the 20th century. The longevity of this maneuver's success is surprising since the Grimm brothers' definition was dismissed as inadequate, overly narrow, and apologetic by a wide range of scholars outside the area of biblical study. Still, a glance at the most widely used introductions to the OT which appeared in the period up to about 1960, or at similarly influential OT theologies from the same years, demonstrates that this remained the case until very recently. The OT introductions of Otto Eissfeldt (1965), Artur Weiser (1961), and Georg Fohrer (1968), for example, introduced generations of students to the OT. Each one of these introductions rehearses, in markedly similar language, the argument that a myth demands a plurality of gods, that those stories which look mythical in the OT are merely the decaying fragments of myths which originated elsewhere, and that there can be no complete myths in the OT (Eissfeldt 1965: 35–37; Weiser 1961: 57–59; and Fohrer 1968: 87). The identical chain of reasoning makes its predictable appearance in the OT theologies of Gerhard von Rad and G. E. Wright, different as these scholars' positions are in other areas. Both von Rad and Wright open their theologies with a version of this old argument, conclude that myths find no authentic role in OT thought, and then go on to contrast sharply the alleged cyclical, naturalistic, and mythical thinking which they see as characteristic of Mesopotamia, Egypt, and Canaan, with the linear, historical, and antimythical thought process they claim to find central to OT religion (Wright 1952: 38–48; and *ROTT* 1: 27–28, 136–41; 2:110–11, 349).

2. New Directions: OT Myths and the Cult. Although the first half of the 20th century largely saw the continuation of the tradition of ignoring the potentially fruitful area of study which might have been opened up by analyzing OT stories as other myths were studied, it would be unfair to characterize the entirety of this period in this way. There were already in this period some voices which wished to expand the horizon of OT study in the direction of mythical analysis. The most important of these came from scholars heavily influenced by the myth-ritual program initiated at the turn of the century by the Cambridge University circle which included Sir James George Frazer, Jane Harrison, and others. In addition, Gunkel had also stressed the origins of numerous religious traditions in the popular settings of groups' rituals; and this stress too led him and others to investigate anew the possible myth-ritual origins for a number of OT texts (Gunkel 1967).

Those scholars who investigated the OT under the general heading of myths and cultic activity tend to be grouped into one of several different schools of thought. There were, for example, a number of Scandinavian scholars, including H. S. Nyberg, S. Mowinckel, J. Pedersen, G. Widengren, I. Engnell, and others, whose work can be seen with fair accuracy as a continuation of that of Gunkel (see North 1951: 59–70). A clear example of the application of such scholars' thought to an OT narrative is the conclusion that Pedersen reached considering the Passover story in Exodus 1–15. For Pedersen, this narrative is not a direct historical report of events which occurred to Israel in the generation of Moses. It is rather a ritual legend, which arose from a cultic ceremony whose function was to give a sense of unity to the early Israelites (see Hahn 1966: 144). As Pedersen wrote, "In forming an opinion about the crossing of the reed sea it must be kept in mind . . . that this story, as well as the whole emigration legend, though inserted as part of an historical account, is quite obviously of a cultic character, for the whole narrative aims at glorifying the god of the people at the paschal feast" (*PI*, 728). Though the contributions of Mowinckel were numerous, his longest lasting conclusions were those that stemmed from inquiry into the Psalms (see Johnson 1951: 189–207). Such Psalms as Pss 40, 65, 82, 90, Mowinckel read as prophetic speeches, suggesting to him and others that the origins of the phenomenon of prophecy were to be sought in combined myth-ritual occasions. It was Mowinckel as well who argued for the decisive role played by an autumnal New Year Festival. On this occasion, according to Mowinckel and others, Yahweh was ritually reenthroned each year. This festival Mowinckel reconstructed largely from Babylonian and post-Israelite evidence; and to it he attributed the creative force which lay behind many OT texts.

The chief British advocate of myth-ritualism, perhaps, was S. H. Hooke (Hooke 1933), while the leading American scholar to pursue this line of inquiry was T. H. Gaster (Gaster 1977; on Gaster see Grimes 1976: 14–17). Gaster was in many ways the most consistent in his continuation of the original goals of the myth-ritual program. For him, myths must always be seen as "part and parcel of ritual procedures" (Gaster 1954: 184). So, too, he argued, "Myth is cosubstantial with Ritual. They are not—as is often supposed—two things, . . . but one thing viewed from two different angles or through two different prisms" (Gaster 1954: 187). Gaster was also probably the leading advocate of the "patternism" aspect of the myth-ritual program, according to which there existed throughout the ancient Mediterranean world a myth-ritual complex which fell into a broad pattern of chaos followed by eventual triumph. Specifically, Gaster found in many ancient Eastern texts a "broad sequence of mortification, purgation, invigoration and jubilation such as indeed characterizes seasonal rites in most parts of the world" (Gaster 1954: 211). This pattern was allegedly to be found already in the Babylonian *Akītu* Festival with its attendant performance of the *Enuma Elish* creation epic, as well as in the Ugaritic poems about Baal whose plot runs "parallel on a transcendental plane to the characteristic program of season rituals" (Gaster 1954: 198). The same pattern was then seen by Gaster and others in a variety of biblical texts, including especially the so-called Enthronement Psalms.

However, the application of myth-ritualism to OT materials did not produce as wide an impact upon biblical studies as its relatively few advocates clearly wished. This was chiefly because the very period in which scholars such as Pedersen, Mowinckel, Hooke, and Gaster were writing also saw the rise of an eventually devastating tide of criticism directed against the entire myth-ritual approach (see this discussion in the previous article). If the foundations of this approach appeared to lie in ruins, then there no longer seemed to be any justification for the approach's application to OT texts. In addition, many of the cultic reconstructions proposed by the biblical myth-ritualists were judged to be highly speculative. As Gerstenberger has written, the reconstructed background of the so-called cultic Psalms, "be it called New Year/Enthronement Festival or Covenant Renewal Festival, at times looks like a specter or a bag of bubbles" (Gerstenberger 1974: 197). For this pair of reasons, no real and lasting turn in the direction of a more thorough application of mythological analysis of the OT resulted from this program of inquiry into the cult and OT myths.

D. Myth and OT in Recent Study

In the last several decades, two forces have combined to return the issue of myth and the OT to the forefront of scholarship. First, the discovery of additional ANE myths with undeniable similarities to OT stories has made it increasingly difficult to maintain the former distinction between mythical thinking and OT religion. This is especially the case for the Canaanite myths first uncovered in 1929 at Ras Shamra-Ugarit (Coogan 1978). These Canaanite texts present us with myths composed in a language very similar to biblical Hebrew and from the very area in which Israel would come into existence as a nation in the early Iron Age. Further, it appears that the earliest OT poems (e.g., Exodus 15, Psalm 68, or Judges 5) are composed in a poetic style that stems directly from that which obtains the Ugaritic myths.

Second, the years since about mid-century witnessed a new willingness to reexamine both older definitions of myth and previously dominant theories for the origin and function of myths. However long the definition of myths as "stories about the gods" had survived in biblical study, its reign was crumbling even here. The definition's demise was inevitable, even if it had outlived what anthropologists, folklorists, and others from outside the confines of biblical scholarship might have predicted, because developments in the broader study of myth demonstrated repeatedly the poverty of a definition for myth which excluded all monotheistic stories. So, too, beginning at about mid-century, a number of scholars, chief among whom is the French anthropologist Claude Lévi-Strauss, proposed to take myths much more seriously as a source of potential knowledge about human mental and social organizations than had been the case since the time of Tylor, Frazer, and others at the end of the 19th century (see previous article).

Once again, perhaps the major impetus for OT scholarship to return to the issue of myth came initially from a NT scholar. Just as Strauss had boldly suggested in the early 19th century that the NT must be seen as mythical throughout, so too the 20th-century NT scholar Rudolf Bultmann (1884–1976) took the lead among biblical scholars in jettisoning the narrow and frankly apologetic definition of myth first formulated by the Grimm brothers. Though Bultmann rarely offers a succinct definition of myth, his understanding of myth is much more in keeping with what anthropologists, folklorists, and historians of religion had been saying on the subject since the end of the 19th century. For Bultmann, as for these scholars in other fields, a myth is one of the ways in which any culture objectifies and symbolizes its entire worldview. Thus understood, it becomes impossible to deny that much biblical narrative is inherently mythological. Certainly, the NT assumption of the physical cosmos as a three-storied edifice (heaven, earth, and hell), as well as that of the earth as the arena of the activity of demons and other supernatural beings, is a mythological assumption. But more than just this serves to indicate the mythological character of biblical thought. For Bultmann, "The whole conception of the world which is presupposed in the preaching of Jesus as in the New Testament generally is mythological" (Bultmann 1958: 15).

Anyone today who wishes to appropriate the message of Jesus must then, according to Bultmann, "demythologize" the NT. Demythologizing does not mean ridding the Bible of mythology, an impossible task in any case; it means, rather, translating this mythology. NT mythology requires translation because of the definition with which Bultmann begins. If a myth is the objectification and symbolization of any culture's worldview, then the myth cannot function for a culture with a radically different worldview.

The demythologizing program of Bultmann prompted, as any student of the scholarly fate of Strauss might ruefully have predicted, a controversy within theological circles similar in shape and intensity to that which Strauss' *Life of Jesus* generated. Critics accused Bultmann of substituting his own brand of existentialist philosophy for biblical thought, and of raising this philosophy to the status of an independent mythology. Behind such criticisms can be seen lurking the hope that myths and biblical narratives might forever remain distinguishable. There must remain, such critics clearly urged, a fundamental difference between biblical thought on the one hand and mythological thought on the other.

Studies by other scholars soon demonstrated that Bultmann did not stand alone. The problem of myth and the Bible had been too long and too easily side-stepped by the maneuver of a simple definition; and, even if much of the criticism of Bultmann was to the point, he had raised issues which refused to subside. By the 1950s, biblical scholars began openly to question the usefulness of the long regnant definition of myths as stories about gods. Thus, G. H. Davies concluded a 1956 study on mythology with the affirmation that "mythology is a way of thinking and imagining about the divine rather than thinking and imagining about a number of gods," so that "the content of myth, whether polytheistic or otherwise is accidental to the nature of myth" (Davies 1956: 88). Two years later, John McKenzie's survey of some of the many theories of myth from scholars in disciplines beyond the biblical field convinced him that the Grimm brothers' definition, despite its long utilization within biblical study, was radically inadequate. Thus, the accompanying claim that the OT was free of myth was no longer defensible (McKenzie 1959: 265–82).

Two important volumes from the last quarter century may serve as markers of the new directions taken by scholars in the investigation of the OT and myth. To the first of these volumes, B. S. Childs' *Myth and Reality in the Old Testament* (1960), belongs the great credit of openly unmasking the inadequacy of defining myths as stories about the gods. Further, Childs goes well beyond this to note how this definition alone was responsible for the long hiatus in inquiry into the function of mythology in the OT. Childs shows that the long-unexamined utilization of the Grimm brothers' definition created a "tendency among those using this definition to fail to see the essential problem of myth in the Old Testament" (Childs 1960: 15). This problem, Childs continues, is one which is perceived *within* the OT itself. *Myth and Reality in the Old Testament* develops the argument that the OT does contain material which is mythical, though it also contains material which is in tension with the mythical.

A second volume, F. M. Cross' *Canaanite Myth and Hebrew Epic* (1973), goes further in this same trajectory. Here, the argument is not driven so much by theoretical concerns which arise from a redefinition of myth as it is rather by the force of newly available evidence. This evidence, which is largely that of the myths uncovered at the ancient Syrian city of Ugarit, persuades Cross of the bankruptcy of all attempts to prove that Israelite religion is discontinuous with the religions of Israel's neighbors, and hence discontinuous with a mythological tradition.

Cross *(CMHE)* goes on to present evidence for a pattern discernible within much OT literature which is based upon the shape of a central, cosmogonic myth of the Canaanites. The threefold pattern is as follows: (1) A divine warrior battles against a god of chaos; (2) the divine warrior is victorious; and (3) the divine warrior becomes king and receives a royal palace. This pattern, according to Cross, appears in some OT texts in its pure, mythical form (e.g., Psalms 29, 89, or 93), while in other texts (e.g., Psalm 77 or Isa 51:9–11) we see a mixture of mythical with historical traditions. Such a combination Cross finds to be characteristic of Israelite religion: "In Israel, myth and history always stood in strong tension, myth serving primarily to give a cosmic dimension and transcendent meaning to the historical, rarely functioning to dissolve history" (*CMHE,* 90).

Cross' notion of a "tension" between mythical thought and historical thought recalls Childs' thesis that mythical material in the Bible often remains "in tension" with an alternate viewpoint. The similarity of these two scholars on this point is of potential significance in marking a particular stage in the development of our thinking about the OT and myth. While both Childs and Cross have left far behind the former insistence that myths play no role in the OT, neither is quite willing to entertain the possibility that mythical thought and mythical literature are at the very heart of Israel's religion. The possibility is a real one, and one which more recent studies of biblical religion have begun to explore. These studies largely dispense with any discussion of the tension between the historical and the mythical in OT texts. Rather, they begin with the assumption that a great many OT stories are plainly myths, and then go on to study these OT myths according to one or several of the theories for the analysis of myth made available by scholars in anthropology, psychology, and other disciplines (see Oden 1987, with the bibliography there).

The recent progress by biblical scholars in returning openly to the issue of the presence of myths in the Bible is quite remarkable and altogether in keeping with the broader trend toward moving biblical study into the mainstream of academic studies. But equally remarkable is the century-long refusal by OT scholars to pay any great heed to those efforts to redefine myth accomplished by scholars from other disciplines, such as anthropology or folklore study. This refusal is fundamentally grounded in the assumption that all things biblical must be firmly and forever distinguished from the nonbiblical and, especially, the mythological world. The forcefulness of this foundational and long unquestioned distinction accounts for the otherwise inexplicable desire to divide the OT from myth.

Bibliography

Bultmann, R. 1958. *Jesus Christ and Mythology.* New York.

Childs, B. S. 1960. *Myth and Reality in the Old Testament.* SBT 27. Naperville, IL.

Coogan, M. D. 1978. *Stories from Ancient Canaan.* Philadelphia.

Davies, G. H. 1956. An Approach to the Problem of Old Testament Mythology. *PEQ* 88: 83–91.

Eissfeldt, O. 1965. *The Old Testament: An Introduction.* Trans. P. R. Ackroyd. New York.

Fohrer, G. 1968. *Introduction to the Old Testament.* Trans. D. E. Green. Nashville.

Fontenrose, J. 1966. *The Ritual Theory of Myth.* University of California Folklore Studies 18. Berkeley.

Frei, H. W. 1974. *The Eclipse of Biblical Narrative.* New Haven and London.

Gaster, T. H. 1954. Myth and Story. *Numen* 1: 184–212.

———. 1977. *Thespis: Ritual, Myth, and Drama in the Ancient Near East.* New York.

Gerstenberger, E. 1974. Psalms. Pp. 179–223 in Hayes 1974.

Grimes, R. R. 1976. Ritual Studies: A Comparative Review of Theodor Gaster and Victor Turner. *RSR* 2: 13–25.

Gunkel, H. 1895. *Schöpfung und Chaos in Urzeit und Endzeit.* Göttingen.

———. 1964. *The Legends of Genesis: The Biblical Saga and History.* Trans. W. H. Carruth. New York.

———. 1967. *The Psalms: A Form-Critical Introduction.* Philadelphia.

Hahn, H. F. 1966. *The Old Testament in Modern Research.* Philadelphia.

Harrison, J. 1903. *Prolegomena to the Study of Greek Religion.* Cambridge.

Hayes, J. H., ed. 1974. *Old Testament Form Criticism.* Trinity University Monograph Series in Religion 2. San Antonio.

Hooke, S. H. 1933. The Myth and Ritual Pattern of the Ancient East. Pp. 1–14 in *Myth and Ritual,* ed. S. H. Hooke. London.

Johnson, A. R. 1951. The Psalms. Pp. 162–209 in Rowley 1951.

Kraus, H.-J. 1969. *Geschichte der historisch-critischen Erforschung des Alten Testaments.* 2d ed. Neukirchen-Vluyn.

McKenzie, J. L. 1959. Myth and the Old Testament. *CBQ* 21: 265–82.

North, C. R. 1951. Pentateuchal Criticism. Pp. 48–83 in *The Old Testament and Modern Study,* ed. H. H. Rowley. Oxford.

Oden, R. A., Jr. 1981. Divine Aspirations in Atrahasis and in Genesis 1–11. *ZAW* 93: 197–216.

———. 1987. *The Bible Without Theology.* San Francisco.

Rogerson, J. W. 1974. *Myth in Old Testament Interpretation.* BZAW 134. New York.

Rowley, H. H., ed. 1951. *The Old Testament and Modern Study.* Oxford.

Schweitzer, A. 1961. *The Quest of the Historical Jesus.* New York.

Strauss, D. F. 1835. *Das Leben Jesu.* Tübingen.

Weiser, A. 1961. *The Old Testament: Its Formation and Development.* Trans. D. M. Barton. New York.

Wright, G. E. 1952. *God Who Acts.* SBT 8. Chicago.

ROBERT A. ODEN, JR.

MYTH IN THE GRECO-ROMAN WORLD

A. Terminology
B. The Sources
C. Characteristics and Functions
D. Religious Etiology
E. The Origins
 1. Indo-European Traditions
 2. Minoan-Mycenaean Mythology
 3. Oriental Influence
F. Theogony and Cosmogony
G. Heroic Mythology, History, and the Epos
 1. Heroic Myths
 2. The Homeric Epos
 3. Genealogical Poetry and the "Catalogue of Women"
 4. New Myths
H. Archaic and Classical Poetry
 1. Choral Lyrics
 2. Tragedy
I. Philosophy and Demythization
 1. The Beginnings
 2. The Sophists and Plato
 3. Later Allegorical Interpretation
K. Myth in Rome

A. Terminology

In early Gk, *mythos* means "word, speech, design." It is more or less synonymous with *epos* ("word, speech, message"), close in meaning to *logos* ("account, talk"): myth is narration, tale-telling. After Pre-Socratic and sophistic philosophy began to doubt the empirical truth of the mythical tradition, the epic, non-Attic word *mythos* was used in the 5th century Attic prose and in Plato as a technical term for an entertaining tale, the truth of which was uncertain or unwarranted (Burkert 1985a: 281). From Plato onward, its contrasting term was *logos,* "the rational, responsible account." Latin *fabula* and its derivatives in the Romance languages (Eng-Fr *fable,* Ital *favola*) took over the meanings of Gk *mythos.* The modern term *myth* (Fr *mythe,* Germ *Mythus,* Ital *mito*) goes back to the neo-Latin *mythus,* coined by Chr. G. Heyne around 1760 in order to express the new appreciation of the inner veracity of myth in contrast to the negative connotations of *fabula.*

B. The Sources

Myth is the content of which Greek and Roman poetry is the form: in this respect, nearly the whole of Greek and Latin poetry is its source. Myth had, to most Greeks and Romans, the status of ancient history; in that respect, the local historians and the travelers (esp. Pausanias, 2d cent. A.D.) who recorded local myths otherwise unknown, are of special interest. In Hellenistic times, mythography developed as a special branch of literature (Henrichs, in Bremmer 1987: 242–77): its earlier authors are lost; among the later, preserved compendia, the most important is the *Library* of Apollodorus (2d cent A.D.).

Pictorial representations of mythical themes, in which Attic ceramography is especially rich, began at an early date (Schefold 1964). Visual art has its own rules, different from those of verbal narration, and Greek and Roman images are more than just illustrations of texts: iconography, though difficult where texts are absent, has its own methods which lead to new and important results (exemplary Sourvinou-Inwood 1987).

C. Characteristics and Functions

In the most widely accepted definition, myth is a traditional tale with social and intellectual relevance. Greek myth has a tradition which, at least in some respects, goes back to the time before the Mycenaean Age (ca. 1550–1150 B.C.). Anthropologists and folklorists tend to view the narrator of a myth as a nonindividual instrument of tradition (earlier generations spoke about "*volksgeist*"); in Greece, already in the Archaic Age (ca. 750–480 B.C.), the narrators of the traditional tales were highly individual poets. Poetical ornamentation of the tradition was accepted and indispensable, innovation was checked by the fact that archaic Greek culture was oral (Gentili 1984): written texts served as a basis for oral performance, and any new poetical version of a traditional theme was, in its ritual "publication" during a festival or a common meal, exposed to the censorship of the entire group.

The relevance of myth lies in its explanatory (etiological) and normative function: myth makes intelligible, to the group it belongs to, the physical, political, and social order; it defines man's position toward the world and the gods; it regulates religious and social behavior. It does so by telling how the present order once came into being. Compared with most other mythologies, Greek mythology is radically anthropomorphic and wanting in the more fantastical elements (Kirk 1970: 172–251); its emphasis on the historical dimension is one aspect of this more general character. As a consequence, scholars were tempted far too often to look for a historical kernel in divine and heroic myths (see, for the first, the case of Dionysos, McGinty 1978, or Delphic Apollo, Sourvinou in Bremmer 1987: 215–41; for the latter, see G below).

D. Religious Etiology

The so-called "Cambridge school" derived myth from ritual, as the spoken text of the enacted performance. Contemporary scholarship has pointed out the difficulties (Kirk 1970: 8–31). Still, myth has a privileged relationship with ritual: there is, at least in ancient Greece, virtually no ritual without a myth to explain its origin and function. In most instances, these myths are recorded only by local historians and travelers: the myths of the poetical tradition often lost the link with ritual.

Greek myth uses many themes whose connections with ritual are well attested outside Greece. The theme of death and rebirth belongs to an initiatory background (Eliade 1958; Brelich 1969); the flood theme, which in Greece is rare and confined to local mythologies, is connected with reversal and periodic renewal (Caduff 1986), as is the myth of the Golden Age (Gatz 1967) or, in some variants, the theme of the Divine Guest (Flückiger Guggenheim 1984). The "Battle Against the Dragon" is a theme connected with the establishment of a perpetual order, especially with New Year and foundation rituals (Trumpf 1958).

Greek myth never explains all details of a ritual: it does so for its most important or strangest details, often only for its general structure and atmosphere. Myth and ritual use different languages: ritual uses the language of symbolical action often conditioned by ethological programs;

myth uses linguistic expressions formed by traditional narrative patterns (Burkert 1979: 1–58). Therefore, a myth may free itself from a ritual as well as attach itself to a new ritual whose structure it shares. The privileged connection between myth and ritual has no genetic root; but ritual, as the central way to organize and condition archaic society, and myth, as the central mode of explaining and validating archaic social forms, naturally go together.

E. The Origins

1. Indo-European Traditions. Although the Greeks are Indo-Europeans (IE), undisputed IE elements in their mythology, as in their religion, are rare. There are common mythical themes, often where common institutions guaranteed the stability of tradition, as in the account of Nestor's youth in the *Iliad* which has its roots in IE initiatory practice and ideology (Bader 1980), or in the mythology of Helen, the background of which might be IE wedding poetry (Bremmer 1987: 2). A few epic formulas for key concepts have parallels in other IE traditions: this points to the existence of an IE tradition of epic poetry (Nagy 1974); similarly, there exist indications in Greek of a common IE tradition of narrative formal prose (Risch 1985): both were the means of transmission for IE myths.

2. Minoan-Mycenaean Mythology. For Minoan mythology, the only source is iconography, mainly gemstones, recently supplemented by the frescoes of Thera (Marinatos 1984). In the absence of written sources, the differentiation between divine and human figures, as between cult and mythological scenes, is often impossible. Non-anthropomorphical, "demonical" figures, however, are extant and point to mythology. Otherwise, female beings are dominant; connections with known Iron Age Greek myths are precarious (Nilsson 1950).

The Mycenaean Linear B tablets demonstrated that the pantheon of LB Age Greece was close to the Iron Age pantheon. Mycenaean mythology, however, is virtually untraceable. The existence of mythological representations in Mycenaean art is disputed (Vermeule 1958–59); the Linear B texts are purely administrative documents without narrative content. There must have existed a narrative explanation for divine names like *dirimijo diwo ijewe* (dat.), "Drimios the Son of Zeus" or *matere teija* (dat.), "Mother of the Gods" (Gérard-Rousseau 1968: 68.138): they point to Mycenanean mythology which in turn could be continued by Greek myths. According to the still widely held theory of Nilsson (1932), Greek heroic mythology originated in Mycenaean times as a transformation of Mycenaean history: this is highly unlikely (Brillante 1981).

3. Oriental Influence. Both in late Mycenaean and in early archaic times, Greece was a marginal part of the Near Eastern cultures. Traces of Oriental influence are manifest in its mythology (Burkert, in Bremmer 1987: 10–40). The Hittite and Mesopotamian parallels to the succession myth in Hesiod's *Theogony* as well as to the myth of the metal races in his *Works and Days* are well known (Walcot 1966). His account of Zeus' battle against Typhon, though belonging to the much wider attested dragon-battle theme, has close Oriental parallels (Fontenrose 1959); later accounts of the same myth took up new Oriental stimuli (Graf 1987: 90). Even closer to the Babylonian Enuma Elish is another early Greek theogony whose traces are found in the *Iliad* (14.201 §302); the beginning of the cyclic *Cypria* recalls another detail of the same Babylonian epos (Burkert 1984: 88–90, 96–98).

The exact circumstances of the underlying cultural contact are debated. Given the relative closeness between the respective Greek and Oriental myths, a contact in the early Iron Age, without too many distortions by a long independent oral tradition, seems the most likely solution. Both itinerant Oriental religious specialists (Burkert 1984: 15–42) and Greek merchants with their trading posts in N Syria (Boardman 1980: 38–54) may have brought the stories to Greece, either orally or in written form.

F. Theogony and Cosmogony

The earliest extant and most influential Greek account of the origins of the existing cosmos is the hexametrical poem *Theogonia (The Coming Into Being of the Gods)*, composed by Hesiod of Ascra in Boetia about 700–675 B.C. (West 1966). It views the origins of our cosmos not as a creation, but as a procreation of its single divine members in a strictly genealogical and sexual form (Philippson 1944: 7–42). Eros, the sexual drive, is among the very first primordial beings; the main elements of the physical world (sky, earth, sea, mountains, rivers) are born in the shape of the respective divinities; parthenogenesis, which is rare, denotes the otherness of the being thus brought forth. In three consecutive generations, the cosmos evolved to its present order, from Gaia (Earth) and Uranos (Sky) via their children the Titans, whose leader Cronus separated Earth and Sky by castrating his father, to the third generation of Cronus' children under the leadership of Zeus, who, after his victory over Cronus, the Titans and Typhon ordered the world by assigning the tasks *(timai)* to the respective gods.

Despite the many Near Eastern influences (see E.3 above), the Hesiodic account is unique in its specific world view. Whereas the Near Eastern myths presuppose a strongly hierarchized society around an absolute monarch and his palace, the Greek myth is modeled on a less rigidly stratified society of partly independent princes around a king, and on a social system in which the genealogical ties were predominant. In Near Eastern myths, man is created by the gods, to relieve them from the toils of working: man exists only as the slave of the gods. In the *Theogony*, what matters is not the physical creation of man but his social and religious position: it is defined, in the Prometheus myth, by sacrifice, which creates a reciprocal tie between gods and humans (Vernant 1974: 177–94), and by marriage, which institutes a firm genealogical order.

Both the cosmogonies of Pre-Socratic philosophy (Kirk, Raven, and Schofield 1983: 7–71) and of later Orphic and related mythological poetry (West 1983) continued cosmogonical speculation. Pre-Socratic philosophy, though often radically distant from tradition, makes use of mythological forms as easily decipherable allegories, as in Empedocles' poem *Peri Physeōs (On Nature)*. Orphic cosmogonical poetry is set apart from Hesiod's in its validity: such poems had no relevance to a wider public but were part of the library of ritual specialists and of closed religious groups as early as the 5th cent. B.C. (Burkert 1982). Concomitantly, Orphic poetry, purportedly the work of the heroical singers Orpheus and Musaeus, is close to apocryphal religious poetry.

G. Heroic Mythology, History, and the Epos

1. Heroic Myths. According to the Greek conception, a hero is a mortal accorded cultic honors after death; heroization of prominent men is still attested in historical times (Burkert 1985a: 312–19). Thus, most heroic cults are local, belonging to the ancestor of a family, a clan, or a polis; widespread hero-cults are rare. Heroes thus are conceptually identical with historical persons: to the Greek mind, the deeds and genealogies of heroes are the early history of Greece (Finley 1975: 11–33).

When heroic mythology becomes manifest to us in early archaic time, it had been transmitted orally over a long time, presumably mostly in the form of local epic poetry about the deeds of a single central hero. A fragment found recently of such a poem about the exploits of Heracles in Cos (late 6th cent. B.C.?) (Lloyd-Jones 1984) confirms earlier hypotheses about the existence of such local "*heldenlieder*."

2. The Homeric Epos. The *Iliad* and the *Odyssey* are firmly rooted in this tradition of oral mythological storytelling whose formulation in smaller local epics sometimes still seems discernible. They draw upon the whole range of divine mythology which Hesiod systematized, and the main heroic personalities of both poems have their own mythical history which Homer alludes to or relates in longer digressions. The same holds true for other myths, which have no immediate connection with the main plot of the epos but are used as paradigms. The main event, of which the *Iliad* and the *Odyssey* narrate only a part, the siege and destruction of Troy, also is a mythical tale, even if its historicity could be proved (Foxhall and Davies 1984): the story of the war is told in traditional narrative patterns which have both Near Eastern parallels (see E.3) and possible ritual correspondences (Bremmer 1978).

According to what the epos itself tells, its function is both to delight the audience and to propagate the glory of the heroes. The former function, common to heroic poetry (Bowra 1952: 29), is always fulfilled in public, during a common meal or in an assembly, with the consent and control of the whole group. The latter function implies a normative aim: the deeds of the heroes are worth being remembered because they are exemplary. Besides, heroic epos shares the etiological function of myth, explaining the actual order of the Greek world by reference to a heroic past. For the 8th cent. B.C. the cult of epic heroes around Mycenaean graves and ruins begins to be attested to such an extent that it must have begun in this period (Coldstream 1977: 341–57). The reference to the major, Panhellenic epic cycles gave to these places and ruins not only an owner and a history, but made them part of a newly felt Greek unity: in the 9th/8th cent., Greece had overcome the local isolation characteristic of the poor conditions during the Dark Ages; the first colonial ventures broadened the horizons and awakened the feeling of a common Greek culture.

3. Genealogical Poetry and the "Catalogue of Women." An important subtype of mythical narrative is genealogy; again, not exact chronology or documentary historical truth, but etiology in the wide sense of the term (Calame, in Bremmer 1987: 153–86). Genealogical poetry was widespread in archaic Greece; the most comprehensive account was the Pseudo-Hesiodeic *Gynaikōn Katalogos (Catalogue of Women)* (West 1985), a continuation of the *Theogony* which supplements the divine genealogies with those of the heroes (first half of the 6th cent. B.C.). Beginning with Prometheus' son Deucalion, his grandson Hellen, the ancestor of all *Hellēnes,* and Hellen's sons Dorus, Xuthus and Aeolus, the ancestors of the three major tribes of Greece, the *Catalogue* combines the genealogies of Greek heroic mythology into one more or less coherent system, ending one generation after the Trojan War. It is significant how emphasis is put on Panhellenic unity by the introduction, at the beginning of the genealogy, of eponymous heroes who are mere narrative constructs without any known cult: again, this points to the task of myth to give the Greek tribes and cities unity through a common descent.

4. New Myths. Since mythical narration represented history, the gap between the end of the heroic tradition and the immediate present also needed filling. In this continuation of earlier myths, the memory of historical fact was conditioned by story patterns and by contemporary needs; despite the relatively short span of time this "oral history" covered, it would be unwise to rely on its historicity or chronological accurateness. Good examples of this are the accounts of the Dark Age migrations, even more so the foundation-legends of the new colonies around the Mediterranean and Black Sea (750–600 B.C.). In the course of not too long a period of oral transmission, historical facts were drastically transformed into mythical themes and patterns (Prinz 1979); only details backed up by institutions were preserved, such as the origin of the colonists (who kept their political ties with the mother-city and took over its religious institutions) or the name of the founder (who had a public cult on the agora); divine agency, foremost of Apollo in Delphi, was invoked as a means to legitimate the conquests.

H. Archaic and Classical Poetry

1. Choral Lyrics. In the course of the 7th cent. B.C., the creative oral performance of the epos became, with the canonization of written Homeric epic, a mere rhapsodic recitation of a fixed text. As a living means of public communication, it was ousted by choral lyrics which, by an impressive combination of word, music, and dance became the main vehicle of mythical narration in archaic Greece. Foremost among the choral poets was Stesichorus of Himera (died ca. 556 B.C.), whom later literary critics regarded as *hōmerikōtatos,* "closest to Homer" (Gentili 1984: 160–66; Burkert 1987: 50–53). His poetry is preserved only in fragments, but they support the information given by ancient sources that it was Stesichorus' treatment of a great number of heroic myths which was to be most influential, especially for Attic tragedy.

The continuant fluidity of myth is shown by its use in the victory odes of Pindar (52/518–after 446 B.C.), the only preserved body of Greek choral verse: he can adapt his version of the tradition to the individual circumstances of victor, victory, and celebration, even to the extent of implicitly contradicting himself or explicitly correcting a traditional account (Köhnken 1971).

2. Tragedy. Tragedy, the last public oral performance of myth (Rösler 1980), continued the etiological function. It often told the origin of Attic institutions and cults, and it took its stand in current politics: by projecting Athenian democracy into the time of the mythical heroes, it extolled and legitimated the democratic order. The tragedians' new emphasis on problematical relationships between members of the same household or clan responded to contemporary feelings (Knox 1979); Euripides, in some plays, even attempted an analysis of female roles and psychology. Finally, the dramatic interplay of gods and mortal heroes elucidated the relationship between man and god, often by stressing the utter incompatibility of the two (Graf 1987: 162–65; Euripides: Eisner 1979).

I. Philosophy and Demythization

1. The Beginnings. Literacy, with its creation of poetical texts, slowly destroyed the nearly limitless adaptability of oral tradition: as social and intellectual conditions changed, a gap opened up between the now fixed texts and their new readers. By the end of the Archaic Period, several strategies were available to deal with myths which seemed no longer acceptable. One was to accept the gist of tradition but to explain away all details which did not fit into a rational or commonsense view. This method was adopted especially by the historians, from its first representative, Hecataeus of Miletus (ca. 550–480 B.C.) to the end of antiquity. A second strategy was to reject tradition, mainly on moralistic grounds, as did the pre-Socratic philosophers Xenophanes of Colophon and Heraclitus of Ephesus (Kirk, Raven, and Schofield 1983: 168, 188, 209). This was much more lethal to myth than the petty rationalizations: they radically did away with the strict anthropomorphic model of Greek mythology. A third way was allegorization, the figurative interpretation. It started in the explanation of Homer toward the end of the 6th century B.C. with Theagenes of Rhegium, a rhapsodist and as such also a professional interpreter of Homer, and with the Pythagoreans (Graf 1987: 176–78), and became the standard procedure to deal with mythology from Hellenistic time onward.

2. The Sophists and Plato. Whereas rationalization of myth became the predilection of historians, philosophy continued to rely on allegorization or rejection. The Sophists of the 5th cent. B.C. rejected myth while retaining its normative aims: they used traditional themes in a new guise or created new myths as vehicles for moral and political education, the best known being the "Choice of Heracles" invented by Socrates' contemporary Prodicus of Ceus (Panofsky 1930). The same Prodicus developed a historical reading of divine myths and explained the gods as divine benefactors: this approach became quickly popular and was systematized around 300 B.C. by Euhemerus of Messene after whom, somewhat unjustifiedly, the whole theory was labeled Euhemerism (Henrichs 1984: 140–52).

Like the Sophists, Plato rejected traditional myths in their poetical shape; they were impious and immoral. At the same time, he could invent myths with an educational aim in the sophistic manner. More important, he used *mythos,* the rationally unverifiable tale, as a way to express things which he could not express by *logos,* in rational argumentation, either because, as with statements about the sensual world, their ontological status made *logos* impossible, or, as with eschatology, because they were beyond human knowledge (Brisson 1982).

3. Later Allegorical Interpretation. The Stoics, less radical than Plato, accepted traditional poetical myth but explained it allegorically, usually in terms of natural phenomena, less often moralistically. Due to the success of Stoicism, allegorical explanation became the most widespread strategy to deal with myth both in antiquity (Lévêque 1959; Pépin 1976) and after until the 18th cent., (Feldman and Richardson 1972).

K. Myth in Rome

Roman tradition had, at an early stage, radical historicized its mythology (Dumézil 1987: 63–93); modern scholarship is still decoding early Roman history as myth (for a survey, see Grant 1971). All the more eagerly the Romans accepted Greek mythology, as part of Greek culture which they imitated and adapted, not as part of a living religious tradition. The great number of etiological myths for Roman cults (collected esp. in Ovid's *Fasti*) seem to be of late and mainly scholarly origin.

The Augustan Age, in its aim of giving new spiritual foundations to Rome, changed the status of myth. Vergil, in his *Aeneid,* expanded the Greek myth of Aeneas into an attempt to give a mythico-religious legitimation to Augustan Rome. The myth itself had been known in Italy in the 6th cent. B.C., in Latium in the 4th cent. B.C. as foundation-legend of a local cult at Lavinium (Horsfall, in Bremmer-Horsfall 1987: 12–24). Ovid, though he was a poet without any belief in mythical normativity, explored the psychological aspects of myth in his *Metamorphoses* with a depth and skill theretofore unknown; myth became a mirror of human behavior. Thus Ovid succeeded in giving myth a new, though precarious, relevance: to European culture up to the present day, the *Metamorphoses* were the main source for Greco-Roman mythology.

Bibliography

Bader, F. 1980. Rhapsodies homériques et irlandaises. Pp. 9–83 in *Recherches sur les religons de l'antiquité classique,* ed. R. Bloch. Geneva.

Boardman, J. 1980. *The Greeks Overseas.* 2d ed. London.

Bonnefoy, Y., ed. 1981. *Dictionnaire des mythologies et des religions des sociétés traditionelles et du monde antique.* Paris.

Bowra, C. M. 1952. *Heroic Poetry.* London.

Brelich, A. 1969. *Paides e Parthenoi.* Rome.

Bremmer, J. N. 1978. Heroes, Rituals, and the Trojan War. *Studi Storico-Religiosi* 2: 5–38.

———. 1987. *Interpretations of Greek Mythology.* London.

Bremmer, J. N., and Horsfall, N. 1988. *Roman Myth and Mythography.* Bulletin of the Institute for Classical Studies Supp. 52. London.

Brillante, C. 1981. *La leggenda eroica e la civiltà micenea.* Rome.

Brisson, L. 1982. *Platon, les mots et les mythes.* Paris.

Burkert, W. 1979. *Structure and History in Greek Mythology and Ritual.* Berkeley.

———. 1982. Craft versus Sect. Vol. 3 pp. 1–22, 183–89 in *Jewish and Christian Self-Definition,* ed. B. F. Meyer and E. P. Sanders. London.

———. 1984. *Die orientalisierende Epoche in der griechischen Religion und Literatur.* SHAW Phil.-Hist. Klasse 5. Heidelberg.

———. 1985a. *Greek Religion Archaic and Classical.* Oxford.
———. 1985b. Mythos, Mythologie. Cols. 281–83 in vol. 6 of *Historisches Wörterbuch der Philosophie,* ed. J. Ritter and K. Gründer. Basle.
———. 1987. The Making of Homer in the Sixth Century B.C. Rhapsodes versus Stesichorus. Pp. 43–62 in *Papers on the Amasis painter and his World.* Malibu, CA.
Caduff, G. A. 1986. *Antike Sintflutsagen.* Hypomnemata 82. Göttingen.
Coldstream, J. N. 1977. *Geometric Greece.* London.
Detienne, M. 1981. *L'invention de la mythologie.* Paris.
Dumézil, G. 1987. *La religion romaine archaïque.* 2d ed. Paris.
Eisner, R. 1979. Euripides' Use of Myth. *Arethusa* 7: 153–74.
Eliade, M. 1958. *Birth and Rebirth.* New York (Repr. 1965).
Feldman, B., and Richardson, R. D., eds. 1972. *The Rise of Modern Mythology 1680–1860.* Bloomington, IN.
Finley, M. I. 1975. *The Use and Abuse of History.* London.
Flückiger-Guggenheim, D. 1984. *Göttliche Gäste. Die Einkehr von Göttern und Heroen in der griechischen Mythologie.* Berne.
Fontenrose, J. 1959. *Python. A Study of Delphic Myth and Its Origins.* Berkeley.
Foxhall, L., and Davies, J. K., eds. 1984. *The Trojan War.* Bristol.
Gatz, B. 1967. *Weltalter, goldene Zeit und sinnverwandte Vorstellungen.* Spudasmata 16. Hildesheim.
Gentili, B. 1984. *Poesia e pubblico nella Grecia antica da Omero al V secolo.* Rome.
Gérard-Rousseau, M. 1968. *Les mentions religieuses dans les tablettes mycéniennes.* Rome.
Graf, F. 1987. *Griechische Mythologie.* 2d ed. Munich.
Grant, M. 1971. *Roman Myths.* London.
Henrichs, A. 1984. The Sophists and Hellenistic Religion. Prodicus as the Spiritual Father of the Isis Aretalogies. *HSCP* 88: 139–58.
Kirk, G. S. 1970. *Myth: Its Meaning and Functions in Ancient and Other Cultures.* Berkeley.
Kirk, G. S.; Raven, J. E.; and Schofield, M. 1983. *The Presocratic Philosophers.* 2d ed. Cambridge.
Knox, B. W. 1979. Myth and Attic Tragedy. Pp. 3–24 in *Word and Action: Essays on the Ancient Theater.* Baltimore.
Köhnken, A. 1971. *Die Funktion des Mythos bei Pindar.* Berlin.
Lévêque, P. 1959. *Aurea Catena Homeri.* Paris.
Lloyd-Jones, H. 1984. The Meropis (SH 903A). Pp. 141–50 in *Atti del XVII congresso internazionale di papirologia.* Naples.
Marinatos, N. 1984. *Art and Religion in Thera.* Athens.
McGinty, P. 1978. *Interpretation and Dionysos.* The Hague.
Nagy, G. 1974. *Comparative Studies in Greek and Indic Meter.* HSCL 33. Cambridge, MA.
Nilsson, M. P. 1932. *The Mycenaean Origin of Greek Mythology.* Berkeley.
———. 1950. *The Minoan-Mycenaean Religion and its Survival in Greek Religion.* 2d ed. Lund.
Panofsky, E. 1930. *Hercules am Scheidewege und andere antike Bildstoffe in der neueren Kunst.* Leipzig.
Pépin, J. 1976. *Mythe et allégorie: Les origines grecques et les contestations judéo-chrétiennes.* 2d ed. Paris.
Philippson, P. 1944. *Untersuchungen über den griechischen Mythos.* Zurich.
Preller, L., and Robert, C. 1894–1926. *Griechisch Mythologie.* 3 vols. 4th ed. Berlin.
Prinz, F. 1979. *Gründungsmythen und Sagenchronologie.* Zetemata 72. Munich.
Risch, E. 1985. Homerisch *ennepo-*, Lakonisch *epheneponti* und die alte Erzählprosa, *Zeitschrift für Papyrologie und Epigraphik* 60: 1–9.
Roscher, W. H. 1884–1937. *Ausführliches Lexikon der griechischen und römischen Mythologie.* 5 vols. Leipzig.
Rösler, W. 1980. *Polis und Tragödie.* Konstanz.
Schefold, K. 1964. *Frühgriechische Sagenbilder.* Munich.
Sourvinou-Inwood, C. 1987. Menace and Pursuit. Pp. 41–58 in *Images et société en Grèce ancienne,* ed. C. Bérard; C. Bron; and A. Pomari. Lausanne.
Trumpf, J. 1958. Stadtgründung und Drachenkampf. *Hermes* 86: 129–57.
Vermeule, E. T. 1958/59. Mythology in Mycenaean Art. *The Classical Journal* 54: 97–108.
Vernant, J. P. 1974. *Mythe et société en Grèce ancienne.* Paris.
Walcot, P. 1966. *Hesiod and the Near East.* Cardiff.
West, M. L. 1983. *The Orphic Poems.* Oxford.
———. 1985. *The Hesiodic Catalogue of Women.* Oxford.
West, M. L., ed. 1966. *Hesiod, Theogony.* Oxford.

FRITZ GRAF

N

NAAM (PERSON) [Heb *nāʿam*]. An individual of the tribe of Judah, the son of Caleb, the son of Jephunneh (1 Chr 4:15).

David Channing Smith

NAAMAH (PERSON) [Heb *naʿămâ*]. **1.** Sister of Tubal-cain; daughter of Cain and Zillah (Gen 4:22). Naamah is mentioned in the J genealogy of Cain (Gen 4:17–22), along with her brother (Tubal-cain) and two half-brothers (Jabal and Jubal). Her inclusion is somewhat enigmatic. Daughters are rarely mentioned in the genealogies of Genesis. Moreover, Naamah's entry lacks the vocational information given for each of her brothers (Jabal as herdsmen; Jubal associated with instrumental musicians; Tubal-cain connected with workers in metal). Some traditions clarify her background by identifying her as Noah's wife *(Gen. Rab.)* and associating her with singers *(Tg. Ps.-J., Gen. Rab.)*. The antiquity of these traditions, however, is hard to verify. The inclusion of Naamah's name in Gen 4:22 may simply indicate an attempt to present the reader with a balanced genealogy—two children for each of Lamech's two wives.

2. Mother of Rehoboam, king of Judah (1 Kgs 14:21 = 2 Chr 12:13; 1 Kgs 14:31). Naamah's name occurs in her son's introductory (1 Kgs 14:21 = 2 Chr 12:13) and concluding (1 Kgs 14:31) regnal formulae. The reference in the latter is unusual and is missing from some versions (Syriac, Ethiopian) and from the parallel account in 2 Chr 12:16. Each reference to Naamah identifies her as "the Ammonitess." This coincides with the tradition in 1 Kgs 11:1, which lists Ammonite women among the foreign wives of Solomon. Moreover, according to 1 Kgs 12:24 (LXX) Naamah was the daughter of Ana, son of Naash, king of the children of Ammon. If this is true, it lends credence to the theory that Solomon's marriage to Naamah was a shrewd attempt to consolidate the territory captured by his father, David. See also REHOBOAM; QUEEN.

Linda S. Schearing

NAAMAH (PLACE) [Heb *naʿămâ*]. Town situated in the Shephelah, or lowlands, of Judah (Josh 15:41), within the same district as Lachish. This settlement, whose name perhaps means "pleasant town" (from *nʿm,* "to be pleasant, delightful"), is listed among the towns within the tribal allotment of Judah (Josh 15:21–62). Although a location in the Sorek valley near Timna has often been proposed (e.g., Abel *GP,* 89), a location farther to the S in the vicinity of Lachish seems more appropriate given Naamah's inclusion in the same district. Unfortunately, its exact location has yet to be identified.

Wade R. Kotter

NAAMAN (PERSON) [Heb *naʿăman*]. The name of two men in the OT; it is derived from the stative verb *nʿm,* "to be pleasant." Other names, such as Naamah and Naomi, share the same origin.

1. A member of the tribal families of Benjamin (Gen 46:21; Num 26:40; 1 Chr 8:4, 7). In one genealogy (Gen 46:21) he is listed as the son of Benjamin, and in another (1 Chr 8:4, 7) as the son of Bela, son of Benjamin. The differences between the genealogies ought to be seen in light of an intention to stress belonging rather than strict heredity (Aufrecht 1988). Outside these three texts, nothing is known of Naaman. From the perspective of genre, Gen 46:21 and 1 Chr 8:4, 7 are part of formal genealogies which received their final form in the postexilic period (Wilson 1977: 188). The first of these appears to be an expression of Gen 35:22b–23 (Johnson 1969: 21). On the other hand Num 26:40 is part of a census list, which, although postexilic in its present form, is based on an early military census of the monarchical period (Mendenhall 1958).

2. Commander-in-chief of the army of Aram-Damascus in the mid 9th century B.C.E., who became a leper and who visited the prophet Elisha for healing (2 Kgs 5:1–27). The biblical story tells of a powerful foreign soldier who had achieved fame on the battlefield, and who was trusted by his king (2 Kgs 5:1). He was, however, a leper. A young Israelite slave girl, captured in one of the Syrian raids on Israel, began the process of healing by telling her mistress, Naaman's wife, that there was a prophet of great power in Israel. Initially, Naaman tried to gain access to the prophet Elisha through normal diplomatic channels (vv 4–7), but a serious misunderstanding by the Israelite king of the Syrian king's intentions almost started a war. Finally, the general found Elisha, but when told, through an intermediary, that all he had to do was bathe himself seven times in the Jordan he was furious (vv 8–12). His servant constrained him to obey the prophet and eventually he was healed (vv 13–14). Naaman's gratitude was great and he tried, unsuccessfully, to offer the prophet a gift. The gift was refused, but Naaman himself returned home with some earth from Israel as a symbol of a newfound faith in Yahweh, the God of Israel. When he, as the trusted aide to the king of Syria, entered the temple of the Syrian god, Rimmon, he would remember Yahweh and Israel (vv 15–19). The story ends with an attempt by Gehazi to trick Naaman out of some of his baggage, and the transfer of Naaman's leprosy to Gehazi as punishment (vv 20–27).

The story is remarkable in many ways. Externally, such a visit of a high-ranking officer of Aram-Damascus to Israel is most unusual against the background of the almost continual conflict between the two countries. The reign of Ahab was a time of warfare with only minor intervals of peace (1 Kgs 20:1–34; 22:1–40). Following Ahab's death Israelite territories on the E side of the Jordan were put in jeopardy (2 Kgs 1:1; 3:1–27), and from this time until the death of Elisha some fifty years later war was the norm rather than the exception (2 Kgs 6:8–7:20; 8:2–9:27; 12:17–18; 13:3–9, 24–25). During this period there were short times of peace, and from the stories of Elisha (2 Kgs 8:7–15) there is an account of a close relationship between the prophet and the king of Aram-Damascus, Ben Hadad. Whether this cordiality extended to the diplomatic level is not clear, but it should be noted that the two sides were not averse to burying their differences in the face of a common enemy. Ahab had fought with a coalition of western kings, including Damascus, against the Assyrians at Qarqar in 853 B.C.E. (*ANET,* 278–79), and in 734 B.C.E. Israel and Damascus teamed up against Ahaz of Jerusalem (2 Kgs 16:5–9). So, while the visit is highly unusual, it need not have been impossible.

Exactly when the visit took place is impossible to say. In the order of the Elisha stories it comes soon after the death of Ahab and the rebellion of Naaman, that is, after 850 B.C.E., and before Elisha's visit to Damascus (2 Kgs 8:7–15), which must have taken place before 843 B.C.E. But the stories of Elisha are not necessarily in chronological order. Note that Gehazi reappears in chap. 8 with no hint of his leprosy or disfavor with Elisha.

Internally, the story is a fascinating example of Hebrew narrative art. Of all the stories associated with the prophet, and which obviously originated from the supporters of the prophet, this one has the most highly developed plot and contains the largest number of characters (Hobbs *2 Kings* WBC, 58–69). The movement from problem (Naaman's condition) to resolution of that problem (the healing) is not direct, but twists and turns down many paths until the denouement. The story also contains what can only be called a comedy of manners, almost bordering on a farce. It is the servants, the slave girl (2 Kgs 5:2–3) and the servants of Naaman (vv 13–14), who aid the process of healing, whereas the important characters, such as the kings, misunderstand the situation and almost start a war.

The nature of Naaman's leprosy is not exactly clear, although it can be assumed from v 27 that it was a disease of the skin. It was therefore not "Hansen's disease" (Cochrane 1963; Pilch 1985) (see also LEPROSY), and not something for which Naaman, unlike Uzziah (2 Kgs 15:5), was forced into quarantine.

In the present collection of Elisha stories, 2 Kings 5 provides a perfect counterpart to 2 Kings 1, and a near parallel to 2 Kings 8. In contrast to the Israelite king, Ahaziah, who sought healing from a foreign god, Baalzebub of Ekron, a foreign dignitary and a foreign king seek help in their sickness from the God of Israel and his prophet. This contrast between the behavior of Israel and the behavior of foreign nations becomes a common theme in the prophetic tradition (Jer 2:10–11). It is to this incident, among others, that Jesus referred in justification of his gentile mission (Luke 4:27).

Bibliography

Aufrecht, W. 1988. Genealogy and History in Ancient Israel. Pp. 205–35 in *Ascribe to the Lord,* ed. L. E. Eslinger and G. Taylor. Sheffield.

Cochrane, R. G. 1963. *Biblical Leprosy.* London.

Cochrane, R. G., and Davey, T. F. 1964. *Leprosy in Theory and Practice.* 2d ed. Bristol.

Johnson, M. D. 1969. *The Purpose of Biblical Genealogies.* SNTSMS 8. Cambridge.

Mendenhall, G. E. 1958. The Census Lists in Numbers 1 and 26. *JBL* 77: 52–66.

Pilch, J. J. 1981. Biblical Leprosy and Body Symbolism. *BTB* 11: 108–13.

Wilson, R. R. 1975. The Old Testament Genealogies in Recent Research. *JBL* 94: 169–89.

———. 1977. *Genealogy and History in the Biblical World.* YNER 7. New Haven.

T. R. Hobbs

NAAMATHITE [Heb *naʿămātî*]. Zophar, one of Job's three friends, is called a Naamathite, i.e., a man from Naamah (Job 2:11; 11:1; 20:9; 42:9). There were various places and tribes called Naamah; e.g., a town in Judah (Josh 15:41), a place in Nejd (central Arabia: *Naʿâmah;* Yaqut n.d., V: 293), and a Sabean clan (*nʿmt,* Harding 1971: 594). Tentatively, one may favor a Sabean background for Zophar. In this case, the homelands of Job's friends encircle the whole Arabian peninsula: Bildad is from Shuah, i.e., the middle Euphrates, NE Arabia; Eliphaz the Temanite comes from either Edom or Tayma, NW Arabia in either case; and Zophar comes from S Arabia (Knauf 1983: 25–26).

The S Arabian origin of Zophar is also assumed by the LXX, which makes him a Minaean (by metathesis *mʿn-* instead of *nʿm-*). This, however, reflects the Minaeans' suzerainty over most of W Arabia, which they gained in ca. 400 B.C. See MEUNIM; MEINIM. Before 400 B.C., at the time of the book of Job's composition, the Sabeans controlled the N Arabian trading cities (cf. Job 6:19). See TEMA (PLACE).

Bibliography

Harding, G. L. 1971. *An Index and Concordance of Pre-Islamic Arabian Names and Inscriptions.* Toronto.

Knauf, E. A. 1983. Supplements Ismaelitica 4. Ijobs Heimat. *BN* 22: 25–29.

Yâqût ar-Rûmî (d. 626/1228). n.d. *Muʾjam al-buldân.* Vol. I–V. Beirut (reprint of the 1955–1957 edition).

Ernst Axel Knauf

NAARAH (PERSON) [Heb *naʿărâ*]. Identified as one of the wives of Ashhur (1 Chr 4:5–6).

H. C. Lo

NAARAH (PLACE) [Heb *naʿărâ*]. Var. NAARAN. A city on the border of Ephraim and Manasseh near Jericho (Josh 16:7). It is probably the same site as Naaran (Heb *naʿărān;* see Boling and Wright *Joshua* AB, 402) in 1 Chr 7:28, though in this list it belongs to Ephraim, suggesting it is inside the border on Ephraim's side.

The site is listed immediately before Jericho, indicating proximity; note also Boling and Wright *Joshua* AB, 402, who take *nʿrth* (MT) as having a directive ending. Consequently, several identifications have been offered for Naarah. Eusebius' *Onomast.* 136.24 describes Noorath as a Jewish settlement 5 Roman miles from Jericho. This would be Roman Jericho near Wâdī el-Qilt. The site of el-Aujeh is ca. 5 miles NE of Jericho.

More commonly, Naarah is identified as the modern Tel el-Jisr (M.R. 190144) ca. 3.5 miles NW of Jericho. Jisr is just below the springs, Ain Nuʿeimeh and Ain Duyuq (the latter preserves the name of Duk, a citadel in the Hasmonean period). These springs qualify as the "waters of Jericho" E of the border referred to in Josh 16:1 (*GTTOT,* 163). Josephus (*Ant* 17.13.1 §340) says Archelaus (ethnarch of Judea, Samaria, and Idumea, 4 B.C.–6 A.D.) rebuilt Jericho. Then he "diverted half the water with which the village of Neara used to be watered" to irrigate the plantations for his new city of Archelais. This locates Neara (Naarah) near Jericho and associates it with a good water supply. The narrative is not decisive but it appears that Naarah is nearer to Jericho than to Archelais. The identification with Tel el-Jisr is based on the discovery in 1918 of a synagogue floor from the 6th century A.D. Jewish villages are not common here, so this has been taken as support for the identification of Naarah with Jisr even though the distance is not quite exact. Avi-Yonah (*EAEHL* 3: 891) cites a midrash, *Lam. Rab.* 45a, which mentions the enmity between Naaran and neighboring Jericho. Jews were still mentioned in the 5th century A.D. *(Life of Saint Chariton)* and the 6th century (Palladius *h. Laus.* 48).

However, Kallai *(HGB)* points out that such late "data" does not support earlier identifications, and there is no archaeological evidence for the earlier site. Glueck (1951) favored the first ruin N of Jericho in the Jordan valley proper, Kh. el-Ayash (because of its Iron I–II pottery) near Wâdī el-Auja. Most identify the nearest Roman ruin, Kh. el-Auja et-Tahta as Herodian Archelais. Kallai (*HGB,* 160, n. 131) notes confusion in the designation of sites, which complicates the identification. Kallai also notes an additional site NE of Kh. el-Mifgir (M.R. 193193). It has Iron Age finds and should be considered as a possible identification for Naarah. It is near enough to Tell el-Jisr to be related to it. Kallai (*HGB,* 165) concludes, however, that there is no conclusive identification.

Bibliography

Glueck, N. 1951. Explorations in Eastern Palestine, IV. Part I: Text. AASOR 25–28: 412–13.

Henry O. Thompson

NAARAI (PERSON) [Heb *naʿăray*]. The son of Ezbai and one of David's mighty men (1 Chr 11:37). In the parallel passage at 2 Sam 23:35 he is called Paarai the Arbite, and it is not possible to decide definitely which is the more original reading. For a discussion of the variants, see EZBAI.

Stephen Pisano

NAATHUS (PERSON) [Gk *Naathos*]. One of the sons of Addi who returned with Ezra (1 Esdr 9:31). While in Codex Alexandrinus the name appears as *naathos,* it appears as *lathos* in Codex Vaticanus. He was one of the Israelites who had married foreign wives and had to put them away with their children in accordance with Ezra's reform. He is possibly the same person as Adna in the parallel list in Ezra 10:30.

Jin Hee Han

NABAL (PERSON) [Heb *nābāl*]. A wealthy sheep-and-goat owner from Maon who was the husband of Abigail (1 Sam 25:2–3). When David, who was fleeing from Saul, heard that Nabal was shearing his sheep in Carmel, where he tended his flocks, he sent ten young men to inform Nabal that he did not harm any of his men while he was with them in the wilderness. David then asked for help from Nabal. Instead of reacting positively, Nabal behaved arrogantly and refused to give any provisions to David's men. At this, David called his men to arms against Nabal but was intercepted by Abigail, who sent gifts of food to David. She pleaded on her husband's behalf, reminding David that Nabal, as his name implied, was a fool (Heb *nābāl,* "foolish, senseless"; cf. Prov 17:7). She then predicted that the Lord would establish David's house and preserve his life from his enemies (1 Sam 25:28–31). Because of her intercession David decided not to kill Nabal. Abigail told Nabal of his reprieve the morning after a banquet when "Nabal's wine had left him," and at this "his heart died within him; he became a stone" (1 Sam 25:37). Ten days later he died and David took Abigail as his wife.

Despite the popular etymology of Nabal's name, it has been suggested that *nābāl* may originally have had another meaning (cf. Akk *niblu,* scion), since "no parents would name their child 'Fool' " although it may have been a nickname (*EDB,* 1589). Levenson (1978: 13–14) suggests that his real name may have been suppressed "in order to give him a name indicative of his character." Nabal is referred to as a Calebite (v 3) and we are told that he was from Maon and his business was in Carmel (v 2). According to the LXX he was a Carmelite (v 5) and Josephus (*Ant* 6.13.6) calls him a Ziphite. These variants reflect the settlement of the clan of Caleb in the fertile area of Judea S of Hebron where Maon, Ziph, and Carmel were located.

McCarter (*1 Samuel* AB, 402) points out that "the story is designed to illustrate the excellent qualities of one of David's wives" and that by marrying Abigail, David extended his base of power into Hebron, where he would become king later on (2 Sam 2:1–4). Nabal's sudden death at the hand of the Lord (1 Sam 25:38) brought to fulfillment Abigail's prediction that the Lord would eliminate David's enemies (1 Sam 25:29).

Bibliography

Levenson, J. D. 1978. 1 Samuel 25 as Literature and History. *CBQ* 40: 11–28.

STEPHEN PISANO

NABARIAH (PERSON) [Gk *Nabarias*]. One of the six men who stood on Ezra's left as he read aloud the law of Moses to the people in the open square before the east gate of the temple (1 Esdr 9:44). His name appears as Nabadias in the Vulgate. Ezra's public reading occurred on the day of the New Year, which was a day of convocation (Num 29:1–6). Josephus connects this event with the Feast of Tabernacles (*Ant* 11.5.5). The name does not appear in the parallel list in Neh 8:4.

JIN HEE HAN

NABATEANS [Gk *Nabataioi*]. People from the Arab kingdom of Nabatea, which played an important role in the history of Palestine as early as the 2d century B.C., supporting the Maccabeans Judas and Jonathan (1 Macc 5:24–28; 9:35). The Nabatean king Aretas IV is mentioned in 2 Cor 11:32–33. This kingdom, with its capital at Petra, flourished during the late Hellenistic and early Roman imperial periods. The Nabateans (or "Nabataeans") designated themselves as the *Nabaṭû (nbṭw),* and are known either as the *Nabataioi* or as "Arabs" by Greek writers. Their territory embraced parts of modern S Syria, Jordan, the Negeb of Israel, the Sinai, portions of the E deserts of Egypt, and the NW region of Saudi Arabia. Within this region, over 1,000 archaeological sites have been cataloged as being Nabatean or containing remains described as Nabatean (Wenning 1987; Gatier and Salles 1988). The expanding corpus of Nabatean Aramaic inscriptions has also reached over 4,000, although most of these are merely graffiti and the longer ones consist mainly of stereotyped funerary phrases. The reconstruction of their history is dependent on Greek, Latin, and Jewish classical sources (Starcky *DBSup* 7: 886–1017; Hammond 1973; and Bowersock 1983 are fundamental).

A. Origins

The prehistory of the Nabateans remains controversial. The relations of the Greco-Roman Nabateans with the earlier Ishmaelite tribe of NEBAIOTH mentioned in the OT has been rejected on linguistic grounds. The discovery of the spelling *Nabayât* in N Arabian texts agrees with that of the Hebrew Bible *(Nabayôt)* and the Assyrian records (*Nabaiati;* with variants), which seems to suggest that this early tribe was unrelated to the later Nabateans, whose name appears as *Nabaṭû* in their Aramaic inscriptions. The absence of the *yod* and presence of the emphatic *ṭet* (rather than *taw*) makes it difficult to assume any relationship between the two. Instead, scholars have sought for the origins of the Nabateans in S Arabia, where the root *nbṭ* appears in the SW Semitic dialects (*DBSup* 7:900), but neither the Nabatean pantheon nor their cultural traits seem typical of this region. Moreover, the root *nbṭ* is known in NW Semitic much earlier than its appearance in S Arabia. Historical and geographical factors also suggest that the Nabateans arose within the Aramaic-speaking world of the so-called "Fertile Crescent." Within this context, it has been proposed they were a subtribe of Qedar (Knauf 1986) or from the sphere of the Persian Gulf (Milik 1982), possibly in the vicinity of the al-Hasa or Hofuf oasis near ancient Gerrha (Graf fc.).

Wherever their origins, by 312 B.C. the Nabateans were centered at Petra, where they defended themselves successfully from an attack by Antigonous the One-Eyed, a veteran commander from Alexander the Great's eastern campaigns (Hieronymus of Cardia *apud* Diodorus Siculus 19.95). This same source also indicates they had already established themselves as merchants engaged in the profitable aromatic trade from S Arabia. In 259 B.C., the Zenon papyri represented them as part of the ethnographic landscape of the Ḥaurān and N Transjordan (*Papiri greci e latini,* 406). By the 2d century B.C., they occupied the coastal areas of the Red Sea, where they harassed Ptolemaic merchant ships (Diodorus 3.43.5). With the eclipse of the Minaean kingdom in S Arabia by 100 B.C., formerly the main transporters of aromatics to the Mediterranean (Strabo 16.4.18), the Nabateans emerged into prominence as the primary conveyors of frankincense and myrrh from S Arabia, no longer just middlemen. In the process, they developed numerous settlements along the caravan routes between the Ḥijāz and Damascus, and between Petra and Gaza.

B. History of the Monarchy

The relations of the Nabatean kings with the Hasmonean and Herodian dynasties of Judea (Kasher 1988) and with the Roman authorities (Bowersock 1983; Funke 1989) are the context in which the few historical facts regarding Nabatea emerge in the ancient sources. However, Nabatean Aramaic inscriptions also have helped establish a more secure chronology and sequence for the Nabatean monarchs.

Aretas I (fl. 170–160 B.C.) is the first known Nabatean monarch, the friend of the Maccabean rulers Judas and Jonathan (1 Macc 5:24–28; 15:22; cf. 2 Macc 12:10–12). He is probably the ruler "Aretas, King of the Nabateans" mentioned in the earliest known Nabatean inscription found at Elusa in the Negeb. See ARETAS. A king named Rabbel I has sometimes been assigned to the long interval between Aretas I and II, but the epigraphic evidence cited in support of this hypothesis is uncertain (*DBSup* 7: 905; cf. Bowersock 1983: 71–73).

During the reign of Aretas II (fl. 100 B.C.), the Nabateans became embroiled with Alexander Jannaeus, the Hasmonean king who captured the port city of Gaza from the Arab monarch. Aretas also is probably the Arab king "Herotimus" who conducted campaigns into Egypt and Syria (Justin 39.5).

Obodas I (ca. 93–85 B.C.) was also in continual conflict with Alexander Jannaeus during his reign, finally defeating him about 90 B.C. (Jos. *Ant* 13.13.5 [375]) and seizing territories in Moab and Galaaditis from him (13.[382]). In 87 B.C., the Seleucid king Antiochus XII was defeated at Cana in S Syria and was killed by the forces of Obodas (*Ant* 13.15.1 [387–91]; *JW* 1.4.7 [99–102]). After Obodas' death, a royal cult developed around him, centered in the Negeb city that bears his name (Negev 1986).

Aretas III (85–62/1 B.C.) was king when the first great expansion of Nabatea took place. Known as the "philhellene" from his coins, Aretas expanded the borders of Nabatea into S Syria as far as Damascus and struggled with Alexander Jannaeus for control of Moab and Gilead in Transjordan. More intimate relations existed between Aretas and the Idumean ruler Antipater, the father of Herod the Great. In 63 B.C. they combined their forces in support of the Hasmonean claimant Hyrcanus before being repelled by the Roman general Pompey. In the aftermath, Nabatea became a client-state of Rome. There is no record of Aretas III after 62 B.C.

A king named Obodas II has been postulated as the successor of Aretas III based on several coins bearing his name and a portrait of an unusual nature. The coins enumerated for the first three years of his reign are placed between 62–60 B.C. (Meshorer 1975: 16–20). This putative predecessor to Malichus I is more problematic now with the publication of the Tell esh-Shuqafiya inscription dated to the 26th year of the reign of Malichus I and the 18th (not 14th) year of Cleopatra VII Philopater (Jones et al. 1988). This text, dated to 35/34 B.C., firmly places the accession year of Malichus I in the year 61/60 B.C., leaving a possible gap of only one year for the hypothesized Obodas, assuming that Aretas III died in 62 B.C., not in 61 B.C.

Malichus I (61–30 B.C.) ruled during the period of civil war and turmoil in Rome, producing shifts in his alliance and diplomatic maneuvering. In 55 B.C., Gabinius, the governor of Syria, attacked Nabatea and exacted tribute from Malichus. In 47 B.C. Malichus supplied military aid to Caesar at Alexandria, but later supported the Parthians who invaded Judea in 40 B.C., rather than Mark Antony, which placed him at odds with Herod the Great and Antony when they were expelled. Afterward, he was forced to pay a large indemnity to Rome (Dio Cassius 48.41.5), and Antony also exacted revenues and territories from Malichus at the request of his lover Queen Cleopatra of Egypt (49.32.5; *Ant* 15.4.1 [92–96]; *JW* 1.[360]). In 31 B.C., Herod attacked Nabatea and defeated the forces of Obodas near Philadelphia (modern Amman). The defeat of Antony and Cleopatra at Actium in the same year marked the transition to Augustan rule in the Near East. Nabatean favor with the new regime was gained by their destroying Cleopatra's ships at the Suez in her abortive attempt to escape from Rome (Plutarch *Ant.* 69.3; Dio 51.7.1).

Obodas III (30–9 B.C.) enjoyed more cordial relations with Rome and Judea. In 26 B.C. he supported the Roman campaign of Aelius Gallus into S Arabia with 1,000 Nabatean troops commanded by Syllaeus, his minister. Nabatean relations with Herod the Great also appear to have been friendly as a result of Syllaeus, who even attempted to marry Salome, Herod's sister, until Herod made the arrangement dependent on his conversion to Judaism (*Ant* 16.7.6 [225]). At Obodas' death, Syllaeus attempted to seize control of Nabatea, but was thwarted by Herod's advisor Nicolaus of Damascus. Augustine later had the ambitious Nabatean minister executed (Strabo 16.4.24).

The lengthy reign of Aretas IV (9 B.C.–40 A.D.) marks the apogee of the Nabatean kingdom. He appears to have been from a collateral branch of the royal house and assumed the throne without the approval of Augustus, embroiling himself in controversy with Rome during the early years of his reign. Afterward, however, Aretas, known as "the lover of his people," brought about the great expansion and development of the Nabatean realm, bringing him into contact and sometimes conflict with the Herodian dynasts and Rome. His rule marks the architectural development of the Nabatean capital at Petra, the establishment of the *entrepôt* at HEGRA in the Ḥijāz, and the flourishing of the cities along the Petra-Gaza road in the Negeb. The political, commercial, and cultural aspects of Nabatea reached a high point under his rule.

Literary references to the reign of Malichus II (A.D. 40–70) are minimal, which has led to it being characterized as one of political and economic decline. However, he appears to have been the Nabatean king mentioned in *Periplus Maris Erythraei* 19, implying that trade was still flowing from the Red Sea port of Leuke Kome to Petra at the time. Commercial and military activity also continued at Hegra in his reign, with its citizens occupying the distant N Arabian oasis of Dumah (Jauf) in the Wâdī Sirhan. In A.D. 67, he provided military assistance of 1,000 cavalry and 5,000 infantry to the Romans during the First Jewish Revolt, 66–73 (*JW* 3.4.2 [68]). A Nabatean inscription discovered at Rome in 1989 also appears to date to his reign.

Rabbel II (A.D. 70–106) came to the throne in his minority, with his mother Shuqailat ruling as regent until A.D. 75. His accession appears to have been marked by turmoil. A certain Damasi, the scion of an important Nabatean aristocratic family at Hegra, led a revolt against the royal house of Petra. Support for the uprising included tribes from the far N of the Nabatean realm as well as the citizens of his Hijazi home. The phrase "who brought life and deliverance to his people" that appears in Rabbel II's titulary from A.D. 75 and afterward probably refers to his participation in quelling the rebellion (Graf 1988: 180–81). During his reign, Bostra became the new center for the royal house or at least an alternative to the traditional capital at Petra. Inscriptions in the Negeb also indicate that there was an important development of the agricultural resources of the region during his reign. For his long rule, two queens are known, Gamilat (A.D. 76–102) and Hagru (A.D. 102–106), who are designated as Rabbel's "sisters," the daughters of Malichus II.

In A.D. 106, the governor of Syria, Cornelius Palma, annexed the Nabatean kingdom to Rome. The failure of Trajan to take the title "Arabicus" and the presence of the phrase *Arabia adquisita* on coins of his reign (rather than *Arabia capta*) is thought to suggest a peaceful annexation; other indications suggest that some force was required and some conflict took place (Bowersock 1983: 79–82; Graf 1989: 378–88). The transition to Roman rule is marked by the Babatha archive, discovered at En-gedi, containing documents that stretch from A.D. 93 to the outbreak of the Bar Kokhba revolt in A.D. 132 (Bowersock 1983: 76–79). There is no trace of the descendants of the Nabatean royal house in these documents or other sources after the annexation. The theory that a putative Malichus III ruled over a truncated portion of the kingdom no longer seems viable (Graf 1988: 176–77). The archive of Babatha does reveal that an Obodas was the crown prince of Nabatea in A.D. 98, but his fate after the annexation remains unknown. Unlike most client-kingdoms annexed by Rome, there is no evidence of any of the descendants of the Nabatean royal family serving in Roman imperial administration or obtaining senatorial status. Trajan did draft six auxiliary units—the *cohortes Ulpiae Petraorum*—from the Nabatean army, although they were assigned to adjacent provinces of the East and soon disappeared (Bowsher 1990). Although Bostra became the capital of the Roman province, Petra received the title of metropolis under Trajan and served as the administrative center for the S region. The tomb of the Roman governor L. Aninius Sextius Florentinus (ca. A.D. 127) is even located at the old Nabatean capital city.

C. Language and Inscriptions

The fundamental study of the grammatical and epigraphical aspects of Nabatean Aramaic remains that of Cantineau (1930–32). The Aramaic language used by the Nabateans has its greatest affinity to that employed earlier as the lingua franca of the Achaemenid Persian period. However, this language was adopted; the native language of the Nabateans was an Arabic dialect akin to classical Arabic. This is reflected in the fact that their personal names are primarily Arabic (Healey 1989), typically spelled according to the orthographic practices of the earlier imperial Aramaic (Diem 1973). The peculiar paleography of the 4,000 Nabatean texts (*DBSup* 7: 924–37) also indicates that it was the basis for the development of the Arab script. Late texts also contain a more substantial Arabic vocabulary and syntactical element, forming the basis for the theory of the gradual Arabization of the language. However, the loanwords represent a rather small specialized vocabulary that is mostly funerary and political in nature (O'Connor 1986). The basic Arabic onomasticon of Nabatea and the presence of nearly classical Arabic in an Aramaic Nabatean text of ca. A.D. 100 (Negev 1986) argues against the progressive Arabization of the language.

The Nabateans were obviously polylingual, writing and speaking in other languages indigenous to the region, as is suggested by bilingual texts in the related but different proto-Arabic dialects of Thamudic and Safaitic. The later texts also mention tribes of the Nabatean realm and petitions to deities known from the Nabatean pantheon (Graf 1989: 358–75). Aramaic apparently was used by the Arab rulers primarily for formal and monumental purposes, but they normally spoke in Arabic. Any future history of Nabatea must now consider this larger corpus of non-Aramaic texts. In similar fashon, Nabatean material culture is diverse. Neither the distinctive "eggshell"-thin pottery finds nor Aramaic inscriptions are necessarily indicators of the presence or extent of the Nabatean realm (cf. Graf 1986). Instead, the fact that the Nabateans preserved the indigenous cults of the Edomites, Moabites, and Syrians, wrote in diverse scripts, and spoke several languages suggests a heterogeneous society in which the indigenous populations of Transjordan, N Arabia, and elsewhere were assimilated under Nabatean hegemony. The term "Nabateans" should then be understood as a vast political alliance of various peoples.

D. Nabatean Relations with Judaism and Christianity

Relations between the Nabatean monarchs and the Hasmonean and Herodian dynasties were generally intimate, but occasionally strained (Kasher 1988). The conflicts of Alexander Jannaeus with the Nabatean kings obviously were a result of their expansionist policies after the collapse of the Hellenistic kingdoms. The struggles with the Herodian dynasty were prompted by similar ambitions. Nevertheless, the relations with the Jews generally appears to have been cordial, as suggested by a Jewish presence at Hegra and by the archive of the Jewess Babatha, whose family had peacefully settled within Nabatean territory (Bowersock 1983: 76–78). In fact, the flourishing of Nabatea under Aretas IV offers an excellent parallel to that of Judea under Herod the Great, whose mother Cypros was herself of Nabatean descent. Both client-kingdoms assimilated substantial influences from Greco-Roman culture, as witnessed by the architecture and art of each realm. This "Hellenized" Nabatea even has been viewed as a model for the world of the NT, particularly the Galilean countryside of Jesus (Schwank 1983). However, such elements are more difficult to locate within Nabatean society at large, outside of the upper strata. The Nabatean hinterland is more a reflection of local and indigenous tradition than a synthesis of native and Greco-Roman culture. It is interesting that at the core of Nabatean art there existed a nonfigurative tradition that apparently produced two iconoclastic reactions against the adoption of Hellenistic figurative representations, one in the reign of Aretas IV, and the other after the annexation in A.D. 106, two periods when foreign influences on Nabatea were substantial (Patrich 1990).

The relations of Nabatea with the rise of Christianity are more obscure. The Church Fathers often associated the "magi" mentioned in the birth narrative of Jesus with Arabia, the land of "frankincense and myrrh" (*1 Clem.* 25.1–2; *Dial. Trypho* 78.1; Tertullian, *Adv. Marcion* 3.13). Consequently, some modern scholars have postulated that the magi were Nabateans from Petra (e.g., Charbel 1985), although most have preferred Babylon or Persia for their home country. More certain is the fact that the daughter of Aretas IV—probably Shaʿudat (*DBSup* 7: 914)—was the wife that Herod Antipas divorced in order to marry Herodias, the wife of his half-brother Herod Philip. This action, condemned by John the Baptist (Matt 14:3–12 and par), led to military conflict between the royal households (*Ant* 18.5.1–3 [109–25]). The only clear allusion to the Nabateans in the NT is in the account of Paul's escape from the governor of Aretas IV and the city of Damascus (2 Cor 11:32–33). Paul's earlier sojourn in Arabia (Gal 1:17) is more difficult to locate, although the Decapolis region has been suggested.

No traces of Nabatean conversion to Christianity appear until the Byzantine period. The Christian scholar Origen of Alexandria participated in a synod at Bostra, an old Nabatean center and the capital of Arabia, whose bishop Beryllus was the subject of a doctrinal inquiry (Eusebius, *Hist. Eccl.* VI.33). Petra was also the home of several prominent Sophist philosophers and rhetoricians at the time (Bowersock 1983: 135). But it is not until the time of Constantine that there is any record of churches at Petra and in the desert hinterland of Arabia (Eus. *Comm. on*

Isaiah 42.11 = PG 24.392). In A.D. 325, bishops from Bostra, Philadelphia (Amman), and Aela (ᶜAqaba) participated in the Council of Nicea, but no bishops from Petra were present. Nevertheless, later in the 4th century, hellenized bishops were active at Petra (*DBSup* 7: 921–23), but by this time Nabatean presence is difficult to trace in Arabia. There are no dated Nabatean inscriptions from Petra or Bostra after the annexation of the kingdom in A.D. 106. Emigration by many Nabateans from the heartland of the province to the peripheral regions of the Sinai, the E deserts of Egypt, and the Arabian peninsula evidently took place. Inscriptions from the postannexation period are from the fringes of the province or border regions (Wenning 1987: 305). The last dated inscription in Nabatean Aramaic is from A.D. 356 in the Ḥijāz (Wenning 1987: 305).

Bibliography

Bowersock, G. W. 1983. *Roman Arabia.* Cambridge, MA.

Bowsher, J. 1990. The Nabataean Army. In *The Eastern Frontier of the Roman Empire,* ed. D. French and C. Lightfoot. Oxford.

Cantineau, J. 1930–32. *Le nabatéen.* 2 vols. Paris.

Charbel, A. 1985. Matteo 2, 1–12: I Magi Nella Corniche del Regno nabateo. *StPat* 32: 81–88.

Diem, W. 1973. Die nabatäischen Inschriften und die Frage der Kasusflexion im Altarabischen. *ZDMG* 123: 227–37.

Funke, P. 1989. Rom und das Nabatäerreich bis zur aufrichtung der Provinz Arabia. *Historisch-Archäologischer Freundeskreis,* 5–27.

Gatier, P., and Salles, J.-F. 1988. Aux frontieres méridionales du domaine nabatéen. Pp. 173–91 in *L'Arabie et ses mers bordieres I.* Travaux de la Maison de l'Orient no. 16. Lyon.

Graf, D. F. 1986. The Nabataeans and the Decapolis. Pp. 785–96 in *The Defense of the Roman and Byzantine East,* ed. P. Freeman and D. Kennedy. BARIS 297. Oxford.

———. 1988. Qura ᶜArabiyya and Provincia Arabia. Pp. 171–211 in *Geographie historique au Proche-Orient.* Notes et Monographies Techniques 23. Paris.

———. 1989. Romans and the Saracens: Reassessing the Nomadic Menace. Pp. 341–400 in *L'Arabie préislamique et son environnement historique et culturel.* Travaux du Centre de Recherche sur le Proche-Orient et la Grèce Antiques 10. Leiden.

———. fc. The Origin of the Nabataeans. *ARAM.*

Hammond, P. 1973. *The Nabataeans—Their History, Culture and Archaeology.* Studies in Mediterranean Archaeology 37. Gothenburg.

Healey, J. F. 1989. Were the Nabataeans Arabs? *ARAM* 1: 38–44.

Jones, R.; Hammond, P.; Johnson, D.; and Feima, Z. 1988. A Second Nabataean Inscription from Tell esh-Shuqafiya. Egypt. *BASOR* 269: 47–57.

Kasher, A. 1988. *Jews, Idumaeans, and Ancient Arabs.* Texte und Studien zum Antiken Judentum 18. Tübingen.

Knauf, E. A. 1986. Die Herkunft der Nabatäer. Pp. 74–86 in *Petra: Neue Ausgrabungen und Entdeckungen,* ed. M. Lindner. Munich.

Meshorer, Y. 1975. *Nabataean Coins.* Qedem 3. Jerusalem.

Milik, J. T. 1982. Origines des nabatéens. Pp. 261–65 in *Studies in the History and Archaeology of Jordan,* ed. A. Hadidi. Amman.

Negev, A. 1986. Obodas the God. *IEJ* 36: 56–60.

O'Connor, M. 1986. The Arabic Loanwords in Nabataean Aramaic. *JNES* 45: 213–29.

Patrich, J. 1990. *The Formation of Nabataean Art.* Jerusalem.

Schwank, B. 1983. Neue Funde in Nabatäerstädten und ihre Bedeutung für die neutestamentliche Exegese. *NTS* 29: 429–35.

Wenning, R. 1987. *Die Nabatäer-Denkmäler und Geschichte. Eine Bestandesaufnahme des archäologischen Befundes.* NTOA 3. Göttingen.

DAVID F. GRAF

NABONIDUS (PERSON). The successor of Labasi-Marduk, who ruled as king of Babylon for seventeen years (556–539 B.C.), and who was on the throne when Cyrus took Babylon in 539 B.C. Nabonidus, the father of Belshazzar, appears only in the book of Daniel, but was confused with the infamous Babylonian king Nebuchadnezzar (Hartman, Di Lella *Daniel* AB, 50). He appears by his proper name (Aram *nbny;* see Milik 1956, 407–11) in an Aramaic document found three decades ago at Qumran, entitled "The Prayer of Nabonidus."

Berossus, in his *Babyloniaca,* notes that Nabonidus was not related to any of his predecessors, although in his own inscriptions he claims to have been a legitimate successor of Nebuchadnezzar (605–562 B.C.) and Neriglissar (560–556 B.C.). The problem of how and when he seized power remains a difficult one to resolve. Neriglissar died shortly after his Cilician campaign in early April of 556 B.C. Yet Berossus says his son and successor, Labasi-Marduk, ruled for another nine months before Nabonidus took control. Unfortunately, the dated cuneiform contract tablets support a reign of only about two months for Labasi-Marduk, after which cities from Nippur to Babylon and Sippar dated their documents to the accession year of Nabonidus. Berossus claims that Labasi-Marduk was put out of the way by a group of "friends" because of "the evil practices he manifested." It has been suggested that Nabonidus' own son, Belshazzar, may have had a hand in the murder of Labasi-Marduk, with the ultimate goal in mind of becoming king himself. Those who support this view point out that Belshazzar had business dealings with prominent banking families that were influential in Babylon during the reigns of Nebuchadnezzar and Neriglissar. Furthermore, he appears to have profited from the confiscation of property belonging to Neriglissar following Labasi-Marduk's death. Despite these circumstances, however, there is no direct evidence to support this conclusion.

Whatever the case, certain of Nabonidus' own inscriptions do support Berossus' contention that he "bore no relation to the royal race." He was, in all probability, of western Aramean origin and was well advanced in age when he ascended the throne. He claims to have been an only child who had no followers and no desire to become king. To a limited extent, this view is supported by the contents of the famous "biography" of his mother, Adad-guppi, which was found several decades ago in Harran (Gadd 1958). While this and other important inscriptions were erected there by Nabonidus himself after his return from Arabia, they nevertheless focus on his restoration of the Ehulhul temple of Sin and his apparent preoccupation with this god. Adad-guppi asserts that she was responsible for Nabonidus' becoming acquainted with Nabopolassar and Nebuchadnezzar and that his advancement was almost entirely due to her talents. Such a contention is probably not an overstatement since, unlike his predecessor, Neriglissar, Nabonidus apparently was not associated with prominent Babylonian business interests and held no position in any temple bureaucracy.

Unfortunately, the sections of the *Nabonidus Chronicle,* the *Verse Account* and other royal inscriptions (see Grayson TCS 5; *ANET,* 305–7; 308–15; 562–63) that we would normally expect to detail events of Nabonidus' early years survive only in fragmentary condition. Nevertheless, we do know that he carried out a campaign into Cilicia, visited a number of temples in Babylonia, and ordered the repair of fortifications surrounding a number of cities. Not only did he excavate the Egipar in Ur and rebuild the Ebabbara in Sippar, but he also restored or reinstated religious practices associated with Marduk in Sippar and Uruk. Nabonidus' royal inscriptions repeatedly emphasize his association with earlier times, despite his forceful seizure of power. He liked to emphasize his Assyrian and Chaldean "ancestry." He portrays his "antiquarian" and even Akkadian interests (as illustrated by his excavations at Agade, Uruk, and Ur) as evidence of respect for his predecessors and of his reign's continuity with the past (Reiner 1985: 1–16). Yet at the same time he engaged in an extensive reorganization of the Eanna temple bureaucracy in Uruk, where opposition to the succession of a number of monarchs apparently emerged at various times. It has been suggested that intervention in temple affairs in Uruk represents the possible influence of Babylonian business interests on the king himself, resulting in greater external control of property held by the Eanna. However, such a conclusion ignores the fact that intervention or control of temple affairs in Babylonia was a fact of life as early as the time of Nebuchadnezzar and the relatively small number of Chaldean administrative documents published to date has distorted our picture of the relations between palace and temple in pre-Achaemenid times.

After returning from a second campaign into Cilicia in 553 B.C., Nabonidus left Babylon for Syria, Anti-lebanon and Arabia. Present evidence suggests that he was away from the capital city for at least ten years, during which time his son, Belshazzar, ruled the kingdom as co-regent. It is likely that Nabonidus was aware of the activities of Cyrus of Persia at the time of his departure, since otherwise it would be difficult to explain such a long absence. Nevertheless, the purpose of his visit to Arabia and the oasis of Tema remains unclear (Lambert 1972). While the evidence from Tema published to date is inconclusive, we do know from other sources that Nabonidus made it his principal residence, enlarged its size and fortifications, and stationed troops there. Records of the Assyrian kings from Tiglath-pileser III (745–727 B.C.) to Esarhaddon (681–669 B.C.) indicate both an awareness of the immense economic resources of northern Arabia and attempts to impose tribute in the form of spices and gold on a number of tribes located there. Although Nabonidus' ties to the worship of Sin in Harran probably were a source of friction between himself and the priesthood of Marduk and could have resulted in a lengthy absence from Babylon, it is likely that control of the trade routes from Arabia to Mesopotamia was more of a motivating factor in his decision to reside in Tema for at least a decade.

By the time he returned to Babylon in 543 B.C., Cyrus of Persia had already conquered the kingdoms of Media and Lydia, which left Babylonia open to invasion from virtually all sides. It appears that Belshazzar, Nabonidus' son and co-regent, remained in the vicinity of Sippar (at the command of a Babylonian army) when Cyrus campaigned in Anatolia. There is no evidence of engagements between Chaldean and Persian forces prior to 543 B.C. Unfortunately, the surviving cuneiform sources are either fragmentary or say nothing of substance about events that may have taken place between 543 and 540 B.C. In fact, Nabonidus' name is strangely missing from what does survive. Nevertheless, it appears now that Nabonidus rebuilt Sin's temple in Harran, the Ehulhul, sometime after his return from Tema, while apparently failing to give proper attention to such important centers as Uruk and its Eanna sanctuary, which he had reorganized in his earlier years (Tadmor 1965). The reasons for these activities may never be known, but the Persians insisted that Nabonidus tried to alter traditional religious beliefs by replacing Marduk with Sin, who now became the supreme God of Babylonia. Whatever the case, Cyrus' armies eventually took Babylon in 539 B.C. and Nabonidus' reign came to an end. Classical sources assert that Nabonidus died in another part of the Persian Empire some time after Babylon fell.

In the available cuneiform material from the Chaldean period (605–539 B.C.), Nabonidus is the subject of more varied characterizations than any other monarch. It must be remembered, of course, that he bore no relationship to the other members of the royal line, a fact that later Classical writers were quick to point out. Hence, he was certain to mean different things to different people; his memory would be preserved by various chroniclers or biographers for altogether dissimilar purposes. To some of his contemporaries, he was the symbol of the traditional devotion of a monarch to his god and to the upkeep of his important temples; to others, his reign stood out as an example never to be repeated again. Since such a variety of description exists in the documents, it is not surprising that a multiplicity of elements can be associated with each one, elements that not only enhance the picture of the individual being described but also preserve a cultural attitude toward such a person in accordance with his peculiar achievements.

In attempting an examination of what survives, it is important to make a distinction between sources written during the king's reign and those composed following the conquest of Babylon by Cyrus I of Persia. Fortunately for us, included in the former group is a rather detailed biographical sketch of Nabonidus' mother, Adad-guppi, which provides us both insights into the life of this rather extraordinary woman, and a picture of some of what took place during her son's reign. Clearly, Nabonidus was a devotee of the god Sin of Harran (presumably the city of his origin). A "local" account of his preoccupation with this god would, therefore, be expected to stress this essential fact. In this inscription we are told that "Nabonidus . . . performed indeed all the forgotten rites of Sin . . . He completed the rebuilding of the temple Ehulhul, led Sin . . . in procession from Babylon . . . [and] installed [him] in gladness and happiness [in] Harran" (Gadd 1958). The same attitude is reflected in a stela of Nabonidus, also found at Harran, which credits the god Sin with establishing his rule over the Chaldean kingdom. "(This is) the great miracle of Sin," Nabonidus notes, "that none of the [other] gods and goddesses knew (how to achieve) . . . Sin, the lord of all the gods and goddesses residing in heaven . . . called me to kingship" (*ANET,* 562). Accounts like these could never appear in an inscription in Babylon, formulaic though they may be. Likewise, a description detailing the setting-up of an image of Sin could not be displayed in the capital city, where devotion to Marduk was fundamental to one's success as a monarch. Nevertheless, these descriptions indicate the existence (in Syria, at least) of a highly favorable attitude concerning Nabonidus, one which portrayed the monarch as a penitent, reverent ruler who had respect for the past. Such a highly positive portrait emphasizing the king's piety stands in dramatic contrast to the largely hostile opinions voiced by the Marduk priests in Babylon following Cyrus' conquest in 539 B.C.

Official chronicles detailing the year-by-year events of the reign of Nabonidus have been known for over a century. The relationship of these chronicles to the substance of the foregoing inscriptions will be dealt with later. However, due to their lack of detailed accounts of the king's accomplishments, it is necessary to examine what survives of the Persian point of view; here, naturally, Nabonidus is blamed not for being inattentive to the responsibility of caring for and restoring temples in various urban centers, but for neglecting Marduk and attempting the worship of a new god (i.e., Sin of Harran) whom no one had even seen in the land. Such an unusually critical attitude appears in the *Verse Account* of Nabonidus, an editorialized inscription composed to justify the end of the Chaldean dynasty and the rise of Persia to prominence. "[He had made the image of a deity] which nobody had (ever) seen in (this country)," the account reads, and "he called it by the name of Nanna." Furthermore, "he let everything go," entrusted his kingdom to his son, Belshazzar, and left Babylon for a ten-year sojourn in Tema. In a similar text, the *Cyrus Cylinder,* these "evil deeds" of the last Neo-Babylonian monarch are detailed, with emphasis being placed on the positive elements in the Achaemenid conquest of Babylonia. "The chief of the gods (Marduk) was enraged. . . . The gods . . . left their sanctuaries, angered that Nabonidus had brought them to Babylon." According to this account, it was only when Marduk "took pity on the people of Sumer and Akkad who had become like corpses" and commanded Cyrus to conquer Babylonia that everything returned to normal.

In examining the Persian sources and considering the contents of Nabonidus' own inscriptions (both in Babylon and Harran), it is not hard to understand why the later Classical writers considered Nabonidus to be only a name in a list, while the Persians viewed him as an example of something never to be repeated again. The Achaemenids did not consider either the construction or restoration of sanctuaries that were characteristic of Nabonidus to be significant, since they were considered the traditional responsibilities of Babylonian monarchs. Instead, the activities of the king amounting to behavior that went contrary to the traditional will of a god had to be emphasized. Cyrus I, of course, had to cast his own image in a favorable light; having taken Babylon through force and betrayal, it was necessary to be propagandistic in justifying his success. Such, therefore, were the circumstances surrounding the creating (by the priest-scribes of Marduk in Babylon) of an account which focused on the outright heretical acts of the last king of the Chaldean period. Nebuchadnezzar's 43-year reign was one in which devotion to Marduk was accepted fact; Nabonidus, on the other hand, not only halted the New Year Festival but also forsook his kingdom for a sojourn in Tema. But the most hated act of all was his preoccupation with the god Sin of Harran, a preoccupation that, as we have just seen, formed an integral part of the king's own elaborate accounts. Thus, while Nabonidus (in one quarter of his kingdom, at least) may have been viewed as a monarch devoted to the worship of Sin and to the care and upkeep of his sanctuaries, to the Babylonians (under Persian rule) and the Jews of the postexilic period) Nabonidus was literally mad, and consequently did not deserve the devotion of his subjects. As a result, many of these hostile characterizations seen in the Achaemenid portrayals were to be incorporated into other sources where they were employed for different reasons.

As noted above, additional information regarding the reign of Nabonidus can be found in the chronicles and contracts datable to the king's reign. These sources differ markedly from those discussed above; the rather one-sided characterizations of the Persian and Syrian sources are totally absent, leaving only the rather dry, event-by-event record of happenings associated with each year. Both the *Nabonidus Chronicle* and the economic texts contain numerous references to the king's journey to Tema; both note the monarch's absence from Babylon during at least a ten-year period of time. What is germane to our investigation is the king's own justification for his deeds. The Persians associated his lengthy journey with a neglect of his kingly responsibilities; anyone devoted to Marduk would hardly have avoided being present during the celebration of the New Year Festival, since it would have necessitated cancellation of such an essential event. This fact was certainly worthy of note in the *Nabonidus Chronicle,* where we read that "[The king] did not come to Babylon [in the month of Nisan]. . . . The [Akitu festival] did [not take place]."

What, then, was the king's justification for his own absence? The answer is to be found in his account displayed in Harran, namely, that he was commanded to do so by his god until a ten-year period of time elapsed, after which he could reenter his capital city. In the words of Nabonidus, he was merely carrying out the orders of Sin; he did only what he was instructed to do by divine command. Thus, while the Persians could exploit the absence of the king from Babylon to their propagandistic advantage, the inhabitants of Harran were witnessing the acts of a perfectly normal monarch doing only what a devout servant of Sin would be expected to do. The accounts of these deeds, then, naturally carry forth the positive tradition that emphasizes the king's piety.

While the name of Nabonidus does not occur anywhere in the OT or in the *Midr. Rab.,* his image is nevertheless preserved in the so-called *Prayer of Nabonidus.* This discovery allowed scholars to reassess information found in the book of Daniel in light of relevant materials found in other cultures. While the date of this manuscript is 1st century, B.C., it contains descriptions that are at least similar to the

Verse Account quoted earlier. It suggests a continuity that spanned several centuries and kept alive a folkloric image that was to be characteristic of several of the Hebrew sources, especially the book of Daniel. It gives us "the words of the prayer that Nabonidus, king of Assyria and Babylon, the [great] king, prayed [when he was smitten] with a bad inflammation by the decree of the [Most High God] in [the city of] Tema. [With a bad inflammation] I was smitten for seven years and from men I was put away. But when I confessed my sins and my faults, He [God] allowed me [to have] a soothsayer. This was a Jewish [man of the exiles in Babylon]."

This astonishing little piece (which is, of course, Midrashic in genre), identifies Nabonidus and Daniel (he must be the Jewish man of the text) and mentions Babylon and Tema—all the aspects of a historical reconstruction. This seems to indicate that the OT in general, and the book of Daniel in particular, assume far greater importance (from both folkloric and historical points of view) than the somewhat imaginary reconstructions found in the *Midr. Rab.* If this is so, then, why is there no mention of Nabonidus in the Apocryphal and the pseudepigraphical works (written in Greek) or in the relevant chapters of the Hebrew OT? Probably because, while the fortification of Babylon was not significant to the Jews, conquest, on the other hand, was. The capture of the city of Jerusalem, the dismantling of the temple of Solomon, and the deportation of captives were acts never to be forgotten; the author of such horrible deeds had to be portrayed in such a way as to not only place emphasis on destruction and wickedness but also to show that the apparent power or might of the king of Babylon was merely the result of Yahweh's punishment of the Hebrews. The king was only a tool to be used in the teaching of a lesson. In this light, a characterization of Nebuchadnezzar had to be richly embellished with elements drawn from a number of sources, folkloric or otherwise. In the process, however, the Hebrew writer made use of historical materials associated with Nabonidus, not because he was "confused" but, rather, because of the fact that Nabonidus appeared in his own and later sources in such a way as to *fit* the situation involving Nebuchadnezzar that was being described. Certainly, the Achaemenids needed to (and did) emphasize Nabonidus' lack of attention to Marduk; when the Hebrews returned to Palestine, they carried with them their own hatred for Nebuchadnezzar plus the Persian hostility toward Nabonidus and, as a consequence, transformed them both into a story of a conqueror-king who would forsake his god and require the worship of another by his subjects (Dan 3:1–3). The subsequent account of the madness of Nebuchadnezzar (Dan 4:33) reflects the contents of the *Lives of the Prophets* and the *Wisdom of Ahiqar,* and also echoes the Prayer of Nabonidus quoted earlier, where the king is said to have lived apart from men for seven years.

Herein lies, then, perhaps as fine an example as can be found of a melding of history and oral tradition. Nabonidus' own inscriptions inform us of his (at least) ten-year absence from Babylon. The *Verse Account,* although it clearly exaggerates this fact for political reasons, essentially preserves historical fact. The *Prayer of Nabonidus,* written in Aramaic, further emphasizes this point while adding a purely folkloric description to the picture. The traditional image of a prisoner is thus superimposed on both a historical figure and an essentially factual account of his activities. The Maccabean author(s) of the book of Daniel, four centuries removed from the Chaldean period, chose to substitute the name of Nebuchadnezzar for that of Nabonidus, not because of an ignorance of history or because the events of the exilic period were forgotten, but due to the fact that Nebuchadnezzar was the architect of the captivity and a didactic commentary could best realize its objectives through a portrayal of a king that combined history and fiction. To the Hebrew writer, it did not matter whether a characterization harmonized with historical accuracy; the events of the reign of Nabonidus could be combined with the destruction of the city of Jerusalem by Nebuchadnezzar in order to construct an image of a king that could be easily related to the rule of any monarch at any point in time. Thus, as with the Arabic sources, everyone who besieges Jerusalem is thought of as a Nebuchadnezzar; the characterization of the figure becomes propagandistic. Not limited by time or space, it becomes applicable to all periods of history (see Sack 1982).

While it is, therefore, interesting to note the many and varied characterizations of Nabonidus that have led to the publication of a number of interesting studies focusing individually on portions of the surviving sources, it is, nevertheless, unfortunate that their contents may result in our knowing relatively little of the true *historical* Nabonidus. The sources do provide us, however, with an understanding of the cultural attitudes of a number of ancient Near Eastern peoples toward a king who represented many things at different periods of time.

Bibliography

Dougherty, R. P. 1922. Nabonidus in Arabia. *JAOS* 42: 305–14.
———. 1929. *Nabonidus and Belshazzar.* New Haven.
———. 1933. Tema's Place in the Egypto-Babylonian World of the Sixth Century B.C. *Mizraim* 1: 140–43.
Foster, B. 1983. Nabonidus at Kesh. *RA* 77: 92–93.
Gadd, C. J. 1958. The Harran Inscriptions of Nabonidus. *AnSt* 8: 35–92.
Lambert, W. G. 1969. A New Source for the Reign of Nabonidus. *AfO* 22: 1–8.
———. 1972. Nabonidus in Arabia. Pp. 53–64 in *Proceedings of the Fifth Seminar for Arabian Studies.* London.
Milik, J. T. 1956. "Prière de Nabonide" et autres écrits d'un cycle de Daniel. *RB* 63: 407–11.
Olmstead, A. T. 1925. The Chaldean Dynasty. *HUCA* 2: 29–55.
Reiner, E. 1985. *Your Thwarts in Pieces Your Mooring Rope Cut.* Ann Arbor.
Röllig, W. 1964. Nabonid und Tema. *CRRA* 11: 21–32.
Sack, R. H. 1982. Nebuchadnezzar and Nabonidus in Folklore and History. *Mesopotamia* 17: 67–131.
Soden, W. von. 1983. Kyros und Nabonid. Propaganda und Gegenpropaganda. Pp. 61–68 in *Archaologische Mitteilungen aus Iran, Ergänzungsband* 10. Berlin.
Tadmor, H. 1965. The Inscriptions of Nabunaid: Historical Arrangement. Pp. 351–64 in *Studies in Honor of Benno Landsberger* 16. Chicago.

RONALD H. SACK

NABONIDUS, PRAYER OF

(4QPrNab). The *Prayer of Nabonidus* (4QPrNab) was published by J. T. Milik in 1956 from three fragments of the first column and a fragment of a later column of a single ms, which is dated paleographically to ca. 75–50 B.C.E. A further fragment of the first column was noted in an addendum. There have been many subsequent reconstructions, of which the most authoritative is that of F. M. Cross. Cross reconstructs the first column as follows:

> (1) The words of the p[ra]yer which Nabonidus, king of [Ba]bylon, the great king pray[ed when he was stricken] (2) with an evil disease by the decree of G[o]d in Teman. [I Nabonidus] was stricken with [an evil disease] (3) for seven years, and from [that] (time) I was like [unto a beast and I prayed to the Most High] (4) and, as for my sin, he forgave it. A diviner—who was a Jew o[f the Exiles—came to me and said:] (5) "Recount and record (these things) in order to give honor to the name of the G[od Most High." And thus I wrote: I] was stricken with an evil disease in Teman [by the decree of the Most High God, and, as for me,] (7) seven years I was praying [to] gods of silver and gold, [bronze, iron,] wood, stone (and) clay, because [I was of the opini]on that th[ey] were gods. . . .

The fragment of a later column published by Milik refers to a dream which disturbed the speaker, and contains the words "how you are like. . . ."

Discussion of this fragmentary work has been primarily concerned with its relation to chap. 4 of the book of Daniel. Scholars had long suspected that the story in Daniel had its origin in a tradition about Nabonidus rather than Nebuchadnezzar, specifically about his absence from Babylon when he sojourned for ten years in Tema in the Arabian desert. 4QPrNab shared with Daniel 4 the following features: (1) A Babylonian king speaks in the first person (the OG of Daniel provides a fuller parallel on this point); (2) he is punished by God for seven years (Dan 4:29; seven times); (3) a Jewish exile interprets the experience; and (4) the king has a disturbing dream. Further, the reference to gods of silver and gold, etc., is paralleled in Dan 5:23. Of course there are differences too: the name of the king, his location at Tema, the nature of his affliction (a skin disease in the *Prayer*; transformation into a beast in Daniel). Yet most scholars have taken 4QPrNab as striking confirmation of the theory which links Daniel 4 with traditions about Nabonidus. The relationship is enhanced by some reconstructions. Cross reconstructs line 3 as "I was like [unto a beast . . .]." R. Meyer thinks the dream in the *Prayer* concerned a great tree, as in Daniel. Milik suggested that the last fragment should be completed "how you are like Daniel" (taking the king as the speaker and an angel as the addressee). However plausible these suggestions may seem, it is well to bear in mind that they are not actually attested in the fragments. Our text retains an older form of the tradition than Daniel, insofar as the king is identified as Nabonidus and his sojourn at Tema is recollected. The relationship with Daniel 4 is not necessarily one of direct literary dependence; the two stories may be different elaborations of a common tradition.

The most disputed issue in the interpretation of the *Prayer* concerns line 4 (Cross: "and as for my sin, he forgave it"). Milik takes the verb *šbq* as "he *granted* me a diviner," but he has to emend *lh* to *ly* to sustain this. Fitzmyer rendered the line: "an exorcist remitted my sins for Him," and took it as a rare Jewish instance of forgiveness through a human agent. The line is too ambiguous, however, to stand as evidence for an idea which is in dispute. It is simpler to take God as the subject.

4QPrNab is part of the corpus of Aramiac writings found at Qumran which has no specifically sectarian characteristics. It is probably older than the 2d century B.C.E. The reminiscence of Nabonidus' stay at Tema suggests that the underlying tradition goes back to the eastern diaspora, wherever this particular work may have been composed.

Bibliography

Cross, F. M. 1984. Fragments of the Prayer of Nabonidas. *IEJ* 34: 260–64.

Fitzmyer, J. A. 1980. The Aramaic Language and the Study of the NT. *JBL* 99: 16.

Meyer, R. 1962. *Das Gebet des Nabonid.* Berlin.

Milik, J. T. 1956. "Prière de Nabonide" et autres écrits d'un cycle de Daniel. *RB* 63: 407–15.

John J. Collins

NABOPOLASSAR (PERSON). Founder and first king of the Neo-Babylonian dynasty of Mesopotamia. Later historians of the Hellenistic period state that he served under the Assyrian king Sin-šarra-iškun (Gk Sarakos) before leading a revolt that led to Babylonian independence from Assyria. These writers further describe him as a Chaldean ruler who made Babylon his capital. There is, unfortunately, no evidence proving that Nabopolassar (Akk *Nabû-apla-uṣur*) and his successors were Chaldeans—that is, representatives of an ethnic group distinct from the Arameans, who flourished in Babylonia at the same time. In his own inscriptions, he refers to himself as the "son of a nobody." It is possible, as Lambert has hinted, that his origins can be traced to the area around Uruk, since he appears in a Babylonian chronicle in a context that suggests he originally came from there. The exact date of Nabopolassar's accession to the throne in Babylonia cannot be determined with accuracy. Although he asserts that he officially began his reign on August 26, 626 B.C., there is some evidence to suggest that Babylonian cities were already dating their contracts to the "accession year of Nabopolassar" at least two months earlier. Whatever the case, both the Babylonian sources and the Classical accounts are in agreement that Assyria was in turmoil during the latter years of Assurbanipal (669–626 B.C.). In fact, the surviving sources provide us with no evidence indicating either the extent of his sovereignty over Babylonia, the dates for the reign of his successor, Aššur-etil-ilani, or the identity of a certain Sin-šarra-iškun, known to the later Hellenistic writers as Sarakos. As a result, Nabopolassar, through an alliance with the Medes and their king, Cyaxeres, took advantage of the unsettled situation to liberate Babylonia from Assyrian control. The Medes and Babylonians united their forces and prepared to engage the Assyrians and their Egyptian allies. Pockets of resistance to the Chaldeans now developed in Babylonia (in Uruk and Nippur), complicating an already confused situation. Focusing on these important strongholds, the Assyrians tried to take advantage of an apparent disunity and held out for almost seven years. By 615 B.C., however, Nippur had fallen into Nabopolassar's hand, freeing him to press his advantage into Assyria in an attempt to take Aššur and Nineveh. The Medes and their Scythian allies actually took Aššur before the Chaldean host could arrive. There, Nabopolassar and Cyaxeres concluded a peace treaty, and two years later, in 612, Nineveh was taken. Although Cyaxeres now had an opportunity to share in the spoils of conquest, he instead retreated to his homeland.

In 609 B.C., the last king of the Assyrian empire, Aššur-uballit II, organized one final, futile attempt to recover lost territory. The northern city of Harran was to be the focal point of such efforts, but it, too, fell and the remaining troops retreated into Syria. The Egyptian monarch Necho II (610–595 B.C.) feared both the Medes and the Chaldeans as much as had his predecessors. Furthermore, the Egyptians had years before become friends of the Assyrians, and the collapse of their empire would disastrously upset the balance of power in Mesopotamia and Syria. To avoid this, in 608, the pharoah marched his armies across Palestine and reached the Euphrates river, where he spent the better part of three years fighting against Nabopolassar's forces in a lost cause. In 605 B.C., the end for the Assyrians finally came at Carchemish.

Nabopolassar's original claim, made twenty-five years earlier, to kingship over Babylonia, had been purely nominal. But by 605 B.C., the reverse was true. Nineveh lay in ruins; the Medes and Egyptians were no longer a threat to anyone, and southern Mesopotamian cities were dating their documents according to the appropriate year of Nabopolassar, "king of Babylon." Yet two decades of war meant that the king could hardly devote the time necessary to pressing affairs in the capital. Now, however, with the independent Chaldean dynasty firmly in control, the supremacy of Marduk of Babylon, the "king of the gods" of the Babylonian Creation Epic, must once again become accepted fact. His temple, the Esagila, and the ziggurat Etemenanki had to be restored, and a fortification wall had to be built. Nabopolassar's own contemporary cuneiform sources (as well as those of his son, Nebuchadnezzar) indicate that he died in his hour of triumph over Assyria, while all of this construction work still lay ahead. Nebuchadnezzar (605–562 B.C.) completed the work over the next several decades.

Bibliography

Borger, R. 1965. Der Aufstieg des neubabylonischen Reiches. *JCS* 9: 59–78.

Brinkman, J. A. 1984. *Prelude to Empire, Babylonian Society and Politics, 747–626 B.C.* Philadelphia.

Lambert, W. G. 1978. *The Background of Jewish Apocalyptic.* London.

Wiseman, D. J. 1961. *Chronicles of Chaldean Kings.* London.

———. 1984. *Nebuchadrezzar and Babylon.* Oxford.

Zawadzki, S. 1987. *The Fall of Assyria and Median-Babylonian Relations in Light of the Nabopolassar Chronicle.* Poznan.

Ronald H. Sack

NABOTH (PERSON) [Heb *nābôt*]. The victim of a judicial murder perpetrated by Jezebel in the name of her husband, King Ahab of Israel (1 Kings 21). According to this account, Ahab sought to acquire Naboth's ancestral property, a vineyard situated in Jezreel. Naboth refused Ahab's overtures out of religious attachment (cf. Lev 25:23; Zakovitch [1984] suggests that the phrase "inheritance of my fathers" is intended as a midrash on Naboth's own name: *Naḥălat ʾĀBŌT*). Ahab did not press the issue; but his Tyrian queen, Jezebel, engineered a conspiracy by which Naboth was accused of lèse-majesté ("Naboth cursed God and the king"), convicted on perjured testimony, and stoned to death. Ahab then took possession of the property he had coveted. See also the related discussion in AHAB (PERSON). The frequency with which Naboth's name appears throughout the story is striking. Even after his death, he is named six times in three verses (21:14–16); he haunts the scene like a ghost that will not be laid to rest. After Naboth's murder, Elijah the prophet was sent by Yahweh to condemn Ahab for what he had done. The king repented, and his punishment—violent death and the obliteration of his whole line—was deferred to the next generation.

Other references to Naboth's death, found in 1 Kgs 22:38 and 2 Kgs 9:21–26, raise questions about both the place and the time of the incident. 1 Kgs 22:38, read together with 21:19, suggests that Naboth's trial and execution took place in Samaria rather than Jezreel. This has led some scholars to locate the vineyard there as well. Timm (1982: 118–21) rehearses the arguments for both locations, and concludes that the evidence is insufficient to choose between the two. Miller (1967: 308–17) argues, on the basis of 2 Kgs 9:26, that the offending king was not Ahab but his son Joram. The reference in that verse seems to go back to a variant account of the Naboth incident, since the sons of Naboth spoken of in 2 Kgs 9:26 are not mentioned in 1 Kings 21. There seem, then, to have been several versions of the Naboth story in circulation, varying in details such as connections to Jezreel or to Samaria; identity of the royal oppressor; involvement of Naboth's sons; perhaps even the spelling of his name (the LXX reads *nabouthai,* which points to an underlying Heb *nbwty*). The story's enduring portrait of a small landowner helpless before the damnable acquisitiveness of the powerful may lie behind Micah's denunciation of similar rapacious land-grabbing in Judah a century or more later (Mic 2:1–2; cf. Mic 6:16).

Bibliography

Bohlen, R. 1978. *Der Fall Nabot.* Trierer Theologische Studien 35. Trier.

Miller, J. M. 1967. The Fall of the House of Ahab. *VT* 17: 307–24.

Timm, S. 1982. *Die Dynastie Omri.* FRLANT 124. Göttingen.

Zakovich, Y. 1984. The Tale of Naboth's Vineyard. Pp. 379–405 in *The Bible from Within,* ed. M. Weiss. Jerusalem.

Jerome T. Walsh

NABRATEIN (M.R. 197267). The Arabic name for Kefar Neburaya of the Palestinian Talmud, located 3 km N of Safed at 650 m above sea level. The site was known to the 19th-century explorers Renan, Wilson, Guérin, and Kitchener. It was systematically surveyed in 1905 by the German team of H. Kohl and C. Watzinger (1916). In 1960, N. Avigad deciphered a synagogue lintel inscription which the Germans had published. The lintel stone with wreath and menorah reads: "(According) to the number four hundred and ninety-four years after the destruction (of the temple), the house was built during the office of Hanina son of Lezer and Luliana son of Yudan" (Avigad 1960: 52). The date equivalent is 564 C.E. and corresponds to the final stratum of Byzantine occupation at the site.

Archaeological excavations were undertaken in 1980 and 1981, and the focal point of the expeditions was the synagogue that had previously been surveyed. In addition, soundings were conducted in the village in several areas to the W of the synagogue. The following occupational history of the site is reflected in the structural remains: Period I—Early Roman (ca. 1–135 C.E.); Period II—Middle Roman (Synagogue 1, ca. 135–250 C.E.); Period III—Late Roman (phase "a": Synagogue 2a, ca. 250–306 C.E.; phase "b": Synagogue 2b, ca. 306–363 C.E.); Gap (ca. 363–500/564 C.E.); and Period IV—Byzantine 2 to Early Arab (Synagogue 3, ca. 564–700 C.E.).

The Period IV occupation is defined by the material associated with the basilican synagogue of eight columns. The structure has a single entrance on the S facade facing toward Jerusalem and another on the N wall. Its external dimensions are 16.8 m by 11.6 m and it is one of the smaller Galilean synagogues. A porch probably was attached to the facade, three columns of which have been found. In all probability a wooden torah shrine stood somewhere on the S wall; its form and structure is suggested by a late Byzantine ceramic depiction found in a nearby room (Meyers, Strange, and Meyers 1982). The lintel inscription, dated to the year 564 C.E., is unique in Jewish epigraphy in taking 70 C.E., i.e., the destruction of the temple in Jerusalem, as its departure point. The stone itself apparently was reused from an earlier, probably Period III, Roman building. What is astonishing about the reuse of such a lintel, however, is the long gap which separates the earlier occupation from the Byzantine resettlement.

The Period III synagogue is a much smaller basilica with only six colums, 13.85 m by 11.2 m. Its grandest phase was the earlier one, ca. 250–306 C.E., when two bemas flanked the S facade wall. On the one in the SW stood a magnificent torah shrine which was destroyed in 306 (Meyers, Strange, and Meyers 1981a) and partially buried within the bema in the SW corner. Its roof tiles were deposited in a plastered burial pit under the floor of phase b alongside it. The pediment bears a striking similarity with other known depictions of arks in ancient Jewish art. Two rampant lions stand astride a peaked roof with a rosette and egg-and-dart carvings just beneath the roof. A scallop-shell carving occupies the center of the pediment and has a hole carved in it where the eternal light hung. This represents the oldest and most definitive proof for the existence of the ark of law. Standing on the raised platform where Scripture was stored and read, it provides eloquent testimony to the importance and authority of the Bible in everyday life. See SYNAGOGUE.

A still earlier, four-columned synagogue from Period II was found beneath this one. It was built on the broadhouse plan, 11.2 m by 9.35 m, with the S wall, the longer wall, occupying the focus of worship in this period as well. Synagogue 1 is the oldest broadhouse ever discovered anywhere and bears some similarities to nearby Khirbet Shemaᶜ. The fact that an early 2d century synagogue of this type could be found in Galilee at the time when the synagogue in general was assuming its architectural form(s) is most significant. It clearly shows how a rigid typology did not influence the early designers of synagogues. Two bemas are located on the S wall in this phase and an imprint of a table or small platform was discovered in the center of the building, suggesting that at this early stage Scripture was read in the center and away from the wall of orientation.

Soundings in the village produced quantities of whole pottery and a number of destroyed architectural fragments with relief sculpture on them—lions, birds, sheep, etc.—that may have been buried in debris after the 306 or 363 earthquakes. Coins reveal a much wider trade network than was expected, especially with E Diaspora cities; but the expected Tyrian coins are still prevalent. A surprisingly well-preserved Period I occupation was excavated, indicating a fairly stable settlement at the end of the Second Temple period. Judging from the architecture and the many pithoi, or large storage jars, that were found in the village, Nabratein might well have been a manufacturing or distribution center for fine Galilean olive oil or wine. A striking feature of the site is the elegance and size of the synagogue relative to the smallness of the settlement itself. It is possible that Nabratein was a kind of way station for traders and travelers going to inland Galilean highland towns or was merely a comfortable stopping-off place for anyone heading S.

Although Nabratein will perhaps always be associated with the wonderful ark pediment found there in 1981, it is also significant for the information it provides about Jewish life in Palestine after the Arab conquest of the 7th century. Also, that Jewish settlers chose to return to the site after a century and a half of abandonment reveals something very important about the Semitic attachment to sacred space. Nabratein was apparently an appropriate place to return to in the 6th century. Where the settlers came from, however, and why they chose to return at this time, are questions we still cannot answer.

Bibliography

Avigad, N. 1960. A Dated Lintel Inscription from the Ancient Synagogue of Nabratein. Pp. 49–56 in *Rabinowitz Bulletin* III. Jerusalem.

———. 1977. Kefar Neburaya. *EAEHL* 3: 710–11.

Chiat, M. J. S. 1982. Nabratein. Pp. 41–45 in *Handbook of Synagogue Architecture.* BJS 29. Chico, CA.

Kohl, H., and Watzinger, C. 1916. Antike Synagogen in Galilaea. *WVDOG,* 101–6.

Meyers, E. M.; Strange, J. F.; and Meyers, C. L. 1981a. The Ark of Nabratein—A First Glance. *BA* 44: 237–43.

———. 1981b. Preliminary Report on the 1980 Excavations at en-Nabratein, Israel. *BASOR* 244: 1–25.

———. 1982. Second Preliminary Report on the 1981 Excavations at en-Nabratein, Israel. *BASOR* 246: 35–54.

ERIC M. MEYERS

NACON (PERSON) [Heb *nakōn*]. Var. CHIDON. Owner of a threshing floor mentioned in 2 Sam 6:6, which the "ark of God" passed on its way to Jerusalem when David was transporting it from the house of Abinadab at Kiriath-jearim.

There has not been agreement as to whether the Hebrew word, *nakōn,* should be taken to be a proper noun referring to a person. It has been argued that the term should be taken to be a participial adjective in the *niphal* of the root *kwn.* In this case the phrase *gōren nakōn* would mean a "certain/definite threshing floor" (Morgenstern 1918; Arnold 1917). This is not an acceptable rendering, since the noun *gōren* is feminine singular, while the form of *nakōn* as a participle is masculine singular (Carlson 1964).

Others have argued that *nakōn* should be taken as a noun derived from the verb *nkh,* which means "to strike" (Tur-Sinai 1951). Thus, the phrase would be translated "the threshing floor of destruction." In this way the name would function as a literary device foreshadowing the incident to follow in vv 6–7, in which Uzza touched the ark to keep it from falling and was "struck" down by Yahweh for such an offense as touching the ark. The suggestion appears to be one of great improbability.

Thus, the term ought to be accepted as a proper name referring to an individual. Similarly, the arguments for resolving the differences between the name found in 2 Samuel 6, Nacon, and that found in 1 Chronicles 13, Chidon, attempt to hypothesize and trace the grammatical development from one of these to the other (see Campbell 1975; Jackson 1962; and McCarter *2 Samuel* AB). In such there is no definitive answer.

Bibliography

Arnold, W. R. 1917. *Ephod and Ark: A Study in the Records and Religion of the Ancient Hebrews.* HTS 3. Cambridge, MA.

Campbell, A. F. 1975. *The Ark Narrative (1 Sam 4:6; 2 Sam 6): A Form-Critical and Traditio-Historical Study.* SBLDS 16. Missoula, MT.

Carlson, R. A. 1964. *David, The Chosen King.* Stockholm.

Jackson, J. J. 1962. The Ark Narratives. An Historical, Textual, and Form-Critical Study of I Samuel 4–6 and II Samuel 6. Th.D. diss. Union Theological Seminary.

Morgenstern, J. 1918. *nkwn. JBL* 37: 144–48.

Tur-Sinai, N. H. 1951. The Ark of God at Beit Shemesh (1 Sam. 6) and Peres Uzza (2 Sam. 6; 1 Chron. 13). *VT* 1: 275–86.

RANDALL C. BAILEY

NADAB (PERSON) [Heb *nādāb*]. Name of 5 persons in the Hebrew Bible and the Apocrypha. The name is a shortened form of names such as Nedebiah (*nědabyāh;* 1 Chr 3:18), "YH(WH) is noble" (Noth *IPN,* 193; Fowler *TPNAH,* 161). Although the name Nadab has yet to appear in extrabiblical sources, longer theophoric names containing the element *ndb* are attested to in preexilic seals and ostraca (Tigay 1986: 57–58; Fowler *TPNAH,* 351).

1. Firstborn son of Aaron according to Num 3:2 (P). Other lists in P always name Nadab first, although they do not explicitly call him the *běkôr,* "firstborn." According to Exod 6:23, his mother was Elisheba, from a prominent family of Judah; this probably symbolizes the interconnection between Judah and the Aaronide priesthood (Galil 1985). Syntactically, Nadab is paired in genealogical lists with his brother Abihu; these lists typically read *nādāb wě'ǎbîhû' 'el 'āzār wě'îtāmār,* "Nadab and Abihu, Eleazar and Ithamar" (Exod 6:23; 28:1; Num 3:2; 26:60; 1 Chr 5:29 [—Eng 6:3]; 24:1). This pairing probably reflects awareness of the story of Lev 10:1, that Nadab and Abihu died when they offered an *'ēš zārâ,* "a foreign fire," to God (cf. Num 3:4; 26:61; 1 Chr 24:2). This is an extremely difficult story, whose meaning was debated already in antiquity (Shinan 1979). The words following "a foreign fire" in Lev 10:1, *'ǎšer lō' siwwâ 'ōtām,* "which (God) had not commanded them," are lacking in the parallel in Num 3:4 and 26:61 and may be an early gloss that explicates "foreign" as "unauthorized" (Gradwohl 1963: 289). Perhaps the "proper" fire should have been taken from the altar (Lev 16:12; cf. Haran 1978: 232), or Nadab and Abihu violated the prohibition of Exod 30:9, that no *qĕṭōret zārâ,* "foreign incense," may be offered (Levine 1989: 59). Alternatively, the ambiguity of the story may reflect the irrationality of God (Greenstein 1989: 56–64). Outside of P, the two brothers are mentioned together in Exod 24:1a and 9–11, in a source related to the revelation at Sinai that singles out Nadab and Abihu as ascending along with Moses and seventy elders and seeing God. They are not given any genealogy there, but it is likely that the incident refers to the same two sons of Aaron. The source-critical analysis of this chapter is very difficult, and these verses cannot with certainty be assigned to J or E (Childs *Exodus* OTL, 500). This source, which elevates the status of Nadab and Abihu by including them among those allowed to ascend and see God (contrast Exod 24:2 or 24:12), is opposite in tone from P's conception, which singles them out for a cultic infraction. This P tradition is probably polemicizing against the inclusion of the clans of Nadab and Abihu among the Aaronide priests by claiming that they do not exist since their eponymous ancestors were killed for a severe cultic infraction, and they died childless (Num 3:4; cf. 1 Chr 24:2). Thus, the P texts and Exod 24:1a, 9–11 reflect the different status of the clans of Nadab and Abihu according to their respective authors (Noth *Leviticus* OTL, 84). For the possible interconnections between this Nadab and Nadab, king of Israel, see #2 below.

2. Second king of the N kingdom, son of Jeroboam (I), who ascended to the throne upon the death of his father (1 Kgs 14:20) in the late 10th century. According to the Bible, he began to reign in Asa's second year (1 Kgs 15:25) and was assassinated by Baasha son of Ahijan at Gibbethon, a Philistine city, while Nadab was leading a campaign against that city (15:27); Baasha then murdered the remaining descendants of Jeroboam (15:27–29). The predominant source of this material is generally seen as the Israelite annals, which have been inserted into a Dtr framework and set within a synchronic chronology. The dating of these annals and their historical accuracy have not been clarified; in any case, the Dtr editing of Nadab's reign is very extensive. No extrabiblical material sheds light on Nadab's reign. Perhaps the battle against the Philistines reflected an attempt to consolidate political power via a military victory (*IJH,* 398). A similar siege against Gibbethon is recounted in 16:15, during the reign of Zimri. Perhaps one of these references to a siege on Gibbethon is incorrect, the result of material which was transferred from one king to another to fill out that king's reign. Alternatively the attempt to conquer Gibbethon by the N kingdom reflected its desire to capture a strategic city, and to "drive a wedge between Judah and Philistia and thus to undermine the economic position of Judah (Yeivin 1960: 218).

There is a similarity between Nadab, son of Jeroboam, and Nadab, son of Aaron, especially in relationship to the account of the golden calf fashioned by Aaron (Exodus 32) and Jeroboam's golden calves (1 Kgs 12:28–33). The extensive similarities in terminology and motif suggest a literary relationship between these texts (Aberbach and Smolar 1967), but the direction of the borrowing and whether it is literary or historical is debated, especially due to the complexity of evaluating the sources and attitudes of these two pericopae (Debus 1967; Childs *Exodus* OTL, 558–62; Hahn 1981). Several possibilities present themselves: (1) Jeroboam patterned his actions after a historical occurrence associated with the desert tradition, the building of ancient golden calves. These calves did not yet have a negative valuation and Jeroboam wanted to give his cultic "innovations" greater prestige by associating them with Aaron's actions. (2) The Jeroboam material is patterned after a form of the golden calf pericope which evaluated that episode negatively; this reflects an attempt by a Judean, anti-Northern author to polemicize against Jeroboam by associating him with a great sin of the past. (3) The golden calf pericope is patterned after Jeroboam's actions; this would then reflect an anti-Aaronide polemic in one of the redactions of Exodus 32. If either 2 or 3 is correct, the similarity in name between Aaron's sons Nadab and Abihu, and Jeroboam's sons Nadab and Abijah (1 Kings 14), all of whom died prematurely (Aberbach and Smolar 1967: 134) may be the result of literary patterning, in which case either Nadab 1 or Nadab 2 did not exist as a historical figure. Furthermore, it is possible that the different valuations in the Priestly and non-Priestly material of Nadab and Abihu, the sons of Aaron, may reflect different attitudes toward the legitimacy of Northern worship as established by Jeroboam.

3. A Judahite, the son of Shammai, father of Seled and Appaim (1 Chr 2:28, 30). This appears in a section of the genealogy dealing with the descendants of Jerahmeel (vv 25–33), who is listed as a great-grandson of Judah (vv 4, 5, 9), but who was originally a clan on Judah's S frontier (Williamson *Chronicles* NCBC, 54). The genealogy is from one of the Chronicler's sources (Williamson 1979). The Jerahmeel section is characterized by the formula *wayyāmot* PN *lōʾ bānîm*, "he died childless" (vv 30, 32), which is not found elsewhere in Chronicles; this suggests a separate source for this section. A similar note is found in 1 Chr 24:2 in relationship to Nadab and Abihu. The brother of this Jerahmeelite Nadab is named Abishur (v 28); it is unclear if the similarity in name to Nadab and Abihu/Abijah is coincidental or the result of patterning.

4. A son of Jeiel (1 Chr 9:36). In 8:30, his father is listed as Avi-Gibeon, but this is an error. See JEIEL #5. Nadab was an early Benjaminite, an ancestor of King Saul, and the settler of the Benjaminite city of Gibeon, according to 1 Chr 9:35. This genealogy is probably preexilic (Demsky 1971), though some see the tie of Benjamin to Gibeon rather than Gibeah and the double mention of Ner and Kish in vv 36 and 39 as an indication that this section of the genealogy is artificial (Malamat 1968: 171). On the repetition of the genealogy in 1 Chronicles 8 and 9, and its structure within the genealogies in Chronicles, see AHAZ.

5. Cousin of Ahikar (Tob 11:18). Tob 14:10 tells of the damnation of Nadab for betraying Ahikar and of the reward to Ahikar for acts of charity. The author of Tobit extensively used some form of the pseudepigraphic book, Ahikar (Simpson *APOT* 1: 189–92). Ahikar, however, does not mention Nadab; Nadab is probably a corruption of Ahikar's Nadin or Nadan, who in Ahikar is the protagonist's nephew rather than cousin (Lindenberger *OTP*, 458 n. 57 and 58). The original Nadin or Nadan is a shortened form of an Akkadian name from the root *nadānu(m)*, "to give." The form of the name Nadab in Tobit is highly variable between different manuscript traditions (Lindenberger *OTP*, 488 n. 57), but most forms are attempts to bring the name "Nadin/Nadan" into line with better known names which are similar graphically or aurally, such as Nadab.

Bibliography

Aberbach, M., and Smolar, L. 1967. Aaron, Jeroboam and the Golden Calves. *JBL* 86: 129–40.

Debus, J. 1967. *Die Sünde Jeroboams*. FRLANT 93. Göttingen.

Demsky, A. 1971. The Genealogy of Gibeon (1 Chronicles 9:35–44): Biblical and Epigraphic Considerations. *BASOR* 202: 16–23.

Galil, G. 1985. The Sons of Judah and the Sons of Benjamin in Biblical Historiography. *VT* 35: 488–95.

Gradwohl, R. 1963. Das "Fremde Feuer" von Nadab und Abihu. *ZAW* 75: 288–96.

Greenstein, E. 1989. Deconstruction and Biblical Narrative. *Prooftexts* 9: 43–71.

Hahn, J. 1981. *Das "Goldene Kalb."* Frankfurt am Main.

Haran, M. 1978. *Temples and Temple Service in Ancient Israel*. Oxford.

Levine, B. 1989. *Leviticus*. Philadelphia.

Malamat, A. 1968. King Lists in the Old Babylonian Period and Biblical Genealogies. *JAOS* 88: 163–73.

Shinan, A. 1979. The Sins of Nadab and Abihu in Rabbinic Literature. *Tarbiz* 48: 201–14.

Tigay, J. H. 1986. *You Shall Have No Other Gods*. HSS 31. Atlanta.

Williamson, H. G. M. 1979. Sources and Redaction in the Chronicler's Genealogy of Judah. *JBL* 98: 351–59.

Yeivin, S. 1960. Did the Kingdom of Israel Have a Maritime Policy? *JQR* 50: 193–228.

MARC Z. BRETTLER

NADABATH (PLACE) [Gk *Nadabath*]. A village or place in the S Transjordan from which a Jambrite wedding party proceeded toward Madaba when it was ambushed by Jonathan and Simon Maccabeus ca. 160 B.C. (1 Macc 9:37). The attack on the procession was an act of revenge against the Jambrites of Madaba, who had captured and executed John Maccabeus as he was transporting the baggage of the Hasmonean forces for safekeeping with the Nabateans at a time when those forces had been forced by the Seleucid Bacchides to retreat.

Josephus provides a parallel account of the ambush, in which there are two key differences (*Ant* 13.1.4 §18–21).

He names the home of the bride "Nabatha" and describes the bride's father as an "Arab noble," rather than as a "noble of Canaan," as the author of Maccabees describes him. Goldstein (*1 Maccabees* AB, 384–85) contends that the reason for the variant is that Josephus knew of no "Nadabath" and so substituted an Aramaic form of "Nebo," which was located in the mountainous country NW of Madaba. Goldstein sees the author of 1 Maccabees as using the toponym Nadabath in an effort to inflate the exploits of the Maccabees so that they might be compared with the military heroes of early Israelite history. The early Israelite leaders had been victorious over Arab peoples of the same region including the "Nodab" (Gk *Nadabaioi*; 1 Chr 5:19). Goldstein contends, on the basis of a simple misreading and an example of this mistake by Symmachus, that "Maon" was misread as "Canaan" and was preserved in the mss of Maccabees. Maon was the home of a longtime foe of ancient Israel and would thus have contributed to the author's efforts in drawing a comparison with earlier history. As a result, Goldstein suggests "that Nadabath, a village named for the Nadabite tribe, lay in the territory of the town of Maon." Thus he locates the site at modern Main, 7 km SW of Madaba (M.R. 219120).

The mountainous terrain from which the ambush was launched and into which the survivors fled is of little use in indicating the specific route of the party and hence the direction of Nadabath from Madaba. This description generally excludes the location of the town from being to the E of Madaba. On the basis of Josephus' account, the site of Nadabath has been identified by some scholars as modern en-Neba, NW of Madaba. Another proposed location is Kh. et-Teim 2 km S of Madaba (M.R. 223123).

ROBERT W. SMITH

NAG HAMMADI (26°03′N; 32°15′E). A site near the Egyptian village of al-Qaṣr (ancient Chenoboskion) where, in late 1945, thirteen leather-bound books (codices) written in Coptic were found buried in a storage jar beneath a large boulder. The codices date to the 4th century and reflect a combination of gnostic and early Christian elements. This entry consists of two articles. The first summarizes the archaeological work that has been accomplished in the Nag Hammadi area, specifically the 4th-century monastic basilica discovered at nearby Faw Qibli. The second article surveys the codices themselves, especially their literary genres and religious character.

ARCHAEOLOGY

Located on the W bank of the Nile, some 500 km S of Cairo and at the beginning of the river's turn to the E, the city of Nag Hammadi has given its name to archaeological excavations on the Nile's opposite or N bank in the village of Faw Qibli. The surrounding area on both sides of the river is rich in archaeological remains and has attracted the interest of excavators from the very first years of European activity in Egypt.

As early as 1843 R. Lepsius inspected the rock tombs from the 6th Dyn. found in the cliff face of the Gebel el-Tarif, across the Nile from present-day Nag Hammadi, and named them after a nearby village, Chenoboskion (1904: 177–81). A few years prior to Lepsius' visit, the English explorer Wilkinson had noted both these tombs and the ancient city of Hou (Diospolis parva) located on the opposite bank just 5 km S of Nag Hammadi (1843: 116–17), where Lepsius also stopped on his return trip in 1845 (1904: 181). At the end of the century Petrie excavated the Roman temple in Hou as well as a predynastic cemetery on its outskirts (1901). Based on earlier topographical surveys (Amélineau 1893; Lefort 1939), Debono conducted a brief but unproductive excavation at the supposed site of a Pachomian monastery in the village of Faw Qibli during the early 1950s (1971). However, it was not until the emergence of the so-called Nag Hammadi Codices at the end of the 1940s that systematic exploration of the area's archaeological remains was seriously contemplated. James M. Robinson, organizer of the team which prepared the Nag Hammadi manuscripts for preservation and study, also focused attention on an archaeological survey in hopes of clarifying the original locus of the codices, which according to all accounts had been brought to light at the base of the Gebel el-Tarif. He first sought to engage the Palestinian archaeologist, Paul Lapp, to lead a team to the site of the manuscript discovery, but the Six-Day War of 1967, and then Lapp's unfortunate accidental death in 1970, interrupted these plans (Robinson 1965/66; Van Elderen and Robinson 1976). It was only in 1975 that protonmagnetometer tests of the manuscript find area along the edge of the cliffs at the Gebel el-Tarif, conducted by Philip Hammond, were undertaken; the results were inconclusive. Later that same year the first official season of the Nag Hammadi excavations was directed under the leadership of B. Van Elderen and T. S. Söderbergh.

Several of the 6th-Dyn. cliff tombs were cleared of rubbish and trenches were laid at the manuscript find site. Though evidence was recovered of late-antiquity usage of the tombs by Christian ascetics, no firm connection to the Nag Hammadi Codices could be established (Van Elderen and Robinson 1976; Habachi 1979).

The next year work was shifted to the site of the basilica from the Pachomian monastery at Pbow, now Faw Qibli, whose remains still littered the surface. This monastery had been the headquarters of the 4th-century network of Pachomian communities in the area and a relationship was suspected to exist between the Nag Hammadi library and this monastic foundation (Robinson 1979). Under the direction of B. Van Elderen, and with the assistance of P. Grossmann, the expedition's main effort was expended on recovering the outside walls and the inner stylobates of the basilica (Van Elderen and Robinson 1976). During the third season, 1977–78, work was completed at the cliff tombs and efforts were redoubled to establish a ground plan of the Pachomian monastic basilica at Faw Qibli; it was now clear that an earlier building, also likely a church, underlay the basilica, and evidence was mounting that an even earlier structure had preceded both of them. Whether any of these constructions were contemporary with the founding of the Pachomian settlement in the second decade of the 4th century could not be confirmed (Van Elderen 1979; Grossmann 1979).

The expedition returned to the field in 1979–80 for a fourth season when work continued on the inner stylobates, the outer walls, and the apse of the basilica (Lease

1980). After an extended interlude, a small team under the direction of P. Grossmann resumed operations in 1986, seeking to clarify the relationship between the basilica and its immediate predecessor (Grossmann fc.). The sixth and last field work at Faw Qibli was completed in 1989, when a skeleton crew under the direction of P. Grossmann confirmed the ground plan of the intermediate church and recovered the ground plan of the site's earliest church building (Grossmann and Lease fc.). All three church structures made heavy use of reused limestone blocks for the foundations of the outside walls and corners, presumably robbed from previous Roman buildings in the immediate area. Burned brick, and in the case of the earliest structure also unfired mud brick, made up the bulk of the walls and stylobates. While the basilica (mid-5th century) was ca. 78 m in length and the intermediate church some 56 m long, the earliest church would have been only ca. 40 m. Thus at each building phase the new church was approximately half again as long as its predecessor.

It would appear that the earliest church, as its two successors, was a five-aisle structure with a very narrow nave, thus indicating that this ground plan was the original form at Pbow. As in the later churches there were also rows of columns in the earliest church which ran along the E, and probably along the W sides. The stylobates for these column rows were of unusual construction, consisting of individual foundations for each column which were connected only at the surface level by marginal rows of bricks. Later the apse was added, and as a consequence, the intercolumnar spaces of the E stylobate closest to the apse were most likely closed. This would have created *pastophoria*-like rooms (Grossmann and Lease fc.).

A major difficulty still remaining is the dating of these churches. While the "great" basilica appears firmly dated to 459 (Van Lantschoot 1934: 31, 45, 51), the intermediate church cannot be precisely dated. Very preliminary ceramic analyses all point to the late 4th or early 5th centuries, but the condition of the sherds is such that a more exact chronological determination may not be possible. This is even more the case for the earliest church. The extensive destruction associated with the erection of the later churches, and the thorough robbing of the site for building materials, have left few, if any, certain indicators for setting the time of its construction. Indeed, one must emphasize that a stratigraphical level associated directly with this earliest church has yet to be established. At the moment, however, one is at least partially justified—based primarily on the size and the primitive design and construction—in identifying the earliest church as possibly the initial one built for the monastic community at Pbow before Pachomius' death (ca. 330–346; Bacht 1983: 25, 30–31). Thus a preliminary construction history of the site at Pbow would posit a first church during Pachomius' lifetime (= phase I; ca. 330–346); a second, or intermediate and larger church (= phase II; post-370s and Athanasius' triumph or post-380s and the official appointment of Christianity as a state religion; or even later?); and a third, final church—the "great" basilica (= phase III; completed in 459).

Problematic, however, remain hints of structures on the site *prior* to the three churches. In the very first square of the Faw Qibli excavations (Square 1, 1976) and in the largest trench of the latest season (Square 39, 1989), fragments of four different walls emerged, only one of which can be explained in connection with one of the known buildings. The other three, running roughly E-W and very roughly parallel to each other, are neither related to each other nor to any of the three known structures (= churches). These wall fragments seem to lie below the level of the identified structures and thus point to an older, prior building on the site. What this may have been—a small chapel, for example, associated with Pachomius' earliest organization there, or nonmonastic constructions from a previous occupation and use of the site by others—is not possible to determine at this time. Perhaps further excavation in the middle of the site, where these wall fragments appear best preserved, will shed some light on this matter.

As to the end of the site's formal monastic use, it should be noted that in all the seasons at Faw Qibli, beginning in 1976, neither traces of fire (almost always associated with violent destruction, whether by war or plunder) nor evidence of earthquake damage (in such a case, large stationary pieces, such as columns, all fall in the same direction, which is certainly not the case at Faw Qibli) could be established. In addition, no ceramic evidence, preliminary as it is, points much beyond the 5th–7th centuries. In the face of this archaeological evidence, or rather lack of evidence, it is difficult to maintain an end to the site through destruction by the Persians (620s) or at the time of the Moslem invasion (post-640s). Even harder to accept is the legendary ascription of the site's destruction to el-Hakim (1009), who, like Nero, had many acts charged to his account long after the fact because he was a convenient figure for explaining such violence (cf., Salih 1895: 282). Closer to the truth may be simply that the Pachomian community at Pbow reached its zenith during the 5th century, began to decline throughout the 6th century, and was abandoned toward the end of the same century (Timm 1984: 949–50).

Before the Persian and Moslem invasions of the 7th century, therefore, the site probably already served as a source of building materials: note the extensive, systematic robber trenches and the almost complete lack of capitals on the site; the first two ever found there only came to light during the 1989 season and were heavily damaged. One did reveal clearly, however, its acanthus leaf and branch design. Since it can be dated firmly to the basilica of 459, it is an important piece of evidence in revising accepted notions of a so-called "Coptic art." Even at such a late date, this capital displays the usual design featured in the imperial Byzantine (= Constantinopolitan) catalog (Severin 1977).

In any case, the archaeological evidence not only says little or nothing about the supposed link between the Pachomian community at Pbow and the Nag Hammadi gnostic literature (as Robinson, *NHL,* 16; but see Robinson 1979: xix), but also indicates that the community, and thus the active use of the site, ended with the whimper of decline and abandonment and not the bang of violent destruction.

It would therefore appear appropriate to change the name and identification of these excavations from "Nag Hammadi," which inaccurately assumes such a connection, to the "Faw Qibli excavations," thus following the general and accepted Egyptian practice of naming an excavation after its *actual* site name.

Bibliography

Amélineau, E. 1893. *La géographie de l'Egypte a l'époque copte.* Paris.

Bacht, H. 1983. *Das Vermächtnis des Ursprungs: Pachomius—der Mann und sein Werk.* Vol. 2. Würzburg.

Debono, F. 1971. La basilique et le monastere de St. Pachome. *BIFAO* 70: 191–220.

Grossman, P. 1978. Zur christlichen Baukunst in Ägypten. *Enchoria* 8: 135–46.

———. 1979. The Basilica of St. Pachomius. *BA* 42: 232–36.

———. 1981. Esempi d'architettura paleocristiana in Egitto dal V al VII secolo. *CorsiRavenna* 28: 149–76.

———. fc. Faw Qibli—1986 Excavation Report (= Fifth Season). *ASAE* 72.

Grossmann, P., and Lease, G. fc. Faw Qibli—1989 Excavation Report (= Sixth Season).

Habachi, L. 1979. Sixth-Dynasty Discoveries in the Jabal al-Tarif. *BA* 42: 237–38.

Lease, G. 1980. The Fourth Season of the Nag Hammadi Excavation. 21 December 1979–15 January 1980. *Göttinger Miszellen* 41: 75–85.

Lefort, L. T. 1939. Les premiers monasteres Pachomiens. Exploration topographique. *Mus* 52: 379–407.

Lepsius, R. 1904. *Denkmäler aus Aegypten und Aethiopien.* Vol. 2, ed. E. Naville. Leipzig.

Petrie, W. M. 1901. *Diospolis parva, the cemeteries of Abadiyeh and Hu, 1898–99.* London.

Robinson, J. M. 1965/66. Nag Hammadi Report. *ASOR Newsletter* 4: 1–5.

———. 1979. Preface. Pp. viii–xxiii in *The Facsimile Edition of the Nag Hammadi Codices: Cartonnage.* Leiden.

Salih, A. 1895. *The Churches and Monasteries of Egypt and Some Neighboring Countries.* Trans. B. T. A. Evetts. Oxford.

Severin, H.-G. 1977. Frühchristliche Skulptur und Malerei in Ägypten. Pp. 243–53 in *Propyläen Kunstgeschichte.* Supplement 1. Frankfurt.

Timm, S. 1984. *Das christlich-koptische Ägypten in arabischer Zeit.* Vol. 2. Wiesbaden.

Van Elderen, B. 1979. The Nag Hammadi Excavation. *BA* 42: 225–31.

Van Elderen, B., and Robinson, J. M. 1976. The First Season of the Nag Hammadi Excavation. 27 November–19 December 1975. *Göttinger Miszellen* 22: 71–79.

Van Lantschoot, A. 1934. Allocution de Timothee d'Alexandrie prononcee a l'occasion de la dedicace de l'eglise de Pachom a Pboou. *Le Museon* 43: 13–56.

Wilkinson, J. G. 1843. *Modern Egypt and Thebes; being a description of Egypt.* Vol. 2. London.

Gary Lease

NAG HAMMADI CODICES

A group of twelve papyrus codices, plus eight leaves from a thirteenth, dating from the 4th century C.E. and inscribed in Coptic. The manuscripts were discovered in 1945 in Upper Egypt, ca. 10 km outside of the modern city of Nag Hammadi. They are now housed in the Coptic Museum in Old Cairo. The standard citation for each of the manuscripts is NHC followed by the number of the tractate in the codex, e.g., *Trim.Prot.* (NHC XIII,*1*). An alternative citation is also in use: CG (Cairensis Gnosticus). NHC I is also called the Jung Codex. Most (but not all) of the 52 tractates in the Nag Hammadi collection are gnostic in character. Hence, the American edition of these and related Coptic texts is called the Coptic Gnostic Library.

A. Discovery and Acquisition of the Nag Hammadi Codices
B. Description of the Nag Hammadi Codices
C. Publication of the Nag Hammadi Codices
D. Contents of the Nag Hammadi Codices
E. Provenience of the Manuscripts
F. Classification of the Tractates
  1. Literary Genres
  2. Religious Character
G. Importance of the Nag Hammadi Codices

A. Discovery and Acquisition of the Nag Hammadi Codices

In December 1945, two brothers, Muḥammad ʿAlī and Abū al Majd, of the al-Sammān clan from the village of al-Qaṣr (ancient Chenoboskion), together with six other fellahin, were digging for *sabakh* (a nitrate soil used for fertilizer) at the base of the Jabal al-Ṭarīf, 9 km W of the ruins of the Basilica of St. Pachomius at Faw Qibli (ancient Pabau). Abū al Majd unearthed a storage jar beneath a large boulder; Muḥammad ʿAlī broke the jar, which contained thirteen leather-bound books (codices). An attempt was made on the spot to divide the find into eight equal lots, a process that involved dismembering some of the codices, but the other fellahin renounced any share in the find, and Muḥammad ʿAlī bundled the codices together and brought them home. There his mother, Umm Aḥmad, burned some of the papyrus leaves as fuel for her bread oven. The story of the find and the subsequent fate of the codices has been pieced together by J. M. Robinson (Robinson 1984: 3–31).

The bulk of Codex I was eventually acquired by a Belgian antiquities dealer in Cairo, Albert Eid, who sent it (except for the cover) out of Egypt. It was eventually purchased for the Jung Institute in 1952, and was officially presented by the director of the institute, Dr. C. A. Meier, to C. G. Jung in Zürich in 1953 and named the Jung Codex. (C. G. Jung had a lifelong interest in Gnosticism and alchemy.) Jung's heirs returned the codex to Egypt, in accordance with an agreement with the Egyptian government. As each portion was published, it was sent to the Coptic Museum; the last installment was received in 1975. The leather cover of Codex I, which had remained in Egypt, was sold to a collector and eventually acquired in 1973 by the Institute for Antiquity and Christianity of the Claremont Graduate School (Claremont, California).

Codex III was acquired by the Antiquities Service for the Coptic Museum in 1946. The director of the museum, Togo Mina, showed it to a young French scholar, Jean Doresse, in 1947, who initiated plans for its publication. However, the political coup d'état in Egypt in 1952 interrupted these plans.

Codices II, IV–XIII, and part of Codex I were eventually acquired by Phocion J. Tano, a Cairo antiquities dealer. Tano brought them to the attention of Étienne Drioton, then director general of the Antiquities Service, and Jean Doresse in 1948. After a period of fruitless negotiations for purchase of the codices, the new government in Egypt headed by Nasser declared them national property in 1952.

One intriguing problem associated with the story of the discovery of the Nag Hammadi Codices is the question of precisely how many codices there are. The discoverer, Muḥammad ᶜAlī, consistently maintains that thirteen bound books were found in the jar. But what is now referred to as NHC XIII consists of eight leaves of papyrus that had been ripped out of a codex in antiquity and stuffed into the cover of Codex VI (Robinson 1972). Our Codex XIII, therefore, cannot count as one of the thirteen separate books found in 1945, for it was then part of Codex VI. Was a complete codex destroyed in Umm Aḥmad's oven, together with leaves of papyrus from other codices now left incomplete? Or will it, or parts of it, eventually turn up on the market (Robinson 1984: 15–24)?

B. Description of the Nag Hammadi Codices

The present numeration of the Nag Hammadi Codices was devised by Martin Krause for the Coptic Museum (see Krause 1962), and has superseded all other numeration systems previously in use. (For a table of correspondences, see Robinson 1984: 31).

All of the Nag Hammadi Codices, with the exception of Codex I (and possibly Codices XII and XIII) are single quire codices. (A "quire" of the kind typically found in 4th-century codices, such as those from Nag Hammadi, consists of a stack of sheets of papyrus, folded once in the center.) Codex I was made up of three quires. Not enough is left of Codices XII and XIII to determine how many quires each comprised.

Of the leather (sheepskin and goatskin) covers in which Codices I–XII were bound, all but that of Codex XII are extant. The leather covers of Codices I, IV–IX, and XI contained "cartonnage." (Cartonnage consists of scraps of discarded papyrus glued into leather bookbindings in order to stiffen them. On the cartonnage from the Nag Hammadi Codices, see below.)

In the table that follows, the basic information is provided for each of the codices regarding: (a) maximum height of the folios (leaves) in cm, (b) maximum width, (c) original number of folios, (d) original number of inscribed pages, (e) original number of uninscribed pages, (f) number of inscribed pages extant, and (g) number of uninscribed pages extant.

	(a)	(b)	(c)	(d)	(e)	(f)	(g)
NHC I:	30.0	14.1	72	140	4	140	0
NHC II:	28.4	15.8	75	145	5	145	3
NHC III:	25.8	16.1	78	147	9	135	3
NHC IV:	23.8	13.4	46	81	11	81	11
NHC V:	24.3	13.3	47	84	10	84	10
NHC VI:	27.9	14.9	40	78	2	78	2
NHC VII:	29.2	17.5	65	127	3	127	3
NHC VIII:	24.2	14.7	72	136	8	132	6
NHC IX:	26.3	15.0	38	75 (76?)	1?	72	0
NHC X:	26.0	12.2	36+	68+	4	54	2
NHC XI:	28.2	14.3	37	72	2	72	2
NHC XII:	?	?	38+	71+	?	20	0
NHC XIII:	27.2	13.9	?	?	?	16	0

A page is represented in this table as extant even if only a single small fragment remains. The figures given, therefore, do not provide an accurate picture of how much material is lost from each codex. Those codices that have sustained the greatest loss are IV, V, VIII, IX, X, XI, and XII. The best preserved is Codex VII. As stated earlier, Codex XIII consists of eight folios of a papyrus codex that had been tucked into the front of the leather cover of Codex VI in antiquity.

The Nag Hammadi Codices are now housed in the manuscript wing of the library of the Coptic Museum in Old Cairo, kept in two storage cabinets designed and built for them. The papyri are conserved in Plexiglas panes, with conjugate leaves rejoined to form the original sheets that were stacked and folded in two to make up the quires. The final conservation was carried out in 1974–75 as a special project directed by J. M. Robinson and funded by the Smithsonian Institution and the American Research Center in Egypt.

Up to fourteen different scribal hands may be represented in the Nag Hammadi Codices. Codices I, II, and XI were each inscribed by two different scribes. There is also some overlapping of scribal hands from one codex to another: the second scribe of Codex I was also the first scribe of Codex XI, and the second scribe of Codex XI was also the scribe of Codex VII. The main scribe of Codex II may also have inscribed Codex XIII. The similarities among the hands of codices IV, V, VI, VIII, and IX presumably reflect the influence of a single scribal school (Emmel 1978: 27–28).

Two main Coptic dialects are represented in the Nag Hammadi Codices: Sahidic (S), with various deviations from the classical form of the language (II–IX; XI,*3–4*; XII–XIII); and Lycopolitan (L, also called Subakhmimic, A^2), with considerable variation from tractate to tractate (I, X, and XI,*1–2*).

The cartonnage taken from the leather covers of Codices I, IV–IX, and XI, consists of documentary Greek papyri of the 3d and 4th centuries (the latest date, attested in the cartonnage of Codex VII, is 348 C.E.), as well as documentary and literary Coptic papyri of the same period. The Coptic papyri include fragments of a Sahidic biblical codex (Genesis 32:5–21 and 42:27–30, 35–38, from the cartonnage of Codex VII), probably of the late 3d or early 4th centuries C.E. (Barns, Browne, and Shelton 1981).

C. Publication of the Nag Hammadi Codices

With the publication in 1977 of the facsimile edition of Codices IX and X (Robinson et al. 1977b) and a one-volume English translation of all of the tractates (Robinson and Meyer 1977; cf. Robinson and Smith 1988), the entire Nag Hammadi collection finally became available in some form to the public, 32 years after its discovery. Until that time several tractates, including two entire codices, remained unpublished.

Codex III was the first of the Nag Hammadi Codices to come into the possession of the Coptic Museum. While the initial plans for publication were cut short by the political events in Egypt in 1952, the text of tractates *1, 3,* and *4* became largely accessible in the *apparatus criticus* to Walter Till's publication of the Berlin Codex (BG, Till 1955). Jean Doresse eventually published III,*2* several years later (Doresse 1966, 1968).

In 1952 C. A. Meier, director of the Jung Institute, invited a team of European scholars to edit Codex I, and the *Gospel of Truth* (excluding pp. 33–36, part of the material from Codex I that had not been taken out of Egypt) was published in 1956 (Malinine et al. 1956). The rest of Codex I was published by this team over the next nineteen years (Malinine et al. 1961; 1963; 1968; Kasser et al. 1973; 1975).

In 1952 some photographs were made by the Egyptian authorities for a facsimile edition of the Nag Hammadi mss that had been sequestered by the government. A first volume was published in 1956 (Labib 1956), containing photos of Codex I, pp. 33–36; 49–50; 59–82; 87–90; and Codex II, pp. 1–110. This volume became the basis for several subsequent publications of texts and translations. That same year the International Committee for Coptic Gnostic Papyri was formed, and further publication plans were laid. Three years later the *Gospel of Thomas* was published as a result of this effort (Guillaumont et al. 1959). A French translation of the *Gospel of Thomas* was included by Jean Doresse as an appendix to a book on the Nag Hammadi Codices published by him (Doresse 1958; 1959; cf. 1960), a work which became the chief source of information on the Nag Hammadi collection for years thereafter.

Martin Krause and Alexander Böhlig worked in the Coptic Museum during the next few years, and several texts were published as a result (Krause and Labib 1962; 1971; Böhlig and Labib 1962; 1963). Meanwhile, in 1961 UNESCO became involved in the plans for publishing a complete facsimile edition; as a result over a thousand photographs were made and shipped to Paris between 1963 and 1966. The International Colloquium on the Origins of Gnosticism held at Messina in 1966 urged the completion of this project (Bianchi 1967: xvi), and J. M. Robinson was appointed secretary of an ad hoc committee of the colloquium. Robinson entered into protracted contact with UNESCO concerning the project. In view of the fact that UNESCO envisioned only a facsimile edition, Robinson organized a team of scholars working under the auspices of the new Institute for Antiquity and Christianity of the Claremont Graduate School to prepare a multivolume English-language edition of the Nag Hammadi Codices to be entitled "The Coptic Gnostic Library."

In 1970 Gamal Mokhtar, President of the Egyptian Antiquities Organization, in consultation with UNESCO, appointed a new international committee for the Nag Hammadi Codices. The committee met in Cairo and drew up the guidelines for the facsimile edition, entrusting to a technical subcommittee (Søren Giversen, Rodolphe Kasser, Martin Krause, and J. M. Robinson [Secretary]) the task of identifying and assembling fragments of papyri for definitive photography. Members of the team of scholars working on the English-language edition participated in work sessions of the technical subcommittee in the Coptic Museum. The first volumes of the facsimile edition were published in 1972 (Codices VI and VII; Robinson et al. 1972a; 1972b). The project was completed in 1984 with the publication of *addenda et corrigenda* as part of an introduction to the facsimile edition (Robinson 1984).

The first volume of the Coptic Gnostic Library was published in 1975, a critical edition of NHC III,*2* and IV,*2* (Böhlig, Wisse and Labib 1975), and the last of the volumes are yet to appear.

While the Coptic Gnostic Library Project of the Institute for Antiquity and Christianity at Claremont was producing tentative transcriptions and translations, a group of doctorands studying Coptic with Hans-Martin Schenke at Humboldt-Universität in East Berlin began to focus their work in a concerted manner on the Nag Hammadi texts. This was the genesis of the Berliner Arbeitskreis für koptisch-gnostische Schriften, directed by Schenke, and over the years a good deal of cooperation has existed between the German and the American groups. The German project involves three phases: (1) publication of translations of selected texts in the *Theologische Literaturzeitung* (the first was by Schenke in 1973); (2) monographs and dissertations on the Nag Hammadi texts (the first was by Beltz in 1970; cf. also Tröger 1973, an important volume of essays); and (3) a projected German translation of the complete collection of texts to be published as volumes 2 and 3 of *Koptisch-Gnostische Schriften* in the series, "Die Griechischen Christlichen Schriftsteller der ersten Jahrhunderte" (Schenke 1978).

In 1974 the Social Sciences and Humanities Research Council of Canada provided an initial grant to a group of scholars associated with the University of Laval in Québec for the production of a complete French-language critical edition of the Nag Hammadi texts, entitled "Bibliothèque copte de Nag Hammadi" (see Ménard 1973). The first volume was published four years later (Ménard 1977), and several have been published since.

Thus, over the years since the first meager publication efforts of the 1950s, a growing number of texts, translations, and studies has accumulated. An enormous bibliography now exists, and no end is in sight (Scholer 1971a, b).

D. Contents of the Nag Hammadi Codices

The following table lists for each tractate the title and abbreviation commonly used in English-language scholarship and the page and line of the ms where it begins and ends (or, in the case of lost material, where it began or ended so far as this can be determined). Pagination is uncertain in the case of Codices X (after p. 10), XII, and XIII (indicated below with asterisks). XII,*3* consists of miscellaneous fragments, and is not an identifiable tractate.

I,*1*:	A,1–B,8. + B,9–10	*The Prayer of the Apostle Paul (colophon)*	*Pr. Paul*
I,*2*:	1,1–16,30.	*The Apocryphon of James*	*Ap. Jas.*
I,*3*:	16,31–43,24.	*The Gospel of Truth*	*Gos. Truth*
I,*4*:	43,25–50,18.	*The Treatise on the Resurrection*	*Treat. Res.*
I,*5*:	51,1–138,27.	*The Tripartite Tractate*	*Tri. Trac.*
II,*1*:	1,1–32,9.	*The Apocryphon of John*	*Ap. John*
II,*2*:	32,10–51,28.	*The Gospel of Thomas*	*Gos. Thom.*
II,*3*:	51,29–86,19.	*The Gospel of Philip*	*Gos. Phil.*
II,*4*:	86,20–97,23.	*The Hypostasis of the Archons*	*Hyp. Arch.*

II,*5*:	97,24–127,17.	*On the Origin of the World*	*Orig. World*
II,*6*:	127,18–137,27.	*The Exegesis on the Soul*	*Exeg. Soul*
II,*7*:	138,1–145,19.	*The Book of Thomas the Contender*	*Thom. Cont.*
	+ 145,20–23	*(colophon)*	
III,*1*:	1,1–40,11.	*The Apocryphon of John*	*Ap. John*
III,*2*:	40,12–69,20.	*The Gospel of the Egyptians*	*Gos. Eg.*
III,*3*:	70,1–90,13.	*Eugnostos the Blessed*	*Eugnostos*
III,*4*:	90,14–119,18.	*The Sophia of Jesus Christ*	*Soph. Jes. Chr.*
III,*5*:	120,1–147,23.	*The Dialogue of the Savior*	*Dial. Sav.*
IV,*1*:	1,1–49,28.	*The Apocryphon of John*	*Ap. John*
IV,*2*:	50,1–81,2.	*The Gospel of the Egyptians*	*Gos. Eg.*
V,*1*:	1,1–17,18.	*Eugnostos the Blessed*	*Eugnostos*
V,*2*:	17,19–24,9.	*The Apocalypse of Paul*	*Apoc. Paul*
V,*3*:	24,10–44,10.	*The (First) Apocalypse of James*	*1 Apoc. Jas.*
V,*4*:	44,11–63,32.	*The (Second) Apocalypse of James*	*2 Apoc. Jas.*
V,*5*:	64,1–85,32.	*The Apocalypse of Adam*	*Apoc. Adam*
VI,*1*:	1,1–12,22.	*The Acts of Peter and the Twelve Apostles*	*Acts Pet. 12 Apost.*
VI,*2*:	13,1–21,32.	*The Thunder: Perfect Mind*	*Thund.*
VI,*3*:	22,1–35,24.	*Authoritative Teaching*	*Auth. Teach.*
VI,*4*:	36,1–48,15.	*The Concept of Our Great Power*	*Great Pow.*
VI,*5*:	48,16–51,23.	*Plato, Republic 588b–589b*	*Plato Rep.*
VI,*6*:	52,1–63,32.	*The Discourse on the Eighth and Ninth*	*Disc. 8–9*
VI,*7*:	63,33–65,7.	*The Prayer of Thanksgiving*	*Pr. Thanks.*
	+ 65,8–14	*(scribal note)*	
VI,*8*:	65,15–78,43.	*Asclepius 21–29*	*Asclepius*
VII,*1*:	1,1–49,9.	*The Paraphrase of Shem*	*Paraph. Shem*
VII,*2*:	49,10–70,12.	*The Second Treatise of the Great Seth*	*Treat. Seth*
VII,*3*:	70,13–84,14.	*The Apocalypse of Peter*	*Apoc. Pet.*
VII,*4*:	84,15–118,7.	*The Teachings of Silvanus*	*Teach. Silv.*
	+ 118,8–9	*(colophon)*	
VII,*5*:	118,10–127,27.	*The Three Steles of Seth*	*Steles Seth*
	+ 127,28–32	*(colophon)*	
VIII,*1*:	1,1–132,6.	*Zostrianos*	*Zost.*
	+ 132,7–9	*(cryptogram)*	
VIII,*2*:	132,10–140,27.	*The Letter of Peter to Philip*	*Ep. Pet. Phil.*
IX,*1*:	1,1–27,10.	*Melchizedek*	*Melch.*
IX,*2*:	27,11–29,5.	*The Thought of Norea*	*Norea*
IX,*3*:	29,6–74,30+.	*The Testimony of Truth*	*Testim. Truth*
X,*1*:	1,1–68*,18.	*Marsanes*	*Marsanes*
XI,*1*:	1,1–21,35.	*The Interpretation of Knowledge*	*Interp. Know.*
XI,*2*:	22,1–44,37.	*A Valentinian Exposition*	*Val. Exp.*
XI,*3*:	45,1–69,20.	*Allogenes*	*Allogenes*
XI,*4*:	69,21–72,33.	*Hypsiphrone*	*Hypsiph.*
XII,*1*:	1*,1–34*,28.	*The Sentences of Sextus*	*Sent. Sextus*
XII,*2*:	39*,?–60*,30.	*The Gospel of Truth*	*Gos. Truth*
XII,*3*:		*Fragments*	*Frm.*
XIII,*1*:	35*,1–50*,24.	*Trimorphic Protennoia*	*Trim. Prot.*
XIII,*2*:	50*,25+.	*On the Origin of the World*	*Orig. World*

Note: Where original titles are lacking in the mss, modern scholars have assigned titles. The titles so assigned are: *Ap. Jas.; Gos. Truth; Tri. Trac.; Orig. World; Disc. 8–9; Pr. Thanks.; Norea; Testim. Truth;* and *Val. Exp.* Of these, *Gos. Truth* is so called from the *incipit,* which served as a title in antiquity (cf. Iren. *Adv. Haer.* 3.11.9). The titles of *Plato Rep.; Asclepius;* and *Sent. Sextus,* while not occurring in the Nag Hammadi mss, are also elsewhere attested.

E. Provenience of the Manuscripts

Three major factors point to a monastic provenience for the Nag Hammadi Codices. First, the site of the discovery: The jar containing the codices had been buried midway up the talus of broken rock at the foot of the Jabal al Ṭārif. There is evidence that the talus was used for burials in the early Byzantine period. Over 150 caves are located in the cliff; the one nearest the site of the discovery (T8) has on one of its walls a Coptic inscription, in red paint, of the opening lines of several OT psalms (Robinson 1979: 213). This area had obviously been frequented by Christians. Did a gnostic community use the cliff area as a retreat, and then bury their library before disappearing without a trace? A more likely possibility is that Christian monks, from one or more of the monasteries nearby in the valley below, used a monastic burial site as a place in which to bury a cache of books, presumably because the content of those books had come under suspicion in the monastic communities (Wisse 1978: 436–37).

Second, the cartonnage found in the leather covers points to a monastic context for the manufacture of the codices. This is at least true in the case of the cartonnage found in Codex VII, which contains fragments of a biblical codex and a homily, as well as private letters indicating a monastic provenience, including one from a "Pachomius" to a "Paphnoute." (For a balanced discussion see Veilleux 1986: 278–83.) If, as seems likely, the books were manufactured in one or more of the Pachomian monasteries in the vicinity of the find (Sheneset-Chenoboskion, Pabau, or Tabennesi), were they also inscribed by Pachomian monks, or were they manufactured and sold uninscribed to unknown purchasers? Our first point indicates a likelihood that the scribes of the codices were members of one or more of the monastic communities in the area.

Third, the colophons and scribal notes in some of the manuscripts (esp. I, II, and VII) containing pious Christian prayers and the like, are indications of a monastic provenience for the actual copying of the manuscripts. The persons who copied the various texts into the codices evidently treated them as edifying religious literature. A purge of heretical books was carried out in the Pachomian monasteries by Pachomius' successor, Theodore, in response to Athanasius' paschal letter of 367 C.E. Such a purge could have resulted in the burial of the books on the part of recalcitrant monks who wished to preserve them from destruction (Wisse 1978: 435–37). Thus the Nag Hammadi Codices were actually not in use for very long. They (or at least Codex VII) must have been manufactured after 348 C.E. and were presumably buried in the late 4th or early 5th century. The bowl used as a lid to close the mouth of the jar in which the codices were found is still extant; it is red slipware of the 4th or 5th century (Robinson 1979: 213).

F. Classification of the Tractates

While the texts in the Nag Hammadi collection number 52 in all (though the fragments constituting XII,*3* may be from more than a single tractate), five tractates are represented by more than a single copy: *Gos. Truth* (I,*3*; XII,*2*),

Ap. John (II,*1*; III,*1*; IV,*1*), *Orig. World* (II,*5*; XIII,*2*); *Gos. Eg.* (III,*2*; IV,*2*); and *Eugnostos* (III,*3*; V,*1*). There are, therefore, 46 different tractates in the Nag Hammadi collection (counting XII,*3* as one). Of the four tractates in the closely related Berlin Codex, two are also represented in the Nag Hammadi collection: *Ap. John* (BG,*2*) and *Soph. Jes. Chr.* (BG,*3*). All of the texts in question are Coptic translations of Greek originals. Three of them (*Plato Rep., Sent. Sextus,* and *Pr. Thanks.*) were already known in their original Greek versions before the Nag Hammadi discovery; one (*Asclepius*) was known in a Latin version. Since the discovery, previously extant Greek fragments have been identified as representing two of the tractates from Nag Hammadi (*Gos. Thom.* and *Soph. Jes. Chr.*). An extensive parallel to part of *Ap. John* is found in Irenaeus, *Adv. Haer.* I.29, but it is not certain that Irenaeus knew *Ap. John* as such. Even so, *Ap. John* was evidently considered to be a very important writing, given its multiple attestation, and is, in fact, a key text for the scholarly study of gnostic mythology.

In what follows, the Nag Hammadi tractates will be classified, first according to literary genre and then according to religious character, especially their relation to Gnosticism. The reader is also referred to the respective articles on the individual tractates treated here.

1. Literary Genres. The Nag Hammadi collection features a number of different genres, and literary classification is complicated by the fact that some tractates display features of more than one literary genre or contain different genres within them. Thus, the following classification should not be regarded as definitive or exhaustive.

a. Apocalypses. Several of the tractates have the term "apocalypse" in their titles: *Apoc. Paul; 1 Apoc. Jas.; 2 Apoc. Jas.; Apoc. Adam;* and *Apoc. Peter.* Many of the other tractates are subject to classification as "apocalypses," in whole or in part, according to the criteria commonly accepted (Collins 1979; Fallon 1979): *Ap. John; Hyp. Arch.; Soph. Jes. Chr.; Asclepius; Paraph. Shem; Zost.; Ep. Pet. Phil.; Melch.; Marsanes; Allogenes;* and *Hypsiphr.* Two of these, *Zost.* and *Allogenes,* were known as "apocalypses" in antiquity (Porph. *Vit. Plot.* 12). One, *Soph. Jes. Chr.*, is an apocalypse that has been created as such out of a previously existing tractate also found in the Nag Hammadi collection, *Eugnostos. Ap. John* is similarly a composite document, but it belongs, in its present form, to the apocalypse genre. *Hyp. Arch.*, also a composite document, contains an apocalypse within it (Pearson 1984: 464–65). In addition, *Ap. Jas.* counts as an apocalypse, though it is introduced as an epistle.

Other tractates share features of the apocalyptic genre. *Steles Seth* is presented as a revelation of the content of three steles inscribed by Seth, a heavenly figure associated in gnostic mythology with the biblical son of Adam. The steles contain prayers addressed to the members of the gnostic divine triad of Father, Mother, and Son. *Acts Pet. 12 Apost.* contains within it a revelation of the risen Lord to the apostles.

Two other categories, here treated separately, could arguably be included in a discussion of gnostic apocalypses: revelation dialogues and revelation discourses. They are, in any case, closely related generically to the gnostic apocalypses already listed, all of which contain revelation dialogues or discourses within them. It must be stressed that the apocalypse genre, including the revelation dialogue and revelation discourse, is a central medium of literary expression in Gnosticism.

Of the gnostic apocalypses here mentioned, *Apoc. Adam* represents typologically a key link in the evolution of gnostic apocalyptic out of Jewish apocalyptic tradition (MacRae 1979: 152).

b. Revelation Dialogues. Three Nag Hammadi tractates can be classified as "revelation dialogues" rather than "apocalypses," since they lack an account of the appearance of the revealer. These are *Thom. Cont.; Dial. Sav.;* and *Disc. 8–9. Dial Sav.* is especially interesting because it appears to have been constructed out of a collection of sayings of Jesus like *Gos. Thom. Thom. Cont.* has recently been adjudged to be a Christian revision of a Hellenistic Jewish pseudepigraphical letter attributed first to the patriarch Jacob (Schenke 1983). *Disc. 8–9* is a typical dialogue of the Hermetic tradition.

c. Revelation Discourses. The genre "revelation discourse" is also known as "wisdom monologue" (Layton 1987: 77–78). Two of the examples from the Nag Hammadi collection feature female revealer-figures: *Thund.* and *Trim. Prot. Thund.* closely resembles a shorter "I am" discourse attributed to Eve now embedded in *Orig. World* (II 114,8–15). *Trim. Prot.* appears to be an expansion of a revelation discourse attributed to "Pronoia" ("Providence") in the longer version of *Ap. John.* Its relationship to the prologue of the Gospel of John is a matter of debate (Robinson 1981). *Treat. Seth* features Jesus Christ as the revealer. *Great Pow.* also belongs to this genre, although it lacks the "I am" self-predication found in the others. The first main section of *Ap. John* can also be called a revelation discourse (Pearson 1984: 458).

d. "Rewritten Bible." In this category, which does not constitute a separate literary genre per se, are included those portions of tractates which consist for the most part of paraphrases or running commentary on the opening chapters of Genesis. *Ap. John; Hyp. Arch.;* and *Orig. World* contain notable examples, wherein the focus is on the story of Adam and Eve and the early history of humankind now retold from a gnostic perspective. Formally, the closest parallels to this kind of literature are some of the OT pseudepigrapha, especially *1 Enoch* 6–11, *Jubilees,* and the *Genesis Apocryphon* from Qumran (1QapGen). (For the term "Rewritten Bible," with reference to these Jewish writings, see Nickelsburg 1984: 89; cf. Pearson 1988: 647–51). In this category should also be included discrete sections of tractates which formally resemble Jewish midrashim, such as the midrash on the serpent-revealer in *Testim. Truth* and the midrash on David and Solomon in the same tractate (Pearson 1984: 457).

e. Gospels. Four of the Nag Hammadi tractates are called "gospels": *Gos. Truth* (its *incipit* is used as a title); *Gos. Thom.; Gos. Phil.;* and *Gos. Eg.* None of these is a gospel of the canonical type, though *Gos. Thom.*, a collection of dominical sayings, resembles in its form the hypothetical "Q" source presumably used by Matthew and Luke. *Gos. Truth* is a homily on the "gospel"; here the term *euangelion* is used in its original Christian sense as "message of salvation" (cf. Rom 1:16; 1 Cor 15:1; etc.). *Gos. Phil.* is an anthology of excerpts from various other works (Layton 1987: 325–26). *Gos. Eg.* (not to be confused with the work of that same name cited by Clement of Alexandria and other patristic writers) is also entitled *The Holy Book of the Great Invisible Spirit,* and consists of a doctrinal treatise to which is added a liturgical service book for a gnostic baptism ceremony. A *Gospel of Mary* is found in the related Berlin Codex (BG,*1*). This text belongs to the "apocalypse" genre.

f. Epistles. One of the Nag Hammadi tractates bears the term "epistle" in its title: *Ep. Pet. Phil.* This tractate receives its title from the letter with which it opens; however, as a whole the tractate belongs more properly to the "apocalypse" genre. Two tractates can be classified as "doctrinal epistles": *Treat. Res.* and *Eugnostos. Ap. Jas.* has an epistolary framework at the beginning and the end, and *Hyp. Arch.* shows epistolary features in its opening passage.

g. Acts. One tractate from the Nag Hammadi collection, *Acts Pet. 12 Apost.,* has the term "Acts" in its title, and resembles in some ways the numerous acts of apostles that constitute part of the NT apocrypha. It is probably a piece of a larger work, containing within its extant portion a revelation of the savior. The Berlin Codex contains a similar text: *The Act of Peter* (BG,*4*).

h. Doctrinal Treatises. To this category belong *Tri. Trac.; Orig. World;* and *Val. Exp.* The last named tractate is a doctrinal exposition, to which have been added liturgical fragments on the sacraments of baptism and the eucharist. *Gos. Eg.* is also a doctrinal treatise with liturgical matter at the end. All of these texts present accounts and interpretations of the basic gnostic myth of cosmogony and salvation, with *Tri. Trac.* and *Val. Exp.* offering different interpretations from the Valentinian school. Two other tractates, *Exeg. Soul* and *Auth. Teach.,* can be treated under the general category of "doctrinal treatises," but of a special type: they consist of allegories on the fall and return of the soul.

i. Wisdom Books. *Sent. Sextus* and *Teach. Silv.* belong to this category. The former is a previously known collection of short aphorisms. The latter is a *logos protreptikos* (hortatory discourse) generically akin to the Wisdom of Solomon in the Greek Bible. Neither of these is "gnostic" in the technical sense of the term.

j. Homilies. To this category belong *Gos. Truth; Interp. Know.;* and, at least partially, *Testim. Truth. Gos. Truth* is a meditative disquisition on the message of salvation, and was probably composed by the heresiarch Valentinus himself (Layton 1987: 250–51). *Interp. Know.,* another Valentinian text, presumes a setting in Christian corporate worship. The first part of *Testim. Truth* is a polemical sermon attacking the beliefs and practices of catholic Christian opponents, to which has been added material made up of various sources and utilized for a polemical purpose. In addition, the second part of *Thom. Cont.* consists of a homily made up of woes and blessings pronounced by the savior. *Zost.* concludes with a brief admonitory sermon.

k. Prayers. Two tractates are so identified in the mss. *Pr. Paul,* with title, has been written into the front flyleaf of Codex I. *Pr. Thanks* is a previously known prayer of the Hermetic tradition appended to *Disc. 8–9.* It is introduced with the words, "This is the prayer that they spoke." In addition, *Steles Seth* consists basically of three prayers of praise offered up by "Seth" to members of the divine triad of Father, Mother, and Son. Prayers of praise, with the formula "Holy are you," are found embedded in *Melch.* (IX 16,16–18,7). Some of the appended liturgical material in *Val. Exp.* consists of prayers. Two liturgical prayers are embedded in *Ep. Pet. Phil* (VIII 133,21–134,9). Prayers of invocation are also found at the end of *Gos. Eg.* in material that actually constitutes a "liturgical service book" (Layton 1987: 101–2). Prayers for individual meditation are embedded in the Hermetic tractate *Disc. 8–9* (VI 55,24–57,25). Some of the colophons in Codices I, II, and VII should be classified as prayers, but they reflect the (monastic) setting of the scribes rather than the content of the tractates copied (see E above).

l. Hymns. Some of the aforementioned prayers could also be construed as hymns, especially those that were apparently meant to be chanted in a worship setting. One entire tractate, *Norea,* can be labeled a "hymn" or "ode" on account of its strophic structure. The Hermetic tractate *Disc. 8–9* refers throughout to the singing of hymns, and hymnic material, including "glossolalia" (*voces mysticae*), is found in it (esp. at VI 60,17–61,17). Similar material occurs in *Gos. Eg.* and *Zost.*

m. Anthologies. One of the tractates labeled a "gospel," *Gos. Phil.,* is really an anthology of mostly unconnected excerpts from other gnostic works. None of these other works is extant. *Orig. World* is almost an anthology in that it contains a number of discrete sources within it. Finally, *Plato Rep.* represents an "anthology" of another kind, for it can safely be assumed that it was not taken directly from book 9 of the great philosopher's masterwork but rather, as was common practice in antiquity, from an anthology of excerpts from ancient writers.

2. Religious Character. The earliest major work on the Nag Hammadi collection treated it as a "library" of "undoubted unity" belonging to a single sect of "Sethian" gnostics (Doresse 1960: 249–51). But over the years it has become clear that it is not a "library" of a single group at all, but a collection of disparate works of various origins. Not all of the texts are "gnostic," and the Gnosticism represented in the texts that are gnostic is of various types, some of which, moreover, are not easily classified by sectarian affiliation according to the catalogs of the great heresiologists of the Church. If one can speak of a unity at all in the collection it would be a unity not of a theological or philosophical sort, but having to do with lifestyle. That is to say, many of the texts in the collection advocate an ascetic lifestyle, and all of them could be read in that light. From this perspective, it is not difficult to understand how these writings could be appreciated in a monastic setting (Wisse 1971; 1978).

However, since most of the texts are, in fact, gnostic, it will be useful to classify the collection in terms of their gnostic or non-gnostic character, as well as in terms of the kinds of Gnosticism represented, to the extent that this is possible.

a. Sethian Gnostic Texts. While Doresse's initial classification of the Nag Hammadi collection must be rejected, scholars meanwhile have noted that there are a number of tractates which appear to be "Sethian" in some sense, and are clearly related to one another in terms of content; that is, they share a common underlying mythological "system" (Schenke 1974; 1981). One of the features of this system is an emphasis on Seth, son of Adam, as a revealer figure and spiritual father of a gnostic "race of Seth." Hence, the classification "Sethian" is suggested by the texts themselves.

The Nag Hammadi texts that belong to this system are: *Ap. John; Hyp. Arch.; Gos. Eg.; Apoc. Adam; Steles Seth; Zost.; Melch.; Norea; Marsanes; Allogenes;* and *Trim. Prot.* To these texts must be added the system described by Irenaeus in *Adversus Haereses* 1.29, which is parallel to part of *Ap. John,* and the untitled tractate from the Codex Brucianus.

Of the Nag Hammadi texts here named, one is definitely a Christian text, *Melch.* (whose gnostic features may be secondary). Others appear to reflect various stages of "Christianization" of originally non-Christian material; these are *Ap. John; Hyp. Arch.; Gos. Eg.;* and *Trim. Prot.* Still others are not Christian at all, but reflect a profound influence from Platonist philosophy: *Steles Seth; Zost.; Marsanes;* and *Allogenes. Apoc. Adam,* another non-Christian text, stands in close relationship with Jewish apocalyptic tradition.

It is to be noted that the system described by Irenaeus (1.29) is expressly associated by him with a group of sectarians called, simply, *gnostikoi* ("gnostics"). Irenaeus does not use the term "Sethian." On the other hand, Hippolytus (*Haer.* 5.19) describes a system that he attributes to a group of "Sethians," and refers to a book of theirs called *The Paraphrase of Seth* (V.22). The content of the Nag Hammadi tractate, *Paraph. Shem,* resembles the system described by Hippolytus, though it does not cohere very well with the other "Sethian" texts already identified. Should it be called, nevertheless, a "Sethian gnostic" tractate? In any case, *Paraph. Shem* is a non-Christian gnostic apocalypse featuring a redeemer called "Derdekeas." The *Paraphrase of Seth* known to Hippolytus was a Christianized version of the mythological system found in *Paraph. Shem.*

Other Nag Hammadi tractates seem in various ways to be related to the Sethian gnostic ones mentioned. *Orig. World* contains material that coheres with such Sethian texts as *Hyp. Arch. Eugnostos,* a non-Christian text, contains teaching concerning the divine world and Anthropos that is akin to the material on the same subject in *Ap. John* and Iren. *Haer.* 1.29 (van den Broek 1981). *Soph. Jes. Chr.* is a Christianized version of *Eugnostos.* Finally, *Treat. Seth,* a Christian gnostic text, reflects in its background a Sethian mythological system (Painchaud 1982: 5–6, 21).

b. Valentinian Texts. The Valentinian school is one of the most important heretical complexes in the ancient Church, and quite a bit was known about it before the Nag Hammadi discovery. Irenaeus expressly says (*Haer.* 1.11) that Valentinus adapted the "gnostic" teachings (described by him in 1.29) in setting up his own school. Thus Valentinus can be said to have been a "reformer" of the (Sethian) gnostic religion represented by *Ap. John* and related texts (Layton 1987: xv).

Given the importance of the Valentinian movement, it is not surprising that a number of Valentinian tractates should show up in the Nag Hammadi find. Four of the five tractates in the Jung Codex (NHC I) are surely of Valentinian origin: *Pr. Paul; Gos. Truth* (probably composed by Valentinus himself); *Treat. Res.;* and *Tri. Trac.* If the Jung Codex represents a Valentinian collection of texts, *Ap. Jas.* (1.2), though not of Valentinian authorship, was considered of value to Valentinian gnostics. Another "James" text, *1 Apoc. Jas.,* seems to reflect some Valentinian influence, and may have been subjected to some Valentinian editing.

Also clearly of Valentinian origin are *Gos. Phil.; Interp. Know.;* and *Val. Exp.* Valentinian influences have been discerned in *Exeg. Soul,* and are possibly present in some other tractates as well, such as *Orig. World* and *Norea. Testim. Truth* contains some Valentinian influences, but also takes a stand against the Valentinian school. It has been suggested that the author of that tractate is the ex-Valentinian Julius Cassianus (Pearson 1981: 116–20).

c. Hermetic Texts. The pagan Greco-Egyptian gnosis featuring "Thrice-Greatest Hermes" as its central revealer is represented in the Nag Hammadi collection by three tractates: *Disc. 8–9; Pr. Thanks.;* and *Asclepius.* The two last named are texts known before the Nag Hammadi discovery. *Disc. 8–9* is new Hermetic work, akin especially to *Corpus Hermeticum* I (*Poimandres*) and XIII, but showing more distinctively Egyptian coloring.

d. Texts of the Thomas Tradition. The Syrian (Edessene) Christian tradition identified with Judas Thomas, Jesus' "twin brother," is represented by two texts from Nag Hammadi: *Gos. Thom.* and *Thom. Cont.* This tradition can be considered "gnostic" only in the broader sense of the term (Layton 1987: 360). *Gos. Thom.* was an especially important work. Fragments of three different copies of that gospel in Greek are included in the vast collection of papyri from Oxyrhynchus. (See H. Attridge's edition in Layton 1989: 95–128.) *Gos. Thom.* may have been utilized by the authors of such Nag Hammadi tractates as *Dial. Sav.* and *Testim. Truth,* and may also have influenced Valentinus and his pupils (Layton 1987: 220, 360).

e. Miscellaneous Gnostic Texts. In the case of several Nag Hammadi tractates it is difficult (if not impossible) to discern any particular sectarian affiliation. Of the Christian gnostic texts in question, some are associated with special apostolic authorities: James, the brother of Jesus, was especially beloved in certain Jewish Christian traditions (*Gos. Thom.* 12), and is the focus of three Nag Hammadi tractates: *Ap. Jas.; 1 Apoc. Jas.;* and *2 Apoc. Jas.* The "Petrine tradition" (Perkins 1980: 113–30) is represented by *Apoc. Pet.* (not to be confused with the apocalypse of the same name preserved in Ethiopic); *Ep. Pet. Phil.;* and *Acts Pet. 12 Apost.* (but the last may not be of gnostic origin). The apostle Paul is credited with an account of a heavenly journey: *Apoc. Paul* (not to be confused with another account of a heavenly journey with the same title preserved in Latin and several other languages).

Other Christian gnostic texts which defy sectarian identification are *Dial. Sav.; Auth. Teach.; Great Pow.; Treat. Seth;* and *Soph. Jes. Chr.*

Two gnostic tractates in this miscellaneous category are evidently not influenced by Christianity: *Thund.* and *Hypsiphr.,* though certainty in the case of the latter is unattainable owing to the fragmentary condition of the ms.

f. Non-gnostic Texts. Two Christian texts from Nag Hammadi are definitely not gnostic: *Teach. Silv.* and *Sent. Sextus.* The latter was known before and is preserved in a number of languages. *Acts Pet. 12 Apost.* is also better included with the non-gnostic apocryphal acts, for there is no firm indication in the extant material of any specifically gnostic features. Of course, there can be no question about the non-gnostic character of Plato's *Republic,* though it is possible that the snippet found at Nag Hammadi in a fractured Coptic translation, *Plato Rep.,* has been subjected to gnostic editorial adjustment in its Coptic stage.

To be sure, the "gnostic" or "non-gnostic" character of many of the texts is not easy to determine, and scholars often differ in their judgments on this point. Some have questioned the "gnostic" character of such texts as *Ap. Jas.; Dial. Sav.; Thund.; Auth. Teach.;* and even *Gos. Truth.* Other scholars, at least initially, assumed the "gnostic" character of *Gos. Thom; Teach. Silv.,* and others. It is evident that much more work needs to be done on the study of this material.

G. Importance of the Nag Hammadi Codices

As one of the most important manuscript finds of the century, comparable in that respect to the discovery of the Dead Sea Scrolls, the Nag Hammadi collection has had an enormous impact on a number of scholarly fields and disciplines.

In the field of NT studies, *Gos. Thom.* alone has spawned a huge bibliography. The most important feature of that text is that it consists of a collection of Jesus' sayings which is probably independent of the canonical gospels and, in the case of some sayings, preserves very ancient gospel tradition. The study of gospel tradition has also been enriched by other texts as well, especially *Dial. Sav.* and *Ap. Jas.* New issues in Johannine scholarship have emerged in the study of such texts as *Trim. Prot.,* particularly its relationship to the prologue of the Gospel of John. Indeed, the whole question of the impact of Gnosticism upon the NT and its world has been reopened by the study of the Nag Hammadi texts, and no credible work can be done on that question without recourse to the new material. As study of these texts proceeds, more critical issues for NT studies continue to emerge.

In the field of early Christian history in general, the Nag Hammadi texts have provided new evidence for the analysis of the relationship between "orthodoxy" and "heresy" in the early Church, and how these came to be defined. The study of the religious character of certain geographical areas of the early Church, especially Syria and Egypt, has been greatly enlarged. The study of the history of the NT canon, and of early Christian literature in general, has new material with which to work and new questions to ask.

The study of early Judaism has also been enlarged, for now there is a quantity of new material that bears upon the question of the connections between Judaism and Gnosticism, and the whole issue of Jewish sectarianism in relation to the eventual consolidation of normative (rabbinic) Judaism. The Nag Hammadi collection has been considered of enough importance on these matters to be included in the purview of an important survey of Jewish writings of the Second Temple period (Pearson 1984); one of the texts, *Apoc. Adam,* is even included in a standard collection of OT pseudigrapha (MacRae *OTP* 1: 707–19).

Needless to say, the study of ancient Gnosticism has now been put on a solid basis as a result of this discovery of original gnostic works. Previous to this discovery, scholars of Gnosticism were, for the most part, dependent upon the patristic heresiologists (the gnostics' enemies) for their source material. Gnosticism, to be sure, is only one of the important currents in Hellenistic-Roman religion and philosophy, and, as an eclectic phenomenon, bears upon the study of other religious traditions. The Nag Hammadi collection has provided new material for the study of Hermeticism, for example, and even for the study of Middle Platonism and Platonism. Indeed, an international conference was held in 1984 devoted to "Neoplatonism and Gnosticism," and the Nag Hammadi texts played a very large role in the papers and discussions (Wallis and Bregman 1989).

The study of the Coptic language has been enormously enlarged by the Nag Hammadi discovery, for it is interest in the Nag Hammadi texts that has drawn significant numbers of students into the study of Coptic who otherwise would not have considered such study. The impact of the Nag Hammadi discovery has also been such that the wider study of the whole range of Coptic literature has been accelerated. In addition, the Nag Hammadi texts themselves provide new material for innovative breakthroughs in Coptic philology, especially in grammar and dialectology. An international society has been organized which is devoted to Coptology in all of its aspects, the International Association for Coptic Studies. Its organizing conference took place in Cairo in 1976, in conjunction with a meeting of the International Committee for the Nag Hammadi Codices.

Finally, the close scrutiny of the Nag Hammadi mss carried out by Robinson and his team has resulted in a number of breakthroughs in codicology and papyrology (Robinson 1978).

These are only some of the areas and disciplines which have been enlarged by the Nag Hammadi discovery. In actual fact, it would be virtually impossible to assess fully the enormous impact upon scholarship made by the random digging of those fellahin from al-Qaṣr at the Jabal al-Ṭarīf on that December day in 1945.

Bibliography

1. The Facsimile Edition.

Robinson, J. M. et al. 1972a. *The Facsimile Edition of the Nag Hammadi Codices—Codex VI.* Leiden.

———. 1972b. *The Facsimile Edition—Codex VII.* Leiden.

———. 1973. *The Facsimile Edition—Codices IX, XII, and XIII.* Leiden.

———. 1974a. *The Facsimile Edition—Codex II.* Leiden.

———. 1974b. *The Facsimile Edition—Codex V.* Leiden.

———. 1975. *The Facsimile Edition—Codex IV.* Leiden.

———. 1976a. *The Facsimile Edition—Codex III.* Leiden.

———. 1976b. *The Facsimile Edition—Codex VIII.* Leiden.

———. 1977a. *The Facsimile Edition—Codex I.* Leiden.

———. 1977b. *The Facsimile Edition—Codex IX and X.* Leiden.

———. 1979. *The Facsimile Edition—Cartonnage.* Leiden.

Robinson, J. M. 1984. *The Facsimile Edition—Introduction.* Leiden.

2. The Coptic Gnostic Library.

Attridge, H. 1985. *Nag Hammadi Codex I (The Jung Codex).* 2 vols. NHS 22–23. Leiden.

Barns, J. W. B.; Browne, G. M.; and Shelton, J. C. 1981. *Nag Hammadi Codices: Greek and Coptic Papyri from the Cartonnage of the Covers.* NHS 16. Leiden.

Böhlig, A.; Wisse, F.; and Labib, P. 1975. *Nag Hammadi Codices III,2*

and IV,2: The Gospel of the Egyptians (The Holy Book of the Great Invisible Spirit). NHS 4. Leiden.
Emmel, S. 1984. *Nag Hammadi Codex III,5: The Dialogue of the Savior.* NHS 26. Leiden.
Hedrick, C. 1990. *Nag Hammadi Codices XI, XII, XIII.* NHS 28. Leiden.
Layton, B. 1989. *Nag Hammadi Codex II,2–7, Together with XIII,2*, Brit Lib. Or. 4926 (1) and P. Oxy. 1, 654, 655.* 2 vols. NHS 20–21. Leiden.
Parrott, D. 1979. *Nag Hammadi Codices V,2–5 and VI with Papyrus Berolinensis 8502,1 and 4.* NHS 11. Leiden.
———. 1989. *Nag Hammadi Codices III,3–4 and V,1 with Papyrus Berolinensis 8502, 3 and Oxyrhynchus Papyrus 1081: Eugnostos and the Sophia of Jesus Christ.* NHS 27. Leiden.
Pearson, B. A. 1981. *Nag Hammadi Codices IX and X.* NHS 15. Leiden.
Schmidt, C., and MacDermot, V. 1978a. *Pistis Sophia.* NHS 9. Leiden.
———. 1978b. *The Books of Jeu and the Untitled Text in the Bruce Codex.* NHS 13. Leiden.
Sieber, J. 1991. *Nag Hammadi Codex VIII.* NHS 31. Leiden.
To be published: NHC II,*1* and IV,*1* (*Ap. John*), ed. F. Wisse. NHC III,*1* and BG,*2* (*Ap. John*), ed. P. Nagel. NHC VII, ed. F. Wisse. NHC VIII, ed. J. Sieber.

3. Bibliography.

Scholer, D. M. 1971a. *Nag Hammadi Bibliography 1948–69.* NHS 1. Leiden.
———. 1971b. Bibliographia Gnostica: Supplementum I. *NovT* 13: 322–36.
———. 1972. Bibliographia Gnostica: Supplementum II. *NovT* 14: 312–21 (with annual supplements in *NovT* thereafter, except for 1976).

4. Other Works Cited.

Beltz, W. 1970. Die Adam-Apokalypse aus Codex V von Nag Hammadi—Jüdische Bausteine in gnostischen Systemen. Theol. Habil. diss. Berlin.
Bianchi, U. 1967. *Le Origini dello gnosticismo: Colloquio di Messina 13–18 Aprile 1966.* SHR 12. Leiden.
Böhlig, A., and Labib, P. 1962. *Die Koptisch-gnostische Schrift ohne Titel aus Codex II von Nag Hammadi im Koptischen Museum zu Alt-Kairo.* Deutsche Akademie der Wissenschaften zu Berlin, Institut für Orientforschung 58. Berlin.
———. 1963. *Koptisch-gnostische Apokalypsen aus Codex V von Nag Hammadi im Koptischen Museum zu Alt-Kairo.* Sonderband, *Wissenschaftliche-Zeitschrift der Martin-Luther-Universität Halle-Wittenberg.*
Broek, R. van den. 1981. Autogenes and Adamas: The Mythological Structure of the Apocryphon of John. Pp. 16–25 in *Gnosis and Gnosticism,* ed. M. Krause. NHS 17. Leiden.
Collins, J. J. 1979. *Apocalypse: The Morphology of a Genre. Semeia* 14. Missoula, MT.
Doresse, J. 1958. *Les livres secrets des gnostiques d'Égypte.* Vol. 1, *Introduction aux écrits gnostiques coptes découverts a Khénoboskion.* Paris.
———. 1959. *Les livres secrets des gnostiques d'Égypte.* Vol. 2, *L'Évangile selon Thomas ou Les paroles secrètes de Jésus.* Paris.
———. 1960. *The Secret Books of the Egyptian Gnostics.* Trans. P. Mairet. New York and London.
———. 1966, 1968. "Le Livre sacré du grand Esprit invisible" ou "L'Évangile des Égyptiens": Texte copte édité, traduit et commenté d'après la Codex I de Nagʾa-Hammadi/Khénoboskion. *JA* 254: 317–435; 256: 289–386.
Emmel, S. 1978. The Nag Hammadi Codices Editing Project: A Final Report. *American Research Center in Egypt, Inc., Newsletter* 104: 10–32.
Fallon, F. 1979. The Gnostic Apocalypses. Pp. 123–58 in Collins 1979.
Guillaumont, A. et al. 1959. *The Gospel according to Thomas.* Leiden, London, and New York.
Kasser, R. et al. 1973. *Tractatus Tripartitus, Pars I, De Supernis: Codex Jung F. XXV^r -F. LII^v (p. 51–104).* Bern.
———. 1975. *Tractatus Tripartitus, Pars II, De Creatione Hominis; Pars III, De Generibus Tribus: Codex Jung F. LII^v -F. LXX^v (p. 194–140).* Bern.
Krause, M. 1962. Der koptische Handschriftenfund bei Nag Hammadi: Umfang und Inhalt. *MDAIK* 19: 106–13.
Krause, M., and Labib, P. 1962. *Die drei Versionen des Apokryphon des Johannes im Koptischen Museum zu Alt-Kairo.* ADAIK 1. Wiesbaden.
———. 1971. *Gnostische und hermetische Schriften aus Codex II und Codex VI.* ADAIK 2. Glückstadt.
Labib, P. 1956. *Coptic Gnostic Papyri in the Coptic Museum at Old Cairo.* Cairo.
Layton, B. 1987. *The Gnostic Scriptures.* Garden City, NY.
MacRae, G. 1979. NHC V,*5*: The Apocalypse of Adam. Pp. 151–95 in Parrott 1979.
Malinine, M. et al. 1956. *Evangelium Veritatis: Codex Jung f. VIII^v–XVI^v (p. 16–32) / f. XIX^r–XXII^r (p. 37–43).* Studien aus dem C. G. Jung-Institut 6. Zurich.
———. 1961. *Evangelium Veritatis (Supplementum): Codex Jung F. XVII^r-F. XVIII^v (p. 33–36).* Studien aus dem C. G. Jung-Institut 6. Zurich and Stuttgart.
———. 1963. *De Resurrectione (Epistula ad Rheginum): Codex Jung F. XXII^r-F. XXV^v (p. 43–50).* Zurich and Stuttgart.
———. 1968. *Epistula Jacobi Apocrypha: Codex Jung F. I^r-F. VIII^v (p. 1–16).* Zurich and Stuttgart.
Ménard, J.-É. 1973. La Bibliothèque copte de Nag Hammadi. Pp. 108–12 in *Nag Hammadi and Gnosis,* ed. R. M. Wilson. NHS 14. Leiden.
———. 1977. *La lettre de Pierre à Philippe.* Bibliothèque copte de Nag Hammadi, Section "Textes" 1. Quebec.
Nickelsburg, G. W. E. 1984. The Bible Rewritten and Expanded. Pp. 89–156 in *Jewish Writings of the Second Temple Period,* ed. M. Stone. CRINT: 2/2. Assen and Philadelphia.
Painchaud, L. 1982. *Le Deuxième Traité du Grand Seth (NH VII,2).* Bibliothèque copte de Nag Hammadi, Section "Textes" 6. Quebec.
Pearson, B. A. 1984. Jewish Sources in Gnostic Literature. Pp. 443–81 in *Jewish Writings of the Second Temple Period,* ed. M. Stone. CRINT 2/2. Assen and Philadelphia.
———. 1988. Use, Authority and Exegesis of Mikra in Gnostic Literature. Pp. 635–52 in *Mikra,* ed. M. J. Mulder. CRINT 2/2. Assen and Philadelphia.
Perkins, P. 1980. *The Gnostic Dialogue.* New York.
Robinson, J. M. 1972. Inside the Front Cover of Codex VI. Pp. 74–87 in *Essays on the Nag Hammadi Texts,* ed. M. Krause. NHS 3. Leiden.
———. 1978. The Future of Papyrus Codicology. Pp. 23–70 in *The Future of Coptic Studies,* ed. R. M. Wilson. Leiden.
———. 1979. The Discovery of the Nag Hammadi Codices. *BA* 42: 206–24.
———. 1981. Sethians and Johannine Thought: The *Trimorphic*

Protennoia and the Prologue of the Gospel of John. Pp. 643–70 in *The Rediscovery of Gnosticism.* Vol. 2, *Sethian Gnosticism,* ed. B. Layton. Leiden.

Robinson, J. M., and Meyer, M., eds. 1977. *The Nag Hammadi Library in English.* Leiden and San Francisco.

Robinson, J. M., and Smith, R., eds. 1988. *The Nag Hammadi Library in English.* 3d rev. ed. Leiden and San Francisco.

Schenke, H.-M. 1973. "Die Taten des Petrus und der zwölf Apostel"—Die erste Schrift aus Nag-Hammadi-Codex VI. *TLZ* 98: 13–19.

———. 1974. Das Sethianische System nach Nag-Hammadi Schriften. Pp. 165–72 in *Studia Coptica,* ed. P. Nagel. Berlin.

———. 1978. Koptisch-Gnostische Schriften, Volumes 2 and 3. Pp. 113–16 in *Nag Hammadi and Gnosis,* ed. R. M. Wilson. NHS 14. Leiden.

———. 1981. The Phenomenon and Significance of Gnostic Sethianism. Pp. 588–616 in *The Rediscovery of Gnosticism.* Vol. 2 of *Sethian Gnosticism,* ed. B. Layton. Leiden.

———. 1983. The Book of Thomas (NHC II.7): A Revision of a Psudepigraphical Letter of Jacob the Contender. Pp. 213–28 in *The New Testament and Gnosis,* ed. A. H. B. Logan and A. J. M. Wedderburn. Edinburgh.

Till, W. 1955. *Die gnostische Schriften des koptischen Papyrus Berolinensis 8502.* Texte und Untersuchungen zur Geschichte der Altchristlichen Literatur 60. Berlin.

Tröger, K.-W. 1973. *Gnosis und Neues Testament.* Berlin.

Veilleux, A. 1986. Monasticism and Gnosis in Egypt. Pp. 271–306 in *The Roots of Egyptian Christianity,* ed. B. A. Pearson and J. E. Goehring. Studies in Antiquity and Christianity 1. Philadelphia.

Wallis, R. T., and Bregman, J. 1989. *Neoplatonism and Gnosticism.* Studies in Neoplatonism: Ancient and Modern 6. Albany, NY.

Wisse, F. 1971. The Nag Hammadi Library and the Heresiologists. *VC* 25: 205–23.

———. 1978. Gnosticism and Early Monasticism in Egypt. Pp. 431–40 in *Gnosis,* ed. B. Aland. Göttingen.

BIRGER A. PEARSON

NAGGAI (PERSON) [Gk *Naggai*]. The father of Esli and son of Maath, according to Luke's genealogy tying Joseph, the "supposed father" of Jesus, to descent of Adam and God (Luke 3:25). Codex D omits Naggai, substituting a genealogy adapted from Matt 1:6–15 for Luke 3:23–31. The name "Naggai" occurs nowhere else in the biblical documents, including Matthew's genealogy, and falls within a list of seventeen otherwise unknown descendants of David's son Nathan (Fitzmyer *Luke 1–9* AB, 500), although there is a Gk *Nage*/Heb *nōgâ* at 1 Chr 3:7, as a son of David. A few NT mss read Gk *Nagai* here (A 1241) (see Hervey 1853: 136). Kuhn (1923: 208–9) argues that two seemingly parallel lists of names—Luke 3:23–26 (Jesus to Mattathias) and 3:29–31 (Joshua/Jesus to Mattatha)—were originally identical, the first perhaps reflecting a Hebrew context and the second an Aramaic context, tracing Mary's line of descent (since it does not mention Joseph as Jesus' father). Naggai in the first list corresponds to Melea in the second list. With no major textual variants for Naggai and Melea to support confusion of the two, Kuhn's theory has little plausibility.

Bibliography

Hervey, A. 1853. *The Genealogies of Our Lord and Saviour Jesus Christ, As Contained in the Gospels of St. Matthew and St. Luke.* Cambridge.

Kuhn, G. 1923. Die Geschlechtsregister Jesu bei Lukas und Matthäus, nach ihrer Herkunft untersucht. *ZNW* 22: 206–28.

STANLEY E. PORTER

NAHAL OREN (M.R. 148241). A site located on the W side of Mt. Carmel on a steep terrace facing S at a height of 46–53 m above sea level. It is near the point where the Nahal Oren stream enters the coastal plain.

The Mt. Carmel region belongs to the Mediterranean plant belt with about 500 mm of rain per year. A perennial spring is located about 100 m E of the site.

During two cycles of excavations held in 1954–57 and 1959–60 (Stekelis and Yisraeli 1963) and 1969–71 (Noy, Legge, and Higgs 1973), about nine levels have been identified representing the Kebarian, the Natufian, and the early Pre-Pottery Neolithic A and B (PPN A and PPN B) cultures. These cultures represent the level of late hunter-gatherer and early farmer which date to ca. 16,000–6800 B.C.E.

The Kebarian culture encompassed two cultural phases. To the earliest belongs a short stone wall founded on bedrock and a rich flint industry and animal bones. Among the flint tools are truncated bladelets, carinated and small-end scrapers, and burins. The upper phase is characterized by extremely small microliths, particularly triangles and crescents (Noy et al. 1973; Kukan 1978).

The Natufian culture reflects the Middle and Late phase (Valla 1981). The middle Natufian phase was mainly uncovered in the lower part of the terrace where a cemetery with about 30 skeletons and varied installations covered most of the area. Studies of the human teeth revealed special nutrition habits (Smith 1970). Some notable elements in the cemetery are large hearths made of white slabs of stone, "pipe mortars" standing near some of the graves, and small elongated cup holes laid near some of the skeletons. Individual or small groups of individuals found in one grave and the northern orientation of the bodies are also characteristic (Noy fc.). The later phase stands out by stone walls crossing the terrace, individual graves, animal figurines carved on stone, and animal horns (Stekelis 1960), a rich flint industry and, in addition, bone tools, limestone vessels, and elongated basalt polishers, some of which are decorated. The small microliths continue to the end of this phase (Henry 1973; Valla 1983).

Several architectural features exist between the late Natufian levels and those of the PPN A, but these are still under investigation and evaluation.

The PPN A village was built on terraces, where 20 round buildings have been uncovered. Even though the major site belonged to one occupation level, other short occupation levels exist. The houses range from 3–4 m in diameter and are built of local stones; their floors are of terre pisee and most are equipped with round hearths built of small stones, cup holes on flat stones, and some local stone vessels. The flint tools include tranche axes (the Tahunian type), elongated sickle blades of the Beit Tamir type, arrowheads of El Khaim points, Hegudud truncations (Bar Yosef, Gopher, and Nadel 1987), and some small obsidian blades from the Gülü Dag source in Anatolia (Yellin, personal communication). These tools represent the Sultanian stage in PPN A. Small human figurines carved from stone were found on house floors and very few burials were below the house floor.

The PPN B is the last occupation of the terrace; most of the architecture suffered natural erosion and human destruction. The earliest stage still has some rounded houses following the tradition of the previous period. The second phase of the PPN B settlement is scattered on the terrace with rectangular houses which were built with medium stone pebbles. Some of the houses were paved with flat square pebble stone. Some skeletons without heads were found buried below the houses (Noy 1973). Two-level grinding stones and upper semi-elliptical stones made from basalt or limestone are common; some of the flint was heated and beautiful color was achieved. Helown, Jericho, and Byblos points, some with Abu Ghosh retouch, are well known (Gopher 1985). Long sickle blades, some with serrated and short tangs, and long pointed blades are unique in shape and length. Minute beads cut from shell were sewn on garments as decoration. In the Kebarian phases, deer and gazelle were the most hunted animals and in the Natufian and PPN A phases the gazelle was the major animal hunted, but in PPN B there was a growing number of goats and sheep (Legge 1973: 90–91). Cultivated plants appear in PPN A and B (Dennell 1973: 91–93).

Bibliography

Bar Yosef, O; Gopher, A.; and Nadel, D. 1987. The "Hagdud Truncation"—A New Tool Type from the Sullaman Industry at Netiv Hagdud, the Jordan Valley. *Mitekufat Haeven* 20: 151*–57*.

Dennell, R. W. 1973. Plant Remains in Recent Excavations at Nahal Oren, Israel. Pp. 75–99 in Noy, Legge, and Higgs 1973.

Gopher, A. 1985. Flint Tools Industries of the Neolithic Period in Israel. Ph.D. diss., Hebrew University, Jerusalem.

Henry, D. 1973. The Natufian at Palestine: Its Material Culture and Ecology. Ph.D. diss., Southern Methodist University, Dallas.

Kukan, G. J. 1978. A Technological and Stylistic Study of Microliths from Certain Levantine Epipaleolithic Assemblages, Vols. I–II. Ph.D. diss., University of Toronto.

Legge, A. T. 1973. The Fauna in Recent Excavations at Nahal Oren, Israel. Pp. 75–99 in Noy, Legge, and Higgs 1973.

Noy, T. 1973. A House and Tombs from the Pottery Neolithic Period. *Qad* 6: 18–19 (in Hebrew).

———. fc. Some Aspects of Natufian Mortuary Behaviors at Nahal Oren. *Second Symposium on Upper Paleolithic, Mesolithic and Neolithic Populations of Europe and the Mediterranean Basin.*

Noy, T.; Legge, A. T.; and Higgs, E. S. 1973. Recent Excavations at Nahal Oren, Israel. *Proceedings of the Prehistoric Society* 39: 75–99.

Smith, P. 1970. Dental Morphology and Pathology in the Natufian. Ph.D. diss., Chicago.

Stekelis, M. 1960. The Mesolithic Art at Eretz Israel. *EI* 6: 2–29 (in Hebrew).

Stekelis, M., and Yisraeli, T. 1963. Excavations at Nahal Oren, Preliminary Report. *IEJ* 13: 1–12.

Valla, F. R. 1981. Les Etablissements Natufian dans le nord d'Israel. Pp. 409–19 in *Prehistoire du Levant,* ed. J. Cauvin, P. Sanlaville. Paris.

———. 1983. *Les industries de silex de Mallaha (Eynan) et du Natufien dans le Levant.* Memoires et Travaux du Centre de Recherche Français de Jerusalem 3. Paris.

TAMAR NOY

NAHALAL (PLACE) [Heb *nahălāl*]. Var. NAHALOL. Fourth Levitical city mentioned in the Zebulun listing (Josh 21:35). There are no parallels to Nahalal in the 1 Chronicles account. Nahalal is mentioned in two other OT accounts, first in the allotment list to Zebulun (Josh 19:15), and, second in the Judges conquest narrative. In the conquest narrative "Zebulun did not drive out the inhabitants of . . . Nahalol, but the Canaanites dwelt among them, and became subject to forced labor" (Judg 1:30). The exact location of biblical Nahalal is unknown; however, two tells have been suggested as possible sites: Tell el-Beida and Tell en-Nahl.

Tell el-Beida (M.R. 168231) has been suggested by J. Simons (*GTTOT,* 202) as biblical Nahalal. Beida is located 1 km S of modern Nahalal, a Moshav-ovedim founded in 1921. No doubt this is one reason why Simons associated biblical Nahalal with Beida. The tell is situated in the N central section of the Esdraelon Plain. It is a rich area with a good water supply. At the S base of the tell there is a spring of water and surrounding Beida there are tributaries of the river Kishon. To the S and W lies the fertile Esdraelon Plain while to the N and E are the lower Galilee hills. The closest trade route is 9 km to the SW at Jokneam, where it passes across the Carmel and meets the Acco-Bethshan route.

None of the early geographers make any reference to Tell el-Beida. The archaeological surveys conducted at el-Beida have shown an occupation during EB, MB, LB, Iron I, Iron II, Persian, Roman, Byzantine, and Arab periods. There are many difficulties in trying to associate biblical Nahalal with Tell el-Beida. First and foremost is the name of the site. The modern moshav, Nahalal, founded in 1921, is hardly evidence to demonstrate a case for "historical memory" of a place name. It is possible the moshav chose the name because of biblical Nahalal of Zebulun, but the relationship goes no further than that.

Tell en-Nahl (M.R. 156245) was first identified as biblical Nahalal by Albright (1923: 26–27). He argued his position on the philological grounds that Nahalal was nearly identical in form with the Nahl in Tell en-Nahl. However, there is a geographical problem that Tell en-Nahl is located in the plain of Acco in the tribe of Asher, whereas Joshua and Judges locate it in the tribal territory of Zebulun. Tell en-Nahl is located 10 km E of the Mediterranean. It lies in the coastal plain, E of Haifa, centrally located between the E hills and the coastline. Acco, Tell en-Nahl, and the pass leading into the Esdraelon Plain fall on a near N–S line. The view from Tell en-Nahl to the N is Acco, to the E one sees the valley stretching to the low hills, to the S is the Carmel range, and to the W Haifa and the sea. The tell is surrounded by fertile agricultural lands. 2 km to the W of Tell en-Nahl flows the Kishon River. There is a small tributary that flows past Tell en-Nahl immediately to the

N. The archaeological surveys which have been conducted at Tell en-Nahl indicate occupation during the EB, MB, LB I, LB II, Iron I, Iron II, Hellenistic, Roman, Byzantine, and Arabic periods.

The one major obstacle, as noted above, to the identification of Tell en-Nahl with biblical Nahalal could be resolved if Zebulun's borders had expanded to include this Levitical city; however, that solution is not entirely satisfactory. While the historical memory of the name is important, yet the tribal location must also be considered seriously. Nevertheless the etymological considerations for Tell en-Nahl are attractive and the pottery stretches over the three Iron II centuries. Tell en-Nahl is therefore tentatively accepted as biblical Nahalal. The geographical location of this city remains troubling and until more is understood about Zebulun's expansion to the sea this identification will have to be regarded as speculative. See also Peterson 1977: 125–39.

Bibliography

Albright, W. F. 1923. Contributions to the Historical Geography of Palestine. *AASOR* 2–3. Cambridge, MA.

Peterson, J. L. 1977. *A Topographical Surface Survey of the Levitical "Cities" of Joshua 21 and I Chronicles 6.* Diss. Seabury-Western Theological Seminary.

Saarisalo, A. 1929. Topographical Researches in Galilee. *JPOS* 9: 37–40.

JOHN L. PETERSON

NAHALIEL (PLACE) [Heb *naḥălîʾēl*]. The location of one of Israel's final encampments prior to entering Canaan (Num 21:19). It is listed after Mattanah and before Bamoth. Its name ("stream of ʾEl") implies that it was a wadi rather than a town. Eusebius (*Onomast.*) located it near the Arnon. Recent identifications have included the Wadi Wala, which feeds into the Arnon from the N, and the Wadi Zerqa Ma'in which flows into the Dead Sea 18 km N of the Arnon.

RANDALL W. YOUNKER

NAHAM (PERSON) [Heb *naḥam*]. Identified as the sister-in-law of Hodiah in the genealogy of Judah (1 Chr 4:19).

H. C. LO

NAHAMANI (PERSON) [Heb *naḥămānî*]. A leader of the Jewish community who returned to Palestine with Zerubbabel shortly after 538 B.C.E., the end of the Babylonian Exile. Neh 7:7 lists Nahamani sixth in a list of twelve names which is headed by the names of Zerubbabel and Joshua (the parallel passage, Ezra 2:2, omits the name). The list introduces a passage which records the divisions of the people of Israel, the priests, the Levites, and the temple servants. Nahamani (Gk *naemani*) is replaced in the later parallel 1 Esdr 5:8 by the name Enenios (which is rendered Bigvai, without warrant, by the RSV, in an effort to reconcile the lists of Ezra and Nehemiah).

STEVEN R. SWANSON

NAHARAI (PERSON) [Heb *naḥăray*]. One of David's mighty men and the armor-bearer of Joab in 2 Sam 23:37 and in the parallel at 1 Chr 11:39. Naharai is called "the Beerothite," and we learn from 2 Sam 4:2–3 that they were Benjaminites who had fled to Gittaim. There is some textual confusion in the LXX of Samuel, as he is called Gelorai in the majority of the Greek manuscripts. The mss of the Lucianic text, which contain what is most likely the OG reading, may witness to an original form close to MT, however, since they have *araia,* perhaps a corrupt form due to the loss of the initial *nu* by haplography from the preceding *anamin.* McCarter (*2 Samuel* AB, 494) explains the Greek form in 2 Sam 23:37 by a series of mutations: "*gelōrai* (Gk **gedōrai* < Heb **gdwry* < **gḥry* < *nḥry*)." The LXX of 1 Chr 11:39, except for minor variants, witnesses to the MT form.

STEPHEN PISANO

NAHARIYEH (M.R. 159267). A small mound on the coast 6 miles N of Acco, at the mouth of the Gaʿaton River. It has remains of the MB, Iron II, and Persian periods, with Roman-Byzantine-Islamic ruins in the vicinity. In excavations in 1947 by I. Ben-Dor, and then in 1954–55 by M. Dothan, the principal discovery was a small cult site about 40 m in diameter and rising just 3 m, right on the dunes of the shoreline ca. 800 m N of the main mound. Despite the potential significance of the cult site, the lack of proper stratigraphic excavation and the absence of any but preliminary reports have robbed the site of its full meaning. The artifacts discussed below, for instance, including the figurines, may be only tentatively attributed to a particular phase (although all are MB; see Negbi 1976: 130–31).

The cult site has five major periods of use. Stratum V ("Str. A/Ph. 5") belongs to the MB I period, ca. 1900–1800 B.C., although a few four-spouted lamps and "Canaanean"-style flints suggest some use already in EB IV (Albright's "MB I" period). To the S of the area was a rectangular, single-room structure ca. 6 × 7 m, with a large pebble pavement adjoining it to the S, identified by the excavators as the earliest phase of a *bāmāh* or "high place." Finds from this phase included typical MB I pottery, including Syrian-style painted wares; seven-spouted lamps; cooking pots; many miniature votive vases; a stone mold for casting a horned "Astarte"-type figurine, as well as five silver and bronze figurines themselves (Negbi 1976: 64); and bones of cattle and sheep-goats.

Strata IV–III ("Str. B/Ph. 4–3") were not well separated, but they appear to date from late MB I, perhaps into MB II. At this time the *bāmāh* paving was expanded to ca. 14 m in diameter, covering the wall stubs of the rectangular structure, and steps to the raised platform were added. A new rectangular broadroom temple was built to the N, ca. 10.7 × 6.2 m, with four column-bases down the center. An intervening courtyard featured an altarlike installation. Finds from this phase included seven-cupped bowls and seven-spouted lamps; hundreds of miniature votives; numerous cooking pot sherds; many beads, items of jewelry, and bronze toggle-pins; animal bones; terra-cotta fenestrated stands; and evidence of metal-working. Of particular interest are three mold-made silver figurines (Negbi 1976: 64).

Strata II–I ("Str. C/Ph. 2–1") is sketchily described by the excavators, and was probably not well discerned stratigraphically. It appears to date to MB III and even into MB III/LB I, ca. 1650–1500 B.C. Several subsidiary rooms were added to the broadroom temple, on both ends. Few finds attributable specifically to this phase are mentioned. The *bāmāh* was raised and expanded again, finally covering the S structure completely. The latest deposits included imported Cypriot wares of the transitional MB III/LB I horizon.

The excavators suggest connecting the Nahariyeh sanctuary with the cult of Asherah, El's consort at Ugarit, known there as *Athiratu-yammi*, "She who Treads/Subdues the Sea." The unique, isolated location right by the seashore and the proliferation of molds and "Mother Goddess" figurines (19 in all; Negbi 1976: 130) makes this connection quite plausible. Dove figurines found by Ben-Dor would corroborate the identification, since Asherah (later, as Tanit) is often associated with doves.

Bibliography

Ben-Dor, I. 1950. A Middle Bronze-Age Temple at Nahariya. *QDAP* 14: 1–43.

Dothan, M. 1956. The Excavations at Nahariyeh, Preliminary Report (Seasons 1954/55). *IEJ* 6: 14–25.

———. 1977. Nahariya. *EAEHL* 3: 908–12.

———. 1981. Sanctuaries along the Coast of Canaan in the MB Period: Nahariyah. Pp. 74–81 in *Temples and High Places in Biblical Times*, ed. A. Biran. Jerusalem.

Negbi, O. 1976. *Canaanite Gods in Metal*. Tel Aviv.

WILLIAM G. DEVER

NAHASH (PERSON) [Heb *nāḥaš*]. King of the Ammonites, whose siege of Jabesh-gilead was broken by a decisive Israelite victory early in Saul's reign (1 Sam 11:1–2). Ammon and Israel had long wrangled over territory east of the Jordan (Judg 11:4–33). Background for Nahash's siege is provided by a passage, possibly original, found just before 1 Sam 11:1 in 4QSam[a] and witnessed to by Josephus, *Ant* 6.5.1 §68–71. This describes a longer pattern of repression by Nahash against Gad and Reuben, of which Jabesh-gilead was simply the last chapter. Nahash had gouged out right eyes indiscriminately, and seven thousand refugees escaped to Jabesh-gilead. MT and LXX pick up the story when, after a month's respite, Nahash besieged the city. Because Nahash wanted to humiliate Israel, he offered the city brutal conditions for the vassal treaty they requested and gave them a week to seek aid from their fellow Israelites. The biblical authors used the story of Saul's subsequent victory, similar to the heroic stories found in the book of Judges, to establish the popularity of Saul's kingship. In another place it is suggested that the oppression of Nahash was Israel's motive for requesting a king (1 Sam 12:12). According to 2 Sam 10:1–2 = 1 Chr 19:1–2, Nahash remained king into the first part of David's reign and was on friendly terms with him, perhaps because of a mutual antipathy for Saul. Nahash's son Hanun picked a disastrous quarrel with David which led to the loss of Ammonite independence. Later, Shobi, another son of Nahash, provided supplies to David during Absalom's rebellion (2 Sam 17:27). A puzzling genealogical reference in 2 Sam 17:25 describes Abigail the sister of Zeruiah (and of David according to 2 Chr 2:16) as Nahash's daughter. If this is not a textual corruption from 2 Sam 17:27 and if one may assume that Nahash king of Ammon is meant, this would indicate that David had a family connection with the Ammonite royal house through his mother's marriage to Nahash. This would help explain Nahash's friendly relations with David, Hanun's suspicion of David's motives (2 Sam 10:2–4), and David's later personal acceptance of the Ammonite crown (2 Sam 12:30).

RICHARD D. NELSON

NAHATH (PERSON) [Heb *naḥat*]. The etymology of this personal name is unclear. It could possibly mean "clear, pure" (cf. Ar *nḥt; cf. also *IPN*, 228).

1. The firstborn son of Reuel, and the grandson of Esau (Gen 36:13, 17; 1 Chr 1:37). According to Gen 36:17 he was one of the "tribal chiefs" (Heb *ʾallûpîm*) of the Edomites, and as such the name probably represents a clan within the Esauite-Edomite tribe of Reuel.

2. Apparently a son of Zophai (or of Elkanah?) listed in the Levite genealogy of 1 Chr 6:11 (—Eng 6:26). The name, however, ought to be read either as Toah, in conjunction with 1 Chr 6:19 (—Eng 6:34), or as Tohu, in accordance with 1 Sam 1:1.

3. A Levite overseer during the reign of King Hezekiah of Judah (2 Chr 31:13).

ULRICH HÜBNER

NAHBI (PERSON) [Heb *naḥbî*]. The name "Nahbi," according to Noth (*IPN*, 229), is related to the Arabic term *nachbun* which means "fearful" or "timid." The personal name "Nahbi" is found only in Num 13:14. The son of Vophsi, Nahbi represented the tribe of Naphtali among the twelve men Moses sent from the wilderness of Paran (Num 12:16) to spy out the land of Canaan. Though not the head of the tribe of Naphtali (Num 1:15; 7:78), he was one of its leading princes (Num 13:2–3). His selection was doubtless based upon his suitability for the mission to be carried out.

JON PAULIEN

NAHOR (PERSON) [Heb *nāḥôr*]. **1.** Descendant of Seth and Shem, son of Serug when Serug was 30, father of Terah at the age of 29, and grandfather of Abraham (Gen 11:22–25). Nahor lived 148 years. In the book of Joshua (24:2), Nahor and Terah are regarded as polytheists. Two issues arise regarding Nahor: the context of his religion and the origin of his name. As to the first, the presumed location of Nahor at Ur of the Chaldees and the subsequent movement of his son, Terah, to Haran, suggest a religion associated with the moon deity, Sin. Sin played an important role at both of these sites (Edzard 1965: 102). As to the origin of Nahor's name, many scholars relate it to Naḫur, a site listed in records from the Mari texts and throughout the 2d millennium B.C., and located near Harran on the plain of the Upper Balikh river (Westermann, *Genesis 1–11* BKAT, 748). See also NAHOR (PLACE). A personal name *na-ḫa-ru-um* appears in the 3d millennium B.C. Ur III period (Schneider 1952: 519–20). It is not clear whether this is more closely related to the Akk *naḫraru/nērāru*, "to help," which is also productive of names in the Mari period (Stamm 1939: 212, n. 4; 367; Rasmussen 1981: 315). Personal names with a W Semitic *nḫr* root appear in the Old Babylonian period at Mari (Birot 1979: 160; ARM 22, p. 197, no. 222, 10) and elsewhere (Gelb 1980: 27, 329), and may be found in some Jewish names from Babylonia of the 1st millennium B.C. (Zadok 1977: 335, 342). However, the root does not appear elsewhere in personal names with a *qatūl/qatōl* form.

2. Brother of Abram, son of Terah when Terah was 70, and husband of Milcah (Gen 11:26–29). His eight sons with Milcah included: Uz, perhaps related to Job; Buz; Kemuel, "the father of Aram"; Chesed; Hazo; Pildash; Jidlaph; and Bethuel, the father of Rebekah (Gen 22:20–24). Nahor's concubine, Reumah, bore him four additional children: Tebah; Gaham; Tahash; and Maacah. Laban is also named as a "son" of Nahor (Gen 29:5), understood as a "descendant" of Nahor. At Mizpah, Jacob and Laban swore by the God of Abraham and by the god(s) [*ʾĕlōhê*] of Nahor (Gen 31:53). The latter may be related to the deities worshipped by Nahor, grandfather of Abram. Several issues emerge concerning Nahor: (1) his relation to his grandfather, Nahor; (2) Nahor's name; (3) his marriage to Milcah, the daughter of his brother Haran; (4) the religion of Nahor; and (5) the meaning of his twelve offspring.

As to (1) Nahor's relation to his grandfather, who bore the same name, it should be noted that this is the only clear instance of papponymy in the book of Genesis. However, the practice does occur elsewhere in the Bible and in the ANE (Wenham *Genesis* WBC, 253). Items (2) and (3) above are treated, respectively, in NAHOR (PERSON) and MILCAH.

The question of (4) the religion of Nahor may be related to the religion of his grandfather. Indeed, the similarity in names may imply an intended relationship. Since both of these figures are associated with Ur and Harran, the cult centers of the lunar deity Sin, it may be that the worship of this deity formed the focus of their religion. By swearing by the god(s) of Nahor, his ancestor who settled in the Harran area, Laban may have been concerned to protect his property. In recently published texts from (LB) Emar, inheritance clauses refer to the heirs invoking the gods of the deceased [DINGIR.MEŠ-*ia* . . . *tu-na(-ab-)bi*] (Huehnergard 1985:429–31). This seems to be a right and an expectation of the heirs which coincides with their possession of the inheritance. Here is a further indication of distinction in property rights and family responsibilities between Laban as Nahor's representative in the Harran area, and Jacob, as Abraham's representative in the region to the south (Morrison 1983: 163). As to (5) the meaning of the twelve offspring, comparisons have been drawn with the twelve sons of Jacob, also mothered through both wives and concubines. If so, the twelve children of Nahor may reflect twelve tribes. This seems to be implied at least for Kemuel, "the father of Aram."

Bibliography

Birot, M. 1979. Noms de personnes. Pp. 43–249 in *Répertoire analytique (2ᵉ volume) Tomes I–XIV, XVIII et textes divers hors-collection. Première partie. Noms propres.* ARM 16/1. Paris.

Edzard, D. O. 1965. Mesopotamian. Die Mythologie der Sumerer und Akkader. Pp. 17–139 in *Wörterbuch der Mythologie. Band I. Götter und Mythen im Vorderen Orient,* ed. H. W. Haussig. Stuttgart.

Gelb, I. J. et al. 1980. *Computer-Aided Analysis of Amorite.* AS 21. Chicago.

Huehnergard, J. 1985. Biblical Notes on Some New Akkadian Texts from Emar (Syria). *CBQ* 47: 428–34.

Morrison, M. 1983. The Jacob and Laban Narrative in Light of Near Eastern Sources. *BA* 46: 155–66.

Rasmussen, C. G. 1981. *A Study of Akkadian Personal Names from Mari.* Diss. Dropsie College.

Schneider, N. 1952. Patriarchennamen in Zeitgenössischen Keilschrifturkunden. *Bib* 33: 516–22.

Stamm, J. J. 1939. *Die Akkadische Namengebung.* MVAG 44. Leipzig.

Zadok, R. 1977. *On West Semites in Babylonia During the Chaldean and Achaemenian Periods.* Jerusalem.

RICHARD S. HESS

NAHOR (PLACE) [Heb *nāḥôr*]. The servant of Abraham journeys to "the city of Nahor" in Aram-naharaim where he searches and finds Rebekah, granddaughter of Nahor, as a wife for Isaac (Gen 24:10). In Genesis 24, the remaining three occurrences of the name "Nahor" (vv 15, 24, 47) refer to the personal name of Nahor, brother of Abraham. See NAHOR (PERSON). Therefore, it is reasonable to assume that "the city of Nahor" is not necessarily a city whose name is Nahor but the city occupied by Nahor. If so, it may refer to Haran, a city in which Abraham sojourned with Nahor before traveling to Canaan (Gen 11:29–31). This is also the city from which shepherds who knew Laban, son of Nahor, came (Gen 29:4–5). On the other hand, there is a city Naḫur which appears in early cuneiform texts. Spelled as *na-ḫu-ur* or as *na-ḫur,* it is found in texts from Mari (Kupper 1979:24) and elsewhere in texts from Old Babylonian (Groneberg 1980:173), Middle Babylonian, and Middle Assyrian sources (Kessler 1980: 91; Nashef 1982: 201). It is not clear that this place name appears in any texts from the lst millennium B.C. (Kessler 1980: 223–24). The city has been located in the area of one of the W branches of the Ḫabur river to the E of Harran.

Bibliography

Groneberg, B. 1980. *Répertoire Géographique des Textes Cunéiformes. Vol. 3, Die Orts-und Gewässernamen der altbabylonischen Zeit.* BTAVO B 713. Wiesbaden.

Kessler, K. 1980. *Untersuchungen zur historischen Topographie Nordmesopotamiens nach keilschriftlichen Quellen des 1. Jahrtausends v. Chr.* BTAVO B 26. Wiesbaden.

Kupper, J.-R. 1979. Noms géographiques. Pp. 1–42 in *Répertoire analytique (2ᵉ volume) Tomes I–XIV, XVIII et textes divers hors-collection. Pt. 1: Noms propres,* ed. M. Birot, J.-R. Kupper, and O. Rouault. ARM 18. Paris.

Nashef, K. 1982. *Répertoire Géographique des Textes Cunéiformes. Vol. 5, Die Orts-und Gewässernamen der mittelbabylonischen und mittelassyrischen Zeit.* BTAVO B 715. Wiesbaden.

RICHARD S. HESS

NAHSHON (PERSON) [Heb *naḥšôn*]. Son of Amminadab and chief (*nāśîʾ*, Num 2:3) of the tribe of Judah during the wilderness sojourn after the Exodus. As the leader of the tribe of Judah, he helped Moses conduct a census of the able-bodied fighting men of Israel prior to their departure from Mt. Sinai (Num 1:7), presented the offerings of the tribe of Judah on the first day of the twelve-day celebration of the dedication of the altar (Num 7:12, 17), and conducted Judah both to its proper place on the E side of the tabernacle in the Israelite camp (Num 2:3) and to its position at the head of the tribes as the Israelites prepared to depart from Mt. Sinai (Num 10:14).

Nahshon is listed in a number of significant biblical genealogies. He is celebrated as the ancestor of David both in the OT genealogies in Ruth 4:18–22 and 1 Chr 2:3–17 and in the genealogies of Jesus Christ (Matt 1:4; Luke 3:32). In the genealogies of Moses and Aaron (Exod 6:14–25), Nahshon is identified as the brother of Elisheba, Aaron's only wife from whom the Aaronic priests descended (Exod 6:23). This marriage between Aaron and Nahshon's sister constituted a covenant between the house of David and the house of Aaron and thereby was regarded by the tradition as linking the royal and priestly lines in Judah (Galil 1985: 493). The name "Nahshon" means "little snake"; it may have been given as a nickname (*IPN*, 229).

Bibliography

Galil, G. 1985. The Sons of Judah and the Sons of Aaron in Biblical Historiography. *VT* 35: 488–95.

DALE F. LAUNDERVILLE

NAHUM (PERSON) [Heb *naḥûm*]. **1.** An Israelite prophet. See NAHUM, BOOK OF.

2. The father of Amos and son of Esli, according to Luke's genealogy tying Joseph, the "supposed father" of Jesus to descent from Adam and God (Luke 3:25). D omits Nahum (Gk *naoum*), substituting a genealogy adapted from Matt 1:6–15 for Luke 3:23–31. The name Nahum as an ancestor of Jesus occurs nowhere else in the biblical documents, including Matthew's genealogy, and falls within a list of seventeen otherwise unknown descendants of David's son Nathan (Fitzmyer *Luke I–IX* AB, 500). Kuhn (1923: 208–9) argues that two seemingly parallel lists of names—Luke 3:23–26 (Jesus to Mattathias) and 3:29–31 (Joshua/Jesus to Mattatha)—were originally identical, the first perhaps reflecting a Hebrew context and the second, in an Aramaic context, tracing Mary's line of descent (since it does not mention Joseph as Jesus' father). Nahum, in the first list, corresponds to Jonam, in the second list. Apart from the OT prophet Nahum (see Nah 1:1; cf. Tob 14:4), for whom there is no evidence of his being a relative of Jesus, nothing further is known of any person with this name in the biblical documents.

Bibliography

Kuhn, G. 1923. Die Geschlechtsregister Jesu bei Lukas und Matthäus, nach ihrer Herkunft Untersucht. *ZNW* 22: 206–28.

STANLEY E. PORTER

NAHUM, BOOK OF. The seventh book of the twelve Minor Prophets in the Hebrew Bible. The superscription of the book reads: "An Oracle concerning Nineveh. The Book of the vision of Nahum the Elkoshite." Outside the Bible, Nahum (*naḥûm*, comfort) is a well-attested NW Semitic name (Cathcart 1979: 1). However, nothing is known about the prophet Nahum, and even the place of his origin, Elkosh, has not been identified. Jerome (CChr 76 A, 526) proposed "Elcesaei," a village in Galilee; Pseudo-Epiphanius (*PG* 43, 409) placed it in Judea; and there have been several attempts by modern scholars to locate the site of the ancient town (for bibliography, see Cathcart 1973: 38).

A. Text

Recently-discovered witnesses of the text of Nahum discovered in modern times include the Pesher of Nahum (4QpNah) found at Qumran; the Hebrew Scroll of the Minor Prophets from Wâdī Murabbaʿât (Mur 88); and fragments of the Greek text of the Minor Prophets from Naḥal Ḥever (8 ḤevXIIgr) (Barthélemy 1963). There are no significant variants in the text of Nahum in these scrolls, and the student of the text should probably pay more attention to linguistic investigation than to dubious textual reconstruction.

Ugaritic studies have alerted us to the precise usage of *ṣārâ* in Nah 1:9, though *BHS* still recommends emendation of the text to *ṣārāyw*. The interpretation of *yōdēaʿ*, "cares for, is friendly to," in 1:7 is further supported by *KTU* 1.114.7 (*il dydʿnn*, "the god friendly to him"); and *pĕlādôt* in 2:4 may mean "blankets," "coverings," or even "caparisons" in the light of Ug *pld*. The word *mnzr* in 3:17 has yet to be satisfactorily explained: if it is a military term, it may be a corruption of *ḫnzr*, a term for some kind of military personnel at Ugarit. However, in the light of recent study of Neo-Assyrian preoccupation with astrology and magic, H. Torczyner (1936: 7) was almost certainly correct in reading *manzāzayik*, since in Neo-Assyrian sources the *manzazē* were officials of the palace, including "astrologers, augurs, magicians" etc. (Parpola 1970–71,I: 2). In that same verse, the parallel term *ṭipsārayik* is equivalent to Akk *ṭupšarru*, a word used for "astrologer" in Neo-Assyrian texts (Parpola 1970–71,I: 2).

The recently discovered bilingual inscription from Tell Fakhariyeh contains the word *qlqltʾ* in line 22 of the Aramaic text, and its equivalent in the Neo-Assyrian text, *tupqinnu*, makes it clear that the meaning is "rubbish dump, refuse heap" (Abou-Assaf et al. 1982: 21, 36). This text, and the occurrence in another Neo-Assyrian text (*AfO* 8 iv 16) of the word *kiqillutu*, "refuse dump" (probably a loanword from W Semitic), may throw light on Nah 1:14, *ʾaśîm qibrekā kî qallôtā*. This new evidence supports the *BHS* apparatus, which suggests reading *qîqālôt* or *qîqālôn*, yielding the translation, "I will make your grave a refuse heap."

Finally, more attention is now being given to techniques in classical Hebrew poetry (Watson 1984), and further research in this area will be useful in the assessment of the results of redaction-criticism and of other methods used in the study of the biblical books.

B. Date

The superscription of the book does not mention any date, but it is clear that the reference to the Assyrian sacking of Thebes (No-Amon; 3:8) in 663 B.C. provides the earliest possible date. There is an impression that Nineveh, which fell in 612, was still standing at the time of the oracles, though it is not impossible that the oracles were composed shortly after it fell. However, there is widespread agreement that a date for the oracles should be sought between 663 and 612, but a more precise dating is very difficult to achieve. Two possibilities have been suggested. The first dates the book to ca. 625 B.C., when Nabopolassar emerged as the leader of an aggressive Babylonia, a development which must have given heart to those peoples who hated the oppressing Assyrians. The second possible date is shortly before 612 B.C., just as the Assyrian empire was entering its death throes, since in 614 B.C. the Medes (under Cyaxares) had already taken Assur and would soon take Nineveh. W. Maier (1959: 31) counters that Nineveh had already become weak and degenerate after the death of Assurbanipal in 626 B.C., and he prefers to date Nahum shortly before 654 B.C., a few years after the sack of Thebes (Maier 1959: 36).

C. Contents

Following the superscription (1:1), the contents may be summarized as follows:

1:2–8	Hymn of Theophany
1:9–2:3(—Eng 2:2)	Threat, Promise, and Judgment
2:4(—Eng 2:3)–3:19	The Fall of Nineveh

1. Hymn of Theophany. The sayings and oracles of Nahum are introduced by a hymn of theophany (1:2–8). There has been much discussion as to the extent of the psalm because of its partial alphabetic acrostic character. According to F. Delitzch (*Psalms* BC^3, 117), this was first noticed by a certain pastor G. Frohnmeyer. Unfortunately, this observation by Frohnmeyer prompted a number of scholars to carry out major critical surgery on the first chapter of Nahum in an attempt to reconstruct a complete alphabetic acrostic, and when G. Bickell (1880: 559–60; 1882: 211–13; 1894) and H. Gunkel (1893: 223–44; 1895: 102–6) presented their reconstructions, W. R. Arnold protested that these scholars had "decapitated a masterpiece of Hebrew literature" (1901: 236). In recent years critics have not been quite so ardent, and few scholars have pursued the acrostic beyond vv 8 or 9 (see, e.g., Christensen 1975: 17–30).

There is considerable debate concerning the date of the psalm. It is unlikely that the psalm was composed by Nahum, but given the incomplete nature of the acrostic, it may be that either Nahum modified an already existing psalm and used it as an introduction to his oracles, or a subsequent editor placed it before Nahum's actual oracles. In any event, the hymn does not reflect any particular historical situation; rather it is a typical hymn of theoph any, and its language is similar to that of the Canaanite descriptions of the theophany of the storm god Baᶜal (Cathcart 1975: 68–71). Of particular interest is the reference in 1:4 to Yahweh's roar at the Sea *(yām)* / Rivers *(nĕhārôt),* which recalls the conflict between Baᶜal and the Sea/Rivers in the texts from Ugarit. Like Baᶜal at Ugarit, Yahweh is portrayed as a storm god, a warrior, and a king, and it is the recognition of these motifs that is important for understanding the book of Nahum as a whole and the relationship between the psalm and the oracles in particular (see below).

2. Threat, Promise, and Judgment. Verses 1:9–2:3 have been adjudged by many critics to be in disorder. Verse 9 seems to be addressed to the enemies of Yahweh in general, but since this verse is probably a link between the psalm and the following oracles, one can safely assume that the Assyrians are the specific enemy. A linguistic argument in favor of taking v 9 as a link-verse is the presence of *klh ᶜśh* ("he will make a full end") in vv 8 and 9, and *ḥšb* ("to plot") in vv 9 and 11.

Verses 10–11 and 14 are further threats against the enemy, but v 11 is clearly directed against Nineveh, while v 14 is directed against the king of Assyria. This series of threats is interrupted by vv 12–13, which are promises to Judah.

Chapter 2 opens with a series of imperatives, typical messenger formulae announced by the *mĕbaśśēr,* the courier of Yahweh the divine warrior, who is about to wage war against the Assyrians. (On the *mĕbaśśēr,* see Miller 1973: 12–23, 66–74; and *CMHE*, 229). In 2:1 (—Eng 1:15) there is a message of salvation to Judah and in 2:2 (—Eng 2:1) a message of judgment to Nineveh. Verse 3 (—Eng v 2) states clearly the objective of Yahweh's war against Assyria, namely to deliver his people and restore "the glory of Jacob, indeed the glory of Israel."

3. The Fall of Nineveh. Nah 2:4–14 (—Eng 2:3–13) and 3:1–19 contain a superb description of the assault on Nineveh and its panic and downfall. Neh 2:4–14 (—Eng 2:3–13) is a self-contained unit, but it is difficult to say the same of 3:1–19. Perhaps with Eissfeldt (1965: 414) we should divide it as follows: 3:1–7 describing the destruction and humiliation of Nineveh; 3:8–17, a passage full of derision and irony, stressing the futility of Nineveh's efforts to defend itself; and finally 3:18–19, a dirge or funeral lament.

D. Interpretation

G. Fohrer (1968: 451) is willing to allow "some genuinely prophetical insights" in Nahum, but he is inclined to view the prophet as a "representative of optimistic prophecy with a strong feeling of nationalism." Because there is no condemnation of Israel or call to repentance in the oracles but, on the contrary, a great exultation over the fall of Nineveh, scholars have attributed a virulent nationalism to Nahum and have even alleged that he tends to exhibit the characteristics of false prophecy. Haldar (1947) believes that the book of Nahum originated in cultic circles and that in it the historical enemy is identified with cosmic foes. In other words, there is an element of propaganda in the book. Haldar's views have been widely rejected, but some of his insights in connection with myth deserve attention. Jeremias (1970: 11–55) and Schulz (1973) have not been convincing, and it seems more sensible to try and interpret the material as we have it, rather than engage in wholesale dismembering and reconstruction of the text (Schulz) or in speculation that some oracles against Nineveh were originally directed against Jerusalem/Israel (Jeremias). However, this does not mean that some editorial or redactional process has not taken place, especially with regard to 1:9–2:3 (see *IOTS*, 444; Coggins 1982: 80).

The introductory hymn of theophany (1:2–8) plays an important role in the book, and scholars have not pursued sufficiently their general observations that in it there is a strong sense of the sovereignty of God and a portrayal of Yahweh's lordship over history. The "Avenging God" (1:2, *ʾēl nōqēm*) is the one who as king and judge will punish the Assyrians to save Israel. The overthrow and sacking of Nineveh were historical acts of war by the Medes and Babylonians, but more importantly they were acts of war by Yahweh. The "scatterer" (2:2, *mēpîṣ*) who attacks Nineveh is "the jealous and avenging God," "the Lord of Wrath," who rages against his enemies. He is a mighty warrior, "great in power" (1:3, *gĕdōl kōaḥ*) who directs the earthly "mighty warriors" (2:4) against Nineveh. The Lord of the Storm who overcomes the Sea (1:3–4) to establish his dominion and assert his kingship is Yahweh the King, who decides the fate of the king of Assyria (1:14; cf. 3:18).

E. Nahum and the Day of Yahweh

Chapters 2 and 3 of Nahum have a number of lines and phrases which are similar to some found in those biblical passages which speak of the Day of Yahweh. It is true that a common "war-language" is to be expected, but, nevertheless, it is remarkable that a number of lines and phrases are found only in Nahum and the classic Day of Yahweh texts (Cathcart 1975: 72–76). (Compare Nah 1:10 with Joel 2:5, Obadiah 18, and Mal 3:19; Nah 2:5 [—Eng 2:4] with Jer 46:9, Joel 2:9, and Amos 5:16; Nah 2:9 [—Eng 2:8] with Jer 46:5, 21; Nah 2:10 [—Eng 2:9] with Isa 2:7; Nah 2:11 with Isa 13:7–8 and Joel 2:6; Nah 3:2 with Joel 2:5; and Nah 3:10 with Isa 13:16, Joel 4:2, and Obadiah 11.)

R. H. Charles spoke of the Day of Yahweh as follows: "This conception is related to the people as a whole, and not to the individual. It means essentially the day on which Yahweh manifests Himself in victory over his foes" (1913: 86–87). It is not surprising therefore that Charles included Nahum in his discussion of the Day of Yahweh, though it seems he is the only scholar who has done so.

The motifs of the Day of Yahweh appear in Nahum, for that "day" was "a day of judgment," when Yahweh punished the guilty because Yahweh as Divine King was also Judge Supreme. The day was also a "day of victory" on which Yahweh asserted his kingship and lordship over creation. If J. Day, after his recent assessment of the Ugaritic and OT evidence, is correct in his view that "the motif of Yahweh's Kingship, and with it the *Chaoskampf* . . . had its *Sitz im Leben* in the Feast of Tabernacles at New Year's eve" (1985: 21), then perhaps some of the work of earlier scholars like P. Humbert, who associated Nahum with the New Year, deserves more attention. See also DAY OF YAHWEH.

Bibliography

Abou-Assaf, A. et al. 1982. *La statue de Tell Fekherye et son inscription bilingue assyro-araméenne.* Paris.

Arnold, W. R. 1901. The Composition of Nahum 1–2:3. *ZAW* 21: 225–65.

Barthélemy, D. 1963. *Les devanciers d'Aquila.* VTSup 10. Leiden.

Bickell, G. 1880. Die hebräische Metrik. *ZDMG* 34: 557–63.

———. 1882. *Carmina Veteris Testamenti Metrice.* Innsbruck.

———. 1894. *Beiträge zur hebräische Metrik I: Das alphabetische Lied in Nahum I,2–II,3.* Vienna.

Cathcart, K. J. 1973. *Nahum in the Light of Northwest Semitic.* BibOr 26. Rome.

———. 1975. The Divine Warrior and the War of Yahweh in Nahum. Pp. 68–76 in *Biblical Studies in Contemporary Thought,* ed. M. Ward. Somerville, MA.

———. 1979. More Philological Studies in Nahum. *JNSL* 7: 1–12.

Charles, R. H. 1913. *A Critical History of the Doctrine of a Future Life in Israel, in Judaism, and in Christianity.* London.

Christensen, D. L. 1975. The Acrostic of Nahum Reconsidered. *ZAW* 87: 17–30.

Coggins, R. 1982. An Alternative Prophetic Tradition. Pp. 77–94 in *Israel's Prophetic Heritage.* Ed. R. Coggins, A. Phillips, and M. Knibb. Cambridge.

Day, J. 1985. *God's Conflict with the Dragon and the Sea.* Cambridge.

Eissfeldt, O. 1965. *The Old Testament: an Introduction.* Tr. P. R. Ackroyd. Oxford.

Fohrer, G. 1968. *Introduction to the Old Testament.* Tr. D. E. Green. New York.

Gunkel, H. 1893. Nahum 1. *ZAW* 13: 223–44.

———. 1895. *Schöpfung und Chaos.* Göttingen.

Haldar, A. 1947. *Studies in the Book of Nahum.* Uppsala.

Humbert, P. 1926. Essai d'analyse de Nahoum 1,2–2,3. *ZAW* 44: 266–80.

———. 1928. La vision de Nahoum 2,4–11. *AfO* 5: 14–19.

———. 1932. Le problème du livre de Nahoum. *RHPR* 12: 1–15.

Jeremias, J. 1970. *Kultprophetie und Gerichtsverkündigung in der späten Königszeit Israels.* WMANT 35. Neukirchen-Vluyn.

Maier, W. A. 1959. *The Book of Nahum.* St. Louis.

Miller, P. D. 1973. *The Divine Warrior in Early Israel.* HSM 5. Cambridge, MA.

Parpola, S. 1970–71. *Letters from Assyrian Scholars to the Kings Esarhaddon and Assurbanipal.* Pts. 1–2. AOAT 5. Neukirchen-Vluyn.

Schulz, H. 1973. *Das Buch Nahum.* BZAW 129. Berlin.

Torczyner, H. 1936. Presidential Address. *JPOS* 16: 1–8.

Watson, W. G. E. 1984. *Classical Hebrew Poetry.* JSOTSup 26. Sheffield.

KEVIN J. CATHCART

NAIDUS (PERSON) [Gk *Naidos*]. An Israelite layperson, one of the descendants of Addi, who was forced to give up his foreign wife during Ezra's reform (1 Esdr 9:31). It is possible that Naidus is an alternate form of one of the names which occur in Ezra 10:30. Its position in the list is parallel to Maaseiah, not Benaiah as *IDB* 3: 499 and *ISBE* 3: 479 suggest (though Maaseiah appears to be linguistically parallel to Moossias). On the other hand, it is also possible that this name is drawn from a different list of individuals. Evidence for the latter is indicated by (1) the lack of a name similar in form to Naidus in Ezra 10:30, and (2) the different ancestors named in these two accounts (Addi in 1 Esdr 9:31; Pahath-moab in Ezra 10:30). However, whether Naidus is an alternate form in a parallel account, or whether it is simply drawn from an alternate list of names available to the compiler of 1 Esdras 9, cannot be known for certain.

JOHN KUTSKO

NAIN (PLACE) [Gk *Nain*]. A village or small town mentioned in Luke 7:11 as a *polis.* The crowd bearing the body of a young man exited the "gate" of the city, which implies a city wall, and Jesus raised him from the dead.

The site today is identified with the Muslim town of Nein (M.R. 183226) in the plain of Jezreel on the N slope of the hill of Moreh, N of modern Afula and about 9.5 air miles from Nazareth. Origen of Caesarea knew of the village about A.D. 200 *sel. in Ps.* 88), and it is mentioned as lying in the territory of the tribe of Issachar in one ancient Jewish source (*Gen. Rab.* 98.12). It is mentioned by Eusebius in the 4th century (*Onomast.* 140:3) as "a village, in which he raised the son of the widow from the dead. And now it is to the south of Tabor at the twelfth mile from En-Dor." Jerome (141:5) corrects Eusebius to read "two miles from Tabor near Aendor." Jerome was aware that there was a church at Nain in his day, but he did not visit it (*Ep.* 46:12; 108:13). Usually commentators conclude that Nain lay off the main road, which accounts for why Jerome stayed away. Egeria, the 4th-century Spanish pilgrim, visited a church at Nain a generation later which was built from, or upon, the house of the widow whose son was raised. She also saw the tomb where he was to be laid (Peter the Deacon P1:4). It is possible that this was a house-church like the "House of St. Peter" at Capernaum. Its situation off the main road may account for the lack of references in the Christian pilgrim literature from Egeria until Eutychius of Alexandria in the 10th century.

A survey by the University of South Florida in 1982 confirmed that the topography apparently includes a ruined and eroded circular wall around the city, completely covered with soil and debris, which would have required a gate as in Luke 7:11. On the NW side of the city is a spring with ancient cut stones and fragments of Roman sarcophagi scattered about. A basin 2.0 × 1.5 m collects the slow-moving water. A cemetery of rock-cut tombs is found on the E side of the village. An intact sarcophagus from the cemetery rests beside the modern church. A small edifice described as early as 1598 as "a building like a small palace" lies in ruins N of the village and about 100 m from the spring. It resembles 13th- or 14th-century structures and is known locally as "the place of the Lord," apparently a mosque.

JAMES F. STRANGE

NAIOTH (PLACE) [Heb *nāyôt*]. The place to which David fled from Saul, having escaped with the help of Michal, his wife and Saul's daughter. David fled to Ramah where Samuel the prophet was, and the two of them dwelt in Naioth (1 Sam 18:18). From here David fled again and later met Saul's son Jonathan in 1 Sam 20:1ff. It was to Naioth that Saul pursued David, first sending messengers and later going himself. In each case the pursuers were overcome with prophetic behavior, most likely some form of ecstatic behavior common to prophecy.

This is the second episode which is said to explain the saying "Is Saul also among the prophets?" The other is 1 Sam 10:12 which concludes the story of Saul's receiving ecstatic gifts as part of his royal commissioning (1 Sam 10:1–13). Because of this duplication of stories about Saul's ecstatic behavior and because Saul is said at an earlier point to have never seen Samuel again (1 Sam 15:35), the episode of Saul pursuing David to Ramah (where Samuel was residing) and there exhibiting prophetic behavior is thought to be secondary to the original account of David's rise to power (see the discussion in McCarter *1 Samuel* AB, 330f.).

Of greater importance in discussing the place Naioth itself is the question of the meaning of the word. As our preliminary definition indicates, Naioth is said to be "in Ramah" (1 Sam 19:19, 22, and 23 [twice]). In addition, Saul's messengers are sent to Ramah, not to Naioth (1 Sam 19:22). Because of this, early scholars tended to identify Naioth as a locality within Ramah (Driver *NHT*, 159). Another view is based on the alternate spelling given in the MT. The text has the consonants in the order *nwyt* while the marginal note (the *qere*) suggests that *nywt* is to be preferred. The RSV follows this suggestion in rendering the place as "Naioth." Following the Aramaic translation of the OT, the Targum, Morton (*IDB* 3: 500) and others (see the comments in *NHT*, 158–59) propose understanding the name to refer to a "house of instruction"—a prophetic school within Ramah. Morton (*IDB* 3: 500) cites 2 Kgs 6:1–7 as evidence for this type of prophetic school. More recent study has given some nuance to this suggestion. A. Malamat (1962: 146) notes in texts from Mari an Akkadian term for "encampment" or pasture settlement (*nāwum*) which has several related words in Hebrew, one of which is *nāyôt*. Malamat (1962:146) thinks it likely that these kinds of settlements on the outskirts of a town housed prophetic fraternities. McCarter (*1 Samuel* AB, 328) follows Malamat on this and accordingly translates "the camps" for *nāyôt* where it occurs. He cites Jer 33:12 (which contains the related term *nĕwēh*, "habitations") as an example of shepherds dwelling in these types of settlements.

Bibliography

Malamat, A. 1962. Mari and the Bible: Some Patterns of Tribal Organization and Structure, *JAOS* 82: 143–50.

JEFFRIES M. HAMILTON

NAME. See FAMILY.

NAMES, CITY. See CITY NAMES; TOPONYMS AND TOPONYMY.

NAMES OF GOD IN THE OT. The God of Israel could be referred to by a number of names, titles, and epithets in the text of the Hebrew Bible. These are significant as indicators of developments in the course of Israel's religious history and as expressions of concepts of the divine held by the ancient Israelites.

A. Function of the Name
B. The Divine Name Yahweh
C. Non-Yahwistic Divine Names and Titles
   1. El (Divinity)
   2. El-Elyôn (God Most High)
   3. El-ʿOlām (Everlasting God)
   4. Shaddai (Almighty)
   5. Abîr (Mighty One)

6. Paḥad (Fear)
7. Elohîm (God)
8. Baal
9. Adôn/Adônai (Lord)
10. Ṣebaoth (Hosts)
11. Conclusion

D. Foreign Divine Names
E. Attenuation of the Divine Name
1. Cosmopolitan Thinking
2. Scrupulous Thinking

F. From Immanence to Transcendance

A. Function of the Name

One should be careful not to interpret OT data related to the theme of the "name of God" simply in the light of our modern conceptions of person, personality, existence, or identity. In doing so, one would run the risk of missing the appropriate approach to the essential dimensions of the biblical faith of ancient Israel. Moreover, OT discourse concerning the "names of God" should always be perceived in its twofold context: In respect to the name of God, Israel did not think in any fundamentally different way than in respect to *human* personal names; Israel's thinking about the "name of God" was carried out in the larger context of the ancient Near Eastern world and its divinities.

The "name" is a "distinguishing mark"; seen in an etymological perspective this is true for the common Semitic word *šumu* and consequently for the Hebrew word *šēm,* "name" (KB, 983; Grether 1934: 1). A "distinguishing mark" makes it possible to differentiate, to structure, and to order. In this respect "to name" or "to designate" belongs to the ordering of creation; thus primordial time preceded naming in the Babylonian epic of creation *Enūma eliš* (1.1 [*ANET*, 60] "when on high the heaven had not been named. . . . , when no gods whatever had been brought into being, uncalled by name. . . ."). The bestowal of names initiates the human ordering of creation in Gen 2:19 ("so out of the ground the Lord God formed every beast of the field . . . and brought them to the man to see what he would call them; and whatever the man called every living creature, that was its name"). This association of the act of naming with creation underlines the fact that the name represents something wholesome and salutary; the knowledge of the name opens up specific human dimensions for communication and for fellowship. The one who knows the name of a god or a human can appeal to them. The knowledge of the name can thereby have effective power. Magic and incantations attempt to use this knowledge through techniques which exploit the influence of the name. Thereby free communication degenerates into a manipulative attempt to dominate. Even when such attempts appear to be effective, they are ultimately completely mistaken because they are based on a simplistic and false identification of the person (whether divine or human) with the "distinguishing mark" (name). Or, to express it in a modern way, they are based on an erroneous equation of existence and identity.

The "distinguishing mark" (name) is not quite identical with what is designated; this little difference allows one to think and to hope that the name will endure. This hope also indicates an aspect of the salutary significance of the name: it juxtaposes the experience of human transience with hope of durability. The durability of the "name" can be manifest in the succession of generations ("name" = son: Deut 25:7; 2 Sam 14:7; Ruth 4:5, 10), or owing to a particular exploit ("name" = fame: "let us make an name for ourselves" Gen 11:4; cf. 2 Sam 8:13).

In the sphere of the "name of God" this little difference between the "distinguishing mark" (name) and what is designated can be of considerable theological significance whenever one attempts to express at the same time God's transcendence (his heavenly existence) and his immanence (his presence appealed to in the temple celebration). This thought is particularly conspicuous in Solomon's prayer for the dedication of the temple (1 Kgs 8:27–30). However, there are reasons to assume that similar features could be found in other ancient Near Eastern cultures. The difference between the divinity and its presence in the cult through the name could indeed occasionally lead to a hypostatization of the name as an independent divine figure, e.g., in the Babylonian divine name Išum and in the Aramaic divine name Ašima (cf. 2 Kgs 17:30 [Amos 8:14]). Both of these names may be a form of the common Semitic word *šumu/šēm,* "name," with a prosthetic *ʾalep* (Grimme 1912: 14–15; bibliography in Barstad 1984: 167–70 and 175–77; somewhat differently Roberts 1972: 40–41). If the Babylonian divinity Išum is represented as a "dieu bifront" (*RLA* 5:213–14; Lipiński 1987: 152; cf. *ANEP*, 693; Furlani 1935: 136–56), then this representation corresponds to the cultic function of the "name of God" mediating between the world of human pronounceability of God and his unpronounceable heavenly existence.

B. The Divine Name Yahweh

In Israel of the biblical tradition only one name of God was cultically appealed to: Yahweh (Heb *yhwh*). See also YAHWEH (DEITY). When one speaks of Yahweh one also speaks of Israel. The oldest texts of the OT start from this relationship between Yahweh and his people Israel, so e.g., in the Song of Deborah (one of the oldest [poetical] texts) after the mention of the name of Yahweh the epithet "God of Israel" follows unpretentiously (Judg 5:5; cf. v 3). In fact "Yahweh, the God of Israel" represents one of the most frequent expressions of OT times. What disappears in the course of time is the self-evidence of the appeal to the name of Yahweh. The loss of this obviousness of a living relationship with God is compensated by an explicit confession of faith.

A case example of one such confession is the book of Deuteronomy, especially in its older form, which comprised chaps. 6–26. It begins in a pointed way by mentioning the name of Yahweh ("Yahweh our God is one Yahweh" [6:4]), and concludes in 26:16–19 with a mutual declaration of a covenant between "Yahweh, the God of Israel" and "Israel, Yahweh's people." In the book of Deuteronomy, the old expression "Yahweh, the God of Israel," conditioned by the literary form of Moses' farewell address to the gathered people, was made personal ("Yahweh, your God") and in this form repeated with an almost tiresome frequency. However, this very strongly emphasized confession of the name of Yahweh and his relationship to Israel is not simply a literary reflexion of the piety of a (small) "Yahweh Alone Party" (Smith 1971: 33; Lang 1983: 13–

59). Rather, one should understand in the light of the larger political, cultic, and religious awakening of the time of Josiah (639–609 B.C. [2 Kgs 22–23]). That the name of Yahweh became a constitutive part of the "Josianic reformation" can be seen from the sudden increase in theophoric names with a Yahwistic component in the generation. The epigraphic evidence which archaeology has put at our disposal is quite unequivocal (Rose 1975: 171–82).

A "confessional situation" is in most cases also a "struggle situation." In a confession of the name of Yahweh it is not only a matter of finding one's security and identity. Rather, in the same time a process of demarcation takes place with respect to those who think differently concerning Yahweh's name and concerning its invocation in the cult. The inner Israelite differentiation of the Josianic reform is manifest, e.g., in the brutal action against the cultic sites in Bethel (2 Kgs 23: 15–20), an ancient Yahweh sanctuary (cf. Gen 28:10–22), which had served as a royal state sanctuary (1 Kgs 12:26–33), during the time of the N kingdom (926–722 B.C.). The difference of the confession of faith in Yahweh of the N kingdom when compared with the confession of the Josianic reform can also be seen in the light of the difference in use of divine names; here again one can have recourse to epigraphic evidence, in particular to the Aramaic texts from Elephantine. See ELPHANTINE PAPYRI.

The documents from this colony show that Elephantine Jews built a Yahweh temple (which lasted until 410 B.C.). The spelling of the divine name *yhw* (with three consonants) found in the papyri presumably represents a form older than biblical *yhwh* (Rose 1978: 16–30). But these texts show combinations of the name of Yahweh which cannot be reconciled with what the biblical texts establish as a norm of the faith in Yahweh: e.g., *ʿntyhw* "Anath-Yahwē" (*CAP* 44.3). (On the divinity *ʾšmbytʾl*[*CAP* 22.124], see BETHEL [DEITY].)

For the historical Israel of the royal period one should assume a diversity of confessional expressions of the faith in Yahweh. To these the book of Deuteronomy opposes as a program and a creed its emphasis on the "one Yahweh!" (6:4) and one central sanctuary chosen by Yahweh (12:5, 11, 13, 14, 18, 21, 26). The old "covenant" relationship between Yahweh and Israel (26:16–19) would thus be realized in a comprehensive way and with ultimate authority only at the one central sanctuary: exclusively in the Jerusalem temple. The Deuteronomic creed and the Josianic reform complement each other.

In the subsequent biblical discussion concerning the "localization" of the "covenant"-relationship, the special name of Yahweh plays a part, but the biblical texts also offer some fundamental reflections concerning the function of the name of God. With the older, shorter form ("the place which Yahweh shall choose" [e.g., Deut 12:14, 18]), one is content to emphasize the choosing of a central sanctuary; the younger, longer form specifies the function of this choosing ("the place which Yahweh shall choose to cause his name to dwell there" [e.g., Deut 12:11], or "the place which Yahweh shall choose to put his name there" [e.g., Deut 12:5, 21]). One could almost speak of a "theology of the name" (von Rad 1947: 25–30; Mettinger 1982: 52–66; 123–32). The presence of the divine name at the cult site serves to emphasize the legitimacy of the appeal to God as it was carried out in the cult; the way and the manner in which the name of Yahweh is appealed to in the central sanctuary (= Jerusalem) represents the only legitimate form which corresponds to the will of God, Yahweh having deposited his name there. Only there (and not, e.g., in Bethel) could one be sure that the name invoked by the priest would be identical with the one which God himself revealed. The legitimacy of the entire cultic service (the word and the sacrifice) depends on the legitimization of the name of God.

The "theology of the name" is then also appropriate in order to facilitate a theological reflection beyond the cultic sphere as it opens the way for a distinction between the earthly "dwelling of the name of God" and the heavenly dwelling of God. This amounts to a theological differentiation between the immanence and transcendence of God.

The old formulaic relationship between Israel and the name of Yahweh ("Yahweh, the God of Israel") did not find an emphasis only in an inner Israelite differentiation, but could also serve as a negation of everything which stood outside of this relationship. What is not comprised by the name of Yahweh should have no justification to exist in Israel. This demarcation (or delimitation towards the outside) finds its radical expression in the first commandment ("Thou shalt have no other god before me [lit., in front of my face, i.e., vis-à-vis the symbol of my cultic presence"]). Where one appeals to the name of Yahweh any other divine presence has to be eliminated (e.g., Deut 12:2–3: ". . . you shall destroy their name out of that place"). The divine name of Yahweh does not tolerate any foreign divine name.

In this way in the Josianic reform and in the Deuteronomic creed the name of Yahweh became the focal point for the representation of what faith in God should mean for Israel. In the final analysis, the book of Deuteronomy is nothing else but a sermonic commentary on the old designation "Yahweh, the God of Israel." The name of the people, *Yiśrāʾēl,* is itself formed with another theophoric element: "El." This incongruity between the name of God and the name of the people allows one to conclude that the "Yahweh-Israel" relationship is a result of a historical development which should not be seen independently from the formation of the national and political entity called "Israel."

In addressing the question of the relationship between "Yahweh" and "El," historical and philological research attempts to clarify the epoch *before* the formation of the biblical tradition. Indeed the biblical tradition itself preserved a memory of the fact that the relationship "Yahweh-Israel" is not primordial, but arose in the course of history, whether it is related to the basic experience of the liberation from Egypt ("I am Yahweh thy God from the land of Egypt" [Hos 12:10—Eng 12:9]), or to the covenant and the Sinai revelation (e.g., Exod 24:8), or to a covenant declaration in the land of Moab (Deut 26:18), or to the completion of the conquest (Joshua 24). The biblical tradition has equally preserved a memory that within the tribes which would later form the people of Israel, other divinities were also worshipped (Josh 24:15: "Choose you this day whom you will serve, whether the gods which your fathers served in the region beyond the river . . . , but as for me and my house, we will serve Yahweh"; cf. v 23:

"Then put away the foreign gods which are among you, and incline your heart to Yahweh"). Since the OT intends to be a document of the faith of *Israel*, the possibility of writing the *pre*-Israelite history of the name of Yahweh in the time of the tribes remains extremely limited. One of the most popular theories on the origin of the name of Yahweh is the Qenite or the Midianite hypothesis: Yahweh was presumably worshipped by these nomadic tribes in the Southern Palestine (cf. e.g., the narrative tradition of Moses' Midianite [or Qenite] father-in-law [Exod 2:16; 3:1; Judg 1:16; 4:11; etc.; cf. the discussion in Kinyongo 1970: 7–19]). One thing is certain: Yahweh does not belong to the autochthonous divinities worshipped in Canaan.

C. Non-Yahwistic Divine Names and Titles

The encounter between the nomadic or half-nomadic migrant groups and the sedentary populations in the region of the arable land out of the convergence of which Israel arose is reflected in the titles and attributes of the biblical god.

1. El (Divinity). One of the oldest such encounters and also the most unproblematic was the one which related faith in Yahweh with the worship of El. According to Gen 33:20, Jacob had built an altar in Shechem and called it "El-Elohe-Israel"; the author of this text assumes an identity of this "El" with Yahweh. Actually, "El" is not a divine name but a common Semitic appellative for the "divinity" (see *TDOT* 1: 242–61). In order to make appeals to the divinity, this "El" required some concrete expression either by being related to a locality (e.g., "El-Bethel," Gen 35:7), or by adding an epithet (e.g., "El of the covenant" [El-Berît], Judg 9:46; El-Roi, Gen 16:13; cf. 22:14). For many worshipping communities with a polytheistic religious structure, "El" could also become a personal divine figure (e.g., the Aramaic inscriptions of Panammuwa [Zincirli; 8th century B.C.] mention "El" alongside the divinities Hadad, Rešef, Rākib-el, Šamaš; *KAI* 214 and 215). As a whole the "international" character of the god "El" and the original appellative function of the name "El" have occasioned the circumstance that this title may refer to the highest god (god-king), to the founding god *(Göttervater)*, or to the god-creator. "El" appears to have this function and form in the texts from Ugarit-Ras Shamra, reflecting an expression of the Canaanite religion at the end of the 2d millennium B.C., but also in the biblical texts like e.g., Genesis 14, where Melchizedek is designated as "the king of Salem" and "the priest of El-Elyôn [RSV: "God Most High"], creator of heaven and earth" (vv 18 and 22).

2. El-Elyôn (God Most High) In the biblical tradition this "El-Elyôn" was naturally identified with Yahweh (Gen 14:22): "I [= Abram] have lifted up my hand unto Yahweh, El-Elyôn, creator of heaven and earth." This identification is facilitated by the fact that both elements of the divine name El-Elyôn can be reduced to the function of the attributes: "the divinity, the most high." The conversion into an epithet of Yahweh is, of course, only the last phase of a long process. In the poetic language which stands even closer to the Canaanite worldview, Deut 32:8–9, speaks of "Elyôn" (as the creator and sustainer) who attributes to different nations a portion of the inhabitable land and assigns a nation to a god (to a divine being, "son of El" [according to the original form of the text; cf. LXX, Qumran]). Then Yahweh had equally acquired "his people as his portion." This text seems to presuppose an even earlier differentiation between the "supernational" creator-god ("Elyôn") and Israel's national god Yahweh (cf. Ps 82:1, 6).

Genesis 14 is the only text in the OT where the terms "El" and "Elyôn" are directly connected ("El-Elyôn"). However, there are numerous instances where "El" and "Elyôn" are mentioned in parallelism, e.g., Ps 73:11 ("and they say, 'How can El know? Is there knowledge in Elyôn?' "); Ps 107:11 ("for they had rebelled against the words of El, and spurned the counsel of Elyôn"). Salem in Genesis 14 is to be identified with Jerusalem (cf. Ps 76:3: Salem = Zion), which supports the assumption that the adoration of El-Elyôn was transmitted to the Israelite tribes by the intermediary of this Canaanite city-state. It would have been transmitted first to the Benjaminites who settled north of Jerusalem (cf. the conjecture "Elyôn" in the blessing of the tribe of Benjamin, Deut 33:12 [Helck 1984: 523–29]), and then after David's conquest of Jerusalem to other groups of the young kingdom (The Davidic connection arises from reading the conjectured "Elyôn" in the last words of David, 2 Sam 23:1: "the oracle of the man who was named by Elyôn"; cf. 1 Sam 2:10 [*HALAT,* 780]). With David and Solomon in the royal (residential) city of Jerusalem, the official and national cult was associated with the name of Yahweh, whereby pre-Israelite traditions were further transmitted and extensively absorbed. In many poetic texts Yahweh is placed in parallelism with Elyôn (e.g., 2 Sam 22:14 = Ps 18:14; Ps 21:8); the last clear identification is expressed in Ps 47:2: "Yahweh-Elyôn is terrible, a great king over all the earth."

With the appropriation of the epithet "(El-)Elyôn" the Yahweh worship, which is of nomadic provenance, has become enriched with the dimensions of world creation and the royalty.

3. El-ᶜOlām (Everlasting God). Gen 21:33 attests this divine epithet for the cultic worship in Beer-sheba but identifies this divinity "El-ᶜolām" quite naturally with Yahweh (cf. Jenni 1952–53: 1–5). Numerous ANE texts show that this epithet is not specific to the biblical tradition. Like "El-Elyôn" this epithet appears regularly in contexts in which the *royal* dimensions of the divinity are emphasized. *ᶜolām* designates the "fullness" (totality) of the experience of time and space. With this concept one attempts to place the concrete and limited human experience into the largest possible frame. Within the world of human experience in the ancient Near East, this "transcendence" was extensively personalized and symbolized in the king. In Israel too, one wished this *ᶜōlām* to the king: "May my lord King David live for ever [*ᶜōlām*]!" (1 Kgs 1:31). In respect to the Davidic dynasty developed a term designating an "*ᶜôlām* covenant" (cf. 1 Sam 20:42; 2 Sam 7:13,16). The *ᶜôlām* character of the king points ultimately to the *ᶜôlām*-quality of god, of which numerous biblical and extrabiblical texts speak. In these texts one cannot always clearly determine whether *ᶜōlām* emphasizes mainly the specificity of god (or of gods respectively) or whether *ᶜōlām* functions as an epithet or even as a proper name (as in El-ᶜolām Gen 21:33). In Ps 75:10, the expression "the God of Jacob" stands in parallelism with *ᶜōlām*: "I will praise *ᶜŌlām* (or: "for ever"), I will sing praises to the God of Jacob."

4. Shaddai (Almighty). It is somewhat more difficult to determine exactly the facts about the title "El-Shaddai." See ALMIGHTY. Only the final result in the process of appropriation, its identification with Yahweh, can be clearly ascertained. Exod 6:3 offers an etiology: "I appeared to Abraham, to Isaac, and to Jacob, as El-Shaddai ('God Almighty'), but by my name Yahweh I was not known to them." All other aspects of the title, its origin (Hebron? [cf. Alt 1929: 12–13 and 54–62]) its history, its function (name or attribute?), even its etymology (cf. Koch 1976: 308, 328) and its meaning still remain uncertain. (The meaning "Almighty" is based on the LXX and the Vg and should be seen as a free rendering of the Heb term which had become obscure.) Besides exilic texts which mention "El-Shaddai" (e.g., Exod 6:3 [P] and Ezek 10:5), there are a few more ancient ones like the oracle of Balaam in Num 24:16: "He knows the knowledge of Elyôn, he sees the vision of Shaddai" (cf. v 4). The conspicuous feature in this text is the parallelism between Elyôn and Shaddai (as in Ps 91:1). One could add to this the mention of El and Shaddai in the blessing of Jacob (Gen 49:25: "By El, thy father, who shall help thee; by Shaddai, who shall bless thee . . .").

In the case of El-Shaddai as well, philological-historical research leads us again to the sphere of the Canaanite religion. The *šdyn* "Shaddayin" in the Aram inscription from Deir ᶜAlla were presumably divine beings of uncertain character. See DEIR ᶜALLA (TEXTS). What is theologically significant, however, is to find out in what manner this tradition has been used for the expression of faith in Yahweh. The key text, Exod 6:3, uses an ancient epithet (which no longer had any cultic usage) to contrast the religion of the patriarchs with the Yahweh religion in such a way that the period of the patriarchs should not be lost for the history of Israel's faith. The faith of the patriarchs reflects genuine experiences of God, for the true God had "appeared" to them (Heb pass. "had been seen"), although this was more an intuitive experience than empirical knowledge ("I was not known to them"); full fellowship with God is possible only where "my name Yahweh" is known.

This late (exilic or postexilic) theological conception of the "Priestly writing" remains essentially in line with the old traditional associations of the name of Yahweh: (1) The name Yahweh is related to *Israel*: it is only to Israel that "I am Yahweh" is emphatically addressed (Exod 6:6: "Say to the people of Israel, 'I am Yahweh . . .' "; v 8: "I will bring you into the land: I am Yahweh"). (2) The *cultic* dimension of the name is evident in the Priestly supposition that before the revelation of the true name of God, Yahweh, no legitimate offerings are conceivable; for the Priestly writing, the time of the patriarchs is a period without cultic offerings. (3) The name of Yahweh was associated with the event of the liberation from Egypt (Exod 6:7: "I am Yahweh your God, who brings you out from under the burden of the Egyptians"); all the rest is prehistory of Israel and, in a sense, the prehistory of Yahweh. For this "prehistory" narrated in the book of Genesis, the Priestly author does not use the divine name Yahweh but prefers the expression "Shaddai" (or "Elohîm").

5. Abîr (Mighty One). Here, too, one deals with an ancient divine epithet, which in the OT text appears particularly in connection with the expression *ʾăbîr yaᶜăqōb* (RSV: "the Mighty One of Jacob"): Gen 49:24; Isa 49:26; 60:16; Ps 132:2, 5. The Hebrew word *ʾăbîr,* however, is not used only for God but also for humans and for animals. The basic etymological meaning of this word (in Hebrew and other Semitic languages) is "might" or "strength." For humans the term *ʾăbîr* serves to designate war heroes (e.g., in Ps 76:5, *ʾăbîr* stands in parallelism with "men of might"), and for animals (e.g., choice stallions or steeds [Judg 5:22; Jer 8:16; 47:3; 50:11]). The quality designated by *ʾăbîr* is perceived to be particularly embodied in the strength of a bull; in the texts from Ugarit-Ras Shamra, *ʾibr* means "bull" (*UT* 3, no. 39); also in biblical texts, bulls can be designated with the term *ʾăbîr* (Isa 34:7; Pss 22:12; 50:13).

Jeroboam I (933–911 B.C.E.) the founder of the first Israelite dynasty, did not seek to introduce any new divinity into Israel when he erected the bull figures in Dan and in Bethel (1 Kgs 12:26–30); rather, his act is to be understood as an attempt to give expression to an old N Israelite tradition (as reflected, e.g., in the old divine epithet "ʾAbîr of Jacob" [cf. Gen 49:24 in the blessing of Joseph]) in the figure of an impressive cultic object (Weippert 1961: 93–117). This representation of the God of Israel could be confused with that of the Canaanite god Baal; consequently, as the polemical demarcation against Baal began, the problem arose, on the one hand, to uphold the old epithet "ʾAbîr of Jacob," and on the other hand, to dissociate the strength *(ʾăbîr)* of a bull from Yahweh, the God of Israel. The Masoretic copyists had recourse to an artifice by introducing a *dāgeš* in the letter *bet* and thus distinguished between two words: *ʾăbîr* was reserved for the divine epithet "ʾAbîr of Jacob" (or Israel, respectively), while all other occurrences of the term were written *ʾabbîr.*

This differentiation, however, does not resolve all the problems. In Ps 78:25, the manna is called "the bread of the *ʾabbîrîm.*" Grammatically the plural *(-îm)* is used; nevertheless, one may question whether it is not an instance of a plural of "majesty" (or of "absolutization") which is often employed in connection with God. The context in Psalm 78 speaks of *God:* Yahweh is "Elyôn" (v 17) and he is equally the *ʾăbîr* par excellence; the Revised Version of 1927 translates the grammatical plural as singular, which is correct in respect to its meaning: "man did eat the bread of the mighty." In the gift of the manna the separation between divine and human existence was overcome. The LXX did not understand this divine epithet any longer and rendered it with a plural: "bread of the angels" (cf. RSV).

6. Paḥad (Fear). As in the case of *ʾăbîr,* the term *paḥad* represents a divine epithet which is mentioned in connection with the patriarchs: Gen 31:42, 53b ("Terror/Dread of Isaac"). See also FEAR OF ISAAC. Alt (1929/1953:24–25) had seen in this epithet a divine name, this has been questioned by other scholars (*CMHE,* 4; Koch, 1980). The meaning of *paḥad* is also debated (Albright proposed "kinsman of Isaac" [*FSAC,* 188–89]; rejected by Hillers 1972); the understanding of *paḥad* as "terror" should be given preference since the term has frequently this meaning in the OT. Many occasions of fright provoked by the encounter with the numinous are explicitly related to God: e.g., 1 Sam 11:7 speaks of "*paḥad* Yahweh" (= the dread which Yahweh causes to fall upon the enemies of Israel). As the might of the "ʾAbîr of Jacob" represents an element of protection and of security for the community which identifies itself as belonging to "Jacob," so the terror-spreading numinous effect of "Isaac's *Paḥad*" represents a warranty of an effective protection for this community, which is comprised under the name of "Isaac."

One can trace a definite dissemination of this divine epithet "Paḥad" in the ANE (Lemaire 1985: 500–1). Different divinities were ascribed the capacity of spreading a numinous dread. In the context of OT texts this ancient divine epithet allows the biblical author to talk of the (tribal) prehistory of Israel and of the (numinous) prehistory of Yahweh without using specific divine *names.*

7. Elohîm (God). "Elohîm" belongs to the linguistic root "El" (god); "El" and "Elohîm" can be understood as parallel and interchangeable terms (e.g., "Sons of El" [Ps 29:1; 89:7] and "Sons of Elohîm [Job 1:6; 2:1; 38:7]). The form "El" is found preponderantly in older (or archaizing) texts in the OT. The origin and function of the medial *"h"* is debated in philological research. Texts from Ugarit-Ras Shamra also show a plural with the medial *"h"* as a particular by-form. However, its main area of distribution is the Aramaic-speaking world. Beginning with the 8th century B.C., Aramaic developed increasingly as the international language of the ANE, and its progressive influence on Israel is beyond doubt (the most recent books of the OT [e.g., Daniel] contain chapters written in Aramaic). The assumption of such an extremely strong influence of the Aramaic language could explain the weighty presence of the term "Elohîm" in the biblical texts: late (montheistic) Israel had found in Elohîm a term to express that the numinous concept which Aramaic designated with "Elohîm" as international and unspecific, was nothing else but the rudimentary form of knowledge of the one and true God, which had been given only to Israel with the name of Yahweh (*TDOT* 1: 267–84).

Grammatically the form "Elohîm" contains the plural ending *-îm.* The function of "Elohîm" as a true plural ("gods") is reflected in numerous biblical texts (e.g., Exod 12:12: "all the gods of Egypt"). In this function "Elohîm" can be preceded by a definite article ("the gods"; e.g., Exod 18:11: "now I know that Yahweh is greater than all the gods"). In Heb "Elohîm" can be accompanied by plural adjectives (e.g., very frequently in Deuteronomy: "other gods") and construed with plural verbal forms (e.g., Ps 97:7: "all gods bow down before him [Yahweh]").

The striking feature of the OT texts lies in the use of this plural form "Elohîm" in order to designate the one God of Israel. One could think of a "plural of majesty"; however, it is most probable that this plural should be understood in the sense of an intensification and eventually as an absolutization: "God of gods," "the highest God," "quintessence of all divine powers," "the only God who represents the divine in a comprehensive and absolute way." In this function the term "Elohîm" can stand as a surrogate for the name of the biblical God; e.g., Gen 1:1 (P): "In the beginning Elohîm created the heaven and the earth." In this sense is the term "Elohîm" used in a systematic way instead of the divine name "Yahweh" in one part of the Psalter (Psalms 42–83); therefore in the scholarly literature this part is called the "Elohistic Psalter (note the two almost identical Psalms 14 [with "Yahweh"] and 53 [with "Elohîm"]).

When in the OT texts the form "Elohîm" is used instead of "Yahweh" in this or similar ways, this mirrors different types of theological reflection, in an attempt to place one's own tradition of faith and of the name of God in a context of an increasing challenge manifest through different religions and other divine names. The differentiation in the Priestly writing between "Elohîm" (= pre- [and extra-?] Israelite) and "Yahweh" (= genuinely Israelite) is only one attempt, in the crisis of Israel's dispersion among the nations (in the time of the Babylonian exile), to transform the faith in one primarily national Yahweh into a new form which tries in a conscious and an increased manner to incorporate into one's own tradition the experience of the supranational and international.

Besides the confrontation with the religions of the surrounding world, in the exilic period there arises an inner Israelite dialogue concerning the way one should deal with the traditions. What now appears as a Priestly layer on the Pentateuch must have once been an independent work, which attempted to offer an alternative to the great Deuteronomistic-Yahwistic historical work (Rose 1981: 320–28; Van Seters 1983: 323). What is called the "Yahwist source" (J) in the Pentateuch by exegetes is in fact distinguished by the fact that (in contrast to the Priestly writing [P]), it employs the divine name "Yahweh" from the beginning and presupposes cultic appeal to the name of Yahweh already for the beginning of human history; cf. Gen 4:26: "To Seth [= the third son of Adam and Eve] also a son was born, and he called his name Enosh [=humanity]. At that time men began to call upon the name of Yahweh." For the theologian "J" (the Yahwist), to invoke the name of Yahweh is not an exclusive right of Israel. Rather, access to this God and to his name is in principle open to all of humanity ("Enosh"). The texts of this author are characterized by a truly extraordinary, but presumably programmatic juxtaposition or even blending of "Yahweh-Elohîm" (in the narrative of creation Gen 2:4b–3:24), but also by the integration of the "Elohistic" material ("E"; e.g., Genesis 20) in his narrative flow, stamped throughout with the name of "Yahweh." The constant interchange between "Yahweh" and "Elohîm" in his story of Joseph (Genesis 37–50) and in his story of Balaam (Numbers 22–24) must appear quite confusing. Yahweh, the God of Israel, is "Elohîm."

What interests the theologian "J" in the God of Israel is not his particularity, which expresses itself in an individual name, but the manifest realization of his function: he accomplishes what one expects of a god *(Elohîm).* His name "Yahweh" does not express anything else but a definition of a true and helpful existence: the author of Exod 3:14 understood "Yhwh" etymologically as "I am that I am." The divine name "YHWH" is thus derived from the Semitic verb *hyy/hwy* "to be" in the sense of a helpful and effective being (*"Da-Sein":* support, manifestation, event [von Soden 1966]; cf. somewhat differently Albright 1924: 370–78; *FSAC,* 15–16: "he causes to be, he creates"; cf. Freedman 1960; *TDOT*). The powerful effectiveness which one expects from every divinity (cf. the etymology of *El/Elohîm,* is realized only by Yahweh as the unique true *Elohîm.* In this way the (particular) name of Yahweh can step behind the (universal) Yahweh function (= *Elohîm*). Vis-à-vis this universalistic ("humanistic") interpretation of the "J" theologian, the theology of the Priestly writing attempts to teach faith in Yahweh in a quite pointed way starting from the particularistic specificity of Israel. Both authors employ the term "Elohîm" virtually as another name for Yahweh; each, however, with a very different theological purpose.

8. Baal. While the largest spheres of the pre- and extra-Israelite *El/Elohîm* tradition could have been integrated into the faith in Yahweh, the process of confrontation between Israel and the Canaanite Baal tradition was on the whole more complicated.

Nevertheless, the starting point is not essentially different insofar as the term *baʿal* did not originally represent a specific divine name but rather an appellative "lord, owner, possessor," which could be used entirely outside the religious language and without a reference to a particular divinity (*TDOT* 2:181–200). Thus every married man is a *baʿal* (possessor, owner) of his wife (e.g., Gen 20:3; Exod 21:3,22, etc.), every family leader was a *baʿal* of his family ("house"); in the same way one could be a *baʿal* of a field or of a herd of cattle. The sphere over which one exercises one's possession is defined by the genitive (*baʿal* of . . .). See also BAAL (DEITY).

In a similar way the sphere over which the ancient Near Eastern divinities exercised their lordship is defined; the biblical texts contain a considerable number of such genitival constructions with the element *baʿal*, e.g., "Baal-Peor" (Num 25:3,5; Deut 4:3; Ps 106:28) is the god who is the owner *(baʿal)* of the sanctuary on Mount Peor in Transjordan (Num 23:28). The divine epithet *baʿal* is attested in the entire Semitic-speaking world and was attributed to a variety of gods. In the West Semitic sphere (Syro-Palestine) a particular development occured. From the middle of the 2d millenium B.C. the original epithet was oriented more and more to function as a divine name: first of all, the name was reserved for a clearly defined type of divinity (the storm god); the individual names (e.g., Hadad) of originally different gods of this type receded into the background, so that eventually the term *baʿal* could assume the function of a divine name.

In the West Semitic sphere this development took place with a varied rapidity: in the areas strongly exposed to international exchange and trade (e.g., Ugarit-Ras Shamra) it certainly occurred much faster than in the hill areas of Samaria and Judah. The use of a widely disseminated divine epithet allowed the cities and regions involved in the exchange to emphasize even more strongly their common features as over against their particularistic traditions with their isolating effect. With this "international" character Baal is comparable to "El"; contrary to "El," however, the term *baʿal* stresses much more the dynamic element, which on the one hand, is due to its heritage from storm god, and on the other hand, to the meaning of the word *baʿal*: the rule or dominion implied must be constantly and actively achieved, exercised and demonstrated.

The Israelite tribes which came into contact with Canaanite Baal worship must have felt or even hailed the affinity between their similarly immensely dynamic, and downright warlike Yahweh tradition (e.g., Exod 17:16: "A hand upon the banner of Yahweh! Yahweh will have war with Amalek from generation to generation!") and the Canaanite Baal. In any case, there are a number of indications showing that the Israelites as well began to worship their god Yahweh using the epithet *baʿal*, which the Canaanites applied to the most dynamic god in their tradition. King Saul named one of his sons "Ishbaal" (= "man of the lord"); by doing this he certainly did not intend to show reverence to the foreign, Canaanite divinity Baal. Rather, the epithet *baʿal* referred to Yahweh, the God of Israel. This assumption is further corroborated by the list in 1 Sam 14:49, where the three sons of Saul are mentioned. The second son, called ISHVI (Heb *yišwî*) (perhaps "man of Yahweh"), should probably be identified with "Ishbaal." The theophoric elements "baʿal" and "Yahweh" in the Israelite personal names are interchangeable since Yahweh is "*baʿal*" (lord). The personal name Baalyah in 1 Chr 12:6 is a confessional name meaning "Yah (= Yahweh) is lord [*baʿal*]." That is to say, whatever one characterized with the epithet *baʿal*, it was fully realized by Yahweh (and only by him!); he is the *baʿal* par excellence.

Under these presuppositions of "Yahweh's baalship" it is not surprising that in the OT psalms Yahweh is worshipped with terminology similar to that used of the Canaanite Baal in the epics from Ugarit-Ras Shamra, that is, as the one "who rides on the clouds" (Ps 68:5; 104:3; Deut 33:26), who manifests himself in thunder and storm (e.g., Ps 18:14–15; 77:19). Behind Psalm 29 could be hidden an entire Canaanite hymn to Baal which was transposed into a hymn to Yahweh. This "baalization" of Yahweh should not be understood as if by it the specific Israelite tradition was abandoned; the epithet *baʿal* does not replace the divine name *Yahweh*. Rather, this entire development reflects the natural attempt of a young nation to learn from the cultural experience of older nations. This cultural and religious process of learning had received an enormous impetus from the fact that David had established the capital of his kingdom in the ancient Canaanite-Jebusite city of Jerusalem, and that his son Solomon had erected there the royal palace and the Yahweh temple with the help of Phoenician builders. In doing so the Phoenicians were not just suppliers and workmen; rather, they conceived and erected the temple in Jerusalem as if they were building a Baal temple in their own homeland, and to Solomon this probably appeared suitable.

After the David/Solomon era began a contrary development which saw it as unbefitting to use the epithet *baʿal* for Yahweh. The end of the unity between Israel and Judah (933) and the subsequent feud between these brother nations led to a significant political weakening which had as its cultural and political consequence the gradual transformation of Palestine into a "backyard" of the Aramaic and Phoenician sphere of influence. King Omri of Israel (886–875 B.C.), himself not of Israelite origin (maybe of Aramaic origin?) initiated a policy of coalition and intermarriage with the royal house of Phoenician Sidon. Through the Sidonian princess Jezebel, Israel came into direct contact with a religion in which the term *baʿal* was not just an epithet but had become the divine name of a Phoenician god. Beginning in the 9th century B.C., the term *baʿal* became for the traditionally oriented worshippers of Yahweh in Israel increasingly the embodiment of everything foreign; therefore, one could no longer address one's own god Yahweh with the honorific title *baʿal.* "Yahweh" and "Baal" had become incompatible alternatives; this is portrayed in the striking narrative of Elijah's confrontation with the prophets of Baal on Mount Carmel (1 Kings 18). The book of Hosea as well is stamped with this opposition; the prophet would like to suppress the word *baʿal* in Israel's future worship of Yahweh: "And in that day, says Yahweh, you will call me, 'My husband,' and no longer will you call me, 'My Baal' " (Hos 2:18—Eng 2:16). Later writers go even further in the suppression of the name Baal by substituting *bōšet* ("shame"; Jer 3:24; 11:13; Hos 9:10) thus deforming the name Ishbaal into "Ishbosheth" (= "man of shame"; 2 Sam 2:8 [for a different view, see Tsevat 1975: 71–81]).

9. Adôn/Adônai (Lord). While the address "my *baʿal*" ("my lord"/"my master") was banned from the religious language in the worship of Yahweh, another term enjoyed an increased popularity: The Heb word *ʾādôn* (see also ADONAI) appears to have a meaning close to that of "*baʿal*"; both words could be rendered "lord." *ʾādôn* differs from *baʿal* in nuance, in that this term does not necessarily designate a relationship of ownership but rather authority. Its antonym is Heb *ʿebed* "subordinate, servant, slave." The pharaoh made Joseph the "*ʾādôn* (lord) of his house" (Gen 45:8; Ps 105:21), the term *baʿal* ("owner") being inappropriate here. Above all, the king is addressed with the deferential *ʾădônî* "my lord." Insofar as God is represented as a heavenly king he can be spoken of as "*ʾādôn*" and appealed to as "my *ʾādôn*." With reference to God, the form *ʾadōnāy* is most frequent; the ending *-āy* is either a personal pronoun on a plural noun ("my lords," "my lordship"), or an emphatic substantival-afformative ("lord par excellence").

The royal tradition in the representation of the divinity was well established in the ANE centuries before the beginning of Israel's history. As Israel grew into this monarchic tradition, Yahwism took over royal imagery and royal titles. David called his fourth son Adoniyah (2 Sam 3:4; 1 Kgs 1–2), an unmistakable sign that for David, Yahweh is to be worshipped as a king and appealed to with the deferential designation *ʾādôn.* On the name, see ADONIJAH (PERSON).

The royal tradition appears in a particularly significant way in the story of Isaiah's call (Isaiah 6), and therefore it is not surprising to find that in this connection the honorific title *Adonai* is employed (v 1: "I saw Adonai [the Lord par excellence] sitting upon a throne, high and lifted up; and his train filled the temple"; cf. vv 8 and 11). The prophets see themselves as called and authorized messengers of the king Yahweh, and therefore show a predilection for the "messenger formula" ("thus speaks XY. . . ."), which legitimizes the word of the messenger as being identical with the formulation given by the king who appointed them. It is not accidental that one finds the royal honorific title "lord" used with a particular frequency in the introductory and concluding formulas of the prophetic speeches ("thus says Adonai, Yahweh of hosts" [e.g., Isa 10:24], and ". . . oracle of Adonai, Yahweh of hosts" [e.g., Isa 3:15]). Moreover, the royal function of the term Adonai in these formulas is implied by its affinity with the expression "Yahweh of hosts": the subordinate stands at the disposal of the ruler (*ʾādôn*) and accomplishes his will.

In the prophetic books the term *Adonai* occurs 320 times out of the total 449 occurrences (for the term's distribution in the OT, see *TDOT* 1:62–64). The book of Ezekiel alone contains 217 occurrences of this term. In the title Adonai, the prophet in the Babylonian exile might have seen a possibility of differentiating between his god Yahweh and the Babylonian divinities who were called *bēl* (< *bʿl*) but not *ʾādôn,* (this was not widespread in Mesopotamia. Thus the same title *Adonai,* which in the West Semitic (Canaanite) world of monarchic Israel was a symbol of a definite integration of Yahwism into the old royal tradition, later in the time of the Exile, could become an expression of differentiation over against foreign religious forms. The divine name *Adonai* does not appear at all in 1–2 Chronicles or Leviticus; this may indicate that in these writings the royal-monarchic tradition is set aside in favor of a priestly-Aaronic point of view.

10. Ṣebaoth (Hosts). "Ṣebaoth" is a plural, which sets again the question to the philologists and the exegetes how to understand it, whether as a "real" plural designating ("the hosts"), or whether here again one meets a plural of "majesty," of "intensity" designating something "absolute." The basic etymological meaning of *ṣebāʾôt* is "force, weight, might" (Eissfeldt 1950: 110–11), with a particular consequence that the subordinate be enlisted to serve. A case example of such an enlistment by a royal sovereign is the recruitment for military service (1 Sam 8:11–12a); but also the recruitment for work could be designated with this term (Exod 38:8; 1 Sam 2:22; cf. 1 Sam 8:12b–13). Consequently "Yahweh Ṣebaoth" is the one who has the absolute power to recruit others into service (cf. "plural of extension and importance" [Tsevat 1965: 49–58]; "name of a god whose principal attribute was royal majesty" [Ross 1967: 76–92]). See also HOSTS, LORD OF.

The "power to recruit into service" comprises several domains: first of all it is Israel who is recruited into service by Yahweh, its highest sovereign. Thus in 1 Sam 17:45, the divine name "Yahweh Ṣebaoth" is placed in apposition with "the God of the armies of Israel." The Song of Deborah (Judges 5) illustrates that Yahweh's power of control reaches widely beyond the "armies of Israel"; for not only the Israelites as "Yahweh's troups" (v 13) fight against Jabin of Hazor and against Sisera the captain of his army (Heb *ṣābāʾ* [4:2, 7]), but the stars as well fight on Yahweh's behest: "from heaven fought the stars, from their courses they fought against Sisera" (5:20). The stars symbolize "the host of heaven" (e.g., Isa 40:26; 45:12), the recruited powers of heaven, which could also be perceived as members of a heavenly court of Yahweh (1 Kgs 22:19: "I saw Yahweh sitting on his throne, and all the host [Heb *ṣābāʾ*] of heaven standing beside him on his right hand and on his left"). This representation has its analogies in other ANE religions; the astronomy of Babylonian science and religion exercised a particular influence which, e.g., during the long reign of Manasseh (687–642 B.C.) should not be underestimated. By contrast (according to 2 Kgs 23:5, 11), his grandson Josiah (640–609 B.C.) followed a policy of emancipating his kingdom from all political and religious vassal conditions; he proscribed every cult having to do with "the sun, the moon, the planets, and all the host of heaven" (23:5).

In confrontation with Babylonian science and religion the view of Israel in respect to the power of the stars became increasingly critical, leading to the rejection of astrology (Deut 17:3; Jer 8:2). Eventually it became a criterion of differentiation between Israel and the nations: Israel is forbidden to worship ". . . the sun and the moon and the stars, all the host of heaven, . . . things which Yahweh your God had allotted to all the [pagan] peoples . . ." (Deut 4:19). The prophet Ezekiel does not employ the divine name "Yahweh Sebaoth," perhaps he wanted to renounce an old tradition which in the meanwhile had become ambiguous. When other biblical texts from the same period still use the term *ṣābāʾ* ("host"), they are careful to indicate that in Yahweh's vicinity all other forces must be categorically devoid of power. When, e.g., the Priestly writing continues to designate Israel as "*ṣebāʾôt* (hosts) of Yahweh," then these *ṣebāʾôt* do not represent a military power but a community on its way to a worship at Sinai (Exod 12:41; cf. 6:26; 12:17, 51); when the heavenly *ṣebāʾôt* (hosts) are mentioned, then these do not represent powers so much as the (peaceful) angels and messengers of God (Ps 148:2: "Praise him, all his angels, praise him, all his host [*ṣābāʾ*]!").

In the period of the Exile (after the downfall of the Judean monarchy), Israel had to find for their theology and for their faith in Yahweh other forms of expression than the traditional ones which were anchored in the context of royal-military imagery. Moreover, in the Persian period (the episode of Zerubbabel, ca. 520 B.C.) arose the expectation of a royal Messiah, and so it is not surprising to find the sudden strong usage of the divine name "Yahweh Sebaoth" by the prophets Haggai and Zechariah, for it elicited memories and hopes of the national power and greatness.

11. Conclusion. All the epithets and titles which in the course of its history the faith of Israel combined with the name of Yahweh, cannot be referred to as original attributes of the Israelite worship of Yahweh; rather, they mirror—both together and individually—the history of the dialogue between the OT faith in God and the ANE world. In the course of history of this dialogue the movement of integration became gradually substituted by an opposite movement of demarcation and exclusivity.

D. Foreign Divine Names

Originally Israel showed a considerable readiness to integrate into its own faith in Yahweh epithets, titles, and other attributes stemming from religions of the surrounding world, while at the same time it refrained from placing the proper names of foreign gods into a relationship with Yahweh's name. Herewith Yahwism clearly differs from Mesopotamian practice; for example, among the 50 different names of Marduk are listed numerous older Sumerian divinities in an attempt to identify and harmonize them with the Babylonian main divinity (*ANET*, 69–72; Bottéro 1977: 5–28).

Although the possibility of identification of Yahweh with other deities remains excluded, it is nevertheless significant to see in what way in different periods, Israel dealt with the names of foreign gods. In an older period it was naturally presupposed that other nations had a god responsible for them in a way similar to Israel. Just as Israel was "the people of Yahweh" so were the Moabites "the people of Chemosh" (Num 21:29; Jer 48:46). The existence of these gods was not doubted; however, their power was deemed to be less than that of Yahweh. 1 Kings 10 narrates how the Syrian king Ben-hadad erred in assuming that Yahweh could be spoken of in a disdainful way as a "mountain god" (vv 23 and 28), whose sphere of influence would be restricted to the hill country of Samaria. Yahweh can confront and engage in battle with any other national god; even the god of the great power of Egypt cannot succeed against Yahweh: "Yahweh Ṣebaoth, the God of Israel, said: 'Behold, I am bringing punishment upon Amon of Thebes' " (Jer 46:25). The depiction of Yahweh's superiority can, in the narrative, acquire traits of a parody; thus 1 Samuel 5 narrates the powerlessness of the god Dagon, the god of the Philistines in Ashdod who must formally fall before Yahweh (cf. Delcor 1964: 136–54).

The derision of the powerlessness of foreign gods can lead to the negation of their existence. The story of God's judgment on Mount Carmel (1 Kings 18) may be mentioned as an example: seen in a historical perspective the issue was the claim to preeminence in Israel contested between Yahweh and the Phoenician Baal (v 36: "Yahweh, let it be known this day that thou art God *in Israel*"); in the narrative development of this event Elijah's scorn for Baal is sharp (v 27: "either he is musing, or he is gone aside, or he is on a journey, or perhaps he is asleep and must be awakened"). Therefore his remark "cry aloud, for he is a god" (v 27) can be understood as irony and negation of Baal's existence.

Altogether one finds very few foreign divine names in the biblical texts (note the list of gods in 2 Kgs 17:30–31); the majority of foreign deities were simply ignored. The names of others, although mentioned, were deformed or altered. Marduk, the main god of the Babylonians became "Merodach" (Jer 50:2; cf. Merodach-Baladan [Isa 39:1], Berodach-Baladan [2 Kgs 20:12 (MT)], Evil-Merodach [2 Kgs 25:27; Jer 52:31]); the vowels of this name might be a case of a dysphemic Masoretic vocalization intended to slander, perhaps by calling to mind the word *meʾōrar* cursed. This practice is comparable to the procedure of replacing "Baal" with *bōšet* "shame." This *bōšet*-dysphemism is probably found in the deformation of the divine name Astarte in Masoretic Ashtoreth (1 Kgs 11:5, 33; 2 Kgs 23:13) and in the construction of a (false) divine name Molech (e.g., Lev 18:21; 20:2–5; 1 Kgs 11:7; cf. *TWAT,* 965–66; somewhat differently Heider 1985: 223–28). Milcom, however, is not originally a divine name (1 Kgs 11:5, 33; 2 Kgs 23:13; Jer 49:1, 3; Zeph 1) but an expanded divine title which expresses the royal function *(mlk)* of the god. The case is similar with the word Asherah, which may originally have represented the divinization of cultic sites (Albright 1925: 100; Deut 16:21 suggests a holy tree or a cultic stake) which only secondarily became a name of a goddess (Albright's theory has been followed; cf. Lipiński 1972; *TDOT* 1: 438–44).

The goddess Anath, Baal's consort, is never mentioned in the biblical texts; her cult must have been of considerable significance in Syria and Palestine (cf. "Anath-Yahweh" in Elephantine); her name is found in numerous place and personal names in Israel: Anathoth (as a place name [e.g., Josh 21:18; Jer 1:1]; as a personal name [1 Chr 7:8; Neh 10:19]), Beth-Anath (Josh 19:38; Judg 1:33), and others.

Israel's relation to the names of foreign gods mirrors its changing attitudes toward foreign religions: finally, the existence of foreign gods was denied. In the list of gods of Solomon's foreign wives (1 Kgs 11:5–8) the word "gods" was eventually replaced with "abomination": "Milcom the abomination of the Ammonites," "Chemosh the abomination of Moab."

E. Attenuation of the Divine Name

When for biblical faith other gods do not exist any longer, the necessity of a name disappears; it is no longer indispensable to have a "distinguishing mark" in order to differentiate one's god from others. In postexilic texts the use of the divine name "Yahweh" clearly diminishes (it does not appear at all in the following books, Esther, the Song of Songs, and Ecclesiastes). Yahweh is the only god; Yahweh and God ("Elohîm") became synonyms. The gradual reduction of the use of the divine name on the basis of its loss of function can lead to its complete removal; in this development with Judaism, two mutually exclusive tendencies were manifest: a cosmopolitan attitude and a scrupulous outlook.

1. Cosmopolitan Thinking. From ancient times the wisdom milieu, in conjunction with its international and interreligious thinking, had preferred the general term "god" over any individual divine name. The wisdom literature of ancient Israel participated in this common Oriental current, for which the wider perspective was more important than any particular concretion. For these circles the "fear of god" (religion) seemed more important than any particular cult of any individual divinity. In the period of a universal dispersal of Israel (the time of the Exile), as the customary sacrificial cult for Yahweh was made impossible, the influence of this sapiential, cosmopolitan thinking reached wider circles in Judaism. The expression "God of heaven" from the diplomatic language of the Persian period came into the vocabulary of the monotheistic faith of Judaism, furthering the abandonment of the name of Yahweh in favor of this title with a universalistic appeal ("God of heaven" appears preponderantly in later texts of the OT: 17 times in Ezra-Nehemiah, 12 times in Daniel, cf. e.g., Jonah 1:9; 2 Chr 36:23; one should also name the 9 occurrences in the Elephantine papyri). The cosmopolitan atmosphere of the Persian period and the subsequent Hellenistic era encouraged a tendency to view particularistic thinking as antiquated and unenlightened; it was inevitable that the particular divine name "Yahweh" would be affected by this "modernistic" tendency as it was adopted by larger circles in Judaism.

2. Scrupulous Thinking. The contrary movement is the strong conservatism of traditional Judaism manifest in the revolt of the Maccabees and later in Qumran. This milieu is characterized by an increasingly rigorous interpretation and application of tradition and the precepts of the Torah (the Pentateuch). The prohibition in the decalogue (see TEN COMMANDMENTS) of misusing the name of Yahweh was originally oriented against magical practices, but in the course of the interpretation of the law it became the occasion of eventually denying *any* use of the divine name. This prohibition was motivated by scrupulous fear and a desire to ensure that it would not be used "in vain" (Exod 20:7; Deut 5:11) either by Jews or non-Jews. Even the cultic use of the name in the temple or the synagogue was eventually affected by this fear: whenever in the biblical texts the name of Yahweh was mentioned, it was read and pronounced as "Adonai ("my lord"). See also KETHIB AND QERE. Thus in the Greek translation of the OT (LXX) the name of Yahweh was rendered throughout with *kyrios* ("Lord"). The Masoretic Hebrew manuscripts of the OT have preserved the consonants Y-H-W-H (the tetragram) but supplied the vocalization "Adonai." The authentic pronunciation of the name of Yahweh thus became lost and only isolated instances can be found in the writings of the Church Fathers (Rose 1978: 6–16).

F. From Immanence to Transcendance

Judaism had secured that the divine name should not be profaned any more. The divine name, once the "distinguishing mark" of divine presence and immanence, had become the essence of God's unapproachable holiness so that in the Jewish tradition "the Name" *(haššēm)* could be synonymous with "God." The nuance of difference between God and his name was lost; God and the divine name were one, and equally holy.

Bibliography

Albright, W. F. 1924. The Name Yahweh. *JBL* 43: 370–78.

———. 1925. The Evolution of the West-Semitic Divinity ʿAn-ʿAnat-ʿAttâ. *AJSL* 41: 73–101.

Alt, A. 1929. *Der Gott der Väter.* BWANT 3/12. Stuttgart. Repr., Vol. 1, pp. 1–78 in *Kleine Schriften zur Geschichte des Volkes Israel.* Munich, 1953. Repr. pp. 21–98 in *Grundfragen der Geschichte des Volkes Israel.* Munich, 1970. (ET 1967).

Barstadt, H. M. 1984. *The Religious Polemics of Amos.* VTSup 34. Leiden.

Baumgärtel, F. 1961. Zu den Gottesnamen in den Büchern Jeremia und Ezechiel. Pp. 1–29 in *Verbannung und Heimkehr. Festschrift für Wilhelm Rudolph,* ed. A. Kuschke. Tübingen.

Besnard, A.-M. 1962. *Le mystère du Nom.* LD 35. Paris.

Blenkinsopp, J. 1986. Yahweh and Other Deities: Conflict and Accommodation in the Religion of Israel. *Int* 40: 354–66.

Bottéro, J. 1977. Les noms de Marduk, l'écriture et la 'logique' en Mésopotamie ancienne. Pp. 5–28 in *Essays on the Ancient Near East in Memory of J. J. Finkelstein,* ed. M. de Jong Ellis. Memoirs of the Connecticut Academy of Arts and Sciences 19, Hamden, CT.

Brownlee, W. H. 1977. The Ineffable Name of God. *BASOR* 226: 39–46.

Delcor, M. 1964. Jahweh et Dagon (ou le Jahwisme face à la religion des Philistins, d'après 1 Sam. V.). *VT* 14: 136–54.

Eissfeldt, O. 1929. Götternamen und Gottesvorstellungen bei den Semiten. *ZDMG* 83: 21–36. Repr. *KlSchr* 1: 194–205.

———. 1950. Jahwe Zebaoth. *Miscellanea Academica Berolinensis* 2/2: 128–50. Repr. *KlSchr* 3: 103–23.

Freedman, D. N. 1960. The Name of the God of Moses. *JBL* 79: 151–56.

———. 1976. Divine Names and Titles in Early Hebrew Poetry. Pp. 55–107 in *Magnalia Dei: The Mighty Acts of God,* ed. F. M. Cross, W. E. Lemke, and P. D. Miller, Jr. Garden City, NY. Repr. pp. 77–129 in *Pottery, Poetry and Prophecy.* Winona Lake, IN, 1980.

Furlani, G. 1935. Dei e demoni bifronti e bicefali dell'Asia occidentale antica. Pp. 136–56 in *Miscellanea ortientalia dedicata A. Deimel.* AnOr 12. Rome.
Grether, O. 1934. *Name und Wort Gottes im Alten Testament.* BZAW 64. Giessen.
Grimme, H. 1912. Die Jahotriade von Elephantine. *OLZ* 15: 11–17.
Heider, G. C. 1985. *The Cult of Molek: A Reassessment.* JSOTSup 43. Sheffield.
Helck, J. D. 1984. The Missing Sanctuary of Deut 33:12. *JBL* 103: 523–29.
Hillers, D. R. 1972. Pahad Yishaq. *JBL* 91: 90–92.
Jenni, E. 1952–53. Das Wort ʿōlām im Alten Testament. *ZAW* 64: 197–248; 65: 1–35.
Kinyongo, J. 1970. *Origine et signification théologique du nom divin Yahvé à la lumière de récents travaux et de tradition sémitico-bibliques (Ex 3,13–15 et 6,2–8).* BBB 35. Bonn.
Koch, K. 1976. Šaddaj. Zum Verhältnis zwischen israelitischer Monolatrie und nordwest-semitischem Polytheismus. *VT* 26: 299–332.
———. 1980. păḥăd jiṣḥaq—eine Gottesbezeichnung? Pp. 107–15 in *Werden und Wirken des Alten Testaments,* ed. R. Albertz, H.-P. Müller, H. W. Wolff and W. Zimmerli. Göttingen.
Lang, B. 1983. *Monotheism and the Prophetic Minority.* SWBA 1. Sheffield.
Lemaire, A. 1985. A propos de *paḥad* dans l'onomastique ouest-sémitique. *VT* 35: 500–1.
Lipiński, E. 1972. The Goddess Atirat in Ancient Arabia, in Babylon, and in Ugarit. *OLP* 3: 101–19.
———. 1987. Ashima. Pp. 152–53 in *Dictionnaire Encyclopédique de la Bible,* ed. P.-M. Bogaert et al. Turnhout.
Mettinger, T. N. D. 1982. *The Dethronement of Sabaoth.* ConBOT 18. Lund.
Metzger, M. 1970. Himmlische und irdische Wohnstatt Jahwes. *UF* 2: 139–59.
Rad, G. von. 1947. *Deuteronomium-Studien.* FRLANT 58. Göttingen.
Rendtorff, R. 1966. El, Baʿal und Jahwe: Erwägungen zum Verhältnis von kanaanäischer und israelitischer Religion. *ZAW* 78: 277–92. Repr. pp. 172–87 in *Gesammelte Studien zum Alten Testament.* TBü 57. Munich, 1975.
Roberts, J. J. M. 1972. *The Earliest Semitic Pantheon.* Baltimore.
Rose, M. 1975. *Der Ausschliesslichkeitsanspruch Jahwes.* BWANT 106. Stuttgart.
———. 1978. *Jahwe. Zum Streit um den alttestamentlichen Gottesnamen.* ThStud 122. Zurich.
———. 1981. *Deuteronomist und Jahwist.* ATANT 67. Zurich.
Ross, J. P. 1967. Yahweh Sᵉbaʾôt in Samuel and Psalms. *VT* 17: 76–92.
Smith, M. 1971. *Palestinian Parties and Politics that Shaped the Old Testament.* New York.
Soden, W. von. 1966. Jahwe "Er ist, Er erweist sich," *WO* 3: 177–87. Repr. pp. 77–88 in *Bibel und Alter Orient,* ed. H.-P. Müller. BZAW Berlin, 1985.
Tsevat, M. 1965. Studies in the Book of Samuel. *HUCA* 36: 49–58.
———. 1975. Ishbosheth and Congeners. *HUCA* 46: 71–88.
Van Seters, J. 1983. *In Search of History.* New Haven.
Weinberg, J. P. 1988. Gott im Weltbild des Chronisten: Die vom Chronisten verschweigenen Gottesnamen. *ZAW* 100, Sup.: 170–89.
Weippert, M. 1961. Gott und Stier. *ZDPV* 77: 93–117.

MARTIN ROSE

NAMES, DOUBLE. Additional names adopted by an individual or bestowed upon him by others. Refer to abbreviations list in the appendix of article (see G below).

A. Introduction
B. Phraseology
C. Types of Double Names
  1. Ethnica
  2. Nickname
  3. Pet Name
  4. Metronymic
  5. A Family Trait
D. Reasons for the Addition of a Byname
  1. Cultural Assimilation
  2. Official/Private Contexts
  3. Status
  4. Religion
  5. Homophony
  6. Punning
E. Further Observations on Usage in the NT
  1. A Semitic Feature
  2. Fluid Examples
F. Related Phenomena
  1. Apocopation
  2. Translation Names
  3. Substitute Names
  4. Change of Name
G. Appendix: Abbreviations of Documentary Publications

A. Introduction

The term "double name" is sometimes also called "byname," *"supernomen,"* or *"signum."* The types of such names and the reasons for their acquisition vary. The assuming of extra names, which sometimes actually replace a birth name (whether intentionally or not), is a phenomenon of the Greco-Roman world which spanned the period of the 2d century B.C. to the 3d century A.D., with a peak of frequency in the 2d century A.D.; though it was not confined to this period absolutely. The examples of this naming feature which fall outside these chronological limits (e.g., Paris/Alexander of Trojan War fame) are considerably less common. The phenomenon is not confined to the Greco-Roman milieu, though that will be the focus of this article. Double names occur in various Semitic languages, e.g., Nabatean (*NDIEC 1976,* 92–93), Hebrew (Jacob/Israel, etc.), Palmyrene (Teixidor 1979: 5), and Egyptian (*CEML* 4: 1012, 1095, 1113). Double names were used by Jews and Christians no more and no less than by others in the Greco-Roman world of the period. The high frequency of attestation of bynames in Egypt and Asia Minor in comparison with other areas merely reflects the relative number of texts recovered from those places. Women possess bynames less often than men; but this may be a reflection of the greater frequency with which males are named in ancient texts. There are some attestations of young children with double names. For a discussion of why the use of double names may have been rather more widespread (at least for Ptolemaic Egypt) than the surviving frequencies may suggest, see Clarysse (1985: 57–66, especially 64 n. 22).

Lest this question seem of antiquarian interest only, it may be observed that double names occur quite commonly in contemporary Western society. At one end of the spectrum is the double name adopted by criminals and others wishing to conceal their birth name. But the pejorative connotation of "alias" is unknown for bynames in antiquity. Similarly, no ancient writer assumed a nom de plume (a disputed case is Xenophon [ca. 428/7–ca. 354 B.C.], who may have written his *Anabasis* under the name of Themistogenes of Syracuse; *Hell.* 1.2.). The attribution of a work to a more famous individual is a separate question: a writer "fathers" his work upon someone else in order to have it achieve wider currency. This phenomenon of literary falsification was prevalent in antiquity, particularly among early Christian pseudepigraphica (Speyer 1971). In our own times, there is often a specifically religious motive leading to the adoption of a new name. Western converts to Islam come to mind, such as Muhammed Ali (formerly, Cassius Clay), or Jusuf Islam (formerly, Cat Stevens). Since these individuals substitute a new name for their former one, we are not looking at an exact parallel to the phenomenon of the double name (see F.4 below). One well-known aspect of the Puritan phenomenon in 17th-century England was the adoption of some quite remarkable first names. This appears to have been a congregationally focused initiative, a very self-conscious attempt to indicate the separated character of the congregation, and an expression of independence from the established church, where, of course "standard" Christian names were common. One of the best-known such individuals was Praise God Barebones, a member of the Long Parliament.

The not very large body of research into double names in Greco-Roman antiquity has rarely been taken fully into account by those considering instances in the NT. Indeed, it is often the case that a single name-combination (Saul/Paul, or Simon/Peter) is examined without particular reference to comparable examples in the NT. While such studies may prove fruitful (Elliott 1972), to view individual instances against a wider canvas provides better perspective and illustrates how the language of the NT is entirely a normal part of its times. For the reason(s) which account for the double name of a Saul/Paul may not be identical with those for a Simon/Peter.

Of the studies by classicists, two may be particularly singled out. M. Lambertz (1913–14) devoted his pair of long articles to the spread of the use of double names in the Roman Empire: his evidence is assembled on a regional basis. Nearly thirty years later R. Calderini (1941–42) chose to concentrate upon Egypt, mainly focusing upon papyrus evidence in her bipartite contribution. Lambertz (1913: 79 n. 4) lists previous bibliography, to which Calderini adds little. W. Kubitschek's brief article in Pauly-Wissowa (PW 2A: 2,448–52) is superseded by their contributions. Deissmann (1979) is not the only one who draws upon documentary parallels for his NT study, which is very brief and confined to Saul/Paul. Cerfaux (1938) drew upon Lambertz's articles and more recent papyrological publications in his study of these names in Acts. Yet he fails to make the point that it is the author of Luke/Acts, far more than any other NT writer, who shows greatest interest in bynames, varying the formulae for stylistic reasons. The single most valuable study since Calderini is Kajanto (1963). Solin (1980) provides useful insights on double names among Jews, a matter which had claimed Cassuto's attention half a century earlier (1932–33).

There still remains a need for a comprehensive onomastic study of the *supernomina* in the NT, set against the wider context of current Jewish and Greco-Roman usage. With the completion of the *Thesaurus Linguae Graecae* the whole range of Greek literature, from Homer to A.D. 600 (including the Fathers), may now be practicably investigated for a subject such as this. When the *Lexicon of Greek Personal Names* is brought to completion (the first volume appeared in 1987) this area of research will be further facilitated. As for the documentary evidence, the sheer bulk of inscriptions and papyri being published annually provides plenty of scope for thorough investigation in this area.

In what follows, the different formulae used to indicate double names will be illustrated by reference to several typical examples, drawn particularly from recently published documentary texts. For these texts, dates are A.D. unless otherwise specified. Further examples to illustrate these formulae may be found in the studies of Lambertz and Calderini. Consideration of types of double names will be followed by examination of the variety of reasons for the assuming of an extra name. NT instances of bynames will be dealt with in each of these sections. Next, attention will be given to two particular features involving double names in the NT. Finally, brief observations will be made on some related onomastic phenomena. Examples listed under one subheading are often relevant to other sections. This article focuses exclusively upon personal names, not uses of double names applying to other contexts (e.g., cities or geographical regions). Almost all of the examples provided here are Greek, but a small number in Latin is included.

B. Phraseology

1. *A ho (hos) kai B* (A also [known as] B). This is by far the most common formula used to indicate a byname, notwithstanding that it occurs only once in the NT (Acts 13:9, Saul/Paul). In a fragmentary list of 54 names in Milne, *IG Aeg.* 33028 (Karnak, ca. 200), seventeen use the *ho kai* style to introduce a double name. Occasionally, the formula is filled out by the addition after the second name of a participle (*epiklētheis, legomenos,* etc.), e.g., Jos. *JW* 1 99; *Ant* 12.43, 385; 13.10, 131; 20.240; *CPJ* 3: 462, M. Clodius Alexander *ho kai* Gaianos *epik(aloumenos)* Thebes in Egypt, 157).

Documentary examples: Iv. Eph. 6:221b, Eutychia/Elpis (1st–2d cent.; 2224; Aurelius Herodes/Zeuxanemios (early 3d); 2249c, Donata/Theusebion (Jewish?; undated); 2253c, Eugamia/Diapherousa (servile?; undated); 7, 1.3010, *P. Statienus* Petronianus/Julianus (ca. 220); Pfuhl/Möbius 1159, Trophimos/Krasos (=Crassus; Christian; Altintaş in Phrygia, later Imperial); 1606, Cornelia Fortunata/Doutouros (Tomi, 3d); *SEG* 29: 781, Aletia/Elpidous (Thasos, Imperial); 1275, Gellia Tertia/Elpis (Apameia in Bithynia, 3d); *CIJ* 1: 694, Cl. Tib. Polycharmos/Achyris (Stobi, late 3d); 2.1238, Pheidon/Epiketeos (N of Jerusalem, undated); 1532, Epitychia/Dionysia (Fayum, 29 B.C.); *P.XV Congr.* 14, Heron/Eirenais and Sisois/Chairemon (Philadelphia in Egypt, 41–48/9); *P.Oxy.Hels.* 12, Apollonios/Euporos (99); 23, Calpurnius Isidoros/Harpokration (212; the same man appears in several other texts); 24, Aur. Ptolemaios/Zeuxianos (217); 26, Aur. Dionysios/Apollonios and Aur. Sarapiades/Hierax (296); *P.Köln* 2.84, Zoilos/Dionysos (Thinites, 143); *BGU* 13:2223, Isidora/Haropkratiane (175).

Sometimes the byname is introduced merely by *Kai,* e.g., *AE* (1979) 612, Aphrodeitos *kai* Eirenaios (Mylasa in Caria, Imperial); cf. note in the first publication *ZPE* 34 [1979]: 215–16); *P.Köln* 2.109 (provenance unknown in Egypt, 4th–5th), Pataor *kai* Loutteos; on this last example, cf. *NDIEC 1979,* 124. A further example is noted below under B. 19. An interesting bilingual epitaph preserves the formula in transliterated Latin letters: Acathocles *(sic) o cae* Rodios (*CIL* 10:11; Rhegium Iulium in Sicily, Imperial). The normal Latin equivalent is *qui et.*

2. *A ho kaloumenos B* (A called B). This participle is not terribly common as a byname formula. It is rather more frequently used to define a person or thing by some attribute, e.g., Rev 12:9 (see *NDIEC 1976,* 92); cf. *I.Kyme* 41:47–48 (1st–2d centuries), in which Isis is "called" *Thesmophoros.* In the NT: Luke 6:15, Simon/Zelotes; 8:2, Mary/Magdalene; 22:3, Judas/Iscariot; Acts 1:23, Joseph/Barsabbas *hos epeklēthē* Justus; 13:1, Simeon/Niger; 15:22, Judas/Barsabbas; 15:37, John/Mark.

Documentary examples: Iv.Eph. 6.2241, Cornelia Saturnina/Lollia (Imperial); 2285a, Dionysios/kallistos (undated); VII, 1.3429.20–21, Olympos/Nikephoros (near Metropolis, 2d century B.C.); 4356, Herais/Thymele (Hypaipa, undated); *I.Smyrna* 1.245, Attalos/Gaius, son of Gaius (undated; here the son's second name is derived from his father's name).

3. *A ho epikaloumenos B* (A additionally called B). A common way to introduce an additional name. NT: Acts 11:13, Simon/Peter (the same formula is a *v.l.* at 10:5); 12:12, John/Mark.

Documentary examples: P.Petaus 53, Pentheus/Pkanpesoul, N./Alektonas, and Maximus/Tene (Ptolemais Hormu, 184/5); of the 22 people listed in the 29-line *P.Petaus* 67, eleven have this formula (185); of the ca. 150 people listed in the 174-line *P.Petaus* 93, 28 have this formula (late 2d).

4. *A ho epiklētheis B* (A additionally called B). A reasonably common way to indicate the *supernomen,* especially when it is—or was in origin—a nickname. NT has Acts 4:36, Joseph/Barnabas.

Documentary examples: Iv.Eph. 5.1609, NN/Graus (apameia in Bithynia?, not dated), very possibly servile in view of the nickname, "old man"; *CIJ* 2: 1435, Alexandros (?)/Borzochoria (= Bar Zachariah) (Alexandria, not dated).

Literary examples: Athenaeus, *Deipn.* 1.5b. Hegemon/Phake; 10.437e Dionysios/Metathemenos ("Shifty"); 13.583e, Synoris/Lychnos ("Lamp"); D.S. frag. 35.33.3, M. Cato/Demonsthenes; Diogenes Laertius 5.84, Demetrios/Ixion, and Demetrios/Stamnos.

5. *A ho klētheis B* (A called B). Parallel to (4) above, but rarer in its use as a byname formula. Not so used in the NT.

Documentary example: Iv.Eph 7.1.3127, Ti. Claudius/Paulinus/Charixenos (Scala Nova, Imperial).

6. *A epiklēn B* (A by name B). Not very common; for the form see LSJM, *s.v.* nowhere used in the NT.

Documentary examples: CIJ 1:108, Hermione/Barseoda (Rome, undated); 2:776, M. Aurelius Alexander/[As?]aph (Hierapolis, 3d?); *SEG* 26: 1214, Julianus/Euteknios (Lyon, 3d–4th); Lifshitz 1967: no. 84, Isaak/Sindouros (Lapethos on Cyprus, 5th A.D.).

Literary example: Jos. *Ant* 20.233, Onias/Menelaus.

7. *A ho legomenos B* (A spoken of [as] B). Not common as a double name formula. NT: Matt 27:17, Jesus/Christ (a title on its way to becoming a name); John 11:16, Thomas/Didymos (a translation name which has become a genuine *supernomen;* also at 20:24; 21:2); Col 4:11, Jesus/Justus.

Documentary example: Reilly, *Slaves* 580 (=977), Hermione/Graus (Kalymna, 2d).

Literary example: Jos. *Ant* 13.320, Salome/Alexandra.

8. *A ētoi B* (A or B). A rare usage not found in the NT.

Documentary examples: P.Oxy. 8.1122, Aurelius Phoibammon/Loukas (407); 46.3295, Aurelia Nike/Taias (295); cf. the Latin inscription *AE* (1976) 419, Paula *sive* (E)ustathia (Gaul, late Imperial).

9. *A anth'hou B* (A instead of/alternatively B). Not common; apparently attested as a byname formula only in nonliterary papyri (a distinctively Egyptian Greek usage?).

Documentary examples: P.Basel 10, Tesenouphis/Horos (Soknopaiu Nesos, 166); *P.Mich.* 4.1.223.3118, Heuremon/Pekmeis (Karanis, 175; the same man—a Jew: see *CPJ* 3:492, nos. 4, 6—is identified as P./H. at *P.Cair.Mich.* 359.691 (Karanis, 175); *P.Petaus* 15, Suchotes/Suchion (Ptolemais Hormou, 194/5); 93.73–74, Pouaris/Kynaros (Ptolemais Hormou, late 2d cent.).

10. *A ho dia logōnB* (A by the name of B). Even less common than the previous type; apparently attested as a byname formula only in nonliterary papyri (a distinctively Egyptian Greek usage?).

Documentary examples: BGU 13:2263, Pabous/P . . . , Stotoetis/Sotas, and Sotas/Satabous (Soknopaiu Nesos, mid-2d); *P.Strasb.* 7.4.775, N/Anoubion, and N/Ptasios (Herakleopolite nome, ca. 300).

11. *A B* (i.e., double name without any formula to indicate it). This type is more common than certain other ways of expressing the byname, but is naturally less easy to detect. NT: Simon Peter is the preferred reading at 2 Pet 1:1 (cf. RSV). In contrast to Judas *ho kaloumenos* Iscariot at Luke 22:3, he is named J. *Iskarioth* at 6:16 (cf. Matt 26:14, *ho legomenos* J. *Iskariotes*).

Documentary examples: P.Mich. 4.1.223.391, 2190, Pekmeis Heuremon (karanis, 175), who at 1.3118 in the same text is designated P. *anth'hou* H.; *I.Bankers* 15, Metrodoros Asbolios is called M. *ho epikaloumenos* A. later in the same inscription (Kourion in Cyprus, 3d); *Iv.Eph* 7.1.3329, Euboulos Kassandros (near Ephesos, undated); *I.Smyrna* 1.247, M. Aurelios Moschos III Poseidonios (3d, or later?); *CPR* 5: 2.14 Aurelius Jonah Skim (Heraklepolis, late 5th); 15, Jacob Symeon (Herakleopolite nome, 477) is a possible example: see ed. n., ad loc. *CIL* 8: 4.26415, Pullaienus Florentius Titinius Pupianus, a man addressed by Cyprian, *Ep.* 66, as Florentius *qui et* Puppianus. *AnSt* 37 (1987) 49–53, no. 1, C. Flavius Chrysippos Panages (Cremna in Pisidia, II) may well be a further example.

12. Double Bynames. Fairly rare. NT: Acts 1:23, Joseph *ho kaloumenos* Barsabbas *hos epeklēthē* Justus. *Documentary example: P.Vindob.Tandem* 11.44–45, Aurelius Theodoros *ho kai* Herakleios *epikaloumenos* Nikon (Herakleopolite nome, 241/2). *Literary example:* Appian, 12.2.10, Mithridates *hōi* Dionysos *kai* Eupator *epōnyma ēn.*

13. Variation of the Formula. It is clear that the various formulae used to mark a double name were interchangeable. The only minor qualification to this is that in the case of double bynames a form of *epikaleisthai* is generally used to introduce the last name, since it is normally a nickname in origin. NT: in Acts, John Mark is designated variously: 12:12, J. *ho epikaloumenos* M.; 12:25, J. *ho epiklētheis* M.; 13:5, simply John; 15:37, J. *ho kaloumenos* M.; 15:39, simply Mark. The single name Mark is the form that won out in the Church, as is clear from the gospel title, presumably to differentiate him from the apostle John. So, too, for Simon Peter. In Matt 4:18 and 10:2 he is described as S. *ho legomenos* P.; Luke 6:14 uses the periphrasis S. *hon kai ōomasen* P.; while in Acts participial and finite verb forms of *epikaloumai* are interchanged (10:5, 18, 32, 11:13), clearly for stylistic variation within that section. As in the case of Paul and Mark, the name Peter eventually ousted his Jewish name (cf. 1 Pet 1:1). As further illustration of the interchangeability of the formulae not that whereas Acts 1:23 gives Joseph *ho kaloumenos* Barsabbas *hos epeklethe* Justus, Papias refers to him as Justus *ho epiklētheis* Barsabbas (*PG* 5:1256).

Documentary examples: P. Petaus 93.73–74, Kronios *epikaloumenos* Samanytis, son of Pouaris *anth'hou* Kynaros (Ptolemais Hormou, late 2d); *I.Bankers* 15 uses both *ho kaloumenos* and *ho epikaloumenos* to refer to Alexander/Luscinius (Kourion in Cyprus, 3d).

Literary examples: 1 Macc 2:1–5, all five sons of Mattathias son of John have *supernomina*: four are *ho kaloumenos,* one is *ho epikaloumenos.* Later the *ho kai* formula is used of Judas Maccabeus (1 Macc 8:20; 2 Macc 5:27; 8:1). Jos. *Ant* 18.35, Joseph *ho (kai)* Caiaphas; at 18:95, J. *ho* C. *epikaloumenos*; but in the Gospels he is simply called Caiaphas. According to Theodoret, *Qu. in Num., PG* 80.368, Moses' father-in-law had the double name *(diōnumos)* Raguel "like Jacob *kai* Israel, like Simon Peter (no intervening formula), like Thomas *ho legomenos* Didymos, like Thaddaios *ho kai* Lebbaios."

14. Reversal of Name Order. *Documentary examples: CPJ* 2:178, Theodotos *ho kai* Niger (Edfu, 79), whereas at 2:249 he is Niger *ho kai* Theodotos (Edfu, 73/4). In a series of texts, *P. Sakaon* 11, 12, 82, 85 (cf. 76), dated between 297–300, we have testimony to an official, probably a Christian, who usually calls himself Aurelius Athanasios *kai* (sic: not *ho kai*) Philadelphos, and who signs his name Aurelius Philadelphos. But in no. 12 he calls himself Aurelius Philadelphos *kai* Athanasios. On this man see *NDIEC 1978,* 77. On the use of *kai* alone to introduce a by-name, see B.1, above.

Literary example: Cyprian of Carthage is designated both Cyprianus *qui et* Thascius (*Ep.* 66, *tit.*), and Thascius *qui et* Cyprianus (*Act. Procons. Cyp.* 3.3).

C. Types of Double Names

1. Ethnica. Used as a byname, as distinct from a descriptive label of origin, this is rare. *Documentary examples: Homm. Sauneron* 2.55–56, Psenosiris *ho kai* Syros (Akoris in Egypt, Hadrianic); Lowey, *IGB* 303, Euprepes *ho kai* Rhod[ios] (Rhodes, Imperial).

2. Nickname. Perhaps the most common type. *Documentary examples: SEG* 26: 1843, C. Julius Capito *hos kai* Odysseus (Cyrenaica, lst cent.), a soldier perhaps so named as a reflection of his mobility while in service; *I.Bankers* 17, epitaph for a young banker which says that his parents called him Synekdemos but everyone else used the crude nickname Billos (Kelenderis in Asia Minor, Imperial); *IGUR* 3.1321, Rufinus whom people used to call Asterion, "starlet" (Rome, 3d or 4th); *Epigraphica Anatolica* 12 (1988) 116 no. 63 Flavius Ktesiphon *ho kai* Sphekas, "wasp" (Stratonikeia in Caria, Imperial); *P.Coll.Youtie* 65.12–13, 29, M. Vibius Horigenes *ho kai* Magnus (Oxyrhynchos, 241; nickname omitted in 1.73). With this last the well-known instance of C. Pompeius Magnus (1st cent. B.C.) provides an obvious parallel. Of other Roman nicknames which became assimilated as *agnomina* perhaps the best known is Q. Fabius Maximus Verrucosus Cunctator (late 3d B.C.).

Literary examples: Jos. *Ant* 12.43, Simon *ho kai* Dikaios *epiklētheis* "because he was pious towards God and good-willed towards his compatriots." Cf. in the NT, Col 4:11, Jesus *ho legomenos* Justus, and the second by-name of Joseph/Barsabbas/Justus at Acts 1:23. Even though no explanation is given for the accession of these names in the NT, we may infer something similar to what Josephus makes explicit for Simon. Note, too, the famous classical example of Aristeides "The Just" (Plut. *Comp.Ar.et Men.* 9); but here it is not a double name. Jos. *Ant* 13.383, Alexander Jannaeus was so cruel that he was given the name *(epiklēthēnai)* Thrakidas by the Jews. Cassius Dio, *Epit.* 80.4.1, P. Valerius Eutychianos *ho kai* Komazon acquired his by-name because of his mimes and laughable behavior. Diogenes Laertius 5.84 mentions that a certain Demetrius was called *(epiklētheis)* Ixion "because he was thought to have acted wrongly with regard to Hera." In the same passage is mentioned another Demetrios *ho epikletheis* Stamnos ("Wine-jar"); but no reason for this nickname is provided. Athen. *Deipn.*, 13.583e, Theokleia *epekaleito* Koronē ("Crow").

3. Pet Name. *Documentary example: IG* 10.2.1.214, at the end of this text which honors C. Antonius Urbanianus Philistos we are told that "his parents themselves (honored) their sweetest child Pierios" (Thessalonike, 240/1 or slightly later).

4. Metronymic. This appears to be very rare, and may be an oddity. *Documentary example: BGU* 13:2251.17, Didymos *epikal(oumenos)* the son of Achllis (Fayum, 2d century).

5. A Family Trait. This is particularly marked to distinguish members of ruling dynasties from the Hellenistic period onward. Various Ptolemies, Seleucids, and Antigonids had differentiating bynames, clearly thought of as such in view of the addition of one of the formulae. Names like Ptolemy Philadelphos, Seleucus Nicator, and Antigonos Monophthalmos come to mind. The Persian Artaxerxes III (359–338 B.C.) was differentiated from homonymous predecessors by the *supernomen* Ochos. Other royal houses employed the device, such as rulers of Cappodocia, Bithynia, and Pontus. It is therefore nothing out of the ordinary to find certain of the Hasmoneans bearing double names: Alexander Jonathan (Jannaeus), and John Hyrcanus. The phenomenon is a feature of Imperial Roman rulers: C. Iulius C.f. Caesar/Augustus, popularly called Octavian; Antoninus/Pius, etc. But the case of Roman emperors' names is more complex than that of members of Hellenistic dynasties and client kingdoms, because of the Roman practice of adoption. Furthermore, from the mid-Republic onwards an *agnomen* was not an uncommon addition to the *tria nomina,* sometimes being added to commemorate some particular achievement. Members of the Scipionic family of 3d–2d centuries B.C. illustrate this, e.g., P. Cornelius P.f. Scipio Africanus, and his brother L. Cornelius P.f. Scipio Asiaticus. Some of the Caecilii Metelli attached *agnomina* to their names, reflecting in somewhat gross fashion their imperialistic outlook: e.g., Macedonicus, Delmaticus. Some other examples have been noted above under "nicknames" (c.2). But it is not only ruling families which might display this accretion of names. One recently published property transfer (161 B.C.) forms part of a larger archive which provides evidence of at least 15 individuals with double names out of some three dozen family members spanning six generations (Ritner 1984: 171–84 and pl. 30). *P.Coll.Youtie* 67 (260/1) includes the name Sarapion *ho kai* Apollonianos, which the editor shows (see the family tree on p. 450) was used by four family members spanning three generations. For discussion of this phenomenon in the papyri see Calderini (1942: 17–20), and Bagnall (1988: 23).

In *P. L. Bat* 22, the editor draws together a private archive of a certain Dionysius who, in nearly 40 documents (both Greek and Demotic) spanning 116–104 B.C., is referred to by two other names as well: Plenis and *Pa-ʿš3*. In the three generations for which his family is attested, five other people out of a total of fourteen have a second, or in one case a third, name.

D. Reasons for the Addition of a Byname

1. Cultural Assimilation. Egyptians, Jews, Lycians, Syrians, and other non-Hellenic individuals frequently adopted a Greek or Latin double name to advertise their identification with Greek mores. This is very possibly the most common reason for the adoption of a byname; certainly it is the easiest to perceive. But it is obvious that this does not account for all instances by any means, since there are many examples of individuals whose double names are ethnically identical with their primary names (e.g., Greek + Greek; Egyptian + Egyptian).

Documentary examples: Teixidor 1979: 20, Male *ho kai* Agrippa (Palmyra, 131); *P.Köln* 2.100, Taarpaesis *he kai* Isidora (Oxyrhynchite nome, 133); *CPJ* 1:126, Apollonios *hos kai* Ionathas *Syristi,* "in Aramaic" (Fayum, 238/7 B.C.); *CIJ* 1:108 Hermione *epiklēn* Barseoda (Rome, undated), an epitaph for an infant less than one year old; 2:776, M. Aurelius Alexander *epikln* [As?]aph; (Hierapolis, Imperial); *IGUR* 3.1231, Theodosia/Kalypso (early Imperial), epitaph for a young Jewish woman aged 18. For the proposal that this text is Jewish see Horsley (1987a). The Jewish examples here provide clear parallels for such NT name combinations as Saul/Paul, Simon/Peter, John/Mark, and Jesus/Justus. Paul, at least, must have had both Jewish and his Latin name from birth (Acts 22:26–29), for which *CIJ* 1:108 above provides a good parallel, as does also the double name of a Christian child who died before reaching the age of two, *AE* (1976) 419 (quoted above at B.8).

Literary example: Diogenes Laertius 4.67, the Carthaginian philosopher Hasdrubal, better known as Kleitomachos, who became head of the academy at Athens in 129 B.C.

2. Official/Private Contexts. It has been suggested recently (Clarysse 1985; Bagnall 1988) that in Ptolemaic Egypt what determined the use of an Egyptian or Greek name was the type of document which the person initiated (Clarysse 1985: 59–60). Private texts (especially those in Demotic) show a preference for Egyptian names, while Greek names preponderate in official documents concerned with government or military administration. One inference drawn from this observation is that double names are largely visible only among those with some official role. Furthermore, at least in the sense of language, the context is Egyptian by choice, and Greek only for official purposes (Bagnall 1988: 23). There is some basis for these propositions, but (as Bagnall allows) they do not account for the whole phenomenon of additional names because of their diversity chronologically and geographically. The motivation cannot have been so single in all cases.

Documentary examples: Erbsteit archives (Pathyris, mid 2d century B.C.), for which see Ritner (1984) and Bagnall's inferences (1988: 23) about the use of double names by the males in the family. See *P. L. Bat* 22 (ca. 40 texts from Akoris in Middle Egypt ranging from 116–104) archive of the family of Dionysius also known as Plenis and *Pa-ʿš3*.

3. Status. A slave with a non-Roman name usually adopted the name of his master upon emancipation. But there are examples where the first name is retained in such a way that it is thought of as forming a byname with the freed-status name.

Documentary examples: SEG 29:781, Aletia Tertulla *he kai* Elpidous (Thasos, Imperial); 1275, Gellia Tertia *he kai* Elpis (Apameia in Bithynia, 3d).

4. Religion. A byname may be adopted to signify a shift in religious adherence. In such a circumstance it is not uncommon for the former name actually to be abandoned (see below, F.4); but those instances cannot then be considered double names.

Documentary examples: CIJ 1:523, Veturia Paulla became a convert to Judaism at the age of 70 and took the name Sara (Rome, undated). *SIRIS* 586, a sarcophagus for Tetratia Isais, who is called Memphius (sic) elsewhere on the same monument (on female *supernomina* in *-ius* see Kajanto, 41). The accompanying epigram makes plain that she was a devotee of Isis (Ravenna, 3d). *BGU* 13:2224, Apollonarion *he kai* Sarapias, sister of Sarapion (175) provides a possible example: the sister adopted the extra name in order to identify more closely with the cult of Sarapis.

5. Homophony. Not especially common; in the NT *Saulos/Paulos* may be an example (cf. Mussies, 361), as may be the substitute name Simeon/Simon.

Documentary examples: Pfuhl/Möbius 1977–79: 1509, Gauros *ho kai* Gaius (Byzantion, probably 2d cent.); *I.Nikaia* 275, Antiochis *he kai* Antonia (undated), may be a further example.

6. Punning. In the NT the double name Simon/Peter involves a pun at one remove (Matt 16:15–18): Cephas was accorded as a punning nickname but the Greek translation (John 1:42) came to predominate.

Documentary examples: Iv.Eph. 7:2.3824, Menekrates *ho kai* Baros (Hypaipa, undated): the latter name in the good sense of "strength" may be playing on *-krat-* in the first name; 3828, Aurelius Sokrates *ho kai* Euphronios (Hypaipa, 3d [?]): here the by-name may well be playing on the name Sokrates, the implication being that this individual was a dullard who didn't live up to the reputation of his great namesake. Note also *IGLS* 6: 2841, [K]onnaros *ho kai* Briares (Baalbek, undated): this is el-Qônera, the Palmyrene god El, who created the earth, whose by-name here means "strong, powerful."

E. Further Observations on Usage in the NT

While it will be clear from the foregoing that the occurrences of double names in the NT fit naturally into the larger Greco-Roman linguistic and cultural context there are two aspects which deserve further comment.

1. A Semitic Feature. The use of a patronymic as a double name which then largely ousts the primary name appears to be a Semitic feature, not confined particularly to Judaism. In the OT the name Bath-sheba at 2 Sam 11:3 appears to be an example, although she is also called there the daughter of Eliam. In Acts 4:36 we are told that Barnabas' first name is Joseph, but he is everywhere called simply Barnabas; and this is the name that survives in the later tradition (as in *Ep. Barn.*). Later, at Acts 13:6–8, we encounter Bar-Jesus, for whom a translation equivalent is given ("Elymas the magician"), but not his primary name. Barabbas in the Gospels provides a further example, though it is uncertain whether the name Jesus preserved by some mss at Matt 27:16–17 was Barabbas's primary name. Other examples in the NT are Bartimaeus (Mark 10:46) and Bartholomew (Mark 3:18, and parallels; Acts 1:13). Barsabbas is interpreted as a name by the author of Acts for two men (1:23 and 15:22). Contrast Matt 16:17 where Bar-Jonah remains a patronymic and is not to be thought of as having become a name in its own right. Beyond the NT other instances may be mentioned. Earlier, the Hebrew subscription to Sirach says that the book was written by Simon Ben Sira; but he was normally referred to merely by the patronymic-become-byname. In the 2d century A.D. Simon Bar Kokhba is rarely referred to as Simon: the patronymic had become a second name. A further example of a Semitic patronymic serving as a byname occurs in *CIJ* 2:1435, noted above at B.4.

Is this double name feature distinctive of Judaism? Although all the examples given above are Jewish, and non-Jewish instances are not easy to locate, the question should perhaps be left open, in view of the oddity quoted above at C.4, where a metronymic occurs as a byname in Egypt.

2. Fluid Examples. In the NT there are a small number of individuals whose possession of a double name is not settled in the tradition. In contrast to Luke 6:15, Simon *ho kaloumenos Zelotes,* the latter word is used as a description of him at Acts 1:13, not as a name (so, too, Chrysostom, *Hom. in Matt.; PG* 57-380). The author of Luke/Acts has employed the Greek equivalent of Aram *qanʾānā,* which Mark 3:18 (= Matt 10:4) has preferred to transliterate as S. *ho Kananaios.* With the double name in Luke 6:15 may perhaps be compared *CIJ* 1:362, Ionios (=Jonah?) *ho kai* Akone (Rome, undated), the latter name being suggested by Frey (ad loc.) to be an attempt to transliterate *qanʾānā.* A second example of this onomastic fluidity is Mary *he kaloumenē* Magdalene at Luke 8:2; contrast 24:10 where Magdalene is merely adjectival. This latter use is standard in other Gospels.

Even more than with the previous feature, we should be cautious about claiming this fluidity as distinctively Jewish, let alone distinctive to the NT. For it is to be expected that certain types of *supernomina* will not become permanently attached to the primary name from their first use. Nicknames and patronymics are two obvious kinds of bynames which would all fit into this category of being in flux for some time.

F. Related Phenomena

Alterations to names may be effected in other ways which do not strictly constitute double names. Some types of these may be noted briefly.

1. Apocopation. This was common in antiquity no less than today. A probable NT example is Epaphroditus/Epaphras (Phil 2:25, 4:18; Col 1:7, 4:32). Yet it is clear that each of these names had a life of its own (*NDIEC 1979,* 5: 21–23).

2. Translation Names. In the NT note Cephas/Peter (John 1:42); Tabitha/Dorcas (Acts 9:36); Thomas/*Didymos.* Only the last of these has become a double name (John 11:16; 20:24; 21:2), though the "Peter" element in the first has been formed into a double name on occasions with Simon/Simeon. In Acts 13:6–8 the author suggests that Elymas is the translation equivalent of Bar-Jesus, but this is doubtful. For some examples from the papyri see Clarysse (1985: 65).

3. Substitute Name. In the NT note Simeon/Simon, Silas/Silvanus, Jason probably for Jesus at Rom 16:21. At 1 Macc 7:5 Alcimus probably replaces Eliakim. The diminutive Priscilla replacing Prisca in Acts shows that the phenomenon is not always due to a desire to replace a Semitic name with one that looks more Greek or Latin.

4. Change of Name. Perhaps the most famous instance in antiquity of the abandonment of the original name in favor of a new one is provided by Amenhotep IV, pharaoh of Egypt in the mid New Kingdom, who altered his name to Akhenaton to promote a unique monotheistic reform in Egypt. *IG* 4:1.123.22–33 (Epidauros, late 4th B.C.) records that Asklepios gave the name Apistos (Unbeliever) to a man who came for a cure but disbelieved that the god could heal him. Only the new name is recorded on the inscription, not the man's original name. Vitruvius 10.2.15 recounts the discovery by the shepherd Pixodaros of the quarry from which the Ephesians were able to take their marble for the temple of Artemis. In recognition of this find the citizens decreed honors to him and changed his name to Evangelus. A number of Christians on trial at Caesarea in 308 bewilder the magistrate because they have renounced their birth-names, which were pagan theophorics. In place of them they chose names to identify with their new faith, such as Elijah and Samuel (Eus. *m.P.* 11.8). In Pfuhl/Möbius 1977–79: 764 the deceased Meteleios says that he changed his name to Teinexeios; yet both are preserved on the epitaph (Prusa ad Olympum, late Imperial). As a final example, Ammianus 16.12.25 mentions the case of Agenarich, whose name was changed to Serapion by his father when the latter became an initiate of Isis.

G. Appendix: Abbreviations of Documentary Publications

CEML	Catalogue des étiquettes de momies du Musée du Louvre: Textes grecs, 4ème partie, by F. Baratte and B. Boyaval, *Cahier de recherches de l'Institut de papyrologie et d'égyptologie de Lille* 5 (1979) 237–339 (text nos. 1000–1209).

CPR	*Corpus Papyrorum Raineri. V. Griechische Texte. II.* Ed. J. Rea and P. J. Sijpesteijm. 2 vols. Vienna, 1976.
Homm. Sauneron	*Hommages à Serge Sauneron, II. Egypte post-pharaonique.* Cairo, 1979.
I.Bankers	*Epigraphica III. Texts on Bankers, Banking and Credit in the Greek World,* ed. R. Bogaert. Textus Minores 47. Leiden, 1976.
IGLS	*Inscriptions grecques et latines de la Syrie.* Vol. 6. Ed. J.-P. Rey-Coquais. Paris, 1967.
IGUR	*Inscriptiones graecae Urbis Romae.* Vol. 3. Ed. L. Moretti. Rome, 1979.
I.Kyme	*Die Inschriften von Kyme,* ed. H. Engelmann. Bonn, 1976.
I.Nikaia	*Katalog der antiken Inschriften der Museums von Iznik (Nikaia),* ed. S. Sahin. 3 vols. Bonn, 1978–81.
I.Smyrna	*Die Inschriften von Smyrna,* Vol. 1. Ed. G. Petzl. Bonn, 1982.
Loewy, *IGB*	*Inschriften griechischer Bildhauer,* by E. M. Loewy. 1885. Repr. Chicago. 1976.
Milne, *IG Aeg.*	*Inscriptiones Graecae Aegypti,* vol. 1, ed. J. G. Milne. Oxford, 1905. Repr. Chicago, 1976.
P.Coll.Youtie	*Collectanea Papyrologica. Texts published in Honor of H.C. Youtie,* ed. A. E. Hanson. 2 vols. Bonn, 1976.
P.Köln II	*Kölner Papyri,* vol. 2, ed. B. Kramer and D. Hagedorn. Papyrologica Coloniensia 7. Opladen 1978.
P.Oxy.Hels.	*Fifty Oxyrhynchus Papyri,* ed. H. Zilliacus et al. Papyrologica Coloniensia 4. Cologne, 1969.
P.Petaus	*Das Archiv des Petaus,* ed. U. Hagedorn et al. Papyrologica Coloniensia 4. Cologne, 1969.
P.Sakaon	*The Archive of Aurelius Sakaon,* ed. G. Paréssoglou. Bonn, 1978.
P.Vindob.Tandem	*Fünfunddreissig Wiener Papyri,* ed. P. J. Sijpesteijn and K. A. Worp. Zutphen, 1976.
P.XV Congr.	*Actes du XVe Congrès international de Papyrologie,* vol. 2, ed. J. Bingen and G. Nachtergael. Papyrologica Bruxellensia 17. Brussels, 1979.
SIRIS	*Sylloge inscriptionum religionis Isiacae et Sarapiacae,* ed. L. Vidman. Berlin, 1969.
ZPE	*Zeitschrift für Papyrologie und Epigraphik.*

Bibliography

Bagnall, R. S. 1988. Greeks and Egyptians: Ethnicity, Status and Culture. Pp. 21–27 in *Cleopatra's Egypt: Age of the Ptolemies,* ed. R. S. Bianchi. New York.

Calderini, R. 1941–42. Ricerche sul doppio nome personale nell'Egitto greco-romano. *Aeg* 21: 221–60; 22: 3–45.

Cassuto, M. 1932–33. La corrispondenza tra nomi ebraisci e greci nell' onomastica giudaica. *Giornale Società Asiatica Italiana* 2: 209–30.

Cerfaux, L. 1938. Le 'supernomen' dans le livre des Actes. *ETL* 15: 74–80

Clarysse, W. 1985. Greeks and Egyptians in the Ptolemaic Army and Administration. *Aeg* 65: 57–66.

Deissmann, G. A. 1979. *Bible Studies.* Repr. Winona Lake.

Elliot, J. K. 1972. Kephas, Simon Peter, Peter: An examination of NT usage. *NovT* 14: 241–56.

Horsley, G. H. R. 1981. The Use of a Double Name. *NDIEC* (1976) 55: 89–96.

———. 1987a. A Jewish Family from Egypt in Rome. *NDIEC* (1979) 113: 221–29.

Kajanto, I. 1963. *Onomastic Studies in the Early Christian.* Helsinki.

Lambertz, M. 1913–14. Zur Ausbreitung des Supernomen oder Signum im römischen Reiche. *Glotta* 4: 78–143; 5: 99–170.

Laminger-Pascher, G. 1973. Zweitnamen, Spitznamen, supernomina. App. 7 in vol. 1 of *Index Grammaticus zu den griechischen Inschriften Kilikiens und Isauriens.* Vienna.

Lifshitz, B. 1967. *Donateurs et fondateurs dans les synagogues juives.* CahRB 7. Paris.

Mussies, G. 1985. Greek as the Vehicle of Early Christianity. *NTS* 29: 356–69.

Pfuhl, E., and Möbius, H. 1977/79. *Die ostgriechischen Gabreliefs.* 2 vols. Mainz.

Reilly, L. C. 1978. *Slaves in Ancient Greece: Slaves from Greek Manumission Inscriptions.* Chicago.

Ritner, R. K. 1984. A Property Transfer from the Erbstreit Archives. Pp. 171–87 in *Grammatika Demotika. Festschrift für E. Lüddeckens zum 15. Juni 1983,* ed. H. -J. Thissen and K. T. Zavzich. Würzburg.

Solin, H. 1980. Juden und Syrer im römischen Reich. Pp. 301–30 in *Die Sprache im römischen Reich der Kaiserzeit. Kolloquium . . . April 1974,* ed. G. Neumann and J. Untermann. Bonner Jahrbücher Beiheft 40. Cologne.

Speyer, W. 1971. *Die literarische Fälschung im heidnischen und christlichen Altertum.* Munich.

Teixidor, J. 1979. *The Pantheon of Palmyra.* EPRO 79. Leiden.

Varinlioğlu, E. 1988. Inschriften von Stratonikeia in Karien. *Epigraphica Anatolica* 12: 79–128.

Youtie, L. C. 1969. Introduction. Pp. 54–63 in *Das Archiv des Petaus (P. Petaus),* ed. U. Hagedorn et al. Pap. Coloniensia 4. Cologne.

G. H. R. HORSLEY

NAMES, HYPOCORISTIC. A hypocoristicon is generally a single-element name resulting from the shortening of an originally longer one. Hebrew names, and Semitic names in general, were often composed of two elements (or, as was often the case in Akkadian names and sometimes the case with West Semitic ones, three elements) which formed a nominal or verbal sentence. It was not uncommon for one of these elements to be dropped, producing this hypocoristic form. Theoretically, any element that occurs in a compound name can be considered hypocoristic when found alone, and it can be assumed that biblical names such as *ʿôbēd,* "servant (of)," or *yākîn,* "(he) will establish," are hypocoristic, the fuller form not being represented. As such, they can be differentiated from one-word names, such as those based on descriptions, plants and animals, the elements of which were rarely employed in compound names. However, names such as *šāʾûl,* "asked (of)," which refers to King Saul over 350 times in the OT and never appears in a "full" or longer form (note also the three lesser known individuals named Saul in the OT and Saul/Paul in the NT), suggest that sometimes these elements were used independently, not as hypocoristica of longer names. Despite the sizable corpus of onomastic evidence from inscriptions as well as in the Bible, there is still not enough known about naming practices in the ancient Semitic world to clearly define the functional conventions regarding hypocoristic names. Were they generally considered informal? Did they receive greater preference in speech than in writing? What role did personal preference, as opposed to cultural convention, play in the use of hypocoristic forms? Does the Bible provide a balanced view of hypocoristic use? To what extent, if any, did neighboring Semitic societies differ in their conventions? Such questions have yet to be fully answered.

A hypocoristicon could be verbal, nominal, or theophoric. It could stand alone, with or without minor changes in vocalization, or have a suffix appended to it (Noth *IPN* 36–41). Examples of the most common suffixes, *-â*, *-āʾ* and *-î*, on nominal and verbal Israelite hypocoristica include: *ʿezrāʾ*, *ʿezrâ* (cf. *ʿēzer, ʿazrîʾēl, ʿăzaryāhû*); *šebnāʾ*, *šebnâ* (cf. *šĕbanyāhû*); *mîkāʾ*, *mîkâ* (cf. *mîkāʾēl, mîkāyāhû*); *ʿabdî* (cf. *ʿebed, ʿabdāʾ, ʿabdĕʾēl, ʿabdîʾēl*); *ʿuzzî* (cf. *ʿuzzāʾ, ʿuzzâ, ʿuzzîʾēl, ʿuzzîyāhû*). Other hypocoristic suffixes include *-ay: ḥelqay* (cf. *ḥēleq, hilqîyāhû*); *-at* (most often associated with feminine names): *šimrāt* (cf. *šemer, šimrî, šĕmaryāhû*); *maḥlat* (cf. *maḥlî, maḥlōn*); *-ôt: šĕmôt; šĕlōmôt* (cf. *šĕlūmîʾēl*); *-o: dôdô* (cf. *dôday*); *šĕlōmōh* (cf. *šĕlūmîʾēl*); *-ān/-ām: šipṭān* (cf. *šĕpaṭyāhû*); *ʾăḥuzzām* (cf. *ʾăḥuzzat, ʾăḥazyāhû*); *-ôn/-ôm: ʿabdôn* (cf. *ʿebed, ʿabdāʾ, ʿabdĕʾēl*); *gēršôm, gēršôn*. Diminutive use of the *-ôn* suffix is probably attested in the names *šimšôn* and *naḥšôn*. Theophoric hypocoristic personal names, based on either a divine name or epithet, were much less common throughout the ancient Semitic world. Examples from the OT, with and without suffixes, include: *ʾēlāʾ* (ʾlʾ [Samaria ostraca]), *baʿal* (*bʿlʾ* [Samaria ostraca]), *gād, gādî, malkām, rešep*, and possibly *yēhûʾ*.

Hypocoristic geographic names are less common, or at least less demonstrable, due to the fact that the majority of known geographic names are sparsely attested. Also, there is a proportionally greater number of one-word geographic names, compared to personal names, both with and without suffixes, which cannot, strictly speaking, be considered hypocoristic. Many of these are descriptive in nature. A name such as *gibʿâ*, "height," cannot automatically be considered a hypocoristicon, even when there are names compounded with this element, such as *gibʿat šāʾûl*, since the term *gibʿâ* is descriptive and can function independently, as compared with a name such as "hears," or "servant [of]." Demonstrable examples of geographic hypocoristica in the OT, for which the hypocoristic and the longer form refer to the same site, include: *yābēš*, "dry" (cf. *yābēš gilʿād*) and *yabneh*, "[deity] causes to build" (cf. *yabnĕʾēl*).

The potential value of biblical parallel passages in studying the use of hypocoristic names is illustrated by comparing 1 Chr 9:16: *ʿōbadyâ ben-šĕmaʿyâ ben-gālāl* ("Obadiah the son of Shemaiah, son of Galal") and Neh 11:17: *ʿabdāʾ ben-šammûaʿ ben-gālāl* ("Abda the son of Shammua, son of Galal"). An interesting display of hypocoristic usage, which exemplifies the present incomplete understanding of hypocoristic conventions, involves Jeremiah's scribe Baruch. He is always called *bārûk* in the MT (23 times), usually with the patronymic *ben-nērîyâ/-yāhû*, and in Jer 36:32 he is referred to as *bārûk ben-nērîyāhû hassōpēr* ("Baruch the scribe, the son of Neriah"). This phrase is identical, except for the hypocoristic form of *bārūk*, to the inscription on an Israelite bulla which reads *brkyhw bn nryhw hspr* (Avigad 1978: 53).

Other ancient Semitic names also evidence this practice of hypocoristic usage, exhibiting both independent and suffixed forms. These latter are similar to those mentioned in reference to the Israelite names listed above and can easily be reviewed in the published studies of major collections of names from the ANE. (See for example: Stamm 1939: 11, 113–14; Benz 1972: 232–35; Gröndahl *PTU*, 49–54; Huffmon *APNM*, 130–40; and Zadok 1977: 148–70). One popular Akk hypocoristic suffix, *-ya*, found also in the cuneiform representations of Ugaritic and Amorite names, induced Jastrow (1894: 101–27) to propose that the Israelite theophoric *-yâ* should be regarded as merely an emphatic suffix. Gray (1896: 150–51), among others, rightly disputed and rejected this theory, noting that Jastrow's explanation might be correct in only a few, rare cases.

Hypocoristic forms of Hebrew, as well as Aramaic, names continued to be employed into the NT period. Examples from the NT, preserved in Greek, include: *Anna* = *ḥannâ*, "grace, favor" (cf. *ḥānān, ḥannîʾēl, Ananias* = *ḥănanyâ*) and *Symeōn* = *šimʿōn, Simōn* = *šimʿōn*, "[deity] has heard" (cf. *šimʿāʾ, šimʿâ, šimʿî, šĕmaʿyāhû*).

Bibliography

Avigad, N. 1978. Baruch the Scribe and Jerahmeel the King's Son. *IEJ* 28: 52–56.

Benz, F. L. 1972. *Personal Names in the Phoenician and Punic Inscriptions.* Studia Pohl 8. Rome.

Borée, W. 1930. *Die alten Ortsnamen Palästinas.* Leipzig.

Gray, G. B. 1896. *Studies in Hebrew Proper Names.* London.

Jastrow, M., Jr. 1894. Hebrew Proper Names compounded with YH and YHW. *JBL* 13: 101–27.

Stamm, J. J. 1939. *Die akkadische Namengebung.* Leipzig.

Zadok, R. 1977. *On West Semites in Babylonia during the Chaldean and Achaemenian Periods.* Jerusalem.

DANA M. PIKE

NAMES, THEOPHORIC. Theophoric names, both personal and geographic, have as one of their elements a divine name or epithet. Since many Semitic names were compounded from two or three elements to form verbal or nominal sentences, theophoric names thus represent declarations about or expressions of petition to the deity mentioned in the name.

The most common divine name found in Israelite theophoric personal names is a form of YHWH, which never occurs in a name in its full form, *yhwh*, but does appear in several standardized ones: *yĕhô-*, *yô-*, *-yāhû*, *-yô*, *-yâ*, and rarely *-yĕhô-* and *-yô-*. This is followed to a lesser extent by the generic *ʾēl*, "god." Examples from the OT and Israelite inscriptions include: *ʾûrîyāhû/ʾwryhw*, "YHWH is my light"; *yĕhônātān/ywntn*, "YHWH has given [the child]"; *yišmāʿēʾl/yšmʿʾl*, "God hears [requests]." Divine epithets, or characterized titles, were most often references to kinship or dominion. Examples of this type of theophoric personal name include: *ʾabnēr/ʾăbînēr*, "(My) [divine] father is a lamp" (cf. *ʾăbîyāhû/ʾbyw*, "YHWH is my [divine] father");

ʾăḥînādāb, "My [divine] brother is noble" (cf. ʾăḥîyāhû/ʾḥyhw, "YHWH is my [divine] brother"); ʾădōnîrām, "My lord is exalted" (cf. ʾădōnîyāhû, "YHWH is my lord"); *malkîrām/mlkrm*, "My [divine] king is exalted" (cf. *malkîyāhû*, "YHWH is my king"). Despite the assimilation of Gk names by the Jews of the Greco-Roman period, Heb and Aram names are recorded in the NT, although they have been preserved in Greek form. Examples of theophoric names from the NT include: *Iōannēs* = *yôḥānān*, "YHWH is gracious"; *Zacharias* = *zĕkaryāhû*, "YHWH has remembered"; and *Gamaliēl* = *gamlîʾēl*, "recompense of God."

Theophoric names in other ancient Semitic societies were generally similar in form to those names already cited, differing in the divine name or epithet employed, although many of the latter were fairly standard among different Semitic groups. Examples of some non-Israelite theophoric names contained in the OT are: *hădadʿezer* = *hddʿzr* [Aram], "Hadad is (a) help(er)" and *nĕbûkadneʾssar/nĕbûkadreʾssar* = *Nabû-kudurri-usur* [Akk], "O Nabu, protect the heir."

Theophoric geographic names are less common and are usually cultic or commemorative in nature. Examples from the OT, not all of which originated with the Israelites, include: *bêt-ʿănāt*, "Temple of Anat"; *bāmôt baʿal*, "High places of Baal/the lord"; *migdal-ʾēl*, "Tower of God"; *naḥălîʾēl*, "Wadi of God"; *baʿal pĕrāsîm*, "Baal/lord of the breaches"; *pĕnûʾēl*, "Face of God." The only place names in the OT which contain the divine name YHWH are early altar names, such as *yhwh šālôm*, "YHWH is peace," and later futuristic names for Jerusalem, such as *kissēʾ yhwh*, "Throne of YHWH."

Since names in the ANE were often chosen for their meaning, theophoric names, especially personal ones from the OT period, prove to be a valuable resource for religious information. (Geographic names, by nature, are long-term identifiers. Many of them continued through a variety of population and cultural changes, thus restricting their value.) The very fact that so many of the names in ancient Semitic societies, including the Israelites, were of a theophoric nature demonstrates a strong disposition toward the role of the divine in the lives of these people. These names indicate what attributes and qualities were associated with a specific deity by the general populace of a society. Although basic qualities, such as being mighty, mindful of worshippers, and hearing and responding to petitions were attributed to most major deities, comparisons can be enlightening. According to Israelite personal names, YHWH was brother, father, god, lord, king; he blessed, created, gave, heard, judged, knew, protected, remembered, saved; was light, good, great, gracious, noble, righteousness, perfection; etc. Hunsberger (1969) felt such information could be employed to demonstrate a correlation between the content of Israelite theophoric personal names and theological shifts due to major sociopolitical events during the course of the OT period.

Theophoric names also provide an indication of which deities were considered important by a given population group. Even in polytheistic societies, where many of the sometimes hundreds of deities which were recognized were actively worshipped, certain divine names were more popular in theophoric personal names than others (see, for example, Fine 1954: 116–34). Interestingly, research has indicated at Ugarit that divine names such as *ʾaṯrt*, *dgn* and *yrḫ*, which are well-known from mythological and cultic texts, were not popular in personal names (de Moor 1970: 222; *PTU*, 103, 123, 145). Concerning ancient Israel, studies have shown that despite the prophetic polemics against the waywardness of the people from the time of the Judges onward, a comparatively large percentage of Israelites had names containing the divine element YHWH, while surprisingly few people had names which contained a non-Yahwistic theophoric element (Tigay 1986, for the inscriptional evidence; Pike 1989, for OT evidence). These are the types of information which theophoric names can provide—information which must be weighed in any evaluation of the religion of ancient Israel.

Bibliography

Borée, W. 1930. *Die alten Ortsnamen Palästinas.* Leipzig.

Fine, H. A. 1954. Studies in Middle-Assyrian Chronology and Religion, Part II. *HUCA* 25: 107–68.

Hunsberger, D. R. 1969. *Theophoric Names in the Old Testament and their Theological Significance.* Ann Arbor.

Moor, J. C. de. 1970. The Semitic Pantheon of Ugarit. *UF* 2: 187–228.

Pike, D. M. 1989. *Israelite Theophoric Proper Names in the Bible: Implications for Religious History.* Ph.D. diss. Pennsylvania.

Tigay, J. H. 1986. *You Shall Have No Other Gods: Israelite Religion in the Light of Hebrew Inscriptions.* HSS 31. Atlanta.

DANA M. PIKE

NANEA (DEITY) [Gk *Nanaia*]. A goddess of Mesopotamian origin whose name in Semitic sources is given as *Nanâ* or *Nanay(a)*. Her syncretistic cult spread far and wide throughout the ancient world, including Greece. In the Greek world she was equated with Artemis or Aphrodite, in Egypt with Isis, and in Iran with Anahita. Her name is attested from Alexandria and the Fayum to Transoxiana, and from Arad to Piraeus. Known Nanaiophorous names include Barnanaios, Bathnanaia, Mekatnanaia, and ʿAbdnanay. From early times Nanea was affiliated with sun and moon, and posed as a deity of love and war.

Of particular interest is a temple of Artemis-Nanea in Dura-Europos built in Roman times. Dedicatory inscriptions identify her as the chief goddess of the city, a status she also enjoyed at Susa already in Seleucid times. Images of Aphrodite, Nike, and Tyche in her temple at Dura-Europos suggest associations with these deities. According to 2 Macc 1:13–18, Antiochus IV (Epiphanes) on his eastern campaign (165–164 B.C.) reached Persia, where he attempted to contract a marriage with Nanea and claim the wealth of her temple as dowry. The priests of the Nanaeion displayed the treasures and thus lured the king inside the precinct. Then from a concealed door in the ceiling they stoned him and his attendants, decapitated them, and tossed their heads to the rest of the royal retinue waiting outside.

Antiochus' attack on the temple is confirmed by Polybius (31, 9), Josephus (*Ant* 12.354) and Appian (*Syr. Wars* 66; cf. 2 Macc 9:1–2). All three locate the temple in Elymais (Elam) and identify the goddess as either Artemis (Polybius, Josephus) or Aphrodite (Appian). 1 Macc 6:1–4, though not naming the goddess, includes among the temple's riches dedicatory offerings left by Alexander the Great (cf. Josephus).

The nature and circumstances of Antiochus' death as depicted in 2 Maccabees 1 are contradicted by all other ancient sources. Confusion with Antiochus III (the Great), who lost his life in an attempt to rob a temple of Belus in Elymais (Diodorus 28, 3, 29, 15; Justin 32, 2; Strabo 16, 1.18) seems likely.

The exact location of the Nanaeion in question is unknown. For discussion see *AI* and Goldstein *Maccabees* AB.

Bibliography

Azarpay, G. 1976. Nanâ, the Sumero-Akkadian Goddess of Transoxiana. *JAOS* 96: 536–42.

Cumont, F. 1926. *Fouilles de Doura-Europos (1922–1923). Texte.* Paris.

Heimpel, W. 1982. A Catalog of Near Eastern Venus Deities. *SMS* 4: 9–22 (15–17).

ALBERT PIETERSMA

NAOMI (PERSON) [Heb *noᶜŏmî*]. The wife of Elimelech, mother-in-law of Ruth (Ruth 1:1–4). The family of Elimelech left Bethlehem-Judah for Moab because of famine in the land. Naomi was bereft of Elimelech and her two sons, Mahlon and Chilion, during their ten-year sojourn in Moab (1:1–5). Her daughters-in-law, Ruth and Orpah, weighed their responsibility to the family, and despite Naomi's resistance Ruth accompanied Naomi back to Bethlehem (1:8–18). Although destitute, Naomi and Ruth survived because of the aid of a relative named Boaz (2:1; 4:3, 5) who subsequently married Ruth and purchased a parcel of land in Naomi's possession (4:3, 9–10). Naomi instructed Ruth to approach Boaz and request him to undertake the role of the family's *gōʾēl* (kinsman-redeemer) in their behalf (3:2, 9). However, there was no clear legal obligation upon Boaz since the law limited a *gōʾēl* marriage to a brother-in-law of the widow (Deut 25:5–10). The familial relationship between Naomi's husband and Boaz must have been distant since Naomi did not know of him until her return to Bethlehem (1:8–16; with 2:20).

Also, scholars are puzzled that Naomi is said to have had land for sale. There is no provision in the OT for land ownership by a widow, and more importantly the story portrays Naomi as penniless without mention of her propriety of land. It is best to conclude that Naomi, since she had no sons, was the only party who could dispense the land to a qualified relative.

Another difficulty regarding Naomi is the ascription of Ruth's child, Obed, to Naomi by the women of Bethlehem: "A son has been born to Naomi!" (4:17). The story assumes that the audience will understand this without explanation. Perhaps the writer interpreted Boaz as a proxy for both Elimelech and Mahlon, making the child both Ruth's and Naomi's.

The name "Naomi" is the only one whose meaning is explained in the story itself (1:20–21). The name means "pleasant" or "my pleasantness," although the former is preferred since *y* is a hypocoristicon. It is related to the root *nᶜm*, "to be pleasant, delightful," and the adjective *nāᶜîm*, "pleasant, delightful." By a play on words Naomi implies this meaning for her name because she contrasts it with "Mara" ("bitterness"). See MARA. She explains to the Bethlehem women that her present condition of sorrow prevents her from being "Naomi."

KENNETH A. MATHEWS

NAPHISH (PERSON) [Heb *nāpîš*]. A son of Ishmael (Gen 25:15; 1 Chr 1:31) and, like all the sons of Ishmael, an Arab tribe (1 Chr 5:19). See ISHMAELITES. According to 1 Chr 5:19, Naphish inhabited N Transjordan (or an adjacent region) in the Persian period. See JETUR; NODAB. Two or three centuries earlier, a chief of this tribe, ᶜAmm-la-yit̲aᶜ (in Akkadian, *Am-le-ta Na-pi-šá-a-a*) is mentioned in a cuneiform letter to Ashurbanipal (CT 53, 289 Rs 8f) in connection with a Massaean (see MASSA) and the "rebellion" of the Kedarite chief Yaut̲aᶜ, which troubled the Assyrian king before 649 B.C. (Knauf 1983).

Zadok (1982: 296) has suggested that the Nephisim/Nephushesim (Ezra 2:50 = Neh 7:52) were prisoners of war from the tribe of Naphish. The various spellings of the Nephusim's name (Ezra 2:50 *npysym* [Ketîb], *npwsym* [Qerê]; Neh 7:52 *npwšsym* [Ketîb], *npyšsym* [Qerê]) caution against this suggestion, although neither the difference of the second syllable's vowel (*û* versus *î*) nor the inconsistent rendering of the sibilant (*s* and *š*) provide insurmountable obstacles against it. Although ancient N Arabian *sin* is generally rendered *šin* in Hebrew and Aramaic, occasional spellings with *samek* occur as early as the 5th century B.C.

For an explanation of the tribal name, cf. Arabic *nafīs* "precious"; as a personal name, Nafīs is attested for Tayma-Thamudic and Safaitic (Knauf 1989: 81).

Bibliography

Knauf, E. A. 1983. Supplementa Ismaelitica 1. *BN* 20: 34–36.

———. 1989. *Ismael.* 2d ed. ADPV. Wiesbaden.

Zadok, R. 1982. Remarks on Esra and Nehemiah. *ZAW* 94: 296–98.

ERNST AXEL KNAUF

NAPHOTH-DOR (PLACE) [Heb *nāpôt̲ dôr*]. A Canaanite city-state situated 12 miles S of Carmel and 9 miles from Caesarea. It lies in the N part of the plains of Sharon and was an important seaport town for many centuries beginning in the LB Age. It maintained links with the Mediterranean world from the 15th or 14th centuries B.C. It is identified with modern Kh. el-Burj (M.R. 142224).

The name Naphoth-dor is found in numerous forms, implying varied connotations. It is likely that the Egyptians named it Tantura, whereas the Sea Peoples called it Naphath-dor and the Assyrians referred to it as Duʾru. The MT uses both the plural form *nāpôt* (Josh 11:2) and the singular *nāpat* (Josh 12:23; 1 Kings 4:11) although the singular form is better attested in the MT and in the versions.

"Naphath" has been understood to mean a "district" or a "dune." The sand dunes in the area would certainly have been the reason for that name. On the other hand, the language of the Sea Peoples who occupied the town in the 12th century suggests an alternative meaning. The cognate in archaic Greek means "a wooded country." This is a semantic equivalent of Sharon, conveying the meaning "Dor of Sharon."

The long history of Naphoth-dor is reflected in the abundant remains from the LB Age down to the Crusader period. Apart from the remains some significant references to it in ancient documents illustrate its importance. After being founded probably by the Egyptians in the 15th century, it continued to serve as a harbor. An inscription of Rameses II from the 13th century B.C. mentions it for the first time. It was destroyed at the hands of the Sea Peoples in that century, and the Tjeker, one of the Sea Peoples, subsequently took control of Dor. Wen-Amon's report makes reference to Beder, king of Tjeker, as being in control of Dor during his visit to the city. It flourished throughout the Iron Age and became the capital of Solomon's fourth district governed by Ben-abinadab, his son-in-law. It was also a customs sanctuary. A seal of a priest called Zekaryahu suggests its links with Yahwism. Tiglath-Pileser III attacked it in 734 B.C. and captured it in 732 B.C. He reorganized the area by forming the District of Duʾru consisting of the region which extended as far as the Philistine border. Later Sargon II formed the Province of Samaria which included the former Province of Duʾru. The Assyrian Eponym List and the list of cities repeatedly mentions this city. It was granted autonomy under the Persians and became a Sidonian colony. Later it became a Ptolemaic royal fortress. Antiochus Sidetes besieged it employing cavalry, infantry and ships, but without success. By the end of the 2d century B.C. it was ruled by the tyrant Zoilus. Alexander Jannaeus was able to acquire it by negotiation and Pompey granted it autonomy in 64 B.C. by returning it to its former owners. It continued to be a free city under Herod and his successors. Josephus remarks that the Gentiles who inhabited it practiced Apollo worship. There is also evidence for the worship of Zeus and Astarte. A synagogue was in existence before the destruction of the Second Temple. There was a church and it became a bishopric during the Byzantine period in the 7th century A.D.

Joshua 11 recounts that the King of Naphoth-dor was a member of the coalition which fought against Joshua. Though the king was defeated the victory over the city was temporary, since Josh 17:11 and Judg 1:27 indicate that this city was one of those that remained to be conquered. The account of the defeat, however, affirms that a famous and powerful city like Naphoth-dor was given into the hands of Israel by the Lord when Israel was an obedient people.

PAUL BENJAMIN

NAPHTALI (PERSON) [Heb *naptālî*]. The sixth son of Jacob and the second son of Bilhah, Rachel's servant, and the eponymous ancestor of the tribe Naphtali. Naphtali is born to Bilhah and Jacob after Rachel suggests to her husband that he should have children by her servant. She is driven to this plan because she is unable to conceive, in contrast to her sister Leah, who at the point of the initiation of Rachel's plan had already had four sons by Jacob. Although born to Bilhah, Rachel has the privilege of naming Naphtali. *Naptālî,* formed from a base involving the *Nipʿal* of *ptl,* a verb that means "to twist" or "to wrestle." In popular etymology the name is associated with the words Rachel speaks upon naming him: "with wrestlings of God I have wrestled with my sister, and I have prevailed" (Gen 30:8). Although barren, Rachel feels a measure of success with the births of two sons to her servant; they do not, however, solve her anguish of childlessness. Only with the birth of her own child, Joseph, can she say that God has removed her reproach.

The book of Judges recounts that the tribe of Naphtali attempted to drive out the people of Beth-shemesh and Beth-anath, but was unsuccessful. They do, however, subject the residents to "forced labor" (Judg 1:33). Naphtali's most noted campaign occurs under the direction of its famous military leader, Barak. Barak, instructed by Deborah to fight Sisera at Mt. Tabor, with the assistance of Naphtali and Zebulun, leads people memorialized as those willing to risk "their lives to the death" (Judg 5:18). Naphtali was also summoned by Gideon to fight the Midianites and Amalekites (Judg 6:33–35). Mayes (*IJH,* 315), however, suggests that this reference is not historical because the list of the tribes who assist Gideon appears differently in Judg 7:23 (although Naphtali does appear both here and in Judg 6:33–35) since Gideon's campaigns were undertaken primarily by his own clan, the Abiezrites. It is uncertain whether Jacob's reference to Naphtali as an "unleashed hind" (Gen 49:21) in his blessing to the tribes is pejorative or a reference to the tribe's resilience in fighting.

Deut 27:11–26 describes Naphtali as one of the tribes who participates in a blessing/curse ceremony on Mt. Gerizim and Mt. Ebal. Naphtali, along with Reuben, Gad, Asher, Zebulun, and Dan, represents the curses that will result if the Israelites break the covenant. Elliger (*IDB* 3: 509) suggests that since it is said that Naphtali "dwelt among the Canaanites," probably has a non-Semitic name, and was probably under the domination of Hazor, it enjoyed a lesser status among the tribes. However, the description in Ps 68:27 which refers to Naphtali as one of only four tribes (along with Benjamin, Judah, and Zebulun) who are participants in a temple procession may counter this suggestion. Naphtali is also cited as the tribe that provides three cities to the Gershonites as a portion of their levitical inheritance (Josh 21:32; 1 Chr 6:76).

The boundaries and cities of Naphtali are given in Josh 19:32–39. This territory consists of the N regions of Israel around the E parts of the Galilee. This area is also indicated by Moses' blessing to Naphtali, who is to possess "the lake and the south" (Deut 33:23). The reference to the S is an enigma since the S regions of the Galilee belonged to Issachar. The exact boundaries of Naphtali are disputed. The region extending from Mt. Tabor to the Jordan, clearly part of the territory of Naphtali, is understood to be the tribe's N border by Noth (1935: 225–26), but the S border by Aharoni (*LBHG,* 238). The N border of this tribe may be missing due to the inability of Israel to clearly demarcate its N territory within Canaanite strongholds (Aharoni *LBHG,* 231). The list of Naphtali's territory appears abbreviated; instead of giving independent border demarcations, the references include only the boundaries of the adjacent territories of Zebulun and Asher. The disputed S boundary touches Zebulun, the W boundary borders Asher, and the E border meets at the Jordan (*LBHG,* 239).

Several cities listed as Naphtali's border cities have been identified. Aznoth-tabor, Heleph, Adami-nekeb, and Jabneel have been identified with, respectively, Khirbet el-Jebeil, Khirbet ʿIrbadeh (both at the foot of Mt. Tabor), Khirbet et-Tell above Khirbet ed-Damiyeh, and Tell en-Naʿam. Lakkum may be Khirbet el-Manṣurah (*LBHG,* 238–39).

Gottwald finds the biblical references to Naphtali's territory and skirmishes tenable since Naphtali existed in mountainous and forested terrain that could have been readily defended (1979: 528). Noth and Gottwald suggest that the city of Hazor, whose destruction is described in Joshua 11, was not destroyed by Joshua but by Naphtali in the 13th century B.C.E. (Gottwald 1979: 154; *NHI,* 149). Naphtali continued to challenge the feudal city-states in the E regions of the upper Galilee. Because of its success there, Naphtali was able to settle the region, or, if their settlement had already begun, to increase its own independence (Gottwald 1979: 528).

During the period of the monarchy, Naphtali is mentioned as one of the regions conquered by Ben-hadad of Syria. Ben-hadad, allied with Asa of Judah against Baasha of Israel, attempted to encroach upon Judah's territory (1 Kgs 15:20). During the reign of Pekah of Israel, Naphtali came to an end. Tiglath-pileser of Assyria captured "all the land of Naphtali, and he carried the people captive to Assyria" (2 Kgs 15:29). Ezekiel hopes for the restoration of Naphtali in the N, alongside Dan and Asher.

Bibliography

Gottwald, N. 1979. *The Tribes of Yahweh.* Maryknoll, NY.

Noth, M. 1935. Studien zu den historisch-geographischen Dokumenten des Josuabuches. *ZDPV* 58: 225–26.

SHARON PACE JEANSONNE

NAPHTHA

NAPHTHA [Gk *naphtha*]. A highly flammable substance mentioned twice in the Apocrypha. It was one of the substances used to heat the furnace into which Azariah (i.e., Abednego), Shadrach, and Meshach had been cast (LXX Addition to Daniel v 23). It was also the common name (Gk *naphthai*) used for the thick liquid that in the time of Nehemiah was used to ignite the sacred fire of the altar sacrifices (according to 2 Macc 1:26). Strabo (16.1, 15) also refers to naphtha as a liquid that ignites if it is brought near fire. These references clearly allude to some petroleum product. The word itself comes from the Akk *napṭu,* which eventually worked its way into Greek as a loanword (Aram *nepṭā/napṭā;* Goldstein, *2 Maccabees* AB, 181). See also NEPHTHAR.

GARY A. HERION

NAPHTUHIM

NAPHTUHIM. The Table of Nations (Gen 10:13) and the parallel genealogy in 1 Chr 1:11 place the Naphtuhim among the descendants of Mizraim (Egypt), son of Ham, son of Noah. These two references have the only occurrences of the name in the Bible. Because of the association with Egypt, scholars have looked in that direction to identify more closely who these people might be.

Kitchen (*NBD,* 815) proposes two Egyptian etymologies for the Hebrew name. One is associated with the delta area of Lower (i.e., northern) Egypt, and the other with the "oasis" area W of the Nile. The former location has merit since in the genealogies the Naphtuhim are closely associated with the Pathrusim, probably to be identified with Upper (i.e., southern) Egypt. Rendsburg (1987) proposes an Egyptian original which reads "those of Ptah." This, he claims, refers to Memphis, headquarters of the worship of that Egyptian god (see *CAH*³ 1/2: 15–17, 52; Kitchen 1973: 187–94). This would locate the Naphtuhim somewhat south of the delta, in Middle Egypt.

The Aramaic Targum on Chronicles reads 1:11 as Pentaskinnai, from the Greek *Pentaschoinon.* This is located in the northeastern delta region of Egypt (*EncMiqr* 5: 905). While an Egyptian identification of the Naphtuhim is sure, the lack of more specific evidence does not allow us to determine the exact area occupied by them.

Bibliography

Kitchen, K. A. 1973. *The Third Intermediate Period in Egypt (1100–650 B.C.).* Warminster.

Rendsburg, G. 1987. Genesis 10:13–14: An Authentic Hebrew Tradition Concerning the Origin of the Philistines. *JNSL* 13: 89–96.

DAVID W. BAKER

NARCISSUS

NARCISSUS (PERSON) [Gk *Narkissos*]. In Rom 16:11, Paul sent greetings to "those of the people of Narcissus who are in the Lord," i.e., the Christians among the slaves or freed(wo)men of Narcissus. Narcissus himself does not receive greetings. Perhaps the Christian Narcissus had died or was absent from Rome (cf. Cranfield *Romans* ICC, 792), or more probably he was *not* a Christian. That only some of the servants of Narcissus' household were Christians supports the latter possibility. And Paul probably would have added some detail about Narcissus, as he did with the other Christians mentioned in Rom 16:3–13, if Narcissus had been a Christian.

The Christian slaves or freed(wo)men of Narcissus formed a house-church in Rome (Lampe *StadtrChr,* 302, 319). Paul mentioned four other groups in Romans 16 which evidently worshiped together: The "house-church" of Prisca and Aquila (v 5), "Asyncritus, Phlegon . . . and the brethren/sisters who are with them" (v 14), "Philologus, Julia . . . and all the saints who are with them" (v 15), and "the (Christians) of the people of Aristobulus" (v 10). The latter were slaves and freed(wo)men again. In addition, Jewish and pagan sources reflect that (freed) slaves of one master formed worship communities without the master belonging to their religion: The Jewish freed(wo)men of Agrippa, of Augustus, and of the *gens Volumnia* established three different synagogues in Rome, as did a group of former Herodian slaves (see the inscriptions in Lampe *StadtrChr,* 367). In the year 61 C.E., Cassius (in Tacitus *Ann.* 14.44) complained about those slaves in distinguished Roman households "who have different rituals, foreign religions." Looking from the pagan side, Cassius confirms Rom 16:10–11.

Since freedmen named Narcissus were numerous in Rome (Lampe *StadtrChr,* 136), it is superfluous to speculate whether Narcissus was the famous imperial freedman under Claudius (*CIL* 15: 7500) as is sometimes proposed. *Acts Pet.* 48:7; 49:15; 53:13; 61:8, 27 (2d century C.E.) portray Narcissus as a Roman presbyter owning a house where Christians met.

PETER LAMPE

NARD. See PERFUMES AND SPICES; FLORA.

NARRATIVE, COURT. See COURT NARRATIVE (2 SAMUEL 9–1 KINGS 2).

NARRATIVE, HEBREW. Narrative communicates meaning through the imitation of human life, the temporal ordering of human speech and action. It constructs a verbal world that centers on human characters, their relations, desires, and actions in time. Time is crucial for narrative. Unlike other kinds of discourse, e.g., lyric poetry, proverbs, or legal codes, which communicate through images, propositions, or admonitions, narrative is distinguished by plot, a sequence of connected action that leads, through varying degrees of dramatic intensity, to some sense of resolution. Narrative interrelates distinct events to form a coherent whole without extraneous incidents.

A. Narrative Portions of the Bible
B. Narrative and Genres
  1. Genres
  2. Narrative
C. Elements of Narrative
  1. Plot Structure
  2. Character
  3. Narrator's Point of View
  4. Language and Meaning
  5. Irony
  6. Reader's Point of View
D. Conclusion

A. Narrative Portions of the Bible

The bulk of the Hebrew Bible is narrative. The primary story extends from Genesis through 2 Kings. The plot is initiated by God, who attempts to establish and sustain a relationship of trust with humankind. A particular family is chosen and promised a land and nationhood, gifts which will come to represent God's pledge of commitment and of presence in the relationship. For its part, the divinely chosen family seeks to realize its vision of land and nationhood with, and sometimes without, God's assistance. God's desire for relationship and human desire for place and identity prove frequently incompatible and provide the ingredients of conflict in the overall story. Though the gifts are gained they are lost finally through the people's failure both to take seriously their own story and to respond to God's desire.

A second major narrative is the book of Chronicles, to which the books of Ezra and Nehemiah form a sequel. Prefaced by a genealogical compendium of Israel's ancestors prior to the monarchy, 1 and 2 Chronicles is an account of the kingdom of Judah from the death of Saul through the Exile and announcement of restoration. The heart of the story is an elaborate account of how King David established a united state, organized its bureaucracy, founded the temple, provided for its functionaries, and promoted the levitical priesthood. What follows is essentially a falling away from this perceived ideal. The narrative traverses the same period as 2 Samuel–2 Kings but presents a distinctive point of view, narrower in its focus and more obvious in its ideology. The two books that follow detail the rebuilding of Jerusalem and the temple and the attempt by both Ezra and Nehemiah to sustain the restored community as a theocratic state in the face of external and internal pressures.

Some of the prophetic books also include narrative, usually retelling the historical circumstances in which the prophet worked and prophesied. Material in Isaiah and Jeremiah virtually duplicates segments of 2 Kings. Other books contain a type of discourse marginally akin to narrative as such: visions and divine speeches often report series of events. Visions, however, often minimize temporality, and divine speeches offer more of a catalogue of events rather than a closely constructed plot in which tension rises and falls.

Of the remaining narratives, the books of Ruth and Jonah fit into the temporal scheme of the primary story, and further develop the theme of God's desire for relationship in ways that are both consonant and contrastive with the larger account. Esther and Daniel 1–6 continue Israel's story after the loss of the land. These narratives capture the crisis of the displaced people dealing with foreign rule. Esther relates the pressures upon national identity in an alien context and Daniel explores the limits of God's sovereignty and God's relationship to the rest of humankind. Of all biblical narrative, Job is the most temporally and geographically elusive. Its distinctiveness lies not only in its present form—a brief narrative framing an extensive poetic dialogue—but also in its interest in an individual whose nationality is obscure and whose relationship to Israel is not, on the surface of the story, of primary importance.

B. Narrative and Genres

Biblical scholars have for several hundred years focused their attention upon the way the narratives have come to be in their present form. They have attempted to recover from the Bible its original sources, written and oral, and to write a history of the development of biblical literature and its conventional literary forms for the purpose of reconstructing the history of Israel and Israelite religion. Despite some impressive early hypotheses, the findings of source analysis have proved mainly inconclusive. Even those critics more interested in the literary characteristics of the material have attended to questions of genre or form rather than to the inner workings of the stories themselves. But while definitions of conventional forms can be helpful, they cannot capture the complexity of meaning produced by biblical stories.

1. Genres. Form critics have designated a variety of genres in Hebrew narrative. The term "saga" has been frequently used of the ancestral narratives in Genesis; "legend" is sometimes used of the narratives about Moses in Exodus and Numbers, or about Elijah and Elisha in 1 and 2 Kings; the Joseph story in Genesis has been termed a "novella," as have the books of Esther, Jonah, and Ruth, and the story of King David's family found in 2 Samuel 9–20 and 1 Kings 1–2. Etiologies, or accounts of origins, are found at various places in Genesis–2 Kings. "Tale" is another term that has been used of shorter story units.

Often the labels are used to indicate some perceived relation to "history," though such relations are extremely difficult to determine. In the case of the primary story (Genesis–2 Kings), scholars have been readier to designate as "history writing" subject matter closer to the exilic period (6th century B.C.E.). A major exception has been the story of King David, often thought to be a reliable historical document from close to the time of David. On the other hand, the Chronicler's story, in part because of its more obvious ideological bias and its later composition, has long been viewed as historically less reliable than Samuel and Kings, despite the fact that it presents itself as "history writing" no less than those books.

It would appear that some useful distinction might be made in terms of "imaginative" genres (saga, legend, novella, etc.) and "recording" genres (anecdote, annalistic extract, memoirs, history writing, etc.). In practice, however, such distinctions are not easily sustained. The difference between fiction and nonfiction, for example, is not always clear, especially where ancient "history-like" writing is concerned. Even where historical records are involved, once events are selected and ordered by an author or editor, particularly when serving a distinctive ideology, a distance is established between the narrative world and the world of "what actually happened." In short, then, genre labels, especially those which are conceived in terms of historiographical purpose, are of limited use.

2. Narrative. Nevertheless, an important distinction can be made between "dialogic" and "monologic" narrative. The former is represented by much of the primary story together with most of the shorter stories such as Ruth, Jonah, Daniel 1–6, and Esther. It is more open to multiple interpretations, entertains within it several ideological points of view or "voices," often in tension, and is characterized by restraint on the part of the narrator and a premium on "showing" through characters' actions and dialogue rather than simply "telling." The latter is represented above all by Chronicles, Ezra, and Nehemiah. It has more in common with the rhetoric of public persuasion such as the political speech or the sermon, tends to elicit a narrower range of responses from the reader, minimizes tensions and ideological plurality, and is characterized by a premium on "telling" through extended monologues from both narrator and characters.

C. Elements of Narrative

If the narrative is thought of as the narrator's construction, what the reader does may be thought of as reconstruction. Plot is the organizing force or principle through which narrative meaning is communicated. But not only is meaning expressed on a time continuum, it is conveyed through different and incomplete sources—the voice of the narrator, the speech and actions of characters. Presented with fragmented but potentially coherent information, the reader must observe, order, and amplify in order to forge meaning.

1. Plot Structure. A reader comprehends a plot both in terms of the simple sequence of action and in terms of the rise and fall of dramatic tension. How the reader discerns the dramatic structure of the plot will determine what is most significant in the sequence. Dramatic structure can be charted with three basic categories. The *exposition* sets up the story world and initiates the main series of events. The situation presented in an exposition is usually characterized by incompleteness, disorder, or unfulfilled desire, from which develops a subsequent *conflict.* The conflict, which may be internal to a character or an external one, between characters, moves through various phases until a climax gives way to some degree of *resolution.* Thus the story of the succession to David in 1 Kings 1–2 establishes that the king is old and senile and that the oldest son, Adonijah, desires and expects to succeed to the throne. Conflict materializes in a rival party backing Solomon, and a climax is reached when Nathan and Bathsheba make a successful preemptive strike on Solomon's behalf. The king yields the throne to the younger son. Resolution follows in stages with the king's death and the eventual execution of Adonijah.

In most cases, however, the plot structure may appear to be more complex. For example, there may be several points of intensity or climax. Sometimes this will depend on which character's point of view is perceived to be predominant in the narrative as a whole. Thus in the story of Jephthah in Judges 10–12, the major climax of the story, from the Israelites' point of view, is Jephthah's victory over the oppressing Ammonites (11:32–33). That, too, could be taken to be the climax, from Jephthah's point of view, if his initial predicament is his expulsion from Gilead. On the other hand, the story of a Jephthah early deprived of a family might be seen to reach a climax in his decision to sacrifice his only child. When the tragic role of the daughter predominates, however, the climax may perhaps lie in her acceptance of death as her lot.

Another factor that complicates biblical plots is the frequency with which narratives are constructed from a number of seemingly separate plots. This factor has often led scholars to postulate the presence of originally independent sources in what they see as a composite rather than unitary final narrative. In terms of the final form, however, irrespective of their origins, these plots usually function as subplots or episodes within a larger plot. Thus the stories of Abraham and Sarah in Egypt (Genesis 12), Sarah and Hagar (Genesis 16 and 21), or the wooing of Rebekah (Genesis 24) are all episodes within the larger story of promised land and nationhood. In the family story of Jacob (see Genesis 37:2) the story of Judah and Tamar becomes a subplot within a larger plot which deals primarily with Joseph but in which, in the fraternal struggle for ascendancy, Judah also plays a prominent role.

In some cases, as with various stories of the ancestors in Genesis, the episodes are not causally connected, but rather linked through association. Genesis 26, Isaac's visit to Gerar, has no immediate connection with the preceding incident involving Jacob and Esau's birthright. Nor does it flow into the next episode which reverts to the rivalry between the brothers. Yet it fits into the larger Genesis story, first, by associating Isaac's behavior with that of his father in Abraham's visits to Egypt and Gerar (chapters 12 and 20) and, second, by foreshadowing, through motifs of deception and strife, the coming struggle within Isaac's own family. In other cases, as with the last chapters of Judges or 2 Samuel (or likewise the fight between Ephraim and Gilead at the end of the Jephthah story), the episodes appear as a kind of coda or epilogue which invites the reader to reflect back on what has preceded and to discover thematic and often ironic associations.

Frequently in the larger narrative complexes the subplots and plot episodes center upon one or two main characters as hero or heroine. When the larger plot is considered, however, the main protagonist (apart from God) generally turns out to be a corporate character such as the ancestral family or the people of Israel. As the complex story unfolds the reader, who keeps shifting focus between the inner and outer plots, maintains a more balanced perception of the whole.

2. Character. A reader's reconstruction of character involves observing, assessing, comparing and contrasting what the characters do, what they say, what the narrator says about them, how other characters respond to them and what other characters say about them. We may usually take what the narrator says about a character as a serious guide to aid us in our understanding of a character, but the narrator seldom tells us all we want to know. Rarely does the narrator describe external appearances or present internal thoughts and emotions. Moreover, what other characters say cannot always be relied upon since characters in biblical narrative, mimicking real life, convey only limited human viewpoints, frequently prejudiced and self-serving. In her speech to David in 1 Samuel 25, Abigail heaps opprobrium upon her husband, Nabal, and pictures David as the angel of God, able only to do good. Yet we may be justified in suspecting her of exaggerating once we have noticed, first, the dubious nature of David's unsolicited "protection" of Nabal's flocks, second, the haste and vehemence with which David orders reprisals against the whole of Nabal's household, and, third, the fact that Abigail is desperately seeking to placate David, even to the extent of offering discreetly to join him ("And when the Lord has dealt well with my lord, then remember your handmaid," v 31).

The relationship of character to plot is not simply that characters enact plot. Desire and ambition motivate the movements and changes that constitute the plot. And desire and ambition are forces within the characters who people the story. To understand the complexity of the character we need to determine the desire. Why does Abram try to pass his wife off as his sister in Genesis 12? After he receives God's promise of land, nationhood, and blessing, Abram sets out to find this land seemingly without a word to his wife Sarai about the divine promise. When famine strikes, he eagerly leaves the land of promise to go to Egypt where he, afraid for his life, presents Sarai as his sister rather than his spouse. Pharaoh takes her as his concubine, paying in exchange for her a rather handsome sum to the man Abram. The reader is left pondering Abram's motivation. Is fear only part of what inspires him to pawn his wife? Does she not become the surety for "blessing"? Did he ever intend for the aged and barren Sarai to share in the divine promise at all? Might "nationhood" require the womb of a younger woman? One of the maidservants provided by Pharaoh, perhaps?

3. Narrator's Point of View. Narrative information is presented through the point of view of the narrator and the characters. These perspectives in conjunction with that of the reader form a system of relationships. The reader's point of view affects and is affected by the relation between the perspectives of the narrator and the characters. The narrator's point of view can be detected in direct narration, comment, and explanation. Alternatively, the narrator may step aside and allow the characters to speak for themselves and so to convey their own point of view. The most common error readers of biblical narratives make is confusing a character's point of view with that of the narrator. This can be avoided by carefully comparing and contrasting what the narrator tells the reader directly with what the characters say.

Take, for example, the exposition of the story of Judah and Tamar in Genesis 38. Judah's sons die, the narrator tells us, because they "do evil in the sight of the Lord." When dealing with their widow, Tamar, who is entitled to marry his third son, Shelah, Judah tells her to return to her father's house. Shelah, he says to her, is not old enough to marry yet, but to himself he says, "lest he, too, die like his brothers." It is clear from this inner speech that he views Tamar to be a jinx, whereas the narrator has made it clear that the deaths are God's responsibility. This distinction between point of view assists the reader in evaluating both the characters, Judah and Tamar. First, the reader is guided to accept the narrator's assessment and to recognize Tamar's innocence. Second, the discrepancy invites the reader to consider Judah's readiness to blame the woman rather than see any fault in his sons. His double standard will become doubly apparent in his subsequent rush to condemn her for a second time when she is found to be pregnant. Ironically, where he sees harlotry, the reader sees radical responsibility. The harlotry is his own.

4. Language and Meaning. All narrative information is, of course, communicated through the medium of language. The language of narrative is often multivalent, carrying more than one meaning at once. There are several different types of verbal ambiguity. Sometimes two or more meanings of unequal force are present in a single word or phrase. A careful reader recognizes the play of both meanings off one another, while the characters usually perceive only one meaning to be intended. In the Judah and Tamar story cited above, Tamar, disguised as a prostitute, bargains with an overly eager Judah for his cord, seal, and staff as a pledge of payment for her sexual services. Judah understands her to be referring to the staff that he is carrying in his hand and he willingly leaves it along with the other articles in her care. An astute reader might note, however, that the Hebrew word for staff also means "tribe" and might muse over the fact that Tamar, in the course of the story, indeed controls the future of Judah's tribe. The phallic shape of the staff also allows sexual connotations to play in an already sexually loaded story. Tamar is essentially bartering for a phallus that will bring her children and security, and with Judah's staff in her possession, she is able to emasculate him publicly when he attempts to have her burned for harlotry.

When meanings of equal force are carried in the same word or phrase, the ambiguity may be recognized by the characters as well as by the reader. The significance of the ambiguity is, nevertheless, usually left to the reader to determine. For example, in Ruth 2 Naomi exclaims upon seeing the grain Ruth has gleaned from Boaz's field, "Blessed be he by Yahweh whose kindness has not forsaken the living or the dead!" It is unclear from the construction whether Naomi is referring to the kindness of Yahweh or that of Boaz. For the reader, this ambiguity underscores a major theological point found in the book of Ruth, namely, that divine and human action are often difficult to distinguish.

When savoring the language of narrative, the reader must take seriously variation in expression. A change in wording can often indicate a different point of view (as indicated above), offer insight into a character's values, or reveal a character's attempt to manipulate others in the story world. To cite another example from Genesis 38, we should not miss there a subtle change of term for the role played by Tamar. When Judah sees her alongside the road, he considers her to be a common prostitute *(zônāh)*. His subsequent dealings with her reflect this assumption. When he sends payment to her by the hand of his friend the Adullamite, the search is made for a *qĕdēšāh*, a "holy woman," a person who engages in sexual activity as cultic ritual. The shift in terminology points again to Judah's double standard. For public consumption he portrays his dealings under a more socially acceptable label.

An example of a deliberate variation in a situation involving persuasion can be found in Judges 19–20. The Levite, having handed over his concubine to a mob intent on raping him, equivocates on the details when he seeks to incite the congregation of Israel to take revenge on Gibeah. He avoids describing himself as the object of homosexual desire; instead, he claims that the men wanted to kill him. He avoids implicating himself in the woman's death; instead, he simply states that she was raped and is dead. His speech reduces a situation of complex culpability to a simple scenario of himself as victim with the entire male population of Gibeah at fault. If his view of the woman as a disposable possession was not already apparent to the reader in the preceding scene, it should be by the end of his speech.

5. Irony. When a narrative situation suggests more levels of meaning than the characters involved can recognize, irony is present. Irony is incongruity of knowledge. Characters think they know what they are doing when in fact they may be doing something rather different. They think they understand the way the world is when in fact it is different. Sometimes the discrepancy of knowledge is contained within the story world, so that some characters know more than others. Both Joab and David are in a position to savor the irony of Uriah carrying the letter which is also his warrant of execution (2 Samuel 11). In such cases the reader is also aware of the irony. At other times the reader alone is in a position to appreciate the irony. To Joab, at the news of Uriah's death, David sends the message, "Do not let this thing be evil in your sight, for the sword devours now one and now another." But to the reader the narrator observes a few verses later, "But the thing that David had done was evil in the sight of Yahweh."

Irony as an ingredient or mode of narration varies within the Hebrew Bible. Genesis–2 Kings is particularly rich in irony, Chronicles much less so. That difference is typical of the difference between dialogic and monologic narrative.

Irony becomes particularly significant as an interpretive strategy when the irony is played out between narrator and reader. "In those days there was no king in Israel; every man did what was right in his own eyes" observes the narrator several times amid the accounts of chaotic self-interest at the end of Judges. Are we to read this as a recommendation of kingship as a cure of ills? But if we do, we must ignore both the story of Abimelech (Judges 9) and most of the resulting history of the monarchy in Samuel and Kings where kingship seems no major barrier to the further exercise of corrosive self-interest.

Likewise we are told in the book of Kings of David's and Solomon's rectitude in such positive terms that we may be led to see in them some absolute standards of behavior. But one key word, "except," creeps into the evaluative statement. David "did what was right in the eyes of the Lord and did not turn aside from anything that he commanded him all the days of his life, except in the matter of Uriah the Hittite" (1 Kings 15:5). That "except" can have a powerful effect on the way we read the sentence if we recognize the matter of Uriah the Hittite to be the pivotal episode in David's life, representing a peak of grasping for whatever was good in his own eyes. Likewise we may be impressed by an apparent encomium of Solomon, who "loved the Lord, walking in the statutes of David his father; except he sacrificed and burnt incense at the high places" (1 Kings 3:3). By the end of his story we are obliged to consider whether that comment might not be ironical. "He had seven hundred wives, princes, and three hundred concubines; and his wives turned away his heart [from God] . . . [he] built a high place for Chemosh the abomination of Moab . . . and so he did for all his foreign wives, who burned incense and sacrificed to their gods" (1 Kings 11:3, 7, 8).

6. Reader's Point of View. Irony often is produced through setting up a conflict of facts or values as in the cases just mentioned. Awareness of irony is then a matter of point of view. Indeed play with the reader's point of view is characteristic of much Hebrew narrative and not just in connection with irony. A common way of effecting this is through allusion to other stories, episodes or characters.

The exposition of the book of Ruth describes a situation structurally reminiscent of the exposition to the Judah and Tamar story in Genesis 38. There is separation from family/homeland, a sojourning elsewhere, marriages to foreign women, deaths of two sons and spouse. In the Genesis story, as noted above, Judah suspects Tamar, the Canaanite widow of his two eldest sons, to be the cause of their death. Without openly accusing her, however, he urges her to return to her father's house. Naomi's attitude toward her daughters-in-law is not openly declared by the narrator but she, too, urges return—each to her mother's house. Struck by the analogy between the stories, a reader might well wonder whether Ruth has become to Naomi what Tamar was to Judah, namely, an albatross around her neck. The reader seeking to understand Naomi's motives is thus prompted to scrutinize her speech and actions with a degree of suspicion instead of taking them simply at face value.

Likewise awareness of the symbolic value of Moab in other stories—the story of Lot and his daughters (Genesis 19) and the sin of Baal-Peor (Numbers 25)—enables a reader of Ruth to align his or her point of view for a moment with that of the Israelites in the story or its implied ancient Israelite reader and detect racial and religious prejudice against Moab. Finally, the depiction of Naomi sending Ruth down to the threshing floor at night to lie with Boaz calls to mind not only the way Laban tricked Jacob into marrying Leah rather than Rachel (Genesis 29) but again the deception of Lot by his daughters and Judah by Tamar. Again, the allusions inculcate suspicion on the part of the reader so that entrapment comes into focus as an explanation for an enigmatic episode.

Sometimes allusion is effected by precise word-choice as well as structure. Jephthah (Judges 11) arriving home after victory and a vow that he will sacrifice the first to meet him encounters his daughter, who has gone out "with timbrels and dancing." The narrator's insistence that she was "an only child *(yĕḥîdâ)*—he had, apart from her, no son or daughter" recalls God's speech to Abraham in Genesis 22: "Take your son, your only child *(yāḥîd)* Isaac, whom you love . . . and offer him as a burnt offering. . . ." Later, in 1 Samuel 14, analogy brings into play a third text, Saul's threat to execute his son Jonathan for violating an oath that Saul had made on behalf of the army.

The parallels help to enlarge a reader's perspective. Why is it that the sons are spared, the daughter killed? Is this the priority of patriarchy? Or, to put it another way, why is the daughter so alone? The angel reaches out to stay Abraham's knife, the people stand between Saul and Jonathan, but no one intervenes on the daughter's behalf, though female companions appear to weep for her virginity upon the mountains. Another narrative analogy reinforces the point: Miriam meets a returning victorious Moses (Exodus 15) accompanied by "all the women . . . with timbrels and dancing." With timbrels and dancing, too, "the women" greet the victorious Saul and David on their return home (1 Samuel 18). By contrast the daughter stands before her father isolated, apparently bound to his will, a patriarchal victim. In turn, her isolation points back to Jephthah's own experience of familial (especially patriarchal) rejection. What we see is a vicious cycle, a cycle of abuse. Ironically, the rejected child, whose desire is for acceptance and security, destroys his own child. Human failure ensures that oppression accompanies Israel's deliverance from oppression.

D. Conclusion

The narrative of the Hebrew Bible is multifaceted and richly rewards the careful and imaginative reader. There are many ways of reading that have found favor with the communities that have treasured these stories. No account can do justice to them all. Rather we have selected some features of the text and pointed to ways of response that both draw upon contemporary understanding of how literature is read and also contribute to the interpretive traditions of the great communities of the book.

Bibliography

Alter, R. 1981. *The Art of Biblical Narrative.* New York.

Berlin, A. 1983. *Poetics and Interpretation of Biblical Narrative.* Sheffield.

Gunn, D. M., and Fewell, D. N. 1989. *Old Testament Narrative.* Oxford.

Sternberg, M. 1985. *The Poetics of Biblical Narrative.* Bloomington, IN.

Trible, P. 1984. *Texts of Terror.* Philadelphia.

Danna Nolan Fewell
David M. Gunn

NAṢBEH, TELL EN- (M.R. 170143). A site situated ca. 12 km N of Jerusalem along the main road which leads from Jerusalem to Shechem/Samaria. The tell is generally identified with biblical MIZPAH of Benjamin (Josh 18:26; cf. 1 Sam 7:5–11); some reject this identification, however, preferring to identify Nabi Samwil (ca. 8 km NW of Jerusalem) with Mizpah. Albright (1948: 203) has alternatively suggested that Tell en-Naṣbeh may have been ancient Ataroth-addar.

A. The Site

Tell en-Naṣbeh lies on a spur (ca. 770–784 m above sea level) which connects with a mountain on the N. Deep valleys surround the site on the other three sides. A fortification wall laid out in a large oval, which measures ca. 265 m N–S and 160 m E–W, encompasses ca. 32 dunams. In addition to its strategic importance along the main N–S central hills road, after the division of the kingdom it became particularly important as a border defensive town.

B. History of the Site

After an initial occupation with a small settlement in the EB, the site was deserted until it was reoccupied ca. 1100 B.C., apparently by the Israelites. The city was the scene of the rallying of Israel's forces in retaliation against Benjamin for the rape-murder of the Levite's concubine (Judges 20). It later was part of the circuit of the prophet Samuel (1 Sam 7:16–17). Following the division of the kingdom, Asa apparently fortified the site in an effort to secure his N border against Israel (1 Kgs 15:17–22; see also below). After Nebuchadnezzar destroyed Jerusalem and appointed Gedaliah governor of Judah, Gedaliah established his residence at Mizpah, where he was later assassinated (2 Kgs 25:22–25; Jeremiah 40–41).

After the Exile, the city became the capital of the district (Neh 3:7), and during the Maccabean revolt, it was where Judas mustered his army against Gorgias (1 Macc 3:46).

C. The Excavations

1. Chalcolithic–EB. The only evidence for these periods is occasional sherds on the site and in caves. The caves, most of which are around the base of the tell, were primarily used for burial, but there is evidence of occupation in some.

2. Iron Age I. The tell was unoccupied through the EB, MB, and LB, but was reoccupied in the 11th century B.C. The excavations have revealed part of the fortification wall, which averaged only about a meter thick, into which were integrated at least two towers. Parts of the domestic area have also been discovered.

3. Iron Age II. a. The Fortification System. An offset-inset defensive wall was traced around the entire 660 m circuit of the tell. Nine or ten towers were incorporated into the system. The outer face of the wall stood ca. 12–14 m above the surface, while the interior stood 8–10 m high. The wall averaged 4 m thick, and the towers added another 2–5 m. The towers were defended with glacis, while several sections of the wall had the added strengthening and protection of buttresses, retaining walls, or glacis. The wall was built of fieldstones, which were only slightly dressed. They were bonded with clay mortar and chinked with small stones. A thick plaster covered the lower sections of the wall (ca. 4.5–5 m) to prevent scaling by the enemy. Beyond the wall was a fosse, 2–5 m wide, which is the only fosse found at an Iron Age site in Palestine.

A peculiar feature of the fortifications is the inconsistent quality of construction. It appears that it was built in sections (indeed some sections are not connected to each other). Perhaps the wall was built by groups of corvée laborers, who were required to meet certain work quotas. Such an inference may be corroborated in the biblical texts describing the strife between Baasha and Asa. Upon Baasha's retreat from Judah's border, "King Asa made a proclamation to all Judah, . . . and they carried away the stones of Ramah and its timber, with which Baasha had been building; and with them King Asa built Geba of Benjamin and Mizpah" (1 Kgs 15:22).

The city gate at Tell en-Naṣbeh is one of the best preserved from ancient Palestine. It was a two-entry gate with an opening 4.2 m wide which was apparently 2.2 m high. Benches lined the cubicles between the piers and along the wall and gate just outside the first set of piers. Sockets in the threshold of the outer piers indicate that two pivoting doors were used to close the gate. The doorjamb of the E pier still preserved the slot in which the bar that locked the gate would be stowed when the gate was open, and the W pier retained the hole in which the end of the bar was placed to lock the door. The gate design is unusual in that it is not a bent right or left access, but is a direct access, which still necessitated an entry route parallel to the city wall.

A large open square (8 by 9 m) stood immediately in front of the gate and another was just inside. A covered channel drained both the squares and the city gate.

Near one of the city gates was a stone pillar, a *maṣṣebah,* like the one (with a basin nearby) found in the town gate of Tell en-Farah (N)—these both certainly had some cultic function. See TIRZAH (PLACE).

The discovery of numerous *lmlk* royal store jar handles testifies to the alignment of the city with Judah, at least in the late 8th century B.C. In contrast, the excavations at Bethel, just 5 km to the N, yielded no such seal impressions.

b. Domestic Remains. About a third of the area within the wall has eroded away completely to bedrock. Because of the absence of cisterns, it would appear that this area was not densely developed, since the presence of cisterns is common in developed areas. From the concentration of houses, it appears that the city may have accommodated a population of ca. 1,000. With few exceptions, no houses were built against the wall, but this area served as a street encircling the houses. Most of the houses of the town were very poorly built; however, some were fairly well-built with either monolithic or stacked drums, which supported the ceiling. The presence of strong pillars and stairs implies that some of the buildings had upper stories.

Three examples of four-room houses were found built against the wall, and separated from the main group of buildings—these may have had a public function of some kind and perhaps were storehouses (for the collection of taxes?) or military structures.

Water was supplied to the site mainly by cisterns, fifty-three of which were discovered on the site. A seasonal spring is on the SE edge of the mound, but it is often dried up during the summer months.

c. Small Finds. Tell en-Naṣbeh has yielded one of the most complete collections of Israelite pottery in the country. Epigraphic finds included seven incised potsherds, various stone weights, and numerous seal impressions, among which were 68 *lmlk* seal impressions and several private seals, the most beautiful of which is the seal of "Jaazaniah servant of the king."

Badè, the original excavator of this site, suggested that Jaazaniah was one of Gedaliah's officials and that he should be identified with Jaazaniah, the captain of the forces mentioned in both 2 Kgs 25:23 and Jer 40:8, but his identification is not absolutely certain. The seal depicts the representation of a cock, the earliest known representation of this bird in Palestine. Other finds include a short dedicatory inscription in Neo-Babylonian, a cylinder seal, and numerous scarabs.

Meager building remains testify to some occupation during the Persian period, and fragments of Attic pottery (ca. 540–420 B.C.) have been found on the site. Among other imported ware was an E Greek Clazomenian vessel, unique in Palestine, dating from 540–530 B.C. From this period numerous stamped seal impressions were found on pottery reading *Yhd* and *Yršlm* and about thirty reading *Mṣh,* which some have suggested is an abbreviation for Mizpah, but this is not convincing. In the inscription deciphered by N. Avigad, the name is written in full, *Mwṣh,* which probably refers to Moṣah, a locality W of Jerusalem.

Wampler dated the Persian period settlement to 587–400 B.C.; he believed the site was abandoned after that time. However, Albright and G. E. Wright have contended that occupation continued at Tell en-Naṣbeh during the first half of the 4th century B.C. Evidence in the form of surface and tomb finds (i.e., sherds and coins) testifies to settlements during the Hellenistic, Roman, and Byzantine periods at nearby Kh. ʿAtara and Kh. Shweikha.

Bibliography

Albright, W. F. 1948. Review of McCown et al. 1947. *JNES* 7/3: 202–5.

Avigad, N. 1958. New Light on the MṢH Seal Impressions. *IEJ* 8: 113–19.

Branigan, K. 1968. The Four Room Buildings of Tell en-Naṣbeh. *IEJ* 16: 206–8.

Cross, F. M. 1969. Two Notes on Palestinian Inscriptions of the Persian Age. *BASOR* 193: 19–24.

Dothan, T. 1982. *Philistines and Their Material Culture.* Jerusalem.

Malamat, A. 1950. The Last Wars of the Kingdom of Judah. *JNES* 9: 218–27.

McCown, C. C. et al. 1947. *Tell en-Naṣbeh.* Vols. 1–2. Berkeley and New Haven.

Stern, E. 1987. *Material Culture of the Land of the Bible in the Persian Period, 538–332 B.C.* Warminster.
Tufnell, O. 1948. Review of McCown et al. 1947. *PEQ* 80: 145–50.
Wampler, J. C. 1941. Three Cistern Groups from Tell en-Nasbeh. *BASOR* 82: 25–43.
Wright, G. E. 1948. Review of McCown et al. 1947. *AJA* 52: 470–72.

M. BROSHI

NASI. See SANHEDRIN.

NATHAN (PERSON) [Heb *nātān*]. Var. NETHANIAH. **1.** A son of David born in Jerusalem to Bath-shua (Bathsheba) (2 Sam 5:14; 1 Chr 3:5; 14:4). Three full brothers of Nathan's are listed: Shammua (Shimea), Shobab, and Solomon. In addition, David had six sons born previously in Hebron to six different wives, and nine born in Jerusalem to unnamed wives, as well as many sons born to his concubines in Jerusalem.

The genealogy of Jesus in Luke 3 includes this Nathan as the son of David through whom Jesus was descended (v 31). Matthew's genealogy traces it through Solomon (1:6). The two genealogies thus diverge at this point, and they converge again (briefly) with Shealtiel and Zerubbabel (Matt 1:12; Luke 3:27). Many solutions have been proposed to the problem of the divergences between these genealogies (see Johnson 1969: 139–252). The one preferred here sees the Matthean genealogy as giving Jesus' legal lineage; the Lukan, his natural lineage (Marshall *Luke* NIGTC, 157–62), but the definitive solution undoubtedly has not yet been advanced.

This Nathan is also mentioned in Zech 12:12, an eschatological passage that lists several houses (i.e., families) that will mourn a messianic figure who has been pierced. Four families are mentioned by name (vv 12–13): David's and his son Nathan's, and Levi's and his grandson Shimei's, representing royal and priestly (i.e., civil and religious) authority, respectively.

Zech 12:12 conceivably could be referring instead to the prophet Nathan (see Mitchell *Haggai and Zechariah* ICC, 333). If so, then royal, prophetic, and priestly traditions all are represented in vv 12–13, and the Shimei there could be Saul's descendant, representing the (failed) dynasty of the first king. This seems less likely than the first proposal, however.

2. A prophet in David's time who figured prominently in events at three critical junctures in David's life: (1) he delivered the dynastic promise to David; (2) he confronted David about his sin involving Bathsheba and Uriah; and (3) he intervened on Solomon's behalf in the struggle for succession to David's throne.

Nathan first appears, with no introduction and no pedigree, in the crucial and much discussed 2 Samuel 7 (paralleled at 1 Chronicles 17), in which he delivers to David the important promise of a perpetual dynasty (see Kaiser 1974; McCarter *2 Samuel* AB, 190–231). His first word to David, delivered on his own authority (v 3)—that David should build a house for YHWH—was overruled by YHWH himself. He appeared to Nathan in a night vision (vv 4, 17), with his message about David's dynasty and his son's place in building YHWH's house. Nathan then delivered this message via the classical prophetic formula ("Thus says YHWH"—vv 5, 17), and David responded with a prayer of thanksgiving (vv 18–29).

Nathan's greatest moments came in his confrontation with David after David's two great sins (2 Samuel 12). Here, he boldly and courageously accused the king of gross sin. He used a fictional legal case to do this, at which David became incensed at the injustice perpetrated (vv 1–6). Nathan dramatically pointed out that David himself was the wrongdoer (vv 7–9), and pronounced a sentence (vv 10–12). (Nathan appears in this role in the superscription to Psalm 51.) David immediately repented, and Nathan pronounced forgiveness, but declared that the child born of the adulterous affair would die (vv 13–14). After this happened, David and Bathsheba were blessed with another son, Solomon, and Nathan was the bearer of a message of comfort to them at this time (vv 24–25).

Nathan next appears as Bathsheba's and Solomon's ally in the struggle for succession to the senile David's throne (1 Kings 1). He was excluded, along with several other officials, from Adonijah's installment as king (vv 7–10), and he helped Bathsheba plan a strategy for having Solomon installed (vv 11–14). Both of them appeared before David, reminding him of a promise he apparently had made to make Solomon king (vv 13, 17, 30). In response, David authorized Solomon's installation as king (vv 28–37); consequently, Nathan and Zadok the priest anointed Solomon king (v 45), and Adonijah was displaced (vv 41–53).

Nathan appears in these texts (especially the first two) as a court prophet with free access to the king, yet as one who spoke with the authority and boldness of the classical prophets of the 8th century and later. He certainly does not appear as beholden to the king in the way the 400 court prophets that Ahab consulted do (1 Kings 22). He also appears as a historian of sorts: the "Chronicles of Nathan the Prophet" are mentioned in 1 Chr 29:29 and 2 Chr 9:29 as being among the historical records for the reigns of David and Solomon. His prophetic authority appears again later, when Hezekiah installed Levites with musical instruments in the temple, according to YHWH's command through "David and Gad the king's seer and Nathan the prophet" (2 Chr 29:25). He also was likely the Nathan of 1 Kgs 4:5 (see 4 below).

3. The father of Igal, who was one of David's select group of thirty mighty men (2 Sam 23:36). He was from Zobah, a region N of Dan. In 1 Chronicles, he is listed as the brother of Joel, rather than as the father of Igal (11:38). McCarter (*2 Samuel* AB, 494–95), emending the verse in Samuel at several points, based upon OG readings and the parallel in 1 Chr 11:38, reads it as follows: "Igal son of Nathan, the commander of the army of the Hagrites."

4. The father of two of King Solomon's officials: Azariah, who was over the district prefects, and Zabud, a priest and the "king's friend" (1 Kgs 4:5). It is impossible to tell whether this Nathan is David's son (see 1 above), or the prophet (see 2 above), or someone else; most scholars see him as either of the first two. Of these, it would appear more plausible that he was the prophet, given (1) the positive role the prophet played in Solomon's accession;

and the facts that (2) Solomon may have been loath to give a brother's (and possible rival's) sons high positions in his administration, and (3) his son Zabud was the "king's friend," an unlikely title for a nephew.

5. The son of Attai and father of Zabad (1 Chr 2:36). His name is found in a lengthy Judahite genealogy (2:3–4:23), specifically, among the descendants of Jerahmeel, son of Hezron (2:25–41). His grandfather was an Egyptian slave, to whom Sheshan gave one of his daughters in marriage, since he had no sons (2:34–35).

6. One of the "leading men" sent by Ezra to Iddo and others at Casiphia (a place otherwise unknown), to ask him to provide Levites for Ezra to perform religious services (Ezra 8:16; 1 Esdr 8:44). Thirty-eight Levites were provided, along with 220 temple servants to attend them (Ezra 8:18–20). This Nathan may have been the same one mentioned in Ezra 10:39, a son of Binnui (MT Bani), one of those who put away their foreign wives and children during the reforms of Ezra (cf. the variant Nethaniah in 1 Esdr 9:34).

Bibliography

Johnson, M. D. 1969. *The Purpose of the Biblical Genealogies.* Cambridge.

Kaiser, W. C., Jr. 1974. The Blessing of David: The Charter of Humanity. Pp. 298–318 in *The Law and the Prophets,* ed. J. H. Skilton. Nutley, NJ.

DAVID M. HOWARD, JR.

NATHAN-MELECH (PERSON) [Heb *nĕtan-melek*]. A chamberlain under Josiah, king of Judah (2 Kgs 23:11). Josiah removed the horses dedicated to Šamaš, the sungod, which were near the chambers of Nathan-melech, as part of his purge of the Jerusalem cult. Nathan-melech is called a *sārîs,* often translated "eunuch," but the term need not be understood in the literal sense. Though similar to the Arabic root *sarisa,* meaning "to be impotent," the term is actually an Aramaic loanword of Akkadian origin *(ša rēši),* which means "he who is at the head (of the king)." The exact status of a *sārîs* is difficult to determine, for the term is given to officials of various standing in the court (Gen 37:36; 1 Kgs 22:9; 2 Kgs 18:17; 20:18; 25:19). The name "Nathan-melech" means "the King has given." It is a theophoric name declaring that the child has been given *(ntn)* by the deity *(mlk).* Melech is not the name of a deity, but a title (king) and may refer to Yahweh as King. However, it is also possible that it refers to Molech, whose worship is mentioned in the Hebrew Scriptures (1 Kgs 11:7; 2 Kgs 23:10; Jer 32:35) or to the Ammonite deity, Milcom (1 Kgs 11:33; Jer 49:1, probably to be identified with Molech). For further discussion see Gray *Kings* OTL; and *IPN.*

PAULINE A. VIVIANO

NATHANAEL (PERSON) [Gk *Nathanael*]. **1.** A priest from the line of Pashhur, required by Ezra to dismiss his foreign wife (1 Esdr 9:22).

2. A relative of the fictional Judith, identified in the opening genealogy of the book's second half (Jdt 8:1). Designed to provide the book's heroine with an exemplary Jewish heritage, there is little point in treating the genealogy, and the reference to Nathanael in particular, as historical (Enslin 1972: 109–10; Lamparter 1972: 161; Zenger 1981: 434). In this case, as in others, the names have been drawn from other biblical texts (cf. Neh 12:21; see Zenger 1981: 485).

Bibliography

Enslin, M. 1972. *The Book of Judith.* Jewish Apocryphal Literature. Leiden.

Lamparter, H. 1972. *Die Apokryphen II: Weisheit Salamos, Tobias, Judith, Baruch.* BAT 25/2. Stuttgart.

Zenger, E. 1981. *Historische und legendarische Erzählungen Das Buch Judith.* JSHRZ 1/6. Gütersloh.

FREDERICK W. SCHMIDT

3. A disciple of Jesus from Cana in Galilee (John 1:45–51; 21:2). Nathanael was brought to Jesus by Philip, who confessed Jesus to be "him of whom Moses in the law and also the prophets wrote, Jesus of Nazareth, the son of Joseph." The testimony, apparently alluding to Deut 18:15, 18, identified Jesus as the prophetic figure expected by some circles within 1st-century Judaism. Philip's testimony was met with disbelief by Nathanael, who responded, "Can anything good come out of Nazareth?" His disbelief was apparently based on the scriptural lore that neither the awaited prophet nor the Messiah would have Galilean origins (John 7:40–44).

The rejoinder identifies Nathanael as a serious student of the scriptures, a trait confirmed by the evangelist's description of him as having been seated under a fig tree prior to Philip's invitation. In rabbinic tradition, fig trees were frequently cited as appropriate locales for teachers to discuss the meaning of the scriptures with their students (Str-B 2. 371). Further indications of Nathanael's scriptural competency are to be found in his use of "Rabbi" to address Jesus and the allusion to Jacob's vision at Bethel (Gen 28:12) at the conclusion of Jesus' dialogue with him.

In the encounter between Jesus and Nathanael, Jesus enigmatically proclaims Nathanael to be a true Israelite and wins his adherence by a demonstration of his superhuman knowledge. As is frequently the case in the fourth gospel, those who come to faith in Jesus because of his superhuman power or knowledge express their faith in a profound christological statement. Nathanael professed Jesus to be the Messiah, "You are the Son of God! You are the King of Israel!"

Nathanael, the true Israelite, is then promised a vision of the Son of Man by Jesus (John 1:51). The verse containing the promise was most probably an originally independent unit of material, appended to the story of Nathanael by the evangelist. In his gospel, it serves to identify Nathanael as a representative disciple (cf. the plural, "you will see") to whom the vision of the Son of Man is promised. Seeing Jesus is characteristic of faith and discipleship in the fourth gospel (John 1:39).

In the promise of the vision of the Son of Man, Jesus offers a self-revelation to Nathanael. The promise's allusion to the vision of Jacob (= Israel; cf. Gen 32:28–30) at Bethel is best understood within the Jewish tradition of paraphrasing the scriptures. In context, Jesus' saying identifies Jesus in glory as the revelation (manifestation) of

God. Thus Nathanael, who has been seen by Jesus, is one who will see who Jesus truly is. In this respect he is a "true Israelite," meriting from Jesus a title of honor which stands in contrast to "the Jews," a title used of Jewish leaders with pejorative connotations in the fourth gospel.

Nathanael is not mentioned in the Synoptic Gospels, but Christian tradition has had a tendency to identify him with BARTHOLOMEW whose name comes after that of Philip in the Synoptics' listing of the Twelve (Matt 10:3; Mark 3:18; Luke 6:14; Acts 1:13). Although Bartholomew is a patronymic name, leaving open the possibility that he had a proper, personal Hebrew name, there is no historical evidence to support the identification of Nathanael and Bartholomew. Most probably the desire to find the name of Nathanael, whose discipleship is celebrated in John 1:45–51, on the list of the twelve disciples led to the confusion between Nathanael and Bartholomew.

Bibliography

Collins, R. F. 1974. The Representative Figures of the Fourth Gospel. *DRev* 94: 26–46, 118–32.

———. 1989. *John and His Witness.* Zacchaeus Studies: New Testament. Wilmington, DE.

Neyrey, J. H. 1982. The Jacob Allusions in John 1:51. *CBQ* 44: 586–605.

Painter, J. 1977. Christ and the Church in John 1, 45–51. Pp. 359–62 in *L'Evangile de Jean: Sources, rédaction, théologie.* BETL 44. Louvain.

Rowland, C. C. 1984. John 1, 51, Jewish Apocalyptic and Targumic Tradition. *NTS* 30: 498–507.

Stichel, R. 1985. *Nathanaël unter dem Feigenbaum.* Stuttgart.

RAYMOND F. COLLINS

NATIONALITY AND POLITICAL IDENTITY.

The term "nation" is commonly employed in OT studies, being the standard translation of Heb *gôy* (as opposed to "people," the standard translation of Heb *ʿam*) (*TWAT* 1: 965–73; *THAT* 2: 290–325; Høgenhavn 1988: 23–42). Yet the modern use of the term and its derivates ("nationality," "nationalism") has special features, not necessarily to be found in the quite different situation of biblical times. The possibility of (unperceived) misunderstandings is a real one; in particular, the current idea that Israel was a "nation" (in its modern sense) is doubtful and in any case the subject for specific research.

As is well known, the terminology and the very same historical reality of the "national states" are the result of the great political movements of the late 18th century: The American declaration of independence (1776) and the French Revolution (1791) established the transfer of sovereignty from kings to peoples, eventually giving birth to the national states, i.e., states coincident with ethnic boundaries (Weil 1938; Kohn 1956; Guyomar 1974, Ranum 1975). European history in the 19th century is largely the history of the progressive constitution of national states—the political movements being deeply embedded in the "romantic" culture of the time (with its positive evaluation of peoples, national traditions, language, etc.). In the 20th century the national idea gained a worldwide extension (being applied to new states emerging from decolonization: Cohen and Middleton 1970). But at the same time it underwent various processes of crisis (cf., e.g., Shafer 1955; Deutsch 1962; Snyder 1968; Mancur 1982; Gellner 1983): application to quite artificial entities, extremization in the form of nationalism (not devoid of racist implications); challenge by the international character of new political movements; and lastly a growing inadequacy to face the needs of an advanced capitalism and a "world-system" market.

The flourishing of nationality as the leading model of political organization seems therefore to be quite limited in time. During the long millennia from the birth of the state to the late 18th century, other models were mostly in use: from the city-state to the universal empire, from the feudal system to the centralized monarchy—with the principle usually well on the fore that the state (including the people) was the personal belonging of its sovereign (be it king or god). The application of the term "nation" to political realities in the old periods of history is possible (cf., e.g., the use of "nation" with reference to ethnic groups at a stateless stage: Mair 1962: 15–16; and case studies like Bailey 1960), but is always in need of a specific definition in order to avoid the suspect of anachronism. On the other hand, the nationalistic trends in past-century Europe were effective in shaping the institutional history of Israel in terms of a search for national unification. (Clements 1976: 142–43; Sasson 1981).

A. Political Identity in the Ancient Near East
   1. The Archaic Counterposition "Us" vs. "The Others"
   2. The Lack of Ethnic Motivations in Political Conflicts
   3. The Territorial State and the Role of the Tribe
   4. The Early Iron Age: From Tribe to "National" State
   5. Evolution and Decline of the National States
B. "National" Identity in Israel
   1. Preliminary Remarks
   2. The "Tribal" Picture
   3. The Monarchic Picture
   4. The Exilic and Postexilic Pictures

A. Political Identity in the Ancient Near East

1. The Archaic Counterposition "Us" vs. "The Others." In the early stages of development of the state in the ANE there is no place for the national state. On the one hand, the prevailing dimension is that of the city-state (so that a single people is often divided into a multitude of states); on the other hand, the processes of unification in Egypt and lower Mesopotamia gave birth to a counterposition between the inhabitants of the more civilized alluvium and the "barbarians" of the surrounding areas—a counterposition more cultural (also cosmological, in a sense) than nationalistic in nature. The Egyptians, by locating the Nile valley at the center of the world, distinguish their own land as *t3* from the neighboring countries as *ḫ3św̌t,* the fertile valley *(kmt)* from the surrounding desert *(dšrt),* and even label only Egyptians as really "men" *(rmt),* and consequently their own language as the only "human language." The same approach is found in the Sumerian world, with the counterposition between the land (= lower Mesopotamia) as KALAM and the hilly seats of the foreigners as KUR.KUR.RA (Limet 1978; Steiner 1982). In both the Egyptian and the Sumerian cultures the feeling of superiority leads to describe the strangers/foreigners as inferior, hardly human, beings—lacking the basic features of culture. This counterposition ("us" vs. "the others") cannot be considered as a kind of nationalism, however; and the various "foreign peoples" (Helck 1964; Limet 1972), albeit listed in stereotyped sequences (e.g., Uphill 1965–66), are just a component of the chaotic periphery threatening the cosmic order established by the god (and maintained by the sovereigns) at the center of the world.

2. The Lack of Ethnic Motivations in Political Conflicts. In lower Mesopotamia, the close contact between Sumerians and Akkadians produced an obvious consciousness of linguistic, ethnic, and cultural differentiations (Sollberger 1960; Kraus 1970; Cooper 1973). It has been observed, however, that ethnic identity was never an important political factor, neither in the inner (political, administrative, religious) relationships, nor even in conflicts between bordering states (Jacobsen 1939). The rise of Sargon of Akkad has been often (in the early stages of research) presented as the result of a new wave of Semitic intruders, as a conscious attempt to establish a Semitic empire over the Sumerian cities, as a climax in the assumed conflict between the two ethnic groups. Such implications are not present in the documents of the time, and the resulting "Akkadization" of the written official records is only the result of the location of the new capital city in a Semitic-speaking area. Quite different is the ethnic and cultural animosity against the barbarian invaders of the Guti dynasty. Again, the so-called "Sumerian renaissance" is well characterized by its use of the Sumerian language in the administration, because of the location of the capital city Ur in the Sumerian area, but any kind of discriminating politics against the Akkadians is lacking—the kings of Ur bearing the title of "kings of Sumer and Akkad." In the following Old-Babylonian (OB) period, Sumerian became a dead language, but the new element of the West-Semitic Amorites kept Mesopotamia in a multilinguistic state, again with no political relevance attached to the ethnic groups. As soon as the Amorites were culturally assimilated, their origin made no difference in their status as members of the state.

The same situation has been studied in N Syria, where Hurrian and West-Semitic groups closely intermingled in the same states, as Alalah (where the Hurrians prevail) or Ugarit (where the Semites prevail). Also in this case, some proposals about an ethnic interpretation of the political relationships have been shown not to be supported by the documents of the time (Paltiel 1981). Even the onomastic habits in the royal houses were not simply the reflection of ethnic affiliation, but took into account political purposes and marriage links (Liverani 1978).

Lastly, the political role of the ethnic groups of Indo-Iranians in the Mitanni kingdom has been clearly overevaluated by the peculiar trends of prewar Germany, and is now quite discredited (Kammenhuber 1968). In any event, the issue of the Indo-Iranians is one of political elitism rather than the formulation of a "national" state.

3. The Territorial State and the Role of the Tribe. During the Bronze Age, i.e., from the "urban revolution" at the end of the 4th millennium to the 13th century B.C., states had a "territorial" nature. Individuals belonged to one state just because they were resident in its territory—with no consideration of their ethnic affiliation or origin. The king, residing in a "palace" in the capital city, was the sovereign of the territory controlled by that city, i.e., he exerted a "monopoly" of taxation on the surrounding villages, he was the head of the administrative organization (in its largest sense, including cult and army), he was recognized as the representative of the local god. The king's subjects were basically divided into two categories: (a) the "free" population, mainly peasants and pastoralists, residing in villages, engaged in food production, owning the means of production (land and cattle), dependent on the king on a fiscal basis only; and (b) the "king's servants," mainly engaged in specialized activities, residing in the capital city, using means of production which belonged to the palace, therefore dependent on the king in their working relationships. The inner structure of the state was socioeconomic; linguistic and ethnic qualifications were irrelevant.

This general picture obtained also in Syria-Palestine (Buccellati 1967), divided during the Bronze Age into a multitude of kingdoms, centered on capital cities and governed by local kings (leaving aside the higher sovereignty imposed in some periods by foreign empires, which did not alter the local political structure). The kingdom was designated by the name of its capital city (e.g., Ugarit), to which the titulary of the king makes reference (e.g., RN king of Ugarit). In the case of a larger kingdom encompassing more cities, the minor ones would be ruled by "vassal" kings, in a system of "Chinese boxes." Quite seldom, in countries devoid of important cities, the kingdoms were named after the country (e.g., Amurru, Nuhashshe). In any case, what was evidenced was a territorial unit, not an ethnic one.

The system outlined above is valid for discussions of the sedentary and urbanized population. The pastoral element had a quite different social and political organization, based on kinship relations instead of residence. The relevance of this "tribal" sector in the "dimorphic" society of the Bronze Age was subject to some fluctuations through time. The apex of their impact on the territorial states took place ca. 2,000 B.C., in the "intermediate period" between EB and MB (Kamp and Yoffee 1980); and was still important during the MB period, when many kingdoms in upper Mesopotamia, Syria, and Palestine had a double designation according to the capital city and the surrounding tribe. So the king of Mari was also king of the Hana (tribe); the king of Tuttul was also king of the Amnanum (tribe); the king of Abattum was also king of the Rabbum (tribe); etc. Even in lower Mesopotamia the Amorite penetration gave origin to similar cases: e.g., the king of Uruk was also king of the Amnanum. The MB kingdoms seem to be composed of two elements, the territorial one (the capital city and its territory) and the tribal one. Their spatial coincidence may have been only partial, and their nature was quite different (residence in one case; kinship in the other).

Later on, during the LB period, the tribal sector became less and less important, its political role completely marginal, and its relations with the king's palace tendentially hostile. The double labeling disappeared in the 17th century. Syria and Palestine in the LB Age were politically shaped according to the "territorial" model in its most "pure" form—the residual tribes (Ahlamu in upper Mesopotamia, Sutu in Syria; the Shasu in Palestine according to the Egyptian sources) were considered outside the reach of the king's control.

4. The Early Iron Age: From Tribe to "National" State. At the end of the Bronze Age, the territorial states underwent a serious inner (socioeconomic) crisis (Strange 1987): the palace organization collapsed, and the tribal element acquired a new preeminence. Peoples of nomadic origin gained control especially of the inner belt (almost abandoned after the flourishing in the EB Age) between the most urbanized coastal plains and the steppe plateau: the Arameans in Syria and in upper Mesopotamia; Ammonites, Moabites, and Edomites in Transjordan. A colonization took place in the hilly country of Cisjordan (Israelites), which was previously unsettled. Arameans and Chaldeans further penetrated the alluvium of lower Mesopotamia, which was subject to an agricultural and demographic crisis and partly reduced to swamps and pasturelands.

The characteristic "model" of the Iron Age state was no longer territorial: it was a state based on tribal kinship. The state took its name from the ruling "house" *(bêt PN)*, and the members of the state were its "sons" *(bĕnê PN)*, as if all the population was a huge "extended family" ultimately going back to a common tribal ancestor. From the old stock of the "Ahlamu Arameans" a number of tribal states came into being in upper Mesopotamia (Bit Adini on the Middle Euphrates, Bit Bahyani in the Habur triangle, Bit Zamani on the Upper Tigris) and in N Syria (Bit Gusi or Bit Agusi in the Aleppo area; cf. also Bit Gabbar as the ruling dynasty in Sam'al); while the Aramean tribes kept their political autonomy in southern Mesopotamia (Bit Yakini, Bit Dakkuri, Bit Ammukani, Bit Sha'alli, Bit Shilani). In Palestine the same picture can be deduced from the names of the *Bĕnê ʿAmmōn* and the *Bĕnê Yiśrāʾēl* themselves. In cases where the new states were named after a regional name (like Moab, Edom, Judah) it is doubtful whether they were topographical or tribal in origin.

Of course, it is not only a matter of names. The implication is that the members of the state were no longer just the inhabitants of a region, but rather individuals belonging to the same tribe—linked together by birth (or "blood") ties, common language, common traditions (as revealed by genealogies and by etiological stories), and the common worship of a tribal god. The counterposition between states acquired nationalistic elements as well. The political belonging and relationships were, in the last analysis, inscribed into the individual's birth; and the "model" state would encompass all the members of the same "nation" and nobody else (unless in the form of foreign residents).

It is lastly to be noticed that the national element was characteristic of the Iron Age states not only in the West Semitic world of Syria and Palestine. Similar trends can be pointed out also on the Anatolia, Armenian, and Iranian highlands: the kingdoms of the Phrygians or the Lydians in Anatolia, or those of the Manneans or the Medians in Iran had a "national" basis and characterization hardly precedented in the Bronze Age.

5. Evolution and Decline of the National States. Of course, the national features of tribal origin were immediately challenged by the remains of the old territorial kingdoms. The passing of time produced a progressive reestablishment of the territorial ties, the sedentary and urban elements recovered their preeminence at the expense of the tribal pastoralists, and the kinship relationships were reshaped in the form of administrative structures. The results were different in different areas: in Syria and Palestine a compromise was reached between territorial and tribal elements; in lower Mesopotamia the tribes remained politically separated from (and antagonistic to) the old temple-cities; in Assyria and in Egypt some kind of "nationalistic" feeling was added to the traditional views of centralization and imperialistic expansion.

Later on, the advancing empires of Assyria, Babylon, and Persia successfully acted in order to destroy the nationalities in the subdued regions—in order to produce a homogeneous texture throughout the territory of the empire. The transformation of the conquered kingdoms into "provinces" (later "satrapies"), the destruction of temples and palaces (the seat of the local cultural and religious traditions), the establishment of a unified administration, and the presence of imperial officials, the recourse to cross-deportations (especially affecting the ruling elites), were all powerful means for the overcoming of the national dimension, and even for the linguistic and cultural unification of the Near East. The residual (or renovated) nationalistic movements were by now framed not more in a pluralistic background of contending nations, but in a context of resistance by the local ethnic groups against an all-embracing and superimposed ideology and government—a situation that was inherited by the Hellenistic and Roman empires.

B. "National" Identity in Israel

1. Preliminary Remarks. When dealing with the topic "Nationality and Political Identity" in ancient Israel, a problem is immediately perceived, which is common to every historical subject in OT studies. Scholars can make use of a more traditional approach, by using the statements contained in the OT books as bits of evidence for the times to which they refer, or they can use a more critical approach, by using the same statements as evidence for the times in which they were written. It is evident how different the two counterposed possibilities are: namely, to accept the institutional evolution outlined in the OT (from tribal confederacy to united kingdom, eventually divided, conquered and exiled, and to be restored as a religious community); or to read it as a series of flashbacks, all of them belonging to the postexilic period, and whose connection with the "real" history of previous periods is quite doubtful. In the present article, the traditional frame will be maintained, but the critical caution will be introduced time and again. In any case, the entire institutional development of ancient Israel takes place within the Iron Age (the patriarchal legends can be left aside, of course), in a period when some kind of "national" identification was historically possible—even though the scenery of the first Iron Age is completely different from those of the Assyrian, Achaemenian or Hellenistic empires.

2. The "Tribal" Picture. The picture provided by the OT traditions of the periods of the conquest and of the Judges fits quite properly into the developmental paradigm "from tribe to state"—and it must be said that these traditions provided a basic contribution to the very building of the paradigm in the Semitic world, along with early

Islamic history (Moscati 1962). The Canaanite city-states are the representatives of the Bronze Age system of territorial states in the sedentary-urbanized component of the population. The league of the twelve tribes, on the other hand, is a case of pastoral groups giving birth to a larger political unit, to which the term "nation" can be applied—with common leaders (Moses, Joshua, the Judges), with a political structure reproducing the kinship relationships, with the national god Yahweh. The "nation" is already existent before the conquest, so that only a territory is needed to establish a national state. The conquest brings about the inclusion of the former local settlements (villages becoming clans of the Israelite tribes), and the destruction (or more seldom the inclusion) of former polities. After the conquest some areas and cities are "left" outside the Israelite league, so that belonging to the Israelite political unit is (at least tendentially) coincident with the ethnic unit itself. Besides Israel, other national polities exist, the result of foreign immigration (Philistines: but their pentapolis has no political unity) or of parallel developments (Ammon, Moab, Edom).

The "classical" reconstruction (Alt 1925, 1930; Noth 1930) has been criticized and has become obsolete on many points: the pastoral nature of the tribe; the league as an "amphictyony" (de Geus 1976); the arrival of Israel from outside Palestine; the nomadic origins. A new paradigm has developed in the USA, in which Israel is constituted following an inner social upheaval rather than an immigration (Mendenhall 1962, 1973; Gottwald 1979). This "new paradigm" is certainly important in many respects, yet it changes very little the institutional picture of the premonarchic period: we are in any case dealing with some kind of "national" unity (whatever the origin of its components and the reasons for its constitution). The underscoring of the early and decisive role played by the covenant (Mendenhall) and by the national worship of Yahweh (Gottwald), as well as the counterposition (be it ethnic or social) to the Canaanites in any case strengthens the national hypothesis.

Much more drastic is the criticism coming from European scholarly circles on the historical reliability of the traditional picture, because of the late date of the documents in which the traditions are embedded (a difficulty surmounted by the Alt-Noth school through a high dating of the documentary sources, and practically ignored by the partisans of the "revolution" hypothesis). A "moderate" solution is that the system of the twelve tribes cannot be earlier than the monarchic period (e.g., de Vaux 1973: 37–65), and its origin should be sought in the administrative partitions of the united monarchy. This solution would mean the overturning of the traditional paradigm: instead of "from tribe to state" we would have "from state to tribe," and the emphasis would be on the artificial (as contrasted to genetic) origin of the tribal links. A more "radical" solution is that the tribal system is basically a forgery of postexilic times, and that the outer origin of the Israelites as well as their conflicts with the former inhabitants of the land are the reflection of what happened when (and after) some exiled groups came back in Palestine (cf. recently Lemche 1985). In both cases, we have no evidence for any national entity "Israel" in the premonarchical period; and the scenario of the book of Judges is a mythical model for the conditions obtaining in Palestine during the Achaemenian and Hellenistic periods.

Apart from the problem of the late date of the texts, some important arguments favor the "negative" position: the artificial nature of the twelve tribes league (the documents more confidently assigned to an early date preserve the memory of different groupings) and of their political system in general; the legendary (even mythical) nature of the stories about the Judges, and the etiological nature of most stories about the Conquest; the late emergence (not before the exilic age) of the role of the covenant and of the traditions about Exodus and Conquest in the Prophets and the Psalms (Lemche 1985: 306–85); lastly the progressive growth of Yahweh toward a role of "national" god which seems anachronistic in the formative period.

Data outside the OT are extremely scanty for the 13th–12th centuries. The mention of Israel in the Merenptah stela (Ahlström and Edelman 1985) cannot prove nor disprove anything; other topographical or tribal names (e.g., the *Yʿqb-ʾl* of Thutmose III or the **Bny Rhm* of the Beth Shan stela) are even more uncertain. The very existence of a political entity "Israel" before the monarchic period must remain a matter of doubt; and even more uncertain is its institutional structure (including the presence or absence of any "national" self-identification). The solution depends largely on the validity attached to later traditions.

3. The Monarchic Picture. Political conditions change around 1000 B.C. with the constitution of a large kingdom in Palestine, a kingdom largely inhabited by Israelites and considered by the Israelite tradition to complete the trend toward a national state. According to the tradition (esp. 1 Samuel 8), a "people" (*ʿam*) of Israel was already at hand, with its kinship structure, its territory, its common cult and law: the only feature necessary to transform the people into a "nation" (*gôy*) like the surrounding ones, was a kingship (*mamlākāh*), i.e., a politically centralized power (Rost 1934; Speiser 1960). At the terminological level, this "institutional" meaning ("nationality" = "people" + "state") is challenged by a prevailing connotative aspect: "we" are *ʿam*, while "the others" are *gôyîm* (Cody 1964; May 1968). This connotation is based on the privileged appreciation of the kinship relations to define a community from within, and of the political appreciation to define the outer communities. Yet it brings about the prevailing ethnic character of Israel (also in the monarchic period), at the expense of its national unity.

In fact, a noteworthy difference exists between Israel's institutional history as seen by later tradition and in contemporary records. According to the tradition, the national unity was accomplished already by Saul, best represented by David and Solomon, but unfortunately disintegrated into the two separate kingdoms of Judah and Israel, to be hopefully reconstituted in the future. Unity would be the norm, division an unfortunate accident. But during most of Israelite history, the "normal" condition of a national unity is a memory from the past and a hope for the future. Moreover, if we reject the possibility of any national consciousness in the period of the Judges, then the following process has to be reformulated accordingly: a progressive compaction as a result of the political vicissitudes.

A diachronical analysis makes the situation more precise but also more problematical. The short-lived kingdom of Saul has a kind of national character, in being basically limited to tribal territory, in keeping a part of the former kinship organization, in rising as a defensive need against surrounding nations—but is basically limited to the northern tribes (Ahlström 1986: 85–99). Under David, the kingdom of Israel can hardly be defined as a national state. The division between Judah and Israel is paramount in the formative process, the capital city is chosen outside the tribal territory, and the extent of the kingdom encompasses non-Israelite elements (from the Canaanite towns to the neighboring peoples). The ideal borders of Israel move from a national horizon ("from Dan to Beersheba") to an imperialistic one (from the Euphrates to the "brook of Egypt"). Even the army shifts from national to professional, and the palace administration is largely a legacy of the Canaanite polities. The composite nature of the Davidic state is inherited by Solomon, whose administrative structuring and building programs may have produced some degree of national self-identification (Ahlström 1982), but had been overevaluated by later traditions. The administrative structure provided a model for inner ethnic relationships, the temple became the focus of the national identity, and the royal dynasty (Ishida 1977) was seen as the privileged guarantee of the divine willingness to preserve Israel's freedom and unity.

But was the idea of a "national kingdom" already operating in David's and Solomon's time? Or was it a flashback to the exilic period? In fact the following story of the divided kingdoms seems to imply a low degree of national consciousness. The northern tribes considered the Jerusalem dynasty as foreign to their own traditions and interests; the conflicts between Judah and Israel were almost endemic, yet quite similar to those with other states; the political structure of both kingdoms focused on the respective capital cities; the cult was multicentered (even if Yahweh was given a privileged status in both kingdoms). It is difficult to maintain that the difference between Judah and Israel was in some way less marked or different in nature from the difference, e.g., between Moab and Edom, or between Damascus and Hama. In the same period, the Philistine and the Phoenician city-states were also politically independent inside an ethnic (not a national) unity. As to the very name "Israel," its application to both Judah and the northern kingdom is quite problematic before Josiah's times (cf. the basic materials in Danell 1946). As to the name "Hebrew," its application to the Jewish nationality is very late (Lemche 1979).

The attempt by Josiah to revive the Davidic model of a unified kingdom certainly had a greater impact than the original Davidic reality. In David's times the unity was basically political, on a variegated ethnic basis; in Josiah's times, on the contrary, the national feeling is evident (if the Deuteronomistic history belongs to this period)—unification of cult, promulgation of the divine law, reconstruction of past history as a process finalized to the national unity, role of the covenant with the national god, and counterposition to other nationalities. It is probably with Josiah's reforms that we can more confidently speak of a "nation" of Israel.

The reason for the change has to be looked for in the Assyrian policy of conquest and deportation affecting the northern kingdom. The foreign immigrants in Palestine produced a situation of "inner boundaries." Inside the same area, groups of different ethnic origin were present, and the attempt to preserve an identity gave rise to a sort of national self-identification. When Assyria collapsed, Josiah's attempt to annex the north Palestinian provinces found its ideological justification in tracing a national unity back to the Davidic model through the "twin" kingdoms of Israel and Judah similarly related to Yahweh's role. By this time, the specific self-identification of Israel as the "people of Yahweh" (von Rad 1929; Lohfink 1971), and the nationalistic stance against the neighboring peoples, had received a coherent shaping—to be further elaborated and partly modified in postexilic times, e.g., by the Deutero-Isaiah (Hollenberg 1969; Orlinsky 1970; Wilson 1986; Høgenhavn 1988).

4. The Exilic and Postexilic Pictures. The process went on with the Babylonian conquest of Jerusalem and the deportation of the Judean political elites. Different from the Israelite exiles in the Assyrian empire, who underwent an affective loss of political identity, cultural traditions, and religious cult, and were substituted in Palestine by newcomers of different origin, the Judean exiles in Babylon were able to keep (thanks to a different attitude of the conquerors and the short time of the Exile) and to improve their national consciousness. And when they were allowed to come back to Palestine, they found the area almost free for a new colonization (the Babylonians did not use any cross-regional transfer of population), and put into being a program of national recovery by adding a racial element (prohibition of mixed marriages) to the religious and cultural elements already conceived in Exile.

The most important "pre-Israelite peoples" found in Palestine by the Moses tribes according to the traditions, are artificial formations from the geographical designations of Syria-Palestine obtaining in Babylonia: Amurru and Hatti (Van Seters 1972; Ishida 1977: 466–68). This forgery of nonexistent "nations," and their fate under Josiah's attacks, are obvious models for the struggle of the Judean immigrants against the other Palestinian groups, a struggle certainly endowed with nationalistic implications quite anachronistic one millennium before.

As a kind of paradox, the national unity of Israel was the result, not so much of a political unification, but of the political disaster of the Exile and the return. The national self-identification was achieved, not when the material conditions were more stable and peaceful, but as a reaction against vicissitudes and conditions conceived in order to destroy any national feeling in the melting-pot of the imperial state. As a consequence of this paradoxical situation, the features were privileged in the shaping of the nationality, that were conceivable outside the land: the unity of cult (the Solomonic temple was never so important in Israelite ideology than after it was destroyed), the common law of divine origin, the historical traditions (providing a model for national recovery), and the assumed ethnic unity (in the form of extended kinship ties). On the contrary, the features were lacking of a territorial seat and of a political unification and independence. Land and kingship (the basic prerequisites for any national entity at the time) were projected toward the future, as something needed in order to (re)establish a full national unity. All the differing attempts which took place in the postexilic period—from the building of the Second Temple to the constitution of the Hasmonean kingdom—were conceived of as a restoration of the past, and necessarily produced the myth of a lost national identity and history. But this "former stage" of the national unity never occurred in reality in the forms later presumed in order to fit the political programs of the postexilic community. So the Israelite nationality assumed its form in the very period of its disintegration, as something projected in the past and in the future—but undergoing "presently" to a state of crisis.

Lastly, since the projects of restoration of some kind of political unity and independence were largely unsuccessful (the imperial order of the Achaemenian and Hellenistic periods being incompatible with anything more than a local community centered on the Jerusalem temple), a further shift took place. From the model of the national state emerged that of a religious community (Causse 1937; Ahlström 1986: 101–18), devoid of any political power and competence, and reusing the previous projects of national recovery as a metaphor for the eschatological salvation. The "national" origin of the Jewish religious community kept important features, however, in the ethnic and racial limitations of its membership—to be eventually overcome by the "universalistic" character of Christianity (under the impact of the Hellenistic-Roman cosmopolitism).

Bibliography

Ahlström, G. 1982. *Royal Administration and National Religion in Ancient Palestine.* Leiden.

———. 1986. *Who Were the Israelites?* Winona Lake, IN.

Ahlström, G., and Edelman, D. 1985. Merneptah's Israel. *JNES* 44: 59–61.

Alt, A. 1925. *Die Landnahme der Israeliten in Palästina.* Leipzig.

———. 1930. *Die Staatenbildung der Israeliten in Palästina.* Leipzig.

Bailey, F. G. 1960. *Tribe, Caste and Nation.* Manchester.

Bertholet, A. 1896. *Die Stellung der Israeliten und der Juden zu den Fremden.* Freiburg-Leipzig.

Buccellati, G. 1967. *Cities and Nations of Ancient Syria.* SS 26. Rome.

Causse, A. 1937. *Du groupe ethnique a la communauté religieuse.* Paris.

Clements, R. E. 1976. *A Century of Old Testament Studies.* Guilford, Surrey, England.

Cody, A. 1964. When Is the Chosen People Called a Gôy? *VT* 14: 1–6.

Cohen, R., and Middleton, J. 1970. *From Tribe to Nation in Africa.* Scranton, PA.

Cooper, J. 1973. Sumerian and Akkadian in Sumer and Addad. *Or* 42: 239–58.

Danell, G. A. 1946. *Studies in the Name Israel in the Old Testament.* Uppsala.

Deutsch, K. W. 1962. *Nationalism and Social Communication.* 2d ed. Cambridge, MA.

Diakonoff, I. M. 1972. Die Arier im Vorderen Orient: Ende Eines Mythos. *Or* 41: 91–120.

Drioton, E. 1957. Le nationalisme au temps des Pharaohs. *Revue du Caire* 198: 81–92.

Fohrer, G. 1968. Israels Haltung gegenüber den Kanaanäern und anderen Völkern. *JSS* 13: 64–75.

Gellner, E. 1983. *Nations and Nationalism.* Cambridge.

Geus, C. H. J. de. 1976. *The Tribes of Israel.* SSN 18. Amsterdam.

Gottwald, N. 1979. *The Tribes of Yahweh.* Maryknoll, NY.

Guyomar, J.-Y. 1974. *L'idéologie nationale.* Paris.

Helck, W. 1964. Die Agypter und die Fremden. *Saeculum* 15: 103–114.

Høgenhavn, J. 1988. *Gott und Volk bei Jesaja.* Acta Theologica Danica 24. Leiden.

Hollenberg, D. E. 1969. Nationalism and "the Nations" in Isaiah 40–55. *VT* 19: 23–36.

Ishida, T. 1977. *The Royal Dynasties in Ancient Israel.* BZAW 142. Berlin.

Jacobsen, T. 1939. The Assumed Conflict between Sumerians and Semites in Early Mesopotamian History. *JAOS* 59: 485–95.

Kammenhuber, A. 1968. *Die Arier im Vorderen Orient.* Heidelberg.

Kamp, K. A., and Yoffee, N. 1980. Ethnicity in Ancient Western Asia During the Early Second Millennium B.C.: Archaeological Assessments and Ethnoarchaeological Prospectives. *BASOR* 237: 85–104.

Kohn, H. 1956. *The Idea of Nationalism.* New York.

Kraus, F. R. 1970. *Sumerer und Akkader, ein Problem der altmesopotamischen Geschichte.* Amsterdam.

Lemche, N. P. 1979. "Hebrew" as a National Name for Israel. *StTh* 33: 1–23.

———. 1985. *Early Israel. Anthropological and Historical Studies on the Israelite Society Before the Monarchy.* VT Sup. 37. Leiden.

Limet, H. 1972. L'étranger dans la société sumérienne. Pp. 128–38 in *Gesellschaftsklassen im Alten Zweistromland,* ed. D. O. Edzard. ABAW Phil.-hist. Klasse, N.F. 75. München.

———. 1978. Etude sémantique de ma.da, kur, kalam. *RA* 72: 1.12.

Liverani, M. 1978. L'élément hourrite dans la Syrie du nord. *RHA* 36: 149–56.

Lohfink, N. 1971. Beobachtungen zur Geschichte des Ausdrucks *ᶜm yhwh.* Pp. 275–305 in *Probleme biblischer Theologie. G. von Rad zum 30. Geburtstag,* ed. H. W. Wolff. München.

Mair, L. 1962. *Primitive Government.* Harmondsworth.

Mancur, O. 1982. *The Rise and Decline of Nations.* New Haven.

May, H. G. 1968. "This People" and "this Nation" in Haggai. *VT* 18: 190–97.

Mendenhall, G. E. 1962. The Hebrew Conquest of Palestine. *BA* 25: 66–87.

———. 1973. *The Tenth Generation.* Baltimore.

Moscati, S. 1962. Dalla tribu allo stato nel Vicino Oriente antico. Pp. 55–65 in *Dalla tribu allo stato.* Quaderni 54. Rome.

Noth, M. 1930. *Das System der zwölf Stämme Israels.* BWANT 4/1. Stuttgart.

Orlinsky, H. M. 1970. Nationalism-Universalism and Internationalism in Ancient Israel. Pp. 206–236 in *Translating and Understanding the Old Testament. Essays in Honor of H. G. May,* ed. H. T. Frank, and W. L. Reed. Nashville.

Paltiel, E. 1981. Ethnicity and the State in the Kingdom of Ugarit. *AbrN* 19: 43–61.

Rad, G. von. 1929. *Das Gottesvolk im Deuteronomium.* BWANT 3/89. Stuttgart.

Ranum, O. 1975. *National Consciousness. History and Political Culture in Early-Modern Europe,* ed. O. Ranum. Baltimore.

Rost, L. 1934. Die Bezeichnungen für Land und Volk im Alten Testament. Pp. 125–48 in *Festschrift O. Procksch.* Leipzig.

Sasson, J. M. 1981. On Choosing Models for Recreating Israelite Pre-Monarchic History. *JSOT* 21: 3–24.

Shafer, B. C. 1955. *Nationalism, Myth and Reality.* London.

Snyder, L. L. 1968. *The New Nationalism.* Ithaca, NY.

Sollberger, E. 1960. Aspects du contact suméro-akkadien. *Genava* 8: 241–314.
Speiser, E. A. 1960. "People" and "Nation" of Israel. *JBL* 79: 157–63.
Steiner, G. 1982. Der Gegensatz "Eigenes Land": "Ausland, Fremdland, Feindland" in den Vorstellungen des alten Orients. Pp. 633–64 in *Mesopotamien und seine Nachbarn,* ed. H.-J. Nissen, and J. Renger. Berlin.
Strange, J. 1987. The Transition from the Bronze Age to the Iron Age in the Eastern Mediterranean and the Emergence of the Israelite State. *Scandinavian Journal of the Old Testament* 1: 1–19.
Uphill, E. 1965–66. The Nine Bows. *JEOL* 19: 393–420.
Van Seters, J. 1972. The Terms "Amorite" and "Hittite" in the Old Testament. *VT* 22: 64–81.
Vaux, R. de. 1973. *Histoire ancienne d'Israël.* Vol. 2. Paris.
Weil, G. 1938. *L'Europe du XIX siecle et l'idée de nationalité.* Paris.
Wilson, A. 1986. *The Nations in Deutero-Isaiah.* Lewiston, NY.
Wiseman, D. J. 1973. Introduction: Peoples and Nations. Pp. xv–xxi in *POTT.*

MARIO LIVERANI

NATIONS [Heb *ʿammîm, gôyim, lĕʾūmmîm*]. The study of the nations within the canonical tradition of ancient Israel leads inevitably to the primary tension between the concepts of nationalism and universalism. On the one hand, particularly within the prophetic literature, there are passages which express the narrowest self-interest and even hatred for Israel's enemies among the nations. But alongside these stand passages expressing an exalted vision of worldwide salvation for "the nations." Scholars are divided as to how deeply embedded within the developing canonical tradition of ancient Israel they choose to see the latter development. Nonetheless, it is clear that "Israel as a light to the nations" is no peripheral theme within the canonical process. The nations are the matrix of Israel's life, the raison d'être of her very existence.

The initial period of world prehistory in the book of Genesis ends with the Flood, after which humanity makes a new start from Noah and his sons and separates into families, languages, lands, and nations. The Table of Nations in Genesis 10 lists some seventy entities, which include the whole of the ancient world, as known to the author, divided roughly into racial groups. It is without parallel in ancient literature, for this interest in the nations reflects accurately the biblical emphasis on history as the vehicle of revelation and the nations as the object of God's redemptive purpose.

A. Terminology
  1. In the Old Testament
  2. In the New Testament
B. Israel Against the Nations
  1. Holy War as a Celebrated Event in Ancient Israel
  2. Egypt and Amalek as Paradigmatic Enemies
  3. The Seven Traditional Enemies of Deuteronomic Tradition
  4. Assyria and Babylon Join Egypt as Paradigmatic Enemies
  5. The Oracles Against the Nations
C. Israel and the Nations in History
  1. The Davidic Empire as Political Ideal
  2. An Era of Transition (ca. 750–700 B.C.E.)
  3. *Pax Assyriaca* (ca. 700–640 B.C.E.)
  4. *Regnum Davidicum redivivum* (ca. 640–609 B.C.E.)
  5. *Imperium Babylonicum* (ca. 626–582 B.C.E.)
D. The Nations in Prophetic Eschatology and Early Apocalyptic Literature
E. A New Israel: The Righteous from All Nations

A. Terminology

1. In the Old Testament. Three words appear in the Hebrew text of the OT which are used more or less synonymously in reference to the nations, each of which may be used in the singular to refer to a particular nation, including Israel.

ʿammîm (cf. Ugaritic *ʿm,* "clan"; Vg. *populi* or *nationes;* LXX *ethnē* or *laoi*), "peoples." The stress is on kinship as the basis of the group, at least in the original meaning of the word. In the singular, the term *ʿam* is used most frequently in reference to Israel as the "people of Yahweh." In such cases the LXX uses *laos.* The LXX uses *ethnē* for the plural in the Pentateuch, Joshua, and Judges; elsewhere both *ethnē* and *laoi* are used.

gôyim (Akkadian loanword from West Semitic, *gaʾu,* "gang" or "group" [e.g., of workmen]; Vg. *gentes;* LXX *ethnē*), "nations"; KJV alternately "heathen." This term stresses political and social rather than kinship bonds.

lĕʾummîm (cf. Akkadian *liʾimmu,* "thousand"; Ugaritic *lʾm,* "people"; Vg. *populi;* LXX *ethnē*), "peoples"; KJV (incorrectly) "the people." Originally the term probably referred to a city which could produce a contingent of soldiers (a "thousand") in time of war. The word is often used in parallel with *gôyim* within the prophetic literature and Psalms.

A fourth term appears in both Hebrew *ʾummôt* (Gen 25:16; Num 25:15) and *ʾummîm* (Ps 117:1) and Aramaic *ʾummâ* (Dan 3:29) and *ʾummayyāʾ* (seven times) with the meaning "nation(s)," "tribe(s)," "people."

2. In the New Testament. The primary term used in the NT is *ethnē* (Vg. *gentes*), taken from LXX usage. "Gentiles" is used in reference to non-Jewish nations in contrast to the Jews (Luke 21:24; Acts 9:15; 1 Cor 1:23), or in contrast to followers of Christ (Matt 6:7, 32; 10:5; 20:19; Eph 2:11–12). "Nations" is used in reference to all nations including the Jews (Matt 24:9, 14; Mark 11:17; Rev 7:9). Exceptions to be noted include Acts 13:19; 14:16; and Gal 3:8.

In the NT the term *laoi,* "peoples" in the plural, occurs only eight times, four of which are in parallel to *ethnē,* indicating either Semitic style or LXX quotation (Luke 2:31; Acts 4:25, 27; Rom 15:11), and four in Revelation within the formula "nations, tongues, and tribes," reminiscent of Genesis 10 and Dan 3:4–7.

B. Israel Against the Nations

1. Holy War as a Celebrated Event in Ancient Israel. The institution of Holy War during the period of the Judges should be distinguished from Yahweh's Holy War as celebrated in the cultus of Ritual Conquest. Yahweh's Holy War is the ritual fusing of the events of the Exodus-Conquest into one great cultic celebration in which the

Divine Warrior marched with his hosts from Sinai to Shittim and then across the Jordan River to Gilgal, the battle camp for the conquest of Canaan. The nature of the institution of holy war as reflected in the Song of Deborah (Judges 5) can be reconstructed, at least in part, from an analysis of Yahweh's Holy War as celebrated in the Ritual Conquest tradition. The ark of the covenant was a battle palladium. The tribal groups had designated positions within the battle camp under priestly organization. Moses and Joshua, as "judges" over Israel, filled the role later assumed by the prophets in delivering war oracles to inspire the troops in battle.

The quotation from the Book of the Wars of the Lord in Num 21:14 presents the Divine Warrior as poised on the edge of the promised land, before the most celebrated battles of the Exodus-Conquest. He has come in the whirlwind with His hosts to the sources of the river Arnon in Transjordan. He marches through the wadis, turning aside to settle affairs with Moab before marching against the two Amorite kings to the north, and then across the Jordan to Gilgal and the conquest of Canaan.

The actual conquest of Canaan was apparently reenacted as part of the annual festival tradition within ancient Israel, from the period of the judges down into the monarchic era, and perhaps beyond, as suggested by the so-called "War Scroll" from the Dead Sea community at Qumran. The tribal units of Israel took up their designated positions around the ark of the covenant at Gilgal. From there they set out to conquer Jericho in ritual tradition as part of the spring festival of Passover each year.

2. Egypt and Amalek as Paradigmatic Enemies. The crossing of the Jordan river in the tradition of Ritual Conquest was set over against the crossing of the Red Sea *(yam sup),* or "Sea of Reeds [or rushes]," in which the people of Israel were delivered from their traditional foe, the Egyptians (cf. Exod 15, the "Song of the Sea," and Ps 114:5). After crossing the sea, Israel's first military encounter was against the Amalekites (Exod 17:8–15). Amalek was defeated and cursed in the name of Yahweh, who pledged "war with Amalek from generation to generation" (Exod 17:16). In later tradition Israel was commanded to "blot out the remembrance of Amalek from under heaven; you shall not forget" (Deut 25:19). Though not much is known about Amalek so far as history is concerned, her traditional enmity with Israel surfaces in the story of Saul's demise because of his refusal to slay Agag, king of Amalek, and again in the story of Esther whose archenemy Haman is identified as the Agagite (Esth 3:1, 10; 8:3, 5; 9:25).

The war with Amalek is the first in a series of wars which, together with the defeat of the Egyptians at the Red Sea, constitute Yahweh's Holy War par excellence. Further battles in this series include the war with the Canaanite king of Arad (Num 21:1–3), the wars with the Amorite kings Sihon and Og (Num 21:21–35), and the war against Midian (Num 31:1–54)—all under the leadership of Moses. After Moses' death, Joshua led the people across the Jordan to the second phase of Yahweh's Holy War against Jericho, Ai, and the Canaanite inhabitants of the promised land.

3. The Seven Traditional Enemies of Deuteronomic Tradition. The full list of "seven nations greater and mightier than (Israel)"—the Hittites, the Girgashites, the Amorites, the Canaanites, the Perizzites, the Hivites, and the Jebusites—appears in three passages (Deut 7:1; Josh 3:10; 24:11). Though some of these "nations" are identifiable, the Perizzites and Girgashites remain obscure. Detailed study of the occurrences of these seven names within the biblical tradition suggests that the complete listing of seven nations is probably traditional in nature. Within the holy war materials of the Deuteronomic tradition these seven nations apparently constitute a roll call of enemies within some sort of cultic context.

4. Assyria and Babylon Join Egypt as Paradigmatic Enemies. In the flow of historical events, the northern kingdom of Israel was eventually destroyed by Assyria under Sargon II (722 B.C.E.), and somewhat later Judah fell to the Neo-Babylonian Empire under Nebuchadnezzar (587–586 B.C.E.). The prophetic books of Nahum and Jonah focus on Nineveh, the capital of Assyria, which became a symbol for the archenemy of God's people. In the book of Judith the city of Nineveh, as the capital of Assyria, was said to be ruled by Nebuchadnezzar, in complete disregard of history as such. Nebuchadnezzar was the ruler of the New Babylonian Empire, which destroyed Jerusalem; Babylon subsequently became another symbol of the archenemy (cf. Rev 18:2).

5. The Oracles Against the Nations. Within the prophetic literature of ancient Israel, the oracles against the nations constitute a large and distinctive block of material. The classical prophets of ancient Israel were apparently political figures, sharing in the rule of the people in some way, alongside the king. Jeremiah's self-description of his call to be "a prophet to the nations" (Jer 1:5) speaks of one aspect of this responsibility.

The establishment of the Davidic monarchy and the centralization of Israel's worship in Jerusalem introduced a powerful impulse to the religion of ancient Israel which tended to reshape earlier tradition. The cultus of the premonarchic Covenant League was retained but was subordinated to a royal cultus administered by dominant priestly families under the control of the king. Yahweh's Holy War, as cultic reenactment of the Exodus-Conquest, was no longer climaxed by mere possession of the land of promise. The ark of the covenant was carried in ritual procession to its "eternal resting place" on Mount Zion in Jerusalem. The climax of the Royal Festival became the enthronement of the Davidic monarch in dynastic covenant. The ark of the covenant was subsequently housed permanently in an elaborate temple, constructed under Solomon, which became the center of Israelite worship until its destruction by Nebuchadnezzar in 587 B.C.E.

Beginning with the oracles against the nations in Amos 1–2, the member nations of the former Davidic empire were judged in a highly stylized manner for violation of the treaty stipulations of their "covenant of brotherhood." Motifs from earlier war songs of Israel's Covenant League were incorporated into this poetic composition, which was essentially a reversal of Yahweh's Holy War as celebrated in the Ritual Conquest traditions. The Divine Warrior was now leading his hosts in battle against his own people because they had spurned their covenant obligations. The framework of the idealized Davidic empire as the legal basis for judgment speeches against the nations was expanded in the developing tradition from Amos to Jeremiah. Isaiah's oracles against Assyria, Egypt, Ethiopia, and the insurgent Arab tribes of the East were based on the concept of the universal sovereignty of Yahweh as suzerain of the nations. The intent of the tradition at the hands of Isaiah, Nahum, Zephaniah, and Jeremiah appears to be primarily political. The major thrust of the oracles against the nations in this period was aimed at shaping foreign policy in Judah with respect to the nations concerned.

C. Israel and the Nations in History

1. The Davidic Empire as Political Ideal. Under David, Israel as a political entity was no longer a loosely federated tribal league, but rapidly became the center of an international empire. After defeating the Philistines (2 Sam 5:17–25; 1 Chr 18:1), David first turned his attention to Moab: he defeated Moab, ruthlessly punished their army, exacted tribute, and became their overlord. Next came the Arameans and the Ammonites. After humiliating David's delegation and thus provoking war with Israel, Hanun king of Ammon summoned his Aramean allies to aid him in battle. David defeated the Arameans and drew up a treaty of peace which made of the Aramean states a kind of province administered from Damascus. He also negotiated a "treaty of friendship" with king Toi of Hamath, making him a vassal within the emerging Davidic empire (cf. 2 Sam 8:9–10). The Ammonite campaign continued under Joab, David's general. When finally forced to capitulate, Ammon became Davidic territory with David ostensibly its king (cf. 2 Sam 12:26–31 and 1 Chr 20:1).

After the Aramean campaign, Edom was attacked and ravaged with dreadful cruelty by Joab and his troops (cf. 2 Sam 8:13-14; 1 Kgs 11:15–17), making David the undisputed master from Egypt to the Euphrates. The Philistines were reduced to their pentapolis and immediate coastal area. David was king of Judah, Israel, Jerusalem, Ammon, and the Canaanite city-states incorporated into Judah and Israel. He ruled through provincial governors or vassal chiefs in Aram, Edom, and Moab and had established treaty relationships with Tyre and Hamath. David had thus become the most powerful ruler in the world of his day, and Israel was transformed from a tribal confederation to suzerain of a league of nations.

Though the Davidic empire as a political reality did not survive the breakup of the United Monarchy in 922 B.C.E., the ideal extent of Israel's suzerainty under David lived on in prophetic circles. Mauchline has demonstrated this persistent belief in the Davidic empire in the 8th and 7th centuries, particularly in the writings of Amos, Isaiah, and Jeremiah. The emergence of both the Assyrian and the Neo-Babylonian empires did not obliterate the prophetic vision of Israel as the kingdom of David at its height in the first half of the 10th century B.C.E. In fact, this political ideal played a formative role in the shaping of the messianic hope of ancient Israel.

At the midpoint of the 8th century, Egypt was divided with numerous petty dynasts competing for the political authority of the decadent 22d Dynasty. Egypt seemed to be moving relentlessly down the road toward disaster and eclipse while Assyria was once again on the rise. From 801 to 746 the Assyrian kings were occupied with difficulties closer to home—north, east, and south of Assyria—and consequently left the West relatively undisturbed. Jeroboam II of Israel was thus able to conquer Damascus and to restore the old Davidic border on the north in eastern Syria (cf. 2 Kgs 14:23–25); while his younger contemporary Uzziah, king of Judah, regained control of the southern desert, the land of Edom, and its sea-trade routes to the south (2 Chr 26:1–15).

To summarize the first half of the 8th century, it may be said that Assyrians, Arameans, and Urarteans fought each other to a standstill in Mesopotamia and Syria. Given the internal stability that chanced to prevail in Judah and Israel at the time, it is no wonder that the divided kingdom briefly regained the economic strength and territorial extent of the Solomonic empire. Assyria's long respite made the people of Israel forget how much the conquests and splendor of Jeroboam's reign were the result of Assyria's maiming Israel's more immediate oppressors. With the rise of Tiglath-pileser III in 745, after the death of Jeroboam II in Israel, things changed. Assyria was now bent on conquest, and Syria-Palestine was a prime target in her march toward Egypt and control of the Near East.

2. An Era of Transition (ca. 750–700 B.C.E.). The accession of the usurper Tiglath-pileser III (745–727) to the throne in Assyria marks the beginning of a new era, for he and his two successors changed the balance of power in the ANE. In 745, Tiglath-pileser found Assyria in a difficult, even desperate military and economic situation; but over the next forty years Assyria recovered and consolidated control of all its old territories, reestablishing itself as the preeminent military and economic power of the Middle East. Tiglath-pileser reorganized the nearer Syrian provinces under direct Assyrian rule and divided the former provinces into smaller prefectures so as to secure centralized control of the empire. At the same time he regulated succession to political power in the middle tier of states, including Israel, and waged war against the more distant ones.

Israel was soon beset with internal crises brought on by the new Assyrian policy, and political prominence in Syria-Palestine apparently passed to Judah. The inscriptions of Tiglath-pileser for the year 738 mention the fact that he fought in Judah. Uzziah's daring attempt to halt the expansion of Assyria failed and the league dissolved. By 738, Tiglath-pileser reached the mountains of Lebanon, founding Assyrian provinces in the former territory of the kingdom of Hamath. The list of kings paying tribute to Assyria at this time includes the kings of Byblos, Tyre, Aram, and Samaria, and even a certain queen of Arabia.

Uzziah died in 735 or 734 and was succeeded by his son, Jotham, who had apparently shared a lengthy coregency with his father. Jotham died in 734 and was succeeded by Ahaz, who was immediately confronted with a political crisis of major proportions: Pekah had usurped the throne in Samaria and, together with Rezin king of Aram, apparently began preparing a new league against Assyria. When Ahaz refused to join this league, the two kings marched against Jerusalem in an attempt to replace him with a certain "son of Tabeel" (Isa 7:6). During the campaign of Rezin and Pekah against Ahaz, the Edomites asserted their independence and invaded Judah from the south (2 Kgs 16:6; 2 Chr 28:17). The people of Philistia also took the opportunity to overcome the cities of the Negeb and the Shephelah of Judah (2 Chr 28:18). If the reconstruction of Aharoni and Avi-Yonah is correct, Rezin, king of Aram, either neutralized Ammon and Moab or engaged their assistance against Judah at this time. Then, in spite of the warnings of Isaiah (Isa 7:4), Ahaz turned to Assyria for aid.

Tiglath-pileser's actions were swift and decisive. From Assyrian inscriptions it is known that he had already set out on a campaign to Philistia in 734. Hanun, king of Gaza, took refuge in Egypt and Tiglath-pileser left troops on the Egyptian border, thus cutting the kings of Palestine off from Egyptian aid. In response to the appeal of Ahaz of Judah, Tiglath-pileser marched against Israel and Aram-Damascus. In the years 734–33, the plains of Esdraelon and Sharon, the region around Mount Carmel, and Gilead in Transjordan were incorporated into the Assyrian provincial system, leaving the city-state of Samaria with only a measure of independence. By 732 the Assyrian victory was complete with the conquest of Damascus and the incorporation of its territory into the Assyrian empire (2 Kgs 16:9). Tiglath-pileser's second western campaign (734–732) was decisive, for from the Taurus mountains in the north to the River of Egypt in the south, the entire Mediterranean littoral now paid him homage, either as province or as vassal kingdom. In 731, Tiglath-pileser's attention was again diverted to other regions with a rebellion in Babylonia, settled in 729 when he set himself up as Pul, king of Babylon (2 Kgs 15:19; 1 Chr 5:26).

Tiglath-pileser died in 727 and his successor, Shalmaneser V (727–722), was occupied for some time securing his throne. Though Israel was not hard-pressed by Assyria, Hoshea continued to pay tribute. Then, in 726, an event to the south altered the situation. 2 Kgs 17:4 records the fact that Hoshea, king of Israel, appealed for aid against Assyria to a certain King "So" in Egypt, who is probably to be identified with Tefnakhte I of Sais. Hoshea, who evidently was no longer as pro-Assyrian as he had been in 732, welcomed the news from Egypt that a new dynasty was emerging in the Delta which promised to unite a badly divided Egypt and return her to her legendary greatness. Reports evidently confirmed the news as Tefnakhte rapidly gained the supremacy of the Delta area and began to move south with his troops. At last the time was right and Hoshea withheld tribute from Assyria, apparently convinced that Tefnakhte would come to his aid.

Tefnakhte's rise to power in the Delta was preceded by the emergence of Piye *(Piʿankhi),* a Cushite ruler in Upper Egypt, whose brother later became the first pharaoh of the Ethiopian 25th Dynasty in Egypt. Piye ordered his troops, which were already in Upper Egypt, northward to besiege Hermopolis, which had just submitted to Tefnakhte. Meanwhile, he dispatched a second army which defeated Tefnakhte's fleet on the Nile and continued on its way to Heracleopolis, the last major city in the Delta still holding out against Tefnakhte. Piye's troops were victorious both by land and by sea, and Tefnakhte saw his empire crumbling even more quickly than it had taken form. When Piye left the Delta to return south, he apparently left the various petty dynasts in their individual cities as vassals. In Upper Egypt his rule continued for an uncertain but brief period.

Meanwhile, Sargon II (722–705) had taken power in Assyria during the siege of Samaria. In his first campaigns following the fall of Israel, he was defeated near Der by Merodach-Baladan, then king of the small kingdom of Bit-Yakin, who had the assistance of the Elamite king Humbanigash. Sargon turned against Syria where, following the death of his brother, Shalmaneser V, the Assyrian rule had collapsed, at least as far north as Hamath. Apparently Piye deemed the time a propitious one to deal a vital blow to Assyria, for on the historic battlefields of Qarqar on the Orontes, Sargon had met the kings of Hamath and Damascus, and others whom the Egyptian general Reʾu (formerly read Sibʾu) had been able to muster. Though the fact that this Egyptian was indeed Piye's general cannot be demonstrated, it seems likely that such was the case. The defeat of the allies was complete, and in 720 Sargon pursued the Egyptian contingent as far as Raphia, whence the Egyptian general fled home, presumably to Ethiopia, for Sargon did not cross the Egyptian border.

In 720 Tefnakhte reemerged as king in Sais, apparently by allying himself with Assyria so as to make a new bid for the control of Egypt and to keep Assyrian forces out of the Delta. In 718 he erected a stela which he dated to his eighth year as pharaoh, considering his reign from his earlier rise to power in 726. Tefnakhte's son Bocchoris, who was recognized by all as a pharaoh of the 24th Dynasty, in 716/15 left a monument dated to his sixth year and reigned until 710/09 when Shabaka, brother of Piye, founded the Ethiopian 25th Dynasty, which was involved in much of the diplomatic intrigue in Palestine in the following decades.

The respite following Sargon's first campaign in the West lasted two years (719–718) during which time Sargon was engaged in the far north. In 717, Carchemish conspired against Assyria and Sargon, unleashing a two-year show of strength in the West, defeated Carchemish and marched south to the Egyptian border where, according to a fragment of a clay prism published in 1941, he received tribute from king Shilkanni (Osorkon IV) of Bubastis, the last king of the so-called 23d Dynasty in Egypt. It is significant that Osorkon is called king *(Lugal)* and not pharaoh *(ᵐPi-ir-'u)* in this inscription. The *Pir'u* (pharaoh) who was king of Egypt in 715, according to the annals of Sargon II, was probably Bocchoris. Osorkon was a king of Egypt in the western Delta in 716, but Tefnakhte of Sais (in 720) and his son Bocchoris (in 715) were recognized as pharaohs by the Assyrians.

In the midst of these events on the Egyptian border, Ahaz of Judah died and was succeeded by Hezekiah (715–687). Sargon was again occupied on his northern frontier until 712, when Palestine once more felt the full impact of the Assyrian arms. The provocation for Sargon's third and last western campaign came from Ashdod, where a certain Yamani had usurped the throne. Yamani had contacted other Philistine cities, Judah, Edom, Moab, and Egypt in an attempt to stir up a rebellion. Anticipating an Assyrian attack, he fortified Ashdod against siege. When news of Ashdod's revolt reached Sargon, he dispatched his army under a commander-in-chief who "came to Ashdod and fought it and took it" (Isa 20:1). Ashdod and her surrounding territory were organized as a new Assyrian province ruled by a governor.

For the rest of his reign (710–705), Sargon was occupied in Mesopotamia and in Anatolia, where his death on a battlefield in 705 triggered widespread rebellion, beginning with Babylonia. Ashkelon and Ekron took an active part in this rebellion, probably because of the ominous proximity of Assyrian authority in the province of Ashdod. Hezekiah intervened in Ekron deposing the loyal Assyrian vassal Padi, taking him captive to Jerusalem. The increasingly aggressive policy of the Ethiopian dynasty in Egypt was no doubt an important factor in the anti-Assyrian stand of Ashkelon and Ekron. For four years Sennacherib (705–681) took no steps to quell the rebellion. Finally in 701, after settling affairs in Babylon, he marched against Philistia and Judah.

Sennacherib's campaign against Judah in 701 is well known, though still the subject of sharp debate among scholars. The records present an unusually complete account from both sides. The problem arises over the very different interpretations given to the biblical and Assyrian evidence. Albright, Bright, and others have argued that there were actually two contests between Sennacherib and Hezekiah and that the Assyrians won the first but lost the second. Hallo, Tadmor, and others reject the two-campaign theory. It is sufficient here to note, with Hallo, that the accession of Sennacherib in 705 symbolized in many ways the start of a new phase in the Assyrian impact on western Asia.

3. *Pax Assyriaca* (ca. 700–640 B.C.E.). The triumph of Assyria and the subsequent *pax Assyriaca* brought an eclipse to the developing tradition of oracles against the nations within the prophetic literature of the OT, for no such material can be dated to this period with any degree of confidence. During the first half of the 7th century Judah, Moab, Ammon, Edom, and Philistia remained subservient to Assyria as vassal kingdoms or nominal Assyrian provinces. The other nations addressed in prophetic materials of the second half of the 7th century reveal a rather stormy history for the so-called *pax Assyriaca.*

The conquest of Phoenicia by Assyria was a drawn-out affair which met continued opposition, particularly from Tyre. When Sennacherib marched against Phoenicia, Luli, king of Sidon, fled to Cyprus where he died. The Assyrians installed Ittobaᶜal II as king in Sidon, who was in turn succeeded by ᶜAbdmilkot. Allying himself with Cilicia, ᶜAbdmilkot revolted against Assyria, and this time the Assyrian conquest was followed by destruction and exile of the population. In 677, Sidon was razed to the ground and replaced by the new city of Kar-Esarhaddon. Tyre was spared and a treaty was drawn up which set up an Assyrian governor alongside King Baᶜal. Six years later (671) Tyre revolted, in league with Taharqa (Tirhakah), king of Egypt. Though Esarhaddon's reign (681–669) in Assyria marked continued decline in Phoenician independence, Tyre remained autonomous under the rule of Baᶜal during the reign of Ashurbanipal (669–630). Sometime after the sack of Thebes (663), Baᶜal rebelled again, and though the revolt was quelled, Tyre was not occupied and merely had to send homage and tribute as a nominal vassal to Assyria.

The emergence of the Ethiopian 25th Dynasty (ca. 710–664) in Egypt set the stage for one of the great power struggles in antiquity. With a direct clash of interest in Lower Egypt and southern Palestine an eventual confrontation with Assyria was inevitable. However, as Gardiner has noted, it was with a third party to this dispute that ultimate victory was destined to lie, namely with Psammetichus (Psamtik) I (663–609), founder of the Saite 26th Dynasty. The campaigns of Esarhaddon and Ashurbanipal from 675 to 663, climaxed by the sack of Thebes, marked the crest of Assyrian expansion. To defeat the Ethiopians, Ashurbanipal apparently used the royal house of Sais to unify Lower Egypt against the Ethiopian king. In so doing the Assyrians set the stage for a second phase in the power struggle. After about a decade on the throne, Psammetichus I shook off the restraint and supervision of the resident Assyrian officials and allied himself with Gyges of Lydia in a successful revolt against Assyria. By the time Ashurbanipal settled affairs with Elam and Kedar around 640, the independence movement of Psammetichus had gone so far that the Assyrian monarch did not care to risk opposing it.

The history of Elam from ca. 700 to 639 is marked by conspiracy, revolt and factional strife, with seven rebellions against Assyria in six decades. It is possible that Egypt (or Ethiopia) was involved in most, if not all, of these revolts, and Judah may have been a party in as many as four of the widespread conspiracies associated with them. In the rebellion of 703–701, Shutruk-nahunte II of Elam (717–699) is singled out as the most prominent ally of Merodach-Baladan of Babylon. Sennacherib put down the revolt, routing the Elamite forces in 703 and again in 700. Between these two conquests of Elam, Sennacherib defeated a coalition of western states including "Hezekiah the Jew," the princes of Egypt, and the "king of Ethiopia." From 694 to 689 B.C. the bitter struggle between Elam and Assyria was resumed, no doubt precipitating revolt in the West again as had occurred earlier in the Elamite revolts of 721–720 and 703–700. The involvement of Egypt in such a revolt is reflected in the biblical reference to Taharqa (Tirhakah) in 2 Kgs 19:9. Unfortunately, the Assyrian records are incomplete for the years immediately following the sack of Babylon in 689. A second campaign in southern Palestine on the part of Sennacherib to quell a revolt in 688 is certainly possible, if not likely. The defeat of Elam in 689 marked the end of political unity and the beginning of an era of factionalism there. Nonetheless, the embers of revolt continued to smolder and burst forth in flames of rebellion twice in connection with the Assyrian conquest of Egypt (ca. 675–663).

When revolt broke out in Babylon in 652 under Ashurbanipal's brother Shamash-shum-ukin, the widespread conspiracy included numerous petty states in Syria-Palestine and pharaoh Psammetichus, who had already freed Egypt from Assyrian rule. If credence is given the Chronicler's account of the Babylonian captivity of King Manasseh (2 Chr 33:10–17), Judah was a member of the conspiracy, as was the case earlier in 701 and probably ca. 688. The Babylonian revolt led to civil war in Elam, which Ashurbanipal put down. By 646 Elam was once more under Assyrian control, at least for the moment. Six years later the stage was set for a final coup which once and for all put an end to an independent Elamite kingdom. In 639 Susa was taken by Assyria and utterly destroyed.

The Kedarites emerged as the dominant power of the desert league of Arab tribes in Syria-Palestine during the closing years of the reign of Sennacherib (ca. 690–688). The years up to the Babylonian revolt in 652 were relatively tranquil for Assyria in the Kedarite controlled area of Syria-Palestine. Kedar joined in the revolt against Assyria in 652, sending troops under Abiyate to assist Shamash-shum-ukin in Babylon. When the Arab reinforcements were defeated, Abiyate went to Nineveh, where he submitted to Ashurbanipal and was appointed king of the Arabs. Some time prior to Abiyate's return to his people, a certain Uaiteʾ "made himself king of Arabia," thus claiming leadership of the Arab confederacy. Around 640 Abiyate apparently deemed it politic to renounce his fealty to Assyria and to join with Natnu of Nabate and with Uaiteʾ in revolt again. In Ashurbanipal's second campaign against the Arabs (639–637), Uaiteʾ and Abiyate were captured and taken to Assyria. After humiliating Uaiteʾ, Ashurbanipal apparently had mercy on him as he did earlier with Necho I of Egypt, Tammaritu of Elam, and Manasseh of Judah, whom he restored as vassal kings after subjecting them to a humiliating ceremony of submission. That this was the case is suggested by the fact that a later inscription makes reference to Nuhur, the son of Uaiteʾ, who came in submission to Ashurbanipal and was granted his father's throne.

Though the details are not certain, it is likely that the assassination of King Amon in Judah in ca. 640 (2 Kgs 21:23–24) was related to the simultaneous revolt against Assyria on the part of Elam, Kedar, and Tyre. Realizing that the time was not yet right for such drastic action, the "people of the land" put the murderers to death and placed the boy Josiah on the throne in Jerusalem. This action forestalled Assyrian intervention and gave Judah the opportunity to revolt at a more opportune moment.

4. *Regnum Davidicum redivivum* (ca. 640–609 B.C.E.). Little is known about the history of Babylon and Assyria from 640 to 630. Ashurbanipal died ca. 630 and was succeeded by his son Asshuretililani, whose rule was challenged early. In 629 Sinsharishkun, another son of Ashurbanipal, was recognized as king in Sippar and Uruk; and a certain Sinshumlishir, commandant of the Nippur garrison, claimed the throne of Assyria in 627/26. That year has also been described as "the year in which there was no king in the land." In the year 626 the diadem of Babylon passed from the hands of Assyria to the Chaldean Nabopolassar (626–605), who organized a new dynasty in Babylon. The death throes of the mighty Assyrian empire were at hand.

With the decline of Assyria after the middle of the 7th century, the stage was set for the restoration of Judah among the nations. From 648 to his death in 642, Manasseh remained a loyal vassal to Assyria; and his son Amon (642–640) apparently continued his father's policy. When Elam, the Arab confederacy, and Tyre were again in revolt against Assyria in 640, pressure was exerted on Judah to join them. The assassination of Amon was probably an attempt on the part of rebel extremists to force Judah to throw off the Assyrian yoke. Instead, a more moderate group, the "people of the land," regained control in Judah, executed the king's murderers, and installed the eight-year-old Josiah (640–609) as king of Judah. This action apparently staved off Assyrian intervention in Judah, though it seems that the advisers of the young king were merely seeking a more opportune time to restore the "kingdom of David."

In the eighth year of his reign, according to 2 Chr 34:3, Josiah "began to seek the God of David his father." In other words, as early as 632 Josiah repudiated the gods of his Assyrian overlords. Four years later he annexed the Assyrian provinces to the N—Samaria, Megiddo, and probably Gilead. Of the three Transjordan states only Moab, which was but a shadow of her former self, escaped direct territorial incursion on the part of Judah. The Negeb in particular was wrested from Edomite control.

Unfortunately for Judah, the international situation in the Levant in the 7th century was only superficially similar to that of the 10th century, such that it was quite impossible to restore the empire of David for any length of time. Egypt was again seeking an Asian empire of her own, and the temporary vacuum formed by the demise of Assyria was soon to be filled by the Neo-Babylonian Empire. Josiah met his death at Megiddo in battle against the Egyptian forces of Neco II (609–594), who was on his way north to Haran to check the progress of the Medo-Babylonian alliance against Assyria. The death of Josiah in 609 marked the beginning of the end for the kingdom of Judah and for the former members of the Davidic League as well. Judah, Moab, Ammon, Edom, Aram, and Phoenicia were soon to be swallowed up by the military might of Nebuchadnezzar the Great (605–561). Philistia, Egypt, Kedar, and distant Elam (Persia) were to share the same fate.

5. *Imperium Babylonicum* (ca. 626–582 B.C.E.). The accession of Nabopolassar (626–605) marks the beginning of a new era in the history of the ANE. The Babylonian Chronicle for 626 begins with a revolt in Babylon in which Nabopolassar routed the Assyrian garrison established by Sinsharishkun. Since his first official act in the chronicle was to return to Susa the gods carried off to Uruk by the Assyrians some twenty years earlier, it is clear that he either had or hoped to have Elamite (or Persian) support in his struggle against Assyria. By November 624, Uruk was retaken by Assyria; but Sinsharishkun's belated foray into Babylonia in 623 appears to be the action of a hard-pressed man who snatched time for temporary measures to control a local insurrection. Aware that the Egyptians were now potential enemies to any force pushing into Syria, Nabopolassar allied himself with the Medes in order to destroy the great citadels of Assyria along the Tigris.

When Nabopolassar engaged the Assyrians in Syria on July 23, 616, they fled in disarray. In a second encounter in September the "army of Egypt" appeared along with the Assyrians. The penetration of Egyptian forces so far into Syria can only mean that the Egyptians were aware of the growing weakness of Assyria and of Nabopolassar's intention of establishing Babylonian control there. In May 615, Nabopolassar besieged Asshur but was forced to retreat before the forces of Sinsharishkun. By midsummer of 614 an army of Medes was advancing toward Nineveh. Again Shinsharishkun repelled the invaders, at least from Nineveh. Turning downstream along the bank of the Tigris, the Medes attacked Asshur, which was poorly defended, since Sinsharishkun had gone to the defense of Nineveh. The city was sacked and its inhabitants massacred. The destruction of Asshur was such a shocking violation of international practice of the time—which usually permitted a city to ransom itself unless it could be termed "rebellious"—that even the Babylonian Chronicler took pains to dissociate Nabopolassar from this act of savagery. An alliance of "peace and cordial relations" was concluded between Umakishtar, king of the Medes, and Nabopolassar, and it apparently remained in effect through the major campaigns against Nineveh (612) and Haran (610). After 609 the Medes disappear from the extant chronicles.

After two unsuccessful assaults on Nineveh in 612, the wall of the city was finally breached and the Medes and Babylonians poured into the city. Sinsharishkun died, as Shamash-shum-ukin before him, in the ruins of the city. Though Nineveh was utterly destroyed, Sinsharishkun's son Asshuruballit II (611–609) managed to escape, making his way to Haran, the final bastion of Assyria. When the combined armies of Babylonia and the Medes marched against Haran in 610, the Assyrians and Egyptians fled and the city was taken. The Egyptian force was a garrison, which was apparently delayed by Josiah's fateful battle at Megiddo in 609. A vain attempt on the part of Asshuruballit to retake Haran in 609, with Egyptian help, failed. The final curtain had fallen on Assyrian power in the ANE.

In March 609, the Babylonians and Medes returned to their own lands, and sometime later, according to tradition, a covenant of friendship between Babylonia and the Medes was sealed by the marriage of Nabopolassar's son Nebuchadnezzar to Umakishtar's daughter Amyntas. With their eastern frontier secured by treaty, the Babylonians gave their attention to affairs in the West.

In the spring of 605 Nabopolassar turned over command of the army to Nebuchadnezzar who, in his first major campaign, took the Egyptians by surprise and defeated them roundly at Carchemish. Though this defeat of the Egyptians marked the beginning of Babylonian dominance in Syria-Palestine, the struggle was by no means over. Entries in the Babylonian Chronicle for the next four years show repeated military expeditions in the West. On August 15, 605, Nabopolassar died and Nebuchadnezzar returned in haste to Babylon to secure his throne. After the ceremonies of accession, he returned to Syria to continue his military exploits. In February 604 he returned to Babylon for the New Year's festival. Later that year he was again in Palestine, where he destroyed Ashkelon. Further campaigns in Palestine in 603 and 602 were designed to eliminate the Egyptian sphere of influence from Gaza north. In December 601, having reduced most of Syria and Palestine, Nebuchadnezzar launched a campaign against the borders of Egypt. In the ensuing battle the Egyptian forces were crippled, but at great cost to Nebuchadnezzar. Nebuchadnezzar was forced to withdraw, and his next year was spent in Babylon rebuilding his army. Egypt, on the other hand, was so seriously weakened that, for the moment, she was reduced to virtual parity with the lesser states of southern Palestine.

From the death of Josiah at the hands of pharaoh Neco in 609 to the second fall of Jerusalem in 587, the kings of Judah and the other Palestinian states held their thrones at the pleasure of Egypt or Babylon. Foreign policy in Jerusalem and other major cities of the area was determined by which of these two powers seemed stronger or more menacing. After the death of Josiah, Judah became an Egyptian vassal. Jehoahaz, a son and successor of Josiah, was deposed, after reigning only three months, by Neco, who installed Eliakim, another son of Josiah, with the crown name Jehoiakim (609/8–597). After the defeat of Egypt at Carchemish in 605, the area as far south as Riblah was placed under tribute. In 604 Nebuchadnezzar extended his exactions to "all the kings of Hatti land," though Jehoiakim, Adon of Ashkelon, and perhaps others, held out for a time. Sometime in 603, probably after the fall of Ashkelon, Judah also became tributary to the Babylonians. This relationship stood until 601.

The decisive battle between Nebuchadnezzar and Neco at "the borders of Egypt" in 601/600 was a blow to the pro-Babylonian faction in Jerusalem. Jehoiakim withheld tribute in a vain attempt to reassert Judean independence. In 599/98 Nebuchadnezzar sent raiding parties from his Syrian bases to plunder the Arabs. The Babylonians sent raiding bands of Syrians, Moabites, and Ammonites against Judah as well, as late as 598. Josephus has reconstructed this raid, perhaps with the aid of additional sources now lost.

Late in November 598 a mixed force of Chaldeans, Syrians, Moabites, and Ammonites appeared before Jerusalem. The death of Jehoiakim at this time was probably the result of a palace revolt in which "his body was thrown outside the gates of Jerusalem, and left there, like the body of an ass" (cf. Jer 22:19 and 36:30). Jehoiakim was succeeded by his eighteen-year-old son, Jehoiachin, who, three months and ten days later, was carried into exile by the Babylonians on March 16, 597; his uncle Mattaniah was installed with the throne name Zedekiah (2 Kgs 24:17). The treasuries of the palace and temple were looted, and the royal family, together with members of the court, soldiers, and artisans, were deported to Babylon (2 Kgs 24:13–16). In Babylon, Jehoiachin was maintained in nominal captivity along with a group of kings from other lands. Meanwhile, in Jerusalem, Zedekiah was regarded as regent for the exiled king of Judah.

Jerusalem was the focus of an anti-Babylonian coalition in 594 when envoys from Edom, Moab, Ammon, Tyre, and Sidon came in a conspiracy (Jer 27:3). For some reason the revolt did not materialize. In 591 Psammetichus II (594–588) made a trip through *Ḫurru* (Phoenicia), which may have had as its purpose the inciting of further rebellion in Palestine. When Zedekiah foolishly withheld, or perhaps reduced, the amount of tribute paid to Babylon in 590 or 589, Babylonian troops appeared before the walls of Jerusalem. An Egyptian army under pharaoh Apries (Hophra) (588–568) came to the aid of Jerusalem, causing the siege to be lifted temporarily, but the Egyptians were routed and the siege was resumed. Finally, in the summer of 587, weakened by siegeworks, famine, and plague, Jerusalem was stormed and methodically destroyed (cf. 2 Kgs 25:8–21; Jer 52:12–27). Booty and prisoners were transported to Mesopotamia.

The catastrophe which struck Judah in 587 did not immediately affect Ammon, Moab, and Edom. By the beginning of the last decade of the 7th century, Ammon had asserted its independence and rapidly became the dominant state of S Transjordan, expanding as far west as the Jordan valley. Nebuchadnezzar's victory at Carchemish in 605 posed a new threat to the petty states of Palestine, and it is probable that the king of Ammon was among the "kings of Hatti" who paid homage to the Babylonian monarch in 604. After three years, Jehoiakim of Judah revolted, though Ammon and Moab remained loyal and fought with the raiding parties dispatched from Syria against Judah (2 Kgs 24:2). The Ammonites and Moabites remained loyal to Babylon in order to secure protection against the Kedarite dominated Arab confederacy which was encroaching upon the borders of all the states in Transjordan. It was not until 594, after the first fall of Jerusalem, that Ammon and Moab were induced to join with Edom, Tyre, and Sidon in a conspiracy against Babylon.

Though the widespread revolt against Babylon did not materialize, Ammon remained in open rebellion, even to the point of interference in the internal affairs of the remnant of Judah after 587. King Baalis of Ammon was involved in the plot to assassinate Gedaliah, the governor of Judah (Jer 40:14). Apparently the Ammonite king was trying to gain control of Judah, possibly in the hope of restoring the kingdom of Josiah, this time under Ammonite rule. Though the subsequent political events in Transjordan from 586 to 582 are obscure, it seems probable that punitive measures were undertaken by Nebuchadnezzar. Josephus records a Babylonian campaign in Coele-Syria against Ammon and Moab "in the fifth year after the sacking of Jerusalem, which was the twenty-third year of the reign of Nebuchadnezzar" (*Ant.* 10.9.7). The biblical account in Jer 52:30 apparently describes the same event, noting that 745 Jews were included in the deportation of 582, which was carried out by Nebuzaradan, the doughty Babylonian general who had also executed the deportation of 587. The devastating punitive action of 582 created a political vacuum in Transjordan into which poured the Arab invaders of the Kedarite League, destroying all organized political activity in the area (cf. Ezek 25:4–5, 8–9). By the middle of the 6th century the Ammonite state had collapsed, as witnessed by archaeological explorations which show that sedentary occupation of Ammon ceased almost completely until the early 3d century.

The situation in Moab was similar to that in Ammon. In 604 the Moabite king submitted to Nebuchadnezzar and remained loyal to Babylon in the revolt of ca. 600–597. Though Moab sent envoys to Jerusalem in the conspiracy of 594, she apparently withdrew and returned to nominal vassalage to Babylon. When Judah was destroyed in 587, Moab was spared. Fugitives who fled from Judah were scorned by the Moabites who, according to the prophet Jeremiah, rejoiced over the fate of Judah and proclaimed their own country to be an impregnable fortress (Jer 48:26–30). The haughtiness of Moab produced a flood of condemnation from the prophets of Judah. In the Babylonian campaign of 582, the voice of Moab, like that of Ammon, was silenced. Some of the Moabites were exiled to Babylonia, while others fled to Egypt. The destruction of the line of Moabite fortresses in the first quarter of the 6th century meant Moab's end. Subsequent Arab encroachment destroyed any surviving sedentary culture in Transjordan.

The kingdom of Edom managed to survive the devastations of 587 and 582 in Palestine. Along with the other petty states of the area, Edom submitted quietly to the Babylonian yoke in 604. Though envoys from Edom were present in Jerusalem in the conspiracy of 594, Edom apparently withdrew. When Babylonian forces besieged and captured Jerusalem in 587, the Edomites joined the forces of Nebuchadnezzar and exulted over the destruction of their ancient enemy (cf. Ps 137:7; Lam 4:21–22; and Obad 10–16). After the deportation of the people of Judah to Babylon in 587 and 582, the Edomites moved northward into southern Judah, making Hebron the capital of a kingdom which eventually came to be known as Idumea. Behind them the Nabateans pressed into former Edomite territory and established a kingdom with Petra as their capital.

The fate of Philistia and Phoenicia at the hands of Nebuchadnezzar is not clear, at least in detail. Only the fall of Ashkelon in 604 can be dated. Gaza, which fell into Egyptian hands in the reign of Neco II (609–594), was later listed as a Babylonian dependency along with Tyre, Sidon, Arvad, and Ashdod. Citing an earlier source of Philostratos, Josephus mentions a thirteen-year siege of Tyre, which apparently began in 587, the year Jerusalem fell, and terminated in 573, when Tyre surrendered.

D. The Nations in Prophetic Eschatology and Early Apocalyptic Literature

The fate of the separate nations addressed in the oracles of the OT prophets has been presented in order to explain the transformation of prophecy in relation to the nations, which took place against this background. The death of Josiah in 609 and the conquests of Nebuchadnezzar from 605 to 597 mark the end of an era in the development of the prophetic literature of ancient Israel, and the beginning of a major transformation of the war oracle in particular. Beginning with Habakkuk and Jeremiah's oracle against Elam (Jer 49:34–39), the focus of attention shifted from contemporary events of political history to the realm of eschatology. The primary intent of this new literary mode was no longer that of shaping foreign policy per se, but the preservation of the people of Israel in the impending crisis by means of hope in events yet to come. The fall of Jerusalem in 597 and its final destruction at the hands of Nebuchadnezzar in 587 served to complete this transformation. Loosed from its moorings in the royal court and temple cult, OT prophecy evolved rather quickly from a focus on prophetic eschatology to that of early apocalyptic.

Within this setting those who assembled the biblical material in its present canonical form turned their attention to the deeper meaning behind the historical events. The nation of Israel was not to be understood in isolation from other nations, even her bitter enemies of times past. One of the most interesting examples of this shift in perspective appears in the book of Isaiah at the conclusion to the oracles against Egypt (19:24–25):

> In that day Israel will be the third with Egypt and
> Assyria,
> a blessing in the midst of the earth,
> whom Yahweh of hosts has blessed, saying:
> "Blessed be Egypt, my people,
> Assyria the work of my hands,
> and Israel my heritage."

Both Assyria and Egypt/Ethiopia here take their place alongside Israel as part of the people of Yahweh.

Isaiah's oracle against Arabia (Isa 21:13–17) does not move beyond the Davidic ideal of earlier tradition, as witnessed by the inclusion of Arab tribes within the roll call of nations in Psalm 83. Arab groups were occupying land within the idealized boundary of the former Davidic empire. Moreover, the agreements formulated between the Queen of Sheba and Solomon placed Arabia within the sphere of influence of the United Monarchy. With Assyria and Egypt/Ethiopia, however, no such rationalization was possible. The new model was found within the holy war traditions of ancient Israel, especially the war songs from the premonarchic era. The Divine Warrior was seen to be the suzerain of all nations, the Lord of history, whose dominion knew no geographical bounds. Even mighty Assyria was but the "rod of Yahweh's anger," as the Divine Warrior chastened his chosen people. Once he was through with this unwitting servant, the Divine Warrior would vent his wrath against Assyria as well, to punish "the arrogant boasting of the king of Assyria and his haughty pride" (Isa 10:5–12).

The resurgence of Assyria in the last half of the 8th century was paralleled by a dramatic recovery on the part of Egypt, which eventually succumbed to invasion from the south and political subjugation to Ethiopia. Though these events in Egypt did not immediately threaten Judah, Isaiah incorporated them within his model of the nations under the suzerainty of Yahweh in a series of oracles (Isa 18–20; 30:1–17; 31:1–3). Yahweh, the Divine Warrior, comes riding upon the stormcloud to Egypt, where her gods tremble before him (Isa 19:1). It is Yahweh who stirs up Egyptians against Egyptians in civil struggle (19:2). It is Yahweh who confounds their plans (19:3) and gives them into the hands of a hard master, a fierce king who will rule over them—probably Piye (Piᶜankhi), or perhaps his brother Shabaka, who founded the Ethiopian 25th Dynasty in Egypt (ca. 710 B.C.E.).

Since these oracles against Egypt already possessed trans-historical elements, it was but a short step to lift them to the realm of eschatology. The judgment of Egypt was portrayed in apocalyptic fashion as the Nile is dried up (19:5–10) and the traditional wisdom of Egypt's sages is turned into confusion such that Egypt staggers "as a drunken man staggers in his vomit" (19:11–15). An altar and a pillar were to be erected in Egypt to Yahweh as a sign and a witness to Yahweh's presence there. When Egypt cries to Yahweh for deliverance from her oppressors, Yahweh will send a savior who "will defend and deliver them" (19:19–20). The picture presented here is indeed remarkable, for Yahweh will one day send a "new Moses" to deliver Egypt from bondage. Yahweh will reveal himself to the Egyptians, who in turn will worship him (19:22). Yahweh will build a highway from Egypt to Assyria for a new exodus, in which both the Egyptians and the Assyrians will participate along with Israel (19:23–25).

The idea of Assyria as "the rod of (Yahweh's) anger" in Isa 10:5 must be understood in terms of its literary context. The "March of Conquest" in 10:27c–34 is more than a description of the approach of Assyrian troops on hapless Jerusalem. It is the Divine Warrior himself who threatens daughter Zion with destruction. The vision continues across the chapter division. In spite of the hewing down of "the thickets of the forest" (10:34), a shoot from the stump of Jesse will become an ensign to the nations (11:1, 10) for an eschatological contest. Although the focus in these passages is on the remnant of Israel, it is clear that Yahweh is Lord of the nations. He will use, however unwittingly, even wicked Assyria to pave the way for a "new Conquest" (11:12–16) which will establish his people in a "new Kingdom" described in messianic terms (11:1–9). We have a transformation of prophetic language and thought which very nearly anticipates that of apocalyptic.

Further evidence of an eschatological transformation that includes the nations within the purview of Yahweh's people is found in Zephaniah. Yahweh's terrifying might "will lay waste all the gods of the earth." They are going to "bow down before him, each in his own place—all the lands of the nations" (Zeph 2:11). The picture is somewhat like that found in Jeremiah's oracle against Elam, in which Yahweh declared that he would establish his throne in that distant land (Jer 49:38). The prophet is projecting his message into the distant future where he sees a new day on the horizon, a day when pagan world powers will submit themselves to Yahweh, the suzerain of the nations.

Cultic gatherings at the Temple in Jerusalem became anticipations of the gathering of all nations to worship Yahweh. Kings from Egypt, Ethiopia, and the kingdoms of the earth, bearing gifts for the temple and singing praises to God, join the procession of the tribes of Israel to the temple in Psalm 68. In Deutero-Isaiah we see the descendants of Israel returning to Zion from exile, in contexts which suggest that the "survivors of the nations" are reckoned among these descendants (Isa 44:1–5; 45:22–25; 49:12–20; 53:10). When, as a result of the suffering and mission of the servant, the peoples at the ends of the earth are waiting for Yahweh's rule, their survivors join themselves to Israel to converge on Jerusalem (55:5). People from nations "of every tongue" join the returning Jews (Zech 8:21–23), and the alienation of the enemy nations is removed when Yahweh changes "the speech of the peoples to a pure speech" so that they may call on his name (Zeph 3:9). Kings lead their nations in a great procession (Isa 60:3, 11), which extends "from sea to sea and from mountain to mountain" (Mic 7:12), bringing the wealth of the nations on camels (Isa 60:5–6), driving before them animals for sacrifice, and carrying the sons and daughters of Israel in their arms (v 4). They join themselves to Yahweh and become his people (Zech 2:11) and go up every year to the Feast of Tabernacles in Jerusalem (14:16).

The destination of this pilgrimage is Mount Zion, which becomes a house of prayer for all nations (Isa 56:7; cf. Mark 11:17). Zion, as the navel of the earth (Ezek 5:5; 38:12) and the throne of Yahweh (Jer 3:17), is also the world mountain symbolizing the supremacy of Yahweh over the nations and their gods (Ps 99:9; Isa 2:2–4 = Mic 4:1–4; Isa 66:20; Dan 2:35). Zion will then be called the birthplace of the nations (Psalm 87). This eschatological pilgrimage will be climaxed by a great "festival banquet on Mount Zion," to which Yahweh will invite "all peoples" as he removes "the veil that is spread over all nations," destroys death, and "take(s) away the reproach of his people" (Isa 25:6–8). Thus will the nations become sons of Abraham and inherit the promised land as their own.

The Jewish mission to the nations in later postexilic times (see PROSELYTE) belongs to this same motif; for the object of the mission was to make Jews of the people of the nations and to bring them to worship Yahweh at Jerusalem. The obvious link with Jewish nationalism and legalism lies behind Jesus' severe condemnation of the proselyte movement (Matt 23:15).

In the exilic period, the motif of dominion over the nations was subordinated to that of the servant who suffers at the hands of the nations and is despised by rulers. In eschatological times, however, kings and rulers will bow down to Israel and serve the servant (Isa 14:1; 49:7, 22–23; 60:10–14; 61:5). Peoples from the nations will come to rebuild Jerusalem as the servants of Israel, and will bring their wealth as tribute (Isa 60:1–3, 10–18) to the glory of Yahweh.

In the postexilic literature the holy war motif reappears, in terms of a new exodus, in which Yahweh will overthrow the nations (Hag 2:7), cast down those who have scattered Judah (Zech 1:21), make the plunderers plunder for Israel (Zech 2:8–9), and trample the people in anger (Isa 63:6). Jerusalem herself will become a cup of reeling to all peoples (Obad 16; Zech 12:2). The eschatological dominion of Israel over the nations is most clearly expressed in Daniel, where the stone "cut out by no human hands," breaks the image into powder and then becomes a great mountain which fills the whole earth (Dan 2:34–35). This stone is God's kingdom, "which shall never be destroyed, nor shall its sovereignty be left to another people" (v 44). In another vision, a Son of Man, who is identified with the "saints of the Most High," is "given dominion and glory and kingdom, that all peoples, nations, and languages should serve him" (Dan 7:13–14).

In early apocalyptic literature (Isa 24–27; Ezek 38–39; Zech 9–14) the enmity of the nations toward Israel grows in intensity until the climactic struggle at Mount Zion, where Yahweh both summons them and punishes them for their violence on Israel. The author of Daniel places this final struggle in the persecution under Antiochus Epiphanes. This literature reveals the extreme enmity between the Jews and the nations, and the cry for revenge and vindication by direct intervention of God, born of intense suffering. The result is a complete polarization between Israel and the nations in contrast to the situation of earlier periods, so that the word *gôyim* ("nations" or "gentiles"), becomes a technical term denoting non-Jews as enemies and aliens. The retention of the term, however, remains a significant link with the earlier tradition and its emphasis on the mission of Israel to the nations.

E. A New Israel: The Righteous from All Nations

The inclusion of the righteous from among all nations within the "New Israel" of prophetic vision appears to be a specific and sustained challenge to a narrow nationalistic conception rooted in ancient legal pronouncements. That ancient nationalistic perspective surfaced again in the "fundamentalist" reforms of Ezra and Nehemiah which excluded all foreigners. Meanwhile, embedded in the very structure of the canon itself is an alternate point of view, perhaps best illustrated in the book of Jonah and its place within the Book of the Twelve (minor prophets). The message of Jonah is clear: Not only does God have a right to show compassion on Nineveh, the capital of wicked Assyria, but Jonah's anger over God's compassion for that great city is dangerous. The moment that Jonah's anger excludes compassion for the object of that anger it becomes a great evil, one that will destroy him (and Israel as well).

A close look at the four central books within the Book of the Twelve—Jonah-Micah and Nahum-Habakkuk—shows the canonical ambivalence which some scholars would remove from Isaiah 40–55. The fact that Nahum and Habakkuk may be described as a single literary unit is suggested by the following outline:

A. Hymn of Theophany (Nahum 1)
  B. Taunt Song against Nineveh (Nahum 2–3)
    C. The Problem of Theodicy (Habakkuk 1)
  B′. Taunt Song against the "Wicked One" (Habakkuk 2)
A′. Hymn of Theophany (Habakkuk 3)

The close relation between the books of Jonah and Micah, on the other hand, is demonstrated by the fact that the missing ending to the book of Jonah is supplied in liturgical use within Jewish tradition by the addition of Mic 7:18–20 to the afternoon reading of Jonah on the Day of Atonement to the present time.

Wicked Nineveh is the subject of both Jonah and Nahum, but in sharply contrasting manner. In Jonah, Nineveh is the focus of God's compassion in what some have called the greatest missionary text in the OT. On the other hand, as Robert Pfeiffer once put it, "Nahum's classic paean on the fall of Nineveh is one of the earliest and by far the best of (the) outbursts of hatred for the heathen kingdoms." The conflicting attitudes of nationalism and universalism could not be put in sharper contrast.

The complementary nature of Jonah-Micah over against Nahum-Habakkuk is also seen in a comparison of the second half of each of these literary constructions. Micah's prophecy of the fall of Jerusalem (3:9–12) sets the stage for Habakkuk's reflections on the profoundly disturbing question of why a just God is "silent when the wicked swallows up the man more righteous than he" (1:13).

The dialectic within the prophetic literature of the OT in terms of nationalism and universalism is part of the very structure of the canon itself. It is not to be removed by scholarly reconstruction of the biblical text, nor is it to be explained away by semantics. Even wicked Assyria is the work of Yahweh's hands (Isa 19:24), and as such she enjoys the same potential relationship to Yahweh as did Israel of old. As a light to the nations, the Servant Israel has a mission to the nations. Those who respond to that message, even among the Assyrians, will constitute the people of Yahweh—a new Israel.

A close look at structural detail within the partriarchal narratives in Genesis suggests a remarkable role for Edom in relation to Israel in the purposes of God.

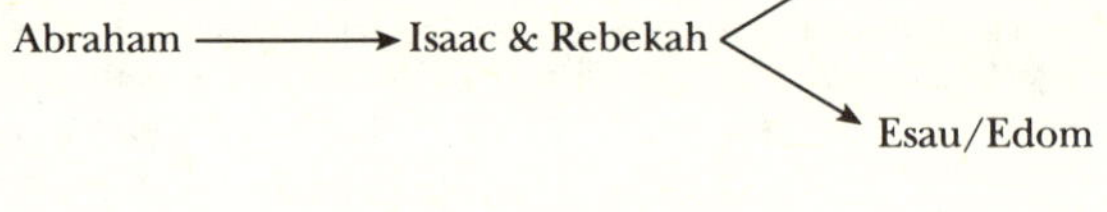

Jacob and Esau are presented as twin brothers and the cponymous ancestors of Israel and Edom, respectively. Z. Weisman has demonstrated the priority of national consciousness as reflected in the Jacob stories over that of the traditions concerning Abraham and Isaac. This observation raises new questions about the canonical process itself in ancient Israel.

It has long been noted that the editorial conclusion for the book of Job places him among the patriarchs in Genesis. From a literary perspective, Job is in effect an adoptive patriarch who takes his place alongside Abraham. The 140 years allotted to Job after his great testing becomes part of a larger structural pattern in which that number is associated with each of the patriarchs. Abraham was 140 years old when his son Isaac married Rebekah. Isaac and Rebekah were in turn married for 140 years; and Jacob was 140 years old at the point of his "wrestling match" at the River Jabbok when his name was changed to Israel (Genesis 32). And, of course, his twin brother Esau/Edom was also 140 years old at this decisive reunion of the estranged brothers. Placing Job within this schema makes of him the literary "twin brother" of Abraham, as suggested in the following diagram:

Job		Jacob/Israel
	Isaac & Rebekah	
Abraham		Esau/Edom

The fact that the home of both Job and his friends is so strongly associated with Edom thus takes on deeper meaning, for Job and Esau are associated structurally. In terms of canonical structure Edom seems to be included within a larger conception of Yahweh's people. As Job and Esau are related in chiastic fashion in the above diagram, so are Abraham and Jacob, both of whom are associated with Aram-Naharaim. In terms of canonical structure, the Arameans, too, belong to the people of Yahweh, as the ancient Deuteronomic confession put it: "A wandering Aramean was my father" (Deut 26:5).

At this juncture it is instructive to take a closer look at Deuteronomic legislation with regard to the nations. Both Egypt and Edom are clearly given precedence over Moab and Ammon, the incestuous offspring of Lot in the Genesis narrative (Gen 19:30–38; cf. Deut 23:7–8). The treatment of Moabites and Ammonites is much harsher (Deut 23:3–6). It is possible to see a historical reason for the different treatment of Egypt and Edom over against Moab and Ammon in terms of the idealized program of political expansion in the time of king Josiah. At this time Edom was within the political sphere of Egypt and both stood outside the scope of Josiah's projected political expansion, which included both the former territory of the northern state of Israel and the Transjordan states of Moab and Ammon.

A close look at the canonical process in ancient Israel suggests another point of view concerning the inclusion of Moab within the "New Israel" of prophetic vision. Both the question of genre and setting for the book of Ruth are subject to renewed debate. Apparently only a foreign woman could embody what the author wanted to say—even a Moabite who, according to Deut 23:4, could never enter into Yahweh's assembly. In short, Ruth is conceived by the author as a kind of matriarch by adoption. It is a literary and canonical challenge to a simplistic reading of the book of Deuteronomy, in a manner somewhat parallel to the book of Job, which may be read as a canonical challenge to a superficial reading of the Deuteronomic theology of history. Job suffers not because he violated the terms of the Covenant, but because he was "a blameless and upright man" (Job 1:8), at least within the folktale frame of the book. And, like Ruth, this man from the land of Uz is a foreigner.

In short, Job and Ruth are to the Patriarchs of earlier tradition what the nations are to Israel within the prophetic literature. While universalism can be qualified as a form of nationalism, as Hollenberg has argued, it can also stand alone. Job was admitted to the patriarchal structure of the book of Genesis because he was a righteous man—"blameless and upright, one who feared God, and turned away from evil" (Job 1:1). He was admitted to the community of faith because of the quality of his life. Thus, universalism need not have national roots as such. But in the end, of necessity, it becomes national because those who swear allegiance to Yahweh, as Ruth did, *are* Israel—that is, the people of Yahweh from among all nations (cf. Isa 19:2).

The covenant community in ancient Israel was open to non-Israelites from the start, according to Deuteronomy, since the resident alien *(ger)* actually participated in the covenant ceremony concluded before Moses' death (Deut 29:10). Even the exiled community of Judahites in Babylonia remained open to foreigners who wished to join it, and there were foreigners who did (cf. Isa 56:2–8). The readiness of strangers to join this politically crushed community is no more astonishing than their acceptance within that community; for it would have been natural for the exiles to have closed ranks tightly. That this did not happen witnesses to the radical hospitality of Israel to foreigners, which was ultimately grounded on a self-conscious representation of God's interest in all the nations.

In the NT there is a consciousness that the promise made first to Abraham was being fulfilled. The evangelists compiled their narratives accordingly. John the Baptist began his preaching with a rebuke to the Jewish nationalists; the children of Abraham are not confined to Israel according to the flesh (Matt 3:9). Jesus is described at the outset as a "light for revelation to the nations" (Luke 2:32); and the early days of his life are placed not in Israel but in Egypt (Matt 2:15). Jesus began his public ministry not in Bethlehem or Jerusalem, but in "Galilee of the nations" (Matt 4:15). During his ministry there, many came to him from among the neighboring peoples (Mark 3:8). Later he made a journey into Tyre and Sidon, beyond the borders of the Jewish state. On this trip he exorcised a demon in the Phoenician girl whose mother recognized him as the giver of the bread of life (Matt 15:21–28; Mark 7:24–30), cured a deaf mute in the Decapolis (Mark 7:31–37), and fed the 4000 in the wilderness (Matt 15:32–39; Mark 8:1–10). Jesus later healed the servant of a Roman centurion, with commendatory words for the faith of this man from the nations (Matt 8:5–13; Luke 7:1–10; cf. John 4:46–54, where this healing is taken as one of the great signs of Jesus' power), and a demoniac in Gerasa, whom he sent as a missionary of God's grace to his own people (Mark 5:19–

20). The mission of the 70 whom Jesus sent out is intended to be to the nations (Luke 10:1–16). Jesus gave his disciples the mission to be the servant of light and the salt of the world (Matt 5:13–14; cf. Isa 42:6; 49:6; and on the fact that salt may imply covenant, cf. Num 18:19; 2 Chr 13:5). The triumphal entry into Jerusalem revealed Jesus as the messianic king who will bring the blessings of peace unto the nations (Matt 21:5; cf. Zech 9:9–10). In short, Jerusalem as the city on a hill whose glory cannot be hidden is the signal for an eschatological pilgrimage of the nations (Matt 5:14; cf. Isa 60:1–3). There is to be a gathering of all nations before the throne of the King (Matt 25:32), and the righteous among the nations will receive their inheritance in the Kingdom of God.

The first Christians knew that the risen Christ had sent them to the nations on a mission in line with the eschatological signs of the earthly ministry of Jesus (Matt 28:19–20; Mark 16:15; Luke 24:47; Acts 1:8), the prophecies of Deutero-Isaiah, the royal (messianic) theology, the Sinai covenant, and the ancient promise to Abraham.

Paul found the very purpose of the death of Jesus to be that "in Christ Jesus the blessings of Abraham might come upon the nations" (Gal 3:14; cf. v 8). This fulfillment of the promise to Abraham in Christ brought Israel to a crisis, however, for it implied the end of her national aspirations. According to Jesus, the nations themselves will judge Israel for her hardness of heart (Matt 12:41–42). Peter quoted the promise to Abraham in order to encourage the Jews to take up their mission to the nations (Acts 3:25–26), and Paul quoted Isa 49:6 as a judgment on the Jews for refusing to see their mission to the nations (Acts 13:47). Paul finally concluded that it was in the providence of God that the very disobedience of Israel after the flesh should mean that the blessing would reach the nations through Christ (Rom 11:11–12).

The final appearance of the mission of Israel to the nations is in the book of Revelation, where in the midst of world catastrophe and the martyrdom of Christians there is an "angel flying in midheaven, with an eternal gospel to proclaim to those who dwell on earth, to every nation and tribe and tongue and people" (Rev 14:6).

In the NT, the line was drawn not so much between Jews and the nations as between the Christian community and the nations. According to the Gospels, the Son of Man would be handed over to the nations (Matt 20:19; Mark 10:33; Luke 18:32), for all nations are at enmity with Jesus and with his disciples (Matt 24:9; cf. 10:7–18; John 15:18–20).

The alliance of Jew and gentile against the followers of Jesus is a prominent theme in the book of Acts (12:1–5; 14:2; 16:10–24; cf. 2 Cor 11:26). Similarly, suffering at the hands of the nations is central in 1 Peter and Revelation, where the nations play a major role in the apocalyptic drama as the enemies of God who trample the Holy City for 42 months (Rev 11:2). Nonetheless, the time has come to destroy the destroyers (Rev 11:18), so that mighty Babylon (Rome), who made the nations drunk (14:8; 18:3, 23; cf. Jer 51:7), will be broken and the nations defeated (16:19). Satan, the deceiver of the nations, will be bound during the reign of the saints (20:3) and then released to deceive the nations once again, prior to the great apocalyptic battle before the "camp of the saints" and the "beloved city" (20:7–9). In the end, the nations are destroyed, Satan is cast into the lake of fire, and the dead are raised for judgment. This marks the end of the nations as enemies of God and the ultimate fulfillment of the OT prophetic vision which foresaw the ingathering of the nations within the kingdom of God.

Bibliography

Bächli, O. 1962. *Israel und die Völker,* ATANT 41. Zurich.

Bertholet, A. 1896. *Die Stellung der Israeliten und der Juden zu den Fremden.* Freiberg.

Bloch, J. S. 1980. *Israel and the Nations.* Berlin.

Causse, A. 1924. *Isräel et la vision de l'humanité.* Paris.

Christensen, D. L. 1975. *Transformations of the War Oracle in Old Testament Prophecy.* Missoula.

———. 1976. The March of Conquest in Isaiah 10:27c–34 *VT* 26: 385–99.

———. 1989. The Identity of "King So" in Egypt (2 Kings 17:4) *VT* 39: 140–53.

Cross, F. M. 1973. *Canaanite Myth and Hebrew Epic.* Cambridge, MA.

Davidson, R. 1963. Universalism in Second Isaiah. *SJT* 16: 166–85.

Donner, H. 1964. *Israel Unten den Völkern.* VTSup 11. Leiden.

Eichrodt, W. 1942. Gottesvolk und die Völker. *Evangelische Missionsmagazin.*

Gottwald, N. K. 1964. *All the Kingdoms of the Earth.* New York.

Greenberg, M. 1971. Mankind, Israel and the Nations in the Hebraic Heritage. Pp. 15–40 in *No Man Is Alien,* ed. J. Nelson. Leiden.

Hallo, W. 1960. From Qarqar to Carchemish: Assyria and Israel in the Light of New Discoveries. *BA* 23: 34–61.

Hanson, P. D. 1975. *The Dawn of Apocalyptic.* Philadelphia.

Hollenberg, D. E. 1969. Nationalism and "The Nations" in Isaiah XL–LV. *VT* 19: 23–36.

Jeremias, J. 1958. *Jesus' Promise to the Nations.* London.

Kitchen, K. 1973. *The Third Intermediate Period in Egypt.* Warminster.

Manson, T. W. 1955. *Jesus and the Non-Jews.* London.

Mauchline, J. 1970. Implicit Signs of a Persistent Belief in the Davidic Empire. *VT* 20: 287–303.

McCullough, W. S. 1972. Israel's Eschatology from Amos to Daniel. Pp. 86–101 in *Studies on the Ancient Palestinian World,* ed. J. Wevers and D. Redford. Toronto.

McKenzie, J. L. 1974. Yahweh and the Nations, and the Future of Israel. Pp. 170–79 and 278–332 in *A Theology of the OT.* Garden City, NY.

Murphy, R. 1977. "Nation" dans l'Ancien Testament. *Concilium* 121: 3–14.

Orlinsky, H. M. 1970. Nationalism-Universalism and Internationalism in Ancient Israel. Pp. 206–236 in *Translating and Understanding the OT,* eds. H. Frank and W. Reed. Nashville.

Rowley, H. H. 1944. *The Missionary Message of the OT.* London.

———. 1950. *The Biblical Doctrine of Election.* London.

Sanders, E. P. 1977. "The Gentiles." Pp. 206–212 in *Paul and Palestinian Judaism.* London.

Schmökel, H. 1934. *Yahweh und die Fremdvölker.* Breslau.

Spieckermann, H. 1982. *Juda und Assur in der Sargonidenzeit.* FRLANT 129. Göttingen.

Stolz, F. 1972. *Jahwes und Israels Kriege.* ATANT 60. Zurich.

Sundkler, B. 1936. Jesus et les païens. *RHPR* 16: 462–99.

Weisman, Z. 1985. National Consciousness in the Patriarchal Promise. *JSOT* 31: 55–73.

Wilson, A. 1986. *The Nations in Deutero-Isaiah.* Lewiston, NY.
Zeissl, H. von. 1944. Athiopen und Assyrer. In *Agypten.* ÄF 14.

DUANE L. CHRISTENSEN

NAVE. See discussion of *hêkāl* in TEMPLE, JERUSALEM.

NAZARAEANS, GOSPEL OF. See NAZORAEANS, GOSPEL OF THE.

NAZARENES. The term "Nazarene" has been used in English for several related Greek and Semitic-language terms found in NT and later writings. Some of these terms are more accurately represented by other spellings, and the ways in which these terms became related remain to some extent a matter of debate. In general, Nazarene means either (1) a person from Nazareth, or (2) a member of a religious group whose name may have other connotations.

Two Greek forms, *Nazōraios* and *Nazarēnos,* are rendered in English versions of the NT as Nazarene, corresponding to the more Hellenistic of the two. (Similarly, English uses Essene for *Essaios* and *Essēnos.*) However, in the Greek NT text, *Nazōraios* is the more frequently used form. That *Nazōraios* is the more Semitic of the two is suggested by the Syriac NT, which renders both forms as *Nāṣrāyā.* Matthew, John, and Acts use *Nazōraios* exclusively; Mark and Luke (once or twice, depending on the manuscript) employ *Nazarēnos.* No other NT books use the name.

In the NT, Nazarene most frequently describes a person—namely, Jesus—from Nazareth. Nazareth is not directly mentioned in Hebrew literature until the liturgical poems of Kallir (7th cent. C.E.?). This, together with philological questions on the link between the town name and Nazarene, led to much speculation on the origin of these names (see Schaeder *TDNT* 4: 874–79). Archaeological excavation has revealed a Jewish settlement in Nazareth in the 1st cent. C.E. (see NAZARETH), and an inscription from about 300 C.E. found in Caesarea confirms the spelling of the town as *NṢRT* (Avi-Yonah 1962). While one might expect the *Ṣ (ṣade)* to be represented in Greek by *s (sigma),* parallel cases using *z (zeta)* are known. Thus questions on the formation of the gentilic remain. In rabbinic literature Jesus is labeled *YŠHW HNWṢRY,* apparently a *nomen agentis* from the root *NṢR,* meaning, e.g., "observer" (of torah). There are at least two cases in the NT where Nazarene means something different than, or additional to, "from Nazareth." Most of Jesus' followers were not from Nazareth, nor, according to Luke 4, was he well received there. These cases are significant for later use of Nazarene as a group name.

Matt 2:23 has puzzled many by asserting that when Jesus' family arrived in Nazareth it fulfilled what was said by the "prophets" (note the plural) "that he shall be called *Nazōraios.*" The text clearly associates Nazareth and *Nazōraios,* but since no Hebrew Scripture mentions Nazareth, readers had to look for other allusions, calling on the Hebrew roots *NṢR* and *NZR.* In the case of *NṢR,* Isa 11:1 prophesies the messianic "shoot *(neṣer)*" from Jesse; additionally *NṢR* as a verb can mean "to observe, to guard." On the other hand, if Matt 2:23 alludes to *NZR,* there are stories of Nazirite vows, consecrating Samson (Judges 13) and others (Samuel in 4Q1 Sam). Jesus was surely not a Nazirite proper, but the LXX associates this root with holiness, and consequently some church writers (e.g., Tertullian, Eusebius) so interpreted the verse. The intention of Matt 2:23 depends in part on the language knowledge and exegetical method of the writer(s) of Matthew (Brown 1977: 207–13). In any case, Matt 2:23 presents *Nazōraios* as a favorable appellation.

In Acts 24:5 Paul appears accused by other Jews as a leader of the "heresy" of the *Nazōraioi.* Though of course he defends his teaching, Paul does not disown the name. Acts also introduces the name Christian *(Christianoi),* which eventually displaced Nazarene as the preferred self-designation of the increasingly Greek and Latin speaking gentile Church. But while those who believed in Jesus as Messiah abandoned the name Nazarene, Jews generally—including Jews who believed in Jesus, but who still observed Mosaic law—kept using Nazarene and its apparent varieties, including Heb *Noṣrim.* Additionally, the name was retained by the churches speaking Syriac *(Nāṣrāyā),* Armenian, and Arabic *(Naṣāra).*

In patristic literature the evolution continued. Writing ca. 200 C.E. Tertullian noted, "the Jews call us *Nazarenos*" (*Against Marcion* 4. 8). A century later Eusebius switched to past tense: "We who are now called Christians received in the past the name *Nazarenoi*" *(onomast.).* Writing about 375 C.E. Epiphanius condemns the *Nazōraioi,* who are not a newly founded group, as a heresy (*Panarion* 29). Jerome followed Epiphanius: ". . . since they want to be both Jews and Christians, they are neither Jews nor Christians" (Epistle 112.13 to Augustine).

Epiphanius and Jerome (in the works cited) also provide the first clear accounts of the practice in some ancient synagogues of condemning the *Noṣrim* in the blessing or curse on heretics *(birkat ha-minim)*: ". . . may the *Noṣrim* and *Minim* speedily perish . . ." (according to Cairo Genizah manuscripts). By this time, Epiphanius and Jerome are not sure whether the curse encompasses all Christians or only Jewish-Christians.

Epiphanius also condemns the *Nasaraioi* (*Panarion* 18) which his sources describe as a pre-Christian, law-observant group. There is no direct evidence that such a group existed. However, Epiphanius may have encountered a claim such as that made by the Mandeans, who call themselves the *Nāṣōrāyā,* the true religious "observers." (This claim parallels that made by other groups, e.g., the Samaritans' self-description as the "true *keepers* of torah.") The Mandeans claim to predate Judaism as well as Christianity.

Another illustration of the question of differing meanings of the terms subsumed by Nazarene appears in the 3d cent. Middle Persian inscription of Kartīr, a Zoroastrian priest who was intolerant of other religions. Kartīr condemned, among others, ". . . Jews . . . and *Nazarai,* and Christians . . ." (lines 9–10; Chaumont). Nazarene here could represent orthodox Christians (if "Christians" in this case refers to Marcionites) or Mandeans or some variety of Jewish-Christians.

To define Nazarene, one must take into account the time, place, language, and religious perspective of the speaker, as well as the meanings of other available religious group names. The development of these names merits further study.

Bibliography

Avi-Yonah, M. 1962. A List of Priestly Courses from Caesarea. *IEJ* 12: 137–39.

Brown, R. 1977. *The Birth of the Messiah.* Garden City, NY.

Chaumont, M.-L. 1960. L'inscription de Kartīr a la "Kaᶜbah de Zoroastra." *JA* 248: 339–80.

Klijn, A. F. J., and Reinink, G. J. 1973. *Patristic Evidence for Jewish-Christian Sects.* Leiden.

Pritz, R. 1982. The Jewish Christian Sect of the Nazarenes and the Mishna. *PWCJS* 8/1: 125–30.

STEPHEN GORANSON

NAZARETH (PLACE). The town of Jesus' youth in Lower Galilee, just N of the valley of Jezreel (M.R. 178234). The Sea of Galilee lies 15 miles to the E while the Mediterranean lies 20 miles to the W. Nazareth is identified by Matthew (2:23) and Luke (1:26; 2:4, 39) as the village of Mary and Joseph, the place where Jesus grew up (Luke 2:39, 51) and the village he left to visit the towns and villages of Galilee to begin his ministry (Mark 1:9). Luke mentions a synagogue in Nazareth (4:16) where Jesus spoke as an adult and where his message was not well received (4:28–30). Evidently later in his ministry, it was well known that Jesus was from Nazareth (Matt 21:11), which did not always evoke an amiable response (cf. John 1:45–46).

The etymology of the Hebrew name of the town is difficult. The formula quotation in Matt 2:23, "He went and dwelt in a city called Nazareth [Gk *Nazaret*], that what was spoken by the prophets might be fulfilled, 'He shall be called a Nazarene [Gk *Nazōraios*]' " calls for an explanation. The usual solution is to appeal to Isa 11:1, ". . . a branch [Heb *nēṣer*] shall grow out of his [Jesse's] roots." In this case Nazareth would mean "branch" or "shoot," indicating the fecundity of the area. But the plays-on-words are more enigmatic than that, and Matthew's formula is used in a form that appears nowhere else in Matthew, suggesting that he is not quoting the OT.

As inferred from the Herodian tombs in Nazareth, the maximum extent of the Herodian and pre-Herodian village measured about 900 x 200 m, for a total area just under 60 acres. Since most of this was empty space in antiquity, the population would have been a maximum of about 480 at the beginning of the 1st century A.D. Nazareth lay beside Yafa or Yafia, a city that Josephus fortified in the first revolt against Rome and in which he lived (*JW* 2.20.6–573; *Life* 52–270). This village was known to be Jewish as late as the 4th century A.D. After the failure of the First Jewish Revolt against Rome, the twenty-four "courses" or divisions of priests from the Temple in Jerusalem fled northward. One priestly family by the name of Hapizez (or Hapises) settled in Nazareth (*Mishmaroth* 18). That Nazareth was the home of a priestly course is repeated in a fragment of a Byzantine period Hebrew inscription, a list of the priestly courses, found at Caesarea in 1962. In the 3d century, Nazareth still had a strong priestly character according to *Midr. Qoh.* 2.8. In the 3d century the Christian martyr Conon from Nazareth of the family of Jesus was killed in Asia Minor (Bagatti 1969: 16).

The next reference to Nazareth is in the 4th century, when Eusebius mentions that Nazareth is fifteen miles E of Legio, near Mount Tabor. Jerome adds that it was merely a tiny village, a "viculus" (rather than "oppidum"), but neither Eusebius nor Jerome mentions a church (*Onomast.* 138.25; 141.1). Epiphanius (*Adv. Haeres.* 30.1—347) tells the story in his memoirs (377 A.D.) of Count Joseph of Tiberias, who appealed to the Emperor Constantine for permission to build a church at Nazareth, among other places. Constantine agreed, and presumably the church was built. When Egeria visited Nazareth about ten years later, however, she was shown "a big and splendid cave in which [Mary] lived." There was also an altar in the cave and a spring to draw water (Peter the Deacon T). Since this text confuses the remains from the Church of Gabriel and the Church of the Annunciation in Nazareth, Peter has presumably confused Egeria's notes. It is possible that the Helenopolis mentioned in A.D. 444 by Sozomen (*Hist. Eccl.* 2.2) refers to Nazareth and Mt. Tabor, cities of special interest to Helena, the mother of the emperor Constantine. She understood the Transfiguration of Jesus to have taken place on Mt. Tabor. The Piacenza Pilgrim in A.D. 570 says that the house of Mary "is now a basilica." This same pilgrim says he visited the synagogue of Jesus. He admired the beautiful Jewish women of Nazareth and hinted that Jewish-Christian relations were at least on a cooperative level (v161.4). Adomnan (Arculf), who lived about A.D. 679–704, visited Nazareth after the Arab conquest. He saw two churches that correspond to the Church of Gabriel and the Church of the Annunciation or perhaps the Church of St. Joseph and the Church of the Annunciation. According to Willibald (Hugeburc 95.20–25), by 808, Christian-Muslim relations had deteriorated so that Christians paid a "ransom" for the Church of the Annunciation to the Muslims.

Nazareth was excavated from 1890 to 1910 within the precincts of the Church of St. Joseph and the Church of the Annunciation. Vlaminek excavated in 1895 and Viaud from 1907–1909. A Neanderthal skull was found near Nazareth in 1934 about 1.5 miles to the SE. Excavations began again in 1954 by Bagatti. Beneath the Church of the Annunciation are some very suggestive archaeological remains. Among them are two small caves with painted plaster, a cross, and inscribed prayers to Jesus in Greek. These could derive from the end of the 3d century, but are most cautiously dated to the early 4th century. These caves are incorporated into a building with mosaic floors that faces S toward Jerusalem. This building, which is oriented N–S, would be interpreted as a synagogue except for a large, equal-armed cross built into its mosaic floor. The excavator interprets this building as a Jewish-Christian synagogue, which may be correct. Between the mosaic floor and the caves, at a level 1.2 m below the main floor of the Jewish-Christian synagogue, is a second 4th-century mosaic with a Greek inscription: "Offering of Conon, Deacon of Jerusalem." This Conon is evidently a namesake of the Conon mentioned above. When the main mosaic in the floor of the synagogue was lifted the excavators discovered a Jewish ritual bath that measures about two m on each side. Seven steps lead down to the water. Since the ritual bath is not oriented either with the synagogue or with its caves, it seems to be earlier than the structure. In the debris that filled the ritual bath was found painted plaster with inscriptions and graffiti scratched onto it in Greek and Syriac. The plaster had belonged to a 4th-century synagogue which was destroyed to give way to the building of a 5th-century church with its attached monastery. In the debris beneath the floor of one of the rooms of the monastery were about seventy architectural fragments that appear to have belonged to the 4th-century synagogue.

In chronological order, the occupational sequence in this area appears to have included: (1) detached caves of indeterminate (perhaps domestic) use, dating before the 3d century; (2) the cutting and use of a ritual bath, perhaps as early as the 2d century but not after the 3d century, perhaps for Jewish-Christians; (3) the building of a synagogue above the ritual bath which incorporated the caves (this was likely the church seen by Egeria and reported by Peter the Deacon); and finally (4) the building of a 5th-century church and monastery which incorporated the caves and floor of the 4th-century synagogue. This may be the church and monastery seen by the Piacenza Pilgrim in A.D. 570. The long continuity of use and incorporation of earlier units in later buildings suggests a continuity of veneration and worship extending back to the Roman period.

Beneath the convent of the Dames de Nazareth about 100 m W of the Church of the Annunciation are remains of houses, a tomb of the Herodian period, and other underground working spaces typical of those found beneath the other churches. It appears that the inhabitants of Nazareth took advantage of the soft limestone to build cisterns, basements, storage bins, and other underground installations, primarily for agricultural use.

The general archaeological picture is of a small village, devoted wholly to agriculture, that came into being in the course of the 3d century B.C. Although there are traces of earlier Bronze Age or Iron Age occupation, none of these suggests a continuity of more than a generation at a time. It is the late Hellenistic period that gives life to Nazareth, as it does with many other sites which have been surveyed or excavated in the Galilee. People have continued to live in Nazareth from the 3d century B.C. to the present day.

Bibliography

Baggati, B. 1969. *Excavations in Nazareth.* Vol. 1. Jerusalem.

Meyers, E. M., and Strange, J. F. 1981. *Archaeology, the Rabbis, and Early Christianity.* Nashville.

JAMES F. STRANGE

NAZORAEANS, GOSPEL OF THE. The name (note the spelling: on the name, see Schrader *TDNT* 4: 874–79, and Klijn and Reinink 1973: 44, n. 2) given by scholars to a presumed Judaic-Christian gospel, now lost. The matter of these Judaic-Christian gospels, namely, the Gospel of the Nazoraeans, the Gospel of the Hebrews, and the Gospel of the Ebionites, has been called the most enigmatic and irritating problem in the NT Apocrypha: enigmatic because all are now lost, and irritating because our knowledge of these early (pre-170 C.E.) gospels comes only indirectly via the Fathers' cryptic and inconsistent remarks. Snippets of text, assigned by scholars to one or the other of these three Judaic-Christian gospels, are quoted by the Fathers (often with no clear attribution) and appear to be preserved *in scholia* (the ZION GOSPEL EDITION). See also HEBREWS, GOSPEL OF THE; EBIONITES, GOSPEL OF THE.

The title "Gospel of the Nazoraeans" is never used by the Fathers. Rather, they speak of a gospel used by the Nazoraeans. It is difficult to ascertain whether this is a distinct gospel or simply the "Gospel of the Hebrews," also cited by the Fathers. The evidence, contradictory and inconclusive, follows.

Epiphanius (*Haer.* 29.7.1–29.9.4) offers the first description of the Nazoraeans and their gospel. According to him, they are like the Jews in everything, save that they accept Jesus as the Messiah. Regarding their origin, Epiphanius appears to know two traditions. According to the first (29.1.2–3; 29.6.23), the name roughly parallels the usage in Acts 24:5, and denotes the earliest (hence Jewish) Christians. According to the second tradition (29.7.7–8), the group originated in Pella, among the Judaic-Christians who fled Jerusalem prior to its destruction in 70 C.E. (cf. Eus. *Hist. Eccl.* 3.5.3). Epiphanius states that they know Hebrew well, and that they possess "the whole *(plērestaton)* gospel of Matthew in Hebrew. It is carefully preserved in Hebrew letters" (29.9.4). Epiphanius, however, never names this gospel, nor does he quote from it. Given his description of the Nazoraeans and their gospel, we may distinguish it from the similar gospel which Epiphanius attributes to the Ebionites, for the Ebionites' gospel "which is called with them 'according to Matthew' which is not complete but falsified and distorted *(oux holō de plērestatō, alla nenotheumenō kai ēkrōtēriasmenō)*, they call it 'the Hebrew gospel' " (30.13.1). Epiphanius further reports that the Ebionites have "removed the genealogies of Matthew" (30.14.3). Moreover, Epiphanius quotes from this Ebionite gospel, and it appears to be a harmonization of the Synoptic Gospels and together with some non-received traditions. Thus, we may say Epiphanius knew two Judaic-Christian gospels: one used by the Nazoraeans, and one used by the Ebionites. Both gospels are related to Matthew, and both appear to be in Hebrew (Aramaic).

Jerome is the second Father to speak of a gospel in use among the Nazoraeans, and certain of his statements confirm what we learned from Epiphanius. Jerome states that "Matthew . . . was the first to compose a gospel of Christ in Judea in Hebrew letters and words for the sake of those of the circumcision who believed. . . . From the Nazoraeans who use this book in Beroia, a city in Syria, I also received the opportunity to copy it" (*de vir. ill.* 3). From time to time in his prolific writings, Jerome refers to a "gospel which the Nazoraeans use," but he never calls it the "Gospel of the Nazoraeans." On the contrary, he sometimes equates it with the "gospel used by the Ebionites," and even calls it the "Gospel according to the Hebrews." Compare the following: (1) "a gospel which the Nazoraeans and the Ebionites use, which we translated from Hebrew to Greek and which is called the authentic text of Matthew by a good many" (*in Matt.* 12.13); (2) "the gospel which is 'according to the Hebrews' which the Nazoraeans are accustomed to read" (*in Hiez.* 18.5–9); (3) "From the 'Gospel according to the Hebrews.' In the 'Gospel according to the Hebrews' which was written in Chaldaic and Syriac language, but with Hebrew letters, and is used up to the present day by the Nazoraeans" (*adv. Pelag.* 3.2).

Scholars have usually assumed that Jerome knew two gospels—(1) the gospel used by the Nazoraeans, and (2) the Gospel of the Hebrews (also quoted by Origen, *in Io.* 2.12)—and that he frequently confused them when quoting. Jerome's quotations are, by and large, brief.

The difficulty in assigning the various fragments quoted by the Fathers or found in the scholia to one or another of these three Judaic-Christian gospels is formidable. A comparison of the assignments made by Preuschen (1901), James (1924), Klostermann (1929), and Vielhauer (*NTApocr*) makes this apparent. It is worth noting that only when reaching the medieval sources (Vielhauer, frag. 24–36) does one find the name "Gospel of the Nazoraeans" used. And of the twenty-three patristic fragments in Vielhauer's reconstruction, all but three come from the Zion Gospel Edition or Jerome—whose sources and attributions are, as we have seen, less than certain. Lagrange questioned the existence of the Gospel of the Nazoraeans, equating it with the Gospel of the Hebrews. Waitz and Vielhauer argue for three distinct gospels. Given our present state of knowledge, it is difficult to say which, if any, theory is correct.

Nevertheless, the testimony of the Fathers and the whole complex of Judaic-Christian gospel quotations—from whichever of the gospels they may come—serve to establish the following: (1) the Nazoraeans apparently had a particular gospel, perceived to be an ancient/original form of Matthew; (2) this gospel was apparently written in Hebrew characters, probably in the Aramaic language; (3) the descriptions of the beliefs of the Nazoraeans, as well as the various appellations given the gospel ("used by the Nazoraeans"; "Gospel of the Hebrews"; "the Jewish gospel") and the citations, show a distinctive perspective, Jewish in outlook, Semitic in character and expression. When compared with our present (Greek) canonical Matthew, many of the fragments appear to be expansions or interpolations. Logically, however, one would expect to find just the opposite: if, indeed, it was equated with the "original" Matthew, and written in a Semitic language, one would expect it to present the shorter, less-developed text. If one is to take the Fathers' reports of the antiquity of the gospel used by the Nazoraeans at face value, then the fact that many of the fragments now assigned to the Gospel of the Nazoraeans seem to be secondary expansions would lead one to question their assignation.

Since Tatian's Diatessaron has numerous readings similar to those found in the various Judaic-Christian gospels (thus providing a *terminus ad quem*), it should not be overlooked in reconstructing these gospels. Similar parallels have also been noted between the gospel of Thomas and the Judaic-Christian gospels (Quispel 1975; 1981); these too bear consideration in future studies of this elusive and vexing subject.

Bibliography

Bardenhewer, O. 1913. *Geschichte der altkirchlichen Literatur.* Vol. 1. 2d ed. Freiburg.

Bardy, G. 1946. Saint Jérome et l'Évangile selon les Hébreux. *MSR* 3: 5–36.

Dibelius, M. 1975. *Geschichte der urchristlichen Literatur.* Rev. ed. by F. Hahn. TBü 58. Munich.

James, M. R. 1924. *The Apocryphal New Testament.* Oxford.

Klijn, A. F. J., and Reinink, G. J. 1973. *Patristic Evidence for Jewish-Christian Sects.* NovTSup 36. Leiden.

Klostermann, E. 1929. *Apocrypha: II. Evangelien.* Kleine Texte für Vorlesungen und Übungen 8. Berlin.

Lagrange, M.-J. 1922. L'Évangile selon les Hébreux. *RB* 31: 161–81; 321–49.

Meyer, E. 1921. *Ursprung und Anfänge des Christentums.* Vol. 1. Stuttgart.

Preuschen, E. 1901. *Antilegomena.* Giessen.

Quispel, G. 1975. *Tatian and the Gospel of Thomas.* Leiden.

———. 1981. The Gospel of Thomas Revisited. Pp. 218–66 in *Colloque international sur les textes de Nag Hammadi,* ed. B. Barc. BCNHE 1. Quebec.

Resch, A. 1906. *Agrapha: aussercanonische Schriftfragmente.* 2d ed. TU 30/3–4. Berlin.

Schmidtke, A. 1911. *Neue Fragmente und Untersuchungen zu den judenchristlichen Evangelien.* TU 37/1. Berlin.

———. 1936. Zum Hebräerevangelium. *ZNW* 36: 24–44.

Schoeps, H. J. 1953. Ebionite Christianity. *JTS* n.s. 4: 219–24.

Waitz, H. 1937. Neue Untersuchungen über die sogenannten judenchristlichen Evangelien. *ZNW* 36: 60–81.

William L. Petersen

NEAH (PLACE) [Heb *nēʿâ*]. A place on the NE border of the territory of the tribe of Zebulun (Josh 19:13), situated between Rimmon and Hannathon, in the vicinity of the Bet Netofa Valley. The precise location of the site, however, remains unknown.

Raphael Greenberg

NEAPOLIS (PLACE) [Gk *Neapolis*]. A common name given to many Greco-Roman towns and cities founded near older sites, meaning simply "new city." The Neapolis mentioned in the NT (Acts 16:11) is certainly the seaport town for Philippi, which was 16 km inland. Located on a promontory on the coast of the Aegean Sea (40°56′ N; 24°23′ E), Neapolis had a harbor on both bays.

The first of several sections of Acts in which the author employs the first person plural begins at Troas prior to the voyage by sea to Neapolis. The mention of the seaport and the island Samothrace are unnecessary detail in the account of the trip to the main destination of Philippi (Acts 16:12; cf. Acts 20:6, "And we sailed from Philippi"), but it is detail that is understandable in an alleged eyewitness account: Samothrace, a small island with a 5000-ft. mountain, was an obvious landmark on the voyage, and one tends to note that place where one touched land again. The apostle set foot in Europe for the first time when he landed in Neapolis on the second missionary journey. From there, the travelers would have gone the short distance to Philippi using a part of the Roman highway called the Egnatian Way, which began here at the Aegean and spanned Macedonia to reach the Adriatic.

The earliest record of Neapolis appears to be in a tribute list of Athens from the 5th century B.C., in which it is treated as a city of Thrace rather than of Macedonia (Finegan *IDB* 3: 527), and part of the Athenian Confederacy. Pliny (*HN* 4.18) also treats it as Thracian, but the geographers Strabo (7.330) and Ptolemy (*Geog.* 3.13) link it with Macedonia, as does the Acts account.

The ships of Brutus and Cassius were moored in the W harbor at Neapolis when the conspirators fought Mark Antony and Octavian at the battle of Philippi in 42 B.C. (Appian *BCiv.* 4.106). The name of the city was changed to Christoupolis in later years. The modern name for the town is Kavalla, and apart from coins and inscriptions found there and in nearby Philippi, there are also the ruins of the Roman aqueduct and a shrine to the locally esteemed goddess Parthenos.

CONRAD GEMPF

NEARIAH (PERSON) [Heb *ne^caryāh*]. A name held by two persons in the Hebrew Bible. The name means "servant of Yah."

1. Neariah was a leader of the tribe of Simeon in the time of Hezekiah king of Judah. He and other tribal leaders, all the sons of Ishi, led a group of Simeonites to Mount Seir, which was at that time in the possession of the Amalekites. These they drove out; then they took possession of the land. The story appears to be an etiology to explain the presence of this group of Simeonites in Mount Seir and to justify their possession of it (1 Chr 4:42).

2. The fourth son of Shemiah, according to the MT (1 Chr 3:22–23). The phrase "and the sons of Shemiah" in v 22 may be a dittography and many scholars delete it. This would make Shemiah the first son of Sheconiah and Neariah the fifth son.

RUSSELL FULLER

NEBAI (PERSON) [Heb *nêbāy*]. A leader of the people and a signatory to the covenant established by Ezra (Neh 10:19; K *nwby*). The meaning of the name is obscure and at least one scholar has suggested that the place-name, Nebo (Ezra 2:29), has been mistaken for a personal name (Brockington *Ezra, Nehemiah and Esther* Century Bible, 181). It is more likely, however, that a family has assumed the name of the village in which they resided (Meyer 1896: 156; Myers *Ezra, Nehemiah* AB, 177; and Williamson *Ezra, Nehemiah* WBC, 324).

Bibliography

Meyer, E. 1896. *Die Entstehung des Judenthums.* Halle.

FREDERICK W. SCHMIDT

NEBAIOTH (PERSON) [Heb *nĕbāyôt, nĕbāyōt*]. A son of Ishmael (Gen 25:13; 28:9; 36:3; 1 Chr 1:29) and, as is the case with all the sons of Ishmael (with the possible exception of KEDEMAH), an Arab tribe (Isa 60:7). The tribe is mentioned in several Assyrian inscriptions from the time of Ashurbanipal; the various Assyrian spellings render ancient N Arabian **Nabayât,* as does the Hebrew form. In the middle of the 7th century B.C., the Nebaioth and the Assyrians entered commercial relations. At the end of his reign, Ashurbanipal claimed to have conquered their "distant" country and to have destroyed their settlements (Eph^cal 1982: 221–23; Knauf 1989: 65–66; 93–96). In Taymanite inscriptions—dated by Winnett (1980) to the 6th century B.C. and by Roschinski, Högemann, and Knauf to the early 4th century B.C. (Knauf 1989: 76–77)—*nbyt* (i.e., **Nabayât*) are mentioned among the enemies of the city of Taymâʾ. The Assyrian and the ancient N Arabian references combined lead to the vicinity of Ḥâʾil (27°35′N; 41°42′E) for the tribe's location.

It has previously been assumed that the Nebaioth may be identical with the Nabateans (*Nabaṭ* in Arabic); but both linguistically and historically this equation is untenable (cf. Eph^cal 1982: 233 n. 33; Knauf 1989: 92 n. 507 contra Broome 1973; Bartlett 1979: 62–63). The Nabateans could have formed a Kedarite clan before they ascended to the dominium over N Arabia after the demise of the Kedarite confederation, ca. 400 B.C. See KEDAR; NABATEANS. It is, however, possible that biblical authors of the 6th and 5th centuries B.C. applied the name "Nebaioth" from the list of the "sons of Ishmael," Gen 25:13–15 (originating in the 7th century B.C., see ISHMAELITES) to the Kedarite clan Nabat whom they encountered in their immediate vicinity, within the borders of Edom (Knauf 1989: 108–9). This assumption would explain why the "daughter of Ishmael" married by Esau is always a "sister of Nebaioth," although her name varies in Gen 28:9 and Gen 36:3. Then the parallelism between the "sheep of Kedar" and the "rams of Nebaioth" (Isa 60:7, from the end of the 6th century B.C.) would become more obvious. Finally, the qualification of Nebaioth as Ishmael's firstborn (Gen 25:13) becomes understandable if Nebaioth refers to the Nabateans and if this qualification forms part of the final redaction of the Pentateuch, ca. 400 B.C. By then the Kedarites had been dispersed; earlier, from the 7th through the 5th centuries B.C., Kedar had been the most powerful tribe among the Ishmaelites, and as such could have claimed "primogeniture" with more right than the "distant" Nebaioth.

The formation of the tribal name with the feminine plural afformative belongs to a class of tribal names which is rare in Classical Arabic but frequent among contemporary Arab tribes and clans. Thus the name **Nabayât* provides an example for the antiquity of some features of "modern" Semitic usage.

Bibliography

Bartlett, J. R. 1979. From Edomites to Nabataeans. A Study in Continuity. *PEQ* 111: 53–66.

Broome, E. C. 1973. Nabaiati, Nebaioth and the Nabataeans: The Linguistic Problem. *JSS* 18: 1–16.

Eph^cal, I. 1982. *The Ancient Arabs. Nomads on the Borders of the Fertile Crescent, 9th–5th Centuries B.C.* Jerusalem.

Knauf, E. A. 1989. *Ismael.* ADPV. Wiesbaden.

Winnett, F. V. 1980. A Reconsideration of Some Inscriptions from the Tayma Area. *Proceedings of the Seminar for Arabian Studies* 10: 133–40.

ERNST AXEL KNAUF

NEBALLAT (PLACE) [Heb *nĕballaṭ*]. A town of Benjamin that was repopulated by returning Judeans in the postexilic period (Neh 11:34). It is listed in conjunction with Lod, and has been identified with Beit Nabala (M.R. 146154; 4 miles NE of Lod), a site that has yielded Iron Age II and Persian period remains. On the basis of the name Sin-uballaṭ, Albright (1924: 106 n. 15) suggested that the name may preserve the memory of a 7th century B.C. Assyrian governor, Nabu-uballiṭ.

Bibliography

Albright, W. F. 1924. *Excavations and Results at Tell el-Ful.* AASOR 4. New Haven.

Gary A. Herion

NEBAT (PERSON) [Heb *nĕbāṭ*]. The father of Jeroboam I, first king of Israel (1 Kgs 11:26). The text uses the patronymic to distinguish this king from Jeroboam II (Jeroboam son of Joash). See JEROBOAM. Nebat (or perhaps only Jeroboam himself) is identified as an "Ephrathite," which most scholars take as a synonym here for "Ephraimite." Since Jeroboam's mother is named (unlike the mothers of other Israelite kings) and she is called a widow, some scholars infer that Nebat died young. Šanda (*1 Kings* EHAT, 317) proposes that the name is not in fact a patronymic but a clan name; however, the suggestion that it means "Nabatean" is surely wrong: The Nabateans do not appear in the region until at least three centuries later. Danielus (1967–68: 211–12) argues that *nbṭ* means "The Lady," and that "Son of Nbṭ" is a throne name taken by Jeroboam I to honor the cow-goddess Hatḥor, whose cult he would have known in Egypt (1 Kgs 11:40) and to whom the sanctuaries he established at Dan and Bethel would have been dedicated (1 Kgs 12:28–30).

Bibliography

Danielus, E. 1967–68. "The Sins of Jeroboam ben-Nebat." *JQR* 58: 95–114, 204–23.

Jerome T. Walsh

NEBIIM. The second section of the Jewish division of the Hebrew Bible meaning "Prophets" (Heb *nĕbîʾîm*). This section is divided, in turn, into two sections, the Former (Heb *rîʾšônîm*) and Latter (Heb *ʾaḥărōnîm*) Prophets. The Former Prophets include the historical books of Joshua, Judges, 1–2 Samuel, and 1–2 Kings. The Latter Prophets include the three "major" prophets (Isaiah, Jeremiah, and Ezekiel) and the so-called twelve Minor Prophets (Hosea, Joel, Amos, Obadiah, Jonah, Micah, Nahum, Habakkuk, Zephaniah, Haggai, Zechariah, Malachi).

NEBO (DEITY) [Heb *nĕbô*]. The name of a Babylonian deity mentioned only in Isa 46:1, a passage which comes from the pen of an exilic Judean in the Babylonian captivity (ca. 550 B.C.). Nebo, or Nabû, was the tutelary deity of the ancient city of Borsippa, some 15 miles S–SW of Babylon. He achieved great popularity throughout Mesopotamia and the surrounding regions during the 1st millennium B.C. The name of this god appears as the theophoric element in at least three Babylonian names mentioned in the OT: the great king Nebuchadnezzar, the Babylonian official Nebushazban, and the military commander Nebuzaradan (some have included Abednego, but with reservations). The meaning of the name has been contested. At the turn of the 19th century many scholars believed that it meant "proclaimer," "prophet," "announcer" (cf. Heb *nabîʾ*). In recent decades, however, most scholars would share the conclusion of Albright (*FSAC*, 231–32) that the correct etymological meaning is "one who is called (by god), one who has a vocation (from god)" (Rassmussen 1981: 103, 310; *AHW* 697b, 699b).

A. Nebo in the Mesopotamian Pantheon

The earliest extant reference to Nebo/Nabû is attested in the Chronicle of Hammurabi, where in the 16th year it is recorded that "the throne of Nabû [was made]" (King 1898–1900, 3: 235, 251). Nabû does not appear in the earliest pantheon of Ur (Roberts 1972: 167–72), nor does his name occur in the royal Assyrian inscriptions before 1115 B.C. *(GARI).* The data concerning Nabû are somewhat meager before 1000 B.C., but they increase dramatically in the Neo-Assyrian and Neo-Babylonian periods, when Nabû became one of the most beloved deities in Mesopotamian religion (see further below).

Late in the 2d millennium B.C. Nabû was considered to be the eldest son of the god Marduk. Accordingly, he was called "Mighty, exalted Lord, who knows all; majestic, ever splendid, the veritable First-born of Marduk" (Ebeling 1953: 13b). Marduk was the son of Enki/Ea (one of the four greatest deities) and the god who had successfully defeated the wicked Tiamat. By virtue of this victory, Marduk received not only the entire universe by right of conquest, but also possession of the sacred Tablets of Destiny (that prescribed the functions of the political, social, and moral order, and that Tiamat had illegally given to her evil ally Kingu) and supremacy over the total assembly of the grateful gods (see *ANET,* 60–62, 501–502). See ENUMA ELISH. As Marduk's firstborn, Nabû enjoyed a most honored status. His mother was the important goddess Sarpanitu, the veritable complement of Marduk, whether as the goddess of childbirth, or in her assistance to the needy and as the source of salvation and life to the perishing (Ebeling 1953: 69; *BWL* 69.34, 38). In Mesopotamian mythology, the family of Marduk maintained high integrity and a loyalty to its regal responsibility and avoided the sorts of scandals that had marred the reputation of the great god Enlil.

According to the myths, Nabû also married well. One of his wives was the eminently prestigious Sumerian goddess Nana, the divine queen of Uruk who brought to the marriage an equally noble heritage as "the first-born of Anu, surpassing great, whose might is the greatest among all the goddesses." In every way her marriage to her "noble spouse Nabû" was beneficial; she was compassionate, helpful to his Majesty, and greatly loved by him (*LAR* 2: 743–51). The other wife was the great lady Tašmetum, a Babylonian goddess who was honored in the Babylonian date formula "The year of Tašmetum" (King 1898–1900, 3: 240–41 n). Their warm and singularly devoted marital relationship is suggested by her association with Nabû in matters of state (e.g., the ratification and guarantee of the treaty between KTK and Arpad in Syria [*ANET,* 659]), her kindly touch with those in need (Langdon 1927: 5; Ebeling 1953: 24, 124–27), and the frequent references to her and

Nabû together. Thus Nabû's marriages and his supreme pedigree helped to convince the Babylonian citizenry of the stability and moral foundation of the Babylonian throne.

In the divine assembly, Nabû shared many of the predicates associated with the ancient and distinguished goddess Nidaba, who was the most famous divine exponent of the scribal craft. Likewise, Nabû came to be regarded as the scribe par excellence, a sort of secretary-general and record-keeper of the heavenly council. As such, he was custodian of the Tablets of Destiny that his father Marduk had wrested from the defeated Tiamat and Kingu. This position gave him great power. As scribe (or secretary-general), he had the task of setting in writing the various destinies that were proclaimed orally and to observe any deviations from the desired goals of the decrees. In certain respects, therefore, he could be regarded as a sort of "power behind the throne" of his father, Marduk. Nabû was eminently qualified for such a responsibility, and despite all the historical vicissitudes of 1st-century Mesopotamia, Nabû (along with Marduk, Sarpanitum, and Tašmetum) was accorded primal responsibility and honor, held in high esteem not only by the Assyrians and the Babylonians, but also later by the conquering Persians.

B. The Cult of Nebo

No summary can replace the animated devotion of the prayers, hymns, dedicatory inscriptions, and other affirmations produced by the devotees of the Nabû cult (many of these may be found in Ebeling 1953 [which brings up to date the monumental work of King 1896]; Falkenstein and von Soden 1953; and Seux 1976). Much additional information concerning prayers and psalms to Nabû (as well as the ceremonies practiced by the Babylonian kings) is available in the Assyrian royal correspondences (Waterman 1930–36), in the historical records *(LAR),* and in the exhaustive studies of the Ashurbanipal era (Streck 1916) and the Neo-Babylonian royal inscriptions (Langdon 1912), supplemented by the results of ongoing archaeological excavation.

The cultic literature of the Nabû rites follows a recognizable literary pattern called a *šu-ila* composition (see esp. King 1896 and Ebeling 1953). The composition generally begins with lavish praise of the nobility, splendor, heritage, accomplishments, etc., of the deity. Then there follows a description of the distress that currently afflicts the suppliant, who then introduces a prayer that distills the thought of the lament. Finally, a vow is proffered to the effect that if deliverance is granted by Nabû, then the grateful suppliant will perform the vow.

Although Nabû's tutelary domain was the city of Borsippa (site of the great temple of Ezida), sumptuous dwellings were provided for Nabû in Calah, Assur, Nineveh, Babylon, and almost every significant city in Mesopotamia (*LAR* 1: 799; Streck 1916, 3: 822–23), an assertion that archaeology has fully substantiated. The worship of Nabû even spread as far as Syria and Syene (Egypt), where some migrant Syrians lived and named the god Nabû more than any other in their correspondences. The liturgies of the Nabû cult were richly devised with numerous and diverse priestly ministrants, each with specific duties. The temple was often the legal center where deeds, contracts, and oaths were recorded, public notices posted, juridical procedures processed, and temple slaves supervised. The temples were also the refuge of the sick; thus exorcists with their extensive practice of caring for the mentally and physically ill mingled there with sacrificers, musicians, choristers, seers, prophets, and custodians.

The major annual festival in the Assyro-Babylonian period was the New Year Festival, in which the basic foundation of the political order was powerfully reaffirmed through myth and ritual. In this paramount drama Marduk and Nabû played the lead roles. After some initiatory ceremonies beginning on the second day of the month Nisannu, the (statue of) the god Nabû boarded his sacred barge in Borsippa and headed for the capital city of Babylon a few miles away. The excitement in Babylon must have been great when the barge came into view and the noble son of Marduk arrived at the home of his father. Over the course of the next ten days the divine father and son presided over rites that reaffirmed the divine rule and legitimacy of Marduk, that purified the temple and the people, that formulated the decrees for the coming year, that vindicated and reinstated the human king of Babylon, and that affirmed the victorious future of Nabû. All this was intended to undergird national unity and reinvigorate the hopes and positive feelings of the Babylonian citizens. See also AKITU.

The Nabû cult outlasted the Babylonian empire. The Persian conqueror Cyrus was personally committed to the survival of the native Babylonian cults (Oppenheim 1985). It is interesting to note that when the Macedonian Antiochus I Soter (280–262/1 B.C.), by right of conquest, became "king of Babylon," he left an inscription eulogizing Nabû, whose temple in Borsippa he rebuilt (*ANET,* 317). Even as late as the 1st century A.D. a temple to Nabû was built in the oasis city of Palmyra (Teixidor 1979: 106). However, the Nabû/Nebo cult was at its peak during the Neo-Babylonian period, the time when the Judean elite lived in exile in Babylon. The author of Isaiah 46, who lived among them, gives witness to the extravagant processions whereby (statues of?) the gods Bel (= Marduk) and Nebo were paraded before their devotees through the streets of Babylon (vv 1–2). This writer was a keen observer of details: the gods mounted on pack animals, the swaying deities, the weary beasts, the priceless array of the gods. But the writer envisioned a day of judgment fierce at hand, when instead of the adulation of the crowd, it would be the despairing cries of frantic people vacating the capital. The priests have laden the beasts of burden with the gods. They shall not escape but shall fall victim to the enemy; the jeweled adornment of the deities will not save them from the looting of the foe. Nebo and Marduk will then be revealed for what they truly are—simply the impotent creations of mere human beings.

Bibliography

Ebeling, E. 1953. *Die akkadische Gebetsseries "Handerhebung."* Berlin.

Falkenstein, A., and von Soden, W. 1953. *Sumerische und Akkadische Hymnen und Gebete.* Stuttgart.

Hallo, W. W. 1968. Individual Prayer in Sumerian: The Continuity of a Tradition. *JAOS* 88: 71–89.

King, L. 1896. *Babylonian Magic and Sorcery.* London.

———. 1898–1900. *The Letters and Inscriptions of Hammurabi.* 3 vols. London.
Langdon, S. 1909. *Sumerian and Babylonian Psalms.* Paris.
———. 1912. *Die Neubabylonsichen Königsinschriften.* VAT 4. Leipzig.
———. 1927. *Babylonian Pentitential Psalms.* OECT 6. Paris.
———. 1935. *Babylonian Menologies and the Semitic Calendars.* London.
Oppenheim, A. L. 1964. *Ancient Mesopotamia.* Chicago. Rev. ed. E. Reiner. 1977.
———. 1985. The Babylonian Evidence of Achaemenian Rule in Mesopotamia. *CHI* 2: 537–54.
Pinckert, J. 1920. *Hymnen und Gebete an Nebo.* Leipzig.
Porten, B. 1968. *Archives from Elephantine.* Berkeley.
Rasmussen, C. G. 1981. *A Study of Akkadian Person Names from Mari.* Diss. Dropsie.
Roberts, J. J. M. 1972. *The Earliest Semitic Pantheon.* Baltimore.
Seux, M.-J. 1976. *Hymnes et priéres aux dieux de Babylonie et d'Assyrie.* Paris.
Soden, W. von. 1971. Die grosse Hymnus an Nabû. *ZA* 44: 44–71.
Streck, M. 1916. *Assurbanipal.* 3 vols. Leipzig.
Teixidor, J. 1979. *The Pantheon of Palmyra.* Leiden.
Waterman, L. 1930–36. *Royal Correspondence of the Assyrian Empire.* Ann Arbor. Repr. 1972.

EDWARD R. DALGLISH

NEBO (PERSON) [Heb *nĕbô*]. The ancestor of several men who were required to divorce their foreign wives during the reforms of Ezra (Ezra 10:43 [LXX *Nabou*]; 1 Esdr 9:35 [Gk *Nooma*]). This may be a reference to the Judean *town* of Nebo. See NEBO (PLACE) #2.

NEBO (PLACE) [Heb *nĕbô*]. **1.** A town in NW Moab and one of the final stages of the Exodus (Num 33:47). Nebo may have been founded by people of Babylonian origin since Nebo is the name of a principal Babylonian deity. After the town was taken from the Amorite king Sihon the tribes of Gad and Reuben requested possession of Nebo because the region was suitable for livestock (Num 32:3, 33–38). The Reubenites rebuilt the city and continued to occupy it (cf. 1 Chr 5:8). According to the Moabite Stone (ll 14–18) the town of Nebo came under Moabite domination, and as such Nebo appears in the doom prophecies of Isaiah (15:2) and Jeremiah (48:1, 22) directed against Moab. Though the exact site of the town is unknown it probably was one of the tells near Mount Nebo. Eusebius and Jerome (Lagarde 1887: 283, 96–100; 142, 1–6) located Nebo 8 Roman miles S of Heshbon. During the present century the town has been tentatively equated with *Khirbet ʿAyûn Mûsā* (e.g., *MBA,* 181), *Luhithu* (cf. Saller and Bagatti 1949: 4–5, 204–207), but mostly with *Khirbet el-Mekhayyat,* which is about 5 miles from *Ḥesbân* (e.g., Kaiser *Isaiah 13–39* OTL, 67; Saller and Bagatti 1949: 207–217).

Khirbet el-Mekhayyat (M.R. 221131) is situated about 2 miles SE of the hill of *Siyâgha,* traditionally associated with the death of Moses, and about 1.25 miles SW of the highest peak of the Nebo ridge called *Jebel en-Neba.* Saller and Bagatti (1949: 207–209) claim that this identification is confirmed by (1) the local tradition represented by the name *Neba,* and especially (2) the testimony of the *Life of Peter the Iberian.*

Excavations carried out since 1933 (and periodically reported in *Liber Annuus*) reveal a wall, and building activity and cisterns both inside and outside the wall. Though our knowledge of the history of the site is sketchy, it appears so far that the two most prosperous periods in the history of the town of Nebo were Iron Ages I and II and the Byzantine period. Due to variant readings in 1 Macc 9:37 it is uncertain whether the author refers to the town of Nebo. See also NEBO, MOUNT.

2. A town of uncertain location referred to in lists of Israelites who returned after the exile from Babylon (Ezra 2:29). Assuming (1) the validity of the reading "the *other* Nebo" in the parallel account in Neh 7:33, and (2) the return of the exiles to Jerusalem and Judah (Ezra 2:1; Neh 7:6) and its placement after the towns of Bethel and Ai, this Nebo is generally located in Judah, though recently the less likely identification of this Nebo with the Nebo in Moab has been suggested (Cogan 1979: 37–39). Scholars generally tentatively identify Nebo with modern *Nûbā* (M.R. 153112) approximately 3 miles NW of Bethzur and 2 miles E of *Khirbet Qeila* (Keilah) (e.g., *GP,* 398). Nebo in Ezra 10:43 and 1 Esdr 9:35 is most likely a reference to a person and not a place.

Bibliography

Cogan, M. 1979. The Men of Nebo-Repatriated Reubenites. *IEJ* 29: 37–39.
Lagarde, P. de. 1887. *Onomastica Sacra.* Hildesheim. Repr. 1966.
Saller, S. J., and Bagatti, B. 1949. *The Town of Nebo (Khirbet El Mekhayyat).* Jerusalem. Repr. 1982.

ARTHUR J. FERCH

NEBO, MOUNT (PLACE) [Heb *nĕbô*]. A mountain in Moab, which was the site of Moses' preview of the promised land and the place where he died and was buried (Deut 32:49–52; 34:1–8). The two and a half Transjordanian tribes name it as part of the territory they requested of Moses (Num 32:3). The toponym "Nebo" is often found in biblical texts as both a mountain and as a town in Moab. See NEBO (PLACE) #1.

A. Biblical Citations

The mountain Nebo is remembered in the traditions tied with the conquest of Transjordan and with the last part of the Exodus before Israel's entrance into the promised land (Num 33:47). The connection of Nebo with Pisgah (Deut 34:1) ties the mountain with the geographical descriptions of S Gilead ("and from Bamoth to the valley lying in the region of Moab by the top of Pisgah which looks down upon the desert" [RSV], or "which is opposite Jeshimon" [MT]; Num 21:20). Num 23:28 adds the toponym "Peor" and reads (MT): "Balak took Balaam to the top of Peor which faces toward Jeshimon." In the description of the territory of the Reubenites and Gadites the area extends "as far as the Sea of the Arabah, under the slopes of Pisgah" (Deut 4:49). The text of Josh 12:3 is inflated: "and the Arabah to the Sea of Chinneroth eastward and in the direction of Beth-jeshimoth, to the sea of the Arabah, the Salt Sea, southward to the foot of the slopes of Pisgah." Consequently, in the list of cities of Reuben one finds in order Beth-peor, the slopes of Pisgah, and Beth-jeshimoth (Josh 13:20).

The toponym "Nebo" as a town recurs among the cities of the same conquered territory (Num 32:3), even though later it is said that Reuben's sons built Nebo (Num 32:38). It was part of the Bela family territory, and formed its boundary with Baal-meon (1 Chr 5:8). In the prophetic texts it is considered a city of Moab (Isa 15:2; Jer 48:1, 22), but in the Mesha Stele (lines 14–18) it is mentioned as a conquered Israelite city (*ANET,* 320).

Later Jewish tradition tells about Jeremiah who, accompanied by the tabernacle and the ark, went to the mountain where Moses had ascended to see the inheritance of God (2 Macc 2:4).

B. Identification

As far as the mountain is concerned, if the Targumic texts are not specific in translating Nebo as the tomb of Moses (Pseudo-Jonathan in Num 32:3, 38; 33:47; Onkelos Num 32:3 and several *midrashim*), Eusebius records that the mountain was on the road from Livias to Esbus (*Onomast.* 16.24) and that it was shown to pilgrims at the sixth mile on the same road W of Esbus (*Onomast.* 136.5). The pilgrim Theodosius (mid 6th century) writes that the death place of Moses could be visited in the neighborhood of Livias (*De Situ* 19). The pilgrim of Piacenza (ca. 570) places the sanctuary eight miles from the Jordan river (*Itinerarium* 18.13). Egeria (end of 6th century) left Jerusalem intending to visit the sanctuary. From Jericho she crossed the Jordan and stopped at Livias. Accompanied by a priest of the city who knew those places well, she took the road from Livias to Esbus on the plateau. At the sixth mile, a detour from the main road led her to the Springs of Moses, from which she climbed to the summit of Nebo to see the Memorial of Moses (*Itinerarium* 10–12). Bishop Peter the Iberian, old and sick and having come to Transjordan to cure himself in the thermal waters of the area, stopped to pray at the sanctuary of Moses where he had once been as a young man before his conversion (*Vita Petri* 85).

An early description of the Siyagha ruins 9 km W of Madaba was given by Le Duc de Luynes in 1864 and subsequently by the members of the American Palestine Exploration Society in 1873 and by the Survey in 1881, who hypothesized its biblical identification. The discovery of Egeria's itinerary in 1884 and of Peter the Iberian's life in 1895 were decisive for the identification of the Siyagha ruins with the sanctuary of Moses. The city of Nebo is apparently mentioned by Eusebius (*Onomast.* 136.14) under the item "Naba, a city of Reuben," which mentions a desert place called Nebo about eight miles S of Esbus. Peter the Iberian's biographer knew a village by that name, inhabited by Christians, which was on the mountain of Nebo (*Vita Petri* 85). In 1863 De Sauky noted the name Khirbet el Mukhayyat, a tell not far from Siyagha that was first explored by the Survey members in 1881 and then by Musil in 1901, who proposed the historical identification with the biblical toponym.

C. Archaeological Exploration

1. The Mountain of Nebo. The mountain Nebo is delimited on the N by wadi Ayoun Mousa and on the S by wadi Afrit, which drains to the W into the Jordan valley. The highest peak is 835 m, and while the others have slightly lower altitudes, none is lower than 700 m. The two most important peaks from a historical point of view are to the N—Siyagha (710 m)—and to the SE—Mukhayyat (790 m). Perennial springs gush into the valleys. The mountain region makes a natural balcony providing a dramatic view which includes the Dead Sea and the Jordan valley; the Judean desert from Tekoa to Jerusalem; and up to the mountains of Samaria.

An early human presence is testified by dolmens and menhir, as well as by megalithic circles. An EB III tomb was found in wadi Abu en-Naml, which is a continuation of wadi Ayoun Mousa further E. There is an MB tomb on the slopes of Khirbet el-Mukhayyat, and ceramics of the LB I have been gathered near some monuments (apparently tombs) on the ridge of el-Mushaqqar and on the N slopes of wadi Ayoun Mousa. Iron Age II sherds were gathered on the surface on the peak el-Mukhayyat.

In 1933, an excavation was conducted on Siyagha under the direction of S. Saller, assisted from 1935 by B. Bagatti. The 1933, 1935, and 1937 campaigns revealed a basilica with mosaics and a monastery that had developed around it. At the same time, a thorough exploration of the mountain was made and several churches of Khirbet el-Mukhayyat were excavated. The results of the work at Siyagha were published in 1941 and those of el-Mukhayyat in 1949. A restoration program of the sanctuary and mosaics at Siyagha was entrusted in 1963 to V. Corbo, who recovered the surface mosaics of the presbytery from the S nave and from the two lateral chapels in the S port to add new elements to the history of the sanctuary. The work, which was interrupted by the Arab-Israeli wars, resumed in 1976 under M. Piccirillo, who continues the investigations.

The original state of the constructions and the beginning of human presence on the summit of Siyagha remain problematic. In spite of some contrary indications, Piccirillo is inclined to believe that the monument as well as its occupation were established in the 4th century with the Christian sanctuary. Originally it had three apses, to which was added an atrium. The cell and the atrium were used for funeral purposes. About the time of abbot Alexis (ca. late 4th century), two funeral chapels were added on the N and S. If the Alexis remembered in the S chapel is the abbot mentioned in the inscription of the presbytery, it would appear that the mosaics were contemporary. The atrium pavement near the S wall was decorated with a braided cross, while the area before the sanctuary, on the highest point of the mountain, consisted of a courtyard surrounded on the N and S by monastery rooms.

In August of 531, the mosaicists Soelos, Kaiomos, and Elias renovated and embellished diaconicon, the baptistry, and the very elegant ciborium. The diaconicon-baptistry stood on the N side of the courtyard and was accessible by stairway in front of the sanctuary.

In 597/98, the sanctuary was completely restructured. The facade of the old church was destroyed and became the presbytery of the new basilica with three naves, which took the place of the courtyard. The mosaic of the central nave with dedicatory inscriptions has been lost. The new sanctuary included a long diaconicon chapel on the N wall which covered the old diaconicon, and a new baptistry along the S wall. During the first decade of the 7th century, the chapel of Theotocos was added. The basilica was supplied with a narthex decorated with mosaics. One approached the basilica by means of five wide steps.

The buildings associated with the renovated basilica are divided into residential blocks around paved courtyards on the N, S, and W sides, and around the church atrium. The excavations revealed that the E sector and perhaps the N one on the steep slopes of Ayoun Mousa were abandoned. The monastery included places cut into the mountain slopes, like the hermitage dug into the rock on the W side, and a complex of rooms covered with mosaics at the time of abbot Procapis (the first decade of the 6th century). For bibliography on Siyagha, see Bagatti 1936; *DBSup* 7: 1122ff.; Corbo 1967; 1970; Piccirillo 1976; Saller 1941–50; and Yonick 1967.

2. The City of Nebo: Khirbet el-Mukhayyat. In 1949 Saller and Bagatti published the mosaics and the inscriptions of four churches. In 1962 J. Ripamouti excavated a small monastery in wadi Afrit, a tower of the Iron Age, and several tombs in the necropolis of the city. From these examinations it is clear that the ruins, which had been naturally fortified, had been inhabited in Iron Age II, in the Hellenistic/Roman period (2d century B.C.–1st century A.D.), and in the Byzantine period (5th–6th centuries).

The acropolis, which was later fortified, includes the churches of St. Georges and of the martyrs Lot and Procopius. The church of St. Georges was built with donations from some village families (ca. 535), and was decorated by the mosaicists Nalium, Kiriacos, and Tomas. Greek inscriptions accompany the mosaic decorations, which include themes of hunting, vine harvest, and agriculture, with personifications of the Seasons and the Earth. There is also an inscription in Christian-Palestinian Aramaic. The church of Sts. Lot and Procopius was built with donations from various women, among whom was Mrs. Roma, and its mosaic work was done at the time of bishop John of Medeba, who resided there in 562. The church preserves one of the most beautiful designs of the Madaba School mosaicists, with symbolic scenes, Nilotic motifs in the intercolumniation, and scenes of hunting, shepherding, and vine harvest in the central area.

The inhabited area of the slopes of wadi Afrit includes a church to which, at the time of bishop John, a chapel was added on the N side. The church of Amos and Casiseos, named after the benefactors whose names are engraved on the small pilasters of the balustrade, is probably the oldest in the village. The chapel of priest John which borders it was built over earlier remains and included new mosaics executed under the supervision of deacon Kaiomos. The mosaics were done by the same team who worked in the church of Sts. Lot and Procopius with donations from the same benefactors. Besides the usual scenes and personifications, there are two portraits of a lady and a clergyman (perhaps priest John) who took care of the work. The monastic complex, known to Arabs as el-Kenish, is made up of three interconnecting rooms forming the head of the chapel, which are on split levels on the wadi slopes. For bibliography, see Milik 1960; Piccirillo 1973; Saller 1966; 1967; and Saller and Bagatti 1949.

3. The Exploration of Wadi Ayoun Mousa. Explorations have identified the milestones from the Roman-Byzantium period which mark the road from Esbus to Livias. Near the fort of Mehatta, the stones of the sixth mile still exist, from which branches a road leading to the springs. Among the vineyards are three monastic complexes. In the summer of 1984, excavations began of the monastery of Kaiano. The church was built at the time of bishop Cyrus of Medeba (early 6th century) by Casiseus in memory of members of his family who were buried in the two tombs below. This attribution is recorded on two inscriptions in Greek and is repeated on an inscription in Christian Palestinian Aramaic. The church was rebuilt and the mosaics redone at the higher altitude with the donations from Salamanus, Paul, Maxim, and Lady Harton, probably at the end of the century. See Piccirillo 1984; Puech 1984.

D. Conclusion

From the archaeological excavation it is clear that the biblical toponym Nebo has been preserved by the city of Nebo. The summit of Siyagha acquires importance with the construction in the 4th century of the sanctuary dedicated by the Christians of the region to the memory of Moses. However, even earlier the mountain was already known by this name, as it is testified by the *Onomasticon.*

Bibliography

Bagatti, B. 1936. Edifici cristiani nella regione del Nebo. *RivArCr* 13: 4–13.

Corbo, V. 1967. Nouvi scave archeologici nella cappella del battistero della basilica del Nebo (Siyagha). *LASBF* 17: 241–58.

———. 1970. Scavi archeologici sotto i mosaici della basilica del monte Nebo (Siyagha). *LASBF* 20: 273–98.

Milik, J. T. 1960. Notes d'épigraphie et de topographie Jordaniennes. *LASBF* 10: 145–84.

Piccirillo, M. 1973. Campagna archeologica a Khirbet el Mukhayyet (città di Nebo). *LASBF* 23: 341–58.

———. 1976. Campagna archeologica nella basilica di Mosé Profeta sul monte Nebo-Siyagha. *LASBF* 26: 281–318.

———. 1977. Campagne archéologique dans la basilique du mont Nébo-Siyâgha. *RB* 84: 246–53.

———. 1984. Una chiesa nell'wadi Ayoun Mousa ai piedi del monte Nebo. *LASBF* 34: 307–18.

Puech, E. 1984. L'inscription christo-palestinienne d'Ayoun Mousa (Mont Nebo). *LASBF* 34: 316–28.

Saller, S. 1941–50. *The Memorial of Moses on Mount Nebo.* 3 pts. Jerusalem.

———. 1966. Iron Age Tombs at Nebo, Jordan. *LASBF* 16: 165–98.

———. 1967. Hellenistic to Arabic Remains at Nebo, Jordan. *LASBF* 17: 5–64.

Saller, S., and Bagatti, B. 1949. *The Town of Nebo.* Jerusalem.

Yonick, S. 1967. The Samaritan Inscription from Siyagha. *LASBF* 17: 162–221.

MICHELE PICCIRILLO

NEBUCHADNEZZAR (PERSON) [Heb *nĕbûkadne(ʾ)ṣṣar*]. Var. NEBUCHADREZZAR. The second king of the Chaldean dynasty of Babylonia, successor to his father Nabopolassar. Nebuchadnezzar (Akk *Nabu-kudurri-uṣur*) ruled for 43 years (605–562 B.C.). Before his reign began, he developed a considerable reputation as a field commander. In early 605 B.C. he took the initiative against Egyptian armies located south of Carchemish on the Euphrates River and won a decisive victory. After word was received of Nabopolassar's death, Nebuchadnezzar returned to Babylon to formally ascend his father's throne. He then left his capital city for Syria where, over the next three years, he forced a number of cities, including Damascus, to accept Babylonian suzerainty and provide tribute. From 601 to 598 B.C., his armies not only fought the Egyptians and their pharaoh Necho II (610–595 B.C.) but also penetrated Arabia, where they were able to carry off much plunder. While it appears that he suffered heavy losses in the engagement with Egypt in 601 B.C., he nevertheless (in 599) prepared to deal with Syria and the kingdom of Judah, whose king Jehoiakim subsequently lost his throne. In March of 597 B.C., Nebuchadnezzar besieged Jerusalem and placed Zedekiah, Jehoiachin's uncle, in control. Josephus, in his *Jewish Antiquities,* and the OT relate an account of a second siege of Jerusalem in 586 B.C. that resulted in the destruction of Solomon's temple and the beginning of the so-called Babylonian Captivity of the Jews that was to last until 538 B.C. Unfortunately, the Babylonian Chronicle breaks off after the entry for 594 and, thus far, no corroboration of this second campaign into Judah can be found in the cuneiform sources. In fact, his later campaigns against Tyre and Egypt referred to by Josephus cannot be precisely dated or completely accounted for in the cuneiform evidence. Nebuchadnezzar died in 562 B.C. and was succeeded by his son Amel-Marduk (OT Evil-Merodach) who, according to Jer 52:31, released the imprisoned Jehoiachin, former king of Judah, and gave him an allowance.

Nebuchadnezzar's reign was also marked by significant building activity in Babylon and elsewhere. Temple restoration projects were organized throughout southern Mesopotamia. No fewer than five walls were built to enclose Babylon. The so-called "Summer Palace" was constructed in the part of the city still carrying the name "Babil." But the S Palace was the most important, not only because of its size, but because it was located near the Ishtar Gate and the Processional Way, one of the many streets that were a feature of the "inner city." Extensive work was done on the Etemenanki, the ziggurat of Babylon that found its way into the OT as the infamous Tower of Babel. According to the classical sources, Nebuchadnezzar married Amytis, daughter of the Median king Astyages, and constructed the royal gardens near the N palace. These Hanging Gardens were created to remind his wife of her mountainous homeland, and were remembered by later writers as one of the seven wonders of the ancient world.

Nebuchadnezzar's own contemporary cuneiform sources (Grayson *TCS* 5), including the important Babylonian Chronicle, are largely incomplete and provide us with relatively little information about the important events of his reign. As a consequence, we know perhaps less about the actual historical events of the reign of Nebuchadnezzar than about those associated with almost any other king of the Chaldean period. Nevertheless, he turns up in more secondary sources for the Chaldean period than any other monarch of his dynasty, and in many of them, descriptions of the king's deeds bear no relationship to historical accuracy. In addition to the books of Jeremiah, 2 Kings, 2 Chronicles and Daniel of the OT, no less than ten of the rabbinic commentaries mention his name. Also, he appears in six books of the Apocrypha, in several Arabic commentaries, and in the extant writings of classical and medieval Greek and Latin authors. These latter sources, ranging from Berossus' *Babyloniaca* to the *Chronicle* of the Venerable Bede, speak not only of Nebuchadnezzar's conquests but also place particular emphasis on his building activities in Babylon. The question, then, that must be addressed concerns the reason for his prominence in these sources. Certainly, one explanation lies in the fact that the Greek mind idolized the monumental. Any famous metropolis that could not easily be visited by anyone was a topic of great interest and it was incorporated as a noteworthy feature into the historian's work. Thus it is not surprising to find that Babylon fascinated nearly everyone. Its imposing walls and ziggurat were, literally, unreal. Since the creation itself was extraordinary, the creator of such a marvel had to be extraordinary also. Thus the classical writers characterized Nebuchadnezzar's building activities in a variety of ways. On the one hand, he emerged (in the writings of Berossus and Megasthenes) as the creator of a monument of imposing size and enduring quality who was given ability by Marduk to restore Babylon and build its walls. On the other hand, writers of the so-called "universal histories" (such as Strabo and Diodorus Siculus) lost Nebuchadnezzar's achievements among those of several other kings who together constituted an image of a "superfigure" who was either a god or godlike. Actual human achievements were cast in the guise of a superhuman with actual historical names being (if at all) of only secondary concern or consideration.

Understandably, the element of conquest was of greater concern to the Hebrews. In Nebuchadnezzar's case, the capture of the city of Jerusalem, the dismantling of the temple of Solomon, and the deportation of captives were acts never to be forgotten. The author of such horrible deeds had to be portrayed in such a way as not only to place emphasis on destruction and wickedness but also to show that the apparent power or might of the king of Babylon was merely the result of Yahweh's punishment of the Hebrews. The book of Daniel is a case in point. The king was only a tool to be used in the teaching of a lesson. In this light, the characterization of Nebuchadnezzar had to be richly embellished with elements drawn from a number of sources, folkloristic or otherwise. In the process, however, the Hebrew writer made use of historical materials associated with the reign of Nabonidus (556–539 B.C.), not because he was confused but, rather, because of the fact that Nabonidus just happened to appear in his own and later sources in such a way as fit the situation involving Nebuchadnezzar that was being described. Nebuchadnezzar's "image" need not harmonize with historical accuracy; indeed, it knew no limits of time or space and was applicable to all periods of history.

Bibliography

Sack, R. H. 1982. Nebuchadnezzar and Nabonidus in Folklore and History. *Mesopotamia* 17: 67–131.

Wiseman, D. J. 1961. *Chronicles of the Chaldean Kings.* London.

———. 1985. *Nebuchadnezzar and Babylon.* Oxford.

RONALD H. SACK

NEBUSHAZBAN (PERSON) [Heb *nĕbûšazban*]. One among a list of Babylonian officials who played a role in taking Jeremiah from imprisonment in the court of the guard and entrusting him to Gedeliah (Jer 39:13–14). Nebushazban held a position entitled Rabsaris. While knowledge of the functions of Babylonian officials is sketchy, the position is thought to be a high military or diplomatic office—in the Neo-Assyrian period he would have been the "chief eunuch," but according to Bright (*Jeremiah* AB, 243) this is no longer a valid designation in the Neo-Babylonian period (see also Carroll, *Jeremiah* OTL, 691). The text does not indicate the specific role Nebushazban may have played either in the capture of Jerusalem or the release of Jeremiah. Another list of Babylonian officials occurs in Jer 39:3 in which SARSECHIM is titled Rabsaris. However, it is widely held that the Hebrew of Jer 39:3 is confused, and the verse is typically reconstructed with the aid of Jer 39:13 to include Nebushazban (Bright, 243). The name in Akkadian would be *Nabû-šūzibanni* "Nabû deliver me" (cf. *IDB* 3: 530).

JOHN M. BRACKE

NEBUZARADAN (PERSON) [Heb *nĕbûzarʾădān*]. A high-ranking Babylonian official who played a key role in the destruction of Jerusalem in 587 B.C.E. and subsequent deportations of portions of the Judean population (2 Kgs 25:8–11, 18–21; Jer 39:–14; 52:30). In addition, Nebuzaradan is identified as the Babylonian official who after the fall of Jerusalem participated in freeing Jeremiah from prison and entrusting him to the care of Gedeliah (Jer 39:11–14; cf. Jer 41:10; 43:6). Nebuzaradan's title was literally "chief butler" ("*rab tabbāḥîm*" cf. Gen 37:36). However, this title is clearly archaic. The functions of Nebuzaradan which are described in 2 Kings and Jeremiah indicate that he was a ranking military official. English translations often identify him as "captain of the guard" (RSV, ASV, KJV). In 2 Kgs 25:8–11, Nebuzaradan is presented as commander of the forces which invaded Jerusalem and the Babylonian official responsible for the destruction of the temple, the king's palace, and other prominent Jerusalem residences. Nebuzaradan oversaw the deportation of the Judean population following the fall of Jerusalem in 587 (2 Kgs 25:11–12, 18–21). Nebuzaradan also is mentioned in connection with a later deportation during the 23d year of Nebuchadnezzar in 582/1 B.C.E. (Carroll, *Jeremiah* OTL, 569–70).

Though the historical accuracy of the accounts of the release of Jeremiah from prison after the fall of Jerusalem are dubious (Bright, *Jeremiah* AB, 244ff; Carroll, 695ff), the narrative in Jer 39:10–14 indicates that Nebuzaradan was charged by Nebuchadnezzar to see that Jeremiah would not be harmed. Nebuzaradan entrusted Jeremiah to Gedeliah, the newly appointed Babylonian governor of Judea. Others in Judea were apparently dealt with similarly by Nebuzaradan (cf. Jer 41:10; 43:6).

Nebuzaradan's name means "'Nabu' has given offspring." In later traditions, he is regarded as a proselyte (perhaps based on Jer 40:2–6; Carroll, 692).

JOHN M. BRACKE

NECKLACE. See JEWELRY.

NECO (PERSON) [Heb *nĕkōh*]. An Egyptian Pharaoh of the 26th Dynasty (Saite), and son of its founder, Psammetichus I (Psamtik; 663–609 B.C.E.). Neco (or Necho) ruled from 609 to 595 B.C.E. He is most well known for his role in the death of Josiah of Judah at Megiddo in 609 (2 Kgs 23:28–30 = 2 Chr 35:20–27), and for his brief control over Syria-Palestine in the closing years of the 7th century B.C.E. According to Babylonian sources, he was a major foe of Babylon during the last years of Assyria in the late 7th century B.C.E.

The sources for Neco's reign are biblical, Akkadian, and classical, and so are written from a perspective which does not reflect the Egyptian point of view. They consist of part of the biblical account of the last decades of the kingdom of Judah (2 Kings 23–24), some highly emotive poetry from the prophetic tradition (Jer 46:1–12), fragments of the neo-Babylonian Chronicles, and the history of Herodotus. Of the sources, Herodotus appears to be the most suspect since he offers no account of Neco's involvement with the great events of the fall of Assyria. However, both the biblical and Akkadian records have a distinct agenda of their own and are also highly selective with their information. The biblical accounts of the involvement of Neco in the death of Josiah do not agree on all details.

From this selective data we can reconstruct the following sketchy outline of Neco's career and the events leading up to it. In the early 7th century B.C.E. Aššurbanipal of Assyria (ca. 668–627 B.C.E.) invaded Egypt and dispersed the princes of the Delta, among them Taharqa and Neco (I) (*ANET,* 294–97), then sacked the capital of the 25th (Ethiopian) Dynasty at Thebes. Neco I was later killed by the Ethiopian Shabaka, but his son, Psamtik I (664–610 B.C.E.), consolidated his power at the new capital Sais with the help of Ionians and Carians, and embarked on campaigns to the N and E. Conflict with Syria-Palestine culminated in the Egyptian capture of Ashdod in 635 B.C.E. (Hdt. 2:157). The son of Psamtik, Neco II, took advantage of a weakened Syria, and expanded Egyptian trade to the E and W (Hdt. 4:42). He then turned to warfare with his eastern neighbors, including the Syrians and Arabs, and captured the border town of Gaza, an event which is probably reflected in Jer 47:1–7.

The activities of Neco impinge more directly upon the history of Judah with a reconstruction of the moves of Neco found in biblical and Akkadian sources. 2 Kgs 23:29–35 (= 2 Chr 35:20–36:4) refer to Neco's move to the N to aid Assyria in 609 B.C.E. From Akkadian sources (Wiseman 1956: 54–63; *ANET,* 305), we learn that Neco had taken an army N to help Aššuruballiṭ retake Harran from a small Babylonian garrison. A Babylonian counterattack, under Nabopolassar was unsuccessful, but with the Assyrians and Egyptians engaged at Harran, the Babylonian army plundered at will in N Assyria. It is possible that Aššuruballiṭ died in this campaign. In any event, he is not heard from again.

By 606 B.C.E. the Egyptian army was now at the gates of Carchemish, but not necessarily under the direct leadership of Neco, and successfully campaigned against Kimuhu (Commagene) and Qaramati. The Babylonian army, now under the crown prince Nebuchadrezzar, attacked in the following year and completely routed the Egyptian force. According to the record, ". . . the Egyptian army withdrew before [Nebuchadrezzar]. He accomplished their defeat and to non-existence [beat] them. As for the rest of the Egyptian army which had escaped from the defeat . . . the Babylonian troops overtook and defeated them so that not a single man escaped to his own country" (Wiseman 1956: 67–69). This complete annihilation of the Egyptian army was celebrated with equal glee by the prophet Jeremiah (Jer 46:2–12). In the following year Nebuchadrezzar attacked the S Levant as far as Ashkelon, but an attack on the border of Egypt was repulsed by Neco in 601 B.C.E. Neco was now confined to his former territory. ". . . the king of Egypt did not come again out of his land, for the king of Babylon had taken all that belonged to the king of Egypt, from the Brook of Egypt (Wadi el-Arish) to the River Euphrates" (2 Kgs 24:7).

It was during the first advance of Neco northwards (609 B.C.E.) that Josiah met him at Megiddo, and died (2 Kgs 23:29–33). After a brief reign by Josiah's son, Jehoahaz, Neco set Eliakim (Jehoiakim), Josiah's younger son, on the throne of Judah, and for the next few years Judah was a tribute-paying vassal of Egypt (2 Kgs 24:31–35). It was presumably during the advance of the Babylonian army in 604 B.C.E. to the borders of Egypt that Jehoiakim changed his allegiance to Babylon. However, Nebuchadrezzar's failure to enter Egypt in 601 B.C.E. encouraged the king to throw off the Babylonian control (2 Kgs 24:1) and to look to the S for support, despite prophetic warnings (Jer 46:14–28). Following the repulsion of the Babylonian army, the two nations of Egypt and Babylon ceased hostilities, and nothing more is heard directly of Neco. He died in 595 B.C.E. and was succeeded by his son, Psammetichus (Psamtik) II.

In 2 Kgs 23:28–30 and clearly in 2 Chr 35:20–27 the impression is given that Josiah died in battle against Neco. Some, however, have doubted this and have argued that Neco arrested and executed Josiah (Cogan, Tadmor *2 Kings* AB, 300–301), who had gone N, not seeking battle, but simply to meet Neco. This is possible but unlikely. The reason for Josiah's move can only be guessed at, but it makes sense for him to fear both a revival of Assyrian power in Judah, and a resurgent Egypt. Strategically, a battle at Megiddo was the best option, but the strategy misfired, and like his predecessor Thutmoses III in 1468 B.C.E., Neco defeated a local force at this important site.

Bibliography

Gardiner, A. 1961. *Egypt of the Pharaohs*. London.

Malamat, A. 1973. Josiah's Bid for Armageddon. *JANES* 5: 267–79.

Wiseman, D. J. 1956. *Chronicles of the Chaldaean Kings (626–556 B.C.) in the British Museum*. London.

T. R. HOBBS

NECROMANCY. See MAGIC.

NEDABIAH (PERSON) [Heb *nedabyāh*].

Nedabiah occurs only in 1 Chr 3:18 where he is listed as the seventh son of Jeconiah/Jehoiachin. Otherwise the name is found in extrabiblical material.

RUSSELL FULLER

NEGEB.

In the Bible the word "Negeb" (Heb *negeb*), or "Negev," refers to one of the main regions of Palestine S of the hill country of Judah, W of the Arabah, and NE of the Sinai peninsula (see Gen 12:9; 13:1). The Hebrew word seems to mean "dry south country." This entry contains three articles, one surveying the archaeological remains of the Negeb in the Bronze Age, the second surveying the archaeological remains in the Iron Age (Israelite period), and the third covering the Hellenistic-Roman period.

BRONZE AGE

A. Environmental Background
B. Settlement History
  1. Northern Negeb
  2. Central Negeb
  3. Southern Negeb
C. Society and Economy
D. The Biblical Narrative
E. Summary

A. Environmental Background

The modern Negeb is a rough triangle with its E border running N from the Gulf of Aqaba/Eilat through the Arabah valley to the Dead Sea; its W border begins at the same point, running NW to Raphiah. The N border, less clearly defined, is sometimes considered coincident with the Nahal Beer-sheba drainage, although for some scholars is as far N as Kiryat Gat and the Nahal Shiqma drainage. However, the hilly regions to the E and the coastal area to the W are excluded. On a general level, the Negeb is an extension of the Arabian-Saharan subtropic desert zone and shows geographic continuity with Sinai. Although the biblical Negeb is generally considered to have incorporated the N Negeb exclusively, the Bronze Age predates most of the biblical narrative, and archaeological remains S of Beer-sheba are of considerable interest and importance.

The physical geographical-climatic divisions of the Negeb played a significant role in determining the nature of settlement in the Bronze Age, so that to a great extent regional contrasts are reflected in the archaeology. Thus settlement in the loessial semi-arid plains of the *N Negeb*, generally above the 200-mm isohyet considered to be the threshold for viable dry farming, is dominated by urban centers and associated villages. In contrast, the arid degraded steppe of the *Central Negeb* Highlands, receiving only between 75 and 150 mm of rainfall yearly, hosted a variety of pastoral nomadic adaptations with much less emphasis on agriculture. Settlement in the harsh desert regime of the *S Negeb* (averaging less than 50 mm of rainfall per annum) is characterized by both pastoral sites and encampments and, apparently, copper mining-trade sites. Significant E–W climatic gradients also affected settlement, so that, for example, there may be major differences in settlement patterns within subregions such as the E versus W halves of the Beer-sheba Basin.

In addition to these physical geographic and climatic factors, there is accumulating evidence of Bronze Age climatic change which may have played an important influencing role in Negeb settlement. Summarizing briefly, the

Chalcolithic period in the N Negeb, preceding the EB Age, shows evidence of wadi alluviation, continuing on a somewhat lesser scale into the early part of the EB. This accords well with other lines of evidence from both the Negeb and the rest of the country indicating a moister phase in this period. The length of this phase is difficult to determine, but it seems to have been followed by a period of unstable climate and subsequently a period of desiccation, corresponding roughly to the EB IV and the MB. This is difficult to demonstrate specifically in the Negeb, but can be seen in adjacent areas, as in Dead Sea lake levels, alluvial fills around Nahal Lachish, and arboreal pollen decline in the Upper Jordan valley. The dry period may have continued into the Iron Age.

B. Settlement History

The chronological sequence in the Negeb during the Bronze Age shows several culture-stratigraphic disconformities and gaps which vary in length and areal scale in the different subregions. See Fig. NEG.01.

1. Northern Negeb. The final phases of the Beer-sheba Chalcolithic culture, dating to ca. 3700 B.C. (calibrated radiocarbon years) are followed by a much less widespread EB I. The chronological span of this phase has not been established. In the NW Negeb, at sites such as En Besor and Gaza H, somewhat later at the Besor Bridge site, and farther N as at Tell AREINI, there seems to have been significant Egyptian presence. In the E, as at ARAD and (small tell) MALHATA, Egyptian influence seems much less evident.

The EB II shows the rise of Tell Arad as a fortified town which clearly played a central role in Negeb economic systems. There appears to be a concomitant decline in the number of smaller sites in the region.

The abandonment/destruction of Tell Arad by the end of the EB II seems to correspond to a shift in urban settlement to the N and W, to such sites as Tell el HESI and Tell HALIF, leaving the Beer-sheba basin with little evidence of occupation in this period, although Tell ᶜIRA shows some EB III occupation. These sites were themselves abandoned in the EB IV; occupation seems to have been on a significantly smaller and non-urban scale in this period.

Reurbanization in the MB centered around the NW Negeb, at sites such as Tell Haror, Tell Nagila, and, closer to the coast, Tell JEMMEH and Tell el FARA (S). In the E, (large) Tell MALHATA and Tell Masos show occupations in this period. In this region one can trace a general line of cultural continuity through the LB, although the Beer-sheba basin shows little evidence of sedentary populations throughout the MB and LB.

2. Central Negeb. Chalcolithic settlement is sparse, but is followed by a major peak in the EB. Literally hundreds of sites, probably related to a system of sheep/goat pastoralism and copper trade, have been discovered as a result of intensive survey work. Although this peak has traditionally been attributed to the EB II to correspond to the rise of Arad as an urban center, there seems no compelling reason to reject an EB I date for some of the sites, especially in light of EB I presence in Sinai. Ceramic evidence is inconclusive, although there are indeed types which may be attributed to the EB I. Attribution to the EB III is somewhat more problematic, since contiguous regions do not show unambiguous evidence of EB III occupation, and ceramic assemblages contain no hints of EB III. This apparent decline in settlement corresponds well with the eclipse of urban Arad and the end of Canaanite outposts in Sinai.

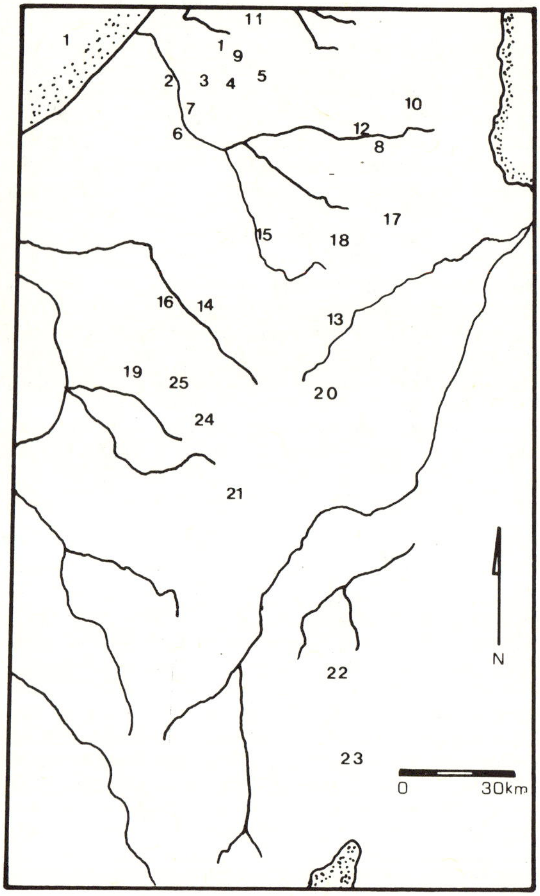

NEG.01. Regional map of the Negeb—Bronze Age. *1,* Hesi; *2,* Jemmeh; *3,* Haror; *4,* Seraᶜ; *5,* Halif; *6,* Fara (S); *7,* Gaza H and En Besor; *8,* Malhata; *9,* Nagila; *10,* Arad; *11,* Areini; *12,* Masos; *13,* Ein Ziq; *14,* Beᵓer Resisim; *15,* Mushabe Sadeh; *16,* Nahal Nizzana; *17,* Har Zayad; *18,* Yeruham; *19,* Kadesh-barnea; *20,* Makhtesh Ramon; *21,* Har Karkom; *22,* Uvda Valley; *23,* Timna Valley; *24,* Har Harif; *25,* Ramat Barnea. *(Map by S. Rosen)*

The tendency to see a settlement hiatus in the EB III in the Central Negeb is supported by the major changes evident in the region in the EB IV. Aside from significant transformations in material culture, including ceramics and stone and metal tools, the EB IV shows marked changes in settlement patterns. Sites such as Ein Ziq, BEER RESISIM, Mushabe Sadeh, Nahal Nizzana, Har Zayad and to a lesser extent, MOUNT YERUHAM, show densely clustered villages of up to 200 structures, far larger than sites from the EB I–II. Furthermore, the focus of settlement shifts from the W edges of the highlands along the axis from Har Karkom–Har Harif to Ramat Barnea (in the EB I–II) further N and E more to the center of the highlands in the EB IV.

Unlike the N Negeb, in the Central Negeb there is virtually no evidence of occupation, permanent, ephemeral, or otherwise, during the MB or LB. The significance of this gap has been debated, one school claiming it reflects a major demographic decline in the region (some claiming total abandonment), and a second suggesting it merely reflects reduced archaeological visibility due to a reversion to more nomadic lifestyles which left few recoverable residues.

3. Southern Negeb. In this region, as exemplified by the TIMNA^c and Uvda valleys, a local culture, sometimes referred to as the Timnian, spans the transition from Chalcolithic to the first stages of the EB. Biqat Uvda sites attributed to the EB II also show N influences, both architecturally and in the ceramic assemblage. The problem of EB III sites is similar to that in the Central Negeb, and the general cultural discontinuity between the EB I–II and the EB IV also resembles that found farther N except in the absence of comparably large EB IV village sites.

As in the Central Negeb, in the S Negeb there is little or no evidence of "indigenous" occupation during the MB and LB. However, in the Timnaᶜ valley impressive remains of LB Egyptian copper mining colonies have been excavated.

C. Society and Economy

During the EB I, as mentioned above, the NW Negeb shows a major Egyptian presence; interpretations range from conquest, colonization, and annexation to Egypt to trade, trade stations, and trade quarters in some sites. Material culture shows a mix of Canaanite elements with locally produced Egyptian types. Most sites have been incompletely excavated and are difficult to characterize. Nevertheless, the settlement system can be generally described as one of hamlets, villages, and perhaps a central town at Areini. Economy was based on village farming and animal husbandry, and given the Egyptian presence, trade can be assumed to have had a significant role as well. In the NE Negeb, EB I society can be characterized as one of village organization and subsistence farming. There is little evidence of large-scale Egyptian presence in the region.

It is difficult to distinguish EB I from EB II in the Central and S Negeb. However, using the local Sinai-Nawamis (Timnian) culture as a comparative base, (possible) EB I sites show affinities to those of Sinai, with hints of Egyptian influences in the ceramics and lithics. Sheep/goat husbandry was the dominant economic mode.

The concomitant development of urban (and fortified) Arad and the organized copper trade from S Sinai in the EB II had its ramifications for the entire Negeb. Egyptian influence wanes in the N, and examples of "Aradian" architecture and ceramics appear at numerous sites throughout the Negeb. The increased Canaanite presence in the Central and S Negeb, almost unquestionably stimulated by copper exploitation both in S Sinai and the Timnaᶜ valley, seems to have effected major growth in the pastoral nomadic population, as well as tying it more closely to the N economy. Thus, this period shows the development of a classic system of urban/village heartland and pastoral nomadic hinterland, with a typical nomadic dependence on the economies of the N. Archaeologically this is reflected in the animal bone assemblages, central pen-attached room architecture, disappearance of arrowheads from the lithic assemblages, and trade items such as some ceramics, metals, shells, and flint tools. Fields of round secondary burial tumuli are often found in association with these pastoral sites and may be a Negeb version of the Nawamis tombs of S Sinai. Possible ritual sites, such as at Har Karkom and in the Ramon Crater (Makhtesh), have also been discovered.

This general framework seems to have collapsed with the decline of Arad and the copper trade. Reasons for this are debated and include invasion and destruction, climatic change, and internal social dissolution. It is possible that reassertion of Egyptian control over SW Sinai also played a role. EB III cities such as at Tell Halif and Tell Hesi, although showing good evidence for Egyptian trade, do not show the desert contacts evident in EB II Tell Arad. As in N Israel, the EB III in the N Negeb is dominated by complex city sites supported by agricultural hinterlands.

The decline of urban civilization in the EB IV has been interpreted as the result of invasion, internal collapse, plague, climatic catastrophe, and various combinations of these factors. EB IV sites in the Negeb as a whole are dwarfed by the large sites of the Central Negeb, which have been viewed as the remains of large seasonal base camps of pastoral nomads. However, their size, the permanent nature of the agriculture, and the proximity of the sites to water suggest they may have been occupied year-round. Typically the sites show round rooms with central columns, often attached to one another in a room-small courtyard complex. Rectangular tumuli are often associated with the larger sites. The subsistence base of this culture is difficult to reconstruct since, aside from the presence of grinding stones, there is little evidence for agriculture; from the presence of ovicaprids and pens, pastoralism clearly played a significant role. Discoveries of caches of copper ingots indicate that the metal trade persisted, if not perhaps on the same scale as in the preceding EB II. Other sites in the S Negeb are considerably smaller and more ephemeral, although showing similar material culture. In the N Negeb, sites from this period have been little investigated.

MB and LB cities in the N Negeb at Tells Masos, Malhata, Nagila, Fara (S), Haror, Seraᶜ, Jemmeh, etc., show impressive and sophisticated fortification systems, public structures, and possibly elite residences. These sites fall into the general mode of the MB–LB Canaanite culture of N and central Palestine. They show international connections, especially with Egypt, and sites such as Malhata, Haror, Fara (S), and Masos may be Egyptian (Hyksos) garrisons. Tombs seem to show status differences within the population. Subsistence economies were based on grain agriculture and animal husbandry. Historical and political events in this period in the N Negeb are tied to the coastal plain and the Shephelah and as such are less associated with the Negeb as a geographical unit. The transition from MB to the LB in this region is marked by the reduction of some of the Egyptian fortresses, but shows essential cultural continuity.

The S Negeb in the LB, at Timna^{c}, again shows Egyptian mining colonies. Of special interest is the temple to Hathor at Timna^{c}. These discoveries can be tied to the Egyptian control of SW Sinai.

D. The Biblical Narrative

It is difficult to tie the biblical narrative to Negeb Bronze Age sites and locations with any certainty, especially in the Central and S Negeb, where there are virtually no written records associated with the sites. Thus, in the N Negeb, Tell Haror can be reasonably associated with GERAR, and Tell el Fara (S) with Sharuhen, but even the identification of Tell Arad with its pre-Iron Age biblical counterpart is problematic, as is the identification of the biblical Besor with Wadi Gaza. In the Central Negeb, if on the one hand identifications such as Ein el Qudeirat with KADESH-BARNEA seem well founded in the Iron Age, they present problems for earlier parts of the biblical narrative. The virtual absence of remains from the MB or LB in this area (and the rest of the Central Negeb) contradict the 38-year Israelite settlement recounted in Exodus. Similar problems attend virtually all attempts to identify specific sites (especially Mt. Sinai) in the Central Negeb with places mentioned in Exodus.

E. Summary

The Negeb in the Bronze Age cannot really be seen as a stable culture-geographic unit. The nature and borders of settlement shift considerably with each archaeological phase, so that in different periods, subregions may be either "abandoned" or incorporated into the N sphere, or may undergo significant shifts in type of settlement. This dynamism, or perhaps better, instability, is a function of basic tensions in man-desert adaptations, stimulated by external historical processes and/or minor climatic changes. Tying the biblical narrative to the archaeological history remains a speculative endeavor except in specific circumstances.

Bibliography

Amiran, R. et al. 1978. *Early Arad.* Jerusalem.

Anati, E. 1984. *Har Karkom, Montagna Sacra Nel Deserto dell'Esodo.* Milan.

Avner, U. 1984. Ancient Cult Sites in the Negev and Sinai Deserts. *TA* 11: 115–31.

Cohen, R. 1986. *The Settlement of the Central Negev in the Light of Archaeology and Literary Sources During the 4th–1st Millennia B.C.E.*, Ph.D. diss., Hebrew University, Jerusalem (in Hebrew).

Cohen, R., and Dever, W. G. 1979. Preliminary Report on the Second Season of the "Central Negev Highlands Project." *BASOR* 236: 41–60.

Dever, W. G. 1980. New Vistas on the EB IV (MB I) Horizon in Syria-Palestine. *BASOR* 237: 35–64.

Evenari, M. 1982. *The Negev: Challenge of a Desert.* Cambridge, MA.

Gerstenblith, P. 1983. *The Levant at the Beginning of the Middle Bronze Age.* ASORDS 5. Winona Lake, IN.

Glueck, N. 1959. *Rivers in the Desert.* Philadelphia.

Goldberg, P., and Rosen, A. M. 1987. The Early Holocene Paleoenvironments of Israel. Pp. 23–34 in *Shiqmim I,* ed. T. E. Levy. BARIS. Oxford.

Gophna, R. 1976. Egyptian Immigration into Southern Canaan in the First Dynasty? *TA* 3: 31–37.

———. 1984. The Settlement Landscape of Palestine in the Early Bronze Age II–III and Middle Bronze Age II. *IEJ* 34: 24–31.

Haiman, M. 1986. *Archaeological Survey of Israel Map of Har Hamran-Southwest (198) 10–00.* Jerusalem.

Kochavi, M. 1969. The Middle Bronze I Period (the Intermediate Bronze). *Qadmoniot* 2: 38–44 (in Hebrew).

Miroschedji, P. de, ed. 1989. *L'Urbanisation de la Palestine a l'Age du Bronze Ancien: Bilan et perspectives des recherches actuelles.* BARIS. Oxford.

Rosen, S. A. 1987. Demographic Trends in the Negev Highlands: Preliminary Results from the Emergency Survey. *BASOR* 266: 45–58.

———. 1988. Notes on the Origins of Pastoral Nomadism: A Case Study from the Negev and Sinai. *Current Anthropology* 29: 498–506.

Rothenberg, B. 1972. *Were These King Solomon's Mines? Excavations in the Timna Valley.* New York.

Thompson, T. L. 1975. *The Settlement of Sinai and the Negev in the Bronze Age.* Weisbaden.

Weinstein, J. 1981. The Egyptian Empire in Palestine: a Reassessment. *BASOR* 241: 1–28.

STEVEN A. ROSEN

IRON AGE

Within its biblical limits, the Negeb embraced mainly the area of the Arad and Beer-sheba valleys, a flat upland region, measuring ca. 40 × 40 km, in S Judah. See Fig. NEG.02. The region is covered by loess soil and has a semi-desert climate, with an annual rainfall of around 200 mm. This amount of rainfall is insufficient for intensive, high-yield agriculture, but permits subsistence cultivation and sheepherding.

The main wadis of the biblical Negeb are Wadi Gerar and Wadi Beer-sheba. These are the two largest tributaries of Wadi Besor, which drains the region into the Mediterranean. Along these streambeds and their tributaries exist active wells, with especially high-yielding wells found in the vicinity of Tel Masos, Tel Malhata, and Tel ʾAroer in the E Negeb.

The name "Negeb" derives from the Hebrew radical *ngb,* meaning "dry" or "dryness." In biblical terminology *negeb* is often synonymous with *darom,* that is, "south" or "southern direction." Throughout the history of Israel, the Negeb has been a region of strategic importance, both as a landbridge and as a buffer between the S deserts of the Negeb mountains and the Sinai, and the settled country in the N. The S deserts were often occupied by hostile wandering tribes, thrusting N into the settled country, sometimes to conquer and displace its population, and sometimes for the purpose of robbery and despoliation. In response to this threat, the central authorities established a series of fortified settlements in the Negeb during the periods of the United Monarchy and after.

The Negeb was part of the tribe of Judah, as well as of the tribe of Simeon, which had been absorbed by the latter (Josh 15:20–32; 19:1–9). The tribe of Judah also absorbed various other tribal elements, including families of the Kenites (Judg 1:16), Jerahmeelites (1 Sam 27:10), and Cherethites (1 Sam 30:14), as well as sons of Caleb (1 Sam

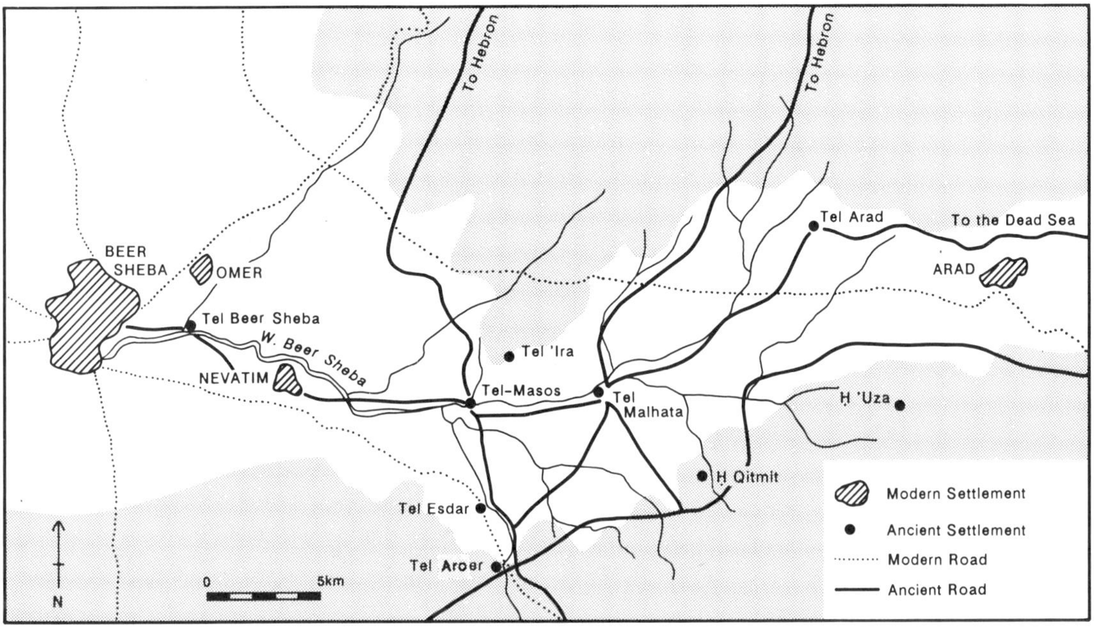

NEG.02. Regional map of E Negeb and Israelite Settlements—Iron Age. *(Courtesy of I. Beit-Arieh)*

30:14). The Kenites apparently lived in the E Negeb, the Jerahmeelites in the SE, the Calebs in the NE, and the Cherethites in the W of the Negeb. These localities were named after the tribal families. The area of the tribe of Simeon is generally located in the central Negeb, though some scholars place it further to the NE.

The earliest occupation evidence for the Israelite period is at Tel Masos, where a settlement was established at the end of the 13th century B.C. However, no remains of Canaanite settlement from the LB have so far been discovered in the region.

This lack of evidence has created difficulties with regard to the biblical accounts of the Israelite settlement and the reported battles with the Canaanites over ARAD and HORMAH, which are described as Canaanite cities (Num 21:1–3; 33:40) and are said to have been destroyed by Joshua (Josh 12:14). Modern scholars have tried to overcome these difficulties in various ways. Glueck (1968: 114–15) suggested that the king of Arad was not the ruler of that city but merely the chieftain of a wandering tribe in the area. On the other hand, Mazar (1965) proposed to identify Arad with Tel Malhata (though no Canaanite remains from the LB were found there either). See MALHATA, TEL. The suggestion that the conquest of Arad is an etiological story reflecting the biblical writer's experience of the ruined early Canaanite city was advanced by Fritz (1966). Aharoni (*LBHG,* 215–16), based on the list of cities conquered by Shishak during his campaign in Canaan in 925 B.C., which mentions two forts named Arad (*Arad rabbâ* and *Arad lĕ bêt yeruhem,* abbreviated for *Arad lĕ bêt yerehmiʾelî*), would identify the former *(Arad rabbâ)* with Tel Arad and the latter *(Arad lĕ bêt yeruhem)* with Tel Malhata. Naʾaman (1980) suggested a location for Ḥormah at Tel Halif (and not at Tel Masos, as frequently proposed), giving as one of his reasons for this identification that Tel Halif has an occupation stratum from the Late Canaanite period (though this stratum is not from the period of Israelite settlement, but dates to the Iron Age period).

During the period of the Judges, the Negeb was only thinly settled, with few permanent settlements. To this period are assigned stratum II at Tel Masos, strata VII–VI at BEER-SHEBA, and stratum III at Tel Esdar. See ESDAR, TEL. Recently a large settlement has been discovered E of Tel Beer-sheba on one of the tributaries of Wadi Yatir; the pottery of this settlement dates apparently to this period (11th century B.C.). The settlement was unfortified, and its population probably engaged in sheepherding, commerce, and perhaps agriculture.

The wars conducted by Saul against the Amalekites were in defense of these border settlements, which, however, were destroyed at the end of the 11th century, perhaps by one of the wandering desert tribes (like the Amalekites) pushing up from the S.

In the 10th century B.C., probably in Solomon's reign, new fortified towns were erected on the destruction layers of the previous settlements. Such new fortified towns were excavated in stratum V at Tel Beer-sheba and at Tel Malhata, while perhaps the fort of stratum XI at Arad belongs to this period. In their layout, planning, and construction, these new fortified towns and forts reflect the official state policy of creating a S defense line, probably as a shield against Egyptian attacks. They were, however, destroyed during Shishak's invasion of Judah.

The settlements of the Negeb highlands (some of which are described as "forts" in the research) are dated by some scholars to the 10th century and by others to the 11th century B.C. It was at this time that the Israelite population apparently began its expansion into the Negeb highlands. Some of these settlements, including those uncovered at RAMAT MATRED, were apparently civilian agricultural estates, while others probably served as garrisons for army personnel commanded to defend this border region. Given the mobile nature of warfare in the desert and against wandering tribes, one would not expect to find fortified settlements of the tower-fortress type; and accordingly the settlements that were erected in strategic places in the lowland and on hilltops are best defined as military garrison forts.

During the 8th and 9th centuries, the Judean occupation of the Negeb remained sparse, confined almost exclusively to fortified settlements, as at Beer-sheba, Tel Malhata, and Arad. In the 8th century, the Negeb borderland was the scene of many Assyrian campaigns against Philistia and Egypt; some scholars believe that in one of his campaigns against Philistia in 720 B.C., Sargon II penetrated the area of Judean settlements, inflicting widespread destruction. The destruction of stratum II at Beer-sheba may be assigned to this year, though Aharoni, the excavator of the site, attributes the destruction of this stratum to Sennacherib's campaign of 701 B.C. Others date the destruction of stratum II as late as Nebuchadnezzar.

In the 7th century, there was an upturn of settlement activity in the Judean Negeb. Only at Beer-sheba was the settlement not revived after its destruction; other destroyed sites were rebuilt. New settlements were also established during this century at Tel ᶜIra, Tel Masos (a small settlement), Horvat ᶜUza, and on the N outskirts of Beer-sheba. See AROER (PLACE), ᶜIRA, TEL; ᶜUZA, HORVAT.

The most prominent of these new settlements was the strategically sited and well-fortified settlement at Tel ᶜIra, which may perhaps be identified with the biblical Ramah of the Negeb. In all probability it became the central town of the Judean Negeb, replacing Beer-sheba, which had ceased to exist at that time.

The settlement pattern of the E Negeb for this period shows great density, resulting probably from the efforts of the central administration to secure this S border against both attacks by Arab tribes and the attempts of Edom to seize parts of the Negeb, which it desired to control the transit routes to the seas. However, this defensive effort of the Judean kingdom was also aimed against Babylonia, which conducted its first military campaign against Judah at the end of the 7th century. There is increasing evidence that the Edomites actively participated in the destruction of the Judean Negeb cities, which significantly weakened Judah before its final demise. Aside from the traditional enmity that existed between Judah and Edom, which is amply attested in the Bible, there is archaeological evidence of hostile Edomite presence in the E Negeb during this period. This evidence includes pottery finds from all the mentioned Judean sites (and especially Qitmit), as well as written documents, of which the most important are Arad ostracon no. 24 (in which the commander of Arad is ordered to send reinforcements to Ramat Negeb "lest Edom arrive there") and the Edomite ostracon from Horvat ᶜUza. The combined archaeological evidence can be taken to indicate that large areas of the E Negeb were annexed at the end of the First Temple period by the Edomites, who perhaps were also responsible for the destruction of the Judean cities during the Babylonian campaign against Jerusalem in 586 B.C., or a few years thereafter.

Bibliography

Fritz, V. 1966. Arad in der biblischen Uberlieferung und in der Liste Schoschenkes I. *ZDPV* 82: 331–42.

Glueck, N. 1968. *Rivers in the Desert.* New York.

Mazar, B. 1965. The Sanctuary of Arad and the Family of Hobab in the Kenite. *JNES* 24: 297–303.

Naʾaman, N. 1980. The Inheritance of the Sons of Simeon. *ZDPV* 96: 136–52.

ITZHAQ BEIT-ARIEH

HELLENISTIC-ROMAN PERIOD

There is growing evidence that the history of the Nabateans in the Negeb did not begin in the Hellenistic period, as formerly thought, but began in the Persian period, if not earlier. Archaeological evidence for this period is extremely scarce, but it is scarce for the Hellenistic period as well. Outstanding are the pits in which Persian pottery was found at Horvat Ritma in the central Negeb. Theoretically these pits mark the arrival of nomadic Arabs to the central Negeb. See also NABATEANS.

In studying the history of the Arabs of the Negeb, known as "Nabatean" from the end of the 4th century B.C.E. onward, scholars have tended to discredit Herodotus' account, limiting it generally to the statement "the Arabs call Dionysus Orotalt; and Aphrodite, Alilat" (3.8). Whereas the identity of Orotalt is disputed, Alilat is identified with al-Ilat, or Allat, the chief goddess of the Nabateans. But Herodotus supplies much more information. In his discussion of Cambyses' campaign against Egypt, Herodotus paid much attention to the matter of water supply: "I will tell of a thing that but few of those who sail to Egypt have perceived. Earthen jars full of wine are brought to Egypt twice a year from all Greece and Phoenicia besides: yet one might safely say that there is not a single empty wine jar anywhere in the country. . . . Each governor of a district must gather in all the earthen pots from his own township and carry them to those waterless lands of Syria; so the earthen pottery that is brought to Egypt and unloaded and emptied there is carried to Syria to join the stock that has already been taken there" (3.6). But the Arabs supplied Cambyses' army with water in a different way: ". . . the Arabian planned and did as I shall show: he filled camel-skins with water and loaded all his live camels with these; which done he drove them to the waterless land and awaited Cambyses' army" (3.9). And as is Herodotus' habit: "I must relate the less credible tale also, since they tell it. There is a great river in Arabia called Corys, issuing into the sea called Red. From this river (it is said) the king of the Arabians carried water by a duct of sewn oxhides and of other hides of a length sufficient to reach to the dry country; and he had many tanks dug in that country to receive and keep the water. It is a twelve days' journey from that river to that desert. By three ducts (they say) he led the water to three several places" (3.9).

Herodotus' account is confirmed by the more recent and more accurate account of Hieronymus of Cardia related by Diodorus. After describing the Nabatean Arabs this source concludes, "Consequently neither the Assyrians of old, nor the kings of the Medes and Persians, nor yet those of the Macedonians have been able to enslave them, they never brought their attempts to a successful conclusion" (2.48.5). This source is more specific on the matter of water supply: "As the earth in some places is clayey and in others of soft stone, they make great excavations in it, the mouths of which they make very small, but constantly increasing the width as they dig deeper, they finally make them of such size that each side has a length of one plethrum. After filling these reservoirs with rain water, they close the openings, making them even with the ground, and they leave signs that are known to themselves but are unknown to others" (19.94.6–8). This notice not only tallies in every detail the description of the cisterns excavated by the Nabateans in the Negeb, but fits well the nature of the lithology of the central Negeb, and not of any other Nabatean region.

The only positive evidence for the presence of the Nabateans in the Negeb in the first half of the 2d century B.C.E. is the Elusa inscription, antedating by half a century the evidence from any other Nabatean site. The other finds at Elusa, Oboda, Nessana, and more recently at Moyet Awad in the Arabah and some sites along the SW shore of the Dead Sea are coins of the Hellenistic period, "Megarian" bowls and Eastern Sigillata wares, and numerous stamped jar handles originating in the Greek islands, the wine jars of Herodotus. As the Nabateans refrained from drinking wine at this early period (cf. Diod. 19.94.3–4), these wine jars were an improvement on the more perishable skins which they used for the transportation of water on their journeys in the desert.

On no site in the central Negeb were discovered any traces of buildings which date earlier than the last quarter of the 1st century B.C.E. This again agrees with Hieronymus'-Diodorus' description: "It is their custom neither to sow corn, plant fruit-bearing trees, use wine, nor construct any house; if anyone is found acting contrary to this, death is his penalty" (19.94.3–4). Only very recently have archaeologists been able to find traces of Nabatean tent encampments of this period.

Most of the 1st century B.C.E. is not represented by any finds in the whole of the central Negeb. The retreat of the Nabateans from the Negeb was an outcome of the aggressive policy of Alexander Jannaeus and his predecessors. Not only did Nabateans lose territories which they held in Moab, but they also lost the harbors of Gaza, Anthedon, Raphia, and Rhinocorura (cf. *Ant* 13.395). It is only with the ascendancy of John Hyrcanus II that the fortunes of the Nabateans began to change (Ant 14.18). Herod apparently restored to the Nabateans use of the S harbors, which brought a new prosperity, and marks the beginning of the Middle Nabatean Period (30 B.C.E.–50 C.E.). During this period the Petra-Oboda-Gaza road was built. The road follows Nahal Neqarot (Wadi es-Siq) necessitating the construction of a caravanserai at Moyet Awad, and forts and water stations at other locations. In some sections the road was cleared of stones and marked by curbstones and unepigraphical milestones. A secondary road led from Petra to Mampsis, joining the Oboda-Gaza road NE of Oboda. This road, too, had a caravansarai and minor stops and water stations along its course. Thus the region which during the Early Nabatean Period had only a few sites, developed no less than six. The main caravan stop, and the backbone of the whole system, must have been at Oboda, and included a large temple, which in addition to its regular religious functions apparently served also as a bank. The army which protected the whole region was stationed in the large camp, and large camel sheds supplied the necessary vehicles for the caravan traffic and its protection. Another temple apparently existed at Elusa, a caravan halt at Mampsis, and a fort at Nessana. The noncombatant population must still have lived in tent encampments, traces of which have been discovered at Elusa, Oboda, and Biqᶜat Uvdah, NW of Eilat, from which a road branched off to Nessana and Gaza. The destruction of this system apparently occurred in 50 C.E., when newly invading Arab tribes, who had been weakened by the loss of international spice trade to the Romans, flooded the Nabatean realm. This historical picture, corroborated by the archaeological finds at Oboda and other Nabatean sites in the Negeb, is now confirmed by the history of Nabatean coinage, which showed a steep decline in silver content in 50 C.E.

The reign of Malichus II (40–70 C.E.) seems to have been a period of decline in the Negeb, as it was elsewhere in the Nabatean realm. The accession to the throne of Rabel II marks the beginning of a new prosperity. The Nabateans, who lost a large share of trade, began to develop agriculture. At first this was based on horse breeding, apparently developing the Arabian horse which became renowned in subsequent centuries. This is mainly attested at Mampsis, but similar stables were found also at Sobata and Oboda. Barley was grown for food in the surrounding valleys. At the beginning the Nabateans terraced narrow valleys only, but they later cultivated wider valleys, depending on the supply of rainwater from much larger catchment areas. This new development was so important that the event was celebrated by religious festivities, and the king was honored by a new title: "He Who Brought Life and Deliverance to His People," which is attested on numerous inscriptions at Oboda and the surrounding hinterland. During this period the Nabateans began to construct spacious dwellings to compensate for the loss of freedom they had enjoyed with their tents. Nothing portrays this change of life better than the production of pottery. The luxurious Middle Nabatean wares, which equaled the quality of their sumptuous architecture, gave way to pottery types better suited to rich farmers. The annexation of the Nabatean kingdom to the Roman empire on March 22, 106 C.E., did not adversely affect the prosperity of the Nabatean Negeb. The construction by Trajan of a new road to connect the *Via Nova* with a road from Jerusalem, Hebron, and Mampsis must have contributed to the well-being of the Negeb. This economic boom continued well into the 3d century C.E., when Palestine was subdivided into three separate provinces and the Negeb formed the backbone of the large new *Palestina Tertia.* Most of the evidence for this period still comes from Oboda. Although Nabatean-Aramaic gave way to Greek, and the old Semitic cults assumed a Roman disguise, the builders of the new temple at Oboda all bore Nabatean names. King Oboda, after whom the city was named, and who was deified after his death, was venerated at this temple as Zeus-Obodas. The work of constructing a new quarter at Oboda was entrusted to a Nabatean architect from Petra, who followed assiduously Nabatean methods of planning and construction. Although the evidence is not as decisive as at Oboda, this prosperity in the post-Nabatean Period was shared also by Elusa, Mampsis, Sobata, and Ruheibah.

The accession to the throne of Diocletian, and the great interest which he took in the E, was a turning point for the towns of the central Negeb. The Nabateans, who were at home in the desert, felt it unnecessary to protect their towns with walls. On the other hand, Diocletian, who consolidated the *limes Palaestinae* along the *Via Nova,* found it necessary to fortify Mampsis, which was the weakest link in the system of the Negeb. Citadels for the protection of the towns people were built at Oboda and at Mampsis. The construction of the wall at Mampsis became an obstacle to further urban development. The policy instituted by Diocletian was apparently followed also by Constantine the Great and his house. In the second half of the 4th century C.E. began the struggle between Semitic-Roman paganism and Christianity. Soon after the middle of the century the first churches were built at Oboda, Mampsis, Sobata, and Nessana. Literary evidence shows that Elusa played an important role in the advent of Christianity, and that opposition to the new religion was stronger in this large town, which had been a center of Roman cultural life. From a study of personal names, it is clear that even in this late period the Nabateans were still the dominant element in local population, and that even in the Church they contributed the rank and file.

Agriculture formed the basis of the local economy, as seen in the large number of papyri found at Nessana which refer to the cultivation of wheat, barley, vegetables, and fruit trees of various kinds. Archaeological data indicate that olive oil production and wine also contributed significantly to the prosperity. The climatic conditions of the region made it possible to produce wine of a quality good enough to compete with the wines of S Europe. Local trade and the pilgrimages to the holy places in S Sinai were factors of lesser economic importance.

In 636 C.E. the Negeb was conquered by the Moslems. Mampsis was apparently destroyed in an earlier raid, and Oboda, which apparently put up a strong opposition, did not survive this conquest. However, the towns in the W part of the region survived at least until the end of the 7th century C.E. Although there was apparently no direct pressure, the necessity to pay heavy taxes for the upkeep of the Islamic army and population weakened these towns, and disturbed the delicate balance between survival and ruin in the Negeb. Another factor which might have sealed the fate of the towns of the Negeb was the loss of a market for the main product of the towns of the Negeb—wine.

Bibliography

Cohen, R. 1981. *Archaeological Survey of Israel.* Jerusalem.

Evenari, M.; Shanan, L.; and Tadmor, N. 1971. *The Negev.* Cambridge, MA.

Meshel, Z., and Tzafrir, Y. 1974. The Nabatean Road from 'Avdat to Sha'ar Ramon. *PEQ* 106: 103–18.

Negev, A. 1966. The Date of the Petra-Gaza Road. *PEQ* 98: 89–98.

———. 1969. The Chronology of the Middle Nabatean Period. *PEQ* 101: 5–14.

———. 1974. The Churches of the Central Negev. An Archaeological Survey. *RB* 81: 397–420.

———. 1976a. The Early Beginnings of the Nabatean Realm. *PEQ* 108: 125–33.

———. 1976b. Permanence et Disparition d'Anciens Toponymes du Negev Central. *RB* 83: 545–57.

———. 1977. The Nabateans and the Provincia Arabia. Pp. 520–686 in *ANRW* 2.8.

———. 1981a. *The Greek Inscriptions from the Negev.* Jerusalem.

———. 1981b. House and City Planning in the Ancient Negev and the Provincia Arabia. Pp. 3–32 in *Housing and Arid Lands,* ed. G. Golani. London.

———. 1982. Numismatics and Nabatean Chronology. *PEQ* 114: 119–28.

———. 1983. *Tempel, Kirchen und Zisternen.* Stuttgart.

———. 1986. *New Avenues in Nabatean Archaeology.* New York.

AVRAHAM NEGEV

NEHELAM (PLACE) [Heb *hanneḥĕlāmî*]. An appellation of Shemaiah, a prophet among the exiles in Babylon who wrote a letter to the religious officials of Jerusalem in which he opposes Jeremiah (Jer 29:24, 31–32). Though the RSV treats this as a proper name, the Hebrew does not seem clearly to support this interpretation. The word in Hebrew is a gentilic formation and appears most likely to be an adjective which modifies the proper name "Shemaiah." A solution to the problem may be found in a possible parallelism between Shemaiah the Nehelam and Jeremiah of Anathoth (Jer 29:24–28). Anathoth in Hebrew also has the gentilic formation—Jeremiah of Anathoth (Heb *bĕyirmĕyāhû hāʿănnĕtōtî;* Jer 29:27). This might indicate that Nehelam is a place name, perhaps the town of Shemaiah's origin. However, no such place is known or referred to elsewhere in the OT, though this does not exclude the possibility that Nehelam refers to an obscure location. Muilenberg (*IDB* 3: 532–33) notes that LXX B reads *ailameiten* (Elamite), but also suggests that Nehelam may be a family name. Carroll (*Jeremiah* OTL, 564) proposes that Nehelam is a "literary creation" to set Shemaiah the Nehelam opposite Jeremiah of Anathoth. Yaure (1960: 306–309), taking Nehelam as a *Nipʿal* form of *ḥlm* "to dream," proposes that Nehelam means "dreamer" (i.e., he is a prophet whose inspiration is derived from dreams). So, Shemaiah is a prototype of Elymas in Acts 13:6–12. However, this proposal has found little support (cf. Carroll, 564; Bright *Jeremiah* AB, 209; *IDB* 3: 533).

Bibliography

Yaure, L. 1960. Elymas-Nehelamite-Pethor. *JBL* 79: 297–314.

JOHN M. BRACKE

NEHEMIAH (PERSON) [Heb *nĕḥemĕyāh*]. **1.** A leader of the Jewish community who returned to Palestine with Zerubbabel shortly after 538 B.C.E., the end of the Babylonian exile. Ezra 2:2 lists this Nehemiah (Gk *neemias/*

neemios) third in a list of twelve names, immediately after the names of Zerubbabel and Joshua. This order is followed in the parallel passages Neh 7:7 (Gk *neemia*) and 1 Esdr 5:8 (Gk *neemiou/neemias*).

2. Neh 3:16 mentions one "Nehemiah the son of Azbuk, ruler of half the district of Beth-zur." It is unclear whether this Nehemiah or his father ruled this half-province. He worked under the direction of Nehemiah ben-Hacaliah on the project to rebuild the city walls of Jerusalem in the 5th century B.C.E.

STEVEN R. SWANSON

3. The son of Hacaliah who is the central figure in the book of Nehemiah and one of the most convincing human personalities in the Bible. The dating of his primary reform activity begins in 445 B.C., the 20th year of Artaxerxes (Neh 1:1; 2:1)—although Josephus refers to Xerxes' 25th year (*Ant* 11.5 §168) and his 28th year (§179; see note in LCL 6: 400). In contrast with Ezra, Nehemiah "was a successful man of action. Through his energy, unselfishness, and cleverness he brought new life to the dying Jewish community in Jerusalem" (Pfeiffer *IDB* 3: 534). This convincingness does not mean that every detail in his transmitted history is unambiguous. Around every great leader cluster legends and midrash. See EZRA-NEHEMIAH, BOOKS OF.

Already in Neh 1:1–2:9 the colorful presentation of Nehemiah's emergence leaves us with one massive uncertainty. In 1:1 was he just "cupbearer," or table servant to the king? The "cupbearer" attested throughout centuries of Persian history and legend was a favorite and trusted youthful official. Such a position would indeed best account for the instant success of his carefully nurtured attack on the monarch's resistance (1:4; 2:1–4; the king's only reply was "How soon will you come back?"). It would also account for the prompt success of his wall building (6:15) and whatever else he later set his hand to (5:6ff.; 13:8, 10, 15, 23).

The "honorable and privileged" dignity of the cupbearer ("wine taster," or at least trusted authority responsible for the king's nutriment reaching him free of poisoning) to Van den Born (*EDB*, 1626–27) "seems to suggest that he was a eunuch." But that was the requirement for the quite different but equally trusted office which we still today call "chamberlain"; though Myers (*Ezra, Nehemiah* AB) from 2:6 concludes that Nehemiah's duties extended to the harem. The real reason for suspecting Nehemiah was a eunuch is of a quite different order. "Eunuch," not cupbearer, is the reading of the usually more reliable Greek texts corresponding to Neh 1:11 (i.e., Esdras-B 11:11 except Alexandrinus and a Sinaiticus corrector). The confusion is quickly seen to be an inner Greek problem; though *oinochoos*, "wine pourer," corresponds to Hebrew *mašqeh* (causative participle of *šāqāh*, "to drink"), it strongly resembles *euno-echos*, "bed-holder." Since "eunuch" was the name of an official probably higher and better known in Greek circles, we may suppose that this term was chosen simply as "trusted high official" without anatomical implications: either as the most primitive rendition of *mašqeh*, or as an early scribal correction of *oinochoos* which won almost complete acceptance. In any case "eunuch" as a physical condition is totally alien to the exuberance and forcefulness shown throughout Nehemiah's career (Yamauchi 1980).

Another dilemma with which the very opening of the book of Nehemiah confronts us is momentous in itself but minor for our portrayal of his personality. The event which prompted his taking action (1:3) was "the wall of Jerusalem broken down and its gates destroyed by fire." Since this is last minute news brought by his brother Hanani, the reference can hardly be to Nebuchadnezzar's destruction of Jerusalem in 2 Chr 36:17 (cf. 2 Kgs 25:10). This wall destroyed only in 446 has been equated to a rebuilding already undertaken by the temple builders (Ezra 4:12, related rather to Ezra himself [rejected by Williamson 1987: 75; *Ezra, Nehemiah* WBC, 59] or to rebellions in the area of Judah attested in secular history (Morgenstern 1957). While keeping open the relevance of these efforts, we see no imperative need to suppose that the Jerusalem disaster which grieved Nehemiah was anything but a local mishap without any international or even political involvements.

Like Gelin in his thumbnail sketch, which is still the best (1960: 23, summarized in *JBC* 24: 100 and *NJBC*), we may take up at once the aspect of Nehemiah's character which most calls for attention and debate. Was he really "vain" (2:10, 18; 5:15; 6:11)? But to "explosively emotional" we will add a more challenging question which Gelin's summary ignores. Was not Nehemiah's "vanity" ultimately a form of separatism and xenophobia?—doubtless an understandable form, as exemplified in an overachiever, yet one which may give us an important key to the place he has earned in history.

His characterization of two Jerusalem locals as "outsiders," Sanballat the Horonite and his toady, Tobiah the Ammonite (2:10, 19), is followed by a confidence in God which excludes that they can "have any part or justification or *zikkārôn*." *Zikkārôn* can mean remembrance, memoir, or monument. Does it hint that Nehemiah is already thinking of the wall as a "monument more enduring than bronze" to his own achievement, or at least to that of the returned exiles? Verse 20 contains a clear implication that the never exiled Jerusalemites might have already wanted, or would eventually desire, to share in the wall building.

Such a desire is admittedly far clearer in Ezra 4:2. Though that verse in its context is related not to the wall but to the Temple building of a century earlier, the continuation is a letter to Artaxerxes protesting *wall* building in Jerusalem (vv 12 and 16; *city* rebuilding in Artaxerxes' answer in v 21). Thus Ezra 4, at least vv 7–22, may well be seen as belonging to the Nehemiah context (6:7 "report to the king"; the alternative transposition of Ezra 4 to Ezra 10, perhaps echoing 9:9, "protection in Judah and Jerusalem," has to suppose that part of Ezra's failure lay in trying to build a wall, *the* wall *later* destroyed [Neh 1:3]).

A radical change within the Sanballat-Tobiah party is recorded: though Nehemiah 4 shows only their taunts and opposition, in Nehemiah 6 they are desirous of dialogue. Neh 6:2 interprets this offer a priori as a plot, and Neh 6:10–13 makes much more explicit a more sinister plot, but one only suspected (though prudently) by Nehemiah. If, however, we make a judicious effort to focus on only the recorded facts, apart from Nehemiah's frankly hostile innuendos, we may find it possible and plausible to maintain that the local low-class inhabitants of Jerusalem were just as Judean and Yahweh-worshiping as those who returned from exile, though mingled among them and in administrative positions were many "Samaritans" (name applicable in general to non-exiled Judah, made subordinate to the province of Samaria). Of these in turn, *some* (though hardly a [Beth-]Horonite from the Samaria-Judah border, or even an Ammonite) might have been in part descendants of the Mesopotamians installed under Sargon in 721 (2 Kgs 17:24; cf. Ezra 4:10). These merit also elsewhere in the Bible the taunt of "foreign captives" (Neh 4:4). The intrenched Jerusalemites, rabble and leaders, despised the wall building project as hopeless at first, then came to fear it as a threat to their "Persian peace," but finally, seeing that it was likely to succeed, sued to have a part in it. But Nehemiah, more than ever after seeing how successful he had been in the face of their opposition, refused to allow all the "people of God in Jerusalem" to unite, and stuck intransigently to his claim that only the upper-class Judeans who had suffered in Babylon were the true Jews.

If this reconstruction of the facts is at least to some extent admissible, it would account for the praise of Nehemiah without Ezra in Sir 49:11 (especially in Cazelles' [1954] view that Ezra's aim was to conciliate the "Samaritans" not only of Judah, and thus bring them to accept "his" Pentateuch). But the more permanent Ezra-glorifying tradition in *m. ʾAbot* 1:1 (Ezra's wall was the Law) fitted a situation in which the "true Judeans" no longer wielded the power, but lived as a resistant minority in the midst of encroaching "non-observers."

To this question of how (pardonably) overbearing or "vain" Nehemiah really was, a further answer is provided by the "Nehemiah-memoir" thesis (von Rad 1964). The (apparent) fact that he wrote his own memoirs at all, and in such a style as to put his achievements in so favorable a light, must indeed be taken to imply a personality forceful and self-assured like Caesar or Churchill; his record, like theirs, is not only justified by the facts it narrates, but also shows considerable literary skill. In comparison with so plausible a "Nehemiah-memoir" thesis, there is hardly likelihood of any "Ezra-memoir" at all.

A further question then becomes relevant: whether the "Nehemiah-memoir" was a religious duty to be walled up in a shrine like our "cornerstone documents," destined to be seen by human eye either never or long past the time for vanity. Though some such religious intention may have been invoked, it seems safe to say that whoever wrote the "Nehemiah-memoir" in first person was guided chiefly by an eye on an immediate readership. On the other hand, the prayerful doxologies of Neh 1:11; 5:19; 6:9, 14; 13:14, 21, while losing nothing of their touching personal sincerity, fit the hypothesis of a secret votive document for the Temple even better than a report to the public.

Amazingly, throughout this belligerent account up through Neh 5:13 the only title under which Nehemiah postures proudly is "cupbearer," or rather his own personal prowess and leaderliness. Also in his admirable but autocratic intervention against usury abuses (5:1–13, where v 10 admits that he himself is one of the guilty), he invokes no title or authority whatever except common sense and good-natured bullying (doubtless as in Neh 13:25). But with Neh 5:14 we learn for the first time, and quite obliquely from a date *twelve years later* than the events described, that he had been appointed not Judah's governor but "*their* governor *(peḥām)* in the land of Judah." Yet in Neh 7:2 he puts his brother Hanani in charge of Jerusalem, not "as governor" nor "to take place as governor," along with Hananiah (who was already *śar* of the citadel, not *peḥâ,* though similarly rendered "governor" in RSV). Only dubiously as associated with Ezra's speech in Neh 8:9, Nehemiah is called *tiršātāʾ* (not *peḥâ*), echoed even more dubiously in Neh 10:2—Eng v 1.

The repopulating of Jerusalem in Neh 11:1, confidently attributed by Pfeiffer (*IDB* 3: 534) to Nehemiah, is in fact an anonymous popular move, mentioning neither him nor any title. And the Zerubbabel-era genealogies which follow end up mysteriously in 12:26, "These were in the days of Joiakim the son of Jeshua son of Jozadak and in the days of Nehemiah the *peḥâ* and of Ezra the priest, the scribe." What follows in Neh 12:27–30 is the dedication of the wall, exactly what we would have expected at Neh 7:1—but here with no mention of Nehemiah at all in either the third (as since 8:9) or first person. But suddenly in 12:31, in the first person Nehemiah intervenes to direct the procession upon the wall (then v 47 mentions him only noncommittally and in the third person). And what follows in 13:1–5 was while Nehemiah (in first person) was not in Jerusalem. Upon his return (with the king's permission, but no mention of old or new title other than his customary bumptiousness [13:6]) he angrily throws furniture around and gets Tobiah thrown out of his choice Temple quarters. He further defends Levite perquisites, but as fact finder and public-spirited citizen accusing the officials (*rîb, sĕgānîm,* 13:11; "I appointed" treasurers in 13:13 MT is an emendation unacknowledged in RSV 13:12). Again in 13:17 he accuses the nobles *(rîb, ḥōrîm),* and takes the law into his own hands—with his personal servants) (v 19), and threatening bodily violence (v 21). All these virtuous even if not nonviolent activities of Nehemiah are as much in the religious as in the civil sphere, and despite some verbs of commanding in the first person account, no mention is made of a title or office.

In the whole book it is patent that the personality and leadership of Nehemiah were relatively independent, not indeed of the Persian king's authority and good will, but of whatever official title Nehemiah may have had; indeed this fact enhances his stature as human being and achiever. Without reopening the debate about civil authority titles in Ezra-Nehemiah (North 1972; see also EZRA-NEHEMIAH, BOOKS OF; McEvenue 1981; Nober 1961), and while noting respectfully that our claim of no civil authority function at all has met with less acceptance for Nehemiah than for Ezra, we may firmly reiterate two basic issues of common sense and universal experience hardly overcome by the exceedingly problematical philology of *peḥâ* and *tiršātāʾ:* (1) Human nature tends inexorably to give people on a higher social level a title safely nobler than what the facts require; and to retain temporary titles long after their actual function. (2) The work Nehemiah is shown doing is that of a building contractor, an amateur but highly endowed contractor; this work itself involved insistence on justice and brotherhood (Nehemiah 5); and his success with these rather religious aspects of his proper task impelled him toward cognate ventures in which either he himself seems to recognize he was overstepping whatever authority he had (e.g., the sabbath in 13:19), or the text is dubious as to whether Ezra or another is acting (mixed marriages 10:1—Eng 9:38; 13:1–3). As for Neh 5:14, its chief thrust is his justified boast that he did not "eat like a lord" *(peḥâ)* among his collaborators; and the undeniably arresting phrase "from the time I was appointed their *peḥâ*" loses much of its force in view of the debates aroused by 5:15 inserting Nehemiah into a series of former governors (including Zerubbabel?; note also Ginzberg 1947: 4.352 "Zerubbabel *was* Nehemiah"; and also Smitten's (1974) defense and Emerton's (1972: 177–79) rejection of Kellermann's (1967: 154–59) claim that Nehemiah was of Davidic lineage). Ultimately even if Nehemiah had some genuine civil function, it plays a negligibly slight role in evaluating the genial personality and self-sacrificing religious devotedness conspicuous in the actual work which he is shown doing.

Bibliography

Alt, A. 1931. Judas Nachbarn zur Zeit Nehemias. *PJ* 27: 66–74. Repr. 1953. *KlSchr* 2: 238–45.

Cazelles, H. 1954. La mission d'Esdras. *VT* 4: 113–40.

Emerton, J. A. 1972. Review of Kellermann 1967. *JTS* 23: 171–85.

Gelin, A. 1960. *Le livre d'Esdras et de Néhémie.* 2d ed. Paris.

Ginzberg, L. 1947. *Legends of the Jews.* 2d ed. Philadelphia.

Kellermann, U. 1967. *Nehemia: Quellen, Überlieferung und Geschichte.* BZAW 102. Berlin.

McEvenue, S. E. 1981. The Political Structure in Judah from Cyrus to Nehemiah. *CBQ* 43: 353–64.

Mayer, R. 1968. Das achämenidische Weltreich und seine Bedeutung in der politischen und religiösen Geschichte des Antiken Orients. *BZ* 12: 1–16.

Morgenstern, J. 1957. Jerusalem—485 B.C. *HUCA* 28: 17–47.

Nober, P. 1961. Notae philologicae [*peḥâ*]. *VD* 39: 110–11.

North, R. 1972. Civil Authority in Ezra. Pp. 377–404 in *Studi in onore di E. Volterra.* Vol. 6. Milan.

Rad, G. von. 1964. Die Nehemia-Denkschrift. *ZAW* 76: 176–87.

Rowley, H. H. 1955. Nehemiah's Mission and its Background. *BJRL* 37: 528–61.

Sánchez Caro, J. M. 1985. Esdras, Nehemías y los orígenes del Judaismo. *Salman* 32: 5–35.

Smitten, W. T. in der. 1974. Erwägungen zu Nehemias Davidizität. *JSJ* 5: 41–48.

Stern, E. 1982. *Material Culture of the Land of the Bible in the Persian Period.* Jerusalem.

Williamson, H. G. M. 1987. *Ezra and Nehemiah.* Old Testament Guides. Sheffield.

Yamauchi, E. M. 1980. Was Nehemiah the Cupbearer a Eunuch? *ZAW* 92: 132–42.

Robert North

NEHEMIAH, BOOK OF. See EZRA-NEHEMIAH, BOOKS OF.

NEHUM (PERSON) [Heb *nĕḥûm*]. One of the first citizens to return to Judah from the captivity of the Babylonian exile (Neh 7:7). This name may, however, be a scribal error. We expect the name "Rehum," which is found in a parallel list in Ezra 2:2 (cf. 1 Esdr 5:8). Note that this is the only occurrence of the name "Nehum," while "Rehum" occurs quite frequently in the books of Ezra and Nehemiah.

Nora A. Williams

NEHUSHTA (PERSON) [Heb *nĕḥuštāʾ*]. Mother of Jehoiachin, King of Judah (2 Kgs 24:8). Nehushta's name occurs in the regnal formula of her son in 2 Kings, but is missing from the parallel account in 2 Chr 36:9. She is the daughter of Elnathan, and one of three queen mothers from Jerusalem (the others being Jecoliah and Jehoaddan). Nehushta is referred to, but not named, in two lists of captives taken from Jerusalem by Nebuchadrezzar in 598/597 B.C.E. (2 Kgs 24:12, 15) and in two passages in Jeremiah (13:18; 29:2). In the latter she is given the title *gebira* ("great lady"), which designates her official position at court. See also JEHOIACHIN; QUEEN.

Linda S. Schearing

NEHUSHTAN [Heb *nĕḥūštān*]. See SERPENT, BRONZE; HEZEKIAH.

NEIEL (PLACE) [Heb *nĕʿēʾēl*]. A town in the allotment of Asher (Josh 19:27). Most scholars identify Neiel with Khirbet Yaʿnin (M.R. 171255), on the E edge of the Plain of Acco (see *LBHG,* 382).

David Salter Williams

NEKODA (PERSON) [Heb *nĕqôdāʾ*]. **1.** Eponymous ancestor of a family of Nethinim, or temple servants (Ezra 2:48). The "sons of Nekoda" (LXX *nekōda*) returned from captivity in Babylon to Jerusalem and Judah with Zerubbabel. They are mentioned in the parallel lists in Neh 7:50 and in 1 Esdr 5:31 (Gk *noeba*). Suggestions for the meaning of the name link it with *nāqōd* "speckled, spotted" or Akk *niqūdu* "moorhen" (*HALAT* 2: 680; cf. IPN 225).

2. Eponymous ancestor of a family of returned exiles (Ezra 2:60). The "sons of Nekoda" were unable to prove their Israelite descent. Probably their family records had been lost or destroyed in the exile (see Fensham *Ezra Nehemiah* NICOT, 55). They were among a group of families that returned under Zerubbabel from exile in Telmelah, Telharsha, Cherub, Addan, and Immer (Ezra 2:59–63). The name also appears in the parallel lists in Neh 7:62 and in 1 Esdr 5:37 (Gk *nekōdan*).

Kenneth Hugh Cuffey

NEMUEL (PERSON) [Heb *nĕmûʾēl*]. Var. JEMUEL. NEMUELITE. Name of two individuals in the Hebrew Bible. The exact meaning of the "Nemuel" or "Jemuel" is uncertain (Fowler *TPNAH,* 121, 123).

1. A head of the tribe of Reuben (Num 26:9), and brother of Dathan and Abiram.

2. A Simeonite and ancestor of the Nemuelites (Num 26:12; 1 Chr 4:24). Nemuel is also called Jemuel in Gen

46:10 and Exod 6:15. This name change probably results from scribal confusion over the Heb *nun* and *yod.* Nemuel is the preferred reading.

JOEL C. SLAYTON

NEOLITHIC. See PREHISTORY.

NEPHEG (PERSON) [Heb *nepeg*]. **1.** A Levite included in the genealogy that functions to legitimate Moses and Aaron (Exod 6:14–27). His father was Izhar, descended from Levi's son Kohath, and his brothers were Korah and Zichri (6:21).

2. One of thirteen sons of David listed as having been born to David's wives in Jerusalem (2 Sam 5:15; 1 Chr 3:7; 14:6), in addition to his six sons born at Hebron. His mother's name is unknown: four of the thirteen were Bathsheba's sons; the remainder were born to unnamed wives. Besides these thirteen, David had numerous (unnamed) sons born to his concubines, according to 1 Chr 3:9. The occurrence of Nepheg's name after NOGAH in both lists in 1 Chronicles and the latter's absence from the MT in Samuel has led to the suggestion that the name Nogah was a corruption of Nepheg. See also DAVID, SONS OF.

DAVID M. HOWARD, JR.

NEPHILIM [Heb *nĕpilîm*]. A group of antediluvians who were the product of the union of the sons of God *(hāʾĕlōhîm)* with the daughters of humans *(hāʾādām)* (Gen 6:1–4). They are described as heroic *(hāggibbōrîm)* and famous *(ʾanšê haššēm).* In Genesis 6, the Nephilim are connected with the multiplication of humanity on the face of the earth (v 1) and with the evil of humanity which brings about God's judgment in the form of the flood (vv 5–7). Verse 4 includes a reference to later (postdiluvian) Nephilim. The majority of the spies who were sent by Joshua to spy out Canaan reported giants whom they called Nephilim, and who are designated in the account as the sons of Anak (Num 13:33). The reference to Nephilim as ancient dead warriors in Ezek 32:27 requires a textual change from the MT's *nōpĕlîm* (Zimmerli, *Ezekiel* Hermeneia, 168, 176; Hendel 1987a: 22).

Their heroic attributes were noted in translating Nephilim in the versions. Both the LXX and the Vulgate render the expression as *gigantes.* The Syriac has *gnbrʾ*. The Samaritan Pentateuch and Targums also follow this custom (Alexander 1972), using either *gybryh* (Samaritan), *gybrym* (Neofiti), or *gbrʾ* (Onkelos). *Targum Pseudo-Jonathan* translates Nephilim with the names of the fallen angels *(šmḥzʾy wʿzʾl)* mentioned in *1 Enoch* as leading the rebellion. Nephilim are referred to as "giants" in the Apocrypha/Pseudepigrapha, usually with reference to their pride and wickedness, and to God's judgment upon them (e.g., Bar 3: 26–28). The fullest development appears in *1 Enoch* 6–19, and this is followed by allusions in the Dead Sea Scrolls, the Midrashim, and the NT (Dimant 1974; Hanson 1977).

2 Peter 2:4 and Jude 6 are the NT allusions to the Nephilim. Here they are identified as angels who rebelled and have been imprisoned by God. They lead a list of biblical examples of rebels and their punishments current in contemporary Jewish paraenisis (Bauckham, *Jude, 2 Peter* WBC, 46–47). Although elements of Greek Titan mythology have been identified here and in Gen 6:1–4 (Kraeling 1947, who separates the *gibbōrîm* from the Nephilim), the presence of a common source for the traditions of *1 Enoch* and those of the Greek world is more likely (Bauckham, *Jude, 2 Peter* WBC, 50–53, 248–49). Speiser (*Genesis* AB, 46) identifies this source as Hurrian. Kilmer (1987) has sought to identify the Nephilim with the *apkallu* of Mesopotamian tradition.

The root *npl,* "to fall," seems to be the basis of Nephilim, i.e., "the fallen ones." This may refer to their fall from heaven, their "fall" into sin, or their fallen status as dead at the time when the events are recorded. The earliest use of the W Semitic *npl* supports the last option. It occurs in a military context, the 14th century B.C.E. letter of Lab'ayu of Shechem to the pharaoh (EA 252, lines 25–27), "Fall under them that they may smite you!" The sons of Anak, who are identified with the later Nephilim in Num 13:33, are also identified with the Rephaim in Deut 2:11. As the Rephaim are understood as ancient warriors slain by Israel and others, so the Nephilim, "the fallen ones," are those who are doomed to die.

Source critics have ascribed Gen 6:1–4 to J, while recognizing it as uncharacteristic (*WPG1,* 329; Gunkel, *Genesis* BKAT, 52; Noth 1948: 29). Recent studies have ascribed the text to a Canaanite origin (Westermann, *Genesis* BKAT, 499–500) or to later editorial activity (Scharbert 1967: 66–78; Schreiner 1981: 65–74). Hendel (1987a; 1987b) argues that the improper mating of deities and humans was the original reason for the Genesis flood. However, later additions to this tradition changed the reason to the matter of a general evil in the imaginations of humanity.

As fathers of the Nephilim, the identity of the sons of God is important in understanding whether the Nephilim of Genesis 6 were semi-divine or completely human. The sons of God *(hāʾĕlōhîm)* have been understood as nonhumans (gods, angels), rulers, or descendants of Seth. The first interpretation is supported by the term's use in Ugaritic myths, in the OT (Ps 29:1; Job 1:6), and in the intertestamental and NT material noted above. It allows for a real contrast with "daughters of men," which would be nonspecific if it were to mean daughters of nonrulers or daughters of the descendants of Cain (Cassuto 1973; van Gemeren 1980–81; Wenham, *Genesis 1–15* WBC, 139–40). Further, the mating of deities with women appears in ANE and Greek mythology (Bartelmus 1979: 36–78). Support of identification with rulers may be found in a similar designation given to the Ugaritic king Keret and to the Davidic king (2 Sam 7:14; Ps 2:7), and in traditional Jewish exegesis (Alexander 1972; Tsukimoto 1979: 19–21). The Sethite interpretation has few modern adherents (Junker 1935; for a reversal of this argument, in which the Sethites are the daughters of man, cf. Eslinger 1979).

For Wenham (*Genesis 1–15* WBC, 141), the key seems to be the limitation of human life span in v 3. The daughters of men willingly cohabited with divine beings in order to produce offspring who would gain much longer life spans and perhaps achieve immortality. By rejecting this attempt, God has established a rigid distinction between the mortal and the immortal (Clines 1979: 33–37; Petersen 1979: 58–

59; Schreiner 1981: 70–72). The mating of the sons of God with the daughters of men became but one example of the "cosmic imbalance" created in Genesis 1–6.

Bibliography

Alexander, P. S. 1972. The Targumim and Early Exegesis of "Sons of God" in Genesis 6. *JJS* 23: 60–71.
Bartelmus, R. 1979. *Heroentum in Israel und seiver Umwelt.* ATANT 65. Zurich.
Cassuto, U. 1973. The Episode of the Sons of God and the Daughters of Man. Pp. 17–28 in *Bible and Oriental Studies. Volume I.* Trans. I. Abrahams. Jerusalem.
Clines, D. J. A. 1979. The Significance of the "Sons of God" Episode (Genesis 6:1–4) in the Context of the "Primeval History" (Genesis 1–11). *JSOT* 13: 33–46.
Dimant, D. 1974. "The Fallen Angels" in the Dead Sea Scrolls and in the Apocryphal and Pseudepigraphic Books Related to Them. Diss., Hebrew University.
Eslinger, L. 1979. A Contextual Identification of the *bene haʾelohim* and *benoth haʾadam* in Genesis 6:1–4. *JSOT* 13: 65–73.
Gemeren, W. A. van. 1980–81. The Sons of God in Genesis 6:1–4 (An Example of Evangelical Demythologization?). *WTJ* 43: 320–48.
Hanson, P. D. 1977. Rebellion in Heaven, Azazel, and Euhemeristic Heroes in 1 Enoch 6–11. *JBL* 96: 195–233.
Hendel, R. S. 1987a. Of Demigods and the Deluge: Toward an Interpretation of Genesis 6:1–4. *JBL* 106: 13–26.
———. 1987b. When the Sons of God Cavorted with the Daughters of Men. *BRev* 3/2: 813, 837.
Junker, H. 1935. Zur Erklärung von Gen. 6, 1–4. *Bib* 16: 205–212.
Kilmer, A. D. 1987. The Mesopotamian Counterparts of the Biblical *Nĕpīlîm.* Pp. 39–43 in *Perspectives on Language and Text: Essays and Poems in Honor of Francis I. Andersen's Sixtieth Birthday,* ed. E. W. Conrad and E. G. Newing. Winona Lake, IN.
Kraeling, E. G. 1947. The Significance and Origin of Gen. 6:1–4. *JNES* 6: 193–208.
Noth, M. 1948. *Überlieferungsgeschichte des Pentateuch.* Stuttgart.
Petersen, D. L. 1979. Yahweh and the Organization of the Cosmos. *JSOT* 13: 47–64.
Scharbert, J. 1967. Traditions- und Redaktionsgeschichte von Gn 6, 1–4. *BZ* n.s. 11: 66–78.
Schreiner, J. 1981. Gen 6, 1–4 und die Problematik von Leben und Tod. Pp. 65–74 in *De la Tôrah au Messie,* ed. M. Carrez et al. Paris.
Tsukimoto, A. 1979. "Der Mensch ist geworden wie unsereiner"—Untersuchungen zum zeitgeschichtlichen Hintergrund von Gen. 3, 22–24 und 6, 1–4. *AJBI* 5: 3–44.

RICHARD S. HESS

NEPHISIM (PERSON) [Heb *nĕpîsîm*]. Var. NEPHUSHESIM. Eponymous ancestor of a family of Nethinim, or temple servants (Ezra 2:50; K *nĕpîsîm,* Q *nĕpûsîm;* LXX *naphisōn*). The "sons of Nephisim" returned from exile in Babylon to Jerusalem and Judah under Zerubbabel. The name occurs in 1 Esdr 5:31 (Gk *naphisi*). In the parallel list in Neh 7:52 it appears as Nephushesim (Heb K *nĕpûšsîm,* Q *nĕpîšsîm;* LXX *nephōsasim*). The form in Nehemiah could result from a superimposition of two variant spellings on each other, one with *ś* (MT understands this as *š*), the other with *s* (*IDB* 3: 536). It is also possible that an *s* was placed as a superscript over *ś* to distinguish it from *š*. A scribe who was not acquainted with this device then incorporated the superscript letter into the text (Honeyman 1944: 47–48). The group may be descended from the Ishmaelite clan of Naphish (cf. Gen 25:15; cf. *HALAT* 2: 669–70).

Bibliography

Honeyman, A. 1944. Traces of an Early Diacritic Sign in Isaiah 8:66. *JBL* 63: 45–50.

KENNETH H. CUFFEY

NEPHTHAR [Gk *nephthar*]. The name that Nehemiah and his associates gave to the precious thick liquid that ignited the sacred fire of the altar sacrifices (2 Macc 1:36). The author relates it to the common word "naphtha," and erroneously implies that it has a Hebrew etymology, perhaps from *pṭr,* "separate, set free," and, by extension [?], "purify" (Goldstein, *2 Maccabees* AB, 181). See also NAPHTHA.

GARY A. HERION

NEPHTOAH (PLACE) [Heb *neptôaḥ*]. A location on the boundary between Judah and Benjamin (Josh 15:9; 18:15). It has been identified with present day Lifta (Arabic name), that is, Me Neftoah (modern Hebrew name), about 3 miles NW of Jerusalem (M.R. 168133). The name appears only in the phrase *maʿyan mê neptôaḥ* ("spring of the waters of Nephtoah"). Scholars have often recognized the name of the Egyptian Pharaoh Merneptah in *mê neptôaḥ.* The entire phrase, then, would mean "the well of Merneptah," which could be identified with the wells of Merneptah referred to in Papyrus Anastasi III ("Journal of a Frontier Official," *ANET,* 258), which dates to about the end of the 13th century B.C.E.

WESLEY I. TOEWS

NEPHUSHESIM (PERSON) [*npwšsym* (Kethib); *nĕpîšsîm* (Qere)]. The "father" of a group of temple servants (Neh 7:52). The parallel list in Ezra 2:50 has *npysym* (Kethib), *nĕpûsîm* (Qere), "Nephisim" (RSV). See also NEPHISIM; NAPHISH.

NER (PERSON) [Heb *nēr*]. **1.** The son of Jeiel, the founder of the postexilic settlement at Gibeon (1 Chr 9:36; Rudolph *Chronikbücher* HAT, 81). The name has accidentally fallen out of the parallel text in 1 Chr 8:30. It is possible that it represents a clan rather than an individual in the genealogy.

2. The son of Abiel (1 Sam 14:51), father of Abner, brother of Kish, and uncle of Saul ben Kish, the first king of Israel (1 Sam 14:50). Nothing is known of his life. His name appears regularly as a patronymic in connection with Abner ("Abner ben Ner"), and is known from the Saulide genealogies in 1 Sam 14:47–51 and 1 Chr 8:29–40; 9:35–44. In the latter two genealogies, Ner is listed as Kish's father instead of as his brother. A plausible explanation of the inconsistency of Ner's status is easily found. In addition to redefining Ner's place in the ramage, the genealogies in 1 Chronicles have omitted the names of the Saulide ancestors Abiel, Zeror, Becorath, and Aphiah, which were readily available from 1 Sam 9:1. It appears that the Chronicler intentionally did so in order to be able to graft the Saulide genealogy onto the postexilic genealogy of Gibeon. The occurrence of the name "Ner" among the postexilic settlers at Gibeon easily allowed the Saulide family tree to be added by identifying the postexilic Ner with Saul's uncle Ner. The move required the elimination of the earliest four ancestors of Saul, and Ner's relocation in the line of descent from a parallel ramage to Saul's direct line of descent.

The association of a clan of Ner with Gibeon seems to have had a long history, which is corroborated by the appearance of the name Ner'a on some wine jar handles excavated from the fill of the great pool at Gibeon (Demsky 1971: 22). The handles are generally dated on the basis of paleography to the 7th–6th century B.C. (Avigad 1959; Cross 1962). The resettlement of Ner in Gibeon in the postexilic period can almost certainly be seen to be a return of the group to its ancestral home, which can be dated as far back as the 11th century B.C., if one is willing to associate Saul's uncle Ner with Gibeon as well.

Bibliography

Avigad, N. 1959. Some Notes on the Hebrew Inscriptions from Gibeon. *IEJ* 9: 130–33.
Cross, F. M. 1962. Epigraphical Notes on Hebrew Documents of the Eighth–Sixth Centuries B.C. III. *BASOR* 168: 18–23.
Demsky, A. 1971. The Genealogy of Gibeon (1 Chronicles 9:35–44): Biblical and Epigraphic Considerations. *BASOR* 202: 16–23.

DIANA V. EDELMAN

NEREUS (PERSON) [Gk *Nēreus*]. A Roman Christian who received greetings from Paul in Rom 16:15. He probably was a gentile Christian (Lampe *StadtrChr*, 58), because Paul usually mentioned specifically if persons in the list of Romans 16 were Jewish-Christian "kins(wo)men" (Rom 16:7, 11, 21). While the latter term is absent in his other letters, Paul in Romans, after chaps. 9–11 (cf. 9:3), was interested in emphasizing Christians' ties to Israel. It can be assumed therefore that he purposefully applied or omitted the label "kins(wo)man" in Romans 16. (The only exception is Aquila at the beginning of the list, about whom so many other characteristics were reported that his Jewish background was passed over.) A member of a Roman house-church (Lampe *StadtrChr*, 301), Nereus, his sister Philologus, Julia, and Olympas were mentioned individually, while the other participants were mentioned only generally as "all the saints who were with them." The five persons therefore may have played leading roles in the house-church. As the inscriptions of the city of Rome show, the name "Nereus" was commonly held by slaves (Lampe *StadtrChr*, 142, 145, 148, 152–53). Thus Nereus was most likely a slave or freedman; so was his sister.

PETER LAMPE

NERGAL (DEITY) [Heb *nērgal*]. The name of the god whose idol and cult were introduced into Samaria by the people of Cuth, who had been deported there by the Assyrians (2 Kgs 17:30). The name of this deity is also an element in the name Nergalsharezer (Jer 39:3, 13). Nergal—Sum [E]N.ERI.GAL, "Lord of the Great City (i.e., of the Underworld)" or *Nergal*$_x$ (KIS.UNU.GAL)—was the Sumerian netherworld god of Kutha, a city about 20 miles NE of Babylon. Kutha was thought to have been the earthly residence of all the underworld deities (Buccellati 1982: 3). The Akkadians identified Nergal with their own underworld deity Erra, so that by the 1st millennium B.C. the names became virtually interchangeable. Both gods were associated with fire, famine, drought, plague, and sudden death.

In one tradition, Nergal's consort was Ereshkigal, sister of Inanna-Ishtar and mistress of the underworld. The fragmentary text *Nergal and Ereshkigal* (*ANET*, 103–104) offers a glimpse into Nergal's domestic behavior: in a quarrel with Ereshkigal, he grabs her by the hair, throws her to the floor, and threatens to cut off her head. In other traditions Nergal's mate is either ominously named Lāṣ, "No Exit," or identified as the mother-goddess Mamma, who was more specifically the wife of Erra (Roberts 1972: 44).

The West Semites identified the Akkadian Nergal with Resheph, also a god of the underworld. By the 4th century B.C. the Cypriots in turn identified Resheph with Apollo in his more negative aspects (Fulco 1976: 49–54). The description of *rešep* and *qeṭeb* in Deut 32:24 (RSV "burning heat" and "pestilence") and of Apollo in the *Iliad* (1.45–52) match very closely the depiction of Nergal's activities as recounted in the 1st millennium B.C. annals of the various Assyrian and Babylonian kings (e.g., *ANET*, 538).

Bibliography

Buccelatti, G. 1982. The Descent of Inanna as a Ritual Journey to Kutha? *SMS* 4: 1–7.
Fulco, W. J. 1976. *The Canaanite God Rešep*. New Haven.
Jacobsen, T. 1976. *The Treasures of Darkness: A History of Mesopotamian Religion*. New Haven.
Roberts, J. J. M. 1971. Erra—Scorched Earth. *JCS* 24: 11–16.
———. 1972. *The Earliest Semitic Pantheon*. Baltimore.
Steinkeller, P. 1987. The Name of Nergal. *ZA* 77: 161–68.

WILLIAM J. FULCO

NERGAL-SHAREZER (PERSON) [Heb *nērgalśar-ʾeṣer*]. Var. NERIGLISSAR. Included in the list of Babylonian officials in Jer 39:3, 13, Nergal-sharezer was connected with the fall of Jerusalem and the subsequent release of the prophet Jeremiah. Nergal-sharezer is thought to be Neriglissar, King of Babylon from 560 to 556 B.C.E.

Regretfully, textual problems in Jer 39:3 make the identification of Nergal-sharezer more difficult. Nergal-sharezer is mentioned twice in this verse: the first mention states that he was the prince of Sin-magir, and the second, which matches Jer 39:13, refers to him as an official whose title is Rabmag. Thompson (*Jeremiah* NICOT, 644) argues that the name is a common one and that two different identically named persons are intended in v 3. By contrast, Bright (*Jeremiah* AB, 243) and Rudolph (*Jeremiah* HAT, 245) believe the two occurrences of Nergal-sharezer refer to the same person who is both prince of Sin-magir, a province in Babylon (Bright, 243), and holder of the title Rabmag. The function of this office is not known (cf. Wiseman (1956: 38, 94).

It is widely held that Nergal-sharezer is the brother-in-law of Nebuchadrezzar's son, Amel-marduk (562–560 B.C.E.), whom Nergal-sharezer succeeds as King of Babylon. It is not clear how Nergal-sharezer came to power, although evidence suggests he may have instituted a revolt and murdered his brother-in-law, Amel-marduk (Wiseman 1985: 10–11; Wiseman 1956: 38–39; Josephus *AgAp; BHI,* 352). *The Chronicles of the Chaldaean Kings* (BM 25142, Wiseman 1956: 75–77) record an account of an extensive and successful military conquest of Neriglissar in 557/6. This campaign pushed into W Cilicia (SW Asia Minor) against King Appuasu to punish an attack on a Babylonian protectorate in that region (Bright *BHI,* 243).

Nergal-sharezer's name includes that of the Babylonian sun god, Nergal. The name means "Nergal, protect the king."

Bibliography

Wiseman, D. J., 1956. *Chronicles of the Chaldaean Kings (626–556 B.C.) in the British Museum:* London.

———. 1985. *Nebuchadrezzar and Babylon.* London.

JOHN M. BRACKE

NERI (PERSON) [Gk *Nēri*]. The father of Shealtiel and son of Melchi, according to Luke's genealogy tying Joseph, the "supposed father" of Jesus, to descent from Adam and God (Luke 3:27). D omits Neri, substituting a genealogy adapted from Matt 1:6–15 for Luke 3:23–31. The name Neri occurs nowhere else in the biblical documents, including Matthew's genealogy, and falls within a list of seventeen otherwise unknown descendants of David's son Nathan (Fitzmyer *Luke 1–9* AB, 500). In 1 Chr 3:17 and Matt 1:12, the father of Shealtiel is said to be Jeconiah, not Neri, which has led to several proposals to explain the apparent discrepancy (for a survey see Marshall 1978: 163–64). Plummer (*Luke* ICC, 104), assuming that Zerubbabel and Shealtiel in Matt 1:12 and Luke 3:27 are the same person, argues that, since Jer 22:30 states that Jeconiah had no children, the line of David could not proceed through him: "The three pedigrees (of Matt 1:12; Luke 3:27; 1 Chr 3:17) indicate that an heir for the childless Jeconiah was found in Shealtiel the son of Neri, who was of the house of David *through Nathan.* Thus the junction of the two lines of descent in Shealtiel and Zerubbabel is fully explained. Shealtiel was the son of Neri of Nathan's line, and also the heir of Jeconiah of Solomon's line; and having no sons himself, he had his nephew Zerubbabel as adopted son and heir." A major problem with this view is that Jer 22:30 on the most plausible reading does not say that Jeconiah was to be childless (cf. 1 Chr 3:17–18, where seven sons are listed), but that, "as far as throne succession was concerned, he was as good as that" (Bright *Jeremiah* AB, 143; cf. Johnson 1969: 183–84). A second proposal (see Johnson 1969: 243–45, where the text is quoted) cites Eusebius *qu. Marin.* 3.2 which records that Eusebius knew of some, possibly including Luke, who thought that Jeconiah was passed over in the genealogy because the curse on Jeconiah made messianic descent through his line impossible. Johnson goes on to emphasize the implications of this for his view that the Lukan genealogy reflects belief in Jesus as prophet (note mention of Nathan) (contra Abel 1974: 209). As Johnson points out, however, it is difficult to know who exactly—Eusebius or Luke—was meant to have believed this theory. A third position, suggested by Jeremias (1969: 295–96), is that even though nowhere else in the OT except 1 Chr 3:17–19 is it said that Zerubbabel was a descendant of Jehoiakim, the author of 1 Chronicles may have "wrongly considered as the grandson of the last reigning king, the restorer of the Temple upon whom for a long time political hopes were concentrated, and upon whose descendants still in later years the messianic hope was fixed." And fourth, Kuhn (1923: 214; see also Hervey 1853: 92–93, 148–49) argues that Neri, as well as several other men in this section, is a corruption, in particular here of Heb *mlkyrm* found in 1 Chr 3:18, on the basis that Gk *nēri* and *melchi* are derived from a single name: Heb *nrymlky* (meaning "my king is my light"), possibly making it into 1 Chronicles through the corrupted intermediate form *mlkynrh* (Kuhn believes he can prove the change from Heb *nry* to *rm*). This proposal has not won widespread acceptance, especially since there is serious question whether the genealogy at this point is based on 1 Chronicles (Marshall 1978: 164; cf. Jeremias 1969: 295–96).

Bibliography

Abel, E. L. 1974. The Genealogies of Jesus O XPICTOC. *NTS* 20: 203–10.

Hervey, A. 1853. *The Genealogies of Our Lord and Saviour Jesus Christ, As Contained in the Gospels of St. Matthew and St. Luke.* Cambridge.

Jeremias, J. 1969. *Jerusalem in the Time of Jesus.* Philadelphia.

Johnson, M. D. 1969. *The Purpose of the Biblical Genealogies, with Special Reference to the Setting of the Genealogies of Jesus.* SNTSMS 8. Cambridge.

Kuhn, G. 1923. Die Geschlechtsregister Jesu bei Lukas und Matthäus, nach ihrer Herkunft untersucht. *ZNW* 22: 206–28.

Marshall, I. H. 1978. *The Gospel of Luke: A Commentary on the Greek Text.* NIGTC. Grand Rapids.

STANLEY E. PORTER

NERIAH (PERSON) [Heb *nērîyāh*]. The son of Mahseiah and father of Seraiah (Jer 51:59) and Baruch, the scribe or secretary of Jeremiah the prophet (Jer 36:4; see also 32:12, 16; 36:8, 14, 32; 43:3, 6; Bar 1:1). Seraiah, an officer of the king (see Keil n.d., 317), seems to have been entrusted with carrying and then reading an oracle from Jeremiah, when Seraiah accompanied Zedekiah, king of Judah, to Babylon (Jer 51:59; cf. v 61). Baruch, Jeremiah's scribe and biographer, usually remains in the background, except in Jer 45:1 and the following verses, where he reveals his despair, presumably brought about by the writing of Jeremiah's scroll of judgment (Bright *Jeremiah* AB, 185). Avigad (1978: 53–56) believes that two recently discovered seals, possibly from an official archive, refer to biblical Neriah. One seal mentions a "Berechiah son of Neriah [Heb *nryhw*] the scribe," and can be interpreted as referring by way of his full name to biblical Baruch as a royal rather than private scribe, and one with access to the temple and royal precincts (cf. Muilenburg 1970: 227–30). The second seal refers to a "Seraiah (ben) Neriah [Heb *nryhw*]," presumably Baruch's brother. On the basis of Baruch and Seraiah both being educated and literate men, possibly each with a public position of importance, it can be speculated that Neriah was a man of not insignificant abilities and probably of some position and means, although he is otherwise unknown to the biblical documents.

Bibliography

Avigad, N. 1978. Baruch the Scribe and Jerahmeel the King's Son. *IEJ* 28: 52–56.

Keil, C. F. n.d. Jeremiah, Lamentations. In vol. 3 of *Commentary on the OT in Ten Volumes,* ed. C. F. Keil, and F. Delitzsch. Grand Rapids. Repr.

Muilenburg, J. 1970. Baruch the Scribe. Pp. 215–38 in *Proclamation and Presence: OT Essays in Honour of Gwynne Henton Davies,* ed. John I. Durham and J. R. Porter. London.

STANLEY E. PORTER

NERO (EMPEROR). Nero was the fifth Princeps to rule Rome under the political system created by Augustus after civil war had ended the Roman Republic. He was also the last Princeps who could claim blood descent from Augustus, for the next round of civil wars, in A.D. 68–70, ended the Julio-Claudian dynasty.

A. Early Life
B. The First Years of Rule
C. Deterioration and Opposition
D. Foreign Policy
E. Provincial Administration
F. The Neronian Persecution
G. The False Neros

A. Early Life

L. Domitius Ahenobarbus, as Nero was called at birth, was the only child of Julia Agrippina, the great-granddaughter of Augustus, and Cn. Domitius Ahenobarbus, whose family belonged to the ancient nobility and whose father had married a niece of Augustus. Born on 15 December A.D. 37, when his uncle Gaius Caesar (Caligula) had been on the throne for less than a year, the young Domitius was soon deprived of his mother, sent into exile by her brother in the autumn of 39, and of his father, who died toward the end of the next year. Within a few months, however, Gaius was murdered, and Claudius, his successor as Princeps, restored the boy's property and recalled his niece Agrippina from the island of Pontia. In 49 Agrippina married her paternal uncle, a type of union previously regarded as incestuous but now authorized by senatorial decree, and, in the next year, Domitius was adopted by his stepfather, acquiring at the age of twelve the name Nero Claudius Caesar Germanicus.

Though the Principate was not an avowed monarchy and there could therefore be no law of succession, Nero had now clearly displaced Claudius' own son Britannicus as the expected political heir. He was not only the older son of the current ruler (adoption had long been common practice in Roman aristocratic families and no distinction was made between adopted and natural sons): he was also a direct descendant of Augustus, a fact that he and his mother never ceased to publicize. Then, in 53, he was married to Octavia, the daughter of Claudius by his former wife Valeria Messallina.

Agrippina saw to it that Nero received a good training in oratory, for the ability to make a good speech was expected of the Princeps, just as it had always been of men in public life. She had prevailed on Claudius to cancel the sentence of banishment he himself had imposed on the distinguished orator, writer, and philosopher Lucius Annaeus Seneca. He now prepared Nero for his oratorical debut in the Senate, where he pleaded for concessions on behalf of various cities of the empire, in Latin or Greek, as appropriate.

When Claudius died on 13 October 54, the way had been prepared for Nero's accession. He was escorted into the camp of the Praetorian Guard by Sextus Afranius Burrus, who owed his position as sole Prefect to Agrippina. The Senate echoed the salutation of the Guard, conferred the necessary powers on Nero, and then declared Claudius a god and Agrippina his priestess. The will of Claudius was suppressed, so that his intentions with regard to Britannicus, like the question of whether his death was natural or contrived, remained a matter for speculation.

B. The First Years of Rule

The ancient tradition is unanimous on the excellence of Nero's initial years of rule. Indeed, two 4th-century writers, Aurelius Victor (5.2–4) and the unknown author of the *Épitome de Caesaribus* (5.2–5) ascribe to the later emperor Trajan the view that, for a quinquennium, Nero surpassed all other Princeps. Though little reliance can be placed on the ascription to Trajan and the five years have been variously located in the first, last, or middle portion of the reign, the contrast made by both authors with the rest of Nero's life suggests that they are alluding to his first years as Princeps, a period hailed as a Golden Age by contemporary poets (Calp. Sic. 1.42; *Carm. Einsidl.* 2.22; Sen. *Apocol.* 4.1, vv. 8–32).

Two of our most important literary sources, the biographer Suetonius and the Greek historian Cassius Dio (whose work is preserved for this period only by Byzantine excerpters), suggest that the young emperor at first left the business of government to his mother. Dio adds that Seneca and Burrus took over control after a few months, leaving the emperor free to concentrate on the pleasures of youth. The Roman historian Tacitus, however, has a more subtle view. He regards the influence of Agrippina, given visible form on coins of December 54 showing the heads of Agrippina and Nero facing each other, as a matter of appearance only, and the role of Nero's contrasting but concordant advisers as one of guiding the young Princeps in government, not of replacing him. Various indications tell in favor of Tacitus' picture, which is substantially the same as that offered for public consumption in Seneca's essay *De Clementia,* published in late 55 or 56. There Seneca explains that Nero will enjoy great security and affection if he perseveres in his liberal and generous conduct, and he portrays Nero as reluctant to sign the death warrants presented by his Praetorian Prefect.

In *De Clementia* Seneca criticizes by implication the cruel and irregular exercise of jurisdiction by Nero's predecessor and thereby endorses the reversal of the Claudian style of government announced in Nero's accession address to the Senate, also written by Seneca. The imperial widow will not have liked that any more than she will have relished the dismissal early in 55 of her ally, Claudius' powerful ex-slave M. Antonius Pallas, from his post as chief accountant *(a rationibus)*.

Earlier still, there had been criticism of Claudius in the *Apocolocyntosis,* Seneca's satirical account of his deification, which was probably presented to the court at the Saturnalia festival in December of 54. This work is revealing not only about the real balance of power, but about Nero's role in government, for it combines the criticism of his predecessor with two themes also found together in contemporary poetry: praise of Nero's artistic interests and political approval of his adherence to legal forms and his protection of senatorial freedom. The young Princeps must then have prided himself on both counts. Indeed, it is possible to view Nero's interest in poetry, music, and chariot-racing, which had overshadowed his traditional training in oratory from his early years, not as a distraction from government but as part of his conception of it. The philhellene emperor clearly felt that he had a mission to civilize the Roman upper classes and bring them to appreciate and practice the esthetic, intellectual and athletic skills that had always been regarded as respectable by their Greek equivalents. Thus in 59 he celebrated the first shaving of his beard with a festival for which the upper classes were encouraged to take lessons in singing and dancing. A year later he introduced for the first time at Rome public games in the Greek fashion, to be celebrated every five years. Men of high rank participated in contests of oratory, poetry, singing, and playing the lyre. It was only at the second celebration of the games in 65 that the Princeps himself performed.

The political message of the new régime had been made clear in Nero's first speech to the Senate (Tac. *Ann.* 13.4; Suet. *Nero* 10). Excesses of court influence were renounced: to the audience that meant that there would be no more commands obtained through powerful secretaries like Narcissus (Suet. *Vesp.* 4.1), no more grants of citizenship secured through bribery (Acts 22:28), no more malicious prosecutions engineered by imperial ladies like Messallina (Tac. *Ann.* 13.43). In fact, not only was Agrippina prevented in the first months of the reign from joining her son on his dais, not only was Pallas dismissed from his post, but the imperial ex-slaves who served the emperor in various secretarial capacities disappear entirely from the ancient accounts until after 61 when we begin to hear of such notorious minions as Polyclitus, Epaphroditus, Patrobius, and Helius.

Nero had also promised to end the practice of exercising imperial jurisdiction behind closed doors, a practice which had facilitated improper influence. Trials of this kind were usually for treason *(maiestas),* an elastic charge even in the Republic. Claudius is credited with keeping a promise to end *maiestas* charges (Dio 60.3.15). If his promise covered all charges under this statute, he had disregarded it, but, more plausibly, it covered only charges involving disrespect to the emperor which the law had come to cover by interpretation since the late reign of Augustus (Tac. *Ann.* 1.72). In that case, he had kept his promise yet undermined justice by showing extreme credulity toward charges of a more orthodox type and by trying such cases *intra cubiculum,* which made convictions easier to obtain. Nero is not known to have tried any cases in this manner or to have allowed *maiestas* charges in the extended sense to be brought until 62 (Tac. *Ann.* 14.48).

The new Princeps had further assured the Senate that he would not monopolize jurisdiction in general—another allusion to Claudius, whose passion for jurisdiction had led him to take cases that would normally have come before other tribunals and to sit among the advisers when ordinary magistrates tried cases. But it would be wrong to conclude (as does Sherwin-White 1963: 110–11) that Nero neglected his judicial duties, for his biographer describes his procedure in detail (Suet. *Nero* 15), while Seneca's treatise *De Clementia* is largely concerned with the administration of justice by the Princeps and closely reflects the freedom, especially in the matter of penalties, that characterized the *cognitio* procedure of the imperial and senatorial courts.

Nero closed his accession manifesto with a general formula for a division of responsibilities between himself and the Senate. The narrative of Tacitus, however, who vouches for the emperor's fidelity to his promises, shows that the formula was understood, not in the sense of a clear constitutional division, but as an assurance that the Princeps would show increased respect for the authority of the Senate. Symbolic of the new attitude was the legend *ex senatus consulto* appearing consistently on the silver and gold coinage. Though it is not clear whether this is an authorization mark of some kind or relates to the types and legends on the coins, some advertisement of respect for the Senate is clearly intended.

C. Deterioration and Opposition

The tradition of the Quinquennium Neronis reflects a contemporary view that the murder of Agrippina, thought to be organized by her son, marked the turning point of the Neronian Principate (Tac. *Ann.* 15.67): Nero's responsibility for the death of Britannicus in 55, though credited by some, was not so widely rumored. For Tacitus, however, the political deterioration of Nero's government, as opposed to his own moral decline, did not begin until 62, when a *maiestas* charge of the dubious kind was admitted, Burrus died, and Seneca withdrew from his active role as adviser. Nero's increased cruelty and exhibitionism coincided with the increased influence of his dissolute friend Ofonius Tigellinus, who took over part command of the Praetorian Guard, and of Nero's paramour Poppaea Sabina, whom he finally married in 62, after divorcing his unloved and barren wife Octavia.

One of Nero's persistent problems, in fact, was the presence of a considerable number of dynastic rivals, as the descendants of Augustus and his successors multiplied. Moreover, the Senate could in theory confer the relevant powers on any appropriate candidate, and Republican nobility still counted for much. That fact was ultimately to be demonstrated in 68 by the successful coup of Servius Sulpicius Galba, but three years earlier there was an abortive conspiracy to replace Nero with C. Calpurnius Piso. It was mounted by senators, *equites,* and officers of the Praetorian Guard, including its other Prefect, Faenius Rufus.

Though there is no sign of the involvement of senatorial army commanders that was later to lead to Nero's overthrow, the causes of dissatisfaction were already present. Nero had extended his crimes outside the palace. The disappointment of his hopes for an heir from Poppaea, who was pregnant when he married her but gave birth to a girl who lived only a few months, had led to fear and persecution of aristocrats related to the imperial house, like the Junii Silani. Nero also offended conservatives by planning to perform in public at Rome at the Neronia scheduled for that summer, having already made his debut in 64 at the Greek city of Naples.

The emperor's popularity with the propertied classes had been further undermined by a natural disaster which devastated the city of Rome and placed the economy under strain. In the early hours of 19 June 64, a fire broke out in shops around the Circus Maximus and spread north through the valley between the Palatine and the Esquiline. It lasted for nine days in all and reduced three of the fourteen regions of the city to rubble, leaving only four regions untouched. The emperor was energetic in providing emergency shelter, clearing debris, and helping with reconstruction. But it soon became clear that he intended a reconstruction of Rome involving not only a new code of safety for building construction, but the use of land, previously in private occupation, for a grand palace and spacious parks in the center of Rome. The precious metal coinage shows the financial strain of Nero's efforts: both the gold and silver were reduced in weight and the silver content of the *denarius* lowered by more than 10% in addition. The ancient authors attest the resentment that Nero's plans aroused. The planned extension of the city, if carried out, would no doubt have relieved the housing shortage caused by his wider streets and by the sprawl of the Golden House which even included a lake where the Colosseum now stands. But Nero never lived to realized his conception, which was probably to provide Rome with a fine center of government open to the public: it must be remembered that emperors, like ordinary Roman magistrates, had always conducted business in their own residences.

The scale and fury of the fire, the fact that its second outbreak occurred on Tigellinus' estates, and perhaps knowledge of Nero's dissatisfaction with the limits of his own first palace the Domus Transitoria, then being built, gave rise to the rumor that Nero had deliberately started the blaze. The Princeps first attempted to quash the story by religious ceremonies to appease the supposed anger of the gods. When this failed, Nero decided to direct popular hostility toward an unpopular minority whose refusal to join in the recent pagan ceremonies may have attracted attention at this point. On the Christians were visited cruel punishments, including one particularly appropriate to the alleged crime: they were crucified and used as living torches to light the Emperor's races in the Vatican Circus (Tac. *Ann.* 15.44; Suet. *Nero* 16.2). A corrupt passage of Juvenal (1.155) suggests that Tigellinus had a hand in the punishment, perhaps taking revenge for the damage to his property.

Though Tacitus says that Nero's cruelty aroused pity for the Christians and though the Domus Aurea displaced houses of the poor as well as of the rich, Nero never seems to have lost his popularity with the ordinary people of Rome, who loved his generosity and his games (Tact. *Hist.* 1.4.3; Suet. *Nero* 57.1). The threat came from the upper classes, and especially from senators who found themselves in positions of authority in provinces where the propertied elite had become discontent. For after the fire at Rome, confiscations are attested in Gaul, Spain, Africa, Britain, Judea, and Egypt, to say nothing of the art treasures that were brought from Greece to adorn the Domus Aurea.

Nero now decided to fulfill his ambition to compete in the traditional Greek games. In September 66 he left for Greece, despite the detection of another conspiracy at Beneventum, a town that he could be expected to visit on his way to Brundisium. Some of the Greek festivals had to be rescheduled, so that the Emperor could compete and win in all of them during his visit. The highpoint was his liberation of Greece from Roman administration and taxation, announced at a special celebration of the Isthmian Games at Corinth on 28 November 67. The text of Nero's speech in Greek is preserved on an inscription (*ILS* 8794).

While in Greece, Nero deposed and executed three senatorial commanders of the highest rank. But disaffection was rumbling in the West. At last Nero, in response to the warnings of his ex-slave Helius, returned to Italy. Soon after, in March of 68, Julius Vindex, the governor of one of the Gallic provinces, rose in arms. Although he was defeated two months later by the governor of Upper Germany, Verginius Rufus, Nero's failure to respond quickly and decisively had encouraged others to defect. The Praetorian Guard were told that he had already fled abroad and declared for Galba. The Senate followed suit, decreeing Nero a public enemy. Nero took refuge in the villa of his ex-slave Phaon, and there he committed suicide, reputedly lamenting, "What an artist dies with me!" (Suet. *Nero* 48–49).

D. Foreign Policy

Nero, like his predecessors, was mainly content to follow the guidelines laid down by Augustus in foreign affairs. Two problems dominated his reign: Britain, of which the southern part had been made a Roman province by Claudius, and the eastern frontier. In Britain Nero's governors set out to end the resistance of the Welsh tribes and of the Druids who were defeated in their stronghold on Anglesey. The most significant fighting, however, came in Norfolk, where the tribe of the Iceni resisted Roman annexation after their king died. They were joined by the Trinovantes who resented the veteran colony, with its expensive cult of Divus Claudius, planted in their midst at Colchester.

In the East, ever since the conquests of Pompey the Great had brought the Roman Empire up against the Parthian dominions, the problem had been to secure stable control of the border kingdom of Armenia, where the Augustan policy was to have a "client king" selected by Rome. Nero's general Domitius Corbulo finally negotiated a new arrangement, in the latter part of 63, by which a member of the Parthian ruling house would hold Armenia, as the Parthians had repeatedly tried to do, but would publicly recognize Roman suzerainty. The new settlement was to prove stable, but it committed Rome to providing more military support in the area than the Augustan arrangement. Further to the N, Nero annexed the kingdom of Pontus and was planning to take personal command of an expedition against the Sarmatians N of the Dariel Pass in the Caucasus. Tribal movements there had already had repercussions as far as the Danube.

E. Provincial Administration

The historian Tacitus found an exception to the excellence of Nero's early years of rule in the laxness with which provincial governors had been brought to justice. Nero's good relations with the Senate led him to cooperate with senatorial reluctance to sentence their peers on the testimony of their subjects. As for the appointment of governors, his record was mixed until his last years, when his fear of giving power to potential rivals led him to install undistinguished, though not necessarily incompetent, men in key military provinces.

His most disastrous appointments were in Judea, where the decision taken by Claudius, after the death of Herod Agrippa I, to return to the Augustan policy of direct rule imposed on Nero the obligation to find *equites* of particular skill and tact to serve as procurators. Antonius Felix, the brother of the influential Pallas, had been appointed as procurator late in Claudius' reign. Despite his tactless marriage to the Jewish princess Drusilla, he was retained by Nero, though it is not clear for how long. It is worth noting, however, that the Eusebian-Jerome date of 56 for the appointment of his successor Porcius Festus accords well with the evidence of Tacitus (*Ann.* 13.14; 21–22) that Pallas was dismissed in 55 but that Agrippina, his political ally, regained some influence at the end of 55. For the decision to remove Felix would, on this chronology, have been taken in 55 and his acquittal, when tried in Rome on charges brought by the Jews of Caesarea, would then fall in 56 and could be plausibly attributed to the influence of Pallas, as Josephus notes (*Ant* 20.182).

Of Nero's four procurators, only Porcius Festus escapes censure from Josephus. Felix is represented as cruel and murderous, Lucceius Albinus as venal, and Gessius Florus as exhibiting the vices of the others in heightened form. All found themselves unable to maintain order in the province. Rebellion finally broke out in the summer of 66 when rebel forces took possession of Masada and massacred the Roman garrison there while others took control of the temple in Jerusalem and banned the daily sacrifices for the Emperor. Nero was in Greece when, on 8 November 66, he heard of the defeat of the governor of Syria Cestius Gallus, who had marched to Jerusalem in hopes of restoring order. Nero appointed the future Emperor Vespasian, then in his entourage, to take command of the Jewish War.

The two Neronian procurators whom Paul encountered are portrayed in a more benign light by the author of Acts than by Josephus. Antonius Felix is shown observing the traditions of Roman criminal justice; moreover, the tribune of the auxiliary unit in Jerusalem who arrests Paul, Claudius Lysias, is punctilious himself and clearly expects his superior to behave similarly. Once Paul revealed his possession of Roman citizenship, the tribune released him from his bonds and asked the Sanhedrin to investigate the Jewish charges against him (22:30). He was consistently concerned to protect his Christian prisoner from mob violence, to the extent of dispatching him in the dead of night to the procurator at Caesarea with a large escort for protection, just on the strength of evidence from Paul's nephew that there was a Jewish plot against his uncle. Lysias sent along a letter to Felix stating that he had uncovered only charges concerning the violation of Jewish law, "nothing deserving execution or imprisonment" (24:29), and that he had told Paul's accusers to go and confront him at Caesarea. Felix, having ascertained that Paul came from Tarsus in Cilicia, an area probably subject to the governor of Syria at that period, decided not to bother the senior senatorial legate, who was also his own superior in times of crisis, but to try the case himself when the Jewish accusers arrived (24:35). Though the advocate for the Jerusalem priests cleverly adduced a charge of fomenting agitation among the Jews throughout the world—a menace that Claudius' Letter to the Alexandrians shows was a real worry to the Roman government—Felix stated that he must wait for the testimony of Claudius Lysias and then kept Paul in comfortable custody, allowing his friends access to him (24:23).

The bad motives attributed to Felix—hope of a bribe from his Christian prisoner and a weak wish to conciliate the Jews (24:26–27)—do not seriously darken the portrait of a man described by the Jewish accuser as a guarantor of peace and a reformer benefiting his Jewish subjects, but also shown as willing to listen to Paul's lecture on morality and the new faith (24:24–25). Even his retention of Paul in custody for two years is understandable: other Roman governors, including the upright Cicero (*ad Att.* 6.1.7), are known to have avoided decisions that could earn them criticism, and Felix will have been aware that two of his predecessors had been recalled for trial. Moreover, Paul seems to have welcomed the chance to harangue the procurator and his Jewish wife, for he did not exercise his right of appeal at this stage (Sherwin-White 1963: 53).

In Acts, Porcius Festus also insists on the Jews coming to Caesarea, the procurator's seat of administration, to accuse Paul (25:5), finds nothing substantial in their charges which mostly concern Jewish law, but hesitates to offend the Jews and suggests a trial at Jerusalem, where he might have allowed an advisory role to members of the Sanhedrin. Scholars are not agreed as to whether Paul's defense, "Neither against the laws of the Jews, nor against the temple, nor against Caesar, have I offended at all" (25:8), is evidence that treason against Rome, if only in the form of causing a riot, was alleged by the Jews. In any case, once Paul expressed his right as a Roman citizen to appeal to Caesar in order to avoid the proposed trial, Festus, having consulted his *consilium* in the traditional Roman way, decided neither to drop the proceedings altogether nor to pursue the trial to an acquittal (which would not have violated the appeal) but to send Paul to Rome for trial (25:12, 21).

Though there is broad agreement among scholars on the type of jurisdiction exercised by Roman governors of all categories, namely *cognitio*, an accusatory procedure not bound by statute and allowing the governor discretion in countenancing charges and in deciding penalties, there is less certainty about the scope and nature of appeal in this period and about Paul's request in particular. The Greek word attributed to Paul in Acts 25:11, *epikaloumai*, is the standard Greek equivalent of the Latin *appello* (Plut. *Marc.* 2.4; Dio 51.19,6), addressed in the Republic to the tribunes of the plebs, but under the Empire to the Princeps when it came to replace the old *provocatio* to the people. Since, however, in the juristic sources, appeal always seems to occur after sentence, an attempt has been made to reinterpret Paul's demand as one for transfer of jurisdiction (Garnsey 1970: 182–85). But the alleged right of *reiectio Romae* is poorly attested (Cotton 1979: 45), and it has been more plausibly argued that appeal could, at least in the early Principate as in the Republic, be laid against a magistrate's authority at various stages in the proceedings, including both before and after sentence (Lintott 1972: 264). See also APPEAL TO CAESAR.

F. The Neronian Persecution

Without firm evidence of the date and circumstances of Paul's martyrdom, it is difficult to relate his two-year imprisonment in Rome, attested in Acts 28:30 to the Neronian persecution of 64. Paul is said to have comforted his fellow passengers on the stormy voyage to Rome by recounting a dream in which an angel tells him that he will survive to stand before Caesar (Acts 24:27; Fox 1987: 430). If we are meant to take this as a true divine prediction, Paul must eventually have been tried by the Emperor. Unless a very late chronology for Paul's journeys is adopted, it will not do to explain the delay by Nero's negligence, for during his years of good rule, as we have seen, Nero was conscientious about jurisdiction. It is better to remember that Paul's trial would not deserve high priority, in Roman terms, and that his accusers may have taken some time to pursue their case, if they ever did.

Nothing suggests that the charge against Paul was Christianity, or anything other than offenses against Jewish law and the fomenting of unrest among the Jews. That will not have been new to the Romans, if we can trust the story in Suetonius of Jewish unrest in Rome under Claudius *impulsore Chresto* (*Claudius* 25.4).

Nero's ability to distinguish Jews from Christians, whom he singled out in 64 as scapegoats, should probably be traced, as Edward Gibbon surmised, to his wife Poppaea, rather than to Paul's accusers. For Poppaea is described by Josephus as *theosebēs* (*Ant* 2.195), and she had recently met Josephus, securing for him the release from custody of some Jewish priests (*Life* 16), and had succeeded in overturning a decision by the procurator of Judea in favor of King Herod Agrippa (*Ant* 20.195). It is ironic that, because of her friendship with the wife of Gessius Florus (*Ant* 20.252), she is held responsible for imposing the last and worst of the Neronian procurators on the people she favored.

For the Christian sources, Nero was the first to persecute the Christians (Melito in Eus. *Hist. Eccl.* 4.26.9; Tert. *Ad Nat.* 1.7.8/9; *Apol.* 5.3/4), and this was the one Neronian practice *(institutum Neronianum)* to survive. The account of Tacitus, however, shows us a very different situation from the later Trajanic one, revealed in Pliny's famous letters (*Ep.* 10.96–97), where the charge is Christianity, and apostasy secures pardon. In 64, Nero, by blaming the fire on the Christians as a group, could then treat a confession of Christianity as proof of incendiarism. On his assumption, that while Christians these people had committed the crime for which they were now to be punished, later apostasy from the religion was clearly irrelevant. When Tacitus says that the Christians were convicted "not so much for the crime of arson as for hatred of the human race" (*Ann.* 15.44), he is not making a statement about the legal position but about the political reality that enabled Nero to punish for arson, people who were already hated for their exclusiveness. The historian's own attitude illustrates the point, for, in going on to describe the Christians as "guilty and deserving of the worse punishments," he is not endorsing Nero's view of the fire (he had already given his own view of its cause) but popular ideas of Christian conduct.

G. The False Neros

The secrecy of Nero's death and burial (Suet. *Nero* 50) lent plausibility to a belief in his survival current in the eastern part of the Empire, where he had enjoyed a certain popularity. In 69 "Achaea and Asia were alarmed by a false report of Nero's return" (Tac. *Hist.* 2.8). The imposter, who resembled Nero facially and was skilled in singing and playing the cithara, collected a following of slaves and impoverished adventurers, but his claim to be supported by the legions of Syria and the East was alarming enough for him to be assassinated by order of the Roman governor of Galatia-Pamphylia. Then, in A.D. 80, an Asiatic named Terentius Maximus made the same claim and won the support of the Parthian King. The Parthians went on to support another imposter in 88–89, and Dio Chrysostom, writing about this time or later, says of opinion in the East (*Or.* 21.10), "Even now his subjects wish he were alive, and most men believe that he is." It is notable that even Greek writers like Plutarch, Philostratus, and Pausanias, whose Roman connections and sympathies led them to share the Roman assessment of Nero's crimes and artistic aspirations, soften their judgments because of his one great act, the liberation of Greece (Plut. *Ant.* 87; *Mor.* 505C, 567F; Philostratus *Apoll.* 5.7; Paus. 7.17.3).

The Jews and Christians, deliberately perverting the Greek hope that the philhellene emperor would return, portrayed him as an avenging spirit who would punish their Roman persecutors. In the Jewish Sibylline oracles, written not long after the destruction of the temple in Jerusalem in 70, Nero has fled to the Parthians and will cross the Euphrates to destroy Rome and the whole world (4.119–24, 138–39; 5.137–52, 362). The Christian oracles see Nero as the antichrist whose persecution of the Christians prepares for the destruction of Rome (8.70, 88–90). The Christian Fathers and later Christian writers continued and established this hostile tradition, thus endorsing the view of Nero's original pagan historians.

Bibliography

Barnes, T. D. 1968. Legislation against the Christians. *JRS* 58: 32ff.
Cotton, H. 1979. Cicero, *ad Familiares* XIII, 26 and 28: evidence for *revocatio* or *reiectio Rommae/Romam? JRS* 69: 39–50.
Fox, R. L. 1987. *Pagans and Christians.* New York.
Garnsey, P. 1970. *Social Status and Legal Privilege in the Roman Empire.* Oxford.
Grant, M. 1970. *Nero.* London.

Griffin, M. T. 1984. *Nero, the End of a Dynasty*. London.
Lintott, A. 1972. Provocatio. From the Struggle of the Orders to the Principate. *ANRW* 1/2: 226–67.
Sherwin-White, A. N. 1963. *Roman Society and Roman Law in the New Testament*. Oxford.
Smallwood, E. M. 1976. *The Jews under Roman Rule*. Leiden.
Warmington, B. H. 1969. *Nero, Reality and Legend*. London.

MIRIAM T. GRIFFIN

NERVA (EMPEROR). Marcus Cocceius Nerva was born in Narnia (Italy) on November 8, probably in A.D. 35, and became emperor after Domitian's assassination (September 18, 96). The Cocceii, despite their faint links with the Julio-Claudians (possibly through Nerva's mother), lacked illustrious lineage, yet they could trace their ancestry back as far as a consul of 36 B.C., and were one of the few lineages able to do so at the end of the 1st century A.D.

Not much is known of Nerva's early career. There is no evidence that he was a jurist like his famous grandfather in the days of the emperor Tiberius (Tac. *Ann* 6.26), nor that he ever commanded an army or governed a province. He was a poet and impressed Nero by his ability, for Nero dubbed him the "Tibullus of the age" (Mart. *Spect.* 8.70.7). Nero was also impressed by his assistance in the detection of the Pisonian conspiracy of 65, which resulted in the execution or forced suicide of many eminent Romans: both he and the praetorian prefect Tigellinus "were awarded triumphal honors . . . and busts of them were placed in the palace in addition to triumphal statues in the Forum" (Tac. *Ann* 15.72). What precisely Nerva did to merit such unparalleled honors is not recorded, nor is there any hint that he was in danger of retribution or retaliation on Nero's death. Quite the contrary, for he managed not only to survive the vicissitudes of the Civil War (A.D. 68–69) but also to emerge as a favorite of the new regime, holding ordinary consulships at critical periods, i.e., in 71 (under Vespasian) and in 90 (under Domitian). Normally these offices were reserved for Vespasian, Titus, Domitian, or some imperial relative, and Nerva is the only non-Flavian to have held two of them in this period. Later writers, possibly in an effort to explain his almost uncanny ability to survive each change of ruler and, at the same time, to acquire even greater honors from the new regime, allege that, during the last years of Domitian's reign, he was banished and that his life was in danger. However, this is regarded as highly unlikely.

More controversial is Nerva's role in Domitian's assassination. His activities at the time of the Pisonian conspiracy, together with his well-rewarded support of Vespasian and Domitian, must surely have rendered him an unlikely confidant of those who planned Domitian's death. Yet Dio Cassius (67.15.5), although not Suetonius, claims that the conspirators warned Nerva of their intentions. Also, support comes from the *Fasti Ostienses,* which show that Nerva speedily replaced Domitian: he was named emperor "on the same day" as the assassination.

Nerva's selection may seem surprising. His "advantages" were negative: he offended no one, he was 60 years old, he had no children and so could not establish a dynasty, he had no connections with the military: essentially, he was safe. But these qualities do not necessarily lead to sound administration.

The quality of his brief sixteen-month reign is debatable. Domitian's memory was officially condemned, his statues melted down or destroyed, his legislation abrogated, and informers prosecuted. A number of measures obviously designed to win support were introduced: the customary donative was paid to the army and the people; the postal service became more the responsibility of the central government, minimizing its burden on local areas and individual cities; the water supply was reorganized; and the *alimenta,* a system of support for poor children, may have been inaugurated at this time rather than in Trajan's reign. So, while Nerva's setting up an economic commission to recommend savings does not prove that a financial or budgetary crisis existed, it need hardly cause surprise if such a crisis did exist.

Even less satisfactory was his relationship with the army. Apart from Nerva's assumption of the title *Germanicus* and references to both a victory in Pannonia and to a war against the Suebi, we have no indication of official military activity during his reign. On the other hand, it is clear that he could control neither the Praetorian guard nor one of the senior military commanders. The result, according to Pliny, was that the "country was in peril and the whole realm tottering to a fall" (*Pan.* 5.5–6). The Praetorian guard, under the command of Casperius Aelianus, demanded the execution of Domitian's murderers: Nerva had to agree to the request and Parthenius and Petronius were killed—an obvious display of the emperor's impotence. Another problem was the attitude of the army commander in Syria. Pliny refers to "someone who was then [i.e., in 97] in the East, at the head of a powerful and celebrated army, about whom serious though unconfirmed rumors were circulating" (*Ep.* 9.13.10). The identity of this "someone . . . in the East" has long puzzled scholars, but it now seems that he was Marcus Cornelius Nigrinus Curiatius Maternus, commanding the 4 legions of Syria. His precise activities have not been discovered, but it is argued that he was later executed by Trajan, as was Casperius Aelianus.

Nerva's attitude toward Judaism and Christianity was less repressive than his predecessor's. Eusebius notes that the apostle John was recalled from exile and resumed residence at Ephesus (*Hist. Eccl.* 3.20); presumably, Domitilla was treated in a similar fashion. On a coin, Nerva also claimed to have removed certain injustices (perhaps false charges) associated with the collection of the Jewish tax. The precise nature of the reform is not known, but, when taken in conjunction with Dio Cassius's statement that "no one was allowed to accuse other people of treason or Jewish life" (68.1.2), it seems clear that Nerva's regime was more tolerant, or at least less harsh, than Domitian's.

As his position deteriorated during the summer of 97, Nerva resorted to the expedient of adoption. He selected (or was persuaded to select) the governor of Upper Germany, Marcus Ulpius Traianus, who was given the title *Caesar;* subsequently the senate conferred on Trajan all the imperial powers, making him virtually co-ruler with Nerva. The decision, whether forced or not, proved to be a wise one, and when Nerva died on January 25, 98, the transfer of power was accomplished smoothly and peacefully.

Bibliography

Alföldy, G., and Halfmann, H. 1973. M. Cornelius Nigrinus Curiatius Maternus, General Domitians und Rivale Trajans. *Chiron* 3: 331–73.

Bruce, I. A. F. 1964. Nerva and the *Fiscus Iudaicus*. *PEQ* 96: 34–45.

Garzetti, A. 1974. *From Tiberius to the Antonines: A History of the Roman Empire A.D. 14–192*. London.

Syme, R. 1958. *Tacitus*. Oxford.

BRIAN W. JONES

NESSANA (M.R. 095031). A town in the W part of the central Negeb, 52 km SW of Beer-sheba, known by the Arabic name *Aujah el-Hafir.*

A. Identification and History

The ancient name of the site is not mentioned in any of the historical sources, and were it not for the discovery of the ancient papyri on the site, the name "Nessana" would not have been known. Its exact meaning is unknown. Perhaps it comes from the Semitic word *niṣan,* meaning "bud."

The site is on one of the major ancient caravan routes, leading from Aila on the Red Sea through the W fringes of the Negeb to Rhinocorura and Gaza, and over Elusa to Beer-sheba, Hebron, and Jerusalem. The earliest remains on the site were sherds: Rhodian, Coan, Pamphylian, and Italian stamped jar handles of the Hellenistic period. Among the comparatively numerous numismatic finds were coins of Ptolemy IV (212 B.C.E.), Ptolemy VII (127–126 B.C.E.), and John Hyrcanus I (134–104 B.C.E.). The excavators did not hesitate to relate these finds to the Nabateans, who had already established in the 3d century B.C.E. a caravan stop at this place. Mistakenly they assigned the Nabatean fort to this period.

From the Middle Nabatean period (30 B.C.E.–50/70 C.E.) came much Nabatean and Early Roman pottery and coins of Aretas IV (9 B.C.E.–40 C.E.), Malichus II (40–70 C.E.) or Rabel II (70–106 C.E.). Probably in this period the fort was built on the N part of the acropolis, and much of the grafitti originated (which the publisher assigned to the 3d century C.E.).

The late 2d–early 3d century C.E. is represented only by two coins of Septimius Severus (193–211 C.E.). The number of coins increases greatly at the beginning of the 4th century, with the accession of the House of Constantine. However, the excavators tend to assign the major construction operations on the acropolis to Theodosius II (408–450 C.E.). This date is based on the assumption that a military unit by the name of "the Most Loyal Theodosians," mentioned in one document at Nessana, was recruited by him and that it was stationed in Nessana. However, the document in question, although found at Nessana, did not originate there, but at Rhinocorura, at which two brothers, "natives of the village Nessana," served in the above-mentioned unit. Moreover, Theodosius I (379–383 C.E.) and not II was an active military monarch, and was probably the one to recruit the unit. In any case, the history of Nessana does not differ much from that of Mampsis and Oboda; the construction of the citadel on the acropolis must be assigned to the times of Diocletian and Constantine. This new date also affects the ecclesiastical history of Nessana. According to the excavators, the North Church formed part of the citadel, and they suggest at least one part of it, identified as a chapel, was built at the same time as the citadel. Should the new date be accepted, the construction of this church must be reassigned to the second half of the 4th century C.E., a date assigned also to the early churches in the other towns of the Negeb.

The Byzantine period was one of great prosperity for Nessana. The acropolis served as a military, ecclesiastical, and possibly an administrative center, and the town extended along the W slope and beyond the wadi on the W. Farms surrounded the town, and the prosperity of Nessana continued until the end of the Byzantine period. The Moslem conquest of Nessana initiated a gradual decline. In addition to the ceramics, evidence for this period comes mainly from the large number of papyri dating to the latter part of the 7th century C.E. Most important for the study of the decline are documents in which the townspeople are requested to pay to the Arab military and civil authorities taxes in wheat, oil, and money. The omission of wine may help explain the fate of Nessana—grape wine must have been the most important product of Nessana, and with the loss of a customer, the Byzantine army, Nessana was doomed.

B. History of Research

E. Robinson (1838) visited Aujah, but identified it with Oboda. After visits by E. H. Palmer in 1871 and P. J. Lagrange in 1897, A. Musil in 1896 and 1902 drew the first detailed plan of the site (1907: 88–109). Musil's description is of great importance, because the Turkish authorities built an administrative center at Aujah el-Hafir that destroyed the ancient lower town, which Musil said was surrounded by a wall with gates. No trace of this wall has survived. When E. Huntington visited the site in 1908 the Turks had completed their work. One of their buildings was erected above a church which had been decorated with multicolored mosaics, and was dedicated in 502 C.E. He described two collonaded streets, each 200 m long. A German team headed by T. Wiegand drew a plan of the North Church in the acropolis and found fragments of Greek papyri. The painted Nabatean pottery they identified as "Coptic," and during their visit the newly built Turkish center had already deteriorated badly. P. H. Haensler, a German physician in the service of the Turko-German army, spent two months at Nessana, describing the extant remains and copying Greek inscriptions found during the looting of the North Church.

J. H. Iliffe visited the site in 1934, and from 1935 to 1937 extensive excavations were conducted. These concentrated only on the acropolis, where there was still hope of salvaging some of the ancient remains. The greatest achievements of the expedition were the excavations of the North Church and the discovery of the unique archive of papyri.

C. Excavations

1. The Nabatean Fort. The fort was on the N end of the acropolis. Since the North Church was built over the fort, few details of the fort are known. It measured 27 × 25 m, and was fortified with round towers and a retaining wall on its S side. From the little-detailed plan, it appears that the rounded towers and retaining wall were meant to support the building after it had been shattered by an earthquake. The rest of the building, which apparently consisted of a central court with a central cistern and with rooms around it, was destroyed almost to its foundations. The stones in the construction of the fort were differently dressed than those of the other buildings at Nessana. According to A. Negev, some stones in the foundations of the court were dressed in typical Nabatean fashion. The excavators dated the fort to the 2d century B.C.E. This date is based on mixed pottery found at the foundations, which included both Hellenistic and Early Roman-Middle Nabatean pottery. It thus seems that it should most probably be dated late 1st century B.C.E. to early 1st century C.E.

2. The Citadel. This large structure (85 × 35 m) occupies the central part of the acropolis. It is strengthened by rectangular corner towers, and two towers on its W side, which face the desert. It had gates on the S and E, facing the lower town. In an early phase, the citadel had eighteen rooms along its W wall; an additional nine rooms were built later on the E. In the SW part of the court is a large, rectangular cistern (ca. 5 × 15 m) covered by a roof resting on seven arches. The excavators suggested that the citadel was used as a headquarters, arsenal, and stables for the military camels, but not as barracks. They also suggested that the large court was used in times of emergency to protect the civilian population. The excavators suggested that after 600 C.E., the citadel was excavated by the military, and was annexed to the North Church to house a monastery.

3. The North Church. The North Church abuts the N wall of the citadel. Because of the steep slope on the W, the entrance to the building was on the E. A long monumental staircase leads from the town below to a narrow atrium (named "East Court"), which has a cistern under its floor. At a later stage, a portico was added E of the atrium. A door in the SW corner of the atrium opens on a narrow corridor ("Room 10"). To the S are two rooms, which the excavators assumed had been a chapel used by the soldiers before the construction of the larger church. This was, however, a mortuary chapel, in which a priest and a deacon were buried in 464 and 475 C.E., respectively. One of the epitaphs mentions a "holy martyrium" and the other a "holy place," which probably refer to the whole church; according to other inscriptions found in the building, it was dedicated to the saints Sergius, Stephen, and Bacchus. A corridor leads to a small court ("South Court") and to Room 8, where the papyri were found; two other doors lead into the basilica. The basilica (10.70 × 19.0 m) is a rectangular hall with a single apse, attached to the back wall by a short support. Within the apse are remains of the bishop's throne and at its sides near the walls of the apse are traces of two small columns. These columns apparently supported small altar tables for the placement of reliquaries. The church was eventually lengthened by 3.0 m. W of the basilica is a baptistry with a semicircular font built into the floor. In addition to the hundreds of papyri found in the church, there were discovered 90 inscriptions, graffiti, and paintings.

4. The South Church. This church (20.8 × 14.1 m) was on a low hill S of the acropolis, and is one of the few churches in the Negeb initially built as a triapsidal church. There is a small atrium of porticoes on the S and E, and the basilica is entered by two doors instead of the usual three. S of the basilica are a chapel with an apse at its E end and three small rooms, one of which is entered by a door behind the apse. One of these rooms, S of the atrium, could have served as a prothesis. There were apparently rooms, or one long hall also N of the basilica. An inscription engraved on a capital reads: "Holy Mary, Mother of God, help and pity thy slave—year 496" (601/2 C.E.).

There were also two churches in the lower town, the East Church or Monastery Church, and the South Church. Both were razed by the Turkish authorities. An inscription in the mosaic floor of the East Church was copied by Huntington in 1909: "For the salvation of the benefactors Sergius, ex-assessor and monk, and Pallus his sister, and John the deacon, her son, curialis of the metropolitan city of Emesa. In the year 496, in the 5th indiction, on the 20th of the month Gorpiaeus" (i.e., September 7, 601 C.E.). It is noteworthy that the 7th century C.E. began at Nessana with the construction of two new churches, or at least with the construction of one, and the laying of a mosaic floor in the other.

5. The Papyri. The discovery of the hundreds of papyri at Nessana—both literary and nonliterary—is certainly the most important contribution to the study of the history of the whole region in the Byzantine and Early Arab periods. Among the literary papyri are a Latin-Greek glossary of the *Aeneid* of Virgil and fragments of *Aeneid* II–VI; a group of ecclesiastical literature includes fragments of the Gospel of John, Acts of St. George, fragments of the Pauline epistles, letter of Abgar to Christ and Christ's reply, the Twelve Chapters of Faith, and another theological fragment. Among the secular literature are a Greek glossary and legal fragments. The nonliterary archive includes 195 documents and fragments of documents. These include contracts referring to everyday life (marriages, divorces, inheritances, divisions of property, sales, loans, receipts, letters on ecclesiastical affairs, allotments of taxes, and accounts of cavalry units). To the period following the Arab conquest belong bilingual Greek-Arabic documents dealing with the payment of taxes, demands to supply guides for journeys to the Holy Mountain (in Sinai), lists of fields and crops, and protests against the payment of heavy taxes. The latest documents found at Nessana are of the late 7th century C.E.

D. Summary

Nessana was founded by the Nabateans at the beginning of the Hellenistic period (Early Nabatean period) as one of three major caravan stops on the routes from N Arabia to the Mediterranean. At the beginning of the Early Roman period (Middle Nabatean period) the Nabateans built a fort on the site. The history of the site in the 2d and 3d centuries C.E. is not at all clear. During the reigns of Diocletian and Constantine, a citadel was built on the site to house units of local militia, apparently soldiers recruited from the local population, who were allotted farms. By the middle of the 4th century at least part of the population was Christian, and the construction of churches began.

The town thrived until after the Islamic conquest, perhaps until the 8th century C.E., when the burden of heavy taxation caused its decline.

Bibliography

Avi-Yonah, M. 1977. Nessana. *EAEHL* 3: 927–30.

Casson, L., and Hettich, E. L. 1950. *Excavations at Nessana.* Vol. 2. Princeton.

Colt, H. D., ed. 1962. *Excavations at Nessana.* Vol. 1. London.

Huntington, E. 1911. *Palestine and its Transfigurations.* London.

Kraemer, C. J. 1958. *Excavations at Nessana.* Vol. 3. Princeton.

Musil, A. 1907. *Arabia Petraea.* Vol. 2. Vienna.

Negev, A. 1976. The Churches of the Central Negev: An Archaeological Survey. *RB* 83: 397–420.

Robinson, E. 1838. *Biblical Researches in the Holy Land.* Vol. 1. London.

Avraham Negev

NETAIM (PLACE) [Heb *nĕṭāʿîm*].

A town of Judah where royal potters resided (1 Chr 4:23). See GEDERAH. Most scholars feel that the site of Netaim is unknown, although Albright (1925: 50) suggested an identification with Khirbet en-Nuweiti, south of the Wadi Elah.

Bibliography

Albright, W. F. 1925. The Administrative Divisions of Israel and Judah. *JPOS* 5: 17–54.

David Salter Williams

NETHANEL (PERSON) [Heb *nĕtanʾēl*].

A personal name meaning "God has given."

1. The son of Zuar, mentioned in chaps. 1, 2, 7, and 10 of Numbers along with the chiefs of the tribes of Reuben, Simeon, Judah, Zebulun, Ephraim, Manasseh, Benjamin, Dan, Asher, Gad, and Naphtali. Nethanel is identified as the chief *(nāśîʾ)* of the tribe of Issachar in Num 1:8, 16; and 2:5b. In the register in Num 1:5–16, Nethanel and the other chiefs are designated as the "summoned ones of the assembly" (*qĕrûʾê hāʿēdâ* [Q]; "the elect of the congregation") who were to assist Moses and Aaron in registering the adult males of their tribes. In Numbers 2, Moses and Aaron were given instructions in (1) the order in which the tribes were to encamp around the tabernacle and (2) the order in which the tribes were to march. Nethanel and the tribe of Issachar were to encamp with the tribes of Judah and Zebulun on the E side of the tabernacle. When camp was broken and the tribes set out, Issachar was to be second in order, following Judah. (See Num 10:11–28, which reports Israel's breaking camp and setting out from Sinai.) The order in which the tribes and their leaders are mentioned in Numbers 7 (which reports the gifts of the tribal chiefs for the tabernacle and altar) and Numbers 10 is the same as that observed in Numbers 2. A different order, unique in the OT, is seen in Num 1:5–16. (Another difference to be noticed in these texts is that the father of Eliasaph the chief of Gad is identified as Reuel in Numbers 2 and as Deuel in Numbers 1, 7, and 10 in the MT and RSV. Eliasaph's father is called Reuel consistently in the LXX [Gk *ragouēl*]. This may well reflect a desire of the LXX translator to achieve consistency rather than bearing witness to another textual tradition.)

2. The fourth son of Jesse, a brother of David, was named Nethanel according to the Chronicler (1 Chr 2:14). That the names of all the children of Jesse are given might be taken as characteristic of the Chronicler's concern with the tribe of Judah and with the family of King David. Braun says that making David the seventh son rather than the eighth may reflect a desire to depict David as a uniquely favored child, but adds that he could point to no other symbolic use of a number in the Chronicler's work (*1 Chronicles* WBC, 34). It should be noted that 1 Sam 16:10–11 and 17:12–14 speak of eight sons of Jesse, and 1 Chr 27:18 mentions a brother of David named Elihu.

3. One of the priests who was to sound a trumpet before the ark as the Levites were bringing it into Jerusalem at David's direction (1 Chr 15:24).

4. A Levite, identified as the father of Shemaiah, the scribe who recorded David's organization of the priests and Levites by ancestral houses (1 Chr 24:6).

5. The fifth son of Obed-edom, listed by the Chronicler as a gatekeeper in 1 Chr 15:16–24 (see also 1 Chr 15:21 and 16:5). This may reflect the changing status of those who claimed Obed-edom as their ancestor.

6. One of the princes sent by Jehoshaphat in the third year of his reign to teach in the cities of Judah (2 Chr 17:7). Myers (*2 Chronicles* AB, 99) proposes that the fact that laymen were mentioned as teachers points to a tradition older than the Chronicler, since the Chronicler considered the Levites to have had the primary responsibility as teachers. He considers 2 Chr 17:8 as a possible addition by the Chronicler. The nature of the "book of the law of Yahweh" which the officials, Levites, and priests took with them is not known. Williamson holds that the Chronicler understood it as primarily religious in character, based on what we now know as the Pentateuch (*1 and 2 Chronicles* NCBC, 282–83) but agrees with Myers' suggestion (*2 Chronicles* AB, 99–100) that the book referred to in the Chronicler's sources may have been a royal law code. Commentators have also discussed the possibility that the report of the teaching mission in 2 Chr 17:7–9 represents another version of the report of judicial reform in 2 Chr 19:4–11.

7. One of the levitical officials who with his brothers Conaniah and Shemaiah offered pascal lambs and cattle for the Levites for the Passover celebrated in the reign of Josiah (2 Chr 35:9). In 1 Esdras 1:9 Nethanel (Gk *Nathanēl*) and the others are identified as commanders of a thousand (Gk *chiliarchoi*) while the LXX of 2 Chr 35:9 calls them chiefs (Gk *archontes*).

8. A priest of the family of Pashhur, he was required to divorce his foreign wife during Ezra's reform (Ezra 10:22). The list of those who divorced their foreign wives and disowned the children born to them may seem "extraordinarily small considering the furor and the census figures in chapter ii" (Myers *Ezra-Nehemiah* AB, 87). Myers discusses three possible explanations: (1) the problem was not as serious as it would seem on the surface; (2) the list preserved is only a partial list perhaps reflecting only the upper classes; or (3) the reform was not successful (ibid., 87–88). Stating that the first explanation can be easily dismissed, he favors the second explanation (ibid., 87–88).

Blenkinsopp, on the other hand, argues that the reform was not successful (*Ezra-Nehemiah* OTL, 197–201).

9. The head of the priestly house of Jedaiah (Neh 12:21).

10. One of the musicians who participated in the dedication of the rebuilt wall of Jerusalem (Neh 12:36). Blenkinsopp (*Ezra-Nehemiah* OTL, 342–43) and Myers (*Ezra-Nehemiah* AB, 200–204) emend the MT of Neh 12:35a, moving the conjunction from the beginning of v 35a to the beginning of 35b in order to show that Zechariah (who is a descendant of Asaph) and the others who used the "musical instruments of David the man of God" were levitical musicians. Nethanel was in the procession led by Ezra the scribe.

KEITH L. EADES

NETHANIAH (PERSON) [Heb *nĕtanyāh; nĕtanyāhû*]. Five people in the Bible bear this name, which means "Yahweh gives." Names compounded with the theophoric element *yāh/yāhû* plus the verb *ntn* produce such nomenclature as Jonathan (see *TPNAH,* 352; cf. the theophoric element *ʾel* in such names as Elnathan, Nathanael, and Nathanel). Of the twenty occurrences in the OT, five have *-yāhû* as the final element and fifteen have *-yāh;* the name appears once also in the deuterocanonical writings (Gk *Nathanias*). The Akkadian equivalent produced with the verb *nadānu,* "to give," and the name of the deity is also common (see CAD 11/1: 42; *AN,* 357).

1. One of the musicians associated with the school of Asaph, adept in percussion and stringed instruments as well as vocal rendition of the liturgy (1 Chr 25:2, 12). Nethaniah and his three associates were members of the larger confederation of the six sons of Jeduthun, and the nine students of Heman forming altogether the masters of the royal choir school. The term prophesy (v 1) is characteristic of temple music; it has its origin in the early prophetic guilds where emotional extravagances were practiced. In this new musical consortium the music would be prophetic, but with the emotional and ecstatic patterns moderated (see Dalglish 1962: 214–20).

2. One of the nine Levites whom Jehoshaphat sent to the citizenry of Judah in his third regal year together with five princes of the realm and two priests to inculcate the basis of Judean religion in the nation (2 Chr 17:8).

3. The father of Jehudi and the son of Shelemiah, the son of Cushi (Jer 36:14). Nothing is properly related of Nethaniah, but it may be inferred that he was present in Jerusalem, if not at the royal palace, when Jehudi read the words of Jeremiah before Jehoiakim, king of Judah, and would therefore be alive in the year 604 B.C. That his son had such immediate entrée to the aristocracy and the royal court appears to confirm what may be drawn from the recital of his genealogy to the fourth generation, that he was ensconced in Judean nobility. That the princes chose Jehudi to be their liaison to Jeremiah suggests that the family was of esteemed fidelity to have one of its members serve as an internuncio between the prophetic and the political in the days when the two parties clashed.

4. The father of Ishmael, a royal military official and the infamous murderer of Gedeliah, the governor of Judea, newly appointed by the high command of the Babylonians. In the twenty-four times that the name Ishmael appears (2 Kgs 25:23, 25; Jeremiah 40 and 41), seven omit the patronymic, while seventeen instances carry the reading "the son of Nethaniah." The text indicates three generations of the family and includes the note that it belonged to the royal family (2 Kgs 25:25). What the relationship was between the tempestuous and irresponsible son and the father is not provided in the narrative.

5. A son of Bani; he was required to put away his foreign wife (and children) during Ezra's reform (1 Esdr 9:34). In the parallel account in Ezra 10:39, he is called Nathan. See NATHAN #6.

Bibliography

Dalglish, E. R. 1962. *Psalm Fifty-One.* Leiden.

EDWARD R. DALGLISH

NETHINIM [Heb *nĕtînîm*]. A class of "temple servants" (RSV) who appear in the postexilic period. The Hebrew Bible has seventeen references to the Nethinim, all in Ezra and Nehemiah (Ezra 2:43, 58, 70; 7:7; 8:17, 20 [2x]; Neh 3:26, 31; 7:46, 60, 73; 10:29—Eng v 28; 11:3, 21 [2x]), with the single exception of a reference in 1 Chr 9:2. In every occurrence, the word has the definite article *(hannĕtînîm)* and never appears in the singular. Etymologically, the word is a past participle of the root *ntn,* "to give." Thus it means, literally, "those who have been given." This is confirmed by the fact that the single instance in which the LXX does not transliterate the Hebrew word (most often as *hoi Nathinim*), it is rendered "the given ones" (Gk *hoi dedomenoi;* 1 Chr 9:2).

The mention of the Nethinim is in the context of those who returned to Jerusalem from exile in Babylon. The first group (Ezra 2:43–54 = Neh 7:46–56 = Esdr 5:29–32) led by Zerubbabel included 392 temple servants and sons of Solomon's servants (Ezra 2:58 = Neh 7:60; cf. 372 in 1 Esdr 5:35). The second wave (Ezra 8:16–20) initiated by Ezra included 220 more members of this clerical order. In Nehemiah 7 this original list is taken up again as the prologue for an appeal by Nehemiah for settlers to move into Jerusalem proper (Myers *Ezra-Nehemiah* AB, 164). There are questions which pertain to the dating, provenance, and purpose of these lists, but they do not affect our discussion of this subject.

The Nethinim are one of the five clerical orders associated with the temple in Ezra-Nehemiah: priests, Levites, gatekeepers, singers, temple servants (Neh 10:28). Ziha and Gishpa are said to be in charge of these temple personnel (Neh 11:21, omitted in the LXX). The temple servants are said to live within a specific precinct on the Ophel in Jerusalem (Neh 3:26, 31; 11:21), as well as in other cities (Ezra 2:70 = Neh 7:73).

The fact that a number of the names of the Nethinim are foreign has led to speculation that they had their origins among groups of prisoners of war or conquered peoples. In Josh 9:23, 27 the Gibeonites are given the task of cutting wood and carrying water "for the house of God," ostensibly because they deceived the Israelites into making a covenant with them. But the story may reflect the practice of using subject peoples for menial tasks (cf. Num 31:30, 47). Though Ezra 8:20 ascribes the origin of the Nethinim to "David and his officials," Ezek 44:7–9 condemns the practice of using foreigners in the temple services (*AncIsr,* 89–90).

Whatever the scruples of Ezekiel, by the time of Ezra and Nehemiah the Nethinim appear to be well-recognized and important members of the religious establishment. The initial disinterest of the levitic families in Ezra's mission appears to be overcome by the active recruitment of significant numbers of the Nethinim to participate in the venture (Myers *Ezra-Nehemiah* AB, 70). There is evidence in the Talmud (*m. Yebam.* 2:4; *m. Qidd.* 4:1) that the Nethinim were viewed as foreigners, and the designation of them by Josephus as *hierodouloi* ("sacred slaves," *Ant* 11.5.1 §128) implies their function as the menial laborers of the temple. Their position in the Ezra-Nehemiah context, however, is more elevated. They are even exempt along with priests and Levites from certain taxes (Ezra 7:24). In 1 Esdr 1:3, the Levites are called *hierodouloi* of Israel, the same term used for the Nethinim by Josephus.

The general impression is that the Nethinim are an accepted and rather well placed group within the religious community and, consequently, in the general community. Though they do not fully belong in the priestly ranks, they are close to the Levites in the hierarchy and are clearly seen to be in a position superior to the "servants of Solomon" and the other groups assigned to more menial tasks.

Bibliography

Ackroyd, P. 1970. *Israel Under Persia and Babylonia.* Oxford.

Cody, A. 1969. *A History of the Old Testament Priesthood.* AnBib 35. Rome.

Haran, M. 1961. The Gibeonites, the Nethinim and the Sons of Solomon's Servants. *VT* 11: 159–69.

Levine, B. A. 1963. The Netînîm. *JBL* 82: 207–12.

———. 1973. Later Sources on the *Netînîm.* Pp. 101–7 in *Orient and Occident,* ed. H. A. Hoffner. AOAT 22. Neukirchen-Vluyn.

Mendelsohn, I. 1942. State Slavery in Ancient Palestine. *BASOR* 85: 14–17.

JOSEPH P. HEALEY

NETOPHAH (PLACE) [Heb *nĕṭōpāh*]. NETOPHATHITES. A town in the hill country of Judah, located near Bethlehem and Anathoth (1 Chr 2:54; Ezra 2:21–23; Neh 7:26).

According to 1 Chr 2:54, the Netophathites were descendants of Caleb through Salma. The town was the home of two of David's "mighty men," Maharai and Heleb (2 Sam 23:28–29; 1 Chr 11:30) who served as captains for the tenth and twelfth military divisions (1 Chr 27:13, 15). 2 Kgs 25:23 suggests that the family of Seraiah, son of Tanhumeth, who supported governor Gedaliah after the latter was appointed by Nebuchadrezzar, was from Netophah. However, a parallel passage in Jer 40:8 indicates that it was the "sons of Ephai" who came from Netophah.

Ezra 2:22 indicates that 56 Netophathites (cf. 1 Esd 5:18, fifty-five) as well as 123 men from Bethlehem joined those who returned with Zerubbabel from Babylonian captivity. The total of these two groups (179) is at variance with Neh 7:26 which says that the total number of men from these two towns was 188. A number of Levites who returned from the Exile settled in the villages of the Netophathites, even though the territory was not originally assigned to them (1 Chr 9:16). Some of these Levites sang at the dedication of the rebuilt wall of Jerusalem (Neh 12:28).

Byzantine sources appear to preserve two forms of the name—*Natoupha* and *Metopa.* Conder believed Kh. Umm Tuba, near Bethlehem, preserved these ancient names. Kolb and Alt, on the other hand, felt that the two Byzantine names must be distinguished and that only the latter be identified with Kh. Umm Tuba. They proposed to identify biblical Netophah with Kh. Bedd Faluh (M.R. 171119), a site which rests on the spur of a ridge created by the conjunction of two valleys ca. 5.5 km (3.5 mi) SE of Bethlehem.

Mazar suggested that Ramat Rahel (M.R. 170127) would make a better candidate because of its proximity to Jerusalem (Neh 12:28), a suggestion maintained by Avi-Yonah. However, Aharoni's failure to find Iron I remains at the site (from the time of David's mighty men), led him to abandon this identification. Most scholars now seem to prefer Alt's original identification with Kh. Bedd Falul. A nearby spring, ʿAin en-Natuf, may preserve the ancient name.

Bibliography

Aharoni, Y. 1956. Ramat Rahel, 1954. *IEJ* 6: 152.

Alt, A. 1933. *PJ* 28:12, 47–54.

Avi-Yonah, M. 1977. *The Holy Land From the Persian Period to the Arab Conquest (536 B.C.–A.D. 640).* Grand Rapids.

Maisler (Mazar), B. 1935. *Qobes* (Mazie Vol.). Jerusalem (in Hebrew).

RANDALL W. YOUNKER

NETS. See ZOOLOGY.

NETWORK. A word appearing in technical descriptions of two sacral appurtenances. First, it translates Heb *rešet* ("net") and refers to the bronze grating on the altar made for the Tabernacle (Exod 27:4–5; 38:4). See also GRATING. Second and more frequently, however, it translates Heb *śĕbākâ* (also "net") and is used in reference to part of the ornamentation on Jachin and Boaz, the two bronze pillars that flanked the entry to the forecourt of Solomon's Temple. Since the Hebrew word denotes a window lattice (2 Kgs 1:2) and is found in parallel with *rešet* (Job 18:8), its general nature as a kind of grillwork around the capitals of the two pillars seems clear. Perhaps it served as a device for hanging the pomegranate decorations (1 Kgs 7:17, 18, 20; 2 Chr 4:12, 13; 2 Kgs 25:17 = Jer 32:22–23); or like *rešet,* it may have been a grating to cover the "bowls," which were also part of the capitals (2 Kgs 7:40, 41; cf. 2 Kgs 25:17 and Jer 52:22–23). Whatever its exact function, it contributes to the intricacy of the metalwork used to decorate the two pillars and so participates in forming the striking visual appearance of these symbolic features of the Temple. See also CAPITAL.

CAROL MEYERS

NEW [Gk *kainos, neos*]. In the NT, the idea of "new" is most commonly represented by the use of two adjectives, *kainos* (42 times) and *neos* (23 times), which in the English language versions of the Bible are generally translated "new." Many scholars, particularly on the basis of the 19th-century lexographical studies of R. C. Trench and H. Cremer, distinguished the meaning of the two adjectives, ascribing a qualitative aspect to *kainos* and a temporal aspect to *neos*. There is, however, ample reason to affirm that in their NT usage the two terms are essentially synonymous. The interchangeability of the two adjectives in such passages as Mark 2:21–22 (Matt 9:16–17; Luke 5:36–39) and Heb 8:8, 13; 9:15; 12:24, as well as the parallelism between and probable dependence of Eph 4:22–24 upon Col 3:10, underscore the essential synonymity of the two terms. *Kainos* represents a more literary usage, while *neos* represents more popular terminology which has made its way into Koine Greek literature.

A. The Profane Use

If a distinction is to be made apropos of the NT usage of these terms, it a distinction between a merely profane (or narrative) use and a more theological use. A profane sense is to be discerned in the gospels' reference to the new tomb in which Jesus was buried (Matt 27:60; John 19:41). A profane sense is also to be discerned in the use of the comparative of *neos (neōteros)* as a pronominal adjective to designate a young person, thus the younger son in the Lukan parable (Luke 15:12, 13), young stretcher bearers (Acts 5:6), the young person cited in a traditional proverb (John 21:18), and the young person as the subject or object of community regulations (1 Tim 5:1, 2; Titus 2:4, 6; 1 Pet 5:5; cf. Luke 22:26). Community regulations on young widows are also found in the NT (1 Tim 5:11, 14). The profane sense of "new" is likewise reflected in the related expression "from youth" (*ek neotētos;* Mark 10:20; Luke 18:21; Acts 26:4).

B. The Theological Use

A manifestly theological connotation of the adjective "new" is found in such NT expressions as new commandment (John 13:34; 1 John 2:7, 8; 2 John 5), new covenant (Luke 22:20; 1 Cor 11:25; 2 Cor 3:6; Heb 8:8, 13; 9:15; 12:24), new creation (2 Cor 5:17; Gal 6:15), new earth (2 Pet 3:13; Rev 21:1), new Jerusalem (Rev 2:12; 21:2), new heavens (2 Pet 3:13; Rev 21:1), new hymn (Rev 5:9; 14:3), new name (Rev 2:17; 3:12), new person (*anthrōpos;* Eph 2:15; 4:24; Col 3:10), new teaching (Mark 1:27), and new tongues (Mark 16:17).

C. Old and New

"New" is a relational term, implying both comparison and contrast. These aspects of the term are most apparent in the expressions "new covenant," "new commandment," and "new creation," especially in those passages (Heb 8:8, 13; 9:15; 1 John 2:7, 8; 2 Cor 5:17) where the NT authors explicitly dwell on the newness of the subjects at hand.

In the letter to the Hebrews, where only the new covenant is explicitly described as new (*kainos* in Heb 8:8, 13; 9:15; *neos* in Heb 12:24), the author introduces the idea of a "new covenant" by citing Jer 31:31–34, in explanation of his own contrast between a first and a second covenant (Heb 8:7). According to the author the new or second covenant is so much better than the old that, in a commentary on the biblical text, he claims that the new covenant has made the old obsolete (Heb 8:13). Jesus Christ is the mediator of this new covenant (Heb 9:15; 12:24), a covenant established in his blood (12:24). Essential to the author's idea of newness are the dimensions of uniqueness and permanence, and thus finality.

Specific reference to the prophecy of Jeremiah is absent from the other NT references to the new covenant, but the language of both the eucharistic passages (Luke 22:20; 1 Cor 11:25; some manuscripts of Matt 26:28; Mark 14:24) and Paul's reference to ministers of a new covenant (2 Cor 3:6) apparently allude to the biblical text. The eucharistic meal and the ministry are realities in a new and definitive, because divinely and ultimately established, order of things.

In this way, "new" acquires an eschatological connotation. This eschatological dimension is related to a Jewish understanding of time and an apocalyptic world view in which all of history is under the direction of God and oriented to its ultimate realization. Newness is characteristic of God's ultimate and definitive action in history.

The eschatological aspect of "new" also is present in the use of the neuter nominative form of the adjective (*kainon,* equivalent to the adverb, in Matt 26:29; Mark 14:25) when Jesus speaks of eating anew in the kingdom, thereby making reference to the traditional motif of the messianic banquet.

Within the Johannine school, the love commandment is described as a new commandment (John 13:34; 1 John 2:7, 8; 2 John 5). The commandment is new because of its christological focus. The commandment is a final gift of the departing Jesus and has Jesus himself as its foundation. The Johannine epistles recognize the traditional nature of the love commandment, affirming that it is part of the baptismal catechesis ("which you have heard from the beginning," 1 John 2:7; 2 John 5) and is, in this respect, an old commandment. Nonetheless the commandment is new precisely because of its christological aspect ("true in him"). As such it is an ultimate reality, belonging to the true light, which is already shining, in contrast to the darkness, which is passing away.

The eschatological dimension of "new," specified by its christological reference and the aspect of finality, is also clearly present when the apostle Paul writes, in an apocalyptic vein, of the new creation (2 Cor 5:17; cf. Gal 6:15). The new creation is "in Christ." It stands in contrast with the old creation which has passed away.

D. Eschatological Aspect

The eschatological aspect of "new" is predominant in the apocalyptic scenarios of the book of Revelation, which speak of the new heavens and the new earth (Rev 21:1; cf. 2 Pet 3:13), the new Jerusalem (Rev 2:12; 21:2), a new hymn (Rev 5:9; 14:3), and a new name (Rev 2:17; 3:12). Elements of comparison and contrast are present in all of these descriptions, but finality is the preeminent aspect. Because of these apocalyptic scenes, R. A. Harrisville (1960: 18–20) cites a dynamic quality as a distinctive aspect of the NT idea of newness.

This eschatological dimension of "new" is also clearly present within the deutero-Pauline writings. Both Ephesians and Colossians speak of the new person (*anthropos;*

Eph 2:15; 4:24; Col 3:10). In these writings the christological reference and the element of finality are integral to the meaning of "new," just as they were in the apostle's own work (1 Cor 11:25; 2 Cor 3:6; 5:17; Gal 6:15).

The eschatological aspect of "new," without, however, its Pauline and Johannine specificity, is clearly apparent in the expression "new tongues," found in the canonical conclusion to Mark, where it is part of an eschatological summary (Mark 16:17–18). There the adjective characterizes the spirit-provoked phenomenon of glossolalia.

E. Contrast

Elsewhere in Mark the element of contrast comes to the fore in the evangelist's use of "new." Jesus' new teaching stands in contrast to the teaching of the scribes (Mark 1:27; cf. v. 22). Matthew, who wants to highlight the continuity between traditional teaching, the teaching of Jesus, and the teaching of the Church (Matt 3:2; 4:17; 10:7), has omitted "new" from his parallel commentary on the reaction to Jesus' teaching (Matt 7:28–29).

The element of contrast also characterizes the use of "new" in a series of metaphorical remarks attributed to Jesus, especially apropos new wine and new wineskins (Matt 9:17; Mark 2:22; Luke 5:37–39), and new patches and new clothes (Mark 2:21; Luke 5:36). In their present context these metaphorical expressions symbolize the radical newness of Jesus' eschatological presence (cf. 1 Cor 5:7). See also *TDNT* 3: 447–51 and 3: 896–901.

Bibliography

Collins, R. F. 1986. "A New Commandment I Give to You, That You Love One Another . . ." (Jn 13:34). Pp. 101–36 in *Christian Morality: Biblical Foundations.* Notre Dame.

Harrisville, R. A. 1955. The Concept of Newness in the New Testament. *JBL* 74: 69–79.

———. 1960. *The Concept of Newness in the New Testament.* Minneapolis.

Raymond F. Collins

NEW COMMANDMENT.

In the Johannine literature a new commandment *(entolē kainē)* is mentioned four times (John 13:34; 1 John 2:7, 8; 2 John 5). John's new commandment of love is of a somewhat different order from the Synoptics' teaching on love, where the focus is on the significance of the law (Matt 5:43–47; 22:39; Mark 12:31; Luke 6:27–28, 32–35; 10:27–37).

Within the Johannine gospel the new commandment is presented as a gift of the departing Jesus to his disciples. As such, it is one of the great realities of salvation given by Jesus, along with the Spirit, the bread of life, living water, eternal life, peace, glory, the word of God, and the power to become children of God. The specificity of the new commandment of love is to be found in its object ("one another," that is, the members of the community) and its christological reference ("as I have loved you"): Jesus is the model, ground, and means of the disciples' love for one another.

The Johannine love commandment is a new commandment because of this christological reference: a new and definitive era of salvation has been inaugurated with the presence of Jesus. A manifestation of this new era is to be found in the love the disciples have for one another, a love which participates in the Father's love for his Son ("*as* I have loved you," cf. John 3:35; 5:20). For John, the new commandment is constitutive of the Church insofar as the disciples of Jesus are recognizable by their mutual love (John 13:35) and insofar as their mutual love binds them together as a community.

The description of the love commandment as a *new* commandment apparently became problematic when the Johannine community was troubled by gnosticizing elements which reveled in a new Christian experience at the expense of Christian tradition. The tension of the situation led the author(s) of 1–2 John to affirm that the new commandment was, in fact, the old commandment. That is, the love commandment had not only been taught in the baptismal catechesis of the Johannine community, it had also been part of the Gospel proclamation from the very outset.

Bibliography

Collins, R. F. 1986. "A New Commandment I Give to You, That You Love One Another . . ." (Jn 13:34). Pp. 101–36 in *Christian Morality: Biblical Foundations.* Notre Dame.

Furnish, V. P. 1972. *The Love Command in the New Testament.* Nashville.

Nereparampil, L. 1983. "A New Commandment I Give You": Johannine Understanding of Love. *Jeev* 13: 104–14.

Raymond F. Collins

NEW COVENANT

[Heb *bĕrît ḥădāšâ*]. A phrase appearing in Jer 31:31, and only there in the OT, which denotes the basis on which a future relationship between God and his people will rest following the collapse of the Mosaic covenant and Israel's loss of nationhood in 587 B.C. This new relationship, which God himself will create, is anticipated in other terms by Jeremiah and also by Ezekiel, Second Isaiah, and Malachi. The new covenant forms the centerpiece of a larger eschatological hope which includes a new act of salvation, a new Zion, and a new Davidic king. The belief in a new covenant existed among the Essenes of Qumran, but it was the Christian Church that laid real claim to Jeremiah's promise, establishing the new covenant finally as its charter of faith. In the NT the phrase "new covenant" appears in Luke 22:20, in Paul's Corinthian correspondence (1 Cor 11:25; 2 Cor 3:6), and in the Letter to the Hebrews (Heb 8:8, 13; 9:15; "fresh covenant" in 12:24). See also COVENANT.

A. Old Testament
B. Literature of Judaism Including Qumran
C. New Testament
D. Patristic Literature to A.D. 325

A. Old Testament

The new covenant prophecy in Jer 31:31–34 is one of four brief eschatological utterances that conclude an earlier edition of Jeremiah's Book of Comfort (chaps. 30–31). A rhetorical structure calls attention to the eschatological nature of these utterances ("Behold the days are coming" in 31:27, 31, 38; cf. 30:3), and indicates that the promised future will contain both continuity and discontinuity with the past (*ʿôd*, "again" in 31:23, 39; and *lōʾ . . . ʿôd*, "not . . . again" in 31:29, 34a, 34b, 40; cf. Lundbom 1975: 32–36). Discontinuity gets the accent in the new covenant passages. Whereas the *tôrâ* remains in the new covenant and the obligation to comply with its demands still exists, conditions for compliance are vastly improved because Yahweh promises to write his *tôrâ* on the human heart.

Scholars have considered two major questions when discussing the concept of a "new" covenant: (1) whether this covenant really is "new," and (2) whether the Mosaic covenant over against which the new covenant is compared continues to be viable. Zimmerli (1965: 80) believes that Jeremiah announces the end of the Mosaic covenant. Von Rad (*ROTT*, 212–13) agrees that the old covenant really was broken; nevertheless, the revelation it contained was not nullified in whole or in part; so far as content goes, the new covenant also neither alters nor expands the old. What may certainly be said is that for Jeremiah the gulf between the new covenant and the old is greater than for any who preceded him. The new covenant will be more than a renewed Mosaic covenant, such as those formalized in the plains of Moab (Deut 5:2–3; 28:69 [—Eng 29:1]), at Shechem (Joshua 24), or in Jerusalem at the climax of the Josianic Reform (2 Kings 23). It is a really "new" covenant, one that marks a new beginning in divine-human relationships and one which is grounded in a wholly new act of divine grace, i.e., the forgiveness of sins (Jer 31:34; cf. Ezek 36:25–28).

The forgiveness of sins did not undergird the Mosaic covenant, in fact it played no part at all in that covenant's understanding—either in the earliest formulation or in the formulation appearing in Deuteronomy. The act of divine grace undergirding the Mosaic covenant was the deliverance from Egypt (Exod 20:2; Deut 5:6). In Deuteronomy the nation is promised life if it obeys the covenant; if it does not obey, Yahweh will rain down a multitude of curses, the most serious of which will be the loss of the land. The essential Deuteronomy (i.e., chaps. 1–28) makes no provision for a restored divine-human relationship once the covenant is broken and the curses have fallen (4:29–31 is exilic or postexilic). Disobedience is simply not the problem for Deuteronomy that it is for Jeremiah and Ezekiel (*ROTT*, 270). Deuteronomic theology is best summed up in Joshua's words to the people at Shechem: If you disobey the covenant Yahweh will *not* forgive your sins; instead he will punish you (Josh 24:19–20). A later theology concludes the Holiness Code in Leviticus 26. There, provisions are made for the forgiveness of sins, after which Yahweh says he will begin again with Israel on the basis of his covenant with Abraham (Isaac and Jacob) and his remembrance of the land (Lev 26:40–45).

The new covenant is new because Yahweh's *tôrâ* will be written on the human heart. The Sinai covenant was written on tablets of stone (Exod 24:12; 31:18; *et passim*). In the homiletical rhetoric of Deuteronomy, however, the *tôrâ* was supposed to find its way into the human heart (Deut 6:6; 11:18). But Deuteronomy knows—as does Jeremiah—that the heart is deceitful and layered with evil (Deut 10:16; 11:16; Jer 4:4). Jeremiah is the more negative in assessing the human condition. He says sin is "engraved" on the tablet of the heart (17:1), that the heart is "deceitful above all things" (17:9). In addition he believes the people have not the ability within themselves to make their relationship with God right again (e.g., 2:25; 13:23; cf. *ROTT*, 216–17). In any case, prior "heart talk" in Deuteronomy and Jeremiah is background for and determines the articulation of the new covenant promise. Jeremiah on another occasion says that Yahweh will give Israel a (new) heart (24:7). Ezekiel expects for Israel a new heart and a new spirit (Ezek 11:19; 36:26); both they were to acquire for themselves (18:31), a demand of course incapable of fulfillment.

According to ancient Hebrew thought, the "will" took up residence within the heart (Johnson 1949: 79). So if the *tôrâ* is written on the human heart, people will have the will to obey it; moreover, they will no longer have to admonish one another to "know Yahweh," for everyone will know him (Jer 31:34). Knowing Yahweh here and elsewhere requires the expanded meaning of "knowing and doing the *tôrâ*" (Hos 4:1–2; Jer 5:4–5). In Deuteronomy the people must continually be told, "Be careful to do (the commands)" (5:1, 32; 6:3, 25; etc.), "Take heed . . . lest you forget the covenant/Yahweh" (4:23; 6:12; 8:11; etc.). The liturgical injunctions in 6:6–9 and 11:18–20 admonish them to keep Yahweh's words in their hearts as well as in other more conspicuous places. In the end, however, admonitions such as these and more from the prophets were made to no avail. Disobedience exceeded all limits and the Mosaic covenant was undone.

In Jer 32:37–41, which is a parallel passage to 31:31–34 (*ROTT*, 214), the covenant of the future is described as an "everlasting covenant" (*bĕrît ʿôlām*). The term "everlasting covenant" appears also in Jer 50:5. Previously, only the unconditional covenants given to Noah, Abraham, Phinehas, and David (Freedman 1964; *TDOT* 2: 270–72), along with a few lesser ones, were taken to be everlasting. Unconditional covenants were at home in southern theology, i.e., in P traditions (Gen 9:16; 17:7, 13, 19; Exod 31:16; Lev 24:8; Num 18:19; 25:13) and psalms from the Jerusalem temple (Pss 89:20–38—Eng 89:19–37; 111:5, 9; cf. 2 Sam 23:5). At some point before the Exile, the covenants to Abraham and David were expanded so as to cover Jerusalem and the temple (Isa 37:33–35 = 2 Kgs 19:32–34; Pss 105:8–11 = 1 Chr 16:15–18; 132:11–18; cf. Isa 31:4–5; Jer 7:1–15). Ezekiel and Second Isaiah look forward to an everlasting covenant between Yahweh and the nation (Ezek 16:60; Isa 55:3; 61:8) which they describe elsewhere as a covenant of "peace" (Ezek 34:25; 37:26; Isa 54:10) or one in which Yahweh's Spirit will indwell the people (Ezek 36:27–28; Isa 59:21). These varied descriptions of the future covenant were part of the larger messianic hope taking shape at that time. The servant figure of Second Isaiah will personally embody the new covenant (Isa 42:6; 49:8), and through this servant other nations will be brought into covenant relation (Isa 55:1–5; Muilenburg, *IB* 5: 405). One finds a universalism in Second Isaiah not existing in Ezekiel. Malachi's "messenger of the covenant," finally, is cast as a priestly figure (Mal 3:1; cf. 2:1–9).

B. Literature of Judaism Including Qumran

In postexilic Judaism the covenant idea contains all the ambiguity characterizing the larger eschatological hope generally. National life has been reconstructed along the old lines, which is to say the Mosaic covenant is again central and the Law (Torah) occupies a position of supremacy. In Nehemiah 9–10 a "faith covenant" (*ʾămānâ* in 10:1—Eng 9:38) is made to walk according to Yahweh's *tôrâ* given through Moses. Ezra prays that the people will thereby return to the "faithful heart" of Abraham (9:7–8). At the same time a new covenant is looked for in the future, at which time the Messianic Age will dawn. Bar 2:35 speaks of an everlasting covenant which will secure Israel's tenure in the land. In *Jubilees,* where the Law has eternal validity and the Messianic Age is thought to have already begun, an everlasting covenant is described in which the people on their part will confess sin, and God on his part will create a holy spirit in the people and will cleanse them (*Jub.* 1:22–24).

Among the Essenes at Qumran the new covenant finds fulfillment in a separated community *(yḥd)* which believes it is living in the "last days." This community has important similarities to the early Church. Members of the Qumran community swore an oath to uphold a covenant variously described as a "covenant of God," an "everlasting covenant," a "covenant of repentance," a "covenant of steadfast love" *(ḥsd),* and a "new covenant." The Essene covenant theology is contained in two sectarian documents found among the Dead Sea Scrolls: the *Manual of Discipline* (1QS), and the *Damascus Document* (CD) which also goes by the name of the Zadokite Document. The latter was known before the Dead Sea discoveries, two fragmentary medieval codices having been found in the genizah of the Cairo Synagogue in 1896. These were published in 1910 (*APOT* 2: 785–834; Rabin 1958). The *Damascus Document* contains three references to a "new covenant" which people have entered into "in the land of Damascus," a cryptonym for their place of exile in the Qumran desert (cf. Amos 5:26–27). The "new covenant" references are 6:19; 8:21 = 19:33/34; and 20:12 in Rabin (also Gaster 1976), and 8:15; 9:28, 37 in *APOT* 2. Seven mss of the *Damascus Document* were found in Cave 4, some tiny fragments also in Caves 5 and 6 (Cross 1961: 82; *IDBSup,* 210). Of these only the Cave 6 fragments have been published. See DEAD SEA SCROLLS. Also in the *Pesher on Habakkuk* found at Qumran (1QpHab) there may originally have been a reference to the "new covenant" in 2:3; however, the MS has a lacuna where scholars think "covenant" once stood, leaving the reading uncertain and opinions about it divided.

The Essene Jews who separated themselves from the rest of Judaism and relocated in the Qumran desert did so in order to be reborn as the New Israel. According to Cross (1961: 80) the word "community" *(yḥd)* as used in the *Manual of Discipline* is eschatological, i.e., it means "Israel of the New Covenant." People entering this new covenant were required to return to a serious study of the Mosaic Law; required also of each member was strict obedience to the Law's demands as understood in light of interpretations given by the priestly hierarchy. At the top of this hierarchy was the Teacher of Righteousness, the original leader of the sect, and also the author, perhaps, of the *Manual of Discipline.* The *Damascus Document* is from a later period after the Teacher's death (Cross 1961: 121). The community bore an unmistakable stamp of legalism; nevertheless that legalism was informed by the prophets whose great legacy at Qumran was the conviction that sin lay deep within each human soul and only through repentance and purification was a restored relationship with God possible. The *Damascus Document* in 19:16 (*APOT* 2:9.15B) called the Qumran covenant a "covenant of repentance" *(bryt hšwbh).* Repentance had to precede purification, which was accomplished in the initiatory baptismal rite (Black 1961: 94).

This new covenant was to be everlasting. Whatever else this signified, it at least meant that anyone entering the covenant was expected to remain within it for life (1QS 3:11–12). The covenant was renewed annually, at which time all members underwent evaluation. This covenant had its obligations, and like the Mosaic covenant, these obligations were fortified with blessings and curses (1QS 2:1–18). The *Manual* reads much like Deuteronomy. The main difference between the two is that in the *Manual* the older corporate sense is gone; the blessings and curses, for example, fall now upon individuals. The *Manual* does not foresee any abrogation of the covenant as a whole nor does it imagine the noncompliance might lead to the whole community being destroyed. The same can also be said of the Church (cf. C below). On the other hand, the individual responsibility presupposed in the *Manual* appears not to result from any inner motivation, at least not the sort Jeremiah envisioned in his new covenant prophecy. God is said to have placed a holy spirit in the people of Qumran (1QS 3:7), but they still need admonitions to obey, as both the *Manual* and the *Damascus Document* make clear.

The new covenant idea undergoes no further development in Judaism. The Midrashim contain merely a few citations of Jer 31:33 for purposes of focusing on the old problem of remembering the Torah. *Midr. Cant.* 8:14 interprets the phrase about God writing the Torah on people's hearts to mean that God recalls for the people what they themselves have forgotten and what has led them into error. More often in the midrashic literature, the Jeremiah verse is given a meaning closer to the one it had originally: that forgetting the Torah can be expected in the Present World, and only in the World to Come, when the Torah is (truly) written on the heart, will people no longer forget it (*Midr. Qoh* 2:1; *Midr. Cant.* 1:2; *Midr. Pesiq.* 107a; *Midr. Yal.* on Jer 31:33; cf. Str.-B. 3: 89–90, 704).

C. New Testament

The Christian Church, from earliest times, claimed the promise of Jer 31:31–34 and understood itself to be the people of the new covenant. It also thought of itself as a new people (1 Pet 2:1–10): Israel reborn, but a more inclusive Israel to which gentiles now belong. It comes as somewhat of a surprise then to find so little said in the NT about a new covenant. G. E. Wright (1971: 986) attributes the paucity of references to legalistic connotations which the term "covenant" had in the NT period. He says "covenant" had come to mean almost exclusively obedience to the law; for this reason NT writers were uncomfortable with the term, using it only to point out that in Christ the covenant was not law but faith or life in the Spirit. NT rhetoric at this point contrasts sharply with Jewish rhetoric and rhetoric found in the Essene sectarian documents from Qumran.

The words "new covenant" are placed on the lips of Jesus only in the longer text of Luke 22:20, where, at the

Last Supper Jesus passes the wine and says, "This cup . . . is the new covenant in my blood." Scholarly opinion is divided about the originality of this reading, though the longer text does have wide support. This Lucan text, in any case, depends most likely upon 1 Cor 11:25, where Paul cites a Last Supper tradition antedating him, perhaps reflecting usage in the Antioch Church (Jeremias 1955: 127–31): "This cup is the new covenant in my blood." Mark 14:24 records Jesus' words as, "This is my blood of the covenant," a modification in the direction of Exod 24:8 (*TDNT* 2: 133; Richardson 1958: 230; cf. Heb 9:20). Matt 28:26 adds "for the forgiveness of sins," which is new covenant language from Jer 31:34 (Dodd 1953: 45). In some ancient mss both the Mark and Matthew texts have the word "new" added. Some form-critics conclude that neither "new" nor "covenant" was spoken by Jesus (*BTNT* 146; Jeremias 1955: 110–15), which is to say the Last Supper liturgy was originally more brief and in each of the synoptic passages has undergone expansion. Even in its most radical reconstruction, the Last Supper liturgy clearly conveys the idea that Jesus' death, or his shedding of blood, seals the new covenant which God now makes with humankind. Sacrificial terminology from Exod 24:3–8, all but absent in the Prophets (but see Zech 9:11), has come to dominate the covenant idea where it takes on fresh new meaning.

Paul refers to himself and the Corinthian laity as "ministers of a new covenant" (2 Cor 3:6) where Jer 31:31–34 appears to be in the back of his mind. This covenant has found expression in the *hearts* of the Corinthians, wherein the "Spirit of the living God" resides (vv 2–3). It therefore contrasts with the "old covenant" of Moses (vv 14–15) which was written on stone (v 3).

Paul might have said more about the new covenant were it not for his concern to establish a more ancient base than Jer 31:31–34 for the new faith in Christ. The important promise for Paul is the one given to Abraham, that through him all the families of the earth would be blessed. Paul grounds the blessings through Christ in the Abrahamic covenant so they may apply equally to Jews and gentiles (Gal 3:14). Paul must short-circuit the Mosaic covenant if he is to realize his goal of evangelizing the gentiles, for the Mosaic covenant was made only with Israel (cf. Rom 9:4; Eph 2:11–13). Moreover, the Mosaic covenant contains the law which is now a burden to everybody—Jew and gentile. In Paul's view the law only brings people under its curses. But Christ, by dying on the cross, becomes himself a curse which redeems those under the law who have faith in him (Gal 3:10–14). The new covenant, therefore, contains only blessings which makes it just like the Abrahamic covenant. The Mosaic covenant serves Paul only for the purpose of making a contrast with the Abrahamic covenant. In his allegory in Gal 4:21–31, Paul sees the Abrahamic covenant (fulfilled through Sarah) leading to freedom, sonship, and the Jerusalem above; the covenant made at Sinai (called Hagar) leads to present Jerusalem, i.e., the Jews and Judaizers, and thus slavery.

As a Christian, Paul has a major problem knowing what to do with the law (Torah). The law is supposed to belong to the new covenant, but the coming of Christ has eclipsed the law. Paul resolves this problem to some extent by adopting a developmental attitude toward the covenants. Among the former covenants the Abrahamic covenant is primary, and it was not annulled by the Mosaic covenant which came later (Gal 3:17). Paul exploits the dual meaning of *diathēkē* as "covenant" and "will" (or "testament") in Gal 3:15–18 in order to make this point. The Mosaic covenant, when originally given, was accompanied with great splendor, though it was a splendor that faded (cf. Exod 34:29–35); now there is no splendor at all associated with the Mosaic covenant because of the surpassing splendor of Christ, whose new covenant is eternal (2 Cor 3:7–11). Paul also betrays a developmental attitude toward the covenants when he views the Mosaic law as a schoolmaster that must discipline a people not yet mature (Gal 3:23–24). With the coming of Christ, however, those having faith are no longer subject to their former schoolmaster (vv 25–26). In Romans, Paul says Christians are discharged from the law (Rom 7:6), that Christ is the end of the law (10:4). Yet Paul does not want to dispense with the law; in fact, he claims to uphold it (3:31). His other statements, however, distance him irrevocably from Judaism, for whom the law is central and eternally binding. For Paul, Christ is central, and the new covenant written by his life-giving Spirit surpasses all other covenants and is eternal.

Paul's law and grace dichotomy (Rom 6:14) stems from the lack of a typology in his thinking between the new covenant in Christ and the Mosaic covenant. Were such a typology made, Paul would have to concede that the Mosaic covenant/law had its own accompanying act of divine grace, which was the Exodus from Egypt.

Paul's views on sin and reconciliation in Romans lack covenant language *per se,* nevertheless they rest almost certainly on broad-based assumptions about the new covenant which existed in the early Church. According to Paul's gospel both Jew and gentile are under the power of sin, both stand in need of forgiveness, and both are reconciled to God by Jesus' death on the cross. In Ephesians too (whether or not it is Pauline) the blood of Christ is said to bring gentiles near to God, even though formerly they were strangers to the covenants of promise (Eph 2:12–13).

In Rom 2:14–15 Paul seeks parity between Jew and gentile by stating that upright gentiles not possessing the Jewish law show nevertheless "that what the law requires is written on their hearts." Such people also possess a "conscience" *(syneidēsis).* The first remark about a law-equivalent "written on the heart" appears to be a borrowing from Jer 31:33 (cf. Str.-B. 3: 89–90); the following remark about a "conscience that bears witness" derives most likely from Stoic or Jewish-Hellenistic philosophy. Paul's precise understanding of how the new covenant manifests itself among the gentiles is by no means transparent in these verses, but one should note that his thinking nevertheless runs parallel to Jeremiah's new covenant passage where the promise of a law written on the heart is followed by the promise of a new inner motivation to know and do the law (Jer 31:34).

In Rom 11:25–32 the new covenant prophecy is given a most extraordinary interpretation, unlike any other in the NT and certainly unlike any made subsequently by the Church Fathers. Elsewhere the referent for the new covenant is the Church, who is the New Israel; here the referent is the Israel that remains hardened to the gospel (Dodd *Romans* MNTC, 182). Paul says that at some future time, when the full number of gentiles have come in and the Parousia of Jesus occurs, *all* Israel will be saved. Isa 59:20 is quoted in support of the Parousia (v 26); next comes the new covenant prophecy: "And this will be my covenant with them, when I will take away their sins" (v 27). The OT passage or passages here quoted cannot be identified with certainty. The first part of v 27, "And this will be my covenant with them," is thought to be a continuation of the previous quotation of Isa 59:20 into v 21a. The second part of the verse, however, "when I take away their sins," has to be from somewhere else. Some suggest this phrase comes from Isa 27:9b, which in the LXX compares nicely, except for the singular "his sin." The plural "their sins" concludes the new covenant passage of Jeremiah (LXX 38:34), where also in v 33 the beginning words are "For this is the covenant." Paul could then be giving a freely rendered abridgment of Jer 31:33–34 (Dodd *Romans* MNTC, 182). An abridgment of this same Jeremiah passage is found in Heb 10:16–17. Regardless of what precise passages make up this florilegium, Paul gives the new covenant promise its most inclusive meaning possible: he believes this covenant really is for everyone.

Paul's lack of a typology between the Mosaic covenant and the new covenant in Christ is compensated for, to some extent, by theology embedded in Matthew and John's gospels. Indirectly, and in different ways, some scholars suggest that both gospel writers draw a parallel between Jesus and Moses. Matthew depicts Jesus as the "new Moses" leading a "new Exodus"; the Sermon on the Mount is Jesus' "new Torah" (Davies 1969: 10–32). Although the new Torah is significantly less burdensome than the old (Matt 11:28–30), no antithesis is intended between the two; the new comes to complete the old (5:17). Matthew does, however, intend an antithesis between the new people of God and the old. Jesus pronounces his "blessings" on the new torah (5:3–11); but on the old he pronounces "woes" (23:13–36). These blessings and woes are structurally balanced in the gospel and most likely constitute an adaptation of the old covenant form found in Deuteronomy (Deut 11:26–32; 28). The language, however, is toned down by Matthew. The words *makarioi* (blessed) and *ouai* (woe) translate the Hebrew *ʾašrê* and *hôy,* both less strong than the covenant words *bārûk* (blessed) and *ʾārûr* (cursed). Jesus does not go so far as to curse the scribes and the Pharisees. Also, with the blessings and woes spoken to different audiences, the new people of God receive neither woes nor curses, only blessings. This amounts to Matthew saying that there can be no abrogation of the new covenant and no destruction of the Church (Matt 16:18).

John in a different way presents Jesus as a "new Moses" (Glasson 1963). But for this gospel writer Jesus gives no new Torah, unless one identifies such in the new commandment to "love one another" (John 13:34). Jesus himself is the Logos. John therefore makes a law/grace dichotomy similar to Paul's: "For the law was given through Moses, grace and truth came through Jesus Christ" (1:17). The Holy Spirit is John's answer to the new inner motivation required to know and do the Torah. He dwells within the believer (14:17) and in Jesus' absence will bring his teachings (torah) to remembrance (14:26). He will also convince the rest of the world of sin, righteousness, and judgment (16:7–11).

In the letter to the Hebrews the new covenant is given its most prominent place in the NT. The new covenant passage from Jeremiah is quoted twice, once in its entirety (8:8–12) and once in abridged form (10:16–17).

For this NT writer, Christ is the great high priest of the heavenly sanctuary (7:26), one who has "obtained a ministry which is as much more excellent than the old as the covenant he mediates is better, since it is enacted on better promises" (8:6). The Mosaic covenant, which is here called the first covenant, was shown to be faulty because people under it turned up faulty (8:7–8a). Reference here is presumably being made to the first covenant's provisions for noncompliance, i.e., the curses. The new covenant prophesied by Jeremiah has better promises: it contains God's unconditional commitment to forgive sins; it is eternal (9:15; 13:20); and Jesus is the covenant's surety (7:22). According to Hebrews, Jeremiah in announcing this new covenant treats the Mosaic covenant as obsolete. That obsolescence is just now being seen as the first covenant is ready to vanish away (8:13).

Jesus is the "mediator of the new covenant" (9:15; "better covenant" in 8:6; "fresh covenant" in 12:24; cf. 1 Tim 2:5–6; Isa 42:6; 49:8). In Judaism the covenant mediator was Moses (cf. Gal 3:19) and after his death the high priest (Richardson 1958: 229). Jesus becomes mediator of the new covenant by virtue of his death on the cross, which the author of Hebrews explains in priestly and sacrificial categories understood within Judaism (9:1–14). Special appropriation is made of the Day of Atonement ritual (Leviticus 16). As the high priest who enters once and once only the Holy Place with his own sacrificial blood, Jesus secures for God's elect their eternal redemption (9:11–12, 24–28; cf. 7:27). This death purifies human consciences (9:14; 10:22; cf. Rom 2:15), something not possible with the earlier sacrifices (9:9).

The Holy Place—or Heavenly Sanctuary (9:24)—is for the elect also the Promised Land of rest and inheritance (4:9–11; 9:15). In raising the subject of inheritance the author of Hebrews uses both meanings of *diathēkē:* "covenant" and "will" (9:15–22; cf. Gal 3:15–18). A will does not take effect until the death of the one who makes it, i.e., the testator. Jesus is therefore the testator of the new covenant. At his death the elect receive their inheritance, which is redemption from transgressions under the first covenant. The blood performs the same function of ratification in the new covenant as it did in the old (9:18–21; cf. Exod 24:6–8). The author echoes a common Rabbinic theme when he says that without the shedding of blood there is no forgiveness of sins, or no atonement with God (9:22; cf. Lev 17:11).

In the abridged quotation from Jeremiah in 10:16–18, the accent is on the concluding words of the new covenant promise which state that God will no longer remember the peoples' sins. Earlier in chap. 10 the author maintained that yearly sacrifices on the Day of Atonement—as well as daily sin offerings—were ineffectual because they had to be repeated. Jewish teachers would find such an argument unconvincing; indeed it is flatly contradicted in *Jub.* 5:17–18. Nevertheless, for this writer Jesus makes the single offering of his body, which for all time perfects the sanctified elect (10:10, 14). Once the forgiveness of sins is granted, there is no longer any sin offering which can be made (10:18, 26).

The "once for all" view of Jesus' sacrifice is matched in Hebrews with a "once for all" view of repentance, enlightenment (baptism), and sanctification of the believer. If one deliberately sins after coming to a knowledge of the truth, that person profanes the blood of the new covenant and has only God's vengeance to look forward to (10:26–31). This exaggerated view of Christian sanctification has the effect of recasting the new covenant in terms of the old, and it also qualifies the "blessings only" promise made to the Church. Although curses are not explicitly placed on individuals who lapse under the new covenant, they are implied (6:1–8; 10:26–31). The idea that deliberate sin makes a sin offering inefficacious is found in Num 15:30–31 (*t. Yoma* 8:9 applies the same principle to the Day of Atonement ritual; cf. Buchanan *Hebrews* AB, 144). But in a closing benediction the author of Hebrews prays that the Lord Jesus, "by the blood of the eternal covenant," will equip the elect to do God's will (13:20–21).

D. Patristic Literature to A.D. 325

The Church of the 2d and 3d centuries carried on its polemic against two major opponents, one external to the Church, the other internal. The external opponent was the Jews from whom an all-gentile Church had now been completely cut off. The Fathers saw the Jews as a rejected people, one which the Church had supplanted in God's economy of salvation. Against the Jews they contrasted the new and old covenants, or the new and old "laws," if topics such as circumcision happened to be at issue (Tert. *Adv. Judaeos* 3). By the end of the 2d century the phrase "New Testament" (= "New Covenant") was the name given to the Gospels and other apostolic writings which the Church took to be Scripture (Iren. *haer.* 4.15.2). The Hebrew Scriptures were called the "Old Testament" (Melito of Sardis fr. 4; Iren. *haer.* 4.15.2), a designation found already in 2 Cor 3:14 where Paul alludes to the *reading* of the "Old Covenant" in the synagogue.

The internal threat to the Church was heresy, above all Gnosticism which peaked in the mid-2d century. The most serious aberration of Christian thought to impact covenant understanding came from Marcion (A.D. 100–160), a gnostic in the minds of some, but for others one who merely had affinities with Gnosticism. Marcion wanted to cut off Christianity from Judaism—completely and for all time. Against Marcion, and others such as Valentinus, who was a true gnostic, the Fathers fought to preserve Christianity's Jewish roots, arguing that the God of the NT was not distinct from the God of the OT, that the Holy Spirit in the NT was the same Holy Spirit found in the OT, and that NT Scripture itself was inextricably bound to OT Scripture—indeed it was a fulfillment of it. Gnostics minimized the historical foundations of Christianity; they were more concerned with creation than covenant, which explains perhaps the noticeable absence of discussion about the covenant in Gnostic treatises, including the horde of texts recently found at Nag Hammadi. In a rare quote of the words of Institution for the wine in *Pistis Sophia* (4.141), the wine and/or blood—along with fire and water—are mysteries which have the ability to purify sin (Schmidt 1978: 366–69).

The Fathers explained the rejection of the Jews by citing the "calf incident" in the wilderness at which time the Mosaic covenant was promulgated (*Ep. Barn.* 4: 14; Iren. *haer.* 4.15.2; Tert. *Adv. Judaeos* 3; cf. Exodus 32). Origen (*Cels.* 74–75) typed the Jews on the basis of this incident, i.e., the incident explained how it happened that the Jews rejected Jesus.

The *Epistle of Barnabas* does not mention the new covenant, but rather "the new law of our Lord Jesus Christ," which contrasts with the older law of sacrifice in that it is "without the yoke of necessity" (*Ep. Barn.* 2 [*PG* 2: 729–30]). The Christian has forgiveness from sins through Jesus' blood (chap. 5). For Barnabas there was only one covenant, received by Moses, but immediately lost due to the sin of the calf. In reality, Israel never had a covenant with God. Christians are heirs to this one covenant through Christ in whom it is sealed upon their hearts. Barnabas thus argues that the one covenant cannot belong to both Jews and Christians (*Ep. Barn.* 4; 13–14; cf. *BTNT*, 98, 110–11). Promises of a future covenant cited from the OT are Ezek 11:19; 36:26 (chap. 6) and Isa 42:6–7 (chap. 14).

Justin Martyr in his *Dialogue with Trypho the Jew* recognizes two laws or covenants (*dial.* 10–12, 67, 118, 122–23). The old through Moses has been abrogated and remains only for the Jews, although Justin asks rhetorically if even this is so since the Jews do not believe their own Scriptures (*Dial.* 29). The new law and covenant through Christ in any case replaces the old; it does not require circumcision along with other lesser observances, and it is final, eternal, and universal in scope (*dial.* 11). Jer 31:31–32 and Isa 51:4–5 point to Christ as the new law and covenant, also to Christians who are the true spiritual Israel (*Dial.* 11; cf. 123). Isa 42:6–7 likewise points to Christ, and its promise of a covenant which will be a "light to the nations" finds fulfillment in illumined gentiles, who under the new covenant are the true proselytes (*dial.* 122).

Irenaeus (*haer.* 4.15.1) says that when the Israelites made the calf they decided in favor of slavery. This did not cut them off from God, but it did subject them to a state of servitude for the future (cf. Gal. 4:21–31). Stephen in Acts 7:38a–43a referred to the calf incident and God's decision to give up the Jews to slavery, and is cited (40.15.1). The old covenant, under which the Jews lived until the coming of Christ, is law; the new covenant under which Christians live, promised in Jer 31:31–32 and Ezek 11:19; 36:26 (4.33.14) and not fulfilled by Zerubbabel when temple worship was restored after the Exile (4.34.4), is gospel, or a "covenant of liberty" (4.9.1–2; 16.5; 33.14; 34.3–4). It was fulfilled in Christ. Both old and new covenants were prefigured in Abraham (4.25.1, 3). The older law predicted the new covenant, which in turn became a fulfillment of it (4.34.2). The new covenant also canceled the old covenant (4.16.5). Irenaeus reflects the typological thinking of Hebrews when he says the old covenant was a *type* of heavenly things—things now existing in the Church (4.32.2). The Bishop of Lyons, however, was also capable of process thinking. In his view divine grace multiplies over time and Christian living is a process of maturation. God's new covenant of liberty bestowed more grace than the old covenant of bondage. Then, as the Christian's love toward God increases, God bestows more and greater gifts

(4.9.2–3). Life under the new covenant also calls for greater faith, which means a higher quality of living (4.16.5; 28.2). Since the new covenant grants real liberty, the Christian is more significantly tested in doing what God requires (4.16.5).

Tertullian cites the new covenant promise of Jeremiah to show the Jews that circumcision is replaced by a new law unlike any previously given (*Adv. Judaeos* 3). The old law made customary the *lex talionis;* the new urges mercy and converts one to peace (cf. Iren. *haer.* 4.34.4 on the new covenant bringing peace). Gentiles are admitted under this new law. In fact, a curious reversal has taken place: the Jews, who were known by God and made the recipients of his many benefits, forgot him and turned to idolatry, i.e., the calf; the gentiles originally did not know God, nevertheless they forsook their idols and converted to him by accepting the new law in Christ. Jer 31:31–32 is quoted against Marcionism to show that the old covenant was only temporary, since it needed changing. Isa 55:3 promises in addition that the old covenant will be replaced by an eternal covenant which will run its course in Christ (*adv. Marc.* 4.1; cf. Just. *dial.* 12; 118 on the new covenant as an eternal covenant).

Clement of Alexandria, who was a Christian philosopher, saw in Jer 31:33–34 an indication that God had implanted his heavenly teaching, or laws, into human minds and hearts. These laws enable all people to know him and to be the recipients of his grace (*Protr.* 11 [*PG* 8, 233–34]). Clement says the old covenant disciplined people with fear, but in the new covenant fear is turned into love (*paed.* 1.7 [*PG* 8: 321–22]; cf. Just. *dial.* 67 who says the new covenant no longer builds on "fear and trembling"). Clement does recognize that the law given through Moses was an ancient grace, but it was only temporary; eternal grace and truth came through Jesus Christ.

Origen (*c. Cels.* 74–75) says the Jews fashioned the calf because they did not believe the marvels of Egypt, the Sea, and the Wilderness. In keeping with their character of disbelief they refused to accept the coming of Jesus and the "second covenant," which were equally marvelous. Christian preachers, says Origen, like the Apostles are to be "ministers of the new covenant" (2 Cor 3:6), i.e., messengers who ascend high mountains by preaching good news to the poor (*comm. in Jo.* 1.11; cf. Isa 52:6–7; 40:9). Paul was a "minister of the new covenant," distinguished not by voluminous writings but by the preaching he did under the power of the Spirit (*comm. in Jo.* 5.3; cf. Rom 15:19). Origen therefore wonders if he himself will qualify as a "minister of the new covenant" with all the writing he is doing (*comm. in Jo.* 5.4).

Lactantius (*Div. Inst.* 4.20) reiterates themes developed by the earlier Fathers. Jer 31:31–32 shows that Jews are disinherited and that Christians—thanks to the death of Jesus—are now heirs to the kingdom. The "House of Judah" in v 31 refers to those called out from among the gentiles. There are two testaments: the old, which is used by the Jews, and the new, which is used by Christians. The new fulfills the old and is more complete than the old. As a result of being adopted under the new covenant, the gentiles are freed from their chains and brought into the light of wisdom (Isa 42:6–7).

Against Marcion and others, the Fathers argued that although there were two covenants (and two peoples), there was but one God (Iren. *haer.* 4.9, 15, 32–33; Tert. *adv. Marc.* 1.20; 4.1; Or. *comm. in Jo.* 1.14). Clement of Alexandria argued against the Valentinians that the Holy Spirit operating in the Church was the same Holy Spirit which operated in the OT (*exc. Thdot.* 24 *PG* 9, 671–72]). Irenaeus saw in both Testaments the same righteousness of God when God takes vengeance, although he believed that in the NT, vengeance was more real, more enduring, and more rigid (*haer.* 4.28.1).

The Marcionite heresy required also from the Fathers a defense of the unity of Scripture. Origen did this with eloquence. He said all the sacred writings were in fact one book (*comm. in Jo.* 5.4; *comm. in Mt.* 2.15), "one perfect and harmonized instrument of God" (*comm. in Mt.* 2.1). The OT was the beginning of the gospel of Jesus Christ; from another point of view, John the Baptist was a *type* of OT (*comm. in Jo.* 1.14–15). If Origen was the most eloquent in defending the unity of Scripture, Tertullian was the most open in acknowledging Scripture's diversity, but he said that amidst all the diversity there was still no inconsistency with one and the same God (*adv. Marc.* 4.1).

Bibliography

Black, M. 1961. *The Scrolls and Christian Origins.* New York.
Cross, F. M., Jr. 1961. *The Ancient Library of Qumran.* Rev. ed. Garden City.
Davies, W. D. 1969. *The Sermon on the Mount.* Cambridge.
Dodd, C. H. 1953. *According to the Scriptures.* New York.
Freedman, D. N. 1964. Divine Commitment and Human Obligation. *Int* 18: 3–15.
Gaster, T. H. 1976. *The Dead Sea Scriptures.* 3d rev. ed. Garden City.
Glasson, T. F. 1963. *Moses in the Fourth Gospel.* London.
Jeremias, J. 1955. *The Eucharistic Words of Jesus.* New York.
Johnson, A. R. 1949. *The Vitality of the Individual in the Thought of Ancient Israel.* Cardiff.
Lundbom, J. R. 1975. *Jeremiah: A Study in Ancient Hebrew Rhetoric.* SBLDS 18. Missoula.
Rabin, C. 1958. *The Zadokite Documents.* 2d rev. ed. Oxford.
Richardson, A. 1958. *An Introduction to the Theology of the New Testament.* New York.
Schmidt, C., ed. 1978. *Pistis Sophia.* NHS 9. Leiden.
Wright, G. E. 1971. The Theological Study of the Bible. Pp. 983–88 in *The Interpreter's One-Volume Commentary on the Bible,* ed. Charles M. Laymon. Nashville and New York.
Zimmerli, W. 1965. *The Law and the Prophets.* Trans. R. E. Clements. New York.

JACK R. LUNDBOM

NEW EARTH, NEW HEAVEN. The expression "new heaven, new earth" (Gk *ouranos kainos kai gē kainē*) is found in the preface to the vision of the new Jerusalem in Rev 21:1 (cf. 20:11). It is an element of the expectation of cosmic upheaval common to apocalyptic literature. It occurs in a partially plural form in 2 Pet 3:12 as "new heavens and a new earth." Its source is probably to be traced to Isaiah, where "new heavens and a new earth" are integral to the prophetic promise of restoration (65:17; 66:22).

It is uncertain if the new heaven and new earth in Rev 21:1 are renewed versions of earth and heaven, or replacements for them that result from the return to primeval chaos and destruction by fire. Both expectations were common to Jewish tradition (Str-B 3:843–44). The renewal tradition is exemplified by *2 Bar.* 57:2 ". . . and the belief in the coming judgment was brought about, and the hope of the world which will be renewed was built at that time . . ." (*OTP;* cf. *2 Bar.* 32:6; 2 Esdr 7:75; *Jub.* 1:29; 1 Cor 7:31; *1 Enoch* 45:3–5). The replacement tradition was adopted by the NT and the early Church and is exemplified by 2 Pet 3:10–13: ". . . the heavens will be kindled and dissolved, and the elements will melt with fire! But according to his promise we wait for new heavens and a new earth in which righteousness dwells" (RSV; cf. Matt 5:18 = Mark 13:31 = Luke 16:17; 1 John 2:17; *Did.* 10:6; *2 Clem.* 16:3; *1 Enoch* 72:1; 83:3–5; 91:15–16; cf. Ps 102:25–27). The most widely accepted interpretation of Rev 21:1 is that it is illustrative of the replacement tradition.

The major distinction between the former heaven and earth and the new heaven and earth is the absence of the sea (Rev 21:1; cf. *T. Mos.* 10:6; *Sib. Or.* 5:447). The sea may symbolize the primeval ocean out of which the first heaven and earth were made. The sea was the source of the beast (13:1) and the great harlot is seated upon many waters (17:1), and thus may symbolize incomplete sovereignty over the powers of chaos and sin. The absence of the sea in the new heaven and new earth indicates that the long awaited purging of sin from creation has been accomplished (Rom 8:18–22; Rev 21:27; 22:14–15). This is echoed in 2 Pet 3:13, where righteousness dwells in the new heavens and new earth.

Bibliography

Minear, P. S. 1962. The Cosmology of the Apocalypse. Pp. 23–37 in *Current Issues in New Testament Interpretation: Essays in Honor of Otto Piper,* ed. W. Klassen and G. F. Snyder. New York.

———. 1968. *I Saw A New Earth: An Introduction to the Visions of the Apocalypse.* Washington.

Stauffer, E. 1955. *New Testament Theology.* Trans. John Marsh. London.

Duane F. Watson

NEW GATE (PLACE) [Heb *šaʿar-yhwh heḥādāš*]. A gate of the Temple's inner or upper court that probably was located to the S of the inner court and led to the royal residences (possibly identified as the Upper Gate and/or the Gate of the Guards). It was at the New Gate that a royal judiciary came to listen to the people's complaints against Jeremiah's prophecy concerning the ruin of Jerusalem and the Temple (Jer 26:10). It was also from the New Gate that Baruch (Jeremiah's scribe) read the prophecies of Jeremiah (36:10), whose words were subsequently read before King Jehoiakim (36:20–26). In close proximity to the New Gate was the chamber of Gemariah, the son of Shaphan the scribe, whose family distinguished themselves in their reverence for the Torah and in their support of Jeremiah (2 Kgs 22:3–20; 2 Chr 34:8–20; Jer 26:24; 29:3; 36:10, 25).

For a time (at least until the reign of Jehoiakim, 597 B.C.E.), the New Gate was so called as it was probably the Upper Gate rebuilt by Jotham (758–743 B.C.E., 2 Kgs 15:35; 2 Chr 27:3), possibly in response to his father's unauthorized intrusion into the Temple (2 Chr 26:16–21; 27:2).

Dale C. Liid

NEW JERUSALEM [Gk *Ierousalēm kainē*]. This expression is found in the Bible only in Rev 3:12 and 21:2. The vision of the New Jerusalem begins in 21:2 with the announcement that it is coming down from heaven to unite the new heaven and the new earth. The New Jerusalem refers to the capital of the new creation in which the presence of God is with humankind (21:3). As indicated by 3:12, where the faithful of the church of Philadelphia are promised that the name of the New Jerusalem will be written upon them, the citizens of the New Jerusalem are those who have not denied Christ, and have remained faithful to his word (cf. 21:7).

The concept of the New Jerusalem derives from the OT exilic and postexilic prophetic expectation of the restoration of Jerusalem, the return of God to his Temple, and his acknowledgment by all the nations. The restoration of Jerusalem is the focus of the promises and the salvation of God (Isa 2:1–5; 49:14–18; 52; 54; 60–62; 65:17–25; Jer 31:38–40; Mic 4:1–4; Zechariah 14). The actual restoration in the Persian Period was disillusioning, and in later Jewish literature the expectation of Jerusalem restored was replaced by Jerusalem supernaturally transformed by God (Tob 13:8–18; *T. Dan* 5:12–13; *Sib. Or.* 5.420–27; *1 Enoch* 90:28–29) or a Jerusalem from heaven which would replace the earthly Jerusalem altogether (2 Esdr 7:26; 10:25–28; 13:36; *2 Bar.* 4; 32:1–4). The idea of a Jerusalem in heaven was appropriated by the NT (Gal 4:26–27; Heb 11:10; 12:22; 13:14; cf. Phil 3:20).

The OT image of the people of God as his bride is often associated with the renewal of Zion, the renewed Jerusalem (Isa 49:10; 54:1–8; 61:10; 62:4–5). The NT contains the image of the Church as the bride of Christ (Eph 5:25–33). In 2 Esdr 10:25–28, Zion, represented as a woman, is transformed into a heavenly city. In light of these images, the imagery of the bride and New Jerusalem present here in Rev 21:2, 9 (cf. 19:7–8) indicates that the New Jerusalem, while distinct from its citizens, partly symbolizes the redeemed.

The New Jerusalem is described in detail in Rev 21:1–22:5. The description contains many details which are similar to descriptions of the restored or transformed Jerusalem of the OT and the Jerusalem from heaven of later Jewish literature (Isa 54:11–12; Tob 13:16–18), as well as descriptions of the heavenly city of the gods found in Babylonian sources. The city is portrayed as the Temple of God (cf. 21:3, 22) and the new Paradise of the recreation anticipated in apocalyptic literature (cf. 22:1–5; *2 Bar.* 4; *4 Ezra* 8:52; *T. Dan* 5:12–13; cf. Ezek 47:1–12).

Bibliography

Court, J. M. 1979. *Myth and History in the Book of Revelation.* Atlanta.

Deutsch, C. 1987. Transformation of Symbols: The New Jerusalem in Rv 21,1–22,5. *ZNW* 78: 106–26.

Georgi, D. 1980. Die Visionen vom himmlischen Jerusalem in Apk 21 und 22. Pp. 351–72 in *Kirche: Festschrift für Gunther Bornkamm zum 75 Geburtstag,* ed. D. Lührmann and G. Strecker. Tübingen.

Rissi, M. 1966. *The Future of the World: An Exegetical Study of Revelation 19:11–22:15.* SBT 2d ser. 23. Naperville, IL.
Schüssler Fiorenza, E. 1972. *Priester für Gott.* NTAbh 7. Munster.
DUANE F. WATSON

NEW MOON. See CALENDARS.

NEW TESTAMENT SEMITICISMS. See SEMITICISMS IN THE NT.

NEW TESTAMENT, OT QUOTATIONS IN THE. The OT quotations in the NT express the historical fact that early Christianity has significant roots in the religion of Judaism, as well as the theological fact that paramount theological statements and arguments of NT writers are made in continuity with the OT, which they call Scripture *(graphē).* In terms of the latter, these quotations are indeed symptomatic of the fundamental fact that the outlook, content, and language of most NT writers are essentially determined by the OT. It is necessary to point out, however, that there is no evidence for an uninterrupted continuity from the OT to the specific theological statements of the NT writers. The gospel of the cross and resurrection of Jesus Christ is more than just the eschatological result of the OT.

A. Fundamental Concerns
B. Quotative Formulas
C. Quotations of Scripture and Midrash
D. Textual Criticism
E. Scripture Quotations in NT Writings
  1. Paul
  2. Deutero-Pauline Letters
  3. Synoptics
  4. Acts
  5. The Gospel of John
  6. Hebrews, James, 1 Peter

A. Fundamental Concerns

The reader of the NT writings is apt to gain the impression of a fundamental continuity, especially because of the frequent appeal of some NT writers to OT sayings which are often introduced by stereotypical *formulae quotationis* (see below). Hence the question arises, whether these quotative formulas are intended to substantiate the NT proclamation by virtue of their OT testimony. To the extent that it represents the Scriptures of early Christianity, the OT is uncontestably authoritative and, in this sense, is cited as holy Scripture. Yet for some of the NT writers, its authority structure in relation to the NT kerygma and to the proclamation of Jesus is only marginally the object of theological reflection. In keeping with ancient Jewish interpretation of Scripture, the interrelationship of the two or three authoritative dimensions (especially the scheme of "promise and fulfillment" and the methods of typology and allegory) reaches a certain balance. In the NT this interrelationship is once again hermeneutically presupposed, rather than delineated.

The crucial theological question is, from what perspective or with what preunderstanding did the NT writers read the OT as Scripture? For almost all NT writers concerned, this preunderstanding may be circumscribed—though individually quite diverse, as follows: the announcement of the eschatological redemptive event which God has accomplished in Jesus Christ, is the content of the OT writings. In this sense they understand the OT as the manifold promise of Christ. This is true a fortiori when they work with the "promise-fulfillment" schema which had already been constitutive for the deuteronomistic historiography and, principally, also when they use the allegorical or typological method. In this regard the manner of Scripture usage is comparable to the interpretation of Scripture practiced at Qumran, though not in terms of content, but in form (cf. e.g. Isa 40:3 in Mark 1:3 and 1QS 8:13ff.). Of course, this kind of interpretation of Scripture diminishes the literal sense, if it does not indeed lose its meaning altogether.

A distinction is therefore to be made between the *Vetus Testamentum per se* and the *Vetus Testamentum in Novo receptum.* Over against the Vetus Testamentum per se, the latter constitutes a new theological entity. It is the task of NT theology to extricate this entity in the individual mosaic pieces and to assemble them so as to show the theological features (Hübner 1990: 37–76). It can be argued that especially the OT quotations in the NT are of considerable importance in such a picture. The text basis of the Vetus Testamentum in Novo receptum, however, is primarily the Septuagint (on certain modifications, see below). Much theological argumentation in which the NT writers engage by means of OT quotations would lose its own power of argument, if it were to be predicated upon the original Hebrew text which differs from the LXX in a given instance (e.g., Deut 27:26 in Gal 3:10). Nevertheless it is constitutive of the theological particularity of the Vetus Testamentum in Novo receptum that it is largely based on the LXX.

B. Quotative Formulas

The larger part of the OT citations begins with an introductory formula (*formula quotationis,* hereafter abbreviated fq., [pl.] fqq.) and is thereby characterized as a quotation in its form. At times the occurrence of a quotation is obvious even in the absence of such a formula.

Beginnings of a fq. occur already in the OT, e.g., 2 Kgs 14:6 "according to what is written in the book of Moses," 4 Kgdms 14:6 (LXX) "as it is written in the book of the laws of Moses." This is paralleled in the Qumranian "as it is written" (1QS 5:15; 8:14; 4QFl 1, 2:12; CD 7:19). Thus the rabbinic *kktwb* (Aram *kdktyb*) as [it] is written) which is not attested until after the NT era, may well have been used in rabbinic exegesis during NT times.

To this exegetical tradition, therefore, belongs the most frequent NT fq. "as it is written" or "thus it is written," "(for) it is written" or similarly (62 times), particularly in the Synoptics and Paul. Next to these we find other forms of *grapho* (to write), e.g., "as it has been written" or variations of "the scripture says." The latter formula provides the transition to the fqq. which are built upon a form of *lego* (to say). In lieu of the Scriptures, their writers may be cited, e.g., Isaiah (John 1:23) or David (Acts 2:25). Apart from those cases in which God, Christ, or the Holy Spirit is introduced as speaker in the quotation, using the first person singular (Romans 9–11, Acts, and Hebrews), God himself is not mentioned as speaker in the fqq. In the Pauline corpus, *kathos eipen ho theos* "as God said" is singular in 2 Cor 6:16. But this citation is part of an interpolation into the Pauline text. In all ten instances, *legei kyrios* "the Lord says" is part of the quotation or an addition to the quotation by the NT writer (Ellis 1978: 182–87).

An exception is found in the fqq. of the fulfillment quotations of Matthew, namely "in order that that which was said by the Lord through the prophets may come to pass saying . . ." or similarly, which are constitutive of his theological conception. John's fulfillment quotations which are also theologically relevant are less stereotypical formulations. Likewise characteristic for Matthew are the Scripture references in Matthew 5 which are introduced with *ekousate hoti errethe (tois archaiois)* "you heard that it was said (by the ancients)" and surpasses or renders ineffective with an antithesis.

Occasionally (especially in Paul, see below) a single fq. introduces combinations of quotations (merging two or more Scripture statements) or mixed quotations (parts of one Scripture statement are inserted into another). Neither of these phenomena is typically Jewish and, consequently, not likely borrowed from Jewish exegesis.

C. Quotations of Scripture and Midrash

The Midrash Jewish exegesis was indeed familiar with collating Scripture statements which were to interpret one another. To date, however, Judaic scholarship (Bloch *DBSup* 5: 1263–81; J. W. Doeve, R. Le Déaut, G. Vermes, and A. G. Wright) has not yet reached a consensus on this. To what extent specific types of midrashim, such as the Proem Midrash (Peticha), do indeed have NT parallels, is difficult to determine in each case (on this, see Ellis 1978: 154–62; Koch 1986: 224–27; Hanson 1974: 201–24). Since the relationship between the method of NT quotation and the Midrashim is still unclear, no further reference will be made.

D. Textual Criticism

Although most NT writers cite the OT from the LXX and an appeal to the Hebrew original warrants serious consideration only in specific cases (e.g., in some of the fulfillment quotations in Matthew), there are frequent divergences between the text of the LXX and the NT quotation. The hypothesis of P. Kahle did not succeed, according to which the history of the LXX did not begin with an original text, but rather with multiple, targum-like Greek translations of Hebraic popular texts. See SEPTUAGINT. It is appropriate to assume with D. Barthélemy, R. Hanhart, and others, that continued recensions of the LXX were made in the direction of content agreement between the Greek translation and Hebrew original, and that this process is also reflected in the quotations in the NT (Hanhart 1984: 400–09).

E. Scripture Quotations in NT Writings

1. Paul. Among the Pauline letters acknowledged as authentic, Scripture quotations are found only in Romans, 1–2 Corinthians, and Galatians, and among the Deutero-Pauline letters only in Ephesians and 1–2 Timothy. But even in the letters of Paul the quotations occur with considerable diversity. One encounters very frequent citations in Galatians 3, Romans 3f. and especially Romans 9–11 (with approx. 25 quotations, i.e., more than half of all the quotations in Romans). 1 Corinthians has only 17 quotations, 2 Corinthians at best 11, while Galatians, with only six chaps., has 10 quotations (with minor variations, depending on the method of counting). Because of the combinations of quotations which are frequently found in Paul, the number of cited Scripture statements is higher than the number of formal quotations.

The issue of which letters contain quotations must also be considered in relation to which of the OT books Paul cites. Isaiah is cited 28 times (in 25 cited texts), the Psalms 20 times (in 29 cited texts), Deuteronomy and Genesis 15 times each (in 13 and 12 cited texts, respectively), and the Minor Prophets 8 times (in 12 cited texts). Five quotations or less are found in Exodus, Leviticus, Proverbs, 1 Kings (LXX) and Job (according to Koch 1986: 33). A negligible number of quotations are disputed with regards to their source (e.g., 1 Cor 2:9). Koch (1986: 35) unjustly argues against Paul's citing of Jer 9:23–24 in 1 Cor 1:31 and 2 Cor 10:7, especially since the use of Bar 3:9–4:4 in 1 Cor 1:18–31 can also be documented (Hübner 1984b: 161).

In the 10 citations in Galatians, Genesis is used four times, Leviticus twice, and Deuteronomy twice, while Isaiah and Habakkuk are used only once. The quotations from Genesis are drawn from the narrower frame of Genesis 12–27, due to the Abrahamic theme, since judaistic opponents of Paul demand the circumcision of the gentile Christian Galatians, presumably by appealing to Genesis 17. Next to Hab 2:4, the central argument for Paul, however, was Gen 15:6. In contrast, six of the 17 quotations in 1 Corinthians (likely written after Galatians) are from Isaiah. Since 2 Corinthians may be composed of five individual letters, little can be determined concerning favorite OT writings in the 10 quotations. The picture in Romans is all the more noteworthy. That the Genesis quotations are found in strategic positions, namely three times in Romans 4 and 9 respectively, can be explained from the theme of these chapters. But apart from Gen 15:6, the Genesis quotations in Romans are not of primary relevance to the theological argument. Notably, none of the three Genesis quotations in Rom 9:6–9 is introduced by a fq. One must ask, therefore, whether Paul actually uses these quotations as Scripture evidence. At any rate, all three quotations are used as a spoken word of God, as an announcement of what he intends to do or of what is to happen, according to his will: *klēthēsetai* in Gen 21:12 (Rom 9:7) is the theological passive ("they will be called"). In Gen 18:10, 14 (Rom 9:9) God speaks in the first person plural; in Gen 25:23 (Rom 9:12) *errethē autē* "it was said to her" is once again in the theological passive. Consequently, because Paul's motive in using all three Genesis quotations was not primarily that they were written in Scripture, but that they were spoken by God (the key term in Rom 9:6–29 is *kalein* "to call"), the quotation of Mal 1:2–3 in Rom 9:13 likewise should not be understood as Scripture evidence in the strict sense of the word, despite the fq. *kathōs gegraptai* "as it is written." A Scripture quotation cannot prove an already spoken word of God; it can only confirm it. The real strength of the "written word" lies in the fact that in it God once again speaks with the divine "I" (on the divergent argumentative functions of Paul's Scripture statements, see Koch 1986: 257–85). On Romans 9–11, see Hübner 1984a).

In the final pericope of Rom 9:6–29, Paul appeals to the prophets exclusively and, significantly, the otherwise stereotypical "as it is written" does not occur here. Since God calls gentiles to be his people, according to Hos 2:25, in Rom 9:25 he is the subject of the fq. "as indeed in Hosea he says." Likewise peculiar are the fqq. in Rom 9:27, 29: "Isaiah cryed out over Israel" and "as Isaiah predicted." Paul most frequently cites from the book of Isaiah. In 16 or 17 quotations, 19 or 20 references from Isaiah are used, 10 or 11 of which occur in Romans 9–11 alone. But the theological relevance of the dominance of Isaiah is not only rendered effective through the formal quotations, but also in 11:26 "and so all Israel will be saved; as it is written . . ." God himself ushers his initially partial redemptive activity regarding Israel (cf. 9:27) into his comprehensive redemptive activity. Rom 11:26 makes implicit reference to Isa 45:25 (see also Isa 45:27; Hübner 1984a: 113). The linguistic circumstances that the semantic field of Isaiah (especially Isa 45–66) is largely identical with Romans 9–11, raises the assumption that Paul read Isaiah from his Christian preunderstanding and such references as Isa 45:17, 25 appeared to him to be revelatory of the mystery mentioned in Rom 11:25. Paul in general, and Romans 9–11 in particular, demonstrates that the observation of the OT context is essential for the exegesis of the Scripture quotations in the NT (Hanson 1983: 7). The independent and theologically productive character of Paul's use of the LXX can be derived symptomatically from the combination of quotations in Rom 3:10–18 (Koch 1986: 180–84; "an intentional composition" of the apostle, comprised predominantly of references from the Psalms).

Thus we find a relationship of interdependence between kerygma and Scripture: Paul reads the Scripture on the horizon of the kerygma, that is on the horizon of his doctrine of justification and interprets it accordingly. Conversely, via reading the Scripture from the vantage point of faith as preunderstanding, he gains such decisive convictions as that of the eschatological redemptive justification of Israel (Rom 4:23–24).

Koch correctly points out that for Paul the Scripture attests to the Gospel, hence it is a word addressed to the present; in this case the Gospel is a precondition for understanding the Scripture, as seen especially in 2 Cor 3:12–18 (1986: 331–41). On the basis of three assumptions, it is possible to lay claim to Scripture as witness of the Gospel (1986: 344–47): (1) Based on a radically changed frame of understanding: Paul assumes the conviction from the pre-Pauline communities that "messianic announcements of Scripture are to be understood as fulfilled in Christ." (2) By means of a distinctly selective use of Scripture: Quotations from Leviticus and Numbers are largely missing. (3) By means of massive changes, in part, in the wording of the Scripture quotations: Paul has changed 52 of the 93 quotations.

Of course, one may be of a different opinion in individual instances, as a purview of his prize example of Rom 10:6–8 shows (Koch 1986: 129–32). There are convincing reasons, in this case, for the argument of W. Sanday and A. Headlam (*Romans* ICC, 286–90) and others, that Paul does not adduce a Scripture quotation when he uses statements from Deut 9:4; 30:12, 14 by introducing them with the fq. "but the righteousness based on faith says, . . ." and then juxtaposes them to the undisputed Mosaic quotation of Lev 18:5, introduced with the fq. "Moses writes concerning the righteousness of the Law thus . . ." (Hübner 1984a: 85–91).

While Paul uses Scripture quotations en masse for his gospel of justification, he is also capable to do entirely without Scripture quotations when he expresses something unique to him. It is striking, for instance, that he cites Scripture only sporadically in Romans 5–8, and not at all when he unfolds the Christian's existence in the Spirit in Rom 8:1–17.

2. Deutero-Pauline Letters. No Scripture quotation is found in Colossians, although its author refers back to authentic Pauline letters which contain formal quotations. To begin with, this is paralleled by the author of Ephesians who likewise forgoes Scripture quotations in chaps. 1–3 which are theologically crucial for him. Not until Eph 4:8 does one encounter Ps 67:19 (LXX). The bulk of this quotation corresponds to the LXX, but diverges significantly in matters of content. Most likely this is not done deliberately against the OT text, since the writer of Ephesians may have taken recourse to a Jewish tradition of exegesis (see commentaries). What is crucial, however, is that the quotation is interpreted christologically in Eph 4:9–11. Except for this quotation, all others in Ephesians are in an immediate, paraenetic context. 2 Thess 1:9–10 is likely not to be construed as a quotation. But the Pastoral Epistles do contain some quotations.

3. Synoptics. a. Jesus and the OT. The question of Jesus' use of Scripture is one of the most disputed in exegetical scholarship. The spectrum of opinions ranges all the way from the argument that Jesus, as a Jew, respected the uninterrupted authority of Scripture, to the assertion that the specifics of his preaching were expressed symptomatically in a view critical of the Scriptures, even in the annulment of the Law's central claims. One must maintain that, apart from the fulfillment quotations in Matthew, in the Synoptic Gospels Jesus himself generally appeals to Scripture. He cites it as the authoritative word of God and, in doing so, uses the invincible term *gegraptai* "written." He cites Moses (Mark 7:10; 10:6–8), the prophets (Mark 7:6–7; 11:17), David (Mark 12:36) and the Psalms (Mark 12:10–11, 36).

In sharp contrast is the fact that in his own authority he relativizes statements of the Law (Mark 10:6 [Gen 1:27; 2:24] against Mark 10:4 [Deut 24:1–4, verbalized by the Pharisees]), exceeds them (Matt 5:21, 27), or even annuls them (Matt 5:31–32, 38–39, 43–44 as annulment is disputed). The annulment of the Levitical food regulations in Mark 7:15, however, is made without reference to Leviticus 11 and Deuteronomy 14.

The more convincing arguments favor the hypothesis that Jesus indeed relativized or even annulled statements of the Law. Such sayings as Matt 5:18 (=Luke 16:17) are not authentic sayings of Jesus. To be sure, Jesus is able to render affirmative quotations of OT sayings. Typically, for instance, he uses the commandment concerning the parents in the Decalogue, Exod 20:12 = Deut 5:16, against the Pharisiac notion that because of Num 30:3 even an immoral qorban pledge dare not be broken. His struggle is not primarily against strange abuses, as manifested in a qorban pledge entered immorally; the issue is the correct understanding of God. One cannot refuse the dissolution of an immoral pledge for the sake of the glory of God, when people are treated unjustly thereby. Jesus appeals to the Decalogue because for him it holds absolute importance as expression of the will of God. Hence, Jesus does not advocate a formal principle of Scripture.

b. Synoptic Gospels. All of the 18 quotations in Mark (with minor variations in number, depending on the computation) are also found in Matthew (yet, if Mark 1:11 is quasi-mixed, this would not be true of Matt 3:17). Luke, however, did not utilize some of these quotations in his gospel because he ignored the particular Markan pericopae for theological reasons. Over and above Mark, Matthew and Luke share from the logia source Q especially the Scripture quotations from the pericope of Jesus' temptation in Matthew 4 (= Luke 4).

Only a small portion of the Markan Scripture quotations in the mouth of Jesus refers to authentic sayings of Jesus. The entire gospel of Mark is predicated upon one fulfillment quotation. According to Mark 1:1–4, the appearance of John the Baptist occurred "in the wilderness" at the beginning of the Gospel, "as it is written in Isaiah the prophet." The quotation introduced with this fq. contains not only Isa 40:3 (LXX), but also the mixed citation from Mal 3:1 and Exod 23:20. The Gospel is then signaled as the fulfillment of the Scriptures from the outset. To begin with, the fulfillment quotation in Mark 1:2–3 focuses primarily on John the Baptist, yet it emphatically points out the path of Jesus; the *hodos* "way" motif is central to the gospel of Mark, drawn up from the perspective of Jesus' passion, with the path of Jesus leading to Jerusalem (Mark 8:27; 9:33–34; 10:17, 32, 52; Steichele 1980: 79–80).

If the question "Who and what is Jesus" (Steichele 1980: 37), central to the fulfillment quotation in Mark 1:2–3, permeates the whole Gospel, it is necessary to ask whether the voice from heaven in Mark 1:11, with its two OT components of Ps 2:7 and Isa 42:1 (Jesus as son of God and servant of God), should not be regarded as more than a mere allusion. God himself cites the sayings of the OT which are messianically understood, and so fulfills his own holy scripture.

This quotation of the Scriptures at the beginning of Mark has its parallel in the quotation of Ps 21:2 (LXX), voiced by the crucified Jesus, in Mark 15:34. The salvation expressed in the thanksgiving hymn of Psalm 21 must be considered here. The resurrection in which the community believed, is the presupposition for describing the passion of Jesus by means of this Psalm (Gnilka 1979: 322). This is further supported by the allusion to Ps 21:19 (LXX) in Mark 15:24. That the passion was prophesied in the OT, in Mark's understanding, can also be seen in the quotation of Zech 13:7 in Mark 14:27 which is introduced by *gegraptai* "written" (cf. Mark 14:49). In the Spirit, David already attested to the majesty of Jesus, Ps 109:1 LXX in Mark 12:36. Further, the quotation of Ps 117:22–23 (LXX) is christologically significant.

Matthew particularly belongs to those writings of the NT whose theology, as far as content is concerned, is essentially determined by the reception of the OT. Of course, the status of the scholarly inquiry continues to be controversial on some crucial points. In general, however, the distinction of two types of OT quotations proposed by H. J. Holtzman, has been accepted: (1) reflection quotations which are joined to a narrative and comment on the narrative as fulfillment of a prophetic promise; (2) context quotations which are themselves an integral part of the narrative. There is, however, no consensus on the precise number of fulfillment quotations. In any case, the following quotations must be considered: Matt 1:22–23; 2:15, 17–18, 23; 4:14–16; 8:17; 12:17–21; 13:35; 21:45; 27:9. The following are subject to debate: 2:5–6; 3:3; 11:10; 13:14–15.

Modern scholarship is fairly unanimous on the issue that the fqq. of the fulfillment quotations are to be traced back to the redactional work of the evangelist, but not on the issue that this also applies to the quotations themselves. The situation which has been noted repeatedly since W. C. Allen (*Matthew* ICC, 281) demands an explanation, namely that, on the one hand, those quotations which the evangelist adopted from Mark or Q, or personally inserted as context quotations, were either left unchanged or only marginally changed, in light of the LXX. On the other hand, the fulfillment quotations, in part, show an affinity to the Hebrew original (occasionally also with a distinct dependence upon the LXX, as e.g., in Matt 1:23, partly as mixed quotations comprised of LXX components and a verbatim translation of the Hebrew original when the latter differs from the LXX). It has been held as unlikely, however, that the same author would strive for as close an affinity to the LXX as possible in one part of his quotations, while favoring more closely the Hebrew original in another part. As an escape from this dilemma, therefore, various forms of a hypothesis have been suggested, according to which the evangelist made use of an existing tradition in his fulfillment quotations. In this case it is highly unlikely that he follows an oral tradition of a liturgical practice familiar to him (Kilpatrick 1946; Matthew is Mark liturgically revised). Likewise, the argument of F. C. Burkitt (1907) and J. R. Harris (1916–20) that the evangelist borrowed the quotations from a collection of testimonia, fails to convince.

Conversely, K. Stendahl's hypothesis of a "School of Matthew" is an attempt at explanation worth discussing. As for E. von Dobschütz (1928: 338–48), if the evangelist was a converted Rabbi and if he actively participated in the life of the Church, it is "tantamount to saying that there was a school at work in the church of Matthew" (Stendahl 1967: 30). The interpretation of Scripture practiced in that church, for Stendahl, was "the Matthean type of midrashic interpretation; . . . it closely approaches . . . the midrash pesher of the Qumran Sect" (1967: 35). The peculiar treatment of the texts of the fulfillment quotations in the school of Matthew, therefore, should be seen as analogous to the commentary of Habakkuk in 1QpHab, in which "a violation of the consonant text" of Habakkuk was carried out with creative liberty (1967: 190–202). Thus Stendahl's hypothesis is certainly capable of providing a plausible explanation for the difference between the extant type of the fulfillment quotations and the text type of the remaining quotations in Matthew.

B. Gaertner (1954: 1), however, has been able to adduce considerable arguments for the fact that Stendahl's hypothesis of a fairly liberal usage of the Habakkuk text is subject to serious doubts. The pesher interpretation in the Qumran commentaries is based on an uninterrupted continuity of the text (that is, in the CD it emerges as previously fixed text segments), while the interpretation of the scripture by Matthew could be named a messianic *interpretatio pūnctūalis*.

But even if these objections to Stendahl are taken seriously, it still remains to be taken into consideration that both the community at Qumran and the writer of Matthew read and interpret the prophetic texts as promises of an already fulfilled presence of salvation, or of one which is being fulfilled. Hence the hermeneutical premise is common to both.

Another presupposition in Stendahl's argument is questionable, namely the assumption of an "unbroken line from the School of Jesus via the 'teaching of the Apostles,' the 'ways' of Paul . . . to the rather elaborate School of Matthew with its ingenious interpretation of the OT as the crown of its scholarship" (1967: 34). Whether we are allowed to understand Jesus as a teacher of a "school," however, is extremely doubtful.

Recently attempts have been made to relativize the discrepancy between the text form of the fulfillment quotations and that of the remaining quotations in Matthew. Thus R. H. Gundry argues as follows: "contrary to former opinion, the Matthaean formula-citations do not stand out from other synoptic quotation material in their divergence from the LXX, but the formal quotations in the Marcan (and parallel) tradition stand out in their adherence to the LXX" (1975: 5). But he encumbers his argument heavily with the hypothesis which has been held prior to him (among them E. J. Goodspeed), that "the Apostle Matthew was a note-taker during the earthly ministry of Jesus . . . from whose material the synoptists drew" (1975: 182–83). His result: "Matthew was his own targumist and drew on a knowledge of the Hebrew, Aramaic, and Greek textual traditions of the OT" (1975: 172). But quite apart from the untenable argument that Matthew had written the words of Jesus in shorthand, even his own evaluation of the text forms of the quotations in Matthew cannot remove the discrepancy under discussion within these quotations; it can at best mitigate it (see especially the summary, 1975: 147–50).

According to G. M. Soares Prabhu, too, all the fulfillment quotations in Matthew have "the same adaptive, context-directed character." From this he concludes that they are "free targumic translations made from the original Hebrew by Matthew, in view of the context into which he has inserted them" (1976: 104). His—albeit quite brief—investigation of the context quotations certainly cautions against too blatant an assertion that the LXX is the Bible of Matthew. But neither has he succeeded in demonstrating the nonexistence of the fact that there are, in principle, two divergent text forms in the OT quotations in Matthew.

While some queries with regard to the construction of the quotations in Matthew remain, statements about the theological intention of the evangelist can be made with greater certainty. Its characteristic expression is found especially in the fqq. of the fulfillment quotations: what took place in the Christ event—e.g., the virgin birth, according to Isa 7:14 (Matt 1:22), or the return from Egypt, according to Hos 11:1 (Matt 2:15)—happened in order to fulfill what the prophets had said. To be sure, this theological intention would be turned on its head, if one were to view the evangelist as a theologian who thinks from the perspective of the OT, that is, of the promises of the OT. Rather, he is thinking from the perspective of the fulfillment in Jesus Christ. Not until Israel's Scripture is read from the perspective of the Christian faith can the former be understood as Scripture of the fulfillment.

The opinion of P. Vielhauer, according to whom the evangelist is not concerned with the fulfillment of the Scripture in Jesus, but rather with the fulfillment of particular sayings in the details of the life of Jesus (1975: 362) is to be rejected. Even the appeal to what the prophets have said in the disputed fulfillment quotation in 2:23 contradicts that, but even more so 26:54, 56: The writings of the prophets must be fulfilled in the passion.

The quotations of Matthew continue to present scholars with extremely difficult tasks. Attention must be given to the inquiry into the extent to which, if at all, the respective OT context is to be considered in understanding the citations (A. T. Hanson's claim), in what sense, if at all, one is allowed to speak of an atomized exegesis by Matthew (against this, Gundry et al.), and to what extent the evangelist, or his school, practiced Jewish exegetical methods.

It is also true of the Lukan writings that the author's appeal to the OT by far exceed what can be read explicitly from the Scripture quotations. Allusions to the LXX occur frequently (as well as some possible traces of a direct use of a semitic text) in the poetic elements of the infancy narratives in Luke 1–2, with features resembling quotations. These hymns are indeed to be regarded as pre-Lukan (see commentaries) and cannot say much, therefore, about the evangelist's attitude to the OT. Characteristic of his theological conception are those quotations which he alone features and in which his theological intention can be discerned.

While Mark presents the pre-Easter Jesus at least in a certain distance to the law of Moses (Mark 7:15 is not in Luke), already in the infancy narratives Luke stresses the faithfulness to the Law by the parents of the Baptist and by the parents of Jesus. As declaration concerning the complete obedience to the Law by the Baptist's parents, Luke 1:6 corresponds to Luke 2:23, a quotation of Exod 13:2, 12, 15 (LXX text only in part), which is introduced with "as it is written in the law of the Lord" followed by a quotation of Lev 5:11 (cf. Lev 12:8), which is introduced with ". . . according to what is said in the law of the Lord." The combination quotation in Mark 1:2–3 which contains a mixed quotation, is rectified by Matthew as well as by Luke (both bring in Mal 3:1 and Exod 23:20 only in the baptist pericope of Matthew 11 = Luke 7). In Luke 3:4–6—a fulfillment quotation, as in Mark 1:2–3—Luke expands the reference from Isaiah and thereby lends it more weight. It is of special programmatic significance that in Luke 4:18–19 Jesus quotes Isa 61:1–2; 58:6 in his inaugural sermon in Nazareth and applies it to himself. Isaiah has promised him as the Christ and stipulated his tasks. More than the other Synoptics, Luke submits the messianic ministry of the earthly Jesus to the prophetic promise. Luke then adds as a commentary "Today the scripture has been fulfilled in your hearing" (v 21).

It is not clear whether or not the statement of Luke 7:22 which consists of several sayings of Isaiah (Isa 29:18; 42:18; 26:19; 61:1), in Jesus' answer to the Baptist, should be regarded as quotation uttered by Jesus. Luke may well have understood it as such, since Isa 61:1 is mentioned again.

Only Luke relates the passion event to Isaiah 53. In Luke 22:37 (Gethsemane scene) Jesus applies Isa 53:12 to himself "and he was reckoned with transgressors." Here Luke varies from the LXX text, a certain proximity to the MT is unmistakable. Holtz (1968: 41–43) considers the LXX "most likely" to be the source; but against this is the fact that not a single LXX manuscript has the text found in Luke. It may be regarded as certain that there is no authentic saying of Jesus here (Rese 1969: 164).

The quotation of Hos 10:8 in Luke 23:30, which comes across as a saying of Jesus, belongs to Luke's own material (LXX text, though with transpositions). From Psalm 21 (LXX), quoted twice in Mark, Luke uses only Ps 21:19 (LXX) (Luke 23:34). Yet the crucified Jesus no longer utters Ps 21:2 (LXX), but instead Ps 31:6 (LXX) (Luke 23:46, the text is almost entirely LXX). The passion which was purposed by God and announced by the prophet Isaiah, cannot afford Jesus to utter a single word of God-foresakenness.

In the same way the resurrected Jesus also instructed the Emmaus disciples, in Luke 24:44, that everything written in the Law of Moses, the Prophets and the Psalms, had to be fulfilled. Jesus himself "opened" their understanding for them to comprehend the Scriptures, that "it is thus written" that Christ suffers and is raised from the dead on the third day. Furthermore, it is written that in his name repentance for the forgiveness of sins will be proclaimed to all people. Hence, Luke 24:44–47 is a programmatic reference which presents the Christ event as the salvific event in keeping with the Scriptures and, at the same time, serves as the transition to the second volume of Luke's two volume work, Luke-Acts. Accordance with the Scriptures constitutes an essential and central element in the theology of the gospel of Luke, which finds its clear expression in the Scripture quotations.

4. Acts. Depending on the count in the book of Acts, most of the slightly more than 20 quotations are used in Peter's speeches and sermons in chaps. 1–3, in Stephen's speech in chap. 7, and in Paul's first speech given in Pisidian Antioch, in chap. 13. James appeals to a Scripture quotation during the Jerusalem council. Most of the quotations are thus encountered in speeches or sermons. In addition, in Acts 8:32–33 the Ethiopian eunuch reads a text from Isaiah aloud (see ETHIOPIAN EUNUCH); Acts 13:22 may possibly have to be viewed as a mixed quotation. Paul documents his faithfulness to the Law and his loyalty to the state with a quotation from the Pentateuch in Acts 23:5, and, finally, a quotation at the end of Acts, intended as a programmatic quotation functioning as Scripture evidence, underscores the mission-theological intention of Luke. It is precisely at the pivotal points of his second work that Luke placed key Scripture references.

In Peter's Pentecost sermon is found the eschatological quotation of Joel 3:1–5 in Acts 2:17–21 and the christological quotations of Ps 15:8–11 (LXX) and 109:1 (LXX) in Acts 2:25–28, 34–35 (prophetic announcement by Deuteronomy, cf. also Luke 20:42–43; according to fq. in Acts 4:25 David speaks "by the Holy Spirit" [see commentaries regarding text-critical problem]).

In Paul's first sermon which expresses the failed announcement of salvation to the Jews by means of a salvation-historical sketch—the christological quotations of Ps 2:7 (LXX); Isa 55:3; Ps 15:10 (LXX) in Acts 13:33–35, and the quotation of Hab 1:5 which is introduced in Acts 13:40–41 by a fq. whose locus is a warning leveled predominantly against the Jews. This quotation has its counterpart in the gospel to the gentiles of Isa 49:6 in Acts 13:47, after the stir: God himself had destined Paul (and Barnabas as well) to be the light for the salvation of the gentiles.

In the speech of James (Acts 15:15–17) Luke quotes Amos 9:11–12 as Scriptural proof for the mission to the gentiles: God will rebuild David's fallen tent (interpreted christologically, since Christ is its referent), in order that "all the peoples" may seek the Lord.

Paul's mission-theological reflection at the end of the book, Acts 28:25–28: Via Isaiah the prophet the Holy Spirit has already announced to the fathers the blindness of the Jews in Isa 6:9–10. Hence "this salvation" (namely the salvation of the Jews) is sent to the gentiles. Acts concludes, then, with the emphatic recognition that the Scriptures of the Jews negate salvation to the same Jews and according it to the gentiles.

Theologically significant is the Ethiopian eunuch's quotation of Isa 53:7–8 in Acts 8:32–33. That which is encountered for the first time in the synoptic tradition in Luke 22:37, namely the quotation of Isa 53:12 which Jesus uses and applies to himself, is continued here: Isaiah 53 refers explicitly to the passion of Jesus.

Which OT books Luke knew, is a matter of dispute. According to T. Holtz, on his own he used only the Minor Prophets, Isaiah, and Psalms recognizably and, with some degree of probability, it may be assumed that he was acquainted with the LXX text of the Book of the Twelve Prophets and of Isaiah, which has affinities to the text type of the codex Alexandrinus (1968: 169). However, Holtz also claims that Luke did not know the Pentateuch (at least Exodus to Deuteronomy), that he used quotations from it only through secondary mediation, and that he stands virtually alone in his lack of knowledge of the Torah (1968: 171). This argument, however, is not uncontested (see Rese 1969: 211).

In Acts the fqq. are conspicuous. Of the Minor Prophets Joel is mentioned by name in Acts 2:18; as for the other two Minor Prophets, Amos and Habakkuk, they are only mentioned as "prophets": Amos in Acts 7:42; 15:45 and Habakkuk in Acts 13:40. Does the reference to the "book of the Prophets" in Acts 7:42 mean the Minor Prophets? In a formal sense, this finds its correspondence in the fq. of Acts 1:20: "for it is written in the book of Psalms" which introduces Ps 68:26 (LXX) and 108:8 (LXX). In Acts 28:25–26 Isaiah is introduced by mention of his name, while the Holy Spirit is explicitly mentioned as the actual speaker. But in Acts 7:48 he is simply introduced with "as the prophet says." Is Isaiah the prophet? In Acts 13:34

and 13:47, however, God is said to be the speaker in these quotations from Isaiah. Elsewhere God appears as the speaker in some references to God's direct address, e.g., to Abraham in Acts 3:25 (Gen 22:18). In quotations from the Psalms, David is mentioned as the speaker several times (Acts 2:25, 34; 4:25). The special introduction of Ps 2:7 in Acts 13:33 is unique: "as it is written in the second Psalm." In the two instances where Deuteronomy 18 is quoted, Moses is the speaker (Acts 3:22; 7:37). It is noteworthy, therefore, that Luke was apparently more concerned to posit important OT characters, such as David, Moses, or Isaiah, or even God himself, or the Holy Spirit, as speakers (note the frequent form of *legein* or *lalein,* "to say") in the formal Scripture quotations. Out of over 20 quotations only 5 are introduced with a fq. in which the term *gegraptai,* "written," occurs. The written character of the quotation, for Luke, seems to be of secondary importance.

5. The Gospel of John. The picture given by the Scripture quotations in John appears to be rather confusing at first glance, because there is no easily recognized pattern by which these quotations were placed within the overall structure of John. A further element of uncertainty is apparent, since the literary-critical questions of John continue to be completely fluid, and since only a literary-critical analysis of this NT writing could indicate where exactly it is the evangelist wants to use a quotation.

Certain structural elements, however, can be discerned clearly. Five quotations are introduced with the fq. *gegrammenon estin,* "it is written," or similarly (John 2:17; 6:31; 45; 10:34; 12:14; see also 8:17, where the evangelist begins with the peculiar fq. "in your law it is written that. . . ." [codex Sinaiticus: *gegrammenon estin,* "it is written"], apparently to introduce Deut 17:6 or Deut 19:15; there are striking differences in comparison with the OT text, however). The fulfillment quotations are notable as well, but these are not encountered until John 12:38, and their fq. is generally something like, "in order that the scripture might be fulfilled" (12:38; 19:24 and 19:36 as the evangelist's remark; 13:18 and 15:25 as Jesus' statement).

If one inquires as to who is the respective speaker in the quotations, no clear direction emerges in this case either. The Baptist produces the first quotation; frequently it is the people, or Jesus, or the evangelist who wrote the Scriptures. Likewise, the inquiry into the underlying text yields no clear answers. Occasionally there is verbal agreement with the LXX text (there are only four clear LXX quotations); in most cases, however, there are considerable modifications with regard to the LXX. Sometimes there may be dependence upon the Hebrew original, while other times neither the LXX nor the Biblia Hebraica can be discerned as the primary text. In some references to the Scriptures it is not possible to determine a clearly verifiable OT reference.

According to Rothfuchs (1969: 153) the evangelist consistently uses *ho logos,* "the word," when the locus of the fulfillment quotation is established with fair accuracy. The fqq. of the fulfillment quotations use *hē graphē,* "the scripture," when no locus is mentioned. Further, the fqq. of most other quotations use neither *ho logos* nor *hē graphē;* instead they merely use forms of *legō* "to say" and *graphō* "to write," while a locus may or may not be given (with the exception of John 7:38). Rothfuchs also correctly observes that by *hē graphē* the evangelist has in mind "the locus of the Scripture reference," all the more so since he uses the plural *hai graphai* "the scriptures" (John 5:39) for the whole scripture. Of the four fqq. using *ho logos,* only two introduce an OT quotation, while the other two refer to a saying of Jesus as fulfilled (John 18:9, 32), without stating explicitly the particular saying of Jesus to which reference is made.

A clear perspective is further obtained from another observation made by Rothfuchs. With the exception of John 12:38–40, all of the fulfillment quotations have to do with Jesus' enemies and their actions (1969: 170). Thus the two quotations from Isaiah in John 12:38–40 take on a more distinct profile. The failure of humanity, expressed in the remaining fulfillment quotations, is ultimately traced back to God himself who blinds their eyes and hardens their hearts. Therefore, as indirect fulfillment quotations Isa 53:1 and 6:10 are of central significance in the framework of the Johannine conception, because they lend clarity to the theological purpose of the remaining fulfillment quotations.

The quotations of Isa 53:1 follow the LXX text verbatim, but the first part of the quotation of Isa 6:10, however, shows major divergences. R. Schnackenburg (1984: 143–52) has demonstrated that the evangelist deliberately changed the text of Isaiah here. He eliminated the idea of hearing and established the sequence of "eyes-heart," in order to show that God's oppressive action begins in the external realm of man and penetrates into his inner being (see also the Pharisees' failure to see in John 9). Hence the evangelist used the LXX text where he deemed it appropriate to his theological conception, and radically changed the biblical text where, in his own estimation, he considered it inappropriate.

The christological conception which is expressed by means of the modification of the text, actually receives its clarity in the commentary on the quotation in John 12:41, where the immediate context of the quotation is given by appealing to Isa 6:1; Isaiah did not see the glory of God, but of Christ (see John 1:18; Schnackenburg 1984: 151). The evangelist's interpretation of the immediate context is an important indication for the assumption that his way of referring to the Scriptures was the result of his independent pursuit of it, all the more so since the same can also be shown elsewhere in John.

Among the climactic statements of the evangelist is John 19:28–30 where the death of Jesus is said to be the triumphant conclusion of his work (see John 12:32, "and I, when I am lifted up from the earth . . ."). In v 28, "to fulfil the scripture" *hina teleiōthē* instead of *hina plērōmē* is predicated upon Jesus' last word "it is fulfilled" *tetelestai* in v 30. The death of Jesus, which is theologically interpreted from the vantage point of his exaltation, is the center of the Johannine "theology of the cross." It is theologically important that precisely this death constitutes the fulfillment and completion of Scripture. The theology of the cross and the theology of Scripture are inseparably intertwined in John. A closer evaluation indicates, therefore, that the picture of the quotations in John, which appeared to be so confusing at first, is actually well thought out and well structured.

The argument of E. D. Freed, according to which the

evangelist was dependent upon the Synoptics in his literary use of Scripture, is to be rejected; his following statement, however, should be given serious consideration: "But in no other writer are the OT quotations so carefully woven into the context and the whole plan of composition as in Jn" (1965: 129).

6. Hebrews, James, 1 Peter. The question of which LXX text the author of Hebrews used has still not been completely resolved. Many quotations are based on the A-text, while some are based on the B-text. Is the source a recension based on traditions which were later taken up in codices A and B? According to E. Ahlborn, the question of which LXX text the quotations in Hebrews follow is often misleading because the mss. in the respective OT books belong to divergent recensions (1966: 10). "An Alexandrian recension as source for Hebrews is out of the question. . . . Likewise Alexandrinus per se as source for the quotations, is eliminated; rather it is plausible that A knew Heb and used it" (1966: 141).

Nowhere among the fqq. does one find *kathōs gegraptai,* "as it is written," or something similar; instead fqq. with forms of the verb *legein,* "to say," are used continuously. It is important that the quotations are spoken; the quotations cite God as the speaker, at times also the Son of God (2:12–14); 10:5–7) and the Holy Spirit (3:7–11; 10:15–17), but rarely one of the OT characters (occasionally Moses; but does 9:19–20 constitute a quotation in the true sense of the word?).

The quotations are used as proof in the framework of christological intention. In Hebrews the support by the spoken word of God is analogous to the support of Scripture in other NT writings. Thus God speaks to his Son (1:5–13) and the Son to his Father (10:5–7). In quotations with a paraenetic purpose the Holy Spirit is introduced as speaker (3:7–11; 10:15–17). Thus God speaks as the Father to the Son (and vice versa) and God as the Holy Spirit to the Church. The dominant role of the Psalms in the quotations in Hebrews is reflected in that the words of the Father to the Son are taken from the Psalms. Among the approximately 30 Scripture quotations there are 15 taken from the Psalms. Pss 2 and 109 (LXX) are particularly important for the theology of Hebrews (Christ as the Son of God and as priests). In contrast to many other NT writings, Isaiah is hardly ever referred to in Hebrews. However, while the exposition of the high priestly office of Jesus in Hebrews constantly alludes to the OT cultic regulations, this cult is hardly deemed worthy of a quotation (only in Exod 25:40 in Heb 8:5, as a cultic instruction from God to Moses, and Exod 24:8 in Heb 9:20, but as a statement of Moses). As high priest, Jesus speaks against the OT cult in 10:5–7 (from Ps 39:7–9 LXX). While his high priestly office is described in cultic categories, in principle it actually denotes the negation of cultic existence. There is a dialectic between the OT cult being surpassed and of being rendered ineffective. The Hebrew writer's method of exegesis is noteworthy because of the way in which quotations are handled. Shorter passages of a longer quotation are repeated and then commented upon individually (see 3:7–9; 10:5–7). In this connection, the current literature tends to point to Jewish exegetical methods as parallels (especially F. Schröger, passim). G. W. Buchanan perceives Hebrews as "homiletic midrash, which is based in Psalm 110" (1972: xix–xxx).

In James, three of the four quotations in James 2 are used in conjunction with the topic of the law (Lev 19:18 in Jas 2:8; two commandments of the Decalogue in Jas 2:11; especially Gen 15:6 in Jas 2:23 against Paul or a misunderstood Paulinism). Of the eight scripture quotations in 1 Peter, three are from Isaiah and three from the Psalms.

Bibliography

Ahlborn, E. 1966. Die Septuaginta-Vorlage des Hebräer. Ph.D. diss. Göttingen.

Amsler, S. 1960. *L'Ancien Testament dans l'Église.* Neuchâtel.

Burkitt, F. C. 1907. *The Gospel History and its Transmission.* Edinburgh.

Daube, D. 1949. Rabbinic Methods of Interpretation and Hellenistic Rhetoric. *HUCA* 22: 239–64.

Dittmar, W. 1899–1903. *Vetus Testamentum in Novo.* 2 vols. Göttingen.

Dobschütz, E. von. 1928. Matthäus als Rabbis und Katechet. *ZNW* 27: 338–48.

Doeve, J. W. 1954. *Jewish Hermeneutics in the Synoptic Gospels and Acts.* Göttinger Theologische Beiträge 24. Assen.

Ellis, E. E. 1957. *Paul's Use of the Old Testament.* London.

———. 1978. *Prophecy and Hermeneutics in Early Christianity.* WUNT 18. Tübingen.

Feld, H. 1985. *Der Hebräerbrief.* Darmstadt.

Freed, E. D. 1965. *Old Testament Quotations in the Gospel of John.* NovTSup 11. Leiden.

Gaertner, B. 1954. The Habakkuk Commentary (DSH) and the Gospel of Matthew. *ST.* 8: 1–14.

Gnilka, J. 1979. *Das Evangelium nach Markus (Mk 8,27–16,20).* EKK 2/2. Zurich and Neukirchen.

Gundry, R. H. 1975. *The Use of the Old Testament in St. Matthew's Gospel.* NovTSup 18. Leiden.

Hanhart, R. 1984. Die Bedeutung der Septuaginta in neutestamentlicher Zeit. *ZTK* 81: 395–416.

Hanson, A. T. 1974. *Studies in Paul's Technique and Theology.* London.

———. 1983. *The Living Utterances of God: The New Testament Exegesis of the Old.* London.

Harris, J. R. 1916–20. *Testimonies.* 2 vols. Cambridge.

Hays, R. B. 1989. *Echoes of Scripture in the Letters of Paul.* London.

Holtz, T. 1968. *Untersuchungen über die alttestamentlichen Zitate bei Lukas.* TU 104. Berlin.

Howard, G. 1968. Hebrews and the Old Testament Quotations. *NovT* 10: 208–16.

Hübner, H. 1984a. *Gottes Ich und Israel.* FRLANT 136. Göttingen.

———. 1984b. Der vergessence Baruch. *SNTU* 9: 161–73.

———. 1990. *Biblische Theologie des Neuen Testaments.* Vol. 1. Göttingen.

Kilpatrick, G. D. 1946. *The Origins of the Gospel According to St. Matthew.* Oxford.

Kistemaker, S. 1961. *The Psalm Citations in the Epistle to the Hebrews.* Amsterdam.

Koch, D.-A. 1986. *Die Schrift als Zeuge des Evangeliums.* BHT 69. Tübingen.

Le Déaut, R. 1969. A propos d'une définition du midrash. *Bib* 50: 395–413.

Lindars, B. 1961. *New Testament Apologetic: The Doctrinal Significance of the Old Testament Quotations.* London.

Michel, O. 1972. *Paulus und seine Bibel.* Darmstadt.

Miller, M. P. 1971. Targum, Midrash and the Use of the Old Testament in the New Testament. *JSJ* 2: 29–82.

Rese, M. 1969. *Alttestamentliche Motive in der Christologie des Lukas.* SNT 1. Gütersloh.
Rothfuchs, W. 1969. *Die Erfüllungszitate des Mt.* BWANT 8. Stuttgart.
Sanday, W., and Headlam, A. C. 1902. *Romans.* ICC. Edinburgh.
Schnackenburg, R. 1984. *Das Johannesevangelium.* HTKNT 4/4. Freiburg, Basel, and Vienna.
Soares Prabhu, G. M. 1976. *The Formula Quotations in the Infancy Narrative of Matthew.* AnBib 63. Rome.
Steichele, A.-J. 1980. *Der leidende Sohn Gottes.* Gütersloh.
Stendahl, K. 1967. *The School of St. Matthew and Its Use of the Old Testament.* 2d ed. ASNU 20. Lund.
Suhl, A. 1965. *Die Function der alttestamentlichen Zitate und Anspielungen im Mk.* Gütersloh.
Ulonska, H. 1963. Die Funktion der alttestamentlichen Zitate und Anspielungen in den paulinischen Briefen. Ph.D. diss. Münster.
Vermes, G. 1974. Bible and Midrash: Early Old Testament Exegesis. Pp. 59–91 in *Post-Biblical Studies,* ed. G. Vermes. SJLA 8. Leiden.
Vielhauer, P. 1975. *Geschichte der urchristlichen Literatur.* Berlin and New York.
Wright, A. G. 1966. The Literary Genre Midrash. *CBQ* 28: 105–38.

HANS HÜBNER
Trans. Siegfried S. Schatzmann

NEW YEAR FESTIVAL. See AKITU.

NEZIAH (PERSON) [Heb *nĕṣîaḥ*]. The name of a family of temple servants who returned to Palestine with Zerubbabel shortly after 538 B.C.E., the end of the Babylonian exile. The name appears in Ezra 2:54 in the phrase "the sons of Neziah" (Gk *nasoue/nasous/nethie*), where the temple servants are distinguished from the people of Israel, the priests, and the Levites. The parallel verse Neh 7:56 (Gk *nisia/n(e)is(e)ie*) and the later parallel 1 Esdr 5:32 (Gk *nasi/nasith*) also list "the sons of Neziah."

STEVEN R. SWANSON

NEZIB (PLACE) [Heb *nĕṣîb*]. Town situated in the Shephelah, or lowlands, of Judah (Josh 15:43), within the same district as Libnah and Mareshah. This settlement, whose name perhaps means "post" or "garrison" (from *nṣb,* "stand, station oneself"), is listed among the towns within the tribal allotment of Judah (Josh 15:21–62). The ancient town is most often identified with modern Khirbet Beit Nesib (e.g., Aharoni *LBHG,* 382), approximately 15 km E and slightly N of Lachish and 12 km NW of Hebron (M.R. 150110). Given that the location is appropriate and that the ancient and modern names are clearly related, this identification seems secure. However, archaeological confirmation of occupation during the appropriate time period has yet to be found.

WADE R. KOTTER

NIBHAZ (DEITY) [Heb *nibḥaz*]. Among the foreigners whom Sargon II settled in Samaria after deporting the local population are listed (2 Kgs 17:30) the people of Avva (var. Ivvah, 2 Kgs 19:13) with their gods Nibhaz and Tartak. The many variations of the first god's name in the ancient sources indicate that the deity was foreign and unfamiliar even to the early editors. There is no satisfactory explanation of Nibhaz's name in contemporary scholarship. One early suggestion (see Cogan and Tadmor *2 Kings* AB, 212), that Nibhaz is the Elamite god Ibnahaza and Avva the Elamite Ama, is unlikely on both geographical and chronological grounds (for context see Edzard *WbMyth* 1).

In the Persian-period Aramaic papyri from Hermopolis, Egypt, the proper name *ʾIsm-madbaḥ* is encountered. The second element, *madbaḥ,* seems to mean "Altar," personified as a deity. As such, it would correspond to the *Dii Madbachō̦* and more fully Gk *Dii Bōmō̦* ("Zeus Altar") of N Syrian inscriptions. Some have proposed that Nibhaz is a miswriting or corruption of *Madbaḥ* (see Gese et al. 1970: 169 and summary in Milik 1967: 577–78, 605).

Milik (1967: 578, 606) makes a yet more plausible suggestion: the LXX variants of the name would indicate that the original form ended in *-r.* If so, the name probably would have been *Nabā-ḥāzer,* "Nabu-Returns." Compound Nabu names were common at the Aramaic-speaking Jewish community at Elephantine, Egypt (Porten *ArchEleph,* 166). The context of 2 Kings 17–19 would suggest a N Syrian background for Avva and Nibhaz[er?], and there is reason to make associations between Aramaic-speaking Syria and Egyptian diaspora communities. See also ASHIMA. The Babylonian Talmud (*Sanh.* 63b) read *nibḥan,* deriving it from the root *NBḤ,* "to bark," and translated it as "dog," an interpretation which fit nicely the anti-idol tenor of the passage.

Bibliography

Gese, H.; Höfner, M.; and Rudolph, K. 1970. *Die Religionen Altsyriens, Altarabiens und der Mandäer.* Vol. 10 pt. 2 of *Die Religionen der Menschhheit,* ed. C. M. Schröder. Stuttgart.
Milik, J. T. 1967. Les papyrus araméens d'Hermoupolis et les cultes syro-phéniciens an Égypte perse. *Bib* 48: 546–622.

WILLIAM J. FULCO

NIBSHAN (PLACE) [Heb *nibšān*]. Town situated in the wilderness of Judah (Josh 15:61), within the same district as En-gedi. This settlement is listed among the towns within the tribal allotment of Judah (Josh 15:21–62). Recent archaeological work in the Buqeiah valley has uncovered three Iron Age fortress farms which may be associated with the towns of this district (Stager 1976). If the list in Jos 15:61–62 runs N to S, then ancient Nibshan is probably to be located at Khirbet el-Maqari, approximately 9 km SW of Khirbet Qumran (Boling and Wright *Joshua* AB, 392; M.R. 186123).

Bibliography

Stager, L. E. 1976. Farming in the Judean Desert During the Iron Age. *BASOR* 221:145–58.

WADE R. KOTTER

NICANOR (PERSON) [Gk *Nikanōr*]. The name Nicanor appears several times in 1 and 2 Maccabees. It is difficult to determine whether there were two or three separate individuals bearing this name.

1. The governor of Cyprus (2 Macc 12:2). Because this Nicanor has a relatively low rank, he is not to be confused with the other references to "Nicanor" in 1 and 2 Maccabees.

2. The soldier who had been in command of the elephant corps and who was appointed by Demetrius I as governor of Judea, charged with the responsibility of capturing and killing Judas Maccabeus, scattering those forces loyal to him and setting up Alcimus as high priest (2 Macc 14:12ff.). Some would distinguish this Nicanor from the Nicanor mentioned in other passages (so Goldstein *I Maccabees, II Maccabees,* AB). However, there are no insurmountable problems with the assumption that all the references to Nicanor in 1–2 Maccabees (except 2 Macc 12:2, which pertains to Nicanor #1 above) allude to the same individual; consequently it seems reasonable to assume (with Abel 1949 and Habicht 1976) that there was only one distinguished person named Nicanor fighting Judas Maccabeus, not two.

On this assumption, Nicanor was therefore the son of Patrocles (1 Macc 8:9). He is usually identified with the close friend of Demetrius I who was with him when he was hostage in Rome (Polybius 31.14(22).4; and cf. *Ant* 12.402). However, Nicanor already held a high position under Antiochus IV, before Demetrius I came to power. He is first mentioned in the battle of Emmaus as one of those (along with Ptolemy and Gorgias) to whom the battle against Judas Maccabeus depicts Gorgias playing the major military role, but in the 2 Maccabees version Nicanor has the leading role. In 2 Maccabees this incongruency is explained by the fact that Gorgias, who was sent to join Nicanor in command, was a commander with military experience (8:9); 2 Maccabees therefore focuses on Nicanor to show him as an example of an enemy to the Jews (8:11) who, with God's help, is punished and defeated (vv 24–28, 34–36). This brought to an end the first phase of Nicanor's involvement with the Jewish revolt.

The second phase came at the time of Demetrius I, who began to rule in 162 B.C.E. Assuming that he is the same Nicanor mentioned in Polybius, then he should have earlier visited Rome and taken part in Demetrius' flight from there and in Demetrius' successful campaign to regain the Seleucid throne. Demetrius then sent Nicanor to quell Judas' revolt: Judas had not acquiesced with the installment of Alcimus as high priest. Again Nicanor is depicted as being extremely inimical to the Jews, but this time by the writer of 1 Maccabees (7:26–35). It seems that his army was not large enough for the task (probably because Demetrius was preoccupied on other military fronts), hence Nicanor tried to overcome Judas not by force but either through strategum (according to 1 Macc 7:27–31) or reconciliation (according to 2 Macc 14:18–25). This proved unsuccessful, and at a battle at Chapharsalama Judas was victorious.

In spite of the discrepancies in our two sources, and probably after the Jews received harsh treatment from the frustrated and hostile Nicanor, the two armies met a second time, this time at Adasa. There, even though he enjoyed some military support (1 Macc 7:39), Nicanor was defeated and killed. The victory was commemorated by an annual holiday on that same day, the 13th of Adar (1 Macc 7:48–49). Some uncertainty exists about the year in which the battle of Adasa occurred, but most commentators date it to 160 B.C.E. This whole event is treated in detail and with much embellishment in 2 Maccabees 15. There Nicanor, the sinner and blasphemer, received from God's hand the retribution he deserved (cf. also *Meg. Taᶜan.* on the 13th of Adar).

Bibliography

Abel, F. M. 1949. *Les livres des Maccabees.* Paris.
Habicht, C. 1976. *2 Makkabäerbuch.* JSHRZ 1/3. Gütersloh.

URIEL RAPPAPORT

NICANOR GATE. See BEAUTIFUL GATE.

NICODEMUS (PERSON) [Gk *Nikodēmos*]. A fairly common Greek name in the 1st century meaning "conqueror of the people." Its Semitic equivalent was "Naqdimon," sometimes shortened to "Naqai." The biblical individual of that name is mentioned only in the gospel of John (3:1,4,9; 7:50; 19:39). Nicodemus is portrayed as a Pharisee who was also part of the ruling class in Judea (3:1), presumably a member of the Sanhedrin. John 19:39 implies that he was quite wealthy, and in 3:10 Jesus addresses him as the preeminent teacher of Israel. The above, combined with the fact that "rulers" and "Pharisees" are distinguished elsewhere in the gospel (cf. 7:48; 12:42), suggests that Nicodemus was a prominent figure within the governing group.

Nicodemus first appears in John 3:1–12, where he visits Jesus by night and is confronted with the "born-again" discourse. About six months before the crucifixion the "chief Priests and Pharisees" seek to have Jesus arrested as a deceiver (7:32, 45–52). Nicodemus protests, arguing that the law required them to give Jesus a fair hearing (7:51). He is accused, in response, of having joined Jesus' Galilean followers (7:52). Nicodemus last appears after Jesus' death, bringing a large quantity of spices to anoint Jesus' body (19:38–42). The three Nicodemus episodes in the Fourth Gospel are connected by editorial marks in 7:50 and 19:39.

Though Nicodemus is often portrayed as timid, Robinson (1985: 284) is probably correct in seeing him as quite courageous. Most likely, Nicodemus came by night, not out of fear, but to avoid the crowds that would have interrupted his interview with Jesus. His reaction to the council's desire to arrest Jesus was boldly calculated to bring out the irony of their lawless act at the very moment in which they were ridiculing the lawless behavior of the "crowd" (7:49–51). And he certainly showed more courage at the Cross than did the absent Disciples of Jesus.

There is no serious reason to doubt that Nicodemus was a historical individual. It is questionable, however, whether the gospel material leads to the conclusion that he became a disciple of Jesus. Brown (*John* AB, 130) sees Nicodemus as the counterpart to Judas: he moves from darkness to light (3:2), just as Judas moved from light to darkness (13:30). Along with him Beasley-Murray (*John* WBC, 47),

Cotterell (1985: 238), King (1986: 45), Morris (*John* NICNT, 210) and Schnackenburg (1980–82, 1: 364–65) understand the actions of 19:38–42 to be those of a secret but committed disciple of Jesus. However, secret discipleship is not a complementary designation in the Fourth Gospel (12:42, 43). And it is possible to understand the extravagance of Jesus' burial not as an act of love and respect as do Bultmann (1971: 680n4) and Schnackenburg (1980–82, 3: 295), or as a pointer to His royalty as do Morris (825) and Brown (60), but as a failure to understand the cross combined with a lack of faith in the resurrection (see De Jonge 1971: 342 and Sylva 1988: 148). Thus, Michel (1981: 231), Pamment (1985: 71, 73), and Sylva (1988: 149) argue that Nicodemus remained on the fence throughout the gospel, never making a positive decision for Jesus.

Considerable study has investigated whether Nicodemus might be equated with one or more individuals in the Talmud or in the writings of Josephus. Helpful summaries of the evidence can be found in Klausner (1929: 29–30), Robinson (1985: 284–87) and Str-B 2:413–19, but the evidence is insufficient at this point to draw any firm conclusions. The total absence of Nicodemus in the Talmud would not be surprising if he indeed became a Christian.

Christian tradition suggests that Nicodemus gave evidence in favor of Christ at the trial before Pilate, was deprived of office and persecuted by hostile Jews as a result, and was ultimately baptized by the apostles Peter and John. The *Acts of Pilate* became known as the *Gospel of Nicodemus* in the Latin tradition after the 14th century.

Numerous parallels between John 3:1–2 and 2:23–25 and the frequent use of plurals in 3:1–12 indicate that within the gospel itself, Nicodemus functions as a representative of those who had a partial faith in Jesus as a result of the "signs" which Jesus did. For the evangelist such individuals are in darkness, not in light (note the genitive usage of "night" in 3:2 cf. 12:37, 42, 43). As a ruler, teacher, and Pharisee, he demonstrates for the author of the gospel that the very best that the Judaism of his day could offer was inadequate to rightly comprehend the significance of Jesus.

On the positive side, however, Nicodemus functions, along with the Samaritan woman, as an illustration of the power of the Christian gospel to attract whoever might believe, regardless of education, wealth, piety, or circumstances (John 3:16; 12:32). The Fourth Gospel reflects a situation at the close of the 1st century where Pharisees were divided over the significance of Jesus as they had been seven decades earlier (cf. 9:16). The Nicodemus episodes appealed to those Pharisees who, like Nicodemus, had only a relative acceptance of Jesus, to come to the "light." (John 3:18–21) Without a more complete decision they would not be able to fully understand Jesus or the nature of the salvation that he brought.

Bibliography

Bultmann, R. 1971. *The Gospel of John.* Trans G. R. Beasley-Murray, R. W. N. Hoare, and J. K. Riches. Philadelphia.

Cotterell, F. P. 1985. The Nicodemus Conversation: A Fresh Appraisal. *ExpTim* 96: 237–42.

Höppl, B. 1983. *Das Nachtgespräch mit Nikodemus.* Münsing.

Jonge, M. de. 1971. Nicodemus and Jesus: Some Observations on Misunderstanding and Understanding in the Fourth Gospel. *BJRL* 53: 337–59.

King, J. S. 1986. Nicodemus and the Pharisees. *ExpTim* 98: 45.

Klausner, J. 1929. *Jesus of Nazareth.* New York.

Mendner, S. 1958. Nikodemus. *JBL* 77: 293–323.

Michel, M. 1981. Nicodème ou le non-lieu de la verité. *RevScRel* 55: 227–36.

Pamment, M. 1985. Focus in the Fourth Gospel. *ExpTim* 97: 71–75.

Robinson, J. A. T. 1985. *The Priority of John.* Ed. J. F. Coakley. London.

Schnackenburg, R. 1980–82. *The Gospel According to St. John.* 3 vols. New York.

Sylva, D. D. 1988. Nicodemus and His Spices (John 19:39). *NTS* 34: 148–51.

Jon Paulien

NICODEMUS, GOSPEL OF. See PILATE, ACTS OF.

NICOLAITANS [Gk *Nikolaïtai*]. A group mentioned in Revelation in the letters to Ephesus (2:6) and Pergamum (2:15). The former reference tells us only that the risen Lord commends the church at Ephesus for joining him in hating the works of the Nicolaitans. The latter reference is more informative, for the risen Lord chastises the church at Pergamum for holding the teaching of the Nicolaitans. By way of a similitude, the teaching of the Nicolaitans is defined as that of Balaam of the OT and Jewish tradition: eating food sacrificed to idols and immorality (Num 25:1–2; 31:16). Since these same two sins are listed at Thyatira as the teaching of a self-proclaimed prophetess named Jezebel (2:20–25), it is probable that, although not specifically named, the Nicolaitans were present there also, and that she was a Nicolaitan prophetess.

The risen Lord presents the Nicolaitans as a great threat to the churches he addresses. He commends the church of Ephesus for hating them (2:6; cf. *Ign. Eph.* 6:2; 9:1), and declares to the church of Pergamum that he will come and war against the Nicolaitans with the sword of his mouth (2:16). To the church of Thyatira he promises that those who refuse their teaching will receive no other burden, and encourages them to hold fast until he comes. As for Jezebel, she will be made sick, her less ardent followers will be thrown into great tribulation unless they repent, and her more ardent followers will be struck dead (2:20–25).

The Nicolaitans are not merely a subgroup in the church who were more lenient toward pagan religion and society. In the letters their thought is called a teaching (Gk *didachē;* 2:14, 15, 20, 24), and they may have claimed inspiration for this teaching (2:20). Their leaders may have called themselves apostles (2:2) and prophets (2:20), and been actively seeking disciples. They were permissive about both eating meat offered to idols and immorality. The former is the purchase of previously consecrated meat at the marketplace or the actual participation in pagan religious festivals where such meat was served. The latter is either a synonym for idolatry, or, as seems more probable in connection with pagan practice at religious festivals, sexual license. Both eating meat offered to idols and immorality were in direct contradiction to the Apostolic Decree, which forbids gentiles to practice either (Acts 15:20, 28–29; 21:25). This antinomianism may be a misrepresentation of the Pauline doctrine of liberty, as was the case with the antinomians of 2 Peter, who are also likened to Balaam (2:15; 3:15–16; cf. Jude 11).

The Nicolaitans appear to have gnostic tendencies. Irenaeus (*Haer.* 3.11.1) states that the Nicolaitans had disseminated doctrine similar in kind to the gnostic heresy of Cerinthus. Their teaching could have been based on a dualism claiming that what was done in the body had no bearing on the soul. Jezebel may have claimed to know the "deep things (of Satan)" (2:24), a claim reminiscent of the gnostic secret knowledge. If Jezebel and her group described the deep things as being "of Satan," then she may have claimed to possess knowledge which prevented being overcome by sin while being a libertine. "Of Satan" may also be an ironic twist added to denigrate the opposition (cf. 2:9, 3:9 for such irony).

Apart from these observations and suggestions, nothing can be confidently known about the Nicolaitans other than what is stated in Revelation. Irenaeus (*Haer.* 1.26.3) basically repeats the biblical material, adding the assertion that the Nicolaitans were heretical followers of Nicolaus, the proselyte of Antioch who was chosen to be one of The Seven (Acts 6:5). Hippolytus (*Haer.* 7.24) underscores Irenaeus, adding that Nicolaus departed from true doctrine. Clement of Alexandria (*Str.* 2.20) claims that Nicolaus was an ascetic, and then current Nicolaitans were not his true followers because they perverted his teaching that it was necessary to abuse the flesh. The *Apostolic Constitutions* (6:8) describe the Nicolaitans as "shameless in uncleanness." Tertullian (*Adv. Marc.* 1.29; *De proescr. haeret.* 33; cf. *De Pudic.* 19) speaks of the lust and luxury of contemporary gnostics he calls Nicolaitans, but distinguishes them from the Nicolaitans of Revelation by calling them another type, a Satanic sect, more specifically called the Gaian heresy. Eusebius (*Hist. Eccl.* 3:29) notes that the Nicolaitans claimed Nicolaus, arose briefly, and died out.

When all this patristic evidence is compiled, we still do not know the connection, if any, of Nicolaus to the Nicolaitans, or the connection of the Nicolaitans in Revelation to later sects of the same name. Contemporary scholarship is skeptical that the 2d century manifestation of the Nicolaitans is linked to the Nicolaitans of Revelation. All that can be said is that the biblical presentation of the Nicolaitans was part of a heresiological tradition associated with later Gnosticism and other heresies.

Perhaps the designation "Nicolaitan" was not the name of the sect in Revelation at all. The close association of Balaam and the Nicolaitans in Rev 2:14–15 may be the result of a wordplay. It has been proposed that Nicolaitan is an etymological play on the Hebrew name "Balaam." Balaam (*bilʿām*) can be the contracted form of *bālaʿʿam* ("he has destroyed the people") or *baʿal ʿam,* ("lord of the people"). Nicolaitan also could be the Greek equivalent of *niką laon* ("he has conquered the people").

In support of this proposal, a similar Hebrew wordplay with the name Balaam is found in *t. b. Sanh.* 105a. There are other wordplays using Balaam in the first century (e.g. Philo, *Cher* 32). Jezebel and Balaam are cryptic descriptions rather than the self-designations of the groups so characterized. Jezebel represents the active promotion of idolatry and immorality for her sanction of Baal worship in Jerusalem. Balaam represents idolatry, immorality, and false teaching for taking Balak's advice and leading the Israelites into idolatry and immorality with the Moabite women. Thus Nicolaitans may be a cryptic name for the sect in Revelation used to associate them with the negative traditions about Balaam.

Bibliography

Brox, N. 1965. Nikolaos und Nikolaiten. *VigChrist* 19:23–30.

Goguel, M. 1937. Les Nicolaites. *RHR* 115: 5–36.

Hemer, C. J. 1986. *The Letters to the Seven Churches of Asia in Their Local Setting.* JSNTSup. 11. Sheffield.

Mackay, W. M. 1973. Another Look at the Nicolaitans. *EvQ* 45: 111–15.

Schüssler Fiorenza, E. 1973. Apocalyptic and Gnosis in the Book of Revelation and Paul. *JBL* 92: 565–81.

DUANE F. WATSON

NICOLAUS (PERSON) [Gk *Nikolaos*] One of the seven Hellenists chosen to supervise the daily distribution for dependent widows in the early Jerusalem church and designated a proselyte from Antioch (Acts 6:5). The name is derived from the Greek verb "conquer" *(nikaō)* and the noun "people" *(laos).*

Since the following narratives indicate that Stephen and Philip were born Jews and the grammar of the sentence clearly applies the description "proselyte" only to Nicolaus, the implication is that the others in the list were born Jews and he alone had come into Judaism from paganism by way of circumcision (Pesch 1986: 229; Kuhn *TDNT* 6: 742–44). Cadbury (1933: 59–74) thought that others in the list might have been gentiles. But this theory is dispelled by Nicolaus' position in the list as last. Gentiles would have been listed after born Jews and proselytes.

It has been conjectured that either Luke or one of his sources was connected with Antioch on the Orontes. The mention of Nicolaus as being from Antioch is sometimes thought to be another example of the city's prominence in Acts in support of this theory.

The notation of Nicolaus as a proselyte may also be significant for Luke's theology. Jack Sanders (1987: 137–39) has argued that the appearance of Nicolaus at this point in Acts is important in terms of understanding Luke's view of the spread of the gospel in ever-widening circles from its Jewish parent. Nicolaus is the first named gentile to come to faith (cf. the implication in Acts 2:10). If Sanders is correct, Nicolaus is, for Luke, part of a "gray area" between Jews and gentiles. He is not totally Jewish and not totally gentile and thus can function as a bridge as Luke moves the gospel away from Judaism toward gentile Christianity.

Early church tradition (Iren. *Her.* 1.26.3; Eus. *Hist. Eccl.* 3.29.1–3) connected this Nicolaus with the later Nicolaitans first mentioned in Rev. 2:6. This connection seems to have arisen by inference from the name and there is no definite knowledge about Nicolaus beyond what is recorded in Acts.

Bibliography

Cadbury, H. J. 1933. The Hellenists. Pp. 59–74 in *The Beginnings of Christianity*. Vol. 5, *Additional Notes to the Commentary*, ed. K. Lake and H. J. Cadbury. London.

Pesch, R. 1986. *Die Apostelgeschichte*. Vol. 1. Zürich.

Sanders, J. 1987. *The Jews in Luke-Acts*. Philadelphia.

THOMAS W. MARTIN

NICOPOLIS (PLACE) [Gk *Nikopolis*]. The name of several cities of the Greco-Roman world that had Greek-speaking populations and were founded in commemoration of military victories. Cities bearing this name were found in Epirus, in most of the provinces of Asia Minor, and in Egypt. Sometime around A.D. 63–65 the apostle Paul arranged to meet Titus in one of these cities (Titus 3:12). The identification of the specific Nicopolis is facilitated not only by Paul's description of it as a good place to spend the winter but also on the basis of Paul's recorded travels.

Nicopolis of Pontus, the location of Pompey's victory over Mithridates in 66 B.C. (Strabo 12.555), was at a strategic position in the Roman communication system and was growing during the 1st century, but it lay far from Crete and from Paul's known journeys. The Nicopolis in Bithynia (Pliny *HN* 5.150), or in Cilicia (Strabo 14.676) would have provided uncomfortable winter quarters. The Nicopolis in the Delta region of Egypt near Alexandria, that had been founded by Caesar Augustus (Josephus *Ant* 5.11.15 § 273) would have provided a comfortable climate, but it also lies outside Paul's reported travels. Some cities named Nicopolis were founded by later Roman leaders and thus would not have been the site of the meeting between Titus and Paul.

The most likely site for the meeting was the Nicopolis in Epirus; this same Nicopolis is also known as Nicopolis of Achaia. This variance has resulted because Tacitus (*Ann.* 2.53) described it as an Achaian town, whereas Ptolemy (*Geog.* 3.13) ascribed it to Epirus. The two terms are designations for large portions of what is today modern Greece. It was located on the W side of the Greek peninsula across the sea from the S end of the Italian peninsula (39°02′N; 20°44′E). The city was built on the isthmus of the Bay of Actium. Augustus founded the city in commemoration of the important naval victory over Mark Anthony in 31 B.C. which took place in the bay. The undisputed Princeps established the city as a Roman colony. The show piece of Nicopolis was a memorial dedicated in 29 B.C. to Neptune and Mars. The monument was decorated with a number of rams from the front of ships captured during the naval conflict. The city dominated the trade of the region and was the venue for a quadrennial festival which rivaled the Olympic games. Herod the Great, in his typical flair for promoting his own position with Augustus, made generous donations toward the construction of a temple there, as well as for numerous other public buildings (Josephus, *Ant* 16.5.3 § 147). The city became the home of the exiled philosopher Epictetus in A.D. 89 (Aulus Gellius *Attic Nights* 15.11.5). The site is occupied today by the modern village of Smyrtoula.

Paul's intention to meet Titus in Nicopolis sometime after being released from prison in Rome would have been a continuation of his evangelistic endeavor. It is widely held that after traveling through Miletus and Corinth, Paul made his way to Nicopolis, where he was arrested and returned to Rome in a second Roman imprisonment.

Codex Alexandrinus appends a note to the epistle to Titus indicating that the letter was sent from Nicopolis, but this note is not attested in other ancient manuscripts. It contrasts with Titus 3:12, which suggests that Paul was *near* Nicopolis, not *in* Nicopolis. Paul is usually thought to have written the letter from Corinth.

ROBERT W. SMITH

NIGER [Gk *Niger*]. The second name of Simeon, who was part of a group of prophets and teachers in the church at Antioch (Acts 13:1). The name is a Graecized form of the Latin word for "black," thus it is assumed that this Simeon was of African origin. This African connection has led to speculation that he is to be identified with Simon of Cyrene (Luke 23:26). It has also been suggested that the grammar of the sentence may specify that Niger was a prophet (with Barnabas and Lucius, Saul and Manean being teachers). But it is more likely that Luke has stylistically varied the list by shifting particles. Another speculation connects this Niger with the Simeon mentioned in Acts 15:14.

The list seems to assume that Niger was an Antiochean. This may reflect Luke's general interest in Acts with this city and perhaps provide a further clue for the provenance of Acts. The list, and Niger's place in it in Acts, illustrates the diversity of the community at Antioch, highlighting the Lucan theme of the universality of the gospel.

THOMAS W. MARTIN

NIGHT HAG. See LILITH (DEITY).

NILE (PLACE) [Heb *yĕʾōr, nāhār; yām*]. The river that essentially defines Egypt. This article consists of two entries. The first surveys OT references to the Nile River, while the second provides a geographical overview of the river's role in constituting Egyptian life.

OLD TESTAMENT

The term most commonly used to refer to the Nile River or its tributaries (particularly the Delta region) in the Hebrew Bible is *yĕʾōr*. This Hebrew word is generally thought to be a loan word from Eg *i(t)rw*, "river, Nile, a river/stream [of the Nile]" (*WbÄS* 1: 146–47; Lesko 1982–89 1: 60; de Buck 1948: 1; Lambdin 1953: 151; see Kadish 1988 for a discussion of the word's possible origin); and is often followed by the adjective *ʿ3(j)*, "great" (i.e., the "Great River") to denote the Nile generally and its central artery within the Delta system (Gardiner 1947: 153*–68*; Bietak 1975: 118–25).

In the Pentateuch, the Nile is most prominent within the story of Joseph (Genesis 41) and the Exodus tradition (Exodus 2, 7–8). In Gen 41:1–3, Pharaoh sees in his dream seven healthy cows emerging from the Nile and feeding on the "reed grass" (Heb *ʾāḥu*, from Eg *3ḫ[w]*, "papyrus thicket"; see Lambdin 1953: 146) near the river. In his recounting of the dream to Joseph, Pharaoh (or rather the narrator) adds the Heb *śĕpat,* "lip, edge," to *yĕʾōr,* i.e., "In my dream I saw myself standing at the edge of the Nile" (v 17). The same phrase (Heb *śĕpat hayĕʾōr*) is also found in Exod 2:3, where the text states that the child (Heb *yeled*) Moses was placed "in the marsh *(sûp)* at the river's edge" (see Ward 1974: 343 for "marsh" instead of RSV "reeds").

Certainly the most celebrated biblical narrative concerning the Nile is that relating the story of the plagues, specifically the first two where the river turns to blood (7:15–24) and frogs emerge from its waters, infesting the land of Egypt (7:25–8:11 [Eng 8:1–15]). According to the text (7:20), Moses lifted his staff and struck the waters of the Nile in the presence of Pharaoh and his servants, whereupon all the waters of the Nile turned to blood. The intended effect of this miracle upon Pharaoh was, however, lessened by the fact that Egypt's "magicians" (Heb *ḥarṭummîm,* a problematic term generally believed to be of Egyptian derivation; see Lambdin 1953: 150–51 and Quaegebeur 1985) were able to do the same (7:22), although one naturally questions how they accomplished this feat. One would have to assume that the miracle was first reversed, i.e., the blood—which was now throughout all the land of Egypt (v 21b)—became water once again, thus allowing them to demonstrate their comparable powers. In the same fashion (but this time Aaron wields the staff), the second plague brings frogs from the "waters of Egypt" (8:6) upon the land. There is some confusion within the text concerning the origin and extent of these two plagues—whether they were restricted to the Nile (as in 7:17, 20–21a; 8:3, 9b, 11) or encompassed all bodies of water (7:19, 24; 8:1–2 [—Eng 8:5–6]; see Fohrer 1964; Childs *Exodus* OTL, 130–62; Zevit 1976 for a discussion of the source-critical problems and final redaction of the plague narrative). With respect to the latter position (i.e., all bodies of water), Zevit (1976: 199–202, 210–11; 1990: 22) has noted that these descriptions echo the language of Genesis 1, and are intended by P to evoke the "undoing" of Yahweh's creation (compare, e.g., "their bodies of waters" [Heb *miqwēh mêmêhem*] in exod 7:19 with "the gathering of waters" [Heb *miqwēh hammayim*] in Gen 1:10).

As with the crossing of the Red Sea, scholars have never tired of seeking natural explanations for these otherwise miraculous events. The most widely cited treatment of the plagues from this perspective is that of Greta Hort (1957–58), who attempts to demonstrate that "the salient features of each plague are also the salient features of one specific natural phenomenon, and that the plagues follow upon each other in the Bible in the sequence which such phenomena would have in nature" (85). Thus, the "blood-red" color of the waters of the Nile was brought about by an abnormally high inundation (contra the earlier view of a low Nile, e.g., Petrie 1911: 35–36), which in turn raised the level of flagellates within the water to a point where the fish could no longer survive. The numerous dead fish then made the water foul and undrinkable, and, according to Hort, at that point the already reddish water of the high inundation "became truly blood-red in colour" (94). As for the plague of frogs that followed, Hort explains that invasion of dry land as the result of the masses of dead and decomposing fish along the banks of the river that threatened the frogs' normal habitat (96–97).

The most frequent objection to Hort's rather elaborate scenario (apparent as she progresses through the plagues) is that she fails seriously to consider the source-critical/redactional history behind the formation of the narrative (e.g., Greenberg 1969: 202). According to Zevit (1976: 195–96), the "plasticity" of the plagues tradition, reflected in their varying order in Psalms 78 and 105, "tells against any attempt to explain the order of the ten plagues as reflecting a connected series of natural catastrophes," although he does not deny the possibility that "some actual natural disasters ultimately lie behind the various traditions" (see also Zevit 1990: 42). (Note also the comments of Beegle 1979: 117–18 and the insightful critiques of Greenberg 1969: 200–3 and de Vaux *EHI,* 360–62.)

While she is not interested in literary analysis per se (e.g., p. 85), Hort's conclusion that the narrative is indeed historical implies some type of unity, even if at the hands of its latest redactor who placed the plagues in their correct historical sequence (note her revealing, if not confusing, statement on the "original account" of the first plague [p. 95]). While she often relies upon the details of the text and, indeed, maintains that it is in these that her case is strongest, Hort must at times "interpret" certain passages. For example, she consistently refers to the "blood-red colour" of the Nile, while the biblical writer(s) state that the Nile actually became blood (note Exod 4:9), and infer that the death of the fish was due to this change (Exod 7:20–21). Ironically, Hort employs natural means to explain what was clearly perceived by the biblical author(s) as a purely miraculous event—one whose sole purpose was to magnify the superior power of their god, Yahweh—and thus defeats the purpose of the biblical text. The writer does not speak in terms of a natural catastrophe, but wishes the reader to understand that this occurrence is strictly beyond the normal course of affairs (high inundations were not previously unknown or unique), and thus evidence of the hand of Yahweh. Ultimately, Hort's rationalistic explanations reveal more about the mind-set of the modern interpreter than the biblical text itself (see also the comments of Childs *Exodus* OTL, 168; Coats 1988: 12–13).

Attempts to support the historicity of the first plague through an appeal to the Egyptian text *Admonitions of Ipuwer* (e.g., Zevit 1990: 20), which states "Lo, the river is blood" (Eg *iw ms itrw m snfw;* see Gardiner 1909: 27 and plate 2, 10; translation from Lichtheim *AEL* 1: 151) overestimate the historical value (and misunderstand the genre) of this text (note esp. the comments of Lichtheim [149–50] on the literary topos "national distress"; also Kemp in *AESH* 74–75). Hort contends (as she must) that this statement in the *Admonitions* refers to "the dreaded calamity of *too high* a rise of the Nile" (92), but elsewhere in the same text one finds passages that indicate otherwise. For example, prior to the above quotation, one reads, "Blood is everywhere, there is no shortage of dead . . . Many dead are buried in the river [*itrw*], the stream [*nwj*] is the grave, the tomb has become a stream" (Gardiner 1909: 25–26; *AEL* 1: 151). Thus, the writer has prepared the reader for what follows, i.e., the numerous dead bodies in the river have turned it to blood.

Aside from this Egyptian text, Hort's treatment of the first two plagues is conspicuous by its absence of reference to ancient Egyptian texts concerning the Nile or inundation—from the 13th century or any other period of Egyptian history—that might support her scenario. (Another Egyptian example of the "water into blood" motif, although unrelated to the Nile, is found in a late demotic text of Roman date; see Montet 1968: 95–96, citing Maspero; Lichtheim *AEL* 3: 148.) The ancient Egyptians kept detailed records of Nile levels (crucial in the modern reconstruction of Egyptian chronology; e.g., von Beckerath 1966) and were fully aware of the destructive consequences of too high an inundation (e.g., the flooding of temples; under Sebekhotpe VIII [13th Dyn.], see Habachi 1974 and discussion in Baines 1974 and 1976; under Osorkon III [23 Dyn.], see Breasted *ARE* 4: 369; von Beckerath 1966: 44–45; Edwards in *CAH*ª 3/1: 567) and modern Egyptologists increasingly recognize the socioeconomic impact of these fluctuating levels upon the course of Egyptian history (e.g., Bell 1975; Butzer 1976: 26–38; 1984). Thus, it is all the more puzzling that such a catastrophic series of events related to the Nile should fail to prompt even the slightest mention in Egyptian texts from the alleged period of their occurrence. The traditional response to this uncomfortable silence has been that it was not in the best interest of the Egyptians to cite such embarrassing "defeats," but one does find other such catastrophes narrated within Egyptian inscriptions (e.g., the account of the destructive storm during the reign of Ahmose [1550/1539–1525/1514 B.C.E.; see Vandersleyen 1967], where no attempt is made to hide the negative effects of the disaster, as one finds, e.g., with the high inundation under Taharqah [690–664 B.C.E.; see Macadam 1949: 27; Kitchen 1986: 388–89]). While highly conservative regarding the historicity of other events recorded in the book of Exodus, it is instructive to note the cautious approach of Sarna, who remarks of the plagues tradition that "the entire account has a didactic and theological purpose, not a historiographic one. In order to underline and emphasize these points, the narrator has devised a literary structure of impressive artistry" (1986: 75, 77). Unlike Sarna, who nevertheless does not rule out the possibility of a historical core behind the tradition (68–70), Van Seters (1986: 38) explains the plagues as a literary creation of the Yahwist (for him of exilic date), who drew from both biblical (prophetic) and ANE (curse) traditions.

Another issue raised regarding the first plague is the Nile's place in Egyptian religion vis-à-vis the biblical statement that Yahweh's actions on behalf of his people constituted a judgment against "all the gods of Egypt" (Exod 12:12; Num 33:4). One frequently finds the statement that the first plague was directed against the Egyptian "Nile god" Hapi (e.g., Finegan 1963: 49; Aling 1981: 106; Sarna 1986: 79; but compare Greenberg 1969: 201). But as Egyptologists have long known, the Eg word *ḥʿpi* refers not to the Nile, but to the inundation. This important distinction between Eg *itrw* (*ʿ3*) as the river and *ḥʿpi* as the inundation was demonstrated by de Buck (1948), who collected numerous examples in support of his thesis (see also Hornung 1982: 77–79; Janssen 1987: 131, note 22; Baines 1985: 112). The term "Nile god," coined with reference to the many offering bearers in Egyptian reliefs associated, but not exclusively so, with the abundance of the inundation, is misleading at best and should be abandoned (see esp. the extensive treatment of Baines 1985, particularly pp. 112–16, who prefers the term "fecundity figures"). However, leaving aside their overt theological biases, one need not assume that the biblical writers' own perception of the Nile in Egyptian thought—however they may have acquired this knowledge—must tally in all respects with that presented in Egyptian texts. It is not impossible that the biblical authors drew from a more "popular" view of Egyptian religion current in the Palestine of their day (the importance of later Egyptian traditions, i.e., from the 7th–6th centuries, in the composition of the Exodus narratives should not be overlooked). Be that as it may, it is clear from the text that the biblical authors/redactors were aware of the extreme importance of the Nile to the welfare of Egypt, and that any serious disruption of its normal agricultural cycle (which revolved around the river), as the first plague was certainly intended to be, would deal a severe blow to the very heart of the Egyptian way of life (compare Isa 19:5–8).

Outside the Pentateuch, the Nile figures most prominently within the prophetic corpus, particularly in the major prophets' oracles against Egypt. In Amos 8:8 and 9:5, the earth trembles (Heb *rgz*) and melts (Heb *mwg*) like the rising and falling of the Nile; at first reading, an apparent reference to the inundation, but there are serious textual problems in these two (not quite parallel) verses. The Heb (*Nipʿal*) verb *grš*, "be tossed/thrown about" (v 8b) is better suited to a violent sea (Isa 57:20), unlike the inundation (see discussion in Andersen and Freedman, *Amos* AB, 811–13). A somewhat similar description of the rising Nile occurs in Jer 46:7–8, where, in his attempt to reassert Egyptian dominance in the N, Pharaoh Neco (Necho II, 610–595 B.C.E.) likens his march into a devastating inundation, the "gushing" or "surging" (Heb *gʿš*) waters of the many Delta rivers (*nĕhārôt*).

In the book of Isaiah (7:18), the predicted invasion of the Egyptian (or rather Kushite) army, summoned by Yahweh as judgment against Judah (cf. 5:26; discussion in Hayes and Irvine 1987: 137–38), is compared to a swarm or plague of flies from the streams/rivers of Egypt (Heb *yĕʾōrê miṣrāyim*, i.e., the Delta of Lower Egypt). Many regard the reference to Egypt here as a later interpolation (e.g., Wildberger *Jesaja 1–12* BKAT, 301–5; brief discussion in Clements *Isaiah 1–39* NCBC, 89–90). Elsewhere (Isa 19:5–8), the downfall of Egypt is symbolized in part by the drying up of the Nile with its streams and canals (here Heb *yām*, *nāhār*, and *yĕʾōr* are all used interchangably; compare Ezek 30:12).

The RSV's "Nile" in Isa 18:2 represents the traditional interpretation of Heb *yām* here; but, as the commentaries reveal, the first two verses of this chapter are fraught with textual and historical difficulties. Others (e.g., Clements *Isaiah 1–39* NCBC, 164; Hayes and Irvine 1987: 254; note also NJPS) prefer "sea" (i.e., the Mediterranean), a reading partially dependent upon one's view of the origin (Kush or Jerusalem?) and destination (Assyria, Jerusalem, or even Kush?) of the messengers of v 2 (discussion in Wildberger *Jesaja 13–27* BKAT, 678–89; Kaiser *Isaiah 13–39* OTL, 89–94; Hayes and Irvine 1987: 252–55; note the interpretation of Ezek 30:9). In his oracle against Tyre, the First

Isaiah (23:1–3) comments upon the productive trade relations between the N Levantine coast and Egypt: "her [Tyre's] revenue came from the grain [lit. "seed"] of Shihor, and from the harvest of the Nile" (Heb *yĕʾôr,* omitted in LXX; on Shihor, see Bietak in *LÄ* 5: 623–26). The RSV rendering of Isa 23:10, "Overflow [Heb *ʿibrî*] your land like the Nile," is generally emended, with support from Qumran and the LXX, to "Till [Heb *ʿibdî*] your land like the Nile" (although the meaning of the verse as a whole is still unclear; see NJPS and the suggestions of Wildberger *Jesaja 13–27* BKAT, 857; Hayes and Irvine 1987: 292).

In 2 Kgs 19:23–24 (= Isa 37:24–25), the Neo-Assyrian monarch, Sennacherib, boasts of his exploits in Lebanon and, following the traditional interpretation, Egypt. Evidence for the latter derives from the phrase *yĕʾōrê māṣôr,* "the streams/rivers of Masor," rendered by RSV and others (NJPS, NEB) as "streams of Egypt." Here *māṣôr* is taken as a variant for *miṣrāyim,* the common term for Egypt. This view, however, has not gone unchallenged (e.g., Calderone 1961). Tawil (1982: 199–202) suggests that Heb *māṣôr* should be identified with the Mesopotamian geographical site *šadê Muṣri,* Mount *Muṣur,* and that the biblical account (19:24 = 37:25) is actually a reference to Sennacherib's construction of irrigation works in this area (modern Jebel Bashiqah, E of Khorsabad) for the city of Nineveh. Although, as he admits (201, note 34), the presence of *yĕʾōrê māṣôr* in Isa 19:6, a clear reference to Egypt, remains unexplained.

The prophet Nahum (3:8–10) compares the fall of Nineveh (612 B.C.E.) to the earlier Assyrian sack of Thebes "that sat by the Nile" in Upper (southern) Egypt (663 B.C.E.). The references to rivers/streams *(yĕʾorîm),* water(s) *(mayim),* and sea *(yām)* in Nahum's portrayal of this S Egyptian city have caused difficulties (although *yām* could refer to the Nile, as in Isaiah 19 above, and Nahum's description may reflect a knowledge of this chapter). As earlier scholars have noted, this description of Thebes is more suited to a typical city of the Delta (see Spiegelberg 1904: 33; Müller 1903; Simons *GTTOT,* 474; on Delta cities, Bietak 1979: 100–1), and later tradition (e.g., Jerome) identified Heb *Nōʾ-ʾāmôn* (Thebes) with Alexandria (see Doorslaer 1949). However, Nahum's description of Thebes as insular and aquatically fortified may draw from his own limited knowledge of Egyptian cities, which included only those of the Delta, as opposed to the lesser-known cities (at least to the inhabitants of Palestine) of Upper (southern) Egypt (but see Schneider 1988, who defends the prophet's description as accurate and possibly reflecting a personal knowledge of the city).

In Ezekiel's oracles against Egypt (Ezekiel 29–32), the pharaoh is like the "great sea creature [Heb *hattannîm haggādôl*] lying [in the sense of "at ease"?] in the midst of his rivers [*yĕʾōrāyw*], who says 'My Nile [MT sg. *yĕʾōri*] is my own, I made it [for?] myself' " (29:3; see Freedy and Redford 1970: 471; Boadt 1980: 26–30; see also v 9 and 32:2–3). Through this statement, the pharaoh proudly asserts his sole ownership of and sovereignty over Egypt, and such hubris, of course, does not go unpunished. To continue the metaphor, Yahweh will hook the animal and leave him to rot out of water, with his carcass as food for the "beasts of the earth and birds of the air" (v 5; note the cosmic dimensions of this event in 32:3–8). While Heb *yĕʾōr* is used exclusively in 29:3–5 and 9, other related passages (32:2, 14) vary with *yām, nāhār,* and *mayim.* There is disagreement over the interpretation of Heb *tannîm* in 29:2 and 32:2 (generally read *tannîn;* see Zimmerli *Ezekiel 2* Hermeneia, 106; Boadt 1980: 26–27). Since the seminal work of Gunkel (*Schöpfung und Chaos in Urzeit und Endzeit,* 1895), a number of scholars have advocated a mythological context for this passage, identifying Ezekiel's *tannîm* with the well-known sea creature or dragon subdued (or requiring subjugation) by Yahweh (e.g., Isa 27:1; 51:9; Ps 74:13; for Gunkel, see translation of selected passages in Anderson 1984: 25–52; discussion in Boadt 1980: 26–27; Day 1985: 94–95). Others (e.g., Cooke *Ezekiel* ICC, 325–26) reject this view, rendering *tannîm* as "crocodile," a creature familiar in Egyptian literature (e.g., Westcar Pap., see Simpson 1973: 17–18, 30; *Admonitions of Ipuwer,* see Lichtheim *AEL* 1: 151; Book of the Dead, see Allen 1974: 29, 41–43, 65, etc.; see Stead 1986: 69 for illustration; in general, Brunner-Traut in *LÄ* 3: 791–801). According to Zimmerli *Ezekiel 2,* 111, this mythological monster has already been demythologized in Ezekiel, and "what should be thought of in the first instance is the crocodile." He then draws attention to the often quoted phrase from the Poetical Stela of Thutmose III, where Amun-Re says of the king, "I let them [the king's enemies] see your majesty as a crocodile [*dpi*], master of terror in the water, unapproached" (*Urk.* IV, 616, line 9; translation from Lichtheim *AEL* 2: 37). However, the relevance of this text for Ezekiel is greatly diminished when one notes that in the same poem, Amun also caused the king's foes to see him as (among other things) a youthful bull, a fearsome lion, a falcon(?) (Eg *nb dm3t,* lit "lord of wing") pouncing on its prey, and a jackal. A more fruitful, although highly speculative, approach to the question of Egyptian parallels might be found in those inscriptions or reliefs assigning royal attributes (e.g., through assimilation with Re, Horus, or Osiris) to the Egyptian deity Sobek (Gk *Suchos*), represented in the form of a crocodile, a human body with a crocodile head, or fetish; not unnaturally, Sobek is also closely associated with the Nile (e.g., "Lord of the Nile") and is protected by its fish (see Brovarski in *LÄ* 5: 995–1031, esp. 999–1000; compare Ezek 29:4–5). But even the existence of suitable Egyptian parallels need not imply conscious borrowing by the biblical writer.

In a handful of passages, *yĕʾōr* is unrelated to the Nile or Egypt: Isa 33:21 (the broad rivers of the restored Zion); Job 28:10 (man-made channels cut through rock); and Dan 12:5–7 (the shore of the Tigris [?], compare 10:4).

Bibliography

Aling, C. F. 1981. *Egypt and Bible History.* Grand Rapids.

Allen, T. G. 1974. *The Book of the Dead.* SAOC 37. Chicago.

Anderson, B. W., ed. 1984. *Creation in the Old Testament.* IRT 6.

Baines, J. 1974. The Inundation Stela of Sebekḥotpe VIII. *AcOr* 36: 39–58.

———. 1976. The Sebekḥotpe Inundation Stela: An Additional Fragment. *AcOr* 37: 11–20.

———. 1985. *Fecundity Figures: Egyptian Personification and the Iconology of a Genre.* Warminster.

Beckerath, J. von. 1966. The Nile Level Records at Karnak and Their Importance for the History of the Libyan Period (Dynasties XII and XIII). *JARCE* 5: 43–55.

Beegle, D. M. 1979. *Moses, the Servant of Yahweh.* Ann Arbor.
Bell, B. 1975. Climate and the History of Egypt: The Middle Kingdom. *AJA* 79: 223–69.
Bietak, M. 1975. *Tell el-Dabʿa.* Vienna.
———. 1979. Urban Archaeology and the "Town Problem" in Ancient Egypt. Pp. 97–144 in *Egyptology and the Social Sciences,* ed. K. R. Weeks. Cairo.
Boadt, L. 1980. *Ezekiel's Oracles against Egypt.* BibOr 37. Rome.
Buck, A. de. 1948. On the meaning of the Name *Ḥʿpj.* Pp. 1–22 in *Orientalia Neerlandica.* Leiden.
Butzer, K. W. 1976. *Early Hydraulic Civilization in Egypt.* Chicago.
———. 1984. Long-Term Nile Flood Variation and Political Discontinuities in Pharaonic Egypt. Pp. 102–12 in *From Hunters to Farmers: The Causes and Consequences of Food Production in Africa,* ed. J. D. Clark and S. A. Brandt. Berkeley and London.
Calderone, P. J. 1961. The Rivers of Maṣor. *Bib* 42: 423–32.
Coats, G. W. 1988. *Moses.* JSOTSup 57. Sheffield.
Day, J. 1985. *God's Conflict with the Dragon and the Sea.* University of Cambridge Oriental Publications 35. Cambridge.
Doorslaer, J. van. 1949. No Amon. *CBQ* 11: 280–95.
Finegan, J. 1963. *Let My People Go.* New York.
Fohrer, G. 1964. *Überlieferung und Geschichte des Exodus: Eine Analyse von Ex 1–15.* BZAW 91. Berlin.
Freedy, K. S., and Redford, D. B. 1970. The Dates in Ezekiel in Relation to Biblical, Babylonian and Egyptian Sources. *JAOS* 90: 462–85.
Gardiner, A. H. 1909. *The Admonitions of an Egyptian Sage.* Leipzig. Repr. Hildesheim, 1969.
———. 1947. *Ancient Egyptian Onomastica.* Vol. 2. Oxford.
Greenberg, M. 1969. *Understanding Exodus.* New York.
Habachi, L. 1974. A High Inundation in the Temple of Amenre at Karnak in the Thirteenth Dynasty. *SAK* 1: 207–14.
Hayes, J. H., and Irvine, S. A. 1987. *Isaiah the Eighth-Century Prophet.* Nashville.
Hornung, E. 1982. *Conceptions of God in Ancient Egypt. The One and the Many.* Trans. J. Baines. Ithaca, NY.
Hort, G. 1957–58. The Plagues of Egypt. *ZAW* 69: 84–103 and 70: 48–59.
Janssen, J. J. 1987. The Day the Inundation Began. *JNES* 46: 129–36.
Kadish, G. E. 1988. Seasonality and the Name of the Nile. *JARCE* 25: 185–94.
Kitchen, K. A. 1986. *The Third Intermediate Period in Egypt (1100–650 B.C.).* 2d ed. Warminster, England.
Lambdin, T. O. 1953. Egyptian Loan Words in the Old Testament. *JAOS* 73: 145–55.
Lesko, L. H. 1982–89. *A Dictionary of Late Egyptian.* 4 vols. Berkeley.
Macadam, M. F. L. 1949. *The Temples of Kawa I. The Inscriptions.* London.
Montet, P. 1968. *Egypt and the Bible.* Trans. L. R. Keylock. Philadelphia.
Müller, W. M. 1903. No, No-Amon. *EncBib,* cols. 3427–29 (1 vol. ed.).
Petrie, W. M. F. 1911. *Ancient Egypt and Ancient Israel.* 2d ed. London.
Quaegebeur, J. 1985. On the Egyptian Equivalent of Biblical *Ḥarṭummîm.* Pp. 162–72 in *Pharaonic Egypt, the Bible and Christianity,* ed. S. Groll. Jerusalem.
Sarna, N. M. 1986. *Exploring Exodus.* New York.
Schneider, T. 1988. Nahum und Theban. Zum topographisch-historischen Hintergrund von Nah 3,8f. *BN* 44: 63–73.
Simpson, W. K., ed. 1973. *The Literature of Ancient Egypt.* New Haven.
Spiegelberg, W. 1904. *Aegyptologische Randglossen zum Alten Testament.* Strassburg.
Stead, M. 1986. *Egyptian Life.* Cambridge, MA.
Tawil, H. 1982. The Historicity of 2 Kings 19:24 (= Isaiah 37:25): The Problem of *Yĕʾōrê Māṣôr. JNES* 41: 195–206.
Vandersleyen, C. 1967. Une tempête sous le règne d'Amosis. *RdÉ* 19: 123–59.
Van Seters, J. 1986. The Plagues of Egypt: Ancient Tradition or Literary Invention? *ZAW* 98: 31–39.
Ward, W. A. 1974. The Semitic Biconsonantal Root *SP* and the Common Origin of Egyptian *ČWF* and Hebrew *SÛP:* "Marsh(-Plant)." *VT* 24: 339–49.
Zevit, Z. 1976. The Priestly Redaction and Interpretation of the Plague Narrative in Exodus. *JQR* 66: 193–211.
———. 1990. Three Ways to Look at the Ten Plagues. *BRev* 4/3: 16–23, 42.

JOHN R. HUDDLESTUN

GEOGRAPHY

The most remarkable of the ancient world's river systems (Hurst 1925; 1957; Hurst and Phillips 1931), the Nile formed an indispensable resource for Egypt and a series of cultures in Nubia and Sudan in Ancient times.

A. Course and Hydrology.
1. White Nile.
2. Blue Nile.
3. Main Nile.
B. Inundation.
C. Nile North of Khartoum.
1. Development.
2. Inundation and occupation.
D. Land and Water.
1. Natural irrigation.
2. Nile and Egyptian Agriculture.
E. Nile in Egyptian Religion.

A. Course and Hydrology

1. White Nile. The sources of the Nile lie 6,671 km from the river's mouths, in the Kagera river system in Central Africa which empties into Lake Victoria, the largest freshwater lake in the Eastern Hemisphere. The Victoria Nile leaves the lake, flowing over the Owen and Ripon falls, and enters shallow and swampy Lake Kioga. The river then flows through more rapids to the edge of the Central African rift at Murchison Falls, entering Lake Albert with a volume of 10.7 G m^3/year (billions of cubic meters). The Albert Nile descends from the lake 153 m in its 156 km course to the Uganda-Sudan border. The river, here known as the Bahr el Gebel (River of the Mountain), flows to the great swampy Sudd (Block) with a volume of 26.5 G m^3/year, where despite the addition of the Bahr el Ghazal (Gazelle River), evaporation and percolation reduce the volume of water that leaves the Sudd as the White Nile (Bahr el-Abyad) to only 14.24 G m^3/year. The Sobat, which rises in the Ethiopian highlands, the last significant tributary to the White Nile, brings the flow to 25.2 G m^3/year, its volume at Khartoum (Kleinschroth 1977: 158–59).

2. Blue Nile. From Lake Tana in the N Ethiopian highland, the Blue Nile (Bahr el-Azraq) flows 900 km to Rosieres Dam in Sudan, descending 1,300 m, partly through a spectacular gorge (Williams and Williams 1980: 212), and receiving numerous tributaries. The rivers Dinder and Rahad join the Blue Nile below Rosieres to make a total flow of some 51.4 G m^3/year (Kleinschroth 1977: 159).

3. Main Nile. The Blue and the White Niles join at Khartoum, and the river receives the addition of the seasonal Atbara north of the Sixth Cataract to make up the annual volume at Aswan of 84 G m^3/year, the last addition to the Nile for 2,700 km when it empties into the Mediterranean (Kleinschroth 1977: 159).

B. Inundation

For nine months, the river's water comes primarily from the White Nile. Most of the Nile's flow occurs in a three-month inundation season from August to October, when monsoon rains in Ethiopia swell the Sobat, the Blue Nile, and the Atbara to make up 95 percent of the Nile's volume for the season, the inundation being more than 80 percent for the entire year. The inundation is quite irregular, and the total volume has varied from a low of 41 G m^3/year in 1913/14 to 151 G m^3/year in 1878–79 (Kleinschroth 1977: 159).

C. Nile North of Khartoum

Six cataracts divide the Nile into moderately sloped navigable reaches and regulate the speed of the inundation. From Aswan, the Nile descends somewhat less than 1 m for every 10 km. The river follows a valley at the edge of the Eastern Desert plateau that varies from the Nile's own width to about 15 km which often encloses the valley between high cliffs (Kleinschroth 1977: 159; Rushdi Said 1975: 12–13 and 31–32). Below the First Cataract, the valley becomes wider, especially north of the great bend at Nag Hammadi. North of Cairo, the cliffs disappear and the Nile divides, now into two branches (Rosetta and Damietta), in ancient times into seven (Bietak 1975: 75–98), forming the great fertile Egyptian Delta, some 150 x 245 km.

1. Development. The Nile Valley, a graben, and the Delta were filled with hundreds of meters of sediment, beginning in mid-Tertiary times (Williams and Williams 1980: 218–20), but the gray-black alluvium that forms the agricultural plain is a thin surface that has been deposited in the last 30,000 years (Rushdi Said 1975: 30–32). The Nile berms are above the plain, which slopes downward toward the edges (Bietak 1975: 53–54; Butzer 1976: 15–17). The banks of different courses generally paralleled the river as natural dikes.

2. Inundation and Occupation. The broad valley and the annual silt-laden inundation make possible a lush vegetation on the floodplain and an almost miraculous agricultural productivity. The inundation (6–8 m above low water) covers the land about 1.5–2 m deep for about 45 days. Its timing is right to allow grain plants to mature in the winter without further watering. The inundation's soaking removes soil-damaging salts and leaves a thin (ca. 1 mm) layer of fresh silt with new nitrogen to renew the land. The silt increased the height of the land about one meter per millennium, broadening the valley floor and filling lower, swampy areas more rapidly than higher ones, an important long-term change (Rushdi Said 1975: 33).

D. Land and Water

Based on the distribution of water, different modes of occupying the Egyptian valley can be characterized as "natural irrigation," basin irrigation, perennial irrigation, and artificial irrigation (Willcocks and Craig 1913: 299–426; Schenkel 1978: 21–23).

1. Natural Irrigation. The simplest agriculture in the valley involved no modification of the flood. As the river receded, a cultivator would follow its progressive fall with rows of plantings. Probably derived from seasonal playa agriculture, this technique appears elsewhere in Africa where shallow seasonal bodies of water occur (McIntosh and McIntosh 1984: 159; Butzer 1976: 19). It was recently used in parts of Nubia and where irrigation is not practicable, and it is sometimes enhanced by terracing or by the erection of small dam-traps which create mud flats in the braided channels of the Second Cataract (Vercoutter 1966: 161–63, pls. XVI–XVII).

The condition of the land could be unpredictable even when floods were normal. The river's eroding meanders and changing bed continuously altered the landscape, and the location of "good" floods would change (Russell 1966: 78–79; see Rushdi Said 1975: 37–38; Butzer 1976: fig. 1), so in a thirty-year period, only a few Niles were ideal, and many were too high or too low. Land usable one year might not be adequately watered, silted, or drained the next. The silt provided sufficient fertility for planting grain only every second year or two years out of five (Girard 1824: 137–48; Baer 1971), and with the variable inundation, a field's fallow cycle could not be anticipated and land ownership would be difficult. Even with irrigation, villages could be difficult to site (Russell 1966: 79).

2. Nile and Egyptian Agriculture. Egypt developed complementary agricultural practices, engineering works, economic arrangements, and administrative measures that formed the basis of its monumental civilization.

a. Agricultural Cycle. Egyptians raised many garden crops and other specialized products, but the agricultural cycle was dominated by the cultivation of grains, generally barley and millet, and raising livestock, goats, sheep, and cattle. These two activities were mutually dependent. Grain was alternated with fallow, but alternation with nitrogen-enriching crops, as done more recently, was apparently not practiced. Animals were fed on straw from the fields and they foraged in the fallow fields, where their droppings helped enrich the soil (Willcocks and Craig 1913: 762; Baer 1971; *LÄ* 2: 934–35).

The population, about 2.5–4.5 million, about 1/5 urban, was supported by cultivation of somewhat less than half the arable land in any one year (for estimates, see Baer 1962: 42–44; 1971; for the fallow cycle, see Girard 1824: 141). Much land was privately owned, but large areas were controlled by the ruler and cults (Baer 1962: 32–33; Hughes 1952: 74). Most cultivators sought favorably inundated land to lease in a single year for about 1/3–1/2 of the crop or other rent, in addition to any land they might possess (Baer 1962: 33–39; 1963: 9–16). Farmers often operated with associates and hired hands in teams

(Hughes 1952: 45, 49 note m, 68–69 note f; Baer 1963: 7; note household rations 18–22).

b. Hydraulic Engineering: The Basin System. The most important element of Egyptian agriculture made the inundation perform more reliably, regulating the natural regime. At its simplest, the banks of the river were reinforced, and transverse dikes were constructed between natural levees enclosing basins, which were carefully leveled to ensure even watering and deposition of silt (Butzer 1976: 20; Baer 1971; Hurst 1957: 38–41; Girard 1824: 10–13). In the 19th century, these generally varied in size from 2,000 to 40,000 acres, averaging about 7,000, but they could be made much smaller (Willcocks and Craig 1913: 301; Baer 1971). An inlet canal, sometimes an abandoned channel, was dug to about halfway between the high and low Nile to lead water onto the fields, and a drain was dug to lead it off again. In Upper Egypt, the same canal could serve for both watering and drainage. At the appropriate time, the high Nile was let into the canal by cutting a closing bank, and 40–45 days later, the drain would be opened to clear the fields for planting. The simplest basin systems would be established by a village or a town (Hurst 1957: 39), but a considerable amount of yearly maintenance was necessary, backed by regular labor obligations (*LÄ* 2: 333-34; Goyon 1982: 64 n. 23). The effectiveness of basin irrigation could be greatly enhanced by large projects and its flexibility improved by complex refinements (Wilcocks and Craig 1913: 299–341). Nevertheless, irrigation, like many mundane but very important functions, is not detailed in Egyptian sources (Baer 1971; Schenkel 1978: 25). Before the end of the New Kingdom, there are few unequivocal references to irrigation apart from some important texts in the First Intermediate Period (Schenkel 1978: 29–36) and the titles of some low-echelon officials in the New Kingdom (Endesfelder 1979: 47–49). Irrigation was largely a local or mundane matter that rarely appears in representations and only occasionally in texts before the Ptolemaic period. Because it is first mentioned in inscriptions during the First Intermediate Period, an irrigation revolution has been postulated (Schenkel 1978; *LÄ* 1: 776–82).

There is substantial evidence for hydraulic works much earlier (Schenkel 1978: 26–27). Before the First Dynasty, the monumental decorated mace-head of Scorpion (third predessor of Narmer) shows a hydraulic event no matter what ceremony was actually depicted. The pharaoh appears with a hoe in his hand attended by a man with a basket and a second man with a sheaf. Below is what seems to be a canal with men, also holding hoes, partly in the water, and a palm revetted against the flood (Smith 1946: 113–14, fig. 30; but see Schenkel 1978: 29; Helck 1987: 97; *LÄ* 1: 1261–63). From Dynasty I, inundation levels were recorded in the annals, a systematic recording later intimately connected with the basin system (Jaritz 1986: 1–2). In the Old Kingdom, canals were built for shipping. Quays at royal mortuary complexes were located on the Memphite canal (*LÄ* 3: 10–12). A large (110 × 98 × 14 m) masonry-faced dam across an Eastern Desert wadi, the Sadd el Kafara, was constructed in the Old Kingdom (Fahlbusch 1986; Garbrecht et al. 1983: Appendix B). Abundant evidence of early hydraulic engineering and careful measurement indicates indirectly that the basin complex was already in existence.

c. Hydraulic Engineering: True Irrigation. As the land rose in ancient times, the canals gradually gained on the higher land and were extended to increase the area that could be irrigated using devices that would lift the water into a garden plot, devices such as the shadoof, lifting up to 3 m (Girard 1824: 17–18; *LÄ* 5: 520–21). In Ptolemaic times, the Archimedes' screw was added, and later a simple ox-turned waterwheel with buckets or chambers *(tambusha)* which could lift water about a meter (Hurst 1957: 44–45). A wheel with a rope chain of pots or buckets *(saqia)* imported by Roman times from Persia was capable of lifting water up to even 10 m, making it possible to water large gardens and palm groves (Girard 1824: 20–22).

Large projects such as the Old Kingdom Sadd el-Kafara were sponsored by the state. The most famous of these was the Lake Moeris (not to be confused with Birket Qarun) probably created in the southern Fayum in the Middle Kingdom (Herodotus 2: 148–50; Garbrecht 1986b: 8–11). In the Ptolemaic period, this region was made much more productive with elaborate works (Bonneau 1981; see also Eck 1986: 5–6).

d. Government, Agriculture and Irrigation. Although not well represented in the texts, irrigation was an essential economic support of the Egyptian state, and the state at least indirectly became necessary for successful irrigation through its concern with agricultural output. Important measures complemented basin complexes and agricultural practices to make Egypt's large population and continuity possible. Security against marauding invaders, animals, and social disorder, the fundamental obligation of the pharaonic state, was needed to keep enough of an active agricultural population (young males) on the land to maintain the dikes and canals or even to prevent deliberate acts of destruction (Schenkel 1978: 27, also 29–31 and 55–87). Measurement of the inundation (Jaritz 1986: 2) together with taxes and rents paid in kind to institutions not only supported their own activities, but provided grain to be stored and available to alleviate famine (Schenkel 1978: 37–49; see Genesis 41; *LÄ* 3: 84). In addition, governments and even officials undertook the resettlement of people on reclaimed land, an "internal colonization" (Goyon 1982: 64; Schenkel 1978: 55–57, 65–67).

e. Nile and Egyptian History. In four millennia, failures were bound to occur (Butzer 1976: 26–38; 1984: 106), and they could lead to famine, starvation, cannibalism, banditry, social disruption, and displacement. It is difficult to attribute specific periods of social disorder to Nile failure because disruption of normal agricultural routines or grain supplies by war or mismanagement would have the same effect, but even some unusual Niles did not cause insuperable difficulties, as indicated by much more complete medieval records (Russell 1966). Relatively low Niles recorded in the Second Dynasty occur in a period of some conflict, but increasing prosperity is also shown in the development of royal complexes and the great private cemetery at Helwan (Butzer 1984: 106, 108; but see Stadelmann 1985). Major disruptions at the end of the Old Kingdom are not accompanied by explicit documentation of poor Niles, but formulistic references to events that occur regularly in Egypt, such as dust storms that appear in the *khamsin* season and shallow water (1 m), occur commonly (Willcocks 1889: 19); a famine at the end of the 11th Dynasty may also have its origin in social or administrative disruption (Bell 1971; Butzer 1984: 106–7, 108–9; see von Beckerath 1965, esp. p. 9). In late Dynasty XII and early Dynasty XIII, records of extremely high water in Nubia under the powerful Amenemhat III are not accompanied by evidence of chaos, despite a change of dynasty (Bell 1975; Butzer 1984: 107, 109; see Bietak 1975: 63 n. 198; Vercoutter 1966). At the end of the New Kingdom, drastic rises in prices are accompanied by official corruption in the grain supply and by invasion and infiltration from Libya and Nubia that repeatedly disrupted work routines as far S as Thebes (*CAH* 2/2: 616–34; Butzer 1984: 107–8, 109–10; Baer 1962: 27–29). Shortage and disruption are correlated in late Ptolemaic and Roman times, attributed to rapacious administration and neglect. In medieval times, long periods of low Niles were accompanied by reduced population and a generalized social weakening, sometimes even plagues, without sudden disruption (Russell 1966: 75, 77–82).

Fragmentary and disputed evidence indicates that quite early, Egyptians developed agricultural practices, some irrigation technology, and institutions for storing and distributing produce that were capable of dealing with almost any variation in the Nile. When these habits and institutions broke down, as when people avoided exactions or pestilence wiped out part of the population, the irrigation works deteriorated rapidly from neglect and Egypt was impoverished (Russell 1966: 71; Bonneau 1971: 189–98; Garbrecht 1986a: 10–11; Eck 1986: 20–22). If fluctuation in the inundation probably had limited effect on the course of Egyptian history, long-term changes may have been more influential. The deposition of silt, concentrated especially in the Delta (Rushdi Said 1975: 33–34; van den Brink et al. 1987), increased the area available there for cultivation so much that it became Egypt's predominant region by the end of the New Kingdom, a position it has occupied to the present day.

E. Nile in Egyptian Religion

Despite its importance to Egypt, the Nile's deity, Hapy, was not numbered among the great gods of the pantheon (Bonneau 1964: 229; *LÄ* 4: 485–88). God of the inundation, Hapy had his own cults (see *LÄ* 4: 498–500), festival, and hymn (*LÄ* 4: 490–96), but was most often seen as the bringer of produce offerings. He is often shown covered with zigzag lines as though under water, a male figure with pendulous breasts, a large stomach, and a beard, wearing a papyrus bundle on his head. He typically appears as a pair of gods who tie the plants of Lower and Upper Egypt together on the side of a throne. Rows of Nile gods, one for each district or nome, alternately red and blue, bring offerings to the chief god of a temple (Bonneau 1964: 223–29). Hapy was identified or clearly associated with many gods in their aspect of fruitfulness, but he was especially close to Nun, the primeval water which was connected to the inundation, as Hapy-Nun (Bonneau 1964: 238–39), and to Osiris, joined with him as Hapy-Osiris (*LÄ* 4: 485–88; see also Bonneau 1964: 243–74). The first rising of the Nile at the Cataract was brought about by Khnum, with his associates Satis and Anukis (Bonneau 1964: 232–33), and the pharaoh was a guarantor of its fruitfulness (Bonneau 1982: 62–63, *LÄ* 6: 831–33).

Bibliography

Baer, K. 1962. An Eleventh Dynasty Farmer's Letters to His Family. *JAOS* 83: 1–19.

———. 1963. The Low Price of Land in Egypt. *JARCE* 1: 25–45.

———. 1971. Land and Water in Ancient Egypt. Paper delivered at the Twenty-eighth International Congress of Orientalists, Canberra.

Beckerath, J. von. 1965. Zur Begrundung der 12. Dynastie durch Ammenemes I. *ZÄS* 92: 4–10.

Bell, B. 1971. The Dark Ages in Ancient History I. The First Dark Age in Egypt. *AJA* 75: 2–25.

———. 1975. Climate and the History of Egypt: The Middle Kingdom. *AJA* 79: 223–69.

Bietak, M. 1975. *Tell ed-Dab'a II; der Fundort im Rahmen einer archaeologisch-geographischen Untersuchung über das ägyptische Ostdelta.* DÖAW 4. Vienna.

Bonneau, D. 1964. *La Crue du Nil.* Paris.

———. 1971. *Le Fisc et le Nil.* Paris.

———. 1981. Le Nil a l'epoque ptolemaique: Administration de l'eau au IIIe siécle avant notre ére. Pp. 103–14 in *L'Homme et l'eau en Mediterranée et au proche orient I,* ed. Metral and P. Sanlavalle. Travaux de la Maison de l'Orient 1. Lyon.

———. 1982. Le Souverain d'Egypte, juge de l'usage de l'eau. Vol. 1, pp. 69–80 in *L'Homme et l'eau en Mediterranée et au proche orient,* ed F. and J. Metral. Travaux de la Maison de l'orient 2. Lyon.

Brink, E. C. M. van den.; Wesemael, B. van; and Dirksz, D. 1987. A Geo-Archaeological Survey in the North-Eastern Nile Delta, Egypt: The First Two Seasons, a Preliminary Report. *MDAIK* 43: 7–31.

Butzer, K. 1976. *Early Hydraulic Civilization in Egypt.* Chicago.

———. 1984. Long-term Nile Flood Variation and Political Discontinuities in Pharaonic Egypt. Pp. 102–12 in *From Hunters to Farmers: The Causes and Consequences of Food Production in Africa,* ed. J. D. Clark and S. A. Brandt. Berkeley.

Eck, W. 1986. Staat und landwirtschaftliches Bewässerungssystem Agyptens in römischer Zeit. Pp. 1–37 (separate pagination) in *Vorträge der Tagung "Geschichtliche Wasserbauten in Agypten" Kairo, 10. bis 17. Februar 1986.* Mitteilungen des Leichtweiss-Instituts für Wasserbau der Technischen Universität Braunschweig 89. Braunschweig.

Endesfelder, E. 1979. Zur Frage der Bewässerung im pharaonischen Agypten. *ZÄS* 106: 37–51.

Fahlbusch, H. 1986. Der Sadd-el-Kafara. Pp. 1–20 (separate pagination) in *Vorträge der Tagung "Geschichtliche Wasserbauten in Agypten" Kairo, 10. bis 17. Februar 1986.* Mitteilungen des Leichtweiss-Institut für Wasserbau der Technischen Universität Braunschweig 89. Braunschweig.

Garbrecht, G. 1986a. Der Nil und Agypten. Pp. 1–20 (separate pagination) in *Vorträge der Tagung "Geschichtliche Wasserbauten in Agypten" Kairo, 10. bis 17. Februar 1986.* Mitteilungen des Leichtweiss-Institut für Wasserbau der Technischen Universität Braunschweig 89. Braunschweig.

———. 1986b. Wasserpeicherung im Fayum (Moris-See), Legende oder Wirklichkeit? Pp. 1–12 (separate pagination) in *Vorträge der Tagung "Geschichtliche Wasserbauten in Agypten" Kairo, 10. bis 17. Februar 1986.* Mitteilungen des Leichtweiss-Institut für

Wasserbau der Technischen Universität Braunschweig 89. Braunschweig.
Garbrecht, G.; Bertram, H.-U.; et al. 1983. *Der Sadd-el-Kafara: Die alteste Talsperre der Welt (2600 v. Chr.)* Mitteilungen des Leichtweiss-institut für Wasserbau der Technischen Universität Braunschweig 81. Braunschweig.
Girard, M. P. S. 1824. Ebauche d'un systeme etatique d'utilisation de l'eau. Egypte pharaonique de l'ancien au nouvel empire. Vol. 1, pp. 61–67 in *L'Homme et l'eau en Mediterranée et au proche orient,* ed. F. and J. Metral. Travaux de la maison de l'Orient 2. Lyon.
Goyon, J. C. 1982. Ebauche d'un systeme etatique d'utilisation de l'eau. Egypte pharaonique de l'ancien au nouvel empire. Pp. 61–67 in *L'Homme et l'eau en Mediterranée et au proche orient I,* ed. J. Metral. Travaux de la Maison de l'Orient 2. Lyon.
Helck, W. 1987. *Untersuchungen zur Thinitenzeit.* ÄA 45. Wiesbaden.
Hughes, G. R. 1952. *Saite Demotic Land Leases.* SAOC 28. Chicago.
Hurst, H. E. 1925. *A Short Account of the Nile and its Basin.* Cairo.
———. 1957. *The Nile: A General Account of the River and the Utilization of Its Waters.* 2d ed. London.
Hurst, H. E., and Phillips, P. 1931. *The Nile Basin.* Vol. 1, *General Description of the Basin, Meteorology, Topography of the White Nile Basin.* Physical Department Paper 28. Cairo.
Jaritz, H. 1986. Wasserstandmessungen am Nil-Nilometer. Pp. 1–23 (separate pagination) in *Vorträge der Tagung "Geschichtliche Wasserbauten in Agypten" Kairo, 10. bis 17. Februar 1986.* Mitteilungen des Leichtweiss-Instituts für Wasserbau der Technischen Universität Braunschweig 89. Braunschweig.
Kleinschroth, A. 1977. Nutzung der Gewässer im sudan. *Osterreichische Wasserwirtschaft* 29 7/8: 157–64.
McIntosh, R. J., and McIntosh, S. K. 1984. Early Iron Age Economy in the Inland Niger Delta (Mali). Pp. 158–72 in *From Hunters to Farmers: The Causes and Consequences of Food Production in Africa,* ed. J. D. Clark and S. A. Brandt. Berkeley.
Rushdi Said. 1975. The Geological Evolution of the River Nile. Pp. 7–44 in *Problems in Prehistory: North Africa and the Levant,* ed. F. Wendorf and A. E. Marks. Dallas.
Russell, J. 1966. The Population of Medieval Egypt. *JARCE* 5: 69–82.
Schenkel, W. 1978. *Die Bewässerungsrevolution im alten Agypten.* Mainz am Rhein.
Smith, W. S. 1946. *History of Egyptian Painting and Sculpture in the Old Kingdom.* London.
Stadelmann, R. 1985. Die Oberbauten der Königsgraber der 2. Dynastie in Saqqara. Pp. 295–307 in *Melanges Gamal eddin Mokhtar,* ed. P. Posener-Krieger. Cairo.
Vercoutter, J. 1966. Semna South Fort and the Records of Nile Levels at Kumma. *Kush* 14: 125–64.
Willcocks, W. 1889. *Egyptian Irrigation.* London.
Willcocks, W., and Craig, J. I. 1913. *Egyptian Irrigation.* 3d ed. London.
Williams, M. A. J., and Williams, F. M. 1980. Evolution of the Nile Basin. Pp. 207–24 in *The Sahara and the Nile: Quaternary Environments and Prehistoric Occupation in Northern Africa,* eds. M. A. J. Williams and H. Faure. Rotterdam.

BRUCE B. WILLIAMS

NIMRIM, THE WATERS OF (PLACE) [Heb *mê-nimrîm*]. Waters located in Moab and mentioned in oracles against Moab (Isa 15:6; Jer 48:34). The once fertile and well-watered region had become desolate and denuded. Eusebius and Jerome equated the Waters of Nimrim with *Bennamerium* N of Zoar (Lagarde 1887: 284, lines 32–34; 143, lines 11–13). Modern scholarship has traced the name Nimrim to locations both NE and SE of the Dead Sea. Most scholars identify the Waters of Nimrim with the homonymic *Wâdī en-Numeirah,* a small stream flowing W just above the *Wâdī el-Ḥesā* into the Dead Sea about 8–10 miles above its S end (e.g., Rudolph *Jeremia,* HAT,[2] 265; Wildberger *Jesaja* BKAT, 616). The ruined site called *Numeirah* (M.R. 201059) which lies at the source of the *Wâdī en-Numeirah* may have been the location of the ancient Moabite town.

Other scholars hold that the ancient biblical name Beth-nimrah (Num 32:36; Josh 13:27), identified by many with *Tell el-Bleibil* (M.R. 2010146), survives in the name of the Roman-Byzantine site called *Tell Nimrîn* (about 1 mile SW of *Tell el-Bleibil*), and suggest that the waters of the *Wâdī Nimrîn* may be a reference to the biblical Waters of Nimrim (e.g., Glueck 1943: 11).

Given the association of the Waters of Nimrim with towns such as Zoar and Horonaim and the apparently southern escape route of the fugitives (cf. Isa 15:1–5), a southerly location of the Waters of Nimrim, while not proven, seems preferable.

Bibliography

Glueck, N. 1943. Some Ancient Towns in the Plans of Moab. *BASOR* 91: 7–26.
Lagarde, P. de. 1887. *Onomastica Sacra.* Göttingen. Repr. Hildesheim, 1966.

ARTHUR J. FERCH

NIMROD (PERSON) [Heb *nimrōd*]. A pre-Israelite hero mentioned in Gen 10:8 (= 1 Chr 1:10), 9–12, and Mic 5:5—Eng 5:6. The Genesis passage, part of the Table of Nations of chap. 10, but marked out from the rest by its narrative, not simply genealogical, character, is regularly assigned to J. It describes Nimrod, the first of the (post-Flood) heroes, as the son of Cush. As a hero he achieves proverbial renown as a hunter, and rules the land of Shinar/Babylonia, with its chief cities, Babylon, Erech/Uruk, and Akkad/Agade. From there he extends his kingdom to Assyria, building Nineveh, Rehoboth-Ir, Calah, and Resen. In Micah the land of Nimrod is put in parallel and thus presumably equated with the land of Assyria.

The identity of Nimrod has been much debated. Three different approaches have been pursued. The first identifies Nimrod as a god, usually the Mesopotamian Ninurta or Marduk. The second would find in Nimrod a legendary Mesopotamian hero, either Gilgamesh or Lugalbanda, or a legendary eponym of Mesopotamia, parallel to the Ninos of Greek tradition. In the third approach, Nimrod has been equated with an historical personage, especially the Mesopotamian kings Sargon of Agade or Tukulti-Ninurta I of Assyria; less often, Nazimaruttash, a Kassite king of Babylonia, the Egyptian pharaoh Amenophis III, or the Aramaean ruler Ben-Hadad.

Deciding among this bewildering variety of identifications is not easy. Since the Genesis text, especially, describes human achievements in a Mesopotamian setting, one would expect a legendary hero, an eponym, or an historical personage of Mesopotamia, not a god, even if the form "Nimrod" fits best as a Hebrew corruption and denigrative reinterpretation ("we will rebel" [*mārad*]) of the divine names Ninurta or Marduk. A way to reconcile these alternatives is to suppose (so Speiser 1958) that Nimrod is a legendary hero, eponym, or historical personage whose name is an abbreviation of one formed with "Ninurta" or "Marduk," like Tukulti-Ninurta I.

In trying to narrow the options further, we may observe that the biblical representation of Nimrod seems to have drawn upon a multiplicity of Mesopotamian traditions. The mention of Babylon, Erech/Uruk, and Akkad/Agade points, on the one hand, to Babylonia. More specifically, the fact that Nimrod is based in Babylonia, from which he then extends his rule over Assyria (construing *ʾaššûr* in Gen 10:11 as the land, in the directional case, viz., "he went out to Assyria"), reflects, at the least, the long-standing cultural superiority of Babylonia over Assyria. But there seems to be an implication of Babylonian political domination as well, for which the best background would be either before 2000 B.C., under the Agade or Ur III dynasties, or ca. 610–539 B.C., under Neo-Babylonian (Chaldean) rule. On the other hand, the likelihood that "Cush," Nimrod's father, stands for the Kassites (Akkadian *Kaššû/Kuššû*) and that "Shinar" reflects "Shanhara," a designation of Kassite Babylonia, points to the use of Babylonian traditions originating in Kassite times, i.e., from the later 2d millennium B.C.

Assyria also forms a part of the imagery of the biblical Nimrod, particularly the Assyria of the Neo-Assyrian period (9th–7th centuries B.C.), when it dominated Babylonia. This is clear from the identification of the land of Nimrod with Assyria by the 8th–7th-century prophet Micah. It also fits the picture of Nimrod as hunter in Genesis 10, for this is a well-known royal motif in Mesopotamian literature and art which became especially prominent with the Neo-Assyrian kings. Finally, a Neo-Assyrian setting explains the Genesis 10 reference to Nineveh, Calah, Rehoboth-Ir, and Resen. Calah (= modern Nimrud), founded apparently in the early 13th century B.C., only became a major capital with its grandiose revival by the Neo-Assyrian king Assurnasirpal II in the early 9th century. "Rehoboth-Ir" seems best explained as Assyrian *rebīt āli,* "the public square of a city"; more specifically, given its position in v 11 next to Nineveh, it should be *rebīt Ninua,* the large square complex of Nineveh which the 8th–7th-century Assyrian king, Sennacherib, boasted of enlarging as part of his great rebuilding of the city and establishment of it as the principal imperial capital. "Resen," in turn, makes good sense as Assyrian *risnu,* an aqueduct or canal, of which we know two major examples in Assyrian history, both Neo-Assyrian: the Patti-hegalli, dug by Assurnasirpal II in the early 9th century in the area of Calah and restored by Esarhaddon in the early 7th; and the huge canal system around Nineveh, dug by Sennacherib in the late 8th–early 7th century. The Resen in Gen 10:12 which is said to be between Nineveh and Calah, could well be an echo, albeit a bit confused, of one or both of these enterprises.

The diverse traditions just sketched make it difficult to look only for one personage whom Nimrod is supposed to represent. Speiser's proposal, for example, that Nimrod is the Middle Assyrian king Tukulti-Ninurta I may account for the connection with Cush, since it was a Kassite ruler whom Tukulti-Ninurta defeated in his conquest of Babylon. But it does not readily explain the hunting motif, as Speiser himself admits, since hunting is not found as a literary or artistic topos in the sources for Tukulti-Ninurta's reign. Nor, obviously, can it fit the identifications of Rehoboth-Ir and Resen discussed above.

It appears, thus, that Nimrod functions for the biblical writers as a legendary—and composite—eponym of Mesopotamia, and as such we should not expect to find any precision of historical reference. The parallel would be with the Ninos of Greek tradition, likewise the eponymous hero-founder of Assyria and its empire and likewise of composite background. Indeed, already in antiquity, Ninos was identified with Nimrod.

Still, the Nimrod portrait does represent a reaction to certain Mesopotamian historical realities, and since the latest of these takes us into the 1st millennium B.C., specifically, the 9th–6th centuries, then perhaps it is this period when at least the present form of our portrait was fashioned. One can speculate that it was the great achievements of the Neo-Assyrian kings of the 9th–7th centuries that served as a particular impetus for the portrait. The reversal of perspective, however, whereby Nimrod moves from Babylonia to dominate Assyria, rather than vice versa, would not be expected if the portrait had been completely fixed in the Neo-Assyrian period. Hence, one may conjecture that the final form of the portrait, with this reversal, reflects the Neo-Babylonian exile. In this regard one may add that all three Babylonian cities in Gen 10:10, although founded much earlier, continued and flourished in Neo-Babylonian times; indeed, Akkad/Agade became the particular focus of efforts to seek out and restore its ancient history.

In postbiblical sources, Jewish, Christian, and Muslim, Nimrod was not forgotten. The attachment of his name to various ancient Mesopotamian ruins in Iraq, especially Calah, was only one aspect of the interest in remembering and elaborating on his hunting and military might. This power, however, was seen mostly negatively: Nimrod being singled out as the greatest sinner since the Flood, whose crowning evils were his claim to be divine and his willingness to sponsor the Tower of Babel. A few sources, however, managed a more positive view, describing his opposition to the building of the Tower. For further discussion see *EncMiqr* 5: 872–73; *RGG* 4: 1496–97; Westermann *Genesis 1-11* BKAT, 686–92.

Bibliography

Abramsky, S. 1980. Nimrod and the Land of Nimrod. *Beth Mikra* 82: 237–55, 321–40 (in Hebrew).

Barnett, R. D. 1975. *A Catalogue of the Nimrod Ivories.* 2d ed. London.

Dossin, G. 1934. Le site de Reḫobot-ʿIr et de Resen. *Mus* 47: 107–21.

Ginzberg, L. 1909–25. *The Legends of the Jews.* Philadelphia.

Jacob, B. 1974. *Das erste Buch der Tora: Genesis.* Repr. New York.

Kraeling, E. G. 1921–22. The Origin and Real Name of Nimrod. *AJSL* 38: 214–20.

Lewy, H. 1952. Nitokris-Naqīʾa. *JNES* 11: 264–86.

Lipiński, E. 1966. Nimrod et Aššur. *RB* 73: 77–93.

Reade, J. 1978. Studies in Assyrian Geography. *RA* 72: 47–72, 157–80.

Sasson, J. M. 1983. Reḥōvōt ʿîr. *RB* 90: 94–96.

Speiser, E. A. 1958. In Search of Nimrod. *EI* 5: 32*–36*. Repr. pp. 41–52 in *Oriental and Biblical Studies. Collected Writings of E. A. Speiser,* ed. J. J. Finkelstein and M. Greenberg. Philadelphia, 1967.

Zadok, R. 1984. The Origin of the Name Shinar. *ZA* 74: 240–44.

PETER MACHINIST

NIMSHI (PERSON) [Heb *nimšî*]. The father or grandfather of Jehu, king of Israel. Jehu is called "son of Nimshi" in 1 Kgs 19:16; 2 Kgs 9:20; and 2 Chr 22:7. He is called "son of Jehoshaphat, son of Nimshi" in 2 Kgs 9:2, 14. See JEHU. The identification of Nimshi as Jehu's grandfather is generally preferred, since the Heb *ben* is broader than the Eng "son," and can be construed as "grandson," "descendant," or the like. It is often inferred that Nimshi was a more prominent figure than Jehoshaphat, though he is otherwise unknown today. Šanda (*2 Kings* EHAT, 93) conjectured that Nimshi might be a clan name, but its appearance as a personal name on a Samarian ostracon makes this hypothesis unnecessary. The etymology of the name is unsure. Šanda (*1 Kings* EHAT, 450) relates it to the same root as "Moses," but this is unlikely; Noth (*IPN,* 230) cites an Arabic cognate for "mongoose."

JEROME T. WALSH

NINEVEH (PLACE) [Heb *nînĕwēh*]. The capital of Assyria in the last few decades of the Assyrian empire. The majority of the biblical references to Nineveh are to this period. Apart from these references there is the narrative in the Bible, Gen 10:11–12, regarding Nimrod, who was "a mighty hunter"; he began his kingdom at Babel (Babylonia) and then went into Assyria where he built four cities, two of which were Nineveh and Calah.

In the Bible, Nineveh was regarded as the seat of the greatest enemy of the kingdoms of Israel and Judah and most biblical references are to its fall. Thus Jonah was commanded by the Lord to go to Nineveh to cry out against it because of its wickedness. See JONAH, BOOK OF. In the book of Jonah we read the prophet's attempts to avoid this divine commission, which included the flight by sea and being swallowed by a whale, before finally accepting his fate. The story of Jonah and Nineveh is referred to in the NT in Matt 12:40–41 and Luke 11:30–32. The tradition has continued at the site of Nineveh to the present time, for on one of the two mounds, Nebi Yunus, there is a mosque dedicated to the prophet Jonah ("Nebi Yunus" in Arabic) and inside this structure there hangs the bone of a whale. With regard to the fall of Nineveh, the entire book of Nahum ("an oracle concerning Nineveh") gloats over this event, calling the Assyrian capital "the bloody city, all full of lies and booty." A brief description of Nineveh's fall is found in Zeph 2:13.

A. Location and Excavation

The ancient site of Nineveh is still part of a major city, now called Mosul, which is the second largest city in the republic of Iraq. The site of Nineveh is on the east bank of the Tigris just a few kilometers downstream from the foothills of the Kurdish mountains. The modern city of Mosul has spread over onto the west bank of the Tigris. This region is an obvious location for a major settlement. The surrounding countryside was and still is a rich agricultural area. From the point of view of trade, Nineveh was on both the N-S trade route going up and down the Tigris and also straddled a major E-W route following along the S foothills of the Kurdish mountains. In its heyday the site of the city Nineveh covered an area with a circumference of approximately 7.75 miles (12.5 km). Within this circumference were two citadels or tells called respectively Kuyunjik and Nebi Yunus, with the river Hosr flowing between them. Only the Kuyunjik mound has been extensively explored since on the other mound, Nebi Yunus, is located the major shrine dedicated to the prophet Jonah (Yunus). Because of the sacred nature of the latter mound it has remained virtually untouched by modern archaeologists.

Although the location of the ancient city of Nineveh was never forgotten in native tradition, being preserved in medieval and modern Arabic sources, European explorers who were ignorant of this tradition remained confused about the location until the mid–19th century. In fact, even Sir Austin Henry Layard, one of the pioneer archaeologists in Assyria, was misled to think that the site of Nimrud farther downstream was the location of ancient Nineveh and it was realized only later that it was actually the site of ancient Calah. Serious digging began at Nineveh in the mid–19th century by French and British explorers and excavation has continued at the site by various nationalities, including Iraqis. Unlike the archaeological work at Asshur and Calah, however, excavations at Nineveh have usually been very sporadic and unsystematic. Nevertheless in the late 19th century the libraries of Ashurbanipal, our most important source for the history and culture of Assyria, were discovered here and taken to the British Museum.

B. History

The history of the city Nineveh is an integral part of the history of Assyria. Nineveh was one of the four great cities of Assyria, the others being ASSHUR, CALAH, and ARBELA. The patron deity of Nineveh was Ishtar, goddess of love and war, who was also the patron deity of Arbela. The site of Nineveh was settled in prehistoric times but nothing is known of its history until the mid–3d millennium B.C. (ca. 2400 B.C.). At this time it was under the political control of the Old Akkadian kings in the south and there is a record that one of these kings, Manishtushu (ca. 2269–2255) rebuilt the temple of Ishtar. Nineveh does not appear prominently in the historical record again until the time of Shamshi-Adad I (ca. 1813–1781 B.C.), who also restored the temple of Ishtar and mentioned the work of his predecessor, Manishtushu. Apart from these periods when Nineveh was ruled by foreign powers it generally was an autonomous city-state with no political links to the other cities in the Assyrian heartland.

In the middle of the 2d millennium B.C. Nineveh came under the control of the kingdom of Mitanni but then was wrested from Mitanni by the rulers of the city-state of Asshur. This was the beginning of the creation of the country Assyria and from the reign of Assur-uballit I

(1363–1328 B.C.) Nineveh, together with the other cities of the Assyrian heartland, was regarded as an intregal part of the land of Assyria. During the period of the Middle Assyrian Empire the great Assyrian kings built extensively at Nineveh, concentrating on the temple of Ishtar. The early kings of the Neo-Assyrian Empire continued this policy of building at Nineveh.

In the 7th century B.C. the city of Nineveh was transformed from being a major metropolis in Assyria to being the capital of the entire country and empire. This was the result of a decision by Sennacherib (704–681 B.C.) (cf. 1 Kings 19; Isaiah 37). See SENNACHERIB. In choosing Nineveh as his capital, Sennacherib launched a massive rebuilding program there. He built a magnificent palace and cut a professional way right through the center of the city from the palace to the bridge crossing the Tigris. His workers constructed an intricate system of aqueducts and canals to bring water into the city to irrigate an extensive garden which he created. The transformed city was surrounded by an enormous wall with several fortified gates, the remains of which are still standing. Thereafter Nineveh remained the capital of Assyria until the fall of the empire and the capture of the city itself in 612 B.C. by a coalition of Medes and Babylonians.

A. KIRK GRAYSON

NINLIL (DEITY). In Sumerian and subsequent Akkadian mythology, a goddess of grain and the wife of the god ENLIL. Her temple was called the Kiʾur, located in Nippur. Although she is the consort of the leading Sumerian god, Enlil, Ninlil does not appear widely in the mythological texts. The two major works in which she figures are *Enlil and Ninlil* (Cooper 1980) and *Enlil and Ninlil: The Marriage of Sud* (Civil 1983). In the former text, Ninlil's mother, Nunbarshegunu, prepares her for marriage with Enlil, but cautions her against meandering about alone. Ninlil disobeys, and Enlil, spotting her alone near a stream, ignores her pleas that she is not adequately prepared and rapes her. The gods brand Enlil a sex offender and banish him from Nippur. He opts to descend to the netherworld in exile.

Ninlil, now pregnant with his child, the moon god Nanna-Suʾen, attempts to follow Enlil. He, disguised as various netherworld functionaries, mates again with Ninlil, apparently wishing to produce chthonic offspring to take the place of Nanna Suʾen in the Underworld. Ninlil does bear three such sons. Jacobsen (1976: 104) suggests that this tale is part of the cult of dying and reviving gods associated with fertility and the agricultural seasons.

In the latter text, Enlil offends Sud and her mother by assuming Sud was a prostitute. However, he becomes infatuated with her and asks her to marry him, but she mocks him and refuses. Enlil sends his messenger to Nanibgal, her mother, and placates them both with many gifts. Nanibgal concedes and allows Enlil to marry Sud, at which point her name is changed to Ninlil.

Bibliography

Civil, M. 1983. Enlil and Ninlil: The Marriage of Sud. *JAOS* 103: 43–66.
Cooper, J. 1980. Critical Review of *Enlil and Ninlil*. *JCS* 32: 175–88.
Jacobsen, T. 1976. *The Treasures of Darkness*. New Haven.
Kramer, S. N. 1963. *The Sumerians*. Chicago.

WILLIAM J. FULCO

NINURTA (DEITY). A Sumero-Akkadian god of the south wind and agriculture, but also of hunting and, especially during the militaristic Assyrian regimes of the early 1st millennium B.C., of warfare (*EncRel* 10:447–48). Early in the Sumerian period he was identified with Ningirsu, the tutelary god of Lagash at the Eninnu temple and the special patron of King Gudea. The myths concerning Ningirsu and those about Ninurta seem eventually to have become interchangeable.

Ninurta figures in a whole cycle of mythological texts, a corpus which has not yet been adequately studied. However, the myths consistently associate Ninurta with one or another aspect of water and its management: life-giving storms, floods, dams, irrigation. The still enigmatic myth of the bird god Zu or Anzu (*ANET,* 11–13, 514–17) deals with Ninurta and hydrology on a more cosmic level (see Jacobsen 1976: 131–34).

Ninurta's mate is either Gula or Baba, the latter more originally Ningirsu's wife. Neither Gula nor Baba is prominent in the extant literature. Albright (*YGC,* 138) and others associated Ninurta with the West Semitic god Ḥoron.

Bibliography

Jacobsen, T. 1976. *The Treasures of Darkness*. New Haven.
Kramer, S. N. 1963. *The Sumerians*. Chicago.
Reisman, D. 1971. Ninurta's Journey to Eridu. *JCS* 24:3–10.

WILLIAM J. FULCO

NIPPUR (32°08′N; 45°03′E). The mounds of Nippur, located in the desert about 150 kms SE of Baghdad, stand today to a height of 18 meters above the alluvial plain. From the time of its establishment as a village along the Euphrates in the 6th millennium B.C. to its abandonment in the 9th century A.D., the site was almost continuously occupied, providing an archaeological record spanning 7,000 years. The Sumerians considered Nippur one of their oldest and most sacred cities, and it was apparently one of the few Mesopotamian cities which had a special legal status involving certain tax-shelter privileges. It is also one of the few great cities of Mesopotamia which retained its ancient name in the memory of man for a thousand years after its abandonment.

As the home of the temple of Enlil, the chief god of the Sumerian pantheon, Nippur was a sacred city of ancient Mesopotamia for thousands of years, but it was never a political capital. Throughout much of its history, control of the city and the sanction of its chief god, Enlil, were necessary to legitimize a ruler's sovereignty over Mesopotamia. Nippur also served as a major scribal center. The approximately 50,000 cuneiform tablets excavated at the site constitute about 80 percent of the Sumerian literary texts known today; also found were administrative, legal, medical, and economic documents of major importance.

The location of the city on the linguistic and ethnic frontier between Sumer and Akkad gives the contents of these texts increased significance.

From 1889–1990 Nippur was the focus of the first American excavation in the Near East, sponsored by the University of Pennsylvania. The excavators made rough plans of several major buildings, uncovered some important artifacts, and found many thousands of clay tablets. From 1948–52, three seasons of joint excavations were conducted by the University of Pennsylvania and the Oriental Institute of the University of Chicago at the Ekur (the Enlil Temple), and on Tablet Hill. From 1953–62, the American Schools of Oriental Research joined with the Chicago team for five seasons of work on the North Temple and the Inanna Temple. Finally, the Oriental Institute conducted ten seasons of work at the site between 1964 and 1989, including excavation of the Parthian fortress at the Ekur, a temple and palace along with other structures on the West Mound, and outlying parts of the site to the SW and NE.

Throughout much of its history, the walled city was an irregular rectangle measuring 1.0 by 1.6 km. The city covered approximately 150 hectares and had about nine gates. Branches of the Euphrates River ran W of the city and through the center of the city during some periods. The three major mounds which make up the site are traditionally called Temple Hill, Tablet Hill, and the West Mound.

The Ekur, or temple precinct of Enlil, was sacred to this deity from at least the late 4th millennium to the mid–1st millennium B.C. The great ziggurat, or temple tower, was built by Ur-Nammu about 2000 B.C. The last major use of the area was as a Parthian fortification in the 1st century A.D. The Inanna Temple, nearby on Temple Hill, was sacred to this goddess from the 3d millennium to Parthian times. The North Temple was built in about 2300 B.C.

Excavations at Tablet Hill have encountered dwellings and administrative buildings. On the West Mound excavators have found dwellings, a temple dating to the 3d to 1st millennium B.C., a Kassite palace (ca. 1300 B.C.), and a Parthian villa. The Islamic settlement was principally on the West Mound.

Throughout its long occupation, the fortunes of the city of Nippur were often reflected by the size and quality of public construction by those in power in Mesopotamia. Strong rulers sponsored major building projects which coincided with times of prosperity. When the country was in a state of conflict or chaos, the economy of the city often suffered, the power of surrounding nomadic groups increased at the expense of urban dwellers, and major building projects ceased.

Although excavations at Nippur have not discovered the prehistoric settlement, the presence of thousands of sherds of the distinctive Hajji Mohammed phase of prehistoric Ubaid pottery attests to settlement by the mid–6th millennium B.C. Similarly, hundreds of ceramic cones of a type used as architectural decoration in Protoliterate temples found at the Enlil temple site attest to temple building here in the 4th millennium. Sumerian texts record a tradition at Nippur of the building of a temple to Enlil called the "Tummel." It was built by Enmebaragesi, a king who is attested in fragmentary inscriptions dating to the ED II period.

With the rise to power of the Semitic Akkadian dynasty under Sargon I (late 3d millennium), the Enlil temple became the focus of major royal building activity, and this central shrine became a repository of objects dedicated by the king. The North Temple was built at this time, and an archive of the Akkadian governor of Nippur has been excavated on the West Mound.

It was not until the Sumerian revival marked by the rise of the Third Dynasty of Ur, however, that royal building projects made a major impact on the site which remains to the present day. Ur-Nammu, the first king of that dynasty, built a three-staged temple tower (ziggurat) for Enlil, as well as a series of courtyards and auxiliary temples which would be repaired and rebuilt on the same plan for the next 1,500 years. The Inanna Temple was also rebuilt during this dynasty, while the building or rebuilding of portions of the city wall set the boundaries for the city that would be maintained throughout the centuries.

With the shift of control of S Mesopotamia to the Amorite Old Babylonian dynasty with its capital at Babylon, building continued at Nippur under kings such as Hammurabi, but there was a shift of religious hegemony from Enlil of Nippur to the god Marduk of Babylon. Over the years, however, a cosmogony evolved in which some of the aspects of Enlil were combined with those of Marduk. Beginning about 1720 B.C. there is also evidence of a major economic crisis at Nippur, probably related to a lack of water, which may have resulted in a temporary abandonment of the city.

The 14th century B.C., when control of S Mesopotamia had passed to a dynasty of Kassite kings which originated outside the country, marked a time of major building and rebuilding of temples at Nippur, as well as the city wall. An unusually vivid record of the city at this time is preserved in a captioned plan drawn on a clay tablet. See Fig. NIP.01. Also attested at Nippur during the Kassite dynasty is a palace on the West Mound. This palace fell into ruin and was abandoned, along with most of the rest of the city, by the mid 13th century, perhaps as a result of an Elamite raid on the city about 1224 B.C. In the ensuing centuries, there is little archaeological or textual evidence for activity at Nippur except at the Ekur. Occupation is attested again by the mid–8th century, however, by an archive of several hundred tablets which portray Nippur as a thriving town surrounded by Chaldaean and Aramaean tribes.

The last major restoration of the precinct of Enlil was in the late 7th century B.C., during the rule of Assurbanipal, king of the N Assyrian dynasty which controlled all of Mesopotamia along with much of the Near East. Assyria's strength at Nippur, which included troops stationed there, enabled it to hold out to the end in the struggle between Assyria and the Chaldean tribes for control of Babylonia, even though it suffered a devastating siege. Nippur supported Assyria until its final defeat by the Chaldeans in 612 B.C.

After the defeat of the Chaldean Babylonians by Cyrus in 539 B.C., Nippur continued to prosper under Achaemenid rule. An archive of tablets of the Murashû family (see MURASHU, ARCHIVE OF) reflects their financial

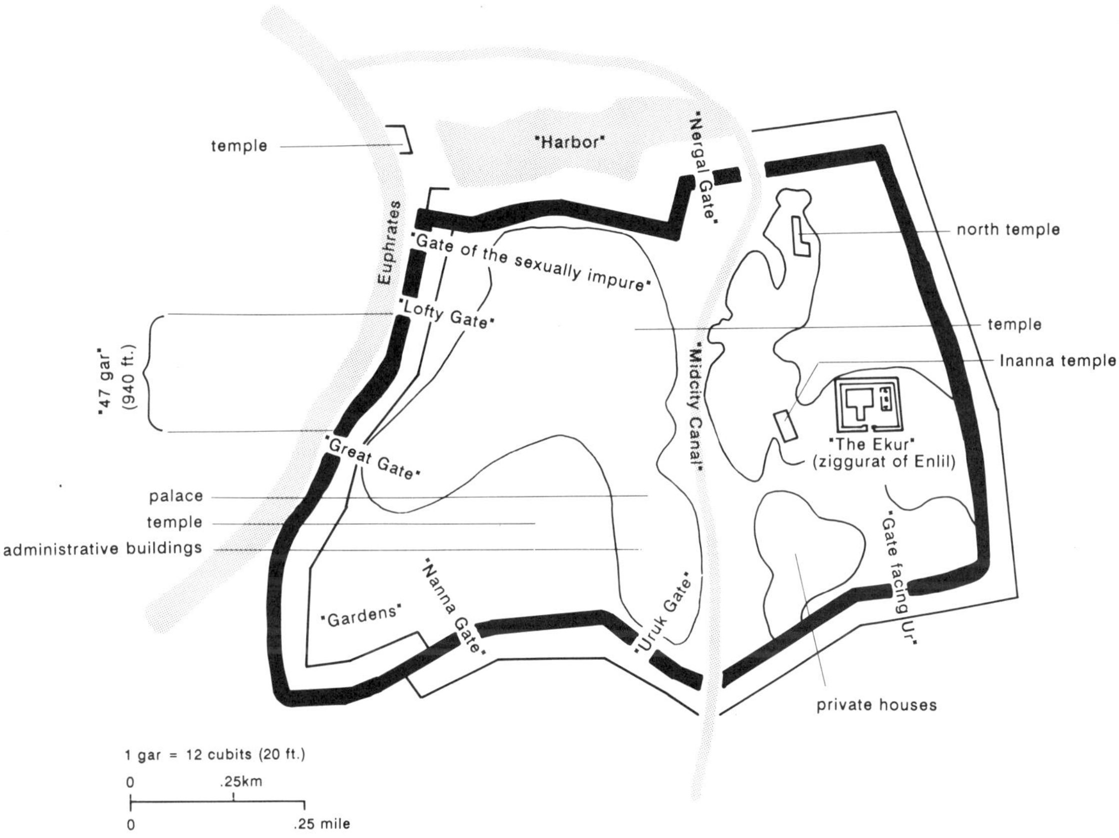

NIP.01. City plan of Nippur, based on excavations and on a Kassite map of ca. 1300 B.C.E. Terms in quotation are translated from the Kassite map. *(Redrawn and translated from McCown, Haines, and Hanson 1967: pl. 4.)*

power at Nippur, where they owned mortgages on much of the land. They rented out canals, cattle, and fisheries, and loaned money at high interest rates to local landowners so that they might pay their taxes.

The city continued to be occupied in the Seleucid period, and in the first centuries before and after the time of Christ it was the focus of massive building operations by the Parthians, who constructed an enormous fortress over and around the remains of the ziggurat and temple complex of Enlil. We know little about the character of occupation of the site during the rule of the Sassanian dynasty in the 3d to 7th centuries A.D., but the presence of potsherds attests occupation, and the Babylonian Talmud notes that important colonies of Jews lived at Nippur as well as at Babylon. A distinctive archaeological feature of this period are hundreds of incantation bowls, more than are known from any other site. While most are found today on the surface of the site, they have been found buried upside down beneath the floors in the corners of houses dating to the Sassanian period. The inner surface of each bowl is covered with an incantation in Syriac, Mandaic, or the "Jewish" dialect of Aramaic, written in a spiral from the center outward. Some of the incantations contain biblical quotations. There is often a crude drawing of a chained demon or spirit in the center of the bowl. These bowls were apparently designed to protect houses and their inhabitants from the demons and evil spirits which are named in the inscriptions.

After several hundred years of Islamic occupation, principally on the West Mound, Nippur's long history as an urban center came to an end. Throughout the 7,000 years in which Nippur was a major settlement, the Euphrates and its branches shifted gradually from the E to the W, and the structure of the city shifted as well. Through time, it became increasingly difficult to divert water to the area; it was abandoned, and eventually became desert.

Bibliography

Fisher, C. S. 1905. *Excavations at Nippur.* Philadelphia.
Gibson, M. 1975. *Excavations at Nippur, Eleventh Season.* Oriental Institute Communication 22. Chicago.
———. 1978. *Excavations at Nippur, Twelfth Season.* Oriental Institute Communication 23. Chicago.
Hilprecht, H. V. 1903. *Explorations in Bible Lands.* Philadelphia.
McCown, D. E.; Haines, R. C., and Biggs, R. D. 1978. *Nippur II.* OIP 97. Chicago.
McCown, D. E.; Haines, R. C.; and Hansen, D. P. 1967. *Nippur I.* OIP 78. Chicago.
Peters, J. P. 1899. *Nippur, or Explorations and Adventures on the Euphrates,* Vols. 1 and 2. New York.
Stone, E. C. 1987. *Nippur Neighborhoods.* SAOC 44. Chicago.

JUDITH A. FRANKE

NISAN [Heb *nîsān*]. The first month of the Hebrew calendar, roughly corresponding to March–April. See CALENDARS (ANCIENT ISRAELITE AND EARLY JEWISH).

NISROCH (DEITY) [Heb *nisrōk*]. According to 2 Kgs 19:37 (Isa 37:38), the god in whose temple Sennacherib was assassinated. The identity of Nisroch is problematic, since Assyrian sources do not attest to any god with such a name. One possible candidate is the god Enlil, whose name was sometimes used as an epithet of the god Ashur, the chief god of Assyria. Another is Ninurta, the Assyrian god of war. But in both cases there are serious difficulties in reconciling the biblical form of the name with the forms preserved in Assyrian sources.

A. KIRK GRAYSON

NOADIAH (PERSON) [Heb *nôᶜadyāh*]. Var. MOETH. A personal name utilizing the verb *yᶜd,* which as *Nipᶜal* can mean "meet by appointment," "appear," or "gather," and the theophoric element *yh.* Translation possibilities include "Yahweh has revealed himself, has become manifest"—particularly through the birth of a child (*IPN,* 184), "Yahweh has met by appointment," "Yahweh has gathered together" (Myers 1987: 766). Brockington (*Ezra, Nehemiah and Esther* Century Bible, 104) suggests "Yahweh has kept his appointment," envisioning a connection with *mōᶜēd* ("appointed meeting") in the designation of the tabernacle as "tent of meeting." Some, such as Odelain and Séguineau (1981: 284), BDB (418), and White (*HDB,* 555), render it "encounter, meeting with Yah." This name is born by two individuals in the Hebrew Bible.

1. The son of Binnui and one of two Levites who were "with them," i.e., Meremoth and Eleazar, when Ezra and those with him brought into "the house of our God" the silver, gold, and vessels and weighed them into Meremoth's hands (Ezra 8:33). Gunneweg (*Esra* KAT, 157) believes these personal names are secondary additions to a tradition in which the personalities were all anonymous. In the 1 Esdr 8:62—Eng 8:63 account of this event, the second of the two Levites is *Mōeth Sabannou,* which Bewer (1922: 78) believes is a corruption of *Nōadeia Banaiou.*

2. The prophetess (MT *hannĕbîᵓāh*) or prophet (LXX *tę̄ prophētę̄*) who, along with other unnamed prophets (MT *hannĕbîᵓîm;* Codex Alexandrinus *tōn prophētōn*) or priests (Codices Vaticanus and Sinaiticus *hiereōn*) contributed to "making me (i.e., Nehemiah) afraid" (Neh 6:14). Elsewhere this charge is levied against (v 13) the one spoken of in v 12 who "spoke the prophecy against me." Where this speaker is understood to be Shemaiah (v 10) some (Brockington *Ezra, Nehemiah, and Esther* Century Bible, 156; Williamson *Ezra, Nehemiah* WBC, 260) find it strange that rather than Shemaiah, elsewhere unknown Noadiah (Codex Alexandrinus *Nōadia;* Codices Vaticanus and Sinaiticus *Noadia*) is mentioned in this imprecation in which God is called upon to "remember" (Heb *zakrāh + lĕ*) the threateners. Clines (*Ezra, Nehemiah, Esther* NCBC, 176) even wonders if Noadiah was Shemaiah's wife! Drawing upon the Lucianic recension of the LXX, which reads "warned" (Gk *enouthetoun,* reflecting Heb *mbynym*) instead of "fearing" (LXX *phoberizontes* = MT *myrᵓym*) and thus changes the imprecation of v 14a to a supplication in v 14b, Batten (*Ezra and Nehemiah* ICC, 258) suggests that Noadiah was working for Nehemiah. However, the miniscule manuscripts representing this Lucianic recension omit the personal name Noadiah and read instead *ge tę̄ ǭdę̄/hodę̄ tę̄ prophētidi,* "the song/way the prophetess." Ehrlich (1914: 198–99) argues that the one being spoken of in vv 10–12 is not Shemaiah, who is only referred to as the owner of the house mentioned in v 10. He believes Noadiah, possibly in a position of high authority, functions as the false prophet (not prophetess!) who speaks the words in v 10 (he believes the verb form *nwᶜd* is a corruption of *nwᶜdyh*) and is referred to in v 12.

Bibliography

Bewer, J. A. 1922. *Der Text des Buches Ezra.* Göttingen.
Ehrlich, A. B. 1914. *Randglossen zur Hebräischen Bibel.* Vol. 7. Leipzig.
Myers, A. 1987. Noadiah. P. 766 in *The Eerdmans Bible Dictionary.* Rev. ed. Grand Rapids, MI.
Odelain, O., and Séguineau, R., eds. 1981. Noadiah. P. 284 in *Dictionary of Proper Names and Places in the Bible.* Trans. M. O'Connell. Garden City, NY.

RODNEY H. SHEARER

NOAH (PERSON) [Heb *nōaḥ, nōᶜâ*]. **1.** The son of Lamech who, along with his family, survived the Flood (Gen 5:28–9:29; Heb *nōaḥ*). See NOAH AND THE ARK.

2. One of the five daughters of Zelophehad son of Hepher of the tribe of Manasseh (Num 26:33; 27:1–11; 36:1–12; Josh 17:3–6; Heb *nōᶜâ;* cf. 1 Chr 7:15). Noah and her sisters petitioned to receive legal status as heirs because their father had no sons (Num 27:1–4). Their request was granted provided that they marry within their father's tribe (Num 27:5–7; 36:1–9). Noah and her sisters followed the divine ruling on their case and married cousins on their father's side (Num 36:12). Hence their inheritance remained in their father's tribe. Scholarly interest in the daughters of Zelophehad has focused on questions related to the prehistory of the story of the daughters (e.g., the relationship of the daughters to places—here the mention of the name Noah as a district in the Samaria Ostracon 50 is relevant [Lemaire 1972]); its sources, development, form, purpose, and historicity; its significance for the study of Israelite case law (Weingreen 1966); the relationship of Manasseh and its subclans of traditions about settlement to the east and west of the Jordan (Snaith 1966); the rights of women (Sakenfeld 1982); and more recently its positioning in terms of the literary and theological shaping of the book of Numbers (Olson 1985).

Bibliography

Lemaire, A. 1972. Le "Pays de Hépher" et les "filles de Zelophehad" à la lumière des Ostraca de Samarie. *Sem* 22: 13–20.

Olson, D. T. 1985. *The Death of the Old and the Birth of the New.* Chico, CA.

Sakenfeld, K. D. 1982. Old Testament Perspectives: Methodological Issues. *JSOT* 22: 13–20.

Snaith, N. H. 1966. The Daughters of Zelophehad. *VT* 16: 124–27.

Weingreen, J. 1966. The Case of the Daughters of Zelophehad. *VT* 16: 518–22.

Marion Ann Taylor
J. Glen Taylor

NOAH AND THE ARK. This entry consists of two articles. The first focuses on the biblical hero of the Flood (Gen 5:28–9:29) who later became the subject of Jewish and Christian legend. The second article focuses on the ark itself and the claims through the ages that its remains have survived.

THE HERO OF THE FLOOD

A. Introduction
1. Name
2. Flood Heroes in Other Ancient Literature
B. Noah in Judeo-Christian Tradition
1. Hebrew Bible
2. Apocrypha
3. *Genesis Apocryphon*
4. New Testament
5. Pseudepigrapha

A. Introduction

In the genealogical reckoning of Gen 5:28–29, Noah is introduced as a son of the 182-year-old Lamech. Noah stands at the end of the era that is now to be destroyed, the era that has lasted more than 1,500 years since the beginning of the world when the first human couple was created.

According to the genealogies of Genesis 4 and 5, there have been 7–10, depending on how we count them, generations starting with that of Adam and Eve up to Noah's generation. However, the narrative tradition hurries through the same 1,656 years in just three generations, beginning with that of Adam and Eve, followed by that of Cain and Abel, and now of Noah and his family. Then the Flood sweeps over—only Noah's family is saved, because "Noah was a righteous man; he was blameless in his time; with God Noah walked" (Gen 6:9). Thus, Noah is the one who is saved, guarded by the covenant of the rainbow, and in turn is destined to save humanity. He is the father of the new era; he is the father of Shem, Ham, and Japheth, whose offspring are going to repopulate the entire world after the Flood (Gen 10:1–32). Noah is an epoch divider figure as well as a bridge between the quasi-mythological history and a more humanly accountable history.

In these early chapters of Genesis a complex image of Noah emerges. The later chapters and books variously refer to Noah specifically by name or obliquely by alluding to many aspects of Noah and the Flood Story. In the following sections the major significance of Noah and his ancient counterparts and some of the more obvious references and allusions to him are examined.

1. Name. No firm etymology for the name Noah (Heb *Nōaḥ,* Gk *Nōe*) has been established, but it is generally derived from the verb root *nwḥ,* to rest, settle down, repose, etc.; thus "Noah" may mean "to rest." Whatever "Noah," spelled consonantally as *nḥ,* may have meant originally, the genealogy (Gen 5:29) gives us a folk etymology that Noah *(nḥ)* is to bring us comfort *(nḥm, Piʿel,* to comfort, console: *Nipʿal,* to be sorry, console oneself); thus *nḥ* is associated aurally to *nḥm,* making Noah the bringer of comfort *(nḥm)* from labor (derived from *ʿśh*) and toil (derived from *ʿṣb*).

It is not fortuitous that when the Flood Story introduces Noah, these very same roots, *nḥm, ʿśh,* and *ʿṣb,* are repeated in the same order: "And the Lord was sorry [*nḥm*] that he had made [*ʿśh*] man on the earth and it grieved [*ʿṣb*] him to his heart"—(Gen 6:6).

The wordplay involving *nḥm* continues; "And the Lord said, 'I will blot out [*mḥh*] man whom I have created' " (Gen 6:7). Here the two key consonants *ḥ* and *m* are reversed. The wordplay still goes on as "Noah [*nḥ*] found favor [*ḥn*] in the eyes of the Lord" (Gen 6:8); note here the two consonants of the name are also reversed. Furthermore, Noah begets a son named Ham (*ḥm,* Gen 6:10), relating assonantally to *nḥm,* "comfort," but substantially to *ḥms,* "violence"; "and the earth was corrupt in the eyes of God and the earth was filled with violence [*ḥms*]" (Gen 6:11). "Noah" *(nḥ)* and "violence" *(ḥms)* are picked up again in Gen 6:13 and the wordplay extends to the word *mḥwṣ,* "outside," in Gen 6:14, as Noah is to "pitch it (the ark) with pitch inside and outside [*mḥwṣ*]."

Moreover, observe that Ham is introduced soon after the initial episode of the story, namely, the sexual involvement of the sons of gods with the daughters of men (Gen 6:1–4), and then he finds himself in a sexual offense against Noah at the final episode of the story (Gen 9:18–29). These two episodes of sexual intrigue frame the story, and Ham is closely associated with both of them.

The notion of *mḥh,* "blotting out," as a result of the Lord's "regret" *(nḥm)* terminates in the central episode of the devastating flood destruction (Gen 7:17–24), where that verb is used both actively and passively: "and he blotted out [*ymḥ*] every living thing that was upon the face of the ground . . . and they were blotted out [*ymḥw*] from the earth" (Gen 7:23). The idea of the name Noah, "rest," is fittingly echoed where the ark securely rests *(tnḥ)* after

150 days of water ordeal, yet the dove *(ywnh)* could not find the place to rest *(mnwḥ)* its foot (Gen 8:9).

Many words that are loosely associated with the name Noah are used in a cluster at the beginning of the story. These same words are then distributed in strategic positions throughout the story, helping to unify the story and to make it unmistakably Noah's Flood Story.

2. Flood Heroes in Other Ancient Literature. a. Mesopotamian. Noah as the Flood hero has many counterparts in ancient literature. To begin with, the Sumerian and Akkadian genealogical material as well as the epic tradition preserved various names of the righteous Flood hero, who stands exactly at the same relative position in world history as Noah, that is, at the end of the mythological, primeval historical era, ushering in a new, more concretely historical era. The Flood, thus, serves as an epoch divider. The main difference between Noah and his Mesopotamian counterparts is that Noah dies, while the other Flood heroes seem to gain immortality (Cohen 1974). See FLOOD.

(1) The Sumerian Deluge Story. The Sumerian counterpart of Noah is Ziusudra (meaning "life of prolonged day(s)"), the son of Ubartutu of Shuruppak. He is the Flood hero and epoch divider who becomes immortal. This is known from both the genealogical tradition found in the Sumerian king list (Jacobsen 1939) and from the narrative tradition as preserved in the Sumerian Deluge Story (*ANET,* 42–44; Civil 1969).

The 6-column text of the Sumerian Deluge Story is badly broken; the major portion of each column is gone. Only about one fourth (approximately 70 out of 300 lines) of the story remains, and even that is preserved imperfectly. But the text includes more than the Flood Story. In column 1, there appears to be one or two episodes of earlier destructions of humankind long before the Flood. The text also recalls the creation by Anu, Enlil, Enki, and Ninhursag of the black-headed people, i.e., the Mesopotamians. The kingship and civilization are established, and the name of five antediluvian cities, which we know from the Sumerian King List and to which different gods are assigned, are listed in column 2. The pious king Ziusudra is praying in column 3 and the impending flood is announced in column 4. The Flood rages, Ziusudra is saved, and he offers a sacrifice in column 5. The earth is repopulated and Ziusudra becomes immortal and lives in Dilmun in column 6. The rest of the tablet is broken off.

(2) Gilgamesh XI. The best preserved Mesopotamian Flood narrative, however, is found in Tablet 11 of the Akkadian Gilgamesh epic. It provides so far the clearest parallel to Noah's flood story. The creator and magician god Enki/Ea cleverly communicates to Utnapishtim (for the meaning of the name, see below), whose nickname is Atrahasis (meaning "exceedingly wise"), about the impending disaster and instructs him to build a cubical ship with six stories and nine sections and to save himself and his family. The Flood rages for seven days; everyone dies except the Utnapishtim family, the seed of all living creatures, and all the craftsmen. The ship rests on the top of the Mount Nasir, a bird is let out to check the water level, and Utnapishtim offers a sacrifice over which the hungry gods gather like flies. Utnapishtim is granted immortality by the gods. According to Anne D. Kilmer (1987b) we perhaps can even recover a rainbow covenant motif from the enigmatic passage describing Ishtar's colorful necklace of lapis lazuli and her promise:

> Then she [Nintu] approached the big flies
> Which Anu had made and was carrying . . .
> Let these flies be the lapis around my neck
> That I may remember it [every(?)] day [and forever(?)]
> (Atrahasis, 3.5.46–6.4)

The parallel passage in Gilgamesh is:

> When at last the Great Goddess arrived,
> She lifted up the great flies [jewels] which Anu had made light-heartedly[?]
> "These gods—verily [by] the lapis round my neck and I shall not forget
> These days—surely I will remember forever and not forget."
> (Gilgamesh XI 162–169)

Enki then chastises Enlil for sending the most destructive flood instead of a less severe disaster, such as a lion or a famine, to "diminish mankind." In response Enlil makes Utnapishtim immortal.

The Flood hero himself, reluctantly at first, narrates this Flood Story to Gilgamesh, who is questing immortality and thinks that he too may obtain it by consulting Utnapishtim. Thus the rest of the Gilgamesh Epic offers no contextual parallel to Genesis, except for some isolated verbal and motif similarities.

(3) The Atrahasis Epic. However, the Atrahasis Epic, though the Flood portion of the text (Tablet III) is quite damaged, presents a narrative account of the Mesopotamian primeval history that parallels Genesis 1–11 inclusively. The Flood Story in Atrahasis (approximately 405 lines) is more than twice the size of the Gilgamesh flood story (approximately 190 lines). Although they seem to tell the same story (cf. Utnapishtim is identified as Atrahasis, "Exceedingly Wise," in Gilgamesh XI.187), the function of the Flood in these two epics is quite different; in Atrahasis it is a population control measure and an epoch divider, whereas in Gilgamesh it explains how immortality was once granted to a mortal. A synoptic outline of the Atrahasis Epic and Genesis 1–11 is as follows:

Atrahasis	Genesis 1–11
A. Creation of Mankind	
(Tablet I.1–248)	(Gen 1:1–2:25)
Summary of Work of Gods	Summary of Work of God
Creation of Mankind	Creation of Mankind
B. People's Numerical Increase	
(I.249–415)	(2:4–3:24)
Attempt to Decrease Numbers	Adam and Eve
Threat of Death by Plague	Near Death

C. Second Attempt to Decrease:	
Double Story (II i.1–vi.55)	(4:1–5:32)
1. Threat of Death: Drought	1. Cain and Abel
2. Severer Means	2. Lamech's Taunt
D. Final Solution	
(II vii–II vi.40)	(6:1–9:29)
Atrahasis' Flood	Noah's Flood
Salvation in Boat	Salvation in *Tēbâ*—Ark
E. Resolution	
(III vi.41–viii.18)	(10:1–11:32)
Compromise between Enlil and Enki	Dispersion—Abram Leaves Ur
"Birth Control"	Exodus Motif

The Atrahasis Epic begins with the creation of humankind because the labor-class gods are fed up with the heavy tasks imposed on them by the management-class gods, and they make much "noise," especially against the chief god, Enlil. As a result, the mother goddess Mami and magician god Enki create procreating people as a substitute for the laboring gods. The people multiplied so much in 1,200 years that they made a great "noise," to the annoyance of Enlil. Enlil tries to exterminate them first by a famine, then 1,200 years later by a drought, and finally, yet another 1,200 years later, by the flood. Three times Enlil's plans are foiled by Enki and his faithful worshipper Atrahasis. Now the thrice failing and furious Enlil convenes a divine assembly where a post-Flood compromise is reached among gods to limit the expanding population. At least three such population control measures (Kilmer 1972) are suggested, presumably by Enki and Mami:

Moreover, a third category let there be among people;
Let there be among people bearing women and barren women!
Let there be among people the *pāšittu*-demon;
Let him snatch the baby
from the lap of the woman who bore it!
Place *Ugbabtu*-priestess, *Entu*-priestess,
and *Igiṣītu*-priestess;
Let them be taboo and
Thus cut off child-bearing!

(Atrahasis III vi.52?–vii.9)

Note Genesis 1–11 topically parallels the Atrahasis Epic but reaches exactly an opposite conclusion. Whereas the Atrahasis Epic suggests "birth control" as means to curb human population, Genesis offers "dispersion" as means to accommodate the expanding population in response to the initial blessing of Gen 1:28, "Be fruitful and multiply and fill the earth." Out of the dispersion of Gen 11:1–9, who but Adam, the first Hebrew, emerges.

Atrahasis may have received immortality in the end. We cannot be sure because of the broken text, but his longevity, known from the unbroken part of the epic and spanning over three generations of 1,200 years each, is extraordinary. This gave rise to the following speculation.

(4) The Enki and Ninmah Story. The longevity of Atrahasis has led to the thought that Atrahasis may be the first man, or at least the first baby. This speculation is based on a Sumerian story called "Enki and Ninmah" (Benito 1969), which deals with the creation of people in two stages (Kikawada 1983). Note in the following story of Enki and Ninmah, the same topics and motifs as in Genesis 1–2 and Atrahasis I.1–351 are found, i.e. in the first stage humanity is invented for the purpose of work, to have dominion over the other living beings (Gen 1:26), and to bear the toil of the gods (Atrahasis I.191), and in the second stage specific persons, Adam and Eve (Gen 2:7, 22) and seven pairs of people (Atrahasis K 3399+3934, Obverse iii 9–13), are created and destined to be self-propagating by establishing marriage (Gen 2:24, Atrahasis I.300–1).

The Enki and Ninmah story begins after the goddess Nammu gives birth to gods who work in different regions of the world. When the work becomes too severe for the worker gods, they complain to the manager gods. The creator god Enki first tries to ignore the complaint by sleeping, but mother Nammu persuades Enki to create "substitutes," namely humanity, for worker gods. Nammu decrees the fate of the new creature; goddess Ninmah imposes work on humankind. Gods become very happy; and have a big feast where Enki and Ninmah get drunk. That is the first stage of creation.

In the second stage, Ninmah proposes a people-making contest to Enki, one to create and the other to decree fate. Ninmah begins and she creates from clay six (could be seven, see Lambert and Millard 1969) creatures with some physical weaknesses. Enki decrees fates for them:

Ninmah's Creature	Enki's Decree
1. One with weak arm	Court officer
2. One with blinking eyes	Singer
3. One with weak feet	?
4. One with uncontrollable semen emission	Made safe
5. One barren	Appointed to harem
6. One sexless person	Court officer

All these creatures of Ninmah are appointed to appropriate stations in the society—hence they gain independence and livelihood. The apex of the second stage is the creation of the procreating woman and her first baby, Umul, who was miraculously sired by Enki, the magician god himself. An irony of this story seems to lie in the fact that Ninmah the mother goddess does not recognize a baby:

She [Ninmah] approached Umul and asked him questions
[but] he did not know how to speak,
She offered him bread for his nourishment
[but] he did not reach out for it,
On the . . . [his] heart could not rest,
he could not sleep,
Standing up he could not sit down,
could not lie down,

a house he could not build[?]
food he could not eat,
Ninmah said with a stammer to Enki,
"The man you have fashioned is
neither alive nor dead,
he cannot carry anything."
(Enki and Ninmah 96–101)

Then Enki advises her to hold him on her lap and assures her that Umul, having Enki's "form," will be a pious man. By the bringing forth of the first baby the model for human procreation is established by Enki, who instructs Ninmah, saying, "pouring the semen of an erected phallus in a woman's womb, that woman will conceive in her womb."

If the Enki and Ninmah story and the Sumerian deluge story are viewed in succession, they together seem to offer a tantalizing parallel to the whole of the Atrahasis Epic (Kilmer 1976). For this reason, Atrahasis is suspected of being the first baby. The other link between Atrahasis and the first baby lies in the meaning of the names. The first Sumerian baby's name, given at birth, is Umul, "my day [of death] is far"—suspiciously a longevity name! Note that Atrahasis' other name is Utnapishtim, reading here as *ūta-napištim,* "I have found life"—a longevity name given at the "end" of life when he is made immortal (Gilgamesh XI.193–95). Perhaps it is even better to read his full name, Utnapishtim the Distant, as *um-napištim-rūqi,* meaning "day of my life is long," which would give us a still closer parallel to the Sumerian hero. Note that the name of the hero in the Sumerian deluge is Ziusudra, which means "life of prolonged day(s)"—a longevity name as well. Mesopotamian Noahs all have longevity names. In sharp contrast (Cohen 1974) to these names, Noah *(nḥ)* may signify eternal "Rest" or "Repose" in Sheol (cf. Isa 57:2 and Job 3:17).

b. Indo-European. (1) Iranian. The *Avesta,* in *Vendidad* Book 2 of the Iranian tradition, preserves a Zoroastrian counterpart to Noah, called Yima/Yama, the first man and first king (Christensen 1943), entrusted with government as well as religion. Yima helps expand the overburdened earth in three stages to accommodate the increasing population. He lives through 1,200 years until he is directed by Ahuramazda to prepare for an impending flood resulting from the melting snow. Ahuramazda gives Yima detailed instructions on how to make an enclosure in the mountain to save himself and "the seed of small and large cattle and the mortals and dogs and birds and the red burning fire" (*Vendidad* 2.25). The end of the story takes on an eschatological tone and it appears as though Yima is still in the enclosure even at the present time. From this story, too, we can recover the overall outline of the primeval history. Yima, like Noah, stands at the demarcation point between the primeval era and the new age to come.

(2) Indian. From India we can observe the Flood hero in both the genealogical and narrative traditions. He is either the seventh (or fourteenth) Manu, the last sage of the primeval era. In genealogical material Manu Vaivasvata stands at the end of the primeval epoch that is terminated by the Flood. The succeeding epoch has a different form of social structure which is reflected in a different type of genealogy (Thapar 1976). The antediluvian genealogy is a linear type wherein only one leader in a given period is accounted for, as in Genesis 4 and 5. After the Flood, the style of genealogy changes to the branched type wherein all the contemporary leaders and their relatives are recorded, i.e., to describe a family tree as in Genesis 10. The same Manu, in a narrative tradition, is saved from the Flood by a giant horned fish, which he found when it was little and helped by giving it successively bigger containers in which to grow. Thus, Manu Vaivasvata, like Noah, is the hero of the epoch-dividing Flood.

(3) Classical. Another Indo-European flood tradition is found in Greco-Roman literature, featuring righteous Deucalion and his pious wife Pyrrha, the best example of which is preserved in Ovid's *Metamorphoses.* This Flood Story is placed in the same relative position in the early history of humankind as in the Mesopotamian tradition and Genesis.

The *Metamorphoses* begins with creation, followed by deterioration of the world in four stages from the Golden Age of the righteous to the Iron Age of evil. Jove then intends to get rid of the evil; he tries this in three stages. First, the household of evil, Lycaon, is blasted by a thunderbolt. Next, Jove wants to do the same thing to the whole earth but he is dissuaded because of the fear that heaven would be burnt up as well. In the third and final stage Jove sends the Flood from which the righteous couple, Deucalion and Pyrrha, are saved; after the Flood the earth is repopulated for the new epoch.

A scholiastic commentary on Homer's *Iliad* (*Il.* 1.5, on *Dios boulēn*) preserves a progression of topics similar to that found in *Metamorphoses.* The commentary also alludes to and summarizes the lost composition by Stasinos, entitled *Cypria,* whose emphasis is on the unburdening of the overpopulated earth in three stages. The motif of overpopulation brings this tradition close to the Mesopotamian and the biblical traditions.

B. Noah in Judeo-Christian Tradition

Both in the Old and New Testaments as well as in the intertestamental literature there are references to Noah. The following are some obvious examples and some speculative specimens.

1. Hebrew Bible. a. Exodus 1–2, 15. Moses is an obvious Noah figure, perhaps even a double Noah figure, in the book of Exodus, although Abraham emerges as an even earlier reflection of the Noah figure in the Sodom and Gomorrah story (cf. 2 Peter 2:5–6 section of this article).

The Hebrew people, now located in Egypt, must go through the threefold trial and tribulation of Pharaoh's effort to diminish their number; note the very close parallel to the outline of the Atrahasis Epic as well as that of Genesis 1–11. First, taskmasters are set up to impose hard work on the Israelites, but the harder they oppress the Israelites, the more the Israelites "multiply" (Exod 1:12, cf. 1:7 where "Be fruitful and multiply and fill the earth" of Gen 1:28 is already echoed and amplified). Then, Pharaoh orders that the infant sons are to be killed by the two midwives Shiprah and Puah. When this plan too fails, the third trial is commanded by Pharaoh, "Every son that is born to the Hebrews you shall cast into the Nile!" (Exod 1:22). This is the Flood in miniature: Moses is saved in the ark *(tēbâ),* the Hebrew word used exclusively for Noah's ark.

The connection is underscored by the language (cf. Exod 2:3 and Gen 6:14), for this is the only time the word *tēbâ* is used outside of Genesis 6–9. The way in which the ark is built is the same in both instances: the one for whom the ark is made, the material of which it is built, and the number of times it is to be "pitched with pitch" are all designated in the same order. Out of this water ordeal there emerges an adult Moses, a hero for the new age, another Noah.

Moses along with the children of Israel, however, goes through another epoch-dividing Flood as depicted in Exodus 15. Here the war imagery of the Lord as a Man of War dominates, but the Flood as the means of salvation for Israel and that of epoch divider is also present. While the pharaoh's army is drowned in the upsurging waters, Moses and Israel emerge as a new entity to be feared among the neighbors such as Philistia, Edom, Moab, and Canaan. A new era for Israel thus begins. Note the change in the form of genealogical reckoning (cf. Thapar 1976) as well. After Noah's Flood up to this point the genealogy has been of the branched type accounting for the lines of brothers and sisters, but now it reverts to the linear type of reckoning, accounting again only for the main line of leadership.

The war image associated with the Noachian Flood is recoverable from the rainbow. Remembering that the biblical Hebrew does not have a special word for "rainbow," what we have in Gen 9:12, 14, 16 is the expression "a bow [the weapon] in the cloud," suggesting, perhaps, that the Lord is declaring a truce after a war by resting his bow in the cloud.

In the following section only a few prophetic reflections of Noah material are brought out, although there may be many other allusions that are hidden in unsuspected places.

b. Isaiah 54. The important verses here are 9 and 10, which read:

> For this is like the days of Noah to me,
> As I swore that the waters of Noah
> Should no more over the earth,
> So I have sworn
> that I will not be angry with you
> and will not rebuke you.
> For the mountain may depart
> and the hills be removed,
> but my steadfast love
> shall not depart from you,
> and my covenant of peace
> shall not be removed,
> says the Lord,
> who has compassion on you.

Along with Noah the Flood and covenant are recalled by Isaiah for the people who are afflicted and not comforted (*nḥm,* Isa 54:11), reminding them of the everlasting kindness and great compassion of God (*rḥmh,* Isa 57:7,8). Isaiah plays on the folk etymology of the name Noah, i.e., *nḥm* of Gen 5:29, and adds *rḥmh,* "compassion," to the continuing wordplay.

Isaiah renames the covenant, changing it from the "everlasting covenant" (Gen 9:16), to the "covenant of peace" in Isa 54:10. This may be seen as a commentary on the rainbow. It is based on a further play on the name Noah *(nḥ),* especially in reference to Isa 54:15–17 in which the Lord has caused the smith to blow *(npḥ)* the fire of coals *(pḥm)* to create weapons. But these weapons will not be used against God's people. Realizing that Hebrew has no special word for rainbow, we understand that the Lord hangs the bow on the cloud, as a sign of the covenant and as a gesture of peace after a battle.

c. Jeremiah 31. In the context of the everlasting covenant, Jeremiah 31 may be appreciated in a new light. While Jeremiah's new covenant (Jer 41:31–34) is explicitly based on the Mosaic covenant, the Noachian covenant may be implicitly referred to in the passage immediately following (Jer 31:35, 36). In it Jeremiah recalls both the creation of sun and moon and the perpetuity of seasons as promised by the rainbow covenant:

> Thus says the Lord,
> who gives the sun for light by day,
> and who the fixed order of the moon,
> and the stars for light by night,
> who stirs up the sea and its waves roar—
> the Lord of hosts is his name,
> "If this fixed order departs from before me,
> says the Lord,
> then shall the descendants of Israel
> cease from being a nation
> from before me all the days."

Note that both Isaiah's reinstatement of the Noachian covenant of perpetual compassion and Jeremiah's updating of the Mosaic covenant of the Law are described in the cosmic setting of mountains and hills (Isa 54:10) and heaven and earth (Jer 31:37). Both prophets seem to invoke the primeval history, the earliest part of cosmic and human history, for the establishment of a new covenant. Perhaps they are recalling the very beginning of the world when and only when the entire creation is described as "good" and "very good," insisting upon making the new covenant firmly based on the primeval goodness of the creation (Cf. Hesse and Kikawada 1984).

d. Ezekiel. The Lord's speech to the Son of Man (Ezek 14:12–20) demands righteousness for salvation, recognizing no act of supererogation. Noah, Daniel, and Job are singled out as exemplary men of righteousness in sinful ages. Ezekiel sees the three men as having survived extraordinary ordeals by their own righteousness.

Noah, as the hero of the epoch-dividing Flood, may be hidden at the end of Ezekiel's first vision (Ezek 1:1–18). The vision moves from "I saw and behold . . ." (Ezek 1:4) and "I saw . . . and behold . . ." (Ezek 1:15) to the audition, "I heard . . ." (Ezek 1:24). Ezekiel hears seven voices *(qwl).* One of the seven voices is that of many waters (Ezek 1:14), perhaps of the Flood. The six voices are clustered in two verses (Ezek 1:24, 25). As the seventh voice is about to be heard, Ezekiel makes a flashing allusion to Noah's Flood by "the bow in the cloud on the day of rain" (Ezek 1:28). The seventh voice, climactically introduced, is none other than the voice of the Lord; and it is heard throughout the rest of the book.

Here, Ezekiel is apparently invoking primeval authority for contemporary speech, as did the poet of Psalm 29. In the Psalm we find the lone reference to the Flood, *mabbûl* (Ps 29:10), outside of the Noah story (Genesis 6–9).

e. Jonah. Within the ironic reversal of the whole narrative structure of primeval history, we find Jonah as another Noah in the episode of the tempest and the great fish. The overall topical outline of the book of Jonah that chiastically parallel Genesis 1–11 (Hesse and Kikawada 1984) is given in the table below.

Jonah is not only Noah (Jonah 1:4–3:4) but also he is Adam (Jonah 4:6–9), and Abel (Jonah 2:5–4:5). Moreover, we may even visualize Moses when Exod 34:6–7 is restated in Jonah 4:9, ". . . for I know that thou art a gracious God and merciful, slow to anger, and abounding in steadfast love, and repentest of evil," or recall Abram when Gen 14:13, 19–22 is echoed in Jonah 1:9, "I am a Hebrew, and I fear the Lord, the God of heaven who made the sea and the dry land," as an answer to his shipmates.

2. Apocrypha. In the Apocrypha of the OT, references to Noah appear in such books as Tobit, Sirah, and the Wisdom of Solomon. In these books Noah takes a minor part in the list of people who are to be commended.

Tobit's advice to his son Tobias (Tob 4:3–21) includes an admonition to marry his own kind as did Noah, Abraham, Isaac, and Jacob (Tob 4:12). Neither the Flood nor the covenant is recalled.

In Sir 44:17–18, Noah appears in the long list of praises to the fathers of old, a list that begins with Enoch and ends with Moses. Noah is regarded as a substitute/continuator in the new age and in the remnant left from the Flood which ended because of the covenant.

Wis 4:10 refers to Noah without using his name, for the main interest of the passage lies in the enumeration of the accomplishments of Wisdom. Adam, Abel, Noah, Abraham, et al. are all alluded to without names. Wisdom saves the earth by "guiding the righteous man's course by a poor piece of wood."

3. *Genesis Apocryphon.* Column II of the *Genesis Apocryphon* preserves fragments of an episode recounting Noah's extraordinary birth. Noah is so extraordinary that his father, Lamech, is frightened and doubts the paternity of the child, suspecting one of the Watchers, the holy ones, or the fallen angels (for an Assyriological view on the Nephilim, cf. Kilmer 1987a). Lamech first goes to his wife, *btʾnws,* who assures him that the child is his, reminding him of her pleasure when the child was conceived. Still discontent, Lamech goes to his father, Methuselah, who in turn proceeds to Enoch, his own father, for explanation. Here the text breaks, but what happens next may be

Jonah		*Genesis*	
A. Fleeing to Tarshish		A. Dispersion	
Not going to Mesopotamia despite God's will	1:1–3	Coming out of Mesopotamia according to God's will	
Nineveh	1:2	Babel/Shinʿar	11:1–32
Hebrew	1:9	Abram, the Hebrew	14:13
B. Flood, *nāhār*	1:4–15	B. Flood, *mabbûl*	6–9
Ship of tribulation	1:5	Ship of salvation	
Jonah = Dove		Dove	8:10–12
Fish, vessel of salvation	2:1	(Cf. Manu and Fish, Indian myth)	
Waves passed over Jonah	2:4	Wind passed over earth	8:1
Těhôm surrounds	2:6	*Těhôm* bursts forth	7:11
Bottoms of the mountains	2:7	Tops of the mountains	8:5
Jonah remembered the Lord	2:8	God remembered Noah	8:1
In 40 days . . .	3:4	End of 40 days . . .	8:6
C. Jonah's anger and		C. Cain's anger and	
Tôb in causative stem	4:4	*Tôb* in causative stem	4:7, 9
Driven out before God	2:5	Driven out of God's face	4:14
Hebel = Abel	2:9	Abel = *hebel*	4:2
Jonah wants to die	4:4	Cain wants to live	4:13–14
Jonah *yšb* east of city	4:5	Cain *yšb* east of Eden	4:16
D. Gourd and Worm	4:6–7	D. Tree and Snake	2:5–3:24
Protection from evil	4:6	Cause for evil	3:22
Glad because of gourd	4:6	Tree is delightful	3:6
Worm causes gourd to wither	4:7	Snake entices to eat of tree	3:4–5
Gourd taken away = test	4:7	Tree given = test	2:17
Jonah wants to die because of gourd	4:9	Eat of tree and surely die	2:17
E. God who cares for both		E. God the Creator of	
Men and beasts	4:11	Beasts and men	1:1–2:3
Seven narrative days		Seven days of creation	
Cf. "God of heaven, who made the sea and the dry land"	1:9		

	ATRAHASIS	GENESIS 1–11	EXODUS 1–2	MATTHEW 1–3
A.	Creation of Man			
	(Tab I. 1–248)	(Gen 1:1–2:25)	(Exod 1:1–7)	(Matt 1:1–17)
	Summary of Work of Gods	Sum of Work of God		
	Creation of Man	Creation of Man	A Genealogy	A Genealogy
B.	Man's Numerical Increase			
	(I. 249–415)	(2:4–3:24)	(1:8–14)	(1:18–25)
	Attempt to Decrease Numbers	Adam and Eve	Hard Labor of Hebrews	Joseph and Mary
	Threat of Death by Plague	Near Death		"Virgin Birth"
C.	Second Attempt to Decrease:			
	Double Story (II. i. 1–vi. 55)	(4:1–5:32)	(1:15–22)	(2:1–18)
	1. Threat of Death: Drought	1. Cain and Abel	1. Two Midwives	1. 3 Wise Men
	2. Severer Means	2. Lamech's Taunt	2. Severer Means	2. Infanticide
D.	Final Solution			
	(II. vii.–III. vi. 40)	(6:1–9:7)	(2:1–10)	(2:19–23)
	Atrahasis' Flood	Noah's Flood	Moses and the Nile	Flight to Egypt
	Salvation in Boat	Salvation in *tēbâ*	Salvation in *tēbâ*	Exodus Motif
E.	Resolution			
	(III. vi. 41–viii. 18)	(9:8–11:32)	(2:11–25)	(3:1–17)
	Compromise between Enlil and Enki	Dispersion—Abram leaves Ur	Moses goes out to Midian	Baptism of John in River Jordan
	"Birth Control"	Exodus Motif	Exodus Motif	Flood Motif

NOA.01. Comparative chart of Primeval History.

supplied from the pseudepigraphic fragment of the book of Noah (= *1 Enoch* 106, see above).

4. New Testament. a. Matthew 24:38 and 1:1–3:17. Matthew uses the Flood as an illustration for the eschatological coming of the Son of Man, who will come stealthily without the knowledge of incorrigible sinners. The Flood is seen here as the epoch divider and the Son of Man event will be analogous to it; the Son of Man is another Noah.

For Matthew, Jesus like Moses is another Noah from the outset (Kikawada 1974). In fact, the outline and themes of Genesis 1–11 and Exodus 1–2 as well as the ancient parallel to them can be seen in the first three chapters of Matthew's gospel. See Fig. NOA.01 All four are relating the primeval history. Atrahasis and Genesis 1–11 are on a macrocosmic scale whereas Exodus 1–2 and Matthew 1–3 are on a microcosmic scale. All four symbolically tell their stories from the very beginning of the world through the epoch-dividing event, and then introduce the new era. In all the biblical examples the dispersion or Exodus motif emerges as a means of salvation in contrast to the Mesopotamian method of salvation, i.e., birth control. The motifs of mass killing of undesirable population and of the "Flood" as an epoch divider are present in all.

Jesus the Savior comes out of the water of salvation. Thereupon, he is met by the dove, linking him to the Flood tradition and making him another Noah.

b. 1 Peter 3:20. In a very enigmatic passage of 1 Peter 3:13–22 in which Peter may be claiming that Christ has preached the gospel to the dead (cf. 1 Pet 4:6), especially to the dead of the time of Noah, the Flood is made analogous to baptism as a means of salvation through water. Quite independently of this passage, however, the baptism of Jesus in Matthew's gospel can be construed as a miniature Flood bearing the significance of an epoch divider within a miniature primeval history in Matthew 1–3.

c. 2 Peter 2:5–6. Peter makes a reference to two Genesis figures, Noah and Lot, both of whom are righteous persons saved from disasters. It is difficult to know how much Peter wished to parallel these figures, but the stories of these two men are astonishingly similar. Consider the following (the present writer owes this observation to his student Hugo Garcia).

The whole area of Sodom and Gomorrah was said to be "like the garden of the Lord" (Gen 13:10); but the people of Sodom were very wicked (Gen 13:13). Despite Abraham's plea on behalf of the people, they were to be destroyed (Gen 18:16–33). From this point on the parallel with Noah becomes closer. In both the Noah and Lot stories the sex offense episodes, including incest and homosexuality, frame the story and the sequence of events concerning the great disaster and salvation from it provides point-by-point contacts between the two:

Sodom and Gomorrah Story	Noah's Flood Story
Sex offense involving "angels" and "daughters"	
Angels—homosexual (19:1–11)	Sons of God (6:1–4)
Announcement of disaster because of wickedness	
To Lot (19:12–14)	To Noah (6:11–13)
"come in [*bo*ʾ]" and "shut [*sgr*]"	
Angels brought Lot (19:10)	All flesh (7:16)
Instruction for salvation of a family	
Lot and daughters 19:15–23	Noah family 6:14–18

"Rain"—*himṭîr* 19:24, *mamṭîr* 7:4	
Brimstone/fire 19:24	40-day rain 7:4
All die but one family	
Lot's family 19:25–29	Noah's family 7:21–23
"God remembered"	
Abraham instead of Lot 19:29	Noah and animals 8:1
Living outside of city	
Cave in hills 19:30	In tent 9:20–21
Drunkenness	
Of Lot 19:32–35	Of Noah 9:21
Sex offense—Incest	
Father/daughters 19:31–38	Father/son, homosexual 9:22–23

Thematically, note that Lot, like Noah, is the epoch-divider figure who, having experienced the end of Sodom and Gomorrah, ushers in the new generation of Moabites and Ammonites. The major difference, however, lies in the fact that Lot is not a covenant figure as is Noah. The reason for this may be that Noah obeys all that God commands (Gen 6:22; 7:5, 9, 16), whereas Lot twice modifies the angel's instruction to flee to the hills—initially Lot wants to go to the little city of Zoar because it is closer than the hills, but eventually he settles *(nwḥ)* in a cave in the hills outside *(mḥwṣ)* of Zoar because he is afraid of the city! On the other hand, Lot's cousin Abraham, the intercessor for Sodom and Gomorrah, is a covenant figure whom "God remembers" (Gen 19:29, cf. 8:1, "God remembers Noah"). Abraham vicariously participates in the "rain" of fire that sweeps over Lot's cities, thus making both Lot and Abraham Noah-like.

d. Hebrews 11:7. In the list of righteous people of faith, Noah is used to illustrate the definition of faith as "the assurance of things hoped for, the conviction of things not seen." Noah's obedience of the divine instruction to construct an ark saves his household and preserves the seed of righteousness for the new generation. Noah is seen as a bridge between the condemned world and the new age.

5. Pseudepigrapha. a. *1 Enoch* 106. Enoch tells the story of Lamech being frightened at the birth of Noah. At birth Noah's "body was as white as snow and red as a rose; the hair of his head as white as wool and his *demdema* [an Ethiopic word describing his hair] beautiful; and as for his eyes, when he opened them the whole house glowed like the sun—[rather] the whole house glowed even more exceedingly" (*1 En.* 106:2). Lamech goes to Methuselah and Methuselah to Enoch; but note that Lamech does not go to his wife for explanation first as he did in the *Genesis Apocryphon.*

Enoch assures Methuselah that Lamech indeed is the child's father, revealing the secret that there will be a Flood to destroy wicked humanity. Enoch advises Methuselah to name the child Noah. He will be saved from the disaster along with his three children (*1 En.* 106:18) and "he will comfort the earth after all the destruction" (*1 En.* 107:3; cf. 106:18). The folk etymology of the name in Gen 5:29 is reflected here also. Apart from the name and its folk etymology, this pseudepigraphic story, like that in the *Genesis Apocryphon,* has nothing to do with the Genesis story, although some connections with the Sumerian and possibly with the Babylonian stories may be adduced in terms of the miraculous birth of the Flood hero (see above).

1 Enoch includes a few more references to Noah. The Most High sends the archangel Uriel to Noah to inform him of the impending Flood, so that Noah may escape the destruction and preserve his seed for the future generations (*1 En.* 10:2). In *1 Enoch* 65, Enoch foretells the destruction of the world and the salvation of Noah in response to Noah's outcry for help because the earth had "sunk down" or "became deformed" (*1 En.* 65:1). One is tempted to speculate here that a tradition of preflood overpopulation as in the Atrahasis Flood Story and of overburdened earth as in Yima's Flood Story may be reflected in this passage.

The word of God comes in *1 Enoch* 67 and tells Noah that he has been "blameless" and "righteous" (cf. Gen 6:9) and that "the angels are working with wood [making an ark]" (*1 En.* 67:2). The divine speech also includes an echo of the blessings of Gen 1:28 and 9:1, "Be fruitful and multiply and fill the earth." In contrast to this passage, *1 En.* 89:1 reports that Noah himself makes the ark, which floats on water to save him.

b. *Book of Jubilees.* From its own peculiar viewpoint of chronology and law, the *Book of Jubilees* recounts the history of the world from creation to Moses, with whom the new age of the Law begins. The Flood Story is retold in much greater detail in *Jub.* 4:28–10:17. Noah also appears in scattered references down to *Jub.* 22:13 in the context of blessing (*Jub.* 9:24, 27; 22:13) and covenant (*Jub.* 14:20). Moses, however, replaces Noah as the epoch divider as in the book of Exodus.

Bibliography

Avigad, N., and Yadin, 1956. *Genesis Apocryphon.* Jerusalem.

Benito, C. A. 1969. "Enki and Ninmah" and "Enki and the World Order." Diss. Pennsylvania.

Cassuto, U. 1949. *Genesis.* Vol. 2. Jerusalem.

Christensen, A. 1943. *Les Types du Premier Himme et du Premier roi.* Archives d'études orientales 14/2. Leiden.

Civil, M. 1969. Sumerian Flood Story. Pp. 138–45 in *Atra-hasis,* ed. W. G. Lambert and A. R. Millard. London.

Cohen, H. H. 1974. *The Drunkenness of Noah.* University, AL.

Hesse, E. and Kikawada, I. M. 1984. Jonah and Genesis 11–1. *AJBI* 10: 3–19.

Humphries, R. 1958. *Ovid: Metamorphoses.* Bloomington, IN.

Jacobsen, T. 1939. *The Sumerian King List.* Chicago.

Kikawada, I. M. 1974. Literary Conventions for Primeval History. *AJBI* 1:3–21.

———. 1983. The Double Creation of Mankind in Enki and Ninmah, Atrahasis I 1–351, and Genesis 1–2. *Iraq* 45: 43–45.

Kikawada, I. M., and Quinn, A. 1985. *Before Abraham Was.* Nashville.

Kilmer, A. D. 1972. The Mesopotamian Concept of Overpopulation and Its Solution as Reflected in the Mythology. *Or* 41: 160–77.

———. 1976. Speculations on Umul, the First Baby. *AOAT* 25: 265–70.

———. 1987a. The Mesopotamian Counterparts of the Biblical Nephilim. Pp. 39–43 in *Perspectives on Language and Text,* ed. E. W. Conrad and E. G. Newing. Winona Lake, IN.

———. 1987b. The Symbolism of the Flies in the Mesopotamian Flood Myth and Some Further Implications. *AOS* 67: 175–80.
Lambert, W. G., and Millard, A. R. 1969. *Atra-hasis: The Babylonian Story of the Flood.* London.
Thapar, R. 1976. Genealogy as a Source of Social History. *The Indian Historical Review* 4.
Wolff, F. 1910. *Avesta, die heiligen Buecher der Pasrsen.* Strassburg.

Isaac M. Kikawada

NOAH'S ARK

Noah's ark (Heb *tēbâ*) was the great boxlike vessel by means of which Noah and his family escaped the waters of the Flood. According to the story, God was dissatisfied with the violence of human creatures and decided to destroy them and cleanse the earth by means of a universal deluge. Because he was a righteous man, Noah was to be the exception. Consequently, God instructed him to construct a huge floatable "box" wherein he and his family could ride out the destructive waters. It was to be made of "gopher wood," the identification of which is a matter of dispute among modern interpreters [Heb *gōper,* possibly the same as Gk *kyparissos,* Eng "cypress"]. The vessel was then to be caulked with pitch (bitumen), divided into three partitioned decks, and provisioned for Noah's family and for pairs of land and flying animals. When it was completed, rain and subterranean waters devastated the earth for 40 days, covering the tops of the highest mountains. Approximately one year later, when the waters had subsided and the earth had become dry, Noah's family disembarked atop one of the mountains of Ararat and repopulation of the earth began.

A. Dimensions of the Ark

The size of the vessel is given in "cubits," the modern estimate for which is approximately 18 inches each. Thus, 300 cubits long, 50 cubits wide, and 30 cubits high converts into 450 feet, 75 feet, and 45 feet, and this yields a rectangular box which was more suitable for floating than for sailing. Its size is astonishing in comparison with some modern vessels (e.g., the English ship *Mayflower* was only ninety feet long).

There is reason to suspect that the dimensions reflect a preoccupation with the number 60, as was commonly the case in Mesopotamian mathematics and occasionally that of the Bible. (For example, the ages of the Mesopotamian antediluvians in the Sumerian King List are given in multiples of 60^2 years and those of the Bible in Genesis 5 are given in multiples of 60 months with the occasional supplement of 7 years.) Thus, the vessel of Utnapishtim, the Mesopotamian flood hero of the Akkadian version, is 120 cubits per side. (Allowing 19.7 inches for a Babylonian cubit, this yields 197 feet per side, for a volume about 5 times that of Noah's boat.) The sides are thus (60×2) cubits, a reflection that Mesopotamian mathematics reckons in a place notation of base 60 (in contrast to the English system of base 10). This means that Utnapishtim's vessel is two ideal (or base) units per side and has an ideal volume of $(60 \times 2)^3$. Good fortune, one may suppose, must thereby smile upon it.

The dimensions of Noah's vessel, likewise, rather than being random or corresponding to actual measurement of Israelite boats, reflects the same idealization. It is 300 (60×5) cubits long and 30 (60/2) cubits high. The third dimension, the width, is a curious 50 cubits, but nonetheless the resultant volume is $(60^3 \times 2) + (60^2 \times 5)$ cubic cubits.

B. Claims that the Ark has Survived

Prior to the beginning of the Common Era, the claim was being made that parts of the Flood Hero's boat yet survived and had been seen: "It is said there is still some parts of this ship in Armenia, at the mountain of the Gordyaeans; and that some people carry off pieces of the bitumen . . . [for] use chiefly as amulets" (Josephus, *Ant* 1.3.6 [1st century, C.E.], quoting the Babylonian priest Berossos [3d century, B.C.E.]). Berossos here speaks of the Sumerian hero, Ziusudra, whom Josephus happily identified with Noah. Thereafter (in Christian, Jewish, and Muslim literature), a number of sites were proposed as the landing place of Noah's ark, most of which were alleged to have produced wooden remnants: in Arabia (Jabal Judi in the ʾAjaʾ Range), on the headwaters of the Tigris in SE Turkey (Cudi Dağ/Jabal Judi in the Gordian Mountains), in the Caucasus Range (Mt. Baris), in W Turkey (near the city of Apamea), in N Iran (Alwand Kuh and Mount Demavand), and in NE Turkey (Masis/Ağri Dağ).

It is the last of these sites, a majestic mountain (39° 42′ N; 44° 18′E) which rises dramatically to a height of 16,900 feet above the plain, that modern ark searchers have designated as "Mount Ararat" (a term which the Bible itself, at Gen 8:4, does not use; rather, it speaks of "the mountains of [the kingdom of] Ararat"). Although the literature of the native Armenian population knows this peak as the landing place only since the 11th–12th centuries C.E., the claim has recently been made (in newspapers, magazines, books, movies, and television programs) that this is undeniably the biblical site. Such claim has been supported by eyewitness testimony to a boat protruding from a glacier, by photographs, and by pieces of handhewn timber which reportedly date to high antiquity (up to 5,000 years of age, which might accord with Archbishop Ussher's literal biblical chronology which puts the Flood around 2450 B.C.E.; Montgomery 1972; Navarra 1974).

None of this alleged evidence for the survival of Noah's vessel has withstood rigid scrutiny (Bailey 1978; 1989). The eyewitnesses fundamentally contradict each other and some accounts have been shown to be fabrications. The photographs are either now missing or have been denounced as fake. The beams, based upon the best scientific evidence, are to be dated to the 7th century C.E. (Bailey 1977). There is no reason, then, to believe that remnants of Noah's ark are to be found anywhere in the world (regardless of one's decision about the historicity of the biblical account of the Flood).

Bibliography

Bailey, L. R. 1977. Wood from "Mt. Ararat": Noah's Ark? *BA* 40: 137–46.
———. 1978. *Where Is Noah's Ark: Mystery on Mt. Ararat.* Nashville.
———. 1989. *Noah.* Columbia, SC.
Montgomery, J. W. 1972. *The Quest for Noah's Ark.* Minneapolis.
Navarra, F. 1974. *Noah's Ark, I Touched It.* Plainfield, NJ.

Lloyd R. Bailey

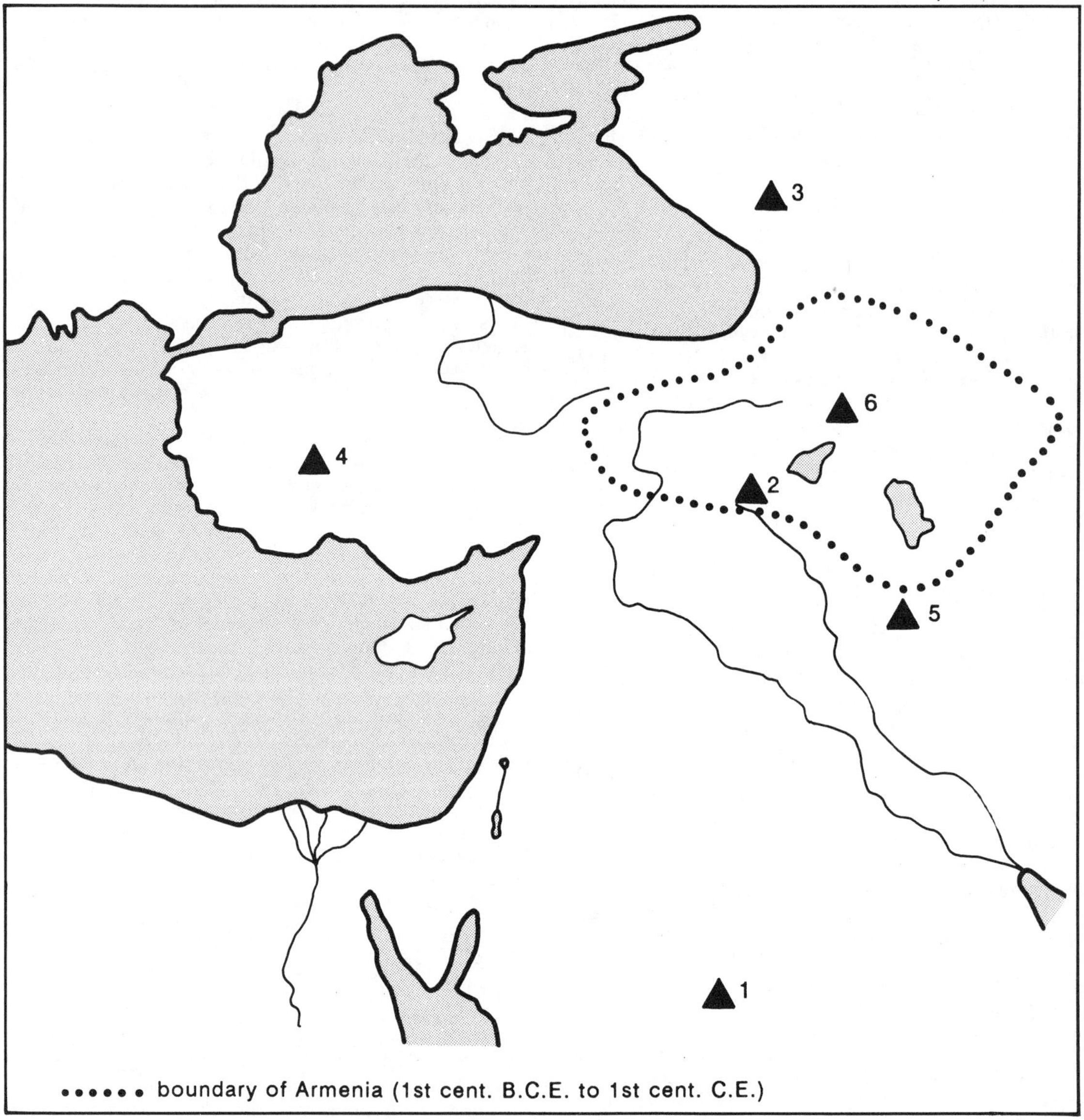

NOA.02. Regional map of proposed sites for "Mt. Ararat." *1,* Jabal Judi in the ʾAjaʾ Range; *2,* Cudi Dağ (Jabal Judi in the Gordian Mountains); *3,* Mount Baris; *4,* near Apamea, on the Marsyas River; *5,* in Adiabene (Pir Omar Gudrun/Pira Magrun); *6,* Büyük Ağri Dağ/Masis.

NOAH, APOCALYPSE OF. A pseudepigraphal book mentioned by name only in *Jub.* 10:13 and 21:10. Some scholars identify portions of this work in *Jub.* 7:20–39 and 10:1–7, as well as *1 En.* 6–11; 54:7–55:2; 60; 65:1–69:25; 106; 107 (Charles, *APOT* 2: 168; Rist, *IDB* 3: 556). Further evidence for its existence is provided by fragments discovered in Cave 1 at Qumran (Dupont-Summer 1962: 299; Rist, *IDB* 3: 556). Its exact date, author, and place of composition are unknown. However, it is clearly earlier than *Jubilees,* which is usually dated between 161 and 140 B.C.E. (Wintermute, *OTP* 2: 44; Rist, *IDB* 3: 556). It was probably composed in Hebrew or Aramaic somewhere in Palestine. While some fragments are apocalyptic, many contain ideas and language that cannot be so classified.

Since all we possess of the *Apocalypse of Noah* are fragments embodied within other works, it is impossible to present a complete and coherent picture of the content or structure of the book. From the extant fragments, it seems that the book focused primarily on the fallen angels (mentioned in Genesis 6). These angels taught magic, medicine, astrology, alchemy, the art of making weapons, and all kinds of evil and injustice that corrupted the earth and brought about the Flood. The names of the angels and a description of their evil deeds are also provided.

One fragment relates information about the primeval monsters Leviathan and Behemoth (cf. Job 40 and 41). Others contain descriptions of the many "hidden things," such as the contents of the first and last heaven, and what is beneath the earth and in the depths. They tell of the mysteries of the winds, lightning, and thunder; God's promise to Noah; and of the punishment of the evil angels. The story of Noah's birth and how he and his family were spared from the Flood is also told in one of the fragments.

Bibliography

Dupont-Sommer, A. 1962. *The Essene Writings from Qumran.* Trans. G. Vermes. New York.

Schmidt, N. 1926. The Apocalypse of Noah and the Parables of Enoch. Pp. 111–23 in *Oriental Studies Dedicated to Paul Haupt,* ed. C. Adler and A. Embler. Baltimore.

DANA ANDREW THOMASON

NOB (PLACE) [Heb *nōb*]. Town N of Jerusalem where David met Abimelech the priest (1 Sam 21:1—Eng 21:2). It was here that David and his companions ate the Bread of the Presence (an episode mentioned in Jesus' dispute with the Pharisees concerning the Sabbath; cf. Matt 12:1–4, Mark 2:23–28, and Luke 6:1–5) and where David received the weapons of Goliath. During this time Nob apparently held the position of the chief sanctuary of YHWH after the fall of Shiloh, Ahimelech being the great-grandson of Eli, the priest at Shiloh (cf. 1 Sam 14:3; see McCarter *Joshua* AB, 349).

Saul hears of this through the information of Doeg the Edomite (1 Sam 22:9). Saul summons Ahimelech and all the priests of Nob (1 Sam 22:11) and eventually razes the city when the priests refuse to disclose David's whereabouts (1 Sam 22:19).

Isaiah lists Nob among the cities overrun by an army advancing on Jerusalem from the north (Isa 10:32). On the difficulties in understanding this passage, see GALLIM and the bibliography listed there. Nob is later listed among the cities to which the Judahites returned after the Exile (Neh 11:32).

The proximity of Nob to Jerusalem is plain in Isa 10:32 where the invader shakes its fist at Jerusalem from Nob. Albright (1925: 139; so also Donner 1968: 50; *NHT,* 172) places Nob on Râs el-Mešârif, a slope of Mount Scopus within sight of Mount Zion. Another slope north of Mount Scopus, Quᶜmeh, has also been named as a possible site (*IDB* 3: 557), though Râs el-Mešârif has the advantage of being more clearly within eyesight of Jerusalem. The exact location of the town, however, remains unidentified.

Bibliography

Albright, W. F. 1925. The Assyrian March on Jerusalem. *AASOR* 4: 134–40.

Donner, H. 1968. Der Feind aus dem Norden: Topographische und archaeologische Erwangungen zu Jes. 10,27b–34. *ZDPV* 84: 46–54.

JEFFRIES M. HAMILTON

NOBAH (PERSON) [Heb *nōbaḥ*]. A male descendant of Manasseh who conquered a league of cities, known as KENATH, at the same time that his relative Jair presumably was campaigning against Og of Bashan (Num 32:47). Other traditions (1 Kgs 4:13 and Deut 3:4) report more generally that all Israel took the land of Og from Bashan and divided it for the half-tribe of Manasseh.

PAUL NIMRAH FRANKLYN

NOBAH (PLACE) [Heb *nōbaḥ*]. **1.** An area of Gilead named after its Manassite conqueror, Nobah (Num 32:40–42). The context of the Numbers passage is a description of Moses' division of the territories of Sihon and Og to the tribes of Reuben, Gad, and Manasseh. Nobah, a leader of Manasseh, subsequently overthrew Kenath and its environs and renamed the area after his own name. In 1 Chr 2:23 the old name Kenath is used. See KENATH. Gray (*Numbers* ICC, 441) suggested that the name Kenath was retained by later generations because the new name failed to establish itself. The site has been identified as modern Qanawat in Hauran at the extreme NE corner of Manasseh's territory.

2. A town near Jogbehah in E Gilead (Judg 8:10–11). Using Nobah and Jogbehah as a surprise travel route, the judge, Gideon, made an attack against the Midianites at Karkor. The exact site is unknown, and this possibly might be the same as Nobah #1 above.

JOEL C. SLAYTON

NOBLES. See PALESTINE, ADMINISTRATION OF (POSTEXILIC JUDEAN OFFICIALS).

NOD (PLACE) [Heb *nôd*]. The name of the land where Cain went after he had killed his brother Abel and Yahweh had put a mark on him to prevent him from being killed in revenge (Gen 4:16). This verse locates it "east of Eden." The land of Nod is not mentioned elsewhere in the Bible. It is unlikely that an actual geographical location is meant. The name seems to be derived from the Hebrew root *nwd,* "to wander." The word *nōd* also appears as a noun in Ps 56:9 (—Eng 56:8) with the meaning "wandering(s)" (RSV "tossings"). Thus, rather than denoting a specific place, the land of Nod symbolizes Cain's fate as "a fugitive and a wanderer (*nād*) on the earth" (Gen 4:12, 14). The same appears to be true for the phrase "east of Eden." Gen 3:24 reports that Yahweh God drove the man out of the Garden of Eden and placed the cherubim and a flaming sword at the E of the garden to prevent access to the tree of life. "East of Eden" simply means outside of the Garden of Eden, and thus banishment from God.

The LXX reads "the land of *Naid*" in Gen 4:16. Unlike "Nod," which fits the context beautifully, "Naid" has no perceptible meaning. It seems to be a corruption of *nôd* due to a confusion of the letter *waw* (representing *ô* in the MT reading) and the letter *yod* (representing the *ai* diphthong of the LXX reading). *Waw* and *yod* were almost identical in appearance for much of the history of the Hebrew language, and confusion of the two letters is common in the Hebrew Bible.

JAMES R. DAVILA

NODAB (PERSON) [Heb *nôdāb*]. A tribe in N Transjordan, 1 Chr 5:19. In 1 Chr 5:18–22, Reuben, Gad, and half of Manasseh conduct war against "the Hagrites, Jetur, Naphis and Nodab" (5:19). 1 Chr 5:10 dates this war to the reign of Saul. See HAGAR; HAGRITES; NAPHISH. As, according to its orthography, the name Jetur cannot have entered the biblical tradition before the 7th century B.C., the date provided by 1 Chr 5:10 must be aberrant. See JETUR. Most probably, the Chronicler (Ephᶜal 1982: 100 n. 337, 239), or one of his redactors (Knauf 1989: 49–52) had contemporary Arab tribes from N Transjordan (and a conflict between them and Jewish settlers?) in mind when he wrote his account, which then dates to the 4th–3d centuries B.C.

It can be argued that Nodab is identical with Adbeel, an Ishmaelite tribe (Gen 25:13; see ISHMAELITES) attested in 734/733 B.C., when Tiglath-pileser III entrusted this tribe with the control of the Egyptian border. The Assyrian king may have encountered Adbeel in southern Syria or northern Transjordan (Knauf 1989: 67). The names Nodab and Adbeel were linked to the same tribe by W. F. Albright (1956: 13). Knauf (1989: 67) derives both names linguistically from **Nadabʾil*, "God has called up, incited." The LXX renders "Adbeel" by *Nabdeêl,* and "Nodab" by *Nabadaioi.* As the sequence *db* is impossible in Greek, and had to be changed to *bd,* the occurrence of the same metathesis in *Nabadaioi* (where *d* and *b* are separated by a vowel) indicates that the two names were regarded as identical by the LXX.

Personal names from *NDB,* "to call up, to incite," occur in biblical Hebrew (Nadab, Nedabjah), Ammonite (ᶜAmminadab), Safaitic, Thamudic, classical Arabic, and Sabaic (Nadab).

Bibliography

Albright, W. F. 1956. The Biblical Tribe of Massa' and Some Congeners. Vol. 1, pp. 1–14 in *Studi orientalistici in onore di Giorgio Levi della Vida.* 2 vols. Rome.

Ephᶜal, I. 1982. *The Ancient Arabs.* Jerusalem.

Knauf, E. A. 1989. *Ismael.* ADPV. Wiesbaden.

ERNST AXEL KNAUF

NOGAH (PERSON) [Heb *nōgah*]. One of thirteen sons of David listed as having been born to David's wives in Jerusalem (1 Chr 3:7; 14:6), in addition to his six sons born at Hebron. His mother's name is unknown: four of the thirteen were Bathsheba's sons; the remainder were born to unnamed wives. Besides these thirteen, David had numerous (unnamed) sons born to his concubines, according to 1 Chr 3:9.

Nogah's name is missing (along with the first occurrence of "Eliphelet") from the list of David's sons born in Jerusalem in 2 Sam 5:13–16. A corrupt dittography with the following name, Nepheg, has been postulated, and the list in 2 Samuel has been seen as the more reliable (e.g., Williamson *1 and 2 Chronicles* NCBC, 56). However, there is evidence that the 2 Samuel list originally carried both names missing in the MT. See ELIPHELET #1. Also, the number of David's sons given in 1 Chr 3:8—nine—requires the presence of Nogah's name, as well as both occurrences of "Eliphelet." Thus, it is most reasonable to accept Nogah as a separate name and person. (See Myers *1 Chronicles* AB, 19.) See also DAVID, SONS OF.

DAVID M. HOWARD, JR.

NOHAH (PERSON) [Heb *nôḥâ*]. The fourth son of Benjamin according to 1 Chr 8:2. Besides 1 Chronicles 8, the sons of Benjamin are listed in three other places: Gen 46:21 (= *Jub.* 44:25); Num 26:38–41; and 1 Chronicles 7. In none of these other lists does Nohah appear. The following table clearly shows the many divergences between these lines.

Gen 46:21	Num 26:38–41	1 Chr 7:6	1 Chr 8:1–2
Bela	Bela	Bela	Bela
Becher		Becher	
Ashbel	Ashbel	*Jediael	Ashbel
Gera	*Ahiram		*Aharah
Naaman	*Shephupham		*Nohah
*Ehi			
*Rosh			*Rapha
*Muppim			
*Huppim	*Hupham		
*Ard			

*Indicates names not appearing in the other lists

The name most closely resembling Nohah is Naaman in Gen 46:21. The presence of the name Naaman later on in the list (1 Chr 8:4, 7), however, argues against simply substituting "Naaman" for "Nohah." Curtis and Madsen (*Chronicles* ICC, 157–58) suggested that "Nohah" is a transcriber's variation of "Ahoah" (v 4), but there is no support for this suggestion. Of these lists, the list reflecting the oldest traditions is the one in Numbers 26, but even that list probably does not list the actual sons of Benjamin, instead giving clan names (Noth *Numbers* OTL, 203–8). Von Rad (*Genesis* OTL, 403) suggested that the list in Genesis 46 is artificial and the product of "very late and theoretical erudition." The great differences among the lists as well as their differing purposes make it difficult, if not impossible, to assert the priority of one list over the others and thereby identify a name like Nohah which occurs only in one.

TOM WAYNE WILLETT

NOPHAH (PLACE) [Heb *nopaḥ*]. "Nophah" appears as the name of a town in the MT of Num 21:30. However, this text has suffered in transmission and was interpreted differently by the versions. In the Masoretic punctuation the last consonant of the word *ʾăšĕr* ("which") is marked with a *punctum extraordinarium* indicating that the *reš* was questioned by the scribes at an early date. The Sam. Pent. and LXX considered the consonants underlying the word "Nophah" to be a verbal form meaning "to breathe," "to set aflame" (a reading followed by Noth 1940–41: 169; Althann 1985: 568–71). Taking the consonants *nph* as a verb and replacing the word *ʾēš* ("fire") for *ʾăšĕr* by omitting the last consonant, the Sam. Pent. and LXX understood the MT reading "unto Nophah which" to mean "further kindled a fire." The latter reading is followed by the RSV whereas the former is retained by the KJV. If "Nophah" is a place-name as in the MT (e.g., Hanson 1968: 306), it refers to an unidentified site in Moab probably S of Heshbon.

Bibliography

Althann, R. 1985. Num 21, 30b in the Light of the Ancient Versions and Ugaritic. *Bib* 66: 568–71.

Hanson, P. D. 1968. The Song of Heshbon and David's *NÎR*. *HTR* 61: 297–320.

Noth, M. 1940–41. Num. 21 als Glied der "Hextateuch"—Erzählung. *ZAW* 58: 161–89.

ARTHUR J. FERCH

NOREA, THOUGHT OF (NHC IX,*2*). The second of three gnostic tractates contained in Nag Hammadi Codex IX (27,11–29,5), inscribed in Sahidic Coptic. It is one of the shortest tractates in the Nag Hammadi corpus, and is found in a relatively undamaged portion of the MS. The title has been assigned to it by modern editors from a phrase occurring in the text at its conclusion (29,3). Another title is in use in German scholarship: *Ode on Norea,* a title which is based on a judgment concerning the literary genre of this tractate. While its strophic structure and diction are reflective of the characteristics of Semitic or "biblical" poetry, the putative Greek text of *Norea* seems to lack the meter that would qualify it as Greek poetry (e.g., the Naassene Psalm preserved by Hippolytus, *Ref.* 5.10.2).

A clear fourfold structure is reflected in this tractate: (1) Norea's invocation of the Father and his divine companions, 27,11–20; (2) Norea's deliverance, 27,21–28,12; (3) Norea's role as savior, 28,12–23; (4) the future salvation of Norea's spiritual progeny, 28,24–29,5.

Norea is a "saved savior" in this and related texts. In the Sethian gnostic system Norea appears as the daughter of Eve and the sister-consort of Seth. She is thus the spiritual mother of the gnostic race. In the *Hypostasis of the Archons* (NHC II,*4*) she is portrayed as the intended victim of rape by the wicked archons, and as "crying out" for help (II 92,33–93,2). The help comes in the form of a heavenly revelation mediated by Eleleth, one of the four "luminaries" in the Sethian system. The tractate *Norea* dovetails with *Hyp. Arch.,* for the invocation comprising its first part is followed by the sentence, "It is Norea who cries out to them" (27,21–22). Norea's deliverance and reintegration into the Pleroma are then treated; this constitutes the second section of the tractate.

Norea's role as savior, highlighted in the third and fourth sections of the text, is a particularly interesting feature of *Norea* and the closely related *Hyp. Arch.* Both documents are included among those gnostic tractates that are associated in modern scholarship with Sethian Gnosticism. But, whereas in most of those texts it is Seth who is the gnostic savior par excellence, in *Norea,* as in *Hyp. Arch.,* the major salvific role is played by Seth's consort, Norea. She thus functions as the feminine counterpart to Seth, as the mother of the gnostic elect. She is a saved savior, and her salvation is paradigmatic of that of her spiritual progeny. This feature of *Norea* would, no doubt, have appealed to female members of a gnostic group; indeed, it is possible that *Norea* was composed by a gnostic woman (Stroumsa 1984: 35–70).

There are no clear indications of Christian influence in *Norea,* unless such technical terms as "Pleroma" and "deficiency" are traceable to Valentinian influence. (Valentinian Gnosticism is, of course, a Christian form of the gnostic religion.) In any case, the figure of Norea itself originates as a gnostic reinterpretation of a Cainite antiheroine in Jewish Haggadah, Naamah (cf. Gen 4:22). The original spelling of "Norea" is "Horaia," a form of the name that occurs in other gnostic sources. *Hōraia* is the semantic equivalent in Greek of Hebrew *naʿămâ* ("pleasing, lovely"). Gnostic traditions revolving around Horaia-Norea probably developed in Jewish gnostic circles, independently of Christianity.

The technical terminology in *Norea,* as well as its allusions to developed gnostic traditions (e.g. "the four holy helpers," 28,27–28), suggest that this tractate represents a comparatively late development of an earlier Jewish Gnosticism. Its original Greek version can be dated to the late 2d or early 3d century. It could well have been composed in Egypt, or in another E Mediterranean region.

Bibliography

Pearson, B. A. 1977. The Figure of Norea in Gnostic Literature. Pp. 143–52 in *Proceedings of the International Colloquium on Gnosticism; Stockholm, August 20–25, 1973,* ed. G. Widengren. Stockholm.

———. 1988. Revisiting Norea. Pp. 265–75 in *Images of the Feminine in Gnosticism,* ed. K. L. King. Studies in Antiquity and Christianity 4. Philadelphia.

Pearson, B. A., and Giverson, S. 1981. NHC IX,*2: The Thought of Norea.* Pp. 87–99 in *Nag Hammadi Codices IX and X,* ed. B. A. Pearson. NHS 15. Leiden.

Roberge, M. 1980. *Noréa (NH IX,2).* Pp. 149–71 in *L'Hypostase des Archontes (NH II,4)* par B. Barc, suivi de *Noréa (NH IX,2)* par M. Roberge. Bibliothèque copte de Nag Hammadi, "Textes" 5. Québec and Louvain.

Stroumsa, G. 1984. *Another Seed: Studies in Gnostic Mythology.* HS 24. Leiden.

BIRGER A. PEARSON

NORTH [Heb *ṣāpôn, śĕmōʾl*]. One of the cardinal compass points in the ANE. But unlike modern Western culture, "north" was not the primary direction for orientation. "East" was the primary direction for orientation, probably from the rising sun. See DIRECTION AND ORIENTATION. Hebrew had two major words for "north," *ṣāpôn,* from a root which meant hidden or dark, and *śĕmōʾl,* literally the left hand. This latter term shows clearly the Hebraic use of the body to gain directions when one faces east.

In addition to the expected use in reference to the direction, "north" comes to have several specific connotations in the OT. "North" is especially the direction from which invaders come (Jer 1:14–15; Isa 14:31). Certainly Israel's position influenced this understanding. Protected by the sea on the W and the Syrian desert on the E, her only major concerns for massive invasion came from the S (Egypt) and the N (Assyria, Babylon, the Hittites, etc.). Especially in the latter period of the monarchy and exilic/postexilic periods, those empires to the N and E were by far the strongest. Perhaps as much symbolically as geographically, "north" is also the direction invaders will come upon Babylon (Jer 50:9; Zech 2:10—Eng 2:6) and the direction from which Gog of Magog will come (Ezek 38:6, 15).

Since the invaders have come out of the N and have carried off exiles, it is only natural that the returning exiles will come from the N (Jer 3:18).

In Ugaritic mythology, *ṣpn* is the name of the holy mountain, used especially as Baal's abode, and was the place of the assembly of the gods. Mt. Ṣapon is usually identified with Mt. Casius, N of Ras Shamra. In other texts Baal calls himself the god of *Ṣpn* and the title-epithet "Baal Ṣpn" appears in several texts. Closely related to this Ugaritic and Canaanite mythology must be the reference to God's abode in the far N (Isa 14:13). Also God appeared to Job out of the N (Job 37:22) and Ezekiel's cherub chariot theophany appeared from the N (Ezek 1:4).

JOEL F. DRINKARD, JR.

NORTH AFRICAN CHRISTIANITY. See CHRISTIANITY (NORTH AFRICAN).

NORTH AFRICAN JUDAISM. See JUDAISM (NORTH AFRICAN).

NORTH COUNTRY, THE (PLACE) [Heb *ʾereṣ ṣāpôn*]. Ominous appellation for the N regions of Mesopotamia and Syria. This designation is used mostly by Jeremiah, but is also found four times in Zechariah.

Jeremiah is told in one of his opening visions that evil is about to break forth from the N against Judah (Jer 1:13–16). In Jeremiah 4–6, Yahweh states that he is about to bring "evil" and "great destruction" from the N. Specifically, he refers to a nation skilled with "bow and spear," a cruel nation who will show no mercy to Zion (Jer 6:22–23, see also 10:22 and 25:9). At the end of his book, Jeremiah sees a great and mighty nation arising again from the North Country, but this time against Babylon. In nearly the same language as Jer 6:22–23, the prophet predicts a nation skilled at warfare will show no mercy to Babylon (Jer 50:41–42, see also 50:3, 9 and 51:48).

The North Country is also the land of the Exile, from which Yahweh will redeem his people. Jeremiah uses the designation in this way, and similar expressions freely (Jer 3:12, 18; 16:15; 23:8; 31:8, etc. and see also Zech 2:6).

Israel's unique geographical features contributed to these perceptions regarding the North Country. With the Mediterranean on her W and desert protecting her E and SE, enemies normally approached from the SW or N. Although the Egyptians and Philistines were to the S and SW, most of Israel's attackers came from the N. Even Assyrian and Babylonian armies were considered northern enemies. The North Country was a designation broad enough to include the NW extremities of Mesopotamia (since it was the site of Egypt's defeat at Carchemish on the Euphrates in 605 B.C., Jer 46:2,10).

The specific identity of Jeremiah's northern foe (Jeremiah 4–6) is a much disputed question. Herodotus reports that the Scythians invaded Syria-Palestine around 625 B.C., near the beginning of Jeremiah's ministry (1.104–6). Proponents of an older "Scythian hypothesis" hold that Jeremiah's descriptions of invaders best fit these Indo-European nomads from the Russian steppes (for recent reviews, see Holladay *Jeremiah* Hermeneia 1: 42–43 and Perdue 1984: 6–10). Recent commentators have tended to deny this position (Bright *Jeremiah* AB, lxxxi–lxxxii; Holladay, 42–43; and Thompson *Jeremiah* NICOT, 86–87). Others have argued that Jeremiah's "foe from the north" carries a definite mythological flavor (Childs 1959: 197–98). Thus, no specific historical group can be identified with the northern army. Recently, it has been suggested, on the basis of cuneiform texts and archaeological evidence, that Scythian mercenaries served as the vanguard of the Chaldean attack against Jerusalem, so that the Scythian theory is not to be entirely dismissed (Yamauchi 1982: 87–99).

Bibliography

Childs, B. S. 1959. The Enemy from the North and the Chaos Tradition. *JBL* 78: 187–98.

Perdue, L. G. 1984. Jeremiah in Modern Research: Approaches and Issues. Pp. 1–32 in *A Prophet to the Nations: Essays in Jeremiah Studies*, ed. L. G. Perdue and B. W. Kovacs. Winona Lake, IN.

Yamauchi, E. 1982. *Foes from the Northern Frontier*. Grand Rapids, MI.

BILL T. ARNOLD

NORTHWEST SEMITIC LANGUAGES. See LANGUAGES (INTRODUCTORY SURVEY).

NOSE RING. See JEWELRY.

NOT MY PEOPLE (PERSON) [Heb *lōʾ ʿammî*]. The third child, a son, born to the prophet Hosea and his wife Gomer (Hos 1:9). At God's command, Hosea gave each of his three children names symbolizing divine judgment against Israel. This last of Hosea's children bears the most drastic of the three sign names. The formula "I will be your God and you shall be my people" lies at the heart of God's covenant with Israel, and thereby at the center of Israel's self-identity (Exod 6:7; Lev 26:12; 2 Sam 7:24; Jer 7:23; etc.). The name of Hosea's first child, JEZREEL, anticipated the impending military defeat of the reigning dynasty. His second child's name, NOT PITIED, indicated God's withholding of love and protection from the house of Israel. "Not My People" signifies that God has repudiated the covenant and utterly rejected the people of Israel. The judgment of Hos 1:9 is reversed in 2:25 (—Eng 2:23). "Not My People" will be renamed "My People" (cf 2:1, 2—Eng 1:10; 2:1). The verse promises that divine judgment of Israel will be followed by the restoration of covenant. See HOSEA, BOOK OF.

CAROLYN J. PRESSLER

NOT PITIED (PERSON) [Heb *lōʾ ruḥāmâ*]. The second child, a daughter, born to the prophet HOSEA and his wife Gomer (Hos 1:6, 8). Her name is explained (v 6) as a sign that God will "no more have pity on the house of Israel." The Hebrew word translated "pitied" *(rḥm)* also has the broader meaning "love." Denial of pity elsewhere in the prophets is associated with judgment, entailing both withdrawal of protection and active destruction. The child's name (like the names of her brothers) thus symbolizes God's refutation of love for and wrathful judgment against Israel. The child later becomes a symbol of renewal and eschatological hope. Hosea 2:25 (—Eng 2:23) promises that God will "have pity on Not Pitied" (cf. 2:3—Eng 2:1). See also HOSEA, BOOK OF; JEZREEL (PERSON); NOT MY PEOPLE (PERSON).

CAROLYN J. PRESSLER

NOVELS, GREEK AND LATIN. The novel, as understood by the modern reader, was not a genre recognized by ancient literary criticism. Traditionally, the depiction of fictional characters and their adventures and emotions was the province of the poets (epic, tragic, comic). Prose fiction emerges relatively late in Greek and Latin literature and, even when it does so, is virtually unnoticed by the arbiters of literary taste. It does not even have a name of its own: *drama* (Photius), *mythoi eroticoi* (Ach. Tat. 1.2.3), and *historia* (Longus 1.1.1) are all used. Its neglect by contemporary intellectuals has tended to lead to a corresponding neglect by scholars, but the recent flowering of critical interest in this branch of literature has opened up many avenues of interest to biblical studies.

A. The Novels

The texts may be divided into two groups, the sentimental or "ideal" romance of love and adventure, and the picaresque or comic. Of the former, five complete texts and numerous fragments survive, all Greek: Achilles Tatius, *Adventures of Leucippe and Cleitophon,* in 8 books (2d century A.D.); Chariton, *Chaereas and Callirhoe,* in 8 books (before A.D. 150: possibly as early as 1st century B.C.); Heliodorus, *Aethiopica,* in 10 books (2d–4th century A.D.); Longus, *Daphnis and Chloe,* in 4 books (end of 2d century A.D.); Xenophon of Ephesus, *Ephesiaca* or *Anthia and Habrocomes,* in 5 books, possibly abridged from 10 (A.D. 150–250) Fragments include those of the *Ninus Romance* (ca. 100 B.C.), *Parthenope and Metiochus,* Iamblichus' *Babyloniaca,* and Lollianus' *Phoenicica.*

Broadly speaking, the 2d century A.D. may be regarded as the heyday of the ideal novel, but the papyrus fragments show that similar tales were circulating in written form at least in the 1st century B.C., almost certainly earlier. Of the complete texts, Chariton and Xenophon (whatever their actual dates) represent the earlier, less sophisticated approach to the genre, while Heliodorus, Longus, and Achilles Tatius reflect a more consciously literary approach influenced by the Second Sophistic. All five texts concern the adventures of a pair of young lovers (hence the name "erotic": but the treatment is on the whole sentimental-romantic rather than pornographic). All but Longus involve a separation at the beginning of the story and a "happy ending" in which the couple are reunited after an impossibly complicated series of adventures including voyages, shipwrecks, capture by pirates, attempted rape, mistaken identity, imprisonment, sacrifice, suicide, and entombment. Longus' story stands alone as a Theocritean pastoral idyll describing the gradual sexual awakening of the young shepherd and shepherdess; there is no voyaging here, but, as in the other novels, the couple are separated by capture (pirates, and an invading army) and finally reunited with the aid of divine intervention.

Of the picaresque type we have only Latin examples. Petronius' *Satyricon* (probably 1st century A.D.) was originally at least 16 books in length: most of books 15 and 16 survive, including the famous scene of Trimalchio's dinner party *(Cena Trimalchionis).* The work is a highly individual and sophisticated composition, drawing on a Roman tradition of satire and probably deliberately parodying the Greek ideal novel (Hägg 1983: 171). Here a travel narrative is used as a framework for a series of comic and scandalous episodes: the antihero, a Greek student accompanied by two rogues, is "a kind of comic reversal of Odysseus or Aeneas in his wanderings" (Hägg 1983: 170). Apuleius' *Metamorphoses* or *The Golden Ass,* in 11 books, dates from the mid or late 2d century A.D. The story relates the adventures of Lucius who, overcurious about magic, is turned into an ass and endures many vicissitudes until his final intiation into the mysteries of Isis and restoration to his own shape. Lucius' wanderings as an ass again provide the framework for a variety of tales, many of the "Milesian" (pornographic) type, but some of the "ideal" type, notably the myth of Cupid and Psyche (4.28–6.24). There is a Greek version of the simple *Story of the Ass* (wrongly attributed to Lucian), to which Apuleius has added a variety of ingredients.

B. Origins

Against a prevailing preoccupation with the "development" of the novel out of earlier Greek literary genres (Alexandrian love elegy, hero tales, degenerate historiography, and mystery texts were all suggested), B. E. Perry, in his classic study *The Ancient Romances* (1967), asserted that "the first romance was deliberately planned and written by an individual author, its inventor. He conceived it on a Tuesday afternoon in July . . . It did not come into being by a process of development on the literary plane" (p. 175). More recent studies, however, have stressed once again that the extant novels cannot be considered in isolation, but must be placed in a context embracing all the varied types of narrative activity taking place in the Hellenistic world and in the Near East. Thus, for example, Scobie (1969) looks at the role of the *aretalogus* and other tellers of "wonder tales" in Roman society. Hägg (1983) examines the Greek novels against a broad background of epic, drama, historiography, popular biography, and fantastic travel tales, but also stresses their continuity with the "historical" romances (Alexander, Apollonius of Tyre) and with the new Christian popular literature of apostles, martyrs, and saints. Anderson (1984) spreads the net wider: like Braun (1938), who had earlier suggested the need to look further east, Anderson points out parallels to the Greek novels in Sumerian tales like *Dumuzi's Dream* and *Enlil and Ninlil,* and finds in Petronius' *Satyricon* "a substantial portion of an Ancient Near Eastern tale-complex about an everyman and his fortunes at the hands of an at least ambiguous companion" (p. 193). Even Apuleius, in this perspective, becomes part of a continuum of oriental storytelling reaching right through from *Gilgamesh* to the *Arabian Nights.*

C. Style

As Perry (followed especially by Reardon) stressed, none of this "background" research should detract from the appreciation of the extant texts as individual works in their own right. Once we have assimilated the fact that much of their plot content is a "given" to these authors, not original invention as might be assumed with a modern novelist, it remains true that the ancient novelists (like Shakespeare) all exercised their individual talent and judgment in the *presentation* of their stories (Hägg 1983: 108, "the goal was originality, not in content but in execution"). Characterization, idealized and often wooden, tends to come second to complicated plot construction, which is often handled in a masterly fashion: Rattenbury (1949) made an apt comparison with film scenarios. The setting of the ideal novels tends to be timeless or archaic; their language leans toward the classicistic even in Chariton, while Achilles Tatius, Heliodorus, and Longus write in the full-blown Atticizing manner associated with the Second Sophistic. All the Greek novelists use the basic narrative as a thread on which to hang learned excurses, geographical or pictorial descriptions, and rhetorical displays. Xenophon is the least artistic of the five: Dalmeyda (1926) believes his infelicities of style and construction are his own, not the result of an incompetent epitomator's work. Petronius and Apuleius, following the centuries-old convention for comedy, depict something more like the real world of their day, and include much racy and idiomatic contemporary diction; but they remain "highly sophisticated authors addressing themselves ostensibly to the learned world of fashion for purposes of their own" (Perry 1967: vi).

D. Audience

If we accept Northrop Frye's definition of popular literature as "what people read without being told to," then the Greek novels must certainly be regarded as popular literature, despite their apparently frigid and mannered styles. The number of papyrus fragments of novels testifies to their wide distribution in an age when the school classics, from Homer downward, must have been losing their appeal. As Reardon (1969) observes, Perry's objective was to stress not only the individual achievement of the novelists but their cultural context, the "broad conditions of society" in which and for which they wrote. Earlier historians had already pointed out that the rise in the novel's popularity in the 2d century A.D. coincided with an era of mass literacy and relative prosperity for the middle classes (Giangrande 1970). Within the broader category there must be distinctions between one end of the spectrum and the other: Perry's "poor in spirit" (1967) perhaps applies more obviously to the audiences of Xenophon or Chariton than to those of Longus or Achilles Tatius who, as Giangrande observes, must have possessed "a notable degree of culture." Nevertheless the very fact that the novels remained outside the canon of accepted literary taste makes them a potentially valuable introduction to the tastes and interests of that widely distributed subculture of the Eastern Empire, scarcely represented in our predominantly aristocratic literary remains, which (while aware of the inadequacies of the term) we can only call "middle class." As Hägg observes (1983: 90), "the people who needed and welcomed the novel are the same as those who were attracted by the mystery religions and Christianity," an observation which seems to be confirmed by the fact that the decline of the novel after the 3d century A.D. apparently coincides with the rise in popularity of the Christian stories of martyrs and saints (p. 161).

E. Religion

One theory sees the novels as originating in the mystery religions: Kerenyi (1927), Merkelbach (1962; 1965). Thus Merkelbach sees Achilles Tatius' novel as a retelling of the myth of Isis and Osiris, with concealed references to the mystery rituals of baptism and mock-mummification: "the narrative symbolizes the fall of the human soul into matter, its wandering through life and its arrival at the safe haven of the Isis religion, or the homecoming of the soul into the kingdom on the other side after death" (1965: 11). Even if this view is not accepted (it has not convinced the majority of scholars, cf. Turcan 1963), it is still true that the ideal novels are both highly moral (chastity and fidelity invariably triumph over all conceivable obstacles) and deeply imbued with religious sentiment. Priests, temples, and processions figure largely, the gods play an active role in the narrative, and the hero and heroine often have a deeply personal relationship with their own private deities. Even the picaresque adventures of Apuleius' *Golden Ass* end in a dramatic conversion to Isis in Bk.11 (for the significance of this scene for our understanding of ancient attitudes to religious conversion, see Nock 1933: chap. 9). Interestingly, the atmosphere of the narrative itself tends to give an archaic or timeless picture of the religious scene, with the new personal deity manifesting himself or herself to the individual against a backdrop of traditional cult and ceremonial: the Isis novels never mention Christianity or Judaism, just as Acts never mentions Isis or Serapis.

F. The Bible

The relevance of all this to the Bible may be described under four heads: motif and incident; embellishment; style and presentation; audience.

1. Motif and Incident. If the Greek and Latin novels are part of a continuum of ancient oriental storytelling, then it should not surprise us if many Bible stories also form part of the same continuum. Extrabiblical parallels to the Daniel story *(Ahiqar, Prayer of Nabonidus)* are already well known; similarly, Joseph, Esther, Tobit, Susannah, even Ecclesiastes and the gospel parables contain motifs which can be paralleled in other Near Eastern tales (Anderson 1984: 103 n. 20, 105 n. 76, 187; *OTP* 2: 487). It is not here a question of direct influence: merely that some biblical stories may be regarded as ladlefuls out of the same "pot of story" (to use Tolkein's phrase) from which the Greek and Latin novelists drew.

2. Embellishment. More direct influence (though not of any of the extant novels) may be seen in those cases where the biblical story has been embellished in extrabiblical tradition in novelistic fashion, most obviously by supplying a romantic interest absent in the original story. The Joseph story has been enhanced in this way in *Joseph and Aseneth* (Burchard 1985: 183–84); Josephus' account of Moses' Ethiopian expedition (*Ant* 2§ 238–53) has also gained an embryonic love interest (252). We may also note here Christian postbiblical stories such as *Paul and Thecla,* which supply the romantic interest (in a sublimated form) which is lacking in the canonical stories (Hägg 1983: 159–60).

3. Style and Presentation. Novelistic influence on the style and presentation of some biblical material has long been suspected, notably in Acts (Norden, Dibelius). Acts is a sober narrative compared with its apocryphal successors, but the detailed account of the shipwreck as well as the inclusion of apparently gratuitous geographical information in the second half of the book seems to point to a wish to gratify an audience whose tastes were, at least in part, molded by the novels (Pervo 1987).* Whether these tastes influenced the *content* of Acts—i.e., whether the author actually invented incidents—is another matter: on the analogy of the extant novels, we can now see that the authors were for the most part working on "given" plot material rather than inventing freely, and this may provide a better model for the biblical writers' approach to their work.

4. Audience. Perhaps the most fruitful line to be pursued in the study of the Greek and Latin novels is for the light they throw on their audiences and their tastes and interests (including religious interests): see D and E above. It is clear that there was in the late Hellenistic and early imperial periods a reading public of armchair travelers who liked "a good yarn" well laced with exotic adventure: the ingredients of love, death, and religion could be combined in many different ways, but the desire to edify while entertaining, and the need to entertain while edifying, were never too far apart. It is surely not too fanciful to suggest that similar needs and desires may have motivated many biblical storytellers as well.

Bibliography

Texts:

Achilles Tatius: S. Gaselee in LCL, 1947.

Apuleius: S. Gaselee, LCL, 1915; R. Graves, Penguin 1950; J. Lindsay, Bloomington, IN, 1962.

Chariton: ed. W. E. Blake, Oxford, 1938 (ET W. E. Blake, London, 1939).

Heliodorus: ed. Rattenbury-Lumb-Maillon. Collection des Universités de France, 3 vols. Paris, 1960 (in French). (ET M. Hadas, Ann Arbor, 1957).

Longus: J. M. Edmonds and S. Gaselee, *Daphnis and Chloe, with Parthenius.* LCL, 1924. P. Turner, Penguin 1956.

Petronius: M. Heseltine, LCL, 1969.

Xenophon: ed. G. Dalmeyda. Collection des Universités de France. Paris, 1926 (in French). (ET M. Hadas, New York, 1953).

Other Works:

Anderson, G. 1984. *The Novel in the Graeco-Roman World.* New Jersey.

Braun, M. 1938. *History and Romance in Graeco-Oriental Literature.* Oxford.

Burchard, C. 1985. Joseph and Aseneth. Pp. 177–247 in *OTP.*

Dalmeyda, G. Ed. and trans. 1926. *Xenophon.* Paris.

Giangrande, G. 1970. Novel, Greek. *OCD,* 739–40.

Hägg, T. 1983. *The Novel in Antiquity.* Oxford.

Kerenyi, K. 1927. *Die griechisch-orientalisch Roman-literatur in religionsgeschichtlicher Bedeutung.* Budapest. Repr. Darmstadt, 1962.

Merkelbach, R. 1962. *Roman und Mysterium in der Antike.* Munich and Berlin.

———. 1965. Achilleus Tatios. P. 11 in *Lexikon der alten Welt.* Zurich.

Nock, A. D. 1933. *Conversion.* Oxford.

Perry, B. E. 1967. *The Ancient Romances.* Berkeley.

Pervo, Richard I. 1987. *Profit with Delight: The Literary Genre of the Acts of the Apostles.* Philadelphia.

Rattenbury, R. 1949. Novel, Greek. *OCD,* 611–12.

Reardon, B. P. 1969. The Greek Novel. *Phoenix* 23: 291–309.

———. 1971. *Courants littéraires grecs des IIe et IIIe siècles ap. J.-C.* Annales Littéraires de l'Université de Nantes, Fasc. 3. Paris.

Scobie, A. 1969. *Aspects of the Ancient Romance and Its Heritage.* Beiträge zur klassischen Philologie 30. Meisenheim am Glan.

Turcan, R. 1963. Review of Merkelbach. 1962. *RHR* 163: 149–99.

LOVEDAY C. A. ALEXANDER

NU. The thirteenth letter of the Greek alphabet.

NUMBERS AND COUNTING. Numbers are often mentioned in the Bible, where they are always expressed in terms of number words. Nevertheless, inscriptions on archaeological objects such as weights, ostraca, and monuments demonstrate that the use of number symbols was common in ancient Israel. The forms of these number symbols reveal foreign influences, in no way unexpected under the given circumstances. Also the literary use of numbers in the Bible demonstrates a fair amount of foreign influence. High numbers are often of a form which is characteristic for numbers originally expressed in the Mesopotamian number system with the base 60. Stylistic comparisons can be made in many cases between passages in the Bible and parallels in Ugaritic or Sumero-Akkadian legends. The religious-literary-historical nature of the Bible explains why computations in the Scripture are very few and unsophisticated. For a proper understanding of the role played by numbers and counting in the cultural environment where the biblical literature arose, it is necessary to look for extraneous sources and influences. How important that role was, and how deep and widely branched its roots, will be demonstrated below. Comparatively little emphasis will be put on numbers occurring in the Bible itself, since detailed discussions exist elsewhere (*IDB* 3: 561–67; *EncJud* 12: 1254–61). See also MATHEMATICS, ALGEBRA, AND GEOMETRY.

A. Number Representations and Arithmetic
1. The Preliterate Middle East
2. Ancient Mesopotamia
3. Ancient Iran
4. Ancient Egypt
5. Ancient Syro-Palestine
B. Numbers in Poetic and Religious Literature
1. Sumero-Akkadian
2. Ugaritic
3. The Bible

A. Number Representations and Arithmetic

1. The Preliterate Middle East. For five millennia before the invention of writing, a uniform method for the recording of numbers was spread over the entire Middle East (Schmandt-Besserat 1977). The method consisted of the use of small "tokens" of clay as representations of numbers and measures. Such tokens have been discovered at practically all excavated sites from Anatolia in the north to Iran in the east and Egypt in the west. Some tokens found in Israel, for instance, can be dated to the 7th millennium B.C. (Jericho), while others are as late as the 2nd millennium B.C. (Megiddo). These tokens come in many shapes, such as cylinders, spheres, disks, cones, ovoids, etc., and in various sizes. It is probable that they were used in trading and commerce, in and between many autonomous regions. The meaning of the various shapes and sizes of the tokens can be inferred, on a tentative basis, from a comparison with the corresponding shapes and sizes of the written number notations which eventually replaced them (see below).

The number representation system based on tokens was used without any apparent modification well into the 4th millennium B.C.. Thereafter the beginning of urban civilization on an unprecedented scale forced the system to undergo a series of profound changes (Schmandt-Besserat 1980; 1981; Le Brun and Vallat 1978; Ifrah 1981. As a first step, perforations allowed tokens to be tied together in groups, forming permanent records. At the same time, many new types of tokens appeared, and the increased use of incised or attached markings on the tokens made possible the recording of ever more complex economic transactions. A second step was to surround groups of tokens by balls of clay, so-called "spherical envelopes," often with imprints of cylinder seals for the further protection and verification of records. Such balls with tokens have been found at sites ranging from Shah Dad in southern Iran to Dumah, near Hebron, in Israel. The next step in this increasingly rapid development was when the use of the tokens was discontinued in favor of a new invention, "impressed" clay tablets with punch marks as number symbols. Reed styli of different diameters were used to punch circular and semioval marks into the clay, in an obvious attempt to imitate the shapes of small and big cylindrical, spherical, and conical tokens. The invention of writing was the logical last step in this chain of innovations. It took place, probably in southern Mesopotamia, some time toward the end of the 4th millennium B.C..

2. Ancient Mesopotamia. The earliest written records unearthed so far are "proto-Sumerian" clay tablets from Uruk in southern Mesopotamia (ca. 3000 B.C.). This archaic Uruk script consists of both word and number signs. Some word signs are pictographic, while others are abstract and can be interpreted only when they are precursors to Sumerian word signs of known meaning. The number signs, punched into the clay with a set of round styli, are easy to distinguish from the word signs. They consist of combinations of small and big, round and semioval marks. Sexagesimal numbers are written by repetition of the signs "small oval, small round, big oval, small round in big oval, big round" with the values 1, 10, 60, 600, 3,600. Number signs can also denote values of measures for grain, length, area, etc., so that one and the same sign can have, for instance, the values 10, 6 grain units, and 1,800 area units, depending on the context (Friberg 1984). Measures of time (days, months, years) are indicated through diverse combinations of number signs with the pictogram for "sun, day." The "administrative" year is, in the early Uruk texts as in later cuneiform texts, a fictive year of 12 months with 30 days each (Englund 1987).

With the evolution of the cuneiform script, the number signs changed form but were still used for both sexagesimal numbers and measures. The end result of the development was the sexagesimal place-value system (ca. 2000 B.C.), which allowed all numbers to be written by repetition of only two number signs, "upright wedge" for "1" and "oblique wedge" *(Winkelhaken)* for "10." A sexagesimal zero was used sparingly, most often in Late Babylonian mathematical and astronomical texts (ca. 300 B.C.).

The oldest known mathematical texts are from the Sumerian city of Shuruppak (Fara), ca. 2650 B.C. They consist of a table of squares, a multiplication exercise, and two division exercises, all with high numbers involved. The later OB period, ca. 1700 B.C., was a time when the teaching of mathematics was intense in the Mesopotamian scribal schools. At the elementary level, this teaching was based on the use of elaborate multiplication tablets, division tables, and tables of measures. At a more advanced level, the curriculum comprised algorithms for the computation of square roots, reciprocals, etc., as well as methods for solving quadratic equations and indeterminate problems, and practical rules for computations having to do with bricks, irrigation, work division, and so forth (Neugebauer and Sachs 1945). During the LB period, ca. 300 B.C., there was a renewed interest in mathematics, coupled with the production of astonishingly sophisticated mathematical division tables or astronomical tables with predictions for the movements of the sun, the moon, and the planets.

3. Ancient Iran. Toward the end of the 4th millennium B.C. the influence from the Late Uruk culture in Mesopotamia reached far into ancient Iran. This was the time of the spherical envelopes and the impressed tablets. Thereafter followed a break in the relations between the two regions, at about the time when the Archaic Uruk script was invented in Mesopotamia. Not much later, an independent "proto-Elamite" script was invented and established in Iran. It was based on a repertory of abstract signs, probably a mixture of word signs and syllable signs, written on clay tablets in lines from right to left. The script turned out to be relatively ephemeral, and is still undeciphered, with one important exception, the sign for "barley, grain." The number signs which are present in practically all proto-Elamite texts are formed in the same way as the number signs on the early Uruk tablets (Friberg 1984). It is possible to show that the notational systems for sexagesimal numbers and grain numbers are nearly identical in the two scripts. There is also, unexpectedly, a third proto-Elamite system of number notations which is decimal, with special signs for "100" and for "1,000." Decimal number signs were probably used to count animals, while sexagesimal numbers were used to count people and inanimate objects. In the Sumerian scripts there were never any special signs for decimal numbers. The words for "hundred" and "thousand" in Sumerian were loanwords from the Semitic language of the Akkadian (Semitic) part of the population of southern Mesopotamia. Special signs for "100" and "1,000" did not exist until a relatively late date, around the end of the 3d millennium B.C. Cuneiform signs for "10,000" appear only in a few texts from peripheral sites (Nuzi, Hattusha, Ugarit). The explanation of the meaning of the proto-Elamite number signs entails an important partial decipherment of many proto-Elamite clay tablets. A majority of the texts can be shown to be simple economic or administrative documents with additions, multiplications, and conversions between various systems of numbers. In this respect there is no great difference between protoliterate texts from ancient Iran and from neighboring Mesopotamia.

4. Ancient Egypt. Available facts suggest that writing was invented in Mesopotamia toward the end of the 4th millennium B.C. Information about the new technique must have spread rapidly, for within a very brief time span two other independent scripts were invented, the proto-Elamite script in Iran and the hieroglyphic script in Egypt. The latter seems to have been fully developed from the beginning, complete with notations for large numbers up to a million (the image of a seated god stretching up both arms). The role of "a million" as a conventional notation for a "vast number" is clear from its frequent appearance in Egyptian myths (*ANET,* 3–36): In *The God and His Unknown Name of Power* it is said about Isis, "Her heart was craftier than a million men; she was choicer than a million gods; she was more discerning than a million of the noble dead." In the *Spell for Not Dying a Second Time,* Atum answers the deceased, "Thou art (destined) for millions of millions (of years), a lifetime of millions." The only whole numbers appearing in the hieroglyphic script are decimal numbers: a single stroke for "1," an arc for "10," a lotus for "100," a finger for "1,000," and a tadpole for "10,000" (Gillings 1972). Hieroglyphic numbers in monumental inscriptions were formed by the additive principle, so that writing a number like 89 required 17 symbols, 8 nines and 9 ones. For everyday practical purposes, the cursive hieratic script was developed, with individual signs for the units 1–9, for the tens 10–90, for the hundreds 100–900, and for the thousands 1,000–9,000 (See *LA,* s.v. Symbolische Zahlen). Place-value notation for decimal numbers and fractions was never introduced.

Three kinds of notations for fractions appear in the hieratic and hieroglyphic scripts, namely "unit fractions" $1/n$, individual signs for the "special fractions" ½, ⅓, ¼, ⅔, and ¾, and signs denoting binary fractions (from ½ to $1/64$) of the basic units of capacity and area measure. In their hieroglyphic forms, the capacity fractions were fashioned as parts of the eye of the falcon god Horus: the inner part (½), the iris (¼), the eyebrow (⅛), etc. The unit fractions $1/n$ were written with the sign *r',* "mouth," as *r'*-5, *r'*-6, etc. Mathematical papyri from the first half of the 2d millennium B.C. show that the concept of common fractions a/b was unknown. This led to great practical difficulties in the course of even the simplest computations involving fractions. The best-known example is constituted by the *Rhind Mathematical Papyrus* (Robins and Shute 1987). A disproportionally large part of this document is occupied by a table with rules for the doubling of unit fractions, from $2 \times 1/3 = 2/3$ to $2 \times 1/101 = 1/101 + 1/202 + 1/303 + 1/606$. Doubling was an important arithmetical operation for the reason that multiplication by any whole number could be replaced by a series of doublings, followed by an addition. So, for instance, since $13 = 1 \times 8 + 1 \times 4 + 0 \times 2 + 1 \times 1$, the product 13×7 can be computed as $(1 \times 8 + 1 \times 4 + 0 \times 2 + 1 \times 1) \times 7 = 1 \times 7 + 0 \times 14 + 1 \times 28 + 1 \times 56 = 105$. The method had the advantage that it could be used equally well for solving division problems. It is possible that Egyptian scribes carried out additions on some kind of primitive abacus. Multiplications, divisions, and operations with fractions were carried out explicitly on the papyrus, sometimes with the use of both black and red ink for the reader's convenience.

Some important late Egyptian mathematical texts (3d century B.C.–2d century A.D.), written in the demotic script, were published by Parker (1972). At this time, the Persian and Greek conquests of Egypt had opened the way for increased cultural contacts between Egypt and Mesopotamia. This fact is obvious in Parker's demotic mathematical texts, which demonstrate a typically Babylonian choice of topics. On the other hand, the conservativeness of Egyptian mathematical traditions manifests itself through the continued use of the unwieldy unit fractions as the sole means of expressing fractions.

A few late Greek mathematical papyri from the middle of the 1st millennium A.D., recovered from sites in Egypt, are other examples of how amazingly tenacious mathematical traditions can be (Knorr 1982). *Papyrus Akhmim,* the most complete of these texts, shows clear similarities with the more-than-2,000-years-older *Rhind Mathematical Papyrus.* It begins with an extensive multiplication table for unit fractions, and continues with 50 arithmetical problems, many solved with techniques related to those used in the construction of the table. The main part of the table lists the products of ⅔ and the unit fractions from ⅓ to $1/10$ with the units, tens, hundreds, and thousands. The products are expressed as sums of unit fractions, as in the example $1/7 \times 1{,}000 = 142\ 1/2\ 1/3\ 1/42$.

The number notations used in the mentioned Greek-Egyptian papyri are Greek alphabetic numerals (Ifrah 1981), using the letters *alpha–theta* for the units, *iota–koppa* for the tens, and *rho–san* for the hundreds. The classical Greek alphabet with its 24 letters is, for this purpose, augmented with three obsolete letters, the *digamma* (6), the *koppa* (90), and the *san* (900). The thousands and the myriads (ten thousands) are denoted by the letters *alpha–theta* with special distinguishing marks. It is difficult to assess the age of this system, but it is documented in a marriage contract on a papyrus from Elephantine 310 B.C., on coins dating from the reign of Ptolemy Philadelphus (286–246 B.C.), and in papyri with multiplication tables and tables of squares from the last part of the 3d century B.C. From this time until the end of the Middle Ages, the Greek alphabetic numerals played nearly the same role in the Near East and around the eastern Mediterranean as the Roman numerals did in western Europe. However, the alphabetic numerals were not the only type of numerals used by the ancient Greeks. In Greek monumental inscriptions from the second half of the 1st millennium B.C. (and also on a famous Greek counting board) one encounters Attic (or Athenian) numbers, with special acrophonic signs for 1, 5, 10, 5 × 10 . . . 5 × 10,000. The Attic number system was of the same structure as the more well known Roman system.

5. Ancient Syro-Palestine. Around the middle of the 3d millennium B.C., Ebla was a flourishing Semitic city-state in Syria. The remains of its rich library were found to contain mostly administrative and economic accounts written in Eblaic on clay tablets using the Old Sumerian cuneiform script. The numbers used in these accounts are decimal. One of the texts is a mathematical exercise, the solution of a division problem involving high numbers (Friberg 1986). It is the oldest known mathematical text with decimal numbers. The problem solved in the text can be formulated as follows: if a month's rations for a man is 10/11 *gu-bar* of barley, then how many *gu-bar* are needed for the daily rations of 260,000 (2 *ma-i-ḫu* 6 *ri-ba*$_x$) men? A clever and efficient algorithm yields the correct answer: 7,879 *gu-bar*. The number in the answer is written in a decimal-sexagesimal hybrid notation which is typical for Semitic cuneiform texts as 7 *li* 8 *mi* 60 + 20 − 1. Another text from Ebla, in Sumerian, contains a brief list of notations for high sexagesimal numbers. It ends with an admission of defeat: the number 60 × 60 × 60 × 60 (= 12,960,000) "cannot be counted," since the scribe cannot think of an appropriate notation for it. In an OB metrological list, the same number is referred to as "the great ŠÁR the hand does not reach."

Mari, a Mesopotamian outpost at the upper Euphrates, has yielded a few OB mathematical texts (Soubeyran 1984). The texts comprise the usual assortment of combined multiplication tables and tables of reciprocals or square roots. There is also a mathematical exercise which contains an early parallel to the famous Indian legend about the reward demanded by the inventor of the game of chess: if one starts with 1 grain of barley, and if the amount of barley is doubled every day, how much barley will there be after 30 days? The answer, correctly computed and expressed in the Mari grain measure system, has one unexpected feature: the words *līmum* and *mētum*, which normally stand for "thousand" and "hundred," have here the sexagesimal values 600 and 60. There exist roughly contemporaneous examples of a similar nature from Mesopotamia, which clearly demonstrate the difficulties caused by the clash between the sexagesimal arithmetics associated with the Sumero-Akkadian cuneiform script and the indigenous decimal number words of the Semitic populations.

The coastal city Ugarit, which flourished between the 15th and 13th centuries B.C., was influenced by the Mesopotamian civilization. This is clearly demonstrated, for instance, by some clay tablets found in Ugarit, on which Sumero-Akkadian metrological lists (lists of notations for measures of capacity, weight, and area) are inscribed in the cuneiform script. In one of these lists, capacity measures are enumerated from 1/3 SÌLA (= ⅓ liter) to 60 SIG$_7$ GUR (= 60 × 60 × 60 × 5 × 60 SÌLAS). In another list, weight measures proceed from ½ grain to 60 talents (= 60 × 60 × 60 shekels = 60 × 60 × 60 × 3 × 60 grains). Texts written in Ugaritic using the Ugaritic cuneiform alphabet often express numbers in terms of Ugaritic number words, and use the local system of weight measures. A good example is offered by a brief text (Liverani 1972), which mentions *šbʿ.kkr.šʿrt?b.kkr.ad̲dd|wbkkr.ugrt ḫmš.kkrm alp.t̲mn mat kbd d mnḥt* "seven talents of wool in the talent of Ashdod, but in the talent of Ugarit five talents one thousand eight hundred [shekels] as tribute." The text seems to imply that the talent of Ashdod was worth only ⅘ of the talent of Ugarit. Indeed, ⅘ × 7 talents = 5⅗ talents = 5 talents 1800 shekels, if 1 Ugarit talent = 3000 shekels. The number word of highest rank in Ugaritic is *rbt*, "myriad," "10,000." For the "special fractions" ½ and ⅓ the usual cuneiform signs are used, but ⅔ was referred to by the Sumerian/Akkadian loanword *šnpt* (Gordon 1965).

The order of the 30 letters in the Ugaritic cuneiform alphabet is known from several alphabetic lists, so-called "spelling books," from about the 14th century B.C. (Ifrah 1981: pl. 95). The oldest known examples of the Phoenician "linear" alphabet, on the other hand, go back no further than the 12th century B.C. The 22 letters of the Phoenician alphabet are arranged in the same familiar ways as the letters in the many alphabets derived from it: Aramaic, Hebrew, early Arabic (see below), Greek, Etruscan, Roman, etc. Moreover, if those 8 letters are removed from the Ugaritic alphabet which have no equivalents in the Phoenician alphabet, then the remaining letters in this alphabet are also arranged in the same order. It is therefore probable that the Ugaritic alphabet was just an expanded variant (in cuneiform) of a primordial Northwest Semitic alphabet dating back at least to the 15th century B.C. This conclusion is important because the ancient Greeks were not the only, and probably not the first, people using alphabetic numerals. Other examples are the Hebrews and the Arabs. (The often repeated attribution of the first use of alphabetic numerals to the Phoenicians has, however, never been confirmed.) In the case of the Hebrew alphabet with its 22 letters, *ʾalep–ṭet* are used for the values 1–9, *yod–ṣade* for 10–90, and *qop–taw* for 100–400 (Ifrah 1981: chap. 17). Higher number units are expressed by combinations of letters. In the case of the Arabic alphabet, the situation is complicated by the fact that the order of the letters in this alphabet is no longer the same as it was when the letters were given their numerical values (Ifrah 1981: chap. 21). The Early Hebrew script is used in inscriptions dating from the time of the kings of Judah and Israel (about the 11th to 6th centuries B.C.). Many such documents in the form of ostraca inscribed with simple receipts or messages reveal that not only number words but also genuine number signs were used to write numbers. Ostraca have been found at Samaria, Lachish, Arad, Kadesh-barnea, and Ophel Hill. In all cases the Early Hebrew number signs are identical with Egyptian hieratic numerals in the form they had during the New

Kingdom (Ifrah 1981: chap. 15). This picture is confirmed by hieratic inscriptions on many Israelite inscribed weights (Aharoni 1966). Since 4 Israelite shekels weighed the same as 5 Egyptian *qedets,* weightstones of 4, 8, 16, and 24 shekels are inscribed with the hieratic numerals for 5, 10, 20, and 30. The best examples of inscribed ostraca with numbers are those from Kadesh-barnea (Lemaire and Vernus 1980; 1983). On one of these ostraca, a simple writing exercise, the number 2,382 is repeated many times. A particularly big ostracon contains on the obverse a list of capacity measures, from 1 to 10 *ʾlpm* (10,000) *kor,* a list of weight measures, from 1 to 10 *ʾlpm* shekels; and a partly unintelligible list of fractions (?).

As a trading and traveling people, the Arameans gradually imposed their culture on the entire Middle East. The Hebrews, who adopted the language and writing of the Arameans, also borrowed their way of denoting numbers, as did the Phoenicians and other Semitic peoples. Aramaic number notations were based on the use of separate signs for 1, 10, 100, 1,000, and 10,000. For the ones and the tens the additive principle was used, so that for instance 70 was written as 7 tens, grouped two by two so that the result looked like 20 + 20 + 20 + 10. For the units of higher rank the multiplicative principle was used, so that 18,000 was written as 1 × 10,000 + 8 × 1,000 (Ifrah 1981: chaps. 19, 25). Examples of Aramaic number notations can be found in many preserved papyri from the Jewish military colony established in the 5th century B.C. on the island of Elephantine, in the Nile. A bilingual ostracon found at Khirbet-el-Kom, a site in Israel between Lachish and Hebron, dates to the 3d century B.C. It mentions twice, once in Greek and once in Aramaic, a sum of 32 drachmas. In the Greek part of the text, 32 is written as *lambda beta,* in the Aramaic part as 20 + 10 + 2.

The oldest examples of the use of Hebrew alphabetic numerals may go as far back as the late 2d and the 1st centuries B.C., namely a single letter *mem* for a year date on a clay seal, and the letter *gimel* as a sheet number on a parchment scroll found at Khirbet Qumran (Ifrah 1981: chap. 18). Other examples are offered by coins with inscriptions such as "Shekel of Israel year 5*(he)*" (struck during the first Jewish rebellion, A.D. 70), and "Year 2 *(bet)* of the liberation of Israel" (from the time of the second Jewish rebellion, A.D. 132–34), etc. The relatively late dates of these first examples suggest that the Hebrew alphabetic numeration was introduced as a result of Greek influence. As a matter of fact, between the 1st century B.C. and the 7th century A.D., when the Hebrew alphabetic numeration became increasingly common in the Jewish world, many Jewish scribes in the Diaspora preferred to use the Greek alphabetic numerals.

B. Numbers in Poetic and Religious Literature

1. Sumero-Akkadian. In the Sumerian myth *Inanna's Descent to the Netherworld* (*ANET,* 55), Inanna has to give up, one by one, her 7 ME-symbols, her crown, her wig, her measuring rod and line, etc., as she enters through the 7 gates to the netherworld. Her corpse is hung from a stake for 3 days and 3 nights, but it comes to life again when "sixty times the food of life, sixty times the water of life, they sprinkled upon it."

Three sources (two OB texts and Berossos' Babylonian history) contain lists of the Sumerian kings who reigned before the Flood, all characterized by an amazing longevity (Langdon 1923). In W.-B. 444, 8 antediluvial kings from five cities are said to have reigned for 8, 10, 12, 8, 10, 8, 8, 5⅚, and 5⅙ ŠÁR (meaning 3,600) years, or for a total of 1 ŠÁR-GAL 7 ŠÁR (=67 × 3,600) years. In W.-B. 62, 10 kings reign for 2 *šár-gal* 7 *šár* years, and Berossos mentions 10 kings reigning for an even 432,000 (2 ŠÁR-GAL) years.

The *Epic of Gilgamesh* enjoyed an unparalleled popularity in the cuneiform literature; its known editions, in four different languages, range in time from the 21st to the 6th centuries B.C., and in provenance from S Mesopotamia to Anatolia (Thompson 1928; Schott and von Soden 1969). One of its distinguishing features is the tendency to use numbers as a literary tool. This tendency is partly a consequence of the important role played by the teaching of mathematics and metrology in the Late Sumerian/Old Babylonian school, the *eduba.* To mention some examples: Gilgamesh, the godlike hero, is "two-thirds divine, one-third human," he is 11 cubits tall. Enkidu, his companion, "dallies six days, seven nights with the courtesan-girl in his mating." The two are each laden with axes and swords weighing 10 talents (600 minas). The gate of Uruk, Gilgamesh's city, has 7 bolts. On their way to the Cedar Forest, the heroes "break their fast after twenty 'double-hours,' rest after thirty"; after 3 days they have covered the distance from Uruk to Lebanon. Humbaba raises 8 winds against them. Ishtar's invitations are refused by Gilgamesh, who accuses the goddess of digging "seven and seven" pits to trap the lion she loves. Ishtar summons the Heavenly Bull, threatening 7 years of famine. The breath of the bull kills 100 men of Uruk, 200, 300. Enkidu lies on his deathbed "for a day, a second day . . . an eleventh and a twelfth." Gilgamesh follows the course of the sun, through the mountain of darkness, for 12 "double-hours." To cross the Waters of Death, he fashions punting poles 5 NINDAN (60 cubits) long and uses one, a second, . . . , a twelfth; after 2 times 60 they are all spent. Utnapishtim tells him how he made his ship 10 NINDAN high, 10 NINDAN square above, divided its innards, and smeared it with 6 times 3,600 measures of bitumen; on the seventh day the work was done. Gilgamesh fails the test for immortality, to avoid sleep for 6 days and 7 nights. The time he is asleep, 7 days in all, is noted on the house wall and marked by the 7 pieces of bread baked for him but not eaten.

The Babylonian *Story of the Flood* (Lambert and Millard 1969) is another example of a cuneiform literary work with interesting numbers. It begins with a description of the misery of the gods, summarized in a difficult passage with the doubtful translation, "The seven great Anunnakū were making the Igigū suffer the work" (see below). Later, it is mentioned how Bēlet-kāla-ilī, Mistress-of-All-the-Gods, "nipped off 14 pieces of clay, 7 she put on the right, 7 on the left . . . 7 and 7 birth-goddesses, 7 produced males, 7 produced females." An oft-repeated motif is the lamentation "2 times 600 years had not yet passed, when the land extended and the peoples multiplied."

The prominence of the number 7 in the quoted examples is evident. Many more examples are quoted by Hehn (1907) from Mesopotamian and other sources. The etymology of the Semitic word for "7" is unclear, and cannot be used to explain the popularity of this particular number. The correct explanation may be simply that 7 is a conveniently sized odd number. It is also the first "non-regular" number in the sense of OB mathematics (it is not divisible exclusively by 2, 3, and 5). Hehn proposes that "7" may have, in many instances, the symbolic meaning "innumerable." The ziggurat of Uruk, for example, had 7 stories. Some lexical or bilingual texts translate "7" (but also "40" and "50") with *kiššatu,* a word meaning "totality." The clearest example is probably the Babylonian-Assyrian ^{d}7-*bi* or ^{il}*si-bit-te,* the "Seven Gods," often mentioned together with, or instead of, the "Great Gods" and all "Known and Unknown Gods." The Seven Gods are associated with the enigmatic Anunnakū and Igigū (see *RLA* s.v. Igigu), which are sometimes responsible for all kinds of unfavorable events, sometimes representative of all gods in the heavens or on the earth. Interesting cryptograms for Anunnakū and Igigū are 1 10 and 5 1 1. The first of these cryptograms may have the value $1(60) \times 10 = 600$, the other both $5(60) \times 2 = 600$ and $5 + 1 + 1 = 7$.

A NB metrological table text from Uruk (von Weiher and Friberg, unpubl.) begins with a table of "mystic numbers" of the gods. After some damaged lines follow the equations ^{d}7 - *bi* = [7], ^{d}I - gi$_4$ - gi$_4$ = 8, ^{d}*A - nun - na - ki* = 9. The table goes on, assigning the numbers 10, 20, 30, 40, 50 to the great gods Bēl, Shamash, Sîn, Ea, and Enlil. This second group of mystic numbers appears also, with a few others, in a NA mystic text (Livingstone 1986: 30) listing "names of Sîn," the moon god. That text assigns to Anu, "father of the gods," the number 1 (or 60). A related text (ibid., 22) starts by mentioning the days of the month associated with Sîn: the 7th day, the 14th day, the day of the full moon *(šapattu),* etc. It continues with a series of "metamathematical" equations. One example will suffice: it is stated that the 22d day is associated with the 14th day, because $14 \times 10 = 140 = 2\ 20$ (base 60), and if the order of the digits is reversed, then 2 20 becomes $20\ (+)\ 2 = 22$. The numbers 40 and 50 appear as ideograms for gods already in texts from the 3d millennium.

Metamathematical reasoning may also lie behind the fact that 3 20 appears as a cryptogram for "king" in cuneiform omen texts. Indeed, 20 (the number of the sun god) is a common ideogram for *šarru,* "king," and $20 \times 10 = 200 = 3\ 20$ (base 60). Other common cryptograms in omen texts are 15 for *imittu,* "right," and 2 30 ($= 15 \times 10$) for *šumēlu,* "left." According to a famous passage in an inscription of the NA king Sargon II, the wall around his city Dur Sharrukin (Khorsabad) measured 4(3,600) 3(600) 1(60) 3(6) 2 cubits. This is also, says Sargon in the inscription, "the number of my name." In an effort to explain this cryptic statement, one may resolve the king's name into its constituent parts *šarru-kīnu.* The first part of the name can be replaced by the cryptogram 3 20, the second part by the sumerogram GUB (the picture of a foot). A sign with the same pronunciation is GUB$_3$ (the picture of a left arm), which is a sumerogram for *šumēlu,* "left" and can be equated with 2 30. In this way, the king's name can be expressed by the cryptogram 3 22 30, a sexagesimal number with 5 "ones" and 5 "tens." The length of the city wall transformed to sexagesimal place-value notation is 4 31 20, another number with 5 "ones" and 5 "tens," and therefore also another cryptogram for "Sharrukin" or "Sargon."

2. Ugaritic. Just like the Mesopotamian *Epic of Gilgamesh,* the Ugaritic poetic texts (Gordon 1949) exhibit a pronounced tendency to use numbers as a literary tool. In the *Baal and Anat Cycle,* for instance, "graded numbers" is a recurring theme: for the decoration of Baal's house, Ḥasis "pours silver by thousands, gold he pours by myriads." Baal declares that "a thousand *šd* the house shall comprise, a myriad *kmn* the palace" (*šiddu* and *kumani* are, respectively, Akkadian and Hurrian loanwords for a certain Ugaritic unit of area and length measure). A variant of this theme involves tens and ones together: Baal's conquests are immense, "He took sixty-six towns, seventy-seven cities, eighty, Baal . . . ninety, Baal." Before descending into the underworld, he impregnates a heifer: "He lies with her seventy-seven times . . . eighty-eight times, so that she conceives." Another recurring theme is the "climactic series of numbers," as when Baal's house is turned into gold and silver by the application of divine fire: "Behold a day and a second . . . a third and a fourth . . . a fifth and a sixth, the fire eats into the house . . . on the seventh day the fire departs from the house." A similar climactic series appears in a passage in the Hittite *Song of Ullikummis* (*ANET,* 122): "They drank once, they drank twice . . . they drank seven times; and Kumarbis began to speak."

The stylistic devices mentioned above are applied also in the *Epic of Keret.* In a dream, El advises king Keret, "For a day and a second, a third day, a fourth day, a fifth day, a sixth day, do not send thine arrows toward the city . . . behold at sunrise on the seventh, king Pbl will not be sleeping." Keret makes a vow: "If I may take Ḥurrai to my house . . . I'll give twice her price in silver, thrice her price in gold." "Vast numbers," starting with 3,000,000, are used in the description "Thine army, a great host: three hundred myriads (*t̲lt̲.mat.rbt*), troops without number, soldiers without reckoning . . . arrayed in twos, look all of them arrayed in threes." The opening lines of the epic are hard to translate. It is usually assumed, perhaps in error, that they mention a sequence of unit fractions that sum up (almost) exactly to 1. The plight of King Keret is described as follows: "Destroyed is the house of the king, who had seven brothers, (there were) eight sons of one mother . . . a third died at birth, a fourth of disease, a fifth the pestilence gathered up, a sixth the sea engulfed, a seventh of them fell by the sword . . . a family is perished." In the *Epic of Aqhat,* a cycle of lean years is described in the words "Seven years may Baal fail, eight the Rider of Clouds, without dew, without rain . . ."

3. The Bible. "Graded numbers" is an often-used stylistic device in the OT. In Deut 32:30, there are two linked pairs of graded numbers: "How should one chase a thousand, and two put ten thousand to flight, except . . . the Lord had shut them up?" In Isa 17:6, the ruining of Damascus is described in the parable "gleaning grapes shall be left in it . . . two or three berries in the top . . . four or five in the outmost fruitful branches." A more elaborate gradation can be found in Gen 4:24, "If Cain shall be avenged sevenfold, truly Lamech seventy-and-seven-fold." In Amos 1:3–2:15, the Lord says, "For three transgressions of Damascus, and for four, I will not turn away the punishment thereof," after which follows a list of 8 transgressions and punishments. A "climactic series of numbers" appears in Genesis 1: "And the evening and the morning were the first day . . . the sixth day . . . and on the seventh day God ended his work which he had made."

Vast numbers occur frequently in the OT. Sometimes they are precise, as in Num 3:43, where the firstborn males of Israel number "twenty and two thousand two hundred and threescore and thirteen," with an excess of 273 over the number of the Levites, an excess which had to be redeemed by 5 × 273 = 1,365 shekels of the sanctuary. Sometimes they are symbolic or hyperbolic, as in Daniel's dream in Dan 7:10: "thousand thousands ministered unto him, and ten thousand times ten thousand stood before him" (cf. Rev 5:11). According to Dahood (1981), the difficult passage Ps 4:8 may be translated, "Put joy in my heart; a hundred thousand fold *(māᶜōt)* be their wheat, and their wine ten thousand fold *(rabbû)*." Similarly in Isa 48:19, "Your offspring would have been like the sand, and the issue of your body like its hundred thousand grains" (cf. Gen 41:49, "And Joseph gathered corn as the sand of the sea, very much, until he left numbering; for it was without number"). Sand as a symbol for the "innumerable" appears also in Gen 23:17, where the Lord promises Abraham, "I will multiply thy seed as the stars of the heaven, and as the sand which is upon the seashore."

Several numbers occur frequently in the Bible and are of symbolic or cultural significance, notably "7" (Gen 41:26, "The seven good kine are seven years; and the seven good ears are seven years; the dream is one"), but also, for instance, "3" (Job was blessed with 7 sons and 3 daughters), "4" (4 rivers issued from the garden of Eden), "10" (the number of righteous men required to save Sodom), "12" (the sons of Jacob were 12), "40" (the number of years the Israelites wandered in the wilderness), "70" (Jer 25:11, "these nations shall serve the king of Babylon seventy years"), "1,000" (see above), and many numbers derived from these. The examples can be multiplied. Besides, many biblical (as well as Talmudic or Midrashic) numbers have a sexagesimal structure (2 Chronicles 2: "And Solomon told out threescore and ten thousand men to bear burdens, and fourscore thousand to hew in the mountain, and three thousand and six hundred to oversee them"; Gen 8:6, "And Noah was six hundred years old when the flood of waters was upon the earth").

Many attempts have been made to find correlations between the antediluvian section of the Sumerian King List and the genealogy in Genesis 5. The futility of such attempts is obvious in view of the fact that there are three bids for the total length of the reigns of the Sumerian kings before the Flood (67, 127, and 120 times 3,600 years), while in the Hebrew Bible the years between the creation and the Flood are 1,656, in the Septuagint 2,262, and in the Samaritan recension 1,307. There is no discernible regularity in the listed ages of the patriarchs at the time when they begat their first son, or at the time of their death. On the other hand, Noah was an even 500 years old when he fathered Shem, Ham, and Japheth, and 600 at the time of the Flood. Lamech lived for 777 years, until 5 years before the Flood, and Methuselah lived for 969 years, only to die in the Flood. Enoch lived for 365 years, or for as many years as there are days in a year.

Many interesting numbers are mentioned in Revelation 7–9. To mention a few examples: "four angels standing on the four corners of the earth, holding the four winds of the earth," "and there were sealed an hundred and forty and four thousand of all the tribes of the children of Israel," "and when he had opened the seventh seal there was silence in heaven about the space of half an hour; and I saw the seven angels which stood before God; and to them were given seven trumpets," "and the fourth angel sounded, and the third part of the sun was smitten," "and the number of the army of the horsemen were two hundred thousand thousand." Even more interesting is the well-known passage in Rev 13:18, "Let him that has the understanding count the number of the beast; for it is the number of a man; and his number is Six hundred threescore and six." It is reasonable to assume that this "number of the beast" should be explained by interpreting the letters of some detested name as alphabetic numerals (Ifrah 1981: 332). The problem has tried the ingenuity of interpreters for centuries, and many different solutions have been proposed. If, for instance, the name of Nero is written as *nrw(n) ḳsr,* then the sum of the values of its letters is equal either to 100 + 60 + 200 + 50 + 200 + 6 = 616, or to 616 + 50 = 666. In order to find the proposed hidden sense of many words or passages in the Scriptures, a kind of numerology called gematria (from Gk *geometria*) was developed in the Talmudic, Midrashic, and Kabbalistic literatures (Ifrah 1981: 321–36). The basic idea was to interpret words, or groups of words, by computing the sums of their constituent letters as alphabetic numerals, and relating words to each other if they added up to the same letter sums. To quote just one example: the difference between letter sums of the Hebrew names of Adam and Eve *(ḥawah)* is (1 + 4 + 40) − (8 + 6 + 5) = 45 − 19 = 26, and 26 is the letter sum of YHWH.

Bibliography

Aharoni, Y. 1966. The Use of the Hieratic Numerals in Hebrew Ostraca and the Shekel Weights. *BASOR* 184: 13–19.

Dahood, M. 1981. Ebla, Ugarit, and the Bible. Afterword in G. Pettinato, *The Archives of Ebla.* Garden City, NY.

Englund, R. K. 1987. Administrative Timekeeping in Ancient Mesopotamia. *JESHO* 31: 121–85.

Friberg, J. 1984. Numbers and Measures in the Earliest Written Records. *Scientific American* 250: 110–18.

———. 1986. Three Remarkable Texts from Ancient Ebla. *Vicino Oriente* 6: 3–25.

Gillings, R. J. 1972. *Mathematics in the Time of the Pharaohs.* New York.

Gordon, C. H. 1949. *Ugaritic Literature.* Rome.

———. 1965. *Ugaritic Textbook.* AnOr 38. Rome.

Hehn, J. 1907. *Siebenzahl und Sabbat, bei den Babyloniern und im Alten Testament.* Leipzig.

Ifrah, G. 1981. *Histoire universelle des chiffres.* Paris.

———. 1985. *From One to Zero: A Universal History of Numbers.* New York.

Knorr, W. 1982. Techniques of Fractions in Ancient Egypt and Greece. *Hist Math.* 9: 133–71.

Lambert, W. G., and Millard, A. R. 1969. *Atra-Ḫasīs: The Babylonian Story of the Flood.* Oxford.

Langdon, S. 1923. *The Weld-Blundell Collection.* Vol. 2, *Historical Inscriptions.* OECT 2. London.

Le Brun, A., and Vallat, F. 1978. L'origine de l'écriture à Suse. *Cahiers de la délégation archéologique Francaise en Iran* 8: 11–59.

Lemaire, A., and Vernus, P. 1980. Les ostraca paléo-hébreux de Qadesh-Barnéa. *Or* 49: 341–45, pl. 71–73.
———. 1983. L'ostracon paléo-hébreu N°6 de Tell Qudeirat (Qadesh-Barnéa). Pp. 302–26, pl. 6 in *Fontes atque Pontes.* ÄAT 5.
Liverani, M. 1972. Il talento di Ashdod. *OrAnt* 11: 193–99.
Livingstone, A. 1986. *Mystical and Mythological Explanatory Works of Assyrian and Babylonian Scholars.* Oxford.
Neugebauer, O., and Sachs, A. 1945. *Mathematical Cuneiform Texts.* AOS 29. Lancaster, PA.
Parker, R. A. 1972. *Demotic Mathematical Papyri.* Providence, RI.
Robins, G., and Shute, C. C. D. 1987. *The Rhind Mathematical Papyrus: An Ancient Egyptian Text.* London.
Schmandt-Besserat, D. 1977. *An Archaic Recording System and the Origin of Writing.* SMS 1. Malibu.
———. 1980. The Envelopes That Bear the First Writing. *Technology and Culture* 21: 357–85.
———. 1981. From Tokens to Tablets: A Reevaluation of the So-Called "Numerical Tablets." *Visible Language* 15: 321–44.
Schott, A., and Soden, W. von. 1969. *Das Gilgamesch-Epos.* Stuttgart.
Soubeyran, D. 1984. Textes mathématiques de Mari. *RA* 78: 19–48.
Thompson, R. C. 1928. *The Epic of Gilgamish.* London.

JÖRAN FRIBERG

NUMBERS, BOOK OF.

The fourth book of the Hebrew Bible.

A. The Title
B. The Subdivisions
C. The Cohesion
D. Alternation of Law and Narrative
E. Structures
F. Redaction
G. The Antiquity of the Priestly Materials
1. Technical Terms
2. Institutions
H. Polemics
I. Realism
J. Theology and Anthropology
1. The Presence of God
2. Sacrifice
3. Intercession
4. Levites
5. Priests
6. Israelites
7. Moses

A. The Title

The Hebrew title of the fourth book of the Torah is called *bĕmidbar,* "In the Wilderness." The English title, *Numbers,* goes back to the Latin *Numeri* and the earlier Greek (LXX) *arithmoi.* However, the LXX title is probably derived from the oldest Hebrew title, *ḥōmeš happĕqqûdîm,* "the Fifth (of the Torah concerning) the Mustered" (*m. Yoma* 7:1; *m. Menaḥ.* 4:3), referring to the several censuses recorded in the book (chaps. 1–4, 26). It was also entitled *wayyĕdabbēr* after the first word (see Rashi on Exod 38:26), as is the case with the other books of the Torah. The present Hebrew title, *bĕmidbar* (the fifth word of the opening verse), seems more apt since it actually encompasses all the events described in the book, which took place "in the wilderness."

B. The Subdivisions

The book of Numbers describes the journey of the Israelites from Mt. Sinai to the borders of Canaan. Their 40-year trek comprises 40 stations (see chap. 33) which can be subsumed under three main stages: the wilderness of Sinai (1:1–10:10), where the preparations for the journey are made; the vicinity of Kadesh (10:11–20:13), where the bulk of the 40 years is spent; and from Kadesh to the steppes of Moab (20:14–36:13), where they prepare for the conquest and settlement of the promised land.

Numbers also subdivides according to temporal as well as spatial criteria. The 40 years embrace two generations, both of whose accounts begin with the census (chaps. 1 and 26). The generation of the Exodus, doomed to die in the wilderness (14:32–34), is finally extinguished by a plague at Baal-peor (25:9, 18–19). Thus, the second census, which follows immediately upon the plague (25:19), states unambiguously: "Among these there was not one of those enrolled by Moses and Aaron the priest when they recorded the Israelites in the wilderness of Sinai. For the Lord has said of them, 'They shall die in the wilderness.' Not one of them survived, except Caleb the son of Jephunneh and Joshua the son of Nun" (26:64–65). The chapters that follow the second census (27–36) differ sharply from the preceding ones, which are informed by murmuring and rebellion (chaps. 11–14; 16–17; 20:1–13; 21:4–9); later ones, however, describe the fidelity and stoutheartedness of the new generation (chap. 32), which, as a reward, does not lose a single life, even in battle (31:49). That these chapters constitute an organic literary block is indicated by the accounts concerning the daughters of Zelophehad which flank them at both ends (27:1–11; 36).

C. The Cohesion

Regardless of how one conceives the overarching organizational structure of the book, it is more important to note the thematic and verbal links that bind the material together. Chaps. 1–10 deal with the preparations for the march through the wilderness: chaps. 1 and 2 constitute the census and camp arrangement predicated upon military criteria. Chaps. 3–4, 7–8 deal with the Levites: they undergo a census for guarding and transporting the tabernacle (chaps 3–4); they receive carts from the tribal chieftains for the tabernacle transport (7:1–9); they are purified prior to their entry into tabernacle service (8:1–22); and they are informed of the retirement regulations (8:23–26).

The laws comprising chaps. 5–6 are inserted into these preparations for the march since they have as their common denominator the prevention and elimination of defilement in Israel's camp. Thus 5:1–4 banish the bearers of severe impurity; 5:5–8 prescribe reparation for the desecration of God's name in a false oath; 5:11–31 ordain a test for the suspected (defiled) adulteress; 6:1–21 highlight the law of the defiled Nazirite. However, the most likely basis for the joining of these pericopes is that in each the priest plays a prominent role: it is the priest who determines and terminates ritual impurity (5:1–4; see Leviticus 13–15), officiates at the reparation sacrifice (5:5–

8), is the recipient of all sanctuary donations (5:8–10), executes the ordeal for the suspected adulteress (5:11–31), officiates at the ritual for the Nazirite (6:1–21), and offers the priestly blessing (6:22–27). If so, then chaps. 5–6—perhaps originally an independent scroll—was inserted here because of its opening law, the impurity of the wilderness camp. Certain words bind the inner chapters: *maʿal*, "trespass" (5:6, 12); *ʾiššâ*, "woman" (5:31; 6:2); *ṭāmēʾ*, "impure" (5:2; 5:13, 14, 19, 20, 28, 29; 6:9) and, of course, *kōhēn*, "priest" (5:8, 9, 10; 5:15–26; 6:10, 11, 16, 19, 20; 6:23 [equivalent]).

Chaps. 11–14, 16–17 detail Israel's rebellions in the wilderness. Ostensibly, chap. 15, a legal miscellany, jarringly interrupts this sequence. However, its thematic and literary links with the previous unit prove otherwise. Chap. 15 begins with two laws that are operative in Canaan (vv 2, 18). They are a reassurance to the Israelites condemned to die in the wilderness that their children will indeed inherit the promised land (14:31). A third law (vv 22–31), bearing no heading, may originally have referred to the two preceding laws. The case of the Sabbath violator follows (vv 32–36) since his punishment is not certain: will he be subject to *kārēt* mentioned in the previous law (vv 30–31; see Exod 31:14) or is he to be put to death, as demanded by Exod 31:15? A fifth and final law, tassels, has no apparent connection with the immediately preceding material but was probably placed here to provide a verbal inclusion to the episode of the scouts (chaps. 13–14): by wearing tassels, Israel will henceforth be warned about "scouting" and "whoring" with sight and thought (14:33–34; 15:39).

Demoralized by the majority report of the scouts and condemned to die in the wilderness, the people are psychologically receptive to demagogic appeals to overthrow their leadership and return to Egypt. Four discrete rebellions have been fused in chap. 16, all attributed to the machinations of Korah. The aftermath vindicates Aaron when his fire pan of incense brings not death (16:35–17:5) but life (17:6–15) and when his rod blossoms miraculously (17:16–26). As a result of their hazardous responsibility in guarding the tabernacle against encroachment, the priests and Levites are granted specific endowments (17:27–18:32).

The position of chap. 19, purification rites for corpse contamination, is an enigma. By dint of its theme, corpse contamination, one would have expected it to have been placed with the other impurity sources described in Leviticus 11–15, or at least with Num 5:1–4, which presumes a knowledge of the laws of corpse contamination (5:2). Why was it placed here? Perhaps the twice-mentioned warning that corpse contamination may pollute the sanctuary (vv 13, 20) made this chapter a natural sequel to the episode of Korah (chaps. 16–18), which deals especially with the issue of the desecration of the sanctuary by encroachment.

The traditions concerning the final stage of the wilderness march from Kadesh to the steppes of Moab are collected in chaps. 20–21. They are grouped in two parallel panels, the first detailing the failure and punishment of Moses and Aaron and the second describing the failure and deliverance of the people. The unifying theme is that God provides water (and all of Israel's needs) even when the leaders fail to do so. The emphasis on God's providence is perhaps what accounts for the insertion of the episode of the bronze serpent (21:4–9) and a new itinerary list (21:12–20), the latter containing two ancient poems (21:14–15, 17–18). A third poem, the Song of Heshbon (21:17–20) has been inserted to justify Israel's conquest of Transjordan (21:17–20).

The "Document of Balaam," as chaps. 22–24 are called in rabbinic tradition, is the largest independent section in Numbers. It has absolutely no verbal or thematic link with the contiguous chapters. The only connecting link is its setting: the steppes of Moab. Perhaps it performs the same function as chap. 15: it reassures Israel that despite her defection she is blessed and she will live through her posterity in the promised land. With the exception of the ass episode (22:22–35), itself an interpolation, these chapters, comprising both prose and poetry, are an integrated, interlocking, artfully structured unity.

The apostasy at Baal-peor (chap. 25) resembles the apostasy of the golden calf (Exodus 32) in context and placement. Both involve illicit worship, the slaughter of the guilty, and the choice of the line of the Levites/Phineas. Both describe the fall of Israel after having previously attained the sublime heights of the Lord's promise of Israel's future greatness (the Sinaitic covenant, Exodus 19–20, 24; Balaam's blessings, Numbers 23–24). According to one tradition (31:16), it was Balaam who plotted the Baal-peor apostasy. If so, it would account for its placement here.

The final 11 chapters of Numbers (26–36) are motivated by a single theme, the immediate occupation of the promised land: a (second) census of able-bodied men for war in the land and for the apportionment of the land (chap. 26); inheritance rights of women in the land (27:1–11; chap. 36); the succession to Moses in the land (27:2–13); the cultic calendar of the land (chaps. 28–29) and the fulfillment of vows (chap. 30); the war against Midian (chap. 31); the allotment of Transjordan (chap. 32); a summary of the wilderness stations (33:1–49); evicting the inhabitants of the land and extirpating their cult (33:50–56); the boundaries of the land (34:1–15); supervisors for the division of the land (34:16–29); the levitical holdings in the land (35:1–8); and preventing the pollution of the land by homicide (35:9–34). The final chapter, further instructions on women's inheritance rights (chap. 36), is an appendix; however, it forms an inclusion with the earlier material on the daughters of Zelophehad (27:11), thereby framing the chapters on the new generation (chaps. 27–36).

D. Alternation of Law and Narrative

A striking feature of Numbers is that law (L) and narrative (N) alternate regularly, as follows: 1:1–10:10 (L); 10:11–14:45 (N); 15 (L); 16–17 (N); 18–19 (L); 20–25 (N); 26:1–27:11 (L); 27:12–23 (N); 28–30 (L); 31:1–33:49 (N); 33:50–36:13 (L).

In the main, the narrative is confined to the wilderness march; the law, to the three main structures of the march: Sinai (1:1–10:10); Kadesh (chaps 15, 18–19); and the steppes of Moab (chaps 28–30, 34–36). However, there are exceptions. Certain events are associated with stations, e.g., the scouts (13–14), the Korahite rebellions (16–17), and the Midianite war and Transjordan settlement (31–32), and some laws arise from test cases, composed in narrative style, e.g. the *pesaḥ* (9:1–14), the wood gatherer (15:32–36), and Zelophehad's daughters (27:1–11). Thus, this alternation is not a matter of whether Israel was stationary or in motion.

The admixture of these two genres is of no surprise for anyone conversant with the ANE vassal treaties which open with a recounting of the suzerain's beneficial actions to his vassal (narrative), followed by the stipulations imposed upon the vassal (law). The book of Deuteronomy is a parade example of this literary type where the law code (chaps. 12–26) is preceded by a recital of God's salvific acts for Israel (chaps. 1–11). Numbers, too, operates in the shadow of Sinai; Israel had accepted the suzerainity of its God and is bound to his law while the narratives continue to manifest divine providence (and Israel's backsliding).

E. Structures

The individual pericopes of Numbers manifest design. Their main structural device is chiasm and introversion. Also evidenced are such artifices as parallel panels, inclusions, subscripts and repetitive resumptions, prolepses, and septenary enumerations. The pericopes are linked not only to each other by associative terms and themes but also to similar narratives in Exodus by the same itinerary formula. The revelation to Moses at Sinai (Exodus 33) is the pivotal center not only for the Exodus and Numbers narratives but also the entire Hexateuch, which takes the shape of a grand introversion in which the events after Sinai repeat the failures and fulfill the promises of the pre-Sinaitic period.

F. Redaction

Despite this unmistakable evidence of recensional activity, one cannot with confidence speak of the redaction of Numbers. Redaction implies a single mind or, if several persons are involved, a single mind-set or school. To be sure, marks left by two editors from the Priestly school have been detected in the account of the scouts (chaps. 13–14), the Korahite rebellions (chap. 16), the war against Midian (chap. 31), and in other pericopes (e.g., chap. 36). However, there is as yet no way to ascertain if these strands were deposited by the same person. And even if they betray the same style and ideology, other pericopes reveal that another (Deuteronomic) school was at work. There are only two places where a Deuteronomic hand can be detected (21:33–35 and 32:7–15), and there is a strong possibility that it represents the last editorial activity in Numbers, even after the Priestly recension had been completed. This possibility will be augmented by the evidence, presented here below, that the Priestly material is of great antiquity. Yet, until new evidence is adduced, it would be more prudent to speak of Numbers' composition rather than its redaction.

One conclusion, however, can be asserted with relative certainty. The interpolations bearing the Priestly trademark show that the Priestly material does not comprise an independent source but is the product of at least two recensions. In other words, two writers of the Priestly school—possibly redactors—added their interpolations to combined Priestly and epic material, thereby composing the book of Numbers.

G. The Antiquity of Priestly Materials

There is scholarly consensus on the antiquity of the poetry and narratives that comprise the non-Priestly stratum in Numbers. The same verdict must be passed on those texts assigned to the priestly stratum as well. The sheer weight of the demonstrably old terms and institutions contained in the Priestly material renders such a conclusion ineluctable. The evidence of technical terms will be marshaled first.

1. Technical Terms. The sociopolitical divisions of ancient Israel are described by (1) *ᶜēdâ*, "congregation"; (2) *môᶜēd*, "(national) assembly"; (3) *maṭṭeh*, "tribe"; (4) *ʾelep*, "clan"; (5) *nāśîʾ*, "chieftain"; terms which cease being used after the 9th century. Even more compelling is the term (6) *ᶜăbōdâ* which in the Tetrateuch (Genesis-Numbers) only means "physical work" and is the occupation not of the priests but of the Levites, whereas in the postexilic literature (e.g. Ezra, Nehemiah, Chronicles) it means "cultic service," the occupation of the priests. However, these two meanings are mutually exclusive: Levites perform cultic service on pain of death. Thus the fact the *ᶜăbōdâ* is ascribed only to Levites in Numbers whereas in the Second Temple period priests alone are permitted to do *ᶜăbōdâ* ineluctably leads to the conclusion that Levitic *ᶜăbōdâ* is a preexilic phenomenon, and since this term proliferates throughout Numbers (chaps. 1, 3, 4, 7, 8, 16, 18), the cultic contexts in which this term is found must all be adjudged old. Similarly the term (7) *mišmeret*, meaning "guard duty" in Numbers, changes to "course of duty" in postexilic texts, a meaning, however, it does not have in Numbers, another indication that its cultic contexts in Numbers must be old. Evidence of another sort is provided by (8) *ʾāšam*, "feel guilt," the Priestly forerunner of prophetic *šāb*, "repent." Since the latter word is totally absent from the Priestly texts, and indeed from the Tetrateuch, it stands to reason that *ʾāšam* is a preexilic term—indeed, one that most likely was current before the 7th and possibly the 8th century when prophetic *šāb* became the prominent term for repentance. Further evidence has been adduced by (9) *mi . . . wāmaᶜălâ*, "from . . . and upward" (1:3) and (10) *yityalĕdû*, "registered," which were replaced in postexilic texts by *mi . . . ûlĕmaᶜălâ* and *hityaḥēs*, respectively. Also (11) *ḥallâ*, "loaf" (6:15, 19; 15:20), which appears only in the Priestly texts and in 2 Sam 6:19, is changed to the frequently attested *kikkār* when the latter passage is cited in 2 Chr 16:3, and (12) *leḥem tāmîd*, "regular bread" (4:7), *leḥem pānîm*, "display bread," in the Priestly texts (e.g., Exod 25:30; 35:13) and in the early narratives (1 Sam 21:5; 1 Kgs 7:48 [= 2 Chr 4:19]) is always referred to in postexilic books by the term *maᶜăreket* (e.g., Neh 10:34; 2 Chr 2:3). Finally (13) *ʾummâ*, a rare word for "tribe" (25:15) attested in the Akkadian of ancient Mari, is usually replaced by *lĕʾōm*.

In addition to the 13 terms above which can be shown to have fallen out of usage by the time of the Babylonian Exile, there remains a host of other technical terms which are attested in literature—especially Mesopotamian—antecedent to the Bible. The term used at ancient Mari for (14) "muster the troops" is the exact cognate of *pāqad ṣābāᶜ* (1:13). (15) None of the 24 names found in the list of chieftains (1:5–15) is compounded of the divine element YH (YHWH), a fact which corresponds with the tradition that the Tetragrammaton was first revealed to Moses. (16) Old Aramaic *ʿdn* and Akkadian *adê* correspond to biblical *ʿēdût,* "pact" (1:53). (17) The word *qārab,* "encroach" (3:10) has an exact cognate in Nuzi (15th century) Akkadian. (18) The word *millēʾyad,* "ordain," also has an older Akkadian equivalent (see 3:3). (19) The word *ṣābāʾ,* "service" (4:3) in Akkadian as well as Hebrew has a military and nonmilitary meaning. Other ancient Akkadian terms surfacing in the priestly texts of Numbers are (20) *ṣāb,* "draught animal" (7:3); (21) *ʿămûd,* "pillar" (14:14), i.e., the "standard" of the deity; (22) *pērēš,* "specify (by oracle)" (15:34); (23) *mišḥâ,* "perquisite, allotted measure" (18:8); (24) *ṣāmad,* "couple (sexually)" (25:2); (25) *mekes,* "tax" (31:27); and (26) *sikkîm,* "pointed object" (33:55). To be sure, this latter group of thirteen terms, though attested in antecedent Mesopotamian literature, could have survived even in late biblical Hebrew. But in their aggregate, and coupled with the preceding thirteen terms which demonstrably did not survive in postexilic Hebrew, they make a strong case for the preexilic provenience of their contexts.

2. Institutions. The antiquity of the terminology is matched by the antiquity of the institutions represented in the Priestly texts:

(1) Israel's camp in the wilderness is square-shaped; in later Israel the war camp was round. The wilderness camp most resembles the war camp of Rameses II, the probable Pharaoh of the Exodus. Not only is the latter square in shape but Pharaoh's tent sanctuary is in its center and is surrounded by thick walls as protection against defilement, a function supplied in Israel's camp by the levitical cordon.

(2) The custody of the tabernacle is shared by the priests who guarded inside the sacred precincts and the Levites who guarded without, a tradition that is found solely in the anterior Hittite cult. In the texts dealing with Solomon's Temple, however, the Levites do not appear at all and only surface in Ezekiel's visionary temple and in the postexilic writings which were influenced by the Torah literature. Moreover, the Levite guards of the tabernacle were armed, ready to strike down any encroacher, a fact which explains the action of Phineas at Baal-peor, who slew the encroaching couple in his capacity as chief of the levitical guards. Armed levitical guards are not, however, attested for the two Jerusalem Temples.

(3) The firstborn originally held a sacred status, possibly as officiants at the worship of the family's ancestors. Their replacement by the nonsacred Levites may reflect an ancient polemic and struggle against ancestral cults in Israel.

(4) The purification offering required of the Nazirite who successfully completed his vow conflicts with the Torah's definition of the *ḥaṭṭāʾt.* Following Rambam, the *ḥaṭṭāʾt* here serves directly to desanctify the Nazirite, a function that is more characteristic of the reparation offering. Like the boiled shoulder eaten by the Nazirite in the sanctuary court (see below), it probably reflects a more ancient usage of the purification offering prior to its differentiation from the reparation offering.

(5) The boiled shoulder of the Nazirite ram (6:19) is at odds with Israel's sacrificial system, which never requires the shoulder, nor that the lay offerer cook his sacrificial portion inside the sacred precincts. However, both practices are attested in pre-Israelite Lachish and pre-Temple Shilo.

(6) The details of form and manufacture of the tabernacle menorah do not correspond with those of Solomon's Temple or of later periods but most closely resemble the design of lampstands of the LB Age.

(7) The use of trumpets for assembling the people to worship as well as to war (10:1–10) is characteristic of the New Kingdom in Egypt.

(8) Ecstatic prophecy as a group phenomenon (11:25) is last attested at the time of Saul (1 Sam 19:20–24).

(9) The rebellions which are conflated in the Korah pericope (chap. 16) are redolent of high antiquity: that of the Reubenites, Dathan, and Abiram against Moses before their tribe lost its firstborn leadership status, and that of the Levites against Aaron before the struggle over which priestly family would control the Temple had been settled.

(10) The account of the war against the Midianites (chap. 31) bears many hallmarks of antiquity, chief of which is the absence of camels from the spoils whereas they predominate in the inventory of booty taken from the Midianites in Gideon's war (Judges 6–8). Thus the Mosaic account must have originated before the 11th century when the Midianites developed a camel cavalry.

(11) Moses permits his soldiers to marry their Midianite captive women (31:18), a precedent which Moses himself had set (Exod 2:16–21) but which was anathema to the postexilic age (for example, Ezra 9).

(12) The boundaries of the promised land (chap. 34) do not conform to any historical situation in Israel's national existence but are congruent with Egypt's Asiatic province during the period of the New Empire (15th–13th centuries). Transjordan, in particular, lies outside the promised land (and the Egyptian province) though it is occupied by Reuben and Gad during the period of conquest and settlement. The book of Deuteronomy, on the other hand, adjusts to historical reality by making the conquest of all of Transjordan a divine command.

(13) Deuteronomy, the product of the 8th and 7th centuries, is familiar with the following Priestly materials in Numbers: (a) details of the scouting expedition attributed to the Priestly strand (for example, 14:31–33; Deut 1:39); (b) the priestly dues (18:20; Deut 18:2); (c) the death of Moses (27:12–14; Deut 32:48–52); (d) the succession of Joshua (27:18; Deut 34:9); (e) the asylum cities (35:13–14; Deut 19:8–9). In addition, Deuteronomy exhibits knowledge of Priestly laws from other Torah books, for example, (f) priests are in charge of leprosy cases (Deut 24:8; Lev 13:2, 9, etc.); (g) blemished sacrifices (Deut 17:1; Lev 22:20); and (h) the reciprocal covenant (Deut 29:12; Exod 6:7; Lev 26:12). To be sure, it can be (and has been) maintained that in all these Deuteronomic passages a later editor interpolated these Priestly elements. However, it can be shown, in many instances, that the so-called additions are too integrated into their contexts to allow for their excision, and furthermore, it is more logical to posit a borrowing of Deuteronomy from the Priestly material than to assume that a later hand reworked so many Deuteronomic passages.

(14) The big bulge in the story of Gad and Reuben (32:7–15) is replete with Deuteronomic phrases. Thus it seems probable that the final redaction of this piece was

done by a Deuteronomist. Of course, it can be maintained that this latter-day Deuteronomist lived in the postexilic period. This, however, is unlikely since it presupposes that the Deuteronomic school extended over several centuries. In any event, the existence of this Deuteronomic bulge proves that the last editorial hand in Numbers is not of the Priestly school.

(15) As Y. Kaufmann has already argued (1960), the absence of priestly sanctums such as the ark, the Urim and Thummim (27:21), and the anointing of oil (4:16) in the postexilic age speaks eloquently for their antiquity. Similarly, the 12:1 ratio of priests to Levites in postexilic times (Ezra 2:36–42; 8:15) cannot be squared with the 1:10 ratio presupposed by the tithe laws (18:26) unless the latter stem from a much earlier period.

In addition, there are many other institutions reflected in the Priestly texts of Numbers which are demonstrably old, as follows: (16) the census (1:2, 3, 49), whose closest model is that of ancient Mari; (17) the golden libation bowls inside the tent (4:8; 28:7), which may reflect a pre-Mosaic usage; (18) the priestly doctrine of repentance, which precedes the prophetic doctrine; (19) the antiquity of the temple tithe, in general, and the tithe of the levitical tithe (18:25–32), in particular (ibid); (20) the letter to Edom (20:14–17), which resembles 2d-millennium diplomatic notes; (21) the copper serpent worshipped by Israel in the wilderness (21:4–9) and that found in a shrine in Timna, approximately the same place and time attributed to the Numbers passage. (22) It is possible that it is the priestly tradition that Balaam seduced Israel to engage in the idolatrous rites at Baal-peor, which is reflected in the 8th-century Deir ʿAlla inscription; (23) the second census (chap. 26) of Israel's clans (and not its tribes) belongs to the premonarchic age; (24) the Manassite clans (26:29–34) are shown by the Samaria ostraca (8th century) to be the names of districts, indicating that the Manassites settled there in a much earlier period; (25) the master itinerary of the wilderness march (chap. 33) most closely resembles, in form, 9th-century Assyrian itineraries; (26) the probability that the original plan for the levitical and asylum towns is to be found in the Priestly (rather than Deuteronomic) texts.

Thus, 11 Priestly terms and 15 Priestly institutions mentioned in Numbers disappear from usage in the postexilic age. In addition, 13 Priestly terms and 10 Priestly institutions, though they may have continued in use in later times, originate in the earliest period of or prior to Israel's national existence. In sum, we have 26 strong reasons and 23 supportive ones for affirming the antiquity of the Priestly material in the book of Numbers.

H. Polemics

Israel's ideological war with its pagan surroundings is reflected in the book of Numbers. Its first encounter with the Baal fertility cult in the steppes of Moab is calamitous, resulting in a devastating plague (25:1–9) and an avenging attack against the Midianites (25:16–19; 31:1–54). Balaam, the foreign diviner who is the instigator of the Baal apostasy—according to one tradition (31:16)—must unlearn his heathen arts before he can qualify for direct revelation from God. First, as he consistently insists to Balak, he is a diviner, not a sorcerer. Second—and here he enters the realm of Israelite prophecy—he discards the divinatory technique and seeks a direct communication from the Lord.

The transformation of Balaam is matched by the transformation of two rituals that were clearly pagan in origin. The ritual of the suspected adulteress (5:11–31), minus the interpolated verse 21, originally called for an incantation ordeal employing magical water but not invoking the name of any deity. The Priestly legislators, however, found the formula unacceptable since it ostensibly attributed the effect of the incantation to the water itself. They therefore inserted a statement affirming that the efficacy of the ritual was due to the God of Israel (v 21b).

An even more striking transformation of a widespread, long-enduring pagan belief is evident in the purification ritual for those contaminated by contact with a corpse (chap. 19). The preparation of the exorcistic medium, the ashes of the heifer, was totally overhauled so as to incorporate it into Israel's monotheistic sacrificial system. Moreover, the hitherto demonic impurity attributed to corpses was devitalized by denying it the automatic power to contaminate the sanctuary.

A polemic against paganism may also lie behind the replacement of the firstborn by the Levites (3:11–14; 8:16–19). That the human firstborn originally held a sacred status is indicated by their being "dedicated, sanctified, transferred, to the Lord" (Exod 13:1, 12; 22:28) and the need to "ransom" them from the Lord (18:15). This terminology may be a reflex of an attested custom in the ANE whereby the firstborn was expected to nurture and worship the spirits of his departed parents and grandparents. Thus the substitution of the firstborn by the Levite may reflect Israel's ancient struggle against the deeply rooted ancestor worship in its environment.

Priestly concerns play a major role in the book of Numbers. It is therefore not surprising that a number of issues addressed in this book express Priestly points of view and thus are brushed with polemical colorations. For example, Num 5:9–10 declares the right of each worshipper to choose the priestly recipient of his donations. The inflated language of this passage betrays its polemical character. The controversy within Priestly circles over the issue of egalitarian division versus worshipper's choice may be reflected here. The law of the temporary Nazirite (6:1–21) may also be a polemic. The priests may have frowned on lifelong Nazirites (e.g. Samuel and Samson) and their asceticism. Instead, they proposed a limited period which could be brought under priestly control (6:1–21). Finally, the possibility should be entertained that the Priestly texts deny that Moses could communicate with God "face to face." Rather, he could only hear God's voice while standing in the outer room of the tent of meeting where the veil blocked his vision of the ark and cherubim onto which the divine fire cloud had descended. Thus the priests may have taught that the privilege Moses received to penetrate the fire cloud at Sinai's summit in order to receive the Decalog was unique: Moses was not vouchsafed the experience again.

I. Realism

It has been frequently averred that the Priestly laws predicate a utopia and do not reflect the existential conditions of Israel's life. Even those who posit that the Priestly laws were written in the Babylonian Exile affirm they are future-oriented—preparing the way for Israel's restoration and reoccupation of its land. To be sure, there can be no doubt that idealism permeates the Priestly legislation (indeed, every code sets forth ideals; otherwise why promulgate it?). Yet it is also true that these laws are permeated by a realism that reflects the social, economic, and political conditions that obtained in ancient Israel, and they thus provide a window on the life of ancient Israel. Evidence will be adduced from several laws in Numbers.

a. The census and organization of Israel's camp (chaps. 1–2) are grounded on military principles that reflect the actual dangers that persons on a trek through the wilderness would encounter.

b. The law of the suspected adulteress (5:11–31) is geared toward curbing the lynch mentality that prevailed in society and was thus meant to protect the hapless woman from the uncontrollable rage of her husband and/or community.

c. As discussed above, the Nazirite law (6:1–21) may be the Priestly countermeasure to the prevailing institution of the lifelong Nazirite.

d. Though the purification procedure for corpse contamination (chap. 19) uses wilderness terminology, it nonetheless reflects settled conditions. The impurity bearer, for example, need not leave his community, as is mandated by the older law of Israel's wilderness camp (5:1–4). This change, therefore, reflects the changed conditions of Israel's national existence—again an instance of law as a mirror of society.

e. The fact that the *šābû*ᶜ*ôt* festival is not called a *ḥag* (28:26) despite its designation as such in the other calendars of the Torah (Exod 23:16; 34:22; Deut 16:10, 16) implies that realism prevailed over idealism: the middle of the harvest season was no time to make a pilgrimage to the sanctuary. Furthermore, that this festival's designation as *ḥag* is missing in the one other Priestly calendar (Lev 23:16–21) proves that the omission of this term is no accident but a clear example of how the Priestly legislator accommodated the law to changing socioeconomic conditions.

f. The levitical settlements are a model of town planning. They allow not only for variations in size at the moment of their settlement but also for their future growth. This is realism at its finest.

g. The appendix to the case of Zelophehad's daughters (chap. 36) reflects the changeover from clan to tribal dominance. Thus the two stages of adjustment to reality are manifested here: the fear that daughters who inherit may marry first outside their clan and then outside the tribe. Once again, the Priestly legislation is shown to have undergone amendment in order to address changing needs.

J. Theology and Anthropology

1. The Presence of God. The principal actor in the book of Numbers, of course, is God. Even under extreme provocation, he keeps his covenant with the Israelites; guides them through the wilderness; and provides for their needs.

Of all of God's attributes, it is on his *ḥesed* that Moses bases his plea that God not destroy Israel (14:18–20). The word *ḥesed* stands for God's constancy, his fidelity to his covenant with Israel. It is this unimpeachable reliability of God's word that Balaam, the heathen prophet, lauds: "God is not man to be capricious / a mortal to change his mind / would he speak and not act / promise and not fulfill?" (23:19).

The high point in Balaam's praise of Israel is reached when he exclaims: "Lo, there is no augury in Jacob / No divination in Israel / Jacob is told at once / Yea Israel, what God has planned" (23:27). Israel, then, is unique among the nations. It needs neither diviners nor divination to learn the deity's will; it has direct access to God. Indeed, the Balaam story is nothing but the education of a prophet. At the outset, having associated himself with the God of Israel, Balaam rejects Balak's request that he curse Israel, an act which would make him a sorcerer who could coerce the deity to accede to his desires. Balaam, however, will only admit to divinatory powers, which, by virtue of God's grace, enable him to discern his will. As Balaam proceeds—blessing Israel—he learns something else: the Lord need not be approached by complex techniques. Balaam then casts aside his divinatory apparatus and becomes a true prophet "who hears God's speech / who beholds visions from the Almighty / Prostrate, but with eyes unveiled" (24:4).

To be sure, there is a qualitative difference between Moses and any other prophet. To the latter, "I make myself known to him in a vision / I speak with him in a dream" (12:6). Not so with Moses: "With him I speak mouth to mouth / Plainly and not in riddles" (12:8). This distinction is also apparent in the degree of approachability to God: when Moses is in the company of Aaron or his people, God's presence—*kābôd* (see below)—is beheld in the tabernacle courtyard (14:10; 17:8, 15; 20:6) to which all of Israel has access. However, when Moses meets with God alone, he is permitted to stand inside the tent, before the veil (7:89; 17:19). Nonetheless, it must be remembered that this distinction is not in kind but in degree. Divination presumes that the deity leaves traces of his plans imprinted upon natural phenomena which the skilled diviner can discern. Not so, proclaims Israel: God will disclose his will to a prophet only when he so desires and he does so directly, eschewing mediation.

The *kābôd* on Sinai's summit has transferred itself to the tabernacle, visible as a cloud by day and as fire by night (9:15–16). Its starts and stops determine Israel's stages and stations. Its constant visibility is a sign to Israel and the nations "that you, O Lord, are in the midst of this people; that you, O Lord, appear in plain sight when your cloud rests over them and when you go before them in a pillar of cloud by day and in a pillar of fire by night" (14:14b). Thus the divine presence will enter with Israel into the promised land. Just as God's presence mandates the purity of his camp (5:1–4; 31:19, 24) so his presence in the land mandates Israel not to pollute in his land (35:34).

Since God's fire cloud descends upon the ark whenever he wishes to address Moses (7:89), the ark also serves as a tangible witness to the divine presence. The sight of the ark in battle holds promise that Israel will be victorious over its enemies (10:35–36; 31:6), while its absence is a sure sign that Israel will be defeated (14:43–44). That the ark is flanked by winged cherubim indicates that it represents a flying chariot, a symbol that God is not confined to his tabernacle-ark except when he descends upon it to communicate with Israel. During the march, the ark, distinguished by its blue cover (4:6), occupies the very center of the camp (10:21), but according to another tradition, it is placed at the head of the camp to lead the march (10:33).

God supplies Israel with all of its nutritional needs: manna and quail (11:14–34) and water, even when rejected by the people at large, or its leadership (20:12–13; 21:5). God also assures Israel's victory over its enemies (21:21–35; 24:8–9, 17–18).

2. Sacrifice. The doctrine of collective responsibility is nowhere better illustrated than in the *ḥaṭṭāʾt,* the purification offering. This sacrifice, brought for severe physical impurity on inadvertent violations, presumes that these offenses give off a miasma that is attracted magnetlike to the sanctuary and accumulates there until God abandons it and his people to their doom. Thus this sacrifice preserves a vivid image of how the individual can affect the commonweal.

The other sacrifice with a totally expiatory function is the *ʾāšām,* the reparation offering (5:5–8). It is brought for the desecration of the sanctums, be they cult objects or God's holy name. The latter offense, even if committed deliberately, may be expiated by this offering provided that remorse and confession have taken place. Thus only unrepented sins are ineligible for sacrificial expiation. Repentance alone, however, cannot absolve sin (in contrast to the later teaching of the prophets). According to priestly theology, repentance must be augmented by sacrifice; otherwise divine forgiveness is unavailable.

3. Intercession. a. Prophetic. The prophet's job is to defend his people before the divine judge. The intercessory role of the prophet is underscored by the Lord's statement to Moses after the scout heresy: "I would fain strike them with pestilence and disown them; let me make of you a nation . . ." (14:12), a statement which is semantically equivalent to the Lord's request of Moses following the apostasy of the golden calf: "now let me be, that my anger may blaze forth against them and that I may destroy them and make of you a great nation" (Exod 32:10). First, by asking Moses not to intercede, God as much as admits that prophetic intercession is effective. Moreover, God seems to be hinting to Moses—perhaps even testing him—that he should intercede if he wants to save Israel. The psalmist, citing a striking image from Ezek 22:30, pays this tribute to Moses' intercessory achievement: "He would have destroyed them, had not Moses, his chosen one, stood in the breach in front of them, to keep his wrath from destroying them" (Ps 106:23). So, indeed, Numbers confirms that Moses interceded for his people at every turn and thereby assuaged the divine wrath (see 11:2; 12:13; 14:13–20; 16:22; 21:7).

b. Priestly. And yet a prophet, even a Moses, can only avert punishment; he cannot expunge the sin. Sin remains suspended over the heads of the sinners, capable of exacting retribution at a future date. Thus Moses' intercession mitigates or postpones the punishment but it does not abolish it: God's anger will take its toll and the sinners will die, be they Korah and his cohort (chap. 16) or the entire generation of the Exodus (chap. 14).

A priest, however, can not only intercede but win absolution as well. Aaron stems the plague by offering incense (17:6–14), and his grandson, Phineas, does the same by force (25:7–8). More typically, however, the priest obtains forgiveness by means of sacrifice (15:22–29). To be sure, sacrifice is not inherently efficacious; it must be accompanied by contrition and confession (for deliberate sins) and, even then, forgiveness is not assumed but is dependent on the grace of God. Still, the impact of the tandem repentance and sacrifice is total: the sin is erased from the divine record. This Priestly teaching predates the subsequent prophetic doctrine that repentance alone can eradicate sin, but it demonstrates that the older Priestly circles fully appreciated the power of repentance, even if they hitched it to the sacrificial system.

That repentance by itself in Numbers (and in the preceding Torah books) is incapable of shriving sin is evident from the fact that Moses never asks his people to repent. He also takes for granted that punishment is the ineluctable consequence of sin. Once only does he ask God for forgiveness, but his request is rejected out of hand (Exod 32:32–33). True, he also asks for reconciliation (*sālaḥ* 14:19), and this time his request is approved (14:20); however, this means only that God will not abandon Israel but will continue to maintain his covenant with it.

4. Levites. The book of Leviticus is the domain of the priests; the Levites do not appear there at all. But they proliferate in Numbers and, indeed, dominate the book. They are expressly excluded from the national census (1:47–53; 2:33) to be mustered separately (chaps. 3–4). They are assigned wagons for their transport duties (7:6–9), undergo purificatory rites when they join the work force (8:5–22), and are assigned guard duty in their retirement years (8:23–28). They march between the tribal units laden with the disassembled tabernacle (10:17, 21). Having joined Korah's rebellion against Aaron (16:7–10) they, henceforth, are represented by Aaron (17:18, 23). They are assigned lethally dangerous guard duties in the tabernacle precincts, for which they are rewarded with the tithe (18:1–6, 21–24). In the second census, they once again are counted apart from the people (26:57–62). They receive a 1/50 share of the spoils (31:30, 47) as well as 48 cities in the settled land, six of which are designated as asylums for unintentional homicides (35:6, 9–15).

The most important function of the Levites, one that invests their entire adult life, is to guard the sanctuary against encroachers. In fact, they are identified by this function—"guardians of the tabernacle of the Lord" (31:30, 47). In the ancient world, the entrances to temples were adorned with images of protector gods to ward off supernal demons. In Israel, where the world of demons has been abolished, the sanctuary remains in danger of defilement by the one creature capable of the demonic—man. His sin can pollute the sacred precincts and his physical encroachment upon the sanctums can bring down the wrath of the deity upon the entire community. The levitical cordon is therefore empowered to strike down the encroacher; moreover, it is made fully responsible if any encroachment occurs. Just as in the human sphere the guard pays with his life if anyone manages to slip through his watch (e.g., 2 Kgs 10:24), so in the divine sphere the levitical guards are guilty of a capital crime before God for failing to prevent encroachment upon the sanctuary. Henceforth, the Israelites need not be concerned that God will punish the entire community; only the encroacher and the negligent levitical cordon will pay the penalty. For Israel's sake, God will compromise his doctrine of collective responsibility. The Levites will be the lightning rod to absorb the divine anger so that Israel may worship at the sanctuary without fear.

5. Priests. The centrality of the priesthood in assuring divine favor for Israel by means of sacrifice has already been discussed. The story of the Korahite rebellions (chaps. 16–17) vindicates the Aaronids as the sole priestly line and declares that any encroacher on their prerogatives is to be put to death (18:3, 7).

In Numbers, the priests are assigned the following roles: (1) to serve as guards at the entrance and in the courtyard of the tabernacle (3:38; 18:5); (2) to dismantle and cover the tabernacle sanctums before the Kohathite Levites carry them (4:1–20); (3) to officiate at the ordeal of the suspected adulteress (5:11–31), the rite terminating the aborted and successfully completed Nazirite period (6:1–21), the priestly blessing (6:22–26), the purification of the levitical work force (8:5–26), blowing the trumpets (10:8), and preparing the ashes of the red heifer (19:1–10).

The high priest is assigned even loftier responsibilities: (1) to intercede for Israel with sacrificial means (17:6–15); (2) to consult the Urim and Thummim oracle (27:21); and (3) to serve by his death as vicarious atonement for the unintentional homicide (35:28).

For their service, the priests are granted the following emoluments: they are assigned sacrificial portions, *ḥērem,* of the firstlings of pure animals, and the redemption price of impure firstlings and human firstborn (18:8–20), a tithe of the levitical tithe (18:25–32); and 1/500th of the spoil (31:30, 41–46). The worshiper is permitted to designate his priestly officiant and recipient of his edible donations (5:9–10).

6. Israelites. All Israelites, men and women alike, are to attach tassels, each containing one violet cord, to the edges of their outer garments (15:37–41). The tassels render their garments *šaʿăṭnēz,* a mixture permitted only to priests. The tassels must contain a violet cord, the emblem of royalty. Thus the tassels remind Israelites that they belong to a royal priesthood (Exod 19:6). Though only priests are holy from birth, all of Israel can aspire to a life of holiness (Lev 19:2). Belonging to royalty, they serve no mortal king; they are servants of God.

Yet Israelites who crave the austere life of the priesthood can do so by retaking the Nazirite vow (6:1–21); but this practice, it seems, is transitory and discouraged. Indeed, even Levites (see above), are not inherently holy. Though they are bound to the sanctuary as much as the priests, in ritual requirements they differ not at all from the laity. The priesthood, then, is the prerogative of the descendants of Aaron. Attempts on the part of the laity to break into this circle lead to disaster (chap. 16). It is enough that Israel's special relationship to God sets it on a path that leads to a life of holiness.

Another tradition in Numbers, however, sets not the priest but the prophet as the ideal and Moses as the paragon (12:6–8). Just as one cannot choose to be a priest, so one cannot be a prophet except by divine election (11:16–17, 23–25). Still, though Eldad and Medad's prophesying is regarded by Joshua as a threat to Moses' leadership, Moses rises to the summit of altruism when he proclaims: "Would that all the Lord's people were prophets, that the Lord put his spirit upon them" (11:29). This teaching is echoed by a later prophet: "After that, I will pour out my spirit on all flesh, your sons and daughters shall prophesy; your old men shall dream dreams, and your young men shall see visions" (Joel 3:1).

7. Moses. One would expect the traditions about a founder of a nation to be embossed with legend and hyperbole. Yet what surprises about Moses, particularly his appearances in Numbers, is his all-too-human, flesh-and-blood character. Betraying a streak of self-doubt (11:14; see Exod 4:10–14), he indulges in self-pity (11:11, 15), and even begins to doubt God (11:21–22); he becomes more intemperate (20:10–11) and—in the plain hearing of his assembled people—he allows his anger to overrun his words and commits the ultimate heresy: he attributes the miracle to himself (20:10). This man Moses we know; we recognize him in ourselves. He is burnt out, worn down by his grueling task, and chaps. 11–20 record his steady decline. Though it is years since his people have been liberated from Egypt, by their hankering after their past material security (11:5) and their panicky fears that the promised land promises only disaster (14:3), they reveal that they still are slaves. Moses cannot handle them. His leadership falters and he cannot be trusted to bring them into the land.

Yet despite these lapses, Moses remains a giant. Indeed, it is in this book that he attains unprecedented moral stature. Though he selflessly intercedes with God for his people whenever the occasion demands it (11:2; 12:13; 14:13–20; 16:22; 21:7), he refuses to utter one word in his own defense when his own family pillories his reputation, producing the editorial comment: "Moses was a humble man, more so than any other man on earth" (12:3). He bears no grudge against his sister Miriam when she defames him (12:1–2); to the contrary, he prays that her punishment be remitted (12:13). Moses brushes aside Joshua's warning that the prophesying of Eldad and Medad is a threat to his leadership: "Are you wrought up on my account? Would that all the Lord's people were prophets" (11:29). The Numbers traditions about Moses thus prove him capable of reaching new spiritual heights. True, he plummets to his nadir, but it is matched by his zenith.

Moses' lapses, though fatal, are few and momentary. Otherwise he is the unfailing leader. He has prepared his people militarily for the Conquest. Organizing them into an effective army (chap. 1), he succeeds in establishing a secure bridgehead on the Jordan by conquering much of the east bank (21:12–22:1) and by crushing the Midianites (chap. 31). His administrative acumen is in evidence when he provides for the succession to Aaron and to himself (20:22–29; 27:12–23) and when he successfully negotiates with the tribes of Reuben and Gad to lead their brethren in the campaign of conquest for the privilege of settling in the conquered Transjordan territory (chap. 32). To the end of his days he functions as covenantal mediator when he renders oracular decisions: the second Passover for impurity bearers (9:1–14), the punishment for the Sabbath violation (15:32–36), inheritance rights for women (27:1–11; 36:1–10). His continued success as prophet-intercessor has already been discussed above. Having consecrated the tabernacle and its clergy (Leviticus 8), Moses no longer officiates as priest (contrast Exod 24:8; and see Ps 99:6). However, he is still credited as the author of Israel's cultic institutions: purificatory rites (5:1–4; 31:19–20, 24), sacrificial accompaniments (15:1–16), priestly gifts (15:17–21; 18:25–32), and the cultic calendar (chaps. 28–29). To be sure, the Priestly tradition refutes the legendary superhuman status accorded to the figure of Moses: it allows Moses an aural but not visual audience with God (7:8a, and despite Exod 33:11) by barring him from the Holy of Holies, but it never denies that he was the greatest of men.

Bibliography

Ben-Barak, Z. 1980. Inheritance by Daughters in the Ancient Near East. *JSS* 25: 22–23.

Brichto, H. C. 1975. The Case of the Sota and a Reconsideration of Biblical Law. *HUCA* 46: 55–70.

Christiansen, D. L. 1974. Numbers 21:14–15 and the Book of Wars of YHWH. *CBQ* 36: 359–60.

Coats, G. W. 1968. *Rebellion in the Wilderness.* Nashville.

Davies, G. J. 1974. The Wilderness Itineraries. *TynBul* 25: 46–81.

Dillmann, A. 1886. *Numeri, Deuteronomium, und Josua.* Leipzig.

Dumbrell, W. J. 1975. Midian—A Land or League? *VT* 25: 323–37.

Evans, G. 1958. Ancient Mesopotamian Assemblies. *JAOS* 78: 1–11, 149–56.

Fishbane, M. 1985. *Biblical Interpretation in Ancient Israel.* Oxford.

Freedman, D. N. 1975. The Aaronic Benedictions. Pp. 35–47 in *No Famine in the Land,* ed. J. L. Flanagan and A. W. Robinson. Missoula and Claremont.

Geus, C. H. J. de. 1976. *The Tribes of Israel.* Aasen.

Gordis, R. 1950. Democratic Origins in Ancient Israel. The Biblical *ʿedah.* Pp. 369–88 in *A. Marx Jubilee Volume.* New York.

Gottwald, N. K. 1979. *The Tribes of Yahweh.* New York.

Greenberg, M. 1959. The Biblical Conception of Asylum. *JBL* 78: 125–32.

———. 1968. Idealism and Practicality in Numbers 35:4–5 and Ezekiel 48. *JAOS* 88: 59–63.

Greenstone, J. H. 1939. *Numbers with Commentary.* Philadelphia.

Hackett, J. A. 1984. *The Balaam Text from Deir ʿAlla.* Chico, CA.

Hanson, P. D. 1968. The Song of Heshbon and David's *Nir. HTR* 61: 297–320.

Hurvitz, A. 1974. The Evidence of Language in Dating the Priestly Code. *RB* 81: 24–56.

Jobling, D. 1978. A Structural Analysis of Numbers 11 and 12. Pp. 29–62 in *The Sense of the Biblical Narrative.* JSOTSup 7. Sheffield.

Kallai, Z. 1986. The Wandering Traditions from Kadesh-Barnea to Canaan. *JJS* 33: 175–88.

Kalsich, M. M. 1877. *Pt.1 of Bible Studies. The Prophecies of Balaam.* London.

Kaufmann, Y. 1960. *The Religion of Israel.* Trans. and abridged M. Greenberg. Chicago.

Kellermann, D. 1970. *Die Priesterschrift von Numeri 1:1 bis 10:10.* BZAW 120. Berlin.

Kuschke, A. 1951. Die Lagervorstellung der priesterliche Erzählung. *ZAW* 63: 74–105.

Levine, B. A. 1965. The Descriptive Tabernacle Texts of the Pentateuch. *JAOS* 85: 307–18.

Licht, J. 1985. *A Commentary on the Book of Numbers I–X.* Jerusalem.

Liver, J. 1961. Korach, Dothan and Abiram. *ScrHier* 8: 201–14.

Loewenstamm, S. E. 1972–73. The Relation of the Settlement of Gad and Reuben in Num XXXII: 1–38. *Tarbiz* 42: 12–26 (in Hebrew).

McNeile, A. H. 1911. *The Book of Numbers.* Philadelphia.

Malamat, A. 1970. The Danite Migration and the Pan Israelite Exodus-Conquest. *Bib* 51: 1–16.

Margaliot, M. 1983. The Transgression of Moses and Aaron—Numbers 20: 1–13. *JQR* 74: 196–228.

Mazar, B. 1965. The Sanctuary of Arad and the Family of Hobeb the Kenite. *JNES* 24: 297–303.

Mendenhall, G. E. 1973. *The Tenth Generation.* Baltimore.

Meyers, C. L. 1976. *The Tabernacle Menorah.* Missoula, MT.

Milgrom, J. 1970. *Studies in Levitical Terminology.* Berkeley.

———. 1976. *Cult and Conscience.* Leiden.

———. 1978. Priestly Terminology and the Political and Social Structure of Pre-Monarchical Israel. *JQR* 69: 65–81.

———. 1981a. The Paradox of the Red Cow (Num XIX). *VT* 31: 62–72.

———. 1981b. *Sancta Contagion and Altar/City Asylum.* VTSup 32: 278–310.

———. 1981c. Vertical Retribution. *Conservative Judaism* 34: 11–16.

———. 1983a. Magic, Monotheism, and the Sin of Moses. Pp. 261–65 in *The Quest for the Kingdom of God,* ed. H. H. Huffmon et al. Winona Lake, IN.

———. 1983b. Of Hems and Tassels. *BARev* 9/3: 61–65.

———. 1983c. The Two Pericopes on the Purification Offering. Pp. 211–15 in *WLSGF.*

Milgrom, J., ed. 1985. *Numbers.* Ramat-Gan (in Hebrew).

Milgrom, J. 1986. The Chieftain's Gift: Numbers, Chapter 7. *HAR* 9: 221–26.

———. 1987a. The Literary Structure of Numbers 8: 5–22 and the Levitic *Kippur.* Pp. 205–9 in *Perspectives in Language and Text,* ed. E. W. Conrad and E. G. Newing. Winona Lake, IN.

———. 1987b. The Structures of Numbers, Chapters 11–12, 13–14 and Their Redaction. Pp. 49–61 in *Judaic Perspectives in Ancient Israel,* ed. J. Neusner et al. Philadelphia.

———. 1988. *The Book of Numbers.* Philadelphia.

Oded, B. 1970. The Settlement of Reuben in the Mishor Region. *Mehqarim* 1: 11–36.

Olsen, D. T. 1985. *The Death of the Old and the Birth of the New.* Chico, CA.

Paran, M. 1983. *Literary Features of the Priestly Code.* Diss., Hebrew University (in Hebrew).

Reviv, H. 1978. The Pattern of the Pan-Tribal Assembly. *JNSL* 8: 85–94.

Rofe, A. 1979. *The Book of Balaam.* Jerusalem (in Hebrew).

———. 1986. The History of the Asylum Cities in Biblical Law. *Beth Mikra* 105: 109–33.

Toeg, A. 1973–74. A Halkhic Midrash in Num 22–31. *Tarbiz* 43: 1–20 (in Hebrew).

Weinfeld, M. 1983. Social and Cultic Institutions in the Priestly Source Against Their Ancient Near Eastern Background. Pp. 95–129 in *Proceedings of the Eighth World Congress of Jewish Studies.* Jerusalem.

Wright, D. P. 1985. Purification from Corpse-Contamination in Numbers XXXI: 19–24. *VT* 25: 213–23.

Yadin, Y. 1963. *The Art of Warfare in Biblical Lands.* 2 vols. New York.
Ziderman, I. 1987. First Identification of Authentic *Tekelet. BASOR* 265: 25–34.

JACOB MILGROM

NUMENIUS (PERSON) [Gk *Nouměnios*]. In 1 Macc 12:16, Numenius, son of Antiochus, is mentioned along with Antipater, the son of Jason, in a letter from the high priest Jonathan the Hasmonean to the Spartans. Numenius and Antipater were to convey greetings to the Spartans, who were en route to Rome on a mission from Jonathan to restore cordial relations between Judea and Rome (ca. 143 B.C.E.). The presence of Greek names in this list should not be surprising given the Hellenistic atmosphere of the Hasmonean court (Tcherikover 1959: 252–53). Numenius is once again mentioned in 1 Macc 14:24 and 15:15 as the envoy of the Hasmonean high priest Simon to Rome. Numenius carried a large gold shield to Rome as a gift to confirm the peace between Judea and Rome (ca. 142 B.C.E.). Numenius' efforts were part of an Hasmonean foreign policy designed to court a growing Roman influence as a hedge against the threat of the Syrian Seleucids. Josephus expands the account in 1 Maccabees 12 by noting that Numenius was a member of the Judean ruling council (*Ant* 13.5.8 §169). Josephus also cites a decree from the Roman senate during the time of Julius Caesar noting the history of diplomatic relations between Rome and Judea (*Ant* 14.8.5 §§145–48). In this decree, reference is made to a Jewish mission to Rome by Alexander, son of Jason, Numenius, son of Antiochus, and Alexander, son of Dorotheus, who present a golden shield to the senate. As both *Ant* 14 and 1 Macc 15:16 agree that the Lucius was Roman consul and as Josephus describes the purpose of the Jewish mission to Rome as the restoration of relations and mention is made of the gift of a golden shield, one cannot escape the conclusion that the subject is the mission described in 1 Maccabees 14 and 15. However, significant differences between the accounts exist. 1 Macc 14:22 names Numenius' colleague as Antipater, son of Jason, while Josephus names him Alexander. Further, in *Ant* 14 the mission takes place during the time of the high priest Hyrcanus (ca. 106 B.C.E.). Josephus' account may reflect a witness independent of 1 Maccabees but which nevertheless confirms Numenius' mission to Rome.

Bibliography

Tcherikover, V. 1959. *Hellenistic Civilization and the Jews.* New York.

MICHAEL E. HARDWICK

NUN. The fourteenth letter of the Hebrew alphabet.

NUN (PERSON) [Heb *nûn*]. Father of Joshua (Exod 33:11; Num 11:28; 14:6; etc.). He is named the father of Hoshea (Num 13:8, 16; Deut 32:44), and the father of Jeshua (Neh 8:17), but these names are variant forms of "Joshua." He is said to be the son of Elishama from the tribe of Ephraim (*nôn* of 1 Chr 7:27 being an alternate form of *nûn*). It may be that the LXX *nauē* preserves a more original form of the Hebrew term *nāweh*; the *nûn* of the MT is a contraction of *nāweh* with the *n* enclitic. The word *nāweh* means "the herds and men comprising a nomad tribe," in contrast to "fish," the meaning of *nûn*. This suggests the possibility that the name is a tribal designation rather than a patronymic. For further discussion see Soggin *Joshua* OTL; and Boling and Wright *Joshua* AB.

PAULINE A. VIVIANO

NUNC DIMITTIS. This is the Latin for "Now you are permitting me to depart," and has become the title of the poem of praise recited by Simeon in Luke 2:29–32. (See Fitzmyer *Luke I–IX* AB, 418–33; Farris 1985: 127–42.)

This poem, together with Simeon's remarks in vv 34–35, plays an important literary role in Luke's total work. The initial word *nyn* (now) echoes the word *sēmeron* (today) in v 11. At the same time it suggests a contrasting period of anxious waiting that finally is resolved in the present assurance of peace. Simeon sees what others have desired to see (Luke 10:24) and his patience is therefore a model for Christians who are to live in expectation of Christ's return (21:19). Unlike many self-styled benefactors (22:25) who do not fulfill promises, God is reliable and keeps faith. What Zachariah prophesied (1:76–79) is now fulfilled. In an echo of Luke 2:11, salvation is here again identified specifically with the person of Jesus. Especially significant is the pandemic perspective. In contrast to "all the people" in the singular (v 10), Simeon speaks of salvation that has been prepared for "all the peoples." This perspective is explored further in v 32. In contrast to the more limited view expressed in the Benedictus (1:78), Jesus is to be "a light for revelation to the Gentiles." This expression apparently means that because of Jesus, gentiles are to be viewed as proper candidates for salvation.

Simeon's statement is replete with allusions to Isaiah's presentation of the Servant of the Lord, whose identity fluctuates from corporate Israel (Isa 43:10; 44:1) to an individual Israelite (42:1; 49:1–6). On the one hand, it is Israel's obligation and high privilege to be a "light to the nations" (42:6). On the other hand, the anticipated extraordinary Israelite appears on the scene in the person of Jesus, whose mission is identical with that of Israel, to be a "light to the nations" (Isa 49:6). The implicit presence of these protagonists gives Simeon's words an intensely dramatic character. Will the two work together in carrying out the assignment? Will corporate Israel recognize that in Jesus, their "glory," they possess their greatest claim to fame? Luke's auditors know the answer, and it is confirmed with pathos in Luke 2:34–35. Nevertheless, as Luke 15 affirms, Jesus endeavors to secure the participation of Israel's caretakers in what ought to be a joint enterprise. In the face of rejection of the Lord's Servant, God is determined that Israel's mission shall be achieved. Among the chief representatives of Israel in the new community of believers are Paul and Barnabas, who declare at Acts 13:47 that they are committed to the assignment given to the Servant (Isa 49:6). Similarly, at Acts 26:17–18 Paul assumes the obligations cited in Isaiah 49, and at Acts

28:28 solemnly confirms that the mission has been discharged. Thus Simeon's prophecy finds it dramatic fulfillment.

The Nunc Dimittis appears as an evening prayer in the *Apostolic Constitutions* 7.48.

Bibliography

Farris, S. 1985. *The Hymns of Luke's Infancy Narratives.* Sheffield.

FREDERICK W. DANKER

NUTS. See FLORA.

NUZI.

One of the provincial administrative centers of the land of Arraphe, the capital of which was located at present-day Kirkuk in the second half of the 2d millennium B.C. This predominantly Hurrian city belonged at least for part of its history to Mitanni, one of the great nations of the Near East at that time. See HURRIANS; MITANNI. Nuzi's fame derives from the over 3,500 cuneiform tablets found there. These texts document the administrative activities of the palace and private estates for the latter part of the community's existence and the social and economic transactions of the city of Nuzi and the neighboring cities over a six-generation period. Especially significant is the information concerning administrative, social, economic, and legal structures and practices at Nuzi and neighboring cities and towns. These materials illustrate vividly the history and daily life of a mid-2d-millennium-B.C. community in the ANE. The customs so amply documented at Nuzi find parallels at other ANE sites and have helped to illuminate materials that otherwise would be poorly understood. Among the Near Eastern cultures compared with that of Nuzi, the world of the OT has received extraordinary attention.

A. Archaeology
B. Nuzi Archives
C. History and Chronology
D. Ethnic Identity
E. Social Structure
F. Military
G. Religion
H. Law
I. Economic Structure
J. Types of Texts
K. Family Structure and Inheritance
L. Nuzi and the Old Testament

A. Archaeology

Ancient Nuzi was located at modern Yorgan Tepe, 13 km SW of Kirkuk in N Iraq. Excavations of the site from 1929–31 exposed a large portion of the main mound of Yorgan Tepe and two small mounds to the N (Starr 1937–39). The site was occupied during the prehistoric, Akkadian, Hurrian, and Partho-Sassanian periods. During the Akkadian period it was named Gasur. Limited excavation to the Akkadian level produced a number of Sargonic texts apparently belonging to a royal estate (Foster *SCCNH* 2: 89–107; Meek 1932; 1935). The site is best known, however, during the Hurrian period of the mid–2d millennium B.C., when it was called Nuzi. For this phase at the site, the main mound yielded the architectural remains of a palace, a temple, administrative buildings, and numerous private residences. On the suburban mounds the homes of more affluent members of the community, including Prince Šilwa-Tešup and the families of Teḫip-tilla, son of Puḫi-šenni and Katiri, were located. Large quantities of ceramics ranging from fine palace ware to crude utilitarian vessels and an array of stone, bone, glass, and metal artifacts were found. Among the more distinctive finds are the ceramic animal figures associated with the temple and fragments of wall painting (Starr 1937–39). Cylinder seals were found at the site, but the corpus of seal impressions on the tablets from Nuzi provides an unparalleled wealth of information for the history of glyptic art and the site of Nuzi itself (Porada 1947).

Archaeological evidence for Nuzi's (and incidentally, Mitanni's) international connections during the second half of the 2d millennium B.C. include the fragmentary "International Style" wall paintings that show Egyptian Hathor head designs, a bull's head, and a Syrian palmette design alternating in a frieze. In addition, Nuzi ware pottery with its characteristic light-on-dark painted designs is found throughout the Mitannian sphere of influence. The inspiration for this style has been traced to the Aegean. Furthermore, the Saustatar seal on *HSS* 9 1 is a superlative example of the Mitanni style in glyptic art, which draws on Syrian and Mesopotamian predecessors but contributes its own unique character (Smith 1965; Porada 1948).

B. Nuzi Archives

Some 3,500 cuneiform tablets were retrieved from buildings throughout the excavated areas of Nuzi. These tablets originate in family and administrative archives found in both the suburban and main mounds. Tablets were kept in family archives to the extent that they continued to have meaning to their owners. Tablets involving real estate passed with the property either through inheritance or sale and were kept as the legal deeds to the property over a number of generations. Non–real estate tablets, those involving personnel, livestock, and consumable goods, probably were transmitted in a similar fashion, but were kept for only as long as the ownership of the property might be questioned. In these cases, the time involved would be far shorter than that for real estate. Because of these practices, Nuzi archives contain many types of texts. In any given archive, however, real estate documents tend to represent the activities of many generations while other types of documents cluster near the end of Nuzi's existence. Similarly, in administrative archives in which the texts are largely ration lists and other documents relating to the daily activities of the palace or an estate the texts relate primarily to the later period of Nuzi. These archive-keeping practices generated materials within families over a number of generations and a vast amount of information concerning activities at Nuzi in its later period. (Morrison *SCCNH* 2:167–213; 1979; Wilhelm 1980; 1986; Maidman 1976; 1979; Mayer 1978; Dosch 1976).

Scribal "families" (especially the family of Apil-Sin) who worked at Nuzi throughout its history have been identified in many archives. These scribal "families" serve as the skeleton for the reconstruction of the internal chronology of Nuzi. Because of the coherence of the individual archives and the numerous cross-references among them, an internal chronology of at least six generations can be established for the Nuzi tablets (Friedman *SCCNH* 2: 109–30; Stein *SCCNH* 2: 225–320; Wilhelm 1970).

C. History and Chronology

An absolute chronology for Nuzi is difficult to establish because there are few references in the texts to events and figures outside the land of Arraphe. The names of at least two kings of Arraphe, Kip-Tešup and his son Itḫi-Tešup (also Ithiya), are known from royal letters, some bearing seal impressions, found in the Nuzi archives of Prince Šilwa-Tešup (Wilhelm 1970). The latter king was a vassal of Saustatar, king of Mitanni, as the famous Saustatar letter (*HSS* 9 1) indicates. A text mentioning Parsatatar (father of Saustatar) (*HSS* 13 165) suggests that Arraphe belonged to Mitanni during the reign of that king as well. Texts from the later period in the Nuzi archives mentioning Assyrian and Kassite activities in the region coincide with evidence from Assyria and Babylonia to suggest that the site was sacked by the Assyrians, perhaps during the reign of Aššur-uballiṭ I (1365–1330 B.C.).

Saustatar's dates remain problematic and the circumstances surrounding Nuzi's demise are not entirely clear, so Nuzi's exact place in ANE history has not been established. It is apparent, however, that the Nuzi archives span the period from Mitanni's dominance of northern Mesopotamia and Syria to the rise of the Middle Assyrian Empire. On the other hand, evidence from the Mari letters suggests that the site was settled by Hurrians and known as Nuzi as early as the reign of Šamši-Adad, when his son Išme-Dagan was embroiled in conflicts with the Hurrians to the north and east of Assyria (Wilhelm 1970).

D. Ethnic Identity

The Nuzi tablets are written in a dialect of Akkadian heavily influenced by Hurrian (Wilhelm 1970; Gordon 1938). The population of Nuzi was predominately Hurrian, but there are references to Assyrians, Babylonians, and others living and working at Nuzi and elsewhere in the land of Arraphe. Furthermore, personal names, though largely Hurrian in origin, include Akkadian, Mitannian, Kassite, and other elements, attesting to the influence of these ethnic groups on the region (Cassin and Glassner 1977; Gelb, Purves, and MacRae 1943).

One group documented in the Nuzi texts that has received special attention is the *ḫab/piru*. These individuals of varied ethnic backgrounds entered the community to work in return for food, clothing, and protection. Typically, they placed themselves and their families in servitude (Akk *wardūtu*) in wealthy households. In some instances, they reserved the right to replace themselves and thereby regain their freedom. Initially, these Nuzi *ḫab/piru* were equated with the Hebrews because of apparent parallels in their behavior. They were foreigners who migrated into settled areas to make lives for themselves just as the Hebrews were doing in Egypt and Canaan. However, the linguistic and historical evidence from Ugarit, Alalakh, and Amarna demonstrates that the *ḫab/piru* cannot be categorized either as an ethnic group or generally as "foreigners" (Greenberg 1955). Instead, they appear to have been individuals who belonged to neither the settled nor the nomadic social orders of the ANE and in different locations were found assimilating to one or the other way of life (Rowton 1976). Indeed, at Nuzi they would appear to be homeless refugees who were trying simply to survive.

E. Social Structure

As would be expected at any urban center of the time, the socioeconomic structure of Nuzi was complex. The king of Arraphe and the royal family, including the queen, numerous *esrītu* women (concubines), and *mārē šarri* and *mārāti šarri* (sons and daughters of the king), stood at the peak of the social ladder. The king of Arraphe was a vassal of Mitanni, at least during the reigns of Parsatatar and Saustatar, but managed the internal affairs of his kingdom. In essence, the king was the head of the military, the economy, the law, and the cult.

At Nuzi the term SAL.LUGAL has been translated as "queen," but whether this term refers only to the chief wife of the king or to highly placed "secondary" wives remains an open question. Women so designated, however, include property owners and entrepreneurs who owned their own estates. A related issue is the existence of *esrītu* women or "concubines" as they are often called. The term is found only during this period in Assyria, the Hittite lands, and Mitanni, and so may have had a Hurrian connection. *Esrītu* women in Mitanni and the Hittite lands were attached to royal households (in Assyria they are found in private households), often owned property and engaged in business, and held high status in the community.

The *mārē šarri*, "sons of the king," were landowners and businessmen who also served in the military, and the *mārāti šarri*, "daughters of the king," appear in the records as landowners with households. Children of the king would inherit according to their rank, but even sons and daughters of "secondary wives" or *esrīti* women could rise to important economic positions in the state (Morrison 1979; Wilhelm 1980; 1986).

Below the royal family, well-to-do private citizens and officials, including judges, mayors, irrigation officers, and the like, formed the *rākib narkabti* ("charioteers," though they may not all have served in that capacity in the military), the equivalent of the *mariyannu* class elsewhere. These individuals had their own estates and business activities that included banking, real estate acquisitions, manufacturing, and trade. Records belonging to a number of such prominent individuals were found at Nuzi, even though their principal estates were located elsewhere in the land of Arraphe. This discovery reinforces our understanding of Nuzi's significance as a provincial administrative center.

The Nuzi archives also attest to a large group of middle-class property owners, professional workers, and small landholders. Such individuals participated to the extent of their means in the social and economic life of the community, buying and selling real estate, trading in various commodities, and making marriage and adoption contracts and wills.

Typically, the *wardus*, "slaves," are considered the lowest social and economic class in the community. Indeed, slaves might have been prisoners of war or personnel traded into Arraphe from the land of Lullu. A great many slaves, however, were people who were forced by economic necessity to join the households of those who could support them. In return for food, clothes, and shelter, these people committed their families and their labor to someone who would take them in, typically the wealthy landlords. They could be sold or given away, but they retained rights to property ownership and could engage in a wide variety of contracts, including land acquisition, adoption, and the like, if they had the means. Indeed, some slaves prospered at Nuzi and had estates far greater than those of the average citizen. Pai-Tešup, the slave of Prince Šilwa-Tešup, was one such individual (Morrison 1983–84; Wilhelm 1980).

Women at Nuzi and Arraphe had more freedom than those in many other ANE nations. Enjoying the right to own property and make most contracts on their own, women engaged actively in real estate and commercial transactions and occupied important social and economic positions in the community. Amminnaya, wife of the king; Winnirke, the wife of Puḫi-šenni and mother of Teḫip-Tilla; and Tulpunaya are perhaps the most famous of Nuzi's real estate baronesses. Others include *esrītu* women and princesses whose royal positions augmented their power and wealth. Often women were protected in marriage documents and wills. For instance, some marriage contracts prohibit the groom from taking a second wife, and some wills appoint the deceased wife or even daughter as executor of the estate with powers of disinheritance over male members of the family. In addition, a son might be entrusted with the care of his mother and sisters after the death of his father. In such instances, stipulations concerning the mother's future behavior and inheritance rights might be made. On the other hand, fathers and brothers, either real or contractual, of women arranged for the marriages of their daughters or sisters and appear in guardian-like roles. There is evidence, however, that the woman involved could refuse the marital choice made for her. In general, then, it appears women at Nuzi had broad freedoms, but certain limitations did exist with respect to women's activities in the larger community. (Grosz *SCCNH* 1: 161–82 and *SCCNH* 2: 131–52; Gordon 1935; 1936).

F. Military

Landowners of all economic levels were responsible for paying taxes and performing or having a substitute perform the *ilku*—military and corvée service—for the state. Those who did so were called the *ālik ilki.* In the military context, they were the infantry. Above them were the *rākib narkabti,* the charioteers, who came from the royal and landed families of Nuzi and other cities of Arraphe. While on duty, these forces were armed and fed by the king. Nuzi produced voluminous inventories and ration lists recording equipment and food distributed to the troops, lists of chariots and horses, and who did and did not report for military service. Further, the palace archives record the manufacture of weapons, armor, and chariots for use by the army both at Nuzi and abroad (Kendall 1975).

G. Religion

Information about the cult is sparse at Nuzi, but palace records do reflect the distribution of rations to cult personnel. Nuzi had at least one major temple, and perhaps smaller ones, but the center of the cult in Arraphe would, of course, have been in the capital city (Jankowska *SCCNH* 1: 195–209). Presumably, the Nuzi records reflect only royal support for the local religious institution(s).

On the common level there are references to "family gods" in the Nuzi texts, and archaeological evidence indicates that residences might have shrines. It is assumed that the "family gods" passed from father to eldest son in the normal course of inheritance. However, the "gods" often appear in wills in which an individual designates either the heir to the gods or the distribution of his gods among his sons or daughters. Disinherited family members are prohibited from approaching the family's gods. There is even a court case concerning a family's gods of whom an outsider had gained possession (*HSS* 14 8). Clearly, the family gods were of great significance to individuals at Nuzi. Indeed, they appear to have represented the identity of the family itself. On the other hand, the father of a family had the power to shape the future identity of his family through various kinds of contracts and his will. Seemingly the allocation of the "family gods" was one of many demonstrations of this authority (Cassin *SCCNH* 1: 37–46; Deller *SCCNH* 1: 47–76; Draffkorn 1957; Greenberg 1962).

H. Law

All citizens in Arraphe, including slaves, were able to seek redress in court, so litigation concerning property ownership and other civil and criminal matters was common. Judges, who were among the *rākib narkabti* class, presided over the courts in the cities of Arraphe and were assisted by various court officials. The parties involved in the cases presented their testimonies, which were recorded on tablets. The judges' decisions appear to have been based on common law that was fairly standard throughout the ANE. Therefore, there are numerous parallels between the law as illustrated by the Nuzi texts and such legal documents as the Code of Hammurabi and the laws of the OT. If the evidence was not sufficient for the judges to render a verdict, they could send the parties to either the "oath of the gods" or river ordeals. In some instances, usually when the local judges could not adjudicate because of conflicting testimony or some other reason, the case was referred to the king for final judgment. The most famous of the Nuzi legal cases is the impeachment trial of the mayor Kušši-ḫarbe for numerous counts of malfeasance and abuse of authority. The testimony of numerous witnesses is preserved on ten tablets and some fragments. In that Kušši-ḫarbe disappears from his office, it appears that he was convicted of the crimes with which he was charged.

I. Economic Structure

The city of Nuzi, like all of the cities in Arraphe, was surrounded by agricultural land divided into districts. Outside of Nuzi proper, there were many towns and villages of varying sizes. These were linked by roads that led from Nuzi to other cities and byways connecting the smaller settlements, each with its own population and urban affiliation. The fields were irrigated by canals, some of which could support traffic, and, of course, natural waterways (Zaccagnini 1979).

Nuzi's economy was agriculturally based with wealth deriving ultimately from the land and what it produced. The "palace" and wealthy landowners held substantial real estate throughout the land of Arraphe and employed large numbers of dependents and slaves in agricultural pursuits. Barley, wheat, and various fruits and vegetables were produced: sheep and goats were used for their wool, meat, and milk; and pigs, large cattle, asses, and horses, used primarily in the chariotry, were raised (Cross 1937; Morrison *SCCNH* 1: 257–96). The produce of these large operations was used to support their personnel and provide a surplus for use in many activities.

Industry at the palace and the large estates included the manufacture of many goods, most notably textiles (both fabric and garments), leather goods, furniture, wooden and metal tools and weapons, stonework, chariots, and the like (Cross 1937; Zaccagnini *SCCNH* 1: 349–61). Professionals in these crafts are found among the dependents of the palace and large estates. Especially prominent among the workers in ration lists are the textile workers, most of whom were women. Many of these manufactured items were luxury goods, trade goods, or equipment used by the state, so references to them do not often appear outside of the archives of the wealthy.

The palace and some large estates (especially those of Prince Šilwa-Tešup and Puḫi-šenni son of Muš-apu) were also banking centers engaged in lending silver, gold, other metals, grain, wood, bricks, livestock, and wool to private individuals and dependents of the estates. Normally, grain loans were necessary to carry the borrowers over until the harvest, after which the loan plus interest was to be repaid. Both the loan documents and the accounting texts recording grain loans have been found (Owen 1969).

Loans involving silver, gold, or other metals as well as horses sometimes were related to the overland trade. Both the palace and private individuals sponsored trade in raw materials and finished products outside Nuzi, including the land of Lullu. All parties involved in this trade expected substantial returns on their investments (Zaccagnini 1977).

Smaller property owners also worked the land and had livestock, but the produce of their holdings was consumed largely by their families with little left over for other activities. Some had the means to make small loans; more often they were borrowers. It is assumed that everyday goods for the use of the family or for sale were produced at home or by craftsmen working in the city and towns. The Nuzi tablets trace the gradual impoverishment and dissolution of these small landowning families and the growth of the large estates (Zaccagnini 1979; Wilhelm 1980; Morrison *SCCNH* 2: 167–213) over the six-generation period they record. There were certainly many and varied reasons for this pattern. In general, many of the freeholds operated on the margin of subsistence, and it did not take much to push a family over the edge into bankruptcy. Poor crops, debt, division of an estate into increasingly smaller and insufficient units, and lack of labor in the family might all have been causes.

The state and private sectors of Nuzi's society and economy coexisted in close interconnection. Repeatedly, it can be shown that high officials responsible for irrigation, land management, and the judiciary first were property owners in their own rights. In mercantile activities there was much interaction among merchants working for the palace and for private individuals. The palace depended on the productivity of the private sector for taxes and personnel for the military and corvée. Further, as a "bank" the palace had a vested interest in the fortunes of its clients. On the other hand, the private sector relied on the state for protection and maintaining order.

J. Types of Texts

While land was inalienable, land acquisition was possible by a number of means. In the *ṭuppi mārūti* ("tablet of sonship") type of contract, a landowner (the seller) adopted an individual who did not belong to his family (the buyer) in order to sell a piece of property. The property purchased was called an "inheritance share" and the price "a gift" (usually movable property such as silver, grain, livestock, clothing, or a combination of such items). Often the texts note who will perform the *ilku* service on the land. The inalienability of land at Nuzi might be attributed to political, religious, or social reasons or to a combination of them. (1) Political: Land was owned by the king and granted in exchange for "feudal service." The land and the responsibility for the service could pass only from father to son as in the OB system. (2) Religious: A family, its land, and its family gods were inextricably bound together. The king granted the land on behalf of his gods who were the ultimate owners of the land and superior to the family gods. Again, only family membership qualified an individual to possess the property in question. (3) Social: Land was granted to a family in common (an "extended family commune") in return for service, and all the individuals within a family were responsible ultimately to the family. Only through adoption into the family could a person acquire land that was part of the family's holdings. Certainly, nobody was fooled by the fiction of this type of adoption. At the very least, the *ṭuppi mārūti* texts demonstrate how close the tie between the family and its land at Nuzi was at one point in time and may be an extension of earlier practices that were indeed legitimate. The motivation for these "real estate adoptions" usually appears to have been financial distress on the part of the seller (Chiera and Speiser 1924–25; Cassin 1938; Lewy 1942; Koschaker 1928; Purves 1945; 1947).

A method of transferring real estate for a limited period of time was the *ṭuppi titennūti* ("tablet of lease") contract. Land was leased for varying periods of time in return for a fee of movable property. The land could be redeemed by its owner at the end of the time indicated or on demand, depending on the terms of the contract, by returning the fee. In the meantime, the lessor reaped the produce of the land. The *titennūtu* type of land transaction may have developed because the transfers effected by the *ṭuppi mārūti* contracts deprived families of their land, and so their source of wealth, permanently. Again, the motivation for this sort of arrangement appears to have been financial difficulty (Speiser 1932).

Ṭuppi aḫḫūti ("tablet of brothership") contracts also exist and serve as another means of passing an "inheritance share" to an individual outside the family (Lewy 1940; Cassin 1962; Skaist 1969; Paradise 1972). All of these real estate arrangements reflect the sale of a birthright, either between a "father" and a "son" or between two "brothers."

The *ṭuppi mārūti* and *ṭuppi titennūti* types of contracts were used for personnel acquisitions as well. In a "real adoption" an individual adopted a son who would inherit his adopted father's property after caring for him (and often his wife) in his old age and "weeping over him and burying him" when he died (Cassin 1938). In personnel leases, a man could place himself, his children, or his slaves into servitude for a predetermined period of time in return for a fee the return of which would redeem the leased person (Eichler 1973).

Other forms of personnel contracts include the *ṭuppi mārtūti* ("tablet of daughtership") whereby an individual adopted a woman as a daughter and agreed to provide for her marriage. A fee was paid to a relative of the woman, and varying arrangements made as to the division of the bride-price. In the *ṭuppi aḫātūti* ("tablet of sistership") a woman was adopted as a sister and the terms were similar to those of the *ṭuppi mārtūti.* The nuances of "daughtership" versus "sistership" are not entirely understood in that the ends of these contracts appear to be essentially the same, i.e., a "guardian" who will arrange for the woman's marriage is appointed. In the first the guardian has the rights of a father and in the second of a brother (Grosz *SCCNH* 1: 161–82 and *SCCNH* 2: 131–52; Eichler 1977).

The marriage contracts *(ṭuppi riksi)* show that fathers or brothers arranged for the marriages of their daughters or sisters. Daughters received dowries from the family's property, usually in the form of silver or movable property. In certain exceptional cases, real estate was included in a dowry. In return the father or brother received a payment normally equivalent to 40 shekels of silver. These marriage contracts might also include clauses prohibiting the groom from taking a second wife or establishing the status of the bride's children as primary heirs to the groom's estate (Gordon 1936; Koschaker 1928).

Wills *(ṭuppi šimti)* describe the distribution of an individual's estate after his death. There are relatively few wills from Nuzi, considering the number of families and amount of property attested at the site. Most likely, wills were drawn up if the testator wished to depart from normal inheritance practices (Paradise 1972).

Among other types of texts that exist, some warrant mention. The *ṭuppi šupeʾulti* ("tablet of exchange") records exchanges of property. The *ṭuppi tamgurtu* ("tablet of agreement") attests to agreements made between parties before witnesses concerning a transaction. The *lišānšu* ("declaration of PN") usually records a statement made by an individual before judges and/or witnesses concerning real estate and other transactions already completed by the parties involved. The relationship of this sort of text to the other types of texts mentioned above is still not clear (Maidman 1976).

K. Family Structure and Inheritance

The kinship terminology of both land and personnel documents at Nuzi stresses how important the family was as the basic unit of the community and provides some insight into the nature of the family at Nuzi. The family structure was patriarchal. The father had complete authority over his wife/wives and children and could disinherit an offending child, sell or lease his children, and arrange for his children's marriages in the sorts of transactions discussed above. Moreover, he could direct the disposition of his estate through a duly witnessed and sealed will.

The family property, especially real estate, passed through the male line with a larger share being given to the chief heir *(māru rābu),* normally the eldest son, and smaller shares to other sons. Typically, it appears, the eldest son also became head of the family with responsibility for his mother and unmarried sisters and kept the family gods. Many wills from Nuzi, however, show that the father could designate his chief heir and head of the family (not always the same individual), divide his property as he chose, and make various stipulations about the use of his property, the ownership of the family gods, and the responsibilities of his wife and children (Paradise 1972).

The institution of "brothership" is not entirely clear at Nuzi. Essentially, "brothership" in the texts appears to indicate guardianship rights over sisters, but these are not identical to a father's rights. It has been suggested that "brothership" at Nuzi indicates that the Hurrians began as a matriarchal society in which the brother of the matriarch was the authority of the family and, hence, was a fratriarch. Through marriage to his sister, the fratriarch became a patriarch and the entire system shifted from the female to the male line. According to this analysis, the marriage and adoption texts in which "brothership" figures are simply vestiges of this form of societal organization. The problem with this explanation is that there is no evidence that the Hurrians ever married their sisters (Koschaker 1928; Skaist 1969).

L. Nuzi and the Old Testament

When the Nuzi tablets were discovered, many scholars found striking parallels between the social, economic, and legal practices at the site and those described in the OT. It is not possible to itemize all of the parallels discussed in the literature, but some of the more famous and enduring ones must be noted. For a thorough treatment of this subject see Gordon 1964; Speiser 1930; 1963a; *Genesis* AB.

A number of episodes in the patriarchal narratives reflect a background of family law that is similar to that demonstrated at Nuzi. In the story of Abraham in Genesis, Abraham adopted Eliezer of Damasacus as his heir because he had no children (Gen 15:2–3). At Nuzi, slaves were adopted by childless couples. Sarah, the chief wife, unable to conceive, provides her handmaid Hagar as a substitute through whom her husband can have children. Subsequently, when a child is born to Sarah, he becomes the principal heir, even though he is younger than Hagar's son (Gen 16; 21:1–21). The Nuzi tablets record similar situations, including inheritance provisions for children born to the chief wife after the handmaiden's. On two occasions Abraham called Sarah his sister to conceal the fact that she was his wife (Gen 12:11–20; chap. 20). Though not entirely clear on the subject themselves, Nuzi materials have been used to explain this "wife-sister motif" (Speiser 1963a).

In the marriage of Isaac, Laban, Rebekah's brother, handled the negotiations (Genesis 28–31), and Rebekah was asked if she consented. Later, Laban arranged his own daughters' marriages to Jacob (Gen 29:15–30), but it appears that the women were not consulted. Typically at Nuzi, a clause concerning the woman's consent is included in marriage contracts drawn up by brothers, but this clause is absent in contracts drawn up by fathers. Furthermore, the gifts proffered in the marriage of Rebekah are reminiscent of marriage prestations at Nuzi. Jacob's arrangements with Laban in return for marriage to Rachel and Leah also find parallels in the Nuzi texts. (Moses' marriage to Zipporah resembles Jacob's situation.) In the treaty reached between Jacob and Laban there are clauses containing terms similar to those of marriage contracts at Nuzi.

Nuzi parallels exist for the institution of levirate marriage, illustrated by the Judah and Tamar story (Genesis 38) and codified in Deut 25: 5–10 (Burrows 1940).

In the Joseph story, Joseph's brothers worry that their father, Jacob, favors Joseph, a younger son, possibly because they fear he will be chosen as primary heir. The Nuzi tablets show that a father could name his heir regardless of his rank of birth. (It is worth noting that Joseph's acquisition of land and "slaves" for the pharaoh in return for food recalls the way the small landowning families of Nuzi gave themselves and their lands up to the large estates.)

Related to matters of family and inheritance is the "deathbed blessing." In biblical material, instances such as Isaac's blessings on Jacob and Esau (Genesis 27), Jacob's on his and Joseph's sons (Genesis 48–49), Moses' on Israel (Deuteronomy 33), and Joshua's (Joshua 23–24) illustrate the importance of the deathbed blessing in shaping the identity and "share" of Israel and its component parts. Though at Nuzi the deathbed blessing is confined to property litigation, it apparently was recognized as valid evidence in courts of law (Speiser 1955).

Rachel's theft of the *tĕrāpîm* is subject to many interpretations ranging from psychological to legal, all attempting to explain her apparent rash behavior. The Nuzi texts demonstrate that the household gods were the very heart of the family and appear to have been passed down through either traditional or willed lines of inheritance. Thus, in nearly all interpretations of this incident, the Nuzi evidence has been cited (Cassin *SCCNH* 1: 37–46; Gordon 1937; Greenberg 1962; Morrison 1983; Speiser *Genesis* AB).

The similarities between the socioeconomic milieus of Nuzi and the patriarchal narratives suggest that the two cultures shared a common background in the ANE in the 2d millennium B.C. While most scholars agree that the patriarchal age predated the Nuzi materials (e.g., *BHI*), others made them contemporaneous (Gordon 1964). Moreover, the widespread distribution of Hurrians was credited with the dissemination of Near Eastern and specifically Hurrian customs throughout the area including Nuzi and the patriarchal setting (Speiser 1967).

More recent studies have demonstrated that the customs described in the Nuzi texts and the Bible are found throughout the Near East in the 2d and 1st millennia B.C. (Indeed, some survive to this day in more rural areas of the Near East.) Moreover, 1st millennium materials may offer better parallels in some cases (Van Seters 1969; 1975). Yet others look to folklore and literary forms to elucidate the biblical text (Thompson 1974; 1978). As a result, Nuzi has receded as an important tool for analyzing the Bible and dating its materials.

While the Nuzi materials are no longer considered important for the chronology of the OT, there is no question that they provide some of the best available evidence for common social, economic, and legal practices in the ANE. These practices were widespread and deeply entrenched throughout the Syro-Mesopotamian sphere of influence. Thus, Nuzi's continued value in biblical studies derives from its illustration of the background against which the OT was written.

Bibliography

Burrows, M. 1940. The Ancient Oriental Background of Hebrew Levirate Marriage. *BASOR* 77: 1–15.

Cassin, E. 1938. *L'adoption à Nuzi.* Paris.

———. 1962. L'influence babylonienne à Nuzi. *JESHO* 5: 113–38.

Cassin, E., and Glassner, J.-J. 1977. *Anthroponymie et Anthropologie de Nuzi.* Vol. 1, *Les Anthroponymes.* Malibu.

Chiera, E., and Speiser, E. A. 1924–25. A New Factor in the History of the Ancient East. Pp. 75–92 in AASOR 6. New Haven.

Cross, D. 1937. *Movable Property in the Nuzi Documents.* AOS 10. New Haven.

Dosch, G. 1976. *Die Texte aus Room A 34 Des Archivs von Nuzi.* Heidelberg.

Draffkorn, A. 1957. Ilani/Elohim. *JBL* 76: 215–24.

Eichler, B. 1973. *Indenture at Nuzi.* YNER 5. New Haven.

———. 1977. Another Look at the Nuzi Sistership Contracts. Pp. 45–59 in *Essays on the Ancient Near East in Memory of J. J. Finkelstein,* ed. M. Ellis. Hamden, CT.

Gelb, I. J.; Purves, I. J.; and MacRae, P. M. 1943. *Nuzi Personal Names.* OIP 57. Chicago.

Gordon, C. 1935. Fifteen Nuzi Tablets relating to Women. Mus 48: 113–32.

———. 1936. The Status of Woman Reflected in the Nuzi Tablets. *Babyloniaca* 16: 1–153.

———. 1937. The Story of Jacob and Laban in the Light of the Nuzi Tablets. *BASOR* 66: 25–27.

———. 1938. The Dialect of the Nuzu Tablets. *Or* n.s. 7: 32–63; 215–32.

———. 1964. Biblical Customs and the Nuzu Tablets. *BAR* 2: 21–33.

Greenberg, M. 1955. *The Hab/biru.* AOS 39. New Haven.

———. 1962. Another Look at Rachel's Theft of the Teraphim. *JBL* 81: 239–48.

Jankowska, N. 1957. The Influence of the Peculiarities of the Social System of Arrapha on Property Deals. *Eos* 48/2.

Kendall, T. 1975. *Warfare and Military Matters in the Nuzi Tablets.* Diss. Brandeis.

Koschaker, P. 1928. *Neue keilschriftliche Rechtsurkunden aus der El-Amarna-Zeit.* ASAW 39/5. Leipzig.

Lewy, H. 1940. The *Titennūtu* Contracts from Nuzi. Pp. 110–11 in *Actes du XXe Congrès Internationale de Orientalistes. Bruxelles 5–10 Septembre 1938.* Louvain.

———. 1942. The Nuzian Feudal System. *Or* n.s. 11: 1–40, 209–50, 297–349.

Maidman, M. 1976. *A Socio-Economic Analysis of a Nuzi Family Archive.* Diss. Pennsylvania.
———. 1979. A Nuzi Private Archive. *Aššur* 1.
Mayer, W. 1978. *Nuzi Studien I: Die Archive des Palastes und die Prosopographie der Berufe,* AOAT 205/1. Neukirchen-Vluyn.
Meek, T. J. 1932. The Akkadian and Cappadocian Texts from Nuzi. *BASOR* 48: 2–5.
———. 1935. *Old Akkadian, Sumerian and Cappadocian Texts from Nuzi.* HSS 10. Cambridge, MA.
Morrison, M. A. 1979. The Family of Šilwa-Tešup *Mār Šarri. JCS* 31: 3–29.
———. 1983. The Jacob and Laban Narrative in Light of Near Eastern Sources. *BA* 46: 155–64.
———. 1983–84. Review of Wilhelm 1980. *AfO* 29/30: 113–21.
Owen, D. I. 1969. *The Loan Documents from Nuzu.* Diss. Brandeis.
Paradise, J. 1972. *Nuzi Inheritance Practices.* Diss. Pennsylvania.
Porada, E. 1947. *Seal Impressions of Nuzi.* AASOR 24. Cambridge, MA.
———. 1948. The Collection of the Pierpont Morgan Library. *Corpus of Ancient Near Eastern Seals in North American Collections.* Bollingen Series 14. Washington, DC.
Purves, P. 1945. Commentary on Nuzi Real Property in the Light of Recent Studies. *JNES* 4: 68–86.
———. 1947. Additional Remarks on Nuzi Real Property. *JNES* 6: 181–85.
Rowton, M. B. 1976. Dimorphic Structure and the Problem of the ᶜApiru-ᶜibrîm. *JNES* 35: 13–20.
Skaist, A. 1969. The Authority of the Brother at Arrapha and Nuzi. *JAOS* 89: 10–17.
Smith, W. S. 1965. *Interconnections in the Ancient Near East.* New Haven.
Speiser, E. A. 1930. *New Kirkuk Documents Relating to Family Laws.* AASOR 10. Cambridge, MA.
———. 1932. New Kirkuk Documents relating to Security Transactions. *JAOS* 52: 350–67.
———. 1955. "I Know Not the Day of My Death." *JBL* 74: 252–56.
———. 1963a. The Wife-Sister Motif in the Patriarchal Narratives. Pp. 15–28 in *Biblical and Other Studies,* ed. A. Altmann.
———. 1963b. Mesopotamian Motifs in the Early Chapters of Genesis. *Expedition* 43/5: 10–19.
———. 1967. The Hurrian Participation in the Civilization of Mesopotamia, Syria and Palestine. Pp. 244–69 in *Oriental and Biblical Studies,* ed. J. J. Finkelstein and M. Greenberg. Philadelphia.
Starr, R. F. S. 1937–39. *Nuzi: Report on the Excavations at Yorgan Tepa Near Kirkuk, Iraq.* Vol. 1. Cambridge, MA.
Thompson, T. L. 1974. *The Historicity of the Patriarchal Narratives.* BZAW. Berlin.
———. 1978. A New Attempt to Date the Patriarchal Narratives. *JAOS* 98: 76–84.
Van Seters, J. 1969. Jacob's Marriage and Ancient Near Eastern Customs: A Reexamination. *HTR* 62: 377–95.
———. 1975. *Abraham in History and Tradition.* New Haven.
Wilhelm, G. 1970. *Untersuchungen zum Hurro-Akkadischen von Nuzi.* AOAT 9. Neukirchen-Vluyn.
———. 1980. *Das Archiv des Šilwa-Teššup,* Heft 2, Rationenlisten I. Wiesbaden.
———. 1986. *Das Archiv des Šilwa-Teššup.* Vol. 3, *Rationenlisten II.* Wiesbaden.
Zaccagnini, C. 1977. The Merchant at Nuzi. *Iraq* 39: 171–89.
———. 1979. *The Rural Landscape of the Land of Arraphe.* Rome.

MARTHA A. MORRISON

NYMPHA (PERSON) [Gk *Nympha*]. Nympha and "the church in her house" are greeted by Paul at the end of Colossians (4:15). It can be inferred from the text that she lived in Laodicea, although there is an ambiguity in the reference which leads some commentators to think her home was in Colossae or Hierapolis. One theory is that by analogy with the sending of greetings to the Laodiceans just previously in 4:15, Nympha's must be the church of Hierapolis since that group is not greeted otherwise in the letter (Gielen 1986: 123–24). By extension of this analogy, it has also been reasoned that just as the Laodicean church is evidently referred to by Paul as the local, thus not partial, church, so must Nympha's house-church be the entire church at Hierapolis (Gielen 1986: 123–24). Assumably Nympha was not only hostess but also leader of that local church.

As a household head, Nympha was likely a widow or single, but it cannot be excluded that she was a rather independently acting married woman. How she came to know Paul is not clear. Since he is not known to have visited Colossae, Laodicea, or Hierapolis, perhaps she met him in Ephesus.

Nympha's place in the NT as a female Christian has been retained only at the cost of some debate. While her gender is assumed to be feminine by the RSV, since her name in Greek is cited only in the accusative case, *Nymphan,* which could refer to a woman named Nympha or a man named Nymphas, other translations have variously interpreted this person. The issue has been complicated by variations in manuscripts for the possessive pronoun modifying "house" in Col 4:15. Some texts read *autēs,* "her," others *autou,* "his," still others, *autōn,* "their." Since the feminine reading is the hardest to explain, it is most likely to be the original. The masculine form was probably a correction of the feminine by copyists who could not envision a woman in such a leadership role. The reading "their" could have been substituted when scribes included in the pronoun the earlier mention of "brethren" in Col 4:15.

Bibliography

Gielen, M. 1986. Zur Interpretation der paulinischen Formel *hē kat' oikon ekklēsia. ZNW* 77: 109–25.
Gillman, F. M. 1989. *Women Who Knew Paul.* Wilmington.

FLORENCE MORGAN GILLMAN

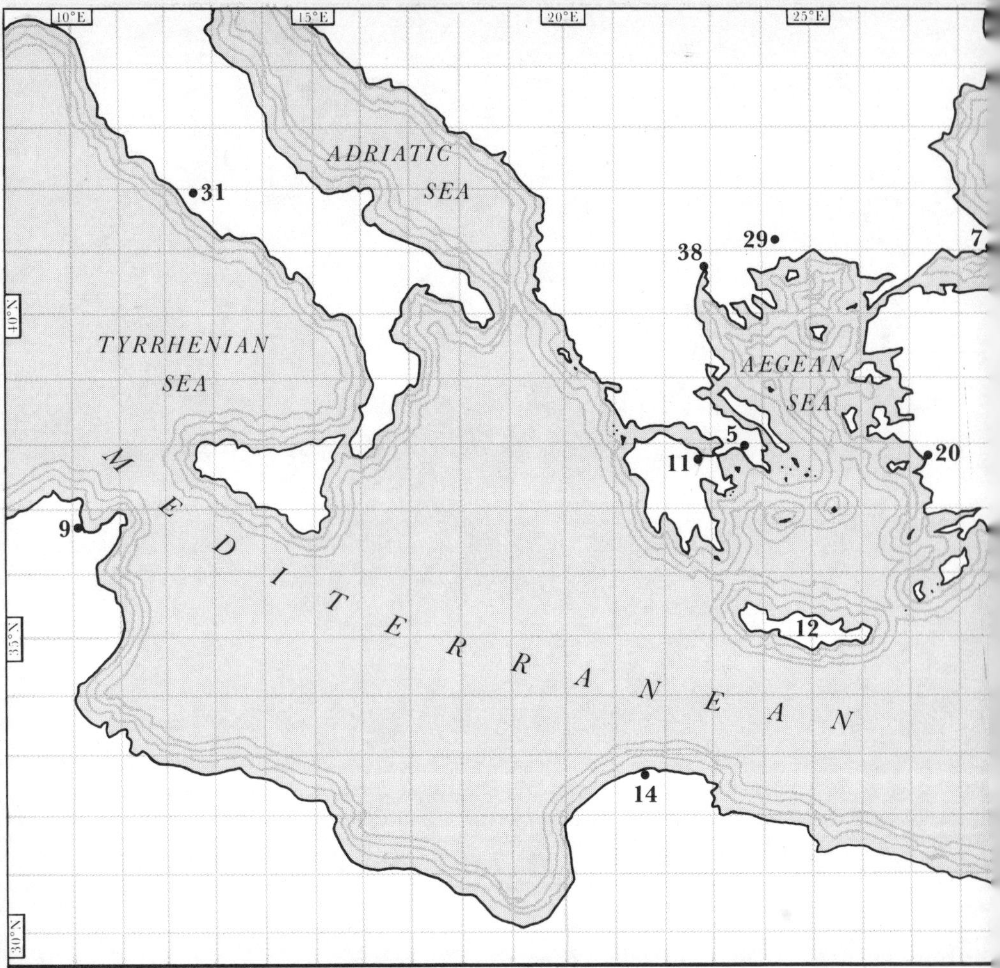

1 **Alexandria** (31°12′N; 29°53′E)
2 **Amarna, Tell el-** (27°38′N; 30°52′E)
3 **Antioch** (36°12′N; 36°10′E)
4 **Assur** (35°27′N; 43°16′E)
5 **Athens** (37°58′N; 23°43′E)
6 **Babylon** (32°33′N; 44°24′E)
7 **Byzantium/Constantinople** (41°01′N; 28°58′E)
8 **Carchemish** (36°49′N; 38°01′E)
9 **Carthage** (36°54′N; 10°16′E)
10 **Colossae** (37°46′N; 29°15′E)
11 **Corinth** (37°56′N; 22°56′E)
12 **Crete**
13 **Cyprus**
14 **Cyrene** (32°48′N; 21°54′E)
15 **Damascus** (33°30′N; 36°18′E)
16 **Dumah/al-Djawf (Jauf)** (29°48′N; 39°52′E)
17 **Dura-Europus** (34°46′N; 40°46′E)
18 **Ebla/Tell Mardikh** (35°48′N; 36°45′E)
19 **Elephantine** (24°05′N; 32°53′E)
20 **Ephesus** (37°55′N; 27°17′E)
21 **Haran** (36°51′N; 39°00′E)
22 **Hattusas/Boghazköy** (40°02′N; 34°37′E)
23 **Mari** (34°33′N; 40°53′E)
24 **Memphis** (29°51′N; 31°15′E)
25 **Nag Hammadi** (26°04′N; 32°13′E)
26 **Nineveh** (36°25′N; 43°10′E)
27 **Nuzi** (35°22′N; 44°18′E)
28 **Persepolis** (29°57′N; 52°5
29 **Philippi** (41°05′N; 24°19′
30 **Qurayya** (28°47′N; 36°00′
31 **Rome** (41°53′N; 12°30′E)
32 **Seleucia** (33°05′N; 44°35′
33 **Sidon** (33°33′N; 35°22′E)
34 **Susa** (32°11′N; 48°15′E)
35 **Tadmor/Palmyra** (34°36′N; 38°15′E)
36 **Tarsus** (36°52′N; 34°52′E)
37 **Thebes/Luxor** (25°42′N;
38 **Thessalonica** (40°38′N; 2
39 **Ugarit/Ras Shamra** (35°35′N; 35°45′E)
40 **Ur** (30°56′N; 46°08′E)
41 **Uruk** (31°18′N; 45°40′E)